WORLD CHRISTIAN ENCYCLOPEDIA

WORLD CHRISTIAN ENCYCLOPEDIA

A comparative survey of churches and
religions in the modern world

SECOND EDITION

David B. Barrett
George T. Kurian
Todd M. Johnson

Volume 2:
The world by segments: religions,
peoples, languages, cities, topics

UNIVERSITY PRESS

2001

OXFORD
UNIVERSITY PRESS

Oxford   New York

Athens   Auckland   Bangkok   Bogotá   Buenos Aires   Calcutta
Cape Town   Chennai   Dar es Salaam   Delhi   Florence   Hong Kong   Istanbul
Karachi   Kuala Lumpur   Madrid   Melbourne   Mexico City   Mumbai
Nairobi   Paris   São Paulo   Shanghai   Singapore   Taipei   Tokyo   Toronto   Warsaw

and associated companies in
Berlin   Ibadan

Copyright © 2001 by David B. Barrett

Published by Oxford University Press, Inc.,
198 Madison Avenue, New York, New York 10016
www.oup.com

Oxford is a registered trademark of Oxford University Press

Library of Congress Cataloging-in-Publication Data

World Christian encyclopedia : a comparative survey of churches
and religions in the modern world / David B. Barrett,
George T. Kurian, Todd M. Johnson.—2nd ed.
p.   cm.
Includes bibliographical references and index.
1. Christianity. 2. Christian sects. 3. Ecclesiastical geography. 4. Christianity—Statistics.
I. Barrett, David B. II. Kurian, George Thomas. III. Johnson, Todd M.
BR157 .W67   2000   230'.003—dc21   99-057323
ISBN 0-19-507963-9 (set)
ISBN 0-19-510318-1 (vol. 1)
ISBN 0-19-510319-X (vol. 2)

1 3 5 7 9 8 6 4 2

Printed in the United States of America
on acid-free paper

TABLE OF CONTENTS

Volume 1. THE WORLD BY COUNTRIES: RELIGIONISTS, CHURCHES, MINISTRIES

Volume 2. THE WORLD BY SEGMENTS: RELIGIONS, PEOPLES, LANGUAGES, CITIES, TOPICS

Summary of the world's 238 countries and their codes

Ref	Country name	Code	Ref	Country name	Code	Ref	Country name	Code
1	Afghanistan	afgh	81	Germany	germ	161	Oman	oman
2	Albania	alba	82	Ghana	ghan	162	Pakistan	paki
3	Algeria	alge	83	Gibraltar	gibr	163	Palau	pala
4	American Samoa	amer	84	Greece	gree	164	Palestine	pale
5	Andorra	ando	85	Greenland	grel	165	Panama	pana
6	Angola	ango	86	Grenada	gren	166	Papua New Guinea	papu
7	Anguilla	angu	87	Guadeloupe	guad	167	Paraguay	para
8	Antarctica	anta	88	Guam	guam	168	Peru	peru
9	Antigua & Barbuda	anti	89	Guatemala	guat	169	Philippines	phil
10	Argentina	arge	90	Guinea	guin	170	Pitcairn Islands	pitc
11	Armenia	arme	91	Guinea-Bissau	gunb	171	Poland	pola
12	Aruba	arub	92	Guyana	guya	172	Portugal	port
13	Australia	aust	93	Haiti	hait	173	Puerto Rico	puer
14	Austria	ausz	94	Holy See	holy	174	Qatar	qata
15	Azerbaijan	azer	95	Honduras	hond	175	Reunion	reun
16	Bahamas	baha	96	Hungary	hung	176	Romania	roma
17	Bahrain	bahr	97	Iceland	icel	177	Russia	russ
18	Bangladesh	bang	98	India	indi	178	Rwanda	rwan
19	Barbados	barb	99	Indonesia	indo	179	Sahara	saha
20	Belgium	belg	100	Iran	iran	180	Saint Helena	saih
21	Belize	beli	101	Iraq	iraq	181	Saint Kitts & Nevis	saik
22	Belorussia	belo	102	Ireland	irel	182	Saint Lucia	sail
23	Benin	beni	103	Isle of Man	isle	183	Saint Pierre & Miquelon	saip
24	Bermuda	berm	104	Israel	isra	184	Saint Vincent & the Grenadines	saiv
25	Bhutan	bhut	105	Italy	ital	185	Samoa	samo
26	Bolivia	boli	106	Ivory Coast	ivor	186	San Marino	sanm
27	Bosnia-Herzegovina	bosn	107	Jamaica	jama	187	Sao Tome & Principe	saot
28	Botswana	bots	108	Japan	japa	188	Saudi Arabia	saud
29	Bougainville	boug	109	Jordan	jord	189	Senegal	sene
30	Brazil	braz	110	Kazakhstan	kaza	190	Seychelles	seyc
31	Britain (UK of GB & NI)	brit	111	Kenya	keny	191	Sierra Leone	sier
32	British Indian Ocean Territory	briy	112	Kirghizia	kirg	192	Singapore	sing
33	British Virgin Islands	briz	113	Kiribati	kiri	193	Slovakia	slok
34	Brunei	brun	114	Kuwait	kuwa	194	Slovenia	slov
35	Bulgaria	bulg	115	Laos	laos	195	Solomon Islands	solo
36	Burkina Faso	burk	116	Latvia	latv	196	Somalia	soma
37	Burundi	buru	117	Lebanon	leba	197	Somaliland	somi
38	Cambodia	camb	118	Lesotho	leso	198	South Africa	soua
39	Cameroon	came	119	Liberia	libe	199	South Korea	souk
40	Canada	cana	120	Libya	liby	200	Spain	spai
41	Cape Verde	cape	121	Liechtenstein	liec	201	Spanish North Africa	span
42	Cayman Islands	caym	122	Lithuania	lith	202	Sri Lanka	sril
43	Central African Republic	cent	123	Luxembourg	luxe	203	Sudan	suda
44	Chad	chad	124	Macedonia	mace	204	Suriname	suri
45	Channel Islands	chan	125	Madagascar	mada	205	Svalbard & Jan Mayen Islands	sval
46	Chile	chil	126	Malawi	mala	206	Swaziland	swaz
47	China	chin	127	Malaysia	malb	207	Sweden	swed
48	Christmas Island	chri	128	Maldives	mald	208	Switzerland	swit
49	Cocos (Keeling) Islands	coco	129	Mali	mali	209	Syria	syri
50	Colombia	colo	130	Malta	malt	210	Taiwan	taiw
51	Comoros	como	131	Marshall Islands	mars	211	Tajikistan	taji
52	Congo-Brazzaville	cong	132	Martinique	mart	212	Tanzania	tanz
53	Congo-Zaire	conz	133	Mauritania	maur	213	Thailand	thai
54	Cook Islands	cook	134	Mauritius	maus	214	Timor	timo
55	Costa Rica	cost	135	Mayotte	mayo	215	Togo	togo
56	Croatia	croa	136	Mexico	mexi	216	Tokelau Islands	toke
57	Cuba	cuba	137	Micronesia	micr	217	Tonga	tong
58	Cyprus	cypr	138	Moldavia	mold	218	Trinidad & Tobago	trin
59	Czech Republic	czec	139	Monaco	mona	219	Tunisia	tuni
60	Denmark	denm	140	Mongolia	mong	220	Turkey	turk
61	Djibouti	djib	141	Montserrat	mont	221	Turkmenistan	turm
62	Dominica	domi	142	Morocco	moro	222	Turks & Caicos Islands	turs
63	Dominican Republic	domr	143	Mozambique	moza	223	Tuvalu	tuva
64	Ecuador	ecua	144	Myanmar	myan	224	Uganda	ugan
65	Egypt	egyp	145	Namibia	nami	225	Ukraine	ukra
66	El Salvador	elsa	146	Nauru	naur	226	United Arab Emirates	unia
67	Equatorial Guinea	equa	147	Nepal	nepa	227	United States of America	usa
68	Eritrea	erit	148	Netherlands	neth	228	Uruguay	uuay
69	Estonia	esto	149	Netherlands Antilles	nets	229	Uzbekistan	uzbe
70	Ethiopia	ethi	150	New Caledonia	newc	230	Vanuatu	vanu
71	Faeroe Islands	faer	151	New Zealand	newz	231	Venezuela	vene
72	Falkland Islands	falk	152	Nicaragua	nica	232	Viet Nam	viet
73	Fiji	fiji	153	Niger	niga	233	Virgin Islands of the US	virg
74	Finland	finl	154	Nigeria	nige	234	Wallis & Futuna Islands	wall
75	France	fran	155	Niue Island	niue	235	Yemen	yeme
76	French Guiana	freg	156	Norfolk Island	norf	236	Yugoslavia	yugo
77	French Polynesia	frep	157	North Korea	nork	237	Zambia	zamb
78	Gabon	gabo	158	Northern Cyprus	norl	238	Zimbabwe	zimb
79	Gambia	gamb	159	Northern Mariana Islands	norm			
80	Georgia	geor	160	Norway	norw			

Part 7

RELIGIOMETRICS

Profiles of the 270 largest of the 10,000 distinct religions worldwide

Great beyond all question is the mystery of our religion.
—Apostle Paul (I Timothy 3:16, Revised English Bible)

The academic disciplines of theology, church history, comparative religion and the like have all been pursued without serious attention to the sciences of missiometrics or religiometrics. Since 5,137 million people on Earth—85% of the world—are religionists who live their lives and livelihood in this context of billions of fellow-believers in over 10,000 different religions, descriptive demographic and numerical analyses of their welfare and their activities are long overdue.

Profiles of the 270 largest of the 10,000 distinct religions worldwide

The usual way in which the world of religions is described numerically is by means of a listing of the 7 largest world religions each followed by a number enumerating its followers. The familiar form in which this is done is naming the followers of the 7 as shown in Table 7-1, which is itself a shorter version of this Encyclopedia's Table 1-1.

While valuable as a succinct global summary, if not expanded further such listings become a gross oversimplification of what is in fact a vast global complex of at least 10,000 distinct and different religions across the world. What is needed is a comprehensive global survey, description, typology and classification of all religions.

With this in mind, there are many different ways in which religions can be defined, described, and classified. They are usually defined by their beliefs, dogmas, doctrines, or systems of belief. Such a comparative approach is intensely interesting and valuable for the understanding of religion that it provides. But this approach often ignores statistical enumeration as of little value in understanding religious issues.

Defining not 'religion' but 'a religion'

The difference depends on whether one is studying the abstract category 'religion' or the more specific category 'a religion'. For any scientific study of the latter, concrete aspects such as size, language, race, ethnicity, location, age, and relation to other religions are just as important as the more philosophical aspects.

This part of the Encyclopedia therefore attempts to present a relational database in which all religions can be listed with comparable variables that can be contrasted, listed, ranked, added, and totaled to give the overall global situation. For this purpose, a religion is defined here in a new and unusual way—in the first instance not by its dogmas, beliefs, or practices, but primarily by its **adherents**, also termed here religionists.

Defining a religion by its adherents

A religion is defined here as a religious community of believers or adherents who hold there to be something unique in their beliefs, and who give their primary religious allegiance and loyalty to that religion.

Table 7–1. Global status of religions, AD 2000: a minimal statement.

The following table demonstrates the minimal statistical information typically offered in global comparative studies of religion. Though useful for those wanting a succinct statement, it represents an oversimplification that calls for a far more complex elaboration. (Source of numbers: Table 1-1 in Part 1 "World Summary".)

Name	Adherents
Religionists	*5,137,000,000*
Christians	1,999,564,000
Muslims	1,188,243,000
Hindus	811,336,000
Buddhists	359,982,000
Ethnoreligionists	228,367,000
Sikhs	23,258,000
Jews	14,434,000
Nonreligionists	*918,249,000*
Agnostics (Nonreligious)	768,159,000
Atheists (Anti-religionists)	150,090,000

Table 7–2. A typology of 10 varieties of the globe's 10,000 distinct religions in AD 2000, with each's global significance, its range of descriptive attributes, and its current contact with Christians and Christianity.

Definition of a religion

A religion is defined in this Encyclopedia not in the first instance by its dogmas but primarily by its adherents. This means that a religion is defined by its adherents' loyalty to it; by their acceptance of it as unique and superior to all other religions, which they in practice ignore (though not necessarily deliberately), even those closely related in beliefs; by its relative autonomy (freedom to manage its own affairs); by its use of its own language, culture, customs, property; and by its adherents' ability in practice to get along without depending on any other religions or their adherents. Similarly, a religion's global significance—its significance in the wider world—is measured by its adherents' size and other attributes. These are defined and measured in particular by any distinctive or unique features among 21 of the religion's attributes or properties. Nine of these are tabulated in the nine columns in Tables 7-4 and 7-5, and are listed here below as columns 1,2,3,4,5,6,7,8,9. Note that other columns with a letter (4a, 5a, 7a, 8a, 8b, 9a-i) are not shown in Tables 7-4 and 7-5 but are available via the related CD.

1. The uniqueness of its **name** or identity, being distinct and distinctive with both collective and individual meanings.
2. Any shared **pedigree** or relationship to existing religions, religious movements, or families or clusters of religions, as shown by a code which indicates each religion's relation vertically and horizontally to other religions (see Part 3 "Codebook" and the database version of Country Tables 1).
3. Its **type** or layer or level (religion, family of religions, macroreligion, etc.) as measured by a scale 1-10 which is also an indicator of order of magnitude, as shown in the box with minitable at the right below.
4. Its history, as illustrated in particular by its year of origin (year **begun**).

4a. Size: the numerical size globally of its followers. This is almost universally known and stated, in one form or another. For many religions the meaningful figure is adult members, which refers to persons over 15 years old. The variable in this column enumerates **adult members** in AD 2000. Their figures are given on the related CD, *World Christian database*, but are not given in the tables below.

5. The more common usage is for a religion to compile and quote a larger category than adults, namely the religion's total **adherents** or total community. This is often called the demographic or census or total population figure. It is defined as the total of its adult members plus their children and infants, and all other varieties of followers. Of these 2 statistics (in columns 4a and 5) the more detailed one is the main one reported by the religion, and the less detailed one, or the more obviously rounded one (rounded to the nearest 100 or 1,000 or 10,000 or 100,000) is an estimate computed here from adult/child ratios in the countries concerned.

5a. The **distinctiveness** of its statistics of adherents, being either unique (not duplicated) in this table (code 1 = numbers not included elsewhere under a different name or category); or not unique (code 0 = numbers already included elsewhere higher or lower in the hierarchy, hence a duplication not to be counted twice when doing a global totaling).

6. Its **extent,** measured as the number of countries worldwide where it is significantly present.
7. Its geographical **location** expressed as its main or major country (shown below in its 4-letter coded form), with sometimes (in the end column) a note on where its HQ is.

7a. Its adherents' identity as a **people:** who and what ethnolinguistic people are in the majority in this religion, or what language the majority speak, as indicated by their 6-character ethnic code and/or 8-character language code as used in this Encyclopedia.

8. Its predominant missiological **World** (A, B, or C), being a measure of its adherents' status of evangelization.

8a. The number of its adherents who can be said to be evangelistically **unreached** or unevangelized. As with variable 4a above, this variable 8a is not shown in the database table printed below but is accessible on the related CD, *World Christian database*.

8b. The current extent of its **contact** with global Christianity and its world mission, or one of its branches, using code 0 = no contact, 1 = sparse or occasional contact, 2 = adequate contact, 3 = extensive contact, 4 = vast contact everywhere, 5 = total contact with extensive dialogue literature.

9. Notes, covering descriptions, background religions of ethnic group, D = Christian denominations present, M = Christian missions present.

Additional names, notes, data, beliefs

9a. Its **beliefs** and belief system involving the divine or the supernatural, the origin of life, human role on earth, and/or related dogmas; names for God in its language.

9b. Its related **behavior**, customs and experiential phenomena.

9c. Its degree of **independence** from other related religions or religious movements, and the separateness of its traditions.

9d. Its variety of autonomy of **institutions** whether few or many.

9e. Its **leadership**, whether lay or ordained, male or female, religious or nonreligious, absolute or localized, hierarchical or democratic, visible or invisible.

9f. Its literature and **bibliography** of descriptive books and articles.

9g. Its **self-understanding** as a unique religion, with unique validity, self-sufficient, claiming to be superior to several, many, most, or even all other religions, hence claiming completeness and needing no religious input from any other religion.

9h. Its **access to the Christian Scriptures** (a scale 0-5: 0 = no contact, up to 5 = Bible available in main language and in wide use).

9i. Its **name for God** (or, names) in the Christian Scriptures, if existing.

Enumerating attributes

For each religion listed in the main table below, the first 9 attributes as described above are presented in the 9 columns of the table, in the same order. Additional attributes are measured or further described in the final columns 9a-i, showing a selection of data illustrating each religion.

Ten levels of religion (column 3, *Type*)

All religions are classified here by *Type* in column 3. Using a 10-point scale, this describes each religion in terms of the various layers or levels composing religions in general and the many ways in which they relate or can be grouped and classified.

Note that the global total of all religions in each *Type* category 1-10, shown in the end column of the minitable immediately below, adds up to the total of all religions. Thus 2 religions may be correctly spoken of as 2 distinct religions even though there may be overlap in adherents, or even with one simply a part of the other. Thus Islam (Muslims) is properly described as a distinct religion; but so also is its excommunicated sect Ahmadiya.

The codes 1-10 shown under *Type* in the large table have the following meanings shown in the minitable below. The additional codes 11-15 are added below for interest and completeness, although they are, by definition, not separate religions and so do not occur in the large table itself.

Note further that the 'Adherents of each religion' column below is simply an approximate guide to numerical size, and is not intended to be a rigid inclusion/exclusion criterion.

Type	*Type: 10 basic types of religions (with alternate descriptions)*	*Adherents of each religion*	*Global total of religions*
	TEN LAYERS OR LEVELS OF RELIGIONS		
1	Cosmoreligion (universal religion open to all, family of macroreligions)	Over 200 million	9
2	Macroreligion (global/worldwide religion, megabloc)	20 to 200 million	35
3	Megareligion (world religion, family of megatraditions)	1 to 20 million	150
4	Megacommunion (megatradition, family of traditions)	Over 10 million	40
5	Communion (family of denominations or religions, confession)	Under 10 million	306
6	Macrodenomination (very large denomination, sect, school)	Over 10 million	50
7	Megadenomination (or paradenomination or network or sect)	1 to 10 million	1,110
8	Tradition (ecclesiastical family of churches)	From 10,000 to 1 billion	300
9	Cluster of related religions (smaller family of religions)	Under 1 million	2,000
10	Local religion (ethnoreligion, tribal religion closed to outsiders)	Under 1 million	6,000
—	Religion = each of the above categories 1-10	Over 100	10,000
	SUBRELIGIONS, SUBCATEGORIES, SUBDIVISIONS		
11	Minireligion (not a religion but a component)	Under 10,000	40,000
12	Denomination (not a religion but a component part)	Under 1 million	60,000
13	Minor denomination	Under 1,000	100,000
14	Congregation (church, temple, mosque, synagogue, assembly)	Up to 1 million	10,000,000
15	Cell (special-interest group, house meeting)	Up to 5,000	50,000,000

Table 7-3.	Ten layers or levels or types of religions, with definitions, examples, orders of magnitude, and global totals of each variety.		

Code	Type	Adherents of each religion	Global total of religions
1.	**Cosmoreligion** (universal religion open to all; gigareligion (>1 billion), global macrofamily of macroreligions). .... *Examples*: Christianity, Islam, Hinduism, Buddhism, Chinese folk-religion, ethnoreligion (the whole complex of smaller folk-religions), nonreligion (agnosticism, secularism, secular humanism, materialism).	Over 200 million	9
2.	**Macroreligion** (global religion, worldwide religion, family of megareligions, megabloc (including any cosmoreligion's subdivision or grouping over 20 million). *Examples*: Sunnis, Shias, Sufis, Mahayana, Hinayana, Tantrayana, Lamaism, African traditional religion (ATR/ethnoreligion), shamanism, Orthodoxy, Catholicism, Anglicanism, Protestantism, Independency, marginal Christianity (O, R, A, P, I, m), Pentecostal/Charismatic Renewal, evangelicalism, Non-White indigenous churches, White-led Postdenominationalism, animism, polytheism, Great Commission Christians, New Religion (Neoreligionists), popular religion, atheism (antireligion, irreligion).	Over 20 million	35
3.	**Megareligion** (world religion, family of megatraditions). .... *Examples*: Sikhism, Jainism, Taoism, Confucianism, Judaism, Ahmadiya, a Sufi order, Methodism, Lutheranism, Presbyterianism, Pentecostalism, CCR, Eastern Orthodoxy, Oriental Orthodoxy, Evangelicalism, Fundamentalism, Baha'i, High Spiritism, folk-Buddhism, folk-Islam, folk-Hinduism, Neopaganism, Korean folk-religion, Afro-American spiritists, Shinto.	From 1 to 20 million	150
4.	**Megacommunion** (world confessional family, megatradition, megacouncil). .... *Examples*: WCC, WEF, Wahhabites, Zaydis, Alawites, Druzes, Ibadis, Hanbalites, Malikites, Shafiites, Hanafites, a Christian world communion, Classical Pentecostalism, SDA, BWA, WMC, LWF, WARC, ACC, Oriental Jews, Orthodox Jews, Reformists, Reconstructionists, Sefardim, Ashkenazim, Vaishnavites, Saivites, Saktists, Neo-Hinduism, Zen Buddhism, Pure Land Buddhism, Ismailis, Ithna-Asharis, UBS.	Over 10 million	40
5.	**Communion** (confession, family of religions, family of ethnoreligions, family of denominations, larger national council of related religions) .... *Examples*: Oneness Pentecostalism, AWCF, Bantu religion, Nilotic religion, CJCLdS, JWs, NAC, Vedantists, Lahoris, Qadianis, Black Muslims, Shrine Shinto, Unity, Reform Hinduism, Digambara Jainism, Svetambara Jainism, Zoroastrianism (Parsiism).	Under 10 million	306
6.	**Macrodenomination** (very large denomination or sect or school). .... *Examples*: EKD, C of E, SBC, ROC, UOC, TSPM, Uniatism, Tijaniya, Shadhiliya, Sanusiya.	Over 10 million	50
7.	**Megadenomination** (large single denomination or sect or school, a subdivision). .... *Examples*: EJCSK, Self-Religionists.	From 1 to 10 million	1,110
8.	**Tradition** (ecclesiastical family or type, family of microtraditions). .... *Examples*: Mennonites, Holiness, Quakers, Episcopalians.	Over 10,000	300
9.	**Cluster of related religions** (smaller religious family, or national council or grouping, group of smaller ethnoreligions). .... *Examples*: Christopaganism, Australian Aboriginal religion, Pygmy religion.	Under 1 million	2,000
10.	**Local religion** (a single ethnoreligion, tribal religion restricted to tribal population). ... *Examples*: Samaritans, Mandeans, Karaites, Bohras, cargo cultists.	Under 1 million	6,000
-	**Religion** (primary religious association); each entity in the above 10 categories. ..... *Examples:* all of the above names are here each called 'a religion'.	Over 100	10,000

What this means is that the basic unit of study and analysis here is a specific religion with its religionists, with a short list of features that can be described and measured.

A distinct religion is defined here by its adherents' loyalty to it. They accept it as in some sense unique and superior to all other religions, even those closely related to it. In practice, adherents ignore other religions, not necessarily wilfully or deliberately. In practice they can get along without depending on the existence of any or all other religions or their adherents.

Likewise a religion's global significance, its impact and influence in the wider world, can be measured by its adherents' size and other attributes. In the database, some 21 attributes—14 being numerical and 7 descriptive—are tabulated for every religion. Further attributes are added in the table's final column 9, where any additional numerical data are added when available for particular religions. All these attributes are listed, defined, and described at the beginning of Table 7-2.

A coded pedigree for each religion
Religions are related to other religions in varying degrees which can then be reduced to a simple code representing its pedigree. This is presented and listed in Tables 7-4 and 7-5 for all values of the code. This code can be regarded as the first or primary identifying feature of any religion. The code describes the religion's pedigree or relationship to other existing religions, religious movements, or clusters or families of religions. The code thus indicates each religion's relation vertically and horizontally to other religions. Meanings of these codes are shown here in Part 3 "Codebook", Table 3-3.

The order of letters in the codes used here is designed to assist the user in memorizing codes that represent complex names. An initial letter 's' before

capitals indicates a specific sect or example or case in a wider category. Thus Japan's Shinshu Ōtani is coded sTPMB meaning that this religion is a sect of True Pure Land Buddhism. Such wider categories may themselves be sects, but still be wide enough to justify a capital letter; thus the Wahhabite school of Sunni Muslims, in Saudi Arabia, is coded WSM. This order of code letters means that to measure the closeness of any 2 religions, the user compares each character in the code, reading from right to left: the final right-hand letter first, then the last but one, and so on. This procedure provides an estimate of distance or religious barriers between 2 populations.

Ethnoreligions
The largest single specific family of religions in the world today is what this Encyclopedia is calling ethnoreligions. These are religions each confined to members of one single ethnolinguistic people, tribe, or culture. No persons outside the tribe may join; no members may leave (although in this present analysis members who have joined another religion, e.g. Christianity or Islam, are no longer enumerated in an ethnoreligion's demographic totals). In most cases an ethnoreligion has a unique name for God, Creator, or a complex of names for God or of gods (see Table 9-12, 'Names for God in 900 languages'). An ethnoreligion is also likely to have unique Creation and Flood and related stories, unique ethics and practices, and usually its own unique language which functions to exclude aliens from other tribes or races. Table 7-4 lists all 90 ethnoreligions each with over 500,000 adherents. Its database records that the total of all ethnoreligions with no restriction due to size is 5,800 different religions. All of these latter are listed with their data on the CD, *World Christian database*.

Eleven levels of religions
Among students and scholars of religion, the term 'religion' is employed at widely different levels. Buddhism is usually thought of by most as a religion; others however regard it as a group of religions; yet others insist that it is in fact a whole family of different religions. Likewise Islam is a religion, but so also is its heretical sect Ahmadiyya; and this in turn consists of 2 rival religions, Qadiani and Lahori. In order to make sense of statistics of their adherents, and to obtain national, regional, continental, and eventually global statistics of each and every religion that can be directly related to demographic populations, it is therefore necessary to clearly define the various levels to avoid double counting and similar misunderstandings.

All religions are thus classified in column 3 of Table 7-4 and 7-5, using the 10-point scale defined in Tables 7-2 and 7-3. The basic unit, *a religion* is there given a technical description meaning that it is a small measurable building block in this study of religions, in much the same way as the molecule, or the atom, or now the quark, has been so regarded in the study of physics.

This basic unit can appear as various larger entities in the following ascending ranking of complexity: a *religion* can take any of 10 forms, sizes, or shapes: a *local religion* (a tribal religion closed to outsiders), a *cluster of related religions*, a *tradition*, a *megadenomination*, a *macrodenomination*, a *communion* (confession, a family of religions), a *megacommunion* (megatradition), a *megareligion* (a family of megatraditions), a *macroreligion* (a global religion or family of megareligions), and even finally a *cosmoreligion* (universal religion open to all, gigareligion, a huge global macrofamily of macroreligions).

For any specific religion, therefore, all of its complexity as described above can be rapidly pinpointed by means of this single digit describing type together with a 2-, 3-, 4-, or 5- character code as listed in the second column of Table 7-2, 7-3, 7-4, or 7-5.

Christianity as a macrofamily of macroreligions
The application of these coding levels to Christianity is complex but provides a rich typology. Clearly Christianity may correctly be termed a single religion; but its adherents would argue that Christians are also composed of many other religions. Roman Catholics are sufficiently different from Seventh-day Adventists or Jehovah's Witnesses for one to agree that these 3 are, in practice, 3 distinct and separate religions. Southern Baptists practice their faith with little or no religious contact with Classical Pentecostals; and so on. In this classification the largest Christian macrodenominations are defined as distinct and separate religions when their adherents each number over 10 million; and those from 1 to 10 million as megadenominations. Macrodenominations (level 6) are included in Tables 7-4 and 7-5, column 3, by the type value 6. Megadenominations are excluded from the tables because they are less significant.

COMPILING A RELIGIOMETRIC DATABASE

Using the typology and method described above, a database was then designed and constructed. The first chart opposite, Table 7-4, presents an initial selection of well-known religions with over 500,000 adherents each, giving each religion one single line in order to facilitate comparative study and analysis. Table 7-4 lists its data alphabetically by name.

Next follows a 2-page collage of photographs illustrating a representative group of today's non-Christian religions.

Lastly, the identical material in Table 7-4 is re-ordered in Table 7-5 ranked by religious pedigree or relationship. Thus all the Buddhist family of religions appear as a single bloc sharing degrees of closeness between the various schools and sects; and so on.

A far larger selection of data on 8,000 or so distinct religions is available on the forthcoming CD *World Christian database*. It is envisaged that scholars and interested persons will continue to augment these data for some time to come.

Table 7-4. Global survey of 270 religions and parareligions with over 500,000 adherents in AD 2000, listed alphabetically by name.

Name of religion/religionists 1	Pedigree 2	Type 3	Date begun 4	Adherents 5	Ext 6	Ctry 7	Wld 8	Descriptions, background religions of ethnic group, D=denominations present, M=missions. 9
Affiliated Christians	AC	2	30	1,888,439,000	238	usa	C	All Christians known to the churches by name; baptized church members.
Afro-American spiritists	AU	3		5,649,000	20	jama	C	Wide range of religions across Caribbean and Latin America. Mostly Blacks.
Agonshu	sN	10	1978	580,000	10	japa	A	Veneration of Buddhist Agama Sutras. F=Kiriyama Seiyu. Annual mass fire ceremony, Kyoto.
Ahir ethnoreligionists	PAT	10		647,000	1	indi	A	Bhils. In Maharashtra and Gujarat States. Animists/polytheists 79%, Hindus 20%.
Ahmadis	AXM	3		7,950,000	70	paki	A	*Ahmadiyah.* Islamic messianic movement (F=Mirza Ghulam Ahmad).
Alawites	LHM	3	c950	1,631,000	50	syri	B	*Nusayris.* A Shiite group in Syria.
Ananda Marga	sH	3	1955	2,000,000	7	indi	B	Self-development Hindu Yoga. F= Anandamuotiji. Also in Europe, USA.
Anglican Church of Nigeria	A-Low-AC	6	1842	17,500,000	50	nige	B	ACN in CPWA until 1979. Mushrooming to 63 Dioceses. M=CMS(UK). 68f,1p,1s,1u.
Anglican Consultative Council	A-FC	4		102,000,000	120	brit	C	*ACC.* HQ London. Representatives of the 36 Churches of the worldwide Anglican Communion.
Anglicans	AAC	2		79,650,000	166	brit	C	102 million professing, 79 million affiliated to Anglican Communion.
Animists	AT	2		216,161,000	130	beni	B	Belief in spiritual beings, mountains, rocks, trees, rivers.
Antaisaka ethnoreligionists	AT	10		679,000	1	mada	B	Southeast coastal strip. Animists 72%, Baha'is 0.1%. D=RCC(D-Farafangana). M=CM.
Antandroy ethnoreligionists	AT	10		563,000	1	mada	B	Extreme south coast of island and inland. Animists 80%. D=RCC(D-Fort-Dauphin). M=CM.
Arya Samaj	sNH	3	1875	1,200,000	30	indi	B	'Society of Honourable Ones'. Reform Hindu body to reconvert Christians to Hinduism.
Ashkenazis	AJ	3		11,080,000	70	isra	B	Yiddish-speaking Judaism. From Germany; Poland, Russia, Ukraine.
Assembleias de Deus	P-Pe2-AC	6	1910	22,000,000	5	braz	C	*Assemblies of God.* 1934,M=AoG,SFM,NPY,FFFM. 30000n,27000mw,20f.
Atheists	a	1		150,090,000	161	chin	B	Militantly nonreligious and antireligious secularists and communists
Badawiya	sUM	3	c1240	1,000,000	20	egyp	B	Major Sufi order in Egypt, centered in Tanta; attracts one million pilgrims every autumn.
Bagri ethnoreligionists	AT	3		1,865,000	1	indi	A	In Punjab, Rajasthan, Pakistan. Nomads across India-Pakistan borders. Animists 99%.
Baha'is	L	3	1863	7,106,000	218	iran	A	Acceptance of all religions under mission of Bahaiullah. In all countries.
Bai ethnoreligionists	PAT	3		1,158,000	2	chin	A	Yunnan, Sichuan, Guizhou. Polytheists 65%, Buddhists 30%. D=TSPM,RCC. M=7.
Bambara ethnoreligionists	AT	10		669,000	3	mali	B	Maliki Muslims 85%, animists 13%. D=RCC(3 Dioceses),EEPM,ECEM,AoG,SDA. M=10.
Baptist World Alliance	B-FC	4		52,000,000	171	usa	C	*BWA.* HQ MacLean, Washington, DC.
Bara ethnoreligionists	AT	10		501,000	1	mada	B	Large inland area in south of island. Animists 50%. D=RCC(3 Dioceses). M=CM,MSF,MS.
Baule ethnoreligionists	AT	10		786,000	1	ivor	B	Literates 10%. Animists 44%, Muslims 3%. D=RCC(D-Bouake),EPEC,EPC,AoG,AICs. M=7
Betsimisaraka ethnoreligionists	AT	3		1,584,000	1	mada	B	Revival center. Animists 77%. D=RCC(2 Dioceses). Eglise du Reveil,FMTA,MET,AICs. M=3.
Bhilala ethnoreligionists	AT	10		644,000	1	indi	A	Bhils. In Gujarat, Madhya Pradesh, Maharashtra, Karnataka, Rajasthan. Animists 99%.
Black Muslims	BXM	3		1,650,000	10	usa	C	*Nation of Islam.* F=Elijah Mohammed. Two rival factions.
Black Tai ethnoreligionists	AT	10		711,000	3	viet	A	North Viet Nam. Animists 95%. D=RCC,ECVN,SDA. M=CMA,UWM,SIL. R=FEBC.
Bodo ethnoreligionists	HAT	10		740,000	1	indi	B	Hinduized animists 93%. D=Goalpara Boro Baptist Ch,North Bank Baptists,RCC,CNI,ICI. M=7.
Buddhists	B	1		359,982,000	126	japa	B	Followers of the way of the Buddha in several hundred schools and sects.
Bulgyohwoi	sKMB	9	1975	563,000	10	souk	B	*SGI Hankuk-Bulgyohwoi*/Korean Buddhist Council. Emphasis upon world peace.
Buzan-ha	sSMB	3		1,372,000	4	japa	B	Larger of 2 main branches of Shingon Buddhism (Shingonshu).
Cao Dai	sSN	3	1926	3,200,000	50	viet	B	*Dai Dao Tam Ky Pho Do* (Great Way of the 3 Epochs of Salvation). Catholicism syncretized.
Catholic Ch in the Philippines	R-Lat-AC	6	1521	56,554,000	25	phil	C	*Iglesia Catolica.* C=34+3+66. 80 dioceses or other jurisdictions, all Latin-rite.
Catholic Charismatic Renewal	r-FC	4	1967	120,000,000	233	holy	C	*CCR.* HQ Vatican City. M=ICCRS/ICCRO.
Catholic Church in India	R-LEr-AC	6	1319	14,286,000	30	indi	B	C=35+15+122. 126 dioceses or other jurisdictions. Sizeable Eastern-rites.
Catholic Church in Nigeria	R-Lat-AC	6	1487	11,689,000	10	nige	B	C=11+4+23. 5p,4s(546). 40 dioceses or other jurisdictions.
Catholic Church in Poland	R-Lat-AC	6	c 950	35,475,000	40	pola	C	*Kosciól Rzymsko-katolicki.* C=35+7+99. 26q,24s. 42 dioceses or jurisdictions.
Catholic Church in the USA	R-LEr-AC	6	1526	56,715,000	100	usa	C	31,820 diocesan priests, 16,770 religious priests, 91,870 nuns/sisters. Annual baptisms 1,090,500
Catholic Church of Canada	R-LEr-AC	6	1534	12,409,000	31	cana	C	*Eglise Catholique.* C=63+17+196. 11q,15s. 6,170 diocesan priests.
Central Bhil ethnoreligionists	AT	3		4,449,000	1	indi	A	Polytheists/animists 95%. D=RCC(D-Ajmer-Jaipur),CNI(D-Jabalpur),DNC,MCSA,CMA,M=11.
Central Gond ethnoreligionists	PAT	3		1,721,000	1	indi	B	Mainly in MP. Hindus 70%, animists 30%. D=Mennonites,Methodists,MPELC. M=12.
Central Shona ethnoreligionists	AT	10		886,000	2	zimb	C	Animists 33%. D=RCC,ACZ/CPCA,AACJM,JWs,AFMSA,GGCZ,SDA,FGC,DRC,AICs. M=15.
Ch of JC of Latter-day Saints	m-FC	4	1830	11,000,000	116	usa	C	*CJCLdS. Mormons.* Rapid growth worldwide with converts ex Protestant churches.
Chiesa Cattolica in Italia	R-LEr-AC	6	c 40	55,750,000	100	ital	C	*Catholic Ch in Italy.* 228 dioceses, 25,800 parishes. 36560n,18930x.
Chinese Buddhists	CMB	2	60	90,000,000	60	chin	A	Violently suppressed in AD 452, 574, and 845.
Chinese folk-religionists	F	1		384,807,000	89	japa	B	A mixture of Confucianism, Taoism, Buddhism, animism, universism.
Chinese Mongolian ethnoreligionists	ST	3		1,368,000	1	chin	A	Nonreligious 50%, shamanists 40%, Lamaists 10%. D=RCC,house churches. M=7.
Chizan-ha	sSMB	3		1,101,000	5	japa	B	One of the 2 main branches of Shingon Buddhism.
Chogyejong	sKMB	3	372	7,001,000	10	souk	B	*Daihan-Bulgyo-Chogyejong* (Korean Buddhist Sect of Chogye). HQ Seoul, 24 regional centers.
Chongwhajong	sKMB	9	1969	712,000	1	souk	B	*Daihan-Bulgyo-Chongwhajong* (Korean Buddhist Sect of Chongwha; Mahayana).
Chontaijong	sKMB	3		1,182,000	1	souk	B	*Daihan-Bulgyo-Chontaijong* (Korean Buddhist Sect of Chontai; Mahayana).
Christians	C	1	AD 30	1,999,564,000	238	usa	C	Followers of Jesus Christ, Son of God, Savior, in 238 countries. D=34,000.
Church of England	A-plu-AC	6	c 100	24,493,000	160	brit	C	Reformed 1558. 1960, Charismatic Renewal, now 12%. 100x,308m,2358w,23s (950).
Church of God in Christ	c-FC	4		10,000,000	40	usa	C	*CoGiC.* HQ Memphis, TN.
Church of Perfect Liberty	sSN	3	1946	2,000,000	10	japa	B	*PL Kyodan.* Liturgical, rituals, monotheistic. Life is art, sports, clubs.
Church of World Messianity	sNN	9	1934	700,000	2	japa	B	*Sekai Kyuseikyo.* Ex Omoto.
Chwabo ethnoreligionists	AT	10		757,000	1	moza	B	Around Quelimane. Animists 76%, Muslims 7%. D=RCC,SDA. M=UBS.
Confucianists	G	3	BC 500	6,299,000	15	chin	B	Founded by Confucius. Highly organized in South Korea, also Japan, Vietnam
Congregation for Bishops	b-FC	4		901,000,000	1	holy	C	Vatican dicastery for administering dioceses, bishops, new appointments.
Conservative Jews	sOJ	3	1854	2,000,000	6	isra	B	*Masorati.* Begun in Germany; USA 1900; opposing Reform Judaism's neglect of Halakhah.
crypto-Christians	CC	2		123,726,000	85	chin	A	All secret believers in Christ unknown to state, society, or hostile religions.
Dan ethnoreligionists	AT	10		677,000	2	ivor	B	Animists 62%, Muslims 10%. D=RCC(D-Daloa),UEESO. M=SIL,SMA,MB,SIM,FMB.
Dhammayut Nikaya	sTB	3	c1870	1,500,000	2	thai	B	Theravada monastic community with 1,500 monasteries.
Divine Light Mission	sFH	3	1965	1,200,000	7	indi	B	Begun in India, 1971 USA (24 ashrams in 24 cities); by 1990, declining to 30,000 in UK, USA.
Druzes	DXM	9	c1050	834,000	10	pale	B	Quasi-Muslims also in Lebanon, Syria, Jordan, Israel. Split ex Ismailis.
East African Revival	-FC	5	1927	3,000,000	20	rwan	C	*Rwanda Revival. Balokole* (Saved Ones). Pietists. Biennial conventions of 50,000 or so.
Eastern Bhil ethnoreligionists	PAT	3		2,676,000	1	indi	A	Polytheists 95%. D=CMA,CNI,RCC. M=IEM,CGMM,BFI,UPM,YWAM.
Eastern Meo ethnoreligionists	PAT	3		1,473,000	1	chin	B	Northeast Yunnan, Guizhou, Guangxi; also Thailand, Viet Nam. Polytheists 94%. D=Chinese Ch.
Eastern Nuer ethnoreligionists	AT	10		856,000	2	suda	B	Nomadic animists 79%, highly resistant to Islam. D=RCC(D-Malakal),CCUN,COC,ECMY.
Eastern Yi ethnoreligionists	PAT	10		861,000	1	chin	A	Southeastern Yi. Guizhou, Weining Autonomous Region. Polytheists 98%. D=TSPM,RCC.
Eglise Cath au Congo-Zaire	R-Lat-AC	6	1482	23,001,000	10	conz	C	*Catholic Ch.* C=37+23+162. 11p,1q,9x(472).
Eglise Catholique de France	R-LEr-AC	6	c 80	48,064,000	150	fran	C	*Catholic Ch in F.* C=71+9+397. 4p,11q,39s.
Ethiopian Orthodox Church	O-Eth-AC	6	332	20,250,000	4	ethi	B	*EOC. Ethiopia Tewahido Bete-Cristian.* 20 Dioceses. 53 bps, 250000n. 200,000 Charismatics.
Ethnoreligionists	T	1		228,367,000	142	nige	B	Tribalists. Tribal religionists, with local religions open only to members of tribe or ethnopeople.
Ev Kirche in Deutschland	P-Uni-AC	6	1946	29,205,000	20	germ	C	*EKD.* 20 Landeskirchen, 8 other denominations. 300p,39s,P=26%,W=6%.
Evangelicals	EAC	2		210,603,000	237	usa	C	Church members affiliated to Evangelical denominations, councils, or agencies.
Falun Gong	sCMB	3		30,000,000	20	chin	A	A Buddhist motivation-based sect. 1999 clashes with Communist regime.
Focolare Movement	sRAC	3	1943	2,000,000	20	ital	C	Catholic lay renewal emphasizing youth, families, humanity, unity. F=Chiara Lubich.
Fon ethnoreligionists	AT	3		1,015,000	74	beni	B	Animists 62%(260 fetish monasteries), Muslims 5%. D=RCC(D-Abomey),EPMB,AoG. M=20.
Freemasons	QY	3	1714	5,900,000	37	brit	C	Largest worldwide secret society. Members men only. In USA, UK, France.
Gedatsukai	sN	10	1929	500,000	10	japa	B	Shingon-derived New Religion. Honor to rising Sun each day. HQ Tokyo.
Gideo ethnoreligionists	AT	10		570,000	1	ethi	B	Animists 69%, Muslims 1%. D=ECMY,WLEC,FGBC,Light of Life Ch,AIC. M=10.
Gormati ethnoreligionists	HAT	3		2,161,000	1	indi	B	AP,MP,HP,TN, 5 other States. Hindus/polytheists 99%. D=20. M=30.
Great Commission Christians	GCC	2		647,821,000	237	usa	C	All church members aware of Christ's Commission and involved in His global mission.
Gurenne ethnoreligionists	AT	10		593,000	2	ghan	B	Animists 83%, Muslims 5%. D=AoG,GBC,RCC(D-Navrongo-Bolgatanga), 15 others. M=20.
Han charismatic house chs	I-3cC-AC	6	c1950	29,740,000	1	chin	B	500 Regional Councils, 5,000 Pastoral Districts. M=Taiwanese/Diaspora short-termers; CCRC.
Han Chinese Three-Self Chs	I-Uni-AC	6	1807	10,500,000	1	chin	B	*TSPM.* 1950, all non-RCs forcibly united. 1966-79, all churches closed. Now 40% registered.
Hanafites	HSM	2	c750	531,418,000	90	turk	A	School of law. In India, Pakistan, Turkey, Afghanistan, Central Asia, Lower Egypt.
Hanbalites	BSM	3	850	2,325,000	30	saud	B	School of law officially accepted in Saudi Arabia.
Hani ethnoreligionists	PAT	3		1,495,000	3	chin	A	Yunnan, Viet Nam, Laos, Burma. Polytheists (animists, ancestor veneration) 95%. D=TSPM.
Hare Krishna	sH	10	1965	800,000	50	indi	B	*ISKCON. International Society for Krishna Consciousness.* In many countries east and west.
High Spiritists	HU	3		3,750,000	30	fran	C	Kardecism and other European non-Christian forms without African features.
Highland Nung ethnoreligionists	PAT	10		958,000	1	viet	A	Closely related to Tho and Southern Zhuang. Polytheists 98%(ancestor worship).
Hindus	H	1		811,336,000	114	indi	B	Based on the Vedas, now with many varieties.
Ho ethnoreligionists	AT	10		783,000	1	indi	A	Animists 69%, Hindus 30%. D=RCC(D-Jamshedpur),CNI. M=SJ,IBT,OFUCPM,IEM,USPG.
Hoa Hao	sSF	3	1939	2,050,000	10	viet	B	*Buo Son Ky Hong.* Millennialist. F=Huynh Phu So, regarded as the Emergent Buddha.
Hommon Butsuryu	sN	10	1857	500,000	2	japa	B	Lay movement in Kyoto. Ex Buddhism. Main feature: Lotus Sutra.
Hossoshu	sNMB	9		600,000	4	japa	B	One of the 6 Nara sects of Japanese Buddhism. 40 temples. In 1945, 57,042 adherents.
Hutu ethnoreligionists	AT	10		846,000	2	rwan	C	Animists 8%, Muslims 8%. D=RCC(6 Dioceses),AC/EAR,SDA,ADEEP,EPR,UEBR. M=14.
I Kuan Tao	sSN	3	1928	3,000,000	30	taiw	C	*Yi Guan Dao. Unity. Unity Way.* Begun in China. Buddhism, Taoism, Christian elements.
Identity Christianity	-FC	5	1925	500,000	10	usa	C	Identification of Anglo-Saxon-European Whites with 10 Lost Tribes of Israel. Violent rhetoric.

Continued overleaf

Table 7-4 continued

Name of religion/religionists 1	Pedigree 2	Type 3	Date begun 4	Adherents 5	Ext 6	Ctry 7	Wld 8	Descriptions, background religions of ethnic group, D=denominations present, M=missions. 9
Iglesia Católica en España	R-Lat-AC	6	c 63	38,057,000	70	spai	C	*Catholic Ch in Spain.* C=62+9+244. 114q,48s.
Iglesia Católica en Chile	R-Lat-AC	6	1541	11,041,000	10	chil	C	*Catholic Ch in Chile.* C=49+4+136. 1090x,12p,3s.
Iglesia Católica en Colombia	R-Lat-AC	6	1512	37,064,000	10	colo	C	*Catholic Ch.* C=46+2+128. 5p,38q,15s(1378),W=63%.
Iglesia Católica en el Ecuador	R-Lat-AC	6	1534	10,803,000	10	ecua	C	*Catholic Ch in E.* C=20+2+37.
Iglesia Católica en el Perú	R-Lat-AC	6	1536	22,590,000	20	peru	C	*Catholic Ch.* 9 Zones. C=40+6+110. 10p,4q,9x(115).
Iglesia Católica en la Argentina	R-LEr-AC	6	1539	31,800,000	20	arge	C	C=60+8+170. (1970: 5326nx,12486w,470504Yy). (1990)
Iglesia Católica en México	R-Lat-AC	6	1518	85,500,000	35	mexi	C	*Catholic Ch.* C=37+3+146.
Iglesia Católica en Venezuela	R-Lat-AC	6	1513	20,657,000	10	vene	C	*Catholic Church.* C=31+3+78. 1q,5s(101),W=10%.
Igreja Católica no Brasil	R-LEr-AC	6	1500	144,000,000	60	braz	C	C=101+14+329.
Ilkwando	sSN	9	1948	844,000	1	souk	B	*Kukje-Dodug Hyophwoi-Ilkwando* (Unified Truth Principle); claiming unity of Buddhism, Taoism.
Independents	IAC	2		385,745,000	221	chin	B	Non-White indigenous Christians; Postdenominationalists, Neocharismatics.
Islamic schismatics	XM	3		14,950,000	160	iraq	A	A large number of splits or secessions from major schools of Islamic law.
Ismailis	IHM	3	909	23,772,000	120	indi	B	'Seveners', Khojas. Shia sect with Aga Khan IV as its imam.
Ithna-Asharis	AHM	2	680	136,655,000	10	iran	A	'Twelvers'. Imamis.
Izumo-taishakyo	qN	3	1873	2,261,000	20	japa	B	One of largest Shinko Shukyo (New Religions). Based on Shinto. HQ Taisha, Izumo shrine
Jains	V	3	BC 550	4,218,000	10	indi	B	Ex Brahmanic Hinduism. 98% in Mysore and Gujarat. Monasteries.
Jehovah's Christian Witnesses	w-FC	4		13,000,000	219	usa	C	*Jehovah's Witnesses.* JWs. IBRA. Watch Tower. In 219 countries.
Jeungsando	sNN	9	1911	767,000	1	souk	B	Total Transformation. Folk religion seeking and believing total change-transformation.
Jews	J	3		14,434,000	134	isra	B	Practitioners of Judaism in 5 main branches. Centered in Israel, USA, Argentina.
Jilliwhoi	SF	3	1925	4,630,000	1	souk	B	*Daisoon Jilliwhoi* (Great & Genuine Truth Assembly).
Karanga ethnoreligionists	AT	10		587,000	4	zimb	C	Animists 30%. D=RCC(D-Gwelo),DRC,ACZ,ZCC,ELCZ, AICs. M=20.
Karijites	KXM	3		1,636,000	10	saud	A	Early Muslim sect (7th-10th centuries), strictly puritanical; now termed Ibadites.
Katholische Kirche Deutschland	R-LEr-AC	6	c 90	28,478,000	30	germ	C	*Catholic Ch in G.* C=44=15=302. 10q,20s(1895).
Kegon	sNMB	9	c700	700,000	3	japa	B	Mutual identity of phenomena and great Buddha Dainichi. HQ Nara. 1945: 50,915 adherents.
Khalkha Mongol shamanists	ST	10		507,000	1	mong	A	Lamaists 30%, shamanists 30%, nonreligious 28% atheists 10%, Muslims 1%. M=115 a
Khandeshi ethnoreligionists	AT	3		1,162,000	1	indi	A	Maharashtra, Gujarat. Dialects: Ahirani, Dangri, Kunbi, Rangari. Animists 70%, Hindus 30%.
Khasi ethnoreligionists	AT	10		546,000	1	indi	B	Animists 50%. D=RCC(D-Silchar),ICFG,CNI(D-Assam),PCNEI. M=PCW,LBI,BFI,TEAM,FMPB.
Khmu ethnoreligionists	AT	10		714,000	3	laos	A	Animists 94%. D=RCC(many catechumens),LEF. M=CMA,ACCM,APM,OMI,MEP. R=FEBC.
Konko-kyo	sTS	9	1859	683,000	2	japa	B	'Religion of Golden Light'. F=Kawate Bunjiro. (1814-1883), now venerated.
Korean shamanists	ST	3		1,619,000	8	chin	B	Shamanists 55%, Mahayana Buddhists 35%. D=TSPM,RCC. M=25 agencies from S. Korea.
Kui ethnoreligionists	AT	10		584,000	1	indi	A	Orissa. Hindus 54%, animists 45%. D=RCC(M-Cuttack), SDA,Baptists,CNI. M=15.
Kurozumi-kyo	sTS	9	1814	574,000	2	japa	B	Faith healing, F=Kurozumi Munetada (1780-1850). Possession by sun goddess Amaterasu.
Kuruba ethnoreligionists	AT	10		708,000	1	indi	A	Animists 80%, Hindus 19%. D=Gospel in Action,Brethren,RCC,CSI,UELCI. M=IEM,IBT,QCI.
Kwanumjong	sKMB	9	1940	618,000	1	souk	B	*Daihan-Bulgyo-Kwanumjong* (Korean Buddhist Sect of Sattva).
Lamaists	LB	3	640	21,490,000	40	chin	B	Tibet, worldwide diaspora. Prayer wheels and mantra 'Om mani padme hum' to ward off evil.
Li ethnoreligionists	PAT	3		1,235,000	1	chin	A	Tropical mountains in Hainan. Polytheists (animists) 100%. D=TSPM. M=5.
Lomwe ethnoreligionists	AT	10		857,000	2	moza	B	Zambezia Province. Animists 65%, Muslims 7%. D=RCC,ICFG,MCSA,SDA,ECM. M=12.
Lutheran World Federation	L-FC	4		80,000,000	150	germ	C	*LWF.* HQ Geneva.
Maasai ethnoreligionists	AT	10		557,000	1	keny	B	Kajiado, Narok, Tanzania. Animists 55%. D=RCC,EFMK,CPK,LCK,AIC,PCEA,BCC. M=18. M=1.
Madariya	sUM	3	c1410	4,000,000	25	indi	B	Mostly in north India but also in Nepal and widespread across South Asia.
Mahayana	MB	2		202,233,000	100	japa	B	'Greater Vehicle of Salvation', larger of the 2 major branches of Buddhism.
Maitili ethnoreligionists	HAT	3		1,575,000	1	indi	A	*Tirahutia.* In Bihar, MP, WB; Nepal. Educated high-caste Hindus 95%. D=RCC,CNI. M=10.
Makua ethnoreligionists	AT	3		1,329,000	4	moza	B	Animists 59%, Muslims 18%. D=RCC(STET),AEC,JWs. M=30.
Makuana ethnoreligionists	AT	3		1,775,000	1	moza	B	Nampula, south of Meeto area. Animists 59%, Muslims 20%. D=RCC.
Malayic Dayak ethnoreligionists	AT	10		573,000	1	indo	B	Kalimantan. West central, to Delang in south. Animists 80%. D=NTM.
Malikites	MSM	2	c790	221,900,000	90	nige	B	School of law. In North, West, and Central Africa, Upper Egypt.
Manchu shamanists	ST	3		2,188,000	1	chin	B	500 Manchu speakers left. Folk-religionists 70%, shamanists 20%, Buddhists 10%. D=TSPM.
Marginal Christians	MAC	3		26,060,000	215	usa	C	*CJCLdS*, JWs, and bodies placing selves on periphery of mainline Christianity.
Mende ethnoreligionists	AT	10		542,000	7	sier	B	Lingua franca. Animists 42%, Muslims 42%. D=UMC,MCSL,WAMC,SLC, 15 others. M=20.
Merina ethnoreligionists	AT	10		556,000	1	mada	C	Animists 12%, Muslims 1%, Baha'is 0.2%. D=70% Protestants,RCC,AICs. M=20.
Mina ethnoreligionists	AT	3		1,086,000	1	indi	A	Aborigines in Rajasthan. Animists 98%(with Hindu elements). M=Tribal Mission,CSI,CCCI,EHC.
Mitajong	sKMB	3	1943	1,026,000	1	souk	B	*Daihan-Bulgyo-Mitajong* (Korean Buddhist Sect of Sattva).
Mitake-kyo	sTS	3		1,648,000	2	japa	B	Mountain-worship. Shinto sect focused on Mount Ontake, a major religious center.
Mon ethnoreligionists	AT	10		792,000	4	myan	A	Animists 75%, Buddhists 20%. D=Ch of Christ,BBC(Mon Baptist Churches Union). M=5.
Mossi ethnoreligionists	AT	3		1,203,000	4	burk	B	Animists 16%, Muslims 61%(Maliki Sunnis; many converts on arrival in cities). D=16. M=25.
Muong ethnoreligionists	AT	3		1,058,000	2	viet	A	Mostly in mountains of north Viet Nam; also Banmethuot in south. Animists 94%. D=RCC.
Muslim Brotherhood	sNXM	3	1928	1,000,000	30	egyp	B	*Ikhwan al-Muslimin.* 30 countries (Egypt 500,000). Fundamentalist, puritan, anti-Christian.
Muslims	M	1		1,188,243,000	204	paki	A	*Islam* (active submission to the will of Allah).
Naqshabandiya	sUM	2	c1200	50,000,000	30	uzbe	A	Great Sufi order, strong in Central Asia, India, Western Europe.
Ndebele ethnoreligionists	AT	10		559,000	2	zimb	B	Animists 36%. D=RCC,AOC,ACZ,CCNZ,ELCZ,AMCZ,BCZ,BiCC,CMCCA, & 20 others. M=30.
Neo-Buddhists	NTB	3	1951	6,000,000	10	indi	B	Buddhism of social protest espoused by B.R. Ambedkar in Maharashtra state.
Neo-Hindus	NH	3		17,385,000	20	indi	B	Large variety of new religions based on revivals of Hinduism.
New Apostolic Church	I-3aX-AC	6		11,000,000	120	germ	C	*NAC/NAK.* HQ Zurich.
New Sect Shintoists	sTS	3		2,000,000	30	japa	B	13 independent sects after shrines banned.
New-Agers	sFN	3	c1870	12,000,000	41	usa	C	Self-religiosity in hundreds of diverse forms. Bookshops, spiritual therapy centers, training.
New-Religionists	N	1		102,356,000	60	japa	B	Recent new non-Christian religions, many syncretizing Christianity with other religions.
Nichiren Shoshu	sNN	3	1930	1,000,000	50	japa	B	*True Nichiren School.* International, this-worldly appeal. 1992, Soka Gakkai splits off.
Nichirenshu	NJMB	3		2,100,000	10	japa	B	'Sun Lotus'. The original movement begun by monk Nichiren (1222-1282).
Nishi-Honganji	sPMB	3		7,379,000	10	japa	B	*Temple of the Original Vow.* Eastern Temple, Kyoto. Leading sect of Shin Buddhism.
Nonreligious	Q	1		768,159,000	236	chin	B	Secularists, materialists, agnostics, with no religion but not militantly antireligious.
North Korean shamanists	ST	3		2,952,000	12	nork	B	Nonreligious 55%, atheists 16%, New-Religionists 13%, shamanists 12%, Buddhists 1.5%. D=6.
Northern Meo ethnoreligionists	PAT	10		828,000	1	chin	A	West Hunan. Agriculturalists. Polytheists 96%. D=Chinese Church,RCC,TSPM. M=3.
Northern Tung ethnoreligionists	PAT	3		2,240,000	1	chin	A	Guizhou. Polytheists(animists) 80%, Buddhists 20%. D=RCC,TSPM. M=IMB, SIL, TELL, FEBC.
Northern Yi ethnoreligionists	PAT	3		1,582,000	5	chin	A	Northern Nosu. Yunnan, Laos, Viet Nam. Polytheists(animists) 90%, Buddhists 5%. D=2. M=22.
Northern Zhuang ethnoreligionists	PAT	3		10,237,000	2	chin	A	Polytheists 80%, Buddhists 19%. D=TSPM(300 churches),RCC,TJC. M=25.
Old Ritualists	I-OBe-TC	8	1666	1,821,860	21	russ	B	*Old Believers. Raskolniki.*
Oomoto	sNN	3	1892	1,500,000	15	japa	A	'Great Origin' Omotokyo. F=peasant woman, Deguchi Nao. Extensive use of mass media.
Organization of African Instituted Chs	I-FC	4		40,000,000	50	keny	C	*OAIC.* HQ Nairobi. African Independent Churches. 92 related national councils.
Oriental Jews	EJ	3		2,378,000	20	isra	B	Jews from diaspora in eastern countries, now mostly in Israel.
Orthodox	OAC	2		215,129,000	135	russ	B	Eastern Orthodox (HQ Constantinople/Istanbul), Oriental Orthodox (5 communions).
Otani	sPMB	3	1602	8,484,000	20	japa	B	Branch of Jodo Shinshu based on East Temple, Kyoto. Otani=name of abbots.
Pentecostal World Conference	Z-FC	4		50,000,000	180	swit	C	*PWC.* No HQ. Triennial conferences of Classical Pentecostal preachers.
Pentecostals/Charismatics	ZAC	2	1900	523,778,000	237	usa	C	Vast Renewal in 3 waves experiencing charismatic gifts of the Holy Spirit.
Protestants	PAC	2		342,002,000	233	usa	C	Vast fragmented sphere of denominations in 150 traditions or communions.
Punu ethnoreligionists	PAT	10		555,000	1	chin	A	Guangxi. Polytheists (animists) 99%, including ancestor worship.
Pure Land Buddhists	PMB	3	c1250	4,521,000	31	japa	B	*Jodo, Jodoshu.* Amitabha (Amida, a god presiding over a Western Paradise) Buddhism.
Puyi ethnoreligionists	PAT	3		2,269,000	1	chin	A	Guizhou, Yunnan. Written. 40 dialects. Polytheists 80%, Buddhists 10%, Taoists 8%. D=1. M=12.
Qadiriya	sUM	3	c1120	20,000,000	50	syri	B	Oldest Sufi order, widespread in 50 countries from Senegal to Malaysia. Miracles claimed.
Quasireligionists	QY	2		60,000,000	20	fran	C	Most members (e.g. Freemasons) belong also to mainline religions listed here.
Reform Hindus	RH	3		4,460,000	20	indi	B	*Arya Samaj,* et alia. Modern attempts to revitalize Hindus and win back converts.
Reform Jews	RJ	3	c1860	1,100,000	30	germ	C	Liberal or Progressive Judaism. USA (300,000 families), UK, Argentina, Brazil, Australia, NZ.
Reiyukai Kyodan	sNN	3	1922	3,000,000	10	japa	B	'Society of Companions of the Spirits'. Rooted in Nichirenshu, family values. F=Kubo Kakutaro.
Rinzai-shu	sZMB	3	1191	3,000,000	10	japa	B	Sect of Japanese Zen. F=Lin Chi (Chinese).
Rissho Koseikai	sNN	3	1938	5,000,000	40	japa	B	'Society for Establishing Righteousness and Harmony'. HQ Tokyo. Goal: perfect Buddhahood.
Roman Catholics	RAC	2		1,057,328,000	235	braz	C	All local churches in communion with Holy See (Vatican, Rome).
Romanian OC, P Bucuresti	O-Rum-AC	6	c 100	19,040,000	10	roma	C	*Biserica Ortodoxa Romana.* The Lord's Army (300,000) are Evangelicals. 20 bps,8545n.
Russian Orthodox Church	O-Rus-AC	6	988	73,998,000	50	russ	B	*ROC. Russkaya Pravoslavnaya Tserkov.* 93 Dioceses, 103 bps, 14000n,60de(5000),82s.
Sakalava ethnoreligionists	AT	10		574,000	2	mada	B	Strongest Muslim presence among Malagasy. Animists 59%, Muslims 7.5%. D=RCC. M=14.
Saktists	KH	3		25,720,000	2	indi	B	Shaktas. Hindu devotees of goddess Devi.
Santal ethnoreligionists	AT	3		1,482,000	3	indi	B	Hindus 78%, animists 21%. D=RCC, (3 dioceses)CNI,NELC,BOBBC,MCSA. M=25.
Sect Shintoists	TS	3	1882	6,000,000	20	japa	B	*Shuha.* Shinto, Kyoha Shinto. 13 Sects. No shrines.
Sefardis	SJ	9		952,000	50	arge	C	Main centers: Latin America, USA, Israel, Spain, Portugal, Balkans.
Segyejunggyo	sNN	9	1957	621,000	1	souk	B	*World True Religion*; folk religion seeking world peace, realization of human ideals (Utopia).
Seicho-no-Ie	sNN	3	1930	3,000,000	2	japa	B	'House of Growth'. Perfection of all things, denial of evil. Literature, lectures.
Sena ethnoreligionists	AT	3		1,053,000	3	moza	B	Animists 60%, Muslims 1%. D=RCC, (D-Beira, Quelimane), CNC,CB,CC,AoG,ICFG. M=5.

Continued opposite

Table 7-4 concluded

Name of religion/religionists 1	Pedigree 2	Type 3	Date begun 4	Adherents 5	Ext 6	Ctry 7	Wld 8	Descriptions, background religions of ethnic group, D=denominations present, M=missions. 9
Seventh-day Adventists	V-FC	4		25,000,000	200	usa	C	*SDA*, General Conference. HQ Washington D.C.
Sgaw Karen ethnoreligionists	AT	3		1,021,000	4	myan	B	Animists 49%, Baha'is. D=BBC(Karen Bap Conv),RCC,CPB,SSKBC,AoG,NAC,SDA. M=10.
Shafiites	SSM	2	810	239,900,000	80	malb	A	School of Islamic law. Popular in Southeast Asia, East Africa, southern Arabia.
Shaivites	SH	2		216,260,000	10	indi	B	Shaivas, devotees of god Shiva.
Shias	HM	2		170,100,000	60	iran	A	Shiites. Followers of Ali, cousin of Mohammed. In Iran, Iraq, Lebanon, India, Pakistan.
Shin-nyo En	sMB	3		2,100,000	2	japa	B	'Garden of the Truth of Buddha'. Lay movement with 500 workers. Focuses on Nirvana Sutra.
Shingonshu	SMB	3	816	11,000,000	6	japa	B	'True Word'. Major form of Tantric Buddhism in Japan: 45 sects, subsects. Chief temple Kyoto.
Shinshu Honganjiha	sPMB	3		7,000,000	10	japa	B	A subgroup of Jodoshinshu, with 10,000 temples.
Shinshu Otani	sTPMB	3		6,000,000	10	japa	B	A major subgroup of Jodoshinshu, with 9,000 temples.
Shintoists	S	3		2,762,000	8	japa	B	Shinto='*The Way of the Gods*'. 80,000 shrines in Japan
Shrine Shintoists	HS	2	1946	62,000,000	40	japa	B	*Jinja Honcho, Jinja Shinto.* 26,000 priests, 77,000 shrines.
Sikhs	K	3	c1500	23,258,000	34	indi	B	Monotheistic revelation to F=Guru Nanak (1469-1539). HQ Amiritsar.
Soka Gakkai	sNN	3	1930	18,000,000	115	japa	B	1975 SG International; 1990 Lay split ex Nichiren Shoshu. Shedding world conversion aims.
Soto	sZMB	3	c1230	6,409,000	20	japa	B	F=Dogen (1200-1253). Popular Buddhist teaching.
Soto-shu	sZMB	3	c1240	6,000,000	15	japa	B	Zen Buddhism with temples, priests, rites, Chinese origin.
South Korean shamanists	ST	3		18,082,000	8	souk	B	Shamanists 16%, Buddhists 15%, New-Religionists 15%, Confucianists 11%. D=100. M=300.
Southern Baptist Convention	P-Bap-AC	6	1845	21,500,000	150	usa	C	*SBC.* 1845 ex North. 99% White. (1970) 31000n,2H,6s,W=39%,409659Y. (1990) 63352n.
Southern Bhil ethnoreligionists	PAT	3		1,260,000	1	indi	A	Polytheists 95%. D=CMA,MCSA,CNI,RCC,Pentecostals. M=IEM,COUNT,CGMM,BFI,UPM,WVI.
Southern Maninka ethnoreligionists	AT	3		1,127,000	1	guin	A	Also in Guinea Bissau, Liberia. Animists 59%, Muslims 39%. D=RCC,EEP. M=10.
Southern Senufo ethnoreligionists	AT	10		622,000	1	ivor	B	Animists 65%, Muslims 30%. D=RCC(D-Korhogo,D-Katiola),ANBC,EPC. M=WEC,CBFMS,BGC.
Southern Yi ethnoreligionists	PAT	10		835,000	1	chin	A	Eastern Yi, Southern Yi. Black Yi. Yunnan, Guizhou, Sichuan. Polytheists 95%. D=RCC,TSPM.
Southern Zhuang ethnoreligionists	PAT	3		4,009,000	1	chin	A	Southwest Guangxi. Polytheists 90%, some Buddhists. D=TSPM,RCC. M=CSI,YWAM,SIL.
Spiritists	U	3		62,334,000	55	braz	C	Very strong in Brazil: Umbanda, Macumba, Candomblé. Many Catholics belong.
Sufis	UM	2	c1150	237,400,000	100	moro	A	Mass movements as Sufi orders/brotherhoods spread from Morocco to Indonesia.
Sukuma ethnoreligionists	AT	3		1,047,000	1	tanz	B	Animists 33%, Muslims 30%. D=RCC,AIC,SDA,CPT,BCT,PCSAT,CWC,KOAB. AICs. M=20.
Sunnis	SM	2		1,002,543,000	180	paki	A	Main body of Islam.
Swaminarayans	sRH	3	1801	5,000,000	30	indi	B	In India, UK, Kenya, USA. HQ Gujarat. F= Sahajananda Swami (1781-1830).
Tai (Shinto Honkyoku)	sTS	3		1,091,000	2	japa	B	*Shintokyo.*
Taigojong	sKMB	3	1356	3,133,000	2	souk	B	*Hankuk-Bulgyo-Taigojong* (Korean Buddhist Sect of Taigo; Mahayana).
Tanala ethnoreligionists	AT	10		504,000	1	mada	B	East of Betsileo. Animists 80%. D=RCC(M-Fianarantsoa),ERSM, and other AICs. M=SJ.
Taoists	D	3		2,655,000	8	chin	B	*Daoists.* China; strong in Taiwan as separate religion. Syncretized with numerous new religions.
Tendai	TMB	3	c800	5,000,000	2	japa	B	*Tendaishu.* Tien-tai(Chinese). A rationalist monastic order, ascetic, meditative. Many sects.
Tenrikyo	sTS	3	1838	3,000,000	10	japa	B	*Religion of Heavenly Wisdom.* Faith-healing.17,000 churches, 20,000 mission stations.
Theravada	TB	2		136,259,000	40	sril	B	'Way of the Elders'. Also termed Hinayana ('Lesser Vehicle of Salvation').
Tho ethnoreligionists	PAT	3		2,246,000	4	viet	A	In China, Laos, USA, France. Polytheists 99%. D=RCC,ECVN. M=CMA,SIL. R=FEBC.
Transcendental Meditation	sNH	3		4,000,000	30	usa	C	Known as TM, or Spiritual Regeneration Movement. In USA, UK (100,000 practicing), India.
Tripuri ethnoreligionists	HAT	10		673,000	2	indi	A	In Assam. Hinduized animists 92%, Muslims 6.5%. D=RCC(D-Silchar),PCNEI. M=10.
True Pure Land Buddhists	TPMB	3	c1270	14,000,000	20	japa	B	*Jodoshinshu.* Also termed Shin Buddhism.
Tsimihety ethnoreligionists	AT	10		950,000	1	mada	B	Animists 85%. D=RCC(3 Dioceses),ERSM,FMTA, and other AICs. M=CSSp,OFMCap,FMB.
Tsonga ethnoreligionists	AT	10		634,000	5	soua	C	In Mozambique. Animists 30%, Muslims, Baha'is. D=RCC,TPC,ZCACSA,DRC, AICs. M=12.
Tswa ethnoreligionists	AT	10		978,000	2	moza	B	Animists 79%. D=UCCSA(ICUM),IMU,RCC,IML,CPSA,AICs. M=UCBWM,FMC,UMC,USPG.
Tujia ethnoreligionists	PAT	3		6,327,000	1	chin	A	Northwest Hunan. Unwritten language. Polytheists/animists 99%. D=TSPM,RCC. R=TWR.
Ukrainian Orth Ch (P Moscow)	O-Ukr-AC	6	991	26,994,000	10	ukra	C	*Russian Orthodox Church, Exarchate of the Ukraine*, under P Moscow. 37 bishops.
Umbanda	sBU	3	c1920	20,000,000	22	braz	C	Afro-American religion, many White followers. Displacing Candomblé and Macumba.
United Methodist Church	P-Met-AC	6	1766	11,091,000	100	usa	C	*UMC.* 1968, EUB merger. 96% White, 4% Black. 81 Confs. 34974n,13s,W=36%.
Vaishnavites	VH	2		549,583,000	30	indi	B	Sri Vaishnavas, devotees of god Vishnu, by bhakti (devotion).
Venda ethnoreligionists	AT	10		573,000	3	soua	B	Animists 65%. D=DRCA,AoG,CPSA,WC,RCC,ABC,CBCSA,ZCC,other AICs. M=15.
Wagdi ethnoreligionists	PAT	3		1,692,000	1	indi	A	Udaipur, Rajasthan, Gujarat. Bhils. Second language Hindi. Animists/polytheists 99%.
Wahhabites	WSM	3	c1780	7,000,000	40	saud	B	Wahhabis follow the Hanbali school of Islamic law.
Walamo ethnoreligionists	AT	3		1,007,000	2	ethi	B	Animists 35%. D=WLEC(strong),ECMY(20%), EOC,FGBC,RCC,SDA,AICs. M=12.
Wallega ethnoreligionists	AT	10		902,000	2	ethi	B	Muslims 40%, animists 25% D=30%: EOC(D-Wallega),BECE,ECMY,SDA. M=SIM,WVI,FMB.
West Makua ethnoreligionists	AT	10		642,000	2	moza	B	Niassa Province. Animists 60%, Muslims 20%. D=CPSA,RCC.
Western Meo ethnoreligionists	AT	3		3,492,000	1	chin	B	Guizhou, Guangxi, Sichuan, Yunnan; Viet Nam, Laos. Polytheists 94%. D=6. M=20.
White Karen ethnoreligionists	AT	10		996,000	3	myan	B	Animists 65%, some Baha'is. D=BBC,SSKBMS,CPB(D-Yangon),AoG,SDA,NAC. M=10.
Won	sSF	9	1916	550,000	10	souk	B	*Won Bulgyo.* Based on modern Buddhism, Confucianism, Taoism, Chondogyo, Christianity.
World Alliance of Reformed Chs	P-FC	4		60,000,000	210	swit	C	*WARC.* HQ Geneva.
World Assemblies of God Fellowship	z-FC	4		43,000,000	140	souk	C	*WAGF.* HQ Seoul, Korea.
World Convention of Chs of Christ	T-FC	4		10,000,000	130	usa	C	*WCCC.*
World Council of Churches	-FC	4		430,000,000	20	swit	C	*WCC.* HQ Geneva.
World Evangelical Fellowship	-FC	4		150,000,000	50	sing	C	*WEF.* HQ Singapore.
World Methodist Council (WMC)	W-FC	4		70,226,000	108	usa	C	*WMC.* HQ Lake Junaluska, NC.
Yao ethnoreligionists	PAT	3		2,415,000	3	chin	A	53% speak Yao. Polytheists/animists(ancestor-worship) 99%. D=RCC,TSPM,TJC. M=10.
Yoruba ethnoreligionists	AT	10		856,000	20	nige	B	Muslims 37%, animists 4%. D=CPN,RCC,CAC,ESOCS,NCF,NBC, & 200 others. M=150.
Zaydis	ZHM	3		8,042,000	40	yeme	A	*Five Shiites.* Shia school of law, in Yemen.
Zezuru ethnoreligionists	AT	10		580,000	6	zimb	C	Animists 28%. D=RCC,AACJM,ACZ/CPCA,SDA,SA,DRC,BCZ,MCZ,UMC,AICs. M=120.
Zoroastrians	Z	3	BC 1000	2,544,000	24	iran	A	*Parsis.* Ancient monotheist religion of Persia. Iran 1,903,000, Afghanistan 304,000, India 100,000.
other religions over 500,000	.			50,000,000				Total other distinct religions with over 500,000 adherents each: around 50.
other religions under 500,000	.			20,000,000				Total distinct religions with under 500,000 each: around 10,000.
doubly-counted				-13,527,299,000				Persons counted under 2, 3, or more overlapping religion levels above.
Global religionists	-	-		5,137,000,000	238			Adherents of the world's 10,000 or so different religions.
Global nonreligionists	Q,a	-		919,933,000	230			Persons with no religion, indifferent to religion, also persons militantly antireligious (atheists).
Global population	-	-		6,055,000,000	238			Total population of world in mid-2000.

Non-Christians: a selection of non-Christian religionists.

Afro-American spiritists. Woman priest of Macumba (Brazil's major Afro-Brazilian cult) at Sta Barbara center whose ceremonies last over 4 hours each.

Ahmadis. Large crowd of Ahmadis at prayers in Saltpond (Ghana) led by world leader of Ahmadiya Movement in Islam. Hazrat Hafiz Mirza Nasir Ahmad, Khalifat-ul-Massih III (center, white turban).

Atheists. Militantly anti-religious Red Guards in Peking (August 1966) hold up Mao's Little Red Book prior to destroying churches and temples.

Baha'is. Brazilian children at Instituto Baha'i de Gravatai, Rio Grande do Sul.

Black Muslims. USA Black women of World Community of Al-Islam in the West/America, formerly Nation of Islam.

Buddhists. World's largest Buddhist monument, a stone polyhedron in Borobudur, Central Java (Indonesia), built AD 800, to which come 500,000 visitors a year. Upper circular terraces hold 72 stupas each containing a Buddha. The whole stupa complex with its 500 Buddhas is a mandala (ritual diagram) or allegory of the universe, representing ascending stages of enlightenment towards nirvana (spiritual freedom).

Hindus. Spiritual head of Hindu religion worldwide, Swami Satya Mitra Nandgiri, from 1960-74 His Holiness Swami Jagatguru Shankar Acharya, Head of Dandi Sanyasis, Head of Central India Math (Bhanpur, Ujjain).

Hindu festival Vijay Dashmi, celebrated annually (here, in Nairobi, Kenya).

Tamil woman imploring Hindu god Subrahmanya for help during festival procession in Saidapet district, Madras (India). At top left are the god's musicians.

Chinese folk-religionists. In See Yeah Temple (Malaysia), Chap Goh Meh (15th Night) is celebrated with glitter, pomp and gaiety, in a blending of Confucianism, Taoism, Buddhism and worship of local deities.

Jains. 25-yearly ceremony of anointing colossal 57 ft. statue of Digambara saint Bahubali (rain god Gomatesvara) with milk, curds and ghee, at Sravana-Belgola, Mysore (India).

Jews. Four UK Jewish leaders are interviewed on BBC-1 television, including Editor of *Jewish Chronicle* (second left) and Chief Rabbi Jakobovits of United Hebrew Congregation of the Commonwealth (right).

Muslims. Orthodox (Sunni) Muslims at Great Prayer of Thursday before ancient mud mosque in Mopti (Mali), during which all streets are closed.

Sufi mosque seating 150 in Cape Town, South Africa. The domes represent the various levels of man's conscience.

Parsis. Zoroastrian or Parsi priests in Fire Temple worship spirit of goodness and light, Ahura Mazda, under form of continually-burning sacred fire. Adherents are declining because no converts are accepted.

Neo-Hindus. Largest neo-Hindu movement is the Divine Light Mission. Here, 20% of its 5 million followers attend annual Hans Jayanti celebration in Delhi commemorating Guru's late father's birthday.

Center of DLM's devotion is Guru Maharaj Ji (born 1958), worshipped as Lord of the Universe, Divine Incarnation, who became Perfect Master in 1966 at age 8.

Reform Hindus. Official opening of new center in Pretoria by Swami Nisreyasananda (left) of the Ramakrishna Mission in Zimbabwe.

New-Religionists. Modern Asiatic syncretistic religions with Christian elements (and over 102 million adherents). (1) *Above*. Viet Nam: *Cao Daist Missionary Church* (Doctrine of the Third Revelation of God), worshippers facing altar and Divine Eye inside Holy See Great Divine Temple.

(2) Japan: *Rissho-koseikai* (Society for Establishment of Righteousness), with worshippers in Great Sacred Hall, Tokyo, facing 10-foot gold image of Sakyamuni Buddha on main altar.

(3) USA: *Nichiren Shoshu of America, NSA* (True Church of Nichiren/Soka Gakkai/Value Creation Society): 20,000 NSA conventioneers in Los Angeles in 1972 stage Salute to America.

Shamanists. North American Indian shaman of Tlingit tribe (northern British Columbia coast), in spirit helper's headdress, attempts with drum (left) and rattle to effect a cure.

Shintoists. In Shinto festival in Japan, young men carry shrines down public street.

Sikhs. Five Sikh swordsmen guarding the Granth Sahib (Holy Scriptures) process through Nairobi.

Table 7-5. Global survey of 270 religions and parareligions with over 500,000 adherents in AD 2000, listed by pedigree.

Name of religion/religionists 1	*Pedigree* 2	*Type* 3	*Date begun* 4	*Adherents* 5	*Ext* 6	*Ctry* 7	*Wld* 8	*Descriptions, background religions of ethnic group, D=denominations present, M=missions.* 9
Atheists	a	1		150,090,000	161	chin	B	Militantly nonreligious and antireligious secularists and communists
Buddhists	B	1		359,982,000	126	japa	B	Followers of the way of the Buddha in several hundred schools and sects.
Lamaists	LB	3	640	21,490,000	40	chin	B	Tibet, worldwide diaspora. Prayer wheels and mantra 'Om mani padme hum' to ward off evil.
Mahayana	MB	2		202,233,000	100	japa	B	'Greater Vehicle of Salvation', larger of the 2 major branches of Buddhism.
Chinese Buddhists	CMB	2	60	90,000,000	60	chin	A	Violently suppressed in AD 452, 574, and 845.
Falun Gong	sCMB	3		30,000,000	20	chin	A	A Buddhist motivation-based sect. 1999 clashes with Communist regime.
Nichirenshu	NJMB	3		2,100,000	10	japa	B	'Sun Lotus'. The original movement begun by monk NIchiren (1222-1282).
Bulgyohwoi	sKMB	9	1975	563,000	10	souk	B	SGI Hankuk-Bulgyohwoi/Korean Buddhist Council. Emphasis upon world peace.
Chogyejong	sKMB	3	372	7,001,000	10	souk	B	Daihan-Bulgyo-Chogyejong (Korean Buddhist Sect of Chogye). HQ Seoul, 24 regional centers.
Chongwhajong	sKMB	9	1969	712,000	1	souk	B	Daihan-Bulgyo-Chongwhajong (Korean Buddhist Sect of Chongwha; Mahayana).
Chontaijong	sKMB	3	594	1,182,000	1	souk	B	Daihan-Bulgyo-Chontaijong (Korean Buddhist Sect of Chontai; Mahayana).
Kwanumjong	sKMB	9	1940	618,000	1	souk	B	Daihan-Bulgyo-Kwanumjong (Korean Buddhist Sect of Sattva).
Mitajong	sKMB	3	1943	1,026,000	1	souk	B	Daihan-Bulgyo-Mitajong (Korean Buddhist Sect of Sattva).
Taigojong	sKMB	3	1356	3,133,000	2	souk	B	Hankuk-Bulgyo-Taigojong (Korean Buddhist Sect of Taigo; Mahayana).
Hossoshu	sNMB	9		600,000	4	japa	B	One of the 6 Nara sects of Japanese Buddhism. 40 temples. In 1945, 57,042 adherents.
Kegon	sNMB	9	c700	700,000	3	japa	B	Mutual identity of phenomena and great Buddha Dainichi. HQ Nara. 1945: 50,915 adherents.
Pure Land Buddhists	PMB	3	c1250	4,521,000	31	japa	B	Jodo, Jodoshu. Amitabha (Amida, a god presiding over a Western Paradise) Buddhism.
Nishi-Honganji	sPMB	3		7,379,000	10	japa	B	*Temple of the Original Vow*. Eastern Temple, Kyoto. Leading sect of Shin Buddhism.
Otani	sPMB	3	1602	8,484,000	20	japa	B	Branch of Jodo Shinshu based on East Temple, Kyoto. Otani=name of abbots.
Shinshu Honganjiha	sPMB	3		7,000,000	10	japa	B	A subgroup of Jodoshinshu, with 10,000 temples.
Shinshu Otani	sTPMB	3		6,000,000	10	japa	B	A major subgroup of Jodoshinshu, with 9,000 temples.
True Pure Land Buddhists	TPMB	3	c1270	14,000,000	20	japa	B	*Jodoshinshu*. Also termed Shin Buddhism.
Shin-nyo En	sMB	3		2,100,000	2	japa	B	'Garden of the Truth of Buddha'. Lay movement with 500 workers. Focuses on Nirvana Sutra.
Shingonshu	SMB	3	816	11,000,000	6	japa	B	'True Word'. Major form of Tantric Buddhism in Japan: 45 sects, subsects. Chief temple Kyoto.
Buzan-ha	sSMB	3		1,372,000	4	japa	B	Larger of 2 main branches of Shingon Buddhism (Shingonshu).
Chizan-ha	sSMB	3		1,101,000	5	japa	B	One of the 2 main branches of Shingon Buddhism.
Tendai	TMB	3	c800	5,000,000	2	japa	B	*Tendaishu*. Tien-tai(Chinese). A rationalist monastic order, ascetic, meditative. Many sects.
Rinzai-shu	sZMB	3	1191	3,000,000	10	japa	B	Sect of Japanese Zen. F=Lin Chi (Chinese).
Soto	sZMB	3	c1230	6,409,000	20	japa	B	F=Dogen (1200-1253). Popular Buddhist teaching.
Soto-shu	sZMB	3	c1240	6,000,000	15	japa	B	Zen Buddhism with temples, priests, rites, Chinese origin.
Theravada	TB	2		136,259,000	40	sril	B	'Way of the Elders'. Also termed Hinayana ('Lesser Vehicle of Salvation').
Neo-Buddhists	NTB	3	1951	6,000,000	10	indi	B	Buddhism of social protest espoused by B.R. Ambedkar in Maharashtra state.
Dhammayut Nikaya	sTB	3	c1870	1,500,000	2	thai	B	Theravada monastic community with 1,500 monasteries.
Christians	C	1	AD 30	1,999,564,000	238	usa	C	Followers of Jesus Christ, Son of God, Savior, in 238 countries. D=34,000.
Affiliated Christians	AC	2	30	1,888,439,000	238	usa	C	All Christians known to the churches by name; baptized church members.
Assembleias de Deus	P-Pe2-AC	6	1910	22,000,000	5	braz	C	*Assemblies of God*. 1934,M=AoG,SFM,NPY,FFFM. 30000n,27000mw,20f.
Han charismatic house chs	I-3cC-AC	6	c1950	29,740,000	1	chin	B	500 Regional Councils, 5,000 Pastoral Districts. M=Taiwanese/Diaspora short-termers; CCRC.
Ethiopian Orthodox Church	O-Eth-AC	6	332	20,250,000	4	ethi	B	*EOC. Ethiopia Tewahido Bete-Cristian.* 20 Dioceses. 53 bps, 250000n. 200,000 Charismatics.
Han Chinese Three-Self Chs	I-Uni-AC	6	1807	10,500,000	1	chin	B	*TSPM*. 1950, all non-RCs forcibly united. 1966-79, all churches closed. Now 40% registered.
Ev Kirche in Deutschland	P-Uni-AC	6	1946	29,205,000	20	germ	C	*EKD*. 20 Landeskirchen, 8 other denominations. 300p,39s,P=26%,W=6%.
Romanian OC, P Bucuresti	O-Rum-AC	6	c 100	19,040,000	10	roma	C	*Biserica Ortodoxa Romana*. The Lord's Army (300,000) are Evangelicals. 20 bps,8545n.
Southern Baptist Convention	P-Bap-AC	6	1845	21,500,000	150	usa	C	*SBC*. 1845 ex North. 99% White. (1970) 31000n,2H,6s,W=39%,409659Y. (1990) 63352n.
Catholic Church in India	R-LEr-AC	6	1319	14,286,000	30	indi	B	C=35+15+122. 126 dioceses or other jurisdictions. Sizeable Eastern-rites.
Catholic Church in the USA	R-LEr-AC	6	1526	56,715,000	100	usa	C	31,820 diocesan priests, 16,770 religious priests, 91,870 nuns/sisters. Annual baptisms 1,090,500
Catholic Church of Canada	R-LEr-AC	6	1534	12,409,000	31	cana	C	*Eglise Catholique*. C=63+17+196. 11q,15s. 6,170 diocesan priests.
Chiesa Cattolica in Italia	R-LEr-AC	6	c 40	55,750,000	100	ital	C	*Catholic Ch in Italy.* 228 dioceses, 25,800 parishes. 36560n,18930x.
Eglise Catholique de France	R-LEr-AC	6	c 80	48,064,000	150	fran	C	*Catholic Ch in F*. C=71+9+397. 4p,11q,39s.
Iglesia Católica en la Argentina	R-LEr-AC	6	1539	31,800,000	20	arge	C	C=60+8+170. (1970: 5326nx,12486w,470504Yy). (1990)
Igreja Católica no Brasil	R-LEr-AC	6	1500	144,000,000	60	braz	C	C=101+14+329.
Katholische Kirche Deutschland	R-LEr-AC	6	c 90	28,478,000	30	germ	C	*Catholic Ch in G*. C=44=15=302. 10q,20s(1895).
Ukrainian Orth Ch (P Moscow)	O-Ukr-AC	6	991	26,994,000	10	ukra	C	*Russian Orthodox Church, Exarchate of the Ukraine*, under P Moscow. 37 bishops.
Russian Orthodox Church	O-Rus-AC	6	988	73,998,000	50	russ	B	*ROC. Russkaya Pravoslavnaya Tserkov*. 93 Dioceses, 103 bps, 14000n,60de(5000),82s.
Catholic Ch in the Philippines	R-Lat-AC	6	1521	56,554,000	25	phil	C	*Iglesia Catolica*. C=34+3+66. 80 dioceses or other jurisdictions, all Latin-rite.
Catholic Church in Nigeria	R-Lat-AC	6	1487	11,689,000	10	nige	B	C=11+4+23. 5p,4s(546). 40 dioceses or other jurisdictions.
Catholic Church in Poland	R-Lat-AC	6	c 950	35,475,000	40	pola	C	*Kosciól Rzymsko-katolicki*. C=35+7+99. 26q,24s. 42 dioceses or jurisdictions.
Eglise Cath au Congo-Zaire	R-Lat-AC	6	1482	23,001,000	10	conz	C	*Catholic Ch*. C=37+23+162. 11p,1q,9x(472).
Iglesia Católica en España	R-Lat-AC	6	c 63	38,057,000	70	spai	C	*Catholic Ch in Spain*. C=62+9+244. 114q,48s.
Iglesia Católica en Chile	R-Lat-AC	6	1541	11,041,000	10	chil	C	Catholic Ch in Chile. C=49+4+136. 1090x,12p,3s.
Iglesia Católica en Colombia	R-Lat-AC	6	1512	37,064,000	10	colo	C	*Catholic Ch*. C=46+2+128. 5p,38q,15s(1378),W=63%.
Iglesia Católica en el Ecuador	R-Lat-AC	6	1534	10,803,000	10	ecua	C	*Catholic Ch in E*. C=20+2+37.
Iglesia Católica en el Perú	R-Lat-AC	6	1536	22,590,000	20	peru	C	*Catholic Ch*. 9 Zones. C=40+6+110. 10p,4q,9x(115).
Iglesia Católica en México	R-Lat-AC	6	1518	85,500,000	35	mexi	C	*Catholic Ch*. C=37+3+146.
Iglesia Católica en Venezuela	R-Lat-AC	6	1513	20,657,000	10	vene	C	*Catholic Church*. C=31+3+78. 1q,5s(101),W=10%.
United Methodist Church	P-Met-AC	6	1766	11,091,000	100	usa	C	*UMC*. 1968, EUB merger. 96% White, 4% Black. 81 Confs. 34974n,13s,W=36%.
Church of England	A-plu-AC	6	c 100	24,493,000	160	brit	C	Reformed 1558. 1960, Charismatic Renewal, now 12%. 100x,308m,2358w,23s (950).
Anglican Church of Nigeria	A-Low-AC	6	1842	17,500,000	50	nige	B	ACN in CPWA until 1979. Mushrooming to 63 Dioceses. M=CMS(UK). 68f,1p,1s,1u.
New Apostolic Church	I-3aX-AC	6		11,000,000	120	germ	C	*NAC/NAK*. HQ Zurich.
Anglicans	AAC	2		79,650,000	166	brit	C	102 million professing, 79 million affiliated to Anglican Communion.
Evangelicals	EAC	2		210,603,000	237	usa	C	Church members affiliated to Evangelical denominations, councils, or agencies.
Independents	IAC	2		385,745,000	221	chin	B	Non-White indigenous Christians; Postdenominationalists, Neocharismatics.
Marginal Christians	MAC	3		26,060,000	215	usa	C	CJCLdS, JWs, and bodies placing selves on periphery of mainline Christianity.
Orthodox	OAC	2		215,129,000	135	russ	B	Eastern Orthodox (HQ Constantinople/Istanbul), Oriental Orthodox (5 communions).
Protestants	PAC	2		342,002,000	233	usa	C	Vast fragmented sphere of denominations in 150 traditions or communions.
Roman Catholics	RAC	2		1,057,328,000	235	braz	C	All local churches in communion with Holy See (Vatican, Rome).
Focolare Movement	sRAC	3	1943	2,000,000	20	ital	C	Catholic lay renewal emphasizing youth, families, humanity, unity. F=Chiara Lubich.
Pentecostals/Charismatics	ZAC	2	1900	523,778,000	237	usa	C	Vast Renewal in 3 waves experiencing charismatic gifts of the Holy Spirit.
crypto-Christians	CC	2		123,726,000	85	chin	A	All secret believers in Christ unknown to state, society, or hostile religions.
Great Commission Christians	GCC	2		647,821,000	237	usa	C	All church members aware of Christ's Commission and involved in His global mission.
East African Revival	-FC	5	1927	3,000,000	20	rwan	C	*Rwanda Revival. Balokole* (Saved Ones). Pietists. Biennial conventions of 50,000 or so.
Identity Christianity	-FC	5	1925	500,000	10	usa	C	Identification of Anglo-Saxon-European Whites with 10 Lost Tribes of Israel. Violent rhetoric.
World Council of Churches	-FC	4	1948	430,000,000	20	swit	C	*WCC*. HQ Geneva.
World Evangelical Fellowship	-FC	4		150,000,000	50	sing	C	*WEF*. HQ Singapore.
Anglican Consultative Council	A-FC	4		102,000,000	120	brit	C	*ACC*. HQ London. Representatives of the 36 Churches of the worldwide Anglican Communion.
Baptist World Alliance	B-FC	4		52,000,000	171	usa	C	*BWA*. HQ MacLean, Washington, DC.
Congregation for Bishops	b-FC	4		901,000,000	1	holy	C	Vatican dicastery for administering diocese, bishops, new appointments.
Church of God in Christ	c-FC	4		10,000,000	40	usa	C	*CoGiC*. HQ Memphis, TN.
Organization of African Instituted Chs	I-FC	4		40,000,000	50	keny	C	*OAIC*. HQ Nairobi. African Independent Churches. 92 related national councils.
Lutheran World Federation	L-FC	4		80,000,000	150	germ	C	*LWF*. HQ Geneva.
Ch of JC of Latter-day Saints	m-FC	4	1830	11,000,000	116	usa	C	*CJCLdS*. Mormons. Rapid growth worldwide with converts ex Protestant churches.
World Alliance of Reformed Chs	P-FC	4		60,000,000	210	swit	C	*WARC*. HQ Geneva.
Catholic Charismatic Renewal	r-FC	4	1967	120,000,000	233	holy	C	*CCR*. HQ Vatican City. M=ICCRS/ICCRO.
World Convention of Chs of Christ	T-FC	4		10,000,000	130	usa	C	*WCCC*.
Seventh-day Adventists	V-FC	4		25,000,000	200	usa	C	*SDA*, General Conference. HQ Washington D.C.
Jehovah's Christian Witnesses	w-FC	4		13,000,000	219	usa	C	*Jehovah's Witnesses*. JWs. IBRA. Watch Tower. In 219 countries.
World Methodist Council (WMC)	W-FC	4		70,226,000	108	usa	C	*WMC*. HQ Lake Junaluska, NC.
Pentecostal World Conference	Z-FC	4		50,000,000	180	swit	C	*PWC*. No HQ. Triennial conferences of Classical Pentecostal preachers.
World Assemblies of God Fellowship	z-FC	4		43,000,000	140	souk	C	*WAGF*. HQ Seoul, Korea.
Old Ritualists	I-OBe-TC	8	1666	1,821,860	21	russ	B	*Old Believers*. Raskolniki.
Taoists	D	3		2,655,000	8	chin	B	Daoists. China; strong in Taiwan as separate religion. Syncretized with numerous new religions.

Continued opposite

Table 7-5 continued

Name of religion/religionists 1	Pedigree 2	Type 3	Date begun 4	Adherents 5	Ext 6	Ctry 7	Wld 8	Descriptions, background religions of ethnic group, D=denominations present, M=missions. 9
Chinese folk-religionists	F	1		384,807,000	89	japa	B	New-Religionists. A mixture of Confucianism, Taoism, Buddhism, animism, universism.
Confucianists	G	3	BC 500	6,299,000	15	chin	B	Founded by Confucius. Highly organized in South Korea, also Japan, Viet Nam
Hindus	H	1		811,336,000	114	indi	B	Based on the Vedas, now with many varieties.
Divine Light Mission	sFH	3	1965	1,200,000	7	indi	B	Begun in India, 1971 USA (24 ashrams in 24 cities); by 1990, declining to 30,000 in UK, USA.
Saktists	KH	3		25,720,000	2	indi	B	*Shaktas.* Hindu devotees of goddess Devi.
Neo-Hindus	NH	3		17,385,000	20	indi	B	Large variety of new religions based on revivals of Hinduism.
Arya Samaj	sNH	3	1875	1,200,000	30	indi	B	'Society of Honourable Ones'. Reform Hindu body to reconvert Christians to Hinduism.
Transcendental Meditation	sNH	3		4,000,000	30	usa	C	Known as TM, or Spiritual Regeneration Movement. In USA, UK (100,000 practicing), India.
Reform Hindus	RH	3		4,460,000	20	indi	B	Arya Samaj, et alia. Modern attempts to revitalize Hindus and win back converts.
Swaminarayans	sRH	3	1801	5,000,000	30	indi	B	In India, UK, Kenya, USA. HQ Gujarat. F= Sahajananda Swami (1781-1830).
Ananda Marga	sH	3	1955	2,000,000	7	indi	B	Self-development Hindu Yoga. F= Anandamuotiji. Also in Europe, USA.
Hare Krishna	sH	10	1965	800,000	50	indi	B	*ISKCON. International Society for Krishna Consciousness.* In many countries east and west.
Shaivites	SH	2		216,260,000	10	indi	B	Shaivas, devotees of god Shiva.
Vaishnavites	VH	2		549,583,000	30	indi	B	Sri Vaishnavas, devotees of god Vishnu, by bhakti (devotion).
Jews	J	3		14,434,000	134	isra	B	Practitioners of Judaism in 5 main branches. Centered in Israel, USA, Argentina.
Ashkenazis	AJ	3		11,080,000	70	isra	B	Yiddiah-speaking Judaism. From Germany; Poland, Russia, Ukraine.
Oriental Jews	EJ	3		2,378,000	20	isra	B	Jews from diaspora in eastern countries, now mostly in Israel.
Conservative Jews	sOJ	3	1854	2,000,000	6	isra	B	*Masorati.* Begun in Germany; USA 1900; opposing Reform Judaism's neglect of Halakhah.
Reform Jews	RJ	3	c1860	1,100,000	30	germ	C	Liberal or Progressive Judaism. USA (300,000 families), UK, Argentina, Brazil, Australia, NZ.
Sefardis	SJ	9		952,000	50	arge	C	Main centers: Latin America, USA, Israel, Spain, Portugal, Balkans.
Sikhs	K	3	c1500	23,258,000	34	indi	B	Monotheistic revelation to F=Guru Nanak (1469-1539). HQ Amiritsar.
Baha'is	L	3	1863	7,106,000	218	iran	A	Acceptance of all religions under mission of Bahaiullah. In all countries.
Muslims	M	1		1,188,243,000	204	paki	A	Islam (active submission to the will of Allah).
Shias	HM	2		170,100,000	60	iran	A	*Shiites.* Followers of Ali, cousin of Mohammed. In Iran, Iraq, Lebanon, India, Pakistan.
Ithna-Asharis	AHM	2	680	136,655,000	10	iran	A	'Twelvers'. Imamis.
Ismailis	IHM	3	909	23,772,000	120	indi	B	'Seveners', Khojas. Shia sect with Aga Khan IV as its imam.
Alawites	LHM	3	c950	1,631,000	50	syri	B	*Nusayris.* A Shiite group in Syria.
Zaydis	ZHM	3		8,042,000	40	yeme	A	Fiver Shiites. Shia school of law, in Yemen.
Sunnis	SM	2		1,002,543,000	180	paki	A	Main body of Islam.
Hanbalites	BSM	3	850	2,325,000	30	saud	B	School of law officially accepted in Saudi Arabia.
Hanafites	HSM	2	c750	531,418,000	90	turk	A	School of law. In India, Pakistan, Turkey, Afghanistan, Central Asia, Lower Egypt.
Malikites	MSM	2	c790	221,900,000	90	nige	B	School of law. In North, West, and Central Africa, Upper Egypt.
Shafiites	SSM	2	810	239,900,000	80	malb	A	School of Islamic law. Popular in Southeast Asia, East Africa, southern Arabia.
Wahhabites	WSM	3	c1780	7,000,000	40	saud	B	Wahhabis follow the Hanbali school of Islamic law.
Sufis	UM	2	c1150	237,400,000	100	moro	A	Mass movements as Sufi orders/brotherhoods spread from Morocco to Indonesia.
Badawiya	sUM	3	c1240	1,000,000	20	egyp	B	Major Sufi order in Egypt, centered in Tanta; attracts one million pilgrims every autumn.
Madariya	sUM	3	c1410	4,000,000	25	indi	B	Mostly in north India but also in Nepal and widespread across South Asia.
Naqshabandiya	sUM	2	c1200	50,000,000	30	uzbe	A	Great Sufi order, strong in Central Asia, India, Western Europe.
Qadiriya	sUM	3	c1120	20,000,000	50	syri	B	Oldest Sufi order, widespread in 50 countries from Senegal to Malaysia. Miracles claimed.
Islamic schismatics	XM	3		14,950,000	160	iraq	A	A large number of splits or secessions from major schools of Islamic law.
Ahmadis	AXM	3		7,950,000	70	paki	A	*Ahmadiyah.* Islamic messianic movement (F=Mirza Ghulam Ahmad).
Black Muslims	BXM	3		1,650,000	10	usa	C	*Nation of Islam.* F=Elijah Mohammed. Two rival factions.
Druzes	DXM	9	c1050	834,000	10	pale	B	Quasi-Muslims also in Lebanon, Syria, Jordan, Israel. Split ex Ismailis.
Karijites	KXM	3		1,636,000	10	saud	A	Early Muslim sect (7th-10th centuries), strictly puritanical; now termed Ibadites.
Muslim Brotherhood	sNXM	3	1928	1,000,000	30	egyp	B	*Ikhwan al-Muslimin.* 30 countries (Egypt 500,000). Fundamentalist, puritan, anti-Christian.
New-Religionists	N	1		102,356,000	60	japa	B	Recent new non-Christian religions, many syncretizing Christianity with other religions.
New-Agers	sFN	3	c1870	12,000,000	41	usa	C	Self-religiosity in hundreds of diverse forms. Bookshops, spiritual therapy centers, training.
Church of World Messianity	sNN	9	1934	700,000	2	japa	B	*Sekai Kyuseikyo.* Ex Omoto.
Jeungsando	sNN	9	1911	767,000	1	souk	B	Total Transformation. Folk religion seeking and believing total change-transformation.
Nichiren Shoshu	sNN	3	1930	1,000,000	50	japa	B	True Nichiren School. International, this-worldly appeal. 1992, Soka Gakkai splits off.
Oomoto	sNN	3	1892	1,500,000	15	japa	A	'Great Origin' Omotokyo. F=peasant woman, Deguchi Nao. Extensive use of mass media.
Reiyukai Kyodan	sNN	3	1922	3,000,000	10	japa	B	'Society of Companions of the Spirits'. Rooted in Nichirenshu, family values. F=Kubo Kakutaro.
Rissho Koseikai	sNN	3	1938	5,000,000	40	japa	B	'Society for Establishing Righteousness and Harmony'. HQ Tokyo. Goal: perfect Buddhahood.
Segyejunggyo	sNN	9	1957	621,000	1	souk	B	*World True Religion*; folk religion seeking world peace, realization of human ideals (Utopia).
Seicho-no-Ie	sNN	3	1930	3,000,000	2	japa	B	'House of Growth'. Perfection of all things, denial of evil. Literature, lectures.
Soka Gakkai	sNN	3	1930	18,000,000	115	japa	B	1975 SG International; 1990 Lay split ex Nichiren Shoshu. Shedding world conversion aims.
Izumo-taishakyo	qN	3	1873	2,261,000	20	japa	B	One of largest Shinko Shukyo (New Religions). Based on Shinto. HQ Taisha, Izumo shrine
Agonshu	sN	10	1978	580,000	10	japa	A	Veneration of Buddhist Agama Sutras. F=Kiriyama Seiyu. Annual mass fire ceremony, Kyoto.
Gedatsukai	sN	10	1929	500,000	10	japa	B	Shingon-derived New Religion. Honor to rising Sun each day. HQ Tokyo.
Hommon Butsuryu	sN	10	1857	500,000	2	japa	B	Lay movement in Kyoto. Ex Buddhism. Main feature: Lotus Sutra.
Jilliwhoi	SN	3	1925	4,630,000	1	souk	B	*Daisoon Jilliwhoi* (Great & Genuine Truth Assembly).
Cao Dai	sSN	3	1926	3,200,000	50	viet	B	*Dai Dao Tam Ky Pho Do* (Great Way of the 3 Epochs of Salvation). Catholicism syncretized.
Church of Perfect Liberty	sSN	3	1946	2,000,000	10	japa	B	*PL Kyodan.* Liturgical, rituals, monotheistic. Life is art, sports, clubs.
Hoa Hao	sSN	3	1939	2,050,000	10	viet	B	*Buo Son Ky Hong.* Millennialist. F=Huynh Phu So, regarded as the Emergent Buddha.
I Kuan Tao	sSN	3	1928	3,000,000	30	taiw	C	*Yi Guan Dao. Unity.* Unity Way. Begun in China. Buddhism, Taoism, Christian elements.
Ilkwando	sSN	9	1948	844,000	1	souk	B	*Kukje-Dodug Hyophwoi-Ilkwando* (Unified Truth Principle); claiming unity of Buddhism, Taoism.
Won	sSN	9	1916	550,000	10	souk	B	*Won Bulgyo.* Based on modern Buddhism, Confucianism, Taoism, Chondogyo, Christianity.
Nonreligious	Q	1		768,159,000	236	chin	B	Secularists, materialists, agnostics, with no religion but not militantly antireligious.
Shintoists	S	3		2,762,000	8	japa	B	Shinto='The Way of the Gods'. 80,000 shrines in Japan
Shrine Shintoists	HS	2	1946	62,000,000	40	japa	B	*Jinja Honcho*, Jinja Shinto. 26,000 priests, 77,000 shrines.
Sect Shintoists	TS	3	1882	6,000,000	20	japa	B	*Shuha.* Shinto, Kyoha Shinto. 13 Sects. No shrines.
Konko-kyo	sTS	9	1859	683,000	2	japa	B	'Religion of Golden Light'. F=Kawate Bunjiro. (1814-1883), now venerated.
Kurozumi-kyo	sTS	9	1814	574,000	2	japa	B	Faith healing, F=Kurozumi Munetada (1780-1850). Possession by sun goddess Amaterasu.
Mitake-kyo	sTS	3		1,648,000	2	japa	B	Mountain-worship. Shinto sect focused on Mount Ontake, a major religious center.
New Sect Shintoists	sTS	3		2,000,000	30	japa	B	13 independent sects after shrines banned.
Tai (Shinto Honkyoku)	sTS	3		1,091,000	2	japa	B	*Shintokyo.*
Tenrikyo	sTS	3	1838	3,000,000	10	japa	B	*Religion of Heavenly Wisdom.* Faith-healing.17,000 churches, 20,000 mission stations.
Ethnoreligionists	T	1		228,367,000	142	nige	B	Tribalists. Tribal religionists, with local religions open only to members of tribe or ethnopeople.
Animists	AT	2		216,161,000	130	beni	B	Belief in spiritual beings, mountains, rocks, trees, rivers.
Ahir ethnoreligionists	PAT	10		647,000	1	indi	A	Bhils. In Maharashtra and Gujarat States. Animists/polytheists 79%, Hindus 20%.
Antaisaka ethnoreligionists	AT	10		679,000	1	mada	B	Southeast coastal strip. Animists 72%, Baha'is 0.1%. D=RCC(D-Farafangana). M=CM.
Antandroy ethnoreligionists	AT	10		563,000	1	mada	B	Extreme south coast of island and inland. Animists 80%. D=RCC(D-Fort-Dauphin). M=CM.
Bagri ethnoreligionists	AT	3		1,865,000	1	indi	A	In Punjab, Rajasthan, Pakistan. Nomads across India-Pakistan borders. Animists 99%.
Bai ethnoreligionists	PAT	3		1,158,000	2	chin	A	Yunnan, Sichuan, Guizhou. Polytheists 65%, Buddhists 30%. D=TSPM,RCC. M=7.
Bambara ethnoreligionists	AT	10		669,000	3	mali	B	Maliki Muslims 85%, animists 13%. D=RCC(3 Dioceses),EEPM,ECEM,AoG,SDA. M=10.
Bara ethnoreligionists	AT	10		501,000	1	mada	B	Large inland area in south of island. Animists 50%. D=RCC(3 Dioceses). M=CM,MSF,MS.
Baule ethnoreligionists	AT	10		786,000	1	ivor	B	Literates 10%. Animists 44%, Muslims 3%. D=RCC(D-Bouake),EPEC,EPC,AoG,AICs. M=7
Betsimisaraka ethnoreligionists	AT	3		1,584,000	1	mada	B	Revival center. Animists 77%. D=RCC(2 Dioceses). Eglise du Reveil,FMTA,MET,AICs. M=3.
Bhilala ethnoreligionists	AT	10		644,000	1	indi	A	Bhils. In Gujarat, Madhya Pradesh, Maharashtra, Karnataka, Rajasthan. Animists 99%.
Black Tai ethnoreligionists	AT	10		711,000	3	viet	A	North Viet Nam. Animists 95%. D=RCC,ECVN,SDA. M=CMA,UWM,SIL. R=FEBC.
Bodo ethnoreligionists	HAT	10		740,000	1	indi	B	Hinduized animists 93%. D=Goalpara Boro Baptist Ch,North Bank Baptists,RCC,CNI,ICI. M=7.
Central Bhil ethnoreligionists	AT	3		4,449,000	1	indi	A	Polytheists/animists 95%. D=RCC(D-Ajmer-Jaipur),CNI(D-Jabalpur),DNC,MCSA,CMA,M=11.
Central Gond ethnoreligionists	PAT	3		1,721,000	1	indi	B	Mainly in MP. Hindus 70%, animists 30%. D=Mennonites,Methodists,MPELC. M=12.
Central Shona ethnoreligionists	AT	10		886,000	2	zimb	C	Animists 33%. D=RCC,ACZ/CPCA,AACJM,JWs,AFMSA,GGCZ,SDA,FGC,DRC,AICs. M=15.
Chinese Mongolian ethnoreligionists	ST	3		1,368,000	1	chin	A	Nonreligious 50%, shamanists 40%, Lamaists 10%. D=RCC,house churches. M=7.

Continued overleaf

Table 7-5 concluded

Name of religion/religionists 1	*Pedigree* 2	*Type* 3	*Date begun* 4	*Adherents* 5	*Ext* 6	*Ctry* 7	*Wld* 8	*Descriptions, background religions of ethnic group, D=denominations present, M=missions.* 9
Chwabo ethnoreligionists	AT	10		757,000	1	moza	B	Around Quelimane. Animists 76%, Muslims 7%. D=RCC,SDA. M=UBS.
Dan ethnoreligionists	AT	10		677,000	2	ivor	B	Animists 62%, Muslims 10%. D=RCC(D-Daloa),UEESO. M=SIL,SMA,MB,SIM,FMB.
Eastern Bhil ethnoreligionists	PAT	3		2,676,000	1	indi	A	Polytheists 95%. D=CMA,CNI,RCC. M=IEM,CGMM,BFI,UPM,YWAM.
Eastern Meo ethnoreligionists	PAT	3		1,473,000	1	chin	B	Northeast Yunnan, Guizhou, Guangxi; also Thailand, Viet Nam. Polytheists 94%. D=Chinese Ch.
Eastern Nuer ethnoreligionists	AT	10		856,000	2	suda	B	Nomadic animists 79%, highly resistant to Islam. D=RCC(D-Malakal),CCUN,COC,ECMY.
Eastern Yi ethnoreligionists	PAT	10		861,000	1	chin	A	Southeastern Yi. Guizhou, Weining Autonomous Region. Polytheists 98%. D=TSPM,RCC.
Fon ethnoreligionists	AT	3		1,015,000	74	beni	B	Animists 62%(260 fetish monasteries), Muslims 5%. D=RCC(D-Abomey),EPMB,AoG. M=20.
Gideo ethnoreligionists	AT	10		570,000	1	ethi	B	Animists 69%, Muslims 1%. D=ECMY,WLEC,FGBC,Light of Life Ch,AIC. M=10.
Gormati ethnoreligionists	HAT	3		2,161,000	1	indi	B	AP,MP,HP,TN, 5 other States. Hindus/polytheists 99%. D=20. M=30.
Gurenne ethnoreligionists	AT	10		593,000	2	ghan	B	Animists 83%, Muslims 5%. D=AoG,GBC,RCC(D-Navrongo-Bolgatanga), 15 others. M=20.
Hani ethnoreligionists	PAT	3		1,495,000	3	chin	A	Yunnan, Viet Nam, Laos, Burma. Polytheists (animists, ancestor veneration) 95%. D=TSPM.
Highland Nung ethnoreligionists	PAT	10		958,000	1	viet	A	Closely related to Tho and Southern Zhuang. Polytheists 98%(ancestor worship).
Ho ethnoreligionists	AT	10		783,000	1	indi	A	Animists 69%, Hindus 30%. D=RCC(D-Jamshedpur),CNI. M=SJ,IBT,OFUCPM,IEM,USPG.
Hutu ethnoreligionists	AT	10		846,000	2	rwan	C	Animists 8%, Muslims 8%. D=RCC(6 Dioceses),AC/EAR,SDA,ADEEP,EPR,UEBR. M=14.
Karanga ethnoreligionists	AT	10		587,000	4	zimb	C	Animists 30%. D=RCC(D-Gwelo),DRC,ACZ,ZCC,ELCZ, AICs. M=20.
Khalkha Mongol shamanists	ST	10		507,000	1	mong	A	Lamaists 30%, shamanists 30%, nonreligious 28% atheists 10%, Muslims 1%. M=115 a
Khandeshi ethnoreligionists	AT	3		1,162,000	1	indi	A	Maharashtra, Gujarat. Dialects: Ahirani, Dangri, Kunbi, Rangari. Animists 70%, Hindus 30%.
Khasi ethnoreligionists	AT	10		546,000	1	indi	B	Animists 50%. D=RCC(D-Silchar),ICFG,CNI(D-Assam),PCNEI. M=PCW,LBI,BFI,TEAM,FMPB.
Khmu ethnoreligionists	AT	10		714,000	3	laos	A	Animists 94%. D=RCC(many catechumens),LEF. M=CMA,ACCM,APM,OMI,MEP. R=FEBC.
Korean shamanists	ST	3		1,619,000	8	chin	B	Shamanists 55%, Mahayana Buddhists 35%. D=TSPM,RCC. M=25 agencies from S. Korea.
Kui ethnoreligionists	AT	10		584,000	1	indi	A	Orissa. Hindus 54%, animists 45%. D=RCC(M-Cuttack), SDA,Baptists,CNI. M=15.
Kuruba ethnoreligionists	AT	10		708,000	1	indi	A	Animists 80%, Hindus 19%. D=Gospel in Action,Brethren,RCC,CSI,UELCI. M=IEM,IBT,QCI.
Li ethnoreligionists	PAT	3		1,235,000	1	chin	A	Tropical mountains in Hainan. Polytheists (animists) 100%. D=TSPM. M=5.
Lomwe ethnoreligionists	AT	10		857,000	2	moza	B	Zambezia Province. Animists 65%, Muslims 7%. D=RCC,ICFG,MCSA,SDA,ECM. M=12.
Maasai ethnoreligionists	AT	10		557,000	1	keny	B	Kajiado, Narok, Tanzania. Animists 55%. D=RCC,EFMK,CPK,LCK,AIC,PCEA,BCC. M=18. M=1.
Maitili ethnoreligionists	HAT	3		1,575,000	1	indi	A	Tirahutia. In Bihar, MP, WB; Nepal. Educated high-caste Hindus 95%. D=RCC,CNI. M=10.
Makua ethnoreligionists	AT	3		1,329,000	4	moza	B	Animists 59%, Muslims 18%. D=RCC(STET),AEC,JWs. M=30.
Makuana ethnoreligionists	AT	3		1,775,000	1	moza	B	Nampula, south of Meeto area. Animists 59%, Muslims 20%. D=RCC.
Malayic Dayak ethnoreligionists	AT	10		573,000	1	indo	B	Kalimantan. West central, to Delang in south. Animists 80%. D=NTM.
Manchu shamanists	ST	3		2,188,000	1	chin	B	500 Manchu speakers left. Folk-religionists 70%, shamanists 20%, Buddhists 10%. D=TSPM.
Mende ethnoreligionists	AT	10		542,000	7	sier	B	Lingua franca. Animists 42%, Muslims 42%. D=UMC,MCSL,WAMC,SLC, 15 others. M=20.
Merina ethnoreligionists	AT	10		556,000	1	mada	C	Animists 12%, Muslims 1%, Baha'is 0.2%. D=70% Protestants,RCC,AICs. M=20.
Mina ethnoreligionists	AT	3		1,086,000	1	indi	A	Aborigines in Rajasthan. Animists 98%(with Hindu elements). M=Tribal Mission,CSI,CCCI,EHC.
Mon ethnoreligionists	AT	10		792,000	4	myan	A	Animists 75%, Buddhists 20%. D=Ch of Christ,BBC(Mon Baptist Churches Union). M=5.
Mossi ethnoreligionists	AT	3		1,203,000	4	burk	B	Animists 16%, Muslims 61%(Maliki Sunnis; many converts on arrival in cities). D=16. M=25.
Muong ethnoreligionists	AT	3		1,058,000	2	viet	A	Mostly in mountains of north Viet Nam; also Banmethuot in south. Animists 94%. D=RCC.
Ndebele ethnoreligionists	AT	10		559,000	2	zimb	B	Animists 36%. D=RCC,AOC,ACZ,CCNZ,ELCZ,AMCZ,BCZ,BiCC,CMCCA, & 20 others. M=30.
North Korean shamanists	ST	3		2,952,000	12	nork	B	Nonreligious 55%, atheists 16%, New-Religionists 13%, shamanists 12%, Buddhists 1.5%. D=6.
Northern Meo ethnoreligionists	PAT	10		828,000	1	chin	A	West Hunan. Agriculturalists. Polytheists 96%. D=Chinese Church,RCC,TSPM. M=3.
Northern Tung ethnoreligionists	PAT	3		2,240,000	1	chin	A	Guizhou. Polytheists(animists) 80%, Buddhists 20%. D=RCC,TSPM. M=IMB, SIL, TELL, FEBC.
Northern Yi ethnoreligionists	PAT	3		1,582,000	5	chin	A	Northern Nosu. Yunnan, Laos, Viet Nam. Polytheists(animists) 90%, Buddhists 5%. D=2. M=22.
Northern Zhuang ethnoreligionists	PAT	3		10,237,000	2	chin	A	Polytheists 80%, Buddhists 19%. D=TSPM(300 churches),RCC,TJC. M=25.
Punu ethnoreligionists	PAT	10		555,000	1	chin	A	Guangxi. Polytheists (animists) 99%, including ancestor worship.
Puyi ethnoreligionists	PAT	3		2,269,000	1	chin	A	Guizhou, Yunnan. Written. 40 dialects. Polytheists 80%, Buddhists 10%, Taoists 8%. D=1. M=12.
Sakalava ethnoreligionists	AT	10		574,000	2	mada	B	Strongest Muslim presence among Malagasy. Animists 59%, Muslims 7.5%. D=RCC. M=14.
Santal ethnoreligionists	AT	3		1,482,000	3	indi	B	Hindus 78%, animists 21%. D=RCC, (3 dioceses)CNI,NELC,BOBBC,MCSA. M=25.
Sena ethnoreligionists	AT	3		1,053,000	3	moza	B	Animists 60%, Muslims 1%. D=RCC, (D-Beira, Quelimane), CNC,CB,CC,AoG,ICFG. M=5.
Sgaw Karen ethnoreligionists	AT	3		1,021,000	4	myan	B	Animists 49%, Baha'is. D=BBC(Karen Bap Conv),RCC,CPB,SSKBC,AoG,NAC,SDA. M=10.
South Korean shamanists	ST	3		18,082,000	8	souk	B	Shamanists 16%, Buddhists 15%, New-Religionists 15%, Confucianists 11%. D=100. M=300.
Southern Bhil ethnoreligionists	PAT	3		1,260,000	1	indi	A	Polytheists 95%. D=CMA,MCSA,CNI,RCC,Pentecostals. M=IEM,COUNT,CGMM,BFI,UPM,WVI.
Southern Maninka ethnoreligionists	AT	3		1,127,000	1	guin	A	Also in Guinea Bissau, Liberia. Animists 59%, Muslims 39%. D=RCC,EEP. M=10.
Southern Senufo ethnoreligionists	AT	10		622,000	1	ivor	B	Animists 65%, Muslims 30%. D=RCC(D-Korhogo,D-Katiola),ANBC,EPC. M=WEC,CBFMS,BGC.
Southern Yi ethnoreligionists	PAT	10		835,000	1	chin	A	Eastern Yi, Southern Yi. Black Yi. Yunnan, Guizhou, Sichuan. Polytheists 95%. D=RCC,TSPM.
Southern Zhuang ethnoreligionists	PAT	3		4,009,000	1	chin	A	Southwest Guangxi. Polytheists 90%, some Buddhists. D=TSPM,RCC. M=CSI,YWAM,SIL.
Sukuma ethnoreligionists	AT	3		1,047,000	1	tanz	B	Animists 33%, Muslims 30%. D=RCC,AIC,SDA,CPT,BCT,PCSAT,CWC,KOAB. AICs. M=20.
Tanala ethnoreligionists	AT	10		504,000	1	mada	B	East of Betsileo. Animists 80%. D=RCC(M-Fianarantsoa),ERSM, and other AICs. M=SJ.
Tho ethnoreligionists	PAT	3		2,246,000	4	viet	A	In China, Laos, USA, France. Polytheists 99%. D=RCC,ECVN. M=CMA,SIL. R=FEBC.
Tripuri ethnoreligionists	HAT	10		673,000	2	indi	A	In Assam. Hinduized animists 92%, Muslims 6.5%. D=RCC(D-Silchar),PCNEI. M=10.
Tsimihety ethnoreligionists	AT	10		950,000	1	mada	B	Animists 85%. D=RCC(3 Dioceses),ERSM,FMTA, and other AICs. M=CSSp,OFMCap,FMB.
Tsonga ethnoreligionists	AT	10		634,000	5	soua	C	In Mozambique. Animists 30%, Muslims, Baha'is. D=RCC,TPC,ZCACSA,DRC, AICs. M=12.
Tswa ethnoreligionists	AT	10		978,000	2	moza	B	Animists 79%. D=UCCSA(ICUM),IMU,RCC,IML,CPSA,AICs. M=UCBWM,FMC,UMC,USPG.
Tujia ethnoreligionists	PAT	3		6,327,000	1	chin	A	Northwest Hunan. Unwritten language. Polytheists/animists 99%. D=TSPM,RCC. R=TWR.
Venda ethnoreligionists	AT	10		573,000	3	soua	B	Animists 65%. D=DRCA,AoG,CPSA,WC,RCC,ABC,CBCSA,ZCC,other AICs. M=15.
Wagdi ethnoreligionists	PAT	3		1,692,000	1	indi	A	Udaipur, Rajasthan, Gujarat. Bhils. Second language Hindi. Animists/polytheists 99%.
Walamo ethnoreligionists	AT	3		1,007,000	2	ethi	B	Animists 35%. D=WLEC(strong),ECMY(20%), EOC,FGBC,RCC,SDA,AICs. M=12.
Wallega ethnoreligionists	AT	10		902,000	2	ethi	B	Muslims 40%, animists 25% D=30%: EOC(D-Wallega),BECE,ECMY,SDA. M=SIM,WVI,FMB.
West Makua ethnoreligionists	AT	10		642,000	2	moza	B	Niassa Province. Animists 60%, Muslims 20%. D=CPSA,RCC.
Western Meo ethnoreligionists	AT	3		3,492,000	1	chin	B	Guizhou, Guangxi, Sichuan, Yunnan; Viet Nam, Laos. Polytheists 94%. D=6. M=20.
White Karen ethnoreligionists	AT	10		996,000	3	myan	B	Animists 65%, some Baha'is. D=BBC,SSKBMS,CPB(D-Yangon),AoG,SDA,NAC. M=10.
Yao ethnoreligionists	PAT	3		2,415,000	3	chin	A	53% speak Yao. Polytheists/animists(ancestor-worship) 99%. D=RCC,TSPM,TJC. M=10.
Yoruba ethnoreligionists	AT	10		856,000	20	nige	B	Muslims 37%, animists 4%. D=CPN,RCC,CAC,ESOCS,NCF,NBC, & 200 others. M=150.
Zezuru ethnoreligionists	AT	10		580,000	6	zimb	C	Animists 28%. D=RCC,AACJM,ACZ/CPCA,SDA,SA,DRC,BCZ,MCZ,UMC,AICs. M=120.
Spiritists	U	3		62,334,000	55	braz	C	Very strong in Brazil: Umbanda, Macumba, Candomblé. Many Catholics belong.
Afro-American spiritists	AU	3		5,649,000	20	jama	C	Wide range of religions across Caribbean and Latin America. Mostly Blacks.
Umbanda	sBU	3	c1920	20,000,000	22	braz	C	Afro-American religion, many White followers. Displacing Candomblé and Macumba.
High Spiritists	HU	3		3,750,000	30	fran	C	Kardecism and other European non-Christian forms without African features.
Jains	V	3	BC 550	4,218,000	10	indi	B	Ex Brahmanic Hinduism. 98% in Mysore and Gujarat. Monasteries.
Quasireligionists	QY	2		60,000,000	20	fran	C	Most members (e.g. Freemasons) belong also to mainline religions listed here.
Freemasons	sQY	3	1714	5,900,000	37	brit	C	Largest worldwide secret society. Members men only. In USA, UK, France.
Zoroastrians	Z	3	BC 1000	2,544,000	24	iran	A	*Parsis.* Ancient monotheist religion of Persia. Iran 1,903,000, Afghanistan 304,000, India 100,000.
other religions over 500,000	.			50,000,000				Total other distinct religions with over 500,000 adherents each: around 50.
other religions under 500,000	.			20,000,000				Total distinct religions with under 500,000 each: around 10,000.
doubly-counted				-13,527,299,000				Persons counted under 2, 3, or more overlapping religion levels above.
Global religionists	–	–		5,137,000,000	238			Adherents of the world's 10,000 or so different religions.
Global nonreligionists	Q,a	–		919,933,000	230			Persons with no religion, indifferent to religion, also persons militantly anti-religious (atheists).
Global population	Gpop	–		6,055,000,000	238			Total population of world in mid-2000.

Part 8

ETHNOSPHERE

Cultures of the world, with 12,600 people profiles

The Lord spoke to Moses: Take a census of the people of Israel. Number the whole community by families. Make a detailed list of them by their tribal hosts.
—Numbers 1:1-2, Revised Standard Version and New English Bible

Before me was a great multitude that no one could count, from every nation, tribe, people and language.
—Revelation 7:9, New International Version

Part 8 enumerates 12,600 ethnolinguistic peoples or cultures and describes and measures them by means of a panel of 38 different instruments.

Cultures of the world, with 12,600 people profiles

1. A WORLD ETHNOCULTURAL CLASSIFICATION

This Encyclopedia presents an ethnolinguistic descriptive enumeration of each country's (1) total population, and (2) total of affiliated Christians, throughout the 20th century. In this Part the methodology is explained and the classification itself is given with its codes and full descriptive data on all peoples arranged by country.

This enumeration is built on the taxonomy and classification of race, races, ethnicity, cultures, peoples, families, with physical/geographical/genetic characteristics as set out in *The new Encyclopedia Britanica*, 15th edition, 1975-2001 versions. These annually updated versions contain lengthy expositions, in 1975 entitled 'Races of Mankind', 10 pages with photographs of faces within 16 geographical races and local races. In 2000, the major articles had become 'Human Evolution' (52 pages), 'Modern Human Populations' (11 pages), and 'The Races of Mankind' (6 pages) with scores of new terms and references listed in the volumes' main Index. The 5–page text below, and Tables 8–1 and 8–2, are all built on this mass of new data, new understandings, and new concepts.

The inclusion of this analysis by races, peoples, tribes, and cultures is an affirmation of the centrality of indigenous cultures to local expressions of Christianity, of the right to exist of minority tribes and peoples, of their autonomy in their own areas, of their importance from the Christian standpoint vis-a-vis the world's dominant peoples and cultures, and of the need to reduce the imperialistic influence of these latter (especially Western culture) in non-Western local churches and lands. It is also an affirmation of the necessity to view people, not primarily as nationals of a given country, but primarily as members of the natural homogeneous units they belong to, through which they may the most effectively be described.

The Bible frequently draws attention to the complex mosaic of peoples who compose the human race. In the Great Commission, the command of Christ is to 'Go and disciple all peoples' (*panta ta ethne*, Matthew 28:19). In attempting to depict this vast diversity of peoples, the Book of Revelation provides descriptive listings at 7 points, each time of 4 entities, as follows (using the RSV text):
1. every tribe and tongue and people and nation (Revelation 5:9);
2. every nation, all tribes and peoples and tongues (7:9);
3. many peoples and nations and tongues and kings (10:11);
4. the peoples and tribes and tongues and nations (11:9);
5. every tribe and people and tongue and nation (13:7);
6. every nation and tribe and tongue and people (14:6);
7. peoples and multitudes and nations and tongues (17:15).

In these 7 listings, 5 points can be noted: (a) 3 of the 4 entities occur in all 7 lists, namely 'nation' (an ethnic term), 'people' (a cultural term), and 'tongue' (a linguistic term); (b) another term, 'tribe' (an ethnocultural term, often with connotations of color or skin pigmentation) occurs in 5 of the lists; (c) another, 'multitudes' illustrates the demographic aspect; (d) a last term, 'kings' (here used to personify 'kingdoms'), invokes the ideas of nationality, citizenship, subject status, and the like; and (e) in other English versions than the RSV, other synonyms emerge such as 'race' for 'nation' in 10:11 (Good News Bible), 'kindred' for 'tribe' (5:9, AV/KJV), 'language' for 'tongue', et alia. The Bible can thus be said to be fully aware of the vast ethnolinguistic diversity of the world and of its importance for the Christian world mission.

From a descriptive or anthropological point of view, therefore, a human population (or an individual) has 6 related but distinct characteristics: race, color, ethnic origin, nationality, culture, and language. Race and color are inherited (passed from generation to generation), whereas culture and language are learned; and ethnic origin is a less clearly-defined characteristic referring to the main name by which a people is usually known. Ethnic groups are often grouped by anthropologists into primary ethnic culture areas. The sixth term, nationality (citizenship), may be inherited or acquired, and unlike the other 5 characteristics may be changed instantaneously and with ease. Of the 5 which cannot be changed, race and language are the clearest-defined concepts, and their worldwide manifestations have been classified by biologists and linguists respectively as follows.

An identity code
This world ethnocultural ethnolinguistic classification can be seen to give a unique code to every segment of population anywhere in the world. Adding geopolitical codes, a population's code identifies it by ethnic group, language, country, continent, region, province, city, religion, megabloc, denomination, and the whole range of ecclesiastico-cultural descriptors.

The 2 main descriptors, or race and language, will now each be further investigated.

Race
From the biological or purely physical or genetic or serological (blood-group) point of view, race (or physical type) is a biological concept referring to the taxonomic (classificatory) unit immediately below the species. Thus, the human race today consists of a single surviving species, Homo Sapiens, and 5 surviving subspecies or races or racial stocks (many others having long become extinct): Australoid, Capoid, Caucasoid, Mongoloid and Negroid. Between these are various hybrid races, known as clines (Negroid-Caucasoid, Mongoloid-Caucasoid, etc). Race covers such physical features as skin color, stature, blood group, head shape and hair type. From the point of view of skin color, all can be given a stylized label each in order to permit approximate numerical analysis. For the 5 races, these are, respectively, (1) Grey (a stylized color combining the concepts 'early', 'aboriginal', non-White, non-Black, non-Yellow), (2) also Grey, (3) White, (4) Yellow, (5) Black. Government censuses often enumerate populations in this way, especially in the use of White and Black. In Portuguese, in the 1960 and 1970 censuses of Mozambique, Chinese persons were classified as 'Yellows', defined there as persons with 4 Yellow grandparents; and in the Angola censuses, there were 'Whites' (Brancos), 'Blacks', (Pretos), etc. In Spanish, the 1903 census of the Philippines enumerated people as Moreno (Brown), Amarillo (Yellow), Blanco (White), Negro (Black), etc. In this classification, in addition, certain geographical races are labeled Tan, Brown, Red. Tan refers to ochre- or olive- or yellow-brown-or light-brown-skinned peoples. Red is a term traditionally in use for American Indians. The result of all these typologies is a series of possible classifications which vary considerably from scholar to scholar but which approximate to the one given here as Table 8-1 entitled PEOPLES OF THE WORLD, especially in the first and third capital letters of each people's coded name.

Where statistics of race are to be gathered, government census and allied bureau often define their terms with great precision. In the USA, employment regulations define the term 'Indian' exactly as (a) members of any recognized Indian tribe now under Federal jurisdiction, (b) descendants of any such members residing within the present boundaries of any Indian reservation, (c) all others of one-half or more of Indian blood of tribes indigenous to the United States, (d) Eskimos and other Aboriginal people of Alaska, and (e) persons of at least one-quarter degree Indian ancestry. In Viet Nam, 'Chinese' are defined as anyone with a Chinese ancestor 5 generations back.

An important extension of race is the concept of geographical race, as popularized and described by *The new Encyclopaedia Britannica* (1975, 2000). (In the 2000 edition the article is virtually unchanged but the actual term has been shortened to 'geographic race'). Geographical race is defined as one of the 13 broad, geographically-delimited races of mankind, a collection of human populations, usually rather similar physically, delimited by some natural boundary, such as an ocean, and tending to have similar heredity, skin color, hair type, language, and the like. Table 8–1 follows these guidelines and in fact utilizes the same nomenclature for the major races.

An important caution needs to be given here. The concept of different races is regarded by many scientists as outdated, for the reasons that the multiple origins of man have not been proven, population movements with resulting interbreeding have been continuous since the origin of man, and that populations today grade into each other to such an extent that no pure stocks exist. There is no such thing as a 'pure' race; instead, there exist almost imperceptible gradations of genetic character from one group of people to the next. For these purposes this classification has some value, it being understood that none of the 5 races and 7 colors are original or pure or isolated stocks and that all overlap to a greater or lesser extent.

Language
In this Encyclopedia, language as a distinct entity separate from race, culture, and ethnicity is described and classified in Part 9 "LinguaMetrics". What follows in the paragraphs below is a discussion of language as a distinct part of the ethnolinguistic definition of peoples and cultures.

Language is the principal means of communicating culture (a word which itself commonly embraces the entire way of life of a people). From the linguistic point of view, the world's 13,000 distinct living languages (excluding dead languages and those no longer spoken) as shown in the classification can be classified into 10-16 major linguistic families (or 24 major phyla or groupings or superstocks, or from 40-100 families according to some classifications), with several minor ones consisting each of one language isolate. Languages are usually classified in the first instance genetically (evolution from a common ancestral language), in some cases with the superimposing of further classification typologically (grammatical or lexical similarities in language structure). The total of languages according to different scholars varies widely, and is clearly dependent on how one differentiates between language and dialect. The index of languages and alternative names in C. F. & F. M. Voegelin's *Classification and index of the world's languages* (New York: Elsevier, 1977, 658p), lists some 28,300 different names. There is considerable variety also in the classifications proposed by linguists, using techniques such as genetic relationship, glottochronology and lexicostatistics, but they all usually include the following families: Indo-European, Hamito-Semitic, Ural-Altaic, Caucasian (Georgian), Sino-Tibetan, Malayo-Polynesian (Austronesian), Dravidian, Amerindian, Nilotic, Sudanese-Guinean, Hottentot-Bushman, and Bantu. A detailed listing of most living languages, with all living dialects and alternate spellings, and also Scripture translation status, is given in *Ethnologue*, ed B. F. Grimes (Wycliffe Bible Translators, 14th edition 2000). This work usually divides living languages into the following 24 phyla: Afro-Asiatic, Austronesian, Austro-Asiatic, Azteco-Tanoan, Australian, Caucasian, Dravidian, Hokan, Indo-European, Indo-European Creole, Kam-Tai, Khoisan, Macro-Algonkian, Macro-Chibchan, Macro-Siouan, Na-Dene, Niger-Kordofanian, Nilo-Saharan, Oto-Manguean, Penutian, Papuan, Paleo-Siberian, Sino-Tibetan, and Ural-Altaic.

There are, therefore, various definitions of language and dialect, some stricter and some looser. For the purposes of this Encyclopedia, a distinct language is defined as one which has, or should have, or is agreed to need to have, its own separate and distinct translation of Holy Scripture, instead of its speakers being satisfied with (or being told by missions or translators to be satisfied with) Scriptures already translated into another tongue which is held to be sufficiently close or comprehensible. In many such cases (2 languages using a single translation), the 2 languages may often be correctly regarded as dialects of each other rather than as separate languages.

In this statistical analysis, the category 'Languages' for a given country is enumerated and quantified here as consisting of mother tongues and lingua francas either (a) native to the country, even if minuscule in size (e.g. Bushmen tribes in Southern Africa with a handful of speakers), or (b) in the case of expatriates, with as speakers a community (not just isolated individuals) numbering at least 0.05% of the country's population, or (c) significant enough for them to be officially listed as languages in use in the country by government censuses or schedules or other similar publications.

Culture
A people is characterized by a distinctive culture based on a distinctive mother tongue. A culture can be described as a group of people who do things together in a patterned way: sharing beliefs and customs with a worldview at the centre, together with values and standards of judgement and conduct, common institutions, a common language with shared proverbs, myths, folk-tales and arts, a common history, and common land or territory. Classifications of peoples using this criterion usually divide peoples into ethnic culture areas. An example of this may be seen in the map and table 'Primary European ethnic culture areas' in *The new Encyclopaedia Britannica* (1975), which divides Europe into 4 major culture areas, 22 culture provinces, and 158 distinct peoples. A different aspect of culture is that it can cover a whole range of social strata or socio-religious stratification, such as India's over 26,000 castes in the 4 categories of Vedic theory.

A single classification
These 3 classifications overlap a good deal, but by no means at all points. There is in fact no precise correlation between race, physical type, color, language and culture. The world distribution of languages does, however, correspond broadly with that of human races. As just noted, the matter is complicated by the fact that, for both race and language, scholars of different nationalities and persuasions have proposed numerous overlapping, often conflicting and even contradictory classifications. For the purposes of this Encyclopedia, however, what is needed is one single stable classification of all living peoples and languages (excluding all now extinct) in which all proper names in use, whether racial, ethnic, national, cultural, linguistic, or pertaining to color, and whether referring to a single people or language or to a major family or grouping, and all their synonyms and alternate names, can be inserted into a single framework which will show the relationships between all names (in their generally-preferred anglicized versions only, excluding forms in other languages), together with population and other data referring to each name. In the main, members of each ethnic group have a similar mother tongue (first language), whatever country they live in or have migrated to. The 3 preceding classifications have therefore been combined, in their various published versions, and have evolved a single classification (here termed ethnolinguistic) of the peoples of the world at 11 progressively more detailed levels: 5 major races (as detailed above, changing the mainly biological ending -oid for the last 3 races, to obtain Caucasian, Mongolian, and Negro) with 7 skin colors; 13 geographical races and 4 sub-races; 71 ethnolinguistic families (sometimes termed microraces, sometimes local races); 432 peoples (or, sub-families or ethnic culture areas); 12,600 constituent peoples and sub-peoples (13,500 languages); and many thousand additional names ranked in 4 further levels of subdivisions. This classification is based on the various extant schemes of nearness of language plus nearness of racial, ethnic, cultural, and culture-area characteristics.

The full classification also contains several thousand synonyms, alternative names, variant spellings, and names in other languages than English. It contains Bantu names with ethnic prefixes (Ama-, Ba-, Ma-, Ovi-, Wa-, etc) and linguistic prefixes (Eki-, Ki-, Lo-, Lu-, etc), though these are omitted in the present classification. The grand total of all such names with all variant spellings must be over 70,000. Over 12,000 of these tribes, language groups, nations, clans and other social division are listed in J. G. Leyburn, *Handbook of ethnography* (New Haven: Yale University Press, 1931); and, as noted above, 28,300 names are listed in Voegelin 1977 in English usage (i.e. in anglicized form), with at least a further 50,000 variations and usages in French, German, Spanish, Portuguese, Italian, Russian and the other major languages of world scholarship. In addition many peoples and languages are named with yet other terms by, and unique to, their surrounding peoples and languages. Altogether, the grand total of all ethnolinguistic names must be over 100,000 distinct terms. A reduced version of the full classification, evolved with special reference to this survey of Christianity, covering the first 6 of the above levels together with codes for the first 5 levels only (races, colors, geographical races, ethnolinguistic families, peoples) is given here in the anglicized listing PEOPLES OF THE WORLD in Table 8–2. In it, each ethnolinguistic family, and most of the world's major peoples, are given a code number and are also classified by race, geographical race and color. Most of the ethnic groups it lists may be seen located geographically in the detailed ethnic maps in *Atlas narodov mira* (Atlas of the peoples of the world, Moscow, 1964–1998). Similar maps, but with a different classification, are found in *Peoples of the earth:* Volume 20, *The future of mankind* (Europa Verlag, 1973–1990).

The reader should note that the classification is neither purely 'ethnic' nor 'racial' nor 'linguistic' nor 'cultural', but is ethnocultural and/or ethnolinguistic; and that on this definition an 'ethnolinguistic people' means an ethnic or ethnocultural or racial group speaking its own language or mother tongue. In the 20th century, mass international migration has therefore sometimes involved, over a generation or two, a change in the way an ethnic group is classified. For example, in 1972 in the USA, 2.2 million people (1.1% of the population) were of Russian origin (*Statistical abstract of the United States*, 1973–2001), but only 334,000 (0.2%) spoke Russian as their mother tongue (1970 Census of Population). This means that large numbers of persons of Russian origin (0.9% of the USA population) no longer speak Russian as their mother tongue and so (on this classification) have now become USA Whites (English-speaking), leaving only the 0.2% to be classified here as Russian-speaking Russians. In the same way, millions of Europeans have emigrated to South America over the last century, including Russians and Ukrainians, but after the first generation or so they have tended to lose their original mother tongues and have become assimilated to what is called the Latin American White race (Spanish- or Portuguese-speaking). Similarly, in countries such as the USA, Brazil, France, et alia, it is necessary to distinguish between (e.g.) Polish-speaking Polish immigrants on the one hand, and, on the other, persons of Polish origin who are now assimilated to the dominant race and culture. Likewise, every year millions of individuals and families who migrate to countries of different language and ethnic group are recorded here in those countries by their original mother-tongue ethnic group until such time (usually one generation) as they have changed their mother tongue and become absorbed in the dominant national group (e.g. Italian families who move permanently to Germany and who eventually become Germans linguistically and culturally). A different set of cases concerns peoples who, through emigration, retain a strong identity but change their mother tongue to a local language (e.g. Chinese who now speak only Indonesian, Mexican Indians who are now monolingual in Spanish only, etc); because such peoples still retain their ethnic identity and culture, they are classified here as still members of their original ethnic group.

The term 'ethnolinguistic people' refers to that group which speaks the language shown as its first or primary or cultural or official language. In France, for instance, 82.0% of the population are French-speaking ethnic Frenchmen. Of these, 13 million

(24.6%) speak for everyday purposes Occitan (Gascon, Languedoc, Provençal), a Romance language closer to Catalan than to French, although they use French as their official and cultural language. In this classification, therefore, the 13 million are classified under the ethnolinguistic term 'French', the only persons coded under 'Occitan' being the handful for whom Occitan and not French is their primary or cultural or only language.

In a few cases, it is difficult to be consistent in classification on a global scale because a name has both ethnic, cultural and religious meanings, all closely related, but applied in different countries and their censuses with differing emphases. The major example of this concerns the Jewish people. In most countries and censuses Jews are regarded as an ethnic group as well as a religious group, and they are treated as such in this survey. In the USA, they are classified not in the general 'USA White' category although they are in fact mostly White and mostly English-speaking, but in the separate category 'Jewish'. The reason is that the main criterion in all ambiguous situations is their answer to the question: 'What is the first, or main, or primary ethnic or ethnolinguistic term by which persons identify themselves, or are identified by people around them?'

The definition of 'language' in this present classification refers to distinct and separate languages excluding near variants and dialects except in a handful of special cases. On this definition, for example, there are about 1,247 Bantu languages in Africa (listed in *Linguasphere*, 1999). On other broader definitions, including major dialects, the total for this group of languages is even larger: 2,770.

Ethnolinguistic composition of all countries, 1970-2000
A voluminous ethnolinguistic analysis of every country's population is given in the large database printed out here country by country as Table 8-2. Readers wanting printouts arranged by any other criteria can obtain these from the related electronic *World Christian database*.

In the section SECULAR DATA, AD 2000 at the start of each country's survey article in Part 4, under the heading 'ETHNOLINGUISTIC GROUPS', the de facto ethnolinguistic composition of the total population is given. These figures were in all cases worked out de novo for the present survey, utilizing population censuses and a host of other sources. These were then prepared in coded form by (a) utilizing the codes given in the classification that here follows, and (b) translating each ethnolinguistic element into an 8- or 9-digit alphanumeric code. For example, '35.0% British' is coded as 350CEW19i, '95.5% Russian' is coded as 955CEW22j, and '1.2% Samoan' is coded as 012MPY55e. The object of this coding is to assist the reader who wishes to make exact numerical comparisons from one country to another, or over a period of time, or to make global or continental analyses using the ethnolinguistic criterion. It also permits the analysis of the total population of the world, and of Christians, by ethnolinguistic family and people.

How data are presented
In each country's survey article in Part 4, the ethnolinguistic data for the secular population are given in one single standardized and precisely-defined format, concerning which the following 11 points should be carefully noticed. (1) In almost all countries, and in most churches, there are 3 categories of ethnolinguistic groups: (a) dominant groups, (b) other sizeable groups over 0.05% in size, and (c) a mass of smaller groups of yet other ethnic origin, often expatriates, under 0.05% in size and tapering off in size down to a single individual or two. Here, the data in their uncoded form report (a), (b) and where significant the largest of (c) also; in coded form, the data cover (a) and (b) only. For each country, these data therefore give its major races and all numerically-significant ethnolinguistic families and peoples, in the period 1900-2025, shown in descending order of size, each as a percentage of total population, to the nearest 0.1 down to 0.1%, with smaller groups (below 0.05% but still numerically significant) in descending order of size at the end. It should thus be remembered that a figure '0.1%' means somewhere in the range 0.05-0.15%. (2) Commas indicate distinct and separate peoples; thus '5% Bantu, Indian' does not imply any relationship between Bantu and Indi-

Paiwan Aborigine.

New Guinea Papuans.

Punjabi labourers.

Twa Pygmies.

Kalahari Bushman.

Arusi Galla girl.

English archbishop.

PEOPLES OF THE WORLD. A selection illustrating widely-different racial and cultural characteristics. The 5 races are represented here by some 15 peoples, shown in the same order as in the classification in Table 8-1.

AUSTRALOID.

CAUCASIAN.

CAPOID

MONGOLIAN.

Jivaro warrior (Amerindian).

Korean girls.

Tibetan (Panchen Lama).

Maori parliamentarian.

NEGRO.

Kabre peasant.

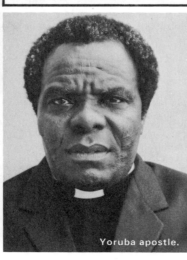

Yoruba apostle.

Ruandese (Tutsi King).

Kikuyu witchdoctor.

ans but merely refers to the presence of 2 distinct groups, one 5% Bantu and the other (less than 0.05%) Indian. (3) Parentheses and brackets indicate a breakdown, usually only partial, of certain larger categories into their major component peoples. (4) The addition 'et alii' refers to the presence of several other smaller peoples in addition to those listed; the addition '&c' refers to the presence of a large number of other smaller peoples. (5) For some minorities, as well as giving the percentage, the actual number of persons in 2000 is given. (6) A slash / indicates a racial mixture between the 2 or more peoples indicated. (7) All percentages given in 'ETHNOLINGUISTIC GROUPS' at the start of a country's article are percentages of the total population of the country. (8) The degree of accuracy of these percentages in those locations is indicated by the presence or absence of a decimal point; where this is absent, percentages are more approximate. (9) Note that the percentages for most countries under Secular Data do not reach a total of 100%, the remainder being usually a number of smaller groupings, aliens of many nationalities, refugees, diplomats, traders, students and the like. (10) Under this procedure, the entire population of a country is assigned to one or other of these ethnolinguistic groups; each group thus includes any and all persons of mixed race or tribe who are closer to the group than to any other group. (11) Any discrepancies between these names and percentages and similar listings published by other sources (anthropologists, linguists, government censuses, etc) are due to either (a) differences in the ethnic or linguistic classifications employed, concerning which there is as yet no universal agreement; or (b) alternative possible ways of classifying a people (e.g. Jews can also be Whites, or British, or Spanish-speaking, or aliens, etc); or (c) the fact that many names, and their alternates, can be used by different types of user (anthropologists, linguists, government officials, missionaries, religious officials) in different senses or ways to cover different though overlapping populations.

Extrapolation to 2025

For the vast majority of countries, the ethnolinguistic composition of either population or Christians has not altered appreciably during the 3 decades 1970-2000, and so the figures shown, which describe the situation in AD 2000 unless otherwise indicated, may be taken to have remained unchanged over the whole period. In those few countries where the composition has changed markedly since 1970, this is described in situ. In the same way, in most countries the ethnolinguistic composition was much the same in the year 1900, and will doubtless be similar in AD 2025. For this reason the tables give the 2025 extrapolations and projections, it being understood that they represent only a first approximation based on current trends.

Obtaining absolute numbers

If the reader wishes to obtain the total number of persons in any particular ethnolinguistic group in any year, he or she should multiply its percentage by the country's population in that year. For countries (the vast majority) whose ethnic composition has remained unchanged from 1970-2000, to obtain the total number of persons in any ethnolinguistic group in 1970 or 1990 or 2025, the reader should multiply its percentage by the country's population in 1970 or 1990 or 2025 (given in Country Tables 1). The resulting figures for the year 2025 will be projected estimates, but they will serve to establish the general order of magnitude of the future situation. It should be noted that the world totals for each people in the year 2025 are likely to be more accurate than national totals because the former will remain unaffected by future migrations across the world. In the same way, world totals for each people in the year 1900, also presented here, are more accurate than national totals based on these percentages because global totals are largely unaffected by the vast migrations of the 20th century.

When calculating sizes of small peoples whose population is shown as '0.2%' or '0.1%', it must again be noted that, because these figures cover the ranges

0.15-0.25%, and 0.05-0.15%, respectively, any totals resulting are only intended to be approximate.

Ethnolinguistic percentages

The data given in this survey enable the presenting of certain clear relationships between the numerical size of peoples and their nations, both total populations and Christian populations. Each ethnolinguistic people, tribe or group in a particular country can be described by 3 main percentage variables, as set out in the next paragraph. These are also related to a variable describing Christians as a percentage of the people's country, defined below. These 4 variables may be grouped into a formula by means of which the reader may use data he or she has to produce but does not have. In parentheses after each variable are shown the locations in this Encyclopedia where values of the data are presented.

Variables

AC_p = people's affiliated Christians as % of people's total population (Table 8-2)
AC_c = country's affiliated Christians as % of country's total population (see Country Tables 1)
ac_p = people's affiliated Christians as % of country's affiliated Christians (Table 8-2)
pop_p = people's total population as % of country's total population (Table 8-2).

Formula for a people or group

This can be spelled out in words as follows:

(People's AC) = (Country's AC) x (People's Christians as % of Country's Christians) ÷ (People's population as % Country's population).

Using the symbols in the previous paragraph, this reduces to the following formula:

$$AC_p = (AC_c) \times (ac_p) \div (pop_p)$$

In practice, though, one can drop the suffixes as unnecessary provided the reader remembers that 'AC' or 'pop' are simply statistical measures whose differing contexts necessitate care in their use.

Clarity in handling statistics

When the reader is either checking any of the computed percentages, or taking the analysis further, he or she needs to remember that a number of these ethnolinguistic terms are enumerated by different users in very different ways (e.g. published statistics for the Yoruba of Nigeria vary from 3 million, referring to the Yoruba proper, to over 20 million Yoruba-speaking persons). A specific name, e.g. Herero, or Mongol, may have different meanings from one denomination to another, from one religion to another, even from one country to another. It may be used to include peripheral sub-tribes in one context, but to exclude them in another. This means that care must be taken to establish exactly what distinct meaning any particular usage has. Having done this, if one is working out a percentage by dividing the total of Yoruba Christians by the total of all Yoruba, both of these 2 totals must use exactly the same definition of the term Yoruba. This principle is observed throughout the present analysis.

The extent to which a people can properly be called a Christian people can be defined in various ways. Firstly, it can be defined in terms of the magnitude of the people's Christian following; secondly, in terms of the years or even centuries of past Christian influence; and thirdly, in terms of the depth of Christian influence upon its language, literature and culture. As a first approximation, for purposes of analysis, one may define a Christian culture as a culture related to a specific ethnolinguistic people or tribe among which affiliated church members number a majority of the total population, defined as over 60% in number.

The analysis can now proceed to derive ethnolinguistico-racial codes, here termed, in the interests of brevity, race codes (which is nothing to do with racism or racist criteria).

CROSS-CULTURAL FRONTIERS OR BARRIERS

The construction of the ethnocultural or ethnolinguistic classification in this Part 8 enables the method to quantify a subject that is of prime concern to the Christian world mission. This is the measurement of distance between various cultures, and the number of frontiers or barriers that Christian workers or missionaries have to cross in order to reach peoples of other cultures.

Cultural distance, C

This distance is defined here as the number of cultural (ethnic, ethnolinguistic, racial, linguistic) frontiers or barriers that exist between a person or group of one culture (especially a Christian worker, missionary or evangelist, or a group of such) and their target individual, group or people. The distance as defined here can have integer values of 0, 1, 2, 3, 4, 5, or 6; and these 7 distances can be labeled ('C-0', 'C-1', etc), tabulated, and explained as follows.

Measuring cultural distance

To measure the cultural distance between a particular individual (e.g. a German foreign missionary in Nigeria) and his target population (e.g. the Yoruba people), it is first necessary to compare their codes as given here. These are obtained from the classification below, or can be most rapidly obtained from Table 8-1. There, German is coded CEW19m; Yoruba is coded NAB59n. Now one compares these 2 codes, answering the identity question with either 0 or 1 or 3 in the end column.

Measuring distances for countries

There are a number of possible usages for this index of cultural distance. It can be used to make people aware of the barriers that exist between themselves and other cultures, and therefore of the efforts that must be made in language learning and cultural awareness before good relations and communication can be effected. Distances can also be computed for whole countries; in particular, one can derive measures, for every country in the world, of the average cultural distance of the population from the world's largest Christian culture at 3 points in time: the years 1900, 1980 and 2000.

Average cultural distance of a country

The idea of an index of this kind is to obtain an approximation for the number of cultural frontiers or barriers between a country's population and global practicing Christianity. As a starting-point in each country, 4 base cultures can now be selected which represent the largest single Christian peoples in each of the years AD 30, 1900, 1970, and 2000. In AD 30 on the birthday of the Christian church, most Christians were Biblical Jews or Hebrews (shown as CMT30 in the code). At the 3 years 1900, 1980 and 2000, the world's largest single Christian ethnolinguistic peoples were, or will be, as follows: in 1900, Russians (with 59 million Christians; coded here CEW22j); in 1980, USA Whites (with 108 million Christians; coded CEW19s); and in 2000, Latin-American Spanish-speaking Mestizos (with 173 million Christians; coded CLN29). This means that at the 4 base years, the world's largest single missionary-minded culture or people were, or will be, respectively, Biblical Jews, Russians, USA Whites, and Latin-American Mestizos; or (in terms of language) in AD 30 Aramaic/Hebrew, in 1900 Russian, in 1980 USA English, and in 2000 Spanish. Using these 4 cultures as bases or starting-points, the average cultural distance of each country can be measured by multiplying each component ethnolinguistic people in the country at each date by its cultural distance from the 4 cultures. For example, a country in AD 2000 composed of 90% Chinese and 10% USA Whites has an average cultural distance from USA Whites of [(90 x 6) + (10 x 0)] ÷ 100, which is 5.4. This distance provides an idea of the comparative cultural difficulty of the Christian task in all countries.

2. COMPILING THE ETHNOCULTURAL DATABASE

This database can be termed by many adjectives. It is an attempt to describe the world of peoples by various overall taxonomic characteristics—ethnic, racial, biogenetic, cultural, linguistic, ethnolinguistic, ethnocultural. It has been built up country by country from a large variety of sources—government censuses, public-opinion polls, sociological or anthropological research, sociopolitical studies, bibliographies and literature, ecclesiastical enquiries and reports of all kinds. These sources number some 800,000 titles or books on ethnolinguistic names and criteria, available on the shelves of the world's 50,000 leading libraries. A small selection are listed in the bibliography below immediately after this cidebook section.

The meaning of the codes and columns in Tables 8-1 and 8-2 will now be given.

CODES FOR ETHNOCULTURAL CLASSIFICATION (TABLE 8-1)

This table 'Peoples of the World' has 9 columns, as follows:

Column 1: A multi-character code
This first column consists of a classification of race and ethnic family, shown below as the 4-page Table 8-1. In it, each ethnolinguistic people (or culture, or microrace) is given a 5- or 6-character alphanumeric code (example: CEW19m) defining its race, geographical race, major culture area, stylized color, ethnocultural family (local race), and its own unique code number as a people. These 6 codes are composed as follows:

Subcolumns
1 *Race (stock, biological grouping)*
   A = Australoid
   B = Capoid
   C = Caucasian (Caucasoid)
   M = Mongolian (Mongoloid)
   N = Negro (Negroid) .
2 *Geographical race (geographic race, continental race)*
   A = African
   E = European
   F = Afro-American
   I = American Indian
   L = Latin American
   M = Middle Eastern
   N = Indo-Iranian
   O = Oceanic
   P = Pacific
   R = Arctic Mongoloid
   S = Asian
   U = Austro-Asiatic
   Y = Early African
3 *Major culture area (stylized color/skin pigmentation, biogenetic pool, culture province)*
   B = Black
   G = Grey
   N = Brown
   R = Red
   T = Tan
   W = White
   Y = Yellow
4-5 *Ethnocultural family (local race, culture area, local breeding population/reproductive isolate, genetically distinct population)*
A 2-digit code numbered 01 to 71 defines each family or local race uniquely (the 3 preceding letters serve merely to further classify the family by race and major culture area/stylized color). The codes for the 71 families are given below in Table 8-1 and in the classification itself in Table 8-2, 'Peoples of the world'.
6 *People (culture, microrace, single breeding population, ethnic group, subfamily)*
In numerous cases where a family is particularly large or important, especially on the Christian scene, its code has been given here a further character subdividing the family into its major component peoples, subfamilies or

other groupings. When this further character is employed, it is added in the form of lower-case letters (a,b,c,d,e,f, etc), as shown below. The letters x, y and z, when used, refer to other remaining tribes and peoples not covered by the preceding a,b,c...series.

This classification can be greatly extended to encompass all lower levels of subdivisions. This is done in Table 8-2 by adding the 8-character language code, as described in Part 9 "LinguaMetrics". The resulting variable, termed 'Identity code', then describes subdivisions of each people, where such exist.

The remainder of the 9 columns of Table 8-1 have the following meanings:

Column 2: Anglicized name of race, people, or culture.

Column 3: Stylized color/skin pigmentation/major culture area/biogenetic pool: see detailed discussion above.

Columns 4-8: Statistical data for each people. The 5 variables enumerated here are:

Column 4: Annual birth rate, % p.a

Column 5: Annual death rate, % p.a.

Column 6: Annual immigration rate, % p.a.

Column 7: Annual natural increase, % p.a. (=columns 4 minus 5 plus 6).

Column 8: Adults as % total population.

Column 9: Main constituent cultures, et alia.

Index of peoples and languages
A comprehensive index to all names in this classification is given in the related *World Christian database*. This index enables readers immediately to locate any name they come across.

Statistical analysis
Using the codes above, the ethnolinguistic compositions of each country's population, and of its affiliated Christians, were then quantified. Two procedures were employed. The first was to add a 3-digit number in front of each code, this number being the percentage (to the first 5 places of decimals, from 0.1% to 99.9%, omitting decimal points) of the country's total population, or its total of affiliated Christians, who belong to the people that follow it. Thus if the composition of a country's population was '80.0% Chinese, 20% British', this was converted to the 2 coded elements '800MSY42a,200CEW19i'.

The second procedure was to calculate, via census statistics where available, the same percentages to 5 places of decimals. These results are then shown in Table 8-2, column 3.

A rule is necessary
The classification as shown in Tables 8-1 and 8-2 is closely printed in order to provide the reader with as complete an overview as possible, in as compact a space as possible. Readers should use a ruler or straight edge to find their way around as quickly as they require, both vertically and horizontally.

Summary description
The following additional points should be noted by way of explanation and summary. (1) Names of the 5 races, 7 colors, 13 geographical races, 71 ethnolinguistic families, 432 major peoples, and 12,600 constituent peoples, subpeoples and additional ethnic groups shown here. These are given in their usual generally-preferred anglicized form (usually giving the singular form only and not the plural; excluding their forms in other languages; and in almost all cases omitting diacritical marks) in strictly alphabetical order by name (their codes, accordingly, are not fully

in alphabetical order throughout). The ethnolinguistic families can then be seen to be numbered 01-71 in numerical sequence. (2) This entire classification gives anglicized (English) names only, together with a handful of non-English terms which have now come into English use also (e.g. Mestizo), or which are necessary here for exact identification or to avoid confusion. Prefixes for Bantu and other peoples (A-, Ama-, Ba-, Ma-, Ovi-, Wa-, &c) are omitted.

A large number of all these anglicized names have equivalents in French, German, Italian, Portuguese, Spanish and other international languages, in addition to names in use in their own local languages. These names in other languages are too numerous to be included below, but are stored in the longer computerized version. In the the same way, derivations and meanings of these anglicized names are not given here but in the computerized version (many in fact mean simply 'people' or 'man'); for a comprehensive reference to meanings, see the *New Encyclopaedia Britannica*. (3) Families (in the second column below, in boldface type) are subdivided into their component peoples in cases where a family is particularly large or important, especially on the Christian scene. (4) The European geographical race as defined here, and the term European, include Whites who have emigrated outside Europe and the Western world for the first generation (30 years) only, but exclude Whites of the second or more generations in the Third World if they have intermarried or assimilated with Non-Whites, and who are therefore here considered to have become separate Third-World peoples by then. (5) Color, a term from physical anthropology describing biological race characteristics, is defined here and given (in the third column) as a stylized typology of 7 terms. Where 2 or 3 terms are given (e.g. 'White/Tan/Brown'), it means that the race or family or people concerned is predominantly White but significant numbers are either Tan or Brown; only the predominant color is included in the code. (6) For each family or people, the last column gives a selection of its major constituent peoples, subpeoples, tribes, languages (on this classification, 13,500 on the world scene) or dialects, with (in parentheses) synonyms or alternative names in use. Slightly-different alternate spellings are only given occasionally where necessary for easy identification. (7) Names in the last column in roman type are ethnic, or are both ethnic and linguistic. (8) The addition 'et alii' refers to the presence of several others groupings; the addition '&c' refers to the presence of a large number of other smaller groupings.

Statistics, 1900-2025
For all ethnolinguistic peoples in this classification, statistics are given here in Table 8-2, with world summary statistics. Full statistics, for all peoples, of total populations, total Christians, professing Christians, affiliated Christians, and practicing Christians (Great Commission Christians)—given both as absolute numbers, as percentages of their total population, and ranked in various ways—are given in the related CD.

Bibliography
Literature on specific peoples is immense. What is provided here is a bibliography of descriptive and analytical literature, mainly books and scholarly articles. Each deals with one people, usually with one people in one country.

CODEBOOK FOR ETHNOSPHERE (TABLE 8-2)

Now that Table 8-1 has been described above and its codes listed there, the larger database shown here as Table 8-2 will be described. These paragraphs should be regarded as an extension of Part 3 "Codebook".

The 230 pages that follow set out the 12,600 distinct and separate peoples (each being a people-in-one-country) who inhabit the world's 238 countries, and each's values for 38 columns. Peoples are set out across 2 facing pages in alphabetical order within countries also in alphabetic sequence. Each people therefore is described on one single line (with the same opening reference number) across the 2 facing pages.

COLUMN
1. ID or reference number (for 1 line on 2 facing pages).
2. Ethnic name of people (people-in-a-country), anglicized.

POPULATION
3. Persons in each people as % country, 1995-2010.
4. Persons in each people, in 1995.
5. Persons in each people, in 2000.
6. Persons in each people, in 2025.

IDENTITY CODE
7. Race/ethnic code (6 characters), as in Table 8-1.
8. Language code (7 characters), as in Table 9-13.

LANGUAGE
9. Autoglossonym (people's own name for language, in most cases this being an *inner-language*, but sometimes an *outer-language*, this being identified by the word *'cluster'*). Note that accents and other diacritical marks in this column are not explained here and may be technical or phonetic, etc. For exact spelling of any name consult Dalby, *Linguasphere* for the code shown.
10. Users of this language in this country, % (selective), both native speakers and non-native users.

CHURCH
11. Affiliated Christians, % of this people.
12. Church members (affiliated persons).

MINISTRY (codes: see before Table 9-13).
13. 'Jesus' Film availability
14. Audio scriptures (a)
15. New Reader Scriptures (y)
16. Braille Scriptures for the blind (u)
17. Hearing-impaired (signed) Scriptures for the deaf (h)
18. Discipleship/discipling (d, 0–10)
19. Work among (agencies at work: wa, 0–10)
20. Cross-cultural mission (xc, 0-16)
21. Mass evangelistic campaigns (mc, 0–5)
22. Mission agencies present (mi, 0–5)

SCRIPTURE
23. Biblioglossonym (official name of language for any translation done or under way). Note: if an asterisk is added, it means there also is an alternate biblioglossonym (usually from WBT/SIL). See full explanation before Table 9-13.

Published scriptures:
24. P=Portion (Gospel; 1 Book), p=near-Portion, . =none.
25. N=New Testament (27 Books), n=near-NT, . =none.
26. B=Bible (whole 66 or 80 Books), b=near-Bible, . =none.
27. Second-language scriptures (usable by over 50% of this people's population) (ss)

EVANGELIZATION
28. Denominations present (with major work among this people, D).
29. Alien Christians (of another culture resident among this people, aC, 0–10)
30. Exponential church growth, % per year, for period AD 1900-2000.
31. Countries broadcasting Christian programs in this language (r, 0–8)
32. E, % of this population now evangelized.
33. U, % of this population unevangelized.
34. Location of this people in World A/B/C trichotomy.

EVANGELISM
35. Evangelistic offers received per capita per year (e, 0–900)
36. Responsiveness to Christianity (R)
37. Targeting variable (T, 1–10)

ADDITIONAL DESCRIPTIVE DATA
38. Locations, civil divisions, literacy, other religions, church history, D=actual number of denominations, dioceses, church growth, M=missions at work, parachurch agencies, ministries, movements.

BIBLIOGRAPHY

This bibliography of 600 items is only a selection from a huge literature. It highlights the wealth of data, information, knowledge, and analysis that exists for individual or particular ethnolinguistic peoples. In most cases an item refers to only one such people. Available bibliographies on any or all peoples may be obtained online via OCLC (Online Computer Library Catalog), which utilizes the names and classification scheme of the USA Library of Congress. Readers using this system should enter as keywords not only the anglicized name of the people being investigated; enter also the French name, German name, Spanish name, and any other alternate spellings and names.

'A bibliography for ethnographic research on Iceland,' F. E. Bredahl-Petersen, Behavior science research, 14, 1 (1979), 1–35.

A bibliography of the Hmong (Miao) of Southeast Asia and the Hmong refugees in the United States. D. P. Olney. 2nd ed. *Southeast Asian refugee studies, Occasional papers*, no. 1. Minneapolis, MN: Center for Urban and Regional Affairs, University of Minnesota, 1983. 75p.

'A brief history and development factors of the Karen Baptist Church of Burma (Myanmar).' S. D. Say. Th.M. thesis, Fuller Theological Seminary, Pasadena, CA, 1990. 206p.

A century of growth: the Kachin Baptist Church of Burma. H. G. Tegenfeldt. South Pasadena, CA: William Carey Library, 1974. 512p.

A church in the wilds: the remarkable story of the establishment of the South American mission amongst the hitherto savage and intractable natives of the Paraguayan Chaco. W. B. Grubb. London: Seeley Service, Dutton, 1914. 287p.

'A comparative survey of Eskimo–Aleut religion,' G. H. Marsh, *Anthropological papers of the University of Alaska*, 3, 1 (1954), 21–36.

'A comparison of Tamil and Chinese Lutheran churches in peninsular Malaysia and Singapore.' D. W. Vierow. D.Miss. thesis, Fuller Theological Seminary, Pasadena, CA, 1976. 283p.

'A cross–cultural communication of Biblical truth in Grebo villages of Maryland County, Liberia.' R. J. Martin. D.Min. thesis, Southeastern Baptist Theological Seminary, Wake Forest, NC, 1990. 130p.

A decade with the Basotho. H. Sleath. Ed., T. Coggin. Johannesburg: Dept. of Public Relations and Communication of the Methodist Church of Southern Africa, 1988. 127p.

A dictionary of black African civilization. G. Balandier & J. Maquet (eds). New York: Leon Amiel, 1974. 350p.

A glossary of the tribes and castes of the Punjab and North–West Frontier Province. D. Ibbetson, E. Maclagan & H. A. Rose. Reprint, New Delhi: Rima, 1985. 3 vols.

A history of Christianity in the Balkans: a study in the spread of Byzantine culture among the Slavs. M. Spinka. *Studies in church history*, 1. Chicago: American Society of Church History, 1933. 202p.

'A history of church growth among the Yalunka tribe of Sierra Leone (1951–1983).' S. M. Harrigan. M.A. thesis, Columbia Graduate School of Bible and Missions, Columbia, SC, 1985. 110p.

A history of the Arab peoples. A. Hourani. Cambridge, MA: Harvard University Press, 1991. 532p.

A history of the Jews in Macedonia. A. Matkovski. Skopje, Macedonia: Madeconian Review Editions, 1982. 223p.

'A history of the Turkman people,' V. V. Barthold, in *Four studies of the history of Central Asia.* Leiden: E. J. Brill, 1962.

'A hundred years of change in Kalabari religion,' R. Horton, in *Black Africa: its peoples and their cultures today*, p.192–211. J. Middleton (ed). London: Macmillan, 1970.

A maternal religion: the rôle of women in Tetum myth and ritual. D. Hicks. *Monograph series on Southeast Asia, Special Report*, no. 22. De Kalb, IL: Northern Illinois University, Center for Southeast Asian Studies, 1984. 141p.

'A missiological strategy for the evangelization of lowland Laotian refugees in the United States.' C. T. Wright. Ph.D. dissertation, Southwestern Baptist Theological Seminary, Fort Worth, TX, 1988. 2 vols.

A Pacific bibliography: printed matter relating to the native peoples of Polynesia, Melanesia and Micronesia. C. R. H. Taylor. 2nd ed. Oxford, UK: Clarendon Press, 1965. 692p.

'A people divided: the tame Nosu of Yunnan and the wild Nosu of Sichuan,' R. R. Covell, chapter 9 in *The liberating gospel in China: the Christian faith among China's minority peoples.* Grand Rapids, MI: Baker, 1995.

A people of migrants: ethnicity, state, and religion in Karachi. O. Verkaaik. *Comparative Asian studies*, 15. Amsterdam: VU University Press, 1994. 89p.

'A renewal strategy of the Karen Baptist Church of Myanmar (Burma) for mission.' S. G. Taw. Th.M. thesis, Fuller Theological Seminary, Pasadena, CA, 1992. 182p.

'A select bibliography of works on the Tamangs of Nepal,' A. Höfer, *Bulletin of the Nepal Studies Association*, 10 (1976), 34–36.

A Solomon Island society: kinship and leadership among the Siuai of Bougainville. D. L. Oliver. Cambridge, MA: Harvard University Press, 1955.

'A strategy for planting churches in Java through the Sangkakala Mission: with special emphasis on the Javanese and Chinese people.' A. Sutanto. Ph.D. dissertation, Fuller Theological Seminary, Pasadena, CA, 1986. 211p.

'A study of how churches grow in Zambia.' C. I. Woodhall. M.A. thesis, Abilene Christian University, Abilene, TX, 1979. 316p.

'A study of Karen Baptist Church growth in Myanmar.' L. Zan. Th.M. thesis, Fuller Theological Seminary, Pasadena, CA, 1993. 115p.

'A study of the growth of the church of Christ among the Tonga tribe of Zambia.' J. S. Shewmaker. M.A. thesis, Fuller Theological Seminary, Pasadena, CA, 1969. 278p.

'A study of the religious customs and practices of the Rajbangshis of North Bengal.' R. H. Clark. Ph.D. dissertation, Hartford Seminary Foundation, Hartford, CT, 1969. 598p.

A Zuni atlas. T. J. Ferguson & E. R. Hart. Norman, OK: University of Oklahoma, 1990. 240p.

'About the original religion of the Creoles in Suriname.' J. Schoffelmeer. *Mededelingen van het Surinaams Museum*, no. 38 (December 1982) 6-48; no. 39 (April 1983) 4-65.

'Adam and Eve on the island of Roti,' J. J. Fox, *Indonesia*, 36 (October 1983), 15–23.

Adat, Islam and Christianity in a Batak homeland. S. R. Siregar. *Papers in international studies, Southeast Asian series*, no. 57. Athens, OH: Ohio University Center for International Studies, Southeast Asia Program, 1981. 108p.

African and African American studies. Middletown, CT: Choice, 1993. 148p. (Bibliographic work with 754 titles).

'Aging, religion, and mastery style among the Quechua of Pocona, Bolivia.' T. L. Schemper. Ph.D. dissertation, Northwestern University, Evanston, IL, 1987. 176p.

Aladura: a religious movement among the Yoruba. J. D. Y. Peel. London: Oxford University Press for the International African Institute, 1968. 338p.

Allons faire le tour du ciel et de la terre: le chamanisme des Hmong vu dans les textes. J. Mottin. Bangkok: White Lotus, 1982. 559p.

Ambivalence et culte de possession: contribution à l'étude du Bori hausa. J. Monfouga-Nicolas. Paris: Anthropos, [1972]. 403p.

Among the Bantu nomads: a record of forty years spent among the Bechuana, a numerous and famous branch of the Central South African Bantu, with the first full description of their ancient customs, manners, and beliefs. J. T. Brown. London: Seeley, Service & Co., 1926. 272p. (Treats religion).

Among the primitive Bakongo: a record of thirty years close intercourse with the Bakongo and other tribes of equatorial Africa, with a description of their habits, customs, and religious beliefs. J. H. Weeks. London: Seely, Service & Co., 1914. 318p.

An African trail. J. K. Mackenzie. West Medford, MA: Central Committee on the United Study of Foreign Missions, 1917. 222p. (Religion of Bulu of Cameroon).

An analytical guide to the bibliographies on modern Egypt and the Sudan. C. L. Geddes. *Bibliographic series*, no. 2. Denver, CO: American Institute of Islamic Studies, 1972. 78p. (Deals with Muslim peoples in Egypt and Sudan).

'An annotated bibliography of the Thakalis,' M. Vinding & K. B. Bhattachan, *Contributions to Nepalese studies*, 12, 3 (1985), 1–24. (140 titles).

'An ethnic geography of Kuwait: a study of eight ethnic groups.' A. B. Al-Ostad. Ph.D. dissertation, Kent State University, Kent, OH, 1986. 257p.

'An ethnography of the Mahorais (Mayotte, Comoro Islands).' J. Breslar. Ph.D. dissertation, University of Pittsburgh, Pittsburgh, PA, 1981. 3 vols

'An eye in the sky, one deep in the earth: elements of Zaose religion,' A. Roberts, in *Ethnologies: hommage à Marcel Griaule*, p.291–306. S. Ganay et al (ed). Paris: Hermann, 1987.

An inquiry into the animism and folk–lore of the Guiana Indians. W. E. Roth. 1915; reprint, New York: Johnson Reprint Corp., [1970]. 453p.

An outline of Dahomean religious belief. M. J. Herskovits & F. S. Herskovits. *Memoirs of the American Anthropological Association*, no. 41. 1933; reprint, New York: Kraus, 1976. 77p.

'Animisme, religion caduque: étude qualitative et quantitative sur les opinions et la pratique religieuse en Basse–Casamance (pays diola),' L. Thomas, *Bulletin de l'IFAN*, 27 (B), 1-2 (1965), 1–41.

Anthropological bibliography of aboriginal Nicaragua. J. A. Lines, E. M. Shook & M. D. Olien. *Tropical Science Center occasional paper*, no. 3. San Jose: Tropical Science Center, 1965. 98p.

Anthropology and ethnography of the peoples of Somalia. N. Puccioni. New Haven, CT: Human Relations Area Files, 1960. 205p. (Translated from Italian).

Anthropology in Indonesia, a bibliographical review. R. M. Koentjaraningrat. *Koninklijk Instituut voor Taal-, Land- en Volenkunde, Bibliographical series*, no. 8. The Hague: Martinus Nijhoff, 1975. 343p.

Anthropology of Southern Africa in periodicals to 1950. N. J. van Warmelo. Johannesburg: Witwatersrand University Press, 1977. 1484p.

Approche de la religion des Birifor. A. Erbs. Paris: Musée de l'Homme, 1975. 75p.

'Arte Nalu,' A. Augusto da Silva, *Boletim Cultural da Guiné Portuguesa*, 11, 44 (1956), 27–47. (Art and religion).

'Asante Catholicism: ritual communication of the Catholic faith among the Akan of Ghana.' J. P. Obeng. Ph.D. dissertation, Boston University, Boston, 1991. 327p.

Asen, iron altars of the Fon people of Benin: October 2–December 21, 1985, Emory University, Museum of Art and Ar-

chaeology, Michael C. Carlos Hall, Emory University, Atlanta, Georgia. E. G. Bay. Atlanta: The Museum, 1985. 48p.

Asian and Asian American studies. Middletown, CT: Choice, 1993. 115p. (Bibliographic work).

Atlas naratov mira (Atlas of the peoples of the world). Moscow: Akademia, 1964.

Atlas of man. J. Gaisford (ed). London: Marshall Cavendish, 1981. 272p.

Atlas of modern Jewish history. E. Friesel. New York: Oxford University Press, 1990. 159p.

Atlas of world cultures: a geographical guide to ethnographic literature. D. H. Price. Newbury Park, CA and London: Sage Publications, 1990. 156p.

Australian Aboriginal religion. R. M. Berndt. *Iconography of religions*, section 5: Australia. Leiden: E. J. Brill, 1974. 4 vols.

'Bakuu: possessing spirits of witchcraft on the Tapanahony,' D. Vernon, *Nieuwe West–Indische Gids*, 54, 1 (1980), 1–38.

Balinese temple festival. C. Hooykaas. *Bibliotheca Indonesica*, no. 15. The Hague: Martinus Nijhoff, 1977. 109p.

Bantu philosophy of life in the light of the Christian message: a basis for an African vitalistic theology. D. R. K. Nkurunziza. Frankfurt: Lang, 1989. 307p.

Banyarwanda et Barundi. R. Bourgeois. Brussels: Institut Royal Colonial Belge, 1954–58. 4 vols. (Vol.1 treats "ethnology," vol. 2 "custom," and vol. 3 "religion and magic").

Basotho religion and Western thought. L. B. B. Machobane. Edinburgh: Centre of African Studies, Edinburgh University, 1995. 57p.

Batek negrito religion: the world–view and rituals of a hunting and gathering people of Peninsular Malaysia. K. Endicott. Oxford, UK: Clarendon Press, 1979. 234p.

'Belize: Black Caribs,' N. L. S. González, in *Witchcraft and sorcery of the American native peoples*, p.279–93. D. E. Walker Jr. (ed). Moscow, ID: University of Idaho Press, 1989.

Bemba–speaking women of Zambia in a century of religious change (1892–1992). H. F. Hinfelaar. Leiden: E. J. Brill, 1994. 238p. (Revision of author's Ph.D. dissertation, University of London, 1989).

Beyond the stream: Islam and society in a West African town. R. Launay. *Comparative studies on Muslim societies*, 15. Berkeley, CA and Los Angeles: University of California Press, 1992. 275p.

'Biblical basis of church growth and its application to the Kachin Baptist church of Burma.' H. Naw. D.Miss. thesis, Trinity Evangelical Divinity School, Deerfield, IL, 1990. 209p.

Bibliografía antropológica aborigen de Costa Rica. J. A. Lines, E. M. Shook & M. D. Olien. *Occasional papers*, no. 7. San José: Tropical Science Center, 1967. 196p.

'Bibliografía antropológica de Costa Rica,' M. E. B. de Wille, *Boletín bibliográfico de antroplogía Americana*, 38, 47 (1976), 63–82.

Bibliographie ethno–sociologique de la Tunisie. A. Louis. *Publications de l'Institut des belles lettres arabes*, 31. Tunis: N. Bascone, 1977. 448p.

'Bibliography of bibliographies on the Inuit,' I. Kleivan, in *Artica 1978: 7th Northern Libraries Colloquy, 19–23 September 1978*, p.39–41. S. Devers (ed). Paris: Éditions du Centre National de la Recherche Scientifique, 1982.

Bibliography of the Ewes. R. Arkaifie. Cape Coast, Ghana: University of Cape Coast, 1976. 81p. (Large section on Christianity).

Bibliography of the peoples and cultures of mainland Southeast Asia. J. F. Embree & L. O. Dotson. New Haven, CT: Yale University, 1950. 821p.

'Bibliography on peoples of Zimbabwe.' M. F. C. Bourdillon & A. Cheater. Computer database and printout, University of Zimbabwe, Harare, Zimbabwe, 1983.

Body of power, spirit of resistance: the culture and history of a South African people. J. Comaroff. Chicago: University of Chicago Press, 1985. 276p. (Treats Barolong boo Ratshidi people and Zion Christian Church).

Breve estudio sobre las tribus moras de Mauritania. A. C. de Laiglesia. *Primer informe*, 10. Madrid: Instituto Hispano-Arabe de Cultura, [1985]. 120p.

Buddhist traditions and culture of the Kathmandu valley (Nepal). K. Vaidya. Kathmandu: Sajha, 1986. 299p.

'Buryat religion and society,' L. Krader, *Southwestern journal of anthropology*, 10, 3 (1954), 322–51.

Bwiti: an ethnography of the religious imagination in Africa. J. W. Fernandez. Princeton, NJ: Princeton University Press, 1982. 731p. (Religion of the Fang).

'Campa cosmology,' G. Weiss, *Ethnology*, 11, 2 (1972), 157–72.

Caribbean ethnicity revisited. S. D. Glazier (ed). New York: Gordon and Breach, 1985. 164p.

Catholics, peasants, and Chewa resistance in Nyasaland, 1889–1939. I. Linden & J. Linden. Berkeley, CA: University of California Press, 1974. 235p.

China's minority nationalities. M. Yin (ed). Beijing: Foreign Languages Press, 1989. 455p.

'Christ in tribal culture: a study of the interaction between Christianity and Semai society of peninsular Malaysia in the context of the history of the Methodist Mission (1930–1983).' H. P. Shastri. Thesis, Universität Heidelberg, 1989. 213p.

'Christian education among the Ovambo people: the house as the center of transmitting culture and tradition.' B. Haileka. S.T.M. thesis, Lutheran Theological Seminary at Gettysburg, Gettysburg, PA, 1994. 245p.

Christian Indians and Indian nationalism, 1885–1950: an interpretation in historical and theological perspectives. G. Thomas. Frankfurt: Lang, 1979. 271p.

Christian response to change in East African traditional societies. G. G. Brown. *Woodbrooke occasional papers*, 4. London: Friends Home Service Committee for Woodbrooke College, 1973. 55p.

'Christianity and culture in Kenya: an encounter between the African Inland Mission and the Marakwet belief systems and culture.' S. K. Elolia. Ph.D. dissertation, Toronto School of Theology, Toronto, 1992. 2 vols.

Christianity and native traditions: indigenization and syncretism among the Inuit and Dene of the western Arctic. A. R. Gualtieri. Notre Dame, IN: Cross Roads Books, 1984. 186p.

Christianity and the Eastern Slavs. B. Gasparov & O. Raevsky-Hughes. *California Slavic studies*, vol. 16. Berkeley, CA: University of California Press, 1993.

Christianity and the Shona. M. W. Murphree. London: Athlone Press, 1969. 200p.

Christianity in northern Malawi: Donald Fraser's missionary methods and Ngoni culture. T. J. Thompson. *Studies in Christian mission*, vol. 15. New York: E. J. Brill, 1995.

'Christianity in South–west Arabia,' J. S. Trimingham, chapter 8 in *Christianity among the Arabs in pre–Islamic times*, p.287–308. London: Longman, 1979.

'Christianity in the Batak culture: the making of an indigenous church.' G. P. Harahap. M.S.T. thesis, Trinity Lutheran Seminary, Columbus, OH, 1982. 196p.

'Christianity, politics, and the Manyika: a study of the influence of religious attitudes and loyalties on political values and activities of Africans in Rhodesia.' N. E. Thomas. Thesis, Boston University, Boston, 1968. 396p.

'Christianizing the Karen.' K. M. Dettmer. M.A. thesis, Arizona State University, Tempe, AZ, 1987. 113p.

Church, state, and people in Mozambique: an historical study with special emphasis on Methodist developments in the Inhambane Region. A. Helgesson. *Studia missionalia Upsaliensia*, 54. Uppsala: Uppsala University Swedish Institute of Missionary Research, 1994. 455p.

Cities and caliphs: on the genesis of Arab Muslim urbanism. N. Al Sayyad. New York: Greenwood Press, 1991. 207p.

Coastal Bantu of the Cameroons. E. Ardener. London: International African Institute, 1956. 116p.

'Communicating the Gospel among the Iban: a resource manual for new cross–cultural missionaries.' J. A. Fowler. D.Min. thesis, Southern Methodist University, Dallas, TX, 1976. 148p.

Consultation of Lutheran Churches on work in West Africa among Fulani speaking people: Dakar, Senegal, January 14–21, 1979. R. Lehtonen (ed). Geneva: Lutheran World Federation, 1979. 108p.

'Contact between the Kipsigis traditional religion and world view and Christianity.' C. C. Cheruiyot. S.T.M. thesis, Drew University, Madison, NJ, 1985. 118p.

'Contribution á l'étude du comportement religieux des Wodaabe Dageeja du Nord–Cameroun,' R. Labatut, *Journal des Africanistes*, 48, 2 (1978), 63–92.

'Conversion to Protestantism and social change in a Bolivian Aymara community.' D. C. Knowlton. M.A. thesis, University of Texas, Austin, TX, 1982. 261p.

Cosmology and social life: ritual exchange among the Mambai of East Timor. E. G. Traube. Chicago: University of Chicago Press, 1986. 273p.

'Crossing religious frontiers: Christianity and the transformation of Bulu society, 1892–1925.' P. R. Dekar. Ph.D. dissertation, University of Chicago, Chicago, IL, 1978. 392p.

Croyances et pratiques religieuses traditionelles des Mossi. P. Ilboudo. *Etudes sur l'histoire et l'archéologie du Burkina Faso*, vol. 3. Stuttgart: Franz Steiner, 1990. 160p.

Cultural anthropology: a guide to reference and information sources. J. Z. Kibbee. Englewood, CO: Libraries Unlimited, 1991. 226p.

Cultural anthropology of the Middle East: a bibliography. R. Strijp. Leiden: E. J. Brill, 1992–. (Multivolume work in progress).

Cultural atlas of China. C. Blunden & M. Elvin. New York: Facts on File, 1983.

Cultural patterns and economic change (anthropological study of Dhimals of Nepal). R. R. Regmi. Delhi: Motilal Banarsidass, 1985. 218p.

Curse, retribution, enmity as data in natural religion, especially in Timor, confronted with scripture. P. Middlekoop. Amsterdam: Jacob van Campen, 1960. 168p.

'Cutting the ancient cords: the Lahu and Wa are liberated from demons,' R. R. Covell, chapter 10 in *The liberating gospel in China: the Christian faith among China's minority peoples.* Grand Rapids, MI: Baker, 1995.

Das Exil der Götter: Geschichte und Vorstellungswelt einer afrokubanischen Religion. S. Palmié. Frankfurt am Main: P. Lang, 1991. 527p.

Deep Mende: religious interactions in a changing African rural society. D. Reeck. *Studies on religion in Africa*, 4. Leiden: E. J. Brill, 1976. 102p.

'De–westernizing Christianity among the Krobo of Ghana.' D. K. Tei-Kwabla. D.Miss. thesis, Fuller Theological Seminary, Pasadena, CA, 1983. 460p.

'Diaspora Indians: church growth among Indians in West Malaysia.' C. D. Thomas. D.Miss. thesis, Fuller Theological Seminary, Pasadena, CA, 1976. 337p.

Dictionary of Celtic religion and culture. B. Maier. Trans., C. Edwards. Woodbridge, UK and Rochester, NY: Boydell Press, 1997. 346p.

Dictionary of Himalayan people. J. C. Regmi & S. Shiwakothi. *Nepal Antiquary*, nos. 50-55. Kathmandu: Office of the Nepal Antiquary, 1983. 220p.

Die Kurumba von Lurum. A. Schweeger-Hefel & W. Staude. Vienna: Verlag A. Schendl, 1972. 532p.

Die Religionen des Hindukusch. K. Jettmar with contributions by S. Jones and M. Klimburg. *Die Religionen der Menschheit*, vol. 4, no. 1. Stuttgart, West Germany: Verlag W. Kohlhammer, 1975. 525p.

Die Toura: zwischen Geisterglaube und Evangelium. I. Bearth-Braun. *Telos-Taschenbucher*, Nr. 7615. Neuheusen-Stuttgart: Hänssler, 1993. 99p.

'Dieux souverains et rois dévots dans l'ancienne royauté de la vallée du Népal,' G. Toffin, *L'homme*, 26, 3 (1986), 71–95. (Deals with Newar kingship).

Disinheriting the Jews: Abraham in early Christian controversy. J. S. Siker. Louisville, KY: Westminster John Kox Press, 1991. 296p.

Divinity and experience: the religion of the Dinka. G. Lienhardt. Oxford, UK: Clarendon, 1961. 328p.

Doing theology with the Maasai. D. Priest Jr. Pasadena, CA: William Carey Library, 1990. 248p.

'Drugs and mysticism: the Bwiti of the Fang,' J. Binet, *Diogènes* (Paris), 86 (Summer 1974), 31–54.

Du gomdé au Verbe incarné: puissance de la parole. E. D. Wedraogo. Ouagadougou, Upper Volta, 1976. 160p.

Du Mvett: essai sur la dynastie Ekang Nna. D. A. Ndoutombe. Paris: L'Harmattan, 1986. 184p. (Deals with religion of the Fang).

Eastern European national minorities, 1919–80: a handbook. S. M. Horak. Littleton, CO: Libraries Unlimited, 1985. 353p.

El cristianismo aymara: inculturación o culturización. L. Jolicoeur. Cochabamba: Universidad Católica Boliviana, 1994. 465p.

El judío en Costa Rica. J. Schifter, L. Gudmundson & M. S. Castro. *Serie estudios sociopolíticos*, no. 4. San José: Editorial Universidad Estatal a Distancia, 1979. 385p.

El monte: igbo–finda, ewe orisha, vititi nfinda: notas sobre las religiones, la magia, las supersticiones y el folklore de los negros criollos y el pueblo de Cuba. L. Cabrera. 7th ed. Miami: Ediciones Universal, 1992. 589p.

El nacimiento y la muerte entre los bribris. M. E. B. Wille. San José: Editorial Universidad de Costa Rica, 1979. 264p.

El sistema religioso de los afrocubanos. R. Lachatañeré. Havana: Editorial de Ciencias Sociales, 1992. 450p.

Elements of Southeastern Indian religion. No. 1 of section 10, *North America*, of *Iconography of religions.* C. Hudson. Leiden: E. J. Brill, 1984. 36p.

Encyclopaedia of peoples of the world. S. Gonen. New York: Holt, Henry, 1993. 704p.

Encyclopaedic dictionary of demography. D. Valentei. New York: State Mutual Book and Periodical Service, 1985. 608p.

Encyclopedia of Jewish history: events and eras of the Jewish people. J. Alpher (ed). New York: Facts on File, 1986. 288p.

Encyclopedia of Native America. T. Griffin-Pierce. New York: Viking Penguin, 1995. 192p.

Encyclopedia of Native American biography: six hundred life stories of important people. D. A. Grindle. New York: Holt, Henry, 1996. 512p.

Encyclopedia of Native American ceremonies. M. A. Pesantubbee. Santa Barbara, CA: ABC-CLIO, 1996.

Encyclopedia of Native American tribes. C. Waldman. New York: Facts on File, 1987. 308p.

Encyclopedia of North American Indian tribes. B. Yenne. New York: Random House, 1988.

Encyclopedia of North American Indians. F. E. Hoxie (ed). HM, forthcoming. 11 vols.

Encyclopedia of the Holocaust. I. Gutman (ed). New York: Macmillan, 1989–1996. 5 vols.

Encyclopedia of the Indians of the Americas. H. Waldman (ed). St. Clair Shores, MI: Scholarly Press, 1981. 7 vols.

Encyclopedia of world cultures. D. Levinson (ed). New York: Macmillan, 1995. 10 vols.; 6,500p.

Encyclopedia Yiddishanica. E. Markowitz. Fredericksburg, VA: Haymark, 1980. 450p.

Eskimos: Greenland and Canada. No. 2 of section 8: *Arctic peoples*, of *Iconography of religions.* I. Kleivan & B. Sonne. Leiden: E. J. Brill, 1985. 52p.

Ethnic groups of insular Southeast Asia. F. M. LeBar et al. New Haven, CT: Human Relations Area Files Press, 1964.

Ethnic groups of mainland Southeast Asia. F. M. LeBar, G. C. Hickey & J. K. Musgrave. New Haven, CT: Human Relations Area Files Press, 1964. 288p.

Ethnic minorities in Belize: Mopan, Kekchi and Garifuna. R. Wilk & M. Chapin. Belize City: SPEAR, 1990. 43p.

Ethnic minorities in Vietnam. D. N. Van, C. T. Son & L. Hung. Hanoi: Foreign Languages Publishing House, 1984. 305p.

Ethnic NewsWatch. SoftLine Information Company, Stamford, CT. (Selected articles from 100 top North American newspapers and magazines. Phone: 203-968-8878).

Ethnicity and nationality in Singapore. C. S. Foon. *Southeast Asia series*, no. 78. Athens, OH: Ohio University Monographs in International Studies, 1987. 229p.

Ethnicity: source of strength? source of conflict? J. M. Yinger. Albany, N.Y.: State University of New York, 1994. 504p.

Ethnographic atlas. G. P. Murdock. Pittsburgh, PA: University of Pittsburgh, 1967.

Ethnographic bibliography of North America. G. P. Murdock. 3rd ed. New Haven, CT: Human Relations Area Files, 1960. 393p.

Ethnographic bibliography of North America, 4th edition. Supplement 1973–1987. M. M. Martin & T. J. O'Leary. New Haven, CT: Human Relations Area Files Press, 1990. 3 vols. (Previously published as *Ethnographic bibliography of North America* . G. P. Murdock, 1960, 1975.).

'Ethnographic notes on the Tamangs of Nepal,' C. von Fürer–Haimendorf, *Eastern anthropologist*, 9 (3–4 March 1956), 166–77.

Ethnographical survey of the Miskito and Sumu Indians of Honduras and Nicaragua. E. Conzemius. Washington, DC: Bureau of American Ethnology, 1932. Bulletin no. 106. 191p.

Ethnography, North Africa (Tunisia, Algeria). R. Herzog. Berlin: Gebrüder Borntraeger, 1981. 46p. (Summaries in English and French).

Ethnography: step by step. D. M. Fetterman. *Applied social research methods series*, 17. Newbury Park, CA and London: Sage Publications, 1989. 156p.

Ethnologie religieuse des Kuta, mythologie et folklore. E. Andersson. Uppsala: Almquist & Wiksell, 1987. 164p.

'Evangelism on the perpendicular among the Lisu people of Yunnan,' R. R. Covell, chapter 6 in *The liberating gospel in China: the Christian faith among China's minority peoples.* Grand Rapids, MI: Baker, 1995.

Events and movements in modern Judaism. R. Patai & E. Goldsmith (eds). New York: Paragon House, 1995. 316p.

Eyes of the night: witchcraft among a Sengalese people. W. S. Simmons. Boston: Little, Brown & Co., 1971. 169p. (Treats Badyaranke).

Faith and the Intifada: Palestinian Christian voices. N. S. Ateek, M. H. Ellis & R. Radford Ruether (eds). Maryknoll, NY: Orbis Books, 1992. 204p.

Festivals, religious practices, and traditions of Telugus in Mauritius. R. Sokappadu. N.p., 1992. 64p.

First fruits of the forest: amongst the Tharus of North India. B. Pritchard. London: Regions Beyond Missionary Union, 1962. 14p.

'Folk religion among the Chinese in Singapore and Malaysia.' L. Tjandra. D.Miss. thesis, Fuller Theological Seminary, Pasadena, CA, 1988. 392p. (Text in Chinese with extended summary in English).

Folk stories of the Hmong: peoples of Laos, Thailand, and Vietnam. N. J. Livo & D. Cha. Englewood, CO: Libraries Unlimited, 1991. 147p.

For the land and the Lord: Jewish fundamentalism in Israel. I. S. Lustick. New York: Council on Foreign Relations, 1988. 227p.

Girkaa: une cérémonie d'initiation au culte de possession bòorii des Hausa de la région de Maradi (Niger). V. Erlmann & H. Magagi. Berlin: Dietrich Reimer Verlag, 1989. 173p.

God: ancestor or creator? Aspects of traditional beliefs in Ghana, Nigeria and Sierra Leone. H. Sawyerr. London: Longman, 1970. 118p.

Good magic in Ovambo. M. Hiltunen. Helsinki: Suomen Antropologinen Seura, 1993. 234p.

Gourmantche ethnoanthropology: a theory of human being. R. A. Swanson. Lanham, MD: University Press of America, 1985. 464p.

'Growth of the Church of God through Ushirika groups among the Luhya in Nairobi, Kenya.' R. E. Edwards. D.Miss. thesis, Fuller Theological Seminary, Pasadena, CA, 1989. 377p.

Guérisseurs et magiciens du Sahel. J. Gibbal. Paris: Presses universitaires de France, 1984. 160p.

Gurkhas. C. J. Morris. 2nd ed. *Handbooks for the Indian Army.* Delhi: Government of India, 1936; reprint, B. R. Publishing, 1985. 182p.

Gypsies: Indians in exile. D. P. Singhal. *Kirpa Dai series in folklore and anthropology,* 5. Berkeley, CA: Folklore Institute, 1982. 170p.

Handbook of Middle American Indians. R. Wauchope et al (ed). Austin, TX: University of Texas Press, 1964–86. 16 vols, plus 4 supplemental vols.

Handbook of North American Indians. W. C. Sturtevant (ed). Washington, DC: Smithsonian Institution, 1978–. (Multivolume).

Handbook of South American Indians. J. H. Steward (ed). Washington, DC: Smithsonian Institution, Bureau of American Ethnology, 1946–59. 7 vols.

Harmony ideology: justice and control in a Zapotec mountain village. L. Nader. Stanford, CA: Stanford University Press, 1990. 343p.

Harvard encyclopedia of American ethnic groups. S. Thernstrom (ed). Cambridge, MA: Harvard University Press, 1980.

Hausa studies: a selected bibliography of B.A., M.A., and Ph.D. papers available in Northern Nigerian universities. E. L. Powe. 2nd ed. Kano, Nigeria: Bayero University, 1983. 29p. (330 items; religion is a main heading).

Hausa women in the twentieth century. C. Coles & B. Mack (eds). Madison, WI: University of Wisconsin Press, 1991. 308p.

Hawks of the sun: Mapuche morality and its ritual attributes. L. C. Faron. Pittsburgh, PA: University of Pittsburgh Press, 1964. 220p.

Headhunters about themselves: an ethnographic report from Irian Jaya, Indonesia. J. H. M. Boelaars. *Koninklijk Instituut voor Taal–, Land– en Volkenkunde, Verhandelingen,* no. 92. The Hague: Martinus Nijhoff, 1981. 296p. (Study of Jaqaj tribe by missionary).

Heart drum: spirit possession in the Garifuna communities of Belize. B. Foster. 2nd rev. ed. Belize: Cubola Productions, 1994. 59p.

Hegemony and culture: politics and religious change among the Yoruba. D. D. Laitin. Chicago: University of Chicago, 1986. 252p.

'Hinduism and Buddhism in the Kathmandu Valley (Nepal),' D. N. Gellner, in *The world's religions,* p.739–55. S. Sutherland et al (eds). London: Croom Helm, 1988. (Deals with Newars).

Historical dictionary of Mongolia. A. J. K. Sanders. *Asian historical dictionaries,* no. 19. Lanham, MD: Scarecrow Press, 1996.

History of the American Baptist Chin Mission: a history of the introduction of Christianity into the Chin Hills of Burma by missionaries of the American Baptist Foreign Mission Society during the years 1899 to 1966. R. G. Johnson. Valley Forge, PA: R. G. Johnson, 1988. 2 vols

'History of the Methodist Church in its Rotuman setting,' J. Langi, in *Island churches: challenge and change,* p.1–73. C. W. Foreman (ed). Suva, Fiji: University of the South Pacific, Institute of Pacific Studies, 1992.

'Hmong ethnohistory: an historical study of Hmong culture and its implications for ministry.' J. Davidson. D.Miss. thesis, Fuller Theological Seminary, Pasadena, CA, 1993. 230p.

Hopi Indian altar iconography. No. 5 of section 10, *North America,* of *Iconography of religions.* A. W. Geertz. Leiden: E. J. Brill, 1987. 39p.

Horses, musicians, & gods: the Hausa cult of possession–trance. F. E. Besmer. South Hadley, MA: Bergin & Garvey, 1983. 290p.

Hunters and herders of Southern Africa: a comparative ethnography of the Khoisan peoples. A. Barnard. Cambridge, UK: Cambridge University Press, 1992. 349p. (Treats religion).

I am a shaman: a Hmong life story with ethnographic commentary. D. Conquergood & P. Thao. *Southeast Asian refugee studies, Occasional paper,* no. 8. Minneapolis, MN: Center for Urban and Regional Affairs, University of Minnesota, 1989. 90p. (Related to the documentary film *Between two worlds: the Hmong shaman in America,* produced by D. Conquergood and T. Siegel [Chicago: Siegel Productions, 1985]).

Iconography of New Zealand Maori religion. No. 1 of section 2, *New Zealand,* of *Iconography of religions.* D. R. Simmons. Leiden: E. J. Brill, 1986. 33p.

'Identity conflict and ceremonial events in a Sereer community of Saalum, Senegal.' K. M. Marcoccio. Ph.D. dissertation, Brandeis University, Waltham, MA, 1987. 347p.

Imperialism, evangelism, and the Ottoman Armenians, 1878–1896. J. Salt. London: Frank Cass and Co., 1993. 198p.

In search of China's minorities. Z. Weiwen & Z. Qingnan. Beijing: New World Press, 1993. 354p.

In search of Genghis Khan. T. Severin. New York: Atheneum, 1992. 232p.

'In search of the Karen king: a study in Karen identity with special reference to 19th century Karen evangelism in Northern Thailand.' A. P. Hovemyr. Doctoral dissertation, University of Uppsala, Uppsala, Sweden, 1989. 207p.

In sorcery's shadow: a memoir of apprenticeship among the Songhay of Niger. P. Stoller & C. Olkes. Chicago: University of Chicago Press, 1987. 252p.

In the wake of martyrs: a modern saga in ancient Ethiopia. A. E. Brant. Langley, British Columbia: Omega Publications, 1992. 300p.

'Inculturation of rites of Christian initiation of the Kewabi people of Papua New Guinea.' M. T. Dwan. M.T.S. thesis, Catholic Theological Union, Chicago, 1993. 81p.

Indianen en kerken in Suriname: identiteit en autonomie in het binnenland. J. Vernooij. Paramaribo: Stichting Wetenschappelijke Informatie, 1989. 178p.

Indians of North America: methods and sources for library research. M. L. Haas. Hamden, CT: Library Professional Publications, 1983. 175p.

Indians of Northeastern North America. No. 7 of section 10, *North America,* of *Iconography of religions.* A. W. Geertz. Leiden: E. J. Brill, 1986. 50p.

'Innocent pioneers and their triumphs in a foreign land: a critical look at the work of the American Baptist Mission in the Chin Hills, 1899–1966 in Burma from a missiological perspective.' Cung Lian Hup. Th.D. thesis, Lutheran School of Theology, Chicago, 1993. 204p.

Introduction à l'ethnographie du Congo. J. Vansina. Kinshasa: Université Lovanium, 1965. 228p.

Introduction au wanzanisme ou au culte ancestral. B. Lala. Bangui, C.A.R.: B. Lala, 1991. 19p.

Inventaire ethnique du Sud–Cameroon. I. Dugast. *Populations,* no. 1. Yaoundé, Cameroon: l'Institut Français d'Afrique Noire, 1949. 159p.

Islam in tribal societies: from the Atlas to the Indus. A. S. Ahmed & D. M. Hart. London: Routledge & Kegan Paul, 1984. 350p.

Islam in tropical Africa. I. M. Lewis (ed). 2nd ed. London: International African Institute in association with Indiana University, 1988. ("Studies presented and discussed at the Fifth International African Seminar, Ahmadu Bello University, Zaria, January 1964").

Islamic Britain: religion, politics and identity among British Muslims. P. Lewis. London and New York: I. B. Tauris, 1994. 256p.

Islamic peoples of the Soviet Union: an historical and statistical handbook. S. Akiner. 2nd ed. London: KPI, 1986. 462p.

Jewish life in Muslim Libya: rivals and relatives. H. E. Goldberg. Chicago: University of Chicago Press, 1990. 197p.

Jewish–American history and culture: an encyclopedia. J. Fischel & S. Pinsker. New York: Garland, 1991.

Jews in the Soviet Union since 1917: paradox of survival. N. Levin. New York: New York University Press, 1988. 2 vols.

Jews of Arab and Islamic countries: history, problems, solutions. H. M. Haddad. New York: Shengold, 1984. 158p.

Kinkirsi, Boghoba, Saba: das Weltbild der Nyonyosi in Burkina Faso. A. Schweeger-Hefel. Vienna: A. Schendl, 1986. 436p.

Kpele lala: Ga religious songs and symbols. M. Kilson. Cambridge, MA: Harvard University, 1971. 313p.

Kunst und Religion der Lobi. P. Meyer. Zurich: Museum Rietberg, 1981. 184p.

Kurdish ethnonationalism. N. Entessar. Boulder, CO: L. Rienner, 1992. 216p.

'La dimension thérapeutique du culte des rab: Ndop, tuuru et samp.,' A. Zempleni, *Psychopathologie Africaine,* 2, 3 (1966), 295–439.

La naissance à l'envers: essai sur le rituel du Bwiti Fang au Gabon. A. Mary. Paris: L'Harmattan, 1983. 384p.

La poésie populaire et les chants religieux du Gabon. S. Swiderski and M.–L. Girou–Swiderski. Ottawa: Editions de l'Université d'Ottawa, 1981. 290p. (Summary in English, French, German, Italian, Polish, and Spanish).

La religion Bouiti. S. Swiderski. *Série culture du Gabon.* Ottawa: Legas, 1989–. In progress to 5 vols. (Summaries in English, Italian, German, Spanish, and Polish).

'La religion musulmane: facteur d'intégration ou d'identification ethnique. Le cas des yarsé du Burkina Faso,' A. Kouanda, in *Les ethnies ont une histoire,* p.125–34. J. P. Chrétien & G. Prunier (eds). Paris: Karthala, 1989.

La religiosidad contemporánea maya–kekchí. L. Pacheco. Quito, Ecuador: Ediciones Abya–Yala, 1992. 225p.

La secta del Bwiti en la Guinea Española. A. de V. Vilaldach. Madrid: Instituto de Estudios Africanos, 1958. 63p.

La structure socio–politique et son articulation avec la pensée religieuse chez les Aja–Tado du Sud–est Togo. K. E. Kossi. *Arbeiten aus dem Seminar für Völkerkunde der Johann Wolfgang Goethe-Universität Frankfurt am Main,* vol. 21. Stuttgart: F. Steiner, 1990. 325p.

La tierra no da así nomás: los ritos agrícolas en la religión de los aymara–cristianos. H. van den Berg. La Paz: HISBOL, 1990. 352p.

L'Angola traditionelle: une introduction aux problèmes magico–religieux. M. L. Rodrigues de Areia. Coimbra, Portugal: Tipografia de Atlántida, 1974.

Language, religion, and ethnic assertiveness: the growth of Sinhalese nationalism in Sri Lanka. K. N. O. Dharmadasa. Ann Arbor, MI: University of Michigan, 1993. 384p.

Latino studies. Middletown, CT: Choice, 1993. 102p. (Bibliographic work with 531 titles).

Le ginnili devin, poète et guerrier afar: (Ethiopie et République de Djibouti). D. Morin. *Langues et cultures africaines,* 16. Paris: Peeters, 1991. 146p. (Summaries in English and Afar).

'Le Harrisme et le Bwiti: deux réactions Africaines à l'impact Chrétien,' R. Bureau, *Recherches de Sciences Religieuses,* 63, 1 (1975), 83–100.

Le Noir du Yatenga: pays Mossi et Gourounsi. L. Tauxier. Paris: Larose, 1912. 796p. (Mossi, Gurunsi, and Fulani peoples, including their religion).

Le paysan limbu, sa maison et ses champs. P. Sagant. *Le monde d'outre mer passé et présent,* 1st series, 41. Paris: Mouton with Ecole des Hautes Etudes en Sciences Sociales, 1976. 404p.

Le pouvoir du Bangré: enquête initiatique à Ouagadougou. K. Fidaali. Paris: Presses de la Renaissance, 1987. 222p.

'Le sens des limites: maladie, sorcellerie, religion et pouvoir chez les Winye, Gourounsi du Burkina Faso.' J. Jacob. Doctoral dissertation, Université de Neuchâtel, 1988. 384p.

Le symbolisme religieux dans l'ethnie Ngambay: approche culturelle de la religion. L. Draman Odial. St.–Paul, Ottawa: Université St.–Paul, 1975–1976. 100p.

Le système religieux des Evhé. A. de Surgy. Paris: L'Harmattan, 1988. 343p.

Le vodu en Afrique de l'Ouest: rites et traditions: le cas des sociétés Guen–Mina (Sud–Togo). I. de La Torre. *Collection anthropologie—Connaissance des hommes.* Paris: L'Harmattan, 1991. 179p.

Lepcha, my vanishing tribe. A. R. Foning. Delhi: Sterling, 1987. 314p. (Treats religion).

'Les activités religieuses des jeunes enfants chez les Bobo,' G. L. Moal, *Journal des Africanistes* (Paris), 51, 1–2 (1981), 235–50.

'Les Bandas de l'Oubangui–Chari (Afrique Equatoriale Française),' R. P. J. Daigre, *Revue internationale d'ethnologie et de linguistiques anthrôpos,* 26 (1932) 647–95, and 27 (1933) 151–81.

Les Bobo: nature et fonction des masques. G. Le Moal. *Travaux et documents de l'ORSTOM,* no. 121. Paris: ORSTOM, 1980. 545p.

Les chemins de Nya: culte de possession au Mali. J. P. Colleyn. *Anthropologie visuelle,* 1. Paris: Editions de l'Ecole des Hautes Etudes en Sciences Sociales, 1988. 221p.

Les Diola: essai d'analyse fonctionelle sur une population de Basse–Casamance. L. Thomas. *Mémoire,* 55. Dakar: IFAN, 1959. 2 vols.

Les êtres surnaturels dans la religion populaire khmère. Ang Chouléan. Paris: Cedorek, 1986. 369p.

Les Gbaya. J. Hilberth. *Studia Ethnographica Upsaliensia,* 19. Uppsala: Studia Ethnographica Upsaliensia, 1962. 142p.

Les Gurungs—une population himalayenne du Népal. B. Pignède. Ed., L. Dumont. *Le monde d'outre mer passé et present,* 3rd series, 21. Paris: Mouton, 1966. 414p.

Les hommes qui cueillent la vie: les Imragen. F. Pelletier. *L'Aventure vécue.* Paris: Flammarion, 1986. 246p.

'Les peuples de la République démocratique du Congo, du Rwanda et du Burundi,' A. Dorsinfang-Smets, in *Ethnologie régionale,* p.566–661, vol. 1. J. Poirier (ed). Paris: Gallimard, 1972.

'Les populations de la côte française des Somalis,' R. Muller, in *Mer Rouge Afrique orientale, études sociologiques et linguistiques: préhistoire—explorations—perspectives d'avenir,* p.45–102. M. Albospeyre et al (ed). *Cahiers de l'Afrique et l'Asie,* no. 5. Paris: J. Peyronnet, 1959.

Les populations païennes du Nord–Cameroun et de l'Adamaoua. B. Lembezat. Paris: Presses Universitaires de France, 1961. 252p.

Les rites beti au Christ: essai de pastorale liturgique sur quelques rites de nos ancêtres. I. Tabi. N.p., 1991. 31p.

Les rites secrets des primitifs de l'Oubangui. A. Vergiat. Paris: Payot, 1936. 308p.

Les Senufo et le christianisme. R. Deniel. Korhogo–Abidjan: Inades, 1979. 67p.

Les symboles divinatoires: analyse socio–culturelle d'une technique de divination des Cokwe d'Angola (Ngombo ya Cisuka). M. L. Rodrigues de Areia. Coimbra, Portugal: Instituto de Antropologia, Universidade de Coimbra, 1985. 555p.

Les Tamangs du Népal—usages et religion. B. Steinman. Paris: Edition Recherche sur les Civilisations, 1987. 310p.

L'Habitation des Fali: montagnards du Cameroun septentrional. J. Lebeuf. Paris: Librairie Hachette, 1961. 607p. (Includes Fali religion).

Life among the Magars. G. Shepherd. Kathmandu: Sahayogi, 1982. 269p.

Like people you see in a dream: first contact in six Papuan societies. E. L. Schieffelin & R. Crittenden. Stanford, CA: Stanford University Press, 1991. 343p.

L'intérieur des choses: maladie, divination et reproduction sociale chez les Bisa du Burkina. S. Fainzang. Paris: L'Harmattan, 1986. 204p.

'L'Islam et les tribus dans la colonie du Niger,' P. Marty, *Revue des études islamiques,* (1930), 333–429.

Living among the Bedouin Arabs. A. R. Johnson. New York: Vantage Press, 1985. 99p.

Llamamiento de Dios al pueblo Gitano. Terrassa: Adolfo Giménez, 1981.

Los nicaro y los chorotega según las fuentes históricas. A. M. Chapman. *Serie historia y geografía,* no. 4. San José: Universidad de Costa Risa, 1960. 115p.

'Maisin Christianity: an ethnography of the contemporary religion of a seaboard Melanesian people.' J. Barker. Ph.D. dissertation, University of British Columbia, 1985. 578p.

Maîtres et possédés: les dieux, les rites et l'organisation sociale chez les Tharu. G. Krauskopff. Paris: Editions du Centre Nationale de la Recherche Scientifique, 1989. 276p.

Man on earth: a celebration of mankind. J. Reader. New York: Harper and Row, 1988. 256p.

'Mande settlement and the development of Islamic institutions in Sierra Leone,' D. E. Skinner, *International journal of African historical studies,* 11, 1 (1978), 32–62.

Manding: focus on an African civilization. International Conference on Manding Studies. London: School of Oriental and African Studies, University of London, 1972. 5 vols.

'Men of the sea: coastal tribes of southern Thailand's west coast,' D. W. Hogan, *Journal of the Siam society*, 60, pt. 1 (1972), 205–234.

Mende religion: aspects of belief and thought in Sierra Leone. A. J. Gittins. *Studia Instituti Anthropos*, vol. 41. Nettetal, Germany: Steyler Verlag-Wort und Werk, 1987. 258p.

Migration across time and nations: population mobility in historical contexts. I. Glazier & L. de Rosa (ed). New York and London: Holmes and Meier, 1986. 392p.

Millennium: tribal wisdom and the modern world. D. Maybury–Lewis. New York: Penguin, 1992. 416p.

Minorities in the Middle East: a history of struggle and self–expression. M. Nisan. Jefferson, NC: McFarland & Co., 1991. 272p.

Minority groups in the Republic of Vietnam. J. L. Schrock et al. Washington, DC: Department of the Army, Pamphlet, no. 550–105, 1966. 1,163p.

Mission impossible: the unreached Nosu on China's frontier. R. Covell. Pasadena, CA: Hope Publishing House, 1990. 319p.

Mission in Burma: the Columban Fathers' forty–three years in Kachin country. E. Fischer. New York: Seabury, 1980. 164p.

Missionaries and western education in the Bechuanaland protectorate 1859–1904: the case of the Bangwato. P. T. Mgadla. *Studies on the church in southern Africa*, no. 2. Gaborone: University of Botswana, 1989. 47p.

Missionaries, miners, and Indians: Spanish contact with the Yaqui nation of Northwestern New Spain, 1533–1820. E. H. Hart. Tuscon, AZ: University of Arizona Press, 1981. 152p.

Modern Kongo prophets: religion in a plural society. W. MacGaffey. *African systems of thought series.* Bloomington, IN: University of Indiana Press, 1983. 285p.

Moeurs et coutumes des indigènes. H. Mayet. 52p.

'Monk, householder and priest: Newar Buddhism and its hierarchy of ritual.' D. N. Gellner. D.Phil. dissertation, Oxford University, Oxford, UK, 1987. 586p.

'Mountain spirits and maize: Catholic conversion and renovation of traditions among the Q'eqchi' of Guatemala.' R. Wilson. Ph.D. dissertation, University of London, 1990. 382p.

Muslim Chinese: ethnic nationalism in the People's Republic. D. C. Gladney. *Harvard East Asian Monographs*, 149. Cambridge, MA and London: Council on East Asian Studies at Harvard University, and Harvard University Press, 1991. 499p. (Treats the Chinese government's response to rising ethnic nationalism among the Hui).

Muslim peoples: a world ethnographic survey. R. V. Weekes (ed). 2nd ed. Westport, CT: Greenwood Press, 1984. 2 vols.

Muslims in Central Asia: expressions of identity and change. J. Gross (ed). Durham, NC: Duke University Press, 1992. 238p.

Muslims of the Soviet Union: a guide. A. Bennigsen & S. E. Wimbush. London: Hurst, 1985. 294p.

Muslims through discourse: religion and ritual in Gayo society. J. R. Bowen. Princeton, NJ: Princeton University Press, 1993. 370p.

'Myths and rituals of the Ethiopian Bertha,' A. Triulzi, in *Peoples and cultures of Ethio–Sudan borderlands.* M. L. Bender (ed). *Committee on Northeast African Studies*, no. 10. East Lansing, MI: African Studies Center, Michigan State University Press, 1981. 214p.

'Nári,' F. Z. Gomes, *Geographica*, 8, 31 (1972), 64–74.

'National minorities in Albania, 1919–1980,' S. M. Horak, in *East European national minorities: 1919–1980: a handbook*, p.309–313. S. M. Horak (ed). Littleton, CO: Libraries Unlimited, 1985.

Native American religions: a geographical survey. J. J. Collins. Lewiston, NY: E. Mellen Press, 1991. 411p.

Native American religions: North America. L. E. Sullivan (ed). *Encyclopedia of religion series.* New York: Macmillan, 1989.

Native American religious action: a performance approach to religion. S. D. Gill. *Studies in comparative religion.* Columbia, SC: University of South Carolina Press, 1987. 199p.

Native American studies. Middletown, CT: Choice, 1993. 54p. (Bibliographic work with 278 titles).

Native peoples of South America. J. H. Steward & L. C. Faron. New York: McGraw Hill, 1959. 479p.

Native peoples of the Russian far north. N. Vakhtin. London: Minority Rights Group, 1992. 38p.

Ndebele religion and customs. W. Bozongwana. Gweru, Zimbabwe: Mambo Press in association with the Literature Bureau, 1983. 56p.

Nepal et ses populations. M. Gaborieau. *Pays et Populations.* Brussels: Editions Complexe, 1978. 308p.

'Newar Buddhist initiation rites,' J. K. Locke, *Contributions to Nepalese studies*, 2, 2 (1975), 1–23.

Ngaju religion: the conception of God among a south Borneo people. H. Schärer. Trans., R. Needham. *Koninklijk Instituut voor Taal-, Land- en Volkenkunde, Translation series*, no. 6. The Hague, Netherlands: Martinus Nijhoff, 1963. 229p. (By missionary).

Nigerian studies, or the religious and political system of the Yoruba. R. E. Dennett. *Cass library of African studies, General studies*, no. 48. 1910; reprint, London: Frank Cass, 1968. 235p.

Nomad: a year in the life of a Qashqa'i tribesman in Iran. L. Beck. Berkeley, CA: University of California Press, 1991. 503p.

Nomads of the world. R. L. Breeden (ed). Washington, DC: National Geographic Society, 1971. 200p.

Nomads of western Tibet: the survival of a way of life. M. C. Goldstein & C. M. Beall. Berkeley, CA: University of California Press, 1990. 191p.

'Nomination, réincarnation et/ou ancêtre tutélaire? Un mode de survie: l'example des Sérèr Ndout (Sénégal),' M. Dupire, *L'Homme*, 22, 1 (1982), 5–31.

'Norway's Gypsy minority,' U. Jørstad, *Scandinavian review*, 58, 2 (1970), 129–37.

Nyabingi: the social history of an African divinity. J. Freedman. Tervuren, Belgium: Musée Royal de l'Afrique Centrale, 1984. 119p.

'Obstructions and strategizing in church planting among the Tamil Hindus in Sri Lanka.' V. Chandy. D.Miss thesis, Fuller Theological Seminary, Pasadena, CA, 1984. 276p.

'Of MAULI, macaws, and other things: what it means to be human among the Rama Indians of eastern Nicaragua,' F. O. Loveland, *Journal of Latin American Indian literatures*, 1, 2 (1985), 137–47.

Of water and the spirit: ritual, magic, and initiation in the life of an African shaman. M. P. Somé. New York: Putnam, 1994. 311p.

Old and new in Southern Shona independent churches. M. L. Daneel. *Monographs under the auspices of the Afrika–Studiecentrum, Leiden.* The Hague: Mouton Atlantic Highlands, 1971–88. 3 vols.

Olódùmarè: god in Yoruba belief. E. B. Idowu. New York: Praeger, 1963. 222p.

One Europe—100 nations. R. N. Pedersen. Clevedon, UK: Channel View Books, 1992. 170p.

One God—two temples: schismatic process in a Kekchi village. J. Schackt. *Occasional papers*, no. 13. Oslo: University of Oslo, 1986. 206p. (Treats cargo system).

Option für die Anderen: Kirche und ursprüngliche Religionen am Beispiel der Kuna–Indianer. A. Wagua. Lucerne, Switzerland: Romero-Haus, 1992. 18p.

Orisha: the gods of Yorubaland. J. Gleason. New York: Atheneum, 1971. 122p.

Ottomans, Turks and the Jewish polity: a history of the Jews of Turkey. W. F. Weiker. Lanham, MD: University Press of America, 1992. 386p.

Outline of world cultures. G. P. Murdock. 3rd ed. New Haven, CT: Human Relations Area Files, 1963.

Oxford illustrated encyclopedia of peoples and cultures. R. Hoggart (ed). Oxford, UK and New York: Oxford University Press, 1992. 399p.

People movements in Southern Polynesia: studies in the dynamics of church–planting and growth in Tahiti, New Zealand, Tonga, and Samoa. A. R. Tippett. Chicago: Moody Press, 1971. 288p.

Peoples and cultures. A. Rogers. Oxford, UK: Oxford University Press, 1992. 256p.

Peoples and cultures of Ethio–Sudan borderlands. M. L. Bender (ed). *Committee on Northeast African Studies*, no. 10. East Lansing, MI: African Studies Center, Michigan State University Press, 1981. 214p.

Peoples and cultures of Kenya. A. Fedders. Nairobi: Transafrica, 1979.

Peoples and cultures of the Middle East. A. Shiloh (ed). New York: Random House, 1969. 506p.

Peoples and cultures of the Middle East: an anthropological reader. L. E. Sweet (ed). Garden City, NY: Natural History Press, 1970. 2 vols.

Peoples and cultures of the Pacific: an anthropological reader. A. P. Vayda (ed). Garden City, NY: Natural History Press, 1968.

Peoples, languages and migrations in Central Asia: a century of Russian rule. C. H. Minges. New York: Columbia University Press, 1967.

Peoples of Africa. J. Middleton. New York: Arco Publishing, 1978. 200p.

Peoples of Central Asia. L. Krader. Bloomington, IN: University of Indiana Press, 1963. 319p.

Peoples of Sierra Leone. M. McCulloch. *Ethnographic survey of Africa: Western Africa*, part 2. 1950; reprinted with supplementary bibliography, London: International African Institute, 1964. 102p.

Peoples of South Asia. C. Maloney. New York: Holt, Rinehart and Winston, 1974. 584p.

Peoples of the earth. E. Evans–Pritchard (ed). Danbury: Grolier, 1973. 20 vols.

Peoples of the Golden Triangle: six tribes in Thailand. P. W. Lewis & E. Lewis. London: Thames and Hudson, 1984. 300p. (Deals with Karen, Hmong, Mien, Akha, Lahu, and Lisu).

Peoples of the Horn of Africa: Somali, Afar and Saho. I. M. Lewis. London: International African Institute, 1969.

Peoples of the world: Africans south of the Sahara: the culture, geographical setting, and historical background of 34 African peoples. J. Moss & G. Wilson. Detroit, MI: Gale Research, 1991. 461p. (For young readers).

Perpetual dilemma: Jewish religion in the Jewish state. S. Z. Abramov. Cranbury, NJ: Associated University Presses, 1976. 432p.

'Perseverance of African beliefs in the religious ideas of the Bosnegers in Surinam,' B. E. Bekier, *Hemispheres*, no. 1 (1985), 93–108.

'Personhood, possession and the law in Ewe gorovodu culture.' J. V. Rosenthal. Ph.D. dissertation, Cornell University, Ithaca, NY, 1993. 389p.

Philippine ethnography: a critically annotated and selected bibliography. S. Saito. *East–West bibliographic series*, no. 2. Honolulu, HI: University Press of Hawaii, 1972. 512p.

'Philosophy, initiation and myths of the Indians of Guiana and adjacent countries,' C. H. de Goeje, in *Internationales Archiv für Ethnographie*, p.1–136, vol. 44. W. D. van Nieuwenhuis et al (eds). Leiden: E. J. Brill, 1943.

Pilgrims in a strange land: Hausa communities in Chad. J. A. Works. New York: Columbia University Press, 1976. 294p.

Poland and the minority races. A. L. Goodhart.

Polish Jewry: history and culture. M. Fuks et al. Trans., B. Pitrowska & L. Petrowicz. Warsaw: Interpress, 1982. 196p.

Prairie and plains Indians. No. 2 of section 10, *North America*, of *Iconography of religions.* Å. Hultkrantz. Leiden: E. J. Brill, 1973. 46p.

Pratique de la tradition religieuse et reproduction sociale chez les Guen/Mina du Sud–est du Togo. E. Adjakly. Geneva: Institut Universitaire d'Études du Développement, 1985. 150p.

'Process of departure of the Uzbek population from religion,' S. M. Mirhasilov, in *Secularization in multi–religious societies: Indo–Soviet perspectives: papers presented at the Indo–Soviet Symposium on Problems of Secularization in Multi–Religious Societies, Tashkent, 1978*, p.241–57. S. C. Dube & V. N. Basilov (ed). New Delhi: Indian Council of Social Science Research, 1983.

Publications in languages of the Micronesian Islands from the libraries of Bernice P. Bishop Museum and Hawaiian Mission Children's Society, Honolulu, Hawaii. P. T. Mochida. Honolulu, 1977. 53p. (Microfilm; chiefly biblical and other religious works in Gilbertese, Kusaie, Marshallese, Mortlock, Nauru and Ponape languages).

Pueblo cultures. No. 4 of section 10, *North America*, of *Iconography of religions.* B. Wright. Leiden: E. J. Brill, 1986. 29p.

Race and culture: a world view. T. Sowell. New York: Basic Books, 1994. 347p.

Rainmaking rites of Tswana tribes. I. Schapera. Cambridge, UK: African Studies Centre, 1971. 144p.

Reference encyclopedia of the American Indian. B. T. Klein. 6th ed. New York: Todd Publications, 1993. 681p.

Religion among the Bantu in South Africa. B. L. Ellis. Johannesburg: University of the Witwatersrand Library, 1968. (Contains bibliography).

'Religion and authority in a Korekore community,' M. F. C. Bourdillon, *Africa* (London), 49, 2 (1979), 172–81.

Religion and custom in a Muslim society: the Berti of Sudan. L. Holy. *Cambridge studies in social and cultural anthropology*, 78. Cambridge, UK: Cambridge University Press, 1991. 239p.

'Religion and ethnicity in the arts of a Limba chiefdom,' S. Ottenberg, *Africa*, 58, 4 (1988), 437–65.

Religion and healing in Mandari. J. Buxton. Oxford, UK: Clarendon Press, 1973. 443p.

Religion and political culture in Kano. J. N. Paden. Berkeley, CA and Los Angeles: University of California Press, 1973. 461p.

'Religion and social organization among a West African Muslim people: the Susu of Sierra Leone.' J. S. Thayer. Ph.D. dissertation, University of Michigan, Ann Arbor, MI, 1981. 386p.

Religion and society among the Tagbanuwa of Palawan Island, Philippines. R. B. Fox. *Monograph series*, no. 9. Manila: National Museum, 1982. 262p.

Religion and society in Arab Sind. D. N. Maclean. *Monographs and theoretical studies in sociology and anthropology*, no. 25. Leiden: E. J. Brill, 1989. 201p.

Religión de los Nicaraos: análisis y comparación de tradiciones culturales Nahuas. M. León–Portilla. *Universidad Autónoma de México.* Mexico City: UNAM, 1972. 116p.

'Religion in a Fante town of Southern Ghana.' H. D. Hornsey. Ph.D. dissertation, University of London, 1979. 354p.

Religion in a Tswana chiefdom. B. A. Pauw. London: Oxford University Press for the International African Institute, 1960. 258p.

Religion in an African society: a study of the religion of the Kono people of Sierra Leone in its social environment with special reference to the function of religion in that society. R. T. Parsons. Leiden: E. J. Brill, 1964. 245p.

Religion in native North America. C. Vecsey (ed). Moscow, ID: University of Idaho Press, 1990. 208p.

Religion in New Zealand. C. Nichol & J. Veitch (eds). 2nd ed. Wellington, NZ: Victoria University, 1983. 313p.

Religion, morality and the person: essays on Tallensi religion. M. Fortes. *Cambridge paperback library. Essays in social anthropology.* Cambridge, UK: Cambridge University Press, 1987. 347p.

'Religion traditionnelle et techniques thérapeutiques des Lébou du Sénégal,' O. Silla, *Bulletin de l'IFAN*, 30 (B) (1968), 1566–80.

Religión y magia entre los indios de Costa Rica de origen sureño. C. H. A. Piedra. *Publicaciones de la Universidad de Costa Rica, Serie historia y geografía*, no. 6. San José: Universidad de Costa Rica, 1965. 83p.

Religious minorities in the Soviet Union: a report. M. A. Bourdeaux. 4th ed. London: Minority Rights Group, 1984. 24p.

Religious practices of the Guji Oromo. J. Van de Loo. Addis Ababa, 1991. 153p.

'Revival Christianity among the Urat of Papua New Guinea: some possible motivational and perceptual antecedents.' S. L. Eyre. Ph.D. dissertation, University of California, San Diego, 1988. 300p.

Rhythms of a Himalayan village. H. R. Downs. San Francisco: Harper & Row, 1980. 228p. (Deals with Sherpa religion).

'Rites d'initiation et vie en société chez les Sérèrs du Sénégal,' H. Gravrand, *Afrique documents* (Dakar), 52 (1960), 129–44.

'Ritual paradoxes in Nepal: comparative perspectives on Tamang religion,' D. Holmberg, *Journal of Asian studies*, 43 (August 1984), 197–222.

'Ritual systems in Cuban Santería.' J. M. Murphy. Ph.D. dissertation, Temple University, Philadelphia, 1981. 396p.

Sacrifice and sharing in the Philippine highlands: religion and society among the Buid of Mindoro. T. Gibson. *London School of Economics monographs in social anthropology*, no. 57. London: Athlone, 1986. 262p.

Sacrifice in Ibo religion. F. A. Arinze. Ed., J. S. Boston. Ibadan, Nigeria: Ibadan University, 1970. 129p.

Samoan village: then and now. L. D. Holmes & E. R. Holmes. 2nd ed. *Case studies in cultural anthropology.* Fort Worth, TX: Harcourt Brace Jovanovich College Publishers, 1992. 176p.

Saturday God and Adventism in Ghana. K. Owusu-Mensa. Frankfurt: P. Lang, 1993. 108p.

Secret societies and the church: an evaluation of the Poro and Sande secret societies and the missionary among the Mano of Liberia. P. J. Harrington. Rome: Pontificia Universitas Gregoriana, Facultas Scientiarum Socialium, 1975. 71p.

'Shadow and substance: a Mopan Maya view of human existence,' A. E. Fink, *Canadian journal of native studies*, 7, 2 (1987), 399–414.

Shamanism and the art of the eastern Tukanoan Indians. No. 1 of section 9, *South America*, of *Iconography of religions.* G. Reichel-Dolmatoff. Leiden: E. J. Brill, 1987. 25p.

Sherpas through their rituals. S. Ortner. *Cambridge studies in cultural systems*, no. 2. Cambridge, UK: Cambridge University Press, 1978. 195p.

'Shona independent churches and ancestor worship,' M. L. Daneel, in *African initiatives in religion*, p.160–70. D. B. Barrett (ed). *21 studies from Eastern and Central Africa*. Nairobi: East African Publishing House, 1971.

Sincretismo religioso de los indigenas de Bolivia. J. Esch-Jakob. La Paz, Bolivia: HISBOL, 1994. 132p.

Sixteen cowries: Yoruba divination from Africa to the New World. W. Bascom. Bloomington, IN: Indiana University, 1980. 790p.

Sketches from the Karen hills. A. Bunker. New York: Revell, 1910. 215p. (American Baptist missionary work).

'Social organizational aspects of religious change among Basotho.' D. Bosko. Ph.D. dissertation, New York University, New York, 1983. 368p.

Société et religion chez les Newar du Népal. G. Toffin. Paris: Centre Nationale de la Recherche Scientifique, 1984. 668p.

'Some developments in Bemba religious history,' D. Werner, *Journal of religion in Africa*, 4 (1971), 1–24.

Songs of life: an introduction to Navajo religious culture. No. 3 of section 10, *North America*, of *Iconography of religions*. S. D. Gill. Leiden: E. J. Brill, 1979. 31p.

Soo Thah: a tale of the making of the Karen nation. A. Bunker. London: Anderson & Ferrier, 1902. 280p. (Deals with a Karen convert to Christianity).

'Sorcery and witchcraft in Bechuanaland,' I. Schapera, *African affairs*, 51, 202 (1952), 41–50. (On Tswana religion).

'Sorcery and witchcraft with the Bayei and Hambukushu: a cross cultural comparison,' T. J. Larson, *South African journal of ethnology*, 12, 4 (1989), 131–36.

Sorcery in its social setting: a study of the Northern Rhodesia Cewa. M. G. Marwick. Manchester, UK: Manchester University Press, 1965. 339p.

South African Jewry: a contemporary survey. M. Arkin. Cape Town: Oxford University Press, 1984. 212p.

'South Asia: the Baluch frontier tribes of Pakistan,' R. G. Wirsing, in *Protection of ethnic minorities: comparative perspectives*, p.277–312. R. G. Wirsing (ed). New York: Pergamon Press, 1981.

'South East Africa (Namibia): a human tapestry,' E. du Pisani, *Namibiana*, 2, 2 (1980), 55–62.

'South West Africa and its indigenous people,' O. Levinson, *South Africa International*, 3 (1972), 19–27.

Southeast Asian tribes, minorities, and nations. P. Kunstadter (ed). Princeton, NJ: Princeton University Press, 1967. 2 vols.

Soviet empire: the Turks of Central Asia and Stalinism. O. K. Caroe. New York: St. Martin's Press, 1953.

'Space, motion and symbol in Tetum,' D. Hicks, in *Indonesian religions in transition*, p.35–47. R. S. Kipp & S. Rodgers (ed). Tucson, AZ: University of Arizona Press, 1987.

Spanish Jesuit churches in Mexico's Tarahumara. P. M. Roca. Tuscon, AZ: University of Arizona Press, 1979. 369p.

Speaking of diversity: language and ethnicity in twentieth–century America. P. Gleason. Baltimore, MD: Johns Hopkins University Press, 1992. 327p.

Spider divination in the Cameroons. P. Gebauer. *Publications in anthropology*, no. 10. Milwaukee, WI: Milwaukee Public Museum, 1964. 157p.

'Spirit possession and deprivation cults,' I. M. Lewis, *Man*, 1, 3 (1966), 307–329.

Spirit possession and personhood among the Kel Ewey Tuareg. S. J. Rasmussen. Cambridge, UK: Cambridge University Press, 1995. 189p.

Spirits of protest: spirit–mediums and the articulation of consensus among the Zezuru of Southern Rhodesia (Zimbabwe). P. Fry. *Cambridge studies in social anthropology*, no. 14. Cambridge, UK: Cambridge University Press, 1976. 145p.

'Spirituality of the Basotho: the values of the reign of God.' M. R. A. Khiba. M.T.S. thesis, Catholic Theological Union, Chicago, 1991. 97p.

'Split–level Christianity in Africa: a study of the persistence of traditional religious beliefs and practices among the Akan Methodists of Ghana.' M. K. Forson. D.Miss. thesis, Asbury Theological Seminary, Wilmore, KY, 1993. 337p.

Storm from the East: from Genghis Khan to Khubilai Khan. R. Marshall. Berkeley, CA: University of California, 1993. 256p. (Companion volume to BBC TV series).

Symbols of change. B. Jules–Rosette. Norwood, NJ: Aldex Publishing, 1984.

Tamang ritual texts, I: preliminary studies in the folk–religion of an ethnic minority in Nepal. A. Höfer. *Beiträge zur Südasienforschung*, vol. 65. Wiesbaden, Germany: Franz Steiner, 1981. 184p.

Taming the wind of desire: psychology, medicine, and aesthetics in Malay shamanistic performance. C. Laderman. *Comparative studies of health systems and medical care*. Berkeley, CA and Los Angeles: University of California Press, 1991. 382p.

'Teach them unto your children: contextualization of Basanga puberty rites in the United Methodist Church.' D. N. Persons. Ph.D. dissertation, Fuller Theological Seminary, Pasadena, CA, 1990. 344p.

'Tharus of Dang: rites de passage and festivals,' D. P. Rajaure, *Kailash*, 9, 2–3 (1982), 177–258.

'Tharus of Dang: Tharu religion,' D. P. Rajaure, *Kailash*, 9, 1 (1982), 61–96.

'Tharus of Dang: the people and the social context,' D. P. Rajaure, *Kailash*, 8, 3–4 (1981), 155–82.

'The adoption and diffusion of Christianity amongst the Khumi–Chin people of the Upper Kaladan river area of Arakan, North–West Burma from 1900 to 1966 (with an appendix up–date to 1988).' A. N. Nason. M.A. thesis, University of Warwick, Coventry, UK, 1988. 170p.

The Akan doctrine of God: a fragment of Gold Coast ethics and religion. J. B. Danquah. 2nd ed. *Cass library of African studies, Africana modern library*, no. 2. 1944; reprint, London: Frank Cass, 1968. 206p.

The Arab Christian: a history in the Middle East. K. Cragg. London: Mowbray, 1992. 303p.

The Armenians in history and the Armenian question. E. Uras. Istanbul: Documentary Publications, 1988. 1064p.

The atlas of mankind. L. Clarke (ed). London: Mitchell Beazley & Rand McNally, 1982. 208p.

The Azerbaijani Turks: power and identity under Russian rule. A. L. Altstadt. Stanford, CA: Hoover Press, 1992. 330p.

The Baluchis and the Pathans. R. G. Wirsing. London: Minority Rights Group, 1981. 23p.

The Bambara. No. 2 of section 7, *Africa*, of *Iconography of religions*. D. Zahan. Leiden: E. J. Brill, 1974. 32p.

The ban of the bori: demons and demon–dancing in West and North Africa. A. J. N. Tremearne. London: Heath Cranton & Ouseley, 1914. 497p.

The Bantu–speaking peoples of Southern Africa. W. D. Hammond-Tooke (ed). London: Routledge & Kegan Paul, 1974. 525p.

The Barbarians of Asia: the peoples of the Steppes from 1600 B.C. S. Legg. 1970; New York: Dorset Press, 1990. 350p.

The Bassa of Liberia: a study of culture, historical development, and indigenization of the Gospel. L. Vanderaa. N.p., 1982. 138p.

The Bauls of Bangladesh: a study of an obscure religious cult. A. S. M. Anwarul Karim. Kushtia: Lalan Academy, 1980. 212p.

The Bedouin of Cyrenaica: studies in personal and corporate power. E. L. Peters. Ed., J. Goody & E. Marx. *Cambridge studies in social and cultural anthropology*, no. 72. Cambridge, UK: Cambridge University Press, 1990. 329p.

The Beja tribes of the Sudan. A. Paul. Cambridge, UK: Cambridge University Press, 1954.

The bruised pearl of Africa: Uganda past and present. M. L. Prentice. Richmond, Australia: Spectrum, 1990. 109p.

The Cape Malays: history, religion, traditions, folk tales: the Malay quarter. I. D. du Plessis. 3rd ed. Cape Town: Balkema, 1972. 97p.

The Cherokees: a population history. R. Thornton. Lincoln, NE: University of Nebraska Press, 1990. 253p.

'The church in Ghana: towards a redemptive African ecclesiology.' R. B. Otchere. D.Min. thesis, Wesley Theological Seminary, Washington, DC, 1990. 157p.

The Church of Christ in The Sudan Among the Tiv: a sociological perspective. A. Dzurgba. Ibadan, Nigeria: Dept. of Religious Studies, University of Ibadan, 1992. 145p.

'The claim of Maori identity on the cultural structure of church and society in New Zealand.' C. B. Turley. D.Min. thesis, School of Theology at Claremont, Claremont, CA, 1977. 141p.

The clash of cultures: Christian missionaries and the Shona of Rhodesia. G. Z. Kapenzi. Washington, DC: University Press of America, 1979. 104p.

The Cossacks. P. Longworth. London: Constable, 1969. 409p.

The countries and tribes of the Persian Gulf. S. B. Miles. 2nd ed. London: Cass, 1966. 643p.

The Crimean Tartars. A. Fisher. Stanford, CA: Hoover Institution Press, 1978. 264p.

The cult of Ifá among the Yoruba. Vol. 1: folk practice and the art. E. M. McClelland. London: Ethnographica, 1982. 125p.

'The cultural politics of religious change: a study of the Kpelle of Liberia.' R. Stakeman. Ph.D. dissertation, Stanford University, Stanford, CA, 1982. 355p.

'The curse on Ham's descendants: its missiological impact on Zairian Mbala Mennonite Brethren.' N. U. Lumeya. Ph.D. dissertation, Fuller Theological Seminary, Pasadena, CA, 1988. 238p.

The Dani of Irian Jaya before and after conversion. D. J. Hayward. Sentani, Irian Jaya, Indonesia: Regions Press, 1980. 233p.

'The despised serfs of southwest China: liberation in Christ of the Miao,' R. R. Covell, chapter 4 in *The liberating gospel in China: the Christian faith among China's minority peoples*. Grand Rapids, MI: Baker, 1995.

'The divining basket of the Ovimbundu,' L. Tucker, *Journal of the Royal Anthropological Institute*, 70, 2 (1940), 171–201.

The drums of affliction: a study of religious processes among the Ndembu of Zambia. V. W. Turner. Oxford, UK: Clarendon Press, 1968. 326p.

'The dual legacy: government authority and mission influence among the Glebo of eastern Liberia, 1834–1910.' J. J. Martin. Ph.D. dissertation, Boston University, Boston, 1978. 479p.

The early years of a Dutch colonial mission: the Karo field. R. S. Kipp. Ann Arbor, MI: University of Michigan Press, 1990. 272p.

'The emergence of a Diola Christianity,' R. M. Baum, *Africa*, 60, 3 (1990), 370–98.

The encyclopedia of Native American religions: an introduction. A. Hirschfelder & P. Molin. New York: Facts on File, 1992. 352p.

The encyclopedia of the peoples of the world. A. Gonen (ed). New York: Holt, Henry, 1993. 703p.

The ethnic origins of nations. A. D. Smith. Oxford, UK and Cambridge, MA: Blackwell Publishers, 1986, 1993. 330p.

The eve of the Holocaust: Shtetl Jews under Soviet rule 1939–1941. B. Pinchuk. Oxford, UK and Cambridge, MA: Blackwell, 1990. 186p.

The Ewe–speaking peoples of the Slave Coast of West Africa, their religion, manners, customs, laws, languages, &c. A. B. Ellis. London: Chapman & Hall, 1890. 331p.

'The expansion of Islam among the Bambara under French rule, 1890–1940.' S. A. Harmon. Ph.D. dissertation, University of California, Los Angeles, 1988. 562p.

The family of man. London: Marshall Cavendish, 1974. 7 vols.

The future of the Jews. D. Vital. Cambridge, MA: Harvard University Press, 1990. 170p.

The Gaia atlas of first peoples: a future for the indigenous world. J. Burger et al. New York and London: Anchor Books of Doubleday, 1990. 191p.

'The Gbaya naming of Jesus: an inquiry into the contextualization of soteriological themes among the Gbaya of Cameroon.' T. G. Christensen. Th.D. thesis, Lutheran School of Theology, Chicago, 1984. 484p.

The gospel according to Bolivia: analogies in Bolivian culture. H. L. Firestone. Cochabamba, Bolivia: Mobile Publishers, 1984. 197p.

The great human diasporas: the history of diversity and evolution. L. L. Cavalli-Sforza & F. Cavalli-Sforza. Trans., S. Thorne. Reading, MA: Helix Books of Addison-Wesley Publishing Company, 1995. 311p.

The Gurkhas. B. Farwell. New York: W. W. Norton, 1984. 317p.

The Gurungs of Nepal. D. A. Messerschmidt. Warminster, UK: Aris & Philips, 1976. 151p.

The Gypsies. A. Fraser. Oxford, UK: Blackwell, 1992. 370p.

The Gypsies in Poland: history and customs. J. Ficowski. Trans., E. Healey. Warsaw: Interpress, 1989. 303p.

The gypsies of Eastern Europe. D. Crowe & J. Kolsti (eds). Armonk, NY and London: M. E. Sharpe, 1991. 200p.

'The Gypsy population of Yugoslavia,' T. P. Vukanovic, *Journal of the Gypsy Lore Society*, 42, 1/2 (1963), 10–27.

The Hausa people: a bibliography. F. A. Salamone with the assistance of J. A. McCain. New Haven, CT: Human Relations Area Files, 1983. 2 vols.

'The history and development of the Church among the Bawm tribe and the future plan for the evangelization of other tribes in Bangladesh.' P. B. Tlung. M.Div. thesis, Asian Center for Theological Studies and Mission, Seoul, Korea, 1987. 194p.

'The history and growth of the churches in Chin State, Myanmar (Burma).' Khuang Nawni. Th.M. thesis, Fuller Theological Seminary, Pasadena, CA, 1990. 184p.

'The history of the Thakaalis according to the Thakaali tradition,' S. Gauchan & M. Vinding, *Kailash*, 5, 2 (1977), 97–184.

The Hmong: an annotated bibliography, 1983–1987. J. C. Smith. *Southeast Asian refugee studies, Occasional papers*, no. 7. Minneapolis, MN: Center for Urban and Regional Affairs, University of Minnesota, 1988. 67p.

The Holy Ghost Fathers and Catholic worship among the Igbo people of eastern Nigeria. D. E. O. Ogudo. Paderborn, Germany: Verlag Bonifatius-Druckerei, 1988. 331p.

The House of Phalo: a history of the Xhosa people in the days of their independence. J. B. Peires. Johannesburg: Ravan Press, 1981. 281p. (Treats Xhosa religion and response to Christianity).

The image of god among the Sotho–Tswana. G. M. Setiloane. Rotterdam, Netherlands: A. A. Balkema, 1976. 298p. (Treats Christianity among Sotho-Tswana).

The impact of Christianity on the tribes of Northeast India. S. Karotemprel. Shillong, India: Sacred Heart Theological College, 1994. 63p.

The Indians of Central and South America: an ethnohistorical dictionary. J. S. Olson. Westport, CT: Greenwood Press, 1991. 504p.

The influence of Islam on a Sudanese religion. J. Greenberg. *Monographs of the American Ethnological Society*, no. 10. Seattle, WA: University of Washington, 1966. 73p.

'The influence of Islam on the Afar.' K. Shehim. Ph.D. dissertation, University of Washington, Seattle, WA, 1982. 230p.

'The influence of Western Christianity on the African culture: the Abaluyia of Western Kenya.' L. N. Shamalla. M.T.S. thesis, Emory University, Atlanta, 1995. 99p.

'The island broken in two halves: sacred land and religious renewal movements among the Maori of New Zealand.' J. E. Rosenfeld. Ph.D. dissertation, University of California, Los Angeles, 1994. 474p.

'The Javanese in Surinam: ethnicity in an ethnically plural society.' P. Suparlan. Ph.D. dissertation, University of Illinois, Urbana–Champaign, 1976. 390p.

The Jews of Arab lands: a history and source book. N. A. Stillman. Philadelphia: Jewish Publication Society of America, 1979. 427p.

The Jews of Islam. B. Lewis. Princeton, NJ: Princeton University Press, 1984. 257p.

The Jews of the Middle East 1860–1972. H. J. Cohen. Jerusalem: Israel Universities Press, 1973. 197p.

The Jews of the Ottoman Empire and the Turkish Republic. S. J. Shaw. New York: New York University Press, 1991. 393p.

The Jews of the Soviet Union: the history of a national minority. B. Pinkus. Cambridge, UK: Cambridge University Press, 1988. 397p.

The Kachins: religion and custom. C. Gilhodes. Calcutta: Catholic Orphan Press, 1922. 304p.

The Kachins: their customs and traditions. O. Hanson. 1913; reprint, New York: AMS, 1982. 225p.

The Kalunga concept in Ovambo religion from 1870 onwards. T. Aarni. Stockholm: Almquist & Wicksell, 1982. 166p.

The Kavango peoples. G. D. Gibson, T. J. Larson & C. R. McGurk. Wiesbaden, Germany: Franz Steiner Verlag, 1981. 275p. (Treats religion).

'The Kavango: the country, its people and history,' K. F. R. Budack, *Namib und Meer*, 7 (1976), 29–42.

'The Kikuyu, Christianity and the Africa Inland Mission.' D. P. Sandgren. Ph.D. dissertation, University of Wisconsin, Madison, WI, 1976. 427p.

The Kurds: a concise history and fact book. M. Izady. Washington, DC: Crane Russak, 1991. 285p.

The Kurds: a contemporary overview. P. G. Kreyenbroek & S. Sperl (eds). London: Routledge, 1992. 262p.

The Kurds: a nation denied. D. McDowall. London: Minority Rights Publications, 1992. 168p.

The Kurds: an unstable element in the Gulf. S. C. Pelletiere. Boulder, CO: Westview Press, 1984. 220p.

The Kurds and Kurdistan. D. Kinnane. London: Oxford University Press, 1964. 91p.

The Kurds of Iraq: tragedy and hope. M. M. Gunter. New York: St. Martin's Press, 1992. 185p.

'The land as body: an essay on the interpretation of ritual among the Manjaks of Guinea–Bissau,' W. V. Binsbergen, *Medical anthropology quarterly*, 2, 4 (1988), 386–401. (Treats religious rituals).

The Lapps. R. Bosi. *Ancient people and places*. London: Thames & Hudson, 1960. 220p. (Discusses Lapp religion).

The Lebanese in the world: a century of emigration. A. Hourani

& N. Shehadi (eds). London: Center for Lebanese Studies/I. B. Tauris, 1993. 741p.
The liberating gospel in China: the Christian faith among China's minority peoples. R. R. Covell. Grand Rapids, MI: Baker, 1995. 288p.
The listening ebony: moral knowledge, religion, and power among the Uduk of Sudan. W. James. Oxford, UK: Clarendon Press, 1988. 391p.
The making of Bamana sculpture: creativity and gender. S. C. Brett-Smith. *RES monographs in anthropology and aesthetics.* Cambridge, UK: Cambridge University Press, 1994. 372p.
'The making of Christianity in a southern African kingdom: GammaNgwato, ca. 1870 to 1940.' P. S. Landau. Ph.D. dissertation, University of Wisconsin, Madison, WI, 1992. 589p.
'The Maya evangelical church in Guatemala.' A. J. Lloret. Th.D. thesis, Dallas Theological Seminary, Dallas, TX, 1976. 357p.
'The Mayahac of the Kekchi Belizeans,' J. Cayetano, *Belizean studies*, 10, 2 (1982), 1–8.
'The Mecca pilgrimage by West African pastoral nomads,' J. S. Birks, *Journal of modern African studies*, 15, 1 (1977), 47–58.
The Mexican Kikapoo Indians. F. A. Latorre & D. L. Latorre. *Texas Pan–American series.* Austin, TX: University of Texas Press, 1976. 401p.
The minorities of northern China: a survey. H. Schwartz. Bellingham, WA: Western Washington University Press, 1984.
The modern Uzbeks: from the fourteenth century to the present: a cultural history. E. A. Allworth. Stanford, CA: Hoover Institution Press, 1990. 424p.
The myth of ritual: a native's ethnography of Zapotec life–crisis rituals. F. E. Gundi & A. H. Jiménez. Tucson, AZ: University of Arizona Press, 1986. 147p.
The Naron: a Bushman tribe of the central Kalahari. D. F. Bleek. Cambridge, UK: University of Cape Town, Publications of the School of African Life and Language, 1928. 67p.
The nationalities question in the Soviet Union. G. Smith (ed). London: Longman, 1990. 389p.
The native tribes of South West Africa. C. H. L. Hahn. Cape Town: Cape Times, 1928. 214p.
'The new people of God: the Christian community in the African Orthodox Church (Karing'a) and the Arathi (Agikuyu spirit churches).' F. K. Githieya. Ph.D. dissertation, Emory University, Atlanta, 1992. 405p.
'The Orang Asli: an outline of their progress in modern Malaya,' A. Jones, *Journal of Southeast Asian history*, 9, 2 (1968), 286–305.
The other Jews: the Sephardim today. D. J. Elazar. New York: Basic Books, 1989. 248p.
'The Ovambo sermon: a study of the preaching of the Evangelical Lutheran Ovambo–Kavango Church in South West Africa.' S. Löytty. Tampereen Keskuspaino thesis, University of Helsinki, Tampere, Finland, 1971. 175p.
The Ovimbundu of Angola. Part 2 of *West Central Africa.* M. McCulloch. *Ethnographic survey of Africa,* D. Forde (ed). London: International African Institute, 1952. 50p.
The Ovimbundu of Angola. W. D. Hambly. *Field Museum of Natural History, Publication no. 329: Anthropological series,* 21, 2. Chicago: Field Museum of Natural History, 1934. 362p. (Treats religion).
'The Paramacca Maroons: a study in religious acculturation.' J. D. Lenoir. Ph.D. dissertation, New School for Social Research, New York, 1973. 213p.
The Penguin atlas of diasporas. G. Chaliand & J. Rageau. Trans., A. M. Berret. New York and London: Viking Penguin, 1995. 204p. (Originally published as Atlas des Diasporas. Editions Odile Jacob, 1991).
'The people,' D. B. Bista, in *Nepal in perspective*, p.35–45. P. S. J. Rana & K. P. Malla (eds). Kathmandu: Centre for Economic Development and Administration, 1973.
The people atlas. P. Steele. Oxford, UK: Oxford University Press, 1991. 64p. (For children).
The people of Nepal. D. B. Bista. 5th ed. Kathmandu: Ratna Pustak Bhandar, 1987. 210p.
The people of the stones: the Chepangs of central Nepal. N. Rai. Kathmandu: Centre for Nepal and Asian Studies, 1985. 125p.
The people of Tibet. C. Bell. Oxford, UK: Clarendon Press, 1928. 319p.
The people time forgot. A. Gibbons. Chicago: Moody Press, 1981. 355p.
The peoples of Africa: an ethnohistorical dictionary. J. S. Olson. Westport, CT: Greenwood press, 1996. 689p.
The peoples of the Soviet Union. V. Kozlov. Trans., P. M. Tiffen. London: Hutchinson, 1988. 262p.
The peoples of the USSR: an ethnographic handbook. R. Wixman. London: Macmillan Reference Books, 1984. 246p.
The peopling of Southern Africa. R. Inskeep. Cape Town: Philip, 1978. 160p.
The pool that never dries up. R. Wynne. London: USPG, 1988. 129p. (Christian missions among the Hambukushu).
'The position of women in the Sisala divination cult,' E. L. Mendonsa, in *The new religions of Africa*, p.57–66. B. Jules–Rosette (ed). Norwood, NJ: Ablex Publishing, 1979.
The possessed and the dispossessed: spirits, identity, and power in a Madagascar migrant town. L. A. Sharp. *Comparative studies of health systems and medical care*, no. 37. Berkeley, CA: University of California Press, 1993. 364p.
'The presence of Islam among the Akan of Ghana: a bibliographic essay,' R. A. Silverman & D. Owusu–Ansah, *History in Africa*, 16 (1989), 325–39.
'The prime mover and fear in Inuit religion: a discussion of "native views",' J. G. Oosten, in *Continuity and identity in native America: essays in honor of Benedikt Hartmann*, p.69-83. M. Jansen et al (eds). Leiden: E. J. Brill, 1988.
'The problem of a female deity in translation,' R. Venberg, *Bible Translator*, 35, 4 (October 1984), 415–417. (Translating the Bible for the Pévé tribe, southwestern Chad. Reprinted from *Bible Translator*, April 1971).
'The Qashqa'i,' R. Weekes, in *Muslim peoples*, p.631–37, vol. 2. Westport, CT: Greenwood Press, 1984. (Lists 25 books and articles on the Qashqa'i).
The Qashqa'i nomads of Fars. P. Oberling. The Hague: Mouton, 1974. 277p.
The Qashqa'i of Iran. L. Beck. New Haven, CT: Yale University Press, 1986. 400p.
'The Raute: notes on a nomadic hunting and gathering tribe of Nepal,' J. Reinhard, *Kailash*, 2, 4 (1974), 233–71.
The realm of the Word: language, gender, and Christianity in a Southern African kingdom. P. S. Landau. *Social history of Africa.* Portsmouth, NH: Heinemann, 1995. 278p.
The rise and fall of the Black Caribs of St. Vincent. I. E. Kirby & C. I. Martin. Kingstown, St. Vincent: St. Vincent Archaeological and Historical Society, 1972. 65p.
The sacred mountain of Colombia's Kogi Indians. No. 2 of section 9, *South America*, of *Iconography of religions.* G. Reichel-Dolmatoff. Leiden: E. J. Brill, 1990. 38p.
The Samaritans. A. D. Crown (ed). Tübingen, Germany: Mohr, 1989. 813p.
'The Seleka–Rolong and the Wesleyan Methodist missionaries, 1823–1884.' R. L. Watson. Ph.D. dissertation, Boston University, Boston, 1974. 237p.
The Sherpas of Nepal—Buddhist highlanders. C. von Fürer–Haimendorf. 1972; reprint, New Delhi: Sterling, 1979. 298p.
The Shona and the Ndebele of Southern Rhodesia. H. Kuper, A. J. B. Hughes & J. van Velsen. London: International African Institute, 1954. 131p.
The Shona peoples: an ethnography of the contemporary Shona, with special reference to their religion. M. F. C. Bourdillon. 3rd ed. Gwelo, Zimbabwe: Mambo Press, 1987. 359p.
The Slovene minority of Carinthia. T. M. Barker with the collaboration of A. Moritsch. *East European Monographs*, no. 169. Boulder, CO: East European Monographs, 1984. 415p.
'The social structure of the Pokot and its implications for church planting: a new paradigm for strategic African missions.' R. G. Lewis. D. Miss. thesis, Biola University, La Mirada, CA, 1991. 260p.
'The southern Methodists and the Atetela: the history of the Methodist Episcopal Church, South, in the central Congo, 1912–1960.' Okenge Owandji Kasongo. Ph.D. dissertation, University of Kentucky, Lexington, KY, 1982. 230p.
The Soviet Germans: past and present. I. Fleischhauer & B. Pinkus. London: Hurst, in association with the Marjorie Mayrock Center for Soviet and East European Research at the Hebrew University, Jerusalem, 1986. 185p.
The spirits and their cousins: some aspects of belief, ritual, and social organization in a rural Hausa village in Niger. R. H. Faulkingham. Amherst, MA: Dept. of Anthropology, University of Massachusetts, 1975. 57p.
The springs of Mende belief and conduct: a discussion of the influence of the belief in the supernatural among the Mende. W. T. Harris & H. Sawyerr. Freetown: Sierra Leone University Press, 1968. 152p.
'The supernatural world of the Badyaranké of Tonghia (Senegal),' W. Simmons, *Journal des africanistes*, 37, 1 (1967), 41–72.
'The Tajik of Afghanistan,' D. B. Barrett, *International journal of frontier missions*, 10 (April 1993), 93–94.
The Talaings. R. Halliday. Rangoon: Superintendent, Government Printing, 1917. 164p. (Treats religion).
The timetables of Jewish history: a chronology of the most important people and events in Jewish history. J. Gribetz et al. New York: Simon & Schuster, 1993. 752p.
The Tshi–speaking peoples of the Gold Coast of West Africa: their religion, manners, customs, laws, language, etc. A. B. Ellis. 1887; reprint, Chicago: Benin Press, 1964. 343p.
'The Tshwa response to Christianity: a study of the religious and cultural impact of Protestant Christianity on the Tshwa of Southern Mocambique.' A. Helgesson. M.A. thesis, University of the Witwatersrand, Johannesburg, 1971. 296p.
The Tswana. I. Schapera. 2nd ed. London: International African Institute, 1976. 93p.
'The Turkmen in the age of imperialism: a study of the Turkmen people and their incorporation into the Russian Empire.' M. Saray. University Society Printing House, 1989.
'The Uighurs of Xinjiang,' A. al–Hada (pseudonym), *International journal of frontier missions*, 2, 4 (1985), 373–83.
'The Uzbeks and their ideas of ultimate reality and meaning,' H. R. Battersby, *Ultimate reality and meaning*, 8, 3 (1985), 172–95.
'The Uzbeks in Afghanistan,' E. Naby, *Central Asian Survey*, 3, 1 (1984), 1–21.
The victim and its masks: an essay on sacrifice and masquerade in the Maghreb. A. Hammoudi. Chicago: University of Chicago Press, 1993. 214p. (Also in French).
The Vlachs: the history of a Balkan people. T. J. Winnifrith. London: Duckworth, 1987. 180p.
The Volga Tatars: a profile in national resilience. A. A. Rorlich. Stanford, CA: Hoover Institution Press, 1986. 288p.
The Yaka and Suku. No. 1 of section 7, *Africa*, of *Iconography of religions.* A. P. Bourgeois. Leiden: E. J. Brill, 1985. 26p
Tibet: Bon religion: a death ritual of the Tibetan Bonpos. No. 13 of section 12, *East and Central Asia*, of *Iconography of religions.*H. P. Kvaerne. Leiden: E. J. Brill, 1985. 34p.
'Tierce, Eglise, ma Mère: ou, la conversion d'une Communauté païenne au Christ.' A. T. Sanon. Thesis, Institut Catholique de Paris, 1970. 294p.
Tin mosques and Ghanatowns: a history of Afghan camel drivers in Australia. C. Stevens. Melbourne: Oxford University Press, 1989. 400p.
Tonga Christianity. S. Shewmaker. South Pasadena, CA: William Carey Library, 1970. 215p.
'Toward a new missionary impulse of the Karen Baptist Church of Myanmar.' S. D. Say. D. Miss. thesis, Fuller Theological Seminary, Pasadena, CA, 1993. 276p.
Toward an African Christianity: inculturation applied. E. Hillman. New York: Paulist Press, 1993. 106p.
'Towards an Aymara church.' D. Llanque Chana. M.Th. thesis, St. John's Seminary, 1979. 146p.
'Tradition and change among the pastoral Harasiis in Oman,' D. Chatty, in *Anthropology and development in North Africa and the Middle East.* Boulder, CO: Westview Press, 1990.
Tradition and Christianity in the Bakossi society: a lecture delivered in the Presbyterian Theological College, Nyasoso, 6 Jan. 1976. S. N. Ejedepang–Koge. N.p., 1976. 23p.
'Traditional religion in Nigeria with particular reference to the Yoruba,' E. A. Odumuyinwa, in *Nigerian life and culture: a book of readings.* O. Y. Oyeneye & M. O. Shoremi (eds). Ago–Iwoye, Nigeria: Ogun State University, 1985.
Tribal communities: issues, analysis and organization: a resource book based on the tribal organizers training programme in Southeast Asia, April–May 1987. Kowloon, Hong Kong: Christian Conference of Asia, 1988. 103p.
Tribes and state formation in the Middle East. P. S. Khoury & J. Kostiner. Berkeley, CA: University of California, 1991. 366p.
Tribes, government, and history in Yemen. P. Dresch. Oxford, UK: Clarendon Press, 1989. 440p.
Tribes in Oman. J. R. L. Carter. London: Peninsular, 1982. 176p.
Tribus, ethnies et pouvoir en Mauritanie. P. Marchesin. Paris: Karthala, 1992. 437p.
'Turkmen,' W. G. Irons, in *Muslim peoples: a world ethnographic survey.* 2nd ed. Westport, CT: Greenwood Press, 1984. Ed. R. V. Weekes.
Two worlds of Judaism: the Israeli and American experiences. C. S. Liebman & S. M. Cohen. New Haven, CT: Yale University Press, 1990. 183p.
'Ukrainian Catholics and Orthodox in Poland,' A. Sorokowski, *Religion in Communist lands*, 14, 3 (1986), 244–61.
Un cycle oral hagiographique dans le Moyen–Atlas marocain. J. Drouin. *Série Sorbonne*, 2. Paris: Publications de la Sorbonne, 1975. 270p.
'Un exemple d'indépendence et de résistance religieuse: les hommes et les dieux Lobi,' M. Cros, *Mondes et Développement* (Paris), 17, 65 (1989), 59–65.
'Un système philosophique sénégalais: la cosmologie des Diola,' L. V. Thomas, *Présence africaine*, 32/33 (1960), 64–76.
Undermining the centre: the Gulf migration and Pakistan. S. Addleton. Oxford, UK: Oxford University Press, 1992. 232p.
Unreached peoples: clarifying the task. H. Schreck & D. B. Barrett (ed). Monrovia, CA: MARC; Birmingham, AL: New Hope, 1987. 310p.
Unreached peoples of Kenya project. K. Shingledecker et al. Nairobi: Daystar Communications, 1982. 13 vols.
Urban anthropology: perspectives on 'Third World' urbanization and urbanism. P. Gutkind. New York: Harper & Row, 1974.
Vanishing diaspora: the Jews in Europe since 1945. B. Wasserstein. Cambridge, MA: Harvard University Press, 1996. 352p.
'Varieties of religion and religious specialists among the Susu of Sierra Leone,' J. S. Thayer, in *Sierra Leone studies at Birmingham, 1983: proceedings of the third Birmingham Sierra Leone Studies Symposium, 15th-17th July 1983, Fircroft College, Birmingham.* P. K. Mitchell & A. Jones (eds). Birmingham, UK: University of Birmingham, Centre of West African Studies, 1984.
Virgin Islands English creoles. G. Sprave. *Microstate studies*, vol. 1. N.p.: Caribbean Research Institute, 1977, p.8–28.
What prize awaits us: letters from Guatemala. B. Kita. Maryknoll, NY: Orbis Books, 1988. 254p.
Wind, sand, and silence: travels with Africa's last nomads. V. Englebert. San Francisco: Chronicle Books, 1992. 181p. (Descriptions of Tuareg, Bororo, Danakil, and Turkana).
'Witchcraft among the Akamba and Africa Inland Church, Kenya.' J. M. Mbuva. M.A. thesis, Fuller Theological Seminary, Pasadena, CA, 1992. 177p.
'Witchcraft among the Tapanahoni Djuka,' W. van Wetering, in *Maroon societies: rebel slave communities in the Americas*, p.370–88. R. Price (ed). Garden City, NY: Anchor Press/Doubleday, 1973.
Witchcraft and sorcery in Ovambo. M. Hiltunen. Helsinki: Finnish Anthropological Society, 1986. 178p.
Witchcraft, oracles and magic among the Azande. E. E. Evans–Pritchard. Oxford, UK: Clarendon, 1937. 558p.
'Women, ecology and Islam in the making of modern Hausa cultural history.' M. W. Bivins. Ph.D. dissertation, Michigan State University, East Lansing, MI, 1994. 265p.
Women of fire and spirit: history, faith and gender in Roho religion in Nyanza. C. H. Hoehler–Fatton. New York: Oxford University Press, 1995.
'Words and blessings: Batak Catholic discourses in North Sumatra.' B. Sutanto. Ph.D. dissertation, Cornell University, Ithaca, NY, 1989. 369p.
World cultures encyclopedia. Human Relations Area Files. New Haven, CT: Yale University with G. K. Hall, 1991–94. 10 vols.
'Yao religion and society,' J. Lemoine, in *Highlanders of Thailand*, p.195–211. J. McKinnon & W. Bhruksasri (eds). Kuala Lumpur, Malaysia: Oxford University Press, 1983.
Yoruba beliefs and sacrificial rites. J. O. Awolalu. London: Longman, 1979. 203p.
Yoruba religion and medicine in Ibadan. G. E. Simpson. Ibadan, Nigeria: Ibadan University, 1980. 195p.
'Yoruba religion in Trinidad: transfer and reinterpretation,' M. W. Lewis, *Caribbean quarterly*, 24, 3–4 (1978), 18–32.
Yoruba religious carving: pagan and Christian sculpture in Nigeria and Dahomey. K. Carroll. London: G. Chapman, 1967. 184p.
Zimbabwe. D. Potts. 2nd ed. *World bibliographical series*, vol. 4. Oxford, UK: CLIO Press, 1993. 402p. (See especially 'Religion,' p.99–109).

Table 8-1. Peoples of the World: an ethnocultural, ethnolinguistico-racial classification.

Code 1	RACE GEOGRAPHICAL RACE **Ethnolinguistic family** People (or sub-family) 2	*Color* 3	*b%* 4	*d%* 5	*m%* 6	*n%* 7	*A%* 8	*Main constituent cultures, additional peoples, tribes, languages, alternative names or synonyms (in parentheses)* 9
	AUSTRALOID (Archaic White)	Grey/Brown						Australoid (Archaic White, Proto-Caucasoid, Classical Australoid)
	AUSTRO-ASIATIC	Grey						Aboriginals in Australasia, Southeast Asia, India; 140 Austro-Asiatic languages, about 360 others
AUG01	**Ainu/Aborigine**	Grey	3.00	1.00	0.00	2.00	75.00	Ainu; also Ainu-like Formosan Aborigine; Ami, Atayal, Bunun, Paiwan, Pyuma, Saisait, Yami; 22 languages
AUG01a	Aborigine	Grey	3.00	1.00	0.00	2.00	75.00	Asian Aborigines, Amis, Bunan, 20 languages
AUG01b	Ainu	Grey	3.00	1.00	0.00	2.00	75.00	Ainu
AUG02	**Australian Aborigine**	Grey	3.00	1.00	0.00	2.00	65.00	Arunta, Bidjandjara, Gunwingguan, Kariera, Mumgin, Pama-Nyungan, Tiwi, Walbiri, Warramunga; 260 languages
AUG03	**Mon-Khmer**	Grey/Yellow						Mon-Khmer, Australoid peoples with Mongoloid admixture; over 105 languages
AUG03a	Khasi	Grey/Yellow	3.50	1.50	0.00	2.00	58.00	Khasi (Standard Khasi; Lyngngam, Synteng, War)
AUG03b	Khmer	Grey/Yellow	3.92	1.42	0.00	2.50	58.20	Khmer (Cambodian)
AUG03c	Mon	Grey/Yellow	3.50	1.50	0.00	2.00	58.00	Mon (Peguan, Talaing), Niakoul
AUG03d	Nicobarese	Grey/Yellow	3.00	1.00	0.00	2.00	57.00	Central (Camorta, Kathcall, Nancowry, Trinkat), North (Bompaka, Car, Chowra, Teressa), South (Coastal Great); Shompe
AUG03z	other Mon-Khmer	Grey/Yellow	3.00	1.00	0.00	2.00	57.00	Bahnar, Bo, Boloven, Brao, Cham Re, Katu, Khmu, Ma, Mnong, Oi, Palaung, Pear, Phuteng, Sedang, So, Suai, Wa, &c
AUG04	**Munda-Santal**	Grey						Munda (Kherwarl): Northern, Southern, Western; 20 languages
AUG04a	Ho	Grey	3.50	1.00	0.00	2.50	58.00	Ho (Lankakol), Lohara
AUG04b	Mundari	Grey	3.50	1.10	0.00	2.40	58.00	Birhor, Mundari (Kol, Horo)
AUG04c	Santal	Grey	3.50	1.00	0.00	2.50	57.00	Karmali (Kohle), Mahili (Mahli), Pahariya (Mal Paharia), Santal (Santali, Satar)
AUG04d	Saora	Grey	3.50	1.00	0.00	2.50	58.00	Saora (Savara, Sora)
AUG04z	other Munda-Santal	Grey	3.50	1.10	0.00	2.40	57.00	Asuri, Bhumij, Chenchu, Gadaba (Gutob), Geta, Juang, Kharia, Koda, Korku, Korwa, Nahari, Remo, Turi, et alii
AUG05	**Negrito** (Oceanic/Asiatic Pygmoid)	Grey/Black	3.00	1.00	0.00	2.00	55.00	Aeta, Andamanese, Baluga, Kadar, Malaccan (Aslian), New Guinea Pygmy (Aiome, Ekari (Kapauku), Tapiro), Semang, Senoi
AUG06	**Pre-Dravidian**	Grey						Proto-Australoid (Pre-Dravidian Aboriginal); 42 languages
AUG06a	Bhil	Grey	3.50	1.00	0.00	2.50	58.00	Bhil (Bhili, with over 20 dialects)
AUG06b	Gond	Grey	3.40	1.00	0.00	2.40	58.00	Gond (Gondi): Adilalad, Betul, Bisonhom Maria, Chhindwara, Hill Maria, Kol, Mandla, Muria
AUG06c	Oraon	Grey	3.50	1.10	0.00	2.40	58.00	Oraon (Kurukh, Kurux, Uraon)
AUG06z	other Pre-Dravidian	Grey	3.50	1.00	0.00	2.50	59.00	Kadir, Kandh, Khond (Kui), Kolami, Kolarian, Kurumba, Malto, Naiki, Paniyan, et alii
AUG07	**Vedda**	Grey/Brown	2.50	1.00	0.00	1.50	58.00	Vedda (Indo-Australoid, Bedda, Veddah, Veddoid, Weddo)
	OCEANIC	Brown						Melanesian, Melanesold, Oceanic Negro, Oceanic Negroid, Papuasian; Heonesian; over 1,180 languages
AON08	**Fijian**	Brown	2.45	0.45	-0.94	1.06	64.90	Fijian (Bauan), Kadavu, Rotuman
AON09	**Melanesian**	Brown/Black						Melanesian (island, coastal); 380 Oceanic Austronesian languages, et alia
AON09a	New Caledonian	Brown/Black	3.23	0.94	0.00	2.15	60.00	New Caledonian: Houailou (Wailu), Lai, Lifu (Lific), Maré (Nengone), Ponérihouen; 18 other languages
AON09b	New Guinea Melanesian	Brown/Black	3.35	1.07	0.00	2.29	60.00	Bwaidoga, Dobu, Graged, Keopara, Kirilwina, Motu, Police Motu, Tuna, Usiai, Yabem; over 190 languages
AON09c	New Hebridean	Brown/Black	3.55	1.10	0.00	2.45	57.00	New Hebridean; Efate, Epi, Malo, Mota, Nguna-Tongoa, Paama, Tanna; 117 languages
AON09d	Solomoni Melanesian	Brown/Black	3.75	0.44	0.00	3.32	56.00	Solomoni: Bambatana, Bugotu, Kerebuto, Kwaio, Lau, Maringe, Nggela, Roviana, Saa, To'abaita, Vaturanga; about 85 languages
AON09e	Western Melanesian	Brown/Black	3.10	1.00	0.00	2.10	58.00	Ambonese, Ceramese, Irianese (Bonggo, Sobei, Tobati, Yamna), other Moluccan and South Moluccan (Samic); 50 languages
AON09f	Neo-Melanesian	Brown/Black	3.10	1.00	0.00	2.10	58.00	Half-Melanesian, Melanesian-Papuan, Solomoni-Papuan
AON10	**Papuan**	Brown						700 Papuan (Indo-Pacific, Non-Austronesian) languages, 450 related to each other, another 50 isolates; Papuasian
AON10a	Irianese Papuan	Brown	3.30	1.00	0.00	2.30	60.00	Asmat, Bentoeni, Damal, Dani, Djabi, Jali, Marind-Anim, Sentani & 340 other tribes
AON10b	New Guinea Papuan (Eastern)	Brown	3.35	1.07	0.00	2.29	60.00	Awa, Chimbu, Enga, Gadsup, Gahuku, Guhu-Samane, Kiwai, New Britain Papuan, Orokaiva, Wabago, & over 450 others
AON10c	North Halmaheran	Brown	3.10	1.00	0.00	2.10	59.00	North Halmaheran: Galelos, Ibu, Kau, Loloda, Makian, Modole, Morotai, Papu, Tabaru, Temate, Tidore, Tobelo, Wai
AON10d	Solomoni Papuan	Brown	3.74	0.44	0.00	3.30	56.00	Solomoni Papuan: Bougainvillian, Rendova, Russell Islander, Santa Cruz, Savosavo, Vella Lavella (Bilua)
AON10e	Timorese Papuan	Brown	3.10	1.00	0.00	2.10	58.20	Alorese, Kisarese, Timorese Papuan; over 20 languages
AON10f	Torres Strait Islander	Brown	2.90	1.10	0.00	1.80	60.00	Torres Strait Islander: Mabuiag, Mer, Saibai, et alii
	CAPOID (Archaic African)	Grey/Brown						Descendants of Early, Paleolithic or Prehistoric Africans
	EARLY AFRICAN	Grey/Brown						Aboriginal descendants of Bushmanoid, Sangoan Pygmy, Pygmoid
BYG11	**Khoisan**	Grey						Khoisan (Bushmanoid, Click): Central Khoisan (Khoe), North (Zhu), South (Kwi); about 47 languages
BYG11a	Bergdama	Grey	3.00	1.00	0.00	2.00	56.00	Bergdama (Damara, Haukoin, Mountain Damara)
BYG11b	East African Bushman	Grey	3.10	1.00	0.00	2.10	55.00	Boni, Dorobo (Asa, Okiek), Kindiga (Hadzapi, Tindiga), Manjo (Bacha, Fuga), Midgan (Ribi), Sandawe, Sanye, Teuso
BYG11c	Hottentot	Grey	3.00	1.10	0.00	1.90	55.00	Cape Hottentot (Grigriqua), Nama (Namaqua)
BYG11d	South African Bushman	Grey	3.00	1.00	0.00	2.00	55.00	Dukwe, Galikwe, Gwi, Heikum, Hiechware, Hukwe, Korana, Koroca, Kung, Namib, Naron, Nusan, Ohekwe, Tannekwe, Xam
BYG12	**Pygmy**	Grey/Brown	3.00	1.10	0.00	1.90	54.00	Pygmy (Negrillo, Pygmoid): Binga (Bongo, Koa, Yaga), Central Twa, Gesera (Twa, Zigaba), Mbuti (Aka, Efe, Twides)
	CAUCASIAN (Caucasoid)	White/Tan/Brown						Caucasian, Caucasoid, Indo-European; about 660 languages
	EUROPEAN	White						European: Alpine, Armenian, Mediterranean, Nordic; about 198 languages
CEW13	**Albanian**	White	2.27	0.53	-0.90	0.84	68.80	Albanian (Shiptar): Gheg (Dukagjin, Malësia), Tosk (Camövia, Labëria, Myzeqe)
CEW14	**Armenian**	White	2.30	0.60	-0.60	2.30	70.00	Armenian (Ashksarhik, Hay, Hayq), Thrace-Phrygian
CEW15	**Baltic**	White						Balt: East Baltic, Baltic-Slavic
CEW15a	Latvian	White	1.39	1.21	-0.46	-0.28	78.40	Latvian (Lett, Lettish)
CEW15b	Lithuanian	White	1.48	1.00	-0.27	0.21	77.70	Lithuanian, Samogit
CEW16	**Basque**	White	1.10	1.00	0.00	0.10	82.00	Basque (Euskarian, Navarrese)
CEW17	**Caucasian**	White						Ibero-Caucasian (Paleocaucasian): about 39 languages
CEW17a	Adygo-Abkhazi	White	1.80	1.00	-0.70	0.10	74.00	Abazinian, Abkhazian, Adyghe, Circassian (Cherkess, Karbardian), Ubykh
CEW17b	Dagestani	White	1.90	1.00	-0.80	0.10	72.00	Aguly, Andi-Tsezi, Avar, Budukh, Dargin, Dargwa, Khinalug, Kryz, Lakk, Lezgin, Rutul, Tabasaran, Tsakhur, Udi, &c
CEW17c	Georgian	White	1.80	0.90	-0.80	0.10	75.00	Georgian (Kartvelian), Laze (Chan, Laz, Zan), Mingrelian, Svan
CEW17d	Nakh	White	1.80	1.00	-0.70	0.10	75.00	Veinakh: Bat, Chechen (Kokhchi, Shishan), Ingush (Galgai), Kist
CEW18	**Celtic**	White						Celtic: Continental (Gaulish), Insular (Brythonic: Breton, Cornish, Welsh; Goidelic: Irish, Manx, Scottish)
CEW18a	Breton	White	1.30	1.00	0.00	0.30	77.00	Breton: Comouaille, Léon, Tréguier, Vannes
CEW18b	Irish	White	1.44	0.92	-0.72	-0.19	75.30	Irish (Gaelic, Erse), Irish Traveller (Nomad, Shelta)
CEW18c	Scotish Gaelic	White	1.40	1.00	0.00	0.40	75.00	Scottish Gaelic (Gaelic, Gael, Goidel, Scots Gaelic)
CEW18d	Welsh	White	1.40	1.00	0.00	0.40	75.00	Welsh (Cymraeg)
CEW18z	other Celtic	White	1.40	1.00	0.00	0.40	75.00	Cornish, Manx
CEW19	**Germanic** (Teutonic)	White						Germanic: North Germanic (Scandinavian), West Germanic (Afrikaans, Dutch, English, Flemish, Frisian, German)
CEW19a	Afrikaner	White	2.00	0.90	0.00	1.10	76.00	Afrikaner (Afrikaans, Boer)
CEW19b	Alsatian	White	1.50	1.10	0.00	0.40	82.00	Alsatian, Lotharingian
CEW19c	Anglo-Australian	White	1.51	0.77	0.68	1.41	78.30	Anglo-Australian (English)
CEW19d	Anglo-Canadian	White	1.42	0.77	0.73	1.38	79.30	Anglo-Canadian (English)
CEW19e	Anglo-New Zealander	White	1.74	0.82	0.00	0.92	77.00	Anglo-New Zealander (English), Pakeha
CEW19f	Austrian	White	1.16	1.12	0.35	0.38	82.40	Austrian (German), Tirolean
CEW19g	Danish	White	1.25	1.16	0.12	0.20	82.90	Danish (Dane)
CEW19h	Dutch	White	1.37	0.87	0.23	0.73	81.30	Dutch (Netherlandic)
CEW19i	English (British)	White	1.39	1.15	0.00	0.24	80.30	British: Briton, English, Scot, Scottish; many regional dialects
CEW19j	Faeroese	White	1.60	1.40	0.00	0.20	78.00	Faeroese (Faroese, Faeroe Islander)
CEW19k	Flemish	White	1.21	1.13	0.04	0.13	82.10	Fleming (Flemish, Netherlandic)
CEW19l	Frisian	White	1.25	1.16	0.00	0.20	82.00	Frisian: East, North, West
CEW19m	German	White	1.13	1.14	0.45	0.44	82.90	German (East Middle, High, Low, West Middle): Bavarian, Franconian, German-Swiss, Rhinelander, Saxon, Swabian
CEW19n	Icelander	White	1.74	0.70	0.00	1.04	75.70	Icelander (Icelandic)
CEW19o	Luxemburger	White	1.23	1.07	0.53	0.69	82.40	Luxemburger (Letzeburgesch)
CEW19p	Norwegian	White	1.47	1.08	0.12	0.51	80.30	Norwegian: New Norwegian (Nynorski, Landsmal), Dano-Norwegian (Bokmal), Russonorsk
CEW19q	Swedish	White	1.40	1.15	0.23	0.48	81.20	Swedish (Swede), Finlander Swede
CEW19r	Ulster Irish	White	1.40	1.20	-0.10	0.10	78.00	Ulster Irish (Northern Irish, English-speaking), British Irish
CEW19s	USA White	White	1.50	0.90	0.40	1.00	78.10	English-speaking USA White (of numerous immigrant ethnic backgrounds, but mother tongue now English)
CEW20	**Greek**	White	1.04	0.98	0.20	0.26	82.70	Hellenic (Romaic): Demotic Greek, Katharevusa; Cretan, Old Athenian, Peloponnesian, Tsakonian; Greek Cypriot, Karakachan
CEW21	**Latin** (Romance)	White						Latin (Romance, Romanic, Italic), Latin European
CEW21a	Catalonian	White	1.70	0.90	0.00	0.80	82.00	Catalonian (Catalán): Andorran, Balearic, East Catalán, Valencian, West Catalán
CEW21b	French	White	1.35	0.98	0.00	0.37	80.20	French, Franco-Swiss, metropolitan French, Monégasque; Bourbonnais, Francien, Gallo, Orléanais, &c
CEW21c	French-Canadian	White	1.40	0.80	0.50	1.10	79.30	French-Canadian (French)
CEW21d	Galician	White	1.20	0.90	0.00	0.30	83.00	Galician (Northern Portuguese, Gallego)
CEW21e	Italian	White	1.00	1.00	0.09	0.09	84.60	Italian, Italo-Swiss, Sanmarinese, Sicilian; Gallo-Italian, Tuscan, Venetan, &c
CEW21f	Moldavian	White	2.10	1.00	-1.10	0.00	72.00	Moldavian (Eastern Daco-Rumanian, Bessarabian)
CEW21g	Portuguese	White	1.16	1.02	-0.11	0.03	81.50	Portuguese: Central, Insular, Northern, Southern
CEW21h	Rhaeto-Romanian	White	2.00	1.00	0.00	1.00	82.90	Rhaeto-Romanian: Friulian, Ladin, Rhaetian, Romansh (Grishun, Rumantsch), Sursilvan, Sutsilvan
CEW21i	Romanian	White	1.57	1.12	-0.19	0.26	77.70	Aromanian (Vlach, Volokh), Romanian (Rumanian): Daco-Rumanian, Transylvanian, Wallachian
CEW21j	Sardinian	White	1.35	1.00	0.00	0.35	84.00	Sard (Sardinian, Sardo): dialects Campidanian, Gallurian, Logudorian, Sassarian
CEW21k	Spanish	White	1.08	0.92	0.00	0.16	82.90	Spaniard Spanish (Castellano, Castillan): Andalusian, Aragonese, Asturias, Leonese, &c
CEW21l	Walloon	White	1.21	1.13	0.04	0.13	82.10	Walloon (French)
CEW21z	other Latin	White	1.30	1.00	0.00	0.30	80.00	Corsican, Franco-Provençal, Gibraltarian, Istriot, Latin, Occitan (Gascon, Languedoc, Provençal), et alii
CEW22	**Slav**	White						Slav (Slavic, Slavonic): East, South, West
CEW22a	Bosnian	White	1.50	0.90	0.00	0.00	77.00	Bosnian (Serbo-Croatian), Muslmani
CEW22b	Bulgar	White	1.25	1.23	-0.25	-0.23	80.70	Bulgar (Bulgarian), Palityan: Central, Eastern, Northeastern, Western
CEW22c	Byelorussian	White	1.60	1.00	-0.50	0.10	74.90	Byelorussian (Belorussian, White Russian): Northeastern, Northwestern, Southwestern
CEW22d	Croatian	White	1.40	1.08	-0.10	0.22	78.50	Croatian (Croat), Serbo-Croatian; Cakavian, Kajkavian
CEW22e	Czech	White	1.40	1.13	0.00	0.27	79.10	Czech: Bohemian, Moravian, Silesian; Hanak, Horak, Yalach, Zahorak
CEW22f	Kashubian	White	1.40	1.00	0.00	0.40	79.00	Kashubian (Pomeranian), Slovincian
CEW22g	Macedonian	White	1.41	0.95	-0.21	0.25	78.50	Macedonian: Armin (Macedo-Rumanian), Bulgarian Macedonian
CEW22h	Montenegrin	White	1.40	1.08	-0.10	0.22	78.50	Montenegrin (Serbo-Croatian)
CEW22i	Polish	White	1.43	1.01	-0.13	0.29	76.50	Polish; Great Polish, Little Polish, Masurich, Mazovian
CEW22j	Russian	White	1.60	1.10	-0.30	0.20	74.90	Russian, Great Russian: Central, Northern, Southern
CEW22k	Ruthenian	White	1.40	1.20	0.00	0.20	74.90	Ruthenian (Carpatho-Russian, Carpatho-Ukrainian, Rusin, Ruthene)

Continued opposite

Table 8-1 continued

Code 1	**RACE** GEOGRAPHICAL RACE **Ethnolinguistic family** People (or sub-family) 2	*Color* 3	*b%* 4	*d%* 5	*m%* 6	*n%* 7	*A%* 8	*Main constituent cultures, additional peoples, tribes, languages, alternative names or synonyms (in parentheses)* 9
CEW22l	Serbian	White	1.40	1.08	-0.10	0.22	78.50	Serbian (Serb, Serbo-Croatian, Shtokavian); Torlakian
CEW22m	Slovak	White	1.40	1.13	0.00	0.27	79.10	Slovak: Central, Eastern, Western
CEW22n	Slovene	White	1.30	1.00	0.00	0.30	79.00	Slovene (Slovenian): Northwestern, Western
CEW22o	Sorb	White	1.20	1.00	0.00	0.20	75.00	Sorb (Lusatian, Sorabian, Sorbian (East, High, Low), Wendish)
CEW22p	Ukrainian	White	1.40	1.20	0.00	0.20	74.90	Ukrainian: Carpathian, Little Russian, Northern, Podolian, Ruthenian, Southeastern, Southwestern, Volhynian
	INDO-IRANIAN	Brown/Tan						Caucasoid peoples from Iran to Indian subcontinent; over 290 Indo-Aryan (Indic), Iranian, Dravidian languages
CNN23	**Dravidian**	Brown/Black						Dravidian (Indo-Dravidian, Paleo-Indian): 50 languages
CNN23a	Kanarese	Brown/Black	3.00	1.00	0.00	2.00	60.00	Kanarese (Kannada): Badaga
CNN23b	Malayali	Brown/Black	3.00	1.00	0.00	2.00	59.00	Malabari, Malayali (Malayalam), Pallyan, Panlyan
CNN23c	Tamil	Brown/Black	3.01	1.00	0.00	2.01	60.00	Tamil: Ceylon Tamil, Indian Tamil, Kling (SE Asia); scripts Grantha, Vattelluttu
CNN23d	Telugu	Brown/Black	3.00	1.00	0.00	2.00	61.00	Andhra, Telugu (Gentoo)
CNN23z	other Dravidian	Brown/Black	3.10	1.00	0.00	2.10	60.00	Brahul (Kur Galli), Ceylon Moor, Coorg, Irula, Koya, Mannan, Parjl, Toda, Tulu, Urali, &c
CNT24	**Iranian**	Tan/White						Iranian (Iranic): Afghani, Baluchi, Kurdish, Ossetian, Persian, Tadzhik, et alii
CNT24a	Afghani	Tan/White	5.28	2.22	3.62	3.06	60.00	Pathan (Pashtun, Pushtu): Afridi, Durrani, Ghilzal, Mahsud, Mangal, Parachi, Shinwari, Waziri, Yusufzal, & 55 other tribes
CNT24b	Baluchi	Tan/White	3.80	1.00	0.00	2.80	61.00	Baluchi (Baluch, Baloch): Kechi, Lotuni, Makrani, Rakhshani, Sarawani
CNT24c	Kurdish	Tan/White	3.60	2.00	-0.10	1.50	57.00	Kurd (Kurdish): Akre, Amadiyah, Dahuk, Kermanji, Kermanshahi, Sulaimani (Mukri), Zaza
CNT24d	Nuristani	Tan/White	4.00	1.20	0.00	2.80	60.00	Nuristani: Ashkun, Kafiri, Kati, Nangalami, Prasun, Tregami, Walgeli, Wai-aia, &c
CNT24e	Ossetian	Tan/White	3.00	1.10	0.00	1.90	59.00	Ossetian (Ossete, Ossetin, Ossetic: Digor, Iron, Tagaur, Tual), Jassic
CNT24f	Persian	Tan/White	3.99	0.70	-0.58	2.71	54.10	Persian (Dari, Farsi): Gabri, Gazi, Khunsari, Natazi, Sivandi, Sol, Tati, Vafsi
CNT24g	Tadzhik	Tan/White	4.00	0.70	-0.80	2.50	57.00	Tadzhik: Farsiwan, Mountain Tajik, Pamir Tadzhik (Bartang, Ishkashin, Khuv, Vakhan, Yazgulem), Selekur, Yaghnobi
CNT24z	other Iranian	Tan/White	4.00	1.00	0.00	3.00	55.00	Bakhtiari, Firozkohi, Galesh, Gilaki, Hazara-Berberi, Jamshidi, Luri, Mazanderani, Munji, Shughni, Talysh, Teymur, et alii
CNN25	**North Indian**	Brown/Tan						North Indian (Indic, Indo-Aryan); Caribbean East Indian, Indo-Mauritian, Indo-Pakistani; subdivided into 30,000 castes
CNN25a	Assamese	Brown/Tan	2.90	1.01	-0.01	1.90	58.00	Assamese Bengali (Eastern, Western)
CNN25b	Bengali	Brown/Tan	3.85	1.36	-0.07	2.41	59.70	Bengali (Calit-Bhasa, Sadhu-Bhasa): caste Bengali (Arzal, Ashraf, &c), outcaste (Namasudra, Pallya, &c); Rajbansi, &c
CNN25c	Bihari	Brown/Tan	2.94	1.02	-0.01	1.92	65.00	non-tribal Bihari: Bhojpuri, Magahi, Maithill (Tirhutia), Nagpuri (Sadani)
CNN25d	Goanese	Brown/Tan	2.91	1.00	-0.01	1.91	66.00	Goanese (Konkani, Gomantaki; Bankoti)
CNN25e	Gujarati	Brown/Tan	2.93	1.01	0.00	1.92	65.00	Gujarati: Barla, Gamadia, Gramya Koll (Kohli), Patidar, Patnuli, Tarimuki, &c
CNN25f	Gypsy	Brown/Tan	3.03	1.03	-0.01	2.00	60.00	Gypsy (Rom, Romany); tribes: Gitano, Kalderash, Lambadi (Banjuri), Lovara, Manush (Sinti), Tschourara
CNN25g	Hindi	Brown/Tan	2.92	1.00	-0.01	1.91	65.20	Hindi: Eastern (Awadhi, Bagheli, Chhattisgarhi, Kosadi, Kosali), Western (Braj Bhasa, Bundell, Kanauji)
CNN25h	Jat	Brown/Tan	2.93	1.01	0.00	1.92	59.00	Awan (Lahnda), Jat (Jhat, Jatki, Multani)
CNN25i	Kashmiri	Brown/Tan	2.90	1.00	0.00	1.90	59.00	Dard (Dardic): Dogra, Kafiri (Western Dardic), Kho, Khowari (Central DArdic), Kishtwari, Kohistani, Pashai, Poguli, Rambani, Shina
CNN25j	Marathi	Brown/Tan	2.91	1.01	0.00	1.90	65.00	Marathi: Dekini, Desi, Kunbi, Maratha, Poona
CNN25k	Nepalese	Brown/Tan	3.75	1.30	0.00	2.45	56.90	Nepalese: Chambiali, Garhwali, Gorkhali, Khas-kura, Kulu, Nepali, Pahari (Jaunsari, Kumauni, Palpa, Parbate), Tarai, Tharu
CNN25l	Oriya	Brown/Tan	2.91	1.00	0.00	1.91	62.00	Oriya (Ordi, Uriya, Utkali): Bhatri, Halbi, Mughalbandi
CNN25m	Parsi	Brown/Tan	2.90	1.00	0.00	1.90	65.00	Parsi (Parsee) (Gujarati)
CNN25n	Punjabi	Brown/Tan	4.06	1.05	-0.35	2.67	56.40	Punjabi: Western (Lahnda), Gurmukhi, Dogri-Kongri, Majhi
CNN25o	Rajasthani	Brown/Tan	2.29	1.00	0.00	1.92	65.00	Rajasthani, Rajput, Thakur: Ahirwati, Harauti, Jalpuri, Malvi, Marwari, Mewati, Nimadi
CNN25p	Sindhi	Brown/Tan	3.62	1.00	-0.20	2.42	59.00	Sindhi: Kachchi, Lari, Lasi, Macharia, Saraiki, Sindh, Thareli, Vicholl
CNN25q	Sinhalese	Brown/Tan	2.08	0.58	-0.23	1.27	69.70	Sinhalese (Cingalese: Low-Country, Up-Country or Kandyan), Maldivian (Divehi)
CNN25r	Urdu	Brown/Tan	3.65	1.03	-0.20	2.60	56.40	Urdu (Hindustani, Khari Boli): Bangaru, Deccani (Dakhni), Deswali, Hariani
CNN25z	other North Indian	Brown/Tan	3.03	1.02	-0.10	1.91	65.00	Anglo-Indian, Arain, Burusho (Burushaski), Ceylon Burgher, Gujar, Julaha, Lamani (Labhani), Lohar, Mussalli, Tarkhan, &c
	LATIN AMERICAN	Tan/Brown						Europeans resident in Latin America for over one generation, or partially assimilated, or of mixed race
CLT26	**Latin-American White** (Branco)	Tan/White	2.20	0.84	0.00	1.36	70.00	Portuguese-speaking White Brazilian of pure Portugese or other European origin
CLT27	**Latin-American White** (Blanco)	Tan/White	2.03	0.86	0.00	1.17	71.70	Spanish-speaking White of pure Spanish or other European origin (Argentinian, Costa Rican, Puerto Rican, &c)
CLN28	**Mestiço** (Portuguese)	Brown	2.33	0.74	0.00	1.59	67.80	Mestiço: mixed Portuguese/Amerindian/African Negro; Caboclo (Portuguese/Amerindina), Mulatto (more White than Black)
CLN29	**Mestizo** (Spanish)	Brown	2.79	0.55	-0.18	2.06	69.60	Chicano, Chilote, Cholo, Ladino, Mestizo, Pachuco; mixed Spanish/Amerindian/African Negro, in Latin America and USA
	MIDDLE EASTERN	Tan/White						Semito-Hamitic (Afrasian, Afro-Asiatic, Erythraic, Erythraen, Hamito-Semitic, Lisramic)
CMT30	**Arab** (Arabic)	Tan/White	3.40	0.70	0.00	2.70	62.00	Bedouin, Copt, Egyptian, Levantine, Meghreb, Palestinian, Saharan (Baggara, Moor, Shoa), Sudanese, Yemeni, Zanzibari, &c
CMT31	**Assyrian**	Tan/White	3.78	0.68	-0.10	3.00	65.00	Aissor, Aramaean, Chaldean, Elkoosh: East Aramaic (Eastern Neo-Assyrian, Syriac), Neo-Syriac, Targumic, West Aramaic
CMT32	**Berber**	Tan/White						Berbero-Libyan (Northern Hamite): Kabyle, Rif, Shawiya, Shluh, Tamazigt, Tuareg, Udalan, Zenati: 38 languages, 110 tribes
CMT32a	Arabized Berber	Tan/White	3.40	0.70	0.00	2.70	55.00	Arabized, Arabic-speaking, detribalized Berber
CMT32b	Beraber	Tan/White	3.23	0.83	0.00	2.40	61.30	Beraber (Tamazigt): Idrassen, Ndhir, Seri, Serruchen, Sokhman, Yafelman, Zaer, Zayan, Zemmur
CMT32c	Kabyle	Tan/White	3.50	0.70	0.00	2.80	58.70	Kabyle (Bergus, Sanhajah, Zouaouah)
CMT32d	Oasis Berber	Tan/White	3.15	0.65	0.00	2.50	56.00	Oasis Berber: Figig, Filala, Gadames, Jalo, Jofra, Mzab, Siwa, Tuat, Wargla, &c
CMT32e	Rif	Tan/White	3.23	0.83	0.00	2.40	61.30	Rif (Riffian): Metalsa, Znassen, & 17 other tribes
CMT32f	Shawiya	Tan/White	3.30	0.80	0.00	2.50	60.00	Shawiya (Chaouyah)
CMT32g	Shluh	Tan/White	3.23	0.83	0.00	2.40	61.30	Shleuh (Shilha, Masmudah, Tashellhayt): Aghbar, Fruga, Glawa, Hawara, Massat, Susiua, & 30 others
CMT32h	Tuareg	Tan/White	3.10	0.70	0.00	2.40	55.00	Tuareg (Tamahaq, Tamashek): Ahaggaren, Air, Antessar, Asben, Aulliminden, Azjer, Ifora, Udalan
CMT32i	Zenaga	Tan	3.10	0.70	0.00	2.40	57.00	Zenaga: Allush, Girganke, Mbarek, Meshduf, Nasser, Sirifou, Tichit
CMT32y	other Moor	Tan/White	3.10	0.70	0.00	2.40	59.00	White Moor, Black Moor, Maure, Bidan
CMT32z	other Berber	Tan/White	3.10	0.70	0.00	2.40	59.00	Atta, Drawa, Guanche, Jerba, Menasser, Nefusa, Uregu, Warain, Zekara, et alii
CMT33	**Cushitic**	Tan/Brown						Cushitic (Eastern Hamite, Hamitic): Eastern Cushitic, Southern Cushitic, West Cushitic (Omotic)
CMT33a	Agau	Tan/Brown	4.40	1.90	0.00	2.50	53.00	Awiya, Awngi, Bilin (Bitin), Bogos, Damot, Falasha (Kaila), Kamta (Hamta), Kemant (Qemant), Khamir (Kamir), Kwara
CMT33b	Galla	Tan/Brown	4.90	1.90	0.00	3.00	55.00	Galla (Oromo): Arusi, Bararetta, Boran, Gabbra, Ittu, Kwottu, Macha, Rendille, Salale, Tulama (Shoa Galla), Wallega, Wallo
CMT33c	Iraqw	Tan/Brown	4.00	1.60	0.00	2.40	56.00	Iraqw (Asa, Erokh, Iraku, Mbulu, Ngomwia)
CMT33d	Sidamo	Tan/Brown	4.90	1.90	0.00	3.00	53.00	Bako, Burji, Darasa, Gibe, Gimira, Hadya, Janjero, Kaffa, Kambatta, Konso-Geleba, Maji, Ometo, Reshiat, Walamo, &c
CMT33e	Somali	Tan/Brown	5.02	1.85	0.00	3.18	52.50	Darod, Digil, Dir, Geri, Hawiya, Ishaak, Issa (Esa), Mijertein, Ogaden, Rahanwein, Sab, West Somali
CMT33z	other Cushitic	Tan/Brown	4.90	1.90	0.00	3.00	54.30	Beja (Ababda, Amarar, Amer, Bisharin, Bogo, Hadendowa), Burungi, Danakil (Afar), Goroa, Mbugu, Saho, Wasi, &c
CMT34	**Ethiopic**	Tan/Brown						Ethiopic (Semitic, Ethiosemitic, African Semitic)
CMT34a	Amhara	Tan/Brown	4.91	1.84	-0.02	3.05	53.50	Amhara (Amharic), Argobba, Harari (Adere); Abyssinian
CMT34b	Tigrai	Tan/Brown	4.90	1.83	-0.02	3.05	53.00	Tigrai (Tigrinya: Habesha)
CMT34c	Tigre	Tan/Brown	4.40	1.90	-0.03	2.47	57.00	Tigre (Hasi, Xassa)
CMT34z	other Ethiopic	Tan/Brown	4.50	1.80	0.00	2.70	53.00	Fuga, Geez (Ethiopic), Gogot (Dobi), Gurage, Maskan, Muher, Soddo, et alii
CMT35	**Jewish**	Tan/White	2.11	0.69	3.22	4.67	71.00	Hebrew: Ashkenazi (American Jew, German Jew, Western, Yiddish), Maghreb (Oriental), Sefardi (Judeo-Spanish, Ladino)
CMT36	**Maltese**	Tan/White	1.52	0.80	0.00	0.72	77.70	Maltese
	MONGOLIAN (Mongoloid, Asiatic)	Yellow/Red						Mongolian (Mongoloid, Asiatic, Oriental)
	AMERICAN INDIAN	Red						Amerindian (American Mongoloid, Amerind), including mixed-blood (Métis, Half-Breed); about 1,700 languages
MIR37	**Central Amerindian**	Red						Meso-American: Azteco-Tanoan, Mayan, Oto-Manguean, Pueblo Indian, Uto-Aztecan; about 270 languages
MIR37a	Aztec	Red	3.45	0.75	0.00	2.70	64.00	Aztec (Nahuati), Nahua (Mexicano, Mexicanero), Pipil
MIR37b	Maya	Red	3.87	0.77	-0.23	2.88	55.70	Chol, Chontal, Chorti, Huastec, Lacandon, Mam, Quiché (Cakchiquel, Kekchi, Uspantec), Teco, Tzeital, Tzotzil, Yucatec
MIR37c	Mixtec	Red	3.40	0.70	0.00	2.70	64.00	Amuzgo, Cuicatec, Mixtec, Trique
MIR37d	Otomí	Red	3.40	0.70	0.00	2.70	64.00	Chichimec (Jonaz), Ixtenco, Matlatzinca, Mazahua, Mezquital, North & South Pame, Ocuiltec, Otomi, Sierra, Tenango
MIR37e	Part-Indian	Red	3.00	0.60	-0.20	2.20	66.00	Indian of mixed blood: Half-Indian, Semi-Indian (non-tribal, detribalized)
MIR37f	Zapotec	Red	3.40	0.70	0.00	2.70	64.00	Chatino, Zapotec (Juárez, South Mountain, Valley, Villalta): Choapán, Etla, Istmo, Mitia, Rincon
MIR37y	Detribalized Amerindian	Red	3.50	0.80	0.00	2.70	65.00	Half-Indian, Part-Indian (Spanish-speaking tribal)
MIR37z	other Central Amerindian	Red	3.50	0.80	0.00	2.70	65.00	Chinantecan, Huichol, Lenca, Mazatec, Miskito, Mixe-Zoque, Sumu, Tarahumara, Tarascan, Tepehua, Totonac, Yaqui &c
MIR38	**Northern Amerindian**	Red						Native Indian (pure Amerindian, registered American Indian); about 195 languages (57 families); also Indian of mixed blood
MIR38a	North American Indian	Red	3.40	0.90	0.00	2.50	70.00	Algonklan (Ojibwa), Creek, Hoka-Slouan (Cherokee, Sioux), Iroqois, Na-Dene (Athabaskan: Apache, Navajo), Penutlan, &c
MIR38b	Part-Indian (Métis)	Red/White	2.90	0.70	0.00	2.20	66.00	Indian/White, Indian/French, Métis (Mixed-Blood, Half-Caste), unregistered or non-status Indian; Creole
MIR38y	Detribalized Amerindian	Red/White	2.90	0.70	0.00	2.20	66.00	Half-Indian (English-speaking), Detribalized urbanite
MIR39	**Southern Amerindian**	Red						Andean-Equatorial; Arawakan, Cariban, Macro-Chibchan, Macro-Ge, Quechumaran, Tucanoan, Tuplan: over 1,230 languages
MIR39a	Arawak	Red	3.00	1.00	0.00	2.00	58.00	Arawak (Arowak): Bauré, Campa, Goajiro, Machiguenga, Mojo, Wapishana, Wiriná, & 120 other languages
MIR39b	Aymara	Red	3.44	0.94	-0.13	2.37	60.30	Aymara (Oruro), Cauqui (Jaqaru), Lupacca, Ubina
MIR39c	Carib	Red	3.02	1.01	-0.01	2.00	58.00	Bakairi, Cannibal, Carib, Cariban, Chocó, Galibi, Guicuru, Island Carib, Makushi, Trio, Waiwai, & 85 others
MIR39d	Jungle Amerindian	Red	3.90	0.70	0.00	3.20	55.00	Auca, Chapacura, Jivaro (Achuale, Murato, &c), Pano, Saparo, Taruma, Tucano, Ve, Witoto; & over 400 others
MIR39e	Lowland Amerindian	Red	3.30	0.64	0.02	2.69	60.40	Bari, Chibcha (Cayapa, Cuna, Guaymi). Chon, Emerillon, Guarani, Lengua, Mataco, Oyampi, Palikur, Toba, Tupi, Wayana, &c
MIR39f	Mapuche	Red	2.60	0.60	0.00	2.00	62.00	Araucanian, Mapuche: Divihet, Huiliche, Manzanero, Mapudungu, Pehuenche, Pichunche, Taluhet
MIR39g	Quechua	Red	2.97	0.69	0.00	2.28	64.50	Quechua: Almaguero, Ancash, Ayachucho, Cajamarca, Huánuco, Junin, Lamano, Ucayall, & 28 others
MIR39y	Detribalized Amerindian	Red	3.00	1.00	0.00	2.00	60.00	Part-Indian (Spanish- or Portuguese-speaking)
MIR39z	other Southern Amerindian	Red	3.00	1.00	0.00	2.00	60.00	Over 400 other tribes and languages unrelated to the 7 major language groups; also Half-Indian
	ARCTIC MONGOLOID	Yellow						Arctic, Arctic Mongoloid, Eskimoid
MRY40	**Eskimo-Aleut**	Yellow						Aleut, Eskaleut, Eskimo
MRY40a	Aleut	Yellow	2.80	0.80	0.00	2.00	60.00	Aleut (Unangan): Atka, Attuan, Unalaskan
MRY40b	Eskimo	Yellow	2.80	0.80	0.00	2.00	63.00	Eskimo (Inuit): Greenlander (Greenlandic), Inupik (Inuk), Polar Eskimo, Siberian Eskimo (Yuit), Yupik, Yupik (Yuk)
	ASIAN	Yellow						Asian, Asiatic (Classical Mongoloid, East Asiatic)
MSY41	**Altaic**	Yellow						Altaic (Altayan): Mongolian, Tungus-Manchu, Turkic (Karluk, Hunnic, Oghuz); over 60 languages
MSY41a	Azerbaijani	Yellow	2.70	0.70	-1.20	0.80	67.00	Azerbaijani (Azerbaijanian, Azeri): Airym, Aynallu, Karapapakh, Qasqay, et alii
MSY41b	Bashkir	Yellow	3.00	0.80	0.00	2.20	70.00	Bashkir: Burzhan, Kuvakan, Yurmaty
MSY41c	Chuvash	Yellow	3.00	0.80	0.00	2.20	70.00	Chuvash (Anatri, Viryal)
MSY41d	Gagauz	Yellow	3.00	0.80	0.00	2.20	69.00	Gagauz (Gagauzi)
MSY41e	Kazakh	Yellow	2.40	0.80	-0.80	0.80	68.00	Kazakh (Hasako, Qazag, Qazagi)
MSY41f	Khalka-Mongol	Yellow	3.40	0.77	0.00	2.63	59.80	Mongolian: Bargu, Chakhar, Dariganga, Khalka-Mongol, Kharchin, Meng, Ordos, Ujumuchin, Urat
MSY41g	Kirgiz	Yellow	3.10	0.70	-1.10	1.30	62.00	Kirgiz (Kirghiz, Kirghizi, Koerhkossu)
MSY41h	Tatar	Yellow	3.00	0.80	0.00	2.20	60.00	Tatar (Tartar): Central, Mishar (Western), Uralian, Siberian Tatar (Baraba, Ishim, Tara, Tom, Tura), &c
MSY41i	Tungus-Manchu	Yellow	3.40	0.80	0.00	2.60	60.00	Manchu-Tungus: Amur, Even (Lamut), Manchu, Nanai (Gold, Hoche, Olcha), Orochon, Sibo, Tungus (Evenki, Solon)
MSY41j	Turkish	Yellow/Tan	2.81	0.71	-0.05	2.05	66.30	Turkish (Osmanli): Anatolian Turk (including Yuruk), Asian Turk, Black Sea Turk, Rumelian Turk
MSY41k	Turkmen	Yellow	3.60	0.80	-0.30	2.50	59.00	Turkmen (Turkman, Turkoman): Erseri, Kizilbash, Sarak, Tekke
MSY41l	Uzbek	Yellow	3.60	0.70	-0.80	2.10	59.00	Uzbek (Uzbeki): Kypchak, Lockhay, Oghuz, Qurama, Sart
MSY41m	Yakut	Yellow	3.00	0.90	0.00	2.10	55.00	Yakut (Dolgan, Jeko, Sakha)

Continued overleaf

Table 8-1 continued

Code	**RACE** GEOGRAPHICAL RACE **Ethnolinguistic family** People (or sub-family)	*Color*	*b%*	*d%*	*m%*	*n%*	*A%*	*Main constituent cultures, additional peoples, tribes, languages, alternative names or synonyms (in parentheses)*
1	*2*	*3*	*4*	*5*	*6*	*7*	*8*	*9*
MSY41y	other Mongolian	Yellow	3.40	0.77	0.00	2.63	60.00	Bayat, Buryat, Dahur (Dagur), Darkhat, Kalmyk, Mogul, Oyrat (Altai), Paongan, Santa, Tu (Mongour), Tunghsiang, &c
MSY41z	other Turkic	Yellow/Tan	3.00	0.80	0.00	2.20	65.00	Afshar, Kajar, Karaim, Karachay, Kara-Kalpak, Khakas, Khoton, Kumyk, Nogay, Shahseven, Tuvinian, Uighur, &c
MSY42	**Chinese**	Yellow						Chinese (Sinitic), including diaspora Chinese (Totok, &c) and overseas non-Chinese-speaking (Peranakan, &c); 68 languages
MSY42a	Han Chinese	Yellow	2.08	0.65	-0.01	1.42	72.70	Han: Mandarin, Cantonese (Yüeh), Hakka, Hsiang (Huanese), Kan, Min, Minnan (Amoy-Swatow, Hoklo, Taiwanese), Wu
MSY42b	Hui	Yellow	2.05	0.65	0.00	1.40	65.00	Hui (Dungan)(Mandarin-speaking): Ho, Hui-tze, Hwei, Khuei, Panghse, Panthay (Panthe)
MSY42c	Sino-Burmese	Yellow	2.05	0.65	0.00	1.40	65.00	Chinese/Burmese mixed races
MSY43	**Eurasian**	Yellow/White	3.00	0.80	0.00	2.20	58.00	Asian/European: Anglo-Burmese, Anglo-Chinese, Injerto (Latin American White/Chinese or Japanese), Macanese, Tay Boi
MSY44	**Indo-Malay**	Yellow						Indonesian-Malayan (Oceanic & Southern Mongoloid, Western Austronesian, Indonesian, Hesperonesian), Chamic
MSY44a	Balinese	Yellow	2.66	0.85	-0.03	1.78	62.00	Balinese
MSY44b	Batak	Yellow	2.68	0.85	-0.03	1.80	65.00	Batak: Angkola, Dairi, Karo, Mandalling, Pakpak, Simalungun, Toba
MSY44c	Buginese	Yellow	2.68	0.85	-0.03	1.80	65.00	Buginese (De, Sindjai)
MSY44d	Chamorro	Yellow	2.09	0.39	0.00	1.70	66.00	Chamorro (Guamanian)
MSY44e	Iban	Yellow	2.86	0.51	0.00	2.35	58.00	Iban (Sea Dayak)
MSY44f	Ilocan	Yellow	3.00	0.70	-0.22	2.07	61.60	Ilocan (Ilocano, Iloko)
MSY44g	Javanese	Yellow	2.66	0.85	-0.03	1.78	66.60	Javanese (Basa Kedatan, Madhya, Ngoko, Pegon): Banjuwangi, Cheribon, Indramaju, Tegal, Tengger, &c
MSY44h	Madurese	Yellow	2.66	0.85	-0.03	1.78	66.60	Madurese: Bangkalan, Bawean, Pamekasan, Sumenep, &c
MSY44i	Makassarese	Yellow	2.80	0.90	-0.03	1.90	60.00	Makassarese (Tawna): Selajar, Tonthian, Turatea
MSY44j	Malagasy	Yellow	4.55	1.27	0.01	3.29	54.30	Antaisaka, Antandroy, Bara, Betsileo, Betsimisaraka, Mahafaly, Merina, Sakalava, Sihanaka, Tanala, Tsimihety
MSY44k	Malay	Yellow	2.80	0.70	0.00	2.10	62.10	Bahasa Indonesia, Cham-Malay, Malay: Baba Malay, Bahasa Malay, Mergui, Pasemah, Pattani, Selung, &c
MSY44l	Minahasan	Yellow	2.65	0.85	0.00	1.80	65.00	Menadonese, Minahasan (Ton): Mongondow, Ratahan, Tombulu, Tomini, Tondano, Tonsawang, Tontemboan: 15 languages
MSY44m	Palawan	Yellow	2.77	0.70	0.00	2.07	65.00	Babuyan, Batah, Palawan (Palawano), Tagbanwa
MSY44n	Sundanese	Yellow	2.66	0.85	-0.03	1.78	66.60	Sundanese: Banten, Priangan
MSY44o	Tagalog	Yellow	3.03	0.68	-0.27	2.07	61.60	Tagalog (Philipino)
MSY44p	Toraja	Yellow	2.70	0.90	0.00	1.80	62.00	Toraja (Koro, Palu, Poso, Sadang): 25 languages
MSY44q	Visayan	Yellow	3.03	0.68	-0.28	2.07	61.60	Visayan (Bisayan, Cebuano): Constantino, Hillgaynon (Ilongo), Kantilan, Samaran (Waray-Waray), Surigaonon
MSY44x	other Filipino	Yellow	3.03	0.68	-0.28	2.07	61.60	Bicol, Bontoc (Igorot), Ibanag, Ifugao, Magindanao, Maranao, Pampangan, Pangasinan, Sulu-Samal; & 100 others
MSY44y	other Indonesian	Yellow	2.66	0.85	-0.03	1.78	58.00	Achinese, Banjarese, Dayak, Dusun (Kadazan), Kenyah, Lampong, Minangkabau, Nias, Sasak, Timorese; & 250 others
MSY44z	other Malaysian	Yellow	2.86	0.51	0.00	2.35	62.00	Bisaya, Cham, Jaral, Kayan, Kedayan, Kelabit, Melanau, Murut, Orang-Laut (Bajau, Moken, Sea Gypsy, Sekah), Tagal; & 50 others
MSY45	**Japanese**	Yellow						Japanese, Okinawan, Ryukyuan; Eastern Altaic
MSY45a	Japanese	Yellow	1.12	0.75	0.00	0.37	83.20	Japanese (Nipponese), Japanese-American (Issei, Kibel, Nisel, Sansei): Nan-oo, Hoku-oo, Satsuma, & many other dialects
MSY45b	Ryukyuan	Yellow	1.12	0.74	0.00	0.38	83.00	Ryukyuan: Central Okinawan, Luchu), Northern (Amami), Southern (Miyako, Sakishima), Hogan
MSY46	**Korean**	Yellow	1.63	0.61	-0.20	0.82	76.00	Korean (Hangul & Choson Muntcha alphabets): 6 dialects: Central, Cheju-do (Southern), NE, NW, SE, SW
MSY47	**Miao-Yao**	Yellow						Meo-Yao: Kelao, Lakwa, Lati, Miao (Meo-Hmong, Hmu), She (Sho), Yao
MSY47a	Miao	Yellow	2.30	0.70	0.00	1.60	60.00	Chi-lao (Kelao), Miao: Black Meo, Blue Meo, Hwa (Flowered) Meo, Red Meo, Striped Meo, White Meo; 80 different groups
MSY47b	Yao	Yellow	2.30	0.70	0.00	1.60	61.00	Laka, Puna, She (Sho), Yao (Iu Mien, Kim Mien, Lingnan Yao, Man, Yu Mien)
MSY48	**Paleoasiatic**	Yellow	2.10	0.70	0.00	1.40	57.00	Aboriginal Siberian (Paleosiberian, Hyperborean): Chukchi, Gilyak, Itelmen, Kerek, Kett, Koryak, Nivkh, Yukaghir (Odul)
MSY49	**Tai**	Yellow						Kam-Tai (Dalc), Thai-Chuang Tai, Tai-Kadal: Central, Northern, Southwestern Tai
MSY49a	Chuang	Yellow	2.05	0.65	0.00	1.40	67.00	N & C Tai: Chinese Nung, Chuang (Zhuang), Chungcha, Molao, Thai Nung, Padi, Phula, Tho, Tu, Tudi, Tujen, Tulao, Wuming
MSY49b	Lao	Yellow	4.52	1.52	0.00	3.00	55.20	Lao (Northeastern Thai, Thai Isan, Thai Lao)
MSY49c	Shan	Yellow	3.25	1.11	0.00	2.14	62.60	Shan: Chinese Shan (Tai Dau), Khamti (Ahom), Nglaw, Shan-Bama (Nglo), Tal Nul, Tal Yal
MSY49d	Thai	Yellow	2.05	0.58	-0.21	1.27	70.80	Tai (Central Thai, Khon-Thai, Siamese), Northern Thai (Kammyang), Southern Thai
MSY49z	other Tai	Yellow	2.05	0.60	-0.20	1.25	61.00	Be, Black Tai, Gial, Kadai, Kam, Khun, Li, Lu, Neua, Nhang, Phutal, Puyl, Red Tai, Sek, Tay, White Tai, Yuan
MSY50	**Tibeto-Burmese**	Yellow						Tibeto-Burmese (Tibeto-Burman), Gyarung-Mishmi, Himalayan; over 240 languages
MSY50a	Bhotia	Yellow	4.00	1.67	0.00	2.33	59.20	Bhotia (Bhote, Bhutia, Bhutanese, Dzongkha), Sikkimese
MSY50b	Burmese	Yellow	3.25	1.11	0.00	2.14	62.60	Burmese: Arakan, Bama, Burman, Maghl, Tenasserim
MSY50c	Chin	Yellow	3.25	1.10	0.00	2.15	60.00	Asho, Chin, Khumi, Kuki Chin (Kukish), Laizo Chin, Mru, Ngawn, Salzang, Siyin, Teizang, Tiddim, Zo, Zomi, Zotung
MSY50d	Garo	Yellow	3.00	1.00	0.00	2.00	65.00	Deori (Chutiya), Garo (Bodo), Hajang, Koch
MSY50e	Gurung	Yellow	3.00	1.00	0.00	2.00	60.00	Gurung, Gurung Gurkha
MSY50f	Kachin	Yellow	3.25	1.10	0.00	2.15	62.60	Kachin: Atzi, Maru, Norra, Nung, Rawang, Singpho (Chingpo, Jinghpaw)
MSY50g	Karen	Yellow	3.25	1.10	0.00	2.15	62.60	Red Karen (Bghai, Bre, Bwe, Geba, Kayah, Padaung, Yinbaw, Zayein), White Karen (Pa-O, Taungthu), Pwo, Sgaw Karen)
MSY50h	Kirati	Yellow	3.20	1.00	0.00	2.20	65.00	Rai, Kirati, Ral Kirati: Athpare, Chamling, Khaling, Saam, Sampange, Thulunge
MSY50i	Lahu	Yellow	3.10	1.10	0.00	2.00	64.00	Hani, Lahu (I, Laku, Musseh, Nakhi (Moso), No), Lolo (Ho, Kopu, Laka, Nosu, Xa), Piseka, Tuchia, Wu-man
MSY50j	Lepcha	Yellow	3.30	1.00	0.00	2.30	57.00	Lepcha (Rong, Rongke)
MSY50k	Limbu	Yellow	3.30	1.00	0.00	2.30	58.00	Limbu (Chang, Monpa, Subah, Tsong): Fagural, Fedopla, Tamarkholea
MSY50l	Lisu	Yellow	3.00	1.00	-0.60	1.40	60.00	Lisu (Hwa (Yawyin), Lasaw, Lishaw): Black Lisu, Flowery Lisu, Shisham, White Lisu
MSY50m	Lushai	Yellow	3.40	1.10	0.00	2.30	65.00	Lushai (Mizo), Mara (Lakher)
MSY50n	Magar	Yellow	3.00	0.80	0.00	2.20	60.00	Gurkha, Magar
MSY50o	Manipuri	Yellow	3.30	1.10	-0.10	2.10	60.00	Manipuri: Meithel, & 25 scheduled hill tribes (Empeo, Kabui, Khoirao, Kwoireng, Maram, et alii)
MSY50p	Naga	Yellow	3.00	0.90	0.00	2.10	58.00	Angami, Ao, Chakesang, Chakru, Chang, Konyak, Lhota, Naga (Tangsa) Pochuri, Rengma, Sema, Zemi-Zeliang, Zheza
MSY50q	Sherpa	Yellow	4.00	1.00	0.00	2.30	60.00	Sherpa
MSY50r	Tibetan	Yellow	3.50	1.67	0.00	2.33	65.00	Bodic: Central (Lhasa), Northern, Southern, Western: Balti, Bod, Bodpa, Kamba, Ladakhi, Lahull, Panaka, Tangut, Tsang, Zargska
MSY50s	Tripuri	Yellow	3.30	1.10	-0.10	2.10	61.00	Chakma, Magh, Riang, Tipura (Tipera), Tripuri, Usipi
MSY50z	other Tibeto-Burmese	Yellow	3.30	1.10	0.00	2.20	60.00	Akha, Bawm, Dafla, Hmar, Kachari, Loba, Mung, Nasi, Newarl, Nu, Pai, Palaychi, Pyen, Sunwar, Tamang, Yi, &c
MSW51	**Uralian**	White/Yellow						Uralic race (a Caucasoid/Mongoloid cline): Finno-Ugric, Neoasiatic, Uralic; 3 families: Finnish, Magyar (Ob-Ugric), Samoyed
MSW51a	Estonian	White	1.40	1.17	-0.38	-0.15	78.30	Estonian: Setu, Tallinn (Reval), Tartu (Dorpat); Vod
MSW51b	Finnish	White	1.28	1.02	0.00	0.26	81.10	Finnish: Hame, Savo
MSW51c	Karelian	White	1.30	1.00	0.00	0.30	80.00	Karelian, Ludic, Olonets, Tver
MSW51d	Komi	White	1.30	1.00	0.00	0.30	80.00	Komi (Zyryan): Komi-Permyak, Yazva
MSW51e	Lapp	White/Yellow	1.20	1.00	0.00	0.20	75.00	Lapp (Lopari, Saamian): Inari, Kola, Lule, Pite, Ruija, Skolt, Southern, Ume
MSW51f	Livonian	White	1.20	1.00	0.00	0.20	75.00	Livonian (Eastern, Western), Liv, Kurlyad
MSW51g	Magyar	White	1.23	1.38	0.00	-0.15	81.50	Magyar (Hungarian), Csango, Siculi
MSW51h	Mari	White	1.30	1.00	0.00	0.30	80.00	Mari (Cheremis): High Mari, Low Mari
MSW51i	Mordvin	White	1.30	1.00	0.00	0.30	80.00	Erzya (Erza), Moksha, Mordvin (Mordoff, Mordovian, Mordva, Mordvinian)
MSW51j	Samoyed	White/Yellow	1.20	1.10	0.00	0.10	70.00	Samoyed: Enets (Yenisei), Kamas, Nenets (Nentsy, Yurak), Nganasan (Tavgi), Selkup (Ostyak-Samoyed)
MSW51k	Udmurt	White	1.30	1.00	0.00	0.30	75.00	Udmurt (Kalmez, Votyak)
MSW51z	other Finno-Ugric	White/Yellow	1.20	1.00	0.00	0.20	77.00	Ingrian, Khanti (Ostyak), Mansi (Vogul), Ob Ugrian, Veps, Votic, et alii
MSY52	**Viet-Muong**	Yellow						Muong, Vietnamese (Kinh, Tonkinese)
MSY52a	Muong	Yellow	2.80	0.80	0.00	2.00	63.00	Muong (Viet-Muong): Pi, Thang, Tong, Wang
MSY52b	Vietnamese	Yellow	2.92	0.85	-0.04	2.03	63.00	Vietnamese (Annamese, Cochinchinese, Ching, Kinh, Quoc-ngu, Tonkinese)
MSY52z	other Viet-Muong	Yellow	2.80	0.80	0.00	2.00	63.00	Arem, Hung Khong Kheng, May, Nguon, Sach, Tay Pong, et alii
	PACIFIC	Yellow/White						Pacific Islander (Eastern Austronesian, Oceanic)
MPY53	**Euronesian**	Yellow/White	3.00	0.80	0.00	2.20	55.80	European/Austronesian: Bislama, Filipino Mestizo, Hawaiian Pidgin, Neo-Melanesian (Pidgin), Part-Samoan, Pitcairner, &c
MPY54	**Micronesian**	Yellow/Black						Micronesian: Nuclear Micronesian (Gilbertese, Marshallese, Ponapese, Trukese, Ulithian), Nauruan, Yapese; 18 languages
MPY54a	Gilbertese	Yellow/Black	3.15	0.63	-0.31	2.21	68.00	Gilbertese
MPY54b	Marshallese	Yellow/Black	3.15	0.63	1.09	3.61	69.00	Marshallese (Ebon; Ralik, Ratak)
MPY54c	Nauruan	Yellow/Black	3.15	0.63	-0.31	2.21	68.00	Nauruan
MPY54d	Ponapese	Yellow/Black	3.15	0.63	0.94	3.46	69.00	Ponapese (Ponapean)
MPY54e	Trukese	Yellow/Black	3.15	0.63	0.94	3.46	70.00	Trukese (Ruk; Falchuk)
MPY54f	Ulithian	Yellow/Black	3.15	0.63	0.78	3.30	68.00	Ulithian (Fals, Ngulu, Sonsoral, Sorol)
MPY54g	Yapese	Yellow/Black	3.15	0.63	0.94	3.46	69.00	Yapese
MPY54z	other Micronesian	Yellow/Black	3.15	0.63	-0.12	2.40	69.30	Banaban, Carolinian, Kusalean, Mortlock, Palauan, Wolean, et alii
MPY55	**Polynesian**	Yellow/White						Polynesian: Hawaiian, Maori, Marquesan, Samoan, Tahitian, Tongan, Uvean; about 34 languages
MPY55a	Hawaiian	Yellow/White	2.80	0.52	0.00	2.28	72.00	Hawaiian, Neo-Hawaiian
MPY55b	Maori	Yellow/White	2.80	0.52	0.00	2.28	70.00	Maori (New Zealand Maori)
MPY55c	Marquesan	Yellow/White	2.80	0.52	0.00	2.28	65.00	Marquesan: Northwest Marquesan, Southeast Marquesan
MPY55d	Rarotongan	Yellow/White	2.80	0.52	-2.41	-0.13	65.00	Cook Islands Maori (Cook Islander, Rarotongan), Manohiki, Mauke, Mitiaro, Pukapukan, Rakahanga
MPY55e	Samoan	Yellow/White	2.80	0.52	-2.13	0.15	65.00	Samoan
MPY55f	Tahitian	Yellow/White	2.79	0.51	0.00	2.28	65.10	Tahitian, Neo-Tahitian, Rurutu
MPY55g	Tongan	Yellow/White	2.80	0.52	-1.73	0.55	65.00	Tongan (Tonga-Uvea): Niuafo'ou, Niuatoputapu
MPY55h	Tuamotuan	Yellow/White	2.80	0.52	0.00	2.28	64.00	Tuamotuan (Pa'umotuan), Napukan
MPY55i	Uvean	Yellow/White	2.80	0.52	-1.28	1.00	66.00	Uvean (Wallisian)
MPY55j	West Uvean	Yellow/White	2.80	0.52	-1.28	1.00	66.00	Loyalty Islander, Haigan, Ouvea
MPY55z	other Polynesian	Yellow/White	2.80	0.52	-1.68	0.60	55.80	Futunan, Niuean, Outier, Solomoni (Nukuria, Pilheni, Rennellese, Sikalana, Tikopian), Tokelauan, Tubualan, Tuvaluan, &c
	NEGROID (Negro, Equatorial)	Black						Negro (Negroid, Equatorial, Black)
	AFRICAN	Black						African: Congold, Nigritic, Niger-Congo (1,450 languages), Nilo-Saharan Macro-Sudanic (210 languages); over 1,660 languages
NAB56	**Bantoid**	Black						Bantoid (=Bantu-like), Broad Bantu, Benue-Congo; about 380 languages
NAB56a	Central Bantoid (Voltaic)	Black	4.37	1.37	-0.10	2.90	55.10	Bariba, Birifor, Bobo, Busa, Dagari, Dogon, Grunshi, Gurma, Kabre, Lobi, Moba, Mossi, Senufo, Somba, Tem, Wala; 85 languages
NAB56b	Eastern Bantoid (Benue)	Black	4.52	1.39	0.00	3.13	53.00	Anyang, Basakomo, Birom, Ekoi, Ibiblo (Efik), Jarawa, Jukun, Katab, Tion, Tiv, Yako, Zumper: Semi-Bantu; 240 languages
NAB56c	Western Bantoid (Atlantic)	Black	4.30	1.60	0.00	2.70	55.50	Balante, Bijogo, Bullom, Diola, Gola, Fulani, Kissi, Limba, Pepel, Serer, Sherbro, Temne, Tenda, Tukulor, Wolof; 56 languages
NAB57	**Bantu**	Black						Bantu-speaking (Benue-Congo); Bantu Proper, Narrow Bantu; about 540 languages
NAB57a	Cameroon Highland Bantu	Black	4.07	1.22	-0.02	2.83	56.00	Bamileke, Fia, Fungum, Fut (Bafut), Kom, Li(Bali), Mum(Bamum), Ndob, Nen, Nsaw(Banso), Nsungil, Tikar, Widekum, Wum
NAB57b	Central Bantu	Black	4.75	1.46	-0.12	3.17	50.80	Bemba, Chewa, Chokwe, Kimbundu, Kongo-Kuba, Lomwe, Makonde, Makua, Ndembu, Nyanja, Sena, Tumbuka, Vill, Yao
NAB57c	Equatorial Bantu	Black	4.47	1.47	0.00	3.00	54.60	Amba, Babwe, Bangi, Bira, Budu, Dzem, Fang, Kaka, Kota, Kumu, Kokele, Maka, Ngala, Rega, Sanga, Topoke
NAB57d	Interlacustrine Bantu	Black	5.10	2.10	0.00	3.00	52.00	Chiga, Ganda, Gusil, Ha, Haya, Konjo, Luhya, Nkole, Nyoro, Ruanda, Rundi, Shi, Soga, Sonjo, Toro, Zinza
NAB57e	Kenya Highland Bantu	Black	4.37	1.03	0.00	3.35	52.60	Chagga, Embu, Kamba, Kikuyu (Gikuyu), Mbere, Meru, Pare (Asu), Shambala (Sambaa), Talta, Tharaka
NAB57f	Luba	Black	4.75	1.46	-0.12	3.17	51.90	Luba (Baluva, Bena Kalundwe, Bena Kanioka), Lulua(Bena Lulua, Lange), Lunda, Mbagani(Kete), Salampasu, Songe, Yeke
NAB57g	Middle Zambezi Bantu	Black	4.64	1.80	0.00	2.84	51.50	East Caprivian, Ila, Koba (Yeye), Lenje, Lozi (Barotse), Lukolwe, Mashasha, Mashi, Mbukushu, Nkoya, Subia, Tonga, Totela
NAB57h	Mongo	Black	4.75	1.46	-0.12	3.17	51.90	Bosaka, Ekonda, Kela, Kutshu, Mbole, Mongo, Ngandu, Ngombe, Nkundo, Songomeno, Tetela
NAB57i	Nguni	Black	3.72	1.04	0.00	2.68	58.00	Angoni (Gomani, Mombera, Mpezeni), Fingo, Laka, Manala, Ndebele, Pondo, Swazi, Tembu, Xhosa, Zulu

Continued opposite

Table 8-1 concluded

Code	RACE / GEOGRAPHICAL RACE / **Ethnolinguistic family** / People (or sub-family)	*Color*	*b%*	*d%*	*m%*	*n%*	*A%*	*Main constituent cultures, additional peoples, tribes, languages, alternative names or synonyms (in parentheses)*
1	*2*	*3*	*4*	*5*	*6*	*7*	*8*	*9*
NAB57j	Northeast Coastal Bantu	Black	4.81	1.46	0.00	3.36	52.00	Bajun, Comorian, Digo, Giriama, Gosha, Hadimu, Nguru, Pemba, Pokomo, Segeju, Shebelle, Shirazi, Swahill, Zaramo, Zigua
NAB57k	Northwestern Bantu	Black	4.35	1.80	0.00	2.55	55.00	Bubi, Duala, Duma, Koko, Kossi, Kpe, Kundu, Lumbo, Mpongwe, Ngumba, Puku, Seke, Shogo, Teke
NAB57l	Shona	Black	4.06	1.10	0.00	2.97	55.40	Kalanga, Karanga (Duma), Korekore (Shangwe), Manyika, Nambya, Ndau (Gova), Tawara (Budjga), Zezuru (Hera, Rozwl)
NAB57m	Sotho	Black	3.44	0.97	0.00	2.47	59.30	Eastern Sotho (Pedi), Northeastern Sotho (Lovedu, Venda), Southern Sotho
NAB57n	Southwestern Bantu	Black	5.13	1.92	0.49	3.72	52.90	Ambo (Ovambo: Kwangali, Ndonga, Okavango), Herero, Mbundu (Ovimbundu), Ndombe, Ngonyelu, Ngumbi, Nyaneka
NAB57o	Tanganyika Bantu	Black	4.81	1.46	0.00	3.36	52.10	Bena, Fipa, Gogo, Hehe, Iramba, Iwa, Kimbu, Nyakuysa, Nyamwezi, Pogoro, Rangi, Safwa, Sagara, Sukuma, Sumbwa, Turu
NAB57p	Tsonga	Black	4.51	1.82	0.13	2.83	55.10	Tsonga (Shangaan): Chopi, Hlengwe, Lenge, Nwanati, Ronga, Tswa, Tsonga (Thonga, Tonga)
NAB57q	Tswana	Black	3.84	0.93	0.00	2.92	55.10	Tswana (Western Sotho): Hurutshe, Kgatla, Kwena, Ngaketse, Ngwato, Rolong, Tlhaping, Tlharu, Tlokwa
NAN58	**Eurafrican** (Coloured)	Brown/Tan	3.00	1.10	0.00	1.90	54.00	Afro-European: Aku, Americo-Liberian (Kwi), Baster, Caboverdian, Cape Coloured, Creole, Krlo, Mistiço, Mulatto, Wescos
NAB59	**Guinean** (Kwa)	Black						Guinean (Kwa); about 170 languages
NAB59a	Akan	Black	4.17	1.17	0.00	3.00	64.70	Volta-Comoe: Akim (Akyem), Akwapim, Anyi-Baule, Ashanti, Attie, Brong, Fanti, Gonja, Guan, Kwahu; Twi
NAB59b	Central Togolese	Black	4.45	1.28	0.00	3.18	54.00	Adele, Akebu, Akposo, Avatime, Basila, Buem, Kebu, Krachi, Logba, Nyangbo, Tafi, Tribu (Ntrubo)
NAB59c	Edo	Black	4.52	1.39	0.00	3.13	53.00	Edo (Bini): Aakwo, Degema, Engenni, Epie, Eruhwa, Ishan (Esa, Isa), Kukuruku (Afenmai), Uhami: 22 languages
NAB59d	Ewe	Black	4.45	1.28	0.00	3.18	54.20	Anglo, Ewe (Elbe, Ephe, Krepe), Gilidyi, Ho
NAB59e	Fon	Black	4.89	1.78	0.00	3.11	52.80	Fon (Dahomean): Adja, Aizo, Djedj, Fongbe, Hwelanu, Mabi, Wachi, Whydah
NAB59f	Ga-Adangbe	Black	4.17	1.17	0.00	3.00	64.70	Adangbe (Adangme), Anima, Awutu, Ga, Gain, Kpone, Krobo, Ningo, Osuduku, Prampram, Se (Shai)
NAB59g	Gun	Black	4.89	1.78	0.00	3.11	52.80	Gun: Egun, Tofinu, Wemenu
NAB59h	Ibo	Black	4.52	1.39	0.00	3.13	53.00	Ibo (Igbo): Abriba, Adda, Ekpeya, Ika, Izi, Ngwa, Ngwo, Onitsha, Owerri
NAB59i	Ijaw	Black	4.52	1.39	0.00	3.13	53.00	Brass (Nembe), Ibani, Ijaw (Ijo), Ikwere, Kabo, Kalabari, Kumbo, Mein, Nkoro, Okurikan, &c
NAB59j	Kru	Black	4.73	1.42	0.00	3.32	54.00	Bakwe (Krumen), Bassa, Bete, Dida, Grebo, Kran (Krahn), Kru (Crau, Krao, Krawi, Nana), Sapo (Pahn), Wobe
NAB59k	Lagoon	Black	4.99	1.47	0.15	3.68	51.00	Abe, Abure, Ajukru, Alladian (Alagya), Ari, Assini, Avikam, Ebrie, Gwa, Mekyibo, Nzima
NAB59l	Popo	Black	4.45	1.28	0.00	3.18	54.00	Popo (Mina): Anecho, Ge, Mina, Peda, Pia
NAB59m	Nupe	Black	4.52	1.39	0.00	3.13	55.00	Bassange (Nge), Batache, Beni, Dibo, Egagi, Ebe, Gbedye, Igbira, Kakanda, Kupa, Kusopa, Nupe, Nupe Zam, &c
NAB59n	Yoruba	Black	4.52	1.39	0.00	3.13	53.00	Ana, Bunu, Egba, Ekiti, Ife, Igala, Igbolo, Igbomina, Ijebu, Ikale, Ilaje, Itsekiri, Nago, Ondo, Owo, Oyo, Yoruba
NAB59z	other Guinean	Black	4.40	1.40	0.00	3.00	58.00	Gade, Gbari, Idoma, Isoko, Urhobo (Abraka, Agbon, Ewu, Olomu, Sobo, Ughelli, Uwherun); Yala, &c
NAB60	**Hausa-Chadic**	Black/Brown						Hausa-speaking Chadic peoples, with over 170 of their own languages also
NAB60a	Hausa	Black/Brown	4.00	1.20	0.00	2.80	51.90	Adarawa, Azna, Hausa (Afuno), Kanawa, Katsenawa, Kurfei, Maguzawa, Mauri, Tazarawa, Zazzagawa, &c
NAB60b	Plateau Chadic	Black	4.52	1.39	0.00	3.13	57.00	Angas, Bura, Gaberi, Gude, Kapsiki, Kirdi, Kotoko, Mandara, Margi, Masa, Matakam, Musgum, Tangale, Tuburi, Wurkum, &c
NAB61	**Kanuri** (Saharan)	Black	4.50	1.40	0.00	3.10	57.00	Beriberi, Berti, Bideyat, Bornu, Bulgeda, Daza, Kanembu, Kanuri (Saharan Negro), Kawar, Kreda, Manga, Teda, Tubu, Zagawa
NAB62	**Nilotic** (Para-Nilotic)	Black						Nilo-Hamitic: East Nilotic, Eastern Sudanic, Prenilote, South Nilotic, West Nilotic; about 100 languages
NAB62a	Acholi	Black	4.30	1.50	0.00	2.80	53.00	Acholi (Gan, Gang, Shuli)
NAB62b	Alur	Black	4.30	1.50	0.00	2.80	53.00	Alur (Alua, Lur, Luri)
NAB62c	Anuak	Black	4.20	1.43	-0.01	2.78	55.00	Anuak (Yambo), Pari
NAB62d	Barea	Black	4.10	1.40	0.00	2.70	57.00	Barea (Barya, Nera)
NAB62e	Bari	Black	4.20	1.43	0.00	2.78	55.00	Bari: Mondari, Nyambara, Nyepu, Polulu
NAB62f	Dinka	Black	4.20	1.43	0.00	2.78	55.00	Agar, Bor, Dinka (Denkawi, Jang), Gok, Luaich, Maluai, Padang, Raik, Ruweng, Twij
NAB62g	Kalenjin	Black	4.00	1.00	0.00	3.00	52.00	Kalenjin: Elgeyo (Keyo), Kipsigis, Marakwet, Nandi, Tatoga, Tugen
NAB62h	Kunama	Black	4.10	1.40	0.00	2.70	58.00	Kunama (Bazen, Cunama)
NAB62i	Lango	Black	4.30	1.50	0.00	2.80	53.00	Lango (Langi, Leb-Lano, Umiro)
NAB62j	Luo	Black	4.20	0.90	0.00	3.30	52.00	Gaya (Girange, Wagela), Luo (Joluo, Dholuo), Nilotic Kavirondo, Nyifwa, Padhola (Dama, JoPadhola)
NAB62k	Maasai	Black	4.00	1.00	0.00	3.00	54.00	Arusha, Elmolo, Kwafi, Lumbwa, Maasai, Njemps, Samburu
NAB62l	Mao	Black	4.10	1.40	0.00	2.70	57.00	Mao (Amam, Anfillo, Mau, Mayo), Busasi
NAB62m	Nubian	Black	4.00	1.40	0.00	2.60	60.00	Nubian: Anag, Barabra (Danagla, Kenuzi, Maha, Nile Nubian, Nubi), Birked, Dair, Dilling, Midobi, Nyimang, Temein
NAB62n	Nuer	Black	4.20	1.43	0.00	2.78	55.00	Atwot, Barr, Gaweir, Jalal, Jl Kany Cien, Lak, Lau, Nuer, Nyuong, Thiang
NAB62o	Shilluk	Black	4.20	1.43	0.00	2.78	55.00	Shilluk; Dembo (Bwodho), Kapango, Shatt (Thuri), Shilluk Luo
NAB62p	Suk	Black	4.20	1.50	0.00	2.70	55.00	Suk (Pokot): Cepleng, Endo, Kimunkon, Upe
NAB62q	Teso	Black	4.10	1.30	0.00	2.80	53.00	Itesyo, Kumam, Teso (Bakedi, Iteso)
NAB62r	Turkana	Black	4.20	1.50	0.00	2.70	54.00	Ngamatak, Nibelai, Nithir, Turkana (Elgume)
NAB62y	other Nilotic	Black	4.20	1.43	0.00	2.78	55.00	Didinga, Fajulu, Ik, Jie, Jur, Kakwa, Karamojong, Latuka, Murle, Sabei (Sabaot), Suri, Surma (Tirma), Tepeth, Topotha, &c
NAB62z	other Prenilote	Black	4.20	1.50	0.00	2.70	55.00	Berta (Shangalla), Burun, Fung, Gule (Hameg), Gumuz, Ingessana (Tabi), Koma, Meban, Mesongo, Uduk, Ulu, &c
NAB63	**Nuclear Mande**	Black						Mande: Bambara, Bozo, Dialonke, Kasonke, Konyanke, Koranko, Malinke, Soninke, Yalunka; about 30 languages
NAB63a	Bambara	Black	5.07	1.91	0.00	3.17	52.60	Bambara (Bamana), Dyangirte, Gan, Kaiongo, Masasi, Nyamosa, Somono, Toro
NAB63b	Bozo	Black	5.07	1.91	0.00	3.17	54.00	Bozo (Sorko, Sorogo)
NAB63c	Dialonke	Black	5.06	2.03	0.00	3.04	55.00	Dialonke (Djalonke, Jallonke, Northern Yalunka)
NAB63d	Kagoro	Black	5.07	1.91	0.00	3.17	56.00	Kagoro (Bagane, Logoro)
NAB63e	Kasonke	Black	5.07	1.91	0.00	3.17	55.00	Kasonke (Kasson, Khasonke, Xasouke)
NAB63f	Konyanke	Black	5.06	2.03	0.00	3.04	52.00	Gyomande, Konyanke (Konianke), Mau
NAB63g	Koranko	Black	5.06	2.03	0.00	3.04	53.00	Koranko (Kuranko), Lele
NAB63h	Malinke	Black	5.06	2.03	0.00	3.04	52.90	Bambugu, Malinke (Mandingo, Mandinka, Maninka, Wangara), Mikifore: Komendi, Konya, Manimo, &c
NAB63i	Nono	Black	5.06	2.03	0.00	3.04	53.00	Djennenke, Nono
NAB63j	Soninke	Black	5.07	1.91	0.00	3.17	54.00	Aser, Aswanik, Diawara, Dyakanke, Gadyaga, Marka, Serahuli, Silabe, Soninke (Sarakole), Toubakal, Wakore, &c
NAB63k	Susu	Black	4.82	2.16	0.00	2.66	55.00	Susu (Soso)
NAB63l	Yalunka	Black	4.82	2.16	0.00	2.66	52.00	Yalunka (Southern Dialonke, Yalun Soso)
NAB63z	other Nuclear Mande	Black	5.00	1.90	0.00	3.10	53.00	Busansi, Diula (Dyula), Huela, Ligbi, Samo, Sya, et alii
NAB64	**Peripheral Mande**	Black						Mande-fu: Dan, Gagu, Gbande, Guro, Kono, Kpelle, Loko, Loma (Toma), Mende, Ngere, Val; about 16 languages
NAB64a	Dan	Black	4.99	1.47	0.15	3.68	51.00	Dan (Da), Gio (San, Yafuba, Yakuba), Tura
NAB64b	Gagu	Black	4.99	1.47	0.15	3.68	51.00	Gagu (Gban)
NAB64c	Gbande	Black	4.73	1.42	0.00	3.32	51.00	Belle, Gbande (Bande, Gbassi), Gbundi, Weima
NAB64d	Guro	Black	4.99	1.47	0.15	3.68	51.00	Guro (Gwio, Kwendre, Kweni, Lo), Mwa, Nwan
NAB64e	Kono	Black	4.82	2.16	0.00	2.66	55.00	Kono (Kolo, Kondo, Konnoh)
NAB64f	Kpelle	Black	4.73	1.42	0.00	3.32	53.00	Kpelle (Gbese, Gerse, Guerze, Kpese, Pessy)
NAB64g	Loko	Black	4.82	2.16	0.00	2.66	55.00	Loko (Landro, Landogo)
NAB64h	Loma	Black	4.99	1.47	0.00	3.68	52.00	Loma (Balu, Buzi, Domor, Gisima, Jokoi, Loghoma, Toa, Toma, Wuboma, &c)
NAB64i	Mende	Black	4.82	2.16	0.00	2.66	55.00	Ko (Comende), Kpa, Mende (Boumpe, Hulo, Kossa, Kosso), Sewa
NAB64j	Ngere	Black	4.73	1.42	0.00	3.32	54.00	Mano, Ngere, Niadrubu, Zague, Zahon
NAB64k	Vai	Black	4.73	1.42	0.00	3.32	55.00	Vai (By, Galdinas, Gallina, Karo, Nai, Vei)
NAB65	**Songhai**	Black						Dendi, Songhai, Zerma (Djerma)
NAB65a	Dendi	Black	5.10	1.90	0.00	3.20	53.00	Dendi (Dandawa)
NAB65b	Songhai	Black	5.10	1.90	0.00	3.26	53.00	Gao, Koroboro, Songhai (Sonhral), Tombmata
NAB65c	Zerma	Black	5.10	1.90	0.00	3.20	54.00	Zerma (Adzerma, Djerma, Dyabarma, Zaberma)
NAB66	**Sudanic**	Black						Sudanic (Central & Eastern Nigritic): Adamawa-Eastern/Ubangian, Surma, et alii; about 230 languages
NAB66a	Azande	Black	4.43	1.83	0.00	2.60	55.00	Azande (Niam-Niam, Sande, Zande), Bandya, Idio
NAB66b	Banda	Black	4.45	1.83	0.00	2.62	54.90	Banda, Belingo, Dakpwa, Langbwasse, Mbanja, Tagbo, Wada, Wasa, Yakwa
NAB66c	Baya	Black	4.45	1.83	0.00	2.62	55.00	Baya (Baja, Gbaya), Bogoto, Chamba, Duru, Jen, Longuda, Mbum, Mumuye, Vere, Yungur
NAB66d	Fur	Black	4.40	1.80	0.00	2.60	54.00	Baygo, Dagu (Daju), Dalinga, Forenga, Fur, Kimr, Kungara, Marait, Sila, Sungor, Tama, Temurka
NAB66e	Madi	Black	4.20	1.43	0.00	2.77	53.00	Bongo, Kreish, Logo, Madi, Mittu
NAB66f	Mandja	Black	4.45	1.83	0.00	2.62	55.00	Mandja (Mangia)
NAB66g	Moru-Mangbetu	Black	4.47	1.69	0.00	2.78	56.00	Moru-Mangbetu: Lendu, Lugbara, Mamvu, Mangbetu, Mayogo, Moru, Okebu, Popoi, Rumbi
NAB66h	Nuba	Black	4.20	1.43	0.00	2.77	54.00	Nuba (Kordofanian): Heiban, Kadugli, Katla, Koalib, Krongo, Mesakin, Moro, Otoro, Tagall, Talodi, Tumtum, & 90 others
NAB66z	other Sudanic	Black	4.20	1.43	0.00	2.77	55.00	Bagirmi, Banziri, Bwaka, Kare, Maba, Masalit, Mbai, Mubi, Mundang, Ndogo, Ngama, Nzakara, Riverine, Sango, Sara, Yakoma, &c
	AFRO-AMERICAN	Black						Black of African or mixed descent: Antillean (Antillese), Black, Cafuso, Coloured, Creole, Mulatto, Negro, Preto, Zambo
NFB67	**Dutch-speaking**	Black						Dutch-speaking Black of African or mixed descent
NFB67a	Black	Black	4.00	0.65	-1.10	3.34	69.00	Bush Negro, Dutch-speaking, Negro
NFB67b	Creole	Black	2.56	0.56	-1.14	1.86	66.00	Antillean, Creole, Mulatto, Papiamento (Spanish/Dutch Creole), Sranan (Taki-Taki, English/Dutch Creole), Surinam Creole
NFB68	**English-speaking**	Black						English-speaking Black of African or mixed descent including speakers of English-based Pidgin-Creoles
NFB68a	Black (African Negro)	Black	2.20	0.62	-0.56	1.02	72.40	African Negro, pure-(full-)blooded Negro, Bush Negro, USA Negro/Black (80% Negro/20% White), West Indian Black
NFB68b	Mulatto	Black	2.51	0.71	-0.86	0.94	67.70	Afro-Asian, Afro-Chinese, Black Carib (Garif), Coloured, Creole, Djuka, Guyanese, Maroon, Mulatto, Saramaccan
NFB69	**French-speaking**	Black						French-speaking Black of African or mixed descent
NFB69a	Black	Black	3.53	1.19	-0.31	2.03	66.00	Black, Boni, Bush Negro, Noir
NFB69b	Creole	Black	3.30	0.80	0.00	2.50	62.00	Antillean (Antillese), Dominican Creole, French (Black) Creole (Creole), French-speaking Mulatto (Mulatre), Haitian Creole
NFB70	**Portuguese-speaking**	Black						Portuguese-speaking Black of African or mixed descent
NFB70a	Black	Black	4.50	1.50	0.00	3.00	67.80	Preto (Black) (African Negro)
NFB70b	Mulato	Black	4.40	1.40	0.00	3.00	65.00	Cafuso (Negro/Amerindian), Crioulo, Mulato (more Black than Portuguese), Portuguese Creole, Quilombola
NFB71	**Spanish-speaking**	Black						Spanish-speaking Black of African or mixed descent
NFB71a	Black	Black	3.90	0.60	0.00	3.30	68.00	Negro, Spanish Black
NFB71b	Mulatto	Black	3.80	0.60	0.00	3.20	66.00	Chinocholo, Criollo of mixed race, Mulatto, Palenquero, Spanish Creole, Zambo (Negro/Amerindian)

Table 8-2. Cultures of the world, with 12,600 people profiles, each described on 1 line across 2 facing pages, with same reference number.

PEOPLE		POPULATION				IDENTITY CODE		LANGUAGE		CHURCH		MINISTRY						SCRIPTURE		
Ref 1	Ethnic name 2	P% 3	In 1995 4	In 2000 5	In 2025 6	Race 7	Language 8	Autoglossonym 9	S 10	AC 11	Members 12	Jayuh 13-17	dwa 18	19	xcmc 20	21	mi 22	Biblioglossonym 23	Pub 24-26	ss 27
	Afghanistan	**100.00000**	**19,663,087**	**22,720,416**	**44,934,122**					**0.03**	**6,894**									
1	Afghani Tajik (Tadzhik)	17.90000	3,519,693	4,066,954	8,043,208	CNT24g	58-AACC-f	dari-t.		0.00	81	1Asu.	1	3	1	0	4	Dari*	PNb	b
2	Afshari	0.03441	6,766	7,818	15,462	MSY41a	44-AABA-fb	south azeri		0.04	3	1a.u.	3	1	1	0	1	Azerbaijani, South	pnb	b
3	Aimaq-Hazara	0.70000	137,642	159,043	314,539	CNT24z	58-AACC-li	qedai-nao-hazara		0.00	0	1csu.	0	1	2	0	0		pnb	n
4	Amulah	0.02600	5,112	5,907	11,683	CNT24d	58-ACAA	ashkund cluster		0.00	0	0....	0	3	2	0	1		...	.
5	Ashkuni (Wamayi)	0.04818	9,474	10,947	21,649	CNT24d	58-ACAA-a	ashkuni		0.00	0	0....	0	2	0	0	1		...	.
6	Balkh Arab	0.03946	7,759	8,965	17,731	CMT30	12-AACF-h	northeast `anazi		0.20	18	1asuh	5	3	2	0	0		pnb	b
7	Bashgari (Kafar, Kamtoz)	0.07945	15,622	18,051	35,700	CNT24d	58-ACBA	bash-gali cluster		0.10	18	0....	5	2	0	0	1		...	.
8	Bashkarik	0.00530	1,042	1,204	2,382	CNN25i	59-AACC-a	kalami		0.00	0	0....	0	2	0	0	0		...	b
9	Berberi	0.78039	153,449	177,308	350,661	CNT24z	58-AACC-l	aimaq		0.00	0	1csu.	0	2	2	0	0		pnb	n
10	Brahui (Kur Galli)	1.24510	244,825	282,892	559,475	CNN23z	49-AAAA-a	bra'uidi		0.10	283	3....	5	3	0	0	0	Brahui	P..	n
11	British	0.00272	535	618	1,222	CEW19i	52-ABAC-b	standard-english	4	79.00	488	3Bsuh	10	8	10	2	0		PNB	b
12	Darwazi (Badakhshani)	0.06623	13,023	15,048	29,760	CNT24z	58-AACC-h	darwazi		0.00	0	1csu.	0	1	0	0	0		pnb	.
13	Firozkohi (Char Aimaq)	0.90000	176,968	204,484	404,407	CNT24z	58-AACC-le	firozhohi		0.00	0	1csu.	0	2	2	0	1		pnb	n
14	Gawar-Bati (Narisati)	0.06005	11,808	13,644	26,983	CNN25i	59-AAAE-b	gawar-bati		0.00	0	0....	0	2	0	0	0		...	b
15	German	0.00681	1,339	1,547	3,060	CEW19m	52-ABCE-a	standard hoch-deutsch		85.00	1,315	2B.uh	10	8	10	2	0	German*	PNB	b
16	Grangali (Nangalami)	0.02648	5,207	6,016	11,899	CNT24d	59-AAAB-d	nangalami		0.00	0	0....	0	0	0	0	0		...	.
17	Guhjali (Wakhi, Wakhani)	0.04395	8,642	9,986	19,749	CNT24z	58-ABDC	wakhi cluster		0.00	0	0....	0	2	0	0	0	Wakhi	...	b
18	Gujur Rajasthani	0.01059	2,082	2,406	4,759	CNN25o	59-AAFG-o	gujuri		0.03	1	1.s..	3	3	0	0	1	Gujari	pn.	.
19	Hazara (Berberi)	8.13460	1,599,513	1,848,215	3,655,211	MSY41z	58-AACC-eo	central hazaragi		0.03	554	1asu.	3	4	2	1	3		pnb	b
20	Hindi	0.50000	98,315	113,602	224,671	CNN25g	59-AAFO-e	general hindi		0.10	114	3Asuh	5	4	0	0	0		pnb	b
21	Italian	0.00454	893	1,032	2,040	CEW21e	51-AABQ-c	standard italiano		84.00	866	2B.uh	10	8	10	2	1	Italian	PNB	b
22	Jamshidi (Char Aimaq)	0.40000	78,652	90,882	179,736	CNT24z	58-AACC-ld	jamshidi		0.00	0	1csu.	0	0	2	0	0		pnb	n
23	Jat (Jatu, Jati, Musali)	0.00627	1,233	1,425	2,817	CNN25h	12-AACJ-a	jakati		0.00	0	0....	0	1	0	0	0		...	.
24	Jewish	0.00060	118	136	270	CMT35	58-ABDA-a	pashto		0.00	0	1As..	0	2	2	0	0		pnb	b
25	Kamdeshi (Shekhani)	0.02703	5,315	6,141	12,146	CNT24d	58-ACBA-d	kam-viri		0.00	0	0....	0	2	0	0	0		...	.
26	Karakalpak	0.01254	2,466	2,849	5,635	MSY41z	44-AABC-b	karakalpak		0.00	0	1c.u.	0	3	0	0	1	Karakalpak	Pn.	b
27	Kazakh	0.01254	2,466	2,849	5,635	MSY41e	44-AABC-c	kazakh		0.00	0	4A.u.	0	3	0	0	1	Kazakh	PN.	b
28	Kho (Citrali, Qasqari)	0.02600	5,112	5,907	11,683	CNN25i	59-AABA-a	kho-war		0.00	0	0....	0	2	0	0	1		...	.
29	Kirghiz	0.00344	676	782	1,546	MSY41g	44-AABC-d	kirghiz		0.01	0	2r.u.	3	3	1	0	1	Kirghiz	PN.	b
30	Kowli Gypsy (Churi-Wali)	0.03000	5,899	6,816	13,480	CNN25f	59-ACAA-a	domari		0.01	1	0....	3	1	0	0	0		...	b
31	Kurdish	0.10000	19,663	22,720	44,934	CNT24c	58-AAAA-c	kurdi		0.01	2	2c...	3	2	2	1	0	Kurdi	PN.	b
32	Malakhel	0.01325	2,605	3,010	5,954	CNT24d	58-ABEA-bc	malakhel		0.00	0	0....	0	0	0	0	1		...	.
33	Moghol	0.02000	3,933	4,544	8,987	MSY41y	44-BAAA-a	mogholi		0.00	0	0....	0	1	0	0	1		...	b
34	Munji-Yidgha (Munjiwar)	0.01731	3,404	3,933	7,778	CNT24z	58-ABDB-a	munji		0.00	0	0....	0	1	0	0	0		...	.
35	Ormuri	0.02179	4,285	4,951	9,791	CNT24d	58-ABEA-b	ormuri		0.00	0	0....	0	1	0	0	1		...	.
36	Pahlavani	0.01000	1,966	2,272	4,493	CNT24f	58-AACC-g	pahlavani		0.00	0	1csu.	0	2	0	0	0		pnb	.
37	Parachi	0.03786	7,444	8,602	17,012	CNT24a	58-ABEA-a	parachi		0.00	0	0....	0	0	0	0	1		...	.
38	Parya (Laghmani)	0.00600	1,180	1,363	2,696	CNT24z	59-AAAD-c	laghmani		0.00	0	0....	0	1	2	0	0		...	b
39	Pashayi (Pashai)	0.70130	137,897	159,338	315,123	CNN25i	59-AAAA	north pashayi cluster		0.00	0	0....	0	2	0	0	0		...	.
40	Pathan (Pukhtun, Afghani)	47.56434	9,352,618	10,806,816	21,372,619	CNT24a	58-ABDA-a	pashto		0.01	1,081	1As..	3	4	5	3	3		pnb	b
41	Persian	3.35000	658,713	761,134	1,505,293	CNT24f	58-AACC-c	standard farsi		0.12	913	1Asu.	5	4	2	1	1		PNB	b
42	Persian (Parsiwan)	0.30000	58,989	68,161	134,802	CNT24f	58-AACC-f	dari-t.		0.20	136	1Asu.	5	4	2	0	0	Dari*	PNb	b
43	Prasuni	0.01377	2,708	3,129	6,187	CNT24d	58-ACBB-a	prasuni		0.00	0	0....	0	0	0	0	1		...	.
44	Punjabi	0.01600	3,146	3,635	7,189	CNN25n	59-AAFE-c	general panjabi		1.00	36	1Asu.	6	4	2	0	1		PNB	b
45	Qizilbash (Kizilbash)	0.90000	176,968	204,484	404,407	CNT24z	58-AACC-f	dari-t.		0.01	20	1Asu.	3	1	2	0	0	Dari*	PNb	b
46	Russian	0.00600	1,180	1,363	2,696	CEW22j	53-AAAE-d	russkiy		31.00	423	4B.uh	9	5	8	2	1	Russian	PNB	b
47	Sanglechi (Eshkashimi)	0.01377	2,708	3,129	6,187	CNT24z	58-ABDD-a	sanglechi		0.00	0	0....	0	2	0	0	0		...	b
48	Sau	0.01987	3,907	4,515	8,928	CNN25i	59-AADA-a	sau		0.00	0	0....	0	0	0	0	1		...	.
49	Shughni (Kushani)	0.10593	20,829	24,068	47,599	CNT24z	58-ABDE-a	shughni-bajuvi		0.00	0	0....	0	0	0	0	1	Shughni	...	b
50	Shumashti	0.00529	1,040	1,202	2,377	CNN25i	59-AAAE-c	shumasti		0.00	0	0....	0	0	0	0	1		...	.
51	Sindhi	0.05300	10,421	12,042	23,815	CNN25p	59-AAFF-a	standard sindhi		0.08	10	1as..	4	3	2	0	1	Sindhi	PNB	b
52	Southern Pathan	1.00000	196,631	227,204	449,341	CNT24a	58-ABDA-a	pashto		0.01	23	1As..	3	5	0	0	0		pnb	b
53	Southern Uzbek	8.09137	1,591,013	1,838,393	3,635,786	MSY41l	44-AABD-b	south uzbek		0.01	184	1c.u.	3	4	2	0	3		pnb	b
54	Taimani (Char Aimaq)	1.80000	353,936	408,967	808,814	CNT24z	58-AACC-lb	taimani		0.00	0	1csu.	0	1	2	0	0		pnb	n
55	Tangshuri	0.00530	1,042	1,204	2,382	CNT24z	58-AACC-i	tangshewi		0.00	0	1csu.	0	3	0	0	1		pnb	b
56	Tatar	0.00223	438	507	1,002	MSY41h	44-AABB-e	tatar		0.47	2	2c.u.	5	1	2	0	1	Tatar: Kazan	Pn.	b
57	Teymur (Timuri)	0.45000	88,484	102,242	202,204	CNT24Z	58-AACC-la	taimuri		0.02	20	1csu.	3	2	2	0	0		pnb	n
58	Tirahi	0.03441	6,766	7,818	15,462	CNN25i	59-AACB-a	tirahi		0.00	0	0....	0	0	0	0	0		...	.
59	Tregami	0.02000	3,933	4,544	8,987	CNT24d	58-ACCA-b	tregami		0.00	0	0....	0	0	2	0	0		...	.
60	Turkmen (Turkoman)	2.51656	494,833	571,773	1,130,794	MSY41k	44-AABA-e	turkmen		0.00	0	3c.u.	0	3	1	0	3	Turkmen	PNb	b
61	USA White	0.00100	197	227	449	CEW19s	52-ABAC-s	general american		78.00	177	1Bsuh	10	8	11	2	2	English*	PNB	b
62	Uighur (Kashgar-Yarkand)	0.02065	4,060	4,692	9,279	MSY41z	44-AABD-d	east uyghur		0.05	2	1r.u.	4	3	1	0	0	Uighur*	PNB	b
63	Urdu (Hindi)	0.05300	10,421	12,042	23,815	CNN25r	59-AAFO-d	standard urdu	7	0.23	28	2Asuh	5	4	2	1	1	Urdu	PNB	b
64	Waigeli (Nuristani)	0.06000	11,798	13,632	26,960	CNT24d	58-ACCA-a	wai-ala		0.00	0	0....	0	2	0	0	1		...	.
65	Warduji	0.02000	3,933	4,544	8,987	CNT24f	58-AACC-m	warduji		0.00	0	1csu.	0	1	2	0	0		pnb	.
66	Western Baluch (Baloch)	1.25392	246,559	284,896	563,438	CNT24b	58-AABA-b	west balochi		0.01	28	3.s..	3	2	3	0	2	Baluchi: Western*	P..	.
67	Western Punjabi (Lahnda)	0.09740	19,152	22,130	43,766	CNN25h	59-AAFE-e	lahnda		0.20	44	1csu.	5	3	2	1	0	Panjabi, Western	PNb	b
68	Wotapuri-Katarqalai	0.02600	5,112	5,907	11,683	CNN25i	59-AACA-a	wotapuri		0.00	0	0....	0	0	0	0	0		...	.
69	Zargari	0.04000	7,865	9,088	17,974	CNT24f	59-ACBA-bl	zargari		0.00	0	1c...	0	0	0	0	1		pn.	b
70	other minor peoples	0.10000	19,663	22,720	44,934	...				0.10	23		5	5	0	0	0			
	Albania	**100.00000**	**3,176,623**	**3,113,434**	**3,819,763**					**34.38**	**1,070,389**									
71	Aromanian (Armini)	1.77000	56,226	55,108	67,610	CEW21i	51-AADB-a	limba armâneasc-a	3	95.00	52,352	0a...	10	6	2	2	2	Romanian: Macedonian*	P..	b
72	Esperanto	0.00000	0	0	0	CEW21z	51-AAAC-a	proper esperanto		5.00	0	0A...	7	5	7	3	0	Esperanto	PNB	b
73	Gheg Albanian (Scutari)	9.18000	291,614	285,813	350,654	CEW13	55-AAAA-b	northwest gheg	99	24.00	68,595	1a.u.	9	5	8	3	2	Albanian: Gheg*	PN.	b
74	Greek	2.29500	72,903	71,453	87,664	CEW20	56-AAAA-c	dhimotiki	10	90.00	64,308	2B.uh	10	7	8	3	2	Greek: Modern	PNB	b
75	Han Chinese (Mandarin)	0.00600	191	187	229	MSY42a	79-AAAB-ba	kuo-yü		0.50	1	2Bsuh	5	3	2	0	0	Chinese: Kuoyu*	PNB	b
76	Jewish	0.01200	381	374	458	CMT35	55-AAAB	tosk cluster		0.00	0	0A...	0	3	1	0	0		PNB	b
77	Macedonian	0.87000	27,637	27,087	33,232	CEW22g	53-AAAH-a	makedonski	2	90.00	24,378	2a.uh	10	6	7	2	3	Macedonian*	PNB	b
78	Montenegrin	0.30000	9,530	9,340	11,459	CEW22h	53-AAAG-a	standard srpski	5	70.00	6,538	1Asuh	10	6	6	3	2	Serbian*	PNB	b
79	Serb	1.00000	31,766	31,134	38,198	CEW22l	53-AAAG-a	standard srpski		70.00	21,794	1Asuh	10	6	8	3	1	Serbian*	PNB	b
80	Tosk Albanian	82.53000	2,621,667	2,569,517	3,152,450	CEW13	55-AAAB-a	standard tosk	99	31.00	796,550	0A...	9	6	9	3	3	Albanian: Tosk*	PNB	b
81	Vlach Gypsy	1.83700	58,355	57,194	70,169	CNN25f	59-ACBA-am	north vlach-albania	3	60.00	34,316	1c...	10	7	6	1	2		pn.	.
82	other minor peoples	0.20000	6,353	6,227	7,640	...				25.00	1,557		9	5	2	1	3			
	Algeria	**100.00000**	**28,058,368**	**31,471,278**	**46,610,551**					**0.29**	**90,877**									
83	Ahaggaren Tuareg (Hoggar)	0.10822	30,365	34,058	50,442	CMT32h	10-AAAB-ad	ta-haggart	1	0.00	0	1....	0	3	2	0	3	Tamahaq, Hoggar	Pn.	.
84	Algerian Arab	59.15111	16,596,836	18,615,610	27,570,658	CMT30	12-AACB-b	east maghrebi	97	0.24	44,677	2A.uh	5	4	7	3	3	Arabic: Algerian*	PNB	b
85	Arabized Berber	3.00000	841,751	944,138	1,398,317	CMT32a	12-AACB-b	east maghrebi		0.10	944	2A.uh	5	4	6	3	3	Arabic: Algerian*	PNB	b
86	Azjer Tuareg (Ajjer)	0.07000	19,641	22,030	32,627	CMT32h	10-AAAB-af	kel-ajjer		0.00	0	1....	0	3	0	0	0		pn.	.
87	Belbali (Idaksahak)	0.00878	2,464	2,763	4,092	NAB65b	01-AABB-a	koranje		0.00	0	0....	0	1	0	0	0		...	b
88	British	0.00200	561	629	932	CEW19i	52-ABAC-b	standard-english	25	79.00	497	3Bsuh	10	7	8	3	2		PNB	b
89	Byelorussian	0.00590	1,655	1,857	2,750	CEW22c	53-AAAE-c	bielorusskiy		70.00	1,300	3A.uh	10	7	8	3	1	Byelorussian*	PNB	b
90	Central Shilha (Beraber)	3.65000	1,024,130	1,148,702	1,701,285	CMT32b	10-AAAC-b	ta-mazight	3	0.02	230	1a...	3	2	2	0	2	Shilha: Central*	Pn.	b
91	Chaamba Bedouin (Shaanba)	0.20900	58,642	65,775	97,416	CMT30	12-AACD	badawi-sahara cluster		0.01	7	0a...	3	1	0	0	0		PN.	b
92	Dui-Menia Bedouin	0.30000	84,175	94,414	139,832	CMT30	12-AACD	badawi-sahara cluster		0.01	9	0a...	3	1	0	0	0		PN.	b
93	Egyptian Arab	0.04500	12,626	14,162	20,975	CMT30	12-AACF-a	masri		20.00	2,832	2Asuh	9	6	9	3	3	Arabic*	PNB	b
94	Figig Berber	0.08370	23,485	26,341	39,013	CMT32d	10-AAAC	north tamazigh cluster		0.02	5	4A...	3	1	0	0	0		PN.	b
95	French	0.11100	31,145	34,933	51,738	CEW21b	51-AABI-d	general français	60	78.00	27,248	1B.uh	10	7	12	3	3	French	PNB	b
96	Gourara Berber	0.07000	19,641	22,030	32,627	CMT32d	10-AAAC-n	gurara		0.01	2	1c...	3	1	2	0	0		pn.	b
97	Greater Kabyle (Western)	6.19036	1,736,914	1,948,185	2,885,361	CMT32c	10-AAAC-h	tha-qabaylith	15	0.37	7,208	1a...	5	4	6	4	3	Kabyle: Greater	PN.	b
98	Hamyan Bedouin	6.98000	1,958,474	2,196,695	3,253,416	CMT30	12-AACD-a	hassaaniyya		0.01	220	0a...	3	1	0	0	0		pn.	b
99	Hausa	0.03000	8,418	9,441	13,983	NAB60a	19-HAAB-a	hausa		0.00	0	4Asu.	0	1	0	0	0	Hausa	PNB	b
100	Ifora Tuareg	0.05000	14,029	15,736	23,305	CMT32h	10-AAAB-a	ta-mahaq		0.00	0	1....	0	3	0	0	0	Tamahaq: Hoggar*	PN.	b
101	Iraqi Arab	0.01000	2,806	3,147	4,661	CMT30	12-AACF-g	syro-mesopotamian		0.70	22	1Asuh	5	4	7	1	0		pnb	b
102	Jewish	0.00180	505	566	839	CMT35	51-AABI-d	general français		0.00	0	1B.uh	0	2	2	0	0	French	PNB	b
103	Laguat Bedouin (Aruat)	0.07000	19,641	22,030	32,627	CMT30	12-AACD	badawi-sahara cluster		0.01	2	0a...	3	3	0	0	2		PN.	b
104	Lesser Kabyle (Eastern)	2.46690	692,172	776,365	1,149,836	CMT32c	10-AAAC-i	east tha-qabaylith		0.20	1,553	1a...	5	4	6	3	3	Kabyle: Lesser	Pn.	b
105	Menasser Berber	0.05000	14,029	15,736	23,305	CMT32z	10-AAAC-g	menasser-metmata		0.00	0	1c...	0	1	0	0	0		pn.	.
106	Moroccan Arab	0.40000	112,233	125,885	186,442	CMT30	12-AACB-a	west maghrebi		0.15	189	1A.uh	5	4	6	3	1		pnb	b
107	Mozabite Berber (Ghardaia)	0.25054	70,297	78,848	116,778	CMT32d	10-AAAC-m	mzab		0.01	8	1c...	3	1	4	0	0		pn.	b
108	Nail Bedouin (Uled Nail)	0.10000	28,058	31,471	46,611	CMT30	12-AACD	badawi-sahara cluster		0.01	3	0a...	3	1	0	0	0		PN.	b
109	Northern Shilha (Riffian)	1.92308	539,585	605,218	896,358	CMT32e	10-AAAC-f	ta-rift		0.02	121	1A...	3	2	2	0	1	Shilha: Northern*	Pn.	b
110	Rom Gypsy (Xoraxai)	0.01000	2,806	3,147	4,661	CNN25f	12-AACB-b	east maghrebi		0.09	3	2A.uh	4	2	6	0	0	Arabic: Algerian*	PNB	b
111	Ruarha Bedouin	0.45360	127,273	142,754	211,425	CMT30	12-AACD	badawi-sahara cluster		0.00	0	0a...	0	1	0	0	0		PN.	b
112	Russian	0.00100	281	315	466	CEW22j	53-AAAE-d	russkiy		70.00	220	4B.uh	10	7	8	2	1	Russian	PNB	b
113	Shawiya (Chaouia)	5.23913	1,470,014	1,648,821	2,441,987	CMT32f	10-AAAC-j	shawiya	3	0.00	0	1c...	0	3	2	1	3	Chaouia	Pn.	b
114	Sidi Bedouin	0.34900	97,924	109,835	162,671	CMT30	12-AACD	badawi-sahara cluster		0.01	11	0a...	3	1	0	0	0		PN.	b
115	Southern Shilha (Shleuh)	2.69231	755,418	847,304	1,254,901	CMT32g	10-AAAC-a	ta-shelhit		0.09	763	4c...	4	2	3	0	3	Shilha: Southern*	Pn.	b
116	Spaniard	0.00500	1,403	1,574	2,331	CEW21k	51-AABB-c	general español	3	96.00	1,511	2B.uh	10	8	11	3	1	Spanish	PNB	b

Continued opposite

Table 8-2: continuation of page opposite, each people getting one line across the 2 pages.

EVANGELIZATION								EVANGELISM			ADDITIONAL DESCRIPTIVE DATA
Ref 1	*D* 28	*aC* 29	*CG%* 30	*r* 31	*E* 32	*U* 33	*W* 34	*e* 35	*R* 36	*T* 37	*Locations, civil divisions, literacy, religions, church history, denominations, dioceses, church growth, missions, agencies, ministries, movements* 38
Afghanistan											
1	0	0	4.49	4	28.00	72.00	A	0.00	508	1.12	Mountain farmers in north and northeast. Bilingual in Pashto. Muslims 100%(Hanafi Sunnis, with Imami and Ismaili Shias). Many believers. Pushto-speaking.
2	0	0	1.10	1	20.04	79.96	A	0.02	246	2	North of Kabul, in Kabul, in Herat. Dari is now replacing Azeri. Muslims 100%(Sunnis). M=IAM. Bible in Persian script, out of print.
3	0	0	0.00	1	15.00	85.00	A	0.00	0	1.11	One of the 4 Char Aimaq semi-nomadic tribes. Muslims 100%(Hanafi Sunnis, Imami Shias).
4	0	0	0.00	0	5.00	95.00	A	0.00	0	1.03	Small rural tribe. Muslims 100%(Sunnis). M=Gospel Recordings.
5	0	0	0.00	0	3.00	97.00	A	0.00	0	1.00	Nuristanis. Pech Valley around Wama. 1987 many flee to Pakistan as refugees. Language unwritten. Muslims 100%(Sunnis).M=GR.
6	0	0	2.93	7	31.20	68.80	A	0.22	319	3	Persianized Arabic. A few villages west of Daulatabad. Muslims 100%. (Sunnis). R=FEBC, TWR.
7	0	0	2.93	0	8.10	91.90	A	0.03	1,397	2	Kamviri. Two areas of Nuristan: upper Alingar valleys, upper Bashgal Valley. A few in Pakistan. Language unwritten. Muslims 100%. M=GR.
8	0	0	0.00	0	2.00	98.00	A	0.00	0	1.02	Immigrants from Upper Swat Kohistan (Pakistan). Majority in Pakistan. Muslims 100% (Sunnis).
9	0	0	0.00	1	15.00	85.00	A	0.00	0	1.11	Lesser Aimaq tribes after the 5 largest. Muslims 100%(Hanafi Sunnis).
10	0	0	3.40	0	11.10	88.90	A	0.04	1,086	2	Pastoralists in south. Majority in Pakistan; a few in Iran, Bangladesh. Muslims 100% (Sunnis). Early work by M=CMS.
11	0	0	1.66	8	99.79	0.21	C	377.73	59	9	Expatriates in education, development. Mainly Anglicans and Presbyterians. Chapel in UK embassy.
12	0	0	0.00	1	11.00	89.00	A	0.00	0	1.08	Town of Darwaz in north; also in Tajikistan. Related to Tajiki. Muslims 100% (Sunnis).
13	0	0	0.00	1	16.00	84.00	A	0.00	0	1.11	'Tribal people', in west, one of the 4 Char Aimaq tribes. Semi-nomadic. Muslims 100%(Hanafi Sunnis). M=GR. R=FEBC (in Dari).
14	0	0	0.00	0	2.00	98.00	A	0.00	0	1.01	Several villages in Kunar Valley, Nuristan. Also in Pakistan. Many refugees. Muslims 100% (Sunnis).
15	0	0	5.00	8	99.85	0.15	C	431.24	121	10	Expatriates in development, business. Mainly Lutherans(EKD and RCC). R=FEBC.
16	0	0	0.00	0	2.00	98.00	A	0.00	0	1.00	Pech river, Digal Valley, Nuristan. Muslims 100%(Sunnis).
17	0	0	0.00	0	2.00	98.00	A	0.00	0	1.03	East of Ishkashim, Pamir Mountains; 64 villages. Also in Pakistan, Tajikistan, China. Tajik used as literary language. Muslims 100%.
18	0	0	0.00	0	11.03	88.97	A	0.01	248	2	Gujur nomads in east; majority in India, some in Pakistan. Pastoralists. Muslims 100%. M=GR.
19	0	0	4.10	4	29.03	70.97	A	0.03	462	2	In Hazarajat. Poor, underdogs. Muslims 100%(95% Ithna-Ashari Shias(Twelvers), 20,000 Ismailis (Seveners), 3% Sunnis). M=IAM,RCC,OD,CSI.
20	0	0	2.46	7	29.10	70.90	A	0.10	326	3	Indian traders and shopkeepers, in all major cities. Hindus 70%, Muslims 27%, Sikhs 3%.
21	1	0	4.56	7	99.84	0.16	C	423.10	110	10	Expatriates in business, development. Embassy and aid officials. D=RCC. Almost all Catholics.
22	0	0	0.00	1	15.00	85.00	A	0.00	0	1.10	One of the 4 Char Aimaq semi-nomadic tribes. Muslims 100%(Hanafi Sunnis).
23	0	0	0.00	0	2.00	98.00	A	0.00	0	1.01	Non-Romany Gypsies, also in former USSR. 90 families in Kabul, Jalalabad, Charikar. All Muslims, 100%(Sunnis): nomads, minstrels, traders, ironsmiths.
24	0	0	0.00	5	25.00	75.00	A	0.00	0	1.11	A few Afghani practicing Jewish families in Kabul and Herat. Declining by emigration.
25	0	0	0.00	0	2.00	98.00	A	0.00	0	1.00	Lower Bashgal Valley. Mountain Valleys. Related to Kati. Second language Pashtu. Muslims 100%(Sunnis).
26	0	0	0.00	1	8.00	92.00	A	0.00	0	1.07	Vast majority in Uzbekistan. Central, northwest. Bilingual in Pashto. Now acculturated. Muslims 100% (Hanafi Sunnis). M=GR.
27	0	0	0.00	4	19.00	81.00	A	0.00	0	1.09	In north, west of Kunduz. Also in former USSR, China, Mongolia, Iran, Turkey, Germany. Muslims 100% (Hanafi Sunnis). M=GR. R=FEBC.
28	0	0	0.00	0	3.00	97.00	A	0.00	0	1.02	In Chitral. Mainly in Pakistan, a few in India. Muslims 96% (93% Hanafi Sunnis, 3% Ismailis). M=GR.
29	0	0	0.00	4	19.01	80.99	A	0.00	0	1.11	Nomadic pastoralists in far north; most fled in 1978 invasion and resettled in Turkey. Also in China, Turkey. Muslims 100%(Hanafi Sunnis). M=GR. R=FEBC.
30	0	0	0.00	7	12.01	87.99	A	0.00	235	1.04	Muslim Gypsies, found from Libya to Turkey and to India. Muslims 100%.
31	0	0	0.70	0	15.01	84.99	A	0.00	493	1.10	Migrants and immigrants from Kurdistan and Iran. Muslims 100%(Shafi Sunnis).
32	0	0	0.00	0	3.00	97.00	A	0.00	0	1.00	Southwest of Kabul in Logar, north of Baraki. Muslims 100%. M=GR.
33	0	0	0.00	0	6.00	94.00	A	0.00	0	1.03	Descendants of Mongol empire. Only 200 speak Mogholi; languages now Pashto, Farsi/Dari. Muslims 100%(Sunnis). M=GR.
34	0	0	0.00	0	2.00	98.00	A	0.00	0	1.00	300 families in Anjaman, Koron, Munjan, Chitral areas. Muslims 100%(Sunnis).
35	0	0	0.00	0	3.00	97.00	A	0.00	0	1.00	In ethnic group, only 50 Ormuri speakers left. Baraki-Barak, Logar. Muslims 100%. M=GR.
36	0	0	0.00	1	11.00	89.00	A	0.00	0	1.08	One village in Chakhansoor Province. Related to Dari. Muslims 100%(Shias).
37	0	0	0.00	0	3.00	97.00	A	0.00	0	1.00	600 Parachi speakers out of large ethnic group. Hindu Kush valley. Muslims 100%(Sunnis). M=GR.
38	0	0	0.00	0	7.00	93.00	A	0.00	0	1.03	Also in former USSR. Bilingual in Tajiki. Muslims 100%.
39	0	0	0.00	0	2.00	98.00	A	0.00	0	1.02	In western Nuristan. Also Sare or Korashi. 4 major languages (NE,NW,SE,SW), 29 dialects. Converted to Sunni Islam with Nuristanis in 1896. All Muslims 100%.
40	0	0	4.79	5	35.01	64.99	A	0.01	549	2	Semi-nomads. Ghilzai nomads, Durani settled population. 2 million refugees flee, 1979-1990. Muslims 100%(all Hanafi Sunnis). M=IAM,YWAM,CSI,FI,SERVE,PI.
41	1	0	4.62	5	35.12	64.88	A	0.15	415	3	Migrants, immigrants, refugees, merchants from Iran. Muslims 97%(Imami Shias/Ithna-Asharis), Baha'is 3%. D=indigenous groupings. M=GR. R=FEBA,AWR,FEBC.
42	0	0	2.64	4	29.20	70.80	A	0.21	313	3	Dari is language of the elite, Afghan Farsi. Language of wider use. Muslims 100%(Sunnis, some Shias). R=FEBA.
43	0	0	0.00	0	3.00	97.00	A	0.00	0	1.00	Parun valley on upper reaches of Pech river, Nuristan. Related to Bashgali. Muslims 100%(Sunnis). M=GR.
44	0	0	3.65	5	36.00	64.00	A	1.31	358	4	Mostly Hindus and Sikhs from India and Pakistan. Merchants, traders. Muslims 80%, Sikhs 20%. M=GR. R=FEBA.
45	0	0	3.04	4	27.01	72.99	A	0.01	410	2	'Redheads'. Also in Pakistan. Merchant group of traders in government service (professionals, lawyers, &c). Muslims 100%(Imami Shias, Hanafi Sunnis).
46	1	0	1.45	7	84.00	16.00	B	95.04	47	6	Advisors and technicians left after decade-long invasion and war. D=ROC. R=FEBC, TWR, HCJB.
47	0	0	0.00	0	5.00	95.00	A	0.00	0	1.03	Shikoshumi. Pamirs. 19 villages, Sanglech Valley. Also in Tajikistan. Bilingual in Persian, Tajiki. Muslims 100%(Ismaili Shias).
48	0	0	0.00	0	3.00	97.00	A	0.00	0	1.01	On Kunar river. Related to Phalura. Muslims 100%. M=GR.
49	0	0	0.00	0	3.00	97.00	A	0.00	0	1.01	Pastoralists, along border in Pamir Mountains. Majority in east Tajikistan. Neo-Ismaili Muslims 100%. M=GR.
50	0	0	0.00	0	3.00	97.00	A	0.00	0	1.00	On Chitral frontier, 60 miles up Kunar river from Gawar-Bati. Muslims 100%. M=GR.
51	0	0	2.33	4	29.08	70.92	A	0.08	314	2	Merchants, traders, immigrants from India, Pakistan. Muslims 100%(Hanafi Sunnis). M=GR. R=FEBA
52	0	0	3.19	5	22.01	77.99	A	0.00	673	1.09	Southwest Pashto, around Kandahar. Mostly in Pakistan, with many migrating to Gulf Arab states. 100% Muslims (Hanafi Sunnis).
53	0	0	2.96	5	24.01	75.99	A	0.00	418	1.12	Also in Turkey, Pakistan, Germany.; Some nomadic. Bilingual in Dari or Pashto; 15% literates. Muslims 100%(Hanafi Sunnis). M=CSI,WEC,IAM,GR.
54	0	0	0.00	1	15.00	85.00	A	0.00	0	1.10	One of the 4 Char Aimaq semi-nomadic tribes. Muslims 100%(Hanafi Sunnis).
55	0	0	0.00	1	15.00	85.00	A	0.00	0	1.11	East of Darwazi on Amu Darya, also in former USSR. Variety of Tajiki. Muslims 100%. M=GR.
56	0	0	0.70	6	24.47	75.53	A	0.42	168	3	Immigrants. Bilingual in Persian or Pashto. Muslims 99%(Sunnis). M=GR.
57	0	0	3.04	1	18.02	81.98	A	0.01	462	2	Semi-sedentary Aimaq tribes (once the most powerful of them all). In Iran also. Muslims 100%(Hanafi Sunnis).
58	0	0	0.00	0	2.00	98.00	A	0.00	0	1.00	Southeast of Jalalabad, west of Khyber Pass, village of Nangahar. Muslims 100%. Language nearly extinct.
59	0	0	0.00	0	4.00	96.00	A	0.00	0	1.01	Nuristani, villages of Katar and Gambir. Muslims 100%.
60	0	0	0.00	1	17.00	83.00	A	0.00	0	1.11	Near Turkmenistan border. Also in Iran, Turkey, Pakistan. Second language Pashto. Devout Muslims 100%(Hanafi Sunnis,Sufi orders). M=CSI, WEC, GR.
61	2	0	2.92	8	99.78	0.22	C	378.65	79	9	Expatriates in development, education, business, diplomacy, UN. D=Anglicans, Protestants.
62	0	0	0.70	4	26.05	73.95	A	0.04	158	2	Mainly in China, Mongolia, Turkey, Pakistan, Iran. Agriculturalists. Muslims (Sunnis, with heavy Sufi influence).
63	0	0	2.26	5	37.23	62.77	A	0.31	242	3	Merchants and traders from Pakistan and India, mainly in towns. Muslims 95%. M=ABC.
64	0	0	0.00	0	3.00	97.00	A	0.00	0	1.00	Southeast Nuristan. Kafirs. Sunni Muslims, converted to Islam in 1896, but retaining ancient animistic religion. Muslims 90%, animists. M=GR.
65	0	0	0.00	1	13.00	87.00	A	0.00	0	1.09	In Werdoge river area west of Ishkashim, in northeast of country. Muslims 100%.
66	0	0	3.39	1	16.01	83.99	A	0.00	751	1.08	Large nomadic, in southwest desert. Majority in Pakistan and Iran. Muslims 100%(Sunnis). M=GR, CSI.
67	0	0	3.86	1	23.20	76.80	A	0.16	575	3	Merchants, traders from India, Pakistan. Refugees in Pakistan 1979-89. Muslims 100%(Hanafi Sunnis).
68	0	0	0.00	0	2.00	98.00	A	0.00	0	1.00	South of Waigali area in Nuristan, towns of Wotapuri and Katarqalai. Muslims 99%(Sunnis).
69	0	0	0.00	1	12.00	88.00	A	0.00	0	1.07	Secret language used among goldsmiths and others, based on a dialect of Persian, related to Balkan Romany. Muslims 100%(Sunnis,Shias). M=GR.
70	0	0	2.47		2.10	97.90	A	0.00	3,223	1.02	Eastern Pathan, and various other small immigrant/migrant groups from surrounding countries.
Albania											
71	2	0	2.55	6	99.95	0.05	C	457.71	76	10	Also in Bulgaria, Serbia, Greece. Distinct from Romanian. Nonreligious 20%. D=AOC,RCC.
72	0	0	0.00	5	48.00	52.00	A	8.76	0	4	Artificial (constructed) language, spoken in 80 countries. Speakers in Albania: 3,500(non mother-tongue).
73	2	0	-0.02	6	70.00	30.00	B	61.32	20	6	Northern Albania; also Bulgaria, Yugoslavia, USA. Nonreligious 25%, Muslims 30%(Hanafi Sunnis), atheists 19%. D=mainly RCC(M-Scutari); some SDA,JWs.
74	2	0	1.19	7	99.90	0.10	C	486.18	40	10	Residents, merchants, traders from Greece. D=Greek Orthodox Ch,AOC.
75	0	0	0.00	7	39.50	60.50	A	0.72	45	3	Remnants of former large military-political Communist Chinese presence. Mostly atheists.
76	0	0	0.00	6	28.00	72.00	A	0.00	0	1.08	Survivors of anti-Jewish and antireligious campaigns; rest emigrated to Israel.
77	4	0	1.65	5	99.90	0.10	C	473.04	49	10	Immigrants, residents from Macedonia (Yugoslavia, Greece). D=Macedonian Orthodox Ch,SOC,GOC,RCC.
78	2	0	1.11	6	99.70	0.30	C	311.71	49	9	Immigrants from neighboring state of Montenegro. Nonreligious 40%. D=Serbian Orthodox Ch, RCC.
79	1	0	4.32	6	99.70	0.30	C	314.26	96	9	Immigrants from Serbia. Nonreligious 30%. D=Serbian Orthodox Ch (Vicariate of Shkoder).
80	4	0	2.00	6	86.00	14.00	B	97.30	81	6	In south; also USA, Egypt, Italy, Turkey. Nonreligious 50%, Muslims 27%(20% Sunnis,7% Shias(250,000 Bektashiyya Sufis), atheists 13%. D=AOC,RCC,SDA,JWs.
81	2	0	8.48	1	92.00	8.00	C	201.48	283	8	Wallachian, Southern Vlach. Mostly Christians in the past. Muslims 25%, nonreligious 15%. D=RCC,AOC.
82	5	0	0.89		45.00	55.00	A	41.06	54	6	Other Europeans (D=AOC,RCC,SDA), Arabs, Turks.
Algeria											
83	1	3	0.00	0	17.00	83.00	A	0.00	0	1.07	People of the Veil. Blue-robed camel-breeding nomads. Marginal Muslims 100%. Tifinagh script. D=RCC(D-Laghouat). M=SDM,WF,GR.
84	4	6	4.67	8	61.24	38.76	B	0.53	240	3	Muslims 99%(Maliki Sunnis, with Qadiriyya order). D=RCC,EPA,30 others; over 15,000 isolated radio believers. M=WF,CSSp,SJ,ERF,CSI,FI,MEM.
85	3	6	3.58	8	58.10	41.90	B	0.21	202	3	Muslims 100%(Maliki Sunnis). D=RCC,EPA,20 others. M=WF,SJ,CSSp,CM,FSC,CSI,MEM. R=network (Arabic). T=SATT,CTU,CBN (Arabic)
86	0	1	0.00	0	9.00	91.00	A	0.00	0	1.04	Northeastern Tuareg country. Camel nomads. Muslims 100%.
87	0	1	0.00	0	8.00	92.00	A	0.00	0	1.02	Black Africans related to Songhai from Niger river. Muslims 100%(Sunnis).
88	2	10	3.98	8	99.79	0.21	C	420.99	96	10	Diplomats, businessmen, technicians. D=Anglican Ch(D-Egypt),JWs.
89	1	8	4.99	5	99.70	0.30	C	337.26	124	9	White Russian exiles from 1917 USSR among 6,000 Russians in Algeria. D=ROC.
90	0	3	3.19	4	29.02	70.98	A	0.02	380	2	Western Algeria, mountain area of Middle Atlas; mainly in Morocco. Transhumance. Muslims 100%(Maliki Sunnis). M=CSI,MEM. R=TWR.
91	0	1	1.96	7	26.01	73.99	A	0.00	280	1.07	Nomads in eastern Algeria (latitude 31 degrees North), south of Atlas Mountains. Several Bedouin tribes. Muslims 100%(Sunnis).
92	0	1	2.22	7	26.01	73.99	A	0.00	308	1.07	Nomads on southwestern border with Morocco. 3 tribes. Muslims 100%(Sunnis).
93	3	6	5.81	8	87.00	13.00	B	63.51	205	6	Migrant workers from Egypt. Muslims 80%, Copts 20%. D=COC,CCC,CEC.
94	0	1	1.62	4	25.02	74.98	A	0.01	249	2	Western Algeria, near Morocco border. 10 fortified date-growing oasis towns. Muslims 100%(Sunnis).
95	4	7	-2.97	8	99.78	0.22	C	427.05	2	10	Settlers from France from 1830, now citizens. D=RCC,EPA,JWs,AoG. M=UMC,SJ,ERF,LBI.
96	0	1	0.70	1	19.01	80.99	A	0.00	195	1.09	Isolated, near Mzab region. Half are bilingual in Arabic and/or French. Muslims 100%(Maliki Sunnis).
97	3	6	7.78	4	48.37	51.63	A	0.65	480	3	Peasant agriculturalists. Latin alphabet, 52% literates. Strong Muslims(99% Maliki Sunnis). D=RCC(D-Constantine),Assemblee Evangelique,Freres Larges.
98	0	1	3.14	7	25.01	74.99	A	0.00	421	1.07	Semi-nomads of the steppes, on Moroccan border. Numerous tribes. Muslims 100%(Maliki Sunnis).
99	0	1	0.00	5	32.00	68.00	A	0.00	0	1.10	Migrant traders from Niger. Muslims 100%(Maliki Sunnis).
100	0	1	0.00	0	10.00	90.00	A	0.00	0	1.05	Iforas region in western Tuareg country. Camel nomads. Muslims 100%.
101	0	6	3.14	7	46.70	53.30	A	1.19	225	4	Migrants, immigrants from Iraq. Muslims 99%(Maliki Sunnis).
102	0	5	0.00	8	39.00	61.00	A	0.00	0	1.12	Small remnant community of practicing Jews. Emigration to Israel since 1948.
103	0	1	0.70	7	28.01	71.99	A	0.01	137	2	Bedouin nomads around Laghouat. Muslims 100%(Sunnis). M=RCC(D-Laghouat),WF.
104	1	6	4.82	4	44.20	55.80	A	0.32	342	3	Muslims 99%(Maliki Sunnis). D=RCC(M-Alger,D-Constantine). M=CMML,WF,LBI,CSI. R=TWR.
105	0	1	0.00	1	11.00	89.00	A	0.00	0	1.06	Beni Menasser, West Metmata. Coastal tribe 70 miles west of Algiers in Cherchel region, and other remnant tribes. Muslims 100%(Sunnis).
106	0	3	4.65	7	44.15	55.85	A	0.24	332	3	Migrants, residents from Morocco. Muslims 100%(Sunnis). M=CSI.
107	0	1	2.10	1	21.01	78.99	A	0.00	359	1.09	Mzab oases, in vicinity of 5 towns. Urban culture. Over 50% speak Arabic, many men speak French also. Muslims 100%(Hanafi Sunnis,Ibadi Kharijites/Seceders).
108	0	1	1.10	7	26.01	73.99	A	0.00	190	1.07	Bedouin semi-nomads of the steppes, central Atlas region. Muslims 100%(Sunnis).
109	0	3	2.52	4	29.02	70.98	A	0.02	316	2	Region of the Rif, mainly in Morocco. Dialects; Arzeu, Igzennaian, Iznacen, Senhaja. Muslims 100%(Sunnis) M=LBI. R=TWR.
110	0	5	1.10	8	47.09	52.91	A	0.15	124	3	Muslims Gypsies. Nomadic life-style. Muslims 100%(Sunnis).
111	0	1	0.00	7	23.00	77.00	A	0.00	0	1.06	Nomadic Bedouins related to 8 major oases in northeastern Algerian Sahara. All Muslims 100%(Sunnis).
112	1	8	3.14	7	99.70	0.30	C	342.37	64	9	Russian exiles from former USSR. Nonreligious 30%. D=ROC.
113	1	3	0.00	1	23.00	77.00	A	0.00	0	1.11	South and east of Grand Kabylie, Aures. Mountains. Muslims 100%(Maliki Sunnis). D=RCC(D-Constantine). M=LBI,SGM,MEM.
114	0	1	2.43	7	26.01	73.99	A	0.00	330	1.07	Uled Sidi Sheikh. Bedouin nomads, with 4 tribes south of Geryville. Muslims 100%(Sunnis).
115	0	3	4.43	4	32.09	67.91	A	0.10	449	3	Susuia. Southern Algeria, also in Morocco. Muslims 100%(Maliki Sunnis). M=LBI,CSI,MEM.
116	1	9	1.20	8	99.96	0.04	C	578.16	35	10	Immigrants from Spain, Spanish Morocco, and Sahara. D=RCC(M-Alger).

Continued overleaf

Table 8-2 continued

PEOPLE		POPULATION				IDENTITY CODE		LANGUAGE		CHURCH		MINISTRY						SCRIPTURE		
Ref 1	Ethnic name 2	P% 3	In 1995 4	In 2000 5	In 2025 6	Race 7	Language 8	Autoglossonym 9	S 10	AC 11	Members 12	Jayuh 13-17	d 18	wa 19	xc 20	mc 21	mi 22	Biblioglossonym 23	Pub 24-26	ss 27
117	Suafa Bedouin	0.31400	88,103	98,820	146,357	CMT30	12-AACD	badawi-sahara cluster		0.01	10	0a...	3	1	0	0	0		PN.	b
118	Tajakant Bedouin	4.10000	1,150,393	1,290,322	1,911,033	CMT30	12-AACD-a	hassaaniyya		0.00	0	0a...	0	2	0	0	0		pn.	b
119	Tidikelt Berber	0.03221	9,038	10,137	15,013	CMT32d	10-AAAC-p	tidikelt		0.03	3	1c...	3	1	0	0	0		pn.	.
120	Tit Berber	0.05000	14,029	15,736	23,305	CMT32z	10-AAAC-pb	tit		0.02	3	1c...	3	1	0	0	0		pn.	.
121	Tougourt Berber	0.02147	6,024	6,757	10,007	CMT32d	10-AAAC-k	tugurt		0.01	1	1c...	3	1	2	0	0		pn.	b
122	Tuat Berber	0.07000	19,641	22,030	32,627	CMT32d	10-AAAC-o	tuat		0.01	2	1c...	3	1	2	0	0		pn.	.
123	Wargla Berber (Ouargla)	0.01789	5,020	5,630	8,339	CMT32d	10-AAAC-l	wargla-ngusa		0.01	1	1c...	3	1	2	0	0		pn.	b
124	Zekara Berber (Zkara)	0.20900	58,642	65,775	97,416	CMT32b	10-AAAC-b	ta-mazight		0.02	13	1a...	3	1	0	0	0	Shilha: Central*	Pn.	b
125	Ziban Bedouin	0.69800	195,847	219,670	325,342	CMT30	12-AACD	badawi-sahara cluster		0.00	0	0a...	0	1	0	0	0		PN.	b
126	other minor peoples	0.40000	112,233	125,885	186,442	...				1.00	1,259		6	4	6	1	0			
	American Samoa	**100.00000**	**56,755**	**68,089**	**142,680**					**81.13**	**55,241**									
127	Euronesian	10.00000	5,676	6,809	14,268	MPY53	52-ABAC-bv	standard oceanian-english	75	80.00	5,447	1Bsuh	10	8	7	4	3		pnb	b
128	Filipino	1.00000	568	681	1,427	MSY44o	31-CKAA-a	proper tagalog		95.00	647	4Bs..	10	9	12	0	0	Tagalog	PNB	b
129	Han Chinese	0.20000	114	136	285	MSY42a	79-AAAL-a	shao-jiang		40.00	54	0a..	9	6	10	0	0	Chinese: Cantonese	PNB	b
130	Japanese	0.30000	170	204	428	MSY45a	45-CAAA-a	koku-go		5.00	10	1B.uh	7	5	9	0	0	Japanese	PNB	b
131	Korean	0.90000	511	613	1,284	MSY46	45-AAAA-b	kukö		60.00	368	2A...	10	9	12	0	0	Korean	PNB	b
132	Samoan	80.81000	45,864	55,023	115,300	MPY55e	39-CAOA	samoa cluster		81.50	44,844	2a.u.	10	8	16	5	1	Samoan	PNB	b
133	Tokelauan	0.37000	210	252	528	MPY55z	39-CAKC	tokelau cluster		80.00	202	0.s..	10	8	13	5	0		...	b
134	Tongan	1.60000	908	1,089	2,283	MPY55g	39-CAPB	tonga cluster		97.00	1,057	4a...	10	8	14	5	0	Tongan	PNB	b
135	USA White	4.62000	2,622	3,146	6,592	CEW19s	52-ABAC-s	general american	75	80.00	2,517	1Bsuh	10	8	13	4	3	English*	PNB	b
136	other minor peoples	0.20000	114	136	285	...				70.00	95		10	7	11	4	0			
	Andorra	**100.00000**	**64,095**	**77,985**	**154,335**					**90.02**	**70,203**									
137	British	1.77000	1,134	1,380	2,732	CEW19i	52-ABAC-b	standard-english		79.00	1,090	3Bsuh	10	8	8	3	1		PNB	b
138	Catalonian	28.40000	18,203	22,148	43,831	CEW21a	51-AABE-bg	andorrès	66	93.00	20,597	1a..h	10	8	15	3	1		pnb	b
139	Filipino	0.30000	192	234	463	MSY44o	52-ABCF-a	nord-bayrisch-t.		95.00	222	0B.uh	10	9	12	0	0		pn.	b
140	French	7.57000	4,852	5,903	11,683	CEW21b	51-AABI-d	general français		87.00	5,136	1B.uh	10	8	12	3	1	French	PNB	b
141	German	0.53000	340	413	818	CEW19m	52-ABCE-a	standard hoch-deutsch		85.00	351	2B.uh	10	10	10	0	0	German*	PNB	b
142	Indo-Pakistani	0.50000	320	390	772	CNN25g	59-AAFO	hindi-urdu cluster		1.00	4	4Asuh	6	6	7	0	0		PNB	b
143	Jewish	0.36000	231	281	556	CMT35	51-AABB-c	general español		0.00	0	2B.uh	0	4	4	1	0	Spanish	PNB	b
144	Moroccan Arab	0.60000	385	468	926	CMT30	52-ABCF-a	nord-bayrisch-t.		2.00	9	0B.uh	6	6	7	0	0		pn.	b
145	Portuguese	11.10000	7,115	8,656	17,131	CEW21g	51-AABA-e	general português		90.00	7,791	2Bsuh	10	9	12	0	0	Portuguese	PNB	b
146	Spaniard	47.03000	30,144	36,676	72,584	CEW21k	51-AABB-c	general español	60	92.70	33,999	2B.uh	10	8	15	3	1	Spanish	PNB	b
147	other minor peoples	1.84000	1,179	1,435	2,840	...				70.00	1,004		10	6	11	2	0			
	Angola	**100.00000**	**10,972,379**	**12,878,188**	**25,106,861**					**84.91**	**10,934,237**									
148	Afrikaner	0.20000	21,945	25,756	50,214	CEW19a	52-ABCB-a	afrikaans	1	82.00	21,120	2B.uh	10	8	12	3	2	Afrikaans	PNB	b
149	Ambo (Ndonga, Ovambo)	2.00000	219,448	257,564	502,137	NAB57n	99-AURL-c	o-ci-ndonga	5	95.00	244,686	1asu.	10	7	13	2	1	Oshindonga*	PNB	b
150	Aukwe (Auen, West Kung)	0.02800	3,072	3,606	7,030	BYG11d	09-ABBB-a	au-kwe		11.00	397	0.s..	8	5	4	0	1	Akhoe	P..	.
151	Bakwe Pygmy	0.08600	9,436	11,075	21,592	BYG12	99-AURG-f	central ki-koongo		25.00	2,769	4as..	9	5	6	0	0	Kongo	PNB	b
152	Bolo (Haka)	0.02000	2,194	2,576	5,021	NAB57n	99-AURI-c	lu-bolo		65.00	1,674	0....	10	6	7	1	2		pnb	.
153	British	0.08600	9,436	11,075	21,592	CEW19i	52-ABAC-b	standard-english	3	79.00	8,749	3Bsuh	10	8	8	3	1		PNB	b
154	Caboverdian Mestico	0.05000	5,486	6,439	12,553	NAN58	51-AACA-a	caboverdense		98.00	6,310	1c...	10	8	11	2	2	Crioulo, Upper Guinea	PNB	b
155	Chokwe (Kioko)	5.00000	548,619	643,909	1,255,343	NAB57b	99-AURP-f	ki-cokwe	12	75.00	482,932	0....	10	6	8	2	3	Chokwe	PNB	.
156	Cuban White	0.41300	45,316	53,187	103,691	CLT27	51-AABB-hi	cubano	7	30.00	15,956	1B.uh	9	5	2	0	1		pnb	b
157	Dhimba	0.05712	6,267	7,356	14,341	NAB57n	99-AURL-de	himba		90.00	6,620	1csu.	10	6	7	2	1	Otjidhimba*	Pnb	.
158	Eurafrican	1.00000	109,724	128,782	251,069	NAN58	51-AABA-e	general português		80.00	103,026	2Bsuh	10	7	8	2	2	Portuguese	PNB	b
159	Eurafrican (Blackigiese)	0.05000	5,486	6,439	12,553	NAN58	51-AACA-d	angolar	21	70.00	4,507	1a...	10	7	7	2	1		pnb	b
160	French	0.05000	5,486	6,439	12,553	CEW21b	51-AABI-d	general français	4	87.00	5,602	1B.uh	10	8	11	3	1	French	PNB	b
161	Gciriku (Shimbogedu)	0.10000	10,972	12,878	25,107	NAB57n	99-AURN-u	ru-gciriku		50.00	6,439	1cs..	10	6	7	2	1	Gciriku*	PNb	.
162	Han Chinese (Mandarin)	0.00950	1,042	1,223	2,385	MSY42a	79-AAAB-ba	kuo-yü		1.05	13	2Bsuh	6	3	6	0	0	Chinese: Kuoyu*	PNB	b
163	Herero	0.80000	87,779	103,026	200,855	NAB57n	99-AURL-d	o-ci-herero	1	95.00	97,874	4asu.	10	7	7	2	3	Otjiherero*	PNB	.
164	Holu (Holo)	0.20733	22,749	26,700	52,054	NAB57b	99-AUHD-a	ki-holu		50.00	13,350	0....	10	6	7	2	1	Kiholo*	P..	.
165	Hukwe (Kwengo, Xu)	0.15030	16,491	19,356	37,736	BYG11d	08-AABF-e	l`kani-kxoe		20.00	3,871	4....	9	6	4	1	1		...	.
166	Kedi (Heikum, San)	0.00500	549	644	1,255	BYG11d	08-ABAA-b	kedi		20.00	129	0....	9	5	5	0	2		...	.
167	Kongo	10.03271	1,100,827	1,292,031	2,518,899	NAB57b	99-AURG-b	ki-fiote	18	88.50	1,143,448	1as..	10	8	11	2	2		PNB	b
168	Kongo (Kituba)	0.10000	10,972	12,878	25,107	NAB57b	99-AURG-ac	mono-ku-tuba	9	99.00	12,749	4as..	10	8	13	2	3	Munukutuba	Pnb	b
169	Kongo (San Salvador)	2.50000	274,309	321,955	627,672	NAB57b	99-AURG-p	ki-shi-koongo		98.00	315,516	1as..	10	8	14	2	3		PNB	b
170	Kung-Ekoka	0.05712	6,267	7,356	14,341	BYG11d	09-ABAA-a	uukualuthi		10.00	736	0.s..	8	5	4	1	1	Kung: Ekoka*	P..	.
171	Kung-Tsumkwe	0.03427	3,760	4,413	8,604	BYG11d	08-AABE-g	tshuma-khoe		10.00	441	0....	8	5	4	1	1	Kung: Tsumkwe*	P..	.
172	Kwadi (Koroca, Vatua)	0.21429	23,513	27,597	53,801	BYG11d	08-BAAA-a	kwise		20.00	5,519	0....	9	5	6	1	1		...	.
173	Kwangali	0.25000	27,431	32,195	62,767	NAB57n	99-AURN-s	si-kwangali	1	90.00	28,976	4as..	10	6	7	2	2	Rukwangali*	PNB	b
174	Kwanyama	4.09711	449,550	527,634	1,028,656	NAB57n	99-AURL-a	o-shi-kwanyama	5	95.00	501,252	3asu.	10	8	7	2	2	Oshikwanyama*	PNB	b
175	Lingala (Zairian)	0.50000	54,862	64,391	125,534	NAB57c	99-AUIF-b	vehicular lingala	5	98.00	63,103	4asu.	10	8	13	2	3	Lingala	PNB	b
176	Lozi	0.03000	3,292	3,863	7,532	NAB57g	99-AUTE-f	si-lozi	2	97.00	3,748	3asu.	10	8	13	2	2	Silozi*	PNB	b
177	Luchazi	2.33565	256,276	300,789	586,408	NAB57b	99-AURP-i	ci-lucazi	8	92.00	276,726	0....	10	7	11	2	2	Chiluchazi*	PNB	.
178	Luimbi	0.33400	36,648	43,013	83,857	NAB57b	99-AURP-d	ci-luimbi		60.00	25,808	0....	10	7	7	2	1	Chiluimbi*	Pnb	.
179	Luyana (Luyi, Luano)	0.24750	27,157	31,874	62,139	NAB57n	99-AURN-a	e-si-luyana		60.00	19,124	1as..	10	7	7	2	1		pnb	.
180	Lwena (Luvale)	8.15762	895,085	1,050,554	2,048,122	NAB57b	99-AURP-h	lwena-luvale	4	90.00	945,498	0....	10	7	7	2	1	Chiluvale*	PNB	.
181	Macanese	0.01000	1,097	1,288	2,511	MSY43	51-AABA-e	general português		95.00	1,223	2Bsuh	10	7	13	3	1	Portuguese	PNB	b
182	Maligo	0.01700	1,865	2,189	4,268	BYG11d	09-AAAA-a	maligo		20.00	438	0....	9	6	6	1	0		...	.
183	Mbangala (Yongo)	0.17000	18,653	21,893	42,682	NAB57b	99-AURI-f	ci-mbangala		50.00	10,946	0....	10	6	7	2	1		pnb	.
184	Mbukushu (Kusso)	0.10020	10,994	12,904	25,157	NAB57g	99-AURN-o	north mbukushu	1	50.00	6,452	1cs..	10	5	2	2	2	Mbukushu	PNb	b
185	Mbunda	1.01550	111,425	130,778	254,960	NAB57b	99-AURP-j	ci-mbunda	1	80.00	104,622	0....	10	6	7	2	1	Chimbunda*	PNb	.
186	Mbundu (Ovimbundu)	25.20084	2,765,132	3,245,412	6,327,140	NAB57n	99-AURJ-a	u-mbundu	55	84.00	2,726,146	0a...	10	8	11	3	3	Umbundu	PNB	.
187	Mbwela (Ambuella)	1.67001	183,240	215,067	419,287	NAB57b	99-AURP-c	shi-mbwela		80.00	172,054	0....	10	6	7	2	1		pnb	.
188	Ndembu (Lunda)	0.05000	5,486	6,439	12,553	NAB57b	99-AURP-k	ci-lunda	1	94.00	6,053	0....	10	8	11	3	2	Lunda	PNB	.
189	Ndombe (Dombe)	0.17000	18,653	21,893	42,682	NAB57b	99-AURJ-b	n-dombe		40.00	8,757	0c...	9	5	7	2	1		pnb	.
190	Ngandyera	0.10000	10,972	12,878	25,107	NAB57n	99-AURL-aj	ngandjera		70.00	9,015	1csu.	10	8	6	3	2		pnb	.
191	Nkangala	0.20000	21,945	25,756	50,214	NAB57b	99-AURP-b	nkangala		40.00	10,303	0....	9	5	7	2	1		pnb	.
192	Nkhumbi (Ngumbi)	0.17000	18,653	21,893	42,682	NAB57b	99-AURK-c	o-lu-nkumbi		70.00	15,325	0.s..	10	5	7	2	1	Nkhumbi	P..	.
193	North Mbundu (Kimbundu)	23.11265	2,536,008	2,976,491	5,802,861	NAB57b	99-AURI-a	ki-mbundu	35	84.00	2,500,252	0....	10	7	11	3	3	Kimbundu: Luanda*	PNB	.
194	Nyaneka (Nhaneca)	3.89275	427,127	501,316	977,347	NAB57n	99-AURK-a	o-lu-nyaneka		90.00	451,184	0.s..	10	7	7	3	1	Nyaneka	p..	.
195	Nyemba (Nyonyelu)	1.67001	183,240	215,067	419,287	NAB57n	99-AURP-a	nyemba		85.00	182,807	0....	10	6	7	2	1	Nyemba	Pnb	.
196	Nyengo	0.07143	7,838	9,199	17,934	NAB57b	99-AURN-i	nyengo		50.00	4,599	1cs..	10	6	7	2	1		pnb	.
197	Okung (North Kung, Xu)	0.04286	4,703	5,520	10,761	BYG11d	09-ABAA-a	uukualuthi		20.00	1,104	0.s..	9	5	4	1	1	Kung: Ekoka*	P..	.
198	Portuguese (Branco)	0.08600	9,436	11,075	21,592	CEW21g	51-AABA-e	general português	45	93.00	10,300	2Bsuh	10	8	14	3	3	Portuguese	PNB	b
199	Ruund (Northern Lunda)	1.34000	147,030	172,568	336,432	NAB57f	99-AURP-n	u-ruund		96.00	165,665	0....	10	8	12	3	1	Uruund*	PNb	.
200	Sama (Kissama)	0.12857	14,107	16,557	32,280	NAB57n	99-AURI-b	ki-sama		65.00	10,762	0....	10	6	7	2	2		pnb	.
201	Songo (Nsongo)	0.68966	75,672	88,816	173,152	NAB57b	99-AURI-e	ki-songo	1	80.00	71,053	0....	10	6	7	2	2	Nsongo	Pnb	.
202	Spaniard	0.05000	5,486	6,439	12,553	CEW21k	51-AABB-c	general español		96.00	6,182	2B.uh	10	8	14	3	1	Spanish	PNB	b
203	Suku	0.10000	10,972	12,878	25,107	NAB57b	99-AURH-bm	north ki-suku		90.00	11,590	0....	10	8	7	3	1	Kisuku*	P..	b
204	Yaka	0.11000	12,070	14,166	27,618	NAB57b	99-AURH-b	south ki-yaka		94.00	13,316	0....	10	8	7	3	1	Iyaka: Congo*	P..	b
205	Yauma	0.13000	14,264	16,742	32,639	NAB57g	99-AURP-jb	yauma		60.00	10,045	0....	10	6	7	2	1	Yauma	Pnb	.
206	Yombe (Bayombe)	0.30000	32,917	38,635	75,321	NAB57b	99-AURG-c	ki-yombe		90.00	34,771	1cs..	10	8	6	3	1	Yombe	Pnb	b
207	other minor peoples	0.20000	21,945	25,756	50,214	...				80.00	20,605		10	6	2	1	0			
	Anguilla	**100.00000**	**7,798**	**8,309**	**10,984**					**86.48**	**7,186**									
208	British	1.50000	117	125	165	CEW19i	52-ABAC-b	standard-english		79.00	98	3Bsuh	10	8	8	4	3		PNB	b
209	Indo-Pakistani	0.50000	39	42	55	CNN25g	59-AAFO-e	general hindi		31.00	13	3Asuh	9	5	5	3	0		pnb	b
210	Mulatto	8.00000	624	665	879	NFB68b	52-ABAF-q	anguillan-creole		80.00	532	1a..h	10	8	8	4	3		pn.	.
211	West Indian Black	89.80000	7,003	7,461	9,864	NFB68a	52-ABAF-q	anguillan-creole		87.50	6,529	1a..h	10	8	11	4	3		pn.	.
212	other minor peoples	0.20000	16	17	22	...				84.00	14		10	8	7	4	0			
	Antarctica	**100.00000**	**3,900**	**4,500**	**10,000**					**75.6**	**3,402**									
213	other minor peoples	100.00000	3,900	4,500	10,000					75.60	3,402		10	8	13	0	0			
	Antigua & Barbuda	**100.00000**	**65,733**	**67,560**	**75,080**					**79.51**	**53,715**									
214	British	1.30000	855	878	976	CEW19i	52-ABAC-b	standard-english		79.00	694	3Bsuh	10	8	8	4	2		PNB	b
215	Indo-Pakistani	0.20000	131	135	150	CNN25g	59-AAFO-e	general hindi		30.00	41	3Asuh	9	5	5	3	0		pnb	b
216	Mulatto	3.50000	2,301	2,365	2,628	NFB68b	52-ABAF-t	antiguan-creole		80.00	1,892	1a..h	10	8	8	4	2		pn.	b
217	USA White	12.00000	7,888	8,107	9,010	CEW19s	52-ABAC-s	general american		78.00	6,324	1Bsuh	10	10	13	0	0	English*	PNB	b
218	West Indian Black	82.40000	54,164	55,669	61,866	NFB68a	52-ABAF-t	antiguan-creole		79.90	44,480	1a..h	10	8	8	4	3		pn.	b
219	other minor peoples	0.60000	394	405	450	...				70.00	284		10	6	8	3	0			
	Argentina	**100.00000**	**34,764,556**	**37,027,297**	**47,150,313**					**91.79**	**33,985,870**									
220	Argentinian White	73.37752	25,509,369	27,169,712	34,597,730	CLT27	51-AABB-hv	argentino		95.40	25,919,905	1B.uh	10	9	10	5	4		pnb	b
221	Armenian	0.02500	8,691	9,257	11,788	CEW14	57-AAAA-b	ashkharik		90.00	8,331	4A.u.	10	8	11	5	2	Armenian: Modern, Eastern	PNB	b
222	Bolivian Guarani	0.04880	16,965	18,069	23,009	MIR39e	82-AAIF-cb	chiriguano		70.00	12,649	3a...	10	8	7	5	1	Guarayu*	PNb	b
223	Brazilian Guarani (Mbya)	0.01567	5,448	5,802	7,388	MIR39e	82-AAIF-g	mbyá		65.00	3,771	1c...	10	6	6	5	1	Guarani: Brazil, Southern*	PNb	b
224	British	0.09800	34,069	36,287	46,207	CEW19i	52-ABAC-b	standard-english	6	79.00	28,667	3Bsuh	10	9	8	5	1		PNB	b
225	Byelorussian	0.01000	3,476	3,703	4,715	CEW22c	53-AAAE-c	bielorusskiy		80.00	2,962	3A.uh	10	8	8	4	2	Byelorussian*	PNB	b
226	Caiwa (Kaiwa, Pan)	0.00158	549	585	745	MIR39e	82-AAIF-f	kaingwá		70.00	410	1c...	10	5	7	3	1	Kaiwa	PNb	.

Continued opposite

Table 8-2 continued

EVANGELIZATION								EVANGELISM			ADDITIONAL DESCRIPTIVE DATA
Ref *1*	*D* *28*	*aC* *29*	*CG%* *30*	*r* *31*	*E* *32*	*U* *33*	*W* *34*	*e* *35*	*R* *36*	*T* *37*	*Locations, civil divisions, literacy, religions, church history, denominations, dioceses, church growth, missions, agencies, ministries, movements* *38*
117	0	1	2.33	7	26.01	73.99	A	0.00	319	1.07	Bedouin nomads, including several oases. Muslims 100%(Sunnis).
118	0	2	0.00	7	20.00	80.00	A	0.00	0	1.07	Nomadic Bedouins(4 tribes) in northern Mauritania, also across border into Algeria. Muslims 100%(Sunnis).
119	0	1	1.10	1	14.03	85.97	A	0.01	342	2	Vicinity of Taourirt, Berga. Muslims 100%(Maliki Sunnis).
120	0	1	1.10	1	14.02	85.98	A	0.01	352	2	Vicinity of Tit in Southern Algeria. Muslims 100%(Maliki Sunnis).
121	0	1	0.00	1	19.01	80.99	A	0.00	94	1.09	Northeast Algeria, vicinity of Touggourt. Nomads. 50% bilingual in Arabic. Muslims 100%(Maliki Sunnis).
122	0	1	0.70	1	16.01	83.99	A	0.00	231	1.08	Southern Algeria, region of Touat and 3 other Saharan oases. Semi-nomadic date cultivators. Muslims 100%(Maliki Sunnis).
123	0	1	0.00	1	19.01	80.99	A	0.00	94	1.09	South of Constantine. Dialects: Ouedghir(Wadi), Temacin. Half are bilingual in Arabic. Formerly led trans-Sahara caravan trade. Muslims 100%(Maliki Sunnis).
124	0	1	2.60	4	20.02	79.98	A	0.01	469	2	Berbers originally from Morocco. Snus(Beni Snous) tribe. Muslims 100%(Sunnis).
125	0	1	0.00	7	23.00	77.00	A	0.00	0	1.06	Nomadic Bedouins in the desert, including 2 oases and town of Biskra. Tent=dwellers. Muslims 100%(Sunnis).
126	0	5	4.95		20.00	80.00	A	0.73	678	3	Other nomads (Angad, Atta Berber), large numbers of Sahrawi refugees from Sahara.
American Samoa											
127	5	10	2.39	8	99.80	0.20	C	429.24	59	10	Mixed-race, European/American/Asian. D=RCC,CCCS,SDA,JWs,CJCLdS.
128	0	0	4.26	5	99.95	0.05	C	506.25	93	10	Immigrants from Philippines. D=Iglesia ni Cristo(Manalista)(Ch of Christ),RCC. M=SJ,FMB.
129	0	0	4.07	7	83.00	17.00	B	121.18	156	7	Immigrants from China. Buddhists/Chinese folk-religionists 60%. D=RCC. M=SJ,OFMCap,FMB.
130	0	0	2.33	7	48.00	52.00	A	8.76	176	4	Expatriates from Japan, in commerce. Japanese Buddhists 95%. D=RCC,UCC.
131	0	0	3.67	6	99.60	0.40	C	236.52	109	8	Buddhists/Confucians/shamanists 40%. D=RCC. M=SJ,OFMCap,PCK-Tonghap,FMB.
132	5	8	2.26	5	99.82	0.18	C	456.62	50	10	Many emigrants to USA, Hawaii, New Zealand, Fiji. Agriculturalists, fishermen. D=CCCS,RCC(D-Samoa & Tokelau),CJCLdS,MCS,AoG. M=UCBWM.
133	0	9	2.51	5	99.80	0.20	C	376.68	64	9	Also in Tokelau, New Zealand, Hawaii (USA).
134	0	9	2.52	5	99.97	0.03	C	587.72	50	10	Also in Tonga, New Zealand, Fiji, Hawaii (USA).
135	5	10	2.54	8	99.80	0.20	C	449.68	61	10	Expatriates in education, development, government, business. D=CCCS,CJCLdS,JWs,SDA,RCC.
136	0	10	2.51		99.70	0.30	C	275.94	64	8	Other Pacific Islanders, Asians, Australasians, Europeans.
Andorra											
137	1	10	3.73	8	99.79	0.21	C	418.10	92	10	Nationals of Britain, education, commerce. D=Anglican Ch.(D-Europe).
138	1	9	2.74	3	99.93	0.07	C	529.54	64	10	40% Spaniards, 30.3% Andorrans. Most live in Spain, also France, Italy, USA. Very extensive literature and culture. D=RCC(D-Urgel).
139	0	0	3.15	8	99.95	0.05	C	475.04	63	10	Immigrants from Philippines. D=Iglesia ni Cristo(Manalista)(Ch of Christ),RCC. M=SJ,FMB.
140	1	10	3.12	8	99.87	0.13	C	498.55	72	10	With Spanish, the original culture/language/political authority. D=RCC(D-Urgal).
141	0	0	3.62	8	99.85	0.15	C	415.73	97	10	Expatriates from Germany, in business. Nonreligious 11%. D=NAC,SDA,JWs,RCC. M=EKD,FMB,&c.
142	0	0	1.40	7	44.00	56.00	A	1.60	149	4	Immigrants from India and Pakistan. Hindus 90%, Muslims 9%(Sunnis, also Ahmadiyya Mission).
143	0	10	0.00	8	48.00	52.00	A	0.00	0	1.13	Small community of practicing Jews dating from early Middle Ages.
144	0	0	2.22	8	35.00	65.00	A	2.55	229	4	Migrant laborers from Morocco. Muslims 98% (Maliki Sunnis,some Ahmadis). M=OM.
145	0	0	6.88	8	99.90	0.10	C	469.75	151	10	Emigres and residents from Portugal, in all professions. D=RCC. M=GST(Japan).
146	1	10	2.53	8	99.93	0.07	C	567.42	56	10	Spaniards from Spain, with lengthy history in Andorra. D=RCC(D-Urgel).
147	0	10	2.79		99.70	0.30	C	273.38	71	8	A few from 30 other nationalities; migrants, immigrants, refugees, also professionals.
Angola											
148	2	10	3.55	5	99.82	0.18	C	454.93	80	10	Immigrants, businessmen from South Africa. D=DRC,AFM.
149	4	6	5.91	5	99.95	0.05	C	537.46	138	10	Ovamboland. Also in Namibia. Literates 75%. Animists 30%. D=ELOC,RCC(D-Silva Porto),CPSA(D-Damaraland),DRCSA. M=FLM.
150	1	3	3.75	0	33.00	67.00	A	13.25	394	5	Khoisan. Also in Namibia. Animists(tribal religionists)89%. D=ELCN(Namibia).
151	0	7	5.78	5	75.00	25.00	B	68.43	251	6	Small Pygmy bands in forest, dislocated by civil war. Animists 75%.
152	2	7	5.25	1	99.65	0.35	C	249.11	187	8	Northwest, Luanda Province. Related to Loanda Mbundu, Nsongo, Sama. Animists 35%. D=RCC,IMUA.
153	1	10	3.84	8	99.79	0.21	C	415.22	95	10	Expatriates from Britain, in education. D=Anglican Ch(D-Damaraland).
154	2	8	2.63	8	99.98	0.02	C	558.01	66	10	Immigrant Caboverdian farmers from Cape Verde Islands. D=Ch of the Nazarene, RCC.
155	4	7	7.29	2	99.75	0.25	C	342.18	192	9	Traditional religionists(animists) 70%. Y=1884. D=RCC(D-Luso,D-Malanje,D-Silva Porto),ECSA,SDA,Mennonites. M=OSB,AEF,CMML,FF(South Africa).
156	1	10	7.65	8	82.00	18.00	B	89.79	284	6	Military personnel from Cuba for 20 years. Nonreligious 70%. D=RCC.
157	3	7	6.71	3	99.90	0.10	C	443.47	175	10	Mainly in Namibia. Animists 40%. D=RCC,DRC,CPSA. M=ELCN.
158	2	10	4.84	8	99.80	0.20	C	426.32	111	10	Black/Whites. Mixed-race persons, African culture. Animists 30%. D=RCC,Protestants.
159	1	10	2.37	8	99.70	0.30	C	316.82	77	9	Persons of mixed race; Portuguese origin and culture. Animists 50%. D=RCC.
160	1	10	2.32	8	99.87	0.13	C	492.20	58	10	Expatriates from France, in education, development. D=RCC(8 Dioceses).
161	1	7	6.68	3	95.00	5.00	B	173.37	248	7	Also in Namibia, mainly along border. Close to Kwangali. Animists 50%. D=RCC.
162	0	10	2.60	7	52.05	47.95	B	1.99	171	4	Merchants, traders from Chinese diaspora. Folk-religionists. Buddhists 90%.
163	3	6	6.20	4	99.95	0.05	C	530.52	145	10	Mainly in Namibia. Animists 40%. D=RCC,NGK,AICs.
164	1	6	7.46	0	83.00	17.00	B	151.47	294	7	Kwango river area. Also in Zaire. Animists 50%. D=RCC.
165	1	7	6.14	0	51.00	49.00	B	37.23	384	5	Mbarakwena, Khwe, Kwengo, Xu, Zama, Schekere, Black Bushmen. In Cuando; some also in Namibia. Traditional religionists(animists) 80%. D=RCC.
166	2	7	2.59	0	48.00	52.00	A	35.04	205	5	Bushmen. Also in Namibia. Nomadic hunter-gatherers. Animists 80%. D=NGK,RCC.
167	5	7	7.32	5	99.89	0.11	C	486.15	160	10	One-third in Zaire, a third in Angola; also Congo. Animists 1%. D=RCC,EJCSK,CBA,IEB,AICs. M=LBI,BMS. R=HCJB.
168	3	7	2.88	5	99.99	0.01	C	585.38	73	10	Creole lingua franca across Zaire river mouth. Animists 20%. D=RCC,EJCSK,AICs.
169	5	7	10.91	5	99.98	0.02	C	583.05	208	10	Traditional religionists(animists) 10%. D=RCC(D-Carmona),IEB,EJCSK,Igreja dos Negros,AICs. M=BMS,AEM,NAM,CBOMB,CMA,WEC,ABFMS,FMB.
170	1	3	4.39	0	33.00	67.00	A	12.04	448	5	Okavango and Ovamboland Territory. Northern Khoisan. Primarily in Namibia. Animists 90%. D=DRCA. M=Lutheran Mission.
171	1	3	3.86	0	32.00	68.00	A	11.68	416	5	Northeast. Animists 90%. D=DRCA. M=Dutch Reformed Church Mission.
172	1	6	6.52	0	48.00	52.00	A	35.04	429	5	Central Khoisan. Bakise, Bacuisso, Bakwisso, Moquisse. Nomads. Animists 80%. D=RCC.
173	2	3	8.30	4	99.90	0.10	C	473.04	194	10	Also in Namibia. Traditional religionists(animists) 50%. D=RCC, Lutheran Ch.
174	4	3	7.71	5	99.95	0.05	C	516.65	177	10	Also in Namibia. Animists 25%. D=RCC(M-Lubango,D-Sa de Bandeira),Anglican Ch/CPSA(D-Damaraland),IEAC/ECCA,AICs. M=AEF,UCC.
175	3	10	5.08	5	99.98	0.02	C	608.09	106	10	Lingua franca in Zaire. Many itinerants, merchants, transients. Animists 25%. D=RCC,ECZ,AICs.
176	2	8	4.52	5	99.97	0.03	C	566.48	108	10	Immigrants from Zambia. Tribal religionists(animists)25%. D=RCC,AICs.
177	2	3	7.65	2	99.92	0.08	C	466.76	180	10	Southeast. Animists 35%. D=SDA,AICs. M=CMML,AEF.
178	1	4	7.43	1	97.00	3.00	C	212.43	251	8	Central. Cuanza river area. Animists 40%. D=RCC. M=CMML.
179	1	7	7.85	4	99.60	0.40	C	238.71	246	8	Majority live in Zambia; some in Botswana, Namibia. Animists 40%. D=RCC.
180	2	3	8.64	4	99.90	0.10	C	440.19	207	10	Southeast provinces. A minority live in Zambia. Animists 40%. D=RCC,AICs. M=CMML.
181	1	10	1.95	8	99.95	0.05	C	568.67	46	10	Macao Chinese, mixed-race(Chinese/European/African). Many nonreligious. D=RCC.
182	0	4	3.85	0	43.00	57.00	A	31.39	309	5	Northern Khoisan. Nomadic hunter-gatherers. Animists 80%.
183	1	6	7.25	1	89.00	11.00	B	162.42	268	7	Related to Suku, Yaka, Sinji, Hungu. Animists 50%. D=RCC.
184	2	3	6.68	3	88.00	12.00	B	160.60	264	7	Also in Namibia, Zambia, Botswana. Traditional religionists(animists) 70%. D=RCC, AC/CPSA.
185	1	5	6.02	1	99.80	0.20	C	347.48	172	9	Southeast. Half in Zambia. Animists 70%. D=RCC.
186	7	6	8.27	4	99.84	0.16	C	441.50	194	10	Benguela District. Animists 30%.D=RCC(M-Lubango,M-Huambo,D-Benguela,D-Silva Porto),IEAC/ECCA,IESA,SDA, Olosanto, Vapostori,other AICs.
187	1	3	10.24	1	99.80	0.20	C	338.72	276	9	Traditional religionists(animists) 40%. D=RCC. M=AEF.
188	2	6	7.00	4	99.94	0.06	C	500.92	159	10	Northeastern. Mainly in Zambia. Animists 10%. D=RCC(D-Luso),AICs. M=CMML,OSB.
189	1	6	7.01	1	78.00	22.00	B	113.88	298	7	South Mbundu area. Animists 60%. D=RCC.
190	2	3	7.04	1	99.70	0.30	C	278.49	225	8	In the south. Related to Kwanyama. Animists 30%. D=RCC,CPSA.
191	2	6	7.18	1	79.00	21.00	B	115.34	300	7	Eastern Angola. Animists 60%. D=RCC(M-Lubango), Methodist Ch. M=UBS.
192	1	6	7.61	1	99.70	0.30	C	268.27	237	8	Animists 30%. D=RCC(M-Lubango).
193	3	8	8.10	4	99.84	0.16	C	435.37	184	10	Northwest, Luanda Province. 5 dialects, 15 ethnic names. Animists 35%. D=RCC(D-Malanje),IMUA,AICs. M=OFMCap,PFM,UMC. R=HCJB.
194	1	7	11.31	2	99.90	0.10	C	420.48	283	10	Southwestern Angola. Animists 30%. D=RCC.
195	3	7	10.31	1	99.85	0.15	C	394.01	264	9	South central Angola. Animists 40%. D=DRC,Evangelical Ch of South Angola,RCC(D-Silva Porto). M=AEF.
196	1	6	6.32	1	91.00	9.00	B	166.07	234	7	Eastern Angola. Tribal religionists(animists)50%. D=RCC.
197	1	3	4.82	0	45.00	55.00	A	32.85	354	5	Northern Khoisan. Nomads, hunter-gatherers. Animists 80%. D=Lutheran Ch.
198	3	10	1.91	8	99.93	0.07	C	570.27	48	10	Expatriates in development, business. Many nonreligious. D=RCC,Portuguese Baptist Convention,AoG. M=APM,UBS,FMB.
199	3	7	6.96	1	99.96	0.04	C	508.08	159	10	Kambove Lunda, Chilu Wunda, Muatiamvua. Also in Zaire. Animists 10%. D=Methodist Ch/IMUA,RCC,AICs. M=UMC.
200	2	3	7.23	1	99.65	0.35	C	244.36	243	8	Northwest, Luanda Province. Related to Loanda Mbundu. Animists 35%. D=RCC,IMUA.
201	1	6	9.27	2	99.80	0.20	C	353.32	243	9	Cuanza river area. Animists 50%. D=RCC. M=CMML,AEF.
202	1	10	2.58	8	99.96	0.04	C	588.67	57	10	Expatriates from Spain, in education, development. D=RCC(8 Dioceses).
203	1	7	7.31	0	99.90	0.10	C	410.62	192	10	Mainly in Zaire. Animists 20%. D=RCC.
204	3	7	7.46	0	99.94	0.06	C	449.46	187	10	Vast majority in Zaire. Animists 20%. Muvungismo sect in 1940. D=RCC,Baptists,AICs. M=UFM.
205	1	6	7.16	1	99.00	1.00	C	216.81	248	8	Southeast corner of Angola, Kwando river area; also in Zambia. Animists 40%. D=RCC.
206	2	6	5.42	5	99.90	0.10	C	450.04	138	10	In Cabinda; also in Zaire and Congo. Animists 20%. D=RCC,AICs. M=LBI.
207	0	4	4.81		98.00	2.00	C	286.16	134	8	Many Namibian refugees from Namibia, also from Zaire and South Africa; also Sekele and Dwankala (Xu) Bushmen.
Anguilla											
208	3	10	0.68	8	99.79	0.21	C	420.99	34	10	Administrators, educators, from Britain. D=Anglican Ch(D-Antigua),JWs,SDA.
209	0	10	0.62	7	84.00	16.00	B	95.04	53	6	Long-time immigrants from India, Pakistan. Hindus, Muslims, Baha'is.
210	3	10	0.68	8	99.80	0.20	C	397.12	28	9	Black/White mixed race persons. D=CPWI/Anglican Ch(D-Antigua),RCC,SDA.
211	5	7	0.61	8	99.88	0.12	C	461.49	23	10	Africa origins. D=CPWI,MCCA,RCC(D-Saint John's),SDA,&c. M=USPG,CSSR,CMML,FSC,MMS.
212	0	10	0.70		99.84	0.16	C	343.39	17	9	Migrants and immigrants from other Caribbean islands.
Antarctica											
213	0	0	6.00		94.60	5.40	C	261.03	174	8	Nonreligious 24%.
Antigua & Barbuda											
214	2	10	0.66	8	99.79	0.21	C	420.99	34	10	Expatriates from Britain, in administration. D=Anglican Ch/CPWI(D-Antigua),MCCA. M=USPG,MMS.
215	0	10	0.67	7	85.00	15.00	B	93.07	54	6	Long-time residents from India and Pakistan. Hindus 40%, Muslims 30%(Sunnis, also Ahmadiyya Mission).
216	6	10	0.66	8	99.80	0.20	C	411.72	27	10	Black/White mixed-race persons. D=CPWI,RCC,MCCA,SDA,SA,&c. M=FSC, FMB.
217	0	0	6.66	8	99.78	0.22	C	370.11	159	9	Expatriates from USA, in professions. Nonreligious 10%. D=SDA,CJCLdS,JWs,UCA.
218	7	7	0.42	8	99.80	0.20	C	407.99	20	10	Persons of Africa ancestry. Ras Tafari Movement. D=CPWI,RCC(D-Saint John's),CCCU,CGP,MCCA,SDA,&c. M=USPG,CMML,FSC,MMS,FMB.
219	0	10	0.66		99.70	0.30	C	263.16	18	8	Migrant workers, businessmen at alii from other Caribbean islands.
Argentina											
220	9	8	2.12	8	99.95	0.05	C	582.90	49	10	D=RCC(55 Dioceses), ADIRELA,ACI,SDA,JWs,CMML,CJCLdS,IEMA,CEB. M=SDB,OFM,SVD,SJ,CMF,PFM,FSC,CAR,EHC,FMB. T=CBN. R=Radio Cultura,AWR.
221	2	8	2.20	6	99.90	0.10	C	525.60	48	10	Gregorians. Refugees from USSR. Y=1880. D=Armenian Apostolic Ch(D-Argentina),Armenian Evangelical Ch,RCC(EA-Latin America & Mexico,Armenian-rite).
222	1	9	2.20	4	99.70	0.30	C	332.15	60	9	From Bolivia. Shamanists 30%, some Baha'is. Many shamans active. D=RCC (many being christopagans). M=CBFMS.
223	2	10	2.20	4	99.65	0.35	C	284.70	65	8	Northeast. Primarily in Brazil, also Paraguay. Shamanists(animists) 35%; many active shamans. D=RCC,EBCA. M=CBFMS.
224	3	10	2.20	8	99.79	0.21	C	441.17	60	10	Expatriates from Britain, in farming, education, commerce. D=Anglican Ch(2 Dioceses),SDA,JWs. M=SAMS.
225	2	10	2.20	5	99.80	0.20	C	429.24	60	10	White Russians. Immigrants from USSR since 1917, 1945. Nonreligious 20%. D=ROC,RCC.
226	1	4	2.21	1	99.70	0.30	C	281.05	71	8	Northeast. Most in Brazil, some in Paraguay. Animists 30%. D=RCC. M=SIL.

Continued overleaf

Table 8-2 continued

PEOPLE		POPULATION				IDENTITY CODE		LANGUAGE		CHURCH		MINISTRY						SCRIPTURE		
Ref	Ethnic name	P%	In 1995	In 2000	In 2025	Race	Language	Autoglossonym	S	AC	Members	Jayuh	d	w	a	xcmc	mi	Biblioglossonym	Pub	ss
1	2	3	4	5	6	7	8	9	10	11	12	13-17	18	19	20	21	22	23	24-26	27
227	Carangas Aymara	0.07900	27,464	29,252	37,249	MIR39b	85-JABA-ad	caranga		55.00	16,088	1.s..	10	6	7	5	1		pnb	b
228	Catalonian	0.50000	173,823	185,136	235,752	CEW21a	51-AABE-b	català		96.00	177,731	2a..h	10	9	15	4	1	Catalan-valencian-balear	PNB	b
229	Central Aymara	0.03000	10,429	11,108	14,145	MIR39b	85-JABA-a	central aymara		92.00	10,220	2.s..	10	8	11	5	3	Aymara*	PNB	b
230	Central Bolivian Quechua	2.63231	915,111	974,673	1,241,142	MIR39g	85-FAAH-ed	sucre		98.85	963,464	1as..	10	9	12	5	1	Quechua: Bolivia	PNB	b
231	Chane (Izozo, Izoceno)	0.00390	1,356	1,444	1,839	MIR39e	82-AAIF-cb	chiriguano		30.00	433	3a...	9	5	6	5	1	Guarayu*	PNb	b
232	Chorote (Eklenjuy)	0.00275	956	1,018	1,297	MIR39e	86-ABAA-a	yofúaha		70.00	713	0....	10	7	6	3	3	Chorote*	P..	b
233	Chorote (Manjuy)	0.00459	1,596	1,700	2,164	MIR39e	86-ABAA-a	yofúaha		75.00	1,275	0....	10	7	6	3	0	Chorote*	P..	b
234	Chulupe (Chunupi)	0.00069	240	255	325	MIR39e	86-ABBA	niwaclé cluster		40.00	102	0....	9	6	6	3	0	Nivacle*	PNB	.
235	Croat	0.01000	3,476	3,703	4,715	CEW22d	53-AAAG-b	standard hrvatski		91.00	3,369	2Asuh	10	8	11	5	1	Croatian	PNB	b
236	Czech	0.02000	6,953	7,405	9,430	CEW22e	53-AAAD-a	czesky		79.00	5,850	2Asuh	10	8	8	5	2	Czech	PNB	b
237	Esperanto	0.00000	0	0	0	CEW21z	51-AAAC-a	proper esperanto		80.00	0	0A...	10	8	7	5	0	Esperanto	PNB	b
238	French	0.03900	13,558	14,441	18,389	CEW21b	51-AABI-d	general français	2	87.00	12,563	1B.uh	10	8	14	5	3	French	PNB	b
239	Galician	1.90000	660,527	703,519	895,856	CEW21d	51-AABA-b	galego		96.00	675,378	1csuh	10	8	12	5	1	Galician	PNB	b
240	German	0.10000	34,765	37,027	47,150	CEW19m	52-ABCE-a	standard hoch-deutsch		88.00	32,584	2B.uh	10	9	12	5	1	German*	PNB	b
241	Greek	0.09800	34,069	36,287	46,207	CEW20	56-AAAA-c	dhimotiki		95.00	34,472	2B.uh	10	9	10	4	1	Greek: Modern	PNB	b
242	Han Chinese	0.00300	1,043	1,111	1,415	MSY42a	79-AAAM-a	central yue		22.00	244	3A.uh	9	5	8	5	1	Chinese, Yue	PNB	b
243	Han Chinese (Taiwanese)	0.00300	1,043	1,111	1,415	MSY42a	79-AAAJ-h	quan-zhang-taiwan		24.00	267	1A..h	9	5	8	5	1	Taiwanese	PNB	b
244	Italian	4.70000	1,633,934	1,740,283	2,216,065	CEW21e	51-AABQ-c	standard italiano	9	97.00	1,688,074	2B.uh	10	9	14	5	1	Italian	PNB	b
245	Japanese	0.07600	26,421	28,141	35,834	MSY45a	45-CAAA-a	koku-go		40.00	11,256	1B.uh	9	5	8	5	1	Japanese	PNB	b
246	Jewish	1.20000	417,175	444,328	565,804	CMT35	51-AABB-hv	argentino		2.10	9,331	1B.uh	6	3	5	5	1		pnb	b
247	Jewish	0.10000	34,765	37,027	47,150	CMT35	52-ABCH	yiddish cluster		1.00	370	0B..h	6	5	6	5	0		PNB	b
248	Kaingang	0.00500	1,738	1,851	2,358	MIR39d	87-PCAA-c	central kaingáng		40.00	741	0....	9	5	7	3	3	Kaingang	PN.	.
249	Kalderash Gypsy (Gitano)	0.15000	52,147	55,541	70,725	CNN25f	59-ACBA-ar	vlach-españa		80.00	44,433	1c...	10	8	8	4	1		pn.	.
250	Korean	0.07500	26,073	27,770	35,363	MSY46	45-AAAA-b	kukö		80.00	22,216	2A...	10	8	13	5	2	Korean	PNB	b
251	Laotian	0.00500	1,738	1,851	2,358	MSY49b	47-AAAC-b	lao		10.00	185	2As..	8	4	8	4	2	Lao	PNB	b
252	Lengua	0.00400	1,391	1,481	1,886	MIR39e	86-CAAA-e	north lengua		90.00	1,333	0....	10	8	11	4	2	Lengua: Northern	PNB	b
253	Levantine Arab	3.30000	1,147,230	1,221,901	1,555,960	CMT30	12-AACF-f	syro-palestinian		39.00	476,541	1Asuh	9	6	9	4	3	Arabic: Lebanese*	Pnb	b
254	Manjuy Chorote	0.02580	8,969	9,553	12,165	MIR39e	86-ABAA-a	yofúaha		80.00	7,642	0....	10	8	7	3	2	Chorote*	P..	b
255	Mapuche (Araucanian)	0.15354	53,377	56,852	72,395	MIR39f	86-GAAA-c	proper mapuche		70.00	39,796	4....	10	8	7	4	1	Mapudungun	P..	.
256	Mestizo	4.00000	1,390,582	1,481,092	1,886,013	CLN29	51-AABB-hv	argentino		97.00	1,436,659	1B.uh	10	9	10	5	3		pnb	b
257	Mocovi	0.01222	4,248	4,525	5,762	MIR39e	86-EBBA-a	moqoyt		40.00	1,810	0.s..	9	6	7	3	3	Mocovi	PN.	.
258	Nocten Mataco (Wichi)	0.00035	122	130	165	MIR39e	86-AAAA-a	noctén		80.00	104	0.s..	10	7	6	3	1	Wichi Lhamtes Nocten	pn.	.
259	Northwest Jujuy Quechua	0.01547	5,378	5,728	7,294	MIR39g	85-FAAH-f	jujuy		94.00	5,384	1as..	10	8	11	5	1		pnb	b
260	Paraguayan Mestizo	2.50000	869,114	925,682	1,178,758	CLN29	82-AAIF-b	vehicular aba-ñeeme		98.00	907,169	1a...	10	9	11	5	3		pnb	b
261	Pilaga Toba	0.00611	2,124	2,262	2,881	MIR39e	86-EBAB-a	toba-pilagá		90.00	2,036	0.s..	10	10	12	5	1	Pilaga*	PN.	b
262	Pilcomayo Mataco	0.00600	2,086	2,222	2,829	MIR39e	86-AAAA-c	güisnay		50.00	1,111	0.s..	10	7	6	5	1	Wichi Lhamtes Guisnay	pn.	b
263	Platine Italian	0.05000	17,382	18,514	23,575	CEW21e	51-AABQ	italiano cluster		87.00	16,107	2B.uh	10	8	13	5	3		PNB	b
264	Polish (Pole)	0.50000	173,823	185,136	235,752	CEW22i	53-AAAC-c	polski		90.00	166,623	2A.uh	10	9	11	5	3	Polish	PNB	b
265	Portuguese	0.03900	13,558	14,441	18,389	CEW21g	51-AABA-e	general português		93.00	13,430	2Bsuh	10	9	15	5	1	Portuguese	PNB	b
266	Puelche (Gennaken)	0.00002	7	7	9	MIR39z	86-HAAA-a	west günüa-küne		80.00	6	0....	10	7	7	4	0		...	.
267	Romanian	0.03900	13,558	14,441	18,389	CEW21i	51-AADC-a	limba românească		84.00	12,130	3A.u.	10	8	10	5	1	Romanian	PNB	b
268	Russian	0.07900	27,464	29,252	37,249	CEW22j	53-AAAE-d	russkiy		70.00	20,476	4B.uh	10	8	8	5	1	Russian	PNB	b
269	Santiago de Estero Quichu	0.24727	85,962	91,557	116,589	MIR39g	85-FAAH-g	santiagueno		94.00	86,064	1as..	10	7	11	3	3		pnb	b
270	Serb	0.01600	5,562	5,924	7,544	CEW22l	53-AAAG-a	standard srpski		85.00	5,036	1Asuh	10	8	10	4	1	Serbian*	PNB	b
271	Slovak	0.02000	6,953	7,405	9,430	CEW22m	53-AAAD-b	slovensky		80.00	5,924	1Asuh	10	8	8	5	2	Slovak	PNB	b
272	Slovene	0.01000	3,476	3,703	4,715	CEW22n	53-AAAF-a	slovensko		95.00	3,518	1a..h	10	8	11	5	1	Slovenian*	PNB	b
273	Spaniard	1.40000	486,704	518,382	660,104	CEW21k	51-AABB-hv	argentino		96.00	497,647	1B.uh	10	9	15	5	3		pnb	b
274	Spanish Jew	0.05000	17,382	18,514	23,575	CMT35	51-AAAB-a	ladino		0.01	2	0....	3	4	6	3	0		pnb	b
275	Tapiete (Guarayo)	0.00031	108	115	146	MIR39e	82-AAIF-cc	tapieté		80.00	92	1c...	10	7	6	3	1		pnb	n
276	Tehuelche (Aoniken)	0.00002	7	7	9	MIR39e	86-HAAA-b	east günüa-küne		80.00	6	0....	10	7	6	3	0		...	.
277	Toba (Com, Toba Sur)	0.05000	17,382	18,514	23,575	MIR39e	86-EBAA	qom cluster		95.00	17,588	0.s..	10	9	7	5	3	Toba	PN.	b
278	Ukrainian	0.07900	27,464	29,252	37,249	CEW22p	53-AAAE-b	ukrainskiy		80.00	23,401	3A.uh	10	8	8	5	1	Ukrainian	PNB	b
279	Uruguayan White	1.89095	657,380	700,168	891,589	CLT27	51-AABB-hu	uruguayo		71.00	497,119	1B.uh	10	9	13	5	3		pnb	b
280	Vejoz Mataco (Wichi)	0.05833	20,278	21,598	27,503	MIR39e	86-AAAA-b	vejoz		85.00	18,358	0.s..	10	8	8	4	2	Mataco*	PN.	b
281	Vilela	0.00010	35	37	47	MIR39d	86-DBAA	vilela cluster		80.00	30	0....	10	8	6	3	0		...	.
282	Welsh	0.03370	11,716	12,478	15,890	CEW18d	50-ABAA-bc	cymraeg-safonol		85.00	10,606	2A.uh	10	8	14	5	2	Welsh	PNB	b
283	other minor peoples	0.10000	34,765	37,027	47,150	...				65.00	24,068		10	8	10	5	0			
	Armenia	**100.00000**	**3,574,105**	**3,519,569**	**3,946,381**					**83.92**	**2,953,692**									
284	Armenian (Ermeni)	94.56000	3,379,674	3,328,104	3,731,698	CEW14	57-AAAA-b	ashkharik	96	87.00	2,895,451	4A.u.	10	9	10	5	3	Armenian: Modern, Eastern	PNB	b
285	Armenian Bosha Gypsy	0.00150	54	53	59	CNN25f	59-AEAA-a	caló		50.00	26	0....	10	3	7	0	0		...	b
286	Assyrian (Aisor)	0.18000	6,433	6,335	7,103	CMT31	12-AAAA-f	aisor		88.00	5,575	4cs..	10	6	10	2	2	Assyrian Neo-aramaic	PNB	b
287	Azerbaijani (Azeri Turk)	0.50000	17,871	17,598	19,732	MSY41a	44-AABA-fa	north azeri		0.00	0	2c.u.	0	3	3	0	2	Azerbaijani*	PNB	b
288	Balkar	0.02300	822	810	908	MSY41z	44-AABB-a	literary karachay-balkar		0.00	0	1c.u.	0	3	3	0	0	Karachay-balkar	PN.	.
289	Byelorussian	0.03200	1,144	1,126	1,263	CEW22c	53-AAAE-c	bielorusskiy		75.00	845	3A.uh	10	7	8	2	3	Byelorussian*	PNB	b
290	Chechen	0.00680	243	239	268	CEW17d	42-BAAA-b	chechen		0.00	0	0....	0	2	2	0	1	Chechen	P..	b
291	Darghinian	0.00720	257	253	284	CEW17b	42-BBBB-a	dargwa		0.01	0	1....	3	3	2	0	1	Dargwa	P..	b
292	Georgian	0.04130	1,476	1,454	1,630	CEW17c	42-CABB-a	kharthuli		40.00	581	2A.u.	9	6	8	2	2	Georgian	PNB	b
293	German	0.00800	286	282	316	CEW19m	52-ABCE-a	standard hoch-deutsch		80.00	225	2B.uh	10	8	9	3	2	German*	PNB	b
294	Greek (Romei, Urum)	0.14100	5,039	4,963	5,564	CEW20	56-AAAA-c	dhimotiki		90.00	4,466	2B.uh	10	8	11	2	2	Greek: Modern	PNB	b
295	Jewish	0.02000	715	704	789	CMT35	52-ABCH	yiddish cluster		0.02	0	0B..h	3	4	6	0	0		PNB	b
296	Kazakh	0.01000	357	352	395	MSY41e	44-AABC-c	kazakh		0.00	0	4A.u.	0	3	3	0	1	Kazakh	PN.	b
297	Kurdish	0.27000	9,650	9,503	10,655	CNT24c	53-AAAE-d	russkiy		4.00	380	4B.uh	6	3	3	0	0	Russian	PNB	b
298	Lithuanian	0.00660	236	232	260	CEW15b	54-AAAA-a	standard lietuvishkai		90.00	209	3A.u.	10	8	11	2	3	Lithuanian	PNB	b
299	Moldavian	0.01600	572	563	631	CEW21f	51-AADC-ab	standard moldavia		82.00	462	1A.u.	10	7	8	2	2		pnb	b
300	Mordvinian	0.01480	529	521	584	MSW51i	41-AADA-a	erzya		65.00	339	2....	10	8	8	2	1	Mordvin: Erzya*	PN.	b
301	Northern Kurd	1.70000	60,760	59,833	67,088	CNT24c	58-AAAA-a	kurmanji		0.50	299	3c...	5	3	3	0	0	Kurdish: Kurmanji*	PN.	b
302	Ossete	0.01000	357	352	395	CNT24e	58-ABBA	oseti cluster		36.00	127	2....	9	5	8	1	1	Ossete*	PN.	b
303	Polish	0.00820	293	289	324	CEW22i	53-AAAC-c	polski		91.00	263	2A.uh	10	8	11	2	3	Polish	PNB	b
304	Russian	1.50000	53,612	52,794	59,196	CEW22j	53-AAAE-d	russkiy	33	62.00	32,732	4B.uh	10	8	8	5	3	Russian	PNB	b
305	Tatar	0.01420	508	500	560	MSY41h	44-AABB-e	tatar		1.50	7	2c.u.	6	4	8	0	0	Tatar: Kazan	Pn.	b
306	Ukrainian	0.25200	9,007	8,869	9,945	CEW22p	53-AAAE-b	ukrainskiy		78.80	6,989	3A.uh	10	7	9	3	3	Ukrainian	PNB	b
307	Uzbek	0.00740	264	260	292	MSY41l	44-AABD-a	central uzbek		0.00	0	1A.u.	0	3	6	1	1	Uzbek*	PNb	b
308	other minor peoples	0.67000	23,947	23,581	26,441	...				20.00	4,716		9	4	3	0	0			
	Aruba	**100.00000**	**81,503**	**102,747**	**250,376**					**92.7**	**95,242**									
309	Antillean Creole	75.00000	61,127	77,060	187,782	NFB67b	51-AACB-e	papiamento		93.90	72,360	1a.u.	10	9	11	4	3	Papiamentu	PNB	b
310	Dutch	5.00000	4,075	5,137	12,519	NFB67b	52-ABCA-a	algemeen-nederlands	80	75.00	3,853	2Bsuh	10	9	10	4	3	Dutch	PNB	b
311	Filipino	0.33000	269	339	826	MSY44o	31-CKAA-a	proper tagalog		93.00	315	4Bs..	10	9	12	0	0	Tagalog	PNB	b
312	Han Chinese	0.32000	261	329	801	MSY42a	79-AAAL-a	shao-jiang		10.00	33	0a...	8	6	8	0	0	Chinese: Cantonese	PNB	b
313	Jewish	0.14000	114	144	351	CMT35	79-AAAL-a	shao-jiang		0.00	0	0a...	0	8	5	0	0	Chinese: Cantonese	PNB	b
314	Turk	0.20000	163	205	501	MSY41j	44-AABA-a	osmanli		0.00	0	1A.u.	0	4	5	0	0	Turkish	PNB	b
315	other minor peoples	19.01000	15,494	19,532	47,596	CEW19i	52-ABAC	english-mainland cluster	98	95.64	18,681	3Bsuh	10	8	9	4	0		PNB	b
	Australia	**100.00000**	**17,939,944**	**18,879,524**	**23,090,790**					**66.71**	**12,595,013**									
316	Aborigine Creole	0.05852	10,498	11,048	13,513	MPY53	52-ABAI-a	australian-creole		75.00	8,286	1csuh	10	7	13	3	3	Kriol	PNb	b
317	Albanian	0.02000	3,588	3,776	4,618	CEW13	55-AAAA-b	northwest gheg		60.00	2,266	1a.u.	10	6	8	2	1	Albanian: Gheg*	PN.	b
318	Alyawarra	0.00875	1,570	1,652	2,020	AUG02	29-XBBA-a	alyawarra		60.00	991	0....	10	6	6	2	3	Alyawarr	P..	.
319	Andilyaugwa	0.00652	1,170	1,231	1,506	AUG02	28-PAAA-a	anindilyakwa		70.00	862	0.s..	10	6	7	2	1	Anindilyakwa	P..	b
320	Anglo-Australian	73.27088	13,144,755	13,833,193	16,918,825	CEW19c	52-ABAC-x	general australian		65.70	9,088,408	1Bsuh	10	9	14	5	3	English	pnb	.
321	Anglo-New Zealander	1.50000	269,099	283,193	346,362	CEW19e	52-ABAC-y	general new-zealand		76.00	215,227	1Bsuh	10	9	14	5	2		pnb	b
322	Anglo-Romani Gypsy (Rom)	0.03094	5,551	5,841	7,144	CNN25f	59-AGAA-a	pogadi-chib		80.00	4,673	0....	10	7	13	4	2		...	b
323	Anmatjirra	0.00521	935	984	1,203	AUG02	29-XBAA-a	anmatjirra		70.00	689	0....	10	7	6	4	0		...	b
324	Arab	0.12000	21,528	22,655	27,709	CMT30	12-AACF-f	syro-palestinian		45.00	10,195	1Asuh	9	5	8	3	3	Arabic: Lebanese*	Pnb	b
325	Armenian	0.10000	17,940	18,880	23,091	CEW14	57-AAAA-b	ashkharik		90.00	16,992	4A.u.	10	9	11	5	2	Armenian: Modern, Eastern	PNB	b
326	Assyrian	0.06270	11,248	11,837	14,478	CMT31	12-AAAA-d	east syriac		88.00	10,417	1as..	10	9	11	4	1	Syriac: Ancient*	PNB	b
327	Austrian	0.30000	53,820	56,639	69,272	CEW19f	52-ABCF-b	donau-bayrisch-t.		90.00	50,975	0B.uh	10	9	12	5	1		pn.	b
328	Basque	0.05000	8,970	9,440	11,545	CEW16	40-AAAA-a	general euskara		94.00	8,873	3....	10	9	14	3	1	Basque	PNB	b
329	British	6.50000	1,166,096	1,227,169	1,500,901	CEW19i	52-ABAC-b	standard-english		77.00	944,920	3Bsuh	10	10	14	5	3		PNB	b
330	Bulgar	0.05000	8,970	9,440	11,545	CEW22b	53-AAAH-b	bulgarski		72.00	6,797	2A.uh	10	8	8	4	1	Bulgarian	PNB	b
331	Burera	0.00293	526	553	677	AUG02	28-NCAA-a	burarra		45.00	249	0.s..	9	5	6	2	1	Burarra	PN.	.
332	Byelorussian	0.02600	4,664	4,909	6,004	CEW22c	53-AAAE-c	bielorusskiy		67.00	3,289	3A.uh	10	7	8	0	0	Byelorussian*	PNB	b
333	Cambodian	0.08000	14,352	15,104	18,473	AUG03b	46-FBAA-a	historical khmer		5.00	755	1c...	7	4	8	0	0	Khmer: Northern	PNb	.
334	Cocos Islands Malay	0.00100	179	189	231	MSY44k	31-PHAL-c	kokos-sabah		10.00	19	0c...	8	3	4	1	0		...	.
335	Croat	0.33000	59,202	62,302	76,200	CEW22d	53-AAAG-b	standard hrvatski		91.00	56,695	2Asuh	10	9	13	5	1	Croatian	PNB	b
336	Czech	0.10000	17,940	18,880	23,091	CEW22e	53-AAAD-a	czesky		79.00	14,915	2Asuh	10	9	11	5	2	Czech	PNB	b
337	Dangu (Djangu)	0.00228	409	430	526	AUG02	29-AADA	dhangu cluster		70.00	301	0....	10	7	6	3	3	Dhangu'mi	P..	b
338	Dayi (Dhayyi)	0.00130	233	245	300	AUG02	29-AAFA-a	dhalwangu		15.00	37	0....	8	4	6	1	1		...	b
339	Detribalized Aborigine	0.78318	140,502	147,861	180,842	AUG02	52-ABAC-x	general australian		70.00	103,502	1Bsuh	10	8	8	5	2		pnb	b
340	Dhuwaya (Wulamba)	0.00326	585	615	753	AUG02	29-AAEB	dhuwal-jambarr cluster		50.00	308	0.s..	10	6	6	3	2		P..	n
341	Djambarrpuyngu	0.00293	526	553	677	AUG02	29-AAEB-a	jambarr-puyngu		25.00	138	0.s..	9	5	6	1	1	Djambarrpuyngu	P..	n
342	Djaru	0.00168	301	317	388	AUG02	29-BBDA-a	jaru		14.88	47	0....	8	5	6	1	1	Jaru	...	.
343	Djinang	0.00165	296	312	381	AUG02	29-AABA-a	jinang		11.98	37	0....	8	5	6	1	1	Djinang	P..	.
344	Dutch	0.26521	47,579	50,070	61,239	CEW19h	52-ABCA-a	algemeen-nederlands		76.00	38,053	2Bsuh	10	9	14	5	2	Dutch	PNB	b

Continued opposite

Table 8-2 continued

EVANGELIZATION								EVANGELISM			ADDITIONAL DESCRIPTIVE DATA
Ref 1	D 28	aC 29	CG% 30	r 31	E 32	U 33	W 34	e 35	R 36	T 37	Locations, civil divisions, literacy, religions, church history, denominations, dioceses, church growth, missions, agencies, ministries, movements 38
227	1	5	2.20	4	99.55	0.45	B	210.78	57	8	Also in Bolivia. Animists 45%. D=98% RCC (half being christopagans).
228	1	10	2.20	4	99.96	0.04	C	585.16	51	10	Settlers from Catalonia, Valencia Provinces, Spain. Strong links with homeland. D=RCC.
229	3	8	2.20	4	99.92	0.08	C	530.56	38	10	Labor migrants from Bolivia. D=97%RCC(many christopagans),AoG,SA.
230	1	10	2.20	4	99.99	0.01	C	601.99	47	10	South Bolivian Quechua. Migrants and temporary laborers from Bolivia. D=95% RCC(many christopagans). M=CBFMS. R=HCJB.
231	1	5	2.20	4	82.00	18.00	B	89.79	95	6	Chane Language extinct, speakers now use Chiriguano. Shamanists(animists) 70%. D=RCC. M=CBFMS.
232	1	7	2.20	0	99.70	0.30	C	275.94	72	8	Northeast Salta Province. River dwellers. 80% monolinguals. Shamanists 30%. D=AC. M=SAMS,LIM,NTM.
233	0	7	2.20	0	99.75	0.25	C	292.91	73	8	Also in Paraguay, a few in Bolivia. 50% monolinguals. Shamanists 25%.
234	0	6	2.16	0	78.00	22.00	B	113.88	98	7	Salta, northeast. Vast majority live in Paraguay. Shamanists(animists) 60%.
235	1	10	2.20	6	99.91	0.09	C	534.76	56	10	Refugees, settlers from Croatia and 10 other countries. Strong Catholic. D=RCC.
236	2	10	2.20	6	99.79	0.21	C	426.75	62	10	Refugees from CSSR (Czechoslovakia) after 1938, 1968. D=RCC, Moravian Ch.
237	0	10	0.00	5	99.80	0.20	C	405.88	0	10	Artificial (constructed) language, in 80 countries. Speakers in Argentina: 86,000(none mother-tongue), of whom 90% Catholic.
238	3	10	2.20	8	99.87	0.13	C	527.13	52	10	Expatriates from France in business, settlers. Nonreligious 13%. D=RCC,ADIRELA,ERF.
239	1	10	2.20	1	99.96	0.04	C	553.63	54	10	Immigrants, settlers from Galicia Province, Spain. Mostly Catholics. D=RCC.
240	7	10	2.20	8	99.88	0.12	C	526.76	56	10	Expatriates from Germany, also settlers. D=IELA,RCC,CEBA,COG,LCMS,IERP,NAC. M=FMB.
241	1	10	2.20	7	99.95	0.05	C	572.13	53	10	Settlers and immigrants from Greece. D=GOC (Iglesia Ortodoxa Griega). M=GOANSA.
242	2	10	2.19	8	90.00	10.00	B	72.27	86	6	Immigrants from Chinese diaspora. Mainly Buddhists 77%. D=RCC,CEB. M=FMB.
243	2	10	2.21	5	85.00	15.00	B	74.46	92	6	Mainly Confucianists 75%. D=RCC,CEB. M=FMB.
244	3	10	2.20	7	99.97	0.03	C	619.58	50	10	Immigrants from Italy. D=RCC,Chiesa Evangelica Valdese,Asamblea Cristiana Italiana. M=SJ.
245	1	10	2.20	7	99.40	0.60	B	156.22	76	7	Settlers from Japan. Buddhists 40%, New-Religionists 20%(Soka Gakkai,et alia). D=RCC. M=Japan Antioch Mission(Japan).
246	0	10	2.04	8	58.10	41.90	B	4.45	129	4	Practicing Jewish communities. 78% Ashkenazi, 22% Sefardi. M=Jews for Jesus. R=Radio Cultura,AWR. T=CBN. R=Radio Cultura,AWR.
247	0	10	2.13	5	57.00	43.00	B	2.08	136	4	Traditional Yiddish-speaking practicing Jews. Ashkenazis, Sefardis.
248	3	8	2.20	0	81.00	19.00	B	118.26	98	7	Main area is in southern Brazil. Bilingual. Animists 60%. D=RCC, Lutherans, et alia.
249	2	10	2.20	1	99.80	0.20	C	370.84	70	9	Nomadic. Rom Gypsies(Vlach) from Europe. D=RCC,IHL. M=GGMS.
250	2	10	2.20	6	99.80	0.20	C	449.68	50	10	1970, attempt to immigrate to USA/Canada, blocked. Now live in Buenos Aires. Buddhists 15%, New-Religionists 5%. D=Presbyterian Ch of Korea (Haptong), CEB.
251	2	5	2.20	5	66.00	34.00	B	24.09	154	5	Refugees from Laos. Theravada Buddhists 90%. D=RCC,Apostolic Christian Nazarene Ch.
252	2	8	2.20	0	99.90	0.10	C	476.32	54	10	Main Lengua area is in Paraguay. Some semi-nomadic, most pastoralists or agriculturalists. Animists 10%. D=RCC, many Protestant churches.
253	4	10	2.20	8	99.39	0.61	B	152.31	74	7	Powerful business influence, controlling 20% of parochial governments. Muslims 57%(Palestinians,Levantines; Arab Islamic Society), nonreligious 11%. D=RCC.
254	2	9	2.20	0	99.80	0.20	C	347.48	65	9	55% monolinguals. Shamanists 20%. D=90% RCC (many christopagans), Anglican Ch. M=SIL,NTM.
255	3	7	2.20	0	99.70	0.30	C	288.71	68	8	Maputongo, Puelche. Mainly in Chile, recent immigration. Shamanists 25%, some Baha'is. D=95% RCC (many christopagans), Anglican Ch/CASA,EBCA. M=SAMS.
256	2	10	2.20	8	99.97	0.03	C	584.18	46	10	Includes Chilean refugees. D=97% RCC,&c. M=SDB,OFM,SVD,SJ,FMB. T=CBN. R=Radio Cultura,AWR.
257	3	7	2.20	0	82.00	18.00	B	119.72	95	7	Northeast Santa Fe. Shamanists(animists) 60%. D=RCC, Mennonite Ch, IEU.
258	1	7	2.18	0	99.80	0.20	C	338.72	67	9	In north. Shamanists 20%. D=AC. M=SAMS.
259	2	7	2.20	4	99.94	0.06	C	528.37	51	10	Northeast Jujuy Province. Many bilingual in Spanish. D=RCC,EBCA. M=SIM.
260	3	10	2.20	5	99.98	0.02	C	579.47	47	10	Mixed-race immigrants from Paraguay. D=RCC,AoG,EBCA(CEBA). M=CBFMS,WBT,SAMS,SJ,SVD,OFM,SDB,FMB.
261	4	7	2.20	0	99.90	0.10	C	463.18	55	10	Formosa Province. Shamanists(animists) 10%. D=RCC,IEUT,IEPA,several other pentecostal bodies. M=SAMS.
262	1	7	2.20	0	92.00	8.00	B	167.90	85	7	Pilcomayo River area. Shamanists 50%. D=AC. M=SAMS.
263	5	10	2.20	8	99.87	0.13	C	527.13	53	10	Settlers with own culture in River Plate area. D=RCC,WC,JWs,AoG, SDA.
264	4	10	2.20	6	99.90	0.10	C	538.74	37	10	Refugees from Poland since 1939. Strong Catholics. D=RCC,PNCC,PMC,PRCE.
265	1	10	2.20	8	99.93	0.07	C	580.46	52	10	Expatriates, settlers from Portugal since 1600. D=RCC.
266	0	0	1.81	0	99.80	0.20	C	303.68	74	9	Northern Tehuelche. In Pampas. Language isolate, nearly extinct.
267	1	10	2.20	6	99.84	0.16	C	469.09	59	10	Refugees from Romania since 1939. D=Romanian Orthodox Ch.
268	1	10	2.20	7	99.70	0.30	C	360.25	43	9	Refugees from USSR since 1917. Nonreligious 30%. D=Russian Orthodox Ch. M=FMB.
269	4	7	2.20	4	99.94	0.06	C	535.23	51	10	Santiago del Estero Province. Agriculturalists. D=RCC,EBCA,Brethren,GCSB.
270	1	10	2.20	6	99.85	0.15	C	471.58	40	10	Refugees from Yugoslavia after 1939. D=Serbian Orthodox Ch.
271	2	10	2.20	6	99.80	0.20	C	432.16	62	10	Settlers, refugees, emigres from Slovakia. Also in 15 other countries. D=RCC,SECC.
272	1	10	2.20	6	99.95	0.05	C	565.20	54	10	Refugees and immigrants from Slovenia after 1939. Mostly Catholics. D=RCC.
273	2	10	2.20	8	99.96	0.04	C	588.67	51	10	Settlers, immigrants, descendants of early Spanish warriors and settlers. Strong Catholics. D=RCC,&c. M=SDB,SVD,OFM,SJ. T=CBN. R=Radio Cultura,AWR.
274	0	10	0.70	1	36.01	63.99	A	0.01	106	2	Refugees and immigrants from Europe after 1937. Traditional Judaism.
275	2	7	2.24	1	99.80	0.20	C	356.24	65	9	Guarani-Nandeva, Nanagua. Shamanists 20%. D=RCC,AC. M=SAMS.
276	0	7	1.81	0	99.80	0.20	C	321.20	61	9	Patagonia. From Chile. Language nearly extinct.
277	3	7	2.20	0	99.95	0.05	C	499.32	54	10	Chaco Department. Shamanists 5%, some Baha'is. D=IEUT(Mennonites,Pentecostals),EBCA,&c. M=SAMS,ACOG,EMCA,FMB.
278	1	10	2.20	6	99.80	0.20	C	432.16	63	10	Refugees from USSR since 1917. Nonreligious 20%. D=Ukrainian Catholic Ch(D-Santa Maria). M=UOCUSA.
279	5	10	2.20	8	99.71	0.29	C	367.99	59	9	Settlers from Uruguay. Nonreligious 32%, atheist 4%, Baha'is. D=RCC,AoG,WC,JWs,&c. T=CBN. R=Radio Cultura,AWR.
280	1	7	2.20	0	99.85	0.15	C	406.42	59	10	In north. Shamanists 15%, some Baha'is. D=Anglican Ch(2 Dioceses; all Matacos). M=SAMS,Swedish Mission.
281	0	7	2.33	0	99.80	0.20	C	321.20	75	9	In Resistencia. Language nearly extinct, being absorbed into Toba.
282	1	10	2.20	5	99.85	0.15	C	490.19	55	10	Settlers from Wales. Farmers. D=Anglican Ch (2 Dioceses). M=Ch in Wales, MCGB.
283	0	10	2.20		99.65	0.35	C	249.11	57	8	Norwegians, Hungarians, Swiss, Swedes, Chileans, Costa Ricans, Guatemalans, a few Chiripa (Nhandeva).
Armenia											
284	2	6	1.86	6	99.87	0.13	C	489.02	44	10	Gregorians. In 28 countries. Nonreligious 25%, atheists 5%. D=Armenian Apostolic Ch(C-Echmiadzin; 6 Dioceses),RCC(25,000 Armenian-rite).
285	0	10	1.89	8	92.00	8.00	B	167.90	87	7	In Armenia, southern Caucasus; also in Syria. Gypsy language influenced by Armenian; assimilation near. Nonreligious 40%, Muslims 10%.
286	2	10	1.91	5	99.88	0.12	C	491.43	46	10	Eastern-Syriac-speaking Assyrians in Armenia and Georgia; also 11 other countries. D=Ancient Ch of the East(P-Tehran),ROC.
287	1	8	0.00	1	31.00	69.00	A	0.00	0	1.12	Turkler, Airumy, Padar. 73% monolingual. 20 dialects. Muslims 80%(70% Shias,30% Hanafi Sunnis), nonreligious 20%. D=ROC. M=IBT,CSI.
288	0	8	0.00	1	21.00	79.00	A	0.00	0	1.09	Mainly in Russia, some in USA. Superficially 100% Muslims(Hanafi Sunnis).
289	3	9	1.91	5	99.75	0.25	C	383.25	57	9	White Russians, mainly in Belorussia. Nonreligious 25%. D=ROC,RCC,Old Ritualist Chs.
290	0	7	0.00	0	18.00	82.00	A	0.00	0	1.05	Nokhchuo. From Chechen Ingush ASSR (Russia). 76% speak Russian. Highly religious Muslims 63%, atheists 20%, nonreligious 17%. M=IBT.
291	0	8	0.00	0	23.01	76.99	A	0.00	0	1.07	In Dagestan (Russia). 65% speak Russian. Muslims 100%(Shafi Sunnis, some Shias). M=IBT.
292	2	9	1.92	4	99.00	1.00	B	144.54	53	7	Mostly in Georgia. Nonreligious/atheists 55%, Muslims 5%(Sunnis, Shias). D=GOC,AUCECB.
293	2	10	1.91	8	99.80	0.20	C	435.08	56	10	Also in Russia and adjacent states. D=German ELC,AUCECB.
294	2	10	1.92	7	99.90	0.10	C	525.60	50	10	Immigrants from Greece. Since 1770, including Turkish-speaking Urums. D=Greek Orthodox Ch, ROC. M=UBS,LBI.
295	0	10	0.00	5	48.02	51.98	A	0.03	0	2	Bilingual in Russian, Armenian. Few practicing Jews. Emigration to Israel, but sizeable numbers return.
296	0	8	0.00	4	35.00	65.00	A	0.00	0	1.10	Muslims 60%(Hanafi Sunnis, with Sufi influence), nonreligious 30%, atheists 10%. M=ROC.
297	0	8	3.70	7	55.00	45.00	B	8.03	284	4	Russified. Muslims 80%(Shias,Yazidis), nonreligious 20%.
298	4	8	1.89	5	99.90	0.10	C	512.46	33	10	From Lithuania; in 19 countries. Nonreligious 10%. D=RCC,ELCL,ERCL,ROC.
299	2	9	1.92	6	99.82	0.18	C	416.02	58	10	From Moldavia, Romania. D=Russian Orthodox Ch, Romanian Orthodox Ch.
300	1	9	1.91	7	99.65	0.35	C	275.21	45	8	From Mordvinia (Russia). Acculturated to Russian. Nonreligious 35%. D=ROC. M=IBT.
301	0	7	4.71	0	30.50	69.50	A	0.55	603	3	Southwest Azerbaijan, also in Armenia, Georgia. Lingua franca. Muslims 99%(Shias,Yazidis,some Sunnis).
302	1	8	1.92	0	77.00	23.00	B	101.17	107	7	Mainly in Russia, Georgia; also in Syria, Turkey. Muslims 40%(Sunnis), nonreligious/atheists 24%. D=ROC.
303	4	10	1.93	6	99.91	0.09	C	531.44	33	10	Expatriates, businessmen from Poland. D=RCC,ROC,CEF,CWE.
304	8	9	1.87	7	99.62	0.38	C	307.76	38	9	In 70 countries. Nonreligious 30%, atheists 8%. D=ROC,RCC,AUCECB,Old Ritualists,CEF,CCECB,SDA,IPKH.
305	0	8	1.96	6	41.50	58.50	A	2.27	182	4	Bilingual in Russian, Armenian. Muslims 83%(Hanafi Sunnis), nonreligious 15%.
306	7	8	1.91	6	99.79	0.21	C	422.22	58	10	In 15 countries. Nonreligious/atheists 20%. D=ROC(E-Ukraine),Ukrainian Catholic Ch,AUCECB,CEF,CCECB,JWs,SDA.
307	0	9	0.00	5	41.00	59.00	A	0.00	0	1.12	55% speak Russian. Literates 100%. Muslims 80%(Hanafi Sunnis), nonreligious/atheists 20%. M=CSI.
308	0	8	5.19		44.00	56.00	A	32.12	323	5	USA Whites, Austrians, Hungarian Gypsies, Swedish, Bulgarians, Estonians, Buryat, Chuvash, Latvians, Tajiks, Kirghiz, Lezgins, Bashkir.
Aruba											
309	6	8	1.92	5	99.94	0.06	C	551.46	42	10	Blacks. D=80% RCC(D-Willemstad),MCCA,CPWI,COG,CGP,JWs. M=MMS,COG(Cleveland),TEAM(Radio Victoria).
310	6	10	2.01	6	99.75	0.25	C	405.15	48	10	Government and other administrators, settlers. D=UPCC,RCC(D-Willemstad),VKK(LCC),MCCA,CGP,JWs.
311	0	0	3.51	5	99.93	0.07	C	488.80	80	10	Immigrants from Philippines. D=Iglesia ni Cristo(Manalista)(Ch of Christ),RCC. M=SJ,FMB.
312	0	0	2.13	7	50.00	50.00	B	18.25	152	5	Chinese from many countries including mainland China. Buddhists/Chinese folk-religionists 95%. Many immigrants from Surinam. D=RCC. M=OP,FSC.
313	0	0	0.00	7	29.00	71.00	A	0.00	0	1.07	Several communities of practicing Jews, with notable synagogue on Curacao.
314	0	0	0.00	8	31.00	69.00	A	0.00	0	1.09	Labor migrants and immigrants from Turkey. Muslims 100%(Hanafi Sunnis).
315	0	10	2.28	8	99.96	0.04	C	578.22	57	10	Other Europeans(Largo Community Ch), other Caribbean islanders.
Australia											
316	0	10	1.62	1	99.75	0.25	C	364.08	50	9	Roper-Bamyili Creole, Roper River Pidgin. Northern Territory. Hunter-gathers, all bilingual in English. M=CMS,SIL,Aborigines Inland Mission.
317	1	10	2.22	6	99.60	0.40	C	249.66	66	8	Refugees and immigrants from Albania since 1946. Muslims 30%. D=AOC.
318	1	10	2.63	0	97.00	3.00	C	212.43	103	8	Lake Nash area, Ali Curung, Northern Territory. Some bilinguals in English. D=LCA. M=ABHM,IAMBS,SIL.
319	0	9	1.62	0	99.70	0.30	C	275.94	66	8	Hunter-gatherers. Groote Eylandt, Anindilyakwa. Northern Territory, Gulf of Carpentaria. Most youths bilingual in English. Animists(tribal religionists)30%. M=CMS.
320	4	8	1.25	8	99.66	0.34	C	335.01	40	9	D=Anglican Ch(26 Dioceses),RCC(29 Dioceses),UCA,300 others. M=MSC,CSSR,OFM,SJ,FMB. R=local stations,HCJB,AWR.
321	2	10	2.75	8	99.76	0.24	C	407.77	67	10	Expatriates from New Zealand, in commerce, professions. D=CPNZ,&c.
322	2	10	1.62	0	99.80	0.20	C	376.68	56	9	Mainly in UK, USA, Canada. English with many Romani words. D=RCC,ACA.
323	0	10	1.63	0	99.70	0.30	C	273.38	67	8	Northern Territory, Stuart Bluff Range, around Aileron. Animists 30%.
324	3	10	5.81	8	99.45	0.55	B	182.31	161	7	Refugees, immigrants, settlers from 30 Arab countries. Muslim 50%(Druze 8%). D=GOC,RCC,ACA.
325	2	10	1.62	6	99.90	0.10	C	535.45	37	10	Refugees from USSR, Turkey, Middle East, since 1900. D=Armenian Apostolic Ch(D-India),RCC.
326	1	10	1.62	5	99.88	0.12	C	497.86	41	10	Nestorians from Iraq. D=Ancient Assyrian Ch of the East.
327	1	10	1.58	8	99.90	0.10	C	509.17	48	10	Expatriates from Austria, in commerce, professions. D=RCC.
328	1	10	1.62	4	99.94	0.06	C	542.09	45	10	Refugees, immigrants from Spain and France. All Catholics. D=RCC.
329	5	10	1.50	8	99.77	0.23	C	438.43	47	10	Expatriates from Britain, in professions, commerce. D=Anglican Ch of Australia,RCC,BUA,SDA,JWs. R=local stations,HCJB,AWR.
330	1	10	1.62	6	99.72	0.28	C	352.15	58	9	Refugees, migrants from Bulgaria. Nonreligious 28%. D=Bulgarian Orthodox Ch.
331	1	8	1.62	0	81.00	19.00	B	133.04	89	7	Maningrida, Arnhem Land, Northern Territory. Coastal hunter-gatherers. Animists 55%. D=UCNA. M=SIL.
332	0	0	1.62	5	99.67	0.33	C	273.89	64	8	White Russians, from Belorussia. Nonreligious/atheists 33%. D=ROC,RCC,Old Ritualist Chs.
333	0	0	4.42	1	33.00	67.00	A	6.02	485	4	Refugees from civil war in Cambodia. Theravada Buddhists 86%, Animists 5%, nonreligious 3%. D=RCC. M=CMA.
334	0	8	1.57	5	41.00	59.00	A	14.96	152	5	Migrants from Cocos (Keeling) Islands. Muslims 90%(Shafi Sunnis).
335	1	10	4.28	6	99.91	0.09	C	544.72	90	10	Refugees, settlers from Croatia's wars since 1939. All Catholics. D=RCC.
336	2	10	2.76	6	99.79	0.21	C	438.29	70	10	Refugees, immigrants from Czechoslovakia since 1938. D=RCC, Unity of Brethren.
337	3	10	1.63	0	99.70	0.30	C	288.71	64	8	Elcho Island, Arnhem Land, NT. Bilingual in Djambarrpuyngu. Forest, coastal. Hunter-gatherers. Animists 30%. D=RCC,ACA,AoG.
338	1	8	1.68	0	47.00	53.00	A	25.73	156	5	Arnhem Land, Roper River, Northern Territory. All speak Dhuwal or English. Animists 85%. D=UCNA.
339	4	10	4.21	8	99.70	0.30	C	350.03	104	9	Throughout urban areas. Pentecostalism especially strong. D=Anglican Ch,AoG,RCC(D-Darwin,D-Broome),&c. M=MSC,UAM.
340	2	10	1.62	0	90.00	10.00	B	164.25	80	7	Roper River, Arnhem Land, Northern Territory. Flourishing, expanding. Bilingual in Djambarrpuyngu. Animists 50%. D=ACA,RCC.
341	1	8	1.61	0	59.00	41.00	B	53.83	121	6	Jambapuing. Elcho Island, Northern Territory. 450 fluent first-language speakers, increasing in numbers. Animists 75%. D=UCNA.
342	1	8	1.67	0	43.88	56.12	A	23.83	167	5	Halls Creek, Western Australia. Animists 85%. D=RCC. M=UAM.
343	1	8	1.68	0	41.98	58.02	A	18.35	175	5	Arnhem Land, Northern Territory. Coastal, river plains. Many bilinguals but limited use of English. Animists 88%. D=UCNA. M=SIL.
344	2	10	0.97	6	99.76	0.24	C	424.42	33	10	Expatriates, immigrants, settlers, in commerce, professions. D=DRC,RCC.

Continued overleaf

Table 8-2 continued

PEOPLE		POPULATION				IDENTITY CODE		LANGUAGE		CHURCH		MINISTRY						SCRIPTURE		
Ref 1	*Ethnic name* 2	*P%* 3	*In 1995* 4	*In 2000* 5	*In 2025* 6	*Race* 7	*Language* 8	*Autoglossonym* 9	*S* 10	*AC* 11	*Members* 12	*Jayuh* 13-17	*d* 18	*wa* 19	*xc* 20	*mc* 21	*mi* 22	*Biblioglossonym* 23	*Pub* 24-26	*ss* 27
345	Eastern Aranda	0.00925	1,659	1,746	2,136	AUG02	29-XBAB-a	west aranda		40.00	699	0....	9	6	7	2	1	Aranda*	PN.	b
346	Eastern Arrernte	0.00671	1,204	1,267	1,549	AUG02	29-XBAC-a	arrernte		70.00	887	0....	10	6	7	3	1	Arrernte, Eastern	...	.
347	Egyptian Arab	0.55000	98,670	103,837	126,999	CMT30	12-AACF-a	masri		30.00	31,151	2Asuh	9	6	7	0	0	Arabic*	PNB	b
348	Esperanto	0.00000	0	0	0	CEW21z	51-AAAC-a	proper esperanto		50.00	0	0A...	10	8	7	5	0	Esperanto	PNB	b
349	Estonian	0.03000	5,382	5,664	6,927	MSW51a	41-AAAC-b	eesti		83.00	4,701	4A.u.	10	9	11	5	2	Estonian: Tallinn	PNB	b
350	Filipino	0.34000	60,996	64,190	78,509	MSY44o	31-CKAA-a	proper tagalog		98.00	62,907	4Bs..	10	9	12	0	0	Tagalog	PNB	b
351	Finnish	0.04000	7,176	7,552	9,236	MSW51b	41-AAAA-bb	vehicular suomi		87.00	6,570	1A.uh	10	9	12	5	1	Finnish	PNB	b
352	French	0.05000	8,970	9,440	11,545	CEW21b	51-AABI-d	general français		87.00	8,213	1B.uh	10	9	13	5	2	French	PNB	b
353	Gaididj (Kaititj)	0.00130	233	245	300	AUG02	29-XAAA-a	gaididj		45.00	110	0....	9	5	6	3	1		...	n
354	Garawa (Karawa)	0.00119	213	225	275	AUG02	28-TAAA	garawa-wanji cluster		40.00	90	0....	9	6	7	3	2	Garawa	P..	.
355	German	1.00000	179,399	188,795	230,908	CEW19m	52-ABCE-a	standard hoch-deutsch		88.00	166,140	2B.uh	10	9	12	5	1	German*	PNB	b
356	Greek	1.60000	287,039	302,072	369,453	CEW20	56-AAAA-c	dhimotiki		95.00	286,969	2B.uh	10	9	12	5	2	Greek: Modern	PNB	b
357	Gugu-Yimidjir	0.00237	425	447	547	AUG02	29-RDAD	guuguu-yimidhirr cluster		70.00	313	0....	10	7	7	4	3	Guguyimidjir	P..	b
358	Guguyalanji	0.00201	361	379	464	AUG02	29-RDAC-a	gugu-yalandyi		19.00	72	0....	8	5	7	2	1	Kuku-yalanji	PN.	.
359	Gumatj	0.00196	352	370	453	AUG02	29-AAEA-c	gumatj		18.00	67	0.s..	8	5	6	2	1	Gumatj	PN.	.
360	Gunavidji (Djeebbana)	0.00059	106	111	136	AUG02	28-NAAA-a	djeebbana		50.00	56	0....	10	6	6	2	0		...	.
361	Gunwinggu (Gunawitji)	0.00293	526	553	677	AUG02	28-ODBA	gunwinggu cluster		70.00	387	0.s..	10	6	7	3	1	Kunwinjku*	P..	.
362	Gupapuyngu (Gobabingo)	0.00300	538	566	693	AUG02	29-AAEA-a	gupa-puyngu		65.00	368	0.s..	10	6	7	2	1	Gupapuyngu	Pn.	.
363	Han Chinese	0.27000	48,438	50,975	62,345	MSY42a	52-ABAC	english-mainland cluster		35.00	17,841	3Bsuh	9	8	8	5	3		PNB	b
364	Han Chinese (Cantonese)	0.73976	132,713	139,663	170,816	MSY42a	79-AAAM-a	central yue	2	21.00	29,329	3A.uh	9	8	8	3	1	Chinese, Yue	PNB	b
365	Han Chinese (Hakka)	0.05548	9,953	10,474	12,811	MSY42a	79-AAAG-a	literary hakka		12.00	1,257	1A...	8	4	8	3	0	Chinese: Hakka, Wukingfu*	PNB	b
366	Han Chinese (Mandarin)	0.04624	8,295	8,730	10,677	MSY42a	79-AAAB-ba	kuo-yü	3	12.00	1,048	2Bsuh	8	8	10	5	1	Chinese: Kuoyu*	PNB	b
367	Hungarian	0.30000	53,820	56,639	69,272	MSW51g	41-BAAA-a	general magyar		85.00	48,143	2A.u.	10	8	13	5	1	Hungarian	PNB	b
368	Indo-Pakistani	0.55000	98,670	103,837	126,999	CNN25g	59-AAFO-e	general hindi		10.00	10,384	3Asuh	8	5	6	0	0		pnb	b
369	Indonesian	0.10000	17,940	18,880	23,091	MSY44k	31-PHAA-c	bahasa-indonesia		8.00	1,510	4Asuh	7	5	7	3	1	Indonesian	PNB	b
370	Irish	0.50000	89,700	94,398	115,454	CEW18b	52-ABAC-i	irish-english		83.00	78,350	1Asuh	10	10	16	5	2		pnb	.
371	Irish Traveller (Gypsy)	0.03200	5,741	6,041	7,389	CNN25f	50-ACAA-a	west sheldruu		75.00	4,531	0....	10	6	11	4	1		...	b
372	Italian	2.20000	394,679	415,350	507,997	CEW21e	51-AABQ-c	standard italiano		84.00	348,894	2B.uh	10	10	15	5	1	Italian	PNB	b
373	Iwaidja (Ibadjo, Jiwadja)	0.00117	210	221	270	AUG02	28-MBBA-a	iwaidja		6.98	15	0....	7	5	6	4	1		...	b
374	Japanese	0.10000	17,940	18,880	23,091	MSY45a	45-CAAA-a	koku-go		5.00	944	1B.uh	7	7	7	5	3	Japanese	PNB	b
375	Javanese	0.05000	8,970	9,440	11,545	MSY44g	31-PIAA-g	general jawa		20.00	1,888	2As.h	9	7	7	5	3	Javanese	PNB	b
376	Jewish	0.02200	3,947	4,153	5,080	CMT35	52-ABCH-a	west yiddish		1.00	42	0B..h	6	5	5	5	1	Yiddish	PNB	b
377	Jewish	0.57800	103,693	109,124	133,465	CMT35	52-ABAC-x	general australian		1.50	1,637	1Bsuh	6	5	5	5	1	English	pnb	b
378	Kitja	0.00065	117	123	150	AUG02	28-DAAA-a	proper kitja		45.00	55	0....	9	6	6	2	1	Kitja	P..	.
379	Korean	0.10000	17,940	18,880	23,091	MSY46	45-AAAA-b	kukö		55.00	10,384	2A...	10	10	12	0	1	Korean	PNB	b
380	Kukatja	0.00196	352	370	453	AUG02	29-BGAK-c	kukatja		40.00	148	0.s..	9	6	2	2	1		p..	b
381	Kunjen	0.00176	316	332	406	AUG02	29-RHED-e	o-kunjen		60.00	199	0....	10	6	7	2	2	Kunjen	P..	b
382	Kurdish (Kurd)	0.07000	12,558	13,216	16,164	CNT24c	58-AAAA-a	kurmanji		1.00	132	3c...	6	4	5	5	1	Kurdish: Kurmanji*	PN.	b
383	Kuuku-Yaku	0.00067	120	126	155	AUG02	29-RHBA-a	kuuku-ya'u		50.00	63	0....	10	6	6	2	1		...	.
384	Latin American	0.46200	82,883	87,223	106,679	CLT27	51-AABB-h	Latin American		86.00	75,012	4B.uh	10	10	14	5	1		pnb	b
385	Latvian (Lett, Lettish)	0.20000	35,880	37,759	46,182	CEW15a	54-AABA-a	standard latviashu		99.00	37,381	3A.u.	10	9	12	5	3	Latvian	PNB	b
386	Macedonian	0.36000	64,584	67,966	83,127	CEW22g	53-AAAH-a	makedonski		91.00	61,849	2a.uh	10	8	11	4	2	Macedonian*	PNB	b
387	Malay	0.10000	17,940	18,880	23,091	MSY44k	31-PHAA-b	bahasa-malaysia		1.00	189	1asuh	6	4	5	4	0	Malay	PNB	b
388	Maltese	0.40000	71,760	75,518	92,363	CMT36	12-AACC-a	maltiya		91.00	68,721	0a.u.	10	9	16	5	1	Maltese	PNB	b
389	Mantjiltjara	0.00421	755	795	972	AUG02	29-BGEA	martu cluster		45.00	358	0....	9	6	6	2	2	Martu Wangka	P..	.
390	Maori	0.08000	14,352	15,104	18,473	MPY55b	39-CAQA-a	standard maori		70.00	10,573	0a.u.	10	10	13	5	3	Maori: New Zealand	PNB	b
391	Maung (Managari)	0.00130	233	245	300	AUG02	28-MBAA-a	maung		70.00	172	0.s..	10	7	6	3	1	Maung	P..	.
392	Miriam (Mer)	0.00205	368	387	473	AON10f	20-ODAA-a	meriam		67.00	259	0....	10	7	7	3	3	Miriam Mir*	P..	b
393	Miriwung	0.00220	395	415	508	AUG02	28-DABA-a	miriwung		6.00	25	0....	7	5	6	2	1		...	n
394	Murinbata	0.00553	992	1,044	1,277	AUG02	28-FAAA-a	proper murrinh-patha		75.00	783	0.s..	10	7	7	2	1	Murrinh-patha	P..	.
395	Nangumiri (Nangiomeri)	0.00167	300	315	386	AUG02	28-FCAA-b	nangi-kurrunggurr		40.00	126	0....	9	6	2	3	1		...	b
396	Neo-Melanesian Papuan	0.70000	125,580	132,157	161,636	MPY53	52-ABAI-c	tok-pisin-creole		80.00	105,725	3asuh	10	9	11	5	3	Tok Pisin	PNB	b
397	Ngalkbun	0.00098	176	185	226	AUG02	28-ODAB-a	ngalk-bun		7.00	13	0....	7	4	6	1	2		...	.
398	Ngarinman (Hainman)	0.00111	199	210	256	AUG02	29-BBBA	ngarinman cluster		16.00	34	0....	8	5	2	1	0		...	n
399	Ngarinyin	0.00054	97	102	125	AUG02	28-CACC-a	ngarinyin		60.00	61	0....	10	6	6	2	2	Ngarinyin	...	.
400	Northern Aborigine Creole	0.01000	1,794	1,888	2,309	MPY53	52-ABAI-a	australian-creole	1	80.00	1,510	1csuh	10	8	7	3	3	Kriol	PNb	b
401	Northern Mabuiag (Dauan)	0.01100	1,973	2,077	2,540	AON10f	29-RGAA-c	saibai		65.03	1,351	0....	10	7	6	3	2	Mabuiag: Saibai	Pn.	.
402	Northern Yolngu (Dhangu)	0.00228	409	430	526	AUG02	29-AADA-a	galpu		14.93	64	0....	8	5	6	1	1		p..	.
403	Nunggubuyu	0.00228	409	430	526	AUG02	28-OHAA-a	nunggubuyu		70.00	301	0....	10	6	7	2	1	Nunggubuyu	P..	.
404	Nyanganyatjara	0.00495	888	935	1,143	AUG02	29-BGAH-d	ngaanya-tjara		60.00	561	0.s..	10	6	6	2	2	Ngaanyatjarra	PN.	.
405	Nyangumarda	0.00304	545	574	702	AUG02	29-BCAC-a	nyangumarta		75.00	430	0....	10	7	6	2	1	Nyangumarta	...	.
406	Persian	0.06033	10,823	11,390	13,931	CNT24f	58-AACC-c	standard farsi		0.20	23	1Asu.	5	5	5	0	0		PNB	b
407	Pintupi (Bindubi)	0.00522	936	986	1,205	AUG02	29-BGGA-a	pintupi		60.00	591	0.s..	10	6	7	2	2	Pintupi-luritja	PN.	.
408	Pitcairner	0.00378	678	714	873	MPY53	52-ABAI-h	pitcairnese		99.00	707	1csuh	10	10	2	5	1		pnb	b
409	Pitjantjatjara	0.00814	1,460	1,537	1,880	AUG02	29-BGAK-a	pitjantja-tjara		90.00	1,383	0.s..	10	10	7	4	3	Pitjantjatjara	P..	.
410	Polish (Pole)	0.60000	107,640	113,277	138,545	CEW22i	53-AAAC-c	polski		90.00	101,949	2A.uh	10	10	14	5	3	Polish	PNB	b
411	Portuguese	0.14800	26,551	27,942	34,174	CEW21g	51-AABA-e	General português		96.00	26,824	2Bsuh	10	9	11	5	1	Portuguese	PNB	b
412	Rabaul Creole German	0.00067	120	126	155	CEW19m	52-ABCE-cb	unserdeutsch-queensland-		90.00	114	1c.uh	10	9	11	4	1		pnb	.
413	Rembarunga	0.00098	176	185	226	AUG02	28-OEAA-a	rembarunga		40.00	74	0....	9	5	7	2	2		...	n
414	Ritarungo (Ridarngo)	0.00196	352	370	453	AUG02	29-AAGA-a	ritarungo		45.00	167	0....	9	6	7	2	1		...	.
415	Romanian	0.07000	12,558	13,216	16,164	CEW21i	51-AADC-a	limba româneasca		84.00	11,101	3A.u.	10	9	10	5	1	Romanian	PNB	b
416	Romanichal Gypsy	0.05000	8,970	9,440	11,545	CNN25f	59-AGAA-ad	anglo-romani-australia		60.00	5,664	0....	10	6	8	4	1		...	.
417	Russian	0.35000	62,790	66,078	80,818	CEW22j	53-AAAE-d	russkiy		70.00	46,255	4B.uh	10	9	8	5	2	Russian	PNB	b
418	Serb	0.20000	35,880	37,759	46,182	CEW22l	53-AAAG-a	standard srpski		70.00	26,431	1Asuh	10	9	11	5	2	Serbian*	PNB	b
419	Slovak	0.06000	10,764	11,328	13,854	CEW22m	53-AAAD-b	slovensky		80.00	9,062	1Asuh	10	9	13	5	1	Slovak	PNB	b
420	Slovene	0.05000	8,970	9,440	11,545	CEW22n	53-AAAF-a	slovensko		95.00	8,968	1a..h	10	9	13	5	1	Slovenian*	PNB	b
421	Southern Mabuiag	0.02074	3,721	3,916	4,789	AON10f	29-RGAA-d	mabuaig		67.00	2,623	0....	10	7	6	4	2	Kala Lagaw Ya	PN.	.
422	Southwest Aborigine Creol	0.05865	10,522	11,073	13,543	AUG02	29-BFBA	nyunga cluster		80.00	8,858	0....	10	9	2	4	3		...	b
423	Spanish	0.08100	14,531	15,292	18,704	CEW21k	51-AABB-c	General español		90.00	13,763	2B.uh	10	10	14	5	1	Spanish	PNB	b
424	Syro-Lebanese Arab	0.38000	68,172	71,742	87,745	CMT30	12-AACF-f	syro-palestinian		55.00	39,458	1Asuh	10	9	6	0	0	Arabic: Lebanese*	Pnb	b
425	Thaayoore (Taior, Behran)	0.00231	414	436	533	AUG02	29-RHEA-q	koko-tayor		5.00	22	0.s..	7	4	6	1	1	Thayore	Pn.	.
426	Thai	0.05000	8,970	9,440	11,545	MSY49d	47-AAAB-d	central thai		0.80	76	3asuh	5	4	7	3	2	Thai*	PNB	b
427	Tiwi	0.00978	1,755	1,846	2,258	AUG02	28-IAAA-a	ngiu		75.00	1,385	0....	10	7	7	2	1	Tiwi	P..	.
428	Torres Strait Islander	0.14051	25,207	26,528	32,445	MPY53	52-ABAI-b	torres-strait-creole		70.00	18,569	1csuh	10	9	7	4	1	Torres Strait Creole	pnb	b
429	Turk	0.30000	53,820	56,639	69,272	MSY41j	44-AABA-a	osmanli		0.20	113	1A.u.	5	3	6	3	1	Turkish	PNB	b
430	USA White	0.40000	71,760	75,518	92,363	CEW19s	52-ABAC-s	general american		78.00	58,904	1Bsuh	10	10	14	5	3	English*	PNB	b
431	Ukrainian	0.23000	41,262	43,423	53,109	CEW22p	53-AAAE-b	ukrainskiy		80.00	34,738	3A.uh	10	9	11	5	2	Ukrainian	PNB	b
432	Vietnamese	0.91000	163,253	171,804	210,126	MSY52b	46-EBAA-ac	general viêt		22.00	37,797	1Asu.	9	8	7	3	1	Vietnamese	PNB	b
433	Wailbri (Walbiri, Ilpara)	0.01778	3,190	3,357	4,106	AUG02	29-BAAA-a	warl-piri		70.00	2,350	0....	10	7	7	2	2	Warlpiri	P..	.
434	Walmatjari (Walmajiri)	0.00593	1,064	1,120	1,369	AUG02	29-BBEA-a	wal-majarri		65.00	728	0a...	10	7	7	2	2	Walmajarri	P..	.
435	Wangada (Wangai)	0.00195	350	368	450	AUG02	29-BGAB-a	pintiini		70.00	258	0....	10	7	7	3	0		...	b
436	Wangurri	0.00127	228	240	293	AUG02	29-AADA-b	wan'guri		70.00	168	0....	10	7	6	2	3	Wangurri	P..	.
437	Warumungu	0.00130	233	245	300	AUG02	29-WAAA-a	warumungu		9.00	22	0....	7	4	6	1	1		...	n
438	Watjari (Wadjeri)	0.00196	352	370	453	AUG02	29-BFAA-a	watjari		5.00	19	0....	7	4	2	1	3		...	n
439	Welsh	0.20000	35,880	37,759	46,182	CEW18d	50-ABAA-bc	cymraeg-safonol		85.00	32,095	2A.uh	10	10	15	5	3	Welsh	PNB	b
440	Western Aranda	0.00671	1,204	1,267	1,549	AUG02	29-XBAB-a	west aranda		70.00	887	0....	10	7	7	3	1	Aranda*	PN.	b
441	Wik-Munkan	0.00214	384	404	494	AUG02	29-RHEA-a	wik-mungkan		70.00	283	0.s..	10	7	7	2	2	Wik-mungkan	PN.	.
442	Wik-Ngathana	0.00085	152	160	196	AUG02	29-RHEA-k	wik-ngatara		70.00	112	0.s..	10	7	7	3	0		pn.	b
443	Worora	0.00012	22	23	28	AUG02	28-CAAA-a	worora		70.00	16	0....	10	7	6	3	2	Worora	P..	b
444	Yankuntatjara	0.00159	285	300	367	AUG02	29-BGAJ-a	yankunta-tjara		50.00	150	0....	10	6	2	2	3		...	p
445	Yanyula (Yanyuwa)	0.00059	106	111	136	AUG02	28-RAAA-a	yanyuwa		15.00	17	0....	8	5	6	1	3	Yanyuwa	P..	b
446	Yindjibarndi	0.00391	701	738	903	AUG02	29-BDCA-a	yindjibarndi		40.00	295	0....	9	6	7	1	1		...	.
447	Yulparitja	0.00134	240	253	309	AUG02	29-BGEA	martu cluster		8.00	20	0....	7	4	6	1	1	Martu Wangka	P..	.
448	other minor peoples	0.15941	28,598	30,096	36,809	...				70.00	21,067		10	7	2	3	2			
	Austria	**100.00000**	**8,000,712**	**8,210,520**	**8,185,725**					**84.16**	**6,909,671**									
449	Arab	0.09000	7,201	7,389	7,367	CMT30	12-AACF-f	syro-palestinian		6.00	443	1Asuh	7	6	8	5	1	Arabic: Lebanese*	Pnb	b
450	Austrian Gypsy	0.12000	9,601	9,853	9,823	CNN25f	52-ABCF-b	donau-bayrisch-t.		80.00	7,882	0B.uh	10	7	8	4	1		pn.	b
451	Bavarian Austrian	86.44800	6,916,456	7,097,830	7,076,396	CEW19f	52-ABCF-b	donau-bayrisch-t.	96	86.25	6,121,879	0B.uh	10	9	13	5	3		pn.	b
452	Bosniac (Muslmani)	0.90000	72,006	73,895	73,672	CEW22a	53-AAAG-a	standard srpski		0.00	0	1Asuh	0	4	4	4	0	Serbian*	PNB	b
453	British	0.05300	4,240	4,352	4,338	CEW19i	52-ABAC-b	standard-english	24	79.00	3,438	3Bsuh	10	9	11	5	1		PNB	b
454	Cambodian (Khmer)	0.01000	800	821	819	AUG03b	46-FBAA	khmer cluster		5.00	41	2A...	7	4	7	0	0		PNB	b
455	Croat	0.20000	16,001	16,421	16,371	CEW22d	53-AAAG-b	standard hrvatski		91.00	14,943	2Asuh	10	7	13	5	1	Croatian	PNB	b
456	Czech	0.10000	8,001	8,211	8,186	CEW22e	53-AAAD-a	czesky		79.00	6,486	2Asuh	10	7	8	5	2	Czech	PNB	b
457	Esperanto	0.00000	0	0	0	CEW21z	51-AAAC-a	proper esperanto	1	70.00	0	0A...	10	8	8	5	0	Esperanto	PNB	b
458	Estonian	0.00700	560	575	573	MSW51a	41-AAAC-b	eesti		70.00	402	4A.u.	10	7	8	5	3	Estonian: Tallinn	PNB	b
459	Filipino	0.10000	8,001	8,211	8,186	MSY44o	31-CKAA-a	proper tagalog		98.00	8,046	4Bs..	10	9	12	0	0	Tagalog	PNB	b
460	French	0.20000	16,001	16,421	16,371	CEW21b	51-AABI-d	general français	5	87.00	14,286	1B.uh	10	9	13	5	1	French	PNB	b
461	German	3.50000	280,025	287,368	286,500	CEW19m	52-ABCE-a	standard hoch-deutsch	60	88.00	252,884	2B.uh	10	9	12	5	1	German*	PNB	b
462	German Swiss (Allemanic)	3.95000	316,028	324,316	323,336	CEW19m	52-ABCG-a	general schwytzer-tütsch		90.00	291,884	0B.uh	10	9	12	5	1	Schwyzerdutsch*	PN.	b
463	Greek	0.15900	12,721	13,055	13,015	CEW20	56-AAAA-c	dhimotiki		95.00	12,402	2B.uh	10	8	10	5	1	Greek: Modern	PNB	b
464	Han Chinese	0.00500	400	411	409	MSY42a	52-ABCE-a	standard hoch-deutsch		19.00	78	2B.uh	8	7	8	5	0	German*	PNB	b
465	Han Chinese (Cantonese)	0.01200	960	985	982	MSY42a	79-AAAM-a	central yue		9.10	90	3A.uh	7	6	8	4	1	Chinese, Yue	PNB	b
466	Han Chinese (Mandarin)	0.01500	1,200	1,232	1,228	MSY42a	79-AAAB-ba	kuo-yü		6.90	85	2Bsuh	7	6	8	4	1	Chinese: Kuoyu*	PNB	b

Continued opposite

Table 8-2 continued

EVANGELIZATION								EVANGELISM			ADDITIONAL DESCRIPTIVE DATA
Ref	*D*	*aC*	*CG%*	*r*	*E*	*U*	*W*	*e*	*R*	*T*	*Locations, civil divisions, literacy, religions, church history, denominations, dioceses, church growth, missions, agencies, ministries, movements*
1	*28*	*29*	*30*	*31*	*32*	*33*	*34*	*35*	*36*	*37*	*38*
345	1	10	1.62	0	78.00	22.00	B	113.88	92	7	Northern Territory, Alice Springs area. Hunter-gatherers on plains, savannah. Animists 60%. D=LCA.
346	1	10	1.62	0	99.70	0.30	C	270.83	68	8	Alice Springs area, Santa Teresa, NT. Hunter-gatherers. Animists 30%. D=RCC. M=SIL.
347	0	0	8.38	8	77.00	23.00	B	84.31	323	6	Labor migrants from Egypt. Muslims 62%(Maliki Sunnis). D=COC,RCC.
348	0	10	0.00	5	99.50	0.50	B	198.92	0	7	Artificial (constructed) language, in 80 countries. Speakers in Australia: 71,000 (none mother-tongue).
349	2	10	1.62	5	99.83	0.17	C	466.54	50	10	Refugees from Estonia. D=Estonian Orthodox Ch in Exile, Estonian ELC in Exile.
350	0	0	9.14	5	99.98	0.02	C	540.12	178	10	Immigrants from Philippines. D=Iglesia ni Cristo(Manalista)(Ch of Christ),RCC. M=SJ.
351	1	10	1.62	5	99.87	0.13	C	492.20	47	10	Immigrants from Finland, in commerce, professions. D=Finnish Evangelical Lutheran Ch.
352	2	10	1.62	8	99.87	0.13	C	514.43	44	10	Expatriates from France, in commerce, professions. Nonreligious 13%. D=RCC,RCF.
353	0	8	1.62	0	78.00	22.00	B	128.11	92	7	North of Alice Springs, Northern Territory. Bilingual in Kriol. Animists 55%. M=ABHM/ABMS.
354	1	8	1.62	0	75.00	25.00	B	109.50	96	7	Borroloola, Northern Territory, and Doomadgee, Queensland. Animists 60%. D=CB(PB). M=AIM,SIL.
355	3	10	1.56	8	99.88	0.12	C	526.76	45	10	Strong Protestant denominations. D=Lutheran Ch of Australia,NAC,ACQ. M=EKD.
356	2	10	1.62	7	99.95	0.05	C	589.47	42	10	Immigrants from Greece, in commerce, finance, professions. D=Greek Orthodox Ch(AD-Australia), JWs.
357	3	9	1.62	0	99.70	0.30	C	291.27	63	8	Hopevale, Queensland. Speakers bilingual in English. Animists 30%. D=Lutheran Ch of Australia,ACA,RCC.
358	2	9	1.65	0	56.00	44.00	B	38.83	130	5	Bloomfield river, Queensland. Coastal laborers, some bilingual in English. Animists 80%. D=Lutheran Ch of Australia,AoG. M=SIL.
359	1	8	1.65	0	53.00	47.00	B	34.82	137	5	Yirrkala, Northern Territory. Coastal hunter-gatherers. Many bilinguals in Gupapuyngu, some in English. Animists 80%. D=UCNA.
360	0	10	1.64	0	81.00	19.00	B	147.82	89	7	West Arnhem Land. Most are bilingual in Gunwinjku. Animists 50%.
361	1	9	1.63	0	99.70	0.30	C	273.38	67	8	Oenpelli, Arnhem Land, Northern Territory, Croker Island. Animists 30%. D=CEA. M=CMS.
362	1	9	1.62	0	99.65	0.35	C	244.36	70	8	Milingimbi, Arnhem Land; Elcho Islands. Coastal hunter-gatherers. 45 related dialects. Some bilinguals. Animists 35%. D=UCNA.
363	3	10	3.52	8	99.35	0.65	B	136.69	107	7	English-speaking Chinese, many being second-generation immigrants. Buddhists 60%. D=CEA,SDA,AoG.
364	7	10	3.60	8	90.00	10.00	B	68.98	129	6	Buddhists/Confucianists 75%. D=Baptist Ch,SDA,Congregationalists,Anglican Ch,Methodist Ch,Pentecostals,RCC. M=CMA(Hong Kong).
365	0	10	1.62	7	72.00	28.00	B	31.53	86	5	Refugees, immigrants, in business, finance. Chinese folk-religionists/ Buddhists/Confucianists 80%.
366	2	10	1.63	7	82.00	18.00	B	35.91	76	5	Immigrants in business, commerce. Chinese folk-religionists/Buddhists 70%. D=RCC,CEA. M=CMA(Hong Kong).
367	1	10	1.62	6	99.85	0.15	C	483.99	53	10	Refugees, immigrants since 1939, 1945, 1957. In professions. D=RCC.
368	0	0	7.19	7	51.00	49.00	B	18.61	440	5	Immigrants from India and Pakistan. Hindus 58%, Muslims 15%(Sunnis, also Ahmadiyya Mission), Sikhs 12%.
369	1	10	1.62	7	72.00	28.00	B	21.02	88	5	Immigrants from Indonesia. Laborers, business. Muslims 80%, Subud. D=RCC.
370	2	10	1.45	8	99.83	0.17	C	469.57	42	10	Strong Irish influence in Australian Catholicism. D=RCC,Cooneyites(Go-preachers).
371	1	10	1.62	8	99.75	0.25	C	350.40	57	9	Gypsies with strong links to Ireland. D=RCC. M=GGMS.
372	1	10	2.16	7	99.84	0.16	C	490.56	54	10	Large numbers of immigrants from Italy. Strong Catholics. D=RCC.
373	1	8	1.62	0	40.98	59.02	A	10.44	175	5	Croker Island, Northern Territory. Bilingual in English. Animists 90%. D=United Ch of North Australia(Methodist). M=SIL.
374	3	10	1.62	7	71.00	29.00	B	12.95	91	5	Immigrants since 1939, 1945. In professions, finance. Buddhists 90%, Sokkai Gakkai and New Religions. D=RCC,UC,CEA.
375	3	10	1.62	5	86.00	14.00	B	62.78	79	6	Immigrants from Java (Indonesia). Muslims 60% (Sunnis), New-Religionists 20%. D=RCC,UC,AoG.
376	0	10	1.43	4	56.00	44.00	B	2.04	104	4	Traditional Jews practicing orthodox Judaism. M=JFJ.
377	1	10	1.64	8	61.50	38.50	B	3.37	104	4	Refugees immigrants since 1937. In finance, professions. Many practice Judaism, but 20% nonreligious. D=Messianic Jews. M=JFJ.
378	0	8	1.62	0	76.00	24.00	B	124.83	94	7	Near Halls Creek, Western Australia. Nomadic hunter-gatherers. Animists 55%. M=UAM.
379	0	0	7.19	6	99.55	0.45	B	212.79	202	8	Immigrants from Korea. Buddhists 10%, shamanists 30%. D=RCC,Presbyterians. M=PCK-Haptong.
380	1	8	1.61	1	73.00	27.00	B	106.58	98	7	Gregory Salt Sea, South Australia. Mixture of Pitjantjatjara and Antiriginya. Animists 60%. D=RCC.
381	3	9	1.62	0	99.60	0.40	C	221.19	71	8	Wrotham Park, Mitchell river, Edward river, Queensland. Bilinguals in English. Animists 40%. D=RCC,CEA,AoG. M=ABOM,SIL.
382	0	10	1.64	0	43.00	57.00	A	1.57	232	4	Refugees from Iraq, Iran, Turkey. Muslims 99% (Sunnis). M=a vast network of mission agencies.
383	1	10	1.59	0	84.00	16.00	B	153.30	84	7	Queensland, northeastern Cape York Peninsula. Bilingual in Torres Strait Creole. Animists 50%. D=Pentecostals.
384	1	10	2.26	8	99.86	0.14	C	508.52	53	10	Immigrants and refugees predominantly from Chile, Argentina, Uruguay. Nonreligious 13%, Jewish 1%. D=RCC.
385	3	10	1.62	5	99.99	0.01	C	625.13	45	10	Refugees from USSR after 1939, 1945. D=ROC,RCC,ELCL.
386	2	10	3.46	5	99.91	0.09	C	531.44	76	10	Immigrants from Yugoslavia. D=Macedonian Orthodox Autocephalous Ch,Self-Independent MOC.
387	0	10	1.62	5	54.00	46.00	B	1.97	118	4	Immigrants from Malaysia, in business, commerce. Muslim 90% (Sunnis).
388	1	10	1.62	5	99.91	0.09	C	534.76	41	10	Immigrants from Malta, in professions. All Catholics. D=RCC. Many charismatics.
389	0	8	1.63	0	77.00	23.00	B	126.47	94	7	Jigalong area, Western Australia. Widely scattered. Animists 55%. M=ACM,SIL.
390	3	10	1.62	4	99.70	0.30	C	357.70	42	9	Expatriates from New Zealand. Animists 30%. Many denominations. D=CEA,RCC,Ratana Ch.
391	1	9	1.63	0	99.70	0.30	C	270.83	68	8	Goulburn Island, Arnhem Land, Northern Territory. Some are bilingual in English. Animists 30%. D=UCNA.
392	2	9	1.62	0	99.67	0.33	C	266.56	68	8	Murray Island, Eastern Torres Strait Islands, Queensland. Also on islands in PNG. Most bilingual in Tok Pisin. Animists 33%. D=CEA,US. M=ABOM,LMS,SIL.
393	1	8	1.62	0	37.00	63.00	A	8.10	194	4	Kununurra, Western Australia. Youths use only Kriol. Becoming extinct. Mostly animists. D=RCC. M=UAM.
394	1	8	1.63	0	99.75	0.25	C	301.12	66	9	Port Keats area, Wadeye, Northern Territory. Animists 25%. D=RCC. M=SIL.
395	1	8	1.63	0	71.00	29.00	B	103.66	101	7	Angomerry. Junction of Flora and Daly rivers, Northern Territory. People use English and Kriol. Animists 60%. D=RCC.
396	4	10	1.62	5	99.80	0.20	C	449.68	43	10	Papuan, New Guinean labor migrants and immigrants from PNG. Almost all Christians, a few animists. D=CEA,UC,RCC,LCA.
397	0	8	1.48	0	35.00	65.00	A	8.94	194	4	Oenpelli, Arnhem Land, Northern Territory. Some bilinguals in Rembarrnga, Gunwinggu, Kriol. Animists 90%. M=CMS,AIM-I.
398	0	8	1.59	0	41.00	59.00	A	23.94	173	5	Victoria river, Jasper Creek, North Australia. People speak Kriol. Animists 84%.
399	1	9	1.64	0	94.00	6.00	C	205.86	77	8	Derby to King river, Kimberley, Western Australia. Coastal hunter-gatherers, now laborers. Animists 40%. D=UCNA. M=UAM,APBM.
400	4	10	1.62	1	99.80	0.20	C	394.20	49	9	Aborigines from many tribes and extinct languages. Virtually all Christians. D=CEA,UC,AoG,RCC.
401	0	8	1.62	0	99.65	0.35	C	242.17	73	8	Torres Strait Islands. Hunters, fishermen. Animists 35%. M=ABOM,SIL.
402	1	8	1.61	0	44.93	55.07	A	24.48	159	5	Elcho Island, Arnhem Land, Northern Territory. Coastal hunter-gatherers, fishermen. Animists 85%. D=UCNA. M=SIL.
403	1	9	1.63	0	99.70	0.30	C	268.27	69	8	Numbulwar, east Arnhem Land, Northern Territory. Some bilinguals in English. Coastal hunter-gatherers. Animists 30%. D=CEA. M=CMS.
404	2	7	1.62	0	98.00	2.00	C	214.62	73	8	Warburton Ranges, Western Australia. Animists 40%. D=UCNA,AAEM.
405	0	8	1.62	0	99.75	0.25	C	290.17	68	8	Marble Bar, Port Hedlund, Western Australia. Animists 25%. M=SIL.
406	0	0	3.19	5	34.20	65.80	A	0.25	256	3	Migrant workers and refugees from Iran (some Imami Shias). Muslims 84%, Zoroastrians 12%, some Baha'is. D=RCC.
407	2	9	1.62	0	99.60	0.40	C	221.19	71	8	Papunya settlement, Northern Territory. Bilinguals in English: 10%. Animists 40%. D=RCC,LCA. M=ABHM,SIL.
408	1	10	1.63	8	99.99	0.01	C	549.25	44	10	Pitcairn-Norfolk Creole. Migrants from Pitcairn, Norfolk Island. Also in New Zealand. D=SDA.
409	3	9	1.62	1	99.90	0.10	C	440.19	54	10	South Australia, Western Australia. Bilinguals in English: 10%. D=UC,CEA,AoG. M=AAEM,APBM,UAM,SIL.
410	3	10	1.53	6	99.90	0.10	C	538.74	26	10	Refugees, immigrants from Poland. D=RCC,Polish Orthodox Ch,PNCC.
411	1	10	2.26	8	99.96	0.04	C	602.69	52	10	Immigrants from Portugal. Predominantly Catholic. Nonreligious 4%. D=RCC.
412	1	10	1.61	1	99.90	0.10	C	459.90	54	10	Southeastern Queensland. A pidginized Standard German dating from German colonial rule over New Britain (PNG). Mixed-race Vunapope. D=RCC.
413	2	8	1.61	0	76.00	24.00	B	110.96	94	7	Roper River area, Maningrida, Northern Territory. Bilinguals in Kriol, Ngalkbun. Animists 60%. D=UCNA,CEA. M=CMS,AIM.
414	1	8	1.63	0	77.00	23.00	B	126.47	94	7	Eastern Arnhem Land, Northern Territory. Some bilinguals in Kriol, some in Djinba. Animists 55%. D=UCNA. M=CMS.
415	1	10	1.62	6	99.84	0.16	C	459.90	50	10	Refugees from Romania. D=Romanian Orthodox Ch. M=FMB.
416	3	10	1.62	0	99.60	0.40	C	221.19	72	8	One of several varieties of Gypsy, mostly nomadic, some settled. Nonreligious 40%. D=RCC,CEA,UC. M=GGMS.
417	2	10	1.34	7	99.70	0.30	C	357.70	26	9	Refugees from USSR after 1917. D=Russian Orthodox Ch, ROCOR.
418	2	10	0.70	6	99.70	0.30	C	355.14	14	9	Migrants from Yugoslavia. D=Serbian Orthodox Ch(D-Western Europe),Free SOC.
419	1	10	1.62	6	99.80	0.20	C	432.16	51	10	Refugees from Slovakia after 1938, 1945, 1968. D=RCC.
420	1	10	1.62	6	99.95	0.05	C	561.73	44	10	Refugees, immigrants from Slovenia. Mostly Catholics. D=RCC.
421	1	8	1.62	0	99.67	0.33	C	261.66	70	8	Kala Yagaw Ya, Kala Lagaw. Western Torres Strait Islands; Townsville. Hunters, fishermen. Animists 33%. D=CEA. M=ABOM,SIL.
422	4	8	1.62	0	99.80	0.20	C	344.56	61	9	English-Nyunga creole, across southwest Australia. Almost all Christians. D=CEA,UC,RCC,AoG.
423	1	10	2.26	8	99.90	0.10	C	551.88	52	10	Immigrants from Spain not including Basques. Predominantly Catholic. Nonreligious 9%. D=RCC.
424	0	0	8.63	8	97.00	3.00	B	194.72	264	7	Levantine Arabs. Muslims 39%(Sunnis, some Shias, Alawis, Druzes, Ismailis). D=RCC.
425	0	8	1.72	0	36.00	64.00	A	6.57	207	4	Between Edward and Coleman rivers, Queensland. Coastal hunter-gatherers. Only 200 Thaayoore speakers left. Virtually all animists. M=ABOM.
426	2	10	1.64	6	57.80	42.20	B	1.68	105	4	Immigrants, refugees from Thailand, Laos. Buddhists 95%. D=UC,RCC.
427	1	8	1.62	0	99.75	0.25	C	301.12	65	9	Bathurst and Melville Islands, Nguiu, Northern Territory. Some bilingual in English. Laborers, craftsmen. Animists 25%. D=RCC. M=SIL.
428	2	8	1.62	1	99.70	0.30	C	309.15	55	9	Torres Strait Islands, Queensland. Animists 30%. D=UCA,Universal World Ch(all Torres Strait Islanders). M=SIL.
429	0	10	2.04	8	52.20	47.80	B	0.38	144	3	Labor migrants and immigrants from Turkey. Muslims 99%(Hanafi Sunnis). M=International Missions.
430	4	10	3.04	8	99.78	0.22	C	441.28	70	10	Expatriates from USA, in professions. D=SDA,CJCLdS,JWs,UCA.
431	2	10	1.62	6	99.80	0.20	C	446.76	51	10	Refugees from USSR after 1917, 1933, 1939, 1945. D=RCC(EA-Australia),UOCUSA(AD-Australia & New Zealand).
432	5	10	3.59	6	83.00	17.00	B	66.64	147	6	Refugees, immigrants from Viet Nam after 1970. Buddhists/New-Religionists 80%. D=RCC,Anglican Ch,Asian Christian Fellowship,SDA,ICFG. M=FMB.
433	0	8	1.62	0	99.70	0.30	C	268.27	68	8	Hooker Creek, Yuendumu, Northern Territory. Nomadic desert hunter-gatherers. Animists 30%. M=ABHM,SIL.
434	3	8	1.63	0	99.65	0.35	C	251.48	68	8	Hunter-gatherers in semi-desert, Fitzroy Crossing area, Western Australia. Animists 35%. D=RCC,AoG,CC. M=SIL,United Aborigines Mission.
435	0	10	1.63	0	99.70	0.30	C	273.38	67	8	Western Australia, north of Nullabor Plain. Second language: Pitjantjatjara or Ngaanyatjarra. Animists 30%.
436	4	7	1.64	0	99.70	0.30	C	270.83	68	8	Elcho Island, Arnhem Land, NT. Dialect of Dhangu. Animists 30%. D=CEA,RCC,UC,AoG.
437	0	8	1.49	0	38.00	62.00	A	12.48	180	5	Tennant Creek area, Northern Territory. People speak Kriol. Animists 90%. M=ABHM.
438	4	8	1.57	0	35.00	65.00	A	6.38	201	4	Mount Magnet to Geraldton, Western Australia. Kriol is normal usage. Animists 93%. D=CEA,RCC,UC,AoG.
439	3	10	1.62	5	99.85	0.15	C	502.60	44	10	Settlers from Wales over last hundred years. In professions. D=UC,AoG,SDA.
440	1	10	1.62	0	99.70	0.30	C	288.71	64	8	Northern Territory, Alice Springs area. Hunter-gatherers on plains and savannah. Animists 30%. D=Lutheran Ch of Australia.
441	1	9	1.63	0	99.70	0.30	C	281.05	66	8	Edward river to Aurukun, Queensland. Some bilinguals in English. Animists 30%. D=UCNA. M=APBM,SIL.
442	0	10	1.64	0	99.70	0.30	C	283.60	65	8	Queensland, Cape York Peninsula, west coast. Animists 30%.
443	2	9	1.69	0	99.70	0.30	C	281.05	67	8	Derby area, Collier Bay, Western Australia. Many bilinguals in English. Animists 30%. D=PCA,UCNA.
444	3	8	1.62	0	83.00	17.00	B	151.47	86	7	Yalata, Musgrave, and Everard Ranges, South Australia. Bilingual in Pitjantjatjara. Animists 50%. D=UC,CEA,RCC.
445	0	9	1.75	0	50.00	50.00	B	27.37	151	5	Hunter-gatherers in Borroloola, Northern Territory, and Doomadgee, Queensland. Bilinguals in English, Garawa. Animists 85%. M=Aborigines Inland Mission,SIL.
446	0	9	1.62	0	71.00	29.00	B	103.66	101	7	Roebourne, Western Australia. Coastal, desert, riverine hunter-gatherers and fishermen. Animists 60%. M=SIL.
447	1	8	1.62	0	37.00	63.00	A	10.80	194	5	Balgo Hills and Fitzroy Crossing, Western Australia. Animists 92%. D=RCC. M=UAM.
448	0	10	1.62		99.70	0.30	C	260.61	44	8	Indo-Mauritians, Franco-Mauritians, also 180 Aboriginal languages now with under 100 speakers or already extinct.
Austria											
449	2	10	4.23	8	67.00	33.00	B	14.67	202	5	Most do not understand High German broadcasts. Egyptians, Syrians, Lebanese, North Africans. Muslims 90%. D=COC,RCC. M=OM.
450	1	10	0.31	8	99.80	0.20	C	397.12	27	9	Many Gypsies speak only German, and many are settled. D=RCC. M=GGMS.
451	1	6	0.16	8	99.86	0.14	C	476.15	23	10	Austro-Bavarian. Central, North, and South Bavarian. D=RCC(11 Dioceses). M=OSB,OCist,SJ,SVD,OFM,FSC,UFM,FMB.
452	0	10	0.00	6	48.00	52.00	A	0.00	0	1.14	Refugees from Bosnian civil war accepted by Austria in 1992. Muslims 90% (Sunnis), nonreligious 10%.
453	1	10	0.31	8	99.79	0.21	C	432.52	27	10	Expatriates from Britain, in commerce, education. D=Ch of England (D-Europe).
454	0	0	3.78	5	44.00	56.00	A	8.03	324	4	Refugees from civil war in Cambodia. Theravada Buddhists 86%, Animists 5%, nonreligious 3%. D=RCC. M=CMA.
455	1	10	0.31	6	99.91	0.09	C	544.72	23	10	In Burgenland and Vienna. Migrant workers from Croatia(Yugoslavia). D=RCC. M=FMB.
456	2	10	0.31	6	99.79	0.21	C	426.75	27	10	Refugees from Czechoslovakia since 1938. D=Evangelical Ch of Czech Brethren, RCC.
457	0	10	0.00	5	99.70	0.30	C	332.15	0	9	Artificial (constructed) language, with no mother-tongue speakers. Spoken in 80 countries.
458	4	10	0.31	5	99.70	0.30	C	355.14	29	9	Refugees from Estonia since 1945. D=ROC,ELCE,RCC,MCE.
459	0	0	6.92	5	99.98	0.02	C	536.55	139	10	Immigrants from Philippines. D=Iglesia ni Cristo(Manalista)(Ch of Christ),RCC. M=SJ.
460	1	10	0.18	8	99.87	0.13	C	511.25	20	10	Expatriates in business, education, administration. D=RCC.
461	2	10	0.31	8	99.88	0.12	C	523.55	24	10	Speakers of Standard German. 1989-91, large number of refugees from East Germany. D=RCC,EKD. M=FMB.
462	1	10	0.31	8	99.90	0.10	C	512.46	25	10	Swiss German(Alemannic) has 70 dialects. Also in Switzerland, Germany. Related to Bavarian, Alsatian, Swabian. D=RCC.
463	1	10	0.31	7	99.95	0.05	C	575.60	21	10	Expatriates from Greece, in industry, commerce. D=Greek Orthodox Ch.
464	0	10	2.08	8	83.00	17.00	B	57.56	90	6	Chinese whose mother tongue now is German. Still Chinese folk-religionists 50%, rest Christians or nonreligious.
465	0	10	2.93	8	72.10	27.90	B	23.94	136	5	Refugees from south China. 90% Buddhists and Confucianists. M=RCC.
466	0	10	3.82	7	69.90	30.10	B	17.60	175	5	Immigrants and refugees from Chinese diaspora in Asia. 93% Buddhists and Confucianists. M=RCC.

Continued overleaf

Table 8-2 continued

Ref 1	Ethnic name 2	P% 3	In 1995 4	In 2000 5	In 2025 6	Race 7	Language 8	Autoglossonym 9	S 10	AC 11	Members 12	Jayuh 13-17	d 18	wa 19	xc 20	mc 21	mi 22	Biblioglossonym 23	Pub ss 24-26 27
	PEOPLE	**POPULATION**				**IDENTITY CODE**		**LANGUAGE**		**CHURCH**		**MINISTRY**						**SCRIPTURE**	
467	Han Chinese (Taiwanese)	0.01000	800	821	819	MSY42a	79-AAAJ-h	quan-zhang-taiwan		6.00	49	1A..h	7	7	8	5	2	Taiwanese	PNB b
468	Hungarian	0.25700	20,562	21,101	21,037	MSW51g	41-BAAA-a	general magyar		81.00	17,092	2A.u.	10	8	8	5	1	Hungarian	PNB b
469	Indo-Pakistani	0.05000	4,000	4,105	4,093	CNN25g	59-AAFO	hindi-urdu cluster		10.00	411	4Asuh	8	5	6	0	0		PNB b
470	Italian	0.10000	8,001	8,211	8,186	CEW21e	51-AABQ-c	standard italiano	3	84.00	6,897	2B.uh	10	9	8	5	1	Italian	PNB b
471	Jewish	0.10500	8,401	8,621	8,595	CMT35	52-ABCE-a	standard hoch-deutsch		0.20	17	2B.uh	5	5	5	4	0	German*	PNB b
472	Kurdish (Kurd)	0.33000	26,402	27,095	27,013	CNT24c	58-AAAA-a	kurmanji		0.10	27	3c...	5	4	4	4	1	Kurdish: Kurmanji*	PN. b
473	Persian	0.08000	6,401	6,568	6,549	CNT24f	58-AACC-c	standard farsi		1.00	66	1Asu.	6	4	5	4	1		PNB b
474	Polish	0.49600	39,684	40,724	40,601	CEW22i	53-AAAC-c	polski		90.00	36,652	2A.uh	10	9	11	0	0	Polish	PNB b
475	Russian	0.20000	16,001	16,421	16,371	CEW22j	53-AAAE-d	russkiy		70.00	11,495	4B.uh	10	8	8	5	2	Russian	PNB b
476	Serb	0.25000	20,002	20,526	20,464	CEW22l	53-AAAG-a	standard srpski		85.00	17,447	1Asuh	10	7	8	5	1	Serbian*	PNB b
477	Sinti Gypsy (Manush)	0.00700	560	575	573	CNN25f	59-ACBB-b	sinti		80.00	460	0....	10	7	7	4	1	Romani: Sinti, Italian	P.. b
478	Slovene	0.38200	30,563	31,364	31,269	CEW22n	53-AAAF-a	slovensko		95.00	29,796	1a..h	10	8	13	5	1	Slovenian*	PNB b
479	Sorb (Lusatian, Wend)	0.05400	4,320	4,434	4,420	CEW22o	53-AAAB	sorb cluster		70.00	3,104	0....	10	8	12	5	2		PNB b
480	Spaniard	0.05000	4,000	4,105	4,093	CEW21k	51-AABB-c	general español	2	96.00	3,941	2B.uh	10	8	15	5	1	Spanish	PNB b
481	Turk	0.90000	72,006	73,895	73,672	MSY41j	44-AABA-a	osmanli		0.10	74	1A.u.	5	6	5	4	1	Turkish	PNB b
482	USA White	0.12000	9,601	9,853	9,823	CEW19s	52-ABAC-s	general american		78.00	7,685	1Bsuh	10	9	13	5	1	English*	PNB b
483	Vietnamese	0.04000	3,200	3,284	3,274	MSY52b	46-EBAA-ac	general viêt		12.00	394	1Asu.	8	8	8	0	0	Vietnamese	PNB b
484	other minor peoples	0.70000	56,005	57,474	57,300	...				67.50	38,795		10	8	8	5	2		
	Azerbaijan	**100.00000**	**7,562,806**	**7,734,015**	**9,402,570**					**4.63**	**357,800**								
485	Armenian (Ermeni)	3.20000	242,010	247,488	300,882	CEW14	57-AAAA-b	ashkharik		68.00	168,292	4A.u.	10	7	11	2	2	Armenian: Modern, Eastern	PNB b
486	Assyrian	0.01667	1,261	1,289	1,567	CMT31	12-AAAA-f	aisor		85.00	1,096	4cs..	10	9	8	0	0	Assyrian Neo-aramaic	PNB b
487	Avar	0.62770	47,472	48,546	59,020	CEW17b	42-BBAA-a	north avar		0.01	5	1....	3	3	2	0	1	Avar	P.. b
488	Azerbaijani (Azeri Turk)	85.68609	6,480,273	6,626,975	8,056,695	MSY41a	44-AABA-fa	north azeri		0.01	663	2c.u.	3	3	3	0	3	Azerbaijani*	PNB b
489	Budug (Budukh)	0.06999	5,293	5,413	6,581	CEW17b	42-BCAC-b	budukh		0.09	5	0....	4	2	3	0	0		p.. b
490	Byelorussian	0.06476	4,898	5,009	6,089	CEW22c	53-AAAE-c	bielorusskiy		75.00	3,756	3A.uh	10	7	8	2	3	Byelorussian*	PNB b
491	Caucasian Mountain Jew	0.19999	15,125	15,467	18,804	CMT35	58-AACG-b	judeo-tat		0.00	0	0....	0	2	2	0	0	Judeo-tat	P.. b
492	Dargin	0.01216	920	940	1,143	CEW17b	42-BBBB-a	dargwa		0.01	0	1....	3	3	2	0	1	Dargwa	P.. b
493	Georgian	0.20220	15,292	15,638	19,012	CEW17c	42-CABB-a	kharthuli		40.00	6,255	2A.u.	9	6	8	2	1	Georgian	PNB b
494	German	0.01065	805	824	1,001	CEW19m	52-ABCE-a	standard hoch-deutsch		80.00	659	2B.uh	10	8	11	3	2	German*	PNB b
495	Jewish	0.17000	12,857	13,148	15,984	CMT35	52-ABCH	yiddish cluster		0.00	0	0B..h	0	4	6	0	0		PNB b
496	Judeo-Kurdish	0.08001	6,051	6,188	7,523	CMT35	58-AAAA-e	judeo-kurdish		0.00	0	1c...	0	1	3	0	0		pn. b
497	Kazakh	0.02334	1,765	1,805	2,195	MSY41e	44-AABC-c	kazakh		0.01	0	4A.u.	3	3	3	0	1	Kazakh	PN. b
498	Khinalug (Ketsh Khalkh)	0.02500	1,891	1,934	2,351	CEW17b	42-BCBA-a	khinalugh		0.00	0	0....	0	1	3	0	0		... p
499	Kryz (Dzhek, Katsy)	0.10093	7,633	7,806	9,490	CEW17b	42-BCAC-c	kryz		0.00	0	0....	0	1	0	0	0		p.. b
500	Kurdish	0.28460	21,524	22,011	26,760	CNT24c	58-AAAA-a	kurmanji		0.01	2	3c...	3	3	3	0	0	Kurdish: Kurmanji*	PN. b
501	Lak	0.01631	1,233	1,261	1,534	CEW17b	42-BBBA-a	lak		0.01	0	1....	3	3	0	0	0	Lak	P.. b
502	Lezgian (Lezghi)	2.37111	179,322	183,382	222,945	CEW17b	42-BCAC	south lezgin cluster		0.01	18	0....	3	4	0	0	1		P.. b
503	Moldavian	0.02728	2,063	2,110	2,565	CEW21f	51-AADC-ab	standard moldavia		82.00	1,730	1A.u.	10	7	10	2	1		pnb b
504	Mordvinian	0.01025	775	793	964	MSW51i	41-AADA-a	erzya		65.00	515	2....	10	8	8	1	1	Mordvin: Erzya*	PN. b
505	Ossete	0.03135	2,371	2,425	2,948	CNT24e	58-ABBA	oseti cluster		36.00	873	2....	9	5	8	1	1	Ossete*	PN. b
506	Persian	0.01378	1,042	1,066	1,296	CNT24f	58-AACC-c	standard farsi		0.00	0	1Asu.	0	3	2	0	0		PNB b
507	Polish	0.01015	768	785	954	CEW22i	53-AAAC-c	polski		91.00	714	2A.uh	10	8	13	3	3	Polish	PNB b
508	Romanian	0.01891	1,430	1,463	1,778	CEW21i	51-AADC-a	limba românească		80.00	1,170	3A.u.	10	9	10	0	0	Romanian	PNB b
509	Russian	3.00000	226,884	232,020	282,077	CEW22j	53-AAAE-d	russkiy	84	60.00	139,212	4B.uh	10	7	9	3	3	Russian	PNB b
510	Tajik	0.01000	756	773	940	CNT24g	58-AACC-j	tajiki		0.00	0	2asu.	0	3	3	0	1	Tajik*	PNB b
511	Talysh (Lenkoran)	1.94000	146,718	150,040	182,410	CNT24z	58-AACE-d	talishi		0.00	0	1....	0	1	3	0	0		... b
512	Tat (Mussulman Tat)	0.30000	22,688	23,202	28,208	CNT24f	58-AACG-a	muslim-tat		1.00	232	0....	6	4	3	0	1	Tat*	P.. b
513	Tatar	0.39906	30,180	30,863	37,522	MSY41h	44-AABB-e	tatar		1.50	463	2c.u.	6	4	8	0	1	Tatar: Kazan	Pn. b
514	Tsakhur (Caxur)	0.18968	14,345	14,670	17,835	CEW17b	42-BCAC-a	tsakhur		0.03	4	0....	3	1	0	0	0	Tsakhur	p.. p
515	Turkish	0.25217	19,071	19,503	23,710	MSY41j	44-AABA-a	osmanli		0.00	0	1A.u.	0	3	2	0	0	Turkish	PNB b
516	Udin (Udi, Alban)	0.05557	4,203	4,298	5,225	CEW17b	42-BCAC-d	udin		90.00	3,868	0....	10	6	11	2	1	Udin	P.. b
517	Ukrainian	0.46067	34,840	35,628	43,315	CEW22p	53-AAAE-b	ukrainskiy		75.00	26,721	3A.uh	10	7	9	3	3	Ukrainian	PNB b
518	Uzbek	0.01964	1,485	1,519	1,847	MSY41l	44-AABD-a	central uzbek		0.00	0	1A.u.	0	3	6	1	3	Uzbek*	PNb b
519	other minor peoples	0.10000	7,563	7,734	9,403	...				20.00	1,547		9	8	0	0	0		
	Bahamas	**100.00000**	**280,386**	**306,529**	**414,631**					**87.06**	**266,851**								
520	Black	67.50000	189,261	206,907	279,876	NFB68a	52-ABAF-n	bahamian-creole		88.80	183,733	1a..h	10	8	11	5	3		pn. b
521	British	12.00000	33,646	36,783	49,756	CEW19i	52-ABAC-b	standard-english		79.00	29,059	3Bsuh	10	9	12	5	1		PNB b
522	Greek	0.30000	841	920	1,244	CEW20	56-AAAA-c	dhimotiki		95.00	874	2B.uh	10	8	11	5	1	Greek: Modern	PNB b
523	Haitian Black	3.00000	8,412	9,196	12,439	NFB69b	51-AACC-b	haitien		95.00	8,736	3As..	10	9	11	5	2	Haitian*	PNB b
524	Han Chinese	0.20000	561	613	829	MSY42a	79-AAAB-ba	kuo-yü		50.00	307	2Bsuh	10	7	8	5	0	Chinese: Kuoyu*	PNB b
525	Jewish	0.30000	841	920	1,244	CMT35	52-ABAE-ce	bahamian-english		0.26	2	0A.uh	5	4	2	5	0		pnb b
526	Mulatto	14.20000	39,815	43,527	58,878	NFB68b	52-ABAF-n	bahamian-creole		88.00	38,304	1a..h	10	8	10	5	3		pn. b
527	USA White	2.40000	6,729	7,357	9,951	CEW19s	52-ABAC-s	general american		76.00	5,591	1Bsuh	10	9	13	5	3	English*	PNB b
528	other minor peoples	0.10000	280	307	415	...				80.00	245		10	7	8	5	0		
	Bahrain	**100.00000**	**557,564**	**617,217**	**858,368**					**10.16**	**62,698**								
529	Arab	1.00000	5,576	6,172	8,584	CMT30	12-AACF-i	kuwayti-qatari		1.00	62	1Asuh	6	4	5	2	0		pnb b
530	Bahraini Arab	63.90000	356,283	394,402	548,497	CMT30	12-AACF-id	`arab-bahraini		1.80	7,099	1Asuh	6	5	5	2	3		pnb b
531	British	2.10000	11,709	12,962	18,026	CEW19i	52-ABAC-b	standard-english		78.00	10,110	3Bsuh	10	8	12	3	1		PNB b
532	Filipino	4.50000	25,090	27,775	38,627	MSY44o	31-CKAA-a	proper tagalog		94.00	26,108	4Bs..	10	6	12	3	2	Tagalog	PNB b
533	Gujarati	2.00000	11,151	12,344	17,167	CNN25e	59-AAFH-b	standard gujaraati		2.00	247	2A.u.	6	5	2	2	0	Gujarati	PNB b
534	Jewish	0.10000	558	617	858	CMT35	12-AACF-i	kuwayti-qatari		0.00	0	1Asuh	0	4	2	1	0		pnb b
535	Korean	0.20000	1,115	1,234	1,717	MSY46	45-AAAA-b	kukö		70.00	864	2A...	10	6	12	3	3	Korean	PNB b
536	Malayali	3.50000	19,515	21,603	30,043	CNN23b	49-EBEB-a	malayalam		60.00	12,962	2Asu.	10	6	8	3	1	Malayalam	PNB b
537	Persian	13.00000	72,483	80,238	111,588	CNT24f	58-AACC-c	standard farsi		0.02	16	1Asu.	3	3	2	1	0		PNB b
538	Tamil	2.80000	15,612	17,282	24,034	CNN23c	49-EBEA-b	tamil		14.00	2,419	2Asu.	8	5	7	3	1	Tamil	PNB b
539	Telugu	2.00000	11,151	12,344	17,167	CNN23d	49-DBAB-a	telugu		11.00	1,358	2Asu.	8	6	7	2	3	Telugu	PNB b
540	USA White	0.30000	1,673	1,852	2,575	CEW19s	52-ABAC-s	general american		78.00	1,444	1Bsuh	10	8	11	3	1	English*	PNB b
541	Urdu	4.50000	25,090	27,775	38,627	CNN25r	59-AAFO-d	standard urdu		0.01	3	2Asuh	3	3	2	1	0	Urdu	PNB b
542	other minor peoples	0.10000	558	617	858	...				0.90	6		5	4	2	1	0		
	Bangladesh	**100.00000**	**118,615,703**	**129,155,152**	**178,751,214**					**0.72**	**931,741**								
543	Anglo-Bengali	0.00900	10,675	11,624	16,088	CNN25z	52-ABAD-af	bangladeshi-english		60.00	6,974	0A.uh	10	8	7	4	2		... .
544	Arab	0.03000	35,585	38,747	53,625	CMT30	12-AACF-g	syro-mesopotamian		0.10	39	1Asuh	5	1	1	1	0		pnb b
545	Arakanese (Maghi, Mogh)	0.13516	160,321	174,566	241,600	MSY50b	77-AABA-b	arakan		3.00	5,237	1csu.	6	4	6	2	2	Maghi*	Pnb .
546	Assamese	0.00800	9,489	10,332	14,300	CNN25a	59-AAFT-sc	standard axamiyaa		0.10	10	1asuh	5	4	7	3	3		pnb b
547	Baluch (Eastern Baloch)	0.00476	5,646	6,148	8,509	CNT24b	58-AABA-a	east balochi		0.00	0	1.s..	0	3	4	0	0	Baluchi: Eastern*	P.. b
548	Bawm Chin (Banjogi)	0.00636	7,544	8,214	11,369	MSY50z	73-DCCA-a	bawm		98.00	8,050	1csuh	10	8	14	4	2	Bawm*	PNB .
549	Bengali	79.06114	93,778,927	102,111,536	141,322,748	CNN25b	59-AAFT-c	standard baanglaa		0.14	142,956	4Asuh	5	4	8	4	4	Bengali	PNB .
550	Bengali (Hindu)	11.70000	13,878,037	15,111,153	20,913,892	CNN25b	59-AAFT-e	west bengali		1.70	256,890	1Asuh	6	4	9	3	3	Bengali: Musalmani*	PNB b
551	Bihari	1.50000	1,779,236	1,937,327	2,681,268	CNN25c	59-AAFO-d	standard urdu		0.01	194	2Asuh	3	2	4	1	0	Urdu	PNB b
552	British	0.00680	8,066	8,783	12,155	CEW19i	52-ABAC-b	standard-english	27	79.00	6,938	3Bsuh	10	8	12	4	3		PNB b
553	Burmese	0.20000	237,231	258,310	357,502	MSY50b	77-AABA-a	bama		0.20	517	4Asu.	5	5	2	3	2	Burmese	PNB b
554	Chak	0.00100	1,186	1,292	1,788	MSY50c	73-DCBA	haka-chin cluster		5.00	65	0as..	7	5	3	1	1		PNB .
555	Chakma	0.31292	371,172	404,152	559,348	MSY50s	59-AAFT-ie	chakma-baanglaa		3.00	12,125	1csuh	6	5	2	2	2	Chakma	PNb .
556	Dalu	0.00960	11,387	12,399	17,160	MSY50d	72-ACAA	proper garo cluster		40.00	4,960	0as..	9	5	6	2	1		PNB .
557	Darlong	0.00400	4,745	5,166	7,150	MSY50c	73-DCFA-a	darlong		54.00	2,790	0....	10	5	5	1	2	Darlong	PN. .
558	Eurasian (Anglo-Indian)	0.05000	59,308	64,578	89,376	CNN25z	52-ABAD-af	bangladeshi-english		40.00	25,831	0A.uh	9	8	8	4	3		... .
559	Falam Chin (Hallam)	0.00135	1,601	1,744	2,413	MSY50c	73-DDDB-a	falam		17.00	296	1.s..	8	6	5	3	0	Chin: Falam*	PNB b
560	Garo (Garrow, Mandi)	0.09937	117,868	128,341	177,625	MSY50d	72-ACAA-c	abeng		85.00	109,090	0as..	10	7	11	4	3	Garo: Abeng	PNB .
561	Gujarati	0.05000	59,308	64,578	89,376	CNN25e	59-AAFH-b	standard gujaraati	4	1.00	646	2A.u.	6	4	2	3	1	Gujarati	PNB b
562	Hadi	0.03660	43,413	47,271	65,423	MSY50d	72-ACAA	proper garo cluster		0.03	14	0as..	3	4	5	1	1		PNB .
563	Hajong (East Bengali)	0.02400	28,468	30,997	42,900	CNN25b	59-AAFT-l	haijong-bangali		1.00	310	1csuh	6	4	2	3	1		pnb .
564	Haka Chin (Tlantlang)	0.00092	1,091	1,188	1,645	MSY50c	73-DCBA-a	haka		35.00	416	0as..	9	6	7	3	2	Chin: Haka*	PNB .
565	Han Chinese	0.00100	1,186	1,292	1,788	MSY42a	52-ABAC	english-mainland cluster		5.00	65	3Bsuh	7	5	6	3	0		PNB b
566	Han Chinese	0.00200	2,372	2,583	3,575	MSY42a	59-AAFO-f	general urdu		0.10	3	1asuh	5	3	6	0	0		pnb b
567	Han Chinese (Cantonese)	0.00200	2,372	2,583	3,575	MSY42a	79-AAAM-a	central yue		2.00	52	3A.uh	6	4	6	1	0	Chinese, Yue	PNB b
568	Han Chinese (Mandarin)	0.00200	2,372	2,583	3,575	MSY42a	79-AAAB-ba	kuo-yü	1	3.00	77	2Bsuh	6	4	6	1	2	Chinese: Kuoyu*	PNB b
569	Hindi	0.30000	355,847	387,465	536,254	CNN25g	59-AAFO-e	general hindi	26	0.50	1,937	3Asuh	5	4	2	1	0		pnb b
570	Ho (Lanka Kol)	0.00136	1,613	1,757	2,431	AUG04a	46-CABA-e	ho		0.61	11	1cs..	5	4	2	1	1	Ho	PNb .
571	Khasi (Khuchia, Khasa, Ky)	0.16115	191,149	208,134	288,058	AUG03a	46-DAAA-a	khasi-war		56.00	116,555	2as..	10	6	7	4	3	Khasi	PNB .
572	Khumi Chin (Khami, Khuni)	0.00131	1,554	1,692	2,342	MSY50c	73-DEAB-a	khumi		60.00	1,015	0.s..	10	7	7	4	3	Chin: Khumi*	PN. .
573	Koch (Banai, Konch)	0.04000	47,446	51,662	71,500	MSY50d	72-ACAC-a	koch		10.00	5,166	0....	8	5	6	1	1		... .
574	Kuki Chin (Thado-Kuki)	0.00481	5,705	6,212	8,598	MSY50c	73-DAAE-a	thado		68.00	4,224	0as..	10	7	7	4	1	Chin, Thado	PNB .
575	Kurukh (Oraon, Dhangar)	0.02034	24,126	26,270	36,358	AUG06c	49-BAAA-b	chota-nagpur kurukh		60.00	15,762	1....	10	7	7	3	1	Kunrukh*	PN. .
576	Lushai (Mizo, Dulien)	0.00115	1,364	1,485	2,056	MSY50m	73-DCAA-a	lushai		98.00	1,456	0asu.	10	8	13	4	2	Lushai	PNB .
577	Mahili (Mahle)	0.01356	16,084	17,513	24,239	AUG04c	46-CABA-ac	mahali		48.00	8,406	1cs..	9	7	8	4	0		pnb b
578	Manipuri (Meithei, Kathe)	0.09937	117,868	128,341	177,625	MSY50o	73-CAAA-ab	manipuri		1.10	1,412	1as..	6	4	2	1	1	Manipuri*	PNB .
579	Migam	0.00500	5,931	6,458	8,938	MSY50d	72-ACAB-j	megam		60.00	3,875	0....	10	7	7	2	2		pn. .
580	Mru (Mro)	0.01961	23,261	25,327	35,053	MSY50c	73-BAAA-a	murung		0.20	51	0....	5	4	6	2	3	Mro*	P.. .
581	Munda (Mandari, Colh)	0.01356	16,084	17,513	24,239	AUG04b	46-CABA-d	mundari		16.00	2,802	3cs..	8	5	8	3	2	Mundari	PNB .
582	Nepalese	0.01274	15,112	16,454	22,773	CNN25k	59-AAFD-b	nepali		0.04	7	2Asu.	3	3	7	1	1	Nepali	PNB b

Continued opposite

Table 8-2 continued

EVANGELIZATION								EVANGELISM			ADDITIONAL DESCRIPTIVE DATA
Ref 1	*D* 28	*aC* 29	*CG%* 30	*r* 31	*E* 32	*U* 33	*W* 34	*e* 35	*R* 36	*T* 37	*Locations, civil divisions, literacy, religions, church history, denominations, dioceses, church growth, missions, agencies, ministries, movements* 38
467	2	10	1.60	5	69.00	31.00	B	15.11	89	5	Migrant workers. 94% Buddhists and Confucianists. D=RCC,Vienna Chinese Christian Fellowship.
468	2	10	0.32	6	99.81	0.19	C	437.56	31	10	Immigrants, migrant workers. D=RCC,EKHB. M=Reformed Ch of Hungary.
469	0	0	3.79	7	54.00	46.00	B	19.71	243	5	Immigrants from India and Pakistan. Hindus 60%, Muslims 15%(Sunnis, also Ahmadiyya Mission), Sikhs 10%.
470	1	10	0.31	7	99.84	0.16	C	466.03	24	10	Expatriates from Italy in business, commerce. All Catholics. D=RCC.
471	0	10	0.27	8	57.20	42.80	B	0.41	46	3	Austrian Jews practicing orthodox Judaism. From many homelands.
472	0	10	0.30	0	39.10	60.90	A	0.14	161	3	Refugees from Iraq, Iran, Turkey. 2,500 speak Sorani, 500 Zaza. Muslims 100% (Sunnis). M=vast network of agencies.
473	1	10	0.98	5	53.00	47.00	B	1.93	87	4	Migrant workers and refugees from Iran(2,000 Imami Shias). Muslims 95%, some Baha'is. D=RCC.
474	0	0	8.55	6	99.90	0.10	C	456.61	169	10	Refugees from Poland. Nonreligious 10%. D=RCC,PNCC,PMC,Polish Orthodox Church Abroad/GOC,PRCE,PELCE.
475	2	10	0.31	7	99.70	0.30	C	365.36	6	9	Refugees from USSR since 1917. D=Russian Orthodox Ch, RCC.
476	1	10	0.31	6	99.85	0.15	C	471.58	6	10	Migrant workers in Vienna and Burgenland. Muslims 15%. D=Serbian Orthodox Ch. M=FMB.
477	1	10	0.38	0	99.80	0.20	C	344.56	33	9	Gypsies also found in Yugoslavia, Italy, France, East and West Germany, Netherlands, Switzerland. D=RCC. M=GGMS.
478	1	10	-0.74	6	99.95	0.05	C	575.60	4	10	Southwest Austria. Citizens, originally from Slovenia(Yugoslavia). D=95% RCC.
479	2	10	0.32	2	99.70	0.30	C	334.70	28	9	Upper Wendish. Originally from East Germany. D=RCC,EKAB.
480	1	10	0.31	8	99.96	0.04	C	602.68	20	10	Expatriates from Spain in commerce, industry. Mostly Catholics. D=RCC.
481	0	10	4.40	8	52.10	47.90	B	0.19	269	3	Migrant workers from Turkey. Muslims 100%(Hanafi Sunnis). M=OM.
482	6	10	0.86	8	99.78	0.22	C	429.89	32	10	Expatriates in business, commerce. D=UMC,RCC,AC-E, EKD,SDA,JWs. M=FMB.
483	0	0	3.74	6	53.00	47.00	B	23.21	237	5	Refugees, immigrants from Viet Nam after 1970. Buddhists/New-Religionists 88%. D=RCC,Anglican Ch,Asian Christian Fellowship,SDA,ICFG.
484	0	10	0.31		99.68	0.32	C	264.85	8	8	Armenians, Bulgarians, Romanians, Assyrians, Koreans(M=PCK-Tonghap), and large numbers of other Eastern Europeans.
Azerbaijan											
485	2	6	0.90	6	99.68	0.32	C	332.58	31	9	Gregorians. In Nagorno-Karabakh AO (civil war from 1987 on), and Baku. Also living in 27 more countries. Nonreligious 25%, atheists 5%. D=Armenian Apostolics.
486	0	0	4.81	5	99.85	0.15	C	397.12	118	9	Refugees from Iraq. D=Ancient Ch of the East(Nestorians: P-Tehran),RCC(Chaldeans: P-Babylon).
487	0	6	1.62	0	21.01	78.99	A	0.00	342	1.07	From Dagestan (Russia). Muslims 100%(Shafi Sunnis). M=IBT.
488	2	5	3.33	1	33.01	66.99	A	0.01	335	2	Turkler, Airumy, Padar. 73% monolingual. 20 dialects. Muslims 90%(70% Shias,30% Hanafi Sunnis), nonreligious 10%. D=Protestants,ROC(D-Stavropol & Baku).
489	0	6	1.62	0	21.09	78.91	A	0.06	340	2	Unwritten; Azerbaijani used as literary language. Muslims 100%(Shafi Sunnis).
490	3	7	1.11	5	99.75	0.25	C	380.51	42	9	White Russians, from Belorussia. Nonreligious/atheists 25%. D=ROC,RCC,Old Ritualist Chs.
491	0	3	0.00	0	13.00	87.00	A	0.00	0	1.05	Also in Dagestan (Russia),Iran. Language: Judeo-Tati, Hebrew Tati. Ethnic name: Bik. Religious Jews, emigrating to Israel or USA.
492	0	6	0.00	0	21.01	78.99	A	0.00	0	1.07	From southern Dagestan (Russia). Muslims 100%(Shafi Sunnis). M=IBT.
493	1	7	1.66	4	96.00	4.00	B	140.16	47	7	Nonreligious/atheists 55%, Muslims 5%(Sunnis, Shias). D=Georgian Orthodox Ch.
494	2	7	1.66	8	99.80	0.20	C	432.16	52	10	Also found in Volga, Altai (Russia), Kirghizia. D=German ELC,AUCECB.
495	0	7	0.00	5	42.00	58.00	A	0.00	0	1.10	Bilingual in Azeri, Russian. Sizeable numbers have emigrated to Israel. Jewish by culture and religion.
496	0	5	0.00	0	20.00	80.00	A	0.00	0	1.08	Across Azerbaijan. Kurdish Jews, influenced by Hebrew.
497	0	7	0.00	4	37.01	62.99	A	0.01	0	2	Muslims 70%(Hanafi Sunnis, with Sufi influence), nonreligious 20%, atheists 10%. M=ROC.
498	0	7	0.00	0	15.00	85.00	A	0.00	0	1.04	On Shahdag Mountain. Unwritten language; Avar used as literary language. All shifting to Azerbaijani as mother tongue. Muslims 100%(Sunnis).
499	0	8	0.00	0	16.00	84.00	A	0.00	0	1.04	Mountain valleys. Unwritten language; Azerbaijani used as literary language. Muslims 100%(Sunnis).
500	0	6	0.70	0	27.01	72.99	A	0.01	274	2	Scattered groups across western Azerbaijan and in cities. Muslims 80%(Shias, Yazidis), nonreligious 20%.
501	0	6	0.00	0	18.01	81.99	A	0.00	0	1.06	From southern Dagestan. Lingua franca. Fluent in Azeri, Kumyk, or Russian. Muslims 100%(Shafi Sunnis).
502	0	7	1.52	0	19.01	80.99	A	0.00	363	1.05	Also in south Dagestan, Russia. 50% understand Russian. Lingua franca. Muslims 100%(Shafi Sunnis). M=IBT.
503	1	7	1.66	6	99.82	0.18	C	413.03	53	10	From Bessarabia, Romania, Bulgaria. Traditionally Orthodox. D=Russian Orthodox Ch.
504	1	7	1.66	7	99.65	0.35	C	268.09	40	8	From northern Mordvinia (Russia). Acculturated to Russian. Nonreligious 35%. D=Russian Orthodox Ch.
505	1	5	1.91	0	74.00	26.00	B	97.23	111	6	From South Ossetian AO (Georgia). Stockbreeders. Muslims 40%(Sunnis), nonreligious/atheists 24%. D=Russian Orthodox Ch.
506	0	5	0.00	5	35.00	65.00	A	0.00	0	1.12	Farsi is mother tongue for 31%. Muslims 90%(Imami Shias), Baha'is 10%.
507	4	7	1.66	6	99.91	0.09	C	531.44	28	10	Poles from western Ukraine, Poland. D=RCC,RDC,CEF,CWE(Polish Pentecostals).
508	0	0	4.88	6	99.80	0.20	C	370.84	129	9	Refugees from Romania since 1989. Nonreligious 20%. D=Romanian Orthodox Ch(P-Bucharest),RCC.
509	8	7	0.79	7	99.60	0.40	C	286.89	17	8	In 70 countries. Nonreligious 30%, atheists 8%. D=ROC,RCC,AUCECB,Old Ritualists,CEF,CCECB,SDA,IPKH.
510	0	6	0.00	4	37.00	63.00	A	0.00	0	1.12	Most are trilingual (with Uzbek, Russian, or Azeri). Muslims 90%(Hanafi Sunnis, some Shias), nonreligious 10%. M=CSI.
511	0	7	0.00	1	19.00	81.00	A	0.00	0	1.06	In southeast corner of Azerbaijan, along Caspian coast south of Viliazh-Chai river. Also in Iran. Bilingual in Azeri. Muslims 100%(Shias).
512	1	5	1.65	0	25.00	65.00	A	0.91	258	4	Workers in oil industry in and around Baku, also Derbent (Russia). Unwritten; Azeri used as literary language. Muslims 99% (Shias,some Sunnis).
513	1	7	1.66	6	42.50	57.50	A	2.32	159	4	70% bilingual in Russian. Muslims 83%(Hanafi Sunnis), nonreligious 15%. D=ROC(Kryashen).
514	0	7	1.40	0	16.03	83.97	A	0.01	410	2	Also in southern Dagestan, and Azerbaijan. Unwritten; Avar used as literary language. Muslims 100%(Shafi Sunnis).
515	0	6	0.00	8	38.00	62.00	A	0.00	0	1.11	Across Central Asia. Muslims 98%(85% Hanafi Sunnis, 15% Alawi Shias).
516	1	7	1.20	0	99.90	0.10	C	430.33	46	10	Vartashen and Nidzh villages in Azerbaijan; also in Georgia. Unwritten; Azeri used as literary language. Muslims 10%(Shias). D=Armenian Apostolic Ch(Gregorian).
517	7	7	1.39	6	99.75	0.25	C	391.46	50	9	In 15 countries. Nonreligious/atheists 21%. D=ROC(E-Ukraine),Ukrainian Catholic Ch,AUCECB,CEF,CCECB,JWs,SDA.
518	3	6	0.00	5	43.00	57.00	A	0.00	0	1.13	Literates 100%. 55% speak Russian. Muslims 80%(Hanafi Sunnis), nonreligious/atheists 20%. D=ROC,AUCECB,SDA.
519	0	0	1.66		33.00	67.00	A	24.09	138	5	Lithuanians, Greeks and many nationalities working in oil industry.
Bahamas											
520	5	9	1.63	8	99.89	0.11	C	504.97	40	10	Afro-American spiritists 1%. D=CPWI,RCC(D-Nassau),BBU,COG,&c. M=USPG,OSB,SFM,CSSp,BMS,FMB.
521	1	10	1.78	8	99.79	0.21	C	438.29	53	10	Speakers of Standard English and also its dialect Bajan(Barbadian English). Settlers, expatriates. D=CPWI(D-Nassau and the Bahamas). M=USPG.
522	1	10	4.57	7	99.95	0.05	C	572.13	92	10	Traders, merchants, from Greece. D=Greek Orthodox AD North & South America.
523	2	7	2.19	4	99.95	0.05	C	551.33	52	10	Refugees from Haiti. Mostly monolinguals. Afro-American spiritists 5%. D=RCC, many Baptists.
524	0	10	3.48	7	99.50	0.50	B	211.70	98	8	Workers in commerce, banking, finance, industry. Chinese folk-religionists 30%, nonreligious 20%.
525	0	10	0.70	8	48.26	51.74	A	0.45	79	3	Mainly of European or North American origin. Orthodox Judaism practised.
526	2	10	1.71	8	99.88	0.12	C	494.64	43	10	Black/White mixed-race persons. Ras Tafari Movement. D=CPWI,RCC(D-Nassau). M=USPG,OSB,SFM,CSSp,FMB.
527	5	8	4.83	8	99.76	0.24	C	410.55	106	10	Large population of expatriates from USA in all walks of life. D=UMC,RCC,PCUSA,CPWI,BBU.
528	0	10	3.25		99.80	0.20	C	338.72	77	9	Haitians, and many other Caribbean islanders; other Europeans, Latin Americans.
Bahrain											
529	0	6	4.21	7	47.00	53.00	A	1.71	286	4	Professionals, internationals. Official language for education, officialdom, international communication. Muslims 98%.
530	3	6	6.79	7	54.80	45.20	B	3.60	375	4	Eastern Colloquial Arabic. Muslims 99%(50% Sunnis,50% Shias). D=ECJME,RCC(VA-Arabia),GOC. M=TEAM,FMB,FI,MEM.
531	1	9	4.32	8	99.78	0.22	C	421.35	101	10	Expatriates from Britain, in government, educated. D=Episcopal Ch in Jerusalem & Middle East(D-Cyprus & The Gulf).
532	2	6	8.19	5	99.94	0.06	C	562.68	148	10	Migrant workers from Philippines. Strong Christians. D=90%RCC (2 congregations), NEC (one congregation).
533	0	6	3.26	6	47.00	53.00	A	3.43	249	4	Migrant workers from Gujarat, India. Hindus 60%, Muslims 37%.
534	0	6	0.00	7	36.00	64.00	A	0.00	0	1.14	European Jews largely, practicing orthodox Judaism.
535	4	6	4.56	6	99.70	0.30	C	350.03	103	9	Migrant workers from South Korea. Buddhists/shamanists 25%. Mostly Christians. D=National Ev Ch of Bahrain, M=PC(H),RCC,&c.
536	4	6	7.43	4	99.60	0.40	C	264.99	191	8	Migrants from Kerala, India. Hindus 35%. D=CSI,Malayalee Christian Congregation,Syrian OC,Mar Thoma SC (total 12 congregations). M=FMB.
537	0	6	2.81	5	37.02	62.98	A	0.02	260	2	Refugees and migrant workers from Iran. Muslims 99% (Imami Shias).
538	3	6	5.64	6	73.00	27.00	B	37.30	249	5	Migrants from south India. Hindus 80%. D=Assemblies(Jehova Shammah), CSI,RCC. Total 6 Tamil congregations. M=FMB.
539	3	6	5.03	5	70.00	30.00	B	28.10	236	5	Migrants from AP, south India. Hindus 85%. D=National Ev Church of Bahrain, RCC,CSI. Total 4 Telugu congregations.
540	2	9	5.10	8	99.78	0.22	C	412.81	113	10	Expatriates from USA, in commerce, industry. D=ECJME,RCC. M=FMB.
541	0	6	1.10	5	42.01	57.99	A	0.01	139	2	Migrant workers from Pakistan, India. Muslims 100%(Hanafi Sunnis).
542	0	6	-2.15		17.90	82.10	A	0.58	15	3	Palestinians (Shafi Sunnis,GOC,RCC), Japanese, Sinhalese, other Arabs, Asians, Europeans.
Bangladesh											
543	2	5	5.10	8	99.60	0.40	C	232.14	158	8	Mixed-race persons (British/Indian). In administration, government. D=RCC,COB.
544	0	4	1.48	7	36.10	63.90	A	0.13	165	3	Traders originally from Arab countries of Middle East. Arabic now compulsory in all primary schools. Muslims 95%.
545	2	5	1.52	1	38.00	62.00	A	4.16	190	4	Morma. Chittagong Hills. Mainly in Burma, a few in India, China. A form of Burmese. Many bilingual in Bengali. Expulsions. Buddhists 90%, some animists.
546	3	8	1.62	4	50.10	49.90	B	0.18	144	3	Hindus 70%, Muslims 30%(Hanafi Sunnis). 14 million other Assamese live in Assam(India); also China, Bhutan. D=RCC,BBU,BUB.
547	0	4	0.00	1	17.00	83.00	A	0.00	0	1.07	Originally from West Pakistan. Only 130 mother tongue speakers, rest use Bengali. Muslims 100%(Sunnis).
548	1	7	1.52	0	99.98	0.02	C	550.85	47	10	Chittagong Hills. Also India, Burma. Tropical forest. Nomads, agriculturalists. D=Bawm Evangelical Christian Ch. M=NEIGM,UBS.
549	4	5	5.68	6	59.14	40.86	B	0.30	326	3	23% literates. Muslims 99%(Hanafi Sunnis; Chistiyya,Qadiriyya). D=RCC(4 Dioceses; 30,000 speak Portuguese),COB,BBU,BUB. M=SX,YWAM,ABWE.
550	2	5	5.64	6	56.70	43.30	B	3.51	338	4	Refugees since 1970 civil war. Hindus 99%. Peasant wet rice cultivators. D=COB,RCC. M=WVI,WMPL,FMB. R=FEBA,VERITAS,AWR.
551	0	5	1.52	5	41.01	58.99	A	0.01	170	2	Refugees from Bihar(India), hated for their ties to Pakistan and massacres of Bengalis in 1971. Muslims 100%(Hanafi Sunnis). R=VERITAS.
552	4	10	1.52	8	99.79	0.21	C	438.29	48	10	Expatriates from Britain, in education, development. D=COB,SDA,JWs,RCC.
553	1	8	1.51	6	51.20	48.80	B	0.37	140	3	Mainly in Burma; also in India, USA. Theravada Buddhists 97%, Muslims 2%(Shafi Sunnis). D=BBC. M=LBI,UBS.
554	0	6	1.55	4	44.00	56.00	A	8.03	165	4	Chittagong Hills. Most in Arakan Blue Mountains (Burma). Tropical forest. Agriculturalists. Animists 95%. M=YWAM.
555	2	6	1.52	1	38.00	62.00	A	4.16	189	4	Southeast, Chittagong Hills; also India. 36 dialects. 60% literates. Guerilla war against Bengali settlers. Buddhists 90% (with sacred texts in Pali and Chakma).
556	1	6	1.52	4	87.00	13.00	B	127.02	79	7	Animists 60%. D=GBU (Garo missionaries).
557	2	5	1.52	0	86.00	14.00	B	169.50	83	7	Also in India. Animists 45%. D=COB,RCC.
558	4	10	1.52	8	94.00	6.00	B	137.24	74	7	Mixed-race persons other than Anglo-Bengalis: Pakistanis, Indians. D=RCC,SDA,JWs,COB.
559	0	5	1.51	0	52.00	48.00	B	32.26	138	5	Mainly in Burma, a few in India. Animists 80%. Mainly Baptists.
560	3	6	3.79	4	99.85	0.15	C	449.86	91	10	Majority in Assam (India). Literates 65%. Animists still 10%. D=Mymensingh Garo Baptist Union,RCC(M-Dhaka),Ch of Sylhet. M=CSC,PCW,ABFMS,FMB.
561	1	5	1.52	6	46.00	54.00	A	1.67	151	4	Migrants from Maharashtra, India. Hindus 60%, Muslims 38%. D=COB.
562	0	4	1.55	4	35.03	64.97	A	0.03	199	2	Animists(tribal religionists) 98%. M=WVI.
563	1	5	1.51	6	36.00	64.00	A	1.31	218	4	Many in India also Hinduized animists 95%. D=Garo Baptist Union. M=WVI. Resistant to Christianity.
564	2	6	1.52	4	85.00	15.00	B	108.58	84	7	Almost all in Burma, some in India. Animists 65%. D=Baptists, COB.
565	0	6	1.55	8	60.00	40.00	B	10.95	100	5	English-speaking Chinese in urban commerce. Folk-religionists/Buddhists 75%.
566	0	6	1.10	5	39.10	60.90	A	0.14	123	3	Urdu-speaking Chinese from several countries of origin. Mostly Buddhists.
567	0	6	1.57	8	52.00	48.00	B	3.79	117	4	Only a few Chinese live in Bangladesh; most in Dacca. South China origins.
568	2	6	1.52	7	57.00	43.00	B	6.24	104	4	Chinese from several parts of Asian diaspora. Mainly in commerce. D=AoG,RCC.
569	0	6	1.52	7	42.50	57.50	A	0.77	162	3	Indians from north India. Hindus 90%.
570	0	5	1.72	1	27.61	72.39	A	0.61	270	3	Vast majority live in India, Animists 80%, Hindus 20%. M=UBS.
571	2	5	4.30	4	99.56	0.44	B	228.92	142	8	In north. Majority in India. Animists 40%. D=COG(Anderson),Ch of Sylhet. M=PCW,COG,LBI,UBS.
572	3	6	1.52	0	99.60	0.40	C	221.19	71	8	Mostly Burma, some in India. Agriculturalists. Tropical forest. Animists 40%. D=ECC,SDA,AoG.
573	1	4	1.52	0	34.00	66.00	A	12.41	203	5	Also in India (Assam, Tripura). Mostly animists 90%. D=Garo Baptist Union. M=FMB.
574	1	6	1.52	4	99.68	0.32	C	295.35	60	8	Great majority in India, some in Burma. Animists 30%. D=Baptist Chs.
575	1	5	1.52	0	96.00	4.00	C	210.24	75	8	Primarily in India. Animists 30%, Hindus 10%. D=BELC.
576	2	6	1.52	4	99.98	0.02	C	558.01	46	10	Mizo Hills. Most in India, some in Burma, China. Tropical forest. D=Baptist Union,Ch of Sylhet. M=BMS,PCW.
577	0	5	1.52	4	90.00	10.00	B	157.68	77	7	Majority in India (Assam, Bihar, Orissa, West Bengal). Related to the Santal. Animists 50%.
578	1	5	1.52	4	40.10	59.90	A	1.61	179	4	Over a million in India, some in Burma. Hindus 85%, animists 7%, Muslims 6%. D=Baptist Ch.
579	2	6	1.52	0	95.00	5.00	C	208.05	73	8	Northeast. Related to Garo. Animists 35%. D=GBU,RCC.
580	2	5	1.55	0	26.20	73.80	A	0.19	277	3	200 villages in Chittagong Hills. Most in Burma, also in India. Animists (with strong Buddhist elements) 99%. D=Bawm Independent Ch,BECC. M=ABWE,NEIGM.
581	1	6	1.52	1	63.00	37.00	B	36.79	114	5	Most in India, also in Nepal. Animists 80%. D=BELC. M=WVI,CNI.
582	3	5	1.96	4	46.04	53.96	A	0.06	194	2	Immigrants, migrants from Nepal and India. Hindus 99%. D=RCC,COB,BUB. M=ABCUSA.

Continued overleaf

Table 8-2 continued

PEOPLE		POPULATION				IDENTITY CODE		LANGUAGE		CHURCH		MINISTRY						SCRIPTURE		
Ref 1	*Ethnic name* 2	*P%* 3	*In 1995* 4	*In 2000* 5	*In 2025* 6	*Race* 7	*Language* 8	*Autoglossonym* 9	*S* 10	*AC* 11	*Members* 12	*Jayuh* 13-17	*d* 18	*wa* 19	*xc* 20	*mc* 21	*mi* 22	*Biblioglossonym* 23	*Pub* 24-26	*ss* 27
583	Oraon Sadri	0.12055	142,991	155,697	215,485	AUG06c	59-AAFQ-l	oraon-sadri		48.00	74,734	1.s..	9	7	7	3	1	Sadri	pn.	.
584	Orisi (Utkali, Vadiya)	0.02519	29,879	32,534	45,027	CNN251	59-AAFS-a	odiaa		1.00	325	3Asu.	6	4	2	1	1	Oriya	PNB	b
585	Paharia	0.00700	8,303	9,041	12,513	AUG04c	46-CABA-ad	paharia		25.00	2,260	1cs..	9	6	8	4	3		pnb	b
586	Pankhu (Panko)	0.00251	2,977	3,242	4,487	MSY50c	73-DCAC-a	pankhu		95.00	3,080	0....	10	7	15	2	1		...	.
587	Parsi	0.00023	273	297	411	CNN25m	58-AACC-a	parsi-i		0.00	0	1Asu.	0	3	5	0	0	Gujarati: Parsi	PNb	b
588	Punjabi	0.01833	21,742	23,674	32,765	CNN25n	59-AAFE-c	general panjabi		1.00	237	1Asu.	6	4	8	1	0		PNB	b
589	Riang (Kau Bru)	0.00095	1,127	1,227	1,698	MSY50s	72-AABA-b	riang		6.00	74	1.s..	7	5	6	3	1	Riang	PNb	.
590	Santal (Satar)	0.32103	380,792	414,627	573,845	AUG04c	46-CABA-a	santali		22.00	91,218	2as..	9	6	10	4	3	Santali	PNB	b
591	Shendu (Khieng)	0.00113	1,340	1,459	2,020	MSY50m	73-DEEA-b	shendu		7.00	102	0.s..	7	5	2	3	0		pn.	.
592	Southern Chin (Asho Chin)	0.00157	1,862	2,028	2,806	MSY50c	73-DEEA-c	asho		60.00	1,217	0.s..	10	7	7	4	3	Chin: Asho*	PN.	b
593	Sylhetti Bengali	4.68595	5,558,273	6,052,146	8,376,193	CNN25b	59-AAFT-k	sylhetti-bengali		0.10	6,052	3csuh	5	4	3	1	0		pnb	b
594	Tajpuri (Rajbansi)	0.01000	11,862	12,916	17,875	CNN25b	59-AAFT-ha	rajbangshi		0.01	1	1csuh	3	4	3	1	0		pnb	b
595	Tangchangya	0.01949	23,118	25,172	34,839	MSY50p	59-AAFT-m	tangchangya-bengali		1.00	252	1csuh	6	4	2	1	0		pnb	.
596	Telugu	0.00680	8,066	8,783	12,155	CNN23d	49-DBAB-a	telugu		10.00	878	2Asu.	8	5	7	2	1	Telugu	PNB	b
597	Tipperah (Tippera-Bengali)	0.09114	108,106	117,712	162,914	MSY50s	73-DDDB-a	falam		1.00	1,177	1.s..	6	4	8	3	3	Chin: Falam*	PNB	b
598	Tripuri (Tripura)	0.07077	83,944	91,403	126,502	MSY50s	72-AABA-a	kok-borok		1.30	1,188	1.s..	6	4	2	2	3	Kok Borok	PNB	.
599	USA White	0.00100	1,186	1,292	1,788	CEW19s	52-ABAC-s	general american		78.00	1,007	1Bsuh	10	10	12	0	0	English*	PNB	b
600	Urdu	0.60000	711,694	774,931	1,072,507	CNN25r	59-AAFO-d	standard urdu	38	0.01	77	2Asuh	3	3	2	1	1	Urdu	PNB	b
601	Ushoi (Unshoi)	0.00442	5,243	5,709	7,901	MSY50s	73-DDDB-a	falam		1.00	57	1.s..	6	3	8	0	0	Chin: Falam*	PNB	b
602	Usipi	0.03000	35,585	38,747	53,625	MSY50s	72-AABA-ae	usipi		1.00	387	1.s..	6	4	5	2	1	Usipi	Pnb	.
603	other minor peoples	0.03000	35,585	38,747	53,625	...				0.50	194		5	5	2	3	0			
	Barbados	**100.00000**	**264,306**	**270,449**	**296,753**					**72.79**	**196,858**									
604	Arab	0.04000	106	108	119	CMT30	12-AACF-f	syro-palestinian		19.00	21	1Asuh	8	5	7	3	0	Arabic: Lebanese*	Pnb	b
605	Barbadian Black	87.08000	230,158	235,507	258,413	NFB68a	52-ABAF-z	bajan		74.10	174,511	1a..h	10	8	10	5	3		pn.	b
606	Black Carib (Garifuna)	0.05100	135	138	151	MIR39c	80-ACAA-d	garifuna		80.00	110	4.s..	10	7	8	4	3	Garifuna	PN.	b
607	British	4.30000	11,365	11,629	12,760	CEW19i	52-ABAC-b	standard-english		79.00	9,187	3Bsuh	10	9	12	5	1		PNB	b
608	Greek	0.10000	264	270	297	CEW20	56-AAAA-c	dhimotiki		95.00	257	2B.uh	10	8	11	5	1	Greek: Modern	PNB	b
609	Han Chinese	0.05000	132	135	148	MSY42a	79-AAAB-ba	kuo-yü		9.00	12	2Bsuh	7	6	2	5	0	Chinese: Kuoyu*	PNB	b
610	Indo-Pakistani	1.10000	2,907	2,975	3,264	CNN25g	59-AAFO-e	general hindi		4.00	119	3Asuh	6	5	4	5	0		pnb	b
611	Jewish	0.01200	32	32	36	CMT35	52-ABAC-b	standard-english		0.00	0	3Bsuh	0	3	2	1	0		PNB	b
612	Mulatto	6.00000	15,858	16,227	17,805	NFB68b	52-ABAF-z	bajan		61.80	10,028	1a..h	10	8	9	5	1		pn.	b
613	USA White	1.20000	3,172	3,245	3,561	CEW19s	52-ABAC-s	general american		78.00	2,531	1Bsuh	10	10	12	0	0	English*	PNB	b
614	other minor peoples	0.06700	177	181	199	...				45.00	82		9	6	2	5	0			
	Belgium	**100.00000**	**10,088,045**	**10,161,164**	**9,917,861**					**83.84**	**8,518,694**									
615	Albanian	0.03300	3,329	3,353	3,273	CEW13	55-AAAB-a	standard tosk		20.00	671	0A...	9	8	6	5	3	Albanian: Tosk*	PNB	b
616	Algerian Arab	0.18000	18,158	18,290	17,852	CMT30	12-AACB-b	east maghrebi		2.00	366	2A.uh	6	5	6	1	1	Arabic: Algerian*	PNB	b
617	Arabized Berber	0.40000	40,352	40,645	39,671	CMT32a	12-AACB-b	east maghrebi	1	1.00	406	2A.uh	6	5	5	1	1	Arabic: Algerian*	PNB	b
618	British	0.30000	30,264	30,483	29,754	CEW19i	52-ABAC-b	standard-english	26	79.00	24,082	3Bsuh	10	9	8	5	1		PNB	b
619	Cambodian	0.03400	3,430	3,455	3,372	AUG03b	46-FBAA-b	khmae		5.00	173	2A...	7	5	5	2	1	Khmer*	PNB	b
620	Dutch	0.60000	60,528	60,967	59,507	CEW19h	52-ABCA-a	algemeen-nederlands	69	76.00	46,335	2Bsuh	10	9	15	5	1	Dutch	PNB	b
621	Egyptian Arab	0.10000	10,088	10,161	9,918	CMT30	12-AACF-a	masri		5.00	508	2Asuh	7	5	7	3	2	Arabic*	PNB	b
622	Esperanto	0.00000	0	0	0	CEW21z	51-AAAC-a	proper esperanto	3	70.00	0	0A...	10	9	6	5	0	Esperanto	PNB	b
623	Fleming (Flemish)	53.65000	5,412,236	5,451,464	5,320,932	CEW19k	52-ABCA-g	oostvlaandersch	69	89.40	4,873,609	1Bsuh	10	9	16	5	3		pnb	b
624	French	2.00000	201,761	203,223	198,357	CEW21b	51-AABI-d	general français	71	86.00	174,772	1B.uh	10	9	14	5	3	French	PNB	b
625	German	1.52000	153,338	154,450	150,751	CEW19m	52-ABCE-a	standard hoch-deutsch	22	88.00	135,916	2B.uh	10	9	13	5	3	German*	PNB	b
626	Greek	0.40000	40,352	40,645	39,671	CEW20	56-AAAA-c	dhimotiki	1	95.00	38,612	2B.uh	10	8	8	4	1	Greek: Modern	PNB	b
627	Han Chinese (Cantonese)	0.08000	8,070	8,129	7,934	MSY42a	79-AAAM-a	central yue		25.10	2,040	3A.uh	9	7	8	4	0	Chinese, Yue	PNB	b
628	Han Chinese (Mandarin)	0.03000	3,026	3,048	2,975	MSY42a	79-AAAB-ba	kuo-yü	1	12.00	366	2Bsuh	8	6	8	4	0	Chinese: Kuoyu*	PNB	b
629	Italian	2.60000	262,289	264,190	257,864	CEW21e	51-AABQ-c	standard italiano	4	90.00	237,771	2B.uh	10	9	15	5	2	Italian	PNB	b
630	Jewish	0.30000	30,264	30,483	29,754	CMT35	51-AABI-d	general français		0.10	30	1B.uh	5	5	4	4	0	French	PNB	b
631	Kabyle	0.50000	50,440	50,806	49,589	CMT32c	10-AAAC-h	tha-qabaylith		5.00	2,540	1a...	7	5	7	4	3	Kabyle: Greater	PN.	b
632	Kurdish (Kurd)	0.26000	26,229	26,419	25,786	CNT24c	58-AAAA-a	kurmanji		0.10	26	3c...	5	5	5	3	1	Kurdish: Kurmanji*	PN.	b
633	Libyan Arab	0.05000	5,044	5,081	4,959	CMT30	12-AACB-b	east maghrebi		0.20	10	2A.uh	5	5	6	3	1	Arabic: Algerian*	PNB	b
634	Lingala (Zairian)	0.21000	21,185	21,338	20,828	NAB57c	99-AUIF-b	vehicular lingala		75.00	16,004	4asu.	10	9	7	5	3	Lingala	PNB	b
635	Luxemburger	0.15200	15,334	15,445	15,075	CEW19o	52-ABCD-b	letzebürgesch-t.		88.00	13,592	0a.uh	10	9	8	5	1	Luxembourgeois	...	b
636	Moroccan Arab	1.30000	131,145	132,095	128,932	CMT30	12-AACB-a	west maghrebi		0.50	660	1A.uh	5	5	5	1	1		pnb	b
637	Persian	0.03500	3,531	3,556	3,471	CNT24f	58-AACC-c	standard farsi		4.00	142	1Asu.	6	5	5	2	2		PNB	b
638	Polish (Pole)	0.40000	40,352	40,645	39,671	CEW22i	53-AAAC-c	polski	1	90.00	36,580	2A.uh	10	9	8	4	1	Polish	PNB	b
639	Portuguese	0.80000	80,704	81,289	79,343	CEW21g	51-AABA-e	general português		93.00	75,599	2Bsuh	10	9	15	4	1	Portuguese	PNB	b
640	Rom Gypsy	0.14500	14,628	14,734	14,381	CNN25f	59-AFAA-a	rodi		80.00	11,787	0B.uh	10	7	8	3	1	Calo	P..	b
641	Russian	0.20000	20,176	20,322	19,836	CEW22j	53-AAAE-d	russkiy	1	70.00	14,226	4B.uh	10	7	8	5	2	Russian	PNB	b
642	Spaniard	0.70000	70,616	71,128	69,425	CEW21k	51-AABB-c	general español	3	96.00	68,283	2B.uh	10	9	15	5	1	Spanish	PNB	b
643	Tunisian Arab	0.12000	12,106	12,193	11,901	CMT30	12-AACB-b	east maghrebi		0.30	37	2A.uh	5	5	5	1	1	Arabic: Algerian*	PNB	b
644	Turk	0.60000	60,528	60,967	59,507	MSY41j	44-AABA-a	osmanli		0.10	61	1A.u.	5	5	5	3	3	Turkish	PNB	b
645	USA White	0.28000	28,247	28,451	27,770	CEW19s	52-ABAC-s	general american		78.00	22,192	1Bsuh	10	10	13	0	0	English*	PNB	b
646	Vietnamese	0.03100	3,127	3,150	3,075	MSY52b	46-EBAA-ac	general viêt		17.00	535	1Asu.	8	7	6	4	1	Vietnamese	PNB	b
647	Walloon (French)	31.60000	3,187,822	3,210,928	3,134,044	CEW21l	51-AABH-f	wallon	71	84.50	2,713,234	0A.uh	10	9	16	5	1	French: Walloon	P..	b
648	other minor peoples	0.39000	39,343	39,629	38,680	...				19.00	7,529		8	8	2	5	3			
	Belize	**100.00000**	**213,332**	**240,709**	**370,035**					**81.9**	**197,139**									
649	Belizean Black	35.40000	75,520	85,211	130,992	NFB68a	52-ABAF-d	belizean-creole	88	82.00	69,873	1a..h	10	9	11	5	3	Belize Creole English	pn.	b
650	Black Carib	6.60000	14,080	15,887	24,422	MIR39c	80-ACAA-d	garifuna		92.23	14,652	4.s..	10	7	7	5	3	Garifuna	PN.	b
651	British	0.70000	1,493	1,685	2,590	CEW19i	52-ABAC-b	standard-english	71	90.00	1,516	3Bsuh	10	9	13	5	2		PNB	b
652	German (Low German)	3.40000	7,253	8,184	12,581	CEW19m	52-ABCC	north deutsch cluster		90.00	7,366	2A.uh	10	9	12	5	1	German: Low*	PNB	b
653	Guatemalan Mestizo	22.05000	47,040	53,076	81,593	CLN29	51-AABB-hc	guatemalteco		83.00	44,053	1A.uh	10	9	10	5	2		pnb	b
654	Guatemalan White	1.00000	2,133	2,407	3,700	CLT27	51-AABB-hc	guatemalteco		96.00	2,311	1A.uh	10	9	11	5	3		pnb	b
655	Han Chinese	0.50000	1,067	1,204	1,850	MSY42a	79-AAAB-ba	kuo-yü		20.11	242	2Bsuh	9	6	8	4	1	Chinese: Kuoyu*	PNB	b
656	Honduran Mestizo	2.50000	5,333	6,018	9,251	CLN29	51-AABB-he	hondureño		97.00	5,837	1A.uh	10	9	10	5	2		pnb	b
657	Indo-Pakistani	3.50000	7,467	8,425	12,951	CNN25g	59-AAFO-e	general hindi		10.05	847	3Asuh	8	6	3	5	0		pnb	b
658	Itza (Icaiche Maya)	0.30000	640	722	1,110	MIR37b	68-ABAB-b	petén-itza		97.00	700	0....	10	8	11	3	3		pn.	b
659	Jewish	1.20000	2,560	2,889	4,440	CMT35	52-ABAE-ca	belizean-english		0.09	3	0A.uh	4	5	3	5	0		pnb	b
660	Kekchi	4.30000	9,173	10,350	15,912	MIR37b	68-AEAA	kekchi cluster		98.00	10,143	4....	10	9	10	5	3	Kekchi	PNB	b
661	Mestizo	3.00000	6,400	7,221	11,101	CLN29	51-AABB-hb	beliceño		95.00	6,860	1A.uh	10	9	8	5	3		pnb	b
662	Mopan Maya	3.70000	7,893	8,906	13,691	MIR37b	68-ABAB-c	mopan		93.00	8,283	0....	10	8	7	5	1	Maya: Mopan*	PN.	b
663	Mulatto	7.96000	16,981	19,160	29,455	NFB68b	52-ABAF-d	belizean-creole		84.00	16,095	1a..h	10	9	10	5	3	Belize Creole English	pn.	b
664	Syrian Arab	0.09000	192	217	333	CMT30	12-AACF-f	syro-palestinian		40.00	87	1Asuh	9	6	7	5	2	Arabic: Lebanese*	Pnb	b
665	USA White	0.60000	1,280	1,444	2,220	CEW19s	52-ABAC-s	general american		78.00	1,127	1Bsuh	10	10	12	0	0	English*	PNB	b
666	Yucatec (Maya)	3.00000	6,400	7,221	11,101	MIR37b	68-ABAA-b	south yucatec		94.00	6,788	1c...	10	8	7	5	3		pnb	.
667	other minor peoples	0.20000	427	481	740	...				74.00	356		10	6	6	5	0			
	Belorussia	**100.00000**	**10,391,327**	**10,236,181**	**9,495,683**					**64.32**	**6,584,078**									
668	Armenian	0.04859	5,049	4,974	4,614	CEW14	57-AAAA-b	ashkharik		70.00	3,482	4A.u.	10	7	9	5	2	Armenian: Modern, Eastern	PNB	b
669	Azerbaijani	0.04934	5,127	5,051	4,685	MSY41a	44-AABA-fa	north azeri		0.00	0	2c.u.	0	3	3	0	2	Azerbaijani*	PNB	b
670	Bashkir	0.01233	1,281	1,262	1,171	MSY41b	44-AABB-g	bashqurt		7.00	88	1A.u.	7	5	7	0	1	Bashkir	Pn.	b
671	Bulgar (Bulgarian)	0.00801	832	820	761	CEW22b	53-AAAH-b	bulgarski		72.00	590	2A.uh	10	6	8	5	1	Bulgarian	PNB	b
672	Byelorussian	78.35416	8,142,037	8,020,474	7,440,263	CEW22c	53-AAAE-c	bielorusskiy		65.50	5,253,410	3A.uh	10	8	9	5	1	Byelorussian*	PNB	b
673	Chuvash	0.03273	3,401	3,350	3,108	MSY41c	44-AAAA-a	chuvash		35.00	1,173	2....	9	6	8	0	1	Chuvash	PN.	b
674	Estonian	0.00792	823	811	752	MSW51a	41-AAAC-b	eesti		71.00	576	4A.u.	10	8	8	5	2	Estonian: Tallinn	PNB	b
675	Georgian	0.02798	2,907	2,864	2,657	CEW17c	42-CABB-a	kharthuli		40.00	1,146	2A.u.	9	6	8	5	1	Georgian	PNB	b
676	German	0.03464	3,600	3,546	3,289	CEW19m	52-ABCE-a	standard hoch-deutsch		80.00	2,837	2B.uh	10	8	13	5	2	German*	PNB	b
677	Jewish	0.60000	62,348	61,417	56,974	CMT35	52-ABCH	yiddish cluster		0.00	0	0B..h	0	3	6	4	0		PNB	b
678	Karelian	0.00904	939	925	858	MSW51c	41-AAAB-a	central karely		67.00	620	1....	10	6	8	5	3	Karelian	P..	b
679	Kazakh	0.02232	2,319	2,285	2,119	MSY41e	44-AABC-c	kazakh		0.00	0	4A.u.	0	3	3	3	2	Kazakh	PN.	b
680	Latvian (Lett)	0.02618	2,720	2,680	2,486	CEW15a	54-AABA-a	standard latviashu		91.00	2,439	3A.u.	10	8	11	5	3	Latvian	PNB	b
681	Lithuanian	0.09845	10,230	10,078	9,349	CEW15b	54-AAAA-a	standard lietuvishkai		85.00	8,566	3A.u.	10	8	12	5	3	Lithuanian	PNB	b
682	Mari (Cheremis)	0.00892	927	913	847	MSW51h	41-AACA-a	cheremis		90.00	822	1....	10	8	11	5	1	Mari: High*	PN.	b
683	Moldavian	0.04890	5,081	5,005	4,643	CEW21f	51-AADC-ab	standard moldavia		82.00	4,105	1A.u.	10	7	10	5	1		pnb	b
684	Mordvinian	0.02581	2,682	2,642	2,451	MSW51i	41-AADA-a	erzya		65.00	1,717	2....	10	8	8	3	1	Mordvin: Erzya*	PN.	b
685	Ossete	0.00785	816	804	745	CNT24e	58-ABBA	oseti cluster		36.00	289	2....	9	5	8	3	1	Ossete*	PN.	b
686	Polish (Pole)	4.11474	427,576	421,192	390,723	CEW22i	53-AAAC-c	polski		91.00	383,285	2A.uh	10	8	11	5	3	Polish	PNB	b
687	Russian	13.22030	1,373,765	1,353,254	1,255,358	CEW22j	53-AAAE-d	russkiy	84	50.00	676,627	4B.uh	10	8	9	5	3	Russian	PNB	b
688	Russian Gypsy (Ruska Roma)	0.10601	11,016	10,851	10,066	CNN25f	59-ACBA-ag	north vlach		70.00	7,596	1c...	10	5	7	0	3	Romani: Latvian	Pn.	b
689	Tatar	0.12250	12,729	12,539	11,632	MSY41h	44-AABB-e	tatar		1.50	188	2c.u.	6	4	8	2	1	Tatar: Kazan	Pn.	b
690	Udmurt (Votyak)	0.01187	1,233	1,215	1,127	MSW51k	41-AAEA-c	udmurt		55.00	668	2....	10	5	8	2	1	Udmurt	Pn.	.
691	Ukrainian	2.86656	297,874	293,426	272,199	CEW22p	53-AAAE-b	ukrainskiy		79.00	231,807	3A.uh	10	8	9	5	3	Ukrainian	PNB	b
692	Uzbek	0.03484	3,620	3,566	3,308	MSY41l	44-AABD-a	central uzbek		0.00	0	1A.u.	0	3	6	2	3	Uzbek*	PNb	b
693	other minor peoples	0.10000	10,391	10,236	9,496	...				20.00	2,047		9	5	8	3	0			
	Benin	**100.00000**	**5,335,830**	**6,096,559**	**11,109,357**					**27.63**	**1,684,195**									
694	Adja	6.33375	337,958	386,141	703,639	NAB59e	96-MAAE	aja cluster	54	25.00	96,535	0....	9	7	9	5	3		...	b
695	Aguna (Awuna)	0.31408	16,759	19,148	34,892	NAB59n	98-AAAA-i	aguna		30.00	5,744	1csu.	9	6	5	5	2		pnb	n
696	Aizo	4.22948	225,678	257,853	469,868	NAB59e	96-MAAF-j	ayizo	53	35.00	90,248	0....	9	7	6	4	2		...	.

Continued opposite

Table 8-2 continued

EVANGELIZATION								EVANGELISM			ADDITIONAL DESCRIPTIVE DATA
Ref 1	*D* 28	*aC* 29	*CG%* 30	*r* 31	*E* 32	*U* 33	*W* 34	*e* 35	*R* 36	*T* 37	*Locations, civil divisions, literacy, religions, church history, denominations, dioceses, church growth, missions, agencies, ministries, movements* 38
583	1	5	4.31	1	84.00	16.00	B	147.16	176	7	Rajshahi Division, also Sylhet. Use of Bengali is limited. Animists 40%, Hindus 10%. D=BELC.
584	1	6	1.52	4	45.00	55.00	A	1.64	153	4	Vast majority in Orissa(India). Hindus 96%, Muslims 2%(Sunnis, some Shias). D=RCC.
585	3	6	1.52	1	74.00	26.00	B	67.52	93	6	Rajshahi District; a plains tribe. Dialect of Santali. Animists 75%. D=NELC,RCC,COB.
586	2	6	1.52	0	99.95	0.05	C	464.64	54	10	Falam area, Chin Hills. Tropical forest. Agriculturalists. Animists 5%. D=Pankho Baptist Union of Bangladesh,BECC. M=NEIGM. Pankhu workers sent to Chakmas.
587	0	0	0.00	4	23.00	77.00	A	0.00	0	1.10	Followers of Parsi religion (Zoroastrianism) in India since AD 750; fire temples. Zoroastrians 100%. M=BFI.
588	0	5	1.51	5	47.00	53.00	A	1.71	149	4	Eastern Punjabi, from India. Mainly Sikhs 90%, Hindus.
589	1	5	1.54	0	40.00	60.00	A	8.76	181	4	Vast majority in India. Hinduized animists 90%, Muslims 4%. D=Baptist Ch.
590	4	6	4.60	4	82.00	18.00	B	65.84	187	6	Mainly India, also Nepal, Illerate, landless, and poor. Animists 70%. D=Northern Ev Lutheran Ch, Ch of Sylhet, RCC(D-Dinajpur),Ch of Bangladesh. M=Santal.
591	0	5	1.50	1	31.00	69.00	A	7.92	230	4	Also found in India (Lushai Hills, Assam). Animists 90%.
592	4	6	1.52	4	99.60	0.40	C	229.95	68	8	Agriculturalists in tropical forest. Also in Burma (Arakan Hills), China. Animists 40%. D=BUB,ECC,ABCUSA,ACBC(Burma).
593	0	6	3.81	1	33.10	66.90	A	0.12	428	3	District of Sylhet (100 miles north of Dacca). Many emigrants to Britain, India. Muslims 100%(Hanafi Sunnis).
594	0	4	0.00	1	26.01	73.99	A	0.00	143	1.15	Districts of Jalpaiguri, Cooch Behar. Also India (West Bengal, Assam), Nepal. Hinduized animists 70%, Muslims 30% (Sunnis).
595	0	6	1.52	1	28.00	72.00	A	1.02	237	4	Agriculturalists, in tropical forest. Related to Chakma. Buddhists 80%, some animists.
596	2	8	1.52	5	65.00	35.00	B	23.72	106	5	Immigrants and migrants from South India. Hindus 85%. D=COB,RCC. M=FMB.
597	1	5	1.94	0	45.00	55.00	A	1.64	185	4	Chittagong Hills, tropical forest. Agriculturalists. Many bilinguals in Bengali. Hinduized animists 70%(with Hindu elements), high-caste Hindus 19%, Muslims 10%.
598	0	5	1.52	0	34.30	65.70	A	1.62	209	4	Chittagong Hills. Mainly in Tripura (India). Hindus 90%, animists 5%. M=ABWE,ECC,FMB,LBI.
599	0	0	4.72	8	99.78	0.22	C	364.41	120	9	North Americans, in business, education. Nonreligious 10%. D=RCC,BBC,SDA,etc.
600	0	5	1.52	5	40.01	59.99	A	0.01	175	2	Indian Muslims 100%, originating in North India. M=WMPL. R=VERITAS
601	0	5	1.49	0	34.00	66.00	A	1.24	209	4	Chittagong Hills, Tropical forest, agriculturalists. Related to Tipera. Hindus 50%, animists 49%.
602	0	5	1.52	0	30.00	70.00	A	1.09	239	4	Majority live in Tripura (India). Hinduized animists 95%. M=ABWE.
603	0	5	1.52		13.50	86.50	A	0.24	309	3	Armenians, Sindhis, Sak, Kado, Brong, Rohingyas (1978 Arakanese refugees from Burma, then back in 1992).
Barbados											
604	0	10	0.97	8	74.00	26.00	B	51.31	62	6	Palestinians and other Levantines; immigrants, migrant workers. Mostly Muslims 80%.
605	2	8	0.17	8	99.74	0.26	C	370.80	16	9	Not strictly a creole but a dialect of English. D=CPWI,RCC(D-Bridgetown-Kingstown). M=USPG,SFM,OP,FMB.
606	3	10	0.34	4	99.80	0.20	C	400.04	27	10	Remnant of original Amerindians. Animists 20%. D=RCC,SDA,ICFG.
607	2	9	0.18	8	99.79	0.21	C	432.52	24	10	Expatriates from Britain, in government, education. D=CPWI,RCC(D-Bridgetown-Kingstown). M=USPG.
608	1	10	0.32	7	99.95	0.05	C	568.67	22	10	Greek-origin citizens in commerce, finance. D=Greek Orthodox Ch.
609	0	9	0.29	7	64.00	36.00	B	21.02	40	5	Chinese immigrants for several generations. Commerce. Mostly folk-religionists/Buddhists 80%.
610	0	9	0.31	7	56.00	44.00	B	8.17	64	4	Immigrants from north India. Muslims 65%, Hindus 30%.
611	0	9	0.00	8	43.00	57.00	A	0.00	0	1.14	Long-standing families practicing orthodox Judaism.
612	2	9	0.20	8	99.62	0.38	C	277.00	20	8	Language a dialect of English. D=CPWI,RCC(D-Bridgetown-Kingstown). M=USPG.
613	0	0	5.69	8	99.78	0.22	C	367.26	140	9	North Americans, in business, education. Nonreligious 10%. D=RCC,BBC,SDA,etc.
614	0	10	0.31		73.00	27.00	B	119.90	12	7	Vincentians, other Caribbean islanders.
Belgium											
615	3	10	4.30	6	84.00	16.00	B	61.32	158	6	Refugees, migrant workers from Albania since 1946. Nonreligious 40%, Muslims 40%. D=AoC,RCC,SDA.
616	1	10	3.67	8	59.00	41.00	B	4.30	203	4	Labor migrants from Algeria, mostly via France. Mainly in Brussels. Muslims 98%(Maliki Sunnis). D=RCC.
617	2	10	3.77	8	58.00	42.00	B	2.11	211	4	Berbers: Moroccans, Egyptians, Algerians, Libyans. Mostly in Brussels. Muslims 99%(Sunnis). D=RCC,GOC. M=GMU.
618	1	10	0.42	8	99.79	0.21	C	426.75	29	10	Expatriates from UK, in education, commerce, industry. D=Ch of England(D-Europe).
619	1	10	2.89	5	60.00	40.00	B	10.95	197	5	Refugees from civil war in Cambodia. Theravada Buddhists 92%, nonreligious 3%. D=RCC. M=CMA.
620	1	10	0.42	6	99.76	0.24	C	421.64	23	10	Expatriates from Holland, in commerce, professions. D=Dutch Reformed Chs(NHK).
621	2	10	4.01	8	69.00	31.00	B	12.59	187	5	Mainly in Brussels; labor migrants from Egypt. Muslims 95%(Maliki Sunnis). D=COC,RCC.
622	0	10	0.00	5	99.70	0.30	C	327.04	0	9	Artificial (constructed) language in 80 countries. Speakers in Belgium 256,000(none mother-tongue).
623	1	10	0.20	6	99.89	0.11	C	536.45	22	10	5 Provinces of Flanders (northern lowlands). Textiles. Nonreligious 6%, atheists 2%. D=97.5% RCC(D-Brugge,D-Gent,D-Hasselt),1% Protestants(GKB,&c).
624	3	10	0.42	8	99.86	0.14	C	517.93	23	10	French nationals, in the whole range of professions. D=RCC,ERF,et alia.
625	4	10	0.42	8	99.88	0.12	C	536.40	26	10	Eastern Cantons, Liege Province, around Eupen (official language). D=EEAB,EELB,EEPLB,NAC.
626	1	10	0.42	7	99.95	0.05	C	565.20	24	10	Greek Cypriots, emigres from Cyprus. D=Greek Orthodox Ch(D-Belgium).
627	0	10	1.80	8	90.10	9.90	B	82.54	75	6	Residents from Chinese diaspora. 70% Confucianists, Buddhists. Some 4,000 in Antwerp, 3,000 in Brussels.
628	0	10	0.96	7	75.00	25.00	B	32.85	59	5	85% Confucianists, Buddhists. Mainly in Antwerp and Brussels.
629	2	10	0.42	7	99.90	0.10	C	551.88	23	10	Expatriates from Italy, in business, commerce, industry. D=99% RCC,AEI.
630	0	10	0.11	8	55.10	44.90	B	0.20	40	3	Mainly urban, in Brussels and Antwerp. Ashkenazi and Sefardi. 45% practicing Judaism.
631	1	10	5.69	4	55.00	45.00	B	10.03	318	5	Migrant workers from Algeria. Muslims 95%(Maliki Sunnis). D=RCC. M=NAM,LBI,GMU.
632	0	10	3.31	0	36.10	63.90	A	0.13	403	3	Northern Kurdish. Labor migrants and refugees from Turkey, Iran, Iraq. Muslims 100%(Sunnis). M=Whole network of agencies.
633	1	10	2.33	8	58.20	41.80	B	0.42	143	3	Refugees, labor migrants from Libya. In Brussels. Muslims 99%(Maliki Sunnis). D=RCC.
634	3	10	7.66	5	99.75	0.25	C	396.93	173	9	Central Africans. Migrant laborers from Zaire. Animists 15%, nonreligious 10%. D=RCC,EJCSK,ECZ.
635	1	10	0.42	8	99.88	0.12	C	462.52	28	10	Luxembourgeois. Area of Arlon, Luxembourg Province. D=RCC.
636	1	10	4.28	7	49.50	50.50	A	0.90	276	3	Labor migrants from Morocco via France, primarily in Brussels. Muslims 99%(Maliki Sunnis). D=RCC.
637	2	10	2.69	5	59.00	41.00	B	8.61	157	4	Refugees from Iran, mostly migrant workers, professionals. Muslims 90%(Shias), Baha'is 5%, Parsis 0.3%. D=RCC,AoG.
638	1	10	0.42	6	99.90	0.10	C	512.46	7	10	Migrant workers and immigrants from Poland. D=RCC.
639	1	10	0.42	8	99.93	0.07	C	577.06	23	10	Expatriates from Portugal, in commerce, business. D=RCC.
640	1	10	0.42	8	99.80	0.20	C	391.28	30	9	Settled Gypsies, with some nomadic. D=Gypsy Evangelical Movement. M=GGMS.
641	2	10	0.42	7	99.70	0.30	C	365.36	8	9	Refugees from USSR in 1917, 1945. Nonreligious/atheists 30%. D=Russian Orthodox Ch(D-Brussel & Belgie),ROCOR.
642	1	10	0.42	8	99.96	0.04	C	606.19	21	10	Expatriates from Spain, in industry, commerce, professions. D=RCC.
643	1	10	3.68	8	55.30	44.70	B	0.60	217	3	Immigrants from Tunisia, mainly in Brussels. Muslims 99%(Maliki Sunnis). D=RCC.
644	0	10	4.20	8	56.10	43.90	B	0.20	240	3	Migrant workers, most in Brussels, some in other cities. Factory and construction workers. Muslims 100%(Hanafi Sunnis). M=GMU,OM,Orthodox Ch.
645	0	0	8.01	8	99.78	0.22	C	375.80	185	9	North Americans, in business, education. Nonreligious 10%. D=RCC,BBC,SDA,etc.
646	1	10	4.06	6	76.00	24.00	B	47.15	177	6	Refugees from wars in Indochina since 1930s. Buddhists/New-Religionists 80%. D=RCC.
647	1	10	0.30	8	99.85	0.15	C	467.26	26	10	5 Provinces of Wallonie. Nonreligious 6%, atheists 2%. D=97.0% RCC(D-Liege,D-Namur,D-Tournai),1% Protestants(ACE,ADB,AEEB,EPLB,ERB,UEEBB,UEELB).
648	0	10	0.42		51.00	49.00	B	35.36	23	5	West Indian Blacks, Koreans(M=PCK-Haptong,WOM), other Zairois, Rwandese, Burundians.
Belize											
649	3	10	2.09	8	99.82	0.18	C	445.95	50	10	Creole understood by 87.6% of country. D=60% RCC(D-Belize),CPWI,MCCA. M=SJ,0SB,USPG,FMB.
650	6	10	1.55	4	99.92	0.08	C	509.10	46	10	Garifuna. Animists 40%, nonreligious 10%, Afro-American spiritists 10%(Obeah). Second language: Creole. D=50% RCC(D-Belize; many being christopagans).
651	4	10	1.89	8	99.90	0.10	C	542.02	50	10	Expatriates from Britain, in government, education. D=Anglican Ch/CPWI(D-Belize),MCCA,CB,JWs. M=USPG,MCFOM(Fiji).
652	1	10	1.88	8	99.90	0.10	C	528.88	51	10	Mennonite Germans. 36% monolingual (15% speak Standard German, 2% English). D=Mennonite Brethren.
653	2	10	2.21	8	99.83	0.17	C	442.30	52	10	Ladinos. Illegal immigrants levelling Belize jungle. D=RCC, and numerous immigrant churches.
654	2	10	1.89	8	99.96	0.04	C	574.65	46	10	Spaniards et alii from Guatemala. D=RCC(D-Belize),CON. M=Methodist Ch in Fiji Overseas Mission,SJ,OSB,GMU.
655	1	9	0.92	7	84.11	15.89	B	61.73	51	6	Long-term Chinese settlers in commerce, finance. Folk-religionists/Buddhists 70%. D=RCC.
656	2	10	1.89	8	99.97	0.03	C	562.94	42	10	Illegal immigrants. Mainly slash-and-burn in Belize jungle. D=RCC, many Protestant immigrant churches.
657	0	9	2.47	7	63.05	36.95	B	23.12	151	5	Laborers, shopkeepers originally from India, Pakistan. Hindus, Muslims.
658	1	7	1.90	0	99.97	0.03	C	499.21	52	10	Peten Itza Maya. Some in Guatemala. Increasingly bilingual in Spanish, and some in English. D=70% RCC(D-Belize;75% christopagans). M=SJ,OSB,WOF.
659	0	10	1.10	8	47.09	52.91	A	0.15	104	3	Citizens from British colonial days, practicing orthodox Judaism.
660	1	7	1.16	0	99.98	0.02	C	558.01	34	10	Mainly in Guatemala. Mayans. D=60% RCC(D-Belize; 50% being christopagans). M=SJ,OSB,WOF.
661	2	10	1.89	8	99.95	0.05	C	554.80	42	10	Mexicans, Central Americans. D=70% RCC(D-Belize), CON. M=MCFOM(Fiji),EMBMC,GMU,CON.
662	5	9	2.04	0	99.93	0.07	C	471.83	55	10	D=RCC(D-Belize; 75% christopagans),Independent Pentecostal Ch,Mennonites,Ch of the Nazarene,Pentecostal Jesus Ch. M=WOF.
663	4	10	1.80	8	99.84	0.16	C	459.90	46	10	Afro-American spiritists(Obeah). D=RCC(D-Belize),CPWI,MCCA,et alia. M=SJ,MMS,OSB,FMB.
664	2	9	2.55	8	99.40	0.60	B	147.46	88	7	Merchants, traders. Muslims 60%(Hanafi Sunnis,Alawis,Druzes). D=RCC,SOC.
665	0	0	4.84	8	99.78	0.22	C	367.26	122	9	North Americans, in business, education. Nonreligious 10%. D=RCC,BBC,SDA,etc.
666	2	6	1.88	0	99.94	0.06	C	476.90	52	10	Mainly in Yucatan State(Mexico). Mayans. D=RCC(D-Belize; 35% christopagans),Presbyterian Ch. M=OSB,SJ,WOF.
667	0	9	1.89		99.74	0.26	C	278.20	50	8	Other Caribbean islanders, Mexicans, other Central Americans.
Belorussia											
668	2	7	0.38	6	99.70	0.30	C	350.03	20	9	Gregorians, from Armenia. Nonreligious 30%. D=Armenian Apostolic Ch, RCC.
669	1	8	0.00	1	34.00	66.00	A	0.00	0	1.12	From Azerbaijan. 73% monolingual. Muslims 80%(70% Shias, 30% Hanafi Sunnis), nonreligious 20%. D=ROC. M=IBT,CSI.
670	1	9	0.38	4	50.00	50.00	B	12.77	65	5	Many speak Tatar as mother tongue. Muslims 72%(Hanafi Sunnis), nonreligious 21%. D=Russian Orthodox Ch.
671	1	10	0.38	6	99.72	0.28	C	360.03	32	9	From Bulgaria. In 14 other countries. Nonreligious 18%, atheists 10%. D=Bulgarian Orthodox Ch. M=LBI.
672	4	8	0.04	5	99.66	0.34	C	321.55	21	9	White Russians. Also in USA, Canada, Poland. Nonreligious/atheists 25%. D=ROC(D-Minsk & Byelorussia),RCC(D-Minsk,D-Pinsk),Old Ritualist Chs(Old Believers).
673	1	9	0.38	0	77.00	23.00	B	98.36	42	6	From Chuvashia (Russia). Muslims 35%(Sunnis), nonreligious 30%. D=Russian Orthodox Church. M=IBT.
674	5	10	0.38	5	99.71	0.29	C	360.21	31	9	Most are bilingual in Russian. Nonreligions 29%. D=Russian Orthodox Ch,ELCE,RCC,MCE,AUCECB. M=UBS,LBI.
675	1	9	0.38	4	99.40	0.60	B	147.46	10	7	From Georgia. Nonreligious/atheists 55%, Muslims 5%(Sunnis, Shias). D=Georgian Orthodox Ch.
676	2	10	0.38	8	99.80	0.20	C	455.52	27	10	Settlers, also in Volga, Altai (Russia), Kirghizia. D=German ELC,AUCECB.
677	0	10	0.00	5	49.00	51.00	A	0.00	0	1.11	Bilingual in Russian, Belorussian. Religious Jews. Many have emigrated to Israel.
678	3	9	0.38	0	99.67	0.33	C	278.78	33	8	Mainly in Karelia (Russia). Bilingual in Russian. D=ROC,RCC,ELC.
679	0	8	0.00	4	39.00	61.00	A	0.00	0	1.11	Muslims 60%(Hanafi Sunnis, with Sufi influence), nonreligious 30%, atheists 10%. M=ROC,CSI.
680	5	9	0.38	5	99.91	0.09	C	538.08	27	10	In 25 countries, mainly Latvia. D=ROC,ELCL,RCC,RCL,CB.
681	3	8	0.66	5	99.85	0.15	C	483.99	12	10	Found in 24 countries. Strong Catholics. D=RCC,ERCL,ROC.
682	1	9	0.38	0	99.90	0.10	C	456.61	27	10	From Mari, Bashkir (Russia). Agriculturalists. Muslims 7%, many shamanists. Traditionally Orthodox. D=ROC. M=IBT.
683	1	9	0.38	6	99.82	0.18	C	427.99	26	10	From Moldavia (Bessarabia), Romania. Nonreligious 18%. D=Russian Orthodox Ch.
684	1	9	0.38	7	99.65	0.35	C	279.95	9	8	Immigrants from Mordvinia (Russia). Acculturated to Russian. Nonreligious 35%. D=ROC. M=IBT.
685	1	8	0.38	0	79.00	21.00	B	103.80	51	7	Mainly found in Russia, Georgia; also Syria, Turkey. Muslims 40%(Sunnis), nonreligious 12%, atheists 12%. D=ROC.
686	4	10	0.38	6	99.91	0.09	C	548.04	6	10	Poles in Western Ukraine. 29% speak Polish as mother tongue. D=RCC(3 Dioceses),ROC,CEF,Polish Pentecostal Movement/CWE.
687	8	9	-0.31	7	99.50	0.50	B	228.12	2	8	In 70 countries. Nonreligious 30%, atheists 8%. D=ROC,RCC,AUCECB,Old Ritualists,CEF,CCECB,SDA,IPKH. R=FEBC,HCJB,TWR,KNLS,AWR.
688	4	10	0.38	1	99.70	0.30	C	291.27	34	8	Romany-speaking Baltic Gypsies, including White Russian Gypsies; also Latvian, Estonian, and Polish Gypsies. Nonreligious 30%. D=RCC,ROC,ELC,AUCECB.
689	1	8	0.39	6	45.50	54.50	A	2.49	72	4	Originating from Tatarstan (Russia). Muslims 83%(Hanafi Sunnis), nonreligious 15%. D=ROC.
690	1	7	0.38	0	93.00	7.00	B	186.69	41	7	From Udmurtia (Russia). Strong shamanists/animists 40%, some Muslims (Besermen). D=ROC.
691	7	8	0.38	6	99.79	0.21	C	432.52	29	10	In 15 countries. Nonreligious/atheists 21%. D=ROC(E-Ukraine),Ukrainian Catholic Ch,AUCECB,CEF,CCECB,JWs,SDA.
692	0	9	0.00	5	44.00	56.00	A	0.00	0	1.12	Turkic. 55% speak Russian. Literates 100%. Muslims 80%(Hanafi Sunnis), nonreligious/atheists 20%. M=ROC,AUCECB,CSI.
693	0	8	0.38		49.00	51.00	A	35.77	21	5	Komi, Greeks, Koreans, Turkmen, Lezgin, Kirghiz.
Benin											
694	7	5	5.47	4	71.00	29.00	B	64.78	280	6	Mono and Atlantique Provinces. Animists 60%, Muslims 20%. D=mostly RCC,EAN,Methodists,AoG,Pentecostals,Baptists,AICs. M=WF,MMS,FMB.
695	2	5	6.56	1	73.00	27.00	B	79.93	298	6	Zou Province. Bilingual in Fon-gbe. Animists 60%, Muslims 20%. D=RCC,EPMB.
696	1	5	9.54	2	69.00	31.00	B	88.14	450	6	Mono and Atlantique Provinces. Animists 80%. D=RCC. M=SIM,FMB.

Continued overleaf

Table 8-2 continued

PEOPLE		POPULATION				IDENTITY CODE		LANGUAGE		CHURCH		MINISTRY						SCRIPTURE	
Ref 1	Ethnic name 2	P% 3	In 1995 4	In 2000 5	In 2025 6	Race 7	Language 8	Autoglossonym 9	S 10	AC 11	Members 12	Jayuh 13-17	d 18	wa 19	xc 20	mc 21	mi 22	Biblioglossonym 23	Pub ss 24-26 27
697	Ana (Ife, Baate)	1.72786	92,196	105,340	191,954	NAB59n	98-AAAA-cg	west ede-ife		30.00	31,602	1csu.	9	6	7	5	1	Ife	Pnb b
698	Bariba (Nikki, Batonu)	7.16080	382,088	436,562	795,519	NAB56a	91-GIAA-a	baatonum		8.00	34,925	3....	7	7	6	5	3	Bariba	PNB .
699	Basa	0.02094	1,117	1,277	2,326	NAB59j	96-FCCD-a	basa		10.00	128	0....	8	5	7	3	1		... .
700	Basila	0.14658	7,821	8,936	16,284	NAB59b	96-GABB	anii cluster		60.00	5,362	0....	10	7	7	4	1		... .
701	British	0.01000	534	610	1,111	CEW19i	52-ABAC-b	standard-english	5	79.00	482	3Bsuh	10	8	11	5	2		PNB b
702	Burba (Berba, Biali)	1.35050	72,060	82,334	150,032	NAB56a	91-GGEA-a	bia-li		6.00	4,940	0....	7	5	6	4	1	Biali	... .
703	Burusa (Bulba)	0.01675	894	1,021	1,861	NAB56a	91-GGAB-a	not-re		5.00	51	0....	7	5	6	2	1		... .
704	Busa (Boko)	1.32956	70,943	81,057	147,706	NAB63z	00-DGDA	busa-boko cluster		15.00	12,159	0....	8	5	7	4	2	Busa	PNB .
705	Cabe	1.67505	89,378	102,120	186,087	NAB59n	98-AAAA-cc	ede-cabe		10.00	10,212	1csu.	8	5	6	3	2		pnb .
706	Chakosi (Anufo)	0.20937	11,172	12,764	23,260	NAB59z	96-FCAD-a	anu-fo		10.00	1,276	0....	8	5	6	4	3	Anufo	P.. .
707	Dendi (Dandawa)	0.58627	31,282	35,742	65,131	NAB65a	01-AAAB-a	dendi	8	0.07	25	1..u.	4	3	2	1	1	Dendi	PNb .
708	Dompago (Logba, Legba)	0.85846	45,806	52,337	95,369	NAB56a	91-GFCB-e	lukpa		10.00	5,234	1c...	8	5	6	4	2	Lokpa*	PN. b
709	Ewe (Ebwe, Eve, Krepi)	0.70000	37,351	42,676	77,765	NAB59d	96-MAAA-a	standard ewe	56	72.70	31,025	4Asu.	10	8	11	5	3	Ewe	PNB b
710	Fon (Fo, Dahomean, Fogbe)	26.04942	1,389,953	1,588,118	2,893,923	NAB59e	96-MAAG-a	standard fon	60	32.00	508,198	2as..	9	8	9	5	3	Fon*	PNb b
711	Foodo	0.36760	19,615	22,411	40,838	NAB59a	96-FDBD-a	foodo		0.02	4	0....	3	4	4	2	1	Foodo	... .
712	French	0.29999	16,007	18,289	33,327	CEW21b	51-AABI-d	general français	37	87.00	15,911	1B.uh	10	8	13	5	2	French	PNB b
713	Fula (Fulani)	4.69011	250,256	285,935	521,041	NAB56c	90-BAAA-l	fula-atakora		1.00	2,859	1as..	6	5	2	4	2	Fulfulde, Benin-togo	pnb b
714	Ga	0.09999	5,335	6,096	11,108	NAB59f	96-LAAA-a	accra		55.00	3,353	1.s..	10	8	11	5	3	Ga*	PNB b
715	Gun (Gu, Egun)	6.15579	328,462	375,291	683,869	NAB59g	96-MAAG-j	gun	55	55.80	209,413	1As..	10	8	11	5	3	Gun-alada*	PNB b
716	Gurma (Gourma)	0.98409	52,509	59,996	109,326	NAB56a	91-GGDA	gurma cluster		7.00	4,200	3.s..	7	5	6	4	3		PN. .
717	Hausa	0.29999	16,007	18,289	33,327	NAB60a	19-HAAB-a	hausa	5	0.10	18	4Asu.	5	4	2	1	0	Hausa	PNB b
718	Ica	0.81659	43,572	49,784	90,718	NAB59n	98-AAAA-cd	southwest ede-ica		5.00	2,489	1csu.	7	5	6	2	0		pnb .
719	Idaca	0.62814	33,516	38,295	69,782	NAB59n	98-AAAA-cf	ede-idaca		3.00	1,149	1csu.	6	4	6	2	0		pnb .
720	Ije (Holi)	0.41877	22,345	25,531	46,523	NAB59n	98-AAAA-ci	ede-ije		5.00	1,277	1csu.	7	5	6	2	2		pnb .
721	Kabre (Cabrais)	0.62814	33,516	38,295	69,782	NAB56a	91-GFCB-a	kabiye		15.00	5,744	3a...	8	8	7	4	3	Kabiye	PN. .
722	Ko	0.41877	22,345	25,531	46,523	NAB59g	96-MAAF-d	ko		5.00	1,277	0....	7	5	6	4	1		... .
723	Kotokoli (Tem)	0.87940	46,923	53,613	97,696	NAB56a	91-GFCC-a	tem		7.00	3,753	2..u.	7	4	4	3	1	Tem	... .
724	Lamba (Namba, Losso)	1.15159	61,447	70,207	127,934	NAB56a	91-GFCB-b	lama		7.00	4,915	1c...	7	5	6	4	1	Lama: Togo	PN. .
725	Mahi (Maxi)	1.36097	72,619	82,972	151,195	NAB59g	96-MAAG-b	maxi		30.00	24,892	1cs..	9	6	7	5	2		pnb n
726	Mandingo	0.09999	5,335	6,096	11,108	NAB63h	00-AAAA-a	mandinka-kango	2	1.00	61	4a...	6	4	2	1	0	Mandinka	PN. b
727	Mbelime (Niendi)	0.51297	27,371	31,274	56,988	NAB56a	91-GGEC-d	mbelime		17.00	5,316	0....	8	6	7	5	1	Mbelime	pn. .
728	Mina (Ge, Popo)	2.40787	128,480	146,797	267,499	NAB591	96-MAAD	gen cluster	53	70.00	102,758	0....	10	8	11	5	1	Mina*	PN. .
729	Monkole (Mokole)	1.37145	73,178	83,611	152,359	NAB59n	98-AAAA-ca	ede-mokole		10.00	8,361	1csu.	8	6	7	4	2	Mokole	pnb .
730	Mossi	0.40000	21,343	24,386	44,437	NAB56a	91-GGAA-a	moo-re		17.00	4,146	2A...	8	5	8	5	2	Moore	PNB b
731	Mulatto	0.02000	1,067	1,219	2,222	NAN58	51-AABI-d	general français		50.00	610	1B.uh	10	8	7	5	1	French	PNB b
732	Nago (Nagot)	3.66415	195,513	223,387	407,064	NAB59n	98-AAAA-cj	ede-nago		57.00	127,331	1csu.	10	6	7	5	3		pnb b
733	Natemba	0.90035	48,041	54,890	100,023	NAB56a	91-GGDF-a	nate-ni		6.00	3,293	0....	7	5	6	4	1	Nateni	... .
734	Pila (Kpila, Temba, Yoba)	1.14111	60,888	69,568	126,770	NAB56a	91-GGCB-a	yo-m	2	7.00	4,870	0....	7	6	6	4	3	Yom*	PN. .
735	Saxwe-Gbe	0.09999	5,335	6,096	11,108	NAB59z	91-GGDE-e	li-gbe-ln		70.00	4,267	0....	10	7	7	5	2		... .
736	Seto	0.09999	5,335	6,096	11,108	NAB59e	96-MAAG-h	seto		2.00	122	1cs..	6	4	5	3	1		pnb .
737	Shanga	0.01848	986	1,127	2,053	NAB63z	00-DGDB-a	shanga		0.02	0	0....	3	4	4	0	0		... b
738	Somba (Tamberma, Niende)	2.51256	134,066	153,180	279,129	NAB56a	91-GGEC-b	di-tammari		17.00	26,041	0....	8	6	7	4	2	Ditamari*	PN. .
739	Songhai (Sonrhai)	0.07400	3,949	4,511	8,221	NAB65b	01-AAAA	songhay-kine cluster	2	0.81	37	0....	5	3	2	1	1	Songhai*	PN. b
740	Soruba (Biyobe, Meyobe)	0.14658	7,821	8,936	16,284	NAB56a	91-GHAA-a	mi-yobe		6.00	536	0....	7	5	6	3	1	Sola	... p
741	Tofin	1.28769	68,709	78,505	143,054	NAB59e	96-MAAF-l	tofin		20.00	15,701	0....	9	5	6	4	1		... .
742	Toli	0.09999	5,335	6,096	11,108	NAB59E	96-MAAF-k	toli		2.00	122	0....	6	4	5	3	1		... .
743	Waama (Yoabu)	0.89086	47,535	54,312	98,969	NAB56a	91-GGEB-a	waa-ma		10.00	5,431	0....	8	6	7	3	1	Waama	PN. .
744	Wachi (Watyi)	2.15663	115,074	131,480	239,588	NAB59e	96-MAAC-a	waci		65.00	85,462	0....	10	6	9	4	1		... .
745	Weme	1.25628	67,033	76,590	139,565	NAB59e	96-MAAG-g	weme-nu		15.00	11,488	1cs..	8	5	5	4	1		pnb .
746	Xweda	1.13065	60,330	68,931	125,608	NAB59e	96-MAAF-h	xweda		4.00	2,757	0....	6	5	4	3	1		... .
747	Xwela (Phera)	0.20000	10,672	12,193	22,219	NAB59e	96-MAAF-g	xwela		5.00	610	0....	7	5	5	3	1		... .
748	Xwla (Phla)	0.62814	33,516	38,295	69,782	NAB59e	96-MAAF-f	xwla		5.00	1,915	0....	7	5	5	3	1		... .
749	Yoruba	6.74126	359,702	410,985	748,911	NAB59n	98-AAAA-a	standard yoruba	17	37.00	152,064	3asu.	9	8	12	5	3	Yoruba	PNB b
750	Zerma (Dyerma)	0.09999	5,335	6,096	11,108	NAB65c	01-AAAB-b	zarma	2	0.50	30	2..u.	5	3	2	1	2	Zarma	PNB .
751	other minor peoples	0.12020	6,414	7,328	13,353	...				20.00	1,466		9	5	6	3	0		
	Bermuda	**100.00000**	**62,000**	**64,590**	**75,613**					**86.2**	**55,675**								
752	British	29.00000	17,980	18,731	21,928	CEW19i	52-ABAC-b	standard-english		81.00	15,172	3Bsuh	10	9	13	5	2		PNB b
753	Jewish	0.03300	20	21	25	CMT35	52-ABAE-b	samaná-english		0.00	0	0A.uh	0	5	3	5	0		pnb b
754	Mulatto	10.00000	6,200	6,459	7,561	NFB68b	52-ABAE-c	caribbean-english		91.00	5,878	0B.uh	10	9	11	5	2		pnb b
755	Portuguese	4.50000	2,790	2,907	3,403	CEW21g	51-AABA-e	general português		93.00	2,703	2Bsuh	10	8	13	5	2	Portuguese	PNB b
756	USA White	6.00000	3,720	3,875	4,537	CEW19s	52-ABAC-s	general american		78.00	3,023	1Bsuh	10	10	12	0	0	English*	PNB b
757	West Indian Black	50.36700	31,228	32,532	38,084	NFB68a	52-ABAE-c	caribbean-english		88.76	28,875	0B.uh	10	9	11	5	2		pnb b
758	other minor peoples	0.10000	62	65	76	...				37.00	24		9	8	3	5	0		
	Bhutan	**100.00000**	**1,847,112**	**2,123,970**	**3,903,897**					**0.45**	**9,651**								
759	Assamese	5.00000	92,356	106,199	195,195	CNN25a	59-AAFT-sc	standard axamiyaa		0.30	319	1asuh	5	5	6	1	2		pnb b
760	Central Bhutanese (Bhotia)	21.08600	389,482	447,860	823,176	MSY50a	70-AACA	kebumtamp cluster		0.05	224	0....	4	3	4	1	1		... .
761	Chali	0.38000	7,019	8,071	14,835	MSY50a	70-AAAB-g	tshalingpa		0.10	8	1.s..	5	2	3	0	0		pn. .
762	Dakpa (Sagtengpa, Brokpa)	4.00000	73,884	84,959	156,156	MSY50a	70-AAAB-l	sagtengpa		0.02	17	1.s..	3	3	3	1	0		pn. .
763	Doya	0.07000	1,293	1,487	2,733	AUG04z	46-CABA	kherwari cluster		0.10	1	3as..	5	1	0	0	0		PNB b
764	Dzalakha	3.19000	58,923	67,755	124,534	MSY50a	70-AADA	sharchagpa cluster		0.10	68	0....	5	2	3	0	0		... .
765	Eastern Bhutanese (Sharchop)	11.20000	206,877	237,885	437,236	MSY50a	70-AADA-a	sharchagpa-kha		0.01	24	0....	3	3	3	1	1		... .
766	Gurtu	6.40000	118,215	135,934	249,849	MSY50a	70-AACA-f	kurtopa-kha		0.10	136	0....	5	2	3	0	0		... .
767	Gurung	2.00000	36,942	42,479	78,078	MSY50e	59-AAFD-b	nepali		0.30	127	2Asu.	5	4	2	1	0	Nepali	PNB b
768	Hindi	1.50000	27,707	31,860	58,558	CNN25g	59-AAFO-e	general hindi		1.00	319	3Asuh	6	5	9	2	1		pnb b
769	Khen	6.39000	118,030	135,722	249,459	MSY50a	70-AACA-c	khen-kha		0.10	136	0....	5	2	3	0	0		... .
770	Kirati Rai	1.50000	27,707	31,860	58,558	MSY50h	71-CCAB-a	kulung		0.05	16	0....	4	4	2	1	0		... .
771	Lepcha (Rong, Nunpa)	1.70500	31,493	36,214	66,561	MSY50j	73-DFAA-a	lepcha		1.00	362	1....	6	5	2	2	0	Lepcha	PN. .
772	Limbu (Monpa)	1.50000	27,707	31,860	58,558	MSY50k	71-CBCC-a	limbu		0.05	16	0a...	4	4	3	1	0	Limbu	... b
773	Loba (Mustang)	0.10000	1,847	2,124	3,904	MSY50z	70-AAAE-a	loyu		0.10	2	0....	5	4	2	1	0		... .
774	Magar (Eastern Magar)	1.00000	18,471	21,240	39,039	MSY50n	71-BABA-b	east magar		0.10	21	0....	5	4	2	2	0	Magar*	PN. .
775	Nepalese (Paharia)	12.00000	221,653	254,876	468,468	CNN25k	59-AAFD-b	nepali		2.00	5,098	2Asu.	6	5	5	1	1	Nepali	PNB b
776	Oraon (Kurux)	0.20000	3,694	4,248	7,808	AUG06c	49-BAAA-a	nepal kurukh		20.00	850	1....	9	6	7	3	1	Kurux*	PN. .
777	Rai	0.90000	16,624	19,116	35,135	MSY50h	59-AAFD-b	nepali		0.05	10	2Asu.	4	4	2	1	0	Nepali	PNB b
778	Sangla	7.11000	131,330	151,014	277,567	MSY50a	70-AADB-a	tsangla		0.01	15	0....	3	3	3	1	0	Tsangla	... .
779	Santal	0.70000	12,930	14,868	27,327	AUG04c	46-CABA-a	santali		10.00	1,487	2as..	8	5	8	2	3	Santali	PNB b
780	Sherdukpen	0.20000	3,694	4,248	7,808	MSY50r	70-AAAG-a	sherdukpen		0.07	3	0....	4	4	2	1	0		... .
781	Sikkimese Bhotia	0.50000	9,236	10,620	19,519	MSY50a	70-AAAB-b	sikkim-bhotia		0.50	53	1.s..	5	3	3	0	1		pn. b
782	Tibetan (Llasa, Lhasa)	0.22000	4,064	4,673	8,589	MSY50r	70-AAAA-cb	urban utsang		0.00	0	0a...	0	4	2	1	0		pnb .
783	Tseku	0.30000	5,541	6,372	11,712	MSY50r	70-AAAA-cf	tseku		0.09	6	0c...	4	2	2	0	0		pnb b
784	Western Bhutanese (Drukpa)	10.80000	199,488	229,389	421,621	MSY50a	70-AAAB-f	dzongkha		0.10	229	1.s..	5	5	4	1	3	Zongkhar*	Pn. b
785	other minor peoples	0.04900	905	1,041	1,913	...				10.00	104		8	3	2	0	0		
	Bolivia	**100.00000**	**7,413,803**	**8,328,665**	**13,131,183**					**93.49**	**7,786,230**								
786	Apolo Quechua	0.40000	29,655	33,315	52,525	MIR39g	85-FAAH-db	apolo		85.00	28,317	1as..	10	8	8	5	3		pnb b
787	Araona	0.00120	89	100	158	MIR39d	84-RCAA-a	proper arao-na		60.00	60	0....	10	9	6	5	3	Araona	P.. .
788	Ayoreo (Moro, Yovai)	0.01909	1,415	1,590	2,507	MIR39z	86-BAAA-a	north ayoré		55.00	874	0....	10	7	8	5	3	Ayore*	PN. .
789	Baure	0.00400	297	333	525	MIR39a	81-BDAA-a	baure		60.00	200	0....	10	7	7	5	2	Baure	P.. .
790	Bolivian Mestizo	26.80000	1,986,899	2,232,082	3,519,157	CLN29	51-AABB-hs	boliviano		97.05	2,166,236	1B.uh	10	9	14	5	3		pnb b
791	British	0.01000	741	833	1,313	CEW19i	52-ABAC-b	standard-english	4	79.00	658	3Bsuh	10	9	13	5	1		PNB b
792	Callawalla	0.00020	15	17	26	MIR39g	85-LAAA-a	callahuaya		80.00	13	0....	10	9	3	5	0		... .
793	Canichana	0.00742	550	618	974	MIR39d	87-AABA-a	canichana		70.00	433	0....	10	8	6	5	1		... .
794	Carangas Aymara	0.20000	14,828	16,657	26,262	MIR39b	85-JABA-ad	caranga		45.00	7,496	1.s..	9	8	12	5	3		pnb b
795	Cavinena	0.02700	2,002	2,249	3,545	MIR39d	84-RBAA-a	cavineña		16.00	360	0....	8	5	6	1	3	Cavinena	PN. .
796	Cayubaba	0.01337	991	1,114	1,756	MIR39d	84-QAAA-a	cayubaba		81.00	902	0....	10	7	6	5	1		... .
797	Central Aymara	17.02303	1,262,054	1,417,791	2,235,325	MIR39b	85-JABA-a	central aymara		88.00	1,247,656	2.s..	10	8	7	5	4	Aymara*	PNB b
798	Central Bolivian Quechua	37.21810	2,759,277	3,099,771	4,887,177	MIR39g	85-FAAH-ed	sucre		97.52	3,022,897	1as..	10	9	14	5	3	Quechua: Bolivia	PNB b
799	Chacobo	0.00718	532	598	943	MIR39d	84-NGBA-a	cháco-bo		70.00	419	0....	10	6	6	3	2	Chacobo	PN. .
800	Chipaya	0.02690	1,994	2,240	3,532	MIR37b	85-MAAB-a	chipaya		75.00	1,680	0....	10	6	7	3	2	Chipaya	PN. .
801	Chiquitano	0.34904	25,877	29,070	45,833	MIR39c	87-BAAA	chiquito cluster		40.00	11,628	0....	9	8	6	4	3	Chiquitano	PN. b
802	Chorote (Manjuy)	0.00020	15	17	26	MIR39e	86-ABAA-a	yofúaha		60.00	10	0....	10	5	7	3	0	Chorote*	P.. b
803	Detribalized Amerindian	0.60000	44,483	49,972	78,787	MIR39z	51-AABB-hs	boliviano		90.00	44,975	1B.uh	10	9	10	5	1		pnb b
804	Eastern Bolivian Guarani	0.20000	14,828	16,657	26,262	MIR39e	82-AAIF-cb	chiriguano		56.00	9,328	3a...	10	9	7	5	3	Guarayu*	PNb b
805	Ese Ejja (Chama, Huarayo)	0.01250	927	1,041	1,641	MIR39d	84-RAAA	ese-ejja cluster		40.00	416	0....	9	8	6	4	3	Ese Ejja	PN. b
806	German	2.37740	176,256	198,006	312,181	CEW19m	52-ABCE-a	standard hoch-deutsch		86.00	170,285	2B.uh	10	8	13	5	1	German*	PNB b
807	Greek	0.03000	2,224	2,499	3,939	CEW20	56-AAAA-c	dhimotiki		95.00	2,374	2B.uh	10	8	11	5	1	Greek: Modern	PNB b
808	Guarayu (Guarayo)	0.10116	7,500	8,425	13,284	MIR39e	82-AAIF-cb	chiriguano		70.00	5,898	3a...	10	8	6	4	3	Guarayu*	PNb b
809	Han Chinese	0.01851	1,372	1,542	2,431	MSY42a	79-AAAB-ba	kuo-yü		50.00	771	2Bsuh	10	6	8	2	1	Chinese: Kuoyu*	PNB b
810	Ignaciano (Moxos)	0.06791	5,035	5,656	8,917	MIR39a	81-BDBA-a	ignaciano		40.00	2,262	0....	9	5	6	3	3	Ignaciano	PN. .
811	Itene	0.00152	113	127	200	MIR39a	84-OBAA-a	proper itene		80.00	101	0....	10	7	6	4	1		... .
812	Itonama	0.00262	194	218	344	MIR39e	84-PAAA-a	itonama		80.00	175	0....	10	7	6	3	1	Itonama	P.. b
813	Japanese	0.17000	12,603	14,159	22,323	MSY45a	45-CAAA-a	koku-go		60.00	8,495	1B.uh	10	7	8	5	1	Japanese	PNB b
814	Jewish	0.03770	2,795	3,140	4,950	CMT35	51-AABB-hs	boliviano		0.12	4	1B.uh	5	4	2	4	0		pnb b

Continued opposite

EVANGELIZATION								EVANGELISM			ADDITIONAL DESCRIPTIVE DATA
Ref 1	D 28	aC 29	CG% 30	r 31	E 32	U 33	W 34	e 35	R 36	T 37	Locations, civil divisions, literacy, religions, church history, denominations, dioceses, church growth, missions, agencies, ministries, movements 38
697	1	7	8.39	5	81.00	19.00	B	88.69	331	6	Zou Province. Half in Togo. Animists 70%. D=Yoruba churches from Nigeria.
698	5	4	8.50	4	58.00	42.00	B	16.93	466	5	Also in Nigeria, Togo. Animists 60%, Muslims 32%(growing slowly). D=EECOA(ECWA),UEEB,AoG,Methodists,RCC(D-Natitingou). M=SMA,FMB,SIM,WF.
699	2	5	2.58	0	39.00	61.00	A	14.23	181	5	Zou Province, 3 villages. Related to Ashanti. All trilingual in Cabe and Fon. Animists 90%. D=RCC,EECOA. M=SIM.
700	1	6	6.49	0	93.00	7.00	C	203.67	229	8	Atakora Province. Also in Togo. Literates 1%. Muslims 20%, animists 20%. D=RCC.
701	2	10	2.18	8	99.79	0.21	C	432.52	61	10	Expatriates from UK, in professions, education. D=CPWA,EPMB.
702	2	5	6.40	2	37.00	63.00	A	8.10	575	4	Atakora Province, also in Burkina Faso. Animists 94%. D=RCC,AoG. M=SIL.
703	1	5	4.01	0	30.00	70.00	A	5.47	491	4	Atakora Province, Tanguieta town. Animists 95%. D=AoG.
704	2	5	7.36	2	60.00	40.00	B	32.85	423	5	Half in Nigeria. Literates 6%. Animists 52%, Muslims 33%(Sunnis). D=RCC,EECOA. M=SIM,EMS.
705	3	5	7.17	1	51.00	49.00	B	18.61	460	5	Borgu and Zou Provinces. Animists 90%. D=RCC,EECOA,EPMB. M=SIM,UMC.
706	3	6	4.97	0	44.00	56.00	A	16.06	397	5	Most in Togo, also in Ghana. Muslims 50%(Maliki Sunnis), animists 40%. D=EPC,RCC,AoG. M=SMA,OFM,UCMWM.
707	0	4	3.27	4	26.07	73.93	A	0.06	543	2	Muslims 100%(Maliki Sunnis). Dendi are actively spreading Islam in the north, using Qadiriyya, Tijaniyya. M=EBM.
708	2	5	6.46	2	49.00	51.00	A	17.88	438	5	Also in Togo. Animists 85%, Muslims 5%(Sunnis). D=EECOA(ECWA),UEEB. RCC. M=WF,SIM.
709	3	7	7.52	4	99.73	0.27	C	370.70	173	9	Mainly in Ghana and Togo. Animists 26%. D=RCC,ECCB,other AICs.
710	4	7	11.44	4	91.00	9.00	B	106.28	398	7	Some in Togo. Animists 62%(260 fetish monasteries), Muslims 5%(Sunnis). D=RCC(D-Abomey),EPMB,AoG,Pentecostals. M=SIM,FMB,UBS,AAC,SMA,MMS,UMC.
711	0	5	1.40	0	18.02	81.98	A	0.01	391	2	Atakora Province, Semere town. Also a few in Ghana. Muslims 100%. M=SIL.
712	2	10	2.36	8	99.87	0.13	C	514.43	56	10	Expatriates from France, in government, education, commerce. D=RCC,EPMB. M=SIM,ERF.
713	2	6	5.82	4	46.00	54.00	A	1.67	442	4	Benin-Togo Fulfulde. Literates 1%. Muslims 97%, animists 2%. D=AoG,EECOA(ECWA; 400 converts). M=SIM,EMS.
714	4	8	6.53	4	99.55	0.45	B	236.88	179	8	Migrants from Ghana. Animists 40%. D=RCC,EPMB,AoG,many AICs.
715	6	8	6.23	4	99.56	0.44	B	248.07	180	8	Animists 50%, Muslims 10%(Sunnis and Ahmadis, spreading rapidly). D=EPMB,AoG,AIC,Cherubim & Seraphim,EAN,other AICs. M=MMS,FMB,UMC,UBS.
716	3	5	6.23	4	51.00	49.00	B	13.03	408	5	Atakora and Borgou Provinces; mainly in Burkina Faso, also Togo. Animists 60%, Muslims 33%. D=RCC,AoG,ECWA. M=SIM,EMS,EBM.
717	0	7	2.93	5	45.10	54.90	A	0.16	251	3	Traders. Lingua franca across West Africa from Senegal to Sudan. Muslims 100%(Maliki Sunnis).
718	0	5	5.67	1	38.00	62.00	A	6.93	509	4	Zou Province. Also in Togo. Animists 95%.
719	0	5	4.86	1	35.00	65.00	A	3.83	489	4	Zou Province. Related to Fon. Animists 97%.
720	0	5	4.97	1	40.00	60.00	A	7.30	436	4	Zou Province. Animists 95%. M=FMB,UMC.
721	2	5	6.56	4	63.00	37.00	B	34.49	345	5	Atakora Province. Mainly in Togo, also Ghana. Lingua franca with 1.3 million speakers. Animists 84%, Muslims 1%. D=RCC(D-Natitingou),AoG. M=SMA,EET,FMB.
722	1	6	4.97	1	35.00	65.00	A	6.38	528	4	Mono Province. Animists 95%. D=RCC. M=SIM.
723	1	5	6.11	0	33.00	67.00	A	8.43	621	4	Majority in Togo, some in Ghana. Muslims 74%, animists 19%. D=RCC. M=SMA.
724	1	5	6.39	1	42.00	58.00	A	10.73	506	5	Mainly in Togo. Atakora Province. Animists 89%, Muslims 4%. D=AoG.
725	1	6	5.09	2	78.00	22.00	B	85.41	241	6	Also in Togo. Language similar to Fon-gbe. Animists 70%. D=EPMB. M=SIM,UMC.
726	0	7	4.20	4	39.00	61.00	A	1.42	438	4	Itinerants, traders across West Africa. Animists 85%, Muslims 11%.
727	2	5	6.48	0	52.00	48.00	B	32.26	414	5	Atakora Province. Related to Ditamari and Tamberma of Togo. Muslims 60%, animists 23%. D=RCC,AoG. M=SMA.
728	7	8	4.42	2	99.70	0.30	C	304.04	131	9	Mainly in Togo, along coast. Lingua franca, with a million speakers. Animists 20%. Mainly Catholics. D=RCC,EPMB,EAN,ECCB,AICs,AoG,Pentecostals. M=UMC.
729	1	5	6.96	2	51.00	49.00	B	18.61	449	5	Borgou Province. Animists 90%. D=EECOA/ECWA. M=SIM,EMS.
730	4	6	6.21	4	74.00	26.00	B	45.91	281	6	Labor migrants from Burkina Faso. Animists 43%, Muslims 40%(Maliki Sunnis). D=RCC,AoG,Apostolic Ch,AICs. M=SMA,FMB.
731	1	10	3.25	8	99.50	0.50	B	208.05	105	8	Mixed-race, Black/French. Many migrate to France. Animists 30%, nonreligious 20%. D=RCC.
732	0	7	9.91	1	99.57	0.43	B	220.53	292	8	Weme and Atakora Provinces. Some bilinguals in Yoruba. Animists 70%, Muslims 10%. M=UMC,SIM,FMB.
733	1	5	5.97	0	34.00	66.00	A	7.44	592	4	Atakora Province. Animists 90%. D=AoG. M=SIL.
734	3	5	6.38	2	45.00	55.00	A	11.49	472	5	Northwest. Literates 2%. Animists 64%, Muslims 29%. D=EPMB,Apostolic Ch of Togo & Benin,RCC. M=SIM,MMS,PEMS,AAC.
735	3	7	6.05	0	99.70	0.30	C	275.94	189	8	Mono Province. Related to Ewe. Animists 30%. D=EPMB/Methodists,AoG,AICs. M=SIM,MMS.
736	1	6	2.53	1	37.00	63.00	A	2.70	319	4	Oueme(Weme)Province. Also in Nigeria. Animists 98%. D=RCC.
737	0	0	0.00	0	9.02	90.98	A	0.00	0	1.03	Immigrants from Sokoto State and city of Shanga, Nigeria. Animists 60%(Bori), Muslims 40%(Maliki Sunnis).
738	2	5	8.18	0	54.00	46.00	B	33.50	485	5	Atakora Province. Muslims 60%, animists 23%. D=AoG(big response),RCC(D-Natitingou). M=SMA,SIM.
739	0	4	3.68	0	20.81	79.19	A	0.61	735	3	Along Niger River. Muslims 99%(Maliki Sunnis). M=EBM.
740	2	5	4.06	0	33.00	67.00	A	7.22	451	4	Solamba. Atakora Province. Also in Togo. Animists 60%, Muslims 34%. D=RCC,AoG. M=SIM.
741	4	5	7.20	1	54.00	46.00	B	39.42	456	5	Weme and Atlantique Provinces. Related to Ewe, Aja. Animists 80%. D=RCC,AoG,EPMB,AICs. M=MMS.
742	1	6	2.53	1	28.00	72.00	A	2.04	248	4	Weme and Atlantique Provinces. Closely related to Aizo. Animists 98%. D=RCC.
743	2	5	6.50	2	46.00	54.00	A	16.79	469	5	Tangamma. Atakora Province. Animists 70%, Muslims 20%. D=AoG,RCC. M=SIL.
744	3	7	7.31	4	99.65	0.35	C	256.23	231	8	Mono Province. Animists 86%. D=AoG,Baptists,AIC. M=FMB.
745	3	5	7.30	1	56.00	44.00	B	30.66	444	5	Weme and Atlantique Provinces. Animists still strong, 85%. D=RCC,EPMB,AICs. M=MMS.
746	3	5	5.78	1	31.00	69.00	A	4.52	668	4	Atlantique Province. Strong animism: animists 96%. D=RCC,EPMB,AICs. M=MMS.
747	1	6	4.20	1	32.00	68.00	A	5.84	512	4	Mono Province. Animists 95%. D=RCC. M=SIM.
748	1	6	5.40	1	33.00	67.00	A	6.02	596	4	Mono, Weme, Atlantique Provinces. Related to Aja. Animists 95%. D=RCC.
749	5	8	4.43	5	99.37	0.63	B	140.45	153	7	Muslims 50%(Maliki Sunnis, plus 500 Ahmadis), animists 5%. D=RCC,Anglican Ch,Baptists,Methodists,AICs. M=FMB,SMA,WF,SIM.
750	0	4	3.46	1	29.50	70.50	A	0.53	498	3	Mainly in Niger, some in Nigeria, few in Burkina Faso. Muslims 75%(Maliki Sunnis), animists 24%. M=Evangelical Baptist Missions,SIM.
751	0	6	3.75		46.00	54.00	A	33.58	223	5	Kanuri, Tienga (Fringe Mandingo), 3,000 refugees from Chad.
Bermuda											
752	2	10	1.18	8	99.81	0.19	C	464.17	41	10	Expatriates from Britain, in government, administration, commerce. D=Anglican Ch of Bermuda(D-Bermuda),Methodist Ch.
753	0	10	0.00	8	44.00	56.00	A	0.00	0	1.12	Long-term residents practicing orthodox Judaism.
754	4	10	1.17	8	99.91	0.09	C	521.47	33	10	Black/White mixed-race persons. Citizens. D=Anglican Ch of Bermuda,RCC(D-Hamilton),SDA,SA. M=CR,FMB.
755	2	10	1.17	8	99.93	0.07	C	577.06	35	10	Expatriates from Portugal, and long-time residents. D=RCC,Portuguese Evangelical Ch.
756	0	0	5.88	8	99.78	0.22	C	370.11	143	9	North Americans, in business, education. Nonreligious 10%. D=RCC,BBC,SDA,etc.
757	5	10	0.91	8	99.89	0.11	C	504.62	27	10	Language is a dialect of English, not a creole. D=Anglican Ch of Bermuda,RCC(D-Hamilton),Methodist Ch,SDA,SA. M=CR,FMB.
758	0	10	1.10		67.00	33.00	B	90.48	45	6	USA Afro-Americans, Caribbean islanders, Chinese.
Bhutan											
759	2	4	3.52	4	39.30	60.70	A	0.43	316	3	Workers from India. Hindus 80%, Muslims 18%(Hanafi Sunnis). D=RCC,CNI.
760	0	4	3.16	0	14.05	85.95	A	0.02	942	2	Khyengpa. In Bumthang and all central Bhutan. Unwritten language. Strict Buddhists (Lamaists) 100%. M=over 4 agencies (TLM,Interserv).
761	0	0	2.10	0	12.10	87.90	A	0.04	854	2	Tshali area of Shongar District in east Bhutan. Related to Dzongkha. Buddhists(Lamaists) 100%.
762	0	5	2.87	0	17.02	82.98	A	0.01	731	2	Sakteng Valley east of Tashigang Dzong. Agriculturalists, semi-nomadic herdsmen. Lamaists.
763	0	5	0.00	4	35.10	64.90	A	0.12	86	3	Aboriginal inhabitants settled in poverty in southwestern corner, Dorokha Dungkhag. Second language Nepali. Animists/Hindu/Buddhist religion.
764	0	0	4.31	0	7.10	92.90	A	0.02	2,308	2	Bodish language. Buddhists(Lamaists) 100%.
765	0	4	3.23	0	12.01	87.99	A	0.00	1,118	1.05	Shashop. Eastern and southeastern Bhutan. Unwritten language. Strict Buddhists (Lamaists) 100%. Many small temples. M=FFFM et alia.
766	0	0	2.64	0	7.10	92.90	A	0.02	1,663	2	Kurthopkha. In central Bhutan, especially Kurto. Buddhists(Lamaists) 100%.
767	0	5	2.57	4	34.30	65.70	A	0.37	285	3	Pastoralists. Animists 80%, Hindu settlers 20%.
768	2	5	3.52	7	51.00	49.00	B	1.86	243	4	Traders. Expatriates from India. Hindus 90%, some Muslims. D=RCC,CNI. M=Ao Baptist Churches Association.
769	0	0	2.64	0	7.10	92.90	A	0.02	1,663	2	Khenkha. In Bumthang and central Bhutan. 92% lexical similarity with Kebumtamp. Buddhists(Lamaists) 100%.
770	0	5	2.81	0	12.05	87.95	A	0.02	866	2	Agriculturalists. Covers 21 dialects/idioms. Animists 60%, Hindus 40%.
771	0	4	3.65	0	20.00	80.00	A	0.73	637	3	Lower valleys in west. Animists 50%(with Lamaist syncretistic features), strict Buddhists(Lamaists) 45%. Own script. 1945 Indian evangelists win converts.
772	0	5	2.81	4	24.05	75.95	A	0.04	434	2	Less strict Buddhists(Lamaists), also Hindus.
773	0	4	0.70	0	12.10	87.90	A	0.04	408	2	Immigrants from Mustang in Nepal. Agriculturalists, pastoralists. Buddhists 100%.
774	0	5	3.09	0	18.10	81.90	A	0.06	589	2	Also in Nepal and India. Animists 90%, Hindus 10%.
775	0	5	6.43	4	45.00	55.00	A	3.28	471	4	Largely settlers in foothills across Bhutan (south central), until vicious deportations. High-caste Hindus 98%. M=Nagaland Missionary Movement(India).
776	1	5	4.54	0	51.00	49.00	B	37.23	303	5	Nepali Kurux. In India, Nepal. Hindus 57%, animists 23%. D=RCC.
777	0	5	2.33	4	33.05	66.95	A	0.06	276	2	One of many Nepoli-speaking groups settled in west. Hindus 99%.
778	0	5	2.75	0	12.01	87.99	A	0.00	1,008	1.05	In southeast. Close to Sharchagpakha. Others in China, a few in India. Lamaist Buddhists 100%.
779	3	5	5.13	4	64.00	36.00	B	23.36	262	5	Settlers from India. Hindus 82%, animists 8%. D=Ebenezer Lutheran Ch(India),RCC,SDA.
780	0	5	1.10	0	12.07	87.93	A	0.03	629	2	Also in India; a Tibetan language from Assam. Less strict Buddhists(Lamaists) 100%.
781	1	5	4.05	0	23.50	76.50	A	0.42	667	3	Sikami. Immigrants from Sikkim. Agriculturalists, pastoralists. Strict Lamaist Buddhists 99%. D=RCC.
782	0	5	0.00	4	22.00	78.00	A	0.00	0	1.09	Mainly in Tibet, Nepal, India. Buddhists(Lamaists) 100%.
783	0	5	1.81	1	19.09	80.91	A	0.06	499	2	Also in Tibet, Nepal, Sikkim, India. Buddhists (Lamaists) 100%.
784	3	4	3.18	0	25.10	74.90	A	0.09	529	2	Ngalong, Ngalop, Bhotia, Bhutani. Elite in power. Strict Buddhists(Lamaists) 100%, with 6,000 monks. D=CNI,Moravians,Tibetan Christian Fellowship. M=SAM.
785	0	5	2.37		24.00	76.00	A	8.76	271	4	Bengalis, Han Chinese, Burmese, Biharis, Adap, Nagas, British.
Bolivia											
786	2	6	1.69	4	99.85	0.15	C	446.76	45	10	Dialect of Northern Quechua. Apolo Region. Animists 15%. D=97% RCC(40% being christopagans),BBU. M=EPMC(Argentina),WOF,SIM,ABCUSA.
787	1	8	1.92	0	98.00	2.00	C	214.62	73	8	Northwest. Animists 39%. D=RCC(VA-Pando,VA-Reyes). M=MM,CSSR,SIL,NTM.
788	1	8	1.69	0	98.00	2.00	B	196.73	75	7	Southeastern region. Animists 45%. D=RCC(VA-Chiquitos,VA-Nuflo de Chavez). M=OFM,SAIM,NTM,EUSA.
789	1	9	1.70	0	99.00	1.00	C	216.81	75	8	Beni department. Becoming extinct. Animists 40%. D=RCC(VA-El Beni). M=OFM,SIL.
790	4	7	1.70	8	99.97	0.03	C	591.74	37	10	D=97% RCC,SDA,AoG,UWM. M=EPMC(Argentina),WOF,WMPL,FMB,SIM. R=AWR.
791	1	10	1.69	8	99.79	0.21	C	435.40	52	10	Expatriates from Britain, in commerce, education, industry. D=AC.
792	0	8	0.49	0	99.80	0.20	C	321.20	29	9	North of La Paz. Language only spoken by men/herbal doctors. Animists 20%.
793	1	10	4.80	0	99.70	0.30	C	273.38	141	8	Lowlands. Animists 30%. D=RCC(VA-Cuevo). M=OFM. Nearly extinct.
794	2	7	1.69	4	99.45	0.55	B	169.17	45	7	Animists 50%. D=97% RCC(of whom 50% are christopagans),AoG. M=OFM,CP,YWAM,SIM.
795	1	7	2.15	0	50.00	50.00	B	29.20	156	5	Northern Bolivia. Animists 84%. D=RCC(VA-Reyes). M=CSSR,SIL,Swiss Indian Mission.(MES).
796	1	10	5.14	0	99.81	0.19	C	348.86	136	9	Beni Department. Animists 19%. D=RCC(VA-El Beni). M=OFM.
797	12	7	1.69	4	99.88	0.12	C	478.58	31	10	Surge of conversions from 1965: Baha'is 8%. D=95% RCC(M-La Paz;50% being strong christopagans),AoG,SA,ECU,SDA,IBS,CON,BBU,IEB,IELB,INELA,ICs.
798	5	6	1.68	4	99.98	0.02	C	599.84	39	10	D=97% RCC(M-Sucre,40% being christopagans),AoG,Bolivian Baptist Union,Union Cristiana Evangelica(ECU),SDA. M=SJ,SDB,CSSR,FSC,WOF,SIM,WMPL.
799	1	10	2.07	0	99.70	0.30	C	281.05	69	8	Northwest Beni, south of Riberalta. Animists 30%. D=RCC. M=SIL,MES.
800	1	9	2.19	0	99.75	0.25	C	317.55	70	9	Oruro Department, Atahuallpa Province. Hunters, fishermen. Animists 25%. D=RCC. M=SIL,SIM.
801	1	8	1.69	4	88.00	12.00	B	128.48	84	7	East of Santa Cruz. Animists 60%, rest practice syncretistic christopaganism. D=99% RCC(VA-Chiquitos,VA-Nuflo de Chavez; almost all christo-pagans). M=OFM.
802	0	9	1.62	0	94.00	6.00	C	205.86	66	8	Southeast, Tarija Department. Mainly in Argentina, also in Paraguay. 80% monolinguals. Animists 40%.
803	1	10	1.69	8	99.90	0.10	C	505.89	48	10	Slumdwellers and urbanites uprooted from original cultures. D=98% RCC.
804	6	8	1.69	4	99.56	0.44	B	241.19	54	8	Shamanists 40%. D=Evangelical Christian Union(GMU),RCC(many christopagans),AoG,COG,Brethren,Brazilian Baptist Convention. M=GMU,SIM,SIL,SAMS.
805	1	6	1.69	0	77.00	23.00	B	112.42	85	7	Northwest, near Brazil and Peru. Animists 60%. D=RCC(VA-Pando,VA-Reyes). M=MM,CSSR,SIL,NTM,Swiss Indian Mission.
806	2	10	1.69	8	99.86	0.14	C	508.51	48	10	Settlers from Europe, farmers, professionals. D=RCC, Protestants. M=EKD.
807	1	10	1.69	7	99.95	0.05	C	575.60	44	10	Settlers in commerce, professions; from Greece. D=GOC(Iglesia Ortodoxa Griega). M=GOANSA.
808	1	6	2.01	4	99.70	0.30	C	314.26	59	9	Northeast. Animists 30%. D=99% RCC(VA-Cuevo,VA-Nuflo de Chavez;most Catholics practice christo-paganism). M=OFM,SIL,WGM,Methodist Mission.
809	1	10	1.69	7	99.50	0.50	B	209.87	56	8	Settlers in commerce, finance, business. Chinese folk-religionists/Buddhists 50%. D=RCC.
810	1	6	1.69	0	77.00	23.00	B	112.42	96	7	South central Beni. Animists 60%. D=RCC(VA-El Beni). M=OFM,SIL,YWAM.
811	1	9	1.68	0	99.80	0.20	C	335.80	64	9	North central Beni. Animists 20%. D=RCC(VA-El Beni). M=OFM. Rapidly becoming assimilated.
812	1	9	1.68	0	99.80	0.20	C	344.56	54	9	Beni Department and Itonamas river. Language isolate. Bilingual in Spanish. Animists 20%. D=RCC. M=SIL.
813	1	10	1.69	7	99.60	0.40	C	278.13	53	8	Buddhists 40%(Sokka Gakkai et alia), with rest converted to Catholicism. D=97% RCC. M=IGM(Japan).
814	0	10	1.40	8	49.12	50.88	A	0.21	117	3	Active in primary and secondary education. Most practice Judaism.

Continued overleaf

Table 8-2 continued

PEOPLE		POPULATION				IDENTITY CODE		LANGUAGE		CHURCH		MINISTRY						SCRIPTURE		
Ref 1	Ethnic name 2	P% 3	In 1995 4	In 2000 5	In 2025 6	Race 7	Language 8	Autoglossonym 9	S 10	AC 11	Members 12	Jayuh 13-17	d 18	wa 19	xc 20	mc 21	mi 22	Biblioglossonym 23	Pub 24-26	ss 27
815	Jora	0.00018	13	15	24	MIR39e	82-AAIA-e	jora		83.00	12	0....	10	7	2	3	1		pn.	.
816	Latin American Branco	0.10000	7,414	8,329	13,131	CLT26	51-AABA-e	general português		95.00	7,912	2Bsuh	10	9	13	5	1	Portuguese	PNB	b
817	Latin American White	4.53689	336,356	377,862	595,747	CLT27	51-AABB-hs	boliviano		85.80	324,206	1B.uh	10	9	14	5	3		pnb	b
818	Leco	0.00300	222	250	394	MIR39g	51-AABB-hs	boliviano		90.00	225	1B.uh	10	7	10	4	1		pnb	b
819	Low German	0.28253	20,946	23,531	37,100	CEW19m	52-ABCC	north deutsch cluster		90.00	21,178	2A.uh	10	8	13	5	2	German: Low*	PNB	b
820	Mororata	0.00000	0	0	0	MIR39z	85-FAAH	south quechua cluster		70.00	0	3As..	10	6	6	4	2	Quechua: Classical*	PNB	b
821	Movima	0.01045	775	870	1,372	MIR39d	87-AAAA-a	movima		70.00	609	0....	10	7	6	4	1	Movima	P..	.
822	Movima	0.01100	816	916	1,444	MIR39d	51-AABB-hs	boliviano		80.00	733	1B.uh	10	6	6	4	1		pnb	b
823	Nocten Mataco (Wichi)	0.02718	2,015	2,264	3,569	MIR39e	86-AAAA-a	noctén		85.00	1,924	0.s..	10	7	8	4	2	Wichi Lhamtes Nocten	pn.	.
824	North Bolivian Quechua	2.21873	164,492	184,791	291,345	MIR39g	85-FAAH-d	apolo-sandia		95.00	175,551	1as..	10	9	13	5	3	Quechua: Bolivia, North*	PNb	b
825	Pacahuara	0.00019	14	16	25	MIR39d	84-NGAA-a	paca-huara		77.00	12	0....	10	7	2	3	1		...	.
826	Pauserna (Guarayu-ta)	0.00040	30	33	53	MIR39e	51-AABB-hs	boliviano		80.00	27	1B.uh	10	7	5	5	1		pnb	b
827	Reyesano	0.00030	22	25	39	MIR39d	84-RCCA-a	proper reyesano		70.00	17	0....	10	7	6	4	2		...	.
828	Reyesano	0.01500	1,112	1,249	1,970	MIR39d	51-AABB-hs	boliviano		80.00	999	1B.uh	10	8	6	5	1		pnb	b
829	Ryukyuan	0.02089	1,549	1,740	2,743	MSY45b	45-CACA-i	luchu		60.00	1,044	0....	10	7	8	4	1	Japanese: Luchu*	P..	b
830	Sirionо	0.00763	566	635	1,002	MIR39e	82-AAIA-a	proper sirionû		70.00	445	0....	10	8	7	4	2	Siriono	PN.	.
831	Southern Aymara	6.50000	481,897	541,363	853,527	MIR39b	85-JABA-b	south aymara		92.00	498,054	1.s..	10	8	11	5	1		pnb	.
832	Tacana	0.05345	3,963	4,452	7,019	MIR39d	84-RCBA	tacana cluster		9.00	401	0....	7	4	5	1	2	Tacana	PN.	.
833	Tapiete	0.00700	519	583	919	MIR39e	82-AAIF-cc	tapieté		80.00	466	1c...	10	8	6	4	1		pnb	n
834	Toba	0.00175	130	146	230	MIR39e	86-EBAA	qom cluster		95.00	138	0.s..	10	8	13	5	2	Toba	PN.	b
835	Trinitario	0.06648	4,929	5,537	8,730	MIR39a	81-BDBA	mojo cluster		8.00	443	0....	7	4	6	1	2	Trinitario	PN.	.
836	Tsimane	0.07313	5,422	6,091	9,603	MIR39d	84-SAAA-a	tsimané		12.00	731	0....	8	5	6	1	2	Chimane*	P..	.
837	USA White	0.03000	2,224	2,499	3,939	CEW19s	52-ABAC-s	general american		78.00	1,949	1Bsuh	10	10	12	0	0	English*	PNB	b
838	Uru	0.00209	155	174	274	MIR37b	80-AFAD-a	puru-coto		70.00	122	0....	10	6	6	4	1		...	.
839	Western Bolivian Guarani	0.06744	5,000	5,617	8,856	MIR39e	82-AAIF-ca	west guaraní-boliviano		60.00	3,370	1a...	10	9	7	5	3	Guarani: Bolivian*	PNb	b
840	Yaminahua (Jaminawa)	0.00300	222	250	394	MIR39d	84-NAFD-a	yami-nahua		8.00	20	0....	7	4	6	1	2	Yaminahua	P..	b
841	Yuqui	0.00200	148	167	263	MIR39e	82-AAIB-a	yuqui		20.00	33	0....	9	5	6	4	1	Yuqui	...	.
842	Yuracare	0.03324	2,464	2,768	4,365	MIR39z	84-MAAA	yuracare cluster		25.00	692	0....	9	5	6	1	1	Yuracare	P..	.
843	other minor peoples	0.20000	14,828	16,657	26,262	...				60.00	9,994		10	6	7	3	3			
	Bosnia & Hercegovina	**100.00000**	**3,415,411**	**3,971,813**	**4,323,818**					**34.89**	**1,385,886**									
844	Arab	0.70000	23,908	27,803	30,267	CMT30	12-AACF-b	sa`idi		5.00	1,390	1Asuh	7	5	6	5	2		pnb	b
845	Balkan Gypsy	0.80000	27,323	31,775	34,591	CNN25f	59-ACBA-bc	arlija		20.00	6,355	1A...	9	5	8	5	1	Romani: Arlija	Pn.	.
846	Bosniac (Muslimani)	52.54000	1,794,457	2,086,791	2,271,734	CEW22a	53-AAAG-a	standard srpski		0.03	626	1Asuh	3	4	5	5	3	Serbian*	PNB	b
847	British	0.01000	342	397	432	CEW19i	52-ABAC-b	standard-english		79.00	314	3Bsuh	10	9	11	5	3		PNB	b
848	Bulgar	0.10000	3,415	3,972	4,324	CEW22b	53-AAAH	bulgarski cluster		71.00	2,820	2A.uh	10	8	8	5	2		PNB	b
849	Croat	11.80000	403,018	468,674	510,211	CEW22d	53-AAAG-b	standard hrvatski		92.90	435,398	2Asuh	10	10	13	5	3	Croatian	PNB	b
850	Croatian Gypsy	0.02000	683	794	865	CNN25f	59-ACBB-bd	southeast sinti		75.00	596	0....	10	7	8	5	1		p..	.
851	French	0.01000	342	397	432	CEW21b	51-AABI-d	general français		87.00	346	1B.uh	10	9	13	5	3	French	PNB	b
852	Greek	0.05000	1,708	1,986	2,162	CEW20	56-AAAA-c	dhimotiki		95.00	1,887	2B.uh	10	9	11	5	3	Greek: Modern	PNB	b
853	Hungarian	0.02000	683	794	865	MSW51g	41-BAAA-a	general magyar		81.00	643	2A.u.	10	9	9	5	3	Hungarian	PNB	b
854	Italian	0.10000	3,415	3,972	4,324	CEW21e	51-AABQ-c	standard italiano		84.00	3,336	2B.uh	10	9	15	5	3	Italian	PNB	b
855	Jewish	0.01000	342	397	432	CMT35	53-AAAG-a	standard srpski		0.20	1	1Asuh	5	3	3	0	0	Serbian*	PNB	b
856	Montenegrin	0.20000	6,831	7,944	8,648	CEW22h	53-AAAG-a	standard srpski		70.00	5,561	1Asuh	10	8	8	5	2	Serbian*	PNB	b
857	Rumelian Turk	1.10000	37,570	43,690	47,562	MSY41j	44-AABA-a	osmanli		0.02	9	1A.u.	3	3	3	1	0	Turkish	PNB	b
858	Serb	21.40000	730,898	849,968	925,297	CEW22l	53-AAAG-a	standard srpski		79.50	675,725	1Asuh	10	10	12	5	3	Serbian*	PNB	b
859	Slovene	0.01000	342	397	432	CEW22n	53-AAAF-a	slovensko		95.00	377	1a..h	10	10	11	5	3	Slovenian*	PNB	b
860	Turk	0.30000	10,246	11,915	12,971	MSY41j	44-AABA-a	osmanli		1.00	119	1A.u.	6	3	2	1	0	Turkish	PNB	b
861	Ukrainian	0.05000	1,708	1,986	2,162	CEW22p	53-AAAE-b	ukrainskiy		80.00	1,589	3A.uh	10	8	9	5	3	Ukrainian	PNB	b
862	Vlach Gypsy (Gurbeti)	10.10000	344,957	401,153	436,706	CNN25f	59-ACBA-a	vlach-romani		60.00	240,692	1a...	10	8	8	5	1	Romani: Finnish*	PN.	b
863	other minor peoples	0.68000	23,225	27,008	29,402	...				30.00	8,102		9	5	5	1	0			
	Botswana	**100.00000**	**1,474,205**	**1,622,220**	**2,241,857**					**46.3**	**751,068**									
864	Afrikaner	1.34500	19,828	21,819	30,153	CEW19a	52-ABCB-a	afrikaans	10	82.00	17,891	2B.uh	10	9	14	5	1	Afrikaans	PNB	b
865	Barakwengo (Hukwe, Gani)	0.10000	1,474	1,622	2,242	BYG11d	08-AABF-e	l`kani-kxoe		10.00	162	4....	8	4	6	1	0		...	.
866	Birwa	0.71400	10,526	11,583	16,007	NAB57q	99-AUTE-aa	birwa		29.00	3,359	1csu.	9	5	4	4	1		pnb	b
867	British	0.32000	4,717	5,191	7,174	CEW19i	52-ABAC-b	standard-english	60	79.00	4,101	3Bsuh	10	9	13	5	2		PNB	b
868	Bukakhwe (Boga)	0.08000	1,179	1,298	1,793	BYG11d	08-AABF-f	boga-kxoe		8.00	104	1....	7	4	4	1	0		...	.
869	Central Kung	0.30000	4,423	4,867	6,726	BYG11d	09-ABCA-a	zhu-hoa		15.00	730	0....	8	5	0	4	0		...	.
870	Central Tshu (Hiechware)	0.07700	1,135	1,249	1,726	BYG11d	08-AABE-d	shua-khoe		15.00	187	0....	8	4	6	1	0		p..	.
871	Central Tswana (Beetjuans)	10.52500	155,160	170,739	235,955	NAB57q	99-AUTE-g	se-tswana	96	63.00	107,565	4Asu.	10	9	12	5	3	Tswana: Central*	PNB	b
872	Detikhwe (Deti)	0.16000	2,359	2,596	3,587	BYG11d	08-AABE-l	deti-khoe		8.00	208	0....	7	4	4	1	0		p..	.
873	East Hua (Eastern Hoa)	0.04700	693	762	1,054	BYG11d	09-ABCB-a	hoa		8.00	61	0....	7	3	4	1	0		...	.
874	East Xong (Kong, Magarwa)	0.05100	752	827	1,143	BYG11d	09-BABD-a	nc'u-l'en		11.00	91	0....	8	4	6	1	0		...	.
875	Eurafrican (Coloured)	0.56700	8,359	9,198	12,711	NAN58	52-ABAE-e	west-african-english		70.00	6,439	0B.uh	10	8	7	5	1		pnb	b
876	Gwikwe	0.10000	1,474	1,622	2,242	BYG11d	08-AABC-h	c'wi-khoe		15.00	243	0....	8	3	6	1	0		...	.
877	Handa (Tsexa)	0.20200	2,978	3,277	4,529	BYG11d	08-AABF-a	handa-khoe		10.00	328	1....	8	3	6	2	0		...	.
878	Herero	1.40000	20,639	22,711	31,386	NAB57n	99-AURL-d	o-ci-herero	2	60.00	13,627	4asu.	10	9	7	5	3	Otjiherero*	PNB	.
879	Hiechware (Gabake-Ntshori)	0.08000	1,179	1,298	1,793	BYG11d	08-AABD-g	c'hai-tsho-ri		14.00	182	0....	8	4	6	2	1		...	.
880	Hurutshe Tswana	0.70000	10,319	11,356	15,693	NAB57q	99-AUTE-gg	hurutshe		40.00	4,542	1asu.	9	9	10	4	1		pnb	b
881	Indo-Pakistani	0.30000	4,423	4,867	6,726	CNN25g	59-AAFO-e	general hindi		35.00	1,703	3Asuh	9	8	2	5	2		pnb	b
882	Jewish	0.02100	310	341	471	CMT35	52-ABAC-u	south-british-african-english		1.00	3	1Bsuh	6	3	2	5	0		pnb	b
883	Kalanga (Kalana)	14.81000	218,330	240,251	332,019	NAB571	99-AUTA-i	chi-kalanga	15	52.00	124,930	1csuh	10	8	6	3	3	Kalanga	Pnb	.
884	Kanakhoe (Ganakhwe)	0.06000	885	973	1,345	BYG11d	08-AABC-g	gl'ana-khoe		10.00	97	0....	8	4	4	1	0		...	.
885	Karanga (Shona)	0.84000	12,383	13,627	18,832	NAB571	99-AUTA-f	chi-karanga	15	34.00	4,633	1asuh	9	9	9	5	3	Chishona: Chikaranga	PNb	b
886	Kgalagadi (Kxhalaxadi)	2.35400	34,703	38,187	52,773	NAB57q	99-AUTE-h	kxalaxari	70	27.00	10,311	1csu.	9	7	7	3	3		pnb	.
887	Kgatla Tswana	4.30000	63,391	69,755	96,400	NAB57q	99-AUTE-gj	kgatla	90	28.00	19,532	1asu.	9	9	10	5	1		pnb	b
888	Kwangali	0.48600	7,165	7,884	10,895	NAB57n	99-AURN-s	si-kwangali		30.00	2,365	4as..	9	6	7	3	2	Rukwangali*	PNB	b
889	Kwena Tswana	9.80000	144,472	158,978	219,702	NAB57q	99-AUTE-ge	kwena		36.00	57,232	1asu.	9	9	10	5	3		pnb	b
890	Lozi	1.10000	16,216	17,844	24,660	NAB57g	99-AUTE-f	si-lozi		75.00	13,383	3asu.	10	8	14	5	3	Silozi*	PNB	b
891	Malete Tswana	1.90000	28,010	30,822	42,595	NAB57q	99-AUTE-gi	me-lete		28.00	8,630	1asu.	9	7	7	4	1		pnb	b
892	Mbukushu (Gova, Kusso)	0.80000	11,794	12,978	17,935	NAB57g	99-AURN-p	south thi-mbukushu		30.00	3,893	1cs..	9	6	7	5	2	Thimbukushu*	PNb	.
893	Nama Hottentot	0.04000	590	649	897	BYG11c	08-AAAA-a	standard nama		50.00	324	1a...	10	9	9	0	0	Nama	PNB	b
894	Ndebele	1.70000	25,061	27,578	38,112	NAB57i	99-AUTF-j	i-si-nrebele	5	43.00	11,858	4asu.	9	10	9	5	2	Ndebele	PNB	b
895	Ngwaketse Tswana	9.60000	141,524	155,733	215,218	NAB57q	99-AUTE-gf	ngwaketse	96	55.00	85,653	1asu.	10	9	12	5	3		pnb	b
896	Ngwato Tswana	21.47300	316,556	348,339	481,394	NAB57q	99-AUTE-gd	si-ngwato	96	47.00	163,719	1asu.	9	10	12	5	4		pnb	b
897	Nharon (Naro, Aikwe, Aisa)	0.22200	3,273	3,601	4,977	BYG11d	08-AABA	nharo cluster		8.00	288	0....	7	3	4	1	0	Naro	...	.
898	Northern Kung (Xu)	0.05300	781	860	1,188	BYG11d	09-ABAA-a	uukualuthi		12.00	103	0.s..	8	4	7	1	2	Kung: Ekoka*	P..	.
899	Nusan (Ng'amani)	0.23500	3,464	3,812	5,268	BYG11d	09-CAAH-a	nc'usa		10.00	381	0....	8	5	5	4	0		...	.
900	Ohekwe (Danisi, Madenassa)	0.01000	147	162	224	BYG11d	08-AABE-f	danisa		7.00	11	0....	7	4	4	1	0		p..	.
901	Pedi (Northern Sotho)	0.90000	13,268	14,600	20,177	NAB57m	99-AUTE-d	se-pedi		60.00	8,760	2asu.	10	9	10	5	1	Sesotho: Northern	PNB	b
902	Rolong Tswana	1.40000	20,639	22,711	31,386	NAB57q	99-AUTE-gn	south se-rolong	95	28.00	6,359	1asu.	9	10	9	5	2	Setswana: Serolong	PNb	b
903	Seleka Tswana	0.40000	5,897	6,489	8,967	NAB57q	99-AUTE-g	se-tswana		29.00	1,882	4Asu.	9	7	8	3	1	Tswana: Central*	PNB	b
904	Shua (Hiechware)	0.03000	442	487	673	BYG11d	08-AABE	shua cluster		14.00	68	0....	8	4	6	2	0	Shua	P..	.
905	Sotho	0.60000	8,845	9,733	13,451	NAB57m	99-AUTE-e	se-sotho	95	70.00	6,813	3asu.	10	9	13	5	3	Sesotho: Southern*	PNB	b
906	Southern Kung (Auen, Ghan)	0.07000	1,032	1,136	1,569	BYG11d	09-ABBB-a	au-kwe		11.00	125	0.s..	8	4	4	1	0	Akhoe	P..	.
907	Subia (Zambezi Tonga)	0.40300	5,941	6,538	9,035	NAB57g	99-AURS-f	ci-ikuhane	2	31.00	2,027	1..u.	9	7	6	4	0		pnb	.
908	Tawana Tswana	5.70000	84,030	92,467	127,786	NAB57q	99-AUTE-gc	tawana	10	40.00	36,987	1asu.	9	7	11	5	1		pnb	b
909	Tlhaping Tswana (SeTlhapi)	0.50000	7,371	8,111	11,209	NAB57q	99-AUTE-gk	thlaping	95	30.00	2,433	1asu.	9	9	10	5	1	Setswana: Setlhaping	PNB	b
910	Tlokwa Tswana	0.50000	7,371	8,111	11,209	NAB57q	99-AUTE-gh	northwest tlokwa	95	30.00	2,433	1asu.	9	9	10	5	1		pnb	b
911	Tsao-Nhai	0.04500	663	730	1,009	BYG11d	08-AABB-c	nc'hai-tse		7.00	51	0....	7	3	4	1	0		...	.
912	Tsaukwe (Tsau, Naron)	0.16000	2,359	2,596	3,587	BYG11d	08-AABB-a	ts'ao-khoe		8.00	208	0....	7	4	4	1	0		...	.
913	USA White	0.04500	663	730	1,009	CEW19s	52-ABAC-s	general american		78.00	569	1Bsuh	10	10	12	0	0	English*	PNB	b
914	Xhosa	0.60000	8,845	9,733	13,451	NAB57i	99-AUTF-a	i-si-xhosa	5	60.00	5,840	2Asu.	10	9	14	5	1	Xhosa	PNB	b
915	Yeye (Koba)	1.27500	18,796	20,683	28,584	NAB57g	99-AURM-a	ci-yei		15.00	3,102	0....	8	5	0	4	1		...	.
916	Zulu	0.30000	4,423	4,867	6,726	NAB57i	99-AUTF-g	i-si-zulu	5	60.00	2,920	3asu.	10	9	14	5	3	Isizulu*	PNB	b
917	other minor peoples	0.20000	2,948	3,244	4,484	...				50.00	1,622		10	7	3	3	0			
	Bougainville	**100.00000**	**184,500**	**198,495**	**286,097**					**93.37**	**185,330**									
918	Anglo-Australian	0.30027	554	596	859	CEW19c	52-ABAC-x	general australian		67.00	399	1Bsuh	10	9	8	5	3		pnb	b
919	Banoni	1.10027	2,030	2,184	3,148	AON09d	36-BEAB-a	banoni		90.00	1,966	0....	10	7	11	3	1		...	.
920	Buin (Uitai)	14.60000	26,937	28,980	41,770	AON10d	27-VCBA-a	proper buin		96.50	27,966	0....	10	10	11	5	3	Buin	P..	b
921	Detribalized Melanesian	3.50027	6,458	6,948	10,014	MPY53	52-ABAI-c	tok-pisin-creole		80.00	5,558	3asuh	10	7	6	4	2	Tok Pisin	PNB	b
922	Eivo	0.87317	1,611	1,733	2,498	AON10d	27-UDAA-a	eivo		92.00	1,595	0....	10	7	11	3	1		...	.
923	Hahon (Hanon)	1.20000	2,214	2,382	3,433	AON09d	36-BCAA-a	hahon		91.00	2,168	0....	10	8	11	4	2		...	b
924	Hako	3.60000	6,642	7,146	10,299	AON09d	36-BAAA-b	haku		97.00	6,931	0....	10	7	11	4	1		pn.	.
925	Halia (Tasi, Tulon)	14.40000	26,568	28,583	41,198	AON09d	36-BAAA-a	hanahan		96.50	27,583	0....	10	10	11	5	3	Halia	PN.	.
926	Han Chinese	0.40000	738	794	1,144	MSY42a	79-AAAB-ba	kuo-yü		30.00	238	2Bsuh	9	6	8	3	1	Chinese: Kuoyu*	PNB	b
927	Keriaka	0.72791	1,343	1,445	2,083	AON10d	27-UBAA-a	keriaka		90.00	1,300	0....	10	7	11	3	1		...	.
928	Konua	1.40000	2,583	2,779	4,005	AON10d	27-UAAA-a	kunua		90.00	2,501	0....	10	8	11	4	1	Kunua	...	.
929	Koromira	0.90027	1,661	1,787	2,576	AON10d	27-VADA-a	koromira		80.00	1,430	0....	10	7	6	4	3		...	.
930	Lantanai	0.17995	332	357	515	AON10d	27-VACA-a	lantanai		80.00	286	0....	10	7	6	4	1		...	.
931	Mortlock Islander (Takuu)	0.18211	336	361	521	MPY55z	39-CACB-a	takuu		60.00	217	0....	10	9	1	3	1		...	.
932	Nagovisi	5.28184	9,745	10,484	15,111	AON10d	27-VAEA-a	nagovisi		97.00	10,170	0....	10	10	11	4	3	Nagovisi	P..	.

Continued opposite

Table 8-2 continued

EVANGELIZATION								EVANGELISM			ADDITIONAL DESCRIPTIVE DATA
Ref 1	D 28	aC 29	CG% 30	r 31	E 32	U 33	W 34	e 35	R 36	T 37	Locations, civil divisions, literacy, religions, church history, denominations, dioceses, church growth, missions, agencies, ministries, movements 38
815	1	10	1.81	0	99.83	0.17	C	354.45	57	9	Language recently extinct, now speak Spanish. All Catholics who still practise christopaganism. D=RCC(VA-El Beni). M=OFM.
816	1	10	1.69	8	99.95	0.05	C	589.47	41	10	Portuguese-speaking Whites, mainly from Brazil. D=99% RCC.
817	3	10	1.69	8	99.86	0.14	C	494.18	44	10	Professionals, wealthy class. D=96% RCC,AoG,SDA. M=OFM,MM,SJ,SDB,CSSR,SIM.
818	1	9	1.69	8	99.90	0.10	C	492.75	43	10	East of Lake Titicaca. Language extinct. D=RCC. M=WGM.
819	2	10	1.69	8	99.90	0.10	C	535.45	48	10	Mennonite Germans, in 12 countries. 35% monolinguals, 6% understand Spanish. D=MCB,OCM.
820	2	10	0.00	5	99.70	0.30	C	337.26	0	9	Animists 30%. D=Union Cristiana Evangelica,RCC. M=CBOMB,Andes Ev Mission.
821	1	7	1.69	0	99.70	0.30	C	265.72	63	8	Central Beni Department, around Santa Ana. Animists 15%. D=RCC. M=SIL. Nearly extinct.
822	1	8	1.69	8	99.80	0.20	C	394.20	49	9	Beni Department. Nonreligious 5%. D=RCC.
823	1	8	1.69	0	99.85	0.15	C	394.01	50	9	North central Tarija Department. D=RCC(VA-Cuevo). M=OFM,SFM.
824	1	6	1.69	4	99.95	0.05	C	551.33	41	10	16% monolinguals, 56% bilingual in Spanish, 28% trilingual in Spanish, Aymara. D=98% RCC(many being christopagans). M=WMPL,SIL,Lutheran Mission.
825	1	10	1.81	0	99.77	0.23	C	303.53	64	9	Northwest Beni. Rubber gatherers. Nearly extinct. D=RCC(VA-Pando). M=MM.
826	1	10	1.70	8	99.80	0.20	C	400.04	47	10	Southeast Beni. A few elderly speakers. D=RCC(VA-Chiquitos). M=OFM.
827	1	8	1.75	0	99.70	0.30	C	268.27	64	8	Beni Department. Most are elderly speakers. D=RCC(VA-Reyes). M=CSSR,NTM. Nearly extinct.
828	1	9	1.69	8	99.80	0.20	C	400.04	48	10	Beni Department. Spanish-speakers. Animists 20%. D=97% RCC.
829	1	10	1.69	0	99.60	0.40	C	219.00	67	8	From Okinawa(Japan). Buddhists 40%, other 60% converted to Catholicism by 1960. D=97% RCC.
830	2	9	1.69	0	99.70	0.30	C	286.16	57	8	Eastern Beni. Animists 30%. D=RCC(VA-Nuflo de Chavez),ICFG. M=OFM,SIL.
831	1	7	1.69	1	99.92	0.08	C	476.83	33	10	In Oruro Department. Mainly in Peru (Lake Titicaca to ocean). Many Baha'is, 8%. D=95% RCC(half being strong christopagans).
832	1	7	1.69	4	44.00	56.00	A	14.45	149	5	Beni and Madre de Dios rivers, jungle, some in foothills. Animists 90%. D=RCC(VA-Reyes). M=CSSR,SIL.
833	1	7	1.69	1	99.80	0.20	C	356.24	52	9	Mainly in Paraguay, also Argentina. Animists 20%. D=98% RCC.
834	2	8	1.68	0	99.95	0.05	C	499.32	44	10	Mainly in Argentina. A few animists left. D=AC,MB. M=SAMS,MB.
835	1	7	1.69	0	40.00	60.00	A	11.68	184	5	South central Beni. Animists 92%. D=99% RCC(VA-El Beni; many christopagans). M=OFM,NTM.
836	1	7	1.69	0	42.00	58.00	A	18.39	156	5	Southwestern Beni Department. Fishermen, hunters. Animists 88%. D=98% RCC(many being christo-pagans). M=SIL,NTM.
837	0	0	5.41	8	99.78	0.22	C	370.11	133	9	North Americans, in business, education. Nonreligious 10%. D=RCC,BBC,SDA,etc.
838	1	9	1.68	0	99.70	0.30	C	268.27	64	8	Oruro Department, Atahuallpa Province. Assimilated to Spanish or Aymara. Animists 30%. D=RCC.
839	1	8	2.23	4	99.60	0.40	C	258.42	67	8	Chuquisaca Department. Shamanists 40%. D=98% RCC (VA-Cuevo,many being christopagans). M=OFM,GMU,SIM,SIL.
840	2	9	1.62	0	40.00	60.00	A	11.68	159	5	Northwest Pando Department. From Brazil; also in Peru. Animists 92%. D=RCC, Brethren.
841	1	9	1.72	0	54.00	46.00	B	39.42	120	5	Foothills north of Cochabamba. Tupi nomads. Animists/shamanists 80%. D=RCC. M=NTM.
842	1	6	1.69	0	54.00	46.00	B	49.27	136	6	Beni and Cochabamba Departments. Language isolate. Animists 75%. D=RCC. M=NTM.
843	0	10	1.69		94.00	6.00	C	205.86	49	8	Latvians, Koreans(M=BPM,PCK-Haptong,PCK-Tonghap), Toromono, other South Americans.
Bosnia & Hercegovina											
844	2	9	1.26	7	63.00	37.00	B	11.49	85	5	Migrant workers from North Africa, Levant, Arabia. Muslims 90%(Sunnis,Shias). D=RCC,GOC.
845	2	8	1.26	6	72.00	28.00	B	52.56	87	6	In 15 countries. Muslims 80%(Hanafi Sunnis). D=RCC,GEM. M=GGMS.
846	0	8	1.28	6	53.03	46.97	B	0.05	113	2	Bosniaks. All are ethnic Muslims, all Hanafi Sunnis. 200,000 killed in 1991-5 civil war; 500,000 refugees resettled in Western Europe. M=RCC,SOC,OCCBH,CAC.
847	5	10	1.26	8	99.79	0.21	C	438.29	43	10	Expatriates from Britain, in business. D=Ch of England(D-Gibraltar),MCY,SDA,SA,JWs.
848	2	10	1.26	6	99.71	0.29	C	357.62	49	9	Workers, settlers from Bulgaria. Dmitrovgrad and Bosiljgrad Districts. Nonreligious/atheists 25%. D=Bulgarian Orthodox Ch(P-Sofia),RCC(in Banat).
849	8	8	0.65	6	99.93	0.07	C	565.93	28	10	In 10 countries. Nonreligious/atheists 6%. Strongly Catholic. D=RCC(19 Dioceses),COGY,COCC,CNOCC,PCCY,ECCBHV,RCCY,CAC. R=TWR.
850	3	10	1.26	0	99.75	0.25	C	317.55	54	9	Related to Sinti Manush. D=nomadic caravan churches,RCC,Gypsy Evangelical Movement. M=GGMS.
851	3	10	1.26	8	99.87	0.13	C	514.43	38	10	Expatriates from France, in business. D=RCC,SDA,JWs. M=OFM,SJ,SDB,OP,OFMConv.
852	4	10	1.26	7	99.95	0.05	C	586.00	36	10	Emigres, traders. D=SOC,MOC,AOC,RCC(Byzantine-rite: D-Krizevci).
853	4	8	1.25	6	99.81	0.19	C	434.60	49	10	Emigres, refugees from Hungary. D=RCC(D-Subotica,AA-Banat),RCCY,ECS,CNC.
854	1	10	1.26	7	99.84	0.16	C	490.56	39	10	Emigres, workers, settlers from Italy. Strong Catholics. D=RCC(D-Porec & Pula). M=OFM,SJ,OP.
855	0	10	0.00	6	47.20	52.80	A	0.34	40	3	Decline from 80,000 in 1925 due to mass murders by Nazis. High percent practicing Jews.
856	2	8	1.26	6	99.70	0.30	C	344.92	47	9	From Montenegro. D=Serbian Orthodox Ch(M-Montenegro & Coastland),RCC(D-Kotor,AD-Bar).
857	0	10	1.10	8	46.02	53.98	A	0.03	108	2	Also in Turkey, Macedonia, Kosovo, and 20 other countries. Muslims 100%(Hanafi Sunnis).
858	6	8	0.83	6	99.80	0.20	C	439.61	15	10	In 18 countries. Nonreligious 11%, atheists 7%, many Muslims. D=Serbian Orthodox Ch(21 Dioceses),RCC(3 dioceses),UBCY,ECS,OCCSV,PCCY. R=TWR.
859	5	8	1.26	6	99.95	0.05	C	565.20	38	10	Also in Slovenia, Italy, Austria, USA, Canada, Hungary. D=RCC(in Slovenian-speaking dioceses),ECCS,OCCS,PCCY,CAC.
860	0	9	1.26	8	48.00	52.00	A	1.75	112	4	Immigrants from Turkey. Muslims 99%(Hanafi Sunnis).
861	4	8	1.26	6	99.80	0.20	C	435.08	45	10	Emigres from Ukraine. Nonreligious/atheists 20%. D=ROC,RCC,SOC,PCCY.
862	3	10	1.26	6	99.60	0.40	C	256.23	54	8	Serbo-Bosnians (Machvano), Southern Vlach, Kalderash. In 20 countries. Mostly sedentarized, many assimilated. Muslims 40%(Hanafi Sunnis). D=Serbian Orth Ch.
863	0	8	1.26		53.00	47.00	B	58.03	65	6	Albanians, Macedonians, Persians, Pomaks, Russians.
Botswana											
864	1	10	4.00	5	99.82	0.18	C	463.91	87	10	Whites from South Africa. D=Dutch Reformed Ch(Mother Church).
865	0	6	2.82	0	39.00	61.00	A	14.23	268	5	Mbarakwengo. Black Bushmen, Water Bushmen. Mainly in Angola, also Namibia. Animists 90%.
866	1	7	5.99	1	72.00	28.00	B	76.21	263	6	Also in South Africa. Related to Shona. Animists 71%. D=AICs.
867	2	10	2.52	8	99.79	0.21	C	444.05	65	10	Expatriates from Britain, in education, development. D=CPCA(D-Botswana),UCCSA.
868	0	6	2.37	0	31.00	69.00	A	9.05	298	4	River Bushmen. Northern Khoe Bushmen. Swamps, Khwai river, Mababe. Animists 92%.
869	0	8	4.38	0	39.00	61.00	A	21.35	378	5	Northwest Botswana, also in Namibia. Northern Bushmen. Animists 85%.
870	0	6	2.97	0	41.00	59.00	A	22.44	265	5	Eastern Khoe Bushmen, in east central Botswana. Animists 23%.
871	1	6	4.59	5	99.63	0.37	C	305.83	114	9	Part of the major ethnic people in Botswana. Animists 23%. D=many AICs. M=CP,FIFM(Zimbabwe),LCMS.
872	0	6	3.08	0	31.00	69.00	A	9.05	361	4	Eastern Khoe Bushmen, in north central Botswana. Animists 92%.
873	0	6	4.20	0	30.00	70.00	A	8.76	475	4	In harshest part of southern Kalahari Desert. Related to Xong. Animists 92%.
874	0	6	4.61	0	36.00	64.00	A	14.45	427	5	In harsh Southern Kalahari Desert. Related to Eastern Hoa. Animists 89%.
875	4	10	2.38	8	99.70	0.30	C	334.70	73	9	Mixed-race, mainly in urban areas. D=CPCA,UCCSA,RCC,and many AICs. M=CP.
876	0	6	3.24	0	40.00	60.00	A	21.90	290	5	Central Khoe Bushmen. Northeast of the Xun language area. Animists 85%.
877	0	6	3.55	0	37.00	63.00	A	13.50	337	5	Eastern Khoe Bushmen. On Khwai River, Mababe. Related to Buka. Animists 90%.
878	4	8	5.22	4	99.60	0.40	C	271.56	158	8	Immigrants from Namibia. Animists 20%. D=ELCSA,Herero Ch,Protestant Unity Ch(Namibia),and other AICs.
879	0	6	2.94	0	41.00	59.00	A	20.95	263	5	Eastern Khoe Bushmen(Tati Bushmen). Motsetse region. Nomadic. Animists 86%. M=Brethren in Christ.
880	2	6	3.65	5	96.00	4.00	B	140.16	131	7	A major Bantu people; also in South Africa. Animists 35%. D=RCC,AICs. M=CP.
881	2	10	5.27	7	95.00	5.00	B	121.36	181	7	Early immigrants from India and South Africa. Workers, now traders. Hindus 50%. D=RCC,DRC.
882	0	10	1.10	8	53.00	47.00	B	1.93	93	4	Small communities of practicing Jews, mainly in capital.
883	2	8	5.04	1	99.52	0.48	B	189.80	168	7	Northeast border with Zimbabwe. Resistant to Tswana acculturating. Animists 40%. D=UCCSA,AICs. M=LMS,SDA,AFM,AoG,FMB,LCMS.
884	0	6	4.68	0	33.00	67.00	A	12.04	472	5	Central Khoe Bushmen. Several dialects. Animists 90%.
885	4	6	4.87	4	94.00	6.00	B	116.65	174	7	Immigrants from Zimbabwe. Animists 41%. D=AACJM,RCC,CPCA,many other AICs.
886	3	6	5.09	5	77.00	23.00	B	75.88	214	6	Oldest Bantu inhabitants of Botswana. Animists 73%. D=UCCSA,RCC,AICs.
887	3	6	2.98	5	87.00	13.00	B	88.91	123	6	Bantu; also in South Africa. Animists 46%. D=DRCA(all Kgatla),many AICs,RCC. M=CP.
888	2	6	5.62	4	87.00	13.00	B	95.26	237	6	Bantu from Angola. Animists 70%. D=RCC,AICs.
889	4	6	3.67	5	97.00	3.00	B	127.45	130	7	Original inhabitants; also in South Africa. Animists 48%. D=UCCSA,CPCA(D-Botswana),RCC,many AICs. M=CP,LCMS,FMB.
890	4	8	7.46	5	99.75	0.25	C	407.88	170	10	Mainly in Western Zambia. Animists 5%. D=SDA(Zambezi Union, Botswana Field),CPCA,RCC,many AICs.
891	2	8	3.28	5	83.00	17.00	B	84.82	139	6	Botswana, from South Africa. Animists 48%. D=RCC,AICs. M=CP.
892	2	6	6.15	4	80.00	20.00	B	87.60	272	6	Also in Namibia, Zambia, Angola. Animists 70%. D=RCC,CPCA. M=CP,YWAM.
893	0	0	3.54	4	91.00	9.00	B	166.07	140	7	Kgalagadi District, south of Makopong on South African border. Animists 50%.
894	2	6	6.59	4	99.43	0.57	B	167.93	195	7	Some 3,000 refugees from Zimbabwe. Animists 37%. D=CPCA,many AICs.
895	5	6	3.98	5	99.55	0.45	B	238.89	113	8	Also in South Africa. Animists 30%. D=UCCSA,RCC(D-Gaborone),SDA,CPCA,AICs. M=LMS(CWM),CP,FMB,USPG,LBI(IBS).
896	4	6	4.05	5	99.47	0.53	B	190.42	123	7	Animists 36%. D=UCCSA,RCC(D-Gaborone),CPCA,AICs. M=LMS(CWM),USPG,LCMS,LWF,LBI,UCBWM,UMC,CP,HM,FIFM(Zimbabwe),FMB.
897	0	6	3.42	0	30.00	70.00	A	8.76	404	4	Western Botswana. Western Khoe(Kwe) Bushmen. Many dialects. Animists 92%.
898	2	6	2.36	0	44.00	56.00	A	19.27	209	5	In northwest Botswana, also Namibia, Angola. Animists 88%. D=ELC,DRC(NGK).
899	0	6	3.71	0	37.00	63.00	A	13.50	349	5	Northern Taa Bushmen. In Kakia. Also in Namibia. Animists 90%.
900	0	6	2.43	0	30.00	70.00	A	7.66	313	4	North central Botswana. Eastern Khoe Bushmen. In Nata. Animists 93%.
901	2	7	8.31	4	99.60	0.40	C	269.37	207	8	From Transvaal. Animists 14%. D=Zion Christian Ch(Lekganyane) from South Africa, & many other AICs; RCC. M=CP.
902	5	8	3.70	5	89.00	11.00	B	90.95	143	6	From South Africa. Animists 46%. D=MCSA,RCC,UCCSA,CPCA,& many AICs. M=CP,LCMS.
903	1	8	3.32	5	91.00	9.00	B	96.32	128	6	Part of the Laka(Black Ndebele) from Transvaal. Animists 51%. D=AICs.
904	0	6	4.31	0	41.00	59.00	A	20.95	355	5	In Nata. Eastern Khoe Bushmen. Many dialects. Animists 86%.
905	4	8	4.66	5	99.70	0.30	C	362.81	109	9	From Lesotho and South Africa. Animists 3%. D=RCC,CPCA,MBBRC,and many other AICs.
906	0	7	2.56	0	37.00	63.00	A	14.85	264	5	Southern Kung. West central Botswana, also in Namibia. Animists 89%.
907	0	6	5.46	4	71.00	29.00	B	80.33	280	6	Chiikuhane. Most in Zambia, also Zimbabwe. Animists 69%.
908	2	6	3.65	5	99.00	1.00	B	144.54	127	7	Northernmost Bantu in Botswana. Animists 40%. D=RCC,AICs. M=CP.
909	4	6	3.35	5	92.00	8.00	B	100.74	127	7	Bantu from South Africa. Animists 38%. D=DRC,ELCSA,and many AICs,RCC. M=CP.
910	4	6	3.35	5	88.00	12.00	B	96.36	133	6	Part of Tswana immigrants from South Africa. Animists 35%. D=DRC,ELCSA,AICs,RCC. M=CP.
911	0	6	4.01	0	29.00	71.00	A	7.41	473	4	Western Khoe Bushmen. Animists 93%.
912	0	6	3.08	0	30.00	70.00	A	8.76	373	4	Western Khoe Bushmen. Animists 92%.
913	0	0	4.12	8	99.78	0.22	C	367.26	107	9	North Americans, in business, education. Nonreligious 10%. D=RCC,BBC,SDA,etc.
914	3	10	5.22	5	99.60	0.40	C	291.27	129	8	Immigrants from South Africa. Animists 10%. D=AGC,many other AICs,RCC. M=CP.
915	1	8	5.90	0	42.00	58.00	A	22.99	502	5	In Okavango swamp. Servants to Batawana. Animists 85%. D=SDA. M=LMS.
916	3	10	5.74	5	99.60	0.40	C	295.65	138	8	Immigrants from South Africa. Animists 12%. D=AGC,Holiness Union Ch,& many other AICs.
917	0	10	4.30		77.00	23.00	B	140.52	153	7	Greeks, other Africans from many nations, other Khoisan peoples, other Europeans.
Bougainville											
918	4	10	0.51	8	99.67	0.33	C	317.91	27	9	Expatriates in development, business. Nonreligious 30%. D=UCPNGSI,SDA,JWs,RCC.
919	1	6	5.42	0	99.90	0.10	C	410.62	128	10	Bougainville, southwest around Empress Augusta Bay. Austronesian. Animists 10%. D=RCC.
920	4	7	5.06	0	99.97	0.03	C	505.44	105	10	Papuans. Buin Sub-Province. Southeast tip of Bougainville. Closest to Siwai. D=RCC(D-Bougainville),UCPNGSI,SDA,also christianized cargo cults(Hahalis).
921	2	9	6.52	5	99.80	0.20	C	405.88	144	10	Urbanized Papuans and others removed from their cultural roots. Animists, nonreligious 30%. D=UCPNGSI,RCC.
922	1	6	5.20	0	99.92	0.08	C	426.46	122	10	Papuans. Mountains of south central Bougainville. Close to Kunua. D=RCC.
923	2	6	5.53	0	99.91	0.09	C	438.43	124	10	Northwest Bougainville. Moderate acculturation. Austronesian. D=RCC,SDA.
924	1	8	6.76	0	99.97	0.03	C	488.58	143	10	Northeastern Buka. Tropical deciduous forest, coastal. Fishermen. D=RCC.
925	4	7	5.78	0	99.97	0.03	C	505.44	119	10	Northern and eastern half of Buka Island. Coastal. Austronesian. Intensive agriculturalists. D=RCC(D-Bougainville),UCPNGSI,SDA,JWs. M=SM,MMB(NZ),SIL,SVO.
926	1	10	3.22	7	93.00	7.00	B	101.83	114	7	Immigrants from several regions & China. Folk Buddhists 70%. D=RCC.
927	1	6	4.99	0	99.90	0.10	C	410.62	119	10	Papuans. Northeast Bougainville coast, southwest of Mount Balbi. D=RCC.
928	2	6	5.68	0	99.90	0.10	C	417.19	132	10	Western northwest Bougainville, south of Kunua town. Papuans. Inland villages. D=UCPNGSI,RCC. M=SIL.
929	3	9	5.09	0	99.80	0.20	C	344.56	128	9	Kieta District, central mountains and southeast coast. Animists 20%. D=RCC,UMC,SDA.
930	1	9	3.41	0	99.80	0.20	C	329.96	93	9	Kieta District, Piruneu village. Animists 20%. D=RCC.
931	0	1	3.13	0	78.00	22.00	C	170.82	128	7	Mortlock village, Mortlock Island (190 miles northeast of Bougainville). Remote. Austronesian. Animists 40%. M=SIL.
932	3	7	4.73	0	99.97	0.03	C	495.67	101	10	Papuans. Buin Sub-Province. D=UCPNGSI,SDA,RCC. M=SIL,North Solomons Bible Translation Association,MCFOM(Fiji).

Continued overleaf

Table 8-2 continued

PEOPLE		POPULATION				IDENTITY CODE		LANGUAGE		CHURCH		MINISTRY						SCRIPTURE		
Ref 1	Ethnic name 2	P% 3	In 1995 4	In 2000 5	In 2025 6	Race 7	Language 8	Autoglossonym 9	S 10	AC 11	Members 12	Jayuh 13-17	d 18	wa 19	xc 20	mc 21	mi 22	Biblioglossonym 23	Pub 24-26	ss 27
933	Nasioi (Kieta, Naasioi)	7.75014	14,299	15,384	22,173	AON10d	27-VAAB-a	proper nasioi		98.00	15,076	0.s..	10	9	11	5	3	Nasioi*	PN.	.
934	Neo-Melanesian Papuan	7.71816	14,240	15,320	22,081	MPY53	52-ABAI-c	tok-pisin-creole	33	93.00	14,248	3asuh	10	9	13	5	2	Tok Pisin	PNB	b
935	Nissan	4.00000	7,380	7,940	11,444	AON09d	36-AAAA	nehan cluster		98.00	7,781	0....	10	7	11	3	1	Nehan	...	.
936	Nukuria Islander (Nahoa)	0.14580	269	289	417	MPY55z	39-CACA-a	nuguria		93.00	269	0....	10	9	11	4	0		...	.
937	Oune (Dapera)	0.04878	90	97	140	AON10d	27-VABA-a	oune		80.00	77	0....	10	8	6	5	0		...	.
938	Papapana	0.12087	223	240	346	AON09d	36-BDAA-a	papapana		90.19	216	0....	10	7	11	3	1		...	.
939	Petats (Matsungan)	1.71274	3,160	3,400	4,900	AON09d	36-BACA-a	petats	13	96.00	3,264	0....	10	8	11	4	1	Petats	P..	b
940	Piva (Nagarige)	0.44499	821	883	1,273	AON09d	36-BEAA-b	nagarige		90.00	795	0....	10	7	11	3	2		...	.
941	Rotokas (Pipipaia)	3.14580	5,804	6,244	9,000	AON10d	27-UCAA	rotokas cluster		98.00	6,119	0....	10	9	11	4	1	Rotokas	PN.	.
942	Saposa	0.72791	1,343	1,445	2,083	AON09d	36-BBAA-a	fa-saposa		97.00	1,402	0....	10	9	11	4	2	Saposa	P..	.
943	Simeku (Kopei)	2.20000	4,059	4,367	6,294	AON10d	27-VAAA	simeku cluster		85.00	3,712	0....	10	7	10	4	0		...	.
944	Siwai (Baitsi)	5.11491	9,437	10,153	14,634	AON10d	27-VBAA-a	proper siwai		96.50	9,797	0....	10	10	11	4	1	Motuna*	PN.	.
945	Solos	2.59079	4,780	5,143	7,412	AON09d	36-BABA-a	solos		95.00	4,885	0....	10	7	7	3	1		...	.
946	Tasman Islander (Nukumanu)	0.14526	268	288	416	MPY55z	39-CACC-a	nukumanu		80.00	231	0....	10	7	1	3	0		...	.
947	Teop (Wainanana)	3.72412	6,871	7,392	10,655	AON09d	36-BCCA-a	teop		97.00	7,170	0....	10	9	11	4	3	Teop	P..	.
948	Tinputz (Vasuii, Wasoi)	2.22005	4,096	4,407	6,351	AON09d	36-BCBA	timputz cluster		95.00	4,186	0....	10	8	11	4	1		P..	.
949	Torau (Rorovana)	0.68022	1,255	1,350	1,946	AON09d	36-BFAA-a	torau		96.00	1,296	0....	10	7	11	3	1		...	b
950	Uisai	1.37995	2,546	2,739	3,948	AON10d	27-VCAA-a	uisai		90.00	2,465	0....	10	7	10	4	2	Uisai	P..	.
951	Uruava	0.00379	7	8	11	AON09d	36-BGAA-a	uruava		85.71	6	0....	10	8	10	3	1		...	.
952	other minor peoples	7.48022	13,801	14,848	21,401	...				81.00	12,027		10	8	6	3	0			
	Brazil	**100.00000**	**159,345,520**	**170,115,463**	**217,929,781**					**91.39**	**155,475,612**									
953	Agavotaguerra	0.00006	96	102	131	MIR39a	81-BGAA-d	agavotaguerra		20.00	20	0....	9	5	4	0	1		...	.
954	Akawaio (Ingariko)	0.00039	621	663	850	MIR39c	80-AFAC-a	acawayo		75.00	498	0....	10	9	6	4	3	Acawaio*	Pn.	.
955	Amahuaca (Sayacu)	0.00013	207	221	283	MIR39d	84-NAFA-a	ama-huaca		70.00	155	0....	10	9	4	3	3	Amahuaca	P..	.
956	Amanaye (Manajo)	0.00004	64	68	87	MIR39e	82-AAAC-a	amanayé		81.00	55	0....	10	9	6	3	2		...	b
957	Anambe	0.00004	64	68	87	MIR39e	82-AAEB-c	anambé		10.00	7	0....	8	8	0	1	2		...	.
958	Apalai	0.00028	446	476	610	MIR39c	80-AGAA-a	apalaí		80.00	381	0....	10	9	6	3	3	Apalai	PN.	.
959	Apapocuva (Chiripa)	0.00302	4,812	5,137	6,581	MIR39e	82-AAIF-dd	apapocuva		30.00	1,541	1c...	9	6	6	3	1		pnb	.
960	Apiaca	0.00005	80	85	109	MIR39e	82-AAGE-a	apiaca		81.00	69	0....	10	8	6	2	2		...	b
961	Apinaye	0.00050	797	851	1,090	MIR39d	87-PACA-a	apinayé		80.00	680	0....	10	9	6	4	3	Apinaye	P..	.
962	Apurina	0.00125	1,992	2,126	2,724	MIR39a	81-BCBA-a	proper apurinya		40.00	851	0....	9	8	6	3	2	Apurina	P..	.
963	Arab	0.13000	207,149	221,150	283,309	CMT30	12-AACF-f	syro-palestinian		20.00	44,230	1Asuh	9	5	8	3	1	Arabic: Lebanese*	Pnb	b
964	Arapaso	0.00017	271	289	370	MIR39d	88-KAAD-ac	arapaso		40.00	116	0....	9	8	6	3	3		pn.	.
965	Arara	0.00035	558	595	763	MIR39e	82-AAGA-g	juma		61.00	363	0....	10	8	6	3	3	Arara, Para	pn.	.
966	Arawete	0.00011	175	187	240	MIR39e	82-AAFA-a	araweté		80.00	150	0....	10	7	6	2	1		...	.
967	Armenian	0.01575	25,097	26,793	34,324	CEW14	57-AAAA-b	ashkharik		90.00	24,114	4A.u.	10	9	11	2	1	Armenian: Modern, Eastern	PNB	b
968	Asheninca Campa	0.00018	287	306	392	MIR39a	81-BBAA-a	ashéni-nga		65.00	199	0....	10	7	7	3	2		pn.	b
969	Asurini	0.00011	175	187	240	MIR39e	82-AABB-b	proper akuawa		80.00	150	0....	10	8	6	3	3	Asurini, Xingu	P..	.
970	Atruahi	0.00021	335	357	458	MIR39c	80-AFCB-a	atruahí		10.00	36	0....	8	5	4	4	3		...	.
971	Ava-Canoeiro (Canoe)	0.00003	48	51	65	MIR39e	82-AAIF-f	kaingwá		10.00	5	1c...	8	5	0	1	1	Kaiwa	PNb	.
972	Aweti	0.00003	48	51	65	MIR39e	82-IAAA-a	awetí		40.00	20	0....	9	6	6	1	1		...	.
973	Bakairi (Bacairi)	0.00035	558	595	763	MIR39c	80-AIBA-a	bakairí		80.00	476	0....	10	8	6	2	3	Bacairi*	P..	b
974	Banawa (Kitiya)	0.00007	112	119	153	MIR39a	88-PAAI-a	banawá		20.00	24	0....	9	5	6	0	1	Banawa	...	.
975	Baniwa (Baniua)	0.00420	6,693	7,145	9,153	MIR39a	81-AGBB-c	south baniwa		70.00	5,001	0....	10	7	6	2	3	Baniua*	PN.	.
976	Bare (Barawana)	0.00002	32	34	44	MIR39a	81-AHAB	baré cluster		69.00	23	0....	10	7	6	2	2		...	b
977	Basque	0.00300	4,780	5,103	6,538	CEW16	40-AAAA-c	gipuzkera		93.00	4,746	1....	10	9	15	2	1	Basque: Guipuzcoan	PNB	b
978	Black Gypsy (Ibero-Romani	0.01000	15,935	17,012	21,793	CNN25f	59-ACBA-at	vlach-brasil		45.00	7,655	1c...	9	6	7	3	2		pn.	.
979	Bora (Boro)	0.00034	542	578	741	MIR39d	84-DAAA-a	muinane-bora		65.00	376	0....	10	6	6	1	1	Bora	PN.	.
980	Bororo (Boe)	0.00053	845	902	1,155	MIR39z	87-CAAA-a	borùro		19.00	171	0....	8	5	5	1	2	Bororo	PN.	.
981	Brazilian Black	11.00000	17,528,007	18,712,701	23,972,276	NFB70a	51-AABA-e	general português		89.50	16,747,867	2Bsuh	10	9	13	5	3	Portuguese	PNB	b
982	Brazilian Guarani (Mbia)	0.00309	4,924	5,257	6,734	MIR39e	82-AAIF-g	mbyá		65.00	3,417	1c...	10	9	10	5	3	Guarani: Brazil, Southern*	PNb	b
983	Brazilian Gypsy	0.20000	318,691	340,231	435,860	CNN25f	51-AABA-e	general português		80.00	272,185	2Bsuh	10	9	8	4	3	Portuguese	PNB	b
984	Brazilian Mestico	12.00000	19,121,462	20,413,856	26,151,574	CLN28	51-AABA-e	general português		94.82	19,356,418	2Bsuh	10	9	13	5	3	Portuguese	PNB	b
985	Brazilian Mulato	22.00000	35,056,014	37,425,402	47,944,552	NFB70b	51-AABA-e	general português		94.00	35,179,878	2Bsuh	10	9	12	5	3	Portuguese	PNB	b
986	Brazilian White (Branco)	51.76626	82,487,216	88,062,413	112,814,097	CLT26	51-AABA-e	general português		91.50	80,577,108	2Bsuh	10	9	12	5	3	Portuguese	PNB	b
987	British	0.00410	6,533	6,975	8,935	CEW19i	52-ABAC-b	standard-english	6	78.00	5,440	3Bsuh	10	9	14	5	3		PNB	b
988	Cafundo Creole	0.00003	48	51	65	NFB70b	51-AACA-f	cafundo		70.00	36	1c...	10	9	6	5	1		pnb	b
989	Cafuso	0.00400	6,374	6,805	8,717	NFB70b	51-AABA-e	general português		60.00	4,083	2Bsuh	10	9	7	5	1	Portuguese	PNB	b
990	Caiwa (Kaiwa, Caingua)	0.00927	14,771	15,770	20,202	MIR39e	82-AAIF-f	kaingwá		60.00	9,462	1c...	10	9	6	4	3	Kaiwa	PNb	.
991	Calo Gypsy (Gitano)	0.07942	126,552	135,106	173,080	CNN25f	59-AFAA-ad	norsk-rodi		90.00	121,595	0c.uh	10	7	10	1	1	Calo	P..	.
992	Canela	0.00163	2,597	2,773	3,552	MIR39d	87-PADA-a	canela		40.00	1,109	0....	9	6	6	2	3	Canela	PN.	.
993	Carapana	0.00004	64	68	87	MIR39d	88-KAAE-ca	carpano		60.00	41	0....	10	6	6	2	2	Carapana	PN.	.
994	Carib (Galibi, Carina)	0.00007	112	119	153	MIR39c	80-ACAA-b	central carib		40.00	48	1.s..	9	6	6	2	2	Carib*	Pn.	b
995	Caritiana	0.00009	143	153	196	MIR39e	82-FAAA-a	caritiana		40.00	61	0....	9	6	6	2	3	Karitiana	P..	.
996	Cashinahua	0.00056	892	953	1,220	MIR39d	84-NAFB-a	cashi-nahua		70.00	667	0....	10	8	6	3	3	Cashinahua	PN.	.
997	Chicao (Txikao, Tonore)	0.00025	398	425	545	MIR39c	80-AIAC-a	txikao		50.00	213	0....	10	5	6	1	1		...	.
998	Cinta Larga	0.00061	972	1,038	1,329	MIR39e	82-EABA-e	cinta-larga		90.00	934	0....	10	9	10	0	0		p..	.
999	Coastal Tupian	0.00268	4,270	4,559	5,841	MIR39z	82-AAIG-a	nhengatu		70.00	3,191	0....	10	9	6	5	3	Nyengato*	PN.	b
1000	Cocama (Kokama)	0.00013	207	221	283	MIR39e	82-AAHA-a	cocama		10.00	22	0....	8	5	4	1	1	Cocama*	P..	b
1001	Cubeo (Cuveo, Kobewa)	0.00011	175	187	240	MIR39d	88-KAAC-a	cubeo		80.00	150	0....	10	8	6	3	3	Cubeo	PN.	.
1002	Culina (Kulina)	0.00053	845	902	1,155	MIR39a	88-PAAM-a	madijá		70.00	631	0....	10	8	6	3	3	Culina	P..	.
1003	Curipaco (Koripako)	0.00050	797	851	1,090	MIR39a	81-AGBA-a	kúrrim		60.00	510	0....	10	7	6	3	3	Curripaco	PN.	.
1004	Deni (Dani)	0.00043	685	731	937	MIR39a	88-PAAK-a	dení		10.00	73	0....	8	5	4	1	2	Deni	...	.
1005	Desano	0.00059	940	1,004	1,286	MIR39d	88-KAAE-ba	desâna		60.00	602	0....	10	7	6	2	2	Desano	PN.	.
1006	Detribalized Amerindian	0.02482	39,550	42,223	54,090	MIR39z	51-AABA-e	general português		39.00	16,467	2Bsuh	9	9	6	4	2	Portuguese	PNB	b
1007	Dutch	0.00504	8,031	8,574	10,984	CEW19h	52-ABCA-a	algemeen-nederlands		76.00	6,516	2Bsuh	10	9	14	5	2	Dutch	PNB	b
1008	Emerillon (Emerenon)	0.00006	96	102	131	MIR39e	82-AAAA-a	emerillon		10.50	11	0....	8	5	4	1	1		...	.
1009	Esperanto	0.00000	0	0	0	CEW21z	51-AAAC-a	proper esperanto		50.00	0	0A...	10	9	6	5	0	Esperanto	PNB	b
1010	French	0.00840	13,385	14,290	18,306	CEW21b	51-AABI-d	general français	7	84.00	12,003	1B.uh	10	9	13	5	1	French	PNB	b
1011	Fulnio (Furnio)	0.00172	2,741	2,926	3,748	MIR39d	89-DAAA-a	fulniù		60.00	1,756	0....	10	8	6	4	2		...	b
1012	Gaviao do Jiparana (Zoro)	0.00029	462	493	632	MIR39e	82-EABA-b	ikoro		30.00	148	0....	9	7	6	3	3	Gaviao*	P..	.
1013	German	0.04306	68,614	73,252	93,841	CEW19m	52-ABCF-q	brazilinien-deutsch		87.00	63,729	0A.uh	10	9	13	5	3		pn.	b
1014	Greek	0.00515	8,206	8,761	11,223	CEW20	56-AAAA-c	dhimotiki		95.00	8,323	2B.uh	10	9	10	5	1	Greek: Modern	PNB	b
1015	Guaja (Guaxare)	0.00022	351	374	479	MIR39e	82-AAAF-a	guajá		40.00	150	0....	9	5	6	1	1		...	.
1016	Guajajara (Tenetehar)	0.00722	11,505	12,282	15,735	MIR39e	82-AABA-e	guajajára		60.00	7,369	0....	10	7	6	4	3	Guajajara	PN.	.
1017	Guanano	0.00033	526	561	719	MIR39d	88-KAAD-b	cûtiria		70.00	393	0....	10	8	6	3	3	Guanano	PN.	.
1018	Guarequena (Urequema)	0.00026	414	442	567	MIR39a	81-AFEA-a	walékhena		60.00	265	0....	10	7	6	3	2		...	b
1019	Guariba Maku	0.00014	223	238	305	MIR39z	88-ICAA-a	guariba		40.00	95	0....	9	6	6	2	1		...	.
1020	Guato	0.00024	382	408	523	MIR39d	87-DAAA-a	guatû		20.00	82	0....	9	6	5	2	1		...	.
1021	Han Chinese	0.01000	15,935	17,012	21,793	MSY42a	51-AABA-e	general português		40.00	6,805	2Bsuh	9	6	11	3	1	Portuguese	PNB	b
1022	Han Chinese (Cantonese)	0.05000	79,673	85,058	108,965	MSY42a	79-AAAM-a	central yue		17.00	14,460	3A.uh	8	5	8	2	3	Chinese, Yue	PNB	b
1023	Han Chinese (Hakka)	0.02000	31,869	34,023	43,586	MSY42a	79-AAAG-a	literary hakka		25.00	8,506	1A...	9	5	8	2	1	Chinese: Hakka, Wukingfu*	PNB	b
1024	Han Chinese (Mandarin)	0.05500	87,640	93,564	119,861	MSY42a	79-AAAB-ba	kuo-yü		21.00	19,648	2Bsuh	9	5	8	2	1	Chinese: Kuoyu*	PNB	b
1025	Han Chinese (Taiwanese)	0.01000	15,935	17,012	21,793	MSY42a	79-AAAJ-h	quan-zhang-taiwan		19.00	3,232	1A..h	8	5	8	2	1	Taiwanese	PNB	b
1026	Hishkalyana (Shereu)	0.00034	542	578	741	MIR39c	80-AHBC-e	hishkaryana		96.00	555	1....	10	9	13	4	2	Hixkaryana	PN.	.
1027	Hungarian	0.01050	16,731	17,862	22,883	MSW51g	41-BAAA-a	general magyar		82.00	14,647	2A.u.	10	9	11	5	2	Hungarian	PNB	b
1028	Hupda Maku	0.00074	1,179	1,259	1,613	MIR39d	88-IBAA-a	proper hupde		40.00	504	0....	9	6	6	2	2	Hupde	...	n
1029	Ingariko (Pemong)	0.00060	956	1,021	1,308	MIR39c	80-AFAB-a	are-cuna		25.00	255	0....	9	6	6	3	3	Pemon	P..	.
1030	Irantxe (Mundu)	0.00011	175	187	240	MIR39a	87-NAAA-b	irántxe		20.00	37	0....	9	5	5	2	1		...	.
1031	Italian	0.13549	215,897	230,489	295,273	CEW21e	51-AABQ-c	standard italiano		84.00	193,611	2B.uh	10	9	15	5	1	Italian	PNB	b
1032	Italo-Mulatto	0.00600	9,561	10,207	13,076	NFB70b	51-AABQ-c	standard italiano		80.00	8,166	2B.uh	10	9	14	5	1	Italian	PNB	b
1033	Jamamadi	0.00012	191	204	262	MIR39a	88-PAAA	proper yamamadí cluster		30.00	61	0....	9	5	6	2	2	Jamamadi	P..	.
1034	Japanese	0.80000	1,274,764	1,360,924	1,743,438	MSY45a	45-CAAA-a	kokıı-go		63.50	864,187	1B.uh	10	9	9	5	3	Japanese	PNB	b
1035	Jarawara	0.00009	143	153	196	MIR39a	88-PAAH-a	jarawara		30.00	46	0....	9	5	6	3	3	Jaruara	...	.
1036	Jewish	0.03000	47,804	51,035	65,379	CMT35	52-ABCH	yiddish cluster		0.07	36	0B..h	4	4	2	3	0		PNB	b
1037	Jewish	0.20000	318,691	340,231	435,860	CMT35	51-AABA-e	general português		0.10	340	2Bsuh	5	4	2	5	0	Portuguese	PNB	b
1038	Juma (Yuma,Kagwahiva)	0.00001	16	17	22	MIR39e	82-AAGA-g	juma		57.00	10	0....	10	7	6	2	1	Arara, Para	pn.	.
1039	Juruna (Jaruna)	0.00009	143	153	196	MIR39e	82-JAAA-a	yurúna		70.00	107	0....	10	7	6	3	2		...	.
1040	Kabixi	0.00007	112	119	153	MIR39d	84-OBBC-a	cabishí		60.00	71	0....	10	8	6	3	2		...	.
1041	Kadiweu (Caduveo)	0.00092	1,466	1,565	2,005	MIR39e	86-EAAA-a	proper kadiwéu		30.00	470	1....	9	6	6	3	3	Kadiweu	P..	.
1042	Kaimbe	0.00090	1,434	1,531	1,961	MIR39z	51-AABA-e	general português		50.00	766	2Bsuh	10	7	6	4	1	Portuguese	PNB	b
1043	Kaingang (Caingang)	0.01222	19,472	20,788	26,631	MIR39d	87-PCAA-c	central kaingáng		60.00	12,473	0....	10	8	6	4	3	Kaingang	PN.	.
1044	Kalapalo	0.00014	223	238	305	MIR39c	80-AIBB-e	kalapalû		30.00	71	0....	9	5	6	1	1		...	.
1045	Kalderash Gypsy (Rom)	0.15000	239,018	255,173	326,895	CNN25f	59-ACBA-a	vlach-romani		75.00	191,380	1a...	10	7	8	1	3	Romani: Finnish*	PN.	b
1046	Kamayura	0.00017	271	289	370	MIR39e	82-AACA-a	kamayurá		60.00	174	0....	10	7	6	1	2		...	.
1047	Kamba (Camba)	0.00144	2,295	2,450	3,138	MIR39e	51-AABB-h	south americano		30.00	735	4B.uh	9	6	5	2	0		pnb	b
1048	Kambiwa	0.00058	924	987	1,264	MIR39z	51-AABA-e	general português		50.00	493	2Bsuh	10	6	6	4	1	Portuguese	PNB	b
1049	Kanamari (Canamari)	0.00039	621	663	850	MIR39d	88-VBBA-a	proper canamarí		30.00	199	0....	9	5	6	2	2	Kanamari	...	.
1050	Kanoe (Canoe)	0.00001	16	17	22	MIR39e	82-GABA-b	guara-tégaya		60.00	10	0....	10	6	6	3	1		...	.
1051	Kapinawa	0.00021	335	357	458	MIR39z	51-AABA-e	general português		50.00	179	2Bsuh	10	7	6	3	1	Portuguese	PNB	b
1052	Karaja (Chamboa)	0.00105	1,673	1,786	2,288	MIR39d	87-OAAA	carajá cluster		60.00	1,072	0....	10	7	6	4	3	Karaja	PN.	.
1053	Karipuna Creole	0.00041	653	697	894	NFB69b	51-AACC	gallo-creole cluster		70.00	488	3As..	10	7	6	3	3		PNB	b
1054	Karutana	0.00022	351	374	479	MIR39a	81-AGBB-g	adaru		70.00	262	0....	10	7	6	2	1		pn.	.

Continued opposite

Table 8-2 continued

EVANGELIZATION								EVANGELISM			ADDITIONAL DESCRIPTIVE DATA
Ref 1	D 28	aC 29	CG% 30	r 31	E 32	U 33	W 34	e 35	R 36	T 37	*Locations, civil divisions, literacy, religions, church history, denominations, dioceses, church growth, missions, agencies, ministries, movements* 38
933	7	7	5.14	0	99.98	0.02	C	522.24	105	10	Papuans. Eastern central Bougainville south of Kieta city. Animists 4%. D=RCC,UCPNGSI,SDA,JWs,AoG,BC,and christianized cargo cults(Hahalis). M=SM,MMB.
934	2	6	7.53	5	99.93	0.07	C	546.51	142	10	Government officials and others from Papua and New Guinea. D=RCC,UCPNGSI.
935	1	6	3.31	0	99.98	0.02	C	475.74	77	10	Nissan Island midway between Buka and New Ireland. Austronesian. Little acculturation. D=RCC.
936	0	6	3.35	0	99.93	0.07	C	427.70	84	10	Fead/Nuguria Atoll, northeast of Bougainville. 2 villages. Austronesian.
937	1	6	4.44	0	99.80	0.20	C	321.20	122	9	Kieta District, central mountains, southeast coast. Not intelligible with Nasioni. Animists 20%. D=RCC.
938	1	7	3.12	0	99.90	0.10	C	412.11	78	10	Northeast coast, central Bougainville. Austronesian. D=RCC.
939	2	6	5.96	0	99.96	0.04	C	480.04	128	10	Buka Passage Sub-Province. Islands west of Buka Island. Austronesian. Lingua franca. D=UCPNGSI,RCC. M=SIL.
940	2	6	4.47	0	99.90	0.10	C	413.91	107	10	West central Bougainville. Town of Amun, Piva river. Austronesian. D=RCC,UCPNGSI.
941	3	7	4.20	0	99.98	0.02	C	504.35	90	10	Papuans. Kieta Sub-Province, central mountains, 28 villages. Forest. D=UCPNGSI,SDA,RCC. M=SIL.
942	2	6	5.07	0	99.97	0.03	C	481.50	111	10	Small islands opposite Hahon language area; Saposa Island. Austronesian. D=UCPNGSI,SDA. M=SIL,PNGBTA.
943	0	9	6.10	0	99.85	0.15	C	375.40	148	9	Kieta District, central mountains. Culturally conservative. Animists 15%.
944	4	7	4.69	0	99.97	0.03	C	491.35	101	10	Papuans. South Bougainville, southwest coast. D=UCPNGSI,RCC,ACPNG,SDA. M=MCFOM(Fiji).
945	1	7	6.39	0	99.95	0.05	C	440.37	147	10	Western half of Buka Island. Austronesian. D=RCC.
946	0	7	3.19	0	99.80	0.20	C	300.76	99	9	Tasman Atoll, Amotu village. Very remote atoll 380 miles northeast of Bougainville. Austronesian.
947	2	7	6.80	0	99.97	0.03	C	488.58	144	10	Northeast Bougainville. Austronesian. 6 dialects. D=UCPNGSI,SDA. M=MCFOM(Fiji),SIL,PNGBTA.
948	1	6	6.22	0	99.95	0.05	C	457.71	138	10	Northern tip of Bougainville near Timputz town. Forest. Austronesian. D=RCC. M=SIL.
949	1	6	4.98	0	99.96	0.04	C	469.53	111	10	Central Bougainville, east coast, north of Kieta. Swampy coast. Austronesian. Acculturated. Declining. D=RCC.
950	2	9	5.66	0	99.90	0.10	C	430.33	128	10	Buin District. Animists 10%. D=RCC,UCPNGSI.
951	1	10	1.81	0	99.86	0.14	C	383.88	50	9	Central Bougainville, on coast west of Kieta. Austronesian. A few elderly speakers at Arawa. Nearly extinct. D=RCC.
952	0	8	7.35		99.81	0.19	C	319.30	186	9	Other Pacific islanders (Polynesian, Melanesian), British, USA Whites, other Asians.
Brazil											
953	1	6	2.33	0	45.00	55.00	A	32.85	203	5	Mato Grosso, Xingu Park. Animists 80%. D=RCC.
954	2	6	2.27	0	99.75	0.25	C	309.33	80	9	Roraima, Rio Branco. Also in Guyana and Venezuela. Close to Macushi. Some bilinguals. Animists 25%. D=RCC,AoG. M=CIMI,OPAM,COMINA,WC.
955	1	6	2.02	0	99.70	0.30	C	260.61	73	8	Amazonas. Also in Peru. Animists 30%. D=RCC. M=CIMI,COMINA,SIL.
956	1	9	2.24	0	99.81	0.19	C	351.82	66	9	Para. Closely assimilated to Portuguese. Animists 19%. D=RCC. M=CIMI,COMINA.
957	1	10	1.96	0	36.00	64.00	A	13.14	198	5	Language nearly extinct: only 6 speakers. Most now speak Portuguese. Animists 90%. D=RCC. M=CIMI,ELMA/ALEM.
958	1	6	2.61	0	99.80	0.20	C	341.64	85	9	Para. 20 villages, 37% literate. Animists 20%. D=RCC. M=SIL,CIMI,COMINA,NTM,Baptists Mission.
959	1	9	2.88	1	73.00	27.00	B	79.93	132	6	Mato Grosso do Sul. Mostly in Paraguay, few in Argentina. Animists 70%. D=RCC.
960	1	9	2.31	0	99.81	0.19	C	348.86	69	9	Northern Mato Grosso, upper Rio Tapajos. Animists 19%. D=RCC. M=CIMI,COMINA.
961	1	6	2.23	0	99.80	0.20	C	335.80	70	9	Goias, near Tocantinopolis. 4 villages. Hunter-gatherers. Animists 20%. D=RCC. M=NTM,SIL,CIMI,COMINA.
962	1	6	2.46	0	72.00	28.00	B	105.12	132	7	Amazonas. Scattered over a thousand miles. Animists 60%. D=RCC. M=SIL,CIMI.
963	4	10	2.27	8	84.00	16.00	B	61.32	97	6	Palestinians, Syrians, Lebanese, Egyptians, and others. Muslims 76%. D=SOC,COC,GOC,RCC. M=FMB.
964	1	9	2.14	0	78.00	22.00	B	113.88	100	7	São Gabriel, Amazonas. Animists 60%. D=RCC. M=CIMI,COMINA,OPAM.
965	1	9	1.92	0	99.61	0.39	C	222.65	70	8	Para State. 2 villages. Hunter-gatherers. Animists 39%. D=RCC. M=CIMI,COMINA,ELBI,SIL.
966	1	9	2.26	0	99.80	0.20	C	329.96	70	9	Amazonas. Large village near Altamira. Monolingual. Animists 20%. D=RCC.
967	1	10	2.27	6	99.90	0.10	C	509.17	51	10	Refugees from USSR. Nonreligious 10%. D=Armenian Apostolic Ch(C-Echmiadzin).
968	1	6	2.27	0	99.65	0.35	C	239.62	89	8	Amazonas. Mainly in Peru. Animists 35%. D=RCC. M=NTM,SIL.
969	1	9	2.04	0	99.80	0.20	C	341.64	63	9	Para, on Tocantins river. Close to Parakana. Animists 20%. D=RCC. M=NTM,UFM,SIL,CIMI.
970	1	7	1.81	0	41.00	59.00	A	14.96	188	5	Amazonas. Animists 90%. D=RCC. M=UFM,CIMI,COMINA,Amazon Evangelical Mission,Worldteam.
971	1	10	1.62	1	45.00	55.00	A	16.42	138	5	Goias, Island of Bananal. Monolinguals. Animists 90%. D=RCC. M=CIMI.
972	1	9	2.33	0	71.00	29.00	B	103.66	115	7	Xingu Park, Mato Grosso. Fishermen, hunter-gatherers. Animists 60%. D=RCC. M=CIMI.
973	1	7	2.36	0	99.80	0.20	C	341.64	79	9	Mato Grosso. Many speak Portugese. Animists 20%. D=RCC. M=SIL,CIMI,OPAM,COMINA.
974	0	10	2.10	0	50.00	50.00	B	36.50	170	5	Amazonas. Tropical forest. Some bilinguals in Jamamadi, or Portuguese. Animists 80%. M=SIL.
975	1	7	2.27	0	99.70	0.30	C	275.94	83	8	Amazonas. Also in Colombia, Venezuela. Animists 30%. D=RCC. M=NTM,CIMI,COMINA. R=TWR.
976	1	9	2.47	0	99.69	0.31	C	266.96	90	8	Amazonas. Most in Venezuela. All speak Nhengatu(Geral), and Portuguese; many know Tucano. Animists 30%. D=RCC. M=CIMI,COMINA.
977	1	10	2.27	3	99.93	0.07	C	522.75	58	10	Long-time residents from Spain. D=RCC. Strong Catholics. M=SJ.
978	1	9	2.27	1	87.00	13.00	B	142.89	104	7	Local or indigenous Gypsies. Many nonreligious 30%. D=RCC. M=COMINA,GMWB.
979	1	7	2.27	0	99.00	1.00	C	234.87	82	8	Amazonas. Also in Colombia. Many animists 35%. D=RCC. M=SIL.
980	1	8	2.40	0	52.00	48.00	B	36.06	179	5	Central Mato Grosso. 7 villages. Animists 80%. D=RCC. M=SIL,CIMI.
981	2	10	2.22	8	99.90	0.10	C	543.91	61	10	Afro-Brazilian spiritists 11%. D=RCC,vast numbers of others. M=COMINA,OP,SJ,OFM,WEC,FMB,&c. T=CBN. R=AWR.
982	1	10	2.78	4	99.65	0.35	C	289.44	77	8	Southwestern Parana. Also in Argentina. Shamanists 35%. D=RCC. M=COMINA,CIMI,OPAM,Caiua Evangelical Mission,SIL.
983	2	10	2.41	8	99.80	0.20	C	438.00	63	10	Widespread semi-nomadic groups, some settled. D=RCC,many others. M=COMINA,GMWB,&c.
984	2	10	2.22	8	99.95	0.05	C	594.65	47	10	Spiritists(high and low) 5%. D=RCC,vast numbers of others. M=OP,SJ,OFM,SDB,UFM,WEC,FMB. T=CBN. R=AWR.
985	2	10	2.25	8	99.94	0.06	C	586.70	58	10	Spiritists 6%. D=RCC,vast numbers of others. M=OP,SJ,SDB,OFM,UFM,WEC,FMB. T=CBN. R=AWR.
986	2	10	2.20	8	99.92	0.08	C	566.08	49	10	High spiritists 4%. D=RCC(250 Dioceses),very many others; JWs(strong). M=OP,SJ,OFM,SDB,CSSR,UFM,WEC,UBS,LBI,FMB. T=CBN. R=AWR.
987	1	10	2.27	8	99.78	0.22	C	438.43	61	10	Expatriates from UK. D=Igreja Episcopal do Brasil. Many charismatics. M=ECUSA,SAMS,FMB.
988	1	9	2.22	1	99.70	0.30	C	301.49	84	9	Near São Paulo. Portuguese-based creole, seen as a secret language. D=RCC.
989	1	10	2.27	8	99.60	0.40	C	275.94	80	8	One of many groups now speaking only Portuguese. Animists 30%. D=RCC. M=COMINA.
990	0	6	2.34	1	99.60	0.40	C	227.76	79	8	Mato Grosso do Sul. Animists 40%. M=Assoc Ev de Catequese dos Indios Caiuas(Kaiwa/Caiua Evangelical Mission),SIL,CIMI,ELBI.
991	1	10	2.27	1	99.90	0.10	C	433.62	69	10	In Europe, Latin America. Widely-scattered settled and nomadic groups. D=RCC.
992	1	7	2.27	0	77.00	23.00	B	112.42	106	7	In Maranhao, southeastern Para, northern Goias. Animists 60%. D=RCC. M=NTM,SIL,CIMI,UFM.
993	1	9	2.35	0	98.00	2.00	C	214.62	85	8	Amazonas. Also in Colombia. Animists 40%. D=RCC. M=CIMI,SIL.
994	1	8	2.29	1	78.00	22.00	B	113.88	116	7	Territory of Amapa. Mainly in Venezuela, Surinam, French Guiana, Guyana. Animists 60%. D=RCC. M=CIMI,SIL.
995	1	10	2.19	0	76.00	24.00	B	110.96	102	7	Rondonia. Animists 60%. D=RCC. M=COMINA,CIMI,SIL,Baptist Mission.
996	1	7	2.28	0	99.70	0.30	C	275.94	76	8	Acre. Also in Peru. Somewhat bilingual. Animists 30%. D=RCC. M=COMINA,CIMI,SIL,NTM.
997	1	10	2.30	0	83.00	17.00	B	151.47	109	7	Xingu Park. Hunter-gatherers, fishermen. Animists 50%. D=RCC. M=CIMI.
998	0	0	4.64	0	99.90	0.10	C	374.49	127	9	Western Mato Grosso. Animists 10%. D=RCC.
999	1	10	2.27	0	99.70	0.30	C	296.38	77	8	Amazonas. Tupi-Guarani Pidgin. Lingua franca. All speak Tucano as second language. Shamanists 30%. D=RCC. M=NTM,CIMI,CEM.
1000	1	8	2.43	0	41.00	59.00	A	14.96	205	5	Amazonas. Bilingual in Spanish. Mostly in Peru. Animists 90%. D=RCC. M=SIL.
1001	1	8	2.26	0	99.80	0.20	C	347.48	68	9	Northwest Amazonas. Mostly in Colombia. Animists 20%. D=RCC. M=CIMI,NTM(Colombia),SIL.
1002	1	8	2.11	0	99.70	0.30	C	270.83	80	8	Amazonas. Also in Peru. Animists 30%. D=RCC. M=NTM,CIMI,SIL.
1003	1	7	1.48	0	98.00	2.00	C	214.62	69	8	Northwest Amazonas. Also in Colombia. Animists 40%. D=RCC. M=COMINA,CIMI,NTM.
1004	1	8	2.24	0	38.00	62.00	A	13.87	234	5	Amazonas. Animists 90%. D=RCC. M=CIMI,NTM.
1005	1	7	1.59	0	96.00	4.00	C	210.24	65	8	Northwest Amazonas. Also Colombia. Animists 40%. D=RCC. M=CIMI,SIL.
1006	1	10	2.27	8	99.39	0.61	B	148.04	86	7	Found across country in urban slums. From many tribes. Animists/nonreligious 40%. D=RCC. M=COMINA,CIMI.
1007	2	10	2.27	6	99.76	0.24	C	421.64	57	10	Dutch immigrants from Holland, especially in Parana State. D=Netherlands Reformed Ch,ELBI.
1008	1	9	2.43	0	38.50	61.50	A	14.75	218	5	Also in French Guiana. Animists 88%. D=RCC. M=CIMI.
1009	0	10	0.00	5	99.50	0.50	B	197.10	0	7	Artificial (constructed) language, in 80 countries Speakers in Brazil: 594,000 (none mother-tongue). Nonreligious 50%.
1010	1	10	2.27	8	99.84	0.16	C	484.42	56	10	Expatriates from France, settlers, in professions, business, commerce. D=RCC.
1011	1	7	2.33	0	98.00	2.00	C	214.62	85	8	In Pernambuco. Bilingual in Portuguese. Subsistence agriculturalists. Animists 40%. D=RCC. M=NTM,CIMI.
1012	1	8	0.98	0	65.00	35.00	B	71.17	68	6	Rondonia, Mato Grosso. Animists 70%. D=RCC. M=COMINA,CIMI,NTM.
1013	5	10	2.27	8	99.87	0.13	C	495.37	60	10	Settlers, farmers, professions from Germany. D=Ev Lutheran Ch,Mennonite Brethren(AIIM),CBB,IDB,NAC.
1014	1	10	2.27	7	99.95	0.05	C	572.13	54	10	Immigrants from Greece, in commerce. D=Greek Orthodox Archdiocese of North & South America.
1015	1	10	3.11	0	72.00	28.00	B	105.12	143	7	Maranhao State. Nomadic hunter-gatherers. Animists 60%. D=RCC. M=CIMI.
1016	2	6	2.27	0	99.60	0.40	C	219.00	80	8	Maranhao State. Animists 40%. D=RCC,AoG. M=UFM,SIL,CIMI,COMINA,EMIB.
1017	1	8	1.95	0	99.70	0.30	C	278.49	67	8	Northwest Amazonas, also Colombia. Animists 30%. D=RCC. M=COMINA,CIMI,SIL.
1018	1	8	2.27	0	94.00	6.00	C	205.86	95	8	Amazonas. Many speak Nhengatu. Animists 40%. D=RCC. M=CIMI,NTM.
1019	1	8	2.28	0	71.00	29.00	B	103.66	127	7	Amazonas. Animists 60%. D=RCC. M=NTM.
1020	1	9	2.49	0	51.00	49.00	B	37.23	171	5	Mato Grosso do Sul and Bolivian border, on banks of Paraguai river. Animists 80%. D=RCC.
1021	1	10	2.27	8	99.40	0.60	B	160.60	73	7	Immigrants, in commerce. Folk-religionists 60%. Still many Buddhists, but Catholics strong. D=RCC. M=COMINA.
1022	3	9	2.27	8	85.00	15.00	B	52.74	94	6	Buddhists/Confucianists 80%. D=RCC,Baptists,Presbyterians. M=Shin Sang Mission,GMU,FMB.
1023	1	9	2.27	7	83.00	17.00	B	75.73	96	6	Immigrants from China. Buddhists/Confucianists 70%. D=RCC.
1024	1	10	2.27	7	87.00	13.00	B	66.68	92	6	Immigrants in business. Buddhists/Confucianists 74%. D=RCC.
1025	1	10	2.27	5	79.00	21.00	B	54.78	101	6	Immigrants from Taiwan, in business. Buddhists/Confucianists 80%. D=RCC.
1026	1	10	2.59	0	99.96	0.04	C	508.08	68	10	Amazonas. Close to Waiwai. D=Igreja Evangelica. M=SIL,NTM. Whole of tribe baptized.
1027	2	10	2.27	6	99.82	0.18	C	457.92	65	10	Refugees from Hungary, 1957 onwards. Nonreligious 15%. D=Christian Reformed Ch,RCC. M=RCH,CRC.
1028	1	8	1.94	0	74.00	26.00	B	108.04	98	7	Northwest Amazonas. Tropical forest. 50% bilingual in Tucano. Animists 60%. D=RCC. M=CIMI,ALEM.
1029	2	8	2.27	0	61.00	39.00	B	55.66	147	6	Roraima State; mainly in Venezuela and Guyana. Animists 75%. D=RCC,Baptist Ch. M=Amazon Evangelical Mission(Brazil),OFM,UFM.
1030	1	10	2.02	0	52.00	48.00	B	37.96	159	5	Mato Grosso, headwaters of Rio Cravari. Some bilinguals in Portugese. Animists 80%. D=RCC. M=CIMI.
1031	2	10	2.27	7	99.84	0.16	C	493.62	56	10	Settlers from Italy. D=RCC,Congregacao Crista do Brasil. M=FMB.
1032	1	10	2.27	7	99.80	0.20	C	440.92	67	10	Long-time Italian community, intermarried with Blacks and Indians. D=RCC.
1033	1	10	2.53	0	65.00	35.00	B	71.17	149	6	Scattered across 200,000 square miles of Amazonas. Animists 70%. D=RCC. M=SIL,CIMI.
1034	9	9	2.27	7	99.64	0.36	C	314.05	61	9	Buddhists 36%(Sokka Gakkai,&c). D=65% RCC,AoG,Episcopal Ch,FMC,Holiness Ch,Sul-America Ch,CBB,FEJB,IEHB. M=CMA,JAC,JELC,UCCJ,UFM,FMB.
1035	1	10	2.24	0	66.00	34.00	B	72.27	135	6	Amazonas, near the Jamamadi. Animists 70%. D=RCC. M=ELMA,YWAM,SIL.
1036	0	10	2.22	5	48.07	51.93	A	0.12	166	3	First introduced by immigrants from Germany and Central Europe. Practicing Jews.
1037	0	10	2.27	8	56.10	43.90	B	0.20	145	3	Communities in Rio de Janeiro, São Paulo, Curitiba, Recife, Belo Horizonte. Orthodox Judaism.
1038	1	10	2.33	0	94.00	6.00	B	195.56	87	7	Amazonas. Tropical forest. Nearly extinct. Animists 43%. D=RCC. M=CIMI.
1039	1	10	2.30	0	99.70	0.30	C	270.83	76	8	Xingu Park. Agriculturalists, fishermen. Animists 30%. D=RCC. M=CIMI,COMINA.
1040	1	9	2.21	0	95.00	5.00	C	208.05	84	8	Mato Grosso. Animists 40%. D=RCC. M=Misao Crista Brasileira,CIMI.
1041	1	7	2.69	0	65.00	35.00	B	71.17	140	6	Mbaya-Guaikuru. In Mato Grosso de Sul. Animists 70%. D=RCC. M=SIL,CIMI,SAM.
1042	1	10	2.27	8	99.50	0.50	B	206.22	79	8	Bahia. Language extinct; only Portuguese spoken by ethnic remnant. Animists 50%. D=RCC.
1043	3	6	2.27	0	99.60	0.40	C	223.38	80	8	São Paulo, Parana, Santa Catarina. Somewhat bilingual. Animists 40%. D=RCC,Lutheran Ch,Cristianismo Decidido. M=NTM,SIL,CIMI.
1044	1	10	2.21	0	62.00	38.00	B	67.89	142	6	Xingu Park, Mato Grosso. Bilingual in Kuikoro, Fishermen. Animists 70%. D=RCC. M=CIMI.
1045	1	10	2.34	6	99.75	0.25	C	353.13	72	9	Widely-dispersed nomads in settled Gypsies. Nonreligious 25%. D=RCC. M=COMINA,GMWB,GGMS.
1046	1	10	2.42	0	94.00	6.00	C	205.86	89	8	Xingu Park. Hunters, fishermen. Animists 40%. D=RCC. M=SIL,CIMI.
1047	0	9	2.27	8	83.00	17.00	B	90.88	96	6	Mato Grosso do Sul. Language extinct; only Spanish used by ethnic remnant. Animists/nonreligious 70%.
1048	1	9	2.27	8	99.50	0.50	B	204.40	80	8	Pernambuco. Language extinct; only Portuguese used by remaining ethnic group. Animists 50%. D=RCC.
1049	1	7	2.10	0	61.00	39.00	B	66.79	126	6	Amazonas, upper regions of Jurua, Jutai, Itaquai rivers. Animists 70%. D=RCC. M=CIMI,NTM.
1050	1	9	-0.18	0	94.00	6.00	C	205.86	13	8	Rondonia, scattered locations. Animists 40%. D=RCC.
1051	1	9	2.38	8	99.50	0.50	B	202.57	83	8	Pernambuco. Language extinct; Portuguese used. Animists 50%. D=RCC.
1052	1	7	1.68	0	99.60	0.40	C	219.00	65	8	Goias, Para, Mato Grosso. Literates 83%. Agriculturalists, hunters. Animists 40%. D=RCC. M=CIMI,NTM,SDA.SIL.
1053	1	10	1.67	8	99.70	0.30	C	342.37	51	9	On French Guiana border. Fishermen, agriculturalists. Animists/nonreligious 30%. D=RCC. M=SIL,COMINA,NTM.
1054	1	7	2.26	0	99.70	0.30	C	265.72	86	8	Northwest Amazonas, near Curripaco. Animists 30%. D=RCC. M=NTM.

Continued overleaf

Table 8-2 continued

PEOPLE		POPULATION				IDENTITY CODE		LANGUAGE		CHURCH		MINISTRY						SCRIPTURE		
Ref 1	Ethnic name 2	P% 3	In 1995 4	In 2000 5	In 2025 6	Race 7	Language 8	Autoglossonym 9	S 10	AC 11	Members 12	Jayuh 13-17	d 18	wa 19	xc 20	mc 21	mi 22	Biblioglossonym 23	Pub 24-26	ss 27
1055	Kashuyana	0.00031	494	527	676	MIR39c	80-AHBB-a	kashuyana		69.00	364	0....	10	7	6	2	1		...	n
1056	Katukina do Jutai	0.00018	287	306	392	MIR39d	51-AABA-e	general português		50.00	153	2Bsuh	10	7	6	2	1	Portuguese	PNB	b
1057	Kaxarari	0.00013	207	221	283	MIR39d	84-NCAA-a	cashar-arí		60.50	134	0....	10	7	6	2	2		...	.
1058	Kayabi	0.00050	797	851	1,090	MIR39e	82-AAEA-a	proper kayabí		70.00	595	1....	10	7	6	2	3	Kayabi	P..	.
1059	Kayapo (Kokraimoro)	0.00251	4,000	4,270	5,470	MIR39z	87-PABA-a	cayapû		60.00	2,562	0....	10	8	6	3	3	Kayapo	PN.	.
1060	Kiriri-Xoko	0.00165	2,629	2,807	3,596	MIR39z	51-AABA-e	general português		50.00	1,403	2Bsuh	10	7	6	2	1	Portuguese	PNB	b
1061	Kohoroxitari	0.00057	908	970	1,242	MIR39d	81-AGBB-d	kohoroxitari		40.00	388	0....	9	5	6	2	1		pn.	.
1062	Korean	0.01050	16,731	17,862	22,883	MSY46	45-AAAA-b	kukö		55.00	9,824	2A...	10	6	8	4	3	Korean	PNB	b
1063	Kraho	0.00083	1,323	1,412	1,809	MIR39d	87-PADA-a	canela		40.00	565	0....	9	6	5	3	1	Canela	PN.	.
1064	Kreen-Akakore	0.00007	112	119	153	MIR39z	87-PAAA-a	kreen-akarore		40.00	48	0....	9	5	6	1	1		...	.
1065	Krikati (Timbira)	0.00025	398	425	545	MIR39d	87-PADA-d	krinkatí		35.00	149	0....	9	5	6	2	2	Krikati-timbira	pn.	.
1066	Kuikuro	0.00016	255	272	349	MIR39c	80-AIBB-a	kuikuro		40.00	109	0....	9	5	6	1	1		...	.
1067	Lovari Gypsy	0.01000	15,935	17,012	21,793	CNN25f	59-ACBA-a	vlach-romani		80.00	13,609	1a...	10	8	8	3	2	Romani: Finnish*	PN.	b
1068	Low German	0.00439	6,995	7,468	9,567	CEW19m	52-ABCC	north deutsch cluster		79.00	5,900	2A.uh	10	9	12	4	2	German: Low*	PNB	b
1069	Macushi (Makuxi)	0.00339	5,402	5,767	7,388	MIR39c	80-AFAA-a	macushi		40.00	2,307	0....	9	6	6	4	3	Makuchi*	PN.	b
1070	Makurapi (Kurateg)	0.00007	112	119	153	MIR39e	82-GADA-a	kurateg		80.00	95	0....	10	7	6	2	2		...	b
1071	Manairisu	0.00032	510	544	697	MIR39d	86-GAAA	mapu-dungun cluster		40.00	218	4....	9	5	6	2	1		P..	b
1072	Manchineri Piro	0.00024	382	408	523	MIR39a	81-BCAA-d	manitenerí		79.80	326	0....	10	7	6	4	3	Piro: Manchineri*	Pn.	.
1073	Maquiritari (Pawana, Soto)	0.00019	303	323	414	MIR39c	80-AEBA-a	proper maquiritari		80.00	259	0....	10	8	6	2	3	Maquiritare*	PN.	.
1074	Marubo (Marova)	0.00036	574	612	785	MIR39d	84-NACC-a	marú-bo		30.00	184	0....	9	5	6	1	2	Marubo	...	.
1075	Matipuhy-Nahukua	0.00002	32	34	44	MIR39c	80-AIBB-b	matipuhy		40.00	14	0....	9	5	6	1	1		...	.
1076	Maxakali (Caposho, Macuni)	0.00045	717	766	981	MIR39z	89-HAAA-a	proper maxakalí		70.00	536	0....	10	6	6	2	2	Maxakali	PN.	.
1077	Mayo	0.00010	159	170	218	MIR39d	84-NABA-a	mayu-bo		0.00	0	0....	0	1	2	0	0		...	.
1078	Mayoruna (Matse)	0.00029	462	493	632	MIR39d	84-NBAA-a	proper matsés		70.00	345	0....	10	7	6	3	3	Matses	PN.	.
1079	Mehinaku (Minaco)	0.00007	112	119	153	MIR39a	81-BGAA-b	mehináku		40.00	48	0....	9	5	6	1	1		...	.
1080	Miriti-Tapuia	0.00003	48	51	65	MIR39d	88-KAAD-ae	mirití		60.00	31	0....	10	6	6	1	1		pn.	n
1081	Monde (Sanamaika)	0.00001	16	17	22	MIR39e	82-EAAA-a	sanamay		40.00	7	0....	9	5	6	1	2		...	.
1082	Morerebi	0.00007	112	119	153	MIR39e	82-AAGA-f	morerebi		5.00	6	0....	7	4	3	0	0		pn.	.
1083	Munduruku	0.00123	1,960	2,092	2,681	MIR39e	82-CAAA-a	proper mundurucu		60.00	1,255	0....	10	8	6	4	3	Munduruku	PN.	.
1084	Mura-Piraha	0.00092	1,466	1,565	2,005	MIR39z	88-RAAA-a	múra-piraha		19.80	310	0....	8	5	5	3	2	Mura-piraha	P..	.
1085	Murui Huitoto	0.00019	303	323	414	MIR39d	84-BAAA-b	central murui		40.00	129	0....	9	6	5	1	1	Huitoto: Murui*	PN.	b
1086	Nadeb Maku (Makunadobo)	0.00022	351	374	479	MIR39z	88-ICBA-a	nadeb-p.		30.00	112	0....	9	5	6	3	3	Nadeb	...	.
1087	Negarote	0.00015	239	255	327	MIR39z	87-GAAA-h	negarotê		40.00	102	1....	9	4	4	1	1		p..	.
1088	Ninam (Yanam, Sape)	0.00042	669	714	915	MIR39d	88-DAAA	ninam cluster		70.00	500	0....	10	7	6	2	2	Ninam	P..	b
1089	Northern Nambiquara	0.00007	112	119	153	MIR39d	87-GAAA-gb	mamaindê		40.00	48	1....	9	6	6	3	3	Mamainde*	P..	.
1090	Nuquini	0.00018	287	306	392	MIR39d	84-NAFB-b	nukuini		20.00	61	0....	9	5	4	2	1		pn.	.
1091	Omagua	0.00017	271	289	370	MIR39e	80-AHAA-b	jianá-coto		20.00	58	0....	9	5	5	3	0		...	b
1092	Oyampipuku	0.00022	351	374	479	MIR39e	82-AAAB-b	oyampi-puku		20.00	75	1....	9	5	4	2	1	Wayampi, Amapari	...	.
1093	Pakaasnovos	0.00115	1,832	1,956	2,506	MIR39a	84-OBCB-a	oro-wari		60.00	1,174	0....	10	6	6	2	2	Pacaas Novos*	P..	.
1094	Palikur	0.00055	876	936	1,199	MIR39a	81-AEAA-a	proper palikúr		60.00	561	0....	10	6	6	3	3	Palikur	PN.	.
1095	Pankarare	0.00074	1,179	1,259	1,613	MIR39z	51-AABA-e	general português		50.00	629	2Bsuh	10	7	6	4	1	Portuguese	PNB	b
1096	Pankararu	0.00227	3,617	3,862	4,947	MIR39z	51-AABA-e	general português		60.00	2,317	2Bsuh	10	7	6	3	3	Portuguese	PNB	b
1097	Panoan Katukina	0.00072	1,147	1,225	1,569	MIR39d	84-NACD	katukina cluster		10.00	122	0....	8	5	0	3	2	Katukina, Panoan	...	.
1098	Papavo	0.00010	159	170	218	MIR39z	88-WAAA-a	papavô		1.00	2	0....	6	1	3	0	0		...	.
1099	Para Arara	0.00006	96	102	131	MIR39c	82-AAGA-g	juma		30.00	31	0....	9	6	6	1	1	Arara, Para	pn.	.
1100	Paraguayan Guarani	0.06000	95,607	102,069	130,758	MIR39e	82-AAIF-b	vehicular aba-ñeeme		80.00	81,655	1a...	10	8	11	4	2		pnb	b
1101	Parakanan	0.00027	430	459	588	MIR39e	82-AABB-a	parakana		60.00	276	0....	10	6	6	1	2	Parakana	p..	.
1102	Paranawat (Majubim)	0.00007	112	119	153	MIR39e	51-AABA-e	general português		10.00	12	2Bsuh	8	5	0	3	1	Portuguese	PNB	b
1103	Paresi (Haliti)	0.00075	1,195	1,276	1,634	MIR39a	81-BFAA-a	paresí		70.00	893	0....	10	7	6	3	2	Parecis	PN.	b
1104	Parintintin (Tenharem)	0.00018	287	306	392	MIR39e	82-AAGA-a	tenharim		80.00	245	0....	10	7	6	3	2	Tenharim	PN.	b
1105	Patamona (Patamuna)	0.00053	845	902	1,155	MIR39c	80-AFAC-c	patamona		70.00	631	0....	10	6	6	2	1	Patamuna*	PN.	.
1106	Pataxo-Hahahai	0.00182	2,900	3,096	3,966	MIR39z	51-AABA-e	general português		50.00	1,548	2Bsuh	10	7	6	3	1	Portuguese	PNB	b
1107	Pato Tapuia	0.00012	191	204	262	MIR39a	81-AGBA-c	ipeca		60.00	122	0....	10	7	6	1	1		pn.	.
1108	Paumari	0.00043	685	731	937	MIR39a	88-PBAA-a	proper paumarí		70.00	512	0....	10	7	6	3	2	Paumari	PN.	.
1109	Piratapuyo (Waikino)	0.00045	717	766	981	MIR39d	88-KAAD-c	pirá-tapuyo		60.00	459	0....	10	7	6	3	3	Piratapuyo	PN.	b
1110	Piro	0.00038	606	646	828	MIR39a	81-BCAA-a	piro		70.00	453	0....	10	7	6	4	3	Piro	PN.	.
1111	Pokanga (Pakang)	0.00008	127	136	174	MIR39d	88-IAAA-e	bará		60.00	82	0....	10	8	6	4	3		p..	.
1112	Polish (Pole)	0.10000	159,346	170,115	217,930	CEW22i	53-AAAC-c	polski		87.00	148,000	2A.uh	10	9	13	5	1	Polish	PNB	b
1113	Portuguese	0.40000	637,382	680,462	871,719	CEW21g	51-AABA-e	general português		92.00	626,025	2Bsuh	10	9	15	5	3	Portuguese	PNB	b
1114	Potiguara (Pitonara)	0.00378	6,023	6,430	8,238	MIR39e	51-AABA-e	general português		70.00	4,501	2Bsuh	10	7	6	3	1	Portuguese	PNB	b
1115	Poyanawa (Puinahua)	0.00019	303	323	414	MIR39d	84-NAEA-b	pui-nahua		69.00	223	0....	10	8	6	3	2		...	.
1116	Rikbaktsa (Canoeiro)	0.00050	797	851	1,090	MIR39z	87-HAAA-a	rikbaktsa		80.00	680	1....	10	7	6	1	2	Rikbaktsa	P..	.
1117	Romanian	0.01008	16,062	17,148	21,967	CEW21i	51-AADC-a	limba românească		80.00	13,718	3A.u.	10	9	8	5	1	Romanian	PNB	b
1118	Russian	0.07352	117,151	125,069	160,222	CEW22j	53-AAAE-d	russkiy		63.00	78,793	4B.uh	10	8	9	5	1	Russian	PNB	b
1119	Sabanes (Sabane)	0.00003	48	51	65	MIR39d	87-GABA-a	sabanê		80.00	41	0....	10	7	6	4	1		...	b
1120	Saluma	0.00010	159	170	218	MIR39d	80-AHAC-a	saluma		20.00	34	0....	9	3	5	0	1		...	.
1121	Sanuma (Guaika, Xamatari)	0.00042	669	714	915	MIR39d	88-DABA	sanumá cluster		60.00	429	0....	10	8	6	4	3	Sanuma	...	.
1122	Sarare (Kabixi)	0.00012	191	204	262	MIR39d	87-GAAB-d	sararé		69.50	142	0....	10	7	6	3	2		pn.	b
1123	Satere (Mawe)	0.00565	9,003	9,612	12,313	MIR39e	82-BAAA	mawe-satere cluster		70.00	6,728	0....	10	8	6	5	3	Satere-mawe	PN.	.
1124	Serb	0.00987	15,727	16,790	21,510	CEW22l	53-AAAG-a	standard srpski		83.00	13,936	1Asuh	10	8	11	5	1	Serbian*	PNB	b
1125	Sharanahua (Marinahua)	0.00025	398	425	545	MIR39d	84-NAFC-a	shara-nahua		70.00	298	0....	10	7	6	3	2	Sharanahua	PN.	b
1126	Slovak	0.00200	3,187	3,402	4,359	CEW22m	53-AAAD-b	slovensky		79.00	2,688	1Asuh	10	8	8	5	1	Slovak	PNB	b
1127	Southern Nambiquara	0.00062	988	1,055	1,351	MIR39d	87-GAAB	sararé-manduca cluster		40.00	422	0....	9	8	6	5	3	Nambikwara*	PN.	b
1128	Spaniard	0.12183	194,131	207,252	265,504	CEW21k	51-AABB-c	general español		95.00	196,889	2B.uh	10	9	15	5	1	Spanish	PNB	b
1129	Surui	0.00010	159	170	218	MIR39e	82-EABA-d	suruí-jiparaná		60.00	102	0....	10	7	6	2	2	Surui*	P..	.
1130	Surui do Para (Akerewe)	0.00008	127	136	174	MIR39e	82-EABA-d	suruí-jiparaná		31.00	42	0....	9	5	6	2	3	Surui*	P..	.
1131	Suya	0.00012	191	204	262	MIR39z	87-PAEA-a	suyá		60.00	122	0....	10	6	6	1	1		...	.
1132	Tapeba (Tabeba)	0.00060	956	1,021	1,308	MIR39z	51-AABA-e	general português		50.00	510	2Bsuh	10	7	6	3	1	Portuguese	PNB	b
1133	Tapirape	0.00015	239	255	327	MIR39e	82-AABC-a	tapirapé		65.00	166	0....	10	6	6	1	1		...	.
1134	Tariano (Taliaseri)	0.00092	1,466	1,565	2,005	MIR39a	81-AGAA-a	tariana		50.00	783	0....	10	7	6	1	2		...	.
1135	Taulipang (Taurepan)	0.00015	239	255	327	MIR39c	80-AFAB-b	taulipang		60.00	153	0....	10	7	6	1	1		p..	.
1136	Tembe	0.00052	829	885	1,133	MIR39e	82-AABA-c	gurupi-tembé		60.00	531	0....	10	6	6	2	1	Tembe	pn.	b
1137	Terena (Etelena)	0.01128	17,974	19,189	24,582	MIR39a	81-BEAA-a	proper terena		45.00	8,635	0....	9	7	6	4	3	Terena	PN.	.
1138	Ticuna	0.00968	15,425	16,467	21,096	MIR39d	88-MAAA-a	ticuna		40.00	6,587	0....	9	8	6	4	3	Ticuna	PN.	.
1139	Tingui-Boto	0.00058	924	987	1,264	MIR39z	51-AABA-e	general português		50.00	493	2Bsuh	10	7	6	2	1	Portuguese	PNB	b
1140	Trio	0.00020	319	340	436	MIR39c	80-AHAB-a	proper tiriyô		70.00	238	0....	10	8	6	3	2	Trio	PN.	.
1141	Truka	0.00027	430	459	588	MIR39z	51-AABA-e	general português		50.00	230	2Bsuh	10	7	6	3	1	Portuguese	PNB	b
1142	Tshom-Djapa	0.00005	80	85	109	MIR39d	88-VBBA-c	chunyuán-dyapá		30.00	26	0....	9	6	5	1	0		...	.
1143	Tubarao (Aikana, Wari)	0.00006	96	102	131	MIR39a	81-AKAA-a	tubarao		50.00	51	0....	10	7	6	2	2	Tubarao	...	.
1144	Tucano	0.00190	3,028	3,232	4,141	MIR39d	88-VBBA-d	tucano-dyapá		50.00	1,616	0....	10	7	6	2	3		...	.
1145	Tupinikin	0.00050	797	851	1,090	MIR39e	51-AABA-e	general português		50.00	425	2Bsuh	10	7	6	3	1	Portuguese	PNB	b
1146	Turk	0.00300	4,780	5,103	6,538	MSY41j	44-AABA-a	osmanli		0.09	5	1A.u.	4	3	1	1	0	Turkish	PNB	b
1147	Tuxa (Tusha, Todela)	0.00055	876	936	1,199	MIR39z	51-AABA-e	general português		10.00	94	2Bsuh	8	5	0	2	2	Portuguese	PNB	b
1148	Tuyuca (Dochkafuara)	0.00028	446	476	610	MIR39d	88-KAAE-ab	tuyuca		60.00	286	0....	10	6	6	3	2	Tuyuca	Pn.	n
1149	USA White	0.01760	28,045	29,940	38,356	CEW19s	52-ABAC-s	general american		77.60	23,234	1Bsuh	10	9	13	5	1	English*	PNB	b
1150	Uamue	0.00241	3,840	4,100	5,252	MIR39e	51-AABA-e	general português		10.00	410	2Bsuh	8	5	0	2	1	Portuguese	PNB	b
1151	Ukrainian	0.01575	25,097	26,793	34,324	CEW22p	53-AAAE-b	ukrainskiy		75.00	20,095	3A.uh	10	8	8	5	1	Ukrainian	PNB	b
1152	Umotina (Barbados)	0.00010	159	170	218	MIR39z	87-CABA-a	umotina		79.00	134	0....	10	7	6	2	1		...	b
1153	Urubu	0.00035	558	595	763	MIR39e	81-AGBB-p	urubu		70.00	417	0....	10	7	6	2	2	Urubu*	PN.	.
1154	Urupa (Chapacura)	0.00014	223	238	305	MIR39a	84-OBCA-a	urupá		40.00	95	0....	9	6	6	2	1		...	.
1155	Vlach Gypsy	0.20000	318,691	340,231	435,860	CNN25f	59-ACBA-at	vlach-brasil		90.00	306,208	1c...	10	8	7	3	1		pn.	.
1156	Waiwai	0.00035	558	595	763	MIR39c	80-AHBC-a	waiwai		60.00	357	1....	10	8	6	4	3	Waiwai	PN.	.
1157	Wapishana (Wapitxana)	0.00108	1,721	1,837	2,354	MIR39a	81-ADAA-a	proper wapishana		60.00	1,102	0....	10	8	6	3	2	Wapishana	P..	b
1158	Wasu (Wacu)	0.00063	1,004	1,072	1,373	MIR39z	51-AABA-e	general português		50.00	536	2Bsuh	10	7	6	2	1	Portuguese	PNB	b
1159	Waura (Aura, Uaura)	0.00015	239	255	327	MIR39a	82-HAAA-c	aura		20.00	51	0....	9	5	4	1	2	Waura	...	.
1160	Wayana (Alukuyana)	0.00011	175	187	240	MIR39c	80-AEDA-a	wayâna		80.00	150	0....	10	8	6	2	2	Wajana*	PN.	.
1161	Xakriaba (Chikriaba)	0.00286	4,557	4,865	6,233	MIR39d	51-AABA-e	general português		50.00	2,433	2Bsuh	10	7	6	3	1	Portuguese	PNB	b
1162	Xavante (Tapacua)	0.00502	7,999	8,540	10,940	MIR39d	87-PBAA-a	proper xavánte		60.00	5,124	1....	10	6	6	1	2	Xavante	P..	.
1163	Xerente (Sherente)	0.00076	1,211	1,293	1,656	MIR39d	87-PBCA-a	xerénte		80.00	1,034	0....	10	8	6	4	3	Xerente	P..	.
1164	Xeta (Sheta, Cheta)	0.00013	207	221	283	MIR39e	82-AAIE-a	xetá		60.00	133	0....	10	8	6	4	1		...	.
1165	Xiriana (Guaica)	0.00053	845	902	1,155	MIR39a	81-AFEC-a	xiriâna-l		20.00	180	0....	9	4	6	1	1		...	.
1166	Xokleng (Aweikoma)	0.00046	733	783	1,002	MIR39z	87-PCAA	kaingáng cluster		25.00	196	0....	9	5	6	4	2		PN.	.
1167	Xoko (Kariri-Xuco)	0.00178	2,836	3,028	3,879	MIR39z	51-AABA-e	general português		10.00	303	2Bsuh	8	5	0	2	1	Portuguese	PNB	b
1168	Yabaana (Yabarana)	0.00022	351	374	479	MIR39a	51-AABA-e	general português		50.00	187	2Bsuh	10	7	6	2	1	Portuguese	PNB	b
1169	Yahup Maku	0.00030	478	510	654	MIR39z	88-IBAA-d	yahup		30.00	153	0....	9	5	6	2	2	Yuhup	P..	.
1170	Yaminahua (Acre)	0.00026	414	442	567	MIR39d	84-NAFD-a	yami-nahua		40.00	177	0....	9	6	6	3	3	Yaminahua	P..	b
1171	Yanomam (Guaharibo)	0.00114	1,817	1,939	2,484	MIR39d	88-DACA-b	east yanomamõ		20.00	388	1....	9	5	6	4	3		pn.	.
1172	Yanomam (Waica, Naomam)	0.01203	19,169	20,465	26,217	MIR39d	88-DACB-b	guaicá		15.00	3,070	0.s..	8	6	4	5	3	Yanomami	...	.
1173	Yawalapiti (Walapiti)	0.00010	159	170	218	MIR39a	81-BGAB-a	yawalapiti		30.00	51	0....	9	4	6	1	1		...	.
1174	Yawanawa	0.00014	223	238	305	MIR39d	84-NAEA-c	yahua-nahua		50.00	119	0....	10	7	6	2	1		...	.
1175	Zuruaha	0.00009	143	153	196	MIR39a	88-PAAN-a	zuruaha		30.00	46	0....	9	5	5	2	2	Suruaha	...	.
1176	other minor peoples	0.02309	36,793	39,280	50,320	...				53.00	20,818		10	5	7	3	0			

Continued opposite

Table 8-2 continued

EVANGELIZATION								EVANGELISM			ADDITIONAL DESCRIPTIVE DATA
Ref 1	D 28	aC 29	CG% 30	r 31	E 32	U 33	W 34	e 35	R 36	T 37	*Locations, civil divisions, literacy, religions, church history, denominations, dioceses, church growth, missions, agencies, ministries, movements* 38
1055	1	10	2.26	0	99.69	0.31	C	264.44	85	8	Northwestern Para. Many bilingual in Trio. Animists 31%. D=RCC. M=CIMI.
1056	1	9	2.28	8	99.50	0.50	B	200.75	74	8	Acre. Language extinct, now speak only Portuguese. Animists 50%. D=RCC. M=NTM.
1057	1	10	2.63	0	95.50	4.50	C	210.88	96	8	Rondonia, Amazonas. Limited bilingualism. Animists 40%. D=RCC. M=CIMI,ELMA.
1058	1	9	2.64	0	99.70	0.30	C	273.38	84	8	Para State, and northern Mato Grosso. Animists 30%. D=RCC. M=SIL,CIMI,ELMA.
1059	1	7	2.74	0	99.00	1.00	C	216.81	104	8	Para State. Animists 40%. D=RCC. M=UFM,SIL,CIMI,EMIB.
1060	1	9	2.14	8	99.50	0.50	B	202.57	78	8	Pernambuco. Xukuru language extinct, Portuguese used. Animists 50%. D=RCC. M=NTM.
1061	1	7	2.27	0	73.00	27.00	B	106.58	111	7	Amazonas. Animists 60%. Prelazia Rio Negro. D=RCC. M=CIMI.
1062	3	9	2.27	6	99.55	0.45	B	246.92	64	8	Immigrants from Korea. Buddhists 35%, shamanists 5%. D=RCC,Presbyterians,JWs(strong). M=BFMGAP(Korea),PCK,FMB.
1063	1	7	2.27	0	74.00	26.00	B	108.04	110	7	Maranhao, southeastern Para, northern Goias. 5 villages. Limited bilingualism. Animists 60%. D=RCC.
1064	1	8	2.52	0	70.00	30.00	B	102.20	138	7	Xingu Park. Hunter-gatherers. Animists 60%. D=RCC. M=CIMI.
1065	1	8	2.26	0	70.00	30.00	B	89.42	116	6	Maranhao, southeastern Para. Animists 65%. D=RCC. M=NTM,CIMI.
1066	1	8	2.32	0	70.00	30.00	B	102.20	130	7	Xingu Park. Fishermen, hunters. Animists 60%. D=RCC. M=CIMI.
1067	1	10	2.27	6	99.80	0.20	C	394.20	67	9	Nomads and settled groups of Gypsies across country. D=RCC. M=COMINA,GMWB.
1068	1	8	2.27	8	99.79	0.21	C	420.99	64	10	Mennonite Germans. Fairly monolingual. D=Mennonite Brethren. M=MB(Canada),SIL.
1069	1	6	2.27	0	81.00	19.00	B	118.26	111	7	Also in Guyana and Venezuela. Many bilinguals in Portuguese. Animists 60%. D=RCC. M=CIMI,UFM,ECUSA,BMM.
1070	1	10	1.00	0	99.80	0.20	C	344.56	38	9	Rondonia. Many use only Portuguese. Animists 20%. D=RCC. M=COMINA,CIMI.
1071	1	9	2.27	0	79.00	21.00	B	115.34	103	7	Mato Grosso. Familiar with Nambikuara. Animists 60%. D=RCC.
1072	1	9	3.20	0	99.80	0.20	C	348.94	96	9	Acre. Also in Peru. Isolated. Dialect of Piro language but separate territory along Acre and Yacu rivers. Animists 20%. D=RCC. M=CIMI,SIL,NTM.
1073	1	8	2.29	0	99.80	0.20	C	344.56	77	9	Roraima. Also in Venezuela. Animists 20%. D=RCC. M=CIMI,UFM,NTM(Venezuela).
1074	1	7	2.10	0	60.00	40.00	B	65.70	128	6	Amazonas, near Peru border. Animists 70%. D=RCC. M=NTM,CIMI.
1075	1	8	0.56	0	70.00	30.00	B	102.20	61	7	Xingu Park. Fishermen, hunters. Animists 60%. D=RCC. M=CIMI.
1076	1	7	2.23	0	99.70	0.30	C	270.83	83	8	Minas Gerais. Literates over 27%. Animists 30%. D=RCC. M=SIL,CIMI.
1077	0	2	0.00	0	8.00	92.00	A	0.00	0	1.03	Also in Peru. No contact by 1990. Virtually all tribal religionists(animists) 99%.
1078	1	8	2.08	0	99.70	0.30	C	278.49	70	8	Amazonas.Also in Peru. Animists 30%. D=RCC. M=CIMI,ABWE,SIL.
1079	1	10	2.10	0	72.00	28.00	B	105.12	118	7	Xingu Park, Mato Grosso. Fishermen, hunters. Animists 60%. D=RCC. M=CIMI.
1080	1	9	1.66	0	97.00	3.00	C	212.43	67	8	Amazonas. Most speak Tucano. Animists 40%. D=RCC. M=CIMI.
1081	1	10	-0.36	0	73.00	27.00	B	106.58	11	7	Rondonia. Animists 60%. D=RCC. M=COMINA,CIMI.
1082	0	7	1.81	0	29.00	71.00	A	5.29	231	4	Amazonas. Contact with outside cultures rejected. Animists 95%.
1083	2	8	2.36	0	99.60	0.40	C	223.38	81	8	Para, Amazonas. Tropical forests. Animists 40%. D=RCC,Baptist Ch. M=SIL,CIMI,BTT.
1084	1	9	4.45	0	52.80	47.20	B	38.15	283	5	Amazonas. Language isolate. Monolingual. Animists 80%. D=RCC. M=SIL,CIMI.
1085	1	7	2.25	0	72.00	28.00	B	105.12	112	7	Amazonas. Mainly found in Peru and Colombia. D=RCC. Animists 60%. M=SIL.
1086	1	9	2.26	0	65.00	35.00	B	71.17	137	6	Amazonas. Animists 70%. D=RCC. M=SIL,CIMI,NTM.
1087	1	7	2.25	0	69.00	31.00	B	100.74	129	7	Mato Grosso. Relatively isolated people. Animists 60%. D=RCC.
1088	1	8	2.27	0	99.70	0.30	C	265.72	78	8	Also in Venezuela. Monolinguals. Animists 30%. D=RCC. M=UFM,CIMI.
1089	1	9	1.58	0	77.00	23.00	B	112.42	81	7	Mato Grosso, near Bolivia border. Tropical forest. Animists 60%. D=RCC. M=CIMI,Shield of Faith Mission International,SIL.
1090	1	7	2.35	0	51.00	49.00	B	37.23	164	5	Northwestern, Acre, from upper Moa to Rio Sungaru. Animists 80%. D=RCC.
1091	0	7	2.29	0	51.00	49.00	B	37.23	157	5	Amazonas. Also in Peru. All bilingual in Spanish or Cocama. Animists 80%.
1092	1	9	2.26	0	51.00	49.00	B	37.23	156	5	Northern Amapa. Animists 80%. D=RCC. M=CIMI.
1093	1	7	2.60	0	94.00	6.00	C	205.86	105	8	Rondonia, Chapacura-Wanham, Madeira. Isolated. Animists 40%. D=RCC. M=NTM,CIMI.
1094	1	8	2.28	0	99.00	1.00	C	216.81	91	8	Amapa, also French Guiana. Somewhat bilingual. Animists 40%. D=RCC. M=NTM,SIL,CIMI.
1095	1	9	1.70	8	99.50	0.50	B	204.40	66	8	Bahia. Language extinct. Monolingual in Portuguese. Animists 50%. D=RCC. M=NTM.
1096	1	6	2.03	8	99.60	0.40	C	264.99	69	8	Pernambuco, Alagoas. Language isolate. Monolingual in Portuguese. Animists 40%. D=RCC. M=NTM,CIMI,COMINA.
1097	1	10	2.19	0	38.00	62.00	A	13.87	208	5	Amazonas, Rio Gregorio. Close to Marubo. Animists 90%. D=RCC. M=NTM,CIMI.
1098	0	6	0.70	0	20.00	80.00	A	0.73	233	3	Taramaca river, Acre. Hostile to outsiders. Limited bilingualism. Animists 99%.
1099	1	9	2.36	0	64.00	36.00	B	70.08	144	6	2 villages in Para. Hunter-gatherers, fishermen. A few speak Portuguese. Animists 70%. D=RCC.
1100	1	6	2.27	5	99.80	0.20	C	397.12	59	9	Mainly in Paraguay; also Argentina. Shamanists 20%. D=RCC. M=CIMI,Caiua Evangelical Mission.
1101	1	7	2.35	0	92.00	8.00	C	201.48	89	8	Xingu Park, Para. Isolated tribe. Animists 40%. D=RCC. M=SIL,CIMI.
1102	1	10	2.52	8	64.00	36.00	B	23.36	135	5	Rondonia. Language now extinct; only Portuguese spoken. Animists 90%. D=RCC. M=CIMI.
1103	1	8	2.59	0	99.70	0.30	C	283.60	89	8	Mato Grosso, spread over 6000 square kilometers. Many bilinguals. Animists 30%. D=RCC. M=SIL,CIMI.
1104	1	9	2.27	0	99.80	0.20	C	356.24	65	9	Kagwahiva. Amazonas. 10% literate. Fairly bilingual. Fishermen. Animists 20%. D=RCC. M=SIL,CIMI.
1105	1	7	2.27	0	99.70	0.30	C	268.27	86	8	Mainly in Guyana. Animists 30%. D=RCC. M=CIMI.
1106	1	9	2.56	8	99.50	0.50	B	204.40	87	8	Minas Gerais, Bahia. Language extinct; all now monolingual in Portuguese. Animists 50%. D=RCC.
1107	1	9	2.26	0	95.00	5.00	C	208.05	94	8	Amazonas. Animists 40%. D=RCC. M=CIMI.
1108	1	9	2.29	0	99.70	0.30	C	278.49	83	8	Amazonas. Fairly bilingual. Animists 30%. D=RCC. M=SIL,CIMI.
1109	1	7	2.26	0	99.60	0.40	C	219.00	81	8	Amazonas, also in Colombia. Second language Tucano. Animists 40%. D=RCC. M=COMINA,CIMI,SIL.
1110	1	8	2.27	0	99.70	0.30	C	281.05	81	8	Acre. Mainly in Urubamba river area, Peru. Animists 30%. D=RCC. M=CIMI,NTM,SIL.
1111	1	10	2.23	0	99.00	1.00	C	216.81	81	8	Amazonas. Upper Tiquie, tributary of Vaupes. Animists 40%. D=RCC. M=CIMI,NTM,ABWE.
1112	1	10	2.27	6	99.87	0.13	C	504.90	39	10	Immigrants and settlers from Poland, especially after 1939 and 1945. Strong Catholics. D=RCC.
1113	4	10	2.27	8	99.92	0.08	C	574.21	53	10	Many Spiritists. Mostly Catholics. D=RCC,Presbyterian Ch, Methodists, Baptists. M=UBS,LBI,SJ. T=CBN. R=AWR.
1114	1	7	2.55	8	99.70	0.30	C	332.15	67	9	Paraiba. Language extinct, only Portuguese now used. Animists 30%. D=RCC. M=CIMI.
1115	1	10	2.44	0	99.69	0.31	C	264.44	82	8	Acre, upper Rio Moa, tributary of Juma. Animists 31%. D=RCC. M=COMINA,CIMI.
1116	1	9	2.22	0	99.80	0.20	C	335.80	77	9	Mato Grosso, tropical forest. Language isolate. Animists 20%. D=RCC. M=SIL,CIMI.
1117	1	10	2.27	6	99.80	0.20	C	429.24	63	10	Refugees after 1945, from Romania. Nonreligious 16%. D=Romanian Orthodox Ch. M=ROME(USA).
1118	1	8	2.27	7	99.63	0.37	C	305.83	47	9	Refugees after 1917 from USSR, and after 1945. Nonreligious 30%. D=Russian Orthodox Ch(D-South America). M=OCA.
1119	1	10	1.94	0	99.80	0.20	C	347.48	61	9	Mato Grosso. Men are trilingual in Portuguese, Northern Nambiquara. Animists 19%. D=RCC. M=CIMI.
1120	1	7	1.94	0	47.00	53.00	A	34.31	154	5	Mato Grosso, within northeastern Nambiquara reserve. Animists 80%. Isolated. D=RCC.
1121	1	8	2.28	0	96.00	4.00	C	210.24	85	8	Mainly in Venezuela. 25% bilingual in Maquiritare. Animists 40%. D=RCC. M=CIMI,UFM,NTM,ORM(Venezuela),independents.
1122	1	10	2.27	0	99.70	0.30	C	282.84	73	8	Mato Grosso. Bilingual in Southern Nambiquara. Animists 30%. D=RCC. M=CIMI,MCB.
1123	2	7	2.73	0	99.70	0.30	C	286.16	82	8	Para, Andira and other rivers. Animists 30%. D=RCC,Baptist Ch. M=SIL,COMINA,CIMI,CSA,YWAM,NTM.
1124	1	10	2.27	6	99.83	0.17	C	454.42	41	10	Refugees from Yugoslavia. Nonreligious and atheists 17%. D=Serbian Orthodox Ch.
1125	1	9	2.29	0	99.70	0.30	C	278.49	75	8	Acre, along upper Envira. Animists 30%. D=RCC. M=CIMI,SIL.
1126	1	10	2.27	6	99.79	0.21	C	409.45	66	10	Refugees from Czechoslovakia, after 1938, 1945, 1968. Nonreligious 20%. D=RCC.
1127	1	8	2.26	0	80.00	20.00	B	116.80	101	7	Mato Grosso, near Bolivia border. Reduced from 10,000 in 1940 by measles. Animists 60%. D=RCC. M=SAM,SIL,CIMI,SFMI,MCB.
1128	1	8	2.27	8	99.95	0.05	C	589.47	51	10	Immigrants from Spain, long-time settlers, farmers, professionals. Strong Catholics. D=RCC.
1129	1	9	1.20	0	95.00	5.00	C	208.05	53	8	Along Rondonia-Mato Grosso border. 10 villages. 5% literate. Animists 40%. D=RCC. M=CIMI,SIL.
1130	1	10	2.38	0	67.00	33.00	B	75.81	124	6	Para.Isolated language. Animists 69%. D=RCC. M=CIMI,SIL,ALEM.
1131	1	10	2.35	0	93.00	7.00	C	203.67	99	8	Xingu Park. Hunters, fishermen, agriculturalists. Animists 40%. D=RCC. M=CIMI.
1132	1	9	3.74	8	99.50	0.50	B	202.57	117	8	Ceara. Language extinct; all speak Portuguese. Animists 50%. D=RCC.
1133	1	10	2.25	0	98.00	2.00	C	232.50	81	8	Mato Grosso. Hunters, fishermen. Animists 35%. D=RCC. M=CIMI.
1134	1	7	2.04	0	81.00	19.00	B	147.82	103	7	Amazonas, also in Colombia. Animists 50%. D=RCC. M=COMINA,CIMI.
1135	1	6	2.28	0	90.00	10.00	C	197.10	100	7	Along Venezuela border. Animists 40%. D=RCC. M=CIMI.
1136	1	8	2.95	0	98.00	2.00	C	214.62	100	8	Maranhao, Gurupi river and Guama. Tembe spoken by 20%; rest use Portugese. Well integrated. Animists 40%. D=RCC. M=CIMI.
1137	1	6	2.27	0	83.00	17.00	B	136.32	108	7	Mato Grosso do Sul. Somewhat bilingual. Animists 55%. D=RCC. M=SAM,SIL,CIMI,Caiua Evangelical Mission,ELBI.
1138	1	6	2.27	0	78.00	22.00	B	113.88	104	7	West Amazonas. Also in Peru, Colombia. Language isolate. Animists 60%. D=RCC. M=ABWE,CIMI,SIL,OBM.
1139	1	9	2.27	8	99.50	0.50	B	200.75	81	8	Alagoas.All are now monolingual in Portuguese. Animists 50%. D=RCC. M=CIMI.
1140	1	8	2.09	0	99.70	0.30	C	275.94	79	8	Para. Mainly in Surinam. Animists 30%. D=RCC. M=CIMI,WT(Surinam).
1141	1	9	2.29	8	99.50	0.50	B	202.57	81	8	Pernambuco, Bahia. Language extinct, now monolingual in Portuguese. Animists 50%. D=RCC.
1142	0	9	2.18	0	58.00	42.00	B	63.51	136	6	Amazonas. Tribal religionists/animists 70%.
1143	1	7	2.35	0	82.00	18.00	B	149.65	112	7	In Rondonia State. Animists 50%. D=RCC. M=BBDWM,ALEM.
1144	1	6	2.27	0	83.00	17.00	B	151.47	98	7	Amazonas. Lingua franca. Animists 50%. D=RCC. M=COMINA,CIMI,SIL.
1145	1	9	2.44	8	99.50	0.50	B	202.57	76	8	Espiritu Santo. Monolingual in Portuguese. Animists 50%. D=RCC. M=CIMI.
1146	0	10	1.62	8	43.09	56.91	A	0.14	148	3	Immigrants from Turkey. Laborers, farmers, urbanites. Muslims 100% (Hanafi Sunnis).
1147	1	10	2.00	8	64.00	36.00	B	23.36	128	5	Bahia. Language extinct, now monolingual in Portuguese. Animists 90%. D=RCC. M=CIMI,NTM.
1148	1	7	1.78	0	98.00	2.00	C	214.62	69	8	Amazonas. Also in Colombia. Second language: Tucano, or Northern Barasano. Animists 40%. D=RCC. M=CIMI,SIL.
1149	4	10	2.62	8	99.78	0.22	C	429.39	64	10	North Americans, in business, education. D=RCC,BBC,SDA,etc. M=FMB.
1150	1	10	3.36	8	63.00	37.00	B	22.99	174	5	Pernambuco. Language extinct, now monolingual in Portuguese. Animists 90%. D=RCC. M=CIMI.
1151	1	10	2.27	6	99.75	0.25	C	391.46	66	9	Refugees from USSR after 1917, 1945. Nonreligious and atheists 25%. D=Ukrainian Autocephalous Orthodox Ch. M=UOCUSA.
1152	1	10	1.73	0	99.79	0.21	C	334.48	64	9	Mato Grosso. All bilingual in Portuguese. Animists 21%. D=RCC. M=CIMI.
1153	1	7	2.27	0	99.70	0.30	C	270.83	75	8	Maranhao.10 scattered villages. 6% literate. Animists 30%. D=RCC. M=SIL,CIMI.
1154	1	8	2.28	0	71.00	29.00	B	103.66	127	7	Txapakura. Rondonia. Animists 60%. D=RCC. M=CIMI.
1155	1	9	2.33	1	99.90	0.10	C	436.90	69	10	Kalderash, Lovari. In Argentina, Colombia, USA, 20 countries in Europe. D=RCC.
1156	1	7	1.91	0	99.60	0.40	C	219.00	80	8	Amazonas, Para, Roraima States. Hunters, fishermen. Animists 40%. D=RCC. M=UFM,CIMI,Amazon Evangelical Mission.
1157	1	7	2.27	0	95.00	5.00	C	208.05	94	8	Roraima. Somewhat bilingual. Animists 40%. D=RCC. M=CIMI,UFM(Guyana).
1158	1	9	1.91	8	99.50	0.50	B	200.75	72	8	Alagoas. Language extinct, now monolingual in Portuguese. Animists 50%. D=RCC.
1159	1	9	2.58	0	50.00	50.00	B	36.50	196	5	Xingu Park. Animists 80%. D=RCC. M=SIL,CIMI.
1160	1	9	2.26	0	99.80	0.20	C	344.56	76	9	Amapa. Also in Surinam and French Guiana. Animists 20%. D=RCC. M=CIMI,WT(Surinam).
1161	1	9	2.48	8	99.50	0.50	B	204.40	78	8	Minas Gerais. Language extinct; all now monolingual in Portuguese. Animists 50%. D=RCC.
1162	1	7	2.28	0	94.00	6.00	C	205.86	87	8	Mato Grosso. Hunter-gatherers. Animists 40%. D=RCC. M=SIL,CIMI.
1163	1	7	2.49	0	99.80	0.20	C	341.64	75	9	Goias. Somewhat bilingual. Animists 20%. D=RCC. M=NTM,Junta Batista Nacional,CIMI,ALEM.
1164	1	10	2.28	0	96.00	4.00	C	210.24	83	8	Parana, close to Kaingang, Tupi. Language virtually extinct; all now use Portuguese. Animists 40%. D=RCC.
1165	1	7	2.27	0	49.00	51.00	A	35.77	183	5	Amazonas, near Venezuela border. Isolated. Animists 80%. D=RCC. M=CIMI.
1166	2	8	2.26	0	64.00	36.00	B	58.40	140	6	Santa Catarina. Somewhat bilingual. Animists 75%. D=RCC,AoG. M=CIMI,SIL.
1167	1	10	2.27	8	63.00	37.00	B	22.99	142	5	Alagoas. Monolingual in Portuguese. Animists 90%. D=RCC. M=CIMI.
1168	1	9	3.69	8	99.50	0.50	B	200.75	117	8	Amazonas. Language extinct; all monolingual in Portuguese. Animists 50%. D=RCC.
1169	1	8	2.28	0	62.00	38.00	B	67.89	145	6	Amazonas. Animists 70%. D=RCC. M=CIMI,ELMA/ALEM.
1170	1	8	2.26	0	75.00	25.00	B	109.50	108	7	Acre. Also in Peru, Bolivia. Animists 60%. D=RCC. M=CIMI,NTM,SIL.
1171	1	8	2.27	0	59.00	41.00	B	43.07	138	6	Amazonas, also in Venezuela. Monolingual. Animists 80%. D=RCC. M=CIMI,NTM,UFM.
1172	1	6	2.27	0	48.00	52.00	A	28.26	170	5	Roraima State. Monolingual, semi-nomadic. Animists 85%. D=RCC. M=UFM,NTM,COMINA,CIMI,Amazon Evangelical Mission,MBC,SIL.
1173	1	10	2.35	0	62.00	38.00	B	67.89	148	6	Xingu Park. Fishermen, hunter-gatherers. Animists 70%. D=RCC. M=CIMI.
1174	1	10	2.24	0	84.00	16.00	B	153.30	96	7	Acre. Animists (tribal religionists) 50%. D=RCC. M=NTM.
1175	1	9	2.24	0	62.00	38.00	B	67.89	143	6	Indios do Coxodoa. Hunters. Animists (traditional religionists) 70%. D=RCC. M=YWAM,CIMI.
1176	0	10	2.49		85.00	15.00	B	164.43	80	7	Angolans, Mozambicans, Argentinians, Australians, Latvians, Nigerians, Putura (riverine aboriginals related to Tupi), Himarima; 50 nearly-extinct languages.

Continued overleaf

Table 8-2 continued

PEOPLE		POPULATION				IDENTITY CODE		LANGUAGE		CHURCH		MINISTRY						SCRIPTURE		
Ref	Ethnic name	P%	In 1995	In 2000	In 2025	Race	Language	Autoglossonym	S	AC	Members	Jayuh	d	wa	xc	mc	mi	Biblioglossonym	Pub	ss
1	2	3	4	5	6	7	8	9	10	11	12	13-17	18	19	20	21	22	23	24-26	27
Britain (UK of GB & NI)		**100.00000**	**58,308,142**	**58,830,160**	**59,960,856**					**66.38**	**39,053,151**									
1177	Afrikaner	0.05000	29,154	29,415	29,980	CEW19a	52-ABCB-a	afrikaans		79.00	23,238	2B.uh	10	8	14	5	3	Afrikaans	PNB	b
1178	Albanian	0.00027	157	159	162	CEW13	55-AAAA-b	northwest gheg		50.00	79	1a.u.	10	8	8	4	3	Albanian: Gheg*	PN.	b
1179	Anglo-Australian	0.11000	64,139	64,713	65,957	CEW19c	52-ABAC-x	general australian		67.00	43,358	1Bsuh	10	9	13	5	3		pnb	b
1180	Anglo-Canadian	0.11100	64,722	65,301	66,557	CEW19d	52-ABAC-r	general canadian		75.00	48,976	1Bsuh	10	9	14	5	3		pnb	b
1181	Anglo-New Zealander	0.05100	29,737	30,003	30,580	CEW19e	52-ABAC-y	general new-zealand		76.00	22,803	1Bsuh	10	9	14	5	3		pnb	b
1182	Anglo-Romani Gypsy	0.15724	91,684	92,505	94,282	CNN25f	59-AGAA-aa	anglo-romani-t.		70.00	64,753	0....	10	7	7	4	3		...	b
1183	Armenian	0.05000	29,154	29,415	29,980	CEW14	57-AAAA-b	ashkharik		85.00	25,003	4A.u.	10	8	11	4	3	Armenian: Modern, Eastern	PNB	b
1184	Assyrian	0.01400	8,163	8,236	8,395	CMT31	12-AAAA-d	east syriac		87.00	7,166	1as..	10	8	10	4	2	Syriac: Ancient*	PNB	b
1185	Austrian	0.04100	23,906	24,120	24,584	CEW19f	52-ABCF-b	donau-bayrisch-t.		90.00	21,708	0B.uh	10	9	13	5	3		pn.	b
1186	Belgian (Fleming)	0.02600	15,160	15,296	15,590	CEW19k	52-ABCA-g	oostvlaandersch		90.00	13,766	1Bsuh	10	9	15	5	1		pnb	b
1187	Bengali	0.50000	291,541	294,151	299,804	CNN25b	59-AAFT-e	west bengali		1.00	2,942	1Asuh	6	5	8	5	1	Bengali: Musalmani*	PNB	b
1188	Bulgar	0.00123	717	724	738	CEW22b	53-AAAH-b	bulgarski		75.00	543	2A.uh	10	8	8	5	1	Bulgarian	PNB	b
1189	Burmese	0.02100	12,245	12,354	12,592	MSY50b	77-AABA-a	bama		1.00	124	4Asu.	6	5	4	4	2	Burmese	PNB	b
1190	Byelorussian	0.00850	4,956	5,001	5,097	CEW22c	53-AAAE-c	bielorusskiy		85.00	4,250	3A.uh	10	8	11	4	3	Byelorussian*	PNB	b
1191	Ceylon Tamil	0.06400	37,317	37,651	38,375	CNN23c	49-EBEA-bn	north sri-lanka-tamil		30.00	11,295	1Asu.	9	8	8	5	3		pnb	b
1192	Coloured (Eurafrican)	0.23600	137,607	138,839	141,508	NAN58	52-ABAE-e	west-african-english		90.00	124,955	0B.uh	10	8	13	5	3		pnb	b
1193	Coloured (Eurasian)	0.20000	116,616	117,660	119,922	MSY43	52-ABAD-a	south-asian-english		90.00	105,894	0B.uh	10	8	11	5	3		...	b
1194	Cornish	0.00060	350	353	360	CEW18z	50-ABBA-b	kernewek-q.		95.00	335	0....	10	8	13	5	0	Cornish	P..	b
1195	Czech	0.01800	10,495	10,589	10,793	CEW22e	53-AAAD-a	czesky		85.00	9,001	2Asuh	10	9	11	5	2	Czech	PNB	b
1196	Danish	0.01700	9,912	10,001	10,193	CEW19g	52-AAAD-c	general dansk		95.00	9,501	2A.uh	10	9	11	5	2	Danish	PNB	b
1197	Dutch	0.04200	24,489	24,709	25,184	CEW19h	52-ABCA-a	algemeen-nederlands	1	76.00	18,779	2Bsuh	10	9	15	5	1	Dutch	PNB	b
1198	English (British)	74.71896	43,567,237	43,957,284	44,802,128	CEW19i	52-ABAC-b	standard-english	100	65.80	28,923,893	3Bsuh	10	9	14	5	3		PNB	b
1199	English Gypsy	0.05000	29,154	29,415	29,980	CNN25f	52-ABAC-b	standard-english		70.00	20,591	3Bsuh	10	8	8	5	1		PNB	b
1200	Eritrean	0.02500	14,577	14,708	14,990	CMT34c	12-ACAB-a	tigre		70.00	10,295	1B...	10	7	7	4	2	Tigre	PNB	b
1201	Esperanto	0.00030	175	176	180	CEW21z	51-AAAC-a	proper esperanto	1	70.00	124	0A...	10	7	7	5	0	Esperanto	PNB	b
1202	Estonian	0.02500	14,577	14,708	14,990	MSW51a	41-AAAC-b	eesti		90.00	13,237	4A.u.	10	9	11	5	2	Estonian: Tallinn	PNB	b
1203	Filipino	0.12775	74,489	75,156	76,600	MSY44o	31-CKAA-a	proper tagalog		98.00	73,652	4Bs..	10	9	12	5	2	Tagalog	PNB	b
1204	Finnish	0.00750	4,373	4,412	4,497	MSW51b	41-AAAA-bb	vehicular suomi		87.00	3,839	1A.uh	10	9	12	5	2	Finnish	PNB	b
1205	French	0.10000	58,308	58,830	59,961	CEW21b	51-AABI-d	general français	22	87.00	51,182	1B.uh	10	9	14	5	3	French	PNB	b
1206	German	0.35000	204,078	205,906	209,863	CEW19m	52-ABCE-a	standard hoch-deutsch	9	88.00	181,197	2B.uh	10	9	13	5	3	German*	PNB	b
1207	Ghanaian (Akan)	0.04000	23,323	23,532	23,984	NAB59a	96-FCCB-c	twi		78.00	18,355	4ssu.	10	8	10	5	3		PNB	b
1208	Gilbraltarian	0.02000	11,662	11,766	11,992	CEW21z	51-AABB-ca	general españa		90.00	10,589	1A.uh	10	8	11	4	3		pnb	b
1209	Goanese	0.01800	10,495	10,589	10,793	CNN25d	59-AAFU-o	konkani-gomantaki		80.00	8,472	3asu.	10	8	8	4	1	Konkani: Goan*	PNb	b
1210	Greek Cypriot	0.40000	233,233	235,321	239,843	CEW20	56-AAAA-c	dhimotiki		94.00	221,201	2B.uh	10	9	10	5	2	Greek: Modern	PNB	b
1211	Gujarati	0.50000	291,541	294,151	299,804	CNN25e	59-AAFH-b	standard gujaraati		2.00	5,883	2A.u.	6	7	8	4	3	Gujarati	PNB	b
1212	Han Chinese	0.03605	21,020	21,208	21,616	MSY42a	52-ABAC	english-mainland cluster		12.00	2,545	3Bsuh	8	8	9	5	2		PNB	b
1213	Han Chinese (Cantonese)	0.13000	75,801	76,479	77,949	MSY42a	79-AAAM-a	central yue		8.00	6,118	3A.uh	7	8	9	5	2	Chinese, Yue	PNB	b
1214	Han Chinese (Hakka)	0.01802	10,507	10,601	10,805	MSY42a	79-AAAG-a	literary hakka		7.00	742	1A...	7	8	9	4	2	Chinese: Hakka, Wukingfu*	PNB	b
1215	Han Chinese (Mandarin)	0.02000	11,662	11,766	11,992	MSY42a	79-AAAB-ba	kuo-yü	1	6.00	706	2Bsuh	7	8	9	5	2	Chinese: Kuoyu*	PNB	b
1216	Hungarian	0.03200	18,659	18,826	19,187	MSW51g	41-BAAA-a	general magyar		90.00	16,943	2A.u.	10	9	12	5	3	Hungarian	PNB	b
1217	Indian Tamil	0.08000	46,647	47,064	47,969	CNN23c	49-EBEA-b	tamil		50.00	23,532	2Asu.	10	8	9	4	3	Tamil	PNB	b
1218	Iranian (Persian)	0.05000	29,154	29,415	29,980	CNT24f	58-AACC-c	standard farsi		0.20	59	1Asu.	5	7	4	3	0		PNB	b
1219	Irish	2.40000	1,399,395	1,411,924	1,439,061	CEW18b	52-ABAC-i	irish-english		82.00	1,157,778	1Asuh	10	9	16	5	3		pnb	.
1220	Irish Gaelic	0.06000	34,985	35,298	35,977	CEW18b	50-AAAA-g	gaeilge		86.00	30,356	2a.uh	10	8	16	4	2	Irish*	PNB	b
1221	Irish Traveller (Gypsy)	0.01000	5,831	5,883	5,996	CNN25f	50-ACAA-a	west sheldruu		80.00	4,706	0....	10	8	8	4	1		...	b
1222	Israeli	0.01300	7,580	7,648	7,795	CMT35	12-AABA-b	ivrit-x.		0.11	8	2B.uh	5	5	3	5	0	Hebrew	PNB	b
1223	Italian	0.34528	201,326	203,129	207,033	CEW21e	51-AABQ-c	standard italiano	2	84.00	170,628	2B.uh	10	9	15	5	3	Italian	PNB	b
1224	Jamaican Black	0.29300	170,843	172,372	175,685	NFB68a	52-ABAF-m	jamaican-creole		80.00	137,898	1c..h	10	9	13	5	1	West Carib Creole English	pn.	b
1225	Japanese	0.08000	46,647	47,064	47,969	MSY45a	45-CAAA-a	koku-go		3.00	1,412	1B.uh	6	5	8	4	0	Japanese	PNB	b
1226	Jewish	0.55000	320,695	323,566	329,785	CMT35	52-ABAC-b	standard-english		0.40	1,294	3Bsuh	5	5	7	5	3		PNB	b
1227	Kashmiri	0.20000	116,616	117,660	119,922	CNN25i	59-AAFA-e	siraji-kashmiri		0.02	24	2....	3	4	4	3	1	Kashmiri	PNB	.
1228	Korean	0.02000	11,662	11,766	11,992	MSY46	45-AAAA-b	kukö		55.00	6,471	2A...	10	8	12	5	1	Korean	PNB	b
1229	Kurd (Kurdish)	0.04000	23,323	23,532	23,984	CNT24c	58-AAAA-a	kurmanji		0.10	24	3c...	5	4	5	3	1	Kurdish: Kurmanji*	PN.	b
1230	Latin American Mestizo	0.05000	29,154	29,415	29,980	CLN29	51-AABB-h	south americano		92.00	27,062	4B.uh	10	8	13	5	1		pnb	b
1231	Latvian (Lett)	0.02000	11,662	11,766	11,992	CEW15a	54-AABA-a	standard latviashu		98.00	11,531	3A.u.	10	9	12	5	1	Latvian	PNB	b
1232	Malayali	0.03500	20,408	20,591	20,986	CNN23b	49-EBEB-a	malayalam		50.00	10,295	2Asu.	10	8	9	5	3	Malayalam	PNB	b
1233	Malaysian Malay	0.08100	47,230	47,652	48,568	MSY44k	31-PHAA-b	bahasa-malaysia		1.00	477	1asuh	6	5	6	3	0	Malay	PNB	b
1234	Maltese	0.07000	40,816	41,181	41,973	CMT36	12-AACC-a	maltiya		91.00	37,475	0a.u.	10	9	16	5	1	Maltese	PNB	b
1235	Mauritian (Morisyen)	0.03800	22,157	22,355	22,785	NAN58	51-AACC-l	morisyen		90.00	20,120	1cs..	10	8	11	4	2	Mauritius Creole*	Pnb	.
1236	Middle East Arab	0.15000	87,462	88,245	89,941	CMT30	12-AACF-f	syro-palestinian		20.00	17,649	1Asuh	9	6	8	5	2	Arabic: Lebanese*	PNB	b
1237	Moroccan Arab	0.05000	29,154	29,415	29,980	CMT30	12-AACB-a	west maghrebi		1.00	294	1A.uh	6	4	6	3	1		pnb	b
1238	North African Berber	0.00500	2,915	2,942	2,998	CMT32c	10-AAAC-h	tha-qabaylith		1.00	29	1a...	6	5	4	3	0	Kabyle: Greater	PN.	b
1239	Norwegian	0.01200	6,997	7,060	7,195	CEW19p	52-AAAC-e	ny-norsk		93.00	6,565	0B.uh	10	9	14	5	1	Norwegian*	PNB	b
1240	Palestinian Arab	0.03000	17,492	17,649	17,988	CMT30	12-AACF-f	syro-palestinian		60.00	10,589	1Asuh	10	8	8	5	3	Arabic: Lebanese*	PNB	b
1241	Pathan	0.15000	87,462	88,245	89,941	CNT24a	58-ABDA-a	pashto		0.20	176	1As..	5	4	4	3	0		pnb	b
1242	Polish	0.23000	134,109	135,309	137,910	CEW22i	53-AAAC-c	polski		95.00	128,544	2A.uh	10	9	13	5	3	Polish	PNB	b
1243	Portuguese	0.02900	16,909	17,061	17,389	CEW21g	51-AABA-e	general português		92.00	15,696	2Bsuh	10	9	15	5	1	Portuguese	PNB	b
1244	Punjabi	0.80000	466,465	470,641	479,687	CNN25n	59-AAFE-c	general panjabi		3.50	16,472	1Asu.	6	5	8	4	3		PNB	b
1245	Romanian	0.00700	4,082	4,118	4,197	CEW21i	51-AADC-a	limba românească		88.00	3,624	3A.u.	10	8	11	5	2	Romanian	PNB	b
1246	Russian	0.12000	69,970	70,596	71,953	CEW22j	53-AAAE-d	russkiy		85.00	60,007	4B.uh	10	8	11	5	2	Russian	PNB	b
1247	Scots Gaelic	0.15950	93,001	93,834	95,638	CEW18c	50-AAAA-b	standard gàidhlig		83.00	77,882	1c.uh	10	9	13	4	3	Gaelic*	PNB	b
1248	Scottish (British)	9.50000	5,539,273	5,588,865	5,696,281	CEW19i	52-ABAC-h	general scottish-english		76.00	4,247,538	1Asuh	10	9	14	5	4	English: Scottish, Lowland	PNb	.
1249	Serb	0.02000	11,662	11,766	11,992	CEW22l	53-AAAG-a	standard srpski		88.00	10,354	1Asuh	10	8	11	4	2	Serbian*	PNB	b
1250	Seychellois (Seselwa)	0.00400	2,332	2,353	2,398	NAN58	51-AACC-k	seselwa		90.00	2,118	1cs..	10	8	11	4	2	Creole: Seychelles*	PNb	b
1251	Sierra Leonian Creole	0.00700	4,082	4,118	4,197	NAN58	52-ABAH-b	krio		85.00	3,500	4.s.h	10	8	10	5	3	Krio	PN.	b
1252	Somali	0.01280	7,463	7,530	7,675	CMT33e	14-GAGA-a	af-soomaali		0.50	38	2A...	5	4	1	3	0	Somali	PNB	b
1253	Spaniard	0.08000	46,647	47,064	47,969	CEW21k	51-AABB-c	general español	3	96.00	45,182	2B.uh	10	9	15	5	1	Spanish	PNB	b
1254	Swedish	0.01200	6,997	7,060	7,195	CEW19q	52-AAAD-r	svea-svensk		73.00	5,154	1A.uh	10	9	13	5	1	Swedish	PNB	b
1255	Swiss German	0.02200	12,828	12,943	13,191	CEW19m	52-ABCG-a	general schwytzer-tütsch		86.00	11,131	0B.uh	10	9	14	5	1	Schwyzerdutsch*	PN.	b
1256	Sylhetti Bengali	0.18000	104,955	105,894	107,930	CNN25b	59-AAFT-k	sylhetti-bengali		0.30	318	3csuh	5	5	5	4	0		pnb	b
1257	Traveller Gypsy	0.03600	20,991	21,179	21,586	CNN25f	50-ACAA-a	west sheldruu		65.00	13,766	0....	10	7	8	4	1		...	b
1258	Turkish Cypriot	0.05100	29,737	30,003	30,580	MSY41j	44-AABA-a	osmanli		0.20	60	1A.u.	5	4	4	3	0	Turkish	PNB	b
1259	USA Black	0.02000	11,662	11,766	11,992	NFB68a	52-ABAE-a	talkin-black		73.00	8,589	0B.uh	10	9	9	5	3		pnb	b
1260	USA White	0.30000	174,924	176,490	179,883	CEW19s	52-ABAC-s	general american		78.00	137,663	1Bsuh	10	9	14	5	3	English*	PNB	b
1261	Ukrainian	0.11000	64,139	64,713	65,957	CEW22p	53-AAAE-b	ukrainskiy		85.00	55,006	3A.uh	10	8	11	5	1	Ukrainian	PNB	b
1262	Ulster Irish	1.80000	1,049,547	1,058,943	1,079,295	CEW19r	52-ABAC-ib	mid-ulster-t.		92.00	974,227	1Asuh	10	9	16	5	4		pnb	.
1263	Urdu	0.30000	174,924	176,490	179,883	CNN25r	59-AAFO-d	standard urdu		0.01	18	2Asuh	3	6	7	0	0	Urdu	PNB	b
1264	Vietnamese	0.04000	23,323	23,532	23,984	MSY52b	46-EBAA-ac	general viêt		12.00	2,824	1Asu.	8	7	8	4	3	Vietnamese	PNB	b
1265	Vlach Gypsy	0.10000	58,308	58,830	59,961	CNN25f	59-ACBA-a	vlach-romani		65.00	38,240	1a...	10	7	8	4	2	Romani: Finnish*	PN.	b
1266	Welsh	1.90000	1,107,855	1,117,773	1,139,256	CEW18d	50-ABAA-bc	cymraeg-safonol		85.10	951,225	2A.uh	10	9	15	5	4	Welsh	PNB	b
1267	Welsh Gypsy (Kala)	0.10000	58,308	58,830	59,961	CNN25f	50-ABAA-bc	cymraeg-safonol		70.00	41,181	2A.uh	10	8	14	5	3	Welsh	PNB	b
1268	West Indian Black	0.70000	408,157	411,811	419,726	NFB68a	52-ABAF	carib-anglo-creol cluster		85.00	350,039	1a..h	10	8	14	5	1	West Carib Creole English	PN.	b
1269	Yemeni Arab	0.05000	29,154	29,415	29,980	CMT30	12-AACF-n	yemeni		0.10	29	1Asuh	5	4	5	3	0		pnb	b
1270	Yoruba	0.04000	23,323	23,532	23,984	NAB59n	98-AAAA-a	standard yoruba		55.00	12,943	3asu.	10	8	11	5	3	Yoruba	PNB	b
1271	other minor peoples	0.10000	58,308	58,830	59,961	...				60.00	35,298		10	7	9	5	0			
British Indian Ocean Territory		**100.00000**	**2,000**	**2,000**	**2,000**					**45**	**900**									
1272	British	2.00000	40	40	40	CEW19i	52-ABAC-b	standard-english	70	80.00	32	3Bsuh	10	9	13	2	1		PNB	b
1273	Creole (Mulatto)	91.70000	1,834	1,834	1,834	NAN58	51-AACC-k	seselwa	97	42.00	770	1cs..	9	8	9	2	1	Creole: Seychelles*	PNb	b
1274	French	1.00000	20	20	20	CEW21b	51-AABI-d	general français	30	85.00	17	1B.uh	10	9	14	2	1	French	PNB	b
1275	USA White	5.00000	100	100	100	CEW19s	52-ABAC-s	general american		78.00	78	1Bsuh	10	9	13	3	1	English*	PNB	b
1276	other minor peoples	0.30000	6	6	6	...				50.00	3		10	6	7	2	0			
British Virgin Islands		**100.00000**	**18,665**	**21,366**	**36,663**					**69.7**	**14,892**									
1277	British	5.00000	933	1,068	1,833	CEW19i	52-ABAC-b	standard-english		66.00	705	3Bsuh	10	9	13	5	3		PNB	b
1278	Indo-Pakistani	0.70000	131	150	257	CNN25g	59-AAFO-e	general hindi		35.00	52	3Asuh	9	6	2	3	2		pnb	b
1279	Mulatto	1.60000	299	342	587	NFB68b	52-ABAF-p	virgin-islands-creole		69.00	236	1c..h	10	8	8	4	3		pn.	.
1280	Portuguese	0.30000	56	64	110	CEW21g	51-AABA-e	general português		93.00	60	2Bsuh	10	9	15	2	1	Portuguese	PNB	b
1281	Syro-Lebanese Arab	0.10000	19	21	37	CMT30	12-AACF-f	syro-palestinian		33.00	7	1Asuh	9	8	2	2	1	Arabic: Lebanese*	PNB	b
1282	USA White	2.00000	373	427	733	CEW19s	52-ABAC-s	general american		78.00	333	1Bsuh	10	9	13	5	2	English*	PNB	b
1283	West Indian Black	90.00000	16,799	19,229	32,997	NFB68a	52-ABAF-p	virgin-islands-creole		70.00	13,461	1c..h	10	8	13	5	2		pn.	.
1284	other minor peoples	0.30000	56	64	110	...				59.00	38		10	7	8	3	0			
Brunei		**100.00000**	**294,347**	**328,080**	**458,972**					**7.5**	**24,592**									
1285	Bisayan Tutong	5.70000	16,778	18,701	26,161	MSY44z	31-IAAA	tutong-maritime cluster		5.00	935	0....	7	4	6	1	2		...	.
1286	British	1.80000	5,298	5,905	8,261	CEW19i	52-ABAC-b	standard-english		65.00	3,839	3Bsuh	10	9	13	3	1		PNB	b
1287	Dusun (Kadazan)	6.90000	20,310	22,638	31,669	MSY44y	31-GBAL-b	monsok-dusun		19.00	4,301	0....	8	7	6	2	3	Dusun: Ranau*	PNB	b
1288	Gurkha (Gurung)	0.40000	1,177	1,312	1,836	MSY50e	70-AABD	east gurung cluster		0.30	4	0....	5	4	2	1	0	Gurung: Eastern*	P..	b
1289	Han Chinese	1.00000	2,943	3,281	4,590	MSY42a	52-ABAC	english-mainland cluster		22.00	722	3Bsuh	9	6	10	2	1		PNB	b
1290	Han Chinese (Cantonese)	1.31600	3,874	4,318	6,040	MSY42a	79-AAAM-a	central yue		15.00	648	3A.uh	8	5	8	2	1	Chinese, Yue	PNB	b
1291	Han Chinese (Fukienese)	1.00000	2,943	3,281	4,590	MSY42a	79-AAAJ-ic	chaozhou		20.00	656	1A..h	9	5	8	2	1	Chinese, Min Nan	PNB	b
1292	Han Chinese (Hakka)	1.12700	3,317	3,697	5,173	MSY42a	79-AAAG-a	literary hakka		26.00	961	1A...	9	5	8	2	1	Chinese: Hakka, Wukingfu*	PNB	b
1293	Han Chinese (Mandarin)	5.64000	16,601	18,504	25,886	MSY42a	79-AAAB-ba	kuo-yü	31	8.00	1,480	2Bsuh	7	5	8	2	1	Chinese: Kuoyu*	PNB	b

Continued opposite

Table 8-2 continued

EVANGELIZATION								EVANGELISM			ADDITIONAL DESCRIPTIVE DATA
Ref 1	D 28	aC 29	CG% 30	r 31	E 32	U 33	W 34	e 35	R 36	T 37	Locations, civil divisions, literacy, religions, church history, denominations, dioceses, church growth, missions, agencies, ministries, movements 38
Britain (UK of GB & NI)											
1177	6	10	0.44	5	99.79	0.21	C	449.82	24	10	White settlers from South Africa. D=DRC/NGK,NHK,GKSA,AFMSA,RCC,CofE.
1178	4	10	4.47	6	99.50	0.50	B	193.45	129	7	Refugees from Albania. Nonreligious 30%, Muslims 20% (Sunnis). D=RCC,AOC,GOC,JWs.
1179	4	10	0.44	8	99.67	0.33	C	339.92	24	9	Settlers, immigrants from Australia. Nonreligious 20%. D=CofE,RCC,CofS,MCGB.
1180	4	10	0.44	8	99.75	0.25	C	405.15	22	10	Settlers from Canada. D=RCC,CofS,CofE,MCGB.
1181	4	10	0.44	8	99.76	0.24	C	413.32	23	10	Settlers from New Zealand. D=CofE,MCGB,BUGBI,RCC.
1182	4	10	0.44	0	99.70	0.30	C	296.38	35	8	Nomadic caravan churches. Nonreligious 20%. D=RCC,CoE,Gypsy Evangelical Movement, BUGB. M=GGMS,BFBS,SGM,GFC.
1183	3	10	0.44	6	99.85	0.15	C	493.29	18	10	Refugees from 1915-20 genocide. D=Armenian Apostolic Ch(Gregorians: D-England),RCC,Armenian Evanglical Ch.
1184	2	10	0.44	5	99.87	0.13	C	479.50	20	10	Refugees from Iraq. D=Ancient Ch of the East(Nestorians: P-Tehran),RCC(Chaldeans: P-Babylon).
1185	3	10	0.44	8	99.90	0.10	C	525.60	27	10	Expatriates, settlers from Austria. D=RCC,NAC,LCGB.
1186	1	10	0.44	6	99.90	0.10	C	528.88	27	10	Expatriates from Belgium on business. D=RCC.
1187	3	10	5.85	6	65.00	35.00	B	2.37	304	4	Immigrants mostly from Bangladesh. Muslims 85%(Hanafi Sunnis), Hindus 10%, Baha'is. D=RCC,SA,BUGBI. M=WEC.
1188	1	10	4.08	6	99.75	0.25	C	383.25	104	9	Refugees from Bulgaria. Nonreligious 25%. D=Bulgarian Orthodox Ch(P-Sofia).
1189	2	10	2.55	6	61.00	39.00	B	2.22	164	4	Immigrants from Burma. Theravada Buddhists 97%, Muslims 2% (Sunnis). D=BUGBI,CoE.
1190	4	10	6.24	5	99.85	0.15	C	487.09	126	10	White Russian refugees from USSR since 1917. Nonreligious 15%. D=Byelorussian Autocephalic Orthodox Ch,ROC,ROCOR,RCC.
1191	4	10	7.28	6	95.00	5.00	B	104.02	239	7	Immigrants from Sri Lanka. Hindus 65%, Muslims 2%, Baha'is. D=RCC,CSI,MCC,CPM.
1192	3	10	0.44	8	99.90	0.10	C	525.60	26	10	Mixed-race refugees and immigrants from African nations. D=RCC,CoE,MCGB.
1193	3	10	0.44	8	99.90	0.10	C	499.32	22	10	Mixed-race immigrants, workers, refugees, from Asian nations. D=RCC,CoE,MCGB.
1194	0	10	0.44	0	99.95	0.05	C	488.91	28	10	Cornwall. Extinct as mother tongue, but reviving for cultural purposes including church services.
1195	2	10	0.44	6	99.85	0.15	C	487.09	27	10	Refugees from CSSR(Czechoslovakia) since 1938, 1945, 1968. D=RCC,Moravian Ch.
1196	2	10	0.44	6	99.95	0.05	C	575.60	26	10	Expatriates from Denmark in business, commerce, industry. D=Ch of Denmark,LCGB.
1197	1	10	0.44	6	99.76	0.24	C	421.64	24	10	Expatriates from Holland, in professions, industry. Nonreligious 20%. D=Dutch Reformed Ch(NHK).
1198	14	8	-0.04	8	99.66	0.34	C	350.16	21	9	50,000 Lamaists, 5,000 Baha'is. D=Ch of England(48 Dioceses),RCC(20 Dioceses),MCGB,BUGBI,SA,URC,CB,JWs,CBE,EPC,FIEC,HCM,RSF,&c. M=over 1,000.
1199	4	10	0.44	8	99.70	0.30	C	360.25	29	9	Largely settled. D=CofE,RCC,MCGB,Gypsy Evangelical Movement. M=GGMS.
1200	2	10	7.18	4	99.70	0.30	C	344.92	184	9	Refugees from Ethiopia civil war. Muslims 30%(Sunnis). D=RCC,EOC.
1201	0	10	0.44	5	99.70	0.30	C	329.59	31	9	Artificial (constructed) language, spoken in 80 countries. Speakers in Britain: 347,000 (very few mother-tongue). Nonreligious 30%.
1202	2	10	7.45	5	99.90	0.10	C	532.17	146	10	Refugees from 1940. D=Estonian Evangelical Lutheran Ch in Exile,Estonian Apostolic Orthodox Ch in Exile.
1203	2	10	9.31	5	99.98	0.02	C	622.39	157	10	Immigrants from Philippines: workers, refugees, some professions. D=RCC,CofE.
1204	2	10	0.44	5	99.87	0.13	C	498.55	25	10	Expatriates from Finland. D=Evangelical Lutheran Ch of Finland,GOC.
1205	2	10	0.44	8	99.87	0.13	C	523.95	24	10	Expatriates from France, in business. Nonreligious 13%. D=RCC(20 Dioceses),Reformed Ch of France. M=OSB,SJ,SDB,OFM,OP.
1206	3	10	0.44	8	99.88	0.12	C	536.40	26	10	Expatriates, settlers from Germany, in professions, commerce, industry. D=RCC,LCGB,NAC.
1207	4	10	7.80	4	99.78	0.22	C	421.35	166	10	Migrant workers, laborers, immigrants, from Ghana. Muslims 10%. D=RCC,C of E,MCGB,&c.
1208	3	10	0.44	8	99.90	0.10	C	525.60	25	10	Immigrants from Gibraltar, in commerce. Christians: 78% Catholics, 8% Anglicans. D=RCC,CofE,&c.
1209	1	10	6.97	4	99.80	0.20	C	408.80	156	10	Immigrants from Goa(India), East Africa. Hindus 15%, Baha'is 5%. D=RCC(with a long Catholic history).
1210	2	10	10.52	7	99.94	0.06	C	572.97	189	10	Refugees from Cyprus. D=Greek Orthodox Ch(AD-Thyateira & Great Britain),Greek Evangelical Ch.
1211	0	10	6.58	6	63.00	37.00	B	4.59	330	4	From Bombay, also East Africa. Hindus 65%, Muslims 30%(Sunnis), Baha'is. M=BMMF,IM,Church Army,WEC.
1212	2	10	0.44	8	84.00	16.00	B	36.79	36	5	Long-term immigrants from China, Hong Kong. Buddhists/Chinese folk-religionists 80%, Mahayana Buddhists 30%, nonreligious 8%. D=RCC,TJC.
1213	1	10	0.44	8	76.00	24.00	B	22.19	39	5	Most are refugees or immigrants from Hong Kong. Folk Buddhists 90%. D=RCC. M=Chinese Overseas Christian Mission,TJC.
1214	2	10	0.43	7	71.00	29.00	B	18.14	42	5	Immigrants from China. Folk Buddhists 90%. D=RCC,TJC.
1215	2	10	0.44	7	74.00	26.00	B	16.20	40	5	Immigrants from Chinese diaspora. Folk Buddhists 91%. D=RCC,TJC.
1216	3	10	0.44	6	99.90	0.10	C	538.74	30	10	Refugees from Hungary after 1945, 1956, in professions, commerce. D=RCC,CofS,PCE.
1217	3	10	8.07	6	99.50	0.50	B	220.82	205	8	From South India. Hindus 45%, Muslims 2%, Baha'is 2%. D=RCC,CSI,CPM.
1218	0	10	4.16	5	47.20	52.80	A	0.34	282	3	Refugees from Iran after 1979. Over 2,400 are students. Muslims 96%(Ithna-Asharis Shias), Baha'is 4%.
1219	9	10	0.42	8	99.82	0.18	C	469.90	23	10	Very strong Catholic parishes and institutions across UK. D=RCC(5 Dioceses in Ulster),Ch of Ireland(5 Dioceses),PCI,MCI,BUI,RPCI,CUI,CofE,CofS. R=local.
1220	2	10	0.44	4	99.86	0.14	C	499.10	23	10	Mainly in Eire, but still spoken in Northern Ireland (Belfast, countries of Fermanagh and Armagh); also USA. D=RCC,Col.
1221	2	10	0.44	8	99.80	0.20	C	382.52	31	9	Of Irish origin. Nomadic caravan churches. D=Gypsy Evangelical Movement,RCC. M=GGMS.
1222	0	10	0.47	5	53.11	46.89	B	0.21	60	3	Mostly non-practicing or secular Jews, expatriates on business, commerce. Jews 60%, nonreligious 38%.
1223	4	10	0.99	7	99.84	0.16	C	502.82	33	10	Settlers, expatriates from Italy. D=RCC(20 Dioceses),Waldensian Ch,CCINE,Italian Pentecostal Ch.
1224	18	10	10.00	8	99.80	0.20	C	426.32	199	10	Immigrants. D=BUGBI,NTCOG,CoGIC,EOC,FUCJCA,UPCI,CofE,RCC,AMEC,AMEZC,ACG,PAW,AFB,CGP,COG,IMA,SDA,30 others. M=JBU.
1225	0	10	5.07	7	63.00	37.00	B	6.89	253	4	Expatriates from Japan, on business, commerce, finance. Buddhists 57%, New-Religionists 24%(Soka Gakkai), nonreligious 16%.
1226	2	10	0.12	8	68.40	31.60	B	0.99	32	3	60% in London area. 77% Orthodox(United Synagogue),8% Liberal,7% Reform,8% nothing. 350 synagogues. D=CofE,Messianic Jews. M=CMJ,HCM,JFJ.
1227	1	10	3.23	0	38.02	61.98	A	0.02	305	2	Refugees after 1947 from Kashmir. Muslims 95%(90% Sunnis,5% Shias), Hindus 5%. D=C of E. M=CMS.
1228	3	10	6.69	6	99.55	0.45	B	254.95	157	8	Migrant workers. Shamanists/Buddhists 40%. D=RCC,Presbyterians,HSAUWC. M=Korean Methodist Ch.
1229	0	10	3.23	0	39.10	60.90	A	0.14	367	3	Refugees from Iraq-Iran wars. Almost all Muslims 99% (Sunnis, Shias). M=numerous mission agencies.
1230	1	10	8.22	8	99.92	0.08	C	554.07	146	10	From all Latin American nations. Mixed-race European/Amerindians. D=RCC. M=many mission agencies at work.
1231	1	10	0.44	5	99.98	0.02	C	600.93	27	10	Refugees from USSR after 1939, 1945. D=Latvian Evangelical Lutheran Ch in Exile.
1232	5	10	7.18	4	99.50	0.50	B	219.00	187	8	Immigrants from Kerala (India). Hindus 35%, Muslims 10% (Sunnis), Baha'is 5%. D=OSCE,MTSC,IPC,CSI,RCC.
1233	0	10	3.94	5	51.00	49.00	B	1.86	212	4	Immigrants from Malaysia, in business, commerce. Muslims 99%(Shafi Sunnis).
1234	1	10	0.44	5	99.91	0.09	C	534.76	21	10	From Malta, in professions, finance, commerce. D=RCC(staunch traditional Catholics). High % are charismatics.
1235	2	10	7.90	8	99.90	0.10	C	499.32	162	10	Mixed-race immigrants from Mauritius, mostly Christians, with some Hindus, Muslims. D=RCC,CofE.
1236	6	10	3.07	8	87.00	13.00	B	63.51	119	6	Levantines, Egyptians, Saudis, Iraqis, Gulf Arabs. Muslims 75%. D=RCC(Maronites,Copts),COC,SOC,GOC,AC,SA. M=GMU,WEC.
1237	1	10	3.44	7	51.00	49.00	B	1.86	222	4	Immigrants from Morocco. Muslims 99%(Maliki Sunnis). D=RCC. M=OFM.
1238	0	10	3.42	4	44.00	56.00	A	1.60	257	4	Various Berber peoples from Morocco, Algeria, Tunisia. Laborers, manual tasks. Muslims 99%(Maliki Sunnis).
1239	1	10	0.44	6	99.93	0.07	C	556.69	25	10	Expatriates, settlers from Norway, in professions, industry. D=Ch of Norway.
1240	3	10	7.21	8	99.60	0.40	C	282.51	168	8	Refugees from Middle East wars. Muslims 30%(Shafi Sunnis,Druzes,Alawis), Baha'is 3%, nonreligious 7%. D=GOC,RCC,CofE.
1241	0	10	2.91	5	44.20	55.80	A	0.32	318	3	From Aghanistan, since 1940. Muslims 100%(Hanafi Sunnis).
1242	6	10	0.44	6	99.95	0.05	C	592.94	7	10	Refugees from Poland. D=RCC,PNCC,PMC,Polish Orthodox Church Abroad/GOC,PRCE,PELCE.
1243	1	10	0.44	8	99.92	0.08	C	570.86	24	10	Expatriates, settlers from Portugal since 1492. In professions, commerce. D=RCC.
1244	2	10	7.69	5	66.50	33.50	B	8.49	360	4	From India. Sikhs 50%(over 50 temples),Hindus 30%,Muslims 17%(5,000 Ahmadis), Baha'is 1%. D=RCC,Asian Ch of Jesus Christ. M=GMU,WT,WEC.
1245	2	10	0.44	6	99.88	0.12	C	510.70	27	10	Refugees from Romania since 1939. D=Romanian Orthodox Ch(P-Bucharest),RCC.
1246	2	10	0.44	7	99.85	0.15	C	499.50	7	10	Refugees from USSR since 1917. Nonreligious 15%. D=ROCOR, Russian Orthodox Ch(PE-Western Europe).
1247	4	10	0.44	1	99.83	0.17	C	448.36	27	10	Spoken in north and central counties of Ross, Hebrides, Skye. Also Canada. Monolinguals 0.5%. D=Ch of Scotland,ECS,FCS,BUS. D=NBSS.
1248	11	9	0.41	8	99.76	0.24	C	418.87	28	10	Literary Scots. Lowlands, Aberdeen to Ayrshire. D=Ch of Scotland(12 Synods),ECS(7 Dioceses),RCC(8 Dioceses),BUS,MCGB,RPCS,CUS,FCS,RPCS,UFCS,CofE.
1249	2	10	2.72	6	99.88	0.12	C	510.70	47	10	Refugees from Yugoslavia. D=Serbian Orthodox Ch(D-Western Europe),SOC(Libertyville).
1250	2	10	5.50	8	99.90	0.10	C	499.32	119	10	Migrant workers from Seychelles. D=RCC,Ch of England.
1251	3	10	6.03	8	99.85	0.15	C	462.27	131	10	West Africans, in business, commerce, industry. D=Ch of England,MCGB,RCC.
1252	0	10	3.70	5	45.50	54.50	A	0.83	334	3	Refugees from Somalia. Muslims 99%(Shafi Sunnis,some Hanafis).
1253	2	10	0.44	8	99.96	0.04	C	609.69	21	10	Expatriates from Spain, settlers. D=RCC(20 Dioceses),Spanish Evangelical Ch. M=AMEN(Peru).
1254	2	10	0.44	6	99.73	0.27	C	383.68	8	9	Expatriates, settlers from Sweden. Nonreligious and atheists 27%. D=Ch of Sweden,LCGB. M=SFM.
1255	1	10	0.44	8	99.86	0.14	C	483.40	28	10	Expatriates in business, professions, from Switzerland. D=Swiss Reformed Churches.
1256	0	10	3.52	1	43.30	56.70	A	0.47	309	3	Immigrants from Bangladesh; in London(East End), Birmingham, Bradford. Restaurant operators, ships' crews. Muslims 99%(Hanafi Sunnis).
1257	5	10	0.44	8	99.65	0.35	C	279.95	34	8	Nomads and settled Gypsies. D=nomadic caravan churches, Gypsy Evangelical Movement,CofE,RCC,MCGB. M=GGMS.
1258	0	10	4.18	8	49.20	50.80	A	0.35	272	3	Refugees from Cyprus civil war since 1950s. Muslims 100%(Hanafi Sunnis).
1259	6	10	0.44	8	99.73	0.27	C	367.70	9	9	In USA churches, with many West Indian followers. D=CoGiC,AMEZC,AMEC,BWCOLJCWW,CC,AOC.
1260	10	10	0.84	8	99.78	0.22	C	441.28	31	10	Expatriates in business. D=MCGB,BUGBI,SA,CB,JWs,CJCLdS,SDA,CCS,CC,WCOG.
1261	2	10	0.44	6	99.85	0.15	C	487.09	29	10	Refugees from USSR after 1917. Nonreligious 15%. D=Ukrainian Autocephalic Orthodox Ch,RCC(Ukrainianrite: EA-Great Britain). M=UOCUSA.
1262	15	9	0.44	8	99.92	0.08	C	560.78	27	10	Northern Ireland. D=Ch of Ireland(5 Dioceses),RCC,PCI,MCI,BUI,BUGBI,SA,RPCI,CUI,Cooneyites,EPCNI,FPCU,NTCOG,CofE,CofS. R=local stations,HCJB,AWR.
1263	0	0	2.93	5	36.01	63.99	A	0.01	301	2	Refugees from Pakistan and India. Muslims 100% (Hanafi Sunnis).
1264	4	10	5.81	6	75.00	25.00	B	32.85	243	5	Refugees from Indochina and its wars, 1950-75. In businesses. Mahayana Buddhists 60%, New Religionists 20%. D=RCC,URC,MCGB,AoG.
1265	2	10	0.44	6	99.65	0.35	C	296.56	32	8	Nomads and settled Gypsies. D=Gypsy Evangelical Movement,AoG.
1266	11	10	0.44	5	99.85	0.15	C	509.71	24	10	1.2% monolingual, 19.9% bilingual, rest English only. D=Ch in Wales(6 Dioceses),RCC,BUWM,MCGB,PCW,Apostolic Ch of GB,SA,UWI,CGF,RSF,CofE.
1267	3	10	0.44	5	99.70	0.30	C	373.03	28	9	Gypsies in England and Wales, many itinerant. D=Gypsy Evangelical Movement, nomadic caravan churches, AoG.
1268	9	10	4.04	8	99.85	0.15	C	480.88	71	10	Migrants, new citizens. D=UPC,NTCOG,PAW,PWHC,FUCJCA,SDA,RTMOC,SA,VCOG. M=WC.
1269	0	10	3.42	7	50.10	49.90	B	0.18	225	3	Refugees, migrant workers from Yemen. Muslims 100%(50% Zaydis, 45% Shafi Sunnis).
1270	5	10	7.43	5	99.55	0.45	B	256.96	189	8	From Nigeria. Migrant workers, residents. Muslims 30% (Sunnis), animists 15%. D=HOC&S,COTLA,CAC,RCC,other AICs.
1271	0	10	0.44		99.00	1.00	C	216.81	12	8	Thais, Sinhalese, Tibetans, West Africans, Algerians, Guyanese(AMEZC), Fante(MDCC), Shona, Hindi; many Ugandan,other refugees. Muslims 20%, Hindus 10%.
British Indian Ocean Territory											
1272	1	10	1.40	8	99.80	0.20	C	435.08	47	10	Administrators from Britain, mainly military. D=Anglican Ch(D-Mauritius).
1273	2	6	1.54	8	96.00	4.00	B	147.16	75	7	Speakers of Seychelles-Chagos Creole French. Mostly transients. Hindus 45%, Muslims 10%. D=Anglican Ch/CPIO(D-Mauritius),RCC(D-Port Louis). M=CPIO.
1274	1	10	1.46	8	99.85	0.15	C	471.58	44	10	Expatriates from France. D=RCC(D-Port Louis). Charismatic groups.
1275	1	10	1.37	8	99.78	0.22	C	415.66	43	10	Administrators and military from USA. D=Anglican Ch/CPIO(D-Mauritius).
1276	0	10	1.10		79.00	21.00	B	144.17	38	7	Reunionese, Seychellois, Mauritians(Morisyen), Africans, Indians. Hindus 20%, Muslims 20%.
British Virgin Islands											
1277	3	10	1.30	8	99.66	0.34	C	337.26	48	9	Expatriates in government, education. D=Anglican Ch(D-Virgin Islands),MCCA,JWs.
1278	2	10	1.48	7	90.00	10.00	B	114.97	76	7	Former citizens of India and Pakistan. Hindus 35%, Muslims 30%. D=RCC,Anglican Ch(D-Virgin Islands).
1279	3	10	1.49	8	99.69	0.31	C	309.77	49	9	Black/White mixed-race persons. Afro-American spiritists. D=RCC(D-Saint John's),Anglican Ch,MCCA.
1280	1	10	1.47	8	99.93	0.07	C	546.51	42	10	Expatriates and settlers from Portugal. D=RCC(D-Saint John's).
1281	1	10	1.26	8	81.00	19.00	B	97.56	66	6	Levantine Arabs. Muslims 67%(Sunnis, some Shias). D=RCC(D-Saint John's).
1282	2	10	-2.47	8	99.78	0.22	C	421.35	2	10	Expatriates, settlers from USA, in administration, professions. D=Baptist Ch,SDA.
1283	4	6	1.38	8	99.70	0.30	C	324.48	43	9	Lesser Antillean Creole English. D=Anglican Ch(D-Virgin Islands),RCC,BMAA,SDA. M=ECUSA,SVD.
1284	0	10	1.45		88.00	12.00	B	189.50	45	7	Other Caribbean islanders, Latin Americans, other Europeans.
Brunei											
1285	2	7	4.64	0	34.00	66.00	A	6.20	415	4	East of Bisaya, south of Tutong, into Sarawak. Dusunic. Muslims 85%(loose Shafi Sunnis), animists 5%. D=RCC,Protestants.
1286	1	10	4.38	8	99.65	0.35	C	322.66	111	9	Expatriates from UK, in government, education, military. D=Anglican Ch(D-Kuching).
1287	2	7	6.25	0	62.00	38.00	B	42.99	314	6	Tribal religionists (animists) 26%, Muslims 50%. D=RCC,Dusun Ch. M=BEM,SAIM,BAS,SIL.
1288	0	8	1.40	0	24.30	75.70	A	0.26	271	3	Military, in British army, then Brunei army. Hindus 70%, Buddhists 20%, animists 10%.
1289	1	8	4.61	8	88.00	12.00	B	70.66	164	6	Confucianists 10%, Buddhists 65%(Mahayana). D=RCC(VA-Miri). M=MHM.
1290	1	8	5.22	8	76.00	24.00	B	41.61	212	6	Chinese folk-religionists 85% (including Mahayana Buddhists). D=RCC(VA-Miri). M=MHM.
1291	1	9	5.96	6	80.00	20.00	B	58.40	226	6	Confucianists 30%, with Mahayana Buddhists 50%. D=RCC(VA-Miri).
1292	1	8	7.11	7	85.00	15.00	B	80.66	250	6	Originally from mainland China. Confucianists 30%, Buddhists 40%(Mahayana). D=RCC(VA-Miri).
1293	1	8	4.70	7	69.00	31.00	B	20.14	212	5	Confucianists 10%, Buddhists 80%(Mahayana). D=RCC(VA-Miri). M=MHM.

Continued overleaf

Table 8-2 continued

PEOPLE		POPULATION				IDENTITY CODE		LANGUAGE		CHURCH		MINISTRY						SCRIPTURE		
Ref 1	Ethnic name 2	P% 3	In 1995 4	In 2000 5	In 2025 6	Race 7	Language 8	Autoglossonym 9	S 10	AC 11	Members 12	Jayuh 13-17	d 18	wa 19	xc 20	mc 21	mi 22	Biblioglossonym 23	Pub 24-26	ss 27
1294	Han Chinese (Min Nan)	3.76000	11,067	12,336	17,257	MSY42a	79-AAAJ-ic	chaozhou		8.50	1,049	1A..h	7	5	8	2	1	Chinese, Min Nan	PNB	b
1295	Han Chinese (Min Pei)	2.25600	6,640	7,401	10,354	MSY42a	79-AAAI-ce	fuzhou		10.00	740	1A...	8	5	8	2	1	Chinese: Foochow	PNB	b
1296	Indo-Pakistani	1.30000	3,827	4,265	5,967	CNN25g	59-AAFO-e	general hindi		14.00	597	3Asuh	8	5	2	2	2		pnb	b
1297	Kayan (Busang)	0.50000	1,472	1,640	2,295	MSY44z	31-JBAA	baram-kayan cluster		9.00	148	0....	7	5	6	4	1	Kayan, Baram	PNB	.
1298	Kenyah(Upper Baram Kenja)	0.40000	1,177	1,312	1,836	MSY44y	31-JCCJ	bakung-kenyah cluster		70.00	919	0....	10	8	8	4	2		PNB	.
1299	Kiput (Belait Jati)	0.80000	2,355	2,625	3,672	MSY44z	31-IAAB-a	long-kiput		0.20	5	0....	5	1	3	0	0		...	b
1300	Korean	0.15000	442	492	688	MSY46	45-AAAA-b	kukö		30.00	148	2A...	9	6	11	4	1	Korean	PNB	b
1301	Land Dayak (Punan)	1.00000	2,943	3,281	4,590	MSY44y	31-LBAA-d	ma'anyan		15.00	492	0.s..	8	5	6	3	3	Dayak: Maanyan*	PN.	.
1302	Low Malay Creole	0.30000	883	984	1,377	MSY44k	31-PHAA-d	malayu-pasar	25	0.40	4	1csuh	5	3	2	0	0	Malay: Low	PNb	b
1303	Malay (Melaja)	1.00000	2,943	3,281	4,590	MSY44k	31-PHAA-b	bahasa-malaysia		0.07	2	1asuh	4	3	6	0	0	Malay	PNB	b
1304	Orang Bukit (Kedayan)	44.95600	132,327	147,492	206,335	MSY44z	31-PHAF-ab	malayu-brunei		0.50	737	0....	5	5	5	4	2		...	b
1305	Sea Dayak (Iban, Birawut)	5.26000	15,483	17,257	24,142	MSY44e	31-PHIA-a	batang-lupar		20.00	3,451	1.s..	9	5	9	4	2		pnb	.
1306	Sinhalese	0.30000	883	984	1,377	CNN25q	59-ABBA-aa	standard sinhala		3.00	30	1asuh	6	3	6	0	0		pnb	b
1307	Southern Bisaya (Visayak)	6.48000	19,074	21,260	29,741	MSY44z	31-GBBB	south bisaya cluster		10.00	2,126	0....	8	5	6	4	1		P..	b
1308	Southern Murut (Belait)	0.18900	556	620	867	MSY44z	31-HAAC-o	lun-bawang		12.00	74	0.s..	8	5	9	4	1	Lun Bawang*	PNB	.
1309	Tutung	2.59000	7,624	8,497	11,887	MSY44z	31-IAAA-a	tutong-maritime		5.00	425	0....	7	1	6	1	2		...	.
1310	West Coast Bajau	3.58000	10,538	11,745	16,431	MSY44z	31-EACD	west-coast-bajau cluster		0.02	2	0....	3	1	3	0	0		...	b
1311	other minor peoples	0.29600	871	971	1,359	...				10.00	97		8	3	2	1	0			
	Bulgaria	**100.00000**	**8,499,244**	**8,225,045**	**7,023,064**					**80.95**	**6,657,951**									
1312	Arab	0.02000	1,700	1,645	1,405	CMT30	12-AACF-k	central `anazi		5.00	82	4Asuh	7	3	2	0	1		pnb	b
1313	Arliski Balkan Gypsy	1.31578	111,831	108,223	92,408	CNN25f	59-ACBA-bc	arlija	4	70.00	75,756	1A...	10	7	4	1	3	Romani: Arlija	Pn.	.
1314	Armenian (Hai)	0.17000	14,449	13,983	11,939	CEW14	57-AAAA-b	ashkharik		80.00	11,186	4A.u.	10	9	11	3	1	Armenian: Modern, Eastern	PNB	b
1315	Aromanian (Aromunen)	0.18000	15,299	14,805	12,642	CEW21i	51-AADB-a	limba armâneasc-a	1	85.00	12,584	0a...	10	8	11	2	2	Romanian: Macedonian*	P..	b
1316	British	0.01000	850	823	702	CEW19i	52-ABAC-b	standard-english		79.00	650	3Bsuh	10	9	13	3	1		PNB	b
1317	Bulgar	79.84430	6,786,162	6,567,230	5,607,516	CEW22b	53-AAAH-b	bulgarski		92.69	6,087,165	2A.uh	10	9	9	2	2	Bulgarian	PNB	b
1318	Bulgarian Gypsy	3.53000	300,023	290,344	247,914	CNN25f	53-AAAH-b	bulgarski		60.00	174,206	2A.uh	10	7	8	1	1	Bulgarian	PNB	b
1319	Crimean Tatar	0.06659	5,660	5,477	4,677	MSY41h	44-AABA-c	crimea-tatar		0.01	1	1c.u.	3	2	7	0	0	Crimean Tatar*	PNb	b
1320	Czech	0.10000	8,499	8,225	7,023	CEW22e	53-AAAD-a	czesky		80.00	6,580	2Asuh	10	8	11	3	2	Czech	PNB	b
1321	Dzambazi Balkan Gypsy	0.26315	22,366	21,644	18,481	CNN25f	59-ACBA-bf	dzambazi		70.00	15,151	1c...	10	7	8	1	1		pn.	b
1322	East Bulgarian Gypsy	0.13200	11,219	10,857	9,270	CNN25f	53-AAAH-bd	southwest bulgarski		70.00	7,600	1c.uh	10	7	8	1	1		pnb	b
1323	Esperanto	0.00011	9	9	8	CEW21z	51-AAAC-a	proper esperanto	14	55.00	5	0A...	10	9	6	3	0	Esperanto	PNB	b
1324	French	0.03000	2,550	2,468	2,107	CEW21b	51-AABI-d	general français		87.00	2,147	1B.uh	10	9	14	3	1	French	PNB	b
1325	Gagauzi Turk	0.13483	11,460	11,090	9,469	MSY41d	44-AABA-b	gagauzi		80.00	8,872	1c.u.	10	7	10	2	2	Gagauz	Pnb	b
1326	German	0.02000	1,700	1,645	1,405	CEW19m	52-ABCE-a	standard hoch-deutsch		88.00	1,448	2B.uh	10	9	13	3	2	German*	PNB	b
1327	Gheg Albanian (Chamurian)	0.02000	1,700	1,645	1,405	CEW13	55-AAAA-b	northwest gheg		60.00	987	1a.u.	10	7	2	2	1	Albanian: Gheg*	PN.	b
1328	Greek	0.10000	8,499	8,225	7,023	CEW20	56-AAAA-c	dhimotiki		90.00	7,403	2B.uh	10	9	10	3	1	Greek: Modern	PNB	b
1329	Italian	0.04000	3,400	3,290	2,809	CEW21e	51-AABQ-c	standard italiano		84.00	2,764	2B.uh	10	9	15	3	1	Italian	PNB	b
1330	Jewish	0.05000	4,250	4,113	3,512	CMT35	53-AAAH-b	bulgarski		0.05	2	2A.uh	4	3	2	0	0	Bulgarian	PNB	b
1331	Kalderash Gypsy	0.00532	452	438	374	CNN25f	59-ACBA-al	south kalderash		70.00	306	1c...	10	7	7	1	2		pn.	.
1332	Karakachan	0.03780	3,213	3,109	2,655	CEW20	56-AAAA-c	dhimotiki		75.00	2,332	2B.uh	10	8	8	2	1	Greek: Modern	PNB	b
1333	Macedonian	2.50000	212,481	205,626	175,577	CEW22g	53-AAAH-a	makedonski		90.00	185,064	2a.uh	10	8	11	2	3	Macedonian*	PNB	b
1334	Nogai	0.02500	2,125	2,056	1,756	MSY41z	44-AABC-a	noghai		0.09	2	1c.u.	4	1	2	0	0	Nogay*	PN.	.
1335	Palityan (Bogomil)	0.01000	850	823	702	CEW22b	53-AAAH-bi	palityan		65.00	535	1c.uh	10	6	8	1	0	Palityan	PNb	.
1336	Polish (Pole)	0.30000	25,498	24,675	21,069	CEW22i	53-AAAC-c	polski		90.00	22,208	2A.uh	10	9	13	3	1	Polish	PNB	b
1337	Pomak	0.91000	77,343	74,848	63,910	CEW22b	53-AAAH-b	bulgarski		1.20	898	2A.uh	6	1	7	0	0	Bulgarian	PNB	b
1338	Portuguese	0.01000	850	823	702	CEW21g	51-AABA-e	general português		93.00	765	2Bsuh	10	8	15	2	1	Portuguese	PNB	b
1339	Romanian	0.06000	5,100	4,935	4,214	CEW21i	51-AADC-a	limba româneasca		84.00	4,145	3A.u.	10	9	11	2	1	Romanian	PNB	b
1340	Rumelian Turk	9.52222	809,317	783,207	668,752	MSY41j	44-AABA-a	osmanli		0.10	783	1A.u.	5	2	2	0	1	Turkish	PNB	b
1341	Russian	0.20000	16,998	16,450	14,046	CEW22j	53-AAAE-d	russkiy		51.00	8,390	4B.uh	10	8	8	2	2	Russian	PNB	b
1342	Serb	0.10000	8,499	8,225	7,023	CEW22l	53-AAAG-a	standard srpski		85.00	6,991	1Asuh	10	9	10	2	1	Serbian*	PNB	b
1343	Spaniard	0.04000	3,400	3,290	2,809	CEW21k	51-AABB-c	general español		96.00	3,158	2B.uh	10	9	15	3	1	Spanish	PNB	b
1344	Tatar (Tartar)	0.08800	7,479	7,238	6,180	MSY41h	44-AABB-e	tatar		1.00	72	2c.u.	6	4	2	0	0	Tatar: Kazan	Pn.	b
1345	Tinsmith Gypsy (Tinner)	0.13158	11,183	10,823	9,241	CNN25f	59-ACBA-bd	romani-tinsmiths	1	70.00	7,576	1c...	10	7	7	1	1		pn.	.
1346	other minor peoples	0.03331	2,831	2,740	2,339	...				5.00	137		7	5	7	1	0			
	Burkina Faso	**100.00000**	**10,414,577**	**11,936,823**	**23,321,336**					**16.62**	**1,984,077**									
1347	Bambara (Bamanakan)	0.03000	3,124	3,581	6,996	NAB63a	00-AAAB-a	bamanan-kan	3	4.00	143	4As..	6	5	8	3	3	Bambara	PNB	b
1348	Bariba (Bargu)	0.13000	13,539	15,518	30,318	NAB56a	91-GIAA-a	baatonum		8.00	1,241	3....	7	6	5	3	2	Bariba	PNB	.
1349	Bedouin Arab	0.10000	10,415	11,937	23,321	CMT30	12-AACD	badawi-sahara cluster	8	0.04	5	0a...	3	1	1	0	0		PN.	b
1350	Bimoba (Moba)	0.01946	2,027	2,323	4,538	NAB56a	91-GGDC-b	bi-moba		4.00	93	0..u.	6	5	6	1	2	Bimoba	PN.	.
1351	Birifor	1.19205	124,147	142,293	278,002	NAB56a	91-GGAA-j	north birifor		13.00	18,498	1c...	8	5	8	3	3	Birifor*	PNb	.
1352	Bissa (Bisa)	3.82339	398,190	456,391	891,666	NAB63z	00-DFAA-a	bisa	5	18.80	85,802	1....	8	5	7	3	3	Bissa	P..	b
1353	Black Bobo (Bobo Fing)	2.70212	281,414	322,547	630,170	NAB63z	00-DHAA-d	sya		25.00	80,637	0.s..	9	5	6	3	3		pn.	.
1354	Ble	0.00791	824	944	1,845	NAB63z	00-AAAF-a	jelkuna		3.00	28	0....	6	4	3	1	1		...	p
1355	Bobo Jula (Zara)	0.10957	11,411	13,079	25,553	NAB63z	00-DHAA-a	zara-dan		0.00	0	0.s..	0	1	3	0	1	Bobo Madare, Southern	PN.	b
1356	Bolon	0.11921	12,415	14,230	27,801	NAB63z	00-AAAC-a	bolon-kan		3.00	427	0....	6	4	5	1	2		...	p
1357	Bozo (Sorogo)	0.02000	2,083	2,387	4,664	NAB63b	00-BBCA-a	tieya-xo		0.00	0	0....	0	2	2	0	0		...	.
1358	British	0.00500	521	597	1,166	CEW19i	52-ABAC-b	standard-english	2	79.00	472	3Bsuh	10	9	13	4	3		PNB	b
1359	Bulsa (Builsa, Bulea)	0.64851	67,540	77,411	151,241	NAB56a	91-GGBA-b	bu-li		5.00	3,871	4....	7	5	7	2	1	Buli	PN.	.
1360	Burba (Berba, Biali)	0.01686	1,756	2,013	3,932	NAB56a	91-GGEA-a	bia-li		6.00	121	0....	7	5	6	2	1	Biali	...	.
1361	Central Senufo (Suppire)	0.27311	28,443	32,601	63,693	NAB56a	91-BAAC-e	sicite		5.00	1,630	1.s..	7	5	7	3	2	Senoufo: Sicite*	Pn.	.
1362	Dagaaba (Dagari)	2.65456	276,461	316,870	619,079	NAB56a	91-GGAA-h	dagaa-ri		20.00	63,374	1c...	9	5	7	3	3	Dagaare*	Pnb	.
1363	Doghosie (Dorosie)	0.21617	22,513	25,804	50,414	NAB56a	91-GEAA	doghose cluster		5.00	1,290	0....	7	5	5	2	2	Doghosie	...	.
1364	Dogon (Habe)	1.34025	139,581	159,983	312,564	NAB56a	91-ACEA-b	toro-so		21.00	33,596	4....	9	5	8	3	3	Dogon	PN.	b
1365	Dogoso	0.05298	5,518	6,324	12,356	NAB56a	91-FAAA-a	dogoso		5.00	316	0....	7	5	4	2	1		...	.
1366	Duun (Duu)	0.01000	1,041	1,194	2,332	NAB63z	00-DGBA-a	duun		0.10	1	0....	5	3	3	1	1		...	b
1367	Dyan (Dian, Djan)	0.15629	16,277	18,656	36,449	NAB56a	91-GBAB-a	jaane		8.00	1,492	0....	7	5	5	2	1		...	.
1368	Eastern Karaboro (Ker)	0.37762	39,328	45,076	88,066	NAB56a	91-BABB-a	kar		9.00	4,057	0....	7	5	6	3	3		pn.	.
1369	Ewe	0.20000	20,829	23,874	46,643	NAB59d	96-MAAA-a	standard ewe		72.00	17,189	4Asu.	10	8	13	4	3	Ewe	PNB	b
1370	French	0.07400	7,707	8,833	17,258	CEW21b	51-AABI-d	general français	30	87.00	7,685	1B.uh	10	9	14	4	2	French	PNB	b
1371	Gouin (Ciraamba)	0.66364	69,115	79,218	154,770	NAB56a	91-GDAB	cer-ma cluster		11.00	8,714	0....	8	5	6	3	3	Cerma	P..	.
1372	Gurenne (Frafra)	0.27815	28,968	33,202	64,868	NAB56a	91-GGAA-e	guren-ge		4.00	1,328	1c...	6	5	6	3	3	Frafra*	PNb	.
1373	Gurma (Gourmance)	3.38024	352,038	403,493	788,317	NAB56a	91-GGDA	gurma cluster		7.00	28,245	3.s..	7	5	8	3	3		PN.	.
1374	Gurma Fulani (Fulbe)	1.50000	156,219	179,052	349,820	NAB56c	90-BAAA-k	fula-gurma		0.20	358	1cs..	5	4	6	2	1	Fulfulde, Gourmantche	pnb	n
1375	Hausa	0.05000	5,207	5,968	11,661	NAB60a	19-HAAB-a	hausa	8	0.10	6	4Asu.	5	4	8	2	0	Hausa	PNB	b
1376	Jaan (Yana, Yanga)	0.17459	18,183	20,840	40,717	NAB56a	91-GGAA-b	yan-ga		2.00	417	1c...	6	4	4	2	0		pnb	.
1377	Jelgooji Fulani	1.00000	104,146	119,368	233,213	NAB56c	90-BAAA-h	fula-jelgooji		0.10	119	1cs..	5	4	6	2	0	Fulfulde, Jelgoore	pnb	b
1378	Jotoni (Jowulu)	0.01325	1,380	1,582	3,090	NAB63z	00-CABA-a	kpango		3.00	47	0....	6	3	6	1	0	Jowulu	...	b
1379	Jula (Dyula)	1.10000	114,560	131,305	256,535	NAB63h	00-AAAB-z	jula-kan	5	1.00	1,313	1cs..	6	4	6	2	3	Jula	PNb	b
1380	Kalamse	0.12147	12,651	14,500	28,328	NAB56a	91-GFAE	samo-kalamse cluster		10.00	1,450	0....	8	5	6	1	1		...	.
1381	Kambe (Gan, Ga, Kaanse)	0.06670	6,947	7,962	15,555	NAB56a	91-GEBA-a	kaan-se		3.00	239	0....	6	4	3	1	2	Kaanse	...	.
1382	Kasem (Kasena)	1.11161	115,769	132,691	259,242	NAB56a	91-GFAD-b	east kasem		10.00	13,269	1....	8	5	6	3	2	Kasem	PN.	.
1383	Khe (Kheso)	0.01722	1,793	2,056	4,016	NAB56a	91-FABA-a	khe		3.00	62	0....	6	4	3	2	1		...	.
1384	Kolsi (Ko, Kols)	0.17219	17,933	20,554	40,157	NAB56a	91-GFBA-a	ko-lsi		5.00	1,028	0....	7	4	3	2	1	Ko	...	.
1385	Komono	0.03311	3,448	3,952	7,722	NAB56a	91-GEAB-a	khi-sa		3.00	119	0....	6	4	5	3	3	Khisa	...	p
1386	Kurumba (Lilse, Fulse)	1.46939	153,031	175,398	342,681	NAB56a	91-GFEA-a	a-kurum-fe		11.00	19,294	0....	8	5	7	3	3		...	.
1387	Lele	2.53904	264,430	303,081	592,138	NAB56a	91-GFAB	lyele cluster		10.00	30,308	0....	8	5	6	3	3	Lyele	P..	.
1388	Liptako Fula (Macina)	3.40136	354,237	406,014	793,243	NAB56c	90-BAAA-j	fula-liptaako		0.70	2,842	1cs..	5	4	6	2	3		pnb	b
1389	Lobi (Lobiri)	2.58219	268,924	308,231	602,201	NAB56a	91-GBAA-a	lobi-ri		0.73	2,250	0....	5	4	6	3	2	Lobiri	PN.	.
1390	Malinke	0.80000	83,317	95,495	186,571	NAB63h	00-AAAA-h	maninka-kan		1.50	1,432	3a...	6	4	5	2	3	Maninka*	PN.	b
1391	Maranse (Kaadeno)	0.02890	3,010	3,450	6,740	NAB65b	01-AAAA-cc	marense		0.01	0	0....	3	3	2	0	0		pn.	.
1392	Marka (Dafi, Dafin)	2.10482	219,208	251,249	490,872	NAB63a	00-AAAC-c	maraka-jalan-kan		12.00	30,150	0....	8	5	7	2	3	Marka	...	.
1393	Mossi (Moshi)	46.36425	4,828,641	5,534,418	10,812,763	NAB56a	91-GGAA-a	moo-re	69	23.20	1,283,985	2A...	9	5	9	3	3	Moore	PNB	b
1394	Nanerge Senufo	0.63476	66,108	75,770	148,035	NAB56a	91-BAAC-f	nane-ri-ge		6.00	4,546	1.s..	7	4	4	2	1	Senoufo, Nanerige	pn.	.
1395	Natioro (Natyoro)	0.02649	2,759	3,162	6,178	NAB56a	91-EAAB	natioro cluster		5.00	158	0....	7	4	4	1	1		...	p
1396	Niangolo Senufo	0.06623	6,898	7,906	15,446	NAB56a	91-BAAC-d	niango-lo		5.00	395	1.s..	7	4	4	2	1		pn.	.
1397	Northern Samo (Sano, Don)	2.59403	270,157	309,645	604,962	NAB63z	00-DGAA	goe cluster	3	16.00	49,543	0....	8	5	8	2	2	Samo	PN.	.
1398	Northern Tusyan (Win)	0.17185	17,897	20,513	40,078	NAB56a	91-CAAA-b	win		5.00	1,026	0....	7	5	6	3	3		...	p
1399	Nunuma (Nuna, Gurunsi)	2.62605	273,492	313,467	612,430	NAB56a	91-GFAC	nuni cluster		13.00	40,751	0....	8	5	6	3	3	Nuni*	P..	.
1400	Padoro (Padogho)	0.00757	788	904	1,765	NAB56a	91-GEBB-a	kpatogo-so		5.00	45	0....	7	5	4	3	1		...	p
1401	Pana (Sama)	0.07947	8,276	9,486	18,533	NAB56a	91-GFAA	pana cluster		3.00	285	0....	6	4	4	1	1		...	.
1402	Puguli (Pwa)	0.11628	12,110	13,880	27,118	NAB56a	91-GFBB-a	phwi		3.00	416	0....	6	4	5	1	1		...	p
1403	Red Bobo (Bobo Wule)	2.43200	253,283	290,304	567,175	NAB56a	91-GFDA	bo-mu cluster	8	28.30	82,156	4.s..	9	5	8	3	3	Boomu*	PN.	.
1404	Samogho (Kpango)	0.15234	15,866	18,185	35,528	NAB63z	00-CABA-a	kpango		0.10	18	0....	5	4	3	2	3	Jowulu	...	b
1405	Siamou (Seme)	0.16393	17,073	19,568	38,231	NAB59j	95-BAAA-a	siamou		5.00	978	0....	7	5	6	1	1	Siamou	...	.
1406	Sininkere (Silanke)	0.01081	1,126	1,290	2,521	NAB56a	91-GGAA-n	sininkere		3.00	39	1c...	6	4	5	2	1		pnb	b
1407	Sisala (Hissala)	0.14051	14,634	16,772	32,769	NAB56a	91-GFBC-a	sisaa-li		10.00	1,677	0....	8	5	5	2	2	Sisaala*	PN.	.
1408	Songhai (Sonrhai)	1.32620	138,118	158,306	309,288	NAB65b	01-AAAA	songhay-kine cluster	3	0.40	633	0....	5	4	6	1	2	Songhai*	PN.	b
1409	Soninke (Serahuli)	0.97276	101,309	116,117	226,861	NAB63j	00-BAAA-a	proper soninke		0.08	93	3....	4	3	1	1	1	Soninke	...	b
1410	Southern Samo (Sembla)	0.16473	17,156	19,664	38,417	NAB63z	00-CAAA-a	senku		22.00	4,326	0....	9	5	6	3	3		...	.
1411	Southern Tusyan	0.17185	17,897	20,513	40,078	NAB56a	91-CAAA-a	proper tusyan		5.00	1,026	0....	7	5	6	2	3	Toussian, Southern	...	p
1412	Tenbo (Lorhon)	0.01325	1,380	1,582	3,090	NAB56a	91-GCAA-a	teen		3.00	47	0....	6	5	3	2	2	Teen	P..	.
1413	Tiefo	0.11765	12,253	14,044	27,438	NAB56a	91-DAAA-a	kumandara		5.00	702	0....	7	5	5	2	2		...	.

Continued opposite

Table 8-2 continued

EVANGELIZATION								EVANGELISM			ADDITIONAL DESCRIPTIVE DATA
Ref 1	*D* 28	*aC* 29	*CG%* 30	*r* 31	*E* 32	*U* 33	*W* 34	*e* 35	*R* 36	*T* 37	*Locations, civil divisions, literacy, religions, church history, denominations, dioceses, church growth, missions, agencies, ministries, movements* 38
1294	2	8	4.76	6	67.50	32.50	B	20.94	220	5	From Swatow. Including Hainanese. Chinese folk-religionists 72%, Buddhists 20%. D=RCC(VA-Miri),Anglican Ch(D-Kuching). M=MHM.
1295	1	8	4.93	6	67.00	33.00	B	24.45	228	5	Confucianists 20%, with Mahayana Buddhists 70%. D=RCC(VA-Miri). M=MHM.
1296	2	8	4.17	7	67.00	33.00	B	34.23	211	5	Originally from India or Pakistan. Hindus 43%, Muslims 20%, Baha'is 23%. D=Anglican Ch(D-Kuching),RCC.
1297	1	8	2.73	0	50.00	50.00	B	16.42	178	5	Also in Sarawak(Malaysia). Agriculturalists, fishermen. Animists 91%. D=Evangelical Ch of Borneo(SIB). M=BEM.
1298	2	7	4.62	0	99.70	0.30	C	298.93	128	8	Also in Kalimantan (Indonesia), Sarawak (Malaysia). Animists 20%, some Muslims. D=Evangelical Ch of Borneo(SIB),RCC.
1299	0	7	1.62	0	22.20	77.80	A	0.16	263	3	Also in Malaysia: south of Seria to Marudi in Sarawak. Muslims 99%.
1300	3	8	2.73	6	96.00	4.00	B	105.12	95	7	Shamanists 25%, Buddhists 15%, New-Religionists 15%, Confucians 10%. D=PCK,AoG,&c. M=WOM(Korea).
1301	4	7	3.97	0	54.00	46.00	B	29.56	245	5	Mainly in Sarawak, Kalimantan (Indonesia). Animists 60%, Muslims 25%. D=RCC,Anglican Ch,ECB(SIB),SDA.
1302	0	6	1.40	5	35.40	64.60	A	0.51	163	3	Many non-standard Malay dialects. Lingua franca of Sabah. Agriculturalists. Muslims 100%(Shafi Sunnis).
1303	0	9	0.70	5	44.07	55.93	A	0.11	87	3	Official language of Brunei. Muslims 100%(Shafi Sunnis).
1304	1	7	4.39	0	31.50	68.50	A	0.57	426	3	Also in Sabah and Sarawak. Close to Malay. Muslims 100% (Shafi Sunnis). D=Evangelical Ch of Borneo(SIB). M=BEM,SIL.
1305	3	8	6.02	1	69.00	31.00	B	50.37	259	6	Bugau. Also in Kalimantan, Sabah, Sarawak. Tribal religionists(animists) 70%, some Muslims 10%. D=Anglican Ch(D-Kuching),Methodist Ch,SDA. M=USPG,ABM.
1306	0	7	3.46	6	47.00	53.00	A	5.14	236	4	Immigrants from Sri Lanka, in commerce. Buddhists 95%(Theravada/Hinayana).
1307	1	7	5.51	0	43.00	57.00	A	15.69	384	5	Bisaya Bukit, Bekiau, Jilama Bawang. West of Seria. Animists 25%, Muslims 65%. D=Evangelical Ch of Borneo(SIB). M=BEM.
1308	1	7	4.40	0	57.00	43.00	B	24.96	236	5	Also in Sabah, Sarawak, Kalimantan. Tribal religionists(animists) 30%, Muslims 58%. D=Ev Ch of Borneo(SIB). M=BEM.
1309	2	7	3.82	0	34.00	66.00	A	6.20	349	4	Around Tutong on coast. Related to Baram, Tinjar. Animists 90%, Muslims 5%. D=RCC,ECB.
1310	0	7	0.70	0	20.02	79.98	A	0.01	166	2	Pitas Bajau, Sandakan Bajaw, Putatan. North of Bandar Seri Begawan. Also in Sabah. Fishermen. Muslims 100% (Sunnis).
1311	0	10	4.68		31.00	69.00	A	11.31	414	5	Filipinos, south Asians, Melanesians, Austronesians. Animists 60%, Muslims 30%.
Bulgaria											
1312	1	10	2.49	7	56.00	44.00	B	10.22	156	5	Immigrants from Middle East. Muslims 95%(mostly Sunnis). D=RCC.
1313	4	7	2.06	6	99.70	0.30	C	304.04	71	9	In Sofia region, also Yugoslavia. Muslims 20%(Hanafi Sunnis), nonreligious 10%. D=BOC,RCC,AoG,COG(many converts from Islam).
1314	1	10	0.01	6	99.80	0.20	C	435.08	11	10	Gregorians. Mainly in Armenia, also Turkey, Syria, Lebanon, and 15 other countries. D=Armenian Apostolic Ch(D-Sofija).
1315	2	9	0.64	6	99.85	0.15	C	437.45	34	10	Distinct from Romanian; also in Greece, southern Yugoslavia. D=BOC, Romanian Orthodox Ch.
1316	1	10	0.60	8	99.79	0.21	C	429.64	32	10	Expatriates from Britain, in business, education, development. D=Ch of England(D-Europe).
1317	6	7	0.82	6	99.93	0.07	C	526.72	36	10	Nonreligious/atheists 7%. D=Bulgarian Orthodox Ch(11 Dioceses),RCC(3 Dioceses),PEC,SDA,PC,MC. M=LBI,FMB. R=TWR(Monaco),AWR.
1318	5	10	2.61	6	99.60	0.40	C	267.18	82	8	Muslims 38%. D=BOC,RCC,AoG,COG, also numerous nondenominational groups. M=WEC.
1319	0	10	0.00	1	36.01	63.99	A	0.01	61	2	Isolated families in northeast Bulgaria; also Russia, Romania, Turkey, USA. Muslims 100%(Hanafi Sunnis).
1320	2	10	0.59	6	99.80	0.20	C	438.00	31	10	Immigrants from Czechoslovakia in 1938, 1945, 1968. Nonreligious 20%. D=RCC, Unity of Brethren.
1321	4	10	2.77	1	99.70	0.30	C	293.82	91	8	Muslims 20%. D=BOC,RCC,COG(numerous converts), AoG. M=WEC.
1322	4	10	2.77	6	99.70	0.30	C	319.37	83	9	Nomadic and settled Gypsies. Muslims 20%. D=BOC,RCC,AoG,COG. M=WEC.
1323	0	10	1.62	5	99.55	0.45	B	222.83	65	8	Artificial (constructed) language, used in 80 countries. Speakers in Bulgaria: 1,243,000. (only 9 mother-tongue). Nonreligious 24%.
1324	1	10	0.66	8	99.87	0.13	C	504.90	28	10	Expatriates from France in education, medicine, business. D=RCC.
1325	2	10	0.62	1	99.80	0.20	C	385.44	29	9	Varna coastal region. Majority in Moldavia; also Romania. Greek Orthodox converts from 15th century on. D=Greek Orthodox Ch,BOC.
1326	2	10	0.68	8	99.88	0.12	C	510.70	31	10	Expatriates from Germany, in professions, commerce. D=Protestant chaplaincies,RCC.
1327	1	9	-0.53	6	99.60	0.40	C	225.57	0	8	Mainly in Albania, Yugoslavia, Greece; also USA. Sunni Muslims 30%. D=Albanian Orthodox Ch.
1328	1	10	0.69	7	99.90	0.10	C	519.03	29	10	Expatriates from Greece, in commerce, finance. D=Greek Orthodox Ch.
1329	1	10	0.62	7	99.84	0.16	C	481.36	28	10	Expatriates from Italy in commerce, business, industry. Strong Catholics. D=RCC.
1330	0	10	0.70	6	46.05	53.95	A	0.08	83	2	Long-term residents practicing Judaism. 3 synagogues, 7 rabbis(1975).
1331	0	10	2.77	1	99.70	0.30	C	281.05	95	8	Also in Serbia, Romania, Poland, Hungary, Albania, Greece, and 20 other countries. Muslims 25%. M=AoG,WEC.
1332	1	10	0.55	7	99.75	0.25	C	383.25	30	9	D=Greek Orthodox Ch.
1333	3	10	0.70	5	99.90	0.10	C	522.31	28	10	From Macedonia. D=Bulgarian Orthodox Ch(D-Nevrokope),SOC,Macedonian Orthodox Ch.
1334	0	10	0.70	1	26.09	73.91	A	0.08	158	2	White, Black, Central Nogai. Descendants of Muslims of the Volga in Russia. Muslims 100%(Sunnis).
1335	0	8	0.46	1	99.65	0.35	C	251.48	44	8	Descendants of Paulicians/Bogomils. Intelligible with Standard Bulgarian. Nonreligious 25%.
1336	1	10	0.69	6	99.90	0.10	C	525.60	12	10	Expatriates and residents from Poland, in commerce. Strong Catholics. D=RCC.
1337	0	10	4.60	6	54.20	45.80	B	2.37	295	4	Bulgarian Muslims converted from Orthodoxy under Ottoman rule; 120 mosques, 100 imams (in 1975). Muslims 99% (Sunnis).
1338	1	10	0.73	8	99.93	0.07	C	553.30	29	10	Expatriates from Portugal in business, education. D=RCC.
1339	1	10	0.62	6	99.84	0.16	C	459.90	32	10	Expatriates from Romania. Business, commerce. D=Romanian Orthodox Ch, BOC.
1340	2	9	4.46	8	49.10	50.90	A	0.17	289	3	Kurdzhali Province. Danubian, Razgrad, Dinler. In eastern and central Bulgaria. Muslims 95%(Hanafi Sunnis), nonreligious 3%. D=COG,AoG(among Turkish).
1341	2	10	0.13	7	99.51	0.49	B	223.38	3	8	Expatriates, immigrants, from Russia. Nonreligious 40%. D=Russian Orthodox Ch,Old Ritualists(Old Believers).
1342	1	8	0.64	6	99.85	0.15	C	459.17	12	10	Expatriates, residents, from Serbia, in commerce, government. D=Serbian Orthodox Ch.
1343	1	10	0.75	8	99.96	0.04	C	585.16	27	10	Expatriates from Spain in business, development. Strong Catholics. D=RCC.
1344	0	10	4.37	6	37.00	63.00	A	1.35	383	4	Descendants of 13th-century Mongols. Muslims 99%(Hanafi Sunnis).
1345	1	10	3.49	1	99.70	0.30	C	283.60	112	8	Central Bulgar Gypsies. In central and northwest Bulgaria. Muslims 20%. D=RCC. M=WEC.
1346	0	9	0.80		29.00	71.00	A	5.29	76	4	Many expatriates, refugees, immigrants from European and Levantine countries. Muslims 70%.
Burkina Faso											
1347	2	8	2.70	4	62.00	38.00	B	9.05	204	4	Migrants, traders, residents from Mali. Muslims 73%(Maliki Sunnis), animists 23%. D=RCC,AoG. M=WF,FSC,CMA.
1348	2	6	4.94	4	52.00	48.00	B	15.18	332	5	Mostly in Benin, also Nigeria. Animists 60%, Muslims 32%(growing steadily). D=RCC,ECCOA(ECWA). M=WF,SIM.
1349	0	5	1.62	7	28.04	71.96	A	0.04	227	2	Nomads, especially in north. Tent-dwellers. Muslims 100%(Sunnis).
1350	2	6	4.64	0	31.00	69.00	A	4.52	531	4	Boulgou Province. Mostly in Togo. Animists 65%, Muslims 30%(Sunnis, Ahmadis). D=RCC,AoG. M=WF,CSSR.
1351	3	6	7.81	4	60.00	40.00	B	28.47	419	5	Southwestern area. Many monolinguals. Animists 86%, Muslims 1%. D=RCC,EEP,MEAO. M=WEC,WF,CSSR,FSC,ACP(MEP),EPNM.
1352	2	6	9.48	3	55.80	44.20	B	38.29	559	5	South central. Also in Ghana, Ivory Coast. Animists 51%, Muslims 30%. D=RCC(D-Koupela),AoG. M=SIL,WF,CSSR,FSC,FSF,FMB.
1353	2	6	9.41	0	61.00	39.00	B	55.66	508	6	Also in Mali. Animists 50%, Muslims 25%. D=RCC,ECEBF. M=CMA,FMB,Apostolic Ch Mission.
1354	1	7	3.39	0	24.00	76.00	A	2.62	604	4	Comoe Province. All speak Jula. Muslims 87% (Sunnis), some animists. D=RCC.
1355	0	6	0.00	0	19.00	81.00	A	0.00	0	1.07	Hauts-Bassins. Bobo Fing who have converted to Islam. Muslims 90% (Sunnis), Animists 10%. M=CMA.
1356	1	6	3.83	1	27.00	73.00	A	2.95	581	4	Black Bolon(Northern), White Bolon(Southern). Bilingual in Jula. Muslims 90%, some animists. D=ECEBF. M=CMA,EMCM.
1357	0	5	0.00	0	8.00	92.00	A	0.00	0	1.03	Kossi Province. Fishing hamlets along Niger river from Mali to Niger. Fishermen. Muslims 99%(Maliki Sunnis).
1358	4	10	3.93	8	99.79	0.21	C	435.40	92	10	Expatriates from Britain, in development, education. D=CPWA,RCC,AoG,JWs.
1359	2	6	6.14	0	40.00	60.00	A	7.30	514	4	Majority live in Ghana. Animists 95%. D=RCC,ECEBF. M=CMA.
1360	1	5	2.52	2	31.00	69.00	A	6.78	344	4	Benin border, Tapoa and Gourma Provinces. Animists 90%. D=AoG.
1361	2	5	5.23	5	43.00	57.00	A	7.84	421	4	Mainly in Mali. Animists 62%, Muslims 33%(expanding fast). D=RCC,ECEBF. M=CMA,AIMM. Converts persecuted.
1362	3	6	9.15	4	66.00	34.00	B	48.18	437	6	Northern Dagari. Animists 55%, Muslims 25%. D=RCC(D-Diebougou),MEAO,EEP. M=WEC,MEP,WF.
1363	1	6	4.98	0	30.00	70.00	A	5.47	580	4	36 villages in southwest. Animists 85%, Muslims 10%. D=RCC. M=WF,WEC.
1364	2	7	8.46	0	64.00	36.00	B	49.05	421	6	Mainly in Mali. Animists 49%, Muslims 30%. D=RCC,ECEM. M=CMA,WF,FSC.
1365	0	6	3.51	0	26.00	74.00	A	4.74	514	4	Near Kaanse and Khe. Somewhat bilingual in Jula. Animists 95%. M=WEC.
1366	0	6	0.00	0	17.10	82.90	A	0.06	304	2	Mainly in Mali. Spoken in Samogho-Gban. No literates. Animists 70%, Muslims 30%. M=CMA.
1367	2	6	5.13	0	33.00	67.00	A	9.63	540	4	Bougouriba Province. Some bilinguals in Jula. Animists 72%, Muslims 20%. D=EEP,RCC. M=MEP.
1368	2	6	6.19	0	41.00	59.00	A	13.46	505	5	Comoe Province. Also in Togo, Ivory Coast, Senegal, Mali. Animists 79%, Muslims 12%. D=RCC,ECEBF. M=SIL,CMA,WF,CSSR,FSC.
1369	3	10	7.73	4	99.72	0.28	C	378.43	171	9	Immigrants from Ghana. Animists 20%. D=RCC,JWs,AICs.
1370	2	10	6.87	8	99.87	0.13	C	495.37	138	10	Expatriates from France, in business, commerce, education, government. D=RCC,JWs. M=WF,CSSR.
1371	3	6	7.00	0	43.00	57.00	A	17.26	533	5	Animists 81%, Muslims 8%. D=ECEBF,MEAO,RCC. M=CMA,WEC,SIL.
1372	1	6	5.01	1	41.00	59.00	A	5.98	426	4	Mainly in Ghana. Animists 71%, Muslims 25%. D=EEP. M=ACP(MEP),LM(Ghana),FMB.
1373	2	6	8.27	4	51.00	49.00	B	13.03	518	5	Also in Benin, Niger, Togo. Animists 53%, Muslims 40%. D=RCC(D-Fada N'Gourma),AEEBF. M=WF,CSSR,FSC,FSF,ECWA,SIM.
1374	1	5	3.64	4	36.20	63.80	A	0.26	397	3	Extends into Niger to Niamey. Speakers use Gurma, Bogande. Muslims 95%(Sunnis). D=AoG. M=SIM.
1375	0	9	1.81	5	52.10	47.90	B	0.19	158	3	Traders from across Africa. Lingua franca. Muslims 99%(Maliki Sunnis).
1376	0	5	3.80	1	29.00	71.00	A	2.11	488	4	Gourma Province; Pama, Comin-Yanga, and Diabo Subdistricts. Also in Togo. Animists 98%.
1377	0	5	2.51	4	35.10	64.90	A	0.12	321	3	Northeast, on edge of Sahara Desert. Semi-nomadic pastoralists. Muslims 99%.
1378	0	6	3.93	0	26.00	74.00	A	2.84	614	4	Mainly in Mali. Men speak Bambara, some French. Animists 97%.
1379	0	5	5.00	4	42.00	58.00	A	1.53	459	4	Widely-travelling traders across West Africa, Mali to Ghana. Muslims 99%(Maliki Sunnis). M=WEC(Hong Kong),FMB,CMA,UBS,Mennonite Mission.
1380	1	6	5.10	0	35.00	65.00	A	12.77	507	5	Sourou Province, Tougan Sub-district. Animists 60%, Muslims 30%. D=RCC.
1381	0	6	3.22	0	22.00	78.00	A	2.40	572	4	Poni Province, Gaoua sub-district. Animists 87%, Muslims 10%. M=WEC,SIL.
1382	1	6	7.46	4	48.00	52.00	A	17.52	504	5	Majority in Ghana. Animists 80%, Muslims 10%. D=AoG. M=FMB,SIL.
1383	0	6	4.21	0	22.00	78.00	A	2.40	695	4	Near Kaanse and Dogoso. Animists 95%. M=WEC.
1384	1	7	4.74	0	28.00	72.00	A	5.11	598	4	Mouhoun Province. Almost entirely monolingual. Animists 75%, Muslims 20%. D=AoG. M=CMA.
1385	3	6	2.51	0	31.00	69.00	A	3.39	343	4	Southwest. Bilingual in Jula. Muslims 77%, animists 20%. D=Free Will Baptists,AoG,WEC.
1386	2	6	7.86	2	45.00	55.00	A	18.06	562	5	Yatenga Province. Animists 81%, Muslims 8%. D=AoG,RCC(D-Ouahigouya). M=WF,CSSR,FSC,FSF,SIL.
1387	3	6	8.35	2	45.00	55.00	A	16.42	592	5	Sangui Province. Animists 85%, Muslims 5%. D=RCC,AoG,EBBF. M=SIL,NBC,FMB.
1388	4	5	5.81	4	42.70	57.30	A	1.09	475	4	Nomads, cattle pastoralists. Liptaako is official Fulani language in Burkina Faso. Muslims 99%. D=RCC(D-Fada N'Gourma),AoG,ECEBF,AEEBF. M=ECWA,SIM.
1389	2	6	5.57	4	34.73	65.27	A	0.92	548	3	Also in Ivory Coast, a few in Ghana. Animists 98%, Muslims 1%. D=RCC(D-Diebougou),MEAO. M=WEC,WF.
1390	1	5	5.09	5	44.50	55.50	A	2.43	438	4	Also in Mali, Guinea, and several other countries. Animists 58%, Muslims 40%. D=AEEBF. M=ECWA,SIM,WEC,IV.
1391	0	5	0.00	0	14.01	85.99	A	0.00	0	1.06	Provinces: Sanmatenga, Yatenga, Bam. Animists 80%, some Muslims 20%.
1392	2	6	8.34	2	45.00	55.00	A	19.71	624	5	Animists 60%, Muslims 28%. D=RCC(D-Nouna-Dedougou),ECEBF. M=CMA,WF,CSSR.
1393	6	6	12.48	4	81.20	18.80	B	68.76	467	6	Formerly imperial rulers. Animists 16%, Muslims 61%(Maliki Sunnis; many converts on arrival in cities). D=RCC,ECEBF,AoG,EEP,EBBF,a few AICs. M=FMB,WF.
1394	2	6	6.31	1	36.00	64.00	A	7.88	585	4	West of Bobo-Dioulasso. Animists 60%, Muslims 34%. D=RCC,AoG. M=AIMM.
1395	0	7	2.80	0	27.00	73.00	A	4.92	423	4	Comoe Province. Living alongside Jula and Senufo; bilingual in Jula. Animists 72%, Muslims 23%. M=CMA.
1396	1	6	3.74	1	33.00	67.00	A	6.02	424	4	Near Ivory Coast border. Animists 65%, Muslims 30%. D=RCC. M=CMA.
1397	2	6	8.88	2	53.00	47.00	B	30.95	557	5	Sourou Province. Animists 54%, Muslims 30%. D=RCC(D-Nouna-Dedougou),ECEBF. M=CMA,FMB.
1398	1	6	4.74	0	34.00	66.00	A	6.20	492	4	Provinces: Comoe, Houet. Fairly bilingual in Jula. Animists 70%, Muslims 25%. D=RCC. M=SIL,WF,CSSR,CMA,AIMM.
1399	3	6	8.67	2	48.00	52.00	A	22.77	573	5	Over 100 villages in Sissili Province. Animists 62%, Muslims 25%. D=RCC(D-Koudougou),EEP,AoG. M=ACP(MEP),EPNM,SIL,WF,CSSR,FSC,FSF,LM(Ghana).
1400	0	7	3.88	0	29.00	71.00	A	5.29	496	4	Bougouriba Province. Bilingual in Jula and Kaanse. Animists 85%, Muslims 10%. M=WEC.
1401	1	7	3.41	0	24.00	76.00	A	2.62	546	4	Sourou Province. Low bilingualism in Jula. Animists 75%, Muslims 22%. D=RCC(D-Nouna-Dedougou). M=WF.
1402	1	6	3.80	0	25.00	75.00	A	2.73	567	4	Bousouriba Province. Jula bilingualism. Animists 72%, Muslims 25%. D=Pentecostals. M=WEC.
1403	3	5	9.43	0	71.30	28.70	B	73.64	415	6	Animists 62%, Muslims 10%. D=RCC(D-Nouna-Dedougou),ECEBF,AoG. M=WF,CSSR,FSC,FSF,CMA,FMB,SIL,MA.
1404	2	6	2.93	0	22.10	77.90	A	0.08	599	2	Kenedougou Province. No literates, except some in Jula. Muslims 90%, animists 10%. D=RCC,ECEBF. M=CMA,SIL,AIMM.
1405	1	6	4.69	0	28.00	72.00	A	5.11	459	4	Kenedougou Province. Some literates in Jula, more in French. Animists 70%, Muslims 25%. D=RCC. M=Africa Inter-Mennonite Mission.
1406	1	5	3.73	1	36.00	64.00	A	3.94	388	4	Sanmatenga Province, near Pensa. Second language is More (Mossi). Traditional religionists(animists) 97%. D=AoG.
1407	1	6	5.26	0	40.00	60.00	A	14.60	454	5	Sissili Province. Animists 60%, Muslims 30%(strong in towns). D=EEP. M=SIL,ACP(MEP).
1408	0	5	4.24	0	27.40	72.60	A	0.40	614	3	Mainly along Niger River in Mali, Niger. Muslims 99%(Maliki Sunnis). M=SIM,EMS.
1409	0	5	4.64	0	16.08	83.92	A	0.04	1,116	2	Mainly in Mali,Senegal,Ivory Coast; also Mauritania,Gambia,Guinea-Bissau. Muslims 80%(Sunnis,most in Sufi Tijaniyya and in Hamali sect), animists 20%. M=FI.
1410	3	6	6.26	2	56.00	44.00	B	44.96	399	6	Comoe Province, also in Mali. Animists 58%, Muslims 20%. D=RCC(D-Nouna-Dedougou),ECEBF,EBBF. M=CMA,NBC,FMB,AIMM.
1411	1	6	4.74	0	33.00	67.00	A	6.02	507	4	Provinces: Comoe, Houet. Bilingual in Jula. Animists 75%, Muslims 20%. D=RCC. M=WBT,WF,CSSR,CMA,AIMM.
1412	3	6	3.93	0	27.00	73.00	A	2.95	538	4	Poni Province. Animists 95%. D=RCC,MEAO,ECEBF. M=WEC,CMA.
1413	1	6	4.34	0	28.00	72.00	A	5.11	559	4	Comoe Province. Many now speak Jula. Animists 95%. D=ECEBF. M=CMA,WEC.

Continued overleaf

Table 8-2 continued

PEOPLE		POPULATION				IDENTITY CODE		LANGUAGE		CHURCH		MINISTRY						SCRIPTURE		
Ref 1	Ethnic name 2	P% 3	In 1995 4	In 2000 5	In 2025 6	Race 7	Language 8	Autoglossonym 9	S 10	AC 11	Members 12	Jayuh 13-17	d 18	wa 19	xc 20	mc 21	mi 22	Biblioglossonym 23	Pub 24-26	ss 27
1414	Tuareg (Udalan, Bella)	0.27021	28,141	32,254	63,017	CMT32h	10-AAAB-a	ta-mahaq		0.00	0	1....	0	3	3	1	2	Tamahaq: Hoggar*	PN.	b
1415	Turka (Tyurama)	0.49984	52,056	59,665	116,569	NAB56a	91-GDAA	cura-ma cluster		5.00	2,983	0....	7	5	5	2	1	Turka	...	.
1416	Vige	0.07417	7,724	8,854	17,297	NAB56a	91-GAAA	viemo cluster		3.00	266	0....	6	4	4	2	1		...	p
1417	Wala (Dagaari Jula)	0.10000	10,415	11,937	23,321	NAB56a	91-GGAA-i	dagaari-jula		0.10	12	1c...	5	2	3	0	0		pnb	.
1418	Wara	0.04768	4,966	5,691	11,120	NAB56a	91-EAAA	wara cluster		7.00	398	0....	7	5	4	3	0		...	p
1419	Western Bobo Wule (Pwe)	0.60527	63,036	72,250	141,157	NAB56a	91-GFDA	bo-mu cluster		25.00	18,063	4.s..	9	5	7	3	3	Boomu*	PN.	.
1420	Western Karaboro	0.33566	34,958	40,067	78,280	NAB56a	91-BABA-b	syer		4.00	1,603	0....	6	4	4	2	1		pn.	.
1421	Western Kusaal (Kusasi)	0.12970	13,508	15,482	30,248	NAB56a	91-GGAC-a	kusaal		7.00	1,084	1....	7	5	6	2	2	Kusaal*	PN.	.
1422	Yarse	1.85735	193,435	221,709	433,159	NAB63h	91-GGAA-a	moo-re		0.00	0	2A...	0	3	4	1	0	Moore	PNB	b
1423	Yoruba	0.35000	36,451	41,779	81,625	NAB59n	98-AAAA-a	standard yoruba		45.00	18,800	3asu.	9	8	13	4	3	Yoruba	PNB	b
1424	Zaore	0.28296	29,469	33,776	65,990	NAB56a	91-GGAA-c	zao-re		2.00	676	1c...	6	4	4	1	0		pnb	.
1425	Zerma (Dyerma, Zaberma)	0.00722	752	862	1,684	NAB65c	01-AAAB-b	zarma		0.20	2	2..u.	5	3	3	1	1	Zarma	PNB	.
1426	other minor peoples	0.20000	20,829	23,874	46,643	...				10.00	2,387		8	5	3	2	0			
	Burundi	**100.00000**	**6,156,197**	**6,695,001**	**11,568,648**					**76.97**	**5,152,841**									
1427	Arab	0.03000	1,847	2,009	3,471	CMT30	12-AACF-f	syro-palestinian	2	0.00	0	1Asuh	0	3	2	1	0	Arabic: Lebanese*	Pnb	b
1428	British	0.00500	308	335	578	CEW19i	52-ABAC-b	standard-english	5	77.00	258	3Bsuh	10	9	13	5	1		PNB	b
1429	French	0.03000	1,847	2,009	3,471	CEW21b	51-AABI-d	general français	35	87.00	1,747	1B.uh	10	9	14	5	1	French	PNB	b
1430	Greek	0.01000	616	670	1,157	CEW20	56-AAAA-c	dhimotiki		95.00	636	2B.uh	10	9	11	4	1	Greek: Modern	PNB	b
1431	Gujarati	0.12000	7,387	8,034	13,882	CNN25e	59-AAFH-b	standard gujaraati		0.60	48	2A.u.	5	4	2	3	0	Gujarati	PNB	b
1432	Hima	0.11000	6,772	7,365	12,726	NAB57d	99-AUSE-fd	o-ro-hima		60.00	4,419	1cs.h	10	8	7	5	2		pnb	b
1433	Hutu	80.86500	4,978,209	5,413,913	9,354,987	NAB57d	99-AUSD-c	i-ki-ruundi	100	76.50	4,141,643	4csu.	10	9	10	5	3	Kirundi*	PNB	b
1434	Lingala (Zairian)	1.60000	98,499	107,120	185,098	NAB57c	99-AUIF-b	vehicular lingala	7	79.00	84,625	4asu.	10	8	12	5	1	Lingala	PNB	b
1435	Ruanda Tutsi	1.60000	98,499	107,120	185,098	NAB57d	99-AUSD-f	i-ki-nya-rwanda	8	86.00	92,123	2Asu.	10	9	11	5	2	Kinyarwanda*	PNB	b
1436	Swahili	0.10000	6,156	6,695	11,569	NAB57j	99-AUSM-b	standard ki-swahili	35	0.00	0	4Asu.	0	2	2	1	0	Kiswahili*	PNB	b
1437	Tutsi	14.00000	861,868	937,300	1,619,611	NAB57d	99-AUSD-c	i-ki-ruundi		85.00	796,705	4csu.	10	9	10	5	2	Kirundi*	PNB	b
1438	Twa (Gesera) Pygmy	1.00000	61,562	66,950	115,686	BYG12	99-AUSD-c	i-ki-ruundi		8.00	5,356	4csu.	7	5	6	2	1	Kirundi*	PNB	b
1439	Walloon	0.03000	1,847	2,009	3,471	CEW21l	51-AABH-f	wallon		92.00	1,848	0A.uh	10	9	15	5	1	French: Walloon	P..	b
1440	other minor peoples	0.50000	30,781	33,475	57,843	...				70.00	23,433		10	7	7	2	0			
	Cambodia	**100.00000**	**9,982,051**	**11,167,719**	**16,526,449**					**1.06**	**118,400**									
1441	Brao (Bru, Love, Laveh)	0.06354	6,343	7,096	10,501	AUG03z	46-FADC-a	brao		1.00	71	0....	6	4	4	1	0	Brao	...	b
1442	British	0.01000	998	1,117	1,653	CEW19i	52-ABAC-b	standard-english		79.00	882	3Bsuh	10	9	13	3	2		PNB	b
1443	Burmese (Myen)	0.03000	2,995	3,350	4,958	MSY50b	77-AABA-a	bama		0.09	3	4Asu.	4	3	2	0	1	Burmese	PNB	b
1444	Campuon (Tampuan)	0.17156	17,125	19,159	28,353	AUG03z	46-FACB-c	tampuan		1.00	192	0.s..	6	4	4	1	0		pn.	b
1445	Central Khmer (Cambodian)	85.17096	8,501,809	9,511,653	14,075,735	AUG03b	46-FBAA-b	khmae		0.63	59,923	2A...	5	4	6	1	3	Khmer*	PNB	b
1446	Central Mnong (Budong)	0.24145	24,102	26,964	39,903	AUG03z	46-FAEA-a	pnong		12.00	3,236	0.s..	8	4	6	1	1		p..	.
1447	Chong (Shong, Xong)	0.07813	7,799	8,725	12,912	AUG03z	46-FCAB-a	chong		1.00	87	0....	6	4	4	1	0		...	.
1448	Eastern Cham	0.00200	200	223	331	MSY44z	31-MBBC-a	east cham		10.00	22	0.s..	8	5	6	2	2	Cham: Eastern*	P..	.
1449	Eastern Pear (Por)	0.01652	1,649	1,845	2,730	AUG03z	46-FCBA-a	pear		2.00	37	0....	6	4	4	1	0		...	.
1450	Eurasian	0.10000	9,982	11,168	16,526	MSY43	51-AABI-d	general français		50.00	5,584	1B.uh	10	7	8	3	3	French	PNB	b
1451	French	0.03000	2,995	3,350	4,958	CEW21b	51-AABI-d	general français	32	77.00	2,580	1B.uh	10	9	14	4	2	French	PNB	b
1452	Han Chinese (Cantonese)	2.00000	199,641	223,354	330,529	MSY42a	79-AAAM-a	central yue		1.00	2,234	3A.uh	6	4	8	3	3	Chinese, Yue	PNB	b
1453	Han Chinese (Hainanese)	0.10000	9,982	11,168	16,526	MSY42a	79-AAAK-c	wanning		1.00	112	1a...	6	4	8	3	3		p..	b
1454	Han Chinese (Hakka)	0.20000	19,964	22,335	33,053	MSY42a	79-AAAG-a	literary hakka		1.20	268	1A...	6	4	6	3	3	Chinese: Hakka, Wukingfu*	PNB	b
1455	Han Chinese (Hokkien)	0.50000	49,910	55,839	82,632	MSY42a	79-AAAJ-ic	chaozhou		1.20	670	1A..h	6	4	6	3	3	Chinese, Min Nan	PNB	b
1456	Han Chinese (Mandarin)	1.11862	111,661	124,924	184,868	MSY42a	79-AAAB-ba	kuo-yü		1.00	1,249	2Bsuh	6	5	8	4	0	Chinese: Kuoyu*	PNB	b
1457	Han Chinese (Teochew)	2.50000	249,551	279,193	413,161	MSY42a	79-AAAJ-ic	chaozhou		1.40	3,909	1A..h	6	4	8	3	3	Chinese, Min Nan	PNB	b
1458	Jarai (Chrai)	0.28000	27,950	31,270	46,274	MSY44z	31-MBAA	jarai cluster		10.00	3,127	0....	8	5	6	2	1	Jorai*	PN.	b
1459	Kaco	0.02400	2,396	2,680	3,966	AUG03z	46-FACB-c	tampuan		1.00	27	0.s..	6	4	4	1	0		pn.	b
1460	Kravet	0.03812	3,805	4,257	6,300	AUG03z	46-FADC-c	kravet		1.00	43	0....	6	4	4	1	0		...	.
1461	Krung	0.34000	33,939	37,970	56,190	AUG03z	46-FADC-d	krung-2		1.00	380	0....	6	4	4	1	0		...	b
1462	Kui (Suai, Kuoy, Kuay)	0.10327	10,308	11,533	17,067	AUG03z	46-FAAB-a	kuy		3.00	346	0....	6	5	6	2	1	Kuy	PN.	.
1463	Lamam (Lmam)	0.01563	1,560	1,746	2,583	AUG03z	46-FACB-b	lamam		1.00	17	0.s..	6	4	4	1	0		pn.	.
1464	Lao (Laotian Tai)	0.60000	59,892	67,006	99,159	MSY49b	47-AAAC-b	lao		1.40	938	2As..	6	4	6	2	1	Lao	PNB	b
1465	Malay	0.10000	9,982	11,168	16,526	MSY44k	31-PHAA-b	bahasa-malaysia		0.20	22	1asuh	5	3	2	1	0	Malay	PNB	b
1466	Rhade (Raday, Rade, Ede)	0.10000	9,982	11,168	16,526	MSY44z	31-MBAC	rhade cluster		41.00	4,579	0....	9	6	6	3	1	Rade	PN.	.
1467	Samre	0.00313	312	350	517	AUG03z	46-FCAA-a	samrê		1.00	3	0....	6	4	4	1	0		...	.
1468	Saoch	0.00781	780	872	1,291	AUG03z	46-FCAB-b	saoch		1.00	9	0....	6	4	4	1	0		...	.
1469	Somray	0.03125	3,119	3,490	5,165	AUG03z	46-FCAA-b	somray		1.00	35	0....	6	4	4	1	0		...	.
1470	Stieng (Budip)	0.03717	3,710	4,151	6,143	AUG03z	46-FAEC-a	stieng		10.00	415	0.s..	8	4	6	1	0	Stieng	Pn.	.
1471	Suoy	0.00313	312	350	517	AUG03z	46-FCAC	suoy cluster		1.50	5	0....	6	4	4	1	0		...	.
1472	Tamil	0.01000	998	1,117	1,653	CNN23c	49-EBEA-b	tamil		9.00	101	2Asu.	7	5	8	3	1	Tamil	PNB	b
1473	Thai (Central Tai)	0.28000	27,950	31,270	46,274	MSY49d	47-AAAB-d	central thai		0.60	188	3asuh	5	4	5	2	0	Thai*	PNB	b
1474	Vietnamese (Annamese)	3.00000	299,462	335,032	495,793	MSY52b	46-EBAA-ac	general viêt		8.00	26,803	1Asu.	7	5	8	3	3	Vietnamese	PNB	b
1475	Western Cham (Cambodian)	2.47808	247,363	276,745	409,539	MSY44z	31-MBBC-b	west cham		0.01	28	0.s..	3	3	0	0	2	Cham, Western	p..	b
1476	Western Pear (Por)	0.01563	1,560	1,746	2,583	AUG03z	46-FCBA	pear cluster		3.00	52	0....	6	4	4	1	0		...	.
1477	other minor peoples	0.20000	19,964	22,335	33,053	...				1.00	223		6	5	4	2	0			
	Cameroon	**100.00000**	**13,182,056**	**15,084,969**	**26,484,402**					**51.45**	**7,761,502**									
1478	Abo	0.01000	1,318	1,508	2,648	NAB57k	99-AUBA-b	ba-nkon		50.00	754	0....	10	7	6	4	1		...	.
1479	Adamawa Fulani (Fula)	8.42331	1,110,365	1,270,654	2,230,863	NAB56c	90-BAAA-q	fula-adamawa	51	1.00	12,707	1cs..	6	4	6	2	3	Fulfulde, Adamawa	PNB	b
1480	Adere (Dzodinka)	0.01748	2,304	2,637	4,629	NAB57a	99-AGEB-ad	dzodinka		50.00	1,318	0....	10	7	6	4	1		pn.	.
1481	Affade	0.10000	13,182	15,085	26,484	NAB60b	18-BBAB-b	afade		4.00	603	0....	6	5	6	3	0		...	.
1482	Age (Essimbi, Isimbi)	0.21923	28,899	33,071	58,062	NAB57a	99-ABGA-a	e-simbi		85.00	28,110	0....	10	7	10	4	2	Esimbi	...	.
1483	Aghem (Wum)	0.17967	23,684	27,103	47,585	NAB57a	99-AGDA-c	a-ghem		85.00	23,038	0....	10	7	10	4	3		p..	.
1484	Akum	0.00578	762	872	1,531	NAB56b	98-IDJA-a	a-kum		50.00	436	0....	10	7	7	4	2		...	.
1485	Akweto (Nsari, Sali)	0.02000	2,636	3,017	5,297	NAB56b	99-AFBA-d	n-sari		50.00	1,508	0....	10	7	6	4	1		...	p
1486	Amasi (Banta, Anta)	0.14907	19,650	22,487	39,480	NAB57a	99-ABJA-a	m-anta		80.00	17,990	0....	10	7	10	4	1		...	.
1487	Ambele	0.01000	1,318	1,508	2,648	NAB56b	99-AGBA-b	n-gamambo		50.00	754	0....	10	7	6	4	0		...	.
1488	Anyang (Nyang, Takamanda)	0.12277	16,184	18,520	32,515	NAB57a	99-AEAA	denya cluster		60.00	11,112	0....	10	7	7	4	1	Denya	...	.
1489	Assumbo (Badzumbo)	0.02113	2,785	3,187	5,596	NAB57a	99-ABEA-a	i-pulo		85.00	2,709	0....	10	8	11	4	2	Ipulo	...	.
1490	Atong	0.01000	1,318	1,508	2,648	NAB57a	99-AGBA-a	a-tong		50.00	754	0....	10	7	6	4	1		...	.
1491	Awing (Mbwewi)	0.07202	9,494	10,864	19,074	NAB57a	99-AGEA-h	awing		70.00	7,605	0....	10	7	7	4	1		...	.
1492	Baba (Bapa)	0.13976	18,423	21,083	37,015	NAB57a	99-AGEI-ac	ba-pakum		45.00	9,487	0....	9	6	6	3	1		pnb	.
1493	Babessi (Pesii, Sii)	0.13537	17,845	20,421	35,852	NAB57a	99-AGDC-d	wushi		50.00	10,210	0....	10	7	6	4	1		pn.	.
1494	Bafanji	0.09317	12,282	14,055	24,676	NAB57a	99-AGEI-bf	ba-fangi		70.00	9,838	0....	10	7	6	4	1		pnb	.
1495	Bafaw (Bafo, Balong)	0.09207	12,137	13,889	24,384	NAB57k	99-AJBA-a	le-fo'		85.00	11,805	0....	10	8	10	4	1		...	b
1496	Bafumen (Mme)	0.05000	6,591	7,542	13,242	NAB57a	99-AGDB-b	m-mem		60.00	4,525	0....	10	7	7	4	1		pn.	.
1497	Baka Pygmy (Eastern Pygmy)	0.28992	38,217	43,734	76,784	BYG12	93-ADDA-a	baka		10.00	4,373	0....	8	5	6	1	1		...	.
1498	Bakoko (Basoo)	0.57783	76,170	87,165	153,035	NAB57k	99-AJAA-c	do-tanga		60.00	52,299	0....	10	7	7	4	2		...	.
1499	Bakole (Bamusso)	0.00329	434	496	871	NAB57k	99-AUIL-f	lo-kole		85.00	422	0....	10	8	10	4	1		pn.	.
1500	Bakossi (Akosi, Nkosi)	0.54807	72,247	82,676	145,153	NAB57k	99-AJBE	akoose cluster		86.20	71,267	0....	10	8	11	4	2	Akoose	...	.
1501	Bakwele	0.14144	18,645	21,336	37,460	NAB57c	99-AUDH-a	be-kwil		70.00	14,935	0....	10	7	6	4	1	Bekwel	...	.
1502	Baldamu (Mbazia)	0.10000	13,182	15,085	26,484	NAB60b	18-EABA-b	balda		4.00	603	0....	6	5	6	1	1		pn.	.
1503	Bali (Bani, Li)	0.54916	72,391	82,841	145,442	NAB57a	99-AGEI-a	mu-nga'ka	2	40.00	33,136	0....	9	6	8	3	1	Mungaka	PNB	.
1504	Balo	0.01500	1,977	2,263	3,973	NAB56b	99-ABJA	manta cluster		45.00	1,018	0....	9	5	6	3	0		...	b
1505	Bamali (Ngoobechop)	0.05809	7,657	8,763	15,385	NAB57a	99-AGEI-bd	ba-mali		70.00	6,134	0....	10	7	7	4	1		pnb	.
1506	Bambalang (Tshirambo)	0.15894	20,952	23,976	42,094	NAB57a	99-AGEI-be	ba-mbalang		70.00	16,783	0....	10	7	5	4	1		pnb	.
1507	Bambili (Bambui)	0.10309	13,589	15,551	27,303	NAB57a	99-AGEA-ca	ba-mbili		60.00	9,331	0....	10	7	7	3	1		...	.
1508	Bamenyam (Bagam)	0.03729	4,916	5,625	9,876	NAB57a	99-AGEI-c	ma-menyan		80.00	4,500	0....	10	7	7	4	1		pnb	.
1509	Bamileke Fefe (Bafang)	1.35591	178,737	204,539	359,105	NAB57a	99-AGEF-b	central fe'fe'		82.00	167,722	0....	10	7	8	4	1		...	.
1510	Bamileke Megaka	0.03000	3,955	4,525	7,945	NAB57a	99-AGED-c	me-gaka		94.00	4,254	0.s..	10	7	8	4	1		pnb	.
1511	Bamileke Ndanda	0.10300	13,578	15,538	27,279	NAB57a	99-AGEG-b	northeast ndanda		94.00	14,605	0....	10	7	6	4	2		...	.
1512	Bamileke-Bakwa (Bakoa)	0.09427	12,427	14,221	24,967	NAB57a	99-AGEH-bb	mi-pa		75.00	10,665	0....	10	7	7	4	1		...	.
1513	Bamileke-Bamenjou	1.08517	143,048	163,698	287,401	NAB57a	99-AGED-dc	ba-menjo		84.00	137,506	0.s..	10	7	8	4	1		pnb	.
1514	Bamileke-Bandjoun	3.00474	396,087	453,264	795,787	NAB57a	99-AGEE-db	ngo-man-jun		82.00	371,677	0....	10	8	11	4	2	Bamileke: Bandjoun*	P..	.
1515	Bamileke-Batcham	0.96135	126,726	145,019	254,608	NAB57a	99-AGED-b	ngyemboong		84.00	121,816	0.s..	10	8	10	4	2	Ngiemboon	PNB	.
1516	Bamileke-Foto	0.39488	52,053	59,568	104,582	NAB57a	99-AGAB-b	ba-ngwe		90.00	53,611	0....	10	7	7	4	1		...	.
1517	Bamileke-Medumba	1.71583	226,182	258,832	454,427	NAB57a	99-AGED-bd	ba-ngang		82.00	212,243	0.s..	10	7	11	4	2	Bamileke: Medumba*	PNB	.
1518	Bamileke-Ngomba (Bamesso)	0.21923	28,899	33,071	58,062	NAB57a	99-AGEA-d	mundum		94.00	31,087	0....	10	7	6	4	1	Ngomba	...	.
1519	Bamileke-Ngombale (Babadou)	0.32884	43,348	49,605	87,091	NAB57a	99-AGED-a	ngombale		90.00	44,645	0.s..	10	7	6	4	1		pnb	.
1520	Bamileke-Tchang	2.36929	312,321	357,407	627,492	NAB57a	99-AGEE-db	ngo-man-jun		80.00	285,925	0....	10	8	10	4	2	Bamileke: Bandjoun*	P..	.
1521	Banagere (Iyon, Messaga)	0.15346	20,229	23,149	40,643	NAB56b	99-ABHA-a	u-gare		80.00	18,520	0....	10	8	6	4	1	Mesaka	...	.
1522	Bangando (Bangantu)	0.03000	3,955	4,525	7,945	NAB66c	93-AAAB	bangandu cluster		50.00	2,263	0....	10	7	7	4	2		...	.
1523	Bango (Bongo, Baca)	0.00621	819	937	1,645	NAB57k	99-ANBD-a	nu-baca		50.00	468	0....	10	7	6	4	1		...	.
1524	Bangolan	0.09098	11,993	13,724	24,096	NAB57a	99-AGEI-bg	ba-ngolan		70.00	9,607	0....	10	7	7	4	1		pnb	.
1525	Barombi (Lambi)	0.01425	1,878	2,150	3,774	NAB57k	99-AUBA-a	ba-rombi		80.00	1,720	0....	10	7	5	4	1		...	.
1526	Bassa (Koko, Bisaa)	2.52110	332,333	380,307	667,698	NAB57k	99-AUBB	basaa cluster		69.50	264,313	2....	10	8	11	4	3	Bassa: Cameroon*	PNB	.
1527	Bassossi (Sosi, Asobse)	0.70000	92,274	105,595	185,391	NAB57k	99-AJBB-b	n-swase		70.00	73,916	0....	10	7	7	4	2		...	.
1528	Bata (Batta, Demsa Bata)	0.05319	7,012	8,024	14,087	NAB60b	18-IBCA-a	gbwata		10.00	802	0....	8	5	6	2	1		p..	n
1529	Batanga (Puku, Banoo)	0.06577	8,670	9,921	17,419	NAB57k	99-AUAC-a	south ba-tanga		80.00	7,937	0....	10	8	7	4	3	Batanga	P..	.
1530	Bati (Bush Bati)	0.01063	1,401	1,604	2,815	NAB57k	99-ASAA-b	li-baati		85.00	1,363	0....	10	8	7	4	1		...	.
1531	Bayaka (Binga) Pygmy	0.02829	3,729	4,268	7,492	BYG12	99-AUID-e	m-binga		10.00	427	0....	8	5	6	1	1		...	.

Continued opposite

Table 8-2 continued

EVANGELIZATION								EVANGELISM			ADDITIONAL DESCRIPTIVE DATA
Ref 1	*D* 28	*aC* 29	*CG%* 30	*r* 31	*E* 32	*U* 33	*W* 34	*e* 35	*R* 36	*T* 37	*Locations, civil divisions, literacy, religions, church history, denominations, dioceses, church growth, missions, agencies, ministries, movements* 38
1414	1	5	0.00	0	18.00	82.00	A	0.00	0	1.09	In Udalan Province, also in Mali. Muslims 100%(Sunnis). D=RCC. M=WF,SIM.
1415	2	5	5.86	0	29.00	71.00	A	5.29	683	4	Comoe Province. Traditional religionists (animists) 95%. D=ECEBF,AoG. M=CMA.
1416	1	6	3.34	0	25.00	75.00	A	2.73	516	4	Houet Province. Second language: Jula. Animists 67%, Muslims 30%. D=ECEBF. M=CMA.
1417	0	6	2.52	1	24.10	75.90	A	0.08	442	2	Dagaari who have converted to Islam. Muslims 90%(Maliki Sunnis), animists 10%.
1418	0	7	3.75	0	30.00	70.00	A	7.66	468	4	Comoe Province. Language close to Natioro. Bilingual in Jula. Animists 70%, Muslims 23%.
1419	2	5	7.79	0	66.00	34.00	B	60.22	380	6	Kossi Province. Literates 2%. Animists 50%, Muslims 25%. D=RCC,ECEBF. M=WF,CSSR,CMA,FMB.
1420	0	6	5.21	0	28.00	72.00	A	4.08	644	4	Southwest. Some bilingualism in Jula. Animists 86%, Muslims 10%. M=CMA.
1421	2	6	4.80	1	40.00	60.00	A	10.22	423	5	Animists 50%, Muslims 43%. D=RCC(D-Koupela),AoG. M=SIL,FMB.
1422	0	9	0.00	4	36.00	64.00	A	0.00	0	1.11	Completely assimilated to Mossi culture. Farmers, traders. Syncretistic Islam. Muslims 90%(Maliki Sunnis), animists 9%.
1423	6	10	7.83	5	99.45	0.55	B	188.88	220	7	Muslims 50%. D=EBBF,RCC,C&S,COTLA,JWs,other AICs. M=ECWA,SIM,CPN,FMB.
1424	0	6	4.30	1	29.00	71.00	A	2.11	536	4	Boulgou and Gourma Provinces, Diabo Subdistrict. Animists 98%.
1425	0	5	0.70	1	28.20	71.80	A	0.20	253	3	Mainly in Niger, also Nigeria, some in Benin. Muslims 75%(Maliki Sunnis), animists 25%. M=EBM.
1426	0	8	5.63		29.00	71.00	A	10.58	532	5	Beninese, Togolese, Ivorians, Ashanti, Brazilians, Banda (Ligbi), Barani Fulani. Muslims 40%, Animists 40%.
Burundi											
1427	0	10	0.00	8	37.00	63.00	A	0.00	0	1.14	Traders, with roots in Kenya-Tanzania coast. Muslims 100%(Shafi Sunnis).
1428	1	10	3.30	8	99.77	0.23	C	407.52	84	10	Teachers, professionals, commerce; from Britain. D=Anglican Ch(EAB).
1429	1	10	4.02	8	99.87	0.13	C	489.02	89	10	Expatriates from France, many in government service. D=RCC.
1430	1	10	4.24	7	99.95	0.05	C	544.39	91	10	Expatriates, settlers from Greece; in commerce. D=Greek Orthodox Church(AD-Central Africa).
1431	0	8	3.95	6	43.60	56.40	A	0.95	312	3	Long-term laborers, now shop-keepers, commerce. Hindus 70%, Muslims 29%(Sunnis, Ismaili Shias, Bohras, Ithna-Asharis, Kharijites).
1432	2	8	6.28	4	99.60	0.40	C	245.28	205	8	Former ruling caste; pastoralists. Animists 30%. D=RCC,EAB.
1433	5	6	13.81	4	99.77	0.23	C	386.72	315	9	Animists 5%, Muslims 1%(Maliki Sunnis). D=RCC(5 Dioceses),EAB,SDA,EDB,AICs. Many in East African Revival. M=WF,SJ,SX,CR,FSCJ,SSS,FMB,RCMS,UBS.
1434	1	8	9.46	5	99.79	0.21	C	415.22	208	10	Zairian expatriates. Variety of employment, business, commerce. D=RCC.
1435	2	10	9.56	4	99.86	0.14	C	477.12	210	10	Refugees from Rwanda over last 30 years. Animists 14%. D=RCC,EAB.
1436	0	9	0.00	5	39.00	61.00	A	0.00	0	1.13	Traders from the Coast. Swahili is widely used as lingua franca. Muslims 100%(Shafi Sunnis).
1437	2	10	11.95	4	99.85	0.15	C	459.17	260	10	Animists 6%. Tall former royal ruling clan. 4,000 killed in 1972 massacres, 300,000 in 1994. D=RCC,EAB. Many Revivalists.
1438	8	9	6.48	4	56.00	44.00	B	16.35	371	5	Animists 92%. D=RCC,Methodist Ch,World Gospel Ch,Friends,Baptists,Pentecostals,Anglicans,SDA. M=FMB.
1439	1	10	5.36	8	99.92	0.08	C	500.34	119	10	Expatriates from Belgium, in government service. D=RCC.
1440	0	10	8.07		97.00	3.00	C	247.83	228	8	Other Zairian and Tanzanian peoples, Flemish-speaking Belgians, and vast numbers fleeing from or to Rwanda, Zaire, or Uganda over period 1962-1995.
Cambodia											
1441	0	6	4.35	0	23.00	77.00	A	0.84	637	3	Montagnards, on Laos border; also in Laos, France, USA. Many fluent in Lao language. Animists 99%.
1442	2	10	4.58	8	99.79	0.21	C	429.64	105	10	Expatriates from Britain, in business, education. D=Anglican Ch(D-Singapore),SDA.
1443	2	10	1.10	6	49.09	50.91	A	0.16	123	3	Immigrants, migrants, refugees from Myanmar. Theravada Buddhists 98%, Muslims 2%. D=RCC,KEC. M=BBC(Burma).
1444	0	6	3.00	1	28.00	72.00	A	1.02	391	4	Northeast border area, Rattanakiri. System of exogamous clans. Many speak Lao; some know Khmer. Close to Bahnar, Lamam. Animists 99%.
1445	3	4	5.12	5	48.63	51.37	A	1.11	368	4	Theravada Buddhists 94%(1970: 2,826 monasteries, 68,145 monks), animists 3%, nonreligious 2%, Baha'is 0.1%. D=RCC,KEC,SDA. M=MEP,OSB,YWAM.
1446	2	6	5.95	4	45.00	55.00	A	19.71	423	5	Pnong. Montagnards, on northeastern border with Laos. Mainly in Viet Nam. Nonliterate. Animists 88%. D=RCC,KEC. M=CMA.
1447	0	6	4.57	0	20.00	80.00	A	0.73	763	3	Montagnards. Thai-Kampuchea border. Some 500 in Thailand. Animists 95%.
1448	2	6	3.14	4	44.00	56.00	A	16.06	227	5	Known as Khmer Islam; along Mekong river. Almost all in Viet Nam. 60% literate. Muslims 50%(Shafi Sunnis), Hindus 40%. D=RCC,KEC. M=MEP,CMA.
1449	0	6	3.68	0	21.00	79.00	A	1.53	611	4	In southwest, Kompong Thom. Montagnards. Animists 98%.
1450	3	6	2.03	8	99.50	0.50	B	202.57	70	8	Mixed race French/Indochinese. Buddhists/New-Religionists 35%, nonreligious 15%. D=RCC(3 Dioceses),KEC,SDA.
1451	2	10	1.25	8	99.77	0.23	C	413.14	42	10	Expatriates from France, in education, business. D=RCC(3 Dioceses),KEC. M=MEP,OSB.
1452	3	8	3.87	8	64.00	36.00	B	2.33	194	4	Traders. Chinese folk-religionists/Buddhists 98%. D=RCC,EC,SDA. M=MEP,OSB,CMA,OMF.
1453	2	8	3.69	0	42.00	58.00	A	1.53	283	4	Chinese folk-religionists/Buddhists 99%. D=RCC,EC. M=MEP,OSB,CMA,OMF.
1454	2	8	4.59	7	57.20	42.80	B	2.50	251	4	Chinese folk-religionists/Buddhists 98%. D=RCC,EC. M=MEP,OSB,CMA,OMF.
1455	3	8	4.02	6	58.20	41.80	B	2.54	220	4	Traders. Chinese folk-religionists/Buddhists 98%. D=RCC,EC,SDA. M=MEP,OSB,CMA,OMF.
1456	0	8	1.82	7	59.00	41.00	B	2.15	115	4	Long-time residents, transients, refugees, migrants. Traders. Buddhists/Chinese folk-religionists 93%.
1457	4	8	2.69	6	61.40	38.60	B	3.13	149	4	Mahayana Buddhists/Chinese folk-religionists 94%. D=RCC,EC,SDA,KEC. M=MEP,OSB,CMA,OMF.
1458	2	6	5.91	4	49.00	51.00	A	17.88	359	5	Montagnards, in east, with great majority in Viet Nam. Rattanakiri Province. Languages known: Vietnamese, Lao. Animists 90%. D=RCC,KEC. M=CMA.
1459	0	6	3.35	1	25.00	75.00	A	0.91	477	3	Rattanakiri Province, north of related language Tampuan. Animists 99%.
1460	0	5	3.83	0	19.00	81.00	A	0.69	697	3	Montagnards. Related to Brao. Animists 99%.
1461	0	6	3.70	0	23.00	77.00	A	0.84	560	3	In northeast. Montagnards. Language almost identical with Brao(Brau). Many use Lao. Animists 99%.
1462	1	6	3.61	0	31.00	69.00	A	3.39	407	4	Old Khmer. Montagnards, in northeast. Also in Thailand, Laos. Nonliterate. Animists 97%. D=KEC. M=CMA.
1463	0	6	2.87	1	25.00	75.00	A	0.91	424	3	Near northeast corner on Viet Nam border. Related to Tampuan. Animists 99%.
1464	1	6	3.50	5	51.40	48.60	B	2.62	268	4	Theravada Buddhists 57%, tribal religionists 33%, nonreligious 8%. D=RCC. M=CSI.
1465	0	7	3.14	5	41.20	58.80	A	0.30	255	3	Migrant workers from Malaysia. Muslims 100%(Shafi Sunnis).
1466	2	6	6.32	4	79.00	21.00	B	118.22	237	7	Montagnards, mainly in Viet Nam. Animists 59%. D=RCC,KEC. M=CMA.
1467	0	6	1.10	0	20.00	80.00	A	0.73	288	3	Montagnards, just north of Siemreap. Related to Saoch, Suoy, Pear. Animists 99%.
1468	0	6	2.22	0	20.00	80.00	A	0.73	441	3	Southwest, near Kompong Som on coast. Montagnards. Related to Samre, Suoy, Pear. Animists 99%.
1469	0	6	3.62	0	20.00	80.00	A	0.73	633	3	In west; north, east, and west of Phum Tasanh. Related to Chong. Animists 99%.
1470	0	6	3.80	4	41.00	59.00	A	14.96	321	5	Montagnards, in east. Mainly in Viet Nam. Animists 90%.
1471	0	6	1.62	0	20.50	79.50	A	1.12	350	4	Central, northwest of Phnom Penh. Montagnards. Animists 98%.
1472	2	10	2.34	6	68.00	32.00	B	22.33	135	5	Residents from South India. Traders. Hindus 85%, Muslims 6%. D=RCC,KEC. M=MEP.
1473	0	6	5.38	6	47.60	52.40	A	1.04	343	4	From Thailand. Theravada Buddhists 97%, Muslims 1%(Shafi Sunnis).
1474	2	7	-0.26	6	67.00	33.00	B	19.56	24	5	Most in Viet Nam. Mahayana Buddhists 61%, nonreligious 14%, Cao-Daists 10%, atheists 5%, Muslims, Baha'is. D=RCC(3 Dioceses),AoG. M=CMA,CSI,WEC.
1475	2	5	3.39	1	20.01	79.99	A	0.00	534	1.08	Khmer Islam. Along Mekong river. Also in Malaysia, Thailand, USA, France, et alia. Partly urbanized. Literate in Khmer. Muslims 88%(Shafi Sunnis), Hindus 10%.
1476	0	6	4.03	0	22.00	78.00	A	2.40	626	4	Southwestern, Kompong Thom. Montagnards. Animists 97%.
1477	0	7	3.15		18.00	82.00	A	0.65	480	3	USA Whites(AC,SDA), Lun, Thmon, Bahnar, Southern Mnong. Animists 70%, Theraveda Buddhists 20%.
Cameroon											
1478	1	8	4.42	0	83.00	17.00	B	151.47	205	7	Littoral Province, north of Douala. Close to Barombi. Animists 50%. D=RCC.
1479	5	6	7.41	4	49.00	51.00	A	1.78	504	4	From Senegal to Sudan. Muslims 96%(Maliki Sunnis), animists 3%. D=RCC(PA-Maroua),UEENC,FFLC,UEBC,EELC. M=OMI,NLM,LBWM,UBS,CSI.
1480	1	8	5.00	0	87.00	13.00	B	158.77	196	7	Village in Nwa Subdivision, North West Province. Animists 50%. D=RCC.
1481	0	6	4.18	0	28.00	72.00	A	4.08	545	4	Makari Subdivision, Far North Province. Also in Nigeria. Muslims 90%, some animists.
1482	1	8	8.27	0	99.85	0.15	C	387.81	208	9	Wum Subdivision, North West Province. Isolated. Animists 15%. D=Presbyterian Ch of Cameroon. Many itinerant catechists. M=North American Baptists,RBMU.
1483	3	8	8.05	0	99.85	0.15	C	400.22	197	10	Around Wum, North West Province. Close to Fungom. Animists 15%. D=RCC,Presbyterian Ch,AICs.
1484	2	8	3.85	0	86.00	14.00	B	156.95	167	7	Near Nigerian border, Menchum Division, North West Province. Animists 50%. D=RCC, Protestants.
1485	1	7	5.14	0	84.00	16.00	B	153.30	213	7	Western part of Nkambe Subdivision, Donga-Mantung Division, North West Province. Bilingual in Eastern Beboid languages. Animists 50%. D=RCC.
1486	1	8	7.78	0	99.80	0.20	C	347.48	207	9	20 villages in Manyu Division, South West Province. Animists 20%. D=RCC.
1487	0	7	4.42	0	80.00	20.00	B	146.00	199	7	10 villages in Batibo Subdivision, North West Province. Animists 50%.
1488	2	8	7.26	1	98.00	2.00	C	214.62	237	8	Central and southern parts of Akwaya Subdivision, South West Province. Animists 40%. D=PCC,AICs. M=SIL.
1489	2	7	5.76	0	99.85	0.15	C	387.81	153	9	South West Province. Nomads, isolated forest region. Also in Nigeria. Agriculturalists. Animists 15%. D=Roman Catholic Ch,PCC. M=RBMU,GR.
1490	1	7	4.42	0	82.00	18.00	B	149.65	188	7	Northwest of Batibo Subdivision, North West Province. Animists 50%. D=RCC.
1491	2	7	6.86	1	99.70	0.30	C	270.83	209	8	Southwest of Ndop, Ndop Plain, Mezam West Province. Related to Mungaka. Animists 30%. D=RCC,EEC. M=PEMS.
1492	1	7	7.10	1	83.00	17.00	B	136.32	275	7	East of Ndop, Ndop Plain, North West Province. Animists 55%. D=RCC.
1493	1	7	7.17	0	87.00	13.00	B	158.77	264	7	Large Bantu people. Closely related to Vengo, Kenswei-Nsei, and Bamunka. Animists 50%. D=RCC.
1494	1	7	7.13	1	99.70	0.30	C	281.05	208	8	South of Ndop, Ndop Plain, North West Province. Animists 30%. D=RCC.
1495	2	7	8.08	0	99.85	0.15	C	394.01	213	9	North of Kumba, South West Province, and Littoral Province. Bilingual in Duala. Animists 15%. D=RCC,PCC. M=SIL.
1496	1	7	6.31	1	98.00	2.00	C	214.62	211	8	Northwest of Fundong, Wum Subdivision, Menchum Division, North West Province. Animists 40%. D=RCC.
1497	2	6	6.27	0	38.00	62.00	A	13.87	531	5	Scattered in southeast of East Province. Forest nomads. Animists 90%. D=Presbyterian Ch,RCC. M=SIL.
1498	2	7	8.94	0	97.00	3.00	C	212.43	303	8	Scattered communities in Littoral Province, south of Douala. Animists 40%. D=RCC(strong),UEBC.
1499	1	8	6.23	0	99.85	0.15	C	387.81	176	9	Ndian Division, South West Province. Bilingual in Bakweri. Animists 15%. D=RCC.
1500	4	6	7.39	0	99.86	0.14	C	400.20	198	10	Bangem and Tombel Subdivisions, South West Province. Baha'is 10%. D=RCC(D-Buea),PCC,UEBC,AICs. M=SIL,MHM.
1501	1	7	7.58	0	99.70	0.30	C	265.72	238	8	Ngoko river, East Province; mainly in Congo, also Gabon. Animists 30%. D=RCC.
1502	0	6	4.18	0	30.00	70.00	A	4.38	509	4	Diamare Division, Far North Province. Muslims 95% (Maliki Sunnis). M=several agencies.
1503	1	6	8.44	1	84.00	16.00	B	122.64	315	7	Bali District, Mezam Division; North West, and West Provinces. Widespread lingua franca. Animists 60%. D=PCC. M=Basel Mission.
1504	0	7	4.73	0	77.00	23.00	B	126.47	218	7	Akwaya Subdivision. Close to Osatu language. Mountainous. Second language Pidgin; literates use English. Animists 55%.
1505	1	7	6.63	1	99.70	0.30	C	283.60	194	8	South of Ndop, Mezam Division, North West Province. Animists 30%. D=RCC.
1506	1	7	7.71	1	99.70	0.30	C	281.05	222	8	Southeast of Ndop, Mezam Division, North West Province. Animists 30%. D=RCC.
1507	1	6	7.08	1	93.00	7.00	C	203.67	245	8	2 villages each of Bamerda, North West Province. Close to Bafut. Animists 40%. D=RCC.
1508	2	7	6.30	1	99.80	0.20	C	356.24	169	9	Around Bamenyam, northwest Galim Subdivision, West Province. Animists 20%. D=RCC,EEC. M=PEMS.
1509	2	7	10.22	0	99.82	0.18	C	356.16	263	9	Upper Nkam Division, also Mifi Division, West Province. Related to Ghomala, Medumba. Animists 5%. D=RCC,EEC. M=PEMS.
1510	1	6	6.24	1	99.94	0.06	C	466.61	150	10	Southern Galim Subdivision, Bamboutos Division, West Province. Animists 5%. D=RCC.
1511	2	7	7.56	0	99.94	0.06	C	446.03	185	10	Upper Nkam, Nde, and Mifi Divisions, West Province. Transitional Bamileke. Animists 5%. D=RCC,EPC.
1512	1	7	7.22	0	99.75	0.25	C	301.12	210	9	Eastern Nkondjok Subdivision, Nkam Division, Littoral Province, also West Province. Animists 25%. D=RCC.
1513	2	6	10.00	1	99.84	0.16	C	392.44	240	9	West of Bafoussam, Mifi Division, West Province. Animists 5%. D=RCC(D-Nkongsamba),EEC. M=PEMS.
1514	2	7	11.10	1	99.82	0.18	C	374.12	270	9	In West Province. Related to Fefe, Medumba. Animists 5%. D=RCC,EEC. M=PEMS,UBS.
1515	2	6	9.86	1	99.84	0.16	C	413.91	225	10	Batcham Subdivision, Bamboutos Division, West Province. Animists 5%. D=RCC,EEC. M=PEMS,SIL.
1516	1	6	8.97	0	99.90	0.10	C	407.34	225	10	Most of Fontem Subdivision, South West Province. Close to Yemba. Animists 10%. D=RCC.
1517	2	7	10.48	1	99.82	0.18	C	404.05	237	10	Most of Nde Division, West Province. Animists 5%. D=Eglise Evangelique du Cameroon,RCC(5 Dioceses). M=UBS,PEMS.
1518	2	7	8.37	1	99.94	0.06	C	446.03	202	10	Southeast of Mbouda, Bamboutos Division, West Province. A Bamileke group. Animists 5%. D=RCC,EEC. M=PEMS.
1519	2	7	8.77	1	99.90	0.10	C	436.90	206	10	Northwest of Mbouda, Bamboutos Division, West Province. Animists 10%. D=RCC,EEC. M=PEMS.
1520	3	7	6.69	1	99.80	0.20	C	359.16	176	9	Menoua Division, West Province. Animists 5%. D=RCC(D-Nkongsamba),EEC,PCC. M=PEMS,SIL.
1521	2	6	7.81	0	99.80	0.20	C	332.88	221	9	Isolated forest area on border northeast of Akwaya, South West Province. Also in Nigeria. Animists 20%. D=RCC,PCC. M=GR.
1522	2	7	5.57	0	86.00	14.00	B	156.95	236	7	Mostly in Cameroon, some in Congo. Moloundou Subdivision, East Province. Animists 50%. D=RCC,EPC.
1523	1	7	3.92	0	82.00	18.00	B	149.65	191	7	Village of Bongo, south of Yangben, Mbam Division, Centre Province. Animists 50%. D=RCC.
1524	1	7	7.11	1	99.70	0.30	C	283.60	206	8	East of Ndop, Mezam Division, North West Province. Close to Bambalang. Animists 30%. D=RCC.
1525	1	7	5.28	0	99.80	0.20	C	327.04	173	9	South West Province, north of Mount Cameroon. Close to Abo. Animists 20%. D=RCC.
1526	4	7	7.46	1	99.70	0.30	C	318.36	202	9	Spread all over Nyong and Kelle Division, Centre Province, also Littoral Province. Animists 15%. D=UEBC,EEC,EPC,RCC(M-Douala).
1527	2	7	9.32	0	99.70	0.30	C	273.38	285	8	Central part of Nguti Subdivision, South West Province. Animists 30%. D=RCC,PCC.
1528	2	7	4.48	0	42.00	58.00	A	15.33	383	5	On Nigerian border. Muslims 50%, animists 40%. D=EELC,EFLC. M=LBWM. Fulani literature used.
1529	3	7	6.90	0	99.80	0.20	C	347.48	200	9	Along coast around Kribi; Ocean Division, South Province. Animists 20%. D=RCC,EPC,AICs.
1530	1	7	5.04	0	99.85	0.15	C	369.19	157	9	Right bank of Sanaga river, Mbam Division, Centre Province, also Littoral Province. Animists 15%. D=RCC.
1531	1	7	3.83	0	37.00	63.00	A	13.50	365	5	East Province. Small forest groups. Also in Gabon, CAR. Animists 90%. D=RCC.

Continued overleaf

Table 8-2 continued

PEOPLE		POPULATION				IDENTITY CODE		LANGUAGE		CHURCH		MINISTRY						SCRIPTURE		
Ref 1	Ethnic name 2	P% 3	In 1995 4	In 2000 5	In 2025 6	Race 7	Language 8	Autoglossonym 9	S 10	AC 11	Members 12	Jayuh 13-17	d 18	wa 19	xc 20	mc 21	mi 22	Biblioglossonym 23	Pub 24-26	ss 27
1532	Baza (Fali, Mizeran)	0.12498	16,475	18,853	33,100	NAB60b	18-GAAD	bana cluster		10.00	1,885	0....	8	5	6	2	2	Bana	...	b
1533	Bebe	0.01000	1,318	1,508	2,648	NAB56b	99-AFBA-a	bebe		50.00	754	0....	10	7	7	4	1		...	.
1534	Bebele	0.50000	65,910	75,425	132,422	NAB57c	99-AUCA-b	be-bele		60.00	45,255	0....	10	7	7	4	1		...	p
1535	Bebil (Bobilis)	0.04902	6,462	7,395	12,983	NAB57c	99-AUCA-a	gbilgbil		50.00	3,697	0....	10	7	7	3	1		...	b
1536	Becheve (Utser, Oliti)	0.03000	3,955	4,525	7,945	NAB56b	99-ABDA-b	i-ceve		85.00	3,847	0....	10	8	11	4	1	Iceve-maci	...	b
1537	Beezen	0.00386	509	582	1,022	NAB56b	98-HBDA-l	beezen		45.00	262	0....	9	7	6	3	1		pn.	.
1538	Bekpak (Kpa, Bafia)	0.49024	64,624	73,953	129,837	NAB57a	99-AMBA-e	ri-kpa'		67.00	49,548	0.s..	10	7	7	4	1		pn.	.
1539	Belip	0.06577	8,670	9,921	17,419	NAB57k	99-ANBC-a	nu-libie		50.00	4,961	0....	10	7	6	4	1		...	.
1540	Benyi (Mmala)	0.05481	7,225	8,268	14,516	NAB57k	99-ANBC-bd	m-maala		50.00	4,134	0....	10	7	7	4	1		...	.
1541	Bete	0.50000	65,910	75,425	132,422	NAB56b	95-ABAU	west bete cluster		80.00	60,340	0....	10	8	10	4	2	Bete*	PN.	.
1542	Betsinga (Sanaga, Oki, Baki)	0.28499	37,568	42,991	75,478	NAB56b	99-ANDA	tuki cluster		80.00	34,393	0....	10	7	10	4	2		...	.
1543	Biba-Befang	0.04000	5,273	6,034	10,594	NAB56b	99-AGAB-a	ge		85.00	5,129	0....	10	8	10	4	1		...	.
1544	Bikele-Bikay	0.10839	14,288	16,351	28,706	NAB57c	99-AUDC-b	be-kol		60.00	9,810	0....	10	7	7	4	1	Makaa	...	.
1545	Bishuo	0.01500	1,977	2,263	3,973	NAB56b	98-HBGA-a	bishuo		50.00	1,131	0....	10	7	7	4	1		...	.
1546	Bitare	0.04056	5,347	6,118	10,742	NAB56b	99-ABBA-a	njwande		80.00	4,895	0....	10	8	8	4	3		...	.
1547	Bobe (Ewota)	0.00750	989	1,131	1,986	NAB57k	99-AUAA-b	bo-bea		85.00	962	0....	10	8	10	4	1		p..	.
1548	Bodomo	0.06992	9,217	10,547	18,518	NAB66c	93-AAAA-kr	mbodomo		55.00	5,801	0.s..	10	7	8	0	0	Mbodomo	pnb	.
1549	Bokwa-Kendem	0.01067	1,407	1,610	2,826	NAB57a	99-AEBA-a	kendem-bokwa		50.00	805	0....	10	7	6	4	2		...	.
1550	Bokyi (Boki, Nki, Nfua)	0.03557	4,689	5,366	9,421	NAB56b	98-IEAG-a	u-ki		80.00	4,293	0.s..	10	8	10	4	2	Bokyi	PNB	b
1551	Bomboko (Bamboko)	0.03125	4,119	4,714	8,276	NAB57k	99-AUAA-c	bo-mboko		85.00	4,007	0....	10	8	7	4	2		p..	.
1552	Bomwali (Lino)	0.04085	5,385	6,162	10,819	NAB57c	99-AUDI-a	bo-mwali		65.00	4,005	0....	10	7	7	4	1		...	.
1553	Bororo Fulani (Mbororo)	0.80000	105,456	120,680	211,875	NAB56c	90-BAAA-o	fula-bororo		0.05	60	1cs..	4	2	5	0	0	Fulfide, Kano-katsina	pnb	b
1554	British	0.03000	3,955	4,525	7,945	CEW19i	52-ABAC-b	standard-english	20	79.00	3,575	3Bsuh	10	9	13	5	3		PNB	b
1555	Bu	0.01000	1,318	1,508	2,648	NAB56b	99-AFAA-b	bu		50.00	754	0....	10	7	6	4	1		...	.
1556	Buduma	0.00169	223	255	448	NAB60b	18-BBBA-a	yidena		0.06	0	0....	4	3	5	0	1	Buduma	...	b
1557	Bulu Fang	4.00000	527,282	603,399	1,059,376	NAB57c	99-AUCC-n	bulu	9	74.50	449,532	1....	10	8	14	4	1	Bulu	PNB	b
1558	Bulu-Ewondo Creole	0.20000	26,364	30,170	52,969	NAB57c	99-AUCC-n	bulu	4	80.00	24,136	1....	10	7	13	4	3	Bulu	PNB	b
1559	Bum	0.10000	13,182	15,085	26,484	NAB57a	99-AGDB-a	bum		80.00	12,068	0....	10	7	7	4	1		pn.	.
1560	Busam	0.01000	1,318	1,508	2,648	NAB57a	99-AGBA-c	bu-sam		50.00	754	0....	10	7	6	4	1		...	.
1561	Buwal	0.05308	6,997	8,007	14,058	NAB60b	18-FAAA-a	ma-buwal		4.00	320	0....	6	5	4	1	1		...	.
1562	Caka	0.05155	6,795	7,776	13,653	NAB56b	99-ABJA-d	caka		40.00	3,111	0....	9	7	7	3	1		...	p
1563	Cameroonian Creole	5.85841	772,259	883,739	1,551,565	NAN58	52-ABAH-f	cameroonian-creole	52	79.00	698,154	4.s.h	10	7	12	5	1	Pidgin: Cameroon*	Pn.	b
1564	Chamba Daka (Samba, Deng)	0.10961	14,449	16,535	29,030	NAB66c	98-JDAA-a	samba-daka		50.00	8,267	0.s..	10	7	7	4	1	Chamba*	P..	.
1565	Chamba Leko (Suntai)	0.20555	27,096	31,007	54,439	NAB66c	92-BDAB-a	proper samba-leko		50.00	15,504	0....	10	7	7	4	2	Samba Leko	...	.
1566	Cung	0.01000	1,318	1,508	2,648	NAB56b	99-AFBA-f	cung		55.00	830	0....	10	7	6	4	1		...	.
1567	Cuvok	0.05308	6,997	8,007	14,058	NAB60b	18-ECCA-a	cuvok		60.00	4,804	0....	10	7	6	4	1		...	.
1568	Daba (Daba Kola)	0.60215	79,376	90,834	159,476	NAB60b	18-FBAC-a	daba		5.00	4,542	0....	7	5	6	1	3	Daba	PN.	.
1569	Dama	0.00600	791	905	1,589	NAB66z	98-HBEA-d	nama		30.00	272	0....	9	5	6	2	0		...	.
1570	Dek	0.02000	2,636	3,017	5,297	NAB66z	99-ANAA-b	ne-dek		30.00	905	0....	9	5	6	2	1		...	.
1571	Dghwede (Hude, Johode, Waa)	0.02000	2,636	3,017	5,297	NAB60b	18-CBBA-a	zeghvana		10.00	302	0....	8	5	7	1	1	Dghwede	PN.	.
1572	Dii (Yag Dii, Duli, Dusru)	0.58065	76,542	87,591	153,782	NAB66c	92-BBAA-e	dii		5.00	4,380	0.s..	7	5	6	1	2	Duru*	P..	.
1573	Dimbong (Bumbong)	0.00114	150	172	302	NAB57k	99-AMBA-d	di-mbong		50.00	86	0.s..	10	6	7	4	1		pn.	.
1574	Djanti (Tibea)	0.01149	1,515	1,733	3,043	NAB57k	99-AMBA-h	ti-bea		45.00	780	0.s..	9	6	7	3	1		pn.	.
1575	Dowayayo (Namshi, Sewe)	0.18842	24,838	28,423	49,902	NAB66z	92-BCBA-a	doyayo		26.00	7,390	0....	9	5	7	2	2	Dooyaayo*	PN.	.
1576	Duala (Uli, Douala)	1.29032	170,091	194,644	341,734	NAB57k	99-AUAB-a	proper duala	3	75.00	145,983	0....	10	8	13	4	2	Duala	PNB	b
1577	Dugwor	0.02000	2,636	3,017	5,297	NAB60b	18-EADC-a	dugwor		10.00	302	0....	8	5	7	1	1		...	.
1578	Duli (Dui)	0.00500	659	754	1,324	NAB66c	92-BBBA-a	duli		5.00	38	0....	7	5	6	1	1		...	.
1579	Dumbule	0.01000	1,318	1,508	2,648	NAB57k	99-ANBA-a	du-mbule		50.00	754	0....	10	7	7	4	1		...	.
1580	Duupa (Nduupa, Dupa)	0.04085	5,385	6,162	10,819	NAB66c	92-BBAA-a	n-duupa		10.00	616	0.s..	8	5	6	1	1	Duupa	P..	.
1581	Dzem (Ndjem, Bajwee)	0.51387	67,739	77,517	136,095	NAB57c	99-AUDF	koozime cluster		65.00	50,386	0....	10	7	7	4	2	Koozime	P..	.
1582	Efik (Calabari)	0.10961	14,449	16,535	29,030	NAB56b	98-ICBA-c	efik		80.00	13,228	1as..	10	7	13	4	1	Efik	PNB	b
1583	Ejagham (Ekoi, Keaka)	0.38365	50,573	57,873	101,607	NAB56b	99-ACCB-b	proper e-jagham		80.00	46,299	0....	10	8	10	4	3	Ejagham	PN.	.
1584	Eman	0.00676	891	1,020	1,790	NAB56b	99-ABFA-a	e-man		40.00	408	0....	9	7	7	3	1		...	p
1585	Eton	0.80000	105,456	120,680	211,875	NAB57c	99-AUCB-a	proper eton		70.00	84,476	0....	10	7	8	4	1		...	.
1586	Evand	0.10309	13,589	15,551	27,303	NAB56b	99-ABCA-a	e-vand		50.00	7,776	0....	10	7	7	3	1		...	p
1587	Ewondo (Beti, Yaunde)	8.10000	1,067,747	1,221,882	2,145,237	NAB57c	99-AUCC-a	ewondo	8	80.50	983,615	1....	10	7	11	4	3	Ewondo	PNb	b
1588	Fang (Ntum, Pahouin, Okak)	0.95000	125,230	143,307	251,602	NAB57c	99-AUCC-v	ntumu		60.00	85,984	1....	10	8	13	5	3		pnb	b
1589	French	0.20000	26,364	30,170	52,969	CEW21b	51-AABI-d	general français	50	87.00	26,248	1B.uh	10	9	14	5	1	French	PNB	b
1590	Furu (Busuu)	0.00008	11	12	21	NAB56b	98-HBDA-c	diyi		45.00	5	0....	9	6	6	3	1	Jukun Takum	PN.	.
1591	Fut (Bafut, Bufe, Fu)	0.48068	63,364	72,510	127,305	NAB57a	99-AGEA-b	bufe		80.00	58,008	0....	10	7	10	4	2		...	.
1592	Gaduwa	0.02000	2,636	3,017	5,297	NAB60b	18-EADE-a	gaduwa		5.00	151	0....	7	5	6	1	1		...	.
1593	Galke	0.00020	26	30	53	NAB66z	92-CDAD-b	ndai		30.00	9	0....	9	5	6	2	0		...	.
1594	Gavar (Gouwar, Kortchi)	0.04103	5,409	6,189	10,867	NAB60b	18-FABA-a	gavar		4.00	248	0....	6	4	4	1	2		...	.
1595	Gbaya	1.44580	190,586	218,098	382,911	NAB66c	93-AAAA-a	vehicular gbaya	5	76.00	165,755	0.s..	10	5	10	2	2	Gbaya: Gbea*	PNB	b
1596	Gemzek	0.07386	9,736	11,142	19,561	NAB60b	18-EADD-a	gemzek		4.00	446	0....	6	4	6	1	2		...	n
1597	Gidar (Guidar, Kada, Lam)	0.81720	107,724	123,274	216,431	NAB60b	17-GAAA-a	gidar	1	25.00	30,819	0.s..	9	5	5	3	2	Guidar*	PN.	.
1598	Gimme (Kompara)	0.03288	4,334	4,960	8,708	NAB66c	92-BCBB-a	gimme		5.00	248	0....	7	5	6	1	2	Gimme	...	.
1599	Gimnime (Kadam, Laame)	0.03290	4,337	4,963	8,713	NAB66c	92-BCBB-b	gimnime		6.00	298	0....	7	5	6	1	2		...	.
1600	Glavda (Guelebda, Vale)	0.03069	4,046	4,630	8,128	NAB60b	18-CABB-a	gelvaxda-xa		10.00	463	0....	8	5	4	1	1	Glavda	P..	.
1601	Greek	0.02000	2,636	3,017	5,297	CEW20	56-AAAA-c	dhimotiki		95.00	2,866	2B.uh	10	9	11	5	1	Greek: Modern	PNB	b
1602	Gude (Cheke, Mubi, Shede)	0.26491	34,921	39,962	70,160	NAB60b	18-IBAA-d	gude		2.00	799	0....	6	4	4	1	3	Gude	P..	b
1603	Gueve (Gey, Gewe)	0.02000	2,636	3,017	5,297	NAB56c	90-BAAA-q	fula-adamawa		1.00	30	1cs..	6	4	6	0	0	Fulfulde, Adamawa	PNB	b
1604	Gulfe (Gulfei, Malgwe)	0.40000	52,728	60,340	105,938	NAB60b	18-BBAB-c	malgbe		10.00	6,034	0....	8	5	5	1	0		...	.
1605	Hausa	1.40000	184,549	211,190	370,782	NAB60a	19-HAAB-a	hausa	2	0.10	211	4Asu.	5	4	2	0	1	Hausa	PNB	b
1606	Hide (Xedi, Xadi)	0.09865	13,004	14,881	26,127	NAB60b	18-CBBA-b	turu-xedi		10.00	1,488	0....	8	5	6	1	1	Hedi	pn.	.
1607	Hijuk	0.00328	432	495	869	NAB57k	99-AMAA-a	hijuk		50.00	247	0....	10	7	6	4	1		...	.
1608	Hina (Mina)	0.07386	9,736	11,142	19,561	NAB60b	18-FBAB-a	besleri		10.00	1,114	0....	8	5	2	1	0		...	n
1609	Hya	0.01000	1,318	1,508	2,648	NAB60b	18-GAAC	hya-za cluster		10.00	151	0....	8	5	6	1	0		...	n
1610	Ibibio	0.20000	26,364	30,170	52,969	NAB56b	98-ICBA-b	ibibio		85.00	25,644	3cs..	10	8	14	4	1	Ibibio	pnb	b
1611	Igbo (Ibo)	0.40000	52,728	60,340	105,938	NAB59h	98-FAAA-a	standard igbo		90.00	54,306	2..u.	10	7	14	5	1	Igbo	PNB	b
1612	Isu	0.08079	10,650	12,187	21,397	NAB57a	99-AGDA-a	e-su		40.00	4,875	0....	9	5	6	3	0	Isu	P..	.
1613	Jimi (Djimi, Malabu)	0.03836	5,057	5,787	10,159	NAB60b	18-IBAA-e	jimjimen		10.10	584	0....	8	5	5	1	1		p..	n
1614	Jina	0.03000	3,955	4,525	7,945	NAB60b	18-BAAB-a	jina		10.00	453	0....	8	5	6	1	0		...	.
1615	Jukun	0.01639	2,161	2,472	4,341	NAB56b	98-HBDA-c	diyi		60.00	1,483	0....	10	6	6	4	3	Jukun Takum	PN.	.
1616	Kaalong	0.10000	13,182	15,085	26,484	NAB57a	99-AMBA-d	di-mbong		70.00	10,559	0.s..	10	6	7	4	1		pn.	.
1617	Kaka	0.51429	67,794	77,580	136,207	NAB57c	99-AUDA-a	east kako		30.00	23,274	0....	9	5	7	2	1	Kako*	P..	.
1618	Kamkam	0.01200	1,582	1,810	3,178	NAB56b	98-JBBA-b	kamkam		79.00	1,430	0....	10	7	6	4	2		...	.
1619	Kamwe (Higi, Vacamwe)	0.04000	5,273	6,034	10,594	NAB60b	18-GAAA	kamwe cluster		10.00	603	0....	8	5	6	2	1	Kamwe	PN.	b
1620	Kapsiki	0.53763	70,871	81,101	142,388	NAB60b	18-GAAB-a	psikye		25.00	20,275	0.s..	9	4	6	1	2	Kapsiki*	PN.	.
1621	Karang (Lakka)	0.13890	18,310	20,953	36,787	NAB60b	92-CDAE-c	karang		10.00	2,095	0.s..	8	5	6	1	2	Karre*	PN.	.
1622	Karre (Kari, Tale)	0.03000	3,955	4,525	7,945	NAB66c	92-CDAE-c	karang		30.00	1,358	0.s..	9	4	6	2	0	Karre*	PN.	.
1623	Kera	0.04791	6,316	7,227	12,689	NAB66z	17-EBAA-a	kera		30.00	2,168	0....	9	4	6	2	1	Kera	P..	.
1624	Kidzom (Kejom, Tungo)	0.04000	5,273	6,034	10,594	NAB57a	99-AGDB-d	ba-banki		80.00	4,827	0....	10	8	6	4	1		pn.	.
1625	Kofa	0.02000	2,636	3,017	5,297	NAB56b	17-ABBA-a	kofa		80.00	2,414	0....	10	7	6	4	0		...	.
1626	Koh (Kuo)	0.02000	2,636	3,017	5,297	NAB66c	92-CDAE-f	kuo		20.00	603	0.s..	9	4	6	1	2	Kuo	Pn.	.
1627	Kolbila (Kolena)	0.02532	3,338	3,820	6,706	NAB66c	92-BDAA-a	kolbila		40.00	1,528	0....	9	4	6	2	2	Kolbila	P..	.
1628	Koma	0.03000	3,955	4,525	7,945	NAB66c	92-BCBB-g	liu		40.00	1,810	0....	9	5	6	2	2		...	.
1629	Kombe (Combe, Ngumbi)	0.01500	1,977	2,263	3,973	NAB57k	99-AUAD-b	kombe		85.00	1,923	0....	10	7	10	4	3	Combe*	PN.	.
1630	Konabem (Kunabeeb)	0.04807	6,337	7,251	12,731	NAB57c	99-AUDG-k	kunabeeb		70.00	5,076	0....	10	7	6	4	2		...	.
1631	Konja (Kwanja)	0.16341	21,541	24,650	43,278	NAB56b	98-JBAA	konja cluster		35.00	8,628	0....	9	5	6	3	2	Kwanja	...	.
1632	Korop (Ododop, Durop)	0.08222	10,838	12,403	21,775	NAB56b	98-IDAA-a	ko-rop		80.00	9,922	0....	10	8	6	4	1		...	b
1633	Kosin	0.02000	2,636	3,017	5,297	NAB56b	99-AFAA-d	kosin		80.00	2,414	0....	10	7	6	4	1		...	.
1634	Kotoko (Moria, Bara)	0.22000	29,001	33,187	58,266	NAB60b	18-BBAA-a	lagwan		10.00	3,319	0....	8	3	0	0	1		...	n
1635	Kotopo (Kutin, Peer, Pere)	0.14000	18,455	21,119	37,078	NAB66c	92-BCAA	peere cluster		40.00	8,448	0....	9	5	5	2	2	Peere	PN.	.
1636	Kpe (Baakpe, Bakwiri)	0.35295	46,526	53,242	93,477	NAB57k	99-AUAA-a	mo-kpwe		85.00	45,256	0....	10	8	10	4	1		p..	b
1637	Kumaju (Dumbo)	0.02000	2,636	3,017	5,297	NAB56b	99-AFBA-b	ke-mezung		80.00	2,414	0....	10	7	10	4	1		...	.
1638	Kundu (Bakundu)	0.71248	93,920	107,477	188,696	NAB57k	99-AJAB	east oroko cluster		50.00	53,739	0....	10	7	7	4	3		...	.
1639	Kuseri (Mser)	0.02000	2,636	3,017	5,297	NAB60b	18-BBAA-b	mser		10.00	302	0....	8	5	5	1	1		...	b
1640	Kutep (Zumper, Mbarike)	0.01350	1,780	2,036	3,575	NAB56b	98-HBFA-e	kentin		70.00	1,426	0....	10	7	7	4	1		pn.	.
1641	Kwaja	0.02000	2,636	3,017	5,297	NAB56b	99-AGEB-be	kwaja		80.00	2,414	0....	10	8	7	4	1		pn.	.
1642	Kwakum (Akpwakum, Abakum)	0.04056	5,347	6,118	10,742	NAB57c	99-AUDB-h	kwakum		60.00	3,671	0....	10	7	6	4	1		...	.
1643	Laimbue	0.03884	5,120	5,859	10,287	NAB57a	99-AGDA-j	nyos		80.00	4,687	0....	10	8	8	0	0		p..	.
1644	Laka (Kabba-Laka)	0.03000	3,955	4,525	7,945	NAB66z	03-AAAE-f	laka		15.00	679	0.s..	8	5	2	2	0	Kabba-laka*	PNb	.
1645	Londo (Balondo)	0.10000	13,182	15,085	26,484	NAB57k	99-AJBD-d	ehobe-be-lon		80.00	12,068	0....	10	8	6	4	0		...	.
1646	Lue (Western Kundu)	0.08222	10,838	12,403	21,775	NAB57k	99-AJAB-b	lo-lue		80.00	9,922	0....	10	8	6	4	1		...	.
1647	Lundu (Bolundu, Londo)	0.25000	32,955	37,712	66,211	NAB56b	99-AJAA	west oroko cluster		70.00	26,399	0....	10	7	7	4	2		...	.
1648	Mabas	0.05155	6,795	7,776	13,653	NAB60b	18-CBBA-e	mabas		5.00	389	0....	7	5	6	1	0		pn.	b
1649	Mada	0.18634	24,563	28,109	49,351	NAB60b	18-EACC-a	mada		4.00	1,124	0....	6	5	6	1	3	Mada: Cameroon	P..	.
1650	Majera (Daa)	0.05150	6,789	7,769	13,639	NAB60b	18-BAAA-a	majera		10.00	777	0....	8	5	6	1	0		...	.
1651	Mambila (Mambere, Tongbo)	0.21923	28,899	33,071	58,062	NAB56b	98-JBCA	mambila cluster		30.00	9,921	0....	9	5	7	2	1	Mambila*	PN.	.
1652	Mandankwe (Nkwen)	0.10309	13,589	15,551	27,303	NAB57a	99-AGEA-g	menda-nkwe		85.00	13,218	0....	10	8	10	4	1		...	.
1653	Mandara (Wandala, Ndara)	0.36559	48,192	55,149	96,824	NAB60b	18-CAAA-j	vehicular wandala		2.00	1,103	0....	6	4	5	1	2	Mandara*	PN.	.
1654	Mandja (Manza)	0.05000	6,591	7,542	13,242	NAB66f	93-AAAA-d	manja		80.00	6,034	0.s..	10	7	10	4	2	Manza	pnb	b
1655	Mangbai (Mambai)	0.02000	2,636	3,017	5,297	NAB66z	92-CDAC-a	mambai		50.00	1,508	0....	10	7	5	4	1		...	.

Continued opposite

Table 8-2 continued

EVANGELIZATION								EVANGELISM			ADDITIONAL DESCRIPTIVE DATA
Ref	*D*	*aC*	*CG%*	*r*	*E*	*U*	*W*	*e*	*R*	*T*	*Locations, civil divisions, literacy, religions, church history, denominations, dioceses, church growth, missions, agencies, ministries, movements*
1	*28*	*29*	*30*	*31*	*32*	*33*	*34*	*35*	*36*	*37*	*38*
1532	4	8	5.38	0	43.00	57.00	A	15.69	431	5	On Nigerian border, Bourrah Subdivision, Far North Province. Majority in Nigeria. Mostly Muslims 85%. D=RCC,EPC,UEBC,EFLC. M=SIL,LBWM.
1533	1	7	4.42	0	83.00	17.00	B	151.47	192	7	West of Nkambe, Donga-Mangung Division, North West Province. Animists 50%. D=RCC.
1534	1	7	8.78	0	96.00	4.00	C	210.24	293	8	Upper Senaga Division, Centre Province. Related to Fang, Bulu. Animists 40%. D=RCC.
1535	1	6	6.09	0	85.00	15.00	B	155.12	244	7	Belabo Subdivision, East Province. Bilingual in Beti and Bebele. Animists 50%. D=RCC.
1536	1	6	6.13	0	99.85	0.15	C	387.81	165	9	Related to Tiv. On Nigeria border, South West Province; also in Nigeria. Animists 15%. D=RCC. M=GR.
1537	1	7	3.32	0	78.00	22.00	B	128.11	165	7	Southwest of Furu-Awa, Menchum Division, North West Province. Animists 55%. D=RCC.
1538	2	7	8.88	1	99.67	0.33	C	264.11	256	8	Deuk District and Bafia Subdivision, Mbam Division, Centre Province. Animists 33%. D=EPC,RCC. M=UBS.
1539	1	7	6.40	0	83.00	17.00	B	151.47	271	7	In Yambasa, southeast of Bokito, Mbam Division, Centre Province. Animists 50%. D=RCC.
1540	1	7	6.21	0	84.00	16.00	B	153.30	261	7	In and south of Bokito, Mbam Division, Centre Province. Animists 50%. D=RCC.
1541	2	7	6.32	2	99.80	0.20	C	367.92	168	9	Centre and South Provinces. Animists 20%. D=RCC(D-Mbalmayo),EPC.
1542	2	7	8.48	0	99.80	0.20	C	350.40	225	9	Along Sanaga river, Mbam Division, Centre Province. Animists 20%. D=RCC,EPC.
1543	1	7	6.44	0	99.85	0.15	C	378.50	176	9	Around Befang, Mezam Division, North West Province. Animists 15%. D=RCC.
1544	1	6	7.13	1	94.00	6.00	C	205.86	251	8	Around Messamena, East Province. Close to South Makaa. Animists 40%. D=RCC.
1545	1	7	4.84	0	84.00	16.00	B	153.30	203	7	West of Furu-Awa, Menchum Division, North West Province. Animists 50%. D=RCC.
1546	3	6	6.39	0	99.80	0.20	C	344.56	181	9	Near Banyo, Mayo-Banyo Division, Adamawa Province. Majority in Nigeria. Animists 20%. D=RCC,Protestants,AICs.
1547	1	7	4.67	1	99.85	0.15	C	381.60	144	9	Limbe District, Fako Division, South West Province. Animists 15%. D=RCC.
1548	0	0	6.57	1	84.00	16.00	B	168.63	274	7	East Province, Ngoura District. In Betare-Oya and Lom and Djerem. Fulfulde used in the markets. Animists 20%, Muslims 5%. D=RCC.
1549	2	7	4.49	0	84.00	16.00	B	153.30	186	7	2 villages east of Mamfe, Manyu Division, South West Province. Bilingual in Kenyang, Denya. Animists 50%. D=PCC,RCC.
1550	2	7	6.25	0	99.80	0.20	C	388.36	157	9	Akwaya Subdivision, Manyu Division, South West Province. Primarily in Nigeria. Animists 20%. D=AICs,RCC.
1551	2	7	6.41	1	99.85	0.15	C	381.60	183	9	West of Buea Subdivision, Menoua Division, West Province. Animists 15%. D=PCC,RCC.
1552	1	6	6.18	0	98.00	2.00	C	232.50	214	8	Malapa village, east of Moloundou. Also in Congo. Animists 35%. D=RCC.
1553	0	5	4.18	4	33.05	66.95	A	0.06	479	2	Nomads in north; also in Nigeria, Niger. Muslims 99%(Maliki Sunnis).
1554	6	10	1.58	8	99.79	0.21	C	446.94	48	10	Expatriates from Britain in education, development. D=PCC,EPC,EEC,RCC,JWs,SDA.
1555	1	7	4.42	0	82.00	18.00	B	149.65	194	7	Villages of Bu, Za, Ngwen; Wum Subdivision, Menchum Division, North West Province. Animists 50%. D=RCC.
1556	1	6	0.00	0	20.06	79.94	A	0.04	0	2	In Lake Chad. Far North Province. Most in Chad, Niger. Warlike. Muslims 100%. D=Eglise Fraternelle Lutherienne Camerounaise. M=SUM.
1557	5	6	6.25	4	99.75	0.25	C	368.45	156	9	Covers Ntem, Dja, and Lobo Divisions, South Province. Language in decline. Animists 20%. D=RCC(M-Yaounde),EPC,SDA,EPCO,AICs. M=UBS.
1558	4	10	4.86	4	99.80	0.20	C	426.32	119	10	Mixed-race and detribalized persons. Urban areas. D=RCC,PCC,AICs,&c.
1559	1	7	7.35	1	99.80	0.20	C	347.48	197	9	Northern part of Fundong Subdivision, Menchum Division, North West Province. Animists 20%. D=Baptist Ch.
1560	1	7	4.42	0	82.00	18.00	B	149.65	188	7	3 villages in Batibo Subdivision, Momo Division, North West Province. Animists 50%. D=RCC.
1561	1	8	3.53	0	28.00	72.00	A	4.08	481	4	South of Mokolo, Mayo-Tsanaga Division, Far North Province. Muslims 70%, animists 25%. D=RCC.
1562	1	6	5.91	0	72.00	28.00	B	105.12	278	7	3 villages in Akwaza Subdivision, South West Province. Second language: Pidgin. Animists 60%. D=RCC.
1563	4	10	11.80	8	99.79	0.21	C	418.10	244	10	Mixed race, primarily in South West and North West Provinces. Major lingua franca(50% of country). Animists 12%. D=RCC,PCC,CBC,&c. M=UBS.
1564	0	7	6.95	0	85.00	15.00	B	155.12	283	7	Along Nigerian border, Northern Province. Majority in Nigeria. Animists 30%, Muslims 20%. M=SUM.
1565	1	7	7.62	0	86.00	14.00	B	156.95	301	7	West of Poli and south of Beka District, North West Province. Also in Nigeria. Muslims 30%, animists 20%. D=EELC. M=LBT,UBS.
1566	1	7	4.52	0	87.00	13.00	B	174.65	186	7	Northeast of Wum, Menchum Division, North West Province. Animists 45%. D=RCC.
1567	1	7	6.37	0	93.00	7.00	C	203.67	229	8	Southeast of Mokolo, Mokolo Subdivision, Far North Province. Muslims 40%. D=RCC.
1568	3	6	6.31	0	39.00	61.00	A	7.11	541	4	Northwest of Guider, North Province. Muslims 90%, animists. D=RCC,EFLC,UEBC(among Kola people). M=EBMS,LBWM,SIL.
1569	0	7	3.36	0	57.00	43.00	B	62.41	230	6	Rey-Bouba Subdivision, Benoue Division, North Province. Related to Mono. Animists 70%.
1570	1	7	4.61	0	59.00	41.00	B	64.60	281	6	In North Province, related to Kari, Mbum. Muslims 60%, animists 10%. D=RCC.
1571	1	7	3.47	0	42.00	58.00	A	15.33	317	5	Mainly over border in Nigeria, in extreme north. Animists 70%, Muslims 20%. D=COCIN(Nigeria).
1572	2	6	6.27	0	35.00	65.00	A	6.38	634	4	North Province, Adamawa Province. Animists 90%, Muslims 5%. D=RCC,EELC. M=American Lutheran Mission,UBS.
1573	1	6	4.56	1	87.00	13.00	B	158.77	200	7	Northwest of Bafia, Mbam Division, Centre Province. Related to Yambeta, Tunen. Animists 50%. D=RCC.
1574	1	6	4.45	1	80.00	20.00	B	131.40	214	7	Northeast of Bafia, Mbam Division, Centre Province. Animists 55%. D=RCC.
1575	2	7	6.83	0	63.00	37.00	B	59.78	359	6	Northern Poli Subdivision, North Province. 20% bilingual in Fulani. Animists 69%, Muslims 5%. D=EELC,RCC. M=SIL,UBS.
1576	6	9	6.26	1	99.75	0.25	C	369.56	164	9	Littoral and South West Provinces. Lingua franca. D=RCC(M-Douala),PCC,EEC,UEBC,NBC,EBC and other AICs. M=Arm of the Lord Ministry (Nigeria),BM.
1577	1	6	3.47	0	37.00	63.00	A	13.50	360	5	West of Tchere Canton, Diamare Division, Far North Province. Closely related to Mofu. Animists 70%, Muslims 20%. D=RCC.
1578	1	6	3.70	0	30.00	70.00	A	5.47	505	4	Near Pitoa, Benoue Division, North Province. Language is nearly extinct. Animists 90%. D=RCC.
1579	1	7	4.42	0	83.00	17.00	B	151.47	205	7	Bokito Subdivision, Mbam Division, Centre Province. Animists 50%. D=RCC.
1580	2	7	4.21	0	40.00	60.00	A	14.60	414	5	East of Poli, Faro, and Benoue Divisions, North Province. Animists 80%, Muslims 10%. D=EELC,RCC. M=UBS.
1581	3	7	8.90	0	99.65	0.35	C	246.74	273	8	Around Lomie, East Province. Also in Congo. Spoken as second language by many Pygmies. Animists 35%. D=RCC(D-Doume),EPC,AICs. M=CSSp,SIL.
1582	4	10	5.60	4	99.80	0.20	C	435.08	129	10	Coast in South West Province. Majority in Nigeria. Major lingua franca. Animists 20%. D=RCC,PCC,COG,AICs. M=LBI.
1583	3	7	8.81	0	99.80	0.20	C	367.92	222	9	In South West Province. Majority in Nigeria. Many dialects. Animists 20%. D=RCC,PCC,CBC. M=FGM,ACM,SIL.
1584	1	6	3.78	0	71.00	29.00	B	103.66	200	7	4 towns in Akwaya Subdivision, South West Province. Second language: Pidgin. Animists 60%. D=RCC.
1585	1	6	9.46	1	99.70	0.30	C	270.83	283	8	Almost all Lekie Division, Centre Province. Closely related to Beti, Fang. Animists 30%. D=RCC(M-Yaounde).
1586	1	6	6.88	0	83.00	17.00	B	151.47	273	7	Akwaya Subdivision, South West Province; a few in Nigeria. Close to Tiv. Second language: Pidgin. Animists 50%. D=RCC.
1587	2	6	12.18	1	99.81	0.19	C	392.25	280	9	Centre Province, South Province. Lingua franca. Animists 18%. D=RCC(M-Yaounde),AICs. M=CSSp,OMI,MHM,SCJ,SJ,OP,CICM,SAC,&c.
1588	3	7	5.29	2	99.60	0.40	C	258.42	157	8	South Province; mainly in Gabon, Congo, Equatorial Guinea. Animists 14%. D=RCC(M-Yaounde),EPC,AICs.
1589	1	10	2.14	8	99.87	0.13	C	511.25	53	10	Expatriates from France, in business, education, government; also mother tongue of many urbanized Blacks. D=RCC.
1590	1	7	1.62	0	79.00	21.00	B	129.75	104	7	West of Furu-Awa, Menchum Division, North West Province. Animists 55%. D=RCC.
1591	2	7	9.05	1	99.80	0.20	C	353.32	233	9	Tuba District, Mezam Division; Manyu Division, North West Province. Animists 20%. D=PCC,RCC(D-Buea). M=MHM,SIL.
1592	1	7	2.75	0	31.00	69.00	A	5.65	366	4	Southwest corner of Mayo-Sava Division, Far North Province. Animists 55%, Muslims 40%. D=RCC.
1593	0	7	2.22	0	57.00	43.00	B	62.41	175	6	Tchollire, Mayo-Rey Division, North Province. Nearly extinct; very few speakers. Muslims 70% (Maliki Sunnis).
1594	2	8	3.26	0	30.00	70.00	A	4.38	425	4	Around Gawar, North Province. Muslims 70%, animists 25%. Becoming islamized. D=RCC,UEBC.
1595	2	6	10.20	4	99.76	0.24	C	355.07	258	9	Scattered across vast area in North Province. Great majority in CAR; also in Nigeria, Congo. Animists 17%, Muslims 5%. Y=1928. D=EELC,Baptist Chs.
1596	2	6	3.87	0	32.00	68.00	A	4.67	450	4	East of Mandara Mountains, Mayo-Sava Division, Far North Province. Bilingual in Zulgwa. Animists 86%, Muslims 10%. D=RCC,UEENC.
1597	3	6	8.36	0	63.00	37.00	B	57.48	424	6	Mayo-Louti Division, North Province. Also in Chad. Animists 25%, Muslims 50%. D=RCC,EFLC,African Lutheran Brethren. M=UBS,LBWM.
1598	2	6	3.26	0	32.00	68.00	A	5.84	436	4	West of Poli, Faro Division, North Province. Close to Kadam. Second language: Fulfulde. Animists 50%, Muslims 45%. D=RCC,EELC.
1599	2	6	3.45	0	33.00	67.00	A	7.22	438	4	Northwest of Poli on Nigerian border, North Province. Animists 50%, Muslims 44%. D=RCC,EELC.
1600	1	8	3.91	0	37.00	63.00	A	13.50	392	5	Koza Subdivision, Far North Province. Vast majority in Nigeria. Animists 86%, Muslims 4%. D=UEENC.
1601	1	10	5.82	7	99.95	0.05	C	572.13	113	10	Long-time settlers in business, commerce; traders. D=Greek Orthodox Ch(D-Accra).
1602	1	5	4.48	0	26.00	74.00	A	1.89	619	4	North and northwest of Dourbeye, Mayo-Tsanaga Division, Far North Province. Most in Nigeria. Animists 98%. D=EFLC. M=SIL,LBWM,EBMS,Nigerian Baptist .
1603	0	6	3.46	4	42.00	58.00	A	1.53	330	4	Gey language extinct; people now speak Fulani. In Benoue Division, North Province. Muslims 90%.
1604	0	5	6.61	0	33.00	67.00	A	12.04	664	5	North of Kousseri, Logone and Chari Division, Far North Province. Also in Chad. Animists 60%, Muslims 30%.
1605	1	10	3.10	5	49.10	50.90	A	0.17	240	3	Scattered from Senegal to Sudan. Traders. Muslims 100%(Maliki Sunnis). D=EELC.
1606	2	6	5.13	0	41.00	59.00	A	14.96	436	5	Village of Tourou, Mokolo Subdivision, Far North Province. A few in Nigeria. Animists70%, Muslims 20%. D=UEENC,RCC. M=SUM.
1607	1	7	3.26	0	82.00	18.00	B	149.65	169	7	Southwest of Bokito, Mbam Division, Centre Province. Animists 50%. D=RCC.
1608	0	10	4.83	0	37.00	63.00	A	13.50	461	5	South of Mokolo, Hina District, Far North Province. Bilingual in Fulfulde. Muslims 50%, animists 40%.
1609	0	6	2.75	0	36.00	64.00	A	13.14	315	5	In Amsa on Nigerian border, Mokolo Subdivision, Far North Province. Close to Kamwe and Psikye. Animists 87%, Muslims 3%.
1610	6	6	5.23	4	99.85	0.15	C	452.96	124	10	Migrants from Nigeria. Animists 15%. D=RCC,PCC,SA,SDA,AICs,&c. M=Pentecostal Mission (Nigeria).
1611	5	10	4.98	4	99.90	0.10	C	512.46	112	10	Migrants from Nigeria. Animists 10%. D=RCC,PCC,AoG,AICs,&c. M=Pentecostal Mission (Nigeria).
1612	0	6	6.38	0	69.00	31.00	B	100.74	302	7	Village of Isu, Wum Subdivision, North West Province. Animists 60%. D=CBC
1613	1	6	4.15	0	38.10	61.90	A	14.04	398	5	On Nigerian border. Mayo-Tsanaga Division, Far North Province. Also in Nigeria. Muslims 50%, animists 40%. D=EFLC. M=LBWM. Christians use Fulani literature.
1614	0	6	3.89	0	34.00	66.00	A	12.41	426	5	In south of Logone-Birni Subdivision, Far North Province. Animists 80%.
1615	4	6	5.13	0	99.60	0.40	C	219.00	179	8	Migrants from Nigeria. Animists 40%. D=COCIN,PCC,AICs,&c.
1616	1	6	7.21	1	99.70	0.30	C	278.49	212	8	Mbam Division, Centre Province. Related to Bafia. Animists 30%. D=EPC.
1617	1	6	8.06	1	63.00	37.00	B	68.98	414	6	Most of Kadey Division, East Province. A few also in CAR and Congo. Animists 70%. D=EPC. M=SIL.
1618	2	8	5.09	0	99.79	0.21	C	331.60	154	9	Near Mambila, Adamawa Province. Also in Nigeria. Animists 21%. D=AICS,RCC.
1619	1	6	4.18	0	41.00	59.00	A	14.96	372	5	Mainly in Nigeria; related to Psikye and Hya. Animists 87%, Muslims 3%. D=RCC.
1620	2	6	7.91	0	61.00	39.00	B	55.66	418	6	Southwestern part of Mokolo Subdivision, Far North Province. Some in Nigeria. Animists 60%. Muslims 15%. D=RCC,EFLC. M=UBS,LBWM.
1621	2	7	5.49	1	46.00	54.00	A	16.79	410	5	Mayo-Rey Division, North Province. Some in Chad. Animists 85%, Muslims 5% and growing. D=RCC,EELC. M=SIL,ALM.
1622	0	7	5.03	1	64.00	36.00	B	70.08	294	6	Around Belel, Vina Division, Adamawa Province. Muslims 60%, animists 10%.
1623	1	6	5.53	0	60.00	40.00	B	65.70	318	6	Southeast of Doukoula, Mayo-Danay Division, Far North Province. Primarily in Chad. Animists 40%, Muslims 30%. D=EFLC. M=LBWM.
1624	1	6	6.37	1	99.80	0.20	C	338.72	179	9	Tuba Subdivision, Mezam Division, North West Province; village of Babanki. Animists 20%. D=RCC.
1625	0	7	5.64	0	99.80	0.20	C	324.12	174	9	Northeast of Nkambe, North West Province. Bilingual in some other Mfumte language. Animists 20%.
1626	3	7	4.18	1	56.00	44.00	B	40.88	294	6	Around Garoua, North Province; mostly in Chad. Many refugees. Animists 80%. D=RCC,EELC,EFLC. M=SFM(Swedish Pentecostals, from Chad),SIL.
1627	1	7	5.16	0	72.00	28.00	B	105.12	266	7	South of Poli, Faro Division, North Province. Related to Voko. Muslims 60%. D=EELC. M=Norwegian Mission Society,UBS.
1628	2	6	5.34	0	71.00	29.00	B	103.66	277	7	North of Kontcha, in Atlantika Mountains, Faro Division, North Province. Also in Nigeria. Animists 60%. D=RCC,EELC.
1629	3	7	5.40	2	99.85	0.15	C	409.53	149	10	Mainly in Equatorial Guinea, along coast. Animists 15%. D=RCC,EPC,AICs.
1630	2	6	6.43	1	99.70	0.30	C	268.27	206	8	South of Yokadouma, Boumba and Ngoko Division, East Province. Close to Mpompo. Animists 30%. D=EPC,RCC.
1631	2	6	6.99	0	67.00	33.00	B	85.59	343	6	South of Mayo-Darle, Mayo-Banyo Division, Adamawa Province. Animists 45%, Muslims 20%. D=RCC,EELC. M=LBT,UBS.
1632	1	6	7.14	0	99.80	0.20	C	327.04	209	9	Northwest of Mundemba, Ndian Division, South West Province. Also in Nigeria. Animists 20%. D=RCC.
1633	1	7	5.64	0	99.80	0.20	C	329.96	170	9	Villages in Wum Subdivision, Menchum District, North West Province. Animists 20%. D=EELC.
1634	1	5	5.98	0	29.00	71.00	A	10.58	696	5	Logone & Chari Division, Far North Province; also Chad, Nigeria. Fishermen, traders, stock-breeders. Muslims 90%(Maliki Sunnis since 16th century). D=UEENC.
1635	1	8	6.97	0	75.00	25.00	B	109.50	321	7	Faro, Deo, Mayo-Banyo Divisions, Adamawa Province. Also Nigeria. Animists 40%; Muslims 20% and growing. D=EELC. M=Norwegian Mission,UBS.
1636	4	6	8.78	1	99.85	0.15	C	400.22	225	10	Fako Division, South West Province. Bilingual in Duala and Wescos. Animists 15%: D=PCC,RCC(D-Buea),NBC,AICs. M=MHM.
1637	1	7	5.64	0	99.80	0.20	C	341.64	165	9	Northwest of Nkambe, Ako District, Donga-Mantung Division, North West Province. Animists 20%. D=RCC.
1638	3	6	8.97	0	88.00	12.00	B	160.60	335	7	Around Kumba, South West Province. Bakundu-Bolne. Animists 50%. D=RCC,PCC,UEBC.
1639	1	7	3.47	0	39.00	61.00	A	14.23	341	5	Klessem Kousseri Subdivision, Logone and Chari Division, Far North Province. Also in Chad. Bilingual in Arabic. Muslims 90%. D=UEENC.
1640	1	8	5.09	0	99.70	0.30	C	275.94	164	8	3 villages near border, Menchum Division, North West Province; mainly in Nigeria. Animists 30%. D=RCC.
1641	1	8	5.64	0	99.80	0.20	C	344.56	163	9	Nkambe Division, North West Province. Bilingual in some Mfumte languages. Animists 20%. D=RCC.
1642	1	7	6.08	0	93.00	7.00	C	203.67	222	8	Dimako and Doume Subdivisions. Upper Nyong Division, East Province. Animists 40%. D=RCC.
1643	0	0	6.34	0	99.80	0.20	C	297.84	203	8	North West province. In Mechum and Fundong. Animists 20%. D=RCC.
1644	0	6	4.31	1	45.00	55.00	A	24.63	350	5	Mostly in Chad, also CAR, near common border point with Cameroon. Animists 85%.
1645	0	6	7.35	0	99.80	0.20	C	324.12	226	9	Littoral, West and South West Provinces. Related to Mbo. Animists 20%
1646	1	6	7.14	0	99.80	0.20	C	327.04	219	9	South West Province. Related to Bakundu-Balue. Animists 20%. D=RCC.
1647	2	6	6.91	0	99.70	0.30	C	270.83	215	8	West Oroko. Central part of Ndian Division, South West Province. Animists 30%. D=RCC,PCC.
1648	0	6	3.73	0	34.00	66.00	A	6.20	413	4	Village on Nigeria border, Mayo-Tsanaga Division, Far North Province. Also in Nigeria. Bilingual in Matakam. Animists 75%, Muslims 20%.
1649	3	6	4.84	0	34.00	66.00	A	4.96	502	4	Mada massif at edge of Mandara Mts, Tokombere Sub-division, Far North Province. Animists 50%, Muslims 46%. D=RCC,UEENC,SDA.
1650	0	6	4.45	0	34.00	66.00	A	12.41	471	5	Around Majera in south of Logone-Birni Subdivision, Logone and Chari Division, Far North Province. Animists 80%, some Muslims 10%.
1651	4	6	7.14	0	66.00	34.00	B	72.27	354	6	On border, Mayo-Banyo Division, Adamawa Province. Stone Age culture. Animists 50%, Muslims 20%. D=EELC,CBC,RCC, Eglise Evanglique Libre. M=SIL.
1652	1	7	7.45	1	99.85	0.15	C	384.71	192	9	North and east of Bamenda, Tuba Subdivision, Mezam Division, North West Province. Related to Bafut, Ngemba, Pinyin. Animists 15%. D=RCC.
1653	1	5	4.82	0	30.00	70.00	A	2.19	567	4	Mayo-Sava Division, Far North Province. Muslims 98%(Maliki Sunnis). D=UEENC. M=SIL,CMF(Nigeria). R=ELWA(Kirdi-Mora).
1654	2	6	6.61	1	99.80	0.20	C	367.92	184	9	Mainly in CAR; some in Chad. Animists 17%, Muslims 3%. D=AIC,EEF. M=BMM,CBM.
1655	1	7	5.14	0	82.00	18.00	B	149.65	220	7	Along Mayo-Kebi river, Benoue Division, North Province. Also in Chad. Animists 40%, Muslims 10%. D=EFLC. M=LBWM.

Continued overleaf

Table 8-2 continued

PEOPLE		POPULATION				IDENTITY CODE		LANGUAGE		CHURCH		MINISTRY						SCRIPTURE		
Ref 1	Ethnic name 2	P% 3	In 1995 4	In 2000 5	In 2025 6	Race 7	Language 8	Autoglossonym 9	S 10	AC 11	Members 12	Jayuh 13-17	d 18	wa 19	xc 20	mc 21	mi 22	Biblioglossonym 23	Pub 24-26	ss 27
1656	Mangisa	0.23725	31,274	35,789	62,834	NAB56b	99-ANCB-a	le-ti		80.00	28,631	0....	10	8	6	4	1		...	b
1657	Masa (Masana, Banana)	1.69892	223,953	256,282	449,949	NAB60b	17-FAAA-a	yagwa	3	20.00	51,256	0....	9	5	7	2	2	Masana	PN.	.
1658	Maslam	0.05200	6,855	7,844	13,772	NAB60b	18-BBAB-a	maslam		2.00	157	0....	6	4	5	1	0		...	.
1659	Matal (Muktile, Balda)	0.19730	26,008	29,763	52,254	NAB60b	18-EABA-a	matal		10.00	2,976	0....	8	5	5	1	2	Matal	PN.	p
1660	Mbaw	0.01000	1,318	1,508	2,648	NAB57a	99-AGEB-ce	mbaw		50.00	754	0....	10	7	5	4	1		pn.	n
1661	Mbedam	0.01500	1,977	2,263	3,973	NAB60b	18-FBAA-a	mbedam		50.00	1,131	0....	10	7	5	4	1		...	.
1662	Mbere Baya (Gbaya)	0.04000	5,273	6,034	10,594	NAB66c	92-CDAE-e	mbere		80.00	4,827	0.s..	10	8	6	4	1	Gbaya: Mbere*	PN.	.
1663	Mbimu (Mpyemo)	0.04085	5,385	6,162	10,819	NAB57c	99-AUDG-f	m-pyemo		70.00	4,314	0....	10	7	7	4	2		...	.
1664	Mbo (Babong, Bareko)	0.90000	118,639	135,765	238,360	NAB56b	99-AJBD	central mbo cluster		78.00	105,896	0....	10	7	7	4	1		...	.
1665	Mboa (Mbonga)	0.01000	1,318	1,508	2,648	NAB56b	99-AAHA-a	m-bonga		25.00	377	0....	9	5	7	3	0		...	.
1666	Mboku (Mbuko)	0.07344	9,681	11,078	19,450	NAB60b	18-EAAB-a	mbuko		10.00	1,108	0....	8	5	5	1	1	Mbuko	...	.
1667	Mbubem (Kakayamba)	0.27403	36,123	41,337	72,575	NAB57a	99-AGEB-c	yamba		50.00	20,669	0....	10	7	6	4	1	Yamba	PN.	n
1668	Mbum (Wuna, Buna, Bum)	0.42157	55,572	63,594	111,650	NAB66c	92-CDAE-k	mbum	2	25.00	15,898	0.s..	9	5	6	3	1	Mboum*	PN.	n
1669	Mefele	0.08207	10,819	12,380	21,736	NAB60b	18-ECBB-a	mefele		10.00	1,238	0....	8	5	5	1	0		...	.
1670	Mekaf (Naki, Bunaki)	0.02892	3,812	4,363	7,659	NAB57c	99-AFAA-a	bu-naki		60.00	2,618	0....	10	7	4	4	2		...	.
1671	Mengisa	0.10000	13,182	15,085	26,484	NAB57k	99-ANCB-a	le-ti		40.00	6,034	0....	9	5	5	3	0		...	b
1672	Menka	0.13702	18,062	20,669	36,289	NAB57a	99-AGBA-bd	me-nka		80.00	16,536	0....	10	8	7	4	1		...	.
1673	Mere (Merey, Meri, Dugur)	0.10961	14,449	16,535	29,030	NAB60b	18-EADB-a	merey		10.00	1,653	0....	8	5	6	1	2	Merey	P..	.
1674	Mijong (Missong)	0.02000	2,636	3,017	5,297	NAB56b	99-AFAA-c	misong		50.00	1,508	0....	10	7	6	4	1		...	.
1675	Mofa (Matakam, Natakan)	2.49462	328,842	376,313	660,685	NAB60b	18-ECAB	central mafa cluster	2	4.00	15,053	1.s..	6	4	6	1	2	Mofa*	PNB	.
1676	Molokwo (Molko)	0.06976	9,196	10,523	18,476	NAB60b	18-EACD-a	melokwo		5.00	526	0....	7	5	5	1	1		...	n
1677	Mono	0.01206	1,590	1,819	3,194	NAB66b	92-CDAD-a	mono		75.00	1,364	0....	10	7	6	4	1		...	.
1678	Mpade (Makari)	0.01000	1,318	1,508	2,648	NAB60b	18-BBAB-d	mpade		50.00	754	0....	10	7	6	4	1		...	.
1679	Mubako (Mumbake, Nyong)	0.16083	21,201	24,261	42,595	NAB66c	92-BDAB-h	nyong		50.00	12,131	0....	10	7	6	4	2		...	.
1680	Mulimba (Limba)	0.04933	6,503	7,441	13,065	NAB57k	99-AUAB-f	mu-limba		80.00	5,953	0....	10	8	6	4	2		pnb	.
1681	Mum (Bamun, Bamoun)	2.48469	327,533	374,815	658,055	NAB57a	99-AGEI-b	shu-pamem	3	8.50	31,859	0....	7	5	5	1	1	Bamun	PNB	b
1682	Mumuye	0.05000	6,591	7,542	13,242	NAB66c	92-BAAE	west mumuye cluster		5.00	377	0....	7	5	5	1	1	Mumuye	PN.	b
1683	Mundang (Lere, Susang)	0.66667	87,881	100,567	176,564	NAB66z	92-CDAB	mundang cluster		40.00	40,227	0..u.	9	5	7	3	3	Mundang	PNB	.
1684	Mundani (Nko)	0.32686	43,087	49,307	86,567	NAB57a	99-AGCA-c	mun-dani		80.00	39,445	0....	10	8	7	4	3	Mundani	P..	.
1685	Mungong	0.02000	2,636	3,017	5,297	NAB56b	99-AFBA	east beboid cluster		70.00	2,112	0....	10	7	6	4	1		...	p
1686	Musei (Bananna, Mussei)	0.19732	26,011	29,766	52,259	NAB60b	17-FAAC-a	mosi		10.00	2,977	0....	8	5	6	2	2	Musey	PN.	.
1687	Musgum (Mulwi)	0.77419	102,054	116,786	205,040	NAB60b	18-AAAA-e	muskum	1	20.00	23,357	0....	9	5	7	2	2	Mousgoum*	PN.	.
1688	Muyang (Myau)	0.16442	21,674	24,803	43,546	NAB60b	18-EACB-a	muyang		3.00	744	0....	6	4	5	1	2		...	.
1689	Ncane	0.01000	1,318	1,508	2,648	NAB56b	99-AFBA-c	n-cane		50.00	754	0....	10	7	6	4	1		...	.
1690	Ncha	0.02000	2,636	3,017	5,297	NAB56b	99-AGEB-bd	ndaktup		80.00	2,414	0....	10	8	6	4	1		pn.	.
1691	Ndaktup (Bitwi)	0.02000	2,636	3,017	5,297	NAB56b	99-AGEB-bd	ndaktup		80.00	2,414	0....	10	7	5	4	1		pn.	.
1692	Ndemli (Bayong)	0.04000	5,273	6,034	10,594	NAB57a	99-AHAA-a	ndem-li		10.00	603	0....	8	5	5	1	0		...	.
1693	Ndop-Bamessing (Ndob)	0.13702	18,062	20,669	36,289	NAB57a	99-AGDC-b	ke-nswei		80.00	16,536	0....	10	7	7	4	1		pn.	.
1694	Ndop-Bamunka (Muka)	0.16661	21,963	25,133	44,126	NAB57a	99-AGDC-c	ba-munka		80.00	20,106	0....	10	7	6	4	1		pn.	.
1695	Ndoro (Nundoro)	0.01425	1,878	2,150	3,774	NAB56b	98-JAAA-a	ndola		85.00	1,827	0....	10	8	6	4	3		...	.
1696	Ndreme (Pelasla, Mbreme)	0.08221	10,837	12,401	21,773	NAB60b	18-EAAA-a	pelasla-gwendele		5.00	620	0....	7	5	5	1	3		...	.
1697	Nen (Banen, Penin, Penyin	0.38693	51,005	58,368	102,476	NAB57a	99-ALAB	tunen cluster		50.00	29,184	0....	10	6	7	4	3		...	.
1698	Nfumte (Mfumte)	0.27074	35,689	40,841	71,704	NAB57a	99-AGEB-b	mfumte		80.00	32,673	0....	10	7	6	4	1		pn.	.
1699	Ngemba	0.76729	101,145	115,745	203,212	NAB57a	99-AGEA-e	proper n-gemba		74.00	85,652	0....	10	7	7	4	1		...	.
1700	Ngi (Angie, Baninge)	0.34066	44,906	51,388	90,222	NAB57a	99-AGCA-ai	n-gie		80.00	41,111	0....	10	8	7	4	3		p..	.
1701	Ngo (Babungo, Vengoo)	0.14798	19,507	22,323	39,192	NAB57a	99-AGDC-a	vengo		70.00	15,626	0....	10	7	7	4	1	Babungo*	PN.	.
1702	Ngossi (Gevoko)	0.36724	48,410	55,398	97,261	NAB60b	18-CABC-a	kudupa-xa		18.00	9,972	0....	8	5	4	1	2	Guduf	P..	.
1703	Ngumba (Mvumbo, Mabea)	0.10319	13,603	15,566	27,329	NAB57k	99-AUDE-a	mvumbo		99.00	15,411	0....	10	9	12	5	2	Ngumba	P..	.
1704	Ngwo (Ngwaw, Ngunu)	0.33980	44,793	51,259	89,994	NAB57a	99-AGCA-a	n-gwo		80.00	41,007	0....	10	8	10	4	1		p..	.
1705	Nimbari	0.03000	3,955	4,525	7,945	NAB66z	92-BEAA-a	nimbari		30.00	1,358	0....	9	5	6	2	1		...	.
1706	Nkom (Kom, Bekom, Bikon)	1.39209	183,506	209,996	368,687	NAB57a	99-AGDB-c	n-kom		68.00	142,798	0....	10	7	7	4	1	Kom	pn.	.
1707	Nomande (Mandi, Pimenc)	0.06577	8,670	9,921	17,419	NAB57k	99-ALBA-a	no-maande		50.00	4,961	0....	10	6	7	4	1	Nomaande	P..	.
1708	Noni	0.28597	37,697	43,138	75,737	NAB56b	99-AFBA-e	noni		50.00	21,569	0....	10	6	7	4	1	Noone	...	.
1709	North Fali	0.17538	23,119	26,456	46,448	NAB66c	92-CEAA	north fali cluster		1.00	265	0....	6	4	5	1	0		...	n
1710	North Gisiga (Gizika)	0.24259	31,978	36,595	64,249	NAB60b	18-EBAA	north giziga cluster		20.00	7,319	0....	9	5	5	2	3	Giziga	P..	.
1711	North Makaa (Mika, Mekye)	0.08581	11,312	12,944	22,726	NAB57c	99-AUDC-a	b-yep		60.00	7,767	0....	10	6	7	4	2		...	.
1712	North Mofu	0.40000	52,728	60,340	105,938	NAB60b	18-EBBA-b	duvangar		5.00	3,017	0....	7	4	6	1	1	Mofu, North	PN.	.
1713	Northern Fungom	0.00776	1,023	1,171	2,055	NAB56b	99-AGDA-h	fungom		50.00	585	0....	10	6	7	4	1		p..	.
1714	Nso (Nsaw, Banso, Lamso)	1.20169	158,407	181,275	318,260	NAB57a	99-AGDB-g	lam-nso		79.00	143,207	0....	10	8	11	4	3	Nso*	PN.	b
1715	Nsungli (Limbum, Wimbum)	0.84364	111,209	127,263	223,433	NAB57a	99-AGEB-a	li-mbum		84.00	106,901	0....	10	8	11	4	1	Limbum	pn.	b
1716	Nyang (Manyang)	0.43850	57,803	66,148	116,134	NAB57a	99-AECA-a	ke-nyang		50.00	33,074	0....	10	6	7	4	1	Kenyang	...	.
1717	Nyen	0.02000	2,636	3,017	5,297	NAB57a	99-AGCA-be	n-jen		5.00	151	0....	7	4	6	2	1		p..	b
1718	Nzak Mbai (Gonge)	0.01000	1,318	1,508	2,648	NAB66c	92-CDAE-a	nzak-mbay		15.00	226	0.s..	8	5	5	2	1	Nzakmbay	PN.	b
1719	Nzanyi (Jeng, Njai)	0.09783	12,896	14,758	25,910	NAB60b	18-IBBA-a	nzanyi		10.00	1,476	0....	8	5	5	1	0		...	b
1720	Obanliku (Abanliku)	0.10000	13,182	15,085	26,484	NAB56b	98-IEAC-d	o-banliku		85.00	12,822	0....	10	8	10	4	3		...	.
1721	Oblo	0.01000	1,318	1,508	2,648	NAB66c	92-CDAE-m	oblo		30.00	453	0.s..	9	5	5	2	2		pn.	.
1722	Oku (Uku, Ekpwo)	0.32682	43,082	49,301	86,556	NAB57a	99-AGDB-f	kuo		70.00	34,510	0....	10	7	5	4	1		pn.	.
1723	Osatu	0.01000	1,318	1,508	2,648	NAB56b	99-ABJA-c	i-hatum		45.00	679	0....	9	5	6	3	2		...	b
1724	Oshie (Ngishe)	0.05160	6,802	7,784	13,666	NAB57a	99-AGCA-ah	n-gishe		70.00	5,449	0....	10	7	7	5	1		p..	.
1725	Pam	0.10000	13,182	15,085	26,484	NAB66c	92-CDAE-j	pondo		40.00	6,034	0.s..	9	6	7	3	2		pn.	.
1726	Pana	0.02000	2,636	3,017	5,297	NAB66z	92-CDAE-h	pana		60.00	1,810	0.s..	10	7	6	4	1	Pana	Pn.	.
1727	Pandama (Sakpu)	0.07673	10,115	11,575	20,321	NAB66c	92-CDAE-d	sakpu		60.00	6,945	0.s..	10	7	6	4	1		pn.	.
1728	Pape (Dugun)	0.04085	5,385	6,162	10,819	NAB66c	92-BBAA-b	panon		40.00	2,465	0.s..	9	6	4	3	1	Dugun*	P..	.
1729	Peve (Lame)	0.03845	5,069	5,800	10,183	NAB60b	17-FABB-i	peve		17.00	986	0.s..	8	5	5	2	1	Peve	PN.	.
1730	Pinyin (Bapinyi)	0.17538	23,119	26,456	46,448	NAB56b	99-AGEA-i	pinyin		80.00	21,165	0....	10	8	9	4	2		...	.
1731	Pobyeng (Mpompo)	0.12057	15,894	18,188	31,932	NAB57c	99-AUDG-e	m-pompo		70.00	12,732	0....	10	7	6	4	2		...	.
1732	Podoko (Podokwo, Parekwa)	0.23957	31,580	36,139	63,449	NAB60b	18-CABA-a	parekwa		10.00	3,614	0....	8	5	5	1	1	Podoko*	PN.	.
1733	Pongpong (Bombo)	0.36768	48,468	55,464	97,378	NAB57c	99-AUDG	mpo cluster		65.00	36,052	0....	10	7	7	4	2		...	.
1734	Pori (Congo Pol)	0.29596	39,014	44,645	78,383	NAB57k	99-AUDB-f	pori		70.00	31,252	0....	10	7	6	4	0		...	.
1735	Sango	0.02000	2,636	3,017	5,297	NAB66z	93-ABBA-a	sango	3	80.00	2,414	4.s..	10	7	11	4	2	Sango	PNB	b
1736	Sara Mbai	0.02000	2,636	3,017	5,297	NAB66z	03-AAAE-h	mbai-kan		60.00	1,810	0.s..	10	6	9	4	2	Mbai: Moissala	PNB	b
1737	Sara Ngambai	0.05234	6,899	7,895	13,862	NAB66z	03-AAAE-a	ngambai		65.00	5,132	0.s..	10	7	9	4	2	Ngambai*	PNB	b
1738	Sari (Saa, Saapa)	0.03836	5,057	5,787	10,159	NAB66z	92-BBAA-e	dii		30.00	1,736	0.s..	9	5	4	2	2	Duru*	P..	.
1739	Sarwa (Sharwa, Tchevi)	0.00580	765	875	1,536	NAB60b	17-DAAA-a	sarwa		1.00	9	0....	6	4	5	3	1		...	.
1740	Shuwa Arab (Baggara)	0.88172	116,229	133,007	233,518	CMT30	12-AACE-a	shuwa	4	0.02	27	0...h	3	3	2	0	0	Arabic: Chad	PN.	b
1741	So (Fo, Sso)	0.07108	9,370	10,722	18,825	NAB57c	46-FAAA-c	mangkong		60.00	6,433	0.s..	10	6	6	4	1		pn.	b
1742	South Fali	0.21923	28,899	33,071	58,062	NAB66c	92-CEAB	south fali cluster		10.00	3,307	0....	8	5	6	1	2	Fali*	PN.	.
1743	South Gisiga	0.49024	64,624	73,953	129,837	NAB60b	18-EBAB-a	mi-muturwa		1.00	740	0.s..	6	3	5	1	1	Giziga, South	PN.	.
1744	South Makaa	0.76908	101,381	116,015	203,686	NAB57c	99-AUDC-b	be-kol		60.00	69,609	0....	10	6	7	4	2	Makaa	...	.
1745	South Mofu (Zidim, Njeleng)	0.50000	65,910	75,425	132,422	NAB60b	18-EBBB-a	gudur		5.00	3,771	0....	7	5	6	1	2	Mofu-gudur*	P..	.
1746	Southern Fungom (Oso)	0.33980	44,793	51,259	89,994	NAB56b	99-AGDA-a	e-su		80.00	41,007	0....	10	7	7	4	2	Isu	P..	.
1747	Su (Isubu, Subu)	0.00877	1,156	1,323	2,323	NAB57k	99-AUAA-d	i-su		79.00	1,045	0....	10	8	5	4	1	Subu	P..	.
1748	Suga (Mengaka, Baghap)	0.10129	13,352	15,280	26,826	NAB56b	98-JCAA	suga cluster		80.00	12,224	0....	10	8	7	4	1		...	.
1749	Taram	0.02960	3,902	4,465	7,839	NAB66z	98-JDAC-a	taram		30.00	1,340	0....	9	5	5	3	1		...	.
1750	Terki (Teleki)	0.01000	1,318	1,508	2,648	NAB60b	18-IBAA-b	chede		4.00	60	0....	6	4	5	1	1		p..	.
1751	Tigon Mbembe (Tikun, Nzare)	0.39461	52,018	59,527	104,510	NAB56b	98-HBEA	tigon cluster		10.00	5,953	0....	8	5	6	1	1		...	.
1752	Tikar (Twumwu, Ndome)	0.21846	28,798	32,955	57,858	NAB57a	99-AIAA	tikari cluster		10.00	3,295	0....	8	5	5	1	2	Tikar	PN.	.
1753	Tuburi (Tupuri, Ndore)	1.12908	148,836	170,321	299,030	NAB60b	92-CDAA	tupuri cluster	3	40.00	68,129	0.s..	9	6	7	3	2	Tupuri	PN.	.
1754	Tuotomb (Bonek)	0.01031	1,359	1,555	2,731	NAB57k	99-ALBA-b	tuo-tomp		50.00	778	0....	10	7	7	4	1		p..	.
1755	Turku Arab (Tekrur, Turkol)	0.05000	6,591	7,542	13,242	CMT30	12-AACG-d	turku	6	0.00	0	0....	0	1	0	0	0		...	b
1756	Twendi	0.00817	1,077	1,232	2,164	NAB56b	98-JBAA	konja cluster		5.00	62	0....	7	4	6	1	0	Kwanja	...	.
1757	Vere (Verre, Kobo)	0.04385	5,780	6,615	11,613	NAB66c	92-BCBB-k	mom-jango		40.00	2,646	0....	9	5	6	3	1		...	b
1758	Vute (Wute, Babute)	0.29597	39,015	44,647	78,386	NAB56b	98-JCBA	bute cluster		50.00	22,323	0....	10	6	7	4	2	Vute	P..	b
1759	Wawa	0.02451	3,231	3,697	6,491	NAB56b	98-JCBA-b	wawa		5.00	185	0....	7	4	6	1	0		p..	b
1760	Weh	0.05360	7,066	8,086	14,196	NAB57a	99-AGDA-b	wi		70.00	5,660	0....	10	7	6	4	1		p..	.
1761	Widekum-Tadkon	1.00543	132,536	151,669	266,282	NAB57a	99-AGCA-ba	iyi-rikum		83.00	125,885	0....	10	7	11	4	2	Meta	p..	.
1762	Woko (Longa, Gobeyo)	0.02631	3,468	3,969	6,968	NAB66c	92-BCCA-a	longto		40.00	1,588	0....	9	6	5	3	1		...	.
1763	Wom	0.14250	18,784	21,496	37,740	NAB66c	92-BDAB-j	wom		40.00	8,598	0....	9	6	6	3	1		...	b
1764	Wuzlam (Uzam)	0.11509	15,171	17,361	30,481	NAB60b	18-EACA-a	wuzlam		4.00	694	0....	6	4	5	1	2	Wuzlam	...	.
1765	Yambasa (Nu Gunu)	0.33647	44,354	50,756	89,112	NAB57k	99-ANBB-b	nu-gunu		80.00	40,605	0....	10	7	7	4	1	Nugunu	...	.
1766	Yambetta (Nedek, Nigii)	0.04056	5,347	6,118	10,742	NAB57k	99-ANAA	nigi cluster		50.00	3,059	0....	10	7	7	4	1		...	.
1767	Yangben	0.01786	2,354	2,694	4,730	NAB57k	99-ANBC-b	nu-yangben		50.00	1,347	0....	10	6	6	4	1		...	.
1768	Yasa (Yassa, Maasa)	0.01000	1,318	1,508	2,648	NAB57k	99-AUAD-a	yasa		80.00	1,207	0....	10	8	5	4	1		pn.	.
1769	Yerwa Kanuri (Beriberi)	0.61931	81,638	93,423	164,021	NAB61	02-AAAA-b	yerwa	1	0.02	19	4....	3	2	5	0	0	Kanuri*	PN.	.
1770	Yukuben (Nyikobe)	0.00916	1,207	1,382	2,426	NAB56b	98-HBFB-a	yukuben		40.00	553	0....	9	5	6	3	0		...	.
1771	Ziziliveken	0.00233	307	351	617	NAB60b	18-IBAA-o	ziziliveken		3.00	11	0....	6	4	5	1	1		p..	.
1772	Zulgo (Zelgwa, Mineo)	0.19730	26,008	29,763	52,254	NAB60b	18-EADA-a	zulgwa		4.00	1,191	0....	6	4	6	1	1	Zulgo*	PN.	.
1773	Zumaya	0.00040	53	60	106	NAB60b	17-FAAB-a	zumaya		20.00	12	0....	9	5	7	2	0		...	.
1774	other minor peoples	2.51527	331,564	379,428	666,154	...				25.00	94,857		9	5	6	2	0			
	Canada	**100.00000**	**29,617,448**	**31,146,639**	**37,896,497**					**64.98**	**20,237,779**									
1775	Abnaki-Penobscot	0.00700	2,073	2,180	2,653	MIR38a	62-AEAC	abenaki cluster		91.70	1,999	0....	10	7	11	4	1	Abenaqui*	P..	b
1776	Acadian (Cajun French)	0.04000	11,847	12,459	15,159	CEW21b	51-AABH-o	acadjin		90.00	11,213	0c.uh	10	8	11	3	1		p..	b
1777	Algonkin	0.01933	5,725	6,021	7,325	MIR38a	62-ADAD-a	anissinapek		96.00	5,780	0....	10	7	11	4	1	Algonquin	P..	b

Continued opposite

Table 8-2 continued

Ref 1	D 28	aC 29	CG% 30	r 31	E 32	U 33	W 34	e 35	R 36	T 37	ADDITIONAL DESCRIPTIVE DATA: Locations, civil divisions, literacy, religions, church history, denominations, dioceses, church growth, missions, agencies, ministries, movements 38
		EVANGELIZATION						EVANGELISM			
1656	1	6	8.29	0	99.80	0.20	C	338.72	229	9	Along Sanaga river, Saa Subdivision, Lekie Division, Centre Province. Related to Beti, Fang. Also speak Leti. Animists 20%. D=RCC.
1657	2	6	8.92	0	57.00	43.00	B	41.61	496	6	Around Yagoua, Mayo-Danay Division, Far North Province. Densely settled area. Animists 55%, Muslims 25%. D=EFLC,RCC. M=LBWM,UBS.
1658	0	6	2.79	0	23.00	77.00	A	1.67	498	4	In Maltam and Saho, Makari Subdivision, Far North Province. Animists 90%, Muslims 8%.
1659	2	6	5.86	0	43.00	57.00	A	15.69	462	5	Eastern edge of Mandara Mts, Mora Subdivision, Far North Province. Related to Podoko. Animists 90%. D=RCC,UEENC.
1660	1	6	4.42	0	85.00	15.00	B	155.12	182	7	Nwa Subdivision, Donga-Mantung Division, North West Province. Language is being replaced by Tikari. Animists 50%. D=RCC.
1661	1	6	4.84	0	81.00	19.00	B	147.82	211	7	Northeast of Hina, Mokolo Subdivision, Mayo-Tsanaga Division, Far North Province. Animists 40%, Muslims 10%. D=RCC.
1662	1	6	6.37	4	99.80	0.20	C	353.32	186	9	Mainly in, and from, Gbaya of CAR. Animists 18%, Muslims 2%. D=RCC.
1663	2	6	6.25	1	99.70	0.30	C	270.83	200	8	Gari-Gombo Subdivision, Boumba and Ngoko Division, East Province. Animists 30%. D=RCC,EPC.
1664	4	6	8.03	0	99.78	0.22	C	324.55	226	9	Moungo Division, Littoral Province, also West and South West Provinces. Animists 20%. D=RCC(D-Nkongsamba),EPC,EEC,PCC. M=SIL.
1665	0	6	3.70	0	53.00	47.00	B	48.36	263	6	Near Betare-Oya, Lom and Djerem Division, East Province. Also in Nigeria. Animists 75%.
1666	1	6	4.82	0	36.00	64.00	A	13.14	473	5	Mbuko massif and plain, Meri Subdivision, Diamare Division, Far North Province. Animists 70%, Muslims 20%. D=UEENC.
1667	2	6	7.93	0	88.00	12.00	B	160.60	285	7	Central Nwa Subdivision, Donga-Mantung Division, North West Province. Seasonal migrants to Nigeria. Animists 50%. D=CBC,EELC. M=SIL.
1668	2	6	7.65	1	65.00	35.00	B	59.31	400	6	Isolated groups around Ngaoundere; some in Chad,CAR. Lingua franca. Bilingual in Fulani. Muslims 60%(Maliki Sunnis,still expanding), animists 15%. D=EELC.
1669	0	6	4.94	0	34.00	66.00	A	12.41	510	5	South and east of Mokolo, Mayo-Tsanaga Division, Far North Province. Animists 70%, Muslims 20%.
1670	2	7	5.73	0	93.00	7.00	C	203.67	212	8	Northeast of Wum, Menchum Division, North West Province. Animists 40%. D=AICs,RCC.
1671	0	6	6.61	0	67.00	33.00	B	97.82	344	6	Leti is secret language of tradition. Along bend of Sanaga river, Saa Sub-Division, Lekie Division, Centre Province. Animists 60%.
1672	1	6	7.69	0	99.80	0.20	C	332.88	214	9	West of Mbwengi, Batibo Subdivision, Momo Division, North West Province. Animists 20%. D=RCC.
1673	2	6	5.24	0	40.00	60.00	A	14.60	454	5	West of Meri, Diamare Division, Far North Province. Animists 70%, Muslims 20%. D=RCC,UEENC.
1674	1	6	5.14	0	82.00	18.00	B	149.65	218	7	Village of Missong, Wum Subdivision, Menchum Division, North West Province. Animists 50%. D=RCC.
1675	4	6	7.59	0	45.00	55.00	A	6.57	547	4	Far North Province; a few in Nigeria. Animists 76%, Muslims 20%. Y=1950. D=RCC,SDA,UEENC,AIC. M=SUM(Swiss,Norwegian),UBS.
1676	1	5	4.04	0	30.00	70.00	A	5.47	496	4	Village of Mokyo, Tokombere Subdivision, Mayo-Sava Division, Far North Province. Over 70% bilingual in Fulani. Muslims 50%, animists 45%. D=SDA.
1677	1	6	5.04	0	99.75	0.25	C	292.91	176	8	North of Rey-Bouba, Mayo-Rey Division, North Province. Related to Dama. Animists 25%. D=RCC.
1678	1	7	4.42	0	82.00	18.00	B	149.65	194	7	Around Lake Chad, Logone and Chari Division, Far North Province. Animists 40%, Muslims 10%. D=RCC.
1679	2	7	7.36	0	86.00	14.00	B	156.95	293	7	North of Ngaoundere, North Province. Also in Nigeria. Muslims 30%, animists 20%. D=AICs,RCC.
1680	2	6	6.60	1	99.80	0.20	C	353.32	190	9	Small pocket north of Edea, Sanaga mouth, Littoral Province. Animists 20%. D=AICs,RCC.
1681	3	5	8.40	1	49.50	50.50	A	15.35	533	5	Noun Division around Foumban, et alia. Own script. Lingua franca. Muslims 90%(Maliki Sunnis), animists 1%. D=RCC,EEC,EELC. M=UBS.
1682	1	6	3.70	0	33.00	67.00	A	6.02	459	4	Migrants from large Nigeria tribe. Literates 5%. Animists 86%, Muslims 9%. D=RCC. M=SUM.
1683	2	6	8.65	0	84.00	16.00	B	122.64	329	7	Kaele Division. Majority in Chad. Animists 40%, Muslims 20%(1962: many Muslims revert to tribal religion). D=EFLC,AIC. M=UBS,LBWM,EET.
1684	2	7	8.63	1	99.80	0.20	C	350.40	225	9	South of Batibo, Manyu Division, South West Province. Mountainous. Animists 20%. D=Presbyterian Ch of Cameroon,EEC. M=Full Gospel Mission,SIL,PEMS.
1685	1	6	5.50	0	99.70	0.30	C	260.61	185	8	Northeast of Wum, Menchum Division, North West Province. Animists 30%. D=RCC.
1686	1	7	5.86	0	44.00	56.00	A	16.06	451	5	Mayo-Danay Division, Far North Province. Great majority are in Chad. Animists 90%. D=EFLC. M=UBS,LBWM.
1687	1	6	8.06	0	56.00	44.00	B	40.88	462	6	Maga Subdivision, Mayo-Danay Division, Far North Province. Also in Chad. Animists 55%, Muslims 25%. D=AIC. M=UBS,LBWM.
1688	2	5	4.40	0	27.00	73.00	A	2.95	588	4	Massifs northeast of Tokombere, Mayo-Sava Division, Far North Province. Animists 60%, Muslims 37%. D=RCC,SDA.
1689	1	6	4.42	0	81.00	19.00	B	147.82	197	7	Misaje village, western Nkambe Subdivision, Donga-Mantung Division, North West Province. Animists 50%. D=RCC.
1690	1	7	5.64	0	99.80	0.20	C	338.72	166	9	Northeast of Nkambe, Donga-Mantung Division, North West Province. Animists 20%. D=RCC.
1691	1	7	5.64	0	99.80	0.20	C	335.80	167	9	Close to Mfumte languages. Northeast of Nkambe, Donga-Mantung Division, North West Province. Animists 20%. D=RCC.
1692	0	6	4.18	0	33.00	67.00	A	12.04	448	5	Nkam Division, Littoral Province. Tribal religionists(animists) 60%, Muslims 30%.
1693	1	6	7.69	0	99.80	0.20	C	341.64	209	9	Village of Bamessing, Ndop Subdivision, Mezam Division, North West Province. Animists 20%. D=RCC. M=SIL.
1694	1	6	7.90	0	99.80	0.20	C	338.72	215	9	Around village of Bamunka, Ndop Subdivision, Mezam Division, North West Province. Animists 20%. D=RCC.
1695	3	6	5.35	0	99.85	0.15	C	375.40	153	9	Dodeo village, Faro and Deo Division, Adamawa Province; also North West Province. Primarily in Nigeria. Animists 15%. D=RCC,AICs,Protestants.
1696	3	6	4.21	0	33.00	67.00	A	6.02	465	4	Southern Mora massif, Mayo-Sava Division, Far North Province. Animists 90%, Muslims 5%. D=RCC,UEENC,SDA.
1697	4	6	8.31	0	88.00	12.00	B	160.60	297	7	Mbam Division, Centre Province. Animists 50%. D=RCC,EPC,UEBC,EEC.
1698	1	7	8.43	0	99.80	0.20	C	341.64	226	9	14 villages east of Nkambe, Nwa Subdivision, North West Province. Animists 20%. D=CBC.
1699	6	6	9.48	1	99.74	0.26	C	299.81	264	8	Tuba and Bamenda Subdivisions, Mezam Division, North West Province. Animists 25%. D=RCC,PCC,CBC,WEBC,EPC,EEC. M=SIL.
1700	3	6	8.68	1	99.80	0.20	C	350.40	226	9	Western Mbengwi Subdivision, Momo Division, North West Province. Animists 20%. D=EPC,RCC,PCC.
1701	2	6	7.63	0	99.70	0.30	C	278.49	222	8	North of Ndop on Ndop Plain, Mezam Division, North West Province. Animists 30%. D=PCC,RCC. M=SIL.
1702	2	7	7.15	0	47.00	53.00	A	30.87	498	5	On Nigerian border, Mokolo Province; also in Nigeria. Animists 62%, Muslims 20%. D=AICs,RCC.
1703	2	6	6.55	0	99.99	0.01	C	513.11	161	10	In forests, Kribi and Lolodorf Subdivisions, Ocean Division, South Province. Also Equatorial Guinea. Animists 1%. D=Eglise Protestante Africaine,EPC.
1704	1	6	8.67	1	99.80	0.20	C	347.48	228	9	Njikwa District, Momo Division, North West Province. Animists 20%. D=RCC.
1705	1	7	5.03	0	60.00	40.00	B	65.70	295	6	Near Pitoa, Benoue and Mayo-Louti Divisions, North Province. Muslims 40%, animists 30%. D=RCC.
1706	3	6	10.04	1	99.68	0.32	C	268.05	286	8	Southern part of Fundong Subdivision, Menchum Division, North West Province. Animists 30%. D=RCC,PCC,CBC. M=SIL.
1707	2	6	6.40	0	85.00	15.00	B	155.12	264	7	Southwest of Bafia, Bokito Subdivision, Mbum Division, Centre Province. Animists 50%. D=RCC,EPC. M=SIL.
1708	3	7	7.98	0	87.00	13.00	B	158.77	295	7	Northwestern Kumbo Subdivision, Bui Division, North West Province. Animists 50%. D=RCC,PCC,CBC. M=SIL.
1709	0	5	3.33	0	23.00	77.00	A	0.84	615	3	Mayo-Oulo Subdivision, North Province. Speakers switching to Fulfulde. Muslim 80%, animists 19%.
1710	4	6	6.82	0	53.00	47.00	B	38.69	424	5	North and west of Maroua, Diamare Division, Far North Province. Animists 80%, falling rapidly to Christianity, rejecting Islam. D=SDA,EFLC,RCC,UEENC. M=UBS.
1711	2	6	6.88	1	96.00	4.00	C	210.24	238	8	North of Upper Nyong Division, East Province. Animists 30%, Muslims 10%. D=RCC,EPC.
1712	2	6	5.88	0	36.00	64.00	A	6.57	553	4	Massifs south of Meri, Diamare Division, Far North Province. Animists 75%, Muslims 20%. D=RCC,EFLC. M=SIL.
1713	1	6	4.15	0	83.00	17.00	B	151.47	183	7	Northeast of Wum, Wum Subdivision, Menchum Division, North West Province. Animists 50%. D=RCC.
1714	4	6	10.04	1	99.79	0.21	C	363.32	245	9	Northeast of Bamenda, Bui Division, North West Province. Animists 20%. D=RCC(D-Buea),PCC,CBC,CC. M=SIL,MHM,UBS.
1715	3	6	9.72	0	99.84	0.16	C	398.58	231	9	Nkambe Subdivision, North West Province. Lingua franca. Animists 15%. D=RCC,PCC,CBC. M=SIL.
1716	2	7	8.44	0	86.00	14.00	B	156.95	308	7	Southwest of Mamfe, Manyu Division, South West Province. Animists 50%. D=PCC,RCC. M=SIL.
1717	1	6	2.75	1	36.00	64.00	A	6.57	302	4	Southeast of Batibo, Momo Division, North West Province. Muslims 50%, animists 45%. D=EFLC. M=LBWM. Fulani literature used.
1718	1	6	3.17	1	50.00	50.00	B	27.37	274	5	Around Touboro, Touboro Subdivision. Animists 85%. D=UEENC.
1719	0	6	5.12	0	34.00	66.00	A	12.41	525	5	Mayo-Oulo Subdivision, Mayo-Louti Division, North Province. 75% live in Nigeria. Muslims 60%, animists 30%.
1720	3	6	7.42	0	99.85	0.15	C	390.91	192	9	Mainly in Calabar (Nigeria). Animists 15%. D=RCC,AoG,AICs.
1721	2	6	3.89	1	64.00	36.00	B	70.08	245	6	Near Tchollire, Mayo-Rey Division, North Province. Muslims 50%, animists 20%. D=RCC,AICs.
1722	2	6	8.49	1	99.70	0.30	C	273.38	249	8	Around Mt Oku, Bui Division, North West Province. Animists 30%. D=RCC,CBC. M=SIL.
1723	2	7	4.31	0	80.00	20.00	B	131.40	195	7	Southeast of Asumbo, Akwaya Subdivision, South West Province. Second language: Pidgin. Animists 55%. D=RCC,AICs.
1724	1	7	6.50	1	99.70	0.30	C	273.38	198	8	East Njikwa Subdivision, Momo Division, North West Province. Close to Ngwo. Animists 30%. D=RCC.
1725	2	6	6.61	1	78.00	22.00	B	113.88	296	7	Near Tchollire, Mayo-Rey Division, North Province. Muslims 40%, animists 20%. D=RCC,AICs.
1726	3	7	5.34	1	99.60	0.40	C	219.00	185	8	In CAR, Chad, Cameroon across junction of borders. Touboro Subdivision, Mayo-Rey Division, North Province. Muslims 25%, animists 15%. D=RCC,EFLC,EELC.
1727	2	6	6.76	1	98.00	2.00	C	214.62	240	8	In Pandjama and Touboro, Mayo-Rey Division, North Province. Close to Karang, Pana. Muslims 20%, animists 20%. D=RCC,EELC. M=ALM.
1728	1	7	5.66	0	71.00	29.00	B	103.66	289	7	Southeast of Poli, Poli Subdivision, Faro Division, North Province. Close to Dii (Duru). Animists 55%, Muslims 5%. D=EELC. M=UBS.
1729	2	7	4.70	0	50.00	50.00	B	31.02	334	5	Northeast of Tchollire, Mayo-Rey Division, North Province. Most in Chad. Animists 75%, a few Muslims. D=EFLC,EELC. M=UBS.
1730	2	7	7.96	1	99.80	0.20	C	350.40	213	9	Southwest of Bamenda Subdivision, Mezam Division, North West Province. Animists 20%. D=RCC,PCC.
1731	2	6	7.41	1	99.70	0.30	C	270.83	230	8	South and west of Yokadouma, East Province. Close to Mpyemo, Konabembe. Animists 30%. D=RCC,EPC.
1732	2	6	6.07	0	41.00	59.00	A	14.96	499	5	Mora Subdivision, Mayo-Sava Division, Far North Province. Animists 90%. D=RCC,UEENC. M=SIL.
1733	2	7	8.53	2	99.65	0.35	C	246.74	263	8	Mbang Subdivision, Kadey Division; Boumba-and-Ngoko Division, East Province. Monolinguals. Animists 35%. D=RCC,EPC.
1734	0	6	8.38	0	99.70	0.30	C	258.05	276	8	East of Doume, Dimako Subdivision, Upper Nyong Division, East Province. Also in Congo, CAR. Animists 30%.
1735	2	7	5.64	4	99.80	0.20	C	414.64	136	10	Speakers of Sango lingua franca from CAR. Animists 20%. D=RCC,EBRCA. R=ELWA.
1736	2	6	5.34	4	99.60	0.40	C	245.28	166	8	Mainly in Chad, also CAR, Nigeria. Literates. Animists 40%. D=Brethren, Baptists.
1737	1	6	6.44	2	99.65	0.35	C	270.46	189	8	Near Chad border, Mayo-Rey Division. Primarily in Chad, some in Nigeria. Muslims 20%, animists 15%. D=EELC. M=EET,TEAM. R=ELWA.
1738	2	7	5.29	0	62.00	38.00	B	67.89	297	6	In isolated massif southeast of Poli, Faro Division, North Province. Related to Pape. Animists 60%, Muslims 10%. D=RCC,EELC.
1739	0	5	2.22	0	24.00	76.00	A	0.87	412	3	Southern Bourrah Subdivision, Mayo-Tsanaga Division, Far North Province. Also in Chad. Muslims 99%. M=EET.
1740	0	5	3.35	7	28.02	71.98	A	0.02	396	2	Black Arabs. Far North Province. Mainly in Nigeria, Chad, Niger. Chad Arabs, Saharan Arabs. Nomads. Lingua franca. Muslims 100%(Maliki Sunnis).
1741	1	6	6.68	1	97.00	3.00	C	212.43	230	8	East of Akonolinga, Nyong and Mfoumou Division, Centre Province. Animists 40%. D=RCC.
1742	2	6	5.97	0	43.00	57.00	A	15.69	497	5	Benoue Division, North Province. Muslims 80%, animists 10%. D=RCC,EFLC. M=SIL,LBWM.
1743	4	5	4.40	0	30.00	70.00	A	1.09	529	4	Southwest of Maroua, Diamare Division, Far North Province. Animists 99%, rejecting Islam. D=EFLC,RCC,UEENC,EELC. M=UBS.
1744	4	6	9.25	1	98.00	2.00	C	214.62	300	8	Northern part of Upper Nyong Division, East Province. Animists 30%, Muslims 10%. D=RCC,PCC,EPC,RCC(D-Douma). M=SIL,CSS.
1745	4	6	6.11	0	35.00	65.00	A	6.38	587	4	Mokolo Subdivision, Far North Province. Animists 75%, Muslims 20% and expanding. D=RCC,UEBC,UEENC,SDA. M=SIL,EBMS.
1746	2	6	8.67	0	99.80	0.20	C	341.64	236	9	East of Wum, Menchum Division, North West Province. Animists 20%. D=Baptists, AICs.
1747	1	7	2.23	1	99.79	0.21	C	325.83	98	9	Around Bimbia estuary, Tiko Subdivision, Fako Division, South West Province. Animists 21%. D=CBC.
1748	1	6	7.37	0	99.80	0.20	C	332.88	211	9	Around Galim, Faro and Deo Division, also Mayo-Banyo Division, Adamawa Province. Animists 15%, Muslims 5%. D=EELC.
1749	1	6	5.02	0	59.00	41.00	B	64.60	300	6	In North Province, also in Nigeria. Animists 60%, Muslims 10%. D=RCC.
1750	1	6	4.18	0	28.00	72.00	A	4.08	545	4	Northeast of Dourbeye, Bourrah Subdivision, Mayo Tsanaga Division, Far North Province. Muslims 96%. D=UEENC.
1751	3	6	6.60	0	39.00	61.00	A	14.23	561	5	North of Nkambe, Ako District, Donga-Mantung Division, North West Province. A few in Nigeria. Animists 90%. D=PCC,CBC,RCC. M=SIL.
1752	3	6	5.97	0	43.00	57.00	A	15.69	458	5	Northwest of Yoko; Centre, Adamawa, and West Provinces. Animists 60%, Muslims 30%(Maliki Sunnis). D=RCC,EELC,EEC. M=SIL,NMS.
1753	2	5	9.23	0	78.00	22.00	B	113.88	373	7	Kaele and Mayo-Danay Divisions, Far North Province. Similar number in Chad. Densely settled. Farmers, stockraisers. Animists 60%. D=RCC,EFLC.
1754	1	6	4.45	0	83.00	17.00	B	151.47	206	7	Village of Bonke, Bafia Subdivision, Mbam Division, Center Province. Many urbanites. Animists 50%. D=RCC.
1755	0	6	0.00	7	19.00	81.00	A	0.00	0	1.04	Arabic-based creole, lingua franca across to Southern Sudan. Muslims 90%, animists 10%.
1756	0	5	4.21	0	27.00	73.00	A	4.92	568	4	Sanga village, north of Bankim, Adamawa Province. Bilingual in Kwanja. Muslims 95%.
1757	1	6	5.74	0	70.00	30.00	B	102.20	296	7	North of Tchamba on border, Beka District, Faro Division, North Province. Mainly in Nigeria. Animists 50%, Muslims 10%. D=RCC.
1758	3	6	8.02	0	88.00	12.00	B	160.60	293	7	In Centre, Adamawa, and East Provinces; a few in Nigeria. Animists 40%, Muslims 10%. D=RCC,EFLC,EELC. M=NMS,SIL.
1759	0	5	2.96	0	31.00	69.00	A	5.65	384	4	West of Banyo, Bankim Subdivision, Adamawa Province. 13 villages. Second language: Fulani. Muslims 90%.
1760	1	7	6.54	0	99.70	0.30	C	265.72	204	8	Village of Weh, Wum Subdivision, Menchum Division, North West Province. Closely related to Aghem, Fungom. Animists 30%. D=Baptists.
1761	2	6	9.90	1	99.83	0.17	C	378.68	244	9	Mbengwi and Batibo Subdivisions, Momo Division, North West Province. Animists 15%. D=PCC,RCC(D-Buea). M=MHM,SIL.
1762	1	7	5.20	0	70.00	30.00	B	102.20	275	7	Around Voko, Faro Division, North Province. Also Nigeria. Related to Kolbila. Muslims 60%. D=EELC.
1763	1	6	6.99	0	70.00	30.00	B	102.20	345	7	Southwest of Garoua, North Province. Also in Nigeria. Closely related to Chamba. Animists 50%, Muslims 10%. D=EELC.
1764	2	6	4.33	0	29.00	71.00	A	4.23	540	4	Wuzlam massif south of Mora, Tokombere Subdivision, Mayo-Sava Division, Far North Province. Animists 80%, Muslims 16%. D=RCC,UEENC.
1765	2	6	8.66	0	99.80	0.20	C	335.80	249	9	Ombessa and Bokito Subdivisions, Mbam Division, Centre Province. Animists 20%. D=RCC,EPC. M=SIL.
1766	1	6	5.89	0	83.00	17.00	B	151.47	254	7	Bafia Subdivision northwest of Bafia, Mbam Division, Centre Province. Animists 50%. D=RCC. M=SIL.
1767	1	7	5.03	0	83.00	17.00	B	151.47	225	7	Yangben canton south of Bokito, Bokito Subdivision, Mbam Division, Centre Province. Related to Dumbule. Animists 50%. D=RCC.
1768	1	7	4.91	1	99.80	0.20	C	338.72	158	9	Campo Subdivision on coast, Ocean Division, South Province; also in Equatorial Guinea. Animists 20%. D=RCC.
1769	0	5	2.99	4	28.02	71.98	A	0.02	429	2	Bomu, Dagara, Mao. Mayo-Sava Division, Far North Province. Mainly in Nigeria, Chad, Sudan, Niger. Muslims 100%(Sunnis).
1770	0	6	4.09	0	67.00	33.00	B	97.82	224	6	Near Nigeria border west of Furu-Awa, Menchum Division, North West Province. Also in Nigeria. Animists 60%.
1771	1	5	2.43	0	26.00	74.00	A	2.84	403	4	Near Nigeria border, Bourrah Subdivision, Mayo-Tsanoga Division, Far North Province. Muslims 97%(Maliki Sunnis). D=UEENC.
1772	2	6	4.90	0	34.00	66.00	A	4.96	507	4	Eastern edge of Mandara Mts, Mayo-Sava Division, Far North Province. Stone Age culture. Animists 86%, Muslims 10%. D=UEENC,SDA. M=SIL.
1773	0	6	2.52	0	47.00	53.00	A	34.31	228	5	Ouro-Lamorde, Maroua Subdivision, Diamare Division, Far North Province. Nearly extinct. Muslims 70%, animists 10%.
1774	0	6	9.59		49.00	51.00	A	44.71	536	6	Tiv, Koreans (Korea Harbor Mission), Europeans(50,000), other Africans(200,000) including 45,000 refugees from Chad. Muslims 65%.
Canada											
1775	1	10	1.73	0	99.92	0.08	C	460.88	52	10	Quebec. 99% use French or English; mother tongue only used by few elderly. D=RCC.
1776	1	10	1.73	2	99.90	0.10	C	456.61	53	10	French-speaking Acadians in north of New Brunswick Province. D=RCC. M=OM.
1777	1	9	1.73	0	99.96	0.04	C	494.06	51	10	Southwest Quebec. Only 60% (mainly adults) now speak language. D=RCC. M=SIL.

Continued overleaf

Table 8-2 continued

PEOPLE		POPULATION				IDENTITY CODE		LANGUAGE		CHURCH		MINISTRY						SCRIPTURE	
Ref 1	Ethnic name 2	P% 3	In 1995 4	In 2000 5	In 2025 6	Race 7	Language 8	Autoglossonym 9	S 10	AC 11	Members 12	Jayuh 13-17	d 18	wa 19	xc 20	mc 21	mi 22	Biblioglossonym 23	Pub ss 24-26 27
1778	Anglo-Canadian	45.48746	13,472,225	14,167,815	17,238,154	CEW19d	52-ABAC-r	general canadian		65.60	9,294,087	1Bsuh	10	9	16	5	3		pnb b
1779	Anglo-Canadian Jew	1.20801	357,782	376,255	457,793	CMT35	52-ABAC-r	general canadian		1.50	5,644	1Bsuh	6	5	6	5	1		pnb b
1780	Armenian	0.07039	20,848	21,924	26,675	CEW14	57-AAAA-b	ashkharik		90.00	19,732	4A.u.	10	9	13	5	2	Armenian: Modern, Eastern	PNB b
1781	Assiniboin	0.01000	2,962	3,115	3,790	MIR38a	64-AACA-a	assiniboine		96.00	2,990	0....	10	7	11	4	0		pnb b
1782	Atikamek	0.01258	3,726	3,918	4,767	MIR38a	62-ADAC	atikamek cluster		96.00	3,762	0....	10	7	11	4	2	Atikamekw	P.. .
1783	Babine	0.00900	2,666	2,803	3,411	MIR38a	61-BAEE-a	babine-hagwilgate		97.00	2,719	0....	10	8	11	4	1	Carrier: Northern*	Pn. b
1784	Beaver (Tsattine, Castor)	0.00223	660	695	845	MIR38a	61-BAED-a	beaver		96.00	667	0....	10	8	11	4	2	Beaver	P.. b
1785	Bella Coola	0.00264	782	822	1,000	MIR38a	63-EAAB	heiltsuk cluster		98.00	806	0....	10	8	11	4	0		... b
1786	Bengali	0.01175	3,480	3,660	4,453	CNN25b	59-AAFT-e	west bengali		0.60	22	1Asuh	5	5	8	3	3	Bengali: Musalmani*	PNB b
1787	Blackfoot (Piegon, Blood)	0.04204	12,451	13,094	15,932	MIR38a	62-AAAA-a	sikasi-ka		96.00	12,570	0a...	10	8	11	4	3	Blackfoot	P.. b
1788	British	3.30000	977,376	1,027,839	1,250,584	CEW19i	52-ABAC-b	standard-english	81	67.00	688,652	3Bsuh	10	9	15	5	3		PNB b
1789	Bulgar	0.00799	2,366	2,489	3,028	CEW22b	53-AAAH-b	bulgarski		79.00	1,966	2A.uh	10	9	11	5	1	Bulgarian	PNB b
1790	Byelorussian	0.00255	755	794	966	CEW22c	53-AAAE-c	bielorusskiy		77.00	612	3A.uh	10	9	11	5	1	Byelorussian*	PNB b
1791	Carrier	0.00812	2,405	2,529	3,077	MIR38a	61-BAEE-c	south carrier		96.00	2,428	0....	10	8	11	4	2		pn. b
1792	Cayuga	0.01000	2,962	3,115	3,790	MIR38a	64-CAAD-b	cayuga		91.90	2,862	0....	10	8	11	4	0		p.. b
1793	Central Cree	0.01100	3,258	3,426	4,169	MIR38a	62-ADAA-d	east swampy-cree		97.00	3,323	1.s..	10	8	12	4	3		pnb b
1794	Central Cree (Moose)	0.01000	2,962	3,115	3,790	MIR38a	62-ADAA-e	moose-cree		97.00	3,021	1.s..	10	8	12	4	1	Cree: Moose*	PNb b
1795	Chilcotin	0.00735	2,177	2,289	2,785	MIR38a	61-BAEE-d	chilcotin		96.00	2,198	0....	10	8	11	4	2	Chilcotin	Pn. b
1796	Chinook Wawa	0.00030	89	93	114	MIR38b	63-JAAC-a	chinook-wawa		90.00	84	0....	10	8	11	4	0	Chinook*	P.. b
1797	Chipewyan	0.02041	6,045	6,357	7,735	MIR38a	61-BAEE-g	chipewyan		96.00	6,103	1....	10	8	11	4	1	Chipewyan	PN. b
1798	Comox	0.00345	1,022	1,075	1,307	MIR38a	63-GAAA-a	comox		92.00	989	0....	10	8	11	4	0		... b
1799	Croat	0.13232	39,190	41,213	50,145	CEW22d	53-AAAG-b	standard hrvatski		91.00	37,504	2Asuh	10	9	13	5	1	Croatian	PNB b
1800	Czech	0.09491	28,110	29,561	35,968	CEW22e	53-AAAD-a	czesky		90.00	26,605	2Asuh	10	9	12	5	2	Czech	PNB b
1801	Dakota (Sioux, Santee)	0.01200	3,554	3,738	4,548	MIR38a	64-AACA-e	east dakota		98.00	3,663	0....	10	9	12	5	3	Dakota	PNB b
1802	Danish (Dane)	0.10463	30,989	32,589	39,651	CEW19g	52-AAAD-c	general dansk		95.00	30,959	2A.uh	10	9	12	5	2	Danish	PNB b
1803	Delaware (Lenni-Lenape)	0.00151	447	470	572	MIR38a	62-AEBB-a	munsee		90.00	423	0....	10	8	11	4	0	Delaware*	P.. b
1804	Detribalized Amerindian	0.51400	152,234	160,094	194,788	MIR38y	52-ABAC-r	general canadian		90.00	144,084	1Bsuh	10	9	12	5	3		pnb b
1805	Dogrib	0.00934	2,766	2,909	3,540	MIR38a	61-BAEC-d	dogrib		95.00	2,764	1....	10	8	11	4	1	Dogrib	pn. .
1806	Dutch	0.59593	176,499	185,612	225,837	CEW19h	52-ABCA-a	algemeen-nederlands		76.00	141,065	2Bsuh	10	9	15	5	1	Dutch	PNB b
1807	Eastern Arctic Eskimo	0.04200	12,439	13,082	15,917	MRY40b	60-ABBD-a	ungava		96.00	12,558	1....	10	8	13	3	1	Inuktitut: Eastern Arctic*	PNB b
1808	Eastern Coastal Cree	0.02242	6,640	6,983	8,496	MIR38a	62-ADAA-f	east cree		97.00	6,774	1.s..	10	8	11	4	0	Cree: East Coast*	Pnb b
1809	Eastern Ojibwa (Chippewa)	0.07000	20,732	21,803	26,528	MIR38a	62-ADAF-a	east ojibwa		96.00	20,931	0....	10	8	11	4	1	Ojibwa, Eastern	Pn. b
1810	Egyptian Arab	0.50000	148,087	155,733	189,482	CMT30	12-AACF-a	masri		60.00	93,440	2Asuh	10	6	8	5	1	Arabic*	PNB b
1811	English Gypsy (Romanichal)	0.01000	2,962	3,115	3,790	CNN25f	52-ABAC-b	standard-english		80.00	2,492	3Bsuh	10	7	7	4	1		PNB b
1812	Eskimo	0.01000	2,962	3,115	3,790	MRY40b	52-ABAC-s	general american		90.00	2,803	1Bsuh	10	8	13	4	3	English*	PNB b
1813	Esperanto	0.00000	0	0	0	CEW21z	51-AAAC-a	proper esperanto		60.00	0	0A...	10	8	6	5	0	Esperanto	PNB b
1814	Estonian	0.05369	15,902	16,723	20,347	MSW51a	41-AAAC-b	eesti		80.00	13,378	4A.u.	10	9	8	5	2	Estonian: Tallinn	PNB b
1815	Finnish (Finn)	0.13714	40,617	42,715	51,971	MSW51b	41-AAAA-bb	vehicular suomi		87.00	37,162	1A.uh	10	9	12	5	2	Finnish	PNB b
1816	Fleming	0.04030	11,936	12,552	15,272	CEW19k	52-ABCA-g	oostvlaandersch		90.00	11,297	1Bsuh	10	9	15	5	1		pnb b
1817	French	0.40000	118,470	124,587	151,586	CEW21b	51-AABI-d	general français	31	87.00	108,390	1B.uh	10	9	14	5	1	French	PNB b
1818	French Cree	0.04000	11,847	12,459	15,159	MIR38b	62-ADBA-a	mitchif		97.00	12,085	0....	10	8	14	4	3		... b
1819	French-Canadian	23.47653	6,953,149	7,312,150	8,896,782	CEW21c	51-AABI-ib	français-du-canada		68.50	5,008,823	1B.uh	10	9	15	5	3		pnb b
1820	Frisian	0.00725	2,147	2,258	2,747	CEW19l	52-ABBA-a	west-frysk		72.00	1,626	0....	10	9	8	5	2		pnb b
1821	German	2.14782	636,129	668,974	813,949	CEW19m	52-ABCE-a	standard hoch-deutsch		88.00	588,697	2B.uh	10	9	13	5	3	German*	PNB b
1822	German Jew	0.20000	59,235	62,293	75,793	CMT35	52-ABCH-a	west yiddish		0.80	498	0B..h	5	4	3	5	0	Yiddish	PNB b
1823	Greek	0.50509	149,595	157,319	191,411	CEW20	56-AAAA-c	dhimotiki		95.00	149,453	2B.uh	10	9	10	5	3	Greek: Modern	PNB b
1824	Haida	0.00400	1,185	1,246	1,516	MIR38a	63-BAAB-a	skidegate		93.20	1,161	0....	10	8	11	4	1	Haida	P.. b
1825	Haisla	0.00400	1,185	1,246	1,516	MIR38a	63-EAAA-a	hais-la		92.00	1,146	0....	10	8	11	4	1		... b
1826	Haitian	0.10000	29,617	31,147	37,896	NFB69a	51-AACC-b	haitien		95.00	29,589	3As..	10	7	12	4	3	Haitian*	PNB b
1827	Halkomelem	0.02888	8,554	8,995	10,945	MIR38a	63-GAAE	halkomelem cluster		90.00	8,096	0....	10	8	10	4	0		... b
1828	Han (Moosehide)	0.00100	296	311	379	MIR38a	61-BAEB-a	han		91.00	283	0....	10	8	11	4	0		pnb b
1829	Han Chinese	3.40000	1,006,993	1,058,986	1,288,481	MSY42a	79-AAAB-ba	kuo-yü		14.00	148,258	2Bsuh	8	5	12	5	2	Chinese: Kuoyu*	PNB b
1830	Heiltsuk	0.00517	1,531	1,610	1,959	MIR38a	63-EAAB-a	proper heiltsuk		91.00	1,465	0....	10	8	11	4	0		... b
1831	Hindi	0.14000	41,464	43,605	53,055	CNN25g	59-AAFO-e	general hindi		0.60	262	3Asuh	5	5	8	5	1		pnb b
1832	Hungarian	0.34393	101,863	107,123	130,337	MSW51g	41-BAAA-a	general magyar		90.00	96,410	2A.u.	10	9	12	5	3	Hungarian	PNB b
1833	Hutterite (Tyrolese)	0.06173	18,283	19,227	23,394	CEW19m	52-ABCF-r	hutterer-deutsch		90.00	17,304	0c.uh	10	9	11	5	1		pn. b
1834	Icelander	0.02245	6,649	6,992	8,508	CEW19n	52-AAAB-a	íslensk		94.00	6,573	0..uh	10	9	13	5	1	Icelandic	PNB b
1835	Inland Eastern Cree	0.00850	2,517	2,647	3,221	MIR38a	62-ADAA-g	southeast cree		95.00	2,515	1.s..	10	8	11	4	2	Cree, Inland Eastern	Pnb b
1836	Irish Gaelic	0.01146	3,394	3,569	4,343	CEW18b	50-AAAA-g	gaeilge		83.00	2,963	2a.uh	10	9	15	5	1	Irish*	PNB b
1837	Israeli Jew	0.03418	10,123	10,646	12,953	CMT35	12-AABA-b	ivrit-x.		0.07	7	2B.uh	4	4	4	5	0	Hebrew	PNB b
1838	Italian	2.17218	643,344	676,561	823,180	CEW21e	51-AABQ-c	standard italiano		84.00	568,311	2B.uh	10	9	15	5	2	Italian	PNB b
1839	Japanese	0.08271	24,497	25,761	31,344	MSY45a	45-CAAA-a	koku-go		2.50	644	1B.uh	6	5	8	5	1	Japanese	PNB b
1840	Kalderash Gypsy (Rom)	0.14000	41,464	43,605	53,055	CNN25f	59-ACBA-a	vlach-romani		70.00	30,524	1a...	10	7	8	3	1	Romani: Finnish*	PN. b
1841	Kaska	0.00323	957	1,006	1,224	MIR38a	61-BADA-b	kaska		90.00	905	0....	10	8	11	4	1		... b
1842	Khmer (Cambodian)	0.01674	4,958	5,214	6,344	AUG03b	46-FBAA-b	khmae		1.00	52	2A...	6	4	8	4	2	Khmer*	PNB b
1843	Korean	0.30000	88,852	93,440	113,689	MSY46	45-AAAA-b	kukö		61.00	56,998	2A...	10	6	11	5	1	Korean	PNB b
1844	Kutchin	0.00500	1,481	1,557	1,895	MIR38a	61-BAEB-b	gwich'in		96.00	1,495	0....	10	8	11	4	0	Gwichin: Western	PNB b
1845	Kutenai	0.00100	296	311	379	MIR38a	63-HAAA	kutenai cluster		92.00	287	0....	10	8	11	4	2		... b
1846	Kwakiutl	0.01422	4,212	4,429	5,389	MIR38a	63-EAAC-a	kwakwa-la		96.00	4,252	0....	10	8	11	4	1	Kwakiutl	P.. b
1847	Lakota	0.04000	11,847	12,459	15,159	MIR38a	64-AACA-d	lakota		90.00	11,213	0....	10	8	11	4	0		pnb b
1848	Lao (Laotian Thai)	0.04000	11,847	12,459	15,159	MSY49b	47-AAAC-b	lao		5.00	623	2As..	7	5	8	4	3	Lao	PNB b
1849	Latvian (Lett)	0.05188	15,366	16,159	19,661	CEW15a	54-AABA-a	standard latviashu		99.00	15,997	3A.u.	10	9	12	5	1	Latvian	PNB b
1850	Lebanese Arab	0.40000	118,470	124,587	151,586	CMT30	12-AACF-f	syro-palestinian		70.00	87,211	1Asuh	10	8	8	5	2	Arabic: Lebanese*	Pnb b
1851	Lillooet	0.01207	3,575	3,759	4,574	MIR38a	63-GCAA-a	leel-wat-ool		93.00	3,496	0....	10	8	11	4	0		... b
1852	Lithuanian	0.05303	15,706	16,517	20,097	CEW15b	54-AAAA-a	standard lietuvishkai		85.00	14,040	3A.u.	10	9	12	5	1	Lithuanian	PNB b
1853	Low German	0.34043	100,827	106,033	129,011	CEW19m	52-ABCC	north deutsch cluster		88.00	93,309	2A.uh	10	9	13	5	1	German: Low*	PNB b
1854	Macedonian	0.04375	12,958	13,627	16,580	CEW22g	53-AAAH-a	makedonski		91.00	12,400	2a.uh	10	9	11	4	1	Macedonian*	PNB b
1855	Malay	0.00822	2,435	2,560	3,115	MSY44k	31-PHAA-b	bahasa-malaysia		0.05	1	1asuh	4	4	8	5	2	Malay	PNB b
1856	Malayali	0.00844	2,500	2,629	3,198	CNN23b	49-EBEB-a	malayalam		63.00	1,656	2Asu.	10	6	8	5	3	Malayalam	PNB b
1857	Malecite	0.00561	1,662	1,747	2,126	MIR38a	62-AEAB	maliseet cluster		96.00	1,677	0....	10	8	11	4	0	Maliseet*	P.. b
1858	Micmac	0.04741	14,042	14,767	17,967	MIR38a	62-AEAA-b	southeast micmac		97.00	14,324	0....	10	8	11	4	2	Micmac	PN. b
1859	Mohawk	0.01401	4,149	4,364	5,309	MIR38a	64-CAAC-a	mohawk		96.00	4,189	0....	10	9	13	5	1	Mohawk	P.. b
1860	Montagnais	0.03479	10,304	10,836	13,184	MIR38a	62-ADAB-b	north montagnais		96.00	10,402	0....	10	8	11	4	1	Montagnais	PN. b
1861	Moroccan Jew	0.00000	0	0	0	CMT35	12-AACH-c	yudi		0.10	0	0c...	5	4	4	4	1		p.. b
1862	Naskapi	0.00296	877	922	1,122	MIR38a	62-ADAB-a	mushau-innuts		70.00	645	0....	10	8	7	4	1	Naskapi	pn. b
1863	Nass-Gitksian	0.02155	6,383	6,712	8,167	MIR38a	63-CAAB-b	gitksian		96.00	6,444	0....	10	8	11	4	0	Gitksian*	P.. b
1864	Nootka	0.01509	4,469	4,700	5,719	MIR38a	63-EABA-a	nootka		92.00	4,324	0....	10	8	11	4	0		... b
1865	North Alaskan Eskimo	0.03000	8,885	9,344	11,369	MRY40b	60-ABBB-b	kobuk		95.00	8,877	0....	10	8	12	5	1		pn. b
1866	Northern Ojibwa	0.03448	10,212	10,739	13,067	MIR38a	62-ADAF-da	northeast ojibwa		96.00	10,310	0....	10	8	11	4	1		pn. .
1867	Norwegian	0.08091	23,963	25,201	30,662	CEW19p	52-AAAC-e	ny-norsk		93.00	23,437	0B.uh	10	9	14	5	1	Norwegian*	PNB b
1868	Okanagon	0.01154	3,418	3,594	4,373	MIR38a	63-GCBA-a	north okanagan		92.00	3,307	0....	10	8	11	4	1		... b
1869	Oneida	0.01400	4,146	4,361	5,306	MIR38a	64-CAAC-b	oneida		92.80	4,047	0....	10	8	11	4	0	Oneida	P.. b
1870	Onondaga	0.00600	1,777	1,869	2,274	MIR38a	64-CAAD-c	onondaga		90.00	1,682	0....	10	8	11	4	0		p.. b
1871	Palestinian Arab	0.35000	103,661	109,013	132,638	CMT30	12-AACF-f	syro-palestinian		75.00	81,760	1Asuh	10	8	10	5	0	Arabic: Lebanese*	Pnb b
1872	Papago-Pima	0.00200	592	623	758	MIR37z	66-BEAA	pima-papago cluster		85.00	529	0A...	10	8	10	4	2	Papago-piman	PN. b
1873	Part-Indian (Metis)	1.80000	533,114	560,640	682,137	MIR38b	52-ABAC-r	general canadian		73.00	409,267	1Bsuh	10	8	10	5	1		pnb b
1874	Pennsylvania Dutch	0.04690	13,891	14,608	17,773	CEW19m	52-ABCF-t	pennsylvanisch-dietsch		90.00	13,147	0c.uh	10	9	14	5	2	German: Pennsylvania*	PN. b
1875	Pentlatch	0.00016	47	50	61	MIR38a	52-ABAC-s	general american		20.00	10	1Bsuh	9	8	6	4	0	English*	PNB b
1876	Persian	0.08000	23,694	24,917	30,317	CNT24f	58-AACC-c	standard farsi		40.00	9,967	1Asu.	9	6	7	5	0		PNB b
1877	Pilipino (Tagalog)	0.32967	97,640	102,681	124,933	MSY44o	31-CKAA-a	proper tagalog		98.00	100,628	4Bs..	10	9	13	5	3	Tagalog	PNB b
1878	Polish (Pole)	0.52565	155,684	163,722	199,203	CEW22i	53-AAAC-c	polski		91.00	148,987	2A.uh	10	9	12	5	2	Polish	PNB b
1879	Portuguese	0.67990	201,369	211,766	257,658	CEW21g	51-AABA-e	general português		93.00	196,942	2Bsuh	10	9	15	5	3	Portuguese	PNB b
1880	Potawatomi	0.01600	4,739	4,983	6,063	MIR38a	62-ADAE-a	potawatomi		91.00	4,535	0....	10	8	11	4	0	Pottawotomi*	P.. b
1881	Punjabi	2.30000	681,201	716,373	871,619	CNN25n	59-AAFE-c	general panjabi		2.50	17,909	1Asu.	6	5	8	5	3		PNB b
1882	Romanian	0.05318	15,751	16,564	20,153	CEW21i	51-AADC-a	limba românească		84.00	13,914	3A.u.	10	9	10	5	2	Romanian	PNB b
1883	Russian	0.12934	38,307	40,285	49,015	CEW22j	53-AAAE-d	russkiy		70.00	28,200	4B.uh	10	9	8	5	3	Russian	PNB b
1884	Sarsi	0.00259	767	807	982	MIR38a	61-BAED-c	sarsi		93.00	750	0....	10	8	11	4	0	Sekani	P.. b
1885	Sechelt	0.00237	702	738	898	MIR38a	63-GAAB-a	sechelt		89.00	657	0....	10	8	10	4	0		... b
1886	Sekani	0.00247	732	769	936	MIR38a	61-BAED-b	sarsi		91.00	700	0....	10	8	11	4	0	Sekani	P.. b
1887	Seneca	0.00070	207	218	265	MIR38a	64-CAAD-a	seneca		90.00	196	0....	10	8	11	4	0	Seneca	P.. b
1888	Seneca	0.02000	5,923	6,229	7,579	MIR38a	52-ABAC-s	general american		95.00	5,918	1Bsuh	10	9	11	4	0	English*	PNB b
1889	Serb	0.02590	7,671	8,067	9,815	CEW22l	53-AAAG-a	standard srpski		85.00	6,857	1Asuh	10	9	10	5	1	Serbian*	PNB b
1890	Shuswap	0.02451	7,259	7,634	9,288	MIR38a	63-GCAB	shuswap cluster		91.00	6,947	0....	10	8	11	4	0		... b
1891	Sinhalese (Cingalese)	0.00378	1,120	1,177	1,432	CNN25q	59-ABBA-aa	standard sinhala		2.80	33	1asuh	6	5	8	5	3		pnb b
1892	Sinti Gypsy	0.01000	2,962	3,115	3,790	CNN25f	59-ACBB-b	sinti		70.00	2,180	0....	10	7	7	4	3	Romani: Sinti, Italian	P.. b
1893	Slave (Tinne, Mountain)	0.02058	6,095	6,410	7,799	MIR38a	61-BAEC-f	slavey		96.00	6,154	1....	10	8	11	4	2	Slavey	PN. .
1894	Slovak	0.08103	23,999	25,238	30,708	CEW22m	53-AAAD-b	slovensky		80.00	20,190	1Asuh	10	9	12	5	2	Slovak	PNB b
1895	Slovene	0.02763	8,183	8,606	10,471	CEW22n	53-AAAF-a	slovensko		95.00	8,176	1a..h	10	9	11	5	1	Slovenian*	PNB b
1896	Spaniard	0.28821	85,360	89,768	109,221	CEW21k	51-AABB-c	general español		96.00	86,177	2B.uh	10	9	15	5	1	Spanish	PNB b
1897	Squamish	0.00867	2,568	2,700	3,286	MIR38a	63-GAAD-a	squamish		92.00	2,484	0....	10	8	11	4	1		... b
1898	Stoney	0.01237	3,664	3,853	4,688	MIR38a	64-AACA-b	iyarhe-nakodabi		96.00	3,699	0....	10	8	11	4	3	Stoney	Pnb b
1899	Straits Salish	0.00600	1,777	1,869	2,274	MIR38a	63-GAAF	saanich-clallam cluster		92.00	1,719	0....	10	8	11	4	2		... b
1900	Swahili	0.00259	767	807	982	NAB57j	99-AUSM-b	standard ki-swahili		0.45	4	4Asu.	5	4	4	5	0	Kiswahili*	PNB b
1901	Swedish	0.07020	20,791	21,865	26,603	CEW19q	52-AAAD-r	svea-svensk		73.00	15,961	1A.uh	10	9	8	5	3	Swedish	PNB b

Continued opposite

Table 8-2 continued

EVANGELIZATION								EVANGELISM			ADDITIONAL DESCRIPTIVE DATA
Ref 1	*D* 28	*aC* 29	*CG%* 30	*r* 31	*E* 32	*U* 33	*W* 34	*e* 35	*R* 36	*T* 37	*Locations, civil divisions, literacy, religions, church history, denominations, dioceses, church growth, missions, agencies, ministries, movements* 38
1778	3	10	1.09	8	99.66	0.34	C	339.04	36	9	D=RCC(68 Dioceses),ACC(28 Dioceses),UCC. M=NMC,CCC,OMI,SFM,FMB. R=local stations. T=CBN,LESEA.
1779	3	10	1.73	8	62.50	37.50	B	3.42	106	4	Jews practicing orthodox or liberal Judaism. D=UCC,ACC/ECC,RCC. M=JFJ.
1780	2	10	1.73	6	99.90	0.10	C	532.17	39	10	1915 refugees. D=Armenian Apostolic Ch(D-Canada),Armenian Ev Union of Chs.
1781	0	10	1.73	0	99.96	0.04	C	508.08	50	10	Central Alberta. Only 5.7% are fluent speakers (most over 60). English widely used.
1782	1	8	1.73	0	99.96	0.04	C	483.55	52	10	Quebec. All speak the language. D=RCC. M=SIL,LBT.
1783	0	9	1.73	0	99.97	0.03	C	506.29	50	10	West central British Columbia. English used, 73% use Babini, 27% do not. M=SIL.
1784	0	8	1.73	0	99.96	0.04	C	487.05	52	10	BC, Alberta. 83% speak Beaver, 17% do not. M=CMS,SIL.
1785	0	10	1.74	0	99.98	0.02	C	500.78	52	10	BC. 21% speak Bella Coola; all speak English.
1786	3	10	3.14	6	62.60	37.40	B	1.37	197	4	Immigrants from Bangladesh. Muslims 95%, some Hindus. D=ACC/ECC,RCC,UCC.
1787	3	10	1.73	0	99.96	0.04	C	529.10	48	10	Alberta. 60% speak Blackfoot. D=RCC,ACC,Native American Ch.
1788	4	10	1.56	8	99.67	0.33	C	359.48	51	9	Expatriates from UK, in professions, commerce, industry. D=ACC/ECC,UCC,SDA,JWs. R=local stations. T=CBN,LESEA.
1789	1	10	1.73	6	99.79	0.21	C	426.75	55	10	Refugees from Bulgaria. Nonreligious 21%. D=Bulgarian Orthodox Ch(P-Sofia).
1790	1	10	1.73	5	99.77	0.23	C	407.52	52	10	White Russian refugees from 1917. Nonreligious 23%. D=Belorussian Autocephalic Orthodox Ch.
1791	0	9	1.73	0	99.96	0.04	C	501.07	50	10	British Columbia. 29% do not speak Carrier. M=YWAM,SIL.
1792	0	10	1.73	0	99.92	0.08	C	455.85	53	10	Ontario. 87% do not speak Cayuga. All speak English.
1793	3	7	1.73	3	99.97	0.03	C	548.77	46	10	Ontario. 10% do not speak Cree. D=ACC(D-Saskatoon),RCC,Native American Ch.
1794	2	7	1.73	3	99.97	0.03	C	541.69	47	10	Ontario. D=ACC,RCC. M=NCEM.
1795	0	9	1.73	0	99.96	0.04	C	501.07	50	10	South central BC. 33% do not speak Chilcotin. M=NCEM,SIL.
1796	0	10	1.74	0	99.90	0.10	C	436.90	50	10	Former lingua franca. Under 100 speakers(Amerindian Pidgin). Widely scattered, nearly extinct.
1797	0	9	1.73	0	99.96	0.04	C	504.57	50	10	Northern Alberta. 20% do not speak Chipewyan. M=NCEM.
1798	0	10	1.73	0	99.92	0.08	C	449.97	54	10	BC, Vancouver. 50% do not speak Comox. All speak English.
1799	1	10	1.73	6	99.91	0.09	C	544.72	47	10	Refugees, immigrants from Croatia wars. D=RCC.
1800	2	10	1.73	6	99.90	0.10	C	538.74	48	10	Refugees, immigrants from Czechoslovakia after 1938, 1945, 1968. D=RCC,Moravians.
1801	4	10	1.73	0	99.98	0.02	C	568.74	45	10	Southern Manitoba, Saskatchewan. Mainly in USA. 17% do not speak Dakota. D=RCC,ACC,Native American Ch, Lutheran Ch.
1802	2	10	1.73	6	99.95	0.05	C	582.54	47	10	Expatriates from Denmark, in professions. D=UCC,Lutherans.
1803	0	10	1.73	0	99.90	0.10	C	436.90	54	10	Southern Ontario. Also in USA. Only 1.4% speak Delaware, 98% do not.
1804	5	10	1.73	8	99.90	0.10	C	528.88	29	10	Amerindians uprooted from their cultures. D=RCC,UCC,ACC,Native American Ch,PAOC.
1805	0	8	1.73	0	99.95	0.05	C	478.51	52	10	Between Great Slave Lake and Great Bear Lake, NWT. Hunters, trappers. M=SIL.
1806	1	10	1.73	6	99.76	0.24	C	421.64	47	10	Immigrants from Holland. Nonreligious and atheists 24%. D=Christian Reformed Chs in Canada.
1807	6	6	1.73	3	99.96	0.04	C	543.12	45	10	All speak Inuit (Eskimo). D=ACC(D-The Arctic),Baptists,CMA,PAOC,UCC,UB. M=NCEM.
1808	0	8	1.73	3	99.97	0.03	C	527.53	48	10	Quebec. 14% do not speak Cree. Most speak English.
1809	1	10	1.73	0	99.96	0.04	C	508.08	50	10	Around Lake Huron and southeastern Ontario. 32% speak Ojibwa, 68% do not. D=ACC. M=NCEM.
1810	1	10	9.57	8	99.60	0.40	C	284.70	216	8	Massive immigration from Egypt. Muslims 40%. D=Coptic Orthodox Ch in Canada.
1811	3	10	1.73	8	99.80	0.20	C	432.16	51	10	Nomadic and settled Gypsies. D=UCC,RCC,GEM. M=GGMS.
1812	4	10	1.73	8	99.90	0.10	C	538.74	42	10	Shamanists 5%. D=ACC/EEC(D-The Arctic,80% of all Eskimos),RCC,Baptists,Lutherans.
1813	0	10	0.00	5	99.60	0.40	C	258.42	0	8	Artificial (constructed) language, in 80 countries. Speakers in Canada: 66,000 (none mother-tongue). Nonreligious and atheists 40%.
1814	2	10	1.73	5	99.80	0.20	C	435.08	53	10	Refugees from Estonia. Nonreligious 20%. D=Estonian Orthodox Ch,Estonian Ev Alliance Ch.
1815	2	10	1.73	5	99.87	0.13	C	501.72	48	10	Immigrants from Finland. D=ELCF,Finnish Orthodox Ch.
1816	1	10	1.73	6	99.90	0.10	C	528.88	49	10	Immigrants from Belgium. Mostly Catholics. D=RCC.
1817	1	10	1.73	8	99.87	0.13	C	514.43	46	10	Expatriates from France, in professions. D=RCC.
1818	4	9	1.73	3	99.97	0.03	C	538.15	44	10	Scattered locations; main home in North Dakota, USA. French creole. D=RCC,UCC,ACC,Native American Ch.
1819	4	10	1.63	8	99.69	0.31	C	363.78	46	9	Long-time settlers from France. D=RCC(36 French Dioceses),French Baptist Union,SA,UCC. M=CNM,CCC,VICS,OMI,PME,SSSA,OM,FMB. R=local stations,AWR.
1820	2	10	1.73	0	99.72	0.28	C	323.24	64	9	Immigrants from Frisia(Germany, Holland). D=RCC,UCC.
1821	3	10	1.73	8	99.88	0.12	C	536.40	47	10	Expatriates, settlers from Germany. D=NABGC,ACPC,New Apostolic Ch. R=HCJB.
1822	0	10	1.74	4	51.80	48.20	B	1.51	129	4	European Jews speaking Yiddish(Judeo-German) as mother tongue. Orthodox Jews.
1823	4	10	1.73	7	99.95	0.05	C	589.47	44	10	D=Greek Orthodox Archdiocese of N&S America, Old Calender GOC, Greek Gospel Ch, Pentecostal Free Evangelical Ch.
1824	1	10	1.73	0	99.93	0.07	C	473.53	52	10	Queen Charlotte Island. Half in Alaska (USA). 30% use Haida as mother tongue, rest use English. D=ACC.
1825	1	10	1.73	0	99.92	0.08	C	460.04	53	10	British Columbia coast. D=UCC.
1826	3	10	8.32	4	99.95	0.05	C	586.00	154	10	Many refugees from Haiti; especially in Montreal. D=RCC,ACC,Evangelical Baptist Church.
1827	0	10	1.73	0	99.90	0.10	C	433.62	55	10	Southwest British Columbia. Only 7% speak Holkomelem.
1828	0	10	1.73	0	99.91	0.09	C	461.68	52	10	Yukon river area. Speakers 20%, nonspeakers 80%.
1829	6	10	3.16	7	89.00	11.00	B	45.47	117	6	Massive immigration from Hong Kong. Chinese folk-religionists (Buddhists/Confucianists) 85%. D=ACC,UCC,RCC,BFC,Chinese Gospel Church,&c. M=HKOM,FMB.
1830	0	10	1.73	0	99.91	0.09	C	445.08	54	10	Central British Columbia coast. Speakers 38%, nonspeakers 62%.
1831	0	10	3.32	7	58.60	41.40	B	1.28	202	4	Immigrants from India. Hindus 90%, Muslims 9%(mostly Hanafi Sunnis). M=FMB.
1832	3	10	1.73	6	99.90	0.10	C	538.74	52	10	Refugees from Hungary in 1939, 1957, and after. D=RCC,ELCA,PCUSA.
1833	1	10	1.73	1	99.90	0.10	C	466.47	55	10	Western Canada, 116 colonies; others across northwest USA. Dialect of Upper German. Bilingual. D=Huterites.
1834	1	10	1.73	2	99.94	0.06	C	528.37	43	10	Immigrants from Iceland. D=United Conference of Icelandic Chs in North America (Unitarians).
1835	4	10	1.73	1	99.95	0.05	C	527.06	47	10	In Quebec. Montagnais. D=ACC,RCC,Baptists,Pentecostals. M=NCEM,SIL.
1836	1	10	1.73	4	99.83	0.17	C	463.51	47	10	Immigrants from Ireland, speaking original Irish language. D=RCC.
1837	0	10	1.96	5	53.07	46.93	B	0.13	137	3	Immigrants, expatriates from Israel. Mostly secular Jews, some religious.
1838	2	10	1.73	7	99.84	0.16	C	496.69	46	10	Immigrants from Italy. D=RCC,Italian Pentecostal Ch of Canada.
1839	1	10	1.73	7	64.50	35.50	B	5.88	105	4	Mahayana Buddhists 97%, including Soka Gakkai and other New Religions. D=Japanese-Canadian Ev Christian Association.
1840	3	10	1.73	6	99.70	0.30	C	321.93	60	9	Nomadic and settled Gypsies. Mostly Christians. D=UCC,RCC,GEM. M=GGMS.
1841	1	10	1.74	0	99.90	0.10	C	440.19	54	10	Southeast Yukon and BC. Speakers 67%, nonspeakers 33%. D=ACC.
1842	2	10	4.03	5	62.00	38.00	B	2.26	241	4	Refugees from Cambodia wars. Theravada Buddhists 96%, nonreligious 3%. D=RCC,UCC. M=OMF,Yonge St Mission.
1843	2	10	9.03	6	99.61	0.39	C	293.89	200	8	Large numbers of immigrants from Korea. Mahayana Buddhists 20%. D=many Presbyterian bodies,Pentecostals. M=FMB.
1844	0	10	1.73	0	99.96	0.04	C	522.09	48	10	Yukon, Northwest Territories, Alaska. 42% do not speak Gwichin.
1845	2	10	1.74	0	99.92	0.08	C	463.40	52	10	Southeast British Columbia. 31% speak Kutenai, 69% do not. D=RCC,ACC.
1846	1	10	1.73	0	99.96	0.04	C	497.56	51	10	Northern Vancouver Island. 30% speak Kwakiutl, 70% do not. D=ACC. M=CMS.
1847	0	10	1.73	0	99.90	0.10	C	459.90	51	10	Manitoba, Saskatchewan. 30% speak Lakota, 70% do not.
1848	3	10	4.22	5	70.00	30.00	B	12.77	225	5	Refugees from Laos and its wars. Theravada Buddhists 80%, nonreligious 10%. D=Church of the Crusaders,RCC,UCC.
1849	1	10	2.95	5	99.99	0.01	C	610.68	67	10	Refugees from Latvia. D=Latvian Ev Lutheran Ch Outside Latvia.
1850	2	10	9.50	8	99.70	0.30	C	350.03	204	9	Massive immigration of Christian Arabs from Lebanon. Muslims 20%. D=Mennonite Brethren,RCC.
1851	0	10	1.73	0	99.93	0.07	C	461.65	53	10	Southern British Columbia. 18% are speakers, 82% are not. Extensive bilingualism.
1852	1	10	3.35	5	99.85	0.15	C	480.88	59	10	Refugees from Lithuania after 1938, 1945. Mostly Catholics. D=RCC.
1853	1	10	1.73	8	99.88	0.12	C	520.34	49	10	Mennonite Germans, Mennoniten Platt. D=Mennonite Brethren. M=SIL.
1854	1	10	1.73	5	99.91	0.09	C	524.79	46	10	Refugees from Yugoslavia. Slavs. D=Macedonian Orthodox Ch.
1855	2	10	0.00	5	59.05	40.95	B	0.10	32	3	Immigrants from Singapore, Malaysia. Muslims 100%(Shafi Sunnis). D=UCC,RCC.
1856	4	10	5.24	4	99.63	0.37	C	301.23	131	9	Immigrants from Kerala(South India), in professions, commerce. Hindus 25%, Muslims 7%. D=OSC,MTC,ACC,RCC.
1857	0	10	1.73	0	99.96	0.04	C	490.56	51	10	New Brunswick. 50% are speakers, 50% not. All speak English.
1858	0	10	1.73	0	99.97	0.03	C	520.45	49	10	Nova Scotia, Prince Edward Island. Speakers 54%, nonspeakers 46%. M=SIL,Native Christian Evangelical Mission.
1859	1	10	1.73	0	99.96	0.04	C	508.08	50	10	Southwest Quebec, southern Ontario. Mohawk speakers 30%, nonspeakers 70%. Armed revolt, during 1990. D=RCC.
1860	2	9	1.73	0	99.96	0.04	C	511.58	49	10	Quebec, Labrador. Speakers 78%, nonspeakers 22%. D=CMA,PAOC. M=SIL.
1861	1	10	0.00	8	42.10	57.90	A	0.15	0	3	Refugees, immigrants from Morocco. D=Beth San Shalom. M=American Board for Mission to Jews.
1862	1	10	1.73	0	99.70	0.30	C	288.71	64	8	Labrador coast, Schefferville and Davis Inlet. Closely related to Montagnais. 52% speak the language. D=ACC. M=SIL.
1863	0	10	1.73	0	99.96	0.04	C	490.56	51	10	West central British Columbia. 50% speak the language, 50% do not. All speak English.
1864	0	10	1.73	0	99.92	0.08	C	453.33	53	10	Western British Columbia. Speakers 14%, nonspeakers 86%. English widespread.
1865	2	10	1.73	4	99.95	0.05	C	520.12	46	10	Mackenzie delta region, Alaska. Speakers 67%. D=ACC(D-The Arctic), Presbyterians. M=SIL.
1866	1	7	1.73	0	99.96	0.04	C	487.05	52	10	Northern Ontario, Manitoba. All speak the language. D=UCC.
1867	1	10	1.73	6	99.93	0.07	C	560.09	47	10	Expatriates, immigrants from Norway, in commerce, professions. D=Lutherans.
1868	1	10	1.73	0	99.92	0.08	C	460.04	53	10	South central British Columbia. 16% speak Okanagon, 84% do not. D=RCC. M=Faith Mission.
1869	0	10	1.73	0	99.93	0.07	C	463.36	53	10	Southern Ontario. 97% do not speak Oneida, only 3% still do.
1870	0	10	1.73	0	99.90	0.10	C	440.19	54	10	Southern Ontario. 7% speak the language, 93% do not.
1871	0	10	9.43	8	99.75	0.25	C	383.25	198	9	Vast numbers of immigrants from Palestine and Middle East. Muslims 24%.
1872	2	10	1.73	0	99.85	0.15	C	431.24	50	10	South central Arizona.; Also in Mexico. D=Protestants,RCC.
1873	5	10	1.73	8	99.73	0.27	C	373.03	48	9	Amerindian/White, detribalized. D=RCC,ACC,UCC,Native American Ch,PAOC. M=Arctic Missions. T=CBN. R=local stations. T=LESEA.
1874	2	10	1.73	1	99.90	0.10	C	486.18	53	10	Pennsylvania Germans. Most are in USA. D=Amish,Non-Amish.
1875	0	10	1.62	8	79.00	21.00	B	57.67	87	6	South Vancouver Island. No speakers of Pentlatch left; all now use English only.
1876	0	10	7.15	5	99.40	0.60	B	146.00	215	7	Refugees from Iran after 1978. Muslims (Ithna-Asharis Shias) 30%, Baha'is 30%. Many Christians.
1877	3	10	2.33	5	99.98	0.02	C	633.12	47	10	Immigrants from the Philippines. Mostly Catholics. D=RCC,INC,PIC.
1878	2	10	1.73	6	99.91	0.09	C	544.72	29	10	Refugees from Poland, from 1910-1990. D=Polish National Catholic Ch of Canada,RCC.
1879	3	10	1.73	8	99.93	0.07	C	594.03	43	10	Expatriates, immigrants from Portugal. D=Baptists,Pentecostals,Portuguese Christian Church.
1880	0	10	1.73	0	99.91	0.09	C	448.40	53	10	Southern Ontario. 7% speak the language, 93% no longer do.
1881	4	10	1.73	5	67.50	32.50	B	6.15	113	4	Vancouver(0.95% Sikh) is second biggest Sikh city in world. Hindus 34%, Muslims 20%, Sikhs 41%. D=Presbyterians,Pentecostals,SDA,Hindu-Punjabi Gospel Ch.
1882	2	10	1.73	6	99.84	0.16	C	475.23	50	10	Refugees from Romania. D=Romanian Orthodox Ch in Canada,Romanian Orthodox Episcopate of America.
1883	5	10	1.73	7	99.70	0.30	C	370.47	33	9	Refugees from USSR, 1917-1990. Nonreligious/atheists 30%. D=Russian Orthodox Ch(P-Moscow),ROCOR,MBCNA,Old Believers ROC,OCA(AD-Canada).
1884	0	10	1.74	0	99.93	0.07	C	461.65	53	10	Alberta. 12.5% speakers, 87.5% do not speak Sarsi.
1885	0	10	1.73	0	99.89	0.11	C	422.30	55	10	British Columbia coast. Under 15 speakers of Sechelt left.
1886	0	10	1.73	0	99.91	0.09	C	445.08	54	10	British Columbia. 25% speak Sekani, 75% do not. Most bilingual in English.
1887	0	10	1.74	0	99.90	0.10	C	436.90	54	10	Six Nations Reserve, Ontario. Bilingual in English.
1888	0	10	1.73	8	99.95	0.05	C	558.26	45	10	Most Seneca no longer speak Seneca language.
1889	1	10	1.73	6	99.85	0.15	C	474.68	31	10	Refugees from Yugoslavia. D=Serbian Orthodox Ch(D-East USA & Canada).
1890	0	10	1.73	0	99.91	0.09	C	445.08	54	10	British Columbia. 16% still speak Shuswap, 84% do not.
1891	3	10	1.72	6	62.80	37.20	B	6.41	100	4	Refugees from Sri Lanka(Ceylon). Theraveda Buddhists 90%. D=RCC,ACC,UCC.
1892	3	10	1.73	0	99.70	0.30	C	288.71	67	8	Nomads, also settled populations. D=RCC,GEM,UCC.
1893	1	9	1.73	0	99.96	0.04	C	501.07	50	10	Northern Alberta, NWT. 80% speak Slavey. D=RCC. M=NCEM,SIL.
1894	2	10	1.73	6	99.80	0.20	C	446.76	51	10	Immigrants from Slovakia, in professions. D=RCC,Protestants.
1895	1	10	1.73	6	99.95	0.05	C	565.20	46	10	Refugees and immigrants from Yugoslavia up to 1992. D=RCC.
1896	1	10	1.73	8	99.96	0.04	C	606.19	42	10	Expatriates and settlers from Spain, most in professions. D=RCC.
1897	1	10	1.74	0	99.92	0.08	C	460.04	53	10	British Columbia. Less than 20 speakers left. D=RCC.
1898	3	8	1.73	0	99.96	0.04	C	522.09	48	10	Southern Alberta. 47% speak Stoney, 53% do not. D=UCC,ICFG, independents.
1899	2	10	1.73	0	99.92	0.08	C	466.76	52	10	Vancouver, British Columbia. Under 40 speakers left. D=UCC,RCC.
1900	0	10	1.40	5	55.45	44.55	B	0.91	141	3	Immigrants from East Africa. Muslims 99%(Shafi Sunnis).
1901	4	10	1.73	6	99.73	0.27	C	381.02	33	9	Expatriates, settlers from Sweden. D=Baptist General Conference,IAG,ACPC,ECCC.

Continued overleaf

Table 8-2 continued

PEOPLE		POPULATION				IDENTITY CODE		LANGUAGE		CHURCH		MINISTRY						SCRIPTURE		
Ref 1	Ethnic name 2	P% 3	In 1995 4	In 2000 5	In 2025 6	Race 7	Language 8	Autoglossonym 9	S 10	AC 11	Members 12	Jayuh 13-17	d 18	wa 19	xc 20	mc 21	mi 22	Biblioglossonym 23	Pub 24-26	ss 27
1902	Syrian Arab	0.05000	14,809	15,573	18,948	CMT30	12-AACF-f	syro-palestinian		28.00	4,361	1Asuh	9	6	8	5	3	Arabic: Lebanese*	Pnb	b
1903	Tagish	0.00041	121	128	155	MIR38a	61-BADA-a	tagish		99.99	128	0....	10	8	11	4	0		...	b
1904	Tahltan	0.00323	957	1,006	1,224	MIR38a	61-BADA-d	tahltan		92.00	926	0....	10	8	11	4	0		...	b
1905	Tamil	0.04000	11,847	12,459	15,159	CNN23c	49-EBEA-b	tamil		11.00	1,370	2Asu.	8	5	8	5	2	Tamil	PNB	b
1906	Telugu	0.00500	1,481	1,557	1,895	CNN23d	49-DBAB-a	telugu		7.00	109	2Asu.	7	5	8	5	2	Telugu	PNB	b
1907	Thai	0.03056	9,051	9,518	11,581	MSY49d	47-AAAB-d	central thai		0.70	67	3asuh	5	5	8	5	0	Thai*	PNB	b
1908	Thompson (Ntlakyapamuk)	0.01200	3,554	3,738	4,548	MIR38a	63-GCAC-a	in-thla-cap-mu-wh		91.00	3,401	0....	10	8	11	4	0		...	b
1909	Tlingit	0.00900	2,666	2,803	3,411	MIR38a	63-AAAA-a	north tlingit		96.00	2,691	0....	10	8	11	4	2	Tlingit	P..	b
1910	Tsimshian	0.00800	2,369	2,492	3,032	MIR38a	63-CAAA-b	southeast tsimshian		94.00	2,342	0....	10	8	11	4	1	Tsimshian: Coastal	P..	b
1911	Turk	0.01684	4,988	5,245	6,382	MSY41j	44-AABA-a	osmanli		0.50	26	1A.u.	5	4	6	5	0	Turkish	PNB	b
1912	Tuscarora	0.00400	1,185	1,246	1,516	MIR38a	64-CAAE-b	tuscarora		89.19	1,111	0....	10	8	11	4	0		...	b
1913	Tutchone	0.00617	1,827	1,922	2,338	MIR38a	61-BACA-b	selkirk		91.08	1,750	0....	10	8	11	4	0		...	b
1914	USA Black	0.14895	44,115	46,393	56,447	NFB68a	52-ABAE-a	talkin-black		73.00	33,867	0B.uh	10	9	11	5	3		pnb	b
1915	USA White	1.80000	533,114	560,640	682,137	CEW19s	52-ABAC-s	general american		78.00	437,299	1Bsuh	10	9	14	5	3	English*	PNB	b
1916	Ukrainian	1.20060	355,587	373,947	454,985	CEW22p	53-AAAE-b	ukrainskiy		82.00	306,636	3A.uh	10	9	11	5	3	Ukrainian	PNB	b
1917	Urdu	0.08000	23,694	24,917	30,317	CNN25r	59-AAFO-d	standard urdu		0.10	25	2Asuh	5	4	6	5	1	Urdu	PNB	b
1918	Vietnamese	0.32367	95,863	100,812	122,660	MSY52b	46-EBAA-ac	general viêt		20.00	20,162	1Asu.	9	5	8	5	2	Vietnamese	PNB	b
1919	Walloon	0.10000	29,617	31,147	37,896	CEW21l	51-AABH-f	wallon		92.00	28,655	0A.uh	10	9	15	5	1	French: Walloon	P..	b
1920	Welsh	0.01103	3,267	3,435	4,180	CEW18d	50-ABAA-bc	cymraeg-safonol		85.00	2,920	2A.uh	10	9	15	5	3	Welsh	PNB	b
1921	West Indian Black	0.30000	88,852	93,440	113,689	NFB68a	52-ABAF	carib-anglo-creol cluster		85.00	79,424	1a..h	10	9	13	5	3	West Carib Creole English	PN.	b
1922	Western Canadian Eskimo	0.03086	9,140	9,612	11,695	MRY40b	60-ABBC-b	copper		95.00	9,131	1....	10	9	11	5	3	Eskimo: Copper*	PNb	b
1923	Western Cree	0.16350	48,425	50,925	61,961	MIR38a	62-ADAA-a	plains-cree		97.00	49,397	1.s..	10	9	11	4	3	Cree: Saskatchewan, North*	PNB	b
1924	Western Ojibwa (Chippewa)	0.08175	24,212	25,462	30,980	MIR38a	62-ADAF-c	southwest ojibwa		96.00	24,444	0....	10	9	12	4	2	Ojibway*	PN.	b
1925	Wyandot (Huron)	0.00500	1,481	1,557	1,895	MIR38a	52-ABAC-r	general canadian		80.00	1,246	1Bsuh	10	8	11	4	0		pnb	b
1926	other minor peoples	1.00000	296,174	311,466	378,965	...				60.00	186,880		10	7	6	5	3			
	Cape Verde	**100.00000**	**380,530**	**427,724**	**670,931**					**95.13**	**406,882**									
1927	Balanta (Brassa, Alante)	10.00000	38,053	42,772	67,093	NAB56c	90-GABA	north balanta cluster		90.00	38,495	0....	10	8	11	5	1	Frase*	P..	n
1928	Caboverdian Mestico	43.36000	164,998	185,461	290,916	NAN58	51-AACA-ab	sotavento	90	98.78	183,199	1c...	10	9	13	5	1		pnb	b
1929	Caboverdian Mestico	26.24000	99,851	112,235	176,052	NAN58	51-AACA-aa	barlavento	90	98.78	110,866	1c...	10	9	13	5	3		pnb	b
1930	Fulani	12.20000	46,425	52,182	81,854	NAB56c	90-BAAA-a	haal-pulaar		80.00	41,746	2As..	10	7	10	5	1	Fula: Pulaar*	Pnb	n
1931	Mandyak (Manjaco)	4.60000	17,504	19,675	30,863	NAB56c	90-FAAA-a	proper mandyak		90.00	17,708	0....	10	8	11	5	1	Manjako*	P..	b
1932	Portuguese	2.00000	7,611	8,554	13,419	CEW21g	51-AABA-e	general português	85	97.00	8,298	2Bsuh	10	9	13	5	1	Portuguese	PNB	b
1933	other minor peoples	1.60000	6,088	6,844	10,735	...				96.00	6,570		10	7	11	5	0			
	Cayman Islands	**100.00000**	**32,000**	**38,371**	**77,938**					**67.29**	**25,821**									
1934	British	19.30000	6,176	7,406	15,042	CEW19i	52-ABAC-b	standard-english		67.00	4,962	3Bsuh	10	9	9	5	3		PNB	b
1935	Indo-Pakistani	0.30000	96	115	234	CNN25g	59-AAFO-e	general hindi		10.50	12	3Asuh	8	5	2	5	0		pnb	b
1936	Jewish	1.90000	608	729	1,481	CMT35	52-ABAE-cb	cayman-islands-english		0.90	7	0A.uh	5	4	2	5	0		pnb	b
1937	Mulatto	51.50000	16,480	19,761	40,138	NFB68b	52-ABAF-l	cayman-creole		66.30	13,102	1c..h	10	8	10	5	2	Dutch Creole	PN.	.
1938	West Indian Black	25.80000	8,256	9,900	20,108	NFB68a	52-ABAF-l	cayman-creole		77.00	7,623	1c..h	10	9	10	5	3	Dutch Creole	PN.	.
1939	other minor peoples	1.20000	384	460	935	...				25.00	115		9	6	2	5	0			
	Central African Republic	**100.00000**	**3,287,816**	**3,615,266**	**5,703,795**					**44.51**	**1,608,998**									
1940	Ali	1.03044	33,879	37,253	58,774	NAB66z	05-AAAD-a	kaana-masala		60.00	22,352	0....	10	8	8	0	0	Masalit	...	b
1941	Bagirmi Fulani	1.24555	40,951	45,030	71,044	NAB56c	90-BAAA-r	fula-bagirmi		0.02	9	1cs..	3	3	2	1	1		pnb	b
1942	Baka Pygmy (Bebayaka)	0.30000	9,863	10,846	17,111	BYG12	93-ADDA-a	baka		10.00	1,085	0....	8	5	6	1	2		...	.
1943	Banda	9.88588	325,030	357,401	563,870	NAB66b	93-ABAB-a	banda-ndele	31	44.00	157,256	0....	9	6	10	5	3	Banda, South Central	...	b
1944	Banganda-Ngombe	0.04268	1,403	1,543	2,434	NAB66z	93-ADDA-f	ngombe-kaka		40.00	617	0....	9	5	4	3	1		...	.
1945	Banu	2.79693	91,958	101,116	159,531	NAB66c	93-AAAA-f	gbanu	6	40.00	40,447	0.s..	9	6	7	4	3	Banu*	Pnb	.
1946	Baya (Gbaya)	22.84372	751,059	825,861	1,302,959	NAB66c	93-AAAA-a	vehicular gbaya	27	53.00	437,706	0.s..	10	8	9	5	3	Gbaya: Gbea*	PNB	b
1947	Bayaka (Yakwa, Yakpa)	0.44161	14,519	15,965	25,189	NAB66b	93-ABAF-f	yakpa		35.00	5,588	0....	9	5	7	2	0		...	b
1948	Benkonjo (Ukhewjo)	0.04415	1,452	1,596	2,518	NAB57k	99-AUDG-f	m-pyemo		70.00	1,117	0....	10	7	6	4	1		...	.
1949	Besme (Huner)	0.06000	1,973	2,169	3,422	NAB60b	92-CCAA-a	besme		30.00	651	0....	9	5	4	2	1		...	.
1950	Binga Pygmy (Bayaka)	0.07000	2,301	2,531	3,993	BYG12	99-AUID-e	m-binga		10.00	253	0....	8	5	4	1	1		...	.
1951	Biri	0.14720	4,840	5,322	8,396	NAB66z	03-AAAE	sara cluster		64.00	3,406	0.s..	10	8	8	0	0		PNB	b
1952	Bofi	0.69187	22,747	25,013	39,463	NAB66c	93-AAAA-h	gbofi		60.00	15,008	0.s..	10	8	8	0	0		pnb	.
1953	Bomitaba (Bamitaba)	0.00804	264	291	459	NAB57c	99-AUFC-a	north m-bomitaba		40.00	116	0....	9	5	5	5	1		...	.
1954	Bororo Fulani	3.35000	110,142	121,111	191,077	NAB56c	90-BAAA-o	fula-bororo		0.05	61	1cs..	4	3	5	0	0	Fulfide, Kano-katsina	pnb	b
1955	British	0.01000	329	362	570	CEW19i	52-ABAC-b	standard-english	5	79.00	286	3Bsuh	10	9	13	5	2		PNB	b
1956	Buraka	0.06135	2,017	2,218	3,499	BYG12	93-ADAB-a	buraka		40.00	887	0....	9	6	4	4	0		...	.
1957	Congo Pol (Pomo)	0.06000	1,973	2,169	3,422	NAB57c	99-AUDB	pol-kwakum cluster		40.00	868	0....	9	5	2	4	1		...	.
1958	Dagba	1.17765	38,719	42,575	67,171	NAB66z	03-AAAE-d	dagba-goré		30.00	12,773	0.s..	9	6	7	0	0		pnb	.
1959	Dakpa	0.27815	9,145	10,056	15,865	NAB66b	93-ABAI-b	dakpwa		50.00	5,028	0....	10	6	8	4	1		...	b
1960	Dendi	0.29441	9,680	10,644	16,793	NAB65a	01-AAAB-a	dendi		50.00	5,322	1..u.	10	6	8	0	0	Dendi	PNb	.
1961	Djingburu	0.03000	986	1,085	1,711	NAB66b	93-ABAB-d	junguru		45.00	488	0....	9	5	8	4	2		...	.
1962	Fertit (Baggara)	0.50000	16,439	18,076	28,519	CMT30	12-AACD	badawi-sahara cluster		0.01	2	0a...	3	2	0	0	0		PN.	b
1963	French	0.62028	20,394	22,425	35,380	CEW21b	51-AABI-d	general français	70	87.00	19,510	1B.uh	10	9	14	5	1	French	PNB	b
1964	Furu	0.11776	3,872	4,257	6,717	NAB66z	03-AABA-c	furu		20.00	851	0....	9	5	7	0	0		...	b
1965	Gabri (Gabere)	0.70000	23,015	25,307	39,927	NAB60b	17-DGBA	gabri cluster		40.00	10,123	0....	9	5	5	4	1	Gabri	...	.
1966	Ganzi Pygmy (Yaka)	0.04122	1,355	1,490	2,351	BYG12	93-ADDA-c	ganzi		70.00	1,043	0....	10	7	4	4	2		...	.
1967	Gbanziri (Banzini)	0.42689	14,035	15,433	24,349	NAB66b	93-ADAA	gbanziri cluster		40.00	6,173	0....	9	5	4	4	0		...	.
1968	Gbaya	0.10000	3,288	3,615	5,704	NAB66c	93-AAAA-a	vehicular gbaya		60.00	2,169	0.s..	10	7	6	4	1	Gbaya: Gbea*	PNB	b
1969	Gubu	0.10000	3,288	3,615	5,704	NAB66b	93-ABAF-g	gubu		30.00	1,085	0....	9	5	6	2	1		...	b
1970	Gula	0.38273	12,583	13,837	21,830	NAB66z	03-AABA-a	mamun-gula		10.00	1,384	0....	8	4	6	0	0		...	.
1971	Gundi Pygmy	0.04604	1,514	1,664	2,626	BYG12	93-ADDA-d	gundi		20.00	333	0....	9	5	0	1	1		...	.
1972	Hausa	0.63382	20,839	22,914	36,152	NAB60a	19-HAAB-a	hausa	3	0.08	18	4Asu.	4	4	2	1	0	Hausa	PNB	b
1973	Jeme	0.01619	532	585	923	NAB66z	93-BAAA-f	geme		65.00	380	1cs..	10	8	8	0	0		pnb	.
1974	Kaba	0.40040	13,164	14,476	22,838	NAB66z	03-AAAF	kaba cluster		30.00	4,343	0....	9	5	5	3	1	Kaba*	PN.	b
1975	Kaba Dunjo (Sara)	0.11775	3,871	4,257	6,716	NAB66z	03-AAAF	kaba cluster		30.00	1,277	0....	9	5	6	3	1	Kaba*	PN.	b
1976	Kabba (Kabba Laka)	0.06034	1,984	2,181	3,442	NAB66z	03-AAAE-f	laka	1	60.00	1,309	0.s..	10	7	6	4	2	Kabba-laka*	PNb	.
1977	Kaka (Yaka)	0.30617	10,066	11,069	17,463	NAB57c	99-AUDA-a	east kako		30.00	3,321	0....	9	5	7	2	1	Kako*	P..	.
1978	Kara	0.14131	4,646	5,109	8,060	NAB66e	93-AAAA-ko	kara		20.00	1,022	0.s..	9	5	6	2	0		pnb	b
1979	Kari (Karre)	2.73803	90,021	98,987	156,172	NAB66z	92-CDAE-c	karang		43.00	42,564	0.s..	9	7	7	5	3	Karre*	PN.	.
1980	Kpagua	0.10304	3,388	3,725	5,877	NAB66b	93-ABAJ-b	kpagua		20.00	745	0....	9	5	7	0	0		...	.
1981	Kpatiri (Patri)	0.13248	4,356	4,790	7,556	NAB66z	93-ABBA-d	kpatili		45.00	2,155	1.s..	9	8	7	5	1		pnb	.
1982	Kreish	0.02628	864	950	1,499	NAB66e	03-AEAA	kpara cluster		15.00	143	0....	8	5	6	4	1		...	.
1983	Langwasi	1.17766	38,719	42,576	67,171	NAB66b	93-ABAH-b	langbashe		30.00	12,773	0....	9	6	6	3	1		...	.
1984	Lele	0.13000	4,274	4,700	7,415	NAB60b	17-DIAA-a	lele		50.00	2,350	0....	10	6	6	3	1	Lele	PN.	.
1985	Linda	2.00283	65,849	72,408	114,237	NAB66b	93-ABAE	linda-jeto cluster		40.00	28,963	0....	9	6	6	3	1		...	b
1986	Lingala (Zairian)	0.28839	9,482	10,426	16,449	NAB57c	99-AUIF-b	vehicular lingala	17	70.00	7,298	4asu.	10	8	13	5	1	Lingala	PNB	b
1987	Manja (Mandja)	6.47709	212,955	234,164	369,440	NAB66f	93-AAAA-d	manja		55.00	128,790	0.s..	10	8	11	5	3	Manza	pnb	b
1988	Maraba	0.03000	986	1,085	1,711	NAB66b	93-ABAG-b	maraba		50.00	542	0....	10	6	5	5	1		...	.
1989	Mayeka	0.06000	1,973	2,169	3,422	NAB57c	99-ASMA-c	ma-yeka		70.00	1,518	0....	10	7	7	5	1		...	.
1990	Mbandza	0.04436	1,458	1,604	2,530	NAB66b	93-ABAK-b	mbanza		70.00	1,123	0....	10	6	6	3	1	Mbanza	P..	b
1991	Mbangi	0.08096	2,662	2,927	4,618	NAB66z	93-ABBA-bc	m-bangi		45.00	1,317	1.s..	9	7	8	0	0		pnb	.
1992	Mbati (Isongo)	1.76648	58,079	63,863	100,756	NAB66z	99-AUFA-a	mbati		10.00	6,386	0....	8	5	7	2	1		...	b
1993	Mbere Gbaya	0.10000	3,288	3,615	5,704	NAB66c	92-CDAE-e	mbere		60.00	2,169	0.s..	10	7	6	4	1	Gbaya: Mbere*	PN.	.
1994	Mbimu (Mbyemo)	0.70660	23,232	25,545	40,303	NAB57c	99-AUDG-f	m-pyemo		70.00	17,882	0....	10	7	6	5	2		...	.
1995	Mbum	0.36801	12,099	13,305	20,991	NAB66c	92-CDAE-k	mbum	10	63.00	8,382	0.s..	10	7	7	4	2	Mboum*	PN.	n
1996	Monjombo (Monzombo)	0.03890	1,279	1,406	2,219	NAB66z	93-ADCA-a	mo-nzombo		10.00	141	0....	8	5	2	2	1		...	.
1997	Ndogo	0.06000	1,973	2,169	3,422	NAB66z	93-ACAB-a	ndogo		45.00	976	0....	9	6	4	3	1	Ndogo	P..	.
1998	Ndri	0.09523	3,131	3,443	5,432	NAB66b	93-ABAC-b	proper ndi		50.00	1,721	0....	10	6	5	5	1		...	b
1999	Nduka (Ruto, Luto)	0.50049	16,455	18,094	28,547	NAB66z	03-AAAG-d	nduka		20.00	3,619	0....	9	5	0	2	1		...	.
2000	Ngala	0.30000	9,863	10,846	17,111	NAB57c	99-AUIF-c	bangala-3		70.00	7,592	1csu.	10	8	7	5	1	Bangala	PNB	b
2001	Ngam	0.52111	17,133	18,840	29,723	NAB66z	03-AAAE-q	ngam		60.00	11,304	0.s..	10	7	8	3	1	Ngam	pnb	b
2002	Ngando (Ngandu)	0.14720	4,840	5,322	8,396	NAB57h	99-AUFB-c	di-ngando		90.00	4,790	0....	10	7	11	4	2		...	.
2003	Ngbaka Gbaya	0.85380	28,071	30,867	48,699	NAB66c	93-AAAA-l	ngbaka-gbaya		70.00	21,607	0.s..	10	8	7	5	1		pnb	b
2004	Ngbaka Mabo (Bwaka, Mwaka)	2.59082	85,181	93,665	147,775	NAB66z	93-ADBA-a	ngbaka-ma'bo		65.00	60,882	0.s..	10	8	11	5	3	Ngbaka: Ma'bo*	Pnb	b
2005	Ngbandi	0.01400	460	506	799	NAB66z	93-ABBA-b	ngbandi		45.00	228	1.s..	9	8	7	5	1	Ngbandi	PNb	b
2006	Ngola	0.10000	3,288	3,615	5,704	NAB66b	93-ABAC-d	ngola		40.00	1,446	0....	9	5	5	5	0		...	b
2007	Ngundi (Ingundi)	0.32288	10,616	11,673	18,416	NAB57c	93-ADDA-d	gundi		20.00	2,335	0....	9	5	4	3	1		...	.
2008	Nzakara (Sakara)	1.47207	48,399	53,219	83,964	NAB66z	93-BAAA-c	kporo-nzakara		85.00	45,236	1cs..	10	8	12	5	1		pnb	.
2009	Pambia	0.86850	28,555	31,399	49,537	NAB66a	93-BABA-a	pa-pambia		50.00	15,699	0....	10	6	7	3	1		...	.
2010	Pana	2.41417	79,373	87,279	137,699	NAB66z	92-CDAE-h	pana		50.00	43,639	0.s..	10	7	7	3	1	Pana	Pn.	.
2011	Pande	0.28558	9,389	10,324	16,289	NAB57c	99-ARAA-a	mambere-pande		30.00	3,097	0....	9	5	2	3	1		...	b
2012	Runga	0.63299	20,812	22,884	36,104	NAB66z	05-AAAE-a	runga		0.00	0	0....	0	3	0	1	0		...	b
2013	Sabanga	0.06001	1,973	2,170	3,423	NAB66z	93-ABAG-a	sabanga		40.00	868	0....	9	5	2	3	1		...	.
2014	Sango	10.30445	338,791	372,533	587,745	NAB66z	93-ABBA-a	sango	95	50.00	186,267	4.s..	10	9	13	5	3	Sango	PNB	b
2015	Sara Majingai-Ngama (Sar)	1.80000	59,181	65,075	102,668	NAB66z	03-AAAE-j	majingai		70.00	45,552	0.s..	10	8	11	5	1	Sara-majingai	PNb	b
2016	Sara Mbai	0.24436	8,034	8,834	13,938	NAB66z	03-AAAE-h	mbai-kan		65.00	5,742	0.s..	10	8	12	5	3	Mbai: Moissala	PNB	b
2017	Sere (Chere, Basiri)	0.00098	32	35	56	NAB66z	93-ACAA	sere cluster		20.00	7	0....	9	5	2	2	1		...	p
2018	Shuwa Arab (Chad Arab)	1.99651	65,642	72,179	113,877	CMT30	12-AACE-a	shuwa	6	0.11	79	0...h	5	3	1	0	0	Arabic: Chad	PN.	b
2019	Somrai	1.71701	56,452	62,074	97,935	NAB60b	17-DFAA-a	somrai		30.00	18,622	0....	9	5	6	2	1	Somrai	...	b

Continued opposite

Table 8-2 continued

EVANGELIZATION								EVANGELISM			ADDITIONAL DESCRIPTIVE DATA
Ref 1	D 28	aC 29	CG% 30	r 31	E 32	U 33	W 34	e 35	R 36	T 37	Locations, civil divisions, literacy, religions, church history, denominations, dioceses, church growth, missions, agencies, ministries, movements 38
1902	3	10	6.27	8	95.00	5.00	B	97.09	201	6	Immigrants from Syria. Muslims 62% (Hanafi Sunnis,some Alawis), nonreligious 10%. D=Syrian OC of Antioch,Antiochian Orthodox Christian AD New York.
1903	0	10	1.73	0	99.99	0.01	C	518.30	51	10	Southern Yukon. Less than 5 speakers left.
1904	0	10	1.73	0	99.92	0.08	C	449.97	54	10	Northwest British Columbia. 13% speak Tahltan, 87% do not.
1905	2	10	5.04	6	77.00	23.00	B	30.91	215	5	Refugees from civil war in Sri Lanka. Hindus 84%, Muslims 5%. D=Ceylonese Tamil Church,Indo-Canadian Church (Baptist General Conference).
1906	2	10	2.42	5	70.00	30.00	B	17.88	134	5	Immigrants from South India, in professions, commerce. Hindus 70%, Muslims 20%, Baha'is 3%. D=RCC,Baptists.
1907	0	10	4.29	6	59.70	40.30	B	1.52	224	4	Immigrants from Thailand, in commerce, industry. Buddhists 95%.
1908	0	10	1.73	0	99.91	0.09	C	445.08	54	10	South central British Columbia. Speakers 11%, nonspeakers 89%.
1909	0	10	1.73	0	99.96	0.04	C	497.56	51	10	BC, Yukon, Alaska. 21% speak Tlingit, 79% do not. Language isolate. M=YBM,SIL.
1910	1	10	1.73	0	99.94	0.06	C	480.34	51	10	Northern BC coast. 64% do not speak Tsimshian. D=ACC.
1911	0	10	3.31	8	53.50	46.50	B	0.97	206	3	Immigrants from Turkey, in variety of employments. Muslims 99%(Hanafi Sunnis).
1912	0	10	1.73	0	99.89	0.11	C	430.33	55	10	Ontario. Only 2% can speak Tuscarora.
1913	0	10	1.73	0	99.91	0.09	C	445.73	54	10	Yukon. Speakers 30%, nonspeakers 70%.
1914	3	10	1.73	8	99.73	0.27	C	375.69	46	9	Expatriates and immigrants from USA and West Indies. D=AMEC,AOC, and many other denominations.
1915	5	10	1.73	8	99.78	0.22	C	441.28	46	10	Expatriates from USA, in professions, industry, commerce. D=UCC,ACC,CJCLdS,CCS,JWs. T=CBN. R=local stations. T=LESEA.
1916	7	10	1.73	6	99.82	0.18	C	469.90	51	10	Immigrants, refugees from USSR after 1917. D=Ukrainian GOC,UOC of America,ACPC,RCC(4 Dioceses),Baptists,Pentecostals,Presbyterians. Many charismatics.
1917	1	10	3.27	5	58.10	41.90	B	0.21	203	3	Immigrants from Pakistan and north India since 1947. Virtually all Muslims 100%(Hanafi Sunnis). D=RCC.
1918	2	10	7.91	6	87.00	13.00	B	63.51	276	6	Refugees, immigrants from Viet Nam. Mahayana Buddhists 59%, New-Religionists 20%. D=RCC,Vietnamese Alliance Church. M=CMA,Chinese Churches.
1919	1	10	1.73	8	99.92	0.08	C	527.20	50	10	Immigrants from French-speaking Belgium; in professions. D=RCC.
1920	3	10	1.73	5	99.85	0.15	C	499.50	46	10	Welsh immigrants, from Wales. Most are Methodists. D=UMC,UCC,ACC.
1921	5	10	9.40	8	99.85	0.15	C	483.99	176	10	Immigrants from many Caribbean Islands.Very numerous in Edmonton. D=New Testament Ch of God,ACC,RCC,UCC,et alia.
1922	3	10	1.73	8	99.95	0.05	C	558.26	43	10	Central Arctic region. 53% speak Inuit. D=ACC,UCC,RCC.
1923	5	10	1.73	4	99.97	0.03	C	577.10	44	10	North central Manitoba. 30% do not speak Cree. D=RCC,UCC,ACC,PAOC,Native American Ch. M=SIL,CMA,NCEM.
1924	6	10	1.73	0	99.96	0.04	C	525.60	48	10	Southern Canada, USA. 58% speak the language, 42% do not. D=ACC,UCC,RCC,PAOC,Native American Ch, Mennonites. M=CMA,UBS.
1925	0	10	1.73	8	99.80	0.20	C	423.40	50	10	Near Quebec City. Wyandot language extinct; no speakers left, all use English.
1926	0	8	1.58		97.00	3.00	C	212.43	45	8	Upper Tanana, Hispanics (Mestizos: M=GMU, RCC), Central Americans, Chileans, Assyrians, Chaldeans, Parsis.
Cape Verde											
1927	1	10	1.83	0	99.90	0.10	C	446.76	69	10	Black Africans from Guinea Bissau. Animists 9%. Muslims 1%. D=RCC.
1928	4	8	1.79	2	99.99	0.01	C	568.87	50	10	Long Catholic tradition. D=RCC(D-Santiago de Cabo Verde),Ch of the Nazarene,SDA,JWs. M=BMAA.
1929	1	9	1.77	2	99.99	0.01	C	572.47	50	10	Brava Island Creole, Portuguese Creole. Also in Guinea Bissau, Senegal, Gambia. D=RCC. M=CSSp,OFMCap,SDB.
1930	1	10	1.83	4	99.80	0.20	C	414.64	66	10	Fulani settlers from mainland. Muslims (Sunnis) 20%. D=RCC.
1931	1	10	1.83	0	99.90	0.10	C	446.76	69	10	Black Africans from Guinea Bissau, Senegal, Gambia. D=RCC.
1932	1	10	1.83	8	99.97	0.03	C	601.88	46	10	Whites from Portugal, or long-term settlers. D=RCC.
1933	0	10	1.84		99.96	0.04	C	469.53	38	10	Goanese missionary clergy from India.
Cayman Islands											
1934	4	10	1.80	8	99.67	0.33	C	342.37	58	9	Expatriates from Britain, professionals, administrators. D=Anglican Ch(D-Jamaica),UCJGC,JWs,CJCLdS.
1935	0	10	2.52	7	64.50	35.50	B	24.72	150	5	Traders, originally from India, Pakistan. Most are Hindus 85%, with some Muslims.
1936	0	10	1.96	8	48.90	51.10	A	1.60	148	4	Long-term settlers or residents, practicing orthodox Judaism.
1937	4	10	1.78	8	99.66	0.34	C	305.64	54	9	Afro-Caribbean Spiritists 20%. D=United Ch of Jamaica & Grand Cayman,COG(Anderson),Baptists,SDA. M=JBU,PHM.
1938	5	10	1.84	8	99.77	0.23	C	385.03	49	9	Including many immigrants. D=Anglican Ch(CPWI),RCC(M-Kingston),UCJGC,IBSA,WPM.
1939	0	10	2.13		52.00	48.00	B	47.45	112	6	From other West Indies countries, especially Jamaica, Filipinos, Arabs. Afro-Caribbean Spiritists 20%, nonreligious 20%.
Central African Republic											
1940	0	0	8.02	0	82.00	18.00	C	179.58	316	7	Boali, Bimbo, Boda, and Yaloke subprefectures. Many children learn Sango. Muslims 5%. D=RCC.
1941	0	6	2.22	4	29.02	70.98	A	0.02	361	2	Nomads in north, related to Bororo Fulani. Muslims 100%(Maliki Sunnis). M=Baptist Ch of Western CAR.
1942	2	6	4.80	0	39.00	61.00	A	14.23	415	5	Forest Pygmies. Also in Cameroon, Gabon, Congo. Animists 90%. D=RCC,EPC.
1943	6	9	10.15	0	91.00	9.00	B	146.14	361	7	Also in Sudan. Sango as lingua franca. Animists 2%, Muslims 16%(spreading rapidly). D=RCC(M-Bangui),EER,EBRCA,EEF,ECAR,AICs. M=BMM,SIL,CSSp.
1944	1	6	4.21	0	67.00	33.00	B	97.82	231	6	Mambere Kadei Prefecture. Animists 50%, some Muslims. D=RCC.
1945	3	6	8.66	1	85.00	15.00	B	124.10	338	7	Dialect of Gbaya, in west of country. Animists 35%, Muslims 5%. D=EEF,UEB,RCC.
1946	7	6	11.28	4	99.53	0.47	B	216.66	321	8	Also Cameroon, Nigeria, Congo. Lingua franca: Sango. Animists 2%, Muslims 10%. D=AoG,SDA,EELRCA,EEF,UEB,RCC,AICs. M=CBM,SBM,OFMCap. R=ELWA.
1947	0	7	6.53	0	64.00	36.00	B	81.76	358	6	Basse-Kotto Prefecture. Also in Zaire; bilingual there. Closest to Gubu. Animists 55%.
1948	1	7	4.83	1	99.70	0.30	C	265.72	175	8	Sangha Province, South of Nola. Animists 29%, Muslims 1%. D=RCC.
1949	1	7	4.26	0	57.00	43.00	B	62.41	272	6	In extreme west. Also in Chad. Animists 60%, Muslims 10%. D=RCC.
1950	0	6	3.28	0	33.00	67.00	A	12.04	364	5	East Province, also in Gabon, Cameroon. Animists 90%. M=Baptist Mission.
1951	0	0	6.00	4	99.64	0.36	C	233.60	204	8	Scattered throughout the southwest. People bilingual in Zande. Animists 5%. D=RCC.
1952	0	0	7.59	1	90.00	10.00	C	197.10	287	7	Boda and Bimbo subprefectures. People bilingual in Sango. Muslims 5%, Nonreligious 5%. D=RCC
1953	1	7	2.48	0	71.00	29.00	B	103.66	152	7	Lobaye Prefecture. Many also in Congo. Related to Bongili. Animists 50%. D=RCC.
1954	0	0	4.20	4	24.05	75.95	A	0.04	661	2	True cattle nomads. Permanently moving. Muslims 100%(Sunnis). M=AIM,EET.
1955	2	10	3.41	8	99.79	0.21	C	438.29	82	10	Expatriates from UK, in development, education. D=UEB,RCC.
1956	0	7	4.59	0	67.00	33.00	B	97.82	233	6	Nearly extinct in Zaire, but scattered groups remain in CAR along Ubangi river. Animists 60%.
1957	1	7	4.56	0	67.00	33.00	B	97.82	247	6	Sangha Mbaere Prefecture. Also in Congo, Cameroon. Animists 60%. D=RCC.
1958	0	0	7.41	1	58.00	42.00	B	63.51	418	6	Batangafo, Kabo, and Bossangoa subprefectures. Animists 70%. D=RCC.
1959	1	8	6.42	0	89.00	11.00	B	162.42	254	7	Related to Banda. Second language: Sango. Animists 30%, Muslims 20%. D=RCC.
1960	0	0	6.48	4	82.00	18.00	B	149.65	280	7	Ouango subprefecture. People bilingual in Sango. Animists 30%. D=RCC.
1961	2	8	3.96	0	81.00	19.00	B	133.04	196	7	Also in Sudan. Close to Banda. Animists 35%, Muslims 20%. D=RCC,EEF.
1962	0	6	0.70	7	27.01	72.99	A	0.01	142	2	In east. Nomadic Bedouin. Muslims 100%(Sunnis).
1963	1	9	6.15	8	99.87	0.13	C	498.55	124	10	Administrators from France, also teachers, government workers, soldiers. D=RCC.
1964	0	0	4.54	0	38.00	62.00	A	27.74	430	5	Mobaye subprefecture. 11 villages. Animists 40%, Muslims 40%. D=RCC.
1965	1	7	7.17	0	72.00	28.00	B	105.12	326	7	Also in Chad. Animists 45%, Muslims 5%. D=Assemblees Chretiennes du Tchad.
1966	1	7	4.76	0	99.70	0.30	C	260.61	157	8	Sangha Prefecture. Pygmies in dense forests. Animists 30%. D=RCC(M-Bangui). M=CSSp,OFMCap.
1967	0	7	6.64	0	68.00	32.00	B	99.28	341	6	A fishing tribe on the Ubangi river. Similar to Buraka. Animists 55%.
1968	6	7	5.53	4	99.60	0.40	C	240.90	183	8	Animists 35%, Muslims 2%. D=SDA,RCC(M-Bangui),AoG,CBM,SBM,AICs. M=OFMCap.
1969	1	7	4.80	0	60.00	40.00	B	65.70	303	6	Also in Zaire. Bilingual in Mono, Sango. Animists 70%. D=RCC. M=GR.
1970	0	0	5.05	0	27.00	73.00	A	9.85	658	4	Birao subprefecture, near Sudan border at Kafia Kingi. Muslims 60%, Animists 30%.
1971	0	6	3.57	0	40.00	60.00	A	29.20	320	5	Pygmies in dense forest. Animists 80%. M=Baptist Mission.
1972	0	10	2.93	5	47.08	52.92	A	0.13	240	3	Nomads in north. Traders across whole sub-Saharan belt of Africa. Muslims 100%(Maliki Sunnis).
1973	0	0	3.70	0	94.00	6.00	C	223.01	150	8	Ndele subprefecture. 2 villages north of Ndele. Sango used as second language. Animists 5%. D=RCC
1974	1	6	6.26	0	63.00	37.00	B	68.98	334	6	Mainly in CAR, also some in Chad. Animists 70%. D=RCC.
1975	1	6	4.97	0	64.00	36.00	B	70.08	274	6	A Sara people in northwest. Animists 60%. D=RCC.
1976	1	6	5.00	1	99.60	0.40	C	223.38	173	8	Also in Chad. Animists 20%. D=EEF. M=NFBC,CMML.
1977	1	6	5.98	1	62.00	38.00	B	67.89	329	6	Gambula town at Cameroon border near Berberati. Also in Congo, Cameroon. Animists 70%. D=RCC.
1978	0	6	4.74	1	58.00	42.00	B	42.34	291	6	Near Sudan border. Many bilinguals in Kresh, Arabic. Animists 40%, Muslims 40%.
1979	3	6	8.72	1	87.00	13.00	B	136.54	320	7	Primarily in Chad, also Cameroon. Animists 47%, Muslims 10%. D=RCC(D-Berberati), EEC,EEF. M=AIM,NFBC,OFMCap.
1980	0	0	4.41	0	38.00	62.00	A	27.74	450	5	Also in Congo-Zaire. Animists 80%. D=RCC.
1981	1	6	5.52	1	87.00	13.00	B	142.89	219	7	Basse-Kotto Prefecture. Animists 55%. D=RCC.
1982	1	6	2.70	0	44.00	56.00	A	24.09	257	5	In east. Majority live in Sudan. Muslims 80%(Sunnis), some animists. D=RCC.
1983	1	6	7.41	0	61.00	39.00	B	66.79	415	6	Southern Ouaka, Kemo Prefectures. Mainly in Zaire. Animists 30%. D=RCC.
1984	1	6	5.61	0	85.00	15.00	B	155.12	226	7	Mainly in Chad. Animists 50%, D=Eglises Evangeliques du Tchad. M=TEAM.
1985	1	6	8.30	0	74.00	26.00	B	108.04	375	7	In and around Bambari, Ippy. Related to Banda. Second language: Sango. Animists 30%, Muslims 10%. D=RCC.
1986	3	10	6.81	5	99.70	0.30	C	362.81	160	9	Lingua franca from Zaire. Animists 30%. D=RCC,EJCSK,other AICs. M=UBS.
1987	4	6	9.93	1	99.55	0.45	B	218.81	296	8	Also in Cameroon, Chad. Lingua franca used: Sango. Animists 2%, Muslims 3%. D=EEC,Comite Baptiste,EBRCA,other AICs. M=BMM,CEM,AIM,NFBC/CBM.
1988	1	6	4.07	0	81.00	19.00	B	147.82	200	7	Ouaka Prefecture, Bakala town. Related to Banda. Second Language: Sango. Animists 40%, Muslims 10%. D=RCC.
1989	1	7	5.15	0	99.70	0.30	C	268.27	173	8	Near Congo/Zaire/CAR border. Animists 30%. D=RCC.
1990	1	6	4.83	0	99.70	0.30	C	260.61	179	8	Almost entirely in Zaire, some in Congo. Animists 30%. D=RCC.
1991	0	0	5.00	1	74.00	26.00	B	121.54	238	7	Bangassou, Ouango, and Alindao subprefectures. People bilingual in Sango. Animists 55%. D=RCC.
1992	1	6	6.67	0	42.00	58.00	A	15.33	528	5	Lobaye Prefecture. Second language: Sango. Animists 80%, some Muslims. D=RCC.
1993	1	7	5.53	4	99.60	0.40	C	223.38	198	8	In west CAR. Animists 30%, some Muslims. D=RCC.
1994	2	7	7.78	1	99.70	0.30	C	275.94	235	8	Mostly in Cameroon. Animists 14%, Muslims 1%. D=RCC(D-Berberati),UEB. M=Orebro Mission,OFMCap.
1995	0	6	6.96	1	99.63	0.37	C	234.54	236	8	Most in Cameroon, some in Chad. Animists 25%, Muslims 12%. M=SUM,ACT.
1996	1	6	2.68	0	33.00	67.00	A	12.04	341	5	Majority in Congo and Zaire. Strong animists 80%. D=RCC.
1997	1	7	4.69	0	74.00	26.00	B	121.54	227	7	In east of CAR. Primarily in Sudan. Animists 40%, some Muslims. D=RCC.
1998	1	6	5.28	0	85.00	15.00	B	155.12	229	7	Ouaka and Kemo Ibingui Prefectures. Closest to Ngola. Second language: Sango. Animists 30%, Muslims 20%. D=RCC.
1999	1	7	6.07	0	44.00	56.00	A	32.12	467	5	Bamingui-Bangoran and Haute-Kotto Prefectures. Also in Chad. Animists 80%. D=RCC.
2000	3	6	6.86	4	99.70	0.30	C	319.37	183	9	Haut-Zaire Region. Also in Zaire. Lingua franca for 4 million. Animists 30%. D=RCC,ECZ,AICs. M=UBS.
2001	1	6	7.28	1	99.60	0.40	C	223.38	234	8	In north, Ouham Prefecture, Kabo Subprefecture. Also in southern Chad. Animists 40%. D=RCC.
2002	2	7	6.37	0	99.90	0.10	C	427.05	165	10	Labaye Prefecture, south of Mbailo. Close to Ngundi. Animists 10%. D=RCC,AICs.
2003	1	7	7.98	1	99.70	0.30	C	298.93	230	8	Mainly in Zaire, some in Congo. Lingua franca: Sango. Animists 20%. D=RCC.
2004	3	6	9.11	0	99.65	0.35	C	272.83	251	8	Primarily in Zaire and Congo. Animists 5%. D=ECZ-CECU,RCC,AICs.
2005	2	6	3.18	1	91.00	9.00	B	149.46	139	7	Migrants from large tribe in Zaire. Bilingual in Lingala. Animists 55%. D=RCC,ECZ(CECU/EFCA,CEUM/ECCA). M=UBS.
2006	0	6	5.10	0	72.00	28.00	B	105.12	264	7	Related to Banda, with Sango as second language. Animists 40%, Muslims 20%.
2007	1	7	5.60	0	49.00	51.00	A	35.77	395	5	Sangha Mbaere Prefecture. Also in Congo. Related to Mbati, Bomitaba. Animists 80%. D=RCC.
2008	1	6	8.78	0	99.85	0.15	C	415.73	209	10	North of border, also in Zaire. Animists 10%. D=RCC. M=BMM.
2009	1	7	7.64	0	84.00	16.00	B	153.30	309	7	Also in Zaire and Sudan. Animists 30%, some Muslims. D=RCC.
2010	1	6	8.74	1	88.00	12.00	B	160.60	317	7	Northwest border, also in Chad, Cameroon, and Nigeria. Muslims 30%, animists 2%. D=RCC(D-Berberati). M=OFMCap.
2011	1	7	5.90	0	60.00	40.00	B	65.70	337	6	Sangha Mbaere Prefecture. Second language: Sango. Animists 70%. D=RCC.
2012	0	6	0.00	0	12.00	88.00	A	0.00	0	1.04	Also in Chad. Traders. Men are bilingual in Arabic. Muslims 80%, animists 20%.
2013	1	7	4.56	0	66.00	34.00	B	96.36	249	6	In west of CAR. Related to Banda. Animists 50%, some Muslims. D=RCC.
2014	2	6	10.33	4	99.50	0.50	B	206.22	285	8	Official national language, with 5.1 million speakers. Heavily christianized. Animists 2%, nonreligious, Muslims. D=RCC(5 Dioceses),EBRCA. M=CSSp,OFMCap..
2015	2	6	8.79	1	99.70	0.30	C	311.71	230	9	Also in Chad. Animists 2%, Muslims 10%. D=EBRCA,AICs. M=BMM.
2016	3	6	6.56	4	99.65	0.35	C	298.93	174	8	Also in Chad, Cameroon, Nigeria. Fairly literate. Animists 5%. D=Brethren,Baptists,Assemblees Chretiennes du Tchad. M=BMM,CMML,TEAM.
2017	1	7	1.96	0	46.00	54.00	A	33.58	202	5	In southern part of CAR. Mainly in Zaire. Bilingual in Ndogo. Animists 70%, some Muslims. D=RCC.
2018	0	6	4.47	7	30.11	69.89	A	0.12	470	3	Shuwa Arabs from northern Chad. Lingua franca across vast territory. Muslims 100%(Sunnis,mostly Tijaniyya).
2019	1	7	7.82	0	61.00	39.00	B	66.79	414	6	In north of country. Some in Chad. Animists 55%. D=RCC. M=WEC.

Continued overleaf

Table 8-2 continued

PEOPLE		POPULATION				IDENTITY CODE		LANGUAGE		CHURCH		MINISTRY						SCRIPTURE		
Ref 1	Ethnic name 2	P% 3	In 1995 4	In 2000 5	In 2025 6	Race 7	Language 8	Autoglossonym 9	S 10	AC 11	Members 12	Jayuh 13-17	d 18	wa 19	xc 20	mc 21	mi 22	Biblioglossonym 23	Pub 24-26	ss 27
2020	Tagba	0.10000	3,288	3,615	5,704	NAB66z	93-ACAB-b	tagbu		40.00	1,446	0....	9	5	6	3	1		p..	.
2021	Tambogo	0.04000	1,315	1,446	2,282	NAB66b	93-ABAB-b	tangbago		45.00	651	0....	9	5	8	3	1		...	b
2022	Tana	0.66000	21,700	23,861	37,645	NAB66z	03-AAAG-e	tana		20.00	4,772	0....	9	5	7	2	2		...	.
2023	Togboh (Tagbo)	0.29413	9,670	10,634	16,777	NAB66z	93-ABAD-a	togbo		30.00	3,190	0....	9	5	6	2	1		...	b
2024	Turku Arab (Tekrur,Turkol)	0.10000	3,288	3,615	5,704	CMT30	12-AACG-d	turku	15	0.00	0	0....	0	3	0	0	0		...	b
2025	Vale	0.15897	5,227	5,747	9,067	NAB66z	03-AAAG-b	vale		30.00	1,724	0....	9	5	4	2	0		...	.
2026	Vodere (Vidri)	0.04000	1,315	1,446	2,282	NAB66b	93-ABAC-e	vidiri		45.00	651	0....	9	5	7	3	1		...	b
2027	Wada	0.05002	1,645	1,808	2,853	NAB66b	93-ABAG-e	wada		40.00	723	0....	9	5	7	3	1		...	.
2028	Wasa	0.04000	1,315	1,446	2,282	NAB66b	93-ABAF-b	wasa		30.00	434	0....	9	5	6	3	1		...	.
2029	Wojo	0.04000	1,315	1,446	2,282	NAB66b	93-ABAF-e	wojo		50.00	723	0....	10	6	8	3	1		...	b
2030	Yakoma	2.94414	96,798	106,438	167,928	NAB66z	93-ABBA-c	yakoma		30.00	31,932	1.s..	9	5	5	3	1		pnb	p
2031	Yangere	0.23584	7,754	8,526	13,452	NAB66b	93-ABAA	yangere cluster		40.00	3,410	0....	9	5	5	5	1		...	.
2032	Yulu (Youlou)	0.11775	3,871	4,257	6,716	NAB66z	03-AABA-d	yulu		30.00	1,277	0....	9	5	5	2	1		...	b
2033	Zande (Azande, Avongara)	1.82535	60,014	65,991	104,114	NAB66a	93-BAAA-a	pa-zande		64.00	42,234	4As..	10	8	11	5	3	Pazande*	PNB	b
2034	other minor peoples	0.20000	6,576	7,231	11,408	...				50.00	3,615		10	5	7	3	0			
	Chad	**100.00000**	**6,707,475**	**7,650,982**	**13,908,122**					**18.8**	**1,438,011**									
2035	Abu Sharib (Abou Charib)	0.72171	48,409	55,218	100,376	NAB66z	05-DABA-b	abu-sharib		0.00	0	0....	0	1	0	0	0		...	b
2036	Adamawa Fulani	1.10000	73,782	84,161	152,989	NAB56c	90-BAAA-s	fula-fellata		1.00	842	1cs..	6	4	6	2	1	Fulfulde, Adamawa	PNB	b
2037	Babalia Arab	0.06551	4,394	5,012	9,111	NAB66z	12-AACG-a	babaliya		0.00	0	0....	0	1	0	0	0		...	b
2038	Bagirmi Fulani	0.74475	49,954	56,981	103,581	NAB56c	90-BAAA-r	fula-bagirmi		0.02	11	1cs..	3	3	1	1	2		pnb	b
2039	Banda	1.00001	67,075	76,511	139,083	NAB66b	93-ABAB-a	banda-ndele	52	50.00	38,255	0....	10	4	8	3	1	Banda, South Central	...	b
2040	Barein	0.06821	4,575	5,219	9,487	NAB66b	17-CAAA-a	barein	50	0.00	0	0....	0	2	1	0	0		...	b
2041	Barma (Bagirmi, Lisi)	0.83533	56,030	63,911	116,179	NAB66z	03-AAAA-a	tar-barma	5	0.01	6	0....	3	3	5	1	1	Bagirmi	...	b
2042	Bediondo Mbai	1.00279	67,262	76,723	139,469	NAB66z	03-AAAE-e	mbai-doba	2	50.00	38,362	0.s..	10	5	4	2	1	Mbai: Doba*	PNB	.
2043	Besme (Huner)	0.02043	1,370	1,563	2,841	NAB66z	92-CCAA-a	besme		30.00	469	0....	9	5	4	2	1		...	.
2044	Bideyat (Beri)	0.06398	4,291	4,895	8,898	NAB61	02-CAAA-a	beri-aa		0.00	0	0....	0	1	0	0	0		...	b
2045	Bidio	0.30569	20,504	23,388	42,516	NAB60b	17-ABDA-a	bidiyo		0.00	0	0....	0	1	0	0	0		...	b
2046	Bilala (Boulala)	2.27328	152,480	173,928	316,171	NAB66z	03-AAAB-b	bilala		0.00	0	0....	0	1	0	0	1		...	n
2047	Birgid (Bergit)	0.13187	8,845	10,089	18,341	NAB60b	17-AADA-a	birgit		0.10	10	0....	5	4	4	0	0		...	b
2048	Bolgo Dugag	0.03001	2,013	2,296	4,174	NAB66b	92-CAAE-a	petit-bolgo	50	30.00	689	0....	9	3	4	1	1		...	.
2049	Bon Gula (Doun)	0.01997	1,339	1,528	2,777	NAB66Z	92-CAAF-b	taat-aal		5.00	76	0....	7	4	2	2	1		...	.
2050	British	0.00200	134	153	278	CEW19i	52-ABAC-b	standard-english	1	78.00	119	3Bsuh	10	9	13	4	3		PNB	b
2051	Bua	0.12823	8,601	9,811	17,834	NAB66z	92-CAAD-a	bua		0.10	10	0....	5	5	3	2	1		...	b
2052	Buduma (Kuri Islander)	0.85855	57,587	65,688	119,408	NAB60b	18-BBBA-a	yidena		0.02	13	0....	3	3	2	1	3	Buduma	...	b
2053	Bulgeda (Kokorda)	0.29000	19,452	22,188	40,334	NAB61	02-AAAA	kanuri cluster		0.00	0	4....	0	3	0	3	0		PN.	p
2054	Buso	0.00134	90	103	186	NAB66z	17-DBAA-a	buso		30.00	31	0....	9	5	0	3	0		...	.
2055	Dai (Dari)	0.83053	55,708	63,544	115,511	NAB66z	92-CBAA-a	day		50.00	31,772	0....	10	6	7	3	3	Day	PN.	.
2056	Daju of Dar Dadju	0.38434	25,780	29,406	53,454	NAB66d	05-EAAA-a	saarong-ge		0.00	0	0....	0	3	0	0	2	Daju, Dar Daju	...	b
2057	Daju of Dar Sila	0.97100	65,130	74,291	135,048	NAB66d	05-EAAB-aa	daju-sila		0.00	0	0....	0	3	0	0	2		...	b
2058	Dam (Ndam, Guli)	0.11449	7,679	8,760	15,923	NAB60b	17-DEAA	ndam cluster		0.10	9	0....	5	4	3	1	2	Ndam	...	.
2059	Dangaleat	0.44923	30,132	34,371	62,479	NAB60b	17-ABFA-a	dangla-korlongo		0.00	0	0....	0	2	0	0	1	Dangaleat	...	b
2060	Daza	4.69670	315,030	359,344	653,223	NAB61	02-BAAA-b	daza-ga		0.00	0	0....	0	1	0	0	0		...	b
2061	Dekakire (Baggara)	0.09000	6,037	6,886	12,517	CMT30	12-AACD	badawi-sahara cluster		0.00	0	0a...	0	1	0	0	0		PN.	b
2062	Fanya (Fagnia, Fanian)	0.01829	1,227	1,399	2,544	NAB66z	92-CAAH-a	proper fania		0.10	1	0....	5	5	1	2	1		...	.
2063	Fongoro (Gelege, Kole)	0.01601	1,074	1,225	2,227	NAB66z	03-AACB-a	gele		0.00	0	0....	0	1	1	0	0		...	.
2064	French	0.10290	6,902	7,873	14,311	CEW21b	51-AABI-d	general français	25	87.00	6,849	1B.uh	10	9	14	4	3	French	PNB	b
2065	Fur	0.03749	2,515	2,868	5,214	NAB66d	05-CAAA-a	bele-for		0.04	1	0....	3	3	0	0	0		...	b
2066	Gadang	0.06156	4,129	4,710	8,562	NAB60b	17-DCAA-a	gadang		0.00	0	0....	0	3	1	0	2		...	.
2067	Gidar (Guidar)	0.19445	13,043	14,877	27,044	NAB60b	17-GAAA-a	gidar		25.00	3,719	0.s..	9	5	5	3	2	Guidar*	PN.	.
2068	Gkelendeng (Mbara)	0.02234	1,498	1,709	3,107	NAB60b	17-FAAA-k	may-mbara		0.20	3	0....	5	4	4	1	0		pn.	.
2069	Golo	0.10000	6,707	7,651	13,908	NAB66z	00-DCAA-a	golo		30.00	2,295	4....	9	5	5	3	0	Gouro*	PNB	p
2070	Gori (Laal)	0.00950	637	727	1,321	NAB66z	91-GFAC-e	go-ri		10.00	73	0....	8	5	2	1	1		p..	.
2071	Goulai (Goulei)	2.71656	182,213	207,844	377,822	NAB66z	03-AAAE-o	gulai		55.00	114,314	0.s..	10	6	7	4	3	Goulei*	Pnb	b
2072	Gula	0.09000	6,037	6,886	12,517	NAB66z	03-AABA-a	mamun-gula		20.00	1,377	0....	9	5	4	3	0		...	.
2073	Gula Iro (Kulaal)	0.06011	4,032	4,599	8,360	NAB66z	92-CAAG	kulaal cluster		10.00	460	0....	8	5	4	3	2		...	.
2074	Gulfe (Ngwalkwe)	0.50000	33,537	38,255	69,541	NAB60b	18-BBAB-c	malgbe		50.00	19,127	0....	10	5	6	3	1		...	.
2075	Hausa	2.00000	134,150	153,020	278,162	NAB60a	19-HAAB-a	hausa	8	0.01	15	4Asu.	3	4	2	1	0	Hausa	PNB	b
2076	Hemat (Baggara)	0.15000	10,061	11,476	20,862	CMT30	12-AACE-b	baggaari		0.00	0	0...h	0	1	0	0	0		pn.	b
2077	Jaya	0.03660	2,455	2,800	5,090	NAB66z	03-AAAC-e	tar-jaie		0.30	8	0....	5	3	5	0	0		...	.
2078	Jongor (Dionkor, Djonkor)	0.02496	1,674	1,910	3,471	NAB60b	17-BAAA	mokulu cluster		1.00	19	0....	6	3	2	1	0	Mokulu	...	b
2079	Jumam	0.05499	3,688	4,207	7,648	NAB66c	92-CCAB-c	jumam		5.00	210	0....	7	4	4	3	1		pn.	n
2080	Kaba (Sara Kaba)	0.06000	4,024	4,591	8,345	NAB66z	03-AAAF	kaba cluster		30.00	1,377	0....	9	5	4	4	1	Kaba*	PN.	b
2081	Kaba Deme	0.66553	44,640	50,920	92,563	NAB66z	03-AAAF	kaba cluster		59.90	30,501	0....	10	5	4	3	1	Kaba*	PN.	b
2082	Kaba Kurumi	0.03001	2,013	2,296	4,174	NAB66z	03-AAAF	kaba cluster		25.00	574	0....	9	5	4	3	1	Kaba*	PN.	b
2083	Kaba Na (Kaba Nar)	0.58234	39,060	44,555	80,993	NAB66z	03-AAAF-o	na		60.00	26,733	0....	10	5	4	3	1	Kaba Na	PN.	.
2084	Kaba-Lai	0.29757	19,959	22,767	41,386	NAB60b	17-DGCA-a	kabalai		20.00	4,553	0....	9	5	4	2	2		...	.
2085	Kado (Dari, Lame)	0.40000	26,830	30,604	55,632	NAB60b	17-FABB-f	herd'e	1	50.00	15,302	0.s..	10	6	7	4	3	Kado*	PN.	.
2086	Kanembu	1.11478	74,774	85,292	155,045	NAB61	02-AAAB-a	kanembu		0.01	9	0....	3	4	2	1	3	Kanembu	...	b
2087	Karang (Lakka)	0.01572	1,054	1,203	2,186	NAB66c	92-CDAE-c	karang		5.00	60	0.s..	7	4	2	2	0	Karre*	PN.	.
2088	Karanga (Kurunga)	1.58065	106,022	120,935	219,839	NAB66z	05-AAAC-a	karanga		50.00	60,468	0....	10	5	7	2	1		...	.
2089	Kendeje	0.02358	1,582	1,804	3,280	NAB66z	05-AAAA	maba cluster		0.01	0	0....	3	2	4	0	0		...	b
2090	Kenga (Kenge, Cenge)	0.49914	33,480	38,189	69,421	NAB66z	03-AAAC-a	tar-cenge		0.30	115	0....	5	3	2	0	2	Kenga	...	b
2091	Kera	0.74079	49,688	56,678	103,030	NAB66z	17-EBAA-a	kera		30.00	17,003	0....	9	5	6	3	3	Kera	P..	.
2092	Kibet	0.45346	30,416	34,694	63,068	NAB66z	05-AAAF	kibeet cluster		0.00	0	0....	0	1	0	0	0		...	b
2093	Kim (Garap, Kolobo)	0.25546	17,135	19,545	35,530	NAB60b	92-CCAB-a	kim		60.00	11,727	0....	10	7	7	4	3	Kim	PN.	.
2094	Kimre (Gabri-Kimre)	0.26417	17,719	20,212	36,741	NAB60b	17-DGAA-a	kimruwa		20.00	4,042	0....	9	5	4	3	1	Kimre	...	.
2095	Koke	0.00998	669	764	1,388	NAB66z	92-CAAD-b	koke		30.00	229	0....	9	5	4	3	2		...	.
2096	Kotoko-Kuseri (Mser)	0.02000	1,341	1,530	2,782	NAB60b	18-BBAA-b	mser		0.20	3	0....	5	3	4	0	0		...	b
2097	Kotoko-Logone	0.20590	13,811	15,753	28,637	NAB60b	18-BBAA-a	lagwan		0.10	16	0....	5	3	0	0	1		...	n
2098	Kreda (Karra)	0.81271	54,512	62,180	113,033	NAB61	02-BAAA-b	daza-ga		0.00	0	0....	0	1	0	0	0		...	b
2099	Kuang (Kwong)	0.27959	18,753	21,391	38,886	NAB60b	17-EAAA-a	kwang		40.00	8,557	0....	9	5	4	3	2	Kwang	...	.
2100	Kujarge	0.02088	1,401	1,598	2,904	NAB66d	05-CAAA	for cluster		0.10	2	0....	5	3	1	0	0		...	b
2101	Kuka	1.27550	85,554	97,588	177,398	NAB66z	03-AAAB-a	kuka		0.00	0	0....	0	2	0	0	0		...	n
2102	Kuo (Koh)	0.15000	10,061	11,476	20,862	NAB66c	92-CDAE-f	kuo		20.00	2,295	0.s..	9	5	4	2	2	Kuo	Pn.	.
2103	Laka (Kabba Laka)	0.96869	64,975	74,114	134,727	NAB66z	03-AAAE-f	laka		20.00	14,823	0.s..	9	5	7	4	2	Kabba-laka*	PNb	.
2104	Lele	0.44652	29,950	34,163	62,103	NAB60b	17-DIAA-a	lele		45.00	15,373	0....	9	6	7	4	2	Lele	PN.	.
2105	Logone	0.06000	4,024	4,591	8,345	NAB60b	18-BBAA-a	lagwan		30.00	1,377	0....	9	5	7	2	1		...	n
2106	Luto	0.03291	2,207	2,518	4,577	NAB66z	03-AAAG-a	ruto		30.00	755	0....	9	6	7	0	0		...	.
2107	Mahamid Baggara	0.15000	10,061	11,476	20,862	CMT30	12-AACE-b	baggaari		0.00	0	0...h	0	1	0	0	0		pn.	b
2108	Maltam (Maslam)	0.10203	6,844	7,806	14,190	NAB60b	18-BBAB-a	maslam		0.10	8	0....	5	4	4	0	0		...	.
2109	Mangbai	0.01500	1,006	1,148	2,086	NAB66z	92-CDAC-a	mambai		50.00	574	0....	10	6	6	3	1		...	.
2110	Mararit	0.70526	47,305	53,959	98,088	NAB66d	05-DABA-a	abiyi		0.01	5	0....	3	3	4	0	0		...	b
2111	Marba (Azumeina, Kulung)	2.06910	138,784	158,306	287,773	NAB60b	17-FAAD-a	marba	2	20.00	31,661	0....	9	5	8	2	3	Azumeina*	PNB	.
2112	Marfa	3.23591	217,048	247,579	450,054	NAB60b	05-AAAB-a	marfa		5.00	12,379	0....	7	5	6	4	0		...	.
2113	Masa (Masana, Banana)	1.81513	121,749	138,875	252,450	NAB60b	17-FAAA-g	bongor	4	30.00	41,663	0....	9	5	7	2	3		pn.	.
2114	Masalit	0.84601	56,746	64,728	117,664	NAB66z	05-AAAD-a	kaana-masala		0.01	6	0....	3	3	4	1	3	Masalit	...	b
2115	Masmaje (Mesmedje)	0.42805	28,711	32,750	59,534	NAB60b	17-AAAA-a	masmaje		20.00	6,550	0....	9	5	7	2	0		...	.
2116	Massalat	0.66397	44,536	50,800	92,346	NAB66z	05-AAAD-a	kaana-masala		0.01	5	0....	3	3	4	0	1	Masalit	...	b
2117	Mawa	0.08319	5,580	6,365	11,570	NAB60b	17-ABGA-a	mahwa		0.01	1	0....	3	2	4	0	0		...	.
2118	Mbororo Fulani	0.45001	30,184	34,430	62,588	NAB56c	90-BAAA-o	fula-bororo		0.02	7	1cs..	3	4	3	2	2	Fulfide, Kano-katsina	pnb	b
2119	Mbum (Wuna, Buna)	0.17613	11,814	13,476	24,496	NAB66c	92-CDAE-k	mbum	2	25.00	3,369	0.s..	9	5	7	4	2	Mboum*	PN.	n
2120	Medogo (Medoga)	0.31877	21,381	24,389	44,335	NAB66z	03-AAAB-c	kodoi		0.03	7	0....	3	3	0	0	0		...	b
2121	Mesme (Zime)	0.33476	22,454	25,612	46,559	NAB60b	17-FABB	zime cluster	1	65.00	16,648	0.s..	10	7	7	4	3	Zime*	PN.	b
2122	Migaama	0.40215	26,974	30,768	55,932	NAB60b	17-ABEA-a	migaama		0.00	0	0....	0	2	0	0	0	Migaama	...	b
2123	Miltu	0.00451	303	345	627	NAB60b	17-DDAA-a	miltu		2.00	7	0....	6	4	4	2	1		...	.
2124	Mime (Mimi)	1.04384	70,015	79,864	145,179	NAB66z	05-BAAA-a	mimi		0.10	80	0....	5	4	4	0	0		...	b
2125	Mimi (Amdang, Mututu)	0.52083	34,935	39,849	72,438	NAB66z	05-CABA-a	simi-andang-ti		0.00	0	0....	0	2	0	0	0		...	b
2126	Mini (Kajakse)	0.20877	14,003	15,973	29,036	NAB60b	17-AACA-a	kajagise		1.00	160	0....	6	4	2	0	0		...	.
2127	Mire	0.02466	1,654	1,887	3,430	NAB60b	17-DEBA-b	mire		1.00	19	0....	6	4	4	1	0		...	.
2128	Mogum	0.16086	10,790	12,307	22,373	NAB60b	17-ABBA-a	kofa		20.00	2,461	0....	9	5	5	2	0		...	.
2129	Mokulu	0.21134	14,176	16,170	29,393	NAB60b	17-BAAA-a	mokilko		0.00	0	0....	0	3	0	0	0		...	b
2130	Moriil (Zan Gula)	0.05324	3,571	4,073	7,405	NAB66z	03-AABA-a	mamun-gula		1.00	41	0....	6	4	4	2	0		...	.
2131	Mubi (Moubi)	0.96515	64,737	73,843	134,234	NAB60b	17-AABA-a	mubi		25.00	18,461	0....	9	5	6	2	1		...	b
2132	Mundang	2.66214	178,562	203,680	370,254	NAB66z	92-CDAB	mundang cluster	2	38.00	77,398	0..u.	9	6	7	3	2	Mundang	PNB	.
2133	Musei (Bananna)	1.94515	130,470	148,823	270,534	NAB60b	17-FAAC-a	mosi		50.00	74,412	0....	10	6	6	3	3	Musey	PN.	.
2134	Musgu (Mulwi, Musgum)	0.49000	32,867	37,490	68,150	NAB60b	18-AAAA-d	mulwi		20.00	7,498	0....	9	5	7	3	2		pn.	.
2135	Nancere (Nanjere)	1.19144	79,916	91,157	165,707	NAB60b	17-DHAA-a	nancere	1	60.00	54,694	0....	10	6	7	3	3	Nangjere*	PNB	.
2136	Ngama (Sarngam)	0.47354	31,763	36,230	65,861	NAB66z	03-AAAE-q	ngam		60.00	21,738	0.s..	10	6	8	2	1	Ngam	pnb	b
2137	Ngede	0.17174	11,519	13,140	23,886	NAB60b	17-FABB-c	ngete		10.00	1,314	0.s..	8	5	7	2	2	Ngete	pn.	.
2138	Nielim (Mjillem)	0.08581	5,756	6,565	11,935	NAB66z	92-CAAB-a	niellim		1.00	66	0....	6	5	4	2	2		...	.
2139	Northern Gabri (Gabere)	0.30913	20,735	23,651	42,994	NAB60b	17-DGBA	gabri cluster		40.00	9,461	0....	9	6	8	4	2	Gabri	...	.
2140	Pana	0.30000	20,122	22,953	41,724	NAB66z	92-CDAE-h	pana		40.00	9,181	0.s..	9	6	7	2	1	Pana	Pn.	.
2141	Peve (Lame, Dari)	0.34347	23,038	26,279	47,770	NAB60b	17-FABB-i	peve	1	40.00	10,512	0.s..	9	6	7	3	3	Peve	PN.	.

Continued opposite

Table 8-2 continued

EVANGELIZATION								EVANGELISM			ADDITIONAL DESCRIPTIVE DATA
Ref 1	D 28	aC 29	CG% 30	r 31	E 32	U 33	W 34	e 35	R 36	T 37	Locations, civil divisions, literacy, religions, church history, denominations, dioceses, church growth, missions, agencies, ministries, movements 38
2020	1	7	5.10	0	72.00	28.00	B	105.12	249	7	Widely scattered along Sudan border, also in Zaire. Related to Ndogo. Animists 45%, Muslims 15%. D=RCC.
2021	1	8	4.26	0	81.00	19.00	B	133.04	206	7	Also in Sudan. Related to Banda. Second language: Sango. Animists 30%, Muslims 25%. D=RCC.
2022	2	6	6.36	0	52.00	48.00	B	37.96	410	5	Northwest. Animists 80%. D=RCC,EBRCA.
2023	1	6	5.93	0	62.00	38.00	B	67.89	325	6	Basse-Kotto Prefecture. Mostly in Zaire, some in Sudan. Second language: Sango. Animists 70%. D=RCC.
2024	0	7	0.00	7	20.00	80.00	A	0.00	0	1.04	Arabic-based creole. Lingua franca from Cameroon to Sudan. Muslims 100%(Sunnis).
2025	0	7	5.28	0	56.00	44.00	B	61.32	328	6	In north. Close to Nduka. Animists 60%, some Muslims. D=RCC
2026	1	7	4.26	0	79.00	21.00	B	129.75	211	7	Ouaka Prefecture, north of Bria. Also in Sudan. Related to Banda. Second language: Sango. Animists 40%, Muslims 15%. D=RCC.
2027	1	7	4.37	0	71.00	29.00	B	103.66	239	7	Kemo Prefecture, west of Sibut. Also in Sudan. Related to Banda. Second language: Sango. Animists 45%, Muslims 15%. D=RCC.
2028	1	7	3.84	0	60.00	40.00	B	65.70	259	6	Haute Kotto Prefecture, near Yalinga. Also in Sudan. Second language: Sango. Animists 70%. D=RCC.
2029	1	8	4.37	0	87.00	13.00	B	158.77	195	7	Closest to Dakpa, Gbi, Golo, Gbaga. Second language: Sango. Animists 30%, Muslims 20%. D=RCC.
2030	1	7	8.40	1	70.00	30.00	B	76.65	385	6	In south. A riverine dialect of Ngbandi in Zaire. Second language: Sango. Animists 50%. D=RCC.
2031	1	6	6.01	0	71.00	29.00	B	103.66	303	7	Ouham Prefecture. Second language: Sango. Animists 40%, Muslims 20%. D=RCC.
2032	1	7	4.97	0	62.00	38.00	B	67.89	283	6	Also in Sudan and Zaire. Many bilingual in Kresh or Arabic. Animists 40%, Muslims 30%. D=RCC.
2033	3	6	8.71	0	99.64	0.36	C	303.68	222	9	Primarily in Zaire. Lingua franca: Sango. Animists 5%. D=Church of Christ,EEC,AICs. M=CMS,AIM,CC.
2034	0	9	6.07		79.00	21.00	B	144.17	211	7	Refugees from Sudan (Kresh,&c) and Chad; a few Bobangi, Pol (Pomo). Muslims 40% (Sunnis), Animists 10%.
Chad											
2035	0	4	0.00	0	9.00	91.00	A	0.00	0	1.02	East central, east of Abeche. On border with Sudan. Dialect of Mararit. Muslims 100%(Sunnis).
2036	1	6	4.53	4	42.00	58.00	A	1.53	400	4	From Senegal to Sudan. Muslims 80%(Maliki Sunnis), animists 19%. D=EFLT. M=LBWM.
2037	0	4	0.00	1	10.00	90.00	A	0.00	0	1.04	West central, northeast of Ndjamena. Most are bilingual in Arabic. Muslims 100%(Sunnis).
2038	0	6	2.43	4	31.02	68.98	A	0.02	356	2	Nomads of Wodaabe lineage; close to Bororo. Also in northern Niger, Cameroon, CAR. Muslims 100%(Sunnis). M=WEC,AIM.
2039	1	7	8.60	0	84.00	16.00	B	153.30	340	7	Varieties of Banda from Central Africa Republic. Animists 20%, Muslims 20%. D=RCC.
2040	0	4	0.00	0	10.00	90.00	A	0.00	0	1.04	South central, south of Mongo, east of Melfi. Arabized islamized animists.
2041	2	4	1.81	0	21.01	78.99	A	0.00	423	1.07	Once Bagirmi state, now peasant farmers. Also in Nigeria. 12% urban. Most bilingual in Arabic. Muslims 100%(Sunnis, since AD 1600; many in Tijaniyya). D=EET.
2042	1	5	8.60	1	89.00	11.00	B	162.42	309	7	Southwest, Moyen-Cahri Prefecture. Related to Sar. Animists 20%, Muslims 15%. D=RCC. M=OFMCap.
2043	1	5	3.92	0	54.00	46.00	B	59.13	271	6	Southwest, Tandjille Prefecture, Kelo Subprefecture. Also in CAR. Animists 60%, Muslims 10%. D=RCC.
2044	0	4	0.00	0	9.00	91.00	A	0.00	0	1.03	Saharan Negroes. Nomadic cattle breeders related to Zaghawa. Mostly bilingual in Arabic. Indifferent Muslims 90%(Maliki Sunnis), animists 10%.
2045	0	4	0.00	0	9.00	91.00	A	0.00	0	1.03	West of Abu Telfan. Most men are bilingual in Arabic. Muslims 100%(Sunnis).
2046	0	4	0.00	0	9.00	91.00	A	0.00	0	1.03	Guera region, north of Lake Fitri. 13% urban. Muslims 100%(Sunnis). M=AIM.
2047	0	5	2.33	0	19.10	80.90	A	0.07	534	2	Southeast. Salamat Prefecture. Related to Dangla. Bilingual in Arabic. Muslims 100% (Sunnis).
2048	1	5	4.32	0	53.00	47.00	B	58.03	318	6	South central, east of the Barein. Muslims 50%, animists 20%. D=EET. M=AIM.
2049	1	5	4.43	0	25.00	75.00	A	4.56	486	4	Southeast, Guera Prefecture, North of Lake Iro. Animists 95%. D=EET. M=AIM.
2050	3	8	2.51	8	99.78	0.22	C	424.20	67	10	Expatriates from UK, in education, professions. D=EET,RCC,JWs.
2051	1	4	2.33	0	21.10	78.90	A	0.07	488	2	Most men bilingual in Arabic. Islamized at sword point by 1900; most reverted. 5% urban. Animists 80%, Muslims 20%. D=EET. M=AIM.
2052	0	5	2.60	0	19.02	80.98	A	0.01	575	2	Around eastern Lake Chad, also Nigeria, Cameroon. Warlike people; fishing, cattle. 12% polygynous. Most are bilingual in Arabic. Muslims 95%, a few pagans.
2053	0	4	0.00	4	21.00	79.00	A	0.00	0	1.08	Saharan Negroes, related to Teda and Daza. Pastoral nomads. Muslims 100%(Maliki Sunnis).
2054	0	8	3.49	0	52.00	48.00	B	56.94	259	6	Chari-Baguirari Prefecture. Mostly popular Islam, Muslims 50%, animists 20%.
2055	1	6	8.40	0	88.00	12.00	B	160.60	306	7	Southwest, Moyen-Chari Prefecture, southwest of Sarh. Muslims 40%, animists 10%. D=Assemblees Chretiennes du Tchad. M=CMML,BMM,EFLC.
2056	0	3	0.00	0	10.00	90.00	A	0.00	0	1.03	Southeast Ouaddai region. Sedentary cultivators. Most are bilingual in Arabic. Muslims 100%(Maliki Sunnis). M=SUM,WEC.
2057	0	3	0.00	0	10.00	90.00	A	0.00	0	1.03	Southeast Ouaddai, also in Sudan. Most are bilingual in Arabic. Muslims 100%(Maliki Sunnis since 15th century; active in Sufi Tijaniyya). M=WEC,SUM.
2058	0	4	2.22	0	17.10	82.90	A	0.06	578	2	Southwest. Forcibly islamized by 1899; much reversion to animism. Muslims 70%, animists 30%. M=AIM,EET.
2059	1	2	0.00	0	9.00	91.00	A	0.00	0	1.04	Around Mongo northwest of Jebel Geira. Most men bilingual in Arabic. Muslims 100%(Sunnis). D=RCC.
2060	0	2	0.00	0	7.00	93.00	A	0.00	0	1.03	Saharan Negroes. Also in Niger. Tubu pastoral nomads with Aza blacksmith caste. Bilingual in Arabic. Muslims 100%(Maliki Sunnis; Sanussiyya).
2061	0	4	0.00	7	24.00	76.00	A	0.00	0	1.07	Northerners. Nomads. All Muslims 100%(Sunnis).
2062	1	4	0.00	0	16.10	83.90	A	0.05	243	2	Southeast, near Singako. Muslims 60%, animists 40%. D=EET. M=AIM.
2063	0	5	0.00	0	8.00	92.00	A	0.00	0	1.03	Along Sudan border. Hunter-gatherers. Becoming extinct. Muslims 100%.
2064	1	10	6.75	8	99.87	0.13	C	498.55	135	10	Expatriates from France: Administrators, educationists. D=RCC(4 Dioceses). M=SJ,OFMCap,OMI.
2065	0	5	0.00	5	18.04	81.96	A	0.02	273	2	Immigrants from Sudan. Settled, nomads, pastoralists, agriculturalists. Muslims 100%(Maliki Sunnis).
2066	0	4	0.00	0	9.00	91.00	A	0.00	0	1.03	Chari-Baguirmi Prefecture. Mostly Muslims 82%, animists 18%. M=AIM,EET.
2067	1	6	6.10	0	59.00	41.00	B	53.83	348	6	Also in Cameroon. Animists 50%, Muslims 25%. D=EFLT. M=CLB,UBS.
2068	0	5	1.10	0	20.20	79.80	A	0.14	338	3	West. Chari-Baguirmi and Mayo-Kebbi Prefectures. Animists 80%, Muslims 20%.
2069	0	6	5.59	2	73.00	27.00	B	79.93	263	6	Also in Sudan. Bilingual in Ndogo(Sudan). Animists 60%, Muslims 10%.
2070	1	4	4.38	1	31.00	69.00	A	11.31	514	5	Southwest, Moyen-Chari Prefecture. Muslims 60% and animists 30%. D=EET. M=AIM.
2071	1	6	9.79	1	99.55	0.45	B	202.75	304	8	Southwest. Lingua franca: Sar. Animists 35%. D=EET. M=SUM,TEAM,BMM.
2072	0	6	5.05	0	45.00	55.00	A	32.85	395	5	Southeast, near mountains. During civil war, evacuated to town of Zan. Muslims 40%, animists 40%. Also in CAR.
2073	2	6	3.90	0	37.00	63.00	A	13.50	395	5	Southwest Moyen-Chari and Salamat Prefectures, northeast of Sarh. Mostly monolinguals. Animists 50%, Muslims 40%. D=RCC,Baptist Chs.
2074	1	6	7.85	0	81.00	19.00	B	147.82	313	7	In west, Chari-Baguirmi Prefecture. Also in Cameroon, Far North. Animists 20%, Muslims 20%. D=RCC.
2075	0	6	2.75	5	41.01	58.99	A	0.01	264	2	Traders from Nigeria. 20% urban. Also in Niger, Cameroon, Togo, Benin, Ghana, Sudan, et alia. Muslims 100%(Maliki Sunnis).
2076	0	5	0.00	7	21.00	79.00	A	0.00	0	1.07	Nomadic Bedouin Arabs; tent-dwellers. All Muslims 100%(Sunnis).
2077	0	0	2.10	0	11.30	88.70	A	0.12	856	3	Central, Guera Prefecture, Bitkine subprefecture. Similar to Kenga and Bilala. Muslims 69%, Animists 31%.
2078	0	5	2.99	0	17.00	83.00	A	0.62	706	3	Central, south of Mongo. Guera and Salamat Prefectures. Muslims 90%(Sunnis).
2079	1	5	3.09	0	33.00	67.00	A	6.02	409	4	Dialect of Kim. Animists 90%, Muslims 5%. D=EFLT. M=LBWM. Masana literature used.
2080	1	5	5.05	0	64.00	36.00	B	70.08	277	6	Also in CAR. Bilingualism in Ngambai. Animists 70%. D=ACT. M=CMML.
2081	1	5	8.35	0	91.90	8.10	B	200.92	292	8	Southeast, Moyan-Chari Prefecture. Animists 35%. D=Baptist Chs. M=BMM.
2082	0	5	4.13	0	53.00	47.00	B	48.36	287	6	South of Lake Iro in southeast, Moyen-Chari Prefecture. Animists 75%. M=BMM.
2083	0	5	8.21	0	91.00	9.00	C	199.29	290	7	Southeast, Moyen-Chari Prefecture. Animists 40%. M=BMM.
2084	2	5	6.31	0	47.00	53.00	A	34.31	449	5	Southwest, Tandjille Prefecture, Lai Subprefecture. Animists 80%. D=RCC,ACT.
2085	2	5	7.61	0	90.00	10.00	B	164.25	274	7	Southwest, also in Cameroon. Animists 45%, Muslims 5%. D=Assemblees Chretiennes du Tchad,EFLC. M=BMM,CMML,YWAM,LBWM.
2086	0	5	2.22	0	19.01	80.99	A	0.00	522	1.06	Northern Lake Chad basin. Also in Niger. 5% literates (using Arabic). Bilingual in Arabic. Muslims 95%(Sunnis,Sufis), animists 5%. M=TEAM,EMS,WVI.
2087	0	5	4.18	1	29.00	71.00	A	5.29	568	4	Southwest. Logone Oriental Prefecture. Mainly in Cameroon. Animists 95%.
2088	1	5	9.10	0	80.00	20.00	B	146.00	361	7	East central, Ouaddai and Batha Prefectures. Animists 20%, Muslims 20%. D=RCC.
2089	0	0	0.00	0	8.01	91.99	A	0.00	0	1.03	Ouaddai Prefecture. Abeche and Adre subprefectures. Bilingualism in Maba and Masalit. Muslims 100%.
2090	2	4	2.47	0	20.30	79.70	A	0.22	526	3	West of Biltine. Most men bilingual in Arabic. Muslims 69%(Sunnis), animists 30%. D=RCC,ACT.
2091	3	6	7.72	0	65.00	35.00	B	71.17	386	6	A few in Cameroon. Animists 50%, Muslims 20%. D=ACT,RCC,EFLT. M=SIL,LBWM,CMML.
2092	0	4	0.00	0	9.00	91.00	A	0.00	0	1.03	Majority bilingual in Arabic. Muslims 100%(Sunnis).
2093	1	6	7.32	0	99.00	1.00	C	216.81	241	8	Southwest, Logone river area. Animists 40%. D=Assemblees Chretiennes du Tchad. M=CMML,YWAM,LBWM.
2094	1	5	6.19	0	46.00	54.00	A	33.58	452	5	Southwest, Tandjile Prefecture. Animists 80%. D=EET.
2095	1	6	3.18	0	57.00	43.00	B	62.41	222	6	South central, north of Sarh. Animists 70%. D=Swedish Pentecostals. M=SIL,SFM.
2096	0	6	1.10	0	20.20	79.80	A	0.14	338	3	Border near Ndjamena, also Cameroon. Bilingual in Arabic. Muslims 95%(Sunnis).
2097	1	4	2.81	0	15.10	84.90	A	0.05	762	2	Southwest, north of Bongor; also in Cameroon and Nigeria. 30% urban. Muslims 100%(Sunnis). D=EET. M=AIM.
2098	0	4	0.00	0	9.00	91.00	A	0.00	0	1.03	Saharan Negroes. Pastoral nomads, east of Ndjamera. Close to Daza. Muslims 100%(Sunnis).
2099	3	4	6.99	0	68.00	32.00	B	99.28	338	6	In southwest. Tandjile Prefecture. Animists 50%, Muslims 10%. D=RCC,ACT,EET. M=CMML,AIM.
2100	0	4	0.70	5	17.10	82.90	A	0.06	401	2	7 villages near Jebel Mirra, among Fur. Second languages: Fur, Daju. Muslims 99%(Sunnis).
2101	0	4	0.00	0	8.00	92.00	A	0.00	0	1.03	Around Ati and Lake Fitri. Muslims 100%(Sunnis).
2102	0	6	5.59	1	51.00	49.00	B	37.23	399	5	Southwest, Logone Oriental Prefecture. Also in Cameroon. Animists 80%. M=SFM(Swedish Pentecostals),SIL.
2103	1	4	7.57	1	60.00	40.00	B	43.80	411	6	Southwest (Paoua to Baibokoum area), also in CAR. Animists 80%. D=EEF(CAR). M=NFBC,CMML.
2104	1	5	7.61	0	81.00	19.00	B	133.04	304	7	Southwest, also in CAR. Literates 10% in French. Animists 55%. D=Eglise Evangelique du Tchad. M=SUM,TEAM.
2105	1	6	5.05	0	59.00	41.00	B	64.60	299	6	West Chari-Baguitmi Prefecture. Also in Cameroon, Nigeria. Muslims 70%. D=RCC.
2106	0	0	4.42	0	47.00	53.00	A	51.46	341	6	Also in CAR. Moyen-Chari Prefecture, Maro Prefecture, south of Ngam. Animists 70%.
2107	0	4	0.00	7	20.00	80.00	A	0.00	0	1.07	Nomadic Baggara Arabs(moderate Negroid ancestry) in northern Wadai. Camel nomads. Muslims 100%(Sunnis).
2108	0	4	2.10	0	15.10	84.90	A	0.05	633	2	West. Chari-Baguirmi Prefecture. Animistic, Muslims 99%.
2109	1	6	4.13	0	79.00	21.00	B	144.17	193	7	Southwest. Mayo-Kebbi Prefecture. Also in Cameroon. Close to Mundang, Besme. Animists 40%, Muslims 10%. D=RCC.
2110	0	4	1.62	0	16.01	83.99	A	0.00	585	1.05	East central, east of Abeche; also in Sudan. Majority bilingual in Arabic. Cattle, camel-breeding. Muslims 100%(Sunnis).
2111	2	6	8.39	0	64.00	36.00	B	46.72	419	6	Southwest, Logone district. 20% urban. Animists 79%, a few Muslims. D=EFLT,ACT(sending out own evangelists). M=LBWM,CMML,UBS.
2112	0	6	7.38	0	32.00	68.00	A	5.84	751	4	East, south of Abeche, Ouaddai Prefecture. Muslims 90%.
2113	4	5	8.69	0	66.00	34.00	B	72.27	418	6	Southwest, also in Cameroon. Animists 65%, Muslims 5%. D=African Independent Ch,EFLT,RCC(M-Ndjamena),ACT. M=LBWM,CMML,SUM,SJ,OFMCap,OMI.
2114	0	4	1.81	0	20.01	79.99	A	0.00	444	1.06	East central, east of Abeche. Majority in Sudan. Bilingual in Arabic. Muslims 100%(Sunnis). M=WEC,SUM,French Mennonites,SIL.
2115	0	6	6.70	0	47.00	53.00	A	34.31	472	5	Central Batha Prefecture. East of Ati, north of the Mubi. Muslims 80%(Sunnis).
2116	0	4	1.62	0	17.01	82.99	A	0.00	491	1.05	East central, south of Abeche. Nearly extinct. Most are bilingual in Arabic. Muslims 100%(Sunnis). M=WEC.
2117	0	0	0.00	0	8.01	91.99	A	0.00	475	1.02	Guera Prefecture. Bitkine subprefecture centered around village of Mahoua. Muslims 100%.
2118	0	5	1.96	4	30.02	69.98	A	0.02	325	2	True cattle nomads, south of Ndjamena to CAR. Permanently moving. Muslims 100%. M=AIM,EET.
2119	2	5	5.99	1	63.00	37.00	B	57.48	340	6	Southwest, most in Cameroon, few in CAR. Muslims 60%(Maliki Sunnis, spreading rapidly), animists 15%. D=EET,ACT. M=SUM,CMML.
2120	0	4	1.96	0	12.03	87.97	A	0.01	772	2	Central. Batha Prefecture. Majority are bilingual in Arabic. Muslims 100%(Sunnis).
2121	2	5	7.70	0	99.65	0.35	C	256.23	231	8	Southwest Chad. Animists 35%, but by 1975 all fully evangelized (aware of Jesus Christ). D=EFLT,EET. M=LBWM,TEAM,UBS.
2122	0	4	0.00	0	9.00	91.00	A	0.00	0	1.03	Most men are bilingual in Arabic. Muslims 100%(Sunnis).
2123	1	6	1.96	0	24.00	76.00	A	1.75	382	4	South central, around town of Miltou. Second language Bagirmi. Muslims 60%, animists 38%. D=EET. M=AIM.
2124	0	4	4.48	0	18.10	81.90	A	0.06	895	2	Eastern, north of Biltine. Also in Dar Fur(Sudan). Bilingual in Arabic. Pastoralists, Muslims 95%.
2125	0	4	0.00	0	9.00	91.00	A	0.00	0	1.03	Also called Mima, in Sudan. Nomads, and sedentary cultivators. Bilingual in Arabic. Muslims 100%(converts from 1665 on).
2126	0	4	2.81	0	15.00	85.00	A	0.54	767	3	East. Ouaddai Prefecture. Hunter-gathers, traders. Muslims 95%(Sunnis).
2127	0	5	2.99	0	19.00	81.00	A	0.69	632	3	Southwest. Tandjile Prefecture. Close to Ndam(second language). Animists 90%.
2128	0	5	5.66	0	44.00	56.00	A	32.12	439	5	Central. Guera Prefecture, Mongo Subprefecture. Animists 60%, Muslims 20%.
2129	0	4	0.00	0	9.00	91.00	A	0.00	0	1.03	Most men are bilingual in Arabic. Muslims 100%(Sunnis).
2130	0	4	3.78	0	19.00	81.00	A	0.69	751	3	Southeast, Guera Prefecture. Some bilinguals in Arabic. Muslims 60%, animists 39%.
2131	1	5	7.81	0	56.00	44.00	B	51.10	450	6	Southeast, east of Mongo. Most are bilingual in Arabic. Muslims 75%(Sunnis). D=RCC.
2132	2	5	9.37	0	79.00	21.00	B	109.57	375	7	Also in Cameroon. Animists 45%, Muslims 7%. D=EFLT,AIC. M=UBS,LBWM.
2133	1	4	9.32	0	85.00	15.00	B	155.12	345	7	Southwest; also in Cameroon. Animists 40%. D=EFLT. M=UBS,EMS(Nigeria),LBWM.
2134	2	5	6.84	0	54.00	46.00	B	39.42	418	5	Mainly in Cameroon. Animists 75%, Muslims 5%. D=EFLT,AIC. M=UBS,LBWM.
2135	0	5	8.99	0	99.60	0.40	C	223.38	279	8	Southwest. Animists 40%. M=TEAM,SUM,UBS,Mission Ev de l'Ubangi(MEDELU).
2136	3	6	7.99	1	99.60	0.40	C	229.95	246	8	Southern Chad south of Sarh. Also in CAR. Lingua franca: Sar. Animists 40%. D=RCC,EBT,AIC. M=BMM.
2137	2	5	5.00	0	43.00	57.00	A	15.69	407	5	Near Peve and Herde peoples. Close to Marba. Animists 89%, a few Muslims. D=EFLT,RCC.
2138	0	5	4.28	0	22.00	78.00	A	0.80	711	3	South central, around Nielim town. Desert. Civil war since 1960 wrecks economy. Converted to Islam in 1900. Muslims 79%, animists 20%. M=AIM,EET.
2139	1	5	7.09	0	72.00	28.00	B	105.12	323	7	Southwest, east of Kim. Animists 55%, Muslims 5%. D=Assemblees Chretiennes du Tchad(sends out own missionaries). M=CMML,YWAM.
2140	1	5	7.06	1	73.00	27.00	B	106.58	319	7	Also in CAR, Cameroon, Nigeria. Muslims 40%, animists 20%. D=RCC.
2141	3	5	7.21	0	79.00	21.00	B	115.34	298	7	In southwest, also in Cameroon. Animists 60%. D=EFLT,ACT,RCC. M=LBWM,CMML,UBS.

Continued overleaf

Table 8-2 continued

PEOPLE Ref 1	Ethnic name 2	POPULATION P% 3	In 1995 4	In 2000 5	In 2025 6	IDENTITY CODE Race 7	Language 8	LANGUAGE Autoglossonym 9	S 10	CHURCH AC 11	Members 12	MINISTRY Jayuh 13-17	dwa xcmc mi 18	19	20	21	22	SCRIPTURE Biblioglossonym 23	Pub 24-26	ss 27
2142	Runga	0.35737	23,971	27,342	49,703	NAB66z	05-AAAE-a	runga		0.00	0	0....	0	3	0	1	0		...	b
2143	Saba	0.04357	2,922	3,334	6,060	NAB60b	17-CACA-a	saba		0.00	0	0....	0	3	0	1	0		...	b
2144	Sango	0.30000	20,122	22,953	41,724	NAB66z	93-ABBA-a	sango	4	50.00	11,476	4.s..	10	8	9	5	1	Sango	PNB	b
2145	Sara Gambai	9.92593	665,779	759,431	1,380,510	NAB66z	03-AAAE-a	ngambai	10	32.00	243,018	0.s..	9	8	9	5	3	Ngambai*	PNB	b
2146	Sara Majingai-Ngama (Sar)	3.05266	204,756	233,558	424,568	NAB66z	03-AAAE-j	majingai	28	45.00	105,101	0.s..	9	8	12	5	3	Sara-majingai	PNb	b
2147	Sara Mbai	2.18007	146,228	166,797	303,207	NAB66z	03-AAAE-h	mbai-kan	3	68.00	113,422	0.s..	10	8	11	5	3	Mbai: Moissala	PNB	b
2148	Sarwa (Sharwa, Sarua)	0.02500	1,677	1,913	3,477	NAB60b	17-DAAA-a	sarwa		1.00	19	0....	6	4	4	2	2		...	.
2149	Shuwa (Chad Arab, Baggara)	16.43783	1,102,563	1,257,655	2,286,193	CMT30	12-AACE-a	shuwa	65	0.01	126	0...h	3	3	5	1	3	Arabic: Chad	PN.	b
2150	Sinyar (Shamya)	0.15625	10,480	11,955	21,731	NAB66z	03-AACA-a	taar-shamyan		0.00	0	0....	0	2	0	0	0		...	b
2151	Sokoro (Tunjur)	0.08086	5,424	6,187	11,246	NAB60b	17-CABA	sokoro cluster		5.00	309	0....	7	5	0	0	1	Sokoro	...	b
2152	Soliman Bedouin	0.20320	13,630	15,547	28,261	CMT30	12-AACD	badawi-sahara cluster		0.03	5	0a...	3	1	0	0	0		PN.	b
2153	Somrai	0.12328	8,269	9,432	17,146	NAB60b	17-DFAA-a	somrai		30.00	2,830	0....	9	5	7	2	2	Somrai	...	b
2154	Southern Gabri	0.20608	13,823	15,767	28,662	NAB60b	17-DGBA	gabri cluster		30.00	4,730	0....	9	6	5	4	1	Gabri	...	.
2155	Sungor (Asungor)	0.39100	26,226	29,915	54,381	NAB66d	05-DAAA-e	a-songor-i		0.00	0	0....	0	3	0	0	1		...	b
2156	Surbakhal	0.10000	6,707	7,651	13,908	NAB66z	05-AAAA	maba cluster		0.01	1	0....	3	3	4	0	0		...	b
2157	Tama (Gimr)	1.04821	70,308	80,198	145,786	NAB66d	05-DAAA-a	tamo-ngo'bo		0.00	0	0....	0	1	0	0	0		...	b
2158	Teda (Tubu, Gorane)	0.47420	31,807	36,281	65,952	NAB61	02-BAAA-a	tuda-ga		0.00	0	0....	0	1	0	0	1		...	b
2159	Torum (Toram)	0.10724	7,193	8,205	14,915	NAB60b	17-AAEA-a	toram		0.10	8	0....	5	3	3	0	0		...	.
2160	Tumak	0.42009	28,177	32,141	58,427	NAB60b	17-DECA-a	tumak		30.00	9,642	0....	9	5	8	2	1	Tumak	PN.	.
2161	Tunya	0.03750	2,515	2,869	5,216	NAB66z	92-CAAC-a	tunya		20.00	574	0....	9	5	0	2	2		...	.
2162	Tupuri (Tuburi)	1.51052	101,318	115,570	210,085	NAB60b	92-CDAA	tupuri cluster		60.00	69,342	0.s..	10	6	7	4	3	Tupuri	PN.	.
2163	Turku Arab (Tekrur, Turkol)	0.20001	13,416	15,303	27,818	CMT30	12-AACG-d	turku	52	0.00	0	0....	0	1	0	0	0		...	b
2164	Ubi	0.01729	1,160	1,323	2,405	NAB60b	18-BBAA	south kotoko cluster		0.01	0	0....	3	3	4	0	0		...	b
2165	Vale	0.01001	671	766	1,392	NAB66z	03-AAAG-b	vale		30.00	230	0....	9	5	4	2	1		...	.
2166	Wadaian (Mabangi, Maba)	2.06079	138,227	157,671	286,617	NAB66z	05-AAAA-a	bura-maba-ng	13	0.04	63	0....	3	4	0	0	3	Maba	...	b
2167	Yalna	0.32351	21,699	24,752	44,994	NAB60b	18-BBAA	south kotoko cluster		0.00	0	0....	0	1	0	0	0		...	b
2168	Yerwa Kanuri (Beriberi)	1.99283	133,669	152,471	277,165	NAB61	02-AAAA-b	yerwa		0.01	15	4....	3	3	5	1	3	Kanuri*	PN.	.
2169	Zaghawa (Zeghawa, Beri)	0.37313	25,028	28,548	51,895	NAB61	02-CAAA-a	beri-aa		0.00	0	0....	0	2	0	0	1		...	b
2170	other minor peoples	0.21889	14,682	16,747	30,443	...				10.00	1,675		8	5	2	3	0			
	Channel Islands	**100.00000**	**147,725**	**152,898**	**173,400**					**65.91**	**100,781**									
2171	British	97.20000	143,589	148,617	168,545	CEW19i	52-ABAC-b	standard-english		66.00	98,087	3Bsuh	10	9	12	5	3		PNB	b
2172	French	2.00000	2,955	3,058	3,468	CEW21b	51-AABI-d	general français		69.00	2,110	1B.uh	10	9	14	5	3	French	PNB	b
2173	Indo-Pakistani	0.16500	244	252	286	CNN25g	59-AAFO-e	general hindi		3.00	8	3Asuh	6	5	2	5	0		pnb	b
2174	Jewish	0.07500	111	115	130	CMT35	52-ABAC-b	standard-english		1.00	1	3Bsuh	6	4	2	1	0		PNB	b
2175	Norman	0.20000	295	306	347	CEW21b	51-AABI-dd	français-de-normandie	1	80.00	245	1c.uh	10	9	7	5	1	French: Norman, Guernsey	Pnb	b
2176	other minor peoples	0.36000	532	550	624	...				60.00	330		10	8	8	5	0			
	Chile	**100.00000**	**14,210,413**	**15,211,294**	**19,547,916**					**87.82**	**13,358,342**									
2177	Alacaluf (Kawesqar)	0.00042	60	64	82	MIR39z	86-IAAA-a	kawaskar		60.00	38	0....	10	7	2	2	1		...	.
2178	Arab	0.02000	2,842	3,042	3,910	CMT30	12-AACF-f	syro-palestinian		70.00	2,130	1Asuh	10	5	8	4	2	Arabic: Lebanese*	Pnb	b
2179	Armenian	0.00500	711	761	977	CEW14	57-AAAA-b	ashkharik		90.00	685	4A.u.	10	9	13	4	1	Armenian: Modern, Eastern	PNB	b
2180	Basque	0.05600	7,958	8,518	10,947	CEW16	40-AAAA-a	general euskara		94.00	8,007	3....	10	9	15	4	1	Basque	PNB	b
2181	British	0.20000	28,421	30,423	39,096	CEW19i	52-ABAC-b	standard-english	14	79.00	24,034	3Bsuh	10	9	13	5	2		PNB	b
2182	Chilean Aymara	0.17391	24,713	26,454	33,996	MIR39b	85-JABA-ad	caranga		70.00	18,518	1.s..	10	8	7	5	1		pnb	b
2183	Chilean Mestizo	72.36147	10,282,864	11,007,116	14,145,159	CLN29	51-AABB-hr	chileno		90.70	9,983,454	1B.uh	10	9	12	5	3		pnb	.
2184	Chilean Quechua	0.03000	4,263	4,563	5,864	MIR39g	85-FAAH	south quechua cluster		75.00	3,423	3As..	10	8	7	5	1	Quechua: Classical*	PNB	b
2185	Chilean White	20.80000	2,955,766	3,163,949	4,065,967	CLT27	51-AABB-hr	chileno		85.30	2,698,849	1B.uh	10	9	11	5	3		pnb	.
2186	Easter Islander	0.02230	3,169	3,392	4,359	MPY55z	39-CARA-a	rapanui		70.00	2,374	0....	10	7	7	1	1	Rapa Nui	...	.
2187	Esperanto	0.00000	0	0	0	CEW21z	51-AAAC-a	proper esperanto		50.00	0	0A...	10	8	6	0	0	Esperanto	PNB	b
2188	French	0.05000	7,105	7,606	9,774	CEW21b	51-AABI-d	general français	4	87.00	6,617	1B.uh	10	9	14	5	1	French	PNB	b
2189	German	0.16000	22,737	24,338	31,277	CEW19m	52-ABCE-a	standard hoch-deutsch	10	88.00	21,418	2B.uh	10	9	13	5	1	German*	PNB	b
2190	Greek	0.10000	14,210	15,211	19,548	CEW20	56-AAAA-c	dhimotiki		95.00	14,451	2B.uh	10	9	10	5	1	Greek: Modern	PNB	b
2191	Han Chinese	0.01070	1,521	1,628	2,092	MSY42a	79-AAAB-ba	kuo-yü		30.00	488	2Bsuh	9	5	5	3	1	Chinese: Kuoyu*	PNB	b
2192	Huilliche (Veliche)	1.20370	171,051	183,098	235,298	MIR39f	86-GAAA-e	huilliche		60.00	109,859	1....	10	7	7	5	1		p..	b
2193	Italian	0.20000	28,421	30,423	39,096	CEW21e	51-AABQ-c	standard italiano		84.00	25,555	2B.uh	10	9	15	5	1	Italian	PNB	b
2194	Jewish	0.24383	34,649	37,090	47,664	CMT35	51-AABB-hr	chileno		0.10	37	1B.uh	5	4	4	5	0		pnb	.
2195	Mapuche (Araucanian)	3.53982	503,023	538,452	691,961	MIR39f	86-GAAA-c	proper mapuche		70.00	376,917	4....	10	8	11	5	3	Mapudungun	P..	.
2196	Russian	0.02000	2,842	3,042	3,910	CEW22j	53-AAAE-d	russkiy		60.00	1,825	4B.uh	10	8	11	5	2	Russian	PNB	b
2197	Serb	0.05000	7,105	7,606	9,774	CEW22l	53-AAAG-a	standard srpski		85.00	6,465	1Asuh	10	9	11	5	1	Serbian*	PNB	b
2198	Spaniard	0.10000	14,210	15,211	19,548	CEW21k	51-AABB-hr	chileno		96.00	14,603	1B.uh	10	9	15	5	1		pnb	.
2199	Turk	0.00500	711	761	977	MSY41j	44-AABA-a	osmanli		1.00	8	1A.u.	6	4	3	4	0	Turkish	PNB	b
2200	USA White	0.04000	5,684	6,085	7,819	CEW19s	52-ABAC-s	general american		78.00	4,746	1Bsuh	10	10	12	0	0	English*	PNB	b
2201	other minor peoples	0.60785	86,378	92,462	118,822	...				36.60	33,841		9	5	8	3	3			
	China	**100.00000**	**1,205,609,036**	**1,262,556,787**	**1,462,931,461**					**7.05**	**88,955,355**									
2202	Abakan Tatar	0.00009	1,085	1,136	1,317	MSY41z	44-AABD-j	khakas		30.00	341	1c.u.	9	6	7	0	0	Khakas	Pnb	.
2203	Achang (Atsang, Monghsa)	0.00244	29,417	30,806	35,696	MSY50f	77-AAAB-a	achang		8.00	2,465	0....	7	3	3	0	1	Achang	PN.	b
2204	Adi (Miri)	0.00500	60,280	63,128	73,147	MSY50z	74-AAAA-a	adi		0.50	316	0....	5	3	0	1	1	Adi	PN.	.
2205	Ai-Cham	0.00021	2,532	2,651	3,072	MSY49a	47-ABAC-c	sui-ai		1.00	27	0....	6	4	3	0	0		...	.
2206	Akha (Aini)	0.01147	138,283	144,815	167,798	MSY50z	77-BBAA-d	akha		5.00	7,241	1....	7	4	6	2	2	Akha	PN.	b
2207	Amdo (Hbrogpa)	0.07140	860,805	901,466	1,044,533	MSY50r	70-AAAA-bd	ambo		0.00	0	0c...	0	3	2	0	2		pnb	.
2208	Angku	0.00050	6,028	6,313	7,315	AUG03z	46-DBBA-d	pou-ma		3.00	189	0....	6	4	7	1	0		...	b
2209	Anglo-Australian	0.00101	12,177	12,752	14,776	CEW19c	52-ABAC-x	general australian		66.00	8,416	1Bsuh	10	9	13	5	1		pnb	b
2210	Asho Chin (Southern Chin)	0.00080	9,645	10,100	11,703	MSY50c	73-DEEA-c	asho		40.00	4,040	0.s..	9	6	7	2	1	Chin: Asho*	PN.	b
2211	Atsi (Atshi, Zaiwa)	0.00617	74,386	77,900	90,263	MSY50f	77-AAAC-c	atsi		5.00	3,895	0....	7	4	3	1	0	Atsi	P..	p
2212	Atuentse	0.04587	553,013	579,135	671,047	MSY50r	70-AAAA-dc	atuence		0.00	0	0c...	0	1	0	0	0		pnb	.
2213	Aynu (Abdal, Aini)	0.00046	5,546	5,808	6,729	MSY41z	45-BAAA	sakhalin-aynu cluster		0.00	0	0....	0	1	3	0	0	Ainu	PN.	b
2214	Ba Pai	0.00253	30,502	31,943	37,012	MSY47b	48-ABAA-d	ba-pai		0.70	224	0.s..	5	3	3	0	0		pn.	.
2215	Bai (Baizi, Whites)	0.14068	1,696,051	1,776,165	2,058,052	MSY50z	77-BGAA-a	minchia		4.50	79,927	0....	6	4	7	1	3	Bai	...	.
2216	Baima	0.00916	110,434	115,650	134,005	MSY50r	70-AAAA-c	utsang		1.00	1,157	0a...	6	4	4	0	0	Tibetan	PNB	b
2217	Bela	0.00021	2,532	2,651	3,072	MSY49z	77-BAAA	lolo-outer-north cluster		0.50	13	0....	5	4	4	0	0		...	.
2218	Biao Mien	0.00182	21,942	22,979	26,625	MSY47b	48-ABAA-c	biao-min		0.70	161	0.s..	5	4	5	0	0		pn.	.
2219	Bisu	0.00052	6,269	6,565	7,607	MSY50z	77-BBBB-a	bisu		1.00	66	0....	6	4	4	0	0		...	.
2220	Biyo (Bio)	0.00882	106,335	111,358	129,031	MSY50z	77-BBAA-j	biyo		2.00	2,227	1....	6	5	5	0	0		pn.	.
2221	Black Lisu (Eastern Lisu)	0.00511	61,607	64,517	74,756	MSY50l	77-BACA-ae	lip'o		48.00	30,968	1cs..	9	6	11	2	3	Lipo	PNb	.
2222	Black Tai (Thai Den)	0.00250	30,140	31,564	36,573	MSY49z	47-AAAD-ab	jinping-dai		2.00	631	0....	6	4	6	1	0		p..	.
2223	British (Mainland China)	0.00060	7,234	7,575	8,778	CEW19i	52-ABAC-b	standard-english		79.00	5,985	3Bsuh	10	8	11	2	3		PNB	b
2224	British (HK, = Hong Kong)	0.00369	44,487	46,588	53,982	CEW19i	52-ABAC-b	standard-english	48	76.00	35,407	3Bsuh	10	9	13	5	2		PNB	b
2225	British (M, = Macao)	0.00017	2,050	2,146	2,487	CEW19i	52-ABAC-b	standard-english		79.00	1,696	3Bsuh	10	9	13	5	3		PNB	b
2226	Bugan	0.00024	2,893	3,030	3,511	AUG03z	46-GAAA	mon cluster		1.00	30	2....	6	4	4	0	0		PNB	b
2227	Bulang (Pula, Samtao)	0.00726	87,527	91,662	106,209	MSY50i	46-DBAC	bulang cluster		0.60	550	0....	5	4	2	2	0	Blang	...	b
2228	Burig (Purig Bhotia)	0.00800	96,449	101,005	117,035	MSY50r	70-AAAC-d	purik		0.10	101	1....	5	3	1	0	1	Purigskad*	PN.	.
2229	Buryat (Northern Mongolia)	0.00649	78,244	81,940	94,944	MSY41y	44-BAAB-b	buryat		1.00	819	3A..h	6	3	5	0	0	Buryat*	PNB	b
2230	Buyang	0.00022	2,652	2,778	3,218	MSY49a	47-AAAH	buyi cluster		1.00	28	0....	6	4	2	0	0		...	b
2231	Central Tibetan (Hsifan)	0.40517	4,884,766	5,115,501	5,927,359	MSY50r	70-AAAA-c	utsang		1.40	71,617	0a...	6	4	7	1	4	Tibetan	PNB	b
2232	Central Yi	0.04001	482,364	505,149	585,319	MSY50i	77-BAGA	yi-central cluster		2.00	10,103	0....	6	5	3	2	2		...	b
2233	Chiang (Qiang)	0.01749	210,861	220,821	255,867	MSY50r	76-CAAA	qiang cluster		0.10	221	0....	5	4	0	0	1		...	.
2234	Chienchiang	0.01000	120,561	126,256	146,293	MSY49a	47-AAAG-a	qian-jang		0.50	631	1c...	5	4	5	1	1		p..	.
2235	Chinese Jew	0.00002	241	253	293	CMT35	79-AAAB-ba	kuo-yü		0.00	0	2Bsuh	0	4	1	0	0	Chinese: Kuoyu*	PNB	b
2236	Chinese Mongolian (Mongol)	0.27090	3,265,995	3,420,266	3,963,081	MSY41f	44-BAAB-e	oyrat		0.05	1,710	1a..h	4	4	7	0	3	Mongolian: Inner*	PNb	b
2237	Chinese Shan (Dai Nuea)	0.02205	265,837	278,394	322,576	MSY49a	47-AAAA-f	tai-neua		0.00	0	1.s..	0	2	2	0	0	Chinese: Shanghai*	PNB	.
2238	Chinese Tajik (Tadzhik)	0.00296	35,686	37,372	43,303	CNT24g	58-ABDE-d	sarikoli		0.01	4	0....	3	3	4	0	0		...	b
2239	Ching (Mak)	0.00100	12,056	12,626	14,629	MSY49z	47-ABAB-a	ching-cham		0.52	66	0....	5	3	4	0	0		pn.	.
2240	Chingpo (Kachin, Jinghpaw)	0.01052	126,830	132,821	153,900	MSY50f	75-AAAA-a	jing-pho		55.00	73,052	2as..	10	6	11	2	2	Kachin: Jinghpaw*	PNB	.
2241	Choni	0.00193	23,268	24,367	28,235	MSY50r	70-AAAA-ba	choni		0.00	0	0c...	0	3	0	0	0		pnb	.
2242	Choni (Northern Tibetan)	0.00200	24,112	25,251	29,259	MSY50r	70-AAAA-ba	choni		0.00	0	0c...	0	3	0	0	0		pnb	.
2243	Chungchia (Yijia, Ichia)	0.02000	241,122	252,511	292,586	MSY49a	47-AAAF-g	zhong-jia		1.00	2,525	0....	6	3	7	0	0		...	.
2244	Cun	0.00616	74,266	77,773	90,117	MSY49a	47-BBAB-a	ngao-fon		8.00	6,222	0....	7	5	7	0	0		...	b
2245	Cun (Han Chinese)	0.00529	63,777	66,789	77,389	MSY42a	47-BBAB-a	ngao-fon		0.10	67	0....	5	4	2	0	0		...	b
2246	Cung	0.00100	12,056	12,626	14,629	MSY49a	47-AAAA-hb	tai-chung		1.00	126	1.s..	6	4	2	0	0		pnb	b
2247	Cunhua	0.00617	74,386	77,900	90,263	MSY49a	47-BBAB-a	ngao-fon		4.00	3,116	0....	6	4	4	2	1		...	b
2248	Daban Yao (Yerong)	0.00003	362	379	439	MSY49a	48-ABAA-f	yerong		1.00	4	0.s..	6	4	3	2	0		pn.	.
2249	Daguor (Dagur, Qiqihar)	0.01070	129,000	135,094	156,534	MSY41y	44-BAAC-a	daur		0.01	14	1....	3	1	0	0	0		...	.
2250	Dananshan Miao	0.00400	48,224	50,502	58,517	MSY47a	48-AAAE-a	danan-shan		4.00	2,020	0....	6	4	6	1	2		...	.
2251	Dutch	0.00010	1,206	1,263	1,463	CEW19h	52-ABCA-a	algemeen-nederlands		76.00	960	2Bsuh	10	9	15	5	1	Dutch	PNB	b
2252	E	0.00257	30,984	32,448	37,597	MSY50f	95-ABAH-a	jede-po		0.50	162	0....	5	2	6	0	0	E Je*	PN.	b
2253	East Yugur	0.00054	6,510	6,818	7,900	MSY41y	44-BAAE-c	shira-yugur		0.10	7	0....	5	1	0	0	0		...	b
2254	Eastern Meo (Black, Heh)	0.12349	1,488,807	1,559,131	1,806,574	MSY47a	48-AAAC-a	qiandong-miao		5.50	85,752	0r...	7	4	12	0	3	Hmong, Northern Qiandong	PN.	.
2255	Eastern Yi	0.06959	838,983	878,613	1,018,054	MSY50i	77-BAGA	yi-central cluster		2.00	17,572	0....	6	4	11	2	2		...	b
2256	Ergong	0.00291	35,083	36,740	42,571	MSY50r	70-AAAA-c	utsang		1.00	367	0a...	6	4	5	0	0	Tibetan	PNB	b
2257	Ersu	0.00108	13,021	13,636	15,800	MSY50r	70-AAAA	phöke cluster		1.00	136	0a...	6	5	5	0	0		PNB	b
2258	Esperanto	0.00000	0	0	0	CEW21z	51-AAAC-a	proper esperanto		20.00	0	0A...	9	5	5	2	0	Esperanto	PNB	b
2259	Esperanto (Hong Kong)	0.00000	0	0	0	CEW21z	51-AAAC-a	proper esperanto		40.00	0	0A...	9	8	2	5	0	Esperanto	PNB	b

Continued opposite

Table 8-2 continued

EVANGELIZATION								EVANGELISM			ADDITIONAL DESCRIPTIVE DATA
Ref 1	D 28	aC 29	CG% 30	r 31	E 32	U 33	W 34	e 35	R 36	T 37	Locations, civil divisions, literacy, religions, church history, denominations, dioceses, church growth, missions, agencies, ministries, movements 38
2142	0	4	0.00	0	10.00	90.00	A	0.00	0	1.04	Salamat Prefecture. Also in CAR. Most men bilingual in Arabic. Traders. Muslims 80%, animists 20%.
2143	0	5	0.00	0	11.00	89.00	A	0.00	0	1.04	Central. Guera Prefecture. Bilingual in Arabic. Arabicized Muslims 100%(Sunnis).
2144	1	6	7.30	4	99.50	0.50	B	197.10	221	7	Official language of Central African Republic, rapidly spreading. Heavily christianized. Animists 50%. D=RCC.
2145	5	6	10.63	2	87.00	13.00	B	101.61	380	7	Some in Cameroon. Muslims 26%, animists 20%. D=RCC(D-Moundou),EET,EBT,ACT,AICs. M=CMML,SUM,TEAM,UBS,OFMCap,EMS(Nigeria),SJ. R=ELWA.
2146	5	6	9.70	1	99.00	1.00	B	162.60	308	7	Also in CAR. Subsistence farmers. 50% urban. Literates 10%. Muslims 20%, animists 15%. 1973, severe state persecution. D=EBT,EET,EDT,RCC,AICs. M=BMM.
2147	3	6	9.79	4	99.68	0.32	C	310.25	246	9	South; also in CAR, Cameroon, a few in Nigeria. Animists 15%, Muslims 4%. D=ACT,EET,RCC. M=CMML,BMM,SJ,UBS.
2148	0	5	2.99	0	22.00	78.00	A	0.80	546	3	Also in Cameroon. In west, Chari-Baguirmi Prefecture. Related to Gadang. Muslims 99%(since AD 1800). M=AIM,EET. M=YWAM.
2149	1	5	2.57	7	35.01	64.99	A	0.01	256	2	Nomadic and semi-sedentary cattle-herders. Also in Nigeria, Niger, Cameroon. Lingua franca. Muslims 95%(Sunnis, mostly in Tijaniyya Sufi brotherhood). D=ACT.
2150	0	4	0.00	0	9.00	91.00	A	0.00	0	1.03	Zimirra. On Sudan border. Pastoral nomads, bilingual in Arabic. Lax Muslims 100%.
2151	1	4	3.49	0	23.00	77.00	A	4.19	581	4	Northeast of Melfi. Tunjur language becoming extinct; most men are bilingual in Arabic. Muslims 50%(Maliki Sunnis), animists 45%. D=ACT; a few Christian villages.
2152	0	4	1.62	7	27.03	72.97	A	0.03	235	2	Nomads in east of country; tent-dwellers. Muslims 100%(Sunnis).
2153	2	5	5.81	0	63.00	37.00	B	68.98	313	6	Southwest Chad, southeast of Bongor. Primarily in CAR. Animists 70%. D=RCC,EET(strong). M=SUM,WEC.
2154	1	5	6.35	0	58.00	42.00	B	63.51	366	6	Southwest, Tandjile and Mayo-Kebbi Prefectures. Animists 70%. D=ACT. M=CMML.
2155	0	4	0.00	0	10.00	90.00	A	0.00	0	1.03	Northeast of Abeche; also in Sudan. Most are bilingual in Arabic. Muslims 100%(Sunnis). M=WEC.
2156	0	0	0.00	0	8.01	91.99	A	0.00	489	1.03	Ouaddai Prefecture. Adre subprefecture between Hadid and Alacha. Bilingualism in Maba and Masalit. Muslims 100%.
2157	0	4	0.00	0	9.00	91.00	A	0.00	0	1.03	Eastern Chad border. Many in Sudan. Bilingual in Arabic. Muslims 100%(Sunnis; Sufi Tijaniyya gaining ground).
2158	0	4	0.00	0	10.00	90.00	A	0.00	0	1.03	Saharan Negroes. Nomads and semi-nomads around Tibesti volcanic massif; also in Libya, Niger. Bilingual in Arabic. Muslims 100%(Maliki Sunnis, Sanussiyya).
2159	0	4	2.10	0	14.10	85.90	A	0.05	678	2	Central Chad, Salamat Prefecture, Abou Dlia Subprefecture. Muslims 99%, some animists.
2160	2	4	7.11	0	63.00	37.00	B	68.98	370	6	Southwest. Tandjile Prefecture. Also in CAR. Related to Somrai. Animists 70%. D=80% RCC,EBT. M=BMM.
2161	2	5	4.13	0	42.00	58.00	A	30.66	363	5	South. Moyen-Chari Prefecture. Muslims 80%. Also in CAR. D=ACT,EBT. M=CMML,BMM.
2162	3	5	9.25	0	99.60	0.40	C	221.19	289	8	Southwest Chad around Fianga; similar number in Cameroon. Animists 30%. D=EFLT,RCC,ACT. M=UBS,LBWM,CMML.
2163	0	4	0.00	7	13.00	87.00	A	0.00	0	1.04	Arabic-based creole. Lingua franca from Cameroon to Sudan. Muslims 100%(Sunnis).
2164	0	0	0.00	0	8.01	91.99	A	0.00	0	1.03	Guera Prefecture. Mongo subprefecture southwest of Tounkoul. Similar to Mawa. Muslims 100%.
2165	1	5	3.19	0	54.00	46.00	B	59.13	234	6	Also in CAR. Related, but unintelligible to, Sara and Ngambai languages. Animists 70%. D=RCC.
2166	0	4	4.23	0	15.04	84.96	A	0.02	1,031	2	East central, near Abeche. Most are bilingual in Chad Arabic. Literates 6%. Muslims 100%(Maliki Sunnis with Sufi orders, since c1650). M=SGM,WEC,SUM.
2167	0	4	0.00	0	9.00	91.00	A	0.00	0	1.03	South central. Related to Sokoro and Barein. Bilingual in Arabic. Muslims 90%, animists 10%.
2168	0	5	2.75	4	31.01	68.99	A	0.01	367	2	Majority in Nigeria; also in Cameroon, Sudan, Niger. Ajami script used. Many speak Arabic. Strong Muslims 100%(Sunnis). M=WEC,AIM,EET.
2169	0	4	0.00	0	10.00	90.00	A	0.00	0	1.03	Northeast of Abeche; large majority are in Sudan, also some in Libya. Settled cattle raisers. Bilingual in Arabic. Muslims 75%(Maliki Sunnis), animists 25%. M=SUM.
2170	0	6	5.25		28.00	72.00	A	10.22	514	5	Mandera, Alwa, Disa, Mawer, Monogoy, Noy, Majera, Mpade, Nzakmbay, et alia. Muslims 60%, Animists 30%.
Channel Islands											
2171	5	6	0.22	8	99.66	0.34	C	342.07	26	9	65% Anglicans. D=Ch of England(D-Winchester),RCC(D-Portsmouth),BUGBI,SA,URC. M=OMI,SJ,FSC,FICP.
2172	1	10	0.61	8	99.69	0.31	C	365.18	30	9	Nonreligious/atheists 31%. D=RCC(Catholic Ch in England & Wales). Mainly on Jersey. M=OMI,FSC,FICP.
2173	0	10	0.70	7	55.00	45.00	B	6.02	85	4	Asians. Hindus 48%, Muslims 47%, a few Buddhists, 2 Baha'i centers.
2174	0	10	0.00	8	55.00	45.00	B	2.00	34	4	One Jewish congregation on Jersey with synagogue in countryside.
2175	1	10	0.61	8	99.80	0.20	C	400.04	32	10	Settlers originating in Normandy (France). Related to French. D=RCC.
2176	0	10	0.61		93.00	7.00	C	203.67	18	8	Greeks, USA Whites.
Chile											
2177	1	10	1.71	0	90.00	10.00	C	197.10	83	7	Isle of Wellengton, western. Patagonia. Fishermen. Monolingual. Some shamanists, but mostly Catholics. D=RCC. M=SAMS.
2178	2	9	5.51	8	99.70	0.30	C	342.37	127	9	Lebanese, Palestinians. Muslims 30%. D=Antiochian Orthodox Ch,Greek Orthodox Ch(P-Antioch).
2179	1	10	4.32	6	99.90	0.10	C	525.60	84	10	Refugees from Middle East and USSR since 1900. D=Armenian Apostolic Ch(D-South America).
2180	1	10	1.65	4	99.94	0.06	C	548.96	45	10	Immigrants from Spain, in commerce, education, professions. D=RCC. M=SJ.
2181	2	10	1.65	8	99.79	0.21	C	455.59	49	10	Expatriates and immigrants from Britain; professionals, commerce, industry. D=Anglican Ch,RCC.
2182	0	10	1.65	4	99.70	0.30	C	316.82	36	9	Mountains in north. Few speakers of Aymara. Christopagans 50%. Animists 25%, some Baha'is. M=SAMS.
2183	7	9	1.58	8	99.91	0.09	C	532.00	36	10	D=82% RCC(24 Dioceses),IMP,IEP,SDA,IDP,IEMPRNJ,IPC. M=SJ,SDB,OSM,OFMCap,FMB,SIM. R=AWR.
2184	1	10	1.65	5	99.75	0.25	C	385.98	45	9	Northern second region. Animists 20%, some Baha'is. D=RCC(67% christopagans). M=FMB.
2185	4	10	1.47	8	99.85	0.15	C	483.51	41	10	Persons of Italian, Spanish descent. D=RCC,IMP,IEP,SDA. R=AWR.
2186	1	10	1.65	0	99.70	0.30	C	286.27	57	8	Rapanuians. Island 3,500 km west of mainland. Fishermen, craftsmen. Also in mainland Chile, Tahiti, USA. D=RCC(VA-Araucania). M=SIL.
2187	0	10	0.00	5	99.50	0.50	B	187.97	0	7	Artificial (constructed) language, in 80 countries. Speakers in Chile: 14,000 (none mother-tongue). Nonreligious 20%.
2188	1	10	1.65	8	99.87	0.13	C	511.25	45	10	Immigrants from France, in the professions, industry. D=RCC.
2189	1	10	1.65	8	99.88	0.12	C	523.55	47	10	Immigrants from Germany, M=FMB. D=IELC.
2190	1	10	1.65	7	99.95	0.05	C	575.60	43	10	In commerce, trade. D=Greek Orthodox AD of N&S America.
2191	0	9	3.96	7	90.00	10.00	B	98.55	140	6	Buddhists (including Confucianists) 70%. M=FMB.
2192	1	9	1.65	0	99.60	0.40	C	227.76	59	8	Araucanian. South of Mapuche. Only 3% speak the language. D=RCC.
2193	1	10	1.65	7	99.84	0.16	C	481.36	46	10	Immigrants from Italy. D=RCC(24 Dioceses). Strong Pentecostalist leadership.
2194	0	10	1.68	8	49.10	50.90	A	0.17	132	3	Several centers for Jewish culture.
2195	5	8	1.65	0	99.70	0.30	C	309.15	51	9	Polytheists 20%, Baha'is 1%. D=80% RCC(71% are christopagans; also many charismatics),CMA,Iglesia Anglicana,IMNC,ICFG. M=SAGM,SAMS,WVI,FMB,SIL.
2196	2	10	5.34	7	99.60	0.40	C	295.65	108	8	Refugees from USSR after 1917, 1945. Nonreligious 30%. D=ROC(P-Moscow),ROCOR.
2197	1	10	6.69	6	99.85	0.15	C	477.78	119	10	Refugees from Yugoslavia. D=Serbian Orthodox Ch(P-Belgrade).
2198	1	10	1.65	8	99.96	0.04	C	578.16	43	10	Immigrants from Spain. D=RCC(24 Dioceses). Strong Pentecostalist leadership. M=FMB.
2199	0	9	2.10	8	53.00	47.00	B	1.93	145	4	Immigrants from Turkey. Muslims 99%(Hanafi Sunnis).
2200	0	0	6.36	8	99.78	0.22	C	370.11	153	9	North Americans, in business, education. Nonreligious 10%. D=RCC,BBC,SDA,etc.
2201	0	9	1.65		73.60	26.40	B	98.32	61	6	Other European refugees and immigrants; Koreans(M=PCK-H,PCK-T), Bolivians, Canadians. Nonreligious 30%.
China											
2202	0	7	3.59	1	64.00	36.00	B	70.08	188	6	Yenisei Tatar. West Xinjiang; mainly in Khakass AO (Russia) around Abakan. Only 10 speakers. Muslims 70%.
2203	1	4	5.66	0	35.00	65.00	A	10.22	529	5	Western Yunnan. Also in Burma. Many bilingual in Chinese, Dai. Buddhists 50%(Hinayana), polytheists 42%. D=Chinese Ch(in nearly every Achang village).
2204	1	4	3.51	0	19.50	80.50	A	0.35	648	3	In Tibet; under Lhoba nationality. Also in Assam(India). Lamaist Buddhists(Tantrists) 99%. D=Baptist Chs.
2205	0	4	3.35	0	17.00	83.00	A	0.62	645	3	Separate language included under Buyi nationality. Polytheists 99%, a few Buddhists.
2206	2	4	6.81	0	37.00	63.00	A	6.75	586	4	Southwest Yunnan and Kengtung State. Under Hani nationality. Also in Burma, Thailand, Laos, Viet Nam. Animists 60%, Buddhists 35%. D=Baptists,RCC.
2207	0	3	0.00	1	18.00	82.00	A	0.00	0	1.08	Qinghai, Sichuan, and Gansu Provinces. Bodic. Lamaist Buddhists 100%. M=CIM/OMF,AFM.
2208	0	4	2.98	0	24.00	76.00	A	2.62	454	4	Yunnan. Also in Burma, Laos, Thailand. Under Blang nationality. Buddhists 95%(Hinayana). Few Christians.
2209	5	10	2.86	8	99.66	0.34	C	322.80	74	9	Expatriates from Australia, in commerce, business. Nonreligious 30%. D=Anglican Ch,RCC,SDA,CCC,JWs. M=FMB.
2210	1	5	4.05	4	78.00	22.00	B	113.88	181	7	Also in Bangladesh and Lower Burma. Animists 60%. D=Baptists Chs.
2211	0	4	6.15	0	25.00	75.00	A	4.56	795	4	Yunnan Province, Tehung Autonomous Chou. Under Jingpo nationality. Also in Burma. Polytheists(animists) 70%, Buddhists 20%.
2212	0	4	-9.99	1	15.00	85.00	A	0.00	18	1.06	Along Yunnan-Tibet border. Under Tibetan nationality. Lamaist Buddhists 100%.
2213	0	3	0.00	0	16.00	84.00	A	0.00	0	1.06	Towns in Kashgar area. Related to Uighurs but despised as 'abdal' (beggars). Bilingual in Uighur. Muslims 100%(Sunnis).
2214	0	0	3.16	0	14.70	85.30	A	0.37	719	3	Part of official Yao nationality. Guangdong and Hunan provinces. Swidden agriculturalists. Polytheists 99%.
2215	1	4	9.40	0	31.50	68.50	A	5.17	913	4	Yunnan, Sichuan, Guizhou. Unwritten. Polytheists(animists) 65%, Mahayana Buddhists/Taoists 30%. Y=c1890(RC missions). D=strong national church(TSPM,RCC).
2216	0	0	4.87	4	32.00	68.00	A	1.16	560	4	Part of official Tibetan nationality. Pingwu county in north central Sichuan. Buddhists (Lamaists) 98%, Muslims 1%.
2217	0	0	2.60	0	11.50	88.50	A	0.21	762	3	Part of official Jingpo nationality. Yunnan province. Also in Myanmar. Agriculturalists. Polytheists 90%, Buddhists 9.5%.
2218	0	0	2.82	0	16.70	83.30	A	0.42	578	3	Part of official Yao nationality. Guangdong province. Swidden agriculturalists. Polytheists 99%.
2219	0	0	4.28	1	14.00	86.00	A	0.51	1,053	3	Bilingual in Dai, Chinese. Xishuangbanna Dai Autonomous Prefecture in Yunnan. Also in Myanmar. Polytheists 59%, Buddhists 40%.
2220	0	4	5.55	0	25.00	75.00	A	1.82	729	4	Yunnan Province, near the Hani. Polytheists 98%, a few Buddhists.
2221	4	5	3.79	1	97.00	3.00	B	169.94	135	7	Around Taku, east Yunnan Province, highland areas. Polytheists/animists 52%. Y=c1890(RC,Protestant missions). D=Gospel Ch(Lisu Ch;pastors trained).
2222	0	4	4.23	1	24.00	76.00	A	1.75	551	4	Southwest Yunnan Province. Vast majority in Viet Nam; also in Laos, Thailand, USA, France. Animists 98%.
2223	3	9	0.80	8	99.79	0.21	C	429.64	36	10	Expatriates from UK, in education, commerce, development, science. D=TSPM,RCC,SDA.
2224	5	10	3.51	8	99.76	0.24	C	421.64	84	10	Expatriates from UK, in business, education. D=Anglican Ch in China(D-Hong Kong & Macao),CCC,EMC,JWs,union churches. M=CMS,FMB.
2225	3	10	3.38	8	99.79	0.21	C	446.94	80	10	Expatriates from Britain, in business. D=Anglican Ch(D-Hong Kong & Macao),SDA,JWs.
2226	0	0	3.46	0	25.00	75.00	A	0.91	489	3	Yunnan province. Live with Han Chinese in 3 villages, by themselves in 4. Colorful printed dresses. Polytheists 99%.
2227	0	4	4.09	0	19.60	80.40	A	0.42	726	3	Southwestern Yunnan Province, living among Va(Wa). A few in Thailand, Burma. An official nationality. Bilingual in Dai, Wa, Chinese. Buddhists 97%(Hinayana). .
2228	0	4	2.34	0	19.10	80.90	A	0.07	575	2	In Tibet; also in India. Muslims 100%(Shias). M=Central Asian Mission.
2229	0	4	4.50	4	42.00	58.00	A	1.53	344	4	Hulun-Buyr District, Inner Mongolia. Lamaist Buddhists(Tantrists) 99%.
2230	0	4	3.39	0	19.00	81.00	A	0.69	583	3	Yunnan Province, Wenshan Zhuang-Miao Autonomous District. Polytheists 99%.
2231	2	3	8.58	4	47.40	52.60	A	2.42	593	4	Lamaist Buddhists 98%(with, in 1950, 100,000 monks (10% of all men) in 5,000 monasteries); some Muslims. D=98% RCC,2% TSPM. M=TCF,LBI,AoG,PI,GRI.
2232	2	4	7.16	0	26.00	74.00	A	1.89	870	4	A separate language in Yi official nationality. Polytheists/animists 98%. D=TSPM,RCC.
2233	1	1	0.98	0	11.10	88.90	A	0.04	654	2	Western Sichuan; also some in Canada. Official nationality. Agriculturalists. Lamaist Buddhists 70%(Tantrists, some Mahayana), polytheists 30%. Y=c1890(RCC).
2234	1	4	4.23	1	24.50	75.50	A	0.44	546	3	Guizhou Province. Related to Puyi (Bouyei). Polytheists 80%, Buddhists 19%. D=RCC.
2235	0	4	0.00	7	34.00	66.00	A	0.00	0	1.12	An ancient community in Kaifeng city, Henan Province, officially recognized. 100% followers of Judaism.
2236	2	4	5.28	4	44.05	55.95	A	0.08	376	2	Inner Mongolia; 16 Provinces (Liaoning, Jilin, Heilongjiang). Nonreligious 50%, shamanists 40%, Lamaist Buddhists(Tantrists) 10%. D=RCC,house churches.
2237	0	4	0.00	1	22.00	78.00	A	0.00	0	1.09	Southwest of Tali in south Yunnan. Also in Burma, Laos, North Viet Nam. Buddhists 100%(Hinayana).
2238	0	2	1.40	0	15.01	84.99	A	0.00	383	1.05	In southwest Sinkiang, in and around Tashkurghan. Official nationality. Some speak Wakhi; Uighur used for writing. Pastoralists. Muslims 100%(Ismaili Shias).
2239	0	5	4.28	0	20.52	79.48	A	0.38	652	3	A few villages in northwestern Lipo in Guizhou, Guangxi, and Guangdong Provinces. Polytheists/animists 99%.
2240	2	5	3.97	5	99.55	0.45	B	228.85	122	8	Western Yunnan. Also in Burma, India. Official nationality. Polytheists(animists) 35%, Buddhists 10%. Y=c1930(RC,Protestant missions). D=RCC,Chinese Ch
2241	0	0	0.00	1	10.00	90.00	A	0.00	0	1.05	Related to Amdo, Golog, and Kham. Yunnan-Tibet border. Buddhists (Lamaists) 100%.
2242	0	3	-9.99	1	14.00	86.00	A	0.00	20	1.06	Northern Tibet, Yunnan-Tibet border. Lamaist Buddhists(Tantrists) 100%.
2243	0	4	5.69	0	22.00	78.00	A	0.80	790	3	Southwest Guizhou and Guangxi Provinces. A dialect of Northern Zhuang. Under Puyi nationality. Polytheists 99%. R=FEBC.
2244	0	0	6.64	0	25.00	75.00	A	7.30	799	4	Part of official Han nationality. South bank of Changhua River, Hainan Island. Chinese folk-religionists 60%, Nonreligious 20%.
2245	0	4	4.29	0	17.10	82.90	A	0.06	792	2	Hainan, south bank of Changhua river. Cun people are classifieds as Han Chinese. Folk-religionists.
2246	0	4	2.57	1	28.00	72.00	A	1.02	315	4	Yunnan, Hani-Yi-Dai Autonomous County. Polytheists.
2247	1	5	5.91	0	27.00	73.00	A	3.94	666	4	Hainan Island. A separate language. Under Han Chinese nationality. Polytheists 90%. D=TSPM.
2248	0	4	1.40	0	23.00	77.00	A	0.84	244	3	In Guangxi Napo County. Offically under Yao nationality. Polytheists 98%.
2249	0	3	2.67	0	10.01	89.99	A	0.00	942	1.04	Inner Mongolia, Xinjiang. Official nationality. Agriculturalists, pastoralists, hunters. Mongolian used as written language. Shamanists 70%, Lamaist Buddhists 30%.
2250	2	4	5.45	0	29.00	71.00	A	4.23	581	4	In Dananshan, northwestern Guizhou Province. Polytheists/animists 96%. D=TSPM,RCC.
2251	1	10	2.85	6	99.76	0.24	C	413.32	68	10	Expatriates from Netherlands in business, oil. D=CCC.
2252	0	0	2.82	1	18.50	81.50	A	0.33	581	3	Part of official Zhuang nationality, but they do not speak Zhuang. Northern Guangxi-Zhuang Autonomous Region. Polytheists 90%, Buddhists 9.5%.
2253	0	2	1.96	0	13.10	86.90	A	0.04	571	2	Northwest Gansu Province. Pastoralists. An official nationality (with West Yugur). Written Chinese is used. Shamanists 60%, Lamaist Buddhists 40%.
2254	4	4	3.75	4	50.50	49.50	B	10.13	241	5	Northeast Yunnan, Guizhou, Guangxi; also in Thailand, Viet Nam. Agriculturalists. Polytheists(animists) 94%. Y=c1900(RC,Protestant missions). D=Chinese Ch.
2255	2	4	7.76	0	34.00	66.00	A	2.48	714	4	Southeastern Yi. Guizhou Province, Weining Autonomous Region. Polytheists/animists 98%. D=TSPM,RCC.
2256	0	0	3.67	4	32.00	68.00	A	1.16	457	4	Part of official Tibetan nationality. Sichuan province. Buddhists (Lamaists) 98%, Muslims 1%.
2257	0	0	2.64	4	32.00	68.00	A	1.16	369	4	Part of official Tibetan nationality. South central Sichuan on Dadu River. Buddhists (Lamaists) 98%, Muslims 1%.
2258	0	6	0.00	5	68.00	32.00	B	49.64	0	6	Artificial (constructed) language, in 80 countries. Speakers in China: 611,000 (none mother-tongue). Buddhists 40%, Nonreligious/atheists 40%.
2259	0	10	0.00	5	92.00	8.00	B	134.32	0	7	Artificial (constructed) language, in 80 countries. Speakers in Hong Kong: 2,500(none mother-tongue). Nonreligious/atheists 30%.

Continued overleaf

Table 8-2 continued

PEOPLE		POPULATION				IDENTITY CODE		LANGUAGE		CHURCH		MINISTRY						SCRIPTURE	
Ref 1	Ethnic name 2	P% 3	In 1995 4	In 2000 5	In 2025 6	Race 7	Language 8	Autoglossonym 9	S 10	AC 11	Members 12	Jayuh 13-17	d 18	wa 19	xc 20	mc 21	mi 22	Biblioglossonym 23	Pub 24-26 ss 27
2260	Eurasian	0.05000	602,805	631,278	731,466	MSY43	79-AAAB-ba	kuo-yü		10.00	63,128	2Bsuh	8	5	6	3	1	Chinese: Kuoyu*	PNB b
2261	Eurasian (in Hong Kong)	0.00152	18,325	19,191	22,237	MSY43	52-ABAD-ca	hong-kong-english		60.00	11,515	0A.uh	10	8	7	5	3		... b
2262	Evenki (Owenke, Tungus)	0.00232	27,970	29,291	33,940	MSY41i	44-CAAB-a	evenki		1.00	293	0....	6	3	3	0	1	Evenki	P.. b
2263	Filipino	0.00607	73,180	76,637	88,800	MSY44o	31-CKAA-a	proper tagalog		98.00	75,104	4Bs..	10	8	13	5	3	Tagalog	PNB b
2264	Filipino (in Hong Kong)	0.00011	1,326	1,389	1,609	MSY44o	31-CKAA-a	proper tagalog		98.00	1,361	4Bs..	10	8	12	0	0	Tagalog	PNB b
2265	Flowery Meo (Miao Hwa)	0.00343	41,352	43,306	50,179	MSY47a	48-AAAA-b	hmong-njua		5.00	2,165	1A...	7	4	11	2	3	Hmong Njua	PN. b
2266	French	0.00010	1,206	1,263	1,463	CEW21b	51-AABI-d	general français		84.00	1,061	1B.uh	10	9	14	5	3	French	PNB b
2267	Gaoshan (Ami)	0.00026	3,135	3,283	3,804	AUG01a	30-KAAA-e	nanshi-amis		50.00	1,641	0....	10	5	7	2	1		pn. b
2268	German	0.00010	1,206	1,263	1,463	CEW19m	52-ABCE-a	standard hoch-deutsch		87.00	1,098	2B.uh	10	9	13	5	2	German*	PNB b
2269	Golden Palaung	0.00008	964	1,010	1,170	AUG03z	46-DCAA	palaung cluster		0.10	1	0r...	5	1	0	0	0	Palaung, Pale	... b
2270	Grass Miao	0.00505	60,883	63,759	73,878	MSY47a	47-ABAA-aa	dong		5.00	3,188	0....	7	6	9	0	0		... .
2271	Groma	0.00100	12,056	12,626	14,629	MSY50r	70-AAAB-c	groma		0.00	0	1.s..	0	1	4	0	0		pn. .
2272	Groma	0.00109	13,141	13,762	15,946	MSY50r	70-AAAB-c	groma		1.00	138	1.s..	6	4	6	0	0		pn. .
2273	Guiqiong	0.00058	6,993	7,323	8,485	MSY50r	70-AAAB	tibetan-south cluster		1.00	73	1.s..	6	4	6	0	0		PN. b
2274	Gurkha	0.00020	2,411	2,525	2,926	MSY50e	59-AAFD-b	nepali		1.00	25	2Asu.	6	4	3	5	2	Nepali	PNB b
2275	Hainan Cham (Huihui)	0.00040	4,822	5,050	5,852	MSY44y	31-MAAA-a	utsat		0.10	5	0....	5	3	3	0	0		... .
2276	Han Chinese	0.00151	18,205	19,065	22,090	MSY42a	77-AABA-a	bama		3.00	572	4Asu.	6	4	8	5	3	Burmese	PNB b
2277	Han Chinese (Cantonese)	4.50370	54,297,014	56,861,770	65,886,044	MSY42a	79-AAAM-a	central yue		3.40	1,933,300	3A.uh	6	5	12	3	4	Chinese, Yue	PNB b
2278	Han Chinese (Cantonese):HK	0.37743	4,550,330	4,765,268	5,521,542	MSY42a	79-AAAM-a	central yue	98	10.30	490,823	3A.uh	8	5	10	5	2	Chinese, Yue	PNB b
2279	Han Chinese (Cantonese):M	0.03384	407,978	427,249	495,056	MSY42a	79-AAAM-a	central yue	99	7.10	30,335	3A.uh	7	5	8	5	3	Chinese, Yue	PNB b
2280	Han Chinese (Hainanese)	0.45000	5,425,241	5,681,506	6,583,192	MSY42a	79-AAAK-c	wanning		0.10	5,682	1a...	5	5	11	2	3		p.. b
2281	Han Chinese (Hakka)	2.50206	30,165,061	31,589,928	36,603,423	MSY42a	79-AAAG-al	jia-ying		0.50	157,950	1a...	5	5	12	2	3	Chinese: Hakka*	PNB b
2282	Han Chinese (Hakka):HK	0.01668	201,096	210,594	244,017	MSY42a	79-AAAG-a	literary hakka		16.00	33,695	1A...	8	5	9	5	3	Chinese: Hakka, Wukingfu*	PNB b
2283	Han Chinese (Hoklo)	0.04681	564,346	591,003	684,798	MSY42a	79-AAAJ-ic	chaozhou		15.00	88,650	1A..h	8	5	9	5	3	Chinese, Min Nan	PNB b
2284	Han Chinese (Hunanese)	3.50288	42,231,038	44,225,849	51,244,734	MSY42a	79-AAAE-a	xiang		2.00	884,517	1....	6	5	11	2	3		... b
2285	Han Chinese (Jinyu)	3.75038	45,214,920	47,350,677	54,865,489	MSY42a	79-AAAB-l	hui-zu		7.00	3,314,547	1Asuh	7	6	8	0	0		pnb b
2286	Han Chinese (Kan)	2.00165	24,132,073	25,271,968	29,282,768	MSY42a	79-AAAF-a	gan		6.00	1,516,318	0....	7	5	11	3	2		... b
2287	Han Chinese (Mandarin)	63.61643	766,965,428	803,193,555	930,664,769	MSY42a	79-AAAB-ba	kuo-yü	92	7.66	61,524,626	2Bsuh	7	7	9	3	1	Chinese: Kuoyu*	PNB b
2288	Han Chinese (Mandarin):HK	0.02527	304,657	319,048	369,683	MSY42a	79-AAAB-ba	kuo-yü		10.00	31,905	2Bsuh	8	7	9	5	3	Chinese: Kuoyu*	PNB b
2289	Han Chinese (Mandarin):M	0.00076	9,163	9,595	11,118	MSY42a	79-AAAB-ba	kuo-yü	60	8.00	768	2Bsuh	7	5	11	5	1	Chinese: Kuoyu*	PNB b
2290	Han Chinese (Min Nan)	2.05000	24,714,985	25,882,414	29,990,095	MSY42a	79-AAAJ-ic	chaozhou		11.00	2,847,066	1A..h	8	6	12	3	3	Chinese, Min Nan	PNB b
2291	Han Chinese (Min Pei)	1.00082	12,065,976	12,635,921	14,641,311	MSY42a	79-AAAI-ce	fuzhou		10.00	1,263,592	1A...	8	6	12	2	2	Chinese: Foochow	PNB b
2292	Han Chinese (Wu)	7.50617	90,495,064	94,769,659	109,810,122	MSY42a	79-AAAD	wu cluster		12.90	12,225,286	1A...	8	6	12	3	3	Chinese, Wu	PNB b
2293	Han Chinese (Wu):HK	0.00708	85,357	89,389	103,576	MSY42a	79-AAAD	wu cluster		11.00	9,833	1A...	8	8	9	5	2	Chinese, Wu	PNB b
2294	Hani (Uni, Ouni)	0.11061	1,333,524	1,396,514	1,618,148	MSY50i	77-BBAA	hani cluster		4.80	67,033	1....	6	5	4	2	1		PN. b
2295	Highland Nung (Thai Nung)	0.00973	117,306	122,847	142,343	MSY49a	47-AAAE-b	tai-nung		0.30	369	0....	6	4	5	2	0	Nung	P.. b
2296	Hu	0.00010	1,206	1,263	1,463	AUG03z	46-DBBA-e	hu		2.00	25	0....	6	3	6	0	0		... .
2297	Hui (Chinese Muslim)	0.00506	61,004	63,885	74,024	MSY42b	79-AAAB-ba	kuo-yü		0.00	0	2Bsuh	0	3	1	1	0	Chinese: Kuoyu*	PNB b
2298	Hui (Dungan, Tunya, Huizui)	0.75885	9,148,764	9,580,912	11,101,455	MSY42b	79-AAAB-ba	kuo-yü		0.00	0	2Bsuh	0	3	3	0	4	Chinese: Kuoyu*	PNB b
2299	Hui (Huizui)	0.00008	964	1,010	1,170	MSY42b	79-AAAB-ba	kuo-yü		0.00	0	2Bsuh	0	3	2	5	0	Chinese: Kuoyu*	PNB b
2300	Humai (Rumai) Palaung	0.00016	1,929	2,020	2,341	AUG03z	46-DCAA-d	rumai		0.01	0	0c...	3	1	0	0	0		... .
2301	Indo-Pakistani	0.00152	18,325	19,191	22,237	CNN25g	59-AAFO-e	general hindi		7.00	1,343	3Asuh	7	5	2	5	1		pnb b
2302	Japanese	0.06900	831,870	871,164	1,009,423	MSY45a	45-CAAA-a	koku-go		1.60	13,939	1B.uh	6	6	5	2	1	Japanese	PNB b
2303	Japanese (Hong Kong)	0.00105	12,659	13,257	15,361	MSY45a	45-CAAA-a	koku-go		1.60	212	1B.uh	6	4	8	5	1	Japanese	PNB b
2304	Javanese	0.00010	1,206	1,263	1,463	MSY44g	31-PIAA-g	general jawa		2.40	30	2As.h	6	4	1	5	2	Javanese	PNB b
2305	Javanese (Hong Kong)	0.00004	482	505	585	MSY44g	31-PIAA-g	general jawa		9.00	45	2As.h	7	5	7	5	1	Javanese	PNB b
2306	Jewish	0.00005	603	631	731	CMT35	52-ABAD-ca	hong-kong-english		0.20	1	0A.uh	5	4	1	3	0		... b
2307	Jiamao	0.00489	58,954	61,739	71,537	MSY49a	47-BBAA-ae	kamau		3.00	1,852	0....	6	4	4	2	0		... .
2308	Jinmen (Mian-Jin)	0.01897	228,704	239,507	277,518	MSY47b	48-ABAA-b	iu-mien		1.00	2,395	0.s..	6	4	2	0	0	Iu Mien	PN. b
2309	Jinuo (Youle)	0.00159	19,169	20,075	23,261	MSY50z	77-BACA-c	jino		1.00	201	1cs..	6	1	0	0	0		pnb .
2310	Jyarung (Rgyarong)	0.00881	106,214	111,231	128,884	MSY50z	76-BAAA-a	jiarong		0.03	33	0....	3	2	0	0	0		... .
2311	Kado (Sak, Thet, Puteik)	0.00880	106,094	111,105	128,738	MSY50i	75-ABAA-a	kado		2.00	2,222	0....	6	2	5	0	1	Kadu*	P.. .
2312	Kaduo	0.00042	5,064	5,303	6,144	MSY50l	77-BBAA-f	kaduo		0.05	3	1....	4	3	5	0	0		pn. .
2313	Kalmyk-Oirat (Kalmytz)	0.01226	147,808	154,789	179,355	MSY41y	44-BAAB-d	kalmyk		0.10	155	2c..h	5	1	1	0	0	Mongolian: Kalmyk*	PNb b
2314	Kang	0.00300	36,168	37,877	43,888	MSY49z	77-BAAA-c	kang-siang-ying		1.00	379	0....	6	2	4	0	0		... .
2315	Kazakh	0.09806	1,182,220	1,238,063	1,434,551	MSY41e	44-AABC-c	kazakh		0.00	0	4A.u.	0	3	1	0	3	Kazakh	PN. b
2316	Keh-deo Meo	0.01030	124,178	130,043	150,682	MSY47a	48-AAAC-i	keh-deo		3.00	3,901	0c...	6	3	5	0	1	Keh-deo	Pn. .
2317	Kelao (Keh-lao, Thu)	0.03863	465,727	487,726	565,130	MSY47a	47-BDAA-a	gelo		0.20	975	0....	5	4	5	0	0	Gelao	P.. .
2318	Kemiehua	0.00008	964	1,010	1,170	AUG03c	46-GAAA	mon cluster		1.00	10	2....	6	4	6	0	0		PNB b
2319	Khabit (Bit, Phsing)	0.00004	482	505	585	MSY50i	46-DDAA-a	kha-bit		1.00	5	0....	6	4	1	0	0		... .
2320	Khalka Mongol (Mongolian)	0.00400	48,224	50,502	58,517	MSY41f	44-BAAB-c	halh		0.04	20	3A..h	3	3	1	0	3	Mongolian: Khalka*	PNb b
2321	Khamba (Khams Bhotia)	0.13521	1,630,104	1,707,103	1,978,030	MSY50r	70-AAAA-d	kham-atuence		0.05	854	0c...	4	2	0	0	0		PNb .
2322	Khmu (Lao Terng)	0.00014	1,688	1,768	2,048	AUG03z	46-DDBA-a	kha-khmu		7.00	124	0....	7	5	6	1	1	Khmu'	P.. .
2323	Khuen	0.00008	964	1,010	1,170	AUG03z	46-DDBA	khmu cluster		7.00	71	0....	7	5	8	0	0		P.. .
2324	Kirghiz	0.01249	150,581	157,693	182,720	MSY41g	44-AABC-d	kirghiz		0.01	16	2r.u.	3	3	1	0	0	Kirghiz	PN. b
2325	Kjang E (Wuse)	0.00088	10,609	11,110	12,874	MSY49a	95-ABAH-a	jede-po		1.00	111	0....	6	4	2	0	0	E Je*	PN. b
2326	Kopu (Ko)	0.03000	361,683	378,767	438,879	MSY50i	77-BADA-aa	ko-p'u		1.00	3,788	1....	6	4	5	0	0	Kopu	Pn. .
2327	Korean (Hong Kong)	0.00025	3,014	3,156	3,657	MSY46	45-AAAA-b	kukö		40.00	1,263	2A...	9	5	9	5	3	Korean	PNB b
2328	Korean (Chaoxian)	0.16941	2,042,422	2,138,897	2,478,352	MSY46	45-AAAA-b	kukö		10.00	213,890	2A...	8	6	12	2	2	Korean	PNB b
2329	Kyerung	0.00050	6,028	6,313	7,315	MSY50r	70-AAAA-cg	kyerung		0.50	32	0c...	5	1	0	0	0		pnb b
2330	Ladakhi	0.00020	2,411	2,525	2,926	MSY50r	70-AAAC-a	ladakhi		0.10	3	1....	5	3	3	0	3	Ladakhi	Pn. .
2331	Lahu (Black/White/Red)	0.03630	437,636	458,308	531,044	MSY50i	77-BBAB-a	lahu		40.00	183,323	4a...	9	7	11	2	1	Lahu*	PNB b
2332	Lahuli (Bhotia of Lahul)	0.00011	1,326	1,389	1,609	MSY50r	70-ABAD-a	tinan		0.07	1	0....	4	3	1	0	1	Lahuli: Tinan*	P.. .
2333	Lahuli (Bunan)	0.00012	1,447	1,515	1,756	MSY50r	70-ABAA-a	bunan		0.11	2	0....	5	1	1	0	0	Lahuli: Bunan*	P.. .
2334	Lahuli (Manchad)	0.00010	1,206	1,263	1,463	MSY50r	70-ABAC-b	manchati		0.10	1	0....	5	1	1	0	0	Lahuli: Manchad	P.. .
2335	Laka (Lakja, Tai Laka)	0.00079	9,524	9,974	11,557	MSY47b	47-ABBA-a	laka		4.00	399	0....	6	6	5	1	1	Laka	P.. .
2336	Lama	0.00026	3,135	3,283	3,804	MSY50i	76-AABA-d	lama		7.00	230	0....	7	6	4	1	0		... .
2337	Laopang	0.00100	12,056	12,626	14,629	MSY50i	77-BBAB-f	laopang		6.00	758	1c...	7	6	6	1	0		pnb .
2338	Lasi (Chashan)	0.00300	36,168	37,877	43,888	MSY50i	77-AAAC-b	lashi		0.10	38	0....	5	1	2	0	0		p.. .
2339	Lati (Tai Lati)	0.00014	1,688	1,768	2,048	MSY47a	47-BCAA-a	lati		6.03	107	0....	7	6	4	1	0		... .
2340	Lhoba (Lho-pa)	0.00083	10,007	10,479	12,142	MSY50r	74-AADA-a	luo-ba		0.00	0	0....	0	2	0	0	0		... b
2341	Lhomi (Shing Saapa)	0.00010	1,206	1,263	1,463	MSY50r	70-AAAA-ce	lhomi		0.00	0	0c...	0	2	0	0	0	Lhomi	PNb .
2342	Li (Paoting)	0.09799	1,181,376	1,237,179	1,433,527	MSY49z	47-BBAA-a	li		0.20	2,474	0....	5	3	4	0	3		... b
2343	Lowland Yao (Mun, Lanten)	0.00486	58,593	61,360	71,098	MSY47b	48-ABAE-e	mun		0.91	558	0.s..	5	2	2	0	1		pn. .
2344	Loyu (Lopa)	0.00020	2,411	2,525	2,926	MSY50r	70-AAAE-a	loyu		0.00	0	0....	0	2	0	0	0		... .
2345	Lu (Pai-I)	0.02205	265,837	278,394	322,576	MSY49z	47-AAAA-g	tai-lü		2.00	5,568	1.s..	6	5	4	1	1	Lu	PNb .
2346	Lushai (Le, Mizo)	0.00010	1,206	1,263	1,463	MSY50m	73-DCAA-a	lushai		90.00	1,136	0asu.	10	8	13	3	2	Lushai	PNB .
2347	Macanese (Creole)	0.00102	12,297	12,878	14,922	MSY43	79-AAAM-a	central yue	30	92.70	11,938	3A.uh	10	8	11	5	3	Chinese, Yue	PNB b
2348	Macanese (Macao Creole)	0.00043	5,184	5,429	6,291	MSY43	51-AACA-i	makista		95.00	5,158	1c...	10	8	12	5	1		pnb .
2349	Mahei (Mahe, Mabe)	0.00100	12,056	12,626	14,629	MSY50i	77-BBAA-i	mahei		2.00	253	1....	6	5	4	1	0		pn. .
2350	Malay (Melaju)	0.00101	12,177	12,752	14,776	MSY44k	31-PHAA-b	bahasa-malaysia		0.02	3	1asuh	3	3	2	3	1	Malay	PNB b
2351	Malu (Lansu, Diso)	0.00110	13,262	13,888	16,092	MSY50i	77-AAAC	maru cluster		0.50	69	0....	5	3	4	1	1	Maru	P.. p
2352	Man Cao Lan	0.00300	36,168	37,877	43,888	MSY49d	47-AAAE-ab	man-cao-lan		0.78	295	0....	5	3	4	1	0		p.. .
2353	Manchu (Man)	0.86631	10,444,312	10,937,656	12,673,522	MSY41i	79-AAAB-ba	kuo-yü		0.02	2,188	2Bsuh	3	4	7	0	3	Chinese: Kuoyu*	PNB b
2354	Mang (Xamang, Bae)	0.00006	723	758	878	AUG03z	46-DEAA	mang cluster		0.50	4	0....	5	2	4	0	0		... .
2355	Manmit	0.00009	1,085	1,136	1,317	AUG03z	46-DBBA-f	man-met		0.50	6	0....	5	2	4	0	0		... .
2356	Maonan	0.00635	76,556	80,172	92,896	MSY49a	47-ABAA-a	mao-nan		6.00	4,810	0....	7	3	4	0	1		... b
2357	Menghwa (Mehua)	0.00030	3,617	3,788	4,389	MSY50i	77-BBAA-a	menghua		0.38	14	1....	5	2	4	0	0		pn. .
2358	Meo Lai	0.00265	31,949	33,458	38,768	MSY47a	48-AAAF-b	pa-heng		3.00	1,004	0....	6	4	4	0	0		... .
2359	Molao	0.01405	169,388	177,389	205,542	MSY49a	47-AACA-a	mu-lao		1.50	2,661	0....	6	3	4	0	2		... b
2360	Monba (Menba, Memba)	0.00265	31,949	33,458	38,768	MSY50r	71-CBCC-d	moinba		0.02	7	0c...	3	1	0	0	0		... b
2361	Muya	0.00125	15,070	15,782	18,287	MSY50r	70-AAAB	tibetan-south cluster		1.00	158	1.s..	6	4	5	0	0		PN. b
2362	Nakhi (Na-Hsi, Moso)	0.02452	295,615	309,579	358,711	MSY50i	77-BABA-a	naxi		1.00	3,096	0....	6	5	4	1	1	Naxi	P.. .
2363	Namuyi	0.00049	5,907	6,187	7,168	MSY50r	70-AAAB	tibetan-south cluster		1.00	62	1.s..	6	3	5	0	0		PN. b
2364	Nanai (Gold, Hoche)	0.00037	4,461	4,671	5,413	MSY41i	44-CAAE-e	olcha		0.52	24	0....	5	2	0	0	0		p.. b
2365	Ngolok (Golog)	0.00847	102,115	106,939	123,910	MSY50r	70-AAAA-bb	golog		0.00	0	0c...	0	1	0	0	0		pnb .
2366	Nhang (Nyang, Dioi)	0.01845	222,435	232,942	269,911	MSY49z	47-AAAF-c	nhang		2.50	5,824	0....	6	5	4	0	0		... .
2367	Norra	0.00050	6,028	6,313	7,315	MSY50f	76-AABA-a	norra		1.50	95	0....	6	5	4	0	0		... .
2368	Northern Meo (Huayuan)	0.06792	818,850	857,529	993,623	MSY47a	48-AAAD-a	xiangxi-miao		3.50	30,013	0r...	6	4	11	0	3		... .
2369	Northern Tung (Dong, Kam)	0.22176	2,673,559	2,799,846	3,244,197	MSY49z	47-ABAA-aa	dong		0.12	3,360	0....	5	3	4	1	3		... .
2370	Northern Uzbek	0.00128	15,432	16,161	18,726	MSY41l	44-AABD-a	central uzbek		1.00	162	1A.u.	6	3	3	0	1	Uzbek*	PNb b
2371	Northern Yi (I, Lolo)	0.13918	1,677,967	1,757,227	2,036,108	MSY50i	77-BAGA	yi-central cluster		3.50	61,503	0....	6	4	12	0	3		... b
2372	Northern Zhuang (Chwang)	1.01348	12,218,606	12,795,761	14,826,518	MSY49a	47-AAAG-n	wu-ming		1.00	127,958	1r...	6	5	5	2	4	Zhuang, Northern	P.. b
2373	Nung (Anoong, Nu)	0.00239	28,814	30,175	34,964	MSY50f	47-AAAE-b	tai-nung		26.00	7,846	0....	9	5	6	1	1	Nung	P.. b
2374	Nusu	0.00075	9,042	9,469	10,972	MSY50i	76-AAAA-a	nung		2.00	189	0.s..	6	4	4	0	0		... .
2375	Oirat (Western Mongul)	0.01627	196,153	205,418	238,019	MSY41y	44-BAAB-e	oyrat		2.00	4,108	1a..h	6	4	6	0	0	Mongolian: Inner*	PNb b
2376	Ongbe (Be)	0.05192	625,952	655,519	759,554	MSY49z	47-BAAA-a	ong-be		0.50	3,278	0....	5	3	5	0	0		... b
2377	Orochon (Oronchon)	0.00061	7,354	7,702	8,924	MSY41i	44-CAAB-d	oroqen		3.00	231	0....	6	4	2	1	1		p.. .
2378	Palaung (Bonglong, Deang)	0.00136	16,396	17,171	19,896	AUG03z	46-DCAA	palaung cluster		1.00	172	0r...	6	4	2	2	0	Palaung, Pale	... b
2379	Palyu (Lai)	0.00085	10,248	10,732	12,435	AUG03z	46-ECAA-a	palyu		1.00	107	0....	6	4	2	0	0		... .
2380	Panang	0.00100	12,056	12,626	14,629	MSY50r	70-AAAA-bg	banag		0.00	0	0c...	0	1	0	0	0		pnb .
2381	Paongan (Pao-an, Bonan)	0.00108	13,021	13,636	15,800	MSY41y	44-BAAE-b	bonan		0.00	4	0....	3	3	0	0	0		... .
2382	Parauk (Va)	0.03105	374,342	392,024	454,240	AUG03z	46-DBAA-e	parauk		25.00	98,006	1....	9	3	7	1	1	Parauk	PN. .
2383	Persian	0.00005	603	631	731	CNT24f	58-AACC-c	standard farsi		0.20	1	1Asu.	5	4	1	3	0		PNB b

Continued opposite

Table 8-2 continued

EVANGELIZATION								EVANGELISM			ADDITIONAL DESCRIPTIVE DATA
Ref 1	*D 28*	*aC 29*	*CG% 30*	*r 31*	*E 32*	*U 33*	*W 34*	*e 35*	*R 36*	*T 37*	*Locations, civil divisions, literacy, religions, church history, denominations, dioceses, church growth, missions, agencies, ministries, movements 38*
2260	1	7	1.51	7	70.00	30.00	B	25.55	90	5	Mixed-race, especially Chinese/Europeans. Mostly in largest cities. Folk-religionists/Buddhists 90%, Taoists. D=RCC. M=SJ. R=FEBC,KNLS,TWR.
2261	7	10	2.86	8	99.60	0.40	C	254.04	86	8	Mixed-race persons. D=RCC,ACC,SDA,JWs,ICFG,AoG,SA.
2262	1	5	3.44	0	24.00	76.00	A	0.87	484	3	Inner Mongolia, Xinjiang Provinces. Also in Russia, Mongolia. 21 dialects. Written Mongolian, Chinese in common use. Shamanists 70%, Lamaist Buddhists 29%.
2263	4	10	5.16	5	99.98	0.02	C	629.55	91	10	Workers from Philippines, including 50,000 Filipino women. D=95% RCC,IFI,INC,JWs. M=AEF(Singapore),AOI(Hong Kong),FMB.
2264	0	0	5.04	5	99.98	0.02	C	532.97	105	10	Immigrants from Philippines. D=Iglesia ni Cristo(Manalista)(Ch of Christ),RCC. M=SJ.
2265	1	5	2.63	4	52.00	48.00	B	9.49	175	4	Small group of Western Meo in Guizhou, Guangxi, Sichuan, Yunnan Provinces. Agriculturalists. Polytheists/animists 95%. D=Chinese Ch. M=OMF,CSI,NTCM.
2266	3	10	2.85	8	99.84	0.16	C	484.42	66	10	Expatriates from France, in business. D=RCC(D-Hong Kong),JWs,CCC. M=SDB,PIME,SJ,MM,OCSO,OFM.
2267	1	6	5.23	0	87.00	13.00	B	158.77	165	7	Mainlanders related to Taiwan aboriginal tribes Ami and Bunun. In Fujian Province. Animists 40%. D=Chinese Ch.
2268	5	10	2.85	8	99.87	0.13	C	517.60	67	10	Expatriates from Germany, in business. D=German Evangelical Lutheran Ch,NAC,RCC,CCC,CRC. M=RM,VEM.
2269	0	4	0.00	4	22.10	77.90	A	0.08	124	2	Yunnan Province. Majority in Burma. Officially listed under Benglong in China. Buddhists 99%(Hinayana).
2270	0	0	5.93	0	24.00	76.00	A	4.38	757	4	Part of official Miao nationality. Guizhou, Hunan, and Guangxi provinces. Chinese used in singing. Polytheists 95%.
2271	0	3	0.00	0	15.00	85.00	A	0.00	0	1.07	Chambi Valley, between Sikkim, Bhutan, Tibet. Also in India (Sikkim). Lamaist Buddhists 100%.
2272	0	0	2.66	0	20.00	80.00	A	0.73	593	3	Part of official Tibetan nationality. Chambi Valley, between Sikkim, Tibet, and Bhutan. Buddhists (Lamaists) 98%, Muslims 1%.
2273	0	0	4.38	0	21.00	79.00	A	0.76	789	3	Part of official Tibetan nationality. West central Sichuan on Dadu River. Buddhists (Lamaists) 98%, Muslims 1%.
2274	2	10	2.56	4	56.00	44.00	B	2.04	174	4	British army soldiers of Nepalese descent. Hindus 80%, Muslims 19%. D=RCC,CCC.
2275	0	4	1.62	0	15.10	84.90	A	0.05	448	2	Small group on southern Hainan Island. Muslims 50%, Buddhists 30%, polytheists 20%.
2276	2	10	5.39	6	68.00	32.00	B	7.44	243	4	Refugees from Burma. Mahayana Buddhists/Chinese folk-religionists 88%. D=RCC,MBC. M=FMB,ABCUSA,BBC.
2277	4	8	2.94	8	74.40	25.60	B	9.23	132	4	Also termed 'Chinese Nung'. Guangdong. Folk-religionists/Buddhists 80%. D=TSPM,RCC,TJC,SDA. M=SJ,BE(CCCI),TEAM,CMA,ICA,IFES,ISI,IVCF,MUP,OD,OM.
2278	3	7	7.05	8	79.30	20.70	B	29.81	266	5	Folk-religionists 52%, Buddhists 18%, nonreligious/atheists 15%, New-Religionists 3%. D=45% RCC,CCC,and 200 others. M=UECP(Philippines),FMB-SBC.
2279	7	9	3.67	8	76.10	23.90	B	19.72	156	5	Mahayana Buddhists/folk-religionists 75%. Y=1557. D=RCC(D-Macao),MBC,SDA,JWs,AoG,FMC,CEZC. M=SAM,SJ,SDB,OFM,CMA(Hong Kong),FMB.
2280	3	5	0.99	0	42.10	57.90	A	0.15	107	3	Mainly Hainan Island. Economically depressed. Folk-religionists/Buddhists 95%. Many house churches. D=TSPM,RCC,TJC. M=SAM,SJ,CSI,NLM.
2281	3	5	2.99	4	57.50	42.50	B	1.04	173	4	Most in east and northeast Guangdong. Folk-religionists 95%. D=TSPM,RCC,TJC. M=SJ,CSI,MUP,YWAM. R=TWR,FEBC,AWR.
2282	4	6	5.70	7	81.00	19.00	B	47.30	215	6	Chinese folk-religionists 80%. D=RCC,Evangelical Hakka Ch(Basel Mission),ELCHK,&c. M=SDB,PIME,SJ,MM,OCSO,OFM.
2283	7	7	5.77	6	81.00	19.00	B	44.34	217	6	Southern Min, Minnan, Amoy. Folk-religionists 85%. D=RCC,CCC,JWCCA,SDA,ICFG,TJC,SFWEM.
2284	3	5	2.05	0	41.00	59.00	A	2.99	180	4	In Hunan only. Bilingual in Mandarin. Folk-religionists 80%, nonreligious 18%. D=TSPM,TJC,RCC. M=SJ,ADF,BE(CCCI),CCRC,CSI,NMS,PRI,YWAM.
2285	0	0	13.55	7	47.00	53.00	A	12.00	828	5	Mainly in Shanxi province. Bilingual in Standard Mandarin for reading literature. Nonreligious 57%, Chinese folk-religionists 17%, atheists 12%, Buddhists 7%.
2286	3	5	3.04	0	46.00	54.00	A	10.07	220	5	Jiangxi and southeastern corner of Hubei. No written form except standard Chinese. Bilingual in Mandarin. Folk-religionists 84%. D=TSPM,RCC,TJC. M=SJ,CSI.
2287	4	4	4.37	7	68.66	31.34	B	19.19	200	5	Includes Jin dialect group. Official language. Nonreligious 57%, folk-religionists 17%, atheists 12%, Buddhists 7%. Y=AD 635(Nestorians). D=TSPM,RCC,TJC.
2288	10	6	3.63	7	78.00	22.00	B	28.47	150	5	Folk-religionists/Buddhists 78%. D=RCC,CCC,ACC,ELCHK,HK Methodist Ch,SA,SDA,ICFG,TJC,union churches.
2289	1	10	4.97	7	75.00	25.00	B	21.90	205	5	Refugees from various countries. Mahayana Buddhists/folk-religionists 83%. D=RCC.
2290	4	8	3.55	6	80.00	20.00	B	32.12	144	5	Southern Fujian. Folk-religionists 60%. D=TSPM,RCC,TJC,house churches(very rapid growth). M=SJ,CCRC,CMA,OD,YWAM. R=FEBC,AWR.
2291	4	8	3.45	6	76.00	24.00	B	27.74	148	5	Northeastern part of Fujian. Folk-religionists 65%. D=TSPM,RCC,TJC,house churches(very rapid expansion). M=SJ,YWAM.
2292	4	5	4.51	6	77.90	22.10	B	36.67	181	5	Used on local radio/TV soap operas, family planning, counseling. Folk-religionists/Buddhists. D=TSPM,RCC,TJC,house churches. M=SJ,BE(CCCI),SDA,YWAM.
2293	2	6	2.86	6	72.00	28.00	B	28.90	134	5	Shanghainese and other Wu languages. Chinese folk-religionists 49%, Buddhists 25%. D=RCC,CCC.
2294	1	4	9.21	0	32.80	67.20	A	5.74	861	4	Ailao Mountains, south Yunnan. Also in Viet Nam, Laos, Burma. Official nationality. Unwritten in China. Polytheists(animists, including ancestor veneration) 95%.
2295	0	4	3.67	1	21.30	78.70	A	0.23	556	3	Vast majority in northern Viet Nam (with some in South; official ethnic community); also Laos. Polytheists 99% (ancestor worship).
2296	0	4	3.27	0	21.00	79.00	A	1.53	557	4	Southwestern Yunnan Province. Buddhists 95%(Hinayana), polytheists 3%.
2297	0	9	0.00	7	40.00	60.00	A	0.00	0	1.14	Settlers since 1880. Muslims 95%(Hanafi Sunnis), with nonreligious/atheists 5%.
2298	0	4	0.00	7	40.00	60.00	A	0.00	0	1.13	Mumin, Jiaomen. Ningxia Province, 5 other countries. Official nationality. Muslims 90%(Hanafi Sunnis),agnostics/nonreligious 10%. Y=1920. M=AOI,CSI,FI,TIME.
2299	0	10	0.00	7	49.00	51.00	A	0.00	0	1.14	Immigrants since 1880s from Western China. Chinese Muslims 100%(Hanafi Sunnis).
2300	0	4	0.00	1	12.01	87.99	A	0.00	0	1.05	Yunnan Province; also in Burma. In China, officially under Benglong. Buddhists 99%(Hinayama).
2301	0	10	5.02	7	61.00	39.00	B	15.58	270	5	From India and Pakistan. Hindus 70%, Muslims 22%. Sects: Hare Krishna,Ananda Marga,&c. M=FMB-SBC.
2302	0	7	1.98	7	54.60	45.40	B	3.18	137	4	Immigrants, residents, refugees, businessmen. Buddhists 60%(Mahayana), New-Religionists 20%. M=FMB. R=HCJB,AWR.
2303	0	10	4.35	7	61.60	38.40	B	3.59	227	4	Expatriates from Japan, in commerce. Buddhists 98% including Soka Gakkai and other New-Religionists. M=FMB-SBC.
2304	2	10	2.75	5	55.40	44.60	B	4.85	178	4	Expatriates from Indonesia. Javanese folk-religionists 50%, Muslims 45%. D=RCC,CCC.
2305	3	10	3.88	5	72.00	28.00	B	23.65	180	5	From Indonesia. Muslims 50%, New-Religionists 40%. D=RCC,MBC,SDA. M=FMB.
2306	0	10	0.00	8	38.20	61.80	A	0.27	49	3	Small communities of practicing Jews.
2307	0	5	5.36	0	24.00	76.00	A	2.62	686	4	Hainan Li-Miao Autonomous Prefecture, near Wuzhi Mountain. Polytheists 96%, a few Buddhists.
2308	0	4	5.63	0	22.00	78.00	A	0.80	788	3	Guangdong, Ru Yuan County. Under Yao nationality. Buddhists 95%.
2309	0	4	3.05	1	24.00	76.00	A	0.87	474	3	40 villages in forests of south Yunnan, Xishuanbanna Dai Autonomous Prefecture; Laos, Burma. Official nationality. No written language. Animists 99%.
2310	0	2	3.56	0	8.03	91.97	A	0.00	1,590	1.03	In Sichuan. Bodic language, 3 dialects. Lamaist Buddhists 99%.
2311	1	5	5.55	0	25.00	75.00	A	1.82	729	4	South Yunnan; also in Laos and Burma. Polytheists 80%, Buddhists. D=Baptists.
2312	0	0	1.10	0	15.05	84.95	A	0.02	382	2	Part of official Mongolian nationality. South central Yunnan province. Also in Laos. Shamanists 60%, Nonreligious 30%, Buddhists 10%.
2313	0	4	2.78	1	25.10	74.90	A	0.09	388	2	Remnants of Mongols from Sinkiang resettled in Volga region (Russia) in 1628. Lamaist Buddhists 60%, shamanists 35%.
2314	0	5	3.70	0	19.00	81.00	A	0.69	620	3	Southwest Yunnan, also in Laos. Officially under Dai nationality. Polytheists 99%.
2315	0	3	0.00	4	29.00	71.00	A	0.00	0	1.10	North Xinjiang, Gansu, Qinghai. Most in Kazakhstan; also China, Mongolia. Official nationality. Muslims 99%(Hanafi Sunnis, with Sufi influence), some shamanists.
2316	0	5	6.15	1	29.00	71.00	A	3.17	647	4	A tribe and dialect of Eastern Meo. In southwest, Guizhou Province. Polytheists/animists 97%. M=CSI.
2317	0	4	1.69	0	18.20	81.80	A	0.13	360	3	In Yunnan, southwest Guizhou, Guangxi, Hunan; also in Viet Nam. Only 1.4% speak Gelo. Official nationality in China, also in Viet Nam. Polytheists(animists) 99%.
2318	0	0	2.33	0	27.00	73.00	A	0.98	389	3	Xishuangbanna Dai Autonomous Prefecture. Jinghong county. Polytheists 69%, Buddhists 30%.
2319	0	4	1.62	0	15.00	85.00	A	0.54	497	3	Near border with Laos; also in Laos. Buddhists 99%(Hinayana).
2320	2	3	3.04	4	38.04	61.96	A	0.05	274	2	Settlers, immigrants, transients, pastoralists, nomads, traders from Mongolia. Nonreligious 50%, shamanists 50%. D=TSPM,RCC. M=SJ,CSI,OD. R=FEBC.
2321	0	3	4.55	1	19.05	80.95	A	0.03	895	2	Eastern Tibet. Related to Tibetans. Youth are monolingual in Chinese. Lamaist Buddhists(Tantrists) 100%.
2322	1	5	2.55	4	36.00	64.00	A	9.19	270	4	Mainly in Laos, also Thailand, Viet Nam, Burma, USA, France. Animists 93%. D=RCC.
2323	0	0	4.35	4	29.00	71.00	A	7.41	505	4	Related to Khmu. Also in Laos and USA. Animists 93%. D=RCC.
2324	0	3	2.81	4	22.01	77.99	A	0.00	437	1.11	West Xinjiang, Heilongjiang; most in Kirghizia. Nomadic pastoralists. Script used: modified Arabic. Muslims 95%(Hanafi Sunnis), Lamaist Buddhists 5%.
2325	0	4	2.44	1	24.00	76.00	A	0.87	353	3	Northern Guangxi-Zhuang Autonomous Region. 20 villages. Agriculturalists. Polytheists 99%.
2326	0	5	6.12	0	25.00	75.00	A	0.91	791	3	A Lolo language of the Northern Yi. Northern Yunnan Province, Luchuan area. Agriculturalists. Polytheists 99%.
2327	4	10	2.85	6	99.40	0.60	B	159.14	87	7	Immigrants, expatriates from Korea. New-Religionists 30%, shamanists/Confucians 15%, Buddhists 15%, D=CCC,RCC,HSAUWC,&c. M=BFMGAP,PCK-H,PCK-T..
2328	3	4	5.75	6	72.00	28.00	B	26.28	242	5	Inner Mongolia, Hyanbian Korean Autonomous District, Jilin, Liaoning. Shamanists 55%, Mahayana Buddhists 35%. D=TSPM,RCC,many house churches.
2329	0	3	3.53	1	19.50	80.50	A	0.35	731	3	Close to Lhasa Tibetan. Also in Nepal. Lamaist Buddhists 99%.
2330	0	4	1.10	0	22.10	77.90	A	0.08	343	2	In Tibet, with main body in Kashmir(India, also Pakistan). Buddhists 70%(Red Hat Lamaists), Muslims 30%. M=KEF,IET,Moravians.
2331	1	5	10.31	4	99.00	1.00	B	144.54	316	7	Southwest Yunnan, Lanaong Lahu Autonomous County; also in Burma, Thailand, Laos. Official nationality. Animists 50%, Mahayana Buddhists 10%. Y=c1930(RC).
2332	0	1	0.00	0	11.07	88.93	A	0.02	413	2	Western Tibet border; mainly in Kashmir(India). Lamaist Buddhists 100%. M=IEM.
2333	0	1	0.70	0	11.11	88.89	A	0.04	585	2	Border of Western Tibet with Punjab(India). Also in India. Lamaist Buddhists 100%.
2334	0	1	0.00	0	11.10	88.90	A	0.04	412	2	Along border of Western Tibet with Kashmir(India). Lamaist Buddhists 100%.
2335	0	5	3.76	0	26.00	74.00	A	3.79	470	4	Tayaoshan Autonomous District, Guangxi Autonomous Region(Zhuang), Yunnan. Polytheists 95%. M=OMF.
2336	0	5	3.19	0	27.00	73.00	A	6.89	435	4	Also in Burma. Closely related to Norra. Polytheists 80%, Lamaist Buddhists 13%.
2337	0	5	4.42	1	37.00	63.00	A	8.10	409	4	Yunnan Province; also in Burma. Related to Lahu. Animists 60%, Mahayana Buddhists 30%.
2338	0	4	3.70	0	15.10	84.90	A	0.05	871	2	Lashi-Maru. Yunnan Province; also in Burma. Officially included under Jingpo nationality. Polytheists/Buddhists 99%.
2339	0	5	2.63	0	26.03	73.97	A	5.72	351	4	Also in Viet Nam. In Gelo nationality. Agriculturalists. Polytheists(animists) 93%.
2340	0	3	0.00	0	9.00	91.00	A	0.00	0	1.02	3 separate languages. Lhunze and Mainling counties in southeast Tibet. Also in Bhutan. Written language: Tibetan. An official nationality. Lamaists.
2341	0	3	0.00	1	15.00	85.00	A	0.00	0	1.06	In Tibet; also Nepal, India. Agriculturalists, pastoralists. Polytheists(animists) 80%, Lamaist Buddhists(Tantrists) 20%.
2342	1	4	5.67	0	24.20	75.80	A	0.17	710	3	Tropical mountains in Hainan. Li is written language; also, written Minnan in common use. Official nationality. Polytheists(animists) 100%. D=TSPM.
2343	1	5	4.64	0	21.91	78.09	A	0.72	668	3	Guangxi and Guizhou Provinces. Also in Laos, Viet Nam. Polytheists(animists) 99%. D=RCC.
2344	0	3	0.00	0	6.00	94.00	A	0.00	0	1.01	Along Tibet border with Nepal. Majority in Nepal. Pastoralists. Buddhists 100%.
2345	0	4	6.53	1	32.00	68.00	A	2.33	611	4	South Yunnan, west of Black River. Also Burma, Laos, Thailand, Viet Nam (an official nationality there). Polytheists 80%, Buddhists 18%. M=American Presbyterian.
2346	2	6	4.85	4	99.90	0.10	C	486.18	110	10	Also in India, Burma, Bangladesh. All now Christians. D=PCNEI,RCC.
2347	5	10	1.24	8	99.93	0.07	C	570.80	33	10	Portuguese-Chinese Eurasians. Macanese (Macao Creole Portuguese) no longer spoken in Macao. D=RCC(D-Macao),MBC,AoG,SDA,JWs.
2348	1	10	2.86	1	99.95	0.05	C	509.72	68	10	Mixed-race persons (Portuguese/Chinese) from Macao, speaking Portuguese-based creole. D=RCC.
2349	0	4	3.28	0	24.00	76.00	A	1.75	500	4	South Yunnan Province; also in Burma. Related to Hani. Animists 70%, Buddhists 28%.
2350	0	10	1.10	5	43.02	56.98	A	0.03	115	2	From Malaysia. Muslims 100%(Shafi Sunnis). M=FMB-SBC.
2351	0	4	4.33	0	19.50	80.50	A	0.35	763	3	Southern Yunnan Province, in Kachin Hills; also in Burma. In China, officially included under Jingpo. Polytheists/Buddhists 99%. M=NEIGM.
2352	0	5	3.44	1	20.78	79.22	A	0.59	530	3	Also in Viet Nam (an official community there). Under Zhuang nationality in China. Polytheists 99%.
2353	2	3	-2.41	7	51.02	48.98	B	0.03	5	2	Only 500 Manchu speakers left in China, in 15 provinces (Liaoning, Hebei). Chinese folk-religionists 70%, shamanists 20%, Mahayana Buddhists 10%. D=TSPM.
2354	0	5	1.40	0	17.50	82.50	A	0.31	376	3	Yunnan, Junping County; also in Viet Nam, Thailand. Agriculturalists, hunters. Forests. Animists 99%.
2355	0	5	1.81	0	17.50	82.50	A	0.31	440	3	Southwestern Yunnan Province. Buddhists 90%(Hinayana).
2356	1	4	6.37	0	30.00	70.00	A	6.57	641	4	Guangxi Zhuang Autonomous Region. Official nationality. Unwritten; bilingual in Zhuang, Chinese. Agriculturalists. Chinese folk-religionists(Taoists)/animists 94%.
2357	0	5	2.67	0	21.38	78.62	A	0.29	483	3	South of Dali, Yunnan Province. Polytheists/animists 90%.
2358	0	4	4.72	0	21.00	79.00	A	2.30	707	4	South border. Also in Viet Nam; official language nationality in both countries. Polytheists 97%.
2359	2	4	5.74	0	26.50	73.50	A	1.45	661	4	North Guangxi Province. An official nationality. Mulao is unwritten; written Chinese widely used. Agriculturalists. Animists 58%, Buddhists 40%. D=TSPM,RCC.
2360	0	3	1.96	1	14.02	85.98	A	0.01	709	2	East of Bhutan, southeast Tibet; also northeast India. Use written Tibetan. Agriculturalists. Lamaist Buddhists(Tantrists) 100%. No missionary visits or attempts.
2361	0	0	2.80	0	20.00	80.00	A	0.73	612	3	Part of official Tibetan nationality. West central Sichuan. Buddhists (Lamaists) 98%, Muslims 1%.
2362	1	4	5.90	0	23.00	77.00	A	0.84	834	3	Yunnan, Sichuan, Xizang; also in Burma. Dongbaists 80%(polytheists/animists), Buddhists 10%(Lamaists, some Mahayana), Taoists 9%, shamanism widespread.
2363	0	0	4.21	0	20.00	80.00	A	0.73	806	3	Part of official Tibetan nationality. Liangshan Yi Autonomous Prefecture. Buddhists (Lamaists) 98%, Muslims 1%.
2364	0	5	3.23	0	14.52	85.48	A	0.27	760	3	Sungchiang river valley, Heilongjiang Province. Most live in Russia. Only 40 Hezhen speakers now. Official nationality. Fishermen, hunters. Shamanists 99%.
2365	0	3	0.00	1	14.00	86.00	A	0.00	0	1.06	Golog Tibetan Autonomous Zone, Qinghai Province. Semi-nomadic pastoralists. Language unintelligible to other Tibetans. Lamaist. Buddhists 100%.
2366	0	5	6.57	0	21.50	78.50	A	1.96	914	4	Southern Yunnan Province; also northwestern Viet Nam (official ethnic community), USA, France, Laos. Polytheists 97%.
2367	0	5	4.66	0	19.50	80.50	A	1.06	809	4	Southwest Yunnan Province; also in north Burma. Polytheists 70%, Lamaist Buddhists 28%.
2368	3	4	8.34	4	42.50	57.50	A	5.42	583	4	West Hunan. Agriculturalists. Polytheists 96%. D=Chinese Ch,RCC,TSPM. M=AoG,SEF,CSI.
2369	2	4	5.99	0	23.12	76.88	A	0.10	781	3	Southeast Guizhou, western Hunan, Guangxi. Written language. Polytheists(animists) 80%, Mahayana Buddhists 20%. Y=c1920(RC,Protestants). D=RCC,TSPM.
2370	0	4	2.82	5	38.00	62.00	A	1.38	254	4	Northwest Xinjiang. Mainly in Uzbekistan. Official nationality. All bilingual in Uighur. Agriculture, commerce. Arabic script. Muslims 99%(Hanafi Sunnis). M=CSI.
2371	2	4	4.10	0	35.50	64.50	A	4.53	401	4	Northern Nosu. Yunnan, Laos, Viet Nam. Polytheists 90%, Mahayana Buddhists 5%. Y=c1890(RC,Prots). D=RCC,TSPM. M=OMF,CSI,NTCM,Revival CC,VIPS.
2372	3	4	9.92	4	42.00	58.00	A	1.53	690	4	Acculturated to Cantonese. Polytheists 80%, Mahayana Buddhists 19%. Y=c1890. D=TSPM(300 churches),RCC,TJC. M=CSI,YWAM,CCCI,SIL,ELA,HKBC.
2373	2	4	3.61	1	58.00	42.00	B	55.04	223	6	Along Nu (Salween) river, Yunnan. Also in Burma, Thailand. Official nationality. Bilingual in Lisu. Polytheists/animists 56%, Lamaist Buddhists 18%. Y=c1890(RC).
2374	0	5	2.98	0	21.00	79.00	A	1.53	532	4	Yunnan Province. Under Nu nationality. Polytheists/animists 98%.
2375	0	4	6.20	4	39.00	61.00	A	2.84	490	4	Xinjiang Mongolian, part of China Mongolian. Shamanists 60%, Lamaist Buddhists 30%, nonreligious 8%.
2376	0	4	5.96	0	21.50	78.50	A	0.39	836	3	North central coast of Hainan. Most are Han Chinese or Zhuang by nationality. Bilinguals. Buddhists/polytheists 99%.
2377	1	5	3.19	0	23.00	77.00	A	2.51	475	4	Olunchun. Dense forests, Heilongjiang Province, also Nei Mongol; some in Russia. Official nationality. Hunters, agriculturalists. Spoken by only 32%. Shamanists.
2378	0	4	2.89	4	28.00	72.00	A	1.02	381	4	Penglung. Borders of Yunnan Province; a few in Burma. An official nationality. Written Dai and Chinese in common use. Agriculturalists. Buddhists 99%.
2379	0	4	2.40	0	16.00	84.00	A	0.58	582	3	On Guangxi-Guizhou border. Hinayana Buddhists 99%.
2380	0	3	0.00	1	14.00	86.00	A	0.00	0	1.07	In Tibet Autonomous Region. Lamaist Buddhists 100%.
2381	0	5	1.40	0	11.03	88.97	A	0.01	539	2	East Qinghai Province, with most in Gansu Province. An official nationality. Muslims 90%(Sunnis), Buddhists 10%.
2382	1	4	9.63	1	59.00	41.00	B	53.83	494	6	Awa Mountains, southwest Yunnan Province. Majority in Burma. In Va official nationality. Close to Wa language. Buddhists 75%(Hinayana). D=Chinese Church.
2383	0	10	0.00	5	46.20	53.80	A	0.33	42	3	Residents from India, Iran since 19th century. Parsis 90%.

Continued overleaf

Table 8-2 continued

PEOPLE		POPULATION				IDENTITY CODE		LANGUAGE		CHURCH		MINISTRY		SCRIPTURE	
Ref 1	*Ethnic name* 2	*P%* 3	*In 1995* 4	*In 2000* 5	*In 2025* 6	*Race* 7	*Language* 8	*Autoglossonym* 9	*S* 10	*AC* 11	*Members* 12	*Jayuh* 13-17	*d wa xc mc mi* 18 19 20 21 22	*Biblioglossonym* 23	*Pub ss* 24-26 27
2384	Portuguese	0.00152	18,325	19,191	22,237	CEW21g	51-AABA-e	general português		92.00	17,656	2Bsuh	10 9 15 5 3	Portuguese	PNB b
2385	Portuguese	0.00015	1,808	1,894	2,194	CEW21g	51-AABA-e	general português	50	93.00	1,761	2Bsuh	10 9 15 5 1	Portuguese	PNB b
2386	Puman	0.00020	2,411	2,525	2,926	AUG03z	46-DBBA-d	pou-ma		3.00	76	0....	6 3 2 0 0		... b
2387	Pumi	0.00454	54,735	57,320	66,417	MSY50z	76-DAAA-a	p'umi		0.20	115	0....	5 3 3 0 0		... .
2388	Punu (Bunu, Yuno)	0.04383	528,418	553,379	641,203	MSY47b	48-AAAF	punu cluster		0.70	3,874	0....	5 4 6 1 0		... .
2389	Pupeo (Kabeo)	0.00003	362	379	439	MSY49a	47-BBBA-a	laqua		1.00	4	0....	6 3 4 0 0		... .
2390	Puyi (Bouyei, Pu-I)	0.22449	2,706,472	2,834,314	3,284,135	MSY49a	47-AAAH-a	bu-yi		2.00	56,686	0....	6 5 7 1 3	Bouyei	... b
2391	Queyu	0.00058	6,993	7,323	8,485	MSY50c	76-AAAC	qiang cluster		1.00	73	0	6 4 5 0 0		... .
2392	Rawang (Qiuce, Nung)	0.00500	60,280	63,128	73,147	MSY50f	76-AAAB-a	rawang		15.00	9,469	0....	8 5 7 2 1	Rawang	PNB .
2393	Red Meo (Meo Do)	0.00515	62,089	65,022	75,341	MSY47a	48-AAAB-a	meo-do		10.00	6,502	0r...	8 5 11 2 3		... .
2394	Riang (Yin)	0.00025	3,014	3,156	3,657	AUG03z	46-DCAB-a	riang-lang		0.00	0	0....	0 3 4 0 0	Riang Lang	P.. b
2395	Rom Gypsy	0.00100	12,056	12,626	14,629	CNN25f	59-ACAA-a	domari		2.00	253	0....	6 4 6 0 0		P.. b
2396	Russian	0.00002	241	253	293	CEW22j	53-AAAE-d	russkiy		70.00	177	4B.uh	10 8 8 5 1	Russian	PNB b
2397	Russian (Olossu, Eluosi)	0.00119	14,347	15,024	17,409	CEW22j	53-AAAE-d	russkiy		20.03	3,009	4B.uh	9 7 8 2 1	Russian	PNB b
2398	Salar	0.00774	93,314	97,722	113,231	MSY41z	44-AABD-e	salar		0.01	10	1c.u.	3 1 0 0 0		pnb b
2399	Samei	0.00010	1,206	1,263	1,463	MSY50i	77-BAEA	samei cluster		0.50	6	0....	5 4 2 1 0		... b
2400	Sangla	0.00091	10,971	11,489	13,313	MSY50a	70-AADB-a	tsangla		0.01	1	0....	3 3 3 1 0	Tsangla	... .
2401	Sansu	0.00100	12,056	12,626	14,629	MSY50i	77-BBAA-h	sansu		3.00	379	1....	6 4 2 1 0		pn. .
2402	Shan (Tai Yay, Sha)	0.01945	234,491	245,567	284,540	MSY49c	47-AAAA-f	tai-neua		0.40	982	1.s..	5 3 7 0 2	Chinese: Shanghai*	PNB .
2403	Sharpa Bhotia	0.00006	723	758	878	MSY50r	70-AAAA-e	sherpa		0.00	0	0c...	0 3 4 0 0	Sherpa*	Pnb .
2404	She	0.05560	670,319	701,982	813,390	MSY47b	48-ABAB	she cluster		0.30	2,106	0a...	5 4 6 2 1		... b
2405	Shui (Sui)	0.03052	367,952	385,332	446,487	AUG03z	47-ABAC-a	sui-chia		0.50	1,927	0....	5 4 5 2 1		... .
2406	Silver Palaung	0.00041	4,943	5,176	5,998	AUG03z	46-DCAA	palaung cluster		0.10	5	0r...	5 3 0 1 1	Palaung, Pale	... b
2407	Sinhalese	0.00005	603	631	731	CNN25q	59-ABBA-aa	standard sinhala		2.70	17	1asuh	6 4 1 5 3		pnb b
2408	Sotati-po	0.00040	4,822	5,050	5,852	MSY50r	70-AAAA-cd	sotati-po		0.00	0	0c...	0 2 0 0 0		pnb .
2409	Southern Lisu (White Lisu)	0.05071	611,364	640,243	741,853	MSY50l	77-BACA-a	lisu		80.00	512,194	4rs..	10 7 14 3 3	Lisu: Central*	PNB b
2410	Southern Yi (Nosu)	0.06959	838,983	878,613	1,018,054	MSY50i	77-BADA-a	nasö		3.00	26,358	1....	6 6 14 1 2	Nosu*	PN. .
2411	Southern Zhuang	0.35283	4,253,750	4,454,679	5,161,661	MSY49a	47-AAAE-a	south huang		1.00	44,547	0....	6 5 5 2 3		P.. b
2412	Sulung	0.00400	48,224	50,502	58,517	MSY50r	70-AAAA	phöke cluster		0.00	0	0a...	0 2 0 0 0		PNB b
2413	Tai Hongjin	0.01250	150,701	157,820	182,866	MSY49z	47-AAAA-hc	tai hongjin		1.00	1,578	1.s..	6 4 6 0 0		pnb .
2414	Tai Ya	0.00337	40,629	42,548	49,301	MSY49a	47-AAAA-h	tai-ya		1.00	425	1.s..	6 4 6 0 0	Tai: Ya	Pnb b
2415	Tatar (Tartar)	0.00043	5,184	5,429	6,291	MSY41h	44-AABB-e	tatar		0.00	0	2c.u.	0 1 0 0 0	Tatar: Kazan	Pn. b
2416	Ten	0.00200	24,112	25,251	29,259	MSY49z	47-ABAD-a	ten		0.52	131	0....	5 3 4 0 0		... .
2417	Thai	0.00096	11,574	12,121	14,044	MSY49d	47-AAAD-d	central thai		0.50	61	3asuh	5 6 8 0 0	Thai*	PNB b
2418	Thami	0.00050	6,028	6,313	7,315	MSY50r	70-ABCA-a	thami		0.00	0	0....	0 1 0 0 0		... .
2419	Tho (Tai Tho)	0.08500	1,024,768	1,073,173	1,243,492	MSY49a	47-AAAA-ae	tai-tho		0.60	6,439	0....	5 4 4 1 0	Tho*	P.. .
2420	Tseku	0.00100	12,056	12,626	14,629	MSY50r	70-AAAA-cf	tseku		0.00	0	0c...	0 1 0 0 0		pnb b
2421	Tu (Monguor, Tu-jen)	0.01690	203,748	213,372	247,235	MSY41y	44-BAAD-a	tu		0.03	64	0....	3 3 0 0 0		... b
2422	Tuerke (T'urk)	0.00001	121	126	146	MSY41z	44-AABD-dc	ili		0.00	0	1c.u.	0 3 1 0 0		pnb .
2423	Tujia (Tuchia)	0.50316	6,066,142	6,352,681	7,360,886	MSY50i	77-BFAA-a	tujia		0.40	25,411	0a...	5 5 5 2 2		... b
2424	Tulung (Trung, Derung)	0.00051	6,149	6,439	7,461	MSY50z	76-AAAA-b	tulung		88.00	5,666	0.s..	10 7 11 2 1		... .
2425	Tunghsiang (Santa, Tung)	0.03298	397,610	416,391	482,475	MSY41y	44-BAAE-a	dongxiang		0.05	208	0....	4 2 0 0 0		... .
2426	Tuvinian (Tuva, Tuba)	0.00004	482	505	585	MSY41z	44-AABD-k	tuvin		1.00	5	2c.u.	6 4 6 0 0	Tuvin	Pnb b
2427	U (Puman)	0.00026	3,135	3,283	3,804	AUG03z	46-DBBA-d	pou-ma		1.00	33	0....	6 3 2 1 0		... b
2428	USA Black	0.00005	603	631	731	NFB68a	52-ABAE-a	talkin-black		73.00	461	0B.uh	10 9 13 5 3		pnb b
2429	USA White	0.00126	15,191	15,908	18,433	CEW19s	52-ABAC-s	general american		77.00	12,249	1Bsuh	10 9 13 5 3	English*	PNB b
2430	USA White	0.00004	482	505	585	CEW19s	52-ABAC-s	general american		78.00	394	1Bsuh	10 9 13 5 3	English*	PNB b
2431	Uighur (Kashgar)	0.63637	7,672,134	8,034,533	9,309,657	MSY41z	44-AABD-d	east uyghur		0.00	0	1r.u.	0 3 3 1 4	Uighur*	PNB b
2432	Va (Kawa, Wa, Wa Pwi)	0.00529	63,777	66,789	77,389	AUG03z	46-DBAA-a	wa		25.00	16,697	4....	9 5 7 2 1	Wa	PN. .
2433	Vietnamese (Gin, Jhing)	0.00400	48,224	50,502	58,517	MSY52b	79-AAAM-a	central yue		75.00	37,877	3A.uh	10 5 13 2 1	Chinese, Yue	PNB b
2434	Vietnamese (Kinh)	0.00506	61,004	63,885	74,024	MSY52b	46-EBAA-ac	general viêt		15.00	9,583	1Asu.	8 5 8 5 1	Vietnamese	PNB b
2435	Wakhi (Vakhan, Wakhigi)	0.00053	6,390	6,692	7,754	CNT24z	58-ABDC	wakhi cluster		0.00	0	0....	0 1 0 0 0	Wakhi	... b
2436	Waxianghua	0.02500	301,402	315,639	365,733	MSY47a	79-AAAP-d	xiang-hua		5.00	15,782	0c...	7 6 7 0 0		pnb .
2437	Western Lawa	0.00662	79,811	83,581	96,846	AUG03z	46-DBAB	lawa cluster		2.00	1,672	0....	6 3 4 0 0	Lawa, Western	PN. n
2438	Western Manchu (Sibo)	0.01525	183,855	192,540	223,097	MSY41i	44-CAAC-be	xibe		0.02	39	0....	3 2 3 0 1		pn. b
2439	Western Meo (Peh, Tak)	0.29267	3,528,456	3,695,125	4,281,562	MSY47a	48-AAAA-a	hmong-daw		5.50	203,232	2A...	7 5 12 2 3	Hmong Daw*	PN. .
2440	Western Yi	0.02609	314,543	329,401	381,679	MSY50i	77-BAGA-a	yi		2.80	9,223	0....	6 6 11 1 1		... b
2441	White Tai (Thai Trang)	0.01300	156,729	164,132	190,181	MSY49z	47-AAAD-b	tai-kao		3.50	5,745	0....	6 5 7 2 1	Tai: White*	P.. .
2442	Woni (Ho, Honi)	0.00882	106,335	111,358	129,031	MSY50z	77-BBAA-k	honi		3.00	3,341	1....	6 4 2 2 0		pn. .
2443	Wutunhua	0.00016	1,929	2,020	2,341	MSY41y	44-BAAD-a	tu		0.03	1	0....	3 5 5 0 0		... b
2444	Ya (Tai Ya)	0.00040	4,822	5,050	5,852	MSY49a	47-AAAA-h	tai-ya		1.00	51	1.s..	6 4 4 1 0	Tai: Ya	Pnb b
2445	Yao (Highland Yao, Man)	0.18824	2,269,438	2,376,637	2,753,822	MSY47b	48-ABAA-ab	tai-pan		0.70	16,636	0.s..	5 5 9 2 2		pn. b
2446	Yellow Lahu (Shi)	0.00049	5,907	6,187	7,168	MSY50i	77-BBAB-b	kutsung		2.00	124	1a...	6 5 5 0 1	Lahu Shi	pnb .
2447	Yellow Uighur (West Yugur)	0.00108	13,021	13,636	15,800	MSY41z	44-AABD-f	west yugur		0.01	1	1c.u.	3 1 0 0 0		pnb b
2448	Yung-Chuun	0.00100	12,056	12,626	14,629	MSY49d	47-AAAE-ad	yung-chun		0.30	38	0....	5 3 2 0 0		p.. .
2449	Yunnanese Shan (Dai)	0.09042	1,090,112	1,141,604	1,322,783	MSY49a	47-AAAA-e	shan		1.00	11,416	3.s..	6 4 5 1 1	Shan*	PNB b
2450	Zangskar (Zaskar)	0.00010	1,206	1,263	1,463	MSY50r	70-AAAC-e	zangskari		0.03	0	1....	3 2 0 0 0	Zangskari	Pn. b
2451	Zauzou	0.00013	1,567	1,641	1,902	MSY50i	77-BEAB-a	zauzou		25.00	410	0....	9 5 6 1 2		... b
2452	Zhaba	0.00064	7,716	8,080	9,363	MSY50r	76-CAAA	qiang cluster		0.50	40	0....	5 3 6 0 0		... b
2453	other minor peoples	0.10000	1,205,609	1,262,557	1,462,931	...				1.00	12,626		6 4 6 1 0		
2454	other minor peoples (HK)	0.00101	12,177	12,752	14,776	...				10.00	1,275		8 5 2 5 0		
2455	other minor peoples (Macao)	0.00011	1,326	1,389	1,609	...				7.00	97		7 5 4 5 0		
	Christmas Island	**100.00000**	**3,300**	**3,424**	**4,117**					**12.94**	**443**				
2456	Anglo-Australian	9.90000	327	339	408	CEW19c	52-ABAC-x	general australian		67.00	227	1Bsuh	10 9 11 4 2		pnb b
2457	Eurasian	2.00000	66	68	82	MSY43	52-ABAD-a	south-asian-english		69.70	48	0B.uh	10 9 11 4 2		... b
2458	Han Chinese (Cantonese)	1.00000	33	34	41	MSY42a	79-AAAM-a	central yue		6.00	2	3A.uh	7 5 8 3 0	Chinese, Yue	PNB b
2459	Han Chinese (Mandarin)	67.50000	2,228	2,311	2,779	MSY42a	79-AAAB-ba	kuo-yü		7.00	162	2Bsuh	7 5 8 3 0	Chinese: Kuoyu*	PNB b
2460	Indo-Pakistani	1.90000	63	65	78	CNN25g	59-AAFO-e	general hindi		0.00	0	3Asuh	0 4 2 3 0		pnb b
2461	Javanese (Orang Jawa)	1.40000	46	48	58	MSY44g	31-PIAA-g	general jawa		4.00	2	2As.h	6 5 2 3 0	Javanese	PNB b
2462	Malay (Cocos Islander)	16.00000	528	548	659	MSY44k	31-PHAL-b	kokos-christmas		0.10	1	0a...	5 4 1 3 0		pnb b
2463	other minor peoples	0.30000	10	10	12	...				10.00	1		8 5 6 3 0		
	Cocos (Keeling) Islands	**100.00000**	**700**	**726**	**873**					**16.8**	**122**				
2464	Anglo-Australian	14.00000	98	102	122	CEW19c	52-ABAC-x	general australian		58.00	59	1Bsuh	10 9 12 4 3		pnb b
2465	British	14.00000	98	102	122	CEW19i	52-ABAC-b	standard-english		60.00	61	3Bsuh	10 9 13 4 2		PNB b
2466	Cocos Islander (Malay)	69.60000	487	505	608	MSY44k	31-PHAL-c	kokos-sabah		0.20	1	0c...	5 4 3 1 0		... .
2467	Han Chinese	1.00000	7	7	9	MSY42a	79-AAAB-ba	kuo-yü		3.50	0	2Bsuh	6 5 8 4 2	Chinese: Kuoyu*	PNB b
2468	other minor peoples	1.40000	10	10	12	...				14.00	1		8 5 6 4 0		
	Colombia	**100.00000**	**38,541,609**	**42,321,361**	**59,757,874**					**96.73**	**40,935,887**				
2469	Achagua	0.00115	443	487	687	MIR39e	81-AFAA-a	achagua		70.00	341	0....	10 7 5 2 1	Achagua	... b
2470	Agualinda Guajibo	0.00049	189	207	293	MIR39d	88-GAAA-d	macaguán		50.00	104	0....	10 6 5 2 1		pn. .
2471	Andoque	0.00102	393	432	610	MIR39d	84-CAAA-a	andoque		60.00	259	0....	10 6 5 2 1		... .
2472	Baniwa (Maniba)	0.00050	193	212	299	MIR39d	81-AGBB-c	south baniwa		70.00	148	0....	10 7 6 2 1	Baniua*	PN. .
2473	Black Gypsy (Calo, Cale)	0.02270	8,749	9,607	13,565	CNN25f	59-AFAA-a	rodi		70.00	6,725	0B.uh	10 7 8 5 1	Calo	P.. b
2474	Bora (Boro)	0.00171	659	724	1,022	MIR39d	84-DAAA-a	muinane-bora		65.00	470	0....	10 7 6 3 1	Bora	PN. .
2475	British	0.01000	3,854	4,232	5,976	CEW19i	52-ABAC-b	standard-english	6	79.00	3,343	3Bsuh	10 9 8 5 1		PNB b
2476	Cabiyari (Cuyare)	0.00010	39	42	60	MIR39a	81-AFBA-a	caviyarí		80.00	34	0....	10 8 5 3 1		... .
2477	Cacua (Macu)	0.00056	216	237	335	MIR39z	88-IAAA	cacua cluster		70.00	166	0....	10 8 6 4 1	Cacua	P.. .
2478	Camsa	0.01190	4,586	5,036	7,111	MIR39z	83-OAAA-a	camsá		40.00	2,014	0....	9 6 6 4 1	Camsa	PN. .
2479	Carabayo (Macusa)	0.00042	162	178	251	MIR39d	88-FAAB	saliba cluster		1.00	2	0....	6 3 3 0 0		... b
2480	Carapana	0.00182	701	770	1,088	MIR39d	88-KAAE-ca	carpano		80.00	616	0....	10 7 6 5 2	Carapana	PN. .
2481	Carijona (Karihona)	0.00041	158	174	245	MIR39c	80-AHAA-a	carijona-vaupés		10.00	17	0....	8 4 4 4 1		... .
2482	Catio (Katio)	0.05556	21,414	23,514	33,201	MIR39e	83-EIAA-d	catío		60.00	14,108	0....	10 7 6 4 2	Catio*	Pn. .
2483	Central Tunebo	0.00556	2,143	2,353	3,323	MIR39e	83-EFAB-a	central tunebo		40.00	941	0....	9 6 5 4 1	Tunebo*	PN. .
2484	Chami	0.03133	12,075	13,259	18,722	MIR39z	83-EIAA-f	chamí		65.00	8,619	0....	10 7 6 4 1	Embera-chami	pn. .
2485	Chimila	0.00588	2,266	2,488	3,514	MIR39c	83-EEAA	chimila cluster		45.00	1,120	0....	9 6 4 4 1	Chimila	... .
2486	Choco Creole	0.03000	11,562	12,696	17,927	MIR39z	51-AACB-b	chocoano		80.00	10,157	1c.u.	10 7 6 5 1		pnb .
2487	Cocama-Cocamilla	0.00007	27	30	42	MIR39e	82-AAHA-a	cocama		81.00	24	0....	10 7 6 5 1	Cocama*	P.. b
2488	Cofan	0.00148	570	626	884	MIR39d	83-FAAA-a	north cofán		8.00	50	0....	7 5 6 1 1	Cofan	PN. .
2489	Cogui	0.01402	5,404	5,933	8,378	MIR39e	83-EDAA-a	cûwgi		65.00	3,857	0....	10 7 6 4 2	Kogui	... .
2490	Colombian Black	6.00000	2,312,497	2,539,282	3,585,472	NFB71a	51-AABB-ho	colombiano		97.60	2,478,339	1B.uh	10 8 13 5 1		pnb b
2491	Colombian Creole	0.50000	192,708	211,607	298,789	NFB68b	52-ABAF-m	jamaican-creole		95.00	201,026	1c..h	10 8 13 5 1	West Carib Creole English	pn. b
2492	Colombian Gypsy	0.10000	38,542	42,321	59,758	CNN25f	51-AABB-ho	colombiano		90.00	38,089	1B.uh	10 7 8 4 1		pnb b
2493	Colombian Mestizo	47.38592	18,263,296	20,054,366	28,316,818	CLN29	51-AABB-ho	colombiano		98.41	19,735,502	1B.uh	10 9 11 5 4		pnb b
2494	Colombian Mulatto	23.00000	8,864,570	9,733,913	13,744,311	NFB71b	51-AABB-ho	colombiano		97.00	9,441,896	1B.uh	10 9 11 5 4		pnb b
2495	Colombian White	20.00000	7,708,322	8,464,272	11,951,575	CLT27	51-AABB-ho	colombiano		96.69	8,184,105	1B.uh	10 9 12 5 4		pnb b
2496	Coreguaje	0.00511	1,969	2,163	3,054	MIR39d	88-KAAA-a	correguaje-tama		20.00	433	0....	9 5 6 4 3	Coreguaje*	PN. .
2497	Coyaima	0.00300	1,156	1,270	1,793	MIR39z	51-AABB-ho	colombiano		80.00	1,016	1B.uh	10 8 13 5 1		pnb b
2498	Creole Islander	0.05682	21,899	24,047	33,954	NFB71b	52-ABAF	carib-anglo-creol cluster		95.00	22,845	1a..h	10 8 11 5 1	West Carib Creole English	PN. b
2499	Cubeo (Cuveo, Pamiwa)	0.01460	5,627	6,179	8,725	MIR39d	88-KAAC-a	cubeo		80.00	4,943	0....	10 8 6 4 3	Cubeo	PN. .
2500	Cuiba	0.01736	6,691	7,347	10,374	MIR39d	88-GAAB-a	proper cuiba		10.00	735	0....	8 5 6 2 2	Cuiba	PN. .
2501	Curipaco	0.00641	2,471	2,713	3,830	MIR39a	81-AGBA-a	kúrrim		60.00	1,628	0....	10 6 6 4 2	Curripaco	PN. .

Continued opposite

Table 8-2 continued

EVANGELIZATION								EVANGELISM			ADDITIONAL DESCRIPTIVE DATA
Ref 1	*D* 28	*aC* 29	*CG%* 30	*r* 31	*E* 32	*U* 33	*W* 34	*e* 35	*R* 36	*T* 37	*Locations, civil divisions, literacy, religions, church history, denominations, dioceses, church growth, missions, agencies, ministries, movements* 38
2384	3	10	4.00	8	99.92	0.08	C	570.86	81	10	Residents, from Portugal. D=RCC(D-Hong Kong),SDA,JWs.
2385	1	10	1.04	8	99.93	0.07	C	563.48	34	10	Expatriates from Portugal, and locally-born. D=RCC(D-Macao).
2386	0	4	4.43	0	21.00	79.00	A	2.30	708	4	Southwestern Yunnan Province. Officially included under Blang minority. Hinayana Buddhists 97%.
2387	0	4	2.47	0	15.20	84.80	A	0.11	644	3	Northwest Yunnan Province. Official nationality. Agriculturalists. Lamaist Buddhists(Tantrists) 100%.
2388	0	4	6.14	0	20.70	79.30	A	0.52	905	3	Guangxi, Guizhou, Hunan, Yunnan Provinces. Ethnically Yao. Polytheists(animists) 99%, including ancestor worship.
2389	0	4	1.40	0	18.00	82.00	A	0.65	312	3	Yunnan, Wenshan Zhuang-Miao Autonomous district. Polytheists 99%.
2390	1	4	9.03	0	32.00	68.00	A	2.33	829	4	Guizhou, Yunnan. Written (40 dialects), but Chinese in common use. Polytheists(animists) 80%, Mahayana Buddhists 10%, Taoists 8%. Y=c1890(RC missions).
2391	0	0	4.38	0	10.00	90.00	A	0.36	1,200	3	Part of official Tibetan nationality. Ganzi Tibetan Autonomous Prefecture. Buddhists (Lamaists) 98%, Muslims 1%.
2392	0	5	3.04	4	56.00	44.00	B	30.66	203	5	Southeast Yunnan, Tibet; also Burma, India. 100 dialects. Polytheists 60%, Buddhists 25%. M=North Burma Christian Mission.
2393	1	4	6.69	4	50.00	50.00	B	18.25	405	5	Also in Viet Nam, Thailand. Agriculturalists. Polytheists(animists) 90%. D=Chinese Ch. M=CSI,NTCM,AoG,SEF.
2394	0	4	0.00	0	12.00	88.00	A	0.00	0	1.05	Yunnan Province; also in Burma. In China, officially under Benglong/Palaung. Buddhists 99%(Hinayana).
2395	0	4	3.28	7	28.00	72.00	A	2.04	422	4	Wandering nomads related to Gypsies in Asia/Europe/Latin America. Polytheists 98%.
2396	1	10	3.28	7	99.70	0.30	C	352.59	65	9	Refugees from former USSR, China. Nonreligious/atheists 30%. D=Russian Orthodox Ch(P-Moscow).
2397	1	7	0.86	7	82.03	17.97	B	59.97	29	6	Russian settlers in north Xinjiang, Heilongjiang, Nei Mongol during last 200 years. Nonreligious 80%. D=Orthodox Ch of China(D-Peking,D-Shanghai).
2398	0	3	2.33	1	20.01	79.99	A	0.00	429	1.11	Gansu, Qinghai Provinces. No Salar script; 100% literacy in Chinese and Uygur. China's most zealous Muslims(100% Hanafi Sunnis, since 1750).
2399	0	5	1.81	0	19.50	80.50	A	0.35	409	3	Yunnan Province. Adults bilingual in Mandarin. Small minority related to Yi. Polytheists 90%.
2400	0	5	0.00	0	15.01	84.99	A	0.00	305	1.05	In south, near Bhutan. Vast majority in Bhutan, some in India. Lamaist Buddhists 100%.
2401	0	5	3.70	0	24.00	76.00	A	2.62	548	4	Southern Yunnan; also in Burma. Related to Hani. Under Hani nationality. Polytheists/animists 97%.
2402	0	4	4.69	1	34.40	65.60	A	0.50	462	3	Town of Dehong Dai in south Yunnan Province; vast majority in Burma, also Thailand. Theravada Buddhists 89%, animists 10%. M=BBC,OMF.
2403	0	5	0.00	1	20.00	80.00	A	0.00	0	1.08	In Tibet; also in Nepal and India. Lamaist Buddhists 100%.
2404	1	4	3.04	0	30.30	69.70	A	0.33	338	3	Fujian, Guangdong, Zhejiang, Jiangxi Provinces. Official nationality. Only 1,000 speak She; rest speak only Hakka. Taoists/animists 89%, Mahayana Buddhists 10%.
2405	1	4	-0.96	0	22.50	77.50	A	0.41	5	3	In Guizhou (Sandu, Libo Districts), Guangxi (Nandan District). Official nationality. Agriculturalists. Polytheists/animists 99%. Y=c1880. D=RCC(30 churches in 1949).
2406	0	3	1.62	4	20.10	79.90	A	0.07	357	2	Yunnan Province. Also in Burma. Agriculturalists. Buddhists 100%(Hinayana). M=BBC(Burma).
2407	3	10	2.87	6	51.70	48.30	B	5.09	183	4	From Sri Lanka. Buddhists 97%(Theravada). D=RCC,CCC,AoG.
2408	0	3	0.00	1	14.00	86.00	A	0.00	0	1.07	Tibet. Related to Tibetan. Lamaist Buddhists (Tantrists) 100%.
2409	2	5	4.47	4	99.80	0.20	C	420.48	104	10	Flowery Lisu(Hwa Lisu), Western Lisu. West Yunnan, Sichuan; also Burma, Thailand. Polytheists/animists 20%. Y=c1890(RC,Protestants). Mass movement.
2410	3	4	8.20	0	44.00	56.00	A	4.81	579	4	Eastern Yi, Southern Yi. Black Yi. Yunnan, Guizhou, southwest Sichuan Provinces. Elite caste. Polytheists/animists 95%. D=RCC,Chinese Church,TSPM.
2411	2	4	8.76	4	36.00	64.00	A	1.31	716	4	Southwest Guangxi and in 14 other Provinces. Polytheists 90%, some Buddhists. D=TSPM,RCC. M=CSI,YWAM,SIL. R=FEBC.
2412	0	3	0.00	4	24.00	76.00	A	0.00	0	1.08	In Tibet Autonomous Region. Also in India. Lamaist Buddhists 100%.
2413	0	0	5.19	1	25.00	75.00	A	0.91	635	3	Related to Dai. Sichuan province north of the Yangtze River at Huili and Takou. Polytheists 59%, Buddhists 40%.
2414	0	0	3.82	1	24.00	76.00	A	0.87	510	3	Related to Dai. Central Yunnan province. Polytheists(animistic) 59%, Buddhists 40%.
2415	0	5	0.00	6	22.00	78.00	A	0.00	0	1.09	Xinjiang, mainly in Kulja, Qoqek, and Urumqi. Also Russia, Romania, Turkey, Bulgaria. Descendants of 13th-century Mongols. Official nationality.
2416	0	5	2.61	0	17.52	82.48	A	0.33	502	3	A few villages in Huishui, south of Guiyang, Guizhou Province. Under Buyi nationality. Polytheists 100%.
2417	0	0	4.20	6	39.50	60.50	A	0.72	332	3	Immigrants from Thailand. Theravada Buddhists 99.5%.
2418	0	3	0.00	0	6.00	94.00	A	0.00	0	1.02	In Tibet. Mainly in Nepal. Lamaist Buddhists 100%.
2419	0	4	6.68	4	23.60	76.40	A	0.51	851	3	Southern China, Qinghai and Gansu Provinces. Also north Viet Nam, USA, France, Laos. Close to Nung and Southern Zhuang. Polytheists 95%.
2420	0	3	0.00	1	17.00	83.00	A	0.00	0	1.08	In Tibet; also Bhutan, Nepal. Related to Tibetan. Lamaist Buddhists(Tantrists) 100%.
2421	0	4	4.25	0	13.03	86.97	A	0.01	1,056	2	East Qinghai Province, also Gansu. An official nationality. Agriculturalists. Tibetan used as written language; 1979, Tu alphabet created. Lamaist Buddhists 100%.
2422	0	4	0.00	1	16.00	84.00	A	0.00	0	1.10	Xinjiang, Ili Valley near Kuldja. Also in Kazakhstan. Youth abandoning Turk for Kazakh or Uighur. Muslims 100%.
2423	2	4	3.64	0	32.40	67.60	A	0.47	401	3	Northwest Hunan, Hubei, Sichuan Provinces. Unwritten; spoken by only 3%; rest use Southwestern Mandarin. Polytheists/animists 99%. Y=c1890(RC,Prots).
2424	1	5	6.54	0	99.88	0.12	C	395.07	170	9	Northwest Yunnan Province. Official nationality. No written language. Polytheists(animists) 12%. Y=c1930(RC). D=Chinese Ch. M=Lisu Ch. Every village visited .
2425	0	4	3.08	0	11.05	88.95	A	0.02	955	2	Southwest Gansu, Xinjiang, Ningxia. Farming. Muslims 100%(Sunnis: in 1945, 595 mosques, 9,000 religious schools, 2,000 religious personnel).
2426	0	6	1.62	1	31.00	69.00	A	1.13	214	4	Part of China Mongolian. Tuvin AO, also in Russia, Mongolia. Cyrillic script. Lamaist Buddhists/shamanists 99%.
2427	0	4	3.56	0	17.00	83.00	A	0.62	735	3	Southwestern Yunnan Province. Officially under Blang nationality though unrelated. Hinayana Buddhists 95%.
2428	4	10	2.84	8	99.73	0.27	C	373.03	68	9	From USA, in business, education. D=UHKCBCA,PHC,AoG,PCG.
2429	8	10	3.86	8	99.77	0.23	C	427.19	86	10	Expatriates from USA, in finance, commerce, business. D=CCC,SDA,CJCLdS,JWs,CCS,AoG,ACC,ICFG.
2430	7	10	3.74	8	99.78	0.22	C	429.89	84	10	Expatriates from USA, in business. D=AoG,SDA,JWs,MBC,AC,FMC,LCMS.
2431	0	3	0.00	4	34.00	66.00	A	0.00	0	1.12	In Xinjiang, Hunan. In 15 countries. Settled agriculturalists. Muslims 100%(Hanafi Sunnis with heavy Sufi influence; 15,000 mosques). Y=1892(SMF,until 1937).
2432	1	4	7.70	4	66.00	34.00	B	60.22	361	6	Awa Mountains, southwest Yunnan; mostly in Burma. Agriculturalists, former headhunters. Related to Parauk (Va). Animists 40%, Buddhists 35%(Hinayana).
2433	1	5	1.92	8	99.75	0.25	C	385.98	54	9	Annamese. Around Dongxing on coast. Also in Viet Nam, Laos, Cambodia, and 8 others. Official nationality. Fishermen, agriculturalists. Taoists/Buddhists 15%.
2434	1	10	6.22	6	77.00	23.00	B	42.15	252	6	Remnant of refugees since 1975, 1985. Buddhists 60%, Cao Daists 18%. D=95% RCC.
2435	0	7	0.00	0	10.00	90.00	A	0.00	0	1.03	Taxkorgan Tajik Autonomous County, Xinjiang. Also in Afghanistan, Tajikistan, Russia, Pakistan. Muslims 99%(Ismaili Shias).
2436	0	0	7.64	1	31.00	69.00	A	5.65	737	4	Related to Miao. Western Hunan province. Wuling mountains. Polytheists (animistic) 95%.
2437	0	5	5.25	0	25.00	75.00	A	1.82	685	4	Mountain Lawa. Southwest Yunnan Province. Mainly in Thailand. Related to Wa, Parauk. In Blang and Va official nationalities. Animists 50%, Buddhists 48%.
2438	0	3	3.73	0	19.02	80.98	A	0.01	653	2	Ili region of Xinjiang Province, also Jilin. Agriculturalists. Xibe is only spoken by 15%, now being replaced by literary Chinese. Official nationality. Shamanists 100%.
2439	4	4	10.43	4	56.50	43.50	B	11.34	540	5	Southwestern Guizhou, Guangxi, Sichuan, Yunnan; also Viet Nam, Laos, Thailand. Polytheists 94%. Y=c1900(RC,Protestants). D=Chinese Ch,TSPM,RCC,TJC.
2440	2	4	7.07	0	34.80	65.20	A	3.55	643	4	Part of official Yi nationality. 65% preliterate. Polytheists 92%, some Mahayana Buddhists. D=RCC,TSPM. M=CSI.
2441	0	4	6.56	4	32.50	67.50	A	4.15	604	4	Vast majority live in Viet Nam; also a few in Laos and USA. Animists 60%, Buddhists 35%. M=SIL.
2442	0	4	5.98	0	25.00	75.00	A	2.73	776	4	Yunnan, near the Hani. Under Hani official nationality. Polytheists 97%.
2443	0	0	0.00	0	10.03	89.97	A	0.01	210	2	Related to Tu nationality. Huangnan Tibetan Autonomous Prefecture. Agriculturalists. Buddhists (Lamaists) 100%.
2444	0	4	4.01	1	28.00	72.00	A	1.02	456	4	South central Yunnan Province, Ya and Chung Districts, Yuanjiang area, Ailao Shan Range. Polytheists 95%.
2445	3	4	7.70	0	37.70	62.30	A	0.96	611	3	In 5 Provinces; also Viet Nam, Thailand, Laos, USA. 53% speak Yao. Written, but Chinese in common use. Polytheists/animists(ancestor-worship) 99%. D=RCC.
2446	0	5	2.55	1	34.00	66.00	A	2.48	294	4	Southern Yunnan Province. Also in Burma, Thailand, Laos, USA. Animists 80%, some Buddhists. M=Chinese Ch(TSPM).
2447	0	2	0.00	1	19.01	80.99	A	0.00	115	1.11	Northwest Gansu. Descendants from 8th-century Uighurs. Official nationality. 30% use Chinese as first language. Lamaist Buddhists 60%, shamanists 40%.
2448	0	5	3.70	1	17.30	82.70	A	0.18	678	3	A Tai people related to the Zhuang. Polytheists/animists 99%.
2449	2	4	7.29	4	43.00	57.00	A	1.57	506	4	Chinese Tai. Southwest Yunnan and Sichuan Provinces; also Thailand. Main city: Xishuangbanna. Official nationality. Agriculturalists. Buddhists 80%(Hinayana).
2450	0	2	0.00	0	15.03	84.97	A	0.01	0	2	In Tibet, related to Tibetan. Majority live in Kashmir(India). People speak Ladakhi and use Central Tibetan literature. Buddhists 99%.
2451	2	4	3.78	0	55.00	45.00	B	50.18	243	6	Yunnan Province. Officially under Nu nationality with Nung, Nusu, Drung. Polytheists 60%, Buddhists 15%. D=TSPM,RCC.
2452	0	0	3.76	0	13.50	86.50	A	0.24	1,102	3	Part of official Tibetan nationality. Ganzi Tibetan Autonomous Prefecture. Buddhists (Lamaists) 100%.
2453	0	6	7.40		24.00	76.00	A	0.87	845	3	Many 'foreign citizens' (naturalized non-Chinese), also many foreigners (aliens), Chinese refugees from Viet Nam. Buddhists 50%, Muslims 25%.
2454	0	10	2.86		35.00	65.00	A	12.77	224	5	Indonesians, Punjabis(Sikhs, since 1840), Norwegians, Nepalese, Chinese Pidgin/Creoles, and peoples from all parts of the world. Muslims 40%.
2455	0	10	2.03		32.00	68.00	A	8.17	174	4	Karens, Han Chinese (Swatow), Filipinos, other Asians, Europeans, Americans. Chinese folk- religionists/Buddhists 72%.
Christmas Island											
2456	2	10	2.04	8	99.67	0.33	C	322.80	58	9	D=Anglican Ch of Australia,RCC(AD-Singapore).
2457	2	10	2.29	8	99.70	0.30	C	322.33	67	9	D=Anglican Ch of Australia(D=Perth),RCC.
2458	0	10	0.70	8	67.00	33.00	B	14.67	55	5	Chinese folk-religionists predominate.
2459	0	9	2.82	7	67.00	33.00	B	17.11	142	5	Chinese folk-religionists and Buddhists 73%, many nonreligious 20%.
2460	0	10	0.00	7	41.00	59.00	A	0.00	0	1.14	Hindus 50%, Muslims 25%, and nonreligious 25%.
2461	0	10	0.70	5	53.00	47.00	B	7.73	80	4	Javanese folk-religionists 50%, Koranic Muslims 45%.
2462	0	9	0.00	5	34.10	65.90	A	0.12	56	3	From Cocos Islands; originally from Malaysia. Muslims 92%(Shafi Sunnis).
2463	0	10	0.00		40.00	60.00	A	14.60	0	5	Individuals from Indonesian islands and other territories. Muslims 60% (Shafi Sunnis), New-Religionists 20%.
Cocos (Keeling) Islands											
2464	3	10	0.55	8	99.58	0.42	B	266.74	29	8	D=Anglican Ch of Australia(D-Perth),RCC(M-Perth),Uniting Ch of Australia.
2465	2	10	1.12	8	99.60	0.40	C	291.27	47	8	D=Anglican Ch of Australia(D-Perth),Uniting Ch of Australia.
2466	0	10	0.00	5	29.20	70.80	A	0.21	66	3	Muslims 94%(Shafi Sunnis), but mixed with animistic practices.
2467	2	10	0.00	7	68.50	31.50	B	8.75	0	4	Chinese folk-religionists 90%. D=RCC,ACA.
2468	0	10	0.00		45.00	55.00	A	22.99	0	5	A few individuals from other Pacific, Indonesian, and Indian Ocean islands. Muslims 66% (Shafi Sunnis).
Colombia											
2469	1	7	3.40	0	99.70	0.30	C	263.16	107	8	Rio Meta, near Puerto Gaitan. Bilingual, acculturated. Close to Piapoco. Animists 30%. D=RCC.
2470	1	7	2.48	0	83.00	17.00	B	151.47	105	7	Semi-nomadic, monolinguals, hunter-gatherers. Animists 50%. D=RCC. M=independents.
2471	1	7	3.42	0	90.00	10.00	C	197.10	125	7	Aduche river. Tropical forest. Rubber gatherers. Extinct in Peru, nearly so in Colombia. Animists 40%. D=RCC. M=independents.
2472	1	7	2.46	0	99.70	0.30	C	268.27	90	8	Mainly in Brazil and Venezuela. Animists 30%. D=RCC. M=NTM.
2473	1	10	2.43	8	99.70	0.30	C	319.37	76	9	Mostly nomadic Gypsies. Itinerant. Animists 30%. D=RCC. M=GGMS.
2474	1	7	2.44	0	99.65	0.35	C	239.62	85	8	Providencia, also in Brazil and Peru. Riverine. Animists 35%. D=RCC. M=SIL.
2475	1	10	2.43	8	99.79	0.21	C	432.52	65	10	Expatriates from UK, in commerce, education. D=AC/EC.
2476	1	7	2.46	0	99.80	0.20	C	324.12	85	9	Cananari river. Much intermarriage with Barasana. Nearly extinct. Animists 20%. D=RCC.
2477	1	7	2.43	0	99.70	0.30	C	265.72	90	8	Wacara. Mostly monolingual nomads, some bilinguals in Cubeo, Desano, Guanano, but not Spanish. Animists 30%. D=RCC. M=SIL.
2478	1	6	2.43	0	76.00	24.00	B	110.96	124	7	Putumayo Region, Sibunday Valley. Language isolate. Mountainous. Animists 60%. D=RCC. M=SIL.
2479	0	6	0.70	0	20.00	80.00	A	0.73	192	3	Amazonas, between San Bernardo and Pure rivers. Hostile area for outsiders. Animists 99%.
2480	1	9	2.43	0	99.80	0.20	C	353.32	71	9	Vaupes Region. Also in Colombia, Brazil. Tropical forest. Animists 20%. D=RCC. M=SIL,GRI.
2481	1	6	2.16	0	38.00	62.00	A	13.87	229	5	In southeast: Upper Vaupes. Hunters, fishermen. Animists 90%. D=RCC.
2482	1	5	2.43	0	97.00	3.00	C	212.43	87	8	Some in Panama. Animists 40%. D=Plymouth Brethren. D=RCC. M=SIL,BLL.
2483	2	6	2.43	0	75.00	25.00	B	109.50	112	7	North slopes of Sierra Nevada. Tropical forest. Animists 60%. D=ICFG,RCC. M=SIL.
2484	2	6	2.37	0	99.65	0.35	C	241.99	91	8	Mountain slopes. Monolingual. Animists 35%. D=RCC,Iglesia Pentecostal Unida. M=SIL.
2485	1	7	4.22	0	76.00	24.00	B	124.83	189	7	Lowlands near Valledupar. Some use Spanish. Animists 55%. D=RCC. M=SIL.
2486	1	7	2.43	1	99.80	0.20	C	362.08	76	9	Mixed-race, half-castes, detribalized Amerindians. Animists 20%. D=RCC.
2487	1	5	2.52	0	99.81	0.19	C	337.04	76	9	Lower Putumayo. Mainly in Peru; also Brazil. Animists 19%. D=RCC.
2488	0	6	2.85	0	37.00	63.00	A	10.80	263	5	Also in Ecuador. Fairly monolingual. Animists 90%. M=SIL.
2489	1	6	2.38	0	99.00	1.00	C	234.87	84	8	Tropical forest, mountains. Animists 35%. D=RCC. M=SAM,SIL.
2490	2	10	2.43	8	99.98	0.02	C	593.49	50	10	West Indies, Caribbean Blacks along north coast of Colombia. D=RCC,AC. M=FMB. R=CBN. R=AWR.
2491	1	9	2.43	8	99.95	0.05	C	533.99	56	10	Mixed-race Blacks, Jamaicans, other Caribbean islanders. D=RCC.
2492	1	10	2.43	8	99.90	0.10	C	496.03	63	10	Spanish-speaking Gypsies, some nomadic, most settled. D=RCC.
2493	1	7	2.65	8	99.98	0.02	C	590.55	53	10	Mixed-race: White/Indian. D=RCC(56 Dioceses). M=MXY,ORSA,IMC,CMF,OFMCap,CSSR,OCD,SDB,CM,SMM,WEC,FMB. T=CBN. R=AWR.
2494	1	10	2.71	8	99.97	0.03	C	587.72	55	10	Black/White. D=RCC. M=MXY,ORSA,IMC,CMF,OFMCap,CSSR,OCD,SDB,CM,SMM,WEC,FMB. T=CBN. R=AWR.
2495	1	9	2.58	8	99.97	0.03	C	584.75	57	10	Descendants of original Spaniards. D=RCC. M=MXY,ORSA,IMC,CMF,OFMCap,CSSR,OCD,SDB,CM,SMM,WEC,FMB. Many Cath charismatics. T=CBN. R=AWR.
2496	2	7	2.44	0	59.00	41.00	B	43.07	146	6	Caqueta Region. Agriculturalists. Animists 80%. D=RCC,Independent Pentecostal Ch. M=Mision de Cristo,GRI,SIL.
2497	1	7	2.43	8	99.80	0.20	C	394.20	70	9	Tolima Region. Tribe has not used Coyaima language for several generations. Animists 20%. D=RCC.
2498	0	9	2.43	8	99.95	0.05	C	537.46	54	10	English-based creole on San Andres & Providencia Islands. 80% literate in English, 90% in Spanish. M=FMB.
2499	1	6	2.43	0	99.80	0.20	C	347.48	72	9	Vaupes Region, also in Brazil. Lingua franca. Animists 20%. D=RCC. M=NTM,WEC,SIL.
2500	1	5	3.22	0	42.00	58.00	A	15.33	256	5	Also in Venezuela. Nomadic bands of hunter-gatherers. Animists 90%. D=RCC. M=TEAM,SIL.
2501	1	6	2.05	0	98.00	2.00	C	214.62	85	8	Also in Brazil and Venezuela. Animists 40%. D=RCC. M=NTM,WEC.

Continued overleaf

Table 8-2 continued

PEOPLE		POPULATION				IDENTITY CODE		LANGUAGE		CHURCH		MINISTRY						SCRIPTURE		
Ref 1	*Ethnic name* 2	*P%* 3	*In 1995* 4	*In 2000* 5	*In 2025* 6	*Race* 7	*Language* 8	*Autoglossonym* 9	*S* 10	*AC* 11	*Members* 12	*Jayuh* 13-17	*d* 18	*wa* 19	*xc* 20	*mc* 21	*mi* 22	*Biblioglossonym* 23	*Pub* 24-26	*ss* 27
2502	Desano	0.00227	875	961	1,357	MIR39d	88-KAAE-ba	desâna		60.00	576	0....	10	6	6	4	1	Desano	PN.	.
2503	Eastern Tunebo	0.00114	439	482	681	MIR39e	83-EFAB-c	east tunebo		60.00	289	0....	10	6	4	4	1		pn.	.
2504	French	0.02000	7,708	8,464	11,952	CEW21b	51-AABI-d	general français	2	83.00	7,025	1B.uh	10	9	14	5	1	French	PNB	b
2505	German	0.01000	3,854	4,232	5,976	CEW19m	52-ABCE-a	standard hoch-deutsch		88.00	3,724	2B.uh	10	9	13	5	2	German*	PNB	b
2506	Guajibo (Guahibo, Guayba)	0.05556	21,414	23,514	33,201	MIR39d	88-GAAA-a	proper guahibo		85.00	19,987	0....	10	8	11	5	3	Guajibo*	PN.	b
2507	Guajiro	0.38460	148,231	162,768	229,829	MIR39a	81-ACAA-a	wayúu		20.00	32,554	0....	9	5	8	4	3	Guajiro*	P..	.
2508	Guambiano	0.03704	14,276	15,676	22,134	MIR39e	83-GAAC-a	wambiano		70.00	10,973	0....	10	7	8	4	2	Guambiano	P..	.
2509	Guanano (Anana)	0.00163	628	690	974	MIR39d	88-KAAD-b	cûtiria		70.00	483	0....	10	7	6	4	3	Guanano	PN.	.
2510	Guaviare Macusa (Macu)	0.00085	328	360	508	MIR39d	88-ICCA-a	guaviare		1.90	7	0....	6	4	4	1	2		...	.
2511	Guayabero	0.00365	1,407	1,545	2,181	MIR39d	88-GAAA-e	guayabero		80.00	1,236	0....	10	8	6	3	2	Guayabero	Pn.	.
2512	Han Chinese	0.02265	8,730	9,586	13,535	MSY42a	79-AAAB-ba	kuo-yü		60.00	5,751	2Bsuh	10	7	8	5	1	Chinese: Kuoyu*	PNB	b
2513	Highland Inga	0.02848	10,977	12,053	17,019	MIR39g	85-FAAA-a	sibundoy		70.00	8,437	0....	10	7	7	4	1	Inga: Highland	PN.	.
2514	Hupda Maku	0.00045	173	190	269	MIR39d	88-IBAA-a	proper hupde		20.00	38	0....	9	5	6	2	1	Hupde	...	n
2515	Ica (Arhuaco)	0.01764	6,799	7,465	10,541	MIR39e	83-EDBA-a	ihka		20.00	1,493	0....	9	5	6	4	2		...	.
2516	Jewish (Greek, Turkish)	0.02704	10,422	11,444	16,159	CMT35	51-AABB-ho	colombiano		0.10	11	1B.uh	5	4	2	1	0		pnb	b
2517	Jungle Inga (Mocoa)	0.02171	8,367	9,188	12,973	MIR39g	85-FAAA-b	caquetá		20.00	1,838	0....	9	5	6	2	1		pn.	.
2518	Macuna	0.00134	516	567	801	MIR39d	88-KAAF-aa	macuna		70.00	397	0....	10	7	6	4	1	Macuna	PN.	.
2519	Malayo	0.00948	3,654	4,012	5,665	MIR39e	83-EDCA-a	wiwa		60.00	2,407	0....	10	7	6	4	2	Malayo	...	.
2520	Meneca Huitoto	0.00484	1,865	2,048	2,892	MIR39d	84-BABA	meneca cluster		65.00	1,331	0....	10	7	6	4	2	Huitoto: Minica*	PN.	b
2521	Motilon	0.00597	2,301	2,527	3,568	MIR39e	83-EHAA-a	barí		70.00	1,769	0....	10	7	6	5	1	Motilon	...	.
2522	Muinane	0.00056	216	237	335	MIR39d	84-BABA-b	muinane-meneca		80.00	190	0....	10	8	6	5	1	Huitoto: Muinani*	PN.	b
2523	Muinane Huitoto	0.00014	54	59	84	MIR39d	84-BABA-a	nüpode		79.00	47	0....	10	8	5	4	1	Huitoto, Nipode	Pn.	n
2524	Muisca Chibcha (Mosca)	0.00500	1,927	2,116	2,988	MIR39e	51-AABB-ho	colombiano		90.00	1,904	1B.uh	10	5	11	2	1		pnb	b
2525	Murui Huitoto (Witoto)	0.00541	2,085	2,290	3,233	MIR39d	84-BAAA-b	central murui		85.00	1,946	0....	10	8	11	5	1	Huitoto: Murui*	PN.	b
2526	Napo Lowland Quichua	0.02000	7,708	8,464	11,952	MIR39g	85-FAAB-ab	napo-m.		90.00	7,618	0....	10	8	11	5	1	Quichua: Napo*	Pn.	.
2527	Natagaimas	0.00040	154	169	239	MIR39d	51-AABB-ho	colombiano		90.00	152	1B.uh	10	8	11	5	1		pnb	b
2528	Northern Barasano (Bara)	0.00170	655	719	1,016	MIR39d	88-KAAF-a	macuna-barasano		40.00	288	0....	9	5	6	4	1	Barasano: Northern*	PN.	.
2529	Northern Embena (Choco)	0.04489	17,301	18,998	26,825	MIR39e	83-EIAA-a	sambú		85.00	16,148	0....	10	8	10	5	2	Embera, Northern	PN.	.
2530	Nukak (Maku)	0.00031	119	131	185	MIR39d	88-ICCA-b	nukak maku		2.00	3	0....	6	4	5	1	2	Nukak Maku	...	.
2531	Ocaina	0.00014	54	59	84	MIR39d	84-BAFA-a	proper ocaina		79.00	47	0....	10	8	6	5	1	Ocaina	P..	.
2532	Paez	0.25812	99,484	109,240	154,247	MIR39e	83-GBAA-a	paez		65.00	71,006	0....	10	7	7	4	3	Paez	PN.	.
2533	Palenquero Bush Negro	0.00773	2,979	3,271	4,619	NFB71b	51-AACB-c	palanquero		97.00	3,173	1c.u.	10	7	11	5	1		pnb	.
2534	Palestinian Arab	0.10000	38,542	42,321	59,758	CMT30	12-AACF-f	syro-palestinian		20.00	8,464	1Asuh	9	6	8	4	2	Arabic: Lebanese*	Pnb	b
2535	Paya-Pucuro Cuna (Kuna)	0.00208	802	880	1,243	MIR39e	83-EGAA-bb	cuna-colombia		70.00	616	1....	10	7	6	5	2	Kuna, Border	PN.	.
2536	Piajao (Pijao)	0.00100	385	423	598	MIR39c	51-AABB-ho	colombiano		90.00	381	1B.uh	10	8	11	5	1		pnb	b
2537	Piapoco	0.01111	4,282	4,702	6,639	MIR39a	81-AFAC-a	tsase		50.00	2,351	0....	10	6	6	5	3	Piapoco	PN.	.
2538	Piratapuyo (Waikino)	0.00153	590	648	914	MIR39d	88-KAAD-c	pirá-tapuyo		60.00	389	0....	10	7	6	3	1	Piratapuyo	PN.	b
2539	Puinave (Puinabe)	0.00823	3,172	3,483	4,918	MIR39d	88-HAAA-a	west puinave		60.00	2,090	0....	10	7	6	4	2	Puinave	PN.	.
2540	Quaiquer	0.06820	26,285	28,863	40,755	MIR39e	83-HAAA-a	coaiquer		65.00	18,761	0....	10	7	6	3	1	Cuaiquer	P..	.
2541	Rio Arauca Guajibo	0.00058	224	245	347	MIR39d	88-GAAA-b	playero		50.00	123	0....	10	6	6	3	1		pn.	b
2542	Saija (Epera)	0.01022	3,939	4,325	6,107	MIR39c	83-EIAA-i	saija		60.00	2,595	0....	10	7	6	4	1	Embera-saija	Pn.	.
2543	Saliba	0.00741	2,856	3,136	4,428	MIR39d	88-FAAB-a	sáliba		55.00	1,725	0....	10	6	6	4	1	Saliba	...	b
2544	Siona (Sioni)	0.00060	231	254	359	MIR39d	88-KAAA-b	piohé-siona		60.00	152	0....	10	7	6	5	1	Siona	PN.	.
2545	Siriano	0.00080	308	339	478	MIR39d	88-KAAE-bb	siriana		70.00	237	0....	10	7	6	5	1	Siriano	Pn.	b
2546	Southern Barasano	0.00108	416	457	645	MIR39d	88-KAAF-ae	south barasano		40.00	183	0....	9	6	6	4	1		pn.	.
2547	Spaniard	0.03000	11,562	12,696	17,927	CEW21k	51-AABB-ho	colombiano		96.00	12,189	1B.uh	10	9	15	5	1		pnb	b
2548	Syro-Lebanese Arab	0.04900	18,885	20,737	29,281	CMT30	12-AACF-f	syro-palestinian		30.00	6,221	1Asuh	9	8	7	0	0	Arabic: Lebanese*	Pnb	b
2549	Tado	0.00298	1,149	1,261	1,781	MIR39c	83-EFAC-a	chibcha		80.00	1,009	0....	10	7	7	4	1		...	.
2550	Tanimuca-Retuama	0.00127	489	537	759	MIR39d	88-KAAA-d	yaúna-opaina		30.00	161	0....	9	5	5	2	1	Tanimuca-retuara	pn.	.
2551	Tariano	0.00090	347	381	538	MIR39a	88-VBBA-d	tucano-dyapá		50.00	190	0....	10	6	6	3	1		...	.
2552	Tatuyo	0.00127	489	537	759	MIR39d	88-KAAE-cc	tatuyo		20.00	107	0....	9	5	5	2	1	Tatuyo	PN.	.
2553	Ticuna	0.01515	5,839	6,412	9,053	MIR39d	88-MAAA-a	ticuna		40.00	2,565	0....	9	5	6	3	1	Ticuna	PN.	.
2554	Tucano	0.00656	2,528	2,776	3,920	MIR39d	88-VBBA-d	tucano-dyapá		60.00	1,666	0....	10	6	6	3	1		...	.
2555	Tupi-Guarani Pidgin	0.01235	4,760	5,227	7,380	MIR39z	82-AAIG-a	nhengatu		90.00	4,704	0....	10	8	12	5	1	Nyengato*	PN.	b
2556	Tuyuca (Tejuca)	0.00099	382	419	592	MIR39d	88-KAAE-ab	tuyuca		60.00	251	0....	10	7	6	4	2	Tuyuca	Pn.	n
2557	USA White	0.04000	15,417	16,929	23,903	CEW19s	52-ABAC-s	general american		78.00	13,204	1Bsuh	10	9	9	5	1	English*	PNB	b
2558	Vlach Gypsy	0.11475	44,226	48,564	68,572	CNN25f	59-ACBA-au	vlach-colombia		90.00	43,707	1c...	10	8	11	4	1		pn.	b
2559	Waunana (Chanco)	0.00725	2,794	3,068	4,332	MIR39c	83-EIAB	noanama cluster		65.00	1,994	0....	10	7	6	3	1	Waunana*	PN.	.
2560	Western Tunebo	0.00200	771	846	1,195	MIR39e	83-EFAA-a	west tunebo		40.00	339	0....	9	6	5	3	1		...	.
2561	Yahuna (Opaina)	0.00007	27	30	42	MIR39d	88-KAAF-aa	macuna		50.00	15	0....	10	7	6	4	0	Macuna	PN.	.
2562	Yari	0.00180	694	762	1,076	MIR39c	80-AHAA-c	yari		1.00	8	0....	6	5	3	1	0		...	.
2563	Yucuna	0.00296	1,141	1,253	1,769	MIR39a	81-AFGA-a	proper yucuna		80.00	1,002	0....	10	8	6	4	1	Yucuna	PN.	.
2564	Yukpa (Northern Motilon)	0.01055	4,066	4,465	6,304	MIR39c	80-AAAA	yucpa cluster		75.00	3,349	0....	10	8	6	4	1	Yukpa	...	.
2565	Yuruti	0.00067	258	284	400	MIR39d	88-KAAE-ce	yuruti		60.00	170	0....	10	7	6	4	1	Yuruti	Pn.	.
2566	Zambo	1.00000	385,416	423,214	597,579	NFB71b	51-AABB-ho	colombiano		90.00	380,892	1B.uh	10	8	11	5	1		pnb	b
2567	other minor peoples	0.20000	77,083	84,643	119,516	...				68.00	57,557		10	7	6	4	2			
	Comoros	**100.00000**	**516,072**	**592,749**	**989,515**					**1.19**	**7,062**									
2568	Arab	0.10000	516	593	990	CMT30	12-AACF-pg	comores	15	0.00	0	1Asuh	0	2	2	0	0		pnb	b
2569	Comorian (Mwali)	4.50000	23,223	26,674	44,528	NAB57j	99-AUSM-t	ki-mwali		0.02	5	1csu.	3	4	0	1	0		pnb	b
2570	Comorian (Ngazija)	48.86000	252,153	289,617	483,477	NAB57j	99-AUSM-s	shi-ngazidya	100	0.02	58	1csu.	3	4	5	1	2	Comorian*	PNb	b
2571	Comorian (Nzwani)	43.74000	225,730	259,268	432,814	NAB57j	99-AUSM-u	shi-nzuani		0.02	52	1csu.	3	4	2	1	2	Comorian	PNb	b
2572	French	0.40000	2,064	2,371	3,958	CEW21b	51-AABI-d	general français	20	80.00	1,897	1B.uh	10	9	14	2	3	French	PNB	b
2573	Makua (Makhua)	1.60000	8,257	9,484	15,832	NAB57b	99-AUSY-a	e-meeto		40.00	3,794	2.s..	9	5	6	2	0		pnb	b
2574	Malay	0.12000	619	711	1,187	MSY44k	31-PHAA-b	bahasa-malaysia		0.90	6	1asuh	5	1	2	0	0	Malay	PNB	b
2575	Reunionese Creole	0.10000	516	593	990	NAN58	51-AACC-m	réunioné		95.00	563	1cs..	10	8	12	2	2		pnb	b
2576	Sakalava	0.11000	568	652	1,088	MSY44j	31-LDAD	west malagasy cluster		28.00	183	0A.u.	9	5	7	2	3		...	b
2577	Swahili	0.13000	671	771	1,286	NAB57j	99-AUSM-b	standard ki-swahili	30	0.00	0	4Asu.	0	3	2	1	0	Kiswahili*	PNB	b
2578	other minor peoples	0.34000	1,755	2,015	3,364	...				25.00	504		9	4	7	1	0			
	Congo-Brazzaville	**100.00000**	**2,560,671**	**2,943,464**	**5,689,140**					**79.26**	**2,332,876**									
2579	Akwa	0.80000	20,485	23,548	45,513	NAB57c	99-AUFF-a	akwa		75.00	17,661	0....	10	7	7	3	1		...	.
2580	Babole	0.18200	4,660	5,357	10,354	NAB57k	99-AUFC-c	southern mbomitaba		80.00	4,286	0....	10	9	8	5	1	Babole	...	b
2581	Bakwele (Bakwili)	0.45000	11,523	13,246	25,601	NAB57c	99-AUDH-a	be-kwil		80.00	10,596	0....	10	5	7	4	0	Bekwel	...	.
2582	Bangi (Bobangi)	2.00000	51,213	58,869	113,783	NAB57c	99-AUFN-a	lo-bo-bangi		75.00	44,152	0....	10	7	7	5	2	Bobangi*	PN.	.
2583	Bangom (Angom)	0.15000	3,841	4,415	8,534	NAB57k	99-AUDJ	ungom cluster		70.00	3,091	0....	10	7	7	4	1	Ngom	P..	.
2584	Bayaka Pygmy (Binga, Aka)	1.00000	25,607	29,435	56,891	BYG12	93-ABAF-f	yakpa		30.00	8,830	0....	9	5	4	2	1		...	b
2585	Bembe (Keenge)	0.10000	2,561	2,943	5,689	NAB57b	99-AUID-d	ma-bembe		70.00	2,060	0....	10	7	7	5	1		...	b
2586	Bomitaba (Bamitaba)	0.31800	8,143	9,360	18,091	NAB57c	99-AUFC-b	central m-bomitaba		75.00	7,020	0....	10	5	5	5	3		...	n
2587	Bomwali (Bumali)	1.10000	28,167	32,378	62,581	NAB57c	99-AUDI-a	bo-mwali		70.00	22,665	0....	10	6	7	4	2		...	.
2588	Bongili (Bokiba, Bongwili)	0.21800	5,582	6,417	12,402	NAB57c	99-AUFD-a	proper bu-ngili		75.00	4,813	0....	10	7	7	5	1	Bungili*	PN.	.
2589	Bonjo	0.10000	2,561	2,943	5,689	NAB66z	93-AAAA-m	bonjo		70.00	2,060	0.s..	10	7	7	4	1		pnb	.
2590	British	0.06000	1,536	1,766	3,413	CEW19i	52-ABAC-b	standard-english		78.00	1,378	3Bsuh	10	9	13	5	1		PNB	b
2591	Buraka-Gbanziri	0.04500	1,152	1,325	2,560	BYG12	93-ADAB-a	buraka		10.00	132	0....	8	5	4	2	2		...	.
2592	Bwaka (Ngbaka Mabo)	3.00000	76,820	88,304	170,674	NAB66z	93-ADBA-a	ngbaka-ma'bo		94.00	83,006	0.s..	10	8	11	5	1	Ngbaka: Ma'bo*	Pnb	b
2593	Central Teke (Aboo, Tyo)	2.06200	52,801	60,694	117,310	NAB57k	99-AURD-l	a-boong		79.00	47,948	0....	10	7	7	5	1	Teke, Central	p..	.
2594	Cuban White	0.00500	128	147	284	CLT27	51-AABB-hi	cubano		20.00	29	1B.uh	9	5	2	3	0		pnb	b
2595	Dondo (Kaamba)	0.10000	2,561	2,943	5,689	NAB57b	99-AURG-e	ki-doondo		60.00	1,766	1cs..	10	7	7	5	1		pnb	b
2596	Eastern Teke	1.20000	30,728	35,322	68,270	NAB57k	99-AURD-w	li-bali		73.00	25,785	0....	10	7	7	5	2	Teke, Eastern	P..	b
2597	Fang (Pangwe)	0.20000	5,121	5,887	11,378	NAB57k	99-AUCC-u	fang		85.00	5,004	1....	10	9	13	5	3	Fang: Gabon*	PNB	b
2598	French	0.40000	10,243	11,774	22,757	CEW21b	51-AABI-d	general français	55	79.00	9,301	1B.uh	10	9	14	5	1	French	PNB	b
2599	Ganzi (Banziri Pygmy)	0.09000	2,305	2,649	5,120	BYG12	93-ADDA-c	ganzi		40.00	1,060	0....	9	5	4	2	1		...	.
2600	Gbaya	0.10000	2,561	2,943	5,689	NAB66c	93-AAAA-a	vehicular gbaya		75.00	2,208	0.s..	10	5	5	5	1	Gbaya: Gbea*	PNB	b
2601	Greek	0.02000	512	589	1,138	CEW20	56-AAAA-c	dhimotiki		95.00	559	2B.uh	10	9	11	5	1	Greek: Modern	PNB	b
2602	Gundi Pygmy	0.10000	2,561	2,943	5,689	BYG12	93-ADDA-d	gundi		65.00	1,913	0....	10	5	6	2	1		...	.
2603	Han Chinese	0.01000	256	294	569	MSY42a	79-AAAB-ba	kuo-yü		2.90	9	2Bsuh	6	3	8	1	0	Chinese: Kuoyu*	PNB	b
2604	Hausa	0.20000	5,121	5,887	11,378	NAB60a	19-HAAB-a	hausa		0.09	5	4Asu.	4	3	2	1	0	Hausa	PNB	b
2605	Japanese	0.01000	256	294	569	MSY45a	45-CAAA-a	koku-go		2.00	6	1B.uh	6	4	2	5	0	Japanese	PNB	b
2606	Kako	0.30000	7,682	8,830	17,067	NAB57k	99-AUDA-a	east kako		60.00	5,298	0....	10	6	7	4	1	Kako*	P..	.
2607	Kongo (Congo)	16.83700	431,140	495,591	957,881	NAB57b	99-AURG-f	central ki-koongo	52	86.04	426,407	4as..	10	9	13	5	3	Kongo	PNB	b
2608	Kongo (Monokutuba)	4.39700	112,593	129,424	250,151	NAB57b	99-AURG-ac	mono-ku-tuba	78	76.40	98,880	4as..	10	9	7	5	3	Munukutuba	Pnb	b
2609	Kota	0.30000	7,682	8,830	17,067	NAB57c	99-AUEA-c	i-kota		70.00	6,181	0....	10	5	6	4	2	Ikota*	P..	.
2610	Koyo (Kuyu)	0.90000	23,046	26,491	51,202	NAB57c	99-AUFG-a	koyo		65.00	17,219	0....	10	5	6	4	1		...	.
2611	Kuba	1.00000	25,607	29,435	56,891	NAB57c	99-AUFI-a	south li-kuba		65.00	19,133	0....	10	6	7	4	1		...	.
2612	Kunyi	8.00000	204,854	235,477	455,131	NAB57b	99-AURG-d	ki-kunyi		90.50	213,107	1cs..	10	7	7	4	2		pnb	b
2613	Kwala (Likouala)	0.80000	20,485	23,548	45,513	NAB57c	99-AUFJ-a	li-kwala		60.00	14,129	0....	10	6	7	4	1		...	.
2614	Lali (Lari)	3.00000	76,820	88,304	170,674	NAB57b	05-CAAA-a	bele-for		69.00	60,930	0....	10	7	7	5	3		...	b
2615	Lebanese Arab	0.02000	512	589	1,138	CMT30	12-AACF-f	syro-palestinian		50.00	294	1Asuh	10	7	1	4	2	Arabic: Lebanese*	Pnb	b
2616	Lingala (Ngala)	3.00000	76,820	88,304	170,674	NAB57c	99-AUIF-b	vehicular lingala	70	73.00	64,462	4asu.	10	9	12	5	1	Lingala	PNB	b
2617	Lobala	1.00000	25,607	29,435	56,891	NAB57c	99-AUFK-a	lo-bala		60.00	17,661	0....	10	6	7	3	2	Lobala	...	b
2618	Lumbu	0.10000	2,561	2,943	5,689	NAB57k	99-AURA-f	i-lumbu		70.00	2,060	0.s..	10	6	7	3	1	Ilumbu*	Pnb	.
2619	Mangala	0.15000	3,841	4,415	8,534	NAB57k	99-AUIF-d	mangala-4		80.00	3,532	1csu.	10	6	7	3	1		pnb	.
2620	Mbamba	0.50000	12,803	14,717	28,446	NAB57k	99-AURC-c	le-mbaama		61.00	8,978	0....	10	7	7	3	2		...	.
2621	Mbangwe	0.05000	1,280	1,472	2,845	NAB57k	99-AUDL-a	m-bangwe		63.00	927	0....	10	7	7	3	1		...	.

Continued opposite

Table 8-2 continued

EVANGELIZATION								EVANGELISM			ADDITIONAL DESCRIPTIVE DATA
Ref 1	*D* 28	*aC* 29	*CG%* 30	*r* 31	*E* 32	*U* 33	*W* 34	*e* 35	*R* 36	*T* 37	*Locations, civil divisions, literacy, religions, church history, denominations, dioceses, church growth, missions, agencies, ministries, movements* 38
2502	1	7	2.24	0	97.00	3.00	C	212.43	83	8	Most live in Brazil. Animists 40%. D=RCC. M=SIL.
2503	1	7	2.44	0	94.00	6.00	C	205.86	90	8	Eastern plains, Andes foothills. Hunter-gatherers, fishermen. Animists 40%. D=RCC.
2504	1	10	2.43	8	99.83	0.17	C	475.63	60	10	Settlers, expatriates from France, in professions, industry. Nonreligious 13%. D=RCC.
2505	2	10	2.43	8	99.88	0.12	C	526.76	60	10	Expatriates from Germany in industry, commerce. Nonreligious 12%. D=Congregaciones Luteranas,NAC.
2506	1	5	2.43	0	99.85	0.15	C	412.63	64	10	Casanare, also in Venezuela. Animists 15%. D=RCC. M=NTM,WEC,SIL,NTMC.
2507	4	6	2.68	0	60.00	40.00	B	43.80	168	6	Many in Venezuela. Pastoralists. Animists 70%. Mass conversions to Baha'i World Faith. D=RCC,ICFG,CBC,Evangelical Ch. M=SIL,SAIM,FMB.
2508	1	6	2.43	0	99.70	0.30	C	275.94	78	8	Central Andes range near Popayan, Cauca. Animists 30%. D=RCC. M=CMA,SIL.
2509	1	8	2.42	0	99.70	0.30	C	281.05	78	8	Vaupes Department, also in Brazil. Fishermen. Strong christopaganism; animists 30%. D=RCC. M=WBT,NTMC,SIL.
2510	0	6	1.96	0	24.90	75.10	A	1.72	293	4	Jungle, Guaviare region. Isolated, evasive hunters. Animists 98%. M=NTM,NTMC.
2511	1	7	2.64	0	99.80	0.20	C	341.64	78	9	Upper Guaviare river. Basically monolingual. Animists 20%. D=RCC. M=NTM,SIL.
2512	1	10	2.43	7	99.60	0.40	C	282.51	65	8	Settlers, in business. Mahayana Buddhists/Chinese folk-religionists 40%. D=RCC.
2513	1	6	2.64	0	99.70	0.30	C	275.94	84	8	Sibundoy Valley. Agriculturalists, craftsmen. Animists 30%. D=RCC. M=SIL.
2514	1	7	2.57	0	50.00	50.00	B	36.50	179	5	Majority live in Brazil. Jungle. Some 50% are bilingual in Tucano. Nomadic. Animists 80%. D=RCC.
2515	2	5	2.43	0	53.00	47.00	B	38.69	159	5	Sierra Nevada. Animists 80%. D=RCC,Iglesia Pentecostal Unida(very strong; schism ex UPCI). M=SAM,SIL.
2516	0	10	2.43	8	46.10	53.90	A	0.16	185	3	Greek, Turkish, and German Jews, refugees from Europe. Ashkenazi, Sefardi, Eastern. 4 synagogues.
2517	1	5	2.43	0	52.00	48.00	B	37.96	164	5	Upper Caqueta and Putumayo rivers. Tropical forest, rolling hills. Agriculturalists. Animists 80%. D=RCC. M=SIL.
2518	1	10	2.43	0	99.70	0.30	C	281.05	78	8	Lower Pira-Parana, Vaupes Region. Also in Brazil. Tropical forest. Animists 30%. D=RCC. M=SIL.
2519	1	7	4.35	0	95.00	5.00	C	208.05	144	8	South and east slopes of Sierra Nevada. Animists 40%. D=RCC. M=SAM,SIL.
2520	2	7	1.88	0	99.65	0.35	C	249.11	67	8	Upper Igara-Parana. Animists 35%. D=RCC,ABWE. M=SIL,GRI.
2521	0	6	2.43	0	99.70	0.30	C	263.16	82	8	Oro river. Animists 30%. M=Mission of the Motilone Indians; independent missionaries.
2522	1	7	2.44	0	99.80	0.20	C	353.32	71	9	Amazonas, Upper Cahuinari. All bilingual. Animists 20%. D=RCC. M=SIL.
2523	1	7	2.49	0	99.79	0.21	C	328.71	77	9	Animists 21%. D=RCC. M=GRI.
2524	1	10	2.43	8	99.90	0.10	C	496.03	56	10	Central highlands. Nearly 1 million before extinction in 18th century. All now speak only Spanish. D=RCC.
2525	1	7	3.12	0	99.85	0.15	C	400.22	81	10	Amazonas, Upper Igara-Parana. Also in Peru, Brazil. Animists 15%. D=RCC. M=GRI.
2526	1	7	2.43	4	99.90	0.10	C	450.04	62	10	Putumayo river, also in Ecuador and Peru. Animists 10%. D=RCC.
2527	1	7	2.41	8	99.90	0.10	C	492.75	57	10	Tribe has used Spanish for several generations. Animists 10%. D=RCC.
2528	1	9	2.43	0	78.00	22.00	B	113.88	110	7	Vaupes. Also in Colombia, Brazil. Riverine. Animists 60%. D=RCC. M=SIL.
2529	2	6	4.29	0	99.85	0.15	C	403.32	104	10	Larger number live in Panama. Animists 15%. D=ICFG,Mennonite Brethren. M=NTM, independents.
2530	0	6	1.10	0	26.00	74.00	A	1.89	190	4	Forest. Mainly in Colombia. Animists 98%. M=Amazon Evangelical Mission(Brazil),NTM(Colombia).
2531	1	7	2.49	0	99.79	0.21	C	328.71	77	9	Amazonas, also in Peru. Bilingual in Murui Huitoto, Bora, or Spanish. Animists 21%. D=RCC.
2532	1	5	3.00	0	99.65	0.35	C	249.11	95	8	Central Andes range near Popayan, Cauca. Animists 35%. D=RCC. M=GMU,CMA,SIL.
2533	1	8	2.43	8	99.97	0.03	C	541.69	54	10	Southeast of Cartagena. Bilingual in Spanish. Zaire (Africa) influences. D=RCC.
2534	2	10	6.97	8	81.00	19.00	B	59.13	259	6	Immigrants from Levant. Muslims 80%(Shafi Sunnis). D=Greek Orthodox AD of N&S America,RCC.
2535	1	7	2.43	0	99.70	0.30	C	281.05	76	8	North coastal Region. Also in Panama. Language isolate. Animists 30%. D=RCC. M=OMS,IAMS.
2536	1	7	2.45	8	99.90	0.10	C	492.75	63	10	Tolima Region. Language extinct in 1950s. Traditional religionists/animists 10%. D=RCC.
2537	1	6	2.44	0	90.00	10.00	B	164.25	105	7	Hunter-gatherers. Animists 50%. D=RCC. M=NTM,SIL,NTMC.
2538	2	7	2.44	0	99.60	0.40	C	219.00	86	8	Lower Vaupes, Amazonas. All bilingual. Animists 40%. D=RCC,AoG. M=SIL.
2539	1	6	2.43	0	98.00	2.00	C	214.62	88	8	Guainia; also in Venezuela. Animists 40%. D=RCC. M=NTM,NTMC.
2540	1	6	2.43	0	99.00	1.00	C	234.87	85	8	Others in Ecuador. Tropical forest, agriculturalists. Animists 35%. D=RCC. M=SIL.
2541	1	7	2.44	0	88.00	12.00	B	160.60	98	7	Venezuela border. Acculturated, bilingual, many literates. Animists 50%. D=RCC.
2542	2	6	2.43	0	97.00	3.00	C	212.43	97	8	South Pacific coast. Fishermen, agriculturalists. Animists 40%. D=RCC,NTMC. M=SIL.
2543	1	7	2.43	0	89.00	11.00	B	178.66	96	7	Also in Venezuela. Monolingual. Animists 45%. D=RCC. M=SIL.
2544	1	7	2.41	0	98.00	2.00	C	214.62	87	8	Putumayo river. Animists 40%. D=RCC. M=Asociacion Pro-Indigenas de Colombia; SIL.
2545	1	10	2.45	0	99.70	0.30	C	288.71	76	8	Also in Brazil. Tropical forest, riverine. Bilinguals. Animists 30%. D=RCC. M=SIL.
2546	1	9	1.90	0	77.00	23.00	B	112.42	93	7	Tropical forest, also in Brazil. Animists 60%. D=RCC. M=SIL.
2547	1	10	2.43	8	99.96	0.04	C	578.16	56	10	Descendants of first Spaniard conquerors. Wealthy families, strong Catholics. D=RCC.
2548	0	0	6.64	8	71.00	29.00	B	77.74	283	6	Levantine Arabs. Muslims 70%(Sunnis, some Shias). D=RCC.
2549	1	6	2.44	0	99.80	0.20	C	332.88	83	9	Near Chami, Andes, Ricaralda Region. Animists 20%. D=RCC. M=SIL.
2550	1	7	2.40	0	62.00	38.00	B	67.89	137	6	Amazonas. Animists 70%. D=RCC. M=SIL.
2551	1	7	2.44	0	82.00	18.00	B	149.65	115	7	Also in Brazil. Animists 50%. D=RCC. M=SIL.
2552	0	7	2.40	0	52.00	48.00	B	37.96	163	5	Vaupes, Pira-Pirana headwaters and Upper Papuri. Tropical forest. Animists 80%. M=SIL.
2553	1	6	2.43	0	75.00	25.00	B	109.50	114	7	Amazon river. Most in Brazil and Peru. Language isolate. Animists 60%. D=RCC.
2554	1	6	2.43	0	92.00	8.00	C	201.48	93	8	Upper Papuri river. Also in Brazil. Lingua franca. Animists 40%. D=RCC. M=SIL.
2555	1	7	2.43	0	99.90	0.10	C	443.47	70	10	Modern Tupi. In Vaupes; also in Brazil, Venezuela. Non-Christian religionists 10%. D=RCC. M=NTM.
2556	1	7	2.38	0	97.00	3.00	C	212.43	87	8	Also in Brazil. Animists 40%. D=RCC. M=GRI,SIL.
2557	4	10	3.14	8	99.78	0.22	C	421.35	75	10	Expatriates in industry, commerce. Nonreligious 10%. D=SDA,JWS,CJCLdS,SBC. M=FMB.
2558	1	10	2.80	1	99.90	0.10	C	466.47	74	10	Originally from Romania, also from Albania, Yugoslavia, Bulgaria, Greece, Poland, and 15 other countries. D=RCC.
2559	1	6	2.43	0	99.65	0.35	C	239.62	93	8	San Juan river basin, also in Panama. Animists 35%. D=RCC.
2560	1	6	2.42	0	69.00	31.00	B	100.74	122	7	Santander del Sur. Hunter-gatherers, agriculturalists. Animists 60%. D=RCC.
2561	0	9	2.75	0	87.00	13.00	B	158.77	109	7	Umuna river, which leads to Piraparana river. Yauna language extinct. Animists 50%.
2562	0	7	2.10	0	22.00	78.00	A	0.80	387	3	Yari river, Caqueta region. Animists 99%. Relatively unreached.
2563	1	7	2.43	0	99.80	0.20	C	344.56	80	9	Amazonas. Tropical forest, riverine. Animists 20%. D=RCC. M=SIL.
2564	2	7	2.43	0	99.75	0.25	C	301.12	86	9	Also in Venezuela. Animists 25%. D=Plymouth Brethren, RCC. M=SIL.
2565	1	7	2.46	0	96.00	4.00	C	210.24	90	8	Upper Paca river. Also in Brazil. Animists 40%. D=RCC. M=SIL.
2566	1	10	2.43	8	99.90	0.10	C	509.17	54	10	Spanish-speaking Blacks(Negro/Amerindian). Non-Christian religionists 10%. D=RCC.
2567	0	10	2.43		99.68	0.32	C	253.16	65	8	Koreans (M=PCK-Tonghap), immigrants from most Central and South American countries.
Comoros											
2568	0	8	0.00	7	36.00	64.00	A	0.00	0	1.13	Traders, immigrants, expatriates. Muslims 100%(Shafi Sunnis).
2569	0	6	1.62	5	29.02	70.98	A	0.02	291	2	Coastal, origin in East Africa; islands of Moheli and Anjouan, also some on Mayotte and Madagascar. Literates 25%. Muslims 100%(Shafi Sunnis).
2570	2	5	4.14	5	38.02	61.98	A	0.02	404	2	Grande Comore Island. Muslims 100%(Shafi Sunnis). D=RCC,EJCC(100 adherents). M=AIM,OFMCap.
2571	2	5	4.03	5	35.02	64.98	A	0.02	430	2	Muslims 100%(Shafi Sunnis). D=RCC,EJCC. M=AIM,OFMCap.
2572	3	10	2.99	8	99.80	0.20	C	440.92	72	10	Expatriates in development. Nonreligious 20%. D=RCC(AA-Comoro Islands),EJCC,SDA.
2573	0	6	6.12	0	79.00	21.00	B	115.34	263	7	Black settlers from mainland. Animists 45%, Muslims 33%.
2574	0	6	1.81	5	37.90	62.10	A	1.24	181	4	All strong Muslims 99%(Shafi Sunnis).
2575	2	10	4.11	8	99.95	0.05	C	530.52	93	10	Immigrants from Reunion. D=RCC(AA-Comoro Islands),SDA.
2576	3	9	2.95	4	75.00	25.00	B	76.65	154	6	Originally from Madagascar. Animists 72%. D=EJCC,SDA,RCC.
2577	0	10	0.00	5	41.00	59.00	A	0.00	0	1.13	Coastal immigrants from East Africa. Muslims 100%(Shafi Sunnis).
2578	0	10	4.00		51.00	49.00	B	46.53	215	6	Other Malagasy peoples(EJCC,RCC), Antalaotra, Seychellois, Morisyen, other Black Africans. Muslims 60%, Animists 10%.
Congo-Brazzaville											
2579	1	8	7.76	0	99.75	0.25	C	303.86	228	9	Cuvette Region, Makoua District. Animists 5%. D=RCC.
2580	2	7	6.25	0	99.80	0.20	C	353.32	182	9	South half of Epera District, northeastern Congo. Animists 20%. D=RCC,Pentecostals. M=UWM.
2581	0	8	7.21	0	99.80	0.20	C	335.80	207	9	Sangha Region along border with Cameroon, from Gabon to Ouesso. Also in Gabon and Cameroon. Traditional religionists(animists) 10%.
2582	3	7	8.76	0	99.75	0.25	C	325.76	236	9	On Congo river, Cuvette Region, Mossaka District. Primarily in Zaire. Animists 5%. D=ECZ-CBFZ,RCC,AICs. M=BMS,UBS.
2583	1	7	5.90	0	99.70	0.30	C	270.83	199	8	Cuvette Region, northwest of Mbomo. Also in Gabon. Animists 30%. D=RCC.
2584	1	7	7.02	0	59.00	41.00	B	64.60	377	6	Nomadic Pygmies in equatorial rain forest. Animists 50%. D=EEL. M=UWM.
2585	1	8	5.47	0	99.70	0.30	C	281.05	173	8	Dialect of Kongo. Bouenza Region, east of Madingou. Animists 30%. D=RCC.
2586	4	7	6.77	0	99.75	0.25	C	314.81	196	9	Likouala Region, Epena District. Also in CAR. Related to Bongili. Animists 25%. D=RCC,EEL,EBCP,AICs. M=UWM,Orebro Mission,SIL.
2587	2	7	8.03	0	99.70	0.30	C	275.94	241	8	Sangasanga. Sangha Region, around Ouesso. Animists 5%. D=RCC,AICs.
2588	2	7	6.37	0	99.75	0.25	C	317.55	185	9	Sangha Region, on and near Sangha river south of Ouesso. Animists 25%. D=Eglise Baptiste du Congo Populaire,RCC. M=Orebro Mission.
2589	1	7	5.47	1	99.70	0.30	C	288.71	167	8	Likouala Region, Dongou and Impfondo Districts. Animists 30%. D=Eglise Evangelique de la Likouala. M=UWM.
2590	1	10	5.05	8	99.78	0.22	C	429.89	113	10	Expatriates from Britain, in education: administrators, teachers. D=EEC.
2591	2	7	2.61	0	39.00	61.00	A	14.23	261	5	Pygmies in equatorial rain forest in north. Also in Zaire, CAR. Animists 90%. D=EEC,RCC.
2592	1	7	9.44	0	99.94	0.06	C	487.20	210	10	Many in CAR, also in Zaire. Animists 1%. D=ECZ(CECU).
2593	1	7	5.52	0	99.79	0.21	C	337.37	171	9	In Ngabe, Djambala Districts, Plateaux Region. A few in Zaire. Animists 1%. D=AICs. M=SIL.
2594	0	10	3.42	8	69.00	31.00	B	50.37	170	6	Remnant of troops and advisers from Cuba. Nonreligious and atheists 80%.
2595	1	7	5.31	1	99.60	0.40	C	238.71	170	8	Bouenza Region, in 4 Districts. Dialect of Kongo. Animists 40%. D=RCC.
2596	2	7	8.17	0	99.73	0.27	C	301.08	242	9	On Congo river, Pool Region, close to Brazzaville. Primarily in Zaire. Animists 2%. D=RCC,AICs.
2597	3	7	6.41	8	99.85	0.15	C	465.37	150	10	Mainly in Gabon, Equatorial Guinea, Cameroon, a few in Congo, in extreme northwest. Animists 5%. D=EEC,RCC,AICs.
2598	1	10	3.12	8	99.79	0.21	C	432.52	75	10	Expatriate government and business employees from France. Nonreligious 13%. D=RCC.
2599	1	7	4.77	0	69.00	31.00	B	100.74	233	7	Pygmies in equatorial rain forest in north. Also in CAR, Zaire. Animists 50%. D=RCC.
2600	1	8	5.55	4	99.75	0.25	C	342.18	162	9	In Sangha Region, scattered areas on Cameroon border. Mainly in CAR, Cameroon, Nigeria. Animists 5%. D=RCC.
2601	1	10	4.83	7	99.95	0.05	C	561.73	98	10	Traders, immigrants from Greece. D=Greek Orthodox Ch(AD-Central Africa, under P-Alexandria).
2602	1	7	5.39	0	97.00	3.00	C	230.13	183	8	Pygmies in equatorial rain forest. Animists 25%. D=RCC.
2603	0	10	2.22	7	57.90	42.10	B	6.12	136	4	Immigrants in business. Chinese folk-religionists/Buddhists 95%. A few nonreligious, a few Christians.
2604	0	10	1.62	5	48.09	51.91	A	0.15	161	3	Traders from francophone North and West Africa. Muslims 100%(Maliki Sunnis).
2605	0	10	1.81	7	53.00	47.00	B	3.86	132	4	New-Religionists from Japan, following Shinto sect Tenrikyo 80%. Begun in Brazzaville in 1966; 4 stations, dispensary.
2606	1	7	6.47	1	97.00	3.00	C	212.43	234	8	Scattered area in north Likouala Region, on Ibenga and Motaba rivers. Also in CAR, Cameroon. Animists 30%. D=RCC.
2607	3	8	5.84	5	99.86	0.14	C	502.59	125	10	Pool Region, west and northwest of Brazzaville. Animists 0.6%, Muslims 5%. D=RCC(3 Dioceses),EBCP,AICs. M=CSSp,LBI,Orebro Mission.
2608	6	8	4.32	5	99.76	0.24	C	394.30	112	9	Lingua franca along roads and railroads; close to Kituba. Animists 0.5%, nonreligious. D=EJCSK,ENAC,SA,ECC,RCC,many AICs. M=SMF,MCCN,CSSp,SIL.
2609	2	7	6.64	2	99.70	0.30	C	278.49	204	8	Cuvette Region, west of Mbomo; Sangha Region, Liouesso area. Primarily in Gabon. Animists 20%. D=EEC,RCC.
2610	1	7	7.74	0	99.65	0.35	C	237.25	252	8	Cuvette Region, Owando District, around Owando. Animists 5%. D=RCC.
2611	1	7	7.85	0	99.65	0.35	C	239.62	253	8	Above mouth of Sangha river on Congo river, Cuvette Region. Animists 5%. D=RCC.
2612	2	8	5.11	5	99.91	0.09	C	483.92	123	10	Bouenza and Niari Regions, south of Makabana to Zaire border. Dialect of Kongo. Animists 0.5%. D=RCC,AICs.
2613	1	7	7.52	0	96.00	4.00	C	210.24	257	8	Cuvette Region, on lower reaches of Likouala-Mossaka/Sangha rivers. Animists 15%. D=RCC.
2614	4	7	3.94	5	99.69	0.31	C	297.18	125	8	Animists 1%. Widespread indigenous churches. D=Mouvement Croix-Koma ('Nailed to the Cross'),EJCSK,SA,RCC(M-Brazzaville).
2615	2	10	3.44	8	99.50	0.50	B	195.27	106	7	Traders. Muslims 50%(Sunnis). D=Greek Orthodox Ch(AD-Central Africa),RCC(Maronites).
2616	2	7	6.17	5	99.73	0.27	C	378.35	147	9	In center and north. Primarily in Zaire, also CAR. Animists 2%. D=RCC,AICs. M=UBS. Major language of evangelization.
2617	2	7	7.76	0	97.00	3.00	C	212.43	261	8	Primarily in Zaire. Cuvette Region. Animists 10%. D=ECZ,RCC.
2618	1	8	5.47	1	99.70	0.30	C	288.71	176	8	Niari Region, Kibangou District near Gabon border. Animists 30%. D=RCC. M=SFM.
2619	1	7	6.04	1	99.80	0.20	C	359.16	175	9	Likouala Region, on west bank of Oubangui river. Animists 20%. D=RCC.
2620	2	7	7.04	0	97.00	3.00	C	215.97	250	8	Lekoumou Region, Bambama District. Also in Gabon. Animists 15%. D=RCC,EEC.
2621	1	8	4.63	0	97.00	3.00	C	223.05	182	8	Lekoumou Region, small groups in Bambama District. Also in Gabon. Animists 37%. D=RCC.

Continued overleaf

Table 8-2 continued

PEOPLE		POPULATION				IDENTITY CODE		LANGUAGE		CHURCH		MINISTRY	SCRIPTURE	
Ref 1	Ethnic name 2	P% 3	In 1995 4	In 2000 5	In 2025 6	Race 7	Language 8	Autoglossonym 9	S 10	AC 11	Members 12	Jayuh dwa xcmc mi 13-17 18 19 20 21 22	Biblioglossonym 23	Pub ss 24-26 27
2622	Mbanza	0.30000	7,682	8,830	17,067	NAB66b	93-ABAK-b	mbanza		80.00	7,064	0.... 10 7 7 3 1	Mbanza	P.. b
2623	Mbede (Mbeti)	2.00000	51,213	58,869	113,783	NAB57c	99-AURC-a	li-mbede		70.00	41,208	0.... 10 6 7 4 1		... .
2624	Mbosi (Mbochi, Mboshe)	5.40000	138,276	158,947	307,214	NAB57c	99-AUFH-c	mbosi		84.50	134,310	4.... 10 6 6 3 1	Mbosi	... .
2625	Mbuku (Mboxo)	0.90000	23,046	26,491	51,202	NAB57c	99-AUFE-a	mboko		65.00	17,219	0.... 10 6 7 3 2		... .
2626	Mbwisi (Bwisi)	0.10000	2,561	2,943	5,689	NAB57k	99-AURA-e	i-bwisi		70.00	2,060	0.s.. 10 7 7 4 1		pnb b
2627	Minduumo (Kuya, Nyani)	0.36000	9,218	10,596	20,481	NAB57k	99-AURC-d	le-nduumu		60.00	6,358	0.... 10 6 7 4 1		... .
2628	Moi	0.10000	2,561	2,943	5,689	NAB57c	99-AUFM	lemoi cluster		80.00	2,355	0.... 10 7 6 4 1		... .
2629	Monjombo (Monzumbo)	0.27000	6,914	7,947	15,361	BYG12	93-ADCA-a	mo-nzombo		50.00	3,974	0.... 10 5 7 4 1		... .
2630	Nchinchege	0.10000	2,561	2,943	5,689	NAB57k	99-AURD-e	nci-ncege		70.00	2,060	0.... 10 7 7 4 1		p.. .
2631	Ndasa	0.15000	3,841	4,415	8,534	NAB57c	99-AUEC-a	ndasa		75.00	3,311	0.... 10 7 7 3 1		... .
2632	Ngala	1.00000	25,607	29,435	56,891	NAB57c	99-AUIF-c	bangala-3		65.00	19,133	1csu. 10 6 7 4 2	Bangala	PNB b
2633	Ngala Boloki	0.20000	5,121	5,887	11,378	NAB57c	99-AUIC	boloki cluster		70.00	4,121	0.... 10 8 7 5 1	Boleki*	P.. b
2634	Ngando (Ngandu)	0.08000	2,049	2,355	4,551	NAB66c	93-AAAB	bangandu cluster		65.00	1,531	0.... 10 7 8 4 2		... .
2635	Ngbaka	0.12100	3,098	3,562	6,884	NAB66z	93-ADBA	ngbaka cluster		80.00	2,849	0.s.. 10 8 11 4 1	Ngbaka	PNB b
2636	Ngiri (Ngwili)	0.05000	1,280	1,472	2,845	NAB57k	99-AUIA-a	ba-loi		70.00	1,030	0.... 10 8 8 4 2		... .
2637	Ngondi	0.10000	2,561	2,943	5,689	NAB57k	99-AQAA-a	i-ngondi		71.00	2,090	0.... 10 8 7 4 1		... .
2638	Ngungwoni	0.20000	5,121	5,887	11,378	NAB57k	99-AURD-d	ngu-ngwoni		70.00	4,121	0.... 10 7 7 4 1		p.. .
2639	Northeast Teke (Ngungwel)	2.38300	61,021	70,143	135,572	NAB57k	99-AURD-c	n-gungwel		75.50	52,958	0.... 10 6 7 4 2		p.. .
2640	Northern Teke	1.63300	41,816	48,067	92,904	NAB57k	99-AURD-a	ka-tege		79.00	37,973	0.... 10 6 7 4 1		p.. .
2641	Nzebi (Njebi, Njevi)	0.20000	5,121	5,887	11,378	NAB57k	99-AURB-c	yi-nzebi		60.00	3,532	0cs.. 10 6 7 4 1	Yinzebi*	PN. .
2642	Nzime (Djimu, Zimu)	1.00000	25,607	29,435	56,891	NAB57k	99-AUDF	koozime cluster		70.00	20,604	0.... 10 7 7 4 1	Koozime	P.. .
2643	Pidgin Bulu	0.10000	2,561	2,943	5,689	NAB57c	99-AUCC-n	bulu	4	40.00	1,177	1.... 9 6 6 5 1	Bulu	PNB b
2644	Pol (Congo Pol)	0.18000	4,609	5,298	10,240	NAB57c	99-AUDB-f	pori		50.00	2,649	0.... 10 6 6 4 1		... .
2645	Portuguese	0.03000	768	883	1,707	CEW21g	51-AABA-e	general português		93.00	821	2Bsuh 10 9 15 5 1	Portuguese	PNB b
2646	Punu (Puno)	0.30000	7,682	8,830	17,067	NAB57k	99-AURA-a	yi-punu		55.00	4,857	0.s.. 10 6 7 4 1	Yipunu*	PNB .
2647	Sango	2.21000	56,591	65,051	125,730	NAB66z	93-ABBA-a	sango	5	70.00	45,535	4.s.. 10 9 8 5 1	Sango	PNB b
2648	South Central Teke (Ifumu)	0.27000	6,914	7,947	15,361	NAB57k	99-AURD-o	i-fuumu-2		50.00	3,974	0.... 10 6 6 4 3		p.. .
2649	Southern Teke (Kukwa)	1.28500	32,905	37,824	73,105	NAB57k	99-AURD-j	ku-kuya	21	65.00	24,585	0.... 10 6 7 4 3		p.. .
2650	Sundi	4.00000	102,427	117,739	227,566	NAB57b	99-AURG-dc	northwest ki-suundi		87.00	102,433	1cs.. 10 8 7 5 3		pnb b
2651	Tsaangi (Tsangui)	0.45000	11,523	13,246	25,601	NAB57c	99-AURB-e	i-caangi		65.00	8,610	0cs.. 10 6 6 5 1	Tsaangi	pn. .
2652	Vili (Fioti, Tsivili)	0.24200	6,197	7,123	13,768	NAB57b	99-AURB-d	i-vili		75.00	5,342	0As.. 10 8 7 5 3		pn. b
2653	Western Kele (Akele)	0.85900	21,996	25,284	48,870	NAB57c	99-AUEA-a	a-kele		93.00	23,514	0.... 10 9 11 4 1	Dikele*	P.. p
2654	Western Teke (Yaka)	3.17800	81,378	93,543	180,801	NAB57k	99-AURD-f	ge-tsaayi		75.00	70,157	0.... 10 7 7 5 1	Teke, Western	P.. .
2655	Wumvu	0.20000	5,121	5,887	11,378	NAB57k	99-AUEB-a	wumvu		75.00	4,415	0.... 10 8 8 4 1		... .
2656	Yombe (Bayombe, Kiombi)	11.52000	294,989	339,087	655,389	NAB57b	99-AURG-c	ki-yombe		89.00	301,787	1cs.. 10 7 7 5 1	Yombe	Pnb b
2657	other minor peoples	4.15500	106,396	122,301	236,384	...				79.00	96,618	10 6 6 5 0		
	Congo-Zaire	**100.00000**	**45,421,244**	**51,654,496**	**104,787,601**					**91.28**	**47,151,530**			
2658	Alur (Lur, Luri)	1.36132	618,328	703,183	1,426,495	NAB62b	04-ACAA-a	dho-aluur	1	94.00	660,992	0.s.. 10 8 11 4 3	Alur	PNB .
2659	Amba (Ruwenzori Kibira)	0.22183	100,758	114,585	232,450	NAB57c	99-ASHA-b	ku-amba		80.00	91,668	0.... 10 7 7 4 1		p.. .
2660	Angba (Hanga, Bangalema)	0.10000	45,421	51,654	104,788	NAB57h	99-ASCA-b	le-angba		95.00	49,072	0.... 10 8 11 4 1		... .
2661	Apakabeti (Apagibete)	0.08140	36,973	42,047	85,297	NAB57c	99-ASAB-j	mo-mveda		51.00	21,444	0.... 10 7 7 5 1	Pagabete	... b
2662	Arab	0.03000	13,626	15,496	31,436	CMT30	12-AACF-f	syro-palestinian	1	2.00	310	1Asuh 6 4 2 5 3	Arabic: Lebanese*	Pnb b
2663	Asua (Aka) Pygmy	0.05000	22,711	25,827	52,394	BYG12	03-BABA-j	asua-ti		50.00	12,914	0.... 10 7 7 2 1		... .
2664	Aushi (Northern Bemba)	0.45773	207,907	236,438	479,644	NAB57b	99-AURR-q	i-c-aushi		95.00	224,616	1.su. 10 8 11 5 1		pnb b
2665	Avukaya	0.07257	32,962	37,486	76,044	NAB66g	03-BAAB-a	avokaya		65.00	24,366	0.... 10 7 7 4 1	Avokaya	P.. b
2666	Baali (Kibala)	0.12845	58,344	66,350	134,600	NAB57b	99-ASEA-a	li-baali		90.00	59,715	0.s.. 10 8 11 5 2	Bali	... .
2667	Baka (Tara Baaka)	0.00410	1,862	2,118	4,296	NAB66e	03-ABAA-a	tara-baaka		83.00	1,758	0.... 10 7 6 2 1	Baka	P.. b
2668	Bamassa Pygmy	0.02000	9,084	10,331	20,958	BYG12	93-ADDA-h	bomassa		20.00	2,066	0.... 9 8 6 2 1		... .
2669	Bamwe	0.06902	31,350	35,652	72,324	NAB57c	99-AUIB-h	ba-mwe		80.00	28,522	0.... 10 7 7 2 1		... b
2670	Banda	0.15000	68,132	77,482	157,181	NAB66b	93-ABAB-a	banda-ndele		80.00	61,985	0.... 10 8 7 4 1	Banda, South Central	... b
2671	Bangba (Abangba)	0.02667	12,114	13,776	27,947	NAB66z	93-AEAB	bangba cluster		40.00	5,511	0.... 9 6 7 2 1		... .
2672	Bangi (Bobangi)	0.10000	45,421	51,654	104,788	NAB57c	99-AUFN-a	lo-bo-bangi		85.00	43,906	0.... 10 8 12 4 2	Bobangi*	PN. .
2673	Bangobango	0.38950	176,916	201,194	408,148	NAB57f	99-AURQ-y	ki-bangubangu		10.00	20,119	1csu. 8 5 5 1 1		pnb .
2674	Banziri Pygmy	0.00947	4,301	4,892	9,923	BYG12	93-ADAA	gbanziri cluster		30.00	1,468	0.... 9 5 6 1 2		... .
2675	Barambu (Amiangba)	0.07189	32,653	37,134	75,332	NAB66a	93-BABB-a	barambu-ro		80.00	29,708	0.... 10 8 7 4 1		... .
2676	Bari	0.03000	13,626	15,496	31,436	NAB62e	04-BAAB-a	kutuk-na-bari		57.00	8,833	1.s.. 10 7 9 4 2	Bari	PNB .
2677	Bari Kakwa (Zaire Kakwa)	0.09243	41,983	47,744	96,855	NAB62y	04-BAAC-a	kakwa		70.00	33,421	0.... 10 9 12 4 3	Kakwa*	PNB .
2678	Baya Ngbaka (Ngbaka)	0.50112	227,615	258,851	525,112	NAB66z	93-AAAA-l	ngbaka-gbaya		96.00	248,497	0.s.. 10 9 9 4 3		pnb b
2679	Bayaka Pygmy (Binga)	0.00631	2,866	3,259	6,612	BYG12	93-ABAF-f	yakpa		20.00	652	0.... 9 5 6 2 2		... b
2680	Beeke	0.00235	1,067	1,214	2,463	NAB57c	99-ASFA-c	i-beeke		80.00	971	0.... 10 7 6 1 1		... .
2681	Belgian (Fleming, Flemish	0.20000	90,842	103,309	209,575	CEW19k	52-ABCA-g	oostvlaandersch		88.00	90,912	1Bsuh 10 9 15 5 3		pnb b
2682	Belgian (Walloon)	0.13000	59,048	67,151	136,224	CEW21l	51-AABH-f	wallon		89.00	59,764	0A.uh 10 9 15 5 3	French: Walloon	P.. b
2683	Bemba	0.58055	263,693	299,880	608,344	NAB57b	99-AURR-h	i-ci-bemba	2	97.00	290,884	4.su. 10 10 12 5 3	Chibemba*	PNB b
2684	Bembe	0.77069	350,057	398,096	807,588	NAB57c	99-AUJE-b	i-beembe	1	80.00	318,477	0.s.. 10 6 7 5 3	Ebembe*	PNB .
2685	Bendi (Mabendi)	0.08712	39,571	45,001	91,291	NAB66g	03-BADB-b	ma-bendi		50.00	22,501	0.... 10 7 6 4 2		... .
2686	Binga	0.00100	454	517	1,048	NAB66z	99-AUID-e	m-binga		40.00	207	0.... 9 6 6 5 1		... .
2687	Binji	0.31888	144,839	164,716	334,147	NAB57f	99-AURQ-f	ci-binji		97.00	159,774	1csu. 10 8 11 4 1	Binji	PNb .
2688	Binza (Monia, Kutu)	0.03156	14,335	16,302	33,071	NAB57c	99-AUIB-b	li-binza-2		80.00	13,042	0.... 10 8 7 4 1		... .
2689	Boba (Likaw)	0.07937	36,051	40,998	83,170	NAB57c	99-AUFL-a	bomboma		80.00	32,799	0.... 10 7 7 4 1		... b
2690	Boko	0.05000	22,711	25,827	52,394	NAB57h	00-DGDA-a	boko		95.00	24,536	0.... 10 8 11 4 1	Boko	PNB .
2691	Bokote	0.20000	90,842	103,309	209,575	NAB57h	99-ATBD	east mbole cluster		95.00	98,144	0.... 10 8 11 4 3		... .
2692	Boloki (River Ruki)	0.01000	4,542	5,165	10,479	NAB57c	99-AUIC	boloki cluster		80.00	4,132	0.... 10 7 7 2 2	Boleki*	P.. b
2693	Bolondo	0.01035	4,701	5,346	10,846	NAB57h	99-AUIE-b	bo-londo		95.00	5,079	0.... 10 8 11 4 1		p.. b
2694	Boma Kasai (Buma)	0.03986	18,105	20,589	41,768	NAB57h	99-AURE-b	ki-boma		90.00	18,531	0.s.. 10 9 11 4 3		p.. .
2695	Bombongo	0.00789	3,584	4,076	8,268	NAB57c	99-AUIB-a	east bo-mboli		50.00	2,038	0.... 10 6 7 4 1		... b
2696	Bosaka (Ekota)	0.92000	417,875	475,221	964,046	NAB57h	99-AUIK-j	bo-saka		97.00	460,965	0.... 10 9 12 4 3		... .
2697	British	0.03000	13,626	15,496	31,436	CEW19i	52-ABAC-b	standard-english	3	78.00	12,087	3Bsuh 10 9 13 5 1		PNB b
2698	Budu	0.49008	222,600	253,148	513,543	NAB57c	99-ASFA-a	e-budu		87.00	220,239	0.... 10 10 7 5 3	Budu	... b
2699	Buela	0.02000	9,084	10,331	20,958	NAB57h	99-AUFO-c	bwela		95.00	9,814	0.... 10 8 11 4 1		... .
2700	Buja (Budza, Budja)	0.73587	334,241	380,110	771,101	NAB57h	99-AUFS-b	buja-itimbiri		99.00	376,309	0.... 10 8 11 4 3		... b
2701	Bulia (Bolia)	0.18750	85,165	96,852	196,477	NAB57h	99-AUII-d	lo-lia		95.00	92,010	0.... 10 7 11 4 3	Bolia	P.. .
2702	Buraka Pygmy	0.00300	1,363	1,550	3,144	BYG12	93-ADAB-a	buraka		10.00	155	0.... 8 5 3 1 1		... .
2703	Bushoong (Mbale, Kuba)	0.31250	141,941	161,420	327,461	NAB57b	99-AUIP-f	bu-shoong		96.00	154,963	0.... 10 8 12 4 3	Bushoong	PNB .
2704	Buya	0.03000	13,626	15,496	31,436	NAB57c	99-AUSF	north nyanza cluster		80.00	12,397	4.s.. 10 7 7 4 2		PNB b
2705	Buyi	0.03000	13,626	15,496	31,436	NAB57b	99-AUJE-c	ki-buyu		90.00	13,947	0.s.. 10 10 11 5 2		pnb .
2706	Buzaba (Budzaba)	0.01898	8,621	9,804	19,889	NAB57c	99-AUIB-d	bu-jaba		50.00	4,902	0.... 10 6 7 2 1		... b
2707	Bwa (Bua, Bobwa, Babwa)	0.47000	213,480	242,776	492,502	NAB57c	99-ASAC-a	li-bwa-li	1	93.00	225,782	0.... 10 8 7 5 3	Libwa*	P.. .
2708	Bwile	0.06273	28,493	32,403	65,733	NAB57b	99-AURR-f	ki-bwile		70.00	22,682	1.su. 10 9 7 5 1		pnb b
2709	Bwissi (Katalinga)	0.06063	27,539	31,318	63,533	NAB57d	99-AURA-e	i-bwisi		80.00	25,054	0.s.. 10 7 7 4 2		pnb b
2710	Central Swahili	0.06000	27,253	30,993	62,873	NAB57j	99-AUSM-b	standard ki-swahili		6.00	1,860	4Asu. 7 5 6 5 3	Kiswahili*	PNB b
2711	Central Teke (Boma)	0.07860	35,701	40,600	82,363	NAB57k	99-AURD-l	a-boong		73.00	29,638	0.... 10 7 7 4 3	Teke, Central	p.. .
2712	Chokwe (Kioko, Djok)	1.54138	700,114	796,192	1,615,175	NAB57b	99-AURP-f	ki-cokwe	3	83.00	660,839	0.... 10 6 9 5 3	Chokwe	PNB .
2713	Dongo	0.02491	11,314	12,867	26,103	NAB66z	93-AGBA-a	dongo-ko		40.00	5,147	0.... 9 6 7 2 2		... .
2714	Dzando (Maboko)	0.02071	9,407	10,698	21,702	NAB57c	99-AUIB-i	dzandu		70.00	7,488	0.... 10 7 7 2 1		... b
2715	Dzing (Ding, Di, Din)	0.30000	136,264	154,963	314,363	NAB57b	99-AURE-h	i-dzing		95.00	147,215	0.s.. 10 8 7 4 1		p.. p
2716	Eastern Teke	0.32812	149,036	169,489	343,829	NAB57k	99-AURD-w	li-bali	1	97.00	164,404	0.... 10 10 7 5 3	Teke, Eastern	P.. b
2717	Efe Pygmy (Amengi)	0.05445	24,732	28,126	57,057	BYG12	03-BACA-a	amengi		55.00	15,469	0.... 10 6 7 4 3		p.. .
2718	Ekonda	3.10000	1,408,059	1,601,289	3,248,416	NAB57h	99-AUII-g	e-konda		99.00	1,585,276	0.... 10 10 11 5 3		p.. .
2719	Esperanto	0.00000	0	0	0	CEW21z	51-AAAC-a	proper esperanto		60.00	0	0A... 10 9 8 5 0	Esperanto	PNB b
2720	Eurafrican	0.20000	90,842	103,309	209,575	NAN58	51-AABI-mo	français-de-zaïre		90.00	92,978	1B.uh 10 9 12 5 3		pnb .
2721	Foma (Fuma)	0.03000	13,626	15,496	31,436	NAB57c	99-ATBC	foma cluster		80.00	12,397	0.... 10 8 7 4 1		... .
2722	Forest Bira	0.09701	44,063	50,110	101,654	NAB57c	99-ASGB-b	ki-bila		21.00	10,523	0.... 9 5 7 4 1		... .
2723	French	0.46000	208,938	237,611	482,023	CEW21b	51-AABI-d	general français	34	84.00	199,593	1B.uh 10 9 14 5 3	French	PNB b
2724	Fuliro (Fulero)	0.74873	340,082	386,753	784,576	NAB57d	99-AUSD-i	i-ki-fuliru	1	98.00	379,018	1csu. 10 9 11 4 3	Kifuliiru*	Pnb .
2725	Furu	0.04015	18,237	20,739	42,072	NAB66z	03-AABA-c	furu		40.00	8,296	0.... 9 6 7 4 1		... b
2726	Gbati-Ri (Gbote)	0.05000	22,711	25,827	52,394	NAB57d	99-ASMA-b	gbati-ri		90.00	23,245	0.... 10 8 11 4 1		... .
2727	Gbendere	0.00947	4,301	4,892	9,923	NAB66z	93-ADCC-a	yango		30.00	1,468	0.... 9 5 7 3 1		... b
2728	Gbi	0.02000	9,084	10,331	20,958	NAB66b	93-ABAI-a	gbi		50.00	5,165	0.... 10 6 8 2 2		... .
2729	Genja (Gendza-Bali)	0.13572	61,646	70,105	142,218	NAB57h	99-AUFR-g	di-baali-ligendza		80.00	56,084	0.... 10 8 7 2 1		... b
2730	Genya (Wagenia, Zimba)	0.02917	13,249	15,068	30,567	NAB57c	99-ATCA-a	c-eenya		80.00	12,054	0.... 10 7 7 4 1		... .
2731	Gilima	0.04021	18,264	20,770	42,135	NAB66z	93-ADBB-b	mbanza-balakpa		70.00	14,539	0.... 10 7 7 3 1		... .
2732	Gobu (Ngobu)	0.04020	18,259	20,765	42,125	NAB66b	93-ABAF-g	gubu		70.00	14,536	0.... 10 8 7 3 1		... b
2733	Greek	0.10000	45,421	51,654	104,788	CEW20	56-AAAA-c	dhimotiki		95.00	49,072	2B.uh 10 9 11 5 1	Greek: Modern	PNB b
2734	Gundi Pygmy	0.00500	2,271	2,583	5,239	BYG12	93-ADDA-d	gundi		20.00	517	0.... 9 5 4 1 1		... .
2735	Hamba	0.03000	13,626	15,496	31,436	NAB57c	99-ASHA-b	ku-amba		90.00	13,947	0.... 10 8 11 4 1		p.. .
2736	Havu (Haavu)	1.21081	549,965	625,438	1,268,779	NAB57d	99-AUSD-l	e-ki-haavu		98.00	612,929	1csu. 10 9 12 4 3		pnb .
2737	High Lugbara (Logbari)	0.69850	317,267	360,807	731,941	NAB66g	03-BAAF-a	uru-leba-ti	2	91.00	328,334	1As.. 10 8 8 4 1	Lugbara	PNB .
2738	Hima	0.00500	2,271	2,583	5,239	NAB57d	99-AUSE-fd	o-ro-hima		90.00	2,324	1cs.h 10 8 11 4 1		pnb b
2739	Holoholo (Kalanga)	0.03600	16,352	18,596	37,724	NAB57b	99-AUJE-d	ki-holoholo		80.00	14,876	0.s.. 10 8 7 2 2	Holoholo	Pnb b
2740	Holu (Holo)	0.02773	12,595	14,324	29,058	NAB57b	99-AUHD-a	ki-holu		60.00	8,594	0.... 10 7 7 4 1	Kiholo*	P.. .
2741	Hunde (Kobi)	0.75824	344,402	391,665	794,542	NAB57d	99-AUSD-m	e-ki-hunde	1	85.00	332,915	1csu. 10 7 7 5 3	Kihunde*	PNb .
2742	Hunganna (Hungaan, Huana)	0.01000	4,542	5,165	10,479	NAB57b	99-AURG-t	hungaan		90.00	4,649	1cs.. 10 8 12 4 1	Kihungana*	Pnb .
2743	Hutu	0.20000	90,842	103,309	209,575	NAB57d	99-AUSD-f	i-ki-nya-rwanda		90.00	92,978	2Asu. 10 10 11 5 2	Kinyarwanda*	PNB b

Continued opposite

Table 8-2 continued

EVANGELIZATION								EVANGELISM			ADDITIONAL DESCRIPTIVE DATA
Ref 1	D 28	aC 29	CG% 30	r 31	E 32	U 33	W 34	e 35	R 36	T 37	Locations, civil divisions, literacy, religions, church history, denominations, dioceses, church growth, missions, agencies, ministries, movements 38
2622	1	7	6.78	0	99.80	0.20	C	335.80	205	9	Extreme north of Likouala Region, close to Oubangui river. Large tribe, almost entirely in Zaire, with some in CAR. Related to Banda. Animists 20%. D=RCC.
2623	1	7	8.68	0	99.70	0.30	C	270.83	262	8	Cuvette Region, Kelle and northern Ewo Districts. Also in Gabon. Related to Ngwii. Animists 2%. D=RCC. M=SIL.
2624	2	7	9.97	0	99.85	0.15	C	380.90	254	9	Cuvette Region, Owando and Mossaka Districts; Plateau Region. Animists 0.5%. D=RCC,AICs. M=SIL.
2625	2	7	7.74	0	99.65	0.35	C	241.99	247	8	Cuvette Region, western part of Makoua District. Related to Mbosi. Animists 15%. D=RCC,EEC.
2626	1	7	5.47	1	99.70	0.30	C	288.71	176	8	Niari Region, Kibangou District, Banda area on Gabon border. Also in Gabon. Animists 30%. D=RCC.
2627	1	7	6.67	0	95.00	5.00	C	208.05	244	8	Lekoumou Region, Bambama District. Primarily in Gabon. Animists 30%. D=RCC.
2628	1	7	5.61	0	99.80	0.20	C	332.88	170	9	West bank of Oubangui river, south of Mossaka. Related to Ntomba. Animists 20%. D=RCC.
2629	1	7	6.17	0	85.00	15.00	B	155.12	234	7	Extreme northeast, on Oubangui river. Also in Zaire, CAR. Animists 40%. D=RCC.
2630	1	8	5.47	0	99.70	0.30	C	273.38	186	8	Plateaux Region, Lekana District, between Leketi river and Gabon border. Animists 30%. D=RCC.
2631	1	8	5.97	0	99.75	0.25	C	301.12	194	9	Lekoumou Region, west of Zanaga. Also in Gabon. Related to Kele. Animists 25%. D=RCC.
2632	2	7	7.85	4	99.65	0.35	C	289.44	209	8	Along west bank of Zaire and Oubangui rivers. Animists 1%. D=RCC,AICs.
2633	1	7	4.43	0	99.70	0.30	C	273.38	151	8	On both banks of Zaire river upstream from Mbandaka. Being replaced by Lingala. Animists 10%. D=RCC.
2634	2	7	5.16	0	99.65	0.35	C	244.36	186	8	Baagato. Also in Cameroon. Animists 35%. D=RCC,EPC.
2635	1	8	5.81	0	99.80	0.20	C	382.52	151	9	Likouala Region, west bank of Oubangui river. Vast majority in Zaire, few in CAR. Animists 20%. D=RCC.
2636	2	7	4.74	0	99.70	0.30	C	275.94	166	8	Along Oubangui river. Mainly in Zaire. Animists 30%. D=RCC,ECZ.
2637	1	7	5.49	0	99.71	0.29	C	274.69	188	8	Sangha Region, east of Ouesso. Also in CAR. Animists 29%. D=RCC.
2638	1	7	6.21	0	99.70	0.30	C	270.83	207	8	Southwest corner of Plateaux Region, southwest of Djambala. Animists 20%. D=RCC.
2639	2	7	8.95	0	99.76	0.24	C	315.53	257	9	Agungwel. Plateaux Province, Gamboma District. Animists 0.5%. D=RCC,AICs.
2640	3	7	8.59	0	99.79	0.21	C	340.25	241	9	Cuvette Region, Ewo and Okoyo Districts; Plateaux Region. Also in Gabon. Animists 1%.D=RCC,EEC,AICs. M=ABMU.
2641	1	7	6.04	2	99.60	0.40	C	225.57	209	8	Niari Province, Mayoko District. Primarily in Gabon. Animists 30%. D=EESG. M=CMA.
2642	1	7	7.93	0	99.70	0.30	C	273.38	249	8	Sangha Region, Souanke District, along Cameroon border. Also in Cameroon. Animists 10%. D=RCC. M=SIL.
2643	1	8	4.06	4	90.00	10.00	B	131.40	168	7	Detribalized persons, creoles. Widespread in Cameroon. Animists 50%, nonreligious 10%. D=RCC.
2644	1	8	5.74	0	85.00	15.00	B	155.12	232	7	Sangha Region, north of Ouesso, Cameroon/CAR border. Also in CAR, Cameroon. Animists 50%. D=RCC.
2645	1	10	4.51	8	99.93	0.07	C	563.48	91	10	Long-time settlers, merchants, from Portugal. D=RCC.
2646	1	7	6.38	2	99.55	0.45	B	206.77	218	8	Primarily in Gabon. Animists 45%. D=EESG. M=CMA.
2647	1	8	8.79	4	99.70	0.30	C	334.70	214	9	Lingua franca of CAR. Animists 30%. D=RCC.
2648	3	8	6.17	0	90.00	10.00	B	164.25	243	7	Pool Region; north of Brazzaville to Lefini river. Animists 50%. D=RCC,EEC,AICs.
2649	3	7	4.89	0	99.65	0.35	C	251.48	173	8	Plateaux Province, Lekana District, east of Leketi river. Animists 5%. D=RCC,EEC,AICs.
2650	3	8	5.19	5	99.87	0.13	C	463.62	125	10	Dialect of Kongo. Animists 3%. Widespread indigenous churches. D=EJCSK,RCC,AICs.
2651	2	7	6.99	1	99.65	0.35	C	253.85	217	8	Niari Region, north and northwest of Mossendjo. Also in Gabon. Animists 20%. D=EEC,SA. M=Swedish Covenant Mission.
2652	4	8	6.48	5	99.75	0.25	C	364.08	164	9	Dialect of Kongo. Kouilou Province, along coast. Also in Gabon. Animists 25%. Y=1920. D=RCC,Lassyism(Nzambi ya Bougie),SA,other AICs.
2653	2	7	8.07	2	99.93	0.07	C	468.44	189	10	Scattered. Also in Gabon. Mabambe(ancestor veneration) is widespread. D=RCC,EEC. M=PEMS.
2654	3	8	9.26	0	99.75	0.25	C	317.55	261	9	Lekoumou Region west, south, and east of Mbama. Also in Gabon. Animists 5%. D=RCC,EEC,AICs. M=Swedish Mission.
2655	1	8	6.28	0	99.75	0.25	C	306.60	198	9	Also in Gabon. Related to Kele. Animists 25%. D=RCC. M=CMA.
2656	5	8	5.77	5	99.89	0.11	C	464.53	139	10	Also in Zaire and Cabinda(Angola). Animists 0.5%. D=RCC,EJCSK,EEC,SA,AICs. M=LBI.
2657	0	10	9.61		99.79	0.21	C	322.95	235	9	Sehwi, Suppire Senoufo, and many Bantu peoples from surrounding countries.
Congo-Zaire											
2658	2	6	11.74	5	99.94	0.06	C	518.08	240	10	Haut-Zaire Region. Also in Uganda. Animists 2%. D=RCC(D-Mahagi-Nioka),ECZ(CECA). M=CICM,SJ,WF,AIM,UBS.
2659	1	6	9.55	4	99.80	0.20	C	347.48	254	9	Kivu Region north of Lake Edward. Also in Uganda. Animists 8%. D=RCC.
2660	1	7	8.87	0	99.95	0.05	C	464.64	211	10	Haut-Zaire Region, Banalia Zone. Closely related to Ngombe and Bwa. Animists 5%. D=RCC.
2661	2	7	7.97	0	91.00	9.00	B	169.39	284	7	Equateur Region, around Businga, Ngakpo. Most are bilingual in Lingala, some in Ngbandi. Animists 23%. D=RCC,ECZ(CEUM). M=ECCA.
2662	3	10	3.49	8	58.00	42.00	B	4.23	198	4	Omani, Egyptian, Zanzibari Arabs. Muslims 94%(Shafi Sunnis). D=Coptic Orthodox Ch,GOC,RCC.
2663	1	6	7.43	0	82.00	18.00	B	149.65	285	7	Haut-Zaire Region, Ituri Forest. Animists 40%. D=ECZ(CECCA). M=WEC.
2664	4	7	4.71	4	99.95	0.05	C	523.59	112	10	Also in Zambia. Animists 3%. D=RCC(D-Sakania-Kipushi),ECZ,EUSJ,other AICs. M=CICM.
2665	1	6	8.11	0	99.65	0.35	C	237.25	269	8	Haut-Zaire Region, Faradje Zone. Primarily in Sudan. Animists 15%. D=RCC. M=SIL.
2666	2	7	9.08	0	99.90	0.10	C	436.90	217	10	Haut-Zaire Region, Bafwasende Zone. Animists 5%. D=RCC,ECZ(CECA). M=ACM,PBT.
2667	1	8	5.31	0	99.83	0.17	C	360.51	155	9	Haut-Zaire Region. Primarily in Sudan. Bilingual in Zande. Animists 5%. D=ECZ. M=SIL.
2668	0	7	5.48	0	49.00	51.00	A	35.77	368	5	In north, in Ubangi. Animists 65%. M=WEC.
2669	1	8	8.28	0	99.80	0.20	C	341.64	228	9	10 villages in Equateur Region, Kungu Zone. Almost all are bilingual in Lingala (50% literates). Animists 5%. D=ECZ(CECU). M=EFCA.
2670	1	10	9.12	0	99.80	0.20	C	353.32	248	9	On northern border; immigrants from largest tribe in CAR. Animists 5%, Muslims 5%. D=RCC(D-Molegbe).
2671	1	6	6.52	0	70.00	30.00	B	102.20	311	7	Haut-Zaire Region, Niangara Zone, northeast of Rungu. 6 dialects. Animists 25%. D=RCC.
2672	3	7	3.54	0	99.85	0.15	C	409.53	104	10	Equateur Region, east of Zaire river. Also in Congo. Animists 3%. D=RCC,ECZ(CBFZ),AICs. M=BMS,UBS.
2673	1	8	7.90	1	48.00	52.00	A	17.52	534	5	Kivu Region, Kabambare Zone. Muslims 90%. D=ECZ(CLMZ,CADEZA). M=MLM.
2674	2	7	5.12	0	61.00	39.00	B	66.79	279	6	Equateur Region, Bosobolo Zone: a few villages along Ubangi river. Also in CAR. Animists 50%. D=RCC,ECZ(CECU). M=EFCA,WEC.
2675	2	6	8.33	0	99.80	0.20	C	335.80	242	9	Haut-Zaire Region, Poko and Niangara Zones. Animists 1%. D=RCC(D-Doruma-Dungu),ECZ(CECCA). M=WEC.
2676	2	9	7.02	0	99.57	0.43	B	226.77	212	8	Haut-Zaire Region. Mainly in Sudan and Uganda. Animists 8%. D=RCC,ECZ(Anglican).
2677	1	7	8.45	1	99.70	0.30	C	314.26	220	9	Haut-Zaire Region, Aru Zone, north of Aru. Muslims 13%, animists 6%. D=RCC. M=CICM,SJ,WF,OFM,SDB.
2678	2	6	10.65	1	99.96	0.04	C	501.07	231	10	Equateur Region, Gemena Zone. Also in CAR, Congo. Lingua franca. Animists 1%. D=RCC,ECZ(CECU,CEUM). M=CICM,WF,SJ,OFM,SDB,UBS,EFCA,ECCA.
2679	1	7	4.27	0	53.00	47.00	B	38.69	278	5	Equateur Region, Bosobolo and Mobaye Zones. Also in CAR. All bilingual, with Yakpa being replaced by Mono, Mbanza, or Lingala. Animists 70%. D=ECZ(CEUM).
2680	1	9	4.68	0	99.80	0.20	C	324.12	152	9	Haut-Zaire Region, Mambasa Zones, 2 villages east of Bafwasende. Close to Ndaaka. Animists 1%. D=RCC.
2681	1	10	9.54	6	99.88	0.12	C	513.92	183	10	Expatriates from Belgium, in development, business. Enormous investment in Zaire. Animists 3%. D=RCC. M=CICM,SJ,WF,SDB,OFM,PFM,FSC.
2682	1	10	9.08	8	99.89	0.11	C	503.51	180	10	Expatriates from Belgium in business, development. Animists 3%. D=RCC. M=CICM,WF,SJ,SDB,OFM,PFM,FSC.
2683	5	10	4.82	8	99.97	0.03	C	601.88	101	10	Southeast Shaba Region. D=RCC,ECZ(CCCA),EEA,EUSJ,other AICs. M=CICM,SJ,AMEC,NLEA,CC(Zambia).
2684	2	7	10.93	0	99.80	0.20	C	379.60	261	9	Kivu Region, Fizi Zone. Animists 8%, Muslims 2%. D=RCC(D-Uvira),ECZ(CADEZA,CLMZ). M=SX,UPMGBI,FMB,AoG,MLM,UBS.
2685	2	7	8.02	0	86.00	14.00	B	156.95	309	7	Haut-Zaire Region, Djugu Zone. Animists 20%. D=RCC,ECZ(CECA). M=NLEA,AIM.
2686	2	9	3.08	0	75.00	25.00	B	109.50	165	7	In Sudan also. Related to Yulu. Animists 40%. D=RCC,CAZ. M=CMS.
2687	1	6	10.16	1	99.97	0.03	C	513.37	220	10	Kasai Occidental Region, Kazumba Zone. D=RCC.
2688	1	6	7.44	0	99.80	0.20	C	332.88	214	9	Equateur Region, Kungu and Bomongo Zorres. Animists 1%. D=RCC. M=EECZ.
2689	2	7	8.43	0	99.80	0.20	C	347.48	228	9	Equateur Region, Kungu Zone. All bilingual in Lingala. Riverine. Animists 2%. D=RCC,ECZ(CECU). M=EFCA.
2690	1	6	8.12	1	99.95	0.05	C	499.32	182	10	Equateur Region, on Zaire river. Animists 1%. D=RCC.
2691	1	6	5.76	0	99.95	0.05	C	468.11	147	10	Equateur and Bandundu Regions. Animists 2%. D=RCC. M=CICM,SJ,OFM,WF,SDB.
2692	2	8	5.16	0	99.80	0.20	C	347.48	153	9	Equateur Region, both sides of Zaire river. Language being replaced by Lingala. Animists 2%. D=RCC,ECZ.
2693	2	8	6.43	0	99.95	0.05	C	481.98	156	10	Equateur Region, Budjala Zone. Riverine. Lingala widely used, also Ngbandi. D=RCC,ECZ(CECU). M=EFCA.
2694	1	7	7.81	0	99.90	0.10	C	436.90	191	10	Related to Yansi. D=RCC. M=CICM,SJ,WF,SDB,OFM.
2695	2	7	5.46	0	88.00	12.00	B	160.60	216	7	Equateur Region, Kungu Zone. Bilingual in Lingala. Riverine. Animists 20%. D=RCC,ECZ(CECU,CDCZ). M=EFCA.
2696	3	6	5.79	0	99.97	0.03	C	495.67	142	10	Few animists. D=RCC,EJCSK,other AICs. M=CICM,OFM,SJ,WF,SDB.
2697	3	10	5.07	8	99.78	0.22	C	435.59	111	10	Expatriates from Britain, in development. Nonreligious 9%, animists 1%. D=CURBZ(CAZ:D-Boga-Zaire),ECZ,JWs. M=CMS.
2698	4	6	10.52	0	99.87	0.13	C	409.64	255	10	Haut-Zaire Region, Wamba Zone. Fairly bilingual in Swahili and Bangala. Animists 10%. D=RCC(D-Wamba),ECZ(CECCA,CADZ),EJCSK,other AICs. M=SCJ,CICM.
2699	1	7	7.13	0	99.95	0.05	C	461.17	177	10	Northwest. Animists 2%. D=RCC.
2700	3	6	11.11	0	99.99	0.01	C	520.34	239	10	Equateur Region. Lingua franca: Lingala (high literacy). D=RCC(D-Lolo,D-Lisala),ECZ(CEUM,CBFZ,CAZ),AICs. M=CICM,WF,OFM,SDB,ECCA,WEC,AoG,CMS.
2701	1	6	9.56	0	99.95	0.05	C	471.58	222	10	Bandundu Region, north of Lake Mai-Ndombe. D=RCC. M=SJ,CICM,OFM.
2702	0	7	2.78	0	33.00	67.00	A	12.04	322	5	Scattered groups along Ubangi river, Equateur Region. Also in CAR. Nearly extinct. Close to Gbanziri. Animists 90%. M=WEC.
2703	2	6	10.13	0	99.96	0.04	C	518.59	215	10	Kasai Occidental Region, Mweka and Ilebo Zones. Animists 1%. D=RCC,AICs. M=CICM,WF,OFM.
2704	2	7	7.38	4	99.80	0.20	C	397.12	178	9	A Broad Bantu people. Animists 5%. D=RCC,ECZ.
2705	2	7	7.51	0	99.90	0.10	C	456.61	177	10	On Lake Tanganjika, Kivu/Shaba border. Animists 2%. D=RCC(D-Kongolo),ECZ(CADEZA). M=CSSp,UPMGBI.
2706	1	7	6.39	0	85.00	15.00	B	155.12	253	7	Equateur Region, Kungu Zone. Bilingual in Lingala (market use). Riverine. Animists 20%. D=ECZ(CECU). M=EFCA.
2707	2	6	10.54	0	99.93	0.07	C	448.07	249	10	Haut-Zaire Region, in 4 Zones. Animists 5%. D=RCC(D-Buta,D-Lolo),ECZ(CECCA,CEHZ,CBBU). M=UFM,WEC,MBN.
2708	1	7	8.03	3	99.70	0.30	C	304.04	219	9	On both sides of border with Zambia near Lake Tanganyika. Dialect of Bemba. Animists 4%. D=RCC.
2709	2	6	8.14	1	99.80	0.20	C	370.84	221	9	Related to Talinga. Kivu Region, Beni Zone. Primarily in Uganda. Bilingual in Runyoro. Animists 2%. D=RCC,ECZ(CECA,CAZ). M=AIM,CMS.
2710	2	8	4.32	5	65.00	35.00	B	14.23	244	5	Traders from East Africa. Lingua franca across to Indian Ocean coast. Muslims 90%(Shafi Sunnis). Animists 3%. D=RCC,ECZ. M=CTD,IGCM(Zambia).
2711	2	7	8.32	0	99.73	0.27	C	298.42	248	8	Bandundu Region, Mushie Zone. Mostly in Congo. Animists 2%. D=RCC,AICs. M=CICM,WF,SDB,OFM,SJ,BMS.
2712	5	6	5.62	2	99.83	0.17	C	412.01	143	10	Kasai Occidental; also in Angola and Zambia. Animists 12%. D=RCC(D-Luebo,D-Kikwit,D-Popokabaka,D-Kamina),ENAC,ESSE,ECZ(CEFMZ,CAES),other AICs.
2713	2	7	6.44	0	73.00	27.00	B	106.58	295	7	Haut-Zaire Region, east of Watsa. Animists 24%. D=RCC,ECZ.
2714	1	8	6.84	0	99.70	0.30	C	270.83	215	8	Equateur Region, Kungu Zone. Bilingual in Lingala. Riverine. Animists 2%. D=ECZ(CECU). M=EFCA.
2715	1	6	10.07	0	99.95	0.05	C	457.71	239	10	Bandundu Region, Idofa Zone. Related to Yansi. Animists 1%. D=RCC(D-Idiofa).
2716	4	7	5.36	0	99.97	0.03	C	499.21	139	10	Kwamouth. Also in Congo. Literates 75%. Trade languages: Lingala, Kituba. Animists 2%. D=RCC(D-Bikoro),ECZ,EDDZ,other AICs. M=NLEA,CBZO/ABCUSA.
2717	2	7	7.62	0	94.00	6.00	B	188.70	254	7	Haut-Zaire Region, west and southwest of Watsa. Pygmies living among the Lese and others. Animists 45%. D=RCC,ECZ(CECA,CAFEZA,CM,CADZ). M=CICM.
2718	4	6	5.25	0	99.99	0.01	C	520.34	128	10	Equateur and Bandundu Regions. D=RCC(D-Inongo,D-Bikoro),ECZ,EJCSK,other AICs. M=BMS,CICM,SJ,WF,SDB.
2719	0	10	0.00	5	99.60	0.40	C	260.61	0	8	Artificial(constructed) language, in 80 countries. Speakers in Zaire: 12,000(none mother-tongue).
2720	3	10	4.25	8	99.90	0.10	C	522.31	92	10	Mixed-race, Black/Whites. Mostly in urban areas. Animists 5%. D=RCC,ECZ,EJCSK.
2721	1	7	7.38	0	99.80	0.20	C	335.80	211	9	Haut-Zaire Region, north side of Zaire river upstream from Basoko. Animists 2%. D=RCC.
2722	2	7	7.21	0	56.00	44.00	B	42.92	425	6	Haut-Zaire Region, Ituri Sub-Region, Mambasa Zone. Animists 57%, Muslims 2%. D=RCC,ECZ(CM). M=MAM.
2723	1	10	3.15	8	99.84	0.16	C	490.56	71	10	Expatriates from France and Belgium, in development, business. Vast investment in Zaire. Nonreligious 13%. D=RCC(48 Dioceses). M=CICM,SJ,WF,SDB,OFM.
2724	2	7	11.12	1	99.98	0.02	C	532.97	243	10	Kivu Region, Uvira Zone, north and northwest of Uvira. D=RCC(D-Uvira),ECZ(CEPZA,CLMZ). M=SX,SFM,MLM.
2725	2	6	6.95	0	76.00	24.00	B	110.96	302	7	Equateur Region; Nord Ubangi, Bosobolo, and Mobaye Zones. Bilingual in Lingala, Sango, Mono, or Gbanziri. Animists 40%. D=RCC,ECZ(CEUM). M=ECCA.
2726	1	8	8.06	0	99.90	0.10	C	427.05	214	10	Haut-Zaire Region, between Isiro and Watsa. D=RCC.
2727	1	7	5.12	0	65.00	35.00	B	71.17	276	6	Equateur Region, Kungu and Libenge Zones. Lingala, Ngbandi, Mbanza widely spoken. Animists 50%. D=ECZ(CECU). M=EFCA.
2728	2	8	6.45	0	86.00	14.00	B	156.95	264	7	Also in CAR. Closest to Dakpa, Gbaga, Golo, Wojo. Animists 30%. D=RCC,ECZ.
2729	2	6	9.02	0	99.80	0.20	C	338.72	248	9	Equateur Region, Bumba Zone. All bilingual and literate in Lingala. Animists 1%. D=RCC,ECZ(CEUM). M=ECCA.
2730	1	7	7.35	0	99.80	0.20	C	335.80	210	9	Fishermen on Lualaba river from Kisangani upriver to Kongolo, Haut-Zaire. Animists 5%. D=RCC.
2731	2	7	7.55	0	99.70	0.30	C	268.27	234	8	Equateur Region, Libenge Zone; also in CAR. Few are bilingual in Lingala. Few literates. Animists 20%. D=RCC,ECZ(CECU). M=EFCA.
2732	2	7	7.55	0	99.70	0.30	C	275.94	238	8	Equateur Region, Bosobolo Zone; also in CAR. Youths bilingual in Lingala or Sango. Few literates. Closest to Togbo and Mono. Animists 21%. D=RCC,ECZ(CECU).
2733	1	10	4.82	7	99.95	0.05	C	575.60	96	10	Traders. D=Greek Orthodox Ch/AGOC(P-Alexandria: AD-Central Africa).
2734	0	7	4.02	0	45.00	55.00	A	32.85	312	5	Pygmies in forests south of river Ubangi, also north in CAR. Animists 80%. M=WEC.
2735	1	9	7.51	4	99.90	0.10	C	446.76	181	10	Kasai Oriental Region, Lodja Zone. D=RCC.
2736	2	6	11.65	1	99.98	0.02	C	532.97	253	10	Kivu Region, Kalehe Zone. Close to Shi. D=RCC(M-Bukavu),ECZ(CEPZA,CEBZE). M=CICM,SJ,WF,OFM,SDB,SFM,CBFMS.
2737	2	6	10.96	1	99.91	0.09	C	481.61	239	10	Haut-Zaire Region, Aru Zone (High Lugbara only). Also in Uganda (High and Low). Animists 5%. D=35% ECZ(CECA),RCC(D-Mahagi-Nioka). M=AIM.
2738	1	10	5.60	4	99.90	0.10	C	486.18	143	10	Aristocratic elite in monarchy days. Also in Burundi. Animists 1%. D=RCC(D-Bunia). M=EECZ.
2739	2	7	7.58	0	99.80	0.20	C	356.24	203	9	Shaba Region, northwest of Kalemie. Also in Tanzania. Animists 3%. D=RCC,ECZ.
2740	1	6	6.99	0	94.00	6.00	C	205.86	246	8	Bandundu Region, extreme southwest corner. Primarily in Angola. Animists 15%. D=RCC(D-Popokabaka).
2741	2	7	10.97	1	99.85	0.15	C	415.73	267	10	Kivu Region, Masisi and Rutshuru Zones. Animists 5%. D=RCC(D-Goma),ECZ(CEPZA,CEBZE). M=SFM,SJ,CICM,WF,CBFMS.
2742	1	8	6.33	1	99.90	0.10	C	459.90	152	10	Bandundu Region, Bulungu Zone. D=RCC.
2743	2	8	9.57	4	99.90	0.10	C	515.74	204	10	Kivu Region. Rundi and Ruanda refugees from 1962-72 and 1994 genocide in Rwanda and Burundi. Animists 5%. D=RCC(D-Goma,D-Uvira),ECZ(CLMZ).

Continued overleaf

Table 8-2 continued

PEOPLE		POPULATION				IDENTITY CODE		LANGUAGE		CHURCH		MINISTRY						SCRIPTURE		
Ref 1	Ethnic name 2	P% 3	In 1995 4	In 2000 5	In 2025 6	Race 7	Language 8	Autoglossonym 9	S 10	AC 11	Members 12	Jayuh 13-17	d 18	wa 19	xc 20	mc 21	mi 22	Biblioglossonym 23	Pub 24-26	ss 27
2744	Indo-Pakistani	0.30000	136,264	154,963	314,363	CNN25g	59-AAFO-e	general hindi		1.00	1,550	3Asuh	6	4	2	2	0		pnb	b
2745	Jewish	0.00090	409	465	943	CMT35	51-AABI-d	general français		0.30	1	1B.uh	5	4	2	1	0	French	PNB	b
2746	Kabwari	0.02000	9,084	10,331	20,958	NAB57b	99-AUSD-j	kabwari		90.00	9,298	1csu.	10	8	11	4	1		pnb	.
2747	Kaiku	0.03000	13,626	15,496	31,436	NAB57c	99-ASGB-d	i-kaiku		80.00	12,397	0....	10	8	7	4	1		...	.
2748	Kakwa (Uganda Kakwa)	0.02000	9,084	10,331	20,958	NAB62y	04-BAAC-a	kakwa		65.00	6,715	0....	10	9	7	4	3	Kakwa*	PNB	.
2749	Kalebwe (Eastern Kalebwe)	0.34660	157,430	179,034	363,194	NAB57f	99-AURQ-ib	ka-lebwe		98.00	175,454	1csu.	10	9	12	4	2	Ikalebwe	PNb	.
2750	Kaliko (Keliko, Madi)	0.02177	9,888	11,245	22,812	NAB66e	03-BAAD-a	keliko-madi		83.00	9,334	0....	10	8	7	4	1	Kaliko	...	.
2751	Kalunda Lunda	0.15000	68,132	77,482	157,181	NAB57b	99-AURP-k	ci-lunda		95.00	73,608	0....	10	10	13	5	3	Lunda	PNB	.
2752	Kango	0.01400	6,359	7,232	14,670	NAB57h	99-ASBA-a	li-kango		90.00	6,508	0....	10	8	11	4	1		...	.
2753	Kanu	0.01744	7,921	9,009	18,275	NAB57c	99-AUJD-h	ki-kaanu		80.00	7,207	0....	10	7	7	4	1		pn.	.
2754	Kanyok (Kanioka)	0.54453	247,332	281,274	570,600	NAB57f	99-AURQ-u	ci-kanyoka		98.00	275,649	1csu.	10	10	12	5	3	Kanyok	PNb	.
2755	Kaonde (Kawonde)	0.08200	37,245	42,357	85,926	NAB57b	99-AURQ-z	ci-kaonde		90.00	38,121	2Asu.	10	8	12	4	1	Kikaonde*	PNB	.
2756	Kari (Kare)	0.00316	1,435	1,632	3,311	NAB57c	99-ASIA-a	li-kari-li		80.00	1,306	0....	10	8	6	4	1		...	.
2757	Kela (Lemba)	0.87083	395,542	449,823	912,522	NAB57h	99-AUIN-a	o-kela		93.00	418,335	0....	10	10	7	5	3	Okela*	P..	.
2758	Kele (Kili, Yakusu)	0.60659	275,521	313,331	635,631	NAB57c	99-ATBB-a	lo-kele	1	85.00	266,331	0....	10	10	7	5	2	Lokele*	PN.	.
2759	Kete (Mbagani)	0.02000	9,084	10,331	20,958	NAB57f	99-AURQ-d	south lu-kete		95.00	9,814	1csu.	10	9	11	5	1		pnb	.
2760	Kinya-Mituku	0.10000	45,421	51,654	104,788	NAB57c	99-ATCA-b	ki-nya-mituku		80.00	41,324	0....	10	9	7	4	1		...	.
2761	Koguru	0.01000	4,542	5,165	10,479	NAB57c	99-ASKB-c	bo-guru		30.00	1,550	0....	9	5	7	2	1		...	.
2762	Kongo (San Salvador)	1.05400	478,740	544,438	1,104,461	NAB57b	99-AURG-p	ki-shi-koongo		98.00	533,550	1as..	10	10	12	5	1		PNB	b
2763	Kongo Creole (Tuba, Leta)	6.46381	2,935,943	3,338,848	6,773,271	NAB57b	99-AURG-a	ki-tuba	16	93.00	3,105,129	4as..	10	5	11	5	3	Kituba	PNB	b
2764	Konjo	0.37531	170,470	193,864	393,278	NAB57d	99-AUSD-r	o-ru-konzo		84.00	162,846	1csu.	10	7	7	4	3	Lhukonzo*	Pnb	b
2765	Kpagua	0.01000	4,542	5,165	10,479	NAB66b	93-ABAJ-b	kpagua		80.00	4,132	0....	10	7	7	3	2		...	.
2766	Kpala (Gbakpwa)	0.00947	4,301	4,892	9,923	NAB66z	93-ADCB-a	kpala		40.00	1,957	0....	9	6	7	4	2		...	b
2767	Kuba (Northern Luba)	0.15781	71,679	81,516	165,365	NAB57b	99-AURQ-s	luna		43.00	35,052	1csu.	9	7	7	5	3	Kuba: Inkongo*	PNB	.
2768	Kumu (Komo, Kuumu)	0.55058	250,080	284,399	576,940	NAB57c	99-ASGA-a	ki-kuumu		85.00	241,739	0.s..	10	7	7	4	3	Komo	P..	b
2769	Kunda (Seba)	0.40000	181,685	206,618	419,150	NAB57h	99-AURR-p	ki-seba		97.00	200,419	1.su.	10	8	11	4	3		pnb	.
2770	Kusu (Kutsu, Kongola)	0.12955	58,843	66,918	135,752	NAB57h	99-AUIN-e	lo-kutsu		85.00	56,881	0....	10	8	7	4	3		p..	.
2771	Kwami (Kwame)	0.02000	9,084	10,331	20,958	NAB57c	99-AUJB-a	ki-kwame		80.00	8,265	0....	10	7	7	4	1		...	.
2772	Kwese (Pindi)	0.13666	62,073	70,591	143,203	NAB57b	99-AUHC-a	ki-kwezo		95.00	67,061	0....	10	9	11	4	3	Kikwese*	P..	.
2773	Lala-Bisa	1.11602	506,910	576,475	1,169,451	NAB57b	99-AURR-t	i-ci-lala		96.50	556,298	1.su.	10	8	12	4	1	Lala-bisa	PNb	.
2774	Lalia	0.13339	60,587	68,902	139,776	NAB57h	99-AUIL-b	lalia		90.00	62,012	0....	10	8	11	4	1		pn.	.
2775	Lamba	0.04000	18,168	20,662	41,915	NAB57b	99-AURR-o	i-ci-lamba		90.00	18,596	1.su.	10	10	12	5	1	Ichilamba*	PNB	.
2776	Langwasi	0.01005	4,565	5,191	10,531	NAB66b	93-ABAH-b	langbashe		70.00	3,634	0....	10	8	7	4	1		...	.
2777	Lega (Shabunda Rega)	1.42293	646,313	735,007	1,491,054	NAB57c	99-AUJD-a	ki-lega-shabunda	2	87.00	639,456	0....	10	7	7	5	3	Kilega*	PN.	.
2778	Leku	0.01000	4,542	5,165	10,479	NAB57c	99-AUIE-ca	i-liku		80.00	4,132	0....	10	8	7	4	2	Eleku	P..	.
2779	Lele (Bashilele)	0.12955	58,843	66,918	135,752	NAB57b	99-AUIP-b	u-si-lele		90.00	60,227	0....	10	8	12	4	1		pnb	.
2780	Lendu (Baledha, Hema)	1.65632	752,321	855,564	1,735,618	NAB66g	03-BADA-b	bale-dha	2	90.00	770,007	0.s..	10	7	7	5	3	Lendu	PN.	.
2781	Lengola (Lengora)	0.10000	45,421	51,654	104,788	NAB57c	99-ATDA-a	ki-lengola		70.00	36,158	0....	10	8	6	5	2		...	.
2782	Lese (Lissi, Mbuti)	0.13613	61,832	70,317	142,647	NAB66g	03-BACA-d	lese-otsodu		55.00	38,674	0....	10	7	7	4	3	Lese	p..	b
2783	Likila (Bangela, Balobo)	0.02000	9,084	10,331	20,958	NAB57h	99-AUIA-c	li-kila		90.00	9,298	0....	10	8	11	4	1		...	.
2784	Liko (Lika, Toriko)	0.17417	79,110	89,967	182,509	NAB57c	99-ASDA-a	li-lika		80.00	71,973	0....	10	8	7	4	1	Lika	...	.
2785	Lingala	4.00000	1,816,850	2,066,180	4,191,504	NAB57c	99-AUIF-b	vehicular lingala	35	93.70	1,936,011	4asu.	10	10	11	5	3	Lingala	PNB	b
2786	Loanda Mbundu (Kimbundu)	0.03000	13,626	15,496	31,436	NAB57b	99-AURI-a	ki-mbundu		65.00	10,073	0....	10	9	10	5	2	Kimbundu: Luanda*	PNB	.
2787	Lobala	0.13804	62,699	71,304	144,649	NAB57c	99-AUFK-a	lo-bala		50.00	35,652	0....	10	7	7	4	1	Lobala	...	b
2788	Logo (Logo Kuli)	0.60958	276,879	314,875	638,764	NAB66e	03-BAAC-a	logo-ti		91.00	286,537	0....	10	8	7	5	1	Logo	P..	.
2789	Loi	0.01000	4,542	5,165	10,479	NAB57h	99-AUIA-a	ba-loi		80.00	4,132	0....	10	7	7	2	1		...	.
2790	Lombi (Rombi, Odyalombito	0.02910	13,218	15,031	30,493	NAB66g	03-BABA-i	odya-lombi-to		55.00	8,267	0....	10	7	7	4	1		...	.
2791	Lombo (Turumbu)	0.04983	22,633	25,739	52,216	NAB57c	99-ATBD-l	l-ombo		80.00	20,592	0....	10	8	7	4	1		...	.
2792	Lonzo	0.00462	2,098	2,386	4,841	NAB57b	99-AURH-bj	ki-lonzo		85.00	2,028	0....	10	8	6	4	1		p..	.
2793	Lower Kongo (Cataract)	1.30000	590,476	671,508	1,362,239	NAB57b	99-AURG-f	central ki-koongo		98.00	658,078	4as..	10	10	10	5	3	Kongo	PNB	b
2794	Luba (Luba-Bambo)	4.10128	1,862,852	2,118,496	4,297,633	NAB57f	99-AURQ-v	ki-luba	14	97.10	2,057,059	2csu.	10	10	11	5	3	Kiluba*	PNB	b
2795	Luba-Hemba (Eastern Luba)	0.35518	161,327	183,466	372,185	NAB57f	99-AURQ-w	ki-hemba		97.00	177,962	1csu.	10	8	13	4	3		pnb	.
2796	Luba-Lulua (Western Luba)	5.20000	2,361,905	2,686,034	5,448,955	NAB57f	99-AURQ-l	vehicular ci-luba	18	93.00	2,498,011	4csu.	10	10	11	5	3	Tshiluba*	PNB	b
2797	Luba-Shankadi	1.00000	454,212	516,545	1,047,876	NAB57f	99-AURQ-l	vehicular ci-luba		96.00	495,883	4csu.	10	8	14	4	3	Tshiluba*	PNB	b
2798	Lwalwa	0.10463	47,524	54,046	109,639	NAB57f	99-AURQ-a	lwalwa		95.00	51,344	1csu.	10	8	11	4	1		pnb	.
2799	Lwena (Luvale)	0.30000	136,264	154,963	314,363	NAB57b	99-AURP-h	lwena-luvale	1	90.00	139,467	0....	10	8	12	5	1	Chiluvale*	PNB	.
2800	Ma	0.01958	8,893	10,114	20,517	NAB66z	93-AGAA-a	a-ma-ro		40.00	4,046	0....	9	7	7	4	1		...	.
2801	Mabaale (Mbali, Banza)	0.10000	45,421	51,654	104,788	NAB57c	99-AUID-a	lo-mabaale		85.00	43,906	0....	10	8	7	4	3		...	.
2802	Madi (Olubo, West Madi)	0.10000	45,421	51,654	104,788	NAB66e	03-BAAI-a	moyo		85.00	43,906	1....	10	8	7	4	1	Madi	PN.	.
2803	Mamvu (Momfu)	0.16336	74,200	84,383	171,181	NAB66g	03-BACA-b	mamvu		55.00	46,411	0....	10	7	7	5	2	Mamvu	P..	.
2804	Mangbele	0.02000	9,084	10,331	20,958	NAB66g	03-BABA-g	mangbele		60.00	6,199	0....	10	7	6	4	1		...	.
2805	Mangbetu (Amangbetu)	1.87009	849,418	965,986	1,959,622	NAB66g	03-BABA-a	na-mangbetu-ti		94.00	908,026	0....	10	7	7	4	3	Mangbetu	...	b
2806	Mangbutu (Wambutu)	0.04084	18,550	21,096	42,795	NAB66g	03-BACB-a	mangbutu-li		50.00	10,548	0....	10	7	7	5	2		...	.
2807	Mayeka	0.05000	22,711	25,827	52,394	NAB57c	99-ASMA-c	ma-yeka		70.00	18,079	0....	10	8	7	4	1		...	.
2808	Mayogo	0.27226	123,664	140,635	285,295	NAB66z	93-AEAA-a	mangbele-mayogo		85.00	119,539	0....	10	10	7	5	3	Mayogo	...	b
2809	Mba (Mbae, Manga)	0.07083	32,172	36,587	74,221	NAB66z	93-AFAA-a	mba-ni		68.00	24,879	0....	10	7	7	5	2		...	.
2810	Mbacca Pygmy	0.00500	2,271	2,583	5,239	BYG12	93-ADBA-a	ngbaka-ma'bo		20.00	517	0.s..	9	5	4	4	1	Ngbaka: Ma'bo*	Pnb	b
2811	Mbala	0.96759	439,491	499,804	1,013,914	NAB57b	99-AUHA	mbala cluster	1	97.00	484,810	0....	10	8	11	4	1	Mbala	P..	b
2812	Mbanja	0.37433	170,025	193,358	392,251	NAB66b	93-ABAK-a	mbanja		92.00	177,890	0....	10	8	7	4	1		p..	.
2813	Mbanza	0.50000	227,106	258,272	523,938	NAB66b	93-ABAK-b	mbanza		94.00	242,776	0....	10	7	7	2	2	Mbanza	P..	b
2814	Mbesa	0.02000	9,084	10,331	20,958	NAB57c	99-ATAA-a	um-mbesa		80.00	8,265	0....	10	7	7	4	1		...	.
2815	Mbo	0.02585	11,741	13,353	27,088	NAB57d	99-ASFA-d	i-mbo		90.00	12,017	0....	10	8	11	4	1		...	.
2816	Mbole	0.49826	226,316	257,374	522,115	NAB57h	99-AUIK-b	west central lo-mbole.		95.00	244,505	0....	10	8	7	4	3		...	.
2817	Mbuti Pygmy (Twa)	0.05000	22,711	25,827	52,394	BYG12	03-BACA-d	lese-otsodu		25.00	6,457	0....	9	6	7	5	1	Lese	p..	b
2818	Mbuti Pygmy (Twa)	0.16175	73,469	83,551	169,494	BYG12	99-ASHA-a	ki-bira		30.00	25,065	0....	9	6	7	5	3	Kibira*	P..	.
2819	Mfinu (Mfunuka)	0.02000	9,084	10,331	20,958	NAB57b	99-AURD-q	m-finu		90.00	9,298	0....	10	9	11	5	1		p..	.
2820	Moingi	0.01000	4,542	5,165	10,479	NAB57c	99-ATBD	east mbole cluster		80.00	4,132	0....	10	8	7	4	1		...	.
2821	Mongo	1.38000	626,813	712,832	1,446,069	NAB57h	99-AUIJ-c	basi-mongo	9	97.00	691,447	4....	10	10	12	5	2		PNB	.
2822	Monjombo (Monzumbo)	0.01578	7,167	8,151	16,535	NAB66z	93-ADCA-a	mo-nzombo		30.00	2,445	0....	9	5	7	4	1		...	.
2823	Mono	0.21779	98,923	112,498	228,217	NAB66b	93-ABAF-a	mono		70.00	78,749	0....	10	7	7	2	2	Mono	...	.
2824	Moru	0.02000	9,084	10,331	20,958	NAB66g	03-BAAA-a	kala-moru		60.00	6,199	1.s..	10	7	6	4	2	Moru	PN.	.
2825	Mpuon (Mbuun, Bunda)	0.79826	362,580	412,337	836,478	NAB57b	99-AURE-g	i-mbuun		96.00	395,844	0.s..	10	8	11	2	3	Gimbunda*	P..	.
2826	Mundu (Mundo, Mondo)	0.00996	4,524	5,145	10,437	NAB66z	93-AEBA-b	mundu-shatt		45.00	2,315	0....	9	7	7	4	1	Mundu	P..	b
2827	Mvuba (Bambuba, Obiye)	0.01000	4,542	5,165	10,479	BYG12	03-BACA-e	mvu'ba		20.00	1,033	0....	9	5	6	4	2		p..	.
2828	Mwenga Lega (Rega)	0.08812	40,025	45,518	92,339	NAB57c	99-AUJC-a	ki-lega-mwenga		40.00	18,207	0....	9	6	7	2	2	Lega-mwenga	...	b
2829	Nande (Nandi, Ndandi)	2.72810	1,239,137	1,409,186	2,858,711	NAB57d	99-AUSD-q	e-ki-nande	5	97.50	1,373,957	4csu.	10	10	10	5	3	Kinandi*	PNB	b
2830	Ndaka (Ndaaka)	0.05875	26,685	30,347	61,563	NAB57c	99-ASFA-b	i-ndaaka		80.00	24,278	0....	10	8	7	4	1		...	.
2831	Ndembu Lunda	0.07009	31,836	36,205	73,446	NAB57b	99-AURP-k	ci-lunda		95.00	34,394	0....	10	10	12	5	2	Lunda	PNB	.
2832	Ndengese (Dengese, Ileo)	0.01667	7,572	8,611	17,468	NAB57b	99-AUIO-b	lo-lengese		90.00	7,750	0....	10	8	11	4	1		p..	b
2833	Ndo (Kebu, Okebu)	1.22000	554,139	630,185	1,278,409	NAB66g	03-BACC-a	ke'bu-tu		96.00	604,977	0....	10	7	7	5	1	Kebu*	PN.	.
2834	Ndobo	0.02000	9,084	10,331	20,958	NAB57h	99-AUIC-c	ndoobo		85.00	8,781	0....	10	8	7	4	1		p..	.
2835	Ndogo	0.01000	4,542	5,165	10,479	NAB66z	93-ACAB-a	ndogo		45.00	2,324	0....	9	6	6	2	1	Ndogo	P..	.
2836	Ndolo (Mosange, Tando)	0.02761	12,541	14,262	28,932	NAB57h	99-AUIE-c	n-dolo		85.00	12,123	0....	10	8	7	4	1		P..	b
2837	Ndunga (Bondonga, Modunga	0.01042	4,733	5,382	10,919	NAB66z	93-AFBA-a	ndunga-le		40.00	2,153	0....	9	6	6	2	0		...	.
2838	Ngala	1.50000	681,319	774,817	1,571,814	NAB57c	99-AUIF-c	bangala-3	18	96.00	743,825	1csu.	10	9	7	5	3	Bangala	PNB	b
2839	Ngando (Ngandu)	0.60289	273,840	311,420	631,754	NAB57h	99-AUIL-d	lo-ngando		98.00	305,191	0....	10	9	12	4	3	Longandu*	PN.	.
2840	Ngbaka Mabo (Bwaka, Gbaka	0.03686	16,742	19,040	38,625	NAB66z	93-ADBA-a	ngbaka-ma'bo	1	85.00	16,184	0.s..	10	10	7	5	1	Ngbaka: Ma'bo*	Pnb	b
2841	Ngbandi (Nabandi, Mbati)	0.64224	291,713	331,746	672,988	NAB66z	93-ABBA-b	ngbandi		93.00	308,524	1.s..	10	6	7	4	3	Ngbandi	PNb	b
2842	Ngbee	0.14948	67,896	77,213	156,637	NAB57c	99-ASJA-a	li-ngbee		80.00	61,771	0....	10	8	7	2	1		...	.
2843	Ngbinda (Bangbinda)	0.01000	4,542	5,165	10,479	NAB57c	99-ASLA	ngbinda cluster		80.00	4,132	0....	10	8	7	2	0		...	.
2844	Ngbundu	0.05361	24,350	27,692	56,177	NAB66b	93-ABAF-m	ngbundu		60.00	16,615	0....	10	7	6	5	1		...	b
2845	Ngeti (South Lendu, Druna	0.02000	9,084	10,331	20,958	NAB66g	03-BADB-ad	ngiti		40.00	4,132	0....	9	6	7	2	3		...	.
2846	Ngoli (Ngul, Ngulu)	0.02000	9,084	10,331	20,958	NAB57b	99-AUGB-a	i-ngul		90.00	9,298	0....	10	8	11	4	1		...	.
2847	Ngombe	0.74738	339,469	386,055	783,162	NAB57h	99-AUIG-b	li-ngombe	1	95.00	366,753	0....	10	10	12	5	3	Lingombe*	PN.	.
2848	Ngongo	0.30000	136,264	154,963	314,363	NAB57b	99-AUIN-d	lo-nkucu		94.00	145,666	0....	10	8	11	2	2		p..	b
2849	Ngubu	0.02000	9,084	10,331	20,958	NAB66b	93-ABAH-c	ngbugu		60.00	6,199	0....	10	7	7	2	1		...	.
2850	Ngundu	0.01000	4,542	5,165	10,479	NAB66b	93-ABAJ-a	ngundu		80.00	4,132	0....	10	8	7	2	2		...	.
2851	Ngwili (Ngiri, Nguili)	0.02500	11,355	12,914	26,197	NAB57h	99-AUIA-a	ba-loi		90.00	11,622	0....	10	8	11	4	2		...	.
2852	Nkundu (Nkundo)	1.85000	840,293	955,608	1,938,571	NAB57h	99-AUIJ-ce	lo-nkundo	5	98.00	936,496	1....	10	9	11	4	3		pnb	.
2853	Nkutu (Nkutshu, Bankutu)	0.19352	87,899	99,962	202,785	NAB57h	99-AUIN-c	lo-nkutu	1	90.00	89,966	0....	10	10	12	5	1	Lonkutu*	P..	.
2854	Ntomba (Ntomba-Bolia)	0.37912	172,201	195,833	397,271	NAB57h	99-AUIJ-b	north lo-ntomba		96.00	187,999	1....	10	10	12	5	1	Lontomba*	Pnb	.
2855	Nyali (Huku, Bombi)	0.10429	47,370	53,870	109,283	NAB57c	99-ASFA-e	li-nyaali		80.00	43,096	0....	10	10	7	5	1		...	.
2856	Nyanga	0.12456	56,577	64,341	130,523	NAB57c	99-AUJA-a	ki-nyanga		45.00	28,953	0....	9	6	7	2	2		...	.
2857	Nyanga-Li	0.11554	52,480	59,682	121,072	NAB57d	99-ASMA-a	li-nyanga-le		95.00	56,698	0....	10	8	11	4	1		...	.
2858	Nyindu	0.02000	9,084	10,331	20,958	NAB57d	99-AUSD-md	e-ki-nyindu		80.00	8,265	1csu.	10	8	7	2	0		pnb	.
2859	Nzakara (Sakara, Zakara)	0.00300	1,363	1,550	3,144	NAB66z	93-BAAA-c	kporo-nzakara		85.00	1,317	1cs..	10	9	7	5	1		pnb	.
2860	Ombo (Songola)	0.02000	9,084	10,331	20,958	NAB57h	99-ATBD-u	lo-ombo		90.00	9,298	0....	10	8	11	4	1		...	.
2861	Omi	0.11466	52,080	59,227	120,149	NAB66e	03-BAAD-a	keliko-madi		60.00	35,536	0....	10	6	7	3	0	Kaliko	...	.
2862	Pambia	0.07301	33,162	37,713	76,505	NAB66a	93-BABA-a	pa-pambia		80.00	30,170	0....	10	8	8	0	0		...	.
2863	Pelende	0.02000	9,084	10,331	20,958	NAB57b	99-AURH-bd	ki-pelende	1	90.00	9,298	0....	10	8	11	4	1		p..	.
2864	Pende (Phende, Pinji)	1.28448	583,427	663,492	1,345,976	NAB57b	99-AUHB-a	gi-phende	1	99.00	656,857	0....	10	10	11	5	2	Giphende*	PNB	.
2865	Peri (Pere, Pili, Ebhele)	0.04354	19,776	22,490	45,625	NAB57c	99-ASGA-b	e-bhele		80.00	17,992	0.s..	10	8	7	4	1	Ipere*	P..	.
2866	Plains Bira (Bera)	0.30045	136,468	155,196	314,834	NAB57c	99-ASHA-a	ki-bira		89.00	138,124	0....	10	5	7	5	3	Kibira*	P..	.
2867	Poke (Topoke, Puki)	0.22920	104,105	118,392	240,173	NAB57c	99-ATAC-h	li-u-twa		97.00	114,840	0....	10	10	12	5	1	Poke	P..	.

Continued opposite

Table 8-2 continued

EVANGELIZATION								EVANGELISM			ADDITIONAL DESCRIPTIVE DATA
Ref 1	D 28	aC 29	CG% 30	r 31	E 32	U 33	W 34	e 35	R 36	T 37	Locations, civil divisions, literacy, religions, church history, denominations, dioceses, church growth, missions, agencies, ministries, movements 38
2744	0	10	5.17	7	50.00	50.00	B	1.82	338	4	Traders from India, Pakistan. Hindus 60%, Muslims 30%(mainly Ismailis), Baha'is 9%.
2745	0	10	0.00	8	49.30	50.70	A	0.54	38	3	One main community, in Lubumbashi, of practicing Jews. Gradual decline by emigration to Israel, Americas.
2746	1	7	7.07	1	99.90	0.10	C	450.04	171	10	Kivu/Shaba Regions. Animists 1%. D=RCC.
2747	1	7	7.38	0	99.80	0.20	C	335.80	211	9	Eastern Zaire. Related to Bira, Huku. Animists 10%. D=RCC.
2748	2	8	6.73	1	99.65	0.35	C	270.46	196	8	Also in Uganda and Sudan. Muslims 13%, animists 10%. D=RCC,ECZ(CECA). M=CICM,WF,SJ,OFM,AIM,UBS.
2749	2	6	10.27	1	99.98	0.02	C	532.97	216	10	Kasai Oriental Region. Dialect of Songe. Animists 1%. D=RCC,AICs.
2750	2	7	7.08	0	99.83	0.17	C	357.48	198	9	Haut-Zaire Region, Aru Zone, south of Nzoro river. Also in Sudan. Animists 6%. D=RCC,ECZ(CECA). M=AIM.
2751	4	7	5.34	4	99.95	0.05	C	537.46	120	10	Southwest Shaba Region. D=RCC(D-Kikwit,D-Popokabaka,D-Kamina),ECZ,EUSJ,other AICs. M=CICM,WF,SJ,OFM,CMML.
2752	1	7	6.69	0	99.90	0.10	C	420.48	174	10	Haut-Zaire Region. A pidginized language, close to Pagabete. D=RCC.
2753	1	7	6.80	0	99.80	0.20	C	341.64	194	9	Kivu Region, Walikale Zone, Kabunga area. Related to Lega. Animists 10%. D=RCC.
2754	3	7	10.77	1	99.98	0.02	C	547.28	219	10	Kasai Oriental Region, Mwene-Ditu Zone. D=RCC,ECZ(CPZA),AICs. M=CICM,WF,SJ,OFM,Baptist Ch of Kinshasa,NLEA,APM.
2755	1	6	8.60	4	99.90	0.10	C	492.75	184	10	Shaba Region, eastern part of Kolwezi Zone. Majority in Zambia. Animists 1%. D=RCC(D-Sakania-Kipushi).
2756	1	9	4.99	0	99.80	0.20	C	335.80	154	9	Scattered groups in northwestern Haut-Zaire Region, north of Uele river. Also in CAR. Animists 10%. D=RCC(D-Bondo).
2757	5	6	11.23	0	99.93	0.07	C	451.46	261	10	Kasai Oriental Region, Lomela Zone. Animists 5%. D=RCC(D-Kole),ECZ(CRS),EJCSK,Kitawala,other AICs. M=SSCC,CICM,SJ,WF,OFM,NSM.
2758	5	7	6.38	0	99.85	0.15	C	397.12	168	9	Likelo. Haut-Zaire Region, Isangi Zone. Animists 5%. D=ECZ(CBFZ,SA),RCC(D-Isangi),EJCSK,ECC/ECA,AICs. M=BMS,NLEA.
2759	3	7	7.13	1	99.95	0.05	C	502.78	162	10	Kasai Occidental Region, northeast of Mweka. D=RCC,Eglise Ste Immanuel,other AICs. M=NLEA.
2760	1	6	8.68	0	99.80	0.20	C	332.88	244	9	Haut-Zaire Region, Ubundu Zone, west of Lualaba river. Animists 4%. D=RCC.
2761	1	6	5.17	0	60.00	40.00	B	65.70	303	6	Haut-Zaire Region, west of Garamba National Park. Related to Bira, Huku. Animists 40%. D=RCC.
2762	4	7	3.29	5	99.98	0.02	C	590.20	79	10	Along Congo river below Kinshasa, also northern Angola. D=RCC(D-Matadi),ECZ(SA,CBZO),EJCSK,other AICs. M=ABFMS.
2763	4	9	5.62	5	99.93	0.07	C	566.88	116	10	Creole lingua franca across Bas-Zaire and southern Bandundu Regions. Close to Munukutuba of Congo. Many nonreligious. D=RCC,ECZ(SA,CBZO),EJCSK,AICs.
2764	2	6	5.21	1	99.84	0.16	C	398.58	154	9	On Ruwenzori Mountains. Animists 10%. D=RCC(D-Butembo-Beni),AICs. M=CICM,WF,OFM,CBFMS.
2765	2	7	6.21	0	99.80	0.20	C	335.80	192	9	Northern Zaire. Closest to Ngundu, in Banda family. Animists 10%. D=RCC,ECZ.
2766	2	6	5.42	0	77.00	23.00	B	112.42	244	7	Equateur Region, in Libenge and Bosobolo Zones. Bilingual in Lingala. Animists 25%. D=RCC,ECZ(CECU,CEUM). M=EFCA,ECCA.
2767	6	6	5.66	1	94.00	6.00	B	147.53	208	7	Kasai Oriental Region, Lusambo Zone. Animists 21%. D=RCC(D-Mweka),ECZ,EJCSK,AACJM,EFMJC,other AICs. M=APCM,WM,SJ,CICM,WF,OFM,NLEA.
2768	6	6	10.62	0	99.85	0.15	C	397.12	259	9	Covers vast area from Kisangani-Kivu-Lubutu-Punia. Bilingual in Swahili. Animists 5%. D=RCC(M-Kisangani),ECZ(CEPZA,CECCA,CEBZ,CFZ,CNCA),EECZ.
2769	2	6	10.41	1	99.97	0.03	C	516.91	223	10	Shaba Region, Kasenga Zone. D=RCC,AICs. M=WF,CICM,SJ.
2770	1	6	9.03	0	99.85	0.15	C	378.50	236	9	Southwestern corner of Kivu Region, Kibombo Zone. Animists 5%. D=RCC. M=SJ,CICM,WF,NLEA.
2771	2	7	6.95	0	99.80	0.20	C	335.80	201	9	North Kivu. Animists 5%. D=RCC,ECZ(CEBZ). M=Berean Evangelical Mission.
2772	2	6	9.21	0	99.95	0.05	C	475.04	213	10	Eastern Bandundu Region, west of Kikwit. Animists 1%. D=RCC(D-Kikwit),ECZ(Mennonites, Baptists). M=CICM,WF,SJ,OFM,Every Child Ministries.
2773	1	7	5.35	1	99.97	0.03	C	512.48	128	10	Extreme southeast of Shaba Region. Primarily in Zambia. Animists 1%. D=RCC(D-Sakania-Kipushi). M=UCZ.
2774	1	6	9.13	0	99.90	0.10	C	430.33	222	10	Southeast corner of Equateur Region, Ikela Zone. D=RCC(D-Bokungu-Ikela).
2775	7	7	7.82	1	99.90	0.10	C	476.32	175	10	Shaba Region; mainly in Zambia. D=RCC(M-Lubumbashi,D-Sakania-Kipushi),ECZ(CAFS),EEA,EUSJ,GOC,AFK,other AICs. M=Baptist Ch of Kinshasa.
2776	2	10	6.07	0	99.70	0.30	C	275.94	200	8	Equateur Region, Nord Ubangi, Bosobolo Zone along Ubangi river. Also in CAR. Fishermen. Few literates. Some men fluent in Lingala and Sango. Animists 5%.
2777	3	6	11.70	0	99.87	0.13	C	412.81	278	10	Kivu Region, Shabunda and Pangi Zones. Animists 10%. Resistant to Christianity. D=RCC(D-Kasongo),ECZ(CELZA,CEBZ),AACJM. M=Berean Evangelical Mission.
2778	2	8	5.59	0	99.80	0.20	C	344.56	164	9	Dialect of Lusengo, on Zaire river. Animists 5%. D=RCC,ECZ.
2779	3	6	9.09	0	99.90	0.10	C	450.04	211	10	Western edge of Kasai Occidental Region. Close to Wongo. D=RCC,EJCSK,AACJM. M=NLEA.
2780	2	6	11.91	1	99.90	0.10	C	440.19	278	10	Hema-Nord. Haut-Zaire Region. Animists 5%. D=RCC(D-Bunia,D-Mahagi-Nioka),ECZ(Communaute Evangelique au Centre de l'Afrique). M=SIL,UBS,EECZ,AIM.
2781	3	7	8.54	0	99.70	0.30	C	275.94	254	8	Haut-Zaire Region, Ubundu Zone, along Lualaba river. Animists 10%. D=RCC,ECZ(CECCA),SDA. M=EECZ,WEC.
2782	2	6	8.61	0	96.00	4.00	B	192.72	294	7	Haut-Zaire Region. Many Pygmy groups coexist with the Lese. Lingua franca: Kingwana (Swahili). Animists 45%. D=RCC,ECZ(CECA,CAFEZA,CM). M=SCJ,AIM.
2783	1	7	7.07	0	99.90	0.10	C	420.48	183	10	Related to Libinza, Baloi. Animists 1%. D=RCC.
2784	2	6	9.29	0	99.80	0.20	C	335.80	256	9	Haut-Zaire Region, Wamba and Rungu Zones. Animists 5%, many Muslims D=RCC(D-Wamba),ECZ(CECCA). M=WEC.
2785	4	8	6.48	5	99.94	0.06	C	566.70	131	10	Major lingua franca along Zaire river. Animists 1%, some nonreligious. D=RCC,ECZ(CBZO),EJCSK,many other AICs. M=CICM,WF,SJ,IGCM.
2786	4	7	7.16	4	99.65	0.35	C	287.07	195	8	Refugees from Angola wars. Animists 3%. D=RCC,ECZ,EJCSK,ECUA. M=OFMCap,PFM.
2787	2	7	8.52	0	89.00	11.00	B	162.42	308	7	Equateur Region, Kungu and Bomongo Zones. Some also in Congo. Bilingual in Lingala. Animists 15%. D=RCC,ECZ(CECU,CDCZ). M=EFCA.
2788	2	6	10.81	0	99.91	0.09	C	425.15	262	10	Haut-Zaire Region, Faradje and Watsa Zones. Also in Sudan. Animists 3%. D=42% ECZ(CECA),RCC(D-Isiro-Niangara,D-Mahagi-Nioka). M=AIM.
2789	1	7	6.21	0	99.80	0.20	C	327.04	188	9	Equateur Region, around Bomongo. Animists 3%. D=RCC.
2790	2	7	6.95	0	90.00	10.00	B	180.67	263	7	Haut-Zaire Region, southern part of Bafwasende Zone. Close to the Mangbetu. Animists 15%. D=RCC,ECZ(CECCA). M=WEC.
2791	1	7	7.93	0	99.80	0.20	C	335.80	224	9	Haut-Zaire Region, along Zaire river in Isangi area. Animists 2%. D=RCC.
2792	1	8	5.46	0	99.85	0.15	C	372.30	158	9	Bandundu Region, Kenge Zone. Animists 4%. D=RCC.
2793	4	8	11.73	5	99.98	0.02	C	593.78	218	10	Lower Congo region around Mbanza Mantake. D=RCC,ECZ(SA),EJCSK,other AICs.
2794	8	7	6.05	1	99.97	0.03	C	563.87	129	10	Luba-Shaba. Used across Katanga. D=RCC(D-Mbuji-Mayi,D-Mweka,&c),ECZ(CL,CEPS,CPS),EJCTSE,EUSE,EFMJC,GOC,ESSE,many other AICs. M=SJ,EECZ.
2795	3	7	4.70	3	99.97	0.03	C	541.69	110	10	Shaba Region around Kongolo. D=RCC(D-Kalemie-Kirungu,D-Kamina,D-Kilwa-Kasenga),SDA,many AICs.
2796	6	7	5.83	3	99.93	0.07	C	539.72	126	10	Used throughout Kasai. D=RCC(M-Kananga,D-Luebo,D-Mweka),ECZ,COSSEUJCA,EUSE,EFMJC,many other AICs. M=SJ,NLEA,APM,UBS,UMC.
2797	4	7	5.77	3	99.96	0.04	C	571.15	122	10	In south. Few animists left. D=RCC,EJCSK,ECZ,many other AICs.
2798	1	7	8.92	1	99.95	0.05	C	495.85	199	10	Kasai Occidental Region, Luiza Zone. Some nonreligious. D=RCC.
2799	1	6	6.44	4	99.90	0.10	C	473.04	150	10	Mainly in Angola, also Zambia. Animists 5%. D=RCC. M=Africa Missionary Evangelistic Committee.
2800	1	7	6.19	0	73.00	27.00	B	106.58	286	7	Haut-Zaire Region, north of Niangara. Close to Dongo,Ngbaka-Mbo. Animists 25%. D=RCC.
2801	3	6	8.75	0	99.85	0.15	C	381.60	228	9	Equateur Region, Ngiri River area. Animists 1%. D=RCC(D-Budjala),EJCSK,other AICs.
2802	1	7	8.75	1	99.85	0.15	C	390.91	221	9	Related to Logo. Northeast corner of Zaire. Muslims 10%(Shafi Sunnis), animists 5%. D=RCC(D-Buta).
2803	2	7	8.81	0	94.00	6.00	B	188.70	306	7	Haut-Zaire Region, Watsa Zone. Animists 20%. D=RCC,ECZ(CADZ,CECA). M=AoG,AIM.
2804	1	6	6.64	0	92.00	8.00	C	201.48	248	8	Haut-Zaire Region, Rungu Zone. Related to Mangbetu. Animists 5%. D=RCC.
2805	2	6	12.09	0	99.94	0.06	C	459.75	282	10	Haut-Zaire Region, 4 Zones. Also in Uganda. 60% bilinguals in Bangala. Animists 2%. D=RCC(D-Buta,D-Isiro-Niangara),ECZ(CNZ,CECCA,CNCA). M=WEC,AoG..
2806	2	6	7.21	0	87.00	13.00	B	158.77	280	7	Haut-Zaire Region, south of Watsa. Animists 8%. D=RCC,ECZ(CECA). M=AIM,AoG.
2807	1	7	7.79	0	99.70	0.30	C	268.27	242	8	Around borders of CAR and Congo with Zaire; also in CAR. Related to Gbati-Ri. Animists 5%. D=RCC.
2808	4	6	9.84	0	99.85	0.15	C	394.01	243	9	Haut-Zaire Region, Isiro area. Lingua franca: Lingala or Bangala. Few animists left. D=RCC,ECZ(CECCA),EEHU/ECC,AICs. M=HAM(WEC),WF,CICM.
2809	2	6	8.13	0	99.68	0.32	C	260.61	249	8	Haut-Zaire Region, Banalia Territory, Banjwade area. Animists 2%. D=African Independent Ch,ECC/ECA. M=BMS,UFM.
2810	1	7	4.02	0	56.00	44.00	B	40.88	251	6	Pygmies in Equateur Region rain-forest. Animists 80%. D=RCC. M=WEC.
2811	2	6	11.39	0	99.97	0.03	C	495.67	251	10	Bandundu Region, Bagata and Bulungu Zones. Fairly bilingual in Kituba. D=RCC(D-Kenge,D-Kikwit),Baptist Chs. M=Every Child Ministries.
2812	1	6	10.28	0	99.92	0.08	C	426.46	261	10	Equateur Region. Animists 3%. D=RCC(D-Molegbe).
2813	2	7	10.62	0	99.94	0.06	C	456.32	256	10	Equateur Region, around Ngbaka language area. Also in Congo and CAR. Bilinguals in Lingala 60%. Animists 3%. D=RCC,ECZ(CECU,CEUM). M=EFCA,ECCA.
2814	1	7	6.95	0	99.80	0.20	C	332.88	202	9	Haut-Zaire Region, northern Yahuma Zone, south of Zaire river. Animists 5%. D=RCC.
2815	1	7	7.35	0	99.90	0.10	C	423.76	201	10	Haut-Zaire Region, southwestern part of Mambasa Zone. Few animists. D=RCC.
2816	3	6	10.63	0	99.95	0.05	C	461.17	249	10	Haut-Zaire Region, southwest of Kisangani. Animists 2%. D=RCC(M-Mbandaka-Bikoro),EJCSK,other AICs. M=CICM,WF,SJ,OFM,DC.
2817	2	7	6.68	0	61.00	39.00	B	55.66	349	6	Haut-Zaire Region. Animists 75%. D=RCC(D-Tshumbe,D-Bunia),ECZ(CCZO,CAFEZA). M=WEC.
2818	2	7	8.14	1	70.00	30.00	B	76.65	362	6	Haut-Zaire Region, Irumu Zone. Animists 60%. D=RCC(D-Tshumbe,D-Bunia),ECZ(CAFEZA,CCZO). M=CMS,SDA,EM,AIM,WEC.
2819	2	7	7.07	0	99.90	0.10	C	430.33	178	10	Bandundu Region. Animists 1%. D=RCC,ECZ. M=CBZO/ABCUSA.
2820	1	7	6.21	0	99.80	0.20	C	332.88	185	9	Haut-Zaire Region, Yahuma Zone, south of Zaire river. Animists 6%. D=RCC.
2821	2	6	5.79	0	99.97	0.03	C	538.15	131	10	Equateur and Bandundu Regions. D=RCC(M-Mbandaka-Bikoro,D-Basankusu,D-Lisala),AICs. M=ABMU,NLEA.
2822	2	7	5.65	0	63.00	37.00	B	68.98	308	6	Equateur Region, east bank of Ubangi river south of Libenge. Also in Congo and CAR. Bilingual in Lingala. Fishermen. Animists 50%. D=RCC,ECZ(CECU).
2823	1	7	9.39	0	99.70	0.30	C	263.16	298	8	Equateur Region, Bosobolo Zone. Most are bilingual in Lingala or Sango. Few literates. Animists 5%. D=ECZ(CEUM,CECU). M=ECCA,EFCA.
2824	2	8	6.64	0	99.60	0.40	C	221.19	226	8	A few refugees, immigrants, and migrants from the Moru in the Sudan. Animists 10%. D=RCC,PECS. M=CMS,FSCJ.
2825	3	7	11.17	0	99.96	0.04	C	483.55	251	10	Bandundu Region, Idiofa Zone. Close to the Yansi. Animists 1%. D=RCC,EJCSK,other AICs.
2826	1	7	5.60	0	78.00	22.00	B	128.11	247	7	Haut-Zaire Region, north and northeast of Faradje. Primarily in Sudan. Lingua franca: Bangala. Animists 35%. D=ECZ(CECA). M=AIM.
2827	1	7	4.75	0	54.00	46.00	B	39.42	297	5	Kivu Region, Beni Zone, around Oicha. Animists 50%. D=ECZ(CECA). M=AIM,WEC.
2828	3	6	7.80	0	77.00	23.00	B	112.42	330	7	Kivu Region, Mwenga Zone. D=RCC,ECZ(CECA),AICs. Animists 30%. M=ACM,PBT.
2829	3	6	12.56	1	99.98	0.02	C	567.62	252	10	North Kivu Sub-Region, Beni and Lubero Zones. Very few animists left. D=RCC(D-Butembo-Beni,D-Goma),ECZ(CBK,CEBK,CEBZE),AICs. M=UFM,CBFMS,UBS.
2830	1	7	8.11	0	99.80	0.20	C	335.80	228	9	Haut-Zaire Region, Epulu area west of Mambasa. Animists 4%. D=RCC(M-Kisangani,D-Wamba). M=SCJ.
2831	3	7	6.51	4	99.95	0.05	C	530.52	143	10	South, southwest Shaba Region. Majority in Zambia, also Angola. D=RCC(D-Kikwit,D-Popokabaka),EUSJ,other AICs. M=CC(Zambia),CMML.
2832	1	7	6.88	0	99.90	0.10	C	433.62	173	10	Kasai Occidental Region, Dekese Zone. Animists 2%. D=RCC.
2833	2	6	11.64	0	99.96	0.04	C	476.54	269	10	Haut-Zaire Region, Mahagi and Aru Zones. A few in Uganda. Animists 2%. D=RCC,ECZ(CCZO/CECA). M=AIM.
2834	1	7	7.01	0	99.85	0.15	C	372.30	193	9	Equateur Region, between Bomongo and Zaire river. Animists 2%. D=RCC.
2835	1	9	5.60	0	78.00	22.00	B	128.11	247	7	A few refugees and immigrants from the Ndogo in the Sudan and CAR. Animists 30%, some Muslims 5%. D=RCC. M=SIL.
2836	2	7	7.36	0	99.85	0.15	C	387.81	193	9	Equateur Region, Budjala Zone. Bilingual in Lingala. Riverine. Animists 2%. D=RCC,ECZ(CECU). M=EFCA.
2837	0	7	5.52	0	68.00	32.00	B	99.28	280	6	Equateur Region, 8 villages in Lisala Zone. Close to the Mba (Kimanga). Animists 40%.
2838	5	6	4.29	4	99.96	0.04	C	539.61	102	10	Lingua franca for Haut-Zaire Region; also in CAR. D=RCC(M-Kinshasa,D-Budjala),ECZ(CECA,CADZ,CECCA),EJCSK,CHS,other AICs. M=AIM,AoG,WEC,UBS.
2839	3	6	10.88	0	99.98	0.02	C	518.66	233	10	Equateur Region, north of Ikela. Related to Lalia. D=RCC(D-Isangi,D-Basankusu),EJCSK,other AICs.
2840	4	6	7.67	0	99.85	0.15	C	409.53	189	10	Equateur Region, Libenge Zone. Majority in CAR and Congo. Most are bilingual in Lingala. Animists 3%. D=RCC(D-Budjala,D-Lolo,D-Molegbe),ECZ(CECU).
2841	2	6	10.89	1	99.93	0.07	C	485.41	236	10	Equateur Region, 4 Zones. Fairly bilingual in Lingala. Animists 2%. D=RCC(D-Budjala,D-Lisala),ECZ(CECU,CEUM). M=EFCA,ECCA,UBS.
2842	1	7	9.12	0	99.80	0.20	C	329.96	257	9	In northeast corner of Zaire, close to Uganda border. Animists 5%. D=RCC.
2843	0	7	6.21	0	99.80	0.20	C	321.20	191	9	Northeast corner of Zaire. Almost extinct. Animists 1%.
2844	2	6	7.70	0	98.00	2.00	C	214.62	266	8	Equateur Region, Sud Ubangi Libenge Zone. Bilingual in Lingala. Animists 5%. D=RCC,ECZ(CECU). M=EFCA.
2845	1	6	6.21	0	72.00	28.00	B	105.12	301	7	Haut-Zaire Region, south of Bunia. Animists 40%. D=ECZ(CECA,CAFEZA,CAZ). M=AIM,CMML,CMS.
2846	1	7	7.07	0	99.90	0.10	C	420.48	183	10	Western Bandundu Region along Kasai river north of Idiofa. Animists 2%. D=RCC.
2847	3	6	6.50	0	99.95	0.05	C	495.85	153	10	Equateur Region, along Zaire river. Animists 1%. D=RCC(D-Basankusu,D-Lisala),Evangelical Ch of Ubanga-Mongali,ECZ(CECU,CEUM,CBFZ). M=BMS,EFCA.
2848	2	6	10.06	0	99.94	0.06	C	466.61	232	10	Bandundu Region. Fairly bilingual in Kituba. Animists 2%. D=RCC,ECZ.
2849	1	7	6.64	0	92.00	8.00	C	201.48	252	8	Also in CAR. Related to Banda. Animists 10%. D=RCC.
2850	2	7	6.21	0	99.80	0.20	C	332.88	193	9	In Northern Zaire. Closest to Kpagua, in Banda family. Animists 5%. D=RCC,ECZ.
2851	2	7	7.31	0	99.90	0.10	C	430.33	183	10	Equateur Region, southern part of Bomongo Zone. Animists 3%. D=RCC,AICs.
2852	3	6	5.80	0	99.98	0.02	C	525.81	135	10	Equateur and Bandundu Regions. In Mongo sphere. D=RCC(M-Mbandaka-Bikoro),EJCSK,other AICs. M=CICM,WF,SJ,OFM,SDB.
2853	3	7	9.53	0	99.90	0.10	C	440.19	225	10	Kivu Region, Kibombo Zone. Animists 1%. D=RCC(D-Tshumbe),ECZ(CECA),AICs. M=AIM.
2854	3	7	10.34	0	99.96	0.04	C	511.58	221	10	Bandundu Region, northeast of Lake Tumba. Animists 2%. D=RCC,ECZ,AICs. M=ABFMS.
2855	2	7	8.73	0	99.80	0.20	C	341.64	239	9	Haut-Zaire Region, Djugu and Irumu Zones. Animists 4%. D=RCC,ECZ(CAFEZA). M=CMML.
2856	1	6	8.30	0	77.00	23.00	B	126.47	348	7	Nord-Kivu Region, Walikale Zone. Close to Kwami, Enya. Animists 20%. D=ECZ(CEPZA,CEBZE). M=SFM,CBFMS.
2857	1	6	9.03	0	99.95	0.05	C	461.17	229	10	Haut-Zaire Region, Watsa Zone. No animists left. D=RCC.
2858	0	6	6.95	1	99.80	0.20	C	344.56	210	9	Sud-Kivu Region, west of Lake Kivu. Close to Lega-Mwenda, and Shi. Animists 5%.
2859	2	8	5.00	0	99.85	0.15	C	406.42	134	10	Haut-Zaire Region, Bondo Zone. Primarily in CAR. Animists 1%. D=RCC,ECZ(CEBIE). M=BMM.
2860	1	7	7.07	0	99.90	0.10	C	420.48	183	10	Kivu Region, northwest of Kindu. Animists 1%. D=RCC. M=WEC.
2861	0	6	8.52	0	91.00	9.00	C	199.29	300	7	Haut-Zaire Region, Aru Zone, south of Nzoro river. Related to Moru. Animists 15%, Muslims 5%.
2862	0	0	8.34	0	99.80	0.20	C	297.84	273	8	Related to Zande. Animists 1%. D=RCC, ECZ, other AICs.
2863	1	7	7.07	0	99.90	0.10	C	423.76	181	10	Bandundu Region, Kenge Zone. Animists 2%. D=RCC.
2864	6	6	11.73	0	99.99	0.01	C	545.63	239	10	Bandundu Region, Idiofa and Gungu Zones. D=RCC(D-Luebo,D-Kikwit),ECZ(CEFMZ/Communaut Freres Mennonites),AACJM,EJCSK,EFMJC,other AICs.
2865	2	7	7.78	0	99.80	0.20	C	344.56	215	9	Kivu Region, Lubero Zone. Close to Komo and Bila peoples. Animists 10%. D=RCC,ECZ(CEBZE). M=CBFMS.
2866	4	6	10.00	1	99.89	0.11	C	422.30	242	10	Haut-Zaire Region, Irumu Zone. Animists 6%, Muslims 2%. D=RCC(D-Butembo-Beni,D-Bunia),ECZ(CAFEZA,CECA),Ch of the Brethren,some AICs.
2867	5	7	9.80	0	99.97	0.03	C	499.21	219	10	Haut-Zaire Region, Isangi Zone. D=RCC(D-Isangi),ECZ(CBFZ,CDCZ),EJCSK,ECC/ECA,other AICs. M=BMS.

Continued overleaf

Table 8-2 continued

PEOPLE		POPULATION				IDENTITY CODE		LANGUAGE		CHURCH		MINISTRY						SCRIPTURE		
Ref 1	*Ethnic name* 2	*P%* 3	*In 1995* 4	*In 2000* 5	*In 2025* 6	*Race* 7	*Language* 8	*Autoglossonym* 9	*S* 10	*AC* 11	*Members* 12	*Jayuh* 13-17	*d* 18	*wa* 19	*xc* 20	*mc* 21	*mi* 22	*Biblioglossonym* 23	*Pub* 24-26	*ss* 27
2868	Portuguese	0.01000	4,542	5,165	10,479	CEW21g	51-AABA-e	general português	1	92.00	4,752	2Bsuh	10	9	15	4	3	Portuguese	PNB	b
2869	Poto (Lusengo)	0.10000	45,421	51,654	104,788	NAB57c	99-AUIE-dn	lipoto-lusengo		80.00	41,324	0....	10	8	7	4	2	Lusengo	P..	.
2870	Ruund (Kambove Lunda)	0.36254	164,670	187,268	379,897	NAB57f	99-AURP-n	u-ruund	2	97.00	181,650	0....	10	10	12	5	1	Uruund*	PNb	.
2871	Sakata (Saka, Lesa, Bai)	0.26680	121,184	137,814	279,573	NAB57b	99-AURF-c	ki-sakata		95.00	130,923	0....	10	10	12	5	2	Kisakata*	P..	b
2872	Salampasu (Bakwaluntu)	0.25000	113,553	129,136	261,969	NAB57f	99-AURP-p	ci-salampahu		98.00	126,554	0....	10	9	11	4	2	Tshisalampasu*	Pnb	.
2873	Samba (Tsaam, Shankadi)	0.01000	4,542	5,165	10,479	NAB57b	99-AUHD-b	u-samba		90.00	4,649	0....	10	9	11	2	1		p..	.
2874	Sanga (Luba Garenganze)	1.31812	598,707	680,868	1,381,226	NAB57f	99-AURQ-x	ki-sanga	1	98.00	667,251	1csu.	10	10	11	5	3	Kisanga*	PNB	.
2875	Sango	0.01000	4,542	5,165	10,479	NAB66z	93-ABBA-a	sango	4	70.00	3,616	4.s..	10	8	6	4	2	Sango	PNB	b
2876	Sanza	0.06900	31,341	35,642	72,303	NAB57d	99-AUSD-rb	e-ki-sanza		70.00	24,949	1csu.	10	8	7	4	1		pnb	b
2877	Sengele (Sengere)	0.04000	18,168	20,662	41,915	NAB57h	99-AUIH-a	ke-sengele		90.00	18,596	0....	10	9	11	4	2	Kesengele*	P..	.
2878	Sere (Sheri, Basiri)	0.01246	5,659	6,436	13,057	NAB66z	93-ACAA	sere cluster		45.00	2,896	0....	9	6	6	4	1		...	p
2879	Shi (Mashi)	2.00012	908,479	1,033,152	2,095,878	NAB57d	99-AUSD-k	a-ma-shi	4	93.00	960,831	4csu.	10	7	7	5	3	Mashi*	PNB	.
2880	Shila	0.17000	77,216	87,813	178,139	NAB57b	99-AURR-g	ki-shila		80.00	70,250	1.su.	10	9	7	5	1		pnb	.
2881	Soko (So, Soa, Turumba)	0.02990	13,581	15,445	31,331	NAB57c	99-ATAB-a	li-ge-sogo		80.00	12,356	0....	10	8	7	4	1	Heso*	PN.	.
2882	Sonde (Soonde)	0.23000	104,469	118,805	241,011	NAB57b	99-AUHB-b	ki-soonde		90.00	106,925	0....	10	8	11	4	1		pnb	.
2883	Songo	0.03000	13,626	15,496	31,436	NAB57b	99-AUIO-d	songo-mene		90.00	13,947	0....	10	8	12	4	1	Songo	P..	.
2884	Songomeno	0.24190	109,874	124,952	253,481	NAB57h	99-AUIO-d	songo-mene		29.00	36,236	0....	9	5	7	5	2	Songo	P..	.
2885	Songora (Songola, Binja)	0.00648	2,943	3,347	6,790	NAB57c	99-ATEA-a	ke-songola		80.00	2,678	0....	10	8	6	4	1		...	.
2886	Songye (Western Kalebwe)	2.72264	1,236,657	1,406,366	2,852,989	NAB57f	99-AURQ-i	ki-songe	3	97.00	1,364,175	1csu.	10	9	10	5	3	Kisongye*	PNb	.
2887	South Hema (Zaire Nyoro)	0.24466	111,128	126,378	256,373	NAB57d	99-AUSE-cb	west o-ru-nyoro		97.00	122,587	1cs.h	10	10	11	5	2		pnb	.
2888	Suku	0.18956	86,101	97,916	198,635	NAB57b	99-AURH-bm	north ki-suku		90.00	88,125	0....	10	10	11	5	3	Kisuku*	P..	b
2889	Sundi	0.70000	317,949	361,581	733,513	NAB57b	99-AURG-cd	west ki-suundi	2	98.00	354,350	1cs..	10	9	12	4	2		pnb	b
2890	Swaga	0.55919	253,991	288,847	585,962	NAB57d	99-AUSD-qc	e-ki-swaga		95.00	274,404	1csu.	10	9	11	4	1		pnb	b
2891	Tabwa (Taabwa)	1.20948	549,361	624,751	1,267,385	NAB57b	99-AURR-e	i-ci-taabwa		96.00	599,761	1.su.	10	10	11	5	3		pnb	.
2892	Tagbo (Tagba)	0.04000	18,168	20,662	41,915	NAB66z	93-ACAB-b	tagbu		45.00	9,298	0....	9	7	6	4	1		p..	.
2893	Tembo	0.01578	7,167	8,151	16,535	NAB57h	99-AUFP	tembo cluster		80.00	6,521	0....	10	8	7	2	2	Chitembo	P..	b
2894	Tembo (Nyabungu)	0.35251	160,114	182,087	369,387	NAB57h	99-AUFP	tembo cluster		90.00	163,879	0....	10	10	11	5	1	Chitembo	P..	b
2895	Tetela (Sungu)	2.29372	1,041,836	1,184,810	2,403,534	NAB57h	99-AUIR-a	sungu	2	94.00	1,113,721	4....	10	10	7	5	3	Otetela*	PNB	.
2896	Tiene (Tende)	0.10208	46,366	52,729	106,967	NAB57b	99-AURE-a	ki-tiene		90.00	47,456	0.s..	10	9	11	5	2		p..	b
2897	Togbo	0.04021	18,264	20,770	42,135	NAB66b	93-ABAD-a	togbo		70.00	14,539	0....	10	8	7	5	1		...	b
2898	Tutsi	0.30000	136,264	154,963	314,363	NAB57d	99-AUSD-f	i-ki-nya-rwanda		95.00	147,215	2Asu.	10	10	11	5	2	Kinyarwanda*	PNB	b
2899	USA White	0.08000	36,337	41,324	83,830	CEW19s	52-ABAC-s	general american		79.00	32,646	1Bsuh	10	9	8	5	3	English*	PNB	b
2900	Vanuma	0.01624	7,376	8,389	17,018	NAB57c	99-ASFA-f	li-vanuma		80.00	6,711	0....	10	8	8	0	0		...	.
2901	Vili (Fioti)	0.10000	45,421	51,654	104,788	NAB57b	99-AURB-d	i-vili	14	90.00	46,489	0As..	10	10	13	5	3		pn.	b
2902	Vira (Joba, Zoba)	0.02903	13,186	14,995	30,420	NAB57d	99-AUSD-h	ki-joba		90.00	13,496	1csu.	10	9	11	5	2		pnb	p
2903	West Kongo (Fioti)	2.00000	908,425	1,033,090	2,095,752	NAB57b	99-AURG-b	ki-fiote	18	99.00	1,022,759	1as..	10	10	11	5	3		PNB	b
2904	Wongo (Gongo, Bakong)	0.02491	11,314	12,867	26,103	NAB57b	99-AUIP-a	ba-wongo		90.00	11,580	0....	10	8	12	4	1	Wongo	Pnb	.
2905	Wuumu	0.03000	13,626	15,496	31,436	NAB57k	99-AURD-m	i-wuumu		73.00	11,312	0....	10	8	7	4	1		p..	.
2906	Yaka (Iaka)	0.25000	113,553	129,136	261,969	NAB57b	99-AURH-b	south ki-yaka	1	99.00	127,845	0....	10	10	12	5	3	Iyaka: Congo*	P..	b
2907	Yakoma	0.02449	11,124	12,650	25,662	NAB66z	93-ABBA-c	yakoma		45.00	5,693	1.s..	9	7	7	4	1		pnb	p
2908	Yamongeri	0.03000	13,626	15,496	31,436	NAB57h	99-AUIE-dj	ya-mongeri		90.00	13,947	0....	10	8	11	4	1		p..	.
2909	Yansi	0.46253	210,087	238,918	484,674	NAB57b	99-AURE-c	i-yans	1	97.00	231,750	0.s..	10	8	11	4	2		p..	.
2910	Yeke	0.00400	1,817	2,066	4,192	NAB57f	99-AUSH-dd	yeke		95.00	1,963	0....	10	9	11	5	1		pn.	.
2911	Yela	0.13750	62,454	71,025	144,083	NAB57h	99-AUIN-b	lo-yela		90.00	63,922	0....	10	8	11	4	1		p..	.
2912	Yira	0.10000	45,421	51,654	104,788	NAB57d	99-AUSD-qg	e-ki-yira		95.00	49,072	1csu.	10	8	11	4	1		pnb	p
2913	Yombe (Bayombe, Mbala)	1.60000	726,740	826,472	1,676,602	NAB57b	99-AURG-c	ki-yombe	4	97.00	801,678	1cs..	10	9	7	4	2	Yombe	Pnb	b
2914	Zaire Swahili (Ngwana)	2.00000	908,425	1,033,090	2,095,752	NAB57j	99-AUSM-z	ki-ngwana	26	74.00	764,487	2Asu.	10	7	11	4	3	Kiswahili: Zaire*	PNB	.
2915	Zande (Azande, Nyamnyam)	2.23255	1,014,052	1,153,212	2,339,436	NAB66a	93-BAAA-a	pa-zande	4	90.00	1,037,891	4As..	10	6	7	5	3	Pazande*	PNB	b
2916	Zimba	0.24913	113,158	128,687	261,057	NAB57c	99-ATEB-a	zimba		94.00	120,966	0....	10	9	7	5	1		...	.
2917	other minor peoples	0.64769	294,189	334,561	678,699	...				77.00	257,612		10	7	7	4	0			
	Cook Islands	**100.00000**	**18,900**	**19,522**	**23,736**					**94.73**	**18,493**									
2918	Anglo-New Zealander	2.40000	454	469	570	CEW19e	52-ABAC-y	general new-zealand		76.00	356	1Bsuh	10	9	14	5	3		pnb	b
2919	Bukabukan	4.50000	851	878	1,068	MPY55d	39-CANA-a	pukapuka		85.00	747	0....	10	8	9	5	1		...	b
2920	Cook Islands Maori (Kuki)	58.90000	11,132	11,498	13,981	MPY55d	39-CAQB-a	rarotonga		96.80	11,131	0....	10	9	13	5	2	Maori: Cook Island*	PNB	b
2921	Euronesian (Park-Maori)	15.40000	2,911	3,006	3,655	MPY53	52-ABAC-bv	standard oceanian-english		95.00	2,856	1Bsuh	10	8	10	5	1		pnb	b
2922	Niuean	1.00000	189	195	237	MPY55z	39-CAPA-a	niue		89.00	174	0.s..	10	8	11	5	3	Niuean	PNB	b
2923	Penrhyn (Tongareva)	3.30000	624	644	783	MPY55z	39-CAQD-a	tongareva		90.00	580	0....	10	8	11	5	1		...	b
2924	Rakahanga-Manihiki	13.90000	2,627	2,714	3,299	MPY55d	39-CAQC	rakahanga cluster		94.00	2,551	0....	10	8	12	5	1		...	b
2925	other minor peoples	0.60000	113	117	142	...				84.00	98		10	8	10	5	0			
	Costa Rica	**100.00000**	**3,553,881**	**4,023,422**	**5,928,508**					**96.19**	**3,870,161**									
2926	Basque	0.20000	7,108	8,047	11,857	CEW16	40-AAAA-a	general euskara		94.00	7,564	3....	10	9	14	5	1	Basque	PNB	b
2927	Bribri	0.17525	6,228	7,051	10,390	MIR39e	83-EBBB-a	bribri		78.00	5,500	0.s..	10	8	7	5	3	Bribri	P..	b
2928	British	0.08000	2,843	3,219	4,743	CEW19i	52-ABAC-b	standard-english	15	79.00	2,543	3Bsuh	10	9	13	5	1		PNB	b
2929	Burunca (Boruca)	0.03239	1,151	1,303	1,920	MIR39e	83-EBAA-a	brunka		85.00	1,108	0....	10	7	10	4	2		...	b
2930	Chirripo (Cabecar)	0.11046	3,926	4,444	6,549	MIR39e	83-EBBA-aa	chirripû		78.00	3,467	0....	10	7	7	4	2	Cabecar: Chirripo	PN.	.
2931	Costarican White	77.72943	2,762,411	3,127,383	4,608,195	CLT27	51-AABB-hg	costarricense		97.88	3,061,082	1A.uh	10	9	13	5	3		pnb	b
2932	French	0.30000	10,662	12,070	17,786	CEW21b	51-AABI-d	general français	4	87.00	10,501	1B.uh	10	9	14	5	1	French	PNB	b
2933	Guatuso	0.01382	491	556	819	MIR39e	83-DAAA-a	maléku-jaíka		80.00	445	0....	10	7	6	4	1		...	.
2934	Han Chinese	0.30000	10,662	12,070	17,786	MSY42a	51-AABB-hg	costarricense		36.00	4,345	1A.uh	9	5	8	5	1		pnb	b
2935	Han Chinese (Cantonese)	1.00000	35,539	40,234	59,285	MSY42a	79-AAAM-a	central yue		35.00	14,082	3A.uh	9	5	8	5	2	Chinese, Yue	PNB	b
2936	Han Chinese (Mandarin)	0.50000	17,769	20,117	29,643	MSY42a	79-AAAB-ba	kuo-yü		30.00	6,035	2Bsuh	9	5	8	5	1	Chinese: Kuoyu*	PNB	b
2937	Han Chinese (Taiwanese)	0.02000	711	805	1,186	MSY42a	79-AAAJ-h	quan-zhang-taiwan		20.00	161	1A..h	9	5	8	5	1	Taiwanese	PNB	b
2938	Jewish	0.12539	4,456	5,045	7,434	CMT35	51-AABB-hg	costarricense		0.10	5	1A.uh	5	4	2	5	0		pnb	b
2939	Low German	0.00526	187	212	312	CEW19m	52-ABCC	north deutsch cluster		90.00	190	2A.uh	10	9	13	5	1	German: Low*	PNB	b
2940	Mestizo	8.60000	305,634	346,014	509,852	CLN29	51-AABB-hg	costarricense		98.50	340,824	1A.uh	10	8	11	5	1		pnb	b
2941	Mulatto	1.00000	35,539	40,234	59,285	NFB68b	52-ABAF	carib-anglo-creol cluster		95.00	38,223	1a..h	10	8	11	5	1	West Carib Creole English	PN.	b
2942	Nicaraguan Mestizo	8.00000	284,310	321,874	474,281	CLN29	51-AABB-hf	nicaragüense		96.00	308,999	1A.uh	10	10	12	5	1		pnb	b
2943	Part-Indian	0.10000	3,554	4,023	5,929	MIR37z	51-AABB-hg	costarricense		80.00	3,219	1A.uh	10	8	7	5	1		pnb	b
2944	Teribe	0.00800	284	322	474	MIR39e	83-EAAA-a	west naso		84.00	270	0....	10	8	5	4	1	Teribe	P..	.
2945	USA White	0.60000	21,323	24,141	35,571	CEW19s	52-ABAC-s	general american		80.00	19,312	1Bsuh	10	9	13	5	3	English*	PNB	b
2946	West Indian Black	1.00000	35,539	40,234	59,285	NFB68a	52-ABAF-g	limûn-coastal-creole		97.40	39,188	1c..h	10	8	12	5	3		pn.	.
2947	other minor peoples	0.10000	3,554	4,023	5,929	...				77.00	3,098		10	7	6	5	0			
	Croatia	**100.00000**	**4,492,906**	**4,472,600**	**4,193,413**					**95.17**	**4,256,385**									
2948	Albanian	0.30000	13,479	13,418	12,580	CEW13	55-AAAA-b	northwest gheg		45.00	6,038	1a.u.	9	9	8	0	0	Albanian: Gheg*	PN.	b
2949	Austrian	0.01000	449	447	419	CEW19f	52-ABCF-b	donau-bayrisch-t.		90.00	403	0B.uh	10	9	13	5	3		pn.	b
2950	Balkan Gypsy (Arliski)	0.40000	17,972	17,890	16,774	CNN25f	59-ACBA-bc	arlija		20.00	3,578	1A...	9	5	8	5	1	Romani: Arlija	Pn.	.
2951	Balkan Gypsy (Dzambazi)	0.10000	4,493	4,473	4,193	CNN25f	59-ACBA-bf	dzambazi		30.00	1,342	1c...	9	5	8	5	1		pn.	b
2952	Bosniac (Muslimani)	1.00000	44,929	44,726	41,934	CEW22a	53-AAAG-a	standard srpski		0.03	13	1Asuh	3	4	5	5	3	Serbian*	PNB	b
2953	British	0.02000	899	895	839	CEW19i	52-ABAC-b	standard-english		79.00	707	3Bsuh	10	9	13	5	3		PNB	b
2954	Croat	82.00000	3,684,183	3,667,532	3,438,599	CEW22d	53-AAAG-b	standard hrvatski		98.40	3,608,851	2Asuh	10	10	11	5	3	Croatian	PNB	b
2955	Croatian Gypsy	0.16000	7,189	7,156	6,709	CNN25f	59-ACBB-bd	southeast sinti		75.00	5,367	0....	10	7	8	5	1		p..	.
2956	Czech	0.30000	13,479	13,418	12,580	CEW22e	53-AAAD-a	czesky		71.00	9,527	2Asuh	10	9	8	5	3	Czech	PNB	b
2957	Esperanto	0.00000	0	0	0	CEW21z	51-AAAC-a	proper esperanto		80.00	0	0A...	10	8	8	5	0	Esperanto	PNB	b
2958	French	0.02500	1,123	1,118	1,048	CEW21b	51-AABI-d	general français		87.00	973	1B.uh	10	9	14	5	3	French	PNB	b
2959	Friulian (Priulian)	0.23000	10,334	10,287	9,645	CEW21h	51-AABM	furlan cluster		85.00	8,744	0....	10	9	13	5	1	Friulian	PN.	b
2960	German	1.50000	67,394	67,089	62,901	CEW19m	52-ABCE-a	standard hoch-deutsch		95.00	63,735	2B.uh	10	9	13	5	3	German*	PNB	b
2961	Greek	0.01000	449	447	419	CEW20	56-AAAA-c	dhimotiki		95.00	425	2B.uh	10	9	11	5	3	Greek: Modern	PNB	b
2962	Hungarian	0.50000	22,465	22,363	20,967	MSW51g	41-BAAA-a	general magyar		81.00	18,114	2A.u.	10	9	9	5	1	Hungarian	PNB	b
2963	Istro-Romanian (Istriot)	3.38000	151,860	151,174	141,737	CEW21z	51-AADA	istro-roman cluster		97.00	146,639	0....	10	9	11	5	3		...	.
2964	Italian	0.30000	13,479	13,418	12,580	CEW21e	51-AABQ-c	standard italiano		86.00	11,539	2B.uh	10	9	15	5	3	Italian	PNB	b
2965	Jewish	0.05000	2,246	2,236	2,097	CMT35	53-AAAG-a	standard srpski		0.20	4	1Asuh	5	3	3	0	0	Serbian*	PNB	b
2966	Macedonian	0.15000	6,739	6,709	6,290	CEW22g	53-AAAH-a	makedonski		70.00	4,696	2a.uh	10	9	9	0	0	Macedonian*	PNB	b
2967	Montenegrin	0.22000	9,884	9,840	9,226	CEW22h	53-AAAG-a	standard srpski		70.00	6,888	1Asuh	10	8	8	5	3	Serbian*	PNB	b
2968	Polish (Pole)	0.40000	17,972	17,890	16,774	CEW22i	53-AAAC-c	polski		87.00	15,565	2A.uh	10	9	12	5	3	Polish	PNB	b
2969	Romanian	0.10000	4,493	4,473	4,193	CEW21i	51-AADC-a	limba românească		84.00	3,757	3A.u.	10	8	8	4	2	Romanian	PNB	b
2970	Rumelian Turk	0.05000	2,246	2,236	2,097	MSY41j	44-AABA-a	osmanli		0.00	0	1A.u.	0	3	3	1	0	Turkish	PNB	b
2971	Russian	0.06000	2,696	2,684	2,516	CEW22j	53-AAAE-d	russkiy		35.00	939	4B.uh	9	8	8	4	3	Russian	PNB	b
2972	Ruthene (Ruthenian, Rusyn)	0.03000	1,348	1,342	1,258	CEW22k	53-AAAD-bn	saris		91.00	1,221	1csuh	10	9	12	5	1		pnb	b
2973	Serb	5.95300	267,463	266,254	249,634	CEW22l	53-AAAG-a	standard srpski		93.00	247,616	1Asuh	10	9	9	5	1	Serbian*	PNB	b
2974	Slovene	0.51000	22,914	22,810	21,386	CEW22n	53-AAAF-a	slovensko		95.00	21,670	1a..h	10	9	13	5	3	Slovenian*	PNB	b
2975	USA White	0.02200	988	984	923	CEW19s	52-ABAC-s	general american		78.00	767	1Bsuh	10	10	12	0	0	English*	PNB	b
2976	Ukrainian	0.02000	899	895	839	CEW22p	53-AAAE-b	ukrainskiy		70.00	626	3A.uh	10	8	8	5	3	Ukrainian	PNB	b
2977	Vlach Gypsy (Gurbeti)	2.00000	89,858	89,452	83,868	CNN25f	59-ACBB-bd	southeast sinti		70.00	62,616	0....	10	8	8	5	1		p..	.
2978	other minor peoples	0.20000	8,986	8,945	8,387	...				45.00	4,025		9	6	6	4	0			
	Cuba	**100.00000**	**10,964,236**	**11,200,684**	**11,798,235**					**43.06**	**4,822,908**									
2979	Basque	0.00500	548	560	590	CEW16	40-AAAA-a	general euskara		94.00	526	3....	10	8	14	3	1	Basque	PNB	b
2980	Black	12.00000	1,315,708	1,344,082	1,415,788	NFB71a	51-AABB-hi	cubano		35.00	470,429	1B.uh	9	6	8	3	3		pnb	b
2981	British	0.01000	1,096	1,120	1,180	CEW19i	52-ABAC-b	standard-english		79.00	885	3Bsuh	10	9	13	4	3		PNB	b
2982	Cuban White	71.68190	7,859,373	8,028,863	8,457,199	CLT27	51-AABB-hi	cubano		44.50	3,572,844	1B.uh	9	8	8	3	3		pnb	b
2983	Esperanto	0.00000	0	0	0	CEW21z	51-AAAC-a	proper esperanto		50.00	0	0A...	10	9	2	0	0	Esperanto	PNB	b

Continued opposite

Table 8-2 continued

EVANGELIZATION								EVANGELISM			ADDITIONAL DESCRIPTIVE DATA
Ref 1	*D 28*	*aC 29*	*CG% 30*	*r 31*	*E 32*	*U 33*	*W 34*	*e 35*	*R 36*	*T 37*	*Locations, civil divisions, literacy, religions, church history, denominations, dioceses, church growth, missions, agencies, ministries, movements 38*
2868	1	10	1.70	8	99.92	0.08	C	557.42	45	10	Refugees from Angola, settlers, expatriates. D=RCC. M=SJ,CICM,SDB,FSC.
2869	2	6	5.16	0	99.80	0.20	C	341.64	155	9	On Zaire river in northeast Equateur Region. Numerous dialects of significant lingua franca. Animists 3%. D=RCC,ECZ(CDCZ). M=AoG,Baptists.
2870	4	6	10.30	1	99.97	0.03	C	520.45	219	10	Northern Lunda. Shaba and Lunda Regions. Also in Angola. No animists left. D=RCC(D-Kikwit,D-Popokabaka,D-Kamina),ECZ,EUSJ,many other AICs. M=UMC.
2871	4	6	9.94	0	99.95	0.05	C	492.38	220	10	Bandundu Region. Lingua franca: Lingala. Animists 1%. D=RCC(D-Inongo),ECZ(CEBB),CHS,other AICs. M=Swedist Baptist Mission,NLEA.
2872	2	6	9.91	1	99.98	0.02	C	518.66	215	10	Southeastern part of Kasai Occidental Region, east of Luiza. D=RCC(M-Kananga,D-Luiza),AICs.
2873	1	7	6.33	0	99.90	0.10	C	417.19	168	10	Bandundu Region, northern part of Kasongo-Lunda Zone. Related to Holu. Animists 1%. D=RCC.
2874	5	7	5.80	1	99.98	0.02	C	554.43	128	10	Southern Luba. Shaba Region, north of Likasi. D=RCC(M-Lubumbashi),GOC,ECZ(CFCG,CMSZ),EEA,other AICs. M=NLEA,CMML,UMC.
2875	1	10	6.07	4	99.70	0.30	C	329.59	159	9	Lingua franca, trade and official language in CAR. Animists 5%. D=RCC. M=CSSp,OFM.
2876	1	7	8.14	1	99.70	0.30	C	298.93	240	8	Dialect of Nande. North Kivu Sub-Region, Beni and Lubero Zones. Animists 5%. D=RCC.
2877	2	7	7.82	0	99.90	0.10	C	433.62	193	10	Bandundu Region, west of Lake Mai-Ndombe. Animists 1%. D=RCC,ECZ(Baptists).
2878	1	8	5.83	0	78.00	22.00	B	128.11	255	7	Among Zande in Haut-Zaire Region, northeast of Ango; also in CAR. Animists 25%. D=RCC.
2879	2	6	12.16	1	99.93	0.07	C	498.99	266	10	Kivu Region around Bukavu. Animists 2%. D=RCC(M-Bukavu),ECZ(CELZA,CEBZE,CEPZA). M=NPY,NLEA,CBFMS,SFM.
2880	2	6	5.58	3	99.80	0.20	C	367.92	153	9	Shaba Region, around Lake Mweru. Also in Zambia. Animists 3%. D=RCC(D-Kilwa-Kasenga),ECZ(Luanza). M=CMML.
2881	1	7	7.38	0	99.80	0.20	C	347.48	204	9	Haut-Zaire Region, north of Basoko. Animists 4%. D=RCC(M-Kisangani).
2882	1	6	9.72	0	99.90	0.10	C	440.19	229	10	Southeastern Bandundu Region. Animists 2%. D=RCC.
2883	1	7	7.51	0	99.90	0.10	C	430.33	188	10	Bandundu Region, Bulungu Zone. Also in Angola. Animists 1%. D=RCC.
2884	3	7	5.24	0	68.00	32.00	B	71.97	270	6	Kasai Occidental Region, Dekese Zone. Animists 40%. D=RCC(D-Kole),ECZ(CRS),AICs. M=SSCC,NSM.
2885	1	8	5.75	0	99.80	0.20	C	332.88	174	9	Kivu Region, Punia and Kindu Zones. Animists 5%. D=RCC(D-Kindu).
2886	4	6	12.55	1	99.97	0.03	C	531.07	256	10	Northeast Luba, Yembe, Lusonge, Luba-Songi. Kasai Oriental Region, Kabinda Zone. D=RCC(D-Kabinda,D-Kongolo),ECZ(CPZ),ESI,other AICs. M=NLEA,ZEM..
2887	2	10	6.52	4	99.97	0.03	C	552.31	151	10	Haut-Zaire Region, Irumu Zone. Animists 1%, Muslims 2%. D=RCC,ECZ(CAZ,CAFEZA). M=CMS,CMML.
2888	2	6	9.51	0	99.90	0.10	C	446.76	221	10	Bandundu Region. Lingua franca: Kituba (limited use). Animists 4%. D=RCC(D-Kenge,D-Kikwit,D-Popokabaka),ECZ(CCEZ). M=CEM,ECM,Baptists.
2889	2	7	5.07	5	99.98	0.02	C	561.58	114	10	Dialect of Kongo. Also in Congo (Brazzaville). No animists. D=RCC(D-Matadi),AICs.
2890	1	6	10.76	1	99.95	0.05	C	502.78	243	10	Dialect of Nandi. North Kivu Sub-Region, Beni and Lubero Zones. Animists 2%. D=RCC.
2891	3	6	5.77	3	99.96	0.04	C	522.09	133	10	Shaba Region, south of Moba. Also in Zambia. Animists 2%, Muslims 1%. Mainly Catholics. D=RCC(D-Kalemie-Kirungu,D-Kilwa-Kasenga),JWs,AICs.
2892	1	9	7.07	0	80.00	20.00	B	131.40	291	7	Widely scattered in north; also in CAR. Closest to Sere and Ndogo. Animists 30%, Muslims 5%. D=RCC.
2893	2	6	6.69	0	99.80	0.20	C	341.64	191	9	Equateur Region, 2 Zones. Bilingual in Lingala. Riverine. Animists 3%. D=RCC,ECZ(CEBZE,CEPZA). M=CBFMS,SFM.
2894	1	6	10.19	0	99.90	0.10	C	427.05	246	10	Kivu Region, west of Lake Kivu. Animists 1%. D=RCC(D-Kongolo). M=CBFMS.
2895	4	6	12.32	0	99.94	0.06	C	507.78	255	10	Kasai Oriental Region. Animists 2%, Muslims 1%. D=RCC(D-Kindu,D-Kabinda,D-Kole,D-Tshumbe),ECZ(CMZC,CRS),EJCSK,other AICs. M=SSCC,NLEA,UBS.
2896	2	7	8.83	0	99.90	0.10	C	450.04	206	10	Bandundu Region. Lingua franca: Lingala (limited use). Animists 1%. D=RCC,ECZ(AoG,Baptist Ch).
2897	1	7	7.55	0	99.70	0.30	C	278.49	236	8	Equateur Region, Bosobolo Zone. Also in CAR and Sudan. Bilingual in Mono; also many speak Lingala, Sango. Animists 5%, Muslims 5%. D=ECZ(CECU).
2898	2	10	10.07	4	99.95	0.05	C	568.67	203	10	Kivu Region. Refugees from 1962-72 and 1994 Rwanda and Burundi genocides. D=RCC(D-Goma),ECZ(CLMZ).
2899	7	10	8.43	8	99.79	0.21	C	429.64	172	10	Expatriates from USA, in development. D=ECZ,RCC,CURBZ,SDA,JWs,CC,CJCLdS.
2900	0	0	6.73	0	99.80	0.20	C	294.92	222	8	Haut-Zaire Region in Tchabi Collectivity. Related to Nyali, Mbo, Ndaka, and Budu. Animists 4%. D=RCC,ECZ(CAFEZA). M=CMML.
2901	4	8	5.28	5	99.90	0.10	C	505.89	120	10	Along coast from south of Angola border to north of Gabon border. D=RCC,ECZ,EJCSK,many other AICs.
2902	2	7	7.47	1	99.90	0.10	C	466.47	185	10	Around Lake Tanganyika, northwest of Uvira. Bilingual in Kifuliro. Animists 1%. D=RCC,ECZ.
2903	7	6	12.23	5	99.99	0.01	C	603.45	225	10	Bas-Zaire Region, also in Congo, Angola. D=RCC(10 Dioceses),EJCSK(9 Regions),ECZ(83 Communauts),ECUA,EAUA,ENAC,many other AICs.
2904	3	8	7.31	0	99.90	0.10	C	456.61	173	10	Kasai Occidental Region (Ilebo and Tshikapa Zones), Bandundu Region. D=RCC,ECZ,AICs. M=UFM.
2905	1	7	7.28	0	99.73	0.27	C	290.43	228	8	Dialect of South Central Teke. Mainly in Congo. Animists 7%. D=RCC.
2906	5	6	3.97	0	99.99	0.01	C	531.18	101	10	Bandundu Region; also in Angola. Lingua franca: Kituba. D=RCC,ECZ(CBMSK,CEK),EJCSK,Dieudonn, other AICs. M=MEB,CBZO/ABCUSA,AMEC,LCZ,NLEA.
2907	1	7	6.55	1	88.00	12.00	B	144.54	248	7	Equateur Region, Yakoma Zone. Dialect of Ngbandi. Fairly bilingual in Lingala. Animists 35%. D=RCC.
2908	1	7	7.51	0	99.90	0.10	C	427.05	189	10	Equateur Region. Related to Buja. Animists 2%. D=RCC.
2909	2	6	10.57	0	99.97	0.03	C	492.13	237	10	Bandundu Region, Bulungu Zone, Loange River area. Animists 1%. D=RCC(D-Kenge),AICs.
2910	4	6	4.08	0	99.95	0.05	C	478.51	110	10	5 small nearly-extinct groupings northeast of Likasi, Shaba Region, interpersed among the Sanga. D=RCC,ECZ,EEA,AICs. M=Garanganze Mission.
2911	1	6	9.16	0	99.90	0.10	C	423.76	226	10	Equateur Region, mainly in Bokungu Zone. D=RCC(D-Bokungu-Ikela).
2912	1	6	8.87	1	99.95	0.05	C	495.85	210	10	Dialect of Nandi. North Kivu Sub-Region. D=RCC.
2913	6	6	6.52	5	99.97	0.03	C	523.99	148	10	Also in Angola and Congo. Animists 1%. D=RCC(D-Boma),ECZ(CEAZ),EJCSK,APROCO,EECM,other AICs. M=LBI,CMA.
2914	3	9	11.90	5	99.74	0.26	C	380.84	260	9	Used throughout Shaba, Kivu, and southeastern Haut-Zaire Regions. Muslims 20%(Shafi Sunnis). D=RCC(D-Kamina),ECZ(CEBZ),AICs. M=SJ,OFM,UMC,BEM.
2915	4	6	12.24	0	99.90	0.10	C	492.75	257	10	Also in Sudan, CAR. Animists 5%. D=28% RCC(D-Bondo,D-Doruma-Dungu,D-Isiro-Niangara),ECZ(CFP,CBBU,CECA,CECCA),MFP,other AICs. M=AIM,CMS.
2916	1	6	9.86	0	99.94	0.06	C	442.59	241	10	Kivu Region, Kasongo Zone. Animists 3%, some Muslims. D=RCC(D-Kasongo). M=Grace Ministries International.
2917	0	8	10.69		99.77	0.23	C	300.72	274	9	Senegalese, Hausa, Fulani, Yoruba, Canadians, Japanese, Chinese, Zyoba, Shona(AACJM),and vast numbers of refugees from Angola, Burundi, Rwanda, Sudan.
Cook Islands											
2918	3	10	0.87	8	99.76	0.24	C	405.00	32	10	Pakeha/Whites, in administration, government, education, professions. D=Anglican Ch(D-Polynesia),CICC,RCC.
2919	1	10	0.87	0	99.85	0.15	C	387.81	30	9	Pukapuka Island, northern Cook Islands; some in Rarotonga, also New Zealand. Related to Samoan. Unwritten. Fishermen. D=CICC.
2920	4	9	0.80	5	99.97	0.03	C	575.20	22	10	Kuki Airani. Also in New Zealand, French Polynesia. D=Cook Islands Christian Ch,RCC(D-Rarotonga),SDA,CJCLdS. M=CWM(LMS),SSCC.
2921	3	10	0.93	8	99.95	0.05	C	558.26	29	10	Persons of mixed race. D=CICC,RCC,SDA. M=SSCC.
2922	4	10	0.87	5	99.89	0.11	C	500.26	25	10	Also in Niue, New Zealand, Tonga. Strong Congregationalists. D=CICC,Niue Christian Ch,CJCLdS,RCC.
2923	1	10	0.86	5	99.90	0.10	C	459.90	27	10	Northern Cook Islands. Language unwritten, disappearing rapidly; second language Rarotongan. D=CICC.
2924	1	10	0.89	0	99.94	0.06	C	483.77	27	10	Northern Cook Islands. Fishermen, agriculturalists. Language unwritten. D=CICC.
2925	0	10	0.85		99.84	0.16	C	374.05	19	9	Other Pacific islanders, Australians, Europeans.
Costa Rica											
2926	1	10	2.56	4	99.94	0.06	C	548.96	61	10	Immigrants from northern Spain, in agriculture, commerce, professions. D=RCC. M=SJ.
2927	3	8	2.65	0	99.78	0.22	C	353.02	73	9	50% read Spanish. Animists 5%. D=RCC,AoG,Evangelical Mennonites. M=CAM,SIL,independents,NTM.
2928	1	10	2.57	8	99.79	0.21	C	438.29	67	10	Expatriates from UK, in business. D=Episcopal Ch(D-Costa Rica).
2929	2	10	2.57	0	99.85	0.15	C	406.42	67	10	Only 5 women spoke the language in 1986, rest Spanish only. Hunter-gatherers. Animists 15%. D=RCC,AoG.
2930	0	8	2.56	0	99.78	0.22	C	335.94	74	9	80% monolinguals. Animists 5%. D=RCC(0.4% christopagans). D=RCC. M=CAM,independents.
2931	7	8	2.51	8	99.98	0.02	C	596.19	55	10	D=RCC(5 Dioceses),AoG,ICFG,JWs,ACRBC,ACAC,&c. M=CM,OFM,LAM,ABA,LCMS,MCFOM(Fiji),FMB. T=CBN. R=AWR.
2932	1	10	2.56	8	99.87	0.13	C	504.90	61	10	Expatriates from France, in business. Nonreligious 13%. D=RCC.
2933	1	10	2.58	0	99.80	0.20	C	338.72	76	9	Chibchan. Agriculturalists. Animists 20%. D=RCC. M=LAM.
2934	1	10	2.56	8	98.00	2.00	B	128.77	90	7	Immigrants from Chinese diaspora. Chinese folk-religionists/Buddhists 64%. D=RCC. M=FMB.
2935	2	10	3.86	8	99.35	0.65	B	135.41	117	7	Chinese folk-religionists/Buddhists 65%. Only 10% still use Chinese, rest Spanish. D=RCC,Protestants. M=FMB,CCM.
2936	1	10	3.57	7	98.00	2.00	B	107.31	118	7	Chinese folk-religionists/Buddhists 70%. D=RCC. M=FMB.
2937	1	10	2.55	5	83.00	17.00	B	60.59	106	6	Immigration from Taiwan sizeable and continuing. Chinese folk-religionists/Buddhists 80%. D=RCC.
2938	0	10	1.62	8	49.10	50.90	A	0.17	129	3	Descendants of immigrants, living mostly in San Jose, most practicing Judaism.
2939	1	10	2.57	8	99.90	0.10	C	532.17	63	10	Mennonite Germans. 36% monolingual. D=Mennonite Brethren.
2940	1	10	2.56	8	99.99	0.01	C	584.22	52	10	Mixed-race persons(White/Black/Amerindian). D=RCC.
2941	2	10	2.56	8	99.95	0.05	C	547.86	57	10	Dialect: Limon Creole (Mekitelyu). Originally from Jamaica. D=Episcopal Ch,RCC. M=FMB.
2942	1	10	2.56	8	99.96	0.04	C	564.14	53	10	Refugees from Nicaraguan fighting and civil war. D=RCC and 20 others.
2943	1	10	2.56	8	99.80	0.20	C	405.88	66	10	Detribalized, half-Indians, mainly in urban areas. D=RCC(many christopagans).
2944	1	10	2.59	0	99.84	0.16	C	367.92	74	9	Practically extinct language and people. Little animism left. D=RCC.
2945	3	10	4.42	8	99.80	0.20	C	455.52	93	10	Expatriates from USA, in business, commerce. D=SDA,JWs,CJCLdS.
2946	6	10	2.56	8	99.97	0.03	C	570.23	54	10	Dialect: Limon Creole (Mekitelyu). D=RCC,ICFG,Episcopal Ch,SDA,CBCR,UMC. M=JBMS,MMS,USPG,BMS,CBHMS,FMB.
2947	0	9	2.56		99.77	0.23	C	303.53	65	9	Many refugees including 6,000 Salvadorans, 2,500 Cubans.
Croatia											
2948	0	0	6.61	6	80.00	20.00	B	131.40	245	7	Immigrants, refugees from Albania, Yugoslavia. Workers. Muslims 25%(Sunnis), Nonreligious/atheists 25%. D=AOC,COC.
2949	3	10	-2.50	8	99.90	0.10	C	519.03	2	10	Emigres. Includes Bavarian-Austrian speakers. D=RCC,ELCA,NAC. M=OFM,SJ,SDB,OP.
2950	2	8	0.47	6	73.00	27.00	B	53.29	56	6	Jerlides. Tinners Romani. In 15 countries. Muslims 80%(Hanafi Sunnis). D=RCC,Gypsy Evangelical Movement. M=GGMS.
2951	2	10	0.47	1	76.00	24.00	B	83.22	54	6	Close to Balkan Romany (Arliski). Muslims 70%(Hanafi Sunnis). D=RCC,Gypsy Evangelical Movement. M=GGMS.
2952	4	8	-0.65	6	57.03	42.97	B	0.06	12	2	All are ethnic Muslims(45% inhabitants of Bosnia), 100% Hanafi Sunnis. D=RCC,SOC,OCCBH,CAC.
2953	5	10	0.47	8	99.79	0.21	C	446.94	29	10	Expatriates from Britain, in business. D=Ch of England(D-Gibraltar),MCY,SDA,SA,JWs.
2954	8	8	0.54	6	99.98	0.02	C	619.19	26	10	Republic of Croatia. In 10 countries. Nonreligious 1%, atheists 0.6%. Strongly Catholic, D=RCC(19 Dioceses),COGY,COCC,CNOCC,PCCY,ECCBHV,RCCY,CAC.
2955	3	10	0.47	0	99.75	0.25	C	323.02	35	9	Slovenian-Croatian Romany. Related to Sinti Manush. Many nonreligious. D=nomadic caravan churches, RCC,Gypsy Evangelical Movement. M=GGMS.
2956	4	10	-0.23	6	99.71	0.29	C	367.99	17	9	Emigres, refugees, immigrants; in commerce. Nonreligious/atheists 29%. D=RCC,Moravian Ch,CHC,Unitas Fratrum.
2957	0	10	0.00	5	99.80	0.20	C	408.80	0	10	Artificial (constructed) language, in 80 countries. Speakers in Croatia: 77,000 (none mother-tongue).
2958	3	10	0.47	8	99.87	0.13	C	520.78	24	10	Expatriates from France, in business. D=RCC,SDA,JWs. M=OFM,SJ,SDB,OP,OFMConv.
2959	1	10	0.47	0	99.85	0.15	C	425.04	29	10	In extreme west. Mainly in Italy. D=RCC.
2960	6	10	0.47	8	99.95	0.05	C	603.34	25	10	Expatriates from Germany, in business. D=RCC,ECCBHV,PCCY,NAC,SDA,JWs(UJWY).
2961	4	10	-1.82	7	99.95	0.05	C	586.00	2	10	Emigres, immigrants from Greece. D=SOC,MOC,AOC,RCC(Byzantine-rite: D-Krizevcil).
2962	4	8	0.69	6	99.81	0.19	C	437.56	38	10	Emigres, refugees from Hungary. In Vojvodina. D=RCC(D-Subotica,AA-Banat),RCCY,ECS,CNC. M=FMB.
2963	3	10	0.47	0	99.97	0.03	C	513.37	28	10	Small geographical area on Istrian peninsula. Distant relation to Romanian. D=Romanian Orthodox Ch,SOC,RCC.
2964	1	10	0.49	7	99.86	0.14	C	514.79	25	10	Emigres, workers, settlers from Italy. D=RCC(D-Porec & Pula). M=OFM,SJ,SDB,OP.
2965	0	10	0.29	6	48.20	51.80	A	0.35	56	3	Decline from 80,000 in 1925 due to mass murders by Nazis. High percent practicing Jews.
2966	0	0	6.35	5	99.70	0.30	C	291.27	175	8	Mainly in Macedonia(former Yugoslavia), also Bulgaria, Albania, Canada. Nonreligious 30%. D=GOC,Macedonian Orthodox Ch. M=SJ,OFMCap.
2967	3	8	1.26	6	99.70	0.30	C	352.59	46	9	Expatriates from Montenegro republic. Nonreligious 30%. D=Serbian Orthodox Ch(M-Montenegro & Coastland),RCC,(D-Kotor,AD-Bar).
2968	2	10	0.47	6	99.87	0.13	C	511.25	8	10	Migrant workers, from Poland. D=RCC,PCCY. M=OFM,SJ,SDB,OP.
2969	2	9	0.47	6	99.84	0.16	C	459.90	29	10	Citizens, migrant workers from Romania. D=Romanian Orthodox Ch(P-Bucharest),PCCY.
2970	0	10	0.00	8	44.00	56.00	A	0.00	0	1.12	In Macedonia and Kossovo; also in 20 other countries. Muslims 100%(Hanafi Sunnis).
2971	3	10	0.59	7	99.35	0.65	B	135.41	15	7	Emigres, refugees from Russia. Nonreligious 50%, atheists 15%. D=Russian Orthodox Ch(P-Moscow),RCC,PCCY.
2972	1	10	0.47	6	99.91	0.09	C	508.19	8	10	Language spoken: not Rusyn, but Eastern Slovak, Sarish dialect. Refugees, immigrants. D=RCC.
2973	6	8	0.10	6	99.93	0.07	C	546.51	2	10	Citizens of Republic of Serbia, also Croatian Serbs. In 18 countries. Nonreligious 3.5%, atheists 1.5%, many Muslims. D=Serbian Orthodox Ch(21 Dioceses),RCC.
2974	5	8	4.50	6	99.95	0.05	C	582.54	90	10	Expatriates of Republic of Slovenia. Also in Yugoslavia, Italy, Austria, USA, Canada, Hungary. D=RCC(4 Slovenian-speaking Dioceses),ECCS,OCCS,PCCY,CAC.
2975	0	0	4.44	8	99.78	0.22	C	367.26	113	9	North Americans, in business, education. Nonreligious 10%. D=RCC,BBC,SDA,etc.
2976	4	10	0.47	6	99.70	0.30	C	357.70	33	9	Emigres from Ukraine pogrom of 1930s. Nonreligious 30%. D=ROC,RCC,SOC,PCCY.
2977	3	10	0.47	0	99.70	0.30	C	291.27	36	8	Serbo-Bosnians (Machvano), Southern Vlach. Kalderash. In 20 countries. Mostly sedentarized, many assimilated. Muslims 30%(Hanafi Sunnis). D=SOC, RCC.
2978	0	10	0.59		75.00	25.00	B	123.18	22	7	Arabs, Belorussians, Slovaks, Swiss, Bulgarians. Muslims 30%, nonreligious 20%.
Cuba											
2979	1	10	1.84	4	99.94	0.06	C	538.66	50	10	Immigrants from north of Spain. In commerce, professions, government. D=RCC. M=SJ.
2980	4	10	1.84	8	98.00	2.00	B	125.19	68	7	Afro-Cuban spiritists 65%(Santeria,Mayombe). D=AOC,IEC,RCC,&c. R=AWR. T=LESEA.
2981	4	10	1.84	8	99.79	0.21	C	444.05	53	10	Expatriates from Britain, in business, schools. D=IEC(Anglican Ch),JWs,RCC,&c.
2982	7	9	1.08	8	99.45	0.55	B	174.60	49	7	51% atheists and nonreligious. D=RCC(6 Dioceses),IEPC,SA,SDA,CBC,IEC,&c. M=SJ,PME,OFM,FMB,and 20 more. R=AWR. T=LESEA.
2983	0	10	0.00	5	99.00	1.00	B	180.67	0	7	Artificial (constructed) language, in 80 countries. Speakers in Cuba: 4,400(none mother-tongue). Nonreligious/atheists 50%.

Continued overleaf

Table 8-2 continued

PEOPLE		POPULATION				IDENTITY CODE		LANGUAGE		CHURCH		MINISTRY						SCRIPTURE		
Ref 1	Ethnic name 2	P% 3	In 1995 4	In 2000 5	In 2025 6	Race 7	Language 8	Autoglossonym 9	S 10	AC 11	Members 12	Jayuh 13-17	d 18	w 19	a 20	xc 21	mi 22	Biblioglossonym 23	Pub 24-26	ss 27
2984	French	0.05000	5,482	5,600	5,899	CEW21b	51-AABI-d	general français		60.00	3,360	1B.uh	10	9	13	4	1	French	PNB	b
2985	Greek	0.02100	2,302	2,352	2,478	CEW20	56-AAAA-c	dhimotiki		95.00	2,235	2B.uh	10	9	11	3	1	Greek: Modern	PNB	b
2986	Han Chinese	0.35860	39,318	40,166	42,308	MSY42a	79-AAAB-ba	kuo-yü		31.60	12,692	2Bsuh	9	5	8	3	1	Chinese: Kuoyu*	PNB	b
2987	Indo-Pakistani	0.30000	32,893	33,602	35,395	CNN25g	59-AAFO-e	general hindi		3.00	1,008	3Asuh	6	4	2	3	0		pnb	b
2988	Jewish	0.01050	1,151	1,176	1,239	CMT35	51-AABB-hi	cubano		0.08	1	1B.uh	4	3	2	1	0		pnb	b
2989	Mulatto	15.00000	1,644,635	1,680,103	1,769,735	NFB71b	51-AABB-hi	cubano		43.00	722,444	1B.uh	9	5	8	3	3		pnb	b
2990	Russian	0.20000	21,928	22,401	23,596	CEW22j	53-AAAE-d	russkiy		31.00	6,944	4B.uh	9	5	7	1	0	Russian	PNB	b
2991	Spaniard	0.03000	3,289	3,360	3,539	CEW21k	51-AABB-hi	cubano		96.00	3,226	1B.uh	10	9	15	4	1		pnb	b
2992	USA White	0.02300	2,522	2,576	2,714	CEW19s	52-ABAC-s	general american		78.00	2,009	1Bsuh	10	9	13	4	3	English*	PNB	b
2993	other minor peoples	0.31000	33,989	34,722	36,575	...				70.00	24,305		10	7	7	2	0			
	Cyprus	**100.00000**	**563,990**	**600,506**	**687,811**					**91.85**	**551,594**									
2994	Armenian (Ermeni, Hai)	3.35000	18,894	20,117	23,042	CEW14	57-AAAA-b	ashkharik		90.00	18,105	4A.u.	10	9	13	4	2	Armenian: Modern, Eastern	PNB	b
2995	Assyrian (Eastern Syriac)	0.01400	79	84	96	CMT31	12-AAAA-d	east syriac		78.00	66	1as..	10	9	8	4	2	Syriac: Ancient*	PNB	b
2996	British	1.40000	7,896	8,407	9,629	CEW19i	52-ABAC-b	standard-english	35	79.00	6,642	3Bsuh	10	9	13	5	1		PNB	b
2997	Cypriot Arab	0.44500	2,510	2,672	3,061	CMT30	56-AAAA-c	dhimotiki		30.00	802	2B.uh	9	5	2	4	1	Greek: Modern	PNB	b
2998	Greek Cypriot	91.89300	518,267	551,823	632,050	CEW20	56-AAAA-c	dhimotiki		93.00	513,195	2B.uh	10	9	11	4	2	Greek: Modern	PNB	b
2999	Jewish	0.03000	169	180	206	CMT35	56-AAAA-c	dhimotiki		0.00	0	2B.uh	0	3	2	1	0	Greek: Modern	PNB	b
3000	Lebanese Arab	2.50000	14,100	15,013	17,195	CMT30	12-AACF-f	syro-palestinian		75.00	11,259	1Asuh	10	7	8	4	1	Arabic: Lebanese*	Pnb	b
3001	Rumelian Turk	0.01800	102	108	124	MSY41j	44-AABA-a	osmanli		0.02	0	1A.u.	3	3	2	0	0	Turkish	PNB	b
3002	USA White	0.30000	1,692	1,802	2,063	CEW19s	52-ABAC-s	general american		78.00	1,405	1Bsuh	10	9	13	5	1	English*	PNB	b
3003	other minor peoples	0.05000	282	300	344	...				40.00	120		9	5	7	2	0			
	Czech Republic	**100.00000**	**10,325,307**	**10,244,177**	**9,512,292**					**47.04**	**4,819,133**									
3004	Arab	0.00300	310	307	285	CMT30	12-AACF-af	barqi		5.00	15	1Asuh	7	5	2	4	3		pnb	b
3005	Austro-Bavarian	0.09000	9,293	9,220	8,561	CEW19f	52-ABCF-b	donau-bayrisch-t.		93.00	8,574	0B.uh	10	9	13	5	3		pn.	b
3006	British	0.00700	723	717	666	CEW19i	52-ABAC-b	standard-english		78.00	559	3Bsuh	10	9	13	5	1		PNB	b
3007	Carpathian Gypsy (Sarvika)	0.30000	30,976	30,733	28,537	CNN25f	59-ACBB-ac	sarvika		60.00	18,440	0....	10	7	8	4	2		p..	.
3008	Croatian (Croat)	0.03000	3,098	3,073	2,854	CEW22d	53-AAAG-b	standard hrvatski		88.00	2,704	2Asuh	10	8	11	5	0	Croatian	PNB	b
3009	Czech (Bohemian)	92.72250	9,573,883	9,498,657	8,820,035	CEW22e	53-AAAD-a	czesky		44.80	4,255,398	2Asuh	9	9	11	5	2	Czech	PNB	b
3010	Esperanto	0.00000	0	0	0	CEW21z	51-AAAC-a	proper esperanto	5	50.00	0	0A...	10	8	2	5	0	Esperanto	PNB	b
3011	French	0.00800	826	820	761	CEW21b	51-AABI-a	historical français		83.00	680	1B.uh	10	9	14	5	1		pnb	b
3012	German	0.06000	6,195	6,147	5,707	CEW19m	52-ABCD-jk	erzgebirgisch-west		84.00	5,163	0A.uh	10	9	13	5	1		...	b
3013	German (High German)	1.28000	132,164	131,125	121,757	CEW19m	52-ABCE-a	standard hoch-deutsch		76.00	99,655	2B.uh	10	9	13	5	1	German*	PNB	b
3014	Hungarian	0.20000	20,651	20,488	19,025	MSW51g	41-BAAA-a	general magyar	8	78.00	15,981	2A.u.	10	9	11	5	2	Hungarian	PNB	b
3015	Italian	0.01000	1,033	1,024	951	CEW21e	51-AABQ-c	standard italiano		82.00	840	2B.uh	10	9	15	5	1	Italian	PNB	b
3016	Jewish	0.07000	7,228	7,171	6,659	CMT35	53-AAAD-a	czesky		0.10	7	2Asuh	5	4	5	5	0	Czech	PNB	b
3017	Jewish	0.01500	1,549	1,537	1,427	CMT35	52-ABCH-a	west yiddish		0.06	1	0B..h	4	3	2	5	0	Yiddish	PNB	b
3018	Lovari Gypsy (Vlach)	0.00050	52	51	48	CNN25f	59-ACBA-a	vlach-romani		70.00	36	1a...	10	7	6	5	2	Romani: Finnish*	PN.	b
3019	Manush Gypsy (Sasitka)	0.05000	5,163	5,122	4,756	CNN25f	59-ACBB-ad	romani-moravia		70.00	3,585	0....	10	7	6	5	2		p..	.
3020	Polish (Pole)	1.00000	103,253	102,442	95,123	CEW22i	53-AAAC-c	polski	8	87.00	89,124	2A.uh	10	9	12	5	3	Polish	PNB	b
3021	Portuguese	0.00700	723	717	666	CEW21g	51-AABA-e	general português		93.00	667	2Bsuh	10	9	15	5	1	Portuguese	PNB	b
3022	Russian	0.33000	34,074	33,806	31,391	CEW22j	53-AAAE-d	russkiy		50.00	16,903	4B.uh	10	8	7	5	1	Russian	PNB	b
3023	Ruthene (Ruthenian)	0.04000	4,130	4,098	3,805	CEW22k	53-AAAE-a	rusyn		89.00	3,647	1c.uh	10	9	11	5	0		pnb	b
3024	Slovak	3.00000	309,759	307,325	285,369	CEW22m	53-AAAD-b	slovensky		78.80	242,172	1Asuh	10	9	8	5	1	Slovak	PNB	b
3025	Spaniard	0.00700	723	717	666	CEW21k	51-AABB-c	general español		96.00	688	2B.uh	10	9	15	5	1	Spanish	PNB	b
3026	Traveller Gypsy	0.07000	7,228	7,171	6,659	CNN25f	50-ACAA-a	west sheldruu		60.00	4,303	0....	10	7	8	4	2		...	b
3027	USA White	0.10000	10,325	10,244	9,512	CEW19s	52-ABAC-s	general american		78.00	7,990	1Bsuh	10	10	12	0	0	English*	PNB	b
3028	Ukrainian	0.10000	10,325	10,244	9,512	CEW22p	53-AAAE-b	ukrainskiy	5	65.00	6,659	3A.uh	10	8	11	5	3	Ukrainian	PNB	b
3029	other minor peoples	0.50000	51,627	51,221	47,561	...				69.00	35,342		10	7	2	5	0			
	Denmark	**100.00000**	**5,224,829**	**5,293,239**	**5,238,499**					**89.76**	**4,751,112**									
3030	Arab	0.07000	3,657	3,705	3,667	CMT30	12-AACF-k	central `anazi		11.00	408	4Asuh	8	5	7	4	2		pnb	b
3031	British	0.25000	13,062	13,233	13,096	CEW19i	52-ABAC-b	standard-english	51	79.00	10,454	3Bsuh	10	9	13	5	1		PNB	b
3032	Ceylon Tamil	0.11000	5,747	5,823	5,762	CNN23c	49-EBEA-bn	north sri-lanka-tamil		30.00	1,747	1Asu.	9	9	9	0	0		pnb	b
3033	Croatian (Croat)	0.01000	522	529	524	CEW22d	53-AAAG-b	standard hrvatski		91.00	482	2Asuh	10	8	11	5	1	Croatian	PNB	b
3034	Danish (Dane)	93.71200	4,896,292	4,960,400	4,909,102	CEW19g	52-AAAD-c	general dansk	100	91.41	4,534,302	2A.uh	10	10	12	5	3	Danish	PNB	b
3035	Danish Traveller	0.06000	3,135	3,176	3,143	CNN25f	59-AGAA-aa	anglo-romani-t.		90.00	2,858	0....	10	8	11	4	0		...	b
3036	Dutch	0.50000	26,124	26,466	26,192	CEW19h	52-ABCA-a	algemeen-nederlands	4	76.00	20,114	2Bsuh	10	9	15	5	2	Dutch	PNB	b
3037	Esperanto	0.00000	0	0	0	CEW21z	51-AAAC-a	proper esperanto	2	50.00	0	0A...	10	8	6	5	0	Esperanto	PNB	b
3038	Faeroe Islander	0.10000	5,225	5,293	5,238	CEW19j	52-AAAB-b	foroysk		98.00	5,187	0..uh	10	9	11	5	1	Faroese	PNB	b
3039	French	0.04000	2,090	2,117	2,095	CEW21b	51-AABI-d	general français	10	87.00	1,842	1B.uh	10	9	14	5	2	French	PNB	b
3040	German	1.10000	57,473	58,226	57,623	CEW19m	52-ABCE-a	standard hoch-deutsch	48	88.00	51,239	2B.uh	10	9	13	5	3	German*	PNB	b
3041	Greenlander (Eskimo)	0.13600	7,106	7,199	7,124	MRY40b	60-ABBC-f	north greenlandic	1	70.00	5,039	1....	10	9	8	5	2	Greenlandic*	PNB	b
3042	Icelander	0.16000	8,360	8,469	8,382	CEW19n	52-AAAB-a	íslensk	1	94.00	7,961	0..uh	10	9	11	5	2	Icelandic	PNB	b
3043	Iranian	0.17000	8,882	8,999	8,905	CNT24f	58-AACC-k	judeo-persian		5.00	450	1asu.	7	5	9	0	0	Panjabi: Persian*	PNB	b
3044	Italian	0.10000	5,225	5,293	5,238	CEW21e	51-AABQ-c	standard italiano	3	84.00	4,446	2B.uh	10	9	15	5	1	Italian	PNB	b
3045	Jewish	0.14200	7,419	7,516	7,439	CMT35	52-AAAD-c	general dansk		0.10	8	2A.uh	5	4	5	5	1	Danish	PNB	b
3046	Kurdish (Kurd)	0.20000	10,450	10,586	10,477	CNT24c	58-AAAA-a	kurmanji		0.10	11	3c...	5	4	5	5	1	Kurdish: Kurmanji*	PN.	b
3047	Norwegian	0.21000	10,972	11,116	11,001	CEW19p	52-AAAC-e	ny-norsk	100	93.00	10,338	0B.uh	10	9	14	5	1	Norwegian*	PNB	b
3048	Polish (Pole)	0.10000	5,225	5,293	5,238	CEW22i	53-AAAC-c	polski		90.00	4,764	2A.uh	10	9	12	5	1	Polish	PNB	b
3049	Portuguese	0.02000	1,045	1,059	1,048	CEW21g	51-AABA-e	general português	3	93.00	985	2Bsuh	10	9	15	5	1	Portuguese	PNB	b
3050	Punjabi	0.08000	4,180	4,235	4,191	CNN25n	59-AAFE-c	general panjabi		3.00	127	1Asu.	6	4	7	5	0		PNB	b
3051	Russian	0.02000	1,045	1,059	1,048	CEW22j	53-AAAE-d	russkiy	1	70.00	741	4B.uh	10	8	8	5	1	Russian	PNB	b
3052	Serbiac (Serb)	1.20000	62,698	63,519	62,862	CEW22l	53-AAAG-a	standard srpski		85.00	53,991	1Asuh	10	8	11	5	1	Serbian*	PNB	b
3053	Spaniard	0.10000	5,225	5,293	5,238	CEW21k	51-AABB-c	general español	3	96.00	5,082	2B.uh	10	9	15	5	1	Spanish	PNB	b
3054	Swedish (Swede)	0.40000	20,899	21,173	20,954	CEW19q	52-AAAD-r	svea-svensk	100	73.00	15,456	1A.uh	10	9	13	5	1	Swedish	PNB	b
3055	Turk	0.58000	30,304	30,701	30,383	MSY41j	44-AABA-a	osmanli		0.05	15	1A.u.	4	4	6	5	0	Turkish	PNB	b
3056	USA White	0.17000	8,882	8,999	8,905	CEW19s	52-ABAC-s	general american		78.00	7,019	1Bsuh	10	9	13	5	3	English*	PNB	b
3057	Urdu	0.06000	3,135	3,176	3,143	CNN25r	59-AAFO-d	standard urdu		0.03	1	2Asuh	3	4	2	5	0	Urdu	PNB	b
3058	other minor peoples	0.20000	10,450	10,586	10,477	...				57.10	6,045		10	6	8	5	0			
	Djibouti	**100.00000**	**600,688**	**637,634**	**1,026,235**					**4.42**	**28,195**									
3059	Amhara	0.50000	3,003	3,188	5,131	CMT34a	12-ACBA-b	general amarinya	7	81.00	2,582	3Asuh	10	7	11	2	1	Amharic	PNB	b
3060	Arab	11.09000	66,616	70,714	113,809	CMT30	12-AACF-l	omani	78	0.11	78	1Asuh	5	4	5	0	0		pnb	b
3061	Danakil (Afar)	35.49000	213,184	226,296	364,211	CMT33z	14-AAAB-a	'afar-af	51	0.01	23	1.s..	3	3	5	0	3	Afar	PN.	b
3062	Eurafrican	3.00000	18,021	19,129	30,787	NAN58	51-AABI-m	français-d'afrique		55.00	10,521	1B.uh	10	5	10	2	3		pnb	b
3063	French	1.63000	9,791	10,393	16,728	CEW21b	51-AABI-d	general français	40	82.00	8,523	1B.uh	10	9	14	3	3	French	PNB	b
3064	Greek	0.40000	2,403	2,551	4,105	CEW20	56-AAAA-c	dhimotiki		95.00	2,423	2B.uh	10	9	11	2	1	Greek: Modern	PNB	b
3065	Indo-Pakistani	0.10000	601	638	1,026	CNN25g	59-AAFO-e	general hindi		0.01	0	3Asuh	3	3	2	0	0		pnb	b
3066	Somali (Issa)	46.07000	276,737	293,758	472,786	CMT33e	14-GAGA-a	af-soomaali	85	0.50	1,469	2A...	5	3	5	0	3	Somali	PNB	b
3067	Tigrai	0.10000	601	638	1,026	CMT34b	12-ACAC-a	tigray	5	80.00	510	2As..	10	7	10	2	1	Tigrinya	PNB	b
3068	other minor peoples	1.62000	9,731	10,330	16,625	...				20.00	2,066		9	5	2	1	0			
	Dominica	**100.00000**	**70,920**	**70,714**	**73,442**					**94.4**	**66,757**									
3069	Black	82.00000	58,154	57,985	60,222	NFB68a	51-AACC-d	dominiquais	98	95.60	55,434	1cs..	10	8	11	5	3		pnb	.
3070	Black Carib	1.70000	1,206	1,202	1,249	MIR39c	51-AACC-d	dominiquais		75.00	902	1cs..	10	7	7	5	3		pnb	.
3071	British	1.00000	709	707	734	CEW19i	52-ABAC-b	standard-english	70	79.00	559	3Bsuh	10	9	13	5	1		PNB	b
3072	Han Chinese	0.20000	142	141	147	MSY42a	79-AAAB-ba	kuo-yü		40.00	57	2Bsuh	9	6	7	5	1	Chinese: Kuoyu*	PNB	b
3073	Indo-Pakistani	1.00000	709	707	734	CNN25g	59-AAFO-e	general hindi		70.00	495	3Asuh	10	7	2	5	0		pnb	b
3074	Japanese	0.10000	71	71	73	MSY45a	45-CAAA-a	koku-go		4.70	3	1B.uh	6	5	7	5	0	Japanese	PNB	b
3075	Mulatto	7.30000	5,177	5,162	5,361	NFB68b	51-AACC-d	dominiquais		95.00	4,904	1cs..	10	7	11	5	2		pnb	.
3076	Syro-Lebanese Arab	0.30000	213	212	220	CMT30	12-AACF-f	syro-palestinian		49.00	104	1Asuh	9	5	7	4	1	Arabic: Lebanese*	Pnb	b
3077	West Indian Black	6.00000	4,255	4,243	4,407	NFB68a	52-ABAF	carib-anglo-creol cluster	75	96.00	4,073	1a..h	10	9	11	5	3	West Carib Creole English	PN.	b
3078	other minor peoples	0.40000	284	283	294	...				80.00	226		10	8	8	5	0			
	Dominican Republic	**100.00000**	**7,823,266**	**8,495,338**	**11,164,412**					**94.48**	**8,026,704**									
3079	Dominican Black	9.40000	735,387	798,562	1,049,455	NFB71a	51-AABB-hj	dominicano		95.00	758,634	1A.uh	10	8	10	5	3		pnb	b
3080	Dominican Mulatto	69.50000	5,437,170	5,904,260	7,759,266	NFB71b	51-AABB-hj	dominicano		95.20	5,620,855	1A.uh	10	8	10	5	3		pnb	b
3081	Dominican White	16.10000	1,259,546	1,367,749	1,797,470	CLT27	51-AABB-hj	dominicano		93.00	1,272,007	1A.uh	10	9	11	5	3		pnb	b
3082	French	0.02000	1,565	1,699	2,233	CEW21b	51-AABI-d	general français	5	86.00	1,461	1B.uh	10	9	14	5	2	French	PNB	b
3083	German Jew	0.00800	626	680	893	CMT35	52-ABCE-a	standard hoch-deutsch		0.20	1	2B.uh	5	4	2	5	0	German*	PNB	b
3084	Haitian Black	2.42200	189,480	205,757	270,402	NFB69a	51-AACC-a	haitien		94.00	193,412	3As..	10	7	10	5	1	Haitian*	PNB	b
3085	Han Chinese	0.10300	8,058	8,750	11,499	MSY42a	79-AAAM-a	central yue	1	25.00	2,188	3A.uh	9	5	8	5	1	Chinese, Yue	PNB	b
3086	Jamaican Black	0.30000	23,470	25,486	33,493	NFB68a	52-ABAF-m	jamaican-creole		90.00	22,937	1c..h	10	8	11	5	1	West Carib Creole English	pn.	b
3087	Japanese	0.02000	1,565	1,699	2,233	MSY45a	45-CAAA-a	koku-go		4.00	68	1B.uh	6	5	6	5	0	Japanese	PNB	b
3088	Lebanese Arab	0.04000	3,129	3,398	4,466	CMT30	12-AACF-f	syro-palestinian		45.00	1,529	1Asuh	9	5	7	5	1	Arabic: Lebanese*	Pnb	b
3089	Spaniard	0.90000	70,409	76,458	100,480	CEW21k	51-AABB-c	general español		96.00	73,400	2B.uh	10	9	15	5	1	Spanish	PNB	b
3090	USA White	0.84000	65,715	71,361	93,781	CEW19s	52-ABAC-s	general american	4	78.00	55,661	1Bsuh	10	9	13	5	1	English*	PNB	b
3091	West Indian Mulatto	0.11400	8,919	9,685	12,727	NFB68b	52-ABAE-b	samaná-english		90.00	8,716	0A.uh	10	8	11	5	1		pnb	b
3092	other minor peoples	0.23300	18,228	19,794	26,013	...				80.00	15,835		10	7	8	5	0			
	Ecuador	**100.00000**	**11,460,088**	**12,646,068**	**17,796,101**					**97.33**	**12,307,788**									
3093	Achuar Jivaro	0.02395	2,745	3,029	4,262	MIR39d	84-EAAA-b	achuara		10.00	303	1....	8	5	6	4	2	Achual*	PN.	.

Continued opposite

Table 8-2 continued

EVANGELIZATION								EVANGELISM			ADDITIONAL DESCRIPTIVE DATA
Ref	D	aC	CG%	r	E	U	W	e	R	T	*Locations, civil divisions, literacy, religions, church history, denominations, dioceses, church growth, missions, agencies, ministries, movements*
1	28	29	30	31	32	33	34	35	36	37	38
2984	1	10	1.84	8	99.60	0.40	C	282.51	60	8	Expatriates from France, in business, trade, schools. Nonreligious 40%. D=RCC.
2985	1	10	1.84	7	99.95	0.05	C	568.67	47	10	Residents, traders, originally from Greece. D=GOC(AD-N&S America).
2986	1	9	1.84	7	97.60	2.40	B	112.57	70	7	From Chinese diaspora. Buddhists/Chinese folk-religionists 68%. Christians are mostly Catholics. D=RCC.
2987	0	9	1.84	7	53.00	47.00	B	5.80	147	4	Immigrant traders from India and Pakistan, since 1947 on. Hindus 69%, Muslims 27%.
2988	0	9	0.00	8	44.08	55.92	A	0.12	43	3	Small communities of Cuban Jews still practicing their faith.
2989	5	10	0.77	8	99.43	0.57	B	166.36	35	7	White/Black mixed races. Afro-Cuban spiritists 57%(Nanaguismo). D=RCC,IEPC,SA,SDA,&c. R=AWR. T=LESEA.
2990	0	9	1.84	7	89.00	11.00	B	100.70	57	7	Former USSR military and advisors. Nonreligious and atheists 69%.
2991	1	10	1.84	8	99.96	0.04	C	571.15	46	10	Immigrants from Spain, in government, administration, commerce, professions. D=RCC.
2992	3	8	0.82	8	99.78	0.22	C	427.05	31	10	Teachers, other professionals from USA. D=IEC,SDA,&c.
2993	0	8	1.84		99.70	0.30	C	260.61	49	8	Citizens of most Latin countries(America, Europe). Nonreligious 30%.
Cyprus											
2994	4	10	1.18	6	99.90	0.10	C	542.02	30	10	Western Armenian. Refugees from Turkey massacres. Most speak Greek. Urban. Some speak Turkish. D=Armenian Apostolic Ch(D-Cyprus),UAEC,RCC,RPC.
2995	2	9	1.20	5	99.78	0.22	C	401.42	37	10	Nestorian and Chaldean refugees from Iraq, Iran. D=Ancient Ch of the East,Chaldean Catholic Ch.
2996	3	9	1.18	8	99.79	0.21	C	441.17	42	10	Expatriates from Britain. D=Anglican Ch/ECJME(D-Cyprus & The Gulf),JWs,RCC. M=OFM.
2997	1	8	1.18	7	87.00	13.00	B	95.26	59	6	2,000 also speak Cypriot Maronite Arabic: (hybrid language with many borrowings). Muslims 70%(mostly Sunnis). D=RCC(Maronite AD-Cyprus.
2998	3	6	1.09	7	99.93	0.07	C	543.12	35	10	Greeks were original colonizers. D=Orthodox Ch of Cyprus,JWs,RCC. M=OFM,FMB.
2999	0	8	0.00	7	43.00	57.00	A	0.00	0	1.13	Ashkenazi, Sefardi, and Eastern/Oriental Jews.
3000	1	10	1.18	8	99.75	0.25	C	380.51	37	9	Refugees from Lebanon civil war. Muslims 25%. D=RCC(mostly Maronites).
3001	0	5	0.00	8	37.02	62.98	A	0.02	0	2	Residual Turks after partition of island. Muslims 100%(Hanafi Sunnis).
3002	5	9	1.18	8	99.78	0.22	C	427.05	38	10	Expatriates from USA: teachers, businessmen, missionaries. D=SDA,RCC,OCC,JWs,&c. M=OFM.
3003	0	8	1.18		66.00	34.00	B	96.36	49	6	Many internal and foreign refugees, from Europe, Levant, North Africa, Eurasia. Muslims 30%, nonreligious 30%.
Czech Republic											
3004	3	10	0.22	7	61.00	39.00	B	11.13	41	5	Refugees, migrant workers, immigrants. Muslims 90%(Sunnis). D=RCC(Maronites),GOC,other Christians.
3005	1	10	0.24	8	99.93	0.07	C	532.93	24	10	Residents, immigrants from Austria, Bavaria. D=RCC. M=OSB,OCist,SJ.
3006	1	10	0.24	8	99.78	0.22	C	427.05	25	10	Expatriates from Britain, in business, schools. D=Anglican Ch(D-Europe).
3007	2	9	0.34	0	99.60	0.40	C	223.38	37	8	Sarvike, or Ungrike. In Moravia, Bohemia. Moravian Romani, Slovakian Romani. D=RCC,many Jehovah's Witnesses.
3008	0	10	0.24	6	99.88	0.12	C	501.07	23	10	From Croatia. Also in Romania, Hungary, Austria, Italy, Turkey, Sweden, Canada, USA, Australia, Greece.
3009	7	7	-0.43	6	99.45	0.55	B	189.35	17	7	Bohemia, Moravia, Silesia. Also Poland, Austria, &c. D=Czechoslovak Hussite Ch(5 Dioceses),RCC(15 Diocese),ECCB,CUA,OCCC,COB,SDA. M=UBS,LBI.
3010	0	10	0.00	5	99.50	0.50	B	182.50	0	7	Artificial (constructed) language, in 80 nations. Speakers in this country: 510,000(non mother-tongue). Nonreligious/atheists 40%.
3011	1	10	0.23	8	99.83	0.17	C	460.48	22	10	Expatriates from France, in business, in schools. D=RCC.
3012	1	10	0.24	8	99.84	0.16	C	444.57	26	10	Expatriates from Germany, in industry, commerce, professions. D=NAC(Bezirk Schweiz).
3013	1	9	-0.09	8	99.76	0.24	C	416.10	19	10	Expatriates from Germany, in many professions. D=NAC(Bezirk Schweiz).
3014	2	9	-2.67	6	99.78	0.22	C	421.35	2	10	Also in Hungary, Russia, Romania, Austria, USA, Canada, Australia, Israel, Yugoslavia. D=RCC(M-Trnava,D-Kosice),RCCS.
3015	1	10	0.24	7	99.82	0.18	C	466.90	22	10	Expatriates from Italy. Strong Catholics. D=RCC.
3016	0	9	0.15	6	55.10	44.90	B	0.20	42	3	Remnants (from 360,000 Jews in 1938) in Prague and Sub-Carpathian Ukraine.
3017	0	9	0.00	4	48.06	51.94	A	0.10	39	3	Residual Jews left after emigration of 1,000 a year since 1950.
3018	2	10	0.25	6	99.70	0.30	C	316.82	28	9	Romungre. In Slovakia; also in 25 other countries. Nonreligious 30%. D=RCC,JWs.
3019	2	10	0.23	0	99.70	0.30	C	283.60	31	8	Sinte Gypsies, in 13 countries. Ethnic group: Sasitka Roma. Nonreligious 30%.D=RCC,JWs.
3020	3	10	0.68	6	99.87	0.13	C	514.43	12	10	Mainly in Poland, also USA, Ukraine, Canada, Germany, Romania. D=RCC,ECCB,Silesian Evangelical Ch.
3021	1	10	0.24	8	99.93	0.07	C	573.67	20	10	Expatriates, immigrant workers from Portugal. D=RCC.
3022	1	9	0.24	7	99.50	0.50	B	217.17	6	8	Refugees from Russia. 1948-1989, mostly nonreligious/atheists in military. D=ROC.
3023	0	9	0.24	6	99.89	0.11	C	474.28	5	10	Carpathians. Eastern Slavs/Ukrainians. Northeast Slovakia, Preshov region. Also Ukraine, Romania, USA. D=RCC(D-Kosice, Slovak-rite D-Presov,OCC.
3024	4	8	-0.53	6	99.79	0.21	C	419.35	11	10	D=Orthodox Ch of Czechoslovakia(4 Dioceses), RCC(5 Dioceses),SECAC,RCCS; D-Presov claimed by both RCC and OCC. M=LBI. R=HCJB.
3025	1	10	0.24	8	99.96	0.04	C	599.18	19	10	Expatriates from Spain; in professions. Strong Catholics. D=RCC.
3026	2	10	0.23	8	99.60	0.40	C	238.71	32	8	Itinerant nomadic Gypsies. D=RCC, many Jehovah's Witnesses.
3027	0	0	6.91	8	99.78	0.22	C	370.11	165	9	North Americans, in business, education. Nonreligious 10%. D=RCC,BBC,SDA,etc.
3028	3	10	-1.37	6	99.65	0.35	C	329.77	2	9	In 20 countries. Nonreligious/atheists 35%. D=Orthodox Ch(D-Olouc-Brno),RCC(D-Spis),ROC.
3029	0	9	0.75		97.00	3.00	C	244.29	21	8	From all European countries, and many others elsewhere.
Denmark											
3030	2	10	3.78	7	74.00	26.00	B	29.71	166	5	Migrant workers from Morocco, Algeria. Muslims 85%(Sunnis). D=RCC(Maronites),GOC.
3031	1	10	0.77	8	99.79	0.21	C	441.17	34	10	Expatriates from Britain, in professions. D=Ch of England(D-Europe).
3032	0	0	5.30	6	70.00	30.00	B	76.65	247	6	Migrant workers from Sri Lanka. Hindus 65%, Muslims 2%, Baha'is 2%.
3033	1	10	3.95	6	99.91	0.09	C	531.44	86	10	New migrant workers and refugees from Croatia. D=RCC(D-Copenhagen).
3034	10	6	0.65	6	99.91	0.09	C	545.21	30	10	Also in Greenland, Iceland, USA, Germany, Canada. D=NCD(ELPCD)(10 Dioceses),RCC,BUD,JWs,ACD,Elim Ch,CJCLdS,PMD,SA,&c. M=SJ,CSSR,OMI,LBI.
3035	0	10	0.77	0	99.90	0.10	C	427.05	38	10	Rom(Romany) Gypsies. Traveller Danish language based on Danish and Northern Romany.
3036	2	10	0.77	6	99.76	0.24	C	427.19	29	10	Expatriates from Holland, in many professions. D=DRC,RCSD.
3037	0	10	0.00	5	99.50	0.50	B	197.10	0	7	Artificial (constructed) language, in 80 countries. Speakers in Denmark: 84,000(none mother-tongue). Nonreligious/atheists 40%.
3038	1	10	0.77	4	99.98	0.02	C	565.16	38	10	Immigrants from Faeroe Islands; in many professions. D=NCD.
3039	2	10	0.77	8	99.87	0.13	C	517.60	29	10	Expatriates from France, in professions. D=RCC,RCSD.
3040	4	10	0.77	8	99.88	0.12	C	536.40	31	10	Expatriates from Germany. In numerous professions. D=EKD,NAC(Bezirk Hamburg),RCC,RCSD.
3041	2	10	0.77	4	99.70	0.30	C	332.15	33	9	Immigrants from Greenland. D=NCD,Apostolic Ch in Denmark. M=Gronlandsmissionen,Ev Mission.
3042	2	10	0.77	2	99.94	0.06	C	528.37	26	10	Citizens, immigrants from Iceland. D=NCD(ELPCD),National Ch of Iceland.
3043	0	0	0.75	5	44.00	56.00	A	8.03	90	4	Migrant workers from Iran. Muslims 93%, Baha'is 2%.
3044	1	10	0.77	7	99.84	0.16	C	487.49	31	10	Expatriates from Italy; in professions. Strong Catholics. D=RCC.
3045	0	10	0.99	6	56.10	43.90	B	0.20	82	3	In Denmark since 1600; mostly in Copenhagen, with 2 synagogues. M=NCD.
3046	0	10	2.43	0	41.10	58.90	A	0.15	295	3	Refugees from Iraq, Iran, Turkey. Muslims 100%(Sunnis). M=whole network of agencies.
3047	1	10	0.82	6	99.93	0.07	C	560.09	32	10	Expatriates from Norway. Professionals. D=Ch of Norway.
3048	1	10	0.77	6	99.90	0.10	C	525.60	13	10	Immigrants from Poland since 1915. D=RCC(D-Copenhagen).
3049	1	10	0.78	8	99.93	0.07	C	573.67	29	10	Migrant workers from Portugal. D=RCC(D-Copenhagen).
3050	0	10	2.57	5	59.00	41.00	B	6.46	168	4	Pakistanis. Migrant laborers. Mostly Muslims 95%(Sunnis, with many Ahmadis/Qadianis).
3051	1	10	0.77	7	99.70	0.30	C	355.14	15	9	Refugees from USSR after 1917. Nonreligious 30%. D=Russian Orthodox Ch.
3052	1	10	8.97	6	99.85	0.15	C	480.88	159	10	Migrant workers from Serbia. Muslims 10%(Sunnis). D=Serbian Orthodox Ch.
3053	1	10	0.77	8	99.96	0.04	C	602.68	27	10	Expatriates from Spain, in commerce, professions. Strong Catholics. D=RCC.
3054	1	10	0.77	6	99.73	0.27	C	383.68	15	9	Swedish immigrants and residents. Professionals. D=Ch of Sweden.
3055	0	10	2.75	8	52.05	47.95	B	0.09	182	2	Migrant workers from Turkey. Muslims 100%(Hanafi Sunnis, and many Ahmadis/Qadianis).
3056	4	10	1.77	8	99.78	0.22	C	435.59	48	10	Expatriates from USA, in professions, industry. D=RCC,SDA,CJCLdS,SA.
3057	0	10	0.00	5	50.03	49.97	B	0.05	56	2	Pakistanis. Muslims 100%(Hanafi Sunnis, and many Ahmadis/Qadianis).
3058	0	10	0.77		91.10	8.90	B	189.86	23	7	Many migrant workers, including Tibetans (Lamaist Buddhists).
Djibouti											
3059	1	8	4.79	5	99.81	0.19	C	431.64	124	10	Christians from Ethiopia. Many nonreligious. D=Ethiopian Orthodox Ch.
3060	0	8	4.45	7	45.11	54.89	A	0.18	313	3	Mostly from Yemen, Oman. Muslims 92%(Shafi,Hanafi,Maliki), nonreligious 7%. Many Christian traders.
3061	0	8	3.19	4	33.01	66.99	A	0.01	422	2	Mainly in Ethiopia, Eritrea, also in Somalia. Pastoral nomads. Muslims 100%(Sunnis). M=RSM,ELC(Ethiopia),OFMCap.
3062	2	9	7.21	8	99.55	0.45	B	236.88	193	8	Mixed-race persons, White/Black/Arabs. Muslims 45%. D=RCC,RCF. M=OFMCap,FSC,FMND.
3063	2	9	5.00	8	99.82	0.18	C	457.92	107	10	Expatriates in military, government, schools. D=RCC,RCF. M=OFMCap,FSC,FMND.
3064	1	9	5.64	7	99.95	0.05	C	561.73	112	10	Long-time residents from Greece, traders, businessmen. D=Greek Orthodox Ch.
3065	0	8	0.00	7	42.01	57.99	A	0.01	0	2	Traders from Pakistan and India. Muslims 80%(Sunnis), Hindus 20%.
3066	1	8	5.12	5	49.50	50.50	A	0.90	386	3	Majority live in Somalia; also Ethiopia, Kenya, Yemen, UAE. Pastoral nomads. Muslims 99%(Shafi Sunnis). D=RCC(D-Djibouti). M=LBI,SIM,OFMCap.
3067	1	8	6.43	4	99.80	0.20	C	411.72	161	10	Christians from Ethiopia. D=Ethiopian Orthodox Ch.
3068	0	8	5.48		41.00	59.00	A	29.93	366	5	Numerous refugees from Somalia, and 45,000 Ethiopians from Harerge region. Muslims 70% (Sunnis).
Dominica											
3069	4	8	0.85	2	99.96	0.04	C	532.48	26	10	Language also known as Lesser Antillean Creole French (Patwa, Patois). 70% monolinguals. D=RCC(D-Roseau),MCCA,CPWI/Anglican Ch,SDA. M=FMI,CSSR.
3070	3	10	0.90	2	99.75	0.25	C	350.40	41	9	Mother tongue (Carifuna, Island Carib) became extinct in 1920. D=Churches of Christ in Christian Union, Maranatha Baptists, Pilgrim Holiness Ch.
3071	2	10	0.90	8	99.79	0.21	C	438.29	37	10	Expatriates from Britain, in education, government, development. D=Anglican Ch(D-Antigua),RCC(D-Roseau). M=USPG.
3072	1	10	4.13	7	99.40	0.60	B	154.76	124	7	Immigrants from Chinese diaspora. Buddhists 30%, folk-religionists 30%. D=RCC.
3073	0	10	3.98	7	99.70	0.30	C	321.93	108	9	Traders from India and Pakistan. Hindus 20%, Muslims 8%, Baha'is 2%.
3074	0	10	1.10	7	63.70	36.30	B	10.92	80	5	Buddhists from Japan, including Sokka Gakkai(Nichiren Shoshu) 95%.
3075	4	10	0.90	2	99.95	0.05	C	527.06	29	10	Mixed-race Black/Whites. D=RCC(D-Roseau),CPWI/Anglican Ch,MCCA,SDA. M=USPG,MMS.
3076	1	10	2.37	8	99.49	0.51	B	194.94	77	7	Traders from Levant. Muslims 50%, Maronites 49%. D=RCC.
3077	4	10	0.90	8	99.96	0.04	C	564.14	26	10	Immigrants from other Caribbean islands. D=CPWI/Anglican Ch(D-Antigua),RCC(D-Roseau),MCCA,SDA. M=FMI,CSSR,USPG,PEMS.
3078	0	10	0.90		99.80	0.20	C	329.96	22	9	Haitians, French(Francais only understood by 10%), Central and South Americans.
Dominican Republic											
3079	5	10	2.69	8	99.95	0.05	C	561.73	56	10	Afro-Caribbean spiritists 4%. D=RCC,CoGiC,AMEC,CBD,IED. M=UFM,SJ,SDB. T=CBN. R=AWR. T=LESEA.
3080	6	9	2.70	8	99.95	0.05	C	563.61	56	10	Afro-Caribbean spiritists 2%. D=RCC(5 Dioceses),CBD,ACC,IED,COG,UPC. M=SJ,SDB,UFM. T=CBN. R=AWR. T=LEASEA.
3081	5	10	2.69	8	99.93	0.07	C	549.90	60	10	Settlers of Spanish origin. D=RCC,CBD,IED,UPC,JWs. M=SJ,SDB,MSC,OFMCap,UFM. T=CBN. R=AWR. T=LESEA.
3082	2	10	2.68	8	99.86	0.14	C	508.51	62	10	Expatriates in government, schools, business. D=RCC,JWs.
3083	0	10	0.00	8	55.20	44.80	B	0.40	34	3	A small colony of practicing German Jews.
3084	1	10	2.69	4	99.94	0.06	C	548.96	66	10	Refugees from political turmoil in Haiti. Voodooism(Vodoun) very strong among immigrants from Haiti, with many others. D=RCC.
3085	1	10	5.54	8	93.00	7.00	B	84.86	182	6	Buddhists/Chinese folk-religionists 75%. D=RCC. M=FMB.
3086	2	10	2.69	8	99.90	0.10	C	489.46	61	10	Immigrants from Jamaica. D=SDA,CBD. M=JBU.
3087	0	10	4.31	7	62.00	38.00	B	9.05	224	4	Japanese farming community. Buddhists 90%.
3088	1	10	5.16	8	99.45	0.55	B	175.74	150	7	Traders. Muslims 55%, rest Christians(Maronites). D=RCC.
3089	1	10	2.69	8	99.96	0.04	C	595.68	58	10	Strong Catholics. D=RCC.
3090	5	10	5.86	8	99.78	0.22	C	432.74	122	10	Expatriates in development. D=SDA,FMC,AoG,CBD,MCA. M=FMB.
3091	1	10	2.69	8	99.90	0.10	C	509.17	60	10	Rastafarians, Afro-Caribbean spiritists. English-based creole used by descendants of ex-USA slaves from 1824. D=RCC. M=JBU.
3092	0	10	2.69		99.80	0.20	C	335.80	64	9	Other Caribbean islanders: Cubans, Puerto Ricans, Trinidadians, et alii.
Ecuador											
3093	2	8	2.07	0	49.00	51.00	A	17.88	155	5	7 villages near Peruvian border; also in Peru. Swidden agriculturalists. Bilingual in Shuar. Animists 90%. D=RCC,IUME. M=GMU,Brethren Mission.

Continued overleaf

Table 8-2 continued

PEOPLE Ref 1	Ethnic name 2	POPULATION P% 3	In 1995 4	In 2000 5	In 2025 6	IDENTITY CODE Race 7	Language 8	LANGUAGE Autoglossonym 9	S 10	CHURCH AC 11	Members 12	MINISTRY Jayuh 13-17	d 18	wa 19	xc 20	mc 21	mi 22	SCRIPTURE Biblioglossonym 23	Pub 24-26	ss 27
3094	Black	5.00000	573,004	632,303	889,805	NFB71a	51-AABB-hp	ecuatoriano		99.00	625,980	1A.uh	10	8	11	5	2		pnb	b
3095	Black	0.01700	1,948	2,150	3,025	NFB71b	51-AACC-c	guadeloupéan		99.00	2,128	1cs..	10	7	12	2	1	Creole French: Lesser Antill	Pnb	b
3096	Bobonaza Lowland Quichua	0.05517	6,323	6,977	9,818	MIR39g	85-FAAB-bb	bobonaza		98.00	6,837	0....	10	7	11	4	1		pn.	.
3097	Calderon Highland Quichua	0.27716	31,763	35,050	49,324	MIR39g	85-FAAC-b	pichincha		99.00	34,699	1.s..	10	7	12	4	1		pnb	b
3098	Canari Highland Quichua	0.92157	105,613	116,542	164,004	MIR39g	85-FAAC-ea	cañar		99.00	115,377	1.s..	10	8	12	5	3	Quichua: Canar*	Pnb	.
3099	Cayapa (Chachilla)	0.05039	5,775	6,372	8,967	MIR39e	83-HBAA-a	cayapa		8.00	510	0....	7	4	6	5	3	Cayapa*	P..	.
3100	Chimborazo Highland Quich	9.44555	1,082,468	1,194,491	1,680,940	MIR39g	85-FAAC-c	chimborazo	33	99.50	1,188,518	3.s..	10	9	10	5	3	Quichua: Chimborazo*	PNB	b
3101	Cofan (Kofan)	0.00680	779	860	1,210	MIR39d	83-FAAA-a	north cofán		30.00	258	0....	9	5	6	4	1	Cofan	PN.	.
3102	Colorado (Tatchila)	0.01814	2,079	2,294	3,228	MIR39e	83-HBBA-a	tsá-fiki		40.00	918	0....	9	5	6	5	2	Colorado	PN.	.
3103	Detribalized Quichua	25.11430	2,878,121	3,175,971	4,469,366	MIR39g	51-AABB-hp	ecuatoriano		99.00	3,144,212	1A.uh	10	8	10	5	4		pnb	b
3104	German	0.30000	34,380	37,938	53,388	CEW19m	52-ABCE-a	standard hoch-deutsch		88.00	33,386	2B.uh	10	9	13	5	3	German*	PNB	b
3105	Han Chinese	0.10780	12,354	13,632	19,184	MSY42a	79-AAAB-ba	kuo-yü	1	6.00	818	2Bsuh	7	4	8	5	1	Chinese: Kuoyu*	PNB	b
3106	Jewish	0.03370	3,862	4,262	5,997	CMT35	51-AABB-hp	ecuatoriano		0.09	4	1A.uh	4	4	2	5	2		pnb	b
3107	Latin American White	10.00000	1,146,009	1,264,607	1,779,610	CLT27	51-AABB-hp	ecuatoriano		93.78	1,185,948	1A.uh	10	9	12	5	3		pnb	b
3108	Mestizo	41.95945	4,808,590	5,306,221	7,467,146	CLN29	51-AABB-hp	ecuatoriano		98.80	5,242,546	1A.uh	10	9	12	5	4		pnb	b
3109	Mulatto (Zambo)	1.00000	114,601	126,461	177,961	NFB71b	51-AABB-hp	ecuatoriano		98.00	123,931	1A.uh	10	8	12	5	2		pnb	b
3110	Napo Lowland Quichua	0.05952	6,821	7,527	10,592	MIR39g	85-FAAB-ab	napo-m.		90.00	6,774	0....	10	8	11	5	1	Quichua: Napo*	Pn.	.
3111	Norwegian	0.10000	11,460	12,646	17,796	CEW19p	52-AAAC-e	ny-norsk		93.00	11,761	0B.uh	10	9	14	5	1	Norwegian*	PNB	b
3112	Otavalo Highland Quichua	4.00000	458,404	505,843	711,844	MIR39g	85-FAAC-a	imbabura	33	99.00	500,784	1.s..	10	9	10	5	3	Quichua: Imbabura*	PNB	.
3113	Quaiquer (Kwaiker, Awa)	0.00952	1,091	1,204	1,694	MIR39e	83-HAAA-a	coaiquer		65.00	783	0....	10	7	6	4	0	Cuaiquer	P..	.
3114	Salasaca Highland Quichua	0.11333	12,988	14,332	20,168	MIR39g	85-FAAC-cc	ambato		90.00	12,899	1.s..	10	8	12	4	2	Quichua, Highland Tungura	pnb	b
3115	Saraguro Highland Quichua	0.24138	27,662	30,525	42,956	MIR39g	85-FAAC-ed	loja		90.00	27,473	1.s..	10	8	11	4	3	Quichua, Highland, Loja	pnb	.
3116	Secoya (Ecuadorian Siona)	0.00345	395	436	614	MIR39d	88-KAAA-bb	secoya		20.00	87	0....	9	5	6	4	1	Secoya	PN.	.
3117	Shuar (Jivaro, Jibaro)	0.36905	42,293	46,670	65,677	MIR39d	84-EAAA-a	shuar		8.00	3,734	1....	7	4	7	4	3	Shuar: Ecuador	PN.	b
3118	Siona	0.00349	400	441	621	MIR39d	88-KAAA-b	piohé-siona		60.00	265	0....	10	7	6	4	1	Siona	PN.	.
3119	Syro-Lebanese Arab	0.01700	1,948	2,150	3,025	CMT30	12-AACF-f	syro-palestinian		20.00	430	1Asuh	9	5	7	5	3	Arabic: Lebanese*	Pnb	b
3120	Tena Lowland Quichua	0.06897	7,904	8,722	12,274	MIR39g	85-FAAB-ba	tena		90.00	7,850	0....	10	8	11	4	2	Quichua: Tena*	PN.	.
3121	Tetete	0.00002	2	3	4	MIR39d	88-KAAA-c	teteté		66.67	2	0....	10	7	6	3	1		pn.	.
3122	USA White	0.15000	17,190	18,969	26,694	CEW19s	52-ABAC-s	general american	6	78.00	14,796	1Bsuh	10	9	9	5	3	English*	PNB	b
3123	Waorani (Auca, Huaorani)	0.00728	834	921	1,296	MIR39d	84-GAAA-g	waorani		40.00	368	0....	9	6	7	4	2	Waorani	PN.	.
3124	Zaparo (Andoa, Kayapwe)	0.00151	173	191	269	MIR39z	84-HABA-c	simicai		75.00	143	0....	10	7	6	4	1		pn.	b
3125	other minor peoples	0.52450	60,108	66,329	93,341	...				20.00	13,266		9	5	8	3	0			
	Egypt	**100.00000**	**62,281,642**	**68,469,695**	**95,615,454**					**15.07**	**10,320,466**									
3126	Ababdah	0.10000	62,282	68,470	95,615	CMT33z	13-AAAA-a	ti-bedaauye		0.01	7	0....	3	1	0	0	0		...	b
3127	Albanian	0.03000	18,684	20,541	28,685	CEW14	55-AAAB-a	standard tosk		1.00	205	0A...	6	4	3	0	2	Albanian: Tosk*	PNB	b
3128	Amhara	0.00380	2,367	2,602	3,633	CMT34a	12-ACBA-b	general amarinya		80.00	2,081	3Asuh	10	7	11	2	1	Amharic	PNB	b
3129	Arab	0.20000	124,563	136,939	191,231	CMT30	12-AACF-a	masri		7.00	9,586	2Asuh	7	5	9	3	2	Arabic*	PNB	b
3130	Arabized Berber	2.00000	1,245,633	1,369,394	1,912,309	CMT32a	12-AACF-a	masri		0.10	1,369	2Asuh	5	3	2	1	0	Arabic*	PNB	b
3131	Arabized Nubian	0.55000	342,549	376,583	525,885	NAB62m	12-AACF-a	masri		0.00	0	2Asuh	0	3	1	0	0	Arabic*	PNB	b
3132	Armenian (Hai, Ermeni)	0.19940	124,190	136,529	190,657	CEW14	57-AAAA-b	ashkharik		89.10	121,647	4A.u.	10	9	12	2	3	Armenian: Modern, Eastern	PNB	b
3133	Bahariya (Beharia)	0.03000	18,684	20,541	28,685	CMT30	12-AACD	badawi-sahara cluster		0.00	0	0a...	0	1	0	0	0		PN.	b
3134	Bedouin	2.00000	1,245,633	1,369,394	1,912,309	CMT30	12-AACD-f	west egyptian		0.00	0	0c...	0	1	0	0	0	Arabic: Egyptian*	PN.	.
3135	Bisharin	0.10000	62,282	68,470	95,615	CMT33z	13-AAAA-a	ti-bedaauye		0.00	0	0....	0	1	0	0	0		...	b
3136	British	0.13200	82,212	90,380	126,212	CEW19i	52-ABAC-b	standard-english	25	66.00	59,651	3Bsuh	10	9	13	4	1		PNB	b
3137	Dakhla (Dachel)	0.03600	22,421	24,649	34,422	CMT30	12-AACD	badawi-sahara cluster		0.00	0	0a...	0	1	0	0	0		PN.	b
3138	Dongolawi Nubian (Barabra)	1.30000	809,661	890,106	1,243,001	NAB62m	05-FABA	kenuz-dongola cluster	3	0.01	89	0....	3	1	2	0	1		P..	b
3139	Egyptian Arab	84.12950	52,397,234	57,603,212	80,440,803	CMT30	12-AACF-a	masri	100	17.00	9,792,546	2Asuh	8	5	9	3	3	Arabic*	PNB	b
3140	Fedicca-Mahas Nubian	0.50000	311,408	342,348	478,077	NAB62m	05-FAAA	nobiin cluster		0.04	137	0....	3	1	2	0	1	Nobiin	P..	b
3141	French	0.09400	58,545	64,362	89,879	CEW21b	51-AABI-d	general français	12	82.00	52,776	1B.uh	10	9	14	4	2	French	PNB	b
3142	German	0.03000	18,684	20,541	28,685	CEW19m	52-ABCE-a	standard hoch-deutsch		88.00	18,076	2B.uh	10	9	13	4	3	German*	PNB	b
3143	Ghagar Rom Gypsy (Nawar)	0.40000	249,127	273,879	382,462	CNN25f	59-ACAA-a	domari		1.00	2,739	0....	6	1	2	0	0		...	b
3144	Greek	0.12000	74,738	82,164	114,739	CEW20	56-AAAA-c	dhimotiki		95.00	78,055	2B.uh	10	9	10	4	3	Greek: Modern	PNB	b
3145	Halebi Gypsy (Nawari)	1.60000	996,506	1,095,515	1,529,847	CNN25f	12-AACF-a	masri		0.01	110	2Asuh	3	1	0	0	0	Arabic*	PNB	b
3146	Indo-Pakistani	0.00500	3,114	3,423	4,781	CNN25g	59-AAFO-e	general hindi		0.09	3	3Asuh	4	3	2	0	0		pnb	b
3147	Italian	0.11280	70,254	77,234	107,854	CEW21e	51-AABQ-c	standard italiano		80.00	61,787	2B.uh	10	9	15	4	1	Italian	PNB	b
3148	Jewish	0.00220	1,370	1,506	2,104	CMT35	12-AACF-a	masri		0.53	8	2Asuh	5	1	2	0	0	Arabic*	PNB	b
3149	Kharga (Selima)	0.04000	24,913	27,388	38,246	CMT30	12-AACD	badawi-sahara cluster		0.00	0	0a...	0	1	0	0	0		PN.	b
3150	Maaza Bedouin	0.02600	16,193	17,802	24,860	CMT30	12-AACD	badawi-sahara cluster		0.00	0	0a...	0	1	0	0	0		PN.	b
3151	Neo-Egyptian Copt	0.01000	6,228	6,847	9,562	CMT30	11-AAAA-a	bohayric	1	99.00	6,778	0....	10	8	13	4	1	Coptic: Bohairic	PN.	b
3152	Palestinian Arab	0.20000	124,563	136,939	191,231	CMT30	12-AACF-f	syro-palestinian		15.00	20,541	1Asuh	8	5	7	2	3	Arabic: Lebanese*	Pnb	b
3153	Russian	0.00200	1,246	1,369	1,912	CEW22j	53-AAAE-d	russkiy		20.00	274	4B.uh	9	5	7	1	2	Russian	PNB	b
3154	Saadi Bedouin	0.02000	12,456	13,694	19,123	CMT30	12-AACD	badawi-sahara cluster		0.00	0	0a...	0	1	0	0	0		PN.	b
3155	Siwa (Oasis Berber)	0.05600	34,878	38,343	53,545	CMT32d	10-AAAD-c	siwa		0.00	0	0....	0	1	0	0	0		...	b
3156	Sudanese Arab	5.50000	3,425,490	3,765,833	5,258,850	CMT30	12-AACF-c	sudani		1.40	52,722	4Asuh	6	3	7	0	2	Arabic: Sudan	PNb	b
3157	Syro-Lebanese Arab	0.09900	61,659	67,785	94,659	CMT30	12-AACF-f	syro-palestinian		30.00	20,335	1Asuh	9	5	8	2	3	Arabic: Lebanese*	Pnb	b
3158	Tulama (Shoa Galla)	0.00380	2,367	2,602	3,633	CMT33b	14-FBAA-a	tulema		30.00	781	1cs..	9	5	7	2	1		pnb	b
3159	Turk	0.05000	31,141	34,235	47,808	MSY41j	44-AABA-a	osmanli		0.02	7	1A.u.	3	1	2	0	0	Turkish	PNB	b
3160	USA White	0.02000	12,456	13,694	19,123	CEW19s	52-ABAC-s	general american		80.00	10,955	1Bsuh	10	9	13	4	3	English*	PNB	b
3161	Upper Egyptian Copt	0.00050	311	342	478	CMT30	11-AAAA	coptic cluster		99.20	340	0....	10	8	13	4	1	Coptic: Sahidic	PN.	b
3162	Yemeni Arab	0.19800	123,318	135,570	189,319	CMT30	12-AACF-n	yemeni		0.01	14	1Asuh	3	1	2	0	0		pnb	b
3163	other minor peoples	0.10000	62,282	68,470	95,615	...				10.00	6,847		8	5	2	1	0			
	El Salvador	**100.00000**	**5,668,595**	**6,276,023**	**9,062,331**					**97.16**	**6,098,021**									
3164	Arab	0.02000	1,134	1,255	1,812	CMT30	12-AACF-f	syro-palestinian		9.00	113	1Asuh	7	4	7	5	3	Arabic: Lebanese*	Pnb	b
3165	German	0.10000	5,669	6,276	9,062	CEW19m	52-ABCE-a	standard hoch-deutsch		88.00	5,523	2B.uh	10	9	13	5	3	German*	PNB	b
3166	Han Chinese (Cantonese)	0.02400	1,360	1,506	2,175	MSY42a	79-AAAM-a	central yue		8.00	120	3A.uh	7	5	7	5	1	Chinese, Yue	PNB	b
3167	Jewish	0.01000	567	628	906	CMT35	51-AABB-hd	salvadoreño		0.20	1	1A.uh	5	3	2	1	0		pnb	b
3168	Kekchi (Quecchi)	0.25400	14,398	15,941	23,018	MIR37b	68-AEAA	kekchi cluster		90.00	14,347	4....	10	8	11	5	1	Kekchi	PNB	b
3169	Lenca	0.74000	41,948	46,443	67,061	MIR37z	69-HAAA-a	proper lenca		80.00	37,154	0....	10	7	6	5	1		...	b
3170	Mestizo	88.31000	5,005,936	5,542,356	8,002,945	CLN29	51-AABB-hd	salvadoreño		98.15	5,439,822	1A.uh	10	8	12	5	3		pnb	b
3171	Nicaraguan Mestizo	0.05000	2,834	3,138	4,531	CLN29	51-AABB-hf	nicaragüense		90.00	2,824	1A.uh	10	8	12	5	1		pnb	b
3172	Part-Indian	4.40000	249,418	276,145	398,743	MIR37z	51-AABB-hd	salvadoreño		88.00	243,008	1A.uh	10	8	12	5	1		pnb	b
3173	Pipil	4.00000	226,744	251,041	362,493	MIR37a	66-BFBB	pipil cluster		96.40	242,003	0A.uh	10	7	11	2	1		...	b
3174	Pocomam (Pokomam)	0.10000	5,669	6,276	9,062	MIR37b	68-AEBA-c	east pokomam		90.00	5,648	0....	10	8	11	5	1	Pocomam: Eastern*	P..	.
3175	Salvadorian White	1.69000	95,799	106,065	153,153	CLT27	51-AABB-hd	salvadoreño		91.20	96,731	1A.uh	10	9	11	5	1		pnb	b
3176	Turk	0.01000	567	628	906	MSY41j	44-AABA-a	osmanli		1.10	7	1A.u.	6	3	2	1	0	Turkish	PNB	b
3177	USA White	0.15000	8,503	9,414	13,593	CEW19s	52-ABAC-s	general american	9	76.00	7,155	1Bsuh	10	9	13	5	3	English*	PNB	b
3178	other minor peoples	0.14200	8,049	8,912	12,869	...				40.00	3,565		9	5	2	5	0			
	Equatorial Guinea	**100.00000**	**399,486**	**452,661**	**794,724**					**87.2**	**394,699**									
3179	Annobonese Eurafrican	0.72000	2,876	3,259	5,722	NAN58	51-AACA-e	fa-d'ambu	15	95.00	3,096	1c...	10	7	11	2	1		pnb	.
3180	Batanga (Puku)	1.74000	6,951	7,876	13,828	NAB57k	99-AUAC-c	ba-puku		95.00	7,482	0....	10	8	11	4	3		p..	.
3181	Bayele (Beyele) Pygmy	0.70000	2,796	3,169	5,563	BYG12	99-AUID-e	m-binga		38.00	1,204	0....	9	5	6	2	1		...	.
3182	Benga	0.70000	2,796	3,169	5,563	NAB57k	99-AUAE-a	benga		90.00	2,852	0....	10	9	12	5	2	Benga	PNB	.
3183	British	0.01000	40	45	79	CEW19i	52-ABAC-b	standard-english	15	78.00	35	3Bsuh	10	9	13	5	3		PNB	b
3184	Bube (Fernandian, Ediya)	10.01000	39,989	45,311	79,552	NAB57k	99-AKAA	bubi cluster		97.00	43,952	0....	10	9	12	5	3	Bube	P..	b
3185	Creole	0.05000	200	226	397	NAN58	52-ABAH-b	krio	15	95.00	215	4.s.h	10	8	11	5	2	Krio	PN.	b
3186	Eurafrican	2.40000	9,588	10,864	19,073	NAN58	51-AABB-g	español-guineo		95.00	10,321	1A.uh	10	8	13	5	2		pnb	.
3187	Fang (Ntumu, Okak, Pahouin)	56.65000	226,309	256,432	450,211	NAB57c	99-AUCC-v	ntumu	88	90.10	231,046	1....	10	9	12	5	3		pnb	b
3188	Fernandino (Creole)	2.36000	9,428	10,683	18,755	NAN58	52-ABAH-bd	fernando-pûo-creole	19	95.00	10,149	1.s.h	10	9	11	5	3		pn.	b
3189	French	0.02000	80	91	159	CEW21b	51-AABI-d	general français	7	86.50	78	1B.uh	10	9	14	5	1	French	PNB	b
3190	Hausa	2.00000	7,990	9,053	15,894	NAB60a	19-HAAB-a	hausa		0.10	9	4Asu.	5	3	2	1	0	Hausa	PNB	b
3191	Ibibio	0.50000	1,997	2,263	3,974	NAB56b	98-ICBA-b	ibibio		90.00	2,037	3cs..	10	9	13	4	3	Ibibio	pnb	b
3192	Igbo (Ibo)	4.00000	15,979	18,106	31,789	NAB59h	98-FAAA-a	standard igbo		90.00	16,296	2..u.	10	9	12	4	3	Igbo	PNB	b
3193	Indo-Pakistani	0.10000	399	453	795	CNN25g	59-AAFO-e	general hindi		0.00	0	3Asuh	0	3	2	0	0		pnb	b
3194	Maka	0.40000	1,598	1,811	3,179	NAB57c	99-AUDC-b	be-kol		80.00	1,449	0....	10	7	7	3	1	Makaa	...	.
3195	Ngumba (Mabi, Mabea)	2.34000	9,348	10,592	18,597	NAB57k	99-AUDE-a	mvumbo		95.00	10,063	0....	10	8	11	4	1	Ngumba	P..	.
3196	Ngumbi (Combe, Kombe)	1.00000	3,995	4,527	7,947	NAB57k	99-AUAD-b	kombe		95.00	4,300	0....	10	8	11	4	2	Combe*	PN.	.
3197	Seke (Seki, Sheke)	2.90000	11,585	13,127	23,047	NAB57k	99-AOAA-a	sekya-ni		95.00	12,471	0....	10	8	11	4	2		...	.
3198	Spaniard	2.80000	11,186	12,675	22,252	CEW21k	51-AABB-g	español-guineo	40	98.00	12,421	1A.uh	10	9	15	5	2		pnb	.
3199	Yasa (Bongwe)	0.20000	799	905	1,589	NAB57k	99-AUAD-a	yasa		90.00	815	0....	10	8	11	3	1		pn.	.
3200	Yoruba	8.00000	31,959	36,213	63,578	NAB59n	98-AAAA-a	standard yoruba		63.40	22,959	3asu.	10	7	9	4	2	Yoruba	PNB	b
3201	other minor peoples	0.40000	1,598	1,811	3,179	...				80.00	1,449		10	7	7	2	0			
	Eritrea	**100.00000**	**3,186,781**	**3,850,388**	**6,680,653**					**50.24**	**1,934,355**									
3202	African -Arabian Arab	0.54462	17,356	20,970	36,384	CMT30	12-AACF-p	zanji		10.00	2,097	1Asuh	8	5	7	2	0		pnb	b
3203	Amhara	0.62633	19,960	24,116	41,843	CMT34a	12-ACBA-b	general amarinya		94.00	22,669	3Asuh	10	9	12	4	3	Amharic	PNB	b
3204	Beni Amer (Bisharin)	2.85924	91,118	110,092	191,016	CMT33z	13-AAAA-a	ti-bedaauye		0.00	0	0....	0	2	2	1	1		...	b
3205	Bilen (Bogos, Bilean)	1.98222	63,169	76,323	132,425	CMT33a	14-BAAA-a	bilin		30.00	22,897	0....	9	5	7	1	1	Bogos*	P..	b
3206	Danakil (Afar, Adali)	8.16926	260,336	314,548	545,760	CMT33z	14-AAAB-a	'afar-af		0.01	31	1.s..	3	4	5	0	3	Afar	PN.	b
3207	Italian	0.05446	1,736	2,097	3,638	CEW21e	51-AABQ-c	standard italiano		82.00	1,719	2B.uh	10	9	15	5	1	Italian	PNB	b
3208	Kunama (Cunama, Diila)	4.18517	133,372	161,145	279,597	NAB62h	05-KAAA-a	marda-kunama		20.00	32,229	0....	9	5	7	1	3	Kunama	PN.	.
3209	Mensa	1.17092	37,315	45,085	78,225	CMT34c	12-ACAB-ad	mensa		65.00	29,305	1c...	10	7	8	2	1		pnb	.

Continued opposite

Table 8-2 continued

EVANGELIZATION								EVANGELISM			ADDITIONAL DESCRIPTIVE DATA
Ref 1	D 28	aC 29	CG% 30	r 31	E 32	U 33	W 34	e 35	R 36	T 37	Locations, civil divisions, literacy, religions, church history, denominations, dioceses, church growth, missions, agencies, ministries, movements 38
3094	2	10	2.07	8	99.99	0.01	C	596.22	44	10	Spanish-speaking Blacks along coast. A few Baha'is, using radio/TV. D=RCC(VA-Esmeraldas),AIEC. M=OMS,FMB. T=CBN. R=AWR. T=LESEA.
3095	1	10	2.08	8	99.99	0.01	C	578.16	46	10	Ecuadorian Blacks. Some Baha'is, using radio/TV. D=RCC.
3096	1	9	2.07	4	99.98	0.02	C	522.24	52	10	Eastern jungle, tropical rainforest. Many in Peru. Animists 2%. D=RCC(christopagans 20%).
3097	1	9	2.07	4	99.99	0.01	C	567.32	48	10	Pichincha Province around Quito. D=RCC(christopagans 20%).
3098	1	9	2.07	4	99.99	0.01	C	567.32	48	10	South, Canar Province. D=RCC(christopagans 20%). M=NLM,GMU,LBT,WMPL,SIL.
3099	1	6	2.07	0	41.00	59.00	A	11.97	181	5	North coastal jungle. Animists 90%. D=RCC. M=SIL,MCA,FSCJ. R=HCJB.
3100	1	9	2.07	4	99.99	0.01	C	590.15	47	10	Central highlands. 80% monolinguals. Some Baha'is, using radio/TV approaches. D=RCC(christopagans 20%). M=GMU,WVI,FMB,SIL,UBS,CMA,UAIM.
3101	1	6	2.59	0	65.00	35.00	B	71.17	139	6	Also in Colombia. Tropical forest. Fairly monolingual. Animists 70%. D=RCC. M=SIL.
3102	2	6	2.07	0	78.00	22.00	B	113.88	95	7	Northwestern jungle. Animists 60%. D=Plymouth Brethren,RCC. M=SIL,FMB.
3103	5	10	2.54	8	99.99	0.01	C	607.06	53	10	Some Baha'is. D=EMUC,ICFG,IEUE,UPCI,SDA. M=OP,FSCJ,SDB,CSJ,OFM,OFMCap,OCD,GMU,WMPL,FMB,SIM. T=CBN. R=AWR. T=LESEA.
3104	3	10	2.07	8	99.88	0.12	C	536.40	53	10	Immigrants from Germany. D=RCC,NAC,Evangelical Lutheran Ch.
3105	1	9	4.50	7	70.00	30.00	B	15.33	202	5	Immigrants from Chinese diaspora. Buddhists/Chinese folk-religionists 90%. D=RCC. M=FMB.
3106	0	9	1.40	8	49.09	50.91	A	0.16	117	3	Small communities of practicing Spanish-speaking Jews. M=SJ,SDB.
3107	5	10	2.07	8	99.94	0.06	C	560.61	49	10	Original European descent. Almost all are baptized Catholics. D=RCC,EMUC,ICFG,SDA,&c. T=CBN. R=AWR. T=LESEA.
3108	8	10	2.08	8	99.99	0.01	C	612.33	42	10	D=RCC(22 Dioceses),EMUC,ICFG,UPCI,SDA,IEUE,CMA,AoG. M=GMU,SDB,SJ,OFM,CSSR,OP,MJ,FSC,WMPL,FMB,SIM. T=CBN. R=AWR. T=LESEA.
3109	2	10	2.07	8	99.98	0.02	C	590.20	44	10	Mixed-race Black/Amerindians. Some Baha'is. D=RCC,AIEC.
3110	1	9	2.07	4	99.90	0.10	C	456.61	54	10	Tropical Forest. Many in Peru and Colombia. Many animists 10%. D=RCC(christopagans 20%). M=SIL.
3111	1	10	2.07	6	99.93	0.07	C	560.09	52	10	Immigrants from Norway; in commerce, professions. D=Evangelical Lutheran Ch.
3112	1	9	2.07	4	99.99	0.01	C	574.54	48	10	North. 60% monolinguals. Animists still widespread. D=RCC(christopagans 20%). M=FMB,CMA,UBS,SIL. M=HCJB
3113	0	6	2.21	0	96.00	4.00	C	227.76	81	8	Extreme north, slopes of Andes. Great majority live in Colombia. Animists 35%.
3114	2	9	2.07	4	99.90	0.10	C	492.75	50	10	15 towns in Salasaca area. Many animists 10%. D=RCC(christopagans 20%),CMA. M=GMU,SIL.
3115	1	9	2.07	4	99.90	0.10	C	479.61	52	10	Northern area of Loja Province. Many animists, 10%. D=RCC(christopagans 20%). M=WMPL,OMSI,SIL.
3116	0	6	2.09	0	54.00	46.00	B	39.42	142	5	Northeastern jungle, tropical forest; also in Peru. Animists 80%. M=SIL.
3117	1	6	2.07	0	49.00	51.00	A	14.30	155	5	Southeastern jungle. Literates 95%. Animists 92%. D=RCC(Radical bishop, D-Riobamba). M=GMU,Christians in Action (Guatemala),SIL.
3118	1	6	2.07	0	96.00	4.00	C	210.24	79	8	Putumayo river. Riverine. Tropical forest. Primarily in Colombia. Animists 40%. D=RCC.
3119	4	9	3.83	8	84.00	16.00	B	61.32	148	6	Immigrants. Muslims 80%. D=RCC(Maronites),AOCUSA,GOC(P-Antioch),SOC.
3120	1	9	2.07	4	99.90	0.10	C	459.90	54	10	Eastern jungle, tropical forest. Animists 10%. D=RCC(christopagans 20%). M=CMML,CMA.
3121	1	6	0.70	0	99.67	0.33	C	244.97	38	8	Eastern jungle, Cofan. Close to Secoya. Nearly extinct. Animists 33%. D=RCC.
3122	6	10	3.21	8	99.78	0.22	C	427.05	75	10	Expatriates from USA, in development, education. D=SDA,CJCLdS,RCC,ICFG,AoG,JWs.
3123	1	6	3.67	0	77.00	23.00	B	112.42	156	7	Eastern jungle between Napo and Curaray rivers. Tropical forest. Some bilinguals in Quichua and Spanish. Animists 60%. D=RCC. M=SIL,MAF.
3124	0	6	2.09	0	99.75	0.25	C	306.60	76	9	Pastaza Province, tropical forest. Riverine. Extinct in Peru. Bilingual in Quichua. Animists 23%. M=EEMA.
3125	0	9	1.66		51.00	49.00	B	37.23	89	5	Japanese (PBA), Costarricans, Koreans, other Latin Americans, Europeans.
Egypt											
3126	0	5	1.96	7	18.01	81.99	A	0.00	587	1.05	Nomads in southeast. Part of Beja nation in Sudan. Muslims 100%(weak Sunnis).
3127	2	6	0.26	6	47.00	53.00	A	1.71	50	4	Immigrants, residents from Albania. Workers. Muslims 99%(Sunnis). D=AOC,COC.
3128	1	10	2.37	5	99.80	0.20	C	426.32	79	10	Refugees, Christians from Ethiopia. Some pagans still, or Muslims. D=Ethiopian Orthodox Ch.
3129	3	6	1.12	8	69.00	31.00	B	17.63	72	5	Modern Standard Arabic: official language, for education, officialdom, international communication. Muslims 93%. D=COC,RCC,CEC. M=UBS,LBI.
3130	0	9	5.04	8	47.10	52.90	A	0.17	334	3	Berbers with Arabic as mother tongue. From across North African tribes; also detribalized. Muslims 100%(Sunnis).
3131	0	6	0.00	8	36.00	64.00	A	0.00	0	1.13	Nubians(some detribalized or deculturated)with Arabic as mother tongue. Muslims 100%(Sunnis).
3132	3	10	0.85	6	99.89	0.11	C	523.92	25	10	Refugees from Turkey in 1915. Gregorians. D=Armenian Apostolic Ch(AD-Cairo),UAECNE,ASB.
3133	0	1	0.00	7	19.00	81.00	A	0.00	0	1.06	Sedentary Bedouins inhabiting oases of Bahariya and Frafra in western desert. Muslims 100%(Sunnis).
3134	0	1	0.00	7	16.00	84.00	A	0.00	0	1.05	Many nomadic Bedouin tribes. Tent-dwellers. Muslims 100%(Sunnis).
3135	0	5	0.00	7	18.00	82.00	A	0.00	0	1.04	Part of the Beja nation of the Sudan. Part in Eritrea. Nomads. Many bilingual or monolingual in Arabic. Muslims 100%(Sunnis).
3136	1	10	1.10	8	99.66	0.34	C	332.44	45	9	Expatriates from Britain, in professions, commerce. D=Episcopal Ch in Jerusalem & Middle East(D-Egypt).
3137	0	1	0.00	7	19.00	81.00	A	0.00	0	1.06	Sedentary inhabitants of Dakhla oasis in western Egypt. Muslims 100%.(Sunnis).
3138	0	6	4.59	0	19.01	80.99	A	0.00	863	1.06	Growing ethnic pride. Widespread prosperity. In Alexandria, Cairo(originally in Upper Egypt). Muslims 100%(Sunnis). M=OM.
3139	7	6	1.71	8	84.00	16.00	B	52.12	79	6	Muslims 82%(Shafi,Maliki,Hanafi Sunnis). D=Coptic Orthodox Ch(24 Dioceses),RCC(7 rites,12 Dioceses),CEV,AoG,ECJME,CB,&c. M=SDB,OFM,SJ.
3140	0	6	2.65	0	19.04	80.96	A	0.02	583	2	Ratana (Nile Nubian). Ethnic consciousness rapidly increasing among adults. Prosperity. 70% bilingual in Arabic. Muslims 100%(Sunnis). M=OM.
3141	2	10	1.70	8	99.82	0.18	C	460.92	48	10	Expatriates from France, in business, education. D=RCC,Eglise de Langue Francaise.
3142	3	10	1.81	8	99.88	0.12	C	520.34	50	10	Expatriates from Germany, in commerce, industry. D=RCC,CEC,NAC.
3143	0	6	5.77	7	29.00	71.00	A	1.05	642	4	Egyptian Gypsies, Muslim Gypsies. Muslims 99%(Hanafi Sunnis).
3144	4	10	0.41	7	99.95	0.05	C	582.54	23	10	Emigrating. D=Greek Orthodox Patriarchate of Alexandria(4 Dioceses),RCC(Melkite P-Alexandria),GEC,Ch of Sinai.
3145	0	5	2.43	8	37.01	62.99	A	0.01	256	2	Egyptian Gypsies, also called Muslim Gypsies. In 10 countries. Muslims 100%(Hanafi Sunnis).
3146	0	10	1.10	7	44.09	55.91	A	0.14	131	3	Traders from India and Pakistan. Muslims 80%(Sunnis, with many Ahmadis/Qadianis), Hindus 20%.
3147	1	10	1.68	7	99.80	0.20	C	440.92	49	10	Expatriates from Italy, in education, commerce. Strong Catholics. D=RCC.
3148	0	10	2.10	8	49.53	50.47	A	0.95	154	3	Remnants of 75,000 Jews in 1950. Continuous emigration to Israel, USA, Western Europe.
3149	0	1	0.00	7	19.00	81.00	A	0.00	0	1.06	Bedouins inhabiting oases of Kharga and Selima. Muslims 100%(Sunnis).
3150	0	1	0.00	7	19.00	81.00	A	0.00	0	1.06	Several Bedouin tribes extending from Sinai Peninsula into western Gulf of Suez shores. Muslims 100%(Sunnis).
3151	1	10	6.74	2	99.99	0.01	C	545.63	135	10	Lower Egypt. Liturgical language of Coptic Orthodox Church, still with mother-tongue speakers. D=COC(30 Dioceses).
3152	3	8	1.60	8	75.00	25.00	B	41.06	84	6	Many refugees from Israel, West Bank. Laborers, professionals. Muslims 85%. D=RCC,ECJME,GOC.
3153	2	10	0.30	7	81.00	19.00	B	59.13	10	6	Military and other advisers. Nonreligious or atheists 80%. D=ROC(P-Moscow),ROCOR.
3154	0	1	0.00	7	19.00	81.00	A	0.00	0	1.06	Several smaller Bedouin tribes in western desert. Muslims 100%(Sunnis).
3155	0	1	0.00	0	7.00	93.00	A	0.00	0	1.02	Isolated villages in northwestern oasis, near Libya border. Muslims 100%(Hanafi Sunnis).
3156	2	7	5.19	7	57.40	42.60	B	2.93	281	4	Immigrants from Sudan over many generations. Muslims 98%(Maliki Sunnis). D=RCC,GOC. M=FMB,SIL.
3157	4	7	1.74	8	91.00	9.00	B	99.64	73	6	Northeastern Colloquial Arabic. Muslims 70%. D=RCC(Maronites),SOC(Jacobites),GOC(P-Antioch),CEC.
3158	1	9	4.45	5	79.00	21.00	B	86.50	220	6	Workers and residents from Ethiopia. Muslims 60%(Shafi Sunnis). D=EOC.
3159	0	8	1.96	8	42.02	57.98	A	0.03	174	2	Workers from Turkey, including numbers in commerce. Muslims 100%(Hanafi Sunnis).
3160	5	10	3.37	8	99.80	0.20	C	449.68	76	10	Expatriates from USA, in education, business, commerce. D=SDA,AoG,RCC,CEC,ECJME.
3161	1	6	3.59	2	99.99	0.01	C	529.36	80	10	Upper Egypt. A few speakers for liturgical language of COC. D=Coptic Orthodox Ch. M=MEM.
3162	0	6	2.67	7	37.01	62.99	A	0.01	249	2	Eastern Colloquial Arabic. Labor migrants from Yemen and nearby countries. Muslims 100%.
3163	0	7	6.75		28.00	72.00	A	10.22	661	5	Assyrians(Chaldean-rite RCs), Saudis, Iraqis, Maghreb Arabs, Karaite Jews, Koreans(PCK), Tigre refugees, Tigrai, North African Arabs. Muslims 80%.
El Salvador											
3164	3	9	2.45	8	70.00	30.00	B	22.99	123	5	Mainly Palestinians, from Holy Land or the diaspora. Muslims 91%(mostly Sunnis). D=RCC(Maronites),GOC,IEE.
3165	4	10	1.80	8	99.88	0.12	C	520.34	50	10	Expatriates From Germany, in professions, commerce. D=ELC,RCC,JWs,&c.
3166	1	9	2.52	8	70.00	30.00	B	20.44	124	5	From Chinese diaspora. Buddhists/Chinese folk-religionists 92%. D=RCC.
3167	0	10	0.00	8	44.20	55.80	A	0.32	43	3	Small communities of Spanish-speaking Jews, long-time residents.
3168	1	8	1.80	0	99.90	0.10	C	486.18	48	10	Also in Guatemala, southern Belize. Animists 10%. D=RCC(christopagans 5%).
3169	1	10	1.80	0	99.80	0.20	C	353.32	59	9	Language nearly extinct: only 1% use it, rest use Spanish. Animists 20%. D=RCC(christo-pagans 5%).
3170	1	7	1.83	8	99.98	0.02	C	580.89	40	10	Large mixed-race population. D=RCC(5 Dioceses; christopagans 3%). M=SDB,SJ,OFM,OAR,OP,MJ,PFM. T=CBN. R=AWR. T=LESEA.
3171	1	10	1.80	8	99.90	0.10	C	502.60	42	10	Refugees from civil war and fighting in Nicaragua. Nonreligious 10%. D=RCC.
3172	6	10	1.80	8	99.88	0.12	C	494.64	46	10	Many detribalized Amerindians. D=RCC,AoG,SDA,IC,CJCLdS,CON. M=15.
3173	1	10	1.81	8	99.96	0.04	C	536.23	46	10	Large Pipil ethnic group, but language nearly extinct; 20 speakers of Pipil in 1987, rest use Spanish. A few Pipil in Honduras. Animists 3%. D=RCC.
3174	1	8	1.80	0	99.90	0.10	C	430.33	54	10	Amerindians. Majority live in Guatemala. Animists 10%. D=RCC.
3175	1	10	1.80	8	99.91	0.09	C	513.30	47	10	Citizens of European origin, in commerce, professions. D=RCC.
3176	0	9	1.96	8	48.10	51.90	A	1.93	152	4	Immigrants from Turkey, many in manual labor. Muslims 99%(Hanafi Sunnis).
3177	5	10	2.52	8	99.76	0.24	C	416.10	62	10	Expatriates from USA, in education, business. D=SDA,CJCLdS,ABEL,ELC,&c.
3178	0	10	1.80		66.00	34.00	B	96.36	75	6	Some Chorotega (Spanish-speaking), Mexicans, other Central Amerindians, West Indian Blacks, other Caribbean islanders.
Equatorial Guinea											
3179	1	8	2.69	2	99.95	0.05	C	492.38	73	10	On Pagalu (Annobon Island). Portuguese-based creole. Closed to outsiders. D=RCC(D-Malabo).
3180	4	8	4.52	0	99.95	0.05	C	481.98	125	10	Scattered groups from north of country up along coastal Cameroon. All Christians. D=IEGE,RCC,Methodists,AICs.
3181	1	7	4.91	0	68.00	32.00	B	94.31	242	6	Forest-dwelling Pygmies. Animists 62%. D=RCC. M=various small missions.
3182	2	8	3.17	0	99.90	0.10	C	469.75	95	10	In Rio Muni(Corsico Island); also in Gabon. Christians since 1850. Animists 10%. D=RCC(D-Bata),IEGE. M=CMF,PCUSA.
3183	3	10	3.62	8	99.78	0.22	C	435.59	85	10	Expatriates from Britain, in education, commerce. D=IEGE,IEEL,Iglesia Metodista.
3184	4	10	3.58	2	99.97	0.03	C	534.61	98	10	On Fernando Poo. Many Baha'is. D=RCC(D-Malabo),Methodists,many JWs,SDA. M=CMF,Primitive Methodists(UK),FMB.
3185	2	10	2.22	8	99.95	0.05	C	551.33	57	10	Nigerians and others, speaking widely-understood Pidgin. D=RCC,AICs.
3186	5	10	3.18	8	99.95	0.05	C	565.20	72	10	Mixed-race persons. All Christians. D=RCC,IEGE,IEEL,Methodists,AICs. M=WEC,CMF,NEM(Nigeria)
3187	4	9	4.59	2	99.90	0.10	C	490.33	111	10	Also in Gabon, Cameroon, Congo. Numerous atheists, militant marxists, some animists. D=RCC(2-Dioceses),IEGE,IEEL,AICs. M=WEC,CMF,FMB,EPC. R=ELWA.
3188	4	10	4.91	1	99.95	0.05	C	527.06	108	10	On Fernando Poo. English-based creole. Almost all Christians, from Sierra Leone. D=RCC(D-Malabo),many JWs,Methodists,SDA.
3189	1	10	1.23	8	99.87	0.13	C	490.95	39	10	Expatriates from France, in education, commerce. D=RCC.
3190	0	10	2.22	5	48.10	51.90	A	0.17	195	3	Expatriate traders from North and West Africa. Muslims 100%(Maliki Sunnis).
3191	3	10	5.46	4	99.90	0.10	C	509.17	121	10	Migrant workers from Calabar(Nigeria). Strong Christians. D=AICs,RCC,IEEL.
3192	3	10	7.68	4	99.90	0.10	C	509.17	160	10	Migrant laborers from Nigeria. Labor unrest, expulsions. D=RCC,IEEL,AICs.
3193	0	8	0.00	7	38.00	62.00	A	0.00	0	1.13	Traders from India and Pakistan. Hindus 50%, Muslims 50%.
3194	1	9	5.10	1	99.80	0.20	C	338.72	155	9	Mainly in Cameroon. Animists 20%. D=RCC.
3195	2	7	7.16	0	99.95	0.05	C	471.58	181	10	Rio Muni but mainly in Cameroon. All Christians. D=RCC,IEGE. M=WEC.
3196	3	8	6.25	2	99.95	0.05	C	495.85	154	10	Rio Muni coast. D=Presbyterians(IEGE),Asamblea de los Hermanos,RCC. M=WEC,FMB.
3197	2	8	4.52	0	99.95	0.05	C	475.04	126	10	Around Cocobeach. Also in Gabon. All Christians. D=RCC,IEGE.
3198	1	10	2.18	8	99.98	0.02	C	593.78	51	10	Expatriates from Spain, in administration, government, commerce. Strong Catholics. D=RCC. M=CMF,National Evangelical Mission(Nigeria).
3199	1	8	4.50	1	99.90	0.10	C	430.33	132	10	Rio Muni, also in Cameroon. Animists 10%. D=RCC.
3200	2	10	8.05	5	99.63	0.37	C	301.75	198	9	Migrant laborers from Nigeria. Muslims 25%(Maliki Sunnis), animists 11%. D=RCC,AICs.
3201	0	8	5.10		99.80	0.20	C	312.44	131	9	Numerous tribes from 10 neighboring nations.
Eritrea											
3202	0	6	5.49	7	58.00	42.00	B	21.17	292	5	Modern Standard Arabic. Saudi Arabs, Egyptian Arabs, Gulf Arabs, North African Arabs. Muslims 89%.
3203	8	6	5.57	5	99.94	0.06	C	545.52	128	10	Main people of Ethiopia. Literates 60%. D=95% EOC,GOC,RCC,ECMY,SDA,WLEC,FCC,FGC.
3204	0	5	0.00	7	19.00	81.00	A	0.00	0	1.06	Beja, Nabtab. Also in Sudan, Egypt. Bilingual in Tigre. Muslims 100%(Sunnis). M=CSI.
3205	4	6	3.90	0	64.00	36.00	B	70.08	248	6	North central Eritrea. Bilinguals: Christians in Tigrinya, Muslims in Tigre and Arabic. Muslims 68%(Sunnis). D=25% RCC,5% Ethiopian Orthodox Ch,ECE,FCC.
3206	3	4	3.49	4	29.01	70.99	A	0.01	509	2	Nomads, also in Ethiopia, Djibouti, Somalia. Literates 8%. Muslims 100%(Sunnis). D=Orthodox Presbyterian Ch,ECMY,RCC. M=SIL,CMML,RSTI,EMBMC,FMB.
3207	1	10	2.17	7	99.82	0.18	C	451.94	58	10	Expatriates from Italy, some settlers from 1930s occupation. Strong Catholics. D=RCC.
3208	4	6	5.21	0	56.00	44.00	B	40.88	323	6	North and west Eritrea. Muslims 75%. Strong Catholics. D=RCC (VA-Asmara of the Latins),ECE,LCE,FCC. M=OFMCap,MEGM,SLM,EFS.
3209	4	6	3.67	4	99.65	0.35	C	260.97	139	8	Dialect of Tigre. Muslims 35%. Strong Christians. D=RCC(D-Asmara),ECE,FCC,FGC. M=EFS.

Continued overleaf

Table 8-2 continued

PEOPLE		POPULATION				IDENTITY CODE		LANGUAGE		CHURCH		MINISTRY						SCRIPTURE	
Ref 1	Ethnic name 2	P% 3	In 1995 4	In 2000 5	In 2025 6	Race 7	Language 8	Autoglossonym 9	S 10	AC 11	Members 12	Jayuh 13-17	d 18	wa 19	xc 20	mc 21	mi 22	Biblioglossonym 23	Pub ss 24-26 27
3210	Nara (Barea, Barya)	1.88333	60,018	72,516	125,819	NAB62d	05-JAAA	nara cluster		5.00	3,626	0....	7	4	2	2	1		... n
3211	Palestinian Arab	0.81692	26,033	31,455	54,576	CMT30	12-AACF-f	syro-palestinian		10.00	3,145	1Asuh	8	5	7	2	2	Arabic: Lebanese*	Pnb b
3212	Saho (Sao, Minifere, Irob)	4.30475	137,183	165,750	287,585	CMT33z	14-AAAA-a	saho		5.00	8,287	0....	7	5	7	1	2		... .
3213	Somali	1.36154	43,389	52,425	90,960	CMT33e	14-GAGA-a	af-soomaali		0.01	5	2A...	3	4	3	0	3	Somali	PNB b
3214	Tigrai	51.83941	1,652,008	1,996,018	3,463,211	CMT34b	12-ACAC-a	tigray		90.54	1,807,195	2As..	10	9	11	5	3	Tigrinya	PNB b
3215	Tigre (Khasa)	17.96070	572,368	691,557	1,199,892	CMT34c	12-ACAB-a	tigre		0.05	346	1B...	4	4	5	5	3	Tigre	PNB b
3216	Yemeni Arab	2.04232	65,084	78,637	136,440	CMT30	12-AACF-n	yemeni		0.05	39	1Asuh	4	3	1	0	2		pnb b
3217	other minor peoples	0.19879	6,335	7,654	13,280	...				10.00	765		8	5	6	0	0		
	Estonia	**100.00000**	**1,485,675**	**1,396,158**	**1,131,222**					**37.95**	**529,874**								
3218	Armenian	0.10700	1,590	1,494	1,210	CEW14	57-AAAA-b	ashkharik		70.00	1,046	4A.u.	10	7	9	2	1	Armenian: Modern, Eastern	PNB b
3219	Azerbaijani	0.07900	1,174	1,103	894	MSY41a	44-AABA-fa	north azeri		0.00	0	2c.u.	0	3	3	0	2	Azerbaijani*	PNB b
3220	Belorussian	1.80000	26,742	25,131	20,362	CEW22c	53-AAAE-c	bielorusskiy		60.00	15,079	3A.uh	10	7	9	0	0	Byelorussian*	PNB b
3221	Chuvash	0.07500	1,114	1,047	848	MSY41c	44-AAAA-a	chuvash		35.00	366	2....	9	6	8	0	1	Chuvash	PN. b
3222	Estonian (Estlased)	3.67900	54,658	51,365	41,618	MSW51a	41-AAAC-bd	setu		60.00	30,819	1A.u.	10	8	11	3	2	Estonian: Setu	Pnb b
3223	Finnish (Finn)	6.36000	94,489	88,796	71,946	MSW51b	41-AAAA-bb	vehicular suomi		67.00	59,493	1A.uh	10	8	12	4	3	Finnish	PNB b
3224	Georgian	0.03900	579	545	441	CEW17c	42-CABB-a	kharthuli		40.00	218	2A.u.	9	6	8	2	1	Georgian	PNB b
3225	German	0.22100	3,283	3,086	2,500	CEW19m	52-ABCE-a	standard hoch-deutsch		80.00	2,468	2B.uh	10	9	13	3	2	German*	PNB b
3226	Ingrian (Izhor)	0.06100	906	852	690	MSW51z	41-AAAB-f	izhor		70.00	596	1....	10	8	8	5	3		p.. b
3227	Jewish	0.21000	3,120	2,932	2,376	CMT35	52-ABCH	yiddish cluster		0.00	0	0B..h	0	3	6	0	0		PNB b
3228	Karelian	0.05600	832	782	633	MSW51c	41-AAAB-a	central karely		67.00	524	1....	10	6	8	0	3	Karelian	P.. b
3229	Latvian (Lett)	0.20000	2,971	2,792	2,262	CEW15a	54-AABA-a	standard latviashu		91.00	2,541	3A.u.	10	8	11	2	3	Latvian	PNB b
3230	Lithuanian	0.16400	2,437	2,290	1,855	CEW15b	54-AAAA-a	standard lietuvishkai		85.00	1,946	3A.u.	10	8	11	2	3	Lithuanian	PNB b
3231	Moldavian	0.07800	1,159	1,089	882	CEW21f	51-AADC-ab	standard moldavia		82.00	893	1A.u.	10	7	10	2	1		pnb b
3232	Mordvinian	0.06300	936	880	713	MSW51i	41-AADA-a	erzya		65.00	572	2....	10	8	8	2	1	Mordvin: Erzya*	PN. b
3233	Northern Estonian	46.97000	697,822	655,775	531,335	MSW51a	41-AAAC-b	eesti		36.50	239,358	4A.u.	9	9	11	3	2	Estonian: Tallinn	PNB b
3234	Polish	0.19200	2,852	2,681	2,172	CEW22i	53-AAAC-c	polski		91.00	2,439	2A.uh	10	8	11	2	2	Polish	PNB b
3235	Russian	28.90000	429,360	403,490	326,923	CEW22j	53-AAAE-d	russkiy	84	25.00	100,872	4B.uh	9	8	8	3	3	Russian	PNB b
3236	Southern Estonian	7.35800	109,316	102,729	83,235	MSW51a	41-AAAC-bc	tartu		40.00	41,092	1A.u.	9	9	10	3	3	Estonian: Tartu	PNB b
3237	Swedish	0.30000	4,457	4,188	3,394	CEW19q	52-AAAD-r	svea-svensk		70.00	2,932	1A.uh	10	8	8	5	2	Swedish	PNB b
3238	Tatar	0.25000	3,714	3,490	2,828	MSY41h	44-AABB-e	tatar		1.50	52	2c.u.	6	4	8	0	1	Tatar: Kazan	Pn. b
3239	Ukrainian	2.70000	40,113	37,696	30,543	CEW22p	53-AAAE-b	ukrainskiy		69.00	26,010	3A.uh	10	8	9	3	3	Ukrainian	PNB b
3240	Uzbek	0.03800	565	531	430	MSY41l	44-AABD-a	central uzbek		0.00	0	1A.u.	0	3	6	1	3	Uzbek*	PNb b
3241	other minor peoples	0.10000	1,486	1,396	1,131	...				40.00	558		9	8	8	3	0		
	Ethiopia	**100.00000**	**55,353,711**	**62,564,875**	**115,382,091**					**49.81**	**31,161,152**								
3242	Alaba	0.16374	90,636	102,444	188,927	CMT33d	14-CABA-c	alaba		70.00	71,711	1.s..	10	7	7	5	1	Alaba	pn. .
3243	Amar (Hamar-Koke, Bunna)	0.04820	26,680	30,156	55,614	CMT33z	16-AAAA-a	hamar-apo		2.00	603	0....	6	3	5	1	1	Hamer-banna	... .
3244	Amhara	31.56135	17,470,378	19,746,319	36,416,146	CMT34a	12-ACBA-b	general amarinya	56	88.80	17,534,731	3Asuh	10	9	11	4	3	Amharic	PNB b
3245	Anuak (Yambo)	0.05129	28,391	32,090	59,179	NAB62c	04-ABAB-a	adongo		3.00	963	0As..	6	5	7	2	1	Anuak	PN. .
3246	Arab	0.01000	5,535	6,256	11,538	CMT30	12-AACF-p	zanji		10.00	626	1Asuh	8	5	7	2	2		pnb b
3247	Arbore	0.00743	4,113	4,649	8,573	CMT33z	14-GABA-a	oho-arbore		2.00	93	0....	6	4	4	2	0		... .
3248	Argobba	0.07122	39,423	44,559	82,175	CMT34a	12-ACBA-c	argobbinya		10.00	4,456	1csuh	8	5	6	2	0		pnb .
3249	Ari (Bako, Ara)	0.21018	116,342	131,499	242,510	CMT33d	16-AABA	aari-shangama cluster		20.00	26,300	0....	9	5	7	5	3	Aari	... .
3250	Armenian	0.00638	3,532	3,992	7,361	CEW14	57-AAAA-b	ashkharik		80.00	3,193	4A.u.	10	9	13	2	1	Armenian: Modern, Eastern	PNB b
3251	Arusi Galla (Oromo)	2.90000	1,605,258	1,814,381	3,346,081	CMT33b	14-FBAA-f	arusi		3.00	54,431	2cs..	6	5	7	4	3	Oromo: Central	Pnb n
3252	Baiso (Bayso)	0.00183	1,013	1,145	2,111	CMT33z	14-GAAA-a	bayso		2.00	23	0....	6	4	4	1	3		... n
3253	Bale	0.00619	3,426	3,873	7,142	NAB62y	05-PABA-b	bale		30.00	1,162	0....	9	5	7	3	3		... .
3254	Basketo (Badditu)	0.26294	145,547	164,508	303,386	CMT33d	16-BAHA-a	basketo		80.00	131,606	0....	10	7	7	2	1		... .
3255	Begi-Mao	0.00544	3,011	3,404	6,277	CMT33d	16-EAAA-a	hozo-wandi		10.00	340	0....	8	5	6	2	1		... b
3256	Beni Amer (Bisharin)	0.01000	5,535	6,256	11,538	CMT33z	13-AAAA-a	ti-bedaauye		0.00	0	0....	0	2	2	1	0		... b
3257	Beni Shangul (Wetawit)	0.08696	48,136	54,406	100,336	NAB62z	05-NAAA-a	ndu-berthu		10.00	5,441	0....	8	5	7	2	1		... .
3258	Boran	0.01300	7,196	8,133	15,000	CMT33b	14-FBAA	oromo cluster	2	4.00	325	2As..	6	5	7	2	2		PNB b
3259	British	0.01700	9,410	10,636	19,615	CEW19i	52-ABAC-b	standard-english	15	79.00	8,402	3Bsuh	10	9	13	5	3		PNB b
3260	Burji	0.14971	82,870	93,666	172,739	CMT33d	14-CBAA-aa	burji		40.00	37,466	0....	9	5	7	3	2	Burji	PN. .
3261	Bussa	0.01089	6,028	6,813	12,565	CMT33d	14-FAAA-a	mosiya		70.00	4,769	0.s..	10	7	6	4	1		p.. .
3262	Central Koma (Hayahaya)	0.00437	2,419	2,734	5,042	NAB62z	05-OBBA-c	madiin		5.00	137	0....	7	5	4	2	1		... .
3263	Central West Gurage (Chaha)	1.30000	719,598	813,343	1,499,967	CMT34z	12-ACEB-b	gura	2	43.00	349,738	1.s..	9	6	7	4	3		PN. b
3264	Chabo	0.00163	902	1,020	1,881	NAB62y	05-PEAA-a	shabo		5.00	51	0....	7	4	5	1	2		... .
3265	Chara	0.03256	18,023	20,371	37,568	CMT33d	16-BAAA-a	chara		40.00	8,148	0....	9	5	4	2	2		... n
3266	Cuban White	0.01000	5,535	6,256	11,538	CLT27	51-AABB-hi	cubano		20.00	1,251	1B.uh	9	5	2	2	1		pnb b
3267	Dache (Gereze)	0.00850	4,705	5,318	9,807	CMT33d	16-BAFA-b	dache		50.00	2,659	1.s..	10	6	6	3	1		pn. .
3268	Danakil (Afar, Adali)	0.84214	466,156	526,884	971,679	CMT33z	14-AAAB-a	'afar-af		0.01	53	1.s..	3	4	5	3	3	Afar	PN. b
3269	Dembiya	0.01000	5,535	6,256	11,538	CMT33a	14-BABA-b	dembiya		5.00	313	0....	7	4	6	2	0		p.. b
3270	Didessa	0.00197	1,090	1,233	2,273	CMT33d	16-DAAA-a	didessa		10.00	123	0....	8	5	6	2	1		... b
3271	Dihina (Tihinte)	0.00596	3,299	3,729	6,877	CMT33z	14-DAAA-f	dihina		2.00	75	1....	6	4	5	1	1		... .
3272	Dime	0.00530	2,934	3,316	6,115	CMT33z	16-AACA-a	dim-'ap		2.00	66	0....	6	4	4	1	1		... .
3273	Dobase (Bussa, Lohu)	0.00948	5,248	5,931	10,938	CMT33d	14-FAAA-c	mashile		12.00	712	0.s..	8	5	6	2	2		p.. .
3274	Donyiro	0.06000	33,212	37,539	69,229	NAB62y	04-BDAA-c	aku-tuk-angi-nyangatom		5.00	1,877	0....	7	4	6	2	1		... n
3275	Dorze	0.00835	4,622	5,224	9,634	CMT33d	16-BAFA-c	dorze		30.00	1,567	1.s..	9	5	5	4	1		pn. .
3276	East Gurage (Ennequor)	0.97256	538,348	608,481	1,122,160	CMT34z	12-ACCB-c	silti		45.00	273,816	0.s..	9	5	7	4	2	Gurage, East	P.. .
3277	Eastern Nuer (Abrigar)	0.17020	94,212	106,485	196,380	NAB62n	04-AABA-d	dar-cieng		5.00	5,324	1A...	7	4	6	3	1	Nuer: Western	Pn. .
3278	Falasha (Black Jew, Kara)	0.02000	11,071	12,513	23,076	CMT33a	14-BBAA-a	awngi		10.00	1,251	0....	8	5	7	2	2		... b
3279	French	0.04000	22,141	25,026	46,153	CEW21b	51-AABI-d	general français	4	80.00	20,021	1B.uh	10	9	14	5	3	French	PNB b
3280	Gaba (Kaapa)	0.00497	2,751	3,109	5,734	CMT33d	14-DAAA-g	gaba		10.00	311	1....	8	5	7	2	0		... .
3281	Gamila	0.00748	4,140	4,680	8,631	NAB62z	05-NAAB-a	gamila		30.00	1,404	0....	9	5	5	3	1		... b
3282	Gamo (Gemu)	0.89473	495,266	559,787	1,032,358	CMT33d	16-BAFB-a	gemu-dona		15.00	83,968	0....	8	5	6	2	1		p.. .
3283	Ganjule	0.00010	55	63	115	CMT33d	16-BAEA-a	ganjule		10.00	6	0....	8	5	6	2	0		... b
3284	Ganza	0.01000	5,535	6,256	11,538	CMT33d	16-FAAA-a	ganza		10.00	626	0....	8	5	6	2	0		... b
3285	Garre (Gurreh)	0.01000	5,535	6,256	11,538	CMT33b	14-FBAA	oromo cluster		2.00	125	2As..	6	4	4	1	2		PNB b
3286	Gawwada (Gauwada)	0.12378	68,517	77,443	142,820	CMT33d	14-DAAA-i	ko-kawwate		2.00	1,549	1....	6	4	5	1	2		... .
3287	Geez (Giiz, Ethiopic)	0.00100	554	626	1,154	CMT34z	12-ACAA-ba	religious ge`ez	3	99.00	619	0....	10	8	11	4	1	Ethiopic*	PNB b
3288	Gergere	0.00552	3,056	3,454	6,369	CMT33d	14-DAAA-h	gergere		20.00	691	1....	9	5	6	3	1		... .
3289	Gibe (Guma)	0.10000	55,354	62,565	115,382	CMT33d	14-FBAA	oromo cluster		10.00	6,256	2As..	8	5	6	2	0		PNB b
3290	Gideo (Darasa, Gedeo)	1.32000	730,669	825,856	1,523,044	CMT33d	14-CADA-a	gede-inke-afa'o	2	30.00	247,757	2....	9	5	9	4	3	Gedeo	PN. .
3291	Gidole	0.01238	6,853	7,746	14,284	CMT33d	14-FAAA-b	kap-dirashat		50.00	3,873	0.s..	10	6	7	4	1		p.. .
3292	Gimira (Bencho, Mer, She)	0.15782	87,359	98,740	182,096	CMT33d	16-BBAA	bench cluster		30.00	29,622	0....	9	5	6	4	1	Gimira*	PN. .
3293	Gobato	0.00291	1,611	1,821	3,358	NAB62z	05-NAAC-a	gobato		30.00	546	0....	9	5	5	3	1		... .
3294	Gobeze (Goraze, Werize)	0.07100	39,301	44,421	81,921	CMT33z	14-DAAA-b	go-beze		2.00	888	1....	6	4	5	1	0		... .
3295	Gofa	0.29695	164,373	185,786	342,627	CMT33d	16-BAFB-b	gofa		30.00	55,736	0....	9	5	7	3	1	Gofa	P.. .
3296	Gollango	0.00662	3,664	4,142	7,638	CMT33d	14-DAAA-d	go-lango		15.00	621	1....	8	5	7	2	1		... .
3297	Gorose (Korrose)	0.00552	3,056	3,454	6,369	CMT33d	14-DAAA-e	go-rose		20.00	691	1....	9	5	7	2	1		... .
3298	Greek	0.01700	9,410	10,636	19,615	CEW20	56-AAAA-c	dhimotiki		95.00	10,104	2B.uh	10	9	11	5	1	Greek: Modern	PNB b
3299	Guba	0.01000	5,535	6,256	11,538	CMT33d	16-BDCA-b	guba		5.00	313	0....	7	4	6	2	0		... .
3300	Guji Galla (Gujji, Oromo)	0.73966	409,429	462,767	853,435	CMT33b	14-FBAA-g	guji		10.00	46,277	1cs..	8	5	7	2	1		pnb n
3301	Gumuz (Hameg, Shankilla)	0.11828	65,472	74,002	136,474	NAB62z	05-LAAA-a	dakunza		10.00	7,400	0....	8	5	6	2	1	Gumuz	... .
3302	Hadiyya (Hadya, Adea)	2.20000	1,217,782	1,376,427	2,538,406	CMT33d	14-CAAA-a	hadiyya	4	30.00	412,928	3.s..	9	8	7	5	2	Hadiyya	PN. .
3303	Hamir (Kamir, Kharmir)	0.02000	11,071	12,513	23,076	CMT33a	14-BACA-c	xamir		60.00	7,508	0....	10	6	7	3	1		... b
3304	Hamta (Khamta, Xamta)	0.02130	11,790	13,326	24,576	CMT33a	14-BACA-b	xamta		60.00	7,996	0....	10	6	7	3	0		... b
3305	Hamtanga (Xamtanga)	0.14531	80,434	90,913	167,662	CMT33a	14-BACA-a	xamtanga		50.00	45,457	0....	10	6	6	3	1		... b
3306	Harari (Adere, Gesinan)	0.06405	35,454	40,073	73,902	CMT34a	12-ACCA-a	ge-sinan		0.00	0	0....	0	4	7	3	3		... b
3307	Harso	0.00795	4,401	4,974	9,173	CMT33d	14-DAAA-c	harso		3.00	149	1....	6	4	6	1	1		... .
3308	Hausa	0.10000	55,354	62,565	115,382	NAB60a	19-HAAB-a	hausa		0.02	13	4Asu.	3	3	1	0	0	Hausa	PNB b
3309	Indagen Gurage	0.08000	44,283	50,052	92,306	CMT34z	12-ACEC-a	indiagegn		40.00	20,021	0....	9	5	7	3	1		... b
3310	Indo-Pakistani	0.01064	5,890	6,657	12,277	CNN25e	59-AAFH-b	standard gujaraati		1.00	67	2A.u.	6	4	2	0	0	Gujarati	PNB b
3311	Innemor Gurage	0.25646	141,960	160,454	295,909	CMT34z	12-ACEB-ca	innamor		45.00	72,204	1.s..	9	5	7	3	1		pn. b
3312	Italian	0.10000	55,354	62,565	115,382	CEW21e	51-AABQ-c	standard italiano	6	84.00	52,554	2B.uh	10	9	15	5	1	Italian	PNB b
3313	Italian Creole	0.01000	5,535	6,256	11,538	CMT34z	51-AABQ-c	standard italiano	4	30.00	1,877	2B.uh	9	5	7	3	1	Italian	PNB b
3314	Ittu (Eastern Galla)	5.20000	2,878,393	3,253,374	5,999,869	CMT33b	14-FBAA-e	qottu		25.00	813,343	1cs..	9	5	7	3	1	Oromo: Eastern*	PNb n
3315	Jewish	0.00150	830	938	1,731	CMT35	12-AABA-b	ivrit-x.		0.00	0	2B.uh	0	1	2	1	0	Hebrew	PNB b
3316	Juba Somali	0.50000	276,769	312,824	576,910	CMT33e	14-GAGA-a	af-soomaali		0.01	31	2A...	3	1	2	0	0	Somali	PNB b
3317	Kachama (Haruro)	0.00124	686	776	1,431	CMT33d	16-BADA-a	kachama		40.00	310	0....	9	5	5	3	1		... n
3318	Kafa (Kefa)	0.41625	230,410	260,426	480,278	CMT33d	16-BDAA-a	kafaa	1	30.00	78,128	0....	9	5	7	3	1	Kafa*	P.. .
3319	Kambata (Kemata)	2.43000	1,345,095	1,520,326	2,803,785	CMT33d	14-CABA-b	kembaata	2	60.00	912,196	1.s..	10	9	10	5	2	Kambaata	PN. .
3320	Karo (Kerre)	0.00186	1,030	1,164	2,146	CMT33d	16-AAAA-c	karo		50.00	582	0....	10	6	5	2	1		... .
3321	Kebena	0.01000	5,535	6,256	11,538	CMT33d	14-CABA-a	timbara-qebena		75.00	4,692	1.s..	10	7	7	2	3		pn. b
3322	Kemant	0.05280	29,227	33,034	60,922	CMT33a	14-BABA-a	kemantenay		50.00	16,517	0....	10	6	8	4	2		p.. b
3323	Kereyu	0.01000	5,535	6,256	11,538	CMT33b	14-FBAA-ab	kereyu		15.00	938	1cs..	8	5	6	2	1		pnb b
3324	Konso (Conso)	0.38565	213,472	241,281	444,971	CMT33d	14-FAAA-f	afa-karatti	1	20.00	48,256	0.s..	9	5	7	2	1	Komso	P.. .
3325	Koorete (Amarro, Kwera)	0.06387	35,354	39,960	73,695	CMT33d	16-BACA-a	koore-nuuna		30.00	11,988	0....	9	5	6	3	1	Koorete	... b
3326	Kullo (Kulo, Konta)	0.31431	173,982	196,648	362,657	CMT33d	16-BAFC-a	kulo-kale		50.00	98,324	0....	10	6	7	4	1		... .
3327	Kunama (Cunama, Diila)	0.08000	44,283	50,052	92,306	NAB62h	05-KAAA-a	marda-kunama		21.00	10,511	0....	9	5	7	2	3	Kunama	PN. .
3328	Kunfel	0.01000	5,535	6,256	11,538	CMT33a	14-BBAA-b	kunfel		50.00	3,128	0....	10	6	6	4	1		... b
3329	Kwegu (Bacha)	0.00122	675	763	1,408	NAB62z	05-PCAA-a	toko-kwegoi		10.00	76	0....	8	5	4	2	1		... .

Continued opposite

Table 8-2 continued

EVANGELIZATION								EVANGELISM			ADDITIONAL DESCRIPTIVE DATA
Ref 1	*D* 28	*aC* 29	*CG%* 30	*r* 31	*E* 32	*U* 33	*W* 34	*e* 35	*R* 36	*T* 37	*Locations, civil divisions, literacy, religions, church history, denominations, dioceses, church growth, missions, agencies, ministries, movements* 38
3210	1	6	6.07	0	28.00	72.00	A	5.11	731	4	Western Eritrea. Bilingual in Tigre. Muslims 80%(Sunnis). D=ECE. M=MEGM.
3211	2	6	5.92	8	63.00	37.00	B	22.99	288	5	Immigrants from Palestine and other Middle East countries. Muslims 90%(Sunnis). D=RCC,GOC.
3212	1	5	6.95	0	30.00	70.00	A	5.47	808	4	Southern Eritrea. Nomads, close to Afar. Muslims 81%. D=RCC. M=FCC,FGC. Irob are strong Catholics.
3213	1	5	1.62	5	38.01	61.99	A	0.01	250	2	Also in Somalia, Ethiopia, Kenya, Djibouti, Yemen, UAE. Muslims 100%(Shafi Sunnis). D=RCC. M=SIM,EMBMC,LBI,FMB.
3214	7	5	3.41	4	99.91	0.09	C	517.31	92	10	Mainly in Ethiopia. Lingua franca. Muslims 4%(Hanafi Sunnis). D=Ethiopian Orthodox Ch(D-Tigre),RCC,ECMY,ECE,LCE,FGC,FCC. M=EFS,SIM,LBI,AFM,MECO.
3215	3	7	3.61	4	52.05	47.95	B	0.09	290	2	Lingua franca. 50% also belong to Beni Amer confederation. Muslims 95%(Sunnis). Geez script. D=EOC(D-Tigre),ECE,LCE. M=SLM-BV,SIM,EFS,FCC,FGC.
3216	1	9	3.73	7	41.05	58.95	A	0.07	296	2	Traders from Yemen and Saudi Arabia. Muslims 95%(50% Zaydis,40% Shafi Sunnis,5% Ismalis). D=RCC. M=WF,OFMCap.
3217	0	6	4.43		27.00	73.00	A	9.85	450	4	French, US Whites, Sudanese, Indo-Pakistanis. Muslims 70%, Hindus 10%, nonreligious 10%.
Estonia											
3218	1	8	0.78	6	99.70	0.30	C	339.81	28	9	Gregorians. Now in 28 countries. Nonreligious 30%. D=Armenian Apostolic Ch.
3219	1	8	0.00	1	34.00	66.00	A	0.00	0	1.12	Turkic. 73% monolingual. Muslims 80%(56% Shias, 24% Hanafi Sunnis), nonreligious 20%. D=ROC. M=IBT,CSI.
3220	0	0	7.59	5	99.60	0.40	C	234.33	220	8	White Russians. Also in USA, Canada, Poland. Nonreligious 25%. D=ROC(D-Minsk & Belorussia),RCC(D-Minsk,D-Pinsk),Old Ritualist Chs(Old Believers),ECB.
3221	1	9	0.77	0	76.00	24.00	B	97.09	57	6	Origin in Chuvashia (Russia). Muslims 35%(Sunnis),nonreligious 30%. D=ROC.
3222	4	9	0.77	5	99.60	0.40	C	269.37	43	8	In south of country. Most speak Russian. Nonreligious 10%. D=ROC,ELCE,RCC,MCE. M=UBS,LBI.
3223	3	10	0.77	5	99.67	0.33	C	339.92	35	9	Immigrants from Finland. Also in 10 countries. Most bilingual in Russian. D=ELC,ROC,FOC.
3224	1	9	0.78	4	97.00	3.00	B	141.62	22	7	Nonreligious/atheists 55%, Muslims 5% (Sunnis, Shias). D=Georgian Orthodox Ch.
3225	2	10	0.77	8	99.80	0.20	C	449.68	34	10	Settlers, long-time residents from Germany, Russia. D=German ELC,AUCECB.
3226	3	10	0.77	0	99.70	0.30	C	293.82	42	8	Baltic area of Estonia; also some in Sweden and Russia. Only 30% speak Ingrian. Nonreligious 30%. D=ROC,ELCE,MCE.
3227	0	10	0.00	5	45.00	55.00	A	0.00	0	1.10	Religious Jews, bilingual in Russian, Estonian. Many have emigrated to Israel.
3228	3	9	0.77	0	99.67	0.33	C	266.56	44	8	From Karelia (Russia). Bilingual in Russian. Nonreligious 33%. D=ROC,RCC,ELCE.
3229	5	9	0.77	5	99.91	0.09	C	528.11	34	10	Residents from Latvia. In 25 countries. D=ROC,ELCL,RCC,RCL,CB.
3230	3	8	0.77	5	99.85	0.15	C	471.58	14	10	From Lithuania. Found in 24 countries. Strong Catholics. D=RCC,ERCL,ROC.
3231	1	9	0.78	6	99.82	0.18	C	416.02	35	10	Immigrants from Bessarabia (Moldavia), also Romania. D=Russian Orthodox Ch.
3232	1	9	0.77	7	99.65	0.35	C	275.21	18	8	Laborers, migrants from Mordvinia (Russia). Heavily russianized. Nonreligious 35%. D=ROC. M=IBT.
3233	5	8	-0.71	5	99.37	0.63	B	139.22	12	7	Over 60,000 expatriates in 10 countries. Nonreligious 23%. D=ROC(D-Tallinn & Estonia),ELCE,RCC(AA-Estonia),MCE,AUCECB. M=UBS,LBI. R=IBRA,TBN.
3234	4	10	0.77	6	99.91	0.09	C	534.76	13	10	Poles from Poland, Ukraine, Belorussia. Most are bi- or trilingual. D=RCC,ROC,CEF,CWE.
3235	8	9	0.54	7	96.00	4.00	B	87.60	15	6	In 70 countries. Nonreligious 35%, atheists 25%. D=ROC,RCC,AUCECB,Old Ritualists,CEF,CCECB,SDA,IPKH.
3236	4	9	0.77	5	99.40	0.60	B	150.38	52	7	One of the 2 southern dialects of Estonian. Most speak Russian also. D=ELC of Estonia,ROC(D-Tallinn & Estonia),RCC(AA-Estonia),MCE.
3237	2	10	0.77	6	99.70	0.30	C	342.37	16	9	Expatriates, settlers from Sweden. Professionals. Nonreligious 20%. D=LCS,ELCE.
3238	1	8	4.03	6	43.50	56.50	A	2.38	304	4	From Tatarstan (Russia). Muslims 83%(Hanafi Sunnis), nonreligious 15%. D=ROC.
3239	7	8	0.64	6	99.69	0.31	C	347.55	37	9	In 15 countries. Nonreligious/atheists 31%. D=ROC(E-Ukraine), Ukrainian Catholic Ch,AUCECB,CEF,CCECB,JWs,SDA.
3240	0	9	0.00	5	43.00	57.00	A	0.00	0	1.12	From Uzbekistan. 55% Russian-speaking. Literates 100%. Muslims 80%(Hanafi Sunnis), nonreligious/atheists 20%. M=ROC,AUCECB,CSI.
3241	0	9	0.77		72.00	28.00	B	105.12	29	7	Bulgarians, Udmurts, Mari, Gypsies, Kazakhs, Bashkir, other Asians, Europeans. Nonreligious 30%, Muslims 10%.
Ethiopia											
3242	2	6	5.98	0	99.70	0.30	C	278.49	198	8	Adjacent to Kambatta. Literates 5%. Muslims 30% and growing. D=Alaba Evangelical Ch,Ethiopian Orthodox Ch. M=SIM.
3243	1	5	4.18	0	22.00	78.00	A	1.60	757	4	Pastoralists around Omo River. Muslims 90%(Sunnis). D=WLEC. M=SIM.
3244	8	6	2.37	5	99.89	0.11	C	498.49	75	10	16 centuries of Christian tradition. Literates 60%. D=95% EOC(14 Dioceses),GOC(D-Aksum),RCC(8 Dioceses),ECMY,BECE,SDA,BEC,WLEC. M=BCMS,SIM.
3245	3	6	4.67	0	39.00	61.00	A	4.27	328	4	In Ilubabor. Many in Sudan. Animists 95%. D=BECE,ECMY,ECE. M=American Presbyterian Mission(PCUSA).
3246	2	6	4.46	7	61.00	39.00	B	22.26	232	5	Modern Standard Arabic. Educated international Arabs from many countries. Muslims 80%. D=GOC,RCC. M=UBS,LBI.
3247	0	6	4.64	0	21.00	79.00	A	1.53	853	4	Near Lake Stefanie, near the Amar. Lingua franca: Konso. Muslims 70%, animists 20%, nonreligious 8%.
3248	0	6	6.29	1	44.00	56.00	A	16.06	506	5	Northern and Southern Argobba. Muslims 90%. Declining demographically, language disappearing.
3249	2	5	3.60	0	54.00	46.00	B	39.42	279	5	South central Gamo Gofa Province. Some bilinguals in Amharic and Gofa(Wolayta). Animists 80%. D=EOC,WLEC. M=SIL,CMF,SIM. Some 90 churches (1978).
3250	1	10	4.22	6	99.80	0.20	C	426.32	90	10	Long-standing community. Nonreligious 20%. D=Armenian Apostolic Ch(V-Addis Ababa).
3251	6	6	3.23	5	52.00	48.00	B	5.69	270	4	South. Pastoralists. Muslims 85%(Shafi Sunnis), animists 12%. D=WLEC,SDA,ECMY,EOC,FGBC,RCC. M=PCUSA,EMBMC,SIM,WVI.
3252	4	7	3.19	0	29.00	71.00	A	2.11	481	4	Bilingual in Wolayta. Mostly animists 95%. D=WLEC,RCC,FGBC,SDA.
3253	2	6	3.20	0	62.00	38.00	B	67.89	205	6	Bomo Plateau. Some bilingual in Suri. Animists 70%. D=Ethiopia Orthodox Ch,WLEC. M=SIM,BGCBWM,BBFI.
3254	1	6	9.95	0	99.80	0.20	C	321.20	295	9	North of Lake Turkana. Most are monolingual; some also speak Wolayta. Animists 20%. D=WLEC. M=SIM.
3255	1	5	3.59	0	37.00	63.00	A	13.50	407	5	Begiarea, western Wallega. Lingua franca: Oromo-Wallega. Close to Bambeshi. Animists 70%, some Muslims 20%. D=ECMY.
3256	0	5	0.00	7	18.00	82.00	A	0.00	0	1.06	Beja, Nabtab. Mainly in Eritrea, Egypt, Sudan. Bilingual in Tigre. Muslims 100%(Sunnis, mainly Khatmiyya Sufis).
3257	1	5	6.50	0	36.00	64.00	A	13.14	609	5	Northwestern Wallega Province. Also in Sudan. Agriculturalists. Animists 70%, Muslims 20%. D=ECMY.
3258	2	5	3.54	5	52.00	48.00	B	7.59	287	4	Southern border; most in Kenya. Muslims 90%(Shafi Sunnis). D=EOC,SDA. M=BCMS,CPK.
3259	1	10	4.09	8	99.79	0.21	C	435.40	95	10	Expatriates from Britain, in education, commerce. D=Anglican Ch(D-Egypt). M=USPG,BCMS,CMJ,CCCS/ICS.
3260	2	5	8.58	0	75.00	25.00	B	109.50	383	7	South of Lake Ciamo, also in Kenya. Animists 50%. D=WLEC,ECMY. M=SIL,SIM.
3261	1	6	5.63	0	99.70	0.30	C	260.61	202	8	Related to Konso, Gidole. Animists 25%, some Muslims. D=ECMY.
3262	1	6	2.65	0	27.00	73.00	A	4.92	421	4	Majority live in Sudan.Close to Uduk. Animists 90%. D=BECE. M=United Presbyterian(PCUSA).
3263	4	6	11.03	5	89.00	11.00	B	139.68	395	7	Southwestern Shoa Province. Animists 27%, Muslims 30%. D=Mekane Yesus Ch,RCC,WLEC,EOC. M=SIL,SIM,UBS.
3264	2	6	4.01	0	29.00	71.00	A	5.29	514	4	Ilubabor Province. Bilingual in Majang or Mocha. Hunter-gatherers. Animists 95%. D=ECMY, Presbyterians.
3265	2	6	6.93	0	69.00	31.00	B	100.74	351	7	Many bilingual in Wolayta, some in Kafa. Agriculturalists. Animists 60%. D=WLEC,ECMY.
3266	1	10	4.95	8	68.00	32.00	B	49.64	234	6	Remnants of former military and advisers from Cuba. Mostly nonreligious or atheists 80%. D=RCC.
3267	1	6	3.73	0	84.00	16.00	B	153.30	184	7	Related to Wolayta. Agriculturalists. Animists 50%. D=ECMY.
3268	3	4	4.05	4	32.01	67.99	A	0.01	509	2	Nomads. Also in Djibouti and Somalia. Literates 8%. Muslims 100%(Sunnis). D=Orthodox Presbyterian Ch,ECMY,RCC. M=SIL,CMML,RSMT,EMBMC,FMB.
3269	0	6	4.46	0	31.00	69.00	A	5.65	562	4	North of Lake Tana, near Gondar. Related to Qimant, Kara. Animists 90%. Fairly bilingual in Amharic.
3270	1	6	2.54	0	38.00	62.00	A	13.87	320	5	Wallega Province. Lingua franca: Oromo-Wallega. Related to Bambeshi. Animists 90%. D=WLEC. M=SIM.
3271	1	6	4.41	0	24.00	76.00	A	1.75	720	4	Gemu-Gofa Province, west of Lake Ciamo. Mostly animists 90%, some Muslims. D=ECMY.
3272	1	6	4.28	0	22.00	78.00	A	1.60	770	4	Near the Amar. History of disease, warfare, and population decline. Most are monolingual. Muslims 90%. D=WLEC. M=SIM.
3273	2	6	4.36	0	41.00	59.00	A	17.95	418	5	Partly intelligible to Komso, Dirasha. Close to Gawwada. Animists 85%. D=ECMY,WLEC.
3274	1	5	5.37	1	31.00	69.00	A	5.65	601	4	Closely related to Toposa and Turkana. Also in Sudan, Kenya. Animists 95%. D=RCC.
3275	1	6	3.94	0	63.00	37.00	B	68.98	254	6	Mostly in Gemu-Gofa Province, also Addis Ababa. Weavers. Animists 70%. D=WLEC. M=SIM.
3276	2	6	10.76	0	80.00	20.00	B	131.40	430	7	Southwestern Shoa Province. Silti is an official literary language. Islam introduced AD 1250. Muslims 53%. D=WLEC,ECMY. M=SIM,WVI.
3277	2	6	6.48	0	41.00	59.00	A	7.48	529	4	Eastern Jikany. Majority in Sudan. Nomadic. Animists 95%, highly resistant to Islam. D=RCC,ECMY. M=APM.
3278	1	6	3.73	0	41.00	59.00	A	14.96	376	5	In Gondar, north of Lake Tana. Agriculturalists. Bilingual in Amharic or Tigrinya. Archaic Judaism 90%. 1984, 1991 mass emigration of 50,000 Falashas to Israel.
3279	1	10	5.73	8	99.80	0.20	C	440.92	122	10	Expatriates from France, in schools, business. D=RCC. M=OFMCap,CM,FSCJ,SJ,FSC.
3280	0	6	3.50	0	35.00	65.00	A	12.77	423	5	Gemu-Gofa Province, west of Lake Ciamo. Animists 80%.
3281	1	6	5.07	0	60.00	40.00	B	65.70	300	6	Between Dabus and Blue Nile rivers. Bilingual in Western Oromo. Related to Berta. Animists 50%, Muslims 20%. D=ECMY.
3282	1	6	7.95	0	43.00	57.00	A	23.54	628	5	Gemu-Gofa Province. Near Lake Abaya. Animists 80%. D=WLEC. M=SIM.
3283	0	6	1.81	0	36.00	64.00	A	13.14	282	5	On island in Lake Ciamo. Bilingual, nearly extinct. Animists 90%.
3284	0	6	4.22	0	36.00	64.00	A	13.14	466	5	Western Wallega, near Blue Nile. Nearly extinct. Lingua franca: Oromo-Wallega. Animists 90%.
3285	0	2	2.56	5	41.00	59.00	A	2.99	298	4	Most in Kenya, also Somalia. Pastoralists, semi-nomadic. Muslims 98% (Sunnis). M=RCC,CMS.
3286	2	6	2.79	0	27.00	73.00	A	1.97	476	4	West of Lake Ciamo. Close to Dobase, Konso. Animists 90%. D=ECMY,WLEC.
3287	1	10	-0.26	0	99.99	0.01	C	542.02	28	10	Ancient Ethiopic. Ancient liturgical language; literary language. D=EOC(14 Dioceses).
3288	1	6	2.89	0	48.00	52.00	A	35.04	273	5	Gemu-Gofa Province, west of Lake Ciamo. Mostly animists 70%. D=WLEC.
3289	0	6	2.79	5	60.00	40.00	B	21.90	214	5	Dialect of Western Oromo. Mainly Bale Province. Many Muslims 30%, animists 60%.
3290	5	7	10.65	0	74.00	26.00	B	81.03	465	6	Central highlands. Animists 69%, Muslims 1%. D=ECMY,WLEC,FGBC,Light of Life Ch,AIC. M=SIL,PCM,SFM,SIM.
3291	1	6	3.02	0	83.00	17.00	B	151.47	162	7	In hills near Lake Ciamo. Many bilingual in Oromo-Borana-Guji or Konso. Animists 50%, some Muslims. D=ECMY.
3292	3	6	3.01	0	66.00	34.00	B	72.27	204	6	Kafa Province. 10% read Amharic. Forests, savannah; agriculturalists. Animists 70%. D=Bethel Evangelical Ch, EOC,ECMY. M=SIM.
3293	1	6	4.08	0	56.00	44.00	B	61.32	273	6	Didessa Valley. Some bilinguals in Western Oromo. Related to Berte. Animists 70%. D=ECMY.
3294	0	6	4.59	0	22.00	78.00	A	1.60	808	4	Also Innxarsi. Southwest of Lake Abaya. Mostly animists 90%.
3295	1	6	9.01	0	61.00	39.00	B	66.79	490	6	Dialect of Wolaytta. Southwest Lake Abaya area. Animists 70%. D=WLEC. M=SIM.
3296	1	6	2.68	0	42.00	58.00	A	22.99	299	5	Gemu-Gofa Province, on west of Lake Ciamo. Mostly animists, 80%. D=WLEC.
3297	1	6	2.54	0	48.00	52.00	A	35.04	253	5	Gemu-Gofa Province, west of Lake Ciamo. Animists 80%. D=WLEC.
3298	1	10	7.16	7	99.95	0.05	C	558.26	139	10	Originally from Greece. Traders. D=Greek Orthodox Patriarchate of Alexandria(D-Aksum).
3299	0	6	3.02	0	27.00	73.00	A	4.92	499	4	In west of country, near Sudan border. Animists 70%, some Muslims 25%.
3300	5	6	8.81	5	56.00	44.00	B	20.44	524	5	Southern border. Pastoral nomads, raising cattle. Muslims 80%(Sunnis). D=EOC,SDA,WLEC,ECMY,RCC. M=SIM.
3301	3	5	6.83	0	37.00	63.00	A	13.50	617	5	Half in Sudan. Animists 86%, Muslims 4%. D=BECE,WLEC,ECMY. M=American Presbyterian Mission(PCUSA).
3302	3	5	1.34	0	72.00	28.00	B	78.84	123	6	Southern Shoa Province. Animists 20%, Muslims 50% and growing. D=WLEC,ECMY,SDA. M=SIL,SIM.
3303	1	6	3.92	0	93.00	7.00	C	203.67	171	8	Avergele District, Lasta and Waag Regions. In a region of majority Amharic and Tigre speakers. Second language: Amharic. Animists 40%. D=EOC.
3304	0	6	2.17	0	91.00	9.00	C	199.29	123	7	Surrounded by Amharic and Tigre speakers in Avergele District, Lasta and Waag Regions. Animists 40%.
3305	1	6	4.96	0	83.00	17.00	B	151.47	226	7	In Amharic/Tigre zones, in Avergele District, Lasta and Wang Regions. Animists 50%. D=EOC.
3306	5	5	0.00	0	25.00	75.00	A	0.00	0	1.06	Preindustrial urbanites from city of Harar. Now 70% in Addis Ababa. Bilingual in Oromo, Somali, Amharic. Muslims 100%(Shafi Sunnis). D=SDA,RCC,EOC.
3307	1	6	2.97	0	26.00	74.00	A	2.84	513	4	West of Lake Ciamo. Related to Gawwada, Tsamai. Animists 90%. D=ECMY.
3308	0	10	2.60	5	42.02	57.98	A	0.03	248	2	Traders from Sudan across to Niger. Muslims 100%(Maliki Sunnis).
3309	1	6	2.08	0	73.00	27.00	B	106.58	146	7	West Gurage. Second language: Amharic, or Chaha(Central West Gurage). Animists 40%, Muslims 20%. D=ECMY.
3310	0	10	4.29	6	45.00	55.00	A	1.64	323	4	Traders, shopkeepers. Hindus 70%, Muslims 29%.
3311	1	6	3.41	1	84.00	16.00	B	137.97	170	7	Part of West Gurage. Second language: Chaha or Amharic. Animists 35%, Muslims 20%. D=WLEC.
3312	1	10	6.72	7	99.84	0.16	C	472.16	137	10	Long history of colonizing Abyssinia. Strong Catholics. D=RCC(M-Addis Ababa,VA-Asmara). M=OFMCap.
3313	1	10	5.37	7	91.00	9.00	B	99.64	216	6	Mixed-race Italian/Ethiopians, dating from 1930s occupation by Italy. Muslims 25%, nonreligious 15%. D=RCC.
3314	3	5	3.87	5	74.00	26.00	B	67.52	214	6	Eastern Oromo, Harar, Harer. East central. Muslims 70%(Shafi Sunnis), animists 5%. D=EOC,SDA,ECMY. M=EMBMC,SIM.
3315	0	8	0.00	5	38.00	62.00	A	0.00	0	1.13	Israeli and European Jews in military or advisory roles.
3316	0	5	3.49	5	36.01	63.99	A	0.01	406	2	Ogaden Province. Refugees, immigrants, long-time residents. Muslims 100%(Shafi Sunnis).
3317	1	7	2.36	0	69.00	31.00	B	100.74	169	7	Islanders. Many bilinguals in Wolayta. Animists 60%. D=ECMY.
3318	3	6	5.46	0	63.00	37.00	B	68.98	320	6	Kafa Region. Some in Sudan. Animists 30%, Muslims 40%. D=25% EOC,WLEC,RCC. M=SIM.
3319	6	6	2.56	0	99.60	0.40	C	229.95	116	8	Southern Shoa Province. Animists 15%, Muslims 5%(some becoming recent converts to ECMY). D=ECMY,WLEC,SDA,Ch of Christ,KEC,AIC. M=SIM,EMBMC.
3320	1	7	4.15	0	77.00	23.00	B	140.52	215	7	Riverside settlements, upstream from Reshiat. Agriculturalists. Close to Hamer-Banna. Animists 30%, Muslims 20%. D=WLEC.
3321	4	6	2.72	0	99.75	0.25	C	317.55	109	9	Shewa Province. Dialect of Kembata. Bilinguals in Gurage, Amharic, Kambatta, Oromo. Animists 20%, Muslims 5%. D=EOC,ECMY,WLEC,SDA.
3322	1	6	2.08	0	88.00	12.00	B	160.60	124	7	North of Lake Tana, Central Gondar Province. Bilingual in Amharic. Animists 40%. D=EOC. M=SIM,BCMS.
3323	1	6	4.16	1	53.00	47.00	B	29.01	313	5	Eastern Oromo area. Dialect of South Central Oromo. Muslims 80%. D=EOC. M=SIM.
3324	2	6	2.89	0	52.00	48.00	B	37.96	252	5	South of Lake Ciamo. Agriculturalists. Animists 80%. D=ECMY,WLEC. M=SIM.
3325	3	6	2.49	0	64.00	36.00	B	70.08	188	6	Islanders, in Amaarro mountain area. Many bilingual. Animists 70%. D=WLEC,ECMY,ELC. M=SIM.
3326	1	6	9.63	0	82.00	18.00	B	149.65	385	7	Kafa and other provinces. Close to Gimira. Animists 40%, some Muslims. D=WLEC. M=SIM.
3327	3	6	3.36	0	58.00	42.00	B	44.45	225	6	North and west and into Eritrea. Muslims 75%. Strong Catholics. D=RCC(VA-Asmara of the Latins),ECE,LCE. M=OFMCap,MEGM,SLM,FCC,EFS.
3328	1	6	3.73	0	83.00	17.00	B	151.47	186	7	Fairly bilingual in Amharic. Related to Awngi. Animists 50%. D=EOC.
3329	0	7	4.43	0	33.00	67.00	A	12.04	492	5	Omo river bank. Agriculturalists, related to Meen, Bodi, Mursi. Animists 90%. M=American Presbyterian Mission.

Continued overleaf

Table 8-2 continued

Ref 1	Ethnic name 2	P% 3	In 1995 4	In 2000 5	In 2025 6	Race 7	Language 8	Autoglossonym 9	S 10	AC 11	Members 12	Jayuh 13-17	d 18	wa 19	xc 20	mc 21	mi 22	Biblioglossonym 23	Pub 24-26	ss 27
PEOPLE		POPULATION				IDENTITY CODE		LANGUAGE		CHURCH		MINISTRY						SCRIPTURE		
3330	Langa (Shita)	0.00866	4,794	5,418	9,992	NAB62z	05-OBBB-a	opo-shiita		10.00	542	0....	8	5	5	2	0		...	b
3331	Libido (Maraqo)	0.19727	109,196	123,422	227,614	CMT33d	14-CAAA-b	libido		1.00	1,234	1.s..	6	4	5	1	1		pn.	.
3332	Macha (Central Galla)	5.40000	2,989,100	3,378,503	6,230,633	CMT33b	14-FBAA	oromo cluster		30.00	1,013,551	2As..	9	7	7	4	3		PNB	b
3333	Maji (Dezi, Dizi)	0.04456	24,666	27,879	51,414	CMT33d	16-CAAA-a	dizi-nuu		70.00	19,515	0....	10	7	7	4	2		...	.
3334	Male	0.03632	20,104	22,724	41,907	CMT33d	16-BAGA-a	male		40.00	9,089	0....	9	5	6	3	1	Male	...	.
3335	Meen (Mekan, Teshenna)	0.09864	54,601	61,714	113,813	NAB62y	05-PBAA-a	tuk-te-me'en-en		35.00	21,600	0....	9	7	6	4	2	Meen	...	.
3336	Melo	0.14531	80,434	90,913	167,662	CMT33d	16-BAGA-a	male		45.00	40,911	0....	9	7	7	0	0	Male	...	.
3337	Mesengo (Majang)	0.05399	29,885	33,779	62,295	NAB62z	05-PDAA-a	ato-majang		30.00	10,134	0....	9	5	6	2	1	Majang	...	.
3338	Mesmes	0.02000	11,071	12,513	23,076	CMT34z	12-ACCB-d	mesmes		40.00	5,005	0.s..	9	5	6	3	1		p..	.
3339	Mocha (Moca)	0.17329	95,922	108,419	199,946	CMT33d	16-BDAA-b	mocha		30.00	32,526	0....	9	5	7	3	1		p..	.
3340	Murle (Murelei)	0.01485	8,220	9,291	17,134	NAB62y	05-PAAB-a	dod-murle		3.00	279	0....	6	4	6	1	0	Murle	PN.	.
3341	Mursi (Murzu)	0.01085	6,006	6,788	12,519	NAB62y	05-PBAB-a	mursi		15.00	1,018	0....	8	5	6	2	3	Mursi	...	.
3342	Nao	0.03038	16,816	19,007	35,053	CMT33d	16-CABA-a	na'o		40.00	7,603	0....	9	5	6	3	1		...	.
3343	North Gurage	0.20516	113,564	128,358	236,718	CMT34z	12-ACEB-bd	chaha		42.00	53,910	1.s..	9	5	10	3	2	Gurage: Chaha	PN.	b
3344	North Koma (Kwama)	0.03713	20,553	23,230	42,841	NAB62z	05-OBBA-c	madiin		5.00	1,162	0....	7	4	4	1	1		...	.
3345	Northern Mao (Bambeshi)	0.01238	6,853	7,746	14,284	CMT33d	16-DABA-a	mao-koole		35.00	2,711	0....	9	5	6	3	1		...	.
3346	Nuer	0.11659	64,537	72,944	134,524	NAB62n	04-AABA-d	dar-cieng		5.00	3,647	1A...	7	4	6	1	1	Nuer: Western	Pn.	.
3347	Oyda	0.00932	5,159	5,831	10,754	CMT33d	16-BAFD-a	oyda		40.00	2,332	0....	9	5	5	4	3		...	n
3348	Raya Galla (Azebu)	0.10000	55,354	62,565	115,382	CMT33b	14-FBAA-c	raya		0.01	6	1cs..	3	4	2	1	1		pnb	b
3349	Reshiat (Dasenech, Marill	0.06380	35,316	39,916	73,614	CMT33d	14-GACA-a	af-dasenach		5.00	1,996	0....	7	5	5	2	1	Daasanech	...	.
3350	Russian	0.00500	2,768	3,128	5,769	CEW22j	53-AAAE-d	russkiy		15.00	469	4B.uh	8	5	8	2	2	Russian	PNB	b
3351	Sadama (Sidamo)	3.06500	1,696,591	1,917,613	3,536,461	CMT33d	14-CACA-a	sidaamo-'afo		37.00	709,517	2.s..	9	7	8	5	1	Sidamo	PN.	.
3352	Saho (Sao, Minifere, Irob	0.14850	82,200	92,909	171,342	CMT33z	14-AAAA-a	saho		5.00	4,645	0....	7	5	7	2	1		...	.
3353	Selale (Salale)	4.20000	2,324,856	2,627,725	4,846,048	CMT33b	14-FBAA	oromo cluster		10.00	262,772	2As..	8	5	5	2	1		PNB	b
3354	Seze	0.00544	3,011	3,404	6,277	CMT33d	16-EAAA-b	sezo-wangi		35.00	1,191	0....	9	7	7	0	0		...	.
3355	Shabelle (Shebelle)	0.02000	11,071	12,513	23,076	NAB57j	14-GAGA-a	af-soomaali		0.00	0	2A...	0	1	0	0	0	Somali	PNB	b
3356	Shanquilla (Birale)	0.00014	77	88	162	CMT33z	07-AAAA-a	ifa-'ongota		5.00	4	0....	7	5	6	1	0		...	.
3357	Sheko	0.07143	39,539	44,690	82,417	CMT33d	16-CACA-c	dorsha		40.00	17,876	0....	9	5	7	3	1		...	.
3358	Shinasha (Bworo, Amuru)	0.00912	5,048	5,706	10,523	CMT33d	16-BDCA-a	boro		40.00	2,282	0....	9	5	5	3	0		...	b
3359	Shuri (Surma, Dhuri)	0.02207	12,217	13,808	25,465	NAB62y	05-PBAB-d	kacipo		30.00	4,142	0....	9	5	6	3	3	Suri	...	.
3360	Somali	3.90000	2,158,795	2,440,030	4,499,902	CMT33e	14-GAGA-a	af-soomaali		0.01	244	2A...	3	4	3	0	3	Somali	PNB	b
3361	South Koma	0.02000	11,071	12,513	23,076	NAB62z	05-OBBA-c	madiin		5.00	626	0....	7	4	4	2	1		...	.
3362	Southern Agau (Awngi, Awi	0.10000	55,354	62,565	115,382	CMT33a	14-BBAA-a	awngi		70.00	43,795	0....	10	7	7	5	1		...	b
3363	Southern Burun (Maban)	0.00456	2,524	2,853	5,261	NAB62z	04-AEAA-e	mabaan		5.00	143	0.s..	7	5	5	2	1	Mabaan	PN.	.
3364	Southern Mao	0.00203	1,124	1,270	2,342	NAB62l	16-BDBA-a	afan-mao		5.00	64	0....	7	5	4	2	2		...	b
3365	Sudanese Arab	0.20000	110,707	125,130	230,764	CMT30	12-AACF-c	sudani	2	2.00	2,503	4Asuh	6	4	2	1	0	Arabic: Sudan	PNb	b
3366	Tabi (Ingessana)	0.00400	2,214	2,503	4,615	NAB62z	05-MBAA-a	kor-e-gaam		0.50	13	0....	5	4	0	0	1		...	.
3367	Tigrai	5.38958	2,983,333	3,371,984	6,218,610	CMT34b	12-ACAC-a	tigray	15	68.00	2,292,949	2As..	10	9	10	5	3	Tigrinya	PNB	b
3368	Tigre	0.02000	11,071	12,513	23,076	CMT34c	12-ACAB-aa	khasa		0.04	5	1B...	3	4	5	5	3		pnb	b
3369	Tirma (Cirma)	0.05449	30,162	34,092	62,872	NAB62y	05-PBAB-b	tirma		30.00	10,227	0....	9	5	6	3	3		...	.
3370	Topotha (Toposa)	0.02915	16,136	18,238	33,634	NAB62y	04-BDAA-b	akero-a-toposa		70.00	12,766	0....	10	6	6	3	2		...	.
3371	Tsamai (Tsamako, Kule)	0.02229	12,338	13,946	25,719	CMT33d	14-DAAB-a	go-tsamakula		40.00	5,578	0....	9	5	6	3	1		...	.
3372	Tulama (Shoa Galla)	7.50000	4,151,528	4,692,366	8,653,657	CMT33b	14-FBAA-a	tulema		40.00	1,876,946	1cs..	9	6	9	5	3		pnb	b
3373	Turkana	0.04000	22,141	25,026	46,153	NAB62r	04-BDAB-a	nga-turkana		3.00	751	1As..	6	4	5	4	1	Turkana	PN.	.
3374	Walamo (Zala, Ometo)	4.60000	2,546,271	2,877,984	5,307,576	CMT33d	16-BAFA-a	welaitta	6	45.00	1,295,093	2.s..	9	7	9	5	1	Wolayta*	PN.	.
3375	Wallega (Western Galla)	5.60000	3,099,808	3,503,633	6,461,397	CMT33b	14-FBAA-b	mecha	36	35.00	1,226,272	2cs..	9	6	7	5	3	Oromo: Western*	PNB	b
3376	Wallo (Central Galla)	0.31914	176,656	199,670	368,230	CMT33b	14-FBAA-d	wello		10.00	19,967	1cs..	8	5	7	4	2		pnb	b
3377	Wambera	0.01000	5,535	6,256	11,538	CMT33d	16-BDDA-a	wambera		5.00	313	0....	7	5	6	2	1		...	.
3378	Wayto (Weyto)	0.00465	2,574	2,909	5,365	NAB62z	12-ACBA-b	general amarinya		0.00	0	3Asuh	0	3	1	0	0	Amharic	PNB	b
3379	West Gurage	0.39455	218,398	246,850	455,240	CMT34z	12-ACEB-cb	ener		46.00	113,551	3.s..	9	6	7	4	1	Gurage, West	PN.	b
3380	Yaju Galla (Yejju)	0.10000	55,354	62,565	115,382	CMT33b	14-FBAA-c	raya		0.01	6	1cs..	3	3	2	1	1		pnb	b
3381	Yemeni Arab	0.03000	16,606	18,769	34,615	CMT30	12-AACF-n	yemeni	4	0.05	9	1Asuh	4	3	1	0	2		pnb	b
3382	Yemma (Yangaro, Janjero)	0.96414	533,687	603,213	1,112,445	CMT33d	16-BCAA-a	yemsa		50.00	301,606	0....	10	6	7	4	1	Yemsa	...	b
3383	Zayse (Zergulla)	0.04951	27,406	30,976	57,126	CMT33z	16-BABA-a	zayse		2.00	620	0....	6	4	4	1	2		...	.
3384	Zilmamo (Bale)	0.00729	4,035	4,561	8,411	NAB62y	05-PABA	zilmamu cluster		5.00	228	0....	7	5	4	2	2		...	.
3385	Zway (Laqi)	0.00913	5,054	5,712	10,534	CMT34z	12-ACCB-a	zway		45.00	2,570	0.s..	9	6	7	4	0		p..	b
3386	other minor peoples	0.79339	439,171	496,383	915,430	...				10.00	49,638		8	5	6	3	0			
	Faeroe Islands	**100.00000**	**44,621**	**42,749**	**36,604**					**92.61**	**39,590**									
3387	Danish (Dane)	2.50000	1,116	1,069	915	CEW19g	52-AAAD-c	general dansk		95.00	1,015	2A.uh	10	9	11	5	1	Danish	PNB	b
3388	Faeroe Islander	97.00000	43,282	41,467	35,506	CEW19j	52-AAAB-b	foroysk		92.60	38,398	0..uh	10	9	14	5	3	Faroese	PNB	b
3389	Norwegian	0.20000	89	85	73	CEW19p	52-AAAC-e	ny-norsk		93.00	80	0B.uh	10	9	14	5	3	Norwegian*	PNB	b
3390	Swedish (Swede)	0.20000	89	85	73	CEW19q	52-AAAD-r	svea-svensk		73.00	62	1A.uh	10	9	9	5	3	Swedish	PNB	b
3391	other minor peoples	0.10000	45	43	37	...				81.00	35		10	7	8	5	0			
	Falkland Islands	**100.00000**	**2,195**	**2,255**	**2,496**					**79.11**	**1,784**									
3392	British	92.70000	2,035	2,090	2,314	CEW19i	52-ABAC-b	standard-english		79.30	1,658	3Bsuh	10	9	14	5	2		PNB	b
3393	Japanese	1.00000	22	23	25	MSY45a	45-CAAA-a	koku-go		63.50	14	1B.uh	10	8	8	0	0	Japanese	PNB	b
3394	Latin American White	3.50000	77	79	87	CLT27	51-AABB-h	south americano		78.00	62	4B.uh	10	9	12	5	2		pnb	b
3395	Mestizo	0.50000	11	11	12	CLN29	51-AABB-h	south americano		80.00	9	4B.uh	10	9	8	5	2		pnb	b
3396	Norwegian	0.30000	7	7	7	CEW19p	52-AAAC-e	ny-norsk		99.00	7	0B.uh	10	9	14	5	2	Norwegian*	PNB	b
3397	other minor peoples	2.00000	44	45	50	...				75.00	34		10	9	7	5	0			
	Fiji	**100.00000**	**767,711**	**816,905**	**1,104,141**					**56.28**	**459,744**									
3398	Anglo-Australian	0.80000	6,142	6,535	8,833	CEW19c	52-ABAC-x	general australian		69.00	4,509	1Bsuh	10	9	13	5	3		pnb	b
3399	Bengali	2.50000	19,193	20,423	27,604	CNN25b	59-AAFT-e	west bengali		5.00	1,021	1Asuh	7	5	7	3	3	Bengali: Musalmani*	PNB	b
3400	Bihari	3.70000	28,405	30,225	40,853	CNN25c	59-AAFQ-a	bhojpuri		4.00	1,209	1.s..	6	4	7	3	1	Bihari: Bhojpuri*	Pn.	b
3401	British	0.20000	1,535	1,634	2,208	CEW19i	52-ABAC-b	standard-english		79.00	1,291	3Bsuh	10	9	13	5	3		PNB	b
3402	Euronesian	1.80000	13,819	14,704	19,875	MPY53	52-ABAC-bv	standard oceanian-english		96.00	14,116	1Bsuh	10	8	11	5	3		pnb	b
3403	Fijian (Bauan, Mbau)	29.55600	226,905	241,444	326,340	AON08	39-BBAA-b	fiji		96.65	233,356	1.s..	10	10	13	5	3	Fijian*	PNB	b
3404	Fijian Hindi	27.00000	207,282	220,564	298,118	CNN25g	59-AAFO-eu	fiji-hindi		17.70	39,040	1csuh	8	5	7	5	3	Hindi, Fijian	pnb	b
3405	Gonedauan	0.08400	645	686	927	AON08	39-BBAJ	gone-dau cluster		80.00	549	0....	10	7	8	4	1		...	.
3406	Gujarati	2.86000	21,957	23,363	31,578	CNN25e	59-AAFH-b	standard gujaraati		10.00	2,336	2A.u.	8	8	8	5	3	Gujarati	PNB	b
3407	Han Chinese	2.50000	19,193	20,423	27,604	MSY42a	79-AAAB-ba	kuo-yü		85.00	17,359	2Bsuh	10	8	13	4	2	Chinese: Kuoyu*	PNB	b
3408	Jewish	0.01400	107	114	155	CMT35	52-ABAC-bv	standard oceanian-english		0.00	0	1Bsuh	0	3	2	3	0		pnb	b
3409	Kadavu (Tavuki)	1.56000	11,976	12,744	17,225	AON08	39-BBAD	kadavu cluster		93.00	11,852	0....	10	8	10	5	3		...	.
3410	Kiribertese (Gilbertese)	0.71700	5,504	5,857	7,917	MPY54a	38-DAAA-a	i-kiribati		97.00	5,681	3.s..	10	8	11	5	1	Kiribati	PNB	b
3411	Lauan (Lau)	2.49600	19,162	20,390	27,559	AON08	39-BBAE	lau cluster		95.00	19,370	0.s..	10	7	10	5	1		...	.
3412	Lomaiviti Islander	0.20000	1,535	1,634	2,208	AON08	39-BBAC	lomaiviti cluster		90.00	1,470	0....	10	7	8	4	3		...	.
3413	Malayali	0.04300	330	351	475	CNN23b	49-EBEB-a	malayalam		40.00	141	2Asu.	9	6	9	5	3	Malayalam	PNB	b
3414	Namosi	0.20000	1,535	1,634	2,208	AON08	39-BABA	namosi-serua cluster		90.00	1,470	0....	10	7	8	4	1		...	.
3415	Punjabi	1.00000	7,677	8,169	11,041	CNN25n	59-AAFE-c	general panjabi		6.00	490	1Asu.	7	5	2	3	2		PNB	b
3416	Rotuman	1.16000	8,905	9,476	12,808	AON08	39-AAAA-a	rotuman		93.00	8,813	0....	10	8	11	3	1	Rotuman	PNB	.
3417	Samoan	0.14000	1,075	1,144	1,546	MPY55e	39-CAOA	samoa cluster		95.00	1,086	2a.u.	10	9	11	5	3	Samoan	PNB	b
3418	Solomoni Creole	0.80000	6,142	6,535	8,833	MPY53	52-ABAI-d	solomonic-creole		94.00	6,143	1csuh	10	8	11	5	3	Pijin: Solomon Islands	PNb	b
3419	Tamil	8.60000	66,023	70,254	94,956	CNN23c	49-EBEA-b	tamil		27.00	18,969	2Asu.	9	5	7	5	2	Tamil	PNB	b
3420	Telugu	3.70000	28,405	30,225	40,853	CNN23d	49-DBAB-a	telugu		25.00	7,556	2Asu.	9	5	7	5	3	Telugu	PNB	b
3421	Tongan	0.15000	1,152	1,225	1,656	MPY55g	39-CAPB	tonga cluster		97.00	1,189	4a...	10	9	12	5	3	Tongan	PNB	b
3422	Tuvaluan (Ellice Islander)	0.06000	461	490	662	MPY55z	39-CAKB-a	funafuti		95.10	466	0....	10	9	12	5	3	Tuvaluan	PNB	b.
3423	USA White	0.50000	3,839	4,085	5,521	CEW19s	52-ABAC-s	general american		78.00	3,186	1Bsuh	10	10	12	0	0	English*	PNB	b
3424	Urdu	0.50000	3,839	4,085	5,521	CNN25r	59-AAFO-d	standard urdu		3.00	123	2Asuh	6	3	5	1	0	Urdu	PNB	b
3425	Wallisian	0.10000	768	817	1,104	MPY55i	39-CALA	uvean cluster		93.00	760	0....	10	8	12	5	1	Wallisian	P..	b
3426	Western Fijian (Nadroga)	6.56000	50,362	53,589	72,432	AON08	39-BAAB-a	nadroga		98.00	52,517	0....	10	8	11	5	3		...	.
3427	other minor peoples	0.50000	3,839	4,085	5,521	...				90.00	3,676		10	8	8	5	3			
	Finland	**100.00000**	**5,107,802**	**5,175,743**	**5,253,863**					**88.48**	**4,579,453**									
3428	Black Gypsy (Kalo, Kaale)	0.10460	5,343	5,414	5,496	CNN25f	59-AFAA-a	rodi		75.00	4,060	0B.uh	10	7	8	4	2	Calo	P..	b
3429	British	0.04000	2,043	2,070	2,102	CEW21b	52-ABAC-b	standard-english	32	79.00	1,636	3Bsuh	10	9	13	5	3		PNB	b
3430	Esperanto	0.00000	0	0	0	CEW21z	51-AAAC-a	proper esperanto	3	50.00	0	0A...	10	8	6	5	0	Esperanto	PNB	b
3431	Estonian	0.11860	6,058	6,138	6,231	MSW51a	41-AAAC-b	eesti		80.00	4,911	4A.u.	10	9	11	5	3	Estonian: Tallinn	PNB	b
3432	Finnish (Finn)	91.90170	4,694,157	4,756,596	4,828,389	MSW51b	41-AAAA-bb	vehicular suomi		90.00	4,280,936	1A.uh	10	10	13	5	3	Finnish	PNB	b
3433	Finnish Gypsy	0.10000	5,108	5,176	5,254	CNN25f	41-AAAA-b	general suomi		80.00	4,141	1A.uh	10	7	8	4	1		PNB	b
3434	Finnish Lapp (Inari Lapp)	0.00800	409	414	420	MSW51e	41-AABB-b	anar		90.00	373	0c...	10	7	10	4	2	Saami: Inari*	P..	b
3435	French	0.02000	1,022	1,035	1,051	CEW21b	51-AABI-d	general français	3	87.00	901	1B.uh	10	9	14	5	1	French	PNB	b
3436	German	0.05500	2,809	2,847	2,890	CEW19m	52-ABCE-a	standard hoch-deutsch	13	88.00	2,505	2B.uh	10	9	13	5	3	German*	PNB	b
3437	Han Chinese	0.02600	1,328	1,346	1,366	MSY42a	79-AAAL-a	shao-jiang		7.00	94	0a...	7	7	8	0	0	Chinese: Cantonese	PNB	b
3438	Iranian (Persian)	0.03600	1,839	1,863	1,891	CNT24f	58-AACC-d	general farsi		8.00	149	1csu.	7	7	7	0	0		pnb	.
3439	Iraqi Arab	0.02500	1,277	1,294	1,313	CMT30	12-AACA	standard arabic cluster		0.50	6	0.su.	5	8	7	0	0		...	.
3440	Italian	0.01000	511	518	525	CEW21e	51-AABQ-c	standard italiano	2	84.00	435	2B.uh	10	9	15	5	1	Italian	PNB	b
3441	Jewish	0.02800	1,430	1,449	1,471	CMT35	41-AAAA-bb	vehicular suomi		0.07	1	1A.uh	4	4	5	5	0	Finnish	PNB	b
3442	Karelian	0.84900	43,365	43,942	44,605	MSW51c	41-AAAB-a	central karely		75.00	32,957	1....	10	8	9	5	2	Karelian	P..	b
3443	Komi-Zyrian	0.02170	1,108	1,123	1,140	MSW51d	41-AAEA-a	komi		60.00	674	2....	10	8	8	5	1	Komi: Zyryan*	PN.	b
3444	Kurdish (Kurd)	0.02500	1,277	1,294	1,313	CNT24c	58-AAAA-a	kurmanji		2.00	26	3c...	6	3	3	5	0	Kurdish: Kurmanji*	PN.	b
3445	Northern Lapp (Ruija Lapp)	0.03240	1,655	1,677	1,702	MSW51e	41-AABA-a	ruija		90.00	1,509	0....	10	7	11	4	1	Saami: Norwegian*	PNB	b

Continued opposite

Table 8-2 continued

EVANGELIZATION								EVANGELISM			ADDITIONAL DESCRIPTIVE DATA
Ref 1	*D* 28	*aC* 29	*CG%* 30	*r* 31	*E* 32	*U* 33	*W* 34	*e* 35	*R* 36	*T* 37	*Locations, civil divisions, literacy, religions, church history, denominations, dioceses, church growth, missions, agencies, ministries, movements* 38
3330	0	6	4.07	0	35.00	65.00	A	12.77	436	5	Also in Sudan. Lingua franca: Oromo-Wallega. Animists 60%, Muslims 30%.
3331	0	6	4.93	0	27.00	73.00	A	0.98	693	3	West central Arusi Province. Muslims 95%. M=SIM.
3332	3	6	2.09	5	92.00	8.00	B	100.74	119	7	Southwest. Western Shoa Province. Muslims 58%(Shafi Sunnis), animists 2%. D=EOC,SDA,ECMY.
3333	2	5	7.87	0	99.70	0.30	C	263.16	260	8	Animists 30%. D=Bethel Evangelical Ch,ECMY. M=United Presbyterian(PCUSA),SIM.
3334	1	6	7.05	0	68.00	32.00	B	99.28	361	6	Near the Amar. Animists 50%, some Muslims. D=WLEC. M=SIM.
3335	2	5	7.98	0	66.00	34.00	B	84.31	391	6	In south. Animists 60%, some Muslims. D=70% Ethiopian Orthodox Ch,WLEC. M=Presbyterian Mission(PCUSA),SIM.
3336	0	0	8.67	0	63.00	37.00	B	103.47	460	7	North Omo Region around Malo-Koza. Related to Ometo language family. Animists 35%. D=EOC.
3337	1	6	7.17	0	58.00	42.00	B	63.51	410	6	Forests, mountains. Hunters, agriculturalists. Animists 70%. D=ECMY. M=Presbyterian Mission(PCUSA).
3338	1	6	4.46	0	70.00	30.00	B	102.20	245	7	Related to East Gurage. Muslims 60%. D=WLEC. M=SIM.
3339	2	6	2.49	0	62.00	38.00	B	67.89	194	6	Ilubabor Administrative Region. Related to Kafa. Animists 60%, Muslims 10%. D=EOC,ECMY. M=United Presbyterian Mission(PCUSA).
3340	0	6	3.38	0	27.00	73.00	A	2.95	488	4	South of Akobo river. Vast majority in Sudan. Pastoralists, agriculturalists. Animists 97%.
3341	1	6	4.73	0	43.00	57.00	A	23.54	393	5	South, near the Amar. Animists 85%. D=WLEC. M=United Presbyterian Mission(PCUSA),SIM,SEM.
3342	1	6	6.86	0	68.00	32.00	B	99.28	353	6	In south, related to Dizi (Maji). Animists 60%. D=ECMY.
3343	1	5	1.02	5	89.00	11.00	B	136.43	87	7	Southwestern Shoa Province. Close to Amharic: highly bilingual. Animists 40%, Muslims 18%(Sufi orders Qadiriyya, Tijaniyya). D=WLEC. M=SIM,WVI.
3344	1	6	4.87	0	27.00	73.00	A	4.92	646	4	Along Sudan border in Wallega Province. Most live in Sudan. Close to Uduk. Animists 90%. D=BECE.
3345	3	6	5.76	0	65.00	35.00	B	83.03	323	6	Fadiro. Western Wallega. Animists 55%, some Muslims. D=EOC,WLEC,ECMY. M=SIM.
3346	2	6	6.08	0	39.00	61.00	A	7.11	528	4	Majority in Sudan. Animists 95%. D=ECMY,SDA. M=United Presbyterian Mission(PCUSA).
3347	5	6	5.60	0	74.00	26.00	B	108.04	278	7	Southwest. Bilinguals in Wolayta. Animists 60%. D=WLEC,ECMY,EOC,RCC,SDA.
3348	1	5	1.81	5	31.01	68.99	A	0.01	328	2	Northern-most Oromo. Muslims 80%(Shafi Sunnis), animists 20%. D=EOC. M=SIM.
3349	1	6	5.44	0	29.00	71.00	A	5.29	694	4	Some in Kenya. Also called Shangilla. Animists 85%, Muslims 10%. Gradual islamization. D=WLEC. M=United Presbyterian Mission(PCUSA).
3350	2	10	3.92	7	75.00	25.00	B	41.06	143	6	Former military advisers from USSR in 1970s. Nonreligious 70%, atheists 15%. D=EOC,ROC.
3351	5	6	11.82	4	83.00	17.00	B	112.09	453	7	Northeast of Lake Abaya. Animists 10%, Muslims 37%(Sunnis). D=Light of Life Ch(Sidamo Free Chs),ECMY,WLEC,FGBC,RCC. M=SIM.
3352	1	5	6.33	0	30.00	70.00	A	5.47	752	4	Most live in southern Eritrea. Nomads, close to Afar. Muslims 81%. D=RCC(D-Adigrat, especially Irob, Minifere peoples).
3353	2	6	3.24	5	62.00	38.00	B	22.63	227	5	Central area. Dialect of South Central Oromo. Muslims 85%, animists 5%. D=EOC,WLEC. M=SIM.
3354	0	0	4.90	0	52.00	48.00	B	66.43	358	6	Western Oromo Region near Begi. Related to Bambassi. Animists 55%, Muslims 10%. D=EOC.
3355	0	1	0.00	5	24.00	76.00	A	0.00	0	1.08	Former Bantu peoples now acculturated to Somali. Refugees from Somalia. Muslims 100%.
3356	0	6	1.40	0	26.00	74.00	A	4.74	348	4	Gemu-Gofa Province. On Lake Weyto. Nearly extinct; people speak Tsamai. Hunters. Animists 95%.
3357	1	6	7.78	0	70.00	30.00	B	102.20	379	7	Gimira Province. Animists 60%. D=ECMY. M=United Presbyterian Mission(PCUSA).
3358	0	6	2.37	0	68.00	32.00	B	99.28	172	6	In Gojjam near Blue Nile river. Somewhat bilingual in Amharic. Animists 40%, Muslims 20%.
3359	2	6	6.21	0	61.00	39.00	B	66.79	343	6	Kafa Province. Also in Sudan. Animists 70%. Closely related to Tirma. D=WLEC,ECMY. M=SIM,SFM,EFS.
3360	2	5	3.25	5	39.01	60.99	A	0.01	358	2	Ogaden Province; also in Somalia, Kenya, Djibouti, Yemen, UAE. Agriculturalists. Muslims 100%(Shafi Sunnis; Sufism strong). D=RCC,WLEC. M=SIM,EMBMC.
3361	1	6	4.22	0	27.00	73.00	A	4.92	580	4	Koma of Begi. Sudan border, Wallega Province. Animists 90%. D=BECE.
3362	2	5	2.42	0	99.70	0.30	C	270.83	112	8	North central Ethiopia. Bilingual in Amharic or Tigrinya. Animists 30%. D=EOC,WLEC. M=SIM.
3363	1	6	2.70	0	33.00	67.00	A	6.02	349	4	Mostly in Sudan. Animists 95%. D=WLEC. M=SIM.
3364	2	6	4.25	0	32.00	68.00	A	5.84	484	4	Anfillo Forest, west of Dembi Dolo. Speakers mainly use Oromo-Wellega. Animists 80%, Muslims 15%. D=EOC,ECMY.
3365	0	5	2.08	7	45.00	55.00	A	3.28	169	4	Traders, refugees, transients from Sudan. Muslims 98%(Sunnis).
3366	0	6	2.60	0	13.50	86.50	A	0.24	832	3	Main area in Sudan. Access difficult here and prohibited in Sudan. Animists 99%. M=SIM.
3367	5	5	1.49	4	99.68	0.32	C	330.10	68	9	South Eritrea, and Tigray Province. Lingua franca. Muslims 15%(Jabarti, or Hanafi Sunni Muslims in Eritrea). Strong Christians. D=80% EOC(D-Tigre),RCC,ECMY.
3368	3	7	-3.70	4	47.04	52.96	A	0.06	6	2	Most in Eritrea, with a few in Sudan. Lingua franca. Muslims 95%(Sunnis). Geez script. D=EOC(D-Tigre),ECE,LCE. M=SLM-BV,SIM,EFS.
3369	1	5	7.18	0	60.00	40.00	B	65.70	393	6	Also some in Sudan. Animists 70%. D=Ethiopian Orthodox Ch. M=United Presbyterian Mission(PCUSA),SEM,SIM.
3370	1	5	7.41	1	99.70	0.30	C	258.05	240	8	Main area is in Sudan; also in Uganda. Pastoralists, agriculturalists. Animists 30%. Resistant to Islam. D=RCC. M=FSCJ,AIM.
3371	2	6	6.53	0	69.00	31.00	B	100.74	335	7	Gemu-Gofa Province, west of Lake Ciamo. Related to Gawwada, Harso. Trade language used: Konso. Animists 60%. D=WLEC,ECMY. M=SIM.
3372	5	6	2.72	5	96.00	4.00	B	140.16	132	7	Central. Shoa Province. Animists 10%, Muslims 35%(Shafi Sunnis). D=EOC,SDA,WLEC,BEC,RCC. M=SIM,WVI,BGC.
3373	2	6	4.41	0	39.00	61.00	A	4.27	415	4	Mainly in northern Kenya. Many immigrants. Animists 97%. D=WLEC,BECE. M=AIM.
3374	7	6	12.49	0	89.00	11.00	B	146.18	443	7	Southwest Lake Abaya area. Animists 35%. D=WLEC(strong),ECMY,20% EOC,FGBC,RCC,SDA,AICs. M=SIM.
3375	4	6	3.29	5	94.00	6.00	B	120.08	151	7	In west. Animists 25%, Muslims 40%(Shafi Sunnis). D=30% EOC(D-Wallega),BECE,ECMY,SDA. M=SIM,WVI,FMB.
3376	2	6	2.79	5	59.00	41.00	B	21.53	218	5	Northeast area. Muslims 70%, animists 20%. D=EOC,SDA.
3377	1	6	3.50	0	29.00	71.00	A	5.29	510	4	Kafa and other Provinces. Related to Gonga. Animists 70%, Muslims 20%. D=WLEC.
3378	0	10	0.00	5	36.00	64.00	A	0.00	0	1.13	Lake Tana. Hunters of hippopotamus, now shot to death. Muslims 100%(Sunnis). Indigenous language. Wayto language has been extinct since 1850.
3379	1	6	5.31	1	89.00	11.00	B	149.43	219	7	Peripheral West Gurage. Close to Amhara; bilingual. Animists 34%, Muslims 20%. D=WLEC.
3380	2	5	1.81	5	31.01	68.99	A	0.01	328	2	Northern area of Galla. Muslims 80%(Shafi Sunnis), animists 20%. D=EOC,SDA. M=SIM.
3381	1	10	2.22	7	42.05	57.95	A	0.07	190	2	Traders from Yemen and Saudi Arabia. Muslims 100%(50% Zaydis, 40% Shafi Sunnis, 5% Ismailis). D=RCC. M=WF,OFMCap.
3382	1	6	10.86	0	85.00	15.00	B	155.12	411	7	South. Youth bilingual in Amharic, older persons in Oromo. Animists 40%, Muslims 10%. D=WLEC. M=SIM.
3383	2	6	4.21	0	24.00	76.00	A	1.75	698	4	Southwest of Lake Abaya. Close to Gidicho, Wolaylta, Ganjule. Animists 98%. D=WLEC, ECMY.
3384	0	7	3.18	0	28.00	72.00	A	5.11	451	4	Southern border with Sudan: close to Murle. Second language: Surma. Animists 95%. M=BGC-BWM,BBFI.
3385	0	6	1.40	0	78.00	22.00	B	128.11	112	7	Southwestern Shoa Province. Related to East Gurage. Highly bilingual in Amharic. Animists 50%, Muslims 5%.
3386	0	9	8.88		35.00	65.00	A	12.77	695	5	Egyptian Arabs(Al-Azhar missionaries), Shona(AACJM from Zimbabwe), Nigerians, Germans; in 1988, 350,000 refugees from Southern Sudan, others fromYemen.
Faeroe Islands											
3387	6	10	1.05	6	99.95	0.05	C	572.13	37	10	Administrators and government personnel from Denmark. D=ELCD(Danish National Church),CB,SA,SDA,JWs,RCC. M=OMI.
3388	6	6	0.97	4	99.93	0.07	C	525.91	42	10	Sheep farmers, fishing industry(dried cod). Language close to Old Norse. D=ELCD(D-Copenhagen),Christian Brethren,SA,SDA,JWs,RCC. M=CMML,IBSA,OMI.
3389	3	10	1.06	6	99.93	0.07	C	563.48	35	10	Expatriates and residents from Norway; professionals. D=ELCD,SA,SDA.
3390	3	10	1.04	6	99.73	0.27	C	375.69	20	9	From Sweden, expatriates, professionals. D=ELCD,SA,SDA.
3391	0	10	1.08		99.81	0.19	C	342.95	26	9	Germans, Americans, British, other Europeans.
Falkland Islands											
3392	4	6	-0.21	8	99.79	0.21	C	440.82	17	10	Nationals; farmers. D=Ch of England in Fl(D-Argentina,CASA),RCC(PA-Falkland Is),UFCFI,JWs. M=MHM,SAMS.
3393	0	0	2.67	7	99.64	0.36	C	251.47	86	8	Immigrants from Japan. Buddhists 20%, New-Religionists(Soka Gakkai,et alia) 16%. D=UCCJ. M=United Ch of Christ in Japan.
3394	1	10	0.91	8	99.78	0.22	C	424.20	33	10	Argentinians, British Hispanics. D=RCC(PA-Falkland Islands). M=MHM,SAMS.
3395	1	10	0.00	8	99.80	0.20	C	429.24	10	10	Chileans and others of mixed race. D=RCC(PA-Falkland Islands). M=SAMS,MHM.
3396	2	10	0.00	6	99.99	0.01	C	617.90	17	10	Expatriates from Norway; professionals. D=UFCFI,CoE in Fl.
3397	0	10	2.46		99.75	0.25	C	301.12	61	9	Individuals from several other nations. Nonreligious 25%.
Fiji											
3398	4	10	1.97	8	99.69	0.31	C	350.07	54	9	Expatriates in professions. Nonreligious 30%. D=Anglican Ch(in CPNZ),Uniting Ch of Australia,SDA,Presbyterian Ch.
3399	3	10	4.73	6	68.00	32.00	B	12.41	245	5	Laborers from India since 1879. Some speak Hindi as mother tongue. Hindus 65%, Muslims 30%. D=RCC,MCF,AC-CPNZ.
3400	1	10	4.91	6	50.00	50.00	B	7.30	325	4	Laborers from India since 1879. Majority now Hindi-speaking. Hindus 76%, Muslims 20%. D=MCF.
3401	4	10	1.93	8	99.79	0.21	C	446.94	54	10	Administrators, teachers. Nonreligious 13%. D=Anglican Ch(D-Polynesia),Methodist Ch in Fiji,SDA,Presbyterian Ch.
3402	8	10	1.98	8	99.96	0.04	C	588.67	45	10	Part-European (mixed race), bilingual in Fijian. D=44% RCC,39% Methodists(MCF-MCA),CJCLdS,SDA,JWs,AoG,AC-CPNZ,et alia.
3403	7	10	1.19	4	99.97	0.03	C	580.84	27	10	All Christians by 1885. D=83% Methodist Ch in Fiji,RCC(M-Suva),AoG,SDA,AC-CPNZ,CJCLdS,JWs. M=MCA,OFMCap,WEC,FMB,UBS.
3404	7	10	4.99	6	76.70	23.30	B	49.55	214	6	Many farmers. Literates 85%. Hindus 66%, Muslims 15%, Sikhs 1%. D=RCC(M-Suva),MCF,AC-CPNZ,SDA,AoG,CJCLdS,JWs. M=MCA,SPEM/WEC,FMB.
3405	1	9	1.94	0	99.80	0.20	C	338.72	56	9	Eastern Fiji, Gone and Dau Islands off western Vanua Levu. Unintelligible to Standard Fijian. D=MCF.
3406	3	8	5.61	6	74.00	26.00	B	27.01	245	5	Laborers from India. Only 26% now use Gujarati at home; rest use Hindi. Hindus 70%, Muslims 20%. D=MCF,AC-CPNZ,RCC.
3407	2	10	3.61	7	99.85	0.15	C	496.40	73	10	Urban; many bilingual in English. Buddhists/Chinese folk-religionists 15%. D=RCC,Anglican Ch(D-Polynesia).
3408	0	10	0.00	8	43.00	57.00	A	0.00	0	1.14	A small community of English-speaking practicing Jews.
3409	5	7	2.05	0	99.93	0.07	C	461.65	50	10	Dialect of Fijian. On Kadavu Island. D=MCF-MCA,RCC,AC-CPNZ,CJCLdS,&c.
3410	3	10	1.99	4	99.97	0.03	C	562.94	45	10	Workers from Kiribati. Also in Kiribati, Tuvalu, Solomons, Nauru, Vanuatu. D=RCC,SDA,AC-CPNZ. M=GIPC.
3411	1	7	1.97	0	99.95	0.05	C	468.11	49	10	Eastern Fiji Islands. Agriculturalists, fishermen. Much traditional religion. D=6 denominations.
3412	3	9	2.06	0	99.90	0.10	C	430.33	43	10	Islands east of Viti Levu. D=MCF,RCC,AC-CPNZ.
3413	4	9	2.68	4	99.40	0.60	B	153.30	96	7	From Kerala (India). Hindus 40%, Muslims 10%. D=MCF,RCC,AC-CPNZ,OSCE.
3414	1	9	2.06	0	99.90	0.10	C	417.19	44	10	South central Viti Levu, Namosi, Serua, Naitasiri Provinces. D=MCF.
3415	2	10	3.97	5	59.00	41.00	B	12.92	233	5	Laborers from India after 1879. Only 14% speak Punjabi; rest now speak Hindi. Hindus 50%, Sikhs 30%, Muslims 14%(Sunnis, also Qadiani Ahmadis). D=RCC.
3416	4	7	2.05	0	99.93	0.07	C	482.01	48	10	On Rotuma Island. D=62% Methodists(MCF-MCA),34% RCC,AC-CPNZ,&c. M=UBS.
3417	3	10	1.93	5	99.95	0.05	C	568.67	41	10	Workers from Samoa, American Samoa; also in New Zealand, USA. D=Congregational Christian Ch(LMS Ch in Fiji),SDA,CJCLdS.
3418	2	10	2.05	4	99.94	0.06	C	521.51	51	10	Expatriates from Solomon Islands. D=Anglican Ch(D-Polynesia),Messiah Club.
3419	3	10	3.93	6	94.00	6.00	B	92.63	144	6	From India after 1879. Only 9% speak Tamil; most now speak Hindi. Hindus 69%. D=RCC,MCF-MCA,&c. M=CM,SSC.
3420	3	10	4.42	5	91.00	9.00	B	83.03	163	6	From India after 1879. 6.6% still use Telugu; rest now speak Hindi. Hindus 70%. D=RCC,AC-CPNZ,&c. M=OFMCap,IMS,PFM.
3421	4	10	1.93	5	99.97	0.03	C	591.26	40	10	From Tonga; also in New Zealand, American Samoa, Hawaii (USA). D=MCF-MCA,RCC,CJCLdS,&c.
3422	3	10	1.94	5	99.95	0.05	C	541.84	43	10	Expatriates from Tuvalu. Also in Nauru, New Zealand. D=MCF-MCA,RCC,&c.
3423	0	0	5.93	8	99.78	0.22	C	367.26	145	9	Immigrants in business, education. Nonreligious 10%. D=RCC,SDA,CJCLdS,JWs.
3424	0	8	2.54	5	52.00	48.00	B	5.69	188	4	Originally from North India. Lingua franca of Fiji Muslims. Muslims 95%.
3425	1	10	1.93	4	99.93	0.07	C	475.23	48	10	Mainly in New Caledonia, Wallis & Futuna, Vanuatu. D=RCC.
3426	3	7	1.99	0	99.98	0.02	C	507.93	47	10	Based on Sigatoka village, southwest area of Viti Levu, Nadroga Province. D=MCF-MCA,RCC,&c.
3427	4	10	1.35		99.90	0.10	C	423.76	29	10	Other South Pacific Islanders.
Finland											
3428	1	9	0.65	8	99.75	0.25	C	353.13	36	9	Also in Sweden. Many Baha'is. D=ELCF. M=Gypsy Evangelical Movement/GGMS(France,Switzerland),FBS.
3429	4	10	1.35	8	99.79	0.21	C	449.82	41	10	Expatriates from Britain, in commerce, professions. D=Ch of England(D-Europe),JWs,SDA,RCC.
3430	0	10	0.00	5	99.50	0.50	B	197.10	0	7	Artificial (constructed) language, in 80 countries. Speakers in Finland: 153,000(none mother-tongue).
3431	3	10	1.34	5	99.80	0.20	C	446.76	45	10	Refugees from former USSR. Diaspora also in USA, Canada, UK, Australia, Sweden. Nonreligious 5%. D=ELCF,OCF,RCC.
3432	2	7	0.54	5	99.90	0.10	C	519.03	27	10	6% bilingual in Swedish. D=92% ELCF(8 Dioceses),1.2% Orthodox Ch of Finland(2 Dioceses),RCC(D-Helsinki),PRF,SA,JWs,FCF,&c. M=SCJ,OP,FIM,FBS.
3433	1	10	0.65	5	99.80	0.20	C	408.80	33	10	Also in Sweden. A number of Baha'is. D=ELCF. M=GGMS.
3434	2	8	0.64	1	99.90	0.10	C	446.76	33	10	In Lapland between Lake Inari and Norway border. All bilingual in Finnish. Numerous Baha'is. D=ELCF(D-Oulu), Orthodox Ch of Finland. M=UBS,FIM.
3435	1	10	0.65	8	99.87	0.13	C	498.55	28	10	Expatriates from France, in commerce, education. D=RCC.
3436	3	10	1.26	8	99.88	0.12	C	523.55	40	10	Expatriates, residents from Germany, in commerce. Mainly Lutherans. D=ELCF(D-Porvoo),JWs,NAC.
3437	0	0	4.65	7	46.00	54.00	A	11.75	316	5	Immigrants in business. Chinese folk religionists 93%.
3438	0	0	2.74	1	34.00	66.00	A	9.92	277	4	Refugees from Iran since 1980. Muslims 88%, Baha'is 4%.
3439	0	0	1.81	8	15.50	84.50	A	0.28	444	3	Refugees from Iraq since 1980. Muslims 100%.
3440	1	10	0.65	7	99.84	0.16	C	475.23	29	10	Residents, expatriates from Italy, in business, professions. Strong Catholics. D=RCC.
3441	0	10	0.00	5	52.07	47.93	B	0.13	36	3	Small practicing Jewish communities, mostly in Helsinki, with synagogues in Turku and Helsinki.
3442	4	8	0.65	0	99.75	0.25	C	336.71	37	9	Oulu Province, et alia. Mainly in Russia. Bilingual in Finnish, Russian. Nonreligious 25%. D=Orthodox Ch of Finland(D-Helsinki,D-Karelia),ELCF,RCC,&c. .
3443	2	9	0.65	0	99.60	0.40	C	229.95	43	8	From North Komi ASSR(ex USSR). Pastoralists, hunters. Nonreligious 30%. D=Russian Orthodox Ch,OCF. M=IBT.
3444	0	10	3.31	0	41.00	59.00	A	2.99	355	4	Refugees from Iraq, Iran, Turkey. A few speak Sorani, a few Zaza. Muslims 98%.
3445	1	8	0.65	2	99.90	0.10	C	476.32	31	10	Great majority in Norway (Norwegian Lapps), also in Sweden. Some Baha'is. D=ELCF(D-Oulu).

Continued overleaf

Table 8-2 continued

PEOPLE		POPULATION				IDENTITY CODE		LANGUAGE		CHURCH		MINISTRY						SCRIPTURE		
Ref 1	Ethnic name 2	P% 3	In 1995 4	In 2000 5	In 2025 6	Race 7	Language 8	Autoglossonym 9	S 10	AC 11	Members 12	Jayuh 13-17	d 18	wa 19	xc 20	mc 21	mi 22	Biblioglossonym 23	Pub 24-26	ss 27
3446	Olonetsian (Livvikovian)	0.10000	5,108	5,176	5,254	MSW51c	41-AAAB-c	olonec		75.00	3,882	1....	10	7	8	4	2	Livvi	P..	b
3447	Polish	0.02300	1,175	1,190	1,208	CEW22i	52-AAAC-c	trondelags-norsk		98.00	1,167	0c.uh	10	9	11	0	0		pnb	.
3448	Romanian	0.01000	511	518	525	CEW21i	51-AADC-a	limba româneasca		80.00	414	3A.u.	10	9	11	0	0	Romanian	PNB	b
3449	Russian	0.20000	10,216	10,351	10,508	CEW22j	53-AAAE-d	russkiy		70.00	7,246	4B.uh	10	8	9	5	3	Russian	PNB	b
3450	Russian Lapp (Skolt Lapp)	0.01000	511	518	525	MSW51e	41-AABB-a	skolt		90.00	466	0A...	10	7	11	4	2	Saami: Russian*	P..	b
3451	Serb	0.05000	2,554	2,588	2,627	CEW22l	53-AAAG-a	standard srpski		80.00	2,070	1Asuh	10	9	11	0	0	Serbian*	PNB	b
3452	Somali	0.06000	3,065	3,105	3,152	CMT33e	14-GAGA-a	af-soomaali		0.01	0	2A...	3	4	7	0	0	Somali	PNB	b
3453	Swedish (Swede)	5.90000	301,360	305,369	309,978	CEW19q	52-AAAD-r	svea-svensk	31	73.00	222,919	1A.uh	10	9	12	5	4	Swedish	PNB	b
3454	Thai	0.02000	1,022	1,035	1,051	MSY49d	47-AAAB-d	central thai		2.00	21	3asuh	6	5	8	0	0	Thai*	PNB	b
3455	Turkish Tatar	0.02600	1,328	1,346	1,366	MSY41j	44-AABB-e	tatar		0.10	1	2c.u.	5	3	5	1	0	Tatar: Kazan	Pn.	b
3456	USA White	0.05000	2,554	2,588	2,627	CEW19s	52-ABAC-s	general american	32	78.00	2,019	1Bsuh	10	9	13	5	3	English*	PNB	b
3457	Vietnamese	0.05000	2,554	2,588	2,627	MSY52b	46-EBAA-ac	general viêt		12.00	311	1Asu.	8	6	9	0	0	Vietnamese	PNB	b
3458	other minor peoples	0.10000	5,108	5,176	5,254	...				70.00	3,623		10	7	8	5	0			
	France	**100.00000**	**58,019,970**	**59,079,709**	**61,661,804**					**69.6**	**41,116,957**									
3459	Afghani	0.06000	34,812	35,448	36,997	CNT24a	58-ABDA-a	pashto		0.50	177	1As..	5	6	6	5	0		pnb	b
3460	Algerian Arab	1.30000	754,260	768,036	801,603	CMT30	12-AACB-b	east maghrebi		0.60	4,608	2A.uh	5	4	4	5	3	Arabic: Algerian*	PNB	b
3461	Alsatian (Alemannic)	2.68870	1,559,983	1,588,476	1,657,901	CEW19b	52-ABCD-j	ostfränkisch-t.		70.00	1,111,933	0A.uh	10	9	14	5	3		...	b
3462	Arabized Berber	0.70000	406,140	413,558	431,633	CMT32a	12-AACB-b	east maghrebi		0.50	2,068	2A.uh	5	4	4	5	3	Arabic: Algerian*	PNB	b
3463	Arliski Balkan Romany	0.01912	11,093	11,296	11,790	CNN25f	59-ACBA-bf	dzambazi		80.00	9,037	1c...	10	8	8	5	2		pn.	b
3464	Armenian	0.45000	261,090	265,859	277,478	CEW14	57-AAAA-b	ashkharik		90.00	239,273	4A.u.	10	9	13	5	3	Armenian: Modern, Eastern	PNB	b
3465	Assyrian (Chaldean)	0.00600	3,481	3,545	3,700	CMT31	12-AAAA-f	aisor		95.00	3,368	4cs..	10	9	11	5	2	Assyrian Neo-aramaic	PNB	b
3466	Bambara	0.07000	40,614	41,356	43,163	NAB63a	00-AAAB-a	bamanan-kan		3.00	1,241	4As..	6	6	6	5	1	Bambara	PNB	b
3467	Basque	1.30000	754,260	768,036	801,603	CEW16	51-AABI-dp	français-basque		76.00	583,708	1A.uh	10	9	15	5	1		pnb	b
3468	Basque (Euzkadi)	0.17013	98,709	100,512	104,905	CEW16	40-AAAA-i	lapurtera		88.00	88,451	1....	10	9	14	5	2	Basque: Labourdin*	PNB	b
3469	Beraber	0.25000	145,050	147,699	154,155	CMT32b	10-AAAC-b	ta-mazight		0.10	148	1a...	5	8	4	5	1	Shilha: Central*	Pn.	b
3470	Black Gypsy (Gitano)	0.03643	21,137	21,523	22,463	CNN25f	59-AFAA-a	rodi		80.00	17,218	0B.uh	10	8	8	5	3	Calo	P..	b
3471	Black Tai (Thai Den)	0.00296	1,717	1,749	1,825	MSY49z	47-AAAD-a	tai-dam		10.00	175	0....	8	6	5	4	1	Tai: Dam*	P..	b
3472	Breton	1.00000	580,200	590,797	616,618	CEW18a	51-AABI-c	standard français		75.00	443,098	4B.uh	10	8	11	5	1	French	PNB	b
3473	Breton	2.25000	1,305,449	1,329,293	1,387,391	CEW18a	50-ABBB-c	leoneg		70.00	930,505	0....	10	8	14	5	3	Breton: Leon	PNB	b
3474	British	0.06000	34,812	35,448	36,997	CEW19i	52-ABAC-b	standard-english	26	79.00	28,004	3Bsuh	10	9	13	5	1		PNB	b
3475	Catalonian	0.49149	285,162	290,371	303,062	CEW21a	51-AABE-b	català		95.00	275,852	2a..h	10	9	15	5	2	Catalan-valencian-balear	PNB	b
3476	Ceylon Tamil	0.05000	29,010	29,540	30,831	CNN23c	49-EBEA-bn	north sri-lanka-tamil		30.00	8,862	1Asu.	9	5	8	5	1		pnb	b
3477	Corsican	0.50000	290,100	295,399	308,309	CEW21z	51-AABP-b	central corsu		81.00	239,273	0....	10	9	14	5	1	Italian: Corsican*	P..	b
3478	Czech	0.02000	11,604	11,816	12,332	CEW22e	53-AAAD-a	czesky		79.00	9,335	2Asuh	10	9	8	5	3	Czech	PNB	b
3479	Danish (Dane)	0.02000	11,604	11,816	12,332	CEW19g	52-AAAD-c	general dansk	4	95.00	11,225	2A.uh	10	9	11	5	1	Danish	PNB	b
3480	Detribalized	0.89000	516,378	525,809	548,790	NAN58	51-AABI-m	français-d'afrique		40.00	210,324	1B.uh	9	8	8	5	1		pnb	b
3481	Dutch	0.17013	98,709	100,512	104,905	CEW19h	52-ABCA-a	algemeen-nederlands	2	76.00	76,389	2Bsuh	10	9	15	5	2	Dutch	PNB	b
3482	Dzambazi Gypsy	0.00100	580	591	617	CNN25f	59-ACBA-bf	dzambazi		80.00	473	1c...	10	8	8	4	3		pn.	b
3483	Esperanto	0.00000	0	0	0	CEW21z	51-AAAC-a	proper esperanto		80.00	0	0A...	10	9	6	5	0	Esperanto	PNB	b
3484	Eurafrican	0.10000	58,020	59,080	61,662	NAN58	51-AABI-d	general français		75.00	44,310	1B.uh	10	8	7	5	1	French	PNB	b
3485	Eurasian	0.10000	58,020	59,080	61,662	MSY43	51-AABI-d	general français		75.00	44,310	1B.uh	10	8	7	5	1	French	PNB	b
3486	Fleming	1.40000	812,280	827,116	863,265	CEW19k	52-ABCA-g	oostvlaandersch	2	88.00	727,862	1Bsuh	10	9	15	5	2		pnb	b
3487	Fon	0.03000	17,406	17,724	18,499	NAB59e	96-MAAG-a	standard fon		60.00	10,634	2as..	10	9	9	5	1	Fon*	PNb	b
3488	Franco-Provencal	1.00000	580,200	590,797	616,618	CEW21b	51-AABJ-e	vaudois		89.00	525,809	0....	10	9	13	5	1	French: Vaudois, Ancient*	PN.	b
3489	Franco-Swiss	0.05000	29,010	29,540	30,831	CEW21b	51-AABI-f	français-suisse		84.00	24,813	1B.uh	10	9	13	5	2		pnb	b
3490	French	45.40941	26,346,526	26,827,747	28,000,261	CEW21b	51-AABI-d	general français	100	76.00	20,389,088	1B.uh	10	10	16	5	3	French	PNB	b
3491	French Gypsy	0.26000	150,852	153,607	160,321	CNN25f	51-AABI-c	standard français		80.00	122,886	4B.uh	10	9	8	5	3	French	PNB	b
3492	Fulani	0.05000	29,010	29,540	30,831	NAB56c	90-BAAA-n	fula-sokoto		1.00	295	1cs..	6	6	6	5	0	Fulfulde	PNB	b
3493	Gascon	0.70000	406,140	413,558	431,633	CEW21z	51-AABF-a	gascou		75.00	310,168	0....	10	8	11	5	1	Gascon	P..	b
3494	Georgian	0.00400	2,321	2,363	2,466	CEW17c	42-CABB-a	kharthuli		90.00	2,127	2A.u.	10	8	11	4	1	Georgian	PNB	b
3495	German	1.00000	580,200	590,797	616,618	CEW19m	52-ABCE-a	standard hoch-deutsch	12	84.00	496,270	2B.uh	10	9	13	5	4	German*	PNB	b
3496	German Swiss	0.06000	34,812	35,448	36,997	CEW19m	52-ABCG-a	general schwytzer-tütsch	12	88.00	31,194	0B.uh	10	9	13	5	3	Schwyzerdutsch*	PN.	b
3497	Greater Kabyle (Western)	1.10000	638,220	649,877	678,280	CMT32c	10-AAAC-h	tha-qabaylith		5.00	32,494	1a...	7	5	11	5	3	Kabyle: Greater	PN.	b
3498	Greek	0.10000	58,020	59,080	61,662	CEW20	56-AAAA-ic	cargese		95.00	56,126	1A.uh	10	9	11	5	1		pnb	b
3499	Han Chinese	0.10000	58,020	59,080	61,662	MSY42a	51-AABI-c	standard français		15.00	8,862	4B.uh	8	5	8	5	0	French	PNB	b
3500	Han Chinese (Cantonese)	0.17000	98,634	100,436	104,825	MSY42a	79-AAAM-a	central yue	2	7.00	7,030	3A.uh	7	5	8	5	3	Chinese, Yue	PNB	b
3501	Han Chinese (Chaozhou)	0.01000	5,802	5,908	6,166	MSY42a	79-AAAJ-ic	chaozhou		4.00	236	1A..h	6	5	8	5	1	Chinese, Min Nan	PNB	b
3502	Han Chinese (Mandarin)	0.06000	34,812	35,448	36,997	MSY42a	79-AAAB-ba	kuo-yü	1	3.00	1,063	2Bsuh	6	5	8	5	1	Chinese: Kuoyu*	PNB	b
3503	Han Chinese (Shanghainese)	0.00800	4,642	4,726	4,933	MSY42a	79-AAAD-b	tai-hu		4.00	189	1A...	6	5	8	5	1		pnb	b
3504	Han Chinese (Wenchow)	0.03000	17,406	17,724	18,499	MSY42a	79-AAAD-hd	wenzhou		4.00	709	1c...	6	5	8	5	1	Chinese: Wenchow	PNb	b
3505	Highland Yao	0.00347	2,013	2,050	2,140	MSY47b	48-ABAA-b	iu-mien		0.70	14	0.s..	5	4	7	0	0	Iu Mien	PN.	b
3506	Hmong-Lao	0.20000	116,040	118,159	123,324	MSY47a	48-AAAA-b	hmong-njua		50.00	59,080	1A...	10	8	8	5	1	Hmong Njua	PN.	b
3507	Italian	1.88324	1,092,655	1,112,613	1,161,240	CEW21e	51-AABQ-c	standard italiano	14	79.00	878,964	2B.uh	10	9	15	5	2	Italian	PNB	b
3508	Jewish	0.40000	232,080	236,319	246,647	CMT35	52-ABCH-a	west yiddish		0.10	236	0B..h	5	4	4	5	0	Yiddish	PNB	b
3509	Jewish	0.80000	464,160	472,638	493,294	CMT35	51-AABI-d	general français		0.30	1,418	1B.uh	5	5	6	5	1	French	PNB	b
3510	Khmer (Cambodian)	0.11000	63,822	64,988	67,828	AUG03b	46-FBAA-b	khmae		1.00	650	2A...	6	4	6	5	2	Khmer*	PNB	b
3511	Languedocian	4.00000	2,320,799	2,363,188	2,466,472	CEW21z	51-AABG	oc cluster		75.00	1,772,391	0A...	10	8	15	5	1		PN.	b
3512	Lao (Laotian Tai)	0.03000	17,406	17,724	18,499	MSY49b	47-AAAC-b	lao		3.00	532	2As..	6	5	8	5	1	Lao	PNB	b
3513	Lesser Antillean Creole	0.40000	232,080	236,319	246,647	NFB69b	51-AACC-e	martiniquais		90.00	212,687	1As..	10	7	11	5	3		pnb	b
3514	Lesser Kabyle (Eastern)	0.10000	58,020	59,080	61,662	CMT32c	10-AAAC-h	tha-qabaylith		4.00	2,363	1a...	6	5	6	4	1	Kabyle: Greater	PN.	b
3515	Ligurian (Genoan)	0.06000	34,812	35,448	36,997	CEW21e	51-AABO-h	ligure		80.00	28,358	0c...	10	9	13	5	1	Ligurian	Pn.	b
3516	Lovari Gypsy (Rom)	0.00400	2,321	2,363	2,466	CNN25f	59-ACBA-a	vlach-romani		70.00	1,654	1a...	10	8	6	4	2	Romani: Finnish*	PN.	b
3517	Luxemburger	0.06000	34,812	35,448	36,997	CEW19o	52-ABCD-b	letzebürgesch-t.		88.00	31,194	0a.uh	10	9	13	5	1	Luxembourgeois	...	b
3518	Malagasy	0.10000	58,020	59,080	61,662	MSY44j	31-LDAA-aa	standard merina		49.00	28,949	1Asu.	9	7	8	5	1		pnb	b
3519	Malinke	0.10000	58,020	59,080	61,662	NAB63h	00-AAAA-b	sijanka-kango		2.00	1,182	1c...	6	6	6	5	1		pn.	b
3520	Mandyak (Manjaco)	0.03846	22,314	22,722	23,715	NAB56c	90-FAAA-a	proper mandyak		19.00	4,317	0....	8	5	5	5	0	Manjako*	P..	b
3521	Moor	0.03000	17,406	17,724	18,499	CMT32a	12-AACD-a	hassaaniyya		0.20	35	0a...	5	6	5	5	0		pn.	b
3522	Moroccan Arab	1.00238	581,581	592,203	618,086	CMT30	12-AACB-a	west maghrebi		0.40	2,369	1A.uh	5	4	5	5	3		pnb	b
3523	Mossi	0.10000	58,020	59,080	61,662	NAB56a	91-GGAA-a	moo-re		50.00	29,540	2A...	10	7	8	5	2	Moore	PNB	b
3524	North Gallo-Romance	11.00000	6,382,197	6,498,768	6,782,798	CEW21z	51-AABG	oc cluster		76.00	4,939,064	0A...	10	10	15	5	0		PN.	b
3525	Northern Kurd	0.13000	75,426	76,804	80,160	CNT24c	58-AAAA-a	kurmanji		0.10	77	3c...	5	3	5	4	0	Kurdish: Kurmanji*	PN.	b
3526	Persian	0.10000	58,020	59,080	61,662	CNT24f	58-AACC-c	standard farsi		2.00	1,182	1Asu.	6	6	8	5	0		PNB	b
3527	Polish (Pole)	0.20000	116,040	118,159	123,324	CEW22i	53-AAAC-c	polski		90.00	106,343	2A.uh	10	9	12	5	2	Polish	PNB	b
3528	Portuguese	1.50000	870,300	886,196	924,927	CEW21g	51-AABA-e	general português	8	91.00	806,438	2Bsuh	10	9	15	5	3	Portuguese	PNB	b
3529	Provencal	4.60000	2,668,919	2,717,667	2,836,443	CEW21z	51-AABG-ba	standard occitan		75.00	2,038,250	0c...	10	9	15	5	1	Provencal	Pn.	b
3530	Provencal (South French)	4.00000	2,320,799	2,363,188	2,466,472	CEW21z	51-AABI-d	general français		75.00	1,772,391	1B.uh	10	9	15	5	1	French	PNB	b
3531	Reunionese	0.02000	11,604	11,816	12,332	NAN58	51-AACC-m	réunioné		95.00	11,225	1cs..	10	8	11	5	2		pnb	b
3532	Riffian	0.20000	116,040	118,159	123,324	CMT32e	10-AAAC-e	senhaja		0.10	118	1c...	5	3	4	4	2		pn.	b
3533	Romanian	0.02000	11,604	11,816	12,332	CEW21i	51-AADC-a	limba româneasca		70.00	8,271	3A.u.	10	9	9	5	3	Romanian	PNB	b
3534	Russian	0.20000	116,040	118,159	123,324	CEW22j	53-AAAE-d	russkiy		70.00	82,712	4B.uh	10	8	9	5	3	Russian	PNB	b
3535	Senufo	0.01000	5,802	5,908	6,166	NAB56a	91-BAAC	senari-cebaara cluster		10.00	591	3.s..	8	7	6	5	1		PN.	b
3536	Serb	0.04000	23,208	23,632	24,665	CEW22l	53-AAAG-a	standard srpski		85.00	20,087	1Asuh	10	8	10	5	1	Serbian*	PNB	b
3537	Shawiya	0.30000	174,060	177,239	184,985	CMT32f	10-AAAC-j	shawiya		0.10	177	1c...	5	3	4	4	1	Chaouia	Pn.	b
3538	Sinti Gypsy (Sasitka)	0.04800	27,850	28,358	29,598	CNN25f	59-ACBB-b	sinti		75.00	21,269	0....	10	8	8	4	3	Romani: Sinti, Italian	P..	b
3539	Soninke (Sarakole)	0.01500	8,703	8,862	9,249	NAB63j	00-BAAA-a	proper soninke		0.01	1	3....	3	4	4	5	1	Soninke	...	b
3540	Spaniard	1.20000	696,240	708,957	739,942	CEW21k	51-AABB-c	general español	13	95.00	673,509	2B.uh	10	9	15	5	1	Spanish	PNB	b
3541	Swedish	0.02000	11,604	11,816	12,332	CEW19q	52-AAAD-r	svea-svensk	2	72.00	8,507	1A.uh	10	9	8	5	1	Swedish	PNB	b
3542	Syro-Lebanese Arab	0.40000	232,080	236,319	246,647	CMT30	12-AACF-f	syro-palestinian		40.00	94,528	1Asuh	9	6	8	5	1	Arabic: Lebanese*	Pnb	b
3543	Tho	0.00300	1,741	1,772	1,850	MSY49a	47-AAAE-ae	tai-tho		3.00	53	0....	6	5	5	4	2	Tho*	P..	.
3544	Tuareg	0.04000	23,208	23,632	24,665	CMT32h	10-AAAB-a	ta-mahaq		0.20	47	1....	5	6	5	5	1	Tamahaq: Hoggar*	PN.	b
3545	Tunisian Arab	0.38993	226,237	230,370	240,438	CMT30	12-AACB-b	east maghrebi		0.30	691	2A.uh	5	4	4	5	3	Arabic: Algerian*	PNB	b
3546	Turk	0.36000	208,872	212,687	221,982	MSY41j	44-AABA-a	osmanli		0.10	213	1A.u.	5	3	5	4	1	Turkish	PNB	b
3547	USA White	0.10000	58,020	59,080	61,662	CEW19s	52-ABAC-s	general american		78.00	46,082	1Bsuh	10	9	13	5	3	English*	PNB	b
3548	Ukrainian	0.03500	20,307	20,678	21,582	CEW22p	53-AAAE-b	ukrainskiy		80.00	16,542	3A.uh	10	8	9	5	1	Ukrainian	PNB	b
3549	Vietnamese	1.00000	580,200	590,797	616,618	MSY52b	46-EBAA-ac	general viêt		25.00	147,699	1Asu.	9	5	9	5	3	Vietnamese	PNB	b
3550	Vlach Romany Gypsy (Rom)	0.01821	10,565	10,758	11,229	CNN25f	59-ACBA-a	vlach-romani		70.00	7,531	1a...	10	8	8	5	1	Romani: Finnish*	PN.	b
3551	Walloon	0.10000	58,020	59,080	61,662	CEW21l	51-AABH-f	wallon	100	92.00	54,353	0A.uh	10	8	15	5	1	French: Walloon	P..	b
3552	Western Cham	0.00173	1,004	1,022	1,067	MSY44z	31-MBBC-b	west cham		1.00	10	0.s..	6	4	7	0	0	Cham, Western	p..	b
3553	White Meo	0.01738	10,084	10,268	10,717	MSY47a	48-AAAA-a	hmong-daw		2.00	205	2A...	6	5	8	0	0	Hmong Daw*	PN.	.
3554	Wolof	0.06283	36,454	37,120	38,742	NAB56c	90-AAAA-a	vehicular wolof		2.00	742	4.s..	6	5	6	4	2	Wolof: Senegal	PN.	b
3555	other minor peoples	0.20000	116,040	118,159	123,324	...				60.00	70,896		10	5	8	5	0			
	French Guiana	**100.00000**	**146,758**	**181,313**	**416,191**					**84.24**	**152,736**									
3556	Antillean	5.00000	7,338	9,066	20,810	NFB69b	51-AACC-e	martiniquais		90.00	8,159	1As..	10	8	11	5	1		pnb	b
3557	Arawak (Lokono)	0.29000	426	526	1,207	MIR39a	81-ACBA	arawák cluster		92.00	484	0....	10	8	11	5	3	Arawak	P..	b
3558	Boni (Bush Negro)	1.12000	1,644	2,031	4,661	NFB68b	52-ABAG-h	aluku		80.00	1,625	1.s..	10	7	7	5	1		pn.	.
3559	Brazilian Mulatto	1.90000	2,788	3,445	7,908	NFB70b	51-AABA-e	general português		88.00	3,032	2Bsuh	10	8	11	5	1	Portuguese	PNB	b
3560	Brazilian White	3.00000	4,403	5,439	12,486	CLT26	51-AABA-e	general português		88.50	4,814	2Bsuh	10	9	11	5	1	Portuguese	PNB	b
3561	Bush Negro (Djuka)	4.00000	5,870	7,253	16,648	NFB68b	52-ABAG-g	ndjuka		90.00	6,527	1.s..	10	7	6	4	1	Aukan*	Pn.	.
3562	Carib (Galibi)	1.19000	1,746	2,158	4,953	MIR39c	80-ACAA-b	central carib		70.00	1,510	1.s..	10	8	8	5	3	Carib*	Pn.	b
3563	Caribbean East Indian	4.00000	5,870	7,253	16,648	CNN25g	59-AAFP-ed	hindi-cayenne		50.00	3,626	1c.u.	10	8	8	5	1		pn.	b
3564	Caribbean Javanese	1.00000	1,468	1,813	4,162	MSY44g	31-PIAA-k	jawa-surinam		35.00	635	1As.h	9	5	6	5	1	Javanese: Caribbean*	Pnb	b
3565	Emerillon (Emerenon)	0.22500	330	408	936	MIR39e	82-AAAA-a	emerillon		10.00	41	0....	8	5	4	4	1		...	.

Continued opposite

Table 8-2 continued

EVANGELIZATION								EVANGELISM			ADDITIONAL DESCRIPTIVE DATA
Ref 1	D 28	aC 29	CG% 30	r 31	E 32	U 33	W 34	e 35	R 36	T 37	Locations, civil divisions, literacy, religions, church history, denominations, dioceses, church growth, missions, agencies, ministries, movements 38
3446	2	8	0.65	0	99.75	0.25	C	325.76	38	9	Scattered around Finland. Mainly in Russia. Close to Karelian, Finnish, Ludic, Veps. Bilingual in Finnish, Russian. D=OCF,ROC.
3447	0	0	4.87	1	99.98	0.02	C	468.58	102	10	Refugees and immigrants from Poland. D=RCC.
3448	0	0	3.79	6	99.80	0.20	C	370.84	106	9	Refugees from Romania since 1985. Nonreligious 20%. D=Orthodox Church.
3449	3	10	1.27	7	99.70	0.30	C	370.47	24	9	Refugees from former USSR. Nonreligious and atheists 30%. D=Russian Orthodox Ch(P-Moscow),Private Greek Catholic Ch,OCF.
3450	2	8	0.64	4	99.90	0.10	C	473.04	31	10	Northwest of Inari Same. Pastoralists, hunters, fishermen. A few Baha'is. D=ELCF(D-Oulu),OCF. M=FIC,FBS.
3451	0	0	5.48	6	99.80	0.20	C	373.76	117	9	Refugees from Yugoslavia since 1989. Nonreligious 20%. D=Serbian Orthodox Church.
3452	0	0	0.00	5	35.01	64.99	A	0.01	0	2	Refugees, migrants from Somalia. Muslims 100%(Shafi Sunnis).
3453	11	10	0.49	6	99.73	0.27	C	397.01	9	9	Citizens and expatriates. Bilingual in Finnish. D=Ch of Sweden(Olaus Petri),SBCF,OCF,ELCF(D-Porvoo),FMCC,FA,SA,SDA,PRF,MCF,MPC.
3454	0	0	3.09	6	43.00	57.00	A	3.13	234	4	Immigrants from Thailand, in commerce, industry. Buddhists 96%, Muslims 1%.
3455	0	10	0.00	6	36.10	63.90	A	0.13	54	3	Migrant laborers from Turkey. Muslims 100%(Hanafi Sunnis).
3456	7	10	1.16	8	99.78	0.22	C	435.59	37	10	Expatriates from USA, in commerce, education. D=SDA,CJCLdS,CCS,JWs,UMC,OCF,ELCF.
3457	0	0	3.50	6	54.00	46.00	B	23.65	221	5	Refugees from Viet Nam since 1970. Buddhists 60%, New Religionists 20%. D=RCC.
3458	0	9	0.65		99.70	0.30	C	263.16	17	8	Immigrants, refugees, from Middle East, other European, Asian, and African countries.
France											
3459	0	10	2.92	5	51.50	48.50	B	0.94	273	3	Refugees from Afghanistan wars. Muslims 99%(Hanafi Sunnis).
3460	3	10	6.32	8	63.60	36.40	B	1.39	302	4	From Algeria; also in Niger, Belgium, Netherlands, Germany. Muslims 99%(Maliki Sunnis). D=RCC,ICFG,EE. M=UFM,WEC,FMB,CSI.
3461	7	9	0.37	8	99.70	0.30	C	350.03	29	9	Citizens in Alsace-Lorraine. 90% bilinguals in French and Standard German. D=RCC(D-Strasbourg,D-Metz),ECAAL,NEC,NAC,ERAL,EEMF,UEE.
3462	1	10	5.48	8	61.50	38.50	B	1.12	275	4	Arabic-speaking immigrants from Algeria, Morocco. Laborers. Muslims 99%(Maliki Sunnis). D=RCC. M=WEC,FMB,CSI.
3463	3	10	0.37	1	99.80	0.20	C	385.44	29	9	Gypsies, also in 12 countries. Muslims 20%. D=nomadic caravan churches(Gypsy Evangelical Movement),AoG,RCC. M=GGMS,SMIE.
3464	3	10	0.37	6	99.90	0.10	C	548.59	16	10	Refugees from Turkey, USSR. Home language of 32%; rest use French. D=Armenian Apostolic Ch(C-Echmiadzin: D-Western Europe),AAC(C-Sis: D-France,RCC.
3465	2	10	5.99	5	99.95	0.05	C	568.67	111	10	Refugees from Middle East. Chaldean Catholics and Nestorians. D=RCC(Chaldean-rite),ACE.
3466	1	10	4.94	4	64.00	36.00	B	7.00	293	4	Muslim immigrants from Mali. Muslims 90%(Sunnis), Animists 7%. D=RCC.
3467	1	7	0.37	8	99.76	0.24	C	399.45	26	9	Basques, mainly in south, who now use French as first language. D=RCC. M=SJ. R=local stations. T=local stations. R=AWR.
3468	1	7	0.37	4	99.88	0.12	C	485.01	25	10	Near French-Spanish border. Departments: Labourd, Basse-Navarre, Soule. Majority in Spain; also in USA, Costa Rica, Philippines, Australia. D=RCC. M=SJ,UBS.
3469	0	10	2.73	4	44.10	55.90	A	0.16	221	3	Migrant workers from Morocco. Muslims 100%(Maliki Sunnis). M=UFM.
3470	4	10	0.37	8	99.80	0.20	C	417.56	27	10	Brazilian Calo. Southern France; also Spain, Portugal, Latin America (mainly Brazil). D=nomadic caravan churches(Gypsy Evangelical Movement),AoG,RCC,JWs.
3471	1	10	2.90	4	51.00	49.00	B	18.61	188	5	Refugees and labor migrants from Viet Nam, from 1953 to 1995. Animists 60%, nonreligious 30%. D=RCC. M=CMA.
3472	1	8	0.37	8	99.75	0.25	C	405.15	25	10	Brittany. Bretons who now use French as first language. D=RCC. M=Mission Evangelique en Bretagne. R=local stations. T=local stations. R=AWR.
3473	2	8	0.37	1	99.70	0.30	C	337.26	28	9	Breiz spoken by 44% (25% literate). D=RCC(D-Ste-Brieuc,D-Quimper),&c; also Celtic Apostolic Orthodox Ch in Brittany. M=SJ,OFMOP,ATT(An Tour-Tan).
3474	3	10	0.37	8	99.79	0.21	C	455.59	26	10	Expatriates from Britain, in education, business, administration. D=Ch of England(D-Europe),Ch of Scotland,JWs. M=CCCS/ICS.
3475	1	8	0.37	4	99.95	0.05	C	575.60	21	10	From Catalonia(Spain); also Sardinia(Italy), Andorra. Workers, professionals. D=RCC. M=FMB,UBS.
3476	1	10	7.02	6	90.00	10.00	B	98.55	244	6	Migrant workers from Sri Lanka and south India. Many Catholics, charismatics. Hindus 55%, Muslims 10%. D=RCC.
3477	1	8	0.37	4	99.81	0.19	C	396.17	28	9	In Corsica, Paris, Marseilles. Also in Canada, Puerto Rico, USA, Venezuela, Cuba, Bolivia, Uruguay. D=RCC(D-Ajaccio).
3478	5	10	0.37	6	99.79	0.21	C	432.52	27	10	Refugees from Czechoslovakia, 1900-1990. Nonreligious 21%. D=RCC,CHC,ECCB,CUA,&c.
3479	1	10	0.37	6	99.95	0.05	C	572.13	25	10	Expatriates, immigrants from Denmark. D=National Church of Denmark.
3480	1	10	0.37	8	99.40	0.60	B	151.84	39	7	Persons from Africa, Asia, and elsewhere who have abandonded their origins and traditions. Mostly urban slumdwellers. Muslims 30%, nonreligious/atheists 30%.
3481	2	10	0.37	6	99.76	0.24	C	427.19	22	10	In northeast France. Also Netherlands, Antilles, Belgium, Surinam, USA. Expatriates. Nonreligious 23%. D=NHK/DRC,RCC.
3482	1	10	0.37	1	99.80	0.20	C	376.68	30	9	Balkan Romany, in 12 countries. Muslims 20%. D=caravan churches(Gypsy Evangelical Movement). M=GGMS,AoGUSA,JWs,SMIE.
3483	0	10	0.00	5	99.80	0.20	C	402.96	0	10	Artificial (constructed) language, in 80 countries. Speakers in France: 240,000(none mother-tongue).
3484	1	10	0.37	8	99.75	0.25	C	383.25	29	9	Mixed-race persons from former French Africa colonies. Nonreligious 20%. D=RCC.
3485	1	10	0.37	8	99.75	0.25	C	383.25	23	9	Mixed European/Asians, mostly Franco-Vietnamese children from Indochina and other former French colonies. D=RCC.
3486	2	8	0.37	6	99.88	0.12	C	510.70	26	10	Belgian expatriates and immigrants from Belgium, in commerce, professions. D=RCC,NHK.
3487	1	10	7.22	4	99.60	0.40	C	269.37	200	8	Immigrants from Benin. Strong fetishist traditions. Animists 20%, Muslims 5%. D=RCC.
3488	1	8	0.37	8	99.89	0.11	C	480.77	25	10	Romand cluster (6 languages). Near border with Italy. Language distinct from Provencal and from French. D=RCC.
3489	2	10	0.37	8	99.84	0.16	C	469.09	24	10	Expatriates and immigrants from French-speaking Switzerland. D=RCC,SRC.
3490	9	9	-0.27	8	99.76	0.24	C	429.97	13	10	Nonreligious 16%, atheists 5%, Muslims 0.6%. D=RCC(95 Dioceses),Eglise Reformee de France,EELF,JWs,AoG,ACA,SDA,CJCLdS,UMC. M=UFM,FMB,WEC.
3491	2	10	0.37	8	99.80	0.20	C	443.84	25	10	French-speaking itinerants. D=Gypsy Evangelical Movement(Eglises Tsiganes/AoG), in nomadic caravan churches. M=GGMS,AoGUSA,Gypsies for Christ,SMIE.
3492	0	10	3.44	4	52.00	48.00	B	1.89	266	4	Immigrants from 10 West African countries. Nomadic traditions. Muslims 98%.
3493	1	8	0.37	8	99.75	0.25	C	353.13	29	9	Aquitaine. Pyrenean Gascon cluster (6 languages). Gascon spoken by 51%. D=RCC.
3494	1	8	0.37	4	99.90	0.10	C	502.60	7	10	Refugees from Georgian SSR(USSR) since 1917. D=Georgian Orthodox Ch.
3495	11	9	0.37	8	99.84	0.16	C	502.82	25	10	Expatriates from Germany, in commerce, professions. D=RCC,EKD,NAC,EELF,ECAAL,ERAL,ERF,EEMF,UAC,UMC,JWs. R=HCJB,AWR.
3496	6	10	0.37	8	99.88	0.12	C	510.70	26	10	Swiss expatriates. D=RCC,NAC,ECAAL,ERAL,Swiss Pentecostal Mission,Eglise Suisse-Allemande.
3497	1	10	8.42	4	64.00	36.00	B	11.68	390	5	Berber immigrant workers from Algeria. Also in Belgium. Muslims 95%(Maliki Sunnis). D=RCC. M=NAM,UFM,FMB-CSI. Kabyle missionaries sent out. R=TWR.
3498	1	10	0.37	6	99.95	0.05	C	554.80	23	10	From Greece, Cyprus. In Corsica; in 15 other countries. All are bilingual in French. D=Greek Orthodox Ch in France(D-France,E-Spain).
3499	0	9	0.36	8	81.00	19.00	B	44.34	34	6	Most reside in Greater Paris. Chinese folk-religionists/Buddhists 85%.
3500	1	9	0.37	8	74.00	26.00	B	18.90	38	5	Most in Paris. Mahayana Buddhists/Confucianists 90%. D=RCC. M=CMA(Hong Kong),Chinese Overseas Christian Mission,FMB.
3501	1	10	0.36	6	65.00	35.00	B	9.49	43	4	Mahayana Buddhists/Confucianists 95%. D=RCC.
3502	1	10	0.37	7	68.00	32.00	B	7.44	41	4	Mostly residents of Greater Paris. Mahayana Buddhists/Confucianists 96%. D=RCC. M=FMB.
3503	1	10	0.37	6	60.00	40.00	B	8.76	47	4	Chinese folk-religionists 96%. D=RCC.
3504	1	10	0.37	6	57.00	43.00	B	8.32	49	4	Confucianists/Buddhists 95%. D=RCC.
3505	0	0	2.67	0	20.70	79.30	A	0.52	446	3	Refugees from Laos. Also in Thailand, China, north Viet Nam. Polytheists 99% (ancestor veneration).
3506	1	10	9.07	4	99.50	0.50	B	197.10	248	7	Refugees after Viet Nam wars. Now a majority are Christians. Animists 35%. D=RCC.
3507	2	10	0.37	7	99.79	0.21	C	452.71	24	10	Expatriates from Italy. Others also live in Ethiopia, Egypt, USA, Australia. Bilingual in French. D=RCC,Eglises Vaudoises d'Italie en France. R=TWR,AWR.
3508	0	10	0.36	4	52.10	47.90	B	0.19	55	3	Traditional religious Jews 90%, secularized Jews 10%, Ashkenazis from Central Europe.
3509	0	10	0.37	8	60.30	39.70	B	0.66	48	3	Increasing due to immigration from North Africa. Mainly Sefardis. M=RCC.
3510	1	9	4.26	5	59.00	41.00	B	2.15	264	4	Refugees from Cambodia. Buddhists(Theravada) 88%, animists 3%, Muslims 2%(Shafi Sunnis). D=RCC. M=UFM,CMA.
3511	1	8	0.37	8	99.75	0.25	C	388.72	26	9	Southern France. Occitan Cluster (10 languages including Provencal) has 12 million speakers (all using French, 85% with French as first language). D=RCC.
3512	1	10	4.05	5	64.00	36.00	B	7.00	238	4	Refugees from Laos. Buddhists 57%, animists 33%, nonreligious 4%. D=RCC.
3513	2	10	0.37	8	99.90	0.10	C	528.88	20	10	From Guadeloupe, Martinique, St Lucia, and Dominica, speaking Lesser Antillean Creole French. D=RCC,Ev Ch of Guadeloupe. M=CBFMS,Worldteam,FMB.
3514	1	10	5.62	4	53.00	47.00	B	7.73	327	4	Immigrants from Algeria. Muslims 96%(Maliki Sunnis). D=RCC. M=CSI.
3515	1	9	0.37	8	99.80	0.20	C	408.80	27	10	Persons originally from Liguria (Italy). Bonifacio, Corsica; also Monaco and northwestern Italy. D=RCC.
3516	2	10	0.37	6	99.70	0.30	C	324.48	30	9	In many countries. Nomads with network of caravan churches. D=Gypsy Evangelical Movement,RCC. M=GGMS,SMIE.
3517	1	10	0.37	8	99.88	0.12	C	478.58	26	10	Expatriates from Luxembourg, in commerce, professions, business. D=RCC.
3518	1	10	8.30	4	99.49	0.51	B	193.15	243	7	Black migrant workers from Madagascar. D=Eglise Protestante Malgache de France.
3519	1	10	4.89	4	48.00	52.00	A	3.50	395	4	Immigrants from several West African countries. Muslims 83%(Sunnis, some Ahmadis), Animists 10%. D=RCC. M=CMA.
3520	0	10	6.26	0	56.00	44.00	B	38.83	385	5	Black migrant workers from Guinea Bissau, Senegal, Gambia, Cape Verde. Animists 60%, Muslims 10%.
3521	0	10	3.62	7	46.20	53.80	A	0.33	256	3	White and Black Moor immigrants from Morocco and Mauritania. Muslims 99%(Maliki Sunnis).
3522	3	10	5.62	7	58.40	41.60	B	0.85	297	3	From Morocco; also in Belgium, Netherlands, Germany. Muslims 99%(Maliki Sunnis). D=RCC,ICFG,EE. M=UFM,WEC,FMB. R=Network of agencies.
3523	2	10	8.32	4	99.50	0.50	B	213.52	227	8	Labor migrants from Burkina Faso. Muslims 30%(Maliki Sunnis), Animists 10%. D=RCC,AoG.
3524	0	10	0.37	8	99.76	0.24	C	396.68	26	9	Northern France. Peripheral Oil cluster (16 languages). Bilingual; 70% speak French as first language.
3525	0	10	4.44	0	39.10	60.90	A	0.14	451	3	Laborers from Turkey. Factory and construction workers. 4,000 speak Zaza, 1,000 Sorani. Muslims 99%(Shafi Sunnis).
3526	0	10	4.89	5	60.00	40.00	B	4.38	255	4	Refugees from Iran persecutions. Muslims 90%(Ithna-Asharis), Baha'is 7%, some Parsees.
3527	2	10	0.37	6	99.90	0.10	C	535.45	6	10	Refugees from Communist Poland since 1945. D=Mariavite Catholic Ch,RCC.
3528	3	10	0.37	8	99.91	0.09	C	574.62	22	10	Labor migrants from Portugal. High illiteracy. D=RCC,Eglise Evangelique Baptiste,Protestant Ch in Paris. M=AMEN(Peru),CBFMS,FMB.
3529	1	8	0.37	8	99.75	0.25	C	375.03	27	9	Southern Provencal. Traditional mother tongue, extensive literature. Bilingual in French. D=RCC. R=local stations. T=local stations. R=AWR.
3530	1	10	0.37	8	99.75	0.25	C	416.10	25	10	Southeast: Provence, et alia. Mother tongue is French, but 38% bilingual in Provencal. D=RCC.
3531	2	10	7.28	8	99.95	0.05	C	558.26	143	10	Migrant workers from Reunion. D=RCC,Pentecostal Chs.
3532	0	10	2.50	1	38.10	61.90	A	0.13	239	3	Migrant workers from Morocco. Muslims 100%(Maliki Sunnis). M=UFM,CSI.
3533	3	10	0.37	6	99.70	0.30	C	360.25	29	9	Refugees from Romania since 1945. Nonreligious 20%. D=Orthodox Ch(AD-France),EOREO(under ROCOR),EREB.
3534	4	10	0.37	7	99.70	0.30	C	373.03	7	9	Refugees from USSR 1917-1990. Nonreligious 30%. D=Orthodox Ch(AD-France),ROC(PE-Western Europe),ROCOR(D-Western Europe),EER.
3535	1	10	4.16	5	61.00	39.00	B	22.26	248	5	Immigrants from Ivory Coast. Muslims 40%(Sunnis), Animists 30%. D=RCC. M=CMA.
3536	1	10	0.37	6	99.85	0.15	C	477.78	7	10	Migrant workers from Yugoslavia. Muslims 12%(Hanafi Sunnis). D=Serbian Orthodox Ch(P-Belgrade).
3537	0	10	2.92	1	34.10	65.90	A	0.12	299	3	Berber migrant workers from Algeria, Morocco. Muslims 100%(Maliki Sunnis). M=UFM.
3538	2	10	0.37	0	99.75	0.25	C	333.97	31	9	Also in Germany, Austria, Italy, Yugoslavia, Netherlands, Switzerland. D=caravan churches(Gypsy Evangelical Movement),RCC. M=GGMS,AoGUSA,SMIE.
3539	0	10	0.00	0	33.01	66.99	A	0.01	159	2	Diakhanke, Aswanik, Azor, Ouadane. Immigrants from western Mali, Niger. 5,000 live in Marseilles. Muslims 95%(Sunnis). M=RSMT.
3540	2	10	0.37	8	99.95	0.05	C	599.87	20	10	Expatriates, migrant workers for Spain. Strong Catholics. D=RCC,Eglise Espagnole. M=AMEN(Peru). R=AWR.
3541	1	10	0.37	6	99.72	0.28	C	360.03	7	9	Expatriates from Sweden, in commerce, professions. D=Eglise Suedoise Lutherienne.
3542	2	10	9.59	8	99.40	0.60	B	153.30	269	7	Levantines. Muslims 60%(Sunnis,Shias). D=RCC(Maronites),Syrian Orthodox Ch(P-Antioch). M=UFM.
3543	2	10	4.05	4	41.00	59.00	A	4.49	314	4	Refugees from Viet Nam. Most still polytheists 80%, Mahayana Buddists 15%. D=RCC,EEV.
3544	1	10	3.93	0	39.20	60.80	A	0.28	324	3	Saharans from Mali, Niger. Muslims 99%(Sunnis). D=RCC.
3545	2	10	4.33	8	61.30	38.70	B	0.67	225	3	From Tunisia; also in Belgium, Netherlands, Germany. Muslims 99%(Maliki Sunnis). D=RCC,ICFG. M=UFM,WEC,FMB,CSI.
3546	0	10	3.11	8	55.10	44.90	B	0.20	190	3	In industrial cities. Migrant laborers from Turkey: in factories, construction. Muslims 100%(Hanafi Sunnis). M=UFM.
3547	6	10	0.37	8	99.78	0.22	C	438.43	23	10	Expatriates from USA, in commerce, education, professions. D=CJCLdS,SDA,JWs,CCS,ABA,CCNA.
3548	1	10	0.37	6	99.80	0.20	C	435.08	29	10	Refugees from USSR since 1917. D=Ukrainian Orthodox Autocephalic Ch. M=UOCUSA.
3549	2	10	10.08	6	94.00	6.00	B	85.77	319	6	Refugees from Viet Nam, after 1953 to present day. Mahayana Buddhists 53%,Cao Daists 11%. D=RCC,EEV. M=CMA,CBFMS,PI.
3550	5	10	0.37	6	99.70	0.30	C	332.15	30	9	In 25 countries. D=nomadic caravan churches(Gypsy Evangelical Movement),GEC,AoG,RCC,JWs. M=GGMS.AoGUSA,SMIE,IGP.
3551	1	10	0.37	8	99.92	0.08	C	527.20	26	10	French-speaking Belgians. D=RCC.
3552	0	0	2.33	1	20.00	80.00	A	0.73	389	3	Refugees from Cambodia since 1980. Theravada Buddhists 88%, Animists 5%. D=CMA,RCC.
3553	0	0	3.07	4	34.00	66.00	A	2.48	304	4	Refugees from Laos since 1980. Polytheists 98%.
3554	1	10	4.40	4	51.00	49.00	B	3.72	322	4	Migrant laborers from Senegal, Mauritania. Muslims 98%(Maliki Sunnis). D=RCC. M=UFM,FMB.
3555	0	10	0.37		95.00	5.00	C	208.05	11	8	Koreans(HSAUWC), Kongo(EJCSK), Hungarians, Norwegians, Egyptians, Libyans, Zairians, Haitians, Yeniche, Azerbaijanis.
French Guiana											
3556	1	10	2.18	8	99.90	0.10	C	515.74	52	10	From Guadeloupe, Martinique, St Lucia, Dominica, speaking Lesser Antillean Creole French. Afro-Caribbean religionists 10%. D=RCC.
3557	3	9	2.18	0	99.92	0.08	C	463.40	63	10	Most in Guyana, Surinam, and Venezuela. Coastal areas. Animists 8%. D=RCC,AoG,SDA.
3558	2	9	2.11	1	99.80	0.20	C	365.00	62	9	Maroons. Afro-American spiritists(Vodoun,Voodoo,Obeah) 20%. D=RCC,AoG. M=CSSp.
3559	1	10	2.18	8	99.88	0.12	C	517.13	61	10	Mixed-race persons from Brazil. A small minority are Afro-American spiritists(Obeah,Umbanda,Quimbanda,Macumba) 12%. D=RCC. M=FMB.
3560	4	10	2.18	8	99.89	0.11	C	528.14	51	10	Expatriates from Brazil, workers, professionals. D=RCC(D-Cayenne),SDA,AoG,JWs. M=FMB.
3561	1	10	2.18	1	99.90	0.10	C	436.90	60	10	Okanisi, Njuka. English-based creole. Refugees fleeing home base in Surinam. Afro-American spiritists(Vodoun) 10%. D=RCC.
3562	3	9	2.18	1	99.70	0.30	C	304.04	73	9	Caribe, Cariha. Mainly in Venezuela, Surinam, Brazil, Guyana. Coastal areas. Animists 30%. D=RCC,AoG,SDA.
3563	1	9	2.18	1	97.00	3.00	B	177.02	90	7	Hindustani, Aili Gaili (Awadhi/Bhojpuri of India). Bilingual. Agriculturalists. Hindus 40%, Bahai's 10%. D=RCC.
3564	1	9	2.19	7	94.00	6.00	B	120.08	89	7	Surinam Javanese. Migrants and residents from Indonesia. Javanese folk-religionists 40%, Muslims 25%. D=RCC.
3565	1	9	2.13	0	41.00	59.00	A	14.96	185	5	Southern border area. A few in Brazil. Animists 90%. D=RCC.

Continued overleaf

Table 8-2 continued

PEOPLE		POPULATION				IDENTITY CODE		LANGUAGE		CHURCH		MINISTRY						SCRIPTURE	
Ref 1	Ethnic name 2	P% 3	In 1995 4	In 2000 5	In 2025 6	Race 7	Language 8	Autoglossonym 9	S 10	AC 11	Members 12	Jayuh 13-17	d 18	wa 19	xc 20	mc 21	mi 22	Biblioglossonym 23	Pub ss 24-26 27
3566	French	8.00000	11,741	14,505	33,295	CEW21b	51-AABI-d	general français		79.00	11,459	1B.uh	10	9	14	5	2	French	PNB b
3567	Guianese Mulatto	37.93500	55,673	68,781	157,882	NFB69b	51-AACC-h	guyanais		98.34	67,639	1cs..	10	8	12	5	3		pnb b
3568	Guianese White	7.00000	10,273	12,692	29,133	CEW21b	51-AACC-h	guyanais		88.00	11,169	1cs..	10	10	11	5	3		pnb b
3569	Haitian Black	8.00000	11,741	14,505	33,295	NFB69a	51-AACC-b	haitien		96.00	13,925	3As..	10	8	11	5	1	Haitian*	PNB b
3570	Han Chinese	5.10000	7,485	9,247	21,226	MSY42a	79-AAAG-a	literary hakka		27.00	2,497	1A...	9	5	8	5	1	Chinese: Hakka, Wukingfu*	PNB b
3571	Hmong-Lao	1.50000	2,201	2,720	6,243	MSY47a	48-AAAA-b	hmong-njua		58.00	1,577	1A...	10	8	8	5	1	Hmong Njua	PN. b
3572	Jewish	0.06000	88	109	250	CMT35	51-AABI-d	general français		0.00	0	1B.uh	0	3	2	4	1	French	PNB b
3573	Lebanese Arab	1.00000	1,468	1,813	4,162	CMT30	12-AACF-f	syro-palestinian		40.00	725	1Asuh	9	5	7	5	1	Arabic: Lebanese*	Pnb b
3574	Oyampi (Wayapi, Wajapi)	0.45000	660	816	1,873	MIR39e	82-AAAB-a	oyapock		20.40	166	1....	9	5	4	4	1	Wayampi, Oiapoque	... .
3575	Palikur	0.68000	998	1,233	2,830	MIR39a	81-AEAA-a	proper palikúr		60.20	742	0....	10	6	6	4	1	Palikur	PN. .
3576	Saramaccan (Bush Negro)	2.00000	2,935	3,626	8,324	NFB68b	52-ABAG-d	saramacca-tongo		85.00	3,082	1.s..	10	7	11	5	1	Saramaccan	PN. .
3577	Surinamese Creole	6.00000	8,805	10,879	24,971	NFB67b	52-ABAG-c	sranan-tongo		82.00	8,921	4.s..	10	9	7	5	1	Sranan	PN. b
3578	Wayana (Oayana, Guayana)	0.20000	294	363	832	MIR39c	80-AEDA-a	wayâna		9.00	33	0....	7	5	5	4	1	Wajana*	PN. .
3579	other minor peoples	0.35000	514	635	1,457	...				54.90	348		10	7	5	0	0		
	French Polynesia	**100.00000**	**215,213**	**235,061**	**324,439**					**84.54**	**198,724**								
3580	Chinese-Tahitian Creole	0.10000	215	235	324	MSY42a	51-AACC-o	chinese tahitian creole	2	50.00	118	1cs..	10	6	7	5	3		pnb .
3581	Cook Islands Maori	0.62500	1,345	1,469	2,028	MPY55d	39-CAQB-a	rarotonga		94.00	1,381	0....	10	9	12	5	3	Maori: Cook Island*	PNB b
3582	Euronesian	17.00000	36,586	39,960	55,155	MPY53	51-AABI-p	français d'océanie		98.00	39,161	1A.uh	10	8	11	5	2		pnb b
3583	French	11.03500	23,749	25,939	35,802	CEW21b	51-AABI-d	general français	91	87.00	22,567	1B.uh	10	9	14	5	2	French	PNB b
3584	Han Chinese (Hakka)	11.30000	24,319	26,562	36,662	MSY42a	79-AAAG-a	literary hakka		24.60	6,534	1A...	9	5	8	5	2	Chinese: Hakka, Wukingfu*	PNB b
3585	Mangarevan	0.94000	2,023	2,210	3,050	MPY55z	39-CAQL-a	mangareva		83.00	1,834	0....	10	8	11	5	3	Mangareva	P.. b
3586	North Marquesan	2.20700	4,750	5,188	7,160	MPY55c	39-CAQF	north marquesan cluster		85.00	4,410	0....	10	8	11	5	3	Marquesan, North	PN. b
3587	Pitcairner	0.10000	215	235	324	MPY53	52-ABAI-h	pitcairnese		98.00	230	1csuh	10	8	11	5	1		pnb b
3588	Pukapukan	0.62700	1,349	1,474	2,034	MPY55d	39-CANA-a	pukapuka		80.00	1,179	0....	10	8	7	5	3		... b
3589	Rapa	0.28800	620	677	934	MPY55f	39-CAQM-a	rapa		93.10	630	0....	10	8	11	5	3		... b
3590	South Marquesan (Fatuhivan)	1.36400	2,936	3,206	4,425	MPY55c	39-CAQG	south marquesan cluster		84.00	2,693	0....	10	8	11	5	3	Marquesan, South	P.. b
3591	Tahitian	41.04300	88,330	96,476	133,159	MPY55f	39-CAQH-b	vehicular tahiti	81	95.00	91,652	0....	10	10	11	5	3	Tahitian	PNB b
3592	Tuamotuan (Paumotu)	8.47100	18,231	19,912	27,483	MPY55h	39-CAQI	pa'umotu cluster		84.00	16,726	0....	10	9	11	5	3		... b
3593	Tubuaian	4.70000	10,115	11,048	15,249	MPY55z	39-CAQK-a	tubuai-rurutu		84.00	9,280	0....	10	9	11	5	3		... b
3594	other minor peoples	0.20000	430	470	649	...				70.00	329		10	7	7	5	0		
	Gabon	**100.00000**	**1,077,275**	**1,226,127**	**1,981,233**					**88.55**	**1,085,760**								
3595	Bakwele (Bekwil)	0.20000	2,155	2,452	3,962	NAB57c	99-AUDH-a	be-kwil		92.00	2,256	0....	10	8	11	4	2	Bekwel	... .
3596	Barama	0.51200	5,516	6,278	10,144	NAB57k	99-AURA-a	yi-barama		80.00	5,022	0.s..	10	8	6	4	1		pnb .
3597	Bayaka (Binga) Pygmy	0.27300	2,941	3,347	5,409	BYG12	93-ADDA-a	baka		10.00	335	0....	8	7	6	3	1		... .
3598	Benga	0.22000	2,370	2,697	4,359	NAB57k	99-AUAE-a	benga		97.00	2,617	0....	10	9	12	5	1	Benga	PNB .
3599	Bhubhi (Pove)	0.42700	4,600	5,236	8,460	NAB57k	99-APBE-a	i-bubi		80.00	4,188	0....	10	8	6	4	1		... .
3600	British	0.05000	539	613	991	CEW19i	52-ABAC-b	standard-english	7	79.00	484	3Bsuh	10	9	13	5	3		PNB b
3601	Bulu-Ewondo Creole	0.01000	108	123	198	NAB57c	99-AUCC-n	bulu	2	95.00	116	1....	10	8	12	5	3	Bulu	PNB b
3602	Duma (Aduma)	0.80000	8,618	9,809	15,850	NAB57k	99-AURB-a	li-duma		97.00	9,515	0cs..	10	9	12	4	2		pn. .
3603	Eshira (Chira, Sira)	3.21000	34,581	39,359	63,598	NAB57k	99-AURA-b	ghi-sira		97.00	38,178	0.s..	10	9	11	4	2	Yichira*	Pnb n
3604	Fang (Ogowe)	23.61000	254,345	289,489	467,769	NAB57c	99-AUCC-w	make	56	95.90	277,620	1....	10	10	10	5	3		pnb b
3605	Fang (Pahouin, Pangwe)	5.00000	53,864	61,306	99,062	NAB57c	99-AUCC-v	ntumu		94.00	57,628	1....	10	9	10	5	3		pnb b
3606	Fon	1.00000	10,773	12,261	19,812	NAB59e	96-MAAG-a	standard fon		57.00	6,989	2as..	10	6	7	4	1	Fon*	PNb b
3607	French	6.67000	71,854	81,783	132,148	CEW21b	51-AABI-d	general français	65	92.00	75,240	1B.uh	10	9	13	5	3	French	PNB b
3608	Fulani	0.40000	4,309	4,905	7,925	NAB56c	90-BAAA-n	fula-sokoto		1.94	95	1cs..	6	4	1	1	0	Fulfulde	PNB b
3609	Gun	1.00000	10,773	12,261	19,812	NAB59g	96-MAAG-j	gun		60.00	7,357	1As..	10	7	7	4	2	Gun-alada*	PNB b
3610	Hausa	0.60000	6,464	7,357	11,887	NAB60a	19-HAAB-a	hausa		0.50	37	4Asu.	5	4	2	3	0	Hausa	PNB b
3611	Kande	0.08500	916	1,042	1,684	NAB57a	99-APBC-a	o-kande		90.00	938	0....	10	9	11	4	1		... b
3612	Kaningi (Bakanike)	0.51200	5,516	6,278	10,144	NAB57k	99-AURC-e	le-kaningi		80.00	5,022	0....	10	8	10	4	1		... .
3613	Kota (Mekambo)	2.78000	29,948	34,086	55,078	NAB57c	99-AUEA-c	i-kota		85.00	28,973	0....	10	8	7	5	1	Ikota*	P.. .
3614	Lebanese Arab	0.20000	2,155	2,452	3,962	CMT30	12-AACF-f	syro-palestinian	1	5.00	123	1Asuh	7	3	2	1	0	Arabic: Lebanese*	Pnb b
3615	Lumbu	1.62000	17,452	19,863	32,096	NAB57k	99-AURA-f	i-lumbu		96.00	19,069	0.s..	10	9	11	4	1	Ilumbu*	Pnb .
3616	Mahongwe	0.20000	2,155	2,452	3,962	NAB57k	99-AUEA-d	ma-hongwe		70.00	1,717	0....	10	8	6	4	1		p.. .
3617	Mbaama (Mbamba)	0.72200	7,778	8,853	14,305	NAB57k	99-AURC-c	le-mbaama		95.00	8,410	0....	10	9	11	4	1		... .
3618	Mbahouin (Mbangwe)	0.30000	3,232	3,678	5,944	NAB57k	99-AUDL-a	m-bangwe		90.00	3,311	0....	10	9	11	4	1		... .
3619	Mbede (Mbeti, Mbere)	3.70000	39,859	45,367	73,306	NAB57c	99-AURC-a	li-mbede		85.00	38,562	0....	10	9	7	5	2		... .
3620	Mbwisi (Bwisi)	0.10000	1,077	1,226	1,981	NAB57k	99-AURA-e	i-bwisi		70.00	858	0.s..	10	7	7	4	1		pnb b
3621	Minduumo (Ndumu, Ndumbo)	0.35000	3,770	4,291	6,934	NAB57k	99-AURC-d	le-nduumu		95.00	4,077	0....	10	9	11	4	2		... .
3622	Miyangho (Yongho)	0.42700	4,600	5,236	8,460	NAB57c	93-ADCC-a	yango		70.00	3,665	0....	10	8	7	5	1		... b
3623	Myene (Galwa)	0.24400	2,629	2,992	4,834	NAB57k	99-APAB-a	o-myene		96.00	2,872	0....	10	9	11	4	3	Omyene*	PNB b
3624	Myene (Omyene, Mpongwe)	4.05300	43,662	49,695	80,299	NAB57k	99-APAA-a	m-pongwe		97.00	48,204	0....	10	9	11	5	2	Omyene: Mpongwe	PN. .
3625	Ndasa (Andasa)	0.20000	2,155	2,452	3,962	NAB57k	99-AUEC-a	ndasa		80.00	1,962	0....	10	8	7	4	1		... .
3626	Ngom (Angom, Bangomo)	0.67000	7,218	8,215	13,274	NAB57k	99-AUDJ	ungom cluster		85.00	6,983	0....	10	9	11	4	2	Ngom	P.. .
3627	Northern Teke	1.28000	13,789	15,694	25,360	NAB57k	99-AURD-a	ka-tege		80.00	12,556	0....	10	8	7	4	1		p.. .
3628	Nzebi (Ndjabi, Bandzabi)	8.89000	95,770	109,003	176,132	NAB57k	99-AURB-c	yi-nzebi		97.00	105,733	0cs..	10	9	11	5	3	Yinzebi*	PN. .
3629	Pinji (Apindje)	0.42700	4,600	5,236	8,460	NAB57k	99-APBB-a	a-pinji		95.00	4,974	0....	10	9	11	4	1		... n
3630	Punu (Puno)	10.22000	110,098	125,310	202,482	NAB57k	99-AURA-d	yi-punu		99.00	124,057	0.s..	10	9	11	5	2	Yipunu*	PNB .
3631	Sake (Asake)	0.20000	2,155	2,452	3,962	NAB57k	99-AUDK-a	a-sake		80.00	1,962	0....	10	8	7	4	1		... .
3632	Sangu (Masangu, Shango)	1.95000	21,007	23,909	38,634	NAB57k	99-AURA-c	yi-sangu		97.00	23,192	0.s..	10	9	11	5	1	Yisangou*	Pnb .
3633	Seki (Sekiyani, Bulu)	0.30000	3,232	3,678	5,944	NAB57c	99-AOAA-a	sekya-ni		90.00	3,311	0....	10	9	11	4	1		... .
3634	Sighu (Mississiou)	0.08500	916	1,042	1,684	NAB57k	99-AUEB-b	le-sighu		80.00	834	0....	10	8	11	4	1		p.. .
3635	Simba	0.25600	2,758	3,139	5,072	NAB57k	99-AURL-de	himba		80.00	2,511	1csu	10	8	7	5	2	otjiDhimba*	Pnb .
3636	Tsangi (Tsaangi)	0.68000	7,325	8,338	13,472	NAB57c	99-AURB-e	i-caangi		80.00	6,670	0cs..	10	8	7	4	1	Tsaangi	pn. .
3637	Tsogo (Mitsogo)	2.64500	28,494	32,431	52,404	NAB57k	99-APBD-a	ge-tsogo		96.00	31,134	0..u.	10	9	11	5	1	Ghetsogo*	PN. .
3638	Vili (Fiote)	0.30000	3,232	3,678	5,944	NAB57b	99-AURB-d	i-vili		90.00	3,311	0As..	10	9	11	4	1		pn. b
3639	Vumbu	0.20000	2,155	2,452	3,962	NAB57k	99-AURA	shira-punu cluster		95.00	2,330	0.s..	10	9	12	5	1		PNB b
3640	Wandji	0.85200	9,178	10,447	16,880	NAB57c	99-AURB-b	wandji		85.00	8,880	0cs..	10	9	11	4	2		pn. n
3641	Western Kele (Akele)	0.75000	8,080	9,196	14,859	NAB57c	99-AUEA-a	a-kele		93.00	8,552	0....	10	9	10	4	1	Dikele*	P.. p
3642	Western Teke (Tsaayi)	2.73000	29,410	33,473	54,088	NAB57k	99-AURD-f	ge-tsaayi		89.00	29,791	0....	10	8	10	4	2	Teke, Western	P.. .
3643	Wolof	0.50000	5,386	6,131	9,906	NAB56c	90-AAAA-a	vehicular wolof		10.00	613	4.s..	8	5	5	3	0	Wolof: Senegal	PN. b
3644	Wumbvu	1.49000	16,051	18,269	29,520	NAB57c	99-AUEB-a	wumvu		85.00	15,529	0....	10	8	11	4	1		... .
3645	other minor peoples	6.10000	65,714	74,794	120,855	...				50.00	37,397		10	7	7	4	3		
	Gambia	**100.00000**	**1,110,630**	**1,305,363**	**2,150,833**					**3.62**	**47,197**								
3646	Aku (Creole, Krio)	0.76000	8,441	9,921	16,346	NAN58	52-ABAH-a	aku	4	60.00	5,952	1.s.h	10	9	8	5	3		pn. b
3647	Balanta (Brassa)	2.00000	22,213	26,107	43,017	NAB56c	90-GABA	north balanta cluster		15.00	3,916	0....	8	5	7	4	1	Frase*	P.. n
3648	Bambara (Bamanakan)	0.47500	5,275	6,200	10,216	NAB63a	00-AAAB-a	bamanan-kan		0.40	25	4As..	5	5	2	4	1	Bambara	PNB b
3649	Bassari	0.00800	89	104	172	NAB56c	90-JAAA-a	o-ni-yan		15.00	16	0....	8	5	6	4	1	Basari	PN. .
3650	Bayot (Felup, Fulup)	0.05000	555	653	1,075	NAB56c	90-EAAA-a	bayot		8.00	52	0....	7	5	6	3	1		... n
3651	British	0.10000	1,111	1,305	2,151	CEW19i	52-ABAC-b	standard-english	60	79.00	1,031	3Bsuh	10	9	13	5	1		PNB b
3652	Diola (Jola, Felupe)	4.33600	48,157	56,601	93,260	NAB56c	90-DAAA-a	proper foonyi		8.00	4,528	4....	7	5	6	4	3	Diola*	P.. b
3653	Eurafrican Creole	0.10000	1,111	1,305	2,151	NAN58	52-ABAH-a	aku	15	60.00	783	1.s.h	10	8	8	5	3		pn. b
3654	French	0.05000	555	653	1,075	CEW21b	51-AABI-d	general français	10	87.00	568	1B.uh	10	9	14	5	1	French	PNB b
3655	Fulakunda	13.57500	150,768	177,203	291,976	NAB56c	90-BAAA-a	haal-pulaar		0.10	177	2As..	5	4	7	3	2	Fula: Pulaar*	PNb n
3656	Gambian Wolof	14.40000	159,931	187,972	309,720	NAB56c	90-AAAA-g	wolof-gambia	75	4.00	7,519	1.s..	6	5	6	5	3	Wolof: Gambia*	Pn. n
3657	Greek	0.02300	255	300	495	CEW20	56-AAAA-c	dhimotiki		90.00	270	2B.uh	10	9	11	5	1	Greek: Modern	PNB b
3658	Hausa	0.50000	5,553	6,527	10,754	NAB60a	19-HAAB-a	hausa	3	1.00	65	4Asu.	6	4	3	3	0	Hausa	PNB b
3659	Igbo (Ibo)	0.30000	3,332	3,916	6,452	NAB59h	98-FAAA-a	standard igbo		70.00	2,741	2..u.	10	9	12	5	3	Igbo	PNB b
3660	Jahanka (Diakhanke)	0.20000	2,221	2,611	4,302	NAB63j	00-BAAA-b	azayr		0.10	3	1....	5	3	3	3	0		... n
3661	Kalanke	0.20000	2,221	2,611	4,302	NAB63h	00-AAAA-d	kalanke-kango		0.01	0	1c...	3	4	4	2	0		pn. .
3662	Karon	0.11300	1,255	1,475	2,430	NAB56c	90-DBAA-a	karoon		5.00	74	0....	7	5	6	3	1		... n
3663	Khasonke (Xasonke)	0.10000	1,111	1,305	2,151	NAB63e	00-AAAA-f	xasonka-xango		0.10	1	1c...	5	3	4	3	0	Kassonke	pn. n
3664	Lebanese Arab	0.20000	2,221	2,611	4,302	CMT30	12-AACF-f	syro-palestinian	4	29.80	778	1Asuh	9	7	3	4	1	Arabic: Lebanese*	Pnb b
3665	Mandinka (Sose)	36.92100	410,056	481,953	794,109	NAB63h	00-AAAA-a	mandinka-kango	69	0.10	482	4a...	5	5	5	3	3	Mandinka	PN. b
3666	Mandyak (Manjaco, Pecixe)	1.59500	17,715	20,821	34,306	NAB56c	90-FAAA-a	proper mandyak		9.00	1,874	0....	7	5	6	4	2	Manjako*	P.. b
3667	Maninka	1.00000	11,106	13,054	21,508	NAB63h	00-AAAA-h	maninka-kan		0.30	39	3a...	5	4	3	3	2	Maninka*	PN. b
3668	Mankanya (Bola)	0.13600	1,510	1,775	2,925	NAB56c	90-FACA-a	mankany		30.00	533	0....	9	5	7	4	1		... n
3669	Maswanka	0.10000	1,111	1,305	2,151	NAB63z	90-KAAA-a	sua		0.10	1	0....	5	4	2	1	1		... n
3670	Moor (Maure)	1.50000	16,659	19,580	32,262	CMT32a	12-AACD-a	hassaaniyya		0.00	0	0a...	0	1	0	1	0		pn. b
3671	Portuguese Creole	1.00000	11,106	13,054	21,508	NAN58	51-AACA-b	guineense		60.00	7,832	4c...	10	9	10	5	1		PNB b
3672	Serere-Sine	2.35300	26,133	30,715	50,609	NAB56c	90-BBAA-a	sine		8.00	2,457	2....	7	5	7	5	2	Seereer*	PN. n
3673	Soninke (Sarakole)	7.30500	81,132	95,357	157,118	NAB63j	00-BAAA-a	proper soninke		0.02	19	3....	3	3	3	1	0	Soninke	... b
3674	Susu (Soso)	0.20000	2,221	2,611	4,302	NAB63k	00-ACAA-a	soso		0.00	0	4....	0	3	4	1	0	Soso*	PN. n
3675	Tukulor (Takarir)	6.66300	74,001	86,976	143,310	NAB56c	90-BAAA-a	haal-pulaar		0.03	26	2As..	3	3	5	3	1	Fula: Pulaar*	Pnb n
3676	Yoruba	0.50000	5,553	6,527	10,754	NAB59n	98-AAAA-a	standard yoruba		25.00	1,632	3asu.	9	9	9	5	3	Yoruba	PNB b
3677	other minor peoples	3.23700	35,951	42,255	69,622	...				9.00	3,803		7	5	5	3	3		
	Georgia	**100.00000**	**5,249,805**	**4,967,561**	**5,178,116**					**60.57**	**3,008,814**								
3678	Abkhazian (Abzhui, Bzyb)	1.77478	93,172	88,163	91,900	CEW17a	44-AABA-a	osmanli		70.00	61,714	1A.u.	10	5	8	1	1	Turkish	PNB b
3679	Armenian	8.09524	424,984	402,136	419,181	CEW14	57-AAAA-b	ashkharik		50.00	201,068	4A.u.	10	7	9	2	1	Armenian: Modern, Eastern	PNB b
3680	Assyrian (Aisor)	0.14678	7,706	7,291	7,600	CEW31	12-AAAA-f	aisor		78.00	5,687	4cs..	10	6	8	2	2	Assyrian Neo-aramaic	PNB b
3681	Avar	0.07832	4,112	3,891	4,056	CEW17b	42-BBAA-a	north avar		0.01	0	1....	3	3	2	0	1	Avar	P.. b

Continued opposite

Table 8-2 continued

EVANGELIZATION								EVANGELISM			ADDITIONAL DESCRIPTIVE DATA
Ref 1	*D* 28	*aC* 29	*CG%* 30	*r* 31	*E* 32	*U* 33	*W* 34	*e* 35	*R* 36	*T* 37	*Locations, civil divisions, literacy, religions, church history, denominations, dioceses, church growth, missions, agencies, ministries, movements* 38
3566	4	10	2.08	8	99.79	0.21	C	444.05	54	10	Massive immigration from France since 1976. Nonreligious 14%. D=RCC,SDA,Eglise Evangelique,JWs. M=CSSp,FMB.
3567	4	10	1.95	8	99.98	0.02	C	589.88	46	10	Maroons. Afro-American spiritists(Vodoun,Voodoo,Obeah)1.5%. D=RCC(D-Cayenne),SDA,EE,JWs. M=CSSp,CMML,Worldteam.
3568	4	10	2.19	8	99.88	0.12	C	501.07	56	10	French born in Guiana. D=RCC(D-Cayenne),EE,SDA,JWs. M=CSSp,CMML,Worldteam.
3569	1	9	2.19	4	99.96	0.04	C	578.16	56	10	Refugees from Haiti. Mostly Catholics. Afro-Caribbean religionists 4%. D=RCC.
3570	1	10	2.18	7	92.00	8.00	B	90.66	84	6	Bilingual. Also related populations in Surinam and Guyana. Chinese folk-religionists/Buddhists 70%. D=RCC.
3571	1	9	5.19	4	99.58	0.42	B	241.33	142	8	Refugees after Viet Nam wars. Recent converts to Christianity. Animists 35%. D=RCC.
3572	0	10	0.00	8	49.00	51.00	A	0.00	0	1.13	Small community of practicing Jews, resident for a number of years. M=RCC.
3573	1	10	4.38	8	99.40	0.60	B	147.46	138	7	From Levant. Muslims 60%(Sunnis,Shias). D=88%RCC(Maronites).
3574	1	9	2.19	0	53.40	46.60	B	39.76	145	5	Southern border area; some in Brazil. Many bilinguals in Patwa. Animists 80%. D=RCC.
3575	1	9	2.18	0	99.20	0.80	C	217.97	88	8	Eastern border area. Half the Palikur live in Brazil. Animists 40%. D=RCC.
3576	2	9	2.18	1	99.85	0.15	C	418.83	59	10	Maroons. Refugees from Surinam. Afro-American spiritists(Vodoun,Voodoo,Obeah) 15%. D=RCC,SDA. M=CSSp.
3577	1	10	2.18	5	99.82	0.18	C	413.03	54	10	Refugees from Surinam strife. Mostly Catholics. Afro-Surinamese religionists 16%. D=RCC.
3578	1	9	2.13	0	44.00	56.00	A	14.45	196	5	Southwest border. Also in Surinam and Brazil. Animists 91%. D=RCC.
3579	0	9	2.19		78.90	21.10	B	158.10	76	7	Guyanese, Guadeloupians, Haitians, St Lucians, many Maroon refugees from Surinam, other islanders.
French Polynesia											
3580	6	10	1.84	1	99.50	0.50	B	182.50	68	7	Mixed-race Chinese/Polynesian persons. China folk-religionists/Buddhists 50%. D=EEPF,RCC,SDA,CJCLdS,JWs,EPP.
3581	4	10	1.87	5	99.94	0.06	C	542.09	41	10	Migrants from Cook Islands; also in New Zealand. 6 dialects. D=CICC,RCC,SDA,CJCLdS.
3582	6	10	1.87	8	99.98	0.02	C	593.78	44	10	Mixed race European-Polynesians. D=RCC,EEPF,CJCLdS,SDA,JWs,RCJCLdS. M=SSCC,FICP.
3583	6	10	1.87	8	99.87	0.13	C	508.08	49	10	Expatriates and settlers; in education, development, commerce, government. D=RCC,EEPF,CJCLdS,SDA,JWs,RCJCLdS. M=SSCC,FICP.
3584	3	10	1.87	7	90.60	9.40	B	81.35	76	6	Many are shifting to Tahitian language. Control over the economy. Buddhists/Chinese folk-religionists 70%, nonreligious 5%. D=RCC,EEPF,EPP. M=SSCC,FICP.
3585	2	8	1.87	0	99.83	0.17	C	393.83	50	9	On Gambier Islands. Agriculturalists, fishermen. 65% understand Tahitian. Animists 10%. D=RCC,EEPF.
3586	3	9	1.87	0	99.85	0.15	C	421.94	48	10	Marquesas Islands. Fishermen, agriculturalists. D=RCC,EEPF,SDA.
3587	1	10	1.87	8	99.98	0.02	C	568.74	46	10	Mixed-race Euronesians, immigrants from Pitcairn Islands. English-based creole. Also in Fiji, Australia, NZ. D=SDA.
3588	3	10	1.86	0	99.80	0.20	C	362.08	53	9	Immigrants from Pukapuka Island, northern Cook Islands; also in New Zealand. Unwritten language. D=RCC,EEPF,SDA.
3589	5	8	1.87	0	99.93	0.07	C	469.28	47	10	2 villages on Rapa Island, Austral Islands; agriculturalists. Second language (church language) Tahitian. Few bilingual in French. D=RCC,EEPF,SDA,CJCLdS,JWs.
3590	3	9	1.87	0	99.84	0.16	C	404.71	50	10	Marquesas Islands, with some in Tahiti. Fishermen, agriculturalists. D=RCC,EEPF,SDA.
3591	6	10	1.66	5	99.95	0.05	C	551.33	37	10	Society Islands. Lingua franca. D=EEPF,RCC(2 Dioceses),CJCLdS,SDA,RCJCLdS,JWs. M=SSCC,FICP,LMS,BM,PEMS,CEVAA.
3592	3	8	1.87	0	99.84	0.16	C	401.64	50	10	On Tuamotu, also Tahiti. 8 dialects. Bilingual in Tahitian. D=RCJCLdS,EEPF,RCC.
3593	4	9	1.86	5	99.84	0.16	C	416.97	48	10	On Austral (Tubuai) Islands. 4 dialects. Bilingual in Tahitian. D=RCC,EEPF,SDA,JWs.
3594	0	9	1.86		99.00	1.00	C	252.94	51	8	Other Polynesian islanders, Micronesians, Melanesians, Europeans.
Gabon											
3595	2	7	5.57	0	99.92	0.08	C	446.61	145	10	Extreme northeast corner, north of Mekambo. Primarily in Congo; also Cameroon. Animists 8%. D=RCC,AICs.
3596	1	7	4.60	1	99.80	0.20	C	356.24	144	9	Ogooue Maritime Province east of Omboue, Nyanga Province west of Moabi. Animists 20%. D=RCC.
3597	1	6	3.57	0	39.00	61.00	A	14.23	328	5	Forest pygmies dispersed in small groups. Also in Cameroon, CAR, Sudan. Animists 90%. D=RCC. M=CMA.
3598	1	7	2.39	0	99.97	0.03	C	523.99	78	10	North of Libreville. Also in Equatorial Guinea. Christians since 1850. D=RCC.
3599	1	7	6.22	0	99.80	0.20	C	332.88	193	9	Ogooue-Lolo Province west of Koulamoutou. Animists 20%. D=RCC. M=CMA.
3600	3	10	2.24	8	99.79	0.21	C	446.94	60	10	Expatriates from Britain, in education, development, commerce. D=EEG,RCC,JWs.
3601	3	10	3.01	4	99.95	0.05	C	554.80	77	10	Mixed-race and detribalized persons. Urban areas. D=RCC,EEG,EESG.
3602	2	7	7.10	1	99.97	0.03	C	513.37	168	10	Upper Ogooue Province, Franceville area near Lastourville. Few animists left. D=RCC,AICs.
3603	3	7	4.35	2	99.97	0.03	C	534.61	112	10	Ngounie Province, west of Mouila. Bilingual in Yipunu. Malumbi(ancestor veneration) widespread. D=RCC(D-Mouila),EESG,AICs. M=CMA,CSSp.
3604	3	7	3.49	2	99.96	0.04	C	531.70	89	10	Animists 3%: Bekon(ancestor veneration) widespread. Bwiti syncretistic movement strong. D=RCC(M-Libreville),EEG,AICs. M=PEMS,SDB,APM.
3605	4	7	3.37	2	99.94	0.06	C	514.65	88	10	Northwest, Estuary, Woleu-Ntem Provinces. Bwiti(Church of the Initiates) strong. D=RCC(M-Libreville,D-Oyem),EEG,EEP,AICs. M=SDB,CSSp,MFSP,APM,PEMS.
3606	1	10	6.77	4	99.57	0.43	B	241.33	202	8	Dahomean labor migrants from Benin. Animists/fetishists 20%, Muslims10%. D=RCC.
3607	3	10	3.35	8	99.92	0.08	C	560.78	71	10	Administrators, government, educators, commerce from France. Language of formal education. D=RCC(M-Libreville),EEG,JWs. M=SDB,CSSp,PEMS.
3608	0	10	4.66	4	43.94	56.06	A	3.11	390	4	Traders, nomads, from Nigeria and West Africa. Muslims 98%(Maliki Sunnis).
3609	2	10	6.82	4	99.60	0.40	C	271.56	190	8	Dahomean labor migrants from Benin. Animists 5%, Muslims 15%. D=AICs,RCC.
3610	0	10	3.68	5	51.50	48.50	B	0.94	260	3	Traders from Niger. Muslims 99%(Maliki Sunnis).
3611	1	7	4.65	0	99.90	0.10	C	430.33	135	10	Ogooue-Ivindo Province, west of Booue. Language nearly extinct. D=RCC.
3612	1	7	6.42	0	99.80	0.20	C	344.56	191	9	Upper Ogooue Province south of Franceville. D=RCC. M=CMA.
3613	3	7	8.30	2	99.85	0.15	C	394.01	211	9	Large area in Ogooue-Iwindo Province; also in Congo. Animists 5%. Fetishism still very strong. D=RCC,EEG,AICs. M=PEMS.
3614	0	10	2.54	8	53.00	47.00	B	9.67	168	4	Traders, from Middle East/Levant countries. Muslims 95%(Sunnis).
3615	2	7	7.85	1	99.96	0.04	C	508.08	182	10	Nyanga Province, southwest coast and Congo border; also in Congo. D=RCC,AICs. M=Swedish Free Mission.
3616	1	7	5.28	1	99.70	0.30	C	270.83	183	8	Northeast corner, Mekambo area. Close to Kota. Animists 30%. D=RCC.
3617	2	7	6.97	0	99.95	0.05	C	468.11	178	10	Upper Ogooue Province, south of Okondja. Also in Congo. A few animists. D=RCC,AICs. M=CMA.
3618	1	7	5.97	0	99.90	0.10	C	423.76	165	10	Upper Ogooue Province, south and west of Franceville. Also in Congo. D=RCC.
3619	2	7	8.61	0	99.85	0.15	C	384.71	223	9	Okondja area, Upper Ogooue Province. Also in Congo. D=RCC,AICs.
3620	1	7	4.55	1	99.70	0.30	C	286.16	155	8	Far south, Nyanga Province on border with Congo. Also in Congo. Animists 30%. D=RCC.
3621	2	7	6.19	0	99.95	0.05	C	471.58	161	10	Franceville area of Upper Ogooue Province; also in Congo. D=RCC,AICs.
3622	1	7	6.08	0	99.70	0.30	C	270.83	195	8	Haute Ogooue around Mamidi and Bakoumba. Animists 10%. D=RCC. M=CMA.
3623	2	7	2.52	0	99.96	0.04	C	529.10	78	10	Lambarene area and westward. Being submerged by Fang. Few animists. D=RCC,EEG. M=CMA,PEMS,APM.
3624	5	7	3.06	2	99.97	0.03	C	520.45	91	10	Ogooue-Maritime, Middle Ogooue Provinces. Many dialects. D=RCC,EEG,EJCSK,JWs,AICs. M=PEMS,APM(PCUSA).
3625	1	7	5.42	0	99.80	0.20	C	335.80	172	9	Ogooue Province, south of Franceville. Also in Congo. Animists 20%. D=RCC. M=CMA.
3626	2	7	6.77	0	99.85	0.15	C	394.01	185	9	Extreme northeast around Mekambo, and in Ogooue-Lolo Province, Koulamoutou area. Also in Congo. Close to Kele. D=RCC,AICs.
3627	1	7	7.40	0	99.80	0.20	C	341.64	215	9	East of Franceville in Upper Ogooue Province. Mainly in Congo. D=RCC. M=CMA.
3628	3	7	9.71	2	99.97	0.03	C	531.07	210	10	Ogooue-Lolo and Ngounie Provinces, west of Franceville. Also in Congo. Animists 5%. D=RCC(D-Mouila),EESG,AICs. M=CSSp,SDB,CMA.
3629	1	7	6.41	0	99.95	0.05	C	471.58	165	10	Ngounie Province, east of Mouila. Bilingual in Getsogho. D=RCC.
3630	3	7	5.53	2	99.99	0.01	C	563.70	129	10	Nyanga and Ngounie Provinces, Tchibanga and Ndende areas. Also in Congo. D=RCC(D-Mouila),EESG,AICs. M=CSSp,CMA.
3631	1	7	5.42	0	99.80	0.20	C	335.80	172	9	Center, Ogooue-Iwindo Province, Booue area. Animists 20%. D=RCC.
3632	3	7	8.06	2	99.97	0.03	C	527.53	181	10	Ngounie Province, Mimongo-Mbigou area. Few animists left. D=RCC,EESG,AICs. M=CMA.
3633	1	7	3.03	0	99.90	0.10	C	423.76	96	10	Northwest coast around Cocobeach. Animists 10%. D=RCC.
3634	1	7	4.52	1	99.80	0.20	C	350.40	144	9	Ogooue-Lolo Province, Koulamoutou-Lastourville area. Animists 20%. D=RCC.
3635	2	7	5.68	3	99.80	0.20	C	332.88	180	9	Ogoue-Lolo Province, between Sindare and Mimongo. Animists 20%. D=RCC,EESG.
3636	3	7	6.72	1	99.80	0.20	C	359.16	182	9	Upper Ogooue Province, west and southwest of Franceville. Also in Congo. D=EEG,RCC,AICs. M=CMA.
3637	2	7	8.38	2	99.96	0.04	C	501.07	195	10	Ngounie Province, north and east of Mouila. D=EESG,AICs. Very few animists left. M=CMA.
3638	2	8	5.97	5	99.90	0.10	C	486.18	138	10	Extreme south, on coast. Mainly in Congo. Dialect of Kikongo. D=RCC,AICs. M=CMA.
3639	1	8	5.60	2	99.95	0.05	C	468.11	150	10	Yetsou area, west of Mouila. Related to Yipunu. Animists 5%. D=RCC.
3640	2	7	7.02	1	99.85	0.15	C	415.73	174	10	Along southern border with Congo. Related to Nzebi. Some animists, 5%. D=RCC,Baptist Ch,AICs
3641	3	7	4.28	2	99.93	0.07	C	465.04	115	10	Scattered groups in and near Middle Ogooue Province. Close to Ngom. Mabambe (ancestor veneration) widespread. D=RCC,EEG,AICs. M=PEMS.
3642	2	7	8.33	0	99.89	0.11	C	425.55	212	10	Upper Ogooue Province, south of Franceville. Majority in Congo. D=RCC,AICs.
3643	0	10	4.20	4	56.00	44.00	B	20.44	284	5	Traders from Senegal. Muslims 90%(Maliki Sunnis).
3644	1	7	7.62	0	99.85	0.15	C	387.81	199	9	Ngounie Province, east of Lebamba. Also in Congo. Animists 5%. D=RCC. M=CMA.
3645	0	10	8.57		86.00	14.00	B	156.95	273	7	Koreans (M=PCK-Tonghap), Africans from large variety of countries, tribes and areas.
Gambia											
3646	6	10	0.71	8	99.60	0.40	C	262.80	41	8	Descendants of freed slaves. D=MCG,Anglican Ch(D-Gambia & Rio Pongas),RCC,ECG,AICs. M=MMS,UMC,WEC.
3647	3	6	6.15	0	51.00	49.00	B	27.92	416	5	Mainly in Guinea Bissau, also Guinea, Senegal. Bilingual in Mandinka. Animists 60%, Muslims 25%. D=RCC,ECG,Protestants. M=WEC.
3648	3	9	3.27	4	53.40	46.60	B	0.78	266	3	Workers from Mali. Muslims 80%(Sunnis), animists 14%. D=RCC,AoG,ECG. M=CSSp.
3649	1	6	2.81	0	48.00	52.00	A	26.28	252	5	Mainly in Guinea, Senegal, Guinea Bissau. Animists 80%, Muslims 5%. D=RCC. M=CSSp.
3650	1	6	4.03	0	37.00	63.00	A	10.80	417	5	Also in Senegal and Guinea Bissau. Animists 80%, Muslims 10%. D=RCC.
3651	2	10	2.53	8	99.79	0.21	C	438.29	66	10	Expatriates in education, government. D=Anglican Ch(D-Gambia & Rio Pongas),MCG. M=MMS.
3652	2	6	3.58	0	48.00	52.00	A	14.01	296	5	Also in Senegal, Guinea Bissau. Muslims 72%(Maliki Sunnis), Baha'is 10%(expanding), animists 10%. D=RCC,ECG. M=CSSp,WEC,CMF(Nigeria),FMB.
3653	4	10	3.42	8	99.60	0.40	C	260.61	104	8	Mixed-race persons. Largely in urban areas. Animists 30%, nonreligious 5%, Muslims 5%. D=RCC,MCG,ECG,AC.
3654	1	10	2.64	8	99.87	0.13	C	495.37	64	10	Expatriates in education, commerce. Nonreligious 13%. D=RCC(D-Banjul). M=CSSp.
3655	2	6	2.92	4	48.10	51.90	A	0.17	257	3	Mainly in Senegal, Guinea, Guinea Bissau. Muslims 98%(Maliki Sunnis), animists 2%. D=RCC,ECG. M=WEC,FMB.
3656	3	8	6.85	1	47.00	53.00	A	6.86	493	4	Muslims 94%(Maliki Sunnis: 60% Tijaniyya, 28% Muridiyya), animists 1%. D=RCC,MCG,ECG. M=MMS,Wesleyan Methodists,CSSp,CMF(Nigeria),WEC,FMB.
3657	1	9	2.64	7	99.90	0.10	C	509.17	64	10	Residents from Greece: traders, commerce. Mostly in Banjul. D=Greek Orthodox Ch(P Alexandria).
3658	0	6	4.26	5	49.00	51.00	A	1.78	305	4	Traders from Niger, Nigeria. Muslims 99%(Maliki Sunnis).
3659	3	9	5.77	4	99.70	0.30	C	342.37	146	9	Migrant workers from Nigeria. D=RCC,Anglican Ch/CPWA,AICs.
3660	0	4	1.10	0	21.10	78.90	A	0.07	391	2	Related to Mandinka. Also in Senegal, Guinea Bissau. Muslims 100%(Maliki Sunnis).
3661	0	5	0.00	1	22.01	77.99	A	0.00	0	1.10	Part of Manding family. Close to Mandinka. Muslims 95%(Maliki Sunnis), Animists 5%.
3662	1	6	4.40	0	34.00	66.00	A	6.20	484	4	Majority live in Senegal. Related to, but distinct from, Diola. Muslims 80%, Animists 15%. D=RCC.
3663	0	5	0.00	1	28.10	71.90	A	0.10	186	3	Mainly in Mali and Senegal. Muslims 95%(Maliki Sunnis), animists 5%.
3664	1	8	2.42	8	82.80	17.20	B	90.06	103	6	Traders from Levant. Muslims 70%. D=RCC(all Maronites).
3665	4	5	3.95	4	43.10	56.90	A	0.15	380	3	Also in Senegal, Sierra Leone, Guinea Bissau. Muslims 89%(Maliki Sunnis, with Ahmadis/Qadianis since 1960),animists 10%. D=RCC,ECG,Church of Christ.
3666	2	6	2.90	0	43.00	57.00	A	14.12	287	5	Mainly in Guinea Bissau and Senegal. Animists 86%, Muslims 5%. D=Methodist Ch in Gambia,ECG. M=MMS,WEC.
3667	0	6	3.73	5	38.30	61.70	A	0.41	412	3	From Senegal, Guinea. Muslims 90%(Maliki Sunnis,Qadianis), animists 10%. M=WEC,FMB.
3668	2	6	4.06	0	64.00	36.00	B	70.08	242	6	Majority live in Guinea Bissau; some in Senegal. Animists 70%. D=RCC,ECG. M=WEC.
3669	1	4	0.00	0	19.10	80.90	A	0.07	273	2	Mainly in Guinea Bissau. 'Mandinkanized Balanta'. Muslims 99%(Maliki Sunnis). D=ECG. M=WEC.
3670	0	4	0.00	7	25.00	75.00	A	0.00	0	1.08	Black Moors, White Moors. Mainly in Mauretania, Senegal, Morocco. Muslims 100%(Maliki Sunnis).
3671	1	7	3.44	8	99.60	0.40	C	271.56	100	8	Portuguese-based creole; also in Guinea Bissau, Senegal, Cape Verde. Refugees. D=RCC(D-Banjul).
3672	4	6	5.66	0	50.00	50.00	B	14.60	398	5	Mainly in Senegal. Muslims 78%, animists 14%. D=RCC,Lutherans,AoG,ECG. M=CSSp,WEC.
3673	0	6	2.99	0	21.02	78.98	A	0.01	639	2	Serahuli. Mainly in Mali, Burkina Faso, Senegal; also Mauritania, Guinea Bissau, Ivory Coast, Niger. Muslims 100%(Sunnis, most in Sufi Tijaniyya or Hamali sect).
3674	0	5	0.00	4	27.00	73.00	A	0.00	0	1.09	Immigrants, laborers from Guinea. Muslims 97%(Maliki Sunnis).
3675	0	6	3.31	4	40.03	59.97	A	0.04	336	2	Futankobe. Mainly in Senegal, Mauritania, Guinea, Burkina Faso, Nigeria, Mali. Muslims 100%(Sunnis, with Sufi Tijaniyya). M=WEC.
3676	1	8	4.40	5	89.00	11.00	B	81.21	178	6	Workers from Nigeria. Muslims 75%(Maliki Sunnis). D=Yoruba AICs. M=RCC,AC,MCG,AICs.
3677	0	7	6.12		36.00	64.00	A	11.82	466	5	Koreans (M=PCK-Haptong),Ashanti, Mori, Senegalese Wolof, Papel. Muslims 86%.
Georgia											
3678	2	9	0.82	8	99.70	0.30	C	339.81	37	9	Black Sea coast, Abkhazia (53% Georgians); 1993 civil war. Also in Turkey. Muslims 23%(Sunnis); most to Turkey in1860s. D=Georgian Orth Ch(D-Sukhumi).
3679	1	8	0.06	6	99.50	0.50	B	208.05	16	8	Gregorians. Based in Armenia. Nonreligious 30%. D=Armenian Apostolic Ch.
3680	2	10	1.06	5	99.78	0.22	C	401.42	34	10	Eastern-Syriac-speaking Assyrians in Armenia and Georgia; also 11 other countries. D=Ancient Ch of the East(P-Tehran),ROC.
3681	0	8	0.00	0	20.01	79.99	A	0.00	0	1.07	Mainly in Dagestan (Russia). Muslims 100%(Shafi Sunnis). M=IBT.

Continued overleaf

Table 8-2 continued

PEOPLE		POPULATION				IDENTITY CODE		LANGUAGE		CHURCH		MINISTRY						SCRIPTURE		
Ref 1	*Ethnic name* 2	*P%* 3	*In 1995* 4	*In 2000* 5	*In 2025* 6	*Race* 7	*Language* 8	*Autoglossonym* 9	*S* 10	*AC* 11	*Members* 12	*Jayuh* 13-17	*d* 18	*wa* 19	*xc* 20	*mc* 21	*mi* 22	*Biblioglossonym* 23	*Pub* 24-26	*ss* 27
3682	Azerbaijani (Azeri Turk)	5.69459	298,955	282,882	294,872	MSY41a	44-AABA-fa	north azeri		0.00	0	2c.u.	0	3	3	0	3	Azerbaijani*	PNB	b
3683	Batsi (Tsova-Tush, Bac)	0.06500	3,412	3,229	3,366	CEW17d	42-BABA-a	bats		0.06	2	0....	4	1	3	0	0		...	.
3684	Bulgarian	0.01242	652	617	643	CEW22b	53-AAAH-b	bulgarski		72.00	444	2A.uh	10	6	8	1	1	Bulgarian	PNB	b
3685	Byelorussian	0.15915	8,355	7,906	8,241	CEW22c	53-AAAE-c	bielorusskiy		70.00	5,534	3A.uh	10	8	8	3	3	Byelorussian*	PNB	b
3686	Chechen (Shishan, Kokhchi)	0.01129	593	561	585	CEW17d	42-BAAA-b	chechen		0.00	0	0....	0	3	2	0	1	Chechen	P..	b
3687	Estonian	0.04288	2,251	2,130	2,220	MSW51a	41-AAAC-b	eesti		75.00	1,598	4A.u.	10	8	8	2	2	Estonian: Tallinn	PNB	b
3688	Georgian (Gruzin, Adzhar)	57.86120	3,037,600	2,874,290	2,996,120	CEW17c	42-CABB-a	kharthuli		77.00	2,213,204	2A.u.	10	6	9	2	1	Georgian	PNB	b
3689	Georgian Jew	0.26503	13,914	13,166	13,724	CMT35	42-CABB-c	judeo-georgian		0.05	7	1A.u.	4	2	3	0	0		pnb	b
3690	German	0.02863	1,503	1,422	1,482	CEW19m	52-ABCE-a	standard hoch-deutsch		80.00	1,138	2B.uh	10	8	9	3	2	German*	PNB	b
3691	Greek (Urum, Urumy)	1.85755	97,518	92,275	96,186	CEW20	44-AABA-a	osmanli		90.00	83,047	1A.u.	10	8	11	2	2	Turkish	PNB	b
3692	Gypsy	0.03230	1,696	1,605	1,673	CNN25f	59-ACBA-a	vlach-romani		20.00	321	1a...	9	4	7	0	1	Romani: Finnish*	PN.	b
3693	Ingiloy	0.15830	8,310	7,864	8,197	CEW17c	42-CABB-ae	ingilo		10.00	786	1c.u.	8	4	4	1	1		pnb	b
3694	Jewish	0.19267	10,115	9,571	9,977	CMT35	52-ABCH	yiddish cluster		0.00	0	0B..h	0	3	6	0	0		PNB	b
3695	Kazakh	0.04872	2,558	2,420	2,523	MSY41e	44-AABC-c	kazakh		0.00	0	4A.u.	0	3	3	0	1	Kazakh	PN.	b
3696	Laz	0.03756	1,972	1,866	1,945	CEW17c	42-CAAB-b	east laz		1.00	19	0....	6	4	6	1	1		...	b
3697	Lezgian	0.06700	3,517	3,328	3,469	CEW17b	42-BCAC	south lezgin cluster		0.00	0	0....	0	4	0	0	1		P..	b
3698	Mingrelian	9.09100	477,260	451,601	470,743	CEW17c	42-CAAA-a	megrel		1.00	4,516	0....	6	4	6	1	1		...	b
3699	Moldavian	0.05263	2,763	2,614	2,725	CEW21f	51-AADC-ab	standard moldavia		82.00	2,144	1A.u.	10	7	11	2	1		pnb	b
3700	Northern Kurd	0.61714	32,399	30,657	31,956	CNT24c	58-AAAA-a	kurmanji		0.06	18	3c...	4	3	3	0	0	Kurdish: Kurmanji*	PN.	b
3701	Ossetian (Ossete, Iron)	3.03757	159,467	150,893	157,289	CNT24e	58-ABBA	oseti cluster		55.00	82,991	2....	10	5	8	1	1	Ossete*	PN.	b
3702	Polish	0.03729	1,958	1,852	1,931	CEW22i	53-AAAC-c	polski		91.00	1,686	2A.uh	10	8	11	2	3	Polish	PNB	b
3703	Pontic	2.20000	115,496	109,286	113,919	CEW20	56-AAAA-j	pontiki		90.00	98,358	1c.uh	10	8	10	0	0		pnb	b
3704	Russian	6.31702	331,631	313,802	327,103	CEW22j	53-AAAE-d	russkiy	84	60.00	188,281	4B.uh	10	8	8	3	3	Russian	PNB	b
3705	Svanetian (Mushwan)	0.76611	40,219	38,057	39,670	CEW17c	42-CBAA-a	svanuri		60.00	22,834	0....	10	6	8	1	1		...	b
3706	Tajik	0.02209	1,160	1,097	1,144	CNT24g	58-AACC-j	tajiki		0.00	0	2asu.	0	3	3	0	1	Tajik*	PNB	b
3707	Tatar	0.07589	3,984	3,770	3,930	MSY41h	44-AABB-e	tatar		1.50	57	2c.u.	6	4	8	0	1	Tatar: Kazan	Pn.	b
3708	Turkish	0.05696	2,990	2,830	2,949	MSY41j	44-AABA-a	osmanli		0.00	0	1A.u.	0	3	2	0	0	Turkish	PNB	b
3709	Udin (Udi, Alban)	0.00172	90	85	89	CEW17b	42-BCAC-d	udin		90.00	77	0....	10	6	11	2	1	Udin	P..	b
3710	Ukrainian	0.97102	50,977	48,236	50,281	CEW22p	53-AAAE-b	ukrainskiy		69.00	33,283	3A.uh	10	8	9	3	3	Ukrainian	PNB	b
3711	Uzbek	0.02415	1,268	1,200	1,251	MSY41l	44-AABD-a	central uzbek		0.00	0	1A.u.	0	3	6	1	1	Uzbek*	PNb	b
3712	other minor peoples	0.10000	5,250	4,968	5,178	...				0.00	0		0	2	6	0	0			
	Germany	**100.00000**	**81,660,965**	**82,220,490**	**80,238,159**					**71.49**	**58,783,225**									
3713	Afghani (Pathan)	0.04000	32,664	32,888	32,095	CNT24a	58-ABDA-a	pashto		1.00	329	1As..	6	6	6	5	0		pnb	b
3714	Albanian	0.04000	32,664	32,888	32,095	CEW13	55-AAAB-a	standard tosk		25.00	8,222	0A...	9	7	8	5	1	Albanian: Tosk*	PNB	b
3715	Amhara	0.00700	5,716	5,755	5,617	CMT34a	12-ACBA-b	general amarinya		91.00	5,237	3Asuh	10	8	10	0	0	Amharic	PNB	b
3716	Arabized Berber	0.10000	81,661	82,220	80,238	CMT32a	12-AACB-b	east maghrebi		0.50	411	2A.uh	5	4	2	3	0	Arabic: Algerian*	PNB	b
3717	Armenian	0.04120	33,644	33,875	33,058	CEW14	57-AAAA-b	ashkharik		90.00	30,487	4A.u.	10	9	13	5	1	Armenian: Modern, Eastern	PNB	b
3718	Austrian	0.30000	244,983	246,661	240,714	CEW19f	52-ABCF-b	donau-bayrisch-t.		90.00	221,995	0B.uh	10	9	13	5	3		pn.	b
3719	Balkan Gypsy (Arliski)	0.00257	2,099	2,113	2,062	CNN25f	59-ACBA-bc	arlija		80.00	1,690	1A...	10	8	6	5	1	Romani: Arlija	Pn.	.
3720	Balkan Gypsy (Dzambazi)	0.00192	1,568	1,579	1,541	CNN25f	59-ACBA-bf	dzambazi		80.00	1,263	1c...	10	7	5	5	1		pn.	b
3721	Basque	0.04000	32,664	32,888	32,095	CEW16	40-AAAA-a	general euskara		94.00	30,915	3....	10	9	14	5	1	Basque	PNB	b
3722	Black African	0.30000	244,983	246,661	240,714	NAB56c	12-AACB-b	east maghrebi		50.00	123,331	2A.uh	10	9	8	5	3	Arabic: Algerian*	PNB	b
3723	Bosniac (Muslmani)	0.35000	285,813	287,772	280,834	CEW22a	53-AAAG-a	standard srpski		0.10	288	1Asuh	5	4	5	5	1	Serbian*	PNB	b
3724	British	0.11000	89,827	90,443	88,262	CEW19i	52-ABAC-b	standard-english	31	79.00	71,450	3Bsuh	10	9	13	5	1		PNB	b
3725	Bulgar	0.00500	4,083	4,111	4,012	CEW22b	53-AAAH-b	bulgarski		78.00	3,207	2A.uh	10	8	8	5	1	Bulgarian	PNB	b
3726	Byelorussian	0.00660	5,390	5,427	5,296	CEW22c	53-AAAE-c	bielorusskiy		70.00	3,799	3A.uh	10	8	8	5	2	Byelorussian*	PNB	b
3727	Catalonian	0.06000	48,997	49,332	48,143	CEW21a	51-AABE-b	català		96.00	47,359	2a..h	10	9	15	5	1	Catalan-valencian-balear	PNB	b
3728	Circassian	0.00257	2,099	2,113	2,062	CEW17a	42-AAAA-a	adyghe		0.01	0	2a...	3	2	2	1	0	Adyghe	PN.	.
3729	Croat	0.40000	326,644	328,882	320,953	CEW22d	53-AAAG-b	standard hrvatski		91.00	299,283	2Asuh	10	8	11	5	1	Croatian	PNB	b
3730	Czech	0.04000	32,664	32,888	32,095	CEW22e	53-AAAD-a	czesky		79.00	25,982	2Asuh	10	9	8	5	2	Czech	PNB	b
3731	Danish (Dane)	0.06319	51,602	51,955	50,702	CEW19g	52-AAAD-c	general dansk		95.00	49,357	2A.uh	10	9	11	5	3	Danish	PNB	b
3732	Dutch	0.20000	163,322	164,441	160,476	CEW19h	52-ABCA-a	algemeen-nederlands	4	76.00	124,975	2Bsuh	10	9	15	5	1	Dutch	PNB	b
3733	Eastern Frisian	0.01390	11,351	11,429	11,153	CEW19l	52-ABBB	east frysk cluster		72.00	8,229	0....	10	9	10	5	2		...	b
3734	Erzgebirgish German	0.42927	350,546	352,948	344,438	CEW19m	52-ABCD-jk	erzgebirgisch-west		65.00	229,416	0A.uh	10	9	11	5	2		...	b
3735	Esperanto	0.00000	0	0	0	CEW21z	51-AAAC-a	proper esperanto		70.00	0	0A...	10	9	7	5	0	Esperanto	PNB	b
3736	Estonian	0.10000	81,661	82,220	80,238	MSW51a	41-AAAC-b	eesti		80.00	65,776	4A.u.	10	9	9	5	2	Estonian: Tallinn	PNB	b
3737	Franconian	6.00000	4,899,658	4,933,229	4,814,290	CEW19m	52-ABCD-j	ostfränkisch-t.		75.00	3,699,922	0A.uh	10	10	10	5	2		...	b
3738	French	0.09130	74,556	75,067	73,257	CEW21b	51-AABI-d	general français	12	87.00	65,309	1B.uh	10	9	14	5	1	French	PNB	b
3739	Galician	0.05000	40,830	41,110	40,119	CEW21d	51-AABA-b	galego		96.00	39,466	1csuh	10	9	15	5	1	Galician	PNB	b
3740	German (High German)	68.91684	56,278,157	56,663,764	55,297,604	CEW19m	52-ABCE-a	standard hoch-deutsch	100	71.40	40,457,927	2B.uh	10	10	14	5	3	German*	PNB	b
3741	German Gypsy	0.50000	408,305	411,102	401,191	CNN25f	52-ABCE-a	standard hoch-deutsch		80.00	328,882	2B.uh	10	8	8	5	2	German*	PNB	b
3742	German Swiss (Alemannic)	0.04120	33,644	33,875	33,058	CEW19m	52-ABCG-a	general schwytzer-tütsch	100	88.00	29,810	0B.uh	10	9	13	5	3	Schwyzerdutsch*	PN.	b
3743	Greek	0.70000	571,627	575,543	561,667	CEW20	56-AAAA-c	dhimotiki	2	95.00	546,766	2B.uh	10	9	10	5	2	Greek: Modern	PNB	b
3744	Han Chinese	0.06000	48,997	49,332	48,143	MSY42a	52-ABCE-a	standard hoch-deutsch		9.00	4,440	2B.uh	7	5	8	5	2	German*	PNB	b
3745	Han Chinese (Cantonese)	0.00300	2,450	2,467	2,407	MSY42a	79-AAAM-a	central yue		10.00	247	3A.uh	8	5	8	5	2	Chinese, Yue	PNB	b
3746	Han Chinese (Mandarin)	0.00200	1,633	1,644	1,605	MSY42a	79-AAAB-ba	kuo-yü	1	7.00	115	2Bsuh	7	5	8	5	1	Chinese: Kuoyu*	PNB	b
3747	Han Chinese (Taiwanese)	0.00200	1,633	1,644	1,605	MSY42a	79-AAAJ-h	quan-zhang-taiwan		8.00	132	1A..h	7	5	8	5	0	Taiwanese	PNB	b
3748	Hungarian	0.08000	65,329	65,776	64,191	MSW51g	41-BAAA-a	general magyar		85.00	55,910	2A.u.	10	9	12	5	3	Hungarian	PNB	b
3749	Italian	1.00000	816,610	822,205	802,382	CEW21e	51-AABQ-c	standard italiano	3	84.00	690,652	2B.uh	10	9	15	5	1	Italian	PNB	b
3750	Japanese	0.03000	24,498	24,666	24,071	MSY45a	45-CAAA-a	koku-go		5.00	1,233	1B.uh	7	5	6	5	2	Japanese	PNB	b
3751	Javanese	0.00300	2,450	2,467	2,407	MSY44g	31-PIAA-g	general jawa		16.00	395	2As.h	8	5	6	5	0	Javanese	PNB	b
3752	Jewish	0.00200	1,633	1,644	1,605	CMT35	52-ABCE-a	standard hoch-deutsch		0.32	5	2B.uh	5	4	5	5	3	German*	PNB	b
3753	Jewish (Judeo-German)	0.06000	48,997	49,332	48,143	CMT35	52-ABCH	yiddish cluster		0.20	99	0B..h	5	4	5	5	3		PNB	b
3754	Korean	0.01900	15,516	15,622	15,245	MSY46	45-AAAA-b	kukö		37.00	5,780	2A...	9	6	9	5	3	Korean	PNB	b
3755	Kurdish (Kurd, Kermanji)	0.66000	538,962	542,655	529,572	CNT24c	58-AAAA-a	kurmanji		0.10	543	3c...	5	4	2	5	3	Kurdish: Kurmanji*	PN.	b
3756	Latvian (Lettish)	0.01120	9,146	9,209	8,987	CEW15a	54-AABA-a	standard latviashu		98.00	9,025	3A.u.	10	9	12	5	1	Latvian	PNB	b
3757	Lithuanian	0.04940	40,341	40,617	39,638	CEW15b	54-AAAA-a	standard lietuvishkai		83.00	33,712	3A.u.	10	9	11	5	2	Lithuanian	PNB	b
3758	Lovari Rom Gypsy	0.00420	3,430	3,453	3,370	CNN25f	59-ACBA-a	vlach-romani		80.00	2,763	1a...	10	8	11	5	1	Romani: Finnish*	PN.	b
3759	Low German (Saxon)	11.30000	9,227,689	9,290,915	9,066,912	CEW19m	52-ABCC	north deutsch cluster	50	91.00	8,454,733	2A.uh	10	9	14	5	2	German: Low*	PNB	b
3760	Luxemburger	0.01800	14,699	14,800	14,443	CEW19o	52-ABCD-b	letzebürgesch-t.		90.00	13,320	0a.uh	10	9	13	5	1	Luxembourgeois	...	b
3761	Mennonite Low German	0.00641	5,234	5,270	5,143	CEW19m	52-ABCC	north deutsch cluster		88.00	4,638	2A.uh	10	9	13	5	2	German: Low*	PNB	b
3762	Moroccan Arab	0.05646	46,106	46,422	45,302	CMT30	12-AACB-a	west maghrebi		1.00	464	1A.uh	6	4	8	4	1		pnb	b
3763	North African Arab	0.18000	146,990	147,997	144,429	CMT30	12-AACB-b	east maghrebi		5.00	7,400	2A.uh	7	5	3	5	2	Arabic: Algerian*	PNB	b
3764	North Indian (Hindi)	0.03129	25,552	25,727	25,107	CNN25g	59-AAFO-e	general hindi		7.00	1,801	3Asuh	7	5	3	5	0		pnb	b
3765	Northern Frisian	0.07664	62,585	63,014	61,495	CEW19l	52-ABBC	northwest frysk cluster		72.00	45,370	0....	10	9	10	5	2	Frisian: Northern*	PNB	b
3766	Northern Sorb (Wend)	0.06400	52,263	52,621	51,352	CEW22o	53-AAAB	sorb cluster		75.00	39,466	0....	10	9	8	5	2		PNB	b
3767	Persian (Irani)	0.12000	97,993	98,665	96,286	CNT24f	58-AACC-c	standard farsi		0.10	99	1Asu.	5	4	6	5	2		PNB	b
3768	Polish (Pole)	0.40000	326,644	328,882	320,953	CEW22i	53-AAAC-c	polski	1	90.00	295,994	2A.uh	10	9	12	5	1	Polish	PNB	b
3769	Portuguese	0.20000	163,322	164,441	160,476	CEW21g	51-AABA-e	general português	1	93.00	152,930	2Bsuh	10	9	15	5	1	Portuguese	PNB	b
3770	Punjabi	0.02000	16,332	16,444	16,048	CNN25n	59-AAFE-c	general panjabi		5.00	822	1Asu.	7	7	7	5	0		PNB	b
3771	Romanian	0.15000	122,491	123,331	120,357	CEW21i	51-AADC-a	limba româneasca		84.00	103,598	3A.u.	10	8	11	5	1	Romanian	PNB	b
3772	Russian	0.62000	506,298	509,767	497,477	CEW22j	53-AAAE-d	russkiy	1	70.00	356,837	4B.uh	10	8	9	5	1	Russian	PNB	b
3773	Russian Jew	0.07500	61,246	61,665	60,179	CMT35	53-AAAE-d	russkiy		1.10	678	4B.uh	6	5	6	0	0	Russian	PNB	b
3774	Serb	0.60000	489,966	493,323	481,429	CEW22l	53-AAAG-a	standard srpski	2	85.00	419,324	1Asuh	10	8	10	5	2	Serbian*	PNB	b
3775	Sinti Gypsy (Manush)	0.04000	32,664	32,888	32,095	CNN25f	59-ACBB-b	sinti		80.00	26,311	0....	10	9	8	5	1	Romani: Sinti, Italian	P..	b
3776	Slovene	0.10000	81,661	82,220	80,238	CEW22n	53-AAAF-a	slovensko		95.00	78,109	1a..h	10	9	11	5	1	Slovenian*	PNB	b
3777	Southern Sorb (Lusatian)	0.25800	210,685	212,129	207,014	CEW22o	53-AAAB-b	hornjo-serbs ina		70.00	148,490	0....	10	9	8	5	2	Sorbian: Upper*	PNB	b
3778	Spaniard	0.50000	408,305	411,102	401,191	CEW21k	51-AABB-c	general español	2	96.00	394,658	2B.uh	10	9	15	5	3	Spanish	PNB	b
3779	Swabian	1.00000	816,610	822,205	802,382	CEW19m	52-ABCF-j	schwäbisch-t.		80.00	657,764	0c.uh	10	10	10	5	0	Swabian	pn.	.
3780	Syrian Aramaic (Eastern)	0.02473	20,195	20,333	19,843	CMT31	12-AAAA-e	sur-oyo		90.00	18,300	4as..	10	9	11	4	3	Syriac	PNB	b
3781	Tamil	0.05000	40,830	41,110	40,119	CNN23c	49-EBEA-b	tamil		25.00	10,278	2Asu.	9	7	9	5	3	Tamil	PNB	b
3782	Tunisian Arab	0.03215	26,254	26,434	25,797	CMT30	12-AACB-b	east maghrebi		0.10	26	2A.uh	5	7	8	0	0	Arabic: Algerian*	PNB	b
3783	Turk	2.70000	2,204,846	2,219,953	2,166,430	MSY41j	44-AABA-a	osmanli	2	0.10	2,220	1A.u.	5	4	6	3	3	Turkish	PNB	b
3784	USA Black	0.05000	40,830	41,110	40,119	NFB68a	52-ABAE-a	talkin-black		84.00	34,533	0B.uh	10	10	11	0	0		pnb	b
3785	USA White	0.11200	91,460	92,087	89,867	CEW19s	52-ABAC-s	general american		78.00	71,828	1Bsuh	10	9	13	5	1	English*	PNB	b
3786	Ukrainian	0.04940	40,341	40,617	39,638	CEW22p	53-AAAE-b	ukrainskiy		80.00	32,494	3A.uh	10	8	8	5	2	Ukrainian	PNB	b
3787	Urdu	0.02146	17,524	17,645	17,219	CNN25r	59-AAFO-d	standard urdu		0.10	18	2Asuh	5	4	7	3	1	Urdu	PNB	b
3788	Vietnamese	0.08000	65,329	65,776	64,191	MSY52b	46-EBAA-ac	general viêt		35.00	23,022	1Asu.	9	8	9	5	1	Vietnamese	PNB	b
3789	Vlach Gypsy (Romany)	0.00610	4,981	5,015	4,895	CNN25f	59-ACBA-a	vlach-romani		80.00	4,012	1a...	10	8	7	4	1	Romani: Finnish*	PN.	b
3790	Yeniche	0.02000	16,332	16,444	16,048	CMT35	52-ABCI	yenish cluster		50.00	8,222	0....	10	7	8	5	2		...	b
3791	other minor peoples	0.10000	81,661	82,220	80,238	...				60.00	49,332		10	7	7	5	0			
	Ghana	**100.00000**	**17,649,225**	**20,212,495**	**36,876,215**					**42.88**	**8,666,968**									
3792	Achode (Atyoti)	0.06448	11,380	13,033	23,778	NAB59a	96-FDFA-a	gi-kyode		4.00	521	0....	6	7	6	2	3	Gikyode	P..	b
3793	Adangme	2.39667	422,994	484,427	883,801	NAB59f	96-LAAC	adangme cluster	5	55.50	268,857	4.s..	10	9	7	5	3	Dangme	PN.	b
3794	Adele (Bedere)	0.05156	9,100	10,422	19,013	NAB59b	96-GAAA	adele cluster		20.00	2,084	0....	9	8	6	5	3	Adele	PN.	.
3795	Ahafo	0.26625	46,991	53,816	98,183	NAB59a	96-FCCB-ck	a-hafo		60.00	32,289	1csu.	10	7	7	5	1		pnb	b
3796	Ahanta	0.60804	107,314	122,900	224,222	NAB59a	96-FCBC-a	a-hanta		65.00	79,885	0....	10	7	7	5	3	Ahanta	...	.
3797	Akpafu	0.10381	18,322	20,983	38,281	NAB59b	96-HABA-a	si-wu		90.00	18,884	0....	10	8	11	5	3		...	.
3798	Akposo (Kposo)	0.03649	6,440	7,376	13,456	NAB59b	96-JABA	i-kposo cluster		90.00	6,638	0....	10	8	11	5	1	Akposo	...	b
3799	Akwamu	0.20916	36,915	42,276	77,130	NAB59a	96-FCCB-cl	a-kwam		60.00	25,366	1csu.	10	7	7	5	3		pnb	.
3800	Akwapim (Akuapem)	2.33954	412,911	472,879	862,734	NAB59a	96-FCCB-cb	a-kuapem	3	69.80	330,070	1csu.	10	9	11	5	3	Twi: Akuapem	PNB	b
3801	Akyem (Akim)	3.02986	534,747	612,410	1,117,298	NAB59a	96-FCCB-ch	a-kyem	4	69.00	422,563	1csu.	10	9	10	5	2		pnb	b

Continued opposite

Table 8-2 continued

EVANGELIZATION								EVANGELISM			ADDITIONAL DESCRIPTIVE DATA
Ref 1	*D 28*	*aC 29*	*CG% 30*	*r 31*	*E 32*	*U 33*	*W 34*	*e 35*	*R 36*	*T 37*	*Locations, civil divisions, literacy, religions, church history, denominations, dioceses, church growth, missions, agencies, ministries, movements 38*
3682	0	8	0.00	1	34.00	66.00	A	0.00	0	1.11	Turkler, Airumy, Padar. 73% monolingual. 20 dialects. Muslims 80%(56% Shias,24% Hanafi Sunnis), nonreligious 20%. M=ROC,GOC,CSI.
3683	0	10	0.70	0	20.06	79.94	A	0.04	232	2	In Zemo-Alvani. Literary language: Georgian. Muslims 100%(Sunnis).
3684	1	10	0.82	6	99.72	0.28	C	349.52	42	9	Residents from Bulgaria. In 12 other countries. Nonreligious 18%, atheists 10%. D=Bulgarian Orthodox Ch. M=LBI.
3685	3	8	0.82	5	99.70	0.30	C	347.48	37	9	White Russians. Also in USA, Canada, Poland, Russia, Ukraine. Nonreligious/atheists 30%. D=ROC,RCC,Old Ritualist Chs.
3686	0	8	0.00	0	19.00	81.00	A	0.00	0	1.05	Nokhchuo. From Chechen, Ingush (Russia). 76% speak Russian. Highly religious Muslims 63%(fervent Hanafi Sunnis, strongly Sufi), atheists 20%.
3687	5	10	0.82	5	99.75	0.25	C	385.98	39	9	Most are bilingual in Russian. Many nonreligious, 20%. D=ROC,ELCE,RCC,MCE,AUCECB. M=UBS,LBI.
3688	3	9	0.47	4	99.77	0.23	C	396.28	9	9	Also in Turkey, Iran, USA. Nonreligious/atheists 18%, Muslims 5%(Sunnis, Shias). D=Georgian Orthodox Ch(15 Dioceses: C-Mtskheta & Tiflis),AUCECB,CEF.
3689	0	9	0.85	4	38.05	61.95	A	0.06	111	2	Oriental and Ashkenazi Jews each living separately in Georgia. Emigrating to Israel.
3690	2	10	0.82	8	99.80	0.20	C	438.00	36	10	Settlers, also in Volga, Altai (Russia), Kirghizia. Nonreligious 20%. D=German ELC,AUCECB.
3691	3	10	0.82	8	99.90	0.10	C	525.60	31	10	Turkish-speaking traders, merchants from Greece, in Abkhazia since 1770. D=Greek Orthodox Ch,ROC,Georgian Orthodox Ch. M=UBS,LBI.
3692	3	10	0.82	6	69.00	31.00	B	50.37	73	6	Romany-speaking Gypsies. Many Muslims 40%, nonreligious 40%. D=RCC,ROC,GOC. M=GGMS.
3693	1	8	0.82	1	48.00	52.00	A	17.52	47	5	Dialect of Georgian. Adopted Islam c1620. Being assimilated into Azerbaijanis. Muslims 90%(Shias). D=Georgian Orthodox Ch.
3694	0	10	0.00	5	45.00	55.00	A	0.00	0	1.10	Bilingual in Russian, Georgian. Religious Jews. Many have emigrated to Israel.
3695	0	8	0.00	4	35.00	65.00	A	0.00	0	1.10	Muslims 60%(Hanafi Sunnis, with Sufi influence), nonreligious 30%, atheists 10%. M=ROC.
3696	1	9	0.87	0	32.00	68.00	A	1.16	74	4	South Caucasus, in Adjar ASSR, Georgia. In 6 countries. Unwritten. Christians from AD 523-1461. Muslims 99%(Shafi Sunnis). D=Georgian Orthodox Ch.
3697	0	7	0.00	0	16.00	84.00	A	0.00	0	1.04	Also in south Dagestan (Russia). Lingua franca. 50% understand Russian. Muslims 100%(Shafi Sunnis). M=IBT.
3698	1	9	0.82	0	33.00	67.00	A	1.20	68	4	Lowland west Georgia. Language unwritten; literary language Georgian. Muslims 99%(Shafi Sunnis). D=Georgian Orthodox Ch.
3699	1	9	0.82	6	99.82	0.18	C	422.01	35	10	From Moldavia (Bessarabia), Romania. D=Russian Orthodox Ch.
3700	0	7	1.52	0	29.06	70.94	A	0.06	332	2	Across Armenia, Georgia. Lingua franca. Muslims 90%(Shias,Yazidis,some Sunnis), nonreligious 9%.
3701	1	6	0.82	0	97.00	3.00	B	194.72	54	7	In Caucasus Mountains, South Ossetian AO. Also in Russia, Syria, Turkey. Stock-breeders. Muslims 40%(Sunnis, all Digor tribe), nonreligious 5%. D=Russian OC.
3702	4	10	0.81	6	99.91	0.09	C	534.76	14	10	Poles from Poland, Ukraine. 29% speak Polish as mother tongue. D=RCC,ROC,CEF,CWE.
3703	0	0	9.63	1	99.90	0.10	C	407.34	234	10	Called 'Rumka'. Do not speak standard Greek. Mainly in Greece. Also in USA. Nonreligious 10%. D=Greek Orthodox Church.
3704	8	9	0.03	7	99.60	0.40	C	289.08	1	8	In 70 countries. Nonreligious 35%, atheists 5%. D=ROC,RCC,AUCECB,Old Ritualists,CEF,CCECB,SDA,IPKH.
3705	1	9	0.82	0	99.00	1.00	C	216.81	23	8	South of Mt Elbrus. Unwritten language; Georgian used as literary language. Close to Mingrelians and Georgians. Nonreligious 40%. D=Georgian Orthodox Ch.
3706	0	8	0.00	4	39.00	61.00	A	0.00	0	1.12	Most are trilingual (Uzbek, Russian, Georgian). Muslims 90%(Hanafi Sunnis, some Shias), nonreligious 10%. M=CSI.
3707	1	8	0.83	6	43.50	56.50	A	2.38	103	4	From Tatarstan (Russia). Muslims 83%(Hanafi Sunnis), nonreligious 15%. D=ROC.
3708	0	6	0.00	8	38.00	62.00	A	0.00	0	1.11	Across Central Asia. Muslims 98%(85% Hanafi Sunnis, 15% Alawi Shias).
3709	1	8	0.82	0	99.90	0.10	C	430.33	38	10	Oktembri village in eastern Georgia. Also in Azerbaijan. Unwritten; Azeri used as literary language. All Udi Muslims have now become Azerbaijanis. D=Georg OC.
3710	7	8	0.82	6	99.69	0.31	C	347.55	40	9	In 15 countries. Nonreligious/atheists 31%. D=Ukrainian Orthodox Ch,ROC(E-Ukraine),Ukrainian Catholic Ch,AUCECB,CEF,CCECB,JWs,SDA.
3711	0	9	0.00	5	41.00	59.00	A	0.00	0	1.12	55% speak Russian. Literates 100%. Muslims 80%(Hanafi Sunnis), nonreligious/atheists 20%. M=CSI.
3712	0	8	0.00		14.00	86.00	A	0.00	0	1.03	Immigrants from neighbouring countries. Muslims 70% (Ithna-Asharis), nonreligious 30%.
Germany											
3713	0	10	3.56	5	53.00	47.00	B	1.93	299	4	Refugees from Afghanistan. Muslims 99%(Hanafi Sunnis).
3714	1	10	0.67	6	88.00	12.00	B	80.30	37	6	Immigrants and refugees from Albania. Muslims 25%(Sunnis, Shias), nonreligious/atheists 50%. D=AOC.
3715	0	0	6.46	5	99.91	0.09	C	461.68	164	10	Immigrants from Ethiopia. D=EOC.
3716	0	8	3.79	8	50.50	49.50	B	0.92	244	3	Moroccans. Berber immigrants, speaking Arabic and German. Muslims 99%.
3717	1	10	0.67	6	99.90	0.10	C	535.45	21	10	Refugees from Turkey, USSR. Gregorians. D=Armenian Apostolic Ch(C-Echmiadzin).
3718	2	10	0.67	8	99.90	0.10	C	522.31	31	10	Expatriates or residents from Austria and other speakers of Bavarian. D=RCC,EKD. M=OSB,OFM,SJ,FMB.
3719	3	10	0.67	6	99.80	0.20	C	394.20	35	9	In 12 countries. Muslims 20% (Hanafi Sunnis). Caravan churches. D=RCC,EKD,Gypsy Evangelical Movement. M=GGMS.
3720	2	10	0.67	1	99.80	0.20	C	362.08	38	9	In over 10 countries across Europe, Middle East. Muslims 20% (Hanafi Sunnis). Caravan churches. D=RCC,GEM. M=GGMS.
3721	1	10	0.67	4	99.94	0.06	C	552.39	28	10	Immigrants from Spain, in commerce, professions. Strong Catholics. D=RCC. M=SJ.
3722	4	10	9.88	8	99.50	0.50	B	217.17	264	8	Assimilated immigrants from Ghana, Kenya, Nigeria, and countries across Africa. Muslims 30%. D=RCC,EKD,NAK,JWs.
3723	0	10	3.42	6	56.10	43.90	B	0.20	211	3	Refugees from Bosnian civil war, accepted by Germany in 1992. Muslims 100%(Sunnis). M=EKD.
3724	4	10	0.67	8	99.79	0.21	C	446.94	32	10	Expatriates from Britain, in education, business. D=Anglican Ch(D-Europe),RCC,Cooneyites,PB. M=FMB.
3725	1	10	0.67	6	99.78	0.22	C	409.96	36	10	Refugees from Bulgaria, laborers, migrant workers. Nonreligious 22%. D=Bulgarian Orthodox Ch(P-Sofia).
3726	2	10	0.67	5	99.70	0.30	C	352.59	33	9	Refugees from White Russia since 1917. Nonreligious 30%. D=Belorussian Autocephalic Orthodox Ch, RCC.
3727	1	10	0.67	4	99.96	0.04	C	588.67	26	10	Migrant workers from Catalonia(Spain). Nonreligious 4%. D=RCC.
3728	0	10	0.00	0	30.01	69.99	A	0.01	0	2	In Munich. Also in former USSR, Turkey, Syria, Jordan, Israel, Iraq, Yugoslavia, USA. Muslims 99%(Hanafi Sunnis).
3729	1	10	0.67	6	99.91	0.09	C	538.08	30	10	Refugees from Yugoslavia since 1945, especially since 1990. D=RCC.
3730	2	10	1.16	6	99.79	0.21	C	429.64	42	10	Refugees from Czechoslovakia since 1938, 1945, 1968. D=RCC,Moravian Ch.
3731	3	10	0.67	6	99.95	0.05	C	586.00	30	10	Expatriates from Denmark, also settlers in south Schleswig. D=National Ch of Denmark,EKD,RCC.
3732	1	10	0.67	6	99.76	0.24	C	421.64	28	10	Expatriates from Holland, in commerce, professions. D=Netherlands Reformed Ch.
3733	2	9	0.67	0	99.72	0.28	C	310.10	42	9	Schleswig-Holstein Ostfriesland; Lower Saxony; Saterland, Jeverland, Butjadingen. Nonreligious/atheists 28%. D=EKD,RCC.
3734	2	10	0.67	8	99.65	0.35	C	301.30	39	9	East Germany. A dialect of Standard German spoken in the Erzgebirge mountain range along Czechoslavakia border. Nonreligious 30%. D=EKD,RCC.
3735	0	10	0.00	5	99.70	0.30	C	319.37	0	9	Artificial (constructed) language, in 80 countries. Speakers in Germany: 1,536,000(none mother-tongue). Nonreligious 30%.
3736	2	10	0.67	5	99.80	0.20	C	438.00	34	10	Refugees from Estonia since 1940. D=Estonian Evangelical Lutheran Ch in Exile,EOC.
3737	2	9	0.67	8	99.75	0.25	C	372.30	36	9	Frankfurt-am-Main region. Only 40% intelligible with Standard German; but bilingual. Nonreligious 25%. D=EKD,RCC.
3738	1	10	0.67	8	99.87	0.13	C	514.43	28	10	Expatriates from France, in commerce, industry, professions. Nonreligious 10%. D=RCC.
3739	1	10	0.67	1	99.96	0.04	C	564.14	27	10	Migrant workers from Galicia(Spain). D=RCC.
3740	7	6	0.24	8	99.71	0.29	C	389.35	25	9	Standard German. Muslims 50,000. D=EKD(20 denominations),RCC/KKD(23 Dioceses),NAK(NAC),JWs,EMKD,BEFGD,&c. M=OSB,OFM,SJ,FMB,UBS,LBI,&c.
3741	6	9	1.96	8	99.80	0.20	C	443.84	54	10	Gypsies with German as mother tongue. D=nomadic caravan churches,Gypsy Evangelical Movement,AoG,other Pentecostals,Mennonites,RCC. M=IZM,GGMS.
3742	3	10	0.67	8	99.88	0.12	C	510.70	31	10	Alsatians(in France). Similar to Swabian. Bilingual in Standard German. D=RCC,SRC,EKD.
3743	2	10	0.67	7	99.95	0.05	C	582.54	27	10	Migrant laborers, from Greece. D=Greek Orthodox Ch(M-Germany),Greek Evangelical Ch. M=MEOS,MSOE.
3744	2	10	1.26	8	77.00	23.00	B	25.29	68	5	Chinese who now speak German as first language. Buddhists 90%. D=RCC,EKD.
3745	2	10	0.68	8	78.00	22.00	B	28.47	47	5	Long-time residents from Chinese diaspora. Buddhists/Chinese folk-religionists 90%. D=RCC,EKD. M=COCM,FMB.
3746	1	10	0.67	7	72.00	28.00	B	18.39	50	5	Buddhists/Chinese folk-religionists 93%. D=RCC.
3747	0	10	0.67	5	67.00	33.00	B	19.56	54	5	Immigrants from Taiwan. Chinese folk-religionists 90%.
3748	4	10	2.27	6	99.85	0.15	C	493.29	63	10	Refugees from Hungary since 1945, 1956. D=RCC,Hungarian ELCE,RCH,Hungarian Free Protestant Ch.
3749	1	10	0.67	7	99.84	0.16	C	490.56	29	10	Expatriates from Italy, in commerce, professions. Strong Catholics. D=RCC. M=FMB. R=TWR,AWR.
3750	1	10	4.93	7	68.00	32.00	B	12.41	229	5	Buddhists 50%, New-Religionists(Soka Gakkai,et alia) 40%. D=UCCJ. M=United Ch of Christ in Japan,FMB.
3751	0	10	3.74	5	76.00	24.00	B	44.38	165	6	Migrant workers. Muslims 49%(Shafi Sunnis), syncretistic Javanese mystical New Religionists 35%.
3752	0	10	-4.51	8	61.32	38.68	B	0.71	4	3	Remnant after 1940-45 Holocaust. Mostly practicing. M=RCC,EKD,et alia.
3753	0	10	-2.33	5	57.20	42.80	B	0.41	5	3	Remnant of 564,000 in 1925. Practicing Jews 84%. M=EKD,RCC,and many agencies.
3754	4	10	6.57	6	99.37	0.63	B	144.50	184	7	Migrant workers. Buddhists 20%, shamanists 20%, Confucians 13%. D=RCC,AoG,HSAUWC,&c. M=KMC,PCK-H,PCK-T,WOM,BFMGAP,FMB.
3755	0	8	4.08	0	38.10	61.90	A	0.13	437	3	Migrant workers and refugees from Turkey, Iraq, Iran. 40,000 speak Zaza, 10,000 speak Sorani. Muslims 99%(Sunnis). M=EKD,CBFMS,FOT,OM,WEC,FMB.
3756	1	10	0.67	5	99.98	0.02	C	597.35	31	10	Refugees from Latvia since 1940. D=Latvian Evangelical Lutheran Ch in Exile.
3757	2	10	0.67	5	99.83	0.17	C	466.54	12	10	Refugees from Lithuania since 1940. D=RCC,Lithuanian Evangelical Lutheran Ch in Exile.
3758	2	10	0.67	6	99.80	0.20	C	405.88	34	10	A Vlach grouping, found in 25 countries including Argentina, Brazil, Colombia. Caravan churches. D=GEM,RCC. M=GGMS.
3759	2	9	0.67	8	99.91	0.09	C	558.01	30	10	Northern Germany, Lower Saxony. 30 unintelligible dialects, widely used. Bilingual in Standard German. D=EKD,RCC. R=AWR.
3760	1	10	0.67	8	99.90	0.10	C	496.03	32	10	Settlers, immigrants from Luxemburg. Bitburg area in West Germany. Also in Luxemburg, Belgium, USA. D=RCC.
3761	2	10	0.67	8	99.88	0.12	C	523.55	30	10	Friesland, Lower Saxony. Also in former USSR, Canada, USA, Mexico, Belize, Paraguay, Bolivia, Brazil, Uruguay, Argentina, Costa Rica. D=EKD,VDMG.
3762	0	10	3.91	7	56.00	44.00	B	2.04	226	4	Migrant workers from Morocco. Muslims 99%(Maliki Sunnis). M=EKD.
3763	0	10	6.83	8	65.00	35.00	B	11.86	317	5	Residents migrant workers from Algeria, Libya, Tunisia, Niger. Muslims 95%(mostly Sunnis). M=EKD,FMB.
3764	0	10	5.33	7	62.00	38.00	B	15.84	280	5	Migrants, immigrants from India. Merchants. Hindus 87%, Muslims 3%, Baha'is 3%.
3765	2	9	0.67	0	99.72	0.28	C	339.01	39	9	Schleswig-Holstein, coastal strip between Eider and Wiedau rivers, adjacent islands. Bilingual in Low and High German. D=EKD,RCC.
3766	2	10	0.67	2	99.75	0.25	C	364.08	34	9	East Germany. In Nieder Lausitz, south of Berlin. Local dialects preserved by hundreds of islands in Spree river. 95% bilinguals in German. D=EKD,RCC.
3767	0	9	4.70	5	52.10	47.90	B	0.19	284	3	Refugees from Iran. Merchants. Muslims 97%(Imami Shias). M=EKD,WEC.
3768	1	10	0.67	6	99.90	0.10	C	528.88	11	10	Refugees from Poland since 1945. Sizeable community in Berlin. Strong Catholics. D=RCC. M=FMB-SBC.
3769	1	10	0.67	8	99.93	0.07	C	580.46	27	10	Immigrants, migrant workers from Portugal, in commerce, professions. D=RCC.
3770	0	0	4.51	5	52.00	48.00	B	9.49	238	4	Immigrants from India and Pakistan. Muslims 75%, Sikhs 20%, some Hindus.
3771	1	10	2.92	6	99.84	0.16	C	472.16	72	10	Refugees from Romania since 1945. D=Romanian Orthodox Ch(P-Bucharest). M=FMB.
3772	2	10	2.52	7	99.70	0.30	C	365.36	48	9	Refugees from USSR since 1917. D=Russian Orthodox Ch(PE-Middle Europe),ROCOR (D-Germany). M=FMB-SBC.
3773	0	0	4.31	7	43.10	56.90	A	1.73	318	4	Immigrant from former Soviet Union since 1980. Jewish 74%, Nonreligious 20%. Some Messianic believers.
3774	2	10	0.67	6	99.85	0.15	C	483.99	12	10	Migrant workers from Serbia. D=Serbian Orthodox Ch(D-Western Europe),SOC-Independent.
3775	4	9	0.67	0	99.80	0.20	C	359.16	38	9	In 10 countries. D=nomadic caravan churches,Gypsy Evangelical Movement,RCC,EKD. M=GGMS.
3776	1	10	0.67	6	99.95	0.05	C	568.67	28	10	Migrant laborers from Slovenia(former Yugoslavia). Strong Catholics. D=RCC.
3777	2	10	0.67	2	99.70	0.30	C	327.04	36	9	East Germany. Lower Lusatian, Saxon Lusatian. In Ober Lausitz, Upper Saxony, in southeast near Austrian border. Many also in Austria. 95% bilingual. D=EKD.
3778	1	10	0.67	8	99.96	0.04	C	613.20	25	10	Migrant workers from Spain and Latin America. D=RCC. M=OSB,OFM,SJ,FMB.
3779	0	9	0.67	8	99.80	0.20	C	382.52	38	9	In southwest. 40% intelligible with Standard German. Bilinguals.
3780	3	10	7.80	5	99.90	0.10	C	528.88	144	10	Syrian Aramaic language. Also in Syria, Iraq, Turkey, USA, Sweden, Netherlands, et alia. D=Syrian Orthodox Ch(Jacobites),ACE(Nestorians),RCC.
3781	4	10	7.18	6	96.00	4.00	B	87.60	233	6	Refugees from civil war in Sri Lanka; also relocated in Canada. Hindus 70%, Muslims 5%(Hanafi Sunnis), Baha'is. D=RCC,EKD,SDA,JWS.
3782	0	0	3.31	8	41.10	58.90	A	0.15	267	3	Immigrants and workers from Tunisia. Muslims 99%.
3783	3	8	5.55	8	56.10	43.90	B	0.20	306	3	Rumelian, Anatolian. Turks. Guest workers (immigrant laborers). Literates 60%. Muslims 99%(Hanafi Sunnis). D=RCC,EKD,Assyrian Orthodox Ch. M=WEC,OM.
3784	0	0	8.49	8	99.84	0.16	C	398.58	179	9	Military personnel from USA. D=NBC,ICFG,AoG,CJCLdS,CCS,SDA,JWs,CCNA.
3785	7	10	0.67	8	99.78	0.22	C	432.74	28	10	Expatriates from USA, military. D=ICFG,AoG,CJCLdS,CCS,SDA,JWs,CCNA. M=FMB-SBC.
3786	3	10	0.67	6	99.80	0.20	C	440.92	34	10	Refugees from USSR since 1917. D=RCC(EA-Germany),UAOCE(M=UOCUSA),UEBCG.
3787	1	10	2.93	5	57.10	42.90	B	0.20	190	3	Migrant workers, immigrants from Pakistan, India. Muslims 99%(Hanafi Sunnis). D=RCC. M=SJ.
3788	1	10	8.05	6	99.35	0.65	B	129.02	241	7	Refugees after Viet Nam war. Buddhists 40%, New-Religionists 10%, Nonreligious 15%. D=RCC. M=CMA.
3789	3	10	0.67	6	99.80	0.20	C	394.20	35	9	In 15 countries. D=nomadic caravan churches,GEM,RCC. M=GGMS.
3790	2	9	0.67	0	94.00	6.00	B	171.55	40	7	A German/Yiddish/Romani/Rotwelsch blend language of urban non-Gypsy nomadic groups; also in Austria, France, Switzerland. Nonreligious. D=RCC,EKD.
3791	0	10	0.67		94.00	6.00	C	205.86	20	8	Punjabis (Qadiani Ahmadis,Sikhs), USA Blacks, Swedish, Irish, Ghanaians, Kenyans, Nigerians, Filipinos, Ceylonese, South Africans, Romanian Gypsies.
Ghana											
3792	3	7	4.03	0	38.00	62.00	A	5.54	375	4	15 remote villages on Togo border. Bilingual in Twi with outsiders. Animists 95%, Muslims 1%. D=95%RCC,EPCG,DHC. M=WEC,SIL,GILLBT,FAME.
3793	4	6	4.97	0	99.56	0.44	B	215.74	158	8	Animists 5%, Muslims 1.5%(Sunnis,Ahmadis). D=RCC(D-Accra),COP,PCG,many AICs. M=SVD,SMA,ACM,BCM,CoF,EEC,HDM,KC,NDMI,YWAM. R=ELWA.
3794	6	7	5.48	0	61.00	39.00	B	44.53	304	6	Remote area. Also in Togo. Animists 76%, Muslims 4%. D=SDA,RCC,Apostolic Revelation Society,EPCG,COP,CA. M=SIL,SVD,GILLBT.
3795	4	6	8.42	2	99.60	0.40	C	240.90	239	8	Dialect of Akan. Animists 10%, Muslims 5%. D=Methodist Ch Ghana,COP,RCC,AICs. M=LBI.
3796	4	7	5.36	0	99.65	0.35	C	249.11	170	8	Southwest corner. Partial bilingualism in Fante and Nzema. Animists 10%. D=RCC,MCG,AICs,&c.
3797	3	6	7.84	0	99.90	0.10	C	436.90	188	10	Southeast. Close to Lolobi linguistically, but politically separate. Animists 10%. D=RCC,MCG,PCG.
3798	3	7	6.71	0	99.90	0.10	C	430.33	167	10	Mostly in Togo. Somewhat bilingual in Ewe. Animists 10%. D=RCC,AoG,JWs. M=GILLBT.
3799	3	6	4.82	2	99.60	0.40	C	238.71	151	8	In south. Part of Akan nation. Animists 15%, some Muslims. D=RCC,COP,AICs.
3800	5	6	4.97	2	99.70	0.30	C	330.69	130	9	Animists 3%, Muslims 5%(Ahmadis). D=Methodist Ch Ghana,COP,RCC,many AICs,AOC(D-Accra). M=LBI,SVD,SMA,AMC.
3801	7	6	4.96	2	99.69	0.31	C	309.77	137	9	Animists 2%, Muslims 7% (large Ahmadi gains). D=RCC(D-Keta-Ho),COP,PCG,SDA,AMEC,Saviour Ch of Ghana,many other AICs. M=EEC,King's Ch.

Continued overleaf

Table 8-2 continued

PEOPLE		POPULATION				IDENTITY CODE		LANGUAGE		CHURCH		MINISTRY						SCRIPTURE		
Ref 1	*Ethnic name* 2	*P%* 3	*In 1995* 4	*In 2000* 5	*In 2025* 6	*Race* 7	*Language* 8	*Autoglossonym* 9	*S* 10	*AC* 11	*Members* 12	*Jayuh* 13-17	*d* 18	*wa* 19	*xc* 20	*mc* 21	*mi* 22	*Biblioglossonym* 23	*Pub* 24-26	*ss* 27
3802	Ana (Atakpame, Ife)	0.12681	22,381	25,631	46,763	NAB59n	98-AAAA-cg	west ede-ife		29.00	7,433	1csu.	9	5	6	5	3	Ife	Pnb	b
3803	Anum-Boso	0.27280	48,147	55,140	100,598	NAB59a	96-FDAB-c	a-num		60.00	33,084	0....	10	7	7	5	1		...	b
3804	Anyi (Agni)	1.14600	202,260	231,635	422,601	NAB59a	96-FCAB-a	central a-nyi	1	55.60	128,789	0....	10	7	7	5	3	Agni*	PN.	b
3805	Anyimere	0.01415	2,497	2,860	5,218	NAB59a	96-IAAA-b	kunda		65.00	1,859	0....	10	7	7	3	3		...	b
3806	Arab	0.01000	1,765	2,021	3,688	CMT30	12-AACF-f	syro-palestinian	2	5.00	101	1Asuh	7	5	2	3	1	Arabic: Lebanese*	Pnb	b
3807	Asen	0.64800	114,367	130,977	238,958	NAB59a	96-FCCB-cf	a-sen	1	60.00	78,586	1csu.	10	7	7	5	2		pnb	.
3808	Ashanti (Akan)	13.73723	2,424,515	2,776,637	5,065,770	NAB59a	96-FCCB-cc	a-sante	20	48.70	1,352,222	1ssu.	9	9	11	5	3	Twi: Asante	PNB	b
3809	Avatime (Sideme, Sia)	0.07480	13,202	15,119	27,583	NAB59b	96-KAAB-a	si-ya-se		90.00	13,607	0....	10	8	11	5	2		...	.
3810	Banafo (Banda, Nafana)	0.28109	49,610	56,815	103,655	NAB56a	91-BBBA	nafaanra cluster		28.00	15,908	0....	9	5	6	5	3	Nafaanra	PN.	.
3811	Banda (Ligbi, Weela)	0.07078	12,492	14,306	26,101	NAB63z	00-AABA-a	ligbi		0.05	7	0....	4	4	2	1	3		...	p
3812	Bassari (Basari, Ncham)	0.68757	121,351	138,975	253,550	NAB56a	91-GGDD-a	n-can-m		15.00	20,846	0..u.	8	5	6	2	2	Ntcham	PN.	.
3813	Bimoba (Moba, Moab)	0.47521	83,871	96,052	175,239	NAB56a	91-GGDC-b	bi-moba	1	34.00	32,658	0..u.	9	5	6	5	3	Bimoba	PN.	.
3814	Bondoukou Kulango (Nkurang)	0.06448	11,380	13,033	23,778	NAB56a	91-GCCA-d	buna		21.00	2,737	0....	9	5	4	4	3		pn.	b
3815	Bouna Kulango	0.10000	17,649	20,212	36,876	NAB56a	91-GCCA-d	buna		25.00	5,053	0....	9	5	7	4	3		pn.	b
3816	Bowili (Tuwili)	0.07080	12,496	14,310	26,108	NAB59b	96-JAAA-a	li-wuli		90.00	12,879	0....	10	8	11	5	2		...	b
3817	British	0.20000	35,298	40,425	73,752	CEW19i	52-ABAC-b	standard-english	38	80.00	32,340	3Bsuh	10	9	13	5	3		PNB	b
3818	Brong	3.91128	690,311	790,567	1,442,332	NAB59a	96-FCCA-b	brong-ahafo	6	34.80	275,117	0....	9	6	7	5	3		...	b
3819	Buem (Lelemi, Lefana)	0.24065	42,473	48,641	88,743	NAB59b	96-HAAA-a	le-lemi		90.00	43,777	0....	10	9	12	5	3	Lelemi	PN.	.
3820	Bulsa (Builsa, Kanjaga)	0.64479	113,800	130,328	237,774	NAB56a	91-GGBA-b	bu-li		7.00	9,123	4....	7	5	6	5	3	Buli	PN.	.
3821	Busansi (Bisa, Busanga)	0.76794	135,535	155,220	283,187	NAB63z	00-DFAA-a	bisa		7.50	11,641	1....	7	5	7	5	3	Bissa	P..	b
3822	Chakali	0.02831	4,996	5,722	10,440	NAB56a	91-GFBE-a	chaka-li		1.50	86	0....	6	3	2	1	1		...	n
3823	Chakosi (Anufo)	0.30367	53,595	61,379	111,982	NAB59z	96-FCAD-a	anu-fo	1	5.00	3,069	0....	7	5	6	4	2	Anufo	P..	.
3824	Chala (Bagon)	0.01415	2,497	2,860	5,218	NAB56a	91-GFCA-a	chala		2.98	85	0....	6	4	4	2	2		...	.
3825	Cherepong (Kyerepon)	0.50125	88,467	101,315	184,842	NAB59a	96-FDAB-a	okere-mmiri	1	60.00	60,789	0....	10	7	6	3	1		...	b
3826	Dagaaba (Dagati)	3.04631	537,650	615,735	1,123,364	NAB56a	91-GGAA-h	dagaa-ri		36.00	221,665	1c...	9	6	7	4	3	Dagaare*	Pnb	.
3827	Dagomba (Dagbamba)	3.09409	546,083	625,393	1,140,983	NAB56a	91-GGAC-e	dagba-ne	5	3.00	18,762	4....	6	5	6	4	3	Dagbani	PN.	.
3828	Dankyira	0.49741	87,789	100,539	183,426	NAB59a	96-FCCB-ce	dankyira	1	60.00	60,323	1csu.	10	7	7	5	2		pnb	b
3829	Deg (Mo, Degha, Mmfo)	0.12160	21,461	24,578	44,841	NAB56a	91-GFBG-a	proper deg		40.00	9,831	0....	9	5	6	5	2	Deg	PN.	b
3830	Dyula (Jula, Wangara)	0.10000	17,649	20,212	36,876	NAB63h	00-AAAB-z	jula-kan	2	1.00	202	1cs..	6	3	1	0	0	Jula	PNb	b
3831	Eastern Kusasi	2.86490	505,633	579,068	1,056,467	NAB56a	91-GGAC-a	kusaal		15.00	86,860	1....	8	5	6	4	3	Kusaal*	PN.	.
3832	Efutu (Awutu)	0.70771	124,905	143,046	260,977	NAB59a	96-FDAA-a	proper a-wutu		60.00	85,828	0....	10	7	7	5	2		...	b
3833	Eurafrican	0.02000	3,530	4,042	7,375	NAN58	52-ABAH	west-coast-creole- cluster	29	80.00	3,234	4.s.h	10	8	8	5	3		PN.	b
3834	Eurafrican (Creole)	0.20000	35,298	40,425	73,752	NAN58	52-ABAH	west-coast-creole- cluster		80.00	32,340	4.s.h	10	8	7	5	3		PN.	b
3835	Ewe (Ebwe, Eve, Krepi)	10.02735	1,769,750	2,026,778	3,697,707	NAB59d	96-MAAA-a	standard ewe	20	75.00	1,520,083	4Asu.	10	9	11	5	3	Ewe	PNB	b
3836	Fante	11.30113	1,994,562	2,284,240	4,167,429	NAB59a	96-FCCB-b	fante	16	48.40	1,105,572	2csu.	9	10	11	5	3	Fante	PNB	b
3837	Fon	0.05010	8,842	10,126	18,475	NAB59e	96-MAAG-a	standard fon		20.00	2,025	2as..	9	5	6	4	2	Fon*	PNb	b
3838	French	0.05000	8,825	10,106	18,438	CEW21b	51-AABI-d	general français	4	65.00	6,569	1B.uh	10	9	8	5	3	French	PNB	b
3839	Ga	2.36220	416,910	477,460	871,090	NAB59f	96-LAAA-a	accra	17	60.68	289,722	1.s..	10	10	13	5	3	Ga*	PNB	b
3840	German	0.02000	3,530	4,042	7,375	CEW19m	52-ABCE-a	standard hoch-deutsch	1	88.00	3,557	2B.uh	10	9	13	5	3	German*	PNB	b
3841	Ghanaian Birifor (Loor)	0.57298	101,127	115,814	211,293	NAB56a	91-GGAA-j	north birifor		15.00	17,372	1c...	8	6	6	3	3	Birifor*	PNb	.
3842	Guang (Gonja, Ngbanyito)	1.43245	252,816	289,534	528,233	NAB59a	96-FDBA	gonja cluster	3	14.00	40,535	1....	8	6	7	4	3	Gonja	PN.	.
3843	Gurenne (Frafra)	3.39351	598,928	685,913	1,251,398	NAB56a	91-GGAA-e	guren-ge		9.00	61,732	1c...	7	5	7	4	3	Frafra*	PNb	.
3844	Gurunsi (Nankani)	0.81955	144,644	165,652	302,219	NAB56a	91-GGAA-e	guren-ge		12.00	19,878	1c...	8	5	7	4	3	Frafra*	PNb	.
3845	Han Chinese	0.00500	882	1,011	1,844	MSY42a	79-AAAB-ba	kuo-yü		2.00	20	2Bsuh	6	4	3	1	1	Chinese: Kuoyu*	PNB	b
3846	Hanga	0.03123	5,512	6,312	11,516	NAB56a	91-GGAC-g	hanga		23.00	1,452	1....	9	4	6	1	2	Hanga	PN.	.
3847	Hausa	0.91767	161,962	185,484	338,402	NAB60a	19-HAAB-a	hausa	13	0.10	185	4Asu.	5	3	2	1	3	Hausa	PNB	b
3848	Ibibio	0.20000	35,298	40,425	73,752	NAB56b	98-ICBA-b	ibibio		90.00	36,382	3cs..	10	8	14	5	1	Ibibio	pnb	b
3849	Igbo (Ibo)	0.20886	36,862	42,216	77,020	NAB59h	98-FAAA-a	standard igbo		85.00	35,883	2..u.	10	9	13	5	2	Igbo	PNB	b
3850	Ijo (Ijaw)	0.15000	26,474	30,319	55,314	NAB59i	97-AADA-a	kalabari		90.00	27,287	0....	10	9	13	5	3	Kalabari	PN.	b
3851	Indo-Pakistani	0.04000	7,060	8,085	14,750	CNN25g	59-AAFO-e	general hindi		1.00	81	3Asuh	6	4	2	3	0		pnb	b
3852	Kabre (Cabrais)	0.15000	26,474	30,319	55,314	NAB56a	91-GFCB-a	kabiye		15.00	4,548	3a...	8	5	7	4	3	Kabiye	PN.	.
3853	Kantonsi (Yadasi)	0.01290	2,277	2,607	4,757	NAB56a	91-GGAA-f	kanto-si		1.00	26	1c...	6	4	2	3	0		pnb	p
3854	Kasena (Awuna)	0.57298	101,127	115,814	211,293	NAB56a	91-GFAD-b	east kasem	1	15.00	17,372	1....	8	5	7	4	3	Kasem	PN.	.
3855	Koma	0.01432	2,527	2,894	5,281	NAB56a	91-GGBA-a	kon-ni		14.00	405	1....	8	4	2	1	2	Konni	pn.	.
3856	Konkomba (Bikpakpam)	2.29192	404,506	463,254	845,173	NAB56a	91-GGDB-g	le-kpekpam	2	15.00	69,488	2A.u.	8	5	7	3	3	Konkomba	PNB	.
3857	Kotokoli (Tem, Temba)	0.06000	10,590	12,127	22,126	NAB56a	91-GFCC-a	tem		7.00	849	2..u.	7	5	6	3	1	Tem	...	.
3858	Krachi	0.42463	74,944	85,828	156,587	NAB59b	96-FDCF	krachi cluster		90.00	77,245	0....	10	9	12	5	3		...	b
3859	Krobo	2.42223	427,505	489,593	893,227	NAB59f	96-LAAB-a	krobo	3	55.00	269,276	0....	10	8	7	5	3		...	.
3860	Kru	0.09663	17,054	19,531	35,633	NAB59j	95-ABAE-g	central klao		70.00	13,672	0....	10	8	7	5	1	Kru*	PN.	b
3861	Kwahu	1.96184	346,250	396,537	723,452	NAB59a	96-FCCB-cj	a-kwahu	2	51.50	204,216	1csu.	10	8	7	5	3		pnb	b
3862	Larteh	0.33256	58,694	67,219	122,636	NAB59a	96-FDAB-b	late		60.00	40,331	0....	10	8	7	5	1		...	b
3863	Lobi (Lobiri)	0.03000	5,295	6,064	11,063	NAB56a	91-GBAA-a	lobi-ri		2.00	121	0....	6	4	6	2	3	Lobiri	PN.	.
3864	Logba	0.03539	6,246	7,153	13,050	NAB59b	91-GFCB-e	lukpa		80.00	5,723	1c...	10	7	7	5	3	Lokpa*	PN.	b
3865	Lolobi	0.04252	7,504	8,594	15,680	NAB59b	96-HABA-b	lo-lobi		80.00	6,875	0....	10	7	7	5	3		...	.
3866	Macina Fulani	0.07000	12,354	14,149	25,813	NAB56c	90-BAAA-e	fula-masina		0.50	71	4cs..	5	4	3	1	3	Fula: Macina*	Pnb	b
3867	Malinke (Mandingo)	0.50000	88,246	101,062	184,381	NAB63h	00-AAAA-a	mandinka-kango	2	2.00	2,021	4a...	6	4	6	1	0	Mandinka	PN.	b
3868	Mamprusi (Manpelle)	1.46238	258,099	295,583	539,270	NAB56a	91-GGAC-d	mampru-li		0.50	1,478	1....	5	5	6	5	3	Mampruli	Pn.	.
3869	Mossi	1.57786	278,480	318,925	581,855	NAB56a	91-GGAA-a	moo-re	3	20.00	63,785	2A...	9	5	7	5	3	Moore	PNB	b
3870	Namnam (Nabt, Nabdem)	0.25938	45,779	52,427	95,650	NAB56a	91-GGAC-b	nab-t		9.00	4,718	1....	7	5	6	4	3		pn.	.
3871	Nanumba (Nunuma)	0.20366	35,944	41,165	75,102	NAB56a	91-GGAC-f	nanu-ne		4.00	1,647	1....	6	4	6	2	1		pn.	.
3872	Nawuri	0.05729	10,111	11,580	21,126	NAB59a	96-FDDA	nawuri cluster		25.00	2,895	0....	9	7	7	5	2	Nawuri	...	b
3873	Nchumbulu	0.00838	1,479	1,694	3,090	NAB59a	96-FDCD-a	n-chumbulu		60.00	1,016	0....	10	7	6	4	2		...	.
3874	Nchumburu (Kyombaron)	0.24986	44,098	50,503	92,139	NAB59z	96-FDCC	chumburung cluster		8.00	4,040	0....	7	7	4	5	3	Chumburung	PN.	.
3875	Nchumunu	0.07077	12,490	14,304	26,097	NAB59a	96-FDCE-a	dwang		60.00	8,583	0....	10	7	7	4	2		...	.
3876	Nkonya	0.14316	25,267	28,936	52,792	NAB59a	96-FDEA-a	n-konya		60.00	17,362	0....	10	7	7	4	1	Nkonya	...	.
3877	Ntrubo (Ntribu, Dilose)	0.06458	11,398	13,053	23,815	NAB59b	91-GFCB-c	delo		90.00	11,748	1c...	10	8	7	5	2	Delo	pn.	.
3878	Nyangbo (Tutrugbu)	0.02515	4,439	5,083	9,274	NAB59b	96-KAAA-b	tu-trugbu		90.00	4,575	0....	10	8	11	5	2		...	.
3879	Nzima (Ndenye, Appolo)	1.84280	325,240	372,476	679,555	NAB59k	96-FCBA-a	nzema	5	62.70	233,542	1.s..	10	9	7	5	3	Nzema	PN.	.
3880	Pepesa-Jwira	0.08308	14,663	16,793	30,637	NAB59k	96-FCBB	jwira-pepesa cluster		60.00	10,076	0....	10	7	7	4	0		...	.
3881	Prang	0.04965	8,763	10,036	18,309	NAB59a	96-FDCA-a	kplang		60.00	6,021	0....	10	7	6	5	2		...	b
3882	Safaliba (Safazo)	0.01718	3,032	3,473	6,335	NAB56a	91-GGAA-g	safala		30.00	1,042	1c...	9	5	5	4	2		pnb	n
3883	Santrokofi (Sele)	0.04246	7,494	8,582	15,658	NAB59b	96-HBAA-a	se-lé		90.00	7,724	0....	10	7	11	5	3		...	.
3884	Sefwi	1.14596	202,253	231,627	422,587	NAB59a	96-FCAC-a	sehwi		65.00	150,558	0....	10	6	7	5	2	Sehwi	...	b
3885	Sekpele	0.09672	17,070	19,550	35,667	NAB59b	96-HBBA-a	se-kpele		90.00	17,595	0....	10	7	11	5	3		...	.
3886	Songhai (Sonrhai)	0.03000	5,295	6,064	11,063	NAB65b	01-AAAA	songhay-kine cluster	1	0.60	36	0....	5	3	5	0	0	Songhai*	PN.	b
3887	Southern Sisala (Sisaala)	0.15579	27,496	31,489	57,449	NAB56a	91-GFBC-f	paasa-li		10.00	3,149	0....	8	5	7	1	3	Pasaale	Pn.	.
3888	Tafi (Tegbo)	0.01870	3,300	3,780	6,896	NAB59b	96-KAAA-a	te-gbo		90.00	3,402	0....	10	8	11	5	2		...	b
3889	Talensi (Tallensi)	0.51470	90,841	104,034	189,802	NAB56a	91-GGAC-c	tal-ne		9.00	9,363	1....	7	5	6	4	3		pn.	.
3890	Tamprusi (Tampele)	0.24231	42,766	48,977	89,355	NAB56a	91-GFBD-a	tampul-ma		23.00	11,265	0....	9	4	5	4	2	Tampulma	PN.	.
3891	Tumulung Sisala	0.78148	137,925	157,957	288,180	NAB56a	91-GFBC-e	gil-baga-le		12.00	18,955	0....	8	5	7	4	3	Sisaala, Tumulung	PN.	.
3892	USA White	0.01700	3,000	3,436	6,269	CEW19s	52-ABAC-s	general american		78.00	2,680	1Bsuh	10	10	12	0	0	English*	PNB	b
3893	Vagla (Paxala)	0.06246	11,024	12,625	23,033	NAB56a	91-GFBF-a	proper vaghla		40.00	5,050	0....	9	5	5	4	3	Vagla	PN.	.
3894	Wala (Waali)	0.63898	112,775	129,154	235,632	NAB56a	91-GGAA-d	waa-li		3.00	3,875	1c...	6	4	5	4	3	Wali	PNb	.
3895	Wasa (Wassaw)	1.12838	199,150	228,074	416,104	NAB59a	96-FCCC	wasa cluster	2	60.00	136,844	0....	10	6	7	5	3		...	b
3896	Western Sisala (Sisai)	0.14154	24,981	28,609	52,195	NAB56a	91-GFBC-b	busil-lu	1	10.00	2,861	0....	8	5	7	4	2	Sisaala, Western	pn.	.
3897	Yoruba	1.49490	263,838	302,157	551,263	NAB59n	98-AAAA-a	standard yoruba	3	29.00	87,625	3asu.	9	5	11	5	2	Yoruba	PNB	b
3898	Zerma (Dyerma, Zabrama)	0.03000	5,295	6,064	11,063	NAB65c	01-AAAB-b	zarma	2	0.50	30	2..u.	5	3	4	0	2	Zarma	PNB	.
3899	other minor peoples	2.59385	457,794	524,282	956,514	...				20.00	104,856		9	5	6	5	0			
	Gibraltar	**100.00000**	**25,983**	**25,082**	**21,393**					**85.19**	**21,367**									
3900	British	10.00000	2,598	2,508	2,139	CEW19i	52-ABAC-b	standard-english		79.00	1,981	3Bsuh	10	9	13	5	3		PNB	b
3901	Gibraltarian	67.70000	17,590	16,981	14,483	CEW21z	51-AABB-ca	general españa		98.87	16,789	1A.uh	10	9	11	5	3		pnb	b
3902	Indo-Pakistani	1.20000	312	301	257	CNN25g	59-AAFO-e	general hindi		0.80	2	3Asuh	5	4	2	5	0		pnb	b
3903	Jewish	2.00000	520	502	428	CMT35	52-ABAC-b	standard-english		0.50	3	3Bsuh	5	4	2	5	0		PNB	b
3904	Moroccan Arab	9.00000	2,338	2,257	1,925	CMT30	12-AACB-a	west maghrebi		6.00	135	1A.uh	7	5	2	5	0		pnb	b
3905	Spaniard	10.00000	2,598	2,508	2,139	CEW21k	51-AABB-c	general español		97.00	2,433	2B.uh	10	9	15	5	2	Spanish	PNB	b
3906	other minor peoples	0.10000	26	25	21	...				96.00	24		10	6	11	5	0			
	Greece	**100.00000**	**10,489,203**	**10,644,744**	**9,862,572**					**94.52**	**10,061,020**									
3907	African Black	0.05700	5,979	6,068	5,622	NAB57j	99-AUSM-b	standard ki-swahili		20.00	1,214	4Asu.	9	5	1	1	2	Kiswahili*	PNB	b
3908	Arab	0.28400	29,789	30,231	28,010	CMT30	12-AACF-b	sa`idi		14.00	4,232	1Asuh	8	5	1	1	2		pnb	b
3909	Armenian (Hai, Ermeni)	0.20000	20,978	21,289	19,725	CEW14	57-AAAA-b	ashkharik		90.00	19,161	4A.u.	10	9	13	4	3	Armenian: Modern, Eastern	PNB	b
3910	Aromanian (Aromunen)	0.55900	58,635	59,504	55,132	CEW21i	51-AADB-a	limba armâneasc-a	3	84.00	49,983	0a...	10	8	11	4	2	Romanian: Macedonian*	P..	b
3911	Arvanite (Albanian)	1.50900	158,282	160,629	148,826	CEW13	55-AAAB-h	south arbanasi		64.80	104,088	0c...	10	7	8	4	2	Albanian, Arvanitika	PNb	b
3912	Balkan Gypsy (Arliski Rom)	0.11400	11,958	12,135	11,243	CNN25f	59-ACBA-bc	arlija		70.00	8,495	1A...	10	7	6	4	1	Romani: Arlija	Pn.	.
3913	Belgian	0.01700	1,783	1,810	1,677	CEW19k	52-ABCA-g	oostvlaandersch		90.00	1,629	1Bsuh	10	10	13	0	0		pnb	b
3914	British	0.10000	10,489	10,645	9,863	CEW19i	52-ABAC-b	standard-english		79.00	8,409	3Bsuh	10	9	13	5	2		PNB	b
3915	Bulgar	0.33900	35,558	36,086	33,434	CEW22b	53-AAAH-b	bulgarski		78.00	28,147	2A.uh	10	8	8	4	1	Bulgarian	PNB	b
3916	Dutch	0.01700	1,783	1,810	1,677	CEW19h	52-ABCA-a	algemeen-nederlands		76.00	1,375	2Bsuh	10	10	13	0	0	Dutch	PNB	b
3917	Esperanto	0.00000	0	0	0	CEW21z	51-AAAC-a	proper esperanto	1	80.00	0	0A...	10	9	2	5	0	Esperanto	PNB	b
3918	French	0.03400	3,566	3,619	3,353	CEW21b	51-AABI-d	general français		84.00	3,040	1B.uh	10	9	13	0	0	French	PNB	b
3919	German	0.08500	8,916	9,048	8,383	CEW19m	52-ABCE-a	standard hoch-deutsch		87.00	7,872	2B.uh	10	10	10	0	0	German*	PNB	b
3920	Greek (Hellenic, Dimotiki)	88.48200	9,281,057	9,418,682	8,726,601	CEW20	56-AAAA-c	dhimotiki		98.78	9,303,774	2B.uh	10	10	10	5	2	Greek: Modern	PNB	b
3921	Greek Gypsy	0.45000	47,201	47,901	44,382	CNN25f	59-ACBA-bc	arlija		75.00	35,926	1A...	10	8	6	4	3	Romani: Arlija	Pn.	.

Continued opposite

Table 8-2 continued

EVANGELIZATION								EVANGELISM			ADDITIONAL DESCRIPTIVE DATA
Ref 1	D 28	aC 29	CG% 30	r 31	E 32	U 33	W 34	e 35	R 36	T 37	Locations, civil divisions, literacy, religions, church history, denominations, dioceses, church growth, missions, agencies, ministries, movements 38
3802	3	6	6.83	5	81.00	19.00	B	85.73	278	6	A Yoruba group from Togo. Animists 40%, Muslims 20%. D=Yoruba AICs,RCC,AC.
3803	3	6	8.44	0	99.60	0.40	C	219.00	263	8	A pocket in the Ewe area. Bilingual in Twi. Animists 20%. D=RCC,EPC,AICs. M=NDMI.
3804	2	6	9.93	2	99.56	0.44	B	208.21	296	8	Most in Ivory Coast. Animists 30%, Muslims 1%(Sunnis,Ahmadis). D=RCC,many AICs. M=SVD,SMA,EEC,FLM.
3805	4	7	5.36	0	99.65	0.35	C	249.11	170	8	In south. Two remote villages. Second language Twi. Animists 35%. D=RCC,MCG,PCG,AC/CPWA.
3806	1	10	2.34	8	56.00	44.00	B	10.22	149	5	Lebanese and other traders. Muslims 90%. D=RCC(Maronites).
3807	2	6	9.38	2	99.60	0.40	C	234.33	270	8	Dialect of Akan. Animists 15%, Muslims 5%. D=MCG,RCC. M=LBI,CETI(Nigeria).
3808	11	6	3.88	4	99.49	0.51	B	200.33	123	8	Leading kingdom. Muslims 28% (massive Ahmadi conversions), animists 6%. D=RCC(D-Kumasi),ECWA,PCG,COP,MCG,SA,SDA,Anglican Ch of Ghana,AMEC.
3809	2	6	7.48	0	99.90	0.10	C	430.33	183	10	Southeast, centered on Amedzofe. Related to Nyangbo, Tafi. Animists 10%. D=RCC,EPC.
3810	6	6	7.65	0	69.00	31.00	B	70.51	358	6	Western border, also in Ivory Coast. Animists 57%, Muslims 5%. D=PCG,RCC,African Faith Tabernacle Church,CAC,MCG,COP. M=BM,UFCSM,SIL,GILLBT.
3811	4	5	1.96	0	22.05	77.95	A	0.04	480	2	In Numasa(northwest), also Ivory Coast and Burkina Faso. Bilingual in Twi Asante. Muslims 85%, animists 15%. Whole tribe sees itself as committed to Islam.
3812	4	6	7.94	0	50.00	50.00	B	27.37	510	5	Also in Togo. 20 clans. Braille Scripture in progress. Animists 73%, Muslims 12%. D=RCC,ECG,AoG,COP. M=WEC,SIL.
3813	7	6	8.43	0	74.00	26.00	B	91.83	363	6	Northeast, Gambaga District. Animists 33%, Muslims 3%(Sunnis,Ahmadis). D=AoG,ELCG,GBC,COP, RCC,Apostolic Ch of Ghana,PCG. M=FMB,SIL,SVD,SMA.
3814	4	6	5.77	1	61.00	39.00	B	46.75	321	6	West central. Most in Ivory Coast. Animists 76%, Muslims 3%. D=MCG,PCG,RCC,COP.
3815	10	7	6.42	1	69.00	31.00	B	62.96	309	6	West central border area. Most in Ivory Coast. Bilingual in Twi. Animists 70%, Muslims 3%. D=RCC,PCG,COP,MCG,AFTC,FWB,SCG,MDCC,SDA,CAC.
3816	2	7	7.42	0	99.90	0.10	C	443.47	177	10	Volta Region, from Volta Lake eastward. 61% bilingual in Ewe. Animists 10%. D=EPC,RCC.
3817	3	10	3.14	8	99.80	0.20	C	458.44	75	10	Expatriates from Britain, in education, business. D=Anglican Ch of Ghana,JWs,MCG.
3818	3	6	10.76	4	79.80	20.20	B	101.36	410	7	Also in Ivory Coast. Largely Muslims 50%(Sunnis,Ahmadis), some animists. D=RCC,COP,AICs. M=AMC,BCM,ESM,FLM,New Testament Assembly,STM.
3819	3	6	8.75	0	99.90	0.10	C	453.33	199	10	Southeast, town of Jasikan. Some bilingualism in Twi. Animists 5%. D=RCC(D-Keta-Ho),EPC,Buem-Krachi Presbyterian Ch(AIC). M=SIL,SVD,SMA,GILLBT.
3820	10	6	7.05	0	49.00	51.00	A	12.52	471	5	Sandema District. Also in Burkina Faso. Animists 92%, Muslims 1%. D=Presbyterian Ch of Ghana,ECWA,GBC,RCC(D-Navrongo-Bolgatanga),AoG,CC,SDA,COP.
3821	3	6	7.31	3	51.50	48.50	B	14.09	490	5	Most in Burkina Faso, also in Ivory Coast, Togo. Some bilingualism in Moore, Hausa, Kusaal, Mampruli. Literates 7%. Animists 67%, Muslims 25%. D=AoG,RCC.
3822	2	7	4.56	0	25.50	74.50	A	1.39	637	4	40 miles southeast of Wa. Bilingual in Wali. Animists 98%. D=RCC,ECG. M=WEC.
3823	5	6	5.89	0	38.00	62.00	A	6.93	526	4	Over half in Togo, some in Benin. Animists 77%, Muslims 18%(Sunnis). D=AoG,EPC,RCC(M-Tamale),CC,Pentecostals. M=SIL,GILLBT.
3824	2	7	4.54	0	28.98	71.02	A	3.15	559	4	3 villages, under Gichode paramount chief (Achode). Related to Ntrubo. Some bilingual in Twi, or Gichode. Animists 95%(fetishism strong). D=RCC,EPCG.
3825	4	6	9.10	0	97.00	3.00	C	212.43	290	8	Between Ga and Twi areas. Bilingual in Twi. Animists 20%. D=AC,MCG,RCC,AICs. M=NDMI.
3826	2	5	10.52	4	83.00	17.00	B	109.06	393	7	Northwest corner. Also in Burkina Faso. Animists 46%, Muslims 3%. D=91%RCC(very strong; D-Wa),BMM. M=SIL,BMM,WF,EM,WEC,GILLBT,UMC.
3827	8	5	7.83	4	47.00	53.00	A	5.14	536	4	Northeast around Tamale. Also in Togo. Literates 2%. Muslims 60%(Sunnis,Ahmadis), animists 37%. D=AoG,ECWA,GBC,PCG,SDA,RCC(M-Tamale),COP,MCG..
3828	6	6	9.09	2	99.60	0.40	C	243.09	253	8	Dialect of Akan. Animists 25%, Muslims 5%. D=RCC,MCG,COP,PCG,ACG,many AICs. M=SVD,SMA.
3829	9	6	7.13	0	82.00	18.00	B	119.72	284	7	Also in Ivory Coast. Widely bilingual in Twi. Animists 50%, Muslims 10%. D=SDA,RCC,MCG,Lutherans,CAC,Pentecostals,Baptist Chs,AFTC,AICs. M=SIL,GILLBT.
3830	0	5	3.05	4	32.00	68.00	A	1.16	435	4	From Mali to Ghana. Muslims 99%. Islam spreads through Dyula traders, with Jula as Mandinka-related lingua franca.
3831	6	5	9.49	1	55.00	45.00	B	30.11	541	5	Northeast corner, Bawku District. Literates 2%. Animists 75%, Muslims 5%. D=RCC(D-Navrongo-Bolgatanga),ELCG,AoG,PCG,ACG,CPWA. M=SIL,Basel Mission.
3832	6	6	3.94	0	99.60	0.40	C	221.19	139	8	On coast, west of Accra. Bilingual in Fante. Animists 10%. D=RCC,PCG,ACG,MCG,many AICs. M=SVD,SMA.
3833	5	10	2.95	8	99.80	0.20	C	411.72	79	10	Mixed-race persons, mostly in urban areas. Nonreligious 10%. D=RCC,MCG,ACG,PCG,many AICs.
3834	5	10	3.25	8	99.80	0.20	C	411.72	85	10	Urban communities of mixed Black/White race. D=MCG,RCC,ACG,PCG,&c.
3835	11	6	5.33	4	99.75	0.25	C	399.67	124	9	Also in Togo. Animists 15%. D=EPC,EPRC,RCC(D-Keta-Ho),AMEZC,MCG,FCG,EET,BCC,COP,ARS,many other AICs. M=Bremen Mission(1847-1914),SVD,SMA.
3836	8	6	4.63	4	99.48	0.52	B	196.79	143	7	Muslims 37% (Ahmadis,2% Sunnis). Massive Ahmadi growth. D=RCC(M-Cape Coast, D-Kumasi),COP,SA,MCG,AMEC,AMEZC,MDCC,many other AICs. M=LBI.
3837	2	6	5.45	4	71.00	29.00	B	51.83	279	6	Migrants from a large traditional-religionist people in Benin. Animists 75%, Muslims 5%. D=RCC,MCG.
3838	1	10	2.85	8	99.65	0.35	C	310.79	80	9	Expatriates from France, in education, commerce. Nonreligious 25%. D=RCC. M=SVD,SMA,WF.
3839	8	7	4.34	4	99.61	0.39	C	271.71	123	8	Animists 5%, Muslims 1.5%(Sunnis,Ahmadis). D=PCG,RCC(D-Accra),BCC,MCG,AoG,COP,DHC,many other AICs. M=LBI,SVD,SMA,ACM,BCM,COF. R=ELWA.
3840	5	10	2.16	8	99.88	0.12	C	529.98	55	10	Expatriates from Germany. D=ELCG,MCG,PCG,RCC,JWs.
3841	5	5	7.75	4	61.00	39.00	B	33.39	410	5	Northwest corner. Also in Ivory Coast, Burkina Faso. Animists 79%, Muslims 1%. D=40%RCC,COP,ACG,MDCC,ECG. M=Upper Volta Mission,WEC,GILLBT,UMC.
3842	7	6	8.66	0	55.00	45.00	B	28.10	490	5	West central. Muslims 48%(Sunnis,Ahmadis), animists 33%. D=Church of Pentecost,PCG,RCC,ECG,AoG,Supreme Healing Home,many other AICs. M=WF,VEA.
3843	11	5	9.12	1	54.00	46.00	B	17.73	532	5	Animists 83%, Muslims 5%. D=AoG,GBC,PCG,RCC(D-Navrongo-Bolgatanga),ECWA,MCG,COP,SDA,CPWA,CC,Bethlehem Revival Ch. M=SIL,SIM,WF,WEC.
3844	5	5	7.89	1	57.00	43.00	B	24.96	445	5	Part of Gurenne people. Animists 81%, Muslims 1%. D=PCG,RCC,ACG,AoG,ECWA. M=SIM,BM,WF.
3845	0	10	3.04	7	55.00	45.00	B	4.01	184	4	Buddhists/Chinese folk-religionists 98%. Traders. M=WEC(Hong Kong).
3846	3	6	5.10	1	60.00	40.00	B	50.37	295	6	North central, Damongo District. Agriculturalists. Animists 72%, Muslims 5%. D=RCC,PCG,ECG. M=WEC,GILLBT.
3847	1	9	2.96	5	51.10	48.90	B	0.18	223	3	Traders. Muslims 100%(Maliki Sunnis). 1970, two-thirds of all Hausas expelled from Ghana. D=Bethlehem Revival Ch. M=EM,SIM,WVI.
3848	2	10	5.24	4	99.90	0.10	C	509.17	117	10	Remnant of larger community of Nigerians deported from Ghana 1969-70. D=RCC,many AICs. M=Christ Church Mission.
3849	4	10	4.46	4	99.85	0.15	C	468.47	106	10	Workers from Nigeria, most expelled back to Nigeria in 1970. D=RCC,ACG,PCG,many AICs. M=SVD,SMA.
3850	5	10	6.95	0	99.90	0.10	C	479.61	157	10	Laborers from Nigeria, most deported back. D=RCC,MCG,PCG,ACG,many AICs.
3851	0	10	4.49	7	50.00	50.00	B	1.82	301	4	Traders, shopkeepers. Hindus 50%, Muslims 49%. Hindu sect Ananda Marga at work.
3852	4	10	6.31	4	69.00	31.00	B	37.77	305	5	North, Atakora Province. Most in Togo, some in Benin. Animists 82%, Muslims 1%. D=EPC,RCC,White Cross Society,and other AICs.
3853	0	9	3.31	1	34.00	66.00	A	1.24	377	4	Sandema District, Navrongo, Kpaliwongo. Close to Gurenne; second language Buli. Muslims 95%.
3854	6	6	7.75	4	60.00	40.00	B	32.85	416	5	North central. Majority in Burkina Faso. Literates 5%. Animists 74%, Muslims 7%. D=RCC(D-Navrongo-Bolgatanga),ECWA,FGNC,AoG,PCG,COP. M=SIL,SIM,WF.
3855	2	7	3.77	0	43.00	57.00	A	21.97	328	5	Remote, isolated, west of Mamprusi. Hunter-gatherers. Widespread blindness. Animists 57%, Muslims 29%. D=ECWA,RCC. M=SIM,GILLBT.
3856	9	5	9.25	0	65.00	35.00	B	35.58	448	5	Northeast. Also in Togo. Animists 79%, Muslims 1%(Sunnis,Ahmadis). D=AoG,PCG,RCC,ECG,EPCG,ELCG,COP,Apostolic Ch of Ghana,AICs. M=SVD,WEC,WF.
3857	1	5	4.54	0	34.00	66.00	A	8.68	476	4	Mainly in Togo, Benin. In Ghana, most in Accra. Muslims 91%(Sunnis,Ahmadis). D=RCC. M=WF.
3858	3	6	9.37	0	99.90	0.10	C	450.04	213	10	Central, near Nchimburu. Many are bilingual in Twi. Some animists. D=EPC,RCC,Buem-Kratchi Presbyterian Ch(AIC).
3859	3	6	4.07	2	96.00	4.00	B	192.72	150	7	Dialect of Ga-Adangme. Animists 20%, Muslims 2%. D=RCC(D-Accra),PCG,United Christians Ch. M=SVD,ACM,BCM,COF,EEC,HDM,KC,NDMI,FIFM(Zimbabwe).
3860	1	10	6.69	4	99.70	0.30	C	306.60	153	9	Migrants from Liberia. Fishermen, other trades. Animists 5%. D=many Kru AICs.
3861	5	6	4.66	2	99.52	0.48	B	194.55	154	7	Dialect of Akan. Animists 10%, Muslims 5%(Ahmadi gains). D=RCC,CCCC,COP,AOC(D-Accra),AICs. M=SVD,SMA,AMC,AOC(USA Blacks).
3862	5	6	8.66	0	99.60	0.40	C	219.00	269	8	Between Ga and Twi areas. Bilingual in Twi. Animists 5%. D=RCC,ACG,PCG,MCG,many AICs. M=NDMI.
3863	2	6	2.52	4	38.00	62.00	A	2.77	280	4	A few villages in northwest. Most in Burkina Faso and Ivory Coast. Animists 97%, Muslims 1%. D=RCC,Free Will Baptist Ch. M=WEC,NTM,WF.
3864	5	5	6.56	2	99.80	0.20	C	373.76	168	9	Southeast. Close to Ewe people. Animists 20%. D=EPC,RCC,MCG,COP,AICs.
3865	3	5	6.75	0	99.80	0.20	C	341.64	188	9	In southeast. Close to Akpafu linguistically, but politically separate. Animists 20%. D=RCC,MCG,PCG.
3866	3	8	4.35	4	45.50	54.50	A	0.83	358	3	Nomads. Primarily in Mali. Muslims 90%(Maliki Sunnis), animists 9%. D=SDA,RCC,PCG.
3867	0	9	5.45	4	44.00	56.00	A	3.21	466	4	In 10 West African countries. Animists 65%, Muslims 30%(Sunnis).
3868	8	5	5.12	1	36.50	63.50	A	0.66	487	3	East and west of Gambaga. Also in Togo. Animists 81%, Muslims 14%(Sunnis,Ahmadis). D=70% Protestants: MCG,AoG,Ghana Baptist Convention,PCG,ACG.
3869	2	10	9.16	4	85.00	15.00	B	62.05	339	6	Labor migrants from Burkina Faso. Animists 44%, Muslims 30%(Maliki Sunnis). D=RCC,AoG. M=SVD,WF,SMA.
3870	7	6	6.35	1	47.00	53.00	A	15.44	450	5	In north, near Bolgatanga. Animists 86%, Muslims 5%. D=RCC,AoG,MCG,GBC,ECWA,SDA,&c.
3871	3	6	5.24	1	37.00	63.00	A	5.40	489	4	Northeast around Tamale. Related to Dagbani. Literates 2%. Animists 89%, Muslims 7%. D=RCC,AoG,EPC. M=WEC.
3872	4	6	5.83	0	64.00	36.00	B	58.40	300	6	East central, west of Ntrubo. Trade language: Twi. Animists 64%, Muslims 1%. D=ECG,RCC,COP,EPC. M=WEC,GILLBT.
3873	2	7	4.73	0	95.00	5.00	C	208.05	170	8	3 villages west of Volta Lake near Prang. Second language: Twi. Animists 39%, Muslims 1%. D=RCC,MCG.
3874	5	6	6.19	0	44.00	56.00	A	12.84	473	5	North bank of Volta Lake. Animists 91%, Muslims 1%. D=RCC,EPCG,COP,ECG,SDA. M=WEC,SIL,GILLBT.
3875	2	6	6.99	0	95.00	5.00	C	208.05	235	8	South of Volta Lake. Some bilingual in Twi. Animists 39%, Muslims 1%. D=RCC,MCG.
3876	3	6	7.74	0	96.00	4.00	C	210.24	254	8	Southeast Ghana, northwest of Ewe. Some bilinguals in Ewe. Animists 40%. D=RCC,MCG,EPC. M=GILLBT.
3877	7	6	7.32	1	99.90	0.10	C	440.19	176	10	Also in Togo. Animists 10%, Muslims 1%. D=Apostolic Revelation Society,Ev Presbyterian Ch,RCC,CFC,GRM,NCC,COP. M=SIL,GILLBT.
3878	2	7	6.32	0	99.90	0.10	C	430.33	159	10	Southeast. Related to Ewe. Animists 9%, some Muslims. D=EPC,RCC.
3879	4	6	5.30	4	99.63	0.37	C	255.63	166	8	Southwest corner. Also in Ivory Coast. Animists 2%. D=RCC,Ch of Pentecost,Methodist Ch Ghana,AICs. M=LBI,UBS,SVD,SMA,AMC,CFC,COF,EEC,GCM,PJEM.
3880	0	6	7.16	0	92.00	8.00	C	201.48	257	8	Southwest corner. Bilingual in Wasa. Accessible by boat. Animists 40%.
3881	2	6	6.61	0	98.00	2.00	C	214.62	218	8	South of Volta Lake, south of Yeji. Bilingual in Twi (Akan); close to Chumburung. Animists 35%. D=RCC,MCG.
3882	2	7	4.76	1	74.00	26.00	B	81.03	227	6	West central, south of Nome. Main trade language: Gonja. Animists 50%, Muslims 20%. D=RCC,Methodist Ch Ghana.
3883	3	6	6.88	0	99.90	0.10	C	433.62	169	10	Southeast, 3 villages. Related to Ewe. Self-taught-literacy programs. Animists 10%. D=EPC,RCC,AICs.
3884	2	6	10.10	0	99.65	0.35	C	249.11	294	8	Southwest. Related to Anyi. Some also in Ivory Coast. Animists 24%, Muslims 1%. D=RCC,many AICs. M=FLM,NDMI.
3885	3	6	7.76	0	99.90	0.10	C	436.90	186	10	Southeast, north of Hohoe. Close to Ewe. Many literates. Animists 10%. D=EPC,MCG,RCC.
3886	0	10	3.65	0	27.60	72.40	A	0.60	551	3	Immigrants from Niger, Mali. Traders. Muslims 99%(Maliki Sunnis).
3887	2	6	5.92	0	44.00	56.00	A	16.06	454	5	North central. Animists 70%, Muslims 20%. D=95%RCC,GBC. M=GILLBT,FMB,BMM,SIM.
3888	2	7	6.00	0	99.90	0.10	C	440.19	149	10	Close to Ewe. Some animists 5%, Muslims 5%. D=EPC,RCC.
3889	3	5	7.08	1	46.00	54.00	A	15.11	503	5	In north, south of Bolgatanga. Animists 86%, Muslims 5%. D=RCC(D-Navrongo-Bolgatanga),AoG,SDA.
3890	4	6	7.28	0	61.00	39.00	B	51.21	389	6	North central, south of Sisala, Damongo District. Animists 71%, Muslims 6%. D=GBC,AoG,PCG,RCC. M=FMB,SIL.
3891	5	5	7.84	0	51.00	49.00	B	22.33	495	5	North central, Tumu District. Animists 68%, Muslims 20%. D=AoG,GBC,RCC(D-Wa),MCG,PCG. M=SIL,BMM,WF,GILLBT,FMB,SIM.
3892	0	0	5.75	8	99.78	0.22	C	367.26	141	9	North Americans, in business, education. Nonreligious 10%. D=RCC,BBC,SDA,etc.
3893	5	6	6.42	0	78.00	22.00	B	113.88	274	7	West central, Damongo District. Literates 10%. Animists 55%, Muslims 5%(Sunnis,Ahmadis). D=RCC,Evangelical Ch of Ghana,ACG,MCG,COP. M=SIL,WEC.
3894	6	5	6.14	1	43.00	57.00	A	4.70	479	4	Northwest corner. Muslims 50%(Sunnis,Ahmadis with strong mission to Ivory Coast), animists 47%. D=RCC,BMM,MCG,COP,ACG,SDA. M=BMM,WEC,AMC.
3895	7	6	5.28	2	99.60	0.40	C	227.76	170	8	Southwest. Close to Brong. Animists 10%, Muslims 20%. D=RCC,CFC,EEC,Original Ch of Christ,LCMS,COP,AICs.
3896	1	5	5.82	0	44.00	56.00	A	16.06	448	5	North central, town of Lambusie. Animists 70%, Muslims 20%. D=RCC(D-Wa). M=BMM,SIM.
3897	5	10	4.59	5	99.00	1.00	B	104.79	166	7	Many deported back to Nigeria in 1970. Muslims 61%(Sunnis,very many Ahmadis), animists 10%. D=RCC,GBC,ACG,CLA(Aladura),&c. M=NBC,FMB.
3898	2	10	3.46	1	38.50	61.50	A	0.70	381	3	Immigrants from Niger, Benin. Muslims 80%(Maliki Sunnis), animists 19%. D=RCC,ECWA.
3899	0	9	9.70		50.00	50.00	B	36.50	532	5	Japanese(Soka Gakkai), Greeks, numerous other African peoples. Muslims 55% (Sunnis, some Ahmadis), Animists 20%.
Gibraltar											
3900	5	10	0.12	8	99.79	0.21	C	449.82	22	10	Expatriates from Britain, in government, military. D=Ch of England(D-Gibraltar),MC,PC,JWs,SDA.
3901	6	9	0.11	8	99.99	0.01	C	609.41	18	10	Local populace 78% Catholics, 8% Anglicans. D=RCC(D-Gibraltar),CofE(D-Gibraltar),MC,PC,SDA,JWs.
3902	0	10	0.70	7	51.80	48.20	B	1.51	90	4	Long-term residents, and immigrants from India and Pakistan. Traders. Hindus 90%, Muslims 9%.
3903	0	10	0.41	8	57.50	42.50	B	1.04	52	4	Practicing Jewish community with 4 synagogues.
3904	0	10	0.16	7	56.00	44.00	B	12.26	42	5	Labor immigrants since 1961. From Morocco. Muslims 94%(Maliki Sunnis).
3905	2	10	0.23	8	99.97	0.03	C	619.58	18	10	Expatriates from Spain: laborers, professionals. Strong Catholics. D=RCC,JWs.
3906	0	10	0.23		99.96	0.04	C	473.04	5	10	Individuals from European or African countries.
Greece											
3907	2	10	4.92	5	77.00	23.00	B	56.21	227	6	Swahili-speaking African Blacks from East Africa. Mostly Muslims 80%. D=GOC,RCC.
3908	2	10	6.23	7	66.00	34.00	B	33.72	288	5	Arab migrant workers, students, refugees from Levant countries. Muslims 84%. D=GOC,RCC.
3909	3	10	1.25	6	99.90	0.10	C	545.31	31	10	Gregorians. Refugees from Turkey, 1860-1930. D=Armenian Apostolic Ch(D-Athens),Union of Armenian Ev Chs in Near East,RCC(O-Greece).
3910	2	10	1.26	6	99.84	0.16	C	438.43	46	10	Northwest Salonika; northern Greece, Pindus Mountains, around Trikala. Also in Albania, Bulgaria, former Yugoslavia. D=GOC,ROC.
3911	3	10	1.26	6	99.65	0.35	C	295.17	39	8	In Attica, Bocotia, southern Euboea, Salamis island, Epyrus region, and Athens. Rural. Chamurians. Muslims 30%(25% Sunnis, 5% Shias). D=AOC,GOC,RCC.
3912	1	10	1.26	6	99.70	0.30	C	311.71	51	9	Related to Greek Romani. Muslims 30%. D=nomadic caravan communities(Gypsy Evangelical Movement). M=GGMS.
3913	0	0	5.23	6	99.90	0.10	C	450.04	127	10	Immigrants from Belgium in business. Nonreligious 10%. D=RCC.
3914	2	10	1.49	8	99.79	0.21	C	444.05	47	10	Expatriates from Britain, in education, business. D=Ch of England(D-Gibraltar),JWs.
3915	1	9	1.26	6	99.78	0.22	C	407.12	48	10	From Bulgaria, in Thrace and Macedonia regions. D=Bulgarian Orthodox Ch(P-Sofia).
3916	0	0	5.05	6	99.76	0.24	C	355.07	127	9	Expatriates from the Netherlands in commerce. Nonreligious 18%. D=RCC.
3917	0	10	0.00	5	99.80	0.20	C	391.28	0	9	Artificial (constructed) language, in 80 countries. Speakers in Greece: 90,000(non mother-tongue).
3918	0	0	5.88	8	99.84	0.16	C	416.97	138	10	Immigrants from France in business and industry. Nonreligious 13%. D=RCC.
3919	0	0	6.90	8	99.87	0.13	C	435.04	161	10	Immigrants from Germany in business. D= EKD,RCC/KKD,NAK(NAC),JWs,EMKD.
3920	8	6	1.36	7	99.99	0.01	C	601.32	38	10	In 30 countries. D=Ch of Greece(78 Dioceses),Ch of Crete,Ch of the Dodecanese,RCC(11 Dioceses),AOCOC,JWs,GEC,FECG. M=UBS,LBI.
3921	2	10	1.26	6	99.75	0.25	C	358.61	48	9	Gypsies with Greek as mother tongue. D=nomadic caravan churches,Gypsy Evangelical Movement. M=GGMS,OFMCap,SJ.

Continued overleaf

Table 8-2 continued

PEOPLE		POPULATION				IDENTITY CODE		LANGUAGE		CHURCH		MINISTRY						SCRIPTURE		
Ref 1	*Ethnic name* 2	*P%* 3	*In 1995* 4	*In 2000* 5	*In 2025* 6	*Race* 7	*Language* 8	*Autoglossonym* 9	*S* 10	*AC* 11	*Members* 12	*Jayuh* 13-17	*d* 18	*wa* 19	*xc* 20	*mc* 21	*mi* 22	*Biblioglossonym* 23	*Pub* 24-26	*ss* 27
3922	Greek Rom Gypsy	0.34000	35,663	36,192	33,533	CNN25f	59-ACBA-bc	arlija		60.00	21,715	1A...	10	7	2	4	2	Romani: Arlija	Pn.	.
3923	Italian	0.04100	4,301	4,364	4,044	CEW21e	51-AABQ-c	standard italiano		84.00	3,666	2B.uh	10	10	14	0	0	Italian	PNB	b
3924	Jewish	0.01000	1,049	1,064	986	CMT35	56-AAAA-c	dhimotiki		0.10	1	2B.uh	5	4	2	1	0	Greek: Modern	PNB	b
3925	Macedonian	1.80800	189,645	192,457	178,315	CEW22g	53-AAAH-a	makedonski		90.00	173,211	2a.uh	10	8	11	4	2	Macedonian*	PNB	b
3926	Meglenite	0.11500	12,063	12,241	11,342	CEW21i	51-AADB-b	meglenitsa		97.00	11,874	0c...	10	8	11	4	1		p..	b
3927	Persian	0.09600	10,070	10,219	9,468	CNT24f	58-AACC-c	standard farsi		0.50	51	1Asu.	5	5	7	0	0		PNB	b
3928	Pomak	0.90000	94,403	95,803	88,763	CEW22b	53-AAAH-b	bulgarski		0.01	10	2A.uh	3	3	2	0	0	Bulgarian	PNB	b
3929	Pontic	1.92700	202,127	205,124	190,052	CEW20	56-AAAA-j	pontiki		90.00	184,612	1c.uh	10	8	11	4	1		pnb	b
3930	Rumelian Turk	1.40000	146,849	149,026	138,076	MSY41j	44-AABA-a	osmanli		0.10	149	1A.u.	5	3	1	0	0	Turkish	PNB	b
3931	Russian	0.12000	12,587	12,774	11,835	CEW22j	53-AAAE-d	russkiy		60.00	7,664	4B.uh	10	7	8	0	0	Russian	PNB	b
3932	Serb	0.30000	31,468	31,934	29,588	CEW22l	53-AAAG-a	standard srpski		80.00	25,547	1Asuh	10	8	9	4	1	Serbian*	PNB	b
3933	Spanish Jew	0.03700	3,881	3,939	3,649	CMT35	51-AAAB-dc	djudezmo-thessaloníki		0.06	2	0....	4	3	1	0	0		pnb	b
3934	Tsakonian	0.10800	11,328	11,496	10,652	CEW20	56-AABA-b	leonidhion-prastos		95.00	10,922	0....	10	9	11	4	2		...	b
3935	USA White	0.50000	52,446	53,224	49,313	CEW19s	52-ABAC-s	general american		78.00	41,515	1Bsuh	10	9	13	5	3	English*	PNB	b
3936	Vlach Gypsy (Lovari)	0.01100	1,154	1,171	1,085	CNN25f	59-ACBA-a	vlach-romani		70.00	820	1a...	10	8	6	4	2	Romani: Finnish*	PN.	b
3937	other minor peoples	0.04000	4,196	4,258	3,945	...				45.00	1,916		9	6	6	3	0			
	Greenland	**100.00000**	**55,798**	**56,156**	**59,634**					**70.07**	**39,350**									
3938	Danish (Dane)	13.60000	7,589	7,637	8,110	CEW19g	52-AAAD-c	general dansk		89.00	6,797	2A.uh	10	9	12	5	1	Danish	PNB	b
3939	Greenland Eskimo	79.10000	44,136	44,419	47,170	MRY40b	60-ABBC-f	north greenlandic		66.50	29,539	1....	10	8	8	5	2	Greenlandic*	PNB	b
3940	USA Black	0.60000	335	337	358	NFB68a	52-ABAE-a	talkin-black		73.00	246	0B.uh	10	9	13	5	3		pnb	b
3941	USA White	6.00000	3,348	3,369	3,578	CEW19s	52-ABAC-s	general american		74.00	2,493	1Bsuh	10	9	13	5	3	English*	PNB	b
3942	other minor peoples	0.70000	391	393	417	...				70.00	275		10	7	8	5	0			
	Grenada	**100.00000**	**92,135**	**93,717**	**104,647**					**96.83**	**90,746**									
3943	Black	51.70000	47,634	48,452	54,102	NFB68a	52-ABAF-w	grenadan-creole	97	98.10	47,531	1c..h	10	9	12	5	3		pn.	.
3944	Black Carib	0.00900	8	8	9	MIR39c	80-ACAA-d	garifuna		78.00	7	4.s..	10	8	7	5	2	Garifuna	PN.	b
3945	British	0.80000	737	750	837	CEW19i	52-ABAC-b	standard-english		79.00	592	3Bsuh	10	9	13	5	3		PNB	b
3946	Creole	2.00000	1,843	1,874	2,093	NFB69b	51-AACC-e	martiniquais	20	90.50	1,696	1As..	10	9	11	5	1		pnb	b
3947	French	0.10000	92	94	105	CEW21b	51-AABI-d	general français		87.00	82	1B.uh	10	9	14	5	2	French	PNB	b
3948	Indo-Pakistani	4.00000	3,685	3,749	4,186	CNN25g	59-AAFO-e	general hindi		75.00	2,812	3Asuh	10	8	7	5	1		pnb	b
3949	Mulatto	40.40000	37,223	37,862	42,277	NFB68b	52-ABAE-cm	grenadan-english		98.50	37,294	0A.uh	10	10	11	5	3		pnb	.
3950	USA Black	0.10000	92	94	105	NFB68a	52-ABAE-a	talkin-black		84.00	79	0B.uh	10	10	11	0	0		pnb	b
3951	USA White	0.80000	737	750	837	CEW19s	52-ABAC-s	general american		78.00	585	1Bsuh	10	10	12	0	0	English*	PNB	b
3952	other minor peoples	0.09100	84	85	95	...				80.00	68		10	7	7	5	0			
	Guadeloupe	**100.00000**	**424,263**	**455,687**	**569,216**					**95.01**	**432,948**									
3953	East Indian (Tamil)	1.00000	4,243	4,557	5,692	CNN23c	49-EBEA-b	tamil		56.00	2,552	2Asu.	10	8	11	4	2	Tamil	PNB	b
3954	French (White)	2.00000	8,485	9,114	11,384	CEW21b	51-AABI-d	general français	95	84.00	7,656	1B.uh	10	9	14	5	3	French	PNB	b
3955	French Creole (Mulatto)	76.70000	325,410	349,512	436,589	NFB69b	51-AACC-c	guadeloupéan	99	96.00	335,531	1cs..	10	9	13	5	3	Creole French: Lesser Antill	Pnb	b
3956	Guadeloupian Black	10.00000	42,426	45,569	56,922	NFB69a	51-AACC-c	guadeloupéan		99.00	45,113	1cs..	10	8	11	5	3	Creole French: Lesser Antill	Pnb	b
3957	Guadeloupian Mestizo	10.00000	42,426	45,569	56,922	NFB69b	51-AACC-c	guadeloupéan		91.40	41,650	1cs..	10	9	12	5	3	Creole French: Lesser Antill	Pnb	b
3958	Syrian Arab	0.20000	849	911	1,138	CMT30	12-AACF-f	syro-palestinian		19.00	173	1Asuh	8	5	7	4	2	Arabic: Lebanese*	Pnb	b
3959	other minor peoples	0.10000	424	456	569	...				60.00	273		10	7	8	5	0			
	Guam	**100.00000**	**151,095**	**167,556**	**227,634**					**93.49**	**156,653**									
3960	Filipino	17.87000	27,001	29,942	40,678	MSY44o	31-CKAA-a	proper tagalog		98.00	29,343	4Bs..	10	9	12	5	2	Tagalog	PNB	b
3961	Guamanian	44.24000	66,844	74,127	100,705	MSY44d	31-UAAA-d	guam-chamorro		97.40	72,199	1.s..	10	10	12	5	3	Chamorro	P..	b
3962	Han Chinese (Cantonese)	0.30000	453	503	683	MSY42a	79-AAAM-a	central yue		40.00	201	3A.uh	9	5	8	5	3	Chinese, Yue	PNB	b
3963	Han Chinese (Mandarin)	1.00000	1,511	1,676	2,276	MSY42a	79-AAAB-ba	kuo-yü		40.00	670	2Bsuh	9	5	8	5	3	Chinese: Kuoyu*	PNB	b
3964	Ilocano	13.00000	19,642	21,782	29,592	MSY44f	31-CBAA-b	vehicular ilocano		99.00	21,564	2A.u.	10	9	12	5	1	Ilokano*	PNB	b
3965	Japanese	1.67000	2,523	2,798	3,801	MSY45a	45-CAAA-a	koku-go		2.00	56	1B.uh	6	9	8	0	0	Japanese	PNB	b
3966	Korean	3.50000	5,288	5,864	7,967	MSY46	45-AAAA-b	kukö		81.00	4,750	2A...	10	9	12	5	3	Korean	PNB	b
3967	Palauan	3.00000	4,533	5,027	6,829	MPY54z	31-SAAA-a	palau		95.00	4,775	1.s..	10	8	11	5	3	Palauan	PN.	b
3968	USA Black	2.00000	3,022	3,351	4,553	NFB68a	52-ABAE-a	talkin-black		89.00	2,982	0B.uh	10	9	11	5	3		pnb	b
3969	USA White	12.62000	19,068	21,146	28,727	CEW19s	52-ABAC-s	general american		90.20	19,073	1Bsuh	10	9	13	5	1	English*	PNB	b
3970	Ulithian (Ulithi-Mall)	0.20000	302	335	455	MPY54f	38-AABB-a	ulithi		90.00	302	0.s..	10	8	11	5	1	Ulithian	PN.	b
3971	Woleaian	0.10000	151	168	228	MPY54z	38-AABC-a	woleai		91.00	152	0....	10	8	11	5	1		...	b
3972	other minor peoples	0.50000	755	838	1,138	...				70.00	586		10	7	7	5	0			
	Guatemala	**100.00000**	**9,975,895**	**11,385,295**	**19,816,134**					**93.84**	**10,684,149**									
3973	Acatenango SW Cakchiquel	0.11775	11,747	13,406	23,333	MIR37b	68-AEDC-f	cakchiquel-acatenango		80.00	10,725	1A...	10	7	8	4	2		pn.	.
3974	Aguacatec	0.18158	18,114	20,673	35,982	MIR37b	68-ADBB-a	aguacatec		85.00	17,572	0....	10	9	10	5	3	Aguacateco	PN.	.
3975	Black Carib (Garifuna)	0.18691	18,646	21,280	37,038	MIR39c	80-ACAA-d	garifuna		85.00	18,088	4.s..	10	9	10	5	3	Garifuna	PN.	b
3976	British	0.05000	4,988	5,693	9,908	CEW19i	52-ABAC-b	standard-english	4	79.00	4,497	3Bsuh	10	9	13	5	1		PNB	b
3977	Central Cakchiquel	1.43743	143,397	163,656	284,843	MIR37b	68-AEDC-c	central cakchiquel	9	93.00	152,200	4A...	10	9	11	5	3	Cakchiquel*	PN.	b
3978	Central Pocomam	0.09351	9,328	10,646	18,530	MIR37b	68-AEBA-a	central pokomam		80.00	8,517	0....	10	8	7	5	2	Pocomam: Central*	P..	.
3979	Central Quiche	2.29122	228,570	260,862	454,031	MIR37b	68-AEDA-e	quiché-chiché		89.00	232,167	1.s..	10	9	11	5	3		pnb	b
3980	Chajul Ixil	0.14532	14,497	16,545	28,797	MIR37b	68-ADCA-a	ixil-chajul		85.00	14,063	1....	10	8	11	5	2	Ixil: Chajul*	P..	.
3981	Chicomuceltec	0.00136	136	155	269	MIR37b	68-AABA-b	east chicomuceltec		90.00	139	0....	10	8	11	5	1		...	.
3982	Chorti	0.34250	34,167	38,995	67,870	MIR37b	68-ACAC-a	chortí		85.00	33,145	0....	10	7	11	4	3	Chorti	PN.	.
3983	Coastal Quiche	2.07254	206,754	235,965	410,697	MIR37b	68-AEDA-ha	quiché-coastal		80.00	188,772	1.s..	10	8	11	5	1		pnb	b
3984	Cubulco Achi	0.19245	19,199	21,911	38,136	MIR37b	68-AEDA-a	achi-cubulco	1	80.00	17,529	1.s..	10	8	11	5	2	Achi: Cubulco*	PNb	.
3985	East Central Quiche	1.05630	105,375	120,263	209,318	MIR37b	68-AEDA-ea	chichicastenango		88.00	105,831	1.s..	10	8	12	5	1		pnb	b
3986	Eastern Cakchiquel	0.93400	93,175	106,339	185,083	MIR37b	68-AEDC-d	east cakchiquel		88.00	93,578	1A...	10	9	11	5	3	Cakchiquel: Eastern*	PN.	b
3987	Eastern Jacalteco	0.11091	11,064	12,627	21,978	MIR37b	68-ADAB-b	east jacaltec		70.00	8,839	1....	10	7	7	5	3	Jacalteco: Eastern*	Pn.	.
3988	Eastern Kanjobal (Conob)	0.21263	21,212	24,209	42,135	MIR37b	68-ADAC-b	east kanjobal		80.00	19,367	0....	10	8	8	5	2	K'anjobal*	PNB	.
3989	Eastern Pocomam	0.13591	13,558	15,474	26,932	MIR37b	68-AEBA-c	east pokomam		80.00	12,379	0....	10	7	7	4	2	Pocomam: Eastern*	P..	.
3990	Eastern Pocomchi	0.26204	26,141	29,834	51,926	MIR37b	68-AEBB-b	east pokomchi'		80.00	23,867	0.s..	10	8	7	4	3	Pocomchi: Eastern*	PN.	.
3991	Eastern Quiche	0.20839	20,789	23,726	41,295	MIR37b	68-AEDA	quiche cluster		85.00	20,167	4.s..	10	8	11	4	2	Quiche: Sacapulas*	PNB	b
3992	Eastern Tzutujil	0.52300	52,174	59,545	103,638	MIR37b	68-AEDB-b	east tzutujil		80.00	47,636	0....	10	9	8	5	3	Tzutujil: Eastern*	PN.	.
3993	Guatemalan White	0.90000	89,783	102,468	178,345	CLT27	51-AABB-hc	guatemalteco	65	81.00	82,999	1A.uh	10	9	13	5	3		pnb	b
3994	Han Chinese	0.14400	14,365	16,395	28,535	MSY42a	51-AABB-hc	guatemalteco	65	71.00	11,640	1A.uh	10	7	8	5	1		pnb	b
3995	Han Chinese (Cantonese)	0.02000	1,995	2,277	3,963	MSY42a	79-AAAM-a	central yue	1	60.00	1,366	3A.uh	10	7	8	5	1	Chinese, Yue	PNB	b
3996	Jewish	0.00900	898	1,025	1,783	CMT35	51-AABB-hc	guatemalteco	65	0.14	1	1A.uh	5	4	2	3	0		pnb	b
3997	Joyabaj Quiche	0.57355	57,217	65,300	113,655	MIR37b	68-AEDA-g	quiché-joyabaj		85.00	55,505	1.s..	10	9	11	5	3	Quiche: Joyabaj*	PNb	.
3998	Kekchi (Quecchi)	3.65119	364,239	415,699	723,525	MIR37b	68-AEAA	kekchi cluster		92.30	383,690	4....	10	10	13	5	3	Kekchi	PNB	b
3999	Ladino (Mestizo)	63.72148	6,356,788	7,254,878	12,627,134	CLN29	51-AABB-hc	guatemalteco	65	97.20	7,051,742	1A.uh	10	10	11	5	3		pnb	b
4000	Mopan Maya	0.02827	2,820	3,219	5,602	MIR37b	68-ABAB-c	mopan		80.00	2,575	0....	10	8	7	5	3	Maya: Mopan*	PN.	b
4001	Nebaj Ixil	0.31395	31,319	35,744	62,213	MIR37b	68-ADCA-c	ixil-nebaj		80.00	28,595	1....	10	8	7	5	2	Ixil: Nebaj*	P..	.
4002	Northern (Cunen) Quiche	0.06670	6,654	7,594	13,217	MIR37b	68-AEDA-c	quiché-cunén		90.00	6,835	1.s..	10	8	11	5	2		pnb	b
4003	Northern Cakchiquel	0.21816	21,763	24,838	43,231	MIR37b	68-AEDC-a	north cakchiquel		80.00	19,871	1A...	10	8	8	5	3	Cakchiquel: Northern*	Pn.	.
4004	Northern Mam	1.69403	168,995	192,870	335,691	MIR37b	68-ADBA-a	mam-huehuetenango	5	88.00	169,726	4.s..	10	9	11	5	3	Mam: Huehuetenango*	PNB	.
4005	Palestinian Arab	0.01000	998	1,139	1,982	CMT30	12-AACF-f	syro-palestinian		19.00	216	1Asuh	8	5	7	5	2	Arabic: Lebanese*	Pnb	b
4006	Rabinal Achi	0.40557	40,459	46,175	80,368	MIR37b	68-AEDA-b	achi-rabinal	1	80.00	36,940	1.s..	10	8	8	5	2	Achi: Rabinal*	Pnb	.
4007	S Sebastian Coatan Chuj	0.20554	20,504	23,401	40,730	MIR37b	68-ADAA-b	chuj-coatán		85.00	19,891	0....	10	8	11	5	3	Chuj: S Sebastian Coatan*	PN.	.
4008	SD Xenacoj Cakchiquel	0.05493	5,480	6,254	10,885	MIR37b	68-AEDC-e	cakchiquel-xenacoj		80.00	5,003	1A...	10	8	8	5	3	Cakchiquel: S. Domingo Xe*	Pn.	.
4009	Sacapulteco Quiche	0.38896	38,802	44,284	77,077	MIR37b	68-AEDA	quiche cluster		90.00	39,856	4.s..	10	8	13	5	1	Quiche: Sacapulas*	PNB	b
4010	Sacatepequez Mam	0.10908	10,882	12,419	21,615	MIR37b	68-ADBA-e	mam-quetzaltenango		85.00	10,556	1.s..	10	7	11	4	1	Mam, Southern	PNb	.
4011	San Juan Cotzal Ixil	0.11626	11,598	13,237	23,038	MIR37b	68-ADCA-d	ixil-cotzal		80.00	10,589	1....	10	9	7	5	3	Ixil: Cotzal*	P..	.
4012	San Mateo Ixtatan Chuj	0.23376	23,320	26,614	46,322	MIR37b	68-ADAA-a	chuj-ixtatán		85.00	22,622	0....	10	7	8	4	1	Chuj: San Mateo Ixtatan*	PN.	b
4013	Santa Maria Cakchiquel	0.10764	10,738	12,255	21,330	MIR37b	68-AEDC-bb	santa-maría		80.00	9,804	1A...	10	7	8	4	3	Cakchiquel, S Maria Jesus	pn.	.
4014	Sipacapa Quiche	0.06338	6,323	7,216	12,559	MIR37b	68-AEDA	quiche cluster		90.00	6,494	4.s..	10	8	11	5	3	Quiche: Sacapulas*	PNB	b
4015	South Central Cakchiquel	0.79700	79,508	90,741	157,935	MIR37b	68-AEDC-h	south central cakchiquel.		88.00	79,852	1A...	10	8	11	5	3	Cakchiquel: South, Central*	Pn.	.
4016	Southern Cakchiquel	0.42873	42,770	48,812	84,958	MIR37b	68-AEDC-i	south cakchiquel		88.00	42,955	1A...	10	9	11	5	3	Cakchiquel: Southern*	PN.	.
4017	Southern Mam	1.32038	131,720	150,329	261,648	MIR37b	68-ADBA-ea	ostuncalco		86.00	129,283	1.s..	10	9	11	5	3	Mam: Ostuncalco	PNb	.
4018	Southern Pocomam	0.29483	29,412	33,567	58,424	MIR37b	68-AEBA-b	south pokomam		80.00	26,854	0....	10	8	7	4	1		p..	.
4019	Southwestern Quiche	4.84047	482,880	551,102	959,194	MIR37b	68-AEDA	quiche cluster		97.00	534,569	4.s..	10	9	10	5	3	Quiche: Sacapulas*	PNB	b
4020	Tacana Mam	0.21126	21,075	24,053	41,864	MIR37b	68-ADBA-g	tacanec		90.00	21,647	1.s..	10	8	11	5	2		pnb	.
4021	Tajumulco Mam	0.35916	35,829	40,891	71,172	MIR37b	68-ADBA-d	mam-tajumulco		80.00	32,713	1.s..	10	8	8	5	3		pnb	b
4022	Tectitan Mam	0.02827	2,820	3,219	5,602	MIR37b	68-ADBA-f	tectitec		90.00	2,897	1.s..	10	8	11	5	3	Tectiteco	pnb	b
4023	Todos Santos Mam	0.23767	23,710	27,059	47,097	MIR37b	68-ADBA-b	mam-cuchumatan		90.00	24,353	1.s..	10	8	11	5	3	Mam: Todos Santos*	Pnb	.
4024	USA White	0.13000	12,969	14,801	25,761	CEW19s	52-ABAC-s	general american		78.00	11,545	1Bsuh	10	10	12	0	0	English*	PNB	b
4025	Uspantec	0.02175	2,170	2,476	4,310	MIR37b	68-AECA-a	uspantec		85.00	2,105	0....	10	7	11	4	2	Uspanteco	P..	.
4026	West Central Quiche	2.42208	241,624	275,761	479,963	MIR37b	68-AEDA-h	quiché-cantel		91.00	250,942	4.s..	10	7	8	4	1		pnb	b
4027	West Indian Black	2.00000	199,518	227,706	396,323	NFB68a	52-ABAF	carib-anglo-creol cluster		89.00	202,658	1a..h	10	9	13	5	3	West Carib Creole English	PN.	b
4028	Western (Central) Mam	1.02617	102,370	116,832	203,347	MIR37b	68-ADBA-g	tacanec		90.00	105,149	1.s..	10	8	11	5	3		pnb	.
4029	Western Cakchiquel	0.72885	72,709	82,982	144,430	MIR37b	68-AEDC-g	cakchiquel-yepocapa		88.00	73,024	1A...	10	9	11	5	3	Cakchiquel: S W Yepocapa*	PN.	.
4030	Western Jacaltec	0.28586	28,517	32,546	56,646	MIR37b	68-ADAB-a	west jacaltec		80.00	26,037	1....	10	8	8	4	2	Jacalteco, Western	PN.	.
4031	Western Kanjobal	0.25390	25,329	28,907	50,313	MIR37b	68-ADAC-a	west kanjobal		80.00	23,126	0....	10	8	8	4	2	K'anjobal: Western*	PNb	.
4032	Western Pocomchi	0.31689	31,613	36,079	62,795	MIR37b	68-AEBB-a	west pokomchi'		70.00	25,255	0.s..	10	6	7	4	2	Pocomchi: Western*	Pn.	.
4033	Western Tzutujil	0.36751	36,662	41,842	72,826	MIR37b	68-AEDB-a	west tzutujil		80.00	33,474	0....	10	9	8	5	3	Tzutujil*	PN.	.
4034	Xinca	0.00257	256	293	509	MIR37z	69-GAAA	xinca cluster		90.00	263	0....	10	8	11	5	1		...	b
4035	Yepocapa SW Cakchiquel	0.15845	15,807	18,040	31,399	MIR37b	68-AEDC-g	cakchiquel-yepocapa		80.00	14,432	1A...	10	8	8	5	3	Cakchiquel: S W Yepocapa*	PN.	.

Continued opposite

Table 8-2 continued

EVANGELIZATION								EVANGELISM			ADDITIONAL DESCRIPTIVE DATA
Ref 1	D 28	aC 29	CG% 30	r 31	E 32	U 33	W 34	e 35	R 36	T 37	Locations, civil divisions, literacy, religions, church history, denominations, dioceses, church growth, missions, agencies, ministries, movements 38
3922	1	10	1.26	6	99.60	0.40	C	240.90	57	8	Balkan Gypsies. Muslims 40%. D=nomadic caravan churches(Gypsy Evangelical Movement). M=GGMS,SJ.
3923	0	0	6.08	7	99.84	0.16	C	420.04	142	10	Expatriates from Italy in business and industry. D=RCC.
3924	0	10	0.00	7	50.10	49.90	B	0.18	38	3	Decrease from 10,000 in 1943. Practicing Jews in Thessalonika.
3925	2	9	1.26	5	99.90	0.10	C	519.03	38	10	Mainly in Macedonia(former Yugoslavia), also Bulgaria, Albania, Canada. D=GOC,Macedonian Orthodox Ch. M=SJ,OFMCap.
3926	1	10	1.06	6	99.97	0.03	C	534.61	40	10	Meglen region, north of Salonika. A distinct language, though related to Romanian. D=GOC.
3927	0	0	4.01	5	36.50	63.50	A	0.66	354	3	Expatriates, refugees, settlers, laborers from Iran. Muslims 99%(Imami Shias).
3928	0	10	1.21	6	45.01	54.99	A	0.01	149	2	In Xanthi, mountains north of Kastoria. Muslims 100%(converts from Bulgarian Orthodoxy under Ottoman rule, immigrants since 1900).
3929	1	7	1.92	1	99.90	0.10	C	466.47	56	10	From Greeks on Black Sea coast of Turkey; also suburbs between Athens, Pireus; also in USA, Canada. Zealous Greeks. D=GOC.
3930	0	8	1.25	8	41.10	58.90	A	0.15	131	3	In eastern Thrace. Steady emigration to Turkey. Muslims 100%(Hanafi Sunnis). 300 mosques.
3931	0	0	6.87	7	99.60	0.40	C	238.71	173	8	Immigrant workers from Russia since 1989. Nonreligious/atheists 40%. D=Russian Orthodox Church, Baptists, Pentecostals.
3932	1	8	1.26	6	99.80	0.20	C	423.40	24	10	Refugees, immigrants from Serbia. Some Muslims. D=Serbian Orthodox Ch.
3933	0	10	0.70	1	29.06	70.94	A	0.06	131	2	Decline by massacre from 75,000 in 1943. Practicing Jews, in Salonika.
3934	2	10	1.26	0	99.95	0.05	C	495.85	43	10	Pastoralists in isolated mountain communities. Eastern coast of Peloponnese. Most are bilingual in Greek. D=GOC,AOCOC.
3935	5	10	2.77	8	99.78	0.22	C	438.43	65	10	Expatriates from USA, in military, education. D=SDA,CJCLdS,JWs,ICFG,GOC.
3936	1	10	1.22	6	99.70	0.30	C	311.71	51	9	Separate from Manush and other Gypsies. Caravan nomads. D=Gypsy Evangelical Movement. M=GGMS,SJ.
3937	0	10	1.26		74.00	26.00	B	121.54	47	7	Assyrians(Nestorians) and numerous other Europeans and Levantines.
Greenland											
3938	2	10	1.58	6	99.89	0.11	C	519.76	47	10	Administrators, educationists. D=LCG(ELC of Denmark),RCC. M=SJ.
3939	1	8	1.41	4	99.67	0.33	C	302.19	49	9	Fishermen. All baptized Christians, with 32% now nominal only; shamanists 1%. D=Lutheran Ch of Greenland. M=SFM,NPY.
3940	3	10	1.59	8	99.73	0.27	C	375.69	43	9	USA troops (soldiers, airmen) in US military. D=SDA,Pentecostals,JWs.
3941	5	10	1.53	8	99.74	0.26	C	402.44	45	10	US military. D=SDA,RCC,LCG,Pentecostals,JWs.
3942	0	10	1.59		99.70	0.30	C	263.16	42	8	Mainly Europeans. D=RCC.
Grenada											
3943	6	10	0.28	8	99.98	0.02	C	573.26	15	10	Lesser Antillean Creole English(Patwa). D=64% RCC(D-St George's),21% Anglican Ch(D-Windward Isles),SDA,MCCA,PCTG,&c. M=OP,SPS,FMB.
3944	2	10	0.56	4	99.78	0.22	C	370.11	33	9	Remnant of original Carib inhabitants. D=RCC(95% christopagans),SDA.
3945	4	10	0.39	8	99.79	0.21	C	444.05	27	10	Expatriates from Britain, in education, business. D=Anglican Ch(D-Windward Isles),RCC,MCCA,JWs. M=CMML,MMS,FMB.
3946	4	10	0.39	8	99.91	0.09	C	513.65	21	10	Creole-speaking Blacks. D=RCC,AC,ECWI,COG. M=WIM.
3947	1	10	0.40	8	99.87	0.13	C	498.55	24	10	Expatriates from France, in commerce, in business. D=RCC. M=OP,SPS.
3948	1	10	5.80	7	99.75	0.25	C	377.77	135	9	Traders. Hindus 17%. D=Presbyterian Ch in Trinidad & Grenada.
3949	10	10	0.40	8	99.99	0.01	C	591.41	18	10	Mixed-race Black/Whites. D=RCC,AC/CPWI,SDA,MCCA,PCTG,PB,Spiritual Baptist Chs,SA,AMEC,PAoW. M=CMML,OP,SPS,FMB.
3950	0	0	4.47	8	99.84	0.16	C	389.38	96	9	Military personnel from USA. D=NBC, RCC, SDA, etc.
3951	0	0	4.15	8	99.78	0.22	C	364.41	108	9	North Americans, in business, education. Nonreligious 10%. D=RCC,BBC,SDA,etc.
3952	0	10	0.39		99.80	0.20	C	324.12	10	9	Arabs, Lesser Antillean Creole French, other Caribbean islanders.
Guadeloupe											
3953	1	10	5.70	6	99.56	0.44	B	255.50	147	8	Spiritist Catholics with Malieman(Hindu-Catholic spirit-possession cult). Hindus 30%. D=RCC. M=CSSp,FSC.
3954	2	10	0.89	8	99.84	0.16	C	484.42	32	10	Expatriates in government, administration. D=RCC(D-Basse-Terre),EEG. M=CSSp,FSC,FMB.
3955	6	9	0.87	8	99.96	0.04	C	567.64	28	10	French-Blacks, speaking Lesser Antillean Creole French(Patwa). D=RCC(D-Basse-Terra),JWs,SDA,AEG(M=WIM),COG,EEG. M=CSSp,FSC,FMB.
3956	4	10	0.92	8	99.99	0.01	C	592.61	35	10	Persons of direct African descent. D=RCC(D-Basse-Terre),JWs,SDA,AEG. M=CSSp,WIM,FMB.
3957	7	10	0.92	8	99.91	0.09	C	535.11	29	10	French-Amerindians. D=RCC,JWs,SDA,AEG,AoG,COG,EEG. M=WIM,FSC,CSSp,FMB.
3958	2	10	2.89	8	80.00	20.00	B	55.48	123	6	Traders. Muslims 81%. D=Syrian Orthodox Ch,RCC. M=CSSp,FSC.
3959	0	10	0.92		93.00	7.00	C	203.67	27	8	Dominicans, Haitians, other Caribbean islanders.
Guam											
3960	2	10	3.74	5	99.98	0.02	C	618.82	70	10	Immigrants from Philippines. D=Iglesia ni Cristo(Manalista)(Ch of Christ),RCC. M=SJ,FMB.
3961	6	10	2.85	5	99.97	0.03	C	545.35	58	10	Also in Northern Mariana Islands. Tropical. D=80% RCC(D-Agana),SDA,JWs,CJCLdS,AoG,COG. M=YWAM,SJ,OFMCap,FMB,UBS,WEO.
3962	1	10	2.86	8	99.40	0.60	B	157.68	89	7	Immigrants from South China. Buddhists/Chinese folk-religionists 60%. D=RCC. M=SJ,OFMCap,FMB.
3963	1	10	2.88	7	99.40	0.60	B	157.68	90	7	Buddhists/Chinese folk-religionists 60%. D=RCC. M=SJ,OFMCap,FMB.
3964	2	10	2.90	4	99.99	0.01	C	603.45	59	10	Immigrants from Philippines. D=Church of Christ(Iglesia ni Cristo-Manalista),RCC(D-Agana). M=FMB.
3965	0	0	4.11	7	42.00	58.00	A	3.06	317	4	Immigrants from Japan in business. Mahayana Buddhists 65%, New Religionists 30%.
3966	1	10	1.99	6	99.81	0.19	C	449.38	47	10	Buddhists/Confucians/shamanists 19%. D=RCC. M=SJ,OFMCap,PCK-Tonghap,FMB.
3967	4	10	2.90	5	99.95	0.05	C	537.46	62	10	Immigrants from Republic of Belau(Palau); also in west Carolines. D=RCC,(D-Agana),Palau Ch(Modekngei healing movement),SDA.
3968	5	10	2.90	8	99.89	0.11	C	503.51	62	10	US military and dependants. D=AoG,SDA,JWS,RCC,COG. M=CBHMS,GBFMS,FMB.
3969	9	10	2.25	8	99.90	0.10	C	537.30	53	10	US military and dependants. D=SDA,JWs,CJCLdS,CCS,RCC,AoG,CRC,COG,ECUSA. M=FMB.
3970	2	10	2.92	2	99.90	0.10	C	466.47	69	10	Workers from eastern Caroline Islands, Micronesia. D=RCC(D-Agana),Protestants. M=Liebenzell Mission.
3971	2	10	2.87	0	99.91	0.09	C	451.72	71	10	Immigrant workers from islands in eastern Carolines, Micronesia. D=RCC(D-Agana),PCCI(Micronesia). M=Liebenzell Mission.
3972	0	10	2.89		99.70	0.30	C	258.05	78	8	Cambodians, Kosreans, Marshallese, Micronesians, Pohnpeians, Yapese, other Pacific islanders.
Guatemala											
3973	2	9	1.92	1	99.80	0.20	C	379.60	57	9	Agriculturalists. Nominal Christians 15%. Evangelical expansion. D=RCC,AoG. M=BTT,FMB.
3974	3	7	1.92	0	99.85	0.15	C	409.53	56	10	Western Huehuetenango. D=RCC,Iglesia del Principe de Paz,COG. M=SIL,CAM,OFM,SJ,BTT.
3975	5	8	1.92	4	99.85	0.15	C	440.55	57	10	Northeast coast. D=RCC(christopagans 40%),CON,Plymouth Brethren,United Brethren in Christ,Mennonites. M=BTT,LCMS,SIL.
3976	1	10	1.92	8	99.79	0.21	C	435.40	56	10	Expatriates. from Britain, in commerce, professions, education. D=ECUSA.
3977	6	9	1.98	4	99.93	0.07	C	539.72	47	10	Southern Guatemala. Rapid Evangelical growth. D=RCC,CBG,AoG,Iglesia del Principe de Paz,Tabernacle of God,CJCLdS. M=CAM,SIL,COGA,OFM,SJ,FSC.
3978	2	10	1.92	0	99.80	0.20	C	353.32	61	9	5 miles north of Guatemala City. Also in El Salvador. D=INPG,RCC. M=SIL,BTT.
3979	2	9	1.92	0	99.89	0.11	C	471.03	51	10	D=RCC(christopagans 30%); rapid Evangelical growth: Iglesia del Principe de Paz,INPG.AoG,CC. M=SIL,UBS,CAM,OFM,SJ,PFM,FSC,BTT,FMB.
3980	4	7	2.34	0	99.85	0.15	C	403.32	66	10	Quiche. D=Church of the Nazarene,Primitive Methodist Ch,RCC,Church of God. M=BTT,SIL.
3981	1	7	1.91	0	99.90	0.10	C	420.48	57	10	Primarily in Mexico(Chiapas). Mayans: Cakchiquel Mam. 100% bilingual in Spanish. D=RCC.
3982	1	10	1.92	0	99.85	0.15	C	412.63	55	10	Border with Honduras. D=RCC. M=SIL,Society of Friends,BTT,FCSYM,WVI.
3983	1	9	1.92	0	99.80	0.20	C	388.36	55	9	Southwest of Lake Atitlan. Fast Evangelical growth. D=RCC(christopagans 30%). M=BTT.
3984	3	7	1.92	0	99.80	0.20	C	385.44	56	9	Baja Verapaz Department. D=AoG,Church of the Nazarene, Prince of Peace Ch. M=SIL,BTT.
3985	1	9	1.92	0	99.88	0.12	C	456.10	52	10	Includes Chichicastenango and Chiche. D=RCC(strong christopaganism).
3986	5	9	1.92	1	99.88	0.12	C	475.37	50	10	Rapid Evangelical growth. D=INPG,AoG,CBG,RCC,CJCLdS. M=CAM,SJ,OFM,FSC,PFM,BTT,WVI,FMB-SBC, SIL.
3987	1	9	1.92	0	99.70	0.30	C	288.71	65	8	Near Mexico border, Huehuetenango Department, Concepcion area, D=RCC. M=CAM,EC,SIL.
3988	2	7	1.92	0	99.80	0.20	C	376.68	57	9	Huehuetenango Department. Also in USA. 26% literates. D=RCC,CAM.
3989	2	10	1.92	0	99.80	0.20	C	353.32	61	9	Jalapa Department. Partially bilingual in Spanish. D=RCC,Society of Friends. M=BTT,SIL.
3990	1	7	1.92	0	99.80	0.20	C	356.24	60	9	Baja Verapaz. D=Church of the Nazarene. M=SIL,Society of Friends,BTT.
3991	1	9	1.92	0	99.85	0.15	C	440.55	52	10	Agriculturalists. D=RCC. M=BTT,SIL.
3992	4	8	1.92	0	99.80	0.20	C	367.92	58	9	Lake Atitlan. Rapid growth of Evangelicals. D=RCC,AoG,Church of God,Iglesia del Principe de Paz. M=CAM,FMB,SJ,OFM,FSC,CMA,BTT,SIL.
3993	3	10	1.93	8	99.81	0.19	C	443.47	51	10	Original settlers, descendants of conquistadors. D=RCC,ICNG,ICG. M=CAM,SJ,OFM,FSC,FMB.
3994	1	10	1.92	8	99.71	0.29	C	347.26	53	9	Buddhists/Chinese folk-religionists 29%. D=RCC.
3995	1	10	1.92	8	99.60	0.40	C	280.32	55	8	Buddhists/Chinese folk-religionists 40%. D=RCC.
3996	0	10	0.00	8	46.14	53.86	A	0.23	41	3	Practicing Jews. Long-time residents. Mostly resident in capital.
3997	1	9	1.92	0	99.85	0.15	C	428.14	53	10	Rapid Evangelical growth. D=RCC(christopagans 30%), Primitive Methodist Ch. M=SIL,SJ,OFM,FSC,BTT.
3998	6	7	2.04	0	99.92	0.08	C	523.19	50	10	Northern Alta Verapaz. D=80% RCC,5% Protestants: ICFG,CON,Mennonites,CJCLdS,ECUSA. M=FMB,AoG,SJ,OFM,FSC,PFM,BTT,EMBMC,WVI.SIL.
3999	9	10	1.97	8	99.97	0.03	C	586.09	42	10	Unaffiliated Christians 1%. D=RCC(13 Dioceses),AoG,NPC,SDA,Ch of the Prince of Peace,CBG,CJCLdS,CON,JWs. M=OFM,SJ,FSC,PFM,EMBMC,FMB.
4000	6	6	1.92	0	99.80	0.20	C	356.24	60	9	Most in Belize. D=AoG,Calvario,RCC,Nazarenes,Mennonites,Iglesia del Principe de Paz.
4001	3	7	1.92	0	99.80	0.20	C	353.32	61	9	Quiche. D=RCC,Primitive Methodist Ch,Ch of God. M=BTT,SIL.
4002	1	9	1.92	0	99.90	0.10	C	469.75	52	10	Quiche Department. D=RCC(christopagans 30%); fast Evangelical growth. M=BTT, LBT.
4003	2	9	1.92	1	99.80	0.20	C	385.44	56	9	Central Highlands. High Evangelical growth rate. D=RCC,AoG. M=BTT,FMB,SIL,CAM.
4004	3	8	1.92	0	99.88	0.12	C	475.37	50	10	Huehuetenango Mam. D=RCC,NPC,CJCLdS. M=CAM,UBS,OFM,SJ,FSC,BTT,WVI,FMB.
4005	2	10	3.12	8	80.00	20.00	B	55.48	131	6	Immigrants from Palestine. Muslims 80%. D=RCC,ECUSA.
4006	2	7	1.92	0	99.80	0.20	C	370.84	58	9	20% bilingual in Spanish. D=RCC,Church of the Nazarene. M=SIL,BTT.
4007	1	7	1.92	0	99.85	0.15	C	406.42	56	10	Central Western Coatan River Area. Literates 22%. D=RCC. M=CAM,SIL,MEA(Guatemala).
4008	1	9	1.92	1	99.80	0.20	C	379.60	57	9	SD=Santo Domingo. West of Guatemala City. Evangelical growth. D=RCC,AoG. M=BTT,FMB,SIL.
4009	1	9	1.92	0	99.90	0.10	C	489.46	49	10	Quiche Department. D=RCC(christopagans 30%); rapid Evangelical growth: Church of Christ. M=BTT.
4010	1	8	1.92	0	99.85	0.15	C	415.73	55	10	In northwest. Agriculturalists. D=RCC. M=BTT.
4011	5	7	2.10	0	99.80	0.20	C	356.24	64	9	Quiche Department. Monolingual. D=RCC,Church of God,Iglesia del Principe de Paz,Primitive Methodist Ch,et alia. M=Salvadorean Evangelical Mission.
4012	1	7	1.92	0	99.85	0.15	C	387.81	59	9	Western Huehuetenango Department. Literates 14%. D=RCC. M=CAM.
4013	2	8	1.92	1	99.80	0.20	C	376.68	57	9	Southeast of Antigua Guatemala. Evangelical growth. D=RCC,AoG. M=BTT,FMB,SIL.
4014	1	9	1.92	0	99.90	0.10	C	486.18	50	10	San Marcos Department. D=RCC(christopagans 30%); fast Evangelical growth. M=CAM,BTT,SIL.
4015	2	9	1.92	1	99.88	0.12	C	459.31	52	10	West of Guatemala City. D=RCC,AoG. Rapid Evangelical growth in new churches. M=BTT,WVI,FMB,SIL,CAM.
4016	6	9	2.16	1	99.88	0.12	C	465.74	55	10	South of Antigua. Rapid Evangelical growth. D=RCC,CBG,ICFG,AoG,Elim,Independent. M=CAM,UPM,SJ,OFM,FSC,BTT,WVI,FMB,SIL.
4017	5	8	1.92	0	99.86	0.14	C	439.46	53	10	Quetzaltenango Department. Literates 37%. D=RCC,NPC,COG,AoG,CJCLdS. M=CAM,OFM,SJ,FSC,PFM,BTT,WVI,FMB,SIL.
4018	1	9	1.92	0	99.80	0.20	C	344.56	62	9	South of Guatemala City. Agriculturalists. D=RCC. M=BTT.
4019	2	9	2.01	0	99.97	0.03	C	552.31	49	10	West Central Quiche(Cantel Quiche). D=RCC(christopagans 25%),rapid growth of Evangelicals: Ch of Christ;CJCLdS. M=SIL,SJ,OFM,FSC,PFM,BTT. R=HCJB.
4020	4	8	1.92	0	99.90	0.10	C	466.47	52	10	Western Guatemala border; also in Mexico. Agriculturalists. D=RCC,NPC,AoG,COG. M=BTT,CAM.
4021	3	8	1.92	0	99.80	0.20	C	388.36	55	9	San Marcos Department, 2 towns. D=RCC,NPC,&c.
4022	2	8	1.92	0	99.90	0.10	C	463.18	52	10	Tectitan area, western Guatemala border. D=RCC,NPC. M=CAM,BTT,SIL.
4023	4	8	1.92	0	99.90	0.10	C	469.75	52	10	Town of Todos Santos Cuchumatan. D=RCC,NPC,Christian Assemblies,Evangelical Ch. M=CAM,Scripture Gift Mission,BTT,SIL.
4024	0	0	7.31	8	99.78	0.22	C	370.11	173	9	North Americans, in business, education. Nonreligious 10%. D=RCC,BBC,SDA,etc.
4025	1	8	1.92	0	99.85	0.15	C	390.91	58	9	Quiche Department. Literates 12%. D=RCC. M=SIL,BTT.
4026	1	9	1.27	0	99.91	0.09	C	465.01	40	10	Quezaltenango and TotTotonnicapan Departments. Agriculturalists. D=RCC. M=BTT.
4027	4	10	1.92	8	99.89	0.11	C	516.51	44	10	Afro-American spiritists 10%, Baha'is 1%. D=RCC(AA-Izabal),ECUSA,AoG,&c.
4028	2	8	1.92	0	99.90	0.10	C	466.47	52	10	San Marcos Department. D=RCC,NPC. M=CAM,SIL,BTT,WVI,FMB.
4029	4	9	1.92	1	99.88	0.12	C	465.74	51	10	Around Lake Atitlan. Rapid growth of Evangelicals. D=RCC,Emmanuel Mission,AoG,Church of God. M=CAM,SJ,OFM,FSC,PFM,BTT,WVI,FMB,SIL.
4030	1	7	1.92	0	99.80	0.20	C	356.24	60	9	Around Jacalteco town, Huehuetenango. Literates 52%. D=RCC. M=CAM,SIL.
4031	1	7	1.92	0	99.80	0.20	C	362.08	59	9	Conob. Some emigrants to USA. D=RCC. M=CAM,SIL.
4032	3	7	1.92	0	99.70	0.30	C	286.16	66	8	Agriculturalists. D=Church of the Nazarene,Presbyterians,. M=SIL,BTT.
4033	4	8	1.92	0	99.80	0.20	C	367.92	58	9	Southwestern shore, Lake Atitlan. D=RCC,AoG,PDP,COG. Very rapid Evangelical growth. M=CAM,FMB,CMA,SJ,OFM,SIL.
4034	1	10	1.93	0	99.90	0.10	C	440.19	56	10	Southeastern. Language almost extinct; all speak Spanish. D=RCC.
4035	2	9	1.92	1	99.80	0.20	C	388.36	55	9	Yepocapa Municipality. Numerous Evangelicals, rapid growth. D=RCC,AoG. M=BTT, FMB,CAM,SIL.

Continued overleaf

Table 8-2 continued

	PEOPLE					IDENTITY CODE		LANGUAGE		CHURCH		MINISTRY	SCRIPTURE	
Ref	Ethnic name	P%	In 1995	In 2000	In 2025	Race	Language	Autoglossonym	S	AC	Members	Jayuh dwa xcmc mi	Biblioglossonym	Pub ss
1	2	3	4	5	6	7	8	9	10	11	12	13-17 18 19 20 21 22	23	24-26 27
4036	Yucatec Maya	0.07700	7,681	8,767	15,258	MIR37b	68-ABAB-b	petén-itza		85.00	7,452	0.... 10 7 11 2 1		pn. b
4037	other minor peoples	0.10000	9,976	11,385	19,816	...				70.00	7,970	10 7 7 5 0		
	Guinea	100.00000	7,152,605	7,430,346	12,496,941					3.11	231,320			
4038	Badyara (Badyaranke, Gola)	0.09950	7,117	7,393	12,434	NAB56c	90-IBAA-a	ba-jar		1.00	74	0.... 6 4 0 1 1	Badyara	... n
4039	Baga	0.54122	38,711	40,215	67,636	NAB56c	90-MAAA	mbulungish cluster		20.00	8,043	0.... 9 5 6 1 2		
4040	Bambara	0.50000	35,763	37,152	62,485	NAB63a	00-AAAB-a	bamanan-kan	8	2.00	743	4As.. 6 5 2 2 1	Bambara	PNB b
4041	Bande (Bandi, Gbandi)	1.27536	91,221	94,764	159,381	NAB64c	00-ABAA-a	bandi		2.80	2,653	1.... 6 4 5 3 2	Bandi	Pnb .
4042	Bassari	0.14500	10,371	10,774	18,121	NAB56c	90-JAAA-a	o-ni-yan		5.00	539	0.... 7 5 4 3 1	Basari	PN. .
4043	Biafada	0.08000	5,722	5,944	9,998	NAB56c	90-IAAA-a	proper bia-fada		5.00	297	0.... 7 5 5 2 1		... .
4044	Black Baga	0.07000	5,007	5,201	8,748	NAB56c	90-MAAA	mbulungish cluster		0.05	3	0.... 4 3 0 0 1		... .
4045	Boin (Tenda Boeni)	0.20000	14,305	14,861	24,994	NAB56c	90-JAAA-a	o-ni-yan		0.00	0	0.... 0 3 0 0 0	Basari	PN. .
4046	British	0.00300	215	223	375	CEW19i	52-ABAC-b	standard-english	4	79.00	176	3Bsuh 10 9 11 4 2		PNB b
4047	Cuban White	0.00100	72	74	125	CLT27	51-AABB-hi	cubano		20.00	15	1B.uh 9 8 2 2 1		pnb b
4048	Dan (Yacouba)	1.19036	85,142	88,448	148,759	NAB64a	00-DBAA-a	dan		15.00	13,267	3.... 8 6 5 5 2	Dan*	PN. b
4049	English Creole	0.02000	1,431	1,486	2,499	NAN58	52-ABAH	west-coast-creole- cluster	5	70.00	1,040	4.s.h 10 8 8 3 3		PN. b
4050	French	0.03000	2,146	2,229	3,749	CEW21b	51-AABI-d	general français	33	87.00	1,939	1B.uh 10 9 14 4 1	French	Pnb b
4051	French Creole	0.04000	2,861	2,972	4,999	NAN58	51-AACC-c	guadeloupéan		70.00	2,080	1cs.. 10 9 8 4 1	Creole French: Lesser Antill	Pnb b
4052	Fula Jalon (Futa Dyalon)	37.03260	2,648,796	2,751,650	4,627,942	NAB56c	90-BAAA-d	futa-jalon	33	0.01	275	2as.. 3 3 5 1 3	Fula: Futa-jalon*	Pnb .
4053	Fulakunda (Fula Cunda)	0.05058	3,618	3,758	6,321	NAB56c	90-BAAA-c	fula-kunda		0.03	1	1as.. 3 3 5 1 3	Pulaar: Fulakunda	Pnb b
4054	Guerze (Kpelle, Pessy)	5.19305	371,438	385,862	648,972	NAB64f	00-ABAC-b	kpelese		36.90	142,383	2.... 9 5 7 4 2	Kpelee*	Pn. .
4055	Hausa	0.05000	3,576	3,715	6,248	NAB60a	19-HAAB-a	hausa		0.11	4	4Asu. 5 3 2 0 0	Hausa	PNB b
4056	Jahanke (Diakhanke)	0.21244	15,195	15,785	26,549	NAB63j	00-BAAA-b	azayr		0.00	0	1.... 0 4 4 1 0		... n
4057	Kissi (Northern Kisi)	4.83056	345,511	358,927	603,672	NAB56c	94-BABA-a	north kisi		8.00	28,714	3.... 7 5 7 4 3	Kisi: Northern*	PN. .
4058	Kono	0.10000	7,153	7,430	12,497	NAB64e	00-AAAE-a	central kono		4.00	297	1.... 6 4 6 2 2	Kono	P. . .
4059	Konyagi (Coniagui, Tenda)	0.05794	4,144	4,305	7,241	NAB56c	90-JAAA-b	wa-meyny		10.00	431	0.... 8 5 6 2 1	Wamei	pn. .
4060	Konyanke	0.20000	14,305	14,861	24,994	NAB63f	00-AAAB-f	konyanka-kan		0.50	74	1cs.. 5 4 5 2 3		pnb n
4061	Koranko	0.93070	66,569	69,154	116,309	NAB63g	00-AAAD-c	wasamandu-kuranko		0.30	207	0.... 5 4 3 2 1	Kuranko	PN. .
4062	Kru	0.05000	3,576	3,715	6,248	NAB59j	95-ABAE-g	central klao		75.00	2,786	0.... 10 9 11 4 3	Kru*	PN. b
4063	Landoma (Landouman)	0.24279	17,366	18,040	30,341	NAB56c	94-AAAA-b	landuma		5.00	902	0.... 7 4 4 2 1		... .
4064	Lele	1.04483	74,733	77,634	130,572	NAB63g	00-AAAD-a	falanko-kuranko		1.00	776	0.... 6 4 4 1 1		pn. n
4065	Levantine Arab	0.02550	1,824	1,895	3,187	CMT30	12-AACF-f	syro-palestinian	8	15.00	284	1Asuh 8 5 2 3 3	Arabic: Lebanese*	Pnb b
4066	Limba (Yimbe)	0.06343	4,537	4,713	7,927	NAB56c	90-PAAC	south limba cluster		4.00	189	0.... 7 5 4 2 0	Limba	PN. .
4067	Loko (Landogo)	0.06000	4,292	4,458	7,498	NAB64g	00-AAAB-b	loko		2.00	89	1.... 6 4 4 2 1	Loko: Sierra Leone	PNB b
4068	Mano (Ngere, Mawe)	0.57663	41,244	42,846	72,061	NAB64j	00-DAAA-a	man-wi		1.50	643	0.... 6 4 5 2 3	Mano	PN. .
4069	Nalu	0.20614	14,744	15,317	25,761	NAB56c	90-LAAA-a	naluu		0.00	0	0.... 0 3 0 0 1		... n
4070	Northern Bullom (Mnani)	0.06000	4,292	4,458	7,498	NAB56c	90-AACA-a	soso		5.00	223	4.... 7 5 7 4 3	Soso*	PN. n
4071	Northwestern Maninka	1.23926	88,639	92,081	154,870	NAB63h	00-AAAA-c	maninka-xanwo		0.50	460	1c.. 5 4 3 0 0		pn. .
4072	Papel (Pepel)	0.04047	2,895	3,007	5,058	NAB56c	90-FABA-a	proper papel		15.00	451	0.... 8 5 7 2 1	Papel	PN. p
4073	Soninke (Serahuli)	0.08000	5,722	5,944	9,998	NAB63j	00-BAAA-b	proper soninke		0.00	0	3.... 0 3 0 0 0	Soninke	... b
4074	Southern Maninka	25.61821	1,832,369	1,903,522	3,201,493	NAB63h	00-AAAA-h	maninka-kan	38	0.30	5,711	3a.. 5 4 5 3 3	Maninka*	PN. .
4075	Susu (Soso)	12.17838	871,071	904,896	1,521,925	NAB63k	00-AACA-a	soso	16	0.20	1,810	0.... 6 4 5 3 3	Soso*	PN. n
4076	Temne	0.20000	14,305	14,861	24,994	NAB56c	94-AACA-a	ka-themne		5.00	743	3.... 7 5 7 3 2	Themne	PN. .
4077	Toma (Loma, Toa, Toale)	2.42454	173,418	180,152	302,993	NAB64h	00-ABAB-b	toma		6.50	11,710	0.... 7 4 7 4 2	Toma	PN. .
4078	Tukulor	0.35239	25,205	26,184	44,038	NAB56c	90-BAAA-a	haal-pulaar		0.02	5	2As.. 3 1 1 0 0	Fula: Pulaar*	Pnb .
4079	USA White	0.00900	644	669	1,125	CEW19s	52-ABAC-s	general american		78.00	522	1Bsuh 10 10 12 0 0	English*	PNB b
4080	Yalunka (Dyalonke)	2.47512	177,036	183,910	309,314	NAB63l	00-AACA-b	yalunka		0.01	18	0.... 3 4 3 0 1	Yalunka	PN. .
4081	other minor peoples	0.20000	14,305	14,861	24,994	...				5.00	743	7 4 4 1 0		
	Guinea-Bissau	100.00000	1,086,037	1,213,111	1,946,020					12.83	155,644			
4082	Badyara (Badyaranke)	0.35571	3,863	4,315	6,922	NAB56c	90-IBAA-a	ba-jar		1.00	43	0.... 6 4 4 1 1	Badyara	... n
4083	Balanta (Bulanda, Belante)	25.00736	271,589	303,367	486,648	NAB56c	90-GABA	north balanta cluster	38	8.00	24,269	0.... 7 5 7 4 3	Frase*	P.. n
4084	Bambara	0.10002	1,086	1,213	1,946	NAB63a	00-AAAA-a	bamanan-kan		0.10	1	4As.. 5 5 4 1 2	Bambara	PNB b
4085	Banyum (Banyun, Bainuk)	0.60973	6,622	7,397	11,865	NAB56c	90-HAAA	bainuk cluster		15.60	1,154	0.... 8 5 5 3 2		... .
4086	Bassari	0.03181	345	386	619	NAB56c	90-JAAA-a	o-ni-yan		6.00	23	0.... 7 5 4 3 1	Basari	PN. .
4087	Bayot	0.15241	1,655	1,849	2,966	NAB56c	90-EAAA-a	bayot		3.50	65	0.... 6 5 4 1 0		... n
4088	Biafada (Biafar, Bidyola)	3.11404	33,820	37,777	60,600	NAB56c	90-IAAA-a	proper bia-fada		6.10	2,304	0.... 7 5 5 2 3		... .
4089	Bijago (Bidyogo, Bugago)	2.38418	25,893	28,923	46,397	NAB56c	90-OAAA	bijogo cluster		20.20	5,842	0.... 9 5 7 4 3	Bijago*	PN. .
4090	Caboverdian Mestico	1.00000	10,860	12,131	19,460	NAN58	51-AACA-a	caboverdense		75.00	9,098	1c... 10 8 12 2 1	Crioulo, Upper Guinea	PNB b
4091	Diola (Jola, Joola)	1.78362	19,371	21,637	34,710	NAB56c	90-DAHA-a	ku-jamut-aay		3.50	757	0.... 6 4 4 2 3		... b
4092	Felup (Fulup, Flup)	1.65432	17,967	20,069	32,193	NAB56c	90-DAHA-a	ku-jamut-aay		3.00	602	0.... 6 4 4 2 1		... .
4093	French	0.06000	652	728	1,168	CEW21b	51-AABI-d	general français	2	87.00	633	1B.uh 10 9 14 4 1	French	PNB b
4094	Fulakunda (Fula Cunda)	17.10741	185,793	207,532	332,914	NAB56c	90-BAAA-c	fula-kunda		0.30	623	1as.. 5 3 1 1 3	Pulaar: Fulakunda	Pnb b
4095	Ganja (Bandal)	0.10000	1,086	1,213	1,946	NAB56c	90-GAAA-a	ganja-blip		6.00	73	0.... 7 5 4 1 1		... .
4096	Guinean Mestico	9.16259	99,509	111,152	178,306	NAN58	51-AACA-b	guineense	51	57.20	63,579	4c... 10 9 12 4 3		PNB b
4097	Jahanke (Diakhanke)	0.50000	5,430	6,066	9,730	NAB63j	00-BAAA-b	azayr		1.00	61	1.... 6 4 4 1 1		... .
4098	Kasanga (Haal)	0.04416	480	536	859	NAB56c	90-HBBA-a	haal		5.00	27	0.... 7 5 4 1 1		... .
4099	Kobiana	0.04060	441	493	790	NAB56c	90-HBAA-a	buy		10.00	49	0.... 8 5 4 1 1		... p
4100	Kunante (Maswanka, Sua)	1.06705	11,589	12,945	20,765	NAB56c	90-KAAA-a	sua		6.00	777	0.... 7 5 4 1 2		... .
4101	Lebanese Arab	0.50000	5,430	6,066	9,730	CMT30	12-AACF-f	syro-palestinian	5	15.00	910	1Asuh 8 5 2 3 1	Arabic: Lebanese*	Pnb b
4102	Malinke (Maninka)	1.00000	10,860	12,131	19,460	NAB63h	00-AAAA-a	maninka-kan		1.00	121	3a.. 6 4 4 3 3	Maninka*	PN. b
4103	Mandinka	9.97563	108,339	121,015	194,128	NAB63h	00-AAAA-b	mandinka-kango		1.00	1,210	4a... 6 4 4 3 3	Mandinka	PN. b
4104	Mandyak (Manjaco, Caio)	12.00326	130,360	145,613	233,586	NAB56c	90-FAAA-a	proper mandyak	19	7.20	10,484	0.... 7 5 7 3 3	Manjako*	P.. b
4105	Mankanya (Mancanha, Bram)	3.04874	33,110	36,985	59,329	NAB56c	90-FACA-a	mankany		25.60	9,468	0.... 9 5 7 4 3		... n
4106	Nalu	0.61806	6,712	7,498	12,028	NAB56c	90-LAAA-a	naluu		0.50	37	0.... 5 3 1 0 1		... n
4107	Papel (Pepel)	6.30079	68,429	76,436	122,615	NAB56c	90-FABA-a	proper papel	8	25.70	19,644	0.... 9 5 7 4 3	Papel	PN. p
4108	Portuguese	0.30000	3,258	3,639	5,838	CEW21g	51-AABA-e	general português	30	73.00	2,657	2Bsuh 10 9 15 4 2	Portuguese	PNB b
4109	Serer	0.50000	5,430	6,066	9,730	NAB56c	90-BBAA-a	sine		15.00	910	2.... 8 5 4 4 1	Seereer*	PN. .
4110	Soninke (Serahuli)	0.48660	5,285	5,903	9,469	NAB63j	00-BAAA-a	proper soninke		0.50	30	2.... 5 3 2 0 0	Soninke	... b
4111	Susu (Soso)	0.29191	3,170	3,541	5,681	NAB63k	00-AACA-a	soso	1	0.30	11	4.... 5 4 1 1 2	Soso*	PN. n
4112	Wolof	0.50000	5,430	6,066	9,730	NAB56c	90-AACA-a	vehicular wolof		1.00	61	4.s.. 6 4 1 2 0	Wolof: Senegal	PN. b
4113	other minor peoples	0.20000	2,172	2,426	3,892	...				5.00	121	7 5 2 2 0		
	Guyana	100.00000	829,852	861,334	1,044,696					43.43	374,036			
4114	Akawaio (Kapon)	0.47700	3,958	4,109	4,983	MIR39c	80-AFAC-a	acawayo		75.00	3,081	0.... 10 7 7 5 3	Acawaio*	Pn. .
4115	Arawak	1.88000	15,601	16,193	19,640	MIR39a	81-ACBA	arawák cluster		92.00	14,898	0.... 10 7 11 5 2	Arawak	P.. b
4116	Arekuna (Pemong)	0.06000	498	517	627	MIR39c	80-AFAB-a	are-cuna		25.33	131	0.... 9 5 6 3 2	Pemon	P.. b
4117	Berbice Creole Dutch	0.00400	33	34	42	NFB67b	52-ABAF-1	cayman-creole		80.00	28	1c..h 10 7 8 4 1	Dutch Creole	PN. .
4118	British	0.40000	3,319	3,445	4,179	CEW19i	52-ABAC-b	standard-english		79.00	2,722	3Bsuh 10 9 8 5 1		PNB b
4119	Bush Negro	0.10000	830	861	1,045	NFB68b	52-ABAG-g	ndjuka		80.00	689	1.s.. 10 7 8 4 1	Aukan*	Pn. .
4120	Carib (Galibi)	0.33900	2,813	2,920	3,541	MIR39c	80-ACAA-b	central carib		70.00	2,044	1.s.. 10 7 8 5 3	Carib*	Pn. b
4121	Detribalized Amerindian	1.69600	14,074	14,608	17,718	MIR39y	52-ABAE-cp	guyanese-english		28.00	4,090	0A.uh 9 5 6 5 3		pnb b
4122	Guyanese Black (Creolese)	32.30000	268,042	278,211	337,428	NFB68a	52-ABAG-a	guyanese		72.50	201,703	1.s.. 10 9 10 5 3		pn. b
4123	Guyanese Mulatto	11.40000	94,603	98,192	119,092	NFB68b	52-ABAG-a	guyanese		89.30	87,686	1.s.. 10 8 10 5 2		pn. b
4124	Han Chinese (Cantonese)	0.40000	3,319	3,445	4,179	MSY42a	79-AAAM-a	central yue	2	14.00	482	3A.uh 8 5 8 4 1	Chinese, Yue	PNB b
4125	Han Chinese (Hakka)	0.20000	1,660	1,723	2,089	MSY42a	79-AAAG-a	literary hakka	1	15.00	258	1A... 8 5 8 4 1	Chinese: Hakka, Wukingfu*	PNB b
4126	Hindi (Hindustani)	41.40000	343,559	356,592	432,493	CNN25g	52-ABAG-a	guyanese		7.70	27,458	1.s.. 7 5 7 5 1		pn. b
4127	Hindi (Hindustani)	4.00000	33,194	34,453	41,787	CNN25g	59-AAFP-eb	guyana		5.00	1,723	1c.u. 7 5 6 5 2		pn. b
4128	Jewish	0.00800	66	69	84	CMT35	52-ABAE-cp	guyanese-english		0.00	0	0A.uh 0 3 2 3 0		pnb b
4129	Macushi (Makuxi)	0.87900	7,294	7,571	9,183	MIR39c	80-AFAA-a	macushi		40.00	3,028	0.... 9 5 7 4 1	Makuchi*	PN. .
4130	Patamona (Patamuna, Kapon)	0.59000	4,896	5,082	6,164	MIR39c	80-AFAC-c	patamona		70.00	3,557	0.... 10 7 7 5 2	Patamuna*	PN. .
4131	Portuguese	1.30000	10,788	11,197	13,581	CEW21g	51-AABA-e	general português		93.00	10,414	2Bsuh 10 9 8 5 2	Portuguese	PNB b
4132	USA Black	0.10000	830	861	1,045	NFB68a	52-ABAG-a	talkin-black		73.00	629	0B.uh 10 10 13 5 2		pnb b
4133	Urdu	0.50000	4,149	4,307	5,223	CNN25r	59-AAFO-d	standard urdu		1.00	43	2Asuh 6 4 6 1 1	Urdu	PNB b
4134	Waiwai (Katawian)	0.10900	905	939	1,139	MIR39c	80-AHBC-a	waiwai		60.00	563	1.... 10 6 7 4 2	Waiwai	PN. b
4135	Wapishana (Vapidiana)	1.10300	9,153	9,501	11,523	MIR39a	81-ADAA-a	proper wapishana		60.00	5,700	0.... 10 6 7 4 2	Wapishana	P.. b
4136	Warrau (Warao)	0.59000	4,896	5,082	6,164	MIR39e	83-PAAA-a	proper guarao		60.00	2,541	0.... 10 6 6 5 1	Warao	PN. .
4137	other minor peoples	0.16500	1,369	1,421	1,724	...				40.00	568	9 6 8 3 0		
	Haiti	100.00000	7,560,366	8,222,025	11,988,232					92.91	7,639,424			
4138	Dominican Mulatto	0.40000	30,241	32,888	47,953	NFB71b	51-AABB-hj	dominicano		86.00	28,284	1A.uh 10 7 11 5 3		pnb b
4139	French	0.00710	537	584	851	CEW21b	51-AABI-d	general français	10	83.00	485	1B.uh 10 9 14 5 3	French	pnb b
4140	Haitian Black	94.28900	7,128,593	7,752,465	11,303,584	NFB69a	51-AACC-b	haitien	100	93.00	7,209,793	3As.. 10 9 10 5 3	Haitian*	PNB b
4141	Haitian Mulatto	5.00000	378,018	411,101	599,412	NFB69b	51-AACC-b	haitien		93.28	383,475	3As.. 10 9 10 5 3	Haitian*	PNB b
4142	Han Chinese	0.00430	325	354	515	MSY42a	79-AAAM-a	central yue		40.00	141	3A.uh 9 6 8 4 1	Chinese, Yue	PNB b
4143	Jewish	0.00240	181	197	288	CMT35	52-ABAE-cp	general français		0.80	2	1B.uh 6 4 7 1 0	French	pnb b
4144	Levantine Arab	0.04720	3,568	3,881	5,658	CMT30	12-AACF-f	syro-palestinian		45.00	1,746	1Asuh 9 5 7 4 1	Arabic: Lebanese*	Pnb b
4145	USA White	0.15000	11,341	12,333	17,982	CEW19s	52-ABAC-s	general american		79.00	9,743	1Bsuh 10 9 13 5 3	English*	PNB b
4146	other minor peoples	0.10000	7,560	8,222	11,988	...				70.00	5,755	10 7 8 5 0		
	Holy See	100.00000	1,000	1,000	1,000					98	980			
4147	Esperanto	0.00000	0	0	0	CEW21z	51-AAAC-a	proper esperanto	4		0	0A.. 10 9 11 5 0	Esperanto	PNB b
4148	Italian	3.00000	30	30	30	CEW21z	51-AAAA-a	lingua-latina	20	98.00	29	0A.u. 10 10 16 5 1	Latin	PNB b
4149	Italian	62.00000	620	620	620	CEW21e	51-AABQ-c	standard italiano		98.00	608	2B.uh 10 10 16 5 1	Italian	PNB b

Continued opposite

Table 8-2 continued

EVANGELIZATION								EVANGELISM			ADDITIONAL DESCRIPTIVE DATA
Ref	*D*	*aC*	*CG%*	*r*	*E*	*U*	*W*	*e*	*R*	*T*	*Locations, civil divisions, literacy, religions, church history, denominations, dioceses, church growth, missions, agencies, ministries, movements*
1	28	29	30	31	32	33	34	35	36	37	38
4036	3	8	1.92	0	99.85	0.15	C	403.32	57	10	Peten Itza Mayas. Mainly in Yucatan State, Mexico. North central jungles. Only 12 elderly Itza speakers left. D=RCC,PC,CON. M=PCUSA.
4037	0	9	1.92		99.70	0.30	C	258.05	52	8	Germans(CNIL-LCMS), other Europeans, other Amerindians, other Latin Americans.
Guinea											
4038	1	3	4.40	0	18.00	82.00	A	0.65	913	3	Also in Senegal, Guinea Bissau. Muslims 80%, animists 19%. D=RCC. M=NTM.
4039	2	5	6.92	0	49.00	51.00	A	35.77	476	5	On coast. 6 varieties of Baga: Binari, Koga, Maduri, Mboteni, Sitemu, Sobane. Animists (islamized)67%, Muslims 13%. D=OBSC,RCC. M=Pioneer Bible Trans.
4040	1	3	4.40	4	47.00	53.00	A	3.43	368	4	Muslims 75%(Maliki Sunnis), animists 23%. D=RCC.
4041	2	3	5.74	1	35.80	64.20	A	3.65	548	4	Also in Liberia. Animists 78%, Muslims 17%. D=RCC,ELP; work begun by Liberian Christians. M=SFM,SIL.
4042	1	6	4.07	0	34.00	66.00	A	6.20	457	4	Also in Senegal, Gambia. Animists 80%, Muslims 15%. D=RCC.
4043	1	6	3.45	0	30.00	70.00	A	5.47	461	4	Northeast coast. Also in Guinea Bissau. Animists 60%, Muslims 35%. D=RCC. M=OFM.
4044	0	6	1.10	0	14.05	85.95	A	0.02	527	2	Muslims 80%, some animists 20%(islamized animists). M=OBSM.
4045	0	5	0.00	0	12.00	88.00	A	0.00	0	1.04	Northern boundary with Senegal, Guinea Bissau. Muslims 80%, animists 20%.
4046	2	10	1.33	8	99.79	0.21	C	429.64	46	10	Expatriates from Britain, in education, development. D=Anglican Ch/CPWA(D-Gambia & Rio Pongas),JWs.
4047	1	10	2.75	8	69.00	31.00	B	50.37	143	6	Remnants of military and anglophone advisers from Cuba, now withdrawn. Nonreligious/atheists 80%. D=RCC.
4048	1	4	7.46	2	57.00	43.00	B	31.20	429	5	Also in Liberia, Ivory Coast. Animists 55%, Muslims 20%. D=RCC. M=SIL,SIM.
4049	3	10	3.61	8	99.70	0.30	C	337.26	98	9	Expatriates from various West African nations. Muslims 10%, nonreligious 10%. D=Anglican Ch,RCC,JWs.
4050	4	10	1.38	8	99.87	0.13	C	504.90	41	10	Expatriates from France, in administration, education. D=RCC(3 Dioceses),ERF,AC-CPWA,JWs. R=ELWA.
4051	1	10	1.67	8	99.70	0.30	C	327.04	59	9	Migrant workers from various francophone West African nations. Muslims 20%, nonreligious 10%. D=RCC.
4052	2	4	3.37	4	38.01	61.99	A	0.01	358	2	Peul(Fulani) nomads. A major Fula geopolitical state. Much Arabic but many monolinguals. Muslims 100%(Maliki Sunnis). D=RCC,EEP. Some response. M=CMA.
4053	2	4	0.00	4	37.03	62.97	A	0.04	118	2	Fulani nomads. A Fula geopolitical state. Mainly in Senegal, Guinea Bissau, Gambia. Muslims 100%(Maliki Sunnis). D=RCC,EEP. M=CMA,CSSp,WEC,FMB.
4054	2	5	10.04	1	76.90	23.10	B	103.57	408	7	Guinea Kpelle. Southeast, also in Liberia (but different). Animists 17%, Muslims 34%(Maliki Sunnis). Resisting Islamic advance. D=RCC(D-N'Zerekore),LCL.
4055	0	3	1.40	5	40.11	59.89	A	0.16	178	3	Traders from Niger. Muslims 100%(Maliki Sunnis).
4056	0	6	0.00	0	17.00	83.00	A	0.00	0	1.06	Related to Mandinka. Strong Islam. Muslims 100%(Maliki Sunnis).
4057	4	5	8.29	5	54.00	46.00	B	15.76	502	5	South central. Also in Sierra Leone. Animists 77%, Muslims 13%. Resistant to advance of Islam. D=RCC(PA-Kankan),EEP,AoG,ELP. M=CMA,SFM,PBT. R=ELWA.
4058	2	6	3.45	4	37.00	63.00	A	5.40	415	4	Also in Sierra Leone. Animists 76%, Muslims 20%. D=RCC(D-N'Zerekore),also other churches from Liberia and Sierra Leone.
4059	1	5	3.84	0	39.00	61.00	A	14.23	382	5	Also in Senegal. Nomads, migrating each year(3,000 from Guinea to Senegal each year). Animists 87%, Muslims 3%. D=RCC.
4060	2	3	4.40	4	38.50	61.50	A	0.70	458	3	Dialect of Maninka. Muslims 60%, animists 39%. D=RCC,EEP. M=CMA,CSSp,AMEC.
4061	1	3	3.08	0	22.30	77.70	A	0.24	628	3	Majority live in Sierra Leone. Animists 70%, Muslims 29%. D=RCC.
4062	4	10	5.79	4	99.75	0.25	C	350.40	124	9	Expatriate laborers from Liberia. Animists 20%, nonreligious 5%. D=RCC,CPWA,EEP,AICs.
4063	1	6	4.60	0	29.00	71.00	A	5.29	586	4	Between upper Rio Nunez and upper Rio Pongas. Muslims 85%, animists 10%. D=RCC. M=NTM.
4064	1	3	4.45	0	25.00	75.00	A	0.91	710	3	Dialect of Maninka. Animists 60%, Muslims 39%. D=RCC. M=CMA.
4065	3	10	4.66	8	71.00	29.00	B	38.87	207	5	Lebanese, Syrians. Traders. Muslims 70% (Sunnis,Shias). D=RCC(Maronites),GOC,SOC.
4066	0	5	2.98	4	33.00	67.00	A	4.81	380	4	Primarily in Sierra Leone. Animists 84%, Muslims 12%.
4067	2	5	4.59	4	40.00	60.00	A	2.92	462	4	Also in Sierra Leone. Closely related to Mende. Animists 86%, Muslims 12%. D=RCC,AoG. M=LBT.
4068	1	5	4.25	1	31.50	68.50	A	1.72	493	4	Primarily in Liberia. Animists 90%, some Muslims. D=RCC. M=WEC,ULIC,CMA.
4069	0	5	0.00	0	9.00	91.00	A	0.00	0	1.03	Also in Guinea Bissau. Muslims 95%, animists 5% (islamized tribal religionists). M=WEC.
4070	1	5	3.15	4	40.00	60.00	A	7.30	325	4	Mostly in Sierra Leone. Muslims 80%, animists 15%. D=CPWA.
4071	0	5	3.90	1	22.50	77.50	A	0.41	722	3	Maninkaized Fulani. Many also in Mali, Ivory Coast, Senegal. Muslims 50%, animists 50%.
4072	1	6	3.88	0	48.00	52.00	A	26.28	313	5	Bissao Island; also in Guinea Bissau. Closely related to Mankanya and Mandjak. Animists 80%, Muslims 5%. D=RCC. M=WEC.
4073	0	7	0.00	0	15.00	85.00	A	0.00	0	1.04	Diakhanke. Muslims 87%(Sunnis), animists 13%.
4074	2	3	6.55	5	41.30	58.70	A	0.45	569	3	Central, Kankan Region. Also in Guinea Bissau, Liberia. Animists 59%, Muslims 39%. D=RCC,EEP. M=CMA,SIM,CSSp,FMB. R=ELWA.
4075	3	4	1.33	4	43.20	56.80	A	0.31	221	3	Sierra Leone, Guinea Bissau. Trade language. Also speak Fulani, Malinke. Muslims 85%(Maliki Sunnis, since 1600; strongly syncretistic Islam), animists 15%.
4076	2	5	2.96	4	45.00	55.00	A	8.21	278	4	Majority live in Sierra Leone. Muslims 70%, animists 25%. D=RCC,CPWA.
4077	4	5	7.32	1	47.50	52.50	A	11.26	507	5	South. Distinct from Loma of Liberia. Animists 67%, Muslims 25%. Resistant barrier to Islam. D=RCC(D-N'Zerekore),LCL,EEP,ELP. M=CMA,CSSp,SFM. R=ELWA.
4078	0	10	1.62	4	35.02	64.98	A	0.02	252	2	Nomads. Mainly in Senegal, Mauritania, Gambia. Extensive literature in Pular. Muslims 100%(Sunnis, with Sufi Tijaniyya).
4079	0	0	4.03	8	99.78	0.22	C	364.41	106	9	North Americans, in business, education. Nonreligious 10%. D=RCC,BBC,SDA,etc.
4080	0	2	2.93	1	18.01	81.99	A	0.00	774	1.08	Yalun Soso. Also in Sierra Leone. Subsistence agriculture. Strong Muslims 99%(Maliki Sunnis); no pagans left since 1955. M=MCA.
4081	0	5	0.97		20.00	80.00	A	3.65	133	4	Other West African tribes, some Europeans, North Africans, Levantines. Muslims 50% (Sunnis), Animists 35%.
Guinea-Bissau											
4082	1	6	3.83	0	24.00	76.00	A	0.87	620	3	Pajadinca. Northeast corner, also Senegal, Guinea. Bilingual in Mandinka. Muslims 80%, animists 19%. D=RCC.
4083	4	6	3.23	0	43.00	57.00	A	12.55	308	5	Animists 81%(strong ancestor cult), Muslims 11%. D=RCC(D-Bissau),IEG(ECGB),AoG,SDA. M=NTM,WEC,OFM,PIME,AoG(Brazil),SIL.
4084	2	6	0.00	4	49.10	50.90	A	0.17	107	3	Immigrants from Mali. Muslims 75%, animists 25%. D=RCC,IEG.
4085	1	6	4.86	0	43.60	56.40	A	24.82	406	5	Northwest. Mainly in Senegal. Animists 84%(ancestral cult,Choro). D=RCC. M=OFM,PIME.
4086	1	6	3.19	0	34.00	66.00	A	7.44	386	4	Mainly in Guinea and Senegal; also Gambia. Animists 90%, Muslims 4%. D=RCC.
4087	0	6	4.26	0	22.50	77.50	A	2.87	714	4	Northwest, south of Ziguinchor. Animists 80%, Muslims 16%. Also in Gambia, Senegal.
4088	1	6	5.59	0	33.10	66.90	A	7.37	595	4	Central south, north of the Nalu. Muslims 70%, animists 20%. D=RCC. M=WEC,OFM,PIME.
4089	2	6	4.20	0	58.20	41.80	B	42.91	273	6	Roxa and Bijago Islands. Few literates. Animists 79%. D=RCC,IEG(ECPG). M=WEC,OFM,PIME.
4090	1	10	2.03	8	99.75	0.25	C	366.82	64	9	Migrants from Cape Verde Islands. D=RCC. M=WEC.
4091	1	6	4.42	0	30.50	69.50	A	3.89	541	4	Muslims 62%(46% Sufi Qadiriyya), animists 34%. D=RCC. M=CSSp,PIME,OFM,WEC.
4092	2	5	4.18	0	25.00	75.00	A	2.73	633	4	Dialect of Diola. Animists 72%, Muslims 25%. D=RCC,ECGB. M=WEC.
4093	1	10	4.14	8	99.87	0.13	C	489.02	91	10	Expatriates from France in education, business. Nonreligious 13%. D=RCC.
4094	1	5	4.22	4	34.30	65.70	A	0.37	465	3	Muslims 100%(Maliki Sunnis). D=RCC. M=OFM,PIME,WEC,YWAM.
4095	1	6	4.38	4	34.00	66.00	A	7.44	482	4	On border with Senegal. Bilingual in Mandinka. Animists 80%, Muslims 14%. D=RCC.
4096	2	10	4.28	8	99.57	0.43	B	261.39	118	8	Portuguese-Blacks. Crioulo is lingua franca throughout country, also Cape Verde, Gambia, Senegal. D=RCC(D-Bissau),AoG. M=AoG(Brazil),WEC,OFM,PIME.
4097	0	6	4.20	0	24.00	76.00	A	0.87	698	3	Also in Gambia, Senegal. Close to Mandinka. Muslims 99%(Maliki Sunnis). M=WEC.
4098	1	6	3.35	0	27.00	73.00	A	4.92	502	4	Remnant near Felupe, also in Senegal. Most are animists, 90%. D=RCC.
4099	1	6	3.97	0	34.00	66.00	A	12.41	449	5	Near Banyun; also in Senegal. Bilingual in Mandyak. Majority animists, 85%. D=RCC.
4100	2	6	4.45	0	32.00	68.00	A	7.00	518	4	North central, also in Gambia. 'Mandinkanized Balanta.' Muslims 90%. D=RCC,IEG.
4101	1	10	4.61	8	66.00	34.00	B	36.13	220	5	Traders from Lebanon. Muslims 65%, Druzes 20%. D=RCC(Maronites).
4102	2	6	2.52	5	41.00	59.00	A	1.49	304	4	Spread over 8 West African nations. Muslims 65%, animists 30%. D=RCC,IEG. M=WEC.
4103	2	6	4.91	4	42.00	58.00	A	1.53	453	4	North central and northeast. Most in Guinea, some in Liberia. Muslims 65%, animists 30%. D=RCC,IEG. M=WEC.
4104	3	7	7.20	0	42.20	57.80	A	11.09	571	5	Most in Guinea Bissau; also Senegal, Gambia, France, Cape Verde. Animists 79%(strong ancestor cult), Muslims 13%. D=RCC,Methodist Ch,IEG(ECGB).
4105	2	6	5.70	0	59.60	40.40	B	55.69	336	6	Northwest of Bissau. Also in Senegal. Animists 72%. D=RCC,IEG. M=OFM,PIME,WEC.
4106	2	4	3.68	0	17.50	82.50	A	0.31	827	3	South near coast, also in Guinea. Bilingual in Susu. Muslims 85%, animists 14%. D=RCC,IEG. M=WEC.
4107	2	6	3.08	0	65.70	34.30	B	61.63	195	6	Bissao Island, also Guinea. Close to Mankanya and Mandyak. Animists 65%(strong ancestor cult), Muslims 9%. D=RCC(D-Bissau),IEG(ECPG). M=WEC,OFM.
4108	1	10	1.74	8	99.73	0.27	C	386.35	52	9	Former colonists from Portugal, now settlers. D=RCC. M=OFM,PIME.
4109	1	9	4.61	0	52.00	48.00	B	28.47	327	5	Immigrants from Senegal. Animists 80%, Muslims 5%. D=-RCC.
4110	0	4	3.46	0	18.50	81.50	A	0.33	795	3	Ligbe. Most in Mali, Senegal, Mauritania, Burkina Faso, Ivory Coast, Gambia, Niger. Also speak Fula and Mandinka. All Muslims, 100%(Sunnis, most Tijaniyya).
4111	2	8	2.43	4	33.30	66.70	A	0.36	378	3	Majority live in Guinea and Sierra Leone. Muslims 67%(Maliki Sunnis), animists 33%. D=RCC,EEP(Guinea). M=CMA,WEC.
4112	1	8	4.20	4	36.00	64.00	A	1.31	441	4	Traders from Senegal. Muslims 99%(Maliki Sunnis). D=RCC. M=PIME,OFM.
4113	0	8	0.93		22.00	78.00	A	4.01	116	4	Some Futa Jalon, Landoma, other anglophone and francophone West African countries, also European and USA peoples. Muslims 70%, Animists 5%.
Guyana											
4114	3	8	1.32	0	99.75	0.25	C	323.02	54	9	Also in Brazil, Venezuela. Animists 25%. D=WCG(Pilgrim Holiness),Anglican Ch/CPWI,SDA.
4115	3	8	2.39	0	99.92	0.08	C	470.12	66	10	Only 30% still speak the language. Animists 8%. D=RCC,AC/CPWI,SDA. M=USPG,SDBMS.
4116	1	8	1.30	0	58.33	41.67	B	53.92	109	6	Southwest on Venezuela border. Animists 74%. D=RCC. M=ORM,independents.
4117	1	8	1.14	8	99.80	0.20	C	379.60	36	9	Berbice river area. Dutch-based creole; all bilingual in Guyanese. D=RCC.
4118	2	10	1.11	8	99.79	0.21	C	423.87	42	10	Expatriates from Britain, in education, administration. D=Anglican Ch(D-Guyana),JWs. M=USPG.
4119	1	7	1.11	1	99.80	0.20	C	347.48	42	9	Afro-American spiritists 20%(Voodoo,Ashanti cults). D=RCC.
4120	3	8	2.89	1	99.70	0.30	C	298.93	91	8	Animists 30%. D=RCC,AC/CPWI,SDA. M=USPG,SJ,SFM,SDBMS.
4121	5	8	1.11	8	85.00	15.00	B	86.87	36	6	Animists 20%, nonreligious 20%. D=RCC,AC,JWs,SDA,CON. M=CMML,SJ,SFM,CGP,FMB.
4122	3	10	0.78	8	99.73	0.27	C	355.92	29	9	Afro-American spiritists 2%(Voodoo). D=RCC(D-Georgetown),Anglican Ch(D-Guyana),EOC. M=SJ,SFM,PI,UFM,FMB.
4123	9	10	1.12	8	99.89	0.11	C	489.89	33	10	Creolese. Afro-American spiritists 10%(Vodoun). D=RCC,AC/CPWI,GCU,LCG,GBM,MCCA,SDA,AoG,WCG. M=UFM,FMB.
4124	1	9	1.11	8	77.00	23.00	B	39.34	63	5	Main body of Chinese. Buddhists/Chinese folk-religionists 86%. D=RCC.
4125	1	9	1.12	7	75.00	25.00	B	41.06	65	6	Buddhists/Chinese folk-religionists 85%. D=RCC.
4126	6	10	0.87	8	61.70	38.30	B	17.34	83	5	Hindus 70%(2% Arya Samajists, making some Black converts each year),some Muslims,Baha'is. D=RCC,AoG,GPC,CON,LCG,SA. M=FMB.
4127	5	9	1.11	6	54.00	46.00	B	9.85	107	4	Hindus 88%, a few Muslims and Baha'is. D=RCC,AoG,GPC,CON,LCG. M=UFM,FMB.
4128	0	10	0.00	8	40.00	60.00	A	0.00	0	1.12	Small community of practicing Jews in capital.
4129	3	8	2.85	0	80.00	20.00	B	116.80	132	7	Southwestern border area. Animists 60%. D=Hallelujah Church(Amerindian prophet movement),UFM,CPWI. M=BMM.
4130	1	8	1.54	0	99.70	0.30	C	283.60	63	8	West central; 13 villages. Animists 30%. D=Wesleyan Church in Guyana.
4131	1	10	1.11	8	99.93	0.07	C	556.69	36	10	Expatriates, settlers from Portugal. D=RCC. M=SJ,SFM.
4132	2	10	0.01	8	99.73	0.27	C	367.70	13	9	Expatriates from USA; in military, business. D=JWs,RCC.
4133	0	10	3.83	5	54.00	46.00	B	1.97	247	4	Offical language of Guyana's Muslims. Muslims 99%(Hanafi Sunnis, plus both Qadiani and Lahori Ahmadis). M=FMB.
4134	1	8	1.11	0	98.00	2.00	C	214.62	59	8	Southwest, on Essequibo river. Also in Brazil. Animists 40%. D=RCC. M=UFM.
4135	1	8	2.11	0	99.60	0.40	C	219.00	85	8	Southwest. A few also live in Brazil. Second language: English. Animists 40%. D=RCC. M=SIL,UFM.
4136	2	8	3.42	0	90.00	10.00	B	164.25	124	7	Northeast, near coast. Majority live in Venezuela, a few in Surinam. Language isolate. Animists 50%. D=RCC,AC/CPWI. M=SDBMS.
4137	0	9	0.96		68.00	32.00	B	99.28	39	6	Skepi Creole Dutch (Essequibo), Surinamese, Africans, other South Americans, Caribbean islanders.
Haiti											
4138	4	10	1.72	8	99.86	0.14	C	489.68	41	10	Migrants from Dominican Republic. D=RCC,COG,Baptists,&c. M=SJ,SMM,UFM.
4139	2	10	1.72	8	99.83	0.17	C	475.63	47	10	Expatriates from France, in government, education. D=RCC(5 Dioceses),JWs. M=SMM,CSSR,SDB,OMI.
4140	2	10	1.81	4	99.93	0.07	C	549.90	51	10	Almost all monolingual. 15,000 Baha'is. D=82% RCC(90% Spiritist Catholics),17% Protestants(Baptists,SDA,&c). M=EMBMC,UFM,FMB,EP,HAFF.
4141	4	10	1.72	4	99.93	0.07	C	545.70	43	10	Mostly monolinguals. Afro-Caribbean spiritists 6%. D=RCC,Baptist Convention of Haiti,SDA,and 150 others. M=UFM,FMB.
4142	1	10	1.71	8	99.40	0.60	B	151.84	62	7	Long-term residents, from Chinese diaspora. Chinese folk-religionists/Buddhists 60%. D=RCC.
4143	0	10	0.70	8	49.80	50.20	A	1.45	76	4	Small community of practicing Jews in Port-au-Prince.
4144	1	10	5.30	8	99.45	0.55	B	172.46	157	7	Traders from Lebanon, Syria since 1880. Muslims 50%(Sunnis,Shias). D=RCC(Maronites).
4145	5	10	4.59	8	99.79	0.21	C	441.17	98	10	Expatriates from USA, in education, development. D=SDA,RCJCLdS,JWs,AoG,SA.
4146	0	10	1.72		99.70	0.30	C	263.16	46	8	British, Germans, Italians, West Indian Blacks, Caribbean islanders, Latin Americans.
Holy See											
4147	0	10	0.00	5	99.90	0.10	C	502.60	0	10	Artificial (constructed) language, in 80 countries. Speakers in Vatican: 40(none mother-tongue).
4148	1	10	3.42	4	99.98	0.02	C	593.78	73	10	Handful of officials who communicate daily through Latin as official language. D=RCC.
4149	1	10	-0.77	7	99.98	0.02	C	618.82	4	10	Officials, clerks, clergy, bishops, cardinals. D=RCC(V-Vatican City).

Continued overleaf

Table 8-2 continued

PEOPLE Ref 1	Ethnic name 2	POPULATION P% 3	In 1995 4	In 2000 5	In 2025 6	IDENTITY CODE Race 7	Language 8	LANGUAGE Autoglossonym 9	S 10	CHURCH AC 11	Members 12	MINISTRY Jayuh 13-17	d 18	wa 19	xc 20	mc 21	mi 22	SCRIPTURE Biblioglossonym 23	Pub 24-26	ss 27
4150	other minor peoples	35.00000	350	350	350	. . .				98.00	343		10	10	16	5	1			
	Honduras	**100.00000**	**5,653,505**	**6,485,445**	**10,656,044**					**93.4**	**6,057,603**									
4151	Armenian	0.02000	1,131	1,297	2,131	CEW14	57-AAAA-b	ashkharik		90.00	1,167	4A.u.	10	9	13	5	1	Armenian: Modern, Eastern	PNB	b
4152	Black Carib (Garifuna)	1.32660	74,999	86,036	141,363	MIR39c	80-ACAA-d	garifuna		85.00	73,131	4.s..	10	7	10	5	3	Garifuna	PN.	b
4153	Black Creole	0.10000	5,654	6,485	10,656	NFB68b	52-ABAF-e	honduran-creole		97.00	6,291	1c..h	10	8	12	5	3		pn.	.
4154	British	0.10000	5,654	6,485	10,656	CEW19i	52-ABAC-b	standard-english	8	79.00	5,124	3Bsuh	10	9	8	5	3		PNB	b
4155	Chorotega (Mangue)	0.00200	113	130	213	MIR37z	67-AIAB-a	chorotega		30.00	39	0....	9	5	6	4	1		...	b
4156	Chorti (Cholti)	0.00700	396	454	746	MIR37b	68-ACAC-a	chortí		97.00	440	0....	10	8	12	5	3	Chorti	PN.	.
4157	Detribalized Amerindian	4.14770	234,490	268,997	441,981	MIR37z	51-AABB-he	hondureño		89.00	239,407	1A.uh	10	8	10	5	3		pnb	b
4158	Han Chinese (Cantonese)	0.07050	3,986	4,572	7,513	MSY42a	79-AAAM-a	central yue	1	9.00	412	3A.uh	7	5	8	4	2	Chinese, Yue	PNB	b
4159	Honduran Black	2.00000	113,070	129,709	213,121	NFB71a	51-AABB-he	hondureño		95.00	123,223	1A.uh	10	8	11	5	3		pnb	b
4160	Honduran White	2.00000	113,070	129,709	213,121	CLT27	51-AABB-he	hondureño		95.50	123,872	1A.uh	10	10	12	5	3		pnb	b
4161	Jamaican Black	0.50000	28,268	32,427	53,280	NFB68a	52-ABAE-cc	jamaican-english		97.00	31,454	0A.uh	10	9	13	5	3		pnb	.
4162	Jewish	0.00580	328	376	618	CMT35	51-AABB-he	hondureño		0.40	2	1A.uh	5	4	2	1	0		pnb	b
4163	Jicaque (Torrupan)	0.01150	650	746	1,225	MIR38a	69-IAAA-a	proper tol		80.00	597	0....	10	8	6	5	1	Tol	PN.	.
4164	Lenca	1.10000	62,189	71,340	117,216	MIR37z	51-AABB-he	hondureño		87.00	62,066	1A.uh	10	8	10	5	3		pnb	b
4165	Lenca	0.00780	441	506	831	MIR37z	69-HAAA-a	proper lenca		50.00	253	0....	10	7	6	4	1		...	b
4166	Mestizo	83.69940	4,731,950	5,428,279	8,919,045	CLN29	51-AABB-he	hondureño		93.95	5,099,868	1A.uh	10	10	10	5	3		pnb	b
4167	Miskito (Misquito)	0.22070	12,477	14,313	23,518	MIR37z	83-AAAA-a	mam		87.00	12,453	1....	10	9	12	5	3	Miskito	PN.	.
4168	Nicaraguan Mestizo	3.00000	169,605	194,563	319,681	CLN29	51-AABB-hf	nicaragüense		95.00	184,835	1A.uh	10	10	11	5	2		pnb	b
4169	Palestinian Arab	0.78340	44,290	50,807	83,479	CMT30	12-AACF-f	syro-palestinian		85.00	43,186	1Asuh	10	8	10	5	2	Arabic: Lebanese*	Pnb	b
4170	Paya (Pech, Seco, Tawka)	0.01400	791	908	1,492	MIR39e	83-BAAA-a	pech		70.00	636	0....	10	7	6	4	1		...	b
4171	Pipil	0.00100	57	65	107	MIR37a	66-BFBB	pipil cluster		81.00	53	0A.uh	10	8	6	4	1		...	b
4172	Sumo (Honduran Sumu)	0.01260	712	817	1,343	MIR37z	83-AABA-a	north sumo		87.00	711	0....	10	8	10	4	3		...	n
4173	Syro-Lebanese Arab	0.05000	2,827	3,243	5,328	CMT30	12-AACF-f	syro-palestinian		70.00	2,270	1Asuh	10	7	8	5	3	Arabic: Lebanese*	Pnb	b
4174	Turk	0.02000	1,131	1,297	2,131	MSY41j	44-AABA-a	osmanli		0.12	2	1A.u.	5	3	2	1	0	Turkish	PNB	b
4175	USA White	0.20000	11,307	12,971	21,312	CEW19s	52-ABAC-s	general american		78.00	10,117	1Bsuh	10	9	13	5	3	English*	PNB	b
4176	West Indian Black	0.50000	28,268	32,427	53,280	NFB68a	52-ABAF-e	honduran-creole		97.00	31,454	1c..h	10	9	12	5	2		pn.	.
4177	other minor peoples	0.10000	5,654	6,485	10,656	. . .				70.00	4,540		10	7	7	5	0			
	Hungary	**100.00000**	**10,226,856**	**10,035,568**	**8,900,388**					**87.19**	**8,749,732**									
4178	Bosniac (Muslmani)	0.52000	53,180	52,185	46,282	CEW22a	53-AAAG-a	standard srpski		0.00	0	1Asuh	0	2	2	4	3	Serbian*	PNB	b
4179	British	0.03000	3,068	3,011	2,670	CEW19i	52-ABAC-b	standard-english	2	79.00	2,378	3Bsuh	10	9	13	5	2		PNB	b
4180	Carpathian Gypsy (Ungrike	0.02800	2,864	2,810	2,492	CNN25f	59-ACBA-ag	north vlach		80.00	2,248	1c...	10	7	8	4	1	Romani: Latvian	Pn.	b
4181	Croat	0.24180	24,729	24,266	21,521	CEW22d	53-AAAG-b	standard hrvatski	1	91.00	22,082	2Asuh	10	8	11	4	1	Croatian	PNB	b
4182	Esperanto	0.00010	10	10	9	CEW21z	51-AAAC-a	proper esperanto	8	73.00	7	0A...	10	8	6	5	0	Esperanto	PNB	b
4183	French	0.20000	20,454	20,071	17,801	CEW21b	51-AABI-d	general français	1	87.00	17,462	1B.uh	10	9	14	5	3	French	PNB	b
4184	German	2.36130	241,487	236,970	210,165	CEW19m	52-ABCE-a	standard hoch-deutsch	8	94.00	222,752	2B.uh	10	9	13	5	2	German*	PNB	b
4185	Hungarian (Magyar)	84.44000	8,635,557	8,474,034	7,515,488	MSW51g	41-BAAA-a	general magyar	99	88.00	7,457,150	2A.u.	10	10	10	5	3	Hungarian	PNB	b
4186	Hungarian Gypsy	5.20000	531,797	521,850	462,820	CNN25f	41-BAAA-a	general magyar		92.00	480,102	2A.u.	10	9	10	5	3	Hungarian	PNB	b
4187	Jewish	0.05000	5,113	5,018	4,450	CMT35	52-ABCH-a	west yiddish		0.05	3	0B..h	4	4	2	4	0	Yiddish	PNB	b
4188	Jewish	0.50000	51,134	50,178	44,502	CMT35	41-BAAA-a	general magyar		0.10	50	2A.u.	5	4	2	5	0	Hungarian	PNB	b
4189	Lovari Gypsy (Romungre)	0.21000	21,476	21,075	18,691	CNN25f	59-ACBA-a	vlach-romani	1	85.00	17,913	1a...	10	8	8	5	1	Romani: Finnish*	PN.	b
4190	Palityan (Bogomil)	0.01000	1,023	1,004	890	CEW22b	53-AAAH-bi	palityan		65.00	652	1c.uh	10	7	8	5	1	Palityan	PNb	.
4191	Polish	0.20000	20,454	20,071	17,801	CEW22i	53-AAAC-c	polski	1	90.00	18,064	2A.uh	10	8	12	5	1	Polish	PNB	b
4192	Romanian	0.98800	101,041	99,151	87,936	CEW21i	51-AADC-a	limba româneasca	1	84.00	83,287	3A.u.	10	8	10	5	2	Romanian	PNB	b
4193	Russian	0.36760	37,594	36,891	32,718	CEW22j	53-AAAE-d	russkiy	3	56.00	20,659	4B.uh	10	8	8	5	1	Russian	PNB	b
4194	Ruthenian (Rusin)	2.90000	296,579	291,031	258,111	CEW22k	41-BAAA-a	general magyar		91.00	264,839	2A.u.	10	9	11	4	1	Hungarian	PNB	b
4195	Serb	0.19350	19,789	19,419	17,222	CEW22l	53-AAAG-a	standard srpski	1	85.00	16,506	1Asuh	10	8	10	5	2	Serbian*	PNB	b
4196	Slovak	0.94770	96,920	95,107	84,349	CEW22m	53-AAAD-b	slovensky	1	80.00	76,086	1Asuh	10	9	9	5	3	Slovak	PNB	b
4197	Slovene (Prekmurian)	0.04060	4,152	4,074	3,614	CEW22n	53-AAAF-a	slovensko		95.00	3,871	1a..h	10	8	11	5	2	Slovenian*	PNB	b
4198	Traveller Gypsy (Tinker)	0.09300	9,511	9,333	8,277	CNN25f	50-ACAA-a	west sheldruu		60.00	5,600	0....	10	7	8	4	1		...	b
4199	USA White	0.07000	7,159	7,025	6,230	CEW19s	52-ABAC-s	general american		78.00	5,479	1Bsuh	10	10	12	0	0	English*	PNB	b
4200	other minor peoples	0.40840	41,766	40,985	36,349	. . .				79.40	32,542		10	7	7	5	0			
	Iceland	**100.00000**	**268,398**	**280,969**	**328,356**					**94.41**	**265,260**									
4201	British	0.25000	671	702	821	CEW19i	52-ABAC-b	standard-english		79.00	555	3Bsuh	10	10	11	0	0		PNB	b
4202	Danish (Dane)	0.80000	2,147	2,248	2,627	CEW19g	52-AAAD-c	general dansk		92.00	2,068	2A.uh	10	9	12	5	1	Danish	PNB	b
4203	Esperanto	0.00000	0	0	0	CEW21z	51-AAAC-a	proper esperanto	6	90.00	0	0A...	10	8	11	5	0	Esperanto	PNB	b
4204	French-Icelandic Creole	2.00000	5,368	5,619	6,567	CEW19n	51-AACC-c	guadeloupéan		90.00	5,057	1cs..	10	9	11	5	1	Creole French: Lesser Antill	Pnb	b
4205	German	0.30000	805	843	985	CEW19m	52-ABCE-a	standard hoch-deutsch		84.00	708	2B.uh	10	10	11	0	0	German*	PNB	b
4206	Icelander	95.03000	255,059	267,005	312,037	CEW19n	52-AAAB-a	íslensk	99	94.90	253,388	0..uh	10	10	12	5	3	Icelandic	PNB	b
4207	Norwegian	0.27000	725	759	887	CEW19p	52-AAAC-e	ny-norsk		93.00	706	0B.uh	10	9	14	5	1	Norwegian*	PNB	b
4208	Swedish (Swede)	0.45000	1,208	1,264	1,478	CEW19q	52-AAAD-r	svea-svensk		73.00	923	1A.uh	10	10	13	0	0	Swedish	PNB	b
4209	USA White	0.50000	1,342	1,405	1,642	CEW19s	52-ABAC-s	general american		76.00	1,068	1Bsuh	10	9	13	5	3	English*	PNB	b
4210	other minor peoples	0.40000	1,074	1,124	1,313	. . .				70.00	787		10	7	7	5	0			
	India	**100.00000**	**933,665,123**	**1,013,661,777**	**1,330,448,707**					**6.14**	**62,256,518**									
4211	Adi (Miri, Abor)	0.04820	450,027	488,585	641,276	MSY50z	74-AAAA-a	adi		2.10	10,260	0....	6	5	5	3	3	Adi	PN.	.
4212	Adi-Galo (Galong)	0.00518	48,364	52,508	68,917	MSY50r	74-AAAA-c	galong		4.55	2,389	0....	6	5	6	3	1	Galong	pn.	.
4213	Adiwasi Girasia (Bhil)	0.01222	114,094	123,869	162,581	AUG06a	59-AAFS-g	adiwasi-oriya		1.00	1,239	1csu.	6	3	4	1	1	Girasia, Adiwasi*	pnb	.
4214	Adiyan	0.00052	4,855	5,271	6,918	CNN23z	49-EBEB	malayalam cluster		1.90	100	2Asu.	6	4	4	1	3		PNB	b
4215	Agariya	0.00215	20,074	21,794	28,605	AUG04z	46-CABA-l	agariya		0.04	9	1cs..	3	3	2	1	1		pnb	.
4216	Ahir (Ahirani)	0.08078	754,215	818,836	1,074,736	CNN25o	59-AAFM-aa	ahirani		0.20	1,638	0....	5	4	2	1	0		...	.
4217	Aimol	0.00002	187	203	266	MSY50z	73-DDCB-a	aimol		80.00	162	0....	10	7	8	5	1		...	.
4218	Aitonia	0.00100	9,337	10,137	13,304	MSY49c	47-AAAA-b	aiton		0.50	51	1.s..	5	4	7	4	0		pnb	.
4219	Ajmeri	0.00013	1,214	1,318	1,730	CNN25o	59-AAFG-i	ajmeri		0.20	3	1.s..	5	4	2	1	1		pn.	.
4220	Allar	0.00004	373	405	532	CNN23z	49-EBEB	malayalam cluster		0.22	1	2Asu.	5	4	0	1	1		PNB	b
4221	Alu (Kurumba)	0.00200	18,673	20,273	26,609	CNN23z	49-EBAB-b	alu-kurumba		10.00	2,027	0....	8	5	3	2	1	Alu	...	b
4222	Anal Naga (Laizo, Mulsom)	0.00157	14,659	15,914	20,888	MSY50p	73-DDAB-a	anal		73.40	11,681	0....	10	7	7	5	2	Anal	PN.	b
4223	Andh (Andha)	0.00922	86,084	93,460	122,667	CNN25j	59-AAFU	marathi cluster		0.20	187	3Asu.	5	3	4	1	1		PNB	b
4224	Anga (Angika)	0.07455	696,047	755,685	991,850	CNN25c	59-AAFQ-i	angikaa		0.02	151	1.s..	3	3	4	1	2		pn.	.
4225	Angami Naga (Gnamei, Monr)	0.01126	105,131	114,138	149,809	MSY50p	73-ABBC-a	angami-naga		62.00	70,766	1....	10	7	9	5	1	Angami Naga*	PNB	.
4226	Anglo-Indian	0.00441	41,175	44,702	58,673	CNN25z	52-ABAD-aa	north indian-english		80.00	35,762	0A.uh	10	8	7	5	3		...	.
4227	Ao Naga (Aorr, Paimi, Uri)	0.01459	136,222	147,893	194,112	MSY50p	72-BAFC-a	ao		98.00	144,935	0a...	10	8	12	5	2	Naga: Ao*	PNB	.
4228	Apatani	0.00230	21,474	23,314	30,600	MSY50z	74-AABA-c	apatani		5.10	1,189	0....	7	4	2	1	1		pn.	.
4229	Arab	0.01000	93,367	101,366	133,045	CMT30	12-AACF-g	syro-mesopotamian		0.10	101	1Asuh	5	2	1	0	0		pnb	b
4230	Arakanese (Maghi, Mogh)	0.00248	23,155	25,139	32,995	MSY50b	77-AABA-b	arakan		0.06	15	1csu.	4	3	4	2	2	Maghi*	Pnb	.
4231	Arakh	0.00100	9,337	10,137	13,304	CNN25j	59-AAFU	marathi cluster		1.00	101	3Asu.	6	4	2	1	1		PNB	b
4232	Aranadan	0.00008	747	811	1,064	CNN23z	49-EBAA	kannada cluster		1.00	8	3Asu.	6	4	0	1	1		PNB	b
4233	Are (Arya)	0.00057	5,322	5,778	7,584	CNN25j	59-AAFU-j	are		1.00	58	1csu.	6	4	2	1	0		pnb	.
4234	Armenian	0.00205	19,140	20,780	27,274	CEW14	57-AAAA-b	ashkharik		90.00	18,702	4A.u.	10	7	13	4	1	Armenian: Modern, Eastern	PNB	b
4235	Assamese	1.58986	14,843,968	16,115,803	21,152,272	CNN25a	59-AAFT-s	axamiyaa		1.10	177,274	3asuh	6	5	8	3	3	Assamese	PNB	b
4236	Asur	0.00074	6,909	7,501	9,845	AUG04z	46-CABA-h	asuri-birjia		10.50	788	1cs..	8	5	5	3	0		pnb	.
4237	Awadhi (Baiswari, Bagheli)	3.68483	34,403,973	37,351,713	49,024,773	CNN25g	59-AAFP-a	awadhi	5	2.50	933,793	1c.u.	6	4	4	3	2	Awadhi	Pn.	b
4238	Badaga	0.01861	173,755	188,642	247,597	CNN23a	49-EBAA-b	badaga		9.80	18,487	3csu.	7	5	5	3	1	Badaga	Pnb	.
4239	Bagata (Bhakta, Bagat)	0.00991	92,526	100,454	131,847	CNN25l	59-AAFS-j	bagata-oriya		0.09	90	1csu.	4	4	4	1	1		pnb	.
4240	Baghati (Bhagati)	0.00088	8,216	8,920	11,708	CNN25k	59-AAFB-j	baghati		0.06	5	0.s..	4	1	0	0	0		p..	.
4241	Bagri (Bahgri, Bagari)	0.18582	1,734,937	1,883,586	2,472,240	CNN25o	59-AAFG-p	bagri		0.10	1,884	1.s..	5	1	5	0	0		pn.	b
4242	Bahawalpuri (Bhawalpuri)	0.00014	1,307	1,419	1,863	CNN25h	59-AAFE-rc	bahawalpuri		1.00	14	1csu.	6	4	0	3	1		pnb	.
4243	Baiga (Baigani)	0.00196	18,300	19,868	26,077	CNN25g	59-AAFR-ad	baigani		5.00	993	1cs..	7	5	4	3	0		p..	.
4244	Balti (Baltistani Bhotia)	0.00707	66,010	71,666	94,063	MSY50r	70-AAAC-c	balti		1.29	924	1....	6	3	0	0	1	Balti	Pn.	b
4245	Bangri (Deswali, Hariani)	1.46988	13,723,757	14,899,612	19,555,999	CNN25g	59-AAFO-h	baangaru		3.60	536,386	1asuh	6	4	0	3	2	Haryanvi	pnb	b
4246	Barel	0.04049	378,041	410,432	538,699	AUG06a	59-AAFL-b	bareli-bhili		0.10	410	0.s..	5	3	0	1	0		p..	.
4247	Bateri	0.00020	1,867	2,027	2,661	CNN25i	59-AACF-c	bateri		0.10	2	0....	5	2	0	0	0		...	p
4248	Bathudi	0.01331	124,271	134,918	177,083	CNN25c	59-AAFT	bengali cluster		2.82	3,805	4Asuh	6	3	0	1	1		PNB	b
4249	Bauria (Babri, Bawari)	0.00173	16,152	17,536	23,017	AUG06a	59-AAFJ-d	wagadi-bhili		0.10	18	1.s..	5	2	2	1	0	Wagdi*	pn.	b
4250	Bawm Chin (Banjogi)	0.00044	4,108	4,460	5,854	MSY50c	73-DCCA-a	bawm		95.00	4,237	0as..	10	8	12	5	2	Bawm*	PNB	.
4251	Bazigar	0.00003	280	304	399	CNN23z	49-EBAA	kannada cluster		1.94	6	3Asu.	6	3	2	1	0		PNB	b
4252	Bedia	0.01148	107,185	116,368	152,736	CNN25c	59-AAFQ-gd	panchpargania		0.01	12	1.s..	3	1	0	0	0		pn.	.
4253	Bellari	0.00020	1,867	2,027	2,661	CNN23z	49-EAAA-b	bellari		1.00	20	1.s..	6	4	2	3	1		pn.	.
4254	Bengali	7.31571	68,304,233	74,156,556	97,331,769	CNN25b	59-AAFT-e	west bengali		2.50	1,853,914	1Asuh	6	5	9	5	3	Bengali: Musalmani*	PNB	b
4255	Berar Marathi (Brahmani)	0.74500	6,955,805	7,551,780	9,911,843	CNN25j	59-AAFU-b	varhaadi		2.00	151,036	1csu.	6	4	5	1	1		pnb	.
4256	Betta Kurumba	0.00044	4,108	4,460	5,854	CNN23c	49-EBAB-d	betta-kurumba		5.00	223	0....	7	5	6	3	1		...	b
4257	Bhadrawahi (Bhadri, Bahi)	0.00708	66,103	71,767	94,196	CNN25k	59-AAFB-f	bhadrawahi		0.10	72	0.s..	5	3	0	1	0		p..	.
4258	Bhalay	0.00100	9,337	10,137	13,304	CNN25j	59-AAFU-k	bhalay		1.00	101	1csu.	6	3	5	1	0		pnb	.
4259	Bharia (Bharat)	0.00095	8,870	9,630	12,639	CNN23z	49-EBEA	wider-tamil cluster		1.60	154	2Asu.	6	3	0	1	1		PNB	b
4260	Bhateali	0.01178	109,986	119,409	156,727	CNN25n	59-AAFE-k	bhateali		0.50	597	1csu.	5	1	2	0	0		pnb	.
4261	Bhatola	0.00050	4,668	5,068	6,652	CNN25j	59-AAFU	marathi cluster		1.00	51	3Asu.	6	3	2	1	0		PNB	b
4262	Bhattiana (Bhatneri)	0.01544	144,158	156,509	205,421	CNN25o	59-AAFC-bi	bhattiani		0.97	1,518	1....	5	3	4	1	0	Bhatneri	PN.	b
4263	Bhattri (Bhatra)	0.01827	170,581	185,196	243,073	CNN25l	59-AAFS-e	bhatri-oriya		0.02	37	1csu.	3	4	0	0	3	Bhatri	pnb	.
4264	Bhilala	0.06351	592,971	643,777	844,968	AUG06a	59-AAFK-k	bhilala		0.01	64	0cs..	3	3	0	1	0		pn.	.
4265	Bhim	0.00254	23,715	25,747	33,793	MSY50s	72-AABA-c	bhim		1.00	257	1.s..	6	4	4	1	0		pnb	.

Continued opposite

Table 8-2 continued

EVANGELIZATION								EVANGELISM			ADDITIONAL DESCRIPTIVE DATA
Ref 1	D 28	aC 29	CG% 30	r 31	E 32	U 33	W 34	e 35	R 36	T 37	Locations, civil divisions, literacy, religions, church history, denominations, dioceses, church growth, missions, agencies, ministries, movements 38
4150	1	10	-0.69		99.98	0.02	C	515.08	2	10	Officials and clergy of non-Italian origin. D=RCC(V-Vatican City).
Honduras											
4151	1	10	4.87	6	99.90	0.10	C	528.88	93	10	Refugees from Turkey and USSR since 1915. D=Armenian Apostolic Ch(C-Echmiadzin).
4152	6	9	2.36	4	99.85	0.15	C	443.65	65	10	Also in 8 other countries. D=RCC(christopagans 95%),Plymouth Brethren,UBC,Mennonites,SDA,ICFG. M=CBHMS,Hondurean Mission to the Unreached,FMB-SBC.
4153	5	10	2.52	8	99.97	0.03	C	559.39	56	10	Coastal Blacks. D=Episcopal Ch,MCCA,WC,SDA,COG(Cleveland).
4154	4	10	2.52	8	99.79	0.21	C	432.52	67	10	Expatriates from Britain, in education, business. D=Episcopal Ch(D-Honduras),JWs,MCCA,RCC.
4155	1	8	2.60	0	65.00	35.00	B	71.17	143	6	Language extinct, but small ethnic group (mainly in Costa Rica), now Spanish-speaking. Animists 70%. D=RCC.
4156	4	8	2.51	0	99.97	0.03	C	513.37	62	10	Mainly in Guatemala. Animists 3%. D=RCC,Episcopal Ch,SDA,ICFG.
4157	4	10	2.52	8	99.89	0.11	C	503.51	59	10	Many Afro-American spiritists. D=RCC(6 Dioceses; 90% christopagans),AoG,ICFG,JWs.
4158	2	10	2.53	8	74.00	26.00	B	24.30	118	5	Long-time immigrants from Chinese diaspora abroad. Buddhists/Chinese folk-religionists 90%. D=RCC,AoG.
4159	5	10	2.52	8	99.95	0.05	C	561.73	53	10	On northern coast. D=Episcopal Ch,COG(Cleveland),MCCA,WC,JWs. M=MMS,CM,SJ.
4160	3	10	2.52	8	99.96	0.04	C	569.92	57	10	Settlers of European descent. D=RCC,AoG,JWs. M=CM,PME,SJ,OFM,CP,SDB,FMB.
4161	5	10	2.52	8	99.97	0.03	C	584.18	52	10	Migrant workers from Jamaica. D=RCC,Episcopal Ch,COG(Cleveland),WC,JWs.
4162	0	10	0.70	8	44.40	55.60	A	0.64	86	3	Small community of practicing Spanish-speaking Jews.
4163	3	8	2.51	0	99.80	0.20	C	350.40	78	9	Francisco Morazan Department. Animists 20%. D=RCC,ICFG,AoG. M=SIL.
4164	3	10	2.52	8	99.87	0.13	C	485.85	59	10	Acculturated, Spanish-speaking Indians. Animists 6%. D=RCC,AoG,JWs.
4165	1	8	2.52	0	86.00	14.00	B	156.95	106	7	Indians speaking own language, though becoming extinct. Animists 50%. D=RCC.
4166	8	8	2.47	8	99.94	0.06	C	545.06	52	10	15,000 Baha'is. D=95% RCC(6 Dioceses),AoG,SDA,COG,ICFG,IC,JWs,HBC. M=CAM,CM,SJ,FMB. T=CBN. R=AWR.
4167	5	8	2.52	0	99.87	0.13	C	438.21	66	10	Gracias a Dios Department. Mainly in Nicaragua. Animists 13%. D=RCC,ICFG,Unity of Brethren,SDA,JWs. M=MCUSA,CM,SJ,FMB.
4168	2	10	2.52	8	99.95	0.05	C	554.80	53	10	Illegal immigrants and refugees from Nicaraguan civil strife. D=RCC,IMN.
4169	2	10	8.73	8	99.85	0.15	C	474.68	169	10	Immigrants from Middle East. Muslims 12%. D=Greek Orthodox Ch(P-Jerusalem),RCC(Maronites,Melkites).
4170	1	8	2.52	0	99.70	0.30	C	270.83	82	8	North central coast. 50% use Paya language, rest only Spanish. Animists 30%. D=RCC.
4171	1	8	2.62	8	99.81	0.19	C	375.47	73	9	Near El Salvador border. No Pipil speakers now. Animists 19%. D=RCC.
4172	2	8	2.52	0	99.87	0.13	C	409.64	71	10	Bilingual in Miskito. Animists 13%. D=RCC,Moravian Ch. M=CM,SJ,UBS.
4173	2	10	5.57	8	99.70	0.30	C	347.48	126	9	Merchants, traders, recent political refugees. Muslims 25%, some Baha'is. D=RCC(Maronites),SOC(P-Antioch). M=PME,CM,SJ.
4174	0	10	0.70	8	44.12	55.88	A	0.19	88	3	Immigrants from Turkey. Muslims 100%(Hanafi Sunnis).
4175	8	10	3.23	8	99.78	0.22	C	435.59	74	10	Expatriates from USA, in military, business. D=SDA,JWs,CJCLdS,COG,AoG,HBC,CON,RCJCLdS.
4176	4	10	2.52	8	99.97	0.03	C	559.39	54	10	Migrants from Caribbean. Bay Islands English(Weka), Calabash Bight. D=Episcopal Ch,COG(Cleveland),MCCA,WC. M=MMS,SJ.
4177	0	10	2.52		99.70	0.30	C	260.61	68	8	Other Central Americans, South Americans, Europeans, Amerindians.
Hungary											
4178	0	10	0.00	6	49.00	51.00	A	0.00	0	1.14	Refugees from Bosnia civil war, accepted by Hungary in 1992. Muslims 99%(Sunnis). M=RCC,RCH,ELCH.
4179	2	10	0.38	8	99.79	0.21	C	444.05	27	10	Expatriates from Britain, in business. D=Ch of England(D-Europe),JWs.
4180	2	10	0.38	1	99.80	0.20	C	367.92	31	9	Mainly in Czechoslovakia, some in USA, Russia, Ukraine, Poland, Romania. Nonreligious. D=nomadic caravan churches(GEM),RCC. M=GGMS.
4181	1	10	0.38	6	99.91	0.09	C	534.76	25	10	Migrant workers, also citizens originally from Croatia, and refugees from 1990s civil war. Strong Catholics. D=RCC.
4182	0	10	0.34	5	99.73	0.27	C	349.05	28	9	Artificial (constructed) language, in 80 countries. Speakers in Hungary: 796,000(only 11 mother-tongue).
4183	5	10	0.38	8	99.87	0.13	C	517.60	23	10	Citizens, and expatriates from France. D=RCC,RCH,ELCH,ECPC,JWs. M=SJ,OSB,OFM.
4184	4	10	0.38	8	99.94	0.06	C	590.13	24	10	Citizens of German origin. D=NAC(Bezirk Schweiz),RCC,ELCH,RCH. M=SJ,OSB.
4185	7	7	0.35	6	99.88	0.12	C	507.49	30	10	Nonreligious 7%, atheists 5%. D=RCC(13 Dioceses),Reformed Ch of Hungary,ELCH,ECPC,BCH,SDA,JWs. M=SJ,OFM,OP,UBS,LBI. R=TWR,AWR.
4186	2	10	0.38	6	99.92	0.08	C	547.35	24	10	73% speak Romani as second language. D=nomadic caravan churches(Gypsy Evangelical Movement),RCC, many new independent charismatic churches.
4187	0	10	0.00	4	48.05	51.95	A	0.08	39	2	Practicing Yiddish communities, orthodox Judaism.
4188	0	10	-0.21	6	51.10	48.90	B	0.18	26	3	Survivors from 800,000 Jews before 1939. 130 synagogues, 26 rabbis. Jews 80% in Budapest.
4189	2	9	0.38	6	99.85	0.15	C	437.45	27	10	Vlach Gypsies, in 20 countries in Europe, Americas. D=nomadic caravan churches(GEM),RCC. M=GGMS.
4190	1	10	0.38	1	99.65	0.35	C	270.46	39	8	Language interintelligible with Bulgarian. Also in Bulgaria and Romania. A few communities remain. Descendants of Paulicians/Bogomils/Bosnians. D=BOC.
4191	1	10	0.38	6	99.90	0.10	C	528.88	6	10	Citizens from Poland, also migrant workers, refugees. Strong Catholics. D=RCC.
4192	2	10	2.26	6	99.84	0.16	C	475.23	60	10	Citizens, migrants, refugees. D=Romanian Orthodox Ch(P-Bucharest),OCH.
4193	1	9	0.38	7	99.56	0.44	B	257.54	8	8	Military until 1990, also refugees from former USSR. Nonreligious/atheists 39%. D=Russian Orthodox Ch(P-Moscow).
4194	1	10	0.38	6	99.91	0.09	C	528.11	7	10	Magyarized Eastern Slavs, Ukrainians. D=RCC(D-Hajdudorog,EA-Miskolc).
4195	2	9	0.38	6	99.85	0.15	C	480.88	7	10	Migrant workers from Yugoslavia. Muslims 10%. D=Serbian Orthodox Ch(D-Budim),OCH.
4196	4	10	0.38	6	99.80	0.20	C	443.84	27	10	Citizens, originally from Slovakia. D=RCC,RCH,ELCH,ECPC.
4197	1	10	0.38	6	99.95	0.05	C	568.67	23	10	Citizens, originally from Slovenia. Majority in Slovenia(Yugoslavia); also Italy, Austria, USA, Canada. D=95% RCC. M=SJ,OFM.
4198	3	10	0.38	6	99.60	0.40	C	238.71	35	8	Nomads, a few settled Gypsies. Dialect of Balkan Romany. Muslims 30%, nonreligious. D=RCC,ECMC,GEM. M=GGMS.
4199	0	0	6.51	8	99.78	0.22	C	370.11	156	9	North Americans, in business, education. Nonreligious 10%. D=RCC,BBC,SDA,etc.
4200	0	9	0.66		99.79	0.21	C	325.74	16	9	Bulgarians(BOC), refugees from Romania and other nearby countries.
Iceland											
4201	0	0	4.10	8	99.79	0.21	C	377.73	110	9	Expatriates from Britain, in business. D=Church of England.
4202	3	10	1.06	6	99.92	0.08	C	550.71	37	10	Citizens of Denmark, in government, education, professions. D=NCI,ELFCI,PMI. M=SFM.
4203	0	10	0.00	5	99.90	0.10	C	502.60	0	10	Artificial (constructed) language, in 80 countries. Speakers in Iceland: 15,000(none mother-tongue).
4204	2	10	1.29	8	99.90	0.10	C	505.89	35	10	Mixed-race persons of French origin. D=NCI,RCC. M=SFM.
4205	0	0	4.35	8	99.84	0.16	C	410.84	112	10	Expatriates from Germany, mainly in business. D=EKD, RCC.
4206	6	6	1.23	2	99.95	0.05	C	536.55	34	10	Also in Denmark, Canada, USA. Non-Christians(pagans,spiritists) 3%. D=99% National Ch of Iceland,ELFCI,PMI,ILC,SDA,RCC. M=SMM,UBS,LBI.
4207	3	10	2.30	6	99.93	0.07	C	560.09	56	10	Expatriates from Norway, in administration, professions. D=NCI,ELFCI,PMI. M=SFM.
4208	0	0	4.63	6	99.73	0.27	C	322.40	105	9	Expatriates from Sweden, in administration, commerce. Nonreligious/atheists 27%. D=Church of Sweden.
4209	6	10	0.59	8	99.76	0.24	C	418.87	27	10	US military. D=US Military Chaplaincy,SDA,CC,JWs,SA,FMB.
4210	0	10	2.35		99.70	0.30	C	260.61	63	8	Bengalis (Sri Chinmoy adherents), other Asians,Europeans, Americans.
India											
4211	3	6	7.18	0	36.10	63.90	A	2.76	628	4	Northern hills, Assam. Also in Tibet, China. Animists/polytheists 98%. D=Siang Baptist Christian Association,CBCNEI,NBBA. M=BGC-BWM,BFI,ABCUSA,BSI.
4212	1	6	5.63	0	33.55	66.45	A	5.57	596	4	Assam, Tibet border, North East Frontier Agency. Animists/polytheists 95%. Polyandry practised. D=CBCNEI. M=ABCUSA.
4213	0	6	4.94	1	31.00	69.00	A	1.13	525	4	Bhils. Gujarat, Banaskantha and Sabarkantha Districts. Animists/polytheists 60%, Hindus 30%. M=IEM.
4214	1	7	2.33	4	46.90	53.10	A	3.25	195	4	Cannanore District, Kerala, Tamil Nadu, Karnataka. Hindus 98%. D=RCC. M=Kerala Tribal Mission,Zoram Baptist Mission,BFI.
4215	1	6	2.22	1	26.04	73.96	A	0.03	349	2	In Bihar, Madhya Pradesh, Maharashtra, Orissa. Hindus 70%, Muslims 30%. D=local fellowship.
4216	0	6	5.23	0	17.20	82.80	A	0.12	992	3	Bhils. In Maharashtra and Gujarat States. Animists/polytheists 79%, Hindus 20%.
4217	1	7	2.82	0	99.80	0.20	C	332.88	94	9	In Assam State and Manipur. Related to Chiru, Purum. Animists 20%. D=several churches.
4218	0	6	4.01	1	33.50	66.50	A	0.61	419	3	Assam. Related to Shan (Burma). Buddhists 90%, Animists 9%.
4219	1	7	1.10	0	24.20	75.80	A	0.17	238	3	In Rajasthan State. Mostly Hindus 90%, some Muslims 10%. D=CNI. M=Bibles for India.
4220	0	7	0.00	4	37.22	62.78	A	0.29	74	3	In Palghat District, Kerala. Animists 70%, Hindus 30%. M=CSI.
4221	1	7	5.46	0	38.00	62.00	A	13.87	466	5	Nonstandard Kannada. Tamil Nadu, eastern Nilgiri Hills. Inadequate bilingualism. Hindus 80%, some Muslims 10%. D=CSI.
4222	2	6	7.32	0	99.73	0.27	C	303.81	199	9	Southeast Manipur. Also in Burma, Bangladesh. Kuki Nagas; close to Mara Chin. Animists 26%. D=CBCNEI(Nagaland BC),NCRC. M=KCCGMS,BFI.
4223	1	7	2.97	4	43.20	56.80	A	0.31	252	3	In AP, MP, Maharashtra. Marathi spoken. Hindus 99%. D=CNI.
4224	2	5	2.75	1	25.02	74.98	A	0.01	413	2	In Bihar State. Related to Bihari. Hindus 99%. D=RCC,CNI.
4225	3	6	9.27	0	99.62	0.38	C	251.19	251	8	Kohima, Manipur, Maharashtra. Animists 35%. D=Angami Baptist Association,CBCNEI,NCRC. M=Bibles for India.
4226	5	6	1.51	8	99.80	0.20	C	382.52	53	9	Mixed-race persons, throughout India. D=RCC,CNI,MCSA,CSI,et alia.
4227	2	6	10.06	4	99.98	0.02	C	561.58	191	10	Northeastern Nagaland, Mokokchung, Assam. Animists 1%. D=CBCNEI(Nagaland Baptist Convention),NCRC. M=ABFMS,BFI.
4228	2	6	4.89	0	30.10	69.90	A	5.60	545	4	In Assam, Arunachal Pradesh, Nagaland. Close to Dafla. Animists 94%. D=RCC,NBBA. M=BGC-BWM.
4229	0	10	2.34	7	38.10	61.90	A	0.13	219	3	Pure Arabs(Usul) are rare; most are Mawalud(mixed race). Muslims 100%.
4230	2	6	2.75	1	31.06	68.94	A	0.06	341	2	Assam, Tripura. Mainly in Burma, Bangladesh, China. Theravada Buddhists 80%, animists 17%, Muslims 3%. D=RCC,CNI.
4231	0	6	2.34	4	41.00	59.00	A	1.49	224	4	MP, Maharashtra, AP. Mostly Hindus 80%, animists 19%. M=BLL.
4232	0	7	2.10	5	41.00	59.00	A	1.49	207	4	In Tamil Nadu, Karnataka, Kerala. Hindus 90%, a few Muslims 9%. M=Kerala Tribal Mission.
4233	0	6	4.14	1	27.00	73.00	A	0.98	523	3	Andhra Pradesh, Maharashtra, Karnataka. Hindus 99%.
4234	1	10	1.33	6	99.90	0.10	C	525.60	33	10	Long history in India. Gregorians. D=Armenian Apostolic Ch(D-India & Far East).
4235	2	5	4.59	4	57.10	42.90	B	2.29	269	4	Hindus 85%, Muslims 10%(Garia, 70% farmers; Hanafi Sunnis; including 2 million Neo-Assamese Bengali immigrants). D=RCC(M-Shillong-Gauhati),CBCNEI.
4236	0	6	4.46	1	44.50	55.50	A	17.05	342	5	Bihar, Raigarh in east MP, Maharashtra, Sambalput, Orissa, West Bengal. Related to Mundari. Animists 75%, Hindus 14%.
4237	1	6	12.13	1	33.50	66.50	A	3.05	1,074	4	Eastern Hindi. In Bihar, MP, UP, Kanpur; emigrants in USA. Hindus 92%, Muslims 5%. D=CNI. M=FMPB,CARWE. R=TWR.
4238	1	6	7.81	1	47.80	52.20	A	17.09	505	5	Tamil Nadu State, Madras-Nilgiri, Kunda Hills. Hindus 90%. D=RCC. M=Indian Bible Translators.
4239	0	6	4.60	1	27.09	72.91	A	0.08	566	2	Andhra Pradesh, Madras, Orissa. Hindus 99%. M=PFM.
4240	0	6	1.62	1	15.06	84.94	A	0.03	531	2	Himachal Pradesh, Haryana, Uttar Pradesh. Hindus 100%.
4241	0	6	5.38	0	24.10	75.90	A	0.08	725	2	In Punjab and Rajasthan. Also in Pakistan. Nomadic people across India-Pakistan borders. Animists 99%.
4242	1	7	2.67	1	30.00	70.00	A	1.09	336	4	Madhya Pradesh, Maharashtra; also Pakistan. Close to Lahnda, Siraiki. Muslims 70%, Hindus 29%. D=CNI.
4243	0	6	4.71	1	32.00	68.00	A	5.84	489	4	Bihar, Maharashtra, MP, Orissa, West Bengal. Eastern Hindi. Hindus 95%.
4244	0	6	4.63	0	23.29	76.71	A	1.09	741	4	Kargil District, Leh District. Jammu, Kashmir, UP. Mainly Pakistan. Balti is spoken form of literary Tibetan. Buddhists before 1370 conversion to Islam. Muslims 99%.
4245	2	6	11.51	5	46.60	53.40	A	6.12	736	4	In Punjab, Karnataka. Western Hindi. Hindus 98%. D=CNI,CSI.
4246	0	6	3.78	0	16.10	83.90	A	0.05	813	2	Bhils. Madhya Pradesh, Maharashtra, northern Dhule District from bilinguals in Marathi. Hindus 100%.
4247	0	5	0.70	0	12.10	87.90	A	0.04	385	2	Near Srinagar, Jammu & Kashmir. 50% of men are bilingual in Kohistani. Muslims 60%, Hindus 40%.
4248	1	7	6.12	6	47.82	52.18	A	4.92	409	4	In Bihar, Orissa, West Bengal. Hindus 97%. D=CNI; Evangelicals strong.
4249	0	6	2.93	0	21.10	78.90	A	0.07	510	2	Bhils. In Gujarat, Himachal Pradesh, MP, UP, Rajasthan. Animists 70%, Hindus 30%.
4250	1	7	6.24	0	99.95	0.05	C	520.12	134	10	In Assam State, Tripura. Also Chittagong Hills, Bangladesh, Burma. Tropical forest. Agriculturalists. D=Bawm Evangelical Christian Ch. M=NEIGM,UBS.
4251	0	7	1.81	5	42.94	57.06	A	3.04	179	4	Gujarat and Himachal Pradesh, Jammu & Kashmir, MP, Karnataka, West Bengal. Hindus 98%.
4252	0	6	2.52	1	17.01	82.99	A	0.00	570	1.08	Bihar, Gujarat, MP, UP, Maharashtra, Karnataka, West Bengal. Hindus 99%.
4253	1	7	3.04	0	27.00	73.00	A	0.98	410	3	South India. Related to Tulu and Koraga. Hindus 99%. D=CSI.
4254	5	6	5.60	6	65.50	34.50	B	5.97	291	4	Hindus 79%(including Bengali sect Ananda Marga), Muslims 18%(Hanafi Sunnis; Koran in Bengali). D=CNI,RCC(3 Dioceses),MCSA,SA,BOBBC. M=AIPF,FEBC.
4255	1	5	10.10	1	34.00	66.00	A	2.48	895	4	In Maharashtra, MP, AP. 12 dialects. Hindus 90%, some Muslims 9%. D=CNI.
4256	1	6	3.15	0	34.00	66.00	A	6.20	334	4	Nonstandard Tamil. Tamil Nadu, Nilgiri District; Karnataka, Mysore District. Hindus 95%. D=CSI.
4257	0	6	4.37	1	17.10	82.90	A	0.06	909	2	Dialects Bhalesi, Padari. Hindus 100%.
4258	0	5	2.34	1	29.00	71.00	A	1.05	317	4	Maharashtra, Amravati District. Hindus 99%.
4259	1	6	2.77	6	41.60	58.40	A	2.42	248	4	Madhya Pradesh, Uttar Pradesh, West Bengal. A scheduled tribe(formerly Outcaste). Hindus 98%. D=CNI. M=Bibles for India.
4260	0	6	4.17	1	24.50	75.50	A	0.44	584	3	In Himachal Pradesh. Related to Panjabi. Hindus 99%.
4261	0	6	4.01	4	40.00	60.00	A	1.46	344	4	In Madhya Pradesh. Hindus 90%, some Muslims 9%.
4262	0	7	5.15	0	28.97	71.03	A	1.02	582	4	Northwest, Bhattiana region; also Pakistan. Mixture of Punjabi and Rajasthani. Muslims 99% (Sunnis).
4263	1	6	3.68	1	24.02	75.98	A	0.01	534	2	In AP, MP, Maharashtra, Orissa States. Close to Halbi. Hindus 100%. D=Methodist Chs. M=IEM,IEA,Indian Bible Translators.
4264	0	6	4.25	1	18.01	81.99	A	0.00	799	1.09	Bhils. In Gujarat, Madhya Pradesh, Maharashtra, Karnataka, Rajasthan. Animists 99%.
4265	0	6	3.30	0	28.00	72.00	A	1.02	431	4	In Tripura. Largely animists 80%, and Hindus 19%.

Continued overleaf

Table 8-2 continued

PEOPLE Ref 1	Ethnic name 2	POPULATION P% 3	In 1995 4	In 2000 5	In 2025 6	IDENTITY CODE Race 7	Language 8	LANGUAGE Autoglossonym 9	S 10	CHURCH AC 11	Members 12	MINISTRY Jayuh 13-17	d 18	w 19	a 20	xcmc 21	mi 22	SCRIPTURE Biblioglossonym 23	Pub 24-26	ss 27
4266	Bhojpuri Bihari (Deswali)	3.55848	33,224,287	36,070,952	47,343,751	CNN25c	59-AAFQ-a	bhojpuri	4	1.02	367,924	1.s..	6	4	6	1	3	Bihari: Bhojpuri*	Pn.	b
4267	Bhottara (Dhotada)	0.03617	337,707	366,641	481,223	CNN23z	49-EBEA	wider-tamil cluster		0.03	110	2Asu.	3	3	4	1	0		PNB	b
4268	Bhoyari (Ojhi)	0.00069	6,442	6,994	9,180	CNN25o	59-AAFU-bi	kumbhari		0.11	8	1csu.	5	3	0	1	1		pnb	.
4269	Bhuiya (Bhumia)	0.00098	9,150	9,934	13,038	CNN25l	59-AAFS-b	bhuiya-oriya		29.00	2,881	1csu.	9	3	0	1	1		pnb	.
4270	Bhumij (Kisan-Bhumij)	0.00718	67,037	72,781	95,526	AUG04z	46-CABA-f	bhumij		0.51	371	1cs..	5	3	4	1	0		pnb	.
4271	Bhunjia (Bunjia)	0.00067	6,256	6,792	8,914	CNN23z	59-AAFR-c	bhunjia		0.00	0	1cs..	0	2	0	0	0		p..	.
4272	Bhutanese (Bhotia)	0.00500	46,683	50,683	66,522	MSY50a	70-AAAB-f	dzongkha		0.01	5	1.s..	3	3	3	1	3	Zongkhar*	Pn.	b
4273	Biete (Bete)	0.00195	18,206	19,766	25,944	MSY50c	73-DDDA-c	biete		20.00	3,953	0....	9	6	6	4	2	Biate*	PN.	.
4274	Bijori (Binjhia, Brijia)	0.00053	4,948	5,372	7,051	AUG04b	46-CABA-hb	birjia		21.00	1,128	1cs..	9	3	6	1	0		pnb	.
4275	Binjhwari	0.00621	57,981	62,948	82,621	CNN25g	59-AAFR-ae	binjhwari		0.03	19	1cs..	3	2	0	0	0		p..	b
4276	Birhor	0.00023	2,147	2,331	3,060	AUG04b	46-CABA-j	birhor		0.05	1	1cs..	4	3	0	1	0		pnb	.
4277	Bison Horn Maria (Dhuru)	0.01696	158,350	171,917	225,644	AUG06b	49-DAAA-cf	dandami-maria		0.05	86	1.s..	4	3	0	1	1	Maria, Dandami	pn.	.
4278	Bodo (Boro, Bodi, Mech)	0.07800	728,259	790,656	1,037,750	MSY50r	72-AAAA-a	bodo		6.49	51,314	2a...	7	5	7	4	3	Boro*	PNB	.
4279	Bodo Parja	0.00534	49,858	54,130	71,046	CNN25l	59-AAFS-g	adiwasi-oriya		1.00	541	1csu.	6	4	6	0	0	Girasia, Adiwasi*	pnb	.
4280	Bombay Jew (Bney Israel)	0.00080	7,469	8,109	10,644	CMT35	59-AAFU-m	deshi-marathi		0.05	4	2Asu.	4	2	2	0	0	Marathi*	PNB	b
4281	Bondo (Bhonda, Remo)	0.00039	3,641	3,953	5,189	AUG04z	46-CBBB-b	remo		0.82	32	0....	5	3	2	1	2		...	b
4282	Braj Bhakha (Antarbedi)	1.77479	16,570,595	17,990,368	23,612,671	CNN25g	59-AAFO-i	braj-kannauji	3	2.50	449,759	4csuh	6	5	7	1	1	Braj Bhasha	PNb	b
4283	British	0.01000	93,367	101,366	133,045	CEW19i	52-ABAC-b	standard-english	27	79.00	80,079	3Bsuh	10	10	13	5	3		PNB	b
4284	Brokpa (Minaro)	0.00043	4,015	4,359	5,721	CNN25i	70-AAAB-l	sagtengpa		0.10	4	1.s..	5	2	2	1	0		pn.	.
4285	Buksa Tharu	0.00284	26,516	28,788	37,785	CNN25k	59-AAFT-n	mahottari-tharu		0.02	6	1csuh	3	3	6	0	0	Tharu, Mahotari*	Pnb	.
4286	Bundelkhandi (Bondili)	1.23464	11,527,403	12,515,074	16,426,252	CNN25g	59-AAFO-j	bundeli	2	1.50	187,726	1asuh	6	5	7	3	4	Bundeli	pnb	b
4287	Burig (Bhotia, Purig-pa)	0.01521	142,010	154,178	202,361	MSY50r	70-AAAC-d	purik		0.23	355	1....	5	3	4	0	1	Purigskad*	PN.	.
4288	Burmese (Myen, Bhama)	0.00500	46,683	50,683	66,522	MSY50b	77-AABA-a	bama		0.17	86	4Asu.	5	5	8	3	2	Burmese	PNB	b
4289	Burusho (Burusho, Khajun)	0.00053	4,948	5,372	7,051	CNN25z	46-AAAA-a	proper burushaski		0.03	2	0....	3	1	2	0	0	Burushaski	...	.
4290	Car Nicobarese	0.00307	28,664	31,119	40,845	AUG03d	46-HAAA-a	car		81.00	25,207	0....	10	8	9	5	2	Nicobarese: Car*	PNB	.
4291	Central Andamanese	0.00001	93	101	133	AUG05	46-JAAD-a	a-pucikwar		30.00	30	0....	9	8	6	5	3		...	.
4292	Central Bhil	0.46200	4,313,533	4,683,117	6,146,673	AUG06a	59-AAFJ-c	giraasiaa-bhili		0.30	14,049	1.s..	5	5	7	1	3	Bhili: Central*	PN.	.
4293	Central Gond (Gondwadi)	0.56754	5,298,923	5,752,936	7,550,829	AUG06b	59-AAFO-e	general hindi		0.58	33,367	3Asuh	5	5	7	1	3		pnb	b
4294	Central Nicobarese	0.00071	6,629	7,197	9,446	AUG03d	46-HAAA-da	nancowry nancoury		85.00	6,117	0....	10	8	10	5	3	Nicobarese: Nancowry	Pnb	.
4295	Chakma	0.03740	349,191	379,110	497,588	MSY50s	59-AAFT-ie	chakma-baanglaa		17.70	67,102	1csuh	8	5	7	4	2	Chakma	PNb	.
4296	Chamari	0.00094	8,776	9,528	12,506	CNN25g	59-AAFO	hindi-urdu cluster		0.51	49	4Asuh	5	4	2	1	3		PNB	b
4297	Chameali Pahari (Chamba)	0.01494	139,490	151,441	198,769	CNN25k	59-AAFB-l	chameali		0.05	76	0.s..	4	4	2	1	1	Chambiali*	P..	.
4298	Champas (Rong, Rupshu)	0.00100	9,337	10,137	13,304	MSY50r	70-AAAC-b	changthang		0.01	1	1....	3	3	0	1	0		PN.	b
4299	Chang Naga (Changyanguh)	0.00320	29,877	32,437	42,574	MSY50p	72-BABA-a	chang-naga		61.00	19,787	0....	10	7	9	5	2	Naga: Chang*	PN.	.
4300	Chaudangsi	0.00018	1,681	1,825	2,395	MSY50r	70-ABBA-c	chaudangsi		0.00	0	0....	0	1	0	0	0		...	.
4301	Chenchu (Chenswar)	0.00224	20,914	22,706	29,802	AUG04z	49-DBAB-b	chenchu		0.35	79	1csu.	5	4	2	1	2		pnb	.
4302	Chero	0.00361	33,705	36,593	48,029	CNN25c	73-DBAA-a	proper chiru		0.01	4	0....	3	1	0	0	0		...	.
4303	Chhattisgarhi (Khatahi)	1.17828	11,001,189	11,943,774	15,676,411	CNN25g	59-AAFR-a	chhattisgarhi	2	1.30	155,269	2as..	6	5	7	3	1	Chhattisgarhi	P..	b
4304	Chik-Barik	0.02840	265,161	287,880	377,847	CNN25c	59-AAFQ-gd	panchpargania		2.37	6,823	1.s..	6	5	4	4	1		pn.	.
4305	Chiru	0.00068	6,349	6,893	9,047	MSY50c	73-DBAA-a	proper chiru		49.60	3,419	0....	9	7	6	5	1		...	.
4306	Chitkhuli (Tsihuli)	0.00017	1,587	1,723	2,262	MSY50r	70-ABAB-b	chikhuli		0.10	2	0....	5	3	0	1	0		p..	.
4307	Chodhari Bhil	0.02466	230,242	249,969	328,089	AUG06a	59-AAFK-a	chodhari-bhili		0.50	1,250	0cs..	5	5	4	3	3	Chodri	pn.	.
4308	Chokri Naga (Chakrima)	0.00230	21,474	23,314	30,600	MSY50p	73-ABBC-b	chokri-naga		65.00	15,154	1....	10	7	9	5	3	Naga, Chokri	pnb	.
4309	Chote Naga	0.00035	3,268	3,548	4,657	MSY50p	72-BAHA-a	chothe-naga		30.00	1,064	0....	9	7	6	5	1		...	.
4310	Chowra	0.00020	1,867	2,027	2,661	AUG03d	46-HAAB-b	tutet		80.00	1,622	0....	10	8	10	5	3		pnb	.
4311	Chulikata (Ida, Midu)	0.00090	8,403	9,123	11,974	MSY50z	74-AAEA-c	chulikata		1.00	91	0....	6	4	0	4	1		...	.
4312	Churahi Pahari	0.01274	118,949	129,141	169,499	CNN25k	59-AAFB-h	kului		0.05	65	0....	4	3	4	0	0	Kului*	P..	b
4313	Cochin Jew	0.00010	934	1,014	1,330	CMT35	49-EBEB-a	malayalam		0.10	1	2Asu.	5	3	0	1	0	Malayalam	PNB	b
4314	Cutch (Kachchi, Cutchi)	0.08291	774,102	840,427	1,103,075	CNN25p	59-AAFF-j	kachchi		1.00	8,404	1cs..	6	5	7	3	0	Kachchi	Pnb	b
4315	Dafla (Nishi, Lel)	0.02703	252,370	273,993	359,620	MSY50z	74-AABA-a	nisi		1.78	4,877	0....	6	4	5	3	3	Nishi*	PN.	.
4316	Dal	0.00125	11,671	12,671	16,631	CNN25l	59-AAFS	oriya cluster		0.05	6	3Asu.	4	3	0	2	0	Mirgan	PNB	b
4317	Dangs Bhil (Dangi, Dangri)	0.01429	133,421	144,852	190,121	AUG06a	59-AAFM	khandesi cluster		1.00	1,449	0....	6	5	5	1	2		...	.
4318	Darimiya	0.00020	1,867	2,027	2,661	MSY50r	70-ABBA-b	darmiya		0.00	0	0....	0	1	4	0	0		...	.
4319	Darlong (Zo)	0.00054	5,042	5,474	7,184	MSY50m	73-DCFA-a	darlong		80.00	4,379	0....	10	9	10	5	2	Darlong	PN.	.
4320	Deccani	1.25541	11,721,325	12,725,611	16,702,586	CNN25r	59-AAFU-m	deshi-marathi		0.00	0	2Asu.	0	3	5	1	3	Marathi*	PNB	b
4321	Degaru	0.00100	9,337	10,137	13,304	CNN25c	59-AAFS-l	degaru		0.11	11	1csu.	5	3	4	1	0		pnb	.
4322	Dehati (Deshiya)	0.00326	30,437	33,045	43,373	CNN25c	59-AAFQ-f	dehati		0.02	7	1.s..	3	3	4	1	0	Maithili, Dehati	pn.	.
4323	Deori (Deuri)	0.00202	18,860	20,476	26,875	MSY50z	72-ABAA-a	deori		0.56	115	0....	5	4	4	1	0		...	.
4324	Dhanwar (Dhanvar)	0.00372	34,732	37,708	49,493	CNN25j	59-AAFP-d	south dhanuwar		1.00	377	1c.u.	6	5	2	3	0		pn.	.
4325	Dhatki Bhil (Thar)	0.00160	14,939	16,219	21,287	AUG06a	59-AAFG-ag	dhatki		0.05	8	1.s..	4	3	0	0	0	Dhatki	pn.	.
4326	Dhodia (Dhobi, Doria)	0.01332	124,364	135,020	177,216	AUG06a	59-AAFK-m	dhodiaa bhili		0.30	405	0cs..	5	5	5	3	1		pn.	.
4327	Dhurwa (Parji, Thakara)	0.01273	118,856	129,039	169,366	AUG06b	49-CABA-a	parji		0.04	52	0....	3	4	2	1	1	Duruwa	...	.
4328	Digaro (Taraon)	0.00344	32,118	34,870	45,767	MSY50z	74-AAEA-a	digaro		1.00	349	0....	6	4	0	1	1		...	.
4329	Dimasa (Hills Kachari)	0.00614	57,327	62,239	81,690	MSY50z	72-AAAB-a	dimasa		89.00	55,393	0.s..	10	8	7	4	3	Dimasa	P..	.
4330	Dimasa Kachari	0.00561	52,379	56,866	74,638	MSY50z	72-AAAB-c	kachari		7.50	4,265	0.s..	7	7	11	4	1	Kachari	p..	.
4331	Dogri (Hindi Dogri)	0.22864	2,134,732	2,317,636	3,041,938	CNN25n	59-AAFE-l	dogri		0.10	2,318	1asu.	5	5	5	1	2	Panjabi: Dogri*	PNb	.
4332	Dorli	0.00428	39,961	43,385	56,943	AUG06b	49-DAAA	gond cluster		1.00	434	1.s..	6	5	5	3	0		PN.	b
4333	Dubla	0.02328	217,357	235,980	309,728	AUG06a	59-AAFK-l	dubli bhili		4.00	9,439	0cs..	6	5	5	5	1		pn.	.
4334	Eastern Baluch	0.00077	7,189	7,805	10,244	CNT24b	58-AABA-a	east balochi		0.10	8	1.s..	5	2	3	1	0	Baluchi: Eastern*	P..	b
4335	Eastern Bhil (Vil)	0.27791	2,594,749	2,817,067	3,697,450	AUG06a	59-AAFJ-c	giraasiaa-bhili		0.10	2,817	1.s..	5	5	6	1	3	Bhili: Central*	PNB	.
4336	Eastern Hindi (Bagheli)	0.04070	380,002	412,560	541,493	CNN25g	59-AAFP-c	bagheli	5	0.40	1,650	1c.u.	5	5	5	3	0	Bagheli	PN.	b
4337	Eastern Magar (Mangari)	0.00010	934	1,014	1,330	MSY50n	71-BABA-b	east magar		0.10	1	0....	5	3	0	0	0	Magar*	PN.	.
4338	Eastern Muria	0.00100	9,337	10,137	13,304	AUG06b	49-BAAA-bb	raigarh		0.05	5	1....	4	3	2	2	0		pn.	.
4339	Eastern Punjabi (Gurmukhi)	4.03912	37,711,855	40,943,016	53,738,420	CNN25n	59-AAFE-d	majhi	4	2.99	1,224,196	1asu.	6	5	9	5	4	Panjabi*	PNB	b
4340	Eastern Tamang	0.00143	13,351	14,495	19,025	MSY50z	70-AABA-c	east tamang		10.00	1,450	0....	8	6	7	5	3	Tamang, Eastern	pn.	.
4341	Esperanto	0.00000	0	0	0	CEW21z	51-AAAC-a	proper esperanto		10.00	0	0A...	8	6	2	5	0	Esperanto	PNB	b
4342	Falam Chin (Tipura)	0.00276	25,769	27,977	36,720	MSY50c	73-DDDB-a	falam		17.00	4,756	1.s..	8	6	6	5	2	Chin: Falam*	PNB	b
4343	Far Western Muria	0.00100	9,337	10,137	13,304	AUG06b	49-DAAA-ca	bhamani-maria		0.06	6	1.s..	4	3	3	2	0		pn.	.
4344	French	0.00300	28,010	30,410	39,913	CEW21b	51-AABI-d	general français		87.00	26,457	1B.uh	10	9	14	5	1	French	PNB	b
4345	Gadaba	0.00399	37,253	40,445	53,085	AUG04z	46-CBBB-a	gutob		0.20	81	0....	5	3	4	0	0	Gadaba	...	.
4346	Gadba	0.00125	11,671	12,671	16,631	CNN23z	49-CABB-a	gadaba		2.00	253	0....	6	5	5	3	0		...	.
4347	Gaddi (Pahari Bharmauri)	0.01236	115,401	125,289	164,443	CNN25z	59-AAFE-j	gaddi		0.03	38	1csu.	3	3	0	0	1		pnb	.
4348	Gamti (Gamit)	0.02398	223,893	243,076	319,042	AUG06a	59-AAFK-b	gamati-bhili		1.50	3,646	0cs..	6	5	6	5	2	Gamit	PN.	.
4349	Gangte	0.00680	63,489	68,929	90,471	MSY50c	73-DAAE-m	gang-te		88.00	60,658	0cs..	10	9	11	5	2	Gangte	PNB	.
4350	Garhwali (Central Pahari)	0.10000	933,665	1,013,662	1,330,449	CNN25k	59-AAFC-b	garhwali		0.03	304	1....	3	4	5	1	3	Garhwali*	PN.	b
4351	Garhwali (Pahari Gashwali)	0.22482	2,099,066	2,278,914	2,991,115	CNN25k	59-AAFC-b	garhwali		0.02	456	1....	3	4	5	1	3	Garhwali*	PN.	b
4352	Garo	0.01000	93,367	101,366	133,045	MSY50d	72-ACAA-c	abeng		35.10	35,580	0as..	9	8	8	5	3	Garo: Abeng	PNB	.
4353	Garo (Mande)	0.05959	556,371	604,041	792,814	MSY50d	72-ACAA-b	achik		38.00	229,536	0as..	9	8	8	5	2	Garo: Achik	PNB	.
4354	Gataq (Didei, Dire)	0.00041	3,828	4,156	5,455	AUG04z	46-CBBC-a	gta'		0.05	2	0....	4	3	4	0	0		...	.
4355	Gawari	0.00371	34,639	37,607	49,360	CNN25c	59-AAFQ-j	gawari		0.02	8	1.s..	3	3	2	0	1		pn.	.
4356	Goanese (Kunkuna)	0.36000	3,361,194	3,649,182	4,789,615	CNN25d	59-AAFU-o	konkani-gomantaki		57.00	2,080,034	3asu.	10	7	13	5	3	Konkani: Goan*	PNB	b
4357	Gormati (Banjara, Labhan)	0.21348	1,993,188	2,163,965	2,840,242	CNN25f	49-DBAB-a	telugu		0.13	2,813	2Asu.	5	5	6	2	4	Telugu	PNB	b
4358	Gowlan	0.00200	18,673	20,273	26,609	CNN25j	59-AAFU-c	gowlan		6.00	1,216	1csu.	7	5	7	3	1	Gowli	pnb	.
4359	Gowli	0.00100	9,337	10,137	13,304	CNN25g	59-AAFU-c	gowlan		5.00	507	1csu.	7	5	7	3	1	Gowli	pnb	.
4360	Greek	0.00020	1,867	2,027	2,661	CEW20	56-AAAA-c	dhimotiki		95.00	1,926	2B.uh	10	9	11	5	1	Greek: Modern	PNB	b
4361	Groma	0.00150	14,005	15,205	19,957	MSY50r	70-AAAB-c	groma		0.02	3	1.s..	3	3	4	1	0		pn.	.
4362	Gujar (Gujuri, Kashmiri)	0.06251	583,634	633,640	831,663	CNN25o	59-AAFG-o	gujuri		0.02	127	1.s..	3	4	4	1	2	Gujari	pn.	.
4363	Gujarati	4.71308	44,004,384	47,774,690	62,705,112	CNN25e	59-AAFH-b	standard gujaraati		2.30	1,098,818	2A.u.	6	5	9	5	3	Gujarati	PNB	b
4364	Gurung	0.00025	2,334	2,534	3,326	MSY50e	70-AABB-b	north gurung		1.30	33	0....	6	2	0	0	0	Gurung	PN.	.
4365	Gypsy (Dom, Sansi, Hampi)	0.00250	23,342	25,342	33,261	CNN25f	59-ACBB-d	fintika-romani		13.00	3,294	0....	8	6	2	3	1	Romani: Lithuanian	P..	.
4366	Hajong (East Bengali)	0.00196	18,300	19,868	26,077	CNN25b	59-AAFT-l	haijong-bangali		0.29	58	1csuh	5	4	4	1	0		pnb	.
4367	Haka Chin (Zotung)	0.00100	9,337	10,137	13,304	MSY50c	73-DCBA-a	haka		60.00	6,082	0as..	10	9	9	5	3	Chin: Haka*	PNB	.
4368	Halbi (Bastari, Halba)	0.07480	698,382	758,219	995,176	CNN25j	59-AAFR-b	halbi		0.01	76	1cs..	3	4	2	3	2	Halbi	P..	.
4369	Han Chinese (Cantonese)	0.00207	19,327	20,983	27,540	MSY42a	79-AAAM-a	central yue		5.00	1,049	3A.uh	7	5	8	5	3	Chinese, Yue	PNB	b
4370	Han Chinese (Hakka)	0.01105	103,170	112,010	147,015	MSY42a	79-AAAG-a	literary hakka		5.00	5,600	1A...	7	6	8	5	3	Chinese: Hakka, Wukingfu*	PNB	b
4371	Han Chinese (Mandarin)	0.00069	6,442	6,994	9,180	MSY42a	79-AAAB-ba	kuo-yü	1	6.00	420	2Bsuh	7	5	8	5	2	Chinese: Kuoyu*	PNB	b
4372	Harauti (Hadauti, Harotee)	0.05886	549,555	596,641	783,102	CNN25o	59-AAFG-j	harauti		0.10	597	1.s..	5	4	5	1	0	Harauti	PN.	.
4373	Hill Maria (Gatte)	0.00232	21,661	23,517	30,866	AUG06b	49-DAAA-cb	abuj-maria		0.05	12	1.s..	4	4	6	3	1		pn.	b
4374	Hindi (Bazaar, Popular)	5.49750	51,328,240	55,726,056	73,141,418	CNN25g	59-AAFO-e	general hindi	7	1.60	891,617	3Asuh	6	5	6	5	3		pnb	b
4375	Hindi (High Hindi)	6.22110	58,084,241	63,060,913	82,768,545	CNN25g	59-AAFO-c	standard hindi	47	2.10	1,324,279	1Asuh	6	5	8	5	3	Hindi	PNB	b
4376	Hindustani	0.10000	933,665	1,013,662	1,330,449	CNN25r	59-AAFO-b	historical hindi	10	0.05	507	1Asuh	4	4	5	5	1	Hindi: Sarnami*	PNB	b
4377	Hmar	0.00518	48,364	52,508	68,917	MSY50z	73-DCDA-a	hmar		98.70	51,825	0....	10	8	14	5	3	Hmar	PNB	.
4378	Ho	0.11169	1,042,811	1,132,159	1,485,978	AUG04a	46-CABA-e	ho		0.55	6,227	1cs..	5	5	7	3	3	Ho	PNb	.
4379	Holiya (Holar, Holu)	0.00068	6,349	6,893	9,047	CNN23a	49-DBAB-c	kannada south		1.00	69	1csu.	6	4	4	3	1		pnb	.
4380	Hrangkhol (Rangkhol)	0.00185	17,273	18,753	24,613	MSY50c	73-DDDA-a	hrangkhol		25.00	4,688	0....	9	6	5	4	2	Hrangkhol	PN.	.
4381	Indian Gypsy	0.02000	186,733	202,732	266,090	CNN25f	59-AAFO-a	domari		1.00	2,027	0....	6	4	4	3	3		...	b
4382	Indian Kachin (Marip)	0.00098	9,150	9,934	13,038	MSY50f	75-AAAA-a	jing-pho		30.00	2,980	2as..	9	6	6	4	1	Kachin: Jinghpaw*	PNB	.
4383	Indo-Portuguese (Damas)	0.00005	467	507	665	CNN25z	51-AACA-g	indo-português		80.00	405	1c...	10	8	10	5	1	Indo-Portuguese	PNb	b
4384	Irula (Eravallon, Irava)	0.01198	111,853	121,437	159,388	CNN23c	49-EBDA-a	irula		3.00	3,643	0....	6	8	4	1	3	Irula	...	.
4385	Jagannathi (Jaga Aad)	0.00029	2,708	2,940	3,858	CNN25l	59-AAFO-i	braj-kannauji		0.50	15	4csuh	5	4	0	1	0	Braj Bhasha	PNb	b
4386	Janggali (Rawat)	0.00029	2,708	2,940	3,858	MSY50r	70-ABAA-h	jangali		0.10	3	0....	5	2	2	0	1		p..	.
4387	Jangshung (Zangram)	0.00034	3,174	3,446	4,524	MSY50r	70-ABAA	bunan-thebor cluster		0.10	3	0....	5	3	0	1	0		P..	.
4388	Jarawa Negrito	0.00003	280	304	399	AUG05	46-KAAB-a	jarawa		10.00	30	0....	8	6	5	3	3		...	.
4389	Jat (Jati, Bangri)	1.20000	11,203,981	12,163,941	15,965,384	CNN25h	59-AAFO-hb	jatu	1	2.60	316,262	1asuh	6	5	7	3	2		pnb	.

Continued opposite

Table 8-2 continued

EVANGELIZATION								EVANGELISM			ADDITIONAL DESCRIPTIVE DATA
Ref 1	D 28	aC 29	CG% 30	r 31	E 32	U 33	W 34	e 35	R 36	T 37	Locations, civil divisions, literacy, religions, church history, denominations, dioceses, church growth, missions, agencies, ministries, movements 38
4266	3	5	11.09	6	40.02	59.98	A	1.49	829	4	Bihar, Assam, MP, UP. Also in Nepal. Hindus 85%, Muslims 14%. D=RCC(D-Varanasi),CNI,IET. M=RBMU,FGFI,IBT,UPM,CSI,YWAM. R=FEBA.
4267	0	6	2.43	6	39.03	60.97	A	0.04	241	2	In Andhra Pradesh, Tamil Nadu, Orissa. Hindus 99%.
4268	1	6	2.10	1	25.11	74.89	A	0.10	338	3	In Maharashtra. Rajasthani grouping. Largely Hindus 90%, some Muslims 9%. D=CNI.
4269	1	6	5.83	1	59.00	41.00	B	62.45	317	6	Bihar, MP, Maharashtra, Orissa, UP, West Bengal. Hindus 71%. D=mostly Evangelicals. M=FECI.
4270	0	6	3.68	1	28.51	71.49	A	0.53	459	3	Primarily in Mayurbhanj District of Orissa; also Assam, Bihar, West Bengal. Hindus 70%, animists 29%.
4271	0	6	0.00	1	13.00	87.00	A	0.00	0	1.07	Raipur, Hoshangabad, Sambalpur, Kalshandi Districts of MP, Maharashtra, Orissa. Related to Halbi. Hindus 99%.
4272	0	7	1.62	0	27.01	72.99	A	0.01	334	2	From Bhutan, in Sikkim and Assam. Strict Lamaists(Tantric Buddhists)100%. M=CNI,RCC,TCF.
4273	2	6	6.16	0	56.00	44.00	B	40.88	355	6	Assam, Cachar Hills. Closest to Hrangkhol. Animists 80%. D=ICFG,Presbyterian Ch.
4274	0	6	4.84	1	56.00	44.00	B	42.92	291	6	In Bihar, MP, Orissa, West Bengal. Related to Kherwari. Hindus 60%, animists 19%.
4275	0	6	2.99	1	19.03	80.97	A	0.02	574	2	Bihar, MP, Maharashtra, West Bengal. Eastern Hindi understood. Hindus 99%.
4276	0	7	0.00	1	24.05	75.95	A	0.04	125	2	In Bihar, MP, Maharashtra, Orissa, West Bengal; Chota Nagpur. Animists 99%(ancestral spirits, clan divinities venerated). Rapid assimilation to Sadani language.
4277	0	6	4.56	0	19.05	80.95	A	0.03	800	2	MP, Maharashtra, Orissa. Gonds. Hindus 70%, animists 30%. M=IEM.
4278	5	6	8.92	4	60.49	39.51	B	14.32	480	5	Assam, West Bengal; also in Nepal. Hinduized animists 93%. D=Goalpara Boro Baptist Ch,North Bank Baptist Ch,RCC,CNI,ICI. M=ABMS,Norwegian Mission.
4279	0	0	4.07	1	23.00	77.00	A	0.84	604	3	Orissa. Koraput District. Peasant agriculturalists, laborers. Hindus 69%, Polytheists 30%.
4280	0	10	1.40	4	39.05	60.95	A	0.07	147	2	Followers of religious Judaism.
4281	0	7	3.53	0	22.82	77.18	A	0.68	556	3	Orissa, Koraput, Bondo Hills. Almost all bilinguals. Hindus 70%, animists 29%. M=IEM,Mission for the Interior.
4282	0	5	11.31	1	43.50	56.50	A	3.96	775	4	Bihar, MP, UP(Agra region), Rajasthan. Western Hindi. Hindus 95%. M=ZBM. R=TWR.
4283	7	10	1.17	8	99.79	0.21	C	446.94	41	10	Expatriates from Britain, in education, development, business. D=CNI,CSI,MCSA,RCC,JWs,SDA,&c.
4284	0	6	1.40	0	21.10	78.90	A	0.07	312	2	Along Indus river in Ladakh and Kargil Districts. Lamaist Buddhists 60%, animists 30%, Muslims 10%.
4285	0	0	1.81	1	20.02	79.98	A	0.01	426	2	Southwestern Nainital District from Ramnagar to Keneshpur. Agriculturalists, pastoralists. Hindus 95%, Animists 5%.
4286	0	5	10.34	6	51.50	48.50	B	2.82	603	4	In UP, MP, Maharashtra. Western Hindi. Hindus 95%. M=CCC(India,Philippines),EHC,MSCT,NSM,Pocket Testament League,EHC,Ev Friends,BS(India),COUNT.
4287	0	6	3.63	0	23.23	76.77	A	0.19	625	3	North Kashmir, Kargil District, mainly Suru Valley. Also west Tibet, China. Closely related to Balti. Few speak Urdu. Muslims 99%(Shias).M=Central Asia Mission.
4288	2	10	4.56	6	60.17	39.83	B	0.37	258	3	From Burma, in Assam. Theravada Buddhists 98%, Muslims 2%(Shafi Sunnis). D=CNI,Goalpara Boro Baptist Union.
4289	0	6	0.70	0	13.03	86.97	A	0.01	362	2	Kashmir, Gilgit; mainly Hunza area of Pakistan. Language isolate. Muslims 100%.
4290	4	7	2.34	0	99.81	0.19	C	387.30	70	9	Car Island, North Nicobar Islands. Animists 15%. D=RCC,CNI(D-Andaman & Nicobar Islands),CPM,CBCNEI. M=USPG,ABCUSA.
4291	3	7	3.46	0	65.00	35.00	B	71.17	188	6	Remnants of several tribes an Andaman Islands, all extinct or nearly so. Hindus 40%, Animists 30%. D=RCC,CPM,MTSCM(D-Bahya Kerala). M=SX,SJ,SISWA.
4292	6	5	7.52	0	34.30	65.70	A	0.37	681	3	Agriculturalists. Polytheists/animists 95%. D=RCC(D-Ajmer-Jaipur),CNI(D-Jabalpur),DNC,MCSA,CMA,Pentecostals. M=IEM,SVD,SAM,TEAM,COUNT,CGMM,BFI.
4293	3	5	4.29	7	50.58	49.42	B	1.07	287	4	Mainly in MP. Hindus 70%, animists 30%. D=Mennonites,Methodists,MPELC. M=IEM,SIL,LBI,SEMS,COUNT,CGMM,IBT,BFI,UPM,WVI. R=FEBA,VERITAS.
4294	3	7	1.83	0	99.85	0.15	C	409.53	59	10	Nicobar Islands. Animists 12%. D=CNI,Shiloh Evangelistic Association,CBCNEI. M=ABCUSA,USPG,LMS,IEM.
4295	3	6	9.21	1	62.70	37.30	B	40.50	451	6	Assam State. Also in Bangladesh. Buddhists 80%. D=Baptists,Presbyterians,ICFG. M=AIPF,ZBM.
4296	1	6	3.97	7	47.51	52.49	A	0.88	287	3	In Madhya Pradesh, Uttar Pradesh, Maharashstra. Western Hindi. Hindus 95%. D=Society of Friends. M=Christian Hospital,ACRA,FMPB,YWAM.
4297	1	6	4.43	1	20.05	79.95	A	0.03	783	2	Himachal Pradesh, Jammu, Kashmir. Hindus 99%. D=CNI.
4298	0	6	0.00	0	20.01	79.99	A	0.00	229	1.08	Nomads, pastoralists, on Tibet border east of Leh. Close to Ladakhi. Multilingual in Urdu, Kashmiri, Hindi, or English. Lamaist Buddhists 100%.
4299	2	6	7.89	0	99.61	0.39	C	229.33	234	8	Assam, east central Nagaland. Animists 38%. D=CBCNEI(Nagaland Baptist Convention),NCRC. M=Tuensang Mission Compound,BFI.
4300	0	5	0.00	0	7.00	93.00	A	0.00	0	1.02	Mahakali Zone near western edge of Nepal. Related to Rangkas, Darmiya, Byangsi (Nepal). Lamaist Buddhists 100%.
4301	1	6	4.47	1	28.35	71.65	A	0.36	538	3	Andhra Pradesh, Tamil Nadu, Karnataka, Orissa. Hindus 99%. D=CSI. M=COUNT,Bibles for India.
4302	0	6	1.40	0	11.01	88.99	A	0.00	602	1.03	In Bihar, Orissa, Uttar Pradesh, West Bengal. Hindus 80%, some Muslims 20%.
4303	1	5	10.13	6	45.30	54.70	A	2.14	673	4	Eastern Hindi, in Bihar, MP, Maharashtra, Orissa. 7 major dialects. Hindus 98%. D=CNI. M=IBT. R=FEBA.
4304	1	6	6.74	1	33.37	66.63	A	2.88	637	4	In Bihar and West Bengal. Related to Maithili. Hindus 95%. D=CNI.
4305	1	6	6.01	0	80.60	19.40	B	145.91	242	7	Assam, Manipur, Nagaland. Animists 45%, some Hindus 5%. D=Baptist Chs.
4306	0	6	0.70	0	15.10	84.90	A	0.05	430	2	Kinnaur District, Baspa river, Sangla Valley. Related to Kanauri. Lamaist Buddhist 50%, Hindus 30%, animists 20%.
4307	0	6	4.95	1	30.50	69.50	A	0.55	535	3	Gujarat State, mainly in Broach and Dangs Districts; also Maharashtra, Karnataka, Rajasthan. Animists 95%. M=FMPB,NIMS,WVI.
4308	3	6	7.60	0	99.65	0.35	C	265.72	208	8	Eastern Angami. Nagaland. Animists 34%. D=Angami Baptist Association,CBCNEI(Nagaland Baptist Convention),NCRC.
4309	1	6	4.78	0	61.00	39.00	B	66.79	255	6	Nagaland, near Burma border. Largely animists 69%. D=Baptist Chs.
4310	3	7	2.12	0	99.80	0.20	C	370.84	67	9	Nicobar Islands, Chaura Island. Animists 20%. D=RCC,CNI,CBCNEI.
4311	1	6	4.61	0	21.00	79.00	A	0.76	745	3	In Assam, Arunachal Pradesh, West Bengal. Close to Digaro, Miju. Animists 90%, some Hindus 9%. D=CBCNEI.
4312	0	6	4.26	1	19.05	80.95	A	0.03	800	2	Himachal Pradesh. Mostly Hindus 95%.
4313	0	6	0.00	4	35.10	64.90	A	0.12	54	3	Followers of religious Judaism, in Kerala.
4314	0	6	6.97	1	36.00	64.00	A	1.31	607	4	In AP, MP, UP, Assam, Gujarat (Kutch area), Kerala, Tamil Nadu, Maharashtra, Karnataka, Orissa. Hindus 70%, Muslims 29%.
4315	2	6	6.39	0	33.78	66.22	A	2.19	608	4	Assam, Darrang, Arunachal Pradesh. Animists 98%. D=North Bank Baptist Association,CBCNEI. M=CNM,BGC-BWM,ABCUSA.
4316	0	6	1.81	4	36.05	63.95	A	0.06	214	2	In Orissa State. Mostly Hindus 99%.
4317	1	6	5.10	0	25.00	75.00	A	0.91	669	3	Gujarat State, Dangs District. Lingua franca. Animists/polytheists 90%. D=CNI. M=FMPB,IEM.
4318	0	5	0.00	0	11.00	89.00	A	0.00	0	1.03	Mahakali Zone, near western Nepal. Related to Rangkas, Chaudangsi. Lamaist Buddhists 100%.
4319	2	6	6.27	0	99.80	0.20	C	356.24	166	9	In Tripura, also in Bangladesh. Animists 20%. D=CBCNEI,CNI. M=AIPF,BMM.
4320	0	5	0.00	4	40.00	60.00	A	0.00	0	1.13	Deccan Plateau. Muslims 100%(Sunnis, with Shias 4%) but close to Hindu society. Related to Marathi language and culture. Small traders,laborers. Saint worship.
4321	0	6	2.43	1	27.11	72.89	A	0.10	349	3	Bihar, West Bengal. Mostly Hindus 99%.
4322	0	5	1.96	1	21.02	78.98	A	0.01	388	2	Bihar; also south Nepal. Differences from Standard Maithili. Mostly Hindus 95%, some Muslims 5%.
4323	0	6	2.47	0	18.56	81.44	A	0.37	527	3	In Assam, Nagaland. Hindus 70%, Buddhists 20%, animists 9%.
4324	0	6	3.70	1	25.00	75.00	A	0.91	516	3	Madhya Pradesh, Maharashtra. Eastern Hindi. Mostly Hindus 99%.
4325	0	6	2.10	0	17.05	82.95	A	0.03	498	2	In Rajasthan; also Sind(Pakistan). Bhils. Related to Marwari. Muslims 65%, Hindus 30%, animists 5%.
4326	0	6	3.77	1	28.30	71.70	A	0.31	462	3	In Maharashtra State, Gujarat, MP, Karnataka, Rajasthan. Bhils. Animists/polytheists 95%. M=ZBM.
4327	1	6	4.03	0	16.04	83.96	A	0.02	859	2	In Bastar(MP), Koraput(Orissa). Some monolinguals. Second language: Halbi. Forests. Lumbermen. Hindus 99%. D=CNI. M=IEM.
4328	1	6	3.62	0	18.00	82.00	A	0.65	718	3	Assam, Arunachal Pradesh. Animists 95%, some Hindus 4%. D=CBCNEI. M=ABCUSA.
4329	4	6	9.00	0	99.89	0.11	C	415.80	216	10	North Cachar District, Assam, Nagaland. D=PCNEI,CNI(D-Assam; formerly Anglican D-Assam),ICI,NBBA. M=Presbyterian Ch of Wales (Calvanistic Methodists).
4330	1	6	6.24	0	42.50	57.50	A	11.63	473	5	North Cachar District, and Cachar Hills, Assam, Nagaland. Animists 90%. D=Presbyterian Ch.
4331	2	5	5.60	5	40.10	59.90	A	0.14	454	3	Jammu, Kashmir, Gurdaspur, Sialkot; and as far as West Bengal. Dialect of Panjabi. Hindus 65%, Muslims 33%, Sikhs. D=RCC(PA-Jammu & Kashmir),CNI.
4332	0	6	3.84	0	31.00	69.00	A	1.13	428	4	In Andhra Pradesh, MP, Maharashtra, Orissa. Gonds. Hindus 70%, animists 29%.
4333	3	6	7.09	1	39.00	61.00	A	5.69	568	4	Gujarat, Maharashtra, Karnataka, Rajasthan. Bhils. Literates 10%. Hindus 94%, Muslims 2%. D=Ch of the Brethren,Presbyterians,RCC. M=FMPB.
4334	0	8	2.10	1	23.10	76.90	A	0.08	368	2	Majority live in Pakistan. Muslims 100%(Sunnis). R=TWR.
4335	5	5	5.80	0	32.10	67.90	A	0.11	580	3	Polytheists/animists 95%. D=CMA,Methodists,CNI,RCC,Pentecostals. M=IEM,COUNT,CGMM,BFI,UPM,YWAM.
4336	0	6	5.24	1	31.40	68.60	A	0.45	545	3	Kawathi, Riwai, Mandal. Vernacular of northeast Madhya Pradesh; Maharashtra, UP. Also in Nepal. Hindus 98%.
4337	0	6	0.00	0	17.10	82.90	A	0.06	128	2	Majority in Nepal; also in Sikkim, Bhutan. Mountainous. Agriculturalists, hunters. Animists 90%, Hindus 10%.
4338	0	6	1.62	0	20.05	79.95	A	0.03	358	2	Madhya Pradesh, eastern Bastar District. Close to Western Muria. Hindus 60%, animists 40%.
4339	3	5	12.43	5	62.99	37.01	B	6.87	586	4	Punjab Haryana, Delhi, Rajasthan, Jammu, Kashmir. Also in Bangladesh, UK, Fiji, UAE, Singapore. Sikhs(10 sects) 47%, Hindus 50%, Muslims 1%(Hanafi Sunnis).
4340	1	6	5.10	0	46.00	54.00	A	16.79	369	5	Around Darjeeling. Vast majority live in Nepal. Animists 38%, Hindus 27%, Buddhists 23%. 1974, indigenous revival, widespread. D=NCF. M=AO,SIL,YWAM.
4341	0	7	0.00	5	57.00	43.00	B	20.80	0	5	Artificial (constructed) language, in 80 countries. Speakers in India: 95,000(none mother-tongue). Hindus 70%, Muslims 20%.
4342	0	6	6.36	0	59.00	41.00	B	36.61	346	5	Assam, Tripura. Also in Burma, Bangladesh. 9 main dialects. Animists 80%. M=Zoram Baptist Mission,NZBMC.
4343	0	6	1.81	0	22.06	77.94	A	0.04	349	2	Maharashtra State, northern Garhichiroli District. Close to Dandami Maria. Hindus 65%, animists 35%.
4344	1	10	1.34	8	99.87	0.13	C	508.08	40	10	Expatriates from France, in business, commerce, education, professions. D=RCC.
4345	0	6	4.49	0	17.20	82.80	A	0.12	891	3	In AP, MP, Tamil Nadu, Maharashtra, Orissa. An Austro-Asiatic Munda language. Hindus 70%, animists 30%.
4346	0	6	3.28	0	24.00	76.00	A	1.75	489	4	Orissa, Koraput District. A Central Dravidian language. Hindus 96%.
4347	0	6	3.70	1	21.03	78.97	A	0.02	615	2	In Himachal Pradesh, MP, UP, Punjab. Hindus 100%. M=Christian Dynamics.
4348	4	6	6.08	1	39.50	60.50	A	2.16	491	4	Gujarat State, Broach, Surat. Well-educated Bhils. Animists/polytheists 98%. D=CNI,Society of Friends,RCC,SDA. M=FMPB,NIMS.
4349	1	6	9.10	1	99.88	0.12	C	449.68	200	10	Assam, central Manipur. Also Burma. Related to Thado Chin. Animists 12%. D=ICFG. M=NEIGM,Bibles for India.
4350	0	6	3.47	0	25.03	74.97	A	0.02	522	2	In Kashmir and Uttar Pradesh. Hindus 100%. M=AGAPE,CARWE,FECI,IEM,YWAM.
4351	2	5	3.89	0	26.02	73.98	A	0.01	547	2	Kashmir and UP. Hindus 100%. D=Methodists,Pentecostals. M=AGAPE,CARWE,FECI,IEM,YWAM. R=WOH.
4352	4	6	8.52	4	92.10	7.90	B	117.99	283	7	Assam, Nagaland, Tripura. Animists 60%. D=North Goalpara Garo Baptist Union,CBCNEI(Garo Baptist Convention),NBBA,RCC. M=ABMS,BGC-BWM,BFI,LBI.
4353	3	6	10.56	4	94.00	6.00	B	130.37	337	7	West Assam, Garo Hills, West Bengal, Tripura. Animists 62%. D=Garo Baptist Union,CBCNEI(Garo Baptist Convention),NBBA. M=BGC-BWM,BFI.
4354	0	6	0.70	0	16.05	83.95	A	0.02	307	2	Orissa, Koraput District. An Austro-Asiatic Munda language. Hindus 70%, animists 30%.
4355	0	6	2.10	1	20.02	79.98	A	0.01	427	2	Maharashtra State, AP, MP, Bihar. Hindus 100%. M=MSCT.
4356	1	6	2.37	4	99.57	0.43	B	251.74	76	8	Southern coastal strip of Maharashtra, Karnataka, Gujarat. Also in UAR, Kenya. Hindus 40%. Long Catholic history. D=RCC(P-Goa). M=SJ,SX,BFI,BSI.
4357	6	5	5.80	5	50.13	49.87	B	0.23	373	3	AP,MP,HP,TN, 5 other States. Hindus/polytheists 99%. D=UELCI,Baptists,CSI-I,Assemblies,CMA,MB. M=IEM,IM,SIL,BMDT,ABCUSA,WVI,PI,BFI,TM,MTI,MSCT.
4358	1	6	4.92	1	43.00	57.00	A	9.41	378	4	Maharashtra, Amravati District, Hoshangabad District. Pastoralists. Few speak Hindi. Nomads, surrounded by Korku. Hindus/animists 94%. D=CNI. M=IEM.
4359	0	6	4.00	1	40.00	60.00	A	7.30	343	4	Maharashtra, Amravati District. In Gowli caste. Hindus 95%. M=IEM.
4360	1	10	5.40	7	99.95	0.05	C	568.67	107	10	Traders, from Greece. D=Greek Orthodox Ch(D-New Zealand, under EP-Constantinople).
4361	0	4	1.10	0	19.02	80.98	A	0.01	399	2	Sikkim. Also in China. Upper and Lower Groma. Buddhists 99%(Lamaists).
4362	0	6	2.57	0	23.02	76.98	A	0.01	425	2	HP,MP,UP,Jammu,Kashmir,Rajasthan. Also in Pakistan, Afghanistan. Nomads, pastoralists. Underdogs. Muslims(Sunnis) 70%, Hindus 30%, but no mingling.
4363	4	5	12.31	6	63.30	36.70	B	5.31	577	4	Hindus 87%, Muslims 6.6%(Shaikhs,Sunni Vohras,Pathans,Momins,Daudi Bohras),Jains 4%. D=RCC,CNI,ELC,&c. M=SJ,AM,AMM,OM,FPCGI,BFI,LCMS,&c.
4364	0	6	3.56	0	19.30	80.70	A	0.91	647	3	West Bengal, Darjeeling. In Sikkim, also Nepal, Burma. Animists 80%, Hindus 19%.
4365	1	7	5.97	0	39.00	61.00	A	18.50	492	5	Hinduized polytheists 89%. Nomadic caravan communities. D=Gypsy Evangelical Movement. M=GGMS.
4366	0	6	4.14	6	33.29	66.71	A	0.35	453	3	Assam, West Bengal. Also in Bangladesh. Hinduized animists 99%.
4367	3	7	6.62	4	99.60	0.40	C	260.61	178	8	Mostly in Burma, a few in Bangladesh. Animists 40%. D=AoG,SDA,CBCNEI.
4368	2	6	4.43	1	25.01	74.99	A	0.00	596	1.11	MP State, Maharashtra, Orissa, Bastar District. A creole language. Agriculturalists. Hindus 99%. D=MCSA,CB. M=IBT,IEM.
4369	3	10	4.76	8	73.00	27.00	B	13.32	203	5	Most in Calcutta. Buddhists/Chinese folk-religionists 95%. D=RCC,True Jesus Ch,CNI.
4370	3	9	6.53	7	69.00	31.00	B	12.59	285	5	Almost all Chinese live in Calcutta. Buddhists/Chinese folk-religionists 95%(Mahayana). D=True Jesus Ch,RCC,CNI.
4371	2	10	3.81	7	71.00	29.00	B	15.54	172	5	Calcutta; few elsewhere in India. Buddhists/Chinese folk-religionists 94%. D=RCC,True Jesus Ch.
4372	0	6	4.17	0	25.10	74.90	A	0.09	564	2	Rajasthan, Kota area. Hindus 84%, Muslims 10%, Jains.
4373	0	7	2.52	0	31.05	68.95	A	0.05	311	2	Madhya Pradesh, Bastar. Gonds. Hindus 60%, animists 40%. M=many Indian mission agencies.
4374	3	6	4.17	7	59.60	40.40	B	3.48	238	4	Laghu Hindi, Colloquial Hindi. Hindus 95%(popular Hinduism). D=CNI,RCC,&c. R=FEBA,HA,VERITAS,AWR.
4375	5	5	4.05	6	63.10	36.90	B	4.83	219	4	Standard Hindi. Lingua franca of half the nation. Hindus 93%. D=CNI,RCC,BOBBC,SA,IET. M=ABFMS,SJ,FPCGI,BFI,WEC,LBI. R=FEBA,HA,VERITAS,AWR.
4376	1	6	4.00	6	50.05	49.95	B	0.09	275	2	Speech of Delhi. Formerly main language of India, now used of recent Muslim immigrants from north to Deccan. D=Hindustani Covenant Ch(M=SMCC). M=BFI.
4377	4	6	8.93	0	99.99	0.01	C	553.71	179	10	Assam, Manipur. Heavily christianized. D=CBCNEI,ICFG,Evangelical Congregational Ch,Independent Ch of India. M=NEIGM,BFTW,AIPF,BFI,WPM.
4378	2	5	6.65	1	39.55	60.45	A	0.79	530	3	Singbhum District, Bihar; Orissa, WB. Also in Bangladesh. Animists 69%, Hindus 30%. D=RCC(D-Jamshedpur),CNI. M=SJ,IBT,OFUCPM,IEM,USPG,EMS,GR.
4379	1	6	4.33	1	33.00	67.00	A	1.20	443	4	In Madhya Pradesh, Maharashtra. Hindus 95%. D=CNI. M=YWAM.
4380	2	6	6.34	0	60.00	40.00	B	54.75	340	6	In Assam, Tripura. Also in Burma. Animists 70%. D=ICFG,ICI.
4381	3	6	5.46	7	36.00	64.00	A	1.31	494	4	Romany Gypsies, in over 12 countries. Muslims 80%, Hindus 10%, animists 9%. D=CNI,RCC,AoG.
4382	1	7	5.86	5	83.00	17.00	B	90.88	230	6	Western or Indian Kachin. Assam (Tirap area), Arunachal Pradesh; also in Burma, China. Animists 70%. D=RCC.
4383	1	10	3.77	1	99.80	0.20	C	385.44	99	9	Portuguese-based creole, still with speakers in Sri Lanka and India. D=RCC. M=BFI.
4384	1	6	6.08	0	27.00	73.00	A	2.95	718	4	Kad Chensu, Yerukala, Erukala. In AP, Kerala, Tamil Nadu, Maharashtra, Karnataka. Few literates. Hindus 95%. D=CSI. M=Christ's Gospel Mission, COUNT.
4385	0	7	2.75	1	29.50	70.50	A	0.53	348	3	Andhra Pradesh, Maharashtra, Karnataka. Related to Oriya. Hindus 99%.
4386	0	4	1.10	0	15.10	84.90	A	0.05	503	2	Tibetans. North of Pithorgarh District, UP. Also in Nepal. Hindus 60%, animists 40%. M=GR.
4387	0	6	1.10	0	15.10	84.90	A	0.05	503	2	Kinnaur District. Related to Kanauri. Lamaist Buddhists 50%, Hindus 30%, animists 20%.
4388	2	6	3.46	0	39.00	61.00	A	14.23	313	5	Andaman Islands. Hunter-gatherers, pastoralists. Animists 90%. D=CBCNEI,RCC. M=Shiloh Evangelistic Mission,SX,SJ,SISWA,CDF,MFGA.
4389	0	5	10.92	5	46.60	53.40	A	4.42	701	4	Punjab Province. Ancestors of Gypsies. Hindus 80%, Sikhs 10%. M=FMPB,INIM.

Continued overleaf

Table 8-2 continued

	PEOPLE					IDENTITY CODE		LANGUAGE		CHURCH		MINISTRY	SCRIPTURE	
Ref	Ethnic name	P%	In 1995	In 2000	In 2025	Race	Language	Autoglossonym	S	AC	Members	Jayuh dwa xcmc mi 13-17 18 19 20 21 22	Biblioglossonym	Pub ss 24-26 27
1	2	3	4	5	6	7	8	9	10	11	12	13-17 18 19 20 21 22	23	24-26 27
4390	Jatapu	0.00643	60,035	65,178	85,548	CNN23z	49-DAAA	gond cluster		0.80	521	3.s.. 5 5 5 5 1		PN. b
4391	Jaunsari (Pahari)	0.00996	92,993	100,961	132,513	CNN25k	59-AAFC-a	jaunsari		0.01	10	1.... 3 3 0 0 1	Jaunsari	Pn. .
4392	Jharia	0.00045	4,201	4,561	5,987	CNN25l	59-AAFS-c	jharia-oriya		0.50	23	1csu 5 3 2 1 0		pnb .
4393	Juango (Puttooas)	0.00271	25,302	27,470	36,055	AUG04z	46-CBAB-a	juang		0.01	3	0.... 3 3 0 1 0		... .
4394	Kabui Naga	0.00525	49,017	53,217	69,849	MSY50p	73-ACAE-bb	kabui		70.00	37,252	0....10 8 9 5 1		pnb .
4395	Kachin (Singpho)	0.00200	18,673	20,273	26,609	MSY50f	75-AAAA-a	jing-pho		70.00	14,191	0....10 8 6 5 0	Kachin: Jinghpaw*	PNB .
4396	Kadar Negrito	0.00010	934	1,014	1,330	AUG05	59-AAFS	oriya cluster		2.50	25	3Asu. 6 4 2 3 0	Mirgan	PNB b
4397	Kahluri Pahari (Pacchmi)	0.03405	317,913	345,152	453,018	CNN25n	59-AAFE-g	kahluri		1.00	3,452	1csu. 6 4 4 3 1		PNB b
4398	Kaikadi	0.00213	19,887	21,591	28,339	CNN23c	49-EBEA	wider-tamil cluster		5.00	1,080	2Asu. 7 4 4 3 0		PNB b
4399	Kamar	0.00178	16,619	18,043	23,682	CNN23z	49-EBAA	kannada cluster		0.07	13	3Asu. 4 3 2 1 1		pnb .
4400	Kanara Konkani (Kokni)	0.02714	253,397	275,108	361,084	CNN25d	59-AAFU-a	konkan-marathi		1.00	2,751	1csu. 6 5 2 3 3	Konkani: Kanara, Southern*	PNb .
4401	Kanarese (Canarese)	3.66471	34,216,119	37,147,765	48,757,087	CNN23a	49-EBAA-a	kannada		5.80	2,154,570	2Asu. 7 7 10 5 4	Kannada	PNB b
4402	Kanashi	0.00015	1,400	1,520	1,996	MSY50r	70-ABAB-a	kanashi		0.10	2	0.... 5 1 2 0 0		p... .
4403	Kanauji (Western Hindi)	0.92598	8,645,552	9,386,305	12,319,689	CNN25g	59-AAFO-ii	proper kannauji	1	1.60	150,181	1csuh 6 5 7 3 1	Kanauji	PNb .
4404	Kanauri (Kanawari)	0.00629	58,728	63,759	83,685	MSY50r	70-ABAB-d	kanauri		0.01	6	0.... 3 3 0 1 2	Kanauri	P... .
4405	Kanikkaran (Kani)	0.00127	11,858	12,874	16,897	CNN23z	49-EBEB-d	malaryan		1.70	219	0.... 6 4 4 3 2		pnb .
4406	Kanjari (Kagari, Kangri)	0.00975	91,032	98,832	129,719	CNN25f	59-AAFE-m	kangri		0.10	99	1csu. 5 1 2 0 0		pnb .
4407	Karmali	0.01659	154,895	168,166	220,721	AUG04c	46-CABA-b	karmali		1.00	1,682	1cs.. 6 4 4 2 0		pnb .
4408	Kashmiri (Keshur)	0.45298	4,229,316	4,591,685	6,026,667	CNN25i	59-AAFA-e	siraji-kashmiri		0.02	918	2.... 3 4 4 3 3	Kashmiri	PNB .
4409	Kashtwari (Kistwali)	0.00214	19,980	21,692	28,472	CNN25i	59-AAFA-f	kishtwari		0.02	4	1.... 3 3 0 2 0		pnb .
4410	Katakari (Katvadi)	0.00109	10,177	11,049	14,502	CNN25d	59-AAFU-e	kaatkari-kaathodi		0.08	9	1as.. 4 4 2 1 1		pnb .
4411	Kawar (Kamari)	0.00430	40,148	43,587	57,209	CNN25l	59-AAFR-e	kawari		0.03	13	1cs.. 3 2 0 1 0		p... .
4412	Keer	0.00037	3,455	3,751	4,923	CNN25o	59-AAFG-s	keer		0.00		1.s.. 0 1 2 0 0		pn. .
4413	Kezhama Naga (Kezami)	0.00237	22,128	24,024	31,532	MSY50p	73-ABBC-a	khezha-naga		65.00	15,615	1....10 7 9 5 2		pnb .
4414	Khamti Shan (Kham-Tai)	0.00007	654	710	931	MSY49c	47-AAAA-d	khamti		0.74	5	1.s.. 5 4 2 2 0		pnb b
4415	Khandeshi	0.16373	1,528,690	1,659,668	2,178,344	CNN25c	59-AAFM-a	khandesi		0.20	3,319	0.... 5 2 2 1 0	Khandesi*	... .
4416	Kharia (Haria, Kharvi)	0.03031	282,994	307,241	403,259	AUG04z	46-CBAA-a	kharia		71.00	218,141	0....10 7 7 5 2	Kharia	P... .
4417	Kharwar (Bihari)	0.02488	232,296	252,199	331,016	CNN25c	46-CABA	kherwari cluster	2	0.02	50	3as.. 3 2 2 1 2		PNB .
4418	Khasi (Khuchia, Khasa)	0.08970	837,498	909,255	1,193,412	AUG03a	46-CABA-a	khasi-war		46.80	425,531	2as.. 9 7 9 5 3	Khasi	PNB .
4419	Khiamngan Naga (Para)	0.00249	23,248	25,240	33,128	MSY50p	73-ADAA	khiamngan-naga cluster		50.00	12,620	0....10 9 5 2	Naga, Khiamngan	PN. .
4420	Khirwar	0.00436	40,708	44,196	58,008	AUG06b	49-DAAA	gond cluster		0.05	22	3.s.. 4 4 2 2 1		PN. b
4421	Khoibu Maring Naga	0.00249	23,248	25,240	33,128	MSY50p	72-BAGA-a	maring-naga		75.00	18,930	0.s..10 8 11 5 2	Naga, Maring*	PN. b
4422	Khoirao Naga (Kolya)	0.00009	840	912	1,197	MSY50p	73-ACAF-a	khoirao		45.00	411	0.... 9 7 7 5 2	Naga, Khoirao	... .
4423	Khowar (Chitrali, Qashqari)	0.00188	17,553	19,057	25,012	CNN25i	59-AABA-a	kho-war		0.02	4	0.... 3 2 0 0 0		... .
4424	Khumi Chin (Khweymi)	0.00365	34,079	36,999	48,561	MSY50c	73-DEAB-a	khumi		60.00	22,199	0.s..10 7 7 5 1	Chin: Khumi*	PN. .
4425	Kirati Rai (Kiranti)	0.00507	47,337	51,393	67,454	MSY50h	71-CCAB-a	kulung		0.10	51	0.... 5 3 4 1 0		pnb .
4426	Kishanganjia (Shripuri)	0.01001	93,553	101,569	133,311	CNN25b	59-AAFT-gd	kishanganjia		0.60	609	1csuh 5 3 4 1 0		pnb .
4427	Kiutze (Chopa, Rawang)	0.00600	56,020	60,820	79,827	MSY50z	76-AAAB-a	rawang		3.00	1,825	0.... 6 4 3 3 1	Rawang	PNB .
4428	Koch	0.00100	9,337	10,137	13,304	CNN25b	72-ACAC-a	koch		0.50	51	0.... 5 4 3 1 0		pnb .
4429	Koch (Kocch, Konch)	0.00244	22,781	24,733	32,463	MSY50d	72-ACAC-a	koch		10.00	2,473	0.... 6 4 2 2 0		pnb .
4430	Koda (Korali, Mudikora)	0.02017	188,320	204,456	268,352	AUG04z	46-CABA-i	koda-khaira		10.00	20,446	1cs.. 8 5 6 3 0		pnb .
4431	Kodagu (Coorg, Khurgi)	0.01321	123,337	133,905	175,752	CNN23z	49-EBCA-a	kodagu		0.20	268	0.... 5 4 4 1 1	Kodagu	pnb .
4432	Koireng (Kwoireng)	0.00023	2,147	2,331	3,060	MSY50o	73-ACAB-ab	kwoireng		70.00	1,632	0....10 8 8 5 1		pnb .
4433	Kol (Kolian, Kolari)	0.01152	107,558	116,774	153,268	AUG05	46-CABA-m	kol		60.00	70,064	1cs..10 7 7 5 2		pnb .
4434	Kolai	0.00100	9,337	10,137	13,304	CNN23z	59-AADB-a	kolai		0.50	51	0.... 5 4 5 1 0	Kohistani, Indus	p... .
4435	Kom Rem (Kom, Komrem)	0.00143	13,351	14,495	19,025	MSY50c	73-DDBA-a	kom		64.00	9,277	0....10 8 7 5 1	Kom Rem	PNB .
4436	Kongri Dogri (Kangra)	0.02000	186,733	202,732	266,090	CNN25n	59-AAFE-l	dogri		0.10	203	1asu. 5 4 4 1 0	Panjabi: Dogri*	PNb .
4437	Konkanese	0.54054	5,046,833	5,479,247	7,191,607	CNN25d	59-AAFU-n	konkan-marathi		2.00	109,585	1csu. 6 4 6 1 1	Konkani: Kanara, Southern*	PNB .
4438	Konyak Naga (Kanyak, Chen)	0.01085	101,303	109,982	144,354	MSY50p	73-BAAA-b	konyak-naga		76.00	83,587	0....10 8 11 5 3	Naga: Konyak*	PNB .
4439	Koraga (Koragara)	0.00019	1,774	1,926	2,528	CNN23z	49-EABA-a	korra		1.34	26	0.... 6 4 2 1 0		... .
4440	Kortha Bihari	0.20000	1,867,330	2,027,324	2,660,897	CNN25c	59-AAFQ-h	kortha		0.01	203	0.... 3 3 4 3 1	Bihari: Kortha	Pn. b
4441	Korwa (Ernga, Singli)	0.00685	63,956	69,436	91,136	AUG04z	46-CABA-g	korwa		0.39	271	1cs.. 5 4 2 1 0	Majhi	pnb .
4442	Kota	0.00022	2,054	2,230	2,927	CNN23z	49-EBBB-a	kota		1.00	22	0.... 6 4 2 1 2	Kota	... .
4443	Kotia (Tribal Oriya)	0.02494	232,856	252,807	331,814	AUG04z	59-AAFS-f	desia-oriya		0.10	253	1asu. 5 5 0 1 3	Oriya: Adiwasi*	Pnb .
4444	Koya (Koi, Kavor)	0.03446	321,741	349,308	458,473	AUG06b	49-DAAA-b	koya		2.00	6,986	1.s.. 6 5 6 2 3	Gondi: Koi*	Pn. .
4445	Kudiya	0.00001	93	101	133	CNN23z	49-EBEB	malayalam cluster		0.00	0	2Asu. 0 2 4 0 0		PNB b
4446	Kui (Khondi, Kond)	0.07438	694,460	753,962	989,588	AUG06z	49-DACA-a	kui	1	1.10	8,294	1.... 7 5 6 3 1	Kui	PN. .
4447	Kuki-Chin (Thado-Kuki)	0.01697	158,443	172,018	225,777	MSY50c	73-DAAE-a	thado		68.00	116,973	0as..10 8 9 5 3	Chin, Thado	PNB .
4448	Kulu Pahari (Kauli)	0.01130	105,504	114,544	150,341	CNN25k	59-AAFE-h	patialwi		0.04	46	1.... 3 3 2 0 1		pnb .
4449	Kumaoni (Central Pahari)	0.21739	2,029,695	2,203,599	2,892,262	CNN25k	59-AAFC-Q	kumauni		0.40	8,814	1.... 5 5 7 1 2	Kumaoni*	Pn. .
4450	Kurichiya	0.00154	14,378	15,610	20,489	CNN23z	49-EBEB	malayalam cluster		1.55	242	2Asu. 6 4 4 2 1		PNB b
4451	Kurku (Kodaku, Bopchi)	0.04958	462,911	502,574	659,636	AUG04z	46-CAAA	korku cluster		10.00	50,257	0.... 8 6 7 4 3	Korku	P... .
4452	Kuruba (Urali, Kurumvari)	0.08727	814,810	884,623	1,161,083	CNN23a	49-EBAB-a	kurumba		1.00	8,846	0.... 6 5 4 4 3	Kurumba	... .
4453	Kurumba	0.00125	11,671	12,671	16,631	CNN23a	49-EBAA-a	kannada		5.00	634	2Asu. 7 6 7 5 1	Kannada	PNB b
4454	Kuvi (Khondi, Kond)	0.03740	349,191	379,110	497,588	AUG06z	49-DACA-b	kuvi		0.78	2,957	1.... 5 5 5 2 1	Kuvi	PN. .
4455	Laccadive Mappilla	0.00585	54,619	59,299	77,831	CMT30	49-EBEB-a	malayalam		0.02	12	2Asu. 3 3 0 1 0	Malayalam	PNB b
4456	Ladakhi (Ladaphi, Hanu)	0.01055	98,502	106,941	140,362	MSY50r	70-AAAC-a	ladakhi		0.10	107	1.... 5 3 0 1 2	Ladakhi	Pn. .
4457	Lahuli (Bunan)	0.00046	4,295	4,663	6,120	MSY50r	70-ABAA-a	bunan		0.11	5	0.... 5 3 2 1 1	Lahuli: Bunan*	P... .
4458	Lahuli (Manchad, Chamba)	0.00042	3,921	4,257	5,588	MSY50r	70-ABAC-b	manchati		0.10	4	0.... 5 3 2 1 1	Lahuli: Manchad	P... .
4459	Lahuli (Tinan)	0.00267	24,929	27,065	35,523	MSY50r	70-ABAD-a	tinan		0.10	27	0.... 5 3 2 1 1	Lahuli: Tinan*	P... .
4460	Lalung	0.00234	21,848	23,720	31,133	MSY50r	72-AACA-a	lalung		0.38	90	0.... 5 4 3 1 0		... .
4461	Lamgang	0.00095	8,870	9,630	12,639	MSY50p	73-DDAA-a	lamkang		40.00	3,852	0.... 9 7 6 5 1	Lamkang	PN. .
4462	Lepcha (Rong, Rongke)	0.00396	36,973	40,141	52,686	MSY50j	73-DFAA-a	lepcha		3.00	1,204	1.... 6 6 7 4 3	Lepcha	PN. .
4463	Lhoba (Luoba)	0.02344	218,851	237,602	311,857	MSY50r	74-AADA-a	luo-ba		0.00	0	0.... 0 2 0 0 0		... .
4464	Lhomi	0.00013	1,214	1,318	1,730	MSY50r	70-AAAA-ce	lhomi		0.00	0	0c.. 0 2 2 0 0	Lhomi	PNb .
4465	Liangmai Naga (Kwoireng)	0.00217	20,261	21,996	28,871	MSY50r	73-ACAB-a	liang-mai		65.00	14,298	0....10 7 11 5 1	Naga: Liangmei*	PNB .
4466	Limbu (Monpa)	0.00288	26,890	29,193	38,317	MSY50k	71-CBCC-a	limbu		0.10	29	0a.. 5 4 2 1 0	Limbu	... b
4467	Lodhi (Lodha)	0.00776	72,452	78,660	103,243	CNN25g	59-AAFO-jl	lodhi		0.10	79	1csuh 5 4 3 1 0		pnb b
4468	Lotha Naga (Chizima)	0.00838	77,307	83,931	110,161	MSY50p	73-AAAA-a	lotha-naga		99.00	83,092	0....10 8 13 5 3	Naga: Kyong*	PNB .
4469	Magadhi Bihari (Maghori)	1.17802	10,998,762	11,941,138	15,672,952	CNN25c	59-AAFQ-g	magahi	2	1.02	121,800	1.s.. 6 4 5 1 1	Bihari: Magahi*	PN. .
4470	Magar (Gurkha)	0.00113	10,550	11,454	15,034	MSY50n	71-BABA-b	east magar		0.03	3	0.... 3 4 4 2 2	Magar*	PN. .
4471	Mahali Pahari	0.05653	527,801	573,023	752,103	CNN25n	59-AAFB-h	kului		0.10	573	0.s.. 5 3 0 1 0	Kului*	P.. b
4472	Mahili (Maithili, Tharu)	0.00691	64,516	70,044	91,934	AUG04c	46-CABA-ac	mahali		30.00	21,013	1cs.. 9 4 4 2 0		pnb b
4473	Maitili (Maithili, Tharu)	3.12092	29,138,942	31,635,573	41,522,240	CNN25c	59-AAFQ-b	maithili		1.02	322,683	1.s.. 6 4 5 3 2	Maithili	Pn. b
4474	Majhi	0.00162	15,125	16,421	21,553	CNN25c	59-AAFE-d	majhi		1.06	174	1asu. 6 4 4 1 1	Panjabi*	PNB b
4475	Majhwar	0.00367	34,266	37,201	48,827	AUG04z	46-CABA-g	korwa		0.06	22	1cs.. 4 3 0 1 0	Majhi	pnb .
4476	Malai Pandaram	0.00006	560	608	798	CNN23z	49-EBEB-b	malapandaram		0.00	0	1csu. 0 3 0 1 1		pnb .
4477	Malankuravan	0.00064	5,975	6,487	8,515	CNN23z	49-EBEB-c	malankuravan		3.25	211	1csu. 6 5 4 3 1		pnb .
4478	Malaryan (Malai Arayan)	0.00060	5,602	6,082	7,983	CNN23z	49-EBEB-d	malaryan		2.93	178	1csu. 6 5 4 3 0		pnb .
4479	Malavedan (Malai Vedan)	0.00025	2,334	2,534	3,326	CNN23z	49-EBEB-e	malavedan		0.68	17	1csu. 6 5 4 1 0		pnb .
4480	Malay (Melaju)	0.00030	2,801	3,041	3,991	MSY44k	31-PHAA-b	bahasa-malaysia		0.02	1	1asuh 3 3 6 3 0	Malay	PNB b
4481	Malayali (Malabari)	3.78806	35,367,795	38,398,116	50,398,195	CNN23b	49-EBEB-a	malayalam		38.00	14,591,284	2Asu. 9 8 13 5 2	Malayalam	PNB b
4482	Maldivian (Mahl, Malki)	0.00089	8,310	9,022	11,841	CNN25q	59-AAFA-a	dhivehi		0.05	5	0.... 4 2 0 0 1		... b
4483	Mali	0.00021	1,961	2,129	2,794	CNN25l	59-AAFS-k	mali-oriya		0.07	1	1csu. 4 2 0 0 0		pnb .
4484	Malto (Malti, Malpaharia)	0.00870	81,229	88,189	115,749	AUG06z	59-BAAB-a	malto		9.00	7,937	0.s.. 7 5 7 3 3	Malto	P... .
4485	Malvi (Ujjaini, Malavi)	0.11337	1,058,496	1,149,188	1,508,330	CNN25o	59-AAFG-l	malvi		9.00	103,427	1.s.. 7 6 7 3 1	Malvi	PN. .
4486	Manda	0.00040	3,735	4,055	5,322	CNN23z	49-DACB-a	manda		0.00	0	0.... 0 3 3 0 0		... .
4487	Mangelas	0.00100	9,337	10,137	13,304	CNN25d	59-AAFU-h	mangelas		0.50	51	1csu. 5 4 6 3 0		pnb b
4488	Manipuri (Meithei, Kathe)	0.13391	1,250,071	1,357,394	1,781,604	MSY50o	73-CAAA-ab	manipuri		1.08	14,660	1as.. 6 5 7 4 4	Manipuri*	PNB .
4489	Manjhi	0.00200	18,673	20,273	26,609	CNN25d	59-AAFE-d	majhi		1.00	203	1asu. 4 4 1 1 1	Panjabi*	PNB b
4490	Manna-Dora	0.00108	10,084	10,948	14,369	CNN23z	49-DABA-b	manna-dora		0.50	55	0.... 5 4 2 1 0		... .
4491	Mannan	0.00110	10,270	11,150	14,635	CNN23z	49-CAAA-a	mannyod		1.00	112	0.... 6 5 2 3 2		... .
4492	Mao Naga (Spowama, Memi)	0.00838	78,241	84,945	111,492	MSY50p	73-AABB-a	mao-naga		85.00	72,203	0....10 8 13 5 2	Mao Naga*	PNB .
4493	Mara Chin (Lakher, Zao)	0.00229	21,381	23,213	30,467	MSY50m	73-DEBA-a	mara		95.00	22,052	0....10 8 13 5 1	Mara*	PNB .
4494	Maram Naga	0.00166	15,499	16,827	22,085	MSY50p	73-ACAA-a	maram-naga		23.78	4,001	0.... 9 6 6 4 2	Naga, Maram	pnb .
4495	Maratha (Maharathi)	7.46133	69,663,836	75,632,650	99,269,169	CNN25j	59-AAFU-m	deshi-marathi		5.20	3,932,898	2Asu. 7 5 9 5 4	Marathi*	PNB b
4496	Maria (Muria)	0.01382	129,033	140,088	183,868	AUG06b	49-DAAA-c	maria		0.05	70	1.s.. 4 4 4 2 2	Maria*	pn. b
4497	Maring Naga	0.00166	15,499	16,827	22,085	MSY50p	72-BAGA-a	maring-naga		28.50	4,796	0.s.. 9 6 6 4 2	Naga, Maring*	PN. b
4498	Marpaharia	0.00200	18,673	20,273	26,609	CNN25b	59-BAAB-a	malto		9.00	1,825	0.s.. 7 5 6 3 2	Malto	P... .
4499	Matia	0.00100	9,337	10,137	13,304	CNN23z	59-AAFS-ga	matia		0.00	0	1csu. 0 3 5 2 0		pnb .
4500	Mavchi (Mawachi)	0.00779	72,733	78,964	103,642	AUG06a	59-AAFK-h	mawchi-bhili		0.10	79	0cs.. 5 4 4 2 3	Mawchi	PN. .
4501	Mayon Naga	0.00100	9,337	10,137	13,304	MSY50p	72-BADA-b	moyon-naga		40.00	4,055	0.... 9 6 6 5 1	Naga, Moyon*	PN. .
4502	Meluri Naga (East Rengma)	0.00050	4,668	5,068	6,652	MSY50p	72-BAJA-a	meluri-naga		60.00	3,041	0....10 7 6 5 2		pnb .
4503	Miju Mishmi (Miji)	0.00100	9,337	10,137	13,304	MSY50r	74-AAEA-b	miju		1.00	101	0.... 6 5 2 2 1		... .
4504	Mikir (Manchati, Karbi)	0.04946	461,791	501,357	658,040	MSY50r	73-CABA-ac	karbi		10.28	51,540	0.... 8 6 7 4 3	Karbi*	PNB .
4505	Mina	0.10374	968,584	1,051,573	1,380,207	CNN25o	59-AAFF-o	mina		0.30	3,155	1.... 6 5 5 3 1		pnb .
4506	Mirdha	0.00129	12,044	13,076	17,163	AUG04z	46-CABA-i	koda-khaira		5.00	654	1cs.. 7 2 0 0 1		pnb .
4507	Mirpur Punjabi	0.10000	933,665	1,013,662	1,330,449	CNN25n	59-AAFE-n	mirpuri		1.00	10,137	1cs.. 5 4 3 2 0		pnb .
4508	Mizo (Lushai, Hualngo)	0.05483	511,929	555,791	729,485	MSY50m	73-DCAA-a	lushai		99.50	553,012	0asu.10 8 14 5 3	Lushai	PNB .
4509	Monba (Memba, Menpa)	0.00475	44,349	48,149	63,196	MSY50r	71-CBCC-d	moinba		1.17	563	0c.. 6 1 0 0 0		... b
4510	Monsang Naga	0.00031	2,894	3,142	4,124	MSY50p	73-BADA-a	monshang-naga		40.00	1,257	0.... 9 6 7 5 1		pn. .
4511	Moyon Naga	0.00036	3,361	3,649	4,790	MSY50p	72-BADA-b	moyon-naga		80.00	2,919	0.... 9 6 6 5 1	Naga, Moyon*	PN. .
4512	Mru (Niopreng, Mrung)	0.00521	48,644	52,812	69,316	MSY50c	73-BAAA-a	murung		0.20	106	0.... 5 5 5 2 2	Mro*	P... .
4513	Mukha-Dora (Reddi)	0.00127	11,858	12,874	16,897	CNN23d	49-DABA-a	konda-dora		0.02	3	0.... 3 3 2 2 0	Konda-dora	... b

Continued opposite

Table 8-2 continued

EVANGELIZATION								EVANGELISM			ADDITIONAL DESCRIPTIVE DATA
Ref 1	D 28	aC 29	CG% 30	r 31	E 32	U 33	W 34	e 35	R 36	T 37	Locations, civil divisions, literacy, religions, church history, denominations, dioceses, church growth, missions, agencies, ministries, movements 38
4390	1	6	4.03	0	33.80	66.20	A	0.98	408	3	Andhra Pradesh, Karnataka, Orissa. A scheduled tribe. Hindus 99%. D=CSI. M=Bibles for India.
4391	0	6	2.33	0	16.01	83.99	A	0.00	621	1.06	In Uttar Pradesh, Jaunsar, and Himachal Pradesh. Hindus 99%. M=AGAPE.
4392	0	6	3.19	1	25.50	74.50	A	0.46	450	3	Orissa, Koraput District. Hindus 98%.
4393	0	6	1.10	0	13.01	86.99	A	0.00	463	1.04	In Orissa, Keonjhar District. Hindus 100%. M=IEM,GFA,SIL.
4394	1	6	8.57	0	99.70	0.30	C	286.16	232	8	Manipur, Imphal city, Satar Hills. Close to Rongmei Naga. Animists 30%. D=CBCNEI.
4395	0	7	7.53	5	99.70	0.30	C	316.82	191	9	Burmese Kachin (several differences from Indian Kachin). Polytheists 25%, Buddhists 5%.
4396	0	7	3.27	4	44.50	55.50	A	4.06	263	4	In Andhra Pradesh, Kerala, Tamil Nadu. Animists 97%.
4397	1	6	6.02	1	34.00	66.00	A	1.24	570	4	Bilaspuri Pahari, Kehloori Pahari. In Andaman & Nicobar Islands, Himachal Pradesh, Tripura, West Bengal. Hindus 98%. D=CNI.
4398	0	6	4.79	6	51.00	49.00	B	9.30	311	4	In Maharashtra and Karnataka. Nomadic. Related to Tamil. Hindus/animists 95%.
4399	0	6	2.60	5	39.07	60.93	A	0.10	252	3	In Madhya Pradesh, Raipur and Rewa Districts. A scheduled tribe. Hindus/animists 99%. M=Bibles for India.
4400	3	6	5.78	4	40.00	60.00	A	1.46	464	4	Dangs District, Gujarat; also Karnataka, Kanara. Hindus 99%. D=RCC,Interdenominational National Ch,CNI. M=NLC,BFI,WVI,IEM,FMPB.
4401	5	6	4.56	5	70.80	29.20	B	14.98	215	5	Hindus 90%. D=RCC(M-Bangalore,6 Dioceses),CSI(D-Karnataka N,S,C),Assemblies(Bakht Singh),WMCI,&c. M=OFMCap,MMS,CMS,LMS,BYM,CFIM,IEM,ISA.
4402	0	5	0.70	0	15.10	84.90	A	0.05	430	2	Himachal Pradesh, Kullu District. Close to Kanauri. Lamaist Buddhists 50%, Hindus 30%, animists 20%.
4403	1	5	10.09	1	39.60	60.40	A	2.31	767	4	In Uttar Pradesh, with 3 dialects: Proper, Transitional, and Tirhari. Hindus 99%. D=CNI. R=TWR.
4404	2	6	1.81	0	17.01	82.99	A	0.00	561	1.06	East of Simla near Tibet border; UP, Punjab, Kashmir, Himachal Pradesh; also Tibet. Hindus 40%, Lamaist Buddhists 40%, animists 20%. D=SA,Moravian Ch.
4405	1	6	3.13	1	34.70	65.30	A	2.15	326	4	In Kerala and Tamil Nadu. A scheduled tribe. Hindus/animists 95%. D=CSI. M=Unreached Peoples Missions, Fellowship of Evangelical Friends.
4406	0	6	4.70	1	24.10	75.90	A	0.08	651	2	Gypsies. Kanghar Bhat. In AP, MP, UP, Rajasthan. Related to Punjabi. Hindus/animists 95%.
4407	0	6	5.26	1	32.00	68.00	A	1.16	536	4	In Bihar, Orissa, West Bengal. Related to Santali. Hindus 79%, animists 20%.
4408	4	5	4.62	0	35.02	64.98	A	0.02	440	2	In Vale of Kashmir. Muslims 95%(95% Sunnis,5% Shias)(90% rural), Hindus 4%(33% of urbanites). D=RCC,CNI,KEF,IET. M=IEM,MHM,GFK,ZEF,WVI,UPM,BFI.
4409	0	4	1.40	0	18.02	81.98	A	0.01	365	2	In Jammu & Kashmir. Muslims 90%, Hindus 10%.
4410	0	6	2.22	1	23.08	76.92	A	0.06	382	2	In Gujarat and Maharashtra. Related to Konkani. Hindus 99%. M=Ramabai Mukti Mission.
4411	0	6	2.60	1	17.03	82.97	A	0.01	579	2	In Madhya Pradesh, Raipur and surrounding Districts, Maharashtra, Orissa. Related to Halbi. Hindus 99%.
4412	0	6	0.00	0	15.00	85.00	A	0.00	0	1.07	In Madhya Pradesh; Raisen, Sehore. Rajasthanis. Hindus 90%, Muslims 10%.
4413	2	6	7.63	0	99.65	0.35	C	260.97	212	8	Eastern Nagaland, Kohima District. Animists 34%. D=CBCNEI(Nagaland Baptist Convention),NCRC.
4414	0	7	1.62	1	27.74	72.26	A	0.74	270	3	In Assam, Anunachal Pradesh, Siang. Also northwest Burma, China. Buddhists 70%, many animists 29%.
4415	0	6	5.98	0	17.20	82.80	A	0.12	1,112	3	Maherashtra, Gujarat. Dialects: Ahirani, Dangri, Kunbi, Rangari. Animists 70%, Hindus 30%.
4416	2	6	10.51	0	99.71	0.29	C	279.88	295	8	Primarily Ranchi District of Bihar, also Raigarh District of MP, Orissa, Assam, West Bengal, Andaman & Nicobar Islands. D=RCC(D-Sambalpur),GELC. M=SVD.
4417	2	6	3.99	4	43.02	56.98	A	0.03	319	2	Southern Standard Bhojpuri. Bihar, Assam, MP, UP. Hindus 70%, Muslims 30%. D=CNI,RCC.
4418	4	6	3.10	4	99.47	0.53	B	182.43	118	7	Tribals in Assam, Khasi-Jaintia Hills, Jammu, Kashmir, Manipur, Punjab. UP, West Bengal; also Bangladesh. Animists 50%. D=RCC(D-Silchar),ICFG,CNI(D-Assam).
4419	2	6	7.40	0	92.00	8.00	B	167.90	247	7	East central Tuensang District, Nagaland. Also Burma. Animists 50%. D=CBCNEI(Nagaland Baptist Convention),NCRC.
4420	1	6	3.14	0	26.05	73.95	A	0.04	435	2	In Madhya Pradesh. Gonds. Hindus 70%, animists 30%. D=CNI.
4421	2	6	7.84	0	99.75	0.25	C	336.71	195	9	Manipur State, southeast, Laiching. Animists 25%. D=CBCNEI,RCRC.
4422	2	7	3.79	0	79.00	21.00	B	129.75	163	7	North Manipur, east of Barak Valley. Animists 54%. D=CBCNEI(Nagaland Baptist Convention),NCRC.
4423	0	4	1.40	0	9.02	90.98	A	0.00	729	1.03	Jammu & Kashmir. Mainly in Pakistan. Muslims 100%.
4424	3	6	8.01	0	99.60	0.40	C	221.19	247	8	Assam. Mainly in Burma, some in Bangladesh. Animists 40%. D=CNI,SDA,AoG. M=NEIGM.
4425	0	6	4.01	0	18.10	81.90	A	0.06	758	2	Sikkim. Covers 21 dialects from Nepal. Animists 60%, Hindus 40%.
4426	0	6	4.19	1	28.60	71.40	A	0.62	532	3	In Bihar State, a Bengali-Assamese language. Hinduized animists 99%.
4427	0	5	5.34	4	37.00	63.00	A	4.05	477	4	Nung Rawang. Near Tibet border. Majority in Burma (Kachin State); also in China (Yunnan and Tibet). 100 dialects. Animists 80%, some Buddhists. M=NBCM.
4428	0	5	4.01	0	16.50	83.50	A	0.30	892	3	West Bengal, Cooch Behar District. A Bengali-Assamese language (Indo-Aryan). Hinduized animists 99%.
4429	0	6	5.67	0	27.00	73.00	A	9.85	677	4	In Assam, Tripura. Also in Bangladesh. A Tibeto-Burman language. Mostly animists 90%.
4430	0	6	7.92	1	47.00	53.00	A	17.15	526	5	In Bihar, eastern MP (Dhangon), mainly Sambalpur District of Orissa, and West Bengal. Hindus 90%.
4431	1	6	3.34	0	20.20	79.80	A	0.14	589	3	Kadagi, Kurja. In Coorg, Karnataka, around Mercara. Hindus 95%. D=CSI. M=IBT.
4432	1	6	5.23	0	99.70	0.30	C	281.05	158	8	Manipur, Nagaland. Animists 30%. D=CBCNEI.
4433	2	6	9.26	1	99.60	0.40	C	232.14	265	8	In Assam, Bihar, MP, Maharashtra, Orissa, West Bengal. Animists 40%. D=CNI,RCC.
4434	0	5	4.01	0	19.50	80.50	A	0.35	704	3	Andhra Pradesh, on Orissa border. Adiwasi Oriya. Hindus 98%.
4435	4	6	7.07	0	99.64	0.36	C	254.62	205	8	In east and central Manipur. Animists 36%. D=ICFG,RCC,CBCNEI,ICI. M=ABMS.
4436	0	6	3.06	5	35.10	64.90	A	0.12	321	3	In Himachal Pradesh, Kanga. Hindus 95%, some Muslims 5%.
4437	1	6	1.49	4	40.00	60.00	A	2.92	171	4	North and central coastal strip of Maharashtra. Standard Konkani, with over 16 dialects. Hindus 98%. D=CNI. R=FEBA.
4438	3	6	9.45	4	99.76	0.24	C	366.16	215	9	Assam, northeast Nagaland, Mon District. 32 dialects. Animists 23%. D=Sema Baptist Association,CBCNEI(Nagaland Baptist Convention),NCRC.
4439	0	7	3.31	0	19.34	80.66	A	0.94	611	3	In Cannanore, Kerala State. Related to Tulu and Bellari. Hindus 98%.
4440	1	5	3.06	1	28.01	71.99	A	0.01	399	2	Southern Bihar (West Bengal border). Hindus 89%, Muslims 10%. D=CNI. M=UFCSM.
4441	0	6	3.35	1	26.39	73.61	A	0.37	462	3	In Bihar, Madhya Pradesh, Maharashtra, Uttar Pradesh. Rapid assimilation to Sadani. Hindus 70%, Muslims 29%.
4442	0	7	3.14	0	21.00	79.00	A	0.76	540	3	In Madras, Nilgiri Hills, mountains of Kotagiri. Hindus 99%. M=Christian Brethren,WVI.
4443	3	6	3.28	4	35.10	64.90	A	0.12	342	3	Andhra Pradesh, Araku Valley. Lingua franca. Animists/Hindus 99%. D=local fellowships,CNI,UELCI. M=IEM,SIL,LBI,Shiloh Evangelistic Association,MTI,IBT.
4444	1	6	6.77	0	34.00	66.00	A	2.48	626	4	In AP, MP. Aborigines in Hyderabad. Animists 78%, Hindus 20%. D=Baptist Bible Believers Assembly. M=EHC,IEM,Christ's Gospel Mission,ITM,MTI,SISWA,BFI.
4445	0	7	0.00	4	34.00	66.00	A	0.00	0	1.12	In Kerala, Karnataka, Tamil Nadu States. A scheduled tribe. Hindus/animists 100%.
4446	5	6	6.95	0	38.10	61.90	A	1.53	572	4	Orissa, Udayagiri area; AP, MP, Tamil Nadu. Hindus 54%, animists 45%. D=RCC(M-Cuttack),independents,SDA,Baptists,CNI. M=IGOSA,OFUCPM,OMM,SLM,IEA.
4447	2	6	9.82	4	99.68	0.32	C	312.73	237	9	Assam, Manipur, Nagaland. Also in Burma. Animists 30%. D=Evangelical Congregational Ch,CBCNEI. M=ABFMS,NEIGM,BFTW,KCCGMS,BFI,BSI,LBI.
4448	1	6	3.90	1	24.04	75.96	A	0.03	593	2	Himachal Pradesh. Some bilinguals in Hindi. Hindus 99%. D=CNI. M=IEM.
4449	1	4	7.02	0	27.40	72.60	A	0.40	832	3	In Kumaon, UP, Assam, Bihar, MP, Delhi, Maharashtra, Nagaland. Also in Nepal. Hindus 99%. D=CNI. M=Christian Academy for Rural Welfare & Evangelism.
4450	1	6	3.24	4	44.55	55.45	A	2.52	261	4	In Kerala, Tamil Nadu. Highest-caste Hindus 97%. D=RCC. M=Kerala Tribal Mission.
4451	2	6	8.90	0	45.00	55.00	A	16.42	609	5	Southern MP, Betul District; northern Maharashtra. Animists 62%, Hindus 28%. D=RCC(D-Indore),Baptist Ch. M=CBFMS,SVD,MSFS,IEM.
4452	5	6	7.02	0	30.00	70.00	A	1.09	732	4	AP, Kerala, Tamil Nadu, Karnataka. Animists 80%, Hindus 19%. D=Gospel in Action Fellowship,Brethren,RCC,CSI,UELCI. M=IEM,IBT,QCI,TM,UPM.
4453	1	6	4.24	5	59.00	41.00	B	10.76	243	5	Tamil Nadu, Coimbatore and Dharmapori Districts. Hindus 90%. D=CSI.
4454	1	6	5.85	0	28.78	71.22	A	0.81	652	3	Orissa, south of the Kui, Andhra Pradesh. Hindus 99%. D=ELC.
4455	0	6	2.52	4	33.02	66.98	A	0.02	267	2	Moplah. Laccadive Islands Hindu-Arabs. Muslims now 100%(Shafi Sunnis). Also 6.2 million Mappilla within Malayalis in Kerala.
4456	1	6	2.40	0	21.10	78.90	A	0.07	529	2	Highest cultivated fields on Earth. Literates 13%. Buddhists 52%(Red Hat Lamaism since BC 100, with multistoried monasteries; also Bon remnants), Muslims 48%.
4457	1	5	1.62	0	18.11	81.89	A	0.07	498	2	In Himachal Pradesh; also west Tibet. Lamaist Buddhists 100%. D=Moravian Ch.
4458	1	5	1.40	0	18.10	81.90	A	0.06	465	2	Manchati. Chamba District, Himachal Pradesh. Lamaist Buddhists 100%. D=Moravian Ch.
4459	1	5	3.35	0	18.10	81.90	A	0.06	760	2	Lahul and Spiti Sub-Division, Himachal Pradesh. Also in China. Lamaist Buddhists 100%. D=Moravian Ch. M=IEM.
4460	0	6	4.60	0	17.38	82.62	A	0.24	899	3	In Assam. Related to Tibetans. Buddhists 99%. M=IEM. Few Christians, scattered.
4461	1	6	6.13	0	75.00	25.00	B	109.50	257	7	Manipur, Nagaland. Related to Naga, Kuki-Chin. Animists 60%. D=CBCNEI. M=LNBA.
4462	1	6	4.91	0	38.00	62.00	A	4.16	426	4	Primarily in Sikkim and Bhutan; a few in Nepal. Agriculturalists, pastoralists. Buddhists 97%. D=CNI. M=IEC,BFI,UBS,FCSM.
4463	0	5	0.00	0	7.00	93.00	A	0.00	0	1.03	Arunachal Pradesh, Kameng District. Lamaist Buddhists 100%.
4464	0	5	0.00	1	18.00	82.00	A	0.00	0	1.07	Darjeeling area. Majority in Nepal; also Sikkim. Buddhists(Lamaists) 50%, animists 50%.
4465	2	6	7.54	0	99.65	0.35	C	270.46	203	8	Nagaland, upper Barak Valley. Animists 35%. D=CBCNEI(Nagaland Baptist Convention),NCRC. M=BFI.
4466	0	6	3.42	4	24.10	75.90	A	0.08	503	2	West Bengal, Darjeeling District; also Sikkim, though vast majority in Nepal. 6 dialects, 3 scripts used. Buddhists(less strict Lamaists) 60%, animists 35%, Hindus.
4467	0	6	4.47	1	29.10	70.90	A	0.10	515	3	Western Hindi. Bihar, Madhya Pradesh, Maharashtra, Orissa, West Bengal. Hindus 99%.
4468	3	6	9.44	0	99.99	0.01	C	552.86	185	10	West central Nagaland. 7 dialects. D=Lotha Association,CBCNEI(Nagaland Baptist Convention),NCRC.
4469	2	5	9.86	1	32.02	67.98	A	1.19	931	4	Southern Bihar, eastern Patna Division, Chotanagpur Division; West Bengal. Liturgical language. Virtually all are Hindus or Jains; Jainism strong. D=CNI,RCC.
4470	1	4	1.10	0	22.03	77.97	A	0.02	236	2	Sikkim. Mainly in Nepal, also Bhutan. Animists 90%, Hindus 10%. D=indigenous churches. M=FMB,UMN.
4471	0	6	4.13	1	20.10	79.90	A	0.07	706	2	Himachal Pradesh, in Simla and Solan Districts. Second language: Hindi. Hindus 100%.
4472	0	6	7.95	4	71.00	29.00	B	77.74	345	6	In Assam, Bihar, Orissa, West Bengal. Related to Santali. Animists 70%.
4473	2	5	10.94	1	37.02	62.98	A	1.37	885	4	Tirahutia. In Bihar, MP, WB; also in Nepal. Spoken by educated high-caste Hindus. A remarkable literature. Hindus 95%. D=RCC(D-Sambalpur),CNI. M=FMPB,SVD.
4474	0	7	2.90	5	45.06	54.94	A	1.74	240	4	Gurdaspur and Amritsar Districts, Punjab. Also Lahore District, Pakistan. Purest form of Punjabi. Hindus 80%, Sikhs 19%. M=IBT.
4475	0	6	3.14	1	23.06	76.94	A	0.05	504	2	Madhya Pradesh, Uttar Pradesh, but mainly in Sikkim. Related to Asuri. Animists 70%, Hindus 30%.
4476	0	7	0.00	1	20.00	80.00	A	0.00	0	1.11	Kottayam. In Kerala State. A scheduled tribe. Hindus/animists 100%. M=Kerala Tribal Mission.
4477	1	6	3.10	1	35.25	64.75	A	4.18	319	4	In Kerala State. Hindus/animists 96%. D=CSI.
4478	0	6	2.92	1	32.93	67.07	A	3.52	326	4	Ernakulam, Kerala. A South Indian people of Dravidian stock. Hindus 97%.
4479	0	6	2.87	1	27.68	72.32	A	0.68	383	3	Vetan, Vettuvan, Vedans. In Kerala State, Tamil Nadu: Ernakulam, Trivandrum. Hindus 99%.
4480	0	7	-9.99	5	42.02	57.98	A	0.03	7	2	Immigrants from Malaysia. Muslims 100%(Shafi Sunnis).
4481	4	6	15.25	4	99.38	0.62	B	145.63	424	7	Kerala. Hindus(Nayars) 48%, Muslims(Sunnis) 14%. D=52% RCC(22 Dioceses),22% Orthodox(OSCE),14% CSI-I and other Protestants,11% indigenous(MTSCM).
4482	1	5	1.62	0	18.05	81.95	A	0.03	334	2	Minicoy Island (Laccadive Islands). Primarily in Maldive Islands. Fishermen. Muslims 99%(Shafi Sunnis). D=SDA.
4483	0	6	0.00	1	21.07	78.93	A	0.05	130	2	In Andhra Pradesh, Maharashtra. Hindus 99%.
4484	2	6	2.20	0	42.00	58.00	A	13.79	209	5	Northeast Bihar, Rajmahal Hills; West Bengal. Related to Kurux. Hindus 60%, animists 30%. D=RCC(D-Bhagalpur),CNI. M=CMS,FMPB,TOR,NLC,UPM.
4485	1	6	9.68	0	44.00	56.00	A	14.45	665	5	Standard dialect of Southeastern Rajasthani. In northwest MP, Maharashtra, Rajasthan. Hindus 80%, Jains 10%, Muslims. D=RCC(D-Indore). M=SVD.
4486	0	6	0.00	4	19.00	81.00	A	0.00	0	1.05	In Kalahandi District, Orissa. Hindus 100%.
4487	0	7	4.01	1	35.50	64.50	A	0.64	387	3	In Maharashtra. Closedly related to Konkani and Gujarati. Hindus 90%, Muslims 8%.
4488	7	6	7.56	4	55.08	44.92	B	2.17	431	4	Assam, Manipur. Hindus 85%, animists 7%, Muslims 6.5%. D=ECC,EFCI,CBCNEI(Manipur Baptist Convention),PCNEI,RCC,ICFG,ICI. M=NEIGM,BFTW,LBI,AIPF.
4489	0	6	3.06	5	43.00	57.00	A	1.57	260	4	Bihar. Also in Nepal. A Magadhan Bihari Indo-Aryan language. Hindus 99%.
4490	0	9	4.09	0	21.50	78.50	A	0.39	649	3	In Andhra Pradesh (East Godavari), Tamil Nadu. A scheduled tribe. Hindus/animists 99%.
4491	0	6	2.45	0	22.00	78.00	A	0.80	430	3	In Kerala, Andhra Pradesh. Hindus 99%. M=Compassion of Agape,Tribal Mission.
4492	2	6	9.29	0	99.85	0.15	C	425.04	204	10	Northwest Manipur, Nagaland. Animists 15%. D=CBCNEI(Nagaland Baptist Convention),NCRC. M=CNM,BFI.
4493	1	6	8.00	0	99.95	0.05	C	502.78	172	10	Mira. Headhunters in Lushai Hills(Assam), also Burma. Close to Anal. D=95% Lakher/Mara Independent Evangelical Ch. M=LPM.
4494	2	6	6.17	0	56.78	43.22	B	49.28	341	6	Assam, north Manipur, Barak Valley. Animists 75%. D=CBCNEI(Nagaland Baptist Convention). M=CNM,TBC.
4495	5	5	5.42	4	67.20	32.80	B	12.75	262	5	Hindus 76%, Muslims 9%(Hindu converts, being 8% Hanafi Sunnis, 1% Ismaili Shias(Khojas,Bohras,Memons), some Shafis), Sikhs 2%, Jains 2%. D=RCC.
4496	0	6	4.34	0	25.05	74.95	A	0.04	584	2	In AP, Assam, Gujarat, MP, Maharashtra. Gonds, related to Abujmaria, Dandami Maria. Hindus 70%, animists 30%. M=CGMM,IEM.
4497	2	6	6.37	0	65.50	34.50	B	68.13	304	6	In Manipur, southeast, Laiching. Animists 71%. D=CBCNEI(Nagaland Baptist Convention),NCRC. M=Tangkhul Baptist Convention,ABCUSA.
4498	2	6	5.34	0	40.00	60.00	A	13.14	459	5	Assam, Bihar, West Bengal. Part of Malto ethnic group. Hindus 60%, animists 30%. D=RCC,CNI.
4499	0	6	0.00	1	24.00	76.00	A	0.00	0	1.12	Andhra Pradesh, near Adiwasi Oriya. Hindus 95%.
4500	2	6	4.47	1	31.10	68.90	A	0.11	482	3	Southwest Gujarat, Maharashtra. Bhils. Animists/polytheists 99%. D=Church of the Brethren,RCC. M=TEAM,IEM,FECI,WVI,PSSS.
4501	1	6	6.19	0	75.00	25.00	B	109.50	259	7	Nagaland, near Burma border. Animists 60%. D=CBCNEI(NYNBA).
4502	2	6	5.88	0	94.00	6.00	C	205.86	198	8	Nagaland. Animists 39%. D=CBCNEI(Nagaland Baptist Convention),NCRC.
4503	1	6	2.34	0	24.00	76.00	A	0.87	393	3	In Assam, Arunachal Pradesh, Kameng. Related to Chulikata, Digaro. Animists 90%, some Hindus 9%. D=CBCNEI.
4504	5	6	8.92	0	55.28	44.72	B	20.74	497	5	Assam, Mikir Hills. Poverty. Hindus 70%, animists 20%. Y=1859. D=Kuki Christian Ch,CBCNEI(Nagaland Baptist Convention),ICFG,Presbyterian Ch,ICI. M=GMU.
4505	0	5	5.92	1	32.30	67.70	A	0.35	587	3	A scheduled tribe. Aborigines in Rajasthan, Madhya Pradesh. Animists 98%(with Hindu elements). M=Tribal Mission,CSI,CCCI,EHC.
4506	1	6	4.27	1	32.00	68.00	A	5.84	460	4	In Orissa State. Hindus 95%. D=Protestants (a majority being Evangelicals).
4507	0	5	7.17	1	32.00	68.00	A	1.16	704	4	Mirpur area, Kashmir near Pakistan border. Also in Pakistan; 35,000 in Britain. Hindus 90%, Sikhs 9%.
4508	3	6	2.02	4	99.99	0.01	C	590.15	53	10	Mizoram, Assam, Manipur, Nagaland, Tripura. Also Bangladesh, China, Burma. 100% animists in 1891; by 1975, 100% Christians. D=BCMD(ZBK),RCC(D-Silchar).
4509	0	4	4.11	1	15.17	84.83	A	0.64	1,044	3	Northeast India, Arunachal Pradesh. Also in Tibet(China). Lamaist Buddhists 98%.
4510	1	6	4.95	0	75.00	25.00	B	109.50	214	7	Nagaland in north, near Burma border. Animists 60%. D=CBCNEI(MNBCA).
4511	2	6	5.84	0	99.80	0.20	C	359.16	150	9	Nagaland, near Burmese border; Manipur State. Animists 20%. D=CBCNEI,NCRC.
4512	2	6	2.39	0	25.20	74.80	A	0.18	379	3	In Mizoram, Assam, West Bengal. Also in Burma, Bangladesh. Animists(with strong Buddhist elements) 99%. D=BECC,BIC.
4513	0	7	1.10	0	19.02	80.98	A	0.01	303	2	Andhra Pradesh, Tamil Nadu. Related to Telugu. Hindus 99%.

Continued overleaf

Table 8-2 continued

PEOPLE		POPULATION				IDENTITY CODE		LANGUAGE		CHURCH		MINISTRY						SCRIPTURE		
Ref 1	*Ethnic name* 2	*P%* 3	*In 1995* 4	*In 2000* 5	*In 2025* 6	*Race* 7	*Language* 8	*Autoglossonym* 9	*S* 10	*AC* 11	*Members* 12	*Jayuh* 13-17	*d wa xcmc mi* 18	19	20	21	22	*Biblioglossonym* 23	*Pub* 24-26	*ss* 27
4514	Multani (Siraiki Hindki)	0.00276	25,769	27,977	36,720	CNN25h	59-AAFE-r	siraiki		1.00	280	2asu.	6	4	4	3	0	Siraiki*	PNb	b
4515	Munda (Colh, Mondari)	0.15976	1,491,623	1,619,426	2,125,525	AUG04b	46-CABA-d	mundari		26.24	424,937	3cs..	9	6	7	4	3	Mundari	PNB	.
4516	Muthuvan (Muthuwan)	0.00089	8,310	9,022	11,841	CNN23z	49-EBEB	malayalam cluster		0.02	2	2Asu.	3	4	0	1	2		PNB	b
4517	Muwasi	0.00385	35,946	39,026	51,222	AUG04z	46-CAAA-bc	mawasi		10.00	3,903	0....	8	5	6	3	1		p..	.
4518	Mzieme Naga	0.00300	28,010	30,410	39,913	MSY50p	73-ACAD-a	mzie-me		70.00	21,287	0....	10	9	11	5	2	Naga: Mzieme*	PNB	.
4519	Naga-Assamese Creole	0.00100	9,337	10,137	13,304	MSY50p	73-ABBC-d	naganese		60.00	6,082	1....	10	8	11	5	3		pnb	b
4520	Nagarchal (Nagarchi)	0.00125	11,671	12,671	16,631	AUG06b	49-DAAA	gond cluster		0.05	6	3.s..	4	4	0	2	1		PN.	b
4521	Nagpuri Bihari (Sadri)	0.20267	1,892,259	2,054,388	2,696,420	CNN25c	59-AAFQ-k	sadani		0.02	411	1.s..	3	3	4	3	2	Bihari: Nagpuria*	PN.	n
4522	Nahari	0.00200	18,673	20,273	26,609	CNN25z	59-AAFR-d	east nahari		0.01	2	1cs..	3	2	2	1	0		p..	.
4523	Nepalese (Gurkhali)	0.80495	7,515,537	8,159,470	10,709,447	CNN25k	59-AAFD-b	nepali		1.05	85,674	2Asu.	6	5	7	4	4	Nepali	PNB	b
4524	Nesang Bhotia	0.00006	560	608	798	MSY50a	70-AAAA-cl	nyam-kat		0.00	0	0c...	0	3	2	0	0		pnb	.
4525	Newari (Newari)	0.00213	19,887	21,591	28,339	MSY50z	71-AAAA-a	newari		0.10	22	0....	5	4	6	3	1	Newari	PN.	.
4526	Nihali (Nahali)	0.00062	5,789	6,285	8,249	AUG04z	46-BAAA-a	kalto		10.00	628	0....	8	5	4	4	0		...	.
4527	Nimadi (Nimari)	0.13982	1,305,451	1,417,302	1,860,233	CNN25o	59-AAFG-n	nimadi		0.10	1,417	1.s..	5	4	5	1	0		pn.	.
4528	Nocte Naga (Borduria)	0.00339	31,651	34,363	45,102	MSY50p	72-BAEA-a	nocte-naga		70.00	24,054	0....	10	8	11	5	2	Naga, Nocte	...	.
4529	Northern Gond (Betul)	0.08449	788,854	856,443	1,124,096	AUG06b	49-DAAA-ab	betul		0.08	685	3.s..	4	5	4	1	3	Gondi: Betul*	PN.	.
4530	Northwestern Kolam (Kulme)	0.00598	55,833	60,617	79,561	AUG06z	49-CAAA	kolami cluster		0.30	182	0....	5	6	5	1	3	Kolami, Northwestern	...	b
4531	Ntenyi Naga	0.00096	8,963	9,731	12,772	MSY50p	72-BADA-b	moyon-naga		65.00	6,325	0....	10	7	11	5	2	Naga, Moyon*	PN.	.
4532	Nuka-Dora	0.00100	9,337	10,137	13,304	CNN23z	49-DABA-b	manna-dora		1.00	101	0....	6	4	6	2	0		...	.
4533	Ojhi	0.00024	2,241	2,433	3,193	CNN23z	59-AAFP-ch	ojhi		0.10	2	1c.u.	5	3	0	0	0		pn.	.
4534	Ollari (Hallari, Kondkor)	0.00018	1,681	1,825	2,395	AUG04z	49-CABB-aa	ollari		10.00	182	0....	8	4	4	3	0		...	.
4535	Ongin (Onge, Jarao, Jarawa)	0.00002	187	203	266	AUG05	46-KAAC-a	onge		10.00	20	0....	8	5	2	4	3		...	.
4536	Oraon (Uraon, Urang)	0.19018	1,775,644	1,927,782	2,530,247	AUG06c	49-BAAA-b	chota-nagpur kurukh		43.00	828,946	1....	9	6	10	5	3	Kunrukh*	PN.	.
4537	Orisi (Utkali, Vadiya)	3.28314	30,653,533	33,279,935	43,680,494	CNN25l	59-AAFS-a	odiaa		1.40	465,919	3Asu.	6	5	7	5	4	Oriya	PNB	b
4538	Pahari	0.00300	28,010	30,410	39,913	CNN25n	59-AAFE-e	lahnda		1.00	304	1csu.	6	3	6	1	0	Panjabi, Western	PNb	b
4539	Pahari Mandeali (Mandiyali)	0.08949	835,537	907,126	1,190,619	CNN23d	59-AAFB-gb	mandeali		0.05	454	0.s..	4	4	7	3	1	Mandiali	P..	.
4540	Paite Chin (Haihte)	0.00465	43,415	47,135	61,866	MSY50c	73-DAAF-a	pai-te		85.70	40,395	0....	10	8	13	5	3	Paite*	PNB	.
4541	Paliyan	0.00021	1,961	2,129	2,794	CNN23b	49-EBFA-a	paniyan		25.60	545	0....	9	6	6	4	2		...	.
4542	Pangi	0.00174	16,246	17,638	23,150	CNN25n	59-AAFB	west pahari cluster		0.10	18	0.s..	5	4	5	0	0		P..	b
4543	Panika	0.00135	12,604	13,684	17,961	CNN25g	49-EBAA	kannada cluster		0.01	1	3Asu.	3	2	2	0	0		PNB	b
4544	Paniyan	0.00111	10,364	11,252	14,768	AUG06z	49-EBFA-a	paniyan		0.16	18	0....	5	4	4	3	3		...	.
4545	Pao	0.00519	48,457	52,609	69,050	MSY50z	73-DAAE-a	thado		0.03	16	0as..	3	4	0	1	0	Chin, Thado	PNB	.
4546	Pardhan	0.00010	934	1,014	1,330	AUG06b	49-DAAA	gond cluster		1.50	15	3.s..	6	5	0	2	1		PN.	b
4547	Pardhi Bhil (Paria)	0.00193	18,020	19,564	25,678	AUG06a	59-AAFL-c	paradhi-bhili		0.10	20	0.s..	5	4	4	1	3		p..	.
4548	Parengi	0.00048	4,482	4,866	6,386	AUG04z	46-CBBA-c	parengi		0.01	0	0.s..	3	4	0	2	1		pnb	.
4549	Parsi	0.02099	195,976	212,768	279,261	CNN25m	58-AACC-a	parsi-i		0.05	106	1Asu.	4	4	2	3	1	Gujarati: Parsi	PNb	b
4550	Patelia	0.00829	77,401	84,033	110,294	CNN25e	59-AAFK-j	patelia-bhili		0.10	84	0as..	5	5	2	2	3	Patelia	pn.	.
4551	Pathan (Afghani)	0.00100	9,337	10,137	13,304	CNT24a	58-ABDA-a	pashto		1.00	101	1As..	6	5	2	5	1		pnb	b
4552	Pawari Bhil	0.03123	291,584	316,567	415,499	AUG06a	59-AAFL-a	pawari-bhili		0.30	950	0.s..	5	4	4	2	3	Pawri*	P..	.
4553	Pengo	0.00028	2,614	2,838	3,725	AUG06z	49-DACB-b	pengo		0.09	3	0c...	4	4	0	1	0	Pengo	...	.
4554	Persian (Irani)	0.00028	2,614	2,838	3,725	CNT24f	58-AACC-c	standard farsi		0.04	1	1Asu.	3	3	6	3	2		PNB	b
4555	Phakey	0.00100	9,337	10,137	13,304	MSY49c	47-AAAA-c	phake		0.50	51	1.s..	5	4	6	4	0		pnb	.
4556	Phom Naga (Tamlu Naga)	0.00349	32,585	35,377	46,433	MSY50p	72-BAAC-a	phom-naga		67.00	23,702	0....	10	10	11	5	3	Naga: Phom*	PN.	.
4557	Pnar (Synteng)	0.00968	90,379	98,122	128,787	AUG03a	46-DAAA-b	pnar		47.00	46,118	1as..	9	6	7	5	1		pnb	.
4558	Pochuri Naga	0.00096	8,963	9,731	12,772	MSY50p	72-BAFB-a	pochuri-naga		50.00	4,866	0....	10	6	7	5	2	Naga: Pochuri*	PNb	.
4559	Porja (Konda-Dora)	0.00331	30,904	33,552	44,038	CNN23d	49-DABA-a	konda-dora		0.88	295	0....	5	5	4	3	3	Konda-dora	...	b
4560	Portuguese	0.00100	9,337	10,137	13,304	CEW21g	51-AABA-e	general português		93.00	9,427	2Bsuh	10	8	15	5	1	Portuguese	PNB	b
4561	Poumei Naga	0.00399	37,253	40,445	53,085	MSY50p	73-ABBB-b	poumei		60.00	24,267	0....	10	7	7	5	2	Naga: Poumei*	PNb	.
4562	Puh Bhotia	0.00067	6,256	6,792	8,914	MSY50a	70-AAAD-a	larkye		0.00	0	0....	0	3	2	0	0		...	.
4563	Puimei Naga	0.00532	49,671	53,927	70,780	MSY50p	73-ABBC-a	angami-naga		70.00	37,749	1....	10	8	11	5	2	Angami Naga*	PNB	.
4564	Rabha (Maitaria)	0.02493	232,763	252,706	331,681	MSY50r	72-ACAB-a	rabha		3.21	8,112	0....	6	6	5	4	3	Rabha	PN.	.
4565	Rajasthani (Bikaneri)	0.10000	933,665	1,013,662	1,330,449	CNN25o	59-AAFG-f	bikaneri		0.12	1,216	1.s..	5	4	5	5	3	Marwari: Bikaneri	PN.	.
4566	Rajasthani (Jaipuri)	0.05000	466,833	506,831	665,224	CNN25o	59-AAFG-h	jaipuri		0.10	507	4.s..	5	4	4	5	0	Jaipuri	Pn.	b
4567	Rajasthani (Marwari)	0.99838	9,321,526	10,120,196	13,282,934	CNN25o	59-AAFG-h	jaipuri	3	1.10	111,322	4.s..	6	5	7	5	3	Jaipuri	Pn.	b
4568	Rajasthani (Mewari)	0.10000	933,665	1,013,662	1,330,449	CNN25o	59-AAFG-k	mewari		0.10	1,014	1.s..	5	4	5	5	3	Marwari: Mewari	Pn.	.
4569	Rajbansi (Tajpuri)	0.00030	2,801	3,041	3,991	CNN25b	59-AAFT-ha	rajbangshi		0.10	3	1csuh	5	4	3	1	0		pnb	b
4570	Rajput Garasia (Dungri)	0.00653	60,968	66,192	86,878	AUG06a	59-AAFJ-e	dungari-bhili		1.00	662	1.s..	6	5	4	1	1	Girasia, Rajput	pn.	.
4571	Rajput Lohar	0.00050	4,668	5,068	6,652	CNN25o	59-AAFG-r	lohari		0.10	5	1.s..	5	4	3	1	0		pn.	.
4572	Ralte	0.00003	280	304	399	MSY50c	73-DAAA-a	ral-te		60.00	182	0....	10	7	6	5	0		...	.
4573	Rangkas	0.00010	934	1,014	1,330	MSY50r	70-ABBA-a	rangkas		0.00	0	0....	0	1	4	0	0		...	.
4574	Reli	0.00197	18,393	19,969	26,210	CNN23z	59-AAFS-gb	reli		1.00	200	1csu.	6	4	4	2	0		pnb	.
4575	Rengma Naga (Unza, Nzong)	0.00352	32,865	35,681	46,832	MSY50p	73-ABAA-a	rengma-naga		58.45	20,855	0....	10	6	11	5	1	Naga: Rengma*	PNB	.
4576	Riang (Tripuri Riang)	0.01443	134,728	146,271	191,984	MSY50s	72-AABA-b	riang		6.00	8,776	1.s..	7	6	6	4	3	Riang	PNb	.
4577	Rongmei Naga (Songbu)	0.00611	57,047	61,935	81,290	MSY50p	73-ACAE	rongmai-naga cluster		70.00	43,354	0....	10	8	11	5	1	Naga: Rongmei*	PNB	.
4578	Russian	0.00200	18,673	20,273	26,609	CEW22j	53-AAAE-d	russkiy		30.00	6,082	4B.uh	9	7	8	5	1	Russian	PNB	b
4579	Saharia (Sor)	0.02219	207,180	224,932	295,227	CNN25g	59-AAFO	hindi-urdu cluster		0.10	225	4Asuh	5	5	4	3	0		PNB	b
4580	Sangla	0.00050	4,668	5,068	6,652	MSY50r	70-AADB-a	tsangla		0.00	0	0....	0	3	3	1	0	Tsangla	...	.
4581	Sangtam Naga (Isachanure)	0.00312	29,130	31,626	41,510	MSY50p	72-BAFB-b	sangtam-naga		77.78	24,599	0....	10	8	12	5	1	Naga: Sangtam*	PNB	.
4582	Sanskrit	0.00086	8,030	8,717	11,442	CNN25z	59-AAFN-a	sanskrit		0.00	0	0a.u.	0	3	2	5	0	Sanskrit	PNB	b
4583	Santal (Sandal, Hor)	0.61780	5,768,183	6,262,402	8,219,512	AUG04c	46-CABA-a	santali		2.00	125,248	2as..	6	5	8	5	4	Santali	PNB	b
4584	Saora (Shabari, Savara)	0.02981	278,326	302,173	396,607	AUG04d	46-CBBA-a	sora		22.47	67,898	0.s..	9	5	7	3	3	Sora	PNB	.
4585	Sema Naga (Simi, Dayang)	0.01363	127,259	138,162	181,340	MSY50p	73-ABBA-a	sema-naga		91.67	126,653	0.s..	10	9	13	5	3	Naga: Sema*	PNB	.
4586	Sentinelese	0.00001	93	101	133	AUG05	46-KAAA-a	sentinel		5.15	5	0....	7	5	4	3	1		...	.
4587	Shendu (Khyen, Khieng)	0.00030	2,801	3,041	3,991	MSY50p	73-DEEA-b	shendu		8.00	243	0.s..	7	5	2	4	0		pn.	.
4588	Sherdukpen	0.00016	1,494	1,622	2,129	MSY50r	70-AAAG-a	sherdukpen		0.06	1	0....	4	3	2	0	0		...	.
4589	Sherpa (Sharpa Bhotia)	0.00202	18,860	20,476	26,875	MSY50q	70-AAAA-e	sherpa		0.11	23	0c...	5	3	4	1	0	Sherpa*	Pnb	.
4590	Shin (Sina, Dardi)	0.00222	20,727	22,503	29,536	CNN25i	59-AADB-b	brokpa		0.02	5	0....	3	3	2	0	1		p..	n
4591	Shobang	0.00002	187	203	266	AUG03d	46-HABA-ab	sho-bang		30.00	61	0....	9	6	2	3	2		...	.
4592	Shompe (Shom Peng)	0.00001	93	101	133	AUG03d	46-HABA-a	shom-peng		35.00	35	0....	9	7	2	3	3		...	.
4593	Siddi (Black African)	0.00083	7,749	8,413	11,043	NAB57j	99-AUSM-b	standard ki-swahili		0.40	34	4Asu.	5	2	2	3	0	Kiswahili*	PNB	b
4594	Sikkimese Bhotia (Sikami)	0.00405	37,813	41,053	53,883	MSY50a	70-AAAB-b	sikkim-bhotia		1.00	411	1.s..	6	3	4	2	3		pn.	b
4595	Simte	0.00221	20,634	22,402	29,403	MSY50c	73-DAAE-n	sim-te		95.00	21,282	0cs..	10	8	12	5	1	Simte	PNB	.
4596	Sindhi (Kachchi, Bhatia)	0.20365	1,901,409	2,064,322	2,709,459	CNN25p	59-AAFF-a	standard sindhi		1.10	22,708	1as..	6	5	6	5	3	Sindhi	PNB	b
4597	Sinhalese	0.01000	93,367	101,366	133,045	CNN25q	59-ABBA-aa	standard sinhala		2.80	2,838	1asuh	6	5	8	5	1		pnb	b
4598	Sondwari	0.00554	51,725	56,157	73,707	CNN25o	59-AAFG-m	sondwari		0.10	56	1.s..	5	4	2	3	0		pn.	.
4599	Sourashtra	0.03216	300,267	325,994	427,872	CNN25e	59-AAFI-a	east saurashtri		1.00	3,260	0....	6	5	6	3	3	Sourashtra*	P..	.
4600	South Central Gond	0.07100	662,902	719,700	944,619	AUG06b	49-DAAA-aa	adilabad		0.05	360	1.s..	4	4	2	3	3	Gondi: Adilabad*	Pn.	.
4601	Southeast Gond (Koi)	0.07000	653,566	709,563	931,314	AUG06b	49-DAAA-b	koya		0.06	426	1.s..	4	4	2	3	2	Gondi: Koi*	Pn.	.
4602	Southeastern Kolam	0.00120	11,204	12,164	15,965	AUG06z	49-CAAA	kolami cluster		1.00	122	0....	6	4	2	1	0	Kolami, Northwestern	...	b
4603	Southern Bhil	0.13082	1,221,421	1,326,072	1,740,493	AUG06a	59-AAFJ-c	giraasiaa-bhili		0.40	5,304	1.s..	5	5	8	4	3	Bhili: Central*	PN.	.
4604	Southern Nicobarese	0.00050	4,668	5,068	6,652	AUG03d	46-HAAA-e	nicobara		80.00	4,055	0....	10	8	10	5	1		pnb	.
4605	Sungnam	0.00017	1,587	1,723	2,262	MSY50r	70-ABAA-f	sungam		0.00	0	0....	0	3	3	0	0		p..	.
4606	Sunwar (Sunbar)	0.00023	2,147	2,331	3,060	MSY50z	71-CAAA-b	sunwar		0.05	1	0....	4	3	4	0	0	Sunwar	PN.	.
4607	Tadvi Bhil (Dhanka)	0.00180	16,806	18,246	23,948	AUG06a	59-AAFK-i	dhanka-bhili		1.80	328	0cs..	6	4	4	4	1		pn.	.
4608	Tamaria (Tumariya)	0.00064	5,975	6,487	8,515	CNN25c	59-AAFQ-gd	panchpargania		0.01	1	1.s..	3	4	0	1	1		pn.	.
4609	Tamil (Madrasi, Tamalsan)	6.37915	59,559,899	64,663,005	84,871,319	CNN23c	49-EBEA-b	tamil		19.50	12,609,286	2Asu.	8	7	11	5	3	Tamil	PNB	b
4610	Tangkhul Naga (Ukhrul)	0.01139	106,344	115,456	151,538	MSY50p	72-BAGB-a	tangkhul-naga		85.09	98,242	0....	10	8	12	5	2	Naga: Tangkhul*	PNB	.
4611	Tangsa Naga (Rangpan)	0.00171	15,966	17,334	22,751	MSY50p	72-BACA-a	tase-nagaland		70.00	12,134	0....	10	8	11	5	2	Naga, Tase	PN.	.
4612	Tarao Naga	0.00007	654	710	931	MSY50p	72-BAIA-a	tarao-naga		30.00	213	0....	9	7	7	5	1		...	.
4613	Telugu (Andhra, Tolangan)	7.21969	67,407,728	73,183,238	96,054,272	CNN23d	49-DBAB-as	vadaga		13.50	9,879,737	1asu.	8	7	10	5	3		pnb	b
4614	Teressa (Bompaka)	0.00020	1,867	2,027	2,661	AUG03d	46-HAAA-ca	teressa		80.00	1,622	0....	10	8	11	5	0		pnb	.
4615	Thakur	0.01260	117,642	127,721	167,637	CNN25j	59-AAFU-l	thakuri		0.01	13	1csu.	3	4	2	2	1		pnb	.
4616	Thebarskad (Sumtsu)	0.00043	4,015	4,359	5,721	MSY50r	70-ABAA-e	sumchu		0.00	0	0....	0	3	3	0	0		p..	.
4617	Thulunge Rai	0.00073	6,816	7,400	9,712	MSY50h	71-CCAB-a	kulung		0.10	7	0....	5	3	2	1	0		...	.
4618	Tibetan (Lhasa, Dalai)	0.01352	126,232	137,047	179,877	MSY50r	70-AAAA-c	utsang		0.30	411	0a...	5	5	4	4	3	Tibetan	PNB	b
4619	Tiddim Chin (Zoukam)	0.01817	169,647	184,182	241,743	MSY50c	73-DAAD-a	tiddim		60.00	110,509	0as..	10	7	7	5	2	Chin: Tiddim*	PNB	b
4620	Toda	0.00017	1,587	1,723	2,262	CNN23z	49-EBBA-a	toda		12.30	212	0....	8	5	5	5	1	Toda	P..	.
4621	Tripuri (Tipura)	0.07163	668,784	726,086	953,000	MSY50s	72-AABA-a	kok-borok		1.30	9,439	1.s..	6	5	7	4	3	Kok Borok	PNB	.
4622	Tulu (Tullu, Thulu, Tal)	0.20205	1,886,470	2,048,104	2,688,172	CNN23z	49-EAAA-a	tulu		1.00	20,481	1.s..	6	5	7	5	1	Tulu	PN.	.
4623	Turi	0.00060	5,602	6,082	7,983	AUG04c	46-CABA-c	turi		10.00	608	1cs..	8	5	7	5	0		pnb	.
4624	USA White	0.01000	93,367	101,366	133,045	CEW19s	52-ABAC-s	general american		78.00	79,066	1Bsuh	10	9	13	5	3	English*	PNB	b
4625	Ullatan (Kattalan, Katan)	0.00019	1,774	1,926	2,528	CNN23z	49-EBEB	malayalam cluster		7.00	135	2Asu.	7	6	4	5	0		PNB	b
4626	Urali (Uraly, Urli)	0.00044	4,108	4,460	5,854	CNN23a	49-EBAB-ab	urali		2.48	111	0....	6	5	4	5	1		...	.
4627	Urdu (Islami, Undri)	4.98307	46,525,187	50,511,476	66,297,190	CNN25r	59-AAFO-d	standard urdu	10	0.15	75,767	2Asuh	5	5	5	5	4	Urdu	PNB	b
4628	Usipi	0.00800	74,693	81,093	106,436	MSY50s	72-AABA-ae	usipi		1.00	811	1.s..	6	5	4	5	1	Usipi	Pnb	.
4629	Vadval	0.00010	934	1,014	1,330	CNN25d	59-AAFU-i	vadval-phudagi		1.00	10	1csu.	6	4	6	1	1		pnb	.
4630	Vaiphei	0.00222	20,727	22,503	29,536	MSY50c	73-DDEA-a	vaiphei		83.35	18,756	0....	10	8	11	5	3	Vaiphei	PN.	.
4631	Valmiki (Kupia)	0.00054	5,042	5,474	7,184	CNN25l	59-AAFS-i	kupia-oriya		1.00	55	1csu.	6	5	2	4	2	Kupia	PNb	.
4632	Varli	0.06677	623,408	676,822	888,341	CNN25d	59-AAFU-f	varli		1.00	6,768	1csu.	6	5	5	5	1	Varli	pnb	.
4633	Vasava	0.03900	364,129	395,328	518,875	AUG06a	59-AAFK-g	vasavi		0.90	3,558	0cs..	5	5	5	4	3	Vasavi	pn.	.
4634	Vishavan	0.00002	187	203	266	CNN23z	49-EBEB	malayalam cluster		9.90	20	2Asu.	7	6	4	5	0		PNB	b
4635	Waddar	0.00632	59,008	64,063	84,084	CNN23d	49-DBAB-at	vadari		5.00	3,203	1csu.	7	5	5	5	0		pnb	b
4636	Wagdi (Wagheri, Vaged)	0.16709	1,560,061	1,693,727	2,223,047	AUG06a	59-AAFJ-d	wagadi-bhili		0.10	1,694	1.s..	5	4	5	3	0	Wagdi*	pn.	b
4637	Wancho Naga (Banpara)	0.00462	43,135	46,831	61,467	MSY50p	72-BAAB-a	wancho-naga		70.00	32,782	0....	10	8	12	5	2	Naga, Wancho	...	.

Continued opposite

Table 8-2 continued

EVANGELIZATION								EVANGELISM			ADDITIONAL DESCRIPTIVE DATA
Ref 1	D 28	aC 29	CG% 30	r 31	E 32	U 33	W 34	e 35	R 36	T 37	Locations, civil divisions, literacy, religions, church history, denominations, dioceses, church growth, missions, agencies, ministries, movements 38
4514	0	6	3.39	4	39.00	61.00	A	1.42	309	4	Southern Punjabi. In Punjab, Maharashtra, AP, MP, UP, Rajasthan, Delhi. Vast majority live in Pakistan. Muslims 99%(Hanafi Sunnis).
4515	6	6	4.05	1	78.24	21.76	B	74.93	180	6	Bihar(Ranchi District), Assam; also Nepal, Bangladesh. Hindus 53%, animists 20%. D=RCC(D-Dumka,D-Jalpaiguri),CNI(D-Assam),MCSA,GELC,Baptists.
4516	0	6	0.70	4	35.02	64.98	A	0.02	133	2	In Kerala; Andhra Pradesh. A scheduled tribe. Hindus/animists 99%. M=Kerala Tribal Mission,Compassion of Agape.
4517	1	6	6.15	0	39.00	61.00	A	14.23	509	5	Southern Madhya Pradesh, Maharashtra. Dialect of Korku. Animists 62%, Hindus 28%. D=RCC.
4518	2	6	7.96	0	99.70	0.30	C	306.60	202	9	Southwestern Nagaland, northeast of Zeme Nagas. Animists 29%. D=CBCNEI(Nagaland Baptist Convention),NCRC.
4519	3	6	6.62	0	99.60	0.40	C	243.09	186	8	Naga Pidgin, Nagassamese, Kachari Bengali, Bodo. In Kohima District; Nagaland's lingua franca. Animists 40%. D=CBCNEI(Nagaland Baptist Conv),NCRC,RCC.
4520	1	6	1.81	0	24.05	75.95	A	0.04	320	2	In Madhya Pradesh, Maharashtra, Rajasthan. Gonds. Hindus 70%, animists 30%. D=CNI. M=WVI.
4521	2	5	3.79	1	30.02	69.98	A	0.02	439	2	Chota Nagpuri. In Assam, Bihar, MP, West Bengal. Related to Bhojpuri. Hindus 69%, Muslims 30%. D=CNI,RCC. R=FEBA.
4522	0	6	0.70	1	19.01	80.99	A	0.00	248	1.10	Rajpur, Bilaspur, Sambalpur Districts of Madhya Pradesh and Orissa. Dialect of Halbi. Hindus 99%.
4523	5	4	9.48	4	57.05	42.95	B	2.18	518	4	Mainly in Nepal. Hindus 99%. D=RCC(D-Darjeeling, D-Patna),CNI,ICFG,PFWBC,Brethren. M=IEM,SJ,CARWE,FECI,INIM,IEC,NLM,PFM,ZBM,BFI,WEC,ABCUSA.
4524	0	4	0.00	1	16.00	84.00	A	0.00	0	1.08	Upper Kanawar Bhotia, related to Puh. Kinnaur District. Lamaist Buddhists 100%.
4525	0	4	3.14	0	25.10	74.90	A	0.09	463	2	Some in Bettiah, Bihar. Primarily in Nepal. Hindus 85%, Buddhists 15%(Mahayana). M=YWAM.
4526	0	6	4.23	0	34.00	66.00	A	12.41	430	5	In Bihar, Madhya Pradesh, Maharashtra, Buldana, Akola, East Nimar, Amravati Districts. Language isolate. Animists/polytheists 90%.
4527	0	5	5.08	0	24.10	75.90	A	0.08	691	2	In Madhya Pradesh, Maharashtra. Hindus 90%, Muslims 10%.
4528	2	6	8.10	0	99.70	0.30	C	281.05	224	8	Northern Nagaland, Namsang, Lakhimpur District. Animists 29%. D=CBCNEI(Nagaland Baptist Convention),NCRC.
4529	2	6	4.32	0	30.08	69.92	A	0.08	485	2	Betul and other Districts in southern Madhya Pradesh. Hindus 55%, animists 45%. D=CNI,ELC. M=EMS,COUNT,CGMM,BFI,UPM,WVI,UFCS,CMS,IBT.
4530	1	6	2.94	0	26.30	73.70	A	0.28	410	3	In AP, MP, Maharashtra. Hindus/animist 90%. D=Free Methodist Ch of India. M=IEM,FMPB,MSCT,WVI,PSSS,MVM,YCLT.
4531	2	6	6.66	0	99.65	0.35	C	256.23	192	8	West central Nagaland, northern section of Rengma, Kotsenyu village. Animists 34%. D=CBCNEI(Nagaland Baptist Convention),NCRC.
4532	0	6	2.34	0	23.00	77.00	A	0.84	398	3	Near Adiwasi Oriya, Andhra Pradesh. Hindus 99%.
4533	0	4	0.70	1	16.10	83.90	A	0.05	289	2	In Madhya Pradesh, Maharashtra, Chhindwara District. Eastern Hindi. Hindus 99%.
4534	0	6	2.94	0	33.00	67.00	A	12.04	335	5	In Orissa, Koraput District. Hindus 90%.
4535	1	7	3.04	0	37.00	63.00	A	13.50	299	5	Southern Andaman Islands, Little Andaman Island. Hunter-gatherers, fishermen. Animists 90%. D=CBCNEI. M=CARE,Shiloh Evangelistic Mission,SX,SJ,SISWA.
4536	7	5	2.14	0	87.00	13.00	B	136.54	102	7	Bihar, MP. Hindus 37%, animists 20%. D=RCC(D-Jalpaiguri),Gossner ELC,MPELC,Brethren in Christ,SDA,CNI(D-Assam),MCSA. M=AIPF,IEC,JKPS.
4537	4	5	2.78	4	57.40	42.60	B	2.93	180	4	In Orissa. Hindus 96%, Muslims 2%('Pathans' or 'Musalmans', Hanafi or Wahhabi Sunnis; some Shias, Ahmadis). D=BOBBC,AOBC(GMOBM),IET,&c. M=ABFMS.
4538	0	6	3.47	1	32.00	68.00	A	1.16	387	4	Foothills of Himalayas from Pakistan to Nepal. Pahari = 'Hill Language'. Hindus 99%.
4539	1	4	3.89	1	25.05	74.95	A	0.04	535	2	In Himachal Pradesh, Uttar Pradesh, Punjab, Haryana. Hindus 99%. D=CNI.
4540	2	6	8.66	0	99.86	0.14	C	433.86	193	10	Siyin, Parte. Assam, Manipur; also in Burma. Animists 14%. D=Evangelical Congregational Ch,ICFG. M=NEIGM,BFTW,AIPF,BFI.
4541	2	7	4.08	0	57.60	42.40	B	53.82	242	6	In Kerala and Tamil Nadu. Related to Malayalam. Hindus 70%. D=RCC,CSI.
4542	0	0	2.93	4	17.10	82.90	A	0.06	638	2	Himachal Pradesh. Lahul-Spiti District on Chenab River. Closely related to Bhadrawahi. Hindus 100%.
4543	0	5	0.00	5	35.01	64.99	A	0.01	78	2	In Shahdol District, Madhya Pradesh. Hindus 100%.
4544	2	6	2.93	0	25.16	74.84	A	0.14	428	3	Kerala, Tamil Nadu. Agricultural workers, woodcutters. Animists 99%. D=RCC,CB. M=Kerala Tribal Mission,Gospel in Action Fellowship,QCI,WVI.
4545	0	5	2.81	4	30.03	69.97	A	0.03	357	2	In Satna District, Madhya Pradesh. Hindus 99%.
4546	1	7	2.75	0	28.50	71.50	A	1.56	361	4	Andhra Pradesh, Madhya Pradesh, Maharashtra. Gonds. Hindus 60%, animists 40%. D=CNI.
4547	0	6	3.04	0	23.10	76.90	A	0.08	479	2	Widely scattered across AP, MP, Gujarat, Maharashtra. Animists 95%. M=COUNT,CGMM,Bibles for India,UPM.
4548	1	6	0.00	2	22.01	77.99	A	0.00	0	1.09	In Orissa, Koraput District, and Andhra Pradesh. Hinduized animists 99%. D=Baptist Ch. M=SIL.
4549	0	6	2.39	4	38.05	61.95	A	0.06	244	2	Followers of Parsi religion(Zoroastrianism) in India since AD 750; fire temples. Mainly in Bombay. Zoroastrians 99%. M=BFI.
4550	0	6	4.53	5	33.10	66.90	A	0.12	459	3	In Gujarat, Maharashtra. Related to Bhil. Animists/polytheists 99%. M=Irish Presbyerian Mission,Kerypura Mission,Rajkot Mission.
4551	0	6	2.34	5	41.00	59.00	A	1.49	305	4	Muslims 99%(all Hanafi Sunnis); many being refugees from Afghanistan. Muslims M=IEM.
4552	1	6	4.66	0	25.30	74.70	A	0.27	613	3	Maharashtra. Animists 98%. D=Pentecostal Chs. M=COUNT,CGMM,FMPB,Bibles for India,UPM.
4553	0	6	1.10	1	15.09	84.91	A	0.05	381	2	Koraput District, Orissa. Hindus 99%.
4554	0	6	0.00	5	46.04	53.96	A	0.06	42	2	Expatriates, refugees, settlers, laborers from Iran. Muslims 95%(Ithna-Asharis). M=YWAM-Pune(India),IEM.
4555	0	6	4.01	1	32.50	67.50	A	0.59	432	3	Assam. Villages along Dihing river. Related to Shan (Burma). Buddhists 99%.
4556	3	6	8.08	0	99.67	0.33	C	276.34	218	8	Northeastern Nagaland; Assiringia village. Animists 32%. D=Ao Naga Baptist Association,CBCNEI(Nagaland Baptist Convention),NCRC.
4557	1	6	8.80	8	99.47	0.53	B	171.55	282	7	In Assam, Khasi and Jaintia Hills. Animists 53%. D=CBCNEI. M=Bibles for India.
4558	2	6	6.38	0	92.00	8.00	B	167.90	217	7	Southeast Nagaland. Animists 50%. D=CBCNEI,NCRC.
4559	0	6	3.44	0	23.88	76.12	A	0.76	509	3	Orissa State (Kubi), AP (Konda-Dora), Assam. Hindus 99%. M=Christian Endeavour for Hill Tribes(among Porja),IEA,IEHC.
4560	1	10	7.09	8	99.93	0.07	C	560.09	135	10	Long-standing residents of Portuguese origin. D=RCC. M=SJ.
4561	2	7	8.11	0	99.60	0.40	C	227.76	237	8	Nagaland. Animists 40%. D=CBCNEI,NCRC.
4562	0	4	0.00	0	8.00	92.00	A	0.00	0	1.03	Upper Kanawar Bhotia. Tibetan, close to Nesang. Lamaist Buddhists 100%.
4563	2	6	8.58	0	99.70	0.30	C	309.15	215	9	In Manipur and Assam. Animists 30%. D=CBCNEI,NCRC.
4564	3	6	6.93	0	37.21	62.79	A	4.36	633	4	West Assam State, Garo Hills, Nagaland. Animists 90%, Hindus 6%. D=CNI,CBCNEI,other Baptists. M=OM,Garo Baptist Convention,ZBM,ABCUSA.
4565	1	6	4.92	0	34.12	65.88	A	0.14	475	3	Northern Marwari, Rajasthan, MP. Hindus 88%, Muslims 7%. D=IET. M=BYM,FPCGI,BFI.
4566	0	6	4.00	0	30.10	69.90	A	0.11	455	3	Dialect of Marwari. In Madhya Pradesh, Rajasthan. Hindus 88%, Muslims 7%.
4567	3	5	9.77	0	42.10	57.90	A	1.69	701	4	Rajasthan, MP, Gujarat. 23 dialects. Hindus 82%, Jains 10%, Muslims 7%(Meos). D=CNI,Pakistan Christian Fellowship,IET. M=BYM,FPCGI,FMPB,BFI. R=TWR.
4568	0	6	4.73	0	32.10	67.90	A	0.11	489	3	Southern Marwari. Gujarat, Rajasthan, MP. Hindus 85%, Jains 8%, Muslims 7%. M=BYM,FPCGI,BFI.
4569	0	6	1.10	1	27.10	72.90	A	0.09	249	2	West Bengal: Jalpaiguri, Cooch Behar, Darjeeling Districts. Also in Nepal, Sikkim, Bangladesh. Hindus 99%.
4570	1	6	4.28	0	27.00	73.00	A	0.98	536	3	Aborigines in Mewar Hills, Rajasthan, Gujarat. Warrior caste Bhils. Hindus/polytheists/animists 99%. D=CNI. M=IEM.
4571	0	5	1.62	0	21.10	78.90	A	0.07	340	2	Rajasthan, Gujarat, MP, Maharashtra, UP, Delhi, Haryana, Punjab. Some are nomadic blacksmiths. Hindus 99%.
4572	0	7	2.94	0	90.00	10.00	C	197.10	123	7	In Assam; also in Burma. Related to Tiddim, Paite, Thado, Zo. Animists 40%.
4573	0	5	0.00	0	11.00	89.00	A	0.00	0	1.03	Close to Nepal border, also in Nepal. Related to Darmiya, Chaudangsi. Lamaist Buddhists 100%.
4574	0	6	3.04	1	30.00	70.00	A	1.09	369	4	In Andhra Pradesh, near Adiwasi Oriya. Hindus 95%.
4575	2	6	7.94	0	99.58	0.42	B	229.23	225	8	West central Nagaland, centered on Tseminyu. Animists 40%. D=CBCNEI(Nagaland Baptist Convention),NCRC. M=ZBAM.
4576	4	6	7.01	0	47.00	53.00	A	10.29	473	5	In Assam and central Tripura; also in Bangladesh. Close to Tripuri. Hinduized animists 90%, Muslims 4%. D=Tripura Baptist Union,Presbyterians,ICFG,ICI.
4577	2	6	8.74	0	99.70	0.30	C	304.04	222	9	Northwest Manipur, Cachar, Nagaland. Animists 28%. D=CBCNEI(Nagaland Baptist Convention),NCRC. M=RCLS.
4578	1	10	6.62	7	97.00	3.00	B	106.21	187	7	Expatriates from Russia, in commerce, professions. D=Russian Orthodox Ch(P-Moscow).
4579	0	6	3.16	7	47.10	52.90	A	0.17	242	3	Tribal people found in Madhya Pradesh (Shivpuri, Morena, Guna Districts), and Rajasthan. Polytheists/animists 99%.
4580	0	5	0.00	0	11.00	89.00	A	0.00	0	1.04	Villages in Arunachal Pradesh. Vast majority in Bhutan. Lamaist Buddhists 100%.
4581	2	6	8.12	0	99.78	0.22	C	362.76	193	9	Southeast Nagaland. Woodworkers. Animists 20%. D=CBCNEI(Nagaland Baptist Convention),NCRC. M=BFI.
4582	0	10	0.00	4	39.00	61.00	A	0.00	0	1.11	Literary and liturgical language, official language. Nearly half a million speakers, all Hindus.
4583	5	6	1.03	4	59.00	41.00	B	4.30	94	4	Hindus 78%, animists 21%. D=RCC(D-Bhagalpur,D-Dumka,M-Ranchi),CNI(D-Chota Nagpur),NELC,BOBBC,MCSA. M=MMS,ABFMS,LBI,TOR,SDB,SJ,CSM.
4584	2	6	9.22	0	67.47	32.53	B	55.33	415	6	Ganjam District, Orissa, AP, MP. Hindus/animists 75%. D=RCC(M-Cuttack),Saora Association of Baptist Chs. M=CBOMB,Christ's Gospel Mission,COUNT,IEA.
4585	3	6	9.91	0	99.92	0.08	C	490.75	202	10	Central and southern Nagaland, Assam. Animists 5%. D=Sema Baptist Association,CBCNEI(Nagaland Baptist Convention),NCRC.
4586	1	7	1.62	0	30.15	69.85	A	5.66	238	4	Southeastern Andaman Islands. Hunter-gatherers, fishermen. Animists 94%. D=CBCNEI. M=ABCUSA.
4587	0	5	3.24	1	33.00	67.00	A	9.63	344	4	Lushai Hills, Assam. Also in Bangladesh. Animists 90%.
4588	0	5	0.00	0	13.06	86.94	A	0.02	350	2	In Assam, Arunachal Pradesh. Also Tibet. Tibetans. Lamaist Buddhists 100%.
4589	0	6	3.19	1	26.11	73.89	A	0.10	440	3	Darjeeling District, Sikkim; also in Nepal, Tibet. Buddhists 100%(Lamaists).
4590	0	6	1.62	0	17.02	82.98	A	0.01	422	2	South Kashmir and Jammu, also Ladakh area. Great majority in Pakistan. Most speak Purik. Buddhists 35%, animists 30%, Muslims 35%(Sunnis,Shias).
4591	2	7	4.20	0	57.00	43.00	B	62.41	250	6	On Andaman and Nicobar Islands; also in Calcutta. Animists 70%. D=RCC,CBCNEI.
4592	1	7	3.62	0	62.00	38.00	B	79.20	204	6	Interior of Great Nicobar Island. Animists 64%. D=CBCNEI. M=CARE,ABCUSA,SEM.
4593	0	6	3.59	5	45.40	54.60	A	0.66	305	3	Descendants of Black slaves imported from East Africa. Mostly Muslims 70%.
4594	7	6	3.79	0	32.00	68.00	A	1.16	468	4	Sikkim. Strict Lamaist Buddhists 98%(in Sikkim, 67 monasteries; 3,000 lamas; Karma-pa/Red Hat sect). D=RCC,Moravian,MTSC,CNI,CBCNEI. M=TLM,TEAM,LBI.
4595	1	6	7.96	1	99.95	0.05	C	509.72	169	10	In southwest Manipur. Related to Thado and Zome. D=CBCNEI. M=Bibles for India.
4596	2	5	8.03	4	55.10	44.90	B	2.21	449	4	Gujarat, Maharashtra, Rajasthan. Also Pakistan, Afghanistan. Hindus 93%, Muslims 3.8%, Sikhs 2%. D=CNI,RCC. M=YWAM-Bombay,CBFMS,UPM,CMS. R=FEBA.
4597	1	10	5.81	6	57.80	42.20	B	5.90	303	4	From Ceylon. Theravada Buddhists 97%; Maha Bodhi Society of Ceylon proselytizes across India. D=RCC.
4598	0	6	4.11	0	23.10	76.90	A	0.08	606	2	In Madhya Pradesh, Rajasthan. Hindus 96%, some Muslims 4%.
4599	0	6	5.96	0	29.00	71.00	A	1.05	659	4	In Tamil Nadu, Madras, and Deccan. Silk weavers. Hindus 99%. M=Sourashtra Mission,Christ The Hope Ministries,FECI,ICGM,IBT,UPM.
4600	2	6	3.65	0	27.05	72.95	A	0.04	471	2	Adilabad District, northern Andhra Pradesh. Hindus 60%, animists 40%. D=CNI,ELC. M=COUNT,CGMM,Bibles for India,UPM,WVI,IEM.
4601	2	6	3.82	0	26.06	73.94	A	0.05	507	2	Strongly influenced by Telugu, in Andhra Pradesh. Hindus 60%, animists 40%. D=CSI,ELC. M=CMS,UPM.
4602	0	6	2.53	0	18.00	82.00	A	0.65	537	3	AP, Adilabad District. Hindus/animists 99%.
4603	5	6	6.47	0	38.40	61.60	A	0.56	533	3	Animists/polytheists 95%. D=CMA,MCSA,CNI,RCC,Pentecostals. M=IEM,COUNT,CGMM,BFI,UPM,WVI.
4604	1	6	1.77	0	99.80	0.20	C	356.24	62	9	Nicobar Islands: Little Nicobar and outer Great Nicobar Islands. Animists 19%. D=CBCNEI. M=ABCUSA.
4605	0	5	0.00	0	11.00	89.00	A	0.00	0	1.04	Kinnaur District. Lamaist Buddhists 100%.
4606	0	4	0.00	0	18.05	81.95	A	0.03	167	2	Sikkim, also in Nepal. Agriculturalists. Animists 70%, Hindus 30%.
4607	0	6	3.55	1	30.80	69.20	A	2.02	405	4	Gujarat, Maharashtra, Karnataka, Rajasthan. Muslims 98%, very few animists. M=BFI.
4608	1	6	0.00	1	20.01	79.99	A	0.00	140	1.10	MP State, Bihar(Ranchi, Singhbhum). Hindus 100%. D=CNI. M=ZBM.
4609	7	6	2.38	6	86.50	13.50	B	61.56	107	6	Hindus 76%, Muslims 4%(Labbais: Hanafi Sunnis). D=RCC(19 Dioceses),CSI-I(7 Dioceses),CPM,FWBCI,TELC,SA,MCSA. 1 million Charismatics. M=CMS,WEC
4610	2	6	9.63	0	99.85	0.15	C	422.66	212	10	Manipur, Ukhrul, Nagaland. Animists 14%. D=CBCNEI(Nagaland Baptist Convention),NCRC. M=ABFMS,CNM.
4611	2	6	7.36	0	99.70	0.30	C	291.27	199	8	Northern Nagaland. Also in Burma. Animists 28%. D=CBCNEI(Nagaland Baptist Convention),NCRC. M=CNM,ABCUSA.
4612	1	6	3.11	0	61.00	39.00	B	66.79	180	6	East and central Manipur. A Kuki-Naga language. Animists 70%. D=CBCNEI(TRNBA).
4613	11	6	2.55	5	73.50	26.50	B	36.21	132	5	Hindus 78%, Muslims, Baha'is. D=RCC(9 Dioceses),CSI(4 Dioceses),CTBC,AELC,SALC,SA,BM,FIGC,IET,Subba Rao Movement,IPCOG. M=MHM,PIME,MSFS.
4614	0	6	1.70	0	99.80	0.20	C	353.32	61	9	Nicobar Islands, Teressa and Bompoka Islands. Animists 20%.
4615	2	6	2.60	1	27.01	72.99	A	0.01	366	2	Related to Konkani. Hindus 90%, Muslims 10%. D=CNI,RCC. M=WVI.
4616	0	5	0.00	1	11.00	89.00	A	0.00	0	1.04	Kinnaur District. Related to Kanauri. Lamaist Buddhists 100%.
4617	0	6	1.96	0	16.10	83.90	A	0.05	504	2	On border, also in Nepal. Agriculturalists, pastoralists. Hindus 100%.
4618	3	6	3.79	4	45.30	54.70	A	0.49	330	3	Assam. Refugees from Tibet (China) from 1949. Lamaist Buddhists 99%. D=RCC(D-Darjeeling,D-Patna), CNI,Moravian Ch. M=YWAM-Pune(India),SJ,CARWE.
4619	0	7	9.76	5	99.60	0.40	C	251.85	259	8	Assam, Manipur. Also northern Chin Hills, Burma, also Bhutan. Lingua franca. Animists 40%. M=FEBC,BFI.
4620	1	6	3.10	0	41.30	58.70	A	18.54	272	5	Orissa, Tamil Nadu. Pastoralists in Nilgiris. Animists 80%(religion based on cattle and milk houses). D=CSI. M=UPM.
4621	4	6	7.09	0	45.30	54.70	A	2.14	495	4	Assam, eastern Tripura. Many in Bangladesh. Hinduized animists 92%, Muslims 6.5%. D=RCC(D-Silchar),PCNEI,Tripura Baptist Christian Union,ICI. M=NZBMS.
4622	1	6	7.92	0	37.00	63.00	A	1.35	661	4	In AP, Kerala, Tamil Nadu, Maharashtra, Karnataka, Mangalore. Hindus 90%. D=CSI. M=Basel Mission. R=FEBA.
4623	0	6	4.19	1	48.00	52.00	A	17.52	296	5	East Madhya Pradesh (Raigarh), Orissa (Sambalpur), and scattered areas. Hindus 90%.
4624	6	10	1.38	8	99.78	0.22	C	432.74	41	10	Expatriates from USA, in education, business. D=CNI,CJCLdS,AoG,SDA,JWs,COG.
4625	0	6	2.64	4	52.00	48.00	B	13.28	192	5	In Kerala State. A Dravidian language. Hindus 90%.
4626	0	6	2.44	0	26.48	73.52	A	2.39	356	4	In Kerala, Tamil Nadu. Animists 95%. M=Zoram Baptist Mission.
4627	2	5	9.34	5	56.15	43.85	B	0.30	506	3	Ethnic groups in Punjab, UP, Bihar. Muslims 98%(Hanafi Sunnis,Shafis,Shias,Sufi orders). D=RCC,CNI. M=OFMCap,PIME,SJ,CFIM,CARWE,HBIC,INIM,BFI,UPM.
4628	1	6	4.49	0	34.00	66.00	A	1.24	450	4	In Tripura; also in Bangladesh. Close to Riang, Tripuri. Hinduized animists 90%, Muslims 6%. D=Baptist Chs. M=ABWE.
4629	1	6	2.33	1	33.00	67.00	A	1.20	276	4	In Maharashtra. Close to Konkani. Hindus 90%. D=CNI.
4630	2	6	7.83	0	99.83	0.17	C	390.47	191	9	Assam, south Manipur. Related to Kuki. Animists 15%. D=Interdenominational Ch,ICFG. M=AIPF,BFI,IPR.
4631	0	6	4.09	1	33.00	67.00	A	1.20	423	4	Andhra Pradesh. Related to Oriya. Hindus 29%, hinduized animists 70%. M=SIL,Christian Endeavour for Hill Tribes.
4632	0	6	6.73	1	36.00	64.00	A	1.31	588	4	In Gujarat State and Maharashtra. Related to Konkani, Gujarati, and Bhili. Hindus 99%. M=FMPB.
4633	0	6	6.05	1	32.90	67.10	A	1.08	587	4	Gujarat State, Maharashtra. Bhil subgroup. Animists/polytheists 99%. M=UPM,CGMM,FMPB,NLC.
4634	0	7	3.04	4	55.90	44.10	B	20.19	198	5	In Kerala State, Ernakulam and Trichur Districts. Hindus 90%.
4635	0	6	5.94	1	43.00	57.00	A	7.84	442	4	In Andhra Pradesh, Karnataka. Related to Telugu. Hindus 95%.
4636	0	5	5.27	0	29.10	70.90	A	0.10	590	3	In southern Udaipur District, Rajasthan, also Gujarat. Bhils. Second language: Hindi. Animists/polytheists 99%.
4637	2	6	8.43	0	99.70	0.30	C	283.60	230	8	Assam, Nagaland. Animists 29%. D=CBCNEI(Nagaland Baptist Convention),NCRC. M=Ao Baptist Churches Association, ABCUSA.

Continued overleaf

Table 8-2 continued

PEOPLE		POPULATION				IDENTITY CODE		LANGUAGE		CHURCH		MINISTRY						SCRIPTURE		
Ref 1	Ethnic name 2	P% 3	In 1995 4	In 2000 5	In 2025 6	Race 7	Language 8	Autoglossonym 9	S 10	AC 11	Members 12	Jayuh 13-17	d 18	wa 19	xc 20	mc 21	mi 22	Biblioglossonym 23	Pub 24-26	ss 27
4638	Western Muria (Jhoria, Raj)	0.00227	21,194	23,010	30,201	AUG06b	49-DAAA-c	maria		0.05	12	1.s..	4	3	2	2	0	Maria*	pn.	b
4639	Western Punjabi	0.00599	55,927	60,718	79,694	CNN25h	59-AAFE-e	lahnda		1.10	668	1csu.	6	5	8	0	0	Panjabi, Western	PNb	b
4640	Wogri Boli (Tamil Nomad)	0.00200	18,673	20,273	26,609	CNN25f	59-AAFA-m	zirak-boli		1.00	203	1....	6	4	4	3	0	Vaagri Boli*	Pnb	.
4641	Yakha	0.00008	747	811	1,064	MSY50z	71-CBCB-a	yakha		0.00	0	0....	0	2	0	0	0		...	.
4642	Yanadi (Yadi)	0.02614	244,060	264,971	347,779	CNN23d	49-DBAB-au	yanadi		0.13	344	1csu.	5	4	4	3	2		pnb	.
4643	Yerava	0.00191	17,833	19,361	25,412	CNN23b	49-EBEB-ao	yerava		15.00	2,904	1csu.	8	6	6	5	2		pnb	b
4644	Yerukala (Erukala)	0.01189	111,013	120,524	158,190	CNN23c	49-EBDA-b	yerukala		1.37	1,651	0....	6	5	5	5	1		...	b
4645	Yimchungru Naga (Tozhuma)	0.00379	35,386	38,418	50,424	MSY50p	72-BAFA-ba	proper yimchungru		76.00	29,198	0....	10	8	12	5	1	Naga: Yimchungru*	PN.	.
4646	Zangskar (Zaskar)	0.00119	11,111	12,063	15,832	MSY50r	70-AAAC-e	zangskari		0.01	1	1....	3	3	0	1	2	Zangskari	Pn.	b
4647	Zeme Naga (Sangrima)	0.00293	27,356	29,700	38,982	MSY50p	73-ACAC-a	ze-mi		70.00	20,790	0....	10	7	12	5	2	Naga: Zeme*	PNB	.
4648	Zome (Zomi Chin)	0.00178	16,619	18,043	23,682	MSY50c	73-DAAB-a	zo-mi		80.00	14,435	0....	10	8	11	5	3	Zomi*	PNB	.
4649	other minor peoples	0.05910	551,796	599,074	786,295	...				5.00	29,954		7	5	6	5	3			
	Indonesia	**100.00000**	**197,464,493**	**212,107,385**	**273,442,120**					**12.43**	**26,364,863**									
4650	Abau (Green River)	0.00070	1,382	1,485	1,914	AON10a	26-BAAA-a	abau		65.00	965	0.s..	10	7	6	5	1	Abau	P..	.
4651	Abui (Barue, Namatalaki)	0.01039	20,517	22,038	28,411	AON10e	20-ABDA-a	kobola		43.00	9,476	0....	9	6	6	4	1		...	.
4652	Abun (Karon Pantai, Manif)	0.00168	3,317	3,563	4,594	AON10a	25-CAAA-c	abun-je		65.00	2,316	0....	10	7	6	4	1	Abun	P..	.
4653	Abung (Northern Lampungese)	0.36043	711,721	764,499	985,567	MSY44y	31-PFAA	abung cluster		0.01	76	0....	3	2	3	0	1		...	b
4654	Achehnese (Aceh, Atjeh)	1.59774	3,154,969	3,388,925	4,368,894	MSY44y	31-NAAA	aceh cluster		0.01	339	2A...	3	4	4	1	4	Aceh	PN.	.
4655	Aghu	0.00174	3,436	3,691	4,758	AON10a	24-KDBH-a	dyair		65.00	2,399	0....	10	7	6	4	1		...	.
4656	Ahe Dayak	0.01742	34,398	36,949	47,634	MSY44y	31-KAAP-a	ahe		10.00	3,695	0....	8	5	5	2	1	Ahe	...	.
4657	Aikwakai	0.00041	810	870	1,121	AON10a	21-BAGA-a	sikari-tai		60.00	522	0....	10	7	8	4	1	Sikaritai	...	.
4658	Airoran (Adora)	0.00026	513	551	711	AON10a	24-FBAA-a	airoran		65.00	358	0....	10	7	6	4	0		...	.
4659	Alas-Kluet Batak	0.04424	87,358	93,836	120,971	MSY44b	31-PEAA	alas-kluet cluster		0.01	9	0....	3	3	3	1	0		...	b
4660	Alune (Sapolewa)	0.00813	16,054	17,244	22,231	MSY44y	32-DGMA	alune cluster		80.00	13,795	0....	10	8	9	4	1	Alune	P..	b
4661	Amahei	0.00003	59	64	82	MSY44y	32-DGOA-a	amahai		40.00	25	0....	9	5	6	3	0		...	b
4662	Amanab	0.00206	4,068	4,369	5,633	AON10a	21-HEAA	amanab cluster		65.00	2,840	0....	10	7	6	4	2	Amanab	...	.
4663	Ambai	0.00474	9,360	10,054	12,961	AON09e	33-ADCK-a	ambai		41.00	4,122	0....	9	8	5	4	1	Ambai	P..	b
4664	Ambelau	0.00315	6,220	6,681	8,613	MSY44y	32-EAAA-a	ambelau		20.00	1,336	0....	9	5	6	3	0		...	b
4665	Amber (Waigeo, Amberi)	0.00021	415	445	574	AON09e	33-ABBC	maya cluster		91.00	405	0....	10	8	11	3	0		...	.
4666	Amberbaken (Dekwambre)	0.00365	7,207	7,742	9,981	AON10a	25-EAAA-a	mpur		65.00	5,032	0....	10	7	3	4	2	Mpur	...	.
4667	Ambonese	0.11615	229,355	246,363	317,603	AON09e	31-PHAI-a	malayu-ambon		91.00	224,190	0....	10	8	13	5	2	Malay, Ambonese	PN.	b
4668	Ampanang	0.01947	38,446	41,297	53,239	MSY44y	31-LCAB-a	ampanang		60.00	24,778	0....	10	6	5	4	0		...	b
4669	Anakalangu	0.00909	17,950	19,281	24,856	AON09e	32-AACD-a	anakalangu		45.00	8,676	0....	9	5	7	3	0		...	.
4670	Andio (Masama, Imbaoo)	0.00091	1,797	1,930	2,488	MSY44y	31-QHBA-a	andio'o		19.50	376	0....	8	5	6	3	0		...	b
4671	Angguruk Yali	0.00799	15,777	16,947	21,848	AON10a	24-FADD-a	angguruk		50.00	8,474	0....	10	5	6	3	1	Yali: Angguruk*	PN.	.
4672	Angkola Batak	0.43558	860,116	923,897	1,191,059	MSY44b	31-PECA-c	angkola	1	15.00	138,585	1.s..	8	5	7	5	3	Batak: Angkola*	PNB	.
4673	Ansus	0.00267	5,272	5,663	7,301	AON09e	33-ADCC-a	ansus		91.00	5,154	0....	10	8	11	4	1		...	.
4674	Arab	0.10000	197,464	212,107	273,442	CMT30	12-AACF-f	syro-palestinian		0.10	212	1Asuh	5	3	2	0	0	Arabic: Lebanese*	Pnb	b
4675	Aralle-Tabulahan	0.00732	14,454	15,526	20,016	MSY44p	31-QBGA	aralle-tabulahan cluster		45.00	6,987	0....	9	5	6	2	1	Aralle-tabulahan	...	b
4676	Arandai (Jaban, Yaban)	0.00058	1,145	1,230	1,586	AON10a	20-HDAB-a	arandai		65.00	800	0....	10	7	6	3	0		...	.
4677	Arguni	0.00014	276	297	383	MSY44y	33-ACAC-a	arguni		15.00	45	0....	8	5	5	2	0		...	.
4678	As	0.00014	276	297	383	AON10a	33-ABDA-a	as		40.00	119	0....	9	5	6	2	0		...	b
4679	Asienara (Madidwana)	0.00048	948	1,018	1,313	AON10a	24-KAAA	asienara cluster		65.00	662	0....	10	7	6	3	0		...	.
4680	Asilulu (Negeri Lima)	0.00509	10,051	10,796	13,918	MSY44y	32-DGOQ-b	asilulu vehicular		8.00	864	0....	7	5	6	2	0		...	b
4681	Ati (Biritai)	0.00006	118	127	164	AON10a	21-BABA-a	obogwi-tai		64.00	81	0....	10	6	6	2	2		...	.
4682	Attingola	0.00974	19,233	20,659	26,633	MSY44x	31-QJAB-a	atinggola		7.00	1,446	0....	7	4	3	3	0		...	b
4683	Auye	0.00017	336	361	465	AUG05	24-DAAC-a	auye		60.00	216	0....	10	7	6	3	2	Auye	...	.
4684	Awera	0.00006	118	127	164	AON09e	25-HAAA-a	awera		55.00	70	0....	10	6	6	3	1		...	.
4685	Awyi (Awye, Njao)	0.00028	553	594	766	AON10a	21-GAAA-a	awyi		64.00	380	0....	10	7	6	3	0		...	.
4686	Awyu (Awya, Avio)	0.01045	20,635	22,165	28,575	AON10a	24-KDBH-c	nohon		65.00	14,407	0....	10	7	9	4	2		...	.
4687	Ayamaru (Brat, Maibrat)	0.01256	24,802	26,641	34,344	AON10a	25-DAAB	brat cluster		4.00	1,066	0....	6	4	6	4	2	Mai Brat	P..	b
4688	Baburiwa (Barua)	0.00025	494	530	684	AON10a	21-BAAA-b	eri-tai		65.00	345	0....	10	7	8	2	1		p..	.
4689	Bacanese Malay	0.00133	2,626	2,821	3,637	MSY44y	31-PHAH-b	malayu-bacan		34.80	982	0....	9	5	6	1	0		...	b
4690	Badui	0.00276	5,450	5,854	7,547	MSY44n	31-PJAB-a	badui		1.00	59	0....	6	4	4	1	1		...	b
4691	Bagusa	0.00017	336	361	465	AON10a	24-FBAB-a	bagusa		10.00	36	0....	8	5	5	0	0		...	.
4692	Baham (Patimuni)	0.00064	1,264	1,357	1,750	AON10a	24-BBAB-a	baham		65.00	882	0....	10	7	6	2	0		...	.
4693	Bahau	0.00208	4,107	4,412	5,688	MSY44z	31-JBAH-a	central bahau		10.00	441	0....	8	5	4	1	0		...	.
4694	Bahau River Kenyah	0.00097	1,915	2,057	2,652	MSY44y	31-JCCE	bahau-kenyah cluster		10.00	206	0....	8	5	5	2	3		...	.
4695	Bahonsuai	0.00011	217	233	301	MSY44y	31-QDEA-a	bahonsuai		1.00	2	0....	6	3	2	0	0		...	b
4696	Bajau (Sea Gypsy, Laut)	0.03527	69,646	74,810	96,443	MSY44z	31-PHCA-a	moken		0.03	22	0....	3	4	2	0	1	Salong	P..	b
4697	Bakumpai	0.02596	51,262	55,063	70,986	MSY44y	31-LABD-a	bakumpai		1.00	551	0....	6	4	4	1	0		...	.
4698	Bakung Kenyah	0.00070	1,382	1,485	1,914	MSY44y	31-JCCJ	bakung-kenyah cluster		1.00	15	0....	6	4	4	0	1		PNB	.
4699	Balaesan	0.00270	5,332	5,727	7,383	MSY44y	31-QFAA-a	balaesan		0.05	3	0....	4	3	3	0	0		...	b
4700	Balantak	0.01331	26,283	28,231	36,395	MSY44y	31-QHCA-a	balantak		20.00	5,646	0....	9	5	6	2	1	Balantak	P..	b
4701	Balinese	1.98256	3,914,852	4,205,156	5,421,154	MSY44a	31-PKAA-a	bali		1.05	44,154	1....	6	4	8	5	3		pnb	b
4702	Banda (Eli-Elat)	0.00174	3,436	3,691	4,758	AON10e	32-DFAA-b	banda-eli		10.00	369	0....	8	4	5	2	0		...	b
4703	Banggai	0.05061	99,937	107,348	138,389	MSY44y	31-QIAA	banggai cluster		1.00	1,073	0....	6	3	6	0	1	Banggai	PN.	b
4704	Banjarese (Banjar Malay)	0.98292	1,940,918	2,084,846	2,687,717	MSY44k	31-PHAF-d	banjar		0.00	0	0....	0	3	2	0	0		...	b
4705	Bantik	0.00714	14,099	15,144	19,524	MSY44y	31-RBAB-a	bantik		30.00	4,543	0....	9	5	7	3	0		...	b
4706	Banyuwangi	0.22719	448,620	481,887	621,233	MSY44g	31-PIAA-i	osing		2.00	9,638	1cs.h	6	4	4	1	0		pnb	b
4707	Bapu	0.00104	2,054	2,206	2,844	AON10a	25-JDAA-a	bapu		65.00	1,434	0....	10	7	6	4	0		...	.
4708	Barakai (Workai)	0.00217	4,285	4,603	5,934	MSY44y	32-DEBA-a	barakai		15.00	690	0....	8	5	6	1	0		...	b
4709	Baras (Ende)	0.00014	276	297	383	MSY44p	31-QEFA-a	bara		1.00	3	0....	6	4	4	1	0		p..	b
4710	Baropasi (Barapasi)	0.00126	2,488	2,673	3,445	AON10a	25-JCCA-a	barapasi		50.00	1,336	0....	10	6	9	2	2	Barapasi	...	.
4711	Basap (Bulungan)	0.01103	21,780	23,395	30,161	MSY44y	31-PHAF-j	labu		35.00	8,188	0....	9	5	6	5	1		...	.
4712	Baso	0.00011	217	233	301	AON10a	25-JCCA	barapasi cluster		50.00	117	0....	10	6	5	2	0		...	.
4713	Bati	0.00194	3,831	4,115	5,305	AON09e	32-DFCB-a	bati		0.50	21	0....	5	3	2	0	0		...	.
4714	Batu	0.01077	21,267	22,844	29,450	MSY44y	31-PCAC-c	batu		65.00	14,849	0.s..	10	7	7	5	2	Batu	Pnb	b
4715	Bauri (Bauzi)	0.00080	1,580	1,697	2,188	AON10a	25-JAAB-a	bauzi		65.00	1,103	0....	10	7	4	5	3	Bauzi	P..	.
4716	Baweanese (Boyanese)	0.00300	5,924	6,363	8,203	MSY44h	31-PHJA-ab	bawean		1.00	64	1.s..	6	3	0	0	0		pnb	b
4717	Bedoanas	0.00018	355	382	492	MSY44y	33-ACAD-a	bedoanas		60.00	229	0....	10	6	7	2	0		...	.
4718	Behoa (Ako, Besoa)	0.00160	3,159	3,394	4,375	MSY44p	31-QEBC-a	besoa		45.00	1,527	0....	9	5	6	2	2	Besoa	p..	b
4719	Bekati (Land Dayak)	0.00232	4,581	4,921	6,344	MSY44y	31-KAAH-a	be-kati		20.00	984	0.s..	9	5	5	2	3	Bakatiq*	P..	.
4720	Beketan (Bakatan, Pakatan)	0.00027	533	573	738	MSY44y	31-IACC-a	bukitan		50.00	286	0....	10	6	7	2	0		...	.
4721	Belagar (Tereweng)	0.00714	14,099	15,144	19,524	MSY44y	20-AADA	blagar cluster		10.00	1,514	0....	8	5	6	1	0		...	.
4722	Bengkulunese Malay	0.03041	60,049	64,502	83,154	MSY44k	31-PHAD-u	bengkulu		0.03	19	0....	3	3	3	0	1		pn.	b
4723	Bengoi (Isal)	0.00019	375	403	520	MSY44y	32-DGDA-b	benggoi		12.00	48	0....	8	5	6	1	0		...	b
4724	Bentong	0.01452	28,672	30,798	39,704	MSY44y	31-QBAB-a	bentong		3.00	924	0....	6	4	6	0	0		...	b
4725	Benyadu (Land Dayak)	0.02900	57,265	61,511	79,298	MSY44y	31-KAAI-a	be-nyadu		20.00	12,302	0....	9	5	5	5	3		p..	.
4726	Berik	0.00061	1,205	1,294	1,668	AON10a	21-DAAA-e	berik		65.00	841	0....	10	7	6	3	1	Berik	PN.	b
4727	Betaf	0.00030	592	636	820	AON10a	21-DAAA	berik cluster		65.00	414	0....	10	6	9	0	0		PN.	b
4728	Biak-Numfor	0.02596	51,262	55,063	70,986	AON09e	33-ADBA	biak-numfor cluster		91.00	50,107	0.s..	10	8	11	4	1	Biak	PN.	.
4729	Biatah (Land Dayak)	0.00400	7,899	8,484	10,938	MSY44y	31-KAAE-a	bi-atah		12.00	1,018	0As..	8	5	7	4	2	Biatah	PN.	.
4730	Biksi	0.00014	276	297	383	AON10a	26-AAAA-a	biksi		65.00	193	0....	10	5	2	2	1		...	.
4731	Bimanese	0.27650	545,989	586,477	756,067	MSY44y	32-AAAA-b	bima		0.01	59	0....	3	4	4	2	1	Bima	...	b
4732	Bintauna	0.00389	7,681	8,251	10,637	MSY44y	31-QJAB-d	bintauna		1.00	83	0....	6	3	2	0	0		...	b
4733	Boano	0.00206	4,068	4,369	5,633	MSY44y	31-QGAE-e	bolano		40.00	1,748	0....	9	5	6	2	0		...	b
4734	Bobot (Atiahu)	0.00290	5,726	6,151	7,930	MSY44y	32-DGBA-a	bobot		30.00	1,845	0....	9	5	6	2	0		...	b
4735	Bolano	0.00128	2,528	2,715	3,500	MSY44y	31-QGAE-e	bolano		0.06	2	0....	4	3	3	0	0		...	b
4736	Bolongan	0.00785	15,501	16,650	21,465	MSY44x	31-IBAD-b	bulungan		70.00	11,655	0....	10	7	6	2	0		...	.
4737	Bonefa	0.00020	395	424	547	AON10a	25-JCDA-b	bonefa		65.00	276	0....	10	7	6	2	0		...	.
4738	Bonerate	0.00546	10,782	11,581	14,930	MSY44y	31-QAAA-a	bonerate		0.05	6	0....	4	3	3	0	0		...	b
4739	Bonerif	0.00007	138	148	191	AON10a	21-DCBA-a	bonerif		65.00	97	0....	10	7	6	2	0		...	p
4740	Bonfia (Masiwang)	0.00055	1,086	1,167	1,504	AON09e	32-DGAA-a	masiwang		91.00	1,062	0....	10	7	11	2	0		...	b
4741	Bonggo (Armopa, Bgu)	0.00032	632	679	875	AON09e	34-AAAB-a	bonggo		91.00	618	0....	10	7	12	4	1		...	.
4742	Borai	0.00058	1,145	1,230	1,586	AON10a	25-FAAB-a	borai		65.00	800	0....	10	6	6	2	0		...	.
4743	Bothar	0.00040	790	848	1,094	AON10a	20-LDAA-a	bothar		60.00	509	0....	10	6	6	2	0		...	.
4744	British	0.00300	5,924	6,363	8,203	CEW19i	52-ABAC-b	standard-english	12	79.00	5,027	3Bsuh	10	9	13	5	3		PNB	b
4745	Buginese (Bugis)	1.55995	3,080,347	3,308,769	4,265,560	MSY44c	31-QBBA	bugis cluster		1.00	33,088	2....	6	4	6	1	3	Bugis	PNB	b
4746	Bukar Sadong (Tebakang)	0.00400	7,899	8,484	10,938	MSY44y	31-KAAE-d	sadong		19.00	1,612	0cs..	8	5	7	2	0	Bukar Sadong	pn.	.
4747	Bukat	0.00026	513	551	711	MSY44z	31-JBDA-a	bukat		2.00	11	0....	6	4	4	1	0		...	.
4748	Bulanga-Uki	0.01299	25,651	27,553	35,520	MSY44y	31-QJAB-e	bolango-uki		4.00	1,102	0....	6	5	3	2	0		...	b
4749	Buli	0.00119	2,350	2,524	3,254	MSY44y	33-AABD-a	buli		30.00	757	0....	9	5	6	4	1		...	b
4750	Bunak (Mare)	0.03527	69,646	74,810	96,443	AON10e	20-DAAA-a	bunak		5.00	3,741	0....	7	2	0	0	2		...	.
4751	Bungku	0.01088	21,484	23,077	29,751	MSY44y	31-QDCF-a	bungku		0.01	2	0....	3	2	5	0	0		...	b
4752	Buol (Bual)	0.04147	81,889	87,961	113,396	MSY44y	31-QGBA-a	buol		0.02	18	0....	3	4	5	4	1		...	b
4753	Burate	0.00006	118	127	164	AON09e	25-JBBA-a	burate		10.00	13	0....	8	5	5	2	1		...	.
4754	Buruese (Masarete)	0.01824	36,018	38,688	49,876	MSY44y	32-EBBA-c	central buru		12.00	4,643	0....	8	5	6	2	1	Buru	P..	b
4755	Burusu	0.00389	7,681	8,251	10,637	MSY44y	31-IBAB-a	burusu		30.00	2,475	0....	9	5	6	4	2		...	.
4756	Busami	0.00036	711	764	984	MSY44y	33-ADCI-b	sasawa-2		15.00	115	0....	8	5	6	4	1		...	.
4757	Busang Kayan (Kajan)	0.00195	3,851	4,136	5,332	MSY44z	31-JBAG	busang-kayan cluster		9.00	372	0....	7	5	6	4	1		...	.
4758	Busoa	0.00027	533	573	738	MSY44y	31-QAHA-a	busoa		3.00	17	0....	6	4	3	2	0		...	b
4759	Butonese (Butung, Lajolo)	0.01628	32,147	34,531	44,516	MSY44y	31-QAEA-a	wolio		0.01	3	0....	3	3	2	0	0		...	b

Continued opposite

Table 8-2 continued

EVANGELIZATION								EVANGELISM			ADDITIONAL DESCRIPTIVE DATA
Ref 1	D 28	aC 29	CG% 30	r 31	E 32	U 33	W 34	e 35	R 36	T 37	Locations, civil divisions, literacy, religions, church history, denominations, dioceses, church growth, missions, agencies, ministries, movements 38
4638	0	6	2.52	0	21.05	78.95	A	0.03	458	2	In Andhra Pradesh, Madhya Pradesh. Gonds. Hindus 60%, animists 40%.
4639	0	0	4.29	1	26.10	73.90	A	1.04	556	4	Punjab, Haryana, Delhi, Rajasthan, Jammu, Kashmir. Also in Bangladesh, UK, Fiji, UAE, Singapore. Sikhs 47%, Hindus 50%, Muslims 1%. D=RCC,SA,IET.
4640	0	6	3.06	0	29.00	71.00	A	1.05	386	4	Indian Gypsies (Domari Romany), linked to Gypsies westward to Libya and Turkey. Arcot District, Tamil Nadu. Hindus 99%.
4641	0	5	0.00	0	7.00	93.00	A	0.00	0	1.02	Sikkim Gurkhas; also in Nepal. Agriculturalists, pastoralists. Buddhists 70%, Hindus 30%.
4642	1	6	3.60	1	32.13	67.87	A	0.15	392	3	AP, Tamil Nadu, Orissa. Hindus 90%, Muslims, Baha'is. D=Convention of Telugu Baptist Chs. M=ABCUSA,Bibles for India.
4643	2	6	5.84	1	59.00	41.00	B	32.30	318	5	In Karnataka, Coorg. Related to Malayalam. Hindus 85%. D=CSI,&c.
4644	1	6	5.24	0	31.37	68.63	A	1.56	545	4	Nomads in Andhra Pradesh, East Godavari. Related to Irula and Tamil. Hindus 95%. D=CSI. M=IEM.
4645	2	6	8.31	4	99.76	0.24	C	343.97	204	9	Northern Nagaland, Tuensang District. Animists 23%. D=CBCNEI(Nagaland Baptist Convention),NCRC. M=AIPF.
4646	0	6	0.00	0	19.01	80.99	A	0.00	241	1.08	Tibetan District, Zaskar Mountains, Kashmir. Also in Tibet. Bilingual in Leh (Ladakhi). Lamaist Buddhists 90%, some Muslims. M=YWAM, Central Asia Mission.
4647	5	6	7.94	0	99.70	0.30	C	311.71	199	9	Manipur, Nagaland, Assam, Barak Valley. Animists 28%. D=Zeme Presbyterian Ch,RCC,CBCNEI(Nagaland Baptist Convention),NCRC,CNI. M=ZBAM,WPM.
4648	1	6	7.55	4	99.80	0.20	C	391.28	177	9	In Manipur. Majority in Burma. Animists 20%, some Baha'is. D=Baptist Chs. M=PCW/WPM,BBC(Zomi Baptist Convention of Burma),BFI. R=FEBC.
4649	0	6	8.33		32.00	68.00	A	5.84	713	4	Germans(NAC), Rajbansi(M=ZBM), Japanese(UCCJ), Karens(BBC), Bene Israel, Juray, Khamyang, Mudu Koraga, Korlai Creole Portuguese, Pangi, Tukpa, &c.
Indonesia											
4650	1	5	4.68	0	98.00	2.00	C	232.50	159	8	Irian Jaya. Mainly in Papua New Guinea(PNG). Animists 35%. D=South Seas Evangelical Church. M=CMML.
4651	1	5	7.09	0	73.00	27.00	B	114.57	304	7	Nusa Tenggara. Central and western Alor in Lesser Sundas. Muslims 40%, animists 17%. D=GMIT.
4652	0	5	5.60	0	96.00	4.00	C	227.76	188	8	Irian Jaya. 20 villages, north coast of central Bird's Head. Animists 35%. M=SIL.
4653	0	5	4.43	0	18.01	81.99	A	0.00	803	1.05	Northeast Lamponger. South Sumatra. Muslims 100%(Shafi Sunnis). M=IRUP.
4654	0	5	3.59	4	35.01	64.99	A	0.01	347	2	Achinese. Aceh Province, north Sumatra. 100% zealous Muslims(strict Shafi Sunnis). M=Gereja Batak Karo Protestan(GBKP),HKBP,GKPI,GKJ,GM,GPK,FMB
4655	0	5	5.63	0	95.00	5.00	C	225.38	191	8	Irian Jaya. South coast along Digul river. Animists 35%. M=Zending Gereformeerde Kerken.
4656	1	6	6.09	0	37.00	63.00	A	13.50	514	5	Kalimantan. Land Dayak. Animists 90%. D=GKE. M=IBS-I.
4657	0	5	4.03	0	91.00	9.00	C	199.29	151	7	Irian Jaya. Lakes Plain area north of Idenburg/Rouffaer rivers juncture. Few bilinguals in Indonesian. Animists 40%. M=RBMU.
4658	0	5	3.64	0	93.00	7.00	C	220.64	137	8	Irian Jaya. Villages east of Mamberamo river near north coast. Animists 35%.
4659	0	6	2.22	0	19.01	80.99	A	0.00	442	1.06	Northern Sumatra. Northeast of Tapaktuan and around Kutacane. Muslims 100%(Sunnis).
4660	0	6	7.50	0	99.80	0.20	C	347.48	192	9	Central Maluku. 5 villages in Seram Barat District, 22 in Kairatu and Taniwel Districts, west Seram. Access by boat from Amban. Muslims 10% (older persons).
4661	0	5	3.27	0	69.00	31.00	B	100.74	164	7	Central Maluku. 4 villages near Masohi, southwest Seram. Nearly extinct. Access by boat. Muslims 60%(Sunnis).
4662	0	6	5.81	0	97.00	3.00	C	230.13	192	8	Irian Jaya. Majority in Papua New Guinea. Animists 35%. M=SIL,CMML.
4663	0	6	6.21	0	74.00	26.00	B	110.74	267	7	Wadapi-Laut. Irian Jaya. 10 villages on Ambai Island. Bilinguals in Indonesian. Muslims 50%. M=SIL.
4664	0	5	5.02	0	50.00	50.00	B	36.50	322	5	Maluku. Ambelau Island; a few on coast of Buru Island; 7 villages. Access by sea. Muslims 80%.
4665	0	6	3.77	0	99.91	0.09	C	411.86	105	10	Irian Jaya. 7 villages on Central Waigeo Island. Animists 9%.
4666	0	5	6.42	0	93.00	7.00	C	220.64	219	8	Irian Jaya. North coast of Bird's Head, west of Manokwari. Most are monolinguals. Animists 35%. M=SIL,TEAM.
4667	6	6	10.54	5	99.91	0.09	C	488.26	215	10	Ambonese Malay. Central Maluku. Ambon Island. Agriculturalists. Strongly Dutch Protestant. D=GPM(Moluccan Protestant Ch),GPIBB,KINGMI,SJA, AoG,CMA.
4668	0	5	8.13	0	92.00	8.00	C	201.48	267	8	Kalimantan. East central, southeast of Tunjung, around Jambu and Lamper. Animists 40%.
4669	0	6	7.00	0	74.00	26.00	B	121.54	296	7	Nusa Tenggara. Sumba Island, southwest coast, east of Wanukaka. Many animists 45%, some Muslims 10%.
4670	0	6	3.69	0	48.50	51.50	A	34.52	256	5	Central Sulawesi. Lamala Sub-District, 2 villages. Muslims 80%.
4671	1	6	6.97	0	85.00	15.00	B	155.12	257	7	Irian Jaya. Central highlands area northwest of Nalca. Animists 50%. D=GKI. M=NRC.
4672	4	3	3.78	0	61.00	39.00	B	33.39	208	5	Batta Angkola. North central Sumatra. Sipirok area. Muslims 85%(Shafi Sunnis; good relations with Christians). D=RCC(M-Medan,&c),HKBP,BNZ,GPI. M=RMS
4673	1	6	6.44	0	99.91	0.09	C	425.15	159	10	Irian Jaya. 4 villages in Miosnun and south coast of Yapen Island. Animists 9%. D=Gereja Keristen Injil.
4674	0	6	3.10	8	40.10	59.90	A	0.14	260	3	Traders, from a number of Islamic countries. Muslims 100%(Shafi Sunnis).
4675	0	5	6.77	0	75.00	25.00	B	123.18	280	7	South Sulawesi. Between Mandar and Kalumpang. Many Muslims, 55%. M=SIL.
4676	0	5	4.48	0	92.00	8.00	C	218.27	163	8	Irian Jaya. Southern Bird's Head. Close to Kampong Baru. Animists 35%.
4677	0	6	3.88	0	39.00	61.00	A	21.35	332	5	Irian Jaya. Northwest coast of Bomberai Peninsula. Animists 85%.
4678	0	5	2.51	0	68.00	32.00	B	99.28	141	6	Irian Jaya. 3 villages on north coast, West Bird's Head. Bilingual in Moi and Indonesian. Animists 60%.
4679	0	5	4.28	0	92.00	8.00	C	218.27	157	8	Irian Jaya. 8 villages on south Bomberai Peninsula. Animists 35%.
4680	0	5	4.56	0	34.00	66.00	A	9.92	436	4	Maluku. 3 villages on northwest Ambon Island. Lingua franca. Muslims 90%.
4681	0	6	4.49	0	93.00	7.00	C	217.24	162	8	Irian Jaya. Lakes Plain, 2 villages. Minority bilingual in Indonesian. Animists 36%. M=SIL,RBMU.
4682	0	4	5.10	0	31.00	69.00	A	7.92	511	4	Northern Sulawesi. North central coast around Attingola, near Gorontalo. Muslims 93% (Sunnis).
4683	0	5	3.12	0	89.00	11.00	C	194.91	127	7	Irian Jaya, Central Highlands, Seriwo river. Monolinguals. Animists 40%. M=SIL,UFM.
4684	0	5	4.34	0	83.00	17.00	B	166.62	176	7	Irian Jaya, village at mouth of Wapoga river. Bilingual in Ansus, minority in Indonesian. Animist 45%. M=UFM.
4685	0	5	3.70	0	91.00	9.00	C	212.57	142	8	Irian Jaya. Northeast near PNG border south of Jayapura. Animists 36%.
4686	1	5	7.54	0	99.65	0.35	C	239.62	232	8	Irian Jaya. South coast east of Bipim. 9 dialects.Minority bilingual in Indonesian. Animists 35%. Strong churches. D=GAK(Bible Ch). M=TEAM,ZGK.
4687	3	1	4.78	0	34.00	66.00	A	4.96	466	4	Central Bird's Head around Ayamaru Lakes, 40 villages. 50% speak Indonesian. Animists 95%. D=GKI/Indonesian Christian Ch,RCC,AoG. Church language.
4688	0	6	3.60	0	96.00	4.00	C	227.76	131	8	Irian Jaya. West of Mamberamo river. Minority bilingual in Indonesian. Animists 35%. M=RBMU.
4689	0	5	4.69	1	62.80	37.20	B	79.76	242	6	North Maluku. Bacan Island west of southern Halmahera. Agriculturalists, rural. Muslims 65%.
4690	0	6	4.16	0	25.00	75.00	A	0.91	549	3	West Java, Mount Kendeng. Dialect of Sunda. Animists 90%(strong), Hindu and Buddhist elements. M=YWAM-Indonesia.
4691	0	6	3.65	0	32.00	68.00	A	11.68	398	5	Irian Jaya, east of Mamberamo. Tropical forest. Hunter-gatherers. Animists 90%.
4692	0	5	4.58	0	91.00	9.00	C	215.89	168	8	Irian Jaya. West Bomberai Peninsula. Close to Iha. Animists 33%, some Muslims.
4693	0	6	3.86	0	32.00	68.00	A	11.68	374	5	Kalimantan. Northeast, north, and southeast of Busang. Animists 90%.
4694	0	6	3.07	0	37.00	63.00	A	13.50	290	5	Kalimantan. Northeast, on Sarawak border around Longkemuat, Iwan river. Animists 90%. M=BEM,REMP,EMBMC.
4695	0	6	0.70	0	21.00	79.00	A	0.76	202	3	Central Sulawesi. Bungku Tengah Subdistrict. One village. Muslims 95%.
4696	1	3	3.14	0	17.03	82.97	A	0.01	587	2	Sama. Throughout Indonesia's islands. Houses on stilts over water. Muslims 100%, lightly islamized. D=GPIBT-2.
4697	0	6	4.09	0	21.00	79.00	A	0.76	645	3	Kalimantan. Kapuas and Barito rivers, northeast of Kualakapuas. Related to Ngaju, Kahayan, Katingan. Animists 95%, some Muslims.
4698	0	6	2.75	0	31.00	69.00	A	1.13	318	4	Kalimantan. Northeast, near Sarawak border, Oga river. Also in Sarawak (Malaysia). Muslims 99%. M=BEM.
4699	0	3	1.10	0	16.05	83.95	A	0.02	333	2	Central Sulawesi. Balaesang Sub-District, 5 villages. Muslims 99%.
4700	0	5	6.54	0	51.00	49.00	B	37.23	397	5	East central Sulawesi: Luwuk, Balantak, Tinangkung, Lamola Sub-Districts, 49 villages. Animists 70%, Muslims 10%. M=SIL.
4701	3	3	4.99	2	46.05	53.95	A	1.76	347	4	Shaivite Hindus 80% (15,000 village temples, also ISKCON), syncretists 15%. D=GKPB(1975 intense persecution),RCC(D-Denpasar),GKI. M=CMA,SVD.
4702	0	5	3.67	0	36.00	64.00	A	13.14	355	5	South Maluku. West and northwestern side of Kei Besar Island, 2 villages. Muslims 90%.
4703	1	4	4.79	0	30.00	70.00	A	1.09	515	4	Islands east of Central Sulawesi. 7 Sub-Districts with 157 villages. Muslims 95%. D=GKLB. M=Indonesian Bible Society.
4704	0	5	0.00	0	13.00	87.00	A	0.00	0	1.04	Kalimantan. Banjarmasin, pockets on east coast. Some in Malaysia (Sabah). Strongly influenced by Javanese. Muslims 100%(strict Shafi Sunnis). R=FEBC.
4705	0	6	6.31	0	62.00	38.00	B	67.89	316	6	Sulawesi. Northern peninsula, northeast section, 3 villages. Animists 70%.
4706	0	6	7.11	1	37.00	63.00	A	2.70	589	4	East Java, east and northeast coast. Regional Javanese, related to East Javanese. Muslims 95%.
4707	0	5	5.09	0	94.00	6.00	C	223.01	178	8	Irian Jaya. North coast area along Mamberamo river. Animists 35%.
4708	0	6	4.33	0	42.00	58.00	A	22.99	338	5	South Maluku. Barakai Island, southeast Aru Islands, 5 villages. Muslims 50%, animists 35%.
4709	0	5	1.10	0	24.00	76.00	A	0.87	228	3	South Sulawesi. South Pasangkayu Sub-District in Mamuju District. Muslims 90%, animists.
4710	0	6	5.02	0	83.00	17.00	B	151.47	199	7	Irian Jaya. East side of Geelvink Bay. Minority bilingual in Indonesian. Animists 50%. M=UFM,SIL.
4711	3	6	6.94	0	69.00	31.00	B	88.14	309	6	West Kalimantan Province. Scattered throughout Bulungan, Sangkulirang, Kutai. Animists 65%. D=Reformed Protestant Ch,RCC,CMA. M=REMP.
4712	0	5	2.49	0	75.00	25.00	B	136.87	128	7	Irian Jaya, Lakes Plain area. Animists 50%.
4713	0	6	3.09	0	16.50	83.50	A	0.30	679	3	Eastern Seram Island. Related to Geser and Watubela. Muslims 92%.
4714	2	6	4.89	0	99.65	0.35	C	265.72	140	8	Sumatra. Batu Island. Dialect of Nias. Animists 35%. D=RCC(PA-Sibolga),BNKP. M=OFMCap,RM.
4715	0	3	4.82	0	95.00	5.00	C	225.38	168	8	Irian Jaya. 8 villages around Lake Holmes. Animists 35%. M=SIL,RBMU,UFM.
4716	0	5	3.11	1	27.00	73.00	A	0.98	402	3	On Bawean Island. Younger generation speaks in Bahasa Indonesian. Muslims 99% (strict Shafi Sunnis, with 2 Sufi brotherhoods; Naqshbandiyya, Qadiriyya).
4717	0	6	3.18	0	88.00	12.00	C	192.72	125	7	Irian Jaya. Northwest coast of Bomberai Peninsula. Animists 40%.
4718	2	5	5.16	0	79.00	21.00	B	129.75	210	7	Northwest portion of central Sulawesi. 29 villages. Animists 50%. D=GKST, Pentecostals.
4719	7	6	4.70	0	53.00	47.00	B	38.69	287	5	Kalimantan. Northwest near Sarawak Border, around Sambas and Selvas. Land Dayaks. Animists 60%, Muslims 20%. D=GKE,RCC(M-Pontianak),PPIK,ICFG.
4720	0	5	3.41	0	77.00	23.00	B	140.52	152	7	Kalimantan. Iwan river, on border; also in Sarawak (Malaysia). Dialects: Punan Ukit, Punan Busang. Animists 50%.
4721	0	5	5.15	0	34.00	66.00	A	12.41	484	5	Nusa Tenggara. Northeast Pantar, Lesser Sundas. Animists 90%.
4722	0	5	2.99	5	26.03	73.97	A	0.02	388	2	Sumatra. Small area around Bengkulu city. Muslims 100%(Shafi Sunnis). M=GEKISUS(occasional contacts). M=IRUP.
4723	0	5	3.95	0	38.00	62.00	A	16.64	346	5	Central Maluku. North coast, east Seram. Mostly animists 78%, a few Muslims 10%.
4724	0	5	4.63	0	26.00	74.00	A	2.84	578	4	South Sulawesi. Southeast corner of peninsula, 4 districts. Closest to Konjo. Muslims 97%.
4725	8	6	7.37	0	57.00	43.00	B	41.61	395	6	Kalimantan, near Sarawak border. Animists 60%, Muslims 20%. D=GKE,ICFG,RCC(M-Pontianak),PPIK,GBIS,GKPI,NTM,CMA. M=USPG,OFMCap,SMM,MSF.
4726	2	5	4.53	0	99.65	0.35	C	241.99	149	8	Irian Jaya. 12 villages in north coast area along Tor river. Bilinguals in Irianese Malay 60%. Animists 30%. D=GKI,CMA. M=SIL.
4727	0	0	3.79	0	90.00	10.00	C	213.52	146	8	Irian Jaya. North coast area east of Sarmi, Jayapura Kabutpaten, Pantai Timur Kecamatan. Animists 35%.
4728	2	6	4.71	0	99.91	0.09	C	448.40	116	10	Irian Jaya. Islands of Biak and Numfor. 30 dialects. D=GKI/Indonesian Christian Ch,RCC. M=IBS-I.
4729	0	5	2.84	4	56.00	44.00	B	24.52	181	5	Northwest Kalimantan. On border, mainly in Malaysia (Sarawak). Animists 86%. M=OMF,BEM.
4730	0	6	3.00	0	89.00	11.00	C	211.15	123	8	Irian Jaya. Headwaters of Upper Sepik. Also in PNG. Monolinguals. Animists 30%. M=UFM.
4731	2	3	4.16	0	21.01	78.99	A	0.00	653	1.07	Nusa Tenggara. East Sumbawa Island. Related to Sawu. Muslims 99%(Sunnis). D=Timorese Ch,CMA. M=IMF.
4732	0	6	4.52	0	21.00	79.00	A	0.76	701	3	Northeast Sulawesi. Around Bintauna. Mostly Muslims 99%(Sunnis).
4733	0	5	5.30	0	69.00	31.00	B	100.74	244	7	Central Maluku. On Boano Island west of Seram. Muslims 60%(on northern Boano), Christians in south.
4734	0	5	5.36	0	59.00	41.00	B	64.60	288	6	Central Maluku. On east Seram; coastal. Muslims 70%.
4735	0	7	0.70	0	20.06	79.94	A	0.04	212	2	Central Sulawesi. Montong Sub-District, Bolano village. Muslims 99%.
4736	0	5	7.32	0	98.00	2.00	C	250.39	224	8	Kalimantan. Northeast, around Tanjungselor, lower Kayan river. Animists 30%.
4737	0	5	3.37	0	91.00	9.00	C	215.89	132	8	Irian Jaya. East side of Geelvink Bay, inland and southeast of Baropasi. Animists 35%.
4738	0	3	1.81	0	16.05	83.95	A	0.02	454	2	South Sulawesi. Bonerate and Karompa Islands, also east end of Kalao Islands. Access by sea. Muslims 99%.
4739	0	3	4.68	0	90.00	10.00	C	213.52	173	8	Irian Jaya. North coast area east of Tor river. Bilingual in Berik. Animists 34%.
4740	0	5	4.78	0	99.91	0.09	C	418.50	126	10	Central Maluku, Seram Island. Almost all Christians.
4741	1	5	4.21	0	99.91	0.09	C	421.83	112	10	Irian Jaya, northeast coast east of Sarmi, west of Demta. D=CMA. M=IMF.
4742	0	5	4.48	0	91.00	9.00	C	215.89	165	8	Irian Jaya. East coast of Bird's Head, around Manokwari. Animists 35%.
4743	0	6	4.01	0	87.00	13.00	C	190.53	158	7	Irian Jaya. Also in Papua New Guinea. Animists 40%.
4744	4	10	1.53	8	99.79	0.21	C	446.94	47	10	Expatriates from UK, in education. D=Anglican Ch(D-Papua New Guinea),DGI-related bodies,JWs,&c.
4745	5	6	8.24	2	48.00	52.00	A	1.75	519	4	South Sulawesi. Muslims 95%(strict Shafi Sunnis,Sufis, forcibly islamized in 1611), 17,000 'Hindus' following Toanni religion. D=RCC,GKSS,GEPSULTRA,GPST.
4746	0	3	5.21	1	49.00	51.00	A	33.98	339	5	Kalimantan. On border; great majority in Sarawak (Malaysia). Land Dayaks. Animists 81%.
4747	0	5	2.43	0	21.00	79.00	A	1.53	384	4	Kalimantan. North central near Sarawak border, Kapuas river, southeast of Mendalam, 3 areas. Animists 98%.
4748	0	5	4.81	0	27.00	73.00	A	3.94	574	4	Northeastern Sulawesi. South coast around Molibagu. Related to Gorontalo. Muslims 96%.
4749	1	3	4.42	0	60.00	40.00	B	65.70	241	6	North Maluku, central Halmahera, east coast, 3 villages. Access by sea only. Coconut plantations. Muslims 70%. D=GMIH. M=IBS-I.
4750	2	8	6.10	0	28.00	72.00	A	5.11	695	4	Nusa Tenggara. Southeast interior Timor Island. Animists 95%. D=RCC,Protestant Chs.
4751	0	3	0.70	0	17.01	82.99	A	0.00	250	1.05	Central Sulawesi. 4 Sub-Districts, 93 villages; also in northern southeast Sulawesi. Muslims 99%.
4752	1	3	2.93	0	23.02	76.98	A	0.01	450	2	Central Sulawesi. 6 Sub-Districts, 68 villages. Similarity to Tolitoli. Muslims 99%. D=GBIBT-2(Protestant Ch of Indonesia in Buol-Tolitoli).
4753	0	6	2.60	0	35.00	65.00	A	12.77	282	5	Irian Jaya, Waropen Bawah near mouth of Wapoga river. Semi-nomadic. Majority are monolingual. Animists 90%. M=UFM.
4754	0	5	6.33	0	42.00	58.00	A	18.39	468	5	Central Maluku. South and southeast Buru Island. Also in Netherlands. Access by sea. Bilingual in Ambonese Malay, Indonesian. Animists 58%, Muslims 30%.
4755	2	6	5.67	0	63.00	37.00	B	68.98	284	6	Kalimantan. Northeast, around Sekatakbunyi, north of Sajau Basap language area. Animists 70%. D=RCC,CMA.
4756	1	6	2.47	0	44.00	56.00	A	24.09	207	5	Irian Jaya. North coast, Yapen Island. 3 dialects. Animists 85%. D=GKI.
4757	0	5	3.68	0	35.00	65.00	A	11.49	328	5	Kalimantan. On upper Mahakam, Oga, and Belayan rivers. Animists 90%. M=BEM.
4758	0	5	2.87	0	25.00	75.00	A	2.73	408	4	Southeast Sulawesi. Batauga District, southwest coast of Buton Island. 7 dialects. Muslims 97%.
4759	0	3	1.10	0	14.01	85.99	A	0.00	381	1.05	Southeast Sulawesi. Southern part of Buton Island. Lingua franca. Sailors. Muslims 99%.

Continued overleaf

Table 8-2 continued

PEOPLE		POPULATION				IDENTITY CODE		LANGUAGE		CHURCH		MINISTRY						SCRIPTURE		
Ref 1	Ethnic name 2	P% 3	In 1995 4	In 2000 5	In 2025 6	Race 7	Language 8	Autoglossonym 9	S 10	AC 11	Members 12	Jayuh 13-17	d 18	wa 19	xc 20	mc 21	mi 22	Biblioglossonym 23	Pub 24-26	ss 27
4760	Campalagian (Tasing)	0.01742	34,398	36,949	47,634	MSY44c	31-QBCA-a	campalagian		1.00	369	0....	6	3	2	0	0		...	b
4761	Casuarina Coast Asmat	0.00484	9,557	10,266	13,235	AON10a	24-KABG	casuarina-asmat cluster		80.00	8,213	0....	10	7	10	2	1	Asmat, Casuarina Coast	...	.
4762	Central Ambonese	0.00226	4,463	4,794	6,180	AON09e	32-DGFA-a	laha-serani		50.00	2,397	0....	10	6	7	2	1		...	b
4763	Central Asmat (Yas)	0.00554	10,940	11,751	15,149	AON10a	24-KABD	central asmat cluster		80.00	9,401	0....	10	7	10	5	3	Asmat, Central	PN.	.
4764	Central Marsela	0.00034	671	721	930	MSY44y	32-BCEE	south masela-babar cluster		80.00	577	0....	10	7	10	2	1		...	b
4765	Citak Asmat (Cicak)	0.00481	9,498	10,202	13,153	AON10a	24-KABF	citak-asmat cluster		55.00	5,611	0....	10	5	9	5	3	Citak	PN.	b
4766	Coastal Konjo (Kajang)	0.06657	131,452	141,200	182,030	MSY44y	31-QBAD	south konjo cluster		0.20	282	0....	5	4	6	0	1		...	b
4767	Coastal Saluan	0.05003	98,791	106,117	136,803	MSY44y	31-QHAA-b	loinang		50.00	53,059	0....	10	6	6	4	2		pn.	b
4768	Cocos Islander (Kukus)	0.00060	1,185	1,273	1,641	MSY44z	31-PHAL	malayu-kokos cluster		5.00	64	0a...	7	4	6	0	0		...	b
4769	Daa (Pekawa, Inde)	0.03720	73,457	78,904	101,720	MSY44p	31-QEFB-b	ledo		10.00	7,890	0....	8	5	6	4	2	Ledo*	P..	b
4770	Dabe	0.00010	197	212	273	AON10a	21-DEAA-a	dabe		65.00	138	0....	10	7	6	2	0		...	.
4771	Dabra	0.00007	138	148	191	AON10a	21-CAAB-a	dabra		64.00	95	0....	10	7	6	2	2		...	.
4772	Dai	0.00052	1,027	1,103	1,422	MSY44y	32-BCFA-a	dai		70.00	772	0....	10	6	6	5	1		...	b
4773	Dairi Batak	0.72088	1,423,482	1,529,040	1,971,190	MSY44b	31-PEAC-a	dairi		68.00	1,039,747	1.s..	10	6	11	5	2	Batak Dairi	PNB	.
4774	Dakka	0.00087	1,718	1,845	2,379	MSY44p	31-QBGA-b	dakka		5.00	92	0....	7	4	5	1	0		...	b
4775	Damal (Amung, Amuy)	0.01004	19,825	21,296	27,454	AON10a	24-DBAA	damal cluster		98.00	20,870	0....	10	8	12	4	1	Damal	PN.	.
4776	Dampal	0.00005	99	106	137	MSY44l	31-QGAD-a	dampal		10.00	11	0....	8	5	5	0	0		...	b
4777	Dampelas	0.00692	13,665	14,678	18,922	MSY44y	31-QGAE	dampelasa-tolitoli cluster		0.06	9	0....	4	3	2	0	0		...	b
4778	Dao	0.00013	257	276	355	AUG05	24-DAAA	ekari cluster		60.00	165	0....	10	6	9	0	0		PN.	b
4779	Davelor	0.00083	1,639	1,760	2,270	MSY44y	32-BCFB	dawera-daweloor cluster		70.00	1,232	0....	10	7	6	2	1		...	b
4780	Dem	0.00058	1,145	1,230	1,586	AON10a	24-EAAA-a	dem		65.00	800	0....	10	7	7	3	1		...	.
4781	Demisa	0.00026	513	551	711	AON09e	25-JBAA-b	vehicular demisa		60.00	331	0....	10	6	3	3	1		...	.
4782	Demta	0.00062	1,224	1,315	1,695	AON10a	24-GAAA-a	demta		65.00	855	0....	10	7	6	4	1		...	.
4783	Djongkang (Land Dayak)	0.03000	59,239	63,632	82,033	MSY44y	31-KAAL-a	djongkang		40.00	25,453	0....	9	5	6	5	2		...	.
4784	Dobel (Kobroor)	0.00354	6,990	7,509	9,680	MSY44y	32-DEBB	dobel cluster		70.00	5,256	0....	10	7	6	2	1	Dobel	P..	b
4785	Doda (Sarudu)	0.00217	4,285	4,603	5,934	MSY44p	31-QEDB-a	sarudu		10.00	460	0....	8	5	5	1	0		...	b
4786	Dondo	0.00799	15,777	16,947	21,848	MSY44y	31-QGAE-d	dondo		2.00	339	0....	6	4	5	1	0		...	b
4787	Dou (Edopi)	0.00050	987	1,061	1,367	AON10a	21-ACAA-a	edopi		65.00	689	0....	10	7	7	4	2	Edopi	...	.
4788	Dubu	0.00009	178	191	246	AON10a	21-SAAA-a	dubu		65.00	124	0....	10	7	7	2	1		...	.
4789	Duriankere	0.00006	118	127	164	AON10a	20-HAAA-a	duriankere		65.00	83	0....	10	7	5	2	0		...	.
4790	Dusner	0.00001	20	21	27	MSY44y	33-ADCB-a	dusner		35.00	7	0....	9	5	6	1	0		...	.
4791	Dusun Deyah	0.01298	25,631	27,532	35,493	MSY44y	31-LBAB-a	dusun deyah		30.00	8,259	0....	9	5	6	1	0		...	.
4792	Dusun Malang	0.00649	12,815	13,766	17,746	MSY44y	31-GBAL-b	monsok-dusun		35.00	4,818	0....	9	5	5	1	0	Dusun: Ranau*	PNB	b
4793	Dusun Witu	0.01623	32,048	34,425	44,380	MSY44y	31-GBAL-b	monsok-dusun		30.00	10,328	0....	9	5	6	1	0	Dusun: Ranau*	PNB	b
4794	Dutch	0.00600	11,848	12,726	16,407	CEW19h	52-ABCA-a	algemeen-nederlands	5	76.00	9,672	2Bsuh	10	9	8	5	0	Dutch	PNB	b
4795	Duvele (Duvre)	0.00044	869	933	1,203	AON10a	21-BADA	duvle cluster		65.00	607	0....	10	7	6	4	1	Duvle	...	p
4796	East Makianese	0.01248	24,644	26,471	34,126	MSY44y	33-AAAA-b	east makian		20.00	5,294	0....	9	5	6	4	2		...	b
4797	East Marsela	0.00034	671	721	930	MSY44y	32-BCEE-d	east masela		80.00	577	0....	10	6	9	2	0		...	b
4798	East Mori (Lower Mori)	0.00760	15,007	16,120	20,782	MSY44y	31-QDFC	mori-bawah cluster		40.00	6,448	0....	9	5	6	3	0		...	b
4799	East Sumbanese	0.11060	218,396	234,591	302,427	AON09e	32-AADA	sumba cluster		91.00	213,478	4.s..	10	9	7	5	1	Sumba	PNB	.
4800	East Toraja (Toala)	0.01872	36,965	39,707	51,188	MSY44p	31-QBEA-a	toala'		0.90	357	0....	5	4	2	4	1		...	b
4801	East Trangan	0.00220	4,344	4,666	6,016	MSY44y	32-DEAB-a	east tarangan		55.00	2,566	0....	10	6	6	1	0		...	b
4802	Eipomek	0.00174	3,436	3,691	4,758	AON10a	21-RACB-c	eipo-mek		65.00	2,399	0....	10	6	7	3	1		...	.
4803	Ekagi (Ekari, Kapauku)	0.06007	118,617	127,413	164,257	AUG05	24-DAAA-a	ekari		93.00	118,494	0....	10	7	11	4	1	Ekari	PN.	b
4804	Elpaputi	0.00020	395	424	547	MSY44y	32-DGOC-a	elpaputih		10.00	42	0....	8	5	6	1	0		...	b
4805	Embaloh (Mbaloh, Pari)	0.00533	10,525	11,305	14,574	MSY44y	31-PAAA-a	embaloh		11.00	1,244	0....	8	5	6	4	1	Embaloh*	...	.
4806	Emplawas	0.00014	276	297	383	MSY44y	32-BCEE-b	emplawas		60.00	178	0....	10	6	6	2	0		...	b
4807	Emumu	0.00064	1,264	1,357	1,750	AON10a	21-TABA-a	emumu		65.00	882	0....	10	7	6	1	0		...	.
4808	Ende Malay (Larantuka)	0.00700	13,823	14,848	19,141	MSY44k	31-PHAJ-a	malayu-larantuka		1.00	148	0....	6	4	5	1	0		...	b
4809	Endehnese (Ata Ja'o)	0.05649	111,548	119,819	154,467	AON09e	32-AAFA-d	ende		50.00	59,910	0....	10	7	6	4	1		...	.
4810	Engganese	0.00065	1,284	1,379	1,777	MSY44y	31-OAAA-a	enggano		75.00	1,034	0....	10	8	8	4	1		...	.
4811	Enim	0.03871	76,439	82,107	105,849	MSY44k	31-PHAD-g	enim		1.00	821	0....	6	3	2	0	0		pn.	b
4812	Enrekang	0.02663	52,585	56,484	72,818	MSY44y	31-QBDB-a	enrekang		0.10	56	0....	5	4	4	0	0		...	b
4813	Erokwanas	0.00018	355	382	492	MSY44y	33-ACAE-a	erokwanas		11.00	42	0....	8	5	6	1	0		...	.
4814	Eurasian (Euronesian)	0.10000	197,464	212,107	273,442	MPY53	31-PHAA-c	bahasa-indonesia		75.00	159,081	4Asuh	10	8	7	5	1	Indonesian	PNB	b
4815	Fayu	0.00021	415	445	574	AON10a	21-AAAA-a	fayu		65.00	290	0....	10	7	7	3	2	Fayu	...	.
4816	Foau	0.00017	336	361	465	AON10a	21-CABA-a	foau		65.00	234	0....	10	7	5	3	1		...	.
4817	Fordat (Fordate)	0.02530	49,959	53,663	69,181	AON09e	32-DDAB-b	north fordata		20.00	10,733	0....	9	7	6	2	1	Fordata	P..	b
4818	Foya	0.00002	39	42	55	AON10a	21-DBAA-a	mander		65.00	28	0....	10	7	6	2	0		...	p
4819	French	0.00200	3,949	4,242	5,469	CEW21b	51-AABI-d	general français	6	87.00	3,691	1B.uh	10	9	14	5	1	French	PNB	b
4820	Galela (Halmahera, Kadai)	0.04287	84,653	90,930	117,225	AON10c	25-AABA	galela cluster		28.00	25,461	0....	9	5	6	5	3	Galela	P..	b
4821	Galumpang (Makki)	0.00639	12,618	13,554	17,473	MSY44p	31-QBEE-a	kalumpang		70.00	9,488	0....	10	7	6	2	0		...	b
4822	Gamkonora	0.00086	1,698	1,824	2,352	AON10c	25-AADB-c	gamkonora		10.00	182	0....	8	5	5	1	0		...	b
4823	Gane	0.00185	3,653	3,924	5,059	MSY44y	33-AAAB-a	gane		0.18	7	0....	5	3	6	0	0		...	b
4824	Gayo (Gajo)	0.09954	196,556	211,132	272,184	MSY44b	31-PBAA	gayo cluster		0.01	21	0....	3	2	2	0	0		...	b
4825	Gebe (Umera)	0.00125	2,468	2,651	3,418	MSY44y	23-FABA-c	gebi		9.00	239	0....	7	5	3	1	0		...	b
4826	German	0.00200	3,949	4,242	5,469	CEW19m	52-ABCE-a	standard hoch-deutsch	2	88.00	3,733	2B.uh	10	9	13	5	3	German*	PNB	b
4827	Gesa (Geser-Goram)	0.02033	40,145	43,121	55,591	AON09e	32-DFCA-d	geser		8.00	3,450	0....	7	5	5	2	0		...	b
4828	Gilika	0.00046	908	976	1,258	AON10a	21-RAAB-a	gilika		60.00	585	0....	10	6	6	2	1		...	.
4829	Goliath (Oranje-Gebergte)	0.00215	4,245	4,560	5,879	AON10a	21-RACA-a	una		65.00	2,964	0....	10	7	8	4	1	Una	...	.
4830	Gorap	0.00052	1,027	1,103	1,422	MSY44k	31-PHAA-e	gorap		1.00	11	1csuh	6	4	2	1	0		pnb	b
4831	Gorontalese (Wau, Watia)	0.49769	982,761	1,055,637	1,360,894	MSY44y	31-QJAA-e	east gorontalo		1.40	14,779	1....	6	4	2	5	2	Gorontalo	PN.	b
4832	Grand Valley Dani (Morip)	0.02000	39,493	42,421	54,688	AON10a	24-FABC-g	hitigima		80.00	33,937	0....	10	6	11	5	3		pn.	.
4833	Gresi	0.00145	2,863	3,076	3,965	AON10a	21-JACA-a	gresi		20.00	615	0....	9	5	7	2	1		...	b
4834	Hahutan (Limera)	0.00076	1,501	1,612	2,078	MSY44y	32-BCDB-a	iliun		13.00	210	0....	8	5	6	1	0		...	b
4835	Han Chinese (Peranakan)	2.65000	5,232,809	5,620,846	7,246,216	MSY42a	31-PHBB-a	paranakan		44.00	2,473,172	0A...	9	6	8	5	3		...	b
4836	Han Chinese (Totok)	0.11453	226,156	242,927	313,173	MSY42a	79-AAAM-a	central yue	2	42.00	102,029	3A.uh	9	6	8	5	3	Chinese, Yue	PNB	b
4837	Han Chinese (Totok)	0.29270	577,979	620,838	800,365	MSY42a	79-AAAB-ba	kuo-yü	5	42.00	260,752	2Bsuh	9	6	8	5	3	Chinese: Kuoyu*	PNB	b
4838	Han Chinese (Totok)	0.10000	197,464	212,107	273,442	MSY42a	79-AAAP-c	east miao-chinese		43.00	91,206	0A...	9	6	8	5	3	Chinese: Swatow*	PNB	b
4839	Han Chinese (Totok)	0.40723	804,135	863,765	1,113,538	MSY42a	79-AAAG-a	literary hakka	1	40.00	345,506	1A...	9	6	9	5	1	Chinese: Hakka, Wukingfu*	PNB	b
4840	Han Chinese (Totok)	0.44541	879,527	944,748	1,217,939	MSY42a	79-AAAJ	min-nan cluster		40.00	377,899	2A..h	9	6	9	5	3	Chinese, Min Nan	PNB	b
4841	Han Chinese (Totok)	0.01273	25,137	27,001	34,809	MSY42a	79-AAAI-c	south min-dong		40.00	10,801	1A...	9	6	8	5	1		PNB	b
4842	Haruku	0.01007	19,885	21,359	27,536	AON09e	32-DGOH-a	hulaliu		4.00	854	0....	6	4	5	1	0		...	b
4843	Hattam (Tinam)	0.00834	16,469	17,690	22,805	AON10a	25-FAAA-a	hatam		65.00	11,498	0....	10	7	9	5	1	Hatam	PN.	b
4844	Havunese (Sawunese)	0.05426	107,144	115,089	148,370	AON09e	32-AADB	sawu cluster		9.00	10,358	1.s..	7	5	1	5	3	Sawunese*	P..	.
4845	Helong	0.00299	5,904	6,342	8,176	MSY44y	32-BBAA-a	helong		50.00	3,171	0....	10	6	6	4	1		...	.
4846	Highland Konjo	0.07989	157,754	169,453	218,453	MSY44y	31-QBAE-a	konjo-pegunungan		5.00	8,473	0....	7	5	6	3	1		...	b
4847	Hila-Seit	0.00591	11,670	12,536	16,160	AON09e	32-DGOP	seit-kaitetu cluster		50.00	6,268	0....	10	6	6	3	0		...	b
4848	Hindi	0.03300	65,163	69,995	90,236	CNN25g	59-AAFO-e	general hindi		0.50	350	3Asuh	5	4	4	1	0		pnb	b
4849	Hitu	0.00927	18,305	19,662	25,348	AON09e	32-DGOO-d	hitu		40.00	7,865	0....	9	5	5	3	0		...	b
4850	Horuru	0.00200	3,949	4,242	5,469	MSY44y	32-DGLC-a	horuru		7.00	297	0....	7	5	6	1	0		...	b
4851	Hoti	0.00001	20	21	27	MSY44y	32-DGDA-e	hoti		8.00	2	0....	7	5	6	1	0		...	b
4852	Huaulu	0.00017	336	361	465	MSY44y	32-DGGB-a	huaulu		2.00	7	0....	6	4	4	1	1	Huaulu	...	b
4853	Hulung	0.00001	20	21	27	MSY44y	32-DGLB-a	hulung		80.00	17	0....	10	7	10	2	0		...	b
4854	Hupla	0.00192	3,791	4,072	5,250	AON10a	24-FABD-a	hupla		65.00	2,647	0....	10	7	7	4	1	Hupla	PN.	.
4855	Ibu	0.00008	158	170	219	AON10c	25-AADB-a	proper ibu		27.50	47	0....	9	5	6	4	2		...	b
4856	Iha (Kapaur)	0.00319	6,299	6,766	8,723	AON10a	24-BBAA-b	kapaur		65.00	4,398	0....	10	7	6	2	0		...	.
4857	Iha (Latu)	0.00288	5,687	6,109	7,875	MSY44y	32-DGOE-b	iha-saparaua		6.00	367	0....	7	4	6	1	0		...	b
4858	Iliwaki (Talur)	0.00037	731	785	1,012	MSY44y	32-BCCH-b	ilwaki		10.00	78	0....	8	5	6	1	1		...	b
4859	Imroing	0.00025	494	530	684	MSY44y	32-BCED-a	imroing		60.00	318	0....	10	6	6	2	0		...	b
4860	Inanwatan (Suabo)	0.00092	1,817	1,951	2,516	AON10a	20-HBAA-a	inanwatan		65.00	1,268	0....	10	6	6	1	0		...	.
4861	Indonesian	1.82691	3,607,499	3,875,011	4,995,541	MSY44k	31-PHAA-c	bahasa-indonesia	75	12.00	465,001	4Asuh	8	5	8	5	3	Indonesian	PNB	b
4862	Interior Saluan	0.00101	1,994	2,142	2,762	MSY44y	31-QHAB-a	kahumamahon		50.00	1,071	0....	10	6	5	1	1	Saluan, Kahumamahon	...	b
4863	Irahutu (Irutu, Kasira)	0.00232	4,581	4,921	6,344	MSY44y	33-ADAA	irarutu cluster		61.00	3,002	0....	10	6	6	2	1	Irarutu	P..	.
4864	Iresim	0.00007	138	148	191	MSY44y	33-ADIA-a	iresim		25.00	37	0....	9	5	6	1	0		...	.
4865	Iria (Kamrau)	0.00081	1,599	1,718	2,215	AON10a	24-KAAB	iria cluster		65.00	1,117	0....	10	6	6	2	1		...	.
4866	Itik (Borto, Betef)	0.00007	138	148	191	AON10a	21-DFAA-a	itik-tor		65.00	97	0....	10	6	6	1	0		...	.
4867	Iwur (Iwoer)	0.00058	1,145	1,230	1,586	AON10a	24-KEAD-a	iwur		65.00	800	0....	10	6	6	1	0		...	.
4868	Jahalatane (Awaiya)	0.00043	849	912	1,176	MSY44y	32-DGJA	yalahatan-haruru cluster		6.00	55	0....	7	4	6	0	1	Yalahatan	...	b
4869	Jakarta Malay (Batavi)	1.40000	2,764,503	2,969,503	3,828,190	MSY44k	31-PHBC-a	bahasa-betawi		8.00	237,560	0A...	7	5	8	5	2		...	b
4870	Jambinese Malay (Batinese)	0.44239	873,563	938,342	1,209,681	MSY44k	31-PHHB-h	djamb		0.00	0	0....	0	3	1	1	1		...	b
4871	Jamden	0.01997	39,434	42,358	54,606	AON09e	32-DCAA	yamdena cluster		91.00	38,546	0....	10	7	11	5	1	Yamdena	...	b
4872	Japanese	0.00500	9,873	10,605	13,672	MSY45a	45-CAAA-a	koku-go		2.30	244	1B.uh	6	4	8	1	1	Japanese	PNB	b
4873	Javanese (Orang Jawa)	25.60355	50,557,920	54,307,020	70,010,890	MSY44g	31-PIAA-g	general jawa		12.85	6,978,452	2As.h	8	5	8	5	3	Javanese	PNB	b
4874	Javanese Indonesian	10.79483	21,315,956	22,896,632	29,517,612	MSY44g	31-PHAA-c	bahasa-indonesia		9.00	2,060,697	4Asuh	7	5	9	5	1	Indonesian	PNB	b
4875	Jewish	0.00008	158	170	219	CMT35	31-PHAA	bahasa-malayu cluster		0.72	1	4Asuh	5	4	2	1	0		PNB	b
4876	Joloano Sulu (Tausug)	0.00779	15,382	16,523	21,301	MSY44x	31-CKGQ-d	vehicular tau-sug		0.50	83	0.s..	5	4	3	1	1	Tausug	PN.	.
4877	Kabola (Pintumbang)	0.00649	12,815	13,766	17,746	AON10e	20-ABEA	kabola cluster		53.00	7,296	0....	10	6	6	2	0		...	.
4878	Kaburi	0.00035	691	742	957	AON10a	20-HDAB	arandai cluster		70.00	520	0....	10	7	8	0	0		...	.
4879	Kadai	0.00025	494	530	684	MSY44y	32-EDAA	kadai cluster		8.00	42	0....	7	5	6	2	0		...	b
4880	Kaeti (Mandobo)	0.00335	6,615	7,106	9,160	AON10a	24-KDCB-d	kambon		65.00	4,619	0....	10	7	9	2	1		...	.
4881	Kafoa	0.00065	1,284	1,379	1,777	AON10e	20-ABBA-a	kafoa		40.00	551	0....	9	5	5	1	0		...	.
4882	Kahaian (Kahajan)	0.02921	57,679	61,957	79,872	MSY44y	31-LABC-a	kahayan		30.00	18,587	0....	9	5	5	1	0		...	.
4883	Kaibubu	0.00031	612	658	848	MSY44y	32-DGOJ-a	kaibobo		80.00	526	0....	10	7	10	2	0		...	b

Continued opposite

Table 8-2 continued

EVANGELIZATION								EVANGELISM			ADDITIONAL DESCRIPTIVE DATA
Ref	D	aC	CG%	r	E	U	W	e	R	T	Locations, civil divisions, literacy, religions, church history, denominations, dioceses, church growth, missions, agencies, ministries, movements
1	28	29	30	31	32	33	34	35	36	37	38
4760	0	5	3.67	0	20.00	80.00	A	0.73	619	3	South Sulawesi. Majene Kabupaten, Polmas, south coast. Coastal plain. Merchants, fishermen, agriculturalists. Muslims 99%.
4761	2	6	6.94	0	99.80	0.20	C	335.80	189	9	Irian Jaya, Casuarina coast. Mostly monolinguals. Animists 20%. D=RCC,TEAM. M=BCFCI.
4762	1	7	5.63	0	85.00	15.00	B	155.12	214	7	Central Maluku. Laha village, et alia, south central coast of Ambon Island. Muslims 40%, animists 10%. D=RCC.
4763	2	1	7.09	0	99.80	0.20	C	347.48	186	9	Irian Jaya. Between Hellwig and Kampong rivers. Large minority bilingual in Indonesian. Animists 20%. D=60%RCC,GAK. M=Crosier Frs,MM,TEAM,BCFCI.
4764	1	5	4.14	0	99.80	0.20	C	335.80	119	9	South Maluku. Marsela and South Babar Islands. D=GPM.
4765	3	5	6.53	0	99.55	0.45	B	202.75	204	8	Irian Jaya. 19 villages on south coasts, west of upper Digul river. 89% bilingual in Indonesian. Animists 45%. D=GAK,DRC(Conservative),DRC(Liberal). M=TEAM.
4766	1	5	3.40	0	24.20	75.80	A	0.17	481	3	South Sulawesi. Southeast tip of peninsula. Resistant to modernity. Fishermen, boat-builders. Muslims 85%, animists 12%. D=GKSS. M=SIL.
4767	2	5	8.96	0	90.00	10.00	B	164.25	299	7	East central Sulawesi. In 9 Sub-Districts, 136 villages, in Luwuk Banggai. Muslims 30%, animists 20%. D=GKLB,NTM.
4768	0	9	4.25	5	42.00	58.00	A	7.66	311	4	Cocos Islands Malay. Mainly in Sabah (Malaysia). Muslims 85%(Shafi Sunnis, mixed with animistic practices).
4769	3	6	6.90	0	47.00	53.00	A	17.15	455	5	Central Sulawesi, with 5,000 Bunggu in South (Mamuju District, Pasangkayu Sub-District). Muslims 90%. D=SA,SDA,DRC. M=UBS,SIL.
4770	0	5	2.66	0	91.00	9.00	C	215.89	110	8	Irian Jaya. Upper Tor river area, north coast east of Sarmi, village of Dabe. Animists 35%.
4771	0	6	4.66	0	93.00	7.00	C	217.24	167	8	Irian Jaya. Lakes Plain, south side of middle Idenburg river. Minority are bilingual in Indonesian. Animists 33%. M=APCM,RBMU.
4772	1	5	4.44	0	99.70	0.30	C	265.72	139	8	Maluku. On Dai Island. Animists 30%. D=GPM.
4773	3	3	3.68	0	99.68	0.32	C	297.84	103	8	Northern Sumatra. Around Sidikalang. Muslims 25%(Shafi Sunnis), animists 5%. D=RCC(M-Medan,&c),HKBP,GPI. M=OFMCap,IBS-I.
4774	0	5	4.63	0	29.00	71.00	A	5.29	522	4	South Sulawesi. Polewali-Mamasa District, Wonomulyo Sub-District. Muslims 95%.
4775	0	5	7.94	0	99.98	0.02	C	497.20	176	10	Irian Jaya. Central highlands west of Western Dani. D=RCC,KINGMI. M=CMA.
4776	0	5	2.43	0	34.00	66.00	A	12.41	264	5	Central Sulawesi. Virtually extinct due to intermarriage. Animists 50%, Muslims 40% (Sunnis).
4777	0	4	2.22	0	16.06	83.94	A	0.03	524	2	Central Sulawesi. 2 Sub-Districts, 8 villages. Muslims 99%.
4778	0	0	2.84	0	85.00	15.00	C	186.15	124	7	Irian Jaya. West central highlands on Dao River. Animists 40%. D=RCC,KINGMI. M=CMA.
4779	1	5	4.93	0	99.70	0.30	C	260.61	155	8	Maluku. South, Dawera and Daweloor Islands. Animists 30%. D=GPM.
4780	1	6	4.48	0	96.00	4.00	C	227.76	156	8	Irian Jaya. Western highlands along upper Rouffaer river north of Damal. Majority monolinguals. Animists 30%. D=KINGMI. M=CMA.
4781	0	6	3.56	0	86.00	14.00	C	188.34	145	7	Irian Jaya. Several villages along coast, Waropen Bawah District. Monolinguals. Lingua franca of many nomads. Animists 40%. M=UFM.
4782	1	6	4.55	0	96.00	4.00	C	227.76	158	8	Irian Jaya. North coast west of Tanamerah Bay, 5 villages. Animists 35%. D=GKI-Tanah Merah Bay.
4783	8	6	8.16	0	76.00	24.00	B	110.96	325	7	Kalimantan. Kapuas river. Animists 40%, Muslims 20%. D=RCC(M-Pontianak),GKE,ICFG,GBIS,GKPI,PPIK,NTM,CMA. M=OFMCap,WEC.
4784	0	6	6.46	0	99.70	0.30	C	263.16	194	8	Maluku. Aru Islands: 20 villages on Koba Island, Wokam Island, et alia. Bilingual in Ambonese Malay. Muslims 30%. M=SIL.
4785	0	6	3.90	0	36.00	64.00	A	13.14	365	5	South Sulawesi, South Pasangkayu District. Fishermen. Muslims 90%.
4786	0	5	3.59	0	25.00	75.00	A	1.82	487	4	Central Sulawesi. Galang, Baolan, Dondo Sub-Districts, 18 villages. Related to Tolitoli, Tomini. Muslims 98%.
4787	1	5	4.32	0	97.00	3.00	C	230.13	150	8	Irian Jaya. Around juncture of Dow and Fou rivers. Majority are monolinguals. Animists 35%. D=KINGMI. M=SIL,CMA.
4788	1	6	2.55	0	95.00	5.00	C	225.38	102	8	Irian Jaya. Border area south of Jayapura, south of Waris, east of Emumu, north of Towei. 3 villages. Monolinguals. Animists 33%. D=KINGMI.
4789	0	6	4.52	0	91.00	9.00	C	215.89	166	8	Irian Jaya. Small island in Raja Ampat islands. Speakers all elderly. Animists 30%.
4790	0	9	1.96	0	63.00	37.00	B	80.48	122	6	Irian Jaya. Dusner town on west coast of Geelvink Bay, Wandaman Bay area. Nearly extinct. Animists 65%.
4791	0	6	6.95	0	56.00	44.00	B	61.32	382	6	Kalimantan. Southeast, Tabalong river northeast of Bongkang. Animists 70%.
4792	0	6	6.37	0	70.00	30.00	B	89.42	283	6	Kalimantan. East central, west of Muarainu. Closest to Maanyan, Paku. Animists 65%.
4793	0	6	7.19	0	67.00	33.00	B	73.36	329	6	Kalimantan. Southeast, regions of Pendang and Buntokecil. Closest to Maanyan, Paku. Animists 70%.
4794	0	10	-1.08	6	99.76	0.24	C	391.13	2	9	Descendants of early colonists. In government, commerce, professions.
4795	1	5	4.19	0	96.00	4.00	C	227.76	148	8	Irian Jaya. Lakes Plain area south of Van Daalen river. Most including children are monolinguals. Animists 35%. Trade language: Wano.D=ECP. M=UFM.
4796	1	5	6.47	0	54.00	46.00	B	39.42	371	5	North Maluku. Eastern Makian Island, Mori, Kayoa Islands, south Halmahera. Animists 60%, Muslims 20%. D=GMIH. M=UMS,MCC.
4797	0	5	4.14	0	99.80	0.20	C	327.04	122	9	South Maluku. 3 villages on Marsela Island. Mostly Christians.
4798	0	5	6.68	0	70.00	30.00	B	102.20	295	7	Central Sulawesi, Petasia and Lembo Subdistricts. 40 villages. Animists 40%, Muslims 20%.
4799	5	6	10.48	0	99.91	0.09	C	474.97	220	10	Nusa Tenggara. Sumba Island (Sandalwood Island). Animists 9%. D=GKS,RCC(D-Weetebula),KINGMI,GMIT,CMA. M=CSSR.
4800	2	8	3.64	0	28.90	71.10	A	0.94	430	3	South Sulawesi. Luwu District from Masamba to coast. Muslims 99%. D=GPIL,GT. M=BAEF. R=FEBC.
4801	0	5	5.70	0	84.00	16.00	B	168.63	214	7	South Maluku. East coast of Trangan Island, south Aru Islands, 13 villages. Muslims 45%.
4802	0	5	5.63	0	95.00	5.00	C	225.38	191	8	Irian Jaya. Eastern highlands area, Eipo river, east of Nalca. Monolinguals. Animists 35%. M=UFM.
4803	2	5	9.83	0	99.93	0.07	C	468.44	215	10	Irian Jaya. West central highlands, Paniai. 50% bilingual in Indonesian. D=RCC,KINGMI. M=CMA.
4804	0	5	3.81	0	36.00	64.00	A	13.14	355	5	Central Maluku. West Seram. Closest to Nusalaut, Amahai. Animists 70%, some Muslims 20%.
4805	2	5	4.94	0	41.00	59.00	A	16.46	387	5	Kalimantan. West central, near Sarawak border. Animists 89%. D=ECB,NTM. M=BEM.
4806	0	5	2.92	0	89.00	11.00	C	194.91	116	7	West Seram, central Maluku. Most also speak Ambonese Malay. Animists 40%.
4807	0	5	4.58	0	90.00	10.00	C	213.52	170	8	Irian Jaya. Border area south of Jayapura, 11 villages. Animists 35%.
4808	0	5	2.73	0	24.00	76.00	A	0.87	392	3	Nusa Tenggara. Flores, Pantar. Muslims 99%(Sunnis).
4809	1	5	9.09	0	82.00	18.00	B	149.65	337	7	Central Flores. Ata Jao, Ata Soge. Muslims 44%(Coastal),Catholics 50%(Mountain). D=RCC(M-Ende,D-Larantuka,D-Ruteng). M=SVD.
4810	1	6	1.94	0	99.75	0.25	C	298.38	70	8	Sumatra. Enggano Island. Animists 25%. D=KPB(Batak Ch). M=IRUP.
4811	0	6	4.51	1	25.00	75.00	A	0.91	571	3	Southern Sumatra, south of Muaraenim. Muslims 95%.
4812	0	5	4.11	0	20.10	79.90	A	0.07	676	2	South Sulawesi. Enrekang and Pinrang Districts. Foothills, plains. Agriculturalists. Muslims 99%.
4813	0	6	3.81	0	35.00	65.00	A	14.05	365	5	Irian Jaya. Northwest coast of Bomberai Peninsula, north of Baham. Animists 88%.
4814	1	10	2.65	7	99.75	0.25	C	394.20	66	9	Mixed-race or detribalized persons, throughout nation. D=RCC.
4815	0	5	3.42	0	95.00	5.00	C	225.38	127	8	Irian Jaya. West of juncture of Dow and Fou rivers. 4 nomadic groups. Most are monolingual. Animists 35%. M=SIL,CMA.
4816	0	6	3.20	0	93.00	7.00	C	220.64	124	8	Irian Jaya. Foa and Mudiay village, east Lakes Plain area. Monolinguals. Animists 31%. M=RBMU.
4817	2	4	7.23	0	53.00	47.00	B	38.69	425	5	Southeast Maluku. Northern Tanimbar Islands, 30 villages. Lingua franca. Muslims 80%. D=GPM,RCC. M=SIL.
4818	0	8	3.39	0	94.00	6.00	C	223.01	128	8	Irian Jaya. Upper Bu river, upper Tor river area. Foya is nearly extinct. People now speak Mander. Animists 35%.
4819	1	10	3.10	8	99.87	0.13	C	498.55	71	10	Expatriates from France, in business, professions, commerce, industry. D=RCC.
4820	1	5	3.41	0	66.00	34.00	B	67.45	183	6	North Maluku. Galela Bay. Bilinguals in Indonesian. Animists 52%, Muslims 20%. D=GMIH(Evangelical Christian Ch in Halmahera). M=SIL,UMS,MCC.
4821	0	6	3.97	0	99.70	0.30	C	258.05	132	8	South Sulawesi. Southeast Mamuju District, Kalumpang Sub-District. Mountains, river valleys. Agriculturalists. Animists 30%
4822	0	6	2.40	0	36.00	64.00	A	13.14	259	5	Maluku. North Halmahera, a few coastal villages. Muslims 90%.
4823	0	3	1.96	0	20.18	79.82	A	0.13	382	3	North Maluku. Halmahera Island, southern peninsula. Close to East Makian. Access by sea only. Muslims 99%.
4824	0	3	3.09	0	14.01	85.99	A	0.00	771	1.05	North Sumatra, Aceh Province, around Genteng town. Muslims 95%(Sunnis, with Sufi influence), animists 5%.
4825	0	4	3.22	0	30.00	70.00	A	9.85	372	4	North Maluku. 4 villages on islands between southern Halmahera and Waigeo Island. Muslims 90%.
4826	3	10	2.54	8	99.88	0.12	C	529.98	61	10	Expatriates from Germany, in education, business. D=RCC,NAC,JWs.
4827	0	6	6.02	0	35.00	65.00	A	10.22	550	5	Maluku. Eastern end of Seram, Seram Laut Islands. Muslims 92%.
4828	1	5	4.15	0	88.00	12.00	C	192.72	160	7	Irian Jaya. Eastern highlands near Yale-Kosarek. Animists 40%. D=GKI.
4829	1	5	5.86	0	98.00	2.00	C	232.50	192	8	Irian Jaya. Eastern highlands east of Korapun. Most are monolinguals. Animists 35%. D=Netherlands Reformed Congregations. M=SIL.
4830	0	5	2.43	1	31.00	69.00	A	1.13	277	4	North Maluku. North Halmahera, southern coast of inner Kao Bay from Dodinga and Morotai eastward, in 6 villages. Many Muslims 49%, Animists 50%.
4831	8	6	4.75	0	38.40	61.60	A	1.96	400	4	North Sulawesi Province. Moderate Muslims 98%(Sunnis, since 1520), Hindus, Buddhists. D=Protestant Bible Ch of Gorontalo,GMAHKT,RCC,GPDI,GPDS,STII.
4832	5	1	8.47	0	99.80	0.20	C	353.32	214	9	Irian Jaya, Central highlands, Baliem Grand Valley. Majority are monolinguals. Animists 20%. D=RCC,GKI,ECC,KINGMI,GGIK. M=ABMS,RBMU,UFM,APCM.
4833	0	5	4.21	0	50.00	50.00	B	36.50	286	5	Irian Jaya. West of Lake Sentani, southeast of Genyem, 6 villages. All bilingual in Indonesian. Many animists, 80%. M=UFM.
4834	0	5	3.09	0	39.00	61.00	A	18.50	277	5	South Maluku. Wetar Island north of Timor Island. Animists 60%, Muslims 27%.
4835	4	9	5.64	7	99.44	0.56	B	163.81	169	7	Indonesia-born Chinese. Mandarin elements. Control 75% of country's private assets and 17 of 25 biggest business groups. Folk- Religionists 30%, Buddhists 15%.
4836	13	10	6.32	8	99.42	0.58	B	176.29	166	7	China-born. Folk-religionists 45%, D=RCC,GK,GIA,GKT,GPPS,PPIK,GGIK,GKIJT,GKMI,GKIJB,GPI,GJJS,GKKB. M=OSC,OFM,SVD,SJ,OFMCap,SX,SCJ,SSCC.
4837	11	10	8.31	7	99.42	0.58	B	176.29	213	7	China-born. Folk-religionists 38%. D=RCC,GK,GKT,GIA,PPIK,GGIK,GKIJT,GKIJB,GKMI,GPI,GJJS. M=OCar,MSC,CM,CICM,OSC,OFM,SVD,SJ,FMB,&c.
4838	12	10	6.20	4	99.43	0.57	B	171.07	172	7	China-born. Folk-religionists 45%. D=RCC,GIA,GK,GKT,GPPS,PPIK,GGIK,GKIJT,GKIJB,GKMI,GPI,GJJS. M=OCar,MSC,CM,CICM,OSC,OFM,SVD,SJ,&c.
4839	8	9	9.38	7	99.40	0.60	B	156.22	257	7	China-born. Folk-religionists 45%. D=RCC(sizeable in 15 Dioceses),GK,GIA,GKT,PPIK,GGIK,GKIJT,GKIJB. M=APCM.
4840	6	9	7.72	6	99.40	0.60	B	160.60	208	7	Hokkien. China-born. Folk-relgionists 44%. D=RCC(M-Jakarta,&c),GK,GIA,GKT,PPIK,GKIJB. M=SVD,OFM,OSC.
4841	12	10	3.96	6	99.40	0.60	B	156.22	118	7	Xinghua. China-born. Folk-religionists 46%. D=RCC,GK,GIA,GKT,GPPS,PPIK,GKIJT,GKMI,GKP,GPI,GJJS,GKKB. M=APCM.
4842	0	5	4.55	0	27.00	73.00	A	3.94	563	4	Central Maluku. Haruku Island, Lease Islands. Muslims 95%.
4843	2	4	7.30	0	99.65	0.35	C	256.23	211	8	Irian Jaya, eastern Bird's Head, northeast of Manikion. Bilingual in Indonesian. Animists 35%. D=GAK(Christian Bible Ch),Ev Christian Ch. M=TEAM.
4844	4	5	0.95	0	41.00	59.00	A	13.46	130	5	Nusa Tenggara. Savu Islands. Animists 80%, Muslims 10%. D=GKS,GMIT,RCC,KINGMI. M=NCRMS(1881),CMA,IMF.
4845	1	9	5.93	0	85.00	15.00	B	155.12	219	7	Nusa Tenggara. Western tip of Timor Island, also villages in Semau. Heavy influence from Rotinese, Timorese. Animists 45%, some Muslims 5%. D=GMIT.
4846	1	5	6.97	0	35.00	65.00	A	6.38	612	4	South Sulawesi. Central mountain area, Sinjai, Bone, Gowa, Bulukumba Districts. Agriculturalists. Muslims 80%, some animists resistant to education. D=GKSS.
4847	0	6	6.65	0	82.00	18.00	B	149.65	256	7	Central Maluku. North coast of Ambon Island, 3 villages. Access by road. Muslims 50%.
4848	0	5	2.63	7	43.50	56.50	A	0.79	229	3	Traders, from India over several centuries. Hindus 95%.
4849	0	6	6.89	0	70.00	30.00	B	102.20	309	7	Central Maluku. Ambon Island, Hitu Peninsula, 4 villages. Access by road. Muslims 60%.
4850	0	4	3.45	0	31.00	69.00	A	7.92	380	4	Central Maluku. On Seram Island. Muslims 70%, animists 23%.
4851	0	5	0.70	0	33.00	67.00	A	9.63	129	4	Central Maluku. On east Seram Island. Only a few elderly speakers. Nearly extinct. Muslims 50%, Animists 42%.
4852	1	5	1.96	0	26.00	74.00	A	1.89	296	4	Central Maluku. East Seram, northwest of Manusela. Animists 98%. D=NTM.
4853	0	5	2.87	0	99.80	0.20	C	329.96	90	9	Central Maluku. West Seram, Hulung village. Related to North and South Wemale. Access by boat. Nearly extinct. Animists 20%.
4854	0	5	5.06	0	99.65	0.35	C	237.25	166	8	Irian Jaya. Central highlands area near east side of Baliem gorge. Monolinguals. Animists 35%. M=RBMU.
4855	1	8	3.93	0	63.50	36.50	B	63.73	213	6	North Maluku. Northern Halmahera, mouth of Ibu river, 2 villages. Animists 50%, Muslims 22%. D=GMIH. M=UMS,MCC.
4856	0	5	6.28	0	92.00	8.00	C	218.27	217	8	Irian Jaya. Bomberai Peninsula, around Fak Fak in west. Close to Baham. Animists 35%.
4857	0	5	3.67	0	31.00	69.00	A	6.78	400	4	Central Maluku. West Seram, 4 villages; originally from Saparua Island. Muslims 94%.
4858	1	5	4.45	0	38.00	62.00	A	13.87	382	5	South Maluku. Wetar Island north of Timor Island. Animists 90%. D=RCC.
4859	0	5	3.52	0	89.00	11.00	C	194.91	135	7	South Maluku, southwest Babar Island. Animists 40%.
4860	0	5	4.96	0	91.00	9.00	C	215.89	179	8	Irian Jaya. South Bird's Head along Maccluer Gulf, 15 villages. Close to Duriankere. Animists 35%.
4861	1	7	5.00	7	79.00	21.00	B	34.60	198	5	Mother-tongue speakers of national language(excluding 32 million others who call themselves Javanese, Sundanese, Madurese, or Malays), Muslims 75%(Shafi).
4862	1	5	4.78	0	80.00	20.00	B	146.00	193	7	East central Sulawesi. Muslims 30%, animists 20%. D=NTM.
4863	1	5	5.87	0	91.00	9.00	C	202.61	202	8	Irian Jaya. 44 villages in east Bomberai Peninsula southwest from Arguni Bay. Tropical forest. Fishermen. Animists 39%. D=RCC. M=SIL.
4864	0	6	3.68	0	50.00	50.00	B	45.62	248	6	Irian Jaya. South Geelvink Bay west of Nabire and around Yamur Lake. Animists 75%.
4865	0	5	4.83	0	93.00	7.00	C	220.64	172	8	Irian Jaya. Southeast Bomberai Peninsula around Kamrau Bay, 9 villages. Related to Asienara. Animists 35%. M=SIL.
4866	0	6	4.68	0	91.00	9.00	C	215.89	171	8	Irian Jaya. North coast east of Tor river, inland. Animists 35%.
4867	0	5	4.48	0	90.00	10.00	C	213.52	167	8	Irian Jaya. Border area in valley of Iwur river, Ok Iwur, to Ok Denom. Animists 35%.
4868	0	4	4.09	0	30.00	70.00	A	6.57	451	4	Central Maluku. 2 villages on west Seram. Animists 80%, Muslims 14%. M=SIL.
4869	3	6	5.89	5	57.00	43.00	B	16.64	317	5	Betawi Asli. Urbanites in capital city who now use Malay as first language; widespread also as trade language. Folk-religionists 50%, Muslims 40%(Shafi Sunnis).
4870	0	5	0.00	5	19.00	81.00	A	0.00	0	1.06	Central Sumatra. Strong Muslims 100%(Shafi Sunnis). M=GEKISUS(occasional contacts).
4871	2	5	8.61	0	99.91	0.09	C	441.76	198	10	Southeast Maluku. Eastern coast of Yamdena Island; 35 villages. Bilingual in Ambonese Malay. D=RCC(27 villages),Protestants(8 villages). M=SIL.
4872	0	10	3.25	7	58.30	41.70	B	4.89	188	4	Buddhists/New-Religionists 60%, especially Nichiren Shoshu(Soka Gakkai). M=FMB.
4873	9	6	5.60	5	78.85	21.15	B	36.98	224	5	Folk-religionists 40%(hinduized,Agami Jawi,Kejawen), Santri(Koranic)Muslims 36%(Shafi), Hindus/Buddhists 8%(ISKCON). D=GKJW,GKJ,SJA,PJA,GKJTU,GPI.
4874	1	6	13.02	7	74.00	26.00	B	24.30	514	5	Javanese who now speak Indonesian as mother tongue. New-Religionists 42%, Muslims 41%. D=GKJW. R=FEBC,VERITAS,AWR.
4875	0	10	0.00	7	51.72	48.28	B	1.35	37	4	Small community of practicing Jews in capital and beyond.
4876	0	5	4.52	0	23.50	76.50	A	0.42	606	3	Kalimantan (northeast coast), also in Sabah and Philippines. Sea dweller immigrants from Sulu. Muslims 100%(Shafi Sunnis). M=SIL.
4877	0	5	6.81	0	80.00	20.00	B	154.76	267	7	Nusa Tenggara. Northwestern Alor Island in Lesser Sundas. Muslims 30%, animists 17%.
4878	0	0	4.03	0	90.00	10.00	C	229.95	153	8	Irian Jaya. Southern Bird's Head. Animists 30%.
4879	0	5	3.81	0	34.00	66.00	A	9.92	376	4	North Maluku. Sula Islands, Taliabu and Mangole Islands, interior mountains. Forced resettlement. Animists 92%.
4880	0	5	6.33	0	96.00	4.00	C	227.76	209	8	Irian Jaya. Border area near Fly river, east side of Digul river. Also in PNG. Monolinguals. Animists 35%. M=ZGK.
4881	0	5	4.09	0	63.00	37.00	B	91.98	221	6	Nusa Tenggara. Alor Island, north of Aluben, between Abui and Kelong languages. Muslims 40%, animists 20%.
4882	0	5	7.82	0	55.00	45.00	B	60.22	432	6	Kalimantan. Kapuas and Kahayan rivers, south central. Related to Ngaju. Animists 70%.
4883	0	5	4.04	0	99.80	0.20	C	329.96	119	9	Central Maluku. West Seram, Piru Bay, Kairatu District, 8 villages. Nearly extinct. Access by boat.

Continued overleaf

Table 8-2 continued

PEOPLE		POPULATION				IDENTITY CODE		LANGUAGE		CHURCH		MINISTRY					SCRIPTURE		
Ref	Ethnic name	P%	In 1995	In 2000	In 2025	Race	Language	Autoglossonym	S	AC	Members	Jayuh	dwa	xcmc	mi	Biblioglossonym	Pub	ss
1	2	3	4	5	6	7	8	9	10	11	12	13-17	18 19	20 21 22		23	24-26	27
4884	Kaidipan (Bolang Itang)	0.01428	28,198	30,289	39,048	MSY44y	31-QJAB	kaidipang-atinggola cluster		7.00	2,120	0....	7 5	6 1 0				... b
4885	Kaimbulawa	0.00080	1,580	1,697	2,188	MSY44y	31-QAHC-a	kaimbulawa		0.50	8	0....	5 4	4 0 0				... b
4886	Kaiwai (Adi, Kowiai)	0.00037	731	785	1,012	AON09e	33-ACCA-a	koiwai		30.00	235	0....	9 6	6 2 1				... b
4887	Kajeli (Kayeli, Gaeli)	0.00044	869	933	1,203	MSY44z	31-EBAA-a	kayeli		9.00	84	0....	7 5	6 1 0				... b
4888	Kalabit	0.00030	592	636	820	MSY44z	31-HAAE	kelabit cluster		60.00	382	0....	10 6	6 4 1		Kelabit	P...	
4889	Kalabra	0.00155	3,061	3,288	4,238	AON10a	25-BDAA-a	kalabra		65.10	2,140	0....	10 6	6 2 0				
4890	Kalao	0.00029	573	615	793	MSY44i	31-QABA-a	kalastoa		1.00	6	0....	6 4	3 0 0				... b
4891	Kaledupa	0.00200	3,949	4,242	5,469	MSY44y	31-QAAC-a	kaledupa		4.00	170	0....	6 4	4 1 0				... b
4892	Kalisusu	0.01118	22,077	23,714	30,571	MSY44y	31-QDBB-a	kulisusu		1.00	237	0....	6 4	5 0 0				... b
4893	Kalitami	0.00087	1,718	1,845	2,379	AON10a	20-HDBA-a	kemberano		65.00	1,199	0....	10 6	5 2 0				
4894	Kamariang	0.00001	20	21	27	MSY44y	32-DGOI-a	kamarian		7.00	1	0....	7 5	6 1 0				
4895	Kamaru	0.00135	2,666	2,863	3,691	MSY44y	31-QAFA-a	kamaru		4.00	115	0....	6 4	4 1 0				
4896	Kamberataro (Dera, Dra)	0.00058	1,145	1,230	1,586	AON10a	21-UAAA	kamberataro cluster		65.00	800	0....	10 6	6 2 0				
4897	Kamoro (Kamora, Mimika)	0.00465	9,182	9,863	12,715	AON10a	24-KABA-d	central kamoro		65.00	6,411	0....	10 7	5 2				
4898	Kampung Baru (Aiso, Kais)	0.00036	711	764	984	AON10a	24-KDBB-a	kampung		70.00	535	0....	10 7	7 2 0				
4899	Kamtuk (Kemtuk)	0.00145	2,863	3,076	3,965	AON10a	21-JACB-a	kemtuik		15.00	461	0....	8 5	5 4 1		Kemtuik	P..	b
4900	Kangean	0.01000	19,746	21,211	27,344	MSY44h	31-PHJB-a	kangean		0.10	21	0....	5 3	3 0 0				
4901	Kaninjal Dayak	0.02033	40,145	43,121	55,591	MSY44y	31-PHAF-ci	keninjal		45.00	19,405	0....	10 5	5 2 1		Keninjal		
4902	Kanum	0.00027	533	573	738	AON10a	20-LCAA	kanum cluster		65.00	372	0....	10 6	6 2 0				
4903	Kapori (Kapauri)	0.00004	79	85	109	AON10a	21-MAAA-a	kapori		65.50	56	0....	10 6	6 2 0				
4904	Karas	0.00014	276	297	383	AON10a	24-BAAA-a	karas		65.00	193	0....	10 6	6 2 0		Batak: Karo*	....	
4905	Karo Batak	0.34846	688,085	739,109	952,836	MSY44b	31-PEAB-a	karo		60.00	443,466	4....	10 6	12 5 3		Batak: Karo*	PNB	b
4906	Karon Dori (Meon)	0.00290	5,726	6,151	7,930	AON10a	25-DAAA-a	mai-yach		65.00	3,998	0....	10 6	6 2 0				
4907	Kasuweri (Samalek)	0.00144	2,843	3,054	3,938	AON10a	20-HCAA-a	kasuweri		60.00	1,833	0....	10 7	6 3 0				
4908	Katingan Dayak	0.02920	57,660	61,935	79,845	MSY44y	31-LABA	katingan cluster		30.00	18,581	0....	9 5	6 2 0				
4909	Kau	0.00019	375	403	520	AON10c	25-AAEC-a	kao		28.00	113	0....	9 5	6 4 2				
4910	Kaugat (Atohwaim)	0.00058	1,145	1,230	1,586	AON10a	24-HAAA	atohwaim cluster		65.00	800	0....	10 6	6 4 1				
4911	Kaur	0.02765	54,599	58,648	75,607	MSY44k	21-NAAB-a	kaure		0.00	0	0....	0 3	1 0 2		Kaure	P..	b
4912	Kaure	0.00022	434	467	602	AON10a	21-NAAB-a	kaure		65.00	303	0....	9 5	5 2 3		Kaure	P..	b
4913	Kauwerawec	0.00023	454	488	629	AON10a	24-FBAE-a	kauwerawec		40.00	195	0....	9 5	5 2 0				
4914	Kavwol	0.00020	395	424	547	AON10a	24-KEBA-a	kauwol		65.00	276	0....	10 6	6 2 0				
4915	Kawe	0.00021	415	445	574	MSY44z	33-ABBB-a	kawe		15.00	67	0....	8 5	6 1 0				
4916	Kayan Mahakam	0.00076	1,501	1,612	2,078	MSY44z	31-JBAF-a	mahakam-kayan		1.00	16	0....	6 4	5 1 0				
4917	Kayan River Kayan	0.00130	2,567	2,757	3,555	MSY44y	31-JBAC-a	uma-lakan		1.50	41	0....	6 4	6 1 0				
4918	Kayan River Kenyah	0.00389	7,681	8,251	10,637	MSY44y	31-JCCF-c	long-bia		95.00	7,838	0.s..	10 7	11 5 3			pn.	
4919	Kaygir (Kayagar)	0.00521	10,288	11,051	14,246	AON10a	24-HABA-a	kaygir		21.00	2,321	0....	9 5	7 4 1				
4920	Kayu Agung	0.02488	49,129	52,772	68,032	MSY44k	31-PFBE-a	kota-agung		0.10	53	0....	5 3	4 0 0				... b
4921	Kayupulau	0.00040	790	848	1,094	AON09e	34-AABB-c	kayupulau		91.00	772	0....	10 7	11 2 0				... b
4922	Kedangese	0.02078	41,033	44,076	56,821	MSY44y	32-BABH-a	kedang		48.00	21,156	0....	9 5	6 4 1				
4923	Keder	0.00032	632	679	875	AON10a	21-DEBA-a	keder		65.10	442	0....	10 6	6 2 0				... b
4924	Kelimuri	0.00004	79	85	109	MSY44y	32-DFCA-c	kelimuri		8.00	7	0....	7 5	6 1 0				... b
4925	Keling (Sindan Kelingi)	0.02765	54,599	58,648	75,607	MSY44k	31-PHAD-f	sindang-kelingi		0.10	59	0....	5 3	4 0 0			pn.	b
4926	Kelinyau Kenyah	0.00078	1,540	1,654	2,133	MSY44y	31-JCCH	kelinyau-kenyah cluster		70.00	1,158	0.s..	10 7	7 4 1				
4927	Kelong (Panggar)	0.00649	12,815	13,766	17,746	AON10e	20-ABAA	kelon cluster		53.00	7,296	0....	10 6	6 2 0				
4928	Kemak	0.00300	5,924	6,363	8,203	MSY44y	32-BCCB-b	kemak		90.00	5,727	0....	10 7	11 2 0				
4929	Kembayan (Land Dayak)	0.02921	57,679	61,957	79,872	MSY44y	31-KAAJ-a	kembayan		40.00	24,783	0....	9 5	7 5 3				
4930	Kendayan Dayak	0.09737	192,271	206,529	266,251	MSY44y	31-PHAF-cb	kendayan-ambayang		45.00	92,938	0....	9 5	5 2 0				
4931	Keo	0.05390	106,433	114,326	147,385	MSY44y	32-AAFA-b	keo		70.00	80,028	0....	10 6	6 2 0				
4932	Kepoq	0.00500	9,873	10,605	13,672	MSY44y	32-AAEF-a	kepo		10.00	1,061	0....	8 5	4 1 0				... b
4933	Kerei (Karey)	0.00048	948	1,018	1,313	MSY44y	32-DEAA-a	karey		49.00	499	0....	9 6	6 1 0				... b
4934	Kerinchi (Mokomoko, Ulu)	0.16590	327,594	351,886	453,640	MSY44y	31-PHHA	lubu cluster		0.00	0	0....	0 2	1 0 1				... b
4935	Kimaghama	0.00174	3,436	3,691	4,758	AON10a	20-JBAA	kimaghama cluster		65.00	2,399	0....	10 6	6 2 0				... b
4936	Kioko	0.00053	1,047	1,124	1,449	MSY44y	31-QAHF-a	kioko		0.10	1	0....	5 2	1 0 0		Kirikiri		
4937	Kirira	0.00016	316	339	438	AON10a	21-AABA-a	kirikiri		65.00	221	0....	10 6	2 2 0		Kirikiri		
4938	Kisarese (Meher)	0.01012	19,983	21,465	27,672	AON09e	32-BCEA-a	meher		91.00	19,533	0....	10 7	11 2 1		Kisar	P..	b
4939	Koba	0.00026	513	551	711	MSY44y	32-DEBC-a	koba		40.00	221	0....	9 5	6 2 0				... b
4940	Kodeoha	0.00080	1,580	1,697	2,188	MSY44y	31-QDDC-a	kodeoha		1.00	17	0....	6 4	5 1 0				... b
4941	Kodi	0.02323	45,871	49,273	63,521	AON09e	32-AABA-a	kodi-bokol		9.00	4,435	0.s..	7 5	6 4 1		Kodi		
4942	Kofei	0.00006	118	127	164	AON10a	25-JCAA-a	kofei		65.00	83	0....	10 6	3 2 1				
4943	Kokoda (Samalek, Tarof)	0.00199	3,930	4,221	5,441	AON10a	20-HCAA-a	kasuweri		65.00	2,744	0....	10 6	6 2 1				
4944	Kola	0.00389	7,681	8,251	10,637	MSY44y	32-DECB-b	kola		17.00	1,403	0....	8 5	6 1 1		Kola		b
4945	Kolana-Wersin (Alorese)	0.02765	54,599	58,648	75,607	AON10e	20-CAAA-a	kolana		54.00	31,670	0....	10 6	6 5 1				
4946	Kombai	0.00215	4,245	4,560	5,879	AON10a	24-KDCA-a	wanggom		65.00	2,964	0....	10 6	8 4 1				
4947	Komering (Njo)	0.38709	764,365	821,046	1,058,467	MSY44k	31-PFBA-a	komering		0.02	164	2....	3 4	3 0 3		Komering		b
4948	Komfana	0.00015	296	318	410	MSY44y	32-DECB-a	kompane		10.00	32	0....	8 5	6 1 0				b
4949	Komodo	0.00033	652	700	902	MSY44y	32-AAAA-e	komodo		1.00	7	0....	6 4	3 0 0				
4950	Konda	0.00028	553	594	766	AON10a	20-IAAA-a	konda		65.00	386	0....	10 6	6 2 0				
4951	Koneraw	0.00021	415	445	574	AON10a	24-KCBA-a	koneraw		62.00	276	0....	10 6	6 2 0				
4952	Kopka	0.00014	276	297	383	AON10a	24-KCBA	koneraw cluster		60.00	178	0....	10 7	6 0 0				
4953	Korapun (Kimyal)	0.00398	7,859	8,442	10,883	AON10a	21-RABA-a	korupun		45.00	3,799	0....	9 5	8 4 1		Kimyal*	P..	b
4954	Koroni	0.00027	533	573	738	MSY44y	31-QDBC-a	koroni		1.00	6	0....	6 4	5 1 0				... b
4955	Korowai	0.00116	2,291	2,460	3,172	AON10a	24-KDBC-a	korowai		60.00	1,476	0....	10 6	4 4 2				
4956	Kosadle (Kosare)	0.00013	257	276	355	AON10a	21-NAAB-b	kosadle		66.00	182	0....	10 6	3 4 1			P..	
4957	Kota Bangun Malay	0.05195	102,583	110,190	142,053	AON10a	31-PHAF-g	kota-bangun		1.00	1,102	0....	6 4	4 0 0				
4958	Kotogut	0.00026	513	551	711	AON10a	24-KDBJ-a	kotogüt		60.00	331	0....	10 6	6 4 1				b
4959	Kubu (Orang Darat, Djambi)	0.00553	10,920	11,730	15,121	AUG05	31-PHHB	kubu cluster		2.00	235	0....	6 4	4 4 2				
4960	Kui-Kramang	0.00200	3,949	4,242	5,469	AON10e	20-ABCA-a	proper kui		54.00	2,291	0....	10 7	10 4 1		Kulawi*	P..	
4961	Kulawi (Moma)	0.00330	6,516	7,000	9,024	MSY44p	31-QEFB-a	moma		80.00	5,600	0....	0 2	0 0 0		Kulawi*	P..	b
4962	Kumberaha	0.00012	237	255	328	AON10a	24-KCBA	koneraw cluster		0.00	0	0....	10 7	10 4 1				
4963	Kupang	0.00400	7,899	8,484	10,938	MSY44y	31-PHAJ-b	basa-kupang		80.00	6,787	0....	10 7	10 4 1		Ketengban	P..	
4964	Kupel (Ketengban)	0.00498	9,834	10,563	13,617	AON10a	21-RBAB	ketengban cluster		65.00	6,866	0....	10 6	7 4 2		Ketengban		
4965	Kur	0.00150	2,962	3,182	4,102	AON09e	32-DDCA-a	kur		3.00	95	0....	6 4	4 1 0			pn.	
4966	Kurima	0.00300	5,924	6,363	8,203	AON10a	24-FABC-g	hitigima		25.00	1,591	0....	9 5	5 1 1				
4967	Kurudu	0.00113	2,231	2,397	3,090	MSY44y	33-ADDB	kurudu-kaipuri cluster		91.00	2,181	0....	10 7	11 4 1				
4968	Kuwani	0.00065	1,284	1,379	1,777	AON10a	25-BDCA-a	kuwani		50.00	689	0....	10 6	6 2 0				....
4969	Kwandang	0.00500	9,873	10,605	13,672	MSY44x	31-QJAA-a	kwandang		1.00	106	1....	6 4	0 1 0			pn.	b
4970	Kwansu	0.00025	494	530	684	AON10a	21-JABA	kwansu-bonggrang cluster		65.00	345	0....	10 6	6 2 0		Kwerba		
4971	Kwerba (Airmati, Koassa)	0.00124	2,449	2,630	3,391	AON10a	24-FBAF-a	proper kwerba		15.00	395	0....	8 5	8 3 2		Kwerba	P..	
4972	Kwerisa (Taogwe)	0.00002	39	42	55	AON10a	21-BACA-a	taogwe		60.00	25	0....	10 6	6 2 0				
4973	Kwesten	0.00116	2,291	2,460	3,172	AON10a	21-DDAA	kwesten cluster		65.00	1,599	0....	10 6	6 2 0				
4974	Lamboya	0.00974	19,233	20,659	26,633	AON09e	32-AACB-a	lamboya		45.00	9,297	0....	9 5	7 1 0				....
4975	Lamma	0.00581	11,473	12,323	15,887	MSY44y	20-AAAA	lamma cluster		8.00	986	0....	7 5	5 1 0				
4976	Lampungese (Lamponger)	0.97365	1,922,613	2,065,184	2,662,369	MSY44y	31-PFBC-a	lampung		0.00	0	0....	0 1	2 0 3		Lampung		b
4977	Lara (Land Dayak)	0.00390	7,701	8,272	10,664	MSY44y	31-KAAB-a	lara		10.00	827	0....	8 5	6 4 2				b
4978	Larike-Wakasihu	0.00729	14,395	15,463	19,934	MSY44y	32-DGOR	larike-wakasihu cluster		51.00	7,886	0....	10 6	6 4 0				b
4979	Lasalimu	0.00135	2,666	2,863	3,691	MSY44y	31-QADA-a	lasalimu		10.00	286	0....	8 5	5 1 0				b
4980	Latu	0.00139	2,745	2,948	3,801	AON09e	32-DGOD-a	latu		4.00	118	0....	6 4	1 1 0				b
4981	Laudje	0.02397	47,332	50,842	65,544	MSY44y	31-QGAB	lauje cluster		0.01	5	0....	3 3	3 4 1		Lauje		
4982	Lawangan Dayak	0.06494	128,233	137,743	177,573	MSY44y	31-LBBA	lawangan-taboyan cluster		30.00	41,323	0.s..	9 5	6 2 0				b
4983	Layolo (Barang-Barang)	0.00061	1,205	1,294	1,668	MSY44i	31-QABB-b	laiyolo		2.00	26	0....	6 4	4 1 0				b
4984	Leboni (Rampi)	0.00421	8,313	8,930	11,512	MSY44p	31-QEBA-a	leboni		85.00	7,590	0....	10 7	11 2 0		Leboni		b
4985	Ledo Kaili (Toraja, Palu)	0.15777	311,540	334,642	431,410	MSY44p	31-QEFB-b	ledo		55.00	184,053	0....	10 6	8 5 2		Ledo*	P..	b
4986	Legenyem	0.00015	296	318	410	MSY44y	33-ABBA	laganyan cluster		16.00	51	0....	8 5	6 2 0				
4987	Lemantang	0.08295	163,797	175,943	226,820	MSY44k	31-PHAD-b	lematang		0.10	176	0....	5 3	0 5 0			pn.	b
4988	Lembak (Orang Sindang)	0.02765	54,599	58,648	75,607	MSY44y	31-PHAD-t	lembak		0.00	0	0....	0 3	2 0 1			pn.	b
4989	Lemolang	0.00094	1,856	1,994	2,570	MSY44y	31-QCAA	lemolang cluster		5.00	100	0....	7 4	5 1 0				b
4990	Lengilu	0.00001	20	21	27	MSY44z	31-HAAB-a	lengilu		20.00	4	0....	5 3	4 1 0				....
4991	Lepki	0.00028	553	594	766	AON09e	34-AABB	yotafa cluster		65.00	386	0....	10 6	8 0 0				....
4992	Leti	0.00379	7,484	8,039	10,363	AON09e	32-BCEA-a	leti		90.00	7,235	0....	10 8	11 4 0			p..	b
4993	Liabuku	0.00053	1,047	1,124	1,449	MSY44y	31-QAHB-a	liabuku		0.30	3	0....	5 3	3 0 0				b
4994	Liambata (Lenkaitahe)	0.00003	59	64	82	MSY44y	32-DGCA-a	salas		50.00	32	0....	10 6	6 4 1		Liana-seti		b
4995	Liana (Seti, Teula)	0.00166	3,278	3,521	4,539	MSY44y	32-DGEA-a	liana		70.00	2,465	0....	10 7	6 2 0		Liana-seti		b
4996	Liliali	0.00001	20	21	27	MSY44y	32-EBAA-b	leliali		2.00	0	0....	6 4	4 1 0				b
4997	Limboto	0.00500	9,873	10,605	13,672	MSY44y	31-QJAA-d	limboto		0.05	5	1....	4 2	0 0 0				b
4998	Linduan	0.00109	2,152	2,312	2,981	MSY44y	31-QECA-a	lindu		55.00	1,272	0....	10 6	8 2 1				b
4999	Lintang	0.03871	76,439	82,107	105,849	MSY44k	31-PHAD-s	lintang		0.50	411	0....	5 3	1 1 0			pn.	b
5000	Lionese (Ata Lio)	0.08442	166,700	179,061	230,840	AON09e	32-AAFA-a	lio		80.00	143,249	0....	10 8	10 4 1				b
5001	Lisabata-Nuniali	0.00116	2,291	2,460	3,172	MSY44y	32-DGLD	lisabata-nuniali cluster		40.00	984	0....	9 5	6 2 0				b
5002	Lisela (North Buru, Rana)	0.00659	13,013	13,978	18,020	MSY44y	32-EBBB	lisela cluster		10.00	1,398	0....	8 5	6 1 0				b
5003	Lola	0.00042	829	891	1,148	MSY44y	32-DEBD-a	lola		6.00	53	0....	7 5	6 1 0				b
5004	Lolak	0.00100	1,975	2,121	2,734	MSY44l	31-QJBA-a	lolak		10.00	212	0....	5 8	1 0				... p
5005	Lolaki (Laki, Tolaki)	0.15124	298,645	320,791	413,554	MSY44y	31-QDDD	tolaki cluster		1.00	3,208	0....	6 4	6 1 0		Tolaki		
5006	Lonchong (Orang Laut)	0.00020	395	424	547	MSY44k	31-EACB	south sama cluster		2.00	8	1.s..	6 4	6 1 0			PN.	n
5007	Lorang	0.00016	316	339	438	MSY44y	32-DEAD-a	lorang		80.00	271	0....	10 7	10 2 0				... b

Continued opposite

Table 8-2 continued

EVANGELIZATION								EVANGELISM			ADDITIONAL DESCRIPTIVE DATA
Ref 1	D 28	aC 29	CG% 30	r 31	E 32	U 33	W 34	e 35	R 36	T 37	Locations, civil divisions, literacy, religions, church history, denominations, dioceses, church growth, missions, agencies, ministries, movements 38
4884	0	4	5.50	0	32.00	68.00	A	8.17	544	4	Northern Sulawesi. Northern coast on both sides of Bolang Itang. Muslims 70%, animists 23%.
4885	0	5	2.10	0	20.50	79.50	A	0.37	394	3	Southeast Sulawesi. Part of Siompu Island. Related to Muna. Muslims 99%.
4886	0	5	3.21	0	56.00	44.00	B	61.32	206	6	Irian Jaya. Bomberai Peninsula, southwest coast, 5 villages. Muslims 65%, some animists. M=SIL.
4887	0	5	4.53	0	34.00	66.00	A	11.16	434	5	Central Maluku. Northeast central coast of Buru Island, southern Namlea Bay. Heavy Ambonese Malay influence. Muslims 90%.
4888	1	5	3.71	0	91.00	9.00	C	199.29	127	7	Kalimantan. Mainly in Sarawak(Malaysia), in remote mountains on Baram river around Ramudu. Hunters. Animists 21%, Muslims 19%. D=Kelabit Ch(ECB).
4889	0	5	5.51	0	92.10	7.90	C	218.84	194	8	Irian Jaya. West Bird's Head, south of Madik language area, east of Moi. Closest to Tehit. Animists 33%.
4890	0	5	1.81	0	21.00	79.00	A	0.76	354	3	South Sulawesi. Eastern Kalao Island south of Selayar Island. Access by sea. Muslims 99%.
4891	0	5	2.87	0	26.00	74.00	A	3.79	392	4	Southeast Sulawesi. Related to Ciacia, Masiri. Mostly Muslims(Sunnis) 96%.
4892	0	5	3.22	0	23.00	77.00	A	0.84	485	3	Southeast Sulawesi, Kulisusu and Bonegunu Subdistricts. Muslims 95%.
4893	0	5	4.90	0	91.00	9.00	C	215.89	178	8	Irian Jaya. Southern Bird's Head along coast; northwest Bomberai Peninsula. Animists 35%.
4894	0	5	0.00	0	32.00	68.00	A	8.17	73	4	Central Maluku. West Seram Island. Under 10 speakers left in 1987; almost extinct. Muslims 70%, Animists 23%.
4895	0	5	2.47	0	26.00	74.00	A	3.79	350	4	Southeast Sulawesi. Southeastern Buton Island. Muslims 96%.
4896	0	5	4.48	0	91.00	9.00	C	215.89	165	8	Irian Jaya. Northeast, south of Jayapura, near Waris, 13 villages. Also in PNG. Animists 35%.
4897	3	5	6.68	0	99.65	0.35	C	246.74	202	8	Irian Jaya. South coast from Etna Bay to Mukamuga river. 6 dialects. Many bilinguals in Indonesian. Animists 35%. D=RCC,Gereja Al Kitab(Bible Ch),GKI.
4898	0	6	4.06	0	98.00	2.00	C	250.39	141	8	Irian Jaya. South Bird's Head area inland along Kais river, 8 villages. Animists 30%.
4899	1	5	3.91	0	46.00	54.00	A	25.18	292	5	Irian Jaya. West of Lake Sentani, 7 villages. Bilingual in Indonesian. Many animists, 85%. D=GKI. M=SIL.
4900	0	5	3.09	0	19.10	80.90	A	0.07	565	2	Eastern Madura area. Close to Madura language. Muslims 99%(Sunnis).
4901	1	5	7.86	0	73.00	27.00	B	119.90	327	7	Kalimantan. West central, Sayan and Melawi rivers, around Nangapinoh. Animists 55%. D=GKE. M=IBS-I.
4902	0	6	3.68	0	92.00	8.00	C	218.27	139	8	Irian Jaya. South coast border area, east of Merauke. Also in PNG. Animists 35%.
4903	0	8	4.11	0	94.50	5.50	C	225.92	148	8	Irian Jaya. Village of Pagai on north bank, upper Idenburg river. Animists 34%.
4904	0	6	3.00	0	92.00	8.00	C	218.27	119	8	Irian Jaya. Karas Island. Animists(traditional religionists) 35%.
4905	7	3	5.96	0	99.60	0.40	C	258.42	158	8	North Sumatra. Strong animists 5%, also Muslims 30%(Shafi Sunnis). 1966, mass conversions to churches. D=GBKP,GMI,GPI,RCC(M-Medan,&c),HKI,SJA,AoG.
4906	0	5	6.17	0	92.00	8.00	C	218.27	214	8	Irian Jaya. Central Bird's Head north of Brat, 4 villages. Closely related to Brat. Animists 35%.
4907	0	5	5.35	0	88.00	12.00	C	192.72	198	7	Irian Jaya. Bird's Head, south coast. Animists 40%.
4908	0	5	7.82	0	57.00	43.00	B	62.41	417	6	Kalimantan. Katingan river, south central. Related to Ngaju, Kahayan. Animists 70%.
4909	1	5	2.45	0	61.00	39.00	B	62.34	155	6	North Maluku. Interior of north Halmahera, Kao town and river. Animists 52%, Muslims 20%. D=GMIH. M=UMS,MCC.
4910	0	5	4.48	0	97.00	3.00	C	230.13	155	8	Irian Jaya. South coast on Cook and Kronkel rivers. Bilinguals in Indonesian 50%. Animists 34%. M=RBMU.
4911	0	3	0.00	0	13.00	87.00	A	0.00	0	1.05	Southern Sumatra. Related to Malay. Farmers. Batak traders present. Animistic Muslims 100%(Sunnis). M=GEKISIA,WEC.
4912	0	5	3.47	0	94.00	6.00	C	223.01	130	8	Irian Jaya. Southwest of Lake Sentani along Nawa river, 10 villages. Monolingual. Animists 35%. M=RBMU,UFM,SIL.
4913	0	5	3.01	0	64.00	36.00	B	93.44	172	6	Irian Jaya. East of mid Mamberamo. Tropical forest. Hunter-gatherers. Animists 60%.
4914	0	5	3.37	0	91.00	9.00	C	215.89	132	8	Irian Jaya. Upper Kauwol Valley, both sides of border with PNG. Closely related to Faiwol. Animists 35%.
4915	0	6	4.29	0	39.00	61.00	A	21.35	361	5	Irian Jaya. West end of Waigeo Island, 4 villages. Animists 85%.
4916	0	5	2.81	0	21.00	79.00	A	0.76	433	3	Kalimantan. North central, Mahakam river, 2 areas. Mixture of Kayan and Ot Danum (Dohoi). Animists 99%.
4917	0	5	3.78	0	22.50	77.50	A	1.23	522	4	Kalimantan. Northeast, Kayan river, 2 areas. Animists 98%.
4918	0	6	6.89	0	99.95	0.05	C	478.51	154	10	Kalimantan. Northeast, Apo Kayan highlands, and around Longbia. A few in Sarawak(Malaysia). M=BEM,REMP,EMBMC.
4919	1	1	5.60	0	48.00	52.00	A	36.79	377	5	Irian Jaya. South coast in Merauke area. 10% literates in Indonesian. Animists 79%. D=RCC. M=RBMU.
4920	0	4	4.05	0	19.10	80.90	A	0.07	681	2	Southern Sumatra, around Kayuagung. Muslims 99%.
4921	0	5	4.44	0	99.91	0.09	C	405.22	122	10	Irian Jaya. Island villages in Jayapura harbor: Kayubatu, Kayupulau. Almost all Christians.
4922	1	4	7.96	0	77.00	23.00	B	134.90	313	7	Northeast Lomblen Island. Animists 27%, Muslims 25%(Sunnis). Y=1922. D=100% RCC. M=SVD.
4923	0	5	3.86	0	91.10	8.90	C	216.46	146	8	Irian Jaya. North coast east of Tor river mouth. Animists 35%.
4924	0	4	1.96	0	32.00	68.00	A	9.34	241	4	Central Maluku. East Seram, Kelimuri village. Muslims 70%, animists 22%.
4925	0	5	4.16	1	25.10	74.90	A	0.09	531	2	Southern Sumatra, around Muaraklingi. Muslims 95%.
4926	0	7	4.87	0	99.70	0.30	C	265.72	151	8	Kalimantan. Northeast, Kinjau river, around Long Laes, Telen river. Animists 30%. M=BEM.
4927	0	5	6.81	0	80.00	20.00	B	154.76	267	7	Nusa Tenggara. Southwestern tip of Alor Island in Lesser Sundas. Muslims 30%, animists 16%.
4928	0	8	6.56	0	99.90	0.10	C	410.62	162	10	Nusa Tenggara. Timor Island, north central. Closely related to Tetum, Mambai, Timorese.
4929	8	3	3.13	4	79.00	21.00	B	115.34	138	7	Northwest Kalimantan. Animists 40%(Kaharingan), Muslims 20%. D=GKE,ICFG,RCC(M-Pontianak),PPIK,GBIS,GKPI,CMA,NTM. M=USPG,OFMCap,CP,SMM.
4930	0	5	9.57	0	71.00	29.00	B	116.61	402	7	Kalimantan. Barat. Northeast of Bengkayang, also jungle areas. Few bilinguals in Indonesian. Animists 55%.
4931	0	5	9.40	0	98.00	2.00	C	250.39	287	8	South central Flores, east of Ngada. Muslims 15%, animists 15%.
4932	0	5	4.77	0	32.00	68.00	A	11.68	481	5	Central Flores, between Manggarai and Rembong. Muslims 50%, animists 40%.
4933	0	5	3.99	0	76.00	24.00	B	135.92	174	7	South Maluku. Village of Karey, east coast of Trangan Island, southern Aru Islands. Muslims 50%.
4934	0	3	0.00	0	11.00	89.00	A	0.00	0	1.04	Sumatra. Western mountains. Muslims 100%(Shafi Sunnis). M=IMF.
4935	0	5	5.63	0	92.00	8.00	C	218.27	197	8	Irian Jaya. Frederik Hendrik Island off southwest. Animists 35%.
4936	0	3	0.00	0	15.10	84.90	A	0.05	154	2	Southeast Sulawesi. Kulisusu and Mowewe Districts. Related to Muna. Muslims 99%.
4937	0	5	3.14	0	94.00	6.00	C	223.01	121	8	Irian Jaya. West of juncture of Dou and Fou rivers. Majority are monolinguals. Animists 35%. M=SIL,CMA.
4938	0	5	7.87	0	99.91	0.09	C	428.47	188	10	South Maluku. Kisar Island east of Timor Island, 22 villages; several hundred in Ambon city. Lingua franca(used by Oirata). M=SIL.
4939	0	5	3.14	0	68.00	32.00	B	99.28	161	6	Southeast Maluku. Aru Island. Close to Dobel language. Muslims 50%, animists 10%.
4940	0	5	2.87	0	24.00	76.00	A	0.87	425	3	Southeast Sulawesi, Kolaka District. Second language Bugis. Muslims 95%.
4941	1	5	6.28	0	38.00	62.00	A	12.48	525	5	Nusa Tenggara. West Sumba, Lesser Sundas. Animists 91%. D=Gereja Kristen Sumba.
4942	0	5	4.52	0	89.00	11.00	C	211.15	170	8	Irian Jaya. East side of Geelvink Bay. One village, also nomads in interior. Monolinguals. Animists 35%. M=UFM.
4943	0	5	5.78	0	93.00	7.00	C	220.64	200	8	Irian Jaya. South coast of Bird's Head along Bintuni Bay. Animists 30%. M=SIL.
4944	0	5	5.07	0	45.00	55.00	A	27.92	360	5	South Maluku. North Aru Islands, around coast of Kola Island and adjacent islands; 22 villages. Muslims 80%. M=SIL.
4945	3	5	8.39	0	89.00	11.00	B	175.41	289	7	Nusa Tenggara. Alor Island, east and southeast coasts. Close to Kelong. Coastal. Muslims 35%, animists 11%. D=Gereja Keristen Indonesia Timor,GMIT,KINGMI.
4946	1	5	5.86	0	98.00	2.00	C	232.50	192	8	Irian Jaya. South coast area east of Senggo around Boma. Mostly monolinguals. Animists 35%. D=ZGK(Zending Gereformeerde Kerken).
4947	0	4	2.84	0	21.02	78.98	A	0.01	461	2	South Sumatra. Muslims 100%(Shafi Sunnis). M=GKJP,Christian Ch of Java,RCC, Bible School Tanjung Enim,IMF,WECAoG(Australia),YWAM. R=FEBC.
4948	0	5	3.53	0	36.00	64.00	A	13.14	333	5	South Maluku. Northeast Aru in Kompane village, east coast of Kongan Island. Close to Kola. Muslims 90%.
4949	0	3	1.96	0	16.00	84.00	A	0.58	481	3	Nusa Tenggara. Komodo Island, between Sumbawa and Flores. Home of Komodo dragons. One village. Muslims 99%.
4950	0	5	3.72	0	91.00	9.00	C	215.89	142	8	Irian Jaya. Southwest Bird's Head along lower Waromge river. Animists 35%.
4951	0	6	3.37	0	89.00	11.00	C	201.40	135	8	Irian Jaya. South coast of Frederik Hendrik Island. Animists 38%.
4952	0	0	2.92	0	80.00	20.00	C	175.20	134	7	Irian Jaya. Lowlands area south of the main ranges. Animists 40%.
4953	0	1	6.12	0	73.00	27.00	B	119.90	267	7	Irian Jaya. Eastern highlands on upper reaches of Erok river. Monolinguals. Animists 55%. M=RBMU.
4954	0	5	1.81	0	24.00	76.00	A	0.87	304	3	Central Sulawesi, Bungku Tengah Subdistrict. Muslims 95%.
4955	2	5	5.12	0	91.00	9.00	C	199.29	184	7	Irian Jaya. South coast area, north of Boma, east of Senggo. Mostly monolinguals. Animists 40%. D=Zending,Gereformeerde Kerken.
4956	0	5	2.94	0	93.00	7.00	C	224.03	116	8	Irian Jaya. At Hulu Atas west of juncture of Nawa and Idenburg rivers. Monolinguals. Animists 34%. M=APCM. M=UFM.
4957	0	4	4.81	0	19.00	81.00	A	0.69	795	3	Kalimantan. Central Mahakam River basin. Muslims 95%.
4958	0	5	3.56	0	89.00	11.00	C	194.91	140	7	Irian Jaya. South coast area on upper Digul river. Animists 40%. M=ZGK.
4959	2	6	3.21	5	36.00	64.00	A	2.62	320	4	Nomadic Kubu, Dawas. South Sumatra. Swampy forest dwellers spread across Jambi, Riau. Animists 80%, Muslims 18%. D=GKP,FIGAL. M=WEC,YWAM.
4960	0	5	5.58	0	81.00	19.00	B	159.65	223	7	Nusa Tenggara. Alor Island, south coast around Batuiolong and 2 enclaves. Muslims 35%, animists.
4961	1	5	6.53	0	99.80	0.20	C	347.48	171	9	Central Sulawesi. Predominantly Christian. D=Indonesian Protestant Ch(GPID). M=Salvation Army.
4962	0	0	0.00	0	2.00	98.00	A	0.00	0	1.00	Sulawesi. Lasalimu subdistrict in southeast Buton Island. Muslims 100%.
4963	1	5	6.74	0	99.80	0.20	C	335.80	181	9	Nusa Tenggara. Southwest tip of Timor and Roti. Related to Malay. D=GMIT.
4964	0	5	6.75	0	98.00	2.00	C	232.50	217	8	Irian Jaya. Scattered slopes in eastern highlands east of Nalca. Tropical forest. Monolinguals. Hunter-gatherers. Animists 35%. M=UFM,SIL.
4965	1	4	4.66	0	26.00	74.00	A	2.84	596	4	South Maluku. Kur Island and nearby islands, western Kei Kecil District. Muslims 95%. D=RCC.
4966	1	4	5.20	0	53.00	47.00	B	48.36	321	6	Irian Jaya. OT and NT both being translated. Animists 75%. D=CMA.
4967	1	5	5.53	0	99.91	0.09	C	421.83	141	10	Irian Jaya. Kurudu Island, 3 villages. D=GKI-Christian Gospel Ch.
4968	0	7	4.32	0	78.00	22.00	B	142.35	187	7	Irian Jaya. South Bird's Head. Related to Moraid. Animists 50%.
4969	0	3	2.39	0	21.00	79.00	A	0.76	401	3	Sulawesi. Northern peninsula, south of Sumalata town. Close to Gorontalo. Muslims 99%.
4970	0	6	3.60	0	95.00	5.00	C	225.38	133	8	Irian Jaya. West of Lake Sentani, north of Gresi language. All bilingual in Indonesian. Animists 35%.
4971	0	5	3.74	0	45.00	55.00	A	24.63	289	5	Irian Jaya. Upper Tor river area, northeast, headwaters of Apawar river. Hunter-gatherers. Animists 85%, strong. M=RBMU,SIL.
4972	0	8	3.27	0	89.00	11.00	C	194.91	131	7	Irian Jaya. Village of Kaiy on lower Rouffaer river. Most speak Kaiy; Kwerisa nearly extinct. Animists 40%.
4973	0	5	5.21	0	92.00	8.00	C	218.27	185	8	Irian Jaya. Lower Tor river, north coast east of Sarmi, 4 villages. Animists 35%.
4974	0	6	7.07	0	72.00	28.00	B	118.26	307	7	Nusa Tenggara. Sumba Island, southwest coast, southwest of Waikabubak. Many animists 44%, some Muslims 11%.
4975	0	4	4.70	0	28.00	72.00	A	8.17	543	4	Nusa Tenggara. Southwestern Pantar Island, Lesser Sundas. Animists 80%, some Muslims.
4976	1	4	0.00	0	16.00	84.00	A	0.00	0	1.05	Lampung Province, southern Sumatra. Bilingual in Indonesian. Latin and Devanagari scripts used. Muslims 100%(Shafi Sunnis). D=Gereja Keristen Lampung.
4977	0	5	4.51	0	38.00	62.00	A	13.87	386	5	Kalimantan. Upper Lundu and Sambas rivers around Bengkayang. Also in Sarawak (Malaysia). Animists 90%. M=CBFMS,translation team.
4978	0	7	6.90	0	83.00	17.00	B	154.50	256	7	Maluku. 10 villages on Ambon Island, West Seram. Closest to Boano. Muslims 49%.
4979	0	5	3.41	0	35.00	65.00	A	12.77	333	5	Southeast Sulawesi. Southeastern part of Buton Island, Lasalimu District. Muslims 90%(Sunnis).
4980	0	5	2.50	0	26.00	74.00	A	3.79	369	4	Central Maluku. Latu village, Elpaputih Bay, southwest Seram Island. Close to Saparua. Muslims 95%.
4981	0	3	1.62	0	20.01	79.99	A	0.00	338	1.06	Sulawesi. Related to Tomini. Muslims 70%, animists 30%. M=NTM.
4982	0	5	8.68	0	58.00	42.00	B	63.51	450	6	Northeast Barito. Southern Kalimantan, around Karau river. Over 17 dialects. Animists 70%.
4983	0	5	3.31	0	24.00	76.00	A	1.75	481	4	South Sulawesi. Southern tip of Salayar Island, 2 villages. Coastal hills. Agriculturalists. Muslims 98%.
4984	0	5	6.86	0	99.85	0.15	C	372.30	177	9	Central Sulawesi (many villages), South Sulawesi (6 villages in Luwu District). Mountains. A few Muslims. Predominantly Christians.
4985	2	3	10.32	0	94.00	6.00	B	188.70	327	7	Central and south Sulawesi. Lingua franca in West Toraja area. Muslims 30%, animists 15%. D=GPID,SA. M=SIL,BAEF. R=FEBC.
4986	0	5	4.01	0	40.00	60.00	A	23.36	333	5	Irian Jaya. Raja Ampat Islands, Waigeo Island in northwest end. Muslims 60%, animists 24%.
4987	0	3	2.91	1	23.10	76.90	A	0.08	428	2	Southern Sumatra, around Muaraenim. Muslims 99%.
4988	0	5	0.00	1	18.00	82.00	A	0.00	0	1.07	South Sumatra. Interior around Lubuklinggau and east of Bengkulu; 2 areas. Related to Malay. Muslims 100%. M=FMB.
4989	0	5	2.33	0	29.00	71.00	A	5.29	300	4	South Sulawesi. Luwu District, inland from northeast coast, around Baebunta village. Base of foothills. Muslims 95%.
4990	0	6	1.40	0	47.00	53.00	A	34.31	111	5	Kalimantan. Northeast, between Saban and Lundayeh. Nearly extinct. Animists 80%.
4991	0	0	3.72	0	85.00	15.00	C	201.66	152	8	Irian Jaya. Jayawijaya Kabupten, west of the Sogber River. Animists 35%.
4992	0	5	6.81	0	99.90	0.10	C	420.48	167	10	Maluku. Leti Island. Close to Luang. Almost all Christians.
4993	0	5	1.10	0	19.30	80.70	A	0.21	277	3	Southeast Sulawesi. North of Baubau in Bungi and Kapontori Districts. Muslims 99%(Sunnis).
4994	1	6	3.53	0	84.00	16.00	B	153.30	143	7	Central Maluku. Seram Island, Salas Gunung village. Second language: Masiwang. Animists 50%. D=GPM.
4995	0	4	5.66	0	99.00	1.00	C	252.94	180	8	Central Maluku. Seram Island. Districts: Seram, Bula, Werinama, Tehoru in interior; 8 villages. Access by boat. Animists 25%, some Muslims 5%.
4996	0	5	0.00	0	24.00	76.00	A	1.75	0	4	Central Maluku. Northeast Buru Island, around Jiku Merasa town. 20 speakers over 60 years (1985). Access by sea, road. Nearly extinct. Muslims 98%.
4997	0	5	1.62	0	19.05	80.95	A	0.03	355	2	Sulawesi. Northern peninsula. Related to Gorontalo. Muslims 99%.
4998	1	3	4.97	0	87.00	13.00	B	174.65	183	7	Central Sulawesi. Kulawi Sub-District, 3 villages. Animists 45%. D=Salvation Army.
4999	0	3	3.79	1	20.50	79.50	A	0.37	600	3	Southern Sumatra between Lahat and Kapahiang. Related to Malay. Muslims 99%.
5000	1	6	10.04	0	99.80	0.20	C	341.64	259	9	Nusa Tenggara. Central Flores. Part of dialect chain with Endeh. Muslims 20%. D=RCC(M-Ende). M=SVD.
5001	0	5	4.70	0	68.00	32.00	B	99.28	224	6	Central Maluku. Spread across north coast of West and North Seram, 5 villages. Muslims 60%. Nuniali are Christians.
5002	0	5	5.06	0	37.00	63.00	A	13.50	438	5	Central Maluku. North Buru Island. Tropical forest; coastal, mountains. Muslims 60%, animists 30%.
5003	0	4	4.05	0	30.00	70.00	A	6.57	448	4	Southeast Maluku. 3 villages on 3 islands east of Kobroor and Baun Islands, Aru Islands. Muslims 90%.
5004	0	4	3.10	0	35.00	65.00	A	12.77	309	5	Northeastern Sulawesi. Town of Lolak on north coast. 3 villages surrounded by Mongondow (second language). Related to Gorontalo. Muslims 90%.
5005	1	4	5.94	0	27.00	73.00	A	0.98	689	3	Southeast Sulawesi. South tip of southeast peninsula. Muslims 95%. D=GPST. M=SGM,SIL.
5006	0	9	2.10	1	34.00	66.00	A	2.48	226	4	Sumatra. Coast dwellers from Rupat Island southwards to Bangka and Belitung Islands. Muslims 98%.
5007	0	6	3.35	0	99.80	0.20	C	332.88	101	9	Maluku. Village of Lorang, center of Aru, on Koba Island. Close to Dobel, Koba, Wokam. Multilingual. Muslims 15%, Animists 5%.

Continued overleaf

Table 8-2 continued

PEOPLE		POPULATION				IDENTITY CODE		LANGUAGE		CHURCH		MINISTRY						SCRIPTURE		
Ref 1	Ethnic name 2	P% 3	In 1995 4	In 2000 5	In 2025 6	Race 7	Language 8	Autoglossonym 9	S 10	AC 11	Members 12	Jayuh 13-17	d 18	wa 19	xc 20	mc 21	mi 22	Biblioglossonym 23	Pub 24-26	ss 27
5008	Loun	0.00002	39	42	55	MSY44y	32-DGLA-a	loun		40.00	17	0....	9	5	6	1	0		...	b
5009	Low Malay Creole	0.70000	1,382,251	1,484,752	1,914,095	MSY44k	31-PHAA-d	malayu-pasar	20	0.01	148	1csuh	3	2	2	0	3	Malay: Low	PNb	b
5010	Lowland Semang (Sakai)	0.00553	10,920	11,730	15,121	AUG05	46-GBAA-be	semang		2.00	235	0....	6	4	4	0	0		...	.
5011	Luang (Letti, Wetan)	0.01012	19,983	21,465	27,672	AON09e	32-BCEC-d	luang		91.00	19,533	0....	10	8	11	4	1	Luang	P..	b
5012	Lubu	0.01947	38,446	41,297	53,239	MSY44y	31-PHHA	lubu cluster		0.00	0	0....	0	3	2	0	0		...	b
5013	Luhu (Kelang)	0.00406	8,017	8,612	11,102	MSY44y	32-DGOL-a	luhu		6.00	517	0....	7	5	6	4	1		...	b
5014	Luwu	0.20000	394,929	424,215	546,884	MSY44c	31-QBEB-b	northeast luwu		0.01	42	0....	3	3	0	5	1		...	b
5015	Maanyak Dayak	0.04544	89,728	96,382	124,252	MSY44y	31-LBAA-d	ma'anyan		30.00	28,914	0.s..	9	5	6	4	3	Dayak: Maanyan*	PN.	.
5016	Maba (Bitjoli)	0.00312	6,161	6,618	8,531	MSY44y	33-AABC-a	maba		16.00	1,059	0....	8	5	6	2	0		...	b
5017	Maden (Sapran, Saparan)	0.00026	513	551	711	AON09e	33-ABBC-i	maden		50.00	276	0....	10	6	6	2	0		...	.
5018	Madole	0.00125	2,468	2,651	3,418	AON10c	25-AAEA	modole cluster		28.00	742	0....	9	5	6	4	2		...	b
5019	Madurese	5.70000	11,255,476	12,090,121	15,586,201	MSY44h	31-PHJA	madura cluster	8	0.20	24,180	1.s..	5	5	5	5	3	Madurese*	PNB	b
5020	Madurese Indonesian	1.50000	2,961,967	3,181,611	4,101,632	MSY44h	31-PHAA-c	bahasa-indonesia		0.50	15,908	4Asuh	5	5	5	5	1	Indonesian	PNB	b
5021	Mahakam Kenyah	0.00454	8,965	9,630	12,414	MSY44y	31-JCCG-a	mahakam		70.00	6,741	0....	10	7	6	4	1		...	.
5022	Mairasi (Faranyao)	0.00164	3,238	3,479	4,484	AON10a	24-CBAB-a	east mairasi		65.00	2,261	0....	10	7	10	2	2	Mairasi	P..	.
5023	Mairiri	0.00019	375	403	520	MSY44y	32-DEBE-a	mariri		6.00	24	0....	7	3	6	1	0		...	b
5024	Maiwa	0.02713	53,572	57,545	74,185	MSY44y	31-QBDA-a	maiwa		1.00	575	0....	6	4	3	3	0		...	b
5025	Makassarese (Macassar)	0.88478	1,747,126	1,876,684	2,419,361	MSY44i	31-QBAC	makassar cluster	2	0.20	3,753	2.s..	5	4	2	1	4	Macassar*	PNB	b
5026	Maklew	0.00007	138	148	191	AON10a	20-KABA-a	maklew		65.00	97	0....	10	7	6	2	0		...	.
5027	Malay (Coast Malay)	1.63139	3,221,416	3,460,299	4,460,907	MSY44k	31-PHAA-b	bahasa-malaysia		0.01	346	1asuh	3	3	2	4	3	Malay	PNB	b
5028	Malay Indonesian	0.70000	1,382,251	1,484,752	1,914,095	MSY44k	31-PHAA-c	bahasa-indonesia		0.10	1,485	4Asuh	5	3	2	4	1	Indonesian	PNB	b
5029	Malayic Dayak	0.33753	666,502	715,926	922,949	MSY44k	31-PHAF-ch	suhaid		20.00	143,185	0....	9	5	7	4	1	Malayic Dayak	...	.
5030	Malimpung	0.00253	4,996	5,366	6,918	MSY44c	31-QBDD	malimpung cluster		1.00	54	0....	6	4	5	1	0		...	b
5031	Mamasa Toraja	0.05326	105,170	112,968	145,635	MSY44p	31-QBEF-b	central mamasa		90.00	101,672	0A...	10	7	11	4	2	Mamasa	P..	b
5032	Mamboru	0.01039	20,517	22,038	28,411	AON09e	32-AACE-a	mamboru		45.00	9,917	0....	9	6	7	2	0		...	.
5033	Mamuju (Udai)	0.03195	63,090	67,768	87,365	MSY44y	31-QBHA-a	mamuju		6.00	4,066	0....	7	5	6	1	0		...	b
5034	Mandailing Batak (Batta)	0.22120	436,791	469,182	604,854	MSY44b	31-PECA-b	mandailing	1	5.00	23,459	1.s..	7	5	6	4	1		pnb	n
5035	Mandarese (Manjar, Napo)	0.11952	236,010	253,511	326,818	MSY44p	31-QBFA	mandar cluster		7.00	17,746	0....	7	5	6	1	0		...	b
5036	Mander	0.00001	20	21	27	AON10a	21-DBAA-a	mander		65.00	14	0....	10	7	6	2	0		...	p
5037	Manem (Jeti, Wembi)	0.00028	553	594	766	AON10a	21-HAAA	manem cluster		60.00	356	0....	10	7	6	2	0		...	.
5038	Manggarai (Ruteng)	0.27650	545,989	586,477	756,067	MSY44y	32-AAEA	manggarai cluster		4.00	23,459	0....	6	4	6	1	1		...	.
5039	Mangole	0.00343	6,773	7,275	9,379	MSY44y	32-ECBA	mangole cluster		8.00	582	0....	7	5	6	1	0		...	b
5040	Manikion (Mantion, Sogh)	0.00697	13,763	14,784	19,059	AON10a	25-GABA-a	manikion		85.00	12,566	0....	10	7	10	4	1	Manikion	PN.	.
5041	Manimo	0.00030	592	636	820	AON10b	25-OADA-a	vanimo		90.00	573	0....	10	7	11	1	2		...	.
5042	Manipa	0.00094	1,856	1,994	2,570	MSY44y	32-DGOS-a	manipa		6.00	120	0....	7	5	6	1	0		...	.
5043	Mapia	0.00100	1,975	2,121	2,734	MPY54e	33-ADBA	biak-numfor cluster		50.00	1,061	0.s..	10	6	2	2	0	Biak	PN.	.
5044	Maporese (Lom, Belom)	0.00003	59	64	82	MSY44y	31-PEDA-a	lom		10.00	6	0....	8	5	0	1	0		...	.
5045	Marau	0.00099	1,955	2,100	2,707	AON09e	33-ADCH-a	marau		91.00	1,911	0....	10	7	11	4	1		...	.
5046	Marengge	0.00003	59	64	82	AON10a	21-DHAA-a	maremgi		65.00	41	0....	10	7	6	2	0		...	.
5047	Maronene	0.01651	32,601	35,019	45,145	MSY44y	31-QDAB-a	moronene		0.01	4	0....	3	3	5	0	1	Moronene	...	b
5048	Masbuar-Tela	0.00057	1,126	1,209	1,559	AON09e	32-BCEE-a	tela-masboar		50.00	605	0....	10	7	6	5	0		...	b
5049	Masenrempulu	0.05060	99,917	107,326	138,362	MSY44y	31-QBDC-a	duri		2.00	2,147	0....	6	4	0	1	1	Duri	...	b
5050	Masimasi	0.00015	296	318	410	AON09e	34-AAAA-e	masimasi		70.00	223	0....	10	7	8	0	0		...	.
5051	Massep	0.00003	59	64	82	AON10a	25-NAAA-a	massep		60.00	38	0....	10	7	6	2	0		...	.
5052	Matbat	0.00029	573	615	793	AON09e	33-ABCA-a	matbat		11.00	68	0....	8	5	6	1	1		...	.
5053	Mawes	0.00051	1,007	1,082	1,395	AON10a	21-EAAA	mawes cluster		70.00	757	0....	10	7	6	2	0		...	.
5054	Meax (Mejah, Mansibaber)	0.00885	17,476	18,772	24,200	AON10a	25-GAAA-a	meah		85.00	15,956	0....	10	7	11	4	1	Meah*	P..	b
5055	Mekongka (Bingkokak)	0.02663	52,585	56,484	72,818	MSY44y	31-QDDA	mekongga cluster		6.00	3,389	0....	7	4	5	1	0		...	b
5056	Mekwei (Menggwei, Mooi)	0.00070	1,382	1,485	1,914	AON10a	21-JADA-a	mekwei		85.00	1,262	0....	10	7	11	2	0		...	b
5057	Menadonese Malay	0.05000	98,732	106,054	136,721	MSY44k	31-PHAG-b	malayu-manado		0.01	11	0....	3	3	2	4	0		...	b
5058	Mendalam Kayan	0.00097	1,915	2,057	2,652	MSY44z	31-JBAE-a	mendalam-kayan		2.00	41	0....	6	4	4	1	0		...	.
5059	Mentawaian (Siberut)	0.02765	54,599	58,648	75,607	MSY44y	31-PDAA	mentawai cluster		80.00	46,918	0.s..	10	7	11	5	3	Mentawai	PN.	.
5060	Meoswar	0.00013	257	276	355	MSY44y	33-ADBB-a	meos-war		35.00	97	0....	9	5	6	1	0		...	.
5061	Mer	0.00011	217	233	301	AON10a	24-CBAC-a	mer		60.00	140	0....	10	6	6	1	0		...	.
5062	Meratus (Bukit Malay)	0.03247	64,117	68,871	88,787	MSY44k	31-GBBB	south bisaya cluster		2.00	1,377	0....	6	4	6	0	0		P..	b
5063	Merau Malay	0.01299	25,651	27,553	35,520	MSY44k	31-PHAF-dh	berau		0.00	0	0....	0	3	3	0	0		...	b
5064	Mid Grand Valley Dani	0.02713	53,572	57,545	74,185	AON10a	24-FABB-a	tulem		80.00	46,036	0....	10	6	13	5	3		pn.	.
5065	Minangkabau (Padang)	2.52078	4,977,645	5,346,761	6,892,874	MSY44k	31-PHGA	minang cluster	6	0.02	1,069	2....	3	4	3	5	3	Minangkabau	PN.	b
5066	Minangkabau Indonesian	1.10000	2,172,109	2,333,181	3,007,863	MSY44k	31-PHAA-c	bahasa-indonesia		0.10	2,333	4Asuh	5	5	3	5	1	Indonesian	PNB	b
5067	Modang	0.00993	19,608	21,062	27,153	MSY44y	31-JBCB-a	long-wai		5.00	1,053	0....	7	5	6	1	0		...	.
5068	Moi	0.00239	4,719	5,069	6,535	AON10a	21-JADA-a	mekwei		65.00	3,295	0....	10	6	6	2	0		...	b
5069	Mokomoko	0.01659	32,759	35,189	45,364	MSY44k	31-PHGA-e	muko-muko		0.10	35	1....	5	4	5	1	0		pn.	.
5070	Molof	0.00014	276	297	383	AON10a	21-OAAA-a	molof		60.00	178	0....	10	6	6	2	0		...	.
5071	Mombum	0.00015	296	318	410	AON10a	24-KCAA-a	mombum		62.00	197	0....	10	6	6	2	0		...	.
5072	Mongondow (Minahassa)	0.49769	982,761	1,055,637	1,360,894	MSY44l	31-QJBB-a	bola'ang-mongondow		50.00	527,819	0....	10	7	8	5	2	Bolaang-mongondow*	P..	b
5073	Moni (Jonggunu)	0.01076	21,247	22,823	29,422	AON10a	31-QEAC-d	to-moni		85.00	19,399	0....	10	7	12	5	2		pn.	.
5074	Mor	0.00004	79	85	109	AON10a	33-ADEA-e	mo'or		67.00	57	0....	10	6	6	4	1		...	.
5075	Mor (Austronesian Mor)	0.00041	810	870	1,121	MSY44y	33-ADEA-e	mo'or		12.00	104	0....	8	5	6	4	1		...	.
5076	Moraid	0.00056	1,106	1,188	1,531	AON10a	25-BCAA-a	moraid		65.00	772	0....	10	6	6	2	0		...	.
5077	Morari (Moraori)	0.00003	59	64	82	AON10a	20-LAAA-a	moraori		60.00	38	0....	10	6	6	2	0		...	.
5078	Morwap	0.00016	316	339	438	AON10a	21-KAAA-a	morwap		68.00	231	0....	10	6	6	2	0		...	.
5079	Moskona (Meninggo)	0.00398	7,859	8,442	10,883	AON10a	25-GAAB-a	moskona		70.00	5,909	0....	10	7	7	4	3	Moskona	...	.
5080	Mualang	0.00649	12,815	13,766	17,746	MSY44e	31-PHIA	iban-sarawak cluster		30.00	4,130	3.s..	9	5	6	2	0	Iban	PNB	.
5081	Muna (Wuna)	0.12553	247,877	266,258	343,252	MSY44y	31-QAHD	muna cluster		1.00	2,663	0....	6	3	0	0	1	Muna	P..	b
5082	Munggui	0.00051	1,007	1,082	1,395	MSY44y	33-ADCH-d	munggui		10.00	108	0....	8	5	6	3	1		...	.
5083	Musi	0.08295	163,797	175,943	226,820	MSY44k	31-PHAD-d	musi		0.00	0	0....	0	3	2	1	1		pn.	b
5084	Nabi	0.00032	632	679	875	MSY44y	33-ADAB-b	nabi		30.00	204	0....	9	5	6	1	0		...	.
5085	Nafri	0.00120	2,370	2,545	3,281	AON10a	24-GDAA-a	nafri		65.00	1,654	0....	10	6	6	2	0		...	.
5086	Nakaela	0.00001	20	21	27	MSY44y	32-DGLE-a	naka'ela		70.00	15	0....	10	7	6	4	0		...	b
5087	Naltya (Nalca)	0.00523	10,327	11,093	14,301	AON10a	21-RAAD-a	hmanggona		65.00	7,211	0....	10	7	8	4	2	Nalca	...	.
5088	Napu	0.00266	5,253	5,642	7,274	MSY44p	31-QEBC-b	napu		45.00	2,539	0....	9	5	6	2	2	Napu	P..	b
5089	Narau	0.00042	829	891	1,148	AON10a	21-NAAA-a	narau		65.00	579	0....	10	6	1	2	1		...	.
5090	Ndaonese	0.00227	4,482	4,815	6,207	AON09e	32-AADC-a	ndao		91.00	4,382	0....	10	7	11	2	0		...	.
5091	Ndom	0.00032	632	679	875	AON10a	20-JCAA-a	ndom		70.00	475	0....	10	6	6	2	0		...	.
5092	Nduga (Dawa, Pesegem)	0.00601	11,868	12,748	16,434	AON10a	24-FADA	nduga cluster		85.00	10,836	0....	10	7	11	4	1	Nduga	PN.	.
5093	Nedebang	0.00065	1,284	1,379	1,777	MSY44y	20-AACA-a	nedebang		5.00	69	0....	7	5	6	1	0		...	.
5094	Ngada	0.03292	65,005	69,826	90,017	MSY44y	32-AAEH-a	bajava		90.00	62,843	0....	10	7	11	2	1		...	.
5095	Ngaju Dayak (Biadju)	0.16228	320,445	344,208	443,742	MSY44y	31-LABB-b	vehicular ngaju	1	60.00	206,525	0.s..	10	7	7	5	1	Dayak: Ngaju*	PNB	b
5096	Ngalum (Sibil)	0.00581	11,473	12,323	15,887	AON10a	24-KEBJ	ngalum cluster		65.00	8,010	0....	10	7	9	5	3	Ngalum	PN.	.
5097	Nggem	0.00161	3,179	3,415	4,402	AON10a	24-FACA-a	nggem		64.00	2,186	0....	10	6	9	4	1	Nggem	P..	.
5098	Niassan	0.26544	524,150	563,018	725,825	MSY44y	31-PCAC	nias cluster		75.00	422,263	0.s..	10	8	9	5	3	Nias	PNB	b
5099	Nila	0.00104	2,054	2,206	2,844	MSY44y	32-BCHB-a	nila		60.00	1,324	0....	10	6	6	2	0		...	b
5100	Nimboran	0.00203	4,009	4,306	5,551	AON10a	21-JAAA-a	nimboran		65.00	2,799	0....	10	7	6	3	1	Nimboran	P..	b
5101	Ninggrum (Kativa, Muyu)	0.00074	1,461	1,570	2,023	AON10a	24-KEAE-a	ninggerum		64.00	1,005	0....	10	6	6	2	0	Ninggerum	...	.
5102	Nisa (Bonefa)	0.00029	573	615	793	AON10a	25-JCDA-a	proper nisa		66.00	406	0....	10	7	6	4	1		...	.
5103	Njadu (Balantian)	0.00523	10,327	11,093	14,301	MSY44y	31-KAAI-b	ba-lantiang		15.00	1,664	0....	8	5	5	1	0	Nyadu	P..	.
5104	Nobuk	0.00015	296	318	410	AON10a	24-FBAC-a	nopuk		10.00	32	0....	8	5	3	0	0		...	.
5105	North Asmat	0.00053	1,047	1,124	1,449	AON10a	24-KABD-b	keenok		80.00	899	0....	10	9	8	0	0		pn.	.
5106	North Babar	0.00083	1,639	1,760	2,270	AON09e	12-AACB-b	east maghrebi		70.00	1,232	2A.uh	10	7	3	4	0	Arabic: Algerian*	PNB	b
5107	North Borneo Murut (Tagal)	0.00116	2,291	2,460	3,172	MSY44z	31-GCAE-b	sumambuq		20.00	492	0.s..	9	5	7	1	0		pn.	.
5108	North Damar	0.00046	908	976	1,258	MSY44y	32-BCGA-a	west damar		60.00	585	0....	10	6	6	2	0		...	b
5109	North Loloda	0.00827	16,330	17,541	22,614	AON10c	25-AABB-a	loda		28.00	4,912	0....	9	5	6	4	2	Loloda	P..	b
5110	North Moluccan Malay	0.00040	790	848	1,094	MSY44k	31-PHAH-a	malayu-ternate		10.00	85	0....	8	5	4	1	0		...	b
5111	North Ngalik (Ninia Yaly)	0.00480	9,478	10,181	13,125	AON10a	24-FADC-a	ninia		35.00	3,563	0....	9	5	6	5	1	Yali, Ninia	PN.	.
5112	North Nuaulu	0.00027	533	573	738	MSY44y	12-AACB-b	east maghrebi		8.00	46	2A.uh	7	5	6	1	1	Arabic: Algerian*	PNB	b
5113	North Tukangbesi (Wakatobi)	0.06073	119,920	128,813	166,061	MSY44y	31-QAAC	north tukang-besi cluster		8.00	10,305	0....	7	5	6	1	0		...	b
5114	North Wemale	0.00314	6,200	6,660	8,586	MSY44y	32-DGKB	north wemale cluster		80.00	5,328	0....	10	8	10	2	0		...	b
5115	Northern Kati (Muju)	0.00465	9,182	9,863	12,715	AON10a	24-KEAC	north kati cluster		65.00	6,411	0....	10	7	2	4	2		...	b
5116	Northwest Marind (Bian)	0.00063	1,244	1,336	1,723	AON10a	24-IBAB	upper marind cluster		64.00	855	0....	10	6	6	2	0		...	.
5117	Nusa Laut	0.00123	2,429	2,609	3,363	MSY44y	31-PHCA	moken cluster		30.00	783	0....	9	6	5	3	0	Moken	P..	b
5118	Ogan	0.16590	327,594	351,886	453,640	MSY44k	31-PFBA-b	ogan		0.00	0	1....	0	3	2	0	1		...	b
5119	Oirata	0.00071	1,402	1,506	1,941	AON10e	20-GAAA-a	oirata		53.00	798	0....	10	6	6	3	0		...	b
5120	Okolod Murut	0.00160	3,159	3,394	4,375	MSY44z	31-GCAF-a	okolod		40.00	1,357	0.s..	9	5	8	1	0	Okolod	...	.
5121	Onin (Sepa)	0.00041	810	870	1,121	MSY44y	33-ACAA	onin cluster		15.00	130	0....	8	5	6	1	0		...	.
5122	Ormu	0.00030	592	636	820	MSY44y	34-AABA	ormu cluster		15.00	95	0....	8	5	6	1	0		...	b
5123	Ot Danum (Dayak, Dohoi)	0.05193	102,543	110,147	141,998	MSY44y	31-LAAA-f	ot-danum		0.50	551	0.s..	5	4	5	5	3	Dohoi	...	.
5124	Ot Siang	0.03895	76,912	82,616	106,506	MSY44y	31-LAAC-a	ot-siang		1.00	826	0....	6	4	5	1	0		...	.
5125	Pago (Pagu)	0.00156	3,080	3,309	4,266	AON10c	25-AAEB-b	proper pagu		27.00	893	0....	9	5	6	5	2		...	b
5126	Pakpak Batak	0.02000	39,493	42,421	54,688	MSY44b	31-PEAC-b	pakpak	1	50.00	21,211	1.s..	10	7	8	5	1	Pakpak Dairi	PNb	n
5127	Paku	0.01298	25,631	27,532	35,493	MSY44y	31-LBAA-c	paku		30.00	8,259	0.s..	9	5	6	2	0		pn.	p
5128	Palamul	0.00013	257	276	355	AON09e	33-ABBC-h	palamul		50.00	138	0....	10	6	6	2	0		...	.
5129	Palembangese	0.27650	545,989	586,477	756,067	MSY44k	31-PIAA-j	jawa-palembang		0.01	59	1cs.h	3	4	3	5	3		pnb	b
5130	Palue	0.00195	3,851	4,136	5,332	AON09e	32-AAFA-f	palu'e		80.00	3,309	0....	10	7	10	2	0		...	.
5131	Panasuan (To Pamosean)	0.00050	987	1,061	1,367	MSY44p	31-QBIB-a	to-panasuan		80.00	848	0....	10	7	11	4	0		...	b

Continued opposite

Table 8-2 continued

EVANGELIZATION								EVANGELISM			ADDITIONAL DESCRIPTIVE DATA
Ref 1	D 28	aC 29	CG% 30	r 31	E 32	U 33	W 34	e 35	R 36	T 37	Locations, civil divisions, literacy, religions, church history, denominations, dioceses, church growth, missions, agencies, ministries, movements 38
5008	0	5	2.87	0	67.00	33.00	B	97.82	152	6	Central Maluku. North central Seram on coast. Nearly extinct. Access by boat. Muslims 30%, Animists 30%.
5009	0	5	2.73	5	34.01	65.99	A	0.01	276	2	Trade language in ports from Sumatra to Philippines. Many regional non-standard Malay dialects. Literates 70%. Agriculturalists. Muslims 100%(Sunnis).
5010	0	5	3.21	0	20.00	80.00	A	1.46	577	4	Sumatra. Bintan Island, Riau Islands southeast of Singapore. Muslims 90%.
5011	2	5	7.87	0	99.91	0.09	C	441.76	183	10	South Maluku. Northwest Baba Islands east of Timor. 17 dialects. D=GPM,AoG. M=SIL.
5012	0	3	0.00	0	8.00	92.00	A	0.00	0	1.04	East Sumatra, central region. Swampy forest dwellers, found as far north as Siabu among Bataks. Related to Kubu. Animists 80%, Muslims 20%.
5013	0	5	4.02	0	35.00	65.00	A	7.66	381	4	Maluku. Luhu village on Hoamoal Peninsula, west Seram and nearby. Access by boat. Muslims 94%. M=REMP.
5014	4	3	3.81	0	21.01	78.99	A	0.00	608	1.06	South Sulawesi. Dialect of Bugis, related also to Toala. Muslims 95%(Shafi Sunnis). D=RCC,GKSS,GEPSULTRA,GPST. M=NMS(NZ).
5015	1	5	8.30	0	68.00	32.00	B	74.46	369	6	Kalimantan. South around Tamianglayang. Animists 70%. D=GKE(Evangelical Ch in Kalimantan). M=UBS,RM,BM,IBS-I.
5016	0	5	4.77	0	44.00	56.00	A	25.69	350	5	North Maluku. Northern coast of southeastern peninsula, Halmhera; also in Wasilei area. Access by sea. Muslims 84%.
5017	0	7	3.37	0	78.00	22.00	B	142.35	154	7	Irian Jaya. Raja Ampat Islands, northwestern Salawati Island. Animists 40%, some Muslims.
5018	1	5	3.98	0	61.00	39.00	B	62.34	224	6	North Maluku. Interior of north Halmahera. Animists 52%, Muslims 20%. D=GMIH(Evangelical Christian Ch in Halmahera). M=UMS,MCC.
5019	6	6	8.10	2	49.20	50.80	A	0.35	498	3	Eastern Java, islands of Madura, Kangean, Sapudi. Muslims 100%(strict Shafi Sunnis). D=GK,GKIJT,RCC(D-Malang),Sidang Persekutuan Injil,GKJW,Lauwang Ch.
5020	1	6	7.65	7	58.50	41.50	B	1.06	398	4	Madurese who now speak Indonesian as mother tongue. Muslims 99%. D=GX. R=FEBC,VERITAS,AWR.
5021	0	5	6.73	0	99.70	0.30	C	255.50	208	8	Kalimantan. Northeast, east of Bahau and on Mahakam river, 5 areas. Animists 30%.M=BEM.
5022	0	5	5.57	0	99.00	1.00	C	234.87	182	8	Irian Jaya. Bomberai Peninsula, southwest coast of neck. Close to Semimi. Monolinguals. Animists 35%. M=TEAM,SIL.
5023	0	5	3.23	0	31.00	69.00	A	6.78	361	4	South Maluku. Eastern Aru on Mariri Island east of Kobroor Island, 1 village. Muslims 94%.
5024	0	4	4.13	0	23.00	77.00	A	0.84	593	3	South Sulawesi, Enrekang and Sidenrang Districts. Lowlands. Pastoralists. Muslims 95%.
5025	5	3	5.55	4	42.20	57.80	A	0.30	419	3	South Sulawesi. Farmers, fishermen. Literates 62%. Muslims 97%(Shafi Sunnis, Sufis; islamized from AD 1605), Mukdiakbar(indigenous religion). D=GPIB,GKSS.
5026	0	7	4.68	0	93.00	7.00	C	220.64	167	8	Irian Jaya. South coast area, west of Marind. Animists 35%.
5027	1	4	3.61	5	44.01	55.99	A	0.01	268	2	In all Provinces. Over 40 major dialects. Muslims 100%(Shafi Sunnis). D=RCC(D-Pangkal Pinang,&c). M=SSCC,WEC,CSI,YWAM,Go Ye Fellowship,FI.
5028	1	4	5.13	7	51.10	48.90	B	0.18	313	3	Coastal Malays who now speak Indonesian as mother tongue. Muslims 100%. D=RCC. R=FEBC,VERITAS,AWR.
5029	1	6	10.04	0	53.00	47.00	B	38.69	555	5	Kalimantan. West central, to Delang in south. Animists 80%. D=NTM.
5030	0	6	4.07	0	25.00	75.00	A	0.91	539	3	South Sulawesi, Patampanua, Bugis Region. Muslims 99%.
5031	2	6	9.67	0	99.90	0.10	C	456.61	208	10	South Sulawesi. Polmas District. Animists 10%. Heavy islamization in adjacent peoples. D=GTM, with intense persecution by Muslims. D=GT. M=NCRMA,SIL.
5032	0	6	5.67	0	73.00	27.00	B	119.90	250	7	Nusa Tenggara. Northwest Sumba Island, coast around Memboro. Many animists 50%, some Muslims 5%.
5033	0	5	6.19	0	32.00	68.00	A	7.00	603	4	South Sulawesi. Mamuju District from Mamuju town to mouth of Budong-Bundong river. Lingua franca. Muslims 94%.
5034	3	3	4.21	0	44.00	56.00	A	8.03	315	4	North Sumatra. Closer to Minangkabau than to Batak. Muslims 95%(Shafi Sunnis). D=RCC,HKBP,GPI. M=OFMCap.
5035	0	3	7.77	0	32.00	68.00	A	8.17	742	4	South Sulawesi. Majene and Polewali-Mamasa Districts. Fishermen. Muslims 93%.
5036	0	7	2.67	0	94.00	6.00	C	223.01	107	8	Irian Jaya. North coast area on upper Bu river. Nomadic. Bilingual in Berik. Animists 35%.
5037	0	5	3.64	0	86.00	14.00	C	188.34	148	7	Irian Jaya. Northeast border area south of Jayapura, 7 villages. Also in PNG. Animists 40%.
5038	1	5	8.07	0	29.00	71.00	A	4.23	843	4	Nusa Tenggara. Western third of Flores. Closely related to Riung. 43 dialects. Muslims 50%, animists 46%. D=RCC.
5039	0	5	4.15	0	33.00	67.00	A	9.63	415	4	North Maluku. Southern coast of Mangole Island, also Sula Islands. Access by sea. Muslims 92%.
5040	2	1	7.40	0	99.85	0.15	C	378.50	189	9	Irian Jaya. East Bird's Head, east of Meyah, 50 villages. Mostly monolinguals. Animists 15%. D=GAK(Bible Ch),GKI. M=TEAM.
5041	2	8	4.13	0	99.90	0.10	C	417.19	112	10	Irian Jaya. Most in PNG. Related to Wutung. Animists 10%. D=RCC,Christian Brethren.
5042	0	5	2.52	0	28.00	72.00	A	6.13	330	4	Central Maluku. Manipa Island west of Seram, 4 villages. Related to Luhu. Access by boat. Muslims 94%.
5043	0	7	4.77	0	80.00	20.00	B	146.00	185	7	Irian Jaya. Mapia Islands. Mapia language is extinct; ethnic group now speaks Biak. Animists 50%.
5044	0	8	1.81	0	30.00	70.00	A	10.95	243	5	Sumatra. Northeast Bangka Island, Belinyu District. Under 50 speakers left; nearly extinct. Animists 30%, Muslims 30%, nonreligious 30%.
5045	1	5	5.39	0	99.91	0.09	C	421.83	138	10	Irian Jaya. South coast of Yapen Island, 5 villages. D=GKI.
5046	0	8	3.78	0	94.00	6.00	C	223.01	139	8	Irian Jaya. North coast inland from Bonggo language area. Animists 35%.
5047	0	3	1.40	0	18.01	81.99	A	0.00	342	1.05	Southeast Sulawesi. Rumbia and Poleang Districts. Formerly a kingdom. Muslims 99%. M=SIL.
5048	0	6	4.19	0	83.00	17.00	B	151.47	171	7	South Maluku. 2 villages on southwest Babar Island. Animists 50%.
5049	0	3	5.52	0	20.00	80.00	A	1.46	873	4	South Sulawesi. Enrekang District and slightly beyond. Agriculturalists. Muslims 80%, animists 18%. M=SIL.
5050	0	0	3.15	0	90.00	10.00	C	229.95	126	8	Irian Jaya. Island off north coast east of the Tor River mouth. Animists 30%.
5051	0	8	3.70	0	89.00	11.00	C	194.91	145	7	Irian Jaya. North coast east of Mamberamo river mouth, west of Sarmi. Language isolate. Animists 40%.
5052	0	5	4.31	0	35.00	65.00	A	14.05	416	5	Irian Jaya. Raja Ampat Islands, Misool Island, Segaf Islands. Animists 89%. M=SIL.
5053	0	5	4.42	0	96.00	4.00	C	245.28	155	8	Irian Jaya. Northeast coast east of Sarmi near mouth of Wirowai river, 3 villages. Animists 30%.
5054	1	5	7.65	0	99.85	0.15	C	390.91	188	9	Irian Jaya. East Bird's Head, north coast, west of Manokwari. Many speak Indonesian, some Mantion. Animists 15%. D=GAK(Bible Ch). M=TEAM.
5055	0	4	6.00	0	30.00	70.00	A	6.57	626	4	Southeast Sulawesi. Near Soroako. Formerly a kingdom. Muslims 94%.
5056	0	5	4.96	0	99.85	0.15	C	372.30	136	9	Irian Jaya. West of Lake Sentani, 10 villages. All bilingual in Indonesian. Animists 15%.
5057	0	4	2.43	5	24.01	75.99	A	0.00	357	1.07	In Minahasa District, Sulawesi, Many second-language speakers. Muslims 99%(Sunnis).
5058	0	5	3.78	0	21.00	79.00	A	1.53	560	4	Kalimantan. North central, northeast of Putus Sibau, Mendalam river. Animists 98%.
5059	2	5	5.28	0	99.80	0.20	C	367.92	133	9	South Sumatra Province. Mentawai Islands. Animists 20%. Baha'i have medical work. D=PKPM,RCC(D-Padang). M=SX,BM,HKBP,RM,VEM,REMP,IBS-I.
5060	0	5	4.68	0	59.00	41.00	B	75.37	257	6	Irian Jaya. Meoswar Island, west Geelvink Bay. Animists 65%.
5061	0	5	2.67	0	85.00	15.00	C	186.15	118	7	Irian Jaya. Central Bird's Head, headwaters of Wosimi and Uremo rivers. Animists 40%.
5062	0	5	5.05	0	24.00	76.00	A	1.75	656	4	Kalimantan, southeast, Sampanahan River. Animists 50%, Muslims 48%.
5063	0	3	0.00	0	12.00	88.00	A	0.00	0	1.04	Kalimantan. East central coastal area. Related to Banjarese. Muslims 99%.
5064	4	7	8.80	0	99.80	0.20	C	376.68	208	9	Irian Jaya. Baliem Valley. Animists 20%. D=RCC,GKI,KINGMI,GGIK. M=ABMS,CMA,UFM,RBMU.
5065	3	4	4.78	2	36.02	63.98	A	0.02	417	2	Sumatra. Strict Muslims 100%(Shafi Sunnis). Baha'i medical work. D=GEKISUS(Evangelical Ch of South Sumatra),Persekutuan Minang Sumbar. M=OMF.
5066	1	5	5.60	7	54.10	45.90	B	0.19	319	3	Minangkabau who now speak Indonesian as mother tongue. Muslims 99%. D=GEKISUS. R=FEBC,VERITAS,AWR.
5067	0	5	4.77	0	28.00	72.00	A	5.11	550	4	Kalimantan. Around Segah, Kelinjau, and Belayan rivers in northeast, 5 areas. Animists 95%.
5068	0	5	5.97	0	92.00	8.00	C	218.27	208	8	Irian Jaya. Salawati Island, west Bird's Head around Sorong, 9 villages. Animists 35%.
5069	0	5	3.62	1	24.10	75.90	A	0.08	491	2	Southern Sumatra, west coast around Mukormuko. Muslims 99%.
5070	0	7	2.92	0	88.00	12.00	C	192.72	122	7	Irian Jaya. South of Jayapura, west of Waris. Animists 40%.
5071	0	7	3.03	0	90.00	10.00	C	203.67	123	8	Irian Jaya. Island next to southeast coast of Frederik Hendrik Island. Closest to Koneraw. Animists 38%.
5072	2	4	9.03	0	90.00	10.00	B	164.25	301	7	Minahasan. Northeast Sulawesi. Muslims 40%(but not very strict or orthodox), many animists. D=GMIBM,RCC(D-Manado). M=MSC,NZG. R=FEBC.
5073	2	4	7.86	0	99.85	0.15	C	397.12	190	9	Irian Jaya. Central highlands northeast of Lake Paniai. Monolinguals. Animists 15%. D=CMA,RCC.
5074	0	8	4.13	0	99.00	1.00	C	242.10	142	8	Irian Jaya. Northwest Bomberai Peninsula, coast of Bintuni Bay. Animists 33%. M=UFM.
5075	0	5	2.37	0	39.00	61.00	A	17.08	226	5	Austronesian Mor. Irian Jaya. Mor Islands in east Geelvink Bay near Nabire. Animists 88%. M=UFM.
5076	0	5	4.44	0	91.00	9.00	C	215.89	164	8	Irian Jaya. West Bird's Head, east of Moi, south of Madik language area, 4 villages. Animists 35%.
5077	0	9	3.70	0	90.00	10.00	C	197.10	143	7	Irian Jaya. South coast border area east of Merauke. Animists 40%.
5078	0	6	3.19	0	95.00	5.00	C	235.79	121	8	Irian Jaya. South of Jayapura, northeast of Kaureh area. Animists 32%.
5079	1	5	6.59	0	99.70	0.30	C	265.72	200	8	Irian Jaya. West of Meah and Mantion, southeast Bird's Head. Monolinguals. Animists 30%. D=GAK(Bible Ch). M=TEAM,BCFCI,SIL.
5080	0	5	6.21	4	74.00	26.00	B	81.03	249	6	Kalimantan. Along Ayak and Belitang rivers, 200 miles upstream from Pontianak. Close to Iban. Animists 70%.
5081	1	3	5.74	0	20.00	80.00	A	0.73	903	3	Southeast Sulawesi. Muna Island, part of Buton Island, and Ambon Island. Muslims 99%. D=RCC. M=SIL.
5082	1	6	2.41	0	38.00	62.00	A	13.87	235	5	Irian Jaya. North coast of Yapen Island, 4 villages. Animists 90%. D=GKI.
5083	0	3	0.00	1	17.00	83.00	A	0.00	0	1.08	South Sumatra. Interior, both sides of Musi river northwest of Sekayu and Palembang. Muslims 100%. M=WEC.
5084	0	5	3.06	0	54.00	46.00	B	59.13	198	6	Irian Jaya. Southwest Bomberai Peninsula, along Nabi river, 16 villages. Close to Irarutu. Animists 70%.
5085	0	5	5.24	0	92.00	8.00	C	218.27	186	8	Irian Jaya. Nafri village, Jayapura area. Animists 35%.
5086	0	6	2.75	0	99.70	0.30	C	260.61	97	8	Central Maluku. Kairatu village, northwest Seram. Access by boat. Nearly extinct.
5087	1	5	6.80	0	99.00	1.00	C	234.87	216	8	Irian Jaya, eastern highlands area northeast of Korapun. Monolinguals: only 1% read Indonesian. Animists 35%. D=ECP. M=UFM,RBMU.
5088	2	5	5.69	0	79.00	21.00	B	129.75	229	7	East central Sulawesi. Lore Utara and Poso Pesisir Sub-Districts, 12 villages. Closest to Besoa. Animists 55%. D=GKST,Pentecostals. M=NBS,SIL.
5089	0	5	4.14	0	87.00	13.00	C	206.40	162	8	Irian Jaya. Kecamatan Kaureh, Jayapura area. Monolinguals. Animists 35%. M=UFM.
5090	0	1	3.27	0	99.91	0.09	C	395.25	98	9	Nusa Tenggara. Lesser Sundas, Ndao Island off Roti. Close to Sawu. Animists 8%.
5091	0	5	3.94	0	96.00	4.00	C	245.28	141	8	Irian Jaya. Frederik Hendrik Island. Closest to Kimaghama, Riantana. Animists 30%.
5092	1	5	7.24	0	99.85	0.15	C	390.91	179	9	Irian Jaya. Jayawijaya, Tiom, central highlands. Mostly monolinguals: some speak Danal, Moni, Indonesian. Animists 15%. D=KINGMI. M=CMA.
5093	0	5	4.33	0	27.00	73.00	A	4.92	526	4	Nusa Tenggara. North central Pantar, south of Kabir. Animists 90%, Muslims 5%.
5094	1	5	9.14	0	99.90	0.10	C	410.62	219	10	Nusa Tenggara. South central Flores. Muslims 10%. D=RCC.
5095	2	4	10.45	0	99.60	0.40	C	236.52	287	8	Kalimantan. Kapuas and 3 other rivers in south. Lingua franca. Animists 40%. D=GKE(Evangelical Ch in Kalimantan),RCC. M=IBS-I.
5096	2	5	6.91	0	99.65	0.35	C	253.85	203	8	Irian Jaya. South of Jayapura. Also in PNG. Most are monolinguals. Animists 35%. D=ECP,RCC. M=UFM,RM,BM.
5097	0	5	5.53	0	98.00	2.00	C	228.92	183	8	Irian Jaya. Along middle Haflifoeri river. Closely related to Walak. All monolinguals. Animists 36%. M=APCM.
5098	5	4	4.53	0	99.75	0.25	C	342.18	118	9	Nias and Batu Islands. Animists 10%, Muslims 10%. Y=1865. D=BNKP,RCC(PA-Sibolga),ONKP,AMIN,GMAHKT. M=RMS,OFMCap,VEM,BAEF,IBS-I.
5099	0	5	5.01	0	90.00	10.00	C	197.10	178	7	Central Maluku. Seram Island. Removed to Seram from Damar Islands due to volcanic activity. Close to Serua. Animists 40%.
5100	0	5	5.80	0	98.00	2.00	C	232.50	190	8	Irian Jaya. North, near PNG border; west of Lake Sentani, 26 villages. Bilingual in Indonesian. Animists 35%. M=SIL.
5101	0	5	4.72	0	91.00	9.00	C	212.57	172	8	Irian Jaya. Border area; majority in PNG. Animists 36%.
5102	0	5	3.77	0	95.00	5.00	C	228.85	138	8	Irian Jaya. Inland from east side of Geelvink Bay. Mostly monolinguals. Animists 34%. M=UFM.
5103	0	5	5.25	0	39.00	61.00	A	21.35	429	5	West Kalimantan. Landak river headwaters, south of Sarawak border. Similar to Lara. Animists 85%.
5104	0	5	3.53	0	29.00	71.00	A	10.58	428	5	Irian Jaya. East of Mamberamo river, in mountains, tropical forest. Hunter-gatherers. Animists 90%.
5105	0	0	4.60	0	99.80	0.20	C	300.76	149	9	Irian Jaya. Near headwaters of Paterle Cocq River. Also Unir River. Animists 20%. D=60%RCC,GAK. M=Crosier Frs,MM,TEAM,BCFCI.
5106	0	5	4.93	8	99.70	0.30	C	316.82	131	9	Maluku. North Babar Islands, east of Timor. 6 villages. Agriculturalists, fishermen. Animists 30%.
5107	0	6	3.97	0	50.00	50.00	B	36.50	246	5	Kalimantan. Along Alumbis river. Great majority in Sabah (Malaysia). 10 dialects. Animists 80%.
5108	0	5	4.15	0	89.00	11.00	C	194.91	154	7	South Maluku. String of small Damar Islands north and east of Roma; 2 villages. Animists 40%.
5109	1	5	6.39	0	63.00	37.00	B	64.38	321	6	North Maluku. Northwest coast of Halmahera. Animists 50%, Muslims 22%. D=GMIH(Evangelical Christian Ch in Halmahera). M=UMS,MCC.
5110	0	5	4.54	5	39.00	61.00	A	14.23	368	5	North Maluku. Halmahera, Sula, Obi Islands. Lingua franca. Muslims 90%.
5111	3	5	6.05	0	72.00	28.00	B	91.98	268	6	Irian Jaya. Central highlands west from Angguruk. Monolinguals. Animists 65%. D=Indonesian Christian Ch,Netherlands Reformed Congregation,CMA. M=RBMU.
5112	0	4	3.90	8	58.00	42.00	B	16.93	224	5	Central Maluku. 2 villages on north coast of central Seram Island. Animists 90%. M=SIL.
5113	0	5	7.18	0	35.00	65.00	A	10.22	629	5	Southeast Sulawesi. Tukangbesi Archipelago with 4 main islands: Wanci, Kaledupa, Tomea, Binongko. Muslims 92%.
5114	0	6	6.48	0	99.80	0.20	C	335.80	175	9	Central Maluku. North coast of Taniwel District; East Seram District; 24 villages. Church language. Access by boat. Muslims 10%.
5115	1	5	6.68	0	96.00	4.00	C	227.76	219	8	Irian Jaya. South coast area around Muyu river. Bilingual in Indonesian. Animists 35%. D=ECP. M=UFM,APCM.
5116	0	5	4.55	0	90.00	10.00	C	210.24	169	8	Irian Jaya. South coast area near Merauke. Animists 36%.
5117	0	4	4.46	0	58.00	42.00	B	63.51	251	6	Central Maluku. Titawai village, Nusa Laut Island, Lease Islands. Close to Amahai. Language nearly extinct. Animists 40%, Muslims (Sunnis) 30%.
5118	0	3	0.00	0	13.00	87.00	A	0.00	0	1.05	South Sumatra. Around Baturaja, Pagerdewa. Muslims 100%(Shafi Sunnis), converted through Sufi Naqshbandiyya order. M=WEC.
5119	0	5	4.48	0	83.00	17.00	B	160.56	181	7	South Maluku. East and west Oirata in southeast Kisar Island; hundreds in Ambon city. Animists 40%, some Muslims 7%.
5120	0	6	5.03	0	69.00	31.00	B	100.74	220	7	Kalimantan. Northeast along Sabah border, east of Lumbis. Some in Malaysia (Sarawak, Sabah). Animists 60%.
5121	0	5	2.60	0	38.00	62.00	A	20.80	249	5	Irian Jaya. North and northwest Bomberai Peninsula. Animists 85%.
5122	0	5	4.66	0	41.00	59.00	A	22.44	368	5	Irian Jaya. North coast area west of Jayapura, north of Cyclops Mountains. Bilingual. Animists 85%.
5123	3	5	4.09	0	30.50	69.50	A	0.55	444	3	Kalimantan. South of Schwaner Range. Animists 99%. D=GKE(Evangelical Ch of Kalimantan),CMA,NTM. M=RM,BM,MBMC,ODM.
5124	0	5	4.51	0	21.00	79.00	A	0.76	699	3	Kalimantan. Central, east of Dohoi area. Related to Dohoi. Animists 98%.
5125	1	5	3.98	0	61.00	39.00	B	60.11	224	6	North Maluku. North Halmahera. Animists 50%, Muslims 23%. D=GMIH. M=UMS,MCC.
5126	2	3	3.36	0	95.00	5.00	B	173.37	121	7	Northern Sumatra. Close to Dairi Batak. Animists 30%, Muslims 20%(Shafi Sunnis). D=RCC(M-Medan,&c),HKBP. M=OFMCap.
5127	0	5	6.95	0	61.00	39.00	B	66.79	350	6	Kalimantan. Southeast, south of Ampah. Closest to Maanyan. Animists 70%.
5128	0	6	2.66	0	77.00	23.00	B	140.52	130	7	Irian Jaya. Raja Ampat Islands, southwestern Salawati Island. Animists 50%.
5129	2	4	4.16	5	41.01	58.99	A	0.01	325	2	Southeast Sumatra. Palembang city and area; coastal, swamps. Strong Muslims 100%(Shafi Sunnis). D=GMI,GMMI. M=SCJ,UMC,MBMC.
5130	0	6	2.88	0	99.80	0.20	C	327.04	95	9	Nusa Tenggara. Palu Island, north of central Flores. Animists 20%.
5131	0	5	4.54	0	99.80	0.20	C	338.72	128	9	South Sulawesi. North of Kalumpany, Mamuju District. Access by river. Animists 20%.

Continued overleaf

Table 8-2 continued

PEOPLE		POPULATION				IDENTITY CODE		LANGUAGE		CHURCH		MINISTRY						SCRIPTURE		
Ref 1	Ethnic name 2	P% 3	In 1995 4	In 2000 5	In 2025 6	Race 7	Language 8	Autoglossonym 9	S 10	AC 11	Members 12	Jayuh 13-17	d 18	wa 19	xc 20	mc 21	mi 22	Biblioglossonym 23	Pub 24-26	ss 27
5132	Pancana (Kapontori)	0.01014	20,023	21,508	27,727	MSY44y	31-QAHE	pancana cluster		0.01	2	0....	3	2	0	0	0		...	b
5133	Pannei	0.00523	10,327	11,093	14,301	MSY44p	31-QBGA-c	pannei		3.00	333	0....	6	4	5	1	0		...	b
5134	Papasena	0.00025	494	530	684	AON10a	21-BBAA-a	papasena		64.75	343	0....	10	6	6	1	1		...	.
5135	Papuma	0.00038	750	806	1,039	AON09e	33-ADCG-a	papuma		91.00	733	0....	10	7	11	4	1		...	.
5136	Pasemah (Malay)	0.22120	436,791	469,182	604,854	MSY44k	31-PHAD-r	pasemah		0.06	282	0....	4	4	2	4	2		pn.	b
5137	Pass Valley Yali	0.00282	5,568	5,981	7,711	AON10a	24-FADD	angguruk cluster		65.00	3,888	0....	10	8	8	0	0		PN.	.
5138	Patani	0.00499	9,853	10,584	13,645	MSY44y	33-AABB-a	patani		12.00	1,270	0....	8	5	6	1	0		...	b
5139	Pattae (Binuang)	0.02100	41,468	44,543	57,423	MSY44p	31-QBEF-a	pattae'		2.00	891	0c...	6	4	5	1	0		p..	b
5140	Pattinjo (Leta, Kassa)	0.03120	61,609	66,178	85,314	MSY44y	31-QBDB-c	pattinjo		3.00	1,985	0....	6	4	5	1	0		...	b
5141	Paulohi	0.00003	59	64	82	AON09e	32-DGOB-a	paulohi-solahua		91.00	58	0....	10	7	11	2	0		...	b
5142	Pauwi	0.00007	138	148	191	AON10a	25-LAAA-a	pauwi		50.00	74	0....	10	6	6	1	0		...	.
5143	Pekal	0.01659	32,759	35,189	45,364	MSY44k	31-PHGA-f	pekal		0.10	35	1....	5	4	4	0	0		pn.	b
5144	Penasak	0.01106	21,840	23,459	30,243	MSY44k	31-PHAD-k	penesak		1.00	235	0....	6	5	6	0	0		pn.	b
5145	Penihing	0.00171	3,377	3,627	4,676	MSY44z	31-JBDD-a	aoheng		2.00	73	0....	6	4	5	1	0		...	.
5146	Perai	0.00015	296	318	410	MSY44y	32-BCDD-b	tutunohan		20.00	64	0....	9	5	6	0	0		...	b
5147	Petapa (Taje)	0.00026	513	551	711	MSY44y	31-QGAA-a	taje		0.04	0	0....	3	4	2	0	0		...	b
5148	Piru	0.00001	20	21	27	MSY44y	32-DGOK-a	piru		80.00	17	0....	10	7	10	4	0		...	b
5149	Pisa	0.00203	4,009	4,306	5,551	AON10a	24-KDBH-d	miaro		65.00	2,799	0....	10	6	7	2	1	Awyu, Miaro	...	.
5150	Pitu Uluna Salu (Tenete)	0.01278	25,236	27,107	34,946	MSY44p	31-QBGB	pitu-ulunna-salu cluster		15.00	4,066	0....	8	5	6	2	1		P..	b
5151	Pom	0.00116	2,291	2,460	3,172	AON09e	33-ADCE-a	pom		91.00	2,239	0....	10	7	11	4	1		...	.
5152	Ponasakan	0.00195	3,851	4,136	5,332	MSY44l	31-QJBC-a	ponosakan		15.00	620	0....	8	5	6	2	0		...	b
5153	Poso Toraja (Baree)	0.07167	141,523	152,017	195,976	MSY44p	31-QEAC-a	to-bau		80.00	121,614	0....	10	7	11	4	2	Pamona	PN.	b
5154	Pubian	0.28800	568,698	610,869	787,513	MSY44y	31-PFBD	pubian cluster		0.01	61	0....	3	3	4	0	0		...	b
5155	Punan	0.00200	3,949	4,242	5,469	AUG05	31-JBDC-a	kereho-uheng		8.00	339	0....	7	5	7	0	2		...	.
5156	Punan Aput	0.00024	474	509	656	MSY44z	31-JBDC-a	kereho-uheng		2.00	10	0....	6	4	5	0	0		...	.
5157	Punan Bungan	0.00053	1,047	1,124	1,449	MSY44z	31-JBDB-a	hovongan		5.00	56	0....	7	5	6	1	2	Hovongan	...	.
5158	Punan Keriau	0.00012	237	255	328	MSY44z	31-JBDC-a	kereho-uheng		2.00	5	0....	6	4	5	0	0		...	.
5159	Punan Merah	0.00009	178	191	246	MSY44z	31-JBDC-a	kereho-uheng		3.00	6	0....	6	4	6	0	0		...	.
5160	Punan Merap	0.00010	197	212	273	MSY44z	31-JBDC-a	kereho-uheng		2.00	4	0....	6	4	5	0	0		...	.
5161	Punan Tubu	0.00130	2,567	2,757	3,555	MSY44y	31-JCAA-a	punan-tubu		4.00	110	0....	6	4	6	0	0		...	.
5162	Puragi	0.00037	731	785	1,012	AON10a	20-HBAB-a	puragi		65.00	510	0....	10	6	6	2	0		...	.
5163	Putoh	0.00389	7,681	8,251	10,637	MSY44z	31-GBAJ-f	kinabatangan-sungai		20.00	1,650	0.s..	9	5	6	1	0		pn.	.
5164	Pyu	0.00004	79	85	109	AON10a	25-RAAA-a	pyu		65.00	55	0....	10	6	1	2	1		...	.
5165	Rahambuu	0.00266	5,253	5,642	7,274	MSY44y	31-QDDB-a	rahambuu		1.00	56	0....	6	4	4	0	0		...	b
5166	Ranau	0.03318	65,519	70,377	90,728	MSY44k	31-GBAL-b	monsok-dusun		0.01	7	0....	3	3	3	0	0	Dusun: Ranau*	PNB	b
5167	Rasawa	0.00012	237	255	328	AON09e	25-HAAB-a	rasawa		80.00	204	0....	10	7	11	2	1		...	.
5168	Ratahan (Bentenan)	0.01659	32,759	35,189	45,364	MSY44l	31-RBAA-a	ratahan		95.00	33,429	0....	10	8	12	5	1	Ratahan	...	b
5169	Rawas	0.08295	163,797	175,943	226,820	MSY44k	31-PHAD-c	rawas		0.01	18	0....	3	3	3	0	0		pn.	b
5170	Rejang	0.64910	1,281,742	1,376,789	1,774,913	MSY44y	31-PGAA	rejang cluster		0.01	138	0....	3	3	2	1	3		...	b
5171	Rembong (Namu)	0.00100	1,975	2,121	2,734	MSY44y	29-BGEA	martu cluster		10.00	212	0....	8	5	6	4	0	Martu Wangka	P..	.
5172	Riantana	0.00078	1,540	1,654	2,133	AON10a	20-JAAA-a	riantana		65.00	1,075	0....	10	6	6	2	0		...	.
5173	Riau (Malay)	1.02000	2,014,138	2,163,495	2,789,110	MSY44k	31-PHAB-e	malayu-riau		0.01	216	0....	3	3	1	4	3		...	b
5174	Ribun (Land Dayak)	0.03000	59,239	63,632	82,033	MSY44y	31-KAAK-a	ribun		40.00	25,453	0....	9	5	5	5	2		...	.
5175	Riung	0.00909	17,950	19,281	24,856	MSY44y	32-AAEC-a	riung		15.00	2,892	0....	8	5	6	4	1		...	.
5176	Roma	0.00091	1,797	1,930	2,488	MSY44y	32-BCEB-a	roma		60.00	1,158	0....	10	6	6	2	1		...	b
5177	Ron	0.00057	1,126	1,209	1,559	MSY44y	33-ADBC-a	roon		15.00	181	0....	8	5	6	1	0		...	.
5178	Rongkong	0.01872	36,965	39,707	51,188	MSY44p	31-QBEB	tae cluster		60.00	23,824	0....	10	7	6	2	1		...	b
5179	Rotinese (Rotti)	0.08309	164,073	176,240	227,203	MSY44y	32-BCAA	roti cluster		80.00	140,992	0....	10	5	12	5	1	Roti*	P..	.
5180	Saban	0.00040	790	848	1,094	MSY44z	31-HAAD-a	sa'ban		20.00	170	0....	9	5	6	2	0	Saban	P..	.
5181	Saberi (Saweri)	0.00104	2,054	2,206	2,844	AON10a	24-FDAA	isirawa cluster		64.90	1,432	0....	10	6	6	2	1	Isirawa	P..	.
5182	Sahu (Sau, Padisua)	0.00431	8,511	9,142	11,785	AON10c	25-AADA	sahu cluster		60.00	5,485	0....	10	7	6	4	1	Sahu	...	b
5183	Sajau Basap	0.00390	7,701	8,272	10,664	MSY44y	31-IBAC-a	sajau-basap		25.00	2,068	0....	9	5	5	2	0		...	.
5184	Salajarese	0.05616	110,896	119,120	153,565	MSY44y	31-QBAA-a	salayar		3.00	3,574	0....	6	4	6	4	1		...	b
5185	Salawati (Samate)	0.00086	1,698	1,824	2,352	AON09e	33-ABBC	maya cluster		91.00	1,660	0....	10	7	12	4	2		...	.
5186	Saleman (Wahai)	0.00265	5,233	5,621	7,246	MSY44y	32-DGIA-e	saleman		4.00	225	0....	6	4	6	0	0		...	b
5187	Samarkena (Tamaja)	0.00025	494	530	684	AON10a	24-FCAA-a	proper samarkena		65.00	345	0....	10	6	6	2	0		...	p
5188	Sanana (Sula, Facei)	0.01248	24,644	26,471	34,126	MSY44y	32-ECAA	sula cluster		0.06	16	0....	4	2	3	0	0		...	b
5189	Sanggau (Land Dayak)	0.03000	59,239	63,632	82,033	MSY44y	31-KAAM-a	sanggau		40.00	25,453	0....	9	5	5	5	2		...	.
5190	Sangirese (Great Sangir)	0.10122	199,874	214,695	276,778	MSY44y	31-RBAD	sangir cluster		97.00	208,254	4....	10	8	11	5	3	Sangirese	PN.	b
5191	Sangke	0.00010	197	212	273	AON10a	25-OAAA-a	sangke		65.00	138	0....	10	6	6	2	0		...	.
5192	Saparua	0.00565	11,157	11,984	15,449	AON09e	32-DGOE	iha-saparua cluster		4.00	479	0....	6	4	5	0	0		...	b
5193	Saponi	0.00001	20	21	27	AON09e	25-HAAC-a	saponi		60.00	13	0....	10	6	1	2	1		...	.
5194	Sara	0.00300	5,924	6,363	8,203	MSY44y	31-KAAO-a	sara		30.00	1,909	0....	9	5	5	4	1	Sara	...	.
5195	Sasak (Lombok)	1.16128	2,293,116	2,463,161	3,175,429	MSY44y	31-PKAB	sasak cluster		0.02	493	1....	3	4	1	4	3	Sasak	PN.	.
5196	Sasawa	0.00014	276	297	383	AON10a	24-FBAD-a	sasawa		66.00	196	0....	10	6	6	2	0		...	p
5197	Sauri	0.00006	118	127	164	AON10a	25-JCBA-a	sauri		65.00	83	0....	10	6	6	2	0		...	.
5198	Sause	0.00015	296	318	410	AON10a	21-LAAA-a	sause		70.00	223	0....	10	6	6	2	1		...	.
5199	Sawai	0.00664	13,112	14,084	18,157	MSY44y	33-AABA-b	sawai		12.00	1,690	0....	8	5	6	4	2	Sawai	P..	b
5200	Saweru	0.00016	316	339	438	AON10b	25-IAAA-o	saweru		65.00	221	0....	10	8	8	0	0		p..	.
5201	Sawuy (Sawi)	0.00182	3,594	3,860	4,977	AON10a	24-KDAA-a	sawi		85.00	3,281	0....	10	7	11	4	1	Sawi	PN.	.
5202	Sea Dayak (Iban, Birawut)	0.11722	231,468	248,632	320,529	MSY44e	31-PHIB	iban-ketungau cluster		51.00	126,802	0A...	10	5	8	5	3		...	.
5203	Seberuang	0.01043	20,596	22,123	28,520	MSY44e	31-PHIC	iban-seberuang cluster		10.00	2,212	0....	8	6	7	0	0	Seberuang	...	.
5204	Segai	0.00130	2,567	2,757	3,555	MSY44x	31-JBCA	segai cluster		5.00	138	0....	7	4	6	1	0		...	.
5205	Seget	0.00068	1,343	1,442	1,859	AON10a	25-BAAA-a	seget		65.00	938	0....	10	6	6	2	0		...	.
5206	Sekar	0.00032	632	679	875	AON09e	33-ACAB-a	sekar		91.00	618	0....	10	7	11	2	0		...	.
5207	Sekayu	0.22120	436,791	469,182	604,854	MSY44y	31-PHAD-e	sekayu		0.01	47	0....	3	3	1	0	0		pn.	b
5208	Seko Padang (Wono)	0.00285	5,628	6,045	7,793	MSY44p	31-QBJB	seko-padang cluster		80.00	4,836	0....	10	7	8	4	1	Seko Padang	...	b
5209	Seko Tengah (Pewanean)	0.00126	2,488	2,673	3,445	MSY44p	31-QBJA	seko-tengah cluster		80.00	2,138	0....	10	7	7	4	0		...	b
5210	Sela	0.00148	2,922	3,139	4,047	AON10a	32-EBBB-a	li-sela		70.00	2,197	0....	10	7	7	4	1		...	.
5211	Selako Dayak	0.06491	128,174	137,679	177,491	MSY44y	31-KAAA-a	silakau		2.00	2,754	0....	6	4	5	1	1		...	.
5212	Selaru	0.00442	8,728	9,375	12,086	AON09e	32-DAAA-a	selaru		91.00	8,531	0....	10	7	11	2	1	Selaru	...	b
5213	Selungai Murut	0.00030	592	636	820	MSY44z	31-GCAG-a	selungai murut		20.00	127	0....	9	5	6	1	0		...	.
5214	Selvasa (Makatian)	0.00188	3,712	3,988	5,141	AON09e	32-DBAA-a	seluwasan		80.00	3,190	0....	10	7	10	1	0		...	b
5215	Semandang (Land Dayak)	0.01947	38,446	41,297	53,239	MSY44y	31-KAAN-a	semandang		40.00	16,519	0....	9	5	5	5	3	Semandang	P..	.
5216	Sembakung Murut	0.00150	2,962	3,182	4,102	MSY44z	31-GCBB-a	sembakung		20.00	636	0....	9	5	6	1	0		...	.
5217	Semendau (Malay, Semendo)	0.05806	114,648	123,150	158,760	MSY44k	31-PHAD-q	semendo		0.02	25	0....	3	3	5	1	1		pn.	b
5218	Semimi (Etna Bay)	0.00053	1,047	1,124	1,449	AON10a	24-CBAD-a	semimi		65.00	731	0....	10	6	6	2	0		...	.
5219	Sempan	0.00058	1,145	1,230	1,586	AON10a	24-KABB-a	proper sempan		60.00	738	0....	10	6	6	4	1		...	.
5220	Senggi	0.00008	158	170	219	AON10a	21-HCAA-a	senggi		66.00	112	0....	10	6	8	4	2		...	.
5221	Sentani (Buyaka)	0.01495	29,521	31,710	40,880	AON10a	24-GCAA-b	central sentani		20.00	6,342	0....	9	5	9	5	2	Sentani	P..	.
5222	Serawai (Serawaj)	0.08295	163,797	175,943	226,820	MSY44k	31-PHAD-v	serawai		6.00	10,557	0....	7	5	5	4	3	Serawai	PN.	b
5223	Serili	0.00022	434	467	602	AON09e	32-BCEF-a	serili		80.00	373	0....	10	7	10	2	1		...	b
5224	Serua	0.00109	2,152	2,312	2,981	MSY44y	32-BCHB-b	serua		60.00	1,387	0....	10	6	6	2	0		...	b
5225	Serui-Laut	0.00058	1,145	1,230	1,586	AON09e	31-PHCA	moken cluster		91.00	1,120	0....	10	7	11	4	2	Moken	P..	b
5226	Siagha-Yenimu (Oser)	0.00174	3,436	3,691	4,758	AON10a	24-KDBD	siagha-yenimu cluster		65.00	2,399	0....	10	6	7	2	1		...	.
5227	Siau Sangirese	0.02900	57,265	61,511	79,298	MSY44y	31-RBAD-a	siau		91.00	55,975	1....	10	7	11	2	0	Sangirese: Siau	PN.	b
5228	Sikhule (Lekon, Tapah)	0.01162	22,945	24,647	31,774	MSY44y	31-PCAB-a	sichule		50.00	12,323	0....	10	5	3	1	1		...	b
5229	Sikkanese	0.09496	187,512	201,417	259,661	AON09e	32-BAAA-a	sara-krow		91.00	183,290	0....	10	7	12	4	1		...	.
5230	Silindung Batak (Batta)	0.20000	394,929	424,215	546,884	MSY44b	31-PECA-a	toba		95.00	403,004	2.s..	10	8	11	5	1	Batak: Toba*	PNB	b
5231	Simalungun Batak (Batta)	0.56424	1,114,174	1,196,795	1,542,870	MSY44b	31-PEBA-a	simalungun	1	50.00	598,397	0.s..	10	7	6	5	3	Batak: Simalungun*	PNB	b
5232	Simalur-Banyak(Long Bano)	0.06491	128,174	137,679	177,491	MSY44y	31-PCAA	simeulue cluster		1.00	1,377	0....	6	4	6	1	0		...	.
5233	Soa	0.00513	10,130	10,881	14,028	MSY44y	32-AAEH-b	soa		90.00	9,793	0....	10	9	8	0	0		...	.
5234	Sobei (Biga, Liki)	0.00107	2,113	2,270	2,926	AON09e	34-AAAA	sobei cluster		91.00	2,065	0....	10	7	11	3	1		...	b
5235	Solorese (Lamaholot)	0.17143	338,513	363,616	468,762	AON09e	32-BABD-a	takä		72.00	261,803	0....	10	7	3	5	2		...	.
5236	Somahai (Sumohai)	0.00157	3,100	3,330	4,293	AON10a	24-KBAA-a	momuna		64.00	2,131	0....	10	6	7	4	3	Momuna	P..	.
5237	South Butonese	0.00871	17,199	18,475	23,817	MSY44y	31-QACA	south buton cluster		4.00	739	0....	6	4	4	1	0		...	.
5238	South Damar	0.00152	3,001	3,224	4,156	MSY44y	32-BCGB-a	east damar		60.00	1,934	0....	10	6	6	2	0		...	b
5239	South Loloda	0.00107	2,113	2,270	2,926	AON10c	25-AABC-a	laba		30.00	681	0....	9	5	6	4	1		...	b
5240	South Mori (Karongsi)	0.00320	6,319	6,787	8,750	MSY44y	31-QDFA-a	padoe		70.00	4,751	0....	10	7	6	4	1		...	b
5241	South Ngalik (Paiyage)	0.00290	5,726	6,151	7,930	AON10a	24-FADB-a	silimo		25.00	1,538	0....	9	5	8	5	1	Silimo	PN.	b
5242	South Nuaulu	0.00075	1,481	1,591	2,051	MSY44y	32-DGHB-a	south nuaulu		8.00	127	0....	7	5	6	1	1	Nuaulu*	P..	b
5243	South Toraja (Rantepao)	0.27132	535,761	575,490	741,903	MSY44p	31-QBED-e	toraja-barat		65.00	374,068	0....	10	7	8	5	3	Toraja*	PNB	b
5244	South Tukangbesi	0.06579	129,912	139,545	179,898	MSY44y	31-QAAB	south tukang-besi cluster		5.00	6,977	0....	7	5	6	4	0		...	b
5245	South Wemale (Tala)	0.00216	4,265	4,582	5,906	MSY44y	32-DGKA-a	tala		80.00	3,665	0....	10	7	10	4	1		...	b
5246	Southeast Babar	0.00184	3,633	3,903	5,031	AON09e	69-BBAA-b	tepehua-puebla		70.00	2,732	0....	10	7	6	2	0	Nahuatl: Puebla, Southeast*	PN.	b
5247	Southeast Marind (Gawir)	0.00407	8,037	8,633	11,129	AON10a	24-IBAA	lower marind cluster		65.00	5,611	0....	10	6	7	2	2		...	b
5248	Southern Kati (Digul)	0.00232	4,581	4,921	6,344	AON10a	24-KEAC	north kati cluster		60.00	2,953	0....	10	6	2	2	2		...	b
5249	Southern Murut	0.01439	28,415	30,522	39,348	MSY44z	31-HAAC-o	lun-bawang		20.00	6,104	0.s..	9	5	8	4	1	Lun Bawang*	PNB	.
5250	Southern Pesisir	0.28834	569,369	611,590	788,443	MSY44y	31-PFBE	pesisir cluster		0.01	61	0....	3	2	2	0	0		...	b
5251	Sowanda (Wanja)	0.00010	197	212	273	AON10b	21-HDAA-a	proper sowanda		75.00	159	0....	10	7	6	2	0		...	.
5252	Straits Chinese (Baba Creol	0.05000	98,732	106,054	136,721	MSY42a	31-PHBA-a	baba-malay	1	6.00	6,363	0....	7	5	6	5	3	Malay: Baba	PN.	b
5253	Suku Batin	0.03871	76,439	82,107	105,849	MSY44y	31-PHAD-z	suku-batin		0.00	0	0....	0	3	3	0	0		pn.	b
5254	Sukubatong (Kimki)	0.00024	474	509	656	AON10a	26-AAAA-b	kimki		65.00	331	0....	10	6	6	2	1		...	.
5255	Sumbawanese	0.16590	327,594	351,886	453,640	MSY44y	31-PKAC-a	sumbawa		0.01	35	0....	3	3	2	4	3		...	.

Continued opposite

Table 8-2 continued

EVANGELIZATION								EVANGELISM			ADDITIONAL DESCRIPTIVE DATA
Ref 1	D 28	aC 29	CG% 30	r 31	E 32	U 33	W 34	e 35	R 36	T 37	Locations, civil divisions, literacy, religions, church history, denominations, dioceses, church growth, missions, agencies, ministries, movements 38
5132	0	3	0.70	0	12.01	87.99	A	0.00	354	1.04	Southeast Sulawesi. Near Muna. Muslims 99%.
5133	0	5	3.57	0	26.00	74.00	A	2.84	471	4	South Sulawesi. Polewali-Mamasa District, Wonomulyo Subdistrict. Muslims 95%.
5134	0	5	3.60	0	90.75	9.25	C	214.47	139	8	Irian Jaya. Lakes Plain area on lower Idenburg river. Mostly monolinguals. Animists 35%. M=RBMU.
5135	1	5	4.39	0	99.91	0.09	C	418.50	117	10	Irian Jaya. South coast of Yapen Island, Papuma village. Animists 9%. D=GKI.
5136	1	4	3.40	5	31.06	68.94	A	0.06	362	2	Sumatra. Central Bukit Barisan highlands. Muslims 87%(Shafi Sunnis), animists 13%. D=GEKISUS. M=IMF,WEC.
5137	0	0	6.14	0	90.00	10.00	C	213.52	217	8	Irian Jaya. Central highlands, east of Angguruk. Related to Yali of Ninia and Yali of Angguruk. Animists 35%.
5138	0	5	4.96	0	39.00	61.00	A	17.08	408	5	North Maluku. Southeastern peninsula of Halmahera, 9 villages. Access by sea. Muslims 88%.
5139	0	5	4.59	0	27.00	73.00	A	1.97	557	4	South Sulawesi. Polmas District, Polewali Subdistrict. Muslims 95%.
5140	0	5	5.43	0	27.00	73.00	A	2.95	637	4	South Sulawesi. Northern half of Pinrang District. Plains. Agriculturalists. Muslims 95%.
5141	0	5	4.14	0	99.91	0.09	C	415.18	113	10	Central Maluku. West Seram, western shore of Elpaputih Bay, 2 villages. Access by sea. Nearly extinct.
5142	0	7	4.40	0	77.00	23.00	B	140.52	192	7	Irian Jaya. Mamberamo river area, west side by Lake Rombebai. Language isolate. Animists 50%.
5143	0	4	3.62	1	24.10	75.90	A	0.08	491	2	Southern Sumatra, west coast. Muslims 99%.
5144	0	5	3.21	1	28.00	72.00	A	1.02	383	4	Southern Sumatra, around Prabumulih. Muslims 95%.
5145	0	5	4.38	0	22.00	78.00	A	1.60	609	4	Kalimantan. North central near Sarawak border. Animists 98%.
5146	0	5	4.25	0	46.00	54.00	A	33.58	304	5	South Maluku. Wetar Island, north of Timor. Animists 70%, Muslims 10%.
5147	0	6	0.00	0	17.04	82.96	A	0.02	0	2	Central Sulawesi. East coast around Marantale, south of Kasimbar language area. Muslims 95%.
5148	0	8	2.87	0	99.80	0.20	C	344.56	86	9	Central Maluku. West Seram, 1 village. Related to Nakaela, Luhu. Access by boat. Nearly extinct.
5149	0	5	5.80	0	94.00	6.00	C	223.01	198	8	Irian Jaya. South coast area, southwest of Wildeman river, east of Kampong river. Mostly monolinguals. Animists 35%. M=TEAM.
5150	0	5	6.19	0	45.00	55.00	A	24.63	432	5	South Sulawesi. Watershed of Maloso and Mapilli rivers, Mambi Sub-District. Muslims 85% (largely in the south). M=SIL.
5151	1	5	5.56	0	99.91	0.09	C	421.83	142	10	Irian Jaya. Miosnum Island and west Yapen Island, 3 villages. Animists 9%. D=GKI.
5152	0	5	2.12	0	42.00	58.00	A	22.99	194	5	Northeast Sulawesi. Around Belang. Close to Mongondow. Animists 80%, some Muslims 5%.
5153	2	4	9.86	0	99.80	0.20	C	365.00	236	9	Central Sulawesi. Over 250 villages. Animists 20%. Surrounding peoples are highly islamized. D=GKST,NTM. M=NZG,IBS-I.
5154	0	5	4.20	0	18.01	81.99	A	0.00	768	1.05	South Sumatra. Close to standard Riau-Johore Malay, also Pesisir. Muslims 100%(Shafi Sunnis).
5155	0	6	3.59	0	33.00	67.00	A	9.63	381	4	West Kalimantan Province. Nomadic forest dwellers, now becoming settled. Animists 92%. M=NTM,REMP.
5156	0	5	2.33	0	21.00	79.00	A	1.53	371	4	Kalimantan. Northeast, west and north of Mt Menyapa. Nomadic forest-dwellers. Animists 98%.
5157	2	6	4.11	0	32.00	68.00	A	5.84	396	4	Kalimantan. North central near Sarawak border, 2 areas. Animists 95%. D=GKE,NTM.
5158	0	5	1.62	0	21.00	79.00	A	1.53	278	4	Kalimantan. North central near Sarawak south of Bukat and Hovongan. Nomadic forest dwellers. Animists 98%.
5159	0	5	1.81	0	23.00	77.00	A	2.51	276	4	Kalimantan. Northeast, Mahakam river. Nomads in forest. Animists 97%.
5160	0	5	1.40	0	21.00	79.00	A	1.53	249	4	Kalimantan. Northeast, east of Longkemuat. Nomadic forest-dwellers. Animists 98%.
5161	0	6	2.43	0	25.00	75.00	A	3.65	359	4	Kalimantan. Northeast, Malinau, Mentarang, Sembakung rivers, 8 locations. Nomads. Animists 96%.
5162	0	5	4.01	0	91.00	9.00	C	215.89	151	8	Irian Jaya. Southwest Bird's Head along Maccluer Gulf, inland. Animists 35%.
5163	0	6	5.24	0	50.00	50.00	B	36.50	315	5	Kalimantan. Northeast, west of Lundayeh and Saban, Mentarang river. Animists 80%.
5164	0	7	4.09	0	89.00	11.00	C	211.15	157	8	Irian Jaya. Border area near headwaters of Sepik river; also in PNG. Monolinguals. Animists 35%. M=UFM.
5165	0	4	4.11	0	21.00	79.00	A	0.76	647	3	Southeast Sulawesi, Kolaka District, Pakue Subdistrict. Muslims 95%.
5166	0	4	1.96	0	26.01	73.99	A	0.00	280	1.08	Southern Sumatra, south of Muaradua. Muslims 90%.
5167	0	5	3.06	0	99.80	0.20	C	327.04	99	9	Irian Jaya. 2 villages near southern coast of Waropen Bawah District. Most are monolingual. Animists 20%. M=UFM.
5168	2	5	2.02	0	99.95	0.05	C	478.51	57	10	Sulawesi. Northeast section of northern peninsula, around Ratahan town. Minahasan. All Christians. D=GMIM,RCC(D-Manado). M=MSC.
5169	0	4	2.93	1	20.01	79.99	A	0.00	497	1.08	Southern Sumatra, around Ambacang. Muslims 90%.
5170	2	3	2.66	0	20.01	79.99	A	0.00	481	1.07	Sumatra. North of Bengkulu. Literates 45%. Muslims 100%(Shafi Sunnis). D=GKII,GEKISUS/GKSS. M=IMF,WEC,FMB,Misi Rahmat(Mercy Mission).
5171	0	5	3.10	0	37.00	63.00	A	13.50	293	5	Nusa Tenggara. North central Flores. Muslims 70%, animists 20%.
5172	0	5	4.79	0	92.00	8.00	C	218.27	172	8	Irian Jaya. Frederik Hendrik Island. Closest to Kimaghama and Ndom. Animists 35%.
5173	1	5	3.12	5	28.01	71.99	A	0.01	374	2	West central Sumatra. Language on which Bahasa Indonesia modeled. Muslims 100%(Shafi Sunnis), a few animists(responsive). D=RCC(D-Pangkal Pinang).
5174	8	5	8.16	0	74.00	26.00	B	108.04	334	7	Kalimantan. North of Kapuas river. Animists 40%, Muslims 20%. D=GKE,ICFG,RCC(M-Pontianak),GBIS,GKPI,PPIK,CMA,NTM. M=OFMCap,WEC.
5175	1	5	5.83	0	44.00	56.00	A	24.09	416	5	Nusa Tenggara. Flores Island, Lesser Sundas. Close to Manggarai. Muslims 50%, animists 35%. D=RCC.
5176	1	5	1.30	0	92.00	8.00	C	201.48	64	8	South Maluku. Romang Island, north of Timor Island, east of Wetar Island. Animists 40%. D=GPM.
5177	0	5	2.94	0	38.00	62.00	A	20.80	273	5	Irian Jaya. Roon Island west of Geelvink Bay. Animists 85%.
5178	0	5	8.09	0	92.00	8.00	C	201.48	268	8	South Sulawesi. Southeast Limbong and Sabbang Subdistricts, Luwu District. Agriculturalists. Muslims 40% (mostly Rongkong Bawah). M=SIL.
5179	4	5	3.13	0	99.80	0.20	C	356.24	89	9	Nusa Tenggara. Roti Island. 9 dialects. Animists 20%. D=GMIT,KINGMI,RCC,Gereja Bethel(Pentecostal). M=CMA.
5180	0	6	2.87	0	47.00	53.00	A	34.31	197	5	Kalimantan. Northeast on Sarawak border, south of Lundayeh. Also in Sarawak (Malaysia). Animists 80%.
5181	2	5	5.09	0	95.90	4.10	C	227.17	174	8	Irian Jaya, Jayapura, Sarmi, north coast, 9 villages. Close to Kwerba. Lingua franca. Animists 35%. D=GKI,CMA. M=SIL.
5182	1	6	3.98	0	95.00	5.00	C	208.05	144	8	North Maluku. Southwestern north Halmahera. Muslims 40%. D=GMIH. M=Indonesian Bible Society.
5183	0	6	5.48	0	51.00	49.00	B	46.53	340	6	Kalimantan. Northeast; northeast of Muaramalinau. 3 dialects. Animists 75%.
5184	1	5	6.06	0	33.00	67.00	A	3.61	574	4	South Sulawesi. Selayar Island off southwest tip. Close to Makassarese. Muslims 97%(Sunnis). D=GKSS.
5185	2	5	5.24	0	99.91	0.09	C	431.79	132	10	Irian Jaya. Raja Ampat Islands, central Waigeo and central Salawati Islands. Animists 8%. D=GKIIJ,GPS.
5186	0	6	3.16	0	28.00	72.00	A	4.08	392	4	Central Maluku. North central Seram, 5 villages. Related to Nuaulu. Access by boat. Muslims 95%.
5187	0	5	3.60	0	92.00	8.00	C	218.27	137	8	Irian Jaya. North coast inland east of Apawar river, west of Sarmi, 4 villages. Bilingual in Airoran, Isirawa, Kwerba. Animists 35%.
5188	0	5	2.81	0	18.06	81.94	A	0.04	555	2	North Maluku. Sula Islands, Sulabesi Island, also Mangole Island, Buru Island. Muslims 99%.
5189	8	5	8.16	0	74.00	26.00	B	108.04	334	7	Kalimantan. Kapuas river. Animists 40%, Muslims 20%. D=GKE,ICFG,RCC(M-Pontianak),PPIK,GBIS,GKPI,NTM,CMA. M=OFMCap,WEC.
5190	2	5	2.36	0	99.97	0.03	C	527.53	59	10	North Sulawesi. Also Philippines. Almost all Christians. D=GMIST,GMAHKT. Large-scale emigration to Java, Mindanao, with own churches. M=NRMB,SDA,SIL.
5191	0	7	2.66	0	93.00	7.00	C	220.64	108	8	Irian Jaya. North coast, southeast of Jayapura. Animists 35%.
5192	0	5	3.94	0	26.00	74.00	A	3.79	521	4	Central Maluku. Saparua and Seram Islands, Lease Islands, 8 villages. Access by boat. Muslims 95%.
5193	0	6	2.60	0	83.00	17.00	C	181.77	119	7	Irian Jaya. Botawa village, interior of Waropen Bawah. Language nearly extinct. Monolinguals. M=UFM.
5194	0	5	5.39	0	58.00	42.00	B	63.51	295	6	Kalimantan. Near Sanggau-Ledo northeast of Ledo. Animists 70%. M=CBFMS.
5195	2	3	3.97	2	26.02	73.98	A	0.01	508	2	Eastern Lombok Island. Agrarian. Muslims 100%, with strong Islamic schools influencing 50% of island. D=GPIB,AoG. M=YWAM-Indonesia,PI,AOGWM.
5196	0	7	3.02	0	95.00	5.00	C	228.85	116	8	Irian Jaya. North coast, Jayapura area on middle Apawar river, Sasawa village. Close to Kwerba, Airoran. Animists 34%.
5197	0	5	4.52	0	91.00	9.00	C	215.89	166	8	Irian Jaya. East side of Geelvink Bay, near Sirami river. Animists 35%.
5198	0	5	3.15	0	97.00	3.00	C	247.83	117	8	Irian Jaya. Southwest of Sentani, northwest of Lereh, 6 villages. Animists 30%. M=RBMU.
5199	1	5	5.26	0	46.00	54.00	A	20.14	364	5	North Maluku. Coastal area between southern peninsulas of Halmahera. Access by sea. Muslims 88%. D=GMIH. M=Indonesian Bible Society,SIL.
5200	0	0	3.14	0	86.00	14.00	C	204.03	134	8	Irian Jaya. Central Serui Island on an island south of Yapen Island near Serui. Geelvink Bay. Animists 35%.
5201	2	5	5.96	0	99.85	0.15	C	390.91	151	9	Irian Jaya. Merauke area. Animists 15%. D=GKIIJ,RCC. M=RBMU.
5202	4	4	9.91	0	94.00	6.00	B	174.98	304	7	Western Kalimantan Province. Also Malaysia (Sabah, Sarawak),and Brunei. Animists 49%. D=GMI,Anglican Ch,GKE,NTM. M=USPG,REMP,WEC.
5203	0	0	5.55	0	28.00	72.00	A	10.22	593	5	Kalimantan. Kapuas River. Animists 90%.
5204	0	5	2.66	0	27.00	73.00	A	4.92	339	4	Kalimantan. Northeast, Kelai river and around Longlaai. Animists 95%.
5205	0	5	4.65	0	91.00	9.00	C	215.89	170	8	Irian Jaya. West Bird's Head southwest of Sorong, 4 villages. Animists 35%.
5206	0	5	4.21	0	99.91	0.09	C	405.22	117	10	Irian Jaya. Northwest Bomberai Peninsula. Animists 9%.
5207	0	1	3.93	1	15.01	84.99	A	0.00	873	1.07	Southern Sumatra. Muslims 90%.
5208	1	5	6.38	0	99.80	0.20	C	338.72	172	9	South Sulawesi. Northeast of Limbong Sub-District, Luwu District. Resettled. Agriculturalists. Animists 15%, some Muslims. D=various churches. M=SIL.
5209	0	5	5.51	0	99.80	0.20	C	329.96	155	9	South Sulawesi. Limbong Subdistricts, Luwu District, also Mamuju District. Second language: Indonesian. Virtually all Christians.
5210	0	6	5.54	0	99.70	0.30	C	260.61	176	8	Irian Jaya. Sela Valley, Thai river, Jayawijaya District. Monolinguals. Animists 30%. M=RBMU.
5211	1	5	5.78	0	25.00	75.00	A	1.82	727	4	Kalimantan. Northwest, around Pemangkat. Animists 98%. D=GKE. M=BEM.
5212	0	5	6.98	0	99.91	0.09	C	421.83	172	10	South Maluku. 8 villages on Selaru, Yamdena, Nus-Wotar Islands. M=SIL.
5213	0	6	2.57	0	45.00	55.00	A	32.85	188	5	Kalimantan. Along upper reaches of Sembakung river, east of Lumbis. Also in Sabah (Malaysia). Animists 80%.
5214	0	6	5.93	0	99.80	0.20	C	332.88	167	9	South Maluku. Southwest coast of Yamdena Island, 3 villages. Hunters. Animists 20%.
5215	8	6	7.69	0	77.00	23.00	B	112.42	304	7	Kalimantan. North of Sandai. Animists 40%, Muslims 20%. D=RCC(M-Pontianak),GKE,ICFG,PPIK,GKPI,GBIS,CMA,NTM. M=OFMCap,WEC,RBMU.
5216	0	6	4.24	0	45.00	55.00	A	32.85	289	5	Kalimantan. North along Sembakung river, from mouth into Sabah (Malaysia). Animists 80%.
5217	1	5	3.27	5	30.02	69.98	A	0.02	362	2	In interior of south Sumatra. 2 areas: west of Baturaja, south of Pajarbulan. Muslims 100%(Shafi Sunnis). D=GKPI. M=PTTE.
5218	0	5	4.39	0	91.00	9.00	C	215.89	162	8	Irian Jaya. Bomberai Peninsula close to Kaniran. Animists 35%.
5219	1	5	4.40	0	90.00	10.00	C	197.10	164	7	Irian Jaya. Middle south coast between Kokonao and Agats. Close to Kamoro and Nefaripi. Animists 40%. D=GAK. M=TEAM.
5220	2	7	2.45	0	99.66	0.34	C	245.71	93	8	Irian Jaya. Border area south of Jayapura, 2 villages. Most are monolinguals. Animists 34%. D=Indonesian Protestant Ch,KINGMI.
5221	3	5	6.67	0	58.00	42.00	B	42.34	362	6	Irian Jaya. East end of Lake Sentani, to the coast, 23 villages. Fishermen, agriculturalists. Mostly monolingual. Animists 80%. D=GKI,SDA,RCC. M=SIL,UFM.
5222	1	4	7.21	5	47.00	53.00	A	10.29	461	5	Sumatra. South Bengkulu coast. Related to Pasemah. Muslims 86%(Shafi Sunnis), animists 8%. D=GEKISUS/GKSS. M=IMF,WEC,FMB.
5223	1	5	3.69	0	99.80	0.20	C	335.80	112	9	South Maluku. Northeast Marsela Island. D=GPM.
5224	0	5	1.68	0	90.00	10.00	C	197.10	77	7	Central Maluku. Seram Island. Relocated from Damar Islands due to volcanic activity. Animists 40%.
5225	2	5	4.83	0	99.91	0.09	C	431.79	123	10	Irian Jaya. South central Yapen Island and Nau Island; 5 villages. D=GKI,CMA.
5226	0	5	5.63	0	94.00	6.00	C	223.01	193	8	Irian Jaya. Southeast near coast, north of lower Digul river. Mostly monolinguals. Animists 35%. M=TEAM.
5227	0	5	1.84	0	99.91	0.09	C	438.43	56	10	North Sulawesi. Great Sangir Island, Siau Island, and north Maluku. Also Philippines.
5228	1	5	7.38	0	79.00	21.00	B	144.17	285	7	Sumatra. Central part of Simeulue Island. Closely related to Nias. Muslims 30%, animists 20%. D=BNKP.
5229	1	5	10.31	0	99.91	0.09	C	428.47	240	10	Nusa Tenggara. Central Flores Island, Lesser Sundas. Muslims 8%. D=RCC.
5230	4	3	3.31	0	99.95	0.05	C	516.65	76	10	North Sumatra. Closely related to Toba Bakaks. Strongly Protestant. D=HKBP,RCC(M-Medan,&c),GPI,HKI. M=OFMCap.
5231	7	3	4.31	0	99.00	1.00	B	180.67	143	7	North Sumatra. Muslims 40%(Shafi Sunnis), animists 10%. Mixed with local Javanese Muslims. D=GKPS,RCC,GMI,GMMI,GSRKI,GPI,GKPI. M=RMS,NBS.
5232	0	5	5.05	0	23.00	77.00	A	0.84	703	3	Sumatra. West and east ends of Simeulue Island, Babi and Banjak Islands. Close to Sikule and Nias. Muslims 99%.
5233	0	0	7.13	0	99.90	0.10	C	364.63	189	9	Nusa Tenggara. Central Flores between Ngad'a and Riung. Muslims 10%. D=RCC.
5234	0	5	5.47	0	99.91	0.09	C	425.15	138	10	Irian Jaya. North coast area east and west of Sarmi, 4 villages. Youth are bilingual in Indonesian and Irianese Malay. M=SIL.
5235	2	5	10.71	0	99.72	0.28	C	273.31	309	8	Solor Island. Dry impoverished land. 3 dialects. Muslims 15%(Shafi Sunnis since AD 1500), animists 13%, Hindus, Buddhists. Y=1561(RCs). D=93% RCC,7% Prot.
5236	0	6	5.51	0	99.00	1.00	C	231.26	180	8	Irian Jaya. Lowlands south of main ranges south of Silimo. No bilinguals. Animists 36%. M=RBMU,SIL,NRC,CMA.
5237	0	5	4.40	0	23.00	77.00	A	3.35	625	4	Southern Butung. Southern Sulawesi. South Buton Island. Muslims 95%.
5238	0	5	2.70	0	90.00	10.00	C	197.10	108	7	South Maluku. String of small Damar Islands north and east of Roma, off Timor; 6 villages. Animists 40%.
5239	1	5	4.31	0	62.00	38.00	B	67.89	235	6	North Maluku, 4 villages in Loloda District. Northwest coast, Halmahera. Animists 50%, Muslims 20%. D=GMIH.
5240	0	5	6.36	0	99.70	0.30	C	263.16	192	8	South Sulawesi. Eastern Luwu District, Nuha and Malili Subdistricts. Mountains. Muslims 30%. M=SIL.
5241	2	5	5.16	0	66.00	34.00	B	60.22	256	6	Irian Jaya. Central highlands west of Baliem river. Bilinguals in Indonesian. Animists 75%. D=Reformed Congregation,CMA. M=RBMU.
5242	1	4	2.57	0	35.00	65.00	A	10.22	268	5	Central Maluku. South Seram Utara, interior, south coast; 6 villages. Indonesian not used. Animists 90%. D=SIL.
5243	4	3	11.10	2	99.65	0.35	C	277.58	281	8	South Sulawesi. Tana Toraja, also Luwu, Districts. Rantepao is prestige dialect. Animists 20%, Muslims 15%. D=RCC(M-Ujung Pandang),GTRMR,GTM,GPST.
5244	0	4	6.77	0	33.00	67.00	A	6.02	633	4	Southeast Sulawesi. Numerous scattered settlements across north Maluku and Irian Jaya. Muslims 90%.
5245	1	5	6.08	0	99.80	0.20	C	344.56	161	9	Central Maluku. West Seram, 15 villages. Access by boat. Muslims 10%. D=GEKISUS.
5246	0	5	5.77	0	99.70	0.30	C	265.72	178	8	South Maluku. Southeast Babar Island. Animists 30%.
5247	0	5	6.53	0	98.00	2.00	C	232.50	211	8	Irian Jaya. South coast near Merauke. 4 dialects. Majority use Indonesian. Animists 35%. M=RBMU,TEAM.
5248	0	5	5.85	0	88.00	12.00	C	192.72	213	7	Irian Jaya. South coast area south of Yiptem; Kao and Muyu rivers. Bilingual in Indonesian. Animists 40%. M=APCM,TEAM.
5249	1	6	6.62	0	64.00	36.00	B	46.72	305	6	Kalimantan, also Brunei, Sabah, Sarawak. Animists 75%. D=CMA. M=BEM.
5250	0	5	4.20	0	16.01	83.99	A	0.00	864	1.05	South Sumatra. Southwest and southeast Lampung. Muslims 100%(Shafi Sunnis).
5251	0	5	2.80	0	99.75	0.25	C	276.48	105	8	Irian Jaya. Northeast border area south of Jayapura; most now in PNG. Animists 25%.
5252	2	8	6.67	5	53.00	47.00	B	11.60	378	5	Babas, anglicized Chinese Malays, mainly in Malacca. Most speak Penang Hokkien. Chinese folk-religionists/Buddhists 90%. D=RCC,&c. M=AMEC,BFBS,CSI.
5253	0	5	0.00	1	18.00	82.00	A	0.00	0	1.07	Southern Sumatra. Muslims 100%.
5254	0	5	3.56	0	92.00	8.00	C	218.27	136	8	Irian Jaya. Border area with PNG near headwaters of Sepik river. Monolinguals. Animists 35%. M=UFM.
5255	1	3	3.62	0	19.01	80.99	A	0.00	644	1.06	Sumbawa Island. Muslims 82%(Shafi Sunnis), animists 18%. D=RCC(D-Weetebula). M=CSSR,CMA,UFM.

Continued overleaf

Table 8-2 continued

PEOPLE		POPULATION				IDENTITY CODE		LANGUAGE		CHURCH		MINISTRY						SCRIPTURE		
Ref 1	Ethnic name 2	P% 3	In 1995 4	In 2000 5	In 2025 6	Race 7	Language 8	Autoglossonym 9	S 10	AC 11	Members 12	Jayuh 13-17	d 18	wa 19	xc 20	mc 21	mi 22	Biblioglossonym 23	Pub 24-26	ss 27
5256	Sundanese (Urang Sunda)	10.60481	20,940,734	22,493,585	28,998,017	MSY44n	31-PJAA-a	central sunda	18	0.08	17,995	1A...	4	5	6	5	4	Sundanese	PNB	b
5257	Sundanese Indonesian	3.10000	6,121,399	6,575,329	8,476,706	MSY44n	31-PHAA-c	bahasa-indonesia		0.90	59,178	4Asuh	5	5	6	5	1	Indonesian	PNB	b
5258	Sungkai	0.00300	5,924	6,363	8,203	MSY44y	31-PFBB-a	sungkai		1.00	64	0....	6	4	6	1	0		...	b
5259	Suwawa	0.00649	12,815	13,766	17,746	MSY44x	31-QJAC-a	suwawa		0.03	4	0....	3	3	2	0	0		...	b
5260	Tabaru	0.00799	15,777	16,947	21,848	AON10c	25-AACA	tobaru cluster		68.00	11,524	0....	10	7	6	4	3	Tabaru	...	b
5261	Tabu	0.00021	415	445	574	AON10a	21-KAAA-a	morwap		65.00	290	0....	10	6	6	2	0		...	.
5262	Tae Toraja	0.13071	258,106	277,246	357,416	MSY44p	31-QBEB-a	to-rongkong		10.00	27,725	0....	8	5	5	1	0		...	b
5263	Tagalog (Pilipino)	0.03000	59,239	63,632	82,033	MSY44o	31-CKAA-a	proper tagalog		98.00	62,360	4Bs..	10	9	14	5	3	Tagalog	PNB	b
5264	Tagulandang	0.00649	12,815	13,766	17,746	MSY44x	31-RBAC-c	tahulandang		15.00	2,065	0....	8	5	7	4	1		...	b
5265	Taikat	0.00041	810	870	1,121	AON10a	21-GBAA-a	taikat		67.00	583	0....	10	6	6	2	0		...	.
5266	Tajio (Kasimbar)	0.00959	18,937	20,341	26,223	MSY44y	31-QGAC-a	tajio		1.00	203	0....	6	3	2	0	0		...	b
5267	Talaud	0.03895	76,912	82,616	106,506	MSY44x	31-RBAE	talaud cluster		90.00	74,354	0....	10	8	11	5	2	Talaud	PN.	b
5268	Taliabo (Mangei, Kadai)	0.00213	4,206	4,518	5,824	MSY44y	32-EDAB-a	taliabu		80.00	3,614	0....	10	7	10	2	1	Taliabu	...	b
5269	Talondo	0.00029	573	615	793	MSY44p	31-QBEC-a	talondo'		70.00	431	0....	10	7	6	4	1		...	b
5270	Taluki	0.00025	494	530	684	MSY44y	31-QDBA	taloki cluster		0.00	0	0....	0	2	5	0	0		...	b
5271	Taluti (Silen)	0.00940	18,562	19,938	25,704	MSY44y	32-DGFA-b	tehoru-haya		9.00	1,794	0....	7	5	6	1	0		...	b
5272	Tamagario (Buru)	0.00203	4,009	4,306	5,551	AON10a	24-HABB	tamagario cluster		70.00	3,014	0....	10	6	6	2	0		...	.
5273	Taman Dayak	0.00293	5,786	6,215	8,012	MSY44y	31-PAAA-a	embaloh		11.00	684	0....	8	5	5	1	1	Embaloh*	...	.
5274	Tamilouw (Sepa)	0.00144	2,843	3,054	3,938	MSY44y	32-DGFB-b	sepa		10.00	305	0....	8	5	5	1	0		...	b
5275	Tamnin Citak	0.00015	296	318	410	AON10a	24-KABE-a	citak-tamnim		60.00	191	0....	10	6	7	2	1	Citak	P..	.
5276	Tanahmerah (Sumeri)	0.00035	691	742	957	AON10a	24-GBAA	tabla cluster		65.00	483	0....	10	6	6	2	0	Tabla	P..	.
5277	Tandia	0.00024	474	509	656	MSY44y	33-ADCA-b	wandamen		19.00	97	0....	8	5	6	1	0	Wandamen	P..	.
5278	Tangkou	0.00004	79	85	109	MSY44y	31-QBIA-a	tongkou		2.00	2	0....	6	4	5	0	0		...	b
5279	Tanglapui	0.00779	15,382	16,523	21,301	AON10a	20-BAAA-a	tanglapui		45.00	7,435	0....	9	5	6	2	0		...	.
5280	Tanimbarese (Kei)	0.04667	92,157	98,991	127,615	AON09e	32-DDBA-c	kei-tanimbar		1.00	990	0....	6	4	6	4	2	Kei	...	b
5281	Taori-Kei	0.00013	257	276	355	AON10a	21-BAFA-a	kaiy		64.00	176	0....	10	6	6	4	1		...	.
5282	Taori-So (Doutai)	0.00017	336	361	465	AON10a	21-BAEA-a	toli-tai		65.00	234	0....	10	6	5	4	1		...	.
5283	Tarof	0.00193	3,811	4,094	5,277	AON10a	20-HCBA-a	tarof		50.00	2,047	0....	10	6	6	3	0		...	.
5284	Tarpia	0.00039	770	827	1,066	AON09e	34-AAAC-b	tarpia		91.00	753	0....	10	7	11	2	0		...	.
5285	Tarunggare (Turunggare)	0.00026	513	551	711	AON10a	25-JAAA-a	tunggare		64.00	353	0....	10	6	7	2	2		...	b
5286	Taurap (Burmeso, Monau)	0.00012	237	255	328	AON10a	25-MAAA-a	burmeso		60.00	153	0....	10	6	8	2	1		...	.
5287	Tause	0.00018	355	382	492	AON10a	21-ABAA-a	tause		50.00	191	0....	10	6	5	2	2		...	.
5288	Tawaelia (Baria)	0.00041	810	870	1,121	MSY44p	31-QEBD-a	sedoa		45.00	391	0....	9	5	6	4	1		...	.
5289	Taworta	0.00007	138	148	191	AON10a	21-CAAA-a	taworta		65.00	97	0....	10	6	4	2	1		...	.
5290	Tawoyan Dayak	0.01299	25,651	27,553	35,520	MSY44y	31-LBBA-g	tabuyan		15.00	4,133	0.s..	8	5	4	1	1		...	.
5291	Tefaro	0.00006	118	127	164	AON10a	25-JBCA-a	tefaro		50.00	64	0....	10	6	6	2	0		...	.
5292	Tehit (Tahit, Kaibus)	0.00459	9,064	9,736	12,551	AON10a	25-BDBA-a	tehit		65.00	6,328	0....	10	6	6	4	2	Tehit	...	.
5293	Tenggarong Malay	0.13636	269,263	289,230	372,866	MSY44k	31-PHAF-fa	kutai-tenggarong		0.10	289	0....	5	3	3	0	0		...	.
5294	Tenggerese	0.27550	544,015	584,356	753,333	MSY44g	31-PIAB-a	tengger		1.00	5,844	0....	6	4	4	5	3		...	b
5295	Teor	0.00064	1,264	1,357	1,750	AON09e	32-DDCB-a	gaur kristen		10.00	136	0....	8	6	6	2	1		...	b
5296	Tepera (Tanahmerah)	0.00203	4,009	4,306	5,551	AON10a	24-GBAA-b	tepera		60.00	2,583	0....	10	6	6	3	1	Tabla	P..	.
5297	Ternatese (Ternatan)	0.02726	53,829	57,820	74,540	AON10c	25-ACAA-b	vehicular ternate		0.01	6	0....	3	4	2	5	3		...	b
5298	Tetum (Belu)	0.04000	78,986	84,843	109,377	AON09e	32-BCCA-a	west tetun		91.00	77,207	1....	10	7	11	4	1		...	b
5299	Teun	0.00065	1,284	1,379	1,777	MSY44y	32-BCHA-a	teun		60.00	827	0....	10	6	6	2	0		...	b
5300	Tewa (Lebang)	0.00325	6,418	6,893	8,887	MSY44y	20-AABA	tewa cluster		15.00	1,034	0....	8	5	6	1	0		...	.
5301	Tidorese	0.01688	33,332	35,804	46,157	AON10c	25-ACAB-c	vehicular tidore		5.00	1,790	0....	7	4	2	4	2	Tidore	...	b
5302	Tidung(Zedong, Camucones)	0.00987	19,490	20,935	26,989	MSY44z	31-GCBC-b	tidong		7.00	1,465	0....	7	5	6	1	0		...	.
5303	Timorese (Atoni, Dawan)	0.42208	833,458	895,263	1,154,145	MSY44y	32-BCBA	uab-atoni-pah-meto cluster		95.00	850,500	0A...	10	9	13	5	3	Timor*	PN.	b
5304	Toba Batak	1.16154	2,293,629	2,463,712	3,176,140	MSY44b	31-PECA-a	toba	2	85.00	2,094,155	2.s..	10	9	13	5	3	Batak: Toba*	PNB	b
5305	Tobada (Bada)	0.00533	10,525	11,305	14,574	MSY44p	31-QEBB-a	to-bada'		60.00	6,783	0....	10	7	7	2	1		...	b
5306	Tobelorese	0.01307	25,809	27,722	35,739	AON10c	25-AAAA	tobelo cluster		51.00	14,138	0.s..	10	6	6	5	3	Tobelo	PN.	.
5307	Tofamna	0.00008	158	170	219	AON10a	21-QAAA-a	tofamna		65.00	110	0....	10	6	1	2	1		...	.
5308	Tolitoli	0.01491	29,442	31,625	40,770	MSY44y	31-QGAE-c	tolitoli		0.06	19	0....	4	4	3	4	2		...	b
5309	Tomadino	0.00032	632	679	875	MSY44y	31-QDEB-a	tomadino		1.00	7	0....	6	3	3	0	0		...	b
5310	Tombelala	0.00055	1,086	1,167	1,504	MSY44y	31-QEAA-a	to-mbelala		0.10	1	0....	5	4	4	0	0		...	.
5311	Tombulu Menadonese	0.03895	76,912	82,616	106,506	MSY44l	31-RACB-a	ton-bulu		93.00	76,833	0....	10	8	11	5	3	Tombulu	P..	b
5312	Tomini	0.02237	44,173	47,448	61,169	MSY44y	31-QGAB-c	tomini		1.00	474	0....	6	4	8	4	2		...	b
5313	Tondanou (Tolour)	0.05972	117,926	126,671	163,300	MSY44l	31-RACA-b	ka'kas		96.00	121,604	0....	10	9	12	5	3	Tondano	...	b
5314	Tonsawang	0.01298	25,631	27,532	35,493	MSY44l	31-RABA-a	ton-sawang		95.00	26,155	0....	10	9	12	5	3		...	b
5315	Tonsea	0.05193	102,543	110,147	141,998	MSY44l	31-RACC-a	kalabat-atas		90.00	99,133	0.s..	10	8	11	5	3		...	b
5316	Tontemboan (Alifur)	0.08140	160,736	172,655	222,582	MSY44l	31-RAAA-b	ton-temboan		95.00	164,023	0....	10	9	12	5	3	Tontemboan	P..	b
5317	Topoiyo	0.00113	2,231	2,397	3,090	MSY44p	31-QEEA-a	to-poiyo		0.10	2	0....	5	3	4	0	0		...	b
5318	Towei	0.00008	158	170	219	AON10a	21-SABA-a	towei		64.00	109	0....	10	6	6	2	0		...	.
5319	Tugun (Mahuan)	0.00065	1,284	1,379	1,777	MSY44y	32-BCDD-a	tugun		20.00	276	0....	9	5	5	3	0	Tugun	...	b
5320	Tugutil (Teluk Lili)	0.00122	2,409	2,588	3,336	AON10c	25-AAAB	tugutil cluster		5.00	129	0....	7	4	5	4	1	Tugutil	...	b
5321	Tulambatu (Mapute)	0.00270	5,332	5,727	7,383	MSY44y	31-QDCC-a	tu-lambatu		5.00	286	0....	7	4	6	1	0		...	b
5322	Tulehu (Northeast Ambonese)	0.01094	21,603	23,205	29,915	AON09e	32-DGON-a	tulehu		30.00	6,961	0....	9	5	6	1	0		...	b
5323	Tumawo (Sko, Sekol)	0.00024	474	509	656	AON10a	25-OABA-a	tumawo		65.00	331	0....	10	6	6	2	0		...	.
5324	Tunjung Dayak	0.03246	64,097	68,850	88,759	MSY44y	31-LCAA	tunjung cluster		20.00	13,770	0.s..	9	5	4	4	2	Tunjung	...	.
5325	Turu (Urundi, Iaw)	0.00059	1,165	1,251	1,613	AON10a	21-ACBC	iau cluster		95.00	1,189	0....	10	7	12	2	3		...	.
5326	Tutunohan (Opotai)	0.00008	158	170	219	MSY44y	32-BCDD-b	tutunohan		15.00	25	0....	8	5	6	1	0		...	b
5327	USA White	0.00700	13,823	14,848	19,141	CEW19s	52-ABAC-s	general american		78.00	11,581	1Bsuh	10	9	8	5	3	English*	PNB	b
5328	Uhei Kachlakin	0.00200	3,949	4,242	5,469	MSY44y	32-DGEA-b	wahakaim		5.00	212	0....	7	4	6	1	0		...	b
5329	Ujir (Udjir)	0.00049	968	1,039	1,340	MSY44y	32-DECA-a	ujir		7.00	73	0....	7	5	6	1	0		...	b
5330	Ulumandak (Ulunda)	0.01758	34,714	37,288	48,071	MSY44y	31-QBGC	ulumanda cluster		0.01	4	0....	3	3	2	0	0		...	b
5331	Uma (Pipikoro)	0.01094	21,603	23,205	29,915	MSY44p	31-QEDA-a	uma		50.00	11,602	0....	10	6	7	2	1	Uma	PN.	b
5332	Umalasa (Ndau)	0.00186	3,673	3,945	5,086	MSY44y	31-QGAE-b	pendau		1.00	39	0....	6	2	3	0	1	Pendau	...	b
5333	Upper Baram Kenyah	0.00030	592	636	820	MSY44y	31-JCCD	baram-kenyah cluster		60.00	382	0....	10	6	5	4	1		...	.
5334	Uria (Warpu, Oria)	0.00096	1,896	2,036	2,625	AON10a	21-FAAA	orya cluster		65.00	1,324	0....	10	6	6	2	1	Orya	P..	.
5335	Uruangnirin (Tubiruasa)	0.00018	355	382	492	AON09e	33-ACBA-a	uruangnirin		45.00	172	0....	9	6	6	5	0		...	.
5336	Usku	0.00008	158	170	219	AON10a	21-PAAA-a	usku		66.00	112	0....	10	6	7	2	1		...	.
5337	Wabo (Woriasi, Nusari)	0.00087	1,718	1,845	2,379	AON09e	33-ADDA	wabo cluster		41.00	757	0....	9	5	6	4	1		...	.
5338	Waelulu	0.00200	3,949	4,242	5,469	MSY44y	32-DGGA	manusela cluster		6.00	255	0....	7	5	6	1	0		...	b
5339	Wahai (Manusela)	0.00387	7,642	8,209	10,582	MSY44y	32-DGGA	manusela cluster		12.00	985	0....	8	5	6	4	1		...	b
5340	Wahau Kayan	0.00032	632	679	875	MSY44z	31-JBAD-a	wahau-kayan		5.00	34	0....	7	5	4	1	0		...	.
5341	Wahau Kenyah	0.00065	1,284	1,379	1,777	MSY44y	31-JCCI-a	wahau		60.00	827	0....	10	6	4	4	1		...	.
5342	Waioli (Wajoli)	0.00172	3,396	3,648	4,703	AON10c	25-AADB-b	waioli		28.00	1,022	0....	9	5	6	4	2		...	b
5343	Wakde	0.00026	513	551	711	AON09e	34-AAAA-d	wakde		70.00	386	0....	10	6	9	0	0		...	.
5344	Walak (Lower Pyramid)	0.00060	1,185	1,273	1,641	AON10a	24-FACB-a	walak		50.00	636	0....	10	6	9	4	2		...	.
5345	Wambon	0.00174	3,436	3,691	4,758	AON10a	24-KDCB	kaeti-wambon cluster		65.00	2,399	0....	10	6	9	2	1		...	.
5346	Wanam (Kosarek)	0.00119	2,350	2,524	3,254	AON10a	21-RAAA	kosarek cluster		64.00	1,615	0....	10	6	6	4	2	Yale: Kosarek*	P..	.
5347	Wandamen (Bentoeni)	0.00260	5,134	5,515	7,109	AON09e	33-ADCA-b	wandamen		91.00	5,018	0....	10	7	11	3	2	Wandamen	P..	.
5348	Wanggom	0.00069	1,363	1,464	1,887	AON10a	24-KDCA-a	wanggom		65.00	951	0....	10	6	9	4	1		...	.
5349	Wano	0.00189	3,732	4,009	5,168	AON10a	24-FAAA-a	wano		30.00	1,203	0....	9	5	7	4	2	Wano	P..	n
5350	Wanukaka	0.00649	12,815	13,766	17,746	MSY44y	32-AACC-a	wanukaka		45.00	6,195	0....	9	5	7	2	0		...	.
5351	Warembori	0.00035	691	742	957	MSY44y	33-ADCH-b	warabori		11.90	88	0....	8	5	6	1	0		...	.
5352	Wares	0.00008	158	170	219	AON10a	21-DGAA-a	wares		64.00	109	0....	10	6	6	2	0		...	.
5353	Waris	0.00058	1,145	1,230	1,586	AON10a	21-HBAA-a	proper waris		60.00	738	0....	10	6	6	3	1	Waris	Pn.	.
5354	Warkay-Bipim	0.00017	336	361	465	AON10a	24-IAAA-a	warkay-bipim		40.00	144	0....	9	6	7	4	1		...	b
5355	Waropen (Wonti)	0.00348	6,872	7,381	9,516	AON09e	33-ADEA-a	aropen		91.00	6,717	0....	10	8	12	4	1	Waropen	...	b
5356	Waru (Mopute)	0.00019	375	403	520	MSY44y	31-QDDF-a	waru		0.10	0	0....	5	4	3	0	0		...	b
5357	Watubela (Wesi, Kasiui)	0.00217	4,285	4,603	5,934	AON09e	32-DFBA-b	watubela		30.00	1,381	0....	9	6	6	2	0		...	b
5358	Watulai (Batuley)	0.00194	3,831	4,115	5,305	MSY44y	32-DEBF-a	batuley		38.00	1,564	0....	9	5	6	2	0		...	b
5359	Wawonii	0.01172	23,143	24,859	32,047	MSY44y	31-QDCA-a	wawonii		1.00	249	0....	6	5	3	1	0		...	b
5360	Weda	0.00137	2,705	2,906	3,746	MSY44y	33-AABA-a	weda		13.00	378	0....	8	5	6	1	0		p..	b
5361	Welemur	0.00200	3,949	4,242	5,469	MSY44y	32-BCDA-b	welemur		6.00	255	0....	7	5	6	1	0		...	b
5362	Weretai	0.00015	296	318	410	AON10a	21-BAHA-a	wari-tai		65.00	207	0....	10	6	9	2	1		...	.
5363	West Makianese	0.00846	16,705	17,944	23,133	AON10c	25-ABAA-a	west makian		28.00	5,024	0....	9	5	6	4	2		...	.
5364	West Marsela	0.00056	1,106	1,188	1,531	AON09e	32-BCEE-f	west masela		80.00	950	0....	10	7	6	5	1		...	b
5365	West Mori (Aikoa)	0.00759	14,988	16,099	20,754	MSY44y	31-QDFB-a	mori-atas		3.00	483	0....	6	4	6	4	1	Mori*	PN.	b
5366	West Trangan	0.00376	7,425	7,975	10,281	MSY44y	32-DEAC	west tarangan cluster		60.00	4,785	0....	10	6	6	2	1	Tarangan, West	...	n
5367	Western Dani (Timorini)	0.09391	185,439	199,190	256,789	AON10a	24-FABA	west dani cluster		85.00	169,312	0....	10	8	13	5	3	Dani: Western*	PN.	.
5368	Western Lampong (Kroe)	0.01494	29,501	31,689	40,852	MSY44y	31-PFBF-a	krui		0.05	16	0....	4	3	2	0	1		...	b
5369	Wetar (Erai)	0.00200	3,949	4,242	5,469	MSY44y	32-BCDB-c	erai		6.00	255	0....	7	5	4	1	0		...	b
5370	Wewewa (West Sumbanese)	0.04868	96,126	103,254	133,112	AON09e	32-AACA-a	weyewa		0.02	21	4.s..	3	3	4	4	2	Wewewa*	PN.	.
5371	Wodani	0.00264	5,213	5,600	7,219	AON10a	24-DAAB-a	wola-ni		45.00	2,520	0....	9	5	5	4	1	Wolani	PN.	.
5372	Woi	0.00076	1,501	1,612	2,078	AON09e	33-ADCD-a	woi		91.00	1,467	0....	10	7	11	4	1		...	.
5373	Woisika (Kamang, Kamot)	0.00779	15,382	16,523	21,301	AON10e	20-ABFA	woisika cluster		53.00	8,757	0....	10	6	6	2	0		...	.
5374	Wokam (Wamar)	0.00378	7,464	8,018	10,336	MSY44y	32-DEAE-a	manobai		60.00	4,811	0....	10	6	5	2	0		...	b
5375	Woria	0.00001	20	21	27	AON10a	25-JBDA-a	woria		70.00	15	0....	10	7	1	4	1		...	.
5376	Wotu	0.00290	5,726	6,151	7,930	MSY44i	31-QAGA-a	wotu		0.09	6	0....	4	3	0	0	0		...	b
5377	Yafi (Jafi Wagarindem)	0.00013	257	276	355	AON10a	21-TAAA-a	yafi		65.00	179	0....	10	6	7	2	1		...	.
5378	Yahadian (Nerigo)	0.00026	513	551	711	AON10a	20-IAAB-b	nerigo		60.00	331	0....	10	8	7	6	2		...	.
5379	Yair	0.00080	1,580	1,697	2,188	AON10a	24-KDBH	awyu cluster		60.00	1,018	0....	10	7	6	4	0	Awyu, Nohon	...	.

Continued opposite

Table 8-2 continued

EVANGELIZATION								EVANGELISM			ADDITIONAL DESCRIPTIVE DATA
Ref 1	*D* 28	*aC* 29	*CG%* 30	*r* 31	*E* 32	*U* 33	*W* 34	*e* 35	*R* 36	*T* 37	*Locations, civil divisions, literacy, religions, church history, denominations, dioceses, church growth, missions, agencies, ministries, movements* 38
5256	7	5	3.53	4	55.08	44.92	B	0.16	218	3	Muslims 50%(strict Shafi Sunnis; regular mosque attenders 55%), Sundanese New-Religionists 48%, animists(Badui) 1%. D=GKP,GPI,GMI,SA,GMAHKT,GGBI,&c.
5257	1	5	9.07	7	58.90	41.10	B	1.93	461	4	Sundanese who now speak Indonesian as mother tongue. Muslims 51%, New Religionists 48%. D=GKP. R=FEBC,VERITAS,AWR.
5258	0	5	4.25	0	25.00	75.00	A	0.91	559	3	South Sumatra. Northeast of Krui, west of Abung. Close to Pubian and Komering. Muslims 99%(Shafi Sunnis).
5259	0	5	1.40	0	16.03	83.97	A	0.01	356	2	Northeastern Sulawesi. Around Suwawa and Pinogu, east of Gorontalo town. Muslims 99%.
5260	1	5	2.99	0	99.68	0.32	C	260.61	104	8	North Maluku. West side of north Halmahera. Access by sea. Muslims 22%, animists 10%. D=GMIH. M=UMS,MCCSIL,IBS-I.
5261	0	5	3.42	0	91.00	9.00	C	215.89	133	8	Irian Jaya, south of Jayapura, northeast of Kaureh. Related to Awyi. Animists 35%.
5262	0	6	8.25	0	38.00	62.00	A	13.87	660	5	South Sulawesi, Luwu District. Agriculturalists. Part Muslim (60%), Animists 30%.
5263	3	10	2.84	5	99.98	0.02	C	633.12	54	10	Expatriates, refugees, immigrants from Philippines, as laborers, in commerce. All Christians. D=RCC,INC,PIC.
5264	1	5	5.47	0	48.00	52.00	A	26.28	351	5	North Sulawesi. Tagulandang and Biaro Islands in Sangihe Islands. Many Muslims 55%, animists 30%. D=GMIST.
5265	0	5	4.15	0	93.00	7.00	C	227.43	152	8	Irian Jaya. Northeast border area, south of Jayapura. Closest to Awyi. Animists 33%.
5266	0	5	3.06	0	20.00	80.00	A	0.73	536	3	Central Sulawesi. Ampibabo and Tinombo Sub-Districts, 4 villages. Muslims 80%.
5267	2	5	2.54	0	99.90	0.10	C	450.04	64	10	North Sulawesi. Talaud Islands. Almost all Christians. D=GMIST,GMAHKT. M=NRMB,SDA.
5268	1	5	6.07	0	99.80	0.20	C	338.72	163	9	North Maluku. Taliabu, Mangole, Sula Islands. Access by sea. Animists 20%. D=NTM.
5269	1	6	3.84	0	99.70	0.30	C	265.72	125	8	South Sulawesi. Mamuju District, Kalumpang Subdistrict, 2 villages. Muslims 30%. D=GPSS.
5270	0	3	0.00	0	14.00	86.00	A	0.00	0	1.04	Southeast Sulawesi. Wakorumba District. Related to Bungku. Muslims 100%(Sunnis).
5271	0	5	5.33	0	35.00	65.00	A	11.49	484	5	Central Maluku. Seram Island. Trade language. Muslims 91%.
5272	0	5	5.87	0	97.00	3.00	C	247.83	194	8	Irian Jaya. South coast area between Gondu and Bapai rivers. Animists 30%.
5273	2	5	4.32	0	36.00	64.00	A	14.45	393	5	Kalimantan. North central, Kapuas river. Related to Embaloh. Animists 89%. D=GKE,NTM. M=IBS-I.
5274	0	5	3.48	0	35.00	65.00	A	12.77	339	5	Central Maluku. Seram Island. Many Muslims 60%, animists 30%.
5275	1	3	2.99	0	88.00	12.00	C	192.72	124	7	Irian Jaya, 4 villages near Senggo. Close to Asmat. Mostly monolingual. Animists 40%. D=DRC. M=TEAM.
5276	0	5	3.95	0	92.00	8.00	C	218.27	147	8	Irian Jaya. North Bomberai Peninsula along Gondu and Bapai rivers. Animists 35%.
5277	0	5	4.68	0	43.00	57.00	A	29.82	352	5	Irian Jaya. Bird's Head neck area south of Wandamen Peninsula. Most Tandia now speak Wandamen. Animists 81%.
5278	0	5	0.70	0	24.00	76.00	A	1.75	177	4	South Sulawesi. Mamuju District, Budong-Budong Subdistrict, 1 village on Budong-Budong river. 50 speakers left. Muslims 95%.
5279	0	6	6.83	0	72.00	28.00	B	118.26	298	7	Nusa Tenggara. Eastern quarter of Alor Island. Muslims 35%, animists 20%.
5280	1	5	4.70	0	31.00	69.00	A	1.13	504	4	South Maluku. Rural, 207 villages on Kei Islands and Kur Islands (used as lingua franca). Animists 54%, Muslims 45%. D=RCC(D-Amboina). M=MSC,SIL.
5281	0	7	2.91	0	95.00	5.00	C	221.92	113	8	Irian Jaya. Lakes Plain area on lower Rouffaer river, 2 villages. Majority are monolingual. Animists 36%. M=RBMU.
5282	0	5	3.20	0	93.00	7.00	C	220.64	124	8	Irian Jaya. Lakes Plain area at Toli-Dou village, southwest of Taiyeve. Monolingual. Animists 35%. M=RBMU.
5283	0	5	5.47	0	78.00	22.00	B	142.35	227	7	Irian Jaya. Middle south coast of Bird's Head along Bintuni Bay. Animists 40%.
5284	0	5	4.42	0	99.91	0.09	C	405.22	122	10	Irian Jaya. North coast area near Demta, 2 villages. Closest to Bonggo.
5285	0	5	3.63	0	96.00	4.00	C	224.25	132	8	Irian Jaya. North central, inland from Waropen group. Close to Bauzi. Bilinguals in Indonesian. Animists 36%. M=UFM,CMA.
5286	0	7	2.77	0	91.00	9.00	C	199.29	114	7	Irian Jaya. Mid-Mamberamo river northeast of Lake Holmes. Language isolate. Minority bilingual in Indonesian. Animists 40%. M=RBMU.
5287	0	6	2.99	0	78.00	22.00	B	142.35	140	7	Irian Jaya. Around Deraposi, southwest of Danau Bira, western Lakes Plain. No Indonesian spoken. Monolingual. Animists 50%. M=RBMU,SIL.
5288	1	5	3.73	0	74.00	26.00	B	121.54	171	7	East central Sulawesi. Lore Utara and Poso Pesisir Sub-Districts, several villages. Some animists 30%, Muslims 25%. D=GKST.
5289	0	5	4.68	0	90.00	10.00	C	213.52	173	8	Irian Jaya. Lakes Plain area, south side of Idenburg river east of Taiyeve. Mostly monolinguals. Animists 35%. M=APCM.
5290	1	5	6.21	0	40.00	60.00	A	21.90	484	5	Kalimantan. Animists 85%. D=GKE. M=IBS-I.
5291	0	6	4.25	0	77.00	23.00	B	140.52	187	7	Irian Jaya. East side of Geelvink Bay, 2 villages. Animists 50%.
5292	2	5	6.66	0	98.00	2.00	C	232.50	214	8	Irian Jaya. South Bird's Head, 35 villages. Closest to Kalabra. Animists 35%. D=GKI,Baptists.
5293	0	4	3.42	0	15.10	84.90	A	0.05	748	2	Kalimantan. Mahakam River basin, east central coastal area. Many dialects. Muslims 99%.
5294	4	5	6.58	5	39.00	61.00	A	1.42	522	4	East Java, slopes of volcanic Mt Bromo. Literates 20%. Hindus 95%(some ISKCON), Muslims 4%. D=GKJW,GBT,Bethany Ch,Pentecostal Chs. M=NZG,BFM.
5295	1	6	2.64	0	40.00	60.00	A	14.60	249	5	South Maluku. Teor and Ut Islands. Close to Kur. Muslims 90%. D=RCC.
5296	1	5	5.71	0	91.00	9.00	C	199.29	202	7	Irian Jaya. Around Jayapura, Demta, Depapre, and 13 villages. Animists 40%. D=GKI. M=SIL.
5297	3	4	1.81	0	26.01	73.99	A	0.00	296	1.07	North Maluku. Homeland of cloves. Lingua franca. Muslims 100%(but not very orthodox,nor strict). D=GCPM,PCG,GMIH. M=PCGUSA,UMS,MCC,UFM.
5298	2	5	2.55	0	99.91	0.09	C	441.76	73	10	Nusa Tenggara. Central Timor, region of Dili and in the south. Part also in separatist Timor. Lingua franca. D=GMIT,RCC. M=IBS-I.
5299	0	5	0.26	0	89.00	11.00	C	194.91	34	7	Central Maluku. Seram Island. Relocated from Damar Islands due to volcanic activity. Animists 30%, Muslims 10%.
5300	0	5	4.75	0	39.00	61.00	A	21.35	393	5	Nusa Tenggara. Central Pantar Island. Many animists 60%, Muslims 25%.
5301	1	4	5.32	0	32.00	68.00	A	5.84	541	4	North Maluku. Close to Ternate. Muslims 95%(but not very strict or orthodox). High divorce rate. D=GMIH. M=UMS,MCC.
5302	0	4	5.11	0	29.00	71.00	A	7.41	531	4	Eastern Kalimantan, along Sembakung and Sibuka rivers. Also in Sabah (Malaysia). Animists 93%.
5303	3	3	1.88	0	99.95	0.05	C	506.25	51	10	On Timor. Animists 4%, Muslims 1%(converted in 1966). Y=1530. 1966, mass revivalism. D=GMIT,RCC(D-Atambua,D-Kupang),GPIBB. M=SVD,NZG,IMF,IBS-I.
5304	14	3	3.20	0	99.85	0.15	C	449.86	77	10	North Sumatra; Samosir Island; Toba Lake. Y=1861. D=HKBP,HKI,GKPI,GPI,HHKJ,HKB,PKB,HKBPL,RCC(M-Medan,&c),KPB,GMI,GMMI,SJA,&c. M=10.
5305	2	4	6.74	0	93.00	7.00	C	203.67	225	8	South Sulawesi. Mamuju District. Only 1 native speaker left (1985). Nearly extinct in Tobada; ethnic people changing to Topoiyo. Animists 40%. D=GKST.
5306	2	7	2.97	0	94.00	6.00	B	174.98	116	7	North Maluku. North Halmahera. Animists 30%, Muslims 19%. D=GMIH,NTM. M=UMS,MCC,Indonesian Bible Society.
5307	1	6	2.43	0	89.00	11.00	C	211.15	106	8	Irian Jaya. Tofamna village, south of Jayapura east of Nawa river. Monolinguals. Animists 35%. D=KINGMI. M=UFM.
5308	2	5	2.99	0	26.06	73.94	A	0.05	404	2	Central Sulawesi. 5 Sub-Districts, 29 villages. Muslims 99%. D=GPIBT-2(Protestant Ch of Indonesia in Buol-Tolitoli),GPIG.
5309	0	4	1.96	0	20.00	80.00	A	0.73	385	3	Central Sulawesi, Bungku Tengah Subdistrict. Muslims 95%.
5310	0	0	0.00	0	11.10	88.90	A	0.04	210	2	Sulawesi. Bungku Tengah subdistrict. 4 villages. Bahasa Indonesian used as second language. Muslims 100%.
5311	6	5	1.75	0	99.93	0.07	C	471.83	51	10	Minahasan. Northeastern Sulawesi. Heavily christianized. D=GMIM,RCC(D-Manado),KGPM,GPIBB,GPM,GMAHKT. M=MSC,NZG,SDA,FMB. R=FEBC.
5312	2	3	3.93	0	32.00	68.00	A	1.16	409	4	Central and north Sulawesi. 42 villages. Muslims 89%(Sunnis, along coast), animists 10%(in mountains). D=GPIBT-2,NTM.
5313	4	4	1.72	0	99.96	0.04	C	494.06	50	10	Minahasan. Northeastern Sulawesi around Tondano. All Christians. D=GMIM,RCC(D-Manado),KGPM,GMAHKT. M=MSC,NZG,SDA.
5314	4	3	1.71	0	99.95	0.05	C	481.98	50	10	Minahasan. Northeast Sulawesi around Tombatu. All Christians. D=GMIM,RCC(D-Manado),KGPM,GMAHKT. M=MSC,NZG,SDA.
5315	4	3	1.71	0	99.90	0.10	C	440.19	52	10	Northeast tip of Sulawesi. Minahasan. Mostly Christians. D=GMIM,RCC(D-Manado),KGPM,GMAHKT. M=NZG,MSC,SDA.
5316	4	5	1.57	0	99.95	0.05	C	492.38	47	10	Sulawesi. Minahasa Peninsula. All Christians. D=GMIM,RCC(D-Manado),KGPM,GMAHKT. M=MSC,NZG,SDA.
5317	0	5	0.70	0	20.10	79.90	A	0.07	218	2	South Sulawesi. Budong-Budong Subdistrict, Mamuju District, inland. Access by sea and river. Close to Sarudu. Agriculturalists. Muslims 90%.
5318	0	8	2.42	0	93.00	7.00	C	217.24	101	8	Irian Jaya. Border area south of Jayapura, south of Dubu, west of Emumu language area. Animists 36%.
5319	0	5	3.37	0	48.00	52.00	A	35.04	241	5	South Maluku. Wetar Island north of Timor. Animists 60%, Muslims 20%.
5320	0	5	2.59	0	33.00	67.00	A	6.02	298	4	North Maluku. North Halmahera, inland. Group of primitive tribes, minimal contact. Animists 95%. M=NTM.
5321	0	5	3.41	0	30.00	70.00	A	5.47	389	4	Southeast Sulawesi. Dialect of Bungku. Muslims 95%.
5322	0	6	6.76	0	59.00	41.00	B	64.60	360	6	Central Maluku. 4 villages on coast of northeast Ambon Island. Muslims 70%.
5323	0	6	3.56	0	92.00	8.00	C	218.27	136	8	Irian Jaya. North coast border area east of Jayapura at mouth of Tami river. Animists 35%.
5324	1	5	7.50	0	51.00	49.00	B	37.23	449	5	Kalimantan. East central, around Adas, Dempar, Melak, Muntaiwan. Animists 80%. D=GKE. M=REMP,IBS-I.
5325	2	6	4.89	0	99.95	0.05	C	464.64	120	10	Irian Jaya. Lakes Plain area, 6 villages. Indonesian not spoken at all. D=ECP,CMA. M=UFM,RBMU,SIL.
5326	0	5	3.27	0	41.00	59.00	A	22.44	275	5	South Maluku. Wetar Island north of Timor Island. Animists 60%, Muslims 25%.
5327	7	10	3.80	8	99.78	0.22	C	421.35	87	10	Expatriates from USA, in business, oil, education. D=SDA,CJCLdS,JWs,RCC,AoG,COG,&c.
5328	0	5	3.10	0	30.00	70.00	A	5.47	361	4	Central Maluku. Seram Island. Many Muslims 70%, animists 25%.
5329	0	5	4.38	0	32.00	68.00	A	8.17	448	4	South Maluku. 2 villages on Ujir and Wokam Islands, northwest Aru Islands. Muslims 93%.
5330	0	5	1.40	0	16.01	83.99	A	0.00	385	1.05	South Sulawesi. Majene, Mamuju, and Polewali-Mamasa Districts. 6 dialects. Muslims 98%.
5331	1	6	7.31	0	89.00	11.00	B	162.42	253	7	Central Sulawesi. Valley of Koro-Lariang river. Agriculturalists. Animists 30%, Muslims 20%. D=SA. M=SIL.
5332	0	4	3.73	0	21.00	79.00	A	0.76	598	3	Central Sulawesi. Balaesang Sub-District, villages of Walandano and Sibayu; also Simatang Island. Muslims 95%. M=SIL.
5333	0	5	3.71	0	88.00	12.00	C	192.72	142	7	Kalimantan. On border, mainly in Sarawak (Malaysia), also in Brunei. Animists 40%. M=BEM.
5334	1	5	5.01	0	95.00	5.00	C	225.38	173	8	Irian Jaya. Southwest of Nimboran, Jayapura District, 15 villages. Animists 35%. D=GKI. M=SIL.
5335	0	6	2.89	0	74.00	26.00	B	121.54	144	7	Irian Jaya. 2 small islands between Karas Island and Bomberai Peninsula. Animists 55%.
5336	1	10	2.45	0	99.66	0.34	C	240.90	95	8	Irian Jaya. Usku village, south of Jayapura, south of Pauwasi. Isolate. Monolinguals. Animists 34%. D=KINGMI.
5337	1	5	4.42	0	70.00	30.00	B	104.75	212	7	Irian Jaya. North and south coast of east Yapen Island, 6 villages. D=GKI. Animists 59%.
5338	0	5	3.29	0	31.00	69.00	A	6.78	366	4	Central Maluku. Seram Island. Many Muslims 70%, animists 24%.
5339	1	5	4.70	0	43.00	57.00	A	18.83	354	5	Central Maluku. 30 villages in east central Seram. Access by boat. Hindus 80%, some animists. D=NTM(among the Huaulu).
5340	0	5	3.59	0	25.00	75.00	A	4.56	449	4	Kalimantan. North of Muara Wahau. Animists 95%.
5341	0	5	4.51	0	87.00	13.00	C	190.53	169	7	Kalimantan. Northeast, north of Muara Wahau. Animists 40%. M=BEM.
5342	1	5	3.02	0	62.00	38.00	B	63.36	178	6	North Maluku. North Halmahera. Animists 52%, Muslims 20%. D=GMIH. M=UMS,MCC.
5343	0	0	3.72	0	91.00	9.00	C	232.50	142	8	Irian Jaya. Wakde Islands off the north coast just east of the Tor River. Animists 30%.
5344	0	7	4.24	0	85.00	15.00	B	155.12	169	7	Irian Jaya. 5 villages. Related to Dani. Mostly monolinguals. Animists 50%. M=APCM,CMA.
5345	0	5	5.63	0	96.00	4.00	C	227.76	189	8	Irian Jaya. South coast area northeast of Kaeti language area. Most are monolingual. Animists 35%. M=ZGK.
5346	1	5	5.22	0	97.00	3.00	C	226.59	176	8	Irian Jaya. Eastern highlands, east of Yali, northwest of Nipsan. Closely related to Nipsan. Animists 36%. D=GKI. M=APCM,SIL.
5347	0	5	6.42	0	99.91	0.09	C	421.83	160	10	Windessi, Wamesa. Irian Jaya. West Geelvink Bay, Manokwari. Literates 25% in Wandamen (50% in Indonesian). M=SIL,TEAM.
5348	0	5	4.66	0	97.00	3.00	C	230.13	160	8	Irian Jaya. South border area on Digul river, west of Kaeti language area. Mostly monolingual. Animists 35%. M=ZGK.
5349	1	6	4.91	0	66.00	34.00	B	72.27	245	6	Irian Jaya. Central highlands area on upper Rouffaer river. Many monolinguals. Animists 70%. Trade language. D=KINGMI. M=UFM,CMA.
5350	0	6	3.25	0	73.00	27.00	B	119.90	154	7	Nusa Tenggara. Sumba Island, southwest coast. Many animists 50%, some Muslims 5%.
5351	0	6	4.58	0	35.90	64.10	A	15.59	414	5	Irian Jaya. North coast, west of mouth of Mamberamo river, several villages. Language isolate. Animists 88%.
5352	0	5	2.42	0	90.00	10.00	C	210.24	104	8	Irian Jaya. North coast area inland from Kwesten language area. Animists 36%.
5353	0	5	4.40	0	91.00	9.00	C	199.29	163	7	Northeast Irian Jaya south of Jayapura. Majority in PNG. Animists 40%. M=SIL-PNG.
5354	1	1	2.70	0	69.00	31.00	B	100.74	147	7	Irian Jaya. South coast area bordering Asmat, 3 villages. 50% bilingual in Indonesian or Asmat. Animists 60%. D=GAK(Bible Ch). M=TEAM.
5355	1	5	6.73	0	99.91	0.09	C	435.11	162	10	Irian Jaya. East Geelvink Bay, south coast of Yapen Island. Bilingual(but only 25% literate) in Indonesian. D=GKI. M=UFM.
5356	0	5	0.00	0	19.10	80.90	A	0.07	0	2	Southeast Sulawesi. Muslims 95%.
5357	0	5	5.05	0	59.00	41.00	B	64.60	281	6	Central Maluku. Watubela Island, north of Kur Island. Related to Masiwang. Muslims 70%.
5358	0	5	5.18	0	67.00	33.00	B	92.92	247	6	South Maluku. 8 villages in Aru on small islands. Muslims 62%(in 5 southern villages).
5359	0	5	3.27	0	22.00	78.00	A	0.80	513	3	Southeast Sulawesi, Wawonii and Menui Islands. Muslims 95%.
5360	0	5	3.70	0	40.00	60.00	A	18.98	312	5	North Maluku. East coast of southern peninsula of Halmahera. Muslims 87%.
5361	0	5	3.29	0	31.00	69.00	A	6.78	366	4	South Maluku. Wetar Island north of Timor Island. Many Muslims 80%, animists 14%.
5362	0	5	3.08	0	95.00	5.00	C	225.38	118	8	Irian Jaya. Lakes Plain area around Taiyeve. Related to Tolitai. Most are monolingual. Animists 35%. M=RBMU.
5363	1	5	3.29	0	62.00	38.00	B	63.36	190	6	North Maluku. Makian, Kayoa Islands, south Halmahera. Animists 52%, Muslims 20%. D=GMIH. M=MCC,UMS.
5364	1	5	4.66	0	99.80	0.20	C	332.88	136	9	South Maluku. 5 villages on Marsela Island. Animists 20%. D=GPM.
5365	1	5	3.95	0	36.00	64.00	A	3.94	365	4	Central Sulawesi. At neck of southeastern peninsula: 3 Sub-Districts, 49 villages. Muslims 90%. D=GKST.
5366	1	6	1.71	0	92.00	8.00	C	201.48	76	8	South Maluku. West coast of Trangan Island, southern Aru Islands. Lingua franca. Muslims 40%. D=RCC. M=SIL.
5367	5	6	10.23	0	99.85	0.15	C	415.73	230	10	Irian Jaya. Central highlands, west of Baliem Grand Valley. 10% read Indonesian. Animists 10%. Y=1955. D=RCC,GKI,KINGMI,ECP,GGIK. M=CMA,UFM,RBMU.
5368	0	4	2.81	0	17.05	82.95	A	0.03	588	2	Southern Sumatra. South Bengkulu Province. Related to Komering. Muslims 100%(Shafi Sunnis). M=I.
5369	0	4	3.29	0	28.00	72.00	A	6.13	405	4	South Maluku. Wetar Island north of Timor. Many Muslims 72%, animists 22%.
5370	2	3	0.10	0	30.02	69.98	A	0.02	100	2	Nusa Tenggara. Lesser Sundas, west Sumba Island. Mostly animists 90%, with many Muslims 10%. D=GMIT,GKS.
5371	1	5	5.69	0	78.00	22.00	B	128.11	235	7	Irian Jaya. Western central highlands along Kemandoga and Mbiyandogo rivers. Monolinguals. Animists 55%. D=KINGMI. M=CMA.
5372	1	5	5.11	0	99.91	0.09	C	421.83	132	10	Irian Jaya. Miosnum and west Yapen Islands, 2 villages. D=GKI.
5373	0	5	7.01	0	80.00	20.00	B	154.76	274	7	Nusa Tenggara. Alor Island, east central, between Abui and Tanglapui. Muslims Muslims 30%, animists 17%.
5374	0	5	1.81	0	89.00	11.00	C	194.91	82	7	Maluku. West coast of Wokam Island, Kobroor, Maikor Islands; 21 villages. Muslims 20%.
5375	0	6	2.75	0	95.00	5.00	C	242.72	108	8	Irian Jaya. Interior of Waropen Bawah, Botawa village. Language nearly extinct. Monolinguals. Animists 30%. M=UFM.
5376	0	3	1.81	0	13.09	86.91	A	0.04	567	2	South Sulawesi. Town of Wotu, Wotu Sub-District, Luwu District. Muslims 98%.
5377	1	7	2.93	0	96.00	4.00	C	227.76	112	8	Northeast Irian Jaya, border area south of Jayapura near Ampas, 5 villages. Monolingual. Animists 35%. D=KINGMI.
5378	0	5	3.56	0	86.00	14.00	C	188.34	145	7	Irian Jaya. South Bird's Head between lower Mintamani river and Sekak river. Animists 40%.
5379	0	5	4.73	0	89.00	11.00	C	194.91	176	7	Irian Jaya. South coast west side of Digul river, south of Kombai. Animists 40%.

Continued overleaf

Table 8-2 continued

PEOPLE		POPULATION				IDENTITY CODE		LANGUAGE		CHURCH		MINISTRY		SCRIPTURE	
Ref 1	*Ethnic name* 2	*P%* 3	*In 1995* 4	*In 2000* 5	*In 2025* 6	*Race* 7	*Language* 8	*Autoglossonym* 9	*S* 10	*AC* 11	*Members* 12	*Jayuh* 13-17	*dwa xcmc mi* 18 19 20 21 22	*Biblioglossonym* 23	*Pub ss* 24-26 27
5380	Yaly (Yali, Nipsan)	0.00130	2,567	2,757	3,555	AON10a	21-RAAC	nipsan cluster		65.00	1,792	0....	10 8 7 5 2		PN. .
5381	Yamna	0.00016	316	339	438	AON09e	34-AAAA-f	yamna		60.00	204	0....	10 6 9 0 0		... .
5382	Yaosakor Asmat	0.00107	2,113	2,270	2,926	AON10a	24-KABH-a	yaosakor-asmat		60.00	1,362	0....	10 6 6 2 1	Asmat, Yaosakor	PN. b
5383	Yaqay (Sohur, Mapi)	0.00581	11,473	12,323	15,887	AON10a	24-IABA-a	yaqay		50.00	6,162	0....	10 6 6 4 1		... b
5384	Yarsun	0.00010	197	212	273	AON09e	34-AAAA-h	yarsun		60.00	127	0....	10 6 9 0 0		... .
5385	Yaur	0.00024	474	509	656	MSY44y	33-ADHA-a	yaur		12.00	61	0....	8 5 6 1 0		... .
5386	Yava (Yapanani, Mora)	0.00348	6,872	7,381	9,516	AON10a	25-IAAA	yawa cluster		65.00	4,798	0....	10 7 6 5 3	Iau	P.. .
5387	Yei	0.00030	592	636	820	AON10a	20-LBAA	yei cluster		60.00	382	0....	10 6 7 2 1		... b
5388	Yelmek (Jab, Jabsch)	0.00028	553	594	766	AON10a	20-KAAA	yelmek cluster		65.00	386	0....	10 6 6 2 0		... .
5389	Yeretuar	0.00017	336	361	465	AON10a	33-ADGA-a	yeretuar		61.00	220	0....	10 6 6 2 0		... .
5390	Yetfa	0.00049	968	1,039	1,340	AON10a	24-KEAB	yonggom cluster		65.00	676	0.s..	10 6 10 0 0		P.. .
5391	Yonggom (Yongom)	0.00116	2,291	2,460	3,172	AON10a	24-KEAB-a	yonggom		60.00	1,476	0.s..	10 6 6 4 1	Yongkom*	P.. .
5392	Yotafa (Tobati)	0.00181	3,574	3,839	4,949	AON09e	34-AABB-a	tobati		91.00	3,494	0....	10 7 11 4 1		... .
5393	other minor peoples	0.16436	324,553	348,620	449,429	...				20.00	69,724		9 9 5 5 3		
	Iran	**100.00000**	**62,324,350**	**67,702,199**	**94,462,501**					**0.46**	**313,991**				
5394	Afghan Persian (Kaboli)	2.80000	1,745,082	1,895,662	2,644,950	CNT24f	58-AACC-f	dari-t.		0.05	948	1Asu.	4 3 2 0 0	Dari*	PNb b
5395	Armenian (Ermini, Hai)	0.28000	174,508	189,566	264,495	CEW14	57-AAAA-b	ashkharik		85.00	161,131	4A.u.	10 9 11 2 1	Armenian: Modern, Eastern	PNB b
5396	Assyrian (Aisor, Chaldean)	0.03000	18,697	20,311	28,339	CMT31	12-AAAA-f	aisor		84.00	17,061	4cs..	10 8 10 2 3	Assyrian Neo-aramaic	PNB b
5397	Assyrian (Syriac)	0.02000	12,465	13,540	18,893	CMT31	12-AAAA-d	east syriac		85.00	11,509	1as..	10 9 10 2 3	Syriac: Ancient*	PNB b
5398	Astiani	0.03000	18,697	20,311	28,339	CNT24z	58-AACD-a	ashtiani		0.03	6	0....	3 2 0 0 0		... b
5399	Azerbaijani (Turk)	15.89559	9,906,823	10,761,664	15,015,372	MSY41a	44-AABA-fb	south azeri		0.00	6	1a.u.	0 3 4 0 1	Azerbaijani, South	pnb b
5400	Azerbaijani Jewish	0.00200	1,246	1,354	1,889	CMT35	12-AAAA-h	kurdit		0.00	0	1cs..	0 2 0 0 0		pnb b
5401	Bakhtiari	1.67901	1,046,432	1,136,727	1,586,035	CNT24z	58-AACA-ad	haft-lang		0.00	0	0....	0 2 2 0 0		... .
5402	Balkan Rom Gypsy	0.04000	24,930	27,081	37,785	CNN25f	59-ACBA-bl	zargari		5.00	1,354	1c...	7 5 2 0 0		pn. b
5403	Bashkardi	0.01000	6,232	6,770	9,446	CNT24b	58-AABA-d	bashkardi		0.00	0	1.s..	0 1 0 0 0		p.. .
5404	Brahui (Kur Galli)	0.02262	14,098	15,314	21,367	CNN23z	49-AAAA-a	bra'uidi		0.20	31	3....	5 2 0 0 1	Brahui	P.. n
5405	British	0.01000	6,232	6,770	9,446	CEW19i	52-ABAC-b	standard-english	7	78.00	5,281	3Bsuh	10 9 13 5 3		PNB b
5406	Central Kurd	1.00000	623,244	677,022	944,625	CNT24c	58-AAAA-cg	mukri	18	0.03	203	1c...	3 3 5 1 3	Kurdish: Mukri	Pn. b
5407	Esperanto	0.00000	0	0	0	CEW21z	51-AAAC-a	proper esperanto		5.00	0	0A...	7 5 2 0 0	Esperanto	PNB b
5408	Fars	0.01000	6,232	6,770	9,446	CNT24z	58-AACB-b	fars		0.00	0	0....	0 1 0 0 0		... .
5409	French	0.01400	8,725	9,478	13,225	CEW21b	51-AABI-d	general français	5	85.00	8,057	1B.uh	10 9 14 5 2	French	PNB b
5410	Gabri	0.01887	11,761	12,775	17,825	CNT24f	58-AACD-i	gabri		0.05	6	0....	4 1 8 0 0		... b
5411	Galeshi	0.10000	62,324	67,702	94,463	CNT24z	58-AACE-bb	galeshi		0.03	20	1....	3 3 0 0 0		... .
5412	Gazi	0.01000	6,232	6,770	9,446	CNT24z	58-AACD-g	gazi		0.00	0	0....	0 1 0 0 0		... .
5413	Georgian (Gruzin)	0.02571	16,024	17,406	24,286	CEW17c	42-CABB-a	kharthuli		25.00	4,352	2A.u.	9 7 7 2 1	Georgian	PNB b
5414	German	0.00100	623	677	945	CEW19m	52-ABCE-a	standard hoch-deutsch		87.00	589	2B.uh	10 9 13 5 3	German*	PNB b
5415	Ghorbati Gypsy (Kowli)	0.20000	124,649	135,404	188,925	CNN25f	59-ACAA-a	domari		0.01	14	0....	3 1 0 0 0		... b
5416	Gilaki	5.08812	3,171,138	3,444,769	4,806,365	CNT24z	58-AACE-b	ghilaki		0.50	17,224	1....	5 3 6 0 1	Gilaki	... b
5417	Gujarati	0.04000	24,930	27,081	37,785	CNN25e	59-AAFH-b	standard gujaraati		0.50	135	2A.u.	5 4 2 0 0	Gujarati	PNB b
5418	Gulf Arab	1.07600	670,610	728,476	1,016,417	CMT30	12-AACB-b	east maghrebi		2.00	14,570	2A.uh	6 4 5 0 0	Arabic: Algerian*	PNB b
5419	Gurani (Bajalani, Hawrami)	0.03000	18,697	20,311	28,339	CNT24z	58-AAAB-c	hawrami		0.08	16	0....	4 1 0 0 0		... .
5420	Harzani	0.04000	24,930	27,081	37,785	CNT24z	58-AACE-f	harzani		0.06	16	1....	4 3 0 0 0		... .
5421	Hazara-Berberi (Teymur)	0.44102	274,863	298,580	416,599	MSY41z	58-AACC-eo	central hazaragi		0.05	149	1asu.	4 3 4 0 1		pnb b
5422	Herki	0.03000	18,697	20,311	28,339	CNT24c	58-AAAA-ae	herki		0.02	4	1c...	3 3 3 0 0		pn. b
5423	Iranian Arab	1.45882	909,200	987,653	1,378,038	CMT30	12-AACF-h	northeast `anazi	4	0.46	4,543	1asuh	5 4 8 2 1		pnb b
5424	Iranian Kurd	6.00000	3,739,461	4,062,132	5,667,750	CNT24c	58-AACC-c	standard farsi		0.03	1,219	1Asu.	3 4 2 0 0		PNB b
5425	Italian	0.01600	9,972	10,832	15,114	CEW21e	51-AABQ-c	standard italiano		83.00	8,991	2B.uh	10 9 15 5 2	Italian	PNB b
5426	Jamshidi (Char Aimaq)	0.05000	31,162	33,851	47,231	CNT24z	58-AACC-ld	jamshidi		0.02	7	1csu.	3 1 0 0 0		pnb n
5427	Jewish	0.03000	18,697	20,311	28,339	CMT35	58-AACC-c	standard farsi		0.05	10	1Asu.	4 3 6 0 0		PNB b
5428	Jewish Tat (Judeo-Tatic)	0.00100	623	677	945	CNT24f	58-AACG-b	judeo-tat		0.00	0	0....	0 2 0 0 0	Judeo-tat	P.. b
5429	Judeo-Persian	0.00500	3,116	3,385	4,723	CMT35	58-AACC-ka	dzhidi		0.02	1	1csu.	3 2 0 0 0		pnb b
5430	Karakalpak	0.06000	37,395	40,621	56,678	MSY41z	44-AABC-b	karakalpak		0.00	0	1c.u.	0 5 0 0 0	Karakalpak	Pn. b
5431	Karingani	0.02470	15,394	16,722	23,332	CNT24z	58-AACE-e	karingani		0.00	0	1....	0 2 0 0 0		... .
5432	Kazakh	0.00708	4,413	4,793	6,688	MSY41e	44-AABC-c	kazakh		0.00	0	4A.u.	0 3 4 0 1	Kazakh	PN. b
5433	Khalaj	0.05987	37,314	40,533	56,555	MSY41z	44-AABA-i	khalaj		0.00	0	1c.u.	0 2 0 0 0		pnb b
5434	Khorasani Turk	1.12464	700,925	761,406	1,062,363	MSY41j	44-AABD-ae	oghuz-2		0.00	0	1c.u.	0 1 1 0 0		pnb b
5435	Khunsari	0.03000	18,697	20,311	28,339	CNT24z	58-AACD-f	khunsari		0.00	0	0....	0 1 0 0 0		... .
5436	Korean	0.02000	12,465	13,540	18,893	MSY46	45-AAAA-b	kukö		30.00	4,062	2A...	9 8 11 2 2	Korean	PNB b
5437	Larestani (Lari)	0.05000	31,162	33,851	47,231	CNT24z	58-AACB-a	lari		0.00	0	0....	0 1 0 0 0		... .
5438	Luri (Lori, Feyli)	7.19340	4,483,240	4,870,090	6,795,066	CNT24z	58-AACA-aa	luri		0.00	0	0....	0 2 4 1 0		... .
5439	Mamasani	0.18519	115,418	125,378	174,935	CNT24z	58-AACA-ae	luri		0.01	13	0....	3 1 0 0 0		... .
5440	Mandaean	0.01300	8,102	8,801	12,280	CMT31	12-AAAA-j	nasoraye		5.00	440	1cs..	7 5 3 2 0		pnb .
5441	Mazanderani (Tabri)	5.08812	3,171,138	3,444,769	4,806,365	CNT24z	58-AACE-a	mazandarani		0.00	0	0....	0 3 6 0 1	Mazanderani	... b
5442	Mussulman Tat	0.01500	9,349	10,155	14,169	CNT24f	58-AACG-a	muslim-tat		0.00	0	0....	0 1 0 0 0	Tat*	P.. b
5443	Natanzi	0.01000	6,232	6,770	9,446	CNT24z	58-AACD-d	natanzi		0.00	0	0....	0 2 0 0 0		... .
5444	Nayini	0.01000	6,232	6,770	9,446	CNT24z	58-AACD-c	nayini		0.00	0	0....	0 2 0 0 0		... .
5445	Northern Kurd	0.45249	282,011	306,346	427,433	CNT24c	58-AAAA-a	kurmanji	18	0.03	92	3c...	3 3 5 0 1	Kurdish: Kurmanji*	PN. b
5446	Persian (Irani)	34.90310	21,753,130	23,630,166	32,970,341	CNT24f	58-AACC-c	standard farsi		0.14	33,082	1Asu.	5 4 7 2 3		PNB b
5447	Persian Bantu	0.03500	21,814	23,696	33,062	NAB57j	58-AACC-c	standard farsi		1.00	237	1Asu.	6 4 0 0 0		PNB b
5448	Punjabi	0.04000	24,930	27,081	37,785	CNN25n	59-AAFE-c	general panjabi		1.00	271	1Asu.	6 4 2 0 0		PNB b
5449	Qashqai (Kashkai)	1.40000	872,541	947,831	1,322,475	MSY41a	44-AABA-j	qashqai		0.00	0	1c.u.	0 1 0 0 1		pnb b
5450	Rashti	0.30000	186,973	203,107	283,388	CNT24z	58-AACE-bc	rashti		0.70	1,422	1....	5 3 4 0 0	Rashti	... b
5451	Russian	0.00300	1,870	2,031	2,834	CEW22j	53-AAAE-d	russkiy		30.00	609	4B.uh	9 7 8 2 1	Russian	PNB b
5452	Semnani	0.03000	18,697	20,311	28,339	CNT24f	58-AACF-a	semnani		0.03	6	0....	3 1 4 0 0		... .
5453	Shikaki	0.04000	24,930	27,081	37,785	CNT24c	58-AAAA-af	shikaki		0.00	0	1c...	0 1 0 0 0		pn. b
5454	Sivandi	0.01000	6,232	6,770	9,446	CNT24z	58-AACD-h	sivandi		0.00	0	0....	0 1 0 0 0		... .
5455	Soi	0.01000	6,232	6,770	9,446	CNT24z	58-AACD-e	soi		0.00	0	0....	0 1 0 0 0		... .
5456	Southern Baluch (Baloch)	0.78932	491,939	534,387	745,611	CNT24b	58-AABA-c	south balochi		0.00	0	1.s..	0 2 2 0 1	Balochi, Southern	P.. b
5457	Southern Kurd (Carduchi)	4.56990	2,848,160	3,093,923	4,316,842	CNT24c	58-AAAA-ch	kermanshahi	18	0.05	1,547	2c...	4 4 5 2 2	Kurdish: Kermanshahi	Pn. .
5458	Southern Kurd (Sorani)	1.00000	623,244	677,022	944,625	CNT24c	58-AAAA-ce	sorani	18	0.02	135	1c...	3 4 5 1 2	Kurdish: Sorani	Pn. .
5459	Tadzhik (Persian Tajiki)	0.10000	62,324	67,702	94,463	CNT24g	58-AACC-j	tajiki		0.03	20	2asu.	3 3 0 0 1	Tajik*	PNB b
5460	Takistani	0.44473	277,175	301,092	420,103	CNT24z	58-AACE-c	takestani		0.00	0	1....	0 3 0 0 0		... b
5461	Talysh	0.17453	108,775	118,161	164,865	CNT24z	58-AACE-d	talishi		0.01	12	1....	3 2 0 0 0		... b
5462	Turk (Osmanli)	0.00900	5,609	6,093	8,502	MSY41j	44-AABA-a	osmanli		0.03	2	1A.u.	3 3 2 0 0	Turkish	PNB b
5463	Turkmen (Turkomani)	1.55838	971,250	1,055,058	1,472,085	MSY41k	44-AABA-e	turkmen		0.00	0	3c.u.	0 3 2 0 2	Turkmen	PNb b
5464	USA White	0.02000	12,465	13,540	18,893	CEW19s	52-ABAC-s	general american		78.00	10,562	1Bsuh	10 9 13 2 3	English*	PNB b
5465	Uighur	0.00700	4,363	4,739	6,612	MSY41z	44-AABD-d	east uyghur		0.06	3	1r.u.	4 3 0 0 1	Uighur*	PNB b
5466	Urdu (Islami, Undri, Urudu)	0.10000	62,324	67,702	94,463	CNN25r	59-AAFO-d	standard urdu	9	0.01	7	2Asuh	3 3 2 1 1	Urdu	PNB b
5467	Vafsi	0.03000	18,697	20,311	28,339	CNT24f	58-AACD-b	vafsi		0.02	4	0....	3 3 4 0 0		... b
5468	Western Baluch (Baloch)	0.91170	568,211	617,241	861,215	CNT24b	58-AABA-b	west balochi		0.00	0	3.s..	0 1 2 0 1	Baluchi: Western*	P.. .
5469	Western Pathan (Afghani)	0.17609	109,747	119,217	166,339	CNT24a	58-ABDA-a	pashto		0.02	24	1As..	3 3 2 0 0		pnb b
5470	Zott Gypsy (Nawar)	1.90000	1,184,163	1,286,342	1,794,788	CNN25f	12-AACF-h	northeast `anazi		0.00	0	1asuh	0 3 2 0 0		pnb b
5471	other minor peoples	0.59000	367,714	399,443	557,329	...				1.00	3,994		6 3 5 1 0		
	Iraq	**100.00000**	**20,094,652**	**23,114,884**	**41,013,588**					**3.14**	**724,662**				
5472	Anatolian Turk	0.10000	20,095	23,115	41,014	MSY41j	44-AABA-a	osmanli		0.02	5	1A.u.	3 1 2 0 0	Turkish	PNB b
5473	Armenian (Ermeni, Hai)	0.36437	73,219	84,224	149,441	CEW14	57-AAAA-b	ashkharik		82.00	69,063	4A.u.	10 8 11 2 2	Armenian: Modern, Eastern	PNB b
5474	Assyrian (Aisor)	0.30000	60,284	69,345	123,041	CMT31	12-AAAA-f	aisor		95.00	65,877	4cs..	10 8 11 2 3	Assyrian Neo-aramaic	PNB b
5475	Azerbaijani (Azeri Turk)	5.60000	1,125,301	1,294,434	2,296,761	MSY41a	44-AABA-fb	south azeri		0.03	388	1a.u.	3 3 0 1 1	Azerbaijani, South	pnb b
5476	Bajelan (Shabak, Gurani)	0.17391	34,947	40,199	71,327	CNT24c	58-AAAB-b	bajalani		0.07	28	0....	4 2 5 0 3		... .
5477	Bedouin	4.40000	884,165	1,017,055	1,804,598	CMT30	12-AACF-j	north `anazi		0.02	203	1csuh	3 4 7 0 0		pnb .
5478	British	0.00300	603	693	1,230	CEW19i	52-ABAC-b	standard-english	15	79.00	548	3Bsuh	10 9 13 2 3		PNB b
5479	Central Kurd	2.00000	401,893	462,298	820,272	CNT24c	58-AAAA-cg	mukri	26	0.05	231	1c...	4 2 5 1 1	Kurdish: Mukri	Pn. b
5480	Chaldean (Kildanean)	1.60000	321,514	369,838	656,217	CMT31	12-AAAA-g	kald-oyo		95.00	351,346	3cs..	10 9 10 2 8	Chaldean: Modern*	Pnb b
5481	Circassian (Cherkess)	0.09766	19,624	22,574	40,054	CEW17a	42-AAAA-b	cherkes		0.02	5	1a...	3 1 2 0 0		pn. b
5482	Egyptian Arab	2.20000	442,082	508,527	902,299	CMT30	12-AACF-a	masri		18.00	91,535	2Asuh	8 7 8 2 3	Arabic*	PNB b
5483	French	0.00200	402	462	820	CEW21b	51-AABI-d	general français		87.00	402	1B.uh	10 9 14 2 1	French	PNB b
5484	Ghorbati Gypsy	0.53442	107,390	123,531	219,185	CNN25f	59-ACAA-a	domari		0.00	0	0....	0 3 2 0 0		... b
5485	Greek	0.00100	201	231	410	CEW20	56-AAAA-c	dhimotiki		95.00	220	2B.uh	10 9 11 2 1	Greek: Modern	PNB b
5486	Han Chinese	0.00600	1,206	1,387	2,461	MSY42a	79-AAAB-ba	kuo-yü		0.55	8	2Bsuh	5 1 2 0 0	Chinese: Kuoyu*	PNB b
5487	Hawrami (Gurani)	0.10000	20,095	23,115	41,014	CNT24c	58-AAAB-c	hawrami		0.02	5	0....	3 2 5 0 0		... .
5488	Herki	0.10000	20,095	23,115	41,014	CNT24c	58-AAAA-ae	herki		0.04	9	1c...	3 2 5 0 3		pn. b
5489	Iraqi Arab	57.58719	11,571,945	13,311,212	23,618,573	CMT30	12-AACF-g	syro-mesopotamian		0.50	66,556	1Asuh	5 5 7 2 3		pnb b
5490	Iraqi Kurd	6.00000	1,205,679	1,386,893	2,460,815	CNT24c	12-AACF-g	syro-mesopotamian		0.05	693	1Asuh	4 5 5 1 3		pnb b
5491	Italian	0.00100	201	231	410	CEW21e	51-AABQ-c	standard italiano		84.00	194	2B.uh	10 9 15 2 1	Italian	PNB b
5492	Jewish	0.00074	149	171	304	CMT35	12-AACH-d	yahudi		0.00	0	0c...	0 1 2 0 0		p.. b
5493	Luri (Lur)	0.30000	60,284	69,345	123,041	CNT24z	58-AACA-aa	luri		0.03	21	0....	3 1 4 0 0		... .
5494	Northern Kurd (Kermanji)	6.50000	1,306,152	1,502,467	2,665,883	CNT24c	58-AAAA-a	kurmanji	26	0.07	1,052	3c...	4 5 5 1 3	Kurdish: Kurmanji*	PN. b
5495	Palestinian Arab	0.50000	100,473	115,574	205,068	CMT30	12-AACF-f	syro-palestinian		11.00	12,713	1Asuh	8 6 8 2 3	Arabic: Lebanese*	Pnb b
5496	Persian	1.12771	226,609	260,669	462,514	CNT24f	58-AACC-ca	west farsi		0.04	104	1asu.	3 3 7 0 0	Farsi, Western	PNB b
5497	Russian	0.00100	201	231	410	CEW22j	53-AAAE-d	russkiy		20.00	46	4B.uh	9 7 8 2 1	Russian	PNB b
5498	Shikaki	0.10000	20,095	23,115	41,014	CNT24c	58-AAAA-af	shikaki		0.10	23	1c...	5 2 5 0 3		pn. b
5499	Southern Assyrian (Alqosh)	0.26000	52,246	60,099	106,635	CMT31	12-AAAA-ga	alqosh		90.00	54,089	1cs..	10 8 11 2 1		pnb .

Continued opposite

Table 8-2 continued

EVANGELIZATION								EVANGELISM			ADDITIONAL DESCRIPTIVE DATA
Ref	*Da*	*C*	*CG%*	*r*	*E*	*U*	*W*	*e*	*R*	*T*	*Locations, civil divisions, literacy, religions, church history, denominations, dioceses, church growth, missions, agencies, ministries, movements*
1	*28*	*29*	*30*	*31*	*32*	*33*	*34*	*35*	*36*	*37*	*38*
5380	4	5	5.33	0	99.65	0.35	C	249.11	165	8	Yali of Pass Valley, Southern Yali. Irian Jaya. Jayawijaya, Kurulu, Kurima. Mostly monolingual. Animists 35%. D=GKI,NHK,CMA,NRC. M=RBMU,ZGK.
5381	0	0	3.06	0	81.00	19.00	C	177.39	137	7	Irian Jaya. Island off the north coast east of the Tor River. Animists 40%.
5382	1	4	5.04	0	95.00	5.00	C	208.05	174	8	Irian Jaya, south coast. Adults and children are bilingual in Indonesian. Animists 40%. D=TEAM.
5383	1	5	6.63	0	84.00	16.00	B	153.30	249	7	Irian Jaya. South coast area north of Odamun river. Many bilingual in Indonesian. Animists 50%. D=GAK(Bible Ch). M=TEAM.
5384	0	0	2.57	0	81.00	19.00	C	177.39	121	7	Irian Jaya. Island off the north coast east of the Biri River. Animists 40%.
5385	0	6	4.20	0	36.00	64.00	A	15.76	384	5	Irian Jaya. Lower end of Geelvink Bay west of Iresim. Animists 88%.
5386	3	5	6.37	0	99.65	0.35	C	241.99	198	8	Irian Jaya. Central Yapen Island, 28 villages. Animists 35%. D=GKPI,Pentecostals, CMA. M=SIL,RBMU,UFM.
5387	0	5	3.71	0	91.00	9.00	C	199.29	142	7	Irian Jaya. Border area of south coast, bordering Marind on east. Also in PNG. Bilingual in Indonesian. Animists 40%. M=TEAM.
5388	0	6	3.72	0	92.00	8.00	C	218.27	141	8	Irian Jaya. South coast area on east side of Marianne Strait. Closest to Maklew. Animists 35%.
5389	0	7	3.14	0	89.00	11.00	C	198.15	127	7	Irian Jaya. Lower Geelvink Bay south of Wandamen language area. Animists 39%.
5390	0	0	4.30	1	90.00	10.00	C	213.52	161	8	Jayawijaya Kabupaten, border area just east of the Sogber River. Animists 35%.
5391	0	5	5.12	1	93.00	7.00	C	203.67	180	8	Irian Jaya. South coast border area. Majority in PNG. Close to Southern Kati. Animists 40%. M=APCM-PNG.
5392	1	5	6.03	0	99.91	0.09	C	421.83	152	10	Irian Jaya. Yotafa Bay, close to Jayapura, 4 villages. D=GKI.
5393	0	6	9.25		49.00	51.00	A	35.77	517	5	Armenians(AAC), Koreans (M=PCK-Haptong), Swiss, Pakistanis,&c. Muslims 70%, Animists 10%.
Iran											
5394	0	4	4.66	4	34.05	65.95	A	0.06	431	2	In Khorasan. Refugees from Afghanistan's 10-year war. Muslims 100%(Hanafi Sunnis). R=FEBA,FEBC,AWR.
5395	7	6	0.62	6	99.85	0.15	C	468.47	22	10	Northern Iran. Khoi, Shahpur, Aher Tabriz, Tehran, Esfahan, Shiraz. Gregorians. D=Armenian Apostolic Ch(3 Dioceses),RCC(Armenian-rite D-Ispahan),UAECNE.
5396	4	5	0.35	5	99.84	0.16	C	441.50	20	10	Nestorians, Chaldeans. D=Ancient Ch of the East(P-Tehran,D-Urmia),RCC(4 Chaldean Dioceses),Assyrian AoG,ECI.
5397	4	6	-0.18	5	99.85	0.15	C	452.96	9	10	Also in Russia, Iraq, Turkey, Israel, Cyprus, Syria, USA. In Rezaiyeh (Urmia), most in Tehran. D=Assyrian Ch of the East,Chaldean Catholic Ch,Assyrian AoG,ECI.
5398	0	3	1.81	0	13.03	86.97	A	0.01	591	2	Tafres area. Very close to Vafsi; transitional central Iranian to Talysh. Bilingual in Farsi. Muslims 100%.
5399	1	3	0.00	1	27.00	73.00	A	0.00	0	1.12	Breadbasket of Iran. 12 main dialects. Muslims 100%(80% Shias, 20% Hanafi Sunnis). Some ministry by D=AAC(D-Tabriz). M=CSI. R=FEBA.
5400	0	4	0.00	1	21.00	79.00	A	0.00	0	1.10	Kurdistan Jewish Aramaic (Judeo-Aramaic, Targumic). Persons of Jewish origin and religion, most of whom have now emigrated to Israel.
5401	0	3	0.00	1	10.00	90.00	A	0.00	0	1.04	Partially nomadic. Muslims 100%(Shias). Political struggles with Tehran regime.
5402	0	6	5.03	1	31.00	69.00	A	5.65	536	4	Also found in Turkey, Yugoslavia, Bulgaria, Greece, and 7 other countries. Muslims 95%.
5403	0	4	0.00	1	12.00	88.00	A	0.00	0	1.06	Related to Baluchi. Muslims 100%(Sunnis).
5404	0	4	3.49	0	20.20	79.80	A	0.14	609	3	Birahui. In east. Great majority in Pakistan; also Oman, UAE. Nomads, pastoralists. In Iran most now speak Baluchi. Muslims 100%(Sunnis). M=CMS.
5405	4	6	1.76	8	99.78	0.22	C	429.89	53	10	Expatriates from Britain, in business. D=ECJME(D-Iran),SDA,JWs,&c.
5406	0	4	3.06	0	25.03	74.97	A	0.02	554	2	In central Kurdish regions around Senna. Muslims 100%(Sunnis,some Shias). M=GOM,ELCA,CSI.
5407	0	6	0.00	5	47.00	53.00	A	8.57	0	4	Artificial (constructed) language, in 80 countries. Speakers in Iran: 12,000(non mother-tongue). Muslims 90% (Ithna-Asharis), Baha'ia 5%.
5408	0	4	0.00	0	8.00	92.00	A	0.00	0	1.02	Southwest Iran. An Indo-Iranian language distinct from Farsi. Related to Lari. Muslims 100%.
5409	2	6	3.13	8	99.85	0.15	C	477.78	73	10	Expatriates from France, in business. Nonreligious 13%. D=RCC,Eglise Evangelique Francaise(Teheran).
5410	0	6	1.81	0	25.05	74.95	A	0.04	275	2	In Yezd and Kerman cities and surrounding. Private language of Persian Zoroastrians. Bilingual in Farsi. Zoroastrians 99%.
5411	0	1	3.04	1	10.03	89.97	A	0.01	1,104	2	In mountains near Gilaki. Unwritten. Close to Mazanderani. Muslims 100%.
5412	0	4	0.00	0	8.00	92.00	A	0.00	0	1.02	Central Iran. Muslims 100%.
5413	1	5	1.26	4	78.00	22.00	B	71.17	44	6	Immigrants from Georgia. Nonreligious/atheists 45%. Muslims 30%(Sunnis,Shias). D=Georgian Orthodox Ch.
5414	3	6	4.16	8	99.87	0.13	C	498.55	92	10	Expatriates from Germany, in oil, business. D=Deutsche Evangelische Kirche(Teheran),NAC,RCC.
5415	0	4	2.67	7	18.01	81.99	A	0.00	563	1.05	Qorbati. Middle Eastern Romany. In Kurbat, western Iran, and 9 other countries. Muslims 100%.
5416	1	4	5.25	1	28.50	71.50	A	0.52	601	3	Gilan Province, coastal plain, south of Talysh. Unwritten, close to Mazanderani. Bilingual in Farsi. Muslims 99%(Shias). D=RCC. M=CSI.
5417	0	5	3.58	6	41.50	58.50	A	0.75	303	3	Traders, from India. Muslims 50%, Hindus 50%.
5418	0	4	7.56	8	51.00	49.00	B	3.72	444	4	Immigrants from Gulf states; mainly in Kamsch, Khuzestan, islands. Muslims 90%. RAWR,FEBA,IBRA. T=SAT7,CTV.
5419	0	1	2.81	0	9.08	90.92	A	0.02	1,150	2	West part of Kordestan Province, near Iraq border. Also in Iraq. Closest to Dimli in Turkey. Muslims 100%.
5420	0	1	2.81	1	11.06	88.94	A	0.02	944	2	Northwest of Tabriz. Close to Karingani and Talysh. Muslims 100%.
5421	0	2	2.74	4	30.05	69.95	A	0.05	323	2	Northern Iran. Mainly in Afghanistan, some in Pakistan. Semi-sedentary pastoralists. Muslims 100%(Imami Shias, Ismailis, some Sunnis). M=CSI.
5422	0	1	1.40	0	16.02	83.98	A	0.01	582	2	In Kermanji area. Also in Iraq and Turkey. Muslims 100%.
5423	4	6	3.53	7	49.46	50.54	A	0.83	234	3	Khuzestan. Mesopotamian, Eastern Colloquial Arabic. Muslims 99%(Shias). D=GOC(P-Antioch,D-Baghdad),Chaldean Catholic Ch,IM(Good Shepherd Ch),ECJME.
5424	0	5	3.81	5	38.03	61.97	A	0.04	419	2	Kurds from Kurdistan who now use Farsi as mother tongue. Settled urbanites. Muslims 100%(Sunnis, Shias). R=FEBA,TWR,AWR.
5425	1	6	3.92	7	99.83	0.17	C	460.48	89	10	Expatriates from Italy, in commerce. Strong Catholics. D=RCC(Latin-rite AD-Ispahan). M=CM,SDB.
5426	0	1	1.96	1	17.02	82.98	A	0.01	477	2	Refugees and migrants from Afghanistan. Semi-nomadic. Muslims 100%(Hanafi Sunnis).
5427	0	5	2.33	5	43.05	56.95	A	0.07	192	2	Sizeable communities of practicing Jews, mainly in Teheran.
5428	0	5	0.00	0	13.00	87.00	A	0.00	0	1.03	People: Bic. Language: Dzhuhuric. Cultural and religious Jews; also 20,000 more in Russia.
5429	0	4	0.00	4	26.02	73.98	A	0.01	73	2	Close to Bukharic, Farsi. Persons of Jewish origin and religion.
5430	0	1	0.00	1	10.00	90.00	A	0.00	0	1.07	Also in Karakalpak (Uzbekistan). Muslims 100%(Hanafi Sunnis).
5431	0	1	0.00	1	7.00	93.00	A	0.00	0	1.03	Northeast of Tabriz. Close to Harzani, Talysh. Muslims 100%.
5432	0	1	0.00	4	29.00	71.00	A	0.00	0	1.09	Gorgan City, Mazandaran Province. Also in 8 other countries. Arabic script. Muslims 100%(Hanafi Sunnis, with Sufi influence). M=CSI.
5433	0	1	0.00	1	16.00	84.00	A	0.00	0	1.09	Northeast of Arak in Central Province. Most are bilingual in Farsi; children often know only it. Muslims 100%.
5434	0	6	0.00	1	22.00	78.00	A	0.00	0	1.11	Northeast Iran, in northern part of Khorasan Province, and northwest of Mashhad. Bilingual in Farsi. Muslims 100%.
5435	0	1	0.00	0	5.00	95.00	A	0.00	0	1.01	In central Iran. Muslims 100%.
5436	1	6	6.19	6	89.00	11.00	B	97.45	209	6	Migrant workers, especially in construction industry. Shamanists 30%. D=Presbyterians(in Teheran,&c). M=PCK-Tonghap,BPM.
5437	0	5	0.00	0	9.00	91.00	A	0.00	0	1.02	In Fars area. Muslims 100%.
5438	0	3	0.00	4	16.00	84.00	A	0.00	0	1.05	Southwest Iran, Lorestan, Ilam; central city Borujerd. Muslims 100%(90% Ithna-Ashari Shias,5% Ali Allahi, 5% Sunnis). R=HCJB.
5439	0	1	2.60	4	12.01	87.99	A	0.00	821	1.03	Dialect of Luri. Southwest Iran, Lorestan, Ilam, Fars Province. Muslims 100%(Shias).
5440	0	4	1.96	1	35.00	65.00	A	6.38	207	4	In Khuzistan, also Iraq. Descendants of Jewish-Christian Gnostics (AD 150). Now called Christians of St John, Dippers, Sabaeans.
5441	0	4	0.00	4	23.00	77.00	A	0.00	0	1.06	Northern Iran near Caspian Sea, southern half of Mazandaran Province. Bilingual in Farsi. Related to Gilaki. Muslims 100%(Shias). M=CSI. R=HCJB.
5442	0	4	0.00	0	12.00	88.00	A	0.00	0	1.04	Also 22,000 in nation of Azerbaijan, where Muslim Tat use Azeri as literary language. Muslims 100%(Shias).
5443	0	3	0.00	0	7.00	93.00	A	0.00	0	1.01	In central Iran. Muslims 100%.
5444	0	3	0.00	0	7.00	93.00	A	0.00	0	1.01	In central Iran. Muslims 100%.
5445	0	4	4.63	0	25.03	74.97	A	0.02	726	2	Eastern Kurds. Mountain villages along Turkey border region, West Azerbaijan Province. Also in 8 countries. Muslims 100%(Shafi Sunnis,some Shias). M=CSI.
5446	4	6	5.83	5	56.14	43.86	B	0.28	319	3	Almost 2 million are in exile in 15 countries. Muslims 90%(Imami Shias/Ithna-Asharis), 2% Baha'is, 8% Parsis (20 centers). D=RCC,ECJME,AoG,ECI. M=CMS,IM.
5447	0	6	3.22	5	38.00	62.00	A	1.38	337	4	Former Black slaves of African origin, now partly assimilated. Muslims 99%.
5448	0	5	3.35	5	42.00	58.00	A	1.53	287	4	Traders, from India. Hindus 65%, Sikhs 30%, Muslims 4%.
5449	0	1	0.00	1	17.00	83.00	A	0.00	0	1.09	Nomadic pastoralists in southwest, Fars Province; Shiraz city. Related to Azeri. Unwritten. Many bilingual literates in Farsi. Rug weavers. Muslims 100%(all Shias).
5450	0	4	5.08	1	23.70	76.30	A	0.60	703	3	Rasht city, capital of Gilan. Close to Gilaki Province. Bilinguals in Farsi. Muslims 99%.
5451	1	6	0.85	7	88.00	12.00	B	96.36	26	6	Refugees since 1917 from USSR. Nonreligious/atheists 60%, Muslims 10%. D=Russian Orthodox Ch Outside Russia(ROCOR).
5452	0	3	1.81	5	19.03	80.97	A	0.02	361	2	In northwest Iran. Muslims 100%.
5453	0	1	0.00	0	13.00	87.00	A	0.00	0	1.06	Kurdistan area, related to Kurdi. Also in Iraq and Turkey. Muslims 100%.
5454	0	3	0.00	0	7.00	93.00	A	0.00	0	1.01	In central Iran. Muslims 100%.
5455	0	3	0.00	0	7.00	93.00	A	0.00	0	1.01	In central Iran. Muslims 100%.
5456	0	4	0.00	1	15.00	85.00	A	0.00	0	1.08	Southern Baluchistan Province. Mostly in Pakistan; also Oman, UAE. Muslims 100%(Sunnis). M=CSI.
5457	2	4	6.14	0	30.05	69.95	A	0.05	742	2	Northwest, northeast Iran. 90% settled urbanites, 10% nomadic. Also in Iraq. Literates 1%. Muslims 98%(Shafi Sunnis,some Shias,500,000 Ahl-i-Haqq/Men of God).
5458	1	4	2.64	0	25.02	74.98	A	0.01	508	2	Around Suleimaniyah and adjacent Kurdestan. Muslims 100%(Shafi Sunnis). D=RCC. M=LBI,CSI. R=TWR.
5459	0	1	3.04	4	29.03	70.97	A	0.03	353	2	Mountain farmers; refugees and migrants from Afghanistan. Muslims 100%. M=CSI.
5460	0	3	0.00	1	12.00	88.00	A	0.00	0	1.04	Towns and villages in Azeri-speaking north from Khalkhal to Saveh. Close to Talysh. Bilingual in Farsi. Muslims 100%.
5461	0	4	2.52	1	16.01	83.99	A	0.00	602	1.05	Along Caspian Sea to Kepri-Chal, northwest Gilan Province along coastal plain. Also in ex-USSR, Azerbaijan. Close to Harzani. Bilingual in Azeri. Muslims 100%.
5462	0	3	0.70	8	38.03	61.97	A	0.04	102	2	Former immigrants and residents from Turkey. Muslims 100%(Hanafi Sunnis).
5463	0	3	0.00	1	24.00	76.00	A	0.00	0	1.11	Northeast, mainly in Mazandaran Province near Turkmenistan. Also in Afghanistan, Turkey, Pakistan. Devout Muslims 100%(Yomut tribe are Hanafi Sunnis).
5464	7	6	4.12	8	99.78	0.22	C	418.50	94	10	Expatriates in oil, business. D=AoG,SDA,CCS,CJCLdS,JWs,ECJME(D-Iran),&c.
5465	0	1	1.10	4	27.06	72.94	A	0.05	192	2	Agriculturalists. Muslims 100%(Sunnis, with heavy Sufi influence). M=CSI.
5466	1	4	1.96	5	42.01	57.99	A	0.01	195	2	From Pakistan. Muslims 100%(Hanafi Sunnis,Shafis, Shias,Sufis). D=RCC.
5467	0	1	1.40	0	15.02	84.98	A	0.01	383	2	In Tafres area, central Iran. Close to Ashtiani. Bilingual in Farsi. Muslims 100%.
5468	0	4	0.00	1	17.00	83.00	A	0.00	0	1.07	Northern Baluchistan Province. Half are nomades, half settled. Also in Pakistan, Afghanistan, former USSR. Influenced by Farsi, though few speak it. Muslims 100%.
5469	0	4	3.23	5	31.02	68.98	A	0.02	481	2	Large numbers of refugees and expatriates from Afghanistan. In Khorasan Province east of Qaen. Muslims 100%(Hanafi Sunnis).
5470	0	5	0.00	7	30.00	70.00	A	0.00	0	1.12	Arab Gypsies, Muslim Gypsies. Nomads. Muslims 100%(Sunnis). T=SAT7,CTV. R=FEBA,AWR,IBRA.
5471	0	6	3.63		20.00	80.00	A	0.73	497	3	Europeans, Indians, other Asians. Muslims 90%.
Iraq											
5472	0	5	1.62	8	40.02	59.98	A	0.02	160	2	Former immigrants, settlers, residents, from Turkey. Muslims 100%(Hanafi Sunnis).
5473	4	6	0.44	6	99.82	0.18	C	445.95	19	10	Gregorians. D=Armenian Apostolic Ch(AD-Baghdad),UAECNE,AESB,RCC(Armenian-rite AD-Baghdad). M=OP,ABCFM.
5474	3	7	-0.10	5	99.95	0.05	C	558.26	10	10	D=Ancient Ch of the East(Nestorians,P-Tehran: 3 Dioceses),rival P-Baghdad; Assyrian Evangelical Chs. M=PCUSA,RCA,OP,OCD,CSSR.
5475	1	5	3.73	1	29.03	70.97	A	0.03	418	2	In Kirkuk City, Arbil, Rowanduz, Mosul region. Also in Jordan, Russia, Iran, et alia. Arabic script. Muslims 100%(80% Shias,20% Sunnis). D=AAC. M=CSI. R=FEBA.
5476	0	3	3.39	0	19.07	80.93	A	0.04	774	2	Language closer to Dimli than to Kurdish. Muslims 100%(Shias,Sunnis). M=WEC,CSI,YWAM,FI.
5477	0	0	3.06	1	23.02	76.98	A	0.01	448	2	In the western desert bordering Syria. Nomads. Muslims 100%.
5478	4	7	2.17	8	99.79	0.21	C	429.64	61	10	Expatriates in military, UN. D=ECJME(D-Cyprus & The Gulf),SDA,RCC,JWs.
5479	0	4	3.19	0	27.05	72.95	A	0.04	526	2	In central autonomous Kurdish regions. Muslims 100%(Shafi Sunnis, some Shias). M=CSI.WEC,FI,OM,YWAM.
5480	0	7	11.03	5	99.95	0.05	C	544.39	204	10	Nestorians now under Rome as Uniatas. D=Chaldean Ch(10 Chaldean-rite Dioceses in Iraq).
5481	0	1	1.62	0	18.02	81.98	A	0.01	398	2	Immigrants from Caucasus. In 10 countries. Muslims 100%(Sunnis).
5482	2	6	5.22	8	79.00	21.00	B	51.90	205	6	Arabs and Copts. Decline from 3 million in 1980s. Muslims 82%(Sunnis). D=Coptic Orthodox Ch(P-Alexandria),Arab Evangelical Churches. M=ABCFM,PCUSA.
5483	1	6	-0.06	8	99.87	0.13	C	476.32	17	10	Expatriates in military, UN, education. D=RCC.
5484	0	3	0.00	7	16.00	84.00	A	0.00	0	1.04	Middle Eastern Romany. Also in Iran, Syria, Turkey, Israel, India, Egypt, Libya, former USSR, Afghanistan. Muslims 100%.
5485	1	7	0.69	7	99.95	0.05	C	540.93	29	10	Traders, originally from Greece. D=Greek Orthodox Ch(P-Antioch,D-Baghdad).
5486	0	6	2.10	7	43.55	56.45	A	0.87	173	3	Traders, in business or commerce. Buddhists/Chinese folk-religionists 95%.
5487	0	3	1.62	0	15.02	84.98	A	0.01	660	2	Near border with Iran, also in Western Iran. Distinct from Kurdish; closest to Dimli (Turkey). Muslims 100%.
5488	0	3	2.22	0	26.04	73.96	A	0.03	444	2	Dialect of Kermanji. Kurdish. Also in Iran, Turkey. Muslims 100%. M=YWAM,WEC,CSI,FI.
5489	4	6	1.51	7	55.50	44.50	B	1.01	109	4	Muslims 99%(60% Shias, 39% Hanafi Sunnis). D=ACE(P-Baghdad,P-Tehran),RCC(4 rites,14 Dioceses),CB,SDA. M=CSI,FI,MEM. T=SAT7,CTV. R=FEBA,AWR.
5490	0	5	4.33	7	44.05	55.95	A	0.08	394	2	Arabized Kurds with Arabic as mother tongue. Becoming assimilated. Muslims 100%(Shafi Sunnis,some Shias). M=CSI,WEC,FI,AoG(Water of Life),OM,YWAM.
5491	1	7	2.91	7	99.84	0.16	C	456.83	72	10	In military and UN. Strong Catholics. D=RCC(Latin-rite AD-Baghdad).
5492	0	6	0.00	7	24.00	76.00	A	0.00	0	1.07	Remnant from 250,000 Jews in Iraq in 1950. Harassment, persecutions, hangings, murders. Judaism (100% Jews).
5493	0	3	3.09	4	18.03	81.97	A	0.02	622	2	Near Iran border. Also in Iran, USA. Nomadic shepherds. Muslims 100%(Imami Shias).
5494	2	4	5.30	0	32.07	67.93	A	0.08	624	2	Northern and eastern Iraq. Also in 10 other countries. Arabic script. Lingua franca. Muslims 100%(Sunnis,Shias). D=ACE,RCC. M=LBI,LOM,OP,OCD,CSI,WEC.
5495	3	6	7.41	8	68.00	32.00	B	27.30	327	5	Muslims 85%(Shafi Sunnis). D=GOC(P-Antioch,D-Baghdad),RCC(Latin-rite AD-Baghdad),SDA.
5496	0	6	2.37	5	40.04	59.96	A	0.05	210	2	Immigrants, residents, refugees from Iran. Muslims 99%(Imami Shias).
5497	1	7	-1.56	7	79.00	21.00	B	57.67	3	6	Military and advisors. Nonreligious, atheists still predominant 80%. D=Russian Orthodox Ch(P-Moscow).
5498	0	3	3.19	0	25.10	74.90	A	0.09	567	2	Kurdistan area, related to Kurdi. Also in Turkey, Iran. Muslims 100%. M=WEC,YWAM,CSI,FI.
5499	1	7	1.74	5	99.90	0.10	C	466.47	47	10	Citizens living in Kurdish mountains between Mosul and Amadia. Special translation of Modern Syriac. D=Ancient Ch of the East. M=ABCFM(UCC).

Continued overleaf

Table 8-2 continued

PEOPLE		POPULATION				IDENTITY CODE		LANGUAGE		CHURCH		MINISTRY						SCRIPTURE		
Ref 1	*Ethnic name* 2	*P%* 3	*In 1995* 4	*In 2000* 5	*In 2025* 6	*Race* 7	*Language* 8	*Autoglossonym* 9	*S* 10	*AC* 11	*Members* 12	*Jayuh* 13-17	*d* 18	*wa* 19	*xc* 20	*mc* 21	*mi* 22	*Biblioglossonym* 23	*Pub* 24-26	*ss* 27
5500	Southern Kurd (Sorani)	8.50000	1,708,045	1,964,765	3,486,155	CNT24c	58-AAAA-c	kurdi		0.10	1,965	2c...	5	5	5	1	3	Kurdi	PN.	b
5501	Surchi	0.05000	10,047	11,557	20,507	CNT24c	58-AAAA-ag	surchi		0.20	23	1c...	5	3	4	0	3		pn.	n
5502	Syrian Arab	0.05000	10,047	11,557	20,507	CMT30	12-AACF-f	syro-palestinian		8.00	925	1Asuh	7	6	8	2	2	Arabic: Lebanese*	Pnb	b
5503	Syrian Aramaic (Syriac)	0.03000	6,028	6,934	12,304	CMT31	12-AAAA-ge	zakho		90.00	6,241	1cs..	10	8	11	2	3	Lishana Deni	pnb	.
5504	Turkmen	1.20000	241,136	277,379	492,163	MSY41k	44-AABA-f	azeri		0.01	28	2a.u.	3	1	2	0	0		PNB	b
5505	Urdu (Islami, Undri, Urudu)	0.01000	2,009	2,311	4,101	CNN25r	59-AAFO-d	standard urdu		0.00	0	2Asuh	0	3	2	0	1	Urdu	PNB	b
5506	Zott Gypsy (Nawar)	0.10000	20,095	23,115	41,014	CNN25f	12-AACF-g	syro-mesopotamian		0.00	0	1Asuh	0	3	0	0	0		pnb	b
5507	other minor peoples	0.10000	20,095	23,115	41,014	...				0.50	116		5	3	2	1	0			
	Ireland	**100.00000**	**3,609,164**	**3,730,239**	**4,403,843**					**89.95**	**3,355,447**									
5508	Arab	0.24200	8,734	9,027	10,657	CMT30	12-AACA	standard arabic cluster		25.00	2,257	0.su.	9	7	9	0	0		...	.
5509	British (English)	1.40000	50,528	52,223	61,654	CEW19i	52-ABAC-b	standard-english		78.00	40,734	3Bsuh	10	9	15	5	3		PNB	b
5510	British (Scottish)	0.30000	10,827	11,191	13,212	CEW19i	52-ABAC-b	standard-english		78.00	8,729	3Bsuh	10	9	15	5	3		PNB	b
5511	Esperanto	0.00000	0	0	0	CEW21z	51-AAAC-a	proper esperanto		80.00	0	0A...	10	8	11	5	0	Esperanto	PNB	b
5512	French	0.03000	1,083	1,119	1,321	CEW21b	51-AABI-d	general français	12	85.00	951	1B.uh	10	8	14	4	1	French	PNB	b
5513	German	0.02000	722	746	881	CEW19m	52-ABCE-a	standard hoch-deutsch	2	87.00	649	2B.uh	10	9	13	4	3	German*	PNB	b
5514	Greek	0.05000	1,805	1,865	2,202	CEW20	56-AAAA-c	dhimotiki		95.00	1,772	2B.uh	10	9	11	4	1	Greek: Modern	PNB	b
5515	Han Chinese	0.01000	361	373	440	MSY42a	79-AAAB-ba	kuo-yü		19.00	71	2Bsuh	8	5	8	5	1	Chinese: Kuoyu*	PNB	b
5516	Irish	68.31800	2,465,709	2,548,425	3,008,617	CEW18b	52-ABAE-i	oceanian-english	100	89.18	2,272,685	0B.uh	10	9	16	5	1		pnb	b
5517	Irish Gaelic	26.72400	964,513	996,869	1,176,883	CEW18b	50-AAAA-g	gaeilge		95.00	947,026	2a.uh	10	9	16	4	2	Irish*	PNB	b
5518	Irish Gypsy	0.48000	17,324	17,905	21,138	CNN25f	52-ABAC-i	irish-english		80.00	14,324	1Asuh	10	7	14	4	3		pnb	.
5519	Irish Traveller (Gypsy)	0.16100	5,811	6,006	7,090	CNN25f	50-ACAA-a	west sheldruu		80.00	4,805	0....	10	7	14	5	3		...	b
5520	Italian	0.03000	1,083	1,119	1,321	CEW21e	51-AABQ-c	standard italiano	1	83.00	929	2B.uh	10	9	15	4	3	Italian	PNB	b
5521	Jewish	0.04800	1,732	1,791	2,114	CMT35	52-ABAC-i	irish-english		0.20	4	1Asuh	5	5	6	5	1		pnb	.
5522	Russian	0.02700	974	1,007	1,189	CEW22j	53-AAAE-d	russkiy		65.00	655	4B.uh	10	8	8	4	2	Russian	PNB	b
5523	Spaniard	0.01000	361	373	440	CEW21k	51-AABB-c	general español	2	96.00	358	2B.uh	10	9	15	4	1	Spanish	PNB	b
5524	USA White	0.80000	28,873	29,842	35,231	CEW19s	52-ABAC-s	general american		77.00	22,978	1Bsuh	10	9	14	5	3	English*	PNB	b
5525	Ulster Irish	1.00000	36,092	37,302	44,038	CEW19r	52-ABAC-ib	mid-ulster-t.		74.00	27,604	1Asuh	10	9	16	5	1		pnb	.
5526	Urdu	0.05000	1,805	1,865	2,202	CNN25r	59-AAFO-d	standard urdu		0.06	1	2Asuh	4	4	5	3	0	Urdu	PNB	b
5527	Welsh	0.20000	7,218	7,460	8,808	CEW18d	50-ABAA-bc	cymraeg-safonol		85.00	6,341	2A.uh	10	9	15	5	3	Welsh	PNB	b
5528	other minor peoples	0.10000	3,609	3,730	4,404	...				69.00	2,574		10	7	8	5	0			
	Isle of Man	**100.00000**	**74,073**	**79,166**	**100,891**					**66.24**	**52,438**									
5529	British	87.62000	64,903	69,365	88,401	CEW19i	52-ABAC-b	standard-english	100	64.00	44,394	3Bsuh	10	9	13	5	3		PNB	b
5530	Irish	10.00000	7,407	7,917	10,089	CEW18b	52-ABAC-i	irish-english		83.00	6,571	1Asuh	10	9	16	5	1		pnb	.
5531	Jewish	0.08000	59	63	81	CMT35	52-ABAC-b	standard-english		1.00	1	3Bsuh	6	5	2	5	0		PNB	b
5532	Manx	0.20000	148	158	202	CEW18z	50-AAAA-kf	manaweg-q.	1	90.00	142	1c.uh	10	7	12	5	1	Manx	PNB	b
5533	other minor peoples	2.10000	1,556	1,662	2,119	...				80.00	1,330		10	8	8	5	0			
	Israel	**100.00000**	**4,516,212**	**5,121,683**	**6,926,755**					**5.74**	**294,078**									
5534	Amharic Jew	0.03000	1,355	1,537	2,078	CMT34a	12-ACBA-b	general amarinya	1	1.00	15	3Asuh	6	6	7	4	1	Amharic	PNB	b
5535	Arabic Jew	5.60000	252,908	286,814	387,898	CMT35	12-AACF-f	syro-palestinian		0.04	115	1Asuh	3	4	6	3	0	Arabic: Lebanese*	Pnb	b
5536	Armenian (Hai, Armiane)	0.01500	677	768	1,039	CEW14	57-AAAA-b	ashkharik		88.00	676	4A.u.	10	8	13	4	1	Armenian: Modern, Eastern	PNB	b
5537	Assyrian (Eastern Syriac)	0.01000	452	512	693	CMT31	12-AAAA-f	aisor		95.00	487	4cs..	10	8	12	2	2	Assyrian Neo-aramaic	PNB	b
5538	Bedouin Arab	1.30000	58,711	66,582	90,048	CMT30	12-AACD	badawi-sahara cluster		0.04	27	0a...	3	3	3	1	0		PN.	b
5539	Berber Jew	0.05000	2,258	2,561	3,463	CMT35	10-AAAC-c	judeo-tamazigh		0.00	0	1c...	0	1	0	1	0		pn.	b
5540	Black Israelite/Hebrew	0.06000	2,710	3,073	4,156	NFB68a	52-ABAE-a	talkin-black		0.00	0	0B.uh	0	3	2	3	0		pnb	b
5541	British	0.03000	1,355	1,537	2,078	CEW19i	52-ABAC-b	standard-english		70.00	1,076	3Bsuh	10	9	13	5	3		PNB	b
5542	British Jew	0.50000	22,581	25,608	34,634	CMT35	52-ABAC-b	standard-english		3.00	768	3Bsuh	6	6	8	5	1		PNB	b
5543	Caucasian Mountain Jew	0.17800	8,039	9,117	12,330	CMT35	58-AACG-b	judeo-tat		0.00	0	0....	0	1	2	0	0	Judeo-tat	P..	b
5544	Central Asian Jew	1.09000	49,227	55,826	75,502	CMT35	58-AACC-kb	bukharik		0.02	11	1csu.	3	3	2	0	0		pnb	b
5545	Circassian (Cherkess)	0.09000	4,065	4,610	6,234	CEW17a	42-AAAA-b	cherkes		0.05	2	1a...	4	1	3	0	0		pn.	b
5546	Cochin Jew	0.19000	8,581	9,731	13,161	CMT35	49-EBEB-a	malayalam		0.10	10	2Asu.	5	4	3	0	0	Malayalam	PNB	b
5547	Dutch Jew	0.04000	1,806	2,049	2,771	CMT35	52-ABCA-a	algemeen-nederlands		1.00	20	2Bsuh	6	4	6	0	0	Dutch	PNB	b
5548	Egyptian Arab	0.17000	7,678	8,707	11,775	CMT30	12-AACF-a	masri		19.00	1,654	2Asuh	8	5	9	2	3	Arabic*	PNB	b
5549	Esperanto	0.00000	0	0	0	CEW21z	51-AAAC-a	proper esperanto	2	1.00	0	0A...	6	4	2	4	0	Esperanto	PNB	b
5550	Falasha (Black Jew)	1.40000	63,227	71,704	96,975	CMT33a	14-BBAA-a	awngi		3.00	2,151	0....	6	4	7	2	2		...	b
5551	French	0.04000	1,806	2,049	2,771	CEW21b	51-AABI-d	general français		84.00	1,721	1B.uh	10	9	14	4	3	French	PNB	b
5552	French Jew	1.20000	54,195	61,460	83,121	CMT35	51-AABI-d	general français		0.05	31	1B.uh	4	4	6	4	0	French	PNB	b
5553	Gazan Arab	0.19000	8,581	9,731	13,161	CMT30	12-AACF-f	syro-palestinian		5.00	487	1Asuh	7	5	7	5	1	Arabic: Lebanese*	Pnb	b
5554	Georgian Jew	0.99000	44,710	50,705	68,575	CMT35	42-CABB-c	judeo-georgian		0.10	51	1A.u.	5	2	2	1	0		pnb	b
5555	German	0.02000	903	1,024	1,385	CEW19m	52-ABCE-a	standard hoch-deutsch		87.00	891	2B.uh	10	9	13	5	3	German*	PNB	b
5556	German Jew	1.30000	58,711	66,582	90,048	CMT35	52-ABCE-a	standard hoch-deutsch		0.05	33	2B.uh	4	4	6	3	0	German*	PNB	b
5557	Greek	0.06000	2,710	3,073	4,156	CEW20	56-AAAA-c	dhimotiki		95.00	2,919	2B.uh	10	9	11	5	2	Greek: Modern	PNB	b
5558	Hungarian Jew	1.40000	63,227	71,704	96,975	CMT35	41-BAAA-a	general magyar		0.08	57	2A.u.	4	4	8	3	0	Hungarian	PNB	b
5559	Iraqi Jew	2.50000	112,905	128,042	173,169	CMT35	12-AACF-g	syro-mesopotamian		0.02	26	1Asuh	3	3	6	0	0		pnb	b
5560	Israeli Jewish (Sabra)	26.36600	1,190,744	1,350,383	1,826,308	CMT35	12-AABA-b	ivrit-x.		0.80	10,803	2B.uh	5	5	5	5	3	Hebrew	PNB	b
5561	Italian	0.03000	1,355	1,537	2,078	CEW21e	51-AABQ-c	standard italiano		83.00	1,275	2B.uh	10	9	15	4	4	Italian	PNB	b
5562	Jewish Tat	0.88000	39,743	45,071	60,955	CNT24f	58-AACG-b	judeo-tat		0.02	9	0....	3	2	6	0	0	Judeo-tat	P..	b
5563	Judeo-Greek	0.00100	45	51	69	CMT35	56-AAAA-k	yevanitika		0.00	0	1c.uh	0	4	0	3	0		pnb	b
5564	Kurdistani Jew (Kurdim)	0.60000	27,097	30,730	41,561	CMT35	12-AAAA-h	kurdit		0.00	0	1cs..	0	2	2	1	0		pnb	b
5565	Lebanese Arab	0.30000	13,549	15,365	20,780	CMT30	12-AACF-f	syro-palestinian		55.00	8,451	1Asuh	10	7	8	5	3	Arabic: Lebanese*	Pnb	b
5566	Libyan Jew	0.67000	30,259	34,315	46,409	CMT35	12-AACB-bh	tarabulusi		0.01	3	1A.uh	3	3	4	0	0		pnb	.
5567	Marathi Jew	0.18000	8,129	9,219	12,468	CMT35	59-AAFU-m	deshi-marathi		0.10	9	2Asu.	5	3	5	0	0	Marathi*	PNB	b
5568	Moroccan Jew	5.27000	238,004	269,913	365,040	CMT35	12-AACH-c	yudi		0.00	0	0c...	0	2	0	1	1		p..	b
5569	Mussulman Gypsy	0.15000	6,774	7,683	10,390	CNN25f	59-ACAA-a	domari		0.00	0	0....	0	1	0	0	0		...	b
5570	Palestinian Arab	14.70000	663,883	752,887	1,018,233	CMT30	12-AACF-f	syro-palestinian		33.20	249,959	1Asuh	9	5	9	5	3	Arabic: Lebanese*	Pnb	b
5571	Persian Jew	1.30000	58,711	66,582	90,048	CMT35	58-AACC-k	judeo-persian		0.03	20	1asu.	3	2	2	1	0	Panjabi: Persian*	PNB	b
5572	Polish Jew	5.73300	258,914	293,626	397,111	CMT35	53-AAAC-c	polski		0.08	235	2A.uh	4	4	8	3	0	Polish	PNB	b
5573	Portuguese Jew	0.03000	1,355	1,537	2,078	CMT35	51-AABA-e	general português		0.15	2	2Bsuh	5	4	8	3	0	Portuguese	PNB	b
5574	Romanian Jew	5.85000	264,198	299,618	405,215	CMT35	51-AADC-a	limba româneasca		0.10	300	3A.u.	5	4	6	3	0	Romanian	PNB	b
5575	Russian Jew	8.96000	404,653	458,903	620,637	CMT35	53-AAAE-d	russkiy		1.10	5,048	4B.uh	6	4	2	3	1	Russian	PNB	b
5576	Samaritan (Shomronim)	0.01000	452	512	693	CMT35	12-AACF-f	syro-palestinian		0.00	0	1Asuh	0	3	0	3	0	Arabic: Lebanese*	Pnb	b
5577	Spaniard	0.03000	1,355	1,537	2,078	CEW21k	51-AABB-c	general español		96.00	1,475	2B.uh	10	9	15	4	1	Spanish	PNB	b
5578	Spanish Jew	2.83000	127,809	144,944	196,027	CMT35	51-AAAB-b	hakitia		0.05	72	0....	4	4	6	3	0	Ladino	PNB	.
5579	Syrian Arab	0.03000	1,355	1,537	2,078	CMT30	12-AACF-f	syro-palestinian		7.00	108	1Asuh	7	5	8	5	1	Arabic: Lebanese*	Pnb	b
5580	Tigrai Jew	0.31700	14,316	16,236	21,958	CMT35	12-ACAC-a	tigray		1.00	162	2As..	6	6	7	4	0	Tigrinya	PNB	b
5581	Tunisian Jew	0.17000	7,678	8,707	11,775	CMT35	12-AACH-b	judeo-tunisian		0.00	0	0A...	0	2	0	1	1	Arabic: Judaeo-tunisian*	P..	b
5582	Turkish Jew	0.70000	31,613	35,852	48,487	CMT35	44-AABA-a	osmanli		0.01	4	1A.u.	3	1	4	0	0	Turkish	PNB	b
5583	USA Jew	0.04000	1,806	2,049	2,771	CMT35	52-ABAC-s	general american		8.00	164	1Bsuh	7	5	9	5	1	English*	PNB	b
5584	Yemeni Jew	1.10000	49,678	56,339	76,194	CMT35	12-AACF-n	yemeni		0.02	11	1Asuh	3	4	4	0	0		pnb	b
5585	Yiddish Jewish	5.00000	225,811	256,084	346,338	CMT35	52-ABCH	yiddish cluster		0.05	128	0B..h	4	4	6	3	0		PNB	b
5586	other minor peoples	0.30000	13,549	15,365	20,780	...				17.00	2,612		8	5	6	5	0			
	Italy	**100.00000**	**57,337,843**	**57,297,886**	**51,269,528**					**81.89**	**46,922,141**									
5587	Armenian	0.00230	1,319	1,318	1,179	CEW14	57-AAAA-b	ashkharik		87.00	1,147	4A.u.	10	9	13	4	1	Armenian: Modern, Eastern	PNB	b
5588	Austrian	0.40000	229,351	229,192	205,078	CEW19f	52-ABCF-b	donau-bayrisch-t.		88.00	201,689	0B.uh	10	9	13	5	2		pn.	b
5589	Balkan Gypsy	0.10000	57,338	57,298	51,270	CNN25f	59-ACBA-b	balkan-romani		50.00	28,649	1A...	10	7	7	5	2		Pn.	b
5590	Balkan Gypsy (Arliski)	0.00886	5,080	5,077	4,542	CNN25f	59-ACBA-bc	arlija		70.00	3,554	1A...	10	8	6	5	1	Romani: Arlija	Pn.	.
5591	Bavarian Austrian	0.05000	28,669	28,649	25,635	CEW19f	52-ABCF-b	donau-bayrisch-t.		84.00	24,065	0B.uh	10	9	13	5	1		pn.	b
5592	Bergamasco	0.22924	131,441	131,350	117,530	CEW21e	51-AABO-dc	bergamasco		89.00	116,901	0c...	10	9	14	5	1	Italian: Bergamasco	Pn.	b
5593	Black African	0.07000	40,136	40,109	35,889	NAN58	12-AACB-b	east maghrebi		70.00	28,076	2A.uh	10	7	10	0	0	Arabic: Algerian*	PNB	b
5594	Bosniac (Muslmani)	0.00542	3,108	3,106	2,779	CEW22a	53-AAAG-a	standard srpski		0.05	2	1Asuh	4	3	8	3	0	Serbian*	PNB	b
5595	British	0.04700	26,949	26,930	24,097	CEW19i	52-ABAC-b	standard-english	19	78.00	21,005	3Bsuh	10	9	13	5	2		PNB	b
5596	Campidanese Sardinian	0.60000	344,027	343,787	307,617	CEW21j	51-AABS-d	campidanese		80.00	275,030	0....	10	9	14	5	1	Sardinian: Cagliaritan*	P..	b
5597	Catalonian	0.03784	21,697	21,682	19,400	CEW21a	51-AABE-b	català		95.00	20,597	2a..h	10	9	15	5	1	Catalan-valencian-balear	PNB	b
5598	Cimbrian	0.30000	172,014	171,894	153,809	CEW19m	52-ABCF-g	zimbrisch-t.		88.00	151,266	0c.uh	10	8	14	5	1		pn.	b
5599	Corsican	0.01000	5,734	5,730	5,127	CEW21z	51-AABP-b	central corsu		80.00	4,584	0....	10	9	13	5	1	Italian: Corsican*	P..	b
5600	Croat	0.04100	23,509	23,492	21,021	CEW22d	53-AAAG-b	standard hrvatski	1	86.00	20,203	2Asuh	10	8	11	5	1	Croatian	PNB	b
5601	Dolomite	0.05841	33,491	33,468	29,947	CEW21h	51-AABK-c	grischun		90.00	30,121	0....	10	8	11	5	1	Romansch: Ladin Sura*	PNB	b
5602	Emilian	0.03000	17,201	17,189	15,381	CEW21e	51-AABO-k	emiliano-romagnolo		85.00	14,611	0c...	10	9	11	5	1	Italian: Romagnuolo	Pn.	b
5603	Eritrean	0.09000	51,604	51,568	46,143	CMT34c	12-ACAC-a	tigray		20.00	10,314	2As..	9	6	10	0	0	Tigrinya	PNB	b
5604	Esperanto	0.00000	0	0	0	CEW21z	51-AAAC-a	proper esperanto	1	80.00	0	0A...	10	8	12	5	0	Esperanto	PNB	b
5605	Filipino	0.02000	11,468	11,460	10,254	MSY44o	31-CKAA-a	proper tagalog		98.00	11,230	4Bs..	10	9	13	0	0	Tagalog	PNB	b
5606	Franco-Provencal (Vaudois)	0.12951	74,258	74,206	66,399	CEW21b	51-AABG-e	oc-cisalpin		86.00	63,818	0c...	10	9	13	5	1		pn.	b
5607	French	0.22000	126,143	126,055	112,793	CEW21b	51-AABI-d	general français	27	84.00	105,886	1B.uh	10	9	14	5	1	French	PNB	b
5608	Friulian	1.07834	618,297	617,866	552,860	CEW21h	51-AABM	furlan cluster		83.00	512,829	0....	10	9	13	5	1	Friulian	PN.	b
5609	German	0.40438	231,863	231,701	207,324	CEW19m	52-ABCE-a	standard hoch-deutsch	6	86.00	199,263	2B.uh	10	9	13	5	1	German*	PNB	b
5610	Greek	0.27000	154,812	154,704	138,428	CEW20	56-AAAA-i	italiot	2	95.00	146,969	1A.uh	10	5	10	4	1		pnb	b
5611	Han Chinese	0.08500	48,737	48,703	43,579	MSY42a	79-AAAB-ba	kuo-yü		8.00	3,896	2Bsuh	7	10	8	5	1	Chinese: Kuoyu*	PNB	b
5612	Italian	41.39835	23,736,921	23,720,379	21,224,739	CEW21e	51-AABQ-c	standard italiano	100	82.48	19,564,569	2B.uh	10	10	16	5	4	Italian	PNB	b
5613	Italian Gypsy	0.04000	22,935	22,919	20,508	CNN25f	51-AABQ-c	standard italiano		80.00	18,335	2B.uh	10	8	11	5	1	Italian	PNB	b
5614	Italo-Albanian	0.80000	458,703	458,383	410,156	CEW13	51-AABQ-c	standard italiano		85.00	389,626	2B.uh	10	8	11	4	1	Italian	PNB	b
5615	Japanese	0.00090	516	516	461	MSY45a	45-CAAA-a	koku-go		2.00	10	1B.uh	6	4	9	3	0	Japanese	PNB	b

Continued opposite

Table 8-2 continued

EVANGELIZATION								EVANGELISM			ADDITIONAL DESCRIPTIVE DATA
Ref 1	D 28	aC 29	CG% 30	r 31	E 32	U 33	W 34	e 35	R 36	T 37	Locations, civil divisions, literacy, religions, church history, denominations, dioceses, church growth, missions, agencies, ministries, movements 38
5500	2	4	5.42	0	32.10	67.90	A	0.11	633	3	Around Suleimanye. Also in Iran. Literates 27%. Muslims 99%(Shafi Sunnis,Ahl-i-Haqq groups,0.9% Yazidis,some Shias). D=ACE,AAC. M=CSI,WEC,LBI,YWAM.
5501	0	3	3.19	0	26.20	73.80	A	0.19	543	3	Related to Kermanji. Muslims 100%. M=WEC,CSI,YWAM.
5502	2	6	1.71	8	63.00	37.00	B	18.39	105	5	Muslims 92%(86% Hanafi Sunnis,14% Alawi Shias). D=Syrian Orthodox Ch(Jacobites; P-Antioch: 3 Dioceses),RCC(Syrian-rite AD-Baghdad,AD-Mosul).
5503	3	8	2.27	1	99.90	0.10	C	466.47	57	10	Modern Syriac, Western Syriac. Also in Turkey, Syria, Sweden, USA, Netherlands, Germany, et alia. D=Syrian Orthodox Ch(Jacobites; P-Antioch),RCC,ACE.
5504	0	3	3.39	1	31.01	68.99	A	0.01	370	2	Immigrants, settlers from Iran, ex-USSR, Turkey. Muslims 100%(Hanafi Sunnis,some Shias,Sufi orders).
5505	1	4	0.00	5	38.00	62.00	A	0.00	0	1.14	From Pakistan, India. Drastic decline from before 1991 Gulf War. Muslims 100%(Hanafi Sunnis,Shafis,Shias,Sufis). D=RCC.
5506	0	3	0.00	7	27.00	73.00	A	0.00	0	1.11	Arab Gypsies, Muslim Gypsies. Nomads. Muslims 100%(Sunnis).
5507	0	3	0.95		11.50	88.50	A	0.21	226	3	A large range of people involved in migrant labor, from many countries. Muslims 90%.
Ireland											
5508	0	0	5.57	8	47.00	53.00	A	42.88	366	6	Levantine Arabs and other immigrants from North Africa and Western Asia. Muslims 70%.
5509	8	10	0.14	8	99.78	0.22	C	449.82	22	10	Declining churchmanship. D=Ch of Ireland(10 Dioceses),Methodist Ch in Ireland,PCI,CJCLdS,SA,CB,BUI,JWs.
5510	6	10	0.14	8	99.78	0.22	C	446.97	23	10	Scots resident in Eire. D=Presbyterian Ch in Ireland,MCI,SA,EPC,CB,JWs.
5511	0	10	0.00	5	99.80	0.20	C	417.56	0	10	Artificial (constructed) language, in 80 countries. Speakers in Ireland: 12,000(none mother-tongue). Nonreligious 20%.
5512	1	10	0.14	8	99.85	0.15	C	487.09	20	10	Expatriates from France, in business, commerce. D=RCC.
5513	3	10	0.14	8	99.87	0.13	C	517.60	22	10	Refugees after World War II. D=Lutheran Ch in Ireland,RCC,CofI.
5514	1	10	0.14	7	99.95	0.05	C	572.13	19	10	Immigrants from Cyprus after 1950. D=Greek Orthodox Ch(AD-Thyateira).
5515	1	10	0.15	7	85.00	15.00	B	58.94	26	6	Long-term residents from various regions of the Chinese diaspora. Chinese folk-religionists/Buddhists 70%. D=RCC.
5516	7	9	0.00	8	99.89	0.11	C	521.39	16	10	D=RCC(22 Dioceses, sending out 9,500 foreign missionaries),CofI(10 Dioceses),PCI,MCI,SA,BUI,CB. M=UFM. R=local stations,HCJB,AWR.
5517	2	10	0.13	4	99.95	0.05	C	582.54	17	10	Western isles and coasts. Marked Gaelic survivals found. D=RCC(M-Tuam,D-Kerry,D-Galway,D-Raphoe),CofI(UD-Limerick).
5518	3	10	0.14	8	99.80	0.20	C	440.92	21	10	Caravan churches, loose attendance at major churches. D=RCC,CofI,Cooneyites(Go-Preachers).
5519	3	10	0.14	8	99.80	0.20	C	402.96	23	10	Nomadic caravan churches. D=RCC,CofI,Cooneyites(Go-Preachers).
5520	1	10	0.14	7	99.83	0.17	C	478.66	20	10	Expatriates from Italy. Strong Catholics. D=RCC. M=SJ,OFMCap,CSSp,OP,OFM,SDB,OESA,CSSR.
5521	0	10	-0.69	8	52.20	47.80	B	0.38	0	3	Small numbers of practicing Jewish communities, with ongoing emigration to Israel. M=CMJ.
5522	2	10	2.31	7	99.65	0.35	C	320.28	47	9	Refugees since 1917 from USSR. Nonreligious/atheists 25%. D=Russian Orthodox Ch(P-Moscow),ROCOR.
5523	1	10	0.14	8	99.96	0.04	C	595.68	17	10	Expatriates, immigrants from Spain. Strong Catholics. D=RCC.
5524	7	10	0.84	8	99.77	0.23	C	432.81	31	10	Expatriates from USA, in business. D=CJCLdS,SDA,JWs,COGA,CCS,AoG,CON.
5525	7	10	0.14	8	99.74	0.26	C	394.34	25	9	Persons originating in Northern Ireland(UK). D=RCC,CofI,PCI,MCI,SA,JWs,CB. M=UFM.
5526	0	10	0.00	5	52.06	47.94	B	0.11	54	3	Immigrants from Indian subcontinent, East Africa, Europe. Muslims 99% (Sunnis).
5527	6	10	0.14	5	99.85	0.15	C	499.50	19	10	Persons originating in Wales(UK). D=CofI,RCC,PCI,MCI,SA,JWs.
5528	0	10	0.14		99.69	0.31	C	259.40	4	8	A large number of individuals from peoples across the world.
Isle of Man											
5529	7	8	0.30	8	99.64	0.36	C	327.04	28	9	Nonreligious 10%. D=62% Ch of England(D-Sodor & Man),Methodist Ch of GB,RCC,URC,SA,BUGBI,JWs.
5530	1	10	0.74	8	99.83	0.17	C	460.48	30	10	Immigrants, settlers, migrant workers from Ireland. D=95% RCC(D-Liverpool).
5531	0	10	0.00	8	59.00	41.00	B	2.15	32	4	One community of practicing Jews.
5532	1	10	0.74	1	99.90	0.10	C	489.46	32	10	Extinct after 1900 but recently revived. 300 Manx second language speakers. Used for some public functions. D=CofE.
5533	0	10	1.57		99.80	0.20	C	332.88	38	9	Individuals from a wide variety of peoples.
Israel											
5534	1	10	2.75	5	58.00	42.00	B	2.11	217	4	Refugees, migrants from Ethiopia. Jews practicing Judaism. D=Ethiopian Orthodox Ch(D-Jerusalem).
5535	0	5	2.70	8	45.04	54.96	A	0.06	206	2	Sefardi and Oriental Jewish immigrants from North Africa, Yemen, et alia.
5536	1	10	2.66	6	99.88	0.12	C	507.49	57	10	Gregorians. Diaspora in 27 countries. D=Armenian Apostolic Ch(P-Jerusalem: V-Haifa,V-Jaffa). M=UBS.
5537	2	8	2.67	5	99.95	0.05	C	551.33	58	10	Nestorian and Chaldean refugees. D=Ancient Ch of the East,Chaldean Catholic Ch.
5538	0	4	3.35	7	33.04	66.96	A	0.04	336	2	Nomadic tribes in south. Tent-dwellers. Muslims 100%(Sunnis).
5539	0	5	0.00	1	19.00	81.00	A	0.00	0	1.09	Immigrants from Morocco, 1950-1960. Jews bilingual in Judeo-Arabic, Hebrew, French.
5540	0	9	0.00	8	41.00	59.00	A	0.00	0	1.12	USA Black immigrants affirming Judaism but in violent conflicts with police.
5541	3	9	2.55	8	99.70	0.30	C	373.03	69	9	Expatriates from Britain, in education, business, commerce. D=ECJME(D-Jerusalem),SDA,JWs.
5542	1	10	2.65	8	69.00	31.00	B	7.55	133	4	Ashkenazi and other Jews from Britain who have moved to Israel. D=numerous Messianic Jews.
5543	0	6	0.00	0	16.00	84.00	A	0.00	0	1.05	Ashkenazis from former USSR.
5544	0	6	2.43	1	27.02	72.98	A	0.02	316	2	Bukharian, Judeo-Tajik. Also in Russia, Central Asia, USA. Related to Tajik Persian. Close to Judeo-Persian. Hebrew script. Sefardis from Central Asia.
5545	0	4	0.70	0	26.05	73.95	A	0.04	179	2	In Galilee. Also in Russia, Turkey, Jordan, Syria, Iraq, USA, Germany, Egypt, Yugoslavia. Muslims 100%(Hanafi Sunnis).
5546	0	0	2.33	4	36.10	63.90	A	0.13	229	3	Almost all former Black Jews from Kerala (India), with some White Jews.
5547	0	0	3.04	6	41.00	59.00	A	1.49	249	4	Ashkenazis from the Netherlands. Religious Jews. Nonreligious 1%.
5548	3	8	2.66	8	83.00	17.00	B	57.56	111	6	Immigrant workers from Egypt. Muslims 80%(Shafi Sunnis). D=Coptic Orthodox Ch(D-Jerusalem),RCC,CEC.
5549	0	10	0.00	5	47.00	53.00	A	1.71	0	4	Artificial (constructed) language, in 80 countries. Speakers in Israel: 81,000(none mother-tongue).
5550	2	7	5.52	0	34.00	66.00	A	3.72	598	4	Immigrants from Ethiopia, changing to Hebrew and Israeli culture. Jews 97% (archaic Judaism). D=Ethiopian Orthodox Ch,ECJME.
5551	1	10	2.67	8	99.84	0.16	C	478.29	64	10	Expatriates from France, in business, education. D=RCC. M=OFM,OCD,OP,SDB,OSB,SJ.
5552	0	5	3.49	8	51.05	48.95	B	0.09	224	2	Ashkenazis from France, Sefardis from North Africa. Practicing Jews. Nonreligious 20%.
5553	0	8	2.67	8	61.00	39.00	B	11.13	151	5	Originally from Gaza Strip. Muslims 93%. M=FMB.
5554	0	6	4.01	4	36.10	63.90	A	0.13	357	3	Ashkenazis from Georgia(ex-USSR). Practicing religious Jews speaking Judeo-Georgian.
5555	3	9	2.67	8	99.87	0.13	C	508.08	65	10	Expatriates from Germany, in education, business. D=RCC,JWs,NAC.
5556	0	5	3.56	8	51.05	48.95	B	0.09	228	2	Ashkenazis from Germany. Religious Jews, many practicing.
5557	2	10	2.66	7	99.95	0.05	C	572.13	60	10	Expatriates from Greece. D=Greek Orthodox Ch(P-Jerusalem),RCC(AD-Acre, Melkites).
5558	0	10	4.13	6	54.08	45.92	B	0.15	244	3	Ashkenazis from Hungary. Practicing religious Jews 100%.
5559	0	0	3.31	7	32.02	67.98	A	0.02	342	2	Immigrants from Iraq. Most speakers over 40. Religious Jews.
5560	5	5	2.23	5	58.80	41.20	B	1.71	136	4	All are Sabras (Israeli-born) abandoning original racial ties. 94% Orthodox Jews, 30% practicing, 2% nonreligious; 0.4% Karaites. D=RCC,BCI,BEM,Messianic Chs.
5561	1	9	2.66	7	99.83	0.17	C	472.60	64	10	Expatriates from Italy. Strong Catholics. D=RCC. M=OFM,OCD,OP,SDB,OSB,AA,SJ,CP,CM,OCSO,OH,FSC.
5562	0	0	2.22	0	13.02	86.98	A	0.01	615	2	Immigrants from Russia and Caucasus Region. Agriculturalists, merchants. Religious Jews.
5563	0	5	0.00	1	24.00	76.00	A	0.00	0	1.12	Jews of Greek origin from the Balkans and Greece. After AD 1000 Yevanic used only in Greek circles.
5564	0	5	0.00	1	25.00	75.00	A	0.00	0	1.12	Judeo-Aramaic, Aramic. Immigrants from persecution in Iran, Iraq, Turkey. Practicing Jews 100%.
5565	5	8	2.66	8	99.55	0.45	B	236.88	78	8	Muslims 45%. D=RCC(AD-Acre: 3,000 Maronites),ECJME,GOC,CB,ABCI. M=EMMC,CMA,FMB.
5566	0	0	1.10	7	29.01	70.99	A	0.01	169	2	Immigrants from Libya. Most speakers over 40. Religious Jews.
5567	0	0	2.22	4	34.10	65.90	A	0.12	234	3	Immigrants from India. Religious Jews.
5568	0	5	0.00	8	24.00	76.00	A	0.00	0	1.07	Judeo-Moroccan Arabs (youths speak Arabic and Hebrew). Many borrowings from Spanish, Ladino, French. Practicing Sefardi Jews. M=CMJ.
5569	0	4	0.00	7	15.00	85.00	A	0.00	0	1.04	Also in Iran, Iraq, Syria, Turkey, Russia, India, Egypt, Libya, Afghanistan. Muslims 100%.
5570	5	8	2.26	8	99.33	0.67	B	121.42	81	7	Northeastern Colloquial Arabic. Muslims 66%(Shafi Sunnis;strong Alawis;1.3% Druzes,1% Ahmadis). D=GOC,RCC,ECJME,ABCI,15 others. M=CMS,JAG(Japan).
5571	0	6	3.04	5	39.03	60.97	A	0.04	262	2	Sefardis from Iran, with Farsi as mother tongue. Practicing religious Jews.
5572	0	10	3.21	6	55.08	44.92	B	0.16	194	3	Ashkenazis from Poland. Practicing religious Jews.
5573	0	10	0.70	8	60.15	39.85	B	0.32	63	3	Ashkenazis from Portugal. Religious Jews.
5574	0	5	3.46	6	49.10	50.90	A	0.17	232	3	Ashkenazis from Romania. Religious Jews.
5575	0	6	6.42	7	54.10	45.90	B	2.17	360	4	Ashkenazis from Russia. Mostly practicing religious Jews, but many nonreligious 25%. M=FMB.
5576	0	8	0.00	8	36.00	64.00	A	0.00	0	1.13	As-Samarah. A Jewish sect dating from 8th century BC. In Holon(Tel-Aviv), Nablus. Samaritan is literary and religious language.
5577	1	10	2.66	8	99.96	0.04	C	599.18	57	10	Expatriates from Spain, in commerce, religious affairs. Strong Catholics. D=RCC.
5578	0	5	4.37	8	40.05	59.95	A	0.07	346	2	Judeo-Spanish, Dzhudezmo, Spanyol. Sefardis from Spain and North Africa.
5579	1	8	2.64	8	65.00	35.00	B	16.60	141	5	Muslims 80%(Hanafi Sunnis,Alawi Shias,Ahmadis). D=Syrian Orthodox Ch(D-Jerusalem).
5580	0	10	2.82	4	57.00	43.00	B	2.08	169	4	Oriental Jews from Ethiopia and Eritrea. Practicing, religious Jews.
5581	0	8	0.00	7	30.00	70.00	A	0.00	0	1.07	Judeo-Tunisian Arabic. Immigrants from Tunisia from 1965-1990. Practicing Sefardi Jews. M=CMJ.
5582	0	0	1.40	8	33.01	66.99	A	0.01	173	2	Immigrants from Turkey. Religious Jews.
5583	1	9	2.84	8	73.00	27.00	B	21.31	132	5	Ashkenazis from USA, immigrants, residents, settlers, many now Israeli citizens. D=Messianic Jews.
5584	0	0	2.43	7	30.02	69.98	A	0.02	285	2	Immigrants from Yemen. Majority of speakers over 50. Religious Jews.
5585	0	5	2.69	5	47.05	52.95	A	0.08	197	2	Judeo-Germans. Ashkenazis speaking Yiddish, from Europe (nearly extinct). Also in Latin America, Australia, South Africa.
5586	0	7	2.60		44.00	56.00	A	27.30	162	5	Russians(ROC), Scandinavians, Polish(RCs), Hungarians(RCs), Romanians(ROC), USA Whites.
Italy											
5587	1	10	0.55	6	99.87	0.13	C	501.72	20	10	Refugees from USSR since 1917. Gregorians. D=Armenian Apostolic Ch(V-Milan).
5588	2	8	0.55	8	99.88	0.12	C	494.64	30	10	Expatriates from Austria, in commerce, industry. Mainly in north. D=RCC,NAC.
5589	2	9	0.55	6	99.50	0.50	B	198.92	40	7	Found in 12 countries in Balkans and eastern Europe. Muslims 50%. D=RCC,GEM.
5590	4	10	0.55	6	99.70	0.30	C	319.37	35	9	Also in Yugoslavia, Bulgaria, Greece, Turkey, France, Germany, Romania, Hungary, Iran. Muslims 30%. D=nomadic caravan churches, Gypsy Ev Movement,RCC.
5591	1	10	0.55	8	99.84	0.16	C	459.90	31	10	Residents from Bavarian Alps, Tyrol, Styria. D=RCC.
5592	1	10	0.55	1	99.89	0.11	C	467.78	29	10	Bergamo city and environs, central Lombardy. All bilingual in Standard Italian. Close to Lombard. D=RCC.
5593	0	0	8.26	8	99.70	0.30	C	306.60	214	9	Immigrant laborers from sub-Saharan Africa. Muslims 20%, Animists 5%, Nonreligious 5%.
5594	0	8	0.70	6	53.05	46.95	B	0.09	83	2	Refugees, migrant workers from Bosnia (ex Yugoslavia). Muslims 100%(Sunnis).
5595	6	10	0.55	8	99.78	0.22	C	441.28	30	10	Expatriates from Britain, in education, business. D=Ch of England(D-Gilbraltar),Ch of Scotland,SA,EMCI,SDA,JWs. M=ECUSA,FMB.
5596	1	8	0.55	0	99.80	0.20	C	376.68	33	9	Cagliaritan. Dialect of Sardinia's capital city, Cagliari. Southern Sardinia. D=RCC.
5597	1	8	0.55	4	99.95	0.05	C	572.13	24	10	Immigrants from Spain. Also in France, Andorra, Spain. D=RCC.
5598	1	8	0.55	1	99.88	0.12	C	452.89	33	10	Northeast Italy, south of Trent, Venetia Province. Dialect of South Bavarian. Church use abandoned about 1880, revived after 1945. D=RCC.
5599	1	10	0.55	4	99.80	0.20	C	388.36	32	9	On Maddalena Island, Sardinia. Majority live in Corsica(France). D=RCC.
5600	1	9	0.55	6	99.86	0.14	C	489.68	29	10	Mainly in south; and in 15 other countries. Migrant workers from Croatia, refugees. Some are Muslims. D=RCC.
5601	1	8	0.55	1	99.90	0.10	C	479.61	29	10	Southern Tyrol in Alto Adige, Dolomites, Bolzano Province, also Trento, Belluno Provinces. Dolomitic Ladin cluster(5 languages). Most know Standard Italian too.
5602	1	8	0.55	1	99.85	0.15	C	418.83	31	10	Northwest Italy. Speakers also know Standard Italian. D=RCC.
5603	0	0	7.19	4	66.00	34.00	B	48.18	377	6	Refugees from Eritrea since 1990. Muslims 80%.
5604	0	10	0.00	5	99.80	0.20	C	420.48	0	10	Artificial (constructed) language, in 80 countries. Speakers in Italy: 382,000(none mother-tongue). Nonreligious 20%.
5605	0	0	7.28	5	99.98	0.02	C	543.70	143	10	Immigrants from Philippines. D=RCC.
5606	1	8	0.55	8	99.86	0.14	C	455.15	29	10	Northwest Italy, Aosta Valley; also in southern Italy (Foggia in Apulia). Also southeast France. D=RCC.
5607	1	8	0.55	8	99.84	0.16	C	481.36	27	10	Expatriates from France, in business, commerce. D=RCC. M=FMB.
5608	1	7	0.55	0	99.83	0.17	C	402.92	32	10	Northern Friuli-Venezia-Giulia on borders of and in Austria, Slovenia. Friulian cluster(3 languages). Bilingual in Standard Italian. D=RCC.
5609	2	8	0.55	8	99.86	0.14	C	502.24	29	10	Residents, immigrants from Germany. Northern, Trentino-Alto-Adige, South Tyrol, Bolzano. D=Evangelical Lutheran Church in Italy(VELKD),RCC. M=FMB.
5610	1	10	0.55	6	99.95	0.05	C	547.86	27	10	Southern, Salento, Calimera, east of Reggio. Migrant workers from Greece. D=Greek Orthodox Ch(D-Austria).
5611	1	10	2.84	7	74.00	26.00	B	21.60	129	5	Immigrants from Chinese diaspora. Triad mafias (5,000) active in crime. Buddhists/Chinese folk-religionists 90%. D=RCC.
5612	8	8	0.12	7	99.82	0.18	C	492.16	19	10	D=RCC(280 Dioceses in 18 Conciliar Regions),ADI(AoG/CEEP),JWs,CEV,CC,SA,UCEBI,& 200 other denominations. M=SDB,OFM,SJ,FSC,PFM,UFM,WEC,FMB.
5613	4	10	0.55	7	99.80	0.20	C	440.92	29	10	Italian-speaking Gypsies. Nonreligious 20%. D=nomadic caravan churches, Gypsy Evangelical Movement,ADI,RCC. M=GGMS.
5614	1	8	0.55	7	99.85	0.15	C	477.78	19	10	Immigrant Albanians now speaking Italian. D=RCC(Italo-Albanian rite: D-Lungro).
5615	0	5	2.33	7	56.00	44.00	B	4.08	151	4	Expatriates, immigrants from Japan. Buddhists/New-Religionists 95%(Soka Gakkai in Rome,Florence,Naples).

Continued overleaf

Table 8-2 continued

PEOPLE Ref 1	Ethnic name 2	POPULATION P% 3	In 1995 4	In 2000 5	In 2025 6	IDENTITY CODE Race 7	Language 8	LANGUAGE Autoglossonym 9	S 10	CHURCH AC 11	Members 12	MINISTRY Jayuh 13-17	d 18	wa 19	xc 20	mc 21	mi 22	SCRIPTURE Biblioglossonym 23	Pub 24-26	ss 27
5616	Jewish	0.05260	30,160	30,139	26,968	CMT35	51-AABQ-c	standard italiano		0.30	90	2B.uh	5	4	6	4	2	Italian	PNB	b
5617	Judeo-Italian	0.00700	4,014	4,011	3,589	CMT35	51-AAAB-f	italkian		0.00	0	0....	0	3	3	1	0		pnb	.
5618	Kalderash Gypsy (Rom)	0.00523	2,999	2,997	2,681	CNN25f	59-ACBA-a	vlach-romani		80.00	2,397	1a...	10	8	11	5	1	Romani: Finnish*	PN.	b
5619	Kurdish (Kurd)	0.02000	11,468	11,460	10,254	CNT24c	58-AAAA-a	kurmanji		2.00	229	3c...	6	3	3	5	0	Kurdish: Kurmanji*	PN.	b
5620	Latin (Old Latin)	0.00000	0	0	0	CEW21z	51-AAAA-a	lingua-latina		90.00	0	0A.u.	10	10	13	5	0	Latin	PNB	b
5621	Ligurian (Genoan)	3.33132	1,910,107	1,908,776	1,707,952	CEW21e	51-AABO-h	ligure		85.00	1,622,460	0c...	10	9	14	5	1	Ligurian	Pn.	b
5622	Logudorese Sardinian	0.70000	401,365	401,085	358,887	CEW21j	51-AABS-a	logudorese		80.00	320,868	0....	10	9	11	5	1	Sardinian: Logudorese*	P..	b
5623	Lombard	15.35497	8,804,209	8,798,073	7,872,421	CEW21e	51-AABO-e	lombardo-siculo		85.00	7,478,362	0c...	10	9	15	5	1		pn.	b
5624	Lovari Gypsy (Rom)	0.00174	998	997	892	CNN25f	59-ACBA-a	vlach-romani		80.00	798	1a...	10	8	11	5	1	Romani: Finnish*	PN.	b
5625	Maltese	0.05000	28,669	28,649	25,635	CMT36	12-AACC-a	maltiya		90.50	25,927	0a.u.	10	9	15	5	1	Maltese	PNB	b
5626	Neapolitan-Calabrian	12.66584	7,262,319	7,257,259	6,493,716	CEW21e	51-AABR-b	campano-molisano		80.00	5,805,807	0....	10	9	13	5	1	Neapolitan-calabrese	P..	b
5627	North African Arab	0.92000	527,508	527,141	471,680	CMT30	12-AACF-af	barqi		1.00	5,271	1Asuh	6	4	2	3	1		pnb	b
5628	Piedmontese	5.39171	3,091,490	3,089,336	2,764,304	CEW21e	51-AABO-f	piemontese		80.00	2,471,469	0c...	10	9	15	5	1	Italian: Piedmontese*	PN.	b
5629	Pomak	0.00361	2,070	2,068	1,851	CEW22b	53-AAAH-b	bulgarski		0.00	0	2A.uh	0	3	2	1	0	Bulgarian	PNB	b
5630	Provencal (Occitani)	0.17525	100,485	100,415	89,850	CEW21z	51-AABG-ba	standard occitan		90.00	90,373	0c...	10	9	13	5	1	Provencal	Pn.	b
5631	Rhaeto-Romansh	0.03730	21,387	21,372	19,124	CEW21h	51-AABK-c	grischun		85.00	18,166	0....	10	9	13	5	1	Romansch: Ladin Sura*	PNB	b
5632	Russian	0.00720	4,128	4,125	3,691	CEW22j	53-AAAE-d	russkiy		70.00	2,888	4B.uh	10	8	8	5	1	Russian	PNB	b
5633	Sardinian (Sard)	0.30000	172,014	171,894	153,809	CEW21j	51-AABQ-d	general italiano		84.00	144,391	1A.uh	10	9	14	5	1		pnb	b
5634	Sassarese Sardinian	0.60000	344,027	343,787	307,617	CEW21j	51-AABP-e	sassarese		80.00	275,030	0....	10	9	14	5	1	Sardinian: Sassarese*	P..	b
5635	Serb	0.00600	3,440	3,438	3,076	CEW22l	53-AAAG-a	standard srpski		85.00	2,922	1Asuh	10	8	11	5	1	Serbian*	PNB	b
5636	Sicilian	8.41235	4,823,460	4,820,099	4,312,972	CEW21e	51-AABR-e	east central siciliano.		83.00	4,000,682	0....	10	9	16	5	1	Italian: Sicilian*	P..	b
5637	Sinti Gypsy (Manush)	0.01742	9,988	9,981	8,931	CNN25f	59-ACBB-b	sinti		80.00	7,985	0....	10	8	11	5	1	Romani: Sinti, Italian	P..	b
5638	Slovene	0.17471	100,175	100,105	89,573	CEW22n	53-AAAF-a	slovensko		93.00	93,098	1a..h	10	9	12	5	1	Slovenian*	PNB	b
5639	Somali	0.08800	50,457	50,422	45,117	CMT33e	14-GAGA-a	af-soomaali		0.20	101	2A...	5	4	7	0	0	Somali	PNB	b
5640	Spaniard	0.10000	57,338	57,298	51,270	CEW21k	51-AABB-c	general español	5	95.00	54,433	2B.uh	10	9	15	5	1	Spanish	PNB	b
5641	Tempiese Sardinian (Sard)	0.50000	286,689	286,489	256,348	CEW21j	51-AABP-d	gallurese		80.00	229,192	0....	10	9	14	5	1	Sardinian: Tempiese*	P..	b
5642	Tosk Albanian	0.45296	259,717	259,537	232,230	CEW13	55-AAAB-k	arbresh		83.00	215,415	0c...	10	6	11	5	1	Albanian, Arbereshe	Pnb	b
5643	USA White	0.20000	114,676	114,596	102,539	CEW19s	52-ABAC-s	general american		77.00	88,239	1Bsuh	10	9	13	5	3	English*	PNB	b
5644	Venetian (Istrian)	3.79127	2,173,832	2,172,318	1,943,766	CEW21e	51-AABN-bd	urban veneziano		90.00	1,955,086	0....	10	9	15	5	1	Italian: Venetian*	P..	b
5645	Yugoslavian Gypsy (Sinte)	0.00697	3,996	3,994	3,573	CNN25f	59-ACBB-b	sinti		70.00	2,796	0....	10	8	6	5	1	Romani: Sinti, Italian	P..	b
5646	other minor peoples (100)	0.10000	57,338	57,298	51,270	...				68.80	39,421		10	7	8	5	0			
	Ivory Coast	**100.00000**	**13,528,350**	**14,785,832**	**23,345,116**					**29.45**	**4,353,885**									
5647	Abe (Abbey)	1.19274	161,358	176,357	278,447	NAB59k	96-BCAA	a-be cluster	2	90.00	158,721	0....	10	8	11	5	3	Abe	P..	.
5648	Abidji (Ari)	0.37924	51,305	56,074	88,534	NAB59k	96-BBAA	abiji cluster		90.00	50,466	0....	10	8	11	5	3	Abidji	P..	.
5649	Abure (Eyive)	0.41394	55,999	61,204	96,635	NAB59k	96-FAAA	a-bule cluster		89.00	54,472	0....	10	8	11	5	2		...	.
5650	Adyukru (Ajukru, Bubari)	0.72319	97,836	106,930	168,830	NAB59k	96-BAAA-a	mo-jukru		90.00	96,237	0.s..	10	9	12	5	3	Adioukrou	P..	.
5651	Aizi (Edeyi)	0.10671	14,436	15,778	24,912	NAB59j	95-ACAA	edeyi cluster		91.00	14,358	0....	10	8	12	5	2		...	p
5652	Aladian (Jack-Jack)	0.17272	23,366	25,538	40,322	NAB59k	96-ABAA-a	a-ladian		90.00	22,984	0....	10	7	11	5	3	Alladian*	P..	.
5653	Anyi (Agni, Samwi, Ton)	4.58000	619,598	677,191	1,069,206	NAB59a	96-FCAB-a	central a-nyi	6	51.50	348,753	0....	10	5	7	5	3	Agni*	PN.	b
5654	Ashanti (Akan)	1.50000	202,925	221,787	350,177	NAB59a	96-FCCB-cc	a-sante	3	66.00	146,380	1ssu.	10	7	12	5	3	Twi: Asante	PNB	b
5655	Attie	2.86000	386,911	422,875	667,670	NAB59a	96-CAAA	atye cluster		88.00	372,130	0.s..	10	8	10	5	3	Attie	PN.	.
5656	Avikam (Brignan, Lahu)	0.15770	21,334	23,317	36,815	NAB59k	96-AAAA-a	a-vikam		90.00	20,986	0....	10	8	11	5	3	Avikam	P..	.
5657	Bakwe	0.07735	10,464	11,437	18,057	NAB59j	95-ABAZ	bakwe cluster		45.00	5,147	0....	9	6	6	5	3	Bakwe	...	.
5658	Bambara (Bamanakan)	5.00000	676,418	739,292	1,167,256	NAB63a	00-AAAB-a	bamanan-kan	25	5.00	36,965	4As..	7	5	7	5	1	Bambara	PNB	b
5659	Banda (Ligbi)	0.03209	4,341	4,745	7,491	NAB63z	00-AABA-a	ligbi		0.96	46	0....	5	3	4	3	1		...	p
5660	Banda (Nafana, Banafo)	0.41000	55,466	60,622	95,715	NAB56a	91-BBBA	nafaanra cluster		5.00	3,031	0....	7	4	6	3	1	Nafaanra	PN.	.
5661	Baule (Bawule)	12.19446	1,649,709	1,803,052	2,846,811	NAB59a	96-FCAA-a	central baule	31	49.00	883,496	4As..	9	5	12	5	3	Baoule*	PNB	.
5662	Birifor	0.03235	4,376	4,783	7,552	NAB56a	91-GGAA-j	north birifor		13.00	622	1c...	8	5	8	4	2	Birifor*	PNb	.
5663	Bobo Fing (Black Bobo)	0.12000	16,234	17,743	28,014	NAB63z	00-DHAA	bobo-fing cluster		5.00	887	0.s..	7	5	5	5	1	Bobo: Madare	PN.	b
5664	Bondoukou Kulango	1.06639	144,265	157,675	248,950	NAB56a	91-GCCA-b	bonduku	2	4.00	6,307	0....	6	5	6	5	1	Kulango, Bondoukou	PN.	.
5665	Bouna Kulango	1.24358	168,236	183,874	290,315	NAB56a	91-GCCA-d	buna		4.00	7,355	0....	6	5	6	4	1		pn.	b
5666	British	0.02000	2,706	2,957	4,669	CEW19i	52-ABAC-b	standard-english	4	79.00	2,336	3Bsuh	10	9	13	5	3		PNB	b
5667	Brong	0.98904	133,801	146,238	230,893	NAB59a	96-FCCA-b	brong-ahafo		40.00	58,495	0....	9	5	7	5	1		...	b
5668	Busansi (Bisa)	0.54963	74,356	81,267	128,312	NAB63z	00-DFAA-a	bisa		20.00	16,253	1....	9	5	7	5	2	Bissa	P..	b
5669	Central Guere (Ngere/ Wee)	2.38000	321,975	351,903	555,614	NAB59j	95-ABAR	wee cluster		15.00	52,785	0....	8	5	7	5	3	Guere*	PN.	b
5670	Daho-Doo	0.04751	6,427	7,025	11,091	NAB59j	95-ABAQ	daho-doo cluster		20.00	1,405	0....	9	5	7	5	1		...	.
5671	Dan (Yakuba, Diabula)	6.00000	811,701	887,150	1,400,707	NAB64a	00-DBAA-a	dan		26.00	230,659	3....	9	5	7	5	3	Dan*	PN.	b
5672	Diamala Senufo	0.09227	12,483	13,643	21,541	NAB56a	91-BACC-g	jama-la		3.00	409	0....	6	4	7	4	2		pn.	.
5673	Dogon (Habbe)	0.10000	13,528	14,786	23,345	NAB56a	91-ACEA-b	toro-so		20.00	2,957	4....	9	5	6	5	3	Dogon	PN.	b
5674	Dyimini Senufo	0.43565	58,936	64,414	101,703	NAB56a	91-BACC	jimini cluster		2.00	1,288	0....	6	4	5	5	3	Djimini*	PN.	.
5675	East Central Bete (Gbadi)	0.05000	6,764	7,393	11,673	NAB59j	95-ABAV-b	gbadi		30.00	2,218	0....	9	5	5	4	1		...	.
5676	Eastern Bete (Gagnoa Bete)	1.29859	175,678	192,007	303,157	NAB59j	95-ABAV-a	proper shyen		35.00	67,203	0....	9	5	5	4	1	Bete, Gagnoa	...	.
5677	Eastern Krahn (Tchien)	0.05000	6,764	7,393	11,673	NAB59j	95-ABAR-d	cien		10.00	739	0....	8	5	6	5	2	Krahn: Tchien*	PN.	.
5678	Ega	0.00218	295	322	509	NAB59j	96-EAAA-a	e-ga		50.00	161	0....	10	6	6	5	1		...	.
5679	Eotile (Mekyibo, Byetri)	0.02859	3,868	4,227	6,674	NAB59k	96-FABA	be-tibe cluster		90.00	3,805	0....	10	8	13	5	1		...	.
5680	Esuma (Essouma)	0.00780	1,055	1,153	1,821	NAB59k	96-DCAA	e-suma cluster		93.00	1,073	0....	10	7	11	5	1		...	n
5681	Ewe	0.07000	9,470	10,350	16,342	NAB59d	96-MAAA-a	standard ewe	1	75.00	7,763	4Asu.	10	6	9	5	1	Ewe	PNB	b
5682	Fante	0.10000	13,528	14,786	23,345	NAB59a	96-FCCB-b	fante		66.00	9,759	2csu.	10	9	9	5	2	Fante	PNB	b
5683	French	0.13000	17,587	19,222	30,349	CEW21b	51-AABI-d	general français	60	87.00	16,723	1B.uh	10	9	14	5	3	French	PNB	b
5684	French Creole	0.30000	40,585	44,357	70,035	NAN58	51-AABI-m	français-d'afrique		60.00	26,614	1B.uh	10	7	11	5	1		pnb	b
5685	Fulani (Fulbe)	2.07431	280,620	306,704	484,250	NAB56c	90-BAAA-n	fula-sokoto		0.10	307	1cs..	5	4	5	2	0	Fulfulde	PNB	b
5686	Gagu (Gban)	0.27482	37,179	40,634	64,157	BYG12	00-DDAA-a	gba	1	10.00	4,063	0....	8	5	5	5	2	Gban*	P..	.
5687	German	0.12000	16,234	17,743	28,014	CEW19m	52-ABCE-a	standard hoch-deutsch		88.00	15,614	2B.uh	10	9	13	5	3	German*	PNB	b
5688	Godie	0.19861	26,869	29,366	46,366	NAB59j	95-ABAY-j	kwadia-kotrohu		50.00	14,683	0....	10	6	7	5	3	Godie	P..	.
5689	Gouin (Ciraamba)	0.01364	1,845	2,017	3,184	NAB56a	91-GDAB	cer-ma cluster		11.00	222	0....	8	5	6	5	3	Cerma	P..	.
5690	Grebo	0.30000	40,585	44,357	70,035	NAB59j	95-ABAL-d	gle-bo		60.00	26,614	0....	10	7	7	5	1		...	.
5691	Guro (Kweni, Oume, Lo)	2.50000	338,209	369,646	583,628	NAB64d	00-DCAA-a	golo	4	19.00	70,233	4....	8	5	7	5	3	Gouro*	PNB	p
5692	Gwa (Mbato)	0.18774	25,398	27,759	43,828	NAB59k	96-DBAA	gwia cluster		90.00	24,983	0....	10	7	11	5	2		...	.
5693	Hausa	0.60000	81,170	88,715	140,071	NAB60a	19-HAAB-a	hausa		0.10	89	4Asu.	5	3	2	3	0	Hausa	PNB	b
5694	Indo-Pakistani	0.07000	9,470	10,350	16,342	CNN25g	59-AAFO-e	general hindi		1.00	104	3Asuh	6	4	2	1	0		pnb	b
5695	Ivorian Malinke	9.00000	1,217,552	1,330,725	2,101,060	NAB63h	00-AAAA-h	maninka-kan		0.30	3,992	3a...	5	4	7	5	2	Maninka*	PN.	b
5696	Jula (Dyula)	4.00000	541,134	591,433	933,805	NAB63h	00-AAAB-z	jula-kan	20	0.03	177	1cs..	3	5	5	5	3	Jula	PNb	b
5697	Karaboro	0.20000	27,057	29,572	46,690	NAB56a	91-BABB-a	kar		3.00	887	0....	6	4	5	1	0		pn.	.
5698	Komono (Kumwenu)	0.04012	5,428	5,932	9,366	NAB56a	91-GEAB-a	khi-sa		1.00	59	0....	6	4	4	4	1	Khisa	...	p
5699	Kong Dyula	1.60000	216,454	236,573	373,522	NAB63z	00-AAAB-z	jula-kan		0.01	24	1cs..	3	5	7	2	0	Jula	PNb	b
5700	Kono	0.10000	13,528	14,786	23,345	NAB64e	00-AAAE-a	central kono		6.00	887	1....	7	5	5	2	0	Kono	P..	.
5701	Konyanke	0.90000	121,755	133,072	210,106	NAB63f	00-AAAB-f	konyanka-kan		0.05	67	1cs..	4	4	6	0	0		pnb	n
5702	Kouya	0.07597	10,277	11,233	17,735	NAB59j	95-ABAT-a	kuya		40.00	4,493	0....	9	6	7	5	3	Kouya	P..	.
5703	Krobu	0.07449	10,077	11,014	17,390	NAB59k	96-FBAA-a	krobu		90.00	9,913	0....	10	7	13	4	2		...	.
5704	Kulele (Coulailai)	0.19576	26,483	28,945	45,700	NAB56a	91-BAEA-a	kule-re		3.00	868	0....	6	4	5	2	1		...	n
5705	Kwadya	0.00628	850	929	1,466	NAB59j	95-ABAY-ja	kwadia		60.00	557	0....	10	5	5	5	1		p..	.
5706	Kyama (Ebrie)	0.67738	91,638	100,156	158,135	NAB59k	96-DAAA-a	cama-ncan		90.00	90,141	0.s..	10	9	13	5	3	Ebrie	PN.	b
5707	Lakota Dida	0.70000	94,698	103,501	163,416	NAB59j	95-ABAX-b	central dida		70.00	72,451	0....	10	9	7	5	3	Dida	P..	.
5708	Levantine Arab	0.24000	32,468	35,486	56,028	CMT30	12-AACF-f	syro-palestinian		45.00	15,969	1Asuh	9	6	8	4	2	Arabic: Lebanese*	Pnb	b
5709	Libyan Arab	0.08000	10,823	11,829	18,676	CMT30	12-AACF-a	masri		0.01	1	2Asuh	3	4	6	0	0	Arabic*	PNB	b
5710	Lobi (Lobiri)	1.17000	158,282	172,994	273,138	NAB56a	91-GBAA-a	lobi-ri		2.00	3,460	0....	6	4	6	5	3	Lobiri	PN.	.
5711	Lomapo	0.05000	6,764	7,393	11,673	NAB56a	91-GCBA-a	loma		3.00	222	0....	6	4	6	1	1		...	.
5712	Macina Fula (Maasina)	0.00963	1,303	1,424	2,248	NAB56c	00-AAAB-z	jula-kan		0.10	1	1cs..	5	4	2	4	1	Jula	PNb	b
5713	Mau (Mahu)	1.27000	171,810	187,780	296,483	NAB63f	00-AAAB-h	mauka-kan		1.00	1,878	1cs..	6	4	6	4	2		pnb	.
5714	Mo (Degha, Aculo)	0.00883	1,195	1,306	2,061	NAB56a	91-GFBG-a	proper deg		23.00	300	0....	9	5	4	3	2	Deg	PN.	b
5715	Mona (Mwan)	0.12035	16,281	17,795	28,096	NAB64d	00-DEAA-a	mwa		24.00	4,271	0....	9	5	5	4	2	Mwan*	P..	.
5716	Moru	0.17361	23,487	25,670	40,529	NAB56a	91-GBBA-a	moru		3.00	770	0....	6	4	4	4	1		...	.
5717	Mossi	11.41600	1,544,396	1,687,951	2,665,078	NAB56a	91-GGAA-a	moo-re	5	44.00	742,698	2A...	9	5	7	4	1	Moore	PNB	b
5718	Nafara Senufo	0.04012	5,428	5,932	9,366	NAB56a	91-BBBA	nafaanra cluster		3.00	178	0....	6	4	4	1	1	Nafaanra	PN.	.
5719	Neyo	0.07000	9,470	10,350	16,342	NAB59j	95-ABAY-k	ne-wole		0.50	52	0....	5	4	4	4	2		p..	.
5720	Ngan (Nguin, Gan, Ben)	0.12766	17,270	18,876	29,802	NAB63z	00-DDBA-a	beng		3.00	566	0....	6	4	0	4	2		...	.
5721	Niarafolo-Niafolo Senufo	0.29467	39,864	43,569	68,791	NAB56a	91-BAAC-t	nyarafolo		4.00	1,743	1.s..	6	4	4	5	3	Senoufo, Niarafolo	pn.	.
5722	Northeastern Krumen	0.15019	20,318	22,207	35,062	NAB59j	95-ABAM-g	te-po		40.00	8,883	0....	9	6	6	4	2	Krumen: Southern*	PN.	.
5723	Northern Bete (Daloua Bete)	0.97627	132,073	144,350	227,911	NAB59j	95-ABAU	west bete cluster		30.00	43,305	0....	9	5	7	5	1	Bete*	PN.	.
5724	Northwestern Maninke	0.11264	15,238	16,655	26,296	NAB63h	00-AAAA-h	maninka-kan		0.50	83	3a...	5	5	7	0	0	Maninka*	PN.	b
5725	Nyabwa-Nyedebwa	0.32000	43,291	47,315	74,704	NAB59j	95-ABAS-a	nya-bwa		40.00	18,926	0....	9	6	7	5	3	Nyabwa	PN.	.
5726	Nzema (Appolo, Nzima)	0.50000	67,642	73,929	116,726	NAB59k	96-FCBA-a	nzema		90.00	66,536	1.s..	10	8	13	5	3	Nzema	PN.	.
5727	Oubi (Ubi, Glio)	0.02006	2,714	2,966	4,683	NAB59j	95-ABAP	glio-ubi cluster		50.00	1,483	0....	10	6	6	4	2		...	b
5728	Palaka Senufo	0.05612	7,592	8,298	13,101	NAB56a	91-BBAA-a	kpalagha		3.00	249	0....	6	4	4	4	3	Senoufo, Palaka	...	.
5729	Sefwi	0.07000	9,470	10,350	16,342	NAB59a	96-FCAC-a	sehwi		50.00	5,175	0....	10	6	7	5	2	Sehwi	...	b
5730	Soninke (Sarakole)	0.80231	108,539	118,628	187,300	NAB63j	00-BAAA-a	proper soninke		0.01	12	3....	3	3	2	0	1	Soninke	...	b
5731	Southern Krumen	0.21252	28,750	31,423	49,613	NAB59j	95-ABAM-g	te-po		80.00	25,138	0....	10	9	12	5	3	Krumen: Southern*	PN.	.
5732	Southern Senufo (Minianka)	6.47000	875,284	956,643	1,510,429	NAB56a	91-BAAC-a	sena-ri	14	5.30	50,702	1.s..	7	5	7	5	3	Senoufo, Shempire	pn.	.
5733	Suppire Senufo	0.67873	91,821	100,356	158,450	NAB56a	91-BAAB-a	supyi-re		2.00	2,007	0....	6	4	3	2	1	Suppire*	P..	.
5734	Tagwana Senufo	1.03710	140,303	153,344	242,112	NAB56a	91-BACA	north tagwana cluster	3	26.00	39,869	0....	9	5	7	5	3	Tagbana*	PN.	.
5735	Tenbo (Lorhon)	0.04894	6,621	7,236	11,425	NAB56a	91-GCAA-a	teen		3.00	217	0....	6	4	4	4	3	Teen	P..	.
5736	Tura	0.28912	39,113	42,749	67,495	NAB64a	00-DBAA-b	ween		18.00	7,695	1....	8	5	5	5	2	Toura	PN.	.
5737	Tyeliri Senufo	0.20000	27,057	29,572	46,690	NAB56a	91-BAAC-g	cebaa-ra		3.00	887	3.s..	6	4	4	3	0	Cebaara*	PN.	n

Continued opposite

Table 8-2 continued

EVANGELIZATION								EVANGELISM			ADDITIONAL DESCRIPTIVE DATA
Ref 1	D 28	aC 29	CG% 30	r 31	E 32	U 33	W 34	e 35	R 36	T 37	Locations, civil divisions, literacy, religions, church history, denominations, dioceses, church growth, missions, agencies, ministries, movements 38
5616	2	10	0.22	7	61.30	38.70	B	0.67	41	3	Ashkenazis in north, Sefardis in central Italy. 22 communities, mainly in Rome(16,000 Jews), Florence, Milan, Trieste. D=RCC, et alia. M=CBFMS,&c.
5617	0	10	0.00	1	25.00	75.00	A	0.00	0	1.08	Spoken by 10% of all Italian Jews. Used in religious services. Religious Jews 100%. Nearly extinct.
5618	3	10	0.55	6	99.80	0.20	C	408.80	31	10	Vlach Romany. Also in 25 countries: Romania, Yugoslavia, UK, Germany, France, Hungary, Sweden, Norway, Bulgaria, Russia, Greece, USA. Nomads. D=GEM.
5619	0	10	3.18	0	41.00	59.00	A	2.99	346	4	Refugees from Turkey, Iran, Iraq(1,300 speaking Sorani, 700 Zaza). Muslims 98%(Sunnis).
5620	0	10	0.00	4	99.90	0.10	C	502.60	0	10	Still widely used for daily communication, worship, scholarship in Roman Catholic Church.
5621	1	8	0.55	8	99.85	0.15	C	452.96	29	10	Liguria, northern Italy. Also in Monaco, Corsica (France). All adequately bilingual in Standard Italian. D=RCC.
5622	1	8	0.55	0	99.80	0.20	C	367.92	34	9	Sard, Sardarese. Central Sardinia. Second official language of Sardinia after Standard Italian. D=RCC.
5623	1	8	0.55	1	99.85	0.15	C	434.35	30	10	Milan, Lombardy, northern Italy. All bilingual in Standard Italian (though Lombard is very different from it). D=RCC.
5624	3	10	0.55	6	99.80	0.20	C	405.88	31	10	Vlach Romany. Also in over 15 countries. Nomads. D=Gypsy Evangelical Movement,ADI,RCC. M=GGMS.
5625	1	10	0.55	5	99.91	0.09	C	526.86	23	10	Expatriates, immigrants from Malta. D=RCC. Many charismatics.
5626	1	10	0.55	0	99.80	0.20	C	382.52	32	9	Campania and Calabria Provinces in south. Many do not know Standard Italian. D=RCC.
5627	1	10	6.47	7	52.00	48.00	B	1.89	378	4	Expatriates, immigrants, refugees. Tunisians, Libyans, et alii. Muslims 99%. D=RCC. M=OM. R=TWR,AWR.
5628	1	8	0.55	1	99.80	0.20	C	397.12	31	9	Northwest Italy, Piedmont. Bilingual in Standard Italian. D=RCC.
5629	0	10	0.00	6	43.00	57.00	A	0.00	0	1.13	100% Bulgarian Muslims, converted from Orthodoxy under Ottoman rule.
5630	1	8	0.55	8	99.90	0.10	C	489.46	29	10	From Ventimiglia in south to Turin in north, Po valley, Calabria. Also in France, Monaco. D=RCC.
5631	1	8	0.55	1	99.85	0.15	C	443.65	30	10	On border and across border in Switzerland. D=RCC.
5632	2	10	3.90	7	99.70	0.30	C	360.25	76	9	Refugees from USSR after 1917. Nonreligious 25%. D=Russian Orthodox Ch(P-Moscow),ROCOR. M=CBFMS.
5633	1	8	0.55	1	99.84	0.16	C	444.57	29	10	Sardinians who now use Italian as mother tongue. In Sardinia and across Italy. D=RCC.
5634	1	8	0.55	1	99.80	0.20	C	379.60	33	9	Sassarese is the dialect of northwestern Sardinia. Influenced by Corsican and Tuscan. D=RCC.
5635	1	10	0.55	6	99.85	0.15	C	477.78	10	10	In Trieste. Refugees from Yugoslavia. D=Serbian Orthodox Ch(under SOCUSA).
5636	1	8	0.55	0	99.83	0.17	C	408.98	31	10	On Sicily, island off southern mainland. French influence. Bilingual in Standard Italian. D=RCC.
5637	4	10	0.55	0	99.80	0.20	C	367.92	34	9	North Italy. Also Yugoslavia, France, Germany, Austria, Netherlands, Switzerland. D=nomadic caravan churches, Gypsy Ev Movement,ADI,RCC. M=GGMS.
5638	1	8	0.55	6	99.93	0.07	C	546.51	26	10	In northeast: Trieste and Gorizia Provinces. Also Hungary, Canada, USA. Citizens of Italy, originally from Slovenia(Yugoslavia). D=95% RCC.
5639	0	0	0.56	5	37.20	62.80	A	0.27	178	3	Refugees, migrants from Somalia. Muslims 100%(Shafi Sunnis).
5640	1	10	0.55	8	99.95	0.05	C	596.41	23	10	Expatriates from Spain, in commerce, professions. Strong Catholics. D=RCC. M=FMB.
5641	1	8	0.55	1	99.80	0.20	C	379.60	33	9	In north of Sardinia. Gallurese is dialect of northeastern Sardinia. D=RCC.
5642	1	8	10.49	6	99.83	0.17	C	427.16	214	10	Recent immigrants in south: Calabria, Sicily. Many are refugees. Most are bilingual in Italian. Muslims 17%(Sunnis). D=RCC(Italo-Albanian rite: D-Lungro).
5643	10	10	3.55	8	99.77	0.23	C	430.00	80	10	Expatriates from USA, in business, education. D=AoG,JWs,SDA,CJCLdS,IEC,COG,CON,SA,CC,CCS.
5644	1	8	0.55	0	99.90	0.10	C	463.18	30	10	Venetia, northern Italy. Venetian cluster(3 languages). Bilingual in Standard Italian. D=RCC.
5645	3	10	0.55	0	99.70	0.30	C	283.60	39	8	Northeast Italy. Also Yugoslavia. Nomads. Nonreligious 20%. D=Gypsy Evangelical Movement,ADI,RCC. M=GGMS.
5646	0	9	0.55		99.69	0.31	C	258.15	15	8	Other Italian languages, also Norwegians, Koreans, Nigerians(CAC), USA Blacks, Bulgarians, Swiss, Iranians , Ethiopians, Romanians, 4,000 Vietnamese.
Ivory Coast											
5647	3	7	10.16	0	99.90	0.10	C	443.47	236	10	Southern Department, Agboville Subprefecture. 70 villages, on coastal plains. Animists 10%. D=RCC,PMCIC,AICs. M=UBS,SIL,UMC.
5648	5	7	7.40	0	99.90	0.10	C	443.47	180	10	Around Abidjan city and Department. Animists 10%. D=PMCIC,AoG,RCC,SDA,AICs. M=SIL,MMS,UMC.
5649	3	6	8.98	0	99.89	0.11	C	425.55	219	10	Southern Department. Some bilingual in Anyi, Attie, Jula, French. Animists 11%. D=PMCIC,RCC,AICs. M=MMS,UMC.
5650	6	7	7.32	2	99.90	0.10	C	456.61	173	10	33 villages in Southern Department, Dabou Subprefecture. Animists 10%. D=strong Harris Ch,PMCIC,RCC,SDA,EPL,other AICs. M=UBS,MMS,UMC,SIL.
5651	2	7	7.26	0	99.91	0.09	C	448.40	147	10	12 villages in Southern Department. Many bilingual in Adjukru, Aladian. Fish merchants. Animists 9%. D=RCC,PMCIC. M=MMS,UMC.
5652	3	7	6.20	0	99.90	0.10	C	443.47	156	10	21 villages in Southern Department, Jacqueville Subprefecture. Animists 10%. D=PMCIC,RCC,AICs. M=UBS,MMS,UMC.
5653	5	7	11.03	2	97.50	2.50	B	183.27	343	7	Many in Ghana. Animists 45%, Muslims 1%. D=RCC(D-Abengourou,D-Bouake),PMCIC,AoG,EPEC,AICs. M=SMA,MMS,SIL,CMA,NAFWB(Bini dialect),UMC.
5654	7	7	10.07	4	99.66	0.34	C	315.57	235	9	Twi-speaking immigrants from Ashanti, Fante(Ghana). Animists 24%, Muslims 6%(Sunnis, Ahmadis). D=RCC,MCG,PCG,ECWA,COP,CPWA,AICs.
5655	5	7	11.10	2	99.88	0.12	C	443.25	244	10	Lagoon. Abidjan and Adzope Departments. Animists 10%. D=very strong Harris Ch,PMCIC,RCC(D-Abengourou),AoG,SDA. M=SIL,MMS,UMC.
5656	4	7	7.67	0	99.90	0.10	C	443.47	186	10	Southern Department. Animists 10%. D=RCC(D-Gagnoa),PMCIC,SDA,AICs. M=SMA,MMS,UMC.
5657	3	6	6.44	0	81.00	19.00	B	133.04	218	7	Southern and West Central Departments. Animists 55%. D=RCC(D-Gagnoa),UEESO,AIC. M=SMA,UFM,MB,SIL.
5658	1	6	8.56	4	61.00	39.00	B	11.13	470	5	Also in Mali, Senegal, Gambia, Burkina Faso. Traders. Muslims 70%(Maliki Sunnis, some Wahhabis), animists 25%. D=RCC. M=LBI.
5659	1	7	3.90	0	24.96	75.04	A	0.87	637	3	Eastern Department, also in Burkina Faso and Ghana. Muslims 50%, animists 49%. D=FWBC. M=NAFWB.
5660	1	6	5.88	0	37.00	63.00	A	6.75	537	4	Most across border in Ghana. Animists 90%, Muslims 5%. D=RCC.
5661	5	7	12.06	4	99.49	0.51	B	209.25	310	8	Widespread across south. Literates 10%. Animists 44%, Muslims 3%(Sunnis; many new converts from Christianity). D=RCC(D-Bouake),EPEC,EPC,AoG,AICs.
5662	2	6	4.22	4	59.00	41.00	B	27.99	260	5	Labor migrants from Burkina Faso, Ghana. Animists 85%, Muslims 2%. D=RCC,EPC. M=WEC,SMA.
5663	1	7	4.59	0	39.00	61.00	A	7.11	456	4	Large numbers of labor migrants from Burkina Faso. Animists 70%, Muslims 25%. D=RCC. M=CMA.
5664	2	6	6.66	4	42.00	58.00	A	6.13	524	4	Eastern Department, Bondoukou Subprefecture. Some in Ghana. Animists 92%, Muslims 4%. D=RCC,FWBC. M=NAFWB.
5665	2	6	6.82	1	37.00	63.00	A	5.40	607	4	Eastern Department, Nassian Subprefecture; some in Ghana. Animists 90%, Muslims 6%. D=RCC,FWBC. M=NAFWB.
5666	4	10	5.61	8	99.79	0.21	C	446.94	119	10	Expatriates from Britain, in education, commerce, professions. D=PMCIC,RCC,SDA,JWs.
5667	3	7	9.06	4	81.00	19.00	B	118.26	346	7	Eastern Department. Majority in Ghana. Some have switched to Kulango. Bilingual in Asante Twi. Animists 50%, Muslims 7%. D=RCC(D-Abengourou),FWBC,AICs.
5668	2	7	7.67	3	62.00	38.00	B	45.26	423	6	Immigrants from Burkina Faso; also found in Ghana, Togo. Animists 50%, Muslims 30%. D=RCC,AoG. M=WF,CSSR.
5669	4	6	8.95	4	63.00	37.00	B	34.49	389	5	Western Department. Some bilingualism in French and Jula. Literates 10%. Animists 75%, Muslims 10%. D=AoG,UEESO,RCC,SDA. M=LBT,BMM,MB,FMB,UFM.
5670	0	7	5.07	0	53.00	47.00	B	38.69	262	5	Western Department, north of Tai, south of Guere. Close to Guere, Wobe. Animists 70%, Muslims 10%. M=Mission Biblique.
5671	2	6	10.57	2	72.00	28.00	B	68.32	458	6	Half in Liberia. Animists 62%, Muslims 10%(ongoing conversions to Islam). D=RCC(D-Daloa),UEESO. M=SIL,SMA,MB,SIM,FMB.
5672	0	6	3.78	1	35.00	65.00	A	3.83	403	4	Dabakala Department, south of Djimini. Animists 60%, Muslims 37%. M=FMB,CBFMS.
5673	2	8	5.85	0	68.00	32.00	B	49.64	291	6	Labor migrants from Mali, Burkina Faso. Animists 50%(secret societies strong), Muslims 30%. D=RCC,ECEM. M=WF,CMA,FSC.
5674	3	6	4.98	2	40.00	60.00	A	2.92	435	4	Dabakala Department. Animists 58%, Muslims 40%. D=RCC(D-Korhogo),ANBC,EPEC. M=CMA,CBFMS,SIL,SMA.
5675	2	5	5.55	0	60.00	40.00	B	65.70	253	6	East central Bete area. Animists 70%. D=RCC,AIC. M=UFM.
5676	2	5	9.21	0	66.00	34.00	B	84.31	382	6	Subprefecture of Gagnoa. Animists 60%. D=RCC,AICs. M=FMB.
5677	2	7	4.40	1	48.00	52.00	A	17.52	251	5	Also in Liberia. Animists 85%, Muslims 1%. D=AoG,RCC. M=BMM,CNEC(PI).
5678	1	6	2.82	0	82.00	18.00	B	149.65	94	7	2 villages in Southern Department, Dies Canton. All bilingual in Dida. Nearly extinct. Animists 20%, Muslims 10%. D=PMCIC. M=UMC.
5679	2	7	6.12	0	99.90	0.10	C	433.62	158	10	Southern Department. Many now use Anyi or Nzema. High bilingualism. Animists 10%. D=RCC,PMCIC. M=MMS.
5680	1	6	4.79	0	99.93	0.07	C	451.46	129	10	Southern Department. Language extinct, replaced by Agni and Nzema. D=PMCIC. M=UMC.
5681	3	7	6.88	4	99.75	0.25	C	375.03	163	9	From Ghana. Animists 25%. D=RCC,EPC(Ghana),many AICs. M=SMA.
5682	4	7	7.13	4	99.66	0.34	C	303.53	180	9	From Ghana. Animists 29%, Muslims 5%(very strong Ahmadis). D=RCC,AMEC,MDCC, many other AICs. M=SMA,SVD.
5683	3	10	4.67	8	99.87	0.13	C	514.43	96	10	Expatriates from France, in government, business. Nonreligious 13%. D=RCC,PMCIC(Protestant Methodist Ch),JWs. M=SMA,MMS,BROM(Ghana),EEC,FMB.
5684	1	10	6.48	8	99.60	0.40	C	271.56	167	8	Mixed-race persons(French/African). Mostly in urban areas. Animists 15%, Muslims 15%, nonreligious. D=RCC.
5685	0	6	3.48	4	41.10	58.90	A	0.15	339	3	Nomadic Fulani cattle peoples from Guinea and across West Africa. Muslims 99%.
5686	4	6	6.19	0	44.00	56.00	A	16.06	454	5	West Central Department. Animists 90%. D=RCC,EPEC,EPC,AoG. M=WEC,CMA.
5687	3	10	7.63	8	99.88	0.12	C	523.55	147	10	Expatriates from Germany, in commerce, in business. D=RCC,EKD,&c.
5688	3	6	7.56	0	90.00	10.00	B	164.25	230	7	In Sassandra, Fresco. Strong animists 50%. D=UEESO,PMCIC,RCC. M=MMS,UFM,SIL.
5689	3	6	3.15	0	46.00	54.00	A	18.46	269	5	Primarily in Burkina Faso. Animists 81%, Muslims 8%. D=RCC,EPEC,EPC. M=SIL,WEC,CMA.
5690	2	7	8.21	1	98.00	2.00	C	214.62	230	8	Labor migrants from Liberia. Animists 40%. D=RCC,AICs. M=SMA.
5691	3	6	9.26	2	72.00	28.00	B	49.93	408	6	West Central and Central Departments. Literates 25%. Animists 75%, Muslims 6%. D=RCC(D-Daloa),EPEC,EPC. M=SMA,WEC,CMA,FMB.
5692	2	6	8.14	0	99.90	0.10	C	430.33	201	10	Southern Department. Some bilingualism in Attie or Anyi. D=PMCIC,RCC. M=MMS,UMC.
5693	0	10	4.59	5	50.10	49.90	B	0.18	317	3	Traders. Muslims 100%(Maliki Sunnis, also Tijaniyya).
5694	0	10	2.37	7	48.00	52.00	A	1.75	192	4	Immigrants from India, Pakistan: traders, commerce. Hindus 80%, Muslims 19%.
5695	3	6	6.17	5	51.30	48.70	B	0.56	438	3	Traders. Many speak Jula, Bambara. Muslims 67%(Maliki Sunnis), animists 31%. D=RCC(D-Korhogo),ANBC,EPC. M=SIM,WEC.
5696	5	6	2.92	4	45.03	54.97	A	0.04	301	2	Traders with lingua franca known from Mali to Ghana. 95% strong Muslims(most speak Arabic also). D=PMCIC,AoG,ANBC,FWBC,EPC. M=CBFMS,SIM,WEC.
5697	0	6	4.59	0	27.00	73.00	A	2.95	605	4	Labor migrants from Burkina Faso. Some bilinguals in Jula. Animists 85%, Muslims 12%.
5698	0	6	4.16	0	25.00	75.00	A	0.91	606	3	Also in Burkina Faso. Muslims 99%(Sunnis). M=NTM.
5699	0	6	3.23	4	35.01	64.99	A	0.01	401	2	A Jula state near Kong town, mixed with Falafala (subjects of Senufo). Muslims 100%.
5700	0	6	4.59	4	35.00	65.00	A	7.66	528	4	Labor migrants from Sierra Leone, Guinea. Animists 84%, Muslims 10%.
5701	0	6	4.29	4	32.05	67.95	A	0.05	540	2	Mainly in Guinea. Related to Maninka. Animists 58%, Muslims 40%.
5702	4	7	6.30	0	79.00	21.00	B	115.34	219	7	12 villages in West Central Department. Somewhat bilingual in Guro. Animists 60%. D=RCC,UEESO,EPC,AEECI. M=WEC,UFM,MB,SIL.
5703	2	7	7.14	0	99.90	0.10	C	433.62	179	10	4 villages in Southern Department. Somewhat bilingual in Baule, some in Abe. D=PMCIC,RCC. M=MMS,UMC.
5704	0	6	4.56	0	28.00	72.00	A	3.06	580	4	Scattered throughout Senufo area; bilingual in Senufo dialects. Wood carvers. Animists 97%. M=CBFMS.
5705	0	9	4.10	0	94.00	6.00	C	205.86	120	8	South central area. Related to Kru. Some animists 20%. M=UFM.
5706	4	7	6.84	2	99.90	0.10	C	479.61	156	10	Abidjan, Bingerville. Many bilingual in French. D=very strong Harris Ch (with its national HQ here),PMCIC,RCC,SDA. M=MMS,SIL,UBS,UMC.
5707	7	7	9.30	2	99.70	0.30	C	288.71	226	8	Animists 20%, Muslims 10%(increasing rapidly by conversions). D=strong Harrist Ch,PMCIC,RCC(D-Gagnoa),SDA,Eglise du Christ(Krastchotche),Eglise Adaiste.
5708	2	10	7.65	8	99.45	0.55	B	179.03	210	7	Traders and merchants mainly from Lebanon, Syria. Muslims 55%. D=RCC(Maronites),SOC.
5709	0	0	0.00	8	37.01	62.99	A	0.01	52	2	Immigrants from Libya. Muslims 100%.
5710	3	6	6.02	4	43.00	57.00	A	3.13	471	4	Eastern Department. Majority in Burkina Faso; some in Ghana. Animists 97%, Muslims 1%. D=RCC,FWBC,EPC. M=WEC,NTM,NAFWB,FMB.
5711	2	6	3.15	0	28.00	72.00	A	3.06	442	4	Eastern Department, near Teen and Kulango areas. Bilingual in Teen. Animists 90%, Muslims 7%. D=RCC,FWBC. M=NTM.
5712	2	5	0.00	4	39.10	60.90	A	0.14	112	3	Mainly in Mali and Burkina Faso. All now speak Jula. Muslims 100%. D=RCC,ECWA. M=SIM.
5713	2	6	5.37	1	41.00	59.00	A	1.49	495	4	Northern Department, Touba Subprefecture. Mandingo. Muslims 99%. D=RCC,EPC. M=WEC,NLM.
5714	2	6	3.46	0	56.00	44.00	B	47.01	236	6	Vast majority live in Ghana. Most bilingual in Twi. Animists 50%, Muslims 27%. D=RCC,SDA.
5715	3	6	6.24	0	58.00	42.00	B	50.80	364	6	Subprefecture of Kongasso. Animists 70%, Muslims 6%. D=RCC,EPC,AEECI. M=WEC,SIL.
5716	1	6	4.44	0	28.00	72.00	A	3.06	569	4	Eastern Department. Animists(traditional religionists) 70%, many Muslims 27%. D=EPEC. M=CMA.
5717	2	6	11.87	4	99.00	1.00	B	158.99	366	7	Urban labor migrants from Burkina Faso. Animists 9%, Muslims 35%(with many converts after arrival in cities). D=RCC,AoG. M=FMB.
5718	0	6	2.92	0	28.00	72.00	A	3.06	420	4	North. Muslims 90%, some animists still. M=CBFMS.
5719	2	5	4.03	0	26.50	73.50	A	0.48	417	3	Southern Department. Animists 95%. D=RCC,UEESO. M=UFM,MB.
5720	1	6	4.12	0	25.00	75.00	A	2.73	660	4	22 villages in Central Department. Somewhat bilingual in Baule, Jula. Animists 50%, Muslims 47%. D=RCC. M=SIL,CMA.
5721	2	6	5.30	1	40.00	60.00	A	5.84	457	4	Around Ferkessedougou. Muslims 90%, some animists. D=RCC(D-Katiola),ANBC. M=SMA,CBFMS,BGC-BWM,FMB,SIL.
5722	2	7	7.03	0	78.00	22.00	B	113.88	247	7	In southwest. Strong animists 60%. D=UEESO,AICs. M=Mission Biblique,NTM.
5723	2	6	8.73	2	71.00	29.00	B	77.74	337	6	West Central Department, Daloua Sub-Prefecture. Animists 69%, Muslims 1%. D=RCC,AIC. M=FMB.
5724	0	0	4.52	5	30.50	69.50	A	0.55	588	3	Across West Africa. Muslims 50%(Sunnis), Animists 49.5%. D=RCC.
5725	3	7	7.84	0	83.00	17.00	B	121.18	259	7	West Central Department, northwest corner. Animists 60%. D=RCC,AoG,UEESO. M=SIL,MB,UFM.
5726	4	7	9.20	4	99.90	0.10	C	479.61	200	10	Southern Department; most (87%) in Ghana. D=PMCIC,RCC,SDA,AICs. M=UBS,LBI,MMS,UMC.
5727	1	7	5.13	0	87.00	13.00	B	158.77	162	7	Western Department; mainly in Liberia. Highly bilingual. Animists 50%. D=UEESO. M=MB,UFM.
5728	1	6	3.27	0	30.00	70.00	A	3.28	424	4	Central Department, around Sikolo. Muslims 80%. D=ANBC. M=CBFMS,FMB,NTM.
5729	2	6	6.45	0	86.00	14.00	B	156.95	243	7	Also in Ghana. Related to Anyi. Animists 49%, Muslims 1%. D=RCC,AICs.
5730	0	5	2.52	0	17.01	82.99	A	0.00	714	1.06	In 8 countries from Senegal eastwards. Animists 75%, Muslims 25%(Sunnis). M=FI.
5731	6	7	8.14	0	99.80	0.20	C	376.68	173	9	Southwest. Animists 20%. D=RCC,PMCIC,AoG,HSAUWC,UEESO,AICs. M=MMS,SIL,MB,FMB.
5732	3	6	8.91	5	51.30	48.70	B	9.92	549	4	Cebaara. In north around Korhogo. Animists 65%, Muslims 30%(expanding slowly). D=RCC(D-Korhogo,D-Katiola),ANBC,EPC. M=WEC,CBFMS,BGC-BWM,SMA.
5733	1	5	5.44	5	30.00	70.00	A	2.19	622	4	North of Tingrela. Vast majority in Mali. Animists 60%, Muslims 38%. D=RCC.
5734	3	6	8.64	0	68.00	32.00	B	64.53	403	6	Central Department, west of Djimini. Muslims 60%. D=RCC(D-Katiola),FWBC,ANBC. M=SMA,CBFMS,NAFWB,FMB.
5735	2	6	3.13	0	32.00	68.00	A	3.50	385	4	Bouna Department; a few in Burkina Faso. Animists 96%. D=FWBC,RCC. M=SIL,NAFWB,NTM.
5736	2	6	6.87	1	56.00	44.00	B	36.79	408	5	Biankouma Department. Animists 80%. D=RCC,UEESO. M=SIL,MB.
5737	0	6	4.59	1	36.00	64.00	A	3.94	454	4	Scattered throughout Senufo area, bilingual in Senufo. Leather workers. Muslims 87%, some animists 10%.

Continued overleaf

Table 8-2 continued

PEOPLE Ref 1	Ethnic name 2	POPULATION P% 3	In 1995 4	In 2000 5	In 2025 6	IDENTITY CODE Race 7	Language 8	LANGUAGE Autoglossonym 9	S 10	CHURCH AC 11	Members 12	MINISTRY Jayuh 13-17	d wa xcmc mi 18 19 20 21 22	SCRIPTURE Biblioglossonym 23	Pub 24-26	ss 27
5738	USA White	0.00800	1,082	1,183	1,868	CEW19s	52-ABAC-s	general american		80.00	946	1Bsuh	10 9 13 5 3	English*	PNB	b
5739	Vagala (Paxala)	0.00055	74	81	128	NAB56a	91-GFBF-a	proper vaghla		3.00	2	0....	6 4 4 4 1	Vagla	PN.	.
5740	Wan (Nwa, Nwan)	0.16521	22,350	24,428	38,568	NAB63z	00-DEBA	nwa cluster		10.00	2,443	0....	8 5 5 5 3		...	.
5741	Wane	0.01577	2,133	2,332	3,682	NAB59j	95-ABAZ-f	ngwane		40.00	933	0....	9 6 6 5 2		...	.
5742	Western Bete (Guiberoua)	0.97700	132,172	144,458	228,082	NAB59j	95-ABAU	west bete cluster	12	41.00	59,228	0....	9 6 7 5 3	Bete*	PN.	.
5743	Western Krahn (Nidru)	0.09161	12,393	13,545	21,386	NAB59j	95-ABAR-h	gbo-bo		4.00	542	0....	6 5 4 2 1	Krahn: Western*	PN.	.
5744	Wobe	1.17378	158,793	173,553	274,020	NAB59j	95-ABAR-v	wobe	1	27.00	46,859	0....	9 5 7 5 3	Wobe	PN.	.
5745	Wolof	0.07000	9,470	10,350	16,342	NAB56c	90-AAAA-a	vehicular wolof		0.30	31	4.s..	5 4 2 5 2	Wolof: Senegal	PN.	b
5746	Yaure	0.19737	26,701	29,183	46,076	NAB63z	00-DCBA-a	yowele		20.00	5,837	0....	9 5 7 5 2	Yaoure	P..	.
5747	Yocoboue Dida	0.76300	103,221	112,816	178,123	NAB59j	95-ABAX-c	south dida		70.00	78,971	0....	10 7 8 5 2	Dida, Yocoboue	P..	.
5748	Yoruba	0.50000	67,642	73,929	116,726	NAB59n	98-AAAA-a	standard yoruba		50.00	36,965	3asu.	10 6 13 5 2	Yoruba	PNB	b
5749	other minor peoples	0.20000	27,057	29,572	46,690	...				15.00	4,436		8 5 6 5 0			
	Jamaica	**100.00000**	**2,472,927**	**2,582,577**	**3,244,840**					**43.43**	**1,121,713**					
5750	Afro-Chinese	0.51400	12,711	13,274	16,678	MSY42a	52-ABAF-m	jamaican-creole		80.00	10,620	1c..h	10 8 7 5 3	West Carib Creole English	pn.	b
5751	Afro-East-Indian	1.60000	39,567	41,321	51,917	CNN25	52-ABAF-m	jamaican-creole		35.00	14,462	1c..h	9 5 7 5 3	West Carib Creole English	pn.	b
5752	Arab	0.07200	1,781	1,859	2,336	CMT30	12-AACF-f	syro-palestinian		15.00	279	1Asuh	8 5 7 5 2	Arabic: Lebanese*	Pnb	b
5753	British	0.40000	9,892	10,330	12,979	CEW19i	52-ABAC-b	standard-english	70	79.00	8,161	3Bsuh	10 9 13 5 2		PNB	b
5754	Cuban White	0.30000	7,419	7,748	9,735	CLT27	51-AABB-hi	cubano		48.00	3,719	1B.uh	9 6 8 5 2		pnb	b
5755	East Indian	1.70000	42,040	43,904	55,162	CNN25g	59-AAFO-e	general hindi		14.20	6,234	3Asuh	8 5 7 5 2		pnb	b
5756	Haitian	2.00000	49,459	51,652	64,897	NFB69b	51-AACC-b	haitien		90.00	46,486	3As..	10 9 11 5 3	Haitian*	PNB	b
5757	Han Chinese (Hakka)	1.22200	30,219	31,559	39,652	MSY42a	79-AAAG-a	literary hakka		84.70	26,731	1A...	10 7 11 5 2	Chinese: Hakka, Wukingfu*	PNB	b
5758	Jamaican Black	77.00200	1,904,203	1,988,636	2,498,592	NFB68a	52-ABAF-m	jamaican-creole	96	41.40	823,295	1c..h	9 7 11 5 3	West Carib Creole English	pn.	b
5759	Jamaican Mulatto	14.60000	361,047	377,056	473,747	NFB68b	52-ABAE-cc	jamaican-english		45.00	169,675	0A.uh	9 7 11 5 3		pnb	.
5760	Jewish	0.02000	495	517	649	CMT35	52-ABAE-ce	bahamian-english		0.09	0	0A.uh	4 4 2 5 0		pnb	b
5761	Portuguese	0.20000	4,946	5,165	6,490	CEW21g	51-AABA-e	general português		93.00	4,804	2Bsuh	10 9 15 5 3	Portuguese	PNB	b
5762	USA White	0.27000	6,677	6,973	8,761	CEW19s	52-ABAC-s	general american		78.00	5,439	1Bsuh	10 9 13 5 3	English*	PNB	b
5763	other minor peoples	0.10000	2,473	2,583	3,245	...				70.00	1,808		10 7 7 5 0			
	Japan	**100.00000**	**125,472,001**	**126,714,220**	**121,150,001**					**2.71**	**3,436,882**					
5764	Ainu	0.01200	15,057	15,206	14,538	AUG01b	45-BAAB	hokkaidoo-aynu cluster		25.00	3,801	0A...	9 5 5 4 1	Ainu	PN.	.
5765	Bengali	0.05600	70,264	70,960	67,844	CNN25b	59-AAFT-e	west bengali		1.00	710	1Asuh	6 5 8 0 0	Bengali: Musalmani*	PNB	b
5766	British	0.01000	12,547	12,671	12,115	CEW19i	52-ABAC-b	standard-english		78.00	9,884	3Bsuh	10 9 13 5 2		PNB	b
5767	Central Ryukyuan	0.77444	971,705	981,326	938,234	MSY45b	45-CACA-i	luchu		2.90	28,458	0....	6 5 9 5 2	Japanese: Luchu*	P..	b
5768	Esperanto	0.00000	0	0	0	CEW21z	51-AAAC-a	proper esperanto		20.00	0	0A...	9 8 2 5 0	Esperanto	PNB	b
5769	Eta	2.00000	2,509,440	2,534,284	2,423,000	MSY45a	45-CAAA-a	koku-go		0.50	12,671	1B.uh	5 4 2 5 0	Japanese	PNB	b
5770	Eurasian	0.10000	125,472	126,714	121,150	MSY43	45-CAAA-a	koku-go		5.00	6,336	1B.uh	7 5 6 5 2	Japanese	PNB	b
5771	Filipino	0.04800	60,227	60,823	58,152	MSY44o	59-AAFT-e	west bengali		98.00	59,606	1Asuh	10 9 12 0 0	Bengali: Musalmani*	PNB	b
5772	French	0.00500	6,274	6,336	6,058	CEW21b	51-AABI-d	general français		84.00	5,322	1B.uh	10 9 14 5 3	French	PNB	b
5773	Han Chinese	0.00200	2,509	2,534	2,423	MSY42a	45-CAAA-a	koku-go		5.00	127	1B.uh	7 6 8 5 0	Japanese	PNB	b
5774	Han Chinese (Cantonese)	0.00974	12,221	12,342	11,800	MSY42a	79-AAAM-a	central yue	2	10.00	1,234	3A.uh	8 6 8 5 0	Chinese, Yue	PNB	b
5775	Han Chinese (Fukienese)	0.01948	24,442	24,684	23,600	MSY42a	79-AAAJ-ic	chaozhou	2	11.00	2,715	1A..h	8 6 8 5 0	Chinese, Min Nan	PNB	b
5776	Han Chinese (Mandarin)	0.10000	125,472	126,714	121,150	MSY42a	79-AAAB-ba	kuo-yü	5	10.00	12,671	2Bsuh	8 7 8 5 1	Chinese: Kuoyu*	PNB	b
5777	Han Chinese(Shanghainese)	0.00200	2,509	2,534	2,423	MSY42a	79-AAAD-b	tai-hu		10.00	253	1A...	8 6 8 5 0		pnb	b
5778	Japanese	95.74757	120,136,392	121,325,786	115,998,182	MSY45a	45-CAAA-a	koku-go	100	2.45	2,972,482	1B.uh	6 5 9 5 3	Japanese	PNB	b
5779	Jewish	0.00080	1,004	1,014	969	CMT35	45-CAAA-a	koku-go		0.08	1	1B.uh	4 4 2 3 0	Japanese	PNB	b
5780	Judeo-Japanese	0.05000	62,736	63,357	60,575	CMT35	45-CAAA-a	koku-go		90.00	57,021	1B.uh	10 4 11 3 0	Japanese	PNB	b
5781	Kikai	0.01028	12,899	13,026	12,454	MSY45b	45-CACA-a	kikai-shima		2.50	326	0....	6 5 5 3 2		p..	b
5782	Korean	0.54694	686,257	693,051	662,618	MSY46	45-AAAA-b	kukö		29.00	200,985	2A...	9 6 12 5 3	Korean	PNB	b
5783	Kunigami	0.09760	122,461	123,673	118,242	MSY45b	45-CACA-h	kunigami		2.80	3,463	0....	6 5 6 5 3		p..	.
5784	Malay	0.00800	10,038	10,137	9,692	MSY44k	31-PHAA-b	bahasa-malaysia		0.10	10	1asuh	5 5 3 0 0	Malay	PNB	b
5785	Northern Amami-Oshima	0.05983	75,070	75,813	72,484	MSY45b	45-CACA-b	north amami		2.40	1,820	0....	6 5 6 4 2		p..	b
5786	Oki-no-erabu	0.01445	18,131	18,310	17,506	MSY45b	45-CACA-e	oki-no-erabu-shima		2.80	513	0....	6 5 6 4 2		p..	.
5787	Persian	0.04000	50,189	50,686	48,460	CNT24f	58-AACC-c	standard farsi		0.10	51	1Asu.	5 5 7 0 0		PNB	b
5788	Punjabi	0.05600	70,264	70,960	67,844	CNN25n	59-AAFE-c	general panjabi		2.00	1,419	1Asu.	6 5 7 0 0		PNB	b
5789	Southern Amami-Oshima	0.01309	16,424	16,587	15,859	MSY45b	45-CACA-c	south amami		2.50	415	0....	6 5 6 4 3		p..	b
5790	Southern Ryukyuan (Miyako)	0.05323	66,789	67,450	64,488	MSY45b	45-CACB-a	miyako		2.70	1,821	0....	6 5 9 4 3		...	.
5791	Thai	0.00800	10,038	10,137	9,692	MSY49d	47-AAAB-d	central thai		1.00	101	3asuh	6 6 8 0 0	Thai*	PNB	b
5792	Toku-no-shima	0.03030	38,018	38,394	36,708	MSY45b	45-CACA-d	toku-no-shima		3.00	1,152	0....	6 5 6 4 3		p..	.
5793	USA White	0.05000	62,736	63,357	60,575	CEW19s	52-ABAC-s	general american		77.00	48,785	1Bsuh	10 9 12 4 1	English*	PNB	b
5794	Yayeyama	0.03748	47,027	47,492	45,407	MSY45b	45-CACB-b	yaeyama		2.00	950	0....	6 5 6 4 3		...	.
5795	Yonaguni	0.00180	2,258	2,281	2,181	MSY45b	45-CACB-c	yonaguni		2.00	46	0....	6 5 6 4 2		...	.
5796	Yoron	0.00597	7,491	7,565	7,233	MSY45b	45-CACA-f	yoron-jima		2.80	212	0....	6 5 6 4 2		p..	.
5797	other minor peoples	0.03000	37,642	38,014	36,345	...				4.00	1,521		6 5 2 5 0			
	Jordan	**100.00000**	**5,733,765**	**6,669,341**	**12,062,895**					**4.1**	**273,519**					
5798	Armenian (Ermeni)	0.30000	17,201	20,008	36,189	CEW14	57-AAAA-b	ashkharik		89.00	17,807	4A.u.	10 8 13 2 3	Armenian: Modern, Eastern	PNB	b
5799	Azerbaijani	0.08000	4,587	5,335	9,650	MSY41a	44-AABA-fb	south azeri		0.10	5	1a.u.	5 5 7 0 0	Azerbaijani, South	pnb	b
5800	Bedouin Arab	12.80000	733,922	853,676	1,544,051	CMT30	13-AAAA-a	ti-bedaauye		0.01	85	0....	3 3 2 0 0		...	b
5801	British	0.01000	573	667	1,206	CEW19i	52-ABAC-b	standard-english	63	75.00	500	3Bsuh	10 9 13 4 3		PNB	b
5802	Chechen (Shishan)	0.07000	4,014	4,669	8,444	CEW17d	42-BAAA-b	chechen		0.10	5	0....	5 3 2 1 0	Chechen	P..	b
5803	Circassian (Cherkess)	1.21500	69,665	81,032	146,564	CEW17a	42-AAAA-b	cherkes		0.02	16	1a...	3 3 2 3 3		pn.	b
5804	Egyptian Arab	0.24100	13,818	16,073	29,072	CMT30	12-AACF-a	masri		25.00	4,018	2Asuh	9 5 8 5 3	Arabic*	PNB	b
5805	Filipino	0.09000	5,160	6,002	10,857	MSY44o	31-CKAA-a	proper tagalog		98.00	5,882	4Bs..	10 9 12 0 0	Tagalog	PNB	b
5806	Greek	0.02000	1,147	1,334	2,413	CEW20	56-AAAA-c	dhimotiki		95.00	1,267	2B.uh	10 9 11 5 2	Greek: Modern	PNB	b
5807	Iraqi Arab	14.00000	802,727	933,708	1,688,805	CMT30	12-AACF-e	syro-mesopotamian		0.01	93	1Asuh	3 5 7 0 0		pnb	b
5808	Jordanian Arab	32.40000	1,857,740	2,160,866	3,908,378	CMT30	12-AACF-f	syro-palestinian	98	2.80	60,504	1Asuh	6 5 7 5 3	Arabic: Lebanese*	Pnb	b
5809	Kurd	0.10000	5,734	6,669	12,063	CNT24c	58-AAAA-c	kurdi		0.08	5	2c...	4 3 2 1 0	Kurdi	PN.	b
5810	Najdi Bedouin	0.90000	51,604	60,024	108,566	CMT30	12-AACF-j	north `anazi		0.01	6	1csuh	3 4 5 0 0		pnb	.
5811	Nuar Gypsy (Zott)	0.10000	5,734	6,669	12,063	CNN25f	59-ACAA-a	domari		20.00	1,334	0....	9 5 5 1 3		...	b
5812	Palestinian Arab	32.15400	1,843,635	2,144,460	3,878,703	CMT30	12-AACF-f	syro-palestinian		7.50	160,834	1Asuh	7 5 8 5 3	Arabic: Lebanese*	Pnb	b
5813	Saudi Arab	0.30000	17,201	20,008	36,189	CMT30	12-AACB-b	east maghrebi		0.40	80	2A.uh	5 4 5 5 1	Arabic: Algerian*	Pnb	b
5814	Syrian Arab	5.00000	286,688	333,467	603,145	CMT30	12-AACF-f	syro-palestinian		6.00	20,008	1Asuh	7 5 8 4 2	Arabic: Lebanese*	Pnb	b
5815	Turkmen	0.10000	5,734	6,669	12,063	MSY41k	44-AABA-e	turkmen		0.04	3	3c.u.	3 2 2 0 0	Turkmen	Pnb	b
5816	USA White	0.02000	1,147	1,334	2,413	CEW19s	52-ABAC-s	general american		70.00	934	1Bsuh	10 10 13 0 0	English*	PNB	b
5817	other minor peoples	0.10000	5,734	6,669	12,063	...				2.00	133		6 3 5 1 0			
	Kazakhstan	**100.00000**	**16,507,152**	**16,222,563**	**17,698,360**					**15.98**	**2,591,802**					
5818	Armenian	0.11600	19,148	18,818	20,530	CEW14	57-AAAA-b	ashkharik		60.00	11,291	4A.u.	10 7 13 2 2	Armenian: Modern, Eastern	PNB	b
5819	Avar	0.01687	2,785	2,737	2,986	CEW17b	42-BBAA-a	north avar		0.01	0	1....	3 3 2 0 1	Avar	P..	b
5820	Azerbaijani	0.54714	90,317	88,760	96,835	MSY41a	44-AABA-fa	north azeri		0.00	0	2c.u.	0 3 3 0 2	Azerbaijani*	PNB	b
5821	Balkar	0.01800	2,971	2,920	3,186	MSY41z	44-AABB-a	literary karachay-balkar		0.00	0	1c.u.	0 3 3 0 0	Karachay-balkar	PN.	.
5822	Bashkir	0.25417	41,956	41,233	44,984	MSY41b	44-AABB-g	bashqurt		7.00	2,886	1A.u.	7 5 7 0 1	Bashkir	Pn.	b
5823	Bulgarian	0.06332	10,452	10,272	11,207	CEW22b	53-AAAH-b	bulgarski		72.00	7,396	2A.uh	10 6 8 1 2	Bulgarian	PNB	b
5824	Byelorussian	1.10906	183,074	179,918	196,285	CEW22c	53-AAAE-c	bielorusskiy		45.00	80,963	3A.uh	9 7 8 2 3	Byelorussian*	PNB	b
5825	Central Asian Jew	0.00483	797	784	855	CMT35	58-AACC-kb	bukharik		0.01	0	1csu.	3 1 2 0 0		pnb	b
5826	Chechen (Shishan, Kokhchi)	0.30069	49,635	48,780	53,217	CEW17d	42-BAAA-b	chechen		0.00	0	0....	0 3 2 0 1	Chechen	P..	b
5827	Chuvash	0.13547	22,362	21,977	23,976	MSY41c	44-AAAA-a	chuvash		35.00	7,692	2....	9 6 8 0 1	Chuvash	PN.	b
5828	Crimean Tatar	0.01925	3,178	3,123	3,407	MSY41h	44-AABA-c	crimea-tatar		0.00	0	1c.u.	0 2 2 0 2	Crimean Tatar*	PNb	b
5829	Dargin	0.01164	1,921	1,888	2,060	CEW17b	42-BBBB-a	dargwa		0.01	0	1....	3 3 2 0 1	Dargwa	P..	b
5830	Dungan (Hui, Huizui)	0.18321	30,243	29,721	32,425	MSY42b	79-AAAB-l	hui-zu		0.00	0	1Asuh	0 1 2 0 0		pnb	b
5831	Estonian	0.02063	3,405	3,347	3,651	MSW51a	41-AAAC-b	eesti		70.00	2,343	4A.u.	10 8 8 3 2	Estonian: Tallinn	PNB	b
5832	Gagauzi Turk	0.00594	981	964	1,051	MSY41d	44-AABA-b	gagauzi		72.00	694	1c.u.	10 7 8 2 1	Gagauz	PNB	b
5833	Georgian	0.05768	9,521	9,357	10,208	CEW17c	42-CABB-a	kharthuli		40.00	3,743	2A.u.	9 6 8 2 1	Georgian	PNB	b
5834	German (Volga German)	2.50000	412,679	405,564	442,459	CEW19m	52-ABCE-a	standard hoch-deutsch		60.00	243,338	2B.uh	10 8 11 3 3	German*	PNB	b
5835	Greek	0.28392	46,867	46,059	50,249	CEW20	56-AAAA-c	dhimotiki		90.00	41,453	2B.uh	10 8 10 2 2	Greek: Modern	PNB	b
5836	Han Chinese	0.02266	3,741	3,676	4,010	MSY42a	79-AAAB-ba	kuo-yü		1.00	37	2Bsuh	6 1 3 1 0	Chinese: Kuoyu*	PNB	b
5837	Ingush	0.12095	19,965	19,621	21,406	CEW17d	42-BAAA-a	ingush		0.01	2	0....	3 2 0 0 1	Ingush	p..	b
5838	Jewish	0.11619	19,180	18,849	20,564	CMT35	52-ABCH	yiddish cluster		0.00	0	0B..h	0 4 6 0 0		PNB	b
5839	Karachai (Alan)	0.01249	2,062	2,026	2,211	MSY41z	44-AABB-a	literary karachay-balkar		0.00	0	1c.u.	0 2 3 0 1	Karachay-balkar	PN.	.
5840	Karakalpak (Black Hat)	0.00842	1,390	1,366	1,490	MSY41z	44-AABC-b	karakalpak		0.00	0	1c.u.	0 3 0 0 1	Karakalpak	Pn.	b
5841	Kazakh	53.45894	8,824,548	8,672,410	9,461,356	MSY41e	44-AABC-c	kazakh		0.03	2,602	4A.u.	3 3 3 0 3	Kazakh	PN.	b
5842	Kazakhstani Gypsy	0.04352	7,184	7,060	7,702	CNN25f	59-ACBB-ba	sinti-volga		1.00	71	0....	6 3 3 0 0		p..	b
5843	Kirghiz	0.08571	14,148	13,904	15,169	MSY41g	44-AABC-d	kirghiz		0.00	0	2r.u.	0 3 3 0 3	Kirghiz	PN.	b
5844	Komi	0.01724	2,846	2,797	3,051	MSW51d	41-AAEA-b	permyat		40.00	1,119	3....	9 6 8 0 1	Komi: Permyak*	Pn.	b
5845	Korean	0.62750	103,582	101,797	111,057	MSY46	45-AAAA-b	kukö		15.00	15,269	2A...	8 6 8 3 1	Korean	PNB	b
5846	Kumyk	0.01039	1,715	1,686	1,839	MSY41z	44-AABB-d	kumyk		0.01	0	1c.u.	3 2 5 0 0	Kumuk*	Pn.	b
5847	Kurdish	0.15442	25,490	25,051	27,330	CNT24c	58-AAAA-a	kurmanji		0.10	25	3c...	5 3 3 0 0	Kurdish: Kurmanji*	PN.	b
5848	Latvian (Lett)	0.02049	3,382	3,324	3,626	CEW15a	54-AABA-a	standard latviashu		91.00	3,025	3A.u.	10 8 11 2 3	Latvian	PNB	b
5849	Lezgian	0.06445	13,940	13,700	14,946	CEW17b	42-BCAC	south lezgin cluster		0.01	1	0....	3 4 0 0 1		P..	b
5850	Lithuanian	0.06646	10,971	10,782	11,762	CEW15b	54-AAAA-a	standard lietuvishkai		85.00	9,164	3A.u.	10 8 11 2 3	Lithuanian	PNB	b
5851	Low German	0.61814	102,037	100,278	109,401	CEW19m	52-ABCC	north deutsch cluster		60.00	60,167	2A.uh	10 8 13 3 3	German: Low*	PNB	b
5852	Mari	0.07411	12,233	12,023	13,116	MSW51h	41-AACA-b	mariy		90.00	10,820	2....	10 8 11 2 1	Mari: Low*	PN.	b
5853	Moldavian	0.20103	33,184	32,612	35,579	CEW21f	51-AADC-ab	standard moldavia		82.00	26,742	1A.u.	10 7 11 2 2		pnb	b

Continued opposite

Table 8-2 continued

EVANGELIZATION								EVANGELISM			ADDITIONAL DESCRIPTIVE DATA
Ref 1	D 28	aC 29	CG% 30	r 31	E 32	U 33	W 34	e 35	R 36	T 37	Locations, civil divisions, literacy, religions, church history, denominations, dioceses, church growth, missions, agencies, ministries, movements 38
5738	6	7	4.65	8	99.80	0.20	C	438.00	101	10	Expatriates from USA, in business. D=SDA,CJCLdS,RCC,JWs,AoG,EPEC.
5739	0	6	0.70	0	31.00	69.00	A	3.39	183	4	Almost all in Ghana. Around town of Vonkoro. Animists 77%, Muslims 20%. M=WEC.
5740	3	6	5.65	0	44.00	56.00	A	16.06	470	5	Subprefectures of Kounahiri, Beoumi. Closest to Guro and Bete. Animists 80%, Muslims 10%. D=RCC,EPEC,EPC. M=SIL,WEC,CMA.
5741	2	6	4.64	0	73.00	27.00	B	106.58	174	7	Southwestern coast. Animists 60%. D=RCC,UEESO. M=UFM,SMA.
5742	7	6	9.08	2	85.00	15.00	B	127.20	293	7	West Central. Animists 50%, Muslims 8% increasing rapidly by conversions. D=AoG,RCC(D-Daloa,D-Gagnoa),Eglise Deimatiste,Eglise de Papa Nouveau,SDA.
5743	0	6	4.07	1	31.00	69.00	A	4.52	360	4	Northern Krahn. Mainly in Liberia. Animists 95%, Muslims 1%. M=BMM.
5744	3	7	8.82	4	74.00	26.00	B	72.92	327	6	Western Department. Animists 71%, Muslims 1%. D=RCC(D-Daloa),AoG,UEESO. M=SMA,Mission Biblique,UFM,SIL,FMB.
5745	3	5	3.49	4	38.30	61.70	A	0.41	364	3	Traders from Senegal. Muslims 99%(Sunnis). D=RCC,AoG,NABC. M=SMA,CBFMS.
5746	3	6	6.58	0	57.00	43.00	B	41.61	408	6	Bouafle Department. 35% urban (in cities). Animists 75%, Muslims 5%. D=RCC,EPC,AEECI. M=WEC,SIL.
5747	2	7	9.39	1	99.70	0.30	C	283.60	232	8	Southern Department, around Guitry. Animists 10%, Muslims 10%. D=RCC,Methodists. M=FMB,SIL.
5748	5	10	8.56	5	99.50	0.50	B	219.00	227	8	From Nigeria since 1930. Muslims 40%(Maliki Sunnis,many Qadiani Ahmadis). Nominal Christians 10%. D=CBN/NBC,C&S,COTLA,AICs,&c. M=NBC(Nigeria),FMB.
5749	0	10	6.28		44.00	56.00	A	24.09	391	5	Koreans(HSAUWC,PCK-Haptong), other Asians, other Europeans, many other African tribes. Muslims 40%, Animists 30%.
Jamaica											
5750	1	10	1.29	8	99.80	0.20	C	397.12	39	9	Patwa(Patois) is mixture of English/Spanish/French. Chinese folk-religionists 20%. D=RCC. M=SJ,CP,OFM.
5751	2	10	1.29	8	91.00	9.00	B	116.25	39	7	Mixed-race persons. Bongo Talk, Quashie Talk. Afro-Caribbean spiritists 60%. D=RCC,CPWI. M=SJ,CP,OFM.
5752	1	10	3.38	8	76.00	24.00	B	41.61	147	6	Syrians, Lebanese, Palestinians. Traders. Muslims 80%. D=RCC(Maronites). M=SJ,OFM.
5753	5	10	1.29	8	99.79	0.21	C	446.94	43	10	Expatriates from Britain, in education, business. D=Anglican Ch/CPWI(D-Jamaica),MCCA,SDA,JBU,JWs. M=MMS. English is mother tongue for 30% of Jamaicans.
5754	1	10	1.28	8	99.48	0.52	B	196.22	52	7	Refugees from Cuba from 1959 onwards, mostly Catholics. Nonreligious/atheists 50%. D=RCC. M=SJ,OFM.
5755	5	10	1.29	7	79.20	20.80	B	41.04	79	6	Traders from India, Pakistan. Hindus 70%(including Ananda Marga), Baha'is 12%, Muslims 3%. D=RCC,JBU(with 3,000 Indians),MCCA,JWs,SDA. M=SJ,CP.
5756	4	10	1.29	4	99.90	0.10	C	538.74	35	10	Refugees from Haiti over 20th century, especially since 1930. Afro-Caribbean spiritists 10%. Mostly Catholics. D=RCC,JBU,SDA,CPWI.
5757	1	10	1.29	7	99.85	0.15	C	481.35	34	10	Immigrants from Chinese diaspora. Chinese folk-religionist/Buddhists 14%. D=RCC(20,000 Chinese). M=SJ,OFM.
5758	7	9	0.54	8	99.41	0.59	B	153.22	31	7	Afro-Caribbean spiritists 7%(Pocomania,Convince,Cumina). Nominal Christians 42%. D=RCC(2 Dioceses),AC/CPWI,JBU,SDA,SA,MCCMA,EOC.
5759	8	10	1.21	8	99.45	0.55	B	182.31	47	7	Black/Whites. Rastafarians 24%. D=RCC,Revival Zion,AC/CPWI(D-Jamaica),JBU,SDA,MCCA,SA,UPC. M=SJ,CP,OFM.
5760	0	10	-9.99	8	47.09	52.91	A	0.15	6	3	Sefardis. United Congregation of Israelites, with synagogues in Kingston.
5761	1	10	1.29	8	99.93	0.07	C	583.85	37	10	Originally from Portugal, now citizens, residents, landowners, in business, commerce, professions. D=RCC. M=SJ,CP,OFM.
5762	10	10	1.59	8	99.78	0.22	C	435.59	45	10	Expatriates in business, education. D=SDA,JWs,AoG,COG,CON,CCCC,ICFG,CGP,CCS,&c.
5763	0	10	1.29		99.70	0.30	C	263.16	34	8	USA Blacks (AMEC,AMEZC,CoGiC,PAoW),Ethiopians(EOC),Germans(NAC),Nigerians(COTLA), other Caribbean islanders.
Japan											
5764	1	6	6.12	0	65.00	35.00	B	59.31	258	6	Hokkaido; also south Sakhalin. Ainu language (an isolate) with 19 dialects (1897 NT) is now extinct. Animists 65%, Baha'is 10%. D=NSKK(D-Hokkaido). M=CMS.
5765	0	0	4.35	6	41.00	59.00	A	1.49	382	4	Immigrant workers from Bangladesh. Muslims 65%, Hindus 34%.
5766	1	10	1.12	8	99.78	0.22	C	432.74	41	10	Expatriates from Britain, in education, business. D=Japan Holy Catholic Ch/NSKK(11 Dioceses). M=CMS,FMB.
5767	5	5	2.35	0	42.90	57.10	A	4.54	197	4	Southern Okinawa Island, Kerama and other islands, Naha and Shuri Cities. Buddhists 96%. D=Japan Holy Catholic Ch/NSKK(D-Okinawa),UCCJ,RCC,OBC,OCA.
5768	0	6	0.00	5	69.00	31.00	B	50.37	0	6	Artificial (constructed) language, in 80 countries. Speakers in Japan: 352,000(none mother-tongue). Buddhists 80%.
5769	0	5	1.97	7	47.50	52.50	A	0.86	157	3	Untouchable outcaste minority at bottom of Japanese social system; sweepers &c. Organized selves in 1922. Buddhists 70%. R=FEBC,AWR.
5770	2	9	-0.29	7	65.00	35.00	B	11.86	21	5	Mixed-race European/Japanese. Mahayana Buddhists 49%, New-Religionists 35%, nonreligious 10%. D=RCC,UCCJ.
5771	0	0	9.08	6	99.98	0.02	C	529.39	181	10	Immigrant workers from Philippines. D=RCC.
5772	1	10	0.91	8	99.84	0.16	C	481.36	33	10	Expatriates from France, in business. D=RCC(16 Dioceses). M=SJ,OFM,SDB,SVD,SMI,MEP,SSC,CICM.
5773	0	10	2.68	7	66.00	34.00	B	12.04	138	5	Immigrants from China, laborers, businessmen, professionals. Long-time Buddhists 95%.
5774	0	9	3.39	8	74.00	26.00	B	27.01	150	5	Expatriates, residents from Hong Kong, Canton. Buddhists/Chinese folk-religionists 90%.
5775	0	9	3.50	6	72.00	28.00	B	28.90	158	5	Recent immigrants from Fukien(China). Buddhists/Chinese folk-religionists 89%.
5776	2	9	6.13	7	78.00	22.00	B	28.47	238	5	From Chinese diaspora. Buddhists/Chinese folk-religionists 90%. D=RCC,True Jesus Ch in Japan. M=FMB.
5777	0	10	3.39	6	66.00	34.00	B	24.09	168	5	Chinese businessmen and others from Shanghai area. Buddhists/Chinese folk-religionists 90%.
5778	4	5	3.01	7	67.45	32.55	B	6.03	153	4	9 major dialects. Mahayana Buddhists 54%(70,000 temples), New-Religionists 22%,nonreligious 10%,Shintoists 2%. D=RCC,UCCJ,NSKK, 180 others.
5779	0	10	0.00	7	50.08	49.92	B	0.14	38	3	Small communities of practicing Japanese-speaking Jews, mainly in Tokyo and other megacities.
5780	0	10	9.03	7	99.90	0.10	C	515.74	170	10	Makuya(Tabernacle)Christians. New Zionists. Japanese who study Hebrew, copy Jewish customs and songs.
5781	2	5	1.98	0	33.50	66.50	A	3.05	222	4	Northeastern Okinawa. Kikai Island, and Kikai town. Youth are bilingual in Japanese. Buddhists 97%. D=RCC,NSKK.
5782	6	10	5.13	6	99.29	0.71	B	109.02	153	7	Long-time residents from Korea, in commerce, education. Buddhists 50%,Confucians 20%. D=HSAUWC,RCC,UCCJ,KCCJ,AoG,SDA. M=BFMGAP,KMC,PCK-H.
5783	6	5	2.09	0	36.80	63.20	A	3.76	211	4	Central and northern Okinawa Island, Iheya, Izena, Ie-jima, Sesoko Islands. Includes Nago City. Buddhists 97%. D=RCC,NSKK,AoG,SDA,OBC,CON.
5784	0	0	2.33	5	36.10	63.90	A	0.13	230	3	Immigrant workers from Malaysia. Muslims 100%.
5785	6	5	1.93	0	37.40	62.60	A	3.27	196	4	Northwestern Okinawa. Includes Naze City. Younger generations fluent in Japanese. Buddhists 96%. D=NSKK,RCC,OBC,CON,SDA,AoG. M=CMS,CIA.
5786	2	5	2.09	0	32.80	67.20	A	3.35	236	4	North central Okinawa. Oki-no-erabu Island. Buddhists 97%. D=RCC,NSKK.
5787	0	0	4.01	5	36.10	63.90	A	0.13	357	3	Immigrant workers from Iran. Muslims 96%, Baha'is 3.6%.
5788	0	0	5.08	5	40.00	60.00	A	2.92	420	4	Immigrant workers from India. Muslims 98% (Hanafi Sunnis 86%, Ithna-Asharis 8%, Ahmadis 4%).
5789	4	5	1.97	0	37.50	62.50	A	3.42	198	4	Northern Okinawa. Southern Amami-Oshima, Kakeroma, Yoro, and Uke Islands. Youth are fluent in Japanese. Buddhists 97%. D=NSKK,RCC,SDA,AoG.
5790	6	5	2.05	7	44.70	55.30	A	4.40	171	4	Southern Okinawa. Miyako and 6 other Islands. Buddhists 97%. D=NSKK,RCC,OBC,AoG,CON,SDA. M=CMS,CIA,FMB.
5791	0	0	2.34	6	42.00	58.00	A	1.53	190	4	Immigrant workers from Thailand, in commerce, industry. Buddhists 96%.
5792	4	5	2.16	0	36.00	64.00	A	3.94	221	4	Northern Okinawa. Toku-no-shima Island. Includes Toku-no-shima town. Buddhists 97%. D=RCC,NSKK,SDA,AoG.
5793	7	10	2.97	8	99.77	0.23	C	418.76	71	10	Expatriates from USA, in commerce, business. D=UCCJ(16 Church Districts),NSKK,CJCLdS,SDA,JWs,CCCC,CCS. M=FMB.
5794	3	5	2.27	1	34.00	66.00	A	2.48	243	4	Southern Okinawa. 8 Islands. Buddhists 98%. D=RCC,NSKK,SDA.
5795	2	5	2.24	1	32.00	68.00	A	2.33	255	4	Southern Okinawa. Yonaguni Island. Mostly Yonaguni town. Buddhists 98%. D=RCC,NSKK.
5796	2	5	2.08	0	32.80	67.20	A	3.35	236	4	North central Okinawa. Yoron Island. Buddhists 97%. D=RCC,NSKK.
5797	0	10	1.75		28.00	72.00	A	4.08	171	4	Indians (Ananda Marga), Pakistanis,Turks, Russians, USA Blacks (CoGiC), Germans (NAC), Mongolians (CGM), Cambodians, Filipinos, Iranians. Buddhists 49%.
Jordan											
5798	3	10	3.34	6	99.89	0.11	C	529.50	66	10	Refugees from Turkey after 1915. Gregorians. D=Armenian Apostolic Ch(V-Amman),RCC,CON. Large-scale emigration.
5799	0	0	1.62	1	26.10	73.90	A	0.09	244	2	From Azerbaijan. Muslims (Sunnis) 100%.
5800	0	7	3.82	7	23.01	76.99	A	0.00	538	1.06	Nomads, speaking rural dialect of Northeastern Colloquial Arabic. Tent-dwellers. Muslims 100%(Sunnis).
5801	4	10	3.27	8	99.75	0.25	C	410.62	81	10	Expatriates from Britain, in education, business. D=ECJME(D-Jerusalem),JBC,SDA,JWs.
5802	0	8	1.62	0	24.10	75.90	A	0.08	298	2	In a few villages mingled with Circassians and Arabs. Primarily in Russia; also in Germany. Muslims 100%(fervent Hanafi Sunnis, with Sufi influence).
5803	3	9	2.81	0	38.02	61.98	A	0.02	275	2	Urban dwellers. Also in Turkey, Israel, Russia, Syria, Iraq, Germany, Yugoslavia, USA. Muslims 100%(Sunnis). D=Greek Orthodox Ch,Free Evangelical Ch.
5804	4	7	3.34	8	94.00	6.00	B	85.77	118	6	Migrant workers, traders, professionals, from Egypt. Muslims 75%. D=COC,RCC/CCC,CEC,AoG.
5805	0	0	6.58	5	99.98	0.02	C	536.55	133	10	Immigrant workers from the Philippines. D=RCC.
5806	2	10	3.33	7	99.95	0.05	C	582.54	70	10	Immigrants from Greece. Traders. D=Greek Orthodox Ch(P-Jerusalem: D-Amman),RCC(Melkites: AD-Petra).
5807	0	0	4.64	7	33.01	66.99	A	0.01	443	2	From Iraq. Muslims (Sunnis) 100%.
5808	5	6	2.42	8	59.80	40.20	B	6.11	143	4	Muslims 96%(Shafi Sunnis,Alawis(Sufi brotherhood strong)). D=RCC(2 Dioceses),GOC,ECJME,JBC,SDA. M=FMB,OFM,FSC,CBFMS,FI,MEM.
5809	0	8	1.62	0	29.08	70.92	A	0.08	341	2	Refugees, immigrants from Kurdish territories elsewhere. Muslims 100%(Sunnis).
5810	0	0	1.81	1	21.01	78.99	A	0.00	327	1.11	In far eastern desert. Nomads. Muslims (Sunnis) 100%.
5811	3	6	3.34	7	59.00	41.00	B	43.07	203	6	Arab Gypsies, Muslim Gypsies. Nomads. Muslims 80%(Sunnis). D=GOC,SOC,RCC.
5812	6	6	3.15	8	69.50	30.50	B	19.02	152	5	Many refugees since 1948, with their descendants. Muslims 86%(Shafi Sunnis, Alawis). D=99% of GOC(D-Amman),RCC(V-Amman),ECJME,JBC,SDA,JWs.
5813	0	6	3.34	8	54.40	45.60	B	0.79	203	3	Saudi expatriates in oil and other industries. Muslims 99%(Sunnis, Wahhabis). M=CSI.
5814	2	7	3.18	8	66.00	34.00	B	14.45	161	5	From Syria. Muslims 94%(including Druzes and Alawis). D=Syrian Orthodox Ch(P-Antioch: D-Jerusalem;Jacobites),RCC.
5815	0	8	1.10	1	31.04	68.96	A	0.04	168	2	From Turkmenistan. Bilingual in Azeri. Devout Muslims 100%(Hanafi Sunnis, some Shias; Sufi orders).
5816	0	0	4.64	8	99.70	0.30	C	311.71	124	9	North Americans, in business, education. Nonreligious 10%. D=RCC,BBC,SDA,etc.
5817	0	9	3.34		23.00	77.00	A	1.67	398	4	Western Aramaic (Malula), individuals from most nearby countries and peoples. Muslims 94% (Shafi Sunnis, Alawis).
Kazakhstan											
5818	2	6	1.96	6	99.60	0.40	C	280.32	55	8	Gregorians. In 28 countries. Long-time residents in Kazakhstan. Nonreligious 30%, atheists 8%. D=Armenian Apostolic Ch, RCC.
5819	0	6	0.00	0	18.01	81.99	A	0.00	0	1.07	From Dagestan (Russia). Muslims 100%(Shafi Sunnis). M=IBT.
5820	1	5	0.00	1	28.00	72.00	A	0.00	0	1.12	73% monolingual. Muslims 80%(56% Shias,24% Hanafi Sunnis), nonreligious 20%. D=ROC. M=IBT,CSI.
5821	0	8	0.00	1	21.00	79.00	A	0.00	0	1.09	Mainly in Russia, some in USA. Superficially 100% Muslims(Hanafi Sunnis).
5822	1	9	1.96	4	51.00	49.00	B	13.03	148	5	Many speak Tatar as mother tongue. Muslims 72%(Hanafi Sunnis), nonreligious 20%. D=ROC.
5823	1	10	6.83	6	99.72	0.28	C	354.78	164	9	Origins in Bulgaria. In 12 other countries. Nonreligious 18%, atheists 10%. D=Bulgarian Orthodox Ch. M=IBT,LBI.
5824	4	7	5.58	5	99.45	0.55	B	179.03	165	7	White Russians, from Belorussia. Nonreligious/atheists 30%. D=ROC,RCC,Old Ritualist Chs,ECB.
5825	0	6	0.00	1	27.01	72.99	A	0.01	0	2	Bukharian. Centered on Bokhara (Uzbekistan). Also in Israel, USA. Religious Jews, many regularly practicing.
5826	0	8	0.00	0	18.00	82.00	A	0.00	0	1.05	Nokhchuo. From Chechen, Ingush (Russia). Highly religious Muslims 63%(fervent Hanafi Sunnis, strongly Sufi), atheists 21%, nonreligious 16%. M=IBT.
5827	1	9	1.96	0	77.00	23.00	B	98.36	98	6	Originally in Chuvashia (Russia). Independence from Russia demanded. Muslims 35%(Sunnis), nonreligious 30%. D=ROC. M=IBT.
5828	0	7	0.00	1	26.00	74.00	A	0.00	0	1.11	Descendants of 13th-century Mongols. 1944 deported to Uzbek SSR. Muslims 100%(Hanafi Sunnis). M=IBT,FI.
5829	0	8	0.00	0	23.01	76.99	A	0.00	0	1.07	In Dagestan (Russia). 65% speak Russian. Muslims 100%(Shafi Sunnis, some Shias). M=IBT.
5830	0	9	0.00	7	37.00	63.00	A	0.00	0	1.13	Dzhunyan, Tungan. Also in Kirghizia, Uzbekistan. Nomads. 100% Chinese Muslims(strict Hanafi Sunnis); migrated here in 1867 from northwest China.
5831	5	7	5.61	5	99.70	0.30	C	342.37	139	9	In 15 countries. Nonreligious 20%. D=Russian Orthodox Ch,ELCE,RCC,MCE,AUCECB. M=UBS,LBI.
5832	1	10	1.96	1	99.72	0.28	C	312.73	64	9	Mainly in Moldavia, Ukraine. Center: Kishinev. Russian-speakers 77%. Nonreligious 20%. D=95% Russian Orthodox Ch(D-Kishinev & Moldavia). M=IBT.
5833	1	9	1.96	4	98.00	2.00	B	143.08	55	7	Nonreligious/atheists 55%, Muslims 5%(Sunnis,Shias). D=Georgian Orthodox Ch.
5834	3	10	5.90	8	99.60	0.40	C	295.65	143	8	Also in Altai, Kirgizia. Nonreligious 34%. D=German Evangelical Lutheran Ch,Old Mennonites,AUCECB. R=FEBC,HCJB.
5835	2	10	3.83	7	99.90	0.10	C	525.60	82	10	Immigrants, merchants from Greece. D=GOC,ROC. M=UBS,LBI.
5836	0	7	2.02	7	51.00	49.00	B	1.86	143	4	Many now use Russian as mother tongue. Few or no links with PR China. Buddhists 30%, atheists 9%, nonreligious 60%.
5837	0	8	0.70	0	17.01	82.99	A	0.00	274	1.05	From Chechen, Ingush (Russia). All deported 1944-57. Muslims 100%(fervent Hanafi Sunnis). M=IBT.
5838	0	10	0.00	5	45.00	55.00	A	0.00	0	1.10	Bilingual in Russian, Kazakh. Emigration to Israel, with many later returning back. 70% are practicing Jews, 30% nonreligious.
5839	0	9	0.00	1	23.00	77.00	A	0.00	0	1.09	Karachi-Cherkess AO. Long history of oppression, deportation, genocide. Muslims 100%(Hanafi Sunnis). M=SIL.
5840	0	7	0.00	1	19.00	81.00	A	0.00	0	1.09	In Kara-Kalpak, from Aral Sea south. Fishermen. 30% urban. Muslims 78%(Hanafi Sunnis; Sufism, Dervishes strong), nonreligious/atheists 22%. M=IBT.
5841	1	10	3.57	4	44.03	55.97	A	0.04	272	2	Muslims 65%(Hanafi Sunnis,with Sufi influence), nonreligious 25%, atheists 10%, occultists. D=house churches. M=ROC(D-Astrakhan & Enotaevka),AUCECB,CAF.
5842	0	4	1.98	0	22.00	78.00	A	0.80	375	3	Ethnic group: Sasitka Roma. In Kazakhstan (formerly Volga till 1941). Bilingual in Tajiki. Also in Germany, Austria, 10 other countries. Muslims 99%.
5843	0	8	0.00	4	32.00	68.00	A	0.00	0	1.10	Mainly in Kirghizia. Also in China, Afghanistan, Turkey. Nomadic pastoralists. 29% speak Russian. Muslims 45%(Hanafi Sunnis), nonreligious 40%, atheists 15%.
5844	1	8	1.96	0	81.00	19.00	B	118.26	100	7	From Komi (Russia). Pastoralists, hunters. Many nonreligious 25%, atheists 5%, and shamanists 30%. D=Russian Orthodox Ch.
5845	1	9	7.61	6	76.00	24.00	B	41.61	296	6	45% now speak Russian only. Nonreligious 40%, shamanists 20%, Buddhists 15%, atheists 5%. D=KMC. M=CSI.
5846	0	9	0.00	1	29.01	70.99	A	0.01	0	2	In southern Dagestan (Russia). Many trilingual in Kumyk, Azeri, Russian. Muslims 100%(Shafi, Hanafi Sunnis).
5847	0	6	3.27	0	28.10	71.90	A	0.10	514	3	Scattered groups across Central Asia and in its cities. Muslims 80%(Shias, Yazidis), nonreligious 20%.
5848	5	8	5.88	5	99.91	0.09	C	524.79	123	10	In 25 countries. Tenacious Christians who resisted 60 years of Communism. D=ROC,ELCL,RCC,RCL,CB.
5849	0	7	0.00	0	19.01	80.99	A	0.00	144	1.05	Also in south Dagestan (Russia). 50% understand Russian. Muslims 100%(Shafi Sunnis). M=IBT.
5850	3	8	7.06	5	99.85	0.15	C	471.58	127	10	Found in 24 countries. Strong Catholics, who fought Communism for 60 years. D=RCC,ERCL,ROC.
5851	3	8	7.23	8	99.60	0.40	C	293.46	171	8	In Alma Ata, Tashkent. Also in Germany, Canada, USA, Mexico, Belize, Paraguay, Bolivia, Brazil, Uruguay, Argentina, Costa Rica. 50% bilingual in Russian.
5852	1	7	1.96	0	99.90	0.10	C	450.04	59	10	From Mari, Bashkir (Russia). Agriculturalists. Muslims 7%, many shamanists. D=ROC. M=IBT.
5853	2	8	1.96	6	99.82	0.18	C	427.99	57	10	Originally in Moldavia (Bessarabia). Nonreligious 15%, atheists 3%. D=Russian Orthodox Ch,Romanian Orthodox Ch.

Continued overleaf

Table 8-2 continued

PEOPLE		POPULATION				IDENTITY CODE		LANGUAGE		CHURCH		MINISTRY						SCRIPTURE		
Ref 1	Ethnic name 2	P% 3	In 1995 4	In 2000 5	In 2025 6	Race 7	Language 8	Autoglossonym 9	S 10	AC 11	Members 12	Jayuh 13-17	d 18	wa 19	xc 20	mc 21	mi 22	Biblioglossonym 23	Pub 24-26	ss 27
5854	Mordvinian	0.18243	30,114	29,595	32,287	MSW51i	41-AADA-a	erzya		65.00	19,237	2....	10	8	8	2	1	Mordvin: Erzya*	PN.	b
5855	Ossete	0.02617	4,320	4,245	4,632	CNT24e	58-ABBA	oseti cluster		36.00	1,528	2....	9	5	8	1	1	Ossete*	PN.	b
5856	Polish	0.36415	60,111	59,074	64,449	CEW22i	53-AAAC-c	polski		71.00	41,943	2A.uh	10	8	11	2	3	Polish	PNB	b
5857	Russian	28.20000	4,655,017	4,574,763	4,990,938	CEW22j	53-AAAE-d	russkiy	84	37.00	1,692,662	4B.uh	9	8	9	3	3	Russian	PNB	b
5858	Tajik	0.15496	25,579	25,138	27,425	CNT24g	58-AACC-j	tajiki		0.00	0	2asu.	0	3	3	0	1	Tajik*	PNB	b
5859	Tatar	1.99200	328,822	323,153	352,551	MSY41h	44-AABB-e	tatar		1.50	4,847	2c.u.	6	4	8	0	1	Tatar: Kazan	Pn.	b
5860	Turkish	0.30000	49,521	48,668	53,095	MSY41j	44-AABA-a	osmanli		0.00	0	1A.u.	0	3	2	0	0	Turkish	PNB	b
5861	Turkmen	0.02336	3,856	3,790	4,134	MSY41k	44-AABA-e	turkmen		0.00	0	3c.u.	0	2	2	0	1	Turkmen	PNb	b
5862	Udmurt	0.09630	15,896	15,622	17,044	MSW51k	41-AAEA-c	udmurt		55.00	8,592	2....	10	5	8	2	1	Udmurt	Pn.	.
5863	Uighur (Kashgar Turki)	1.76970	292,127	287,091	313,208	MSY41z	44-AABD-d	east uyghur		0.05	144	1r.u.	4	3	2	0	3	Uighur*	PNB	b
5864	Ukrainian	3.00000	495,215	486,677	530,951	CEW22p	53-AAAE-b	ukrainskiy		60.00	292,006	3A.uh	10	7	9	3	3	Ukrainian	PNB	b
5865	Uzbek	2.30000	379,664	373,119	407,062	MSY41l	44-AABD-a	central uzbek		0.00	0	1A.u.	0	3	6	1	3	Uzbek*	PNb	b
5866	other minor peoples	0.20000	33,014	32,445	35,397	...				0.00	0		0	3	6	0	0			
	Kenya	**100.00000**	**27,215,533**	**30,080,372**	**41,755,990**					**74.72**	**22,477,364**									
5867	Ajuran	0.13231	36,009	39,799	55,247	CMT33b	14-FBAA-hg	ajuran		0.01	4	1As..	3	3	2	0	1		pnb	b
5868	Ariaal Rendille	0.02827	7,694	8,504	11,804	CMT33b	04-BCAB-a	sampur		3.00	255	0....	6	4	6	4	3		...	b
5869	Bajun (Shirazi)	0.24100	65,589	72,494	100,632	NAB57j	99-AUSM-d	ki-tikuu		0.01	7	1csu.	3	3	5	1	1		pnb	b
5870	Baluch	0.00200	544	602	835	CNT24b	58-AABA-c	south balochi		0.00	0	1.s..	0	2	2	0	0	Balochi, Southern	P..	b
5871	Bengali	0.00300	816	902	1,253	CNN25b	59-AAFT-e	west bengali		0.90	8	1Asuh	5	4	2	1	0	Bengali: Musalmani*	PNB	b
5872	Boni (Aweera)	0.01280	3,484	3,850	5,345	BYG11b	14-GAFA-a	aweera		0.50	19	0....	5	4	4	0	1		...	.
5873	Boran (Borana)	0.55590	151,291	167,217	232,122	CMT33b	14-FBAA-ha	proper borana	1	8.00	13,377	1As..	7	5	6	5	3	Borana-oromo*	PNB	b
5874	British	0.26000	70,760	78,209	108,566	CEW19i	52-ABAC-b	standard-english	41	77.50	60,612	3Bsuh	10	9	13	5	3		PNB	b
5875	Bukusu (Kitosh)	2.55183	694,494	767,600	1,065,542	NAB57d	99-AUSF-b	u-lu-bukusu	3	80.00	614,080	1.s..	10	8	11	5	1	Lubukusu*	PNb	b
5876	Burji	0.07000	19,051	21,056	29,229	CMT33d	14-CBAA-aa	burji		20.00	4,211	0....	9	5	2	4	1	Burji	PN.	.
5877	Burji (Bambala)	0.02560	6,967	7,701	10,690	CMT33d	14-FBAA-ha	proper borana		10.00	770	1As..	8	5	2	1	0	Borana-oromo*	PNB	b
5878	Central Luhya	7.69856	2,095,204	2,315,755	3,214,610	NAB57d	99-AUSF-f	standard o-lu-luyia	18	91.00	2,107,337	1.s..	10	10	10	5	1	Oluluyia	PNB	b
5879	Chagga	0.04000	10,886	12,032	16,702	NAB57e	99-AUNA-f	ki-mashami		70.00	8,423	0....	10	9	13	5	1	Chagga: Machame	PN.	b
5880	Chonyi	0.44253	120,437	133,115	184,783	NAB57j	99-AUSL-c	ki-conyi		22.00	29,285	1....	9	5	7	4	0		pnb	b
5881	Chuka	0.42080	114,523	126,578	175,709	NAB57e	99-AUMA-d	cuka		40.00	50,631	1cs..	9	5	11	4	1		pnb	b
5882	Coast Arab	0.25500	69,400	76,705	106,478	CMT30	12-AACF-pe	kenya	1	0.01	8	1Asuh	3	3	2	5	3		pnb	b
5883	Cutchi Indian	0.14972	40,747	45,036	62,517	CNN25p	59-AAFF-j	kachchi		0.10	45	1cs..	5	3	5	3	0	Kachchi	Pnb	b
5884	Dabida Taita	0.89253	242,907	268,476	372,685	NAB57e	99-AUOA	dawida cluster		68.00	182,564	1....	10	8	11	5	3	Taita	PNB	b
5885	Dahalo	0.01390	3,783	4,181	5,804	BYG11b	15-BAAA-a	guo-garimani		0.11	5	0....	5	3	2	1	1		...	b
5886	Digo	0.79491	216,339	239,112	331,923	NAB57j	99-AUSL-i	ki-digo		0.12	287	4....	5	4	7	5	3	Kidigo*	Pnb	b
5887	Donyiro (Toposa)	0.00600	1,633	1,805	2,505	NAB62y	04-BDAA-c	aku-tuk-angi-nyangatom		5.00	90	0....	7	5	2	5	2		...	n
5888	Duruma	0.90335	245,852	271,731	377,203	NAB57j	99-AUSL-h	ki-duruma		34.40	93,475	1....	9	5	7	5	3	Duruma	Pnb	b
5889	El Molo	0.01462	3,979	4,398	6,105	NAB62k	04-BCAB-a	sampur		3.00	132	0....	6	5	6	5	2		...	b
5890	El Molo	0.00004	11	12	17	NAB62k	14-GADA-a	guru-pawa		11.00	1	0....	8	5	6	5	2		...	b
5891	Elgeyo	0.66684	181,484	200,588	278,446	NAB62g	04-CAAD-c	keyyo		68.40	137,202	1cs..	10	5	7	5	1		pnb	b
5892	Embu	1.56898	427,006	471,955	655,143	NAB57e	99-AUMA-b	ki-embu	3	72.00	339,808	1cs..	10	9	14	5	3	Embu	pnb	b
5893	Endo Marakwet (Merkweta)	0.21000	57,153	63,169	87,688	NAB62g	04-CAAB-b	endo		44.30	27,984	0....	9	6	9	5	2	Endo	...	b
5894	Eurafrican	0.03900	10,614	11,731	16,285	NAN58	52-ABAE-gb	kenyan-english		70.00	8,212	0A.uh	10	7	11	5	3		pnb	b
5895	French	0.00400	1,089	1,203	1,670	CEW21b	51-AABI-d	general français	1	87.00	1,047	1B.uh	10	9	14	5	3	French	PNB	b
5896	Gabbra	0.19096	51,971	57,441	79,737	CMT33b	14-FBAA-he	gabra		9.50	5,457	1As..	7	5	7	5	3		pnb	b
5897	Ganda	0.10000	27,216	30,080	41,756	NAB57d	99-AUSE-r	o-lu-ganda	2	70.00	21,056	3Bs.h	10	9	14	5	3	Luganda*	PNB	b
5898	Garreh	0.25275	68,787	76,028	105,538	CMT33b	14-FBAA-hb	garre		0.02	15	1cs..	3	3	2	0	3		pnb	b
5899	Giriama	1.58078	430,218	475,505	660,070	NAB57j	99-AUSL-a	ki-giryama		35.30	167,853	2....	9	5	7	5	3	Kigiryama*	PNB	b
5900	Goanese	0.01761	4,793	5,297	7,353	CNN25d	59-AAFU-o	konkani-gomantaki		95.00	5,032	3asu.	10	8	13	4	1	Konkani: Goan*	PNb	b
5901	Gosha	0.06000	16,329	18,048	25,054	NAB57j	14-GAGA-a	af-soomaali		0.14	25	2A...	5	2	2	0	0	Somali	PNB	b
5902	Gujarati	0.41400	112,672	124,533	172,870	CNN25e	59-AAFH-b	standard gujaraati		0.05	62	2A.u.	4	4	5	3	3	Gujarati	PNB	b
5903	Gujarati Creole	0.00400	1,089	1,203	1,670	CNN25e	99-AUSM-x	ki-hindi		0.14	2	1csu.	5	4	2	3	0		pnb	b
5904	Hindi	0.01300	3,538	3,910	5,428	CNN25g	59-AAFO-e	general hindi		0.08	3	3Asuh	4	4	2	3	3		pnb	b
5905	Indo-Mauritian (Creole)	0.00100	272	301	418	CNN25g	51-AACC-lb	indo-mauritian		30.00	90	1cs..	9	5	6	5	1		pnb	.
5906	Jewish	0.00625	1,701	1,880	2,610	CMT35	52-ABAE-gb	kenyan-english		0.09	2	0A.uh	4	3	2	0	0		pnb	b
5907	Jibana	0.07000	19,051	21,056	29,229	NAB57j	99-AJSL-d	ki-jibana		20.00	4,211	1....	9	5	6	4	0		pnb	b
5908	Kalenjin	0.10000	27,216	30,080	41,756	NAB62g	04-CAAD-a	standard kalenjin	11	53.70	16,153	4As..	10	6	11	5	3	Kalenjin	PNB	b
5909	Kamba	10.74000	2,922,948	3,230,632	4,484,593	NAB57e	99-AUMA-i	ki-kamba	19	85.90	2,775,113	1cs..	10	8	10	5	3	Kikamba*	PNB	b
5910	Kambe	0.04500	12,247	13,536	18,790	NAB57j	99-AUSL-e	ki-kambe		20.00	2,707	1....	9	5	6	4	0		pnb	b
5911	Kasigau Taita	0.02220	6,042	6,678	9,270	NAB57e	99-AUOC-a	ki-kasigau		60.00	4,007	0....	10	7	13	5	2		...	b
5912	Kauma	0.06097	16,593	18,340	25,459	NAB57j	99-AUSL-b	ki-kauma		20.00	3,668	1....	9	5	6	4	0		pnb	b
5913	Kikuyu	19.00000	5,170,951	5,715,271	7,933,638	NAB57e	99-AUMA-a	gi-gikuyu	32	92.00	5,258,049	3as..	10	10	10	5	3	Gigikuyu*	PNB	b
5914	Kipsigis	2.83465	771,465	852,673	1,183,636	NAB62g	04-CAAD-f	ngalek-ap-kipsigiis		70.40	600,282	1cs..	10	9	13	5	3	Kipsigis	PNb	b
5915	Kisii (Gusii)	6.25988	1,703,660	1,882,995	2,613,875	NAB57d	99-AUKA-a	i-ki-gusii	8	86.50	1,628,791	3....	10	8	11	5	3	Ekegusii*	PNB	b
5916	Konso	0.01000	2,722	3,008	4,176	CMT33d	14-FAAA-f	afa-karatti		20.00	602	0.s..	9	5	7	2	1	Komso	P..	.
5917	Korokoro (Munyo, Orma)	0.03300	8,981	9,927	13,779	CMT33b	14-FBAA-ib	munyo		0.07	7	1cs..	4	3	2	0	0		pnb	.
5918	Kuria (Tende)	0.49373	134,371	148,516	206,162	NAB57d	99-AUSG-a	e-ke-koria	1	51.70	76,783	0a...	10	7	10	5	3	Igikuria*	PN.	b
5919	Lower Pokomo (Malachini)	0.10606	28,865	31,903	44,286	NAB57j	99-AUSK-c	malachini		20.70	6,604	1....	9	5	8	5	3	Pokomo, Lower	PN.	b
5920	Luhya (Hanga, Wanga)	0.81169	220,906	244,159	338,929	NAB57d	99-AUSF-g	o-lu-wanga		90.00	219,743	2.s..	10	10	11	5	3	Oluhanga	PNb	b
5921	Luhya (Nyore)	0.72150	196,360	217,030	301,269	NAB57d	99-AUSF-d	o-lu-nyore		92.00	199,667	1.s..	10	10	11	5	3	Lunyore*	PNb	b
5922	Luhya (Ragoli)	0.88975	242,150	267,640	371,524	NAB57d	99-AUSF-r	u-lu-logooli		90.00	240,876	4.s..	10	10	11	5	3	Lulogooli*	PNB	b
5923	Luhya (Tiriki)	1.38205	376,132	415,726	577,089	NAB57d	99-AUSF-q	lu-tiriki		91.00	378,310	1.s..	10	9	10	5	3		pnb	b
5924	Luo	13.27094	3,611,757	3,991,948	5,541,412	NAB62j	04-ACCA-b	dho-luo	24	91.30	3,644,649	2As..	10	10	10	5	4	Dholuo*	PNB	b
5925	Maasai (Masai)	2.26217	615,662	680,469	944,591	NAB62k	04-BCAA-a	enkutuk-oo-l-maasai	3	40.00	272,188	4As..	9	5	9	5	3	Maasai	PNB	b
5926	Maasai Dorobo	0.05200	14,152	15,642	21,713	BYG11b	04-BCAA-a	enkutuk-oo-l-maasai		7.00	1,095	4As..	7	5	7	1	2	Maasai	PNB	b
5927	Makonde	0.00700	1,905	2,106	2,923	NAB57b	99-AUSQ-d	ci-makonde		8.00	168	1.s..	7	5	0	4	2	Makonde	pnb	b
5928	Malakote (Ilwana)	0.15031	40,908	45,214	62,763	NAB57j	99-AUQA	ilwana cluster		15.00	6,782	0....	8	5	7	4	1	Malakote	...	.
5929	Malayali	0.00100	272	301	418	CNN23b	49-EBEB-a	malayalam		60.00	180	2Asu.	10	9	8	5	3	Malayalam	PNB	b
5930	Maratha	0.00100	272	301	418	CNN25j	59-AAFU-m	deshi-marathi		1.10	3	2Asu.	6	4	2	1	0	Marathi*	PNB	b
5931	Masaba (Gisu)	0.12600	34,292	37,901	52,613	NAB57d	99-AUSF-a	u-lu-masaba		65.00	24,636	3.s..	10	7	13	5	3	Lumasaaba*	PNb	.
5932	Mbere	0.37112	101,002	111,634	154,965	NAB57e	99-AUMA-c	mbeere		34.00	37,956	1cs..	9	5	11	5	3		pnb	b
5933	Meru	5.56434	1,514,365	1,673,774	2,323,445	NAB57e	99-AUMA-g	ki-meru	8	81.00	1,355,757	2cs..	10	10	9	5	3	Kimeru*	PNB	b
5934	Midgan	0.00500	1,361	1,504	2,088	BYG11b	14-GAGA-a	af-soomaali		0.55	8	2A...	5	4	2	1	0	Somali	PNB	b
5935	Mwimbi	0.42088	114,545	126,602	175,743	NAB57e	99-AUMA-e	nithi		40.00	50,641	1cs..	9	6	10	5	3		pnb	.
5936	Nandi	1.57509	428,669	473,793	657,694	NAB62g	04-CAAD-d	ngalek-ap-naandi		74.30	352,028	1cs..	10	6	11	5	1	Nandi	PNB	b
5937	Ndigiri	0.00600	1,633	1,805	2,505	BYG11b	99-AUMA-a	gi-gikuyu		7.00	126	3as..	7	5	6	3	2	Gigikuyu*	PNB	b
5938	Njemps (Chamus)	0.06000	16,329	18,048	25,054	NAB62k	04-BCAB-b	chamus		12.00	2,166	0....	8	5	7	5	3		...	.
5939	Nubian (Sudanese)	0.05556	15,121	16,713	23,200	NAB62b	12-AACG-c	ki-nubi		0.01	2	0....	3	3	2	1	0		...	b
5940	Okiek (Dorobo)	0.12025	32,727	36,172	50,212	BYG11b	04-CAAE	okiek cluster		3.00	1,085	0....	6	4	6	5	3		...	b
5941	Okiek (Ndorobo)	0.00030	82	90	125	BYG11b	04-CABA-a	omotik		4.00	4	0....	6	5	1	5	3		...	.
5942	Omani Arab	0.05300	14,424	15,943	22,131	CMT30	12-AACF-l	omani		0.01	2	1Asuh	3	5	7	0	0		pnb	b
5943	Orma (Orma Galla)	0.13016	35,424	39,153	54,350	CMT33b	14-FBAA-i	orma		0.01	4	1cs..	3	3	4	5	3	Orma	pnb	b
5944	Oromo (Southern Galla)	0.10000	27,216	30,080	41,756	CMT33b	14-FBAA-i	orma		5.00	1,504	1cs..	7	5	2	0	0	Orma	pnb	b
5945	Padhola (Dama)	0.10000	27,216	30,080	41,756	NAB62j	04-ACCA-a	dho-p-adhola		85.00	25,568	4cs..	10	7	11	5	3	Dhopadhola*	Pnb	b
5946	Pare	0.01000	2,722	3,008	4,176	NAB57e	99-AUSJ-b	ci-athu		38.00	1,143	0....	9	5	10	5	1	Chasu*	PN.	b
5947	Parsi	0.00242	659	728	1,010	CNN25m	58-AACC-a	parsi-i		0.00	0	1Asu.	0	2	2	0	0	Gujarati: Parsi	PNb	b
5948	Pokot (Eastern Suk)	0.96552	262,771	290,432	403,162	NAB62p	04-CAAA-a	ngal-ap-pokot	1	15.50	45,017	0.s..	8	5	6	5	3	Pokoot	PN.	.
5949	Punjabi	0.13050	35,516	39,255	54,492	CNN25n	59-AAFE-c	general panjabi		0.15	59	1Asu.	5	4	4	1	1		PNB	b
5950	Rabai	0.26332	71,664	79,208	109,952	NAB57j	99-AUSL-g	ki-rabai		30.00	23,762	1....	9	5	9	4	2		pnb	b
5951	Rendille	0.11373	30,952	34,210	47,489	CMT33b	14-GAEA-a	afi-rendille		5.00	1,711	1....	7	5	6	4	3	Rendille	P..	.
5952	Reshiat (Dasenach, Geleb)	0.01503	4,090	4,521	6,276	CMT33d	14-GACA-a	af-dasenach		5.00	226	0....	7	5	6	4	3	Daasanech	...	.
5953	Ribe	0.02000	5,443	6,016	8,351	NAB57j	99-AUSL-f	ki-ribe		22.00	1,324	1....	9	5	9	4	1	Kinyika: Ribe	Pnb	b
5954	Ruandese	0.47918	130,411	144,139	200,086	NAB57d	99-AUSD-f	i-ki-nya-rwanda		90.00	129,725	2Asu.	10	9	11	5	2	Kinyarwanda*	PNB	b
5955	Rundi	0.10000	27,216	30,080	41,756	NAB57d	99-AUSD-c	i-ki-ruundi		90.90	27,343	4csu.	10	9	11	5	2	Kirundi*	PNB	b
5956	Saamia	1.51303	411,779	455,125	631,781	NAB57d	99-AUSF-e	o-lu-saamia		92.00	418,715	1.s..	10	8	11	5	1	Saamia	Pnb	b
5957	Sab	0.00500	1,361	1,504	2,088	CMT33e	14-GAGA-a	af-soomaali		0.11	2	2A...	5	2	2	0	0	Somali	PNB	b
5958	Sabaot (Elgon Maasai)	0.52299	142,335	157,317	218,380	NAB62y	04-CAAC-a	ku-p-sabiny		77.50	121,921	1....	10	7	11	4	2	Kupsapiny*	PN.	b
5959	Sagalla Taita	0.04000	10,886	12,032	16,702	NAB57e	99-AUPA-a	ki-saghala		37.00	4,452	0....	9	5	11	5	3	Kisagalla*	PN.	b
5960	Sakuye	0.04063	11,058	12,222	16,965	CMT33b	14-FBAA-hf	sakuye		0.17	21	1cs..	5	4	5	4	3		pnb	.
5961	Samburu (Burkeneji)	0.53433	145,421	160,728	223,115	NAB62k	04-BCAB-a	sampur		14.00	22,502	0....	8	5	6	5	3		...	b
5962	Samburu Ndorobo	0.02000	5,443	6,016	8,351	BYG11b	04-BCAB-a	sampur		0.50	30	0....	5	4	2	1	2		...	b
5963	Sanye (Waata, Ariangulu)	0.03006	8,181	9,042	12,552	BYG11b	14-FBAA-ic	waata		0.41	37	1cs..	5	4	2	1	3		pnb	.
5964	Segeju (Dhaiso)	0.20000	54,431	60,161	83,512	NAB57j	99-AUMB-a	ki-daiso		0.01	6	0....	3	2	3	4	1		...	b
5965	Seychellese Creole	0.00400	1,089	1,203	1,670	NAN58	51-AACC-k	seselwa		95.00	1,143	1cs..	10	8	10	4	2	Creole: Seychelles*	PNb	b
5966	Shabelle	0.00500	1,361	1,504	2,088	NAB57j	14-GAGA-a	af-soomaali		0.00	0	2A...	0	2	2	0	0	Somali	PNB	b
5967	Sindhi	0.00650	1,769	1,955	2,714	CNN25p	59-AAFF-a	standard sindhi		0.08	2	1as..	4	2	2	1	0	Sindhi	PNB	b
5968	Sinhalese	0.00100	272	301	418	CNN25q	59-ABBA-aa	standard sinhala		10.00	30	1asuh	8	5	2	4	1		pnb	b
5969	Somali	1.67044	454,619	502,475	697,509	CMT33e	14-GAGA-a	af-soomaali		0.02	100	2A...	3	3	5	1	3	Somali	PNB	b
5970	Somali Ajuran	0.02850	7,756	8,573	11,900	CMT33b	14-GAGA-h	southeast af-ajuran		1.00	86	1c...	6	4	2	3	1		pnb	b
5971	Suba	0.18900	51,437	56,852	78,919	NAB57d	99-AUSG-aa	suba		91.00	51,735	0c...	10	7	11	5	3	Suba	Pn.	b
5972	Suba (Luo Suba)	0.20000	54,431	60,161	83,512	NAB57d	04-ACCA-b	dho-luo		92.00	55,348	2As..	10	8	12	5	3	Dholuo*	PNB	b
5973	Swahili (Coastal)	0.32700	88,995	98,363	136,542	NAB57j	99-AUSM-i	ki-mvita		0.03	30	1Asu.	3	3	4	1	3		pnb	b
5974	Swahili (Urban)	0.10000	27,216	30,080	41,756	NAB57j	99-AUSM-b	standard ki-swahili	76	20.00	6,016	4Asu.	9	5	13	5	1	Kiswahili*	PNB	b
5975	Talai Marakwet	0.12420	33,802	37,360	51,861	NAB62g	04-CAAB	marakwet cluster		43.00	16,065	0....	9	6	9	4	3		...	b

Continued opposite

Table 8-2 continued

EVANGELIZATION								EVANGELISM			ADDITIONAL DESCRIPTIVE DATA
Ref 1	*D 28*	*aC 29*	*CG% 30*	*r 31*	*E 32*	*U 33*	*W 34*	*e 35*	*R 36*	*T 37*	*Locations, civil divisions, literacy, religions, church history, denominations, dioceses, church growth, missions, agencies, ministries, movements 38*
5854	1	8	1.96	7	99.65	0.35	C	277.58	46	8	Migrants, residents from Mordvinia (Russia). Acculturated to Russian. Nonreligious 30%. D=ROC. M=IBT.
5855	1	7	1.96	0	74.00	26.00	B	97.23	113	6	Mainly found in Russia, Georgia; also Syria, Turkey. Muslims 40%(Sunnis), nonreligious 20%. D=ROC.
5856	4	10	8.70	6	99.71	0.29	C	367.99	168	9	Poles. 29% speak Polish as mother tongue. Strong Christians who resisted USSR for 60 years. D=RCC,ROC,CEF,CWE.
5857	8	9	2.92	7	99.37	0.63	B	148.55	73	7	In 70 countries. Long-time settlers and colonizers. Nonreligious 43%, atheists 18%. D=ROC,RCC,AUCECB,Old Ritualists,CEF,CCECB,SDA,IPKH.
5858	0	6	0.00	4	37.00	63.00	A	0.00	0	1.12	Most are trilingual (with Uzbek, Azeri, Russian). Muslims 90%(Hanafi Sunnis, some Shias), nonreligious 10%. M=CSI.
5859	1	7	3.99	6	43.50	56.50	A	2.38	302	4	70% bilingual in Russian. Muslims 83%(Hanafi Sunnis), nonreligious 15%. D=ROC(Kryashen).
5860	0	6	0.00	8	37.00	63.00	A	0.00	0	1.11	Across Central Asia. Muslims 98%(83% Hanafi Sunnis, 15% Alawi Shias).
5861	0	7	0.00	1	27.00	73.00	A	0.00	0	1.11	In and around Kara Kum Desert, Iran, Afghanistan, Uzbekistan, et alia. Devout Muslims 95%(Hanafi Sunnis), nonreligious 5%. M=IBT.
5862	1	7	1.96	0	94.00	6.00	B	188.70	86	7	From Udmurtia (Russia). Strong shamanists/animists 40%, some Muslims. D=ROC.
5863	0	6	2.43	4	38.05	61.95	A	0.06	233	2	Also in Kirghizia, Uzbekistan. In 15 countries. Settled agriculturalists. Muslims 100%(Hanafi Sunnis, with heavy Sufi influence). M=IBT,CSI,UBS.
5864	8	8	7.71	6	99.60	0.40	C	282.51	189	8	In 15 countries. Nonreligious/atheists 35%. D=ROC(E-Ukraine),UOC,Ukrainian Catholic Ch,AUCECB,CEF,CCECB,JWs,SDA. R=FEBC,HCJB,AWR,VERITAS.
5865	0	9	0.00	5	43.00	57.00	A	0.00	0	1.12	55% Russian-speaking. Literates 100%. Muslims 80%(Hanafi Sunnis), nonreligious/atheists 20%. M=ROC,AUCECB,CSI,FI.
5866	0	7	0.00		13.00	87.00	A	0.00	0	1.03	Czechs, Romanians, Hungarians, Finns, Buryat, Kalmyk, Tabasaran, Parsis. Nonreligious 50%, atheists 20%, Muslims 18%, Zoroastrians 10%, Buddhists 2%.
Kenya											
5867	0	4	1.40	5	34.01	65.99	A	0.01	266	2	Mandera and Wajir Districts, also in Ethiopia and Somalia. Nomadic pastoralists. Literates 2%. Muslims 100%(Shafi Sunnis). M=DMA.
5868	2	6	3.29	1	37.00	63.00	A	4.05	384	4	Marsabit District. Pastoralists living among the Samburu. Animists 95%, some Muslims. D=AIC,RCC. M=SIL,LM,SIM.
5869	0	8	1.96	5	37.01	62.99	A	0.01	253	2	Fishermen, agriculturalists on northeast coast, also in Somalia. Muslims 100%(Shafi Sunnis). M=Nairobi Lighthouse Church.
5870	0	10	0.00	1	19.00	81.00	A	0.00	0	1.08	Immigrants from Baluchistan(Pakistan, Afghanistan). Muslims 100%(Sunnis).
5871	0	10	2.10	6	47.90	52.10	A	1.57	198	4	Early immigrants from Bengal(India) as laborers. Traders. Hindus 75%, Muslims 23%, Baha'is 1%.
5872	0	7	2.99	0	20.50	79.50	A	0.37	533	3	Hunter-gatherers in forests. Monolinguals, with some bilinguals in Somali, Orma, or Swahili. Muslims 70%, animists 29%. M=AIC.
5873	3	6	7.46	5	65.00	35.00	B	18.98	395	5	Pastoral nomads. Many in Ethiopia. Muslims 80%(Shafi Sunnis), animists 10%. D=AIC,CPK,RCC. M=BCMS,SIM,LM,BSK,AIM,DMA,BTL,SLM.
5874	6	10	4.39	8	99.78	0.22	C	437.04	98	10	Expatriates from Britain, in education, administration. D=CPK(11 Dioceses),MCK,PCEA,RCC,JWs,SDA. M=CMS,AIM,FMB.
5875	7	8	11.66	1	99.80	0.20	C	397.12	277	9	Bungoma District, Western Province. Animists 15%. D=RCC(D-Eldoret),CPK,Judah Israel Mission,RCEA,EAYMF,BCK,other AICs. M=BSK.
5876	1	6	6.23	0	51.00	49.00	B	37.23	437	5	Around Marsabit in north. Most in Ethiopia. Muslims 75%, some animists. D=Ev Lutheran Ch in Ethiopia/ECMY.
5877	0	6	4.44	5	52.00	48.00	B	18.98	334	5	In north. Burji becoming assimilated to the Boran. Muslims 85%(Shafi Sunnis).
5878	10	6	13.04	4	99.91	0.09	C	501.54	275	10	Baha'is 4%, Muslims 2%, animists 2%. D=RCC,CPK,AOCK,EAYM,SDA,PAG,COGA,PEFA,SA,many AICs. M=CMS. Strong in East African Revival since 1938.
5879	2	10	6.97	0	99.70	0.30	C	311.71	180	9	Labor migrants from Tanzania. Animists 30%. D=ELCK,RCC. M=ELCT.
5880	0	7	8.70	0	64.00	36.00	B	51.39	435	6	Kilifi District, Coast Province. Related to Giriama; part of the Mijikenda. Animists 68%, Muslims 10%.
5881	3	9	8.90	1	95.00	5.00	B	138.70	286	7	Southern Meru District, Eastern Province. Close to Tharaka. Animists 60%. D=CPK,RCC,BCK. M=FMB.
5882	4	6	2.10	7	48.01	51.99	A	0.01	160	2	Almost totally resistant to Christianity for 150 years. Muslims 100%(Shafi Sunnis). D=RCC,CPK,BCK,MCK. M=CMS,IM,FMB,YWAM.
5883	0	6	3.88	1	35.10	64.90	A	0.12	381	3	85% of Asians in Kenya. Merchants. Second language: English, Swahili. Hindus 70%, Muslims 20%.
5884	5	8	8.49	0	99.68	0.32	C	315.21	205	9	Taita District. All bilingual in Swahili. Muslims 20%(Shafi Sunnis), animists 12%. Y=1883. D=CPK,RCC(D-Mombasa),LMC,MRFPC,AICs. M=CMS,CSSp,FMB.
5885	0	9	1.62	0	24.11	75.89	A	0.09	298	2	Near mouth of Tana river. Bilingual in Swahili, highly assimiliated. Animists 95%, few Muslims. M=AIC.
5886	6	7	4.13	0	46.12	53.88	A	0.20	332	3	Kwale District. Many in Tanzania. Literates in Swahili 45%. Muslims 91%(Shafi Sunnis), animists 9%. D=CPK,RCC,AIC,EAPC,BCK,CB. M=CMS,NLM,CBFMS.
5887	2	3	4.60	1	32.00	68.00	A	5.84	516	4	Donyiro: dialect of Toposa; mainly in Ethiopia and Sudan. Animists 95%. D=RCC(D-Meru),AIC.
5888	3	8	8.93	0	84.40	15.60	B	105.97	337	7	West Kwale District, Coast Province. In Mijikenda. Literates in Swahili 13%. Animists 40%, Muslims 25%(Shafi Sunnis). D=MCK,RCC(D-Mombasa),SA. M=CSSp.
5889	2	6	2.61	1	37.00	63.00	A	4.05	267	4	Southeastern shore of Lake Turkana. Semi-arid desert. Fishermen. Animists 97%. D=RCC,AIC. M=WMPL,AIM.
5890	2	9	0.00	0	49.00	51.00	A	19.67	56	5	Nearly extinct: speakers are all over 50 years old. Fishermen. Animists 89%. D=RCC,AIC.
5891	2	8	10.00	1	99.68	0.32	C	298.09	252	8	Animists 25%. D=AIC,RCC(D-Eldoret). M=AIM.
5892	7	8	9.18	1	99.72	0.28	C	349.52	210	9	Embu District. Bilingual in Kikuyu, and some in Swahili. Animists 25%. D=RCC(D-Meru),CPK,PCEA,AEPC,NICA,NAC,other AICs. M=IMC,CMS,CSM,FMB.
5893	3	8	8.26	1	89.30	10.70	B	144.39	284	7	Pastoralists; high education. Language has low intelligibility with Kalenjin. Animists 54%. At least 18 known churches. D=AIC,RCC,FGCK. M=AIM,BTL.
5894	6	10	6.51	8	99.70	0.30	C	344.92	154	9	Mixed-race persons, largely urban. Muslims 10%, Baha'is 5%. D=RCC,CPK,PCEA,MCK,PAG,&c.
5895	1	10	5.30	8	99.87	0.13	C	514.43	106	10	Expatriates from France, in education, business. Nonreligious 13%. D=RCC(13 Dioceses). M=OCSO,SPS,SM,MM,CP,CSSp.
5896	3	2	6.50	5	61.50	38.50	B	21.32	374	5	Pastoral nomads. Animists 70%, Muslims 20%(Shafi Sunnis). D=AIC,CPK,RCC. M=DMA-CPK,SIM,AIM.
5897	4	10	7.95	4	99.70	0.30	C	378.14	186	9	Immigrants and refugees from Uganda. Muslims 20%(Shafi Sunnis), animists 10%. D=CPK,RCC,CBC,AICs. M=CMS,FMB,CU.
5898	0	1	2.75	5	29.02	70.98	A	0.02	439	2	Pastoral nomads in Mandera and Wajir Districts. Literates 2%. Muslims 100%(Shafi Sunnis). M=DMA-CPK,RCC,AIC.
5899	6	7	9.85	0	89.30	10.70	B	115.05	347	7	Coastal hinterland north of Mombasa. In Mijikenda. Bilingual in Swahili. Animists 45%, Muslims 8.5%(Shafi Sunnis). D=CPK,RCC,SA,AIC,BCK,&c. M=CMS.
5900	1	8	6.42	4	99.95	0.05	C	544.39	129	10	Mainly in Goa(India), also United Arab Emirates. Second language English. Trade, commerce. D=95% RCC. M=SJ.
5901	0	3	3.27	5	35.14	64.86	A	0.18	369	3	Somali nomads, pastoralists. Muslims 100%(Shafi Sunnis).
5902	0	10	4.21	6	53.05	46.95	B	0.09	270	2	Long-time residents; early laborers, now traders, in commerce. Hindus 80%, Shia Muslims 10%(Khojas or Nizari Ismailis), Bohras 3%, Jains 3%, Baha'is 2%.
5903	0	10	0.70	1	35.14	64.86	A	0.18	133	3	Swahili-based creole. Gujaratis from Zanzibar, speaking Asian Swahili. Second language: English. Muslims 100%(Ismailis,Ithna-Asharis).
5904	0	10	1.10	7	50.08	49.92	B	0.14	115	3	Long-time laborers from India. In commerce, business. Hindus 63%, Muslims 5%, Baha'is 2%. M=IM,CBFMS,FMB.
5905	3	10	4.60	8	84.00	16.00	B	91.98	183	6	From Mauritius, in business, commerce. Muslims 70%(Hanafis,Shafis,Ahmadis). D=RCC,CPK,JWs. M=SJ.
5906	0	10	0.70	8	41.09	58.91	A	0.13	93	3	A few communities of practicing English-speaking Jews, mainly in Nairobi.
5907	0	7	6.77	0	60.00	40.00	B	43.80	376	6	Coastal. Most understand Swahili, Giriama. Animists 70%, Muslims 10%(Shafi Sunnis).
5908	4	10	7.67	1	99.54	0.46	B	244.41	191	8	Rift Valley peoples, throughout country. Animists 45%. D=AIC,RCC,CPK,FGCK. M=AIM,CMS,FFFM,FMB,BSK.
5909	6	6	7.31	4	99.86	0.14	C	457.44	157	10	Eastern Province. Animists 5%, Muslims 2%, Baha'is 1%, some Hindus. D=CPK,AIC,RCC,SA,ABC,many AICs. M=CSSp,CMS,SPS,AIM,FMB,BSK,LBI. R=IBRA.
5910	0	8	7.04	0	61.00	39.00	B	44.53	382	6	In Mijikenda. Coastal. Understand Giriama, Swahili. Animists 70%, Muslims 10%(Shafi Sunnis).
5911	3	8	6.18	0	99.60	0.40	C	236.52	183	8	Taita District, Coast Province. Dialect of Sagalla Taita. Animists 20%, Muslims 20%(Shafi Sunnis). D=CPK,RCC(D-Mombasa),AIC. M=CMS,CSSp.
5912	0	8	6.08	0	61.00	39.00	B	44.53	339	6	Coastal. Use Giriama, Swahili. Animists 70%, Muslims 10%(Shafi Sunnis).
5913	8	6	8.54	4	99.92	0.08	C	537.28	164	10	Animists 1%, Baha'is 1%, Muslims 1%, 2,000 Hindu converts(Arya Samaj). D=AIPCA(4 Dioceses),RCC,CPK,PCEA,AIC,AOCK,BCK,many other AICs. M=IMC,CMS.
5914	6	8	11.63	1	99.70	0.30	C	337.64	263	9	In Kalinjin cluster, Rift Valley and west. Animists 20%. D=AIC,RCC,CPK,AGC,AGUC,many other AICs. M=WGM,AIM,CMS,MHM.
5915	8	6	12.75	4	99.87	0.13	C	465.69	276	10	Kisii District. Animists 5%. D=RCC(D-Kisii),CGEA,LCK,SDA,PAG,MCK,CBC,many AICs. M=SLM,SIM,PAOC,GNF,FMB,BSK.
5916	1	6	4.18	0	51.00	49.00	B	37.23	327	5	Migrants in Marsabit District from Ethiopia. Bilingual in Boran. Animists 80%. D=ECMY.
5917	0	6	1.96	1	25.07	74.93	A	0.06	422	2	Upper Tana river. Dialect of Orma Galla. Agriculturalists, fishermen. Muslims 99%(Shafi Sunnis).
5918	3	7	9.36	4	99.52	0.48	B	201.34	294	8	Kuria District. Most in Tanzania. Animists 46%. D=RCC(D-Kisii),PEFA,CPK. M=FMB,SLM,BSK,Mennonites.
5919	7	8	6.71	0	68.70	31.30	B	51.90	326	6	Lower Tana river. Bilinguals in Swahili 75%. Muslims 78%(Shafi Sunnis). D=MCK,EAPC,ELCK,RCC,PEFA,CPK,AIC. M=MMS,AICMS,FMB,BTL.
5920	5	8	10.51	1	99.90	0.10	C	489.46	232	10	Baha'is 4%, Muslims 2%. D=RCC,CPK,COGA,SA,&c including many AICs. M=CMS,AIM,MHM,FMB,BSK,LBI.
5921	5	8	10.41	1	99.92	0.08	C	503.70	229	10	Also in Uganda. Baha'is 5%, Muslims 2%. D=RCC,CPK,COGA,SA,&c including many AICs. M=CMS,AIM,MHM,BSK,LBI.
5922	8	8	10.62	1	99.90	0.10	C	505.89	226	10	Kakamega District. Baha'is 3%, Muslims 2%. D=RCC,CPK,COGA,EAYMF,SA,AICN,ACHS,many other AICs. M=CMS,AIM,MHM,FMB.
5923	6	8	11.12	1	99.91	0.09	C	488.26	246	10	Kakamega District. Baha'is 4%, Muslims 2%. D=RCC,CPK,COGA,SA,CCA,many other AICs. M=CMS,MHM,AIM.
5924	8	6	13.66	4	99.91	0.09	C	534.19	249	10	Kavirondo. Animists 1%, Muslims 1%, Baha'is 1%. D=CPK,RCC(D-Kisumu),MLA,SDA,AIC,FGCK,CCA,many other AICs. M=CMS,MHM,AIM,SLM,FFFM,LBI,LM.
5925	9	9	10.75	4	99.40	0.60	B	156.22	301	7	Kajiado and Narok Districts; also Tanzania. Animists 55%. D=RCC,EFMK,CPK,LCK,AIC,PCEA, Pentecostals,BCC,&c. M=AIM,CMS,MHM,CSM,EMBMC,PI,YWAM.
5926	2	10	4.81	4	64.00	36.00	B	16.35	249	5	Forest-dwelling nomadic hunter-gatherers. Animists 93%. D=RCC,AIC.
5927	2	10	2.86	1	45.00	55.00	A	13.14	263	5	From Mozambique, Tanzania. Muslims 90%(Shafi Sunnis). D=RCC,CPK.
5928	1	7	6.74	0	47.00	53.00	A	25.73	478	5	Tana river north of Pokomo. Agriculturalists, fishermen. Muslims 85%(Shafi Sunnis). D=RCC. M=BTL.
5929	4	10	2.93	4	99.60	0.40	C	275.94	85	8	Traders, businessmen from Kerala(India). Hindus 35%, some Muslims. D=CPK,RCC,AOCK,&c.
5930	0	10	1.10	4	47.10	52.90	A	1.89	123	4	From India, in business, commerce, professions. Hindus 56%, Muslims 10%.
5931	3	7	8.12	1	99.65	0.35	C	291.81	228	8	Around Mount Elgon; also in Uganda. Animists 20%(Dini ya Msambwa),Baha'is 10%, Muslims 5%. D=RCC,CPK,&c.
5932	5	9	8.59	1	92.00	8.00	B	114.17	287	7	Embu District. Dialect of Embu. Animists 66%. D=RCC,CPK,PCEA,AEPC,many AICs. M=AIM,CMS,CSM,FMB.
5933	7	6	11.24	1	99.81	0.19	C	416.86	238	10	Meru District. Animists 10%, Muslims 1%, Baha'is 1%. D=RCC(D-Meru),PCEA,CPK,MCK,EAPC,NICA,other AICs. M=IMC,KFM,MMS,CMF,CMS,CSM,FMB,BSK.
5934	0	3	2.10	5	36.55	63.45	A	0.73	232	3	One of several Somali-speaking nomadic peoples in east. Muslims 100%(Shafi Sunnis).
5935	4	6	8.90	1	91.00	9.00	B	132.86	299	7	Central Meru District, Eastern Province. Animists 60%. D=RCC,MCK,CPK,EAPC.
5936	5	9	11.04	1	99.74	0.26	C	366.92	244	9	Rift Valley Province. In Kalenjin cluster, Rift Valley and west. Animists 15%. D=AIC,RCC(D-Kisumu),CPK,RCEA,AICs. M=AIM.MHM,CMS,FMB.
5937	2	10	2.57	4	62.00	38.00	B	15.84	158	5	East African hunters. Forest-dwelling nomadic hunter-gatherers, partially acculturated to Kikuyu. Animists 93%. D=AIC,DMA.
5938	5	9	5.53	1	52.00	48.00	B	22.77	344	5	Samburu District. Pastoralists, nomads. Animists 88%. D=AIC,RCC,New Apostolic Ch,FGCK,PAG.
5939	0	10	0.70	1	23.01	76.99	A	0.00	262	1.07	In Kibera(Nairobi), and other towns; also in Uganda. Former language of soldiers from Sudan. Muslims 100%(Maliki Sunnis).
5940	8	8	4.80	1	42.00	58.00	A	4.59	378	4	Hunters in East Mau Escarpment, Nakuru District. Bilingual in Nandi. Animists 97%. D=RCC,COGA,AIC,AGC,FGCK,SDA,CPK,&c. M=AIM,CMS,FFFM,UBS.
5941	3	5	1.40	0	30.00	70.00	A	4.38	219	4	Hunters in forests of Narok District, all over 50 years old. Nearly extinct. Animists 96%. D=RCC,AIC,CPK.
5942	0	0	0.70	7	32.01	67.99	A	0.01	120	2	Immigrants from Oman. Muslims (Shafi Sunnis) 100%.
5943	3	5	1.40	5	40.01	59.99	A	0.01	226	2	Garissa and Tana River Districts. Pastoral nomads. Muslims 100%(Shafi Sunnis). D=AIC,RCEA,RCC. M=AIM,MM,Life Ministry,BTL,FMB.
5944	0	6	5.14	5	41.00	59.00	A	7.48	470	4	Pastoralists, related to Galla of Ethiopia. In east Kenya. Muslims 95%(Shafi Sunnis).
5945	3	8	8.16	4	99.85	0.15	C	462.27	167	10	Jopadhola. Migrants, refugees from western Uganda. Animists 10%. D=RCC,CU,CPK. M=CMS,FMB,UBS.
5946	2	10	4.85	0	86.00	14.00	B	119.28	187	7	From northern Tanzania. Animists 32%, Muslims 30%(Sunnis). D=ELCK,RCC. M=ELCT(Tanzania).
5947	0	10	0.00	4	35.00	65.00	A	0.00	0	1.12	Long-time residents, from India(Gujarat). All Parsis by religion(Zoroastrians).
5948	7	7	8.78	0	57.50	42.50	B	32.53	490	5	Also in Uganda. Semi-nomadic half-pastoralists. Animists 84%. Y=1927(BCMS). D=CPK,AGC,RCC,ELCK,RCEA,AICs,& and 19 other demominations. M=BCMS.
5949	0	10	4.16	5	48.15	51.85	A	0.26	296	3	Early laborers from India. Traders, commerce. Sikhs 70%, Hindus 27%, Muslims 1%, Baha'is 1%. M=FMB.
5950	2	7	7.06	0	78.00	22.00	B	85.41	299	6	Coastal. In Mijikenda: dialect of Duruma. Bilingual in Swahili. Muslims 50%, Animists 10%. D=CPK,MCK.
5951	2	3	5.28	1	37.00	63.00	A	6.75	532	4	Marsabit District. Semi-arid and desert. Pastoralists. Animists 95%. D=RCC,AIC. M=SIL,LM,SIM,BTL.
5952	2	5	3.17	0	35.00	65.00	A	6.38	397	4	Shangilla. Northeast of Lake Turkana. Majority in Ethiopia. Desert pastoralists. Animists 95%. D=RCC(D-Marsabit),AIC. M=AIM,Master's Mission,BTL.
5953	1	8	6.71	0	68.00	32.00	B	54.60	329	6	Coastal, related to Mijikenda. Bilingual in Swahili. Muslims 50%, Animists 10%. D=CPK.
5954	2	10	9.93	4	99.90	0.10	C	522.31	207	10	Refugees from Rwanda (originator of East African Revival in 1927) since 1962, massacres. Virtually all Tutsi Christians(10% nominal). D=RCC,CPK.
5955	2	10	8.24	4	99.91	0.09	C	523.88	179	10	Refugees from Burundi since 1972 massacres. Virtually all Christians(9% nominal). D=RCC,CPK.
5956	3	6	11.23	1	99.92	0.08	C	486.91	252	10	Busia District. Many in Uganda. Baha'is 3%, Muslims 2%. D=RCC,CPK,COGA. M=BSK.
5957	0	1	0.70	5	33.11	66.89	A	0.13	211	3	Refugees, migrants from Somalia. Muslims 100%(Shafi Sunnis).
5958	2	8	9.87	1	99.78	0.22	C	363.49	241	9	On Mount Elgon. Pastoralists. Animists 15%. D=CPK,RCC. M=BTL,SIL.
5959	5	8	6.83	0	87.00	13.00	B	117.49	248	7	Taita District. Animists 43%, Muslims 20%(Shafi Sunnis). D=CPK,RCC(D-Mombasa),LMC,Pentecostals,AICs. M=CSSp,CMS,BSK.
5960	3	5	3.09	5	42.17	57.83	A	0.26	324	3	Marsabit and Isiolo Districts, Eastern Province. Dialect of Boran. Muslims 99%. D=AIC,RCC,CPK.
5961	7	6	8.02	1	54.00	46.00	B	27.59	458	5	Samburu District. Pastoralists. Animists 86%. D=CPK,AIC,EAPC,RCC,PCEA,FGCK,PAG. M=BCMS,CCM,IMC,Church Army,LM,ACA,WMPL,DMA,FMB,IFM.
5962	2	3	3.46	1	22.50	77.50	A	0.41	543	3	Forest-dwelling nomadic hunter-gatherers in north. Animists 99%. D=RCC,AIC.
5963	0	3	3.68	1	27.41	72.59	A	0.41	468	3	Walenguru. Forest dwellers in lower parts of Tana river. Animists 50%, Muslims 49%. M=indigenous missionaries,AIC,ACA,FMB,DMA.
5964	1	3	1.81	0	21.01	78.99	A	0.00	426	1.07	Southeast coast, also in Tanzania. Bilingual in Swahili. Muslims 100%(Shafi Sunnis). D=RCC.
5965	2	6	4.85	8	99.95	0.05	C	533.99	106	10	Workers from Seychelles. Bilingual in French. Nominal Christians. D=RCC,CPK.
5966	0	1	0.00	5	28.00	72.00	A	0.00	0	1.09	Refugees, migrants from Somalia. Muslims 100%(Shafi Sunnis).
5967	0	10	0.70	4	43.08	56.92	A	0.12	108	3	Long-time residents, laborers, traders. Hindus 90%, Muslims 6%, Sikhs 2%, Baha'is 1%.
5968	1	10	3.46	6	60.00	40.00	B	21.90	184	5	From Ceylon. Theravada Buddhists 90%. D=RCC. M=CPM.
5969	4	6	2.33	5	46.02	53.98	A	0.03	249	2	Northeastern Province. Nomads. Muslims 100%(Shafi Sunnis). Y=1914. D=RCC,AIC,Mennonites,CPK. M=SIM,LM,EMBMC,UPM,FMB,BSK,LBI,CSI,FI.
5970	4	6	4.56	5	41.00	59.00	A	1.49	432	4	Somali-speaking nomads. Muslims 99%(Shafi Sunnis). D=RCC,Protestants,AICs, M=TAC.
5971	4	10	8.93	1	99.91	0.09	C	484.93	207	10	Southeast shores of Lake Victoria. Bilingual in Luo. All Christians(9% nominal). D=CPK,SDA,RCC,AICs.
5972	4	7	9.00	4	99.92	0.08	C	533.92	191	10	On Lake Victoria. Also in Tanzania. Monolinguals, now speaking only Luo. All Christians(8% nominal). D=CPK,SDA,RCC,many AICs.
5973	3	9	3.46	5	46.03	53.97	A	0.05	293	2	Pure Waswahili on coast. Literates 51%. Muslims 100%(Shafi Sunnis). Scarcely any converts since Y=1844. D=RCC,CPK,BSK. M=CMS,AIM,MMS,FMB,CGM.
5974	5	10	7.90	5	92.00	8.00	B	67.16	279	6	Children of mixed marriages in towns. Muslims 80%(Sunnis). D=RCC,CPK,PCEA,PAG,CGM(Nigeria). M=ICB(Burma).
5975	3	8	7.66	1	88.00	12.00	B	138.11	270	7	Rift Valley Province. Low intelligibility with Kalenjin language. Animists 57%. D=AIC,RCC,FGCK.

Continued overleaf

Table 8-2 continued

PEOPLE		POPULATION				IDENTITY CODE		LANGUAGE		CHURCH		MINISTRY						SCRIPTURE		
Ref 1	*Ethnic name 2*	*P% 3*	*In 1995 4*	*In 2000 5*	*In 2025 6*	*Race 7*	*Language 8*	*Autoglossonym 9*	*S 10*	*AC 11*	*Members 12*	*Jayuh 13-17*	*d 18*	*wa 19*	*xc 20*	*mc 21*	*mi 22*	*Biblioglossonym 23*	*Pub 24-26*	*ss 27*
5976	Tamil	0.00100	272	301	418	CNN23c	49-EBEA-b	tamil		20.00	60	2Asu.	9	5	2	5	0	Tamil	PNB	b
5977	Taveta (Tubeta)	0.06300	17,146	18,951	26,306	NAB57e	99-AUSJ-a	ki-tuveta		68.00	12,886	0....	10	8	13	5	2	Kitaveta*	PN.	b
5978	Terik	0.05000	13,608	15,040	20,878	NAB62g	04-CAAD-e	terik		50.00	7,520	1cs..	10	6	7	5	3		pnb	b
5979	Teso (Iteso)	0.79658	216,793	239,614	332,620	NAB62q	04-BDAE-a	a-teso	1	77.50	185,701	3.s..	10	7	11	5	1	Ateso*	PNB	b
5980	Teuso (Ik)	0.00300	816	902	1,253	BYG11b	07-BAAA-a	ik		80.00	722	0....	10	7	7	5	2		...	n
5981	Tharaka	0.40961	111,478	123,212	171,037	NAB57e	99-AUMA-h	ki-tharaka		37.20	45,835	1cs..	9	6	13	4	2	Kitharaka*	Pnb	b
5982	Tugen	0.66701	181,530	200,639	278,517	NAB62g	04-CAAD-b	kalenjin-tugen		56.20	112,759	1cs..	10	6	7	4	1	Kalenjin	PNB	b
5983	Turkana	1.24348	338,420	374,043	519,227	NAB62r	04-BDAB-a	nga-turkana	2	20.00	74,809	1As..	9	5	6	3	3	Turkana	PN.	.
5984	USA White	0.04000	10,886	12,032	16,702	CEW19s	52-ABAC-s	general american		80.00	9,626	1Bsuh	10	9	13	5	3	English*	PNB	b
5985	Upper Pokomo	0.12434	33,840	37,402	51,919	NAB57j	99-AUSK-a	ki-pokomo		24.00	8,976	1....	9	5	8	5	1	Kipokomo	PN.	b
5986	Yaaku (Mukogodo)	0.00020	54	60	84	BYG11b	14-EAAA-a	yaaku		11.00	7	0....	8	5	4	4	1		...	b
5987	Yaaku (Ndorobo)	0.00134	365	403	560	BYG11b	04-BCAA-a	enkutuk-oo-l-maasai		6.00	24	4As..	7	5	6	5	2	Maasai	PNB	b
5988	Yemeni Arab	0.07000	19,051	21,056	29,229	CMT30	12-AACF-n	yemeni		0.01	2	1Asuh	3	4	5	0	0		pnb	b
5989	Zanzibari (Hadimu)	0.01000	2,722	3,008	4,176	NAB57j	99-AUSM-q	ki-unguja		0.00	0	1Asu.	0	3	3	1	0		pnb	b
5990	other minor peoples	0.20262	55,144	60,949	84,606	...				30.00	18,285		9	5	7	5	0			
	Kirghizia	**100.00000**	**4,571,432**	**4,699,337**	**6,096,197**					**9.91**	**465,664**									
5991	Armenian	0.09336	4,268	4,387	5,691	CEW14	57-AAAA-b	ashkharik		70.00	3,071	4A.u.	10	7	13	2	1	Armenian: Modern, Eastern	PNB	b
5992	Avar	0.02316	1,059	1,088	1,412	CEW17b	42-BBAA-a	north avar		0.01	0	1....	3	3	2	0	1	Avar	P..	b
5993	Azerbaijani	0.37050	16,937	17,411	22,586	MSY41a	44-AABA-fa	north azeri		0.00	0	2c.u.	0	3	3	0	2	Azerbaijani*	PNB	b
5994	Balkar	0.05005	2,288	2,352	3,051	MSY41z	44-AABB-a	literary karachay-balkar		0.00	0	1c.u.	0	3	3	0	0	Karachay-balkar	PN.	.
5995	Bashkir	0.09456	4,323	4,444	5,765	MSY41b	44-AABB-g	bashqurt		7.00	311	1A.u.	7	5	7	0	1	Bashkir	Pn.	b
5996	Bulgar (Bulgarian)	0.01426	652	670	869	CEW22b	53-AAAH-b	bulgarski		72.00	482	2A.uh	10	6	10	1	1	Bulgarian	PNB	b
5997	Byelorussian	0.21577	9,864	10,140	13,154	CEW22c	53-AAAE-c	bielorusskiy		70.00	7,098	3A.uh	10	8	10	3	3	Byelorussian*	PNB	b
5998	Central Asian Jew	0.00813	372	382	496	CMT35	58-AACC-kb	bukharik		0.00	0	1csu.	0	1	2	0	0		pnb	b
5999	Chechen	0.06748	3,085	3,171	4,114	CEW17d	42-BAAA-b	chechen		0.00	0	0....	0	3	2	0	1	Chechen	P..	b
6000	Chuvash	0.04883	2,232	2,295	2,977	MSY41c	44-AAAA-a	chuvash		35.00	803	2....	9	6	8	0	1	Chuvash	PN.	b
6001	Crimean Tatar	0.06867	3,139	3,227	4,186	MSY41h	44-AABA-c	crimea-tatar		0.00	0	1c.u.	0	1	2	0	1	Crimean Tatar*	PNb	b
6002	Dargin	0.05822	2,661	2,736	3,549	CEW17b	42-BBBB-a	dargwa		0.01	0	1....	3	3	2	0	1	Dargwa	P..	b
6003	Dungan (Hui, Huizui)	0.86731	39,648	40,758	52,873	MSY42b	79-AAAB-l	hui-zu		0.00	0	1Asuh	0	1	3	0	0		pnb	b
6004	Estonian	0.01010	462	475	616	MSW51a	41-AAAC-b	eesti		70.00	332	4A.u.	10	8	8	2	2	Estonian: Tallinn	PNB	b
6005	Georgian	0.02685	1,227	1,262	1,637	CEW17c	42-CABB-a	kharthuli		40.00	505	2A.u.	9	6	8	2	1	Georgian	PNB	b
6006	German (Volga German)	0.75000	34,286	35,245	45,721	CEW19m	52-ABCE-a	standard hoch-deutsch		80.00	28,196	2B.uh	10	8	11	3	3	German*	PNB	b
6007	Greek	0.04714	2,155	2,215	2,874	CEW20	56-AAAA-c	dhimotiki		90.00	1,994	2B.uh	10	8	11	2	2	Greek: Modern	PNB	b
6008	Ingush	0.01390	635	653	847	CEW17d	42-BAAA-a	ingush		0.00	0	0....	0	2	0	0	1	Ingush	p..	b
6009	Jewish	0.13298	6,079	6,249	8,107	CMT35	52-ABCH	yiddish cluster		0.00	0	0B..h	0	3	6	0	0		PNB	b
6010	Kalmyk (Western Mongolian	0.11861	5,422	5,574	7,231	MSY41y	44-BAAB-d	kalmyk		1.00	56	2c..h	6	3	6	0	0	Mongolian: Kalmyk*	PNb	b
6011	Karachai (Alan)	0.05893	2,694	2,769	3,592	MSY41z	44-AABB-a	literary karachay-balkar		0.00	0	1c.u.	0	2	3	0	1	Karachay-balkar	PN.	.
6012	Kazakh	0.87647	40,067	41,188	53,431	MSY41e	44-AABC-c	kazakh		0.00	0	4A.u.	0	3	3	0	2	Kazakh	PN.	b
6013	Khalka Mongol (Mongolian)	0.00200	91	94	122	MSY41f	44-BAAB-c	halh		0.00	0	3A..h	0	1	3	0	0	Mongolian: Khalka*	PNb	b
6014	Kirghiz	59.82796	2,734,995	2,811,517	3,647,230	MSY41g	44-AABC-d	kirghiz		0.02	562	2r.u.	3	3	3	0	3	Kirghiz	PN.	b
6015	Korean	0.43110	19,707	20,259	26,281	MSY46	45-AAAA-b	kukö		20.00	4,052	2A...	9	6	13	3	1	Korean	PNB	b
6016	Kurdish	0.33497	15,313	15,741	20,420	CNT24c	58-AAAA-a	kurmanji		0.02	3	3c...	3	3	3	0	0	Kurdish: Kurmanji*	PN.	b
6017	Lezgin	0.05855	2,677	2,751	3,569	CEW17b	42-BCAA-a	lezgin		0.01	0	1....	3	4	0	0	1	Lezgi	P..	b
6018	Lithuanian	0.01158	529	544	706	CEW15b	54-AAAA-a	standard lietuvishkai		85.00	463	3A.u.	10	8	11	2	3	Lithuanian	PNB	b
6019	Moldavian	0.04404	2,013	2,070	2,685	CEW21f	51-AADC-ab	standard moldavia		82.00	1,697	1A.u.	10	7	10	2	1		pnb	b
6020	Mordvinian	0.08967	4,099	4,214	5,466	MSW51i	41-AADA-b	moksha		65.00	2,739	1....	10	8	8	2	1	Mordvin: Moksha*	Pn.	b
6021	Ossete	0.01780	814	836	1,085	CNT24e	58-ABBA	oseti cluster		36.00	301	2....	9	5	8	1	1	Ossete*	PN.	b
6022	Polish	0.03262	1,491	1,533	1,989	CEW22i	53-AAAC-c	polski		91.00	1,395	2A.uh	10	8	9	2	3	Polish	PNB	b
6023	Russian	16.00000	731,429	751,894	975,392	CEW22j	53-AAAE-d	russkiy	84	45.00	338,352	4B.uh	9	8	10	3	3	Russian	PNB	b
6024	Tadzhik (Persian Tajik)	0.78722	35,987	36,994	47,990	CNT24g	58-AACC-j	tajiki		0.00	0	2asu.	0	3	3	0	0	Tajik*	PNB	b
6025	Tatar	1.64566	75,230	77,335	100,323	MSY41h	44-AABB-e	tatar		1.50	1,160	2c.u.	6	4	8	0	1	Tatar: Kazan	Pn.	b
6026	Turkish	0.50012	22,863	23,502	30,488	MSY41j	44-AABA-a	osmanli		0.00	0	1A.u.	0	3	2	0	0	Turkish	PNB	b
6027	Turkmen	0.02111	965	992	1,287	MSY41k	44-AABA-e	turkmen		0.00	0	3c.u.	0	3	2	0	2	Turkmen	PNb	b
6028	Udmurt	0.01651	755	776	1,006	MSW51k	41-AAEA-c	udmurt		55.00	427	2....	10	5	8	2	1	Udmurt	Pn.	.
6029	Uighur (Kashgar Turki)	0.86381	39,488	40,593	52,660	MSY41z	44-AABD-d	east uyghur		0.00	0	1r.u.	0	3	2	0	2	Uighur*	PNB	b
6030	Ukrainian	1.90000	86,857	89,287	115,828	CEW22p	53-AAAE-b	ukrainskiy		75.00	66,966	3A.uh	10	7	11	3	3	Ukrainian	PNB	b
6031	Uzbek	13.20000	603,429	620,312	804,698	MSY41l	44-AABD-a	central uzbek		0.00	0	1A.u.	0	3	6	1	3	Uzbek*	PNb	b
6032	other minor peoples	0.20000	9,143	9,399	12,192	...				50.00	4,699		10	5	8	2	0			
	Kiribati	**100.00000**	**77,658**	**83,387**	**119,324**					**92.74**	**77,331**									
6033	British	0.59000	458	492	704	CEW19i	52-ABAC-b	standard-english	8	79.00	389	3Bsuh	10	9	13	5	1		PNB	b
6034	Euronesian	1.30000	1,010	1,084	1,551	MPY53	52-ABAC-bv	standard oceanian-english		92.00	997	1Bsuh	10	8	11	5	2		pnb	b
6035	Han Chinese	0.10000	78	83	119	MSY42a	79-AAAB-ba	kuo-yü		54.00	45	2Bsuh	10	6	10	4	3	Chinese: Kuoyu*	PNB	b
6036	Kiribertese (Gilbertese)	97.31000	75,569	81,144	116,114	MPY54a	38-DAAA-a	i-kiribati		92.90	75,383	3.s..	10	9	12	5	1	Kiribati	PNB	b
6037	Tuvaluan	0.50000	388	417	597	MPY55z	39-CAKB-a	funafuti		92.00	384	0....	10	8	13	5	2	Tuvaluan	PNB	b
6038	other minor peoples	0.20000	155	167	239	...				80.00	133		10	7	8	5	0			
	Kuwait	**100.00000**	**1,689,533**	**1,971,634**	**2,974,454**					**12.55**	**247,536**									
6039	Arabized Black	1.60000	27,033	31,546	47,591	NAB57j	12-AACF-p	zanji		5.00	1,577	1Asuh	7	5	2	1	0		pnb	b
6040	Armenian	1.00000	16,895	19,716	29,745	CEW14	57-AAAA-b	ashkharik		90.00	17,745	4A.u.	10	9	13	5	2	Armenian: Modern, Eastern	PNB	b
6041	Assyrian (Aisor, Chaldean	0.20000	3,379	3,943	5,949	CMT31	12-AAAA-d	east syriac		78.00	3,076	1as..	10	8	10	5	2	Syriac: Ancient*	PNB	b
6042	British	0.30000	5,069	5,915	8,923	CEW19i	52-ABAC-b	standard-english	60	79.00	4,673	3Bsuh	10	9	13	5	1		PNB	b
6043	Egyptian Arab	0.50000	8,448	9,858	14,872	CMT30	12-AACF-a	masri		24.00	2,366	2Asuh	9	8	8	4	1	Arabic*	PNB	b
6044	French	0.20000	3,379	3,943	5,949	CEW21b	51-AABI-d	general français	5	87.00	3,431	1B.uh	10	9	14	5	1	French	PNB	b
6045	Greek	0.04000	676	789	1,190	CEW20	56-AAAA-c	dhimotiki		95.00	749	2B.uh	10	9	11	5	2	Greek: Modern	PNB	b
6046	Iraqi Arab	3.50000	59,134	69,007	104,106	CMT30	12-AACF-g	syro-mesopotamian		0.70	483	1Asuh	5	3	8	1	2		pnb	b
6047	Jordanian Arab	9.58000	161,857	188,883	284,953	CMT30	12-AACF-f	syro-palestinian		12.00	22,666	1Asuh	8	5	8	3	3	Arabic: Lebanese*	Pnb	b
6048	Kurdish (Kurd)	9.60000	162,195	189,277	285,548	CNT24c	58-AAAA-c	kurdi		0.03	57	2c...	3	3	2	1	1	Kurdi	PN.	b
6049	Kuwaiti Arab	30.00000	506,860	591,490	892,336	CMT30	12-AACF-i	kuwayti-qatari		7.40	43,770	1Asuh	7	4	7	5	3		pnb	b
6050	Lebanese Arab	3.30000	55,755	65,064	98,157	CMT30	12-AACF-f	syro-palestinian		45.00	29,279	1Asuh	9	8	8	5	1	Arabic: Lebanese*	Pnb	b
6051	Mahra (Mehri)	0.75000	12,671	14,787	22,308	CMT30	12-ABAA-a	mahri		0.02	3	0....	3	2	2	0	0	Mehri	P..	b
6052	Malayali	6.80000	114,888	134,071	202,263	CNN23b	49-EBEB-a	malayalam		42.00	56,310	2Asu.	9	8	9	5	2	Malayalam	PNB	b
6053	Najdi Bedouin	9.00000	152,058	177,447	267,701	CMT30	12-AACF-j	north `anazi		0.01	18	1csuh	3	4	6	0	0		pnb	.
6054	Omani Arab	0.50000	8,448	9,858	14,872	CMT30	12-AACF-l	omani		0.10	10	1Asuh	5	3	4	0	0		pnb	b
6055	Palestinian Arab	17.00000	287,221	335,178	505,657	CMT30	12-AACF-f	syro-palestinian		17.00	56,980	1Asuh	8	5	8	5	1	Arabic: Lebanese*	Pnb	b
6056	Persian	4.20000	70,960	82,809	124,927	CNT24f	58-AACC-c	standard farsi		0.04	33	1Asu.	3	3	3	1	0		PNB	b
6057	Punjabi	0.30000	5,069	5,915	8,923	CNN25n	59-AAFE-c	general panjabi		2.00	118	1Asu.	6	4	8	3	0		PNB	b
6058	Saudi Arab	0.30000	5,069	5,915	8,923	CMT30	12-AACF-k	central `anazi		0.41	24	4Asuh	5	4	4	5	0		pnb	b
6059	Syrian Arab	0.50000	8,448	9,858	14,872	CMT30	12-AACF-f	syro-palestinian		7.30	720	1Asuh	7	5	8	4	1	Arabic: Lebanese*	Pnb	b
6060	Tamil	0.11000	1,858	2,169	3,272	CNN23c	49-EBEA-b	tamil		11.70	254	2Asu.	8	7	8	5	2	Tamil	PNB	b
6061	Telugu	0.02000	338	394	595	CNN23d	49-DBAB-a	telugu		9.00	35	2Asu.	7	7	8	5	2	Telugu	PNB	b
6062	USA White	0.20000	3,379	3,943	5,949	CEW19s	52-ABAC-s	general american		78.00	3,076	1Bsuh	10	9	13	5	3	English*	PNB	b
6063	Urdu	0.10000	1,690	1,972	2,974	CNN25r	59-AAFO-d	standard urdu		0.10	2	2Asuh	5	4	2	1	0	Urdu	PNB	b
6064	Yemeni Arab	0.20000	3,379	3,943	5,949	CMT30	12-AACF-n	yemeni		0.06	2	1Asuh	4	3	5	1	0		pnb	b
6065	other minor peoples	0.20000	3,379	3,943	5,949	...				2.00	79		6	4	2	5	0			
	Laos	**100.00000**	**4,773,323**	**5,433,036**	**9,652,526**					**2.07**	**112,561**									
6066	Akha (Kaw, Khako)	0.13569	6,477	7,372	13,098	MSY50z	77-BBAA-d	akha		5.00	369	1....	7	5	5	1	0	Akha	PN.	b
6067	Alak	0.09138	4,362	4,965	8,820	AUG03z	46-FACB-a	south alak		3.00	149	0.s..	6	3	4	0	0		pn.	.
6068	Angku	0.10000	4,773	5,433	9,653	AUG03z	46-DBBA-d	pou-ma		4.00	217	0....	6	4	7	1	0		...	b
6069	Arem	0.01400	668	761	1,351	MSY52z	46-EABA-d	arem		1.00	8	0....	6	4	4	0	0		...	.
6070	Bit	0.04256	2,032	2,312	4,108	AUG03z	46-DDAA-a	kha-bit		1.00	23	0....	6	4	4	0	0		...	.
6071	Black Lahu (Musso)	0.07440	3,551	4,042	7,181	MSY50i	77-BBAB-a	lahu	3	40.00	1,617	4a...	9	6	13	4	2	Lahu*	PNB	b
6072	Black Tai (Tribal Tai)	0.80000	38,187	43,464	77,220	MSY49z	47-AAAD-a	tai-dam		4.00	1,739	0....	6	4	6	2	2	Tai: Dam*	P..	b
6073	Blue Meo (Miao)	1.70000	81,146	92,362	164,093	MSY47a	48-AAAA-bd	tak		7.00	6,465	1A...	7	5	9	5	3		pn.	.
6074	Bo	0.06092	2,908	3,310	5,880	AUG03z	46-EAAA	muong-bo cluster		1.54	51	0as..	6	4	6	2	0		P..	.
6075	Boloven (Love, Laweenjru)	0.76150	36,349	41,373	73,504	AUG03z	46-FADA-a	laven		2.00	827	0....	6	4	4	2	0		...	.
6076	Brao (Proue, Love)	0.30400	14,511	16,516	29,344	AUG03z	46-FADA-a	laven		1.00	165	0....	6	4	4	4	3		...	.
6077	British	0.00700	334	380	676	CEW19i	52-ABAC-b	standard-english	10	79.00	300	3Bsuh	10	9	13	5	3		PNB	b
6078	Cambodian (Central Khmer)	0.29579	14,119	16,070	28,551	AUG03b	46-FBAA-b	khmae		0.10	16	2A...	5	4	8	5	3	Khmer*	PNB	b
6079	Cambodian Cham (West Cham	0.30000	14,320	16,299	28,958	MSY44z	31-MBBC-b	west cham		0.04	7	0.s..	3	3	0	1	1	Cham, Western	p..	b
6080	Chinese Shan	2.60000	124,106	141,259	250,966	MSY49a	47-AAAA-f	tai-neua		0.00	0	1.s..	0	3	5	0	0	Chinese: Shanghai*	PNB	.
6081	Con	0.06563	3,133	3,566	6,335	AUG03z	46-DBCA-a	con		1.00	36	0....	6	4	4	1	0		...	.
6082	Eastern Bru (Vankieu)	1.42207	67,880	77,262	137,266	AUG03z	46-FAAA-ea	bru-laos		1.00	773	0.s..	6	4	4	5	2	Bru, Eastern	PN.	.
6083	Flowery Meo (Miao Hwa)	1.15000	54,893	62,480	111,004	MSY47a	48-AAAA-b	hmong-njua	2	7.00	4,374	1A...	7	5	9	4	2	Hmong Njua	PN.	b
6084	French	0.03000	1,432	1,630	2,896	CEW21b	51-AABI-d	general français	35	87.00	1,418	1B.uh	10	9	8	5	2	French	PNB	b
6085	Halang	0.09921	4,736	5,390	9,576	AUG03z	46-FACA-c	halang		1.50	81	0....	6	4	4	4	1	Halang	P..	.
6086	Halang Doan (Duan)	0.04444	2,121	2,414	4,290	AUG03z	46-FACA-g	doan		1.00	24	0....	6	4	4	1	0		p..	.
6087	Han Chinese (Cantonese)	1.00000	47,733	54,330	96,525	MSY42a	79-AAAM-a	central yue	2	0.80	435	3A.uh	5	8	8	5	0	Chinese, Yue	PNB	b
6088	Han Chinese (Mandarin)	0.71104	33,940	38,631	68,633	MSY42a	79-AAAB-ba	kuo-yü	6	0.70	270	2Bsuh	5	9	8	5	1	Chinese: Kuoyu*	PNB	b
6089	Hani (Ho, Haw, Woni)	0.63260	30,196	34,369	61,062	MSY50i	77-BBAA	hani cluster		5.00	1,718	1....	7	5	5	1	0		PN.	b
6090	Highland Nung (Thai Nung)	1.00000	47,733	54,330	96,525	MSY49a	47-AAAE-b	tai-nung		0.70	380	0....	5	4	4	1	1	Nung	P..	b
6091	Highland Yao (Mien, Myen)	1.22905	58,667	66,775	118,634	MSY47b	48-ABAA-b	iu-mien		1.64	1,095	0.s..	6	4	6	1	2	Iu Mien	PN.	b

Continued opposite

Table 8-2 continued

EVANGELIZATION								EVANGELISM			ADDITIONAL DESCRIPTIVE DATA
Ref 1	D 28	aC 29	CG% 30	r 31	E 32	U 33	W 34	e 35	R 36	T 37	Locations, civil divisions, literacy, religions, church history, denominations, dioceses, church growth, missions, agencies, ministries, movements 38
5976	0	10	4.18	6	75.00	25.00	B	54.75	189	6	From South India. Hindus 74%, Muslims 5%, Baha'is 1%.
5977	4	9	7.23	0	99.68	0.32	C	302.80	186	9	Taita District. Also in Tanzania. Bilingual in Swahili. Animists 17%, Muslims 15%. D=CPK(D-Mombasa),RCC(D-Mombasa),LMC,MRFPC. M=CMS,CSSp.
5978	3	6	6.85	1	99.50	0.50	B	184.32	213	7	Nandi District, Rift Valley Province. Animists 45%. D=AIC,RCC,CPK.
5979	4	8	10.33	1	99.78	0.22	C	383.29	235	9	Busia District. Majority in Uganda. Animists 19%. D=RCC(D-Kisumu),CPK,SA,GAK. M=MHM.
5980	2	9	4.37	0	99.80	0.20	C	344.56	125	9	Refugees from northeast Karamoja(Uganda). Animists 18%. D=CPK,RCC.
5981	7	9	8.80	1	95.20	4.80	B	129.26	283	7	Eastern Meru District. Close to Meru. Animists 61%. D=RCC,MCK,CPK,PCEA,AIC,EAPC,AICs. M=BSK,BTL.
5982	2	8	9.78	1	99.56	0.44	B	226.05	268	8	West central Kenya. Related to Kalenjin. Animists 30%. D=AIC,RCC. M=AIM.
5983	9	6	9.33	0	66.00	34.00	B	48.18	450	6	West & south of Lake Turkana. Nomads, pastoralists in semi-arid desert. Animists 87%. D=AIC,SA,FGCK,LCK,RCC,UPEC,EFMK,CPK,RCEA. M=IMC,SFM,LM,PI.
5984	7	10	7.11	8	99.80	0.20	C	449.68	143	10	Expatriates from USA, in education, business. D=SDA,AoG,CPK,RCC,CJCLdS,JWs,CCS.
5985	3	8	7.04	0	70.00	30.00	B	61.32	333	6	Upper Tana river, flood plain. Agriculturalists, fishermen. Muslims 75%(Shafi Sunnis). D=MCK,EAPC,RCC. M=FMB.
5986	2	2	1.96	0	38.00	62.00	A	15.25	213	5	Hunter-gatherers, nomads. Nearly extinct. All bilingual, all over 40 years old. Animists 89%. D=CPK,EAPC. M=DMA-CPK.
5987	4	8	3.23	4	64.00	36.00	B	14.01	181	5	Mukogodo Forest west of Doldol. Hunter-gatherers, nomads. Animists 94%. D=PCEA,CPK,RCC,EAPC. M=CMS,DMA-CPK.
5988	0	0	0.70	7	30.01	69.99	A	0.01	128	2	Immigrants from Yemen. Muslims (Shafi Sunnis) 100%.
5989	0	10	0.00	5	37.00	63.00	A	0.00	0	1.13	Immigrants from Zanzibar island, Tanzania. Muslims 100%(Shafi Sunnis).
5990	0	10	5.90		62.00	38.00	B	67.89	261	6	Shona(ACJM), Germans(NAC), Kongo(EJCSK), Koreans(HSAUWC,PCK-H), Egyptians(COC), Amhara(SIM), Nigerians. Muslims 40%, Jains 20%, Animists 5%.
Kirghizia											
5991	1	8	3.39	6	99.70	0.30	C	347.48	80	9	Gregorians, from Armenia. Nonreligious 30%. D=Armenian Apostolic Ch.
5992	0	8	0.00	0	19.01	80.99	A	0.00	0	1.07	Mainly in Dagestan (Russia). Muslims 100%(Shafi Sunnis). M=IBT.
5993	1	5	0.00	1	27.00	73.00	A	0.00	0	1.12	73% monolingual. Muslims 80%(60% Shias, 30% Hanafi Sunnis 20%), nonreligious 20%. D=ROC. M=IBT,CSI.
5994	0	8	0.00	1	20.00	80.00	A	0.00	0	1.09	Mainly in Russia, some in USA. Superficially 100% Muslims(Hanafi Sunnis).
5995	1	9	2.95	4	49.00	51.00	A	12.52	210	5	Many speak Tatar as mother tongue. Muslims 72%(Hanafi Sunnis), nonreligious 20%. D=Russian Orthodox Ch.
5996	1	8	3.95	6	99.72	0.28	C	346.89	108	9	From Bulgaria; also in 12 other countries. Nonreligious 18%, atheists 10%. D=Bulgarian Orthodox Ch. M=LBI.
5997	4	7	3.83	5	99.70	0.30	C	347.48	97	9	White Russians. Also in Russia, Ukraine, Baltic states, USA, Canada, Poland. Nonreligious 30%. D=Russian Orthodox Ch,RCC,Old Ritualist Chs,ECB.
5998	0	6	0.00	1	23.00	77.00	A	0.00	0	1.12	Bukharian. Centered on Bokhara (Uzbekistan). Also in Israel, USA. Religious Jews, many practicing.
5999	0	8	0.00	0	18.00	82.00	A	0.00	0	1.05	Nokhchuo. From Chechen, Ingush (Russia). 76% speak Russian. Highly religious Muslims 63%(Hanafi Sunnis, strongly Sufi), atheists 20%, nonreligious 17%.
6000	1	8	4.48	0	74.00	26.00	B	94.53	196	6	From Chuvashia (Russia). Muslims 35%(Sunnis), nonreligious 30%. D=Russian Orthodox Ch. M=IBT.
6001	0	7	0.00	1	25.00	75.00	A	0.00	0	1.11	Descendants of 13th-century Mongols. 1944 deported to Uzbek SSR. Muslims 100%(Hanafi Sunnis). M=IBT.
6002	0	8	0.00	0	22.01	77.99	A	0.00	0	1.07	In Dagestan (Russia). 65% speak Russian. Muslims 100%(Shafi Sunnis, some Shias). M=IBT.
6003	0	9	0.00	7	38.00	62.00	A	0.00	0	1.13	Dzhunyan, Tungan. Also in Uzbekistan, Kazakhstan. Nomads. 100% Chinese Muslims(strict Hanafi Sunnis); migrated here in 1867 from northwest China.
6004	5	9	3.56	5	99.70	0.30	C	339.81	97	9	Most are bilingual in Russian. Nonreligious 20%. D=Russian Orthodox Ch,ELCE,RCC,MCE,AUCECB. M=UBS,LBI.
6005	1	8	4.53	4	95.00	5.00	B	138.70	131	7	From Georgia. Nonreligious/atheists 55%, Muslims 5%(Sunnis, Shias). D=Georgian Orthodox Ch.
6006	3	9	5.70	8	99.80	0.20	C	446.76	122	10	Also Altai, Kazakhstan. Nonreligious 20%. D=German Evangelical Lutheran Ch,Old Mennonites,AUCECB.
6007	2	9	2.93	7	99.90	0.10	C	519.03	68	10	Immigrants, merchants from Greece. D=GOC,ROC. M=UBS,LBI.
6008	0	8	0.00	0	16.00	84.00	A	0.00	0	1.04	From Chechen, Ingush (Russia). All deported 1944-57. Muslims 100%(fervent Hanafi Sunnis). M=IBT.
6009	0	8	0.00	5	42.00	58.00	A	0.00	0	1.10	Bilingual in Russian. Religious Jews. Many have emigrated to Israel, then returned.
6010	0	8	4.11	1	38.00	62.00	A	1.38	352	4	From Kalmykia on Volga (Russia). Buddhists 70%(Lamaists), nonreligious 30%.
6011	0	9	0.00	1	22.00	78.00	A	0.00	0	1.09	Karachi-Cherkess AO. Muslims 100%(Hanafi Sunnis). M=SIL.
6012	0	7	0.00	4	34.00	66.00	A	0.00	0	1.10	Muslims 60%(Hanafi Sunnis, with Sufi influence), nonreligious 30%, atheists 10%. M=ROC,CSI.
6013	0	7	0.00	4	35.00	65.00	A	0.00	0	1.11	Also in Buryatia (Russia). From Mongolia. Nonreligious 50%, shamanists 30%, atheists 16%, Lamaist Buddhists 3%.
6014	0	7	4.11	4	33.02	66.98	A	0.02	399	2	Also in China, Afghanistan, Turkey. Nomadic pastoralists. 29% speak Russian. Muslims 74%(Hanafi Sunnis), nonreligious 20%, atheists 5%, shamanists, Lamaists.
6015	1	8	6.19	6	84.00	16.00	B	61.32	222	6	45% now speak Russian only. Nonreligious 40%, shamanists 20%, Buddhists 15%, atheists 5%. D=KMC. M=CSI.
6016	0	6	1.10	0	25.02	74.98	A	0.01	339	2	Scattered groups across Central Asia and in its cities. Muslims 80%(Shias, Yazidis), nonreligious 20%.
6017	0	7	0.00	0	19.01	80.99	A	0.00	0	1.06	Also in south Dagestan (Russia). 50% understand Russian. Muslims 100%(Shafi Sunnis). M=IBT.
6018	3	8	3.91	5	99.85	0.15	C	465.37	71	10	Found in 24 countries. Strong Catholics. Nonreligious 15%. D=RCC,ERCL,ROC.
6019	1	7	5.27	6	99.82	0.18	C	410.04	125	10	From Moldavia (Bessarabia). Nonreligious 15%. D=Russian Orthodox Ch.
6020	1	7	6.31	1	99.65	0.35	C	251.48	163	8	Residents from Mordvinia (Russia). Acculturated to Russian. Nonreligious 30%. D=ROC. M=IBT.
6021	1	7	3.46	0	75.00	25.00	B	98.55	167	6	Mainly in Russia, Georgia; also Syria, Turkey. Muslims 55%(Sunnis), nonreligious 9%. D=ROC.
6022	4	9	3.27	6	99.91	0.09	C	521.47	57	10	Poles. 29% speak Polish as mother tongue. D=RCC,ROC,CEF,CWE.
6023	8	9	3.58	7	99.45	0.55	B	192.17	84	7	In 70 countries. Nonreligious 37%, atheists 15%. D=ROC,RCC,AUCECB,Old Ritualists,CEF,CCECB,SDA,IPKH. R=FEBC,HCJB,TWR,KNLS,VERITAS,AWR.
6024	0	7	0.00	4	36.00	64.00	A	0.00	0	1.12	Also in Uzbekistan, Tajikistan. Most are trilingual (with Uzbek, Russian). Muslims 90%(Hanafi Sunnis,also some Shias), nonreligious 10%.
6025	1	7	4.87	6	42.50	57.50	A	2.32	366	4	70% bilingual in Russian. Muslims 83%(Hanafi Sunnis), nonreligious 15%. D=ROC(Kryashen).
6026	0	6	0.00	8	36.00	64.00	A	0.00	0	1.11	Across Central Asia. Muslims 98%(83% Hanafi Sunnis,15% Alawi Shias).
6027	0	7	0.00	1	27.00	73.00	A	0.00	0	1.11	In Turkmenistan, Iran, Afghanistan, Uzbekistan, et alia. Devout Muslims 95%(Hanafi Sunnis), nonreligious 5%. M=IBT,AFM.
6028	1	7	3.83	0	92.00	8.00	B	184.69	144	7	From Udmurtia (Russia). Strong shamanists/animists 40%, nonreligious 5%. D=ROC.
6029	0	6	0.00	4	32.00	68.00	A	0.00	0	1.11	Also in Kazakhstan, Uzbekistan. In 15 countries. Settled agriculturalists. Muslims 100%(Hanafi Sunnis, with heavy Sufi influence). M=IBT,WEC.
6030	7	8	2.55	6	99.75	0.25	C	396.93	71	9	In 15 countries. Nonreligious/atheists 25%. D=ROC(E-Ukraine),Ukrainian Catholic Ch,AUCECB,CEF,CCECB,JWs,SDA.
6031	0	8	0.00	5	41.00	59.00	A	0.00	0	1.12	55% Russian-speaking. Literates 100%. Muslims 80%(Hanafi Sunnis), nonreligious/atheists 20%. M=ROC,AUCECB,CSI. R=HCJB,FEBC,KTWR.
6032	0	7	6.35		76.00	24.00	B	138.70	229	7	Czechs, Hungarians, Romanians, Iranians, Arabs, Indians, Parsis. Muslims 30%, nonreligious 10%, Zoroastrians 10%.
Kiribati											
6033	3	10	1.41	8	99.79	0.21	C	438.29	46	10	Expatriates from Britain, in education, business. D=Anglican Ch(D-Polynesia),JWs,SDA. M=CPNZ.
6034	6	10	1.41	8	99.92	0.08	C	530.56	38	10	Mixed-race Polynesian/European. D=RCC,GIPC,AC,SDA,JWs,COG. M=MSC,CPNZ.
6035	5	10	1.42	7	99.54	0.46	B	248.34	45	8	Immigrants from Chinese diaspora. Nonreligious 33%, Buddhists. 13%. D=RCC,GIPC,AC,SDA,JWs.
6036	4	6	1.34	4	99.93	0.07	C	528.63	35	10	Also in Solomons, Nauru, Fiji, Tuvalu, Vanuatu. Literates 90%. Baha'is 5%. D=Gilbert Islands Protestant Ch,RCC(D-Tarawa),SDA,COG. M=MSC.
6037	2	10	1.42	5	99.92	0.08	C	520.49	34	10	From Tuvalu. Immigrants, laborers, professionals. D=GIPC,RCC.
6038	0	10	1.40		99.80	0.20	C	327.04	34	9	Indians, other Pacific Islanders.
Kuwait											
6039	0	8	5.19	7	51.00	49.00	B	9.30	357	4	Black Africans: immigrants, slaves, descendants of slaves. Islamized. Muslims 95%(Sunnis).
6040	2	10	6.49	6	99.90	0.10	C	542.02	118	10	Refugees from Turkey after 1915. Gregorians. Nonreligious 10%. D=Armenian Apostolic Ch(V-Kuwait),RCC(Armenian-rite).
6041	2	10	3.76	5	99.78	0.22	C	415.66	83	10	Many migrants from Iraq. Nestorians. D=Ancient Ch of the East,RCC(Chaldean-rite: VA-Kuwait).
6042	3	10	5.11	8	99.79	0.21	C	444.05	111	10	Expatriates from Britain, in education, business. D=Anglican Ch/ECJME(D-Cyprus & The Gulf),CB,NECK. M=RCA.
6043	1	10	6.00	8	91.00	9.00	B	79.71	202	6	Migrant workers from Egypt. Muslims 75%. D=Coptic Orthodox Ch(P-Alexandria).
6044	1	10	6.01	8	99.87	0.13	C	501.72	121	10	Expatriates from France, in business. Nonreligious 13%. D=RCC(VA-Kuwait). M=OCD.
6045	2	10	4.78	7	99.95	0.05	C	579.07	95	10	Traders from Greece. D=RCC(Melkites),Greek Orthodox Ch(P-Antioch).
6046	2	10	3.95	7	55.70	44.30	B	1.42	229	4	Migrant workers from Iraq. Muslims 99%(60% Shias,39% Hanafi Sunnis). D=RCC,GOC.
6047	3	9	8.42	8	76.00	24.00	B	33.28	329	5	Migrant workers from Jordan. Muslims 88%. D=RCC,ECJME,GOC.
6048	1	9	4.13	0	28.03	71.97	A	0.03	599	2	Refugees from Iran-Iraq wars. Muslims 100%(Shafi Sunnis). D=NECK.
6049	3	7	8.75	7	68.40	31.60	B	18.47	379	5	Eastern Colloquial Arabic. Muslims(Maliki and other Sunnis) 92%. D=RCC(VA-Kuwait),GOC,NECK. M=RCA,OCD,FMB,FI,MEM. R=FEBA,AWR.
6050	1	10	8.11	8	99.45	0.55	B	179.03	221	7	Traders from Lebanon. Muslims 45%. D=RCC(Maronites). M=OCD.
6051	0	8	1.10	0	18.02	81.98	A	0.01	274	2	Originally from Al-Mahrah (Yemen) between Hadramaut and Oman. Vast majority live in Oman; also in Yemen, Saudi Arabia. Muslims 100%(Sunnis).
6052	4	10	9.02	4	99.42	0.58	B	168.63	250	7	From Kerala(India). Hindus 38%, Muslims 19%. D=Orthodox Syrian Ch of India,MTSC(D-Bahya Kerala),NECK,RCC. M=CSI,OSCE. 10% of all Christian workers.
6053	0	0	2.93	1	22.01	77.99	A	0.00	452	1.11	In desert regions. Nomads. Muslims (Shafi Sunnis) 100%.
6054	0	8	2.33	7	44.10	55.90	A	0.16	188	3	Migrant workers from Oman. Muslims 100%(Sunnis).
6055	5	8	8.28	8	80.00	20.00	B	49.64	308	6	Migrant workers from Palestinian diaspora. Muslims 80%(Shafi Sunnis). D=RCC(VA-Kuwait),GOC(P-Antioch),Anglican Ch/ECJME,NECK,CB. M=OCD.
6056	0	10	3.56	5	45.04	54.96	A	0.06	259	2	Workers from Iran. Muslims 98%(Imami Shias), Baha'is 2%.
6057	0	10	2.50	5	57.00	43.00	B	4.16	171	4	Workers from India and Pakistan. Sikhs 50%, Hindus 26%, Muslims 22%.
6058	0	8	3.23	7	52.41	47.59	B	0.78	205	3	Migrant workers from Saudi Arabia. Muslims 100%(Shafis,Malikis,Hanbalis).
6059	1	10	5.10	8	66.30	33.70	B	17.66	240	5	Migrant workers from Syria. Muslims 92%(Hanafi Sunnis,Alawi Shias). D=Syrian Orthodox Ch.
6060	3	10	3.29	6	77.70	22.30	B	33.18	151	5	From Tamil Nadu, South India. Hindus 82%, Muslims 5%. D=RCC,NECK,CB. M=OCD,RCA.
6061	3	10	3.62	5	73.00	27.00	B	23.98	173	5	From Andhra Pradesh, South India. Hindus 84%. D=RCC,NECK,CB. M=OCD,RCA.
6062	4	10	5.90	8	99.78	0.22	C	435.59	122	10	Expatriates from USA, in commerce, education. D=NECK,RCC,ECJME,CB.
6063	0	8	0.70	5	46.10	53.90	A	0.16	103	3	Workers from Pakistan, India. Muslims 100% (Sunnis, some Shias).
6064	0	8	0.70	7	45.06	54.94	A	0.09	85	2	Migrant workers from Yemen. Muslims 100%(Zaydi Shias,Shafi Sunnis,Ahmadis).
6065	0	9	4.47		24.00	76.00	A	1.75	510	4	Other Arabs, Europeans, Asians, Africans. Muslims 95%.
Laos											
6066	0	6	3.67	0	31.00	69.00	A	5.65	422	4	North and northwest. Mainly in Burma, China, Thailand, also Viet Nam. Animists 30%, Theravada Buddhists 65%.
6067	0	6	2.74	1	26.00	74.00	A	2.84	394	4	Southern Laos, mainly Saravane Province. Closest to Bahnar, Tampuan, Lamam. Montagnards. 10% literates. Animists 97%.
6068	0	4	3.13	0	24.00	76.00	A	3.50	472	4	Along west bank of Mekong river. Also in Burma, China, Thailand. Buddhists 95%(Hinayana).
6069	0	6	2.10	0	19.00	81.00	A	0.69	418	3	West central, both sides of border with Viet Nam, west of Phuc Trach. Many ethnic names. Animists 99%.
6070	0	6	3.19	0	19.00	81.00	A	0.69	604	3	Near northern border with China, southeast of Nam Tha. Related to Khao. Animists 99%.
6071	2	6	5.22	4	99.40	0.60	B	147.46	171	7	Black/Red/Yellow Lahu, Southern Lahu. Mainly in China, Burma; also Thailand. Animists 50%, Mahayana Buddhists 10%. D=TSPM,RCC. M=OMF,ABMS. R=FEBC.
6072	2	6	5.29	4	36.00	64.00	A	5.25	448	4	Majority in Viet Nam; also China, USA, France. Animists 95%. Ancestor veneration plays essential role in traditional cultus. D=RCC,LEF. M=SIL,CMA.
6073	3	5	6.69	4	55.00	45.00	B	14.05	368	5	Also in Thailand, France, north Viet Nam, Burma, southwestern China, USA. Animists 90%. D=RCC,ACCM,LEF. M=OMF,CMA,CSI. R=FEBC.
6074	0	6	4.01	4	33.54	66.46	A	1.88	409	4	Central Laos inland from bend of Mekong, Nhang river around Nape. Animists 98%.
6075	0	6	4.51	0	22.00	78.00	A	1.60	686	4	Montagnards. Southwestern Laos, Boloven Plateau, near the Alak. Also in USA. Animists 98%.
6076	1	6	2.84	0	27.00	73.00	A	0.98	390	3	On border with Cambodia; also in USA. Montagnards. Animists 99%. D=RCC. M=MEP,OMI,SIL.
6077	3	10	3.46	8	99.79	0.21	C	441.17	83	10	Expatriates from Britain, in development. D=Anglican Ch(D-Singapore),JWs,RCC.
6078	1	6	2.81	5	52.10	47.90	B	0.19	222	3	Refugees from Cambodia. Also in Thailand, France, Viet Nam, USA. Theravada Buddhists 91%, animists 4%, nonreligious 3%, Baha'is 2%. D=RCC. M=KEC,MEP.
6079	1	5	1.96	1	16.04	83.96	A	0.02	422	2	Also called Khmer Islam. Mainly in Cambodia; also in Viet Nam, Malaysia, Thailand, USA, France, Saudi Arabia. Muslims 85%(Shafi Sunnis), Hindus 15%. D=RCC.
6080	0	4	0.00	1	24.00	76.00	A	0.00	0	1.09	Northwestern Laos. Majority in southern Yunnan (China); also Burma, north Viet Nam. Buddhists 100%(Hinayana).
6081	0	6	3.65	0	20.00	80.00	A	0.73	637	3	Northwestern corner, southwest of Vieng Pou Kha. Related to Lamet. Animists 99%.
6082	1	6	4.44	4	36.00	64.00	A	1.31	414	4	Savannehkhet Province. Also Thailand, USA. Montagnards. Animists 99%. D=RCC(with many catechumens). M=MEP,OMI.
6083	2	6	6.27	4	54.00	46.00	B	13.79	354	5	Also in Viet Nam (northwest Tonkin Province), Thailand, China (Guizhou, Guangxi, Sichuan, Yunnan). Polytheists 93%. D=RCC,LEF. M=BCM,CSI. R=FEBC.
6084	2	10	5.08	8	99.87	0.13	C	482.67	109	10	Expatriates from France, in development, business. D=RCC,LEF.
6085	0	6	4.49	4	29.50	70.50	A	1.61	510	4	Attopeu Province, southern Laos. Primarily in Viet Nam. Close to Jeh. Animists 98%. M=SIL.
6086	0	6	3.23	4	25.00	75.00	A	0.91	464	3	Attopeu Province, Kasseng Plateau. Also in Viet Nam. Animists 99%.
6087	0	10	3.84	8	59.80	40.20	B	1.74	206	4	Immigrants, long-time residents from China. In commerce. Folk-religionist/Buddhists 95%.
6088	1	10	3.35	7	61.70	38.30	B	1.57	178	4	Residents, immigrants from China in business. Chinese folk-religionists 80%, Taoists/Buddhists 18%. D=Christian Association.
6089	0	6	5.28	0	32.00	68.00	A	5.84	546	4	Vast majority in south Yunnan(China); also Burma, Viet Nam. Polytheists 64%(ancestor veneration), some Buddhists 31%.
6090	0	6	3.70	1	21.70	78.30	A	0.55	549	3	Mainly on both sides of Viet Nam/China border. Related to Tho, Southern Zhuang. Polytheists 99%(ancestor-worship). M=SIL.
6091	0	6	4.81	0	30.64	69.36	A	1.83	493	4	Also in Thailand, China, north Viet Nam. Polytheists 98% (ancestor veneration). M=OMF,ACCM. R=HCJB.

Continued overleaf

Table 8-2 continued

PEOPLE		POPULATION				IDENTITY CODE		LANGUAGE		CHURCH		MINISTRY						SCRIPTURE		
Ref 1	Ethnic name 2	P% 3	In 1995 4	In 2000 5	In 2025 6	Race 7	Language 8	Autoglossonym 9	S 10	AC 11	Members 12	Jayuh 13-17	d 18	wa 19	xc 20	mc 21	mi 22	Biblioglossonym 23	Pub 24-26	ss 27
6092	I (Yi, Lolo)	0.10000	4,773	5,433	9,653	MSY50i	77-BADA-a	nasô		1.00	54	1....	6	4	2	1	1	Nosu*	PN.	.
6093	Ir	0.31201	14,893	16,952	30,117	AUG03z	46-FABC-a	kha-in		0.10	17	0....	5	4	4	0	0		...	.
6094	Jeh	0.10000	4,773	5,433	9,653	AUG03z	46-FACA-b	jeh		1.00	54	0....	6	4	4	1	2	Jeh	P..	p
6095	Jeng (Cheng)	0.16448	7,851	8,936	15,876	AUG03z	46-FADE-c	cheng		1.00	89	0....	6	4	4	1	0		...	.
6096	Kado (Sak, Ganan)	0.20000	9,547	10,866	19,305	MSY50i	75-ABAA-a	kado		2.00	217	0....	6	4	5	0	0	Kadu*	P..	.
6097	Kaduo	0.15230	7,270	8,275	14,701	MSY50i	77-BBAA-f	kaduo		25.00	2,069	1....	9	4	5	1	0		pn.	.
6098	Kang	0.10000	4,773	5,433	9,653	MSY49z	77-BAAA-c	kang-siang-ying		1.80	98	0....	6	4	4	0	0		...	.
6099	Kantu (High Katu, Pilu)	1.15357	55,064	62,674	111,349	AUG03z	46-FABF-a	kantu		0.10	63	0....	5	4	4	0	0		pn.	.
6100	Kasseng	0.18276	8,724	9,929	17,641	AUG03z	46-FABH-a	kaseng		1.50	149	0....	6	4	4	1	0		...	.
6101	Katang (Kataang)	0.30460	14,540	16,549	29,402	AUG03z	46-FACA-d	kayong		0.10	17	0....	5	4	4	1	0		p..	.
6102	Katu (Teu, Kao, Thap)	0.50000	23,867	27,165	48,263	AUG03z	46-FABF-b	katu		2.00	543	0....	6	4	5	2	3	Katu	PN.	.
6103	Khatin (Tin, Mal, Lua)	0.38886	18,562	21,127	37,535	AUG03z	46-DDCA-a	mal		2.00	423	0....	6	4	4	4	3	Mal	PN.	.
6104	Khlor (Lor)	0.18393	8,780	9,993	17,754	AUG03z	46-FABD-c	khlor		5.00	500	0....	7	4	4	1	0		...	.
6105	Khmu (Lao-Theng)	10.84199	517,523	589,049	1,046,526	AUG03z	46-DDBA-a	kha-khmu		6.00	35,343	0....	7	5	10	5	3	Khmu'	P..	.
6106	Khmuic Pong	0.03046	1,454	1,655	2,940	AUG03z	46-EAAA-e	kha-pong		10.00	165	0cs..	8	5	6	2	0		p..	.
6107	Khouen (Kween)	0.10000	4,773	5,433	9,653	AUG03z	46-DDBA-b	khuen		1.00	54	0....	6	4	4	0	0	Khuen	p..	.
6108	Khua	0.10000	4,773	5,433	9,653	AUG03z	46-FAAA-d	khua		1.00	54	0.s..	6	4	4	0	0		pn.	.
6109	Kui (Sui, Old Khmer)	1.20000	57,280	65,196	115,830	AUG03z	46-FAAB-a	kuy		1.50	978	0....	6	4	5	4	1	Kuy	PN.	.
6110	La-Ven (Loven)	0.60000	28,640	32,598	57,915	AUG03z	46-FADA-a	laven		1.00	326	0....	6	4	4	0	1		...	.
6111	Lamet (Lemet)	0.39938	19,064	21,698	38,550	AUG03z	46-DBCA	lamet-khamet cluster		1.00	217	0....	6	4	4	0	0	Lamet	...	.
6112	Lao (Laotian Tai, Lao-Lu)	48.59915	2,319,794	2,640,409	4,691,046	MSY49b	47-AAAC-b	lao	95	0.80	21,123	2As..	5	4	9	5	3	Lao	PNB	b
6113	Lao Phuan	2.01000	95,944	109,204	194,016	MSY49z	47-AAAB-c	phuan		1.80	1,966	1csuh	6	4	4	0	0		pnb	b
6114	Leun (Muong Leung)	0.10000	4,773	5,433	9,653	AUG03z	46-FAAA-g	leung		1.00	54	0.s..	6	4	4	0	0		pn.	.
6115	Lower Taoih (Tong)	0.30000	14,320	16,299	28,958	AUG03z	46-FABB-a	ta'-oih		3.00	489	0....	6	4	5	1	0	Taoih, Upper	...	.
6116	Lowland Yao (Mun)	0.07374	3,520	4,006	7,118	MSY47b	48-ABAA-e	mun		1.50	60	0.s..	6	4	4	1	0		pn.	.
6117	Lu	0.71111	33,944	38,635	68,640	MSY49z	47-AAAA-g	tai-lü		1.80	695	1.s..	6	4	5	4	1	Lu	PNb	.
6118	Makong	0.06092	2,908	3,310	5,880	AUG03z	46-FAAA-c	mangkong		0.20	7	0.s..	5	4	5	1	0		pn.	b
6119	May	0.02000	955	1,087	1,931	MSY52z	46-EABA-b	may		1.00	11	0....	6	4	4	1	0		...	.
6120	Muong	0.07000	3,341	3,803	6,757	MSY52a	46-EAAA-a	muong		5.00	190	0as..	7	5	4	1	1	Muong	P..	.
6121	Muong Pong	0.01520	726	826	1,467	AUG03z	46-EAAA-e	kha-pong		3.00	25	0cs..	6	4	4	1	0		p..	.
6122	Ngeq (Nkriang)	0.12184	5,816	6,620	11,761	AUG03z	46-FABD-b	ngeq		65.00	4,303	0....	10	5	8	2	1	Ngeq	...	.
6123	Nguon	0.02500	1,193	1,358	2,413	MSY52z	46-EAAA-bb	nguồn-laos		5.00	68	0cs..	7	5	4	2	0		p..	.
6124	Northern Tai (Yuan)	0.17778	8,486	9,659	17,160	MSY49d	47-AAAB-a	yuan		1.00	97	1csuh	6	4	4	1	1	Tai, Northern	PNB	b
6125	Nyaheun	0.12200	5,823	6,628	11,776	AUG03z	46-FADB-a	nya-heun		2.00	133	0....	6	4	4	4	1		...	.
6126	Odu	0.00476	227	259	459	AUG03z	46-DDBA-c	hat		5.00	13	0....	7	4	4	0	0		p..	.
6127	Oy (Riyao)	0.32288	15,412	17,542	31,166	AUG03z	46-FADD-a	oi		1.50	263	0....	6	4	4	1	1		...	.
6128	Pacoh (Bo)	0.44000	21,003	23,905	42,471	AUG03z	46-FABE-a	pa-cùh		1.50	359	0....	6	4	4	4	1	Pacoh	P..	.
6129	Pakatan	0.01523	727	827	1,470	MSY52z	46-EACA	pakatan cluster		2.00	17	0....	6	4	4	1	0		...	.
6130	Phana	0.15230	7,270	8,275	14,701	MSY50i	77-BBAA-e	phana		5.00	414	1....	7	5	4	1	0		pn.	b
6131	Phon Sung	0.01530	730	831	1,477	AUG03z	77-AAAA-a	hpon		2.00	17	0....	6	4	5	0	0		...	.
6132	Phu Thai (Phuthai)	2.50000	119,333	135,826	241,313	MSY49z	47-AAAB-d	central thai		1.80	2,445	3asuh	6	4	4	1	0	Thai*	PNB	b
6133	Prai (Phai, Pray)	0.10000	4,773	5,433	9,653	AUG03z	46-DDCB-a	kha-phai		7.00	380	0....	7	5	6	2	2	Phai	p..	.
6134	Punoi	0.40000	19,093	21,732	38,610	MSY50i	77-BBBA-a	phunoi		1.00	217	0....	6	4	4	0	0		...	.
6135	Puok (Xinh Mul)	0.06020	2,874	3,271	5,811	AUG03z	46-DDEA-a	kha-puok		2.00	65	0....	6	4	4	1	0		...	.
6136	Red Tai (Tribal Tai)	0.58658	27,999	31,869	56,620	MSY49z	47-AAAD-c	tai-deng		2.00	637	0....	6	4	5	2	0		p..	.
6137	Ruc	0.01600	764	869	1,544	MSY52z	46-EABA-a	ruc		5.00	43	0....	7	5	4	1	0		...	.
6138	Russian	0.13912	6,641	7,558	13,429	CEW22j	53-AAAE-d	russkiy		30.00	2,268	4B.uh	9	5	11	4	1	Russian	PNB	b
6139	Saek (Tai Sek)	0.59000	28,163	32,055	56,950	MSY49z	47-AAAF-aa	saek-laos		0.20	64	0....	5	4	4	4	1		...	b
6140	Sapoin	0.05000	2,387	2,717	4,826	AUG03z	46-FAAA-h	sapoin		2.00	54	0.s..	6	4	5	1	0		pn.	.
6141	Sapuan	0.07310	3,489	3,972	7,056	AUG03z	46-FADE-b	sapuan		0.50	20	0....	5	4	4	4	1		...	.
6142	Sila	0.45690	21,809	24,824	44,102	MSY50i	77-BBCA-a	sila		1.00	248	0....	6	4	4	1	0		...	.
6143	So (Kah So, So Makon)	2.17096	103,627	117,949	209,552	AUG03z	46-FAAA	so-bru cluster		0.20	236	0.s..	5	4	4	4	3	So	PN.	b
6144	So Tri	0.13158	6,281	7,149	12,701	AUG03z	46-FAAA-c	mangkong		0.10	7	0.s..	5	4	4	1	0		pn.	b
6145	Sok	0.04874	2,327	2,648	4,705	AUG03z	46-FADE-a	sok		1.00	26	0....	6	4	4	1	0		...	.
6146	Sou	0.04444	2,121	2,414	4,290	AUG03z	46-FADC-b	su		1.00	24	0....	6	4	4	0	0		...	.
6147	Tai Loi (Doi, Wakut)	0.02000	955	1,087	1,931	AUG03z	47-AAAA-gb	lü		4.00	43	1.s..	6	5	7	1	0		pnb	.
6148	Talieng	0.10000	4,773	5,433	9,653	AUG03z	46-FACA	east bahnaric cluster		1.50	81	0....	6	4	4	0	0		P..	p
6149	Tareng	0.15230	7,270	8,275	14,701	AUG03z	46-FABG-a	tariang		2.00	165	0....	6	4	5	0	0		...	.
6150	Tay Pong (Tribal Tai)	0.50538	24,123	27,457	48,782	MSY52z	46-EAAA-e	kha-pong		2.00	549	0cs..	6	4	4	0	0		p..	.
6151	Thai (Central Tai)	2.00000	95,466	108,661	193,051	MSY49d	47-AAAB-d	central thai		0.60	652	3asuh	5	4	5	5	3	Thai*	PNB	b
6152	Thavung	0.01523	727	827	1,470	MSY52z	46-EACA-b	thavung		2.00	17	0....	6	4	4	1	0		...	.
6153	The(Thae)	0.06667	3,182	3,622	6,435	AUG03z	46-FADD-b	the		1.50	54	0....	6	4	4	1	0		...	.
6154	Tum	0.01520	726	826	1,467	AUG03z	46-EADA-c	tum		2.00	17	0....	6	4	4	0	0		...	.
6155	Upper Taoih (Taoy, Kantua	0.78003	37,233	42,379	75,293	AUG03z	46-FABB-a	ta'-oih		1.50	636	0....	6	4	4	5	2	Taoih, Upper	...	.
6156	Vietnamese (Gin, Kinh)	1.70000	81,146	92,362	164,093	MSY52b	46-EBAA-ac	general viêt	19	5.00	4,618	1Asu.	7	5	12	5	3	Vietnamese	PNB	b
6157	White Meo (Striped Miao)	1.10000	52,507	59,763	106,178	MSY47a	48-AAAA-a	hmong-daw		6.00	3,586	2A...	7	5	10	4	3	Hmong Daw*	PN.	.
6158	White Tai (Thai Trang)	0.80000	38,187	43,464	77,220	MSY49z	47-AAAD-b	tai-kao		2.00	869	0....	6	4	5	4	1	Tai: White*	P..	.
6159	Yellow Leaf	0.00066	32	36	64	MSY52z	46-EAAA-c	kha-tong-luang		3.00	1	0cs..	6	4	4	1	0	Luang	P..	.
6160	Yoy	0.03000	1,432	1,630	2,896	MSY49z	47-AAAC-ad	yo		1.80	29	1cs..	6	4	4	4	1	Nyaw	pnb	b
6161	Yumbri (Mrabri)	0.00400	191	217	386	AUG03z	46-DDDA-a	mlabri		1.00	2	0....	6	4	4	4	1	Mlabri	...	.
6162	other minor peoples	0.20008	9,550	10,870	19,313	...				2.00	217		6	4	4	3	0			
	Latvia	**100.00000**	**2,536,694**	**2,356,508**	**1,936,009**					**66.9**	**1,576,426**									
6163	Armenian	0.11500	2,917	2,710	2,226	CEW14	57-AAAA-b	ashkharik		70.00	1,897	4A.u.	10	7	13	2	1	Armenian: Modern, Eastern	PNB	b
6164	Azerbaijani	0.10400	2,638	2,451	2,013	MSY41a	44-AABA-fa	north azeri		0.00	0	2c.u.	0	3	3	0	2	Azerbaijani*	PNB	b
6165	Bashkir	0.02400	609	566	465	MSY41b	44-AABB-g	bashqurt		7.00	40	1A.u.	7	5	7	0	1	Bashkir	Pn.	b
6166	Bulgar (Bulgarian)	0.01600	406	377	310	CEW22b	53-AAAH-b	bulgarski		72.00	271	2A.uh	10	6	10	1	1	Bulgarian	PNB	b
6167	Byelorussian	4.05000	102,736	95,439	78,408	CEW22c	53-AAAE-c	bielorusskiy		59.00	56,309	3A.uh	10	8	11	3	3	Byelorussian*	PNB	b
6168	Chuvash	0.05700	1,446	1,343	1,104	MSY41c	44-AAAA-a	chuvash		35.00	470	2....	9	6	8	0	1	Chuvash	PN.	b
6169	Estonian	0.12200	3,095	2,875	2,362	MSW51a	41-AAAC-b	eesti		70.00	2,012	4A.u.	10	9	10	3	2	Estonian: Tallinn	PNB	b
6170	Finnish	0.01700	431	401	329	MSW51b	41-AAAA-bb	vehicular suomi		91.00	365	1A.uh	10	8	12	4	2	Finnish	PNB	b
6171	Georgian	0.05200	1,319	1,225	1,007	CEW17c	42-CABB-a	kharthuli		40.00	490	2A.u.	9	6	8	2	1	Georgian	PNB	b
6172	German	0.09000	2,283	2,121	1,742	CEW19m	52-ABCE-a	standard hoch-deutsch		80.00	1,697	2B.uh	10	9	13	3	2	German*	PNB	b
6173	Greek	0.01200	304	283	232	CEW20	56-AAAA-c	dhimotiki		90.00	255	2B.uh	10	8	11	2	2	Greek: Modern	PNB	b
6174	Hungarian	0.01300	330	306	252	MSW51g	41-BAAA-a	general magyar		85.00	260	2A.u.	10	9	11	3	1	Hungarian	PNB	b
6175	Jewish	0.60000	15,220	14,139	11,616	CMT35	52-ABCH	yiddish cluster		0.03	4	0B..h	3	3	6	0	0		PNB	b
6176	Karelian	0.01600	406	377	310	MSW51c	41-AAAB-a	central karely		67.00	253	1....	10	6	12	0	3	Karelian	P..	b
6177	Kazakh	0.03900	989	919	755	MSY41e	44-AABC-c	kazakh		0.00	0	4A.u.	0	3	3	0	1	Kazakh	PN.	b
6178	Komi	0.01700	431	401	329	MSW51d	41-AAEA-b	permyat		40.00	160	3....	9	6	10	0	1	Komi: Permyak*	Pn.	b
6179	Latgalian (Upper Latvian)	21.78300	552,568	513,318	421,721	CEW15a	54-AABA-ac	latgale		77.00	395,255	1A.u.	10	9	10	3	3	Latgalian	PNb	b
6180	Latvian (Lett, Lettish)	32.59000	826,709	767,986	630,945	CEW15a	54-AABA-a	standard latviashu		78.00	599,029	3A.uh	10	9	10	2	3	Latvian	PNB	b
6181	Latvian Gypsy	0.29500	7,483	6,952	5,711	CNN25f	59-ACBA-ag	north vlach		61.00	4,241	1c...	10	7	6	1	3	Romani: Latvian	Pn.	b
6182	Lezgin	0.01000	254	236	194	CEW17b	42-BCAA-a	lezgin		0.01	0	1....	3	4	0	0	1	Lezgi	P..	b
6183	Lithuanian	1.30000	32,977	30,635	25,168	CEW15b	54-AAAA-a	standard lietuvishkai		90.00	27,571	3A.u.	10	9	11	2	3	Lithuanian	PNB	b
6184	Livonian	0.05600	1,421	1,320	1,084	MSW51f	41-AAAC-c	liiv		70.00	924	1c.u.	10	9	10	2	3	Livonian: Eastern	PNb	b
6185	Mari (Cheremis)	0.01800	457	424	348	MSW51h	41-AACA-a	cheremis		90.00	382	1....	10	8	8	2	1	Mari: High*	PN.	b
6186	Moldavian	0.12100	3,069	2,851	2,343	CEW21f	51-AADC-ab	standard moldavia		82.00	2,338	1A.u.	10	7	8	2	3		pnb	b
6187	Mordvinian	0.04000	1,015	943	774	MSW51i	41-AADA-a	erzya		65.00	613	2....	10	8	8	2	1	Mordvin: Erzya*	PN.	b
6188	Ossete	0.01800	457	424	348	CNT24e	58-ABBA	oseti cluster		36.00	153	2....	9	5	8	1	1	Ossete*	PN.	b
6189	Polish (Pole)	2.26600	57,481	53,398	43,870	CEW22i	53-AAAC-c	polski		91.00	48,593	2A.uh	10	8	11	2	3	Polish	PNB	b
6190	Romanian	0.03500	888	825	678	CEW21i	51-AADC-a	limba românească		85.00	701	3A.u.	10	8	8	3	3	Romanian	PNB	b
6191	Russian	32.79700	831,960	772,864	634,953	CEW22j	53-AAAE-d	russkiy	84	50.00	386,432	4B.uh	10	8	10	5	3	Russian	PNB	b
6192	Tajik	0.01300	330	306	252	CNT24g	58-AACC-j	tajiki		0.00	0	2asu.	0	3	3	0	1	Tajik*	PNB	b
6193	Tatar	0.18100	4,591	4,265	3,504	MSY41h	44-AABB-e	tatar		1.50	64	2c.u.	6	4	8	0	1	Tatar: Kazan	Pn.	b
6194	Udmurt	0.01800	457	424	348	MSW51k	41-AAEA-c	udmurt		55.00	233	2....	10	5	8	2	1	Udmurt	Pn.	.
6195	Ukrainian	2.98000	75,593	70,224	57,693	CEW22p	53-AAAE-b	ukrainskiy		64.00	44,943	3A.uh	10	8	10	3	3	Ukrainian	PNB	b
6196	Uzbek	0.03500	888	825	678	MSY41l	44-AABD-a	central uzbek		0.00	0	1A.u.	0	3	6	1	3	Uzbek*	PNb	b
6197	other minor peoples	0.10000	2,537	2,357	1,936	...				20.00	471		9	5	7	1	0			
	Lebanon	**100.00000**	**3,008,704**	**3,281,787**	**4,399,649**					**52.86**	**1,734,821**									
6198	Armenian (Ermeni, Armiane	6.80000	204,592	223,162	299,176	CEW14	57-AAAA-b	ashkharik		90.00	200,845	4A.u.	10	9	12	5	1	Armenian: Modern, Eastern	PNB	b
6199	Assyrian (Aisor, Chaldean	0.50000	15,044	16,409	21,998	CMT31	12-AAAA-d	east syriac		95.00	15,588	1as..	10	8	10	5	2	Syriac: Ancient*	PNB	b
6200	British	0.04000	1,203	1,313	1,760	CEW19i	52-ABAC-b	standard-english	18	79.00	1,037	3Bsuh	10	9	13	5	3		PNB	b
6201	French	0.50000	15,044	16,409	21,998	CEW21b	51-AABI-d	general français	25	87.00	14,276	1B.uh	10	9	14	5	2	French	PNB	b
6202	Greek	0.10000	3,009	3,282	4,400	CEW20	56-AAAA-c	dhimotiki		95.00	3,118	2B.uh	10	9	11	5	1	Greek: Modern	PNB	b
6203	Iraqi Arab	0.40500	12,185	13,291	17,819	CMT30	12-AACF-g	syro-mesopotamian		0.70	93	1Asuh	5	4	8	5	3		pnb	b
6204	Italian	0.10000	3,009	3,282	4,400	CEW21e	51-AABQ-c	standard italiano		84.00	2,757	2B.uh	10	9	15	5	3	Italian	PNB	b
6205	Jewish	0.03000	903	985	1,320	CMT35	12-AACF-f	syro-palestinian		0.09	1	1Asuh	4	3	6	3	1	Arabic: Lebanese*	Pnb	b
6206	Lebanese Arab	71.21700	2,142,709	2,337,190	3,133,298	CMT30	12-AACF-f	syro-palestinian	100	61.50	1,437,372	1Asuh	10	10	12	5	2	Arabic: Lebanese*	Pnb	b
6207	Northern Kurd (Kermanji)	6.16000	185,336	202,158	271,018	CNT24c	58-AAAA-a	kurmanji		0.03	61	3c...	3	3	5	3	1	Kurdish: Kurmanji*	PN.	b
6208	Palestinian Arab	12.10000	364,053	397,096	532,358	CMT30	12-AACF-f	syro-palestinian		9.00	35,739	1Asuh	7	5	10	5	3	Arabic: Lebanese*	Pnb	b
6209	Portuguese	0.05000	1,504	1,641	2,200	CEW21g	51-AABA-e	general português		93.00	1,526	2Bsuh	10	9	15	5	1	Portuguese	PNB	b
6210	Spaniard	0.05000	1,504	1,641	2,200	CEW21k	51-AABB-c	general español		96.00	1,575	2B.uh	10	9	15	5	1	Spanish	PNB	b
6211	Spanish Jew	0.03000	903	985	1,320	CMT35	51-AAAB-a	ladino		0.05	0	0....	4	4	6	4	0		pnb	b

Continued opposite

Table 8-2 continued

EVANGELIZATION								EVANGELISM			ADDITIONAL DESCRIPTIVE DATA
Ref 1	*D* 28	*aC* 29	*CG%* 30	*r* 31	*E* 32	*U* 33	*W* 34	*e* 35	*R* 36	*T* 37	*Locations, civil divisions, literacy, religions, church history, denominations, dioceses, church growth, missions, agencies, ministries, movements* 38
6092	1	6	4.07	0	25.00	75.00	A	0.91	567	3	Mainly live over border in China. Polytheists 90%, Buddhists 8%. D=RCC.
6093	0	6	2.87	0	17.10	82.90	A	0.06	620	2	Saravane Province, east of Saravane. Animists 98%.
6094	0	6	4.07	4	28.00	72.00	A	1.02	496	4	Basin of Poko, Se Kamane, and Dak Main rivers. Mainly in Viet Nam. Close to Halang. Animists 99%. M=SIL,OMF.
6095	0	6	4.59	0	20.00	80.00	A	0.73	766	3	North of Attopeu. Related to Oy, Sapuan, Sok. Montagnards. Animists 99%.
6096	0	5	3.13	0	21.00	79.00	A	1.53	552	4	Mainly in Burma; also China(south Yunnan). Polytheists/Buddhists 98%.
6097	0	6	5.48	0	53.00	47.00	B	48.36	335	6	North central on China border, north of Mong Ou Tay. Related to Axi, Sani, Lahu, Lisu. Polytheists/animist 75%.
6098	0	6	4.69	0	19.80	80.20	A	1.30	732	4	Also in southwest Yunnan(China). Animists 98%.
6099	0	6	4.23	1	21.10	78.90	A	0.07	679	2	East central near Viet Nam border, east of Pa Leng. Close to Katu. Animists 99%.
6100	0	6	2.74	0	20.50	79.50	A	1.12	500	4	Southern Laos near Viet Nam border, Boloven Plateau north of Attopeu. Montagnards. Animists 98%.
6101	0	6	2.87	1	20.10	79.90	A	0.07	528	2	Southern Laos near Taoih and Bru peoples, around Muong Nong. Animists 99%.
6102	0	5	4.08	4	33.00	67.00	A	2.40	422	4	Upper Se Kong river along Laos/Viet Nam watershed; also in Viet Nam. Animists 98%. M=SIL,CMA,WEC.
6103	0	6	3.82	0	31.00	69.00	A	2.26	426	4	Also in Thailand and USA. Close to Lua, Phai(Prai). Animists 98%. M=NTM,ACCM (Thailand),CCT.
6104	0	6	3.99	0	25.00	75.00	A	4.56	547	4	Saravane Province, south of Ir and Ong. Closest to Ngeq. Animists 95%.
6105	2	5	8.51	4	47.00	53.00	A	10.29	554	5	Scattered across north. Also in Thailand, Burma, USA, France, China, Viet Nam. Animists 94%. D=RCC(many catechumens),LEF. M=CMA,ACCM,APM,OMI,MEP.
6106	0	6	2.84	1	38.00	62.00	A	13.87	277	5	Northeast, Neun river, around Hua Muong. Related to Puoc and Khang. Animists 90%.
6107	0	6	4.07	1	21.00	79.00	A	0.76	662	3	Near Lamet people. Also in USA. Animists 99%.
6108	0	6	4.07	1	24.00	76.00	A	0.87	579	3	East central, northwest of Boualapha. Also in Viet Nam. Related to Bru. Animists 99%.
6109	1	6	4.69	0	30.50	69.50	A	1.67	511	4	Saravane and Sedone Provinces. Also in Cambodia, Thailand. Monolinguals 80%. Animists 98%. D=LEF. M=CMA-Thailand
6110	1	6	3.55	0	21.00	79.00	A	0.76	594	3	Montagnards. Also in Animists 99%. D=RCC.
6111	0	6	3.13	0	19.00	81.00	A	0.69	596	3	Northwestern Laos, in Khmu area. Also Thailand, USA. Animists 99%.
6112	2	5	1.29	5	56.80	43.20	B	1.65	136	4	Monolinguals 100%. Theravada Buddhists 80%(1,900 pagodas), animists 10%, nonreligious 8%. Y=1630. D=RCC,GCL/LEF. M=FMB,CMA,LBI,SB,WGC,CSI,BL.
6113	0	6	2.47	1	30.80	69.20	A	2.02	273	4	Closest to Central Tai, Northern Tai, Song, Tai Dam; close to Lao. Also in Thailand. Animists 66%, Buddhists 30%.
6114	0	6	4.07	1	24.00	76.00	A	0.87	579	3	Saravane Province. Animists(tribal religionists) 99%.
6115	0	5	3.97	0	22.00	78.00	A	2.40	619	4	Saravane Province. Some bilinguals in Upper Taoih. Animists 97%.
6116	0	6	4.18	0	24.50	75.50	A	1.34	546	4	4 villages in northwestern Laos. Also in China, Viet Nam. Polytheists 89%, many Buddhists.
6117	1	6	4.33	1	36.80	63.20	A	2.41	367	4	Western Phong Saly. Vast majority in China, Burma; also Thailand, Viet Nam. Animists 40%, Theravada Buddhists 58%. D=RCC.
6118	0	5	1.96	1	23.20	76.80	A	0.16	350	3	East central, northeast of Kouang to Viet Nam border. Related to Bru, Khua, Leun. Animists 99%.
6119	0	6	2.43	0	20.00	80.00	A	0.73	443	3	West central, both sides of Viet Nam/Laos border, east of Phuc Trach, southeast of Arem. Animists 99%.
6120	1	6	2.99	4	37.00	63.00	A	6.75	281	4	Almost all live in mountains of north central Viet Nam. Animists 93%. D=RCC.
6121	0	5	3.27	1	25.00	75.00	A	2.73	468	4	Northeast central, on Viet Nam border, south of Hung language area (Viet Nam). Animists 97%.
6122	1	6	6.25	0	96.00	4.00	C	227.76	207	8	Southern Laos, in Muong Phine-Bung Sai area. 70% monolinguals. Closest to Khlor. Montagnards. Animists 35%. D=RCC.
6123	0	6	4.31	1	30.00	70.00	A	5.47	467	4	West central, south of Bai Dinh. Also in Viet Nam. Closest to Muong. Animists 95%.
6124	0	6	1.29	6	43.00	57.00	A	1.57	119	4	Haut Mekong and Sayaboury Provinces. Vast majority are in Thailand. Animists 95%. M=CC(Thailand).
6125	1	6	2.62	0	26.00	74.00	A	1.89	381	4	Eastern part of Boloven Plateau near Saravane and Paksong. Montagnards. Animists 98%. D=GCL/LEF. M=GR.
6126	0	0	2.60	1	19.00	81.00	A	3.46	519	4	Found in the North. Also in Viet Nam (official ethnic community). Animists 95%. D=RCC.
6127	0	6	3.32	0	21.50	78.50	A	1.17	551	4	South, foot of Boloven Plateau and Pakse. Related to Jeng, Sapuan. 80% monolinguals. Montagnards. Animists 98%. M=GR.
6128	0	6	3.65	0	25.50	74.50	A	1.39	500	4	Also in Viet Nam. Related to Phuong. Montagnards. Animists 98%. M=SIL.
6129	0	6	2.87	0	21.00	79.00	A	1.53	479	4	Theun river. Related to Thavung and Phon Sung. Animists 98%.
6130	0	7	3.79	0	33.00	67.00	A	6.02	406	4	One village in north Laos; many near Yunnan border. Adults speak some Lahu. Animists 95%.
6131	0	5	2.87	0	20.00	80.00	A	1.46	530	4	Central, around and east of Theun river, south of Thavung language area. Animists 98%.
6132	0	6	3.22	6	45.80	54.20	A	3.00	229	4	Many also in Thailand; some in north Viet Nam. Agriculturalists. Animists 98%.
6133	0	6	3.70	0	33.00	67.00	A	8.43	390	4	Also in Thailand refugee camps; many more now in USA. Closely related to Tin(Khatin). Animists 93%. M=OMF,NTM.
6134	0	5	3.13	0	18.00	82.00	A	0.65	644	3	North central around Phony Saly. Some in Thailand. Closely related to Bisu, Pyen, Mpi. Animists 99%.
6135	0	6	4.26	0	21.00	79.00	A	1.53	686	4	Northwest, Het river, along border. Half in Viet Nam. Related to Khang. Animists 98%.
6136	0	6	4.24	1	25.00	75.00	A	1.82	530	4	In north central Laos. Mostly in Viet Nam; some in USA. Animists 98%.
6137	0	6	3.83	0	25.00	75.00	A	4.56	507	4	Viet Nam border area, north of Sach, south of May. Austro-Asiatic. Animists 95%.
6138	1	8	5.57	7	97.00	3.00	B	106.21	157	7	Military and civilian advisers from former USSR. Nonreligious 60%, atheists 10%. D=ROC.
6139	0	6	4.25	0	25.20	74.80	A	0.18	527	3	Central Laos near Viet Nam border. Also in northeast Thailand. Second language: Lao. Animists 99%. M=NTM.
6140	0	5	4.07	1	26.00	74.00	A	1.89	534	4	Saravane Province. An Austo-Asiatic language. Related to So, Bru. Animists 96%.
6141	0	6	3.04	0	22.50	77.50	A	0.41	492	3	Banks of Se Kong and Se Kamane, Attopeu Province, southern Laos. Montagnards. Animists 99%. M=OMF.
6142	0	5	3.26	0	19.00	81.00	A	0.69	629	3	North central, north of Muong Hai. Animists 99%.
6143	0	6	3.21	4	33.20	66.80	A	0.24	347	3	Along Mekong river, Thakhek and Savannakhet Provinces; also in Thailand. Montagnards. Ceremonial dances. Buddhists 90%, animists 10%. M=OMF,CMA,NTM.
6144	0	6	1.96	1	23.10	76.90	A	0.08	351	2	Half in Thailand. Close to So language. Montagnards. Animists 99%.
6145	0	6	3.31	0	20.00	80.00	A	0.73	590	3	Attopeu Province, southern Laos. Related to Oy, Sapuan, Jeng. Montagnards. Animists 99%.
6146	0	6	3.23	0	19.00	81.00	A	0.69	610	3	In Attopeu Province, southern Laos. Montagnards. Animists 99%.
6147	0	4	3.83	1	33.00	67.00	A	4.81	401	4	Northwest corner; also in Burma, China. Hinayana Buddhists 90%, some animists.
6148	0	6	4.49	4	24.50	75.50	A	1.34	614	4	Muong Phine-Bung Sai area. Related to Trieng (Hre) in Viet Nam. Animists 98%.
6149	0	5	2.84	0	20.00	80.00	A	1.46	526	4	West of Viet Nam border, east of Kayong, north of Chavane and Thia. Animists 98%.
6150	0	5	4.09	1	23.00	77.00	A	1.67	583	4	Northeast, Neun river, east of Sam Thong. Also in Viet Nam. Animists 98%.
6151	3	6	-0.32	6	56.60	43.40	B	1.24	13	4	Mainly live in Thailand. Theravada Buddhists 98%, Muslims 1%. D=RCC,CCT,SDA.
6152	0	5	2.87	0	20.00	80.00	A	1.46	503	4	Central, Theun river, east and south of Lake Sao. Related to Pakatan, Phon Sung. Animists 98%.
6153	0	6	4.07	0	20.50	79.50	A	1.12	678	4	Attopeu Province, southern Laos. Close to Oy. Monolingual Montagnards. Animists 98%.
6154	0	5	2.87	0	19.00	81.00	A	1.38	558	4	Central, Nhang river, northeast of Nape. Closely related to Hung, Pong-2. Animists 98%.
6155	2	6	4.24	0	28.50	71.50	A	1.56	504	4	Saravane Province. Also in Viet Nam, USA. Monolinguals 70%. Montagnards. Animists 98%. D=RCC,GCL. M=OMF,CMA.
6156	2	6	1.83	6	68.00	32.00	B	12.41	108	5	Ching. 71% foreign military personel. Mahayana Buddhists 60%, nonreligious 14%, Cao-Daists 10%, atheists 7%, animists 2%, Muslims 1%, Baha'is 1%. D=RCC.
6157	2	6	3.13	4	56.00	44.00	B	12.26	187	5	Mainly now in USA; also Thailand, Viet Nam, France, China. Animists 93%. D=RCC,GCL/LEF. M=CSI,CMA,NTM. R=FEBC.
6158	1	6	4.57	4	32.00	68.00	A	2.33	443	4	Northeastern Laos. Majority in Viet Nam; also in China, USA. Many bilinguals in Tai Dam. Animists 20%, Buddhists 78%. D=RCC. M=SIL.
6159	0	5	0.00	1	25.00	75.00	A	2.73	88	4	Phi Tong Luang. Central, on Viet Nam border, Mu Gia Pass. Animists 97%.
6160	0	6	3.42	1	37.80	62.20	A	2.48	291	4	A Tai language, found also in Thailand. Second language Lao. Animists 90%, some Buddhists 8%. M=NTM.
6161	0	6	0.70	0	24.00	76.00	A	0.87	194	3	Yellow Leaf. Thai border area; also in Thailand. Remote forest. Montagnards, nomads. Animists 99%. M=NTM.
6162	0	7	3.13		20.00	80.00	A	1.46	429	4	A few Indian shopkeepers remain(Tamils, Telugus, Gujaratis). Hindus 40%, Muslims 30%, nonreligious 20%, Animists 8%.
Latvia											
6163	1	8	5.39	6	99.70	0.30	C	350.03	120	9	Gregorians; in 28 countries. Nonreligious 30%. D=Armenian Apostolic Ch.
6164	1	8	0.00	1	31.00	69.00	A	0.00	0	1.12	73% monolinguals. Muslims 80%(56% Shias, 24% Hanafi Sunnis), nonreligious 20%. D=ROC. M=IBT,CSI.
6165	1	9	3.76	4	51.00	49.00	B	13.03	245	5	Many speak Tatar as mother tongue. Muslims 72%(Hanafi Sunnis), nonreligious 20%. D=Russian Orthodox Ch.
6166	1	10	0.68	6	99.72	0.28	C	354.78	39	9	From Bulgaria. Nonreligious 18%, atheists 10%. D=Bulgarian Orthodox Ch. M=LBI.
6167	3	8	0.57	5	99.59	0.41	B	277.80	33	8	White Russians. Nonreligious/atheists 36%. D=ROC,RCC,Old Ritualist Chs.
6168	1	9	0.68	0	76.00	24.00	B	97.09	53	6	From Chuvashia (Russia). Muslims 35%(Sunnis), nonreligious 30%. D=ROC. M=IBT.
6169	5	8	0.65	5	99.70	0.30	C	350.03	36	9	From Estonia; also in 10 other countries. Nonreligious 30%. D=Russian Orthodox Ch,ELCE,RCC,MCE,AUCEC. M=UBS,LBI.
6170	2	10	0.65	5	99.91	0.09	C	528.11	29	10	Immigrants from Finland; also in 9 other countries. Most are bilingual in Russian. D=ELC,ROC.
6171	1	9	3.97	4	97.00	3.00	B	141.62	112	7	Nonreligious/atheists 55%, Muslims 5%(Sunnis,Shias). D=Georgian Orthodox Ch.
6172	2	10	0.22	8	99.80	0.20	C	449.68	24	10	Long-time residents from Germany, Russia. Nonreligious 20%. D=German ELC,AUCECB.
6173	2	10	0.66	7	99.90	0.10	C	522.31	28	10	Traders from Greece. D=Greek Orthodox Ch,ROC. M=UBS,LBI.
6174	2	10	0.67	6	99.85	0.15	C	468.47	37	10	Immigrants, refugees from Hungary. Nonreligious 15%. D=RCC,RCH. M=LBI.
6175	0	10	0.29	5	48.03	51.97	A	0.05	56	2	Religious Jews, bilingual in Russian, Latvian. Many have emigrated to Israel, many return.
6176	3	9	0.70	0	99.67	0.33	C	276.34	41	8	From Karelia (Russia). Bilingual in Russian. Nonreligious 30%. D=ROC,RCC,ELC.
6177	0	8	0.00	4	35.00	65.00	A	0.00	0	1.10	Muslims 60%(Hanafi Sunnis, with Sufi influence), nonreligious 30%, atheists 10%. M=ROC.
6178	1	8	0.65	0	82.00	18.00	B	119.72	55	7	From Komi (Russia). Pastoralists. Shamanists 40%, nonreligious 20%. D=Russian Orthodox Ch.
6179	4	9	0.20	1	99.77	0.23	C	385.03	28	9	In eastern part of Latvia. Literary language. D=ROC,ELCL,RCC,RCL.
6180	6	9	0.21	5	99.78	0.22	C	415.66	27	10	Western Latvian. In 25 countries. D=LOC(D-Riga & Latvia),ELC of Latvia,RCC(2 Dioceses),Reformed Ch in Latvia, CB,AUCECB. R=IBRA,Riga.
6181	3	10	0.78	1	99.61	0.39	C	233.78	47	8	Ethnic term: Lotfitka Roma. Part of over 100,000 Romani-speaking Baltic Gypsies, largely nomadic. Many nonreligious. D=RCC,ROC,ELCL.
6182	0	7	0.00	0	20.01	79.99	A	0.00	0	1.06	In south Dagestan (Russia). 50% understand Russian. Muslims 100%(Shafi Sunnis). M=IBT.
6183	3	8	0.67	5	99.90	0.10	C	519.03	12	10	Found in 24 countries. Nonreligious 10%. Strong Catholics. D=RCC,ERCL,ROC.
6184	3	10	0.67	1	99.70	0.30	C	316.82	37	9	Western Livonian. 8 coastal villages west of Kolkasrags, also Riga. Eastern Livonian now extinct. Nonreligious 30%. D=ELC of Latvia,ROC,RCC.
6185	1	9	0.70	0	99.90	0.10	C	436.90	35	10	Residents from Mari (Russia). Muslims 7%, many shamanists. D=ROC. M=IBT. Traditionally Orthodox.
6186	3	9	0.67	6	99.82	0.18	C	425.00	32	10	In Bessarabia (Moldavia), also Romania. Nonreligious 18%. D=Russian Orthodox Ch,Romanian Orthodox Ch,RCC.
6187	1	9	0.68	7	99.65	0.35	C	275.21	16	8	Migrants, laborers from Mordvinia (Russia). Heavily russianized. Nonreligious 30%. D=ROC. M=IBT.
6188	1	6	0.65	0	75.00	25.00	B	98.55	64	6	Originally from Ossetia (Russia) and AO (Georgia). Stock-breeders. Muslims 40%(Sunnis), nonreligious 24%. D=ROC.
6189	4	10	0.67	6	99.91	0.09	C	538.08	11	10	Poles, from Poland and Western Ukraine. 29% speak Polish as mother tongue. D=RCC(3 Dioceses),ROC,CEF,Polish Pentecostal Movement/CWE.
6190	3	10	0.67	6	99.85	0.15	C	471.58	32	10	Expatriates, settlers from Romania. Nonreligious 15%. D=Romanian Orthodox Ch,RCC,Russian Orthodox Ch.
6191	8	9	0.64	7	99.50	0.50	B	229.95	14	8	In 70 countries. Nonreligious 41%, atheists 9%. D=ROC,RCC,AUCECB,Old Ritualists,CEF,CCECB,SDA,IPKH. R=FEBC,HCJB,TWR,KNLS,VERITAS,AWR,IBRA.
6192	0	8	0.00	4	39.00	61.00	A	0.00	0	1.12	Most are trilingual (Uzbek, Russian, Latvian). Muslims 90%(Hanafi Sunnis), nonreligious 10%. M=CSI.
6193	1	8	4.25	6	43.50	56.50	A	2.38	318	4	From Tatarstan (Russia). Muslims 83%(Hanafi Sunnis), nonreligious 15%. D=ROC.
6194	1	7	0.69	0	93.00	7.00	B	186.69	50	7	Migrants, from Udmurtia (Russia). Strong shamanists/animists 40%, Muslims 5%(Besermen). D=ROC.
6195	7	8	0.52	6	99.64	0.36	C	313.02	35	9	In 15 countries. Nonreligious/atheists 36%. D=ROC(E-Ukraine),Ukrainian Catholic Ch,AUCECB,CEF,CCECB,JWs,SDA.
6196	0	9	0.00	5	43.00	57.00	A	0.00	0	1.12	55% Russian-speaking. Literates 100%. Muslims 80%(Hanafi Sunnis), nonreligious/atheists 20%. M=ROC,AUCECB,CSI.
6197	0	6	0.67		43.00	57.00	A	31.39	43	5	Koreans, Turkmen, other Europeans, other Asians. Nonreligious 35%, Muslims 20%, Buddhists 5%.
Lebanon											
6198	4	10	2.00	6	99.90	0.10	C	538.74	43	10	Refugees from Turkey. D=Armenian Apostolic Ch(C-Sis: AD-Beirut),RCC(D-Beirut),UAECNE,AESB. M=AMAA.
6199	2	10	2.06	5	99.95	0.05	C	568.67	46	10	Refugees over last 100 years. D=Ancient Ch of the East(Nestorians: D-Beirut),RCC(Chaldeans: D-Beirut).
6200	5	10	5.72	8	99.79	0.21	C	449.82	121	10	Expatriates from Britain, in business. D=Anglican Ch/ECJME(D-Jerusalem),CB,RCC,JWs,BCC.
6201	2	10	6.08	8	99.87	0.13	C	520.78	118	10	Expatriates from France, in government, commerce. D=RCC(Latin-rite VA-Beirut),FEC.
6202	2	10	2.06	7	99.95	0.05	C	579.07	50	10	Traders. D=Greek Orthodox Ch(P-Antioch: 6 Dioceses),RCC(7 Melkite Dioceses). M=FMB.
6203	3	10	1.71	7	61.70	38.30	B	1.57	107	4	Immigrants from Iraq. Muslims 99%(60% Shias,39% Hanafi Sunnis). D=ACE(D-Beirut),RCC,GOC.
6204	1	10	5.78	7	99.84	0.16	C	484.42	118	10	Expatriates from Italy. Strong Catholics. D=RCC(Latin-rite VA-Beirut). M=OFMCap,OCD,OP,SJ,CM,SDB.
6205	0	10	0.00	8	52.09	47.91	B	0.17	36	3	'The Community of Moses.' Practicing Jews; decline by immigration from 10,000 in 1956. M=PCG.
6206	5	7	1.65	8	99.62	0.38	C	295.18	49	8	Muslims 34%(Sunnis,Alawis,Darqawiyya(Sufis),Druzes 13%). D=RCC(8 Maronite Dioceses),GOC(P-Antioch: 6 Dioceses),NESSL,NEC,LBC. M=FMB,MEM.
6207	0	4	4.20	0	28.03	71.97	A	0.03	606	2	Refugees. Also in Turkey, Iran, Iraq, Syria, Germany, Belgium. Muslims 100%(Sunnis, Shias). M=large network of missions.
6208	3	10	2.71	8	77.00	23.00	B	25.29	121	5	Refugees. Muslims 84%(Shafi Sunnis,Alawis,Druzes). D=Anglican Ch/ECJME,RCC,NESSL.
6209	1	10	5.16	8	99.93	0.07	C	566.88	101	10	Expatriates from Portugal, in commerce. D=RCC(VA-Beirut).
6210	1	10	5.19	8	99.96	0.04	C	592.17	99	10	Expatriates from Spain, in business, commerce. Strong Catholics. D=RCC(VA-Beirut).
6211	0	10	0.00	1	38.05	61.95	A	0.06	0	2	Ladino(Dzhudezmo)=main language of Sefardic Jewry. All trilingual. Mostly practicing Jews.

Continued overleaf

Table 8-2 continued

PEOPLE		POPULATION				IDENTITY CODE		LANGUAGE		CHURCH		MINISTRY	SCRIPTURE	
Ref 1	*Ethnic name* 2	*P%* 3	*In 1995* 4	*In 2000* 5	*In 2025* 6	*Race* 7	*Language* 8	*Autoglossonym* 9	*S* 10	*AC* 11	*Members* 12	*Jayuh dwa xcmc mi* 13-17 18 19 20 21 22	*Biblioglossonym* 23	*Pub ss* 24-26 27
6212	Syrian Arab	0.81000	24,371	26,582	35,637	CMT30	12-AACF-f	syro-palestinian		7.50	1,994	1Asuh 7 5 13 5 1	Arabic: Lebanese*	Pnb b
6213	Turk	0.10000	3,009	3,282	4,400	MSY41j	44-AABA-a	osmanli		0.10	3	1A.u. 5 3 6 1 0	Turkish	PNB b
6214	USA White	0.10000	3,009	3,282	4,400	CEW19s	52-ABAC-s	general american		78.00	2,560	1Bsuh 10 9 12 5 3	English*	PNB b
6215	West Aramaic	0.54200	16,307	17,787	23,846	CMT31	12-AAAA-b	west neo-aramaic		78.00	13,874	1cs.. 10 7 8 4 1	Aramaic: Ancient	PNb b
6216	other minor peoples	0.36600	11,012	12,011	16,103	...				20.00	2,402	9 5 6 5 0		
	Lesotho	**100.00000**	**1,926,409**	**2,152,553**	**3,506,420**					**67.14**	**1,445,328**			
6217	Afrikaner	0.11000	2,119	2,368	3,857	CEW19a	52-ABCB-a	afrikaans	40	80.70	1,911	2B.uh 10 9 13 5 1	Afrikaans	PNB b
6218	British	0.10000	1,926	2,153	3,506	CEW19i	52-ABAC-b	standard-english	70	75.00	1,614	3Bsuh 10 9 13 5 3		PNB b
6219	Coloured (Eurafrican)	0.05000	963	1,076	1,753	NAN58	52-ABAE-fd	lesotho-english		80.00	861	0A.uh 10 8 11 5 3		pnb b
6220	French	0.01000	193	215	351	CEW21b	51-AABI-d	general français	5	87.00	187	1B.uh 10 9 14 5 1	French	PNB b
6221	Indo-Pakistani	0.10000	1,926	2,153	3,506	CNN25g	59-AAFO-e	general hindi		8.00	172	3Asuh 7 5 5 5 0		pnb b
6222	Mine Kaffir (Fanagalo)	0.30000	5,779	6,458	10,519	NAB57i	99-AUTF-h	fanakolo	40	65.00	4,197	1csu. 10 7 7 5 3		pnb b
6223	Phuthi	2.00000	38,528	43,051	70,128	NAB57m	99-AUTF-c	phuthi		80.00	34,441	1csu. 10 7 8 5 3		pnb .
6224	Seroa	0.00500	96	108	175	BYG11d	09-CBAC	seroa cluster		60.00	65	0.... 10 7 6 4 0		... .
6225	Southern Sotho (Sutu)	80.32500	1,547,388	1,729,038	2,816,532	NAB57m	99-AUTE-e	se-sotho	100	68.50	1,184,391	3asu. 10 10 11 5 3	Sesotho: Southern*	PNB b
6226	Taung	1.50000	28,896	32,288	52,596	NAB57m	99-AUTE-ed	northeast taung		75.00	24,216	1csu. 10 8 9 5 3		pnb .
6227	Xhosa (Tembu, Thembu)	1.00000	19,264	21,526	35,064	NAB57i	99-AUTF-a	i-si-xhosa	25	62.00	13,346	2Asu. 10 9 13 5 3	Xhosa	PNB b
6228	Zulu	14.40000	277,403	309,968	504,924	NAB57i	99-AUTF-g	i-si-zulu	50	57.70	178,851	3asu. 10 9 12 5 3	Isizulu*	PNB b
6229	other minor peoples	0.10000	1,926	2,153	3,506	...				50.00	1,076	10 7 7 5 3		
	Liberia	**100.00000**	**2,090,147**	**3,154,001**	**6,617,526**					**29.55**	**932,060**			
6230	Americo-Liberian	2.44553	51,115	77,132	161,834	NAN58	52-ABAH-c	kroo-english	65	73.00	56,306	1.s.h 10 9 11 5 1		pn. b
6231	Ashanti	0.70000	14,631	22,078	46,323	NAB59a	96-FCCB-cc	a-sante		52.00	11,481	1ssu. 10 8 12 5 3	Twi: Asante	PNB b
6232	Bandi (Bande)	2.66266	55,654	83,980	176,202	NAB64c	00-ABAA-a	bandi		10.00	8,398	1.... 8 5 7 5 3	Bandi	Pnb .
6233	Barclayville Grebo	0.89131	18,630	28,112	58,983	NAB59j	95-ABAF-c	wede-bo		60.00	16,867	0.... 10 7 8 5 3		... .
6234	Bassa	13.07258	273,236	412,309	865,081	NAB59j	95-ABAB-a	central basoo		46.00	189,662	0.... 9 8 12 5 3	Bassa: Liberia	PN. b
6235	British	0.30000	6,270	9,462	19,853	CEW19i	52-ABAC-b	standard-english	51	79.00	7,475	3Bsuh 10 9 13 5 3		PNB b
6236	Cape Palmas Creole	0.01000	209	315	662	NAN58	52-ABAH-c	kroo-english	1	90.00	284	1.s.h 10 9 11 5 2		pn. b
6237	Dan (Da, Yakuba)	3.30128	69,002	104,122	218,463	NAB64a	00-DBAA-a	dan		23.00	23,948	3.... 9 6 8 5 1	Dan*	PN. b
6238	Dewoin (Dei, De)	0.30463	6,367	9,608	20,159	NAB59j	95-ABAA-a	dewen-wulu		42.00	4,035	0.... 9 6 7 5 2		... b
6239	Eastern Krahn (Tchien)	1.76758	36,945	55,749	116,970	NAB59j	95-ABAR-d	cien	4	25.00	13,937	0.... 9 5 8 5 3	Krahn: Tchien*	PN. .
6240	Ewe	0.50000	10,451	15,770	33,088	NAB59d	96-MAAA-a	standard ewe		80.00	12,616	4Asu. 10 8 13 5 3	Ewe	PNB b
6241	Fante	1.00000	20,901	31,540	66,175	NAB59a	96-FCCB-b	fante		53.00	16,716	2csu. 10 8 11 5 3	Fante	PNB b
6242	Fopo-Bua Grebo	0.63182	13,206	19,928	41,811	NAB59j	95-ABAG	fopo-bua cluster		55.00	10,960	0.... 10 6 8 5 2		... .
6243	French	0.05000	1,045	1,577	3,309	CEW21b	51-AABI-d	general français	5	87.00	1,372	1B.uh 10 9 14 5 3	French	PNB b
6244	Gbeapo Grebo	1.79767	37,574	56,699	118,961	NAB59j	95-ABAH-a	jede-po		49.00	27,782	0.... 9 7 8 5 2	E Je*	PN. b
6245	Gbii (Gbee)	0.21061	4,402	6,643	13,937	NAB59j	95-ABAD-c	gbii		40.00	2,657	0.... 9 6 7 5 1		... b
6246	Gboloo Grebo	2.11734	44,256	66,781	140,116	NAB59j	95-ABAJ	gboloo cluster		38.90	25,978	0.... 9 7 9 5 3	Grebo, Gboloo	... .
6247	Gio	4.10000	85,696	129,314	271,319	NAB64a	00-DBAA-a	dan		4.00	5,173	3.... 6 5 7 5 3	Dan*	PN. b
6248	Glaro-Twabo (Krahn)	0.14667	3,066	4,626	9,706	NAB59j	95-ABAO	glaro-twabo cluster		42.00	1,943	0.... 9 6 7 5 3	Glaro-twabo	... .
6249	Glebo Grebo	1.07935	22,560	34,043	71,426	NAB59j	95-ABAL-d	gle-bo		54.00	18,383	0.... 10 7 8 5 3		... .
6250	Glio (Oubi, Ubi)	0.13163	2,751	4,152	8,711	NAB59j	95-ABAP	glio-ubi cluster		40.00	1,661	0.... 9 6 5 5 1		... b
6251	Globo Grebo	1.00000	20,901	31,540	66,175	NAB59j	95-ABAK-e	glo-bo		49.00	15,455	0.... 9 7 8 5 2		... b
6252	Gola	3.73449	78,056	117,786	247,131	NAB56c	94-BBAA	gola cluster		2.10	2,474	0.... 6 4 5 5 3	Gola	... b
6253	Jabo Grebo	1.00000	20,901	31,540	66,175	NAB59j	95-ABAL-a	ja-bo		44.00	13,878	0.... 9 8 9 5 2		... .
6254	Kpelle	18.94514	395,981	597,530	1,253,700	NAB64f	00-ABAC-a	kpele	25	25.00	149,382	1.... 9 7 8 5 3	Kpelle*	PN. .
6255	Kru	6.91989	144,636	218,253	457,926	NAB59j	95-ABAE-g	central klao		51.00	111,309	0.... 10 9 13 5 3	Kru*	PN. b
6256	Kru Creole	0.01000	209	315	662	NAN58	52-ABAH-c	kroo-english	2	90.00	284	1.s.h 10 9 11 5 1		pn. b
6257	Kuwaa (Belle, Kwaa)	0.48138	10,062	15,183	31,855	NAB59j	95-AAAA-a	kuwaa		45.00	6,832	0.... 9 6 6 5 1	Kuwaa	PN. n
6258	Lebanese Arab	1.00000	20,901	31,540	66,175	CMT30	12-AACF-f	syro-palestinian		75.00	23,655	1Asuh 10 8 8 5 2	Arabic: Lebanese*	Pnb b
6259	Liberian Creole	0.02000	418	631	1,324	NAN58	52-ABAH-c	kroo-english	10	90.00	568	1.s.h 10 9 11 5 1		pn. b
6260	Loma (Toma, Bouze)	5.33283	111,464	168,198	352,901	NAB64h	00-ABAB-a	loma		15.00	25,230	0.... 8 5 10 5 3	Loma	PN. .
6261	Maninka (Wangara)	1.27115	26,569	40,092	84,119	NAB63h	00-AAAA-h	maninka-kan		4.00	1,604	3a... 6 4 6 4 2	Maninka*	PN. b
6262	Mano (Mah, Maa, Mawe)	6.08686	127,224	191,980	402,800	NAB64j	00-DAAA-a	man-wi		5.00	9,599	0.... 7 5 7 5 2	Mano	PN. .
6263	Manya (Manya Kan)	1.70740	35,687	53,851	112,988	NAB63h	00-AAAB-d	manya-kan	4	0.03	16	1cs.. 3 4 2 5 3		pnb b
6264	Mende (Boumpe)	0.74088	15,485	23,367	49,028	NAB64i	00-ABAA-c	mende		20.00	4,673	3.... 9 5 9 5 1	Mende	PNB b
6265	Northeastern Grebo	0.74840	15,643	23,605	49,526	NAB59j	95-ABAI-c	nitia-bo		40.00	9,442	0.... 9 7 10 5 2		... .
6266	Sapo (Bush Kru)	1.18842	24,840	37,483	78,644	NAB59j	95-ABAR-e	sa-po		30.00	11,245	0.... 9 6 7 5 2	Sapo	Pn. .
6267	Seaside Grebo	1.13200	23,660	35,703	74,910	NAB59j	95-ABAL-a	ja-bo		54.00	19,280	0.... 10 7 11 5 3		... .
6268	Southern Kissi (Kisi)	3.80218	79,471	119,921	251,610	NAB56c	94-BABA-b	south kisi	4	9.50	11,392	1.... 7 5 8 5 3	Kisi: Southern*	PN. .
6269	Southern Krumen	0.10000	2,090	3,154	6,618	NAB59j	95-ABAM-g	te-po		50.00	1,577	0.... 10 8 11 5 2	Krumen: Southern*	PN. .
6270	Tajuasohn	0.36104	7,546	11,387	23,892	NAB59j	95-ABAE-d	tajuoson		40.00	4,555	0.... 9 6 9 4 2	Tajuasohn	pn. .
6271	USA Black	0.20000	4,180	6,308	13,235	NFB68a	52-ABAE-a	talkin-black		90.00	5,677	0B.uh 10 9 11 5 3		pnb b
6272	USA White	1.00000	20,901	31,540	66,175	CEW19s	52-ABAC-s	general american		75.00	23,655	1Bsuh 10 9 13 5 3	English*	PNB b
6273	Vai (Vy)	3.36593	70,353	106,161	222,741	NAB64k	00-AAAE-a	vai		0.70	743	4.... 5 4 3 5 3	Vai	P.. .
6274	Western Krahn	1.79767	37,574	56,699	118,961	NAB59j	95-ABAR-h	gbo-bo		19.00	10,773	0.... 8 5 8 4 2	Krahn: Western*	PN. .
6275	Yoruba	0.40000	8,361	12,616	26,470	NAB59n	98-AAAA-a	standard yoruba		34.00	4,289	3asu. 9 7 13 5 3	Yoruba	PNB b
6276	other minor peoples	0.43368	9,065	13,678	28,699	...				50.00	6,839	10 7 7 5 3		
	Libya	**100.00000**	**4,966,915**	**5,604,722**	**8,646,769**					**3.04**	**170,349**			
6277	Arabized Berber	4.20000	208,610	235,398	363,164	CMT32a	12-AACB-bh	tarabulusi		0.02	47	1A.uh 3 2 2 0 2		pnb .
6278	Arabized Black	1.80000	89,404	100,885	155,642	NAB61	12-AACB	maghrebi cluster		0.01	10	2A.uh 3 2 2 0 0		PNB b
6279	Awjilah Berber	0.04000	1,987	2,242	3,459	CMT32d	10-AAAD-b	wajili		0.02	0	0.... 3 3 6 0 0		... b
6280	British	0.26500	13,162	14,853	22,914	CEW19i	52-ABAC-b	standard-english	15	65.00	9,654	3Bsuh 10 9 11 4 1		PNB b
6281	Bulgar	0.05000	2,483	2,802	4,323	CEW22b	53-AAAH-b	bulgarski		72.00	2,018	2A.uh 10 7 8 2 1	Bulgarian	PNB b
6282	Croat	0.30000	14,901	16,814	25,940	CEW22d	53-AAAG-b	standard hrvatski		83.00	13,956	2Asuh 10 8 8 4 1	Croatian	PNB b
6283	Cyrenaican Arab	26.27900	1,305,256	1,472,865	2,272,284	CMT30	12-AACF-af	barqi		0.35	5,155	1Asuh 5 3 4 3 2		pnb b
6284	Egyptian Arab	7.70000	382,452	431,564	665,801	CMT30	12-AACF-a	masri		16.00	69,050	2Asuh 8 9 8 4 3	Arabic*	PNB b
6285	Fezzan Bedouin	3.09600	153,776	173,522	267,704	CMT30	12-AACB	maghrebi cluster		0.02	35	2A.uh 3 3 2 0 0		PNB b
6286	French	0.10000	4,967	5,605	8,647	CEW21b	51-AABI-d	general français	5	87.00	4,876	1B.uh 10 9 12 4 1	French	PNB b
6287	Gadames Berber	0.08900	4,421	4,988	7,696	CMT32d	10-AAAC-v	ghudamis		0.05	2	1c... 4 2 0 0 0		pn. b
6288	Greek	0.10000	4,967	5,605	8,647	CEW20	56-AAAA-c	dhimotiki		95.00	5,324	2B.uh 10 9 11 4 2	Greek: Modern	PNB b
6289	Halebi Gypsy (Nawari)	0.60000	29,801	33,628	51,881	CNN25f	59-ACAA-a	domari		0.00	0	0.... 0 1 0 0 0		... b
6290	Han Chinese	0.03100	1,540	1,737	2,680	MSY42a	79-AAAB-ba	kuo-yü		1.00	17	2Bsuh 6 3 2 1 0	Chinese: Kuoyu*	PNB b
6291	Italian	0.41700	20,712	23,372	36,057	CEW21e	51-AABQ-c	standard italiano	10	80.00	18,697	2B.uh 10 9 12 4 1	Italian	PNB b
6292	Jalo Berber	0.61900	30,745	34,693	53,524	CMT32d	12-AACF-af	barqi		0.01	3	1Asuh 3 2 0 0 0		pnb b
6293	Jewish	0.00200	99	112	173	CMT35	12-AACH-c	yudi		0.00	0	0c... 0 1 5 0 0		p.. b
6294	Jofra Berber	0.41000	20,364	22,979	35,452	CMT32d	12-AACF-ns	wadi-al-jawf		0.02	5	1csuh 3 2 0 0 0		pnb .
6295	Korean	0.20000	9,934	11,209	17,294	MSY46	45-AAAA-b	kukö		25.00	2,802	2A... 9 8 12 0 0	Korean	PNB b
6296	Kufra Bedouin	0.41300	20,513	23,148	35,711	CMT30	12-AACD	badawi-sahara cluster		0.02	5	0a... 3 3 2 0 0		PN. b
6297	Maltese	0.10000	4,967	5,605	8,647	CMT36	12-AACC-a	maltiya		95.00	5,324	0a.u. 10 9 13 5 1	Maltese	PNB b
6298	Nefusa Berber (Jemmari)	0.80000	39,735	44,838	69,174	CMT32z	10-AAAC-u	nefusi		0.00	0	1c... 0 3 3 0 0		pn. b
6299	Palestinian Arab	1.00000	49,669	56,047	86,468	CMT30	12-AACF-f	syro-palestinian		10.00	5,605	1Asuh 8 5 8 2 2	Arabic: Lebanese*	Pnb b
6300	Punjabi	1.00000	49,669	56,047	86,468	CNN25n	59-AAFE-c	general panjabi		2.40	1,345	1Asu. 6 4 4 2 0		PNB b
6301	Riyah Bedouin	0.51600	25,629	28,920	44,617	CMT30	12-AACD	badawi-sahara cluster		0.03	9	0a... 3 3 2 0 0		PN. b
6302	Sanusi Bedouin	9.28800	461,327	520,567	803,112	CMT30	12-AACF-af	barqi		0.01	52	1Asuh 3 3 2 0 2		pnb b
6303	Sawknah (Sokna)	0.10300	5,116	5,773	8,906	CMT32d	10-AAAD-a	sokna		0.06	3	0.... 4 2 0 0 0		... b
6304	Serb	0.32500	16,142	18,215	28,102	CEW22l	53-AAAG-a	standard srpski		80.00	14,572	1Asuh 10 8 8 4 1	Serbian*	PNB b
6305	Sinhalese	0.20000	9,934	11,209	17,294	CNN25q	59-ABBA	sinhala cluster		1.00	112	2asuh 6 5 8 0 0		PNB b
6306	Sirtican Bedouin	0.51600	25,629	28,920	44,617	CMT30	12-AACD	badawi-sahara cluster		0.03	9	0a... 3 3 2 0 0		PNB b
6307	Sudanese Arab	3.50000	173,842	196,165	302,637	CMT30	12-AACF-c	sudani		0.30	588	4Asuh 5 4 6 2 0	Arabic: Sudan	PNb b
6308	Teda (Tubu)	0.59600	29,603	33,404	51,535	NAB61	02-BAAA-ab	gunda		0.03	10	0.... 3 4 0 0 2		... b
6309	Tripolitanian Arab	30.93300	1,536,416	1,733,709	2,674,705	CMT30	12-AACB-bh	tarabulusi	100	0.32	5,548	1A.uh 5 3 4 3 3		pnb .
6310	Tuareg (Hoggar, Ghat)	0.33700	16,739	18,888	29,140	CMT32h	10-AAAB-a	ta-mahaq		0.00	0	1.... 0 3 2 0 1	Tamahaq: Hoggar*	PN. b
6311	Tunisian Arab	2.91700	144,885	163,490	252,226	CMT30	12-AACB-b	east maghrebi		0.11	180	2A.uh 5 4 2 1 2	Arabic: Algerian*	PNB b
6312	USA White	0.10000	4,967	5,605	8,647	CEW19s	52-ABAC-s	general american		75.00	4,204	1Bsuh 10 9 12 5 2	English*	PNB b
6313	Wadshili	0.10300	5,116	5,773	8,906	CMT32d	10-AAAD-b	wajili		0.06	3	0.... 4 2 0 0 0		... b
6314	Zaghawa (Soghaua)	0.15500	7,699	8,687	13,402	NAB61	02-CAAA-a	beri-aa		0.06	5	0.... 4 3 1 0 0		... b
6315	Zuara (Zwara, Zuraa)	0.60000	29,801	33,628	51,881	CMT32z	10-AAAC-s	jerba		0.01	3	1c... 3 3 0 0 0		pn. b
6316	other minor peoples	0.20000	9,934	11,209	17,294	...				10.00	1,121	8 4 2 2 0		
	Liechtenstein	**100.00000**	**30,790**	**32,843**	**41,252**					**82.37**	**27,052**			
6317	Austrian	65.07000	20,035	21,371	26,843	CEW19f	52-ABCF-b	donau-bayrisch-t.		83.00	17,738	0B.uh 10 10 16 5 3		pn. b
6318	German (High German)	4.87000	1,499	1,599	2,009	CEW19m	52-ABCE-a	standard hoch-deutsch	97	88.00	1,408	2B.uh 10 9 13 5 3	German*	PNB b
6319	German Swiss	20.70000	6,374	6,799	8,539	CEW19m	52-ABCG-a	general schwytzer-tütsch		89.00	6,051	0B.uh 10 9 14 5 3	Schwyzerdutsch*	PN. b
6320	Italian	3.88000	1,195	1,274	1,601	CEW21e	51-AABQ-c	standard italiano		90.00	1,147	2B.uh 10 9 14 0 0	Italian	PNB b
6321	Jewish	0.13000	40	43	54	CMT35	52-ABCE-a	standard hoch-deutsch		0.00	0	2B.uh 0 3 2 5 0	German*	PNB b
6322	other minor peoples	5.35000	1,647	1,757	2,207	...				40.30	708	9 8 8 5 0		
	Lithuania	**100.00000**	**3,725,595**	**3,670,269**	**3,398,950**					**87.55**	**3,213,397**			
6323	Armenian	0.04504	1,678	1,653	1,531	CEW14	57-AAAA-b	ashkharik		70.00	1,157	4A.u. 10 7 13 2 1	Armenian: Modern, Eastern	PNB b
6324	Azerbaijani	0.03576	1,332	1,312	1,215	MSY41a	44-AABA-fa	north azeri		0.00	0	2c.u. 0 3 3 0 0	Azerbaijani*	PNB b
6325	Baltic Gypsy	0.07396	2,755	2,715	2,514	CNN25f	59-ACBA-ag	north vlach		70.00	1,900	1c... 10 7 6 1 3	Romani: Latvian	Pn. b

Continued opposite

Table 8-2 continued

EVANGELIZATION								EVANGELISM			ADDITIONAL DESCRIPTIVE DATA
Ref 1	D 28	aC 29	CG% 30	r 31	E 32	U 33	W 34	e 35	R 36	T 37	Locations, civil divisions, literacy, religions, church history, denominations, dioceses, church growth, missions, agencies, ministries, movements 38
6212	2	10	1.27	8	74.50	25.50	B	20.39	72	5	Traders. Muslims 90%(many Alawis). D=Syrian Orthodox Ch(Jacobites; p-Antioch: D-Beirut),RCC(Syrian VP-Lebanon). M=LEM.
6213	0	10	1.10	8	52.10	47.90	B	0.19	95	3	Immigrants, expatriates from Turkey, in commerce. Muslims 100%(Hanafi Sunnis).
6214	10	10	5.70	8	99.78	0.22	C	432.74	119	10	Expatriates from USA, in business, finance. D=NESSL,SDA,CJCLdS,JWs,LBC,COGA,ECON,ICFG,CMA,PCG.
6215	1	7	1.45	1	99.78	0.22	C	367.26	45	9	Also in Syria, Jordan, Palestine. Bilingual in Northeastern Colloquial Arabic. Muslims 22%. D=RCC(Maronites).
6216	0	8	5.63		49.00	51.00	A	35.77	315	5	Egyptian Arabs(COC,CEC), Germans(NAC,GEC), Russians (ROC,ROCOR), Muslim Gypsies(Nawar/Kurbat). Muslims 40%, Nonreligious 20%.
Lesotho											
6217	1	10	1.87	5	99.81	0.19	C	440.94	51	10	Expatriates from South Africa, in government, business. D=DRC/NGK.
6218	5	10	1.73	8	99.75	0.25	C	410.62	53	10	Expatriates from Britain, in education, government, business. D=Anglican Ch in Lesotho/CPSA,RCC,LEC,JWs,MCSA.
6219	4	10	4.67	8	99.80	0.20	C	426.32	108	10	Mixed-race persons(Black/White), mostly in urban areas. D=RCC,CPSA,LEC,AICs.
6220	1	10	1.13	8	99.87	0.13	C	501.72	37	10	Expatriates from France, in commerce, education. D=RCC(4 Dioceses).
6221	0	10	2.89	7	62.00	38.00	B	18.10	172	5	Long-time residents, immigrants from India, Pakistan. Traders. Hindus 60%, Muslims 30%, Baha'is.
6222	4	10	6.23	1	99.65	0.35	C	272.83	173	8	Xhosa-based pidgin, used in towns and mining areas by Zulu/Xhosa/other tribes/mixed-race persons. D=RCC,LEC,AICs,&c.
6223	3	8	4.84	5	99.80	0.20	C	391.28	119	9	Immigrants originating in Swaziland. Workers. Dialect of Swazi and of Sotho. D=AICs,LEC,RCC.
6224	0	9	4.26	0	91.00	9.00	C	199.29	158	7	Bushmen. Also in South Africa. A few bands, rapidly becoming assimilated or extinct. Animists 40%.
6225	9	8	3.92	5	99.69	0.31	C	346.28	97	9	Animists 3.5%, Baha'is 1%. D=RCC(4 Dioceses),LEC,CPSA,AMEC,AoG,NGK,MBBRC,ZCC,many other AICs. M=OMI,PEMS,SM,FMB.
6226	3	8	4.42	5	99.75	0.25	C	355.87	114	9	Workers, citizens. Dialect of Sotho. D=RCC,LEC,AICs.
6227	6	10	4.57	5	99.62	0.38	C	305.50	114	9	Migrant workers from South Africa. Animists 30%. D=RCC,LEC,CPSA,SDA,JWs,many Xhosa AICs.
6228	6	10	5.46	5	99.58	0.42	B	273.15	137	8	Migrants from South Africa. Also in Swaziland, Zimbabwe, Malawi. Animists 32%. D=RCC,LEC,CPSA,SDA,AMEC,many Zulu AICs.
6229	0	9	6.06		83.00	17.00	B	151.47	200	7	USA Whites(COG,AoG,SDA,JWs,PHC), Koreans(M=PCK-Haptong), other Southern Africans, other Africans. Nonreligious 15%, Animists 5%.
Liberia											
6230	4	6	0.87	8	99.73	0.27	C	349.05	41	9	Descendants of returned USA slaves. D=LBC,Lighthouse Fellowship of Chs,many other AICs, M=FMB.
6231	5	9	7.30	4	99.52	0.48	B	225.86	195	8	Migrant workers from Ghana. Animists 32%, Muslims 6%. D=RCC,ECWA,COP,MCG,AICs.
6232	5	6	6.97	1	54.00	46.00	B	19.71	426	5	Northwest. Animists 80%, Muslims 10%. D=ECL,FPC,UHOP,JWs,other AICs. M=SFM,SIM,many other AICs,Order of the Holy Cross,LBT,LCMS.
6233	4	8	7.71	0	99.60	0.40	C	223.38	207	8	Grand Gedeh County; southeast coast and inland. Animists 20%. D=Baptists,Pentecostals,Methodists,AICs.
6234	10	6	4.59	4	99.46	0.54	B	167.90	126	7	Grand Bassa County. Animists 32%. Vast numbers of Bassa AIC schisms. D=RCC(strong work), Bible Faith Christian Ch,ULIC,CoGIC,COTLA,PAW,SDA,UMCL.
6235	5	10	3.27	8	99.79	0.21	C	446.94	78	10	Expatriates from Britain, in education, business. D=Episcopal Ch of Liberia,UMCL,JWs,SDA,RCC.
6236	2	7	3.40	8	99.90	0.10	C	473.04	86	10	Mixed-race persons(Black/White). Almost all Christians. D=RCC,AICs.
6237	3	6	8.09	2	69.00	31.00	B	57.92	380	6	North central Liberia. Majority in Ivory Coast. Animists 75%, Muslims 2%. Ongoing conversions to Islam. D=RCC,ULIC,AoG. M=WEC.
6238	6	6	4.51	0	81.00	19.00	B	124.17	153	7	Montserrado County near coast. Literates 5%. Many bilingual in English. Animists 40%, some Muslims 15%. D=RCC,FPC,PAW,LBC,Ch of God by Faith,other AICs.
6239	6	6	7.51	1	69.00	31.00	B	62.96	298	6	Northeast; near border. Animists 34%. Muslims 1%. D=RCC,UMCL,AoG,FBHCOGA,GARBC,many other AICs. M=BMM,ENIM,SMA,SIM,FMB.
6240	3	6	7.40	4	99.80	0.20	C	440.92	158	10	Migrants from Ghana, Togo. Animists 10%. D=RCC,MCG,AICs.
6241	4	6	7.70	4	99.53	0.47	B	224.40	210	8	From Ghana. Animists 12%, Muslims 5%. D=RCC,ECL,MDCC(Army of the Cross of Christ Ch),many other AICs.
6242	2	8	5.02	0	95.00	5.00	B	190.71	145	7	Southeast. Animists 35%. Many pastors, using Eh Je scriptures. D=Assemblies of God,AICs.
6243	1	10	3.90	8	99.87	0.13	C	514.43	83	10	Expatriates from France, in business. D=RCC(2 Dioceses). M=SMA,WF,FSC.
6244	2	6	4.89	1	91.00	9.00	B	162.75	147	7	Southeast. Grand Gedeh and Maryland Counties. Animists 40%. D=Baptist Chs,AICs. M=FMB,LBT.
6245	1	6	5.74	1	77.00	23.00	B	112.42	204	7	Inaccessible. Nimba County, central Liberia. Many bilingual in Bassa, English. Animists 60%. D=GARBC. M=BMM.
6246	7	6	4.65	1	79.90	20.10	B	113.44	159	7	Maryland County, Eastern Province. Tropical forest. Animists 50%. D=RCC,CoGiC,ECL,UPAG,HOP,many other AICs,JWs. M=SMA,LBT,WEC,NTM.
6247	6	6	6.45	2	47.00	53.00	A	6.86	462	4	Dialect of Dan. Animists 90%, Muslims 5%. Ongoing conversions to Islam. D=RCC,UMCL,ULIC,GARBC,SDA,AICs. M=LIM/WEC,MLBM,FMB.
6248	3	6	5.41	1	80.00	20.00	B	122.64	185	7	Grand Gedeh County, northeastern Liberia. Tropical forest. Animists 45%. D=RCC,AoG,AICs. M=LBT,SIM,NTM.
6249	5	8	7.81	1	97.00	3.00	B	191.18	221	7	Maryland County. Coastal. Animists 25%. D=Baptist Chs,UMC,ECL,RCC,AICs.
6250	2	7	5.25	0	73.00	27.00	B	106.58	197	7	Northeast. Also in Ivory Coast. Animists 60%. D=AoG,AICs. M=Mission Biblique.
6251	2	8	5.25	0	88.00	12.00	B	157.38	163	7	Eastern border. Many animists, 40%. D=RCC,many AICs.
6252	1	6	5.67	1	33.10	66.90	A	2.53	602	4	West. Some in Sierra Leone. Recently islamized: Muslims 75%(Maliki Sunnis), animists 22%. D=Fire Baptized Holiness Ch of God of Africa. M=LBT,SIM,CCMAHK.
6253	8	6	5.13	1	84.00	16.00	B	134.90	167	7	Grand Gedeh County, in southeast. Animists 40%. D=AoG,RCC,ECL,UMCL,LBC,LCL,JWs,AICs. M=LBT,WEC.
6254	8	5	10.09	1	69.00	31.00	B	62.96	457	6	Central. Resistant to Islam. Animists 43%, Muslims 25%. D=LCL,UMCL,SDA,FPC,GARBC,COTLA,ULIC,several other AICs. M=SFM,SIM,WEC,BMM,FMB.
6255	8	7	9.77	4	99.51	0.49	B	201.04	248	8	Eastern Province. Also in many ports (Lagos,Freetown,Accra). Animists 3%. D=RCC,UMCL,ECL,Liberia AoG,LBC,many other Protestant denominations, AICS.
6256	1	10	5.08	8	99.90	0.10	C	476.32	117	10	Regional lingua franca, spoken by mixed-race Black/White multitribal speakers. D=AICs.
6257	3	6	6.74	1	86.00	14.00	B	141.25	215	7	Lofa County. Literates 5%. Many bilinguals in Bandi, Loma, Kpelle. Animists 34%, Muslims 1%. D=LCL,United Pentecostal Ch of Liberia,AICs. M=LBT.
6258	2	10	8.08	8	99.75	0.25	C	385.98	171	9	Traders. Muslims 20%. D=RCC(Maronites),ECWA. M=SIM,FMB.
6259	1	10	4.66	8	99.90	0.10	C	486.18	107	10	Mixed-race Liberian/Americans. Lingua franca used by 68% of nation. English-based pidgin. D=AICs.
6260	3	5	8.15	3	61.00	39.00	B	33.39	432	5	Loffa County in northwest, also in Ivory Coast, Guinea. Resistant to Islam. Animists 60%, Muslims 25%. D=LCL,UMCL,FPC. M=SFM,ELCA,LCMS,FMB,LBT.
6261	0	5	5.21	5	50.00	50.00	B	7.30	397	4	Mandingo traders. Most in Guinea, Guinea Bissau, et alia. Muslims 50% (Maliki Sunnis), animists 46%. M=SIM,WEC.
6262	6	6	7.11	1	44.00	56.00	A	8.03	531	4	Nimba County; also Guinea. Animists 95%. D=RCC(strong work),UMCL,ULIC,AoG,GARBC,several AICs. M=LIM/WEC,WEC(Hong Kong).
6263	0	6	2.81	5	39.03	60.97	A	0.04	340	2	Related to Maninka, but indigenous to Liberia. Muslims 99%(Maliki Sunnis). M=LBT,SIM,WEC. R=ELWA.
6264	4	6	6.34	4	77.00	23.00	B	56.21	302	6	In west. Also in Sierra Leone. Animists 50%, Muslims 30%(Maliki Sunnis). D=UMCL,SDA,LCL,AICs. M=LCMS.
6265	2	8	4.68	0	80.00	20.00	B	116.80	160	7	Grand Gedeh County. Animists 30%. D=Assemblies of God,AICs.
6266	4	6	7.28	1	71.00	29.00	B	77.74	281	6	Eastern Liberia. Animists 60%. D=LBC,FPC,Liberian Christian AoG,many AICs. M=IAOG(Scandinavia),FMB.
6267	5	8	5.00	1	99.54	0.46	B	197.10	137	7	Maryland County; southeast corner. Animists 25%. D=Baptist Chs,ECL,UMC,Pentecostals,AICs.
6268	6	6	7.29	1	52.50	47.50	B	18.20	464	5	Lofa County, in northwest. Also in Sierra Leone. Literates 15%. Animists 79%, Muslims 10%. D=FPC,ECL,RCC,AoG,LCL,JWs. M=LCMS,SFM,FMB,LBT.
6269	2	9	5.19	0	97.00	3.00	B	177.02	147	7	Southeast. Mainly in Ivory Coast. Animists 20%. D=RCC,many AICs.
6270	1	6	6.31	1	79.00	21.00	B	115.34	219	7	Sino County, north of Greenville. Related to Klaoh, Eh Je Grebo. Animists 60%. D=AICs. M=NTM,FMB.
6271	6	10	3.72	8	99.90	0.10	C	512.46	76	10	Afro-Americans from USA, in development. D=Liberian Baptist Convention,PAOW,AMEC,AMEZC,CoGiC,&c.
6272	8	10	3.33	8	99.75	0.25	C	410.62	77	10	Expatriates from USA, in education, business. D=UMCL,LCL,LBC,ECL,LAoG,SDA,JWs,CCCC.
6273	2	3	4.40	1	30.70	69.30	A	0.78	519	3	Western. Also in Sierra Leone. Indigenous script since 1830. Literates 10%. Muslims 90%(Sunnis with some Ahmadis), animists 9%. Y=1850. D=LBC,ECL.
6274	1	8	7.23	1	60.00	40.00	B	41.61	330	6	Northern Krahn. Also in Ivory Coast. Animists 80%, Muslims 1%. D=AICs. M=LBT,FMB.
6275	4	10	6.25	5	99.34	0.66	B	131.54	197	7	Traders from Nigeria. Muslims 40%(Maliki Sunnis,very many Ahmadis), animists 6%. D=RCC,NBC,CLA,many Yoruba AICs.
6276	0	7	4.82		82.00	18.00	B	149.65	161	7	Koreans(M=PCK-Haptong), Kono, Temne, Fulani, other West Africans. Muslims 10%, nonreligious 10%.
Libya											
6277	0	8	3.93	7	38.02	61.98	A	0.02	334	2	Berber peoples now acculturated. Muslims 100% (Hanafi,Shafi,and Maliki Sunnis). M=RCC,CSI.
6278	0	8	2.33	8	42.01	57.99	A	0.01	243	2	African Blacks now assimilated. Muslims 100%(Hanafi,Shafi,and Maliki Sunnis).
6279	0	0	0.00	0	12.02	87.98	A	0.00	0	1.03	Eastern desert regions. Nomads. Most men are bilingual. Muslims (Ibadis) 100%.
6280	1	10	4.95	8	99.65	0.35	C	320.28	124	9	Expatriates from Britain, in oil industry. Nonreligious 20%. D=Anglican Ch/ECJME(D-Egypt). M=ICS.
6281	1	10	2.38	6	99.72	0.28	C	346.89	75	9	Expatriates from Bulgaria. Nonreligious 25%. D=Bulgarian Orthodox Ch(P-Sofia).
6282	1	10	7.51	6	99.83	0.17	C	445.33	160	10	Expatriates from Croatia, in industry. D=RCC(4 jurisdictions).
6283	0	6	6.44	7	45.35	54.65	A	0.57	431	3	Western Colloquial Arabic. Agriculturalists. Muslims 100%(Maliki Sunnis with strong Sanusiyya Sufi brotherhood). M=CSI,FI.
6284	3	7	2.43	8	81.00	19.00	B	47.30	106	6	From Egypt. Muslims 84%(Shafi Sunnis). D=Coptic Orthodox Ch(P-Alexandria: D-North Africa),RCC(Coptic-rite),CEC.
6285	0	1	3.62	8	35.02	64.98	A	0.02	338	2	Nomads, tent-dwellers around oases of Fezzan, also in Murzuk town. Muslims 100%(Maliki Sunnis).
6286	1	10	3.53	8	99.87	0.13	C	501.72	78	10	Expatriates from France, in industry. D=RCC(4 jurisdictions). M=OFM.
6287	0	1	0.70	1	18.05	81.95	A	0.03	205	2	Indigenous Berbers, mostly nomadic, around oasis of Gadames. Muslims 100%(Ibadis/Kharijites).
6288	2	10	1.22	7	99.95	0.05	C	579.07	36	10	Traders from Greece. D=Greek Orthodox Ch(D-Carthage),RCC(Melkites).
6289	0	2	0.00	7	16.00	84.00	A	0.00	0	1.04	Muslim Gypsies. Nomads. Muslims 100%(Hanafi Sunnis).
6290	0	10	2.87	7	53.00	47.00	B	1.93	182	4	Expatriates from Chinese diaspora, in industry. Buddhists, Chinese folk-religionists 90%.
6291	1	10	3.22	7	99.80	0.20	C	435.08	78	10	From Italy. Expelled, allowed back, expelled, &c. Strong Catholics. D=RCC(4 jurisdictions). M=OFM.
6292	0	1	1.10	7	31.01	68.99	A	0.01	155	2	Indigenous nomadic Berbers, with sedentary tribes around Jalo oasis. Muslims 100%(Ibadis/Kharijites).
6293	0	10	0.00	8	32.00	68.00	A	0.00	0	1.17	Small remnant of practicing Arabic/Hebrew/Italian-speaking Jews(decline from 35,000 in 1948). Youths use Arabic.
6294	0	1	1.62	1	7.02	92.98	A	0.00	886	1.02	Indigenous nomadic Berbers, with sedentary inhabitants around oases of Forgha and Jofra. Muslims 100%(Ibadis/Kharijites).
6295	0	0	5.80	6	73.00	27.00	B	66.61	241	6	Expatriate workers from Korea. Engineers. Mahayana Buddhists 70%. D=Presbyterian Church.
6296	0	1	1.62	7	25.02	74.98	A	0.01	254	2	Nomads, tent-dwellers in oases of Kufra and Wanyanga. Muslims 100%(Maliki Sunnis).
6297	1	10	3.16	5	99.95	0.05	C	558.26	67	10	Migrant workers from Malta. Maltese is related to Arabic. D=RCC. M=OFM.
6298	0	4	0.00	1	20.00	80.00	A	0.00	0	1.09	Isolated Berbers in Tripolitania. In Jebel Nafusa oasis on Tunisia border. Muslims 100%(Ibadi/Kharijite sect predominates).
6299	2	10	2.07	8	68.00	32.00	B	24.82	112	5	From Palestine. Muslims 90%(Shafi Sunnis,some Alawis,some Druzes). D=GOC,RCC.
6300	0	10	5.02	5	53.40	46.60	B	4.67	311	4	Expatriates from India, Pakistan. Muslims 85%, some Hindus 9% and Sikhs 3%.
6301	0	1	2.22	7	25.03	74.97	A	0.02	320	2	Nomadic Arabs. Several Bedouin tribes in western desert. Muslims 100%(Maliki Sunnis).
6302	0	1	4.03	7	32.01	67.99	A	0.01	405	2	Nomadic tent-dwellers Arabs. Muslims 100%(Maliki Sunnis in Sanusiyya brotherhood). M=CSI,FI.
6303	0	2	1.10	0	13.06	86.94	A	0.02	367	2	Isolated Berbers in Tripolitania. Muslims 100%(Ibadis).
6304	1	10	7.56	6	99.80	0.20	C	426.32	142	10	Migrant workers from Serbia. D=Serbian Orthodox Ch(P-Belgrade).
6305	0	0	2.45	6	41.00	59.00	A	1.49	202	4	Expatriate workers from Sri Lanka. Theravada Buddhists 99%.
6306	0	1	2.22	7	25.03	74.97	A	0.02	320	2	Nomads, tent-dwelling Arabs. Several Bedouin tribes on arid Sirtican coast. Muslims 100%(Maliki Sunnis).
6307	0	7	4.16	7	48.30	51.70	A	0.52	276	3	Immigrants, migrant workers from Sudan. Muslims 100%(Maliki Sunnis).
6308	0	1	2.33	0	13.03	86.97	A	0.01	784	2	Saharan Negroes. Nomads around oases, on southwestern border. Also Chad, Niger. Bilingual in Arabic. Transhumance; some slavery. Muslims 100%(Malikites).
6309	0	6	6.52	7	45.32	54.68	A	0.52	437	3	Western Colloquial Arabic. Agriculturalists. Muslims 100%(Hanafi and Shafi Sunnis, also Sanusiyya Malikis). M=YWAM-Italy,CSI,FI,MEM.
6310	0	3	0.00	0	18.00	82.00	A	0.00	0	1.07	West Libyan oases around Ghat. Muslims 100%(Sunnis). M=Sahara Desert Mission.
6311	0	10	2.93	8	49.11	50.89	A	0.19	203	3	From Tunisia. Muslims 99%(Maliki Sunnis). M=CSI,FMB.
6312	5	10	6.23	8	99.75	0.25	C	405.15	132	10	Expatriates from USA, related to oil industry. D=SDA,ECJME,BC,CC,Union Ch of Tripoli. M=OFMCap,FMB-SBC.
6313	0	2	1.10	0	13.06	86.94	A	0.02	367	2	Isolated Berbers in Cyrenaica. Muslims 100%(Ibadis).
6314	0	1	1.62	0	13.06	86.94	A	0.02	634	2	Mainly in Sudan and Chad. Majority bilingual in Arabic. Muslims 95%(Maliki Sunnis), animists 5%.
6315	0	2	1.10	1	18.01	81.99	A	0.00	274	1	Berbers in coastal area near Tripoli in Zuwa. Muslims 100%(Ibadis/Kharijis strong).
6316	0	3	4.83		26.00	74.00	A	9.49	509	4	Russians(8 ROC chapels), Lebanese(Maronites), Armenians(AAC), other Europeans, other Africans, Asians. Muslims 85%, Baha'is 5%.
Liechtenstein											
6317	4	8	0.78	8	99.83	0.17	C	460.48	34	10	Expatriates, residents from Austria. D=RCC(part of D-Chur/Switzerland),EKFL,AELCSL,SDA.
6318	3	10	3.39	8	99.88	0.12	C	517.13	77	10	Residents from Germany. Whole population understands Standard German (official language). D=RCC(D-Chur),AELCSL,SDA.
6319	4	10	1.75	8	99.89	0.11	C	513.26	50	10	Residents of Swiss origin. D=RCC(D-Chur),EKFL,AELCSL,SDA.
6320	0	0	4.86	7	99.90	0.10	C	463.18	114	10	Expatriates, residents from Italy. D=RCC.
6321	0	10	0.00	8	48.00	52.00	A	0.00	0	1.13	A small community of practicing German-speaking Jews.
6322	0	10	2.97		73.30	26.70	B	107.82	111	7	French(RCC), other Europeans, Americans. Muslims 50%.
Lithuania											
6323	1	8	4.87	6	99.70	0.30	C	350.03	109	9	Gregorians; based in Armenia. Nonreligious 30%. D=Armenian Apostolic Ch.
6324	0	8	0.00	1	28.00	72.00	A	0.00	0	1.11	From Azerbaijan. 73% monolinguals. Muslims 80%(56% Shias,24% Hanafi Sunnis), nonreligious 20%.
6325	3	10	0.58	1	99.70	0.30	C	291.27	39	8	Part of over 100,000 Romani-speaking Baltic Gypsies, largely nomadic, mainly in Poland. Some animists or nonreligious. D=RCC,ROC,ELCL.

Continued overleaf

Table 8-2 continued

PEOPLE Ref 1	Ethnic name 2	POPULATION P% 3	In 1995 4	In 2000 5	In 2025 6	IDENTITY CODE Race 7	Language 8	LANGUAGE Autoglossonym 9	S 10	CHURCH AC 11	Members 12	MINISTRY Jayuh 13-17	d 18	wa 19	xc 20	mc 21	mi 22	SCRIPTURE Biblioglossonym 23	Pub 24-26	ss 27
6326	Bashkir	0.01143	426	420	389	MSY41b	44-AABB-g	bashqurt		7.00	29	1A.u.	7	5	7	0	1	Bashkir	Pn.	b
6327	Byelorussian	1.71898	64,042	63,091	58,427	CEW22c	53-AAAE-c	bielorusskiy		70.00	44,164	3A.uh	10	8	10	3	3	Byelorussian*	PNB	b
6328	Chuvash	0.01869	696	686	635	MSY41c	44-AAAA-a	chuvash		35.00	240	2....	9	6	8	0	1	Chuvash	PN.	b
6329	Estonian	0.01627	606	597	553	MSW51a	41-AAAC-b	eesti		61.00	364	4A.u.	10	9	8	3	2	Estonian: Tallinn	PNB	b
6330	Georgian	0.01791	667	657	609	CEW17c	42-CABB-a	kharthuli		40.00	263	2A.u.	9	6	8	2	1	Georgian	PNB	b
6331	German	0.05600	2,086	2,055	1,903	CEW19m	52-ABCE-a	standard hoch-deutsch		80.00	1,644	2B.uh	10	9	13	3	2	German*	PNB	b
6332	Jewish	0.16721	6,230	6,137	5,683	CMT35	52-ABCH	yiddish cluster		0.03	2	0B..h	3	3	6	0	0		PNB	b
6333	Karaite (Karaim)	0.05000	1,863	1,835	1,699	MSY41z	44-AABB-h	karaim		0.00	0	1c.u.	0	2	3	0	0	Karaite*	PN.	b
6334	Kazakh	0.01804	672	662	613	MSY41e	44-AABC-c	kazakh		0.00	0	4A.u.	0	3	3	0	2	Kazakh	PN.	b
6335	Latvian	0.11508	4,287	4,224	3,912	CEW15a	54-AABA-a	standard latviashu		91.00	3,844	3A.u.	10	9	10	2	3	Latvian	PNB	b
6336	Lithuanian	75.80861	2,824,322	2,782,380	2,576,697	CEW15b	54-AAAA-a	standard lietuvishkai		91.50	2,545,878	3A.u.	10	9	11	2	2	Lithuanian	PNB	b
6337	Moldavian	0.03946	1,470	1,448	1,341	CEW21f	51-AADC-ab	standard moldavia		82.00	1,188	1A.u.	10	7	8	2	1		pnb	b
6338	Mordvinian	0.01336	498	490	454	MSW51i	41-AADA-a	erzya		65.00	319	2....	10	8	8	2	1	Mordvin: Erzya*	PN.	b
6339	Polish (Pole)	7.02062	261,560	257,676	238,627	CEW22i	53-AAAC-c	polski		91.00	234,485	2A.uh	10	8	11	2	3	Polish	PNB	b
6340	Russian	9.37343	349,216	344,030	318,598	CEW22j	53-AAAE-d	russkiy	84	62.00	213,299	4B.uh	10	8	10	3	3	Russian	PNB	b
6341	Samogit (Lithuanian)	3.88786	144,846	142,695	132,146	CEW15b	54-AAAA-a	standard lietuvishkai		90.00	128,425	3A.u.	10	8	11	2	1	Lithuanian	PNB	b
6342	Tajik	0.01420	529	521	483	CNT24g	58-AACC-j	tajiki		0.00	0	2asu.	0	3	3	0	1	Tajik*	PNB	b
6343	Tatar	0.13974	5,206	5,129	4,750	MSY41h	44-AABB-e	tatar		1.50	77	2c.u.	6	4	8	0	1	Tatar: Kazan	Pn.	b
6344	Ukrainian	1.21881	45,408	44,734	41,427	CEW22p	53-AAAE-b	ukrainskiy		75.00	33,550	3A.uh	10	8	11	3	3	Ukrainian	PNB	b
6345	Uzbek	0.03954	1,473	1,451	1,344	MSY41l	44-AABD-a	central uzbek		0.00	0	1A.u.	0	3	6	1	1	Uzbek*	PNb	b
6346	other minor peoples	0.10000	3,726	3,670	3,399	...				70.00	2,569		10	8	8	5	0			
	Luxembourg	**100.00000**	**406,900**	**430,615**	**463,356**					**93.51**	**402,673**									
6347	Arab	1.23000	5,005	5,297	5,699	CMT30	12-AACA	standard arabic cluster		18.00	953	0.su.	8	8	7	0	0		...	.
6348	British	1.00000	4,069	4,306	4,634	CEW19i	52-ABAC-b	standard-english	35	79.00	3,402	3Bsuh	10	9	13	5	2		PNB	b
6349	Dutch	0.90000	3,662	3,876	4,170	CEW19h	52-ABCA-a	algemeen-nederlands	5	76.00	2,945	2Bsuh	10	9	15	5	2	Dutch	PNB	b
6350	Esperanto	0.00000	0	0	0	CEW21z	51-AAAC-a	proper esperanto	6	70.00	0	0A...	10	9	7	5	0	Esperanto	PNB	b
6351	Fleming	0.90000	3,662	3,876	4,170	CEW19k	52-ABCA-g	oostvlaandersch	5	91.00	3,527	1Bsuh	10	9	15	5	2		pnb	b
6352	French	2.10000	8,545	9,043	9,730	CEW21b	51-AABI-d	general français	92	87.00	7,867	1B.uh	10	9	14	5	3	French	PNB	b
6353	German (High German)	2.40000	9,766	10,335	11,121	CEW19m	52-ABCE-a	standard hoch-deutsch	97	88.00	9,095	2B.uh	10	9	13	5	3	German*	PNB	b
6354	Greek	0.10000	407	431	463	CEW20	56-AAAA-c	dhimotiki		95.00	409	2B.uh	10	9	11	5	1	Greek: Modern	PNB	b
6355	Italian	7.30000	29,704	31,435	33,825	CEW21e	51-AABQ-c	standard italiano	11	94.00	29,549	2B.uh	10	9	15	5	3	Italian	PNB	b
6356	Jewish	0.18000	732	775	834	CMT35	52-ABCE-a	standard hoch-deutsch		0.30	2	2B.uh	5	4	6	5	0	German*	PNB	b
6357	Luxemburger	67.99000	276,651	292,775	315,036	CEW19o	52-ABCD-b	letzebürgesch-t.		95.90	280,771	0a.uh	10	10	13	5	3	Luxembourgeois	...	b
6358	Portuguese	12.60000	51,269	54,257	58,383	CEW21g	51-AABA-e	general português		95.00	51,545	2Bsuh	10	9	12	0	0	Portuguese	PNB	b
6359	USA White	0.50000	2,035	2,153	2,317	CEW19s	52-ABAC-s	general american		78.00	1,679	1Bsuh	10	9	13	5	2	English*	PNB	b
6360	Walloon	0.90000	3,662	3,876	4,170	CEW21l	51-AABH-f	wallon		92.00	3,565	0A.uh	10	9	15	5	1	French: Walloon	P..	b
6361	other minor peoples	1.90000	7,731	8,182	8,804	...				90.00	7,364		10	8	8	5	0			
	Macedonia	**100.00000**	**1,963,488**	**2,023,580**	**2,257,977**					**63.61**	**1,287,191**									
6362	Arab	0.30000	5,890	6,071	6,774	CMT30	12-AACF-f	syro-palestinian		5.00	304	1Asuh	7	5	6	5	2	Arabic: Lebanese*	Pnb	b
6363	Aromanian (Aromunen)	5.00000	98,174	101,179	112,899	CEW21i	51-AADB-a	limba armâneasc-a		84.00	84,990	0a...	10	9	8	5	3	Romanian: Macedonian*	P..	b
6364	Balkan Gypsy (Jerides)	5.20000	102,101	105,226	117,415	CNN25f	59-ACBA-bc	arlija		10.00	10,523	1A...	8	5	8	5	0	Romani: Arlija	Pn.	.
6365	Bosniac (Muslimani)	1.80000	35,343	36,424	40,644	CEW22a	53-AAAG-a	standard srpski		0.03	11	1Asuh	3	4	5	5	3	Serbian*	PNB	b
6366	Bulgar	1.00000	19,635	20,236	22,580	CEW22b	53-AAAH-b	bulgarski		71.00	14,367	2A.uh	10	8	8	5	2	Bulgarian	PNB	b
6367	Croat	2.00000	39,270	40,472	45,160	CEW22d	53-AAAG-b	standard hrvatski		90.00	36,424	2Asuh	10	9	11	5	3	Croatian	PNB	b
6368	French	0.02000	393	405	452	CEW21b	51-AABI-d	general français		85.00	344	1B.uh	10	9	14	5	3	French	PNB	b
6369	German	0.01000	196	202	226	CEW19m	52-ABCE-a	standard hoch-deutsch		87.00	176	2B.uh	10	9	13	5	3	German*	PNB	b
6370	Greek	1.00000	19,635	20,236	22,580	CEW20	56-AAAA-c	dhimotiki		95.00	19,224	2B.uh	10	9	10	5	3	Greek: Modern	PNB	b
6371	Hungarian	0.10000	1,963	2,024	2,258	MSW51g	41-BAAA-a	general magyar		81.00	1,639	2A.u.	10	9	10	5	3	Hungarian	PNB	b
6372	Italian	0.05000	982	1,012	1,129	CEW21e	51-AABQ-c	standard italiano		84.00	850	2B.uh	10	9	15	5	3	Italian	PNB	b
6373	Jewish	0.05000	982	1,012	1,129	CMT35	53-AAAG-a	standard srpski		0.20	2	1Asuh	5	3	3	0	0	Serbian*	PNB	b
6374	Kosovar (Albanian)	18.00000	353,428	364,244	406,436	CEW13	55-AAAA-c	kosove		25.00	91,061	2c.u.	9	5	5	2	3		pn.	b
6375	Macedonian	53.87000	1,057,731	1,090,103	1,216,372	CEW22g	53-AAAH-a	makedonski		89.00	970,191	2a.uh	10	10	10	5	3	Macedonian*	PNB	b
6376	Meglenite (Vlasi)	0.30000	5,890	6,071	6,774	CEW21i	51-AADB-b	meglenitsa		83.00	5,039	0c...	10	9	8	5	1		p..	b
6377	Montenegrin	0.20000	3,927	4,047	4,516	CEW22h	53-AAAG-a	standard srpski		66.00	2,671	1Asuh	10	8	8	5	2	Serbian*	PNB	b
6378	Pomak	0.10000	1,963	2,024	2,258	CEW22b	53-AAAH-b	bulgarski		1.00	20	2A.uh	6	3	3	0	2	Bulgarian	PNB	b
6379	Romanian	0.50000	9,817	10,118	11,290	CEW21i	51-AADC-a	limba româneasca		84.00	8,499	3A.u.	10	8	10	4	2	Romanian	PNB	b
6380	Rumelian Turk	2.90000	56,941	58,684	65,481	MSY41j	44-AABA-a	osmanli		0.02	12	1A.u.	3	3	3	1	0	Turkish	PNB	b
6381	Serb	2.10000	41,233	42,495	47,418	CEW22l	53-AAAG-a	standard srpski		80.00	33,996	1Asuh	10	9	9	5	3	Serbian*	PNB	b
6382	Serbian Rom Gypsy	0.10000	1,963	2,024	2,258	CNN25f	59-ACBA-b	balkan-romani		60.00	1,214	1A...	10	7	8	4	1		Pn.	b
6383	Turk	4.80000	94,247	97,132	108,383	MSY41j	44-AABA-a	osmanli		0.05	49	1A.u.	4	3	2	1	0	Turkish	PNB	b
6384	Ukrainian	0.10000	1,963	2,024	2,258	CEW22p	53-AAAE-b	ukrainskiy		76.00	1,538	3A.uh	10	8	10	5	3	Ukrainian	PNB	b
6385	other minor peoples (15)	0.50000	9,817	10,118	11,290	...				40.00	4,047		9	6	6	4	0			
	Madagascar	**100.00000**	**13,744,268**	**15,941,727**	**28,963,663**					**47.86**	**7,629,264**									
6386	Antaifasy	0.65710	90,314	104,753	190,320	MSY44j	31-LDAB-e	an-taifasy		14.20	14,875	0A.u.	8	5	7	4	1		...	.
6387	Antaimanambondro	0.27600	37,934	43,999	79,940	MSY44j	31-LDAA-g	taimanambondro		24.00	10,560	1Asu.	9	5	6	4	1		pnb	.
6388	Antaimoro	3.52190	484,059	561,452	1,020,071	MSY44j	31-LDAB-b	an-taimoro		43.90	246,477	0A.u.	9	6	8	4	2		...	.
6389	Antaisaka	5.91800	813,386	943,431	1,714,070	MSY44j	31-LDAB-f	an-taisaka		25.90	244,349	0A.u.	9	5	7	4	1		...	.
6390	Antaivato	0.40400	55,527	64,405	117,013	MSY44j	31-LDAA-eb	an-taiva		30.00	19,321	1Asu.	9	5	6	4	1		pnb	.
6391	Antambahoaka	0.36440	50,084	58,092	105,544	MSY44j	31-LDAB-a	an-tambahoaka		15.00	8,714	0A.u.	8	5	7	4	1		...	.
6392	Antandroy	4.40000	604,748	701,436	1,274,401	MSY44j	31-LDAC-a	an-tandroy		19.80	138,884	0A.u.	8	5	7	4	2		...	.
6393	Antankarana	0.69600	95,660	110,954	201,587	MSY44j	31-LDAF-a	an-tankarana		13.40	14,868	0A...	8	5	8	4	1		...	.
6394	Antanosy	2.45060	336,817	390,668	709,784	MSY44j	31-LDAB-g	an-tanosy		49.70	194,162	0A.u.	9	6	8	4	1		...	.
6395	Antetsimatra	0.14900	20,479	23,753	43,156	MSY44j	31-LDAA	central malagasy cluster		40.00	9,501	2Asu.	9	5	6	4	1	Malagasy	PNB	b
6396	Bara	3.36460	462,440	536,375	974,511	MSY44j	31-LDAC-g	bara-mikaty		43.20	231,714	0A.u.	9	6	7	4	3		...	.
6397	Betsileo	11.34000	1,558,600	1,807,792	3,284,479	MSY44j	31-LDAA-j	betsileo		91.80	1,659,553	1Asu.	10	9	10	5	3		pnb	.
6398	Betsimisaraka	7.67900	1,055,422	1,224,165	2,224,120	MSY44j	31-LDAA-c	north betsimisaraka		22.00	269,316	1Asu.	9	5	8	4	3		pnb	.
6399	Betsimisaraka (Betanimena	5.74500	789,608	915,852	1,663,962	MSY44j	31-LDAA-c	north betsimisaraka		29.00	265,597	1Asu.	9	5	11	4	2		pnb	.
6400	Bezanozano	0.71870	98,780	114,573	208,162	MSY44j	31-LDAA-e	bezanuzanu		26.00	29,789	1Asu.	9	5	7	4	1		pnb	.
6401	British	0.01500	2,062	2,391	4,345	CEW19i	52-ABAC-b	standard-english	5	79.00	1,889	3Bsuh	10	9	13	4	1		PNB	b
6402	Comorian (Ngazija)	0.50000	68,721	79,709	144,818	NAB57j	99-AUSM-s	shi-ngazidya		0.02	16	1csu.	3	4	2	1	2	Comorian*	PNb	b
6403	French	0.60000	82,466	95,650	173,782	CEW21b	51-AABI-d	general français	35	87.00	83,216	1B.uh	10	9	14	5	3	French	PNB	b
6404	Gujarati	0.32000	43,982	51,014	92,684	CNN25e	59-AAFH-b	standard gujaraati		0.10	51	2A.u.	5	4	3	3	0	Gujarati	PNB	b
6405	Han Chinese	0.25000	34,361	39,854	72,409	MSY42a	79-AAAB-ba	kuo-yü	2	70.00	27,898	2Bsuh	10	8	10	4	1	Chinese: Kuoyu*	PNB	b
6406	Jewish	0.00150	206	239	434	CMT35	51-AABI-d	general français		0.00	0	1B.uh	0	4	2	1	0	French	PNB	b
6407	Karimbola	0.53200	73,120	84,810	154,087	MSY44j	31-LDAA	central malagasy cluster		20.00	16,962	2Asu.	9	5	6	4	1	Malagasy	PNB	b
6408	Kimoso	0.10640	14,624	16,962	30,817	BYG12	31-LDAA	central malagasy cluster		5.00	848	2Asu.	7	5	6	2	1	Malagasy	PNB	b
6409	Lohanosy	0.06380	8,769	10,171	18,479	MSY44j	31-LDAB-g	an-tanosy		70.00	7,120	0A.u.	10	7	7	4	1		...	.
6410	Mahafaly	1.50510	206,865	239,939	435,932	MSY44j	31-LDAC-b	mahafale		24.90	59,745	0A.u.	9	5	7	4	1		...	.
6411	Makua (Makhua, Makoa)	1.07430	147,655	171,262	311,157	NAB57b	99-AUSY-a	e-meeto		4.40	7,536	2.s..	6	5	8	4	1		pnb	b
6412	Malay	0.11800	16,218	18,811	34,177	MSY44k	31-PHAA-b	bahasa-malaysia		0.10	19	1asuh	5	3	5	0	0	Malay	PNB	b
6413	Marofotsy	0.10640	14,624	16,962	30,817	MSY44j	31-LDAA	central malagasy cluster		33.00	5,597	2Asu.	9	5	6	4	1	Malagasy	PNB	b
6414	Masianaky	0.17020	23,393	27,133	49,296	MSY44j	31-LDAA	central malagasy cluster		15.00	4,070	2Asu.	8	5	6	4	1	Malagasy	PNB	b
6415	Mauritian	0.01250	1,718	1,993	3,620	CNN25g	59-AAFQ-a	bhojpuri		4.00	80	1.s..	6	5	7	4	1	Bihari: Bhojpuri*	Pn.	b
6416	Merina (Hova, Imerina)	16.28970	2,238,900	2,596,860	4,718,094	MSY44j	31-LDAA-aa	standard merina	100	85.00	2,207,331	1Asu.	10	10	10	5	3		pnb	b
6417	Merina (Vakinankaratra)	7.66000	1,052,811	1,221,136	2,218,617	MSY44j	31-LDAA-aa	standard merina		79.00	964,698	1Asu.	10	8	10	5	3		pnb	b
6418	Mikea	0.01060	1,457	1,690	3,070	BYG12	31-LDAD	west malagasy cluster		4.96	84	0A.u.	6	5	5	3	0		...	b
6419	Morisyen	0.03000	4,123	4,783	8,689	NAN58	51-AACC-l	morisyen		92.00	4,400	1cs..	10	8	8	0	0	Mauritius Creole*	Pnb	.
6420	North Korean	0.05770	7,930	9,198	16,712	MSY46	45-AAAA-bc	north onmun		0.90	83	1A...	5	4	8	3	0	Korean	PNB	b
6421	Onjatsy	0.21300	29,275	33,956	61,693	MSY44j	31-LDAA	central malagasy cluster		20.00	6,791	2Asu.	9	5	6	4	1	Malagasy	PNB	b
6422	Reunionese	0.40000	54,977	63,767	115,855	NAN58	51-AACC-m	réunioné		95.00	60,579	1cs..	10	8	10	4	1		pnb	b
6423	Russian	0.11000	15,119	17,536	31,860	CEW22j	53-AAAE-d	russkiy		20.00	3,507	4B.uh	9	5	8	4	1	Russian	PNB	b
6424	Sahafatra	0.63800	87,688	101,708	184,788	MSY44j	31-LDAA-i	sahafatra		30.00	30,512	1Asu.	9	5	6	4	1		pnb	.
6425	Sahavoay	0.19150	26,320	30,528	55,465	MSY44j	31-LDAA	central malagasy cluster		15.00	4,579	2Asu.	8	5	6	4	1	Malagasy	PNB	b
6426	Saint-Marien	0.24810	34,100	39,551	71,859	MSY44j	31-LDAA	central malagasy cluster		40.00	15,821	2Asu.	9	6	7	4	1	Malagasy	PNB	b
6427	Sakalava	3.82210	525,320	609,309	1,107,020	MSY44j	31-LDAD	west malagasy cluster		32.00	194,979	0A.u.	9	5	11	5	3		...	b
6428	Sakalava (Behosy)	0.21300	29,275	33,956	61,693	MSY44j	31-LDAD	west malagasy cluster		33.00	11,205	0A.u.	9	5	10	5	3		...	b
6429	Sakalava (Masikoro)	0.63800	87,688	101,708	184,788	MSY44j	31-LDAD	west malagasy cluster		33.00	33,564	0A.u.	9	5	10	5	2		...	b
6430	Sakalava (Vezo)	1.27600	175,377	203,416	369,576	MSY44j	31-LDAD	west malagasy cluster		30.00	61,025	0A.u.	9	5	10	5	1		...	b
6431	Sihanaka	2.27470	312,641	362,626	658,836	MSY44j	31-LDAA-b	sihanaka		26.70	96,821	1Asu.	9	5	8	4	1		pnb	.
6432	Swahili	0.02000	2,749	3,188	5,793	NAB57j	99-AUSM-b	standard ki-swahili	2	0.00	0	4Asu.	0	3	2	1	0	Kiswahili*	PNB	b
6433	Tanala	3.95500	543,586	630,495	1,145,513	MSY44j	31-LDAA-h	tanala		20.10	126,730	1Asu.	9	5	8	4	1		pnb	.
6434	Tanosimboahangy	0.21300	29,275	33,956	61,693	MSY44j	31-LDAB-g	an-tanosy		20.00	6,791	0A.u.	9	5	6	4	0		...	.
6435	Tsimihety	7.00970	963,432	1,117,467	2,030,266	MSY44j	31-LDAE-c	tsimihety		14.00	156,445	0A.u.	8	5	10	4	3	Malagasy: Tsimihety*	P..	b
6436	Vazimba	0.63800	87,688	101,708	184,788	MSY44j	31-LDAA	central malagasy cluster		50.00	50,854	2Asu.	10	6	7	4	0	Malagasy	PNB	b
6437	Vorimo	0.10640	14,624	16,962	30,817	MSY44j	31-LDAA-f	vorimo		18.00	3,053	1Asu.	8	5	6	4	0		pnb	.
6438	Yemeni Arab	0.20000	27,489	31,883	57,927	CMT30	12-AACF-n	yemeni	1	0.01	3	1Asuh	3	2	2	0	0		pnb	b
6439	Zafisoro	0.42600	58,551	67,912	123,385	MSY44j	31-LDAB-c	zafisoro		14.00	9,508	0A.u.	8	5	6	4	0		...	.
6440	other minor peoples	0.30000	41,233	47,825	86,891	...				15.00	7,174		8	5	7	3	0			
	Malawi	**100.00000**	**9,670,315**	**10,925,238**	**19,958,349**					**64.37**	**7,032,259**									
6441	Afrikaner	0.02000	1,934	2,185	3,992	CEW19a	52-ABCB-a	afrikaans	3	80.00	1,748	2B.uh	10	9	14	5	2	Afrikaans	PNB	b

Continued opposite

Table 8-2 continued

EVANGELIZATION								EVANGELISM			ADDITIONAL DESCRIPTIVE DATA
Ref 1	D 28	aC 29	CG% 30	r 31	E 32	U 33	W 34	e 35	R 36	T 37	Locations, civil divisions, literacy, religions, church history, denominations, dioceses, church growth, missions, agencies, ministries, movements 38
6326	1	9	3.42	4	51.00	49.00	B	13.03	227	5	Tatar spoken by many as mother tongue. Muslims 72%(Hanafi Sunnis), nonreligious 21%. D=Russian Orthodox Ch.
6327	3	8	0.58	5	99.70	0.30	C	355.14	31	9	White Russians. Nonreligious/atheists 30%. D=Russian Orthodox Ch,RCC,Old Ritualist Chs.
6328	1	9	0.58	0	76.00	24.00	B	97.09	50	6	From Chuvashia (Russia). Muslims 35%(Sunnis), nonreligious 30%. D=ROC. M=IBT.
6329	5	8	0.58	5	99.61	0.39	C	278.31	38	8	In Estonia and 10 other countries. Nonreligious/atheists 39%. D=Russian Orthodox Ch,ELCE,RCC,MCE,AUCECB. M=UBS,LBI.
6330	1	9	3.32	4	97.00	3.00	B	141.62	94	7	Nonreligious/atheists 55%, Muslims 5%(Sunnis,Shias). D=Georgian Orthodox Ch.
6331	2	10	0.58	8	99.80	0.20	C	449.68	31	10	Long-time residents from Germany, Russia. Nonreligious 20%. D=German ELC,AUCECB.
6332	0	10	0.00	5	48.03	51.97	A	0.05	39	2	Religious Jews, bilingual in Russian, Lithuanian. Many have emigrated to Israel, many return.
6333	0	10	0.00	1	26.00	74.00	A	0.00	0	1.10	In Crimea (city of Galiche), as well as Lithuania. 'Readers of the Scriptures'. Heretical Jewish sect rejecting Talmud. Almost russified. 1842: OT published.
6334	0	8	0.00	4	36.00	64.00	A	0.00	0	1.10	Muslims 60%(Hanafi Sunnis, with Sufi influence), nonreligous 30%, atheists 10%. M=ROC,CSI.
6335	5	9	0.58	5	99.91	0.09	C	524.79	31	10	From Latvia; in 25 countries. D=ROC,RCC,ELCL,RCL,CB.
6336	4	8	0.49	5	99.92	0.08	C	532.69	8	10	In 24 countries. Nonreligious 8%. D=RCC(6 Dioceses),ELCL,ERCL,ROC(D-Vilnius); 50-year history of vicious state persecution by USSR. M=UBS,IBT.
6337	1	9	0.58	6	99.82	0.18	C	413.03	31	10	From Bessarabia, Romania. Nonreligious 18%. D=Russian Orthodox Ch, Moldavian Orthodox Ch.
6338	1	8	0.58	7	99.65	0.35	C	272.83	14	8	Migrants, residents from Mordvinia (Russia). Acculturated to Russian. Nonreligious 35%. D=ROC. M=IBT.
6339	4	10	0.58	6	99.91	0.09	C	538.08	10	10	Poles in Western Ukraine. 29% speak Polish as mother tongue. D=RCC(3 Dioceses),ROC,CEF,Polish Pentecostal Movement/CWE.
6340	8	9	0.58	7	99.62	0.38	C	300.97	12	9	In 70 countries. Nonreligious 28%, atheists 10%. D=ROC,RCC,AUCECB,Old Ritualists,CEF,CCECB,SDA,IPKH.
6341	1	8	0.58	5	99.90	0.10	C	505.89	10	10	Kaunas area, southeast Lithuania. Dialect of Lithuanian, with own Bible in Samogit. Nonreligious 10%. D=RCC.
6342	0	9	0.00	4	40.00	60.00	A	0.00	0	1.12	Mainly in Tajikistan, Uzbekistan, Kirghizia. Trilingual (with Uzbek, Russian). Muslims 90%(Hanafi Sunnis), nonreligious 10%. M=CSI.
6343	1	8	0.58	6	43.50	56.50	A	2.38	87	4	From Tatarstan (Russia). Muslims 83%(Hanafi Sunnis), nonreligious 15%. D=ROC.
6344	7	8	0.58	6	99.75	0.25	C	399.67	33	9	In 15 countries. Nonreligious/atheists 25%. D=ROC(E-Ukraine)UOC,UAOC,Ukrainian Catholic Ch,AUCECB,CEF,CCECB,JWs,SDA.
6345	0	9	0.00	5	41.00	59.00	A	0.00	0	1.12	Literates 100%. 55% speak Russian. Muslims 80%(Hanafi Sunnis), nonreligious 20%. M=CSI.
6346	0	10	0.58		99.70	0.30	C	273.38	15	8	Other West Europeans, Americans, Asians, Africans, Arabs. Nonreligious 25%, Muslims 5%.
Luxembourg											
6347	0	0	4.66	8	36.00	64.00	A	23.65	408	5	Migrant workers from North Africa, Levant, and Western Asia. Muslims 82%. D=RCC.
6348	2	10	0.60	8	99.79	0.21	C	444.05	31	10	Expatriates from Britain. D=Communaute Protestante Anglaise,Ch of England(D-Europe).
6349	2	10	0.60	6	99.76	0.24	C	424.42	26	10	Expatriates from Holland, in business, commerce. Nonreligious 20%. D=NPG,RCC.
6350	0	10	0.00	5	99.70	0.30	C	329.59	0	9	Artificial (constructed) language, in 80 countries. Speakers in Luxembourg: 22,000(none mother-tongue). Nonreligious 30%.
6351	2	10	0.60	6	99.91	0.09	C	541.40	29	10	Dutch-speaking Belgians, working in government, administration. D=NPG,RCC.
6352	4	10	0.60	8	99.87	0.13	C	523.95	26	10	Expatriates from France, in administration. D=RCC,EPC,SDA,JWs. M=OSB,SCJ,CSSR,SJ,WF,CS,OMI,SDB.
6353	7	10	0.60	8	99.88	0.12	C	533.19	29	10	Expatriates from Germany. Standard German. D=EPGDL,RCC(D-Luxembourg),CP-CECA,NAC,RAG,SDA,JWs.
6354	1	10	0.60	7	99.95	0.05	C	572.13	26	10	Migrant workers from Greece. D=Greek Orthodox Ch(D-Belgium).
6355	1	10	0.60	7	99.94	0.06	C	590.13	25	10	Expatriates from Italy. All Catholics. D=RCC(D-Luxembourg). M=SJ,OSB,&c.
6356	0	10	0.70	8	59.30	40.70	B	0.64	64	3	Small community of practicing German-speaking Jews(70% citizens).
6357	6	9	0.37	8	99.96	0.04	C	559.70	25	10	Letzburgisch, Moselle Franconian. Also speakers in Belgium, Germany(Bitburg area), USA. D=RCC(D-Luxembourg),EPGDL,JWs,NAC,CP-CECA,&c. M=EMBMC.
6358	0	0	8.92	8	99.95	0.05	C	516.65	183	10	Expatriates, residents from Portugal. D=RCC.
6359	2	10	2.30	8	99.78	0.22	C	429.89	58	10	Expatriates from USA, in business, commerce. D=SDA,JWs.
6360	1	10	0.60	8	99.92	0.08	C	523.84	30	10	French-speaking Belgians, employed in Luxembourg. D=RCC.
6361	0	10	0.78		99.90	0.10	C	417.19	17	10	Russians(ROCOR), Danes, other Europeans, Americans, Asians, some Africans.
Macedonia											
6362	2	9	3.47	8	64.00	36.00	B	11.68	179	5	Migrant workers from North Africa, Levant, Arabia. Muslims 90%(Sunnis,Shias). D=RCC,GOC.
6363	3	10	1.23	6	99.84	0.16	C	438.43	45	10	Armini. In Macedonia, southern Yugoslavia. Also in northern Greece, Bulgaria. Nonreligious 15%. D=ROC,MOC,RCC.
6364	0	8	1.23	6	60.00	40.00	B	21.90	103	5	Arlija, Dzambazi. Tinner's Romany. Also in southern Serbia. Muslims 90%(Hanafi Sunnis).
6365	0	8	2.43	6	54.03	45.97	B	0.05	169	2	All are 100% ethnic Muslims(45% of inhabitants of Bosnia), all Hanafi Sunnis. M=RCC,SOC,OCCBH,CAC.
6366	2	10	1.23	6	99.71	0.29	C	362.81	48	9	Workers, settlers from Bulgaria. Dmitrovgrad and Bosiljgrad Districts. Nonreligious 25%. D=Bulgarian Orthodox Ch(P-Sofia),RCC(in Banat).
6367	8	8	1.22	6	99.90	0.10	C	535.45	39	10	Republic of Croatia. In 10 countries. Nonreligious 7%, atheists 3%. Strongly Catholic. D=RCC(19 Dioceses),COGY,COCC,CNOCC,PCCY,ECCBHV,RCCY,CAC.
6368	3	10	1.23	8	99.85	0.15	C	502.60	37	10	Expatriates from France, in business. Nonreligious 13%. D=RCC,SDA,JWs. M=OFM,SJ,SDB,OP,OFMConv.
6369	6	10	1.23	8	99.87	0.13	C	520.78	40	10	Expatriates from Germany, in business. D=RCC,ECCBHV,PCCY,NAC,SDA,JWs(UJWY).
6370	4	10	1.23	7	99.95	0.05	C	589.47	36	10	Emigres from Greece, in business, commerce. D=GOC,SOC,MOC,AOC,RCC(Byzantine-rite: D-Krizevcil).
6371	4	8	1.23	6	99.81	0.19	C	443.47	48	10	Emigres, refugees from Hungary. Related to majority: In Vojvodina(Serbia). D=RCC(D-Subotica,AA-Banat),RCCY,ECS,CNC.
6372	1	10	1.23	7	99.84	0.16	C	490.56	38	10	Emigres, workers, settlers from Italy. D=RCC(D-Porec & Pula). M=OFM,SJ,SDB,OP.
6373	0	10	0.70	6	48.20	51.80	A	0.35	79	3	Decline from 80,000 in 1925 due to mass murders by Nazis. High percent practicing Jews.
6374	3	8	1.25	6	75.00	25.00	B	68.43	65	6	Militant northern Albanians connected with Kosovo(Serbia). Muslims 75%(Hanafi Sunnis). D=AOC,MOC,RCC.
6375	6	9	0.81	5	99.89	0.11	C	516.51	30	10	In 8 countries. 3 dialects. D=Macedonian Orthodox Ch(5 Dioceses),RCC(D-Skopje-Prizren),SOC(D-Skopje),MCY,UBCY,COGY. R=TWR9Monaco),IBRA.
6376	1	10	1.23	6	99.83	0.17	C	405.95	48	10	Megleno-Romanian, from Meglen region (Greece). D=Greek Orthodox Ch.
6377	2	8	1.23	6	99.66	0.34	C	317.98	48	9	From Montenegro. Nonreligious 30%. D=Serbian Orthodox Ch(M-Montenegro & Coastland),RCC(D-Kotor,AD-Bar).
6378	2	10	1.21	6	54.00	46.00	B	1.97	124	4	Bulgarian Muslims converted from Orthodoxy under Ottoman rule. Muslims 99% (Hanafi Sunnis). Some converts to Protestantism. D=COG(Anderson),AoG.
6379	2	9	1.23	6	99.84	0.16	C	466.03	42	10	Citizens, migrant workers from Romania. Nonreligious 15%. D=Romanian Orthodox Ch(P-Bucharest),PCCY.
6380	0	10	1.10	8	47.02	52.98	A	0.03	105	2	In Macedonia and Kosovo; also in 20 other countries. Muslims 100%(Hanafi Sunnis).
6381	6	8	2.87	6	99.80	0.20	C	438.00	52	10	Migrant workers from Serbia. Others in 18 countries. Nonreligious 11%, atheists 7%, many Muslims. D=Serbian Orthodox Ch(21 Dioceses),RCC(3 Dioceses).
6382	3	8	1.23	6	99.60	0.40	C	249.66	54	8	Closely related to Sinti Manush. Muslims 20%(Hanafi Sunnis), many nonreligious 20%. D=RCC,SOC,GEM. M=GGMS.
6383	0	9	3.97	8	46.05	53.95	A	0.08	278	2	Migrant workers from Turkey, refugees from Bulgaria. Muslims 99%(Hanafi Sunnis).
6384	4	8	1.23	6	99.76	0.24	C	407.77	45	10	Emigres from Ukraine. Nonreligious 20%. D=UOC,ROC,RCC,SOC,PCCY.
6385	0	9	1.23		69.00	31.00	B	100.74	49	7	Armenians, Georgians, Azerbaijanis, Russians, other Europeans, Africans, Asians. Muslims 40%, nonreligious 10%.
Madagascar											
6386	1	7	4.57	4	54.20	45.80	B	28.09	295	5	Animists 80%, Baha'is 0.2%. D=RCC(D-Farafangana). M=CM.
6387	1	7	3.26	4	72.00	28.00	B	63.07	172	6	Animists 75%. D=RCC.
6388	1	7	3.36	4	86.90	13.10	B	139.24	146	7	Superficially islamized. Animists 50%, Muslims 2%, Baha'is 0.2%(increasing fast). D=RCC(2 Dioceses). M=CM,MEP.
6389	1	7	3.18	4	66.90	33.10	B	63.24	182	6	Southeast coastal strip. Animists 72%, Baha'is 0.1%. D=RCC(D-Farafangana). M=CM.
6390	1	7	2.96	4	78.00	22.00	B	85.41	149	6	Animists 70%. D=RCC.
6391	1	7	3.19	4	54.00	46.00	B	29.56	226	5	Somewhat islamized. Animists 80%, Muslims 2%, Baha'is 0.2%. D=RCC.
6392	1	7	3.78	4	60.80	39.20	B	43.94	228	6	Extreme south coast of island and inland. Animists 80%. D=RCC(D-Fort-Dauphin). M=CM,FMB.
6393	1	8	3.08	4	56.40	43.60	B	27.58	211	5	Strongly islamized. Animists 80%, Muslims 6%. D=RCC.
6394	1	7	3.07.	4	91.70	8.30	B	166.34	130	7	Superficially islamized. Animists 45%, Muslims 2%. D=RCC(D-Fort-Dauphin). M=CM.
6395	1	6	3.26	4	91.00	9.00	B	132.86	136	7	Animists 60%. D=RCC.
6396	1	7	3.15	4	86.20	13.80	B	135.92	140	7	Large inland area in south of island. Animists 50%. D=RCC(3 Dioceses). M=CM,MSF,MS.
6397	6	8	1.93	4	99.92	0.08	C	508.63	58	10	South center of island. Animists 7%, Baha'is 0.2%(increasing fast). Early Revival center. D=RCC(5 Dioceses),FPPM,Fifohazana,Eglise du Reveil,FMTA,other AICs.
6398	1	8	3.89	4	75.00	25.00	B	60.22	189	6	Northeast coastal strip. Revival center. Animists 77%. D=RCC(2 Dioceses). Eglise du Reveil,FMTA,MET,other AICs. M=CSSp,SMM,FMB.
6399	2	8	4.17	4	85.00	15.00	B	89.97	175	6	Animists 70%(Tangalamena leaders officiate at ancestral cult). D=RCC(2 Dioceses),AICs. M=CSSp,SMM.
6400	1	8	3.53	4	76.00	24.00	B	72.12	173	6	Animists 73%. D=RCC(D-Ambatondrazaka). M=OSST.
6401	1	10	2.77	8	99.79	0.21	C	429.64	72	10	Expatriates from Britain, in development, business. D=EEM(3 Dioceses). M=USPG.
6402	0	9	2.81	5	36.02	63.98	A	0.02	325	2	Comoro Islanders. Muslims 95%(Shafi Sunnis), many Baha'is. M=AIM,EJCM.
6403	1	10	1.70	8	99.87	0.13	C	504.90	46	10	Expatriates from France, in business, government. D=RCC(17 Dioceses). M=AA,CM,CSSp,MEP,MS,MSF,OC,&c.
6404	0	9	4.01	6	47.10	52.90	A	0.17	292	3	Muslims 80%(5,000 Bohoras, 3,000 Khojas), Hindus 15%(including Divine Light Mission).
6405	1	10	8.26	7	99.70	0.30	C	355.14	176	9	Mahayana Buddhists/folk-religionists 30%. D=RCC.
6406	0	10	0.00	8	43.00	57.00	A	0.00	0	1.13	Small community of practicing French-speaking Jews.
6407	1	7	3.07	4	73.00	27.00	B	53.29	163	6	Animists 75%. D=RCC.
6408	1	7	3.51	4	52.00	48.00	B	9.49	243	4	Animists 95%. D=RCC.
6409	1	7	2.18	4	99.70	0.30	C	283.60	85	8	Animists 30%. D=RCC.
6410	1	7	3.00	4	65.90	34.10	B	59.89	178	6	Small area along southwest coast of island. Animists 75%. D=RCC(D-Tulear). M=AA.
6411	1	7	6.85	0	43.40	56.60	A	6.97	525	4	Animists 80%, Muslims 15%. D=RCC(D-Ambanja). M=OFMCap.
6412	0	7	2.99	5	43.10	56.90	A	0.15	235	3	Migrants from Malaysia. Muslims 100% (Shafi Sunnis).
6413	1	6	3.59	4	84.00	16.00	B	101.17	159	7	Animists 65%. D=RCC.
6414	1	6	3.19	4	65.00	35.00	B	35.58	188	5	Animists 85%. D=RCC.
6415	1	10	4.48	6	46.00	54.00	A	6.71	326	4	From Mauritius, Bhojpuri immigrant workers. Hindus 80%, Muslims 10%, Baha'is 5%. D=RCC.
6416	3	8	1.78	4	99.85	0.15	C	449.86	58	10	Subsistence agriculturalists. Main literary language. Animists 12%, Muslims 1%(Sunnis), Baha'is 0.2%. D=70% Protestants(EJCM/FJKM,ELM/FLM),RCC,AICs.
6417	4	8	2.21	4	99.79	0.21	C	397.92	69	9	North center of island. Animists 30%. Whole Merina area is center of Fifohazana Revival, from 1894. D=FMTA,1930 FBMB,1955 MET,1958 ERSM.
6418	0	6	4.53	4	34.96	65.04	A	6.32	441	4	A small forest tribe of hunter-gatherers in the west. Animists 95%.
6419	0	0	6.28	8	99.92	0.08	C	433.18	157	10	Mixed-race immigrants from Mauritius. D=RCC.
6420	0	10	4.52	6	53.90	46.10	B	1.77	261	4	Military and political advisors. Nonreligious 76%, atheists 23%.
6421	1	6	3.26	4	71.00	29.00	B	51.83	175	6	Animists 80%. D=RCC.
6422	1	10	3.74	8	99.95	0.05	C	537.46	86	10	From Reunion island. D=RCC.
6423	2	10	6.04	7	84.00	16.00	B	61.32	197	6	Military and political advisors. Nonreligious 60%, atheists 20%. D=ROC,ROCOR. M=FMB.
6424	1	6	2.96	4	77.00	23.00	B	84.31	151	6	Animists 70%. D=RCC.
6425	1	6	3.19	4	65.00	35.00	B	35.58	188	5	Animists 80%. D=RCC.
6426	1	7	3.26	4	94.00	6.00	B	137.24	132	7	Animists 55%. D=RCC.
6427	1	7	2.32	4	80.00	20.00	B	93.44	123	6	Strongest Muslim presence among Malagasy peoples. Animists 59%, Muslims 7.5%. D=RCC(6 Dioceses). M=OFMCap,CSSp,MSF,MS,AA,OSST,FMB.
6428	1	6	2.35	4	79.00	21.00	B	95.15	126	6	Northwest Madagascar. Animists 60%. D=RCC(D-Ambanja,D-Majunga). M=OFMCap,CSSp,MSF,MS,AA,OSST.
6429	2	6	2.35	4	79.00	21.00	B	95.15	126	6	Northwestern coastal area. Animists 60%. D=RCC, also from 1895 many Sakalava AICs. (Diocese of the North, ERSM).
6430	1	6	2.25	4	74.00	26.00	B	81.03	130	6	Animists 65%. D=RCC.
6431	2	8	2.84	4	78.70	21.30	B	76.69	143	6	North central, east of Merina. Animists 72%. D=RCC(D-Ambatondrazaka),also AICs(ERIM,FMTA). M=OSST.
6432	0	9	0.00	5	41.00	59.00	A	0.00	0	1.13	Muslims 100%(Shafi Sunnis).
6433	3	8	3.08	4	73.10	26.90	B	53.63	163	6	East center to east of Betsileo. Animists 80%. D=RCC(M-Fianarantsoa),ERSM, and other AICs. M=SJ.
6434	0	6	3.07	4	56.00	44.00	B	40.88	212	6	Animists 80%.
6435	4	7	3.42	4	65.00	35.00	B	33.21	198	5	Near extreme north central. Animists 85%. D=RCC(3 Dioceses),ERSM,FMTA, and other AICs. M=CSSp,OFMCap,FMB.
6436	0	7	2.36	4	99.50	0.50	B	187.97	97	7	Animists 50%.
6437	0	6	3.68	4	61.00	39.00	B	40.07	222	6	Animists 80%.
6438	0	9	1.10	7	39.01	60.99	A	0.01	126	2	Muslims 100%(Zaydi Shias,Shafi Sunnis,Ismailis,Ahmadis).
6439	0	6	3.12	4	49.00	51.00	A	25.03	245	5	Animists 85%.
6440	0	8	5.05		40.00	60.00	A	21.90	346	5	Somalis(Shafi Sunnis). Muslims 30%, nonreligious 30%, animists 5%.
Malawi											
6441	2	10	3.21	5	99.80	0.20	C	440.92	75	10	Whites from South Africa, in government, business, missions. D=DRC,CCAP.

Continued overleaf

Table 8-2 continued

PEOPLE		POPULATION				IDENTITY CODE		LANGUAGE		CHURCH		MINISTRY						SCRIPTURE		
Ref 1	Ethnic name 2	P% 3	In 1995 4	In 2000 5	In 2025 6	Race 7	Language 8	Autoglossonym 9	S 10	AC 11	Members 12	Jayuh 13-17	d 18	wa 19	xc 20	mc 21	mi 22	Biblioglossonym 23	Pub 24-26	ss 27
6442	Bemba	1.35000	130,549	147,491	269,438	NAB57b	99-AURR-h	i-ci-bemba	5	89.00	131,267	4.su.	10	9	14	5	3	Chibemba*	PNB	b
6443	British	0.20000	19,341	21,850	39,917	CEW19i	52-ABAC-b	standard-english	37	79.00	17,262	3Bsuh	10	9	13	5	1		PNB	b
6444	Chewa (Western Nyanja)	34.73280	3,358,771	3,794,641	6,932,093	NAB57b	99-AUSX-ac	standard ci-cewa	85	64.20	2,436,160	1.su.	10	10	11	5	3	Chichewa	PNB	b
6445	Fipa	0.50000	48,352	54,626	99,792	NAB57o	99-AUSA-k	i-ci-fipa		90.00	49,164	1....	10	8	8	5	3	Ichifipa*	PNB	.
6446	French	0.01000	967	1,093	1,996	CEW21b	51-AABI-d	general français	1	87.00	950	1B.uh	10	9	14	5	2	French	PNB	b
6447	Greek	0.03000	2,901	3,278	5,988	CEW20	56-AAAA-c	dhimotiki		95.00	3,114	2B.uh	10	9	11	4	1	Greek: Modern	PNB	b
6448	Gujarati	0.29700	28,721	32,448	59,276	CNN25e	59-AAFH-b	standard gujaraati		0.10	32	2A.u.	5	4	2	4	1	Gujarati	PNB	b
6449	Jewish	0.00180	174	197	359	CMT35	52-ABAC	english-mainland cluster		0.00	0	3Bsuh	0	5	5	0	0		PNB	b
6450	Kokola	1.82740	176,715	199,648	364,719	NAB57b	99-AUSY-hc	kokola		40.00	79,859	1.s..	9	5	7	4	3		pnb	.
6451	Kunda	0.07000	6,769	7,648	13,971	NAB57b	99-AUSX-e	south ci-kunda		27.00	2,065	1.su.	9	5	7	4	1	Kunda	Pnb	.
6452	Lambya (Wandya)	0.45760	44,251	49,994	91,329	NAB57o	99-AUSA-e	i-ci-lambya		42.00	20,997	4....	9	6	7	5	2		pnb	b
6453	Lomwe (Ngulu, Nguru)	7.71100	745,678	842,445	1,538,988	NAB57b	99-AUSY-g	i-lomwe	15	66.00	556,014	1.s..	10	9	10	5	3	Ilomwe*	PNb	.
6454	Makua	2.00000	193,406	218,505	399,167	NAB57b	99-AUSY	makhua cluster		21.00	45,886	2.s..	9	6	7	5	0	Kimakhua	PNB	b
6455	Mpoto (Nyasa)	0.38000	36,747	41,516	75,842	NAB57o	99-AUSR-b	ci-mpoto		42.00	17,437	0....	9	6	8	4	3	Chimpoto*	Pn.	.
6456	Ndau	1.00000	96,703	109,252	199,583	NAB57l	99-AUTA-h	chi-shanga		40.00	43,701	1csuh	9	6	9	5	3	Chixanga	PNb	b
6457	Ngonde (Konde, Mombe)	3.54000	342,329	386,753	706,526	NAB57o	99-AUSV	nyakyusa-ngonde cluster	5	85.00	328,740	1....	10	8	13	5	2	Nyakyusa-ngonde	PNB	b
6458	Ngoni (Mombera, Gomani)	9.00000	870,328	983,271	1,796,251	NAB57i	99-AUSX-c	south ci-ngoni		67.00	658,792	1.su.	10	8	14	5	3	Ngoni	Pnb	b
6459	Nyanja (Lake Nyanja)	0.79000	76,395	86,309	157,671	NAB57b	99-AUSX-aa	standard ci-nyanja	1	85.00	73,363	1.su.	10	9	14	5	3	Nyanja	PNB	b
6460	Nyungwe	0.10000	9,670	10,925	19,958	NAB57b	99-AUSX-h	ci-nyungwe		25.00	2,731	1.su.	9	5	7	4	2	Chinyungwi*	Pnb	.
6461	Portuguese	0.10000	9,670	10,925	19,958	CEW21g	51-AABA-e	general português	10	93.00	10,160	2Bsuh	10	9	15	5	2	Portuguese	PNB	b
6462	Sena	2.82340	273,032	308,463	563,504	NAB57b	99-AUSX-i	ci-sena	8	56.60	174,590	1.su.	10	8	7	5	3	Chisena*	PNb	.
6463	Shona	0.50000	48,352	54,626	99,792	NAB57l	99-AUTA-a	standard chi-shona		62.00	33,868	3csuh	10	5	13	5	2	Shona: Standard	PNB	b
6464	Southern Nyanja (Maravi)	12.17000	1,176,877	1,329,601	2,428,931	NAB57b	99-AUSX-d	ci-manganja	36	81.00	1,076,977	1.su.	10	10	11	5	3		pnb	b
6465	Swahili	0.02000	1,934	2,185	3,992	NAB57j	99-AUSM-b	standard ki-swahili	1	0.00	0	4Asu.	0	4	2	3	0	Kiswahili*	PNB	b
6466	Tonga (Western Nyasa)	2.62260	253,614	286,525	523,428	NAB57b	99-AUSW-d	east ci-tonga	4	83.70	239,822	1....	10	9	12	5	3	Chitonga: Malawi*	PNB	b
6467	Tumbuka (Phoka)	7.86530	760,599	859,303	1,569,784	NAB57b	99-AUSW-c	ci-tumbuka	31	88.00	756,186	3....	10	10	11	5	3	Chitumbuka*	PNB	b
6468	Yao (Ajao, Ajawa)	7.86680	760,744	859,467	1,570,083	NAB57b	99-AUSQ-f	ci-yao	12	16.30	140,093	4.s..	8	5	10	5	3	Chiyao*	PNB	.
6469	Zimba	0.06000	5,802	6,555	11,975	NAB57l	99-AUTA-cj	kwa-zwimba		29.00	1,901	1csuh.	9	5	7	4	1		pnb	.
6470	Zulu	0.91970	88,938	100,479	183,557	NAB57i	99-AUTF-g	i-si-zulu		73.00	73,350	3asu.	10	8	14	5	1	Isizulu*	PNB	b
6471	other minor peoples	1.03460	100,049	113,033	206,489	...				49.57	56,030		9	5	6	5	0			
	Malaysia	**100.00000**	**20,108,395**	**22,244,062**	**30,968,453**					**7.96**	**1,771,183**									
6472	Abai Sungai	0.00346	696	770	1,072	MSY44z	31-GBAJ-f	kinabatangan-sungai		1.00	8	0.s..	6	4	4	1	0		pn.	.
6473	Arab	0.05000	10,054	11,122	15,484	CMT30	12-AACF-f	syro-palestinian		0.10	11	1Asuh	5	3	2	0	0	Arabic: Lebanese*	Pnb	b
6474	Bajau Bukit (Papar)	0.00450	905	1,001	1,394	MSY44z	31-GBBB	south bisaya cluster		5.00	50	0....	7	5	5	0	0		P..	b
6475	Bajau Kagayan	0.02000	4,022	4,449	6,194	MSY44z	31-EACE-a	mapun		0.01	0	0....	3	3	2	1	1	Mapun*	PN.	.
6476	Bakong Kenyah	0.00600	1,207	1,335	1,858	MSY44y	31-JCCJ	bakung-kenyah cluster		5.00	67	0....	7	5	5	5	1		PNB	.
6477	Balau	0.03546	7,130	7,888	10,981	MSY44e	31-PHIA-c	balau		30.00	2,366	1.s..	9	5	6	4	1		pnb	.
6478	Balinese	0.02000	4,022	4,449	6,194	MSY44a	31-PKAA-a	bali		1.00	44	1....	6	4	6	4	2		pnb	b
6479	Banggi Dusun (Kadazan)	0.00759	1,526	1,688	2,351	MSY44y	31-CJEF-a	bonggi		21.00	355	0....	9	5	6	5	3	Bonggi	P..	.
6480	Banjarese (Banjay Malay)	1.10000	221,192	244,685	340,653	MSY44k	31-PHAF-d	banjar		0.02	49	0....	3	3	2	0	0		...	b
6481	Baokan	0.01244	2,501	2,767	3,852	MSY44z	31-GCBA-a	baukan		20.00	553	0....	9	5	5	2	1	Baukan	...	.
6482	Baram Kayan	0.01500	3,016	3,337	4,645	MSY44z	31-JBAA	baram-kayan cluster		60.00	2,002	0....	10	7	10	5	2	Kayan, Baram	PNB	.
6483	Bateq (Kleb, Nong)	0.00496	997	1,103	1,536	AUG05	46-GBAB-c	batek		4.00	44	0....	6	4	6	4	1		...	.
6484	Batu Punan	0.00035	70	78	108	AUG05	31-PCAC-c	batu		8.00	6	0.s..	7	5	6	4	1	Batu	Pnb	b
6485	Beketan (Manketa)	0.00130	261	289	403	MSY44y	31-IACC-a	bukitan		70.00	202	0....	10	7	9	5	1		...	.
6486	Bengali	0.10000	20,108	22,244	30,968	CNN25b	59-AAFT-e	west bengali		0.40	89	1Asuh	5	4	8	5	3	Bengali: Musalmani*	PNB	b
6487	Berawan (Long Pata)	0.00617	1,241	1,372	1,911	MSY44z	31-IAAC	berawan cluster		5.00	69	0....	7	5	6	1	0		...	.
6488	Biatah (Bideyu, Siburan)	0.09550	19,204	21,243	29,575	MSY44y	31-KAAE-a	bi-atah		52.00	11,046	0As..	10	6	8	2	2	Biatah	PN.	.
6489	Bintulu	0.02979	5,990	6,627	9,226	MSY44z	31-IABA-a	bintulu		10.00	663	0....	8	5	6	1	0		...	.
6490	Bisaya (Sabah Bisaya)	0.07121	14,319	15,840	22,053	MSY44z	31-GBBA-a	central bisaya		1.00	158	0....	6	4	5	1	3		...	.
6491	Bisaya (Visayak)	0.04632	9,314	10,303	14,345	MSY44z	31-GBBB	south bisaya cluster		12.00	1,236	0....	8	5	6	5	1		P..	b
6492	Bisingai (Singhi)	0.03404	6,845	7,572	10,542	MSY44y	31-KAAD-a	singgi		10.00	757	0....	8	5	5	1	0		...	.
6493	British	0.10000	20,108	22,244	30,968	CEW19i	52-ABAC-b	standard-english	60	66.00	14,681	3Bsuh	10	9	13	5	3		PNB	b
6494	Buginese	2.83688	570,451	631,037	878,538	MSY44c	31-QBBA	bugis cluster		1.00	6,310	2....	6	3	6	0	2	Bugis	PNB	b
6495	Bukar Sadong (Bidayuh)	0.15000	30,163	33,366	46,453	MSY44y	31-KAAE-d	sadong		39.00	13,013	0cs..	9	5	6	3	3	Bukar Sadong	pn.	.
6496	Bundu Dusun (Kadazan)	0.23890	48,039	53,141	73,984	MSY44y	31-GBAL-b	monsok-dusun		70.00	37,199	0....	10	6	9	5	3	Dusun: Ranau*	PNB	b
6497	Burmese (Myen, Bhama)	0.10000	20,108	22,244	30,968	MSY50b	77-AABA-a	bama		0.17	38	4Asu.	5	4	8	4	2	Burmese	PNB	b
6498	Butonese	0.06000	12,065	13,346	18,581	MSY44y	31-QAEA-a	wolio		0.01	1	0....	3	2	2	0	0		...	b
6499	Central Dusun (Kadazan)	0.76638	154,107	170,474	237,336	MSY44y	31-GBAI-k	ranau		50.00	85,237	1.s..	10	6	9	5	3	Dusun, Central	PNB	.
6500	Central Murut (Keningau)	0.03151	6,336	7,009	9,758	MSY44z	31-GCAC	keningau-murut cluster		50.00	3,505	0....	10	6	9	5	3		...	.
6501	Central Sama (Sinama)	0.20000	40,217	44,488	61,937	MSY44x	31-EACB-a	siasi		0.01	4	1.s..	3	2	2	0	0	Sinama	PN.	.
6502	Chavacano (Chabakano)	0.00300	603	667	929	MPY53	51-AACB-a	chavacano		90.00	601	1c.u.	10	8	8	4	1	Chavacano	PNb	.
6503	Chewong (Siwang)	0.00220	442	489	681	AUG05	46-GBBA-a	che'wong		0.50	2	0....	5	4	2	4	1		...	.
6504	Coastal Kadazan (Papar)	0.37939	76,289	84,392	117,491	MSY44y	31-GBAO	west kadazan cluster		40.00	33,757	0....	9	5	7	5	3	Kadazan, Coastal	P..	.
6505	Cocos Islander (Kukus)	0.02447	4,921	5,443	7,578	MSY44k	31-PHAL-c	kokos-sabah		6.00	327	0c...	7	5	6	1	0		...	.
6506	Daro-Matu	0.05390	10,838	11,990	16,692	MSY44z	31-IADC	daro-matu cluster		10.00	1,199	0....	8	5	5	1	1		...	.
6507	Duano (Desin Dola)	0.01363	2,741	3,032	4,221	MSY44z	31-PHEA-a	duano'		1.00	30	0....	6	4	4	1	0		...	.
6508	Dumpas	0.00485	975	1,079	1,502	MSY44y	31-GBAA-a	dumpas		9.00	97	0....	7	5	6	1	0		...	b
6509	Dusun Segama	0.00324	652	721	1,003	MSY44y	31-GBAL-b	monsok-dusun		70.00	504	0....	10	7	8	5	1	Dusun: Ranau*	PNB	b
6510	Dusun-Murut	0.00712	1,432	1,584	2,205	MSY44y	31-GCAC-d	dusun-murut		50.00	792	0....	10	6	7	5	1		...	.
6511	Eastern Kadazan (Labuk)	0.09264	18,628	20,607	28,689	MSY44y	31-GBAJ-a	labuk-kadazan		55.00	11,334	0.s..	10	6	7	5	3	Kadazan:Labuk-kinabatangan*	PN.	.
6512	Euronesian (Eurasian)	0.20000	40,217	44,488	61,937	MSY43	52-ABAD-b	southeast-asian-english		75.00	33,366	0B.uh	10	8	10	5	3		...	b
6513	Garo	0.00583	1,172	1,297	1,805	MSY44y	31-GBAE-d	talantang		60.00	778	0....	10	6	6	2	1		...	.
6514	Gujarati	0.10000	20,108	22,244	30,968	CNN25e	59-AAFH-b	standard gujaraati		0.60	133	2A.u.	5	4	4	1	1	Gujarati	PNB	b
6515	Han Chinese (Cantonese)	5.43493	1,092,877	1,208,949	1,683,114	MSY42a	79-AAAM-a	central yue		7.00	84,626	3A.uh	7	5	8	5	1	Chinese, Yue	PNB	b
6516	Han Chinese (Hainanese)	1.52671	306,997	339,602	472,798	MSY42a	79-AAAK-c	wanning		5.00	16,980	1a...	7	5	8	5	2		p..	b
6517	Han Chinese (Hakka)	7.16148	1,440,059	1,593,004	2,217,800	MSY42a	79-AAAG-a	literary hakka		9.00	143,370	1A...	7	5	8	5	2	Chinese: Hakka, Wukingfu*	PNB	b
6518	Han Chinese (Hokchiu)	1.49686	300,995	332,962	463,554	MSY42a	79-AAAH-a	min-bei		10.00	33,296	0A...	8	5	8	5	2	Chinese, Min Bei	PN.	b
6519	Han Chinese (Hokkien)	8.71025	1,751,491	1,937,513	2,697,430	MSY42a	79-AAAJ-ic	chaozhou		9.00	174,376	1A..h	7	5	8	5	3	Chinese, Min Nan	PNB	b
6520	Han Chinese (Hsiang)	0.27817	55,936	61,876	86,145	MSY42a	79-AAAE-a	xiang		9.00	5,569	1....	7	5	8	5	3		...	b
6521	Han Chinese (Kwangsi)	0.73529	147,855	163,558	227,708	MSY42a	79-AAAL-a	shao-jiang		10.00	16,356	0a...	8	5	8	5	3	Chinese: Cantonese	PNB	b
6522	Han Chinese (Mandarin)	3.84290	772,746	854,817	1,190,087	MSY42a	79-AAAB-ba	kuo-yü	38	12.00	102,578	2Bsuh	8	5	11	5	3	Chinese: Kuoyu*	PNB	b
6523	Han Chinese (Teochew)	3.90747	785,730	869,180	1,210,083	MSY42a	79-AAAP-c	east miao-chinese		10.00	86,918	0A...	8	5	8	5	3	Chinese: Swatow*	PNB	b
6524	Hindi	0.20000	40,217	44,488	61,937	CNN25g	59-AAFO-e	general hindi		0.50	222	3Asuh	5	4	8	1	1		pnb	b
6525	Hui	0.05000	10,054	11,122	15,484	MSY42b	79-AAAB-ba	kuo-yü		0.00	0	2Bsuh	0	2	0	0	0	Chinese: Kuoyu*	PNB	b
6526	Idahan Dusun (Kadazan)	0.03706	7,452	8,244	11,477	MSY44y	31-FAAA-a	ida'an		20.00	1,649	0.s..	9	5	6	5	2	Idaan	P..	.
6527	Illanun Maranao (Ilanon)	0.04255	8,556	9,465	13,177	MSY44x	31-CKPA-a	ma-ranao		0.13	12	2.s..	5	2	6	0	0	Maranao	PN.	.
6528	Indonesian	1.00000	201,084	222,441	309,685	MSY44k	31-PHAA-c	bahasa-indonesia		0.05	111	4Asuh	4	3	8	0	1	Indonesian	PNB	b
6529	Jah Hut (Cheres)	0.01732	3,483	3,853	5,364	AUG05	46-GDAA-a	jah-hut		2.00	77	0....	6	4	6	4	1		...	.
6530	Jahai	0.00887	1,784	1,973	2,747	AUG05	46-GBAB-a	jehai		1.00	20	0....	6	4	6	4	1		...	.
6531	Jakun (Djakun)	0.06950	13,975	15,460	21,523	AUG05	31-PHFB-a	orang-hulu		1.00	155	0....	6	4	6	1	0		...	.
6532	Japanese	0.05000	10,054	11,122	15,484	MSY45a	45-CAAA-a	koku-go		5.60	623	1B.uh	7	4	8	5	3	Japanese	PNB	b
6533	Javanese (Orang Jawa)	3.10000	623,360	689,566	960,022	MSY44g	31-PIAA-g	general jawa		13.00	89,644	2As.h	8	6	10	5	3	Javanese	PNB	b
6534	Kalabakan Murut	0.01003	2,017	2,231	3,106	MSY44z	31-GCBB-d	kalabakan		10.00	223	0....	8	5	5	1	0		...	.
6535	Kalabit (Kelabit)	0.00500	1,005	1,112	1,548	MSY44z	31-HAAE	kelabit cluster		60.00	667	0....	10	7	9	4	1	Kelabit	P..	.
6536	Kanarese (Canarese)	0.20000	40,217	44,488	61,937	CNN23a	49-EBAA-a	kannada		3.00	1,335	2Asu.	6	4	7	5	3	Kannada	PNB	b
6537	Kanowit	0.00121	243	269	375	MSY44z	31-IADG-a	kanowit		5.00	13	0....	7	5	6	4	0		...	b
6538	Kayaman (Kejaman)	0.00355	714	790	1,099	MSY44z	31-IACA	kajaman-sekapan cluster		5.00	39	0....	7	5	6	4	0		...	.
6539	Kedayan (Orang Bukit)	0.28056	56,416	62,408	86,885	MSY44z	31-PHAF-ab	malayu-brunei		15.00	9,361	0....	8	5	9	5	2		...	b
6540	Keningau Dusun	0.01295	2,604	2,881	4,010	MSY44y	31-GBAN-a	ganaq		20.00	576	0....	9	5	8	4	2		...	b
6541	Kimaragan (Tandek)	0.06045	12,156	13,447	18,720	MSY44y	31-GBAC	kimaragang cluster		50.00	6,723	0.s..	10	6	8	5	1	Kimaragang	...	.
6542	Kinabatangan Sungai	0.05195	10,446	11,556	16,088	MSY44z	31-GBAJ-f	kinabatangan-sungai		10.00	1,156	0.s..	8	5	4	3	0		pn.	.
6543	Kintaq	0.00040	80	89	124	AUG05	46-GBAA-bh	kintaq-bong		1.30	1	0....	6	4	4	4	1		...	.
6544	Kiput (Long Kiput)	0.01200	2,413	2,669	3,716	MSY44z	31-IAAB-a	long-kiput		0.10	3	0....	5	2	5	0	0		...	b
6545	Klias River Kadazan	0.00662	1,331	1,473	2,050	MSY44y	31-GBAP-a	klias		25.00	368	0....	9	5	7	3	0		...	.
6546	Kolod Murut (Kolur)	0.00710	1,428	1,579	2,199	MSY44z	31-GCAF-a	okolod		7.00	111	0.s..	7	5	6	4	0	Okolod	...	.
6547	Kwijau Dusun (Kadazan)	0.03560	7,159	7,919	11,025	MSY44y	31-GBAM-a	kuijau		25.00	1,980	0....	9	5	6	5	1		...	b
6548	Lahanan	0.00248	499	552	768	MSY44z	31-IACB-a	lahanan		0.00	0	0....	0	2	0	0	0		...	.
6549	Lanas Lobu	0.01770	3,559	3,937	5,481	MSY44z	31-GAAD	lanas-lobu cluster		20.00	787	0....	9	5	5	5	1		...	.
6550	Land Dayak	0.35587	71,560	79,160	110,207	MSY44y	31-KAAE-c	bi-deyu		50.00	39,580	0cs..	10	6	8	5	3	Bideyu*	PN.	.
6551	Lanoh	0.00212	426	472	657	AUG05	46-GBCA-a	lanoh		1.00	5	0....	6	4	4	4	1		...	.
6552	Lara (Land Dayak)	0.05100	10,255	11,344	15,794	MSY44y	31-KAAB-a	lara		10.00	1,134	0....	8	5	8	3	1		...	.
6553	Lelak	0.00156	314	347	483	MSY44z	31-IAAD-a	lelak		0.00	0	0....	0	2	2	0	0		...	.
6554	Linkabau	0.02128	4,279	4,734	6,590	MSY44z	31-GAAB-d	lingkabau-sugut		50.00	2,367	0.s..	10	6	6	2	1		p..	.
6555	Low Malay Creole	0.50000	100,542	111,220	154,842	MSY44k	31-PHAA-d	malayu-pasar	30	0.01	11	1csuh	3	3	2	1	0	Malay: Low	PNb	b
6556	Lower Murut (Bukau)	0.01004	2,019	2,233	3,109	MSY44z	31-GCAA	beaufort-murut cluster		10.00	223	0....	8	5	5	2	0		...	.
6557	Madang (Badang, Lepo Tau)	0.01000	2,011	2,224	3,097	MSY44y	31-JCCB-a	madang		60.00	1,335	0....	10	7	7	5	1	Kenya: Lepo'tau	PN.	.
6558	Mah Meri (Sisi, Besisi)	0.00962	1,934	2,140	2,979	AUG05	46-GCAB-a	besisi		0.90	19	0....	5	4	5	4	1	Besisi	PN.	.
6559	Malacca Portuguese Creole	0.00588	1,182	1,308	1,821	MSY43	51-AACA-ha	malaquense		70.00	916	1c...	10	7	10	4	1	Malaccan Creole Portuguese	Pnb	b
6560	Malay (Melaju, Melayu)	33.06049	6,647,934	7,353,996	10,238,322	MSY44k	31-PHAA-b	bahasa-malaysia	81	0.65	47,801	1asuh	5	4	6	1	3	Malay	PNB	b
6561	Malayali	0.60000	120,650	133,464	185,811	CNN23b	49-EBEB-a	malayalam		30.00	40,039	2Asu.	9	6	11	5	1	Malayalam	PNB	b
6562	Melanau (Belanau)	0.17957	36,109	39,944	55,610	MSY44z	31-IADB-c	dalat		5.00	1,997	0....	7	5	6	5	2		...	.
6563	Mendriq	0.00089	179	198	276	AUG05	46-GBAB-b	mendriq		1.30	3	0....	6	4	4	4	1		...	.

Continued opposite

Table 8-2 continued

EVANGELIZATION								EVANGELISM			ADDITIONAL DESCRIPTIVE DATA
Ref 1	D 28	aC 29	CG% 30	r 31	E 32	U 33	W 34	e 35	R 36	T 37	Locations, civil divisions, literacy, religions, church history, denominations, dioceses, church growth, missions, agencies, ministries, movements 38
6442	6	8	9.24	8	99.89	0.11	C	519.76	183	10	From Zambia. Animists 2%, many Baha'is. D=RCC,CPCA,JWs,NAC,AICs,&c.
6443	6	10	3.47	8	99.79	0.21	C	438.29	83	10	Expatriates from Britain, in development. D=Anglican Ch in Malawi/CPCA(2 Dioceses),CCAP,SDA,JWs,AoG,many AICs. M=USPG.
6444	12	7	6.31	5	99.64	0.36	C	298.06	167	8	Animists 1%, Muslims 20%(Shafi Sunnis). D=RCC(7 Dioceses),ACM,CCAP,LCCA,EBCM,NAC,SDA,JWs,CC,AMEC,AoG,many AICs. M=NAC(Burma),FIFM.
6445	3	6	8.87	0	99.90	0.10	C	456.61	204	10	From southwest Tanzania. Animists 10%. D=RCC,JWs,AICs.
6446	1	10	3.22	8	99.87	0.13	C	501.72	73	10	Expatriates from France, in business. D=RCC(7 Dioceses). M=SMM,WF.
6447	1	10	4.53	7	99.95	0.05	C	551.33	95	10	Settlers, traders from Greece. D=Greek Orthodox Ch(AD-Rhodesia).
6448	1	10	3.53	6	49.10	50.90	A	0.17	253	3	Traders from India. Hindus 72%, Muslims 25%(Sunnis, Shias). D=RCC.
6449	0	0	0.00	8	33.00	67.00	A	0.00	0	1.11	Small community of English-speaking Jews in Lilongwe. Jewish 100%.
6450	4	6	9.40	0	83.00	17.00	B	121.18	359	7	Majority live in Tanzania; same language as Nyiha. Animists 40%. D=RCC,ELCT,CPT,PHA.
6451	1	6	5.47	1	65.00	35.00	B	64.05	292	6	Mainly in Mozambique and Zambia. Animists 73%. D=RCC.
6452	2	6	7.95	0	86.00	14.00	B	131.83	300	7	Majority in Tanzania; same language as Nyiha. Animists 38%. D=RCC,PHA. M=WF,PHC.
6453	7	7	11.55	0	99.66	0.34	C	279.44	307	8	Mainly in Mozambique. Animists 19%. D=RCC(M-Blantyre,D-Chikwawa,D-Zomba),CCAP,BMCA,EBCM,CC,PIM,SDB. M=SMM,NBCUSA,FCSM,FMB,CC(UK).
6454	0	9	8.80	0	70.00	30.00	B	53.65	402	6	Refugees from Mozambique wars. Animists 50%, Muslims 20%(Shafi Sunnis).
6455	3	7	7.06	0	82.00	18.00	B	125.70	285	7	Northeast shores of lake Nyasa. Largely in Tanzania. Animists 58%. D=RCC,CPCA,CCAP.
6456	3	7	8.74	1	93.00	7.00	B	135.78	290	7	Mostly refugees from Mozambique civil wars. Animists 25%. D=RCC,AC/CPSA,AICs.
6457	4	6	10.96	0	99.85	0.15	C	428.14	247	10	Northern tip. Most live in Tanzania (known as Nyakyusa there). Animists 10%. D=CCAP(S-Livingstonia),Moravian Ch,RCC,AICs. M=FCSM,MCT.
6458	5	7	7.67	5	99.67	0.33	C	310.57	188	9	Speakers originally spoke Zulu. Animists 13%. D=RCC(4 Dioceses),CCAP,ACM(D-Southern Malawi),SDB,AICs. M=WF,USPG,FCSM,FIFM(Zimbabwe),FMB.
6459	7	8	6.21	5	99.85	0.15	C	465.37	140	10	Southeast. Animists 15%. D=RCC(D-Chikwawa),BMCA,CCAP,SDA,CC,ECM,many AICs. M=SMM,CSM,TEAM,FMB,LBI,UBS.
6460	2	6	5.77	1	65.00	35.00	B	59.31	305	6	Mainly in Mozambique. Animists 75%. D=RCC,CPCA.
6461	1	10	3.61	8	99.93	0.07	C	573.67	75	10	Expatriates from Portugal, Mozambique. D=RCC. M=SMM,WF.
6462	3	6	10.26	1	99.57	0.43	B	211.96	313	8	Also in Mozambique. Animists 30%. D=RCC(D-Chikwawa),AECM,ICFG. M=AEF(SAGM),SMM,UPM,UBS.
6463	2	9	8.71	4	99.62	0.38	C	289.66	210	8	Migrants from Zimbabwe. Animists 10%. D=AACJM,other AICs from Zimbabwe.
6464	7	8	6.83	5	99.81	0.19	C	413.91	162	10	Central and southern. Animists 1%. D=RCC(D-Chikwawa),AECM,BMCA,CCAP,CON,CC,many AICs. M=AEF(SAGM),SMM,FMB,CSM,FIFM(Zimbabwe).
6465	0	10	0.00	5	43.00	57.00	A	0.00	0	1.13	Traders from Swahili coast(Somalia to Mozambique). Muslims 100%(Shafi Sunnis).
6466	5	6	5.89	0	99.84	0.16	C	426.79	144	10	West shore of Lake Malawi, Northern Province. Animists 5%. D=CCAP,RCC(D-Mzuzu),ACM,Bantu Ch,many other AICs. M=CSM,WF,FMB.
6467	8	6	6.68	0	99.88	0.12	C	456.10	157	10	Northern Province. Also in Zambia and Tanzania. Animists 4%. D=CCAP,RCC(D-Nzuzu),ACM,AoG,SDA,CC,ACC,& many other AICs. M=CSM,WF,FMB,UBS.
6468	9	6	10.02	4	73.30	26.70	B	43.61	429	6	Also in Tanzania, Mozambique, Zimbabwe. Muslims 83%(Shafi Sunnis), many animists. D=ACM,CCAP,RCC(M-Blantyre,D-Zomba),EBCM,PIM,BMCA,LCCA,ICFG.
6469	1	6	5.39	4	72.00	28.00	B	76.21	247	6	In extreme south, also in Mozambique north of Sena. Animists 70%. D=AECM. M=AEF(SAGM).
6470	1	10	8.50	5	99.73	0.27	C	378.35	184	9	Migrant workers from South Africa. Animists 2%, nonreligious 8%. D=large numbers of Zulu AICs.
6471	0	7	7.08		75.57	24.43	B	136.72	257	7	Germans(NAC), Mwanga(from Zambia), South Africans(ZCC,&c), Nsenga, Mozambicans; by 1988 some 630,000 had entered as refugees from north Mozambique.
Malaysia											
6472	0	5	2.10	0	25.00	75.00	A	0.91	286	3	Sabah. Lower reaches of Kinabatangan river. Access by boat. Fishermen. Muslims 90%.
6473	0	7	2.43	8	42.10	57.90	A	0.15	204	3	Lengthy history as traders, imperialists, proselytizers. Muslims 100%(Shafi Sunnis).
6474	0	5	3.99	0	30.00	70.00	A	5.47	411	4	Sabah. Kuala Penyu District. Bilingual in Malay and Tatana. Muslims 95%.
6475	1	5	0.00	1	22.01	77.99	A	0.00	0	1.09	Cagayan de Sulu. In Sabah, east coast. Also in Philippines. Muslims 100%. D=RCC. M=SIL.
6476	2	5	4.29	0	44.00	56.00	A	8.03	320	4	Sarawak. South central, near Kalimantan border. Mainly in Indonesia. Muslims 85%, many animists. D=ECB(SIB),RCC. M=BEM.
6477	1	5	5.62	1	70.00	30.00	B	76.65	240	6	Sarawak. Close to Iban. Animists 65%, many Baha'is. D=MCM.
6478	2	6	3.86	2	40.00	60.00	A	1.46	323	4	Immigrants from Bali Island (Indonesia). Hindus 90%. D=RCC,GKPB.
6479	4	5	3.63	0	57.00	43.00	B	43.69	215	6	Sabah. Banggi Island in Kudat District. Close to Molbog. Animists 79%. D=RCC,ACM,BCC/PCS,Evangelical Ch of Borneo. M=BEM,MHM,BM.
6480	0	5	3.97	0	14.02	85.98	A	0.01	913	2	Sabah; most in Indonesia, from south Kalimantan. Muslims 100%(strict Shafi Sunnis).
6481	1	5	4.09	0	47.00	53.00	A	34.31	268	5	Sabah. Keningau and Kinabatangan Districts. Close to Keningau Murut. Animists 80%. D=ACM.
6482	2	6	5.44	0	99.60	0.40	C	240.90	148	8	Sarawak. Baram river area, Upper Sarawak. Also in Brunei. Access by river. Animists 40%. D=RCC,ECB. M=BEM,UBS.
6483	1	5	3.86	0	31.00	69.00	A	4.52	430	4	Malaya. Northern Pahang, Kelantan, Trengganu. Animists 63%, Muslims 33%. D=RCC. M=MHM.
6484	1	5	1.81	0	43.00	57.00	A	12.55	179	5	Sarawak. Nomads. Animists 59%, Muslims 33%. D=RCC. M=MHM.
6485	2	5	3.05	0	99.70	0.30	C	270.83	101	8	Sarawak. Kapit, 7th Division. Also Kalimantan (Indonesia). Animists 30%. D=ECB,RCC. M=BEM.
6486	3	7	4.59	6	61.40	38.60	B	0.89	266	3	Originally laborers from Bengal (India). Hindus 75%, Muslims 23%. D=ELCMS,RCC,ACM.
6487	0	5	4.33	0	28.00	72.00	A	5.11	474	4	Sarawak. Tutoh and Baram rivers in north. Animists 95%.
6488	2	5	4.82	4	99.52	0.48	B	191.69	154	7	Sarawak. 1st Division, Kuching District, 10 villages. Also in Kalimantan (Indonesia). Land Dayak. Agriculturalists. Literates 45%. Animists 40%, Muslims 8%.
6489	0	5	4.28	0	34.00	66.00	A	12.41	386	5	Sarawak. Northeast coast around Sibuti. Coastal. Animists 90%.
6490	3	5	2.80	0	28.00	72.00	A	1.02	324	4	Sabah. On coast, north and around Brunei Bay, mainly along Padas river. Little secondary education. Muslims 90%. D=RCC,TJC,ECB.
6491	4	6	4.93	0	47.00	53.00	A	20.58	317	5	Sarawak Bisaya, southeast of Marudi, 5th Division. Animists 58%, Muslims 30%. D=Bisaya Ch,RCC,ECB,TJC. M=BEM.
6492	0	5	4.42	0	33.00	67.00	A	12.04	438	5	Southwest Sarawak. Southwest of Santubong. Land Dayak. Related to Jagoi. Animists 80%, Muslims 10%.
6493	6	10	2.02	8	99.66	0.34	C	346.89	60	9	Expatriates from Britain, in business. D=Anglican Ch of Malaysia(3 Dioceses),RCC,MCM,SDA,JWs,SA.
6494	2	6	6.66	2	42.00	58.00	A	1.53	490	4	Sabah. Originally from Sulawesi (Indonesia). Muslims 98%(Sunnis, Sufis), some Hindus. D=TJC,RCC.
6495	3	5	7.43	1	80.00	20.00	B	113.88	284	7	Sarawak. Serian, 1st Division, 35 villages. Also in Indonesia. Land Dayak. Animists 50%. D=ACM,RCC,SDA.
6496	5	4	8.57	0	99.70	0.30	C	306.60	215	9	Sabah. Beaufort and other Districts. Animists 30%. D=RCC,ACM,ECB,SDA,TJC. M=BEM,CMS,FMB.
6497	2	10	3.70	6	63.17	36.83	B	0.39	209	3	Immigrants, migrant workers from Burma. Theravada Buddhists 97%, Muslims 3%. D=ACM,MSBC.
6498	0	5	0.00	0	14.01	85.99	A	0.00	166	1.05	Sabah. Immigrants from Buton Islands, Sulawesi (Indonesia). Lingua franca. Sailors. Muslims 99%.
6499	5	5	9.47	0	99.50	0.50	B	187.97	275	7	Sabah. Beaufort and 12 other Districts. Animists 34%, Muslims 1%(much Qadiani Ahmadiyya activity). D=RCC,ACM,SDA,ECB,TJC. M=CMS,BEM,FMB,UBS.
6500	3	6	6.03	0	91.00	9.00	B	166.07	197	7	Sabah. Keningau District along Pegalan river. Animists 50%. D=RCC,ECB,PCS(Basel Christian Ch of Malaysia). M=SIL,BEM,BM.
6501	0	5	1.40	1	21.01	78.99	A	0.00	271	1.09	Coastal Sabah. Also Sulu Province (Philippines). Muslims 100%.
6502	1	6	4.18	1	99.90	0.10	C	436.90	103	10	Sabah. One village in Semporna, speaking Spanish-based creole. From throughout Philippines. D=RCC.
6503	1	6	0.70	0	23.50	76.50	A	0.42	198	3	Malaya. Just south of Semai, Pahang. Animists 66%, Muslims 33%. D=RCC. M=MHM.
6504	3	5	8.46	0	79.00	21.00	B	115.34	323	7	Sabah. West coast, Penampang and Papar Districts. Animists 50%. D=RCC,SDA,TJC.
6505	0	5	3.55	5	35.00	65.00	A	7.66	333	4	Sabah. Tawau and Lahad Datu. Few left on Cocos Islands, also Christmas Island. Muslims 94%(Shafi Sunnis,animistic practices).
6506	1	5	4.90	0	36.00	64.00	A	13.14	412	5	Sarawak. Matu river from Rejang area to sea. Muslims 50%, animists 40%. D=RCC.
6507	0	5	3.46	0	21.00	79.00	A	0.76	518	3	Malaya. South coast around Pontian Kecil. Muslims 50%, animists 49%.
6508	0	6	4.68	0	36.00	64.00	A	11.82	421	5	Sabah. Perancangan village in Labuk-Sugut District. Language dying out due to intermarriage. Muslims 45%, animists 45%.
6509	3	5	4.00	0	99.70	0.30	C	296.38	115	8	Sabah. Segama river area of Lahad Datu District. Animists 30%. D=RCC,ECB,SDA. M=BEM.
6510	3	5	4.47	0	85.00	15.00	B	155.12	171	7	Sabah. Central Keningau area around Ambual, Liau Laut. Bilingual in Nabay. Animists 50%. D=ECB,RCC,SDA. M=BEM.
6511	5	5	7.29	0	99.00	1.00	B	198.74	225	7	Tindakon, Mangkaak. In northeast Sabah. Animists 35%, Muslims 10%. D=Dusun Ch(ECB),RCC,ACM,SDA,PCS. M=BEM,GRI,BM,SIL.
6512	1	10	3.75	8	99.75	0.25	C	375.03	91	9	Mixed-race. Malacca is seat of Eurasian Catholicism. Almost all Catholics. D=95% RCC(M-Kuala Lumpur,D-Malacca-Johore). M=MEP,CSSR,SJ,OFMCap,CDD,OMI.
6513	1	6	4.45	0	90.00	10.00	C	197.10	161	7	Sabah. Kota Marudu District. Agriculturalists. Bilingual in Kimaragang. Animists 40%. D=SIB/ECB.
6514	0	7	2.62	6	47.60	52.40	A	1.04	209	4	Early laborers from India. Settlers, immigrants, businessmen. Hindus 48%, Muslims 49%. M=FMB.
6515	6	8	3.04	8	74.00	26.00	B	18.90	137	5	94% in West Malaysia, 3% in Sarawak, 2% in Sabah. Mahayana Buddhists/Chinese folk-religionists 91%. D=RCC,MCM,TJC,ACM,CB,ECB. M=CMA(Hong Kong).
6516	4	8	3.58	0	53.00	47.00	B	9.67	219	4	Many individual believers but no churches. Folk Buddhists 93%. D=RCC,ACM,MCM,CB. M=MEP,MHM.
6517	3	8	4.07	7	74.00	26.00	B	24.30	175	5	78% in Malaya, 11% in Sarawak, 9% in Sabah. Buddhists/folk religionists 89%. D=Basel Christian Ch(Protestant Ch in Sabah),BPC,ECB. M=BM(since 1882),MEP.
6518	5	8	3.86	6	68.00	32.00	B	24.82	182	5	59% in Sarawak, 41% in Malaya. Folk Buddhists 90%. D=RCC,ACM,TJC,MCM,CB. M=MEP,MHM.
6519	5	8	3.17	6	75.00	25.00	B	24.63	140	5	Totoks 94% in Malaya. Folk Buddhists 89%. D=RCC,ACM,MCM,CB,ECB. M=CMS,MEP,MHM,FMB. Many churches.
6520	5	8	4.13	0	52.00	48.00	B	17.08	252	5	Urban dwellers. Buddhists/folk-religionists 90%. D=RCC,MCM,ACM,CB,ECB.
6521	6	8	4.23	7	75.00	25.00	B	27.37	178	5	Urban dwellers. Folk Buddhists 90%. D=ACM,RCC,CB,PCM,MSBC,ECB. M=FMB,MEP,MHM.
6522	5	8	5.16	7	85.00	15.00	B	37.23	187	5	Totoks. Mostly urban. Mahayana Buddhists 86%, New-Religionists 2%(HVHC). D=RCC,MCM,ACM,TJC,ECB. M=MEP,MHM,CMA(Hong Kong),FMB. R=FEBC.
6523	5	8	3.51	4	73.00	27.00	B	26.64	156	5	Urban dwellers. Chinese control 75% of all Malaysia's economic/commercial power. Folk Buddhists 90%. D=RCC,TJC,MCM,ACM,CB. M=CMML,MEP,MHM.
6524	0	8	3.15	7	52.50	47.50	B	0.95	217	3	Originating from India. Hindus 90%(Ramakrishna Mission,&c), Muslims 9%. M=FMB.
6525	0	6	0.00	7	39.00	61.00	A	0.00	0	1.12	100% Chinese Muslims, immigrants from Western China over last 100 years.
6526	5	5	5.24	0	57.00	43.00	B	41.61	293	6	Sabah. East coast, 3 Districts. Animists 50%, Muslims 30%. D=RCC,ECB,SDA,ACM,MCB. M=BEM,SIL.
6527	0	5	2.52	0	27.13	72.87	A	0.12	323	3	Sabah. From Mindanao (Philippines) in 1850. 17 villages around Lahad Datu and Kota Belud Districts. Fishermen. Muslims 98%.
6528	1	9	2.44	7	57.05	42.95	B	0.10	151	3	Mostly Muslims 69%, New-Religionists 25%, nonreligious, Baha'is. D=RCC. M=FMB.
6529	1	3	4.44	0	27.00	73.00	A	1.97	552	4	Malaya. South of main body of Semai, Kuala Krau, Pahang. Animists 65%, Muslims 33%. D=RCC. M=MHM.
6530	1	6	3.04	0	29.00	71.00	A	1.05	382	4	Malaya. Northeastern Perak, western Kelantan. Animists 66%, Muslims 33%. D=RCC. M=MHM.
6531	0	5	2.78	0	23.00	77.00	A	0.84	450	3	Aboriginal Malays, in Malaya. East coast and inland, Pairang river area. Animists 99%.
6532	3	10	4.22	7	72.60	27.40	B	14.83	188	5	From Japan: settlers, immigrants, businessmen. Buddhists 57%, New-Religionists 24%, nonreligious 12%. D=RCC,ACM,MCM.
6533	3	6	9.53	5	81.00	19.00	B	38.43	351	5	Mainly in Sabah. Immigrants from Java (Indonesia). Muslims 50%, New-Religionists 35%. D=RCC,MCM,PCSM.
6534	0	5	3.15	0	33.00	67.00	A	12.04	304	5	Sabah. Tawau District along Kalabakan river. Mostly animists 80%, a few Muslims.
6535	1	3	4.29	0	93.00	7.00	C	203.67	141	8	Sarawak, in remote northern mountains. Also in Indonesia. Animists 21%, Muslims 19%. D=Kelabit Ch(ECB). M=BEM.
6536	3	10	3.40	5	67.00	33.00	B	7.33	180	4	Long-time residents from Karnataka(India). Hindus 96%. D=RCC,ACM,MCM.
6537	0	6	2.60	0	35.00	65.00	A	6.38	243	4	Sarawak. Middle Rejang river, below Tanjong language area, 3rd Division. Being absorbed by Iban. Animists 95%.
6538	0	4	3.73	0	30.00	70.00	A	5.47	387	4	Sarawak. Near Belaga on Baloi river, 7th Division. Animists 95%.
6539	3	5	7.08	0	52.00	48.00	B	28.47	400	5	Sabah, Sarawak; also in Brunei. Agriculturalists. Muslims 85%(Sunnis). D=RCC,ECB,TJC. M=SIL,BEM.
6540	2	5	4.14	0	57.00	43.00	B	41.61	240	6	Sabah. Minusut and Kuangoh, Keningau District. Second language: Sabah Malay. Animists 75%. D=RCC,ECB.
6541	3	6	6.73	0	89.00	11.00	B	162.42	233	7	Sandayo. In Sabah. Kota Marudu and Pitas Districts. Agriculturalists. Muslims 30%, animists 20%. D=PCS,SDA,TJC. M=BM.
6542	0	6	4.86	0	40.00	60.00	A	14.60	368	5	Sabah. Kinabatangan and Sandakan Districts, villages along Kinabatangan river. Muslims 80%.
6543	1	6	0.00	0	27.30	72.70	A	1.29	100	4	Malaya. Kedah-Perak border area, Thai border. Animists 65%, Muslims 33%. D=RCC. M=MHM.
6544	0	5	1.10	0	19.10	80.90	A	0.07	231	2	Sarawak. Northeast around Marudi and north into Brunei. Related to Narom, Lelak. Muslims 90%, some animists.
6545	0	5	3.67	0	53.00	47.00	B	48.36	234	6	Sabah. Klias river area, Beaufort District. Agriculturalists. Animists 50%, Muslims 25%.
6546	0	5	2.44	0	34.00	66.00	A	8.68	238	4	Sarawak, some in Sabah. Primarily in Kalimantan (Indonesia). Animists 93%.
6547	3	5	5.43	0	62.00	38.00	B	56.57	278	6	Sabah. Keningau District 12 miles north/west of Keningau town. Second language; Sabah Malay. Animists 75%. D=RCC,ECB,SDA. M=BEM.
6548	0	5	0.00	0	9.00	91.00	A	0.00	0	1.02	Sarawak. Central, east of Belaga, southwest of Long Murum. Closest to Kayaman. Animists 100%.
6549	4	5	4.46	0	52.00	48.00	B	37.96	262	5	Sabah. Keningau District near Lanas. Agriculturalists. Animists 80%. D=ACM,RCC,ECB,SDA. M=BEM.
6550	4	3	4.77	4	98.00	2.00	B	178.85	157	7	Sarawak. 28 dialects in west; mainly in Kalimantan (Indonesia). Animists 30%, Muslims 10%. D=RCC,ACM,ECB,SDA. M=BEM,CMS,FMB.
6551	1	6	1.62	0	27.00	73.00	A	0.98	266	3	Malaya. North central Perak. Animists 66%, Muslims 33%. D=RCC. M=MHM.
6552	2	6	4.84	0	43.00	57.00	A	15.69	363	5	Sarawak. Extreme west. 2 small villages on Pasir river, Lundu, 1st Division. Also in Indonesia (Kalimantan). Related to Bukar-Sadong. Animists 90%. D=RCC,SDA.
6553	0	5	0.00	0	11.00	89.00	A	0.00	0	1.03	Sarawak. Northeast, east of Sibuti (Dali) and Tinjar river (Lelak). Related to Narom, Kiput. Muslims 100%.
6554	1	5	5.62	0	82.00	18.00	B	149.65	205	7	Sabah. Southern Kota Marudu District, headwaters of Lingkabau river. Few literates. Muslims 30%, animists 20%. D=TJC.
6555	0	5	2.43	5	33.01	66.99	A	0.01	260	2	Many non-standard Malay dialects. Lingua franca of Sabah, and parts from Sumatra to Philippines. Agriculturalists. Muslims 100%(Shafi Sunnis).
6556	0	5	3.15	0	34.00	66.00	A	12.41	295	5	Sabah. Beaufort District along Bukau and Padas rivers. Animists 60%, Muslims 30%.
6557	2	5	5.02	0	99.00	1.00	C	216.81	162	8	Sarawak. Tinjar river, 4th Division. Literates 25%. Animists 25%, Muslims 15%. D=ECB(SIB),RCC. M=BEM.
6558	1	5	2.99	0	29.90	70.10	A	0.98	366	3	Malaya. Selangor coast, Malacca. Animists 66%, Muslims 33%. D=RCC. M=MHM.
6559	1	10	-0.32	8	99.70	0.30	C	329.59	10	9	Malayo-Portuguese. Malaguense. 10% in Kuala Lumpur and Singapore. Trankera and Hilir, Melaka, Straits of Malacca. Fishermen. D=RCC.
6560	8	7	8.84	5	55.65	44.35	B	1.32	470	4	Muslims 100%(Shafi Sunnis; also proselytic Dakwah). D=MSBC,RCC,Brethren Assemblies,ACM,MCM,PCM,LRGM,FGCM. M=OMI,FMB,FI,OMF,YWAM. R=FEBC.
6561	4	8	2.78	4	97.00	3.00	B	106.21	107	7	From South India. Hindus 50%, Muslims 19%(Hanafi Sunnis). D=RCC,OSCE,MTSC,IPCG. M=MEP.
6562	2	7	5.44	0	39.00	61.00	A	7.11	418	4	Coastal area, Rejang delta, northwest Sarawak. In 1900, Muslims 33%; by 1964, Muslims 55%(loose Shafi Sunnis), animists 40%. D=RCC,Protestants.
6563	1	6	1.10	0	27.30	72.70	A	1.29	211	4	Malaya. Southeast Kelantan. Animists 65%, Muslims 33%. D=RCC. M=MHM.

Continued overleaf

Table 8-2 continued

PEOPLE		POPULATION				IDENTITY CODE		LANGUAGE		CHURCH		MINISTRY						SCRIPTURE		
Ref 1	Ethnic name 2	P% 3	In 1995 4	In 2000 5	In 2025 6	Race 7	Language 8	Autoglossonym 9	S 10	AC 11	Members 12	Jayuh 13-17	dwa 18	xcmc 19	20	21	mi 22	Biblioglossonym 23	Pub 24-26	ss 27
6564	Millikin	0.02837	5,705	6,311	8,786	MSY44e	31-PHIA-d	milikin		20.00	1,262	1.s..	9	5	6	2	0		pnb	.
6565	Minangkabau (Orang Negeri	2.12766	427,838	473,278	658,903	MSY44k	31-PHGA-i	minangkabau-negeri-sembilan		0.02	95.00	1....	3	2	3	0	0		pn.	b
6566	Minokok Dusun (Kadazan)	0.01418	2,851	3,154	4,391	MSY44y	31-GBAL-b	monsok-dusun		35.00	1,104	0....	9	5	6	5	2	Dusun: Ranau*	PNB	b
6567	Mintil	0.00033	66	73	102	AUG05	46-GBAB-f	mintil		1.70	1	0....	6	4	5	4	1		...	.
6568	Molbog	0.01000	2,011	2,224	3,097	MSY44x	31-CJEE-a	molbog		0.10	2	0....	5	2	4	0	0	Molbog	P..	b
6569	Murik Kayan	0.00794	1,597	1,766	2,459	MSY44z	27-EAAA-a	murik		5.00	88	0....	7	5	6	5	1		...	.
6570	Narom	0.01716	3,451	3,817	5,314	MSY44z	31-IAAE-a	narom		5.00	191	0....	7	5	6	1	0		...	.
6571	Northern Sakai (Pie)	0.08222	16,533	18,289	25,462	AUG05	46-GBCA-b	temiar		5.50	1,006	0....	7	5	6	1	1		...	.
6572	Northern Sinama (Bajau)	0.23332	46,917	51,900	72,256	MSY44z	31-EACA-a	balingingi		0.01	5	0.s..	3	2	2	0	0	Sama: Balangingi*	P..	.
6573	Orang Kanaq	0.00024	48	53	74	AUG05	31-PHFB-a	orang-hulu		5.00	3	0....	7	5	5	1	1		...	.
6574	Orang Seletar	0.00384	772	854	1,189	AUG05	31-PHFB-a	orang-hulu		6.00	51	0....	7	5	4	1	0		...	.
6575	Pandewan Murut	0.00860	1,729	1,913	2,663	MSY44z	31-GCAD-f	pandewan		5.00	96	0....	7	5	5	3	0		...	.
6576	Pathan (Afghani)	0.02000	4,022	4,449	6,194	CNT24a	58-ABDA-a	pashto		0.03	1	1As..	3	2	2	0	0		pnb	b
6577	Peluan (Sook Murut)	0.02515	5,057	5,594	7,789	MSY44z	31-GCAD-a	paluan		8.00	448	0....	7	5	6	1	1		...	b
6578	Penan (Punan-Nibong)	0.05298	10,653	11,785	16,407	MSY44z	31-JCCC-c	kakus-penan		10.00	1,178	0....	8	5	6	3	1	Penan	PN.	.
6579	Peranakan (Straits Chines	1.00000	201,084	222,441	309,685	MSY42a	31-PHBB-a	paranakan	16	18.00	40,039	0A...	8	5	13	5	3		...	b
6580	Punjabi	0.40000	80,434	88,976	123,874	CNN25n	59-AAFE-c	general panjabi		1.10	979	1Asu.	6	4	6	4	2		PNB	b
6581	Rejang Kayan (Lisum)	0.02149	4,321	4,780	6,655	MSY44y	31-JBAB-a	ma'-aging		15.00	717	0....	8	5	6	5	1		...	.
6582	Rejang Punan (Bah-Biau)	0.00319	641	710	988	MSY44z	31-IAEA	punan-bah-biau cluster		10.00	71	0....	8	5	7	4	1		...	.
6583	Riau Malay	0.40000	80,434	88,976	123,874	MSY44k	31-PHAB-e	malayu-riau		0.01	9	0....	3	3	2	0	1		...	b
6584	Rungus Dusun (Momogun)	0.08182	16,453	18,200	25,338	MSY44y	31-GBAB-a	rungus		60.00	10,920	0.s..	10	7	9	5	2	Momogun*	PN.	.
6585	Saban	0.00500	1,005	1,112	1,548	MSY44z	31-HAAD-a	sa'ban		15.00	167	0....	8	5	7	4	1	Saban	P..	.
6586	Sabum	0.00400	804	890	1,239	AUG05	46-GBCA-ab	sabubn		0.60	5	0....	5	4	4	4	0		...	.
6587	Sarawak Dayak (Bau-Jagoi)	0.13475	27,096	29,974	41,730	MSY44y	31-KAAC-a	jagoi		18.00	5,395	0A...	8	5	6	1	0	Jagoi	...	.
6588	Sea Dayak (Iban)	1.98610	399,373	441,789	615,064	MSY44e	31-PHIA	iban-sarawak cluster		43.00	189,969	3.s..	9	5	13	5	3	Iban	PNB	.
6589	Sebuyau (Sabuyan)	0.06383	12,835	14,198	19,767	MSY44z	31-PHIA-e	sibuyau		5.00	710	1.s..	7	5	6	3	0		pnb	.
6590	Sekapan	0.00532	1,070	1,183	1,648	MSY44z	31-IACA	kajaman-sekapan cluster		45.00	533	0....	9	6	6	4	1		...	.
6591	Selekau (Land Dayak)	0.02695	5,419	5,995	8,346	MSY44y	31-KAAA-a	silakau		9.00	540	0....	7	5	6	5	2		...	.
6592	Selungai Murut	0.00168	338	374	520	MSY44z	31-GCAG-a	selungai murut		15.00	56	0....	8	5	5	2	0		...	.
6593	Semai (Sakai, Sengoi)	0.12998	26,137	28,913	40,253	AUG05	46-GBCB-a	semai		5.50	1,590	0.s..	7	5	6	5	2	Senoi*	P..	.
6594	Semang Negrito (Kensiu)	0.01985	3,992	4,415	6,147	AUG05	46-GBAA-b	kensiu		1.30	57	0....	6	4	4	5	2	Kensiu	...	.
6595	Semaq Beri	0.01475	2,966	3,281	4,568	AUG05	46-GCAA-a	semaq-beri		3.00	98	0....	6	4	6	4	1		...	.
6596	Sembakung Murut	0.03000	6,033	6,673	9,291	MSY44z	31-GCBB-a	sembakung		10.00	667	0....	8	5	5	2	0		...	.
6597	Semelai	0.01902	3,825	4,231	5,890	AUG05	46-GCAA-b	semelai		4.00	169	0....	6	4	6	4	1		...	.
6598	Semnam	0.00300	603	667	929	AUG05	46-GBCA-ad	semnam		1.00	7	0....	6	4	4	4	0		...	.
6599	Serudung Murut	0.00573	1,152	1,275	1,774	MSY44z	31-GCBB-c	serudung		10.00	127	0....	8	5	5	2	0		...	.
6600	Sian	0.00050	101	111	155	MSY44z	31-IACC-b	sian		5.00	6	0....	7	5	6	0	0		...	.
6601	Sibop Kenyah (Sabup)	0.01227	2,467	2,729	3,800	MSY44y	31-JCBA	sebob-kenyah cluster		15.00	409	0....	8	5	6	5	1		...	.
6602	Siduan (Seduan, Sibu)	0.00298	599	663	923	MSY44z	31-IADF	sibu cluster		5.00	33	0....	7	5	6	1	0		...	.
6603	Sinabu	0.00550	1,106	1,223	1,703	MSY44z	31-GAAH-a	sinabu		40.00	489	0.s..	9	6	6	5	3		...	.
6604	Sindhi	0.10000	20,108	22,244	30,968	CNN25p	59-AAFF-a	standard sindhi		1.10	245	1as..	6	4	5	0	0	Sindhi	PNB	b
6605	Sinhalese	0.10000	20,108	22,244	30,968	CNN25q	59-ABBA-aa	standard sinhala		2.80	623	1asuh	6	4	6	4	2		pnb	b
6606	Sino-Native	0.10000	20,108	22,244	30,968	MSY42a	79-AAAB-ba	kuo-yü		6.00	1,335	2Bsuh	7	5	11	2	0	Chinese: Kuoyu*	PNB	b
6607	Sonsogon (Kimaragang)	0.01324	2,662	2,945	4,100	MSY44y	31-GBAD-a	marudu-sonsogon		10.00	295	0....	8	5	5	5	1		...	.
6608	Southern Kota Marudu	0.00809	1,627	1,800	2,505	MSY44y	31-GBAE-a	marudu-tinagas		20.00	360	0....	9	5	5	4	0		...	.
6609	Southern Murut (Belait)	0.09446	18,994	21,012	29,253	MSY44z	31-HAAC-o	lun-bawang		50.00	10,506	0.s..	10	5	10	5	2	Lun Bawang*	PNB	.
6610	Southern Sama (Bajau)	0.12353	24,840	27,478	38,255	MSY44z	31-EACB-e	si-butuq		0.01	3	1.s..	3	2	2	0	0	Sama: Southern*	Pn.	n
6611	Sugut Kadazan	0.05502	11,064	12,239	17,039	MSY44y	31-GBAE	tinagas-talantang cluster		35.00	4,284	0....	9	5	6	5	2		...	.
6612	Sungai Dusun (Kadazan)	0.17200	34,586	38,260	53,266	MSY44y	31-GBAL-b	monsok-dusun		35.00	13,391	0....	9	5	7	5	1	Dusun: Ranau*	PNB	b
6613	Tagal Murut	0.20728	41,681	46,107	64,191	MSY44z	31-GCAE-d	tagal		60.00	27,664	0.s..	10	5	9	5	3	Murut: Tagal*	PN.	.
6614	Tagalog (Pilipino)	0.10000	20,108	22,244	30,968	MSY44o	31-CKAA-a	proper tagalog		98.00	21,799	4Bs..	10	9	14	5	1	Tagalog	PNB	b
6615	Tambanua (Paitan)	0.10909	21,936	24,266	33,783	MSY44z	31-GAAB	tambanua cluster		20.00	4,853	0.s..	9	5	4	1	2	Tombonuwo	P..	.
6616	Tambunan Dusun	0.07000	14,076	15,571	21,678	MSY44y	31-GBAL-b	monsok-dusun		60.00	9,343	0.s..	10	7	7	5	1	Dusun: Ranau*	PNB	b
6617	Tamil	7.10000	1,427,696	1,579,328	2,198,760	CNN23c	49-EBEA-b	tamil		8.00	126,346	2Asu.	7	5	10	5	3	Tamil	PNB	b
6618	Tampias Lobu	0.01165	2,343	2,591	3,608	MSY44z	31-GAAE-a	tampias-lobu		20.00	518	0....	9	5	6	5	1		...	b
6619	Tanjong	0.00071	143	158	220	MSY44z	31-IADH-a	tanjong		5.00	8	0....	7	5	6	1	0		...	.
6620	Tatana	0.03810	7,661	8,475	11,799	MSY44z	31-GBAQ-a	tatanaq		12.00	1,017	0....	8	5	5	4	1	Tatana	...	.
6621	Tausug (Sulu, Suluk)	0.76193	153,212	169,484	235,958	MSY44x	31-CKGQ-d	vehicular tau-sug		0.50	847	0.s..	5	3	3	1	1	Tausug	PN.	.
6622	Telugu	0.40000	80,434	88,976	123,874	CNN23d	49-DBAB-a	telugu		9.20	8,186	2Asu.	7	5	10	5	3	Telugu	PNB	b
6623	Temoq	0.00248	499	552	768	AUG05	46-GCAA-e	temoq		1.30	7	0....	6	4	5	4	1		...	.
6624	Tempasuk Dusun (Kadazan)	0.04255	8,556	9,465	13,177	MSY44y	31-GBAG-a	tempasuk		30.00	2,839	0....	9	5	7	5	3		...	.
6625	Temuan (Benua, Niap)	0.06604	13,280	14,690	20,452	AUG05	31-PHFA-a	temuan		6.00	881	0....	7	5	6	4	1		...	.
6626	Thai	0.10000	20,108	22,244	30,968	MSY49d	47-AAAB-d	central thai		0.60	133	3asuh	5	4	6	3	1	Thai*	PNB	b
6627	Tidung (Nonukan, Zedong)	0.06788	13,650	15,099	21,021	MSY44z	31-GCBC-b	tidong		27.00	4,077	0....	9	5	2	2	0		...	.
6628	Timogun Murut	0.05445	10,949	12,112	16,862	MSY44z	31-GCAB	timugon-murut cluster		10.00	1,211	0.s..	8	5	4	1	0	Timugon Murut	P..	.
6629	Tobilang	0.01324	2,662	2,945	4,100	MSY44y	31-GBAF-a	tebilung		40.00	1,178	0....	9	6	7	2	0		...	.
6630	Tonga	0.00050	101	111	155	AUG05	46-GBAA-a	tonga		1.00	1	0....	6	4	4	1	0		...	.
6631	Tring (Tringus)	0.00248	499	552	768	MSY44y	31-KAAC-m	tringus		8.00	44	0c...	7	5	4	1	0		...	.
6632	Tuaran Dusun (Lotud)	0.03237	6,509	7,200	10,024	MSY44y	31-GBAL-b	monsok-dusun		21.00	1,512	0....	9	5	6	5	2	Dusun: Ranau*	PNB	b
6633	Tudan Dusun (Kadazan)	0.05000	10,054	11,122	15,484	MSY44y	31-GBAL-b	monsok-dusun		30.00	3,337	0....	9	5	6	5	2	Dusun: Ranau*	PNB	b
6634	Tungara (Tingara)	0.00194	390	432	601	MSY44z	31-GCBA-c	tengara		60.00	259	0....	10	7	5	2	0		...	.
6635	Tutoh Kenyah (Lugat)	0.00426	857	948	1,319	MSY44y	31-JCCJ	bakung-kenyah cluster		80.00	758	0....	10	7	10	5	1		PNB	.
6636	Tutong	0.08300	16,690	18,463	25,704	MSY44z	31-IAAA	tutong-maritime cluster		25.00	4,616	0....	9	5	6	4	2		...	.
6637	USA White	0.03000	6,033	6,673	9,291	CEW19s	52-ABAC-s	general american		77.00	5,138	1Bsuh	10	9	13	5	3	English*	PNB	b
6638	Ukit	0.00085	171	189	263	MSY44z	31-IACC-e	southeast punan-ukit		5.00	9	0....	7	5	6	5	1		...	.
6639	Upper Baram Kenyah	0.01000	2,011	2,224	3,097	MSY44y	31-JCCD	baram-kenyah cluster		80.00	1,780	0....	10	7	10	5	1		...	.
6640	Upper Kinabatangan	0.03536	7,110	7,866	10,950	MSY44z	31-GAAG-a	kalabuan		50.00	3,933	0.s..	10	6	8	5	3		p..	.
6641	Urdu	0.05000	10,054	11,122	15,484	CNN25r	59-AAFO-d	standard urdu		0.01	1	2Asuh	3	3	5	0	0	Urdu	PNB	b
6642	West Coast Bajau (Laut)	0.27707	55,714	61,632	85,804	MSY44z	31-EACD-d	pitas-bajau		0.30	185	0....	5	4	0	1	0		...	.
6643	Western Kenyah (Lunan)	0.00887	1,784	1,973	2,747	MSY44y	31-JCCC-e	lunan		60.00	1,184	0....	10	7	8	5	1		pn.	.
6644	Yacan	0.04855	9,763	10,799	15,035	MSY44z	31-EABA-a	yakan		0.10	11	0.s..	5	3	2	1	1	Yakan	PN.	.
6645	other minor peoples	2.22000	446,406	493,818	687,500	...				14.00	69,135		8	5	6	5	3			
	Maldives	**100.00000**	**249,060**	**286,223**	**501,456**					**0.12**	**357**									
6646	Arab	0.13000	324	372	652	CMT30	12-AACF-g	syro-mesopotamian		1.00	4	1Asuh	6	4	2	0	0		pnb	b
6647	British	0.04000	100	114	201	CEW19i	52-ABAC-b	standard-english		66.00	76	3Bsuh	10	8	13	3	2		PNB	b
6648	Gujarati	0.20000	498	572	1,003	CNN25e	59-AAFH-b	standard gujaraati		0.70	4	2A.u.	5	4	2	3	0	Gujarati	PNB	b
6649	Malay	0.08000	199	229	401	MSY44k	31-PHAA-b	bahasa-malaysia		0.90	2	1asuh	5	4	2	0	0	Malay	PNB	b
6650	Malayali	0.16000	398	458	802	CNN23b	49-EBEB-a	malayalam		25.00	114	2Asu.	9	5	13	3	3	Malayalam	PNB	b
6651	Maldivian (Malki, Mahl)	98.46000	245,224	281,815	493,734	CNN25q	59-ABAA-a	dhivehi		0.01	28	0....	3	3	2	1	3		...	b
6652	Sinhalese	0.68000	1,694	1,946	3,410	CNN25q	59-ABBA-aa	standard sinhala		3.00	58	1asuh	6	4	13	1	2		pnb	b
6653	Tamil	0.15000	374	429	752	CNN23c	49-EBEA-b	tamil		8.00	34	2Asu.	7	5	13	3	2	Tamil	PNB	b
6654	other minor peoples	0.10000	249	286	501	...				13.00	37		8	4	2	3	0			
	Mali	**100.00000**	**9,943,980**	**11,233,821**	**21,295,460**					**2**	**224,368**									
6655	Bambara (Bamanakan)	30.56518	3,039,395	3,433,638	6,508,996	NAB63a	00-AAAB-a	bamanan-kan	78	2.00	68,673	4As..	6	5	9	5	3	Bambara	PNB	b
6656	Banka	0.04710	4,684	5,291	10,030	NAB63h	00-AAAA	west mandekan cluster		1.00	53	4a...	6	4	5	0	0		PN.	b
6657	Berabish Bedouin	1.00000	99,440	112,338	212,955	CMT30	12-AACD-a	hassaaniyya		0.01	11	0a...	3	2	2	0	0		pn.	b
6658	Black Bobo (Bobo Fing)	0.16210	16,119	18,210	34,520	NAB63z	00-DHAA	bobo-fing cluster		5.00	911	0.s..	7	5	4	5	3	Bobo: Madare	PN.	b
6659	Bozo (Hain, Xan)	0.10000	9,944	11,234	21,295	NAB63b	00-BBDA-a	hainya-xo		0.00	0	0....	0	3	0	1	3		...	.
6660	British	0.00700	696	786	1,491	CEW19i	52-ABAC-b	standard-english		79.00	621	3Bsuh	10	9	13	5	3		PNB	b
6661	Dafi (Marka)	0.06500	6,464	7,302	13,842	NAB63a	00-AAAC-c	maraka-jalan-kan		12.00	876	0....	8	5	4	2	0	Marka	...	.
6662	Dialonke (Yalunka)	0.10000	9,944	11,234	21,295	NAB63c	00-AACA-b	yalunka		0.10	11	1....	5	3	2	1	0	Yalunka	PN.	.
6663	Dogon (Habbe, Kado)	4.27963	425,566	480,766	911,367	NAB56a	91-ACEA-b	toro-so	12	12.00	57,692	4....	8	5	8	5	3	Dogon	PN.	b
6664	Duun (Samogho, Duu)	0.73630	73,218	82,715	156,798	NAB63z	00-DGBA-a	duun		0.02	17	0....	3	3	4	4	1		...	b
6665	French	0.10000	9,944	11,234	21,295	CEW21b	51-AABI-d	general français	35	80.00	8,987	1B.uh	10	9	14	5	2	French	PNB	b
6666	Fula Kita (Peuhala)	0.35000	34,804	39,318	74,534	NAB56c	90-BAAA-b	futa-tooro		0.76	299	1cs..	5	4	2	5	3		pnb	.
6667	Fula Macina (Niafunke)	9.58452	953,083	1,076,708	2,041,068	NAB56c	90-BAAA-e	fula-masina		1.00	10,767	4cs..	6	4	2	5	4	Fula: Macina*	Pnb	b
6668	Futa Jalon Fulani	0.52593	52,298	59,082	111,999	NAB56c	90-BAAA-d	futa-jalon		0.00	0	2as..	0	3	0	1	0	Fula: Futa-jalon*	Pnb	.
6669	Idaksahak	0.32421	32,239	36,421	69,042	CMT32h	01-AABA-a	daksahaq		0.00	0	0....	0	3	0	1	0	Tadaksahak	...	.
6670	Jeeri Fulani	0.37053	36,845	41,625	78,906	NAB56c	90-BAAA-b	futa-tooro		0.00	0	1cs..	0	3	0	1	0		pnb	.
6671	Jotoni (Jowulu)	0.09572	9,518	10,753	20,384	NAB63z	00-CABA-a	kpango		5.00	538	0....	7	3	4	1	0	Jowulu	...	b
6672	Jula (Dyula, Kong Jula)	0.52593	52,298	59,082	111,999	NAB63h	00-AAAB-z	jula-kan	15	1.00	591	1cs..	6	4	6	1	0	Jula	PNb	b
6673	Kagoro (Logoro)	0.22615	22,488	25,405	48,160	NAB63d	00-AAAA-g	kakolo-qango		1.00	254	1c...	6	4	4	4	2		pn.	b
6674	Khasonke (Kasonke)	1.26233	125,526	141,808	268,819	NAB63e	00-AAAA-f	xasonka-xango		2.70	3,829	1c...	6	4	4	5	3	Kassonke	pn.	n
6675	Kunta Bedouin	0.30000	29,832	33,701	63,886	CMT30	12-AACD-a	hassaaniyya		1.00	337	0a...	6	4	3	1	0		pn.	b
6676	Mamara Senufo (Minianka)	5.25928	522,982	590,818	1,119,988	NAB56a	91-BAAA	mamara cluster	8	1.50	8,862	1....	6	4	3	5	3	Senoufo, Mamara	P..	.
6677	Moor (Maure, Bidan)	2.90000	288,375	325,781	617,568	CMT30	12-AACD-a	hassaaniyya	5	0.01	33	0a...	3	3	1	1	3		pn.	b
6678	Mossi (Moshi)	0.50000	49,720	56,169	106,477	NAB56a	91-GGAA-a	moo-re	4	7.60	4,269	2A...	7	5	10	5	2	Moore	PNB	b
6679	Nimadi	0.00200	199	225	426	CMT32i	10-AAAA-b	nimadi		0.00	0	0....	0	2	0	0	0		...	.
6680	Northwestern Maninka	6.59118	655,426	740,441	1,403,622	NAB63h	00-AAAB-e	wasulunka-kan	16	2.00	14,809	1cs..	6	4	3	5	3		pnb	.
6681	Pana (Sama)	0.03846	3,824	4,321	8,190	NAB56a	91-GFAA	pana cluster		2.00	86	0....	6	4	4	1	1		...	.
6682	Red Bobo (Bobo Wule)	3.21553	319,752	361,227	684,762	NAB56a	91-GFDA	bo-mu cluster		6.00	21,674	4.s..	7	5	8	5	3	Boomu*	PN.	.
6683	Red Bobo (Bwamu)	0.10000	9,944	11,234	21,295	NAB56a	91-GFDA-a	ouarkoye		6.00	674	1.s..	7	5	4	5	3	Bwamu*	Pn.	.

Continued opposite

Table 8-2 continued

EVANGELIZATION								EVANGELISM			ADDITIONAL DESCRIPTIVE DATA
Ref 1	D 28	aC 29	CG% 30	r 31	E 32	U 33	W 34	e 35	R 36	T 37	Locations, civil divisions, literacy, religions, church history, denominations, dioceses, church growth, missions, agencies, ministries, movements 38
6564	0	5	4.96	1	56.00	44.00	B	40.88	268	6	Sarawak. Southwest, south of Simunjan. Animists 79%, some Baha'is.
6565	0	4	4.66	1	22.02	77.98	A	0.01	667	2	Negeri Sembilan Malay. In Malaya (Peninsular Malaysia). Southeast of Kuala Lumpur. From Sumatra. Muslims 100% (Shafi Sunnis).
6566	2	5	4.82	0	79.00	21.00	B	100.92	197	7	Sabah. Headwaters of Kinabatangan river. Animists 65%. D=RCC,SDA.
6567	1	7	0.00	0	29.70	70.30	A	1.84	92	4	Malaya. Tamun river, Pahang. Animists 65%, Muslims 33%. D=RCC. M=MHM.
6568	0	5	0.70	0	19.10	80.90	A	0.07	198	2	On Banggi Island, Sabah. Mainly in Philippines. Close to Palawano. Muslims 100% (syncretistic practices).
6569	2	5	4.58	0	35.00	65.00	A	6.38	398	4	Sarawak. Below Long Miri (Banyuq) and Lio Mato (Semiang) on Baram river. Animists 95%. D=RCC,ECB. M=BEM.
6570	0	5	2.99	1	29.00	71.00	A	5.29	331	4	Sarawak. South of mouth of Baram river around Miri and south. Mostly Muslims 90%, some animists 5%.
6571	1	5	4.72	0	31.50	68.50	A	6.32	498	4	Aboriginals. Malaya. Mostly in Perak and Kelantan, also Pahang. Semi-nomadic. Animists 61%, Muslims 33%. D=RCC. M=MHM.
6572	0	4	1.62	1	16.01	83.99	A	0.00	365	1.07	Sabah. East Coast Bajaw. Muslims 99%.
6573	0	5	1.10	0	28.00	72.00	A	5.11	206	4	Aboriginal Malays. Malaya. Southeast, northeast of Mawai. Animists 80%, some Muslims 15%. M=Brethren Mission(South Thailand).
6574	0	5	4.01	0	27.00	73.00	A	5.91	508	4	Aboriginals. Malaya. Southeast coast around Kukuo, Jahore Bahru; north coast of Singapore. Coastal. Animists 94%.
6575	0	6	4.67	0	30.00	70.00	A	5.47	473	4	Sabah. Pensiangan District. Close to Keningau Murut (Nabay). Animists 95%.
6576	0	5	0.00	5	35.03	64.97	A	0.03	174	2	Refugees, migrants, from Afghanistan. Muslims 100%(Hanafi Sunnis).
6577	1	5	3.88	0	36.00	64.00	A	10.51	334	5	Sabah. 4 Districts: Sabah, Tenom, Keningau, Pensiangan. Bilingual in Tagal, Sabah Malay. Muslims 50%, animists 42%. D=RCC.
6578	2	5	4.88	0	44.00	56.00	A	16.06	336	5	Sarawak. Upper Baram and Balui rivers. 3 villages. Nomads, semi-nomads in 10-million-year-old tropical rain-forest. Hunter-gatherers. Muslims 50%, animists 40%.
6579	5	8	8.65	7	79.00	21.00	B	51.90	323	6	Babas, anglicized Chinese Malays in Malacca, Penang. Bilingual. Only 3% speak Baba; rest Penang Hokkien. Chinese folk-religionist/Buddhists 70%.
6580	1	8	4.69	5	56.10	43.90	B	2.25	280	4	Muslims 58%, Sikhs 40%(from Indian Punjab). D=RCC. M=MEP,FMB. No churches.
6581	2	5	4.37	0	46.00	54.00	A	25.18	311	5	Sarawak. Rejang, Balui river areas. Animists 85%. D=RCC,ECB. M=BEM.
6582	1	5	4.35	0	40.00	60.00	A	14.60	333	5	Sarawak. Central, around Merit, Rejang river, 7th Division. Nomadic hunter-gatherers. Animists 90%. D=ECB. M=BEM.
6583	1	4	2.22	5	23.01	76.99	A	0.00	348	1.07	Dialect of Malay from Sumatra. Off Malaya coast. Muslims 100%(Shafi Sunnis). D=RCC. M=SSCC.
6584	3	5	3.34	0	99.60	0.40	C	229.95	109	8	Sabah. Kudat, Pitas, Labuk-Sugut. Animists 35%, Muslims 5%(many Qadiani Ahmadis). D=Protestant Ch in Sabah,ACM,TJC. M=BM,CMS.
6585	1	5	2.86	0	46.00	54.00	A	25.18	201	5	Sarawak. Northeast on border (4th Division), also in Kalimantan (Indonesia). Animists 85%. D=ECB. M=BEM.
6586	0	6	1.62	0	23.60	76.40	A	0.51	304	3	North central Perak. Closest to Lanoh and Semnam. Animists 60%, Muslims 39%.
6587	0	5	6.49	0	48.00	52.00	A	31.53	419	5	Sarawak. 20 villages, Bau, 1st Division, Sadong, Samarahan, and Lundu rivers. Animists 60%, Muslims 22%.
6588	4	5	6.41	4	99.43	0.57	B	164.79	181	7	Sarawak, Brunei, Indonesia. Literates 35%. Animists 51%, Baha'is 4%(mass conversions from 1962, under strong state pressure). D=MCM,ACM(D-Kuching).
6589	0	5	4.35	1	39.00	61.00	A	7.11	341	4	Sarawak. Lundu, 1st Division, mouth of Lupa river, west bank around Sebuyau. Related to Iban. Animists 95%.
6590	1	5	4.06	0	75.00	25.00	B	123.18	167	7	Sarawak. Belaga, 7th Division, 1 village. Animists 55%. D=ECB. M=BEM.
6591	2	5	4.07	0	40.00	60.00	A	13.14	337	5	Sarawak. 22 villages in Saak, Lundu, 1st Division. Land Dayaks. Animists 91%. D=ACM,RCC.
6592	0	5	4.11	0	39.00	61.00	A	21.35	325	5	Sabah. Pensiangan District, 7 villages along Sapulut river. Also in Kalimantan (Indonesia). Animists 85%.
6593	4	4	5.20	0	39.50	60.50	A	7.93	430	4	Malaya. Northwest Pahang and southern Perak, Selangor, Negri Sembilan, central mountain area. Animists 61%, Muslims 33%. D=RCC,MCM,MBC,ELCM.
6594	1	6	4.13	0	29.30	70.70	A	1.39	480	4	Malaya. Northeast Kedah. Also in Thailand. Aboriginal nomads in forests. Animists 65%, Muslims 33%. D=RCC. M=MHM,GKPI(Indonesia).
6595	1	6	4.69	0	31.00	69.00	A	3.39	503	4	Malaya. Pahang, Trengganu, Kelantan. Animists 65%, Muslims 32%. D=RCC. M=MHM.
6596	0	5	4.29	0	34.00	66.00	A	12.41	387	5	Tinggalum. In Sabah. Sembakung river; also in Kalimantan (Indonesia). Animists 90%.
6597	1	3	2.87	0	29.00	71.00	A	4.23	366	4	Malaya. Between Segamat and Pahang river. Animists 63%, Muslims 33%. D=RCC. M=MHM.
6598	0	6	1.96	0	25.00	75.00	A	0.91	324	3	North central Perak. Close to Lanoh and Sabum. Animists 66%, Muslims 33%.
6599	0	5	2.57	0	34.00	66.00	A	12.41	248	5	Sabah. Tawau District along Serudung river; village near Tawau town. Animists 90%.
6600	0	5	1.81	0	27.00	73.00	A	4.92	235	4	Sarawak. Belaga, 7th Division. Related to Bukitan. Animists 95%.
6601	2	5	3.78	0	46.00	54.00	A	25.18	276	5	Sarawak, in north. On upper Tinjar river, 4th Division; several large villages. Muslims 70%(mainly Lirong), many animists 15%. D=RCC,ECB. M=BEM.
6602	0	7	3.56	0	30.00	70.00	A	5.47	372	4	Sarawak. Sibu, 3rd Division, Rejang river. Muslims 50%, animists 45%.
6603	1	6	3.97	0	75.00	25.00	B	109.50	164	7	Sabah. Maligatan, Minusu, Tongud, Kinabatangan. Agriculturalists. Animists 40%, Muslims 20%. D=Anglican Ch of Malaysia (D-Sabah). M=CMS(Australia).
6604	0	7	3.25	4	46.10	53.90	A	1.85	253	4	From India, Pakistan. Migrant workers. Hindus 93%, Muslims 4%, Sikhs 2%.
6605	0	7	4.22	6	48.80	51.20	A	4.98	270	4	Workers from Ceylon. Theravada Buddhists 95%.
6606	0	6	5.25	7	66.00	34.00	B	14.45	245	5	Mixed-race persons(Malay/Chinese), mainly in urban areas. Buddhists/folk-religionists 70%, Muslims 24%.
6607	2	5	3.44	0	40.00	60.00	A	14.60	294	5	Sabah. Hills in southern Pitas, southeast Kota Marudu. Monolinguals in remotest areas. No literates. Hunters. Animists 80%, Muslims 10%. D=PCS,SDA. M=BM.
6608	0	5	3.65	0	47.00	53.00	A	34.31	262	5	Sabah. Southern Kota Marudu and Parong, a migrant village in northern Kota Marudu. Animists 79%, Muslims 1%.
6609	4	6	7.20	0	99.50	0.50	B	187.97	205	7	Sabah, also Sarawak. Southwest border; also in Brunei, and northern Kalimantan (Indonesia). Animists 50%. D=RCC,ACM,ECB,TJC. M=BEM,CMS.
6610	0	5	1.10	1	20.01	79.99	A	0.00	220	1.10	Sea Gypsies, Sea Nomads. Southern Bajau. Sabah, east coast. Majority live in Philippines (southern Sulu). 15 dialects. Muslims 100%.
6611	2	5	6.25	0	69.00	31.00	B	88.14	282	6	Sabah. Headwaters of Sugut river, Labuk-Sugut District. Animists 60%, Muslims 5%. D=RCC,SDA.
6612	4	5	7.47	0	81.00	19.00	B	103.47	281	7	Sabah. Animists 30%, Muslims 35%(Shafi Sunnis, many Ahmadis). D=RCC,ACM,SDA,TJC. M=CMS.
6613	4	3	8.25	0	99.60	0.40	C	227.76	231	8	Sabah. 4 Districts over southwest; also in Kalimantan (Indonesia). Animists 30%. D=RCC,TJC,ACM,Tagal Ch(ECB). M=BEM,CMS,BM,SIL,UBS.
6614	1	10	7.99	5	99.98	0.02	C	622.39	137	10	Immigrants, settlers, refugees, migrant workers, businessmen, from Philippines. D=RCC. M=FMB.
6615	2	5	6.38	0	50.00	50.00	B	36.50	378	5	Sabah. Labuk-Sugut and Pitas Districts. Muslims 50%, animists 30%. D=ACM,PCS/BCC.
6616	3	6	7.08	0	99.60	0.40	C	240.90	198	8	Sabah. Across Tambunan District and parts of Keningau. Highly educated. Agriculturalists. Muslims 30%, animists 10%. D=ECB,RCC,SDA. M=BEM.
6617	7	7	3.57	6	75.00	25.00	B	21.90	167	5	Low-caste farmers from South India. Hindus 86%, Muslims 4%(Hanafi Sunnis). D=ACM/CCEA(3 Dioceses),RCC,ELCMS,MCM,PCM,MTSC,ACC. M=CPM,CMS.
6618	3	6	4.03	0	57.00	43.00	B	41.61	218	6	Sabah. 3 villages in Ranau around Tampias. Most bilingual in Central Dusun. Plantation agriculturalists. Animists 80%. D=RCC,ECB,SDA. M=BEM.
6619	0	5	2.10	0	28.00	72.00	A	5.11	255	4	Sarawak. Rejang river above Kanowit language area, below Song village, Kapit, 7th Division. Animists 95%.
6620	1	6	4.73	0	42.00	58.00	A	18.39	342	5	Sabah. In Kuala Penyu District. Animists 70%, Muslims 18%. D=RCC. M=SIL.
6621	0	5	4.54	0	24.50	75.50	A	0.44	584	3	Sabah (5 Districts). Majority in Philippines; also Kalimantan (Indonesia). Dominant Muslim ethnic group in Sulu. Muslims 100%(Shafi Sunnis). M=SIL.
6622	2	8	4.69	5	74.20	25.80	B	24.91	210	5	Low-caste farmers from South India. Hindus 875, Muslims 3%(Hanafi Sunnis). D=RCC,ACM(D-Sabah). M=CMS,MEP,FMB.
6623	1	7	1.96	0	29.30	70.70	A	1.39	277	4	Malaya. Jeram river, southeast Pahang. Animists 66%, Muslims 33%. D=RCC. M=MHM.
6624	3	5	5.81	0	67.00	33.00	B	73.36	272	6	Sabah. Around Tempasuk village, Kota Belud. Animists 60%, Muslims 10%. D=RCC,SDA,TJC.
6625	1	1	4.58	0	30.00	70.00	A	6.57	510	4	Malaya. Scattered settlements in south. Animists 61%, Muslims 33%. D=RCC.
6626	1	7	2.62	6	54.60	45.40	B	1.19	161	4	Immigrants, expatriates from Thailand; workers. Theravada Buddhists 97%, Muslims 2%. D=RCC.
6627	0	5	6.19	0	50.00	50.00	B	49.27	367	6	Tarakan. Sabah. Districts: Sabah, Labuk-Sugut, Sandakan, Tawau. Also northeast coast of Kalimantan. Animists 60%, Muslims 13%.
6628	0	5	4.91	0	35.00	65.00	A	12.77	424	5	Kapagalan, Poros. In Sabah. Tenom District along Padas river. Bilingual in Malay. Muslims 50%, animists 40%.
6629	0	5	4.88	0	68.00	32.00	B	99.28	231	6	Sabah. Kota Marudu District. Animists 50%, Muslims 10%.
6630	0	6	0.00	0	22.00	78.00	A	0.80	125	3	Malaya. Northwest tip north of Kaki. Primarily in Thailand. Close to Kensiu. Animists 85%, Muslims 14%.
6631	0	5	3.86	0	30.00	70.00	A	8.76	430	4	Sarawak. Lower Tutoh river. Close to Jagoi. Animists 85%, Muslims 7%.
6632	4	5	5.15	0	66.00	34.00	B	50.58	249	6	Sabah. Tuaran District, north of Kota Kinabalu. Agriculturalists. Animists 69%, Muslims 10%. D=RCC,PCS,ECB,SDA. M=BEM,BM.
6633	2	5	5.98	0	74.00	26.00	B	81.03	253	6	Sabah. Agriculturalists. Animists 70%. D=RCC,SDA.
6634	0	5	3.31	0	86.00	14.00	C	188.34	122	7	Sabah. Headwaters of Penangah river. Dialect of Baukan. Similar to Tarakan (Tidong). Animists 40%.
6635	2	5	4.42	0	99.80	0.20	C	370.84	114	9	Sarawak. Northeast, Tutoh river. Animists 20%. D=ECB,RCC. M=BEM.
6636	2	6	6.33	0	59.00	41.00	B	53.83	318	6	Sarawak. Along lower Limbang river. Also in Brunei. Animists 65%, some Muslims. D=RCC,ECB.
6637	5	10	4.95	8	99.77	0.23	C	427.19	105	10	Expatriates from USA, in business, commerce. D=MCM,SDA,CJCLdS,JWs,CC.
6638	2	5	2.22	0	35.00	65.00	A	6.38	214	4	Sarawak. Upper Rajom and Tatau rivers, Baleh, 7th Division. Animists 95%. D=ECB,RCC. M=BEM.
6639	2	5	5.32	0	99.80	0.20	C	344.56	143	9	Sarawak. Upper Baram river near border, also in Kalimantan (Indonesia) and Brunei. Animists 20%. D=ECB,RCC. M=BEM.
6640	4	6	6.16	0	92.00	8.00	B	167.90	199	7	Sabah. Upper reaches of Kinabatangan river. Agriculturalists. Muslims 30%, animists 20%. D=ACM,RCC,SDA,TJC.
6641	0	7	0.00	5	45.01	54.99	A	0.01	63	2	From Pakistan, immigrants and migrant workers. Muslims 99%(Hanafi Sunnis).
6642	0	5	2.96	0	15.30	84.70	A	0.16	621	3	Sabah. West coast, northern and eastern areas. Also in Brunei. High educational level. Fishermen. Muslims 100%(Sunnis).
6643	2	5	4.89	0	99.00	1.00	C	216.81	159	8	Sarawak. Balui, Belaga, Kalua, Kemena rivers. Literates 25%. Hunters, fishermen. Animists 30%, Muslims 10%. D=ECB,RCC. M=BEM.
6644	1	5	2.43	1	25.10	74.90	A	0.09	321	2	Sabah. Mainly in Philippines. Migrant workers. Literates 5%. Muslims 99%. D=RCC.
6645	0	6	5.24		44.00	56.00	A	22.48	326	5	Oceanians(CJCLdS), Germans(NAC), Koreans(M=Korea Methodist Ch); 90,000 Filipino Muslim refugees, and some Vietnamese.
Maldives											
6646	0	3	1.40	7	37.00	63.00	A	1.35	156	4	Traders, workers from worldwide Arab diaspora. Muslims 99%(Sunnis, some Shias).
6647	2	10	4.43	8	99.66	0.34	C	327.62	112	9	Expatriates from Britain, in administration, development. Nonreligious 24%. D=SDA,RCC.
6648	0	8	1.40	6	45.70	54.30	A	1.16	144	4	Traders from India. Mostly Muslims 80%, some Hindus 15% and Baha'is 4%.
6649	0	8	0.70	5	41.90	58.10	A	1.37	92	4	Migrant workers, teachers from Malaysia. Muslims 100%(Shafi Sunnis).
6650	3	10	2.46	4	92.00	8.00	B	83.95	103	6	Expatriates from Kerala(India). Mostly Muslims 64%, some Hindus 8%, some Baha'is 3%. D=RCC,SDA,CSI.
6651	0	5	3.39	0	19.01	80.99	A	0.00	572	1.06	On 220 inhabited islands. Mostly fishermen. Muslims 100%(Shafi Sunnis). Highest divorce rate in world (85%). M=SDA,FI,CSI.
6652	2	5	4.14	6	55.00	45.00	B	6.02	235	4	From Sri Lanka. Theravada Buddhists 95%. D=RCC(M-Colombo),SDA.
6653	2	10	3.59	6	73.00	27.00	B	21.31	172	5	Traders from South India. Mostly Muslims 61%, some Hindus 26% and Baha'is 5%. D=RCC,SDA.
6654	0	10	3.68		34.00	66.00	A	16.13	297	5	Other Asians, Europeans, Americans, Africans. Muslims 76%, nonreligious 11%.
Mali											
6655	5	5	5.76	4	64.00	36.00	B	4.67	328	4	Muslims 85%(Maliki Sunnis,with some Wahhabis;80% in towns;also Tijaniyya,Qadiriyya),animists 13%. D=RCC(3 Dioceses),EEPM,ECEM,AoG,SDA. M=WF,FSC.
6656	0	0	4.05	5	31.00	69.00	A	1.13	537	4	North of Sikasso in Danderesso Administrative District. Bambara spoken as second language. Muslims 80%, Animists 19%.
6657	0	2	2.43	7	27.01	72.99	A	0.01	318	2	Nomad Bedouins, tent-dwellers, northwest of Timbuktu. Muslims 100%(Sunnis).
6658	2	6	4.62	0	40.00	60.00	A	7.30	447	4	Most in Burkina Faso. Sya is prestige dialect. Animists 50%, Muslims 45%(Maliki Sunnis). D=RCC(D-San),ECEM. M=WF,FSC,CMA,WVI.
6659	1	5	0.00	0	13.00	87.00	A	0.00	0	1.04	Fishing hamlets along Niger river. Also in Burkina Faso, Niger. Fishermen. Muslims 100%(Maliki Sunnis). D=EEPM. M=SIL,GMU,CMA.
6660	3	10	4.75	8	99.79	0.21	C	444.05	105	10	Expatriates from Britain, in business, education. D=RCC,ECEM,EEPM.
6661	0	5	4.57	2	36.00	64.00	A	15.76	493	5	Most Marka live in Burkina Faso. Muslims 70%(Maliki Sunnis), animists 18%.
6662	0	4	2.43	1	21.10	78.90	A	0.07	579	2	West of Bamako. Muslims 99%(Maliki Sunnis).
6663	2	6	9.05	0	57.00	43.00	B	24.96	501	5	Around Bandiagara on edge of Sahara; also in Burkina Faso. Agriculturalists with caste system. Animists 48%, Muslims 30%(Sunnis). Secret societies strong.
6664	1	5	2.87	0	24.02	75.98	A	0.01	544	2	Kadiolo and Sikasso Circles, also in Burkina Faso. Bilingual in Bambara, some in French. Animists 50%, Muslims 50%(Sunnis). No literates. D=ECEM. M=CMA.
6665	1	10	3.09	8	99.80	0.20	C	440.92	74	10	Expatriates from France, in administration. D=RCC(6 Dioceses). M=WF,FSC.
6666	1	4	3.46	4	36.76	63.24	A	1.02	377	4	Distinct from Fula Macina. Muslims 95%(Maliki Sunnis). D=RCC. M=WF,FSC,Torchbearers(Ghana),PI,CMA,FI.
6667	2	4	7.23	4	45.00	55.00	A	1.64	538	4	A major Fula geopolitical state. Pastoralists. Muslims 95%(Maliki Sunnis). D=ECEM,RCC. M=CMA,CRWM,NLM,WF,FSC,Torchbearers(Ghana),FMB,SIL.
6668	0	5	0.00	4	26.00	74.00	A	0.00	0	1.10	In Western Mali. Majority live in Guinea, Sierra Leone, Senegal, Guinea Bissau, Gambia. Muslims 100%(Maliki Sunnis).
6669	0	5	0.00	0	9.00	91.00	A	0.00	0	1.03	'Sons of Isaac'. In 7th Region. Also some live in Algeria. Wide travellers. Close to Tuareg. Muslims 100%(Maliki Sunnis).
6670	0	5	0.00	4	22.00	78.00	A	0.00	0	1.10	Majority live in Senegal, some in Gambia. Muslims 100%(Maliki Sunnis).
6671	0	4	4.07	0	27.00	73.00	A	4.92	606	4	Kadiolo Circle; and in Burkina Faso. Men also speak Bambara, some French. Animists 95%.
6672	0	5	4.16	4	39.00	61.00	A	1.42	435	4	Traders from Mali to Ghana. Lingua franca. Strong Muslims 99%(Maliki Sunnis; most also speak Arabic).
6673	1	5	3.29	4	38.00	62.00	A	1.38	375	4	Related to Bambara, Khasonke. Animists 98%. D=RCC. M=WF,FSC.
6674	2	5	6.13	1	37.70	62.30	A	3.71	584	4	Also in Senegal, Gambia. Muslims 92%(Maliki Sunnis), animists 4%. D=RCC(D-Kayes),EPK. M=UWM,WF,FSC,NPM,FI.
6675	0	5	3.58	7	33.00	67.00	A	1.20	355	4	Nomadic Bedouins, tent-dwellers, northwest of Timbuktu. Close to Berabish. Muslims 100%(Sunnis).
6676	2	5	7.02	5	36.50	63.50	A	1.99	630	4	Northern Senufo. Animists 43%, Muslims 55%. Many fetish houses(temples). D=RCC(D-Sikasso),ECEM. M=CMA,SIL,FSC,WF,FMB.
6677	0	4	3.56	7	29.01	70.99	A	0.01	402	2	Nioro and Nara. Primarily in Mauritania and Morocco, also Niger, Senegal. Black Moors, also White Moors(Bidan). Muslims 100%(Maliki Sunnis). M=RSMT.
6678	2	8	6.24	4	66.60	33.40	B	18.47	313	5	Migrant workers from Burkina Faso. Animists 49%, Muslims 40%(Maliki Sunnis). D=RCC,AoG. M=WF,FSC.
6679	0	2	0.00	0	5.00	95.00	A	0.00	0	1.02	From Timbuktu across to Mauritania. Nomads, hunter-gatherers. Related to Zenaga. Animists 90%, nominal Muslims 10%.
6680	3	5	7.57	4	45.00	55.00	A	3.28	585	4	Wasulunka. Also in Senegal, Guinea. Muslims 67%(Maliki Sunnis), animists 30%. D=RCC(D-Kayes),EEPM,EPK. M=UWM,GMU,FMB,WF,FSC,WVI,NPM.
6681	1	6	4.56	0	24.00	76.00	A	1.75	677	4	South of Bandiagara. Majority live in Burkina Faso. Animists 75%, Muslims 23%. D=RCC.
6682	2	5	7.98	0	50.00	50.00	B	10.95	512	5	Southeast. Also in Burkina Faso. Animists 42%, Muslims 52%(Maliki Sunnis). D=RCC(D-San),ECEM. M=CMA,WF,FSC,WVI.
6683	2	7	4.30	0	42.00	58.00	A	9.19	370	4	Mainly in Burkina Faso. Animists 64%, Muslims 30% (Maliki Sunnis). D=RCC(D-San),ECEM. M=WF,CMA,WVI.

Continued overleaf

Table 8-2 continued

Ref 1	Ethnic name 2	P% 3	In 1995 4	In 2000 5	In 2025 6	Race 7	Language 8	Autoglossonym 9	S 10	AC 11	Members 12	Jayuh 13-17	dwa xcmc mi 18 19 20 21 22	Biblioglossonym 23	Pub ss 24-26 27
6684	Saharan Arab	1.40000	139,216	157,273	298,136	CMT30	12-AACD-a	hassaaniyya	8	0.00	0	0a...	0 2 2 0 0		pn. b
6685	Shenara Senufo	1.43578	142,774	161,293	305,756	NAB56a	91-BAAC-a	sena-ri		5.00	8,065	1.s..	7 5 3 5 3	Senoufo, Shempire	pn. .
6686	Songhai (Sonrhai)	6.31114	627,578	708,982	1,343,986	NAB65b	01-AAAA	songhay-kine cluster	8	0.20	1,418	0....	5 3 4 1 2	Songhai*	PN. b
6687	Soninke (Sarakole)	7.42390	738,231	833,988	1,580,954	NAB63j	00-BAAA-a	proper soninke		0.01	83	3....	3 3 3 1 2	Soninke	... b
6688	Sorogama Bozo	1.05186	104,597	118,164	223,998	NAB63b	00-BBBA	sorogama cluster		0.02	24	0....	3 3 1 1 1	Boso, Sorogama	... .
6689	Southern Samo (Sambla)	0.03000	2,983	3,370	6,389	NAB63z	00-CAAA-a	senku		15.00	506	0....	8 5 8 4 1		... .
6690	Suppire Senufo	3.82876	380,731	430,116	815,352	NAB56a	91-BAAB-a	supyi-re		2.00	8,602	0....	6 4 3 2 2	Suppire*	P.. .
6691	Tahoua Tuareg (Aulliminde	1.99853	198,733	224,511	425,596	CMT32h	10-AAAB-bc	east ta-wllemmet		0.01	22	1....	3 3 3 0 3		pn. .
6692	Tiema Ciewe Bozo	0.02630	2,615	2,954	5,601	NAB63b	00-BBAA-a	tiema-ciewe		0.10	3	0....	5 3 0 1 0		... .
6693	Tieyaxo Bozo	0.06000	5,966	6,740	12,777	NAB63b	00-BBCA-a	tieya-xo		0.10	7	0....	5 3 0 1 0		... .
6694	Timbuktu Tuareg (Antessar	2.62964	261,491	295,409	559,994	CMT32h	10-AAAB-ba	ta-nslemt		0.01	30	1....	3 3 3 1 3		pn. .
6695	Tukulor (Takarir)	1.42001	141,206	159,521	302,398	NAB56c	90-BAAA-a	haal-pulaar		0.03	48	2As..	3 3 0 0 0	Fula: Pulaar*	Pnb n
6696	Udalan Tuareg	2.40000	238,656	269,612	511,091	CMT32h	10-AAAB-bc	east ta-wllemmet		0.00	0	1....	0 3 3 1 3		pn. .
6697	White Bobo (Bobo Gbe)	0.05000	4,972	5,617	10,648	NAB56a	91-GFDB	chan cluster		5.00	281	0....	7 5 8 4 2		... .
6698	Wolof	0.40000	39,776	44,935	85,182	NAB56c	90-AAAA-a	vehicular wolof		0.50	225	4.s..	5 4 6 4 1	Wolof: Senegal	PN. b
6699	other minor peoples	0.20000	19,888	22,468	42,591	...				0.80	180		5 4 4 4 0		
	Malta	**100.00000**	**375,025**	**388,544**	**429,847**					**95.58**	**371,381**				
6700	Arab	2.00000	7,501	7,771	8,597	CMT30	12-AACF-a	masri		70.00	5,440	2Asuh	10 4 5 5 3	Arabic*	PNB b
6701	British	2.10000	7,876	8,159	9,027	CEW19i	52-ABAC-b	standard-english		79.00	6,446	3Bsuh	10 9 15 5 3		PNB b
6702	Esperanto	0.00000	0	0	0	CEW21z	51-AAAC-a	proper esperanto	3	90.00	0	0A...	10 9 8 5 0	Esperanto	PNB b
6703	French	0.05000	188	194	215	CEW21b	51-AABI-d	general français		87.00	169	1B.uh	10 9 14 5 3	French	PNB b
6704	Greek	0.03000	113	117	129	CEW20	56-AAAA-c	dhimotiki		95.10	111	2B.uh	10 9 11 5 2	Greek: Modern	PNB b
6705	Indo-Pakistani	0.01500	56	58	64	CNN25g	59-AAFO-e	general hindi		2.00	1	3Asuh	6 4 2 3 0		pnb b
6706	Italian	1.45000	5,438	5,634	6,233	CEW21e	51-AABQ-c	standard italiano		84.00	4,732	2B.uh	10 9 15 5 3	Italian	PNB b
6707	Jewish	0.01500	56	58	64	CMT35	12-AACC-a	maltiya		2.00	1	0a.u.	6 4 6 1 0	Maltese	PNB b
6708	Maltese	93.84000	351,923	364,610	403,368	CMT36	12-AACC-a	maltiya		96.80	352,942	0a.u.	10 10 16 5 3	Maltese	PNB b
6709	USA White	0.20000	750	777	860	CEW19s	52-ABAC-s	general american		78.00	606	1Bsuh	10 10 14 0 0	English*	PNB b
6710	other minor peoples	0.30000	1,125	1,166	1,290	...				80.00	933		10 8 7 5 0		
	Marshall Islands	**100.00000**	**54,700**	**64,220**	**127,147**					**93.59**	**60,103**				
6711	Marshallese	88.50000	48,410	56,835	112,525	MPY54b	38-CAAA	rälik-ratak cluster		95.10	54,050	0.s..	10 10 12 5 2	Marshallese	PNB b
6712	USA White	6.50000	3,556	4,174	8,265	CEW19s	52-ABAC-s	general american		85.00	3,548	1Bsuh	10 9 13 5 3	English*	PNB b
6713	other minor peoples	5.00000	2,735	3,211	6,357	...				78.00	2,505		10 7 7 5 0		
	Martinique	**100.00000**	**378,819**	**395,362**	**450,094**					**94.44**	**373,371**				
6714	French	2.30000	8,713	9,093	10,352	CEW21b	51-AABI-d	general français	95	84.70	7,702	1B.uh	10 9 14 5 2	French	PNB b
6715	French Creole	0.70000	2,652	2,768	3,151	CEW21b	51-AACC-e	martiniquais		90.00	2,491	1As..	10 9 12 5 2		pnb b
6716	Han Chinese	0.15000	568	593	675	MSY42a	79-AAAB-ba	kuo-yü		55.00	326	2Bsuh	10 7 8 5 2	Chinese: Kuoyu*	PNB b
6717	Mulatto	93.40000	353,817	369,268	420,388	NFB69b	51-AACC-e	martiniquais	99	95.51	352,688	1As..	10 10 12 5 3		pnb b
6718	Syrian Arab	0.15000	568	593	675	CMT30	12-AACF-f	syro-palestinian		22.00	130	1Asuh	9 5 7 5 2	Arabic: Lebanese*	PNB b
6719	Tamil (East Indian)	1.90000	7,198	7,512	8,552	CNN23c	51-AACC-e	martiniquais		85.00	6,385	1As..	10 8 11 5 1		pnb b
6720	Vietnamese	0.10000	379	395	450	MSY52b	46-EBAA-ac	general viêt		50.00	198	1Asu.	10 7 7 4 2	Vietnamese	PNB b
6721	West Indian Black	0.30000	1,136	1,186	1,350	NFB69a	51-AACC-e	martiniquais		91.00	1,079	1As..	10 8 11 5 2		pnb b
6722	other minor peoples	1.00000	3,788	3,954	4,501	...				60.00	2,372		10 7 8 5 0		
	Mauritania	**100.00000**	**2,329,214**	**2,669,547**	**4,766,399**					**0.24**	**6,527**				
6723	Arabized Berber	9.67000	225,235	258,145	460,911	CMT32a	12-AACD-a	hassaaniyya		0.05	129	0a...	4 3 1 0 1		pn. b
6724	Bambara	0.50000	11,646	13,348	23,832	NAB63a	00-AAAB-a	bamanan-kan	8	2.00	267	4As..	6 4 7 2 1	Bambara	PNB b
6725	Berabish Bedouin	1.50000	34,938	40,043	71,496	CMT30	12-AACD-a	hassaaniyya		0.00	0	0a...	0 1 2 0 0		pn. b
6726	Black Moor (Maure)	24.00000	559,011	640,691	1,143,936	CMT32y	12-AACD-a	hassaaniyya		0.00	0	0a...	0 3 4 0 3		pn. b
6727	British	0.01000	233	267	477	CEW19i	52-ABAC-b	standard-english	3	67.00	179	3Bsuh	10 9 13 5 1		PNB b
6728	Delim Bedouin	4.50000	104,815	120,130	214,488	CMT30	12-AACD-a	hassaaniyya		0.00	0	0a...	0 1 2 0 0		pn. b
6729	Diola (Dyola, Jola)	0.10000	2,329	2,670	4,766	NAB56c	90-DAAA-a	proper foonyi		3.00	80	4....	6 5 6 1 1	Diola*	P.. b
6730	Duaish (Idaouich)	0.20000	4,658	5,339	9,533	CMT32i	10-AAAA-a	znaga		0.00	0	0....	0 2 0 0 0		... b
6731	French	0.15000	3,494	4,004	7,150	CEW21b	51-AABI-d	general français	35	75.00	3,003	1B.uh	10 9 12 5 1	French	PNB b
6732	Fula (Fulakunda)	1.10000	25,621	29,365	52,430	NAB56c	90-BAAA-c	fula-kunda	14	1.00	294	1as..	6 4 2 1 1	Pulaar: Fulakunda	Pnb b
6733	Imragen (Aita, Foikat)	0.02000	466	534	953	CMT30	12-AACD-a	hassaaniyya		0.00	0	0a...	0 2 0 0 0		pn. b
6734	Malinke	0.30000	6,988	8,009	14,299	NAB63h	00-AAAA-a	mandinka-kango		2.00	160	4a...	6 4 5 1 1	Mandinka	PN. b
6735	Masna	0.06000	1,398	1,602	2,860	CMT32	10-AAAA	znaga cluster		0.00	0	0....	0 2 0 0 0		... b
6736	Nimadi (Ikoku)	0.01000	233	267	477	CMT32y	10-AAAA-b	nimadi		0.00	0	0....	0 1 0 0 0		... .
6737	Regeibat	4.00000	93,169	106,782	190,656	CMT30	12-AACD-a	hassaaniyya		0.00	0	0a...	0 1 2 0 0		pn. b
6738	Serer	0.10000	2,329	2,670	4,766	NAB56c	90-BBAA-a	sine		20.00	534	2....	9 5 10 2 2	Seereer*	PN. n
6739	Soninke (Sarakole)	2.80000	65,218	74,747	133,459	NAB63j	00-BAAA-a	proper soninke		0.06	45	3....	4 3 2 0 1	Soninke	... b
6740	Spaniard	0.01000	233	267	477	CEW21k	51-AABB-c	general español		90.00	240	2B.uh	10 9 15 5 1	Spanish	PNB b
6741	Tasumsa (Hadj, Hassan)	3.50000	81,522	93,434	166,824	CMT32z	12-AACD-a	hassaaniyya		0.00	0	0a...	0 2 2 0 0		pn. b
6742	Trarza (Brakna)	8.50000	197,983	226,911	405,144	CMT30	12-AACD-a	hassaaniyya		0.00	0	0a...	0 2 2 0 0		pn. b
6743	Tuareg	2.82000	65,684	75,281	134,412	CMT32h	10-AAAB-a	ta-mahaq		0.01	8	1....	3 2 3 0 0	Tamahaq: Hoggar*	PN. b
6744	Tukulor (Takarir)	7.20000	167,703	192,207	343,181	NAB56c	90-BAAA-a	haal-pulaar		0.03	58	2As..	3 3 0 1 0	Fula: Pulaar*	Pnb n
6745	White Moor (Bidan)	20.00000	465,843	533,909	953,280	CMT32y	12-AACD-a	hassaaniyya	90	0.00	0	0a...	0 3 4 0 3		pn. b
6746	Wolof	6.80000	158,387	181,529	324,115	NAB56c	90-AAAA-a	vehicular wolof	10	0.40	726	4.s..	5 4 6 4 3	Wolof: Senegal	PN. b
6747	Zenaga	1.15000	26,786	30,700	54,814	CMT32i	10-AAAA-a	znaga		0.01	3	0....	3 3 0 0 1		... b
6748	other minor peoples	1.00000	23,292	26,695	47,664	...				3.00	801		6 4 5 2 0		
	Mauritius	**100.00000**	**1,112,017**	**1,156,498**	**1,377,463**					**31.94**	**369,432**				
6749	British (English, Scot)	0.06000	667	694	826	CEW19i	52-ABAC-b	standard-english	58	79.00	548	3Bsuh	10 9 13 5 3		PNB b
6750	Comorian	0.40000	4,448	4,626	5,510	NAB57j	99-AUSM-s	shi-ngazidya	2	0.10	5	1csu.	5 3 7 3 0	Comorian*	PNb b
6751	Franco-Mauritian	5.70000	63,385	65,920	78,515	CEW21b	51-AABI-mu	français-d'île-maurice	85	91.00	59,988	1A.uh	10 10 12 5 2		pnb .
6752	Franco-Mauritian Mulatto	21.67000	240,974	250,613	298,496	NAN58	51-AACC-l	morisyen	98	93.00	233,070	1cs..	10 9 12 5 3	Mauritius Creole*	Pnb .
6753	French (Metropolitan)	0.20000	2,224	2,313	2,755	CEW21b	51-AABI-d	general français		84.00	1,943	1B.uh	10 9 14 5 2	French	PNB b
6754	Han Chinese (Mandarin)	1.20000	13,344	13,878	16,530	MSY42a	79-AAAB-ba	kuo-yü	5	50.00	6,939	2Bsuh	10 7 10 5 3	Chinese: Kuoyu*	PNB b
6755	Ilois (Islander)	0.17000	1,890	1,966	2,342	NAN58	51-AACC-k	seselwa		45.00	885	1cs..	9 6 7 5 2	Creole: Seychelles*	PNb b
6756	Indo-Mauritian	20.37000	226,518	235,579	280,589	CNN25g	51-AACC-lb	indo-mauritian	1	4.30	10,130	1cs..	6 6 8 5 3		pnb .
6757	Indo-Mauritian (Bengali)	0.30000	3,336	3,469	4,132	CNN25b	59-AAFT-e	west bengali	1	2.00	69	1Asuh	6 4 5 4 1	Bengali: Musalmani*	PNB b
6758	Indo-Mauritian (Bihari)	2.00000	22,240	23,130	27,549	CNN25c	59-AAFQ-a	bhojpuri	3	7.70	1,781	1.s..	7 5 7 4 1	Bihari: Bhojpuri*	Pn. b
6759	Indo-Mauritian (Goan)	0.30000	3,336	3,469	4,132	CNN25d	59-AAFU-o	konkani-gomantaki	1	80.00	2,776	3asu.	10 8 12 4 1	Konkani: Goan*	PNb b
6760	Indo-Mauritian (Gujarati)	0.10000	1,112	1,156	1,377	CNN25e	59-AAFH-b	standard gujaraati	1	2.00	23	2A.u.	6 4 6 5 0	Gujarati	PNB b
6761	Indo-Mauritian (Hindi)	30.83000	342,835	356,548	424,672	CNN25g	59-AAFO-k	bhojpuri-mauritius	73	2.80	9,983	1csuh	6 5 7 5 1	Bhojpuri	PNB b
6762	Indo-Mauritian (Hindi)	0.50000	5,560	5,782	6,887	CNN25g	59-AAFO-e	general hindi	71	1.00	58	3Asuh	6 4 5 5 1		pnb b
6763	Indo-Mauritian (Marathi)	1.06000	11,787	12,259	14,601	CNN25j	59-AAFU-m	deshi-marathi	2	2.00	245	2Asu.	6 4 4 5 1	Marathi*	PNB b
6764	Indo-Mauritian (Punjabi)	2.20000	24,464	25,443	30,304	CNN25n	59-AAFE-c	general panjabi	3	21.00	5,343	1Asu.	9 6 8 5 2		PNB b
6765	Indo-Mauritian (Tamil)	2.57000	28,579	29,722	35,401	CNN23c	49-EBEA-b	tamil	7	35.30	10,492	2Asu.	9 7 8 5 2	Tamil	PNB b
6766	Indo-Mauritian (Telugu)	0.96000	10,675	11,102	13,224	CNN23d	49-DBAB-a	telugu	2	31.50	3,497	2Asu.	9 7 8 5 2	Telugu	PNB b
6767	Indo-Mauritian (Urdu)	5.81000	64,608	67,193	80,031	CNN25r	59-AAFO-d	standard urdu	58	0.50	336	2Asuh	5 4 5 5 0	Urdu	PNB b
6768	Malagasy	0.40000	4,448	4,626	5,510	MSY44j	31-LDAA-aa	standard merina	4	47.00	2,174	1Asu.	9 6 10 5 2		pnb b
6769	Sino-Mauritian (Hakka)	1.78000	19,794	20,586	24,519	MSY42a	79-AAAG-a	literary hakka	4	55.00	11,322	1A...	10 7 10 5 3	Chinese: Hakka, Wukingfu*	PNB b
6770	Sino-Mauritian (Kreol)	0.56000	6,227	6,476	7,714	MSY42a	51-AACC-l	morisyen		50.00	3,238	1cs..	10 7 9 5 3	Mauritius Creole*	Pnb .
6771	Sino-Mauritian (Yueh)	0.66000	7,339	7,633	9,091	MSY42a	79-AAAM-a	central yue	4	51.00	3,893	3A.uh	10 7 8 5 3	Chinese, Yue	PNB b
6772	other minor peoples	0.20000	2,224	2,313	2,755	...				30.00	694		9 5 6 5 0		
	Mayotte	**100.00000**	**90,000**	**101,621**	**186,507**					**1.84**	**1,865**				
6773	Arab	0.10000	90	102	187	CMT30	12-AACF-pg	comores	15	2.00	2	1Asuh	6 2 2 0 0		pnb b
6774	Comorian (Mauri,Mahorais)	92.31000	83,079	93,806	172,165	NAB57j	99-AUSM-v	shi-maore	100	0.02	19	1csu.	3 3 2 5 2		pnb b
6775	French	1.76000	1,584	1,789	3,283	CEW21b	51-AABI-d	general français	80	69.00	1,234	1B.uh	10 9 14 5 1	French	PNB b
6776	Makonde	0.60000	540	610	1,119	NAB57b	99-AUSQ-d	ci-makonde		0.90	5	1.s..	5 4 2 5 2	Makonde	pnb b
6777	Makua (Makhua)	1.00000	900	1,016	1,865	NAB57b	99-AUSY-a	e-meeto		8.00	81	2.s..	7 5 2 4 1		pnb b
6778	Malay	0.10000	90	102	187	MSY44k	31-PHAA-b	bahasa-malaysia		0.00	0	1asuh	0 2 2 0 0	Malay	PNB b
6779	Reunionese Creole	0.20000	180	203	373	NAN58	51-AACC-m	réunioné		94.00	191	1cs..	10 8 11 4 1		pnb b
6780	Sakalava	0.60000	540	610	1,119	MSY44j	31-LDAD	west malagasy cluster		53.00	323	0A.u.	10 5 9 4 1		... b
6781	Swahili	3.23000	2,907	3,282	6,024	NAB57j	99-AUSM-b	standard ki-swahili	40	0.00	0	4Asu.	0 3 1 0 0	Kiswahili*	PNB b
6782	other minor peoples	0.10000	90	102	187	...				10.00	10		8 4 2 3 0		
	Mexico	**100.00000**	**91,145,272**	**98,881,289**	**130,196,156**					**94.87**	**93,806,920**				
6783	Afro-Seminole Creole	0.01000	9,115	9,888	13,020	NFB68b	52-ABAF-c	afro-seminole-creole		80.00	7,911	1c..h	10 7 6 2 1		pn. .
6784	Ahuatempan Popoloca	0.00833	7,592	8,237	10,845	MIR37z	67-ADAA-c	ahuatempan		90.00	7,413	1....	10 7 11 2 1	Popoloca: Ahuatempan*	Pn. .
6785	Albarradas Zapotec	0.00610	5,560	6,032	7,942	MIR37f	67-AHBD-a	albarradas		80.00	4,825	1c...	10 7 7 5 1	Zapoteco, Albarradas	pn. b
6786	Amoltepec Mixtec	0.00616	5,615	6,091	8,020	MIR37c	67-AFAF-f	amoltepec		90.00	5,482	0c...	10 7 11 4 2		pn. .
6787	Atlatlahuca Mixtec	0.01419	12,934	14,031	18,475	MIR37c	67-AFAD-b	atatlahuca		93.00	13,049	1....	10 7 11 4 2	Mixteco: Atatlahuca*	PN. n
6788	Atepec Zapotec	0.00473	4,311	4,677	6,158	MIR37f	67-AHBB-da	atepec		91.00	4,256	1c...	10 8 11 5 3	Zapoteco: Sierra Juarez*	PN. .
6789	Atzingo Matlatzinca	0.00260	2,370	2,571	3,385	MIR37d	67-ABBA-a	matlatzinca		90.00	2,314	0....	10 7 11 5 2		... .
6790	Ayotzintepec Chinantec	0.00442	4,029	4,371	5,755	MIR37z	67-AEAB-i	ozumacín		90.00	3,933	1....	10 7 11 4 1	Chinanteco: Ozumacín*	Pn. .
6791	Basque	0.02000	18,229	19,776	26,039	CEW16	40-AAAA-a	general euskara		95.00	18,787	3....	10 9 15 5 3	Basque	PNB b
6792	Black Gypsy (Calo, Cale)	0.02000	18,229	19,776	26,039	CNN25f	59-AFAA-a	rodi		70.00	13,843	0B.uh	10 7 8 3 1	Calo	P.. b
6793	British	0.01000	9,115	9,888	13,020	CEW19i	52-ABAC-b	standard-english	9	78.00	7,713	3Bsuh	10 9 13 5 1		PNB b

Continued opposite

Table 8-2 continued

EVANGELIZATION								EVANGELISM			ADDITIONAL DESCRIPTIVE DATA
Ref 1	D 28	aC 29	CG% 30	r 31	E 32	U 33	W 34	e 35	R 36	T 37	Locations, civil divisions, literacy, religions, church history, denominations, dioceses, church growth, missions, agencies, ministries, movements 38
6684	0	4	0.00	7	23.00	77.00	A	0.00	0	1.08	Nomads as well as agriculturalists. Muslims 100%(Sunnis).
6685	2	5	6.92	5	44.00	56.00	A	8.03	516	4	South of Duun language area. Animists 60%, Muslims 33%(Maliki Sunnis, expanding fast). D=RCC,ECEM. M=WF,FSC,CMA,FMB,Pain de Vie.
6686	1	5	5.08	0	26.20	73.80	A	0.19	730	3	Along Niger river from Timbuktu downstream. Lingua franca. Muslims 100%(Maliki Sunnis). D=UEEB. M=CMA,EBM.
6687	0	4	4.52	0	19.01	80.99	A	0.00	927	1.07	Also in Burkina Faso, Senegal, Mauritania. Muslims 80%(Sunnis, most in Sufi Tijaniyya and in Hamali sect), animists 20%. M=RSMT,FI.
6688	1	5	3.23	0	15.02	84.98	A	0.01	938	2	Between Bani and Niger rivers. Some bilinguals in Songhai, Fulfulde, Bambara. Fishermen, sedentary agriculturalists. Muslims 100%(Maliki Sunnis). D=EEPM.
6689	1	5	4.00	2	47.00	53.00	A	25.73	344	5	Also in Burkina Faso. Animists 65%, Muslims 20%. D=RCC.
6690	1	5	6.99	5	31.00	69.00	A	2.26	739	4	Around Sikasso; also in Ivory Coast. Animists 50%, Muslims 48%. D=RCC. M=CMA,SIL.
6691	2	5	3.14	0	23.01	76.99	A	0.00	457	1.08	Aulliminden, Tamasheq. East Mali, Gao region. Muslims 100%(Sunnis). D=RCC,UEEB. M=WF,EBM,SIL,CMA,SIM.
6692	0	5	1.10	0	14.10	85.90	A	0.05	585	2	Youwarou Cercle. Second languages: Fulfulde, Songhai. Fishermen. Muslims 100%(Maliki Sunnis).
6693	0	5	1.96	0	14.10	85.90	A	0.05	752	2	From Koa to Mierou on Niger river. Fishermen on all large West African rivers. Muslims 100%(Maliki Sunnis).
6694	1	5	3.46	0	23.01	76.99	A	0.00	495	1.09	Antessar Timbuktu area. 30,000 massacred in 1963-4. Muslims 100%(Sunnis). D=RCC. M=WF,EBM,CMA,FMB,SIL,WVI,GR.
6695	0	5	3.95	4	29.03	70.97	A	0.03	524	2	Haalpulaar, in 5 countries. Futankobe. Muslims 100%(Sunnis, with Sufi Tijaniyya). Witchcraft persists.
6696	1	5	0.00	0	20.00	80.00	A	0.00	0	1.08	South of Niger river. Several tribes including Gossi, Igwadaren. Muslims 100%(Sunnis). D=RCC. M=WF,EBM,FMB,SIL.
6697	1	7	3.39	0	37.00	63.00	A	6.75	352	4	In southeast Mali. Animists 60%, Muslims 35%(Sunnis). D=RCC(D-San). M=WF,FSC.
6698	1	8	3.16	4	41.50	58.50	A	0.75	314	3	Expatriates from Senegal, migrant workers. Muslims 98%(Sunnis: Tijaniyya, Muridiyya, Qadiriyya). D=RCC.
6699	0	6	2.93		18.80	81.20	A	0.54	427	3	Senegalese, Gambians, Nigerians, Ghanaians, other West Africans. Muslims 80%, Animists 10%.
Malta											
6700	4	10	6.50	8	99.70	0.30	C	357.70	141	9	Expatriates from Arab countries. Muslims 18%. D=RCC,GOC,CofE,JWs.
6701	5	9	0.63	8	99.79	0.21	C	452.71	31	10	Expatriates from Britain, in education, development. D=Ch of England(D-Gibraltar),MCGB,SA,JWs,CoS.
6702	0	10	0.00	5	99.90	0.10	C	492.75	0	10	Artificial (constructed) language, in 80 countries. Speakers in Malta: 11,000(none mother-tongue).
6703	2	10	0.62	8	99.87	0.13	C	508.08	27	10	Expatriates in business. D=RCC(2 Dioceses),JWs. M=OP,SJ,OC,OFM.
6704	2	10	0.63	7	99.95	0.05	C	580.02	26	10	Traders from Greece. D=Greek Orthodox Ch(AD-Thyateira, under EP-Constantinople),JWs.
6705	0	10	0.00	7	52.00	48.00	B	3.79	53	4	Indian traders. Hindus 70%, a few Muslims 28%.
6706	1	10	0.63	7	99.84	0.16	C	493.62	28	10	Many citizens, some expatriates from Italy. D=RCC(2 Dioceses). M=OFMCap,OP,SJ,OC,OFM,OSA,SDB.
6707	0	10	0.00	5	50.00	50.00	B	3.65	38	4	Small remnant of practicing Jews with synagogue in Valletta. Lengthy history in Malta.
6708	2	6	0.63	5	99.97	0.03	C	585.80	24	10	Also in Australia, Canada, UK, USA. All baptized Catholics. D=RCC(M-Malta,D-Gozo),JWs. M=OFMCap,OP,SJ,OC,OFM,OSA,GRI. Very strong charismatics.
6709	0	0	4.19	8	99.78	0.22	C	372.95	106	9	North Americans, in business, education. Nonreligious 10%. D=RCC,BBC,SDA,etc.
6710	0	10	0.63		99.80	0.20	C	327.04	15	9	Other Europeans, Middle Easterners, North Africans, Asians.
Marshall Islands											
6711	5	7	2.54	2	99.95	0.05	C	541.84	56	10	Also on Nauru. Predominantly Protestant. D=UCCMI,RCC(VA-Marshall Islands),AoG,JWs,AMIC. M=UCBWM,SJ.
6712	4	10	2.43	8	99.85	0.15	C	496.40	57	10	Expatriates from USA, in government, business, education. D=UCCMI,AoG,AMIC,JWs.
6713	0	8	2.22		99.78	0.22	C	310.32	56	9	Filipinos, Chinese, Japanese, Trukese, Ponapeans, Chamorro, Yapese, Palauans, &c.
Martinique											
6714	3	10	0.64	8	99.85	0.15	C	490.62	28	10	Metropolitan French in government, business. Nonreligious 7%. D=RCC,SDA,ERF. M=CSSp,OSB.
6715	3	10	0.64	8	99.90	0.10	C	519.03	28	10	Martinique Whites, speaking Lesser Antillean Creole French. Nonreligious 10%. D=RCC,SDA,ERF. M=CSSp,OSB.
6716	2	10	0.64	7	99.55	0.45	B	250.93	28	8	Chinese folk-religionists 40%. D=RCC,SDA.
6717	6	7	0.59	8	99.96	0.04	C	566.52	23	10	Black/French/Chinese/Indian/Vietnamese. D=RCC(M-Fort-de-France),SDA,JWs,CEL,IBC,AoG. M=CSSp,OSB,EBM.
6718	2	10	2.60	8	85.00	15.00	B	68.25	106	6	Immigrants from Syria. Muslims 78%(Sunnis, Alawis, Ismailis). D=SOC,RCC.
6719	1	10	6.67	8	99.85	0.15	C	462.27	141	10	South Indians, now declining by repatriation. D=RCC. All are Catholics but with Hindu cult of Maldevidan. Hindus 12%. D=RCC. M=CSSp.
6720	1	10	3.03	6	99.50	0.50	B	206.22	94	8	Refugees from Viet Nam. Buddhists 40%, Cao Daists 5%. D=RCC. M=CSSp,OSB.
6721	4	10	0.64	8	99.91	0.09	C	524.79	32	10	From several Caribbean nations. D=RCC,AoG,SDA,JWs. M=CSSp,OSB.
6722	0	10	0.64		94.00	6.00	C	205.86	19	8	Other Caribbean islanders, Europeans, Americans.
Mauritania											
6723	0	8	2.59	7	35.05	64.95	A	0.06	257	2	Uprooted and detribalized Berbers in cities, towns, and slums. Many Sahrawi refugees from Sahara. M=WEC. Muslims 100%(Sunnis). M=WEC. R=ELWA.
6724	1	10	3.34	4	60.00	40.00	B	4.38	240	4	Migrant workers from Mali. Muslims 66%(Maliki Sunnis), animists 32%. D=RCC.
6725	0	4	0.00	7	27.00	73.00	A	0.00	0	1.08	Nomadic Bedouin tribe, mainly in Mali northwest of Timbuktu. Tent-dwellers. Muslims 100%(Sunnis).
6726	0	5	0.00	7	33.00	67.00	A	0.00	0	1.08	Lowest class of Moorish society: 2 varieties of slaves. Muslims 100%(Maliki Sunnis). M=WEC,CSSp,FI,AWM,CRS,LWR,WVI.
6727	1	10	2.93	8	99.67	0.33	C	339.92	80	9	Expatriates from Britain, in development. D=RCC.
6728	0	5	0.00	7	28.00	72.00	A	0.00	0	1.08	Moors/Maures, Bedouin Arab nomads with Berber history. Several tribes. Half are in Sahara republic/Morocco. Muslims 100%.
6729	1	9	4.48	0	36.00	64.00	A	3.94	463	4	Immigrants from large tribe in Senegal. Muslims 63%(Sunnis), animists 30%. D=RCC.
6730	0	2	0.00	0	6.00	94.00	A	0.00	0	1.03	Semi-sedentary Berber millet cultivators and shepherds. Muslims 100%(Sunnis).
6731	1	7	4.18	8	99.75	0.25	C	385.98	100	9	Expatriates from France, in government, business. Nonreligious 20%. D=RCC(D-Nouakchott). M=CSSp.
6732	0	6	3.44	4	40.00	60.00	A	1.46	345	4	Nomads, across whole of Africa along Saharan edge. Muslims 99%(Maliki Sunnis). M=FI.
6733	0	5	0.00	7	26.00	74.00	A	0.00	0	1.07	A Moorish fishing culture along Atlantic shores. Several nomadic Bedouin tribes. Muslims 100%(Sunnis).
6734	1	6	2.81	4	42.00	58.00	A	3.06	316	4	Across West Africa. Muslims 98%(Sunnis). D=RCC.
6735	0	2	0.00	0	6.00	94.00	A	0.00	0	1.03	Central Mauritania. A Berber people with own language. Muslims 100%(Sunnis).
6736	0	0	0.00	0	4.00	96.00	A	0.00	0	1.00	Moors, Nomadi. Nomadic desert hunter-gatherers in southeast and in Mali. Symbiosis with settled Blacks. Nominal Muslims 60%, animists 40%.
6737	0	5	0.00	7	28.00	72.00	A	0.00	0	1.08	Moors, Bedouin Arabs. Large nomadic group of 10 interior tribes spread over center and north of country; also in Sahara republic, with large number as refugees.
6738	2	9	4.06	0	64.00	36.00	B	46.72	242	6	Blacks from Senegal. Muslims 72%(Sunnis), animists 8%. D=RCC,AoG.
6739	0	5	3.88	0	19.06	80.94	A	0.04	832	2	Chamama region, also Mali, Burkina Faso, Senegal, Gambia, Ivory Coast, Niger. Muslims 90%(Sunnis), animists 10%. M=FI.
6740	1	10	3.23	8	99.90	0.10	C	542.02	69	10	Expatriates from Spain. Strong Catholics. D=RCC(D-Nouakchott). M=CSSp.
6741	0	5	0.00	7	28.00	72.00	A	0.00	0	1.08	Semi-nomadic. 3 Berber tribes near coast, part of Trarza culture. Only 45% still speak Tasumsa Berber, rest Hassaniya. Muslims 100%(Sunnis).
6742	0	5	0.00	7	28.00	72.00	A	0.00	0	1.08	Large semi-nomadic Bedouin Arabic nation in southwest. Muslims 100% (Sunnis).
6743	0	0	2.10	0	14.01	85.99	A	0.00	548	1.06	Eastern region. Some from Mali. Muslims (Sunnis) 100%.
6744	0	5	4.14	4	31.03	68.97	A	0.03	507	2	Futankobe. Also in Senegal, Gambia, Mali, Guinea, Burkina Faso, Nigeria. Muslims 100%(Sunnis, with Sufi Tijaniyya). Persistent witchcraft.
6745	0	5	0.00	7	33.00	67.00	A	0.00	0	1.08	Topmost of 4 major divisions of Moors: light-skinned Berber-Arab nomads. Muslims 100%(Maliki Sunnis, with Sufi Qadiriyya, Tijaniyya). M=CSSp,WEC,FI,AWM.
6746	4	8	4.38	4	46.40	53.60	A	0.67	353	3	Mainly in Senegal, also Gambia, France, across West Africa. Muslims 99%(Sunnis: 60% Tijaniyya, 29% Muridiyya, 10% Qadiriyya). D=RCC,AoG,SDA,JWs.
6747	0	5	1.10	0	13.01	86.99	A	0.00	379	1.04	Between Mederdra and Atlantic coast. Arabized Berbers/Bedouins, speaking Hassaniya. 10 tribes. Pastoralists. Muslims 100%(Sunnis). M=CSSp. R=ELWA.
6748	0	5	4.48		21.00	79.00	A	2.30	585	4	Senegalese, Togolese, Dahomeans, Nigerians, Ivorians, Guineans.
Mauritius											
6749	4	10	-0.54	8	99.79	0.21	C	444.05	11	10	Expatriates from Britain, in development, education. D=Anglican Ch/CPIO(D-Mauritius),CoS/ERIIM,SDA,JWs.
6750	0	9	1.62	5	44.10	55.90	A	0.16	191	3	Immigrant workers from Comoro Islands. Muslims 100%(Shafi Sunnis).
6751	1	10	0.75	8	99.91	0.09	C	518.15	30	10	Local-born French Whites. Nonreligious 6%. D=RCC(D-Port-Louis). M=SJ,CSSp.
6752	5	10	0.92	8	99.93	0.07	C	536.33	35	10	Morisyen. Creoles(French/Black). D=RCC,AC/CPIO,SDA,JWs,AoG. M=CSSp,SJ,FMB,UBS.
6753	1	10	0.96	8	99.84	0.16	C	475.23	34	10	Expatriates from France, in government, development. Nonreligious 13%. D=RCC. M=CSSp,SJ.
6754	3	10	6.76	7	99.50	0.50	B	226.30	164	8	Folk-religionists 29%, nonreligious 21%. D=RCC,Chinese Christian Fellowship of Mauritius, Sino-Mauritian Evangelical Ch.
6755	2	10	1.02	8	99.45	0.55	B	165.89	58	7	Islanders, evicted from Diego Garcia air base and islands. Hindus 45%, Muslims 10%. D=RCC,CPIO(D-Mauritius).
6756	4	10	3.43	8	61.30	38.70	B	9.62	198	4	Creoles(mixed-race). Muslims 32%(Hanafi,Shafi,Ahmadi), Hindus 63%. D=RCC(D-Port-Louis),AC/CPIO,CoS,JWs. M=CSSp,SJ,PI,FMB.
6757	1	9	3.60	6	57.00	43.00	B	4.16	238	4	Mauritians of Bengali ancestry. Muslims 45%, Hindus 50%. D=RCC.
6758	1	9	6.29	6	54.70	45.30	B	15.37	366	5	Immigrants from Bihar(North India). Muslims 50%, Hindus 40%. D=RCC. M=SJ.
6759	1	10	1.01	4	99.80	0.20	C	417.56	39	10	Goanese ancestry. Almost all Roman Catholics. D=RCC. M=SJ.
6760	0	10	2.47	6	57.00	43.00	B	4.16	167	4	Long-time residents from Gujarat. Hindus 75%, Muslims 18%(Sunnis,Shias,many Ahmadis), Baha'is 5%.
6761	4	10	7.15	6	60.80	39.20	B	6.21	367	4	Bhojpuri immigrant workers. Hindus 84%, Muslims 12% (Sunnis,Shias,20,000 Qadiani Ahmadis), Baha'is 5%. D=JWs,SDA,RCC,AC/CPI0. M=FMB.
6762	1	10	4.14	7	57.00	43.00	B	2.08	247	4	Hindi-speaking immigrants. Hindus 95%(75% Sanatanists/idol-worshippers,25% Arya Samajists). D=JWs.
6763	1	10	2.77	4	56.00	44.00	B	4.08	185	4	Marathi-ancestry workers. Muslims 70%, Hindus 20%. D=JWs.
6764	4	10	3.11	5	86.00	14.00	B	65.91	133	6	From Punjab(India, Pakistan). Hindus and Sikhs 40%. D=RCC,AC/CPIO,JWs,SDA. M=SJ,CSSp.
6765	3	10	4.07	6	99.35	0.65	B	133.09	134	7	From South India. Hindus 50%, Muslims 9%. D=JWs,RCC,SDA. M=CSSp,SJ.
6766	2	10	6.03	5	96.50	3.50	B	110.95	200	7	Immigrants from Andhra Pradesh. Hindus 49%, Muslims 10%. D=JWs,RCC. M=SJ,CSSp.
6767	0	9	3.58	5	53.50	46.50	B	0.97	236	3	Official language of Mauritian Muslims. Muslims 94%(76% Hanafi Sunnis,10% Ahmadis,7% Shafis,1% Shias).
6768	3	10	1.76	4	99.47	0.53	B	186.99	76	7	Expatriates, residents from Madagascar. Traditional religionists (animists) 50%. D=RCC,FJKMK,FLM. M=CSSp,SJ.
6769	4	9	4.11	7	99.55	0.45	B	252.94	104	8	Buddhists/folk-religionists 37%. D=RCC(D-Port-Louis,which is 6% Chinese),AC,ICPIO,JWs. M=CSSp,SJ,FMB.
6770	2	9	2.77	8	99.50	0.50	B	195.27	88	7	Creoles (Chinese/French/Mulatto). Chinese folk-religionists 32%, nonreligious 10%. D=RCC,AC/CPI0. M=CSSp.
6771	1	10	4.01	8	99.51	0.49	B	225.24	106	8	Cantonese-speaking Creoles. Buddhists/folk-religionists 22%, nonreligious 16%. D=RCC. M=CSSp,SJ,FMB.
6772	0	10	3.91		59.00	41.00	B	64.60	182	6	Reunionese, USA Whites(SDA,JWs,CCS,AoG), Seychellois, Africans.
Mayotte											
6773	0	10	0.70	7	46.00	54.00	A	3.35	83	4	Traders, from various Arab countries. Muslims 98%(Shafi Sunnis).
6774	2	6	2.99	5	39.02	60.98	A	0.02	312	2	Muslims 100%(Shafi Sunnis). D=RCC(AA-Comoro Islands),EJCC. M=AIM,OFMCap.
6775	2	10	3.79	8	99.69	0.31	C	352.59	93	9	Expatriates from France, military and in government. Nonreligious 12%. D=RCC,EJCC. M=OFMCap.
6776	2	8	1.62	1	39.90	60.10	A	1.31	212	4	A Muslim Bantu people from Tanzania/Mozambique. Muslims 92%(Shafi Sunnis). D=RCC,EJCC.
6777	1	8	4.49	0	46.00	54.00	A	13.43	354	5	Black settlers from mainland. Muslims 50%, animists 42%. D=RCC.
6778	0	10	0.00	5	39.00	61.00	A	0.00	0	1.13	Immigrants from Indonesia, Malaysia. All strong Muslims 100%(Shafi Sunnis).
6779	1	10	2.99	8	99.94	0.06	C	518.08	74	10	Immigrants from Reunion. D=RCC(AA-Comoro Islands).
6780	1	10	3.54	4	99.53	0.47	B	197.31	129	7	Immigrants from northern Madagascar. Animists 40%. D=EJCC.
6781	0	10	0.00	5	41.00	59.00	A	0.00	0	1.12	Coastal immigrants from East Africa. Muslims 100%(Shafi Sunnis).
6782	0	8	2.33		30.00	70.00	A	10.95	213	5	Several Malagasy peoples, other Black Africans, Europeans, Asians. Muslims 50%, nonreligious 20%, animists 10%.
Mexico											
6783	1	7	2.00	1	99.80	0.20	C	347.48	62	9	English-based creole, similar to Sea Islands Creole (USA) and Bahamas Creole. D=RCC.
6784	1	7	2.13	0	99.90	0.10	C	430.33	61	10	Puebla State. Agriculturalists. D=RCC.
6785	1	7	2.10	0	99.80	0.20	C	362.08	62	9	Central Oaxaca. Zapoteco. D=RCC.
6786	2	8	2.00	0	99.90	0.10	C	446.76	54	10	Oaxaca State. Mixtecs. D=RCC,UIEI(Union of Evangelical Independent Chs).
6787	2	8	2.46	0	99.93	0.07	C	485.41	61	10	West central Oaxaca. Mixtecs. Agriculturalists. D=RCC,UIEI.
6788	3	8	3.26	0	99.91	0.09	C	471.65	76	10	Northern Oaxaca. Zapotecs. D=RCC,SDA,Pentecostal Chs. M=UFM,WBT,SIL.
6789	2	7	2.00	0	99.90	0.10	C	433.62	56	10	State of Mexico. Several villages. Otomis. D=UIEI,RCC.
6790	1	7	2.00	0	99.90	0.10	C	436.90	58	10	3 villages in North Oaxaca. Agriculturalists. D=RCC.
6791	1	10	4.28	4	99.95	0.05	C	572.13	88	10	Settlers from Spain. D=RCC. M=SJ,OFM,SDB,MSpS,OSA,MJ,OP,PFM.
6792	2	10	2.00	8	99.70	0.30	C	319.37	66	9	Iberian Romani. In many Latin countries. Nomadic. D=IEF/GEM,RCC. M=GGMS.
6793	1	10	2.00	8	99.78	0.22	C	429.89	57	10	Expatriates in development. D=Episcopal Ch in Mexico. M=ECUSA.

Continued overleaf

Table 8-2 continued

PEOPLE		POPULATION				IDENTITY CODE		LANGUAGE		CHURCH		MINISTRY						SCRIPTURE		
Ref 1	Ethnic name 2	P% 3	In 1995 4	In 2000 5	In 2025 6	Race 7	Language 8	Autoglossonym 9	S 10	AC 11	Members 12	Jayuh 13-17	d 18	wa 19	xc 20	mc 21	mi 22	Biblioglossonym 23	Pub 24-26	ss 27
6794	Camotlan Mixe	0.00694	6,325	6,862	9,036	MIR37z	69-FAAB-a	mixe-coatlán		90.00	6,176	1....	10	8	11	5	3	Mixe: Camotlan*	PN.	.
6795	Catalonian	0.05000	45,573	49,441	65,098	CEW21a	51-AABE-b	català		95.00	46,969	2a..h	10	9	15	5	3	Catalan-valencian-balear	PNB	b
6796	Centr Villa Alta Zapotec	0.00387	3,527	3,827	5,039	MIR37f	67-AHBB-fd	tabaa		93.00	3,559	1c...	10	7	11	4	1	Zapoteco: Tabaa*	PN.	.
6797	Central Aztec (Nahuatl)	0.07758	70,711	76,712	101,006	MIR37a	66-BFBA-ba	central nahuatl		95.00	72,876	1c...	10	10	13	5	3	Nahuatl: Central	PN.	.
6798	Central Chichimeca Pame	0.00514	4,685	5,082	6,692	MIR37d	67-ABAB-a	chichimeca pame		90.00	4,574	1....	10	8	11	5	1	Chichimeca: S Maria Acap*	P..	.
6799	Central Miahuatlan Zapote	0.11111	101,272	109,867	144,661	MIR37f	67-AHBE-c	central miahuatlán		90.00	98,880	0a...	10	8	11	5	2	Zapoteco: Miahuatlan*	PN.	b
6800	Central Nochistlan Mixtec	0.01005	9,160	9,938	13,085	MIR37c	67-AFAE-c	diuxi-tilantongo		90.00	8,944	1a...	10	7	11	5	1	Mixteco: Diuxi-tilantongo*	P..	.
6801	Central Puebla Mixtec	0.00189	1,723	1,869	2,461	MIR37c	69-BBAA-b	tepehua-puebla		90.00	1,682	0....	10	7	11	5	3	Nahuatl: Puebla, Southeast*	PN.	b
6802	Central Tarahumara	0.05553	50,613	54,909	72,298	MIR37z	66-BEBA-d	samachique		70.00	38,436	4....	10	8	8	5	3	Tarahumara: Samachique*	PN.	.
6803	Chamula Tzotzil	0.15382	140,200	152,099	200,268	MIR37b	68-ACBB-a	chamula		90.00	136,889	1a...	10	9	11	5	2	Tzotzil: Chamula*	PN.	.
6804	Chan Santa Cruz Yucatec	0.04733	43,139	46,801	61,622	MIR37b	68-ABAA-a	yucatec-maya		95.00	44,460	2c...	10	7	12	5	1	Maya	PNB	n
6805	Chayucu Mixtec	0.04580	41,745	45,288	59,630	MIR37c	67-AFAF-ia	chayuco		93.00	42,117	0c...	10	7	11	5	1		pn.	.
6806	Chenalho Tzotzil	0.04141	37,743	40,947	53,914	MIR37b	68-ACBB-b	chenalhû		90.00	36,852	1A...	10	8	11	5	1	Tzotzil: Chenalho*	PN.	.
6807	Chichicapan Zapotec	0.00884	8,057	8,741	11,509	MIR37f	67-AHBC-cc	tilquiapan		80.00	6,993	0a...	10	7	7	5	1		pn.	b
6808	Chicomuceltec	0.00208	1,896	2,057	2,708	MIR37b	68-AABA	chicomuceltec cluster		90.00	1,851	0....	10	7	11	5	1		...	b
6809	Chihuahua Pima Bajo	0.00115	1,048	1,137	1,497	MIR37z	66-BEAC-a	southeast pima		70.00	796	0....	10	7	6	5	1	Pima Bajo, Sonora	P..	.
6810	Chiltepec Chinantec	0.00118	1,076	1,167	1,536	MIR37z	67-AEAA-b	chiltepec		92.00	1,073	0c...	10	7	11	5	1		pn.	b
6811	Chimalapa Zoque	0.00532	4,849	5,260	6,926	MIR37z	69-FABB-a	zoque-tabasco		91.00	4,787	0a...	10	7	11	3	1	Zoque: Ostuacan	P..	b
6812	Choapan Zapotec	0.02653	24,181	26,233	34,541	MIR37f	67-AHBB-cb	choapan		90.00	23,610	1c...	10	7	11	4	1	Zapoteco: Choapan*	PN.	.
6813	Chocho	0.00142	1,294	1,404	1,849	MIR37z	67-ADAA-g	chocho		90.00	1,264	1....	10	7	11	4	1		pn.	b
6814	Coastal Guerrero Mixtec	0.01005	9,160	9,938	13,085	MIR37c	67-AFAA-a	ayutla		93.00	9,242	1....	10	7	12	5	1	Mixteco: Ayutla	P..	.
6815	Coastal Mixtec	0.02366	21,565	23,395	30,804	MIR37c	67-AFAF-h	west jamiltepec		90.00	21,056	0c...	10	7	11	5	1		pn.	.
6816	Coatecas Altas Zapotec	0.00332	3,026	3,283	4,323	MIR37f	67-AHBF-e	coatecas-altas		80.00	2,626	1....	10	7	6	4	1	Zapoteco, Coatecas Altas	...	.
6817	Coatepec Aztec (Nahuatl)	0.00165	1,504	1,632	2,148	MIR37a	66-BFBA-bg	coatepec		95.00	1,550	1c...	10	9	12	5	1		pn.	.
6818	Coatzospan Mixtec	0.00544	4,958	5,379	7,083	MIR37c	67-AFAC-d	teotitlán-de-camino		91.00	4,895	1....	10	7	11	5	2		pn.	.
6819	Cocopa (Kikima)	0.00020	182	198	260	MIR38a	63-VDCA-a	cocopa		90.00	178	0....	10	7	11	3	1	Cocopa	P..	.
6820	Coicoyan Mixtec	0.01984	18,083	19,618	25,831	MIR37c	67-AFAA-b	metlatonoc		90.00	17,656	1....	10	7	11	5	2	Mixteco: Metlatonoc*	P..	.
6821	Comaltepec Chinantec	0.00236	2,151	2,334	3,073	MIR37z	67-AEAB-h	comaltepec-1		90.00	2,100	1....	10	7	11	3	1	Chinanteco: Comaltepec*	Pn.	.
6822	Copainala Zoque	0.01183	10,782	11,698	15,402	MIR37z	69-FABB-a	zoque-tabasco		93.00	10,879	0a...	10	7	11	3	1	Zoque: Ostuacan	P..	b
6823	Cora	0.00888	8,094	8,781	11,561	MIR37z	66-BEFB	cora cluster		92.00	8,078	1....	10	8	11	5	1	Cora	P..	b
6824	Coyotepec Popoloca	0.00828	7,547	8,187	10,780	MIR37z	67-ADAA-d	coyotepec		89.00	7,287	1....	10	7	11	4	1		pn.	b
6825	Coyutla Totonac	0.04861	44,306	48,066	63,288	MIR37z	69-BAAA-f	totonac-coyutla		90.00	43,260	0....	10	7	11	4	1	Totonaco: Coyutla*	PN.	.
6826	Detribalized Amerindian	10.50754	9,577,126	10,389,991	13,680,413	MIR37y	51-AABB-ha	mexicano		94.96	9,866,335	1B.uh	10	7	10	5	1		pnb	b
6827	Diegueno	0.00025	228	247	325	MIR38a	63-VDCA-b	diegueño		92.00	227	0....	10	7	11	3	1		p..	b
6828	East Highland Chatino	0.01301	11,858	12,864	16,939	MIR37f	67-AHAD-c	nopala		93.00	11,964	0....	10	7	12	3	2	Chatino, Nopala	pn.	.
6829	East Juxtlahuaca Mixtec	0.01419	12,934	14,031	18,475	MIR37c	67-AFAC-1b	juxtlahuaca		93.00	13,049	1....	10	7	11	5	1	Mixteco, San Juan Mixtepec	Pn.	.
6830	East Miahuatlan Zapotec	0.00774	7,055	7,653	10,077	MIR37f	67-AHBE-d	east miahuatlán		90.00	6,888	0c...	10	7	11	3	1	Zapoteco: Mixtepec*	Pn.	.
6831	East Tlacolula Zapotec	0.01499	13,663	14,822	19,516	MIR37f	67-AHBD-cc	quiatoni		60.00	8,893	1c...	10	7	6	3	1	Zapoteco, Eastern Tlacolula	pn.	.
6832	East Valley Zapotec	0.01987	18,111	19,648	25,870	MIR37f	67-AHBD-cb	mitla		85.00	16,701	1c...	10	7	7	5	1	Zapoteco: Mitla*	PN.	b
6833	Eastern Jamiltepec Mixtec	0.01351	12,314	13,359	17,590	MIR37c	67-AFAF-i	east jamiltepec		90.00	12,023	0c...	10	7	11	5	2	Mixteco: Jamiltepec, E.*	PN.	.
6834	Eastern Mixtec	0.01301	11,858	12,864	16,939	MIR37c	67-AFAD-g	peñoles-tepantepec		93.00	11,964	1....	10	7	11	5	1	Mixteco: Penoles*	PN.	.
6835	Eastern Ocotlan Zapotec	0.00903	8,230	8,929	11,757	MIR37f	67-AHBC-cc	tilquiapan		90.00	8,036	0a...	10	7	11	3	1		pn.	b
6836	Eastern Popoloca	0.00553	5,040	5,468	7,200	MIR37z	67-ADAA-e	east popoloc		90.00	4,921	1....	10	7	11	3	1	Popoloca: Eastern*	PN.	.
6837	Eastern Putla Mixtec	0.00128	1,167	1,266	1,667	MIR37c	67-AFAF-e	itundujia		92.00	1,164	0c...	10	7	11	5	2		pn.	.
6838	Eastern Zimatlan Zapotec	0.00694	6,325	6,862	9,036	MIR37f	67-AHBC-bd	lachixio		90.00	6,176	0c...	10	7	11	3	1	Zapoteco: Lachixio*	Pn.	.
6839	Esperanto	0.00000	0	0	0	CEW21z	51-AAAC-a	proper esperanto		90.00	0	0A...	10	7	11	5	0	Esperanto	PNB	b
6840	Filomeno Mata Totonac	0.01528	13,927	15,109	19,894	MIR37z	69-BAAA-d	totonac-coahuitlán		91.00	13,749	0....	10	7	11	5	2		pn.	.
6841	Francisco Leon Zoque	0.02366	21,565	23,395	30,804	MIR37z	69-FABD-e	zoque-francisco-leûn		93.00	21,758	1a...	10	7	11	3	1	Zoque: Francisco Leon*	PN.	.
6842	Francisco Matlatzinca	0.00118	1,076	1,167	1,536	MIR37d	67-ABBA-a	matlatzinca		90.00	1,050	0....	10	7	11	5	2		...	.
6843	French	0.01000	9,115	9,888	13,020	CEW21b	51-AABI-d	general français		84.00	8,306	1B.uh	10	9	14	5	1	French	PNB	b
6844	Galician	0.01000	9,115	9,888	13,020	CEW21d	51-AABA-b	galego		95.00	9,394	1csuh	10	9	14	5	1	Galician	PNB	b
6845	German	0.01000	9,115	9,888	13,020	CEW19m	52-ABCE-a	standard hoch-deutsch		87.00	8,603	2B.uh	10	9	13	5	3	German*	PNB	b
6846	German Jew	0.05300	48,307	52,407	69,004	CMT35	52-ABCH	yiddish cluster		0.20	105	0B..h	5	4	4	3	0		PNB	b
6847	Greek	0.00800	7,292	7,911	10,416	CEW20	56-AAAA-c	dhimotiki		92.00	7,278	2B.uh	10	9	11	5	2	Greek: Modern	PNB	b
6848	Guarijio (Varihio)	0.00544	4,958	5,379	7,083	MIR37z	66-BEBB	varohio cluster		90.00	4,841	0....	10	7	12	3	1	Huarijio	P..	.
6849	Guerrero Amuzgo	0.03472	31,646	34,332	45,204	MIR37c	67-AGAB-b	amuzgo-guerrero		93.00	31,928	1c...	10	7	11	5	1	Amuzgo: Guerrero*	PN.	.
6850	Guerrero Aztec	0.33161	302,247	327,900	431,743	MIR37a	66-BFBA-bl	guerrero		95.00	311,505	1c...	10	10	11	5	1	Nahuatl, Guerrero	PN.	b
6851	Han Chinese	0.00600	5,469	5,933	7,812	MSY42a	51-AABB-ha	mexicano		80.00	4,746	1B.uh	10	8	8	4	1		pnb	b
6852	Han Chinese (Cantonese)	0.02000	18,229	19,776	26,039	MSY42a	79-AAAM-a	central yue		70.00	13,843	3A.uh	10	8	8	4	1	Chinese, Yue	PNB	b
6853	Han Chinese (Mandarin)	0.01000	9,115	9,888	13,020	MSY42a	79-AAAB-ba	kuo-yü		70.00	6,922	2Bsuh	10	8	8	4	1	Chinese: Kuoyu*	PNB	b
6854	Hidalgo Aztec	0.45320	413,070	448,130	590,049	MIR37a	66-BFBA-bc	central huesteca		95.00	425,724	3A...	10	9	10	5	3		pn.	.
6855	Highland Chinantec	0.00721	6,572	7,129	9,387	MIR37z	67-AEAB-f	quiotepec		90.00	6,416	1....	10	7	11	3	1	Chinanteco: Quiotepec*	PN.	.
6856	Highland Guerrero Mixtec	0.02248	20,489	22,229	29,268	MIR37c	67-AFAA-c	alacatlatzala		90.00	20,006	1....	10	7	11	5	1	Mixteco, Alacatlatzala	P..	.
6857	Highland Mazatec	0.08519	77,647	84,237	110,914	MIR37z	67-ADBA-b	upper mazatec		93.00	78,340	1c...	10	8	11	5	2	Mazateco, Huautla Jimenez	PN.	.
6858	Highland Oaxaca Chontal	0.00425	3,874	4,202	5,533	MIR37b	69-DAAA-b	tequistlatec		91.00	3,824	0....	10	8	11	5	1	Chontal: Oaxaca, Highland*	PN.	.
6859	Highland Popoluca	0.03160	28,802	31,246	41,142	MIR37z	69-FABA-a	popoluca-sierra		90.00	28,122	1....	10	7	11	3	1	Popoluca: Highland*	PN.	b
6860	Highland Totonac	0.16667	151,912	164,805	216,998	MIR37z	69-BAAA-e	totonac-sierra		93.00	153,269	0....	10	7	11	5	2	Totonaco: Highland*	PN.	.
6861	Highland Tzeltal	0.22215	202,479	219,665	289,231	MIR37b	68-ACBA-b	oxchuc		90.00	197,698	1A...	10	7	12	5	2	Tzeltal: Oxchuc*	PNB	.
6862	Huajuapan Mixtec	0.00100	911	989	1,302	MIR37c	67-AFAC-g	huajuapan		90.00	890	1....	10	7	11	5	2		pn.	.
6863	Huehuetla Tepehua	0.00417	3,801	4,123	5,429	MIR37z	67-ABCA-d	huehuetla		71.00	2,928	1c...	10	7	6	3	1	Tepehua, Huehuetla*	PN.	.
6864	Huichol	0.02366	21,565	23,395	30,804	MIR37z	66-BEFA-b	east huichol		1.00	234	1....	6	4	2	5	1	Huichol	PN.	.
6865	Huicot Aztec (Mexicanero)	0.00118	1,076	1,167	1,536	MIR37a	66-BFBA-ca	durango		95.00	1,108	1c...	10	9	12	5	1	Nahuatl, Durango	pn.	b
6866	Huixtan Tzotzil	0.02366	21,565	23,395	30,804	MIR37b	68-ACBB	tzotzil cluster		90.00	21,056	1A...	10	8	11	5	1	Tzotzil: Huixtan*	PN.	.
6867	Isthmus Aztec (Nahuatl)	0.05527	50,376	54,652	71,959	MIR37a	66-BFBA-de	mecayapán		95.00	51,919	1c...	10	9	12	5	2	Nahuatl: Isthmus*	Pn.	.
6868	Isthmus Mixe (Eastern)	0.02367	21,574	23,405	30,817	MIR37z	69-FAAB-b	mixe-istmo		90.00	21,065	1....	10	8	11	5	2		PN.	.
6869	Isthmus Zapotec	0.10057	91,665	99,445	130,938	MIR37f	67-AHBG-c	zapotec-istmo		93.00	92,484	4a...	10	7	11	3	1	Zapoteco: Isthmus*	PN.	.
6870	Italian	0.02000	18,229	19,776	26,039	CEW21e	51-AABQ-c	standard italiano		84.00	16,612	2B.uh	10	9	15	5	3	Italian	PNB	b
6871	Jalieza Zapotec	0.00200	1,823	1,978	2,604	MIR37f	67-AHBC-e	jalieza		60.00	1,187	0c...	10	6	6	2	1		pn.	b
6872	Japanese	0.04000	36,458	39,553	52,078	MSY42a	45-CAAA-a	koku-go		5.00	1,978	1B.uh	7	5	8	5	1	Japanese	PNB	b
6873	Jewish	0.06946	63,310	68,683	90,434	CMT35	51-AABB-ha	mexicano		0.40	275	1B.uh	5	4	5	1	0		pnb	b
6874	Jonaz Chichimeca Pame	0.00183	1,668	1,810	2,383	MIR37d	67-AAAA-a	chichimec		90.98	1,646	0....	10	8	11	5	3		...	b
6875	Juquila Mixe	0.01666	15,185	16,474	21,691	MIR37z	69-FAAB-c	mixe-juquila		90.00	14,826	1....	10	7	11	5	2	Mixe: Juquila*	PN.	.
6876	Kalderash Gypsy (Rom)	0.04000	36,458	39,553	52,078	CNN25f	59-AFAA-a	rodi		80.00	31,642	0B.uh	10	7	8	2	3	Calo	P..	b
6877	Kikapoo	0.00034	310	336	443	MIR38a	62-ADCB-b	kikapoo		90.00	303	0....	10	7	11	3	1	Kikapoo	p..	.
6878	Kiliwa (Kiliwi)	0.00003	27	30	39	MIR38a	63-VDCC-a	kiliwi		70.00	21	0....	10	7	6	2	1		...	.
6879	Lacandon	0.00070	638	692	911	MIR37b	68-ABAA-d	lacandûn		90.00	623	1a...	10	9	6	5	1	Lacandon: Lacanja	PNb	.
6880	Lachao-Yolotepec Chatino	0.00222	2,023	2,195	2,890	MIR37f	67-AHAC	yolotepec cluster		90.00	1,976	0....	10	7	11	4	1		...	b
6881	Lachiruaj Zapotec	0.00555	5,059	5,488	7,226	MIR37f	67-AHBB-h	lachiruaj		80.00	4,390	1c...	10	7	7	5	1	Zapoteco, S Cristobal Lachir	pn.	.
6882	Lalana Chinantec	0.01360	12,396	13,448	17,707	MIR37z	67-AEAB-k	lalana		91.00	12,238	1....	10	7	11	3	1	Chinanteco: Lalana*	PN.	.
6883	Lealao Chinantec	0.00236	2,151	2,334	3,073	MIR37z	67-AEAC-a	lealao		93.00	2,170	0....	10	7	11	3	1	Chinanteco: Lealao*	PN.	.
6884	Lebanese Arab	0.40000	364,581	395,525	520,785	CMT30	12-AACF-f	syro-palestinian		93.20	368,629	1Asuh	10	9	11	5	3	Arabic: Lebanese*	Pnb	b
6885	Levantine Jew	0.01000	9,115	9,888	13,020	CMT35	12-AACF-f	syro-palestinian		0.10	10	1Asuh	5	3	4	1	0	Arabic: Lebanese*	Pnb	b
6886	Low German	0.07775	70,865	76,880	101,228	CEW19m	52-ABCC	north deutsch cluster		87.00	66,886	2A.uh	10	8	11	5	1	German: Low*	PNB	b
6887	Lowland Mazatec	0.01736	15,823	17,166	22,602	MIR37z	67-ADBA-c	lower mazatec		90.00	15,449	1a...	10	7	11	5	2	Mazateco: Jalapa De Diaz*	PN.	.
6888	Lowland Oaxaca Chontal	0.00112	1,021	1,107	1,458	MIR37b	69-DAAA-a	huamelula		90.00	997	0....	10	7	11	5	1	Chontal: Oaxaca, Lowland*	Pn.	.
6889	Lowland Totonac	0.11111	101,272	109,867	144,661	MIR37z	69-BAAA-g	totonac-papantla		91.00	99,979	0....	10	7	11	5	2	Totonaco: Papantla*	PN.	.
6890	Lowland Tzeltal	0.11107	101,235	109,827	144,609	MIR37b	68-ACBA-a	bachajon		90.00	98,845	1c...	10	7	11	4	2	Tzeltal: Bachajon*	PNb	.
6891	Mayo	0.06757	61,587	66,814	87,974	MIR37z	66-BEDA-b	mayo		90.00	60,133	1....	10	7	11	5	2	Mayo: Sonora	Pn.	b
6892	Mazahua	0.38877	354,345	384,421	506,164	MIR37d	67-ABCB-a	central mazahua		93.00	357,511	3....	10	9	11	5	3	Mazahua	PN.	.
6893	Mazatlan Mixe	0.01943	17,710	19,213	25,297	MIR37z	69-FAAB-d	mixe-mazatlán		80.00	15,370	1....	10	7	6	4	1		pn.	.
6894	Metlatonoc Mixtec	0.07395	67,402	73,123	96,280	MIR37c	67-AFAA-b	metlatonoc		90.00	65,810	1....	10	9	9	0	0	Mixteco: Metlatonoc*	P..	.
6895	Mexican Black	0.50000	455,726	494,406	650,981	NFB71a	51-AABB-ha	mexicano		93.00	459,798	1B.uh	10	8	12	5	1		pnb	b
6896	Mexican Mestizo	54.64889	49,809,879	54,037,527	71,150,754	CLN29	51-AABB-ha	mexicano	98	96.96	52,394,786	1B.uh	10	10	10	5	1		pnb	b
6897	Mexican White	15.00000	13,671,791	14,832,193	19,529,423	CLT27	51-AABB-ha	mexicano		92.86	13,773,175	1B.uh	10	10	11	5	3		pnb	b
6898	Mezquital Otomi	0.11832	107,843	116,996	154,048	MIR37d	67-ABCA-b	mezquital		95.00	111,147	1s...	10	8	12	5	1	Otomi: Mezquital*	PN.	.
6899	Michoacan Aztec (Nahuatl)	0.00354	3,227	3,500	4,609	MIR37a	66-BFBA-cb	michoacán		95.00	3,325	1c...	10	9	12	5	2	Nahuatl: Michoacan*	PN.	b
6900	Mitlatongo Mixtec	0.00195	1,777	1,928	2,539	MIR37c	67-AFAG	cuicatec cluster		90.00	1,735	1....	10	9	9	0	0		PN.	b
6901	Mocho	0.00019	173	188	247	MIR37b	68-ADAD-a	proper motozintlec		90.00	169	0....	10	7	11	4	1		...	b
6902	Morelos Aztec	0.01774	16,169	17,542	23,097	MIR37a	66-BFBA-bj	morelos		85.00	14,910	1c...	10	7	11	4	1		pn.	b
6903	NW Pochutla Zapotec	0.00267	2,434	2,640	3,476	MIR37f	67-AHBF-b	west loxicha		65.00	1,716	2....	10	7	6	4	1		...	b
6904	NW Tehuantepec Zapotec	0.00763	6,954	7,545	9,934	MIR37f	67-AHBG-b	lachiguiri		90.00	6,790	1c...	10	7	11	4	1	Zapoteco, N W Tehuantepec	pn.	b
6905	NW Tlaxiaco Mixtec	0.01527	13,918	15,099	19,881	MIR37c	67-AFAC-ra	ñumi		90.00	13,589	1....	10	7	11	5	2		pn.	b
6906	NW Yautepec Zapotec	0.00174	1,586	1,721	2,265	MIR37f	67-AHBD-e	yautepec		92.00	1,583	1c...	10	7	11	3	1	Zapoteco, S Catarina Quieri*	Pn.	b
6907	Nochixtlan Mixtec	0.00106	966	1,048	1,380	MIR37c	67-AFAE-b	tidaa		92.00	964	1c...	10	7	11	5	2		p..	b
6908	North C Zimatlan Zapotec	0.00292	2,661	2,887	3,802	MIR37f	67-AHBC-bb	asunciûn		92.00	2,656	0c...	10	7	11	2	1		pn.	b
6909	North Puebla Aztec	0.07099	64,704	70,196	92,426	MIR37a	66-BFBA-be	north puebla		95.00	66,686	1a...	10	9	11	5	3	Nahuatl: Puebla, Northern*	PN.	.
6910	North Villa Alta Zapotec	0.02083	18,986	20,597	27,120	MIR37f	67-AHBB-fa	north rincûn		93.00	19,155	1c...	10	7	11	2	1	Zapoteco: Rincon	PN.	.
6911	NorthE Miahuatlan Zapotec	0.00663	6,043	6,556	8,632	MIR37f	67-AHBE-ba	logueche		91.00	5,966	0c...	10	7	11	2	1		pn.	.
6912	NorthE Yautepec Zapotec	0.00305	2,780	3,016	3,971	MIR37f	67-AHBD-e	yautepec		91.00	2,744	1c...	10	7	11	2	1	Zapoteco, S Catarina Quieri*	Pn.	b
6913	Northeast Pochutla Zapote	0.13500	123,046	133,490	175,765	MIR37f	67-AHBF-c	east loxicha		91.00	121,476	1....	10	7	11	3	1	Zapoteco, Western Pochutla	...	.
6914	Northeastern Mixe	0.02425	22,103	23,979	31,573	MIR37z	69-FAAA-a	mixe-totontepec		70.00	16,785	0....	10	7	6	3	1	Mixe, Totontepec*	PN.	.
6915	Northeastern Otomi	0.01419	12,934	14,031	18,475	MIR37d	67-ABCA-c	texcatepec		95.00	13,330	1c...	10	8	12	5	2		pn.	.
6916	Northern Chatino	0.00946	8,622	9,354	12,317	MIR37f	67-AHAA-a	proper zenzontepec		90.00	8,419	0....	10	8	11	4	1	Chatino, Zenzontepec	...	b
6917	Northern Chichimeca Pame	0.00184	1,677	1,819	2,396	MIR37d	67-ABAA-a	north pame		91.00	1,656	0....	10	7	11	5	2		...	.

Continued opposite

Table 8-2 continued

EVANGELIZATION								EVANGELISM			ADDITIONAL DESCRIPTIVE DATA
Ref 1	D 28	aC 29	CG% 30	r 31	E 32	U 33	W 34	e 35	R 36	T 37	Locations, civil divisions, literacy, religions, church history, denominations, dioceses, church growth, missions, agencies, ministries, movements 38
6794	3	7	2.00	0	99.90	0.10	C	456.61	55	10	East central Oaxaca State. D=RCC,CGP,CEC.
6795	1	10	3.53	4	99.95	0.05	C	586.00	72	10	Settlers from Catalonia(Spain). D=RCC. M=SJ,SDB,OSA,OP,PFM.
6796	1	7	2.00	0	99.93	0.07	C	468.44	54	10	Oaxaca State. Zapotecs. D=RCC. M=SIL.
6797	5	9	2.00	0	99.95	0.05	C	520.12	50	10	Aztecs. 35% bilinguals in Spanish. Traditional religion strong. Zoroastrians 5%. D=RCC(20% christopagans),UIEM,UIEI,NBCM/CNBM,ARPC. M=MIM,CIOM,SIL.
6798	2	7	2.05	0	99.90	0.10	C	436.90	57	10	San Luis Potosi. Otomis. D=UIEI,RCC. M=SIL.
6799	2	7	2.00	0	99.90	0.10	C	473.04	51	10	South central Oaxaca. Zapotecs. 55% bilinguals in Spanish. D=RCC,NBCM/CNBM. M=SIL,CBFMS.
6800	2	8	1.19	0	99.90	0.10	C	453.33	38	10	Oaxaca. Mixtecs. D=RCC,UIEI. M=SIL.
6801	3	8	0.56	0	99.90	0.10	C	466.47	24	10	Puebla State. Mixtecs. D=UIEI,NBCM/CNBM,RCC.
6802	4	8	2.26	0	99.70	0.30	C	309.15	69	9	Chihuahua. D=RCC,MEM,IAFCJ,NBCM/CNBM. M=EMC,SIL,OM,GRI,FMB.
6803	5	7	2.64	0	99.90	0.10	C	469.75	65	10	West central Chiapas. Mayans. D=83% RCC,7% Protestants(National Presbyterian Ch of Mexico,SDA),UIEI,MCGC,IAFCJ and other Mexican indigenous chs.
6804	1	7	2.04	0	99.95	0.05	C	527.06	51	10	Quintana Roo. Mayans. Bilinguals in Yucatec of Yucatan. D=RCC.
6805	2	8	2.00	0	99.93	0.07	C	475.23	53	10	Southwest Oaxaca. Mixtecs. D=RCC,UIEI. M=CIOM.
6806	3	7	3.15	0	99.90	0.10	C	469.75	75	10	Chiapas. Mayans. D=71% RCC,19% Protestants (Presbyterians),IAFCJ. M=SIL.
6807	1	7	2.00	0	99.80	0.20	C	367.92	59	9	Central Oaxaca. East Ocotlan Zapotecs. D=RCC.
6808	1	7	2.00	0	99.90	0.10	C	436.90	57	10	Chiapas. Mayans: Cakchiquel Mam. 100% bilingual in Spanish. D=RCC.
6809	1	7	2.00	0	99.70	0.30	C	268.27	73	8	Chihuahua-Sonoran border. Agriculturalists. Limited bilingualism. D=RCC.
6810	1	7	0.81	0	99.92	0.08	C	466.76	32	10	Oaxaca State. Bilingual in Spanish. D=RCC.
6811	1	7	1.76	0	99.91	0.09	C	445.08	52	10	Oaxaca. Santa Maria Chimalapa, San Miguel Chimalapa. D=RCC. M=SIL.
6812	1	7	2.00	0	99.90	0.10	C	446.76	54	10	North central Oaxaca, and Veracruz. Zapotecs. D=RCC. M=SIL.
6813	1	7	1.00	0	99.90	0.10	C	446.76	36	10	Oaxaca. Bilingual in Spanish. D=RCC.
6814	2	8	2.50	0	99.93	0.07	C	468.44	64	10	In Guerrero. Mixtecs. D=UIEI,RCC. M=SIL.
6815	2	8	2.32	0	99.90	0.10	C	450.04	60	10	Oaxaca. Mixtecs. D=RCC,NBCM/CNBM. M=SIL.
6816	1	7	2.00	0	99.80	0.20	C	335.80	64	9	Oaxaca State, Ejutla. Closest to San Gregorio Ozolotepec. D=RCC.
6817	4	8	0.81	0	99.95	0.05	C	499.32	30	10	State of Mexico. Aztecs. D=UIEM,RCC,UIEI,NBCM/CNBM. M=MIM.
6818	2	8	2.69	0	99.91	0.09	C	458.36	67	10	Oaxaca. Mixtecs. D=UIEI,RCC. M=FMB,SIL.
6819	1	7	0.65	0	99.90	0.10	C	420.48	33	10	Baja California. Hunter-gatherers, agriculturalists. Speakers 90%, nonspeakers 10%. D=RCC.
6820	2	8	1.90	0	99.90	0.10	C	446.76	52	10	Eastern Guerrero. Mixtecs. D=UIEI,RCC.
6821	1	7	2.20	0	99.90	0.10	C	433.62	62	10	North Oaxaca. Agriculturalists. D=RCC. M=SIL.
6822	1	7	2.42	0	99.93	0.07	C	475.23	63	10	Chiapas. 90% bilinguals in Spanish. D=RCC. M=SIL.
6823	2	7	1.26	0	99.92	0.08	C	463.40	41	10	Sinaloa State. 55% bilingual in Chinese. D=RCC,IAFCJ. M=SIL.
6824	1	7	4.67	0	99.89	0.11	C	438.54	111	10	Puebla State. Bilingual in Spanish. D=RCC.
6825	1	7	2.00	0	99.90	0.10	C	440.19	57	10	Puebla State. D=RCC. M=SIL.
6826	1	10	2.17	8	99.95	0.05	C	554.42	37	10	Vast numbers of Amerindians uprooted from tribal cultures. Urbanites, slumdwellers. D=RCC. T=CBN. R=AWR. T=TBN,LESEA.
6827	1	7	2.01	0	99.92	0.08	C	446.61	60	10	Baja California. Bilingual in English. D=RCC.
6828	1	7	1.94	0	99.93	0.07	C	465.04	53	10	Southeast Oaxaca. Peasant agriculturalists. Zapotecs. D=RCC. M=SIL,UIM.
6829	2	8	1.75	0	99.93	0.07	C	475.23	48	10	Oaxaca. Mixtecs. D=UIEI,RCC. M=SIL.
6830	1	7	2.00	0	99.90	0.10	C	433.62	56	10	Southern Oaxaca. Pastoralists, peasant agriculturalists. Zapotecs. D=RCC. M=SIL.
6831	1	7	2.31	0	98.00	2.00	C	214.62	84	8	Central Oaxaca. Zapotecs. Animists 40%. D=RCC. M=SIL.
6832	1	7	2.00	0	99.85	0.15	C	406.42	56	10	Oaxaca. East Central Tlacolula Zapotecs. Mountains, plains. D=RCC.
6833	2	8	2.00	0	99.90	0.10	C	456.61	53	10	Southwest Oaxaca. Peasant agriculturalists. Mixtecs. D=RCC,UIEI. M=FMB,SIL.
6834	2	8	1.67	0	99.93	0.07	C	478.62	46	10	West central Oaxaca. Mixtecs. D=UIEI,RCC. M=SIL.
6835	1	7	2.00	0	99.90	0.10	C	443.47	55	10	Central Oaxaca. Zapotecs. Pastoralists. D=RCC. M=SIL.
6836	1	7	2.00	0	99.90	0.10	C	436.90	58	10	Puebla State. D=RCC. M=SIL.
6837	2	8	0.23	0	99.92	0.08	C	466.76	18	10	Oaxaca. Mixtecs. D=UIEI,RCC.
6838	1	7	2.00	0	99.90	0.10	C	433.62	56	10	Western Oaxaca. Zapotecs. D=RCC. M=SIL.
6839	0	10	0.00	5	99.90	0.10	C	502.60	0	10	Artificial (constructed) language, in 80 countries. Speakers in Mexico: 20,000(none mother-tongue).
6840	2	7	2.00	0	99.91	0.09	C	455.04	56	10	Veracruz State. D=RCC,FIPC.
6841	1	7	3.26	0	99.93	0.07	C	478.62	79	10	Chiapas. D=RCC. M=SIL.
6842	2	7	2.90	0	99.90	0.10	C	433.62	75	10	One town in State of Mexico. Otomis. D=UIEI,RCC.
6843	1	10	2.00	8	99.84	0.16	C	484.42	52	10	Expatriates from France, in commerce. D=RCC.
6844	1	10	2.80	1	99.95	0.05	C	547.86	64	10	Expatriates from northwest Spain, in business. D=RCC.
6845	4	10	3.47	8	99.87	0.13	C	523.95	58	10	Immigrants from Germany. D=German Evangelical Congregations in Mexico,Iglesia Menonita,NAC,RCC.
6846	0	10	2.38	5	51.20	48.80	B	0.37	164	3	Practicing Yiddish-speaking Ashkenazi Jews, mostly in Mexico City.
6847	2	10	2.53	7	99.92	0.08	C	554.07	58	10	Immigrants from Greece. D=Greek Orthodox Ch(AD-N&S America),JWs.
6848	1	7	1.98	0	99.90	0.10	C	427.05	59	10	West central Chihuahua. D=RCC. M=SIL.
6849	4	7	2.00	0	99.93	0.07	C	482.01	52	10	Guerrero State. Peasant agriculturalists. Mixtecs. D=UIEI,Spiritual Christian Evangelical Ch,RCC,Presbyterian Ch. M=SIL.
6850	1	9	2.00	0	99.95	0.05	C	509.72	51	10	Balsas river, Guerrero. Bilingual in Spanish. D=RCC.
6851	1	10	4.60	8	99.80	0.20	C	417.56	101	10	Assimilated Spanish-speaking Chinese. Folk Buddhists 20%. D=RCC.
6852	1	10	5.00	8	99.70	0.30	C	355.14	111	9	Long-time immigrants from Guangdong(China). Buddhists/folk-religionists 30%. D=RCC.
6853	1	10	5.05	7	99.70	0.30	C	352.59	113	9	Residents, from Chinese diaspora. Folk Buddhists 30%. D=RCC.
6854	4	9	2.00	0	99.95	0.05	C	527.06	50	10	In San Luis Potosi and Hidalgo. Aztecs. D=UIEM,RCC,UIEI,NBCM/CNBM. M=MIM,UFM,GR.
6855	1	7	2.04	0	99.90	0.10	C	436.90	59	10	Northwest Oaxaca. D=RCC. M=SIL.
6856	2	8	2.29	0	99.90	0.10	C	443.47	61	10	Eastern Guerrero. Mixtecs. D=UIEI,RCC. M=SIL.
6857	2	7	1.51	0	99.93	0.07	C	482.01	45	10	Oaxaca State. D=RCC,NBCM/CNBM. M=FMB,SIL.
6858	2	7	1.50	0	99.91	0.09	C	451.72	46	10	Oaxaca. Mayans. D=RCC,NBCM/CNBM. M=SIL.
6859	1	7	2.00	0	99.90	0.10	C	450.04	56	10	Veracruz. Half are bilingual in Spanish. D=RCC. M=SIL.
6860	2	7	2.00	0	99.93	0.07	C	475.23	55	10	Veracruz, Puebla States. D=RCC,FIPC. M=UFM,SIL.
6861	2	7	3.82	0	99.90	0.10	C	492.75	84	10	East central Chiapas, Oxchuc area. Mayans. D=RCC,strong Presbyterian work. M=SIL,Potter's House.
6862	2	8	0.86	0	99.90	0.10	C	446.76	31	10	Oaxaca. Mixtecs. D=UIEI,RCC.
6863	1	7	2.00	0	99.71	0.29	C	285.06	70	8	Northeast Hidalgo. Peasant agriculturalists. Animists 25%. D=RCC. M=SIL.
6864	3	6	3.20	0	33.00	67.00	A	1.20	332	4	Western Mexico, Jalisco State. Resistant for centuries, evicted missions, now 99% animists with own culture. D=RCC,IAFCJ,SDA. M=SIL.
6865	4	8	2.09	0	99.95	0.05	C	509.72	53	10	Southern Durango. Aztecs. Bilingual in Spanish. D=UIEM,RCC,UIEI,NBCM/CNBM. M=MIM.
6866	3	7	2.78	0	99.90	0.10	C	469.75	68	10	Chiapas, Huistan region. Mayans. D=85% RCC,5% Protestants(Presbyterians/INPL),IAFCJ. M=SIL.
6867	4	9	2.00	0	99.95	0.05	C	509.72	51	10	Southern Veracruz. Aztecs. D=UIEM,UIEI,NBCM/CNBM,RCC. M=MIM,SIL.
6868	6	7	2.27	0	99.90	0.10	C	456.61	61	10	Northeast Oaxaca. D=RCC,National Presbyterian,Ch of Mexico,CGP,SDA,Pentecostals. M=SIL,CEC.
6869	4	7	1.97	0	99.93	0.07	C	495.59	50	10	Oaxaca. Zapotecs. 30% bilinguals in Spanish. D=RCC,CON,Baptists,Pentecostals. M=SIL.
6870	1	10	2.97	7	99.84	0.16	C	496.69	67	10	Settlers from Italy. Strong Catholics. D=RCC. M=SJ,OFM,SDB,OSA,OP,PFM,FSC.
6871	1	7	2.01	0	99.00	1.00	C	216.81	75	8	Oaxaca. All bilingual in Spanish. Animists 30%. D=RCC.
6872	1	10	3.37	7	69.00	31.00	B	12.59	160	5	Buddhists 58%, New-Religionists 26%(Soka Gakkai, &c), nonreligious 11%. D=RCC.
6873	0	10	3.37	8	49.40	50.60	A	0.72	225	3	Practicing Spanish-speaking Ashkenazi and Sefardi Jews, mostly in Mexico City.
6874	3	7	2.00	0	99.91	0.09	C	458.20	54	10	Guanajuato State. Otomis. Bilingual in Spanish. D=UIEI,ARPC,RCC.
6875	2	7	2.48	0	99.90	0.10	C	453.33	65	10	East central Oaxaca State. D=RCC,CGP. M=CEC,SIL.
6876	3	10	2.00	8	99.80	0.20	C	408.80	59	10	Romany Gypsies across country. D=nomadic caravan churches,RCC,GEM.
6877	1	7	1.39	0	99.90	0.10	C	420.48	49	10	Coahuila. 67% in USA. D=RCC. M=SIL.
6878	1	7	0.34	0	99.70	0.30	C	258.05	34	8	Baja California, south of Paipai and Tipai. D=RCC.
6879	2	10	1.94	0	99.90	0.10	C	459.90	53	10	Northeast Chiapas. Mayans. D=RCC,UIEI. M=SIL.
6880	1	7	2.30	0	99.90	0.10	C	433.62	62	10	Southeast Oaxaca. Chatinos. D=RCC.
6881	1	7	2.11	0	99.80	0.20	C	353.32	64	9	Oaxaca. San Cristobal Lachiruaj Zapotecs. D=RCC.
6882	1	7	3.03	0	99.91	0.09	C	448.40	78	10	Oaxaca-Veracruz border. Peasant agriculturalists. D=RCC. M=SIL.
6883	1	7	2.71	0	99.93	0.07	C	458.25	71	10	North Oaxaca. Agriculturalists. D=RCC. M=SIL.
6884	3	10	8.29	8	99.93	0.07	C	561.97	149	10	Muslims 6%. D=RCC(Maronites),Catholic Apostolic Orthodox Ch,AOCUSA.
6885	0	10	2.33	8	48.10	51.90	A	0.17	172	3	Immigrant from Levantine countries. Most are practicing religious Jews.
6886	1	10	6.54	8	99.87	0.13	C	504.90	132	10	Chihuahua, Durango. D=Mennonites et alii. 22% speak Standard German, 30% Spanish. 60% literates.
6887	2	7	2.00	0	99.90	0.10	C	466.47	54	10	Oaxaca, Veracruz States. D=RCC,NBCM/CNBM. M=FMB,SIL.
6888	3	7	-0.18	0	99.90	0.10	C	440.19	12	10	Southeast Oaxaca. Mayans. D=RCC,NBCM/CNBM,Pentecostals. M=SIL.
6889	2	7	2.00	0	99.91	0.09	C	458.36	56	10	Veracruz State. D=RCC,FIPC. M=SIL,UFM.
6890	1	7	3.33	0	99.90	0.10	C	459.90	80	10	Chiapas State. Mayans. D=RCC. M=SIL,Potter's House.
6891	2	7	2.00	0	99.90	0.10	C	459.90	55	10	Southern Sonora. D=RCC,NBCM/CNBM. M=SIL,FMB.
6892	6	7	1.85	0	99.93	0.07	C	492.20	48	10	State of Mexico. Otomis. D=RCC,UIEI,CGP,CON,FCOGN,FIPC. M=YWAM,ABCUSA(Agape Association),FMB.SIL.
6893	1	7	1.64	0	99.80	0.20	C	347.48	56	9	Oaxaca State. D=RCC. M=MBS.
6894	0	0	9.19	0	99.90	0.10	C	381.06	234	9	Eastern Guerrero in Metlatonoc and San Rafael. Mountainous region. D=RCC.
6895	1	10	2.00	8	99.93	0.07	C	539.72	45	10	African-heritage former-slave ancestry, linked with Caribbean Blacks. D=RCC.
6896	10	10	1.94	8	99.97	0.03	C	587.33	41	10	Cult of Virgin of Guadalupe(2 million pilgrims a year). D=RCC(66 Dioceses),UIEI,CJCLdS,JWs,NPC,SDA,IAFCJ,COG,BGC,&c. M=WMPL. T=CBN. R=AWR.
6897	6	10	1.93	8	99.93	0.07	C	551.99	47	10	Descendants of conquistadores. D=RCC(50 Dioceses),UIEI,JWs,SDA,COG,BGC. T=CBN. R=AWR. T=TBN,LESEA.
6898	2	9	2.07	0	99.95	0.05	C	509.72	52	10	Hidalgo. Otomis. Christopaganism and Indian religion strong. D=RCC,UIEI. M=SIL.
6899	4	9	2.39	0	99.95	0.05	C	520.12	57	10	Michoacan. Aztecs. All bilingual, in Spanish. D=UIEI,NBCM/CNBM,UIEM,RCC. M=MIM,SIL.
6900	0	0	5.29	0	99.90	0.10	C	387.63	139	9	Oaxaca. Altitude 7,000 ft. Agriculturalists (maize, beans). Some children learn Spanish. D=RCC.
6901	1	7	0.70	0	99.90	0.10	C	430.33	31	10	Chiapas. Mayans. Mainly in Guatemala. Mayans. Most now use Spanish. D=RCC.
6902	1	8	0.09	0	99.85	0.15	C	415.73	17	10	Morelos. Aztecs. All bilingual in Spanish. D=RCC.
6903	1	7	2.00	0	99.65	0.35	C	246.74	71	8	Oaxaca. Mountainous. Bilinguals in Spanish. D=RCC.
6904	1	7	2.00	0	99.90	0.10	C	450.04	54	10	Oaxaca. Zapotecs. Mountains. Many bilinguals in Spanish. D=RCC.
6905	2	8	2.00	0	99.90	0.10	C	453.33	54	10	Oaxaca, Tlaxiaco District. Mixtecs. D=UIEI,RCC.
6906	1	7	2.00	0	99.92	0.08	C	453.33	55	10	Eastern Oaxaca. Zapotecs. Bilingual in Spanish. D=RCC.
6907	2	8	0.93	0	99.92	0.08	C	470.12	32	10	Oaxaca. Mixtecs. Bilinguals in Spanish. D=UIEI,RCC.
6908	1	7	3.72	0	99.92	0.08	C	456.68	89	10	Central Oaxaca, southwest of Oaxaca City. Bilinguals in Spanish. Zapotecs. D=RCC.
6909	5	9	1.88	0	99.95	0.05	C	523.59	48	10	Naupan, northern Puebla. Aztecs. D=UIEI,NBCM/CNBM,UIEM,RCC,Independent Pentecostals. M=MIM,WMPL,SIL.
6910	1	7	2.00	0	99.93	0.07	C	465.04	54	10	Northern Oaxaca. Zapotecs. D=RCC. M=SIL.
6911	1	7	2.00	0	99.91	0.09	C	438.43	56	10	Southern Oaxaca. San Cristobal Amatlan. Zapotecs. Forest, mountains. Sedentary pastoralists, agriculturalists. D=RCC.
6912	1	7	2.00	0	99.91	0.09	C	441.76	56	10	Oaxaca. Mostly monolingual. Zapotecs. D=RCC.
6913	1	7	2.00	0	99.91	0.09	C	435.11	56	10	Oaxaca. 80% are monolingual. Zapotecs. D=RCC. M=independents.
6914	1	7	3.63	0	99.70	0.30	C	275.94	112	8	Northeastern Oaxaca. Agriculturalists. D=RCC.
6915	2	9	2.28	0	99.95	0.05	C	506.25	56	10	Northeastern Veracruz. Otomis. D=UIEI,RCC.
6916	1	7	1.61	0	99.90	0.10	C	433.62	48	10	Southeast Oaxaca. Agriculturalists. Zapotecs. Bilingual in Spanish. D=RCC. M=UIM.
6917	2	7	2.00	0	99.91	0.09	C	441.76	56	10	San Luis Potosi. Otomis. D=UIEI,RCC.

Continued overleaf

Table 8-2 continued

PEOPLE		POPULATION				IDENTITY CODE		LANGUAGE		CHURCH		MINISTRY						SCRIPTURE		
Ref 1	*Ethnic name* 2	*P%* 3	*In 1995* 4	*In 2000* 5	*In 2025* 6	*Race* 7	*Language* 8	*Autoglossonym* 9	*S* 10	*AC* 11	*Members* 12	*Jayuh* 13-17	*d* 18	*wa* 19	*xc* 20	*mc* 21	*mi* 22	*Biblioglossonym* 23	*Pub* 24-26	*ss* 27
6918	Northern Isthmus Zapotec	0.01069	9,743	10,570	13,918	MIR37f	67-AHBG-c	zapotec-istmo		90.00	9,513	4a...	10	7	11	5	1	Zapoteco: Isthmus*	PN.	.
6919	Northern Mam	0.00123	1,121	1,216	1,601	MIR37b	68-ADBA-a	mam-huehuetenango		90.00	1,095	4.s..	10	7	11	4	1	Mam: Huehuetenango*	PNB	.
6920	Northern Mixe	0.00615	5,605	6,081	8,007	MIR37z	69-FAAA-a	mixe-totontepec		93.00	5,656	0....	10	8	11	5	2	Mixe, Totontepec*	PN.	.
6921	Northern Popoloca	0.00677	6,171	6,694	8,814	MIR37z	67-ADAA-b	north popoloc		90.00	6,025	1....	10	7	11	3	2	Popoloca: Northern	PN.	.
6922	Northern Tarahumara	0.00166	1,513	1,641	2,161	MIR37z	66-BEBA-a	ariseachi		70.00	1,149	1....	10	8	6	5	2		pn.	b
6923	Northern Tepehuan	0.00946	8,622	9,354	12,317	MIR37z	66-BEAD-a	north tepehuán		5.00	468	0....	7	5	2	2	2	Tepehuan: Northern*	PN.	b
6924	Northern Tlaxiaco Mixtec	0.01656	15,094	16,375	21,560	MIR37c	67-AFAC-ra	ñumi		80.00	13,100	1....	10	7	7	4	1		pn.	b
6925	Northern Totonac	0.01389	12,660	13,735	18,084	MIR37z	69-BAAA-a	totonac-juárez		90.00	12,361	0....	10	7	11	5	1	Totonaco: Northern*	PN.	.
6926	Northwest Oaxaca Mixtec	0.00295	2,689	2,917	3,841	MIR37c	67-AFAC-f	northwest oaxaca		90.00	2,625	1....	10	7	11	4	1	Mixteco, Northwest Oaxaca	pn.	b
6927	Northwestern Otomi	0.03904	35,583	38,603	50,829	MIR37d	67-ABCA-a	queretaro		95.00	36,673	1c...	10	7	11	5	2	Otomi, Western	pn.	.
6928	Oaxaca Amuzgo	0.00473	4,311	4,677	6,158	MIR37c	67-AGAB-a	san-pedro-amuzgos		90.00	4,209	1a...	10	7	11	5	1	Amuzgo: Oaxaca*	PN.	.
6929	Ojitlan Chinantec	0.02603	23,725	25,739	33,890	MIR37z	67-AEAA-a	ojitlán		93.00	23,937	0c...	10	7	11	3	1	Chinanteco: Ojitlan*	PN.	.
6930	Oluta Popoluca	0.01183	10,782	11,698	15,402	MIR37z	69-FAAC-a	popoluca-oluta		90.00	10,528	0....	10	7	11	2	1		pn.	.
6931	Ometepec Aztec (Nahuatl)	0.00051	465	504	664	MIR37a	66-BFBA-bm	ometepec		95.00	479	1c...	10	9	12	5	1		pn.	.
6932	Orizaba Aztec (Nahuatl)	0.13265	120,904	131,166	172,705	MIR37a	66-BFBA-dc	orizaba		95.00	124,608	1c...	10	9	12	5	1	Nahuatl, Orizaba	Pn.	.
6933	Ozolotepec Zapotec	0.00743	6,772	7,347	9,674	MIR37f	67-AHBF-d	ozolotepec		90.00	6,612	1....	10	7	11	2	1	Zapoteco, Ozolotepec	...	.
6934	Ozumatlan Totonac	0.00473	4,311	4,677	6,158	MIR37z	69-BAAA-c	totonac-ozumatlán		90.00	4,209	0....	10	7	6	2	1		pn.	.
6935	Paipai (Akwaala)	0.00035	319	346	456	MIR38a	63-VDCB-a	paipai		90.00	311	0....	10	6	11	2	1		...	.
6936	Palantla Chinantec	0.01419	12,934	14,031	18,475	MIR37z	67-AEAB-a	palantla		93.00	13,049	1....	10	6	11	2	1	Chinanteco: Palantla*	PN.	.
6937	Palestinian Arab	0.20000	182,291	197,763	260,392	CMT30	12-AACF-f	syro-palestinian		59.00	116,680	1Asuh	10	7	8	5	2	Arabic: Lebanese*	Pnb	b
6938	Papago-Pima	0.00150	1,367	1,483	1,953	MIR37z	66-BEAA	pima-papago cluster		93.00	1,379	0A...	10	7	11	2	1	Papago-piman	PN.	b
6939	Part-Indian (Half-Indian)	9.73693	8,874,751	9,628,002	12,677,109	MIR37e	51-AABB-ha	mexicano		95.00	9,146,602	1B.uh	10	8	10	5	2		pnb	b
6940	Patla Totonac	0.00709	6,462	7,011	9,231	MIR37z	69-BAAA-h	totonac-patla		80.00	5,609	0....	10	7	8	4	2	Totonaco: Patla*	PN.	.
6941	Pima Bajo (Mountain Pima)	0.00115	1,048	1,137	1,497	MIR37z	66-BEAC-a	southeast pima		93.00	1,058	0....	10	7	11	4	1	Pima Bajo, Sonora	P..	.
6942	Pisa Flores Tepehua	0.00473	4,311	4,677	6,158	MIR37z	69-BBAA-b	tepehua-puebla		70.00	3,274	0....	10	7	6	3	1	Nahuatl: Puebla, Southeast*	PN.	b
6943	Quetzaltepec Mixe	0.02763	25,183	27,321	35,973	MIR37z	69-FAAB-fg	quetzaltepec		65.00	17,759	1....	10	7	6	2	1		pn.	.
6944	Rayon Zoque	0.01230	11,211	12,162	16,014	MIR37z	69-FABD-d	zoque-rayûn		70.00	8,514	1c...	10	7	6	2	1		pn.	.
6945	Russian	0.08000	72,916	79,105	104,157	CEW22j	53-AAAE-d	russkiy		81.00	64,075	4B.uh	10	8	11	5	1	Russian	PNB	b
6946	S Catarina Quieri Zapotec	0.00442	4,029	4,371	5,755	MIR37f	67-AHBE-e	quioquitani		80.00	3,496	0c...	10	7	7	4	1	Zapoteco: Quioquitani	Pn.	.
6947	S Catarina Xanaguia Zapot	0.00295	2,689	2,917	3,841	MIR37f	67-AHBE-g	xanaguia		85.00	2,479	0c...	10	7	10	4	1	Zapoteco: Xanaguia*	Pn.	.
6948	S Francisco del Mar Huave	0.00444	4,047	4,390	5,781	MIR37z	69-EAAA-ba	san-francisco		90.00	3,951	1....	10	7	11	4	1		pn.	b
6949	S Juan Colorado Mixtec	0.01597	14,556	15,791	20,792	MIR37c	67-AFAF-c	colorado		90.00	14,212	0c...	10	7	11	5	1	Mixteco: S Juan Colorado*	PN.	.
6950	S Maria Ipalapa Amuzgo	0.00141	1,285	1,394	1,836	MIR37c	67-AGAB-b	amuzgo-guerrero		85.00	1,185	1c...	10	7	10	4	0	Amuzgo: Guerrero*	PN.	.
6951	S Maria Petapa Zapotec	0.00946	8,622	9,354	12,317	MIR37f	67-AHBG-a	petapa		90.00	8,419	1c...	10	7	11	4	1		pn.	b
6952	S Martin Itunyoso Trique	0.00270	2,461	2,670	3,515	MIR37c	67-AFBB-b	itunyoso		75.00	2,002	0....	10	7	7	5	2	Trique: S Martin Itunyoso*	PN.	.
6953	S Matatlan Zapotec	0.00568	5,177	5,616	7,395	MIR37f	67-AHBD-da	matatlán		90.00	5,055	1c...	10	7	11	5	1		pn.	.
6954	S Miguel Tilquiapan Zapot	0.00319	2,908	3,154	4,153	MIR37f	67-AHBC-cc	tilquiapan		75.00	2,366	0a...	10	7	7	4	1		pn.	b
6955	S Raymundo Xalpan Zapotec	0.00270	2,461	2,670	3,515	MIR37f	67-AHBC-aa	xalpan		70.00	1,869	0c...	10	7	6	4	1		pn.	b
6956	S Tomas Mazaltepec Zapote	0.00646	5,888	6,388	8,411	MIR37f	67-AHBB-d	ixtlán		90.00	5,749	1c...	10	7	11	4	1	Zapoteco, Western Ixtlan	PN.	b
6957	S Tomas Ocotepec Mixtec	0.00903	8,230	8,929	11,757	MIR37c	67-AFAD-e	ocotepec		90.00	8,036	1....	10	7	11	5	1	Mixteco: Ocotepec*	PN.	.
6958	SBart Zoogocho Zapotec	0.00099	902	979	1,289	MIR37f	67-AHBB-a	zoogocho		92.00	901	1a...	10	7	11	5	1	Zapoteco: S Bart Zoogocho*	PN.	.
6959	SE Yautepec Zapotec	0.00106	966	1,048	1,380	MIR37f	67-AHBD-ee	tlacoculita		90.00	943	1c...	10	8	11	5	2		pn.	b
6960	SE Zimatlan Zapotec	0.00264	2,406	2,610	3,437	MIR37f	67-AHBC-ab	zegache		80.00	2,088	0c...	10	6	6	4	1	Zapoteco, S E Zimatlan	Pn.	.
6961	San Andres Trique	0.00833	7,592	8,237	10,845	MIR37c	67-AFBB-a	chicahuaxtla		90.00	7,413	0....	10	7	11	5	1	Trique: Chicahuaxtla*	PN.	.
6962	San Andres Tzotzil	0.05916	53,922	58,498	77,024	MIR37b	68-ACBB-d	larrainzar		93.00	54,403	1a...	10	8	11	5	2	Tzotzil: San Andres*	PN.	.
6963	San Antonio Mixtec	0.00473	4,311	4,677	6,158	MIR37c	67-AFAD-k	huitepec		90.00	4,209	1....	10	8	11	5	2		pn.	.
6964	San Bartolome Mixtec	0.00060	547	593	781	MIR37c	67-AFAD-cb	teita		85.00	504	1....	10	7	10	4	1	Mixteco, San Juan Teita	pn.	b
6965	San Jeronimo Mazatec	0.04023	36,668	39,780	52,378	MIR37z	67-ADBA-da	san-jerûnimo-tecoatl		93.00	36,995	1c...	10	7	11	5	2	Mazateco, S Jeronimo Teco*	Pn.	.
6966	San Juan Copala Trique	0.01774	16,169	17,542	23,097	MIR37c	67-AFBA-a	copala		91.00	15,963	1....	10	8	11	5	1	Trique: San Juan Copala*	PN.	.
6967	San Juan Mazatec	0.00295	2,689	2,917	3,841	MIR37z	67-ADBA-e	chiquihuitlan		90.00	2,625	1c...	10	7	11	5	1	Mazateco: Chiquihuitlan*	PN.	b
6968	San Luis Potosi Huastec	0.08282	75,487	81,893	107,828	MIR37b	68-AAAA-a	west huastec		93.00	76,161	1....	10	8	11	5	3	Huasteco: San Luis Potosi*	PN.	.
6969	San Mateo Ixtatan Chuj	0.01100	10,026	10,877	14,322	MIR37b	68-ADAA-a	chuj-ixtatán		90.00	9,789	0....	10	7	11	5	1	Chuj: San Mateo Ixtatan*	PN.	b
6970	San Mateo del Mar Huave	0.01419	12,934	14,031	18,475	MIR37z	69-EAAA-a	west huave		90.00	12,628	1....	10	8	11	5	1	Huave*	PN.	.
6971	San Miguel Mixtec	0.01183	10,782	11,698	15,402	MIR37c	67-AFAD-da	san-miguel-el-grande		90.00	10,528	1....	10	7	11	5	1	Mixteco: San Miguel*	PN.	n
6972	San Pedro Mazatec	0.01301	11,858	12,864	16,939	MIR37z	67-ADBA-a	ixcatlan		93.00	11,964	1c...	10	7	11	5	2	Mazateco, S Pedro Ixcatlan	pn.	b
6973	Santiago Apoala Mixtec	0.00930	8,477	9,196	12,108	MIR37c	67-AFAE-aa	apoala		92.00	8,460	1c...	10	7	11	4	2		p..	.
6974	Santiago Lapaguia Zapotec	0.00500	4,557	4,944	6,510	MIR37f	67-AHBE-h	lapaguía		70.00	3,461	0c...	10	7	5	4	1		pn.	b
6975	Santiago Xanica Zapotec	0.00295	2,689	2,917	3,841	MIR37f	67-AHBE-f	xanica		85.00	2,479	0c...	10	7	11	4	0	Zapoteco, Santiago Xanica	pn.	.
6976	Santiago Yosondua Mixtec	0.00591	5,387	5,844	7,695	MIR37c	67-AFAF-a	yosondua		90.00	5,259	0a...	10	7	11	5	1	Mixteco: Santiago Yosondua*	PN.	.
6977	Santo Domingo Zapotec	0.00216	1,969	2,136	2,812	MIR37f	67-AHBD-a	albarradas		90.00	1,922	1c...	10	7	11	5	1	Zapoteco, Albarradas	pn.	b
6978	Sayula Popoluca	0.00473	4,311	4,677	6,158	MIR37z	69-FAAC-b	popoluca-sayula		91.00	4,256	0....	10	7	11	5	1	Popoluca: Sayula*	PN.	b
6979	Seri	0.00079	720	781	1,029	MIR38a	63-VEAA-a	seri-tiburûn		70.00	547	0....	10	6	6	4	1	Seri	PN.	.
6980	Sierra (Eastern) Otomi	0.02366	21,565	23,395	30,804	MIR37d	67-ABCA-d	huehuetla		95.00	22,226	1c...	10	8	12	5	1	Tepehua, Huehuetla*	PN.	.
6981	Sierra Aztec (Nahuatl)	0.16892	153,963	167,030	219,927	MIR37a	66-BFBA-da	zacapoaxtla		95.00	158,679	1c...	10	9	11	5	2	Nahuatl: Puebla, Highland*	PN.	.
6982	Silacayoapan Mixtec	0.01893	17,254	18,718	24,646	MIR37c	67-AFAC-l	silacayoapan		90.00	16,846	1....	10	8	11	5	1	Mixteco: Silacayoapan*	PN.	.
6983	Sochiapan Chinantec	0.00415	3,783	4,104	5,403	MIR37z	67-AEAB-b	sochiapan		90.00	3,693	1....	10	7	11	4	1	Chinanteco: Sochiapan*	PN.	.
6984	South C Zimatlan Zapotec	0.00106	966	1,048	1,380	MIR37f	67-AHBC-b	zimatlán		90.00	943	0c...	10	7	11	4	1		Pn.	b
6985	South E Ixtlan Zapotec	0.00680	6,198	6,724	8,853	MIR37f	67-AHBB-db	yavesia		90.00	6,052	1c...	10	7	11	4	1		pn.	b
6986	South Nochixtlan Mixtec	0.00212	1,932	2,096	2,760	MIR37c	67-AFAE	mixtec-nochixtlán cluster		91.00	1,908	1a...	10	8	11	5	3		P..	b
6987	South Villa Alta Zapotec	0.01181	10,764	11,678	15,376	MIR37f	67-AHBB-fe	cajonos		93.00	10,860	1a...	10	7	11	4	2	Zapoteco: Cajonos*	Pn.	b
6988	Southeast Puebla Aztec	0.14370	130,976	142,092	187,092	MIR37a	66-BFBA-db	chilac		85.00	120,779	1c...	10	7	7	5	2	Nahuatl, Southeast Puebla	Pn.	.
6989	Southeast, Nochixtlan Mix	0.00828	7,547	8,187	10,780	MIR37c	67-AFAD-i	nuxaá		80.00	6,550	1....	10	7	7	4	1	Mixteco, S E Nochixtlan	pn.	b
6990	Southeastern Otomi	0.00633	5,769	6,259	8,241	MIR37d	67-ABCA-f	ixtenco		95.00	5,946	1c...	10	8	11	5	2		pn.	.
6991	Southeastern Tepehuan	0.01005	9,160	9,938	13,085	MIR37z	66-BEAE-b	southeast tepehuán		70.00	6,956	0....	10	7	6	4	1	Tepehuan, Southeastern	P..	.
6992	Southern (Coatlan) Mixe	0.00694	6,325	6,862	9,036	MIR37z	69-FAAB-a	mixe-coatlán		90.00	6,176	1....	10	8	11	5	3	Mixe: Camotlan*	PN.	.
6993	Southern Ejutla Zapotec	0.00287	2,616	2,838	3,737	MIR37f	67-AHBB-fb	south rincûn		90.00	2,554	1c...	10	7	11	4	2	Zapoteco: Rincon, Southern*	PN.	.
6994	Southern Popoloca	0.00222	2,023	2,195	2,890	MIR37z	67-ADAA-f	south popoloc		92.00	2,020	1....	10	7	11	4	1		pn.	.
6995	Southern Puebla Mixtec	0.00157	1,431	1,552	2,044	MIR37c	69-BBAA-b	tepehua-puebla		93.00	1,444	0....	10	8	11	5	1	Nahuatl: Puebla, Southeast*	PN.	b
6996	Southern Putla Mixtec	0.00680	6,198	6,724	8,853	MIR37c	67-AFAF-d	south putla		90.00	6,052	0c...	10	7	11	5	2	Mixteco: Southern Putla*	Pn.	.
6997	Southern Rincon Zapotec	0.01419	12,934	14,031	18,475	MIR37f	67-AHBB-fb	south rincûn		80.00	11,225	1c...	10	7	7	4	1	Zapoteco: Rincon, Southern*	PN.	.
6998	Southwest Tarahumara	0.00014	128	138	182	MIR37z	66-BEBA-f	tubare		90.00	125	1....	10	8	11	5	1		pn.	.
6999	Southwest Tlaxiaco Mixtec	0.00709	6,462	7,011	9,231	MIR37c	67-AFAD-a	nuyoo-yucuhiti		90.00	6,310	1....	10	7	11	5	2	Mixteco, S W Tlaxiaco	pn.	.
7000	Southwestern Tepehuan	0.00828	7,547	8,187	10,780	MIR37z	66-BEAE-a	southwest tepehuán		70.00	5,731	0....	10	7	6	4	1	Tepehuan, Southwestern	p..	.
7001	Spaniard	0.32000	291,665	316,420	416,628	CEW21k	51-AABB-ha	mexicano		93.00	294,271	1B.uh	10	9	15	5	3		pnb	b
7002	State of Mexico Otomi	0.01183	10,782	11,698	15,402	MIR37d	67-ABCA-g	san-felipe		95.00	11,113	1c...	10	10	11	0	1	Otomi: San Felipe Santiago*	PN.	.
7003	Syrian Arab	0.40000	364,581	395,525	520,785	CMT30	12-AACF-f	syro-palestinian		49.00	193,807	1Asuh	9	6	8	5	2	Arabic: Lebanese*	Pnb	b
7004	Tabasco Aztec (Nahuatl)	0.00040	365	396	521	MIR37a	66-BFBA-d	nahuat		95.00	376	1c...	10	9	12	5	1		PN.	b
7005	Tabasco Chontal	0.06948	63,328	68,703	90,460	MIR37b	68-ACAB-a	chontal-tabasco		90.00	61,832	0....	10	8	11	5	1	Chontal: Tabasco*	PN.	.
7006	Tabasco Zoque	0.00097	884	959	1,263	MIR37z	69-FABB-a	zoque-tabasco		90.00	863	0a...	10	7	11	4	1	Zoque: Ostuacan	P..	b
7007	Tacana Mam (Southern)	0.00141	1,285	1,394	1,836	MIR37b	68-ADBA-g	tacanec		91.00	1,269	1.s..	10	7	11	4	1		pnb	.
7008	Tamazunchale Aztec	0.44215	402,999	437,204	575,662	MIR37a	66-BFBA-bb	tamazunchale		95.00	415,343	1A...	10	9	11	5	3	Nahuatl: Huasteca, West*	PN.	.
7009	Tarascan	0.14199	129,417	140,402	184,866	MIR37z	69-AAAA	tarasco cluster		93.00	130,573	1....	10	8	11	5	1	Tarascan*	PN.	.
7010	Tataltepec Chatino	0.00473	4,311	4,677	6,158	MIR37f	67-AHAB-a	tataltepec		90.00	4,209	0....	10	7	11	4	1	Chatino: Tataltepec*	PN.	.
7011	Tectitan Mam (Teco Mam)	0.00113	1,030	1,117	1,471	MIR37b	68-ADBA-f	tectitec		90.00	1,006	1.s..	10	7	11	4	1	Tectiteco	pnb	b
7012	Temoaya Otomi	0.04378	39,903	43,290	57,000	MIR37d	67-ABCA-i	temoaya		70.00	30,303	1s...	10	7	6	5	1	Otomi, Temoaya	pn.	b
7013	Tenango Otomi	0.01183	10,782	11,698	15,402	MIR37d	67-ABCA-e	tenango		95.00	11,113	1c...	10	7	11	5	1	Otomi: Tenango*	PN.	.
7014	Teotitlan del Valle Zapot	0.00200	1,823	1,978	2,604	MIR37f	67-AHBD-b	teotitlán-de-valle		70.00	1,384	1c...	10	7	6	4	1		pn.	.
7015	Tepetotutla Chinantec	0.00437	3,983	4,321	5,690	MIR37z	67-AEAB-e	tepetotutla		90.00	3,889	1....	10	7	11	4	1	Chinanteco: Tepetotutla*	PN.	.
7016	Tepeuxila Cuicatec	0.01183	10,782	11,698	15,402	MIR37c	67-AFAG-a	tepeuxila		90.00	10,528	1....	10	7	11	5	1	Cuicateco: Tepeuxila*	PN.	b
7017	Tepinapa Chinantec	0.00946	8,622	9,354	12,317	MIR37z	67-AEAB-j	tepinapa		91.00	8,512	1....	10	7	11	4	1		pn.	b
7018	Tetelcingo Aztec (Nahuatl	0.00414	3,773	4,094	5,390	MIR37a	66-BFBA-bk	tetelcingo		95.00	3,889	1a...	10	9	11	5	2	Nahuatl: Tetelcingo*	PN.	b
7019	Teutila Cuicatec	0.01161	10,582	11,480	15,116	MIR37c	67-AFAG-c	teutila		90.00	10,332	1....	10	8	11	5	1	Cuicateco: Teutila*	PN.	b
7020	Texistepec Popoluca	0.01867	17,017	18,461	24,308	MIR37z	69-FABA-b	popoluca-texistepec		90.00	16,615	1....	10	7	11	4	1		pn.	b
7021	Texmelucan Zapotec	0.00464	4,229	4,588	6,041	MIR37f	67-AHBA-a	texmelucan		92.00	4,221	0....	10	7	11	4	1	Zapoteco: Texmelucan*	PN.	.
7022	Tezoatlan Mixtec	0.00733	6,681	7,248	9,543	MIR37c	67-AFAC-n	tezoatlan-yucuñuti		70.00	5,074	1....	10	7	6	4	2	Mixteco: Tezoatlan*	Pn.	.
7023	Tila Chol	0.04437	40,441	43,874	57,768	MIR37b	68-ACAA-a	tila		93.00	40,802	1c...	10	8	11	5	2	Chol: Tila*	PNb	.
7024	Tilapa Otomi	0.00047	428	465	612	MIR37d	67-ABCA-h	tilapa		95.00	442	1c...	10	7	11	5	2		pn.	b
7025	Tipai	0.00023	210	227	299	MIR38a	63-VDCA-d	tipai		65.00	148	0....	10	6	6	4	2		p..	.
7026	Tlacoatzintepec Chinantec	0.00236	2,151	2,334	3,073	MIR37z	67-AEAB-c	tlacoatzintepec		90.00	2,100	1....	10	7	11	4	1	Chinanteco, Tlacoatzintepec	pn.	.
7027	Tlapanec	0.03592	32,739	35,518	46,766	MIR38a	67-ACAA	tlapanec cluster		93.00	33,032	4....	10	7	11	4	2		PN.	.
7028	Todos Santos Mam	0.01105	10,072	10,926	14,387	MIR37b	68-ADBA-b	mam-cuchumatan		90.00	9,834	1.s..	10	6	11	4	1	Mam: Todos Santos*	Pnb	.
7029	Tojolabal (Chanabal)	0.04259	38,819	42,114	55,451	MIR37b	68-ACBC-a	tojolabal		93.00	39,166	1....	10	7	11	4	1	Tojolabal	PN.	.
7030	Tumbala Chol	0.10205	93,014	100,908	132,865	MIR37b	68-ACAA-c	tumbalá		93.00	93,845	1A...	10	8	11	5	1	Chol: Tumbala*	PNB	.
7031	Tututepec Mixtec	0.00309	2,816	3,055	4,023	MIR37c	67-AFAF-j	tututepec-acatepec		90.00	2,750	0c...	10	7	11	5	2		pn.	.
7032	USA Black	0.01000	9,115	9,888	13,020	NFB68a	52-ABAE-a	talkin-black		90.00	8,899	0B.uh	10	9	10	5	1		pnb	b
7033	USA White	0.20000	182,291	197,763	260,392	CEW19s	52-ABAC-s	general american		79.00	156,232	1Bsuh	10	9	13	5	1	English*	PNB	b
7034	Usila Chinantec	0.01064	9,698	10,521	13,853	MIR37z	67-AEAA-c	usila		90.00	9,469	0a...	10	7	11	4	1	Chinanteco: Usila*	PN.	.
7035	Valle Nacional Chinantec	0.00177	1,613	1,750	2,304	MIR37z	67-AEAB-d	valle-nacional		90.00	1,575	1....	10	7	11	4	1		pn.	b
7036	Veracruz Huastec	0.05916	53,922	58,498	77,024	MIR37b	68-AAAA-b	east huastec		70.00	40,949	4....	10	6	6	4	2	Huasteco: Veracruz*	Pn.	.
7037	Veracruz Tepehua	0.00486	4,430	4,806	6,328	MIR37z	68-AAAA-b	east huastec		70.00	3,364	4....	10	7	6	4	1	Huasteco: Veracruz*	Pn.	.
7038	Villa Alta Zapotec	0.00600	5,469	5,933	7,812	MIR37f	67-AHBB-b	yatzachi		90.00	5,340	1c...	10	7	11	4	1	Zapoteco: Yatzachi*	PN.	.
7039	W Sola de Vega Zapotec	0.00277	2,525	2,739	3,606	MIR37f	67-AHBA-c	zaniza		92.00	2,520	0....	10	7	11	4	1		pn.	b
7040	West Highland Chatino	0.00863	7,866	8,533	11,236	MIR37f	67-AHAD-a	panixtlahuaca		91.00	7,765	0....	10	7	11	2	1	Chatino: West Highland*	PN.	.
7041	West Miahuatlan Zapotec	0.00382	3,482	3,777	4,973	MIR37f	67-AHBC-cc	tilquiapan		90.00	3,400	0a...	10	7	11	4	0		pn.	b

Continued opposite

Table 8-2 continued

EVANGELIZATION								EVANGELISM			ADDITIONAL DESCRIPTIVE DATA
Ref 1	D 28	aC 29	CG% 30	r 31	E 32	U 33	W 34	e 35	R 36	T 37	Locations, civil divisions, literacy, religions, church history, denominations, dioceses, church growth, missions, agencies, ministries, movements 38
6918	2	7	2.00	0	99.90	0.10	C	469.75	52	10	Eastern Oaxaca. Zapotecs. D=RCC,CON. M=SIL.
6919	1	8	3.11	0	99.90	0.10	C	476.32	73	10	Chiapas. Mayans. 99% in Guatemala. D=RCC. M=CAM.
6920	2	7	1.93	0	99.93	0.07	C	471.83	54	10	Northeastern Oaxaca State. Peasant agriculturalists. D=RCC,CGP. M=CEC,SIL.
6921	1	7	2.00	0	99.90	0.10	C	440.19	57	10	Puebla State. D=RCC. M=SIL,FMB.
6922	4	7	3.01	0	99.70	0.30	C	293.82	91	8	Chihuahua. Many converts to Baha'i World Faith 20%. D=RCC,MEM,IAFCJ,NBCM/CNBM. M=EMC,OM.
6923	1	6	2.04	0	36.00	64.00	A	6.57	216	4	Southern Chihuahua. 50% bilinguals in Spanish. D=RCC. In 1956 many RCs began traditionalist fertility cult rejecting christopaganism and Mexican culture.
6924	1	6	2.05	0	99.80	0.20	C	356.24	62	9	Oaxaca, Tlaxiaco District, Teposcolula District. D=RCC.
6925	2	7	2.00	0	99.90	0.10	C	446.76	56	10	In Puebla, Veracruz. 55% bilingual in Spanish. D=RCC,FIPC. M=SIL.
6926	1	7	2.62	0	99.90	0.10	C	446.76	67	10	In northwest Oaxaca. Mountains. Peasant agriculturalists. D=RCC. M=independents.
6927	2	9	1.90	0	99.95	0.05	C	502.78	49	10	Hidalgo. Otomis. D=UIEI,RCC.
6928	2	7	1.39	0	99.90	0.10	C	459.90	41	10	Southwest Oaxaca. Mixtecs. D=UIEI,RCC. M=SIL.
6929	1	7	2.77	0	99.93	0.07	C	465.04	71	10	Northern Oaxaca State. D=RCC. M=SIL.
6930	1	7	6.37	0	99.90	0.10	C	430.33	150	10	Southeastern Veracruz. D=RCC.
6931	4	8	0.54	0	99.95	0.05	C	495.85	25	10	Southern Guerrero. Aztecs. D=UIEI,UIEM,RCC,NBCM/CNBM. M=MIM.
6932	4	9	2.00	0	99.95	0.05	C	506.25	52	10	Veracruz. Aztecs. D=UIEI,UIEM,RCC,NBCM/CNBM. M=MIM.
6933	1	7	2.00	0	99.90	0.10	C	420.48	58	10	Oaxaca, Southeastern Miahuatlan. Many monolinguals. Zapotecs. D=RCC.
6934	1	7	3.11	0	99.90	0.10	C	410.62	86	10	Puebla State. Monolingual. D=RCC.
6935	1	7	1.84	0	99.90	0.10	C	413.91	60	10	Northern Baja California, south of Diegueno. D=RCC.
6936	1	7	1.97	0	99.93	0.07	C	461.65	56	10	In Palantla, Oaxaca. Agriculturalists. D=RCC. M=SIL.
6937	2	10	7.92	8	99.59	0.41	B	271.34	187	8	Muslims 35%. D=Greek Orthodox Ch(AD-N&S America),RCC(Latins, Melkites).
6938	1	6	2.00	0	99.93	0.07	C	468.44	56	10	Some in Mexico, but mainly in south central Arizona (USA). D=RCC.
6939	2	10	2.83	8	99.95	0.05	C	561.73	58	10	Large numbers of mixed-race(Amerindian/Spanish) persons, in urban areas. D=RCC,UIEI. T=CBN. R=AWR. T=TBN,LESEA.
6940	2	9	2.24	0	99.80	0.20	C	362.08	67	9	Northeastern Puebla State. D=RCC,Pentecostal Chs.
6941	1	6	2.00	0	99.93	0.07	C	448.07	58	10	Central Sonora-Chihuahua border. D=RCC. M=NTM.
6942	1	7	1.77	0	99.70	0.30	C	273.38	66	8	Puebla State. Close to Huehuetla Tepehua. Limited bilingualism. Animists 25%.D=RCC.
6943	1	7	2.00	0	99.65	0.35	C	241.99	75	8	Northeastern Oaxaca. D=RCC. M=MBS.
6944	1	7	4.09	0	99.70	0.30	C	273.38	125	8	Chiapas. Peasant agriculturalists. Mostly monolinguals. D=RCC.
6945	1	10	6.50	7	99.81	0.19	C	458.25	115	10	Refugees from USSR. D=Orthodox Catholic Ch(under OCA-USA).
6946	1	8	2.00	0	99.80	0.20	C	350.40	62	9	Oaxaca, Yautepec. Close to Eastern Miahuatlan. D=RCC.
6947	1	7	2.38	0	99.85	0.15	C	394.01	66	9	Oaxaca, southeastern Miahuatlan. 3 towns. Mountains. D=RCC.
6948	1	7	1.21	0	99.90	0.10	C	446.76	40	10	Coastal Oaxaca State. Fishermen. 12% Huave speakers, 88% nonspeakers. D=RCC.
6949	1	8	1.99	0	99.90	0.10	C	450.04	54	10	Oaxaca. Mountains. Peasant agriculturalists. D=RCC.
6950	0	7	1.34	0	99.85	0.15	C	394.01	44	9	Oaxaca State. Agriculturalists. Some bilingual in Spanish.
6951	1	7	2.02	0	99.90	0.10	C	450.04	54	10	Oaxaca. Zapotecs. Bilingual in Spanish. D=RCC.
6952	2	8	2.00	0	99.75	0.25	C	323.02	63	9	Oaxaca. Sedentary pastoralists. D=Mennonite Chs,RCC.
6953	1	8	2.00	0	99.90	0.10	C	446.76	54	10	Oaxaca, on Pan American highway. Pastoralists. D=RCC. Peasants.
6954	1	7	5.62	0	99.75	0.25	C	320.28	148	9	Central Oaxaca. Distant from surrounding Zapotecs. D=RCC.
6955	1	7	2.00	0	99.70	0.30	C	283.60	67	8	Oaxaca. Language dying out, replaced by Spanish. D=RCC.
6956	1	7	2.00	0	99.90	0.10	C	453.33	54	10	Western Oaxaca Valley. Zapotecs. Bilingual in Spanish. D=RCC.
6957	2	8	2.00	0	99.90	0.10	C	450.04	54	10	West central Oaxaca. Mixtecs. D=UIEI,RCC. M=SIL.
6958	1	7	2.00	0	99.92	0.08	C	470.12	53	10	Oaxaca. Peasant agriculturalists. Zapotecs. D=RCC. M=SIL.
6959	2	7	1.05	0	99.90	0.10	C	456.61	34	10	Eastern Oaxaca. Zapotecs. Bilingual in Spanish. D=RCC,IAFCJ.
6960	1	7	1.29	0	99.80	0.20	C	344.56	46	9	Central Oaxaca, Zimatlan District. D=RCC.
6961	3	7	2.00	0	99.90	0.10	C	446.76	54	10	Oaxaca State. Mixtecs. D=UIEI,MCGC,RCC. M=SIL.
6962	3	6	2.04	0	99.93	0.07	C	492.20	53	10	West Central Chiapas. Mayans. Forests, mountains, plains. Agriculturalists. D=92% RCC,1% Protestants,IAFCJ. M=FMB,SIL.
6963	2	8	1.87	0	99.90	0.10	C	450.04	51	10	Oaxaca. Huitepec Mixtecs. D=UIEI,RCC.
6964	1	7	1.09	0	99.85	0.15	C	400.22	38	10	Oaxaca State. Bilinguals in Spanish numerous, though all prefer Mixtec. D=RCC.
6965	2	7	1.67	0	99.93	0.07	C	478.62	48	10	Oaxaca, Puebla States. D=RCC,NBCM/CNBM. M=FMB,SIL.
6966	3	7	2.48	0	99.91	0.09	C	461.68	63	10	Oaxaca. Mixtecs. D=RCC,UIEI,MCGC. M=SIL.
6967	2	7	1.52	0	99.90	0.10	C	459.90	45	10	Oaxaca State. D=RCC,NBCM/CNBM. M=SIL.
6968	2	8	2.14	0	99.93	0.07	C	485.41	56	10	In San Luis Potosi. Mayans. Agriculturalists. D=RCC(D-Ciudad Valles),ARPC. M=SIL,UFM,FMB.
6969	1	7	3.19	0	99.90	0.10	C	450.04	79	10	Chiapas State. Mayans. Bilingual in Spanish. D=RCC.
6970	4	7	1.84	0	99.90	0.10	C	453.33	52	10	Oaxaca. D=Baptists,Nazarenes,Pentecostals,RCC. M=SIL.
6971	2	8	2.68	0	99.90	0.10	C	459.90	66	10	West central Oaxaca. Mixtecs. D=RCC,UIEI. M=SIL.
6972	2	7	1.85	0	99.93	0.07	C	488.80	50	10	Oaxaca State. D=RCC,NBCM/CNBM.
6973	1	8	2.33	0	99.92	0.08	C	456.68	61	10	Oaxaca State. Mixtecs. D=RCC. M=independent missionaries,SIL.
6974	1	7	2.94	0	99.70	0.30	C	281.05	91	8	Oaxaca, southeastern Miahuatlan. 4 towns. Monolingual. D=RCC.
6975	0	7	1.82	0	99.85	0.15	C	390.91	55	9	Oaxaca, southeastern Miahuatlan. 4 towns. Coffee-growing. Zapotecs.
6976	2	7	0.63	0	99.90	0.10	C	456.61	26	10	Oaxaca. Mixtecs. D=RCC,UIEI. M=SIL.
6977	1	7	2.00	0	99.90	0.10	C	443.47	55	10	Central Oaxaca. Zapotecs. Agriculturalists. D=RCC.
6978	1	7	1.43	0	99.91	0.09	C	458.36	44	10	Coastal Veracruz. Mostly bilingual in Spanish. D=RCC. M=SIL.
6979	1	7	2.18	0	99.70	0.30	C	273.38	79	8	Coast of Sonora State. Fishermen. Many converts to Baha'i 15%. D=RCC. M=SIL.
6980	2	9	1.91	0	99.95	0.05	C	506.25	49	10	Hidalgo. Otomis. Almost all monolinguals. D=UIEI,RCC. M=SIL.
6981	3	9	2.00	0	99.95	0.05	C	509.72	51	10	Northeast Puebla. Aztecs. Pastoralists. D=UIEI,RCC,NBCM/CNBM. M=MIM,WMPL.
6982	2	8	1.91	0	99.90	0.10	C	453.33	52	10	Oaxaca. Mixtecs. D=RCC,UIEI. M=SIL.
6983	1	7	2.00	0	99.90	0.10	C	440.19	57	10	North Oaxaca. Agriculturalists. D=RCC. M=SIL.
6984	1	7	0.18	0	99.90	0.10	C	443.47	18	10	Western Oaxaca. Zapotecs. Bilinguals in Spanish. D=RCC.
6985	1	7	1.61	0	99.90	0.10	C	450.04	46	10	Northern Oaxaca, Yavesia. Zapotecs. Bilinguals in Spanish. D=RCC.
6986	3	8	0.97	0	99.91	0.09	C	471.65	32	10	Oaxaca. Mixtecs. D=UIEI,RCC,Presbyterian Ch.
6987	1	7	2.00	0	99.93	0.07	C	492.20	51	10	Northern Oaxaca. 4 towns. Zapotecs. Craftsmen, merchants. D=RCC. M=SIL,UIM.
6988	1	7	2.00	0	99.85	0.15	C	397.12	59	9	In southeast Puebla, Chilac, San Sebastian Zinacatepec. Intensive agriculturalists. 40% bilinguals in Spanish. D=RCC. M=WMPL,SIL.
6989	1	7	2.05	0	99.80	0.20	C	356.24	62	9	Santo Domingo Nuxaa Mixtecs. Oaxaca, Nochixtlan District. Agriculturalists. D=RCC.
6990	2	9	3.23	0	99.95	0.05	C	499.32	75	10	Tlaxcala. Otomis. D=UIEI,RCC.
6991	1	7	2.38	0	99.70	0.30	C	268.27	83	8	Southern Durango. Pastoralists. Animists 25%. D=RCC. M=SIL.
6992	2	7	2.00	0	99.90	0.10	C	453.33	56	10	East central Oaxaca State. Agriculturalists. D=RCC,CGP. M=CEC,SIL,MBS.
6993	2	7	2.20	0	99.90	0.10	C	450.04	58	10	Oaxaca, 90 km south of Oaxaca City. Zapotecs. D=RCC,Baptist Ch.
6994	1	7	2.38	0	99.92	0.08	C	453.33	65	10	Puebla State. Close to Eastern Popoloca. D=RCC.
6995	3	8	1.01	0	99.93	0.07	C	485.41	33	10	Puebla State. Mixtecs. Children and youth monolingual in Spanish. D=RCC,UIEI,NBCM/CNBM. M=SIL.
6996	2	8	2.72	0	99.90	0.10	C	450.04	68	10	Oaxaca. Mixtecs. D=RCC,UIEI.
6997	1	7	2.26	0	99.80	0.20	C	356.24	66	9	Oaxaca. Some bilinguals in Spanish. D=RCC. M=SIL.
6998	3	7	2.02	0	99.90	0.10	C	443.47	57	10	Chihuahua State. D=RCC,IAFCJ,NBCM/CNBM. M=OM.
6999	2	8	1.72	0	99.90	0.10	C	450.04	48	10	Oaxaca. Mixtecs. D=RCC,UIEI.
7000	1	7	2.09	0	99.70	0.30	C	268.27	75	8	Southwest Durango. Traditional religion still strong: animists 30%. D=RCC.
7001	2	10	2.70	8	99.93	0.07	C	560.09	60	10	Includes refugees from 1936 Spanish Civil War. D=RCC,Iglesia Cristiana Unida. M=FMB,UBS,&c.
7002	2	9	2.20	0	99.95	0.05	C	485.45	57	10	Otomis. D=UIEI,RCC. M=SIL.
7003	2	10	8.25	8	99.49	0.51	B	205.67	213	8	Immigrants from Syria. Muslims 40%. D=Syrian Orthodox Ch,RCC.
7004	4	9	2.00	0	99.95	0.05	C	513.19	51	10	State of Tabasco; Cupilco, Tecominoacan towns. Aztecs. D=UIEI,NBCM/CNBM,UIEM,RCC. M=MIM. Nearly extinct.
7005	2	7	2.49	0	99.90	0.10	C	446.76	66	10	North central Tabasco. Mayans. D=RCC,NBCM/CNBM. M=SIL.
7006	1	7	2.00	0	99.90	0.10	C	446.76	56	10	Ayapa in Tabasco. Close to Popoluca. Bilingual in Spanish. D=RCC. M=SIL.
7007	1	7	2.10	0	99.91	0.09	C	458.36	57	10	Chiapas. Mayans. Also in Guatemala. D=RCC.
7008	4	9	2.00	0	99.95	0.05	C	527.06	50	10	San Luis Potosi, Hidalgo. Western Huasteca Aztecs. D=UIEI,NBCM/CNBM,UIEM,RCC. M=MIM,UFM,GR,SIL.
7009	3	7	2.48	0	99.93	0.07	C	478.62	64	10	Michoacan State. D=RCC,UIEI/IPCCM,FIPC. M=SIL.
7010	1	7	2.32	0	99.90	0.10	C	436.90	62	10	Southeast Oaxaca. Agriculturalists. Zapotecs. D=RCC. M=SIL.
7011	1	7	3.65	0	99.90	0.10	C	459.90	87	10	Chiapas, also in Guatemala. Mayans. Bilingual in Spanish. D=RCC.
7012	1	7	2.13	0	99.70	0.30	C	293.82	67	8	Central Otomis. Forest, mountains. Peasant agriculturalists, city laborers. D=RCC. M=SIL.
7013	2	8	2.07	0	99.95	0.05	C	499.32	53	10	Otomis. D=UIEI,RCC. M=SIL.
7014	1	7	2.00	0	99.70	0.30	C	278.49	68	8	Central Oaxaca. Closest to San Juan Guelavia. D=RCC.
7015	1	7	3.08	0	99.90	0.10	C	440.19	79	10	North Oaxaca. D=RCC. M=SIL.
7016	2	7	1.77	0	99.90	0.10	C	459.90	48	10	Northwest Oaxaca. Mixtecs. Mostly bilingual in Spanish. D=UIEI,RCC. M=SIL.
7017	1	7	3.16	0	99.91	0.09	C	455.04	79	10	Oaxaca. Agriculturalists. D=RCC.
7018	4	9	2.00	0	99.95	0.05	C	527.06	50	10	Morelos State. Aztecs. Most are bilingual in Spanish. D=UIEI,UIEM,RCC,NBCM/CNBM. M=MIM,SIL.
7019	2	7	2.00	0	99.90	0.10	C	459.90	53	10	Oaxaca. Mixtecs. Bilingual in Spanish. D=UIEI,RCC. M=SIL.
7020	1	7	4.09	0	99.90	0.10	C	450.04	98	10	Southeastern Veracruz. Bilingual in Spanish. D=RCC.
7021	1	7	2.11	0	99.92	0.08	C	453.33	57	10	Western Oaxaca. Zapotecs. 95% monolinguals. D=RCC. M=SIL.
7022	2	7	2.09	0	99.70	0.30	C	281.05	69	8	Oaxaca. Some bilinguals, many monolinguals. D=Ch of the Nazarene,RCC.
7023	5	7	1.96	0	99.93	0.07	C	495.59	51	10	Chiapas State. Mayans. D=SDA,RCC,CGP,NBCM/CNBM,Independents. M=WBT/SIL,CBFMS.
7024	2	9	2.87	0	99.95	0.05	C	506.25	67	10	One town in State of Mexico. Otomis. Nearly extinct. D=UIEI,RCC.
7025	2	7	2.02	0	99.65	0.35	C	239.62	79	8	Baja California. Animists 15%. D=Pentecostal Chs,RCC.
7026	3	7	2.58	0	99.90	0.10	C	443.47	69	10	Oaxaca. Agriculturalists. D=RCC,Pentecostals,Baptists. M=SIL.
7027	1	7	1.46	0	99.93	0.07	C	482.01	46	10	Guerrero. D=RCC. M=SIL,independent missionaries.
7028	1	7	2.00	0	99.90	0.10	C	450.04	55	10	Most live in Guatemala. Peasants. D=RCC.
7029	1	7	3.01	0	99.93	0.07	C	468.44	75	10	Chiapas. Mayans. D=RCC. M=SIL.
7030	5	8	2.40	0	99.93	0.07	C	519.35	57	10	Chiapas State. Mayans. D=RCC,National Presbyterian Ch of Mexico,CGP,NBCM/CNBM,SDA. M=WBT/SIL.
7031	2	8	2.00	0	99.90	0.10	C	450.04	54	10	Oaxtaca. Mixtecs. D=UIEI,RCC.
7032	1	10	2.00	8	99.90	0.10	C	499.32	47	10	African-Americans from USA, in business, commerce. D=RCC.
7033	3	10	2.64	8	99.79	0.21	C	441.17	63	10	Expatriates from USA, in commerce, education, government. D=SBC,UMC,RCC. M=FMB.
7034	1	7	2.33	0	99.90	0.10	C	450.04	63	10	San Felipe, Oaxaca. Peasant agriculturalists. D=RCC. M=SIL.
7035	1	7	0.96	0	99.90	0.10	C	446.76	35	10	North Oaxaca. Closest to Chiltepec. Bilingual in Spanish. D=RCC.
7036	1	7	2.20	0	99.70	0.30	C	288.71	72	8	Northern Veracruz. Peasant agriculturalists. Animists 15%. D=RCC. M=FMB,SIL.
7037	1	7	2.00	0	99.70	0.30	C	283.60	69	8	Veracruz. Agriculturalists. Animists 25%. D=RCC. M=SIL.
7038	2	7	2.46	0	99.90	0.10	C	446.76	64	10	North central Oaxaca; also in Los Angeles, California (USA). Zapotecs. D=RCC,Presbyterian Ch. M=SIL.
7039	1	7	2.00	0	99.92	0.08	C	460.04	54	10	Western Oaxaca. Zapotecs. 40% use the language daily. Bilingual in Spanish. D=RCC.
7040	1	7	1.65	0	99.91	0.09	C	438.43	49	10	Southeast Oaxaca. Zapotecs. D=RCC. M=SIL.
7041	0	7	2.00	0	99.90	0.10	C	450.04	54	10	Southern Oaxaca near Chatino region. Bilinguals in Spanish. Zapotecs.

Continued overleaf

Table 8-2 continued

PEOPLE		POPULATION				IDENTITY CODE		LANGUAGE		CHURCH		MINISTRY						SCRIPTURE		
Ref 1	Ethnic name 2	P% 3	In 1995 4	In 2000 5	In 2025 6	Race 7	Language 8	Autoglossonym 9	S 10	AC 11	Members 12	Jayuh 13-17	d 18	wa 19	xc 20	mc 21	mi 22	Biblioglossonym 23	Pub 24-26	ss 27
7042	Western Ejutla Zapotec	0.00417	3,801	4,123	5,429	MIR37f	67-AHBC-d	ayoquesco		70.00	2,886	0c...	10	6	7	4	1		pn.	b
7043	Western Ixtlan Zapoteco	0.00833	7,592	8,237	10,845	MIR37f	67-AHBB-dm	aloapam		93.00	7,660	1c...	10	7	11	4	1	Zapoteco: Aloapam*	Pn.	.
7044	Western Jacaltec	0.01216	11,083	12,024	15,832	MIR37b	68-ADAB	jacaltec cluster		80.00	9,619	1....	10	7	8	4	1	Jacalteco	PN.	b
7045	Western Mixe	0.00553	5,040	5,468	7,200	MIR37z	69-FAAA-b	mixe-tlahuitoltepec		93.00	5,085	0....	10	7	11	5	2	Mixe: Tlahuitoltepec*	PN.	.
7046	Western Ocotlan Zapotec	0.01666	15,185	16,474	21,691	MIR37f	67-AHBC-c	ocotlán		93.00	15,320	0a...	10	7	11	5	1	Zapoteco: Ocotlan*	PN.	b
7047	Western Popoloca	0.00667	6,079	6,595	8,684	MIR37z	67-ADAA-a	west popoloc		90.00	5,936	1....	10	7	11	5	2	Popoloca: Western*	Pn.	b
7048	Western Tarahumara	0.01774	16,169	17,542	23,097	MIR37z	66-BEBA-b	rocoroibo		70.00	12,279	1....	10	9	7	5	3	Tarahumara: Western*	Pn.	.
7049	Western Tlacolula Zapotec	0.04167	37,980	41,204	54,253	MIR37f	67-AHBD-dd	san-baltazar-guelavia		93.00	38,320	1a...	10	7	11	4	1	Zapoteco: Guelavia*	PN.	b
7050	Western Yautepec Zapotec	0.00354	3,227	3,500	4,609	MIR37f	67-AHBD-ea	quiegolani		70.00	2,450	1c...	10	7	6	4	1		pn.	.
7051	Western Zimatlan Zapotec	0.00119	1,085	1,177	1,549	MIR37f	67-AHBC-ba	totomachapan		90.00	1,059	0c...	10	7	11	4	1		pn.	.
7052	Xadani Zapotec	0.01000	9,115	9,888	13,020	MIR37f	67-AHBF-f	xadani		90.00	8,899	1....	10	7	11	4	1		...	b
7053	Yaitepec Chatino	0.00272	2,479	2,690	3,541	MIR37f	67-AHAD-b	yaitepec		91.00	2,448	0....	10	8	11	5	1	Chatino: Yaitepec*	Pn.	b
7054	Yalalag Zapotec	0.00591	5,387	5,844	7,695	MIR37f	67-AHBB-g	yalalag		90.00	5,259	1c...	10	7	11	4	1	Zapoteco: Yalalag*	Pn.	b
7055	Yaqui	0.01777	16,197	17,571	23,136	MIR37z	66-BEDA-a	yaqui		90.00	15,814	1....	10	7	11	4	1	Yaqui	PN.	b
7056	Yecuatla Totonac	0.00054	492	534	703	MIR37z	69-BAAA-i	totonac-yecuatla		90.00	481	0....	10	7	11	4	1		pn.	b
7057	Yucatec (Maya)	0.82829	754,947	819,024	1,078,402	MIR37b	68-ABAA-a	yucatec-maya		95.00	778,073	2c...	10	8	12	5	1	Maya	PNB	n
7058	Zacatepec Chatino	0.00118	1,076	1,167	1,536	MIR37f	67-AHAC-c	san-marcos-zacatepec		90.00	1,050	0....	10	7	11	4	1	Chatino, Zacatepec	...	.
7059	Zinacanteco Tzotzil	0.02958	26,961	29,249	38,512	MIR37b	68-ACBB	tzotzil cluster		93.00	27,202	1A...	10	8	11	5	1	Tzotzil: Huixtan*	PN.	.
7060	other minor peoples	0.30389	276,981	300,490	395,653	...				69.00	207,338		10	7	6	5	0			
	Micronesia	**100.00000**	**107,239**	**118,689**	**189,609**					**91.55**	**108,661**									
7061	Carolinian	2.80000	3,003	3,323	5,309	MPY54z	31-UAAA-a	saipan		95.00	3,157	1.s..	10	8	13	5	1		p..	b
7062	Chamorro	1.00000	1,072	1,187	1,896	MSY44d	31-UAAA-d	guam-chamorro		93.00	1,104	1.s..	10	9	12	5	1	Chamorro	P..	b
7063	Han Chinese	0.50000	536	593	948	MSY42a	79-AAAB-ba	kuo-yü		40.00	237	2Bsuh	9	5	12	5	1	Chinese: Kuoyu*	PNB	b
7064	Japanese	0.80000	858	950	1,517	MSY45a	45-CAAA-a	koku-go		5.00	47	1B.uh	7	4	3	5	2	Japanese	PNB	b
7065	Kapingamarangian	2.41000	2,584	2,860	4,570	MPY55z	39-CABA-a	kapingamarangi		92.00	2,632	0....	10	7	11	5	1		...	.
7066	Kosraen (Kusaie)	5.20000	5,576	6,172	9,860	MPY54z	38-BAAA	kusaie cluster		96.00	5,925	0....	10	9	13	5	2	Kusaien*	PNB	b
7067	Mokilese	1.17000	1,255	1,389	2,218	MPY54d	38-AACB-a	mokil		91.00	1,264	0....	10	7	11	4	2		...	n
7068	Mortlockese	5.60000	6,005	6,647	10,618	MPY54z	38-AABI	mortlock cluster		97.00	6,447	0....	10	7	12	5	1	Mortlock*	PN.	.
7069	Namonuito	0.89000	954	1,056	1,688	MPY54e	38-AABF-a	namonuito		90.00	951	0....	10	7	11	4	1		...	.
7070	Ngatik	0.56000	601	665	1,062	MPY54d	38-AACA-c	ngatik		90.00	598	0....	10	7	11	4	1		pnb	n
7071	Nukoro (Nukuoro)	0.61000	654	724	1,157	MPY55z	39-CAAA-a	nukuoro		90.00	652	0.s..	10	7	11	5	2	Nukuoro	PN.	n
7072	Paafang	1.25000	1,340	1,484	2,370	MPY54e	38-AABG-a	paafang		92.00	1,365	0....	10	7	11	4	2		...	.
7073	Pingilapese (Pingelap)	1.44000	1,544	1,709	2,730	MPY54d	38-AACC-a	pingelap		91.00	1,555	0....	10	7	11	4	2		...	.
7074	Ponapean	24.90000	26,703	29,554	47,213	MPY54d	38-AACA	ponape cluster		96.30	28,460	0....	10	7	13	5	2	Pohnpeian*	PNB	n
7075	Puluwat	1.29000	1,383	1,531	2,446	MPY54e	38-AABE-a	puluwat		92.00	1,409	0....	10	7	11	4	2		...	.
7076	Satawalese	0.46000	493	546	872	MPY54e	38-AABD-a	satawal		90.00	491	0....	10	7	11	4	1		...	.
7077	Trukese	28.03000	30,059	33,269	53,147	MPY54e	38-AABH-b	vehicular truk		95.50	31,771	1.s..	10	9	14	5	3	Trukese*	PNB	b
7078	USA White	4.50000	4,826	5,341	8,532	CEW19s	52-ABAC-s	general american		78.00	4,166	1Bsuh	10	9	13	5	3	English*	PNB	b
7079	Ulithian	3.30000	3,539	3,917	6,257	MPY54f	38-AABB-a	ulithi		97.00	3,799	0.s..	10	9	13	5	1	Ulithian	PN.	b
7080	Woleaian (Wolean)	1.62000	1,737	1,923	3,072	MPY54z	38-AABC-a	woleai		97.00	1,865	0....	10	9	11	5	1		...	b
7081	Yapese	10.60000	11,367	12,581	20,099	MPY54g	31-TAAA-a	yap		77.50	9,750	0.s..	10	9	7	5	0	Yapese	PN.	.
7082	other minor peoples	1.07000	1,147	1,270	2,029	...				80.00	1,016		10	7	7	5	0			
	Moldavia	**100.00000**	**4,375,750**	**4,380,492**	**4,546,842**					**63.89**	**2,798,560**									
7083	Armenian	0.06627	2,900	2,903	3,013	CEW14	57-AAAA-b	ashkharik		88.00	2,555	4A.u.	10	7	12	2	2	Armenian: Modern, Eastern	PNB	b
7084	Azerbaijani	0.06094	2,667	2,669	2,771	MSY41a	44-AABA-fa	north azeri		0.00	0	2c.u.	0	3	3	0	1	Azerbaijani*	PNB	b
7085	Balkan Gypsy	2.30700	100,949	101,058	104,896	CNN25f	59-ACBA-ba	ursari		10.00	10,106	1c...	8	4	6	0	1	Romani, Balkan	Pn.	.
7086	Bashkir	0.01407	616	616	640	MSY41b	44-AABB-g	bashqurt		7.00	43	1A.u.	7	5	7	0	1	Bashkir	Pn.	b
7087	Bulgarian	8.16000	357,061	357,448	371,022	CEW22b	53-AAAH-b	bulgarski		72.00	257,363	2A.uh	10	6	8	1	1	Bulgarian	PNB	b
7088	Byelorussian	0.45228	19,791	19,812	20,564	CEW22c	53-AAAE-c	bielorusskiy		60.00	11,887	3A.uh	10	7	8	2	3	Byelorussian*	PNB	b
7089	Chuvash	0.02777	1,215	1,216	1,263	MSY41c	44-AAAA-a	chuvash		35.00	426	2....	9	6	8	0	1	Chuvash	PN.	b
7090	Crimean Turk	0.04200	1,838	1,840	1,910	MSY41h	44-AABA-c	crimea-tatar		0.10	2	1c.u.	5	4	7	0	0	Crimean Tatar*	PNb	b
7091	Czech	0.01363	596	597	620	CEW22e	53-AAAD-a	czesky		77.00	460	2Asuh	10	8	8	2	1	Czech	PNB	b
7092	Gagauzi Turk	4.20000	183,782	183,981	190,967	MSY41d	44-AABA-b	gagauzi		72.20	132,834	1c.u.	10	7	8	1	1	Gagauz	Pnb	b
7093	Georgian	0.02542	1,112	1,114	1,156	CEW17c	42-CABB-a	kharthuli		40.00	445	2A.u.	9	6	8	2	1	Georgian	PNB	b
7094	German	0.16919	7,403	7,411	7,693	CEW19m	52-ABCE-a	standard hoch-deutsch		79.00	5,855	2B.uh	10	8	13	3	2	German*	PNB	b
7095	Greek (Romei, Urum)	0.01386	606	607	630	CEW20	56-AAAA-c	dhimotiki		90.00	546	2B.uh	10	8	11	2	2	Greek: Modern	PNB	b
7096	Jat Gypsy (Jati, Jatu)	3.86650	169,188	169,372	175,804	CNN25h	12-AACJ-a	jakati		1.00	1,694	0....	6	1	3	0	0		...	.
7097	Jewish	1.58858	69,512	69,588	72,230	CMT35	52-ABCH	yiddish cluster		0.00	0	0B..h	0	3	6	0	0		PNB	b
7098	Kazakh	0.02556	1,118	1,120	1,162	MSY41e	44-AABC-c	kazakh		0.00	0	4A.u.	0	3	3	0	1	Kazakh	PN.	b
7099	Latvian (Lett)	0.01089	477	477	495	CEW15a	54-AABA-a	standard latviashu		91.00	434	3A.u.	10	8	11	2	3	Latvian	PNB	b
7100	Lithuanian	0.02184	956	957	993	CEW15b	54-AAAA-a	standard lietuvishkai		90.00	861	3A.u.	10	8	12	2	3	Lithuanian	PNB	b
7101	Moldavian	48.20924	2,109,516	2,111,802	2,191,998	CEW21f	51-AADC-ab	standard moldavia		69.00	1,457,143	1A.u.	10	7	10	2	1		pnb	b
7102	Mordvinian	0.02510	1,098	1,100	1,141	MSW51i	41-AADA-b	moksha		65.00	715	1....	10	8	8	2	1	Mordvin: Moksha*	Pn.	b
7103	Ossete	0.00930	407	407	423	CNT24e	58-ABBA	oseti cluster		36.00	147	2....	9	5	8	1	1	Ossete*	PN.	b
7104	Polish	0.10931	4,783	4,788	4,970	CEW22i	53-AAAC-c	polski		89.00	4,262	2A.uh	10	8	11	2	3	Polish	PNB	b
7105	Romanian	3.22500	141,118	141,271	146,636	CEW21i	51-AADC-a	limba româneasca		80.00	113,017	3A.u.	10	8	10	3	3	Romanian	PNB	b
7106	Rumelian Turk	0.30000	13,127	13,141	13,641	MSY41j	44-AABA-a	osmanli		0.04	5	1A.u.	3	2	2	0	0	Turkish	PNB	b
7107	Russian	12.92276	565,468	566,080	587,577	CEW22j	53-AAAE-d	russkiy	84	60.00	339,648	4B.uh	10	8	9	3	3	Russian	PNB	b
7108	Tajik	0.01366	598	598	621	CNT24g	58-AACC-j	tajiki		0.00	0	2asu.	0	3	3	0	1	Tajik*	PNB	b
7109	Tatar	0.07824	3,424	3,427	3,557	MSY41h	44-AABB-e	tatar		1.50	51	2c.u.	6	4	8	0	1	Tatar: Kazan	Pn.	b
7110	Udmurt	0.01534	671	672	697	MSW51k	41-AAEA-c	udmurt		55.00	370	2....	10	5	8	2	1	Udmurt	Pn.	.
7111	Ukrainian	13.84812	605,959	606,616	629,652	CEW22p	53-AAAE-b	ukrainskiy		75.00	454,962	3A.uh	10	7	10	3	3	Ukrainian	PNB	b
7112	Uzbek	0.03200	1,400	1,402	1,455	MSY41l	44-AABD-a	central uzbek		0.00	0	1A.u.	0	3	6	1	3	Uzbek*	PNb	b
7113	Vlach Gypsy (Rusurja)	0.04613	2,019	2,021	2,097	CNN25f	59-ACBA-a	vlach-romani		70.00	1,415	1a...	10	5	7	0	1	Romani: Finnish*	PN.	b
7114	other minor peoples	0.10000	4,376	4,380	4,547	...				30.00	1,314		9	5	8	1	0			
	Monaco	**100.00000**	**31,813**	**33,597**	**40,692**					**92.57**	**31,100**									
7115	Arab	0.60000	191	202	244	CMT30	12-AACA	standard arabic cluster		21.00	42	0.su.	9	7	8	0	0		...	.
7116	British	4.50000	1,432	1,512	1,831	CEW19i	52-ABAC-b	standard-english		79.00	1,194	3Bsuh	10	9	13	5	1		PNB	b
7117	Fleming	0.80000	255	269	326	CEW19k	52-ABCA-g	oostvlaandersch		91.00	245	1Bsuh	10	8	15	5	1		pnb	b
7118	French	45.80000	14,570	15,387	18,637	CEW21b	51-AABI-d	general français		96.50	14,849	1B.uh	10	9	14	5	3	French	PNB	b
7119	German	1.90000	604	638	773	CEW19m	52-ABCE-a	standard hoch-deutsch		87.00	555	2B.uh	10	9	10	0	0	German*	PNB	b
7120	Greek	0.70000	223	235	285	CEW20	56-AAAA-c	dhimotiki		95.00	223	2B.uh	10	9	11	4	1	Greek: Modern	PNB	b
7121	Jewish	1.70000	541	571	692	CMT35	51-AABI-d	general français		0.20	1	1B.uh	5	4	3	5	0	French	PNB	b
7122	Ligurian (Genoan)	17.20000	5,472	5,779	6,999	CEW21e	51-AABO-h	ligure		97.00	5,605	0c...	10	8	14	5	1	Ligurian	Pn.	b
7123	Monegasque (Provencal)	16.90000	5,376	5,678	6,877	CEW21b	51-AABO-ha	monegasc		98.60	5,598	0c...	10	10	15	5	3		pn.	b
7124	Portuguese	1.70000	541	571	692	CEW21g	51-AABA-e	general português		94.00	537	2Bsuh	10	9	12	0	0	Portuguese	PNB	b
7125	Russian	0.90000	286	302	366	CEW22j	53-AAAE-d	russkiy		70.00	212	4B.uh	10	8	11	4	1	Russian	PNB	b
7126	Spaniard	0.80000	255	269	326	CEW21k	51-AABB-c	general español		96.00	258	2B.uh	10	9	15	5	1	Spanish	PNB	b
7127	USA White	3.00000	954	1,008	1,221	CEW19s	52-ABAC-s	general american		84.00	847	1Bsuh	10	9	13	5	1	English*	PNB	b
7128	Walloon	1.50000	477	504	610	CEW21l	51-AABH-f	wallon		92.00	464	0A.uh	10	8	15	5	1	French: Walloon	P..	b
7129	other minor peoples	2.00000	636	672	814	...				70.00	470		10	7	8	5	0			
	Mongolia	**100.00000**	**2,451,434**	**2,662,020**	**3,708,989**					**1.25**	**33,392**									
7130	Bayad (Bait, Bayit)	2.10000	51,480	55,902	77,889	MSY41y	44-BAAB-cc	bayit		0.05	28	1c..h	4	2	0	0	0		pnb	b
7131	British	0.00500	123	133	185	CEW19i	52-ABAC-b	standard-english		79.00	105	3Bsuh	10	9	13	3	1		PNB	b
7132	Dariganga	1.70000	41,674	45,254	63,053	MSY41f	44-BAAB-ch	dariganga		0.03	14	1c..h	3	3	0	0	0		pnb	b
7133	Darkhan	0.52900	12,968	14,082	19,621	MSY41y	44-BAAB-e	oyrat		0.00	0	1a..h	0	2	0	1	0	Mongolian: Inner*	PNb	b
7134	Durbet (Dorwot)	2.90000	71,092	77,199	107,561	MSY41f	44-BAAB-cd	dorbet		0.03	23	1c..h	3	2	1	0	0		pnb	b
7135	Dzakhchin (Zahchin)	1.30100	31,893	34,633	48,254	MSY41y	44-BAAB-ce	dzakhachin		0.05	17	1c..h	4	2	0	0	0		pnb	b
7136	Evenki (Tungus, Solon)	0.11300	2,770	3,008	4,191	MSY41i	44-CAAB-a	evenki		1.00	30	0....	6	4	2	1	0	Evenki	P..	b
7137	Han Chinese (Mandarin)	1.50000	36,772	39,930	55,635	MSY42a	79-AAAB-ba	kuo-yü		0.10	40	2Bsuh	5	4	2	3	1	Chinese: Kuoyu*	PNB	b
7138	Kazakh (Qazaq)	5.44000	133,358	144,814	201,769	MSY41e	44-AABC-c	kazakh		0.01	14	4A.u.	3	4	2	3	1	Kazakh	PN.	b
7139	Khalkha Mongol	63.54100	1,557,666	1,691,474	2,356,729	MSY41f	44-BAAB-c	halh		1.30	21,989	3A..h	6	4	3	3	3	Mongolian: Khalka*	PNb	b
7140	Khoton (Hui, Dungan)	0.11300	2,770	3,008	4,191	MSY41y	79-AAAB-l	hui-zu		0.00	0	1Asuh	0	3	0	0	0		pnb	b
7141	Mingat	0.27600	6,766	7,347	10,237	MSY41y	44-BAAB-cf	mingat		0.10	7	1c..h	5	3	0	0	0		pnb	b
7142	Northern Mongolian	2.69000	65,944	71,608	99,772	MSY41y	44-BAAB-b	buryat		1.00	716	3A..h	6	4	0	1	2	Buryat*	PNB	b
7143	Russian	1.00000	24,514	26,620	37,090	CEW22j	53-AAAE-d	russkiy		19.00	5,058	4B.uh	8	7	11	3	1	Russian	PNB	b
7144	Southeastern Mongolian	5.00000	122,572	133,101	185,449	MSY41y	44-BAAB-e	oyrat		1.00	1,331	1a..h	6	4	0	1	0	Mongolian: Inner*	PNb	b
7145	Tuvinian (Tannu-Tuva)	1.29500	31,746	34,473	48,031	MSY41z	44-AABD-k	tuvin		1.00	345	2c.u.	6	4	4	1	0	Tuvin	Pnb	b
7146	Uighur	0.05700	1,397	1,517	2,114	MSY41z	44-AABD-d	east uyghur		0.20	3	1r.u.	5	4	3	0	2	Uighur*	PNB	b
7147	Ukrainian	0.30000	7,354	7,986	11,127	CEW22p	53-AAAE-b	ukrainskiy		42.00	3,354	3A.uh	9	7	11	3	3	Ukrainian	PNB	b
7148	Uzbek	0.81000	19,857	21,562	30,043	MSY41l	44-AABD-a	central uzbek		0.10	22	1A.u.	5	3	6	0	1	Uzbek*	PNb	b
7149	Western Mongol (Oirat)	9.13000	223,816	243,042	338,631	MSY41y	44-BAAB-d	kalmyk		0.10	243	2c..h	5	2	4	0	3	Mongolian: Kalmyk*	PNb	b
7150	other minor peoples	0.20000	4,903	5,324	7,418	...				1.00	53		6	4	2	1	0			
	Montserrat	**100.00000**	**10,764**	**10,629**	**10,658**					**95.68**	**10,170**									
7151	Black	95.30000	10,258	10,129	10,157	NFB68a	52-ABAF-u	montserrat-creole		96.50	9,775	1c..h	10	8	11	5	3		pn.	.
7152	British	2.70000	291	287	288	CEW19i	52-ABAC-b	standard-english		79.00	227	3Bsuh	10	9	8	5	1		PNB	b
7153	French	0.50000	54	53	53	CEW21b	51-AABI-d	general français		87.00	46	1B.uh	10	9	14	5	1	French	PNB	b
7154	German	0.20000	22	21	21	CEW19m	52-ABCE-a	standard hoch-deutsch		89.00	19	2B.uh	10	9	13	5	3	German*	PNB	b
7155	Indo-Pakistani	0.20000	22	21	21	CNN25g	59-AAFO-e	general hindi		30.00	6	3Asuh	9	5	4	5	2		pnb	b

Continued opposite

Table 8-2 continued

EVANGELIZATION								EVANGELISM			ADDITIONAL DESCRIPTIVE DATA
Ref 1	*D* 28	*aC* 29	*CG%* 30	*r* 31	*E* 32	*U* 33	*W* 34	*e* 35	*R* 36	*T* 37	*Locations, civil divisions, literacy, religions, church history, denominations, dioceses, church growth, missions, agencies, ministries, movements* 38
7042	1	6	2.00	0	99.70	0.30	C	283.60	67	8	Oaxaca. Closest to Western Ocotlan Zapotec. Bilingual in Spanish. D=RCC.
7043	1	7	2.00	0	99.93	0.07	C	465.04	54	10	Northern Oaxaca. Zapotecs. Pastoralists. D=RCC. M=SIL.
7044	1	7	4.35	0	99.80	0.20	C	362.08	113	9	Chiapas, Concepcion Saravia. Mayans, 90% in Guatemala. Bilingual in Spanish. D=RCC.
7045	2	7	2.00	0	99.93	0.07	C	471.83	55	10	Northeastern Oaxaca State. Agriculturalists. D=RCC,CGP. M=CEC,SIL.
7046	1	7	1.48	0	99.93	0.07	C	482.01	42	10	Central Oaxaca, Ocotlan. Zapotecs. Peasants. D=RCC. M=SIL.
7047	1	7	1.26	0	99.90	0.10	C	453.33	41	10	20 villages in Puebla State. 90% bilingual in Spanish. D=RCC. M=SIL,FMB.
7048	4	7	2.58	0	99.70	0.30	C	293.82	81	8	Chihuahua. Semi-nomadic pastoralists. Many converts to Baha'is. D=RCC,MEM,IAFCJ,NBCM/CNBM. M=EMC,SIL,OM,FMB,independents.
7049	1	7	2.00	0	99.93	0.07	C	492.20	51	10	Central Oaxaca (mountains). Zapotecs. Agriculturalists. D=RCC. M=SIL.
7050	1	7	2.15	0	99.70	0.30	C	278.49	72	8	Central Oaxaca. Zapotecs. Traditional religion permeates much of life: animists 30%. D=RCC.
7051	1	7	1.74	0	99.90	0.10	C	436.90	50	10	Western Oaxaca. Zapotecs. Bilinguals in Spanish. D=RCC.
7052	1	7	2.00	0	99.90	0.10	C	436.90	56	10	Oaxaca. Zapotecs. Bilingual in Spanish. D=RCC.
7053	1	7	1.83	0	99.91	0.09	C	455.04	51	10	Southeast Oaxaca. Zapotecs. Bilingual in Spanish. D=RCC. M=SIL.
7054	2	7	1.84	0	99.90	0.10	C	453.33	50	10	Oaxaca. Zapotecs. Bilingual in Spanish. D=RCC,Pentecostal Chs. M=SIL.
7055	1	7	2.21	0	99.90	0.10	C	453.33	60	10	In Sonora, also Arizona (USA). Pastoralists, hunters. Many bilinguals in Spanish, English. D=RCC. M=SIL.
7056	1	7	1.66	0	99.90	0.10	C	440.19	50	10	Veracruz. Bilingual in Spanish. D=RCC.
7057	2	6	1.82	0	99.95	0.05	C	520.12	47	10	Yucatan State. Mayans. D=RCC,INPM. M=Presbyterian Mission.
7058	1	7	2.45	0	99.90	0.10	C	423.76	67	10	Southeast Oaxaca. Agriculturalists. Zapotecs. D=RCC.
7059	2	6	2.95	0	99.93	0.07	C	488.80	71	10	West central Chiapas. Mayans. D=91% RCC,2% Protestants: National Presbyterian Ch of Mexico. M=SIL.
7060	0	8	6.15		99.69	0.31	C	251.85	169	8	Hindis, Gujaratis, some 42,000 Guatemalan immigrants and 120,000 unregistered Salvadoran refugees.
Micronesia											
7061	1	8	1.48	2	99.95	0.05	C	499.32	40	10	On Saipan, Pagan, and Agrihan Islands, Carolines. Fishermen, agriculturalists. Bilingual in Chamorro, English. Many Baha'is 2%. D=RCC.
7062	1	7	1.56	5	99.93	0.07	C	485.41	37	10	Immigrants from Guam, Mariana Islands. A trade language. D=RCC.
7063	1	10	2.02	7	99.40	0.60	B	159.14	67	7	Long-time residents, and immigrant laborers from Chinese diaspora. Folk-religionists 60%. D=RCC.
7064	2	10	3.93	7	63.00	37.00	B	11.49	204	5	Expatriates from Japan, in commerce. Buddhists 50%, New Religionists 45%. D=RCC,UCC.
7065	1	8	1.99	2	99.92	0.08	C	446.61	52	10	On Kapingamarangi, also on Ponape (Porakiet village). Intermarriage with Nukuoro. D=RCC.
7066	2	7	1.38	5	99.96	0.04	C	546.62	35	10	Kusaie Island, Caroline Islands. Also on Nauru, Ponape. Predominantly Protestant. D=PCET,UCC.
7067	2	6	1.95	0	99.91	0.09	C	435.11	54	10	Mokil Atoll, east of Carolines. 32% monolinguals; 72% bilinguals in Ponape. D=UCCP,RCC.
7068	1	7	1.66	0	99.97	0.03	C	495.67	45	10	Mortlock Islands, southeast of Truk. Close to Trukese. D=RCC.
7069	1	7	2.12	0	99.90	0.10	C	413.91	60	10	Magur, Ulul Islands, Carolines. D=RCC.
7070	1	6	2.01	1	99.90	0.10	C	440.19	54	10	Ngatik Atoll, east of Carolines. Close to Ponapean. Agriculturalists, fishermen. D=RCC.
7071	2	6	1.91	0	99.90	0.10	C	443.47	49	10	Nukuoro Island, Carolines. Also on Ponape. Many bilinguals in Ponapean. Fishermen. D=UCC,RCC.
7072	2	7	1.43	0	99.92	0.08	C	439.89	43	10	Halls Islands, Carolines. D=UCC,RCC.
7073	2	6	1.45	0	99.91	0.09	C	428.47	44	10	55% monolingual, 45% bilingual in Ponape. D=RCC,UCCP.
7074	2	7	1.51	5	99.96	0.04	C	542.35	38	10	Ponape Island, Carolines. Predominantly Protestant. D=UCCP,RCC.
7075	2	7	1.38	0	99.92	0.08	C	439.89	42	10	Puluwat, Pulap, Pulusuk Islands, Carolines. D=RCC,UCC.
7076	1	7	2.27	1	99.90	0.10	C	417.19	63	10	Satawal Island, Carolines. D=RCC.
7077	3	7	1.59	2	99.96	0.04	C	552.49	38	10	Truk Islands. Some on Ponape. Close to Mortlockese. Lingua franca. Mainly Protestant. D=UCC,RCC,PCET.
7078	5	10	1.90	8	99.78	0.22	C	429.89	51	10	Administrators, educators, commerce from USA. D=UCCP,SDA,JWs,PCET,RCC.
7079	2	6	1.49	2	99.97	0.03	C	509.83	40	10	Ulithi, Ngulu, Sorol, Fais Islands, eastern Carolines. Some traditional religionists(animists), 10%. D=RCC,PCCI. M=LM.
7080	2	6	1.50	0	99.97	0.03	C	477.96	43	10	Woleai and other Islands, eastern Carolines. D=RCC,PCCI. M=Liebenzell Mission.
7081	0	7	1.71	2	99.78	0.22	C	329.54	55	9	Yap Island, 10 islands, Carolines. Agriculturalists, fishermen. Many animists 20%. Predominantly D=RCC.
7082	0	6	2.34		99.80	0.20	C	312.44	60	9	Other Pacific Islanders, Asians, Australasians, Filipinos.
Moldavia											
7083	2	8	1.21	6	99.88	0.12	C	501.07	32	10	Gregorians; in 28 countries. Nonreligious 10%. D=Armenian Apostolic Ch,RCC.
7084	1	8	0.00	1	30.00	70.00	A	0.00	0	1.12	73% monolinguals. Muslims 78%(54% Shias,324%Hanafi Sunnis), nonreligious 20%. D=ROC. M=CSI.
7085	1	8	1.21	1	46.00	54.00	A	16.79	133	5	Romani-speaking Balkan Gypsies, in 15 countries. Many speak Moldavian as mother tongue. Muslims 50%, nonreligious 30%. D=ROC.
7086	1	9	1.20	4	50.00	50.00	B	12.77	110	5	From Bashkiria (Russia). Many speak Tatar as mother tongue. Muslims 70%(Hanafi Sunnis), nonreligious 21%. D=ROC.
7087	1	10	1.21	6	99.72	0.28	C	354.78	50	9	Originally from Bulgaria. In 12 other countries. Nonreligious 18%, atheists 10%. D=Bulgarian Orthodox Ch. M=LBI.
7088	3	9	1.21	5	99.60	0.40	C	278.13	48	8	White Russians, from Belorussia. Nonreligious 30%. D=ROC,RCC,Old Ritualist Chs.
7089	1	9	1.21	0	76.00	24.00	B	97.09	72	6	Originally from Chuvashia (Russia). Muslims 35%(Sunnis), nonreligious 30%. D=ROC. M=IBT.
7090	0	0	0.70	1	24.10	75.90	A	0.08	171	2	Immigrants from Russia. Muslims 97% (Hanafi Sunnis and some Alawis).
7091	5	10	1.20	6	99.77	0.23	C	399.09	45	9	Residents from Czechoslovakia. Nonreligious 20%. D=RCC,ROC,SDA,JWs,AUCECB. M=UBS.
7092	1	10	1.21	1	99.72	0.28	C	316.76	46	9	Turkic Christians. Also in Ukraine, Kazakhstan. Center: Kishinev. Russian-speakers 77%. Nonreligious 20%. D=95% Russian Orthodox Ch(D-Kishinev & Moldavia).
7093	1	9	1.21	4	97.00	3.00	B	141.62	34	7	Also in Georgia, Turkey, Iran, USA, Central Asian countries. Nonreligious/atheists 55%, Muslims 5%(Sunnis,Shias). D=Georgian Orthodox Ch. M=IBT.
7094	2	10	1.21	8	99.79	0.21	C	441.17	42	10	Settlers, also in Volga, Altai (Russia). Nonreligious 20%. D=German ELC,AUCECB.
7095	3	10	1.20	7	99.90	0.10	C	525.60	37	10	Traders, merchants from Greece. D=Greek Orthodox Ch,ROC,Georgian Orthodox Ch. M=UBS,LBI.
7096	0	8	1.21	0	23.00	77.00	A	0.84	264	3	Nomadic non-Romany (pre-Romany) Gypsies. Also in Ukraine, Russian Asia, Afghanistan. Related to Arabic, Bangaru. Muslims 98%.
7097	0	10	0.00	5	45.00	55.00	A	0.00	0	1.10	Religious Jews, bilingual in Moldavian, Russian. Many have emigrated to Israel, then returned.
7098	0	8	0.00	4	34.00	66.00	A	0.00	0	1.10	Muslims 60%(Hanafi Sunnis,with Sufi influence), nonreligious 30%, atheists 10%. M=ROC.
7099	5	9	1.21	5	99.91	0.09	C	524.79	42	10	From Latvia. In 25 countries. D=ROC,ELCL,RCC,RCL,CB.
7100	3	8	1.20	5	99.90	0.10	C	515.74	21	10	Found in 24 countries. Strong Catholics. D=RCC,ERCL,ROC.
7101	1	9	0.60	6	99.69	0.31	C	324.88	34	9	Bessarabia (annexed by USSR in 1945, independent 1991). Also in Romania, Yugoslavia, Greece, Bulgaria. Traditionally Orthodox. Nonreligious 19%. D=ROC
7102	1	9	1.20	1	99.65	0.35	C	256.23	30	8	Laborers, migrants from Mordvinia (Russia). Heavily russianized. Nonreligious 30%. D=ROC. M=IBT.
7103	1	8	1.21	0	74.00	26.00	B	97.23	86	6	Mainly found on Russia-Georgia border; also in Syria, Turkey. Muslims 40%(Sunnis), nonreligious 24%. D=ROC.
7104	4	10	1.21	6	99.89	0.11	C	516.51	21	10	Poles. 29% speak Polish as mother tongue. D=RCC,ROC,CEF,CWE.
7105	3	10	1.21	6	99.80	0.20	C	440.92	42	10	Expatriates, citizens. Closely related to Moldavians. D=Romanian Orthodox Ch,RCC(D-Iasi),ROC.
7106	0	8	1.62	8	42.04	57.96	A	0.06	152	2	Anatolian Turks. In Bessarabia, also across Central Asia. Muslims 98%(85% Hanafi Sunnis,15% Alawi Shias).
7107	8	9	1.17	7	99.60	0.40	C	291.27	24	8	In 70 countries. Nonreligious 30%, atheists 8%. D=ROC,RCC,AUCECB,Old Ritualists,CEF,CCECB,SDA,IPKH. R=FEBC,HCJB,TWR,KNLS,VERITAS,AWR.
7108	0	9	0.00	4	40.00	60.00	A	0.00	0	1.12	Mainly in Tajikistan, Uzbekistan, Kirghizia. Trilingual (Uzbek, Russian). Muslims 90%(Hanafi Sunnis), nonreligious 10%. M=CSI.
7109	1	7	4.01	6	42.50	57.50	A	2.32	310	4	70% bilingual in Russian. Muslims 83%(Hanafi Sunnis), nonreligious 15%. D=ROC(Kryashen).
7110	1	7	1.20	0	93.00	7.00	B	186.69	65	7	From Udmurtia (Russia). Strong shamanists/animists 40%, some Muslims. D=ROC.
7111	7	8	1.21	6	99.75	0.25	C	396.93	46	9	In 15 countries. Nonreligious/atheists 25%. D=ROC(E-Ukraine),Ukrainian Catholic Ch,AUCECB,CEF,CCECB,JWs,SDA. R=FEBC,HCJB,VERITAS,AWR.
7112	0	9	0.00	5	43.00	57.00	A	0.00	0	1.12	55% Russian-speaking. Literates 100%. Muslims 80%(Hanafi Sunnis), nonreligious/atheists 20%. M=ROC,AUCECB,CSI.
7113	1	8	1.21	6	99.70	0.30	C	298.93	52	8	Also in Ukraine, western Russia. In 25 countries. Ethnic groups: Sarvi, Voloxuja, Chache, Lovari. Muslims 20%, nonreligious 10%. D=ROC.
7114	0	8	1.20		57.00	43.00	B	62.41	58	6	Estonians, Mari, Komi, Hungarians, Albanians, Koreans, Turkmen, Kirghiz. Nonreligious 39%, Muslims 20%.
Monaco											
7115	0	0	0.80	8	41.00	59.00	A	31.42	100	5	Immigrant workers from North Africa and Western Asia. Muslims (Sunnis) 75%.
7116	1	10	1.60	8	99.79	0.21	C	438.29	50	10	Expatriates from Britain, in business, commerce. D=Anglican Ch(D-Gibraltar).
7117	1	10	1.25	6	99.91	0.09	C	531.44	41	10	Residents from Belgium, in commerce, industry, education. D=RCC.
7118	2	10	0.50	8	99.97	0.03	C	614.63	23	10	Citizens, and residents from France. D=RCC(D-Monaco),ERM. M=ERF,SJ,OFM,OCD.
7119	0	0	4.10	8	99.87	0.13	C	431.86	106	10	Expatriates from Germany in business. Nonreligious 13%. D=EKD, RCC.
7120	1	10	1.34	7	99.95	0.05	C	568.67	39	10	Residents from Greece. D=Greek Orthodox Ch.
7121	0	10	0.00	8	55.20	44.80	B	0.40	34	3	Community of French-speaking practicing Jews.
7122	1	10	0.74	8	99.97	0.03	C	559.39	30	10	From northern Italy and Corsica (France). D=RCC.
7123	2	10	0.89	8	99.99	0.01	C	588.78	31	10	Citizens of Principality of Monaco. D=RCC(D-Monaco),ERM. M=OFM,OCD,SJ,OSFS,FSC.
7124	0	0	4.06	8	99.94	0.06	C	500.92	95	10	Expatriates from Portugal, in commerce. D=RCC.
7125	1	10	0.77	7	99.70	0.30	C	360.25	15	9	Residents from Russia, in business. Nonreligious 30%. D=Russian Orthodox Ch(P-Moscow).
7126	1	10	0.55	8	99.96	0.04	C	599.18	24	10	Expatriates from Spain, in business. Strong Catholics. D=RCC.
7127	2	10	0.78	8	99.84	0.16	C	475.23	30	10	Expatriates from USA, in commerce. D=ERM,RCC. M=ERF.
7128	1	10	1.29	8	99.92	0.08	C	520.49	43	10	Residents from Belgium (French-speaking), in commerce. D=RCC.
7129	0	10	3.44		99.70	0.30	C	263.16	92	8	Individuals from many countries and peoples of Europe and Middle East. Nonreligious 30%.
Mongolia											
7130	0	1	3.39	1	22.05	77.95	A	0.04	517	2	Ethnic group within Khalkha Mongol. Nonreligious 40%, shamanists 30%, Lamaist Buddhists 20%, and atheists 10%.
7131	1	9	2.38	8	99.79	0.21	C	426.75	65	10	Expatriates from Britain, in business, commerce, development. D=embassy services.
7132	0	1	2.67	1	21.03	78.97	A	0.02	448	2	Ethnic group related to Khalkha Mongol. Nonreligious 50%, shamanists 30%, atheists 16%, Lamaists 4%.
7133	0	1	0.00	4	26.00	74.00	A	0.00	0	1.10	Hovsgol Aimag, north Mongolia, around Lake Khubsugul. Oirats. All literate, bilingual in Halh. Shamanists 80%, Lamaists 20%.
7134	0	1	3.19	1	22.03	77.97	A	0.02	493	2	Ethnic group related to Khalkha Mongol. Shamanists 70%, Lamaists 25%, atheists 5%.
7135	0	1	2.87	1	22.05	77.95	A	0.04	452	2	Ethnic group within Khalkha Mongol. Nonreligious 50%, atheists 26%, shamanists 20%, some Lamaists 4%.
7136	0	5	3.46	0	23.00	77.00	A	0.84	507	3	Selenge Aimag, in north Mongolia. Also in Russia, China. Literate in Halh. Shamanists 80%, Lamaist Buddhists 15%, nonreligious 4%.
7137	0	3	3.76	7	47.10	52.90	A	0.17	257	3	From PR China. All literate in Halh. Chinese folk-religionists 40%, Buddhists 30%, nonreligious 30%. M=CICM.
7138	0	3	2.67	4	35.01	64.99	A	0.01	272	2	Majority live in Kazakhstan, China, Iran, Afghanistan, Turkey, Germany. Official, literary. Muslims 60%(Hanafi Sunnis), nonreligious 30%, atheists 10%.
7139	0	5	8.00	4	47.30	52.70	A	2.24	508	4	Nonreligious 28%, shamanists 30%, atheists 10%, Lamaists 30%, Muslims 1% in west. M=115 agencies by 1994: CICM,CGM,TEAM,CWM,PI,CSI,CCCI,ISS,AO.
7140	0	5	0.00	7	32.00	68.00	A	0.00	0	1.12	Northwest Mongolia. Also China(Hui) and Russia(Dungan). Nomads in northeast Gobi Desert. Now speak Mongol Darbet. Literate in Halh. Muslims 100%(Sunnis).
7141	0	5	1.96	1	27.10	72.90	A	0.09	276	2	Ethnic group within Khalkha Mongol. Nonreligious 50%, atheists 20%, shamanists 20%, some Lamaists 10%.
7142	0	3	4.36	4	43.00	57.00	A	1.57	327	4	Buriat-Mongolians. Northeast border with Russia. Literate in Halh. Nonreligious 43%, shamanists 41%, atheists 10%, Lamaists 5%. M=CICM,5 other agencies.
7143	1	5	2.53	7	83.00	17.00	B	57.56	84	6	30,000 military, advisors, plus long-term residents. Most nonreligious 60%, atheists 20%, occultists. D=Orthodox Ch(remnants after 1937 suppression).
7144	0	3	5.01	4	36.00	64.00	A	1.31	440	4	Vast majority live in China. Most are bilingual and literate in Halh. Nonreligious 29%, shamanists 40%, atheists 10%, Lamaist Buddhists 20%.
7145	0	1	3.60	1	29.00	71.00	A	1.05	416	4	Also in Russia, China. Tuba, Tuva, Soyon, Soyot. Literate in Halh. Lamaists 32%, shamanists 30%, nonreligious 30%.
7146	0	3	1.10	4	37.20	62.80	A	0.27	140	3	Mainly China, Russia, Afghanistan, Turkey, Pakistan. Traders. Literate in Halh, assimilated to Halh culture. Muslims 100%(Sunnis). M=CSI,&c.
7147	3	6	3.55	6	99.42	0.58	B	167.09	119	7	Military, advisors after 1990 withdrawal of 200,000 USSR troops. Nonreligious/atheists 55%. D=UOC,ROC,RCC.
7148	0	4	3.14	5	40.10	59.90	A	0.14	262	3	Mainly in Russia, also China, Afghanistan, USA, Australia, Germany. Muslims 100%(Hanafi Sunnis). M=CSI.
7149	0	5	3.24	1	36.10	63.90	A	0.13	304	3	Sart-Kalmyk. Ethnic group within Khalkha Mongol. Nonreligious, shamanists. M=CCCI,CICM,TEAM.
7150	0	5	0.54		15.00	85.00	A	0.54	99	3	Kharchin-Tumut, Khorchin, Uzemchin, Barga, Olot, Torghut, USA Whites, Europeans, Amerindians. Nonreligious 49%, Shamanists 40%, Lamaists 9%, Baha'is 1%.
Montserrat											
7151	5	6	-0.06	8	99.97	0.03	C	530.09	10	10	West Indians. D=Anglican Ch/CPWI(D-Antigua),MCCA,RCC,SDA,JWs. M=USPG,MMS,FSC.
7152	4	10	-0.14	8	99.79	0.21	C	418.10	19	10	Expatriates from Britain, in administration. D=Anglican Ch/CPWI(D-Antigua),MCCA,SDA,JWs. M=USPG.
7153	3	10	-0.14	8	99.87	0.13	C	504.90	14	10	Expatriates from France, in business, commerce. D=RCC(D-Saint John's),SDA,JWs. M=FSC.
7154	4	10	-0.15	8	99.89	0.11	C	529.50	17	10	Expatriates from Germany, in business, development. D=AC/CPWI,RCC,SDA,JWs.
7155	2	10	1.81	7	88.00	12.00	B	96.36	87	6	Traders from India, Pakistan. Hindus 50%, some Baha'is 20%. D=RCC,AC/CPWI.

Continued overleaf

Table 8-2 continued

PEOPLE		POPULATION				IDENTITY CODE		LANGUAGE		CHURCH		MINISTRY						SCRIPTURE		
Ref 1	Ethnic name 2	P% 3	In 1995 4	In 2000 5	In 2025 6	Race 7	Language 8	Autoglossonym 9	S 10	AC 11	Members 12	Jayuh 13-17	d 18	wa 19	xc 20	mc 21	mi 22	Biblioglossonym 23	Pub 24-26	ss 27
7156	Mulatto	0.70000	75	74	75	NFB68b	52-ABAF	carib-anglo-creol cluster		83.00	62	1a..h	10	8	11	5	1	West Carib Creole English	PN.	b
7157	Spaniard	0.20000	22	21	21	CEW21k	51-AABB-c	general español		96.00	20	2B.uh	10	9	15	5	1	Spanish	PNB	b
7158	other minor peoples	0.20000	22	21	21	...				71.00	15		10	7	6	5	0			
	Morocco	**100.00000**	**25,837,244**	**28,220,843**	**38,529,890**					**0.62**	**174,476**									
7159	Algerian Arab	0.70000	180,861	197,546	269,709	CMT30	12-AACB-b	east maghrebi		0.15	296	2A.uh	5	4	6	2	1	Arabic: Algerian*	PNB	b
7160	Arabized Berber	12.35896	3,193,215	3,487,803	4,761,894	CMT32a	12-AACB-a	west maghrebi		0.14	4,883	1A.uh	5	4	5	2	3		pnb	b
7161	Atta Berber(Yahia)	0.40000	103,349	112,883	154,120	CMT32b	10-AAAC-b	ta-mazight		0.02	23	1a...	3	1	0	0	0	Shilha: Central*	Pn.	b
7162	Berber Jewish	0.00500	1,292	1,411	1,926	CMT35	10-AAAC-c	judeo-tamazigh		0.00	0	1c...	0	2	0	0	0		pn.	b
7163	Black Moor (Sudani)	2.00000	516,745	564,417	770,598	CMT32y	12-AACD-a	hassaaniyya		0.00	0	0a...	0	2	0	0	0		pn.	b
7164	British	0.02000	5,167	5,644	7,706	CEW19i	52-ABAC-b	standard-english	7	79.00	4,459	3Bsuh	10	9	12	5	3		PNB	b
7165	Byelorussian	0.00200	517	564	771	CEW22c	53-AAAE-c	bielorusskiy		70.00	395	3A.uh	10	7	11	2	1	Byelorussian*	PNB	b
7166	Central Shilha (Berraber)	7.39357	1,910,295	2,086,528	2,848,734	CMT32b	10-AAAC-b	ta-mazight		0.10	2,087	1a...	5	4	2	2	3	Shilha: Central*	Pn.	b
7167	Drawa Berber	1.32000	341,052	372,515	508,595	CMT32g	10-AAAC-a	ta-shelhit		0.01	37	4c...	3	1	0	0	0	Shilha: Southern*	Pn.	b
7168	Filala Berber	0.99000	255,789	279,386	381,446	CMT32d	10-AAAC-a	ta-shelhit		0.01	28	4c...	3	1	0	0	0	Shilha: Southern*	Pn.	b
7169	French	0.30000	77,512	84,663	115,590	CEW21b	51-AABI-d	general français	35	60.50	51,221	1B.uh	10	9	12	5	1	French	PNB	b
7170	Ghomara Berber	0.20000	51,674	56,442	77,060	CMT32e	10-AAAC-d	ghomara		0.01	6	1c...	3	1	2	0	0		pn.	.
7171	Gil Bedouin (Beni Guil)	0.13000	33,588	36,687	50,089	CMT30	12-AACD	badawi-sahara cluster		0.01	4	0a...	3	2	2	0	0		PN.	b
7172	Haratine (Black/Berber)	0.15000	38,756	42,331	57,795	CMT32z	12-AACB	maghrebi cluster		0.03	13	2A.uh	3	2	2	0	0		PNB	b
7173	Jebala (Rif)	4.30000	1,111,001	1,213,496	1,656,785	CMT32a	12-AACB-a	west maghrebi		0.03	364	1A.uh	3	3	6	0	0		pnb	b
7174	Judeo-Berber	0.00500	1,292	1,411	1,926	CMT35	12-AACH-c	yudi		0.10	1	0c...	5	3	2	0	0		p..	b
7175	Levantine Arab	1.50000	387,559	423,313	577,948	CMT30	12-AACF-f	syro-palestinian		10.00	42,331	1Asuh	8	5	10	2	0	Arabic: Lebanese*	Pnb	b
7176	Maghrebi Jewish	0.05000	12,919	14,110	19,265	CMT35	12-AACH-c	yudi		0.06	8	0c...	4	2	2	0	2		p..	b
7177	Moroccan Arab	41.59633	10,747,345	11,738,835	16,027,020	CMT30	12-AACB-a	west maghrebi	85	0.26	30,521	1A.uh	5	4	6	2	4		pnb	b
7178	Northern Shilha (Riffian)	5.83703	1,508,128	1,647,259	2,249,001	CMT32e	10-AAAC-f	ta-rift		0.16	2,636	1A...	5	4	6	2	3	Shilha: Northern*	Pn.	b
7179	Russian	0.00200	517	564	771	CEW22j	53-AAAE-d	russkiy		70.00	395	4B.uh	10	7	11	2	1	Russian	PNB	b
7180	Shawiya	0.07000	18,086	19,755	26,971	CMT32f	10-AAAC-j	shawiya		0.03	6	1c...	3	3	6	1	0	Chaouia	Pn.	b
7181	Southern Shilha (Shleuh)	8.95011	2,312,462	2,525,796	3,448,468	CMT32g	10-AAAC-a	ta-shelhit		0.16	4,041	4c...	5	4	5	2	3	Shilha: Southern*	Pn.	b
7182	Spaniard	0.10000	25,837	28,221	38,530	CEW21k	51-AABB-b	standard castellano	10	96.00	27,092	1A.uh	10	9	12	5	3		pnb	b
7183	Tekna Berber	1.65000	426,315	465,644	635,743	CMT32g	10-AAAC-a	ta-shelhit		0.01	47	4c...	3	1	0	0	0	Shilha: Southern*	Pn.	b
7184	USA White	0.01000	2,584	2,822	3,853	CEW19s	52-ABAC-s	general american		85.00	2,399	1Bsuh	10	9	12	5	1	English*	PNB	b
7185	Uregu Berber (Feqqus)	0.20000	51,674	56,442	77,060	CMT32b	10-AAAC-b	ta-mazight		0.02	11	1a...	3	2	0	0	0	Shilha: Central*	Pn.	b
7186	Warain Berber	0.86000	222,200	242,699	331,357	CMT32b	10-AAAC-b	ta-mazight		0.01	24	1a...	3	2	0	0	0	Shilha: Central*	Pn.	b
7187	White Moor (Bidan)	8.00000	2,066,980	2,257,667	3,082,391	CMT32y	12-AACD-a	hassaaniyya		0.00	0	0a...	0	3	2	0	0		pn.	b
7188	Yahi Bedouin	0.30000	77,512	84,663	115,590	CMT30	12-AACD	badawi-sahara cluster		0.01	8	0a...	3	3	2	0	0		PN.	b
7189	Zekara Berber(Bekhti)	0.20000	51,674	56,442	77,060	CMT32b	10-AAAC-b	ta-mazight		0.02	11	1a...	3	2	0	0	0	Shilha: Central*	Pn.	b
7190	other minor peoples	0.40000	103,349	112,883	154,120	...				1.00	1,129		6	4	6	1	0			
	Mozambique	**100.00000**	**17,387,823**	**19,680,456**	**30,611,842**					**32.83**	**6,460,529**									
7191	British	0.01000	1,739	1,968	3,061	CEW19i	52-ABAC-b	standard-english	7	78.00	1,535	3Bsuh	10	9	13	5	1		PNB	b
7192	Central Shona	0.50000	86,939	98,402	153,059	NAB571	99-AUTA-a	standard chi-shona		64.00	62,977	3csuh	10	9	12	5	3	Shona: Standard	PNB	b
7193	Changa (Xanga, Sanga)	1.00000	173,878	196,805	306,118	NAB571	99-AUTA-h	chi-shanga	3	35.00	68,882	1csuh	9	6	9	5	3	Chixanga	PNb	b
7194	Chopi	2.75258	478,614	541,720	842,615	NAB57p	99-AUTC-c	shi-copi		34.00	184,185	0.s..	9	6	9	5	3	Txopi*	Pn.	.
7195	Chwabo (Xuabo)	5.49218	954,971	1,080,886	1,681,257	NAB57b	99-AUSY-h	ci-cuabo	5	18.00	194,559	1.s..	8	5	9	5	1	Chwabo	PNb	.
7196	Coastal Makhuwa (Maka)	2.29659	399,327	451,979	703,029	NAB57b	99-AUSY-c	e-mwuikari		20.00	90,396	1.s..	9	6	9	5	2		pnb	.
7197	Cuban White	0.01000	1,739	1,968	3,061	CLT27	51-AABB	español cluster		20.00	394	4B.uh	9	5	2	4	2		PNB	b
7198	French	0.00500	869	984	1,531	CEW21b	51-AABI-a	historical français	4	84.00	827	1B.uh	10	9	14	5	2		pnb	b
7199	German	0.01000	1,739	1,968	3,061	CEW19m	52-ABCE-a	standard hoch-deutsch		87.00	1,712	2B.uh	10	9	13	5	3	German*	PNB	b
7200	Goanese	0.05000	8,694	9,840	15,306	CNN25d	59-AAFU-o	konkani-gomantaki		90.00	8,856	3asu.	10	8	13	4	2	Konkani: Goan*	PNb	b
7201	Greek	0.03000	5,216	5,904	9,184	CEW20	56-AAAA-c	dhimotiki		95.00	5,609	2B.uh	10	9	10	5	1	Greek: Modern	PNB	b
7202	Gujarati	0.10000	17,388	19,680	30,612	CNN25e	59-AAFH-b	standard gujaraati		0.60	118	2A.u.	5	4	2	3	0	Gujarati	PNB	b
7203	Han Chinese	0.05000	8,694	9,840	15,306	MSY42a	79-AAAB-ba	kuo-yü		17.00	1,673	2Bsuh	8	5	9	4	1	Chinese: Kuoyu*	PNB	b
7204	Hindi	0.10000	17,388	19,680	30,612	CNN25g	59-AAFO-e	general hindi		0.10	20	3Asuh	5	4	2	1	0		pnb	b
7205	Jewish	0.00100	174	197	306	CMT35	51-AABA-e	general português		0.00	0	2Bsuh	0	2	2	0	0	Portuguese	PNB	b
7206	Karanga (Shona)	0.50000	86,939	98,402	153,059	NAB571	99-AUTA-f	chi-karanga		40.00	39,361	1asuh	9	6	12	5	3	Chishona: Chikaranga	PNb	b
7207	Korean (North Korean)	0.10000	17,388	19,680	30,612	MSY46	45-AAAA-b	kukö		0.90	177	2A...	5	4	2	0	0	Korean	PNB	b
7208	Koti	0.34136	59,355	67,181	104,497	NAB57b	99-AUSY-f	e-koti		30.00	20,154	1.s..	9	6	7	5	2		pnb	.
7209	Kunda	0.10000	17,388	19,680	30,612	NAB57b	99-AUSX-e	south ci-kunda		27.00	5,314	1.su.	9	5	7	5	3	Kunda	Pnb	.
7210	Lomwe (Ngulu, Nguru)	7.08257	1,231,505	1,393,882	2,168,105	NAB57b	99-AUSY-g	i-lomwe	15	34.70	483,677	1.s..	9	5	9	5	3	Ilomwe*	PNb	.
7211	Makonde	1.85754	322,986	365,572	568,627	NAB57b	99-AUSQ-d	ci-makonde		37.30	136,358	1.s..	9	6	8	5	2	Makonde	pnb	b
7212	Makua (Makhua, Meto)	9.07000	1,577,076	1,785,017	2,776,494	NAB57b	99-AUSY-a	e-meeto	43	17.30	308,808	2.s..	8	5	9	5	4		pnb	b
7213	Makuana	15.29000	2,658,598	3,009,142	4,680,551	NAB57b	99-AUSY-d	i-makhuani		15.00	451,371	1.s..	8	6	7	5	1	Makhuwa-makhuwana	PNB	.
7214	Manyika	1.01626	176,705	200,005	311,096	NAB571	99-AUTA-e	central chi-manyika	2	42.00	84,002	1csuh	9	6	12	5	3	Chishona: Chimanyika*	PNb	b
7215	Marenje	3.03081	526,992	596,477	927,787	NAB57b	99-AUSY-h	ci-cuabo		18.00	107,366	1.s..	8	6	7	5	1	Chwabo	PNb	.
7216	Matengo	0.01000	1,739	1,968	3,061	NAB57o	99-AUSR-c	ci-matengo		40.00	787	0....	9	6	7	4	0		pn.	.
7217	Maviha (Mawia)	0.02000	3,478	3,936	6,122	NAB57b	99-AUSQ-e	ci-mabiha		20.00	787	1.s..	9	5	7	2	0		pnb	.
7218	Mestico	1.50000	260,817	295,207	459,178	NAN58	51-AABA-e	general português		87.00	256,830	2Bsuh	10	8	11	4	1	Portuguese	PNB	b
7219	Mwani (Ibo, Quimuane)	0.63873	111,061	125,705	195,527	NAB57j	99-AUSN	mwani cluster	1	10.00	12,570	0....	8	5	6	5	2	Mwani	...	b
7220	Ndau (Sofala, Njao)	0.67769	117,836	133,372	207,453	NAB571	99-AUTA-g	chi-ndau	1	37.00	49,348	1csuh	9	6	12	5	2	Chindau*	PNB	b
7221	Ngoni (Angoni, Sutu)	0.22966	39,933	45,198	70,303	NAB57i	99-AUSX-c	south ci-ngoni		26.00	11,752	1.su.	9	5	12	5	2	Ngoni	Pnb	b
7222	Northern Shona (Korekore)	0.60000	104,327	118,083	183,671	NAB571	99-AUTA-b	chi-korekore		61.00	72,030	1csuh	10	9	13	5	3		pnb	b
7223	Nsenga	0.22468	39,067	44,218	68,779	NAB57b	99-AUSX-f	ci-nsenga	1	27.00	11,939	1.su.	9	5	7	5	2	Chinsenga*	PNb	.
7224	Nyanja (Cewa, Maravi)	2.19038	380,859	431,077	670,516	NAB57b	99-AUSX-ac	standard ci-cewa	8	47.80	206,055	1.su.	9	6	13	5	1	Chichewa	PNB	b
7225	Nyasa (Nyanja)	0.50000	86,939	98,402	153,059	NAB57b	99-AUSX-af	ci-nyasa		80.00	78,722	1.su.	10	7	11	5	3		pnb	b
7226	Nyungwe (Tete, Yungwe)	2.16995	377,307	427,056	664,262	NAB57b	99-AUSX-h	ci-nyungwe	9	25.00	106,764	1.su.	9	5	7	5	2	Chinyungwi*	Pnb	.
7227	Palma	0.16500	28,690	32,473	50,510	NAB57j	99-AUSN-e	west mwani		10.00	3,247	0....	8	7	8	0	0		...	.
7228	Podzo (Puthsu)	0.46778	81,337	92,061	143,196	NAB57p	99-AUSX-m	ci-podzo		51.00	46,951	1.su.	10	6	7	2	1	Shiputhsu*	Pnb	.
7229	Portuguese	1.16665	202,855	229,602	357,133	CEW21g	51-AABA-e	general português	20	92.00	211,234	2Bsuh	10	9	13	5	3	Portuguese	PNB	b
7230	Romanian	0.00300	522	590	918	CEW21i	51-AADC-a	limba românească		47.00	277	3A.u.	9	6	8	4	1	Romanian	PNB	b
7231	Ronga	3.50390	609,252	689,583	1,072,608	NAB57p	99-AUTD-d	shi-ronga	15	70.00	482,708	1.s..	10	7	11	5	3	Shironga*	PNB	b
7232	Russian	0.01000	1,739	1,968	3,061	CEW22j	53-AAAE-d	russkiy		20.00	394	4B.uh	9	5	10	4	1	Russian	PNB	b
7233	Sakaji	0.09843	17,115	19,371	30,131	NAB57b	99-AUSY-e	e-sakaji		20.00	3,874	1.s..	9	5	7	5	1		pnb	.
7234	Sena	7.97925	1,387,418	1,570,353	2,442,595	NAB57b	99-AUSX-i	ci-sena	6	31.00	486,809	1.su.	9	5	9	5	3	Chisena*	PNb	.
7235	Senji	0.07000	12,171	13,776	21,428	NAB571	99-AUTA-g	chi-ndau		30.00	4,133	1csuh	9	5	6	5	1	Chindau*	PNB	b
7236	Swahili	0.05047	8,776	9,933	15,450	NAB57j	99-AUSM-b	standard ki-swahili	8	0.00	0	4Asu.	0	3	1	1	0	Kiswahili*	PNB	b
7237	Swazi	0.20000	34,776	39,361	61,224	NAB57i	99-AUTF-e	i-si-swati		52.00	20,468	2csu.	10	6	13	5	3	Siswati*	PNB	b
7238	Tawara (Barwe, Wesa)	0.40000	69,551	78,722	122,447	NAB571	99-AUTA-bd	tavara	1	37.00	29,127	1csuh	9	6	13	5	2		pnb	b
7239	Tonga (Shengwe)	1.85177	321,982	364,437	566,861	NAB57p	99-AUTC-a	gi-tonga		50.00	182,218	0.s..	10	6	9	5	2	Gitonga*	PN.	.
7240	Tsonga (Shangaan)	8.58099	1,492,047	1,688,778	2,626,799	NAB57p	99-AUTD-c	shi-shangana	24	70.70	1,193,966	3.s..	10	7	11	5	3	Tsonga	PNB	b
7241	Tswa (Hlengwe)	5.74555	999,026	1,130,750	1,758,819	NAB57p	99-AUTD-a	shi-tswa	6	16.00	180,920	1.s..	8	5	9	5	3	Xitshwa*	PNB	b
7242	West Makua (Chirima)	5.44000	945,898	1,070,617	1,665,284	NAB57b	99-AUSY-b	i-ngulu		20.00	214,123	1.s..	9	6	8	5	2		pnb	.
7243	Yao	1.60485	279,048	315,842	491,274	NAB57b	99-AUSQ-f	ci-yao	5	19.50	61,589	4.s..	8	5	7	5	2	Chiyao*	PNB	.
7244	Zezuru	2.00000	347,756	393,609	612,237	NAB571	99-AUTA-c	chi-zezuru		47.00	184,996	1csuh	9	8	11	5	3	Chishona: Chizezuru	PNb	b
7245	Zimba	0.50000	86,939	98,402	153,059	NAB571	99-AUTA-cj	kwa-zwimba		40.80	40,148	1csuh	9	7	7	5	3		pnb	.
7246	Zulu	0.20000	34,776	39,361	61,224	NAB57i	99-AUTF-g	i-si-zulu		59.70	23,498	3asu.	10	9	12	5	3	Isizulu*	PNB	b
7247	other minor peoples	0.40538	70,487	79,781	124,094	...				30.00	23,934		9	5	7	5	0			
	Myanmar	**100.00000**	**42,876,572**	**45,611,177**	**58,120,485**					**8.2**	**3,741,467**									
7248	Akha (Ekaw, Khako)	0.46991	201,481	214,331	273,114	MSY50z	77-BBAA-d	akha		15.00	32,150	1....	8	5	8	5	3	Akha	PN.	b
7249	Anal Naga	0.01400	6,003	6,386	8,137	MSY50c	73-DDAB-a	anal		73.00	4,661	0....	10	7	13	4	2	Anal	PN.	b
7250	Angku (Amok)	0.00200	858	912	1,162	AUG03z	46-DBBA-d	pou-ma		3.00	27	0....	6	4	5	1	0		...	b
7251	Anu	0.00183	785	835	1,064	MSY50c	76-AAAA-a	nung		40.00	334	0.s..	9	5	6	2	0		...	.
7252	Arakanese (Maghi, Mogh)	4.20000	1,800,816	1,915,669	2,441,060	MSY50b	77-AABA-b	arakan		1.00	19,157	1csu.	6	4	2	5	1	Maghi*	Pnb	.
7253	Asho Chin (Khyeng, Sho)	0.02350	10,076	10,719	13,658	MSY50c	73-DEEA-c	asho		60.00	6,431	0.s..	10	7	11	5	2	Chin: Asho*	PN.	b
7254	Atsi (Szi, Atsi-Maru)	0.03661	15,697	16,698	21,278	MSY50f	77-AAAC-c	atsi		7.00	1,169	0....	7	5	4	5	0	Atsi	P..	p
7255	Bawm Chin (Banjogi)	0.00750	3,216	3,421	4,359	MSY50c	73-DCCA-a	bawm		95.00	3,250	0as..	10	8	13	5	1	Bawm*	PNB	.
7256	Bengali	0.51000	218,671	232,617	296,414	CNN25b	59-AAFT-e	west bengali		0.40	930	1Asuh	5	4	7	2	2	Bengali: Musalmani*	PNB	b
7257	Black Karen (Pao Karen)	1.55323	665,972	708,446	902,745	MSY50g	78-AAAA-a	pa'o		35.00	247,956	0....	9	6	13	5	2	Pa'o*	PN.	.
7258	Black Lisu (Eastern Lisu)	0.01000	4,288	4,561	5,812	MSY501	77-BACA-b	taku		40.00	1,824	1cs..	9	6	14	5	2		pnb	.
7259	Blang (Pula, Bulang)	0.07000	30,014	31,928	40,684	MSY50i	46-DBAC	bulang cluster		6.00	1,916	0....	7	5	2	1	0	Blang	...	b
7260	Brek Karen	0.04604	19,740	20,999	26,759	MSY50g	78-AABA-a	brek		80.00	16,800	0....	10	7	6	4	0		...	.
7261	British	0.01000	4,288	4,561	5,812	CEW19i	52-ABAC-b	standard-english	9	77.00	3,512	3Bsuh	10	9	13	5	1		PNB	b
7262	Burmese (Myen, Bhama)	55.87037	23,955,299	25,483,133	32,472,130	MSY50b	77-AABA-a	bama	82	0.87	221,703	4Asu.	5	4	9	5	3	Burmese	PNB	b
7263	Burmese Shan (Thai Yai)	6.52163	2,796,251	2,974,592	3,790,403	MSY49c	47-AAAA-e	shan	17	0.60	17,848	3.s..	5	4	10	4	1	Shan*	PNB	b
7264	Central Thai	0.08000	34,301	36,489	46,496	MSY49d	47-AAAB-d	central thai		0.60	219	3asuh	5	10	8	5	3	Thai*	PNB	b
7265	Chak	0.00263	1,128	1,200	1,529	MSY50c	73-DCBA	haka-chin cluster		10.00	120	0as..	8	5	3	1	0		PNB	.
7266	Chaungtha	0.33755	144,730	153,961	196,186	MSY50b	77-AABA-h	chaungtha		0.10	154	1csu.	5	4	2	1	0		pnb	.
7267	Chindwin Chin	0.05436	23,308	24,794	31,594	MSY50c	73-DEFA-ac	ütbü		10.00	2,479	0....	8	5	8	2	0		...	.
7268	Chinese Shan (Tai Neua)	0.20081	86,100	91,592	116,712	MSY49a	47-AAAA-f	tai-neua		0.10	92	1.s..	5	4	5	1	0	Chinese: Shanghai*	PNB	.
7269	Cho Chin	0.07049	30,224	32,151	40,969	MSY50c	73-DAAE	thado-chin cluster		60.00	19,291	0as..	10	7	7	2	0	Chin, Cho	PNB	.
7270	Dai Chin	0.06585	28,234	30,035	38,272	MSY50c	73-DEDA-a	daai		12.00	3,604	0....	8	5	0	5	2	Dai Chin*	PN.	.
7271	Danau (Danaw)	0.02717	11,650	12,393	15,791	MSY50b	46-DCAC-a	danau		50.00	6,196	0....	10	6	8	5	2		...	.
7272	Eastern Shan (Yunnanese)	0.02000	8,575	9,122	11,624	MSY49c	47-AAAA-f	tai-neua		0.50	46	1.s..	5	4	8	5	1	Chinese: Shanghai*	PNB	.
7273	Eurasian (Anglo-Burmese)	0.10000	42,877	45,611	58,120	MSY43	52-ABAD-a	south-asian-english		90.00	41,050	0B.uh	10	8	11	5	3		...	b

Continued opposite

Table 8-2 continued

EVANGELIZATION								EVANGELISM			ADDITIONAL DESCRIPTIVE DATA
Ref *1*	*D* *28*	*aC* *29*	*CG%* *30*	*r* *31*	*E* *32*	*U* *33*	*W* *34*	*e* *35*	*R* *36*	*T* *37*	*Locations, civil divisions, literacy, religions, church history, denominations, dioceses, church growth, missions, agencies, ministries, movements* *38*
7156	7	10	-0.14	8	99.83	0.17	C	430.18	11	10	West Indians. D=AC/CPWI,RCC,MCCA,SDA,JWs,PAWI,CGP. M=PHC.
7157	1	10	-0.18	8	99.96	0.04	C	588.67	12	10	Settlers from Spain. D=RCC(D-Saint John's). M=FSC.
7158	0	10	-0.13		99.00	1.00	C	256.55	3	8	Individuals from other Caribbean islands, Central and South America.
Morocco											
7159	1	6	3.45	8	53.15	46.85	B	0.29	214	3	Muslims 95%(Malaki Sunnis). D=Greek Orthodox Ch(P-Alexandria). M=CSI.
7160	1	5	6.39	7	48.14	51.86	A	0.24	404	3	Muslims 99%(Maliki Sunnis), many Baha'is(severely persecuted). D=GOC. M=YWAM-Spain,GMU,GRI,FI. R=network of agencies.
7161	0	1	3.19	4	20.02	79.98	A	0.01	550	2	Berbers term themselves Imazighen ('Free Men') tribes. Nomads on southern border. Transhumant pastoralists. Muslims 100%(Maliki Sunnis).
7162	0	1	0.00	1	14.00	86.00	A	0.00	0	1.07	High Atlas range. Multilingual in Judeo-Moroccan, Arabic, French. Once numerous, but most long since emigrated to Israel.
7163	0	5	0.00	7	26.00	74.00	A	0.00	0	1.07	Lower of the 2 Moor classes, originally from Mauritania. In southwest. Muslims 100%(Maliki Sunnis).
7164	4	9	1.52	8	99.79	0.21	C	444.05	48	10	Expatriates from Britain, in development, business. D=Anglican Ch(D-Gibraltar),SDA,JWs,CB. M=BCMS,CMML,FMB.
7165	1	9	3.74	5	99.70	0.30	C	342.37	97	9	White Russian refugees (1917), in Casablanca. D=Byelorussian Orthodox Ch.
7166	0	5	5.49	4	37.10	62.90	A	0.13	467	3	Middle Atlas range. Transhumance practised. 12 tribes, the most arabized of Berbers. Muslims 100%(Maliki Sunnis), many Baha'is(severely persecuted). M=GMU.
7167	0	1	3.68	4	20.01	79.99	A	0.00	618	1.08	In south, on Dra river. Western Atlas. Agriculturalists; 4 tribes. Muslims 100%(Maliki Sunnis).
7168	0	1	3.39	4	20.01	79.99	A	0.00	553	1.08	Southeastern corner on Algerian border. 4 river oases, hundreds of walled towns. Muslims 100%(Maliki Sunnis).
7169	4	9	0.89	8	99.61	0.39	C	290.38	39	8	Expatriates and residents from France. Nonreligious 20%, Muslims 16%. D=RCC(2 Dioceses),EEAM,SDA,JWs. M=ERF.
7170	0	5	1.81	1	20.01	79.99	A	0.00	361	1.09	Small region near Xauen, north and west of Tamazight. Intelligible with Tarifit. Muslims 100%(Maliki Sunnis).
7171	0	6	1.40	7	30.01	69.99	A	0.01	192	2	Bedouin nomads in eastern steppe region on border with Algeria. Muslims 100%(Maliki Sunnis).
7172	0	6	2.60	8	40.03	59.97	A	0.04	226	2	Also Berber-speaking. Cultivators, tanners, well-diggers, builders. Muslims 100%(Maliki Sunnis).
7173	0	5	3.66	7	37.03	62.97	A	0.04	323	2	Bedouins and arabized Berbers in north. Covers Ceuta enclave. Muslims 100%(Maliki Sunnis), Baha'is(persecuted). R=Network of agencies.
7174	0	7	0.00	8	31.10	68.90	A	0.11	61	3	Remnant of Judeo-Berbers after 1950-60 mass emigration to Israel. High Atlas range, Tifnut and other communities.
7175	0	7	4.50	8	67.00	33.00	B	24.45	213	5	Immigrants from Levant(Syria, Lebanon, Jordan). Muslims 90%(Sunnis, Shias).
7176	0	7	2.10	8	32.06	67.94	A	0.07	238	2	Judeo-Moroccan Arabs (youths speak only Arabic); 67% in Casablanca. Decline by emigration from 250,000 in 1952. Sefardis, some Arabic- and Berber-speaking.
7177	1	5	4.41	7	48.26	51.74	A	0.45	290	3	Large numbers live in France, Belgium, Netherlands, Germany. Muslims 98%(Maliki Sunnis). D=RCC(2 Dioceses). M=OFM,FSC,PFM,YWAM-Spain,GMU,NAM.
7178	0	5	5.73	4	42.16	57.84	A	0.24	426	3	Northern Atlas up to coast. Muslims 100%(Maliki Sunnis), Baha'is. 1920, Berber Republic of the Rif. Mass revolts against kingdom. M=GMU,FI,CSI,MEM. R=TWR.
7179	1	9	3.74	7	99.70	0.30	C	352.59	74	9	Emigres from USSR after 1917. Nonreligious 30%. D=Russian Orthodox Ch(P-Moscow).
7180	0	5	1.81	1	25.03	74.97	A	0.02	286	2	Sedentary population south of Casablanca. Muslims 100%(Maliki Sunnis).
7181	0	5	6.73	4	37.16	62.84	A	0.21	557	3	Western Atlas, Anti-Atlas ranges. 25 tribes. Settled agriculturalists. Muslims 100%(Maliki Sunnis), many Baha'is(severely persecuted). M=GMU,FI,FMB,CSI.
7182	1	9	1.40	8	99.96	0.04	C	578.16	39	10	Expatriates and residents from Spain. D=RCC(2 Dioceses, in particular AD-Tanger). M=OFM,FSC,PFM.
7183	0	1	3.93	4	20.01	79.99	A	0.00	652	1.08	Extreme southern boundary with Sahara republic. Nomads. 28 tribes. Muslims 100%(Maliki Sunnis).
7184	6	9	5.63	8	99.85	0.15	C	483.99	115	10	USA military, also expatriates in business. D=RCC,AoG,SDA,JWs,CC,UEM. M=FMB.
7185	0	1	2.43	4	20.02	79.98	A	0.01	446	2	In northern Rif area. Sedentary tillers on Moulouya river in east. Muslims 100%(Maliki Sunnis).
7186	0	1	3.23	4	20.01	79.99	A	0.00	556	1.08	A Berber people in north, eastern Middle Atlas mountains. Semi-nomadic. Muslims 100%(Maliki Sunnis).
7187	0	5	0.00	7	28.00	72.00	A	0.00	0	1.08	Upper caste of Moors, originally from Mauritania. In southwest. Muslims 100%(Maliki Sunnis: 3 main tariqas: Qadiriyya, Tijaniyya, Shadhiliyya).
7188	0	6	2.10	7	30.01	69.99	A	0.01	256	2	Nomadic Bedouins in northern Rif mountains. Muslims 100%(Maliki Sunnis).
7189	0	1	2.43	4	20.02	79.98	A	0.01	446	2	In northern Rif mountains. Also in Algeria. Semisedentary. Muslims 100%(Maliki Sunnis).
7190	0	6	1.29		21.00	79.00	A	0.76	168	3	Egyptian Arabs, Libyan Arabs, other Bedouin Arabs(Dui-Menia), Berbers (Gontafa, Senhaja, Haha, Zayan, Ndhir, Yafelmao),Canadians. Muslims 90% (Sunnis).
Mozambique											
7191	3	10	3.50	8	99.78	0.22	C	432.74	84	10	Expatriates from Britain, in development. D=Anglican Ch/CPSA(D-Lebombo),SDA,JWs. M=USPG.
7192	3	6	9.14	4	99.64	0.36	C	296.67	221	8	Mainly live in Zimbabwe. Animists 36%. D=many AICs,CPSA,RCC.
7193	4	6	8.20	1	86.00	14.00	B	109.86	296	7	Coastal Ndau. Animists 61%. D=AACJM,RCC,AC/CPSA,many other AICs. M=USPG,FF,FIFM.
7194	7	6	7.14	0	78.00	22.00	B	96.79	315	6	Southern coast. 57 dialects. Literates 10%. Animists 65%. D=RCC(D-Inhambane),UCCSA(ICUM),IML,AC,IPM,CBM,AICs. M=Finnish Mission,UCBWM,FMC,USPG.
7195	2	6	6.23	0	63.00	37.00	B	41.39	334	6	Around Quelimane. Animists 76%, Muslims 7%. D=RCC,SDA. M=UBS.
7196	2	6	9.54	0	66.00	34.00	B	48.18	457	6	Coast from Moma to Mozambique Island. Animists 60%, Muslims 20%. D=CPSA,RCC.
7197	1	10	3.74	8	79.00	21.00	B	57.67	160	6	Military and advisers from Cuba. Nonreligious/atheists 70%. D=RCC. M=OFM,SJ.
7198	1	10	1.89	8	99.84	0.16	C	469.09	51	10	Expatriates from France, in development, business. D=RCC(9 Dioceses). M=SJ,FSCJ.
7199	3	10	1.95	8	99.87	0.13	C	511.25	53	10	Expatriates from Germany, in business. D=RCC,MCSA,NAC.
7200	1	10	3.96	4	99.90	0.10	C	509.17	88	10	Mostly Catholics, from Goa(India). D=RCC. M=SJ,OFM.
7201	1	10	6.53	7	99.95	0.05	C	568.67	125	10	Traders, originally from Greece. D=Greek Orthodox Ch(P-Alexandria: AD-Rhodesia).
7202	0	10	2.50	6	48.60	51.40	A	1.06	198	4	Long-time residents, workers from India. Hindus 68%, Muslims 30%, some Baha'is.
7203	1	10	4.25	7	83.00	17.00	B	51.50	162	6	After 1977 expulsion of Chinese traders by regime, Communist Chinese advisers entered. Nonreligious/atheists 83%. D=RCC.
7204	0	10	3.04	7	46.10	53.90	A	0.16	240	3	Traders from India. Hindus 90%, Muslims 9%, Baha'is.
7205	0	10	0.00	8	45.00	55.00	A	0.00	0	1.13	Small remnant of Portuguese-speaking practicing Jews.
7206	3	7	7.60	4	99.40	0.60	B	147.46	236	7	A Bantu people living mainly in Zimbabwe. Animists 60%. D=AACJM,AC/CPSA,RCC.
7207	0	10	2.92	6	43.90	56.10	A	1.44	220	4	Military, advisers from North Korea. Nonreligious 70%, atheists 29%.
7208	2	6	7.91	0	74.00	26.00	B	81.03	347	6	Nampula Province, Angoche District. Animists 70%. D=RCC,AoG.
7209	3	6	6.48	1	72.00	28.00	B	70.95	302	6	Also in Zimbabwe, Zambia. Animists 72%. D=RCC,SDA,ICFG.
7210	7	6	11.39	0	83.70	16.30	B	106.01	421	7	Zambezia Province. Also in Malawi. Animists 65%, Muslims 7%. D=RCC,ICFG,MCSA,SDA,ECM,ICM,CC. M=AEF,CCAP,FF(South Africa),Baptists,UBS. R=TWR.
7211	2	6	9.99	1	83.30	16.70	B	113.40	377	7	Mainly in Tanzania. Isolated. Woodcarvers. Muslims 44%(Shafi Sunnis), animists 12%. D=RCC(D-Pemba),AC/CPSA.
7212	3	6	10.89	0	66.30	33.70	B	41.86	510	6	Animists 59%, Muslims 18%(Shafi Sunnis). D=RCC(4 Dioceses),AEC,JWs. M=OFM,SMP,FSCJ,IMC,SJ,OFMCap,SCJ,CM,IEME,USPG,FF,CSM,GR,AEF. R=TWR.
7213	1	6	11.31	0	60.00	40.00	B	32.85	583	5	Nampula, south of Meeto area. Animists 59%, Muslims 20%. D=RCC.
7214	4	7	9.46	4	99.42	0.58	B	157.89	281	7	Most live in Zimbabwe. Animists 57%, Muslims 1%. D=AACJM,CNC,RCC,many other AICs.
7215	1	6	9.73	0	60.00	40.00	B	39.42	511	5	Related to Makua. Closest to Chwabo. Animists 73%, Muslims 7%. D=RCC.
7216	0	6	4.46	0	72.00	28.00	B	105.12	225	7	Northwest corner; primarily in Tanzania, some in Malawi. Animists 60%.
7217	0	6	4.46	1	56.00	44.00	B	40.88	290	6	Most in Tanzania. Closely related to the Makonde. Muslims 45%, animists 35%.
7218	1	10	4.45	8	99.87	0.13	C	495.37	97	10	Mixed-race persons(Black/White). Mostly in urban areas. Nonreligious 10%. D=RCC(9 Dioceses).
7219	2	6	7.40	0	47.00	53.00	A	17.15	517	5	Cabo Delgado Province, on coast. Isolated. Second language Portuguese. Muslims 80%. D=RCC,AoG.
7220	4	7	6.87	4	97.00	3.00	B	130.99	225	7	Southeast Shona; many in Zimbabwe. Animists 63%. D=AACJM,RCC,AC/CPSA,many other AICs. M=Frontline Fellowship(South Africa),FIFM(Zimbabwe).
7221	2	7	6.30	5	83.00	17.00	B	78.76	242	6	Pockets in central Cabo Delgado Province. Related to Zulu. Animists 73%. D=RCC(D-Tete),AC/CPSA.
7222	3	6	9.29	4	99.61	0.39	C	264.95	239	8	Dialect of Shona. Mainly in Zimbabwe. Animists 39%. D=AICs,CPSA,RCC.
7223	2	6	7.34	1	72.00	28.00	B	70.95	335	6	Also in Zambia and Zimbabwe. Animists 73%. D=AC/CPSA,RCC.
7224	3	7	6.06	5	99.48	0.52	B	186.33	193	7	Animists 42%. D=Anglican Ch/CPSA(D-Lebombo),RCC(D-Lichinga,D-Quelimane),AICs. M=USPG.
7225	3	7	9.39	5	99.80	0.20	C	397.12	219	9	Early name for peoples around Lake Nyasa. Animists 20%. D=RCC,CPSA,many AICs.
7226	3	6	9.72	1	70.00	30.00	B	63.87	438	6	Banks of Zambezi. Some in Malawi. Closely related to Sena. Animists 75%. D=RCC,CNC,ICFG. M=WVI,UBS.
7227	0	0	5.95	0	29.00	71.00	A	10.58	700	5	Cabo Delgado Province on the coast north of Pemba. Most men speak Swahili. Muslims 80%, Nonreligious 10%.
7228	1	6	8.62	1	91.00	9.00	B	169.39	314	7	Maputo river area, in south. Zambezia and Sofala Provinces. Close to Sena, Chwabo. Animists 49%. D=RCC.
7229	5	10	3.71	8	99.92	0.08	C	564.14	77	10	Settlers originally from Portugal: decline from 250,000 in 1971. D=RCC(9 Dioceses),IEP,CBM,AoG,NAC(Burma). M=CBP,CBB,OFM,SMP,SJ,IMC,FIFM(Zimbabwe).
7230	1	10	3.38	6	99.47	0.53	B	181.84	116	7	Military, advisers from Romania until 1989. Some stayed on. Nonreligious 50%. D=GOC.
7231	5	6	7.38	5	99.70	0.30	C	332.15	194	9	South, coastal areas. Also in South Africa. Animists 20%. D=RCC,CBM,IPM,AC/CPSA,AICs. M=SM,CPB,CBB,USPG,MCSA,HTI.
7232	1	10	3.74	7	85.00	15.00	B	62.05	121	6	Military, advisers from Russia. Nonreligious 60%, atheists 20%. D=GOC.
7233	1	6	6.14	0	61.00	39.00	B	44.53	341	6	Coastal tribe north of Angoche, Sangange Peninsula. Related to Makua. Animists 60%, Muslims 20%. D=RCC.
7234	8	6	9.89	1	80.00	20.00	B	90.52	389	6	Also in Malawi. Animists 60%, Muslims 1%. D=RCC(D-Beira,D-Quelimane),CNC,CB,CC,AoG,Baptists,ICFG,indigenous pentecostal chs. M=FF(South Africa),FIFM.
7235	3	7	6.21	4	82.00	18.00	B	89.79	244	6	Related to Changa, Ndau. Animists 70%. D=AACJM,RCC,IMU. M=UMC.
7236	0	9	0.00	5	41.00	59.00	A	0.00	0	1.13	Traders from Somalia to Mozambique. Major lingua franca across East Africa. Muslims 100%(Shafi Sunnis).
7237	4	8	4.04	5	99.52	0.48	B	227.76	116	8	Immigrants from Swaziland. Related to Zulu. Animists 28%. D=AICs,CPSA,RCC,&c.
7238	2	7	8.30	4	93.00	7.00	B	125.59	277	7	Partly in Zimbabwe. Related to Shona. Animists 63%. D=AACJM,other AICs.
7239	3	7	5.46	0	96.00	4.00	B	175.20	208	7	South, Inhambane area. Animists 50%. D=AC/CPSA,RCC,AICs. M=USPG,UBS.
7240	11	7	8.01	5	99.71	0.29	C	350.18	198	9	Many in South Africa. Animists 13%, Muslims 1%. D=AC/CPSA,RCC(3 Dioceses),IPM,UCCSA(ICUM),CON,IML,MCSA,Pentecostal Chs,CBM,ILA,other AICs.
7241	6	7	7.36	4	72.00	28.00	B	42.04	349	6	Southern region, also Transvaal (South Africa), Zimbabwe. Animists 79%. D=UCCSA(ICUM),IMU,RCC,IML,AC/CPSA,AICs. M=UCBWM,FMC,UMC,USPG,HTI.
7242	2	6	10.49	0	65.00	35.00	B	47.45	504	6	Niassa Province. Animists 60%, Muslims 20%. D=CPSA,RCC.
7243	2	6	8.00	4	73.50	26.50	B	52.31	353	6	Most in Malawi, Tanzania. Civil war areas. Muslims 80%(Shafi Sunnis), animists 1%. Much syncretism. D=Anglican Ch/CPSA(D-Lebombo),RCC(D-Lichinga).
7244	4	7	10.32	4	99.47	0.53	B	183.55	292	7	Main element of Shona language; most in Zimbabwe. Animists 53%. D=AACJM,AC/CPSA,RCC,many other AICs.
7245	4	6	8.65	4	91.80	8.20	B	136.70	291	7	In Maravi cluster, on lower Zambezi. Animists 58%. D=AACJM,AC/CPSA,RCC,other AICs.
7246	3	8	6.30	5	99.60	0.40	B	284.80	154	8	Immigrant, migrant workers from South Africa. Animists 20%, some Muslims. D=Anglican Ch/CPSA(D-Lebombo),RCC,very many AICs.
7247	0	9	8.09		61.00	39.00	B	66.79	363	6	Comorians, Pakistanis, Mauritians, Macanese, and many other Bantu peoples. Muslims 30% (Sunnis), Animists 20%, nonreligious/atheists 15%.
Myanmar											
7248	4	5	8.41	0	56.00	44.00	B	30.66	465	5	Kengtung Shan State; and 4 other countries. Animists 50%, Theravada Buddhists 35%. D=BBC(Pangwai Baptist Conferences),RCC(D-Myitkyina),AoG,SDA.
7249	2	5	6.34	0	99.73	0.27	C	317.07	171	9	Also in India and Bangladesh. Close to Mara Chin. Closest to Lamgang. Animists 27%. D=LIEC,Baptist Chs.
7250	0	5	3.35	0	22.00	78.00	A	2.40	542	4	Along west bank of Mekong river. Also in Laos, China, Thailand. Buddhists 90%(Hinayana).
7251	0	6	3.57	0	66.00	34.00	B	96.36	194	6	A small Sino-Tibetan people, related to Anal, Nung Rawang. Polytheists 36%, some Buddhists 24%.
7252	3	7	7.85	1	38.00	62.00	A	1.38	646	4	Also in India, Bangladesh, China. Theravada Buddhists 80%, animists 17%, Muslims 2%, Hindus. D=RCC,Anglican Ch/CPB,PCB. M=LEM(Baptists).
7253	4	7	2.36	4	99.60	0.40	C	247.47	84	8	Lower Burma. Irrawaddy river lowlands; also Bangladesh, China. Bilingual in Burmese. Animists 40%. D=BBC(Asho Chin Baptist Conference),CPB(D-Yangon).
7254	0	5	4.88	0	33.00	67.00	A	8.43	497	4	Kachin State. Also Yunnan (China). Lingua franca. Jingpo. Close to Lashi, Maru. Forest. Polytheists (animists) 70%, Buddhists 20%.
7255	1	10	2.66	0	99.95	0.05	C	530.52	67	10	Falam area, Chin Hills. Also India, Bangladesh. D=BECC. M=UBS.
7256	2	6	4.64	6	49.40	50.60	A	0.72	333	3	In Akyab District, Arakan Province. Hindus 47%, Muslims 44%(Hanafi Sunnis). D=AoG,SDA.
7257	5	6	1.92	0	81.00	19.00	B	103.47	102	7	Southwest Shan State; also Thailand. Black dress. Buddhists 42%, animists 22%, some Baha'is. D=BBC(Shan States Home Mission Society),AoG,NAC,SDA,CPB.
7258	3	6	5.34	1	92.00	8.00	B	134.32	189	7	Northern Burma; on China border. Polytheists/animists 60%. D=Lisu Ch,AoG,SDA. M=MEC,OMF.
7259	0	5	5.40	0	24.00	76.00	A	5.25	742	4	Southeast Shan State. Also in China, Thailand. Agriculturalists. Buddhists 90%(Hinayana).
7260	0	7	2.19	0	99.80	0.20	C	324.12	81	9	Mountains of Kantarawady and Kyebogyi Districts, Kayah State. Buddhists/animists 20%.
7261	1	10	-0.35	8	99.77	0.23	C	415.95	15	10	Expatriates from Britain, in education, business. D=Ch of Province of Burma(4 Dioceses).
7262	9	7	4.34	6	61.87	38.13	B	1.96	241	4	Theravada Buddhists 97%, Muslims 2.2% (Zerbadees,Arakanese;Shafi Sunnis), many Baha'is. D=BBC,CPB(4 Dioceses),RCC(8 Dioceses),AoG,EFCB,EPCB.
7263	2	5	3.32	4	49.60	50.40	A	1.08	245	4	Tai Shan. In Shan States, in southeast Burma; also in Thailand, China. Theravada Buddhists 99%. D=BBC,CBP. M=BCMS.
7264	3	8	3.13	6	58.60	41.40	B	1.28	173	4	Immigrants from Thailand. Theravada Buddhists 98%, Muslims 1%. D=BBC,CCT,RCC.
7265	0	6	2.52	4	49.00	51.00	A	17.88	202	5	Most in Arakan Blue Mountains. Also in Bangladesh. Tropical forest. Agriculturalists. Animists 90%.
7266	0	6	2.77	1	25.10	74.90	A	0.09	424	2	People of the Valley. Related to Lolo, Burmese. Buddhists/animists 99%.
7267	0	5	5.67	0	36.00	64.00	A	13.14	515	5	Kanpetlet and 3 other townships. Buddhists/animists 90%.
7268	0	4	4.63	1	30.10	69.90	A	0.11	481	3	Vast majority in south Yunnan, China; also Laos, Viet Nam. Buddhists(Hinayana) 99%.
7269	0	6	7.86	4	99.60	0.40	C	236.52	227	8	A Kuki-Chin language. Animists 40%.
7270	3	6	3.39	0	43.00	57.00	A	18.83	286	5	Matupi, Paletwa, Kanpetlet townships. Forest. Animists 88%. D=RCC,Anglican Ch/CPB,EFB(Nazarenes). M=Evangelical Baptist Conference,MCHMC.
7271	2	7	2.71	6	93.00	7.00	B	169.72	113	7	Also in Thailand and China. Closest to Riang-Lang, Pale Palaung. Buddhists 50%. D=AoG,SDA.
7272	2	6	3.90	1	42.50	57.50	A	0.77	323	3	From Yunnan (China). Theravada Buddhists 80%, many animists 19%. D=BCC(Kengtung Shan Baptist Association),CPB. M=MEC.
7273	4	10	2.31	8	99.90	0.10	C	492.75	57	10	Mixed-race(Burmese/European) persons, mostly urban. D=CPB,RCC,AoG,SDA.

Continued overleaf

Table 8-2 continued

PEOPLE		POPULATION				IDENTITY CODE		LANGUAGE		CHURCH		MINISTRY						SCRIPTURE		
Ref 1	*Ethnic name* 2	*P%* 3	*In 1995* 4	*In 2000* 5	*In 2025* 6	*Race* 7	*Language* 8	*Autoglossonym* 9	*S* 10	*AC* 11	*Members* 12	*Jayuh* 13-17	*d* 18	*wa* 19	*xc* 20	*mc* 21	*mi* 22	*Biblioglossonym* 23	*Pub* 24-26	*ss* 27
7274	Gante (Gangte)	0.01250	5,360	5,701	7,265	MSY50c	73-DAAE-m	gang-te		60.00	3,421	0cs..	10	7	7	3	0	Gangte	PNB	.
7275	Geba Karen	0.11122	47,687	50,729	64,642	MSY50g	78-AABB-a	geba		80.00	40,583	0....	10	7	7	4	1		...	.
7276	Gheko Karen	0.02635	11,298	12,019	15,315	MSY50g	78-AABC-b	gekho		70.00	8,413	0....	10	7	7	4	2		p..	.
7277	Golden Palaung (Shwe)	0.42482	182,148	193,765	246,907	AUG03z	46-DCAA-b	shwe		1.00	1,938	0c...	6	4	5	1	0		...	b
7278	Gujarati	0.07000	30,014	31,928	40,684	CNN25e	59-AAFH-b	standard gujaraati		0.70	223	2A.u.	5	4	8	4	1	Gujarati	PNB	b
7279	Haka Chin (Baungshe)	0.23496	100,743	107,168	136,560	MSY50c	73-DCBA-a	haka	1	60.00	64,301	0as..	10	7	11	5	1	Chin: Haka*	PNB	.
7280	Hallam Chin (Laiso Chin)	0.26087	111,852	118,986	151,619	MSY50c	73-DDDB-a	falam	2	60.00	71,392	1.s..	10	7	8	5	1	Chin: Falam*	PNB	b
7281	Han Chinese	0.64870	278,140	295,880	377,028	MSY42a	77-AABA-a	bama		4.00	11,835	4Asu.	6	4	8	5	3	Burmese	PNB	b
7282	Han Chinese (Cantonese)	0.28860	123,742	131,634	167,736	MSY42a	79-AAAM-a	central yue		2.00	2,633	3A.uh	6	4	9	4	0	Chinese, Yue	PNB	b
7283	Han Chinese (Hakka)	0.07120	30,528	32,475	41,382	MSY42a	79-AAAG-a	literary hakka		3.00	974	1A...	6	4	8	4	0	Chinese: Hakka, Wukingfu*	PNB	b
7284	Han Chinese (Mandarin)	1.15252	494,161	525,678	669,850	MSY42a	79-AAAB-ba	kuo-yü	3	2.00	10,514	2Bsuh	6	4	9	5	1	Chinese: Kuoyu*	PNB	b
7285	Han Chinese (Min Nan)	0.35980	154,270	164,109	209,118	MSY42a	79-AAAJ-ic	chaozhou		2.00	3,282	1A..h	6	4	8	4	0	Chinese, Min Nan	PNB	b
7286	Hani (Putu, Pudu)	0.39512	169,414	180,219	229,646	MSY50i	77-BBAA	hani cluster		10.00	18,022	1....	8	5	2	2	0		PN.	b
7287	Hindi	0.25000	107,191	114,028	145,301	CNN25g	59-AAFO-e	general hindi		0.50	570	3Asuh	5	4	2	1	0		pnb	b
7288	Hkun (Khun Shan, Khuen)	0.23995	102,882	109,444	139,460	MSY49z	47-AAAA-ec	khyn		2.00	2,189	1.s..	6	4	2	0	1	Khun	Pnb	b
7289	Hrangkhol	0.01700	7,289	7,754	9,880	MSY50c	73-DDDA-a	hrangkhol		25.00	1,938	0....	9	5	8	2	2	Hrangkhol	PN.	.
7290	Hsifan (Muli)	0.01000	4,288	4,561	5,812	MSY50z	77-BCAA-a	proper hsifan		0.10	5	0a...	5	4	1	1	0		...	.
7291	Hui (Panthay)	0.01600	6,860	7,298	9,299	MSY42b	79-AAAB-ba	kuo-yü		0.00	0	2Bsuh	0	2	0	0	0	Chinese: Kuoyu*	PNB	b
7292	Intha	0.39136	167,802	178,504	227,460	MSY50b	77-AABA-c	intha		0.10	179	1csu.	5	4	2	1	0		pnb	.
7293	Jewish	0.00080	343	365	465	CMT35	52-ABAD-a	south-asian-english		1.00	4	0B.uh	6	1	2	0	0		...	b
7294	Kachin (Chingpo, Singpo)	1.47251	631,362	671,629	855,830	MSY50f	75-AAAA-a	jing-pho	7	60.00	402,977	2as..	10	8	12	5	3	Kachin: Jinghpaw*	PNB	.
7295	Kado (Asak, Thet)	0.35641	152,816	162,563	207,147	MSY50i	75-ABAA-a	kado		5.00	8,128	0....	7	5	6	1	1	Kadu*	P..	.
7296	Kayah (Red Karen)	0.54782	234,886	249,867	318,396	MSY50g	78-AABE-a	kayah		25.00	62,467	0....	9	5	10	4	1	Kayah, Western*	...	p
7297	Khamti Shan (Khampti)	0.00887	3,803	4,046	5,155	MSY49c	47-AAAA-d	khamti		0.70	28	1.s..	5	4	6	1	0		pnb	b
7298	Khiamngan Naga (Para)	0.00500	2,144	2,281	2,906	MSY50p	73-ADAA	khiamngan-naga cluster		30.00	684	0....	9	5	7	3	1	Naga, Khiamngan	PN.	.
7299	Khmu (Pouteng, Phsin)	0.20000	85,753	91,222	116,241	AUG03z	46-DDBA-a	kha-khmu		10.00	9,122	0....	8	5	11	2	0	Khmu'	P..	.
7300	Khumi Awa Chin (Coastal)	0.08000	34,301	36,489	46,496	MSY50c	73-DEAA-a	khumi-awa		60.00	21,893	0....	10	7	12	5	1	Chin: Khumi, Awa*	P..	.
7301	Khumi Chin (Khami, Khuni)	0.21274	91,216	97,033	123,646	MSY50c	73-DEAB-a	khumi		60.00	58,220	0.s..	10	7	13	5	3	Chin: Khumi*	PN.	.
7302	Kiorr	0.02000	8,575	9,122	11,624	AUG03Z	46-DBBA-a	kiorr		1.00	91	0....	6	4	5	1	0		...	.
7303	Konyak Naga	0.00300	1,286	1,368	1,744	MSY50p	72-BAAA-b	konyak-naga		76.00	1,040	0....	10	8	13	5	2	Naga: Konyak*	PNB	.
7304	Kuki Chin (Thado-Kuki)	0.07267	31,158	33,146	42,236	MSY50c	73-DAAE-a	thado		70.00	23,202	0as..	10	8	9	5	1	Chin, Thado	PNB	.
7305	Lahta Karen	0.02000	8,575	9,122	11,624	MSY50g	78-AABD-b	lahta		5.00	456	0....	7	5	8	2	0		...	.
7306	Lahu (Black, Red)	0.28029	120,179	127,844	162,906	MSY50i	77-BBAB-a	lahu		75.00	95,883	4a...	10	9	9	5	2	Lahu*	PNB	b
7307	Lama	0.00943	4,043	4,301	5,481	MSY50i	76-AABA-d	lama		15.00	645	0....	8	5	4	2	0		...	.
7308	Lao (Laotian Tai)	0.04600	19,723	20,981	26,735	MSY49b	47-AAAC-b	lao		3.00	629	2As..	6	4	7	2	1	Lao	PNB	b
7309	Laopang	0.02000	8,575	9,122	11,624	MSY50i	77-BBAB-f	laopang		14.00	1,277	1c...	8	5	6	2	0		pnb	.
7310	Lashi (Letsi, Acye)	0.15394	66,004	70,214	89,471	MSY50i	77-AAAC-b	lashi		0.01	7	0....	3	3	5	1	1		p..	.
7311	Lopi	0.01000	4,288	4,561	5,812	MSY50i	77-BBDA-a	lopi		16.00	730	0....	8	5	2	1	0		...	.
7312	Lu (Tai Lu, Lue)	0.57864	248,101	263,925	336,308	MSY49z	47-AAAA-g	tai-lü		2.00	5,278	1.s..	6	4	4	2	1	Lu	PNb	.
7313	Lushai (Mizo, Whelngo)	0.03467	14,865	15,813	20,150	MSY50m	73-DCAA-a	lushai		95.00	15,023	0asu.	10	9	13	5	2	Lushai	PNB	.
7314	Mahei	0.02579	11,058	11,763	14,989	MSY50i	77-BBAA-i	mahei		5.00	588	1....	7	5	2	1	0		pn.	.
7315	Maingtha (Achang)	0.00472	2,024	2,153	2,743	MSY50f	77-AAAB-a	achang		20.00	431	0....	9	5	7	2	0	Achang	PN.	b
7316	Malay	0.05000	21,438	22,806	29,060	MSY44k	31-PHAA-b	bahasa-malaysia		0.03	7	1asuh	3	3	1	1	0	Malay	PNB	b
7317	Malayali	0.04600	19,723	20,981	26,735	CNN23b	49-EBEB-a	malayalam		32.00	6,714	2Asu.	9	5	11	5	3	Malayalam	PNB	b
7318	Manipuri (Ponna, Mitei)	0.05000	21,438	22,806	29,060	MSY50o	73-CAAA-ab	manipuri		1.10	251	1as..	6	4	8	4	1	Manipuri*	PNB	.
7319	Manumanaw Karen	0.01241	5,321	5,660	7,213	MSY50g	78-AABG-a	manumanaw		80.00	4,528	0....	10	7	9	2	0		...	.
7320	Mara Chin (Lakher, Zao)	0.02700	11,577	12,315	15,693	MSY50m	73-DEBA-a	mara		95.00	11,699	0....	10	9	9	5	1	Mara*	PNB	.
7321	Maru (Laungwaw, Zi)	0.27376	117,379	124,865	159,111	MSY50f	77-AAAC	maru cluster		6.00	7,492	0....	7	5	7	2	2	Maru	P..	p
7322	Mindat	0.07173	30,755	32,717	41,690	MSY50c	73-DAAE-o	minat		5.00	1,636	0cs..	7	5	5	1	0		pnb	.
7323	Moken (Sea Gypsy, Salon)	0.01569	6,727	7,156	9,119	MSY44z	31-PHCA	moken cluster		0.05	4	0....	4	3	1	4	2	Moken	P..	b
7324	Mon (Talaing, Mun)	2.31625	993,129	1,056,469	1,346,216	AUG03c	46-GAAA-c	mon-te		0.90	9,508	2....	5	4	7	5	2	Mon	PNB	b
7325	Mru (Mro)	0.09458	40,553	43,139	54,970	MSY50c	73-BAAA-a	murung		0.20	86	0....	5	4	5	2	0	Mro*	P..	.
7326	Mun Chin (Chinbok)	0.13340	57,197	60,845	77,533	MSY50c	48-ABAA-e	mun		6.00	3,651	0.s..	7	5	4	2	2		pn.	.
7327	Nepalese (Gurkhali)	0.54000	231,533	246,300	313,851	CNN25k	59-AAFD-b	nepali		0.04	99	2Asu.	3	3	5	1	1	Nepali	PNB	b
7328	Ngawn Chin	0.04076	17,476	18,591	23,690	MSY50c	73-DEGA-a	ngawn		60.00	11,155	0....	10	7	11	4	1	Chin: Ngawn*	P..	.
7329	Norra (Nora, Noza, Byabe)	0.01300	5,574	5,929	7,556	MSY50f	76-AABA-a	norra		2.00	119	0....	6	4	5	2	0		...	.
7330	Nung (Anoong, Nu, Lu)	0.04000	17,151	18,244	23,248	MSY50f	47-AAAE-b	tai-nung		3.00	547	0....	6	4	2	2	0	Nung	P..	b
7331	Orisi (Oriya)	0.23000	98,616	104,906	133,677	CNN25l	59-AAFS-ȧ	odiaa		1.00	1,049	3Asu.	6	4	2	2	0	Oriya	PNB	b
7332	Padaung Karen	0.11344	48,639	51,741	65,932	MSY50g	78-AABD-a	pa-daung		20.00	10,348	0....	9	5	11	2	0		...	.
7333	Paite Chin	0.02469	10,586	11,261	14,350	MSY50c	73-DAAF-a	pai-te		86.00	9,685	0....	10	7	12	2	1	Paite*	PNB	.
7334	Paku Karen (Mopwa, Pagu)	0.01470	6,303	6,705	8,544	MSY50g	78-AABF-b	pa-ku		25.00	1,676	1.s..	9	5	10	4	1		pnb	b
7335	Palu	0.01000	4,288	4,561	5,812	MSY50z	77-AABA-i	palu		0.40	18	1csu.	5	4	11	1	0		pnb	.
7336	Phun (Phon, Samong)	0.00472	2,024	2,153	2,743	MSY50f	77-AAAA-a	hpon		1.00	22	0....	6	4	10	1	0		...	.
7337	Punjabi	0.11600	49,737	52,909	67,420	CNN25n	59-AAFE-c	general panjabi		1.10	582	1Asu.	6	4	13	1	0		PNB	b
7338	Purum	0.00094	403	429	546	MSY50c	73-DDCA-a	purum		12.00	51	0....	8	5	2	1	0		...	.
7339	Pyen	0.00231	990	1,054	1,343	MSY50z	77-BBBB-c	pyen		1.00	11	0....	6	4	6	1	0		...	.
7340	Ralte	0.03000	12,863	13,683	17,436	MSY50c	73-DAAA-a	ral-te		60.00	8,210	0....	10	7	7	5	2		...	.
7341	Rawang (Nung, Taron)	0.13000	55,740	59,295	75,557	MSY50f	76-AAAB-a	rawang		60.00	35,577	0....	10	7	7	5	2	Rawang	PNB	.
7342	Red Karen (Bghai Karen)	0.04355	18,673	19,864	25,311	MSY50g	78-AABC-a	bghai		25.00	4,966	0....	9	5	9	5	1	Karen: Bghai*	P..	.
7343	Riang-Lang (Black Yang)	0.10224	43,837	46,633	59,422	AUG03z	46-DCAB-a	riang-lang		2.00	933	0....	6	4	4	1	0	Riang Lang	P..	b
7344	Rohingya	0.60000	257,259	273,667	348,723	MSY50b	77-AABA-b	arakan		0.00	0	1csu.	0	3	1	0	0	Maghi*	Pnb	.
7345	Rumai Palaung	0.24000	102,904	109,467	139,489	AUG03z	46-DCAA	palaung cluster		2.00	2,189	0r...	6	4	2	1	0	Palaung, Pale	...	b
7346	Samtuan (Samtao)	0.02000	8,575	9,122	11,624	AUG03z	46-DBAC-a	samtau		5.00	456	0....	7	5	5	2	0		...	.
7347	Sansu	0.01000	4,288	4,561	5,812	MSY50i	77-BBAA-h	sansu		5.00	228	1....	7	5	2	1	0		pn.	.
7348	Senthang Chin	0.05048	21,644	23,025	29,339	MSY50c	73-DCDA-a	senthang		11.00	2,533	0....	8	5	5	2	1		...	.
7349	Sgaw Karen (Paganyaw)	3.56327	1,527,808	1,625,249	2,070,990	MSY50g	78-AABF-a	sgaw		48.60	789,871	3.s..	9	6	13	5	2	Sgaw Kayin*	PNB	b
7350	Silver Palaung (Bonglong)	0.15283	65,528	69,708	88,826	AUG03z	46-DCAA	palaung cluster	4	0.20	139	0r...	5	4	1	4	1	Palaung, Pale	...	b
7351	Sino-Burmese	0.03000	12,863	13,683	17,436	MSY42c	77-AABA-a	bama		1.00	137	4Asu.	6	4	6	4	0	Burmese	PNB	b
7352	Siyin Chin (Sizang)	0.02350	10,076	10,719	13,658	MSY50c	73-DAAF-d	siyin		80.00	8,575	0....	10	7	13	3	1	Chin, Siyin	PNb	.
7353	Southern Lisu (Flowery)	0.32191	138,024	146,827	187,096	MSY50l	77-BACA-a	lisu		80.00	117,462	4rs..	10	9	12	5	2	Lisu: Central*	PNB	b
7354	Striped Karen (Yinchia)	0.01342	5,754	6,121	7,800	AUG03z	46-DCAB-b	yinchia		20.00	1,224	0....	9	5	11	4	1		p..	.
7355	Striped Meo (Blue, Green)	0.02551	10,938	11,635	14,827	MSY47a	48-AAAA-ac	hmong-qua-mba		12.00	1,396	1A...	8	5	10	4	1		pn.	.
7356	Tailoi (Loi, Angku)	0.00300	1,286	1,368	1,744	AUG03z	47-AAAA-gb	lü		3.00	41	1.s..	6	4	2	1	0		pnb	.
7357	Taman	0.02600	11,148	11,859	15,111	MSY50i	31-PAAA-b	taman		6.00	712	0....	7	5	4	1	1		...	.
7358	Tamil	0.27000	115,767	123,150	156,925	CNN23c	49-EBEA-b	tamil		9.00	11,084	2Asu.	7	5	11	5	3	Tamil	PNB	b
7359	Tangsa Naga (Rangpan)	0.11600	49,737	52,909	67,420	MSY50p	72-BACA-a	tase-nagaland		70.00	37,036	0....	10	8	12	5	2	Naga, Tase	PN.	.
7360	Taungyo (Dawe)	1.22982	527,305	560,935	714,777	MSY50b	77-AABA-da	taungnyo		0.50	2,805	1csu.	5	4	2	4	0		pnb	b
7361	Tawr Chin	0.00183	785	835	1,064	MSY50c	73-DCEA-a	tawr		13.00	109	0....	8	5	5	2	0		...	.
7362	Telugu	0.25000	107,191	114,028	145,301	CNN23d	49-DBAB-a	telugu		6.00	6,842	2Asu.	7	5	11	5	3	Telugu	PNB	b
7363	Tiddim Chin	0.45375	194,552	206,961	263,722	MSY50c	73-DAAD-a	tiddim	1	60.00	124,176	0as..	10	7	13	5	3	Chin: Tiddim*	PNB	b
7364	Tulung (Trung)	0.12500	53,596	57,014	72,651	MSY50z	76-AAAA-b	tulung		50.00	28,507	0.s..	10	7	8	2	0		...	.
7365	Va (Wa, Baraog)	0.96633	414,329	440,754	561,636	AUG03z	46-DBAA-e	parauk		36.00	158,672	1....	9	6	11	2	0	Parauk	PN.	.
7366	Vaiphei	0.01500	6,431	6,842	8,718	MSY50c	73-DDEA-a	vaiphei		82.00	5,610	0....	10	7	11	4	1	Vaiphei	PN.	.
7367	Wa (Kawa, Va, Vo)	1.33800	573,689	610,278	777,652	AUG03z	46-DBAA-a	wa		10.00	61,028	4....	8	5	6	5	1	Wa	PN.	.
7368	Welaung	0.02000	8,575	9,122	11,624	MSY50z	77-BBAA	hani cluster		0.40	36	1....	5	4	4	1	0		PN.	b
7369	Wewaw	0.05000	21,438	22,806	29,060	MSY50g	78-AABJ-a	wewaw		25.00	5,701	0....	9	5	8	4	1		...	.
7370	White Karen (Pwo Karen)	3.35552	1,438,732	1,530,492	1,950,244	MSY50g	78-AAAB-a	pwo		37.00	566,282	3.su.	9	5	12	5	1	Pwo Kayin*	PNB	.
7371	Yangbye (Yangye)	2.24746	963,634	1,025,093	1,306,235	MSY50b	77-AABA-g	yangbye		0.50	5,125	1csu.	5	4	2	1	0		pnb	.
7372	Yellow Lahu (Kutsung)	0.02635	11,298	12,019	15,315	MSY50i	77-BBAB-b	kutsung		10.00	1,202	1a...	8	5	11	1	0	Lahu Shi	pnb	.
7373	Yimchungru Naga (Tozhuma)	0.01000	4,288	4,561	5,812	MSY50p	72-BAFA-ba	proper yimchungru		75.00	3,421	0....	10	7	11	5	2	Naga: Yimchungru*	PN.	.
7374	Yinbaw Karen	0.02025	8,683	9,236	11,769	MSY50g	78-AABE-b	yinbaw		30.00	2,771	0....	9	5	6	1	0		...	.
7375	Yintale Karen	0.02000	8,575	9,122	11,624	MSY50g	78-AABH-a	yintale		5.00	456	0....	7	5	6	1	0		...	.
7376	Yos	0.00943	4,043	4,301	5,481	MSY50c	73-DAAC-a	yo-te		15.00	645	0....	8	5	4	1	0		...	.
7377	Zayein Karen	0.02579	11,058	11,763	14,989	MSY50g	78-AABI-a	zayein		20.00	2,353	0....	9	5	6	2	0		...	.
7378	Zome (Zomi Chin)	0.07665	32,865	34,961	44,549	MSY50c	73-DAAB-a	zo-mi		80.00	27,969	0....	10	8	13	5	1	Zomi*	PNB	.
7379	Zotung Chin	0.09598	41,153	43,778	55,784	MSY50c	73-DCBA-d	banjogi		60.00	26,267	0cs..	10	7	12	4	1	Chin: Zotung*	Pnb	.
7380	other minor peoples	0.20000	85,753	91,222	116,241	...				4.00	3,649		6	4	2	3	0			
	Namibia	**100.00000**	**1,543,411**	**1,725,868**	**2,337,592**					**78.18**	**1,349,209**									
7381	Afrikaner	8.10000	125,016	139,795	189,345	CEW19a	52-ABCB-a	afrikaans	71	90.00	125,816	2B.uh	10	10	12	5	1	Afrikaans	PNB	b
7382	Aukwe (Auen, West Kung)	0.15000	2,315	2,589	3,506	BYG11d	09-ABBB-a	au-kwe		11.00	285	0.s..	8	5	6	4	1	Akhoe	P..	.
7383	Baster (Rehobother)	2.21000	34,109	38,142	51,661	NAN58	52-ABCB-a	afrikaans		95.00	36,235	2B.uh	10	8	11	5	2	Afrikaans	PNB	b
7384	Bergdama (Mountain Damara	4.50000	69,453	77,664	105,192	BYG11a	08-AAAA-q	east damara		90.00	69,898	1a...	10	8	11	5	3		pnb	.
7385	British	0.60000	9,260	10,355	14,026	CEW19i	52-ABAC-b	standard-english	46	80.00	8,284	3Bsuh	10	9	13	5	3		PNB	b
7386	Coloured (Eurafrican)	14.54600	224,505	251,045	340,026	NAN58	52-ABCB-a	afrikaans		82.00	205,857	2B.uh	10	9	10	5	3	Afrikaans	PNB	b
7387	Dhimba (Simba, Zemba)	0.10000	1,543	1,726	2,338	NAB57n	99-AURL-de	himba		85.00	1,467	1csu.	10	8	10	5	3	Otjidhimba*	Pnb	.
7388	East Kung (Xu, Ekoka)	0.30000	4,630	5,178	7,013	BYG11d	09-ABAA-a	uukualuthi		12.00	621	0.s..	8	5	6	4	1	Kung: Ekoka*	P..	.
7389	East Kung (Xu, Gobabis)	0.18000	2,778	3,107	4,208	BYG11d	09-ABAA-a	uukualuthi		12.00	373	0.s..	8	5	6	4	1	Kung: Ekoka*	P..	.
7390	East Kung (Xu, Tsumkwe)	0.14000	2,161	2,416	3,273	BYG11d	09-ABAA-a	uukualuthi		50.00	1,208	0.s..	10	6	6	5	3	Kung: Ekoka*	P..	.
7391	Fwe	1.60000	24,695	27,614	37,401	NAB57g	99-AURS-g	fwe		80.00	22,091	1..u.	10	5	8	0	0		pnb	.
7392	Gciriku	0.60000	9,260	10,355	14,026	NAB57n	99-AURN-u	ru-gciriku		80.00	8,284	1cs..	10	7	10	4	2	Gciriku*	PNb	.
7393	German	2.80000	43,216	48,324	65,453	CEW19m	52-ABCE-a	standard hoch-deutsch	5	95.00	45,908	2B.uh	10	10	13	5	3	German*	PNB	b
7394	Griqua (Cape Hottentot)	0.00500	77	86	117	BYG11c	52-ABCB-a	afrikaans		70.00	60	2B.uh	10	7	7	4	3	Afrikaans	PNB	b
7395	Heikum (San)	1.45500	22,457	25,111	34,012	BYG11d	08-ABAA-a	hai-nl'um		10.00	2,511	0....	8	5	6	5	1		...	.

Continued opposite

Table 8-2 continued

EVANGELIZATION								EVANGELISM			ADDITIONAL DESCRIPTIVE DATA
Ref 1	D 28	aC 29	CG% 30	r 31	E 32	U 33	W 34	e 35	R 36	T 37	Locations, civil divisions, literacy, religions, church history, denominations, dioceses, church growth, missions, agencies, ministries, movements 38
7274	0	7	3.32	1	99.60	0.40	C	225.57	118	8	Also in India. Related to Thado Chin. Animists 40%.
7275	1	6	2.19	0	99.80	0.20	C	329.96	80	9	Northern Kayah State, Mobye State, in southern Shan States. Literature in Geba. Animists 20%. D=RCC.
7276	2	6	2.35	1	99.70	0.30	C	270.83	89	8	Yamethin and Toungoo Districts, Mobye State. Animists 30%. Mostly Christian. D=BBC,RCC.
7277	0	6	5.41	1	27.00	73.00	A	0.98	650	3	Northern Shan State, centered in Nam Hsan. Also in China. 15 dialects in Burma. Lingua franca: Shan. Buddhists 90%.
7278	1	8	3.52	6	54.70	45.30	B	1.39	227	4	Traders from Gujarat(India). Hindus 88%, some Muslims 9%. D=AoG.
7279	3	7	2.50	4	99.60	0.40	C	262.80	82	8	Chin Hills, Haka area. Also in India, Bangladesh. Animists 40%. D=BBC,AoG,SDA. M=ABFMS.
7280	4	7	9.28	0	99.60	0.40	C	240.90	259	8	Falam District, Chin Hills. Also in Tripura(India), Bangladesh. Animists 40%. D=Anglican Ch/CPB,AoG,BBC,SDA. M=Baptist Mid Missions.
7281	5	6	7.33	6	64.00	36.00	B	9.34	342	4	Buddhists 93%. D=BBC,RCC,CPB,Methodists,Independent Methodist Ch. OMF,MEC,SDA.
7282	0	6	5.73	8	59.00	41.00	B	4.30	296	4	Chinese folk-religionists/Buddhists(Mahayana) 89%.
7283	0	6	4.69	7	52.00	48.00	B	5.69	281	4	Confucianists/Buddhists(Mahayana) 90%.
7284	3	6	7.21	7	65.00	35.00	B	4.74	331	4	Confucianists/Buddhists(Mahayana) 95%. D=Church of Christ(from Yunnan),AoG,SDA. M=MEC. R=FEBC,KNLS,TWR,HA.
7285	0	6	5.96	6	52.00	48.00	B	3.79	348	4	Confucianists/Buddhists(Mahayana) 90%.
7286	0	5	7.78	0	36.00	64.00	A	13.14	676	5	North Shan State. Also in China, Viet Nam, Laos. Polytheists (animists) 60%, Muslims 30%.
7287	0	8	4.13	7	43.50	56.50	A	0.79	323	3	Traders from north India. Hindus 96%, Muslims 1%.
7288	1	6	5.54	1	30.00	70.00	A	2.19	561	4	Main Kengtung Valley in center of Burmese Shan State. Closely related to Lu and Northern Tai. Buddhists 98%. D=Baptist Ch.
7289	2	6	5.41	0	61.00	39.00	B	55.66	292	6	Most in Burma; some in Assam (India). Closest to Biate. Animists 70%. D=CBCNEI,Presbyterians.
7290	0	5	1.62	4	22.10	77.90	A	0.08	337	2	Refugees, settlers from Tibet, most since 1950. Lamaist Buddhists 99%.
7291	0	5	0.00	7	36.00	64.00	A	0.00	0	1.12	Huizui, or Chinese Muslims. Muslims 100%(Hanafi Sunnis), from Yunnan Province (China).
7292	0	6	2.93	1	25.10	74.90	A	0.09	441	2	Near Inle Lake, southern Shan State. Fishermen, agriculturalists. Buddhists 60%, animists 40%.
7293	0	10	1.40	8	35.00	65.00	A	1.27	164	4	One synagogue in Rangoon(Yangon); community of practicing Jews.
7294	4	6	2.03	5	99.60	0.40	C	273.75	69	8	Kachin State; also India, China. Polytheists 30%, Buddhists 10%. D=BBC(Kachin Baptist Convention),RCC(D-Kengtung),SDA,Independent Anglican Ch. R=FEBC.
7295	1	6	6.93	0	31.00	69.00	A	5.65	710	4	Also in China(south Yunnan) and Laos. Polytheists 85%, Buddhists 10%. D=Baptist Chs.
7296	1	6	9.13	4	64.00	36.00	B	58.40	438	6	Kayah and Karen States. Also in Thailand. Related to Bwe Karen. Animists 75%. D=BBC.
7297	0	6	3.39	1	32.70	67.30	A	0.83	377	3	Northwest Burma. Also in Assam (India), China. Related to Shan. Trilingual in Burmese, Kachin. Buddhists 90%, many animists.
7298	1	6	4.32	0	63.00	37.00	B	68.98	227	6	Northwest. Also in India. Animists(tribal religionists) 70%. D=BBC.
7299	0	5	7.05	4	44.00	56.00	A	16.06	501	5	Also in Laos, Thailand, Viet Nam, China, France, USA. Animists 90%.
7300	3	7	3.32	0	99.60	0.40	C	225.57	118	8	Arakan Hills, coast areas. Animists 40%. D=CPB,AoG,SDA. M=BCMS.
7301	4	7	2.61	0	99.60	0.40	C	240.90	92	8	Arakan Hills, Akyab area. Also in India, Bangladesh. Animists 39%, some Baha'is. D=Anglican Ch(CPB/D-Yangon),AoG,BBC,SDA. M=NEIGMs,BCMS,UCCB.
7302	0	6	4.61	0	21.00	79.00	A	0.76	601	3	Related to Polaungis(Angkuic) languages. Buddhists 98%, animists.
7303	3	7	2.43	4	99.76	0.24	C	368.94	69	9	Immigrants from Nagaland (India). Animists 24%. D=BBC,RCC,PCB. M=CBCNET,NORC.
7304	3	7	2.05	4	99.70	0.30	C	327.04	67	9	Mainly in India. Related to Kamhau, Ralte, Paite, Zo. Animists 30%. D=Methodist Ch/Upper Burma,BBC,EBC. M=MMS.
7305	0	6	3.89	0	30.00	70.00	A	5.47	456	4	In Mobye State, southern Shan States. Animists 70%, Buddhists 25%.
7306	5	5	9.60	4	99.75	0.25	C	369.56	217	9	Shan State, Kengtang area. Animists 25%. D=BBC(Kengtung Lahu Baptist Association,Pangwai Baptist Conference),RCC(D-Myitkyina),Ch of Christ,AoG,SDA.
7307	0	5	4.25	0	36.00	64.00	A	19.71	407	5	Also in China. Closely related to Norra. Polytheists 60%, Lamaist Buddhists 25%.
7308	1	6	4.23	5	54.00	46.00	B	5.91	292	4	Migrants, refugees, settlers from Laos. Theravada Buddhists 54%, animists 33%, nonreligious 9%. D=RCC.
7309	0	5	4.97	1	47.00	53.00	A	24.01	354	5	Also in China(Yunnan); related to Lahu. Animists 60%, Mahayana Buddhists 26%.
7310	0	5	1.96	0	18.01	81.99	A	0.00	466	1.06	Htawgan Subdivision, Kachin State. Also in China. Polytheists 90%, Buddhists 10%. M=Missionary Evangelistic Crusade.
7311	0	5	4.38	0	34.00	66.00	A	19.85	442	5	Also in China. Related to Lolo. Animists 83%, some Buddhists.
7312	1	5	6.47	1	34.00	66.00	A	2.48	570	4	Kengtung District. Half in China; also in Thailand, Laos, Viet Nam. Animists 60%, Buddhists 38%. D=SDA.
7313	5	6	2.14	4	99.95	0.05	C	540.93	57	10	Also India, Bangladesh, China. Almost entirely Christians. D=Presbyterian Ch of Burma,Methodist Ch Burma,Independent Ch of Burma,AoG,BCBC. M=IBPM,CNM.
7314	0	5	4.16	0	26.00	74.00	A	4.74	554	4	Also in China. Related to Hani. Polytheists/animists 95%.
7315	0	7	3.84	0	54.00	46.00	B	39.42	251	5	Along China border. Known as Achang in China. Related to Phun, Maru, Lashi, Tsaiwa. Polytheists/animists 70%, Buddhists 10%(Hinayana). Strong church.
7316	0	6	1.96	5	37.03	62.97	A	0.04	197	2	Immigrants, residents, workers from Malaysia, Thailand. Muslims 100%(Shafi Sunnis).
7317	3	8	1.74	4	98.00	2.00	B	114.46	77	7	Immigrant from South India. Traders. Hindus 67%, some Muslims. D=OSCE,CPB,IPC.
7318	1	6	2.79	4	49.10	50.90	A	1.97	217	4	Vast majority in India; also Bangladesh. Hindus 85%, animists 7%, Muslims 7%. D=Mara Christian Ch(strong across border in Assam also).
7319	0	7	1.96	0	99.80	0.20	C	324.12	76	9	Western Kyebogyi part of Kayah State. Animists 20%. Mostly Christian.
7320	3	7	2.14	0	99.95	0.05	C	499.32	62	10	Also in India (Lushai Hills, Assam). Whole of former headhunting tribe are now Christians. D=MIEC/Lakher Independent Evangelical Ch,AoG,SDA. M=LPM.
7321	0	6	6.84	0	34.00	66.00	A	7.44	640	4	Kachin State, eastern border area, north Burma. Also in China. Related to Kachin. Polytheists/animists 90%. M=MEC,NEIGM.
7322	0	7	5.23	1	37.00	63.00	A	6.75	469	4	In west. Related to Chin languages. Polytheists/animists 90%.
7323	0	6	1.40	0	20.05	79.95	A	0.03	261	2	Mergui Archipelago, Dung and other islands. Also Thailand. Boat-dwellers. Animists 80%, Muslims 20%. M=Karen Baptist Convention,CPB.
7324	2	6	3.02	0	45.90	54.10	A	1.50	270	4	Eastern delta from Rangoon to Ye. Bilingual in Burmese. Animists 75%, Buddhists 20%. D=Ch of Christ,BBC(Mon Baptist Churches Union). M=ABMU.
7325	0	6	4.56	0	21.20	78.80	A	0.15	732	3	Arakan Hills and adjacent area. Also Bangladesh, India. Buddhists 95%, some animists.
7326	2	6	6.08	0	36.00	64.00	A	7.88	546	4	Related to Dai Chin, Ngmen. Animists 90%. D=RCC,CPB.
7327	1	7	4.70	4	44.04	55.96	A	0.06	373	2	Immigrants from Nepal and India. Hindus 99%. D=RCC.
7328	1	8	2.90	0	99.60	0.40	C	219.00	110	8	Chin Hills, Falam area. Animists 40%. D=BBC.
7329	0	5	2.51	0	22.00	78.00	A	1.60	450	4	On Burma-Tibet border. Also in China(Yunnan). Polytheists 70%, Lamaist Buddhists 28%.
7330	0	5	4.08	1	22.00	78.00	A	2.40	645	4	North Burma. Also in China (Yunnan), Thailand. 16 dialects. Close to Mutwang. Polytheists 80%, Lamaist Buddhists 17%.
7331	0	7	4.76	4	46.00	54.00	A	1.67	343	4	Immigrants, settlers, transients from Orissa (India). Hindus 96%, Muslims 2%.
7332	0	7	7.19	0	53.00	47.00	B	38.69	429	5	Kayah State, Mobye State, town of Phekon. A few in Thailand. Animists 60%, Buddhists 20%.
7333	1	6	2.26	0	99.86	0.14	C	411.20	70	10	Tiddim District, Chin Hills. Majority in India. Related to Thado, Tiddim, Ralte, Zo. Animists 14%. D=Baptist Chs. M=NEIGM.
7334	1	6	3.13	1	71.00	29.00	B	64.78	163	6	Monnepwa. Southern hills east of Taungoo in Kayah State. Closely related to Sgaw Karen. Animists 75%. D=BBC.
7335	0	5	2.93	1	33.40	66.60	A	0.48	331	3	A small hill tribe. Polytheists/animists 95%.
7336	0	6	3.14	0	26.00	74.00	A	0.94	447	3	Small tribe related to Lolo. Polytheists/animists 98%.
7337	0	8	4.15	5	55.10	44.90	B	2.21	259	4	Mostly Sikhs and Hindus from India, decreasing by repatriation. Sikhs 15%, Hindus 74%, Muslims 10% (Sunnis).
7338	0	8	4.01	0	33.00	67.00	A	14.45	424	5	Related to Chiru, Aimol, Langrong. Hill tribes. Animists 85%.
7339	0	6	2.43	1	23.00	77.00	A	0.84	421	3	East central, 2 enclaves near Laos border. Closely related to Phunoi, Bisu, Mpi. Animists 99%.
7340	2	6	6.94	0	95.00	5.00	C	208.05	232	8	Near border, with a few in India (Assam). Animists 40%. D=AoG,SDA.
7341	4	6	8.52	4	99.60	0.40	C	243.09	237	8	Kachin State, highlands. Also in China (Tibet, Yunnan), India. 100 dialects. Second language Burmese, also English. Polytheists 40%. D=BBC,Ch of Christ,AoG.
7342	4	6	2.00	4	66.00	34.00	B	60.22	129	6	Kyebogyi area, Kayah State. Also in Thailand. Animists 74%, some Baha'is. D=BBC(Karen Baptist Convention,Shan States HMS),AoG,SDA,NAC). M=ABM.
7343	0	6	4.64	0	25.00	75.00	A	1.82	618	4	Shan State, in southeast Burma. Also in China. Bilingual in Shan. Buddhists 90%, animists.
7344	0	5	0.00	1	17.00	83.00	A	0.00	0	1.11	Arakanese Muslims 100%, descendants of Arabs, Moors, Moghuls and Bengalis who settled in Arakan; 1978 expelled from Burma by regime; deported back.
7345	0	3	5.54	4	24.00	76.00	A	1.75	747	4	Southern Shan State. Also in China. Closely related to Shwe and Pale Palaung. Buddhists 95%.
7346	0	6	3.89	0	27.00	73.00	A	4.92	496	4	Eastern Shan State. Angkuic language. Buddhists 90%.
7347	0	5	3.18	0	26.00	74.00	A	4.74	451	4	A Hani group, north Shan State; also in China. Related to Lolo. Polytheists/animists 95%.
7348	1	0	2.81	0	31.00	69.00	A	12.44	346	5	Haka, Chin Hills. Animists 85%. D=BBC.
7349	7	5	2.91	4	99.49	0.51	B	196.19	99	7	Irrawaddy Delta area, Tenasserim, Pegu range. Animists 49%, some Baha'is. D=BBC(Karen Baptist Convention),RCC,CPB,SSKBC,AoG,NAC,SDA. M=PIME.
7350	1	3	2.67	4	24.20	75.80	A	0.17	416	3	Southern Shan State area near Kalaw. Also in China. Forest, mountains. Buddhists 99%. D=BBC(Shweli Valley Baptist Association).
7351	0	7	2.65	6	51.00	49.00	B	1.86	142	4	Mixed-race persons with Chinese and Burmese parents. Mostly in urban areas. Theravada Buddhists 95%, some Mahayana Buddhists.
7352	1	6	6.99	0	99.80	0.20	C	362.08	179	9	Chin Hills. Close to Paite. Animists 20%. D=Baptist Chs. M=NEIGM.
7353	5	6	9.82	4	99.80	0.20	C	420.48	206	10	Around Lashio, in Wa State, around Loilem in Shan States. Also in China, Thailand. Polytheists/animists 20%. D=AoG,BBC(Shan States Home Mission Society).
7354	1	6	4.92	0	56.00	44.00	B	40.88	290	6	Black Riang. Shan State south. Language related to Riang-Lang, Wa. Animists 75%. D=BBC.
7355	1	7	5.06	1	56.00	44.00	B	24.52	282	5	Tak Meo. Also in China, Thailand, Laos, Viet Nam, France, USA. Polytheists 88%. D=PCB.
7356	0	6	3.78	1	29.00	71.00	A	3.17	452	4	Northeast corner near Laos and China borders. Also in Laos and China. Hinayana Buddhists 90%, some animists.
7357	1	5	4.36	0	27.00	73.00	A	5.91	554	4	Related to Kachin. Polytheists/animists 90%. D=BBC.
7358	5	8	7.26	6	76.00	24.00	B	24.96	298	5	Long-time residents from South India. Hindus 88%. D=CPB,St Gabriel's Church Union,BBC(BBIC),ILC,SDA.
7359	5	6	3.48	0	99.70	0.30	C	296.38	103	8	Tase, Hkaluk. Northwest. Most in India (Nagaland). Animists (nat/spirit-worshippers) 30%. D=BBC,RCC,AoG,PCB,SDA. M=CBCNEI,NCRC.
7360	0	7	5.80	1	33.50	66.50	A	0.61	565	3	Southeast, near border with Thailand. Dialect of Burmese. Theravada Buddhists 99%.
7361	0	6	2.42	0	36.00	64.00	A	17.08	268	5	Falam, Haka, Chin Hills. Animists 85%.
7362	3	8	6.75	5	71.00	29.00	B	15.54	299	5	Long-time residents from South India. Hindus 90%. D=BBC(Burma Baptist Indian Convention),ILC,SDA.
7363	4	7	2.78	5	99.60	0.40	C	280.32	83	8	Chin Hills, Tiddim area. Also in India (Assam), Bhutan. Lingua franca. Animists 40%. D=AoG,BBC,EBC,SDA.
7364	0	5	8.28	0	80.00	20.00	B	146.00	321	7	A smaller number of Tulung live over border in Yunnan (China). Polytheists (animists) 50%.
7365	0	7	10.16	1	75.00	25.00	B	98.55	408	6	Shan State, upper Salween river area. Also in China. Related to Lawa. Hinayana Buddhists 64%.
7366	1	7	6.53	0	99.82	0.18	C	368.13	170	9	Immigrants from India (south Manipur, Assam). Related to Kuki. Animists 18%. D=ICFG.
7367	4	6	9.11	4	55.00	45.00	B	20.07	504	5	Shan State, upper Salween river area, Kengtung City. Also in China. Animists 60%, Buddhists 30%. D=BBC(Northern Lahu Wa Mission),Ch of Christ,AoG,SDA.
7368	0	5	3.65	0	22.40	77.60	A	0.32	581	3	A small hill tribe. Polytheists/animists 95%.
7369	1	6	6.55	0	57.00	43.00	B	52.01	368	6	Hill people, related to Karen. Animists 75%. D=BBC.
7370	6	6	2.72	4	94.00	6.00	B	126.94	111	7	Irrawaddy Delta. Also in Thailand. Animists 65%, some Baha'is. D=BBC(Pwo Karen Baptist Conference),SSKBMS,CPB(D-Yangon),AoG,SDA,NAC. M=ABM.
7371	0	7	6.44	1	27.50	72.50	A	0.50	752	3	Related to Lolo. Theravada Buddhists 90%, animists.
7372	0	5	4.91	1	50.00	50.00	B	18.25	329	5	Kengtung District. Also in China, Thailand, Laos, USA. Distantly related to Akha, Lahu. Animists 60%, Buddhists 30%.
7373	3	7	2.42	4	99.75	0.25	C	339.45	73	9	Immigrants from northern Nagaland (India). Animists 25%. D=BBC,RCC,PCB. M=CBCNEI,NCRC.
7374	0	6	2.60	1	56.00	44.00	B	61.32	181	6	Shan Plateau of eastern Mobye State, and in Bawlakhe of southwest Kayah State. Buddhists 40%, animists 30%.
7375	0	6	3.89	0	27.00	73.00	A	4.92	506	4	Bawlakhe part of Kayah State. Buddhists 50%, animists 45%.
7376	0	6	4.25	0	36.00	64.00	A	19.71	407	5	Small hill people related to Kuki Chin. Animists 85%.
7377	0	6	2.90	0	46.00	54.00	A	33.58	238	5	Between towns of Mobye and Phekon in southern Shan State. Animists 50%, Buddhists 30%.
7378	6	6	2.19	4	99.80	0.20	C	397.12	66	9	Chin State, Tiddim, Chin Hills. Also Manipur (India). Animists 15%, some Baha'is. D=BBC(Zomi Baptist Convention),People's Church Movements,AoG,BCBC,SDA.
7379	1	6	3.35	1	99.60	0.40	C	234.33	114	8	Chin Hills, Haka area. Related to Haka language. Animists 40%. D=BBC.
7380	0	6	2.19		20.00	80.00	A	2.92	300	4	Assamese, other Indians, Bangladeshi, Chinese. Animists 48%, Buddhists 20%, Hindus 10%, nonreligious 10%.
Namibia											
7381	4	10	6.31	5	99.90	0.10	C	532.17	122	10	Whites: expatriates and citizens. D=DRCN(NGK,Whites only),AFMSA,CRC(NHK),Blourokkies. M=FF(South Africa).
7382	1	6	3.41	0	42.00	58.00	A	16.86	288	5	Ovamboland Territory. Also in Angola. Bushmen. Animists 89%. D=ELCN. M=BSM.
7383	9	10	3.82	5	99.95	0.05	C	568.67	82	10	Basters(mixed-race). D=DRCN(Coloured Ch),IRMSA,CPSA,CA,MCSA,SDA,UCCSA,RCC,AICs. M=OSFS,FMB.
7384	5	7	9.26	3	99.90	0.10	C	486.18	190	10	South central, Great Namaland. Bushmen. Animists 4%, some Baha'is. D=DRCN,ELCN,RCC,CPSA(D-Damaraland),AICs. M=RM,VEM,OMI,BSM,FMB.
7385	8	10	4.20	8	99.80	0.20	C	455.52	94	10	Expatriates from Britain, in development. D=CPSA(D-Damaraland),MCSA,RCC,UCCSA,PCSA,SDA,JWs,BUSA.
7386	8	10	6.38	5	99.82	0.18	C	460.92	133	10	Mixed-race persons; urban areas. D=DRCN(Coloured Ch),CPSA,CA,AFMSA,MCSA,SDA,RCC(VA-Keetmanshoop),UCCSA. M=OSFS,BSM,FMB.
7387	4	8	5.11	3	99.85	0.15	C	431.24	139	10	Mixed in Angola. Animists 12%, some Baha'is. D=Anglican Ch,Dutch Reformed Ch,RCC,ELCN.
7388	1	6	4.22	0	43.00	57.00	A	18.83	333	5	Bushmen in Okavango and Ovamboland Territory; also in Angola. Animists 88%. D=ELCN.
7389	1	6	3.69	0	43.00	57.00	A	18.83	299	5	Bushmen in north Ovamboland Territory. Animists 88%. D=DRCA.
7390	3	6	4.91	0	89.00	11.00	B	162.42	182	7	Zhuoasi. Northeast, also in Angola. Bushmen. Animists 50%. D=ELCN,NGK,UECN.
7391	0	0	8.00	1	99.80	0.20	C	318.28	246	9	Related to Subia. Animists 10%.
7392	2	6	6.95	3	99.80	0.20	C	382.52	186	9	Also in Angola, and along border. Close to Kwangali. Animists 20%. D=RCC,AICs.
7393	5	10	2.67	8	99.95	0.05	C	599.87	60	10	Long-term settlers. D=GELCN,UECN,NAC,Horpenites(from Saxony),RCC. M=RM,VEM,OSFS.
7394	3	10	-2.22	5	99.70	0.30	C	339.81	2	9	Bushmen. Remnant of original Hottentots. D=DRCN,CPSA,UCCSA.
7395	4	6	5.68	0	43.00	57.00	A	15.69	426	5	Grootfontein, and in Ovambo, also Angola. Bushmen. Animists 90%. D=ELCN,ELOC,DRCN,RCC. M=FMB.

Continued overleaf

Table 8-2 continued

PEOPLE		POPULATION				IDENTITY CODE		LANGUAGE		CHURCH		MINISTRY		SCRIPTURE	
Ref	Ethnic name	P%	In 1995	In 2000	In 2025	Race	Language	Autoglossonym	S	AC	Members	Jayuh	dwa xcmc mi	Biblioglossonym	Pub ss
1	2	3	4	5	6	7	8	9	10	11	12	13-17	18 19 20 21 22	23	24-26 27
7396	Herero	5.50000	84,888	94,923	128,568	NAB57n	99-AURL-e	mbandieru		91.80	87,139	1csu.	10 8 11 5 2		pnb .
7397	Hukwe (Barakwengo, Gani)	0.18200	2,809	3,141	4,254	BYG11d	08-AABF-e	l`kani-kxoe		10.00	314	4....	8 5 6 5 1		... .
7398	Jewish	0.12000	1,852	2,071	2,805	CMT35	52-ABAE-fi	namibian-english		0.30	6	0A.uh	5 4 2 1 0		pnb b
7399	Kwambi	3.73200	57,600	64,409	87,239	NAB57n	99-AURL-b	kwambi		80.00	51,528	1csu.	10 7 10 2 2	Otjikwambi*	PNb b
7400	Kwanyama (Ovambo)	11.28700	174,205	194,799	263,844	NAB57n	99-AURL-a	o-shi-kwanyama		80.00	155,839	3asu.	10 10 11 5 3	Oshikwanyama*	PNB b
7401	Luyana (Kwangali, Kavango	9.10000	140,450	157,054	212,721	NAB57n	99-AURN-s	si-kwangali		82.00	128,784	4as..	10 9 12 5 2	Rukwangali*	PNB b
7402	Mbukushu (Gova, Kusso)	0.33000	5,093	5,695	7,714	NAB57g	99-AURN-o	north mbukushu		81.00	4,613	1cs..	10 7 11 5 2	Mbukushu	PNb b
7403	Nama Hottentot (Namaqua)	4.42300	68,265	76,335	103,392	BYG11c	08-AAAA-a	standard nama		95.00	72,518	1a...	10 8 11 5 3	Nama	PNB b
7404	Namib (Ganin, Nossub)	0.01000	154	173	234	BYG11d	08-AABF	north tshu cluster		1.00	2	4....	6 4 2 4 0		... .
7405	Ndonga (Ambo, Ovambo)	23.10000	356,528	398,676	539,984	NAB57n	99-AURL-c	o-ci-ndonga		67.50	269,106	1asu.	10 10 12 5 2	Oshindonga*	PNB b
7406	Nharon (Nhai)	0.10000	1,543	1,726	2,338	BYG11d	08-AABA	nharo cluster		8.00	138	0....	7 5 5 4 0	Naro	... .
7407	Nusan (Gao)	0.05000	772	863	1,169	BYG11d	09-CAAH-a	nc'usa		7.00	60	0....	7 5 5 4 0		... .
7408	Nusan (Ng'amani, Auni)	0.01700	262	293	397	BYG11d	09-CAAH-a	nc'usa		8.00	23	0....	7 5 5 4 0		... .
7409	Nusan (West Xo)	0.04000	617	690	935	BYG11d	09-BABD-a	nc'u-l'en		7.00	48	0....	7 5 5 4 0		... .
7410	Subia	0.95000	14,662	16,396	22,207	NAB57g	99-AURS-f	ci-ikuhane		85.00	13,936	1..u.	10 7 7 5 0		pnb .
7411	Tswana	0.66300	10,233	11,443	15,498	NAB57q	99-AUTE-g	se-tswana	8	80.00	9,154	4Asu.	10 10 13 5 3	Tswana: Central*	PNB b
7412	Yeye	0.11000	1,698	1,898	2,571	NAB57g	99-AURM-a	ci-yei		64.00	1,215	0....	10 7 7 5 0		... .
7413	other minor peoples	3.00000	46,302	51,776	70,128	...				50.00	25,888		10 6 7 5 0		
	Nauru	**100.00000**	**10,500**	**11,519**	**17,821**					**72.4**	**8,340**				
7414	Anglo-Australian	6.20000	651	714	1,105	CEW19c	52-ABAC-x	general australian		67.00	478	1Bsuh	10 9 13 5 2		pnb b
7415	Filipino	0.50000	53	58	89	MSY44o	31-CKAA-a	proper tagalog		90.00	52	4Bs..	10 9 13 5 1	Tagalog	PNB b
7416	Han Chinese (Cantonese)	13.00000	1,365	1,497	2,317	MSY42a	79-AAAM-a	central yue		6.80	102	3A.uh	7 5 10 5 1	Chinese, Yue	PNB b
7417	Kiribertese (Gilbertese)	19.25000	2,021	2,217	3,431	MPY54a	38-DAAA-a	i-kiribati		87.00	1,929	3.s..	10 8 13 5 2	Kiribati	PNB b
7418	Kusaiean (Kosraen)	1.00000	105	115	178	MPY54z	38-BAAA	kusaie cluster		91.00	105	0....	10 7 12 5 0	Kusaien*	PNB b
7419	Marshallese	1.00000	105	115	178	MPY54b	38-CAAA	rälik-ratak cluster		95.00	109	0.s..	10 8 13 5 0	Marshallese	PNB b
7420	Nauruan	48.00000	5,040	5,529	8,554	MPY54c	38-EAAA-a	nauru		80.50	4,451	0.s..	10 10 12 5 3	Nauru*	PNB b
7421	Tuvaluan	6.85000	719	789	1,221	MPY55z	39-CAKB-a	funafuti		95.20	751	0....	10 8 13 5 3	Tuvaluan	PNB b
7422	other minor peoples	4.20000	441	484	748	...				75.00	363		10 5 8 5 0		
	Nepal	**100.00000**	**21,271,772**	**23,930,490**	**38,010,174**					**2.41**	**576,060**				
7423	Athpare Rai (Rai Kirati)	0.25000	53,179	59,826	95,025	MSY50h	71-CBAA-c	arthare		0.07	42	0....	4 3 4 0 0		... .
7424	Awadhi (Abadhi, Ambodhi)	2.68830	571,849	643,323	1,021,828	CNN25g	59-AAFP-a	awadhi		1.00	6,433	1c.u.	6 4 4 1 1	Awadhi	Pn. b
7425	Bagheli (Riwai, Kawathi)	0.03000	6,382	7,179	11,403	CNN25g	59-AAFP-c	bagheli		0.40	29	1c.u.	5 4 5 1 0	Bagheli	PN. b
7426	Bantawa Rai	0.17673	37,594	42,292	67,175	MSY50h	71-CBBA-a	bantawa		0.10	42	0....	5 3 2 0 0		... .
7427	Baragaunle (Mustang)	0.00993	2,112	2,376	3,774	MSY50z	70-AAAE-a	loyu		0.00	0	0....	0 3 3 0 0		... .
7428	Barhamu	0.00179	381	428	680	MSY50r	70-ABCA-b	baraamu		0.00	0	0....	0 2 0 0 0		... b
7429	Bengali	0.30000	63,815	71,791	114,031	CNN25b	59-AAFT-e	west bengali		0.60	431	1Asuh	5 4 8 1 2	Bengali: Musalmani*	PNB b
7430	Bhojpuri Bihari	7.85102	1,670,051	1,878,788	2,984,186	CNN25c	59-AAFQ-a	bhojpuri		0.02	376	1.s..	3 4 6 1 1	Bihari: Bhojpuri*	Pn. b
7431	Bhotia (Bhutani, Sikami)	0.10000	21,272	23,930	38,010	MSY50a	70-AAAB-f	dzongkha		0.10	24	1.s..	5 3 2 0 0	Zongkhar*	Pn. b
7432	Bodo (Boro, Mache)	0.00987	2,100	2,362	3,752	MSY50r	72-AAAA-a	bodo		8.00	189	2a...	7 5 5 0 0	Boro*	PNB .
7433	Bote-Majhi	0.03547	7,545	8,488	13,482	CNN25z	59-AAFQ-c	bote-majhi		1.00	85	1.s..	6 4 4 0 0		pn. .
7434	British	0.01000	2,127	2,393	3,801	CEW19i	52-ABAC-b	standard-english	16	79.00	1,891	3Bsuh	10 8 13 2 2		PNB b
7435	Byangsi	0.01182	2,514	2,829	4,493	MSY50r	70-ABBA-d	byangsi		0.00	0	0....	0 2 0 0 0		... .
7436	Chamlinge Rai	0.04562	9,704	10,917	17,340	MSY50h	71-CBAA-a	chamling		0.10	11	0....	5 3 4 0 0		... .
7437	Chaudangsi (Tsaudangsi)	0.00500	1,064	1,197	1,901	MSY50r	70-ABBA-c	chaudangsi		0.00	0	0....	0 3 0 0 0		... .
7438	Chaurasia (Tsaurasya)	0.03000	6,382	7,179	11,403	MSY50h	71-CAAB-a	tsaurasya		0.10	7	0....	5 1 2 0 0		... .
7439	Chentel Magar	0.02365	5,031	5,660	8,989	MSY50n	70-ADAA-a	chentel-magar		0.01	1	0....	3 2 2 0 0		... .
7440	Chepang (Eastern Tsepang)	0.11480	24,420	27,472	43,636	MSY50r	71-BAAB-a	chepang		6.00	1,648	0....	7 1 0 0 0	Chepang	PN. .
7441	Chhathar Limbu	0.07700	16,379	18,426	29,268	MSY50k	71-CBCC-c	chhathar		0.09	17	0c...	4 1 2 0 0		... .
7442	Chhulung	0.00500	1,064	1,197	1,901	MSY50h	71-CCAB	kulung-pelmung cluster		0.00	0	0....	0 2 0 0 0		... .
7443	Chitwan Tharu	0.14981	31,867	35,850	56,943	CNN25k	59-AAFT-n	mahottari-tharu		0.02	7	1csuh	3 2 4 0 0	Tharu, Mahotari*	Pnb .
7444	Dang Tharu (Dangha)	1.49226	317,430	357,105	567,211	CNN25k	59-AAFP-b	dang-tharu		0.02	71	1c.u.	3 2 4 0 0		pn. .
7445	Danuwar Rai	0.08669	18,440	20,745	32,951	CNN25j	71-CCAB-a	kulung		1.00	207	0....	6 4 2 1 1		... .
7446	Darai	0.02420	5,148	5,791	9,198	CNN25z	59-AAEB-a	darai		1.00	58	0....	6 1 3 0 0	Darai	... .
7447	Darmiya	0.00500	1,064	1,197	1,901	MSY50r	70-ABBA-b	darmiya		0.00	0	0....	0 1 0 0 0		... .
7448	Dehati Maithili	0.03000	6,382	7,179	11,403	CNN25c	59-AAFQ-f	dehati		0.02	1	1.s..	3 3 4 1 0	Maithili, Dehati	pn. .
7449	Deokri Tharu	0.52360	111,379	125,300	199,021	CNN25k	59-AAFT-q	deokri-tharu		0.02	25	1csuh	3 1 4 0 0		pnb b
7450	Dhimal	0.08619	18,334	20,626	32,761	MSY50r	71-DAAA-a	dhimal		0.00	0	0....	0 3 0 0 0		... .
7451	Dolpa Tibetan	0.02956	6,288	7,074	11,236	MSY50r	70-AAAA-f	dolpo-tichurong		0.00	0	0c...	0 3 0 0 1		pnb .
7452	Eastern Gurung (Gurkha)	0.35471	75,453	84,884	134,826	MSY50e	70-AABD-aa	daduwa		0.02	17	0....	3 2 2 0 0		p.. .
7453	Eastern Magar (Gurkha)	1.35000	287,169	323,062	513,137	MSY50n	71-BABA-b	east magar		0.03	97	0....	3 4 4 2 2	Magar*	PN. .
7454	Eastern Tamang	1.78743	380,218	427,741	679,405	MSY50z	70-AABA-c	east tamang		12.00	51,329	0....	8 6 13 3 3	Tamang, Eastern	pn. .
7455	French	0.01000	2,127	2,393	3,801	CEW21b	51-AABI-d	general français		84.00	2,010	1B.uh	10 8 14 2 1	French	PNB b
7456	Galle Gurung (Ghale)	0.10526	22,391	25,189	40,010	MSY50e	70-AABF-a	ghale		0.02	5	0....	3 3 2 0 0	Ghale, Southern	... .
7457	Gamale Kham	0.05484	11,665	13,123	20,845	MSY50h	71-BADA-a	gamale		0.02	3	0....	3 2 4 0 0		... .
7458	German	0.01000	2,127	2,393	3,801	CEW19m	52-ABCE-a	standard hoch-deutsch		87.00	2,082	2B.uh	10 8 13 2 1	German*	PNB b
7459	Han Chinese	0.07000	14,890	16,751	26,607	MSY42a	79-AAAB-ba	kuo-yü		0.30	50	2Bsuh	5 4 10 0 0	Chinese: Kuoyu*	PNB b
7460	Helambu Sherpa	0.05912	12,576	14,148	22,472	MSY50r	70-AAAA-e	sherpa		0.10	14	0c...	5 2 2 0 0	Sherpa*	Pnb .
7461	Hindi	1.10000	233,989	263,235	418,112	CNN25g	59-AAFO-e	general hindi		1.07	2,817	3Asuh	6 5 10 2 2		pnb b
7462	Humla Bhotia	0.01000	2,127	2,393	3,801	MSY50r	70-AAAA-fe	humla		0.00	0	0c...	0 3 0 0 0		pnb .
7463	Janggali (Dzanggali)	0.09621	20,466	23,024	36,570	MSY50r	70-ABAA-h	jangali		0.02	5	0....	3 2 2 0 1		p.. .
7464	Jerung	0.00800	1,702	1,914	3,041	MSY50h	71-CCAB	kulung-pelmung cluster		0.00	0	0....	0 2 0 0 0		... .
7465	Jirel	0.02956	6,288	7,074	11,236	MSY50r	70-AAAB-a	jirel		0.00	0	1.s..	0 2 0 0 0	Jirel	PN. .
7466	Kagate Bhotia (Syuwa)	0.00532	1,132	1,273	2,022	MSY50r	70-AAAA-ch	kagate		0.00	0	0c...	0 2 0 0 0	Kagate	Pnb .
7467	Kaike	0.01000	2,127	2,393	3,801	MSY50e	70-AAEA-a	tarali-kham		0.09	2	0....	4 4 3 0 0		... .
7468	Kalinge Rai	0.08068	17,162	19,307	30,667	MSY50h	71-CABA-a	khaling		0.07	14	0....	4 3 4 0 0	Khaling	PN. .
7469	Kathoriya Tharu	0.40000	85,087	95,722	152,041	CNN25k	59-AAFT-n	mahottari-tharu		0.00	0	1csuh	0 3 0 0 0	Tharu, Mahotari*	Pnb .
7470	Kayort	0.10000	21,272	23,930	38,010	CNN25b	59-AAFT-q	deokri-tharu		0.30	72	1csuh	5 3 4 0 0		pnb b
7471	Kham-Magar (Kham, Wali)	0.08226	17,498	19,685	31,267	MSY50n	71-BAFA-a	takale		0.06	12	0....	4 4 4 1 0	Kham, Takale	PN. .
7472	Kharia (Haria)	0.02000	4,254	4,786	7,602	AUG04z	46-CBAA-a	kharia		70.00	3,350	0....	10 6 11 2 3	Kharia	P.. .
7473	Koi	0.00591	1,257	1,414	2,246	MSY50h	71-CABA-c	koi		0.10	1	0....	5 2 4 0 0		pn. b
7474	Kulunge Rai (Pelmung)	0.07600	16,167	18,187	28,888	MSY50h	71-CCAB-a	kulung		0.07	13	0....	4 3 4 0 0		... .
7475	Kumaoni (Kumauni)	0.40000	85,087	95,722	152,041	CNN25k	59-AAFC-d	kumauni		0.04	38	1....	3 4 5 0 1	Kumaoni*	Pn. .
7476	Kumhali	0.02000	4,254	4,786	7,602	CNN25z	59-AAFD	east pahari cluster		1.00	48	2Asu.	6 2 4 0 0		PNB b
7477	Kutang Bhotia	0.01578	3,357	3,776	5,998	MSY50r	70-AAAD-a	larkye		0.00	0	0....	0 1 0 0 0		... .
7478	Kyerung	0.02000	4,254	4,786	7,602	MSY50r	70-AAAA-cg	kyerung		0.00	0	0c...	0 1 0 0 0		pnb b
7479	Lepcha (Lapche, Rongke)	0.01339	2,848	3,204	5,090	MSY50j	73-DFAA-a	lepcha		7.00	224	1....	7 5 9 1 2	Lepcha	PN. .
7480	Lhomi (Shing Saapa)	0.02365	5,031	5,660	8,989	MSY50r	70-AAAA-ce	lhomi		0.00	0	0c...	0 1 0 0 0	Lhomi	PNb .
7481	Limbu	1.15000	244,625	275,201	437,117	MSY50k	71-CBCC-a	limbu		0.10	275	0a...	5 4 7 1 0	Limbu	... b
7482	Loba (Mustang)	0.11824	25,152	28,295	44,943	MSY50z	70-AAAE-a	loyu		0.00	0	0....	0 3 0 0 0		... .
7483	Lohorong (Pidisoi)	0.07094	15,090	16,976	26,964	MSY50z	71-CBCA-a	lohorong		0.00	0	0....	0 2 0 0 0		... .
7484	Lumba-Yakkha	0.00500	1,064	1,197	1,901	MSY50h	71-CCAB	kulung-pelmung cluster		0.00	0	0....	0 2 0 0 0		... .
7485	Mahotari Tharu	0.20944	44,552	50,120	79,609	CNN25k	59-AAFT-n	mahottari-tharu		0.02	10	1csuh	3 2 4 0 0	Tharu, Mahotari*	Pnb .
7486	Maikoti Kham	0.01200	2,553	2,872	4,561	MSY50n	71-BAHA-a	maikoti		0.00	0	0....	0 2 4 0 0		... .
7487	Maitili (Tirahutia)	10.79515	2,296,320	2,583,332	4,103,255	CNN25c	59-AAFQ-b	maithili		0.20	5,167	1.s..	5 4 6 2 1	Maithili	Pn. b
7488	Majhi	0.06205	13,199	14,849	23,585	CNN25n	59-AAFE-d	majhi		1.00	148	1asu.	6 4 4 1 0	Panjabi*	PNB b
7489	Malayali	0.03000	6,382	7,179	11,403	CNN23b	49-EBEB-a	malayalam		32.00	2,297	2Asu.	9 7 13 3 2	Malayalam	PNB b
7490	Mugali	0.01556	3,310	3,724	5,914	MSY50r	70-AAAA-fd	mugali-kham		0.00	0	0c...	0 1 0 0 0		pnb .
7491	Munda (Horo, Colh)	0.03000	6,382	7,179	11,403	AUG04b	46-CABA-d	mundari		21.00	1,508	3cs..	9 5 8 3 3	Mundari	PNB .
7492	Musasa	0.04000	8,509	9,572	15,204	CNN25z	59-AAFQ-e	musasa		1.00	96	1.s..	6 4 4 0 0		pn. .
7493	Nachering	0.01000	2,127	2,393	3,801	MSY50h	71-CCAB	kulung-pelmung cluster		0.07	2	0....	4 1 3 0 0		... .
7494	Nawa Sherpa	0.00296	630	708	1,125	MSY50r	70-AAAA-cj	naapa		0.10	1	0c...	5 2 2 0 0		pnb p
7495	Nepalese (Eastern Pahari)	55.76179	11,861,521	13,344,070	21,195,153	CNN25k	59-AAFD-b	nepali	84	3.10	413,666	2Asu.	6 5 9 3 4	Nepali	PNB b
7496	Newange Rai	0.01771	3,767	4,238	6,732	MSY50h	71-CBCA-ab	balali		0.10	4	0....	5 3 4 0 0		... .
7497	Newar	2.95596	628,785	707,376	1,123,566	MSY50z	71-AAAA-a	newari	10	0.13	920	0....	5 4 8 2 3	Newari	PN. .
7498	Nisi Kham	0.05000	10,636	11,965	19,005	MSY50h	71-BACA-a	sheshi		0.02	2	0....	3 1 4 0 0		... .
7499	Northern Ghale	0.01265	2,691	3,027	4,808	MSY50e	70-AABF-a	ghale		0.00	0	0....	0 2 0 0 0	Ghale, Southern	... .
7500	Northern Gurung	0.02910	6,190	6,964	11,061	MSY50e	70-AABB-a	manangba		0.09	6	0....	4 3 2 0 0		pn. .
7501	Northwestern Tamang (Tama	1.28000	272,279	306,310	486,530	MSY50z	70-AABA-a	murmi		17.00	52,073	0....	8 7 13 3 3	Tamang, Northwestern	PN. .
7502	Oraon (Dhangar)	0.04000	8,509	9,572	15,204	AUG06c	49-BAAA-a	nepal kurukh		43.00	4,116	1....	9 7 10 3 3	Kurux*	PN. .
7503	Palpa Pahari	0.03160	6,722	7,562	12,011	CNN25k	59-AAFD-a	palpa		0.04	3	1csu.	3 3 2 0 0	Palpa	PNb .
7504	Puma	0.01518	3,229	3,633	5,770	MSY50h	71-CCAB	kulung-pelmung cluster		0.00	0	0....	0 2 0 0 0		... .
7505	Punjabi	0.05000	10,636	11,965	19,005	CNN25n	59-AAFE-c	general panjabi		2.00	239	1Asu.	6 4 10 1 0		PNB b
7506	Rajbansi (Tajpuri)	0.58078	123,542	138,983	220,755	CNN25b	59-AAFT-ha	rajbangshi		0.50	695	1csuh	5 4 4 1 0		pnb b
7507	Raji	0.01766	3,757	4,226	6,713	MSY50n	71-BABB-a	raji		0.00	0	0....	0 1 0 0 0		... .
7508	Rana Thakur Tharu	1.26973	270,094	303,853	482,627	CNN25k	59-AAFT-p	rana-thakur-tharu		0.00	0	1csuh	0 3 4 0 0		pnb .
7509	Rangkas	0.00170	362	407	646	MSY50r	70-ABBA-a	rangkas		0.00	0	0....	0 1 2 0 0		... .
7510	Raute	0.00118	251	282	449	MSY50h	71-BAGA-a	raute		0.00	0	0....	0 3 0 0 0		... .
7511	Rumdali Rai (Bainge Rai)	0.04302	9,151	10,295	16,352	MSY50h	71-CCAB-a	kulung		0.10	10	0....	5 3 4 0 0		... .
7512	Saam Rai	0.20000	42,544	47,861	76,020	MSY50h	71-CCAB-a	kulung		0.10	48	0....	5 1 3 0 0		... .
7513	Sampange Rai	0.03037	6,460	7,268	11,544	MSY50h	71-CCAB-a	kulung		0.10	7	0....	5 3 4 0 0		... .
7514	Santal (Hor, Har)	0.23648	50,303	56,591	89,886	AUG04c	46-CABA-a	santali		0.78	441	2as..	5 5 8 3 3	Santali	PNB b
7515	Saptari Tharu	0.39270	83,534	93,975	149,266	CNN25k	59-AAFT-o	saptari-tharu		0.02	19	1csuh	3 3 4 0 0		pnb .

Continued opposite

Table 8-2 continued

EVANGELIZATION								EVANGELISM			ADDITIONAL DESCRIPTIVE DATA
Ref 1	D 28	aC 29	CG% 30	r 31	E 32	U 33	W 34	e 35	R 36	T 37	Locations, civil divisions, literacy, religions, church history, denominations, dioceses, church growth, missions, agencies, ministries, movements 38
7396	7	7	4.93	3	99.92	0.08	C	488.53	129	10	Damaraland, Kaokoveld. Animists 8%, some Baha'is. D=ELCN,NGK Sendingkerk,RCC,Oruuano(Herero Ch),PUC,AFMSA,other AICs. M=RM,FMB.
7397	2	6	3.51	0	45.00	55.00	A	16.42	275	5	Black Bushmen, Water Bushmen, Xu, Mbarakwena. In Okavango. Most in Angola. Animists 90%. D=DRCN,RCC. M=BSM.
7398	0	10	1.81	8	43.30	56.70	A	0.47	158	3	Small communities of English-speaking practicing Jews.
7399	2	7	8.92	1	99.80	0.20	C	382.52	227	9	North Ovamboland; some in Angola. Animists 10%. D=RCC,AICs.
7400	8	7	7.49	5	99.80	0.20	C	435.08	173	10	Northern Okavangoland. Primarily in Angola. Literates 50%. Animists 4%, Baha'is. D=ELOC,DRCN,RCC(VA-Windhoek),AEF,CPSA(D-Damaraland),AFMSA,AICs.
7401	5	7	9.93	4	99.82	0.18	C	454.93	214	10	Also in Angola. Animists 5%, some Baha'is. D=RCC(VA-Windhoek),CPSA,ELOC,NGK Sendingkerk,AICs. M=OMI,FF(South Africa).
7402	2	10	6.33	3	99.81	0.19	C	416.86	158	10	Northeast Okavango area; also Zambia, Botswana, Angola. Animists 19%. D=RCC,AC/CPSA.
7403	5	10	4.04	4	99.95	0.05	C	558.26	87	10	Great Namaland; also in South Africa. Khoisan. Animists 1%, some Baha'is. D=DRCN(Coloured Ch),AMEC,ELCN,RCC,other AICs. M=RMS,VEM,AMEC(USA).
7404	0	5	0.70	0	25.00	75.00	A	0.91	186	3	Bushmen. Remnant of origal Khoisan inhabitants. Virtually extinct. Animists 99%.
7405	7	6	7.09	5	99.68	0.32	C	328.91	185	9	Ovamboland; some in southern Angola. Literates 75%. Animists 4%, some Baha'is. D=ELOC,RCC(VA-Windhoek),CPSA(D-Damaraland),AFMSA,JWs,DRC,AICs.
7406	0	6	2.66	0	33.00	67.00	A	9.63	304	4	Remnant of original Bushmen. Animists 92%.
7407	0	6	4.18	0	32.00	68.00	A	8.17	444	4	Last remnant of original inhabitants, Bushmen. Animists 93%.
7408	0	6	3.19	0	33.00	67.00	A	9.63	348	4	Also in South Africa, Botswana. Bushmen. Many dialects. Animists 92%.
7409	0	6	3.95	0	32.00	68.00	A	8.17	424	4	Bushmen. Language and people virtually extinct. Animists 93%.
7410	0	7	7.51	4	99.85	0.15	C	400.22	198	10	Mainly in Zambia (dialect of Tonga). Animists 10%.
7411	3	10	4.25	5	99.80	0.20	C	452.60	92	10	Also in Botswana, South Africa, Zimbabwe. Animists 20%. D=ELCN,NGK Sendingkerk,RCC.
7412	0	9	4.92	0	99.00	1.00	C	231.26	186	8	Okavango Swamp. Mainly in Botswana. Animists 36%.
7413	0	8	9.17		81.00	19.00	B	147.82	310	7	USA Whites(CJCLdS,JWs), Luchazi (Ev Ch in Zambia), Chokwe(FMB), Lozi, Portuguese, Mbundu, Vasekela Bushmen.
Nauru											
7414	2	10	2.06	8	99.67	0.33	C	330.14	57	9	Whites from Australia. Nonreligious 30%. D=Anglican Ch(D-Polynesia),RCC(D-Tarawa,Nauru,& Funafuti).
7415	1	10	4.03	5	99.90	0.10	C	535.45	79	10	Laborers from Philippines. D=RCC. M=MSC.
7416	1	10	2.35	8	73.80	26.20	B	18.31	111	5	Laborers from Hong Kong. Half now use English, Mandarin, or Nauru. Buddhists/Chinese folk-religionists 91%. D=RCC.
7417	4	10	3.18	4	99.87	0.13	C	495.37	67	10	Immigrants from Kiribati. Baha'is 10%. D=NPC,RCC,AC,SDA. M=GIPC,MSC.
7418	0	10	2.38	5	99.91	0.09	C	498.22	55	10	Immigrants from Micronesia. Bilingual in Nauru.
7419	0	10	2.53	2	99.95	0.05	C	530.52	45	10	Immigrants from Marshall Islands. Bilingual in Nauru.
7420	3	10	4.45	2	99.81	0.19	C	424.57	96	10	All bilingual in English. Lingua franca. Fishermen. Baha'is growing. Nominal Christians 40%. D=Nauru Congregational Ch(NPC),RCC,AC. M=LMS,MSC,CPNZ.
7421	4	10	2.43	5	99.95	0.05	C	560.13	50	10	Laborers from Tuvalu. D=NPC,RCC,AC,SDA.
7422	0	10	3.66		99.75	0.25	C	295.65	93	8	Other Pacific Islanders, Chinese creoles (Pidgin English), Mandarin.
Nepal											
7423	0	3	3.81	0	12.07	87.93	A	0.03	1,092	2	Dhankuta District, Koshi Zone. Hindus 80%, some Buddhists 10%, animists 10%.
7424	2	5	6.68	1	30.00	70.00	A	1.09	701	4	Eastern Hindi. Majhkhanda, Khajahani. Vast majority in India; some in USA. Hindus 98%. D=RCC,AoG. M=SJ.
7425	0	6	3.42	1	27.40	72.60	A	0.40	442	3	Eastern Hindi. Morang District, Koshi Zone. Majority in India. Trade language (lingua franca). Hindus 99%.
7426	0	5	3.81	0	13.10	86.90	A	0.04	1,006	2	Bhojpur District, Koshi Zone; western Dhankuta District, Khotang District. Many villages. Pastoralists. Animists 95%, some Lamaist Buddhists.
7427	0	5	0.00	0	9.00	91.00	A	0.00	0	1.02	Northern Mustang. Close to Lopa and Dolpo. Lamaist Buddhists 100%.
7428	0	4	0.00	0	8.00	92.00	A	0.00	0	1.02	North Gorkha District, Gandaki Zone, Takhu village. Related to Thami. Second language Nepali. Animists 70%, Hindus 30%.
7429	3	7	3.84	6	53.60	46.40	B	1.17	266	4	Workers from India and Bangladesh. Hindus 73%, Muslims 25%(Hanafi Sunnis). D=RCC,SDA,AoG. M=CNI,SJ.
7430	1	5	3.69	6	32.02	67.98	A	0.02	403	2	Birgunj area. Most in India. Traders, settlers from India. Bilingual in Hindi and Maitili. Hindus 79%, Muslims 21%. D=RCC.
7431	0	5	3.23	0	18.10	81.90	A	0.06	742	2	Drukke, Zongkhar, Zonkar. Sikkimese, Bhutanese. Traders, shopkeepers. Strict Lamaists(Tantric Buddhists) 100%.
7432	0	5	2.98	4	46.00	54.00	A	13.43	277	5	Jhapa. Almost all in India(Assam, West Bengal). Hindus 50%, hinduized animists 42%.
7433	0	5	4.54	1	23.00	77.00	A	0.84	662	3	Mainly Chitawan District, near Kumhali. Fishermen, boatmen on rivers. Hindus 90%.
7434	3	10	5.38	8	99.79	0.21	C	429.64	120	10	Expatriates from Britain, in development, education. D=RCC,AoG,SDA. M=SJ,UMN.
7435	0	5	0.00	0	6.00	94.00	A	0.00	0	1.01	Tibetans. Far west, Mahakali Zone. Related to Rangkas, Darmiya, Chaudangsi. Lamaist Buddhists 100%.
7436	0	5	2.43	0	15.10	84.90	A	0.05	622	2	Rawa Valley, Khotang District, Sagarmatha Zone. Hindus 70%, animists 30%.
7437	0	5	0.00	0	6.00	94.00	A	0.00	0	1.01	Tibetans. Mahakali Zone, far west. Also in India. Related to Rangkas. Lamaist Buddhists 100%.
7438	0	5	1.96	0	13.10	86.90	A	0.04	619	2	Dhankuta District. Hindus 70%, animists 30%.
7439	0	4	0.00	0	10.01	89.99	A	0.00	219	1.03	Myagdi District, Chawalagiri Zone, Kali Gandaki River Valley. Closest to Kham, Thakali. Animists 70%, Buddhists 30%.
7440	0	4	5.24	0	23.00	77.00	A	5.03	823	4	Inner Terai, Makwanpur District. Agriculturalists. Animists 94%(with Hindu overlay). 4 major churches.
7441	0	5	2.87	1	14.09	85.91	A	0.04	753	2	Dhankuta District, far east. Hindus 50%, animists 40%, Buddhists 10%.
7442	0	0	0.00	0	0.00	100.00	A	0.00	0	1.00	Ankhisalla Panchayat, Dhankuta District. Speakers know moderate amount of Nepali. Animists 70%, Hindus 30%.
7443	0	5	1.96	1	23.02	76.98	A	0.01	388	2	Southern strip of low country in Rapti Valley, Chitwan District. Agriculturalists. Animists 95%, Hindus 5%.
7444	0	5	4.35	1	18.02	81.98	A	0.01	859	2	West of Bhairawa-Butwal, north of India border. Agriculturalists, pastoralists. Animists 80%, Hindus 20%.
7445	1	5	3.08	0	18.00	82.00	A	0.65	623	3	Eastern hills and plain, inner Terai south of Kathmandu. Hindus 98%, animists. D=RCC. M=SJ.
7446	0	5	4.14	0	16.00	84.00	A	0.58	884	3	Inner Terai, Chitawan District. Hindus 80%, animists 19%.
7447	0	4	0.00	0	5.00	95.00	A	0.00	0	1.01	Tibetans. Mahakali Zone, far west. Also in India. Related to Rangkas, Chaudangsi. Hindus 50%, animists 30%, Buddhists 20%.
7448	0	5	0.00	1	20.02	79.98	A	0.01	140	2	Some districts of south Nepal bordering Bihar. Mostly Hindus 95%, Muslims 5%.
7449	0	5	3.27	1	23.02	76.98	A	0.01	544	2	On eastern border with India. Agriculturalists, pastoralists. Animists 95%, Hindus 5%.
7450	0	4	0.00	0	5.00	95.00	A	0.00	0	1.01	Jhapa, Biratnagar, eastern Terai. Some bilinguals in Nepali or Hindi. Lamaist Buddhists 100%.
7451	0	5	0.00	1	15.00	85.00	A	0.00	0	1.06	Tibetans. Northern Dolpa District, Karnali Zone. Close to Lopa, Tichurong. Lamaist Buddhists 100%. M=YWAM.
7452	0	5	2.87	0	12.02	87.98	A	0.00	882	1.05	Lamjung and Gorkha Districts, centered on Daduwa town. Pastoralists. Animists 80%, Hindus 20%.
7453	1	4	4.68	0	21.03	78.97	A	0.02	714	2	Central mountains, east of Bagmati river, Tanahu. Also in Sikkim, Bhutan, India. Some bilinguals in Nepali. Animists 90%, Hindus 10%. D=indigenous chs.
7454	1	5	8.92	0	51.00	49.00	B	22.33	538	5	Kathmandu eastwards, southeast. Also Sikkim, Darjeeling (India). Animists 38%, Hindus 27%, Buddhists 23%. 1974, indigenous revival begins, now widespread.
7455	1	10	5.45	8	99.84	0.16	C	466.03	116	10	Expatriates from France, in business. D=RCC(D-Patna). M=SJ.
7456	0	5	1.62	0	11.02	88.98	A	0.00	651	1.03	Western hills, Gorkha. Agriculturalists. Hindus 94%, Buddhists 5%, some animists.
7457	0	4	1.10	0	12.02	87.98	A	0.00	479	1.03	Gam Khola, western hills, Rukum and Rolpa Districts. Monolinguals. Hindus 90%, animists 5%, Buddhists 5%.
7458	3	10	5.48	8	99.87	0.13	C	498.55	116	10	Expatriates from Germany, in development. D=RCC,AoG,SDA. M=SJ.
7459	0	9	3.99	7	54.30	45.70	B	0.59	234	3	From China. In trade, business, commerce. Buddhists/Chinese folk-religionists 99%.
7460	0	5	2.67	1	21.10	78.90	A	0.07	564	2	Nuwakot and Sindhupalchok Districts, Bagmati Zone. Related to Kagate. Few bilinguals in Nepali. Lamaist Buddhists 90%, some animists.
7461	3	7	5.80	7	58.07	41.93	B	2.26	321	4	In south of country. Traders from India. Hindus 90%, about 3,000 Baha'is, many Muslims also. D=RCC,SDA,AoG. M=SJ,FMB.
7462	0	4	0.00	1	13.00	87.00	A	0.00	0	1.06	Bajura District, Seti Zone; Humla District, Karnali Zone. Low literacy in Tibetan. Lamaist Buddhists 100%.
7463	0	4	1.62	0	12.02	87.98	A	0.00	750	1.05	Tibetans. Mahakali Zone, far west. Also in India (Himachal Pradesh). Hindus 50%, animists 50%. M=GR.
7464	0	0	0.00	0	0.00	100.00	A	0.00	0	1.00	Near mouth of Melungkhola River. Similar to Chourase. Young people do not speak jero. Hindus 70%, Animists 30%.
7465	0	5	0.00	0	12.00	88.00	A	0.00	0	1.06	Tibetans. Dolakha District, Janakpur Zone, Jiri Valley, eastern hills. Animists 60%, Lamaist Buddhists 40%.
7466	0	4	0.00	1	13.00	87.00	A	0.00	0	1.07	Ramechhap District. Agriculturalists, pastoralists. Lamaist Buddhists 100%.
7467	0	6	0.70	0	14.09	85.91	A	0.04	331	2	Dhawalagiri Zone; Dolpa District, Karnali Zone. Hunter-gatherers. Animists 90%, Buddhists 10%.
7468	0	5	2.67	0	18.07	81.93	A	0.04	556	2	Solu Khumbu District, Sagarmatha Zone, eastern hills. Hindus 95%, animists.
7469	0	0	0.00	1	10.00	90.00	A	0.00	0	1.09	Kailali District near the Dangora River. Also in India. Related to Dang and Rana. Animists 99%, Hindus 1%.
7470	0	5	4.37	1	28.30	71.70	A	0.31	555	3	Koshi Zone, Morang District, Dakuwa Danga, near Rajbangsi language area. Related to Bengali. Hindus 99%.
7471	0	4	2.52	0	18.06	81.94	A	0.04	504	2	Rukum, Rolpa Districts, western hills. Pastoralists. Animists 70%, Lamaist Buddhists 27%, some Hindus. Small groups of Christians worship in villages.
7472	1	6	5.99	0	99.70	0.30	C	270.83	183	8	Expatriates, migrant workers from India. Animists 15%, Hindus 15%. D=RCC(D-Patna). M=SJ,SVD,GELC/GMS.
7473	0	4	0.00	0	20.10	79.90	A	0.07	136	2	South Kotang District. Becoming bilingual in Nepali. Hindus 50%, animists 50%.
7474	0	5	2.60	0	14.07	85.93	A	0.03	701	2	Solu Khumbu, eastern hills. Agriculturalists. Related to Khambu. Animists 99%, some Hindus.
7475	1	4	3.70	0	19.04	80.96	A	0.02	720	2	Mahakali Zone. Also in India. Hindus 99%. D=CNI.
7476	0	5	3.95	4	38.00	62.00	A	1.38	358	4	Nawalpur, Gorkha District, Gandaki Zone. Agriculturalists, pastoralists, fishermen. Some bilinguals in Nepali. Hindus 70%, animists 29%.
7477	0	5	0.00	0	6.00	94.00	A	0.00	0	1.01	North Gorkha District, Gandaki Zone, along the Buri Gandalei river. Some bilinguals in Nepali. Lamaist Buddhists 100%.
7478	0	4	0.00	1	16.00	84.00	A	0.00	0	1.07	Rasuwa District, Bagmati Zone. Also in Tibet. Close to Tibetan (Lhasa). Lamaist Buddhists 100%.
7479	5	6	3.16	0	41.00	59.00	A	10.47	278	5	Ilam District, also Sikkim,Bhutan,India. Farmers, cattle breeders. Strict Lamaist Buddhists 70%, animists/shamanists with Lamaist syncretistic features 23%.
7480	0	4	0.00	1	14.00	86.00	A	0.00	0	1.07	Tibetans. Eastern hills, Sankhuwasawa District, Koshi Zone, near Arun river. Animists 70%, Lamaist Buddhists 30%.
7481	0	4	3.37	4	26.10	73.90	A	0.09	459	2	Eastern hills, Dankuta Terhathum District. Some in Sikkim, India. Less-strict Buddhists(Lamaists) 70%, Hindus 20%, animists 10%.
7482	0	5	0.00	0	6.00	94.00	A	0.00	0	1.01	Dawalagiri Zone, Dolpa and Mustang Districts. Salt traders, agriculturalists, pastoralists. Lamaist Buddhists 100%.
7483	0	4	0.00	0	5.00	95.00	A	0.00	0	1.01	Upper Arun Valley, Sankhuwasawa District, Koshi Zone. Rai group related to Limbu, Yakha. Hindus 70%, animists 27%, some Buddhists.
7484	0	0	0.00	0	0.00	100.00	A	0.00	0	1.00	North Dhankuta District around Lakhshmikhola. Related to Yakkha and Chhulung. Buddhists 70%, Hindus 30%.
7485	0	5	2.33	1	23.02	76.98	A	0.01	432	2	Mahottari District, Janakpur Zone. Agriculturalists, pastoralists. Animists 98%, some Hindus.
7486	0	3	0.00	0	8.00	92.00	A	0.00	0	1.02	Western Hills, Rukum and Rolpa Districts. Hindus 50%, Buddhists 30%, animists 20%.
7487	1	5	6.45	1	31.20	68.80	A	0.22	656	3	Eastern Terai; also in India. A very extensive and lengthy literature. High-caste Hindus 99%, Muslims 1%. D=RCC(D-Patna). M=SJ.
7488	0	5	2.73	5	38.00	62.00	A	1.38	273	4	Eastern hills, Dolakha. Also in India. Hindus 90%, a few animists.
7489	3	8	5.59	4	96.00	4.00	B	112.12	188	7	From Kerala. Hindus 48%, Muslims 19%, Baha'is 10%. D=OSCE,MTSC,RCC. M=PCB,MTSEA.
7490	0	4	0.00	1	13.00	87.00	A	0.00	0	1.06	Mugu, Karnali. Close to Humla Bhotia. Pastoralists. Lamaists Buddhists 100%.
7491	2	6	5.14	1	70.00	30.00	B	53.65	244	6	Mainly in India, Bangladesh. Hindus 53%, animists 26%. D=RCC(D-Patna),SDA. M=SJ,CNI,MCSA,GELC.
7492	0	5	4.67	1	23.00	77.00	A	0.84	678	3	Sindhuli Garhi District, Morang District, Koshi Zone; Dolakha District, Janakpur Zone. Hindus 99%.
7493	0	0	0.70	0	7.07	92.93	A	0.01	659	2	Upper northeastern Khotang District near Rawakhola Valley. Related to Kulung and Sangpang. Animists 99%, Hindus 1%.
7494	0	5	0.00	1	22.10	77.90	A	0.08	207	2	Sankhuwasawa District, Koshi Zone. Interspersed among Lhomi (bilinguals). Animists 50%, Lamaist Buddhists 50%.
7495	8	4	11.22	4	59.10	40.90	B	6.68	580	4	Hindus 87%, Buddhists 8%, Muslims 3.5%. D=CNN,RCC(D-Patna),PCK,SDA,UUA,NCC,INF,AoG. M=UMN(50 agencies),TEAM,OM,SJ,LBI,NEB,WEC,IEC,NMM.
7496	0	4	1.40	0	14.10	85.90	A	0.05	466	2	Sankhuwasawa District, Koshi Zone, upper Arun Valley, eastern. Agriculturalists, pastoralists. Hindus 70%, animists 20%, Buddhists 10%.
7497	0	4	4.63	0	27.13	72.87	A	0.12	579	3	In Kathmandu, midlands. Also in Bihar (India). Agriculturalists. Widespread. Hindus 80%(70 castes), Buddhists 20%(Mahayana). M=UMN,FMB,YWAM.
7498	0	4	0.70	0	12.02	87.98	A	0.00	388	1.03	Western hills, Rukum and Rolpa Districts. Hindus 75%, Buddhists 15%, animists 10%.
7499	0	0	0.00	0	0.00	100.00	A	0.00	0	1.00	Gandaki Zone, Gorkha District. Forest and mountains. Swidden agriculturalists. Buddhists (Lamaists) 100%.
7500	0	5	1.81	0	15.09	84.91	A	0.05	510	2	Manang District, Gandaki Zone, northern. Traders. Animists 60%, Hindus 40%.
7501	3	5	8.93	0	59.00	41.00	B	36.61	466	5	West of Kathmandu. Nuwakot District, central mountain strip. Altitude 8000 ft. Animists 35%, Hindus 25%, Buddhists 23%. 1974, widespread revival begins.
7502	2	5	6.20	0	82.00	18.00	B	128.69	244	7	Nepali Kurux. Eastern Terai, Dhanusa. Hindus 37%, animists 20%. D=RCC(D-Patna),SDA. M=SJ,CNI,GELC,MCSA.
7503	0	5	1.10	1	21.04	78.96	A	0.03	313	2	Western, town of Palpa. Related to Nepali and Kumaoni. Hindus 95%, animists 5%.
7504	0	0	0.00	0	0.00	100.00	A	0.00	0	1.00	Northwestern slopes of the Rapcha Range and Shwahkola Valley. Buddhists (Lamaists) 100%.
7505	0	7	3.22	5	51.00	49.00	B	3.72	229	4	Traders from India. Sikhs 70%, Hindus 27%, Muslims 1%.
7506	0	5	4.33	1	26.50	73.50	A	0.48	588	3	Jhapa, Morang. Also in Bangladesh and India. Agriculturalists, pastoralists. Hindus 99%.
7507	0	5	0.00	0	6.00	94.00	A	0.00	0	1.01	Banke-Kailali, Surkhet area, Bardia Districts. Also India. Hunter-gatherers, fishermen, boatmen. Animists 90%, Hindus 10%.
7508	0	4	0.00	1	19.00	81.00	A	0.00	0	1.12	On eastern border with India. Agriculturalists, pastoralists. Animists 99%.
7509	0	5	0.00	0	8.00	92.00	A	0.00	0	1.02	Mahakali Zone, far western. Also India. Related to Darmiya, Chaudangsi, Byangsi. Lamaist Buddhists 100%.
7510	0	6	0.00	0	7.00	93.00	A	0.00	0	1.02	Achham District, Seti Zone; Surkhet District, Bheri Zone. Nomadic. Animists 95%, some Hindus.
7511	0	5	2.33	0	15.10	84.90	A	0.05	604	2	Sagarmatha Zone, Okhaldunga, eastern. Related to Umbule, Sunwar. Pastoralists. Hindus 85%, Buddhists 10%, animists 5%.
7512	0	5	3.95	0	14.10	85.90	A	0.05	962	2	Sankhuwasawa District, eastern. Hindu 70%, animists 30%.
7513	0	5	1.96	0	15.10	84.90	A	0.05	537	2	Khotang District, Sagarmatha Zone, Phali, near Dingla, eastern. Hindus 90%, some animists 10%.
7514	2	6	3.86	4	52.78	47.22	B	1.50	252	4	Jhapa, Morang. Settlers from India, Bangladesh. Bilinguals in Maithili, Nepali. Hindus 78%, animists 21%. D=RCC,SDA. M=SJ,CNI,NELC.
7515	0	5	2.99	1	23.02	76.98	A	0.01	511	2	Saptari District, Sagarmatha Zone. Agriculturalists, pastoralists. Animists 98%, some Hindus.

Continued overleaf

Table 8-2 continued

PEOPLE		POPULATION				IDENTITY CODE		LANGUAGE		CHURCH		MINISTRY						SCRIPTURE		
Ref 1	Ethnic name 2	P% 3	In 1995 4	In 2000 5	In 2025 6	Race 7	Language 8	Autoglossonym 9	S 10	AC 11	Members 12	Jayuh 13-17	d 18	wa 19	xc 20	mc 21	mi 22	Biblioglossonym 23	Pub 24-26	ss 27
7516	Sherpa (Sharpa Bhotia)	0.14869	31,629	35,582	56,517	MSY50q	70-AAAA-e	sherpa	1	0.11	39	0c...	5	3	4	1	2	Sherpa*	Pnb	.
7517	Sheshi Kham	0.05000	10,636	11,965	19,005	MSY50h	71-BAEA-a	nisi		0.02	2	0....	3	1	4	0	0		...	.
7518	Sonha	0.05912	12,576	14,148	22,472	CNN25k	59-AAFP	east hindi cluster		0.02	3	2A.u.	3	2	4	0	0		PN.	b
7519	Southwestern Tamang	0.53600	114,017	128,267	203,735	MSY50z	70-AABA-b	southwest tamang		15.00	19,240	0....	8	7	13	3	0	Tamang	PN.	.
7520	Sunwar (Sunbar)	0.17740	37,736	42,453	67,430	MSY50z	71-CAAA-b	sunwar		0.05	21	0....	4	3	4	0	0	Sunwar	PN.	.
7521	Tamachhange Rai	0.20000	42,544	47,861	76,020	MSY50h	71-CCAB-a	kulung		0.10	48	0....	5	3	4	0	0		...	.
7522	Thakali	0.03600	7,658	8,615	13,684	MSY50e	70-AABE-a	thakali		0.01	1	0....	3	2	2	0	1		...	.
7523	Thami	0.11824	25,152	28,295	44,943	MSY50r	70-ABCA-a	thami		0.00	0	0....	0	2	0	0	0		...	.
7524	Thudam Bhotia	0.00752	1,600	1,800	2,858	MSY50a	70-AAAF-a	thudam-bhotia		0.00	0	0....	0	1	0	0	0		...	.
7525	Thulunge Rai	0.11000	23,399	26,324	41,811	MSY50h	71-CCAB-a	kulung		0.07	18	0....	4	3	2	0	0		...	.
7526	Tibetan (Bhotia)	0.48407	102,970	115,840	183,996	MSY50r	70-AAAA-c	utsang		0.05	58	0a...	4	4	4	1	2	Tibetan	PNB	b
7527	Ticherong	0.01010	2,148	2,417	3,839	MSY50r	70-AAAA-f	dolpo-tichurong		0.00	0	0c...	0	2	0	0	0		pnb	.
7528	Tilung	0.00500	1,064	1,197	1,901	MSY50h	71-CCAB	kulung-pelmung cluster		0.00	0	0....	0	3	2	0	0		...	.
7529	Tseku	0.02000	4,254	4,786	7,602	MSY50r	70-AAAA-cf	tseku		0.00	0	0c...	0	2	0	0	0		pnb	b
7530	Tsum	0.02000	4,254	4,786	7,602	MSY50r	70-AAAA	phöke cluster		0.00	0	0a...	0	1	0	0	0		PNB	b
7531	USA White	0.00500	1,064	1,197	1,901	CEW19s	52-ABAC-s	general american		77.00	921	1Bsuh	10	9	13	3	1	English*	PNB	b
7532	Urdu	0.01000	2,127	2,393	3,801	CNN25r	59-AAFO-d	standard urdu		0.13	3	2Asuh	5	4	2	0	0	Urdu	PNB	b
7533	Vayu	0.01181	2,512	2,826	4,489	MSY50z	71-BAAA-a	vayu		0.00	0	0....	0	1	0	0	0		...	.
7534	Walungchung Gola	0.06530	13,890	15,627	24,821	MSY50r	70-AAAA-ci	olangchung-gola		0.00	0	0c...	0	1	4	0	0		pnb	.
7535	Western Chepang (Gharti)	0.01275	2,712	3,051	4,846	MSY50z	71-BAAB-c	gharti-2		0.13	4	0....	5	1	2	0	0		pn.	.
7536	Western Gurung	0.53207	113,181	127,327	202,241	MSY50c	70-AABC	southwest gurung cluster		0.02	25	0....	3	2	4	0	0		...	.
7537	Western Magar	1.00000	212,718	239,305	380,102	MSY50n	71-BABA-a	west magar		0.03	72	0....	3	2	4	1	0		pn.	.
7538	Yakha	0.04555	9,689	10,900	17,314	MSY50z	71-CBCB-a	yakha		0.00	0	0....	0	2	0	0	0		...	.
7539	Yamphu Rai	0.02000	4,254	4,786	7,602	MSY50z	71-CCAB	kulung-pelmung cluster		0.00	0	0....	0	3	0	0	0		...	.
7540	other minor peoples	0.22500	47,861	53,844	85,523	...				0.10	54		5	4	2	1	0			
	Netherlands	**100.00000**	**15,458,750**	**15,785,699**	**15,781,965**					**65.14**	**10,282,853**									
7541	Ambonese (Moluccan)	0.26860	41,522	42,400	42,390	AON09e	31-PHAI-a	malayu-ambon		95.00	40,280	0....	10	9	14	5	3	Malay, Ambonese	PN.	b
7542	Antillean Creole	0.24282	37,537	38,331	38,322	NFB67b	51-AACB-e	papiamento		88.00	33,731	1a.u.	10	8	13	5	3	Papiamentu	PNB	b
7543	Arabized Berber	0.15000	23,188	23,679	23,673	CMT32a	12-AACB-b	east maghrebi		0.50	118	2A.uh	5	4	4	4	1	Arabic: Algerian*	PNB	b
7544	Bosniac	0.08000	12,367	12,629	12,626	CEW22a	53-AAAG-a	standard srpski		0.10	13	1Asuh	5	5	7	0	0	Serbian*	PNB	b
7545	British	0.12280	18,983	19,385	19,380	CEW19i	52-ABAC-b	standard-english	53	79.00	15,314	3Bsuh	10	9	13	5	2		PNB	b
7546	Caboverdian	0.08000	12,367	12,629	12,626	NAN58	51-AACA-a	caboverdense		98.00	12,376	1c...	10	9	9	0	0	Crioulo, Upper Guinea	PNB	b
7547	Caribbean Javanese	0.05000	7,729	7,893	7,891	MSY44g	31-PIAA-k	jawa-surinam		18.00	1,421	1As.h	8	5	7	5	0	Javanese: Caribbean*	Pnb	b
7548	Dutch	81.08138	12,534,168	12,799,263	12,796,235	CEW19h	52-ABCA-a	algemeen-nederlands	99	67.00	8,575,506	2Bsuh	10	10	15	5	2	Dutch	PNB	b
7549	Dutch Gypsy	0.13500	20,869	21,311	21,306	CNN25f	52-ABCA-a	algemeen-nederlands		60.00	12,786	2Bsuh	10	7	10	4	2	Dutch	PNB	b
7550	Dutch Jewish	0.13000	20,096	20,521	20,517	CMT35	52-ABCA-a	algemeen-nederlands		0.20	41	2Bsuh	5	4	6	4	0	Dutch	PNB	b
7551	East Indian (Hindi)	0.70000	108,211	110,500	110,474	CNN25g	59-AAFP-e	caribbean-hindi		2.10	2,320	2A.u.	6	4	6	5	0	Hindi, Caribbean	Pn.	b
7552	Esperanto	0.00000	0	0	0	CEW21z	51-AAAC-a	proper esperanto	1	70.00	0	0A...	10	9	10	0	0	Esperanto	PNB	b
7553	Eurasian (Euronesian)	0.40000	61,835	63,143	63,128	MPY53	52-ABCA-a	algemeen-nederlands		80.00	50,514	2Bsuh	10	8	13	5	3	Dutch	PNB	b
7554	Fleming	0.30000	46,376	47,357	47,346	CEW19k	52-ABCA-g	oostvlaandersch	99	91.00	43,095	1Bsuh	10	9	15	5	3		pnb	b
7555	French	0.10000	15,459	15,786	15,782	CEW21b	51-AABI-d	general français	16	87.00	13,734	1B.uh	10	9	14	5	1	French	PNB	b
7556	Frisian (Western Frisian)	5.08499	786,076	802,701	802,511	CEW19l	52-ABBA-a	west-frysk		72.00	577,945	0....	10	7	13	5	1		pnb	b
7557	German	0.84400	130,472	133,231	133,200	CEW19m	52-ABCE-a	standard hoch-deutsch	61	88.00	117,244	2B.uh	10	9	13	5	3	German*	PNB	b
7558	Greek	0.03000	4,638	4,736	4,735	CEW20	56-AAAA-c	dhimotiki		95.00	4,499	2B.uh	10	9	11	5	1	Greek: Modern	PNB	b
7559	Groningen Dutch	3.75000	579,703	591,964	591,824	CEW19h	52-ABCC-ab	gronings-noorddrents		75.00	443,973	1A.uh	10	10	16	5	1	Dutch: Groningen	Pnb	b
7560	Han Chinese (Cantonese)	0.45795	70,793	72,291	72,274	MSY42a	79-AAAM-a	central yue		25.00	18,073	3A.uh	9	5	11	5	1	Chinese, Yue	PNB	b
7561	Han Chinese (Mandarin)	0.17450	26,976	27,546	27,540	MSY42a	79-AAAB-ba	kuo-yü	1	12.00	3,306	2Bsuh	8	5	11	5	0	Chinese: Kuoyu*	PNB	b
7562	Han Chinese (Wenchow)	0.01000	1,546	1,579	1,578	MSY42a	79-AAAD-hd	wenzhou		8.00	126	1c...	7	5	8	5	0	Chinese: Wenchow	PNb	b
7563	Han Chinese(Shanghainese)	0.01300	2,010	2,052	2,052	MSY42a	79-AAAD-b	tai-hu		10.00	205	1A...	8	5	11	5	0		pnb	b
7564	Indonesian	0.80000	123,670	126,286	126,256	MSY44y	31-PHAA-c	bahasa-indonesia		40.00	50,514	4Asuh	9	6	11	5	2	Indonesian	PNB	b
7565	Iranian	0.03500	5,411	5,525	5,524	CNT24f	58-AACC-d	general farsi		2.00	110	1csu.	6	5	4	0	0		pnb	.
7566	Italian	0.04000	6,184	6,314	6,313	CEW21e	51-AABQ-c	standard italiano	3	84.00	5,304	2B.uh	10	9	15	5	3	Italian	PNB	b
7567	Javanese	0.20000	30,918	31,571	31,564	MSY44g	31-PIAA-g	general jawa		30.00	9,471	2As.h	9	7	7	0	0	Javanese	PNB	b
7568	Kalderash Gypsy (Rom)	0.00380	587	600	600	CNN25f	59-ACBA-a	vlach-romani		70.00	420	1a...	10	7	6	5	2	Romani: Finnish*	PN.	b
7569	Korean	0.02000	3,092	3,157	3,156	MSY46	45-AAAA-b	kukö		70.00	2,210	2A...	10	7	12	5	3	Korean	PNB	b
7570	Kurdish (Kurd)	0.33000	51,014	52,093	52,080	CNT24c	58-AAAA-a	kurmanji		1.00	521	3c...	6	5	4	5	1	Kurdish: Kurmanji*	PN.	b
7571	Moroccan Arab	0.69377	107,248	109,516	109,491	CMT30	12-AACB-a	west maghrebi	1	0.30	329	1A.uh	5	4	6	4	1		pnb	b
7572	Portuguese Jewish	0.06000	9,275	9,471	9,469	CMT35	51-AABA-e	general português		1.00	95	2Bsuh	6	4	3	1	0	Portuguese	PNB	b
7573	Russian	0.03000	4,638	4,736	4,735	CEW22j	53-AAAE-d	russkiy	2	80.00	3,789	4B.uh	10	8	11	5	2	Russian	PNB	b
7574	Sinti Gypsy (Manush)	0.00770	1,190	1,215	1,215	CNN25f	59-ACBB-b	sinti		70.00	851	0....	10	7	8	5	2	Romani: Sinti, Italian	P..	b
7575	Spaniard	0.02000	3,092	3,157	3,156	CEW21k	51-AABB-c	general español	3	96.00	3,031	2B.uh	10	9	15	5	1	Spanish	PNB	b
7576	Surinamese Creole	1.47200	227,553	232,365	232,311	NFB67b	52-ABAG-c	sranan-tongo		88.00	204,482	4.s..	10	8	13	5	3	Sranan	PN.	b
7577	Syrian Arab	0.02616	4,044	4,130	4,129	CMT30	12-AACF-f	syro-palestinian		30.00	1,239	1Asuh	9	5	10	5	1	Arabic: Lebanese*	Pnb	b
7578	Syrian Aramaic	0.02000	3,092	3,157	3,156	CMT31	12-AAAA-e	sur-oyo		95.00	2,999	4as..	10	9	11	5	3	Syriac	PNB	b
7579	Tamil	0.04500	6,956	7,104	7,102	CNN23c	49-EBEA-b	tamil		30.00	2,131	2Asu.	9	7	10	0	0	Tamil	PNB	b
7580	Tunisian Arab	0.39253	60,680	61,964	61,949	CMT30	12-AACB-b	east maghrebi		0.21	130	2A.uh	5	4	4	3	0	Arabic: Algerian*	PNB	b
7581	Turk	1.25600	194,162	198,268	198,221	MSY41j	44-AABA-a	osmanli		0.05	99	1A.u.	4	4	6	3	3	Turkish	PNB	b
7582	USA White	0.10000	15,459	15,786	15,782	CEW19s	52-ABAC-s	general american		78.00	12,313	1Bsuh	10	9	13	5	3	English*	PNB	b
7583	Vietnamese	0.05000	7,729	7,893	7,891	MSY52b	46-EBAA-ac	general viêt		25.00	1,973	1Asu.	9	7	9	0	0	Vietnamese	PNB	b
7584	Vlach Gypsy (Rom)	0.00300	464	474	473	CNN25f	59-ACBA-a	vlach-romani		70.00	331	1a...	10	7	6	5	2	Romani: Finnish*	PN.	b
7585	Walloon	0.05000	7,729	7,893	7,891	CEW21l	51-AABH-f	wallon		92.00	7,261	0A.uh	10	9	15	5	1	French: Walloon	P..	b
7586	other minor peoples	0.14000	21,642	22,100	22,095	...				30.00	6,630		9	5	8	5	0			
	Netherlands Antilles	**100.00000**	**205,184**	**216,775**	**258,459**					**85.3**	**184,912**									
7587	Antillean Creole	81.18000	166,568	175,978	209,817	NFB67b	51-AACB-e	papiamento	96	88.10	155,037	1a.u.	10	10	12	5	3	Papiamentu	PNB	b
7588	British	0.90000	1,847	1,951	2,326	CEW19i	52-ABAC-b	standard-english		79.00	1,541	3Bsuh	10	10	12	0	0		PNB	b
7589	Dutch	5.30000	10,875	11,489	13,698	CEW19h	52-ABCA-a	algemeen-nederlands		70.00	8,042	2Bsuh	10	10	15	5	2	Dutch	PNB	b
7590	East Indian Hindi	0.26000	533	564	672	CNN25g	59-AAFP-e	caribbean-hindi		1.00	6	2A.u.	6	4	8	4	1	Hindi, Caribbean	Pn.	b
7591	French	1.00000	2,052	2,168	2,585	CEW21b	51-AABI-d	general français		86.00	1,864	1B.uh	10	9	14	5	3	French	PNB	b
7592	French West Indian	2.00000	4,104	4,336	5,169	NFB69b	51-AACC-e	martiniquais		91.00	3,945	1As..	10	8	13	5	2		pnb	b
7593	Han Chinese	0.68000	1,395	1,474	1,758	MSY42a	79-AAAM-a	central yue		4.00	59	3A.uh	6	4	8	4	2	Chinese, Yue	PNB	b
7594	Jewish	0.38000	780	824	982	CMT35	52-ABCA-a	algemeen-nederlands		0.27	2	2Bsuh	5	4	2	3	0	Dutch	PNB	b
7595	Levantine Arab	0.20000	410	434	517	CMT30	12-AACF-f	syro-palestinian		15.00	65	1Asuh	8	5	7	5	2	Arabic: Lebanese*	Pnb	b
7596	Portuguese	0.60000	1,231	1,301	1,551	CEW21g	51-AABA-e	general português		93.00	1,210	2Bsuh	10	9	15	5	3	Portuguese	PNB	b
7597	Surinamese Creole	2.90000	5,950	6,286	7,495	NFB67b	52-ABAG-c	sranan-tongo		78.00	4,903	4.s..	10	8	8	5	3	Sranan	PN.	b
7598	USA White	1.00000	2,052	2,168	2,585	CEW19s	52-ABAC-s	general american		78.00	1,691	1Bsuh	10	9	13	5	3	English*	PNB	b
7599	Venezuelan Mestizo	0.50000	1,026	1,084	1,292	CLN29	51-AABB-hn	venezolano		87.00	943	1B.uh	10	9	11	5	3		pnb	b
7600	West Indian Black	2.90000	5,950	6,286	7,495	NFB68a	52-ABAF	carib-anglo-creol cluster		85.00	5,344	1a..h	10	8	11	5	1	West Carib Creole English	PN.	b
7601	other minor peoples	0.20000	410	434	517	...				60.00	260		10	7	7	5	0			
	New Caledonia	**100.00000**	**193,008**	**214,029**	**285,515**					**75.54**	**161,683**									
7602	Aeke	0.06900	133	148	197	AON09a	37-BBDA-e	haeke		95.00	140	0....	10	7	11	4	2		...	.
7603	Ajie (Wai, Wailu)	3.44800	6,655	7,380	9,845	AON09a	37-CAAC-b	wailu		88.00	6,494	0....	10	8	11	5	3	Houailou*	PN.	b
7604	Ara	0.19400	374	415	554	AON09a	37-CAAB-a	arha		90.00	374	0....	10	7	11	4	1		...	n
7605	Arab	0.30000	579	642	857	CMT30	12-AACF-g	syro-mesopotamian		10.00	64	1Asuh	8	5	3	4	1		pnb	b
7606	Aragure (Haragure, Thio)	0.65500	1,264	1,402	1,870	AON09a	37-CACB	xaragure cluster		95.00	1,332	0....	10	7	11	4	1		...	.
7607	Aro	0.37900	732	811	1,082	AON09a	37-CAAA-a	arhö		90.00	730	0....	10	7	11	4	1		...	n
7608	Aveke	0.20700	400	443	591	AON09a	37-BBDA-d	haveke		90.00	399	0....	10	7	11	4	2		...	.
7609	Caac (Moenebeng)	0.51700	998	1,107	1,476	AON09a	37-BAAD	caac cluster		90.00	996	0....	10	7	11	4	1		...	.
7610	Camuhi (Camuki)	1.72400	3,327	3,690	4,922	AON09a	37-BCAA	cemuhi cluster		97.00	3,579	0....	10	8	11	5	3	Cemuhi	...	.
7611	Dubea (Drubea)	0.96600	1,864	2,068	2,758	AON09a	37-CBAA	dubea cluster		94.00	1,943	0....	10	7	11	4	2		...	.
7612	East Futunan	1.92300	3,712	4,116	5,490	MPY55z	39-CAMA-a	east futuna		90.00	3,704	0....	10	9	13	4	1	Futuna, East	...	.
7613	Euronesian	5.00000	9,650	10,701	14,276	MPY53	51-AABI-p	français d'océanie		74.00	7,919	1A.uh	10	9	12	5	3		pnb	b
7614	French	24.03900	46,397	51,450	68,635	CEW21b	51-AABI-d	general français		61.00	31,385	1B.uh	10	10	14	5	3	French	PNB	b
7615	French Melanesian	0.40000	772	856	1,142	AON09a	51-AABI-c	standard français		90.00	771	4B.uh	10	8	13	4	1	French	PNB	b
7616	Fwai	0.69000	1,332	1,477	1,970	AON09a	37-BBAC-a	fwai		90.00	1,329	0....	10	7	11	4	1		...	.
7617	Half-Melanesian	5.42400	10,469	11,609	15,486	AON09f	51-AABI-c	standard français		75.00	8,707	4B.uh	10	9	13	5	3	French	PNB	b
7618	Hameha	0.20800	401	445	594	AON09a	37-CABB-b	ha-mea		90.00	401	0....	10	7	11	4	1		...	.
7619	Han Chinese	0.10000	193	214	286	MSY42a	79-AAAB-ba	kuo-yü		55.00	118	2Bsuh	10	6	8	4	1	Chinese: Kuoyu*	PNB	b
7620	Iaian (Uvean, Halgan)	1.51700	2,928	3,247	4,331	AON09a	37-DAAA-a	iaai		97.00	3,149	0....	10	7	11	4	3	Iai: New Caledonia*	PNB	.
7621	Italian	3.00000	5,790	6,421	8,565	CEW21e	51-AABQ-c	standard italiano		84.00	5,394	2B.uh	10	9	15	5	3	Italian	PNB	b
7622	Javanese	4.47200	8,631	9,571	12,768	MSY44g	31-PIAA-l	jawa-nouméa		15.00	1,436	1As.h	8	5	12	5	1		pnb	.
7623	Kaldosh Euronesian	0.50000	965	1,070	1,428	MPY53	51-AACC-n	caldoche		70.00	749	1cs..	10	7	7	4	1		pnb	b
7624	Kwenyi (Kapone, Numee)	1.24100	2,395	2,656	3,543	AON09a	37-CBAD-a	naa-kwenyii		96.00	2,550	0....	10	7	11	4	1		...	.
7625	Lifuan (Dehu, Deu)	8.82400	17,031	18,886	25,194	AON09a	37-DABA	dehu cluster		85.00	16,053	0....	10	9	12	5	3	Dehu	PNB	.
7626	Moaeke (Hmwaeke)	0.10300	199	220	294	AON09a	37-BBDA-a	vamale		91.00	201	0....	10	7	11	4	2		...	.
7627	Moaveke	0.20600	398	441	588	AON09a	37-BBDA-b	hmwaveke		95.00	419	0....	10	7	11	4	2	Hmwaveke	...	.
7628	Neku	0.13800	266	295	394	AON09a	37-CAAE-a	neku		90.00	266	0....	10	7	11	4	1		...	.
7629	Nemi	0.41400	799	886	1,182	AON09a	37-BBAB	nemi cluster		97.00	859	0....	10	7	12	4	1		...	.
7630	Nenema	0.62000	1,197	1,327	1,770	AON09a	37-BAAB-b	fwa-kumak		96.00	1,274	0....	10	7	11	4	3		...	.
7631	Nengonese (Mare)	4.17200	8,052	8,929	11,912	AON09a	37-DACA-a	maré		85.00	7,590	0....	10	8	12	5	3	Mare*	PNB	.
7632	Njawe (Ubach)	0.62700	1,210	1,342	1,790	AON09a	37-BBAA	jawe cluster		95.00	1,275	0....	10	7	11	4	2		...	.
7633	Nyua-Bonde (Thuanga)	1.17600	2,270	2,517	3,358	AON09a	37-BAAC	yuaga cluster		98.00	2,467	0....	10	7	12	4	1		...	.

Continued opposite

Table 8-2 continued

EVANGELIZATION								EVANGELISM			ADDITIONAL DESCRIPTIVE DATA
Ref 1	*D* 28	*aC* 29	*CG%* 30	*r* 31	*E* 32	*U* 33	*W* 34	*e* 35	*R* 36	*T* 37	*Locations, civil divisions, literacy, religions, church history, denominations, dioceses, church growth, missions, agencies, ministries, movements* 38
7516	0	5	3.73	1	26.11	73.89	A	0.10	496	3	Solu Khumbu District, northern mountains. Also in Sikkim, India, China. All are strict Lamaist Buddhists, 99%. M=Pioneers,GRI.
7517	0	4	0.70	0	12.02	87.98	A	0.00	388	1.03	Western hills, Rukum and Rolpa Districts. Hindus 70%, Buddhists 20%, animists 10%.
7518	0	5	1.10	6	29.02	70.98	A	0.02	227	2	Along Karnali river in western Nepal, Kailali District, Seti Zone; Mahakali Zone. Gold panners, agriculturalists. Animists 80%, Hindus 20%.
7519	0	5	7.86	0	51.00	49.00	B	27.92	481	5	Nuwakot District. Animists 35%, Hindus 25%, Buddhists 25%. D=NCF.
7520	0	4	3.09	0	17.05	82.95	A	0.03	673	2	Eastern hills, Ramechhap District, Janakpur Zone. Some bilinguals in Nepali. Agriculturalists, gold-panners. Animists 70%, Hindus 30%.
7521	0	4	3.95	0	14.10	85.90	A	0.05	962	2	Chirkuwa Valley, Dingla, eastern. Animists 70%, Hindus 30%.
7522	0	4	0.00	0	11.01	88.99	A	0.00	249	1.03	Mustang District. Some bilinguals in Nepali. Buddhists 50%, animists 50%. M=YWAM.
7523	0	4	0.00	0	5.00	95.00	A	0.00	0	1.01	Dolakha. Also in China. Related to Baraamu. Stone-cutters, hunters, pastoralists. Animists 80%, Hindus 20%.
7524	0	5	0.00	0	6.00	94.00	A	0.00	0	1.01	Tibetans. Mechi Zone, Taplejung, northern. Lamaist Buddhists 100%.
7525	0	5	2.93	0	12.07	87.93	A	0.03	892	2	Eastern hills, Solu Khumbu and Okhaldunga Districts, Sagarmatha Zone. Also in India. Agriculturalists, pastoralists. Hindus 99%, some animists.
7526	0	4	4.14	4	34.05	65.95	A	0.06	468	2	Mainly refugees from Tibet (China); also found in India, Bhutan, USA, Switzerland, Taiwan, UK, Norway. Lamaists(Tantric Buddhists) 100%. M=YWAM,WEC.
7527	0	5	0.00	1	14.00	86.00	A	0.00	0	1.06	Dolpa District, Karnali Zone. Close to Dolpa Tibetan. Lamaist Buddhists 100%.
7528	0	4	0.00	0	7.00	93.00	A	0.00	0	1.03	Okhaldhunga District, Sagarmatha Zone. Animists 90%, some Hindus.
7529	0	4	0.00	1	13.00	87.00	A	0.00	0	1.07	Mechi Zone, far east. Also in Tibet, China, Bhutan, India, Sikkim. Lamaist Buddhists 100%.
7530	0	0	0.00	4	18.00	82.00	A	0.00	0	1.06	North Gorkha District, Gandaki Zone. Chekampar village. Minimal bilingualism in Nepali. Literacy<10%. Buddhists (Lamaists) 100%.
7531	6	10	4.63	8	99.77	0.23	C	404.71	105	10	Expatriates from USA, in development, education. D=AoG,CCN,SDA,UUA,NCC,RCC. M=SJ.
7532	0	6	1.10	5	40.13	59.87	A	0.19	145	3	Immigrants, traders from India. Muslims 100%(Sunnis).
7533	0	4	0.00	0	5.00	95.00	A	0.00	0	1.01	Ramechhap, Sindhuli Garhi Districts. Animists 90%, some Hindus.
7534	0	3	0.00	1	16.00	84.00	A	0.00	0	1.07	Tibetans. Sankhuwasawa District, Koshi Zone. Lamaist Buddhists 99%, some animists.
7535	0	5	1.40	0	16.13	83.87	A	0.07	425	2	Tanahun, south side of Chimkesori Peak, near Magar. Culturally similar to Chepang. Mountainous. Animists 90%, Hindus 10%.
7536	0	5	3.27	0	13.02	86.98	A	0.01	920	2	Southern Gurung. Central mountains, western Gurung area, Kaski and Syangja Districts. Also India. Animists 60%, Hindus 40%.
7537	0	4	4.37	0	16.03	83.97	A	0.01	884	2	West of Pokhara, Tansen highway; Surkhet, Banke and Dialekh Districts, Bheri Zone, Koshi Zone. Some bilinguals in Nepali. Animists 70%, Hindus 30%.
7538	0	5	0.00	0	6.00	94.00	A	0.00	0	1.02	Tehrathum District, Sankhuwasawa District, Koshi Zone; Dhankuta District. Also Gurkhas in Sikkim. Agriculturalists, pastoralists. Buddhists 70%, Hindus 30%.
7539	0	4	0.00	0	5.00	95.00	A	0.00	0	1.02	Eastern hills, upper Arun Valley. Hindus 70%, animists 30%.
7540	0	7	4.07		12.10	87.90	A	0.04	922	2	Assamese, many other Indian peoples, other Chinese, Burmese, other Europeans. Hindus 46%, Buddhists 30%, Animists 15%, Muslims 5%, nonreligious 3%.
Netherlands											
7541	4	10	8.66	5	99.95	0.05	C	547.86	168	10	Refugees in 1950 from Indonesia (80% remain in Ambon, Indonesia). Bilinguals in Dutch, Malay. D=90% Moluccan Protestant Ch/GPM(1950),SDA,JWs,AoG.
7542	4	10	4.37	5	99.88	0.12	C	513.92	84	10	Curassese (Curacoleno). Immigrants from Netherlands Antilles. Also in US Virgin Islands, Puerto Rico. D=RCC,UPCC,MCC,SDA.
7543	1	10	2.50	8	57.50	42.50	B	1.04	152	4	Migrant laborers from Morocco, Algeria. Muslims 98%. D=RCC.
7544	0	0	2.60	6	38.10	61.90	A	0.13	252	3	Refugees and migrant workers from Bosnia since 1990. Muslims 100%.
7545	1	10	1.12	8	99.79	0.21	C	444.05	40	10	Expatriates from Britain, in business. D=Ch of England(D-Europe). M=ICS,MTS.
7546	0	0	7.38	8	99.98	0.02	C	507.93	164	10	Immigrants from Cape Verde. D=RCC.
7547	0	10	3.12	7	77.00	23.00	B	50.58	141	6	Surinam Javanese (1975 immigrants). Muslims 45%, Javanese New-Religionists 37%.
7548	1	7	0.64	6	99.67	0.33	C	347.26	29	9	Nominal Christians 16%, nonreligious 14%, atheists 1.6%. D=61.5% RCC(M-Utrecht and 6 Dioceses), 29% NHK(11 Church Provinces),GKN,GKV,GGN,SA,CGK.
7549	3	10	1.12	6	99.60	0.40	C	284.70	45	8	Many Gypsies are now settled. Nonreligious 20%. D=nomadic caravan churches,Gypsy Evangelical Movement,AoG. M=GGMS,SMIE.
7550	0	10	1.16	6	57.20	42.80	B	0.41	89	3	Some 30 communities of Dutch-speaking practicing Jews.
7551	0	10	5.60	6	52.10	47.90	B	3.99	347	4	Caribbean/Sarnami Hindi. Immigrants from Surinam. Hindus 80%, Muslims 18%.
7552	0	10	0.00	5	99.70	0.30	C	314.26	0	9	Artificial (constructed) language, in 80 countries. Speakers in Netherlands: 185,000(none mother-tongue). Nonreligious 30%.
7553	2	10	1.12	6	99.80	0.20	C	449.68	34	10	Mixed-race(Dutch/Black/Amerindian/Asian). D=NHK,RCC. M=OFM,MHM,SJ.
7554	7	10	1.12	6	99.91	0.09	C	551.36	37	10	Dutch-speaking Belgians. Nonreligious 9%. D=RCC,NHK,GKN,GKV,GGN,CGK,SA.
7555	1	10	1.12	8	99.87	0.13	C	514.43	36	10	Expatriates from France, in commerce, industry, business. D=RCC.
7556	5	10	1.12	0	99.72	0.28	C	339.01	48	9	57% live in Friesland. Also in Germany, Denmark, Canada, USA. Bilingual in Dutch, nonliterate in Frisian. Nonreligious 10%. Many nominal Christians, 18%.
7557	3	10	1.12	8	99.88	0.12	C	536.40	37	10	Residents, settlers, both citizens and expatriates. D=Evangelical Ch in Germany(EKD),NAC,RCC.
7558	1	10	1.12	7	99.95	0.05	C	565.20	35	10	Migrant workers, traders. D=Greek Orthodox Ch(EP-Constantinople: D-Belgium).
7559	6	10	1.12	6	99.75	0.25	C	402.41	37	10	Groningen Province in northeast. Nominal Christians 14%, nonreligious 11%, D=RCC,NHK,GKN,SA,ELK,&c. M=AMEN. R=local programs.
7560	2	10	4.98	8	98.00	2.00	B	89.42	157	6	Folk-Buddhists 65%, nonreligious 5%. D=Chinese Christian Evangelical Ch,RCC. M=Chinese Overseas Christian Mission.
7561	0	10	3.73	7	80.00	20.00	B	35.04	150	5	Chinese from worldwide diaspora. Folk Buddhists 78%.
7562	0	10	1.13	6	57.00	43.00	B	16.64	86	5	Wu-speaking Chinese. Folk Buddhists 87%.
7563	0	10	1.12	6	69.00	31.00	B	25.18	70	5	Han Chinese originating in Shanghai. Folk Buddhists 85%.
7564	2	10	3.53	7	99.40	0.60	B	167.90	104	7	Refugees from Indonesia since 1960, migrant workers, immigrants, settlers, businessmen, other aliens. Muslims 50%(Shafi), Indonesian New-Religionists 10%.
7565	0	0	2.43	1	24.00	76.00	A	1.75	357	4	Immigrant laborers from Iran. Muslims 90%, Baha'is 7%, Zoroastrians 1%.
7566	1	10	1.12	7	99.84	0.16	C	493.62	36	10	Expatriates from Italy, in commerce, industry. All Catholics. D=RCC(7 Dioceses). M=OFM,MHM,SJ,CSSp,MSC.
7567	0	0	4.58	5	74.00	26.00	B	81.03	201	6	Immigrants from Indonesia. Muslims 50%(Shafi Sunnis), New Religionists 20%. D=RCC.
7568	2	10	1.12	6	99.70	0.30	C	316.82	48	9	Vlach Romany Gypsies, in over 26 countries. D=RCC,AoG. M=GGMS,SMIE.
7569	4	10	5.55	6	99.70	0.30	C	360.25	120	9	Migrant laborers from Korea. Buddhists/shamanists 20%, nonreligious 10%. D=RCC,Presbyterian Chs,HSAUWC,AoG.
7570	2	10	4.03	0	44.00	56.00	A	1.60	376	4	Refugees from Iraq, Iran, Turkey. 8,000 speak Sorani, 2,000 Zaza. Muslims 99%(Sunnis). D=NHK,RCC. M=a whole network of agencies.
7571	1	10	3.56	7	50.30	49.70	B	0.55	232	3	Migrant workers from Morocco. Muslims 100%(Maliki Sunnis). D=RCC. M=OM.
7572	0	10	0.60	8	55.00	45.00	B	2.00	64	4	Some 20 communities of Portuguese-speaking practicing Jews.
7573	2	10	3.33	7	99.80	0.20	C	452.60	59	10	Refugees from USSR since 1917. D=Russian Orthodox Ch(AD-Belgium & Netherlands),ROCOR.
7574	2	10	1.12	0	99.70	0.30	C	286.16	53	8	Nomadic Gypsies (Romany), in 10 European countries. D=RCC,AoG. M=GGMS,SMIE.
7575	1	10	1.12	8	99.96	0.04	C	602.68	32	10	Expatriates from Spain, in commerce, professions. Strong Catholics. D=RCC(7 Dioceses). M=AMEN(Peru).
7576	4	10	5.55	5	99.88	0.12	C	497.86	108	10	1975 mass immigration from Surinam. An English-based creole (Taki-Taki). Lingua franca. D=Moravian Ch in Netherlands,RCC,SDA,JWs.
7577	1	10	4.94	8	92.00	8.00	B	100.74	168	7	Migrant laborers from Syria. Muslims 70%. D=Syrian Orthodox Ch(Jacobites, under P-Antioch: M-Netherlands).
7578	3	10	5.87	5	99.95	0.05	C	575.60	108	10	Western Syriac. Refugees from eastern Syria, southeast Turkey, northern Iraq. D=Syrian Orthodox Ch(Jacobites), Ancient Ch of the East,RCC.
7579	0	0	5.51	6	76.00	24.00	B	83.22	235	6	Immigrants from South India. Hindus 55%, Muslims 10%. D=Church of South India.
7580	0	10	2.60	8	51.21	48.79	B	0.39	177	3	Migrant workers from Tunisia. Muslims 99%(Maliki Sunnis).
7581	0	10	4.70	8	53.05	46.95	B	0.09	279	2	Migrant workers from Turkey. Muslims 99%(Hanafi Sunnis). M=YWAM,Reformed League,Pentecostal Missions,OM.
7582	6	10	7.38	8	99.78	0.22	C	438.43	147	10	Expatriates from USA, in business, commerce, industry. D=AoG,SDA,CJCLdS,JWs,CCS,CC.
7583	0	0	5.43	6	69.00	31.00	B	62.96	249	6	Refugees and immigrants from Vietnam. Mahayana Buddhists 53%, New Religionists 11%, Nonreligious 11%. D=RCC.
7584	2	10	1.12	6	99.70	0.30	C	316.82	48	9	Vlach Romany Gypsies, in over 25 countries including Latin America. D=RCC,AoG. M=GGMS,SMIE.
7585	1	10	1.12	8	99.92	0.08	C	523.84	40	10	French-speaking Belgians. Trilingual in French and Dutch also. D=RCC(7 Dioceses).
7586	0	10	1.46		63.00	37.00	B	68.98	63	6	Thais(Theravada monks), Tibetans(Lamaists), Danes, Finns, Norwegians, Swedes, Portuguese, many other European and Asian peoples. nonreligious 25%.
Netherlands Antilles											
7587	11	8	1.80	5	99.88	0.12	C	498.74	42	10	Blacks. D=RCC(D-Willemstad),UPCC,MCCA,SDA,SA,JWs,COG,CGP,COGA,SA,SDA. M=TEAM,OP,FSC,MMS,NHK,TWR,FMB.
7588	0	0	5.17	8	99.79	0.21	C	383.50	130	9	Expatriates, residents from Britain involved in commerce. D=Church of England.
7589	8	10	1.85	6	99.70	0.30	C	378.14	50	9	Settlers from Holland, in government, administration, education, business. Nonreligious 15%. D=UPCC,NHK,VKK(LCC),GK,GKV,RCC,SA,SDA. M=OP,FSC.
7590	1	10	1.81	6	53.00	47.00	B	1.93	145	4	Caribbean/Sarnami Hindi. Immigrants from Surinam. Hindus 80%, Muslims 10%, Baha'is. D=RCC.
7591	2	10	1.93	8	99.86	0.14	C	511.65	49	10	Expatriates from France, in commerce. D=RCC(D-Willemstad),JWs. M=OP,FSC,FMB.
7592	3	10	1.93	8	99.91	0.09	C	531.44	47	10	Black/French Creoles from Martinique, Guadeloupe. D=RCC,SDA,JWs. M=OP,FSC.
7593	1	10	4.16	8	68.00	32.00	B	9.92	194	4	Chinese from many countries including mainland China. Buddhists/Chinese folk-religionists 95%. Many immigrants from Surinam. D=RCC. M=OP,FSC.
7594	0	10	0.70	6	52.27	47.73	B	0.51	73	3	Several communities of practicing Jews, with notable synagogue on Curacao.
7595	3	10	4.26	8	78.00	22.00	B	42.70	174	6	Immigrants from Syria, Lebanon, and Surinam. Muslims 85%. D=RCC(Maronites),SOC,GOC. M=OP,FSC.
7596	3	10	2.35	8	99.93	0.07	C	590.64	53	10	Settlers originally from Portugal D=RCC(D-Willemstad),SDA,JWs.
7597	5	10	1.93	5	99.78	0.22	C	387.19	50	9	Immigrants from Surinam. Afro-Surinamese religionists 20%. D=RCC,UPCC,EBGS(Moravian),SDA,JWs. M=OP,FSC,NHK.
7598	6	10	2.16	8	99.78	0.22	C	435.59	55	10	Expatriates from USA, in development, broadcasting. D=UPCC,SDA,JWs,CC,MCC,WHC.
7599	1	10	1.23	8	99.87	0.13	C	482.67	32	10	Migrant workers from Venezuela. D=RCC. M=OP,FSC,FMB.
7600	1	10	1.93	8	99.85	0.15	C	452.96	48	10	From many Caribbean islands. Numerous Afro-American spiritists. D=Anglican Ch/CPWI(D-Antigua).
7601	0	10	1.94		92.00	8.00	C	201.48	58	8	Arubans, Dominicans, Haitians, and many other Caribbean and South American peoples.
New Caledonia											
7602	2	6	2.19	0	99.95	0.05	C	464.64	64	10	Voh-Kone: Baco. Nearly extinct. D=RCC(M-Noumea),EEA. M=SM,OCSO.
7603	7	6	1.46	0	99.88	0.12	C	443.25	48	10	East coast Moneo to Kouaoua and inland valleys. Regional language. D=RCC,EENCIL,AoG,SDA,JWs,EEL,EEA. M=OCSO,SM,PFM,PEMS.
7604	1	9	1.55	0	99.90	0.10	C	433.62	52	10	Poya, upper valleys. Bilingual in Ajie. D=RCC.
7605	1	10	4.25	7	64.00	36.00	B	23.36	212	5	Migrant workers from various Muslim nations. Muslims 90%. D=RCC.
7606	1	6	1.73	0	99.95	0.05	C	461.17	55	10	Thio, east coast, and Ouinane on west coast. D=RCC.
7607	1	6	1.55	0	99.90	0.10	C	423.76	53	10	Poya, south central Balabio Island, 2 villages. Bilingual in Ajie. Nearly extinct. D=RCC.
7608	2	6	1.59	0	99.90	0.10	C	423.76	54	10	Voh-Kone: Gatope, Oundjo, Tieta. D=RCC,EEL.
7609	1	6	1.54	0	99.90	0.10	C	417.19	54	10	Pouebo, northeast coast. D=RCC.
7610	5	6	1.45	0	99.97	0.03	C	495.67	47	10	Touho: east coast from Congouma to Wagap and inland valleys. D=RCC,EENCIL,SDA,EEL,EEA.
7611	1	6	1.48	0	99.94	0.06	C	456.32	50	10	Paitais, west coast; Ounia, east coast. D=RCC. M=OCSO,SM.
7612	1	10	1.49	2	99.90	0.10	C	446.76	40	10	As many in New Caledonia as in Wallis & Futuna. Distinct from Futuna-Aniwa in Vanuatu. Migrant workers. D=RCC.
7613	5	10	1.87	8	99.74	0.26	C	383.54	52	9	Mixed-race persons. D=RCC(M-Noumea),EENCIL,SDA,AoG,JWs. M=OCSO,SM,PFM.
7614	3	10	1.45	8	99.61	0.39	C	311.71	48	9	Settlers, expatriates from France in government. Mainly in Noumea. Nonreligious 17%. D=RCC(M-Noumea),EENCIL,Eglise Evangelique Libre. M=SM,OCSO.
7615	1	10	1.60	8	99.90	0.10	C	538.74	42	10	Blacks, of various races including Melanesians. D=RCC.
7616	1	8	1.50	0	99.90	0.10	C	427.05	51	10	Hienghene east coast: Ouenguip to Pindache and lower valleys. D=RCC.
7617	4	10	1.38	8	99.75	0.25	C	424.31	24	10	Mixed-race (French/Melanesian). D=RCC,EENCIL,SDA,JWs. M=OCSO,CM,PFM,PEMS.
7618	1	6	1.60	0	99.90	0.10	C	417.19	55	10	La Foa: upper valleys. Intermingled with Tiri. D=RCC.
7619	1	10	2.08	7	99.55	0.45	B	244.91	61	8	Chinese from China, Taiwan, and diaspora. Merchants. Folk Buddhists 45%. D=RCC.
7620	3	6	1.51	0	99.97	0.03	C	527.53	45	10	Ouvea Island, Loyalty Islands. D=RCC,EEA,EEL.
7621	1	10	1.53	7	99.84	0.16	C	493.62	43	10	Expatriates from Italy, in commerce. Strong Catholics. D=RCC(M-Noumea). M=OCSO,SM,PFM.
7622	1	10	1.51	5	76.00	24.00	B	41.61	85	6	Labor migrants from Indonesia over 1900-1938. Muslims 50%(Shafi Sunnis), New-Religionists 35%. D=RCC.
7623	1	10	1.49	1	99.70	0.30	C	306.60	52	9	Southern, Ploum, Mont-Dore, Saint-Louis near Noumea. French-based creole, not intelligible with French. D=RCC.
7624	1	6	1.45	0	99.96	0.04	C	469.53	49	10	Yate, Touaouru, and Goro on main island south coast, Ouen, Pines Islands. D=RCC.
7625	6	7	1.35	0	99.85	0.15	C	437.45	45	10	Lifou, Loyalty Islands. D=RCC,EENCIL,EEA,SDA,AoG,JWs. M=SM,OCSO,PEMS,PFM,LMS.
7626	2	6	1.60	0	99.91	0.09	C	431.79	54	10	East coast: Teganpaik, Tiouande; west coast: Voh, Tieta. Nearly extinct. D=RCC,EEL.
7627	2	6	1.47	0	99.95	0.05	C	464.64	49	10	Voh: Tieta. Dialect of Voh-Kone. D=RCC,EEL.
7628	1	6	1.53	0	99.90	0.10	C	417.19	53	10	Bourail, lower valley. D=RCC.
7629	1	6	1.47	0	99.97	0.03	C	477.96	49	10	East coast: upper valleys north of Hienghene; west coast at Voh. D=RCC.
7630	3	6	1.62	0	99.96	0.04	C	483.55	51	10	Northwest coast Koumac and Poum. D=RCC,EEA,EEL.
7631	7	7	1.34	0	99.85	0.15	C	434.35	45	10	Mare, Loyalty Islands. Iwatenu is a dialect of respect. D=RCC,EENCIL,EEA,EEL,SDA,AoG,JWs. M=PEMS,OCSO,SM,PFM,LMS/CWM.
7632	2	6	1.66	0	99.95	0.05	C	468.11	53	10	Northeast coast from Tchamboenne to Tao and upper valleys. D=RCC,EEA.
7633	1	6	1.42	0	99.98	0.02	C	490.04	47	10	Inland valleys between Gomen and Bonde. D=RCC.

Continued overleaf

Table 8-2 continued

PEOPLE		POPULATION				IDENTITY CODE		LANGUAGE		CHURCH		MINISTRY						SCRIPTURE		
Ref 1	Ethnic name 2	P% 3	In 1995 4	In 2000 5	In 2025 6	Race 7	Language 8	Autoglossonym 9	S 10	AC 11	Members 12	Jayuh 13-17	d 18	wa 19	xc 20	mc 21	mi 22	Biblioglossonym 23	Pub 24-26	ss 27
7634	Orowe (Boewe)	0.51700	998	1,107	1,476	AON09a	37-CAAD-a	orowe		90.00	996	0....	10	7	11	4	2	Orowe	...	.
7635	Pati (Ponerihouen, Ci)	3.79300	7,321	8,118	10,830	AON09a	37-BCBA-a	ponerihouen		86.00	6,982	0....	10	10	12	5	3	Ponerihouen*	P..	.
7636	Pinje	0.06900	133	148	197	AON09a	37-BBAD-a	pije		85.00	126	0....	10	7	7	4	1		...	.
7637	Poamei	0.25200	486	539	719	AON09a	37-BBCA	pwaamei cluster		96.00	518	0....	10	7	11	4	2		...	.
7638	Poapoa	0.09000	174	193	257	AON09a	37-BBBA-a	pwapwa		90.20	174	0....	10	7	11	4	2		...	.
7639	Portuguese	0.30000	579	642	857	CEW21g	51-AABA-e	general português		95.10	611	2Bsuh	10	7	15	4	3	Portuguese	PNB	b
7640	Sirhe (Zire, Zira, Nere)	0.02100	41	45	60	AON09a	37-CABA-a	zire		94.00	42	0....	10	7	11	5	1		...	n
7641	Spanish	1.00000	1,930	2,140	2,855	CEW21k	51-AABB-c	general español		94.00	2,012	2B.uh	10	9	15	5	2	Spanish	PNB	b
7642	Tahitian	4.82800	9,318	10,333	13,785	MPY55f	39-CAQH-b	vehicular tahiti		88.00	9,093	0....	10	9	11	5	2	Tahitian	PNB	b
7643	Tiri (Ciri)	0.41400	799	886	1,182	AON09a	37-CABB-a	ha-tiri		90.00	797	0....	10	7	11	4	1		...	.
7644	Vanuatu Melanesian	0.82800	1,598	1,772	2,364	AON09c	52-ABAI-e	bislama		84.60	1,499	4ssuh	10	8	12	4	1	Bislama	PNB	b
7645	Vietnamese (Kinh)	3.33300	6,433	7,134	9,516	MSY52b	46-EBAA-ac	general viêt		41.20	2,939	1Asu.	9	6	10	5	3	Vietnamese	PNB	b
7646	Voh-Kone	0.20900	403	447	597	AON09a	37-BBDC-a	bwatoo		90.00	403	0....	10	7	11	4	3		...	.
7647	Wallisian (East Uvean)	6.42900	12,408	13,760	18,356	MPY55i	39-CALA	uvean cluster		88.00	12,109	0....	10	8	13	5	3	Wallisian	P..	b
7648	West Uvean (Halgan)	1.29000	2,490	2,761	3,683	MPY55j	39-CAJA-a	faga-uvea		97.00	2,678	0....	10	7	13	4	3		...	.
7649	Xaracuu (Canala, Haraneu)	2.41400	4,659	5,167	6,892	AON09a	37-CACA-d	xaracuu-c		97.00	5,012	0....	10	7	11	4	2		...	.
7650	Yalayu	0.87000	1,679	1,862	2,484	AON09a	37-BAAA-b	n-yaalayu		80.00	1,490	0....	10	7	6	4	1		...	.
7651	other minor peoples	0.09000	174	193	257	...				70.00	135		10	7	6	5	0			
	New Zealand	**100.00000**	**3,671,351**	**3,861,905**	**4,694,964**					**66.35**	**2,562,218**									
7652	Anglo-Australian	1.70000	62,413	65,652	79,814	CEW19c	52-ABAC-x	general australian		67.00	43,987	1Bsuh	10	10	13	5	3		pnb	b
7653	Anglo-Canadian	0.11300	4,149	4,364	5,305	CEW19d	52-ABAC-r	general canadian		73.00	3,186	1Bsuh	10	9	15	5	3		pnb	b
7654	Anglo-New Zealander	69.41000	2,548,285	2,680,548	3,258,775	CEW19e	52-ABAC-y	general new-zealand		66.00	1,769,162	1Bsuh	10	10	15	5	2		pnb	b
7655	Anglo-Romani Gypsy	0.03000	1,101	1,159	1,408	CNN25f	59-AGAA-a	pogadi-chib		70.00	811	0....	10	7	8	4	1		...	b
7656	Arab	0.12000	4,406	4,634	5,634	CMT30	12-AACF-f	syro-palestinian		30.00	1,390	1Asuh	9	5	8	5	3	Arabic: Lebanese*	Pnb	b
7657	Austrian	0.03500	1,285	1,352	1,643	CEW19f	52-ABCF-b	donau-bayrisch-t.		89.00	1,203	0B.uh	10	9	13	5	3		pn.	b
7658	British (English)	7.00000	256,995	270,333	328,647	CEW19i	52-ABAC-b	standard-english		66.00	178,420	3Bsuh	10	9	13	5	3		PNB	b
7659	British (Scottish)	2.10000	77,098	81,100	98,594	CEW19i	52-ABAC-b	standard-english		70.00	56,770	3Bsuh	10	9	13	5	3		PNB	b
7660	Bukabukan	0.01000	367	386	469	MPY55d	39-CANA-a	pukapuka		80.00	309	0....	10	7	8	5	3		...	b
7661	Cook Islands Maori (Atiu)	0.75000	27,535	28,964	35,212	MPY55d	39-CAQB-a	rarotonga		85.00	24,620	0....	10	9	12	5	3	Maori: Cook Island*	PNB	b
7662	Croat	0.09000	3,304	3,476	4,225	CEW22d	53-AAAG-b	standard hrvatski		90.00	3,128	2Asuh	10	8	11	4	1	Croatian	PNB	b
7663	Danish (Dane)	0.07800	2,864	3,012	3,662	CEW19g	52-AAAD-c	general dansk		94.00	2,832	2A.uh	10	9	11	5	2	Danish	PNB	b
7664	Dutch	0.80000	29,371	30,895	37,560	CEW19h	52-ABCA-a	algemeen-nederlands		73.00	22,554	2Bsuh	10	9	15	5	3	Dutch	PNB	b
7665	Esperanto	0.00000	0	0	0	CEW21z	51-AAAC-a	proper esperanto	1	70.00	0	0A...	10	9	10	5	0	Esperanto	PNB	b
7666	Fijian	0.08000	2,937	3,090	3,756	AON08	39-BBAA-b	fiji		84.00	2,595	1.s..	10	9	12	5	3	Fijian*	PNB	b
7667	German	0.07800	2,864	3,012	3,662	CEW19m	52-ABCE-a	standard hoch-deutsch		87.00	2,621	2B.uh	10	9	13	5	3	German*	PNB	b
7668	German Swiss	0.03500	1,285	1,352	1,643	CEW19m	52-ABCG-a	general schwytzer-tütsch		87.00	1,176	0B.uh	10	9	13	5	3	Schwyzerdutsch*	PN.	b
7669	Greek	0.07000	2,570	2,703	3,286	CEW20	56-AAAA-c	dhimotiki		95.00	2,568	2B.uh	10	9	11	5	1	Greek: Modern	PNB	b
7670	Han Chinese	0.07400	2,717	2,858	3,474	MSY42a	52-ABAC	english-mainland cluster		60.00	1,715	3Bsuh	10	7	8	5	3		PNB	b
7671	Han Chinese (Cantonese)	0.87000	31,941	33,599	40,846	MSY42a	79-AAAM-a	central yue	2	51.00	17,135	3A.uh	10	6	10	5	3	Chinese, Yue	PNB	b
7672	Han Chinese (Mandarin)	0.26000	9,546	10,041	12,207	MSY42a	79-AAAB-ba	kuo-yü	3	20.00	2,008	2Bsuh	9	5	9	5	3	Chinese: Kuoyu*	PNB	b
7673	Han Chinese (Shanghainese)	0.20000	7,343	7,724	9,390	MSY42a	79-AAAD-b	tai-hu		27.00	2,085	1A...	9	5	9	5	3		pnb	b
7674	Hungarian	0.07000	2,570	2,703	3,286	MSW51g	41-BAAA-a	general magyar		85.00	2,298	2A.u.	10	9	11	5	3	Hungarian	PNB	b
7675	Indo-Pakistani	0.75500	27,719	29,157	35,447	CNN25g	59-AAFO-e	general hindi		7.00	2,041	3Asuh	7	5	7	5	1		pnb	b
7676	Irish	0.60000	22,028	23,171	28,170	CEW18b	52-ABAC-i	irish-english		83.00	19,232	1Asuh	10	9	16	5	1		pnb	.
7677	Italian	0.03500	1,285	1,352	1,643	CEW21e	51-AABQ-c	standard italiano		84.00	1,135	2B.uh	10	9	15	5	3	Italian	PNB	b
7678	Japanese	0.09000	3,304	3,476	4,225	MSY45a	45-CAAA-a	koku-go		20.00	695	1B.uh	9	7	8	0	0	Japanese	PNB	b
7679	Jewish	0.17000	6,241	6,565	7,981	CMT35	52-ABAC-y	general new-zealand		0.30	20	1Bsuh	5	4	6	5	0		pnb	b
7680	Maori (Rotorua-Taupo)	9.99400	366,915	385,959	469,215	MPY55b	39-CAQA-a	standard maori		67.20	259,364	0a.u.	10	10	13	5	3	Maori: New Zealand	PNB	b
7681	Niuean	0.28000	10,280	10,813	13,146	MPY55z	39-CAPA-a	niue		89.00	9,624	0.s..	10	8	11	5	3	Niuean	PNB	b
7682	Persian (Iranian)	0.01000	367	386	469	CNT24f	58-AACC-c	standard farsi		10.00	39	1Asu.	8	5	8	5	1		PNB	b
7683	Pitcairner	0.00500	184	193	235	MPY53	52-ABAI-h	pitcairnese		98.00	189	1csuh	10	7	12	5	2		pnb	b
7684	Polish (Pole)	0.09000	3,304	3,476	4,225	CEW22i	53-AAAC-c	polski		88.00	3,059	2A.uh	10	8	11	4	3	Polish	PNB	b
7685	Rakahanga-Manihiki	0.08000	2,937	3,090	3,756	MPY55d	39-CAQC	rakahanga cluster		85.00	2,626	0....	10	7	8	5	3		...	b
7686	Romanian	0.01000	367	386	469	CEW21i	51-AADC-a	limba românească		80.00	309	3A.u.	10	8	8	4	1	Romanian	PNB	b
7687	Russian	0.07000	2,570	2,703	3,286	CEW22j	53-AAAE-d	russkiy		74.00	2,000	4B.uh	10	9	11	5	3	Russian	PNB	b
7688	Samoan	2.00000	73,427	77,238	93,899	MPY55e	39-CAOA	samoa cluster		93.00	71,831	2a.u.	10	9	15	5	2	Samoan	PNB	b
7689	Serb	0.03000	1,101	1,159	1,408	CEW22l	53-AAAG-a	standard srpski		82.00	950	1Asuh	10	8	10	5	2	Serbian*	PNB	b
7690	Slovene	0.04000	1,469	1,545	1,878	CEW22n	53-AAAF-a	slovensko		95.00	1,468	1a..h	10	8	11	4	1	Slovenian*	PNB	b
7691	Tahitian	0.00800	294	309	376	MPY55f	39-CAQH-b	vehicular tahiti		90.00	278	0....	10	8	12	5	3	Tahitian	PNB	b
7692	Tokelauan	0.08000	2,937	3,090	3,756	MPY55z	39-CAKC	tokelau cluster		79.00	2,441	0.s..	10	8	10	5	2		...	b
7693	Tongan	0.53000	19,458	20,468	24,883	MPY55g	39-CAPB	tonga cluster		97.00	19,854	4a...	10	9	12	5	3	Tongan	PNB	b
7694	Tuvaluan (Ellice Islander	0.01600	587	618	751	MPY55z	39-CAKB-a	funafuti		95.00	587	0....	10	8	13	5	3	Tuvaluan	PNB	b
7695	USA White	0.32400	11,895	12,513	15,212	CEW19s	52-ABAC-s	general american		77.00	9,635	1Bsuh	10	9	13	5	3	English*	PNB	b
7696	Ukrainian	0.01000	367	386	469	CEW22p	53-AAAE-b	ukrainskiy		77.00	297	3A.uh	10	8	13	5	2	Ukrainian	PNB	b
7697	Vietnamese	0.50000	18,357	19,310	23,475	MSY52b	46-EBAA-ac	general viêt		14.00	2,703	1Asu.	8	7	9	0	0	Vietnamese	PNB	b
7698	Welsh	0.20000	7,343	7,724	9,390	CEW18d	50-ABAA-bc	cymraeg-safonol		85.00	6,565	2A.uh	10	9	15	5	3	Welsh	PNB	b
7699	other minor peoples	0.10000	3,671	3,862	4,695	...				70.00	2,703		10	7	8	5	2			
	Nicaragua	**100.00000**	**4,425,627**	**5,074,194**	**8,696,054**					**95.73**	**4,857,435**									
7700	Black Carib (Garifuna)	0.05100	2,257	2,588	4,435	MIR39c	80-ACAA-d	garifuna		85.00	2,200	4.s..	10	8	8	5	3	Garifuna	PN.	b
7701	British	0.01000	443	507	870	CEW19i	52-ABAC-b	standard-english	7	78.00	396	3Bsuh	10	9	13	5	1		PNB	b
7702	Detribalized Amerindian	0.80000	35,405	40,594	69,568	MIR37z	51-AABB-hf	nicaragüense		93.60	37,996	1A.uh	10	9	11	5	3		pnb	b
7703	Han Chinese (Mandarin)	0.20000	8,851	10,148	17,392	MSY42a	79-AAAB-ba	kuo-yü		15.00	1,522	2Bsuh	8	5	8	4	1	Chinese: Kuoyu*	PNB	b
7704	Jewish	0.01000	443	507	870	CMT35	51-AABB-hf	nicaragüense		0.00	0	1A.uh	0	3	2	1	0		pnb	b
7705	Levantine Arab	0.01000	443	507	870	CMT30	12-AACF-f	syro-palestinian		30.00	152	1Asuh	9	5	3	5	2	Arabic: Lebanese*	Pnb	b
7706	Matagalpa	0.66200	29,298	33,591	57,568	MIR37z	51-AABB-hf	nicaragüense		70.00	23,514	1A.uh	10	5	6	4	1		pnb	b
7707	Mestizo (Ladino)	63.16700	2,795,536	3,205,216	5,493,036	CLN29	51-AABB-hf	nicaragüense		98.50	3,157,138	1A.uh	10	10	11	5	3		pnb	b
7708	Miskito	3.05000	134,982	154,763	265,230	MIR37z	51-AABB-hf	nicaragüense		95.00	147,025	1A.uh	10	9	13	5	3		pnb	b
7709	Miskito (Mosquito)	3.75000	165,961	190,282	326,102	MIR37z	83-AAAA	miskitu cluster	7	90.00	171,254	4....	10	9	13	5	3	Miskito	PN.	b
7710	Monimbo	0.34800	15,401	17,658	30,262	MIR37z	51-AABB-hf	nicaragüense		80.00	14,127	1A.uh	10	5	6	5	3		pnb	b
7711	Nicaraguan Black	4.00000	177,025	202,968	347,842	NFB68a	52-ABAF-f	miskito-coastal-creole		94.00	190,790	1c..h	10	8	11	5	3		pn.	b
7712	Nicaraguan Sumu	0.22600	10,002	11,468	19,653	MIR37z	83-AABA-b	south sumo		85.00	9,748	0....	10	8	7	5	3	Sumo	...	.
7713	Nicaraguan White	14.00000	619,588	710,387	1,217,448	CLT27	51-AABB-hf	nicaragüense		96.05	682,327	1A.uh	10	10	10	5	3		pnb	b
7714	Rama (Ramaquie)	0.02200	974	1,116	1,913	MIR39e	52-ABAF-fb	rama-cay-creole		85.00	949	1c..h	10	7	7	4	1		pn.	.
7715	Rom Gypsy	0.20000	8,851	10,148	17,392	CNN25f	59-AFAA-a	rodi		80.00	8,119	0B.uh	10	7	7	4	2	Calo	P..	b
7716	Spaniard	0.02000	885	1,015	1,739	CEW21k	51-AABB-c	general español		96.00	974	2B.uh	10	9	15	5	3	Spanish	PNB	b
7717	Subtiaba	0.17400	7,701	8,829	15,131	MIR37z	51-AABB-hf	nicaragüense		10.00	883	1A.uh	8	5	6	4	2		pnb	b
7718	USA White	0.10000	4,426	5,074	8,696	CEW19s	52-ABAC-s	general american		77.00	3,907	1Bsuh	10	9	13	5	3	English*	PNB	b
7719	West Indian Black	4.00000	177,025	202,968	347,842	NFB68a	52-ABAF	carib-anglo-creol cluster		94.00	190,790	1a..h	10	9	12	5	3	West Carib Creole English	PN.	b
7720	Zambo (Mulatto)	5.00000	221,281	253,710	434,803	NFB68b	52-ABAF-f	miskito-coastal-creole		81.00	205,505	1c..h	10	8	8	5	3		pn.	b
7721	other minor peoples	0.20000	8,851	10,148	17,392	...				80.00	8,119		10	7	6	5	0			
	Niger	**100.00000**	**9,150,191**	**10,730,102**	**21,495,434**					**0.54**	**58,269**									
7722	Adarawa Hausa	6.00000	549,011	643,806	1,289,726	NAB60a	19-HAAB-a	hausa		0.01	64	4Asu.	3	4	4	5	3	Hausa	PNB	b
7723	Air Tuareg (Air)	1.85267	169,523	198,793	398,239	CMT32h	10-AAAB-be	ta-yrt	21	0.01	20	1....	3	4	2	0	3	Tamahaq: Air	Pn.	.
7724	Algerian Arab	1.25251	114,607	134,396	269,232	CMT30	12-AACB-b	east maghrebi		0.01	13	2A.uh	3	3	0	0	0	Arabic: Algerian*	PNB	b
7725	Anglo-Canadian	0.01000	915	1,073	2,150	CEW19d	52-ABAC-r	general canadian		75.00	805	1Bsuh	10	9	15	5	1		pnb	b
7726	Arabized Tuareg	2.00000	183,004	214,602	429,909	CMT32a	12-AACB-b	east maghrebi		0.01	21	2A.uh	3	3	1	0	2	Arabic: Algerian*	PNB	b
7727	Asben Tuareg (Kel Air)	1.40000	128,103	150,221	300,936	CMT32h	10-AAAB-be	ta-yrt		0.01	15	1....	3	3	2	0	3	Tamahaq: Air	Pn.	.
7728	Bambara (Bamanakan)	0.20000	18,300	21,460	42,991	NAB63a	00-AAAB-a	bamanan-kan		4.00	858	4As..	6	5	10	2	3	Bambara	PNB	b
7729	British	0.00300	275	322	645	CEW19i	52-ABAC-b	standard-english	4	78.00	251	3Bsuh	10	9	13	5	1		PNB	b
7730	Buduma	0.05174	4,734	5,552	11,122	NAB60b	18-BBBA-a	yidena		0.02	1	0....	3	2	4	0	0	Buduma	...	b
7731	Daza (Dazaga)	0.18788	17,191	20,160	40,386	NAB61	02-BAAA-b	daza-ga		0.01	2	0....	3	3	2	0	1		...	b
7732	Dendi (Dandawa)	0.52981	48,479	56,849	113,885	NAB65a	01-AAAB-a	dendi	2	0.07	40	1..u.	4	3	1	0	1	Dendi	PNb	.
7733	French	0.07000	6,405	7,511	15,047	CEW21b	51-AABI-d	general français	17	75.00	5,633	1B.uh	10	9	14	5	3	French	PNB	b
7734	Gurma (Gourmantche)	0.56363	51,573	60,478	121,155	NAB56a	91-GGDA	gurma cluster		27.00	16,329	3.s..	9	5	7	5	3		PN.	.
7735	Hoggar Tuareg (Ahaggaren)	0.10000	9,150	10,730	21,495	CMT32h	10-AAAB-ad	ta-haggart		0.00	0	1....	0	3	1	0	3	Tamahaq, Hoggar	Pn.	.
7736	Kanembu	0.12865	11,772	13,804	27,654	NAB61	02-AAAB-b	kanembu		0.02	3	0....	3	3	3	0	0	Kanembu	...	b
7737	Kawar	0.50000	45,751	53,651	107,477	NAB61	02-AAAA-b	yerwa		0.00	0	4....	0	3	2	0	0	Kanuri*	PN.	.
7738	Kurfei (Soudie)	1.90000	173,854	203,872	408,413	NAB60a	19-HAAB-a	hausa		0.01	20	4Asu.	3	4	3	4	2	Hausa	PNB	b
7739	Lebanese Arab	0.06000	5,490	6,438	12,897	CMT30	12-AACF-f	syro-palestinian		40.00	2,575	1Asuh	9	6	10	2	1	Arabic: Lebanese*	Pnb	b
7740	Manga Kanuri	3.82453	349,952	410,376	822,099	NAB61	02-AAAA-a	manga		0.00	0	1....	0	3	4	0	2		pn.	p
7741	Mauri (Maouri)	3.50000	320,257	375,554	752,340	NAB60a	19-HAAB-a	hausa		0.07	263	4Asu.	4	4	3	4	2	Hausa	PNB	b
7742	Moor (Maure)	1.59569	146,009	171,219	343,000	CMT32y	12-AACD-a	hassaaniyya		0.00	0	0a...	0	3	1	4	3		pn.	b
7743	Mossi	0.90000	82,352	96,571	193,459	NAB56a	91-GGAA-a	moo-re	3	8.00	7,726	2A...	7	5	10	5	1	Moore	PNB	b
7744	North Hausa (Arewa, Arawa	6.60000	603,913	708,187	1,418,699	NAB60a	19-HAAB-a	hausa	85	0.01	71	4Asu.	3	4	4	5	3	Hausa	PNB	b
7745	Shuwa Arab (Baggara)	0.62625	57,303	67,197	134,615	CMT30	12-AACE-a	shuwa	20	0.00	0	0...h	0	3	2	4	1	Arabic: Chad	PN.	b
7746	Sokoto Fulani	11.10000	1,015,671	1,191,041	2,385,993	NAB56c	90-BAAA-n	fula-sokoto	19	0.10	1,191	1cs..	5	4	7	5	3	Fulfulde	PNB	b
7747	Songhai (Sonrhai)	4.88477	446,966	524,141	1,050,003	NAB65b	01-AAAA	songhay-kine cluster	13	0.44	2,306	0....	5	4	7	5	2	Songhai*	PN.	b
7748	Tahoua Tuareg	4.38377	401,123	470,383	942,310	CMT32h	10-AAAB-bc	east ta-wllemmet		0.01	47	1....	3	4	3	0	3		pn.	.
7749	Tazarawa	14.90000	1,363,378	1,598,785	3,202,820	NAB60a	19-HAAB-a	hausa		0.01	160	4Asu.	3	4	6	5	3	Hausa	PNB	b
7750	Teda (Tubu)	0.50100	45,842	53,758	107,692	NAB61	02-BAAA	teda-daza cluster		0.01	5	0....	3	3	0	1	3	Daza*	...	b
7751	USA White	0.01000	915	1,073	2,150	CEW19s	52-ABAC-s	general american		75.00	805	1Bsuh	10	9	13	5	3	English*	PNB	b

Continued opposite

Table 8-2 continued

EVANGELIZATION								EVANGELISM			ADDITIONAL DESCRIPTIVE DATA
Ref 1	D 28	aC 29	CG% 30	r 31	E 32	U 33	W 34	e 35	R 36	T 37	Locations, civil divisions, literacy, religions, church history, denominations, dioceses, church growth, missions, agencies, ministries, movements 38
7634	2	7	1.50	0	99.90	0.10	C	427.05	51	10	Bourail upper valleys: Ni, Pothe, Bouirou. D=RCC,EEL.
7635	7	7	1.36	0	99.86	0.14	C	414.34	48	10	East coast between Poindimie and Ponerihouen and inland valleys. D=RCC(M-Noumea),EENCIL,EEA,EEL,SDA,AoG,JWs. M=OCSO,SM,PFM,PEMS.
7636	1	7	2.09	0	99.85	0.15	C	369.19	70	9	Hienghene: Tipindje, Tiendanite, Pouepai. D=RCC.
7637	2	6	1.46	0	99.96	0.04	C	473.04	49	10	Voh: Ouelis, Temala, Tieta. D=RCC,EEL.
7638	2	6	1.84	0	99.90	0.10	C	425.36	59	10	Voh: Boyen. D=RCC,EEL.
7639	1	10	1.59	8	99.95	0.05	C	597.38	42	10	Settlers originally from Portugal or Macao. D=RCC. M=OCSO,SM,PFM.
7640	1	6	3.81	0	99.94	0.06	C	459.75	97	10	Bourail, coastal plain. Nearly extinct. Speakers bilingual in neighboring languages. D=RCC.
7641	1	10	1.43	8	99.94	0.06	C	586.70	38	10	All Catholics, settlers from Spain. D=RCC. M=SM,OCSO.
7642	4	10	1.40	5	99.88	0.12	C	488.22	34	10	Mainly in Noumea. Immigrants from French Polynesia. Also in New Zealand. D=RCC,EENCIL,SDA,JWs. M=OCSO,PEMS.
7643	1	6	1.48	0	99.90	0.10	C	417.19	52	10	La Foa: lower valleys. Close to Mea. D=RCC.
7644	1	10	1.55	4	99.85	0.15	C	468.12	48	10	Immigrants from Vanuatu. English-based creole. Mainly in Noumea. D=RCC.
7645	1	10	1.44	6	99.41	0.59	B	159.70	59	7	Annamese. In Noumea. Immigrants, refugees from Viet Nam. Folk Mahayana Buddhists 40%, nonreligious 10%, Cao Daists 9%. D=RCC. M=OCSO,SM,PFM.
7646	3	6	1.49	0	99.90	0.10	C	430.33	51	10	Voh-Kone: Baco, Gatope, Oundjo; Poya: Nepou. D=RCC,EEA,EEL.
7647	1	10	1.34	4	99.88	0.12	C	462.52	35	10	In Noumea. Migrant workers from Wallis & Futuna Islands. D=93% RCC(M-Noumea). M=SM,OCSO,PFM,FMB.
7648	1	5	1.53	0	99.97	0.03	C	488.58	30	10	Ouvea (Uvea) Atoll, Loyalty Islands. Fishermen, hunters, agriculturalists. D=RCC. M=OCSO,PFM,PEMS,SM.
7649	1	6	1.64	0	99.97	0.03	C	481.50	52	10	Canala, east coast and inland valleys. D=RCC. M=OCSO,SM.
7650	1	5	1.57	0	99.80	0.20	C	327.04	61	9	Northeast tip and Balabio Island and Belep Islands. D=RCC.
7651	0	10	1.28		99.70	0.30	C	258.05	35	8	British(CPM), USA Whites(RCJCLdS,SDA).
New Zealand											
7652	6	10	1.57	8	99.67	0.33	C	339.92	46	9	Residents, settlers from Australia. Nonreligious/atheists 30%. D=RCC,CPNZ,MCNZ,PCNZ,CJCLdS,&c.
7653	4	10	1.57	8	99.73	0.27	C	397.01	43	9	Immigrants from Canada, as settlers, or in commerce, professions. D=RCC,CPNZ,PCNZ,&c.
7654	8	9	1.12	8	99.66	0.34	C	332.49	39	9	Pakeha(Whites). Agriculture, sheep-farming. D=CPNZ(Anglicans, 7 Dioceses),RCC (4 Dioceses),PCNZ,MCNZ,BUNZ,CJCLdS,SA,ACCNZ(Disciples). M=SOMA.
7655	3	9	1.57	0	99.70	0.30	C	278.49	65	8	Rom Gypsies, in origin from Britain. D=CPNZ,RCC,GEM. M=GGMS.
7656	3	10	1.57	8	97.00	3.00	B	106.21	64	7	Refugees from Lebanon, Syria, Iraq, Egypt, North Africa. Muslims 70%. D=RCC,COC,GOC.
7657	3	10	4.91	8	99.89	0.11	C	503.51	107	10	Immigrants from Austria, in commerce, industry. D=RCC,LCNZ,NAC.
7658	10	10	1.40	8	99.66	0.34	C	346.89	49	9	Settlers from England. D=CPNZ(7 Dioceses),PCNZ,MCNZ,BUNZ,CB,SDA,JWs,SA,UFCC,&c.
7659	8	10	1.46	8	99.70	0.30	C	378.14	48	9	Immigrants from Scotland. D=PCNZ,MCNZ,BUNZ,CB,SA,JWs,SDA,CPNZ.
7660	4	10	1.57	0	99.80	0.20	C	359.16	47	9	Migrant workers from Pukapuka Island, northern Cook Islands. Unwritten language, related to Samoan. D=CICC,RCC,SDA,CJCLdS.
7661	4	10	1.58	5	99.85	0.15	C	471.58	38	10	Rarotongan workers from Cook Islands; also in French Polynesia. D=CICC/PCNZ,RCC,SDA,CJCLdS.
7662	1	10	5.91	6	99.90	0.10	C	522.31	120	10	Refugees from Croatia(Yugoslavia) since 1948. D=RCC.
7663	2	10	1.57	6	99.94	0.06	C	566.11	45	10	Immigrants from Denmark, in agriculture, farming. D=LCNZ,PCNZ.
7664	3	10	1.57	6	99.73	0.27	C	407.66	44	10	Immigrants from Holland, in industry, professions. D=PCNZ,RCNZ,RCC.
7665	0	10	0.00	5	99.70	0.30	C	337.26	0	9	Artificial (constructed) language, in 80 countries. Speakers in NZ: 33,000(none mother-tongue). Nonreligious 30%.
7666	0	10	0.56	4	99.84	0.16	C	453.76	19	10	Migrant workers from Fiji. M=MCNZ,RCC,AoG,SDA,CPNZ,CJCLdS,JWs.
7667	3	10	1.57	8	99.87	0.13	C	523.95	45	10	Immigrants from Germany. D=LCNZ,NAC,RCC.
7668	4	10	1.57	8	99.87	0.13	C	498.55	47	10	Settlers from Switzerland. D=RCC,PCNZ,LCNZ,NAC.
7669	1	10	1.57	7	99.95	0.05	C	575.60	42	10	Immigrants from Greece. Traders. D=Greek Orthodox Ch(D-New Zealand).
7670	5	10	1.57	8	99.60	0.40	C	295.65	45	8	From China, Taiwan, and diaspora. Folk Buddhists 40%. D=CPNZ,RCC,PCNZ,MCNZ,Chinese Ch.
7671	5	10	3.37	8	99.51	0.49	B	236.41	87	8	Originating in Guangdong, China. Buddhists/folk-religionists 48%. D=CPNZ,RCC,PCNZ,BUNZ,Chinese Ch.
7672	3	10	3.21	7	93.00	7.00	B	67.89	114	6	Folk Buddhists 80%. D=CPNZ,RCC,PCNZ.
7673	4	10	3.00	6	92.00	8.00	B	90.66	109	6	From Shanghai region, China. Folk Buddhists 73%. D=CPNZ,RCC,PCNZ,Chinese Ch.
7674	4	10	1.57	6	99.85	0.15	C	487.09	51	10	Refugees from Hungary in 1948, 1957. D=RCC,LCNZ,PCNZ,UFCC.
7675	0	10	5.46	7	67.00	33.00	B	17.11	264	5	Immigrants from India, Pakistan. Hindus 75%, Muslims 12%, Baha'is 5%. M=LBI.
7676	1	10	1.57	8	99.83	0.17	C	463.51	45	10	Immigrants from Ireland. Most White Catholics are Irish. D=RCC(7 Dioceses).
7677	1	10	1.57	7	99.84	0.16	C	493.62	44	10	Immigrants from Italy. Strong Catholics. D=RCC(4 Dioceses). M=SM2,CSSR,IC,AA,PFM,CFC,FSC,OH.
7678	0	0	4.33	7	64.00	36.00	B	46.72	217	6	Immigrants from Japan. Mahayana Buddhists 60%, New Religionists 10%, Nonreligious 10%.
7679	0	10	3.04	8	55.30	44.70	B	0.60	185	3	Small communities of practicing Jews, immigrants from Europe.
7680	7	9	1.57	4	99.67	0.33	C	334.07	42	9	North, east coast. Only 30% speak Maori. All are bilingual in English. Traditional religionists 5%. ¢D=CPNZ(D-Aotearea),RCC,CJCLdS,Ratana Ch,Ringatu Ch.
7681	3	10	1.99	5	99.89	0.11	C	503.51	44	10	Labor migrants from Niue Island; also in Tonga, Cook Islands. D=CUNZ,Niue Christian Ch,CJCLdS.
7682	0	10	3.73	5	70.00	30.00	B	25.55	173	5	Refugees from Iran after 1979 revolution. Muslims 88%(Shias), Baha'is. M=LBI.
7683	2	10	1.59	8	99.98	0.02	C	583.05	40	10	Laborers from Pitcairn Islands; also on Norfolk Island, Fiji, and in Australia. English-based creole. D=SDA,CUNZ.
7684	1	10	1.57	6	99.88	0.12	C	507.49	27	10	Refugees from Poland after 1948. All Catholics. D=RCC. M=CSSR,PFM,FSC.
7685	4	10	1.57	0	99.85	0.15	C	409.53	43	10	Migrant workers from northern Cook Islands. Language unwritten. D=CICC,RCC,SDA,CJCLdS.
7686	1	10	3.49	6	99.80	0.20	C	420.48	88	10	Refugees from Romania since 1948. D=Romanian Orthodox Ch.
7687	3	10	4.57	7	99.74	0.26	C	407.85	83	10	Refugees since 1917, 1945. Nonreligious 20%. D=ROCOR(AD-Australia & New Zealand),Old Believers ROC,ROC(P-Moscow).
7688	2	10	1.87	5	99.93	0.07	C	563.48	39	10	Workers from Samoa; also in American Samoa, Fiji, USA. D=CCCSNZ,AoGNZ.
7689	2	10	4.66	6	99.82	0.18	C	451.94	85	10	Refugees from Yugoslavia since 1948. D=Serbian Orthodox Ch,Free Serbian Orthodox Ch.
7690	1	10	5.12	6	99.95	0.05	C	561.73	104	10	Refugees from Slovenia (Yugoslavia) since 1948. D=RCC.
7691	5	10	1.51	5	99.90	0.10	C	509.17	36	10	Migrant workers from French Polynesia; also in New Caledonia. D=EEPF,PCNZ,RCC,CJCLdS,SDA.
7692	2	10	1.98	5	99.79	0.21	C	380.62	52	9	Labor migrants from Tokelau Island; also in American Samoa, USA(Hawaii). D=CUNZ,CCCS.
7693	3	10	3.02	5	99.97	0.03	C	608.96	56	10	Laborers from Tonga; also in Fiji, American Samoa. D=CUNZ,MCNZ,CJCLdS.
7694	3	10	1.56	5	99.95	0.05	C	558.26	35	10	Ellice Islanders. Laborers from Tuvalu. Also in Fiji, Nauru. D=Tuvalu Ch,RCC,SDA.
7695	9	10	2.55	8	99.77	0.23	C	427.19	62	10	Expatriates, from USA. In commerce, education, industry. D=CJCLdS,SDA,JWs,AoGNZ,CON,UPC,CCS,CGP,CC.
7696	2	10	3.45	6	99.77	0.23	C	421.57	85	10	Refugees from USSR since 1917, 1945. Nonreligious 20%. D=Ukrainian Orthodox Ch,RCC.
7697	0	0	5.76	6	57.00	43.00	B	29.12	318	5	Refugees and immigrants from Viet Nam. Mahayana Buddhists 60%, New Religionists 26%. D=RCC.
7698	4	10	1.57	5	99.85	0.15	C	499.50	44	10	Settlers from Wales, in agriculture, farming. D=PCNZ,MCNZ,RCC,CPNZ.
7699	0	10	1.57		99.70	0.30	C	270.83	41	8	Punjabis(Sikhs), Pacific Islanders(CUNZ), Syrians, French, Creole Maoris, Koreans(M=BPM,PCK-T).
Nicaragua											
7700	4	10	2.35	4	99.85	0.15	C	440.55	65	10	Garif, Garifuna. Descendants of original inhabitants. D=RCC,Episcopal Ch of USA(D-Nicaragua),JWs,SDA.
7701	4	10	2.34	8	99.78	0.22	C	432.74	63	10	Expatriates from Britain, in development. D=Episcopal Ch(D-Nicaragua),SDA,JWs,RCC. M=ECUSA.
7702	5	10	4.01	8	99.94	0.06	C	552.09	82	10	Secularized, urban dwellers. D=RCC(7 Dioceses),MC,AoG,SDA,ICFG. M=CAM,OFM,SJ.
7703	1	10	4.73	7	81.00	19.00	B	44.34	182	6	Chinese from worldwide diaspora. Buddhists/Chinese folk-religionists 80%, nonreligious 5%. D=RCC.
7704	0	10	0.00	8	40.00	60.00	A	0.00	0	1.13	Small community of practicing Jews, in capital and other towns.
7705	2	10	2.76	8	89.00	11.00	B	97.45	107	6	Refugees from Lebanon, Syria, and Middle East. Muslims 70%. D=RCC(Maronites),GOC.
7706	1	10	2.34	8	99.70	0.30	C	327.04	67	9	Subsistence agriculturalists. Language extinct, all now speak Spanish. Animists 30%. D=RCC.
7707	9	10	2.31	8	99.99	0.01	C	602.20	47	10	Mixed-race persons. D=RCC(7 Dioceses),MC(IMN),AoG,NBCN,ICFG,CON,IAFCJ,SDA,and 70 others (many indigenous). M=ABHMS,OFM,SJ,SP,SDB.
7708	3	8	2.34	8	99.95	0.05	C	572.13	52	10	Many high spiritists. D=Moravian Ch(Nicaragua Province),RCC,EC. M=Unity of Brethren,OFM,SJ,SP,SDB.
7709	3	8	2.99	0	99.90	0.10	C	489.46	70	10	Many massacred in 1980s civil war. Lingua franca. Many animists. D=Moravian Ch(Nicaragua Province),RCC,EC. M=Unity of Brethren,SJ,OFM,SP,UBS.
7710	3	10	2.34	8	99.80	0.20	C	417.56	60	10	Language extinct, all now speak Spanish. Assimilated. D=RCC,AoG,Baptist Ch.
7711	9	10	2.34	8	99.94	0.06	C	545.52	51	10	Persons of African descent. D=Moravian Ch/IMN,RCC(7 Dioceses),ECUSA,MC,AoG,SDA,ICFG,JWs,many indigenous churches.
7712	3	9	2.35	0	99.85	0.15	C	394.01	68	9	Hunter-gatherers. Many high spiritists 9%, many animists 6%. D=CNBN,IEMC,Moravian Ch. M=ABCUSA,CAM,UBS.
7713	4	10	2.34	8	99.96	0.04	C	571.62	54	10	Descendants of White(Spanish) settlers. D=RCC(7 Dioceses),AoG,SDA,JWs. M=OFMCap,SJ,SP,SDB,FSC. T=CBN. R=AWR.
7714	2	9	2.32	8	99.85	0.15	C	421.94	60	10	Only 20 speakers of Rama left; rest speak Creole. Animists 15%. D=RCC,IEMC. M=CAM.
7715	2	10	6.93	8	99.80	0.20	C	394.20	162	9	Latin American Gypsies. D=RCC,GEM.
7716	1	10	2.34	8	99.96	0.04	C	595.68	53	10	Expatriates, settlers from Spain. Strong Catholics. D=RCC(7 Dioceses). M=OFMCap,SJ,SP,SDB,OFM,FSC.
7717	2	10	2.34	8	66.00	34.00	B	24.09	130	5	Plains of Leon. Language extinct; all now speak Spanish. Animists 50%, Afro-American spiritists 20%. D=RCC,AoG.
7718	10	10	4.00	8	99.77	0.23	C	427.19	88	10	Expatriates from USA, in development. D=MC(IMN),AoG,CJCLdS,JWs,NBCN,ICFG,CON,SDA,CC,COG.
7719	6	10	2.34	8	99.94	0.06	C	552.39	50	10	Laborers from Caribbean islands(100,000 Jamaicans). D=Moravian Ch/IMN,ECUSA(D-Nicaragua),RCC,SDA,JWs,many indigenous churches.
7720	4	10	2.48	8	99.81	0.19	C	413.91	62	10	Mixed-race persons: Black/Amerindians. D=RCC,AoG,SDA,&c. M=OFM,SJ,SP,CAM.
7721	0	10	2.48		99.80	0.20	C	327.04	61	9	Palestinian Arabs(Muslims), Mexicans(IAFCJ), Germans(ELCN), Puerto Ricans(pentecostals), 7,000 refugees from El Salvador.
Niger											
7722	4	4	4.25	5	51.01	48.99	B	0.01	293	2	Northwestern Hausa(including Azna, Gubei, Tulumi), north of N'Konni. Traders. Lingua franca. Muslims 100%(Maliki Sunnis). D=RCC(D-Niamey),ECWA,JWs,AICs.
7723	2	5	3.04	0	21.01	78.99	A	0.00	488	1.08	Central, Agadez area. Muslims 100%(Sunnis). D=RCC,ECWA. M=SDM,EBM,SIM,YWAM,WVI,Calvary M,BIM,GR.
7724	0	3	2.60	8	36.01	63.99	A	0.01	251	2	Immigrants, transients, seasonal workers or fighters from Algeria. Muslims 100% (Sunnis).
7725	4	10	4.49	8	99.75	0.25	C	399.67	99	9	Canadian White expatriates in development. D=RCC,Methodist Ch,ECWA,JWs. M=SIM.
7726	0	5	3.09	8	39.01	60.99	A	0.01	266	2	Arabic speakers with Tamasheq as second language, around Agadez and northwest Niger. Muslims 100%. M=SIM,FI.
7727	2	5	2.75	0	21.01	78.99	A	0.00	450	1.08	Southeast Tuareg country. Muslims 100%(Sunnis). D=RCC,ECWA. M=BIM,SIM,Ch of the Open Door,SDM,EMS,GR,FI. R=ELWA.
7728	3	5	4.55	4	62.00	38.00	B	9.05	285	4	Migrants from Mali. Muslims 73%(Maliki Sunnis), animists 23%. D=RCC,EEPM,AoG.
7729	4	10	3.28	8	99.78	0.22	C	427.05	81	10	Expatriates from Britain, in development work. D=Methodist Ch,ECWA,RCC,JWs. M=SIM.
7730	0	5	0.00	0	14.02	85.98	A	0.01	272	2	In Lake Chad. Fishing, cattle-raising. Muslims 95%, many animists 5%.
7731	0	4	0.70	0	12.01	87.99	A	0.00	479	1.05	Also in Chad. Tubu pastoral agriculturalists; commerce. Little bilingualism in Arabic. Muslims 100%(Maliki Sunnis; Sanusiyya). M=SIM.
7732	1	7	3.76	4	27.07	72.93	A	0.06	573	2	Primarily in Benin and Nigeria. Muslims 100%(Maliki Sunnis). D=RCC. M=EBM.
7733	1	10	6.54	8	99.75	0.25	C	399.67	141	9	Expatriates from France, in administration. Nonreligious 25%. D=RCC(D-Niamey). M=CSSR,FSC,FMB.
7734	1	7	7.68	4	75.00	25.00	B	73.91	331	6	Majority live in Burkina Faso; some also in Benin, Togo. Animists 31%, Muslims 42%. D=RCC. M=EBM,SIM,WF.
7735	1	5	0.00	0	16.00	84.00	A	0.00	0	1.07	Pastoralists. Muslims 100%(Sunnis). D=RCC. M=SDM,FI,SIM.
7736	0	4	1.10	0	15.02	84.98	A	0.01	456	2	Majority in Chad. Most are bilingual in Arabic. Muslims 95%(Maliki Sunnis), animists 5%.
7737	0	3	0.00	4	19.00	81.00	A	0.00	0	1.07	Saharan Negroes, partly Teda/Kanembu/Kanuri. History of caravan trade. Muslims 100%(Sunnis).
7738	1	5	3.04	5	44.01	55.99	A	0.01	264	2	Animists 95%, Muslims 5%. Resistant to Islam and Christianity. D=ECWA. M=SIM,EMS.
7739	1	10	5.71	8	97.00	3.00	B	141.62	181	7	Traders. Muslims 60%(Sunnis, Shias). D=RCC(Maronites).
7740	0	4	0.00	1	17.00	83.00	A	0.00	0	1.08	Most Kanuri are in Nigeria. Main Kanuri center in Niger is in Yerwa. Literates 30%. Muslims 100%(Maliki Sunnis). M=SIM,EMS.
7741	1	5	3.32	5	45.07	54.93	A	0.11	275	3	Animists 99%. Resistant to Islam as well as to Christianity. D=ECWA. M=SIM,EMS.
7742	0	3	0.00	7	30.00	70.00	A	0.00	0	1.09	Primarily Mauritania, Senegal, Mali; scattered east to Chad. Black, White Moors. Muslims 100%(Maliki Sunnis). M=SIM,ECWA,EMS.
7743	3	10	6.88	4	71.00	29.00	B	20.73	318	5	Labor migrants from Burkina Faso. Animists 45%, Muslims 44%(Maliki Sunnis). D=RCC,ECWA,AICs. M=EMS.
7744	2	4	4.35	5	50.01	49.99	B	0.01	304	2	Northern dialect of mainline Hausa, mostly in Nigeria. Muslims 100%(Maliki Sunnis). D=RCC(D-Niamey),ECWA. M=SIM,CSSR,EMS.
7745	0	5	0.00	7	26.00	74.00	A	0.00	0	1.09	Chad Arabs, Saharan Arabs. Lingua franca. Muslims 100%(Maliki Sunnis). M=SIM.
7746	2	6	4.90	4	51.10	48.90	B	0.18	349	3	Wodaabe lineage from Nigeria. Muslims 99%(Maliki Sunnis). D=RCC,ECWA. M=SIM,CSSR,FSC,EMS.
7747	3	6	5.59	0	35.44	64.56	A	0.56	579	3	Along Niger river. Also in Mali, Burkina Faso. Muslims 99%(Maliki Sunnis). D=RCC,UEEB,Cherubim & Seraphim. M=EBM,SIM.
7748	3	5	3.93	0	23.01	76.99	A	0.00	551	1.08	Aulliminden. Pastoralists, agriculturalists. Muslims 100%(Sunnis). D=RCC,UEEB,ECWA. M=EBM,CSSR,FSC,SDM,SIM,YWAM,FMB,SIL,GR,FI.
7749	4	4	2.81	5	53.01	46.99	B	0.01	207	2	Northeastern Hausa(Tegamawa), reaching to Zinder. Main traders and trade language of Niger. Muslims 100%(Maliki Sunnis). D=RCC(D-Niamey),ECWA,JWs,AICs.
7750	0	4	1.62	0	16.01	83.99	A	0.00	517	1.05	Nomads around oases. Also in Libya. Trilingual in Daza and Arabic. Muslims 100%(Maliki Sunnis; some Sanusi influence). M=BIM,SIM,FI.
7751	5	10	4.49	8	99.75	0.25	C	402.41	100	10	Expatriates from USA, in development. D=Methodist Ch,RCC,ECWA,UEEB,JWs. M=SIM,CSSR,FSC,EMS.

Continued overleaf

Table 8-2 continued

PEOPLE		POPULATION				IDENTITY CODE		LANGUAGE		CHURCH		MINISTRY						SCRIPTURE		
Ref 1	Ethnic name 2	P% 3	In 1995 4	In 2000 5	In 2025 6	Race 7	Language 8	Autoglossonym 9	S 10	AC 11	Members 12	Jayuh 13-17	d wa xcmc mi 18	19	20	21	22	Biblioglossonym 23	Pub 24-26	ss 27
7752	Udalan Tuareg	0.20000	18,300	21,460	42,991	CMT32h	10-AAAB-bb	west ta-wllemmet		0.01	2	1....	3	3	3	0	3		pn.	.
7753	Western Fulani (Bororo)	2.00000	183,004	214,602	429,909	NAB56c	90-BAAA-o	fula-bororo		0.02	43	1cs..	3	4	4	1	3	Fulfide, Kano-katsina	pnb	b
7754	Yerwa Kanuri (Beriberi)	0.62625	57,303	67,197	134,615	NAB61	02-AAAA-b	yerwa	8	0.01	7	4....	3	3	4	0	3	Kanuri*	PN.	.
7755	Yoruba	0.40000	36,601	42,920	85,982	NAB59n	98-AAAA-a	standard yoruba		29.00	12,447	3asu.	9	6	13	5	2	Yoruba	PNB	b
7756	Zaghawa	0.43838	40,113	47,039	94,232	NAB61	02-CAAA-a	beri-aa		0.00	0	0....	0	3	2	0	0		...	b
7757	Zerma (Dyerma)	25.73672	2,354,959	2,761,576	5,532,220	NAB65c	01-AAAB-b	zarma	22	0.05	1,381	2..u.	4	4	6	5	3	Zarma	PNB	.
7758	other minor peoples	0.96275	88,093	103,304	206,947	...				5.00	5,165		7	3	2	3	0			
	Nigeria	**100.00000**	**98,951,865**	**111,506,095**	**183,041,179**					**45.71**	**50,965,008**									
7759	Abanyom (Bakor)	0.01461	14,457	16,291	26,742	NAB56b	99-ACAB-c	a-banyom		70.00	11,404	0....	10	7	7	5	0		pn.	.
7760	Abong	0.00102	1,009	1,137	1,867	NAB56b	99-ACCA-b	north e-tung		50.00	569	0....	10	6	6	5	0		...	.
7761	Abua	0.02437	24,115	27,174	44,607	NAB56b	98-IABB-a	central abua		70.00	19,022	0....	10	7	7	5	2	Abuan	PN.	.
7762	Achipa	0.00649	6,422	7,237	11,879	NAB56b	98-GAEA-a	ta-cep		20.00	1,447	0....	9	5	6	5	3		...	.
7763	Adamawa (Eastern) Fulani	0.77039	762,315	859,032	1,410,131	NAB56c	90-BAAA-q	fula-adamawa	2	3.00	25,771	1cs..	6	4	6	4	3	Fulfulde, Adamawa	PNB	b
7764	Aduge	0.00186	1,841	2,074	3,405	NAB59c	98-EACJ	proper edo cluster		27.00	560	0....	9	7	9	0	0		PNB	.
7765	Affade	0.01904	18,840	21,231	34,851	NAB60b	18-BBAB-b	afade		0.10	21	0....	5	3	2	1	0		...	.
7766	Agoi (Ibami)	0.01143	11,310	12,745	20,922	NAB56b	98-IDBB-d	a-goi		70.00	8,922	0....	10	7	7	5	0		...	.
7767	Agwagwune (Akurakura)	0.02031	20,097	22,647	37,176	NAB56b	98-IDCD-a	a-gwa-gwune		70.00	15,853	0....	10	7	7	5	1	Agwagwune	P..	.
7768	Ake	0.00030	297	335	549	NAB56b	98-HADE-a	ake		50.00	167	0....	10	6	6	4	0		...	.
7769	Akpa-Yache	0.02362	23,372	26,338	43,234	NAB59z	98-BCDA-b	i-yace		70.00	18,436	0....	10	7	7	4	1	Ekpari	P..	.
7770	Akpes	0.00979	9,687	10,916	17,920	NAB59n	98-CAAA	akpes cluster		30.00	3,275	0....	9	5	7	2	0		...	b
7771	Akpet-Ehom	0.01000	9,895	11,151	18,304	NAB56b	98-IDEA	ukpet-ehom cluster		70.00	7,805	0....	10	7	7	2	0		...	.
7772	Alago (Idoma Nokwu)	0.05512	54,542	61,462	100,892	NAB59z	98-BCBB	alago cluster		16.70	10,264	0....	8	5	7	4	2	Alago	P..	b
7773	Alege	0.00122	1,207	1,360	2,233	NAB56b	98-IEAC-a	a-lege		70.00	952	0....	10	7	6	2	0		...	.
7774	Amana	0.01000	9,895	11,151	18,304	NAB56b	99-ABFA-a	e-man		40.00	4,460	0....	9	6	7	2	0		...	p
7775	Amegi (Buseni)	0.00676	6,689	7,538	12,374	NAB59i	97-AABA-b	amegi		70.00	5,276	0....	10	7	8	5	1		...	.
7776	Amon (Amap)	0.18371	181,784	204,848	336,265	NAB56b	98-GBCA-a	ti-map		20.00	40,970	0....	9	5	6	2	0		...	.
7777	Anaang (Western Ibibio)	1.04000	1,029,099	1,159,663	1,903,628	NAB56b	98-ICBA-a	anaang		96.00	1,113,277	1cs..	10	10	10	5	3		pnb	.
7778	Angas	0.15748	155,829	175,600	288,253	NAB60b	19-FBAA	angas cluster		60.00	105,360	0....	10	9	9	5	3	Angas	PN.	.
7779	Arum-Chessu	0.01000	9,895	11,151	18,304	NAB56b	98-HBAA-b	arum-cesu		50.00	5,575	0....	10	6	6	2	0		...	.
7780	Ashingini	0.07000	69,266	78,054	128,129	NAB56b	98-GACB-a	ci-shingini		15.00	11,708	0....	8	7	9	0	0	Kambari*	P..	.
7781	Atakat	0.01456	14,407	16,235	26,651	NAB56b	98-HAGB-d	a-takat		65.00	10,553	1....	10	7	7	5	2		p..	.
7782	Auna-Agaraiwa Kambari	0.04475	44,281	49,899	81,911	NAB56b	98-GACA	west kambari cluster		15.00	7,485	0....	8	5	6	5	3		...	.
7783	Awak	0.00454	4,492	5,062	8,310	NAB66z	92-AABA-a	yiin-yebu		5.00	253	0....	7	5	5	1	1		...	.
7784	Ayu	0.00406	4,017	4,527	7,431	NAB56b	98-HAEA-a	ayu		5.00	226	0....	7	5	5	1	0		...	.
7785	Baangi	0.01304	12,903	14,540	23,869	NAB56b	98-GACB-d	ci-baangi		15.00	2,181	0....	8	7	9	0	0		p..	.
7786	Bachama (Abacama)	0.14687	145,331	163,769	268,833	NAB60b	18-IBCA-h	bacama		65.00	106,450	0....	10	7	9	5	3	Bacama	P..	.
7787	Bache (Rukuba, Inchazi)	0.07874	77,915	87,800	144,127	NAB56b	98-HACE-a	ku-che		40.00	35,120	0....	9	6	7	3	2	Che	P..	.
7788	Bada (Badawa, Jar)	0.01015	10,044	11,318	18,579	NAB56b	99-AADA-e	m-bada		10.00	1,132	0....	8	5	6	3	1		p..	.
7789	Bade	0.23749	235,001	264,816	434,704	NAB60b	19-DABA-c	bade-kado		0.02	53	0....	3	3	2	4	1		...	b
7790	Bagirmi (Lisi, Tar Barma)	0.00240	2,375	2,676	4,393	NAB66z	03-AAAA-a	tar-barma		0.01	0	0....	3	3	2	1	2	Bagirmi	...	b
7791	Bakpinka (Uwet)	0.00300	2,969	3,345	5,491	NAB56b	98-IDAA-a	i-yoniyong		60.00	2,007	0....	10	7	6	3	0		...	b
7792	Bali (Boli)	0.01363	13,487	15,198	24,949	NAB66z	92-BABD-a	bali		0.07	11	0....	4	4	9	1	0		...	b
7793	Bambuka (Kanawa)	0.01015	10,044	11,318	18,579	NAB66z	92-ABAC-a	kyak		10.00	1,132	0....	8	5	6	2	0		...	.
7794	Banagere (Messaga, Iyon)	0.00200	1,979	2,230	3,661	NAB56b	99-ABDA-b	i-ceve		85.00	1,896	0....	10	7	8	5	2	Iceve-maci	...	b
7795	Banda-Minda (Jinleri)	0.01604	15,872	17,886	29,360	NAB56b	98-HBCA	shoo-minda cluster		40.00	7,154	0....	9	7	8	2	0		...	.
7796	Banga (Bangawa)	0.01260	12,468	14,050	23,063	NAB56b	98-GADB	lyase cluster		5.00	702	0....	7	5	5	1	0		...	.
7797	Bangwinji	0.00587	5,808	6,545	10,745	NAB66z	92-AAAC-a	bangwinji		0.04	3	0....	3	3	2	1	0		...	b
7798	Bariba (Bargu, Burku)	0.05699	56,393	63,547	104,315	NAB56a	91-GIAA-a	baatonum		8.00	5,084	3....	7	5	6	5	3	Bariba	PNB	.
7799	Barke (Burkanawa, Lipkawa	0.00561	5,551	6,255	10,269	NAB60b	19-DBGA-a	veran		2.00	125	0....	6	4	5	1	0		...	.
7800	Bashar (Basharawa, Bashir	0.02747	27,182	30,631	50,281	NAB56b	98-HBAC-a	bashar		20.00	6,126	0....	9	5	7	2	0		...	.
7801	Bassa-Kaduna (Bassa Kuta)	0.01800	17,811	20,071	32,947	NAB56b	98-GAGA	basa-kaduna cluster		30.00	6,021	0....	9	5	6	5	2		...	.
7802	Bassakomo (Abatsa, Abacha	0.15748	155,829	175,600	288,253	NAB56b	98-GAGC-a	ru-bassa		50.00	87,800	0....	10	6	9	5	3	Rubassa*	PN.	b
7803	Bata (Gbwata, Dunu)	0.14687	145,331	163,769	268,833	NAB60b	18-IBCA-a	gbwata		10.00	16,377	0....	8	5	6	4	1		p..	n
7804	Batu	0.02539	25,124	28,311	46,474	NAB56b	99-ABBA-b	batu		30.00	8,493	0....	9	5	7	2	0		...	.
7805	Bauchi Fulani	0.54000	534,340	602,133	988,422	NAB56c	90-BAAA-n	fula-sokoto		0.40	2,409	1cs..	5	3	6	1	3	Fulfulde	PNB	b
7806	Baushi (Kushi)	0.01958	19,375	21,833	35,839	NAB56b	98-GAFA-a	baushi		10.00	2,183	0....	8	5	5	1	1		...	.
7807	Bekworra (Yakoro)	0.09522	94,222	106,176	174,292	NAB56b	98-IEAA-a	proper be-kwarra		20.00	21,235	0....	9	5	7	5	3	Bekwarra	PN.	.
7808	Berom (Birom, Gbang)	0.28499	282,003	317,781	521,649	NAB56b	98-HAFB	berom cluster		88.00	279,647	4....	10	9	8	5	3	Berom	PN.	.
7809	Bete	0.00293	2,899	3,267	5,363	NAB56b	98-IDLA-a	north bete		81.00	2,646	0....	10	7	6	2	0		...	b
7810	Bette-Bende (Mbete, Dama)	0.07931	78,479	88,435	145,170	NAB56b	98-IEAD-a	south bete		70.00	61,905	0....	10	7	8	5	1	Bette*	PN.	.
7811	Bile (Billanchi, Bille))	0.02937	29,062	32,749	53,759	NAB56b	99-AAFB-a	bile		50.00	16,375	0....	10	6	6	2	0		...	.
7812	Binawa	0.00315	3,117	3,512	5,766	NAB56b	92-ADAB-a	e-buna		10.00	351	0....	8	5	5	1	0		...	.
7813	Bitare (Yukutare)	0.04720	46,705	52,631	86,395	NAB56b	99-ABBA-a	njwande		80.00	42,105	0....	10	7	7	2	0		...	.
7814	Boghom (Burma)	0.07874	77,915	87,800	144,127	NAB60b	19-EEAC-a	boghom		10.00	8,780	0....	8	5	7	4	1	Boghom	P..	.
7815	Bokkos	0.27623	273,335	308,013	505,615	NAB60b	19-GBAA-g	bokkos		49.00	150,927	0....	9	5	6	4	1	Ron	p..	.
7816	Boko	0.03580	35,425	39,919	65,529	NAB63z	00-DGDA-a	boko		15.00	5,988	0....	8	4	9	0	0	Boko	PNB	.
7817	Bokyi (Nki, Okii)	0.13331	131,913	148,649	244,012	NAB56b	98-IEAG-a	u-ki		80.00	118,919	0.s..	10	7	9	5	3	Bokyi	PNB	b
7818	Bolewa (Bole)	0.10400	102,910	115,966	190,363	NAB60b	19-BABA-a	bara		20.00	23,193	0....	9	5	7	4	1		...	b
7819	British	0.10000	98,952	111,506	183,041	CEW19i	52-ABAC-b	standard-english	46	74.00	82,515	3Bsuh	10	9	13	5	3		PNB	b
7820	Buduma (Yedina)	0.00276	2,731	3,078	5,052	NAB60b	18-BBBA-a	yidena		0.02	1	0....	3	3	4	1	2	Buduma	...	b
7821	Bumaji	0.01000	9,895	11,151	18,304	NAB56b	98-IEAE-a	bu-maji		70.00	7,805	0....	10	7	7	5	0		...	.
7822	Bura (Pabir, Babur)	0.24532	242,749	273,547	449,037	NAB60b	18-GBBD-a	bura-pabir		35.00	95,741	4.s..	9	5	7	5	2	Bura*	PN.	b
7823	Burak	0.00391	3,869	4,360	7,157	NAB66z	92-ABAA-a	burak		0.10	4	0....	5	4	2	1	0		...	b
7824	Busa (Zogbe, Bokhobaru)	0.04027	39,848	44,904	73,711	NAB63z	00-DGDA	busa-boko cluster		15.00	6,736	0....	8	5	5	5	2	Busa	PNB	.
7825	Buta-Ningi (Butawa)	0.01468	14,526	16,369	26,870	NAB56b	98-GBAB	gamo-ningi cluster		0.02	3	0....	3	3	3	1	0		...	b
7826	Cameroonian Creole	0.00500	4,948	5,575	9,152	NAN58	52-ABAH-f	cameroonian-creole	2	80.00	4,460	4.s.h	10	7	10	5	3	Pidgin: Cameroon*	Pn.	b
7827	Central Idoma	0.23000	227,589	256,464	420,995	NAB59z	98-BCBA-bb	oturkpo		68.00	174,396	0....	10	6	9	5	2		pnb	.
7828	Central-Western Ijaw	0.46525	460,374	518,782	851,599	NAB59i	97-AAAA-p	kolokuma	2	94.00	487,655	0....	10	8	9	5	3	Ijo: Central*	P..	.
7829	Chamba Daka (Deng)	0.09623	95,221	107,302	176,141	NAB66c	98-JDAA-a	samba-daka		20.00	21,460	0.s..	9	5	7	5	1	Chamba*	P..	.
7830	Chamba Leko(Ndii, Suntai)	0.05447	53,899	60,737	99,703	NAB66c	92-BDAB-a	proper samba-leko		50.00	30,369	0....	10	6	7	4	1	Samba Leko	...	.
7831	Chara (Fachara, Pakara)	0.00100	990	1,115	1,830	NAB56b	98-HAFC-a	n-fa-chara		30.00	335	0....	9	5	5	2	0		...	.
7832	Chawai (Cawe)	0.04886	48,348	54,482	89,434	NAB56b	98-GBDB-a	atsam		20.00	10,896	0....	9	5	7	5	3	Chawai*	P..	.
7833	Chip (Ship, Cip)	0.00609	6,026	6,791	11,147	NAB60b	19-FBCA-a	mi-ship		10.00	679	0....	8	5	5	2	0		...	.
7834	Chokobo (Izora, Azora)	0.00163	1,613	1,818	2,984	NAB56b	98-GBAF-a	i-zora		5.00	91	0....	7	5	4	4	1		...	.
7835	Chomo-Karim (Shomoh)	0.01000	9,895	11,151	18,304	NAB56b	98-HBCB	como-karim cluster		10.00	1,115	0....	8	5	5	2	0		...	.
7836	Cross River Mbembe (Okam)	0.11628	115,061	129,659	212,840	NAB56b	98-IDHA-a	a-dun		88.00	114,100	0....	10	7	10	4	2	Mbembe: Adun*	PN.	.
7837	Dadiya (Dadianci)	0.00362	3,582	4,037	6,626	NAB66z	92-AACA-a	loo-diya		0.10	4	0....	5	3	2	1	0		...	b
7838	Daffo-Batura (Chala)	0.01000	9,895	11,151	18,304	NAB60b	19-GBAA-a	daffo-batura		5.00	558	0....	7	5	5	1	0		p..	.
7839	Dakka (Dirim, Dirin)	0.00881	8,718	9,824	16,126	NAB66z	98-JDAA-c	dirim		4.00	393	0.s..	6	5	5	4	2		p..	.
7840	Dass	0.00897	8,876	10,002	16,419	NAB60b	19-EDAA-a	zumbul		2.00	200	0....	6	4	5	1	0		...	.
7841	Defaka (Afakani)	0.00097	960	1,082	1,775	NAB59i	97-BAAA-a	defaka		40.00	433	0....	9	6	6	2	1		...	.
7842	Degema (Atala)	0.01015	10,044	11,318	18,579	NAB59c	98-EAEC-a	u-dekama		27.00	3,056	0....	9	5	7	2	0		...	.
7843	Dendi (Dandawa)	0.00180	1,781	2,007	3,295	NAB65a	01-AAAB-a	dendi		0.10	2	1..u.	5	3	2	0	0	Dendi	PNb	.
7844	Deno (Denawa)	0.01575	15,585	17,562	28,829	NAB60b	19-BBCA	deno cluster		10.00	1,756	0....	8	5	6	1	0		...	.
7845	Dera (Kanakuru)	0.03150	31,170	35,124	57,658	NAB60b	19-AAAA	dera cluster		50.00	17,562	0....	10	6	7	2	0	Dera	P..	.
7846	Detribalized	0.90509	895,603	1,009,231	1,656,687	NAN58	52-ABAH-e	nigerian-creole		60.00	605,538	1.s.h	10	7	8	5	3	Pidgin, Nigerian	Pn.	b
7847	Dijim (Cam, Mona)	0.01470	14,546	16,391	26,907	NAB66z	92-AADA	dijim cluster		40.00	6,557	0....	9	5	7	5	0		...	.
7848	Dirya (Diriyawa, Sago)	0.00632	6,254	7,047	11,568	NAB60b	19-DBCA	diri cluster		10.00	705	0....	8	5	5	2	0		...	.
7849	Doka	0.01000	9,895	11,151	18,304	NAB56b	98-HAAB-a	doka		1.00	112	0....	6	4	4	1	0		...	.
7850	Doko-Uyanga (Basanga)	0.00020	198	223	366	NAB56b	98-IDBB-a	u-yanga		70.00	156	0....	10	7	6	3	2		...	.
7851	Dong (Donga)	0.00671	6,640	7,482	12,282	NAB66z	92-BDAB-i	dong		0.10	7	0....	5	3	2	1	0		...	b
7852	Dughwede (Toghwede, Waa)	0.03724	36,850	41,525	68,165	NAB60b	18-CBBA-a	zeghvana		10.00	4,152	0....	8	5	6	4	3	Dghwede	PN.	.
7853	Duguri (Dugurawa)	0.01890	18,702	21,075	34,595	NAB56b	99-AADA-d	duguri		5.00	1,054	0....	7	5	5	1	0		p..	.
7854	Duguza	0.00315	3,117	3,512	5,766	NAB56b	98-GBAH-a	duguza		2.00	70	0....	6	4	4	1	1		...	.
7855	Dukawa (Dukkawa, Kirho)	0.08787	86,949	97,980	160,838	NAB56b	98-GADD	duka cluster		2.00	1,960	0....	6	4	5	4	3	Dukanci	P..	b
7856	Dulbu	0.00013	129	145	238	NAB56b	99-AADB-a	dulbu		10.00	14	0....	8	5	4	1	0		...	.
7857	Dungi (Dunjawa)	0.00097	960	1,082	1,775	NAB56b	98-GBBG-a	dungi		5.00	54	0....	7	5	5	1	0		...	.
7858	Duwai	0.01000	9,895	11,151	18,304	NAB60b	19-DACA-a	duwai		0.05	6	0....	4	3	2	1	0		...	b
7859	East Gbari (Gwari Matai)	0.62409	617,549	695,898	1,142,342	NAB59z	98-BAAB-b	gbagyi		74.00	514,965	2....	10	10	8	5	3	Gbagyi: Gayegi*	PN.	.
7860	Eastern Ijaw	0.24545	242,877	273,692	449,275	NAB59i	97-AACA-a	kalabari		89.00	243,586	0....	10	10	10	5	3	Kalabari	PN.	b
7861	Ebughu (Oron)	0.00551	5,452	6,144	10,086	NAB56b	98-ICAC-a	o-ron		90.00	5,530	0....	10	8	10	0	0		...	.
7862	Edo (Bini)	0.98129	971,005	1,094,198	1,796,165	NAB59c	98-EACJ-a	proper edo	2	78.00	853,475	0....	10	10	7	5	4	Edo	PNB	.
7863	Efai	0.00555	5,492	6,189	10,159	NAB56b	98-ICBA-c	efik		90.00	5,570	1as..	10	8	10	0	0	Efik	PNB	b
7864	Efik (Calabar)	0.34280	339,207	382,243	627,465	NAB56b	98-ICBA-c	efik	6	90.00	344,019	1as..	10	10	13	5	3	Efik	PNB	b
7865	Efutop	0.01575	15,585	17,562	28,829	NAB56b	99-ACAD-a	e-futob		70.00	12,294	0....	10	7	7	2	1		...	.
7866	Egba	2.91800	2,887,415	3,253,748	5,341,142	NAB59n	98-AAAA-cl	ede-egba		86.00	2,798,223	1csu.	10	10	9	5	3		pnb	b
7867	Eggon	0.12932	127,965	144,200	236,709	NAB56b	98-HADD-a	mada-eggon		50.00	72,100	0....	10	6	7	5	1	Eggon	PN.	.
7868	Ejagham (Ekoi)	0.05233	51,782	58,351	95,785	NAB56b	99-ACCB-b	proper e-jagham		85.00	49,598	0....	10	7	7	5	3	Ejagham	PN.	.
7869	Ekajuk	0.03508	34,712	39,117	64,211	NAB56b	99-ACAB-b	e-kajuk		70.00	27,381	0....	10	7	7	4	1	Ekajuk	PN.	.
7870	Eket	0.21427	212,024	238,924	392,202	NAB56b	98-ICBB-a	ekit		70.00	167,247	0....	10	7	7	2	3		...	.
7871	Ekpari	0.01163	11,508	12,968	21,288	NAB59z	98-BCDA-b	i-yace		40.00	5,187	0....	9	6	6	5	2	Ekpari	P..	.
7872	Ekpeye	0.04724	46,745	52,675	86,469	NAB59h	98-FABA	ekpeye cluster		67.00	35,293	0....	10	7	7	4	1		...	.
7873	Eleme	0.05397	53,404	60,180	98,787	NAB56b	98-IBAA-a	eleme		60.00	36,108	0....	10	7	7	5	2	Eleme	P..	.

Continued opposite

Table 8-2 continued

EVANGELIZATION								EVANGELISM			ADDITIONAL DESCRIPTIVE DATA
Ref 1	D 28	aC 29	CG% 30	r 31	E 32	U 33	W 34	e 35	R 36	T 37	Locations, civil divisions, literacy, religions, church history, denominations, dioceses, church growth, missions, agencies, ministries, movements 38
7752	1	5	0.70	0	21.01	78.99	A	0.00	183	1.08	Nomads, tent-dwellers. Camel economy. Muslims 100%(Sunnis). D=RCC. M=SDM,SIM,SIL.
7753	0	5	3.83	4	34.02	65.98	A	0.02	437	2	Kano-Katsina Fulani. Muslims 100%(Maliki Sunnis). M=SIM,EMS,CCTDC.
7754	2	5	1.96	4	31.01	68.99	A	0.01	297	2	Main Kanuri, primarily in Nigeria. Also in Chad, Cameroon, Sudan. Muslims 100%(Maliki Sunnis). D=ECWA,RCC. M=SIM,CSSR,EMS.
7755	6	9	7.39	5	99.00	1.00	B	104.79	243	7	Long-time immigrants from Nigeria. Traders. Muslims 55%(Maliki Sunnis), animists 15%. D=RCC,UEEB,JWs,C&S,HCC,other AICs. M=CSSR,EBM.
7756	0	3	0.00	0	7.00	93.00	A	0.00	0	1.04	Majority live in Sudan; many also in Chad, Libya. Semi-nomadic, also settled cattle-raisers. Muslims 75%(Maliki Sunnis), animists 25%.
7757	3	5	5.05	1	41.05	58.95	A	0.07	464	2	Also in Nigeria, Burkina Faso, Benin. Agriculturalists. Muslims 80%(Maliki Sunnis), animists 20%. Talking drums(possession dances). D=RCC,UEEB,ECWA.
7758	0	7	6.45		23.00	77.00	A	4.19	768	4	Other Nigerians, Malians, Chadians, Ivorians, Senegalese, Beninois, Burkinabe, Togolese, Soninke. Muslims 74%, Animists 18%.
Nigeria											
7759	0	6	7.29	0	99.70	0.30	C	270.83	224	8	Cross River State, Ikom LGA(Local Government Area). Tribal religionists(animists) 30%.
7760	0	6	4.12	0	80.00	20.00	B	146.00	189	7	Gongola State, Sardauna LGA, Abong town. Animists 50%.
7761	1	6	7.84	0	99.70	0.30	C	281.05	230	8	Rivers State, Degema and Ahoada LGAs. Animists 30%. D=AICs. M=SIL,NBTT.
7762	3	6	5.10	0	56.00	44.00	B	40.88	318	6	Sokoto State, Zuru LGA, also in Niger State. Literates 10%. Animists 60%, Muslims 20%. D=ECWA,NBC,UMCA.
7763	1	5	8.17	4	53.00	47.00	B	5.80	505	4	Gongola State (center: Yola). Also in Cameroon, Sudan. Nomads. Muslims 97%(Maliki Sunnis). D=CRCN. M=EFLC(Cameroon),MBE/EBMS,FMB,CSI,JCMWA.
7764	0	0	4.11	2	59.00	41.00	B	58.14	255	6	Kware State, Oyi LGA. Animists 73%.
7765	0	5	3.09	0	16.10	83.90	A	0.05	762	2	Borno State,Ngala LGA. Also in Cameroon. Muslims 90%, animists 10%.
7766	0	6	7.03	0	99.70	0.30	C	260.61	226	8	Cross River State, Obubra LGA. Animists 30%.
7767	1	6	4.90	0	99.70	0.30	C	270.83	163	8	Cross River State, Akamkpa LGA. Animists 30%. D=AICs. M=FCS.
7768	0	6	2.86	0	79.00	21.00	B	144.17	147	7	Plateau State, Lafia LGA. Animists 50%.
7769	2	7	7.81	0	99.70	0.30	C	273.38	236	8	Benue State, Otukpo LGA. Animists 30%. D=ELCN,AICs. M=LCMS.
7770	0	7	5.96	0	62.00	38.00	B	67.89	325	6	Ondo State, Akoko North LGA. Lingua franca: Yoruba. Animists 40%, Muslims 30%.
7771	0	6	6.89	0	99.00	1.00	C	252.94	229	8	Cross River State,Akamkpa LGA. Animists 30%.
7772	2	6	7.18	0	54.70	45.30	B	33.34	430	5	Plateau State, Lafia LGA. Literates 5%. Second language Hausa. Animists 73%, Muslims 10%. D=ECWA,DLBC. M=EMS,SIM.
7773	0	7	4.66	0	98.00	2.00	C	250.39	169	8	Cross River State, Obudu LGA. Animists 30%.
7774	0	6	6.29	0	68.00	32.00	B	99.28	309	6	Cross River State, Obudu LGA. Animists 60%.
7775	1	7	6.47	0	99.70	0.30	C	270.83	203	8	Rivers State, Degema and Bonny LGAs. Related to Ijo. Animists 30%. D=AICs.
7776	0	6	8.67	0	48.00	52.00	A	35.04	574	5	Plateau State, Bassa LGA; Kaduna State, Saminaka LGA. Animists 60%, Muslims 20%.
7777	5	6	5.72	2	99.96	0.04	C	525.60	130	10	Akwa Ibom State. Animists 4%. Nominal Christians 20%. D=RCC(D-Ikot Ekpene),Christ Army Ch,CPN,SDA,many AICs. M=BFM,FGBCA,Holiness,WGMI,&c.
7778	3	6	9.71	0	99.60	0.40	C	229.95	290	8	Plateau State, Pankshin LGA. Animists 30%, Muslims 10%. D=RCC(D-Jos),CON,COCIN. M=CMS,SIL,SMA,NBTT.
7779	0	6	6.53	0	78.00	22.00	B	142.35	278	7	Plateau State, Akwanga LGA. Animists 50%.
7780	0	0	7.32	0	37.00	63.00	A	20.25	645	5	Niger State, Magama and Mariga LGAs. Primarily rural. 20% literate in Hausa. Animists 60%, Muslims 25%.
7781	2	6	7.21	0	99.65	0.35	C	246.74	227	8	Kaduna State, Kachia and Jemaa LGAs. Dialect of Katab. Animists 30%, Muslims 5%. D=RCC,ECWA.
7782	3	6	6.84	0	50.00	50.00	B	27.37	451	5	Kwara State and Sokoto State. Animists 65%, Muslims 20%. D=NBC,RCC,United Missionary Ch of Africa. M=FMB,CRAM,CMF,EMS,MCA.
7783	1	5	3.28	0	28.00	72.00	A	5.11	461	4	Bauchi State, Billiri-Kaltungo LGA. Animists 90%. D=ECWA.
7784	0	6	3.17	0	27.00	73.00	A	4.92	463	4	Kaduna State, Jemaa LGA. Animists 50%, Muslims 45%.
7785	0	0	5.53	0	36.00	64.00	A	19.71	527	5	Northern Niger State. Animists 60%, Muslims 25%. D=NBC,RCC,UMC.
7786	3	6	9.72	0	99.65	0.35	C	253.85	284	8	Adamawa State, Numan LGA. Agriculturalists, fishermen. Animists 30%, many Muslims. D=RCC(D-Yola),CAC,TEKAN. M=SUM,LBI,OSA,Bible Faith Mission, CETI.
7787	1	6	8.51	0	74.00	26.00	B	108.04	367	7	Plateau State, Bassa LGA. Animists 50%, Muslims 10%. D=ECWA. M=SIM,Bible Faith Mission.
7788	0	6	4.84	0	39.00	61.00	A	14.23	438	5	Plateau State, Kanam LGA. Animists 90%. M=SUM.
7789	1	5	4.05	0	22.02	77.98	A	0.01	677	2	Borno State, Bade LGA. Bilingual in Hausa, Kanuri, or Fulani. Muslims 99%. D=ECWA,CDCIW. M=SIM,dlbc,nem.
7790	0	3	0.00	0	14.01	85.99	A	0.00	0	1.06	Borno State, Maidugiri, LGA. Mainly in Chad. Muslims 100%. M=WEC,AIM.
7791	0	6	5.44	0	92.00	8.00	C	201.48	203	8	Cross River State, Akamkpa LGA. Language dying out. Animists 40%.
7792	0	6	2.43	0	26.07	73.93	A	0.06	406	2	Adamawa State, Numan LGA, at Bali. Animists 50%, Muslims 50%. Y=1943. D=LCCN,AC,CAC,ECWA,RCC.
7793	0	5	4.84	0	35.00	65.00	A	12.77	491	5	Gongola State, Karim Lamido LGA. Animists 50%, Muslims 40%. D=ECWA,RCC,UMCN,DLBC,AC,EKAN.
7794	2	6	5.38	0	99.85	0.15	C	387.81	148	9	Cross River State, Obudu LGA. Mainly in Cameroon forests. Close to Tiv. Animists 10%. D=COCIN,RCC.
7795	0	6	6.79	0	69.00	31.00	B	100.74	325	7	Bandawa. Taraba State. Karim Lamido LGA. Animists 60%. D=EKAN,RCC,UMCN,ECWA,AC,DLBC,NBC.
7796	0	6	4.34	0	27.00	73.00	A	4.92	581	4	Kebbi State, Sakaba LGA. Assimilation to Hausa or Lela. Animists 85%, Muslims 10%.
7797	0	5	1.10	0	17.04	82.96	A	0.02	407	2	Bauchi State, Balanga and Billiri-Kaltungo LGAs. Animists 60%, Muslims 40%.
7798	5	6	6.43	4	59.00	41.00	B	17.22	362	5	Kwara State. Mainly in Benin. Also called Busa. Muslims 50%, animists 42%. D=ECWA,AoG,MCN,NBC,RCC. M=SIM,ICB(Burma),CRAM,FMB.
7799	0	6	2.56	0	23.00	77.00	A	1.67	471	4	Bauchi State, Darazo LGA. Animists 50%, Muslims 48%.
7800	0	6	6.63	0	48.00	52.00	A	35.04	458	5	Plateau State, Langtang and Wase LGAs. Animists 80%.
7801	1	6	6.61	0	63.00	37.00	B	68.98	348	6	Niger State, Chanchaga LGA. Language nearly extinct. Animists 60%. D=ECWA. M=QIM,SIM.
7802	6	6	9.51	0	98.00	2.00	B	178.85	305	7	States: Benue, Plateau, Niger, Kwara. Literates 5%. Animists 49%, Muslims 1%. D=AICs,RCC,ECWA,CB,CPN,NBC. M=CMS,SIL,QIM,SIM,EMS,CMML,UBS,BCF.
7803	1	5	7.68	0	41.00	59.00	A	14.96	606	5	Adamaawa State; also in Cameroon. Largely animists 70%, Muslims 20%. Y=1913. D=COCIN/LCCN,CAC,RCC,TF,YM. M=SUM.
7804	0	6	6.98	0	58.00	42.00	B	63.51	395	6	Gongola State, Sardauna LGA. Batu town. Animists 50%, Muslims 20%.
7805	0	5	5.64	4	41.40	58.60	A	0.60	479	3	Nomads. Muslims 100%. M=CETI,JCMWA,CRCM,SCCM,EMS,SIM. R=ELWA.
7806	1	6	5.53	0	36.00	64.00	A	13.14	527	5	Niger State, Rafi LGA. Animists 85%. D=EKAN. M=SUM.
7807	1	6	7.96	0	60.00	40.00	B	43.80	427	6	Cross River State, Ogoja LGA. Animists 80%. D=AoG. M=WGMI,NBTT,SIL.
7808	5	6	10.78	0	99.88	0.12	C	436.83	245	10	Plateau State, JosLGA. Animists 10%. D=RCC(D-Jos),SDA,ECWA,COCIN,AICs. M=SUM,SMA,SIM,Bible Faith Mission,CETI,CRAM,NBTT,SIL.
7809	0	8	5.74	0	99.81	0.19	C	337.04	171	9	TARABA State, Takum LGA. Bete town. Nearly extinct. Most speak Jukun. A few animists. Y=1919. D=CRC,RCC.
7810	3	6	9.12	0	99.70	0.30	C	286.16	257	8	Cross River State, Obudu LGA. Animists 30%. D=AoG,ECWA,AICs. M=EMS.
7811	0	6	7.68	0	79.00	21.00	B	144.17	315	7	East of Numan, along Benue river; Gongola State. Animists 40%, Muslims 10%. D=LCCN,AC,ECWA,CAC,RPM,CA(ETEO).
7812	0	6	3.62	0	33.00	67.00	A	12.04	416	5	Kaduna State, Saminaka LGA. Animists 50%, Muslims 40%.
7813	0	6	8.70	0	99.80	0.20	C	321.20	251	9	Gongola State, Sardauna LGA; also in Cameroon. Animists 20%.
7814	1	5	7.01	0	41.00	59.00	A	14.96	561	5	Plateau State, Kanam, Wase and Shendam LGAs. Animists 80%, Muslims 10%. D=COCIN. M=SUM.
7815	0	6	10.10	0	81.00	19.00	B	144.86	389	7	Plateau State, Barakin Ladi and Mangu LGAs. Animists 40%, Muslim 10%. M=NBTT.
7816	0	0	6.60	1	46.00	54.00	A	25.18	506	5	Niger State, Borgu LGA. Kebbi State, Bagudo LGA. Also in Benin. Animists 50%, Muslims 35%.
7817	4	7	9.84	0	99.80	0.20	C	388.36	231	9	Cross River State; also in Cameroon. Animists 20%. D=RCC(D-Ogoja),ELCN,SDA,AICs. M=SPS,LCMS,CETI.
7818	0	6	8.06	0	55.00	45.00	B	40.15	471	6	Bauchi and Yobe States. All Muslims 60% (Sunnis, with small but aggressive Izala Shias). Few open animists 20%. Y=1960. D=EYN,ECWA,NBC,DLBC.M=EMS.
7819	7	10	2.09	8	99.74	0.26	C	407.85	59	10	Expatriates from Britain, in development. D=Ch of the Province of Nigeria(18 Dioceses),MCN,PCN,RCC,AoG,JWs,DLBC. M=FMB,CMS,SOMA.
7820	0	5	0.00	0	21.02	78.98	A	0.01	181	2	Shores and islands of Lake Chad. Most live in Chad. Warlike fishermen, cattle-herders. Muslims 100%. M=SUM,TEAM.
7821	0	7	6.89	0	99.70	0.30	C	263.16	220	8	Cross River State, Obudu LGA, Bumaji town. Animists 30%.
7822	1	6	9.60	0	82.00	18.00	B	104.75	367	7	Borno State, Biu LGA. Mulsims 35%, animists 30%. Y=1922. D=EKAS,EYN,NBC,RCC,ECWA,WLGC,DLBC,RPM. M=CBM,UBS. R=ELWA.
7823	0	5	1.40	0	19.10	80.90	A	0.07	406	2	Bauchi State, Billiri-Kaltungo LGA. Animists 70%, Muslims 30%.
7824	4	6	6.73	2	60.00	40.00	B	32.85	394	5	Half in Benin. Literates 10%. Animists 50%, Muslims 35%. D=MCN,RCC,ECNA,NBC. M=EMS,SIM.
7825	0	4	1.10	0	17.02	82.98	A	0.01	401	2	Bauchi State. Hausa is replacing Buta-Ningi language. Muslims 60%, animists 40%.
7826	4	10	6.29	8	99.80	0.20	C	423.40	140	10	Mixed-race persons near Cameroon borders. Major lingua franca. Animists 20%. D=RCC,AICs,MCN,&c.
7827	2	6	10.26	2	99.68	0.32	C	285.43	278	8	Benue State, Otukpo LGA. Animists 30%. D=RCC,MCN. M=UBS,Primitive Methodists.
7828	6	6	5.22	2	99.94	0.06	C	473.47	131	10	States: Rivers, Bendel, Ondo. Animists 5%. Nominal Christians 20%. D=ELCN,CAC,AICs,RCC,DLBC,&c. M=CMS,SMA,GRI,FMB.
7829	1	6	7.97	0	56.00	44.00	B	40.88	480	6	Taraba State, also in Cameroon. Literates 3%. Animists 66%, Muslims 14%. D=EKAS,RCC(D-Yola),SDA. M=SUM,OSA.
7830	1	6	8.35	0	84.00	16.00	B	153.30	332	7	Adamawa State. Also in Cameroon. Muslims 35%, animists 15%. Y=1906.D=LCCN,CPN,NEM,DLBC,AoG,AC,RCC(D-Yola). M=OSA.
7831	0	6	3.57	0	55.00	45.00	B	60.22	247	6	Plateau State, Bassa LGA. Animists 40%, Muslims 30%.
7832	2	6	7.24	0	58.00	42.00	B	42.34	408	6	Kaduna State, Kachia LGA. Animists 80%. D=ECWA,RCC. M=AMS,CMS,SIM.
7833	0	6	4.31	0	34.00	66.00	A	12.41	459	5	Plateau State, Pankshin LGA. Animists 70%, Muslims 20%.
7834	0	7	4.61	0	31.00	69.00	A	5.65	530	4	Plateau State, Bassa LGA. Animists 80%, some Muslims 15%. M=EMS.
7835	0	6	4.83	0	35.00	65.00	A	12.77	487	5	Gongola State. Related to Jukun. Animists 85%.
7836	1	6	9.79	0	99.88	0.12	C	417.56	236	10	Cross River State, Obubra and Ikom LGAs; Anambra State. Animists 10%. D=AICs. M=NBTT,SIL.
7837	0	6	1.40	0	20.10	79.90	A	0.07	386	2	Bauchi and Gongola States. Related to Jen. Animists 80%, Muslims 20%.
7838	0	6	4.10	0	28.00	72.00	A	5.11	537	4	Plateau State, Mangu LGA. Animists 60%, Muslims 35%.
7839	1	6	3.74	0	33.00	67.00	A	4.81	429	4	Gongola State, Bali LGA. Most live in inaccessible locations. Animists 79%, Muslims 17%. D=EKAS. M=SUM,EMS.
7840	0	6	3.04	0	23.00	77.00	A	1.67	528	4	Bauchi State, Toro and Dass LGAs. Many dialects. Animists 60%, Muslims 38%.
7841	1	7	3.84	0	69.00	31.00	B	100.74	208	7	Rivers State, Bonny LGA; in Niger Delta. Related to Ijo. Animists 60%. D=AICs.
7842	0	6	5.89	0	55.00	45.00	B	54.20	363	6	Rivers State, Degema LGA. Animists 70%.
7843	0	4	0.70	4	25.10	74.90	A	0.09	284	2	Sokoto State. Mainly in Benin, some in Niger. Muslims 100%(Maliki Sunnis). Dendi are actively spreading Islam.
7844	0	6	5.30	0	35.00	65.00	A	12.77	524	5	Bauchi State, Darazo LGA. Animists 60%, Muslims 30%.
7845	0	6	7.76	0	81.00	19.00	B	147.82	310	7	Adamawa and Borno States. Many animists 35%, some Muslims 15%. Y=1951. D=ECWA,EYN,LCCN,RCC,AC,NBC.
7846	5	10	11.64	8	99.60	0.40	C	264.99	288	8	Urban slum dwellers who have lost or abandoned tribal roots, culture, language. Muslims 32%, animists 2%, nonreligious 5%. D=RCC,CPN,MCN,SA,many AICs.
7847	0	6	6.70	0	71.00	29.00	B	103.66	314	7	States: Bauchi, Gongola. Close to Lotsu-Piri. Animists 50%.
7848	0	6	4.35	0	34.00	66.00	A	12.41	463	5	Bauchi State, Ningi and Darazo LGAs. Animists 70%, Muslims 20%.
7849	0	6	2.45	0	21.00	79.00	A	0.76	501	3	Kaduna State, Kachia LGA. Kajura District. Animists 50%, Muslims 49%.
7850	2	7	2.79	0	99.70	0.30	C	263.16	111	8	Cross River State, Akamkpa LGA. Animists 30%. D=AICs,RCC.
7851	0	5	1.96	0	19.10	80.90	A	0.07	486	2	Gongola State, Zing and Mayo Belwa LGAs. Muslims 60%, animists 40%.
7852	1	6	6.21	0	46.00	54.00	A	16.79	453	5	Azagvana. State, Gwoza LGA. Animists 70%, Muslims 20%. Occultism strong. D=EKAS/COCIN,EYN. M=Basel Mission,NBTT,SIL.
7853	0	6	4.77	0	29.00	71.00	A	5.29	582	4	Bauchi and Plateau States. In Jarawa dialect cluster. Animists 70%, Muslims 25%.
7854	1	6	4.34	0	24.00	76.00	A	1.75	654	4	Bauchi State, Toto LGA. Jamaa District. Animists 90%. D=ECWA.
7855	2	6	5.42	0	36.00	64.00	A	2.62	518	4	Kebbi and Niger States. Becoming Hausaized. Literates 2%. Animists 88%, Muslims 10%(Maliki Sunnis). D=UMCA,COCIN. M=UMS,EMS,MCA.
7856	0	9	2.67	0	35.00	65.00	A	12.77	318	5	Bauchi State, Bauchi LGA. Animists 90%.
7857	0	7	4.07	0	28.00	72.00	A	5.11	534	4	Kaduna State, Saminaka LGA, Dungi town. Animists 80%, Muslims 15%.
7858	0	5	1.81	0	18.05	81.95	A	0.03	486	2	Borno State, Bade LGA; Kano State. Muslims 60%, animists 40%.
7859	4	6	11.46	0	99.74	0.26	C	324.12	294	9	States: Niger, Plateau, Kaduna, Kwara. Animists 20%, Muslims 5%. D=RCC,ECWA,NBC,DLBC. M=LBI,SMA,SIM,EMS,AGM,CRAM,CGM,CMF,MCA,FMB.
7860	8	6	6.13	0	99.89	0.11	C	448.29	149	10	Rivers State, Degemaard Bonny LGAs. Animists 10%. D=AICs,CPN(D-Niger Delta),UNAC,SDA,CAC,RCC,NBC,DLBC. M=SMA,BWM,CRM,CGM,CMF,NEM.
7861	0	0	6.52	0	99.90	0.10	C	371.20	192	9	Akwa Ibom State, Mbo and Oron LGAs. Animists 5%. D=AICs.
7862	8	7	5.75	2	99.78	0.22	C	372.95	149	9	Bendel State. Nominal Christians 30%. Animists 20%. D=CPN(3 Dioceses),RCC(D-Benin City),NBC,Aruosa,CAC,SA,DLBC,AICs. M=SMA,CMS,BWM,CGCM.
7863	0	0	6.53	4	99.90	0.10	C	436.90	163	10	Akwa Ibom State, Mbo LGA. Also in Cameroon. Animists 5%. D=AICs.
7864	11	8	6.48	4	99.90	0.10	C	528.88	134	10	Cross River State. Animists 5%. D=RCC(D-Calabar),MCN,CAC,COG,CJCLdS,CC,New Ch,PCN,SA,DLBC,other AICs. M=GCNC(UK),CSM,PCC,QIM,BWM.
7865	1	6	7.37	0	99.70	0.30	C	260.61	235	8	Cross River State, Ikom LGA. Animists 30%. D=AICs.
7866	10	7	6.44	5	99.86	0.14	C	455.15	148	10	Animists 25%. D=CPN,RCC,MCN,PCN,NBC,ESOCS,CCC,CAC,DLBC,many more AICs. M=CMS,Holiness Assembly,WLM.
7867	2	6	9.29	0	90.00	10.00	B	164.25	325	7	Plateau State, Akwanga and Lafia LGAs. Animists 45%, Muslims 5%. D=COCIN,RCC. M=SUM.
7868	3	6	5.84	0	99.85	0.15	C	397.12	155	9	Cross River State, also in Cameroon. Animists 10%. D=RCC,CPN,many AICs. M=United Evangelical Mission,WGMI,LCMS.
7869	1	6	8.24	0	99.70	0.30	C	275.94	244	8	Cross River State, Ogoja LGA. Animists 30%. D=AICs. M=SIL.
7870	5	6	6.92	0	99.70	0.30	C	270.83	215	8	Akwa Ibom State. Close to Efik. Animists 30%. D=RCC,MCN,PCN,CAC,vast numbers of AICs.
7871	2	6	6.45	0	75.00	25.00	B	109.50	287	7	Cross River State, Ojoja LGA. Animists 60%. D=RCC,ELCN. M=UBS,LCMS.
7872	0	6	7.07	0	99.67	0.33	C	244.55	232	8	Rivers State, Ahoada and Yenagoa LGAs. Close to Ibo. Many animists, 30%. M=Day of Deliverance Ministry.
7873	4	6	5.47	0	99.00	1.00	C	216.81	190	8	Rivers State, Otelga LGA. Animists 40%. D=CPN,MCN,RCC,ELCN. M=LCMS,UBS.

Continued overleaf

Table 8-2 continued

PEOPLE		POPULATION				IDENTITY CODE		LANGUAGE		CHURCH		MINISTRY						SCRIPTURE	
Ref 1	Ethnic name 2	P% 3	In 1995 4	In 2000 5	In 2025 6	Race 7	Language 8	Autoglossonym 9	S 10	AC 11	Members 12	Jayuh 13-17	d 18	wa 19	xc 20	mc 21	mi 22	Biblioglossonym 23	Pub ss 24-26 27
7874	Eloyi (Afo)	0.02539	25,124	28,311	46,474	NAB56b	98-BCAA	afo cluster		1.00	283	0....	6	4	5	5	2	Eloyi	... .
7875	Emai (Ivbiosakon)	0.11360	112,409	126,671	207,935	NAB59c	98-EACH-b	emai		27.00	34,201	0....	9	5	7	2	0	Emai-iuleha-ora	P.. .
7876	Engenni	0.02483	24,570	27,687	45,449	NAB59c	98-EAEA-a	proper ngene		26.00	7,199	0....	9	5	6	5	2	Engenni	PN. .
7877	Epie	0.01890	18,702	21,075	34,595	NAB59c	98-EAEB-a	epie		28.00	5,901	0....	9	5	6	2	0		... b
7878	Eruwa	0.05000	49,476	55,753	91,521	NAB59c	98-EADD-a	eruwa		30.00	16,726	0....	9	5	6	2	0		... b
7879	Esan (Ishan, Isa, Esa)	0.31496	311,659	351,200	576,506	NAB59c	98-EACI-a	proper esan		80.00	280,960	0....	10	7	7	5	3	Esan	P.. .
7880	Etebi	0.01607	15,902	17,919	29,415	NAB56b	98-ICBA-c	efik		90.00	16,127	1as..	10	8	10	0	0	Efik	PNB b
7881	Etulo (Turumawa)	0.01103	10,914	12,299	20,189	NAB59z	98-BCCA-a	e-tulu		60.00	7,379	0....	10	7	7	4	1		... .
7882	Evant (Badzumbo, Balegete	0.00869	8,599	9,690	15,906	NAB56b	99-ABCA-a	e-vand		70.00	6,783	0....	10	7	7	2	0		... p
7883	Ewe	0.30000	296,856	334,518	549,124	NAB59d	96-MAAA-a	standard ewe	1	96.00	321,138	4Asu.	10	8	12	5	3	Ewe	PNB b
7884	Ezaa	0.28347	280,499	316,086	518,867	NAB59h	98-FAAG	northeast igbo cluster		78.00	246,547	0..u.	10	7	7	5	1	Izi-ezaa-ikwo-mgbo	PN. .
7885	Fali (Bana)	0.09399	93,005	104,805	172,040	NAB60b	18-GAAD	bana cluster		3.00	3,144	0....	6	4	6	5	3	Bana	... b
7886	Fam	0.00123	1,217	1,372	2,251	NAB66z	98-JEAA-a	fam		40.00	549	0....	9	7	9	0	0		... .
7887	Firan	0.00151	1,494	1,684	2,764	NAB56b	98-HAGC-f	fi-ran		50.00	842	0....	10	7	9	0	0		p.. .
7888	French	0.00400	3,958	4,460	7,322	CEW21b	51-AAAI-d	general français	2	84.00	3,747	1B.uh	10	9	14	5	3	French	PNB b
7889	Fyam (Fem)	0.03357	33,218	37,433	61,447	NAB56b	98-HAJA-a	fyam		50.00	18,716	0....	10	6	7	2	0		... .
7890	Fyer	0.00305	3,018	3,401	5,583	NAB60b	19-GAAA-a	fyeer		10.00	340	0....	8	5	5	1	0		... .
7891	Gaanda	0.04210	41,659	46,944	77,060	NAB60b	18-HBAA-a	ga'anda		50.00	23,472	0....	10	6	7	2	0		... b
7892	Gade (Gede)	0.08415	83,268	93,832	154,029	NAB59z	98-BABA-a	gade		15.00	14,075	0....	8	5	7	5	3		... .
7893	Galambi (Galambawa)	0.01899	18,791	21,175	34,760	NAB60b	19-BBDA-a	galambu		10.00	2,118	0....	8	5	5	1	0		... .
7894	Gamargu (Abewa)	0.01816	17,970	20,250	33,240	NAB60b	18-CAAA-a	gamargu		2.00	405	0....	6	4	5	4	1		pn. b
7895	Gasi	0.00900	8,906	10,036	16,474	NAB60b	19-AAAA-b	gasi		15.00	1,505	0....	8	5	8	4	0		p.. .
7896	Gaunu (Kuma, Koma Ndera)	0.03047	30,151	33,976	55,773	NAB66c	92-BCBB-g	liu		40.00	13,590	0....	9	6	5	4	3		... .
7897	Gbari Gayegi	0.02000	19,790	22,301	36,608	NAB59z	98-BAAB-b	gbagyi		30.00	6,690	2....	9	5	7	5	3	Gbagyi: Gayegi*	PN. .
7898	Gbaya (Baya, Gbea)	0.00500	4,948	5,575	9,152	NAB66c	93-AAAA-a	vehicular gbaya		40.00	2,230	0.s..	9	6	7	2	3	Gbaya: Gbea*	PNB b
7899	Gbo (Imaban, Itigidi)	0.04724	46,745	52,675	86,469	NAB56b	98-IDGA-a	le-gbo		70.00	36,873	0....	10	7	7	5	1		... .
7900	Geji (Gezawa, Zaranda)	0.00447	4,423	4,984	8,182	NAB60b	19-ECAA-a	geji		3.00	150	0....	6	4	4	4	2		... .
7901	Gengle	0.01000	9,895	11,151	18,304	NAB66z	92-BAAC-a	gengle		0.04	4	0....	3	3	5	1	0		... b
7902	Gera (Gerawa)	0.02243	22,195	25,011	41,056	NAB60b	19-BBEA-a	gera		1.00	250	0....	6	4	5	1	0		... .
7903	German	0.00200	1,979	2,230	3,661	CEW19m	52-ABCE-a	standard hoch-deutsch		87.00	1,940	2B.uh	10	9	13	5	3	German*	PNB b
7904	Geruma (Geremawa)	0.00793	7,847	8,842	14,515	NAB60b	19-BBFA-b	geruma-darazo		2.00	177	0....	6	4	5	1	0		... .
7905	Ghotuo	0.02609	25,817	29,092	47,755	NAB59c	98-EACD-a	ghotuo		30.00	8,728	0....	9	5	7	2	0		... .
7906	Glavda (Ametsa, Gelebda)	0.02500	24,738	27,877	45,760	NAB60b	18-CABB-a	gelvaxda-xa		9.00	2,509	0....	7	6	6	5	3	Glavda	P.. .
7907	Goemai (Ankwe)	0.25000	247,380	278,765	457,603	NAB60b	19-FBDA-a	goemai		0.03	84	0....	3	4	2	5	3		... b
7908	Gokana	0.08504	84,149	94,825	155,658	NAB56b	98-IBBA-a	gokana		70.00	66,377	0....	10	7	7	5	1	Gokana	PN. .
7909	Gongla (Bomla)	0.01000	9,895	11,151	18,304	NAB66c	92-BAAD-a	gongla		10.00	1,115	0....	8	5	5	2	0		... .
7910	Gubi (Gubawa)	0.00094	930	1,048	1,721	NAB56b	99-AACA-a	gubi		10.00	105	0....	8	5	4	1	0		... .
7911	Gude (Cheke, Mapuda)	0.07725	76,440	86,138	141,399	NAB60b	18-IBAA-d	gude		50.00	43,069	0....	10	6	7	5	3	Gude	P.. b
7912	Gudu (Kudo)	0.00474	4,690	5,285	8,676	NAB60b	18-IAAA-a	gudu		2.00	106	0....	6	4	4	1	1		... .
7913	Guduf (Gudupe, Gvoko)	0.03261	32,268	36,362	59,690	NAB60b	18-CABC-a	kudupa-xa		1.00	364	0....	6	4	5	1	0	Guduf	P.. .
7914	Gun (Gu, Alada, Egun)	0.03000	29,686	33,452	54,912	NAB59g	96-MAAG-j	gun		38.00	12,712	1As..	9	6	11	5	1	Gun-alada*	PNB b
7915	Gure-Kahugu (Gura)	0.01449	14,338	16,157	26,523	NAB56b	98-GBBE-b	niragu		2.00	323	0....	6	4	5	4	1		... .
7916	Gurma	0.02000	19,790	22,301	36,608	NAB56a	91-GGDA	gurma cluster		7.00	1,561	3.s..	7	5	6	4	1		PN. .
7917	Gurmana	0.00321	3,176	3,579	5,876	NAB56b	98-GAFB-a	gurmana		10.00	358	0....	8	5	5	2	0		... .
7918	Guruntum (Guruntawa)	0.01607	15,902	17,919	29,415	NAB60b	19-EBAA	guruntum-mbaaru cluster		5.00	896	0....	7	5	5	4	1		... .
7919	Gwa	0.00169	1,672	1,884	3,093	NAB56b	99-AABB-a	gwa		5.00	94	0....	7	5	4	1	0		... .
7920	Gwandara	0.04724	46,745	52,675	86,469	NAB60b	19-HAAA-b	kyankyara		2.00	1,054	0....	6	4	5	5	3		... .
7921	Gwomu	0.00180	1,781	2,007	3,295	NAB66z	92-ABAE-a	gwomu		0.07	1	0....	4	3	2	1	0		... b
7922	Gyem (Gyemawa)	0.00017	168	190	311	NAB56b	98-HAJA-a	fyam		5.00	9	0....	7	5	4	1	0		... .
7923	Haabe Fulani (Town Fulani	1.70000	1,682,182	1,895,604	3,111,700	NAB56c	90-BAAA-nb	kano-katsina	9	0.40	7,582	1cs..	5	4	8	5	3	Fulfulde, Kano-katsina	pnb b
7924	Han Chinese	0.00182	1,801	2,029	3,331	MSY42a	79-AAAB-ba	kuo-yü		6.00	122	2Bsuh	7	5	8	2	0	Chinese: Kuoyü*	PNB b
7925	Han Chinese (Cantonese)	0.00454	4,492	5,062	8,310	MSY42a	79-AAAM-a	central yue		5.00	253	3A.uh	7	5	8	2	0	Chinese, Yue	PNB b
7926	Han Chinese (Shanghainese	0.00272	2,691	3,033	4,979	MSY42a	79-AAAD-b	tai-hu		5.00	152	1A...	7	5	8	2	0		pnb b
7927	Hausa (Hausawa)	17.22174	17,041,233	19,203,290	31,522,876	NAB60a	19-HAAB-a	hausa	48	0.10	19,203	4Asu.	5	4	10	5	4	Hausa	PNB b
7928	Hausa Ajami	0.01600	15,832	17,841	29,287	NAB60a	19-HAAB-a	hausa		0.01	2	4Asu.	3	4	4	5	3	Hausa	PNB b
7929	Horom	0.00079	782	881	1,446	NAB56b	98-HAJC-a	horom		40.00	352	0....	9	6	5	2	0		... .
7930	Hyam (Jabba, Ham, Hum)	0.09219	91,224	102,797	168,746	NAB56b	98-HABD-a	hyam		5.00	5,140	0....	7	5	6	5	3	Hyam*	P.. .
7931	Hyide (Gra, Tur, Xedi, Xadi)	0.00881	8,718	9,824	16,126	NAB60b	18-CBBA-a	turu-xedi		10.00	982	0....	8	5	6	1	1	Hedi	pn. .
7932	Ibani (Bonny, Ubani)	0.05888	58,263	65,655	107,775	NAB59i	97-AADA-b	i-bani		60.00	39,393	0....	10	7	8	4	2	Ibani	Pn. .
7933	Ibeno	0.00952	9,420	10,615	17,426	NAB56b	98-ICAB-a	ibino		70.00	7,431	0....	10	7	7	2	1		... .
7934	Ibibio	3.04051	3,008,641	3,390,354	5,565,385	NAB56b	98-ICBA-b	ibibio		99.00	3,356,450	3cs..	10	10	12	5	4	Ibibio	pnb b
7935	Ibuoro	0.00560	5,541	6,244	10,250	NAB56b	98-ICBA	ibibio-efik cluster		90.00	5,620	3as..	10	8	10	0	0		PNB b
7936	Icen	0.04406	43,598	49,130	80,648	NAB56b	98-HBBB-a	i-cen		20.00	9,826	0....	9	5	6	2	0		... .
7937	Idere	0.00570	5,640	6,356	10,433	NAB56b	98-ICAB-a	ibino		90.00	5,720	0....	10	8	10	0	0		... .
7938	Idoani	0.02165	21,423	24,141	39,628	NAB59c	98-EABB-b	iyayu		30.00	7,242	0....	9	7	9	0	0		... .
7939	Idon (Idong)	0.01000	9,895	11,151	18,304	NAB56b	98-HAAC-a	i-don		5.00	558	0....	7	5	5	2	0		... .
7940	Igala (Igara)	0.78503	776,802	875,356	1,436,928	NAB59n	98-AAAC-a	i-gala	1	57.50	503,330	4.s..	10	7	7	5	3	Igala	PNB .
7941	Igbirra (Ebira)	1.07139	1,060,160	1,194,665	1,961,085	NAB59m	98-BBAA-a	central e-bira	1	24.00	286,720	0....	9	6	10	5	3	Ebira	PN. .
7942	Igbo (Ibo)	13.29790	13,158,520	14,827,969	24,340,633	NAB59h	98-FAAA-ea	isu-ama	23	98.00	14,531,410	1..u.	10	10	12	5	4		pnb .
7943	Igbo (Ungwana)	0.04000	39,581	44,602	73,216	NAB59h	98-FAAF	east igbo cluster		85.00	37,912	0....	10	10	12	5	3		... .
7944	Igbo (Upper, Onitsha)	0.05000	49,476	55,753	91,521	NAB59h	98-FAAA-d	north central igbo.		86.00	47,948	1..u.	10	10	12	5	3		pnb .
7945	Igboro Fulani	0.40000	395,807	446,024	732,165	NAB56c	90-BAAA-n	fula-sokoto		0.20	892	1cs..	5	4	6	5	3	Fulfulde	PNB b
7946	Igede (Egede, Alawu)	0.22289	220,554	248,536	407,980	NAB59z	98-BCBC-a	o-ju		60.00	149,122	0....	10	6	7	5	2	Igede	PN. .
7947	Ika	0.02000	19,790	22,301	36,608	NAB59h	98-FAAB-a	ika		57.00	12,712	0....	10	7	7	2	1		... b
7948	Iko	0.00565	5,591	6,300	10,342	NAB56b	98-IDBB-c	i-ko		90.00	5,670	0....	10	8	10	0	0		... .
7949	Ikpeshe	0.00467	4,621	5,207	8,548	NAB59c	98-EACG-a	ikpeshi		27.00	1,406	0....	9	5	6	2	0		... .
7950	Iku	0.01000	9,895	11,151	18,304	NAB56b	98-HAAE	gora-ankwa cluster		5.00	558	0....	7	5	5	1	0		... .
7951	Ikulu	0.01879	18,593	20,952	34,393	NAB56b	98-HAAF-a	i-kulu		6.00	1,257	0....	7	5	5	2	0		... .
7952	Ikwere	0.31496	311,659	351,200	576,506	NAB59z	98-FAAE	ikwere cluster		40.00	140,480	0....	9	5	6	5	3		... .
7953	Ikwo	0.23622	233,744	263,400	432,380	NAB59h	98-FAAG	northeast igbo cluster		95.00	250,230	0..u.	10	7	7	5	2	Izi-ezaa-ikwo-mgbo	PN. .
7954	Ilue	0.00450	4,453	5,018	8,237	NAB56b	98-ICAB	ibino cluster		90.00	4,516	0....	10	8	10	0	0		... .
7955	Irigwe (Aregwe)	0.04202	41,580	46,855	76,914	NAB56b	98-HAGD-a	nka-rigwe		25.00	11,714	0....	9	5	6	4	3	Rigwe*	P.. .
7956	Isekiri (Jekri, Warri)	0.45470	449,934	507,018	832,288	NAB59n	98-AAAA-h	i-shekiri	1	93.00	471,527	1csu.	10	7	6	5	3	Isekiri	PNb .
7957	Isoko	0.13373	132,328	149,117	244,781	NAB59z	98-EADB-b	isoko		94.00	140,170	0....	10	8	11	5	2	Isoko	PNB .
7958	Ito	0.00580	5,739	6,467	10,616	NAB59z	98-BCBC-b	i-to		90.00	5,821	0....	10	8	10	0	0		... .
7959	Itu Mbon Uzo	0.00575	5,690	6,412	10,525	NAB56b	98-ICAB	ibino cluster		90.00	5,770	0....	10	8	10	0	0		pn. .
7960	Ivbie North	0.03150	31,170	35,124	57,658	NAB59c	12-AACB-b	east maghrebi		50.00	17,562	2A.uh	10	7	7	2	0	Arabic: Algerian*	PNB b
7961	Izarek (Afusare, Jarawa)	0.04749	46,992	52,954	86,926	NAB56b	98-HAGC	zere cluster		50.00	26,477	0....	10	7	7	4	3		P.. .
7962	Izi	0.31496	311,659	351,200	576,506	NAB59h	98-FAAG	northeast igbo cluster		93.00	326,616	0..u.	10	9	7	5	3	Izi-ezaa-ikwo-mgbo	PN. .
7963	Jaku (Jakun, Jakawa, Labi	0.01000	9,895	11,151	18,304	NAB56b	99-AADC-a	labir		10.00	1,115	0....	8	5	5	2	0		... .
7964	Janji (Anafejanzi, Jenji)	0.00101	999	1,126	1,849	NAB56b	98-GBAJ-a	ti-janji		50.00	563	0....	10	6	6	2	0		... .
7965	Janjo (Jen)	0.01768	17,495	19,714	32,362	NAB66z	92-ABBA	dza cluster		60.00	11,829	0....	10	7	7	2	1		... .
7966	Jara	0.04062	40,194	45,294	74,351	NAB60b	18-HABA-a	jara		10.00	4,529	0....	8	5	6	2	0		... .
7967	Jarawa (Kogi, Bada)	0.14741	145,865	164,371	269,821	NAB56b	99-AADA	jar cluster		25.00	41,093	0....	9	5	7	5	3	Jarawa	P.. b
7968	Jera	0.03622	35,840	40,388	66,298	NAB56b	98-GBAG	jera-moro cluster		40.00	16,155	0....	9	6	6	4	1		... .
7969	Jewish	0.00080	792	892	1,464	CMT35	52-ABAC-b	standard-english		0.46	4	3Bsuh	5	4	2	1	0		PNB b
7970	Jibu (Jibawa)	0.02453	24,273	27,352	44,900	NAB56b	98-HBDA	njikum-jibu cluster		6.00	1,641	0....	7	5	6	4	1	Jibu	PN. .
7971	Jidda-Abu (Nakare)	0.01000	9,895	11,151	18,304	NAB56b	98-HADB-a	i-but		40.00	4,460	0....	9	6	6	2	0		... .
7972	Jilbe	0.00179	1,771	1,996	3,276	NAB60b	18-BBAC-a	jilbe		3.00	60	0....	6	6	7	0	0		... .
7973	Jimbin (Jimbinawa)	0.00253	2,503	2,821	4,631	NAB60b	19-DBHA-a	zumbun		10.00	282	0....	8	5	5	1	0		... .
7974	Jimi	0.00063	623	702	1,153	NAB60b	18-IBAA-e	jimjimen		9.90	70	0....	7	5	4	1	0		... .
7975	Jiru (Zhiru)	0.00300	2,969	3,345	5,491	NAB56b	98-HBCC-a	jiru		20.00	669	0....	9	5	5	1	0		p.. n
7976	Jorto	0.01518	15,021	16,927	27,786	NAB60b	19-FBBC-a	jorto		10.00	1,693	0....	8	5	5	1	0		... .
7977	Ju	0.00085	841	948	1,556	NAB60b	19-EBBA-a	ju		4.95	47	0....	6	4	4	1	0		... .
7978	Jukun Kona	0.00275	2,721	3,066	5,034	NAB56b	98-HBDA-g	kona		50.00	1,533	0....	10	6	8	2	1	Jukun: Kona*	Pn. .
7979	Jukun Wase	0.02000	19,790	22,301	36,608	NAB56b	98-HBDA-b	wase		20.00	4,460	0....	9	5	6	4	2		pn. .
7980	Jukun Wukari	0.09449	93,500	105,362	172,956	NAB56b	98-HBDA-i	wapan		60.00	63,217	0....	10	7	9	3	1	Wapan	PN. .
7981	Jukun Wurkum	0.02300	22,759	25,646	42,099	NAB56b	98-HBDA-k	wurkum		50.00	12,823	0....	10	6	7	4	2	Wurkum*	Pn. .
7982	Kadara (Kufana, Adara)	0.06515	64,467	72,646	119,251	NAB56b	98-HAAA	adara cluster		18.00	13,076	0....	8	5	7	5	3		... .
7983	Kafanchan	0.00360	3,562	4,014	6,589	NAB56b	98-HAGB-b	ka-fanchan		60.00	2,409	1....	10	7	6	5	2		p.. .
7984	Kagoma	0.02230	22,066	24,866	40,818	NAB56b	98-HABF-a	ka-goma		5.00	1,243	0....	7	5	5	2	0		... .
7985	Kagoro	0.01600	15,832	17,841	29,287	NAB56b	98-HAGB-c	ka-goro		60.00	10,705	1....	10	7	7	5	2		p.. .
7986	Kaivi (Kaibi)	0.00204	2,019	2,275	3,734	NAB56b	98-GBBF-a	kaivi		2.00	45	0....	6	4	4	1	0		... .
7987	Kaje (Jju, Kache)	0.29530	292,205	329,277	540,521	NAB56b	98-HAGA-a	j-ju		54.70	180,115	0....	10	6	7	5	3	Jju	PN. .
7988	Kakihum	0.01305	12,913	14,552	23,887	NAB56b	98-GACB-c	tsi-gadi		15.00	2,183	0....	8	6	8	0	0		p.. .
7989	Kam (NYIWOM)	0.00474	4,690	5,285	8,676	NAB66z	92-BFAA-a	kam		30.00	1,586	0....	9	5	5	2	1		... .
7990	Kamantan (Angan)	0.01629	16,119	18,164	29,817	NAB56b	98-HABE-a	ka-manton		9.00	1,635	0....	7	5	5	4	1		... .
7991	Kambari (Yauri)	0.06955	68,821	77,552	127,305	NAB56b	98-GACB-c	tsi-gadi	1	15.00	11,633	0....	8	5	7	5	3		p.. .
7992	Kambu (Winbum)	0.00400	3,958	4,460	7,322	NAB66c	92-CDAE-k	mbum		75.00	3,345	0.s..	10	6	10	5	0	Mboum*	PN. n
7993	Kamkam (Bunu)	0.00100	990	1,115	1,830	NAB56b	98-JBBA-b	kamkam		80.00	892	0.s..	10	7	5	5	2		... .
7994	Kamo	0.00305	3,018	3,401	5,583	NAB66z	92-AABB-a	kamo		5.00	170	0....	7	5	5	4	1		... .
7995	Kamuku (Jinda)	0.02685	26,569	29,939	49,147	NAB56b	98-GAEB	kamuku cluster		10.00	2,994	0....	8	5	7	5	3		... b
7996	Kamwe (Higi)	0.29374	290,661	327,538	537,665	NAB60b	18-GAAA	kamwe cluster		40.00	131,015	0....	10	6	7	5	3	Kamwe	PN. b
7997	Kanembu	0.00100	990	1,115	1,830	NAB61	02-AAAB-a	kanembu		0.00	0	0....	0	2	4	0	2	Kanembu	... b

Continued opposite

Table 8-2 continued

EVANGELIZATION								EVANGELISM			ADDITIONAL DESCRIPTIVE DATA
Ref	*D*	*aC*	*CG%*	*r*	*E*	*U*	*W*	*e*	*R*	*T*	*Locations, civil divisions, literacy, religions, church history, denominations, dioceses, church growth, missions, agencies, ministries, movements*
1	*28*	*29*	*30*	*31*	*32*	*33*	*34*	*35*	*36*	*37*	*38*
7874	2	6	3.40	0	30.00	70.00	A	1.09	437	4	Plateau State, Awe and Nassarawa LGAs. Literates in Hausa: 5%. Animists 94%, Muslims 5%. D=ECWA,CB. M=SIM,EMS.
7875	0	6	8.48	0	57.00	43.00	B	56.17	474	6	Kunibum. Bendel State, 6 LGAs. Many animists, 66%.
7876	1	6	6.80	0	63.00	37.00	B	59.78	356	6	Rivers State, Ahoada and Yenagoa LGAs. Animists 74%. D=Baptist Chs. M=SIL,NBTT.
7877	0	6	6.59	0	58.00	42.00	B	59.27	377	6	Rivers State, Yenagoa LGAs. Bilingual in Ijo. Animists 72%.
7878	0	6	5.47	0	61.00	39.00	B	66.79	308	6	Bendel State, Isoko LGA. Most are bilingual in Central Isoko, which is replacing Erohwa. Animists 70%.
7879	7	7	10.79	2	99.80	0.20	C	359.16	271	9	Bendel State. Animists 5%, Muslims 15%. D=CPN,RCC(D-Benin City,D-Oyo),AoG,NBC,DLBC,many AICs,&c. M=SMA,WF,CMS,UBS,LBI,CMORM,FMB.
7880	0	0	7.67	4	99.90	0.10	C	440.19	185	10	Akwa Ibom State, Uquo Ibeno LGA. Animists 5%.D=AICs.
7881	0	6	6.83	0	92.00	8.00	C	201.48	245	8	Benue State, Gboko LGA, and Gongola State, Wukari LGA. Animists 40%. M=UBS.
7882	0	6	6.74	0	99.00	1.00	C	252.94	225	8	Cross River State, Obudu LGA. Mainly in Cameroon. Animists 30%.
7883	5	10	10.93	4	99.96	0.04	C	595.68	197	10	Migrants from Ghana(fishermen, laborers). Animists 4%. D=RCC,EPC,PCN,DLBC,many AICs.
7884	3	7	10.64	0	99.78	0.22	C	338.79	277	9	States: Anambra, Imo. Animists 40%. D=RCC,PCN,AoG. M=NBTT.
7885	2	6	5.92	0	38.00	62.00	A	4.16	527	4	Adamawa State, Mubi and Michika LGAs. Also in Cameroon. Animists 17%, Muslims 80%. D=NBC,CB,RCC,FT,CDM,DLBC. M=CBM,FMB,CMML,ALBM.
7886	0	0	4.09	0	60.00	40.00	B	87.60	252	6	Taraba State, Bali LGA. Animists 50%, Muslims 4%.
7887	0	0	4.53	0	72.00	28.00	B	131.40	225	7	Plateau State, Barkin Ladi LGA. Related to Izere. Animists 50%. D=ECWA,COCIN. M=SIM,EMS,NBTT.
7888	1	10	1.78	8	99.84	0.16	C	487.49	48	10	Expatriates from France, in business. D=RCC. M=CSSp,SMA,SPS.
7889	0	6	7.83	0	80.00	20.00	B	146.00	316	7	Plateau State, in Jos and 2 other LGAs. Animists 40%, Muslims 10%.
7890	0	6	3.59	0	33.00	67.00	A	12.04	413	5	Plateau State, Mangu LGA. Animists 60%, Muslims 30%.
7891	0	6	8.07	0	83.00	17.00	B	151.47	312	7	Adamawa State, Gombi LGA. Animists 40%, some Muslims. Y=1939. D=LCCN,RCC.
7892	2	6	7.52	0	51.00	49.00	B	27.92	479	5	Plateau State, Nassarawa LGA. Animists 75%, Muslims 10%. D=NBC,ECWA. M=SUM,FMB,EMS,SIM.
7893	0	7	5.50	0	35.00	65.00	A	12.77	539	5	Bauchi State, Bauchi LGA. Chadic. Muslims 60%, animists 30%.
7894	1	6	3.77	0	34.00	66.00	A	2.48	416	4	Borno and Gongola States. Muslims 95%(Maliki Sunnis). Y=1958. D=COCIN,RCC,DLBC,NEM,EYN/CBM. M=SUM.
7895	0	5	5.14	0	45.00	55.00	A	24.63	398	5	Borno State, Shani LGA. Animists 65%, Muslims 20%. Y=1954. D=ECWA(rapid growth).
7896	1	6	7.48	0	73.00	27.00	B	106.58	349	7	Adamawa State, Ganye LGA. Minority in Cameroon. Animists 60%, Muslims 5%. Y=1963. D=LCCN(77 churches),ECWA,RCC,CC. D=ECWA. M=EMS,KHM,SIM.
7897	1	6	6.72	0	71.00	29.00	B	77.74	313	6	Dialect of Gbani Yamma. Animists 37%, Muslims 33%. D=ECWA. M=SMA,SIM,EMS,GOWE,NEM,MCA.
7898	3	6	5.56	4	89.00	11.00	B	129.94	228	7	Gongola State, Bali LGA. Mainly in CAR; also in Cameroon, Congo. Animists 50%. D=RCC,CPN,&c.
7899	1	6	8.56	7	99.70	0.30	C	286.16	243	8	Imo State, Afikpo LGA: Cross River State, Obubra LGA. Animists 30%. D=AICs.
7900	1	8	2.75	0	31.00	69.00	A	3.39	366	4	Bauchi State, Bauchi LGA. Animists 70%, Muslims 27%. D=ECWA. M=SIM,EMS.
7901	0	6	1.40	0	21.04	78.96	A	0.03	369	2	Adamawa State, Mayo Belwa and Fufore LGAs. Animists 90%, Muslims 10%. Y=1948. D=LCCN.
7902	0	6	3.27	0	22.00	78.00	A	0.80	580	3	Bauchi State, Bauchi LGA. Animists 88%, Muslims 10%.
7903	3	10	5.41	8	99.87	0.13	C	520.78	109	10	Expatriates from Germany, in business. D=New Apostolic Ch,PCN,RCC.
7904	0	6	2.92	0	23.00	77.00	A	1.67	513	4	Bauchi State, Toro and Darazo LGAs. Animists 85%, Muslims 13%.
7905	0	6	7.01	0	58.00	42.00	B	63.51	397	6	Bendel State, Owan and Akoko-Edo LGAs. Animists 70%.
7906	3	6	5.68	0	44.00	56.00	A	14.45	440	5	Borno State, Gwoza LGA. Also in Cameroon. Literates 5%. Animists 87%, Muslims 4%(expanding rapidly). D=EYN,EKAS,RCC,CC.
7907	4	5	4.53	0	27.03	72.97	A	0.03	600	2	Plateau State, 3 LGAs (Shendam, Awe, Lafia). Lingua franca: Hausa. Animists 89%, Muslims 11%. D=RCC(D-Jos),CPN,NBC,COCIN. M=SUM,SMA. Mainly RCs.
7908	1	6	6.37	0	99.70	0.30	C	278.49	195	8	Rivers State, Bori LGA. Animists 30%. D=ELCN. M=LCMS.
7909	0	6	4.83	0	35.00	65.00	A	12.77	521	5	Gongola State, Zing and Mayo Belwa LGAs. Animists 85%, Muslims 5%.
7910	0	8	2.38	0	34.00	66.00	A	12.41	304	5	Bauchi State, Bauchi LGA. Jarawan. Animists 60%, Muslims 30%.
7911	2	6	8.73	0	92.00	8.00	B	167.90	301	7	Adamawa State, Mubi LGA. Also in Cameroon. Strong animists 50%. D=NBC,EFLC,EYN,RCC,C&S,DLBC,LCCN,ECWA,TF,FT,CA,MCF. M=FMB,SIL,LBWM.
7912	0	6	2.39	0	23.00	77.00	A	1.67	450	4	Adamawa State, Song LGA. Muslims 23%, animists 75%. Virtually no Christians. M=LCCN.
7913	0	6	3.66	0	23.00	77.00	A	0.84	602	3	Borno State, Gwoza LGA. Also in Cameroon. Animists 96%, some Muslims 3%. D=EYN/CBM,COCIN,RCC,DLBC.
7914	2	6	7.41	4	98.00	2.00	B	135.92	257	7	Lagos State, Badagry LGA; also in Benin. Migrant laborers from Benin. Animists 50%, Muslims 10%(Sunnis, Ahmadis). D=MCN,AICs. M=MMS.
7915	0	6	3.54	0	27.00	73.00	A	1.97	500	4	Kaduna State, Saminaka LGA. Muslims 90%. M=SIM.
7916	1	6	5.18	4	48.00	52.00	A	12.26	374	5	Immigrants from Benin, Togo, Niger, Burkina Faso. Animists 53%, Muslims 40%. D=ECWA. M=SIM.
7917	0	6	3.64	0	34.00	66.00	A	12.41	405	5	Niger State, Rafi LGA. Animists 60%, Muslims 30%.
7918	1	6	4.60	0	32.00	68.00	A	5.84	513	4	Bauchi State, Bauchi LGA. Animists 90%. D=ECWA. M=EMS.
7919	0	6	4.65	0	26.00	74.00	A	4.74	637	4	Bauchi State, Toro LGA. Animists 75%, Muslims 20%.
7920	2	6	4.77	0	33.00	67.00	A	2.40	511	4	States: Niger, Kaduna, Plateau. Animists 88%, Muslims 10%. D=ECWA,NBC. M=SIM,CMF,EMS,FMB.
7921	0	6	0.00	0	19.07	80.93	A	0.04	205	2	Gongola State, Karim Lamido LGA. Muslims 50%, animists 50%.
7922	0	9	2.22	0	29.00	71.00	A	5.29	341	4	Bauchi State, Toro LGA, Animists 70%, Muslims 25%.
7923	1	6	6.86	4	48.40	51.60	A	0.70	479	3	Fulbe Siire. Former slaves. Muslims 99%(Maliki Sunnis). D=ECWA. M=EMS,SIM,LCMS,GOWE,ARCM,BBCM,FMB,JCMWA,SCCM. R=ELWA.
7924	0	10	2.53	7	65.00	35.00	B	14.23	134	5	Long-time residents. Traders. Buddhists/Chinese folk-religionists 80%, nonreligious 10%.
7925	0	10	3.28	8	64.00	36.00	B	11.68	168	5	Chinese from Guangdong, China. Buddhists, folk-religionists 95%.
7926	0	10	2.76	6	56.00	44.00	B	10.22	167	5	Chinese from Shanghai area. Folk Buddhists 90%.
7927	7	6	7.85	5	62.10	37.90	B	0.22	399	3	In 20 nations. Muslims 100%(Maliki Sunnis, also Tijaniyya). Many Isawa(People of Jesus). D=ECWA,CPN,NBC,COCIN/TEKAS,DLBC,Chad Brothers,UMCA.
7928	0	6	0.70	5	51.01	48.99	B	0.01	102	2	Hausa who use traditional Ajemi script. Muslims 100%(Maliki Sunnis). M=CMS,EMS,GOWE.
7929	0	7	3.63	0	66.00	34.00	B	96.36	208	6	Plateau State, Mangu LGA. Animists 50%, Muslims 10%.
7930	3	6	6.44	0	40.00	60.00	A	7.30	536	4	Kaduna State, Kachia and Jemaa LGAs. Animists 95%. D=NBC,CPN,ECWA. M=CMS,SIM,FMB,LBI.
7931	1	6	4.69	0	39.00	61.00	A	14.23	427	5	Adamawa State, Sardauna LGA, also Cameroon border. Most live in Cameroon. Animists 70%, Muslims 20%. D=RCC,EYN/CB. M=SUM.
7932	2	6	5.05	0	99.60	0.40	C	219.00	176	8	Rivers State, Bonny and Dagema LGAs. Related to Ijaw. Animists 40%. D=CPN,AICs.
7933	1	6	5.15	0	99.70	0.30	C	258.05	177	8	Akwa Ibom State, Uquo-Ibeno LGA. Animists 30%. D=AICs.
7934	9	7	5.95	4	99.99	0.01	C	592.61	123	10	Akwa Ibom State. Literary language: Efik. Trade language. Animists 1%. Nominal Christians 10%. D=RCC(D-Calabar),MCN,PCN,SA,SDA,CAC,ELCN,FPEC,AICs.
7935	0	0	6.54	4	99.90	0.10	C	443.47	161	10	Akwa Ibom State, Itu and Ikono LGAs. Animists 5%. D=AICs.
7936	0	6	7.13	0	47.00	53.00	A	34.31	497	5	Taraba State, Takum and Sardauna LGAs. Animists 70%, some Muslims. Y=1936. D=CRCN.
7937	0	0	6.56	0	99.90	0.10	C	371.20	159	9	Akwa Ibom State, Itu LGA. Animists 5%. D=AICs.
7938	0	0	6.81	0	51.00	49.00	B	55.84	441	6	Ondo State, one-quarter of Idoani town. Animists 60%, Muslims 10%.
7939	0	6	4.10	0	28.00	72.00	A	5.11	537	4	Kaduna State, Kachia LGA. Animists 75%, Muslims 20%.
7940	5	6	11.43	5	99.58	0.42	B	244.50	302	8	States: Benue, Bendel, Anambra. Animists 32%, Muslims 10%. D=RCC(D-Lokoja,D-Idah),ICFG,ECWA,CB,DLBC. M=CSSp,QIM,SIM,CMML,UBS,CETI.
7941	6	6	6.62	0	69.00	31.00	B	60.44	318	6	Kwara State. Literates 25%. Muslims 50%, animists 26%. D=CPN(D-Ondo),RCC(D-Lokoja),ECWA,AICs,NBC,DLBC. M=CSSp,CMS,SIL,CUMO,SIM,LBI,CUMO.
7942	10	6	6.32	5	99.98	0.02	C	554.43	136	10	In 4 States. Animists 1%. Nominal Christians 33%. D=RCC,CPN,AoG,BHM,ELCN,CC,MCN,PCN,DLBC/DCLM,many AICs. M=OP,SMA,WF,SPS,CSSp,LCMS.
7943	8	6	5.84	5	99.85	0.15	C	415.73	148	10	Animists 10%. D=RCC,CPN,AoG,BHM,COG,SA,CJCLdS,CAC. M=SMA,WF,SPS.
7944	13	6	6.59	5	99.86	0.14	C	445.73	154	10	Animists 9%. D=CPN,RCC,AoG,MCN,PCN,SDA,UNAC,CAC,SA,COG,CJCLdS,CC,ZMCN. M=SMA,WF,SPS,CSSp,QIM.
7945	3	6	4.59	4	48.20	51.80	A	0.35	352	3	Muslims 99% (Maliki Sunnis). D=ECWA,American Lutheran Ch,Sudan United Ch. M=ALC,SUM,JCMWA. R=ELWA.
7946	4	6	10.09	0	99.60	0.40	C	223.38	309	8	Benue State, Cross River State. Animists 40%. D=MCN,AoG,DLBC,other AICs. M=NBTT,SIL.
7947	0	6	6.91	0	91.00	9.00	B	189.32	250	7	Bendel State, 2 LGAs. Related to Igbo. Animists 40%. M=FMB.
7948	0	0	6.55	0	99.90	0.10	C	371.20	193	9	Akwa Ibom State, Ikot Abasi LGA. 3 villages. Culturally related to Obolo. Animists 5%. D=RCC, CPN.
7949	0	6	5.07	0	54.00	46.00	B	53.21	328	6	Bendel State, Etsako LGA. Animists 73%.
7950	0	6	4.10	0	27.00	73.00	A	4.92	557	4	Kaduna State, Kachia LGA. Animists 60%, Muslims 35%.
7951	0	6	4.95	0	30.00	70.00	A	6.57	579	4	Kaduna State, Kachia LGA. Animists 70%, many Muslims 24%.
7952	2	6	10.02	0	76.00	24.00	B	110.96	412	7	Rivers State, 3 LGAs. Animists 60%. D=CPN(D-Niger Delta),DLBC. M=Bible Way Mission,GMFI,HGM.
7953	5	6	10.66	0	99.95	0.05	C	471.58	243	10	Bendel State. Animists 5%. D=RCC,PCN,AoG,DLBC,other AICs. M=Life Transformers' Mission, NBTT.
7954	0	0	6.30	0	99.90	0.10	C	371.20	186	9	Akwa Ibom State, Oron LGA. Diminishing in size. Animists 5%. D=AICs.
7955	1	6	7.32	0	60.00	40.00	B	54.75	398	6	Plateau State, Saminaka LGA. Many animists 65%, Muslims 10%. D=ECWA. M=LBI,SIM,NBTT,FMB.
7956	6	6	6.59	1	99.93	0.07	C	478.62	155	10	Bendel State, 3 LGAs. Animists, 6%. D=CPN,RCC,CAC,NBC,DLBC,other AICs. M=CGCM,UBS,FMB.
7957	4	6	5.60	1	99.94	0.06	C	504.35	130	10	Bendel State, Ndokwa and Isoko LGAs. Animists 5%. D=RCC(D-Benin),CPN(many charismatic youth movements),DLBC,otherAICs. M=CMS,UBS.
7958	0	0	6.57	0	99.90	0.10	C	381.06	188	9	Akwa Ibom State, Akampa LGA. Animists 5%. D=AICs.
7959	0	0	6.56	0	99.90	0.10	C	371.20	193	9	Akwa Ibom State, Ikono LGA. Animists 5%. D=AICs.
7960	0	6	7.76	8	99.50	0.50	B	191.62	239	7	Bendel State, Etsako and Akoko-Edo LGAs. Animists 50%.
7961	2	6	8.20	0	88.00	12.00	B	160.60	299	7	Plateau State, Jos LGA, and Kaduna State, Jemaa LGA. Many animists 50%. D=ECWA,COCIN. M=SIM,EMS,NBTT.
7962	6	6	10.95	0	99.93	0.07	C	458.25	250	10	States: Anambra, Imo. Animists 40%. D=AoG,Deeper Life,BCRCC,PCN,ELCN,other AICs. M=SU,LCMS,NBTT,SIL.
7963	0	6	4.83	0	35.00	65.00	A	12.77	487	5	Bauchi State, Bauchi LGA. Animists 70%, Muslims 20%.
7964	0	7	4.11	0	78.00	22.00	B	142.35	193	7	Plateau State, Bassa LGA. Animists 40%.
7965	1	6	7.33	0	92.00	8.00	C	201.48	261	8	Gongola State, Numan and Karim Lamido LGAs. Jentown. Animists 30%, Muslims. D=COCIN. M=SUM.
7966	0	6	6.31	0	36.00	64.00	A	13.14	586	5	Borno State, Kwaya Kusar LGA. Many Muslims 60%, animists 30%. One Christian (a pastor). D=ECWA.
7967	3	0	8.68	0	61.00	39.00	B	55.66	452	6	States: Bauchi, Gongola, Plateau. Men are bilingual in Hausa. Animists 55%, Muslims 20%. D=SDA,ECWA,EKAS. M=SIM,EMS,SUM.
7968	1	6	7.67	0	72.00	28.00	B	105.12	345	7	Plateau State and Bauchi State. Animists 60%. D=ECWA. M=SIM.
7969	0	10	1.40	8	52.46	47.54	B	0.88	109	3	Small communities of English-speaking practicing Jews.
7970	1	6	5.23	0	39.00	61.00	A	8.54	465	4	Taraba State, Sardauna LGA. Animists 90%. Y=1962. D=EKAS/CRCN. M=SIL.
7971	0	6	6.29	0	67.00	33.00	B	97.82	314	6	Plateau State, Akwanga LGA. Animists 55%, some Muslims.
7972	0	0	4.18	0	18.00	82.00	A	1.97	848	4	Borno State, Jilbe town on border with Cameroon. May be related to Zizliveken. Muslims 97%.
7973	0	6	3.40	0	33.00	67.00	A	12.04	398	5	Bauchi State, Darazo LGA. Animists 80%, Muslims.
7974	0	8	4.34	0	33.90	66.10	A	12.25	463	5	Bauchi State, Darazo LGA. Majority animists 85%.
7975	0	7	4.29	0	45.00	55.00	A	32.85	346	5	Gongola State, Karim Lamido LGA. Animists 80%.
7976	0	7	5.27	0	35.00	65.00	A	12.77	521	5	Plateau State, Shendam LGA. Animists 80%, Muslims 10%.
7977	0	9	3.93	0	27.95	72.05	A	5.05	522	4	Bauchi State, Bauchi LGA. Animists 95%.
7978	1	6	5.16	0	85.00	15.00	B	155.12	211	7	Taraba, Plateau, Bauchi. Animists 50%. D=COCIN. M=SUM.
7979	1	6	6.29	0	55.00	45.00	B	40.15	383	6	Plateau State, Shendam and Langtang LGAs. Animists 80%. D=COCIN/Christian Reformed Ch. M=SUM,NEM.
7980	0	6	9.15	0	98.00	2.00	C	214.62	295	8	Taraba State (Wukari LGA), Plateau State (4 LGAs). Muslims 25%, animists 15%. Y=1918(SUM). D=CRCN(in every village),AC,DLBC,ZPC,ACF,JP,WT.
7981	1	6	7.42	0	88.00	12.00	B	160.60	274	7	Taraba State, in 3 LGAs. Animists 50%. Y=1923. D=COCIN/Christian Reformed Ch,UMCN,DLBC,NBC,RCC,ECWA. M=SUM,NEM.
7982	3	6	7.44	0	55.00	45.00	B	36.13	440	5	Kaduna State, Kachia LGA, and Niger State. Literates 20%. Animists 77%, Muslims 5%. D=ECWA,Baptists,RCC(M-Kaduna). M=SMA,EMS,SIM.
7983	2	6	5.64	0	97.00	3.00	C	212.43	199	8	Kaduna State, Kachia LGA. Dialect of Katab. Animists 30%, Muslims 10%. D=RCC,ECWA.
7984	0	6	4.94	0	29.00	71.00	A	5.29	598	4	Kaduna State, Jemaa LGA. Animists 60%, Muslims 35%.
7985	2	6	7.22	0	99.00	1.00	C	216.81	238	8	Kaduna State, Kachia and Jemaa LGAs. Dialect of Katab. Animists 35%, some Muslims. D=RCC(D-Jos),ECWA. M=SMA,SIM.
7986	0	7	3.88	0	23.00	77.00	A	1.67	628	4	Kaduna State, Saminaka LGA. Animists 60%, Muslims 38%.
7987	2	6	10.29	0	96.70	3.30	B	193.06	331	7	Kaduna State, Kachia and Jemaa LGAs. Animists 30%, Muslims 14%. D=ECWA,NBC. M=SIM,NBTT,SIL.
7988	0	0	5.53	0	35.00	65.00	A	19.16	542	5	Northern Niger State. Kambari language. Animists 60%, Muslims 25%.
7989	0	6	5.20	0	57.00	43.00	B	62.41	319	6	TARABA State, Bali LGA, 2 villages. Animists 50%, Muslims 20%. Y=1957. D=UMCN. M=NLFA.
7990	1	6	5.23	0	37.00	63.00	A	12.15	490	5	Kaduna State, Kachia LGA. Animists 91%. D=CPN. M=CMS.
7991	3	6	7.31	0	53.00	47.00	B	29.01	450	5	States: Niger, Sokoto, Kwara. Literates 15%. Animists 60%, Muslims 25%(Maliki Sunnis). D=NBC,RCC,UMC. M=FMB,CRAM,CMF,EMS,UMS,NBTT.
7992	0	6	5.98	1	99.75	0.25	C	317.55	184	9	Taraba State, Sardauna LGA. Animists 22%, Muslims 3%. D=RCC,NBC,PCN,RPM,DLBC.
7993	2	7	4.59	0	99.80	0.20	C	332.88	144	9	Taraba State, Sardauna LGA, Kamkam town. Also in Cameroon. Muslims 75%, animists 20%. D=CBC,LCCN,CRCN,DLBC,African Independent Ch,ECWA.
7994	0	6	2.87	0	31.00	69.00	A	5.65	380	4	Bauchi State, Billiri-Kaltungo and Akko LGAs. Animists 90%. M=YWAM.
7995	3	6	5.87	0	46.00	54.00	A	16.79	432	5	States: Niger, Kaduna, Sokoto. Literates 10%. Animists 70%, Muslims 20%. D=ECWA,NBC,UMCA. M=FMB,UMS,SIM.
7996	2	5	9.94	0	83.00	17.00	B	121.18	374	7	Adamawa State, Michika LGA. Animists 57%, Muslims 3%. D=EKAN/EYN,RCC(D-Maiduguri,D-Yola),NEM,PC,DLBC,AC,CPN. M=OSA,FMB,SIL.
7997	0	5	0.00	0	17.00	83.00	A	0.00	0	1.04	Around Lake Chad, mainly in Chad, Niger. Bilingual in Arabic. Muslims 100%(Sunnis, Sufis). M=TEAM,EMS.

Continued overleaf

Table 8-2 continued

PEOPLE		POPULATION				IDENTITY CODE		LANGUAGE		CHURCH		MINISTRY						SCRIPTURE		
Ref 1	Ethnic name 2	P% 3	In 1995 4	In 2000 5	In 2025 6	Race 7	Language 8	Autoglossonym 9	S 10	AC 11	Members 12	Jayuh 13-17	d 18	wa 19	xc 20	mc 21	mi 22	Biblioglossonym 23	Pub 24-26	ss 27
7998	Kanufi (Karshi)	0.00910	9,005	10,147	16,657	NAB56b	98-HACD	kanufi-nidem cluster		10.00	1,015	0....	8	5	5	2	0		...	.
7999	Kapsiki	0.01174	11,617	13,091	21,489	NAB60b	18-GAAB	kapsiki cluster		30.00	3,927	0.s..	9	7	9	0	0		PN.	.
8000	Karfa	0.00081	802	903	1,483	NAB60b	19-GBAC-a	karfa		40.00	361	0....	9	5	5	2	0		...	.
8001	Kariya (Lipkawa)	0.00452	4,473	5,040	8,273	NAB60b	19-DBFA-a	vinahe		10.00	504	0....	8	5	5	1	0		...	.
8002	Katab	0.12349	122,196	137,699	226,038	NAB56b	98-HAGB-e	ka-tab		65.00	89,504	4....	10	7	7	5	3	Katab	P..	.
8003	Kerai-Kerai (Karekare, Jalalum	0.08055	79,706	89,818	147,440	NAB60b	19-CAAA	kere-kere cluster		10.00	8,982	0....	8	5	7	4	3		...	b
8004	Kiballo (Vono)	0.00079	782	881	1,446	NAB56b	98-GBBH-a	kiballo		5.00	44	0....	7	4	4	1	0		...	.
8005	Kila	0.01000	9,895	11,151	18,304	NAB56b	98-JBBA-c	somyewe		10.00	1,115	0....	8	5	5	1	0		...	.
8006	Kilba (Huba, Chobba)	0.17135	169,554	191,066	313,641	NAB60b	18-GBAA	huba cluster		60.00	114,639	0....	10	7	8	4	3	Kilba*	P..	.
8007	Kinuku (Kinuka)	0.00079	782	881	1,446	NAB56b	98-GBBJ-a	kinuku		5.00	44	0....	7	5	4	1	0		...	.
8008	Kiong	0.00050	495	558	915	NAB56b	98-IDAB-a	ki-yong		70.00	390	0....	10	6	5	5	0		...	b
8009	Kir-Balar (Kirr)	0.00289	2,860	3,223	5,290	NAB60b	19-EEAA	kir-bala cluster		10.00	322	0....	8	5	4	1	0		...	.
8010	Kirawa	0.01689	16,713	18,833	30,916	NAB60b	18-CAAA-g	kirawa		2.00	377	0....	6	4	5	4	1		pn.	.
8011	Kirifi (Kirifawa)	0.02245	22,215	25,033	41,093	NAB60b	19-BBAA-a	giiwo		10.00	2,503	0....	8	5	6	2	1		...	.
8012	Kitimi (Tumi)	0.00199	1,969	2,219	3,643	NAB56b	98-GBBD-a	ki-timi		5.00	111	0....	7	5	4	1	0		...	.
8013	Koenoem	0.00500	4,948	5,575	9,152	NAB60b	19-FBFA-a	koenoem		30.00	1,673	0....	9	5	6	1	0		...	.
8014	Kofyar (Jibiyal, Bwol)	0.15829	156,631	176,503	289,736	NAB60b	19-FBBB	kofyar-gworam cluster		10.00	17,650	0....	8	5	6	5	1		...	.
8015	Kohumono (Bahumono)	0.02857	28,271	31,857	52,295	NAB56b	98-IDCC-b	e-diba		70.00	22,300	0....	10	7	7	2	1		...	.
8016	Kono	0.00485	4,799	5,408	8,877	NAB56b	00-AAAE-a	central kono		5.00	270	1....	7	5	5	1	0	Kono	P..	.
8017	Koro	0.27588	272,988	307,623	504,974	NAB56b	98-HABA	koro cluster		10.00	30,762	0....	8	5	6	5	3		...	.
8018	Kotoko (Makari)	0.02374	23,491	26,472	43,454	NAB60b	18-BBAA-a	lagwan		0.01	3	0....	3	2	5	3	0		...	n
8019	Kotopo (Potopo, Peer)	0.00474	4,690	5,285	8,676	NAB66c	92-BCAA	peere cluster		30.00	1,586	0....	9	4	5	4	1	Peere	PN.	.
8020	Kpan (Yorda, Abakan)	0.01000	9,895	11,151	18,304	NAB56b	98-HBBA	kpan cluster		20.00	2,230	0....	9	5	6	2	0		...	.
8021	Kubi (Kubawa)	0.00142	1,405	1,583	2,599	NAB60b	19-BBBA-a	kubi		10.00	158	0....	8	5	4	1	0		...	.
8022	Kuda (Kudawa, Kuda-Chamo)	0.00412	4,077	4,594	7,541	NAB56b	98-GBAA	kudu-camo cluster		5.00	230	0....	7	5	5	0	0		...	b
8023	Kugama (Yamale)	0.00300	2,969	3,345	5,491	NAB66z	92-BABC-a	kugama		10.00	335	0....	8	7	5	1	0		...	.
8024	Kugbo	0.00315	3,117	3,512	5,766	NAB56b	98-IAAD-a	kugbo		60.00	2,107	0....	10	7	6	2	1		...	.
8025	Kukele (Ukele, Bakele)	0.09046	89,512	100,868	165,579	NAB56b	98-IDDA	ukele cluster		80.00	80,695	0....	10	7	10	5	1	Kukele	PN.	.
8026	Kulere (Korom Boye)	0.01434	14,190	15,990	26,248	NAB60b	19-GBAD	kulere cluster		50.00	7,995	0....	10	6	7	2	0		...	.
8027	Kulung (Bambur, Wurkum)	0.01523	15,070	16,982	27,877	NAB56b	99-AAEA-a	ku-kulung		60.00	10,189	0....	10	7	7	2	0	Kulung	P..	.
8028	Kumba	0.00300	2,969	3,345	5,491	NAB66z	92-BABB-d	kumba		30.00	1,004	0....	9	5	6	2	0		...	.
8029	Kupto	0.00268	2,652	2,988	4,906	NAB60b	19-ADAA-a	kupto		10.00	299	0....	8	5	5	1	0		...	.
8030	Kurama (Bagwama, Akurumi)	0.03538	35,009	39,451	64,760	NAB56b	98-GBBA-a	ti-kurami		15.00	5,918	0....	8	5	6	4	2		...	.
8031	Kushi	0.00520	5,145	5,798	9,518	NAB60b	19-ACAA-b	chonge		10.00	580	0....	8	5	5	1	0		p..	.
8032	Kuteb (Zumper, Mbarike)	0.03916	38,750	43,666	71,679	NAB56b	98-HBFA	kutep cluster		65.00	28,383	0....	10	7	6	4	3	Kuteb*	PN.	.
8033	Kuturmi (West Yamma)	0.00924	9,143	10,303	16,913	NAB56b	98-HAAD-a	kuturmi		20.00	2,061	0....	9	5	6	4	1		...	.
8034	Kuzamani (Rishuwa)	0.00157	1,554	1,751	2,874	NAB56b	98-GBBM-a	ku-zamani		5.00	88	0....	7	5	4	1	0		...	.
8035	Kwa (Ba, Kwah)	0.00685	6,778	7,638	12,538	NAB66z	92-ACAA	longura-ma cluster		20.00	1,528	0....	9	5	5	1	0		PN.	.
8036	Kwami (Kwamanchi)	0.00300	2,969	3,345	5,491	NAB60b	19-AEAA-a	kwaami		10.00	335	0....	8	5	5	1	0		...	.
8037	Kwanka (Kadun)	0.20624	204,078	229,970	377,504	NAB56b	98-HACF	kwanka-legeri cluster		3.00	6,899	0....	6	4	5	1	0		...	.
8038	Kyibaku (Chibuk)	0.09499	93,994	105,920	173,871	NAB60b	18-GBBA-a	cibak		10.00	10,592	0....	8	5	6	4	1		...	b
8039	Laamang (Gbuhwe, Waha)	0.03799	37,592	42,361	69,537	NAB60b	18-CBAB	central laamang cluster		10.00	4,236	0....	8	5	6	1	1		...	.
8040	Lakka (Lao Habe)	0.00447	4,423	4,984	8,182	NAB66c	92-CDAE	karang-mbum cluster		5.00	249	0.s..	7	4	4	1	0		PN.	b
8041	Lame	0.00315	3,117	3,512	5,766	NAB56b	99-AABA	lame cluster		20.00	702	0....	9	5	5	1	0		...	.
8042	Lamja	0.00300	2,969	3,345	5,491	NAB66z	98-JDAB-a	lamja		20.00	669	0....	9	5	5	1	0		...	.
8043	Laru (Larawa)	0.00448	4,433	4,995	8,200	NAB56b	98-GAAA-b	laru		30.00	1,499	0....	9	5	5	1	0		...	.
8044	Lebanese Arab	0.02000	19,790	22,301	36,608	CMT30	12-AACF-f	syro-palestinian		50.00	11,151	1Asuh	10	6	7	4	2	Arabic: Lebanese*	Pnb	b
8045	Lela (Dakakari, Lalawa)	0.08549	84,594	95,327	156,482	NAB56b	98-GADC-a	chi-lela		50.00	47,663	0....	10	6	7	2	2	Lela	P..	.
8046	Lelau	0.00300	2,969	3,345	5,491	NAB66z	92-ABAD-a	lee-lau		40.00	1,338	0....	9	5	5	2	0		...	.
8047	Libo (Kan)	0.00979	9,687	10,916	17,920	NAB66c	92-ADCA-a	libo		40.00	4,367	0....	9	6	6	2	0		...	.
8048	Limoro (Anowuru, Anemoro)	0.01054	10,430	11,753	19,293	NAB56b	98-GBAG-a	e-moro		40.00	4,701	0....	9	6	6	4	1		...	.
8049	Lo	0.00783	7,748	8,731	14,332	NAB66z	92-ABAA-b	lo		20.00	1,746	0....	9	5	6	1	0		...	.
8050	Lola	0.05000	49,476	55,753	91,521	NAB66z	96-HABA	akpafu-lolobi cluster		9.00	5,018	0....	7	5	5	5	0		...	b
8051	Longuda (Jessu, Nyuwar)	0.05039	49,862	56,188	92,234	NAB66c	92-ACAA-c	nya-guyuwa		45.00	25,285	0....	9	6	7	4	2	Longuda: Guyuk	PN.	.
8052	Lopawa (Lupa)	0.00179	1,771	1,996	3,276	NAB56b	98-GAAA-a	kirikjir		40.00	798	0....	9	6	5	2	0		...	b
8053	Lotsu-Piri (Kitta)	0.00580	5,739	6,467	10,616	NAB66z	92-AADB-a	lotsu		60.00	3,880	0....	10	7	7	2	0		...	.
8054	Lubila (Kabila)	0.01000	9,895	11,151	18,304	NAB56b	98-IDFC-a	lu-bila		70.00	7,805	0....	10	7	7	2	0		...	.
8055	Lufu	0.00244	2,414	2,721	4,466	NAB56b	98-HBDA	njikum-jibu cluster		60.00	1,632	0....	10	6	9	5	1	Jibu	PN.	.
8056	Lungu	0.01629	16,119	18,164	29,817	NAB56b	98-HABB-a	i-dun		10.00	1,816	0....	8	5	5	4	1		...	.
8057	Luri	0.00005	49	56	92	NAB60b	19-EBEA-a	luri		10.00	6	0....	8	5	4	1	0		...	.
8058	Mabo-Barkul (Kaleri)	0.00500	4,948	5,575	9,152	NAB56b	98-HAJB	mabo-barkul cluster		40.00	2,230	0....	9	6	6	2	0		...	.
8059	Madda (Mada, Yidda)	0.09450	93,510	105,373	172,974	NAB56b	98-HACA-a	mada		50.00	52,687	0....	10	6	7	5	3	Mada: Nigeria	P..	.
8060	Magha (Maha)	0.00949	9,391	10,582	17,371	NAB60b	19-BAAA-a	maaka		10.00	1,058	0....	8	3	4	1	0		...	.
8061	Magu	0.01040	10,291	11,597	19,036	NAB56b	98-JBBA-a	mvanon		45.00	5,218	0....	9	6	6	2	0		...	.
8062	Maguzawa	0.10000	98,952	111,506	183,041	NAB60a	19-HAAB-a	hausa		1.00	1,115	4Asu.	6	4	8	5	3	Hausa	PNB	b
8063	Mama	0.03150	31,170	35,124	57,658	NAB56b	99-AAAA	mama cluster		20.00	7,025	0....	9	5	6	4	1		...	.
8064	Mambila (Mambere)	0.09449	93,500	105,362	172,956	NAB56b	98-JBCA	mambila cluster		33.30	35,086	0....	9	5	7	5	3	Mambila*	PN.	.
8065	Mandara (Wandala, Abewa)	0.01899	18,791	21,175	34,760	NAB60b	18-CAAA-j	vehicular wandala		2.00	424	0....	6	4	5	4	1	Mandara*	PN.	.
8066	Manga Kanuri	0.47499	470,011	529,643	869,427	NAB61	02-AAAA-a	manga		0.00	0	1....	0	4	4	5	3		pn.	p
8067	Mangas	0.00030	297	335	549	NAB60b	19-EEAB-a	mangas		10.00	33	0....	8	5	4	1	0		...	.
8068	Marghi Central (Lassa)	0.25000	247,380	278,765	457,603	NAB60b	18-GBAC	central margi cluster		57.00	158,896	1....	10	6	7	5	2	Margi*	PN.	p
8069	Marghi South (Uba)	0.12500	123,690	139,383	228,801	NAB60b	18-GBAB	south margi cluster		58.00	80,842	0....	10	6	7	4	1		...	b
8070	Matakam (Bula, Bulahai)	0.00431	4,265	4,806	7,889	NAB60b	18-ECAB	central mafa cluster		4.00	192	1.s..	6	4	5	5	1	Mofa*	PNB	.
8071	Mboa (Mbonga)	0.00100	990	1,115	1,830	NAB56b	99-AAHA-a	m-bonga		30.00	335	0....	9	5	6	1	0		...	.
8072	Mboi	0.01860	18,405	20,740	34,046	NAB66c	92-ADBA-a	mboi		15.00	3,111	0....	8	5	5	1	0		...	.
8073	Mbula-Bwazza (Bere)	0.03562	35,247	39,718	65,199	NAB56b	99-AAFA-a	mbula		40.00	15,887	0....	9	6	6	4	1		...	.
8074	Megili (Migili)	0.05252	51,970	58,563	96,133	NAB56b	98-HAIA-a	li-jili		50.00	29,282	0....	10	6	7	2	2	Migili*	PN.	.
8075	Mgbo	0.09921	98,170	110,625	181,595	NAB59h	98-FAAG	northeast igbo cluster		90.00	99,563	0..u.	10	7	7	5	1	Izi-ezaa-ikwo-mgbo	PN.	.
8076	Mini	0.00300	2,969	3,345	5,491	NAB56b	98-IAAC-a	mini		70.00	2,342	0....	10	7	6	2	1		...	.
8077	Miya (Miyawa)	0.00877	8,678	9,779	16,053	NAB60b	19-DBEA	miya cluster		3.00	293	0....	6	4	5	4	1		...	b
8078	Montol	0.02014	19,929	22,457	36,864	NAB60b	19-FBEC-a	montol		30.00	6,737	0....	9	5	6	2	0		...	.
8079	Mumuye (Lankaviri, Yoro)	0.37999	376,007	423,712	695,538	NAB66c	92-BAAE	west mumuye cluster	1	10.00	42,371	0....	8	5	7	5	3	Mumuye	PN.	b
8080	Mundat	0.00700	6,927	7,805	12,813	NAB60b	19-GBAB-b	mundat		30.00	2,342	0....	9	5	6	2	0		...	.
8081	Munga	0.00268	2,652	2,988	4,906	NAB66z	92-ABBB-a	munga		50.00	1,494	0....	10	6	6	2	0		...	.
8082	Nandu-Tari	0.00630	6,234	7,025	11,532	NAB56b	98-HAHA	nandu-tari cluster		50.00	3,512	0....	10	6	6	2	0		...	.
8083	Naragutawa (Iguta)	0.00564	5,581	6,289	10,324	NAB56b	98-GBAI-a	i-guta		40.00	2,516	0....	9	6	6	2	0		...	.
8084	Nde (Ekamtulufu, Udom)	0.02215	21,918	24,699	40,544	NAB56b	99-ACAC-a	n-de		70.00	17,289	0....	10	7	7	2	2		...	.
8085	Ndoe (Anep, Anyep)	0.00845	8,361	9,422	15,467	NAB56b	99-ACBB-a	e-kparagbong		70.00	6,596	0....	10	7	7	2	1		...	.
8086	Ndoro (Ndola)	0.01000	9,895	11,151	18,304	NAB56b	99-JAAA-a	ndola		50.00	5,575	0....	10	6	7	4	1		...	.
8087	Ngamo (Ngamawa, Gamo)	0.05699	56,393	63,547	104,315	NAB60b	19-BACA-a	ngamo		11.00	6,990	0....	8	5	6	5	2		...	b
8088	Ngizim (Ngizmawa)	0.07599	75,194	84,733	139,093	NAB60b	19-DAAA-a	ngezem		5.00	4,237	0....	7	5	6	2	1		...	b
8089	Ngohi (Nggwahyi, Ngwaxi)	0.00500	4,948	5,575	9,152	NAB60b	18-GBBB-a	ngwahyi		5.00	279	0....	7	5	5	1	1		...	.
8090	Ngoshe Sama (Nggweshe)	0.02080	20,582	23,193	38,073	NAB60b	18-CBCA-b	ngweshe		30.00	6,958	0....	9	5	6	2	0		...	.
8091	Ngwaba (Gombi)	0.00948	9,381	10,571	17,352	NAB60b	18-IBAA-j	ngwaba		10.00	1,057	0....	8	5	6	2	0		p..	.
8092	Ngwoi (Ngwe, Ungwe)	0.00179	1,771	1,996	3,276	NAB56b	98-GAEC-a	hungworo		30.00	599	0....	9	5	5	2	0		...	.
8093	Nigerian Creole	0.01000	9,895	11,151	18,304	NAN58	52-ABAH-e	nigerian-creole	32	50.00	5,575	1.s.h	10	7	6	5	0	Pidgin, Nigerian	Pn.	b
8094	Ninzam (Ninzo, Gbhu)	0.05512	54,542	61,462	100,892	NAB56b	98-HACB-a	ninzam		5.00	3,073	0....	7	5	6	2	0		...	b
8095	Nkem-Nkum (Ndok, Ogoja)	0.03919	38,779	43,699	71,734	NAB56b	99-ACAA-a	n-kem		70.00	30,589	0....	10	7	7	5	2	Nkem-nkum	...	.
8096	Nkoro (Eastern Ijaw)	0.00433	4,285	4,828	7,926	NAB59i	97-AADB-a	nkoroo		65.00	3,138	0....	10	7	7	5	1		...	.
8097	Nkukoli	0.00157	1,554	1,751	2,874	NAB56b	98-IDFA-a	lo-ku-koli		70.00	1,225	0....	10	7	6	5	1		...	.
8098	Nnam	0.00340	3,364	3,791	6,223	NAB56b	99-ACAB-a	n-nam		70.00	2,654	0....	10	7	6	5	2		pn.	.
8099	North Hausa (Arawa)	0.22000	217,694	245,313	402,691	NAB60a	19-HAAB-a	hausa		0.50	1,227	4Asu.	5	4	4	5	3	Hausa	PNB	b
8100	North Idoma (Agatu)	0.25170	249,062	280,661	460,715	NAB59z	98-BCBA-a	north i-doma		69.00	193,656	0....	10	6	7	5	3		PNb	.
8101	Northeast Central Ijaw	0.01154	11,419	12,868	21,123	NAB59i	97-AABA-a	proper biseni		65.00	8,364	0....	10	7	11	5	1		...	.
8102	Northern Akoko	0.05000	49,476	55,753	91,521	NAB59n	98-AAAB	north akoko cluster		30.00	16,726	0....	9	5	7	4	1		...	.
8103	Nten (Ganawuri, Jal)	0.04413	43,667	49,208	80,776	NAB56b	98-HAFA-a	ten		50.00	24,604	0....	10	6	6	2	0	Aten	P..	.
8104	Numana (Sanga)	0.01523	15,070	16,982	27,877	NAB56b	98-HACC	numana-gwantu cluster		5.00	849	0....	7	5	5	4	1		...	.
8105	Nungu (Rindre, Gudi)	0.02577	25,500	28,735	47,170	NAB56b	98-HADC	nungu cluster		30.00	8,621	0....	9	5	6	2	0		...	.
8106	Nupe (Ganagana, Nufawa)	0.98129	971,005	1,094,198	1,796,165	NAB59m	98-BAAA-a	ezi-nupe	2	2.80	30,638	4....	6	5	8	5	3	Nupe	PNB	.
8107	Nyikuben (Yukuben)	0.01468	14,526	16,369	26,870	NAB56b	98-HBFB-a	yukuben		40.00	6,548	0....	9	6	6	2	0		...	.
8108	Nyima (Anyima, Inyima)	0.01000	9,895	11,151	18,304	NAB56b	98-IDGA-c	le-nyima		60.00	6,690	0....	10	7	7	2	0		...	.
8109	Nzanyi (Nzangi, Paka)	0.07314	72,373	81,556	133,876	NAB60b	18-IBBA-a	nzanyi		10.00	8,156	0....	8	5	6	2	1		...	b
8110	Obanliku (Abanliku)	0.06189	61,241	69,011	113,284	NAB56b	98-IEAC-d	o-banliku		85.00	58,659	0....	10	7	10	5	3		...	.
8111	Obolo	0.09213	91,164	102,731	168,636	NAB56b	98-ICAA-e	ibot-obolo		94.00	96,567	4....	10	7	7	4	1	Obolo	PN.	b
8112	Obulom	0.00300	2,969	3,345	5,491	NAB56b	98-IAAE-b	proper o-bulom		70.00	2,342	0....	10	7	6	2	0		...	.
8113	Ododop (Korop, Erorup)	0.00900	8,906	10,036	16,474	NAB56b	98-IDAA-a	ko-rop		80.00	8,028	0....	10	7	10	2	1		...	b
8114	Odual	0.01714	16,960	19,112	31,373	NAB56b	98-IABA-a	o-dual		70.00	13,379	0....	10	7	7	3	1	Odual	PN.	.
8115	Odut	0.00241	2,385	2,687	4,411	NAB56b	98-IDAC-a	o-dut		70.00	1,881	0....	10	7	6	3	0		...	.
8116	Ogba (Ogbah)	0.16149	159,797	180,071	295,593	NAB59h	98-FAAD-b	ogba		50.00	90,036	0....	10	6	6	4	1	Ogbah	...	.
8117	Ogbia (Ogbinya)	0.19045	188,454	212,363	348,602	NAB56b	98-IAAB-a	proper o-gbia		94.00	199,622	0....	10	7	7	3	1	Ogbia	...	b
8118	Ogbogolo	0.00895	8,856	9,980	16,382	NAB56b	98-IAAA-a	o-gbogolo		60.00	5,988	0....	10	7	7	2	0		...	.
8119	Ogbronuagum (Bukuma)	0.00180	1,781	2,007	3,295	NAB56b	98-IAAE-a	o-gbronuagum		50.00	1,004	0....	10	6	6	2	0		...	.
8120	Ogoni (Kana, Khana)	0.19045	188,454	212,363	348,602	NAB56b	98-IBBB	khana cluster		88.00	186,880	0....	10	6	7	5	1	Khana*	PNB	.
8121	Ogori-Magongo	0.00952	9,420	10,615	17,426	NAB59m	98-DAAA	ogori-osayen cluster		2.00	212	0....	6	4	5	1	0		...	.

Continued opposite

Table 8-2 continued

EVANGELIZATION								EVANGELISM			ADDITIONAL DESCRIPTIVE DATA
Ref 1	*D* 28	*aC* 29	*CG%* 30	*r* 31	*E* 32	*U* 33	*W* 34	*e* 35	*R* 36	*T* 37	*Locations, civil divisions, literacy, religions, church history, denominations, dioceses, church growth, missions, agencies, ministries, movements* 38
7998	0	6	4.73	0	35.00	65.00	A	12.77	479	5	Kaduna State, Jemaa LGA. Many dialects. Animists 50%, Muslims 40%.
7999	0	0	6.16	0	56.00	44.00	B	61.32	369	6	Adamawa State in the Mandara mountains. Low literacy rate. Animal husbandry. Animists 57%, Muslims 3%.
8000	0	6	3.65	0	65.00	35.00	B	94.90	212	6	Plateau State, Akwanga LGA, Kerifa village. Animists 50%, Muslims 10%.
8001	0	6	4.00	0	33.00	67.00	A	12.04	448	5	Bauchi State, Darazo LGA. Animists 60%, Muslims 30%.
8002	2	6	9.53	0	99.65	0.35	C	256.23	277	8	Kaduna State, in 3 LGAs (Kachia, Saminaka, Jemaa). Animists 30%, some Muslims 5%. D=RCC(M-Kaduna),ECWA. M=LBI,SMA,SIM,EMS.
8003	1	6	7.04	0	46.00	54.00	A	16.79	502	5	Bauchi State, Yobe State. Animists 60%, Muslims 30%. Y=1935. D=ECWA,RCC,COCIN. M=SIM,EMS,FMB.
8004	0	8	3.86	0	28.00	72.00	A	5.11	514	4	Kaduna State, Saminaka LGA. Animists 50%, Muslims 45%.
8005	0	6	4.83	0	34.00	66.00	A	12.41	501	5	Taraba State, Sardauna LGA. Blacksmiths. Animists 70%, Muslims 20%.
8006	2	6	9.80	0	99.00	1.00	C	216.81	310	8	Adamawa State, Gombi LGA. Animists 30%, Muslims 10%. Y=1922.D=Ch of the Brethren/COCIN,Lutherans/LCCN,ECWA,NBC,C&S,AC,NEM,FTC,other AICs.
8007	0	8	3.86	0	28.00	72.00	A	5.11	514	4	Kaduna State, Saminaka LGA. Animists 85%, Muslims 10%.
8008	0	9	3.73	0	99.70	0.30	C	268.27	134	8	Cross River State, Odukpani and AkamkpaLGAs. Nearly extinct, spoken only by old people, being replaced by Efik. Animists 20%.
8009	0	8	3.53	0	34.00	66.00	A	12.41	396	5	Bauchi State, Bauchi LGA. Animists 80%, Muslims 10%.
8010	1	6	3.70	0	31.00	69.00	A	2.26	450	4	Borno and Gongola States. Dialect of Wandala. Muslims 98%(Maliki Sunnis). D=COCIN. M=SUM.
8011	0	6	5.68	0	37.00	63.00	A	13.50	524	5	Bauchi State, in 3 LGAs. Muslims 60%, animists 30%. M=EMS.
8012	0	6	2.44	0	26.00	74.00	A	4.74	404	4	Kaduna State, Saminaka LGA. Animists 70%, Muslims 25%.
8013	0	6	5.25	0	56.00	44.00	B	61.32	325	6	Plateau State, Shendam LGA. Animists 60%, Muslims 10%.
8014	2	6	7.76	0	43.00	57.00	A	15.69	583	5	Plateau State, 3 LGAs: Shendam, Mangu, Lafia. Many dialects. Animists 80%, Muslims 10%. D=RCC,COCIN. M=SUM.
8015	1	6	8.01	0	99.70	0.30	C	260.61	253	8	Cross River State, Obubra LGA. Animists 30%. D=AICs.
8016	0	6	3.35	4	33.00	67.00	A	6.02	394	4	Kaduna State, Saminaka LGAs, Kona village. Animists 70%, Muslims 25%.
8017	3	6	8.36	0	46.00	54.00	A	16.79	581	5	Kaduna State, Kachia LGA. Animists 70%, Muslims 20%. D=NBC,ECWA,RCC(M-Kaduna). M=SMA,SIM,EMS.
8018	0	5	1.10	0	19.01	80.99	A	0.00	359	1.06	Borno State, Ngala and Dikwa LGAs. Muslims 100%. Y=1964. D=COCIN.
8019	1	6	5.20	0	64.00	36.00	B	70.08	301	6	Adamawa State, Fufore LGA. Also in Cameroon. Muslims 5%, animists 65%. D=LCCN,EFLC(Cameroon). M=LBM.
8020	0	6	5.56	0	47.00	53.00	A	34.31	405	5	Gongola State, in several LGAs. Animists 80%.
8021	0	8	2.80	0	34.00	66.00	A	12.41	338	5	Bauchi State, Darazo LGA. Muslims 60%, animists 30%.
8022	0	6	3.19	0	29.00	71.00	A	5.29	433	4	Bauchi State, Ningi LGA. Language nearly extinct. Animists 70%, Muslims 25%.
8023	0	6	3.57	0	33.00	67.00	A	12.04	415	5	Adamawa State, Fufore LGA. Animists 80%, Muslims 10%. D=LCCN.
8024	1	6	6.23	0	90.00	10.00	C	197.10	232	7	Rivers State, Brass LGA. Animists 40%. D=AICs.
8025	2	6	9.41	0	99.80	0.20	C	359.16	241	9	Cross River State (Ogoja LGA), Anambra State(Abakaliki LGA). 10 dialects. Animists 20%. D=ELCN,RCC. M=LCMS.
8026	0	6	6.91	0	79.00	21.00	B	144.17	288	7	Plateau State, Mangu LGA. Animists 40%, Muslims 10%.
8027	0	6	7.17	0	91.00	9.00	C	199.29	258	7	Taraba State, Wukari LGA. Animists 40%. Y=1923. D=UMCN,NBC,DLBC,RCC.
8028	0	6	4.72	0	57.00	43.00	B	62.41	296	6	Gongola State, Mayo Belwa LGA. Animists 60%, Muslims 10%.
8029	0	6	3.46	0	33.00	67.00	A	12.04	403	5	Bauchi State, Dukku LGA. Animists 60%, Muslims 30%.
8030	1	6	6.59	0	46.00	54.00	A	25.18	475	5	Kaduna State (Saminaka LGA), Kano State. Animists 65%, Muslims 20%. D=ECWA. M=EMS,SIM.
8031	0	6	4.14	0	34.00	66.00	A	12.41	446	5	Bauchi State, Billiri-Kaltungo LGA, Kushi village. Animists 60%, Muslims 30%.
8032	1	6	8.28	0	99.65	0.35	C	246.74	255	8	Taraba State, Takum LGA. Animists 35%. Y=1915. D=COCIN,CRCN, Pentecostals,RCC. M=SUM,NEM,UBS.
8033	1	6	5.47	0	51.00	49.00	B	37.23	369	5	Kaduna State, Kachia LGA. Animists 60%, Muslims 20%. D=ECWA. M=EMS.
8034	0	6	4.58	0	26.00	74.00	A	4.74	629	4	Bauchi State, Toko LGA. Animists 60%, Muslims 35%.
8035	0	6	5.16	0	49.00	51.00	A	35.77	369	5	Adamawa State, Numan LGA. Tradesmen, butchers. Animists 70%, Muslims 10%. Y=1947. D=LCCN,CAC,RCC.
8036	0	6	3.57	0	33.00	67.00	A	12.04	412	5	Bauchi State, Gombe LGA. Animists 70%, Muslims 20%.
8037	0	6	6.75	0	25.00	75.00	A	2.73	892	4	Plateau State (Mangu LGA), Bauchi State. Animists 60%, Muslims 37%.
8038	1	6	7.21	0	44.00	56.00	A	16.06	536	5	Borno State, Damboa LGA. Muslims strong, 10%, animists 80%. Y=1937. D=EYN/Ch of the Brethren,DLBC,RCC. M=CBM.
8039	0	6	6.24	0	36.00	64.00	A	13.14	581	5	In 2 States: Borno, Adamawa. Strong animists 70%, Muslims 20%(expanding). Y=1938. D=COCIN,EYN. M=NBTT.
8040	0	8	3.27	4	37.00	63.00	A	6.75	378	4	Gongola State, Yola LGA. Also in Cameroon. Muslims 60%, animists 35%.
8041	0	6	4.34	0	44.00	56.00	A	32.12	357	5	Bauchi State, Toto LGA. Animists 60%, Muslims 20%.
8042	0	6	4.29	0	44.00	56.00	A	32.12	356	5	Adamawa State. Related to Chamba Daka. Animists 65%, Muslims 15%. Y=1960. D=LCCN.
8043	0	7	5.14	0	56.00	44.00	B	61.32	320	6	Kwara State, Borgu LGA(on banks of Niger river). Animists 60%, Muslims 10%.
8044	2	10	7.27	8	99.50	0.50	B	208.05	192	8	Traders from Lebanon. Muslims 50%(mostly Shias). D=RCC(Maronites),GOC(D-Accra).
8045	2	6	8.84	0	85.00	15.00	B	155.12	330	7	Niger and Kebbi States. Animists 50%. D=RCC,AICs.
8046	0	6	5.02	0	66.00	34.00	B	96.36	268	6	Gongola State, Karim Lamido LGA. Animists 50%, Muslims 10%.
8047	0	6	6.27	0	67.00	33.00	B	97.82	331	6	Adamawa State, Guyuk LGA. Animists 50%, Muslims 10%. Y=1947. D=LCCN,RCC,NBC.
8048	1	6	6.35	0	71.00	29.00	B	103.66	299	7	Plateau State (Bassa LGA), Bauchi State (Toro LGA). Animists 50%, Muslims 10%. D=ECWA. M=EMS.
8049	0	6	5.30	0	46.00	54.00	A	33.58	401	5	Gongola State, Karim Lamido LGA. Animists 65%, Muslims 15%.
8050	0	6	6.42	0	39.00	61.00	A	12.81	552	5	Adamawa State, Gombi LGA. Animists 90%, few Muslims. Y=1955. D=LCCN/EYN.
8051	0	6	8.15	0	82.00	18.00	B	134.68	333	7	Adamawa State (Guyuk LGA), Bauchi State. Many animists 54%, Muslims 1%. Y=1922. D=LCCN,NBC,DLBC,RPM,PC. M=SIL,NBTT.
8052	0	7	4.48	0	69.00	31.00	B	100.74	233	7	Kwara State, Borgu LGA; Sokoto State, Yauri LGA. On islands in Niger river. Hausaized. Muslims 60%(Maliki Sunnis).
8053	0	6	6.14	0	89.00	11.00	C	194.91	233	7	Gongola State, Numan LGA. Animists 30%, Muslims 10%.
8054	0	6	6.89	0	99.00	1.00	C	252.94	229	8	Cross River State, Akamkpa LGA. Animists 30%.
8055	0	6	5.23	0	99.00	1.00	C	216.81	183	8	Taraba State, Takum LGA. Language mostly used by elders only. Animists 40%(strong). Y=1943. D=CRCN. M=SUM.
8056	1	6	5.34	0	39.00	61.00	A	14.23	473	5	Kaduna State, Jemaa LGA. Animists 90%. D=CPN. M=CMS.
8057	0	9	1.81	0	35.00	65.00	A	12.77	251	5	Bauchi State, Bauchi LGA. Animists 90%.
8058	0	6	5.56	0	67.00	33.00	B	97.82	284	6	Plateau State, Mangu LGA. Animists 58%, some Muslims.
8059	2	6	8.95	0	89.00	11.00	B	162.42	318	7	Plateau State, Kaduna State. Animists 40%, Muslims 10%. D=NBC,RCC. M=SUM,SIM,FMB,NBTT.
8060	0	6	4.77	0	33.00	67.00	A	12.04	511	5	Yobe State, Gujba LGA. Hunters, fisherman. Islam entered from 1770. Muslims 60%, Animists 30%.
8061	0	6	6.46	0	72.00	28.00	B	118.26	299	7	Gongola State, Sardauna LGA. Animists 50%, some Muslims.
8062	4	6	4.83	5	60.00	40.00	B	2.19	275	4	`Pagan Hausa' in North. A tribe of Hausa, 90% animists. Y=1920. D=NBC,CPN,ECWA,RCC. M=CMS,EMS,SCCM.
8063	1	6	6.77	0	51.00	49.00	B	37.23	438	5	Plateau State, Akwanga LGA. Animists 60%, Muslims 20%. D=COCIN. M=SUM.
8064	2	6	8.51	0	74.30	25.70	B	90.30	365	6	Nigerian Mambila. Taraba State, Sardauna LGA. Animists 50%, Muslims 17%. Y=1938. D=MBC(80 churches),RDM,DLBC,CPN,RCC,LCCN,CRCN,NBC.
8065	1	5	3.82	0	31.00	69.00	A	2.26	460	4	Borno State. Most in Cameroon. Muslims 98%(Maliki Sunnis). Y=1958. D=COCIN,RCC,DLBC,NEM,EYN. M=SUM,CMF. R=ELWA.
8066	3	5	0.00	1	29.00	71.00	A	0.00	0	1.10	Yobe State. Part of larger Kanuri nation, centered on Yerwa. Majority in Niger. Lingua franca. Muslims 100%(Maliki Sunnis). D=NBC,ECWA,COCIN.
8067	0	8	3.56	0	34.00	66.00	A	12.41	399	5	Bauchi State, Bauchi LGA. Animists 80%, Muslims 10%.
8068	3	6	10.16	0	99.57	0.43	B	208.05	316	8	Borno State, Adamawa State. Muslims 10%, animists 33%. Y=1927. D=RCC(D-Maiduguri),EYN/Ch of the Brethren,COCIN,HEM,CoGM,DLBC,AoG,NEM,LCCN.
8069	1	6	9.41	0	95.00	5.00	B	201.11	311	8	Adamawa and Borno States. Muslims 15%, animists 3%. Y=1952. D=EYN. D=RCC(D-Maiduguri),CoGM,DLBC,AoG,CPN. M=OSA.
8070	3	6	3.00	0	45.00	55.00	A	6.57	267	4	Borno State, Gwoza LGA, densely populated. Majority in Cameroon. Animists 91%, Muslims 5%. D=EYN,COCIN,SDA,AIC. M=SUM(Swiss, Norwegian).
8071	0	6	3.57	0	55.00	45.00	B	60.22	247	6	Along border with Cameroon. Related to Jarawa. Animists 70%.
8072	0	6	5.91	0	39.00	61.00	A	21.35	544	5	Adamawa State, Song LGA. Animists 75%, Muslims 10%. Y=1962. D=LCCN.
8073	0	6	7.65	0	71.00	29.00	B	103.66	349	7	Adamawa State, in 3 LGAs. Animists 60%. D=LCCN,RCC,GFM,ECWA,RCC,AC,AoG,DLBC,JGM. M=LBI.
8074	0	6	8.31	0	86.00	14.00	B	156.95	309	7	Plateau State, Awe and Lafia LGAs. Animists 40%, Muslims 10%. M=SIL,NBTT.
8075	3	6	9.64	0	99.90	0.10	C	427.05	232	10	States: Anambra, Imo. Animists 10%. D=RCC,PCN,AoG. M=NBTT.
8076	1	7	5.61	0	99.70	0.30	C	258.05	190	8	Rivers State, Brass LGA. Animists 30%. D=AICs.
8077	1	6	3.44	0	32.00	68.00	A	3.50	414	4	Bauchi State, Darazo LGA. Second language Hausa. Animists 96%, Muslims 1%. D=ECWA. M=SIM.
8078	0	6	6.73	0	57.00	43.00	B	62.41	390	6	Plateau State, Shendam LGA. Many animists 60%, some Muslims.
8079	3	5	8.71	0	53.00	47.00	B	19.34	545	5	Taraba State, in 4 LGAs, also in Cameroon. Literates 5%. Animists (reviving) 81%, Muslims 9%. Y=1932. D=RCC(D-Yola),COCIN/EKAS,CC,UMCN(EUB),ECWA.
8080	0	6	5.61	0	57.00	43.00	B	62.41	336	6	Plateau State, Mangu LGA. Mangu LGA. Animists 55%, Muslims 15%.
8081	0	6	5.13	0	78.00	22.00	B	142.35	230	7	Gongola State, Karim Lamido LGA. Animists 45%, some Muslims.
8082	0	6	6.04	0	78.00	22.00	B	142.35	261	7	Kaduna State, Jemaa LGA. Animists 30%, Muslims 20%.
8083	0	6	5.68	0	67.00	33.00	B	97.82	289	6	Plateau State, Bassa LGA. Animists 50%, Muslims 10%.
8084	2	6	7.74	0	99.70	0.30	C	265.72	241	8	Cross River State, Ikom LGA. Several dialects. Animists 30%. D=RCC,AICs.
8085	1	6	6.71	0	99.70	0.30	C	258.05	220	8	Cross River State, Ikom LGA. Animists 30%. D=AICs.
8086	1	6	6.53	0	83.00	17.00	B	151.47	261	7	Taraba State, in 4 LGAs; also in Cameroon. Animists 50%, very few Muslims. Y=1943. D=EKAS/CRCN.
8087	2	6	6.77	0	47.00	53.00	A	18.87	476	5	Yobe State, Bauchi State. Muslims 10%, animists 79%. Y=1951. D=ECWA,RCC. M=SIM,EMS,NLFA.
8088	1	6	6.24	0	35.00	65.00	A	6.38	597	4	Yobe State, in 3 LGAs. Muslims 80%, animists 15%. D=ECWA. M=EMS.
8089	0	6	3.38	0	28.00	72.00	A	5.11	467	4	Borno State, Askira-Uba LGA. Muslims 65%, animists 30%. M=EYN.
8090	0	6	6.76	0	57.00	43.00	B	62.41	392	6	Borno State, Adamawa State. Animists 60%, Muslims 10%. D=COCIN.
8091	0	6	4.77	0	37.00	63.00	A	13.50	456	5	Adamawa State, Gombi LGA. Animists 40%, Muslims 50%. D=EYN,RCC,LCCN,NBC,NEM,AC,CPN,DLBC,ECWA.
8092	0	7	4.18	0	56.00	44.00	B	61.32	273	6	Niger State, Rafi LGA. Animists 60%, Muslims 10%.
8093	0	10	6.53	8	99.50	0.50	B	186.15	205	7	Lingua franca, mainly used in southern states and in sabon garis in north. Novels, plays, radio. Muslims 40%, animists 9%.
8094	0	6	5.90	0	33.00	67.00	A	6.02	605	4	Kaduna State (Jemaa LGA), Plateau State (Akwanga LGA). Bilingual in Hausa. Many animists 50%, Muslims 45%.
8095	2	6	8.36	0	99.70	0.30	C	273.38	250	8	Cross River State, Ogoja LGA. Animists 30%. D=AICs,RCC. M=CUMO,CETI.
8096	1	6	5.64	0	99.00	1.00	C	234.87	195	8	States: Rivers, Cross River. Animists 35%. D=AICs. D=CPN,RCC,AICs.
8097	1	7	4.93	0	99.70	0.30	C	265.72	167	8	Cross River State, in 3 LGAs. (Ikom, Obubra, Akamkpa). Animists 30%. D=AICs.
8098	2	6	5.74	0	99.70	0.30	C	275.94	181	8	Cross River State, Ikom and Ogoja LGAs. Animists 30%. D=RCC,AICs.
8099	3	5	4.93	5	56.50	43.50	B	1.03	297	4	Northern Nigeria, also in southern Niger. Traders. Muslims 100%(Maliki Sunnis). D=RCC,CoN,ECWA.
8100	4	6	10.37	1	99.69	0.31	C	292.14	278	8	Plateau and Benue States. Animists 30%. D=MCN,CB,ECWA,DLBC. M=SIM,EMS,CETI,CMML,UBS,CEFN.
8101	2	6	6.96	0	99.65	0.35	C	246.74	220	8	States: Rivers, Bendel, Ondo. Animists 35%. D=RCC,CAC. M=SMA.
8102	5	7	7.70	0	66.00	34.00	B	72.27	377	6	Ondo State, Akoko North LGA. Animists 50%, Muslims 20%. D=RCC,CON,PCN,MCN,AICs. M=CUMO.
8103	0	6	8.12	0	80.00	20.00	B	146.00	326	7	Plateau State, Barakin Ladi LGA; Kaduna State. Animists 40%, some Muslims.
8104	1	6	4.54	0	32.00	68.00	A	5.84	508	4	Kaduna State (Jemaa LGA), Plateau State (Akwanga LGA). Animists 60%, Muslims 35%. D=ECWA. M=EMS.
8105	0	6	6.99	0	57.00	43.00	B	62.41	403	6	Plateau State, Akwanga LGA. Animists 60%, Muslims 10%.
8106	5	6	4.67	5	57.80	42.20	B	5.90	287	4	States: Niger, Kwara. Literates 60%. Muslims 92%(weak Maliki Sunnis,syncretized), animists 5%. Y=1860. D=CPN,UMCA,SDA,ECWA,DLBC. M=CMS,SIM,EMS.
8107	0	6	6.70	0	67.00	33.00	B	97.82	331	6	Uhumkhegi. Taraba State, Takum LGAs. Also in Cameroon. Animists 60%. Y=1932. D=CRCN,DLBC,RCC.
8108	0	6	6.72	1	90.00	10.00	C	197.10	247	7	Cross River State, Obubra LGA. Animists 40%.
8109	0	6	6.93	0	40.00	60.00	A	14.60	570	5	Adamawa State, in 2 LGAs. Also in Cameroon. Trade language Fulfulde. Muslims 50%, animists 40%. Y=1949. D=LCCN,NBC,C&S,DLBC,RCC,Agape Ch. M=FMB.
8110	3	6	9.06	0	99.85	0.15	C	394.01	225	9	Cross River State, Obudu LGA. Animists 15%. D=AoG,RCC,AICs.
8111	6	6	9.61	0	99.94	0.06	C	483.77	214	10	Rivers State, Akwa Ibom State. Trade languages Ibo, Ibibio. Riverine fishermen. Animists 5%. D=RCC,CPN,PCN,MCN,AoG,many AICs. M=NBTT.
8112	0	6	7.32	0	98.00	2.00	C	250.39	244	8	Rivers State, Otelga LGA, Abuloma town. Animists 30%.
8113	1	6	6.92	0	99.80	0.20	C	341.64	195	9	Cross River State, Akamkpa LGA. Also in Cameroon. Bilingual in Efik. Animists 20%. D=AICs.
8114	1	6	7.46	0	99.70	0.30	C	273.38	227	8	Rivers State, Ahoada LGA. Animists 30%. D=CPN.
8115	0	7	5.38	0	99.70	0.30	C	255.50	185	8	Cross River State, Odukpani LGA. Animists 30%.
8116	2	6	7.64	0	87.00	13.00	B	158.77	284	7	Rivers State, Ahoada LGA. In Igbo language cluster. Animists 50%. D=RCC,CPN. M=UBS.
8117	3	6	10.41	0	99.94	0.06	C	442.59	251	10	Rivers State, Brass LGA. English little used. Animists 5%. D=RCC,CPN,&c. M=UBS.
8118	0	6	6.60	0	89.00	11.00	C	194.91	246	7	Rivers State, Ahoada LGA. Animists 40%.
8119	0	7	4.72	0	79.00	21.00	B	144.17	212	7	Rivers State, Degema LGA, Bukuma village near Buguma. Animists 50%.
8120	2	6	10.34	0	99.88	0.12	C	430.40	240	10	Rivers State, 3 LGAs; Cross River State. Animists 10%. D=CPN(D-Niger Delta),ELCN. M=LCMS.
8121	0	7	3.10	0	24.00	76.00	A	1.75	513	4	Kwara State, Okene LGA. Animists 90%, Muslims 8%.

Continued overleaf

Table 8-2 continued

PEOPLE		POPULATION				IDENTITY CODE		LANGUAGE		CHURCH		MINISTRY						SCRIPTURE		
Ref 1	Ethnic name 2	P% 3	In 1995 4	In 2000 5	In 2025 6	Race 7	Language 8	Autoglossonym 9	S 10	AC 11	Members 12	Jayuh 13-17	d 18	wa 19	xc 20	mc 21	mi 22	Biblioglossonym 23	Pub 24-26	ss 27
8122	Okobo	0.05046	49,931	56,266	92,363	NAB56b	98-ICAD-a	o-kobo		70.00	39,386	0....	10	7	7	2	0		...	.
8123	Okordia	0.00490	4,849	5,464	8,969	NAB59i	97-AABB-a	o-kodia		60.00	3,278	0....	10	7	8	5	2		...	.
8124	Okpamheri	0.04724	46,745	52,675	86,469	NAB59c	98-EAAA	okpamheri cluster		27.00	14,222	0....	9	5	7	3	0		...	.
8125	Okpe	0.02233	22,096	24,899	40,873	NAB59c	98-EAAB	okpe-akuku cluster		28.00	6,972	0....	9	5	6	2	0		...	.
8126	Okpe	0.00500	4,948	5,575	9,152	NAB59c	98-EAAB	okpe-akuku cluster		27.00	1,505	0....	9	5	5	2	0		...	.
8127	Okrika	0.22198	219,653	247,521	406,315	NAB59i	97-AADA-c	o-krika		80.00	198,017	0....	10	7	10	4	1	Okrika	Pn.	b
8128	Olulumo-Ikom (Okuni)	0.08570	84,802	95,561	156,866	NAB56b	98-IDIA-a	o-lu-lumo		80.00	76,449	0....	10	7	10	3	3		...	.
8129	Oron	0.07100	70,256	79,169	129,959	NAB56b	98-ICAC-a	o-ron		70.00	55,419	0....	10	7	7	2	0		...	.
8130	Orri (Oring, Korrin)	0.07142	70,671	79,638	130,728	NAB56b	98-IDDC-a	proper o-ring		75.00	59,728	0....	10	7	7	3	0		...	.
8131	Oruma	0.00447	4,423	4,984	8,182	NAB59i	97-AACA-a	o-ruma		60.00	2,991	0....	10	7	9	0	0		...	.
8132	Ososo	0.01672	16,545	18,644	30,604	NAB59c	98-EACA-a	ososo		30.00	5,593	0....	9	5	6	2	0		...	.
8133	Paa (Afawa, Afanci, Paawa	0.01328	13,141	14,808	24,308	NAB60b	19-DBDA-a	fuucaka		5.00	740	0....	7	5	5	4	2		...	b
8134	Pabir (Babur)	0.16000	158,323	178,410	292,866	NAB60b	18-GBBD-a	bura-pabir		0.03	54	4.s..	3	4	5	2	0	Bura*	PN.	b
8135	Pai	0.00315	3,117	3,512	5,766	NAB56b	98-HACH-a	pai		30.00	1,054	0....	9	5	5	2	0		...	.
8136	Pana (Pani)	0.00400	3,958	4,460	7,322	NAB66c	92-CDAE-h	pana		60.00	2,676	0.s..	10	7	7	5	3	Pana	Pn.	.
8137	Panso (Nso, Nsaw)	0.00300	2,969	3,345	5,491	NAB57a	99-AGDB-g	lam-nso		20.00	669	0....	9	6	9	5	0	Nso*	PN.	b
8138	Panyam	0.00500	4,948	5,575	9,152	NAB66z	92-ABAB-a	lee-mak		40.00	2,230	0....	9	6	6	2	0		...	.
8139	Passam (Kpasham, Manyan)	0.01468	14,526	16,369	26,870	NAB66z	92-BABA-a	kpasam		30.00	4,911	0....	9	5	5	2	0		...	b
8140	Pero	0.03150	31,170	35,124	57,658	NAB60b	19-ACAA-a	peero		50.00	17,562	0....	10	6	7	3	0	Pero	P..	.
8141	Piti	0.00486	4,809	5,419	8,896	NAB56b	98-GBDA-a	piti		5.00	271	0....	7	5	5	4	1		P..	.
8142	Piya (Ambandi, Kukulim)	0.00489	4,839	5,453	8,951	NAB60b	19-ACAB-a	ambandi		30.00	1,636	0....	9	5	5	2	0	Piya	P..	.
8143	Polci (Palci, Palchi)	0.01037	10,261	11,563	18,981	NAB60b	19-ECBA-a	pelci		15.00	1,734	0....	8	5	6	4	1		...	.
8144	Pongu (Pongo)	0.02206	21,829	24,598	40,379	NAB56b	98-GAEE-a	pongu		30.00	7,379	0....	9	5	6	2	0		...	.
8145	Puku (Faka, Aror)	0.02362	23,372	26,338	43,234	NAB56b	98-GADA	puku-wipsi cluster		1.00	263	0....	6	4	5	5	2		...	.
8146	Pyapun	0.00350	3,463	3,903	6,406	NAB60b	19-FBEB-a	pyapun		40.00	1,561	0....	9	6	6	2	0		...	.
8147	Pyapun	0.01518	15,021	16,927	27,786	NAB60b	19-FBEB-a	pyapun		30.00	5,078	0....	9	6	8	0	0		...	.
8148	Reshe (Gungawa, Reshawa)	0.04724	46,745	52,675	86,469	NAB56b	98-GABA	reshe cluster		10.00	5,268	0....	8	5	6	2	1	Reshe	P..	b
8149	River Jukun (Abinsi)	0.02000	19,790	22,301	36,608	NAB56b	98-HBDA-j	abinsi		10.00	2,230	0....	8	5	6	2	0		pn.	.
8150	Roba (Gworam)	0.04369	43,232	48,717	79,971	NAB66c	92-ADAA-b	lala		20.00	9,743	0....	9	5	6	2	0		...	.
8151	Rumaya (Amala)	0.00582	5,759	6,490	10,653	NAB56b	98-GBBC-a	mala		5.00	324	0....	7	5	5	1	0		...	.
8152	Ruruma (Turama)	0.00711	7,035	7,928	13,014	NAB56b	98-GBBB-a	tu-ruma		5.00	396	0....	7	5	5	1	0		...	.
8153	Sanga (Asanga, Gusu)	0.00787	7,788	8,776	14,405	NAB56b	98-GBAG-b	i-sanga		1.00	88	0....	6	4	4	1	0		...	.
8154	Sara Mbai	0.00700	6,927	7,805	12,813	NAB66z	03-AAAE-h	mbai-kan		60.00	4,683	0.s..	10	7	7	4	1	Mbai: Moissala	PNB	b
8155	Sasaru	0.01094	10,825	12,199	20,025	NAB59c	98-EACE	sasaru-enwan cluster		30.00	3,660	0....	9	5	6	1	0		...	.
8156	Saya (Sayawa, Sigidi)	0.07874	77,915	87,800	144,127	NAB60b	19-EDCA	saya cluster		25.00	21,950	0....	9	5	6	4	2		...	.
8157	Seto-Gbe	0.00100	990	1,115	1,830	NAB59e	96-MAAG-h	seto		20.00	223	1cs..	9	5	6	5	0		pnb	.
8158	Sha	0.00051	505	569	934	NAB60b	19-GBAB-a	sha		40.00	227	0....	9	6	5	3	0		...	.
8159	Shagawu (Chala, Nafunfia)	0.02031	20,097	22,647	37,176	NAB60b	19-GBAA-d	maleni		10.00	2,265	0....	8	5	6	4	1	Shagawu	P..	b
8160	Shal (Shall-Zwall)	0.00700	6,927	7,805	12,813	NAB56b	98-HACG	shall-zwall cluster		20.00	1,561	0....	9	5	6	3	0		...	.
8161	Shama	0.00447	4,423	4,984	8,182	NAB56b	98-HABD-c	shamang		10.00	498	0....	8	6	7	0	0		p..	.
8162	Shanga (Shangawa)	0.00671	6,640	7,482	12,282	NAB63z	00-DGDB-a	shanga		0.02	1	0....	3	3	2	1	0		...	b
8163	Shani	0.00036	356	401	659	NAB56b	98-GBAE-a	sheni		5.00	20	0....	7	5	4	1	0		...	.
8164	Sholio (Asholio)	0.01660	16,426	18,510	30,385	NAB56b	98-HAGB-f	a-sholio		60.00	11,106	1....	10	7	7	5	2		p..	.
8165	Shuwa Arab (Baggara)	0.15748	155,829	175,600	288,253	CMT30	12-AACE-a	shuwa	3	0.10	176	0...h	5	3	2	1	2	Arabic: Chad	PN.	b
8166	Siri (Sirawa)	0.00284	2,810	3,167	5,198	NAB60b	19-DBBA	siri cluster		20.00	633	0....	9	5	5	1	0		...	.
8167	Sokoto Fulani	1.70000	1,682,182	1,895,604	3,111,700	NAB56c	90-BAAA-n	fula-sokoto	8	0.10	1,896	1cs..	5	3	6	1	0	Fulfulde	PNB	b
8168	Songhai (Sonrhai)	0.20000	197,904	223,012	366,082	NAB65b	01-AAAA	songhay-kine cluster		0.40	892	0....	5	3	6	1	0	Songhai*	PN.	b
8169	South Idoma (Igumale)	0.07000	69,266	78,054	128,129	NAB59z	98-BCBA-e	south i-doma	1	70.00	54,638	0....	10	9	7	5	3		pnb	.
8170	Southeast Ijaw	0.09821	97,181	109,510	179,765	NAB59i	97-AAEA-a	nembe		93.00	101,844	0....	10	7	10	5	2	Ijo: Brass*	PNB	.
8171	Sukur (Sakul, Gemasakun)	0.01447	14,318	16,135	26,486	NAB60b	18-DAAA-a	sukur		10.00	1,613	0....	8	5	6	2	0		...	b
8172	Sura (Mwaghavul, Mupun)	0.28499	282,003	317,781	521,649	NAB60b	19-FBBA	mwaghavul cluster		77.00	244,692	4....	10	7	7	5	2		PN.	.
8173	Surubu (Zurubu)	0.00630	6,234	7,025	11,532	NAB56b	98-GBBL-a	surubu		5.00	351	0....	7	5	6	1	0		...	.
8174	Syrian Arab	0.01000	9,895	11,151	18,304	CMT30	12-AACF-f	syro-palestinian		9.00	1,004	1Asuh	7	5	5	5	2	Arabic: Lebanese*	Pnb	b
8175	Takum Jukun	0.00001	10	11	18	NAB56b	98-HBDA-d	diyi		67.00	7	0....	10	7	7	5	2	Jukun Takum	PN.	.
8176	Tal	0.01575	15,585	17,562	28,829	NAB60b	19-FBEA	tal-kwabzak cluster		30.00	5,269	0....	9	5	6	2	0		...	.
8177	Tala	0.00094	930	1,048	1,721	NAB60b	19-EBDA-a	tala		20.00	210	0....	9	5	5	1	1		...	.
8178	Tambas	0.00473	4,680	5,274	8,658	NAB60b	19-GAAA	fyeer-tambas cluster		20.00	1,055	0....	9	5	5	2	0		...	.
8179	Tambo	0.01600	15,832	17,841	29,287	NAB56b	99-AAFA-b	bwazza		14.00	2,498	0....	8	5	7	3	0		...	b
8180	Tangale	0.15748	155,829	175,600	288,253	NAB60b	19-ABAA-a	tangle		60.00	105,360	4....	10	6	7	4	3	Tangle*	PN.	.
8181	Tapshin (Tapshinawa)	0.00010	99	112	183	NAB56b	98-HBHA-a	tapshin		10.00	11	0....	8	5	4	1	0		...	.
8182	Tarok (Yergam, Appa)	0.14249	140,997	158,885	260,815	NAB56b	98-HBAB	tarok cluster		67.10	106,612	4....	10	7	7	4	2	Tarok	PN.	.
8183	Teda	0.00200	1,979	2,230	3,661	NAB61	02-BAAA-b	daza-ga		0.00	0	0....	0	1	0	0	0		...	b
8184	Teme	0.00300	2,969	3,345	5,491	NAB66z	92-BAAB-a	teme		40.00	1,338	0....	9	5	5	2	0		...	.
8185	Tera	0.08837	87,444	98,538	161,753	NAB60b	18-HAAA	tera cluster		50.00	49,269	0....	10	6	7	4	2	Tera	P..	.
8186	Teteka (Mumbake, Mubako)	0.00910	9,005	10,147	16,657	NAB66c	92-BDAB-h	nyong		20.00	2,029	0....	9	5	6	2	0		...	.
8187	Tigon Mbembe (Akonto)	0.02272	22,482	25,334	41,587	NAB56b	98-HBEA-a	nzare		10.00	2,533	0....	8	5	5	1	0		...	.
8188	Tita	0.00300	2,969	3,345	5,491	NAB56b	98-IDKA-a	tita		40.00	1,338	0....	9	5	5	2	0		...	.
8189	Tiv	2.57213	2,545,171	2,868,082	4,708,057	NAB56b	99-ABAA-a	dzwa-tiv	3	94.60	2,713,205	4s...	10	10	11	5	3	Tiv	PNB	.
8190	Toroobe Fulani	4.90000	4,848,641	5,463,799	8,969,018	NAB56c	19-HABA-a	hausa		0.30	16,391	4Asu.	5	4	8	4	3	Hausa	PNB	b
8191	Tsagu (Sago)	0.00259	2,563	2,888	4,741	NAB60b	19-DBCB-a	ciwoogai		10.00	289	0....	8	5	5	5	0		...	.
8192	Tuareg (Aulliminden)	0.01800	17,811	20,071	32,947	CMT32h	10-AAAB-bb	west ta-wllemmet		0.00	0	1....	0	3	2	1	1		pn.	.
8193	Tula (Dadia, Kutele)	0.02992	29,606	33,363	54,766	NAB66z	92-AAAB-a	tula		10.00	3,336	0....	8	5	6	4	2	Kutele*	P..	.
8194	Turkwam	0.00945	9,351	10,537	17,297	NAB56b	98-HBAA-a	turkwam		30.00	3,161	0....	9	5	6	2	0		...	.
8195	Tyenga	0.00358	3,542	3,992	6,553	NAB63z	00-DGDB-a	shanga		0.02	1	0....	3	3	4	0	0		...	b
8196	Ubaghara (Biakpan)	0.03151	31,180	35,136	57,676	NAB56b	98-IDCA-c	biakpan		60.00	21,081	0....	10	7	7	4	2	Ubaghara	P..	.
8197	Ubang	0.00300	2,969	3,345	5,491	NAB56b	98-IEAF-a	u-bang		60.00	2,007	0....	10	7	6	2	0		...	.
8198	Ucinda	0.02760	27,311	30,776	50,519	NAB56b	98-GAEB-a	te-gina		10.00	3,078	0....	8	5	6	5	3		...	b
8199	Uda	0.01104	10,924	12,310	20,208	NAB56b	98-ICBA	ibibio-efik cluster		90.00	11,079	3as..	10	8	8	0	0		PNB	b
8200	Uhami	0.01193	11,805	13,303	21,837	NAB59c	98-EABB-a	uhami		30.00	3,991	0....	9	5	6	2	0		...	.
8201	Ukaan (Ikan)	0.02835	28,053	31,612	51,892	NAB59c	98-CBAA	ukaan cluster		30.00	9,484	0....	9	5	6	3	0		...	b
8202	Ukpe-Bayobiri	0.01890	18,702	21,075	34,595	NAB56b	98-IEAC-b	u-kpe		70.00	14,752	0....	10	7	7	3	1		...	.
8203	Ukue-Ehuen	0.02488	24,619	27,743	45,541	NAB59c	98-EABA	ukue-ehuen cluster		30.00	8,323	0....	9	5	5	2	0		...	.
8204	Ukwuani-Aboh (Kwale)	0.15231	150,714	169,835	278,790	NAB59h	98-FAAC	west igbo cluster		90.00	152,851	0....	10	6	7	4	3		...	.
8205	Ulukwumi	0.00979	9,687	10,916	17,920	NAB59n	98-AAAC-ae	u-lukwumi		50.00	5,458	1.s..	10	6	6	2	0		pnb	.
8206	Umon	0.01790	17,712	19,960	32,764	NAB56b	98-IDCB-a	u-mon		70.00	13,972	0....	10	7	6	4	2	Umon	P..	.
8207	Uneme	0.01743	17,247	19,436	31,904	NAB59c	98-EACB-a	uneme		30.00	5,831	0....	9	5	6	2	0		...	.
8208	Ura (Fungwa)	0.00086	851	959	1,574	NAB56b	98-GAED-a	fungwa		30.00	288	0....	9	5	5	1	0		...	.
8209	Urhobo	0.53543	529,818	597,037	980,057	NAB59z	98-EADB-a	urhobo		95.00	567,185	0....	10	8	11	5	3	Urhobo	PNB	.
8210	Usakade	0.01040	10,291	11,597	19,036	NAB56b	98-ICBA-c	efik		90.00	10,437	1as..	10	8	8	0	0	Efik	PNB	b
8211	Utange (Otank)	0.00472	4,671	5,263	8,640	NAB56b	99-ABKA-a	o-tank		50.00	2,632	0....	10	6	6	2	0		...	.
8212	Utugwang (East Mbube)	0.01890	18,702	21,075	34,595	NAB56b	98-IEAB-b	o-tugwang		70.00	14,752	0....	10	7	7	3	2		...	.
8213	Uvbie (Evrie)	0.01739	17,208	19,391	31,831	NAB59c	98-EADC-a	uvbie		60.00	11,635	0....	10	6	6	2	0		...	.
8214	Uzekwe	0.00787	7,788	8,776	14,405	NAB56b	98-IDDB-a	u-zekwe		70.00	6,143	0....	10	7	7	2	0		...	.
8215	Vemgo (Mabas)	0.00950	9,400	10,593	17,389	NAB60b	18-CBBA-e	mabas		5.00	530	0....	7	5	6	1	0		pn.	b
8216	Vere (Verre)	0.01649	16,317	18,387	30,183	NAB66c	92-BCBB-k	mom-jango		18.00	3,310	0....	8	5	6	5	3		...	b
8217	Vimtim (Fali of Mubi)	0.00447	4,423	4,984	8,182	NAB60b	18-IBAA-n	vin		3.00	150	0....	6	4	4	1	0		p..	.
8218	Vute (Wute, Fute, Mbute)	0.00157	1,554	1,751	2,874	NAB56b	98-JCBA	bute cluster		50.00	875	0....	10	6	6	4	1	Vute	P..	b
8219	Waja (Wagga, Wuya)	0.04724	46,745	52,675	86,469	NAB66z	92-AAAA-a	waja		10.00	5,268	0....	8	5	6	4	2	Wuya*	P..	.
8220	Waka	0.00489	4,839	5,453	8,951	NAB66z	92-AAAA-a	waka		20.00	1,091	0....	9	5	5	1	0		...	.
8221	Warji (Warjawa)	0.09296	91,986	103,656	170,155	NAB60b	19-DBAA-a	serza-kway		2.00	2,073	0....	6	4	6	4	1		...	.
8222	Wedu	0.00170	1,682	1,896	3,112	NAB60b	18-GAAB	kapsiki cluster		30.00	569	0.s..	9	7	7	0	0		PN.	.
8223	West Gbari (Gwari Yamma)	0.26747	264,667	298,245	489,580	NAB59z	98-BAAB-a	gbari		35.00	104,386	1....	9	5	7	5	3	Gbari	Pn.	.
8224	West Idoma	0.25000	247,380	278,765	457,603	NAB59z	98-BCBA-c	west i-doma		79.00	220,225	0....	10	6	7	2	1		pnb	.
8225	West Marghi (Putai)	0.00100	990	1,115	1,830	NAB60b	18-GBAC	central margi cluster		50.00	558	1....	10	6	6	1	0	Margi*	PN.	p
8226	Western Fulani (Bororo)	1.50000	1,484,278	1,672,591	2,745,618	NAB56c	90-BAAA-o	fula-bororo		0.05	836	1cs..	4	3	5	5	3	Fulfide, Kano-katsina	pnb	b
8227	Western Mbube (Mbe)	0.02252	22,284	25,111	41,221	NAB56b	99-ADAA-a	m-be		60.00	15,067	0....	10	7	7	4	2	Mbe	P..	.
8228	Whana (Hwana, Fiterya)	0.03150	31,170	35,124	57,658	NAB60b	18-HBBA-a	tuftera		10.00	3,512	0....	8	5	6	2	0		...	b
8229	Widala	0.00195	1,930	2,174	3,569	NAB66z	92-AAAA	waja cluster		0.07	2	0....	4	4	3	0	0		P..	.
8230	Wom (Pereba, Zagau)	0.00489	4,839	5,453	8,951	NAB66c	92-BDAB-j	wom		40.00	2,181	0....	9	6	6	2	0		...	b
8231	Wula (Lying)	0.01100	10,885	12,266	20,135	NAB60b	18-GAAB-c	wula		30.00	3,680	0.s..	9	5	7	5	0		pn.	.
8232	Yache	0.01000	9,895	11,151	18,304	NAB56b	98-BCDA-b	i-yace		60.00	6,690	0....	10	7	7	4	1	Ekpari	P..	.
8233	Yako (Ugep, Loko)	0.11427	113,072	127,418	209,161	NAB56b	35-FAAC-b	loko		93.00	118,499	0....	10	8	7	5	1	Loko: Papua New Guinea	P..	.
8234	Yala	0.07874	77,915	87,800	144,127	NAB59z	98-BCBD-a	i-yala		47.00	41,266	0....	9	7	7	5	3	Iyala*	PN.	.
8235	Yamba (Kaka)	0.01000	9,895	11,151	18,304	NAB57a	99-AGEB-c	yamba		70.00	7,805	0....	10	6	8	5	0	Yamba	PN.	n
8236	Yandang (Nyandang, Yundum	0.07116	70,414	79,348	130,252	NAB66z	92-BABB-a	proper yendang		10.00	7,935	0....	8	5	6	2	0		...	.
8237	Yashi	0.00041	406	457	750	NAB56b	98-HADA-a	yashi		40.00	183	0....	9	5	5	1	0		...	.
8238	Yekhee (Etsako, Afenmai)	0.24525	242,679	273,469	448,908	NAB59c	98-EACC	yekhee cluster		79.00	216,040	0....	10	6	7	5	3	Etsako*	P..	.
8239	Yerwa Kanuri (Beriberi)	3.08880	3,056,425	3,444,200	5,653,776	NAB61	02-AAAA-b	yerwa	6	0.01	344	4....	3	4	5	5	3	Kanuri*	PN.	.
8240	Yeskwa	0.02047	20,255	22,825	37,469	NAB56b	98-HABC-a	yeskwa		5.00	1,141	0....	7	5	5	4	1		...	.
8241	Yigha (Ayiga, Asiga)	0.00952	9,420	10,615	17,426	NAB56b	98-IDGB-a	le-yigha		60.00	6,369	0....	10	7	7	2	2		...	.
8242	Yiwom (Gurka, Gerkanchi)	0.01260	12,468	14,050	23,063	NAB60b	19-FAAA-a	yiwom		30.00	4,215	0....	9	5	5	2	0		...	.
8243	Yoruba (Oyo, Ekiti, Ijebu	17.53425	17,350,467	19,551,757	32,094,898	NAB59n	98-AAAA-a	standard yoruba	25	58.38	11,414,316	3asu.	10	10	11	8	3	Yoruba	PNB	b
8244	Yungur (Binna)	0.09301	92,035	103,712	170,247	NAB66c	92-ADAB	yungur cluster		10.00	10,371	0....	8	5	6	2	0		...	.
8245	Zangwal	0.00009	89	100	165	NAB60b	19-EBCA	zangwal cluster		30.00	30	0....	9	5	6	2	1		...	.

Continued opposite

Table 8-2 continued

EVANGELIZATION								EVANGELISM			ADDITIONAL DESCRIPTIVE DATA
Ref 1	*D* 28	*aC* 29	*CG%* 30	*r* 31	*E* 32	*U* 33	*W* 34	*e* 35	*R* 36	*T* 37	*Locations, civil divisions, literacy, religions, church history, denominations, dioceses, church growth, missions, agencies, ministries, movements* 38
8122	0	6	6.02	0	99.70	0.30	C	255.50	203	8	Akwa Ibom State, Okobo LGA. Animists 30%.
8123	2	6	5.96	0	97.00	3.00	C	212.43	208	8	Rivers State, Yenagoa LGA. Related to Ijaw. Animists 40%. D=RCC,CAC.
8124	0	6	7.53	0	57.00	43.00	B	56.17	429	6	Bendel State, Akoko-Edo LGA. Very many dialects. Many animists, 73%.
8125	0	6	6.20	0	55.00	45.00	B	56.21	378	6	Northwestern Edo. Bendel State, Akoko-Edo LGA. Animists 60%, Muslims 12%.
8126	0	6	5.14	0	53.00	47.00	B	52.23	338	6	Southwestern Edo. Bendel State, Okpe LGA. Animists 60%, Muslims 13%.
8127	1	6	7.39	0	99.80	0.20	C	359.16	196	9	Rivers State, in 4 LGAs. Related to Ijaw. Animists 20%. D=CPN.
8128	3	6	9.35	0	99.80	0.20	C	350.40	245	9	Cross River State, Ikom LGA. Animists 20%. D=AICs,RCC,&c.
8129	0	6	4.44	0	99.70	0.30	C	255.50	160	8	Akwa Ibom State, Oron LGA. Animists 30%.
8130	0	6	9.08	0	99.75	0.25	C	290.17	271	8	Benue State (Okpokwu LGA), Anambra State (Ishielu LGA). Still numerous animists, 25%.
8131	0	0	5.87	0	82.00	18.00	C	179.58	243	7	Rivers State, Brass LGA. One town. Within the Ijo language cluster. Animists 40%.
8132	0	6	6.53	0	57.00	43.00	B	62.41	381	6	Bendel State, Akoko-Edo LGA. Animists 70%.
8133	1	6	4.40	0	36.00	64.00	A	6.57	441	4	Bauchi State, Ningi and Darazo LGAs. Second language Hausa (literates 1%). Animists 76%, Muslims 19%. D=ECWA. M=SIM,EMS.
8134	0	6	4.07	0	31.03	68.97	A	0.03	482	2	Borno State, Biu LGA. Muslims 98% (1920, entry of Islam). Y=c1935. D=EYN.
8135	0	6	4.77	0	56.00	44.00	B	61.32	301	6	Plateau State, Pankshin LGA. Animists 60%, Muslims 10%.
8136	3	6	5.75	1	99.60	0.40	C	225.57	202	8	Mainly in Cameroon, CAR, Chad. Urban areas of Nigeria and Cameroon. Muslims 25%, animists 15%. D=RCC,EFLC,EELC. M=OFMCap,UBS,LBM,NMS,ELCA.
8137	0	6	4.29	1	60.00	40.00	B	43.80	252	6	Taraba State, Sardauna LGA. Animists 78%, Muslims 2%. D=NBC,RCC,RPM,DLBC.
8138	0	6	5.56	0	67.00	33.00	B	97.82	286	6	Gongola State, Karim Lamido LGA. Animists 40%, Muslims 20%.
8139	0	6	6.39	0	59.00	41.00	B	64.60	363	6	Adamawa State, Numan LGA. Animists 60%, Muslims 10%. Y=1942. D=LCCN,AC,CAC,DLBC,MF,Pentecostals.
8140	0	6	7.76	0	82.00	18.00	B	149.65	306	7	Bauchi State, Alkaleri LGA. Many animists 40%. D=UMCN,ECWA,COCIN.
8141	0	6	3.35	0	31.00	69.00	A	5.65	419	4	Kaduna State, Saminaka LGA. Close to Chawai. Animists 90%, some Muslims. M=GRI.
8142	0	6	5.23	0	57.00	43.00	B	62.41	318	6	Taraba State, Karim Lamido LGA. Animists 60%, Muslims 10%. D=UMCN,ECWA,NBC,COCIN.
8143	1	6	5.29	0	45.00	55.00	A	24.63	407	5	Bauchi State, Bauchi LGA. Animists 60%, Muslims 25%. D=ECWA. M=EMS.
8144	0	6	6.83	0	57.00	43.00	B	62.41	395	6	Niger State, Rafi LGA. Animists 60%, Muslims 10%.
8145	2	6	3.32	0	30.00	70.00	A	1.09	430	4	Kebbi State, Zuru LGA. Animists 84%, Muslims 15%. D=UMCA,RCC. M=UMS,MCA.
8146	0	6	5.18	0	67.00	33.00	B	97.82	269	6	Plateau State, Shendam LGA. Shendam District. Animists 56%, some Muslims.
8147	0	0	6.43	0	50.00	50.00	B	54.75	429	6	Plateau State, Shendam LGA. Related to Tal and Montol. Animists 60%, Muslims 10%.
8148	1	6	6.47	0	42.00	58.00	A	15.33	513	5	`Island Dwellers' (in Niger river), Sokoto State. Rapidly becoming Hausaized. High divorce rate. Muslims 70%(Maliki Sunnis), animists 20%. D=UMCA. M=UMS.
8149	0	6	5.56	0	39.00	61.00	A	14.23	488	5	Gongola State (Wukari LGA), Benue State. Animists 90%.
8150	0	6	7.12	0	47.00	53.00	A	34.31	522	5	Gongola State, in 3 LGAs: Song, Gombi, Suyuk. Animists 60%, Muslims 20%.
8151	0	6	3.54	0	27.00	73.00	A	4.92	500	4	Kaduna State, Saminaka LGA. Animists 50%, Muslims 45%.
8152	0	6	3.75	0	27.00	73.00	A	4.92	522	4	Kaduna State, in Saminaka LGA. Animists 55%, Muslims 40%.
8153	0	6	4.58	0	21.00	79.00	A	0.76	779	3	Bauchi State, Toro LGA. Animists 60%, Muslims 39%.
8154	1	6	6.34	4	99.60	0.40	C	243.09	192	8	Borno State. Mainly in Chad, CAR, Cameroon. Animists 38%, Muslims 2%. D=RCC. M=SJ.
8155	0	6	6.08	0	56.00	44.00	B	61.32	365	6	Bendel State, Akoko-Edo LGA. Animists 70%.
8156	1	6	8.00	0	58.00	42.00	B	52.92	444	6	Bauchi State, Tafewa Balewa LGA. Animists 65%, Muslims 10%. D=ECWA. M=SIM,EMS.
8157	0	5	3.15	1	58.00	42.00	B	42.34	233	6	Lagos State, Badagry LGA. Also in Benin. Animists 65%, Muslims 15%.
8158	0	7	3.17	0	67.00	33.00	B	97.82	186	6	Plateau State, Mangu LGA, Sha town. Animists 50%, Muslims 10%.
8159	1	6	5.57	0	44.00	56.00	A	16.06	433	5	Plateau State, Mangu LGA. Lingua franca: Hausa. Animists 60%, Muslims 30%. D=COCIN. M=SUM.
8160	0	6	5.18	0	48.00	52.00	A	35.04	375	5	Bauchi State, Dass LGA. Animists 55%, Muslims 25%.
8161	0	0	3.99	0	28.00	72.00	A	10.22	526	5	Niger State, Rafi and Mariga LGAs. Kaduna State, Birnin Gwari LGA. Animists 70%, Muslims 10%.
8162	0	6	0.00	0	18.02	81.98	A	0.01	289	2	Sokoto State. On islands in Niger river, and city of Shanga. Animists 60%(Bori), Muslims 40%(Maliki Sunnis).
8163	0	8	3.04	0	28.00	72.00	A	5.11	434	4	Kaduna State, Saminaka LGA. Animists 60%, Muslims 35%.
8164	2	6	7.26	0	99.00	1.00	C	216.81	239	8	Kaduna State, Kachia and Jemaa LGAs. Dialect of Katab. Animists 35%, Muslims 5%. D=RCC,ECWA.
8165	0	5	2.91	7	30.10	69.90	A	0.11	329	3	Chad Arabs, mainly in Chad, Niger, and Cameroon. Borno State. Muslims 100%. M=COCIN,WEC,CMML. R=ELWA.
8166	0	6	4.24	0	44.00	56.00	A	32.12	351	5	Bauchi State, Darazo and Ningi LGAs. Animists 60%, Muslims 20%.
8167	0	6	5.38	4	45.10	54.90	A	0.16	424	3	Sokoto State, also in Niger. Fulani rulers ruling Hausas; one of the major Fulani geopolitical units in Africa. Muslims 100%(Maliki Sunnis). M=JCMWA,SCCM,SIM.
8168	0	5	4.59	0	24.40	75.60	A	0.35	729	3	Also in Mali, Niger. Along Niger river. Muslims 100%(Maliki Sunnis).
8169	5	6	8.99	2	99.70	0.30	C	298.93	243	8	Benue State. Animists 26%. D=RCC,Primitive Methodist Ch,MCN,ICFG,ECWA. M=SIM,MMS,EMS,CETI.
8170	3	6	5.51	0	99.93	0.07	C	488.80	131	10	Rivers State, Brass LGA. Animists 5%. D=RCC,CAC,DLBC. M=SMA,FMB.
8171	0	6	5.21	0	39.00	61.00	A	14.23	464	5	Adamawa State, Michika LGA; a few in Cameroon. In Mandara mountains. Animists 80%, Muslims 5%. D=EYN/CBM,RCC. Housa used in their 16 churches.
8172	1	6	10.63	0	99.77	0.23	C	340.07	272	9	Plateau State, Mangu LGA. Lingua franca. Animists 13%, Muslims 10%. D=COCIN. M=SUM,NBTT.
8173	0	5	3.62	0	27.00	73.00	A	4.92	508	4	Kaduna State, Saminaka LGA. Animists 65%, Muslims 30%.
8174	2	10	4.72	8	65.00	35.00	B	21.35	228	5	Traders from Syria. Muslims 90%(Sunnis, Alawi Shias). D=SOC,RCC.
8175	1	6	1.96	0	99.67	0.33	C	256.77	87	8	Lingua franca with few mother-tongue speakers. Gongola State. D=COCIN. M=SUM,UBS.
8176	0	6	6.47	0	57.00	43.00	B	62.41	378	6	Plateau State, Shendam LGA. Animists 60%, Muslims 10%.
8177	1	6	3.09	0	46.00	54.00	A	33.58	267	5	Bauchi State, Bauchi LGA. Animists 80%. D=ECWA.
8178	0	6	4.77	0	46.00	54.00	A	33.58	367	5	Plateau State, Mangu LGA. Animists 60%, Muslims 20%.
8179	0	6	5.68	0	45.00	55.00	A	22.99	430	5	Adamawa State, Song LGA. Animists 84%, few Muslims. Y=1955. D=LCCN,GFF.
8180	1	6	9.71	0	99.60	0.40	C	227.76	292	8	Bauchi State, Akko and Billiri-Kaltungo LGAs. Animists 35%, Muslims 5%. D=ECWA. M=EMS,SIM(East Asia),CETI,FMB.
8181	0	8	2.43	0	34.00	66.00	A	12.41	308	5	Bauchi and Plateau States, Pankshin LGA. Mostly animists 90%.
8182	1	6	9.72	0	99.67	0.33	C	269.65	276	8	Plateau State, in 3 LGAS: Langtang, Kanam, Wase. Animists 30%. D=COCIN. M=SUM,NBTT.
8183	0	0	0.00	0	2.00	98.00	A	0.00	0	1.01	Borno State. Also in Niger, Chad, and Libya. Muslims 100%.
8184	0	6	5.02	0	66.00	34.00	B	96.36	268	6	Adamawa State, Mayo Belwa LGA. Animists 55%(with organized opposition to missions), Muslims 5%. Y=1954. D=LCCN.
8185	1	6	8.87	0	86.00	14.00	B	156.95	327	7	Bauchi State (Gombe LGA), Borno State (Biu LGA). Animists 45%, Muslims 5%. D=ECWA,RCC. M=SIM,EMS.
8186	0	6	5.46	0	47.00	53.00	A	34.31	425	5	Adamawa State, Mayo Belwa LGA. A few in Cameroon. Animists 40%, Muslims 40%. Y=1954. D=LCCN(8 churches).
8187	0	6	5.69	0	34.00	66.00	A	12.41	571	5	Taraba State, Sardauna LGA. Mainly in Cameroon forests. Animists 90%. (reviving, due to youths). Y=1944. D=CRCN.
8188	0	6	5.02	0	66.00	34.00	B	96.36	266	6	Gongola State, Jalingo LGA. Animists 60%.
8189	7	5	13.33	2	99.95	0.05	C	537.27	259	10	Nominal Christians 43%, animists 4%. Y=1911. D=NKST(Tiv Church; many charismatics),RCC(D-Makurdi),CPN,SDA,ECWA,DLBC,other AICs. M=SUM,NGK.
8190	5	6	7.68	5	60.30	39.70	B	0.66	422	3	Aristocrats, schooled in Islamic law and politics. Muslims 99%(Maliki Sunnis, also Qadiriyya). D=RCC,ECWA,CAC,DLBC,et alia. M=EMS,SIM,FMB,JCMWA,SCCM.
8191	0	9	3.42	0	40.00	60.00	A	14.60	329	5	Bauchi State, near the Diri. Animists 70%, Muslims 20%.
8192	2	5	0.00	0	18.00	82.00	A	0.00	0	1.08	Primarily in Niger and Mali. Nomadic pastoralists. Muslims 100%(Sunnis). D=RCC,UEEB. M=EBM.
8193	1	6	5.98	0	42.00	58.00	A	15.33	483	5	Bauchi State, Billiri-Kaltungo LGA. Animists 80%, Muslims 10%. D=ECWA. M=SIM,LBI.
8194	0	6	5.92	0	57.00	43.00	B	62.41	351	6	Plateau State, Akwanga LGA. Animists 70%.
8195	0	0	0.00	0	9.02	90.98	A	0.00	577	1.03	Kebbi State. Also in Benin. Most speak Hausa or Dendi. Animists 60%, Muslims 40%.
8196	1	6	6.21	0	96.00	4.00	C	210.24	217	8	Cross River State, Akamkpa LGA. Animists 40%. D=Presbyterian Ch of Nigeria. M=UBS,BCAS.
8197	0	7	5.44	0	89.00	11.00	C	194.91	210	7	Cross River State, Obudu LGA. Animists 40%.
8198	3	6	5.90	0	48.00	52.00	A	17.52	416	5	States: Niger, Sokoto, Kaduna. Literates 10%. Second language Hausa. Animists 70%, Muslims 20%. D=ECWA,NBC,UMCA.
8199	0	0	7.26	4	99.90	0.10	C	440.19	177	10	Akwa Ibom State, Mbo LGA. Animists 5%. D=AICs.
8200	0	6	6.17	0	57.00	43.00	B	62.41	363	6	Ondo State, Owo and Akoko South LGAs. Animists 60%, Muslims 10%.
8201	0	6	7.10	0	61.00	39.00	B	66.79	381	6	Ondo State (Akoko North LGA). Lingua franca: Yoruba. Animists 65%, Muslims 5%.
8202	1	6	7.57	0	99.70	0.30	C	263.16	238	8	Cross River State, Obudu and Ikom LGAs. Animists 30%. D=AICs.
8203	0	7	6.96	0	57.00	43.00	B	62.41	401	6	Ondo State, Akoko South LGA. Animists 65%, Muslims 5%.
8204	3	6	10.11	0	99.90	0.10	C	420.48	246	10	Rivers and Bendel States. Animists 10%. D=RCC,DLBC,many other AICs. M=CGCM,RTEM,FMB.
8205	0	6	6.51	1	87.00	13.00	B	158.77	249	7	Bendel State, Aniocha and Oshimili LGA. Animists 30%, Muslims 20%.
8206	1	7	5.62	0	99.70	0.30	C	270.83	181	8	Cross River State, Akamkpa LGA, 25 villages. Animists 30%. D=AICs. M=KHM,CSM.
8207	0	6	6.58	0	57.00	43.00	B	62.41	383	6	Bendel State, 3 LGAs (Etsako, Agbazko, Akoko-Edo). Animists 60%, Muslims 10%.
8208	0	7	3.42	0	55.00	45.00	B	60.22	240	6	Niger State, Rafi LGA. Animists 50%, Muslims 20%.
8209	7	6	5.53	2	99.95	0.05	C	520.12	127	10	Bendel State, Erhiope and Ughelli LGAs. Animists 5%. D=RCC(D-Ondo),CAC,SA,CPN(3 Dioceses),SDA,DLBC,many AICs. M=UBS,CMS,ABFMS,SMA,CGCM.
8210	0	0	7.20	4	99.90	0.10	C	433.62	149	10	Cross River State, Odukpani LGA. Mainly in Cameroon. Animists 5%. D=AICs.
8211	0	6	5.73	0	78.00	22.00	B	142.35	250	7	Cross River State (Obudu LGA), Benue State (Kwande LGA). Mountainous. Close to Tiv. Animists 50%.
8212	2	6	7.57	0	99.70	0.30	C	268.27	234	8	Cross River State, Obudu and Ogoja LGAs. Animists 30%. D=AICs,RCC.
8213	0	6	6.95	0	89.00	11.00	C	194.91	257	7	Bendel State, Ethiope LGA. Related to Urhobo. Animists 40%.
8214	0	6	6.63	0	99.00	1.00	C	252.94	222	8	Cross River State, Ogoja LGA. Animists 30%.
8215	0	6	4.05	0	34.00	66.00	A	6.20	438	4	Adamawa State, Michika LGA. Close to Hedi, Lamang. Animists 75%, Muslims 20%. D=EYN/CBM(4 churches),RCC.
8216	2	6	5.97	0	55.00	45.00	B	36.13	389	5	Adamawa State, Fufore and Yola LGAs. Also in Cameroon. Animists 77%, Muslims 5%. Very open to Christianity. Y=1949. D=LCCN(21 stations),RCC.
8217	0	6	2.75	0	24.00	76.00	A	2.62	473	4	Gongola State, Mubi LGA. Muslims 50%, animists 47%.
8218	0	6	4.57	0	81.00	19.00	B	147.82	202	7	Gongola State. Mainly in Cameroon. Muslims 30%, animists 20%. M=SIL.
8219	1	6	6.47	0	42.00	58.00	A	15.33	515	5	Adamawa and Bauchi States. Animists 70%, Muslims 20%. D=EYN/CMB,COCIN,ECWA. M=SIM,FMB.
8220	0	6	4.80	0	45.00	55.00	A	32.85	379	5	Gongola State, Karim Lamido LGA. Animists 70%, Muslims 10%.
8221	1	6	5.48	0	30.00	70.00	A	2.19	627	4	Bauchi State, Darazo and Ningi LGAs. Literates 10%. Animists 88%, Muslims 10%. D=ECWA. M=SIM.
8222	0	0	4.12	0	53.00	47.00	B	58.03	285	6	Plateau State, Pankshin, Kanam, and Langtang LGAs. Related to Tal. Animists 60%, Muslims 10%.
8223	3	6	9.69	0	77.00	23.00	B	98.36	395	6	Western Gbagyi, in Niger and Plateau States. Animists 40%, Muslims 25%. D=ECWA,RCC,CPN. M=SIM,CMS,SMA,EMS,GOWE,NEM,MCA.
8224	3	6	10.52	2	99.79	0.21	C	348.90	270	9	Benue State. Animists 20%. D=RCC,MCN,Primitive Methodist Ch. M=UBS.
8225	0	7	4.10	0	83.00	17.00	B	151.47	181	7	Borno State, Damboa LGA. Language dying out, replaced by Kanuri. Animists 30%, Muslims 20%.
8226	0	5	4.53	4	38.05	61.95	A	0.06	441	2	Kano-Katsina-Bororro Fulfulde. Borno State. Fully nomadic, light-skinned, with large cattle herds. Muslims 100%(Maliki Sunnis). M=EMS,ARCM,CETI,GOWE,SIM.
8227	1	6	7.59	0	96.00	4.00	C	210.24	256	8	Cross River State, Ogoja LGA. Animists 40%. D=ELCN. M=UBS,LCMS.
8228	0	6	6.04	0	39.00	61.00	A	14.23	522	5	Adamawa State, Gombi LGA. Animists 40%, Muslims 50%. D=EYN/CBM,NBC,LCCN.
8229	0	0	0.70	0	10.07	89.93	A	0.02	580	2	Taraba State, Karim Lamido LGA. Muslims 50%, Animists 50%.
8230	0	6	5.53	0	70.00	30.00	B	102.20	288	7	Adamawa State, Fufore LGA. Most in Cameroon. Animists 50%, Muslims 10%. D=LCCN,RCC. Much syncretism.
8231	0	5	6.09	0	64.00	36.00	B	70.08	320	6	Adamawa State, on Mandara mountains south of Madagali. Farmers. Animists 66%, Muslims 4%. D=RCC,SDA,EYN.
8232	1	6	6.72	0	94.00	6.00	C	205.86	236	8	Cross River State, Ogoja LGA. Animists 40%. D=ELCN. M=LCMS.
8233	4	6	9.83	0	99.93	0.07	C	444.68	235	10	Cross River State, Obubra LGA. Animists 5%. D=AoG,Apostolic Ch of Nigeria, West African Episcopal Ch,other AICs. M=SIL.
8234	4	6	8.68	0	89.00	11.00	B	152.68	310	7	Cross River State, 3 LGAs (Ogoja, Obubra, Ikom). Animists 53%. D=RCC(D-Ogoja),AoG,ELCN,Apostolic Ch of Nigeria. M=SPS,LCMS,UBS.
8235	0	6	6.89	0	99.70	0.30	C	273.38	208	8	Taraba State, also in Cameroon. Animists 25%, Muslims 5%. Y=1938. D=CBC/Mambila Baptists),NBC,RPM,DLBC.
8236	0	6	6.90	0	36.00	64.00	A	13.14	634	5	Adamawa State, in 3 LGAs: Mayo Belwa, Numan, Karim Lamido. Animists 80%, Muslims 10%. Y=1948. D=LCCN,UMCN,ECWA,CAC,DLBC,RCC,AC.
8237	0	8	2.95	0	66.00	34.00	B	96.36	180	6	Plateau State, Akwanga LGA. Animists 55%, Muslims 5%.
8238	4	6	10.50	0	99.79	0.21	C	343.13	274	9	Bendel State, in 3 LGAs. Also called Kukuruku (derogatory). Animists 50%. D=RCC(D-Benin City),CPN,ACN,AICs. M=SMA,Christ for the Whole World,CREM.
8239	5	5	3.60	4	39.01	60.99	A	0.01	351	2	In 5 nations. Muslims 100%(Maliki Sunnis). Y=1936.D=NBC,National Ev Association,ECWA,COCIN,CPN,DLBC,CRCN, and 70 others. M=SUM,SIM,EMS,NEM.
8240	1	6	4.85	0	33.00	67.00	A	6.02	518	4	Kaduna State, Jemaa LGA; Plateau State, Keffi LGA. Animists 60%, Muslims 35%. D=ECWA. M=SIM.
8241	2	6	6.67	0	93.00	7.00	C	203.67	237	8	Cross River State, Obubra LGA. Animists 40%. D=AICs,RCC.
8242	0	6	6.23	0	56.00	44.00	B	61.32	373	6	Plateau State, Shendam and Langtang LGAs. Animists 40%, Muslim 30%.
8243	13	6	6.52	5	99.58	0.42	B	273.56	169	8	Muslims 37%(Malikis,Sufis,Ahmadis), animists 4%. Y=1841. Nominal Christians 13%. D=CPN,RCC,CAC,ESOCS,NCF,NBC,MCN,PCN,SDA,SA,C&S,DLBC,AICs.
8244	0	6	7.19	0	37.00	63.00	A	13.50	668	5	Adamawa State, Guyuk and Song LGAs. Animists 60%, Muslims 30% (several mosques opened recently). Y=1932. D=LCCN,NBC,DLBC.
8245	1	6	3.46	0	58.00	42.00	B	63.51	229	6	Bauchi State, Bauchi LGA. Animists 70%. D=ECWA.

Continued overleaf

Table 8-2 continued

Ref 1	PEOPLE: Ethnic name 2	POPULATION: P% 3	In 1995 4	In 2000 5	In 2025 6	IDENTITY CODE: Race 7	Language 8	LANGUAGE: Autoglossonym 9	S 10	CHURCH: AC 11	Members 12	MINISTRY: Jayuh 13-17	d 18	wa 19	xc 20	mc 21	mi 22	SCRIPTURE: Biblioglossonym 23	Pub 24-26	ss 27
8246	Zari (Zariwa, Zakshi)	0.00800	7,916	8,920	14,643	NAB60b	19-EDBB-a	zari		10.00	892	0....	8	5	5	2	0		...	.
8247	Zeem	0.00300	2,969	3,345	5,491	NAB60b	19-EDAF	zeem-tulai cluster		5.00	167	0....	7	5	5	1	0		...	.
8248	Zerma (Dyerma)	0.07874	77,915	87,800	144,127	NAB65c	01-AAAB-b	zarma		0.01	9	2..u.	3	4	4	4	2	Zarma	PNB	.
8249	other minor peoples	0.30000	296,856	334,518	549,124	...				60.00	200,711		10	5	2	5	0			
	Niue Island	**100.00000**	**2,061**	**1,876**	**1,442**					**92.59**	**1,737**									
8250	Anglo-New Zealander	2.60000	54	49	37	CEW19e	52-ABAC-y	general new-zealand		80.00	39	1Bsuh	10	9	14	5	3		pnb	b
8251	Han Chinese	0.60000	12	11	9	MSY42a	79-AAAB-ba	kuo-yü		40.00	5	2Bsuh	9	6	8	5	2	Chinese: Kuoyu*	PNB	b
8252	Niuean	93.30000	1,923	1,750	1,345	MPY55z	39-CAPA-a	niue		93.50	1,637	0.s..	10	10	13	5	2	Niuean	PNB	b
8253	other minor peoples	3.50000	72	66	50	...				85.00	56		10	7	8	5	0			
	Norfolk Island	**100.00000**	**2,000**	**2,075**	**2,495**					**65.2**	**1,353**									
8254	Anglo-Australian	31.00000	620	643	773	CEW19c	52-ABAC-x	general australian		62.00	399	1Bsuh	10	10	13	5	1		pnb	b
8255	Anglo-New Zealander	13.80000	276	286	344	CEW19e	52-ABAC-y	general new-zealand		72.00	206	1Bsuh	10	9	14	5	1		pnb	b
8256	British	10.10000	202	210	252	CEW19i	52-ABAC-b	standard-english		69.00	145	3Bsuh	10	9	13	5	2		PNB	b
8257	Euronesian	3.20000	64	66	80	MPY53	52-ABAC-bv	standard oceanian-english		70.00	46	1Bsuh	10	8	11	5	3		pnb	b
8258	Norfolker (Pitcairner)	41.40000	828	859	1,033	MPY53	52-ABAI-i	norfolk-island-creole	70	64.00	550	1csuh	10	9	11	5	3		pnb	b
8259	other minor peoples	0.50000	10	10	12	...				67.00	7		10	8	7	5	0			
	North Korea	**100.00000**	**22,238,653**	**24,039,193**	**29,387,635**					**2.08**	**500,213**									
8260	British	0.00100	222	240	294	CEW19i	52-ABAC-b	standard-english	5	79.00	190	3Bsuh	10	9	13	5	2		PNB	b
8261	French	0.00200	445	481	588	CEW21b	51-AABI-d	general français		87.00	418	1B.uh	10	9	14	5	1	French	PNB	b
8262	Han Chinese (Mandarin)	0.70000	155,671	168,274	205,713	MSY42a	79-AAAB-ba	kuo-yü		0.10	168	2Bsuh	5	3	2	0	0	Chinese: Kuoyu*	PNB	b
8263	Khalka Mongol	0.03000	6,672	7,212	8,816	MSY41f	44-BAAB-c	halh		0.05	4	3A..h	4	3	2	0	0	Mongolian: Khalka*	PNb	b
8264	North Korean	99.04700	22,026,719	23,810,099	29,107,571	MSY46	45-AAAA-bc	north onmun		2.08	495,250	1A...	6	4	7	2	1	Korean	PNB	b
8265	Russian	0.02000	4,448	4,808	5,878	CEW22j	53-AAAE-d	russkiy		37.00	1,779	4B.uh	9	5	9	2	0	Russian	PNB	b
8266	other minor peoples	0.20000	44,477	48,078	58,775	...				5.00	2,404		7	5	2	2	0			
	Northern Cyprus	**100.00000**	**180,000**	**185,045**	**212,470**					**8.7**	**16,106**									
8267	Greek Cypriot	8.00000	14,400	14,804	16,998	CEW20	56-AAAA-c	dhimotiki		88.00	13,027	2B.uh	10	9	11	5	1	Greek: Modern	PNB	b
8268	Turkish Cypriot	89.50000	161,100	165,615	190,161	MSY41j	44-AABA-a	osmanli		1.20	1,987	1A.u.	6	3	6	1	0	Turkish	PNB	b
8269	Yoruk	0.50000	900	925	1,062	MSY41j	44-AABA-a	osmanli		0.01	0	1A.u.	3	3	5	0	0	Turkish	PNB	b
8270	other minor peoples	2.00000	3,600	3,701	4,249	...				29.50	1,092		9	5	7	1	0			
	Northern Mariana Islands	**100.00000**	**58,846**	**78,356**	**245,191**					**88.39**	**69,260**									
8271	Carolinian	5.40000	3,178	4,231	13,240	MPY54e	38-AABD-b	saipan		98.00	4,147	0....	10	8	13	5	0		...	b
8272	Chamorro	29.00000	17,065	22,723	71,105	MSY44d	31-UAAA-d	guam-chamorro		99.00	22,496	1.s..	10	10	12	5	3	Chamorro	P..	b
8273	Filipino	33.60000	19,772	26,328	82,384	MSY44o	31-CKAA-a	proper tagalog		98.00	25,801	4Bs..	10	8	11	4	0	Tagalog	PNB	b
8274	Han Chinese	9.00000	5,296	7,052	22,067	MSY42a	79-AAAB-ba	kuo-yü		40.00	2,821	2Bsuh	9	7	9	4	0	Chinese: Kuoyu*	PNB	b
8275	Japanese	2.50000	1,471	1,959	6,130	MSY45a	45-CAAA-a	koku-go		5.00	98	1B.uh	7	4	3	5	0	Japanese	PNB	b
8276	Korean	8.10000	4,767	6,347	19,860	MSY46	45-AAAA-b	kukö		81.00	5,141	2A...	10	8	12	5	0	Korean	PNB	b
8277	Palauan	3.70000	2,177	2,899	9,072	MPY54c	31-SAAA-a	palau		98.00	2,841	1.s..	10	10	8	0	0	Palauan	PN.	b
8278	USA White	4.00000	2,354	3,134	9,808	CEW19s	52-ABAC-s	general american		75.00	2,351	1Bsuh	10	9	13	5	0	English*	PNB	b
8279	Woleaian	2.10000	1,236	1,645	5,149	MPY54z	38-AABC-a	woleai		99.00	1,629	0....	10	10	9	0	0		...	b
8280	other minor peoples	2.60000	1,530	2,037	6,375	...				95.00	1,935		10	7	7	5	0			
	Norway	**100.00000**	**4,345,593**	**4,461,033**	**4,812,063**					**94.18**	**4,201,263**									
8281	Arctic Lapp (Ume)	0.02000	869	892	962	MSW51e	41-AABC-a	ume		80.00	714	0....	10	8	9	4	1		...	.
8282	British	0.10000	4,346	4,461	4,812	CEW19i	52-ABAC-b	standard-english	59	78.00	3,480	3Bsuh	10	9	13	5	1		PNB	b
8283	Danish (Dane)	0.30000	13,037	13,383	14,436	CEW19g	52-AAAD-c	general dansk	100	94.00	12,580	2A.uh	10	9	11	5	3	Danish	PNB	b
8284	Esperanto	0.00000	0	0	0	CEW21z	51-AAAC-a	proper esperanto	2	80.00	0	0A...	10	9	9	5	0	Esperanto	PNB	b
8285	Finnish (Finn)	0.24300	10,560	10,840	11,693	MSW51b	41-AAAA-bb	vehicular suomi	1	87.00	9,431	1A.uh	10	9	12	5	2	Finnish	PNB	b
8286	French	0.05000	2,173	2,231	2,406	CEW21b	51-AABI-d	general français	10	84.00	1,874	1B.uh	10	9	14	5	3	French	PNB	b
8287	German	0.10000	4,346	4,461	4,812	CEW19m	52-ABCE-a	standard hoch-deutsch	34	87.00	3,881	2B.uh	10	9	13	5	1	German*	PNB	b
8288	Greek	0.04000	1,738	1,784	1,925	CEW20	56-AAAA-c	dhimotiki		95.00	1,695	2B.uh	10	9	10	5	0	Greek: Modern	PNB	b
8289	Han Chinese	0.08000	3,476	3,569	3,850	MSY42a	79-AAAB-ba	kuo-yü		6.00	214	2Bsuh	7	8	8	5	0	Chinese: Kuoyu*	PNB	b
8290	Jewish	0.02300	999	1,026	1,107	CMT35	52-AAAD-db	riks-mâl		0.21	2	1B.uh	5	4	6	5	0		pnb	b
8291	Kurdish (Kurd)	0.10000	4,346	4,461	4,812	CNT24c	58-AAAA-a	kurmanji		1.00	45	3c...	6	5	4	5	1	Kurdish: Kurmanji*	PN.	b
8292	Latin American	0.17000	7,388	7,584	8,181	CLT27	51-AABB-h	south americano		92.00	6,977	4B.uh	10	8	13	5	0		pnb	b
8293	Middle East Arab	0.17000	7,388	7,584	8,181	CMT30	45-CAAA-a	koku-go		20.00	1,517	1B.uh	9	9	9	0	0	Japanese	PNB	b
8294	Northern Lapp (Samish)	0.25000	10,864	11,153	12,030	MSW51e	41-AABA-a	ruija		98.00	10,930	0....	10	8	12	4	1	Saami: Norwegian*	PNB	b
8295	Norwegian (Dano-Norwegian)	69.77000	3,031,920	3,112,463	3,357,376	CEW19p	52-AAAC-e	ny-norsk	100	97.63	3,038,697	0B.uh	10	10	14	5	3	Norwegian*	PNB	b
8296	Norwegian (New Norse)	24.00000	1,042,942	1,070,648	1,154,895	CEW19p	52-AAAC-e	ny-norsk	100	98.20	1,051,376	0B.uh	10	10	14	5	3	Norwegian*	PNB	b
8297	Norwegian Gypsy	0.07000	3,042	3,123	3,368	CNN25f	52-AAAC-e	ny-norsk		70.00	2,186	0B.uh	10	8	8	4	1	Norwegian*	PNB	b
8298	Norwegian Traveller	0.02000	869	892	962	CNN25f	59-AGAA-ad	anglo-romani-australia		70.00	625	0....	10	7	8	4	2		...	.
8299	Pite Lapp	0.02500	1,086	1,115	1,203	MSW51e	41-AABA-c	pite		90.00	1,004	0....	10	8	11	4	1	Saami, Pite	PNB	.
8300	Punjabi	0.35000	15,210	15,614	16,842	CNN25n	59-AAFE-c	general panjabi		3.50	546	1Asu.	6	5	8	4	0		PNB	b
8301	Russian	0.06000	2,607	2,677	2,887	CEW22j	53-AAAE-d	russkiy		60.00	1,606	4B.uh	10	9	8	0	0	Russian	PNB	b
8302	Southern Lapp	0.06000	2,607	2,677	2,887	MSW51e	41-AABC	south saame cluster		90.00	2,409	0....	10	8	11	4	1	Saami, Southern	...	b
8303	Spaniard	0.02000	869	892	962	CEW21k	51-AABB-c	general español	3	96.00	857	2B.uh	10	9	15	5	3	Spanish	PNB	b
8304	Swedish (Swede)	0.50000	21,728	22,305	24,060	CEW19q	52-AAAD-r	svea-svensk	100	73.00	16,283	1A.uh	10	9	13	5	1	Swedish	PNB	b
8305	Swedish Lapp (Lule Lapp)	0.02600	1,130	1,160	1,251	MSW51e	41-AABA-b	lule		98.00	1,137	0....	10	8	12	4	1	Saami: Swedish*	PNB	b
8306	Tattare Gypsy (Lovari)	0.01200	521	535	577	CNN25f	59-ACBA-a	vlach-romani		80.00	428	1a...	10	8	8	5	2	Romani: Finnish*	PN.	b
8307	Turk	0.05600	2,434	2,498	2,695	MSY41j	44-AABA-a	osmanli		0.20	5	1A.u.	5	5	4	0	0	Turkish	PNB	b
8308	USA White	0.30000	13,037	13,383	14,436	CEW19s	52-ABAC-s	general american		77.00	10,305	1Bsuh	10	9	13	5	3	English*	PNB	b
8309	Urdu	0.33500	14,558	14,944	16,120	CNN25r	59-AAFO-d	standard urdu		0.01	1	2Asuh	3	5	7	0	0	Urdu	PNB	b
8310	Vietnamese	2.41000	104,729	107,511	115,971	MSY52b	46-EBAA-ac	general viêt		12.00	12,901	1Asu.	8	7	8	4	0	Vietnamese	PNB	b
8311	West African	0.18000	7,822	8,030	8,662	NAN58	98-AAAA-d	central yoruba		55.00	4,416	1csu.	10	8	8	5	0		pnb	.
8312	other minor peoples	0.16000	6,953	7,138	7,699	...				44.00	3,141		9	5	8	5	0			
	Oman	**100.00000**	**2,155,142**	**2,541,739**	**5,351,885**					**4.8**	**121,915**									
8313	Bengali	4.40000	94,826	111,837	235,483	CNN25b	59-AAFT-e	west bengali		0.01	11	1Asuh	3	5	7	0	0	Bengali: Musalmani*	PNB	b
8314	British	0.20000	4,310	5,083	10,704	CEW19i	52-ABAC-b	standard-english		72.00	3,660	3Bsuh	10	9	12	5	1		PNB	b
8315	Egyptian Arab	1.65000	35,560	41,939	88,306	CMT30	12-AACF-a	masri		18.00	7,549	2Asuh	8	7	9	0	0	Arabic*	PNB	b
8316	Filipino	2.10000	45,258	53,377	112,390	MSY44o	31-CKAA-ab	vehicular tagalog		96.00	51,241	1cs..	10	9	11	0	0		pnb	.
8317	Gujarati	1.20000	25,862	30,501	64,223	CNN25e	59-AAFH-b	standard gujaraati		0.58	177	2A.u.	5	4	6	1	0	Gujarati	PNB	b
8318	Gulf Arab	3.21000	69,180	81,590	171,796	CMT30	12-AACF-ih	buraimi		4.20	3,427	1Asuh	6	4	6	3	0		pnb	b
8319	Hindi	2.40000	51,723	61,002	128,445	CNN25g	59-AAFO-e	general hindi		0.60	366	3Asuh	5	4	6	1	0		pnb	b
8320	Jordanian Arab	0.40000	8,621	10,167	21,408	CMT30	12-AACF-f	syro-palestinian		6.00	610	1Asuh	7	7	9	0	0	Arabic: Lebanese*	Pnb	b
8321	Korean	0.03000	647	763	1,606	MSY46	45-AAAA-b	kukö		55.00	419	2A...	10	9	12	0	0	Korean	PNB	b
8322	Kumzari	0.15000	3,233	3,813	8,028	CNT24z	58-AACA-b	kumzari		0.00	0	0....	0	1	0	0	0		...	b
8323	Mahra	2.00000	43,103	50,835	107,038	CMT30	12-ABAA-a	mahri		0.01	5	0....	3	2	0	0	0	Mehri	P..	b
8324	Malayali	1.70000	36,637	43,210	90,982	CNN23b	49-EBEB-a	malayalam		40.00	17,284	2Asu.	9	5	10	3	0	Malayalam	PNB	b
8325	Omani Arab	48.11000	1,036,839	1,222,831	2,574,792	CMT30	12-AACF-l	omani		1.00	12,228	1Asuh	6	3	5	1	3		pnb	b
8326	Persian	2.80000	60,344	71,169	149,853	CNT24f	58-AACC-ca	west farsi		0.04	28	1asu.	3	3	8	0	0	Farsi, Western	PNB	b
8327	Punjabi	2.20000	47,413	55,918	117,741	CNN25n	59-AAFE-c	general panjabi		1.30	727	1Asu.	6	4	7	1	0		PNB	b
8328	Saudi Arab	1.00000	21,551	25,417	53,519	CMT30	12-AACF-k	central `anazi		0.09	23	4Asuh	4	3	5	1	1		pnb	b
8329	Shahari (Jibbali)	1.25000	26,939	31,772	66,899	CMT30	12-ABAA-d	jibbali		0.00	0	0....	0	3	1	1	0		p..	b
8330	Singhalese	0.80000	17,241	20,334	42,815	CNN25q	59-ABBA-a	historical sinhala		4.00	813	2asuh	6	7	8	0	0		PNB	b
8331	Southern Baluch	15.00000	323,271	381,261	802,783	CNT24b	58-AABA-ce	balochi-émigré		0.01	38	1.s..	3	3	1	1	2		p..	b
8332	Sudanese Arab	0.45000	9,698	11,438	24,083	CMT30	12-AACF-c	sudani		0.50	57	4Asuh	5	4	8	0	0	Arabic: Sudan	PNb	b
8333	Tamil	2.50000	53,879	63,543	133,797	CNN23c	49-EBEA-b	tamil		27.00	17,157	2Asu.	9	5	10	3	0	Tamil	PNB	b
8334	USA White	0.10000	2,155	2,542	5,352	CEW19s	52-ABAC-s	general american		74.00	1,881	1Bsuh	10	9	12	5	2	English*	PNB	b
8335	Urdu	2.25000	48,491	57,189	120,417	CNN25r	59-AAFO-d	standard urdu		0.01	6	2Asuh	3	3	2	1	0	Urdu	PNB	b
8336	Yemeni Arab	0.50000	10,776	12,709	26,759	CMT30	12-AACF-n	yemeni		0.06	8	1Asuh	4	3	6	0	0		pnb	b
8337	Zanzibari	2.50000	53,879	63,543	133,797	NAB57j	99-AUSM-q	ki-unguja		0.01	6	1Asu.	3	2	2	0	0		pnb	b
8338	other minor peoples	1.10000	23,707	27,959	58,871	...				15.00	4,194		8	4	6	1	0			
	Pakistan	**100.00000**	**136,244,357**	**156,483,155**	**262,999,723**					**2.44**	**3,812,242**									
8339	Afghani Tajik (Tadzhik)	0.76847	1,046,997	1,202,526	2,021,074	CNT24g	58-AACC-fc	tajiki-afghanistan		0.01	120	1Asu.	3	3	5	3	4		pnb	b
8340	Anglo-Pakistani	0.03000	40,873	46,945	78,900	CNN25z	52-ABAD-ad	pakistani-english		30.00	14,083	0A.uh	9	8	10	4	3		...	b
8341	Arab	0.10000	136,244	156,483	263,000	CMT30	12-AACF-g	syro-mesopotamian		0.20	313	1Asuh	5	3	3	0	0		pnb	b
8342	Arhagar Gypsy	0.01000	13,624	15,648	26,300	CNN25f	59-ACBA-a	vlach-romani		0.20	31	1a...	5	3	2	0	0	Romani: Finnish*	PN.	b
8343	Badeshi	0.00200	2,725	3,130	5,260	CNT24z	59-AADB-g	ushojo		0.05	2	0....	4	2	0	0	0		p..	b
8344	Bagri	0.15044	204,966	235,413	395,657	CNN25o	59-AAFG-p	bagri		1.00	2,354	1.s..	6	4	4	1	1		pn.	b
8345	Balmiki	0.01759	23,965	27,525	46,262	CNN25p	59-ACAA-a	domari		1.00	275	0....	6	4	4	1	3		...	b
8346	Baltistani Bhotia	0.20879	284,465	326,721	549,117	MSY50r	70-AAAC-c	balti		0.01	33	1....	3	4	3	0	3	Balti	Pn.	b
8347	Bashgar (Kafari, Kamtoz)	0.00384	5,232	6,009	10,099	CNT24d	58-ACBA	bash-gali cluster		0.10	6	0....	5	3	3	0	0		...	.
8348	Bateri	0.01921	26,173	30,060	50,522	CNN25i	59-AACF-c	bateri		0.10	30	0....	5	2	0	0	0		...	p
8349	Bengali	0.16000	217,991	250,373	420,800	CNN25b	59-AAFT-e	west bengali		0.60	1,502	1Asuh	5	4	8	2	2	Bengali: Musalmani*	PNB	b
8350	Bhattiana (Bhatneri)	0.01000	13,624	15,648	26,300	CNN25o	59-AAFC-bi	bhattiani		1.00	156	1....	6	4	4	1	0	Bhatneri	PN.	b
8351	Black Kafir	0.00290	3,951	4,538	7,627	CNN25i	59-AABA-a	kho-war		0.10	5	0....	5	4	4	1	2		...	.
8352	Brahui (Kur Galli, Kalat)	1.68752	2,299,151	2,640,685	4,438,173	CNN23z	49-AAAA-a	bra'uidi		0.20	5,281	3....	5	4	4	1	2	Brahui	P..	n
8353	British	0.00800	10,900	12,519	21,040	CEW19i	52-ABAC-b	standard-english	35	79.00	9,890	3Bsuh	10	9	13	4	3		PNB	b

Continued opposite

Table 8-2 continued

EVANGELIZATION								EVANGELISM			ADDITIONAL DESCRIPTIVE DATA
Ref 1	*D* 28	*aC* 29	*CG%* 30	*r* 31	*E* 32	*U* 33	*W* 34	*e* 35	*R* 36	*T* 37	*Locations, civil divisions, literacy, religions, church history, denominations, dioceses, church growth, missions, agencies, ministries, movements* 38
8246	0	6	4.59	0	34.00	66.00	A	12.41	482	5	Bauchi State, Toro and Tafawa Bolewa LGAs. Muslims 60%, animists 30%.
8247	0	6	2.86	0	27.00	73.00	A	4.92	431	4	Bauchi State, Toro LGA. Muslims 50%, animists 45%.
8248	0	5	2.22	1	33.01	66.99	A	0.01	342	2	Sokoto State, Arungu LGA. Also in Niger, Benin, Burkina Faso. Muslims 75%(Maliki Sunnis), animists 25%. M=EBM,EMS.
8249	0	8	10.41		86.00	14.00	C	188.34	332	7	Egyptians(COC), Jamaicans, Greeks(GOC), USA Whites and Blacks(SDA,CCS,JWs), Ghanaians(MDCC), Koreans(PCK-H,SIM), Aduge, Barawa, Bele, Chobbo.
Niue Island											
8250	5	10	-0.75	8	99.80	0.20	C	435.08	1	10	Expatriates from New Zealand, in commerce, development. D=Anglican Ch/CPNZ(D-Polynesia),NCC,CJCLdS,RCC,SDA.
8251	2	10	-0.69	7	99.40	0.60	B	156.22	3	7	Traders, laborers. Some folk-religionists 35%, some Baha'is 20%. D=RCC,AC/CPNZ.
8252	6	6	-0.89	5	99.94	0.06	C	527.27	2	10	Also in New Zealand, Tonga, Cook Islands. D=Niue Christian Ch,CJCLdS,RCC(D-Rarotonga),JWs,SDA,AC. M=SM2,LMS/CWM.
8253	0	10	-0.47		99.85	0.15	C	359.89	2	9	Other Pacific Islanders, Europeans, Euronesians.
Norfolk Island											
8254	2	10	0.32	8	99.62	0.38	C	291.92	23	8	Administrators, from Australia. Nonreligious 38%. D=Anglican Ch of Australia,SDA. M=MM.
8255	2	10	0.76	8	99.72	0.28	C	367.92	31	9	Expatriates from New Zealand, in education. Nonreligious 28%. D=ACA,SDA. M=MM.
8256	3	10	0.67	8	99.69	0.31	C	362.66	35	9	Expatriates from Britain, in development. Nonreligious 26%. D=Anglican Ch of Australia(D-Sydney),MC,SDA. M=MM,SM2.
8257	4	10	0.70	8	99.70	0.30	C	352.59	30	9	Mixed-race persons, mostly in urban center. D=RCC,ACA,SDA,MC.
8258	3	10	0.06	1	99.64	0.36	C	287.32	19	8	Originally from Pitcairn Islands. Also second generation in Australia, New Zealand. English-based creole. Bilingual in English. D=ACA,RCC(M-Sydney),SDA.
8259	0	10	1.96		99.00	1.00	C	242.10	54	8	Other Pacific Islanders, European, Asians.
North Korea											
8260	2	10	1.80	8	99.79	0.21	C	441.17	53	10	Expatriates from Britain, in business. D=PCK,RCC.
8261	1	10	1.80	8	99.87	0.13	C	498.55	49	10	Expatriates from France, in business. D=RCC.
8262	0	1	1.81	7	41.10	58.90	A	0.15	164	3	From Communist China. Military, advisors. Nonreligious 76%, atheists 15%.
8263	0	1	1.40	4	34.05	65.95	A	0.06	175	2	From Mongolia. Nonreligious 60%, atheists 36%, Buddhists 4%.
8264	5	1	3.70	6	50.08	49.92	B	3.80	236	4	Also in China, Russia, Japan, Singapore, Thailand, Guam. Nonreligious 55%, atheists 16%, New-Religionists 13%, shamanists 12%, Buddhists 1.5%. D=PCK.
8265	0	3	1.99	7	92.00	8.00	B	124.24	59	7	From USSR; military, advisors. Nonreligious 48%, atheists 15%.
8266	0	8	1.81		25.00	75.00	A	4.56	198	4	Other Asians, Europeans. Nonreligious/atheists 70%, Buddhists 15%, Muslims 5%.
Northern Cyprus											
8267	1	7	4.99	7	99.88	0.12	C	504.28	104	10	Residual Greeks in Turkish-ruled northern republic of Cyprus. D=GOC.
8268	0	7	4.09	8	52.20	47.80	B	2.28	252	4	Great majority now in northern republic. Muslims 99%(Hanafi Sunnis).
8269	0	7	0.00	8	45.01	54.99	A	0.01	0	2	Turks. All Muslims 100%(Hanafi Sunnis).
8270	0	7	4.45		54.50	45.50	B	58.68	224	6	Other Europeans, Arabs, Asians. Muslims 53%, nonreligious 10%.
Northern Mariana Islands											
8271	0	8	3.80	2	99.98	0.02	C	515.08	84	10	Immigrants from the Caroline Islands. Fishermen, agriculturalists. Bilingual in Chamorro, English. Baha'is 2%. D=RCC.
8272	2	9	2.75	5	99.99	0.01	C	567.32	55	10	Majority of Chamorros live on Guam. 30% bilinguals in English. Lingua franca. D=99%RCC(D-Agana),almost all practicing Catholics. M=SJ,Pioneers,UBS.
8273	0	10	3.65	5	99.98	0.02	C	586.62	72	10	Immigrant workers from the Philippines. D=RCC.
8274	0	10	6.54	7	99.40	0.60	B	148.92	193	7	Immigrant workers from Hong Kong, some wealthy. Mahayana Buddhists 40%, Chinese folk-religionists 20%.
8275	0	10	4.69	7	61.00	39.00	B	11.13	244	5	Immigrants from Japan. Mahayana Buddhists 50%, New Religionists 45%.
8276	0	5	6.44	6	99.81	0.19	C	413.91	138	10	Immigrant workers from South Korea. Shamanists 10%, Buddhists 5%, Confucianists 4%. D=Presbyterian.
8277	0	0	5.81	5	99.98	0.02	C	468.58	135	10	Immigrants from Palau. D=Palau Ch(Modekngei,healing movement),RCC(D-Carolines-Marshalls), SDA,AoG,PCCI.
8278	0	10	4.16	8	99.75	0.25	C	391.46	97	9	North Americans, in business, education. Nonreligious 15%. D=RCC,BBC,SDA,etc.
8279	0	0	3.55	0	99.99	0.01	C	440.84	94	10	Immigrants from Woleai and other Islands, eastern Carolines. D=RCC,PCCI.
8280	0	10	5.41		99.95	0.05	C	443.84	116	10	Other Pacific Islanders (SDA,JWs,CJCLdS,&c).
Norway											
8281	1	10	0.70	2	99.80	0.20	C	353.32	38	9	Between Arctic Circle and 66 degrees N southeast from Mo i Rana town. Also in Sweden. D=Ch of Norway(D-Nord Halogaland).
8282	6	10	0.70	8	99.78	0.22	C	435.59	33	10	Expatriates from Britain, in business. D=Ch of England(D-Europe),MCN,CB,SDA,JWs,SA. M=UMC.
8283	4	10	0.70	6	99.94	0.06	C	576.40	30	10	Expatriates from Denmark. D=Ch of Norway,RCC,MCN,JWs.
8284	0	10	0.00	5	99.80	0.20	C	411.72	0	10	Artificial (constructed) language, in 80 countries. Speakers in Norway: 91,000(none mother-tongue).
8285	2	10	0.71	5	99.87	0.13	C	498.55	30	10	Expatriates from Finland. D=Ch of Norway,GOC(D-Swedia). M=ELCF,OCF.
8286	3	10	0.70	8	99.84	0.16	C	487.49	29	10	Expatriates from France, in business. D=RCC(3 Dioceses),SA,JWs. M=OSB,OP,OCSO,OFM,SJ,SM,SSCC,MSF.
8287	4	10	0.70	8	99.87	0.13	C	508.08	32	10	From Germany, in business, commerce, industry. D=Ch of Norway,MCN,RCC,NAC. M=SJ.
8288	0	10	5.27	7	99.95	0.05	C	551.33	108	10	Expatriates from Greece, most involved in commerce. D=GOC.
8289	0	10	3.11	7	65.00	35.00	B	14.23	158	5	Immigrant workers from Hong Kong, China, and Taiwan. Buddhists 60%, Chinese folk-religionists 31%.
8290	0	10	0.70	6	52.21	47.79	B	0.40	73	3	Small community of practicing Jews, most in Oslo. Nonreligious 20%.
8291	1	10	3.88	0	43.00	57.00	A	1.57	375	4	Refugees from Iraq, Iran, Turkey. 300 speak Sorani, 200 ZaZa. Muslims 99%(Sunnis). D=CON. M=whole network of agencies.
8292	0	10	4.72	8	99.92	0.08	C	530.56	97	10	Immigrant workers from Latin America. Afro-American spiritists 6%. D=RCC.
8293	0	0	5.15	7	66.00	34.00	B	48.18	243	6	Immigrant workers from the Middle East. Muslims 75%. D=Orthodox Church, RCC.
8294	1	10	0.70	2	99.98	0.02	C	550.85	30	10	Norwegian Lapps. Sea Lapps. Mainly in Norway: Lapland in Finnmark, Troms, Nordland, Ofoten. Also in Finland, Sweden. D=CON(D-Nord Halogaland).
8295	10	9	0.62	6	99.98	0.02	C	618.73	27	10	Norwegian form of Danish. Primarily urban. Also in USA, Canada. D=Ch of Norway(10 Dioceses),SA,NPY,MCN,ELFCN,NBU,MCCN,JWs,SDA,RCC(3 Dioceses).
8296	6	10	0.69	6	99.98	0.02	C	627.96	28	10	Official language. Primarily rural. D=Ch of Norway,SA,NPY,MCN,ELFCN,&c.
8297	2	10	0.70	6	99.70	0.30	C	337.26	36	9	Partly settled. D=nomadic caravan churches,Gypsy Evangelical Movement. M=GGMS.
8298	2	9	0.70	0	99.70	0.30	C	278.49	43	8	Gypsies. Norwegian-Northern Romany language. D=GEM,CON.
8299	1	9	0.70	2	99.90	0.10	C	469.75	33	10	Between Saltenfjord and Ranenfjord in Norway. Also in Sweden. D=CON(D-Nord Halogaland).
8300	0	10	4.08	5	55.50	44.50	B	7.09	253	4	Immigrant workers from India. Muslims 96.5% (Sunnis, Ahmadis).
8301	0	0	5.21	7	99.60	0.40	C	238.71	131	8	Refugees and immigrant workers from Russia since 1990. Nonreligious 30%, Atheists 10%. D=ROC.
8302	1	9	0.70	2	99.90	0.10	C	446.76	34	10	Hatfjelldalen and Wefsen, south to Roros in Norway. Also in Sweden. D=CON(D-Nord Halogaland). M=NLM.
8303	1	10	0.70	8	99.96	0.04	C	606.19	26	10	Expatriates from Spain, in commerce. Strong Catholics. D=RCC(3 Dioceses). M=OSB,OP,OFM,OCSO,SJ,SSCC,SM,MSF.
8304	4	10	0.70	6	99.73	0.27	C	389.01	13	9	Expatriates from Sweden. D=Ch of Norway,MCN,RCC,SA. M=COS.
8305	1	10	0.70	2	99.98	0.02	C	558.01	30	10	Tysfjord, Hamaroy, and Folden. Also in Sweden. Hunters, fishermen, reindeer herders. D=CON(D-Nord Halogaland).
8306	3	9	0.70	6	99.80	0.20	C	397.12	35	9	Nomadic caravan communities; in 25 countries. D=Gypsy Evangelical Movement,SA,NPY. M=GGMS,NBS.
8307	0	0	1.62	8	35.20	64.80	A	0.25	181	3	Immigrant workers from Turkey (many via Berlin, Germany). Muslims 100%.
8308	7	10	3.25	8	99.77	0.23	C	430.00	74	10	Expatriates from USA, in business, education. D=MCN,JWs,CJCLdS,SDA,CC,CCS,SA.
8309	0	0	0.00	5	36.01	63.99	A	0.01	78	2	Immigrant workers from Pakistan and India. Muslims 100%.
8310	0	10	7.43	6	69.00	31.00	B	30.22	329	5	Refugees and immigrants from Viet Nam. Mahayana Buddhists 60%, New Religionists 20%. D=RCC.
8311	0	10	6.28	5	99.55	0.45	B	210.78	193	8	Immigrant workers from Nigeria and other West African countries. Muslims 30%, Animists 15%. D=CPN, RCC.
8312	0	9	0.70		76.00	24.00	B	122.05	25	7	Pakistanis(Muslims), Tibetans(Lamaists), Italians(RCs), Greeks(GOC), Ghanaians, Russo-Norwegian creoles(Russonorsk). Muslims 10%, Buddhists 8%.
Oman											
8313	0	0	2.43	6	36.01	63.99	A	0.01	185	2	Immigrant workers from Bangladesh. Muslims 100%.
8314	1	10	6.32	8	99.72	0.28	C	378.43	142	9	Expatriates from Britain, in development. D=Anglican Ch(D-Cyprus & The Gulf).
8315	0	0	6.85	8	65.00	35.00	B	42.70	318	6	Immigrant workers from Egypt. Muslims 82%. D=Coptic Orthodox Church.
8316	0	0	8.92	1	99.96	0.04	C	462.52	199	10	Immigrant workers from the Philippines, many in domestic work. D=RCC.
8317	0	9	2.92	6	50.58	49.42	B	1.07	213	4	Workers from Gujarat. Traders. Hindus 88%, Muslims 8%, Baha'is.
8318	0	9	6.01	7	56.20	43.80	B	8.61	327	4	Workers from Gulf states. Muslims 96%(Sunnis,Wahhabis).
8319	0	9	3.67	7	50.60	49.40	B	1.10	253	4	Workers from India. Traders. Hindus 90%, Muslims 9%, Baha'is.
8320	0	0	4.20	8	46.00	54.00	A	10.07	292	5	Immigrant workers from Jordan. Muslims 94%. D=Orthodox, RCC.
8321	0	0	3.81	6	99.55	0.45	B	206.77	118	8	Immigrant workers from South Korea. Shamanists 20%, Buddhists 15%, New Religionists 10%. D=Presbyterians.
8322	0	3	0.00	1	11.00	89.00	A	0.00	0	1.04	Spoken only on Musandam Peninsula, northern Oman. Related to Luri (Iran). Muslims 100%.
8323	0	3	1.62	0	14.01	85.99	A	0.00	454	1.05	Dhofar. Between Hadramaut and Oman. Pre-Arab. Also in Saudi Arabia, Yemen, Kuwait. Muslims 100%(Sunnis).
8324	0	9	7.74	4	99.40	0.60	B	147.46	237	7	From Kerala(India). Hindus 40%, Muslims 18%, Baha'is. D=OSCE,MTSC.
8325	1	5	7.37	7	51.00	49.00	B	1.86	434	4	Eastern Colloquial Arabic. In Arabia, Gulf, Iran, Iraq, Ethiopia, Somalia, USA, Canada, Djibouti. Muslims 99%(Hinawis,Ibadi Kharijites,Ghafiris).
8326	0	5	3.39	5	43.04	56.96	A	0.06	260	2	Immigrants from Iran. Muslims 97%(Imami Shias/Ithna-Asharis), Baha'is 3%.
8327	0	9	4.38	5	52.30	47.70	B	2.48	284	4	Traders from India. Muslims, Sikhs 40%, Hindus 30%, Baha'is 9%.
8328	0	9	3.19	7	50.09	49.91	B	0.16	213	3	Immigrants from Saudi Arabia. Muslims 100%(Shafi,Maliki,and Hanbali Sunnis). M=CSI.
8329	0	4	0.00	0	14.00	86.00	A	0.00	0	1.06	In Dofar, mountains north of Al-Salala. Kuria Muria. 3 dialects. Many bilingual in Arabic. Muslims 100%(Sunnis).
8330	0	0	4.50	6	44.00	56.00	A	6.42	316	4	Traders from Sri Lanka. Theravada Buddhists 95%.
8331	0	4	3.70	1	22.01	77.99	A	0.00	585	1.10	Long-time residents from Baluchistan. Most remain in Pakistan; also UAE, Iran. Muslims 100%(Sunnis). M=RSTI,CSI.
8332	0	0	4.13	7	40.50	59.50	A	0.73	327	3	Immigrant workers from Northern Sudan. Muslims 99.5%.
8333	0	9	7.73	6	87.00	13.00	B	85.73	275	6	Traders from south India. Hindus 55%, Muslims 18%.
8334	2	10	5.18	8	99.74	0.26	C	394.34	114	9	Expatriates from USA, in development. D=Protestant Ch in Oman,RCC. M=RCA,OFMCap.
8335	0	5	1.81	5	41.01	58.99	A	0.01	190	2	Migrant workers from Pakistan. Also living in India, Afghanistan, Bahrain, Qatar, Fiji, South Africa, Germany. Muslims 100%(Hanafi Sunnis).
8336	0	7	2.10	7	44.06	55.94	A	0.09	174	2	Migrant workers from Yemen. Muslims 100%(50% Zaydis,40% Sunnis,5% Ismailis, 5% Ahmadis).
8337	0	9	1.81	5	38.01	61.99	A	0.01	236	2	Coast Province. Also in Tanzania, Kenya, Uganda, Mayotte, Rwanda, Burundi, South Africa, USA. Blacks from Zanzibar (originally as slaves). Muslims 100%(Shafi).
8338	0	7	6.22		38.00	62.00	A	20.80	448	5	Afars, Palestinians(Shafis,Alawis,Druzes), Black Africans, Bantu, Baharahs, other Europeans, other Asians. Muslims 80% (55% Sunnis, 20% Shias, 5% Druzis).
Pakistan											
8339	0	6	2.52	4	43.01	56.99	A	0.01	205	2	Eastern Farsi(Dari). Southeast Chitral, Shishi Koh Valley. Refugees from Afghanistan war, now permanent. Muslims 100%(Hanafi Sunnis). M=CP,RCC,OM,TEAM.
8340	3	10	2.43	8	90.00	10.00	B	98.55	105	6	Mixed-race persons, including Anglo-Indians. Majority are Muslims, 60%; some Baha'is. D=RCC,COP,UPCP.
8341	0	7	3.50	7	41.20	58.80	A	0.30	279	3	Immigrants, traders, workers from numerous Arab nations. Muslims 98%.
8342	0	6	3.49	6	31.20	68.80	A	0.22	397	3	Nomadic Muslim Gypsies in Kalderash tradition. Muslims 99%.
8343	0	5	0.70	0	16.05	83.95	A	0.02	290	2	Swat Kohistan, upper reaches of Chail Valley, east of Madyan, one village. Second language: Pashto. Muslims 99%(Sunnis).
8344	1	5	5.61	0	31.00	69.00	A	1.13	584	4	Nomads between Pakistan (Sindh) and India (Punjab, Rajasthan). Bilingual in Sindhi, Urdu. Specialized beggars. Strong Hindus 95%. D=ICF. M=CBFMS.
8345	2	6	3.37	7	36.00	64.00	A	1.31	333	4	Punjabi sweeper caste in Attock District. Dialect of Lahnda. Strong Hindus 95%, resisting Islam. D=RCC,COP. M=OFM,OP,CMS.
8346	0	4	3.56	0	23.01	76.99	A	0.00	623	1.08	Northeastern Pakistan (Baltistan, Skardu). Also India (Jammu, Kashmir, UP). Balti is spoken form of literary Tibetan. Shia Muslims 100%(strong Sufi influence).
8347	0	5	1.81	0	16.10	83.90	A	0.05	512	2	In lower Chitral, Afghan border, mountain valleys. Language unwritten. Muslims 100%(Sunnis).
8348	0	5	3.46	0	14.10	85.90	A	0.05	867	2	Southern corner of Kohistan District, Batera area. A few in India. 50% of men are bilingual in Pashto, Shina, or Kohistani. Muslims 100%.
8349	2	10	5.14	6	59.60	40.40	B	1.30	299	4	Refugees from East Pakistan in 1947, 1972. Muslims 82%, Hindus 10%. D=COP,RCC.
8350	0	5	2.79	0	25.00	75.00	A	0.91	415	3	Northeast Pakistan. A few in northwest India. Rajputs. Muslims 99%.
8351	0	4	1.62	0	19.10	80.90	A	0.07	376	2	In Chitral. Animists 99%, with priest-shamans, worshipping Imra as supreme creator. M=AoG,WEC.
8352	1	4	6.47	0	25.20	74.80	A	0.18	812	3	In Quetta and Kalat region (no cities). Transhumance and some nomadism. Some bilingual in Baluchi. Pastoralists. Muslims 100%(Sunnis). D=Ch of Pakistan.
8353	3	10	0.31	8	99.79	0.21	C	444.05	26	10	Expatriates from Britain, in development, commerce. D=Ch of Pakistan,SDA,JWs.

Continued overleaf

Table 8-2 continued

PEOPLE		POPULATION				IDENTITY CODE		LANGUAGE		CHURCH		MINISTRY		SCRIPTURE	
Ref	Ethnic name	P%	In 1995	In 2000	In 2025	Race	Language	Autoglossonym	S	AC	Members	Jayuh dwa xcmc mi		Biblioglossonym	Pub ss
1	2	3	4	5	6	7	8	9	10	11	12	13-17 18 19 20 21 22		23	24-26 27
8354	Burig (Purig-pa)	0.26033	354,685	407,373	684,667	MSY50r	70-AAAC-d	purik		0.20	815	0.... 5 4 3 0 0		Purigskad*	PN. .
8355	Burusho (Burusho, Hunza)	0.06188	84,308	96,832	162,744	CNN25z	46-AAAA-a	proper burushaski		0.03	29	0.... 3 3 4 1 3		Burushaski	. . . .
8356	Central Pathan	1.10000	1,498,688	1,721,315	2,892,997	CNT24a	58-ABDA-ch	mahsudi		0.10	1,721	1cs. 5 4 3 2 0			pnb .
8357	Damel (Shintari, Swati)	0.00386	5,259	6,040	10,152	CNT24z	59-AAAE-a	dameli		0.03	2	0.... 3 2 3 0 0			. . . .
8358	Deghwari	0.00933	12,712	14,600	24,538	CNT24z	58-AACC-n	dehwari		0.00	0	1csu. 0 1 0 0 0			. . . .
8359	Dhatki Marwari (Bhil)	0.09335	127,184	146,077	245,510	CNN25o	59-AAFG-a	sindhi-marwari		0.20	292	1.s.. 5 4 3 0 2		Marwari	PN. .
8360	Dogri	0.60000	817,466	938,899	1,577,998	CNN25n	59-AAFE-1	dogri		2.00	18,778	1asu. 6 5 6 2 1		Panjabi: Dogri*	PNb .
8361	Dumaki (Dom, Bericho)	0.00042	572	657	1,105	CNN25i	59-AADB-k	dumaki		0.02	0	0.... 3 2 4 0 0			p. . .
8362	Eastern Baluch	1.94627	2,651,683	3,045,585	5,118,685	CNT24b	58-AABA-a	east balochi	5	0.00	0	1.s.. 0 4 4 0 3		Baluchi: Eastern*	P.. b
8363	Eastern Pathan	7.99118	10,887,532	12,504,851	21,016,781	CNT24a	58-ABDA-c	pakhto	14	0.21	26,260	1as.. 5 5 7 1 4		Pashto*	PNB b
8364	French	0.00200	2,725	3,130	5,260	CEW21b	51-AABI-d	general français		87.00	2,723	1B.uh 10 9 14 3 3		French	PNB b
8365	Gagre	0.04286	58,394	67,069	112,722	CNT24z	58-ABDC	wakhi cluster		5.00	3,353	0.... 7 6 6 2 1		Wakhi	... b
8366	Galo	0.00177	2,412	2,770	4,655	CNN25i	59-AADB-ca	chilas		0.02	1	0.... 5 1 3 2 0 0			p. . .
8367	Goanese	0.03308	45,070	51,765	87,000	CNN25d	59-AAPU-o	konkani-gomantaki		37.00	19,153	3asu. 9 9 13 4 3		Konkani: Goan*	PNb b
8368	Gowro (Gabaro)	0.00016	218	250	421	CNN25i	59-AACC-a	kalami		0.01	0	0.... 3 2 2 0 0			. . . .
8369	Guhjali (Wakhani, Khik)	0.00699	9,523	10,938	18,384	CNT24z	58-ABDC	wakhi cluster		0.02	2	0.... 3 3 2 0 0		Wakhi	... b
8370	Gujarati (Bajania)	0.60000	817,466	938,899	1,577,998	CNN25e	59-AAFH-b	standard gujaraati		2.99	28,073	2A.u. 6 5 8 3 1		Gujarati	PNB b
8371	Gujuri Rajasthani	0.23054	314,098	360,756	606,320	CNN25o	59-AAFG-o	gujuri		0.80	2,886	1.s.. 5 4 4 2 2		Gujari	pn. .
8372	Han Chinese	0.00496	6,758	7,762	13,045	MSY42a	79-AAAB-ba	kuo-yü		0.11	9	2Bsuh 5 3 2 3 0		Chinese: Kuoyu*	PNB b
8373	Hazara (Afghan Persian)	0.05265	71,733	82,388	138,469	MSY41z	58-AACC-eo	central hazaragi		0.05	41	1asu. 4 3 2 1 3			pnb .
8374	Hindi	0.20000	272,489	312,966	525,999	CNN25g	59-AAFO-e	general hindi		0.50	1,565	3Asuh 5 4 8 1 3		Hindi	pnb b
8375	Indus Kohistani	0.16548	225,457	258,948	435,212	CNN25i	59-AACE-a	maiya		0.00	0	0.... 4 1 2 0 0			. . . .
8376	Jat (Awan)	0.01000	13,624	15,648	26,300	CNN25h	59-AAFF-i	jad-gali		2.10	329	1cs.. 6 5 3 1 0			pnb .
8377	Jewish	0.00058	790	908	1,525	CMT35		standard urdu		0.00	0	2Asuh 0 2 2 0 0		Urdu	. . . b
8378	Kalash (Kalashamon)	0.00356	4,850	5,571	9,363	CNN25i	59-AABA-b	kalasha		0.10	6	0.... 5 3 2 0 2		Kalasha	. . . .
8379	Kalkoti	0.00326	4,442	5,101	8,574	CNN25i	59-AACD-a	kalkoti		0.01	1	0.... 3 2 2 0 0			. . . .
8380	Kamdeshi (Shekhani)	0.00134	1,826	2,097	3,524	CNT24d	58-ACBA-d	kam-viri		0.00	0	0.... 3 0 2 0 0			. . . .
8381	Kanauri (Kanawari)	0.00300	4,087	4,694	7,890	MSY50r	70-ABAB-d	kanauri		0.01	0	0.... 3 3 3 0 2		Kanauri	P.. .
8382	Kashmiri	0.07898	107,606	123,590	207,717	CNN25i	59-AAFA-e	siraji-kashmiri		0.36	445	2..... 5 4 4 1 2		Kashmiri	PNB .
8383	Khetrani	0.01000	13,624	15,648	26,300	CNN25n	59-AAFE-rd	khetrani		1.00	156	1csu. 6 3 6 0 0			pnb n
8384	Kho (Chitrali, Khowar)	0.17229	234,735	269,605	453,122	CNN25i	59-AABA-a	kho-war		0.01	27	0.... 3 1 0 0 0			. . . .
8385	Khistani (Garwi)	0.03734	50,874	58,431	98,204	CNN25i	59-AACC-a	kalami		0.04	23	0.... 3 4 5 0 3			. . . b
8386	Kolai (Kohistani-Shina)	0.22501	306,563	352,103	591,776	CNN25i	59-AADB-e	kolai		0.01	35	0.... 3 2 2 0 0		Kohistani, Indus	p... .
8387	Kongri Dogri (Kangra)	0.03000	40,873	46,945	78,900	CNN25n	59-AAFE-1	dogri		2.00	939	1asu. 6 4 4 1 1		Panjabi: Dogri*	PNb .
8388	Kutchi Kohli (Lohar)	0.06405	87,265	100,227	168,451	CNN25p	59-AAFF-k	wadiyara-koli		0.60	601	1cs.. 5 5 6 2 1		Koli, Kachi	Pnb .
8389	Ladakhi (Budhi, Leh)	0.00500	6,812	7,824	13,150	MSY50r	70-AAAC-a	ladakhi		0.10	8	1.s.. 5 3 3 0 1		Ladakhi	Pn. .
8390	Lassi	0.00700	9,537	10,954	18,410	CNN25p	59-AAFF-e	lasi		0.00	0	1cs.. 0 3 0 0 0			pnb .
8391	Majhi	0.00010	136	156	263	CNN25n	59-AAFE-d	majhi		2.00	3	1asu. 6 4 5 1 0		Panjabi*	PNB b
8392	Meghwar Bhil (Chamar)	0.14002	190,769	219,108	368,252	AUG06a	59-AAFG-e	marwari-bhil		1.00	2,191	1.s.. 6 5 5 2 1			pn. b
8393	Narisati (Arandui)	0.00125	1,703	1,956	3,287	CNN25i	59-AAFE-p	gawar-bati		0.01	0	0.... 3 2 3 0 0			. . . .
8394	Northern Hindko (Hindki)	2.10944	2,873,993	3,300,918	5,547,821	CNN25o	59-AAFE-p	hindko		1.00	33,009	1csu. 6 4 6 1 1		Hindko*	PNb b
8395	Northern Marwari	0.03860	52,590	60,402	101,518	CNN25n	59-AAFG-h	jaipuri		1.00	604	4.s.. 6 4 5 0 2		Jaipuri	Pn. b
8396	Od (Oad)	0.03734	50,874	58,431	98,204	CNN25f	59-AAFF-n	od		2.00	1,169	1csu. 6 4 4 1 1			pnb b
8397	Palula (Dangarik)	0.00075	9,605	11,032	18,541	CNN25i	59-AADA-b	phalura		0.12	13	0.... 5 3 3 0 0			. . . .
8398	Parkari Kachchhi	0.17585	239,586	275,176	462,485	CNN25o	59-AAFF-m	parkari-koli		1.00	2,752	1cs.. 6 4 5 1 0		Koli: Parkari*	PNb b
8399	Persian	0.10000	136,244	156,483	263,000	CNT24f	58-AACC-f	dari-t.		0.05	78	1cs.. 4 4 2 0 1		Dari*	PNb b
8400	Persian	0.04000	54,498	62,593	105,200	CNT24f	58-AACC-c	standard farsi		0.04	25	1Asu. 3 2 2 0 0			PNB b
8401	Prasuni	0.00300	4,087	4,694	7,890	CNT24d	58-ACBB-a	prasuni		0.00	0	0.... 0 1 2 0 0			. . . .
8402	Punjabi	0.10000	136,244	156,483	263,000	CNN25z	59-AAFE-c	general panjabi	95	4.00	6,259	1Asu. 6 5 9 4 1		Panjabi*	PNB b
8403	Punjabi Pahari	0.01000	13,624	15,648	26,300	CNN25h	59-AAFE-a	religious panjabi		0.50	78	1csu. 5 4 4 1 0			pnb .
8404	Rajkoti	0.01000	13,624	15,648	26,300	CNN25i	59-AACC-a	kalami		0.00	0	0.... 3 2 0 0 0			. . . b
8405	Sansi Bhil	0.33751	459,838	528,146	887,650	AUG06a	59-AAFG-ec	sansi		1.00	156	1.s.. 6 5 3 0 0			pn. .
8406	Shina (Dras, Shin)	0.37754	459,838	528,146	887,650	CNN25i	59-AADB-c	chilas-darel		0.02	106	0.... 3 3 4 0 1			p... .
8407	Shumashti	0.01000	13,624	15,648	26,300	CNN25i	59-AAAE-c	shumasti		0.02	3	0.... 3 1 2 0 1			. . . .
8408	Sindhi	11.66818	15,897,237	18,258,736	30,687,281	CNN25p	59-AAFF-a	standard sindhi		0.01	1,826	1as.. 3 4 6 1 3		Sindhi	PNB b
8409	Southern Baluch	1.62610	2,215,469	2,544,573	4,276,638	CNT24b	58-AABA-c	south balochi		0.00	0	1.s.. 0 2 4 0 3		Balochi, Southern	P.. b
8410	Southern Hindko	0.70315	958,002	1,100,311	1,849,283	CNN25o	59-AAFE-p	hindko		1.00	11,003	1csu. 6 4 5 0 1		Hindko*	PNb b
8411	Southern Marwari (Meghwar)	0.04200	57,223	65,723	110,460	CNN25o	59-AAFG-dc	sirohi		0.20	131	1.s.. 5 4 4 2 1		Marwari, Southern	pn. b
8412	Southern Pathan	0.96059	1,308,750	1,503,162	2,526,349	CNT24a	58-ABDA-a	pashto		0.20	3,006	1as.. 5 5 6 1 1			PNB b
8413	Southern Punjabi	9.80000	13,351,947	15,335,349	25,773,973	CNN25n	59-AAFE-r	siraiki		4.30	659,420	2asu. 6 6 7 4 2		Siraiki*	PNb b
8414	Southern Uzbek	0.40000	544,977	625,933	1,051,999	MSY41l	44-AABD-b	south uzbek		0.01	63	1c.u. 3 3 2 0 2			pnb b
8415	Tharadari Koli	0.03517	47,917	55,035	92,497	CNN25p	59-AAFF-1	tharadari-koli		1.00	550	1cs.. 6 3 5 0 0			pnb .
8416	Turk	0.00300	4,087	4,694	7,890	MSY41j	44-AABA-a	osmanli		0.03	1	1A.u. 3 3 1 3 3		Turkish	PNB b
8417	Turkmen	0.00600	8,175	9,389	15,780	MSY41k	44-AABA-e	turkmen		1.00	0	3c.u. 0 3 1 0 2		Turkmen	PNb b
8418	Turvali	0.05601	76,310	87,646	147,306	CNN25i	59-AACF	torwali cluster		0.00	0	0.... 0 4 5 1 2			... b
8419	Uighur	0.00500	6,812	7,824	13,150	MSY41z	44-AABD-d	east uyghur		0.05	4	1r.u. 4 4 5 1 0		Uighur*	PNB b
8420	Urdu	7.46763	10,174,224	11,685,583	19,639,846	CNN25r	59-AAFO-d	standard urdu	65	0.01	1,169	2Asuh 3 4 6 2 3		Urdu	PNB b
8421	Urmuri (Ormui)	0.00352	4,796	5,508	9,258	CNT24a	58-ABEA-b	ormuri		0.50	28	0.... 5 3 4 0 1			. . . .
8422	Ushojo (Ushuji)	0.00154	2,098	2,410	4,050	CNN25i	58-AADB-g	ushojo		0.00	0	0.... 0 3 4 0 0			p.. b
8423	Vaghri Koli	0.00234	3,188	3,662	6,154	CNN25p	59-AAFF-je	vagdi		1.00	37	1cs.. 6 3 3 0 0			pnb .
8424	Wadiyara Koli	0.08793	119,800	137,596	231,256	CNN25p	59-AAFF-ka	wadiyara		1.00	1,376	1cs.. 6 3 3 0 0			pnb .
8425	Wanetsi	0.06916	94,227	108,224	181,891	CNT24a	58-ABDA-e	wanechi		0.00	0	1cs.. 0 3 0 0 0			. . . b
8426	Western Baluch	0.69196	942,756	1,082,801	1,819,853	CNT24b	58-AABA-b	west balochi		0.00	0	3.s.. 0 3 3 0 2		Baluchi: Western*	P... .
8427	Western Pathan (Afghani)	3.10000	4,223,575	4,850,978	8,152,991	CNT24a	58-ABDA-a	pashto		0.10	4,851	1As.. 5 4 3 2 1			pnb b
8428	Western Punjabi (Lahnda)	42.69493	58,169,433	66,810,373	112,287,548	CNN25n	59-AAFB-p	panjabi-pahari		4.40	2,939,656	2Asuh 6 6 7 4 3			P.. b
8429	Yudgha (Yidga)	0.00435	5,927	6,807	11,440	CNT24z	58-ADB-b	yidgha		0.09	6	0.... 4 4 5 0 0			. . . .
8430	Zangskar (Zaskar)	0.00400	5,450	6,259	10,520	MSY50r	70-AAAC-e	zangskari		0.03	2	1.... 3 2 0 0 0		Zangskari	Pn. .
8431	other minor peoples	0.20000	272,489	312,966	525,999	...				0.10	313	5 5 3 3 0			
Palau		**100.00000**	**17,225**	**19,426**	**33,228**					**94.57**	**18,371**				
8432	Filipino	9.70000	1,671	1,884	3,223	MSY44o	31-CKAA-a	proper tagalog		97.00	1,828	4Bs.. 10 10 12 0 0		Tagalog	PNB b
8433	Palauan	77.30000	13,315	15,016	25,685	MPY54c	31-SAAA-a	palau		96.00	14,416	1.s.. 10 9 13 5 3		Palauan	PN. b
8434	Sonsorolese	5.00000	861	971	1,661	MPY54f	38-AABA	sonsorol cluster		90.00	874	0.... 10 9 9 0 0			. . . .
8435	USA White	3.00000	517	583	997	CEW19s	52-ABAC-s	general american		90.00	525	1Bsuh 10 9 13 5 3		English*	PNB b
8436	other minor peoples	5.00000	861	971	1,661	...				75.00	728	10 9 7 5 0			
Palestine		**100.00000**	**1,955,251**	**2,215,393**	**4,132,562**					**8.5**	**188,290**				
8437	Armenian	0.20000	3,911	4,431	8,265	CEW14	57-AAAA-b	ashkharik		88.00	3,899	4A.u. 10 9 13 5 3		Armenian: Modern, Eastern	PNB b
8438	Assyrian (Aisor, Chaldean)	0.10000	1,955	2,215	4,133	CMT31	12-AAAA-d	east syriac		85.00	1,883	1as.. 10 9 8 5 2		Syriac: Ancient*	PNB b
8439	Bedouin	0.05000	978	1,108	2,066	CMT30	12-AACD	badawi-sahara cluster		0.10	1	0a... 5 3 2 1 0			PN. b
8440	British	0.05000	978	1,108	2,066	CEW19i	52-ABAC-b	standard-english		78.00	864	3Bsuh 10 9 13 5 2			PNB b
8441	Circassian	0.08500	1,662	1,883	3,513	CEW17a	42-AAAA-b	cherkes		0.12	2	1a... 5 3 2 0 0			pn. b
8442	Egyptian Arab	1.50000	29,329	33,231	61,988	CMT30	12-AACF-a	masri		15.00	4,985	2Asuh 8 5 10 5 2		Arabic*	PNB b
8443	French	0.10000	1,955	2,215	4,133	CEW21b	51-AABI-d	general français		84.00	1,861	1B.uh 10 9 14 5 1		French	PNB b
8444	German	0.10000	1,955	2,215	4,133	CEW19m	52-ABCE-a	standard hoch-deutsch		86.00	1,905	2B.uh 10 9 13 5 1		German*	PNB b
8445	Greek	0.08500	1,662	1,883	3,513	CEW20	56-AAAA-c	dhimotiki		95.00	1,789	2B.uh 10 9 11 5 2		Greek: Modern	PNB b
8446	Italian	0.10000	1,955	2,215	4,133	CEW21e	51-AABQ-c	standard italiano		83.00	1,839	2B.uh 10 9 15 5 3		Italian	PNB b
8447	Jewish	10.50000	205,301	232,616	433,919	CMT35	12-AABA-b	ivrit-x.		0.10	233	2B.uh 5 4 6 5 0		Hebrew	PNB b
8448	Nawar Gypsy (Kurbat)	0.23000	4,497	4,431	8,265	CNN25f	59-ACAA-a	domari		10.00	443	0a... 6 5 1 3 0			. . . b
8449	Palestinian/Gazan Arab	82.93100	1,621,509	1,837,248	3,427,175	CMT30	12-AACF-f	syro-palestinian		8.80	161,678	1Asuh 7 5 12 5 1		Arabic: Lebanese*	Pnb b
8450	Romanian	0.04200	821	930	1,736	CEW21i	51-AADC-a	limba româneasca		80.00	744	3A.u. 10 7 10 4 1		Romanian	PNB b
8451	Russian	0.07600	1,486	1,684	3,141	CEW22j	53-AAAE-d	russkiy		70.00	1,179	4B.uh 10 8 11 5 2		Russian	PNB b
8452	Russian Jew	3.00000	58,658	66,462	123,977	CMT35	53-AACF-d	russkiy		2.10	1,396	4B.uh 6 4 2 3 0		Russian	PNB b
8453	Samaritan (Shomronim)	0.03100	606	687	1,281	CMT35	12-AACF-f	syro-palestinian		0.00	0	1Asuh 0 4 2 4 1 0		Arabic: Lebanese*	pnb b
8454	Syrian Arab	0.50000	9,776	11,077	20,663	CMT30	12-AACF-f	syro-palestinian		7.00	775	1Asuh 7 5 7 5 1		Arabic: Lebanese*	Pnb b
8455	USA White	0.05000	978	1,108	2,066	CEW19s	52-ABAC-s	general american		74.00	820	1Bsuh 10 9 13 5 3		English*	PNB b
8456	West Aramaic	0.10000	1,955	2,215	4,133	CMT31	12-AAAA-b	west neo-aramaic		60.00	1,329	1cs.. 10 7 8 4 1		Aramaic: Ancient	PNb b
8457	other minor peoples	0.20000	3,911	4,431	8,265	...				10.00	665	8 5 7 3 0			
Panama		**100.00000**	**2,630,993**	**2,855,683**	**3,779,174**					**86.04**	**2,457,064**				
8458	Bribri	0.07000	1,842	1,999	2,645	MIR39e	83-EBBB-a	bribri		75.00	1,499	0.s.. 10 7 7 5 2		Bribri	P.. b
8459	Buglere (Bogota)	0.11200	2,947	3,198	4,233	MIR39e	83-ECAB	buglere cluster		75.00	2,399	0.... 10 7 11 4 1		Buglere	PN. .
8460	Catio (Katio)	0.00200	53	57	76	MIR39e	83-EIAA-d	catio		92.00	53	0.... 10 7 11 4 1		Catio*	Pn. .
8461	Colombia Cuna (Paya)	0.02800	737	800	1,058	MIR39e	83-EGAA-ba	paya-pucuro		70.00	740	0.... 10 7 10 4 1		Kuna: Paya-pucuro*	PN. .
8462	East Indian	4.00000	105,240	114,227	151,167	CNN25g	59-AAFO-e	general hindi		10.00	11,423	3Asuh 8 5 6 2 0			pnb b
8463	Eastern Guaymi	1.30000	34,203	37,124	49,129	MIR39e	83-ECAA-b	east ngobere	3	70.00	25,987	0.... 10 7 7 5 3		Guaymi: Eastern	P... .
8464	French	1.00000	26,310	28,557	37,792	CEW21b	51-AABI-d	general français	4	84.00	23,988	1B.uh 10 9 14 5 3		French	PNB b
8465	Greek	0.08000	2,105	2,285	3,023	CEW20	56-AAAA-c	dhimotiki		95.00	2,170	2B.uh 10 9 11 5 1		Greek: Modern	PNB b
8466	Guaymi (Chiriqui)	2.60000	68,406	74,248	98,259	MIR39e	83-ECAA-a	west ngobere		92.00	68,308	0.... 10 9 12 5 3		Guaymi	P.. b
8467	Half-Indian (Part-Indian)	3.10000	81,561	88,526	117,154	MIR37e	51-AABB-hh	panameño		90.70	80,293	1B.uh 10 9 16 5 3			pnb b
8468	Han Chinese (Cantonese)	0.79000	20,785	22,560	29,855	MSY42a	79-AAAM-e	central yue	2	34.00	7,670	3A.uh 9 6 8 5 2		Chinese, Yue	PNB b
8469	Han Chinese (Hakka)	0.67000	17,628	19,133	25,320	MSY42a	79-AAAJ-h	literary hakka		28.00	5,357	1A.. 9 5 8 4 1		Chinese: Hakka, Wukingfu*	PNB b
8470	Han Chinese (Taiwanese)	0.03000	789	857	1,134	MSY42a	79-AAAJ-h	quan-zhang-taiwan		22.00	188	1A.. 9 5 8 4 1		Taiwanese	PNB b
8471	Italian	0.50000	13,155	14,278	18,896	CEW21e	51-AABQ-c	standard italiano		83.00	11,851	2B.uh 10 9 15 5 3		Italian	PNB b

Continued opposite

Table 8-2 continued

EVANGELIZATION								EVANGELISM			ADDITIONAL DESCRIPTIVE DATA
Ref 1	D 28	aC 29	CG% 30	r 31	E 32	U 33	W 34	e 35	R 36	T 37	Locations, civil divisions, literacy, religions, church history, denominations, dioceses, church growth, missions, agencies, ministries, movements 38
8354	0	4	4.50	0	20.20	79.80	A	0.14	837	3	North Kashmir, near border; also in India and Tibet. All Shia Muslims 100%.
8355	0	4	3.42	0	18.03	81.97	A	0.02	675	2	Hunza-Nagir area. A few in India. Literates 20%. Some bilingual in Khowar. Muslims 100%(66% Ismaili/Nizari,33% other Shia). M=OM,SERVE,UP,FI.
8356	0	6	5.28	1	30.10	69.90	A	0.11	683	3	Waziristan, Bannu, Karak. Distinct from other Pashto languages. Muslims 99%(Sunnis).
8357	0	5	0.70	0	14.03	85.97	A	0.01	332	2	In Damel Valley, east side of Kunar river. Second language: Khower. Pastoralists in southern Chitral. Muslims 100%.
8358	0	4	0.00	1	16.00	84.00	A	0.00	0	1.09	Central Baluchistan Province, in Kalat and Mastung. Influenced by Brahui. Muslims 100%.
8359	0	6	3.43	0	26.20	73.80	A	0.19	463	3	Lower Sindh in Tharparkar and Sanghar Districts. Related to northern Marwari. Some use Sindhi, Urdu. Muslims 80%, Hindus 20%. M=Indus Christian Fellowship.
8360	2	6	4.93	5	47.00	53.00	A	3.43	349	4	Foothills of Jammu and Kashmir. Muslims 90%, a few Hindus, Sikhs. D=COP,RCC(PA-Jammu & Kashmir). M=MHM.
8361	0	5	0.00	0	16.02	83.98	A	0.01	0	2	Gilgit Agency. Related to Shina. Close to Gilgit language. Musicians and blacksmiths. Muslims 80%, animists 10%, Buddhists 10%.
8362	0	4	0.00	1	21.00	79.00	A	0.00	0	1.08	Northeast Baluchistan Province, NW Sindh, SW Punjab; 20% in Karachi slums. 7% literate. Muslims 100%(Hanafi Sunnis, Zigri sectarians). M=Red Sea Team.
8363	1	6	8.19	5	53.21	46.79	B	0.40	536	3	North West Frontier Province. Many in UAE. Muslims 99%(Hanafi Sunnis,some Shias). D=COP. M=ABC,DPM,Legaspia Ch(Mexico),OM,WBM,WVI,WEC,WMPL.
8364	1	10	2.44	8	99.87	0.13	C	508.08	59	10	Expatriates from France, in development. D=RCC(6 Dioceses). M=SJ,OP,OFM,MHM,FSC.
8365	4	6	5.99	0	34.00	66.00	A	6.20	563	4	Tribals, largely animists 90%. D=Brethren,COP,Pentecostals,SDA. M=PCUSA.
8366	0	4	0.00	0	13.02	86.98	A	0.01	210	2	Koli, Palas, Jalkot area of Indus Kohistan: scattered families. Integrated into Shina. Muslims 80%(Sunnis), animists 10%, Buddhists 10%.
8367	1	8	1.89	4	99.37	0.63	B	136.40	78	7	Hindus 50%, strong Catholics 37%, in Karachi. D=RCC(M-Karachi). M=SJ,OFM,OP,MHM,FIC,PFM.
8368	0	5	0.00	0	13.01	86.99	A	0.00	0	1.05	Indus Kohistan on eastern bank near Koli and Palas; originally from Swat. Related to Shina. Muslims 80%, animists 10%, Buddhists 10%.
8369	0	5	0.70	0	13.02	86.98	A	0.01	358	2	Northeast Chitral; glacier area. Also in former USSR, Afghanistan, China. Many refugees. Muslims 100%.
8370	1	8	5.35	6	59.99	40.01	B	6.54	290	4	Lower Punjab, Sindh; mainly in India, also Bangladesh. Close to Patani. Muslims 75%, Hindus 25% and still strong in some areas (Bajania,&c). D=Ch of Pakistan.
8371	1	6	7.11	0	29.80	70.20	A	0.87	746	3	Kashmir Gujuri. Chitral, Swat Kohistan. Also Afghanistan, India. Home area Gujranwala. Nomads, pastoralists. Low literacy. Muslims 69%(Sunnis), Hindus 30%.
8372	0	9	2.22	7	51.11	48.89	B	0.20	154	3	Originally from China. Traders, merchants. Buddhists/Chinese folk-religionists 100%.
8373	0	6	3.78	4	36.05	63.95	A	0.06	348	2	Quetta. Mainly in Afghanistan, Iran. Related to Dari. Agriculturalists, pastoralists. Muslims 100%(Imami Shias, some Ismailis, few Sunnis). M=TEAM,OM.
8374	3	8	0.94	7	57.50	42.50	B	1.04	92	4	Hindi-speaking Muslims from India after 1947. Muslims 60%, Hindus 40%. D=COP,RCC,SA.
8375	0	4	0.00	0	9.00	91.00	A	0.00	0	1.03	Indus Kohistan District on western bank of Indus river. Muslims 80%, animists 10%, Buddhists 10%.
8376	0	6	3.56	1	31.10	68.90	A	2.38	403	4	Southeast Baluchistan Province, southwest Sindh. (Also, 20% of all Punjabis are called Jats). Nomads, traders, camel drivers. Muslims 90%, Hindus 7%.
8377	0	10	0.00	5	41.00	59.00	A	0.00	0	1.13	Small community of practicing Jews, with synagogue in Karachi.
8378	0	5	1.81	0	17.10	82.90	A	0.06	450	2	Chitral District, Rumbur, Bumboret, Birir Valleys. Related to Kohwar. Pastoralists, agriculturalists. Animists 50%(in north), Muslims 50%(in south). M=GRI,OM.
8379	0	5	0.00	0	13.01	86.99	A	0.00	211	1.04	Dir Kohistan, in Kalkot village. Close to second language Kalami. Muslims 99%(Sunnis).
8380	0	1	0.00	0	4.00	96.00	A	0.00	0	1.00	Southern Chitral District; mountain valley. Majority in Afghanistan. Some bilinguals in Pashto. Muslims 100%(Sunnis).
8381	2	5	0.00	0	19.01	80.99	A	0.00	0	1.06	Near Tibet border; also in Tibet and India. Hindus 40%, Lamaist Buddhists 40%, animists 20%. D=Moravian Ch,SA.
8382	2	6	3.87	0	35.36	64.64	A	0.46	377	3	Jammu, Kashmir south of Shina. Majority in India. Muslims 100%(94% Sunnis,6% Shias). D=COP,RCC. R=TWR.
8383	0	5	2.79	1	32.00	68.00	A	1.16	329	4	Northeast Baluchistan Province. Related to Siraiki, influenced by Baluchi. Muslims 99%.
8384	0	4	3.35	0	10.01	89.99	A	0.00	1,191	1.03	Major language of Chitral; lingua franca. Also in India. Sizeable Pathan minority lives on their land. Muslims 99%(95% Hanafi Sunnis,4% Ismailis).
8385	0	5	3.19	0	22.04	77.96	A	0.03	521	2	Bashkarik. Upper Swat Kohistan from Peshmal and Kalam north, also Dir Kohistan. Bilingual in Pashto. Muslims 98%(Sunnis). M=Christian Brethren,TEAM,SFM.
8386	0	5	3.62	0	14.01	85.99	A	0.00	904	1.05	Kolai-Palas area of Indus Kohistan. Main language in Kohistan. Muslims 98%(mainly Sunnis).
8387	2	6	4.65	5	42.00	58.00	A	3.06	372	4	Foothills of Jammu and Kashmir. All Muslims since 1947(when local Hindus fled to India) 98%. D=COP,RCC(PA-Jammu & Kashmir). M=MHM.
8388	6	5	4.18	1	35.60	64.40	A	0.78	399	3	Lower Sindh around Hala and Tando Adam. Hindus 90%, many animists and Muslims. D=COP,RCC,SDA,National Ch of Pakistan,Swedish Pentecostal Ch,UPCP.
8389	1	5	2.10	0	22.10	77.90	A	0.08	467	2	In far east of Kashmir near China border. Most in Indian Kashmir, few in Tibet. Literates 15%. Buddhists 52%(Red Hat Lamaists), Muslims 47%. D=Moravian Ch.
8390	0	4	0.00	1	17.00	83.00	A	0.00	0	1.08	Southeast Baluchistan Province, Las Bela District. Influenced by Baluchi, Sindhi. Muslims 100%.
8391	0	5	1.10	5	45.00	55.00	A	3.28	131	4	Lahore District. Also in India. Purest form of Panjabi. Muslims 98%.
8392	6	6	4.19	0	33.00	67.00	A	1.20	431	4	Northern Bhil tribes, in Sindh. 2% literates in Sindhi or Urdu. Hindus 90%, many Muslims. D=COP,RCC,ICF,SDA,ARPC,Pentecostals. M=CBFMS.
8393	0	5	0.00	0	17.01	82.99	A	0.00	0	1.05	In southern Chitral, south of Kalasha, on left bank of Kunar river; also villages in Afghanistan. Second language: Pashto. Muslims 100%(Sunnis).
8394	0	5	8.44	1	38.00	62.00	A	1.38	681	4	Hazara Division up to Kohistan. Few bilinguals. Muslims 99%(Sunnis). M=TEAM.
8395	0	6	4.19	0	34.00	66.00	A	1.24	418	4	South Punjab north of Dadu and Nawabshah. Many bilinguals in Sindhi, also Urdu. Hindus 86%, some Muslims. M=CBFMS,Indus Christian Fellowship.
8396	2	6	4.88	1	39.00	61.00	A	2.84	415	4	Widely scattered in Sindh, some in south Punjab. Bilinguals in Sindhi, Urdu. Brickmakers. Hindus 90%, Muslims 8%. D=RCC,ICF. M=CBFMS.
8397	0	5	2.60	0	16.12	83.88	A	0.07	612	2	Villages on east lower Chitral Valley, Dir Kohistan. Muslims 100%(Sunnis).
8398	0	5	5.78	1	33.00	67.00	A	1.20	563	4	Tharparkar District, especially Nagar Parkar town. Hindus 92%, some animists, some Muslims.
8399	0	6	4.45	4	36.05	63.95	A	0.06	391	2	Afghanis, from Afghanistan. Muslims 80%, Baha'is 10%, Zoroastrians 10%. M=WVI.
8400	0	6	3.27	5	38.04	61.96	A	0.05	286	2	Refugees, merchants from Iran. Muslims 60%(Imami Shias), Baha'is 40%.
8401	0	5	0.00	0	10.00	90.00	A	0.00	0	1.03	From Nuristan. Muslims 100%(Sunnis, though with animistic elements).
8402	0	6	3.78	5	58.00	42.00	B	8.46	228	4	Indian Punjabis using Gurmukhi script. Muslims 94%(82% Hanafi Sunnis,8% Ithna-Ashari Shias,4% Ahmadis). M=YWAM.
8403	0	5	4.45	1	27.50	72.50	A	0.50	544	3	Himalayas foothills from Pakistan to Nepal. A string of divergent dialects. Muslims 99%.
8404	0	1	0.00	0	4.00	96.00	A	0.00	0	1.02	Dir Kohistan, in Rajkot and Patrak villages. Some bilinguals in Pashto. Muslims 100%.
8405	0	5	2.79	0	28.00	72.00	A	1.02	371	4	Northwestern Sindh. Bhils by caste. Second language: Sindhi, then Urdu and Panjabi. Professional beggars. Muslims 80%, Hindus 15%.
8406	0	5	2.39	0	17.02	82.98	A	0.01	546	2	Gilgiti. Upper Indus mountains. Some in India. Few literates. Muslims 80%(56% Sunnis,24% Shias), animists 10%, Buddhists 10%(Brokpas). M=Central Asian M.
8407	0	5	1.10	0	14.02	85.98	A	0.01	410	2	On Chitral frontier. Muslims 100%(Sunnis). M=GR.
8408	3	6	5.35	4	49.01	50.99	A	0.01	355	2	70% cultivators. Muslims 99%(Hanafi Sunnis, many being Mujahir (migrants from India); with sects Memons, Bohras, Shia Khojas). D=RCC(D-Hyderabad),COP,ICF.
8409	0	4	0.00	1	21.00	79.00	A	0.00	0	1.08	Baluchistan, south Sindh, Karachi. Also Oman, Iran, UAE. Literates 7%. Muslims 100%(Hanafi Sunnis; 32%(700,000) Zigri sectarians/semi-Muslims). M=WEC,FI.
8410	0	5	7.25	1	36.00	64.00	A	1.31	632	4	Attock District, Punjab Province; Hazara division, NWFP. Bilingual in Urdu, Pashto, Punjab. Plains, low hills. Muslims 99%(Sunnis). M=TEAM. R=FEBA.
8411	4	6	2.61	0	32.20	67.80	A	0.23	307	3	Sindh between Tando Mohammed Khan/Tando Ghulam Ali/Nawabshah. Bilingual in Sindhi, Urdu. Hindus 98%, many Muslims. D=COP,RCC,SDA,ICF. M=CBFMS.
8412	0	5	5.87	5	44.20	55.80	A	0.32	502	3	Quetta, Khost area; Baluchi Pashto. Unintelligible to Eastern Pushtu. Muslims 100%(Hanafi Sunnis). M=CMS,TEAM,FI. R=FEBA,TWR.
8413	6	6	3.86	4	57.30	42.70	B	8.99	235	4	Saraiki, Bahawalpuri. Strong literary tradition. Muslims 96%(Hanafi Sunnis,some Shias). Many converts to churches since 1960. D=RCC,COP,UPCP,SA,ARPC,BM. .
8414	0	4	4.23	5	29.01	70.99	A	0.01	466	2	Refugees from Afghanistan war. Most in Afghanistan; also Germany, Turkey. Muslims 95%(Hanafi Sunnis). M=CSI,WEC. R=HCJB,FEBC,KTWR.
8415	0	6	4.09	1	31.00	69.00	A	1.13	450	4	Lower Thar Desert, west to Mirpur Khas. Hindus 90%, animists 5%, Muslims 4%.
8416	6	8	0.00	8	50.03	49.97	B	0.05	39	2	From Turkey. Muslims 100%(Hanafi Sunnis, with some Shias). D=RCC,COP,UPCP,SA,ARPC,BM.
8417	0	4	0.00	1	24.00	76.00	A	0.00	0	1.11	Many refugees from Afghanistan, Iran; also in Turkey, USA, Germany. Carpet weavers, merchants. Muslims 100%(Hanafi Sunnis). M=CSI,WEC.
8418	0	5	0.00	0	19.00	81.00	A	0.00	0	1.05	Swat Kohistan, both sides of Swat river from Madyan north to Asrit, and Chail Valley. Men bilingual in Pashto, fewer in Urdu. Muslims 100%(Sunnis). M=AoG,TEAM.
8419	0	4	1.40	4	37.05	62.95	A	0.06	163	2	Gilgit. Also in China, Russia, Iran, Afghanistan, Mongolia, Turkey, Taiwan. Traders. Muslims 99%(Hanafi Sunnis).
8420	1	6	4.88	5	51.01	48.99	B	0.01	317	2	Most in India; also Bahrain, Oman, Qatar, Fiji, Germany, Afghanistan, Mauritius, UAE. Muslims 100%(Hanafi Sunnis). D=RCC(D-Hyderabad). M=YWAM.
8421	0	5	3.39	0	18.50	81.50	A	0.33	831	3	Kaniguram northwest of Dera Ismail Khan, Waziristan. Muslims 100%(Sunnis). M=GR.
8422	0	4	0.00	0	12.00	88.00	A	0.00	0	1.05	Upper reaches of Bishigram(Chail) Valley, east of Madyan, Swat Kohistan. Second language Pashto; Urdu limited. Muslims 99%(Sunnis).
8423	0	6	3.68	1	29.00	71.00	A	1.05	442	4	Sindh. 500 families. Some literate in Sindhi, Urdu, Gujarati. Masons, fruit vendors. Hindus 90%, animists 6%, some Muslims 3%.
8424	0	6	5.05	1	30.00	70.00	A	1.09	553	4	Sindh, bounded by Hyderabad/Tando Allahyar/Mirpur Khas, and Matli/Jamesabad. Hindus 90%, animists, some Muslims.
8425	0	1	0.00	1	14.00	86.00	A	0.00	0	1.07	Northeast Baluchistan Province. Close to Pashto. Muslims 100%.
8426	0	4	0.00	1	18.00	82.00	A	0.00	0	1.07	Northwest Baluchistan Province. Also in Iran, Afghanistan. Muslims 100%(Hanafi Sunnis, Zigri sectarians). M=FI,CSI. R=TWR,FEBA.
8427	0	6	6.38	5	42.10	57.90	A	0.15	560	3	From 1979, vast influx of 3 million refugees from Afghanistan. Muslims 100%(Hanafi Sunnis). M=many agencies. R=FEBA,TWR.
8428	9	6	3.93	4	48.40	51.60	A	7.77	282	4	Muslims 96%(84% Hanafi Sunnis,8% Ithna-Ashari Shias,4% Ahmadis). D=RCC(6 Dioceses),COP(4 Dioceses),UPCP,SA,NVCP,LCC,NMCP,ARPC,AOC. M=CMS.
8429	0	5	1.81	0	15.09	84.91	A	0.05	510	2	Upper Lotkuh Valley of Chitral. Majority in Afghanistan(called Munji there). Mountain valleys. Muslims 100%(Ismailis).
8430	0	5	0.70	0	15.03	84.97	A	0.01	432	2	In Kashmir, India, Tibet. Lamaist Buddhists 95%, some Muslims.
8431	0	6	2.56		19.10	80.90	A	0.07	367	2	Parsis(in Karachi), USA Whites(CC,SDA,JWs), Irish(Cooneyites), Filipinos(OMF), Tajiks(OM). Many Qizilbash. Muslims 70%, Hindus 10%, nonreligious 7%.
Palau											
8432	0	0	5.35	5	99.97	0.03	C	527.53	111	10	Immigrants from the Philippines. D=RCC.
8433	5	7	2.02	5	99.96	0.04	C	550.12	46	10	D=Palau Ch(Modekngei,healing movement begun 1912, now 30% of population),RCC(D-Carolines-Marshalls), SDA,AoG,PCCI. M=UCC,CAMACOP(Philippines).
8434	0	0	4.57	2	99.90	0.10	C	367.92	127	9	Tobi, Pulo Anna, Merir, Helen, and Sonsorol Islands. Some on Saipan. Related to Ulithi. D=RCC.
8435	3	6	1.83	8	99.90	0.10	C	525.60	47	10	Expatriates from USA in administration, government, military. D=AoG,SDA,RCC.
8436	0	6	3.66		99.75	0.25	C	281.96	97	8	Other Pacific Islanders, Japanese, Koreans, Chinese. Buddhists 17%, folk-religionists 5%.
Palestine											
8437	3	10	2.04	6	99.88	0.12	C	526.76	44	10	Gregorians. D=Armenian Apostolic Ch(P-Jerusalem; also rival C-Sis, in Gaza),RCC,CON.
8438	2	10	2.01	5	99.85	0.15	C	468.47	49	10	East Syrians. Nestorian and Chaldean refugees. D=Ancient Ch of the East(P-Tehran),Chaldean Catholic Ch.
8439	0	3	0.00	7	30.10	69.90	A	0.11	64	3	Nomadic tribes, tent-dwellers. Muslims 100%(Sunnis).
8440	1	10	3.61	8	99.78	0.22	C	429.89	86	10	Expatriates from Britain in development, commerce, industry. D=Episcopal Ch/ECJME(D-Jerusalem). M=CMS,JEM.
8441	0	6	0.70	0	28.12	71.88	A	0.12	166	3	In 10 countries. Muslims 100%(Hanafi Sunnis).
8442	2	9	2.24	8	85.00	15.00	B	46.53	95	6	Northeastern Colloquial Arabic. Immigrant workers. Muslims 80%(Shafi Sunnis). D=Coptic Orthodox Ch(D-Jerusalem),RCC.
8443	1	10	4.40	8	99.84	0.16	C	475.23	95	10	Expatriates from France, in development, commerce. D=RCC(P-Jerusalem of the Latins). M=OFMCustody.
8444	3	10	5.39	8	99.86	0.14	C	499.10	113	10	Expatriates from Germany, in business. D=ELCJ,NAC,RCC. M=BJ.
8445	2	10	2.12	7	99.95	0.05	C	582.54	51	10	From Greece. Traders. D=Greek Orthodox Ch(P-Jerusalem),RCC(P-Jerusalem of the Melkites).
8446	1	10	1.99	7	99.83	0.17	C	475.63	52	10	Expatriates from Italy, in business. D=RCC(P-Jerusalem of the Latins). M=OFMCustody,OCD,OP,SJ,AA.
8447	0	10	3.20	5	56.10	43.90	B	0.20	190	3	Recent Israeli settlers in West Bank, 95% Orthodox Jews(progressively secularized).
8448	0	9	3.86	7	42.00	58.00	A	15.33	319	5	Palestinian Gypsies. Arab Gypsies, Muslim Gypsies. Nomadic. Muslims 90%.
8449	5	6	1.76	8	72.80	27.20	B	23.38	93	5	Northeastern Colloquial Arabic. Muslims 86%(Shafi Sunnis, Druzes, strong Alawis(Sufi brotherhood, Ahmadis). D=GOC,RCC,ELCJ,ECJME,BM. M=FMB-SBC.
8450	1	10	4.40	6	99.80	0.20	C	417.56	106	10	From Romania. D=Romanian Orthodox Ch(P-Bucharest).
8451	2	10	4.89	7	99.70	0.30	C	362.81	94	9	From USSR since 1917. Nonreligious 25%. D=ROC(P-Moscow),ROCOR.
8452	0	6	5.06	7	51.10	48.90	B	3.91	308	4	Massive influx of new settlers from USSR, 1986-92; many settled on West Bank. Only 30% practicing Jews. Nonreligious 38%.
8453	0	10	0.00	8	43.00	57.00	A	0.00	0	1.14	As-Samarah. A Jewish sect dating from 8th century B.C. In Nablus; mainly based on West Bank, but some in Israel.
8454	2	9	1.39	8	69.00	31.00	B	17.63	83	5	From Syria in origin. Muslims 87%(Hanafi Sunnis,Alawi Shias,Ahmadis). D=SOC(D-Jerusalem),RCC.
8455	7	10	4.51	8	99.74	0.26	C	399.74	100	9	Expatriates from USA, in development, industry, commerce. D=ELCJ,ECJME,CGP,SDA,COG,JWs,CON.
8456	1	10	5.01	1	99.60	0.40	C	247.47	138	8	In and around Nablus. Also in Lebanon and Syria. Bilingual in Arabic. Muslims 40%. D=RCC(Maronites).
8457	0	10	4.29		43.00	57.00	A	23.54	273	5	Amhara(EOC), Lebanese Arabs(Maronites), Jordanian Arabs(Melkites), other Europeans, Asians. Muslims 69%.
Panama											
8458	2	8	2.69	0	99.75	0.25	C	317.55	79	9	Amerindian tribe primarily in Costa Rica. Animists 20%, some Baha'is. D=RCC,SDA.
8459	3	7	2.69	0	99.75	0.25	C	320.28	78	9	Western mountains. Animists 24%, a few Baha'is. D=RCC(D-David),SDA,COG. M=OAR,SIL.
8460	1	10	2.62	0	99.92	0.08	C	456.68	66	10	Almost all live in Colombia(animists very numerous there). Animists 8%. D=RCC.
8461	3	7	2.70	0	99.70	0.30	C	288.71	81	8	Southeastern Panama. About half live in Colombia. Animists 20%, many Baha'is. D=RCC(VA-Darien),SDA,FWBC. M=CMF,NAFWB,FMB,NTM,IAMS,SIL.
8462	0	10	7.29	7	67.00	33.00	B	24.45	339	5	Traders from India. Muslims 78%, Hindus 8%, Baha'is 4%.
8463	5	7	2.69	0	99.70	0.30	C	286.16	81	8	Western provinces. Animists 20%, many Baha'is. D=RCC(6 Dioceses),SDA,COG,CJCLdS,ICFG. M=OAR,SJ,CMF.
8464	3	10	2.69	8	99.84	0.16	C	490.56	63	10	Expatriates from France, in business. D=RCC(6 Dioceses),SDA,JWs.
8465	1	10	5.53	7	99.95	0.05	C	575.60	107	10	Traders, Panama City. D=Greek Orthodox Ch (AD-North & South America).
8466	5	7	2.69	0	99.92	0.08	C	456.68	67	10	Ngabere. Many Baha'is, few animists. D=RCC(D-David),SDA,COG,CJCLdS,ICFG. M=OAR,SJ,CMF,GMU,SIL,NTM,MMS,PAMS,Baptist Mission.
8467	3	10	3.98	8	99.91	0.09	C	515.45	81	10	Mixed-race persons, mostly urban. Many Baha'is. D=RCC,SDA,CJCLdS. M=LCMS.
8468	2	10	5.48	8	99.34	0.66	B	129.06	162	7	Merchants in towns. Buddhists/Chinese folk-religionists 56%, nonreligious 10%. D=RCC,et alia. M=Chinese Christian Mission,FMB-SBC.
8469	1	10	4.36	7	92.00	8.00	B	94.02	149	6	Immigrants from mainland China. Folk Buddhists 62%, nonreligious 10%. D=RCC.
8470	1	10	2.71	5	84.00	16.00	B	67.45	110	6	From Taiwan. Folk Buddhists 76%, some nonreligious. D=RCC.
8471	1	10	2.69	7	99.83	0.17	C	487.75	63	10	Expatriates from Italy, in business. D=RCC(6 Dioceses). M=CMF,OAR,SJ,FSC.

Continued overleaf

Table 8-2 continued

PEOPLE		POPULATION				IDENTITY CODE		LANGUAGE		CHURCH		MINISTRY						SCRIPTURE		
Ref 1	Ethnic name 2	P% 3	In 1995 4	In 2000 5	In 2025 6	Race 7	Language 8	Autoglossonym 9	S 10	AC 11	Members 12	Jayuh 13-17	d 18	wa 19	xc 20	mc 21	mi 22	Biblioglossonym 23	Pub 24-26	ss 27
8472	Jamaican Black	4.60000	121,026	131,361	173,842	NFB68a	52-ABAF-m	jamaican-creole		55.00	72,249	1c..h	10	6	8	5	1	West Carib Creole English	pn.	b
8473	Japanese	0.05000	1,315	1,428	1,890	MSY45a	45-CAAA-a	koku-go		8.00	114	1B.uh	7	5	8	5	0	Japanese	PNB	b
8474	Jewish	0.13500	3,552	3,855	5,102	CMT35	51-AABB-hh	panameño		0.10	4	1B.uh	5	4	2	5	0		pnb	b
8475	Lebanese Arab	0.20000	5,262	5,711	7,558	CMT30	12-AACF-f	syro-palestinian		54.00	3,084	1Asuh	10	7	8	5	2	Arabic: Lebanese*	Pnb	b
8476	Northern Embera (Empera)	0.36700	9,656	10,480	13,870	MIR39e	83-EIAA-a	sambú		85.00	8,908	0....	10	10	10	5	3	Embera, Northern	PN.	.
8477	Palestinian Arab	0.20000	5,262	5,711	7,558	CMT30	12-AACF-f	syro-palestinian		25.00	1,428	1Asuh	9	5	8	5	0	Arabic: Lebanese*	Pnb	b
8478	Panamanian Black	0.20000	5,262	5,711	7,558	NFB68a	52-ABAF-i	colûn-creole		97.00	5,540	1c..h	10	9	10	5	2		pn.	.
8479	Panamanian Mestizo	58.09600	1,528,502	1,659,038	2,195,549	CLN29	51-AABB-hh	panameño		94.30	1,564,472	1B.uh	10	10	13	5	3		pnb	b
8480	Panamanian Mulatto	9.40000	247,313	268,434	355,242	NFB68b	52-ABAF-i	colûn-creole		96.00	257,697	1c..h	10	10	9	5	3		pn.	.
8481	Panamanian White	4.64000	122,078	132,504	175,354	CLT27	51-AABB-hh	panameño		84.90	112,496	1B.uh	10	10	13	5	1		pnb	b
8482	San Blas Cuna (Kuna)	2.00000	52,620	57,114	75,583	MIR39e	83-EGAA-a	cuna-sanblas		85.00	48,547	4....	10	10	8	5	3	Kuna: San Blas*	PN.	.
8483	Spaniard	1.00000	26,310	28,557	37,792	CEW21k	51-AABB-hh	panameño		95.00	27,129	1B.uh	10	10	15	5	3		pnb	b
8484	Syrian Arab	0.20000	5,262	5,711	7,558	CMT30	12-AACF-f	syro-palestinian		7.00	400	1Asuh	7	5	8	5	2	Arabic: Lebanese*	Pnb	b
8485	Teribe (Quequexque)	0.08000	2,105	2,285	3,023	MIR39e	83-EAAA-b	east naso		65.00	1,485	0....	10	8	6	5	2	Teribe	P..	.
8486	USA Black	0.16000	4,210	4,569	6,047	NFB68a	52-ABAE-a	talkin-black		90.00	4,112	0B.uh	10	9	11	5	3		pnb	b
8487	USA White	4.04000	106,292	115,370	152,679	CEW19s	52-ABAC-s	general american	15	87.00	100,372	1Bsuh	10	9	13	5	1	English*	PNB	b
8488	Waunana (Nonama)	0.12000	3,157	3,427	4,535	MIR39e	83-EIAB	noanama cluster		65.00	2,227	0....	10	10	6	5	3	Waunana*	PN.	.
8489	West Indian Black	0.13000	3,420	3,712	4,913	NFB68a	52-ABAF	carib-anglo-creol cluster		90.00	3,341	1a..h	10	9	11	5	3	West Carib Creole English	PN.	b
8490	other minor peoples	0.10000	2,631	2,856	3,779	...				60.00	1,713		10	7	6	5	3			
	Papua New Guinea	**100.00000**	**4,116,728**	**4,608,145**	**7,173,798**					**82.15**	**3,785,526**									
8491	Abaga	0.00473	195	218	339	AON10b	24-OEAA-a	abaga		90.00	196	0....	10	7	11	5	2		...	n
8492	Abasakur	0.02400	988	1,106	1,722	AON10b	22-HABA-a	abasakur		80.00	885	0....	10	7	7	4	1		...	.
8493	Abau (Green River)	0.14333	5,901	6,605	10,282	AON10b	26-BAAA-a	abau		84.00	5,548	0.s..	10	8	7	5	2	Abau	P..	.
8494	Abie (Abia, Mori, Jari)	0.01678	691	773	1,204	AON10b	23-GACB	aneme-wake cluster		80.00	619	0....	10	7	7	5	1	Aneme Wake	PN.	b
8495	Abulas (Ambulas, Maprik)	0.42573	17,526	19,618	30,541	AON10b	26-HCBA-b	maprik	1	86.00	16,872	0....	10	8	7	5	1	Ambulas: Maprik	PN.	.
8496	Abulas (Wosera)	1.10999	45,695	51,150	79,628	AON10b	26-HCBA	ambulas cluster	1	93.00	47,569	0....	10	8	7	5	3	Ambulas	PN.	.
8497	Adjora (Adjoria)	0.06657	2,741	3,068	4,776	AON10b	26-PBAC-a	proper abu		80.00	2,454	0....	10	7	7	5	2	Abu	P..	.
8498	Aeka (Aiga)	0.06307	2,596	2,906	4,525	AON10b	23-ABCA-a	aeka		85.00	2,470	0....	10	7	7	4	1		...	p
8499	Agala (Sinale)	0.00946	389	436	679	AON10b	24-KGCA-a	agala		40.00	174	0....	9	6	3	4	0		...	.
8500	Agarabi (Agarabe)	0.40363	16,616	18,600	28,956	AON10b	24-PACB-a	agarabi	1	88.00	16,368	0....	10	7	7	5	1	Agarabi	P..	n
8501	Agi	0.01779	732	820	1,276	AON10b	27-HBBA-a	agi		80.00	656	0....	10	7	6	4	0		...	.
8502	Agob (Upiala-Bituri, Dabu	0.09527	3,922	4,390	6,834	AON10b	20-MAAB-a	agöb		80.00	3,512	0....	10	7	7	5	1		...	b
8503	Aiku (Menandon, Wiaki)	0.02583	1,063	1,190	1,853	AON10b	27-HBDA-a	aiku		85.00	1,012	0....	10	7	9	4	0		...	.
8504	Aimele	0.01577	649	727	1,131	AON10b	24-KIGA-b	aimele		10.00	73	0....	8	5	3	4	1		p..	.
8505	Ainbai	0.00338	139	156	242	AON10b	21-IAAC-a	ainbai		80.00	125	0....	10	7	7	5	2		...	.
8506	Aiome Pygmy (Ayom)	0.02368	975	1,091	1,699	AUG05	26-VABA-a	aiome		80.00	873	0....	10	7	7	5	2		...	.
8507	Aion	0.02703	1,113	1,246	1,939	AON10b	26-PBAA-a	aion		85.00	1,059	0....	10	7	9	5	2		...	.
8508	Ak	0.00262	108	121	188	AON10b	26-CBAA-a	ak		30.00	36	0....	9	5	6	4	0		...	.
8509	Akolet	0.02930	1,206	1,350	2,102	AON09b	35-FAAC-f	a-kolet		90.00	1,215	0....	10	7	11	5	3		p..	.
8510	Akrukay	0.00602	248	277	432	AON10b	26-TDCA-a	akrukay		90.00	250	0....	10	7	11	4	1		...	.
8511	Alamblak (Alambuk)	0.04051	1,668	1,867	2,906	AON10b	26-KAAA	alamblak cluster		30.00	560	0....	9	5	6	5	3	Alamblak	P..	n
8512	Alatil (Aruop, Aru, Eru)	0.00394	162	182	283	AON10b	27-HBGA-a	alatil		90.00	163	0....	10	7	11	4	0		...	.
8513	Alauagat	0.01056	435	487	758	AON10b	27-HBFA-a	bragat		90.00	438	0....	10	7	11	4	0		...	.
8514	Ama (Apaka, Abi, Aboa)	0.01293	532	596	928	AON10b	25-WAAA-a	ama		30.00	179	0....	9	5	6	5	1	Ama	PN.	.
8515	Amaimon	0.01154	475	532	828	AON10b	22-JAAA-a	amaimon		90.00	479	0....	10	7	11	4	1		...	.
8516	Amal	0.01224	504	564	878	AON10b	26-BBBA-a	amal		30.00	169	0....	9	5	6	4	0		...	.
8517	Amanab	0.12285	5,057	5,661	8,813	AON10b	21-HEAA	amanab cluster		80.00	4,529	0....	10	7	7	4	2	Amanab	...	.
8518	Ambasi (Tain-Daware)	0.03784	1,558	1,744	2,715	AON10b	23-ABBB-a	ambasi		85.00	1,482	0....	10	7	8	4	1		...	p
8519	Ambul (Palik)	0.01296	534	597	930	AON09b	35-FAAC-d	a-palik		76.00	454	0....	10	7	6	4	0		p..	p
8520	Amele (Amere, Amale)	0.14313	5,892	6,596	10,268	AON10b	22-PDDA-a	amele		95.00	6,266	0....	10	7	6	4	1	Amele	PN.	.
8521	Ampale (Safeyoka)	0.07738	3,186	3,566	5,551	AON10b	24-RABA	ampeeli cluster		75.00	2,674	0....	10	8	6	5	1	Ampeeli*	PN.	n
8522	Amto	0.00725	298	334	520	AON10b	25-VAAA-a	amto		20.00	67	0....	9	5	3	4	1		...	.
8523	Andarum	0.03418	1,407	1,575	2,452	AON10b	26-TAAA-a	andarum		80.00	1,260	0....	10	7	7	4	1		...	.
8524	Andra-Hus (Ahus)	0.02840	1,169	1,309	2,037	AON09b	35-BADB	andra-hus cluster		80.00	1,047	0....	10	7	7	4	1		...	.
8525	Anem	0.01387	571	639	995	AON10b	27-NAAA-a	anem		90.00	575	0....	10	7	11	4	1		...	.
8526	Angaatiha (Langimar)	0.03071	1,264	1,415	2,203	AON10b	24-RBAA-a	angaatiha		75.00	1,061	0....	10	7	7	4	2	Angaatihe*	P..	.
8527	Angaua	0.05045	2,077	2,325	3,619	AON10b	22-CAAA-a	nent		80.00	1,860	0....	10	8	7	5	1	Nend	...	.
8528	Angave (Wunavai, Buu)	0.04321	1,779	1,991	3,100	AON10b	24-RAFA	ankave cluster		20.00	398	0....	9	5	4	5	1	Ankave	PN.	.
8529	Anggor (Watapor, Senagi)	0.03446	1,419	1,588	2,472	AON10b	21-UABA	angor cluster		80.00	1,270	0....	10	7	7	4	2	Anggor*	P..	.
8530	Anglo-Australian	1.30000	53,517	59,906	93,259	CEW19c	52-ABAC-x	general australian		75.00	44,929	1Bsuh	10	9	13	5	3		pnb	b
8531	Angoram (Pondo)	0.19552	8,049	9,010	14,026	AON10b	27-DCAA-a	angoram		95.00	8,559	0....	10	7	7	4	1		...	.
8532	Annaberg (Rao)	0.15608	6,425	7,192	11,197	AON10b	26-UAAA-a	rao		50.00	3,596	0.s..	10	5	3	4	1	Rao	P..	.
8533	Anor	0.02129	876	981	1,527	AON10b	26-VAAA-a	anor		90.00	883	0....	10	7	11	4	1		...	.
8534	Anuki (Gabobora)	0.01709	704	788	1,226	AON09b	34-FCBA-a	gabo-bora		90.00	709	0....	10	7	11	4	1		...	.
8535	Aomie (Upper Managalasi)	0.02971	1,223	1,369	2,131	AON10b	23-CBBA-b	asapa		80.00	1,095	0....	10	7	7	4	1	Omie	PN.	.
8536	Arafundi (Meakambut)	0.02312	952	1,065	1,659	AON10b	26-OAAA-a	alfendio		10.00	107	0....	8	5	3	4	0		...	.
8537	Aramba (Serki)	0.01849	761	852	1,326	AON10a	20-LDCA-a	aramba		30.00	256	0....	9	5	4	4	2	Aramba	...	.
8538	Aramo (Aramaue)	0.00946	389	436	679	AON10b	24-MDAA-a	hagahai		40.00	174	0....	9	5	3	4	1		...	.
8539	Arawe (Arove)	0.06938	2,856	3,197	4,977	AON09b	35-FAAA-e	a-rawe		80.00	2,558	0....	10	7	7	5	3	Solong	...	.
8540	Arawum	0.00237	98	109	170	AON10b	22-UCAA-a	arawum		90.00	98	0....	10	7	11	3	0		...	.
8541	Aregerek (Musar)	0.02157	888	994	1,547	AON10b	22-GGAA-a	musar		90.00	895	0....	10	7	11	4	1		...	.
8542	Ari (Waruna)	0.03571	1,470	1,646	2,562	AON10b	24-JBBA-a	ari		30.00	494	0....	9	5	6	4	1		...	n
8543	Arifama-Miniafia	0.07528	3,099	3,469	5,400	AON09b	34-FAAA	miniafia-arifama cluster		80.00	2,775	0....	10	7	7	3	1	Miniafia*	P..	.
8544	Arinua (Lolopani,Ruruhip)	0.04975	2,048	2,293	3,569	AON10b	27-IEBA-c	heyo		80.00	1,834	0....	10	7	7	3	2		...	.
8545	Arop (Waropu)	0.05550	2,285	2,558	3,981	AON09b	34-BFAA-b	arop-malala		80.00	2,046	0....	10	7	7	4	1	Arop-lokep	P..	.
8546	Aruek (Djang)	0.01936	797	892	1,389	AON10b	27-JAAA-a	aruek		90.00	803	0....	10	7	11	3	0		...	.
8547	Arufe (Nambo)	0.05401	2,223	2,489	3,875	AON10b	20-LEAA-a	nambu		80.00	1,991	0....	10	8	6	5	1	Arufe*	P..	.
8548	Aruop (Lauisaranga)	0.01862	767	858	1,336	AON10b	27-HBEA-a	aruop		90.00	772	0....	10	7	11	3	0		...	.
8549	Asaro (Upper Asaro, Kongi	0.81015	33,352	37,333	58,119	AON10b	24-OBAA-a	dano	1	88.00	32,853	0....	10	8	7	5	2	Dano	PN.	.
8550	Asas (Kow)	0.01050	432	484	753	AON10b	22-RCAA-a	asas		90.00	435	0....	10	7	11	3	0		...	.
8551	Asat	0.03545	1,459	1,634	2,543	AON10b	24-SBBG-a	asat		90.00	1,470	0....	10	7	11	5	2		...	.
8552	Atemble (Atemple)	0.00205	84	94	147	AON10b	22-CABA-a	atemble		95.00	90	0....	10	7	11	3	0		...	.
8553	Aturu (Atura)	0.00696	287	321	499	AON10b	20-NAAB-a	aturu		90.00	289	0....	10	7	11	4	1		...	.
8554	Au	0.12614	5,193	5,813	9,049	AON10b	27-HADA-a	au		90.00	5,231	0....	10	7	7	5	3	Au	PN.	.
8555	Aunalei (Onele, Oni, Seta	0.06957	2,864	3,206	4,991	AON10b	27-GAAA-a	aunalei		80.00	2,565	0....	10	7	6	5	1		...	.
8556	Avau (Awau)	0.18000	7,410	8,295	12,913	AON09b	35-FAAE-a	a-vau		90.00	7,465	0....	10	7	10	5	1		...	.
8557	Awa (Mobuta)	0.05642	2,323	2,600	4,047	AON10b	24-PAAA	awa cluster		60.00	1,560	0....	10	5	5	4	1	Awa	PN.	.
8558	Awar	0.02122	874	978	1,522	AON10b	26-RBBA-b	nubia		90.00	880	0....	10	7	11	5	2		...	.
8559	Awara	0.04000	1,647	1,843	2,870	AON10b	24-SEAA-a	awara		80.00	1,475	0....	10	7	8	0	0	Awara	...	.
8560	Awin (West Awin, Aekyom)	0.21604	8,894	9,955	15,498	AON10b	24-KFAA	awin cluster		90.00	8,960	0.s..	10	7	6	4	1	Aekyom	PN.	.
8561	Awiyaana (Auyana)	0.24110	9,925	11,110	17,296	AON10b	24-PABA-a	awiyaana		84.00	9,333	0....	10	7	7	5	1	Awiyaana	PN.	.
8562	Awun	0.01211	499	558	869	AON10b	26-CCAA-a	awun		30.00	167	0....	9	5	5	4	0		...	.
8563	Azera (Adzera, Acira)	0.55833	22,985	25,729	40,053	AON09b	34-CABB	central adzera cluster	1	90.00	23,156	0....	10	8	7	5	2	Adzera	PN.	.
8564	Bagupi	0.00183	75	84	131	AON10b	22-PCBA-a	bagupi		95.00	80	0....	10	7	11	4	1		...	.
8565	Bagwa Zimakani	0.03872	1,594	1,784	2,778	AON10b	24-ICAB-a	proper zimakani		30.00	535	0....	9	5	6	4	1	Zimakani	PN.	.
8566	Bahinemo (Gahom, Wogu)	0.01009	415	465	724	AON10b	26-JBAA-a	bahinemo		90.00	418	0....	10	7	11	4	2	Bahinemo	P..	n
8567	Baibai	0.00855	352	394	613	AON10b	25-QAAA-a	baibai		30.00	118	0....	9	5	6	3	0		...	.
8568	Baimak	0.01391	573	641	998	AON10b	22-PCHA-a	baimak		80.00	513	0....	10	7	7	4	1		...	.
8569	Baining (Makakat)	0.17148	7,059	7,902	12,302	AON10b	27-RAAC	qaqet cluster		89.00	7,033	0....	10	7	7	5	2	Baining: Qaqet*	PN.	.
8570	Baiyer Enga (Kyaka)	0.48464	19,951	22,333	34,767	AON10b	24-LDAB-k	kyaka		87.00	19,430	0.s..	10	8	7	5	3	Enga: Kyaka*	PN.	.
8571	Bali	0.19483	8,021	8,978	13,977	AON09b	35-DCAB-a	bali		90.00	8,080	0...h	10	7	7	5	2		...	.
8572	Baluan-Pam	0.03071	1,264	1,415	2,203	AON09b	35-BDAA	baluan-pam cluster		80.00	1,132	0....	10	7	7	5	2		...	.
8573	Bam	0.01341	552	618	962	AON10b	24-SEBA-a	bam		90.00	556	0....	10	7	11	3	0		...	.
8574	Bam (Biem)	0.04588	1,889	2,114	3,291	AON09b	34-BBCA-d	biem		85.00	1,797	0....	10	7	7	3	1		...	.
8575	Bamu (Kiwaibora, Sisiame)	0.11517	4,741	5,307	8,262	AON10b	20-PACA-a	wakau		95.00	5,042	0....	10	7	7	4	1	Bamu	P..	.
8576	Banaro	0.06266	2,580	2,887	4,495	AON10b	26-QAAA-a	banaro		80.00	2,310	0....	10	8	7	5	1	Banaro	...	.
8577	Bao (Psokok, Sokhok)	0.03394	1,397	1,564	2,435	AON09b	35-GAAA-e	psokhok		95.00	1,486	0....	10	7	11	5	2		p..	.
8578	Barai (Mogoni, Umwate)	0.11128	4,581	5,128	7,983	AON10b	23-CBAA-b	barai		80.00	4,102	0....	10	7	6	5	2	Barai	PN.	.
8579	Baramu	0.01657	682	764	1,189	AON10b	20-NAAA	lewada-dewara cluster		90.00	687	0....	10	8	8	0	0	Tirio	P..	.
8580	Bariai	0.02826	1,163	1,302	2,027	AON09b	34-BJCC-a	bariai		80.00	1,042	0....	10	7	7	4	1	Bariai	...	.
8581	Bariji	0.00990	408	456	710	AON10b	23-GAAA-a	bariji		90.00	411	0....	10	7	11	4	1		...	b
8582	Barim	0.01135	467	523	814	AON09b	34-BFAC-a	barim		90.00	471	0....	10	7	11	4	1		...	.
8583	Barok (Komalu, Kanapit)	0.06424	2,645	2,960	4,608	AON09b	35-CFAA-a	barok		80.00	2,368	0....	10	7	7	5	1	Barok	P..	.
8584	Baruga (Tugari)	0.04243	1,747	1,955	3,044	AON10b	23-ABGA-a	songadi-karisoa		80.00	1,564	0....	10	7	6	5	1	Baruga	...	b
8585	Baruya (Barua, Usirampia)	0.17965	7,396	8,279	12,888	AON10b	24-RAAB-b	baruya		87.00	7,202	0....	10	8	7	5	1	Baruya	PN.	.
8586	Bau	0.06636	2,732	3,058	4,761	AON10b	22-PDAB-b	bau		80.00	2,446	0....	10	7	7	4	1		...	.
8587	Bauwaki	0.01347	555	621	966	AON10b	23-GBAA	bauwaki cluster		90.00	559	0....	10	7	11	4	1		...	b
8588	Beami (Bedamuni, Mougulu)	0.13245	5,453	6,103	9,502	AON10b	24-KIAA	beami cluster		70.00	4,272	0....	10	5	5	4	1	Bedamuni*	PN.	.
8589	Bebeli	0.03225	1,328	1,486	2,314	AON09b	35-GAAB	kapore-bebeli cluster		90.00	1,338	0....	10	7	11	4	1		...	.
8590	Beli	0.04778	1,967	2,202	3,428	AON10b	27-IBAA-a	beli		80.00	1,761	0....	10	7	7	5	1		...	.
8591	Bemal (Kein)	0.01890	778	871	1,356	AON10b	22-PEBA-a	bemal		10.00	87	0....	8	5	5	1	1		...	.
8592	Bembi	0.05007	2,061	2,307	3,592	AON10b	25-PAAA-a	fas		50.00	1,154	0....	10	6	6	2	0		...	.
8593	Benabena (Bena-Bena)	0.64065	26,374	29,522	45,959	AON10b	24-OBBA-a	benabena	1	89.00	26,275	0....	10	8	7	5	1	Bena-bena*	PN.	.

Continued opposite

Table 8-2 continued

EVANGELIZATION								EVANGELISM			ADDITIONAL DESCRIPTIVE DATA
Ref 1	*D* 28	*aC* 29	*CG%* 30	*r* 31	*E* 32	*U* 33	*W* 34	*e* 35	*R* 36	*T* 37	*Locations, civil divisions, literacy, religions, church history, denominations, dioceses, church growth, missions, agencies, ministries, movements* 38
8472	4	10	2.69	8	99.55	0.45	B	224.84	81	8	Migrant laborers from Jamaica. Afro-American spiritists 10%. D=CBP,EC,IAPN,RCC. M=FMB-SBC.
8473	0	10	2.46	7	69.00	31.00	B	20.14	127	5	Expatriates from Japan, in commerce. Buddhists/New-Religionists 92%(Nichiren Shoshu).
8474	0	10	1.40	8	50.10	49.90	B	0.18	114	3	Small communities of Spanish-speaking practicing Jews.
8475	2	10	5.90	8	99.54	0.46	B	236.52	151	8	Traders, merchants from Lebanon. Muslims 40%. D=RCC(Maronites,Melkites),GOC.
8476	7	6	2.69	0	99.85	0.15	C	406.42	70	10	Jungles near Colombian border. Animists 14%, many Baha'is. D=RCC(VA-Darien),IEU,SDA,FWBC,COG,CJCLdS,ICFG. M=CMF,OAR,SJ,MB,NAFWB,RCM,ICs.
8477	0	10	5.09	8	86.00	14.00	B	78.47	184	6	Recent immigrants from Holy Land. Muslims 72%(Shafi Sunnis,Druzes).
8478	5	10	2.69	8	99.97	0.03	C	552.31	58	10	Persons of African origin. West Indian Blacks. D=RCC,EC,SDA,IAPN,MCCA. M=ECUSA,MMS.
8479	7	10	2.50	8	99.94	0.06	C	572.39	50	10	Mixed-race White/Amerindians. D=RCC(6 Dioceses),ICFG,Episcopal Ch,SDA,CBP,IAPN,COG. M=CMF,OAR,SJ,USPG,FMB,LCMS. R=AWR. T=LESEA.
8480	12	10	2.69	8	99.96	0.04	C	550.12	59	10	Black/White mixed-race persons. D=RCC,ICFG,EC,SDA,CBP,CB,SA,IAPN,CON,COG,MCCA,CBM. M=CMF,SJ,MMS,CBFMS,LCMS,FMB.
8481	2	10	2.69	8	99.85	0.15	C	473.81	64	10	Originally from Spain, descendants of conquistadores. D=RCC,IEU. M=MB.
8482	7	7	2.69	0	99.85	0.15	C	418.83	68	10	San Blas Islands. Language isolate. Animists 10%, many Baha'is. D=RCC(VA-Darien),SDA,FWBC,COG,CJCLdS,ICFG,MEP. M=CMF,NAFWB,SJ,PAMS,RCM.
8483	1	10	2.69	8	99.95	0.05	C	575.60	60	10	Long-time citizens originally from Spain. D=RCC. M=SJ,CMF,FSC,FMB,UBS,LBI.
8484	2	10	3.76	8	69.00	31.00	B	17.63	177	5	From Syria. Muslims 80%(Hanafi Sunnis,Alawis,Ahmadis). D=SOC,RCC.
8485	3	8	2.69	0	99.65	0.35	C	249.11	87	8	Northwestern area. Animists 30%, Baha'is. D=RCC(PN-Bocas del Toro),SDA,COG. M=OAR,SIL.
8486	4	10	2.69	8	99.90	0.10	C	515.74	58	10	Expatriates from USA in military, business. D=CBP,COG,CoGiC,NBCA.
8487	10	10	2.69	8	99.87	0.13	C	511.25	61	10	Expatriates in business, commerce. D=RCC,ICFG,EC,SDA,CBP,SA,CJCLdS,JWs,CC,CGP. M=FMB.
8488	7	7	2.69	0	99.65	0.35	C	256.23	84	8	In southeast lowlands. Animists 30%, many Baha'is. D=RCC(VA-Darien),IEU,SDA,COG,CJCLdS,ICFG,FWBC. M=CMF,OAR,MB,SJ,NAFWB,RCM,SIL.
8489	4	10	2.69	8	99.90	0.10	C	509.17	59	10	Migrant workers from Caribbean islands. D=RCC,IAPN,EC,MCCA. M=ECUSA,MMS,FMB.
8490	0	8	2.69		96.00	4.00	C	210.24	77	8	Germans(ELCP), Brazilians(ICAB,RCC), Nicaraguans, Colombians, Dutch(M=MCFOM), French Creoles, Costarricans, Guyanese.
Papua New Guinea											
8491	2	7	3.02	0	99.90	0.10	C	427.05	86	10	Eastern Highlands Province, Goroka District. Bilingual in Kamano, Benabena. D=SDA,ELCPNG.
8492	1	6	4.59	0	99.80	0.20	C	321.20	141	9	Madang Province. Sawai river. Related to Koguman. Nominal Christians 20%. D=Evangelical Lutheran Church of Papua New Guinea.
8493	2	5	6.52	0	99.84	0.16	C	364.85	175	9	Sandaun Province, Sepik and Green rivers in 28 villages southwest of Namie. Also in Irian Jaya. Animists 2%. D=CB,SSEC(few). Many churches, much activity.
8494	2	6	4.21	0	99.80	0.20	C	347.48	122	9	Oro Province, both sides of Owen Stanley Range. Bilingual in Motu and Yareba. D=Anglican Ch of PNG,RCC. M=SIL.
8495	5	6	7.71	0	99.86	0.14	C	392.37	192	9	East Sepik Province, Maprik District. Tropical forest. Animists 2%. D=60% New Apostolic Ch; also AoG,RCC,SDA,SSEC,NTM. M=SIL.
8496	5	6	8.84	0	99.93	0.07	C	454.86	203	10	East Sepik Province, Maprik District. Related to Kaunga. 80 villages. D=AoG,RCC,SDA,SSEC,NTM.
8497	2	6	5.66	0	99.80	0.20	C	335.80	160	9	Madang and East Sepik Provinces, Ramu river. D=Lutheran Ch(ELCPNG),RCC.
8498	1	6	5.66	0	99.85	0.15	C	362.99	158	9	Oro Province around Kikinonda village. Close to Orokaiva language. Swamps and foothills. D=Anglican Church of PNG.
8499	0	7	2.90	0	64.00	36.00	B	93.44	170	6	Western Province, Upper Strickland river. Closest to Kalamo and Konai. Animists 55%.
8500	3	5	3.55	0	99.88	0.12	C	401.50	101	10	Eastern Highlands Province, Kainantu District. Close to Gadsup. Savannah. Animists 2%. D=ELCPNG,SDA,et alia. M=SIL.
8501	0	7	4.27	0	99.80	0.20	C	315.36	135	9	Sandaun Province. Many nominal Christians.
8502	4	7	6.04	0	99.80	0.20	C	344.56	165	9	Western Province. Savannah. 3 government schools. D=UCPNG,ECP,SDA,One Way. Motu and Kiwai used. M=APCM/UFM.
8503	0	6	4.73	0	99.85	0.15	C	359.89	137	9	Sandaun Province, Maimai Namblo Division, Wemil village, more in West Palei Division.
8504	1	6	4.38	0	35.00	65.00	A	12.77	427	5	Southwest corner of Southern Highlands Province, moved to Wawoi Falls area. Animists 90%. Relatively unevangelized. D=ECP. M=APCM/UFM.
8505	2	6	2.56	0	99.80	0.20	C	329.96	88	9	Sandaun Province, Vanimo District, south of Bewani station; 2 villages. Related to Pagi. D=RCC,SDA.
8506	2	6	4.57	0	99.80	0.20	C	329.96	135	9	Madang Province, 70 miles west of Madang city. Scattered houses. Mountains, valleys. Agriculturalists. Animists 20%. D=Anglican Church of PNG,RCC.
8507	2	6	4.77	0	99.85	0.15	C	375.40	132	9	East Sepik Province. D=ELCPNG,RCC.
8508	0	7	3.65	0	57.00	43.00	B	62.41	227	6	Sandaun Province. Closest to Namia and Awun. Animists 70%.
8509	3	6	4.92	0	99.90	0.10	C	430.33	125	10	West New Britain Province, southwest coast. Tropical forest, coral coast. Dialect chain. D=RCC,Anglican Ch of PNG,SDA.
8510	1	6	3.27	0	99.90	0.10	C	407.34	96	10	Madang Province. D=RCC.
8511	2	5	4.11	0	62.00	38.00	B	67.89	229	6	East Sepik Province, Angoram District. 13 villages. Animists 20%. D=RCC,Evangelical Brotherhood Ch. M=Swiss Evangelical Brotherhood Mission,SVD,SIL.
8512	0	7	2.83	0	99.90	0.10	C	404.05	87	10	Sandaun Province. Many nominal Christians.
8513	0	6	3.85	0	99.90	0.10	C	400.77	110	10	Sandaun Province. A number of Christians are nominal.
8514	2	6	2.93	0	64.00	36.00	B	70.08	171	6	East Sepik Province, Ambunti District, south of Namia. 8 villages. Animists 70%. D=NTM,SDA. M=SIL.
8515	1	6	3.94	0	99.90	0.10	C	407.34	111	10	Madang Province. D=ELCPNG.
8516	0	6	2.87	0	56.00	44.00	B	61.32	193	6	East Sepik Province, Wagana river near confluence with Wanibe Creek. Animists 70%.
8517	1	5	6.31	0	99.80	0.20	C	324.12	182	9	Sandaun Province, Amanab District. Also in Irian Jaya (Indonesia). Forest, mountains. Animists 3%. D=CB. Bible school, center for work in area. M=SIL,CMML.
8518	1	6	5.13	0	99.85	0.15	C	366.09	144	9	Oro Province, a few villages on coast. Close to Binandere language. D=Anglican Church of PNG.
8519	0	6	3.89	0	99.76	0.24	C	291.27	129	8	West New Britain Province, southwest coast and inland. In dialect chain with Gimi, Moewehafen. Animists 6%.
8520	1	5	3.09	0	99.95	0.05	C	443.84	89	10	Madang Province, in hills above Astrolabe Bay. D=Evangelical Lutheran Church of PNG. Nominalism strong. M=SIL.
8521	4	5	5.75	0	99.75	0.25	C	309.33	165	9	Morobe Province; Kaiapit, Lae-Wamba, Menyamya Districts. Bilingual in Tok Pisin, Yabim. Polygamy strong. Animists 2%. D=ELCPNG,some SDA,EMA.
8522	0	6	4.29	0	44.00	56.00	A	32.12	334	5	Sandaun Province, Amanab District, south of Upper Sepik river. Acculturating rapidly. Animists 80%. Relatively unreached tribe. M=CMML.
8523	1	6	4.96	0	99.80	0.20	C	324.12	149	9	Madang Province. Related to Igom. D=RCC.
8524	1	6	4.76	0	99.80	0.20	C	324.12	144	9	Andra and Hus Islands off Manus. Bilingual in Kurti. Close to Ponam. D=RCC.
8525	1	6	4.13	0	99.90	0.10	C	407.34	115	10	West New Britain Province, northwest coast and inland. D=RCC.
8526	1	6	4.77	0	99.75	0.25	C	295.65	148	8	Morobe Province, Menyamya District. Tropical forest, mountains. Agriculturalists. Animists 5%. D=ELCPNG. M=SIL,PNGBTA.
8527	2	6	5.36	0	99.80	0.20	C	329.96	156	9	Madang Province, central, 1 village. D=ELCPNG,RCC. M=PBT.
8528	2	6	3.75	0	52.00	48.00	B	37.96	254	5	Gulf Province in valleys of Mbwei and Swanson rivers. No villages but family hamlets. Animists 60%. D=RCC,SDA. M=SIL.
8529	1	6	4.96	0	99.80	0.20	C	329.96	146	9	Sandaun Province, Amanab District, 11 villages. Forest. D=Plymouth Brethren(work in Tok Pisin; church weak). M=CMML,SIL.
8530	4	10	3.88	8	99.75	0.25	C	394.20	88	9	Expatriates from Australia, in government, business. D=ACPNG(5 Dioceses),RCC(15 Dioceses),UCPNGSI,SDA.
8531	1	5	6.99	0	99.95	0.05	C	433.43	177	10	East Sepik Province, along lower Sepik river near coast, Angoram Sub-Province. D=RCC.
8532	1	5	6.06	0	78.00	22.00	B	142.35	250	7	Madang Province, Keram River area, 80 miles west of Madang city. Swamp. Animists 40%. Relatively unevangelized. D=CC. M=PBT.
8533	1	6	4.58	0	99.90	0.10	C	407.34	125	10	Madang Province. D=RCC.
8534	1	6	4.35	0	99.90	0.10	C	407.34	120	10	Milne Bay Province: north coast, Cape Vogel. Animists 10%. D=Anglican Ch of PNG. Traditional magic strong, hence syncretism widespread.
8535	1	5	4.81	0	99.80	0.20	C	332.88	141	9	Oro Province, Kokoda District, northwest of Managalasi. Forest, mountains. D=Anglican Ch of PNG. M=SIL.
8536	0	5	2.40	0	31.00	69.00	A	11.31	307	5	East Sepik Province on Arafundi river. Animists 90%. Relatively unevangelized.
8537	2	6	3.30	0	58.00	42.00	B	63.51	203	6	Upper Morehead. Western Province, Morehead District, southwest of Suki. 4 primary schools. Related to Rouku. Swamp, savannah. Animists 70%. D=ECP.
8538	0	6	2.90	0	64.00	36.00	B	93.44	170	6	Enga, East Sepik. Related languages: Haruai, Pinai, Wapi. Some speak Tok Pisin. Hunter-gatherers. Declining pop due to poor health. Animists 60%. M=ABFM.
8539	3	5	5.70	0	99.80	0.20	C	335.80	161	9	West New Britain Province, southwestern coast. Tropical forest, coral coast. 3 primary schools. Dialect chain. D=Anglican Ch of PNG,RCC,SDA.
8540	0	7	4.69	0	99.90	0.10	C	400.77	129	10	Madang Province, on coast near Rimbo. Related to Siroi, Pulabu, Kolom, Lemio.
8541	1	6	4.60	0	99.90	0.10	C	407.34	125	10	Madang Province, inland, west of Tokain. Related languages: Kowaki, Mawak, Hinihon, Wanambre. D=RCC.
8542	1	5	3.98	0	59.00	41.00	B	64.60	235	6	Western Province, Aramia River area, 2 villages. Bilingual in Gogodala. Animists 20%. D=ECP. M=APCM/UFM.
8543	1	6	5.79	0	99.80	0.20	C	324.12	169	9	Coast of Oro Province, Tufi District, Cape Nelson to Collingwood Bay. Tropical forest. Fishermen with 25 villages. Literates 10%. D=ACPNG. M=SIL.
8544	2	6	5.35	0	99.80	0.20	C	327.04	157	9	Sandaun Province, Wan Wan Division. Hills, plains, sago swamp. Some use of Tok Pisin. Older women are monolingual. Animists 5%. D=RCC,SSEC.
8545	2	6	5.47	0	99.80	0.20	C	329.96	159	9	Madang Province, half on Long Island, half on mainland between Saidor and Seure. Close to Lukep. D=ELCPNG,RCC. M=SIL.
8546	0	6	4.48	0	99.90	0.10	C	397.48	126	9	Sandaun Province, north of Kombio. Many nominal Christians.
8547	2	6	5.44	0	99.80	0.20	C	329.96	158	9	Western Province, Morehead river. Related to Kanum, Aramba, Bothar, Peremka, Rouku, Dorro. D=ECP,UCPNGSI. M=APCM/UFM.
8548	0	6	4.44	0	99.90	0.10	C	397.48	125	9	Sandaun Province, near Om river.
8549	8	5	8.43	0	99.88	0.12	C	407.92	205	10	Eastern Highlands Province, Goroka Sub-Province. Mountains. 50 villages. Animists 1%. D=ELCPNG,SEBC,RCC,SA,ICFG,SDA,ABWE,JWs. M=SIL,ABM.
8550	0	6	3.84	0	99.90	0.10	C	397.48	111	9	Madang Province, near Koropa. Related to Sinsauru, Sausi, Kesawai, Dumpu.
8551	2	6	5.12	0	99.90	0.10	C	420.48	133	10	Madang Province. D=ELCPNG,RCC.
8552	0	7	4.60	0	99.95	0.05	C	440.37	122	10	Madang Province. All are Christians.
8553	1	7	3.42	0	99.90	0.10	C	410.62	98	10	Western Province, Fly River estuary. Animists 5%. D=ECP. M=APCM/UFM.
8554	3	6	6.46	0	99.90	0.10	C	427.05	159	10	Sandaun Province, Lumi District, 19 villages in Torricelli foothills. Hunter-gatherers. Animists 10%. D=RCC,SDA,CON. M=OFM,CMML,SIL.
8555	2	6	5.70	0	99.80	0.20	C	327.04	166	9	Sandaun Province, 11 villages. Limited Christian work. D=Christian Brethren,RCC. M=CMML.
8556	1	7	6.84	0	99.90	0.10	C	413.91	172	10	West New Britain Province. Tropical forest, inland from Gasmata. Animists 5%. D=RCC.
8557	0	6	5.18	0	92.00	8.00	C	201.48	186	8	Eastern Highlands Province, Okapa and Kainantu Districts. Tropical forest, mountains. Agriculturalists. Animists 20%. M=SIL.
8558	2	6	4.58	0	99.90	0.10	C	417.19	122	10	Madang Province. D=RCC,SDA.
8559	0	0	5.12	0	99.00	1.00	C	289.08	171	8	Morobe Province, Lae District, near the Wantoat. Tropical forest, mountainous region. D=ELCPNG(Lutheran),et alia.
8560	1	5	7.03	0	99.90	0.10	C	407.34	179	10	Western Province, Kiunga area, Upper Fly river. Animists 2%. D=ECP. M=APCM/UFM.
8561	2	6	7.08	0	99.84	0.16	C	370.98	185	9	Eastern Highlands Province, Kainantu and Okapa Districts, 15 villages. Tropical forest; agriculturalists. Animists 4%. D=ELCPNG,SDA. M=SIL.
8562	0	6	2.86	0	55.00	45.00	B	60.22	196	6	Sandaun Province, round Abrau town, east of Namia. Related to Namia and Ak. Animists 70%.
8563	2	5	3.42	0	99.90	0.10	C	420.48	96	10	Morobe Province, Markham Valley, Kaiapit District. Dialect chain. Strong Lutherans. D=GLC,ELCPNG. Lutheran prophet on Markham river spreads cargo cult.
8564	1	7	4.48	0	99.95	0.05	C	450.77	117	10	Madang Province, inland from Madang. 18 closely-related languages. D=ELCPNG.
8565	1	6	4.06	0	62.00	38.00	B	67.89	227	6	Western Province, Lake Murray. Close to Kuni(Boazi). Animists 10%. D=ECP. M=APCM/UFM.
8566	2	6	3.80	0	99.90	0.10	C	423.76	103	10	East Sepik Province, Hunstein Range, Ambunti District, 6 villages. Tropical forest, mountains. Bilingual in Tok Pisin. Strong animism, 10%. D=AoG,NTM.
8567	0	6	2.50	0	55.00	45.00	B	60.22	178	6	Sandaun Province, Amanab District. Animists 70%.
8568	1	6	4.02	0	99.80	0.20	C	321.20	127	9	Madang Province, 20 miles west of Madang city. Related to Gal. D=ELCPNG.
8569	2	6	6.78	0	99.89	0.11	C	412.56	169	10	East New Britain Province, Gazelle Peninsula. Several schools. Swamps. Animists 1%. D=UCPNGSI,RCC. M=SIL,PNGBTA.
8570	5	5	7.87	1	99.87	0.13	C	409.64	190	10	Enga Province. Animists 1%. D=ELCPNG,EBM,SDA,RCC,Baptist Ch(major revival under way).
8571	2	6	6.92	0	99.90	0.10	C	410.62	175	10	West New Britain Province, islands off northwest coast. D=RCC,SDA.
8572	2	6	4.84	0	99.80	0.20	C	332.88	142	9	Manus Province, Baluan and Pam Islands. Many bilinguals in Lou and Titan. D=SDA,RCC.
8573	0	6	4.10	0	99.90	0.10	C	397.48	117	9	Morobe Province. Numerous nominal Christians.
8574	1	5	5.33	0	99.85	0.15	C	353.68	154	9	East Sepik Province, on Schouten Islands east of Wewak. An Austronesian language. D=ELCPNG.
8575	2	5	6.42	0	99.95	0.05	C	440.37	162	10	Western Province, mouth of Bamu to 50 miles upriver. Closely related to Wabuda. D=Bamu River Mission(Australia), with 1 launch. M=SIL.
8576	4	5	5.59	0	99.80	0.20	C	329.96	161	9	Madang and East Sepik Provinces; 2 villages. Animists 20%. D=ELCPNG,RCC,Ch of Christ,SDA. M=PBT.
8577	2	8	5.13	0	99.95	0.05	C	471.58	125	10	West New Britain Province, southwest coast to northwest. In Kaulong dialect chain. D=RCC,Anglican Ch of PNG.
8578	2	5	6.20	0	99.80	0.20	C	338.72	172	9	Inland Oro Province, Afore District. Owen Stanley Mountains. Forests. D=Anglican Ch of PNG,SDA. M=SIL,PNGBTA.
8579	0	0	4.32	0	99.90	0.10	C	358.06	135	9	Western Province, Baramula and Tirio villages. Animists 5%. D=ELCPNG.
8580	1	5	4.76	0	99.80	0.20	C	321.20	145	9	West New Britain Province, east of Cape Gloucester, northwest coast. D=RCC.
8581	1	6	3.79	0	99.90	0.10	C	417.19	105	10	Oro Province, south bank of Bariji river. Bilingual in Hiri Motu. D=SDA.
8582	1	6	3.93	0	99.90	0.10	C	407.34	110	10	Morobe Province, 4 villages on mainland near Wasu, 3 on Umboi Island. Coastal. All nominally Lutherans; D=ELCPNG.
8583	2	5	5.62	0	99.80	0.20	C	329.96	162	9	New Ireland, south central, east and west coasts; 15 villages. D=RCC,UCPNGSI. M=PNGBTA.
8584	2	6	5.18	0	99.80	0.20	C	335.80	149	9	Oro Province, east of Managalasi, between Gaina and Korafe. Some bilingualism in Tok Pisin or Hiri Motu. D=SDA,Anglican Ch of PNG. M=SIL.
8585	4	6	6.80	0	99.87	0.13	C	396.93	173	9	Eastern Highlands Province, Marawaka District. Tropical forest, mountains. Animists 3%. D=Lutheran Ch,NTM,SDA,Baptists. Response slow. M=SIL.
8586	1	5	5.65	0	99.80	0.20	C	321.20	167	9	Madang Province. Related to Sihan, Gumalu, Isebe, Amele, Panim. D=ELCPNG.
8587	1	6	4.11	0	99.90	0.10	C	417.19	112	10	Central Province, mainly at Amau (Mori River). Bilingual in Magi, Suau, Motu, or English. D=UCPNGSI.
8588	1	5	6.24	0	99.70	0.30	C	260.61	196	8	Western Province, east of Nomad, into Southern Highlands Province. Animists 10%. D=ECP. M=APCM/UFM.
8589	1	6	5.02	0	99.90	0.10	C	410.62	133	10	West New Britain Province, Stettin Bay, Cape Hoskins area. D=RCC.
8590	2	6	5.31	0	99.80	0.20	C	329.96	155	9	Sandaun Province, west of Mehek. D=RCC,CB. M=CMML.
8591	1	6	4.57	0	33.00	67.00	A	12.04	468	5	Madang Province, Trans-Gogol Sub-Province. Related to Girawa, Munit. Tropical forest. Agriculturalists. Animists 90%. D=ELCPNG.
8592	0	5	4.86	0	75.00	25.00	B	136.87	217	7	Sandaun Province, east and southeast of Kilmeri language area. Language isolate. Animists 10%.
8593	3	5	3.32	0	99.89	0.11	C	412.56	95	10	Eastern Highlands, Goroka District. Animists 1%. D=ELCPNG,SDA,et alia. M=SIL.

Continued overleaf

Table 8-2 continued

PEOPLE		POPULATION				IDENTITY CODE		LANGUAGE		CHURCH		MINISTRY						SCRIPTURE		
Ref 1	Ethnic name 2	P% 3	In 1995 4	In 2000 5	In 2025 6	Race 7	Language 8	Autoglossonym 9	S 10	AC 11	Members 12	Jayuh 13-17	d 18	wa 19	xc 20	mc 21	mi 22	Biblioglossonym 23	Pub 24-26	ss 27
8594	Bepour	0.00180	74	83	129	AON10b	22-GBAA-a	bepour		95.00	79	0....	10	7	11	3	0		...	.
8595	Biaka (Nai)	0.01514	623	698	1,086	AON10b	25-QABA-a	nai		90.00	628	0....	10	6	11	4	2		...	.
8596	Biangai (Yongolei)	0.03532	1,454	1,628	2,534	AON10b	23-BAAA	biangai cluster		80.00	1,302	0....	10	7	7	4	1	Biangai	PN.	.
8597	Bibasa	0.01000	412	461	717	AON10b	25-XAAA-a	bibasa		90.00	415	0....	10	7	11	3	0		...	.
8598	Bibling (Aria)	0.03687	1,518	1,699	2,645	AON09b	35-EAAA	amara cluster		80.00	1,359	0....	10	7	7	4	2		...	.
8599	Big Sepik (Iatmul, Nyaura	0.33287	13,703	15,339	23,879	AON10b	26-HFAA	iatmul cluster		90.00	13,805	0....	10	8	7	5	1	Ngepma Kwundi*	PN.	.
8600	Bikaru (Bikau, Bugalu)	0.00315	130	145	226	AON10b	24-LDAE-a	east pikaru		10.00	15	0....	8	5	3	1	1		pn.	.
8601	Biksi	0.00520	214	240	373	AON10b	26-AAAA-a	biksi		65.00	156	0....	10	7	6	2	0		...	.
8602	Bilakura	0.00107	44	49	77	AON10b	22-ICAA-a	bilakura		95.00	47	0....	10	7	11	3	0		...	.
8603	Bilbil	0.02208	909	1,017	1,584	AON09b	34-BCAE-a	bilbil		85.00	865	0....	10	7	7	4	1		...	.
8604	Biliau (Yamai)	0.01766	727	814	1,267	AON09b	34-BEBA-a	biliau		90.00	732	0....	10	7	11	4	1	Awad Bing	P..	.
8605	Bilur	0.05000	2,058	2,304	3,587	AON09b	35-CFDB-a	bilur		90.00	2,074	0....	10	8	8	0	0		...	.
8606	Bimin	0.05045	2,077	2,325	3,619	AON10b	24-KEBE-a	bi-min		80.00	1,860	0....	10	7	7	4	1	Bimin	...	.
8607	Binahari	0.02587	1,065	1,192	1,856	AON10b	23-GBBA-a	neme-da'a		80.00	954	0....	10	7	7	5	2		...	n
8608	Binandere	0.14895	6,132	6,864	10,685	AON10b	23-ABBA-a	binandere		75.00	5,148	0....	10	7	7	4	1	Binandere	P..	b
8609	Bine (Oriomo, Pine)	0.05401	2,223	2,489	3,875	AON10b	20-OBAA	northeast bine cluster		80.00	1,991	0....	10	7	7	5	1	Bine	PN.	p
8610	Binumarien	0.00979	403	451	702	AON10b	24-PBAA-a	binumarien		90.00	406	0....	10	7	11	4	1	Binumarien	PN.	.
8611	Bisis	0.01485	611	684	1,065	AON10b	26-JDAA-a	bisis		40.00	274	0....	9	6	3	4	1		...	n
8612	Bisorio (Iniai, Pikaru)	0.00763	314	352	547	AON10b	24-LDAE-b	bisorio		75.00	264	0....	10	7	7	4	1	Bisorio	PN.	.
8613	Bitara	0.00766	315	353	550	AON10b	26-JAAA-a	bitara		95.00	335	0....	10	7	11	4	1		...	n
8614	Biwat (Mundugumor)	0.06091	2,507	2,807	4,370	AON10b	26-MCCB-a	biwat		60.00	1,684	0....	10	5	3	1	0		...	.
8615	Biyom	0.01195	492	551	857	AON10b	22-ECAA-a	biyom		90.00	496	0....	10	7	11	3	0		...	.
8616	Bo (Po)	0.00649	267	299	466	AON10b	25-WABC-a	bo		10.00	30	0....	8	5	3	1	0		...	.
8617	Boanaki (Boanai)	0.06092	2,508	2,807	4,370	AON09b	34-FCDB-a	boianaki		80.00	2,246	0....	10	7	7	4	1		...	.
8618	Bohuai (Pohuai, Pelipowai	0.04300	1,770	1,982	3,085	AON09b	35-BBBB-e	bohuai		90.00	1,783	0....	10	7	11	5	2		...	.
8619	Bohutu	0.04206	1,731	1,938	3,017	AON09b	34-FIAL-a	buhutu		80.00	1,551	0....	10	7	7	5	1	Buhutu	...	n
8620	Boikin (Nucum, Yengoru)	1.11019	45,704	51,159	79,643	AON10b	26-HDAF	boikin cluster		89.00	45,532	0....	10	8	7	5	1	Boiken: Yangoru*	P..	.
8621	Bola (Bakovi)	0.23178	9,542	10,681	16,627	AON09b	35-DBAA-a	bola		80.00	8,545	0....	10	7	7	5	2	Bola	PN.	.
8622	Bom (Bogadjim, Anjam)	0.03606	1,484	1,662	2,587	AON10b	22-TAAA-a	anjam		80.00	1,329	0....	10	7	7	4	1	Anjam	P..	.
8623	Bongos	0.07454	3,069	3,435	5,347	AON10b	26-FBCA-a	bongos		65.00	2,233	0....	10	7	8	0	0		pn.	.
8624	Bongu	0.01539	634	709	1,104	AON10b	22-TCAA-a	bongu		90.00	638	0....	10	8	11	4	1		...	.
8625	Bonkiman	0.00465	191	214	334	AON10b	24-SCBG-a	yupna		90.00	193	0....	10	7	11	4	1	Yupna*	P..	n
8626	Bosavi (Kaluli)	0.06212	2,557	2,863	4,456	AON10b	24-KIHA-a	kaluli		40.00	1,145	0.s..	9	5	3	4	2	Kaluli	...	.
8627	Bosilewa	0.01382	569	637	991	AON09b	34-FCLA-a	bosilewa		90.00	573	0....	10	7	11	5	2		...	b
8628	Bosngun	0.02659	1,095	1,225	1,908	AON10b	26-RBAA-a	bosman		80.00	980	0....	10	7	7	5	2		...	n
8629	Bothar	0.00230	95	106	165	AON10a	20-LDAA-a	bothar		70.00	74	0....	10	7	6	5	2		...	.
8630	Bouye	0.02129	876	981	1,527	AON10b	26-DAAA-a	bouye		30.00	294	0....	9	5	5	1	1	Pouye	...	.
8631	Breri	0.03051	1,256	1,406	2,189	AON10b	26-TDBB-a	breri		80.00	1,125	0....	10	7	6	3	0		...	.
8632	British	0.17000	6,998	7,834	12,195	CEW19i	52-ABAC-b	standard-english	28	79.00	6,189	3Bsuh	10	9	13	5	3		PNB	b
8633	Budibud	0.00671	276	309	481	AON09b	34-FDBA-a	budibud		90.00	278	0....	10	7	11	4	1		...	n
8634	Bukawa (Kawa)	0.33085	13,620	15,246	23,735	AON09b	34-BLAB-a	bukaua		90.00	13,721	0....	10	7	7	4	1	Bugawac	...	n
8635	Bulgebi	0.00164	68	76	118	AON10b	24-SBBA-a	bulgebi		95.00	72	0....	10	7	11	3	0		...	.
8636	Bulu	0.01738	715	801	1,247	AON09b	35-DBBA-a	bulu		90.00	721	0....	10	7	11	4	1		...	n
8637	Bumbita Arapesh (Urita)	0.09939	4,092	4,580	7,130	AON10b	27-JCAA	muhiang cluster		80.00	3,664	0....	10	7	6	5	2	Mufian	PN.	.
8638	Bun	0.00612	252	282	439	AON10b	26-MCCA-a	bun		40.00	113	0....	9	6	3	1	0		...	.
8639	Buna	0.01863	767	858	1,336	AON10b	27-LBAA	buna cluster		30.00	258	0....	9	5	6	1	0		...	.
8640	Bunabun (Bububun)	0.01847	760	851	1,325	AON10b	22-LAAA-a	bunabun		90.00	766	0....	10	7	11	5	2		...	.
8641	Bunama (Barabara)	0.10170	4,187	4,686	7,296	AON09b	34-FCQB-a	bunama		80.00	3,749	0....	10	7	7	5	2	Bunama	PN.	.
8642	Bungain	0.09091	3,743	4,189	6,522	AON10b	27-LABA-a	bungain		80.00	3,351	0....	10	7	6	2	0		...	.
8643	Burui	0.00556	229	256	399	AON10b	26-HEAC-a	burui		75.00	192	0....	10	7	6	2	0		...	p
8644	Burum-Mindik (Somba)	0.18484	7,609	8,518	13,260	AON10b	24-TDBA	burum-mindik cluster		70.00	5,962	0....	10	5	5	4	1	Burum-mindik	PN.	b
8645	Busa	0.00968	398	446	694	AON10b	25-UAAA-a	busa		20.00	89	0....	9	5	5	4	1		...	.
8646	Bwadji (Mbagu)	0.05444	2,241	2,509	3,905	AON10b	34-GCAA-a	kuni		65.00	1,631	0....	10	5	5	4	2		...	b
8647	Bwaidoga (Mataitai)	0.14909	6,138	6,870	10,695	AON09b	34-FCFB-a	bwaidoka		95.00	6,527	0....	10	8	7	5	1	Bwaidoka	P..	.
8648	Central Buang (Mapos)	0.22751	9,366	10,484	16,321	AON09b	34-DABD-d	mapos		90.00	9,436	0....	10	7	7	4	1	Buang: Central*	PN.	.
8649	Chambri (Tchambuli)	0.04289	1,766	1,976	3,077	AON10b	27-DAAA-a	chambri		10.00	198	0....	8	5	3	4	2		...	n
8650	Changriwa	0.01570	646	723	1,126	AON10b	26-MAAA-a	changriwa		30.00	217	0....	9	5	6	1	0		...	.
8651	Chenapian (Zenap)	0.00590	243	272	423	AON10b	26-BCAA-a	chenap		10.00	27	0....	8	5	3	1	0		...	n
8652	Chimbu (Kuman, Nagane)	1.98800	81,841	91,610	142,615	AON10b	24-NCBA-a	kuman	6	89.00	81,533	0....	10	8	7	5	3	Kuman	P..	.
8653	Chuave (Tjuave, Sua)	0.72870	29,999	33,580	52,275	AON10b	24-NCDA-a	chuave		90.00	30,222	0....	10	8	7	5	1	Chuave	PN.	.
8654	Daga	0.15136	6,231	6,975	10,858	AON10b	23-IAAA	daga cluster		80.00	5,580	0....	10	7	7	5	1	Daga	PN.	.
8655	Dahating	0.02983	1,228	1,375	2,140	AON10b	24-SBAA-a	dahating		70.00	962	0....	10	7	7	5	1	Dahating*	P..	.
8656	Dambi	0.01543	635	711	1,107	AON09b	34-DABB-a	dambi		70.00	498	0....	10	7	8	0	0		...	.
8657	Dami (Ham)	0.04715	1,941	2,173	3,382	AON09b	34-BDAA-b	dami		60.00	1,304	0....	10	5	6	4	1	Dami	...	.
8658	Danaru	0.00363	149	167	260	AON10b	22-QCAA-a	danaru		90.00	151	0....	10	7	11	3	0		...	.
8659	Daonda	0.00508	209	234	364	AON10b	21-HBAB-a	daonda		90.00	211	0....	10	7	11	5	2		...	.
8660	Daribi (Elu, Dadibi)	0.26288	10,822	12,114	18,858	AON10b	20-YBAA	dadibi cluster		90.00	10,903	0....	10	8	7	5	2	Dadibi	PN.	n
8661	Dawawa	0.06212	2,557	2,863	4,456	AON09b	34-FJBA-a	manubada		80.00	2,290	0....	10	7	7	4	1	Dawawa	P..	b
8662	Dedua	0.12614	5,193	5,813	9,049	AON10b	24-UBDA	dedua cluster		80.00	4,650	0....	10	7	7	4	1	Dedua	P..	.
8663	Degenan	0.01328	547	612	953	AON10b	24-SBBE-a	degenan		90.00	551	0....	10	7	11	5	2		...	.
8664	Dengalu	0.00478	197	220	343	AON09b	34-DABA-h	dengalu		70.00	154	0....	10	7	5	4	1		pn.	.
8665	Detribalized	5.87455	241,839	270,708	421,428	MPY53	52-ABAI-c	tok-pisin-creole		80.00	216,566	3asuh	10	10	10	5	3	Tok Pisin	PNB	b
8666	Dia (Alu)	0.07267	2,992	3,349	5,213	AON10b	27-HAHA-a	dia		70.00	2,344	0....	10	7	6	5	1		...	.
8667	Dimir (Bosiken)	0.04716	1,941	2,173	3,383	AON10b	22-MAAA-a	dimir		80.00	1,739	0....	10	7	7	4	1		...	p
8668	Diodio (Iauiaula)	0.04739	1,951	2,184	3,400	AON09b	34-FCGA-b	diodio-molata		80.00	1,747	0....	10	7	7	5	2		...	p
8669	Dobu (Galuewa, Sanaroa)	0.21604	8,894	9,955	15,498	AON09b	34-FCOA	dobu cluster	2	95.00	9,458	0..u.	10	9	7	5	2	Dobu	PNB	b
8670	Doga	0.00742	305	342	532	AON09b	34-FCAA-b	doga		90.00	308	0....	10	7	11	4	1		...	b
8671	Dogoro	0.00375	154	173	269	AON10b	23-ABHA-a	dogoro		95.00	164	0....	10	7	11	4	1		...	.
8672	Dom	0.29819	12,276	13,741	21,392	AON10b	24-NCBD-a	dom		91.00	12,504	0....	10	8	7	5	3	Dom	...	.
8673	Domu	0.02056	846	947	1,475	AON10b	23-GBAB-a	domu		90.00	853	0....	10	7	11	5	2		...	b
8674	Domung	0.05322	2,191	2,452	3,818	AON10b	24-SCBB-a	domung		90.00	2,207	0....	10	7	11	4	1		...	.
8675	Doromu (Koriko, Doram)	0.03051	1,256	1,406	2,189	AON10b	23-FAAA-b	doromu		80.00	1,125	0....	10	6	6	5	2		...	.
8676	Dorro	0.00223	92	103	160	AON10b	20-LEBA-a	dorro		90.00	92	0....	10	7	11	3	0		...	.
8677	Doura	0.02523	1,039	1,163	1,810	AON09b	34-GBDA-a	doura		80.00	930	0....	10	7	6	5	2		...	b
8678	Duau (Lomitawa, Sipupu)	0.09448	3,889	4,354	6,778	AON09b	34-FCPA-a	duau-pwata		90.00	3,918	0....	10	7	7	5	2		...	b
8679	Duduela	0.01479	609	682	1,061	AON10b	22-SCAA-a	duduela		90.00	613	0....	10	7	11	4	1		...	.
8680	Duke of York Islander	0.23224	9,561	10,702	16,660	AON09b	35-CFCA	ramuaina cluster		90.00	9,632	0....	10	7	7	5	1	Ramoaaina	P..	.
8681	Dumun (Bai)	0.00132	54	61	95	AON10b	22-VAAA-a	dumun		95.00	58	0....	10	7	11	3	0		...	.
8682	Duna	0.27750	11,424	12,788	19,907	AON10b	24-KHAB-a	duna		89.00	11,381	0....	10	9	7	5	3	Duna	PN.	.
8683	Duranmin (Suarmin)	0.00625	257	288	448	AON10b	27-ABAA-a	suarmin		35.00	101	0....	9	6	4	4	1		...	p
8684	E	0.00158	65	73	113	AON09b	35-BCAB-c	e		95.00	69	0....	10	7	11	4	1		pn.	.
8685	East Angal (Mendi)	0.40371	16,620	18,604	28,961	AON10b	24-LBCC-a	mendi		88.00	16,371	0.s..	10	8	7	5	1	Mendi*	P..	.
8686	East Kewa	0.76781	31,609	35,382	55,081	AON10b	24-LBBB-a	east kewa	1	91.00	32,197	0....	10	8	7	5	1	Kewa: East*	P..	.
8687	Edawapi	0.15341	6,315	7,069	11,005	AON10b	21-HBAB	daonda cluster		70.00	4,949	0....	10	5	6	3	0		...	.
8688	Eitiep	0.01243	512	573	892	AON10b	27-JACA-a	eitiep		90.00	516	0....	10	7	11	3	0		...	.
8689	Elepi (Samap)	0.00470	193	217	337	AON10b	27-LAFA-a	elepi		90.00	195	0....	10	7	11	3	0		...	.
8690	Elkei	0.04523	1,862	2,084	3,245	AON10b	27-HACA-a	elkei		70.00	1,459	0....	10	7	7	4	1		...	.
8691	Elu	0.00647	266	298	464	AON09b	35-BCAB-h	elu		70.00	209	0....	10	8	6	5	3		pn.	.
8692	Emerum	0.01584	652	730	1,136	AON10b	22-DAAA	apal cluster		80.00	584	0....	10	7	6	3	1	Apali	P..	.
8693	Emira (Mussau)	0.11966	4,926	5,514	8,584	AON09b	35-CAAA-a	mussau		90.00	4,963	0....	10	7	7	4	1	Mussau-emira	...	.
8694	Enga (Endakali, Wabag)	4.90000	201,720	225,799	351,516	AON10b	24-LDAB-f	mae		87.00	196,445	0.s..	10	9	14	5	3	Enga	PN.	.
8695	Ere	0.03487	1,436	1,607	2,502	AON09b	35-BCAB-a	ere		70.00	1,125	0....	10	8	6	5	1		pn.	.
8696	Erima (Ogea, Ato)	0.01706	702	786	1,224	AON10b	22-SBAA-a	ogea		90.00	708	0....	10	7	11	5	2	Ogea	P..	.
8697	Etoro	0.02460	1,013	1,134	1,765	AON10b	24-KIBA-a	etoro		65.00	737	0....	10	7	5	3	1	Edolo	...	.
8698	Euronesian	0.08600	3,540	3,963	6,169	MPY53	52-ABAE-ic	papua-new-guinea-english		80.00	3,170	0B.uh	10	9	8	5	3		pnb	b
8699	Ewage-Notu	0.36704	15,110	16,914	26,331	AON10b	23-ABEA-a	ewage-notu		89.00	15,053	0....	10	7	7	4	1	Ewage-notu	PN.	.
8700	Faita	0.00180	74	83	129	AON10b	22-EAAA-a	faita		95.00	79	0....	10	7	11	3	0		...	.
8701	Faiwol (Faiwolmin)	0.12152	5,003	5,600	8,718	AON10b	24-KEBD-a	faiwol-min		80.00	4,480	0....	10	7	7	5	2	Faiwol	PN.	.
8702	Fas	0.05036	2,073	2,321	3,613	AON10b	25-PAAA-a	fas		50.00	1,160	0....	10	5	5	4	2		...	.
8703	Fasu (Namome, Namumi)	0.03784	1,558	1,744	2,715	AON10b	24-KJAA-b	proper fasu		30.00	523	0....	9	5	5	4	1	Fasu	PN.	.
8704	Finungwan	0.01601	659	738	1,149	AON10b	24-SFBB-a	finungwa		35.00	258	0....	9	5	5	4	0		...	.
8705	Fiwaga	0.00946	389	436	679	AON10b	20-XAAB	fiwaga cluster		30.00	131	0....	9	5	5	4	0		...	.
8706	Foi (Kutubu, Mubi, Ifigi)	0.09073	3,735	4,181	6,509	AON10b	20-XAAA	foi cluster		65.00	2,718	0....	10	5	6	4	1	Foe*	PN.	.
8707	Forak	0.00514	212	237	369	AON10b	24-SBBD-a	forak		90.00	213	0....	10	7	11	3	0		...	.
8708	Foran (Kamba)	0.04161	1,713	1,917	2,985	AON10b	22-PABB-a	wagi		80.00	1,534	0....	10	7	7	4	1		...	.
8709	Fuyuge (Fujuge, Mafufu)	0.44728	18,413	20,611	32,087	AON10b	23-BEAA	fuyuge cluster		91.00	18,756	0.s..	10	7	7	4	1	Fuyuge	P..	.
8710	Gabadi (Kabadi)	0.05564	2,291	2,564	3,992	AON09b	34-GBEA-a	kabadi		80.00	2,051	0....	10	7	6	5	2		...	.
8711	Gabutamon	0.00952	392	439	683	AON10b	24-SCBA-a	gabutamon		40.00	175	0....	9	6	3	3	0		...	.
8712	Gadsup (Oyana)	0.23737	9,772	10,938	17,028	AON10b	24-PACA-a	gadsup		89.00	9,735	0....	10	8	7	5	1	Gadsup	PN.	.
8713	Gahuku (Kahuku)	0.50782	20,906	23,401	36,430	AON10b	24-OBAB-a	alekano	1	95.00	22,231	0.s..	10	9	7	5	1	Alekano	PN.	.
8714	Gaikunti	0.02596	1,069	1,196	1,862	AON10b	26-HEAD-a	gaikundi		85.00	1,017	0....	10	7	6	5	2	Gaikundi	P..	.
8715	Gaina	0.03052	1,256	1,406	2,189	AON10b	23-ABFA-b	gaina		80.00	1,125	0....	10	7	6	4	1		...	.
8716	Gaktai	0.05941	2,446	2,738	4,262	AON10b	27-RAAE-a	mali		80.00	2,190	0....	10	7	7	4	1		...	.
8717	Gal	0.00706	291	325	506	AON10b	22-PCGA-a	gal		90.00	293	0....	10	7	11	5	2		...	.

Continued opposite

Table 8-2 continued

EVANGELIZATION								EVANGELISM			ADDITIONAL DESCRIPTIVE DATA
Ref 1	*D* 28	*aC* 29	*CG%* 30	*r* 31	*E* 32	*U* 33	*W* 34	*e* 35	*R* 36	*T* 37	*Locations, civil divisions, literacy, religions, church history, denominations, dioceses, church growth, missions, agencies, ministries, movements* 38
8594	0	7	4.47	0	99.95	0.05	C	440.37	120	10	Madang Province. Related to Mauwake, Moere.
8595	1	6	4.23	0	99.90	0.10	C	410.62	116	10	Sandaun Province, Amanab District; 3 large villages. Hills, plains. D=Christian Brethren. Weak church, no vernacular work. M=CMML,SIL.
8596	1	6	4.99	0	99.80	0.20	C	335.80	144	9	Morobe Province, Wau Sub-Province, headwaters of Bulolo river; 7 villages. D=ELCPNG. M=SIL.
8597	0	6	3.80	0	99.90	0.10	C	397.48	110	9	Western Province. Language isolate. Animists 10%.
8598	2	5	5.03	0	99.80	0.20	C	327.04	149	9	West New Britain Province, northwest interior. D=RCC,NTM.
8599	3	6	7.50	0	99.90	0.10	C	423.76	182	10	East Sepik Province, Sepik River villages, Ambunti and Angoram Sub-Provinces; 50 villages. Animists 2%. Mainly RCs. D=RCC,SDA,AoG. M=SIL.
8600	1	7	2.75	0	35.00	65.00	A	12.77	299	5	East Sepik Province, headwaters of April river. Unreached nomads until first contacted 1983, by helicopter. Animists 90%. D=SSEC. M=SSEM.
8601	0	6	2.79	0	90.00	10.00	C	213.52	118	8	Also in Irian Jaya (Indonesia). On border. Animists 35%.
8602	0	7	3.93	0	99.95	0.05	C	440.37	108	10	Madang Province, Gilagil river. Related languages: Wanuma, Yaben, Yarawata, Parawen, Ukuriguma.
8603	1	6	4.56	0	99.85	0.15	C	356.78	134	9	Madang Province, coast south of Madang city and to its south. D=ELCPNG.
8604	1	6	4.39	0	99.90	0.10	C	410.62	120	10	Madang Province, 7 villages west of Saidor, Astrolabe Bay area. 4 dialects. D=ELCPNG. M=SIL.
8605	0	0	5.48	0	99.90	0.10	C	358.06	165	9	East New Britain Province, Gazelle Peninsula. 9 villages. Animists 5%. D=ELCPNG.
8606	1	6	5.36	0	99.80	0.20	C	324.12	159	9	Sandaun Province, Bak-Bimin District, also a few in Western Province. Close to Faiwol. D=Baptist Church. Much intermarriage with Oksapmin. M=SIL.
8607	2	6	4.66	0	99.80	0.20	C	335.80	137	9	Central Province, both sides of hills near Cloudy Bay. Close to Morawa. Bilingual in Magi, Suau, Hiri Motu, or English. D=UCPNGSI,SDA.
8608	2	6	6.44	0	99.75	0.25	C	303.86	185	9	Oro Province, along Eia, Ope, Mambere, and Kumusi rivers; also Morobe Province. Swamp. Bilinguals. Animists 2%. D=Anglican Church of PNG, since 1902.
8609	2	6	5.44	0	99.80	0.20	C	344.56	151	9	Western Province, south of Fly river, Daru District. Forest, swamp. 10 villages. Animists 5%. D=UCPNGSI,Maranatha(One Way). 20% speak Motu, 30% Kiwai.
8610	1	6	3.77	0	99.90	0.10	C	420.48	104	10	Eastern Highlands Province, Kainantu District. Tropical forest. 35% literates. D=ELCPNG. M=SIL.
8611	1	6	3.37	0	67.00	33.00	B	97.82	182	6	East Sepik Province, between Lower Solumei river and Chambri Lake, 3 villages. Highly bilingual in Tok Pisin. Animists 60%. D=RCC.
8612	1	6	3.33	0	99.75	0.25	C	298.38	111	8	East Sepik Province, headwaters of Karawari, Wagupmeri, Korosameri rivers; 3 villages. Animists 20%. D=NTM.
8613	1	7	3.57	0	99.95	0.05	C	457.71	96	10	East Sepik Province, April river, 2 villages. Many bilingual in Tok Pisin. Animists 5%. Being evangelized by D=AoG and Bahinemo Christians.
8614	0	5	5.26	0	81.00	19.00	C	177.39	214	7	East Sepik Province, Lower and Middle Yuat river. Related to Kyenele, Changriwa, Mekmek, Miyak, Bun. Animists 20%. Relatively unevangelized.
8615	0	7	3.98	0	99.90	0.10	C	400.77	113	10	Madang Province, southeast of Gende. Related languages: Isabi, Tauya, Faita.
8616	0	6	3.46	0	29.00	71.00	A	10.58	428	5	Sandaun Province, 5 villages. Isolated. Animists 90%. Relatively unevangelized.
8617	1	6	5.56	0	99.80	0.20	C	324.12	164	9	Milne Bay Province. Bilingual in Wedau. Literates. Syncretism and traditional magic strong. Animists 10%. D=Anglican Ch of PNG.
8618	2	6	5.32	0	99.90	0.10	C	420.48	137	10	Manus Province, Bohuai, Peli Island, Pelipowai. Bilingual in Kurti, Titan, Ere. D=RCC, Makasol cargo cult.
8619	2	6	5.17	0	99.80	0.20	C	335.80	149	9	Milne Bay Province, eastern tip. 90% bilingual in Suau. D=UCPNGSI,RCC. M=SIL.
8620	3	5	8.79	1	99.89	0.11	C	406.06	216	10	East Sepik Province, Yangoru District. Animists 1%. D=RCC,SDA,AoG. M=SIL.
8621	2	5	6.98	0	99.80	0.20	C	341.64	189	9	West New Britain Province, northeast coast. Many Baha'is 16%, spreading in Talasea area. D=RCC,SDA. NT has become too old, out of print.
8622	1	6	5.01	0	99.80	0.20	C	327.04	149	9	Madang Province, Astrolabe Bay, 4 villages. Tropical forest, coast. Cargo cults 15%. D=ELCPNG. M=SIL.
8623	0	0	5.56	0	87.00	13.00	C	206.40	209	8	East Sepik Province, Maprik District. Tropical forest. Swidden agriculturalists. Animists 10%. D=ELCPNG.
8624	1	6	4.24	0	99.90	0.10	C	407.34	117	10	Madang Province, Astrolabe Bay, Rai Coast. D=ELCPNG(begun early 1900s).
8625	1	6	3.00	0	99.90	0.10	C	417.19	88	10	Madang, Morobe Provinces. Second language Tok Pisin. D=ELCPNG. M=SIL.
8626	1	5	4.85	0	67.00	33.00	B	97.82	242	6	Southern Highlands Province. Mountainous. Animists 30%. D=ECP. M=APCM/UFM,SIL. Relatively unevangelized.
8627	2	6	4.13	0	99.90	0.10	C	427.05	110	10	Milne Bay Province, north shore of Fergusson Island. Bilingual in Iamalele, some in Dobu. D=UCPNGSI,RCC.
8628	2	6	4.69	0	99.80	0.20	C	335.80	137	9	Madang Province. Second language Tok Pisin. D=ELCPNG,RCC.
8629	2	6	4.40	0	99.70	0.30	C	260.61	145	8	Western Province, Morehead area. Also in Irian Jaya (Indonesia). Swamp, savannah. 4 primary schools. Related to Aramba, Kanum. Animists 30%. D=ECP.
8630	0	6	3.44	0	53.00	47.00	B	58.03	233	6	East Sepik Province, near Yellow river. Related languages: Kamnum, Karawa. Animists 70%. M=SIL.
8631	0	6	4.84	0	99.80	0.20	C	312.44	151	9	Madang Province, lower Ramu Valley, 80 miles west of Madang City. Swampy plain. Related languages: Kominimung, Igana, Itutang. Animists 5%.
8632	5	10	6.64	8	99.79	0.21	C	441.17	140	10	Expatriates from Britain, in education, development. D=ACPNG(5 Dioceses),RCC,UCPNGSI,SDA,JWs.
8633	1	7	3.38	0	99.90	0.10	C	417.19	96	10	Milne Bay Province, Lachlan Islands. Bilingual in Muyuw. Animists 10%. Strong syncretism. D=UCPNGSI.
8634	1	5	7.49	0	99.90	0.10	C	404.05	191	10	Morobe Province, coast. Closely related to church language Yabim. Animists 1%. D=ELCPNG. M=LBT.
8635	0	7	4.37	0	99.95	0.05	C	440.37	117	10	Madang Province, on Nankina river, 10 miles southeast of Saidor.
8636	1	7	4.37	0	99.90	0.10	C	417.19	117	10	West New Britain Province, Willaumez Peninsula. Bilingual in Bola. D=RCC.
8637	2	5	6.08	0	99.80	0.20	C	338.72	169	9	East Sepik Province, Torricelli Mountains, south of Wom. Mountains. Pigs. D=SDA(church and educational work),SSEC.
8638	0	7	2.45	0	61.00	39.00	B	89.06	158	6	East Sepik Province, on Yuat river. Related languages: Changriwa, Mekmek, Biwat, Miyak. Animists 60%.
8639	0	6	3.30	0	53.00	47.00	B	58.03	226	6	East Sepik Province, Angoram Sub-Province. Animists 20%.
8640	2	6	4.43	0	99.90	0.10	C	417.19	119	10	Madang Province. D=ELCPNG,RCC.
8641	2	6	6.11	0	99.80	0.20	C	344.56	167	9	Milne Bay Province, southern Normanby Island. Animists 20%. Syncretism strong. D=UCPNGSI,RCC. M=SIL,PNGBTA.
8642	0	6	5.99	0	99.80	0.20	C	309.52	182	9	East Sepik Province. Animists 10%. Many nominal Christians.
8643	0	6	3.00	0	99.75	0.25	C	276.48	110	8	East Sepik Province, Ambunti Sub-Province. Most are fluent in Gaikundi. Animists 20%.
8644	1	5	6.60	0	99.70	0.30	C	260.61	206	8	Morobe Province, Burum River valley. Forest, mountains. Animists 10%. 4 Burum cargo cults. D=ELCPNG. Poor response to gospel. M=SIL.
8645	0	6	4.59	0	46.00	54.00	A	33.58	337	5	Sandaun Province, Amanab District, west of Namia; 3 villages. Hunter-gatherers. Animists 80%. M=CMML.
8646	1	6	5.23	0	95.00	5.00	C	225.38	182	8	Western Province, Lake Murray area. Swampy, lagoons. Isolated, resistant to outsiders. Some educated. Related to Zimakani. Animists 20%. D=ECP. M=APCM.
8647	2	6	6.70	0	99.95	0.05	C	447.30	165	10	Milne Bay Province, Goodenough/Fergusson Islands. Some bilinguals in Dobu. D=UCPNGSI,RCC; both extensive. Bwaidoga is trade and church lingua franca.
8648	1	5	7.09	0	99.90	0.10	C	407.34	180	10	Morobe Province, Upper Snake River area, Mumeng District, 10 villages. Tropical forest. Few animists. D=ELCPNG. Little spiritual life. M=SIL.
8649	2	5	3.03	0	37.00	63.00	A	13.50	304	5	East Sepik Province, by Chambri Lake. Marsh dwellers. Bilingual in Tok Pisin. Animists 40%. D=RCC,NTM.
8650	0	6	3.13	0	53.00	47.00	B	58.03	217	6	East Sepik Province, south of Sepik river. Related languages: Mekmek, Miyak, Biwat, Bun. Animists 70%.
8651	0	6	3.35	0	31.00	69.00	A	11.31	391	5	East Sepik Province, 1 village. Relatively unreached tribe; some mission contact. Many speak Tok Pisin, some English. Animists 90%.
8652	5	6	4.08	1	99.89	0.11	C	415.80	110	10	Simbu Province, Kundiawa District, into Western Highlands Province. Lingua franca. Animists 15%. D=GLC,Independents,RCC,NTM,SDA. M=SEBM,NGLM/LCMS.
8653	4	6	8.34	1	99.90	0.10	C	427.05	198	10	Simbu Province, Chuave District. Savannah, mountains. Animists 1%. D=ELCPNG,NTM,RCC,SDA. M=SIL.
8654	2	6	6.53	0	99.80	0.20	C	341.64	178	9	Milne Bay Province, Rabaraba District; Central Province, Abau District. Related languages: Bagoi, Galeva. Animists 5%. Strong cargo cult. D=Anglican Ch PNG.
8655	2	6	4.67	0	99.70	0.30	C	263.16	153	8	Madang Province, Saidor District, several villages south of Saidor. Related languages: Bulgebi, Guiarak, Forak, Yagomi. Animists 25%. D=ELCPNG,RCC. M=SIL.
8656	0	0	3.99	0	88.00	12.00	C	224.84	158	8	Morobe Province, Madang District. Tropical forest. Swidden agriculturalists. Animists 20%. D=ELCPNG.
8657	1	6	4.99	0	90.00	10.00	C	197.10	184	7	Madang Province, Madang District, 10 villages. Tropical forest. Animists 20%. D=ELCPNG. M=SIL.
8658	0	7	2.75	0	99.90	0.10	C	400.77	86	10	Madang Province, near Ramu river. Related languages: Usino, Urigina, Sumau. Animists 10%.
8659	2	7	3.10	0	99.90	0.10	C	420.48	89	10	Sandaun Province, Amanab District near Imonda. Animists 5%. D=RCC,SDA.
8660	4	6	7.24	1	99.90	0.10	C	436.90	171	10	Southern Simbu Province, Kundiawa District, 28 villages. Forest. Few animists. D=ELCPNG,SDA,ICFG,RCC(very few). Missions use Tok Pisin. M=SIL,SEBM.
8661	2	6	5.58	0	99.80	0.20	C	338.72	157	9	Milne Bay Province, west and inland from Wedau. Bilingual in Wedau(church language), Motu, English. Animists 10%. D=Anglican Ch of PNG,SDA. M=SIL.
8662	1	5	6.33	0	99.80	0.20	C	324.12	183	9	Morobe Province, headwaters of Masaweng river. Mountains. Animists 2%. D=ELCPNG. M=SIL.
8663	2	6	4.09	0	99.90	0.10	C	417.19	111	10	Madang Province. Animists 10%. D=ELCPNG,RCC.
8664	1	5	2.77	0	99.70	0.30	C	255.50	105	8	Morobe Province. Related to Mumeng. Animists 20%. D=ELCPNG.
8665	3	10	4.80	5	99.80	0.20	C	438.00	102	10	Individuals from many tribal backgrounds but now rootless urbanites. D=ELCPNG,RCC,UCPNGSI.
8666	1	5	5.61	0	99.70	0.30	C	255.50	183	8	Sandaun Province. Animists 30%. Cargo cult area. Mainly Roman Catholics, few Protestants(CMML). D=RCC. M=CMML.
8667	1	6	5.29	0	99.80	0.20	C	327.04	156	9	Madang Province. Bilingual. Animists 15%. D=RCC.
8668	2	6	5.30	0	99.80	0.20	C	335.80	152	9	Milne Bay Province, west coast of Goodenough Island. Bilingual in Bwaidoga (church language). High literacy. Isolated. Animists 15%. D=UCPNGSI,RCC.
8669	3	5	7.09	1	99.95	0.05	C	492.38	157	10	Milne Bay Province, 500 villages on 6 islands. Lingua franca. Bilingual in Motu, English. Few animists. D=UCPNGSI(official language of Papuan Islands Region).
8670	1	7	3.49	0	99.90	0.10	C	420.48	98	10	Milne Bay Province, north coast of Cape Vogel. 60% of youths know English, others Anuki and Dima. Traditional magic and syncretism strong. Animists 7%.
8671	1	7	2.84	0	99.95	0.05	C	450.77	82	10	Oro (Northern) Province, Dyke Ackland Bay, 2 villages. Animists 5%. D=Anglican Ch of PNG.
8672	4	6	7.39	1	99.91	0.09	C	428.47	180	10	Simbu Province, south of Wahgi river from Kundiawa west of Sinasina area. Few animists 3%. D=ELCPNG,RCC,SDA,NTM.
8673	2	6	4.55	0	99.90	0.10	C	427.05	118	10	Central Province, coast east of Cape Rodney and inland. Bilingual in Mailu, Suau, Hiri Motu, English. Few animists left 5%. D=UCPNGSI,SDA.
8674	1	6	5.55	0	99.90	0.10	C	410.62	145	10	Madang Province, Tapen. Animists 8%. D=ELCPNG.
8675	2	6	4.84	0	99.80	0.20	C	329.96	143	9	Central Province, south of Mount Obree, west of Mount Brown. Animists 15%. D=RCC,UCPNGSI.
8676	0	7	4.63	0	99.90	0.10	C	400.77	128	10	Western Province, on coast round Mari, and inland 10 miles. Related to Kanum, Aramba, Bothar, Nambu, Peremka, Rouku. Animists 5%.
8677	2	6	4.64	0	99.80	0.20	C	335.80	136	9	Central Province, around Galley Reach. Many also speak Motu, Hiri Motu. Animists 15%. D=UCPNGSI,RCC.
8678	2	6	6.15	0	99.90	0.10	C	417.19	156	10	Milne Bay Province, Normanby Islands and others. D=UCPNGSI,RCC; use Dobu. Strong syncretism.
8679	1	6	4.20	0	99.90	0.10	C	407.34	116	10	Madang Province, south of Madang City. In Mumeng dialect chain. Animists 10%. D=ELCPNG.
8680	2	5	7.11	0	99.90	0.10	C	404.05	182	10	East New Britain Province, Kokopo District. 8 dialects. Tropical forest, coastal. Fishermen. Few animists. D=RCC,UCPNGSI(Wesleyan Methodists). M=SIL.
8681	0	7	4.14	0	99.95	0.05	C	440.37	112	10	Madang Province, on coast at Gowar river. Related languages: Yabong, Ganglau, Saep. Few animists left, 5%.
8682	6	6	7.29	0	99.89	0.11	C	422.30	176	10	Western Highlands Province, Lake Kopiago District, also Southern Highlands Province, Korobo District. D=GLC,RCC,SDA,Pentecostals,Apostolic Ch,UCPNGSI.
8683	1	7	2.34	0	63.00	37.00	B	80.48	148	6	Sandaun Province, Telefomin District, a few hamlets. Youth bilingual in Telefol. Animists 65%. D=BUWH. M=ABMS.
8684	1	8	4.33	0	99.95	0.05	C	464.64	110	10	Manus Province, south center of Manus Island. Close to Nane. Coconut trees, copra. Few animists left, 5%. D=RCC.
8685	5	5	7.68	1	99.88	0.12	C	401.50	192	10	Southern Highlands Province, Mendi Valley. Few animists 2%. D=ELC,EBM,SDA,RCC,UCPNGSI(Mendi is official language of Highlands Region). M=MCFOM(Fiji).
8686	6	5	8.41	0	99.91	0.09	C	418.50	206	10	Southern Highlands Province, Ialibu and Kagua Districts. Few animists. D=ECP,RCC,UCPNGSI,ELCPNG,EBM,et alia. M=SIL.
8687	0	5	6.40	0	96.00	4.00	C	245.28	213	8	Sandaun Province. Animists (traditional religionists) 10%.
8688	0	7	4.02	0	99.90	0.10	C	400.77	114	10	East Sepik Province, southwest of Kombio, also in Sandaun Province. Animists 10%.
8689	0	7	3.01	0	99.90	0.10	C	400.77	92	10	East Sepik Province; coast around Samap town. Animists 10%.
8690	1	6	5.11	0	99.70	0.30	C	258.05	168	8	Sandaun Province. Animists 30%. Cargo cult area. D=RCC. Entirely Roman Catholics; no other missions.
8691	3	6	3.09	0	99.70	0.30	C	273.38	107	8	Manus Province, north coast of Manus Island. Most are bilingual in Kurti. Animists 30%. D=RCC(New Life charismatics),SDA,Paliau Ch(New Way).
8692	0	5	4.15	0	99.80	0.20	C	312.44	134	9	Madang Province, upper Ramu river area, Angguna village. Animists 20%. M=PBT.
8693	1	6	6.40	0	99.90	0.10	C	397.48	169	9	Northern New Ireland, Mussau or St Matthias Islands. Bilingual in Tenis. Few animists. D=SDA.
8694	6	6	4.46	1	99.87	0.13	C	435.04	111	10	Enga Province. 13 dialects (Mae is standard). Few animists. D=GLC(Wabag Lutheran Ch),BUWH,RCC,ACC(Apostolic),SDA,ELCPNG. M=ABMS,NGLM/LCMS.
8695	4	6	4.84	0	99.70	0.30	C	270.83	153	8	Manus Province, south coast, 9 villages. Some bilinguals in Kele. Animists 25%. D=RCC(New Life charismatics),SDA,MEC,Paliau Ch(New Way). M=MEM.
8696	2	6	4.35	0	99.90	0.10	C	420.48	116	10	Madang Province, Astrolabe Bay, 4 villages. Related languages: 6, including Usu, Duduela, Kwato, Yangulam. Tropical forest. Animists 5%. D=ELCPNG,ICFG.
8697	1	6	4.39	0	92.00	8.00	C	218.27	163	8	Southern Highlands Province, southwest of Mount Sisa. Close to Beami. Animists 35%. D=ECP. M=SIL.
8698	6	10	5.93	8	99.80	0.20	C	411.72	131	10	Mixed-race White/Melanesians. Many animists 10%. D=RCC,ACPNG,ELCPNG,UCPNGSI,JWs,&c.
8699	1	5	7.59	1	99.89	0.11	C	406.06	190	10	Oro Province, coast between Bakumbari and Pongani. Tropical forest; fishermen. Few animists. D=ACPNG(Anglican work well established). M=SIL.
8700	0	7	4.47	0	99.95	0.05	C	440.37	120	10	Madang Province, well inland on Ramu river. Related languages: Biyom, Isabi, Tauya. Animists 5%.
8701	2	5	6.29	0	99.80	0.20	C	341.64	172	9	Western Province, Tabubil District, headwaters of Fly and Palmer rivers. Many dialects. Forest. Animists 3%. D=Baptist Union WH,RCC. Nominalism. M=SIL,ABMS.
8702	0	5	4.87	0	78.00	22.00	B	142.35	209	7	Sandaun Province, Amanab District. Language isolate. Hunter-gatherers. Animists 80%. M=CMML,SIL.
8703	0	6	4.04	0	60.00	40.00	B	65.70	233	6	Southern Highlands Province, Nipa District. Animists 20%. M=SIL.
8704	0	6	3.30	0	60.00	40.00	B	76.65	200	6	Morobe Province. Animists 65%.
8705	0	6	2.61	0	55.00	45.00	B	60.22	183	6	Southern Highlands Province, Hegigo river, northeast of Tama. Animists 70%.
8706	1	5	5.77	0	98.00	2.00	C	232.50	191	8	Gulf and Southern Highlands Provinces, east and south of Lake Kutubu and Mubi river. Animists 10%. D=ECP. M=APCM/UFM.
8707	0	7	3.11	0	99.90	0.10	C	400.77	94	10	Madang Province, near coast at Seure. Animists 10%.
8708	1	6	5.16	0	99.80	0.20	C	324.12	154	9	Madang Province, 7 miles northwest of Madang City; 5 villages. Forest, mountains. Animists 20%. D=ELCPNG. M=PBT.
8709	1	5	7.83	0	99.91	0.09	C	411.86	197	10	Central Province, southeastern Goilala District, into Oro Province. Animists 4%. D=RCC. M=SIL.
8710	2	6	5.47	0	99.80	0.20	C	329.96	159	9	Central Province, north of Galley Reach. Closest to Doura. Animists 20%. D=UCPNGSI,RCC.
8711	0	6	2.90	0	62.00	38.00	B	90.52	175	6	Madang Province, west of Gali. Related languages and dialects: Yupna, Mebu, Wandabong, Nokopo, Kewieng. Animists 60%.
8712	3	5	7.12	0	99.89	0.11	C	409.31	178	10	Eastern Highlands Province, Kainantu District. Tropical forest, mountains. Few animists. D=ELCPNG,SDA,et alia. M=SIL.
8713	7	6	8.01	1	99.95	0.05	C	471.58	183	10	Eastern Highlands Province, Goroka District. 75 villages. 90% Lutherans. D=ELCPNG,ICFG,SEBM,SDA,RCC,WOM,ABWE. M=SIL.
8714	2	7	4.73	0	99.85	0.15	C	372.30	132	9	East Sepik Province, Ambunti District. Close to Sawos. Animists 10%. D=RCC,AoG.
8715	1	6	4.84	0	99.80	0.20	C	321.20	147	9	Oro Province, next to the Baruga, around Iwuji. Sago swamp. Animists 20%. D=SDA.
8716	1	6	5.54	0	99.80	0.20	C	324.12	163	9	East New Britain Province, eastern Gazelle Peninsula. Related to Baining. Animists 10%. D=RCC.
8717	2	6	3.44	0	99.90	0.10	C	417.19	97	10	Madang Province, Gogol river. Animists 5%. D=ELCPNG,RCC.

Continued overleaf

Table 8-2 continued

PEOPLE		POPULATION				IDENTITY CODE		LANGUAGE		CHURCH		MINISTRY						SCRIPTURE		
Ref 1	Ethnic name 2	P% 3	In 1995 4	In 2000 5	In 2025 6	Race 7	Language 8	Autoglossonym 9	S 10	AC 11	Members 12	Jayuh 13-17	d 18	wa 19	xc 20	mc 21	mi 22	Biblioglossonym 23	Pub 24-26	ss 27
8718	Galeya (Garea, Wadalei)	0.07409	3,050	3,414	5,315	AON09b	34-FCNB-b	garea		80.00	2,731	0....	10	7	7	5	3		...	b
8719	Gamei (Borewar)	0.05163	2,125	2,379	3,704	AON10b	26-RAAB	borei cluster		80.00	1,903	0....	10	7	7	4	1	Borei	...	.
8720	Ganglau	0.00486	200	224	349	AON10b	22-VCAA-a	ganglau		90.00	202	0....	10	7	11	4	1		...	.
8721	Ganja (Ganjawo, Kandawo)	0.12424	5,115	5,725	8,913	AON10b	24-NBBA-b	kandawo		89.00	5,095	0.s..	10	7	7	5	1	Kandawo	Pn.	.
8722	Gants	0.05941	2,446	2,738	4,262	AON10b	24-MBAA-a	gants		75.00	2,053	0....	10	5	5	3	0		...	.
8723	Gapun	0.00258	106	119	185	AON10b	27-FAAA-a	gapun		90.00	107	0....	10	7	11	3	0		...	.
8724	Garuh (Butelkud-Guntabak)	0.06054	2,492	2,790	4,343	AON10b	22-PABA-a	garuh		80.00	2,232	0....	10	7	7	5	1	Nobanob	PN.	.
8725	Garus	0.04720	1,943	2,175	3,386	AON10b	22-PAAA-a	garus		80.00	1,740	0....	10	7	7	5	2		...	.
8726	Garuwahi	0.00889	366	410	638	AON09b	34-FHBA-a	garuwahi		90.00	369	0....	10	7	11	4	1		...	b
8727	Gasmata	0.00633	261	292	454	AON09b	35-FAAD-a	gasmata		90.00	263	0....	10	7	11	4	1		...	.
8728	Gawanga (Kwanga)	0.01068	440	492	766	AON10b	26-FBCA	kwanga cluster		89.00	438	0....	10	7	7	5	2	Kwanga	PN.	.
8729	Gele (Kele)	0.01843	759	849	1,322	AON09b	35-BCAB-e	kele		80.00	679	0....	10	8	7	5	3		pn.	.
8730	Genagane (Genogani)	0.03154	1,298	1,453	2,263	AON10b	24-NCBC-a	nagane		80.00	1,163	0....	10	7	6	3	0		...	p
8731	Gende (Gendeka)	0.21604	8,894	9,955	15,498	AON10b	24-OAAA-a	gende		90.00	8,960	0....	10	7	7	4	1	Gende	...	.
8732	Gidra	0.06489	2,671	2,990	4,655	AON10b	20-OAAC	gidra-dongori cluster		80.00	2,392	0....	10	7	6	5	2	Gidra	...	b
8733	Gimi	0.70839	29,162	32,644	50,818	AON10b	24-OFAA	gimi cluster		89.00	29,053	0....	10	7	7	5	1	Gimi	PN.	.
8734	Ginuman	0.03129	1,288	1,442	2,245	AON10b	23-KAAA-a	ginuman		80.00	1,154	0....	10	7	7	4	1		...	.
8735	Gira	0.01453	598	670	1,042	AON10b	24-SADA-a	gira		90.00	603	0....	10	7	11	4	1		...	.
8736	Girawa (Bagasin)	0.12624	5,197	5,817	9,056	AON10b	22-PECA-a	girawa		80.00	4,654	0....	10	7	6	4	1	Girawa	PN.	.
8737	Gizra (Waidoro, Togo)	0.02523	1,039	1,163	1,810	AON10b	20-OCAA	west gizra cluster		90.00	1,046	0....	10	7	11	4	1	Gizra	...	b
8738	Gnau	0.03091	1,272	1,424	2,217	AON10b	27-HAGA-a	gnau		80.00	1,140	0....	10	7	6	5	1		...	.
8739	Gobasi	0.04300	1,770	1,982	3,085	AON10b	24-KGAA-f	gobasi		30.00	594	0....	9	5	5	4	1		p..	.
8740	Gogodala	0.25227	10,385	11,625	18,097	AON10b	24-JBCA-a	gogodala		75.00	8,719	0.s..	10	5	6	4	1	Gogodala	PN.	.
8741	Golin (Simbu, Marigl)	1.61164	66,347	74,267	115,616	AON10b	24-NCBE-c	golin		91.00	67,583	0....	10	8	7	5	2	Golin	PN.	.
8742	Gorova	0.00158	65	73	113	AON10b	26-PCAA-a	gorovu		95.00	69	0....	10	7	11	4	1		...	.
8743	Graged (Star, Tiara, Sek)	0.10252	4,220	4,724	7,355	AON09b	34-BCAD-a	gedaged	3	80.00	3,779	0....	10	7	7	5	1	Bel*	PN.	.
8744	Grass Koiari	0.06958	2,864	3,206	4,992	AON10b	23-CABB-b	east koiari		80.00	2,565	0....	10	7	6	5	2		...	.
8745	Greek	0.01250	515	576	897	CEW20	56-AAAA-c	dhimotiki		85.00	490	2B.uh	10	9	11	5	1	Greek: Modern	PNB	b
8746	Guhu-Samane (Paiawa, Bia)	0.21464	8,836	9,891	15,398	AON10b	23-AAAA	guhu-samane cluster		88.00	8,704	0....	10	7	7	4	2	Guhu-samane	PN.	.
8747	Guiarak	0.00413	170	190	296	AON10b	24-SBBB-a	guiarak		90.00	171	0....	10	7	11	3	0		...	.
8748	Gumalu	0.00855	352	394	613	AON10b	22-PDBA-a	gumalu		90.00	355	0....	10	7	11	3	0		...	.
8749	Gumasi (Gumawana)	0.00987	406	455	708	AON09b	34-FCMA-a	gumasi		90.00	409	0....	10	7	11	5	1	Gumawana	P..	.
8750	Guntai	0.00568	234	262	407	AON10b	20-LDBA	tonda cluster		30.00	79	0....	9	5	8	0	0		...	.
8751	Guramalum	0.00011	5	5	8	AON09b	35-CFGA-a	guramalum		70.00	4	0....	10	7	6	3	0		...	.
8752	Guriaso	0.01000	412	461	717	AON10b	25-PACA-a	guriaso		80.00	369	0....	10	7	6	3	0		...	.
8753	Gusan	0.02573	1,059	1,186	1,846	AON10b	24-SFCA-a	gusan		80.00	949	0....	10	7	6	3	1		...	.
8754	Gusap (Yanko Wan)	0.01899	782	875	1,362	AON10b	22-WAAA-a	wasembo		90.00	788	0....	10	7	11	4	1		...	.
8755	Guwet	0.01239	510	571	889	AON09b	34-CDAA-a	guwot		90.00	514	0....	10	7	11	4	1		...	.
8756	Gwedena (Gweda, Gvede)	0.06481	2,668	2,987	4,649	AON10b	23-JAAA-a	north umanakaina		80.00	2,389	0....	10	7	7	4	1	Umanakaina	PN.	.
8757	Hakoa	0.18547	7,635	8,547	13,305	AON10b	24-OCAB-a	hakoa		85.00	7,265	0....	10	7	7	3	0		...	.
8758	Han Chinese	0.25920	10,671	11,944	18,594	MSY42a	79-AAAB-ba	kuo-yü	1	10.00	1,194	2Bsuh	8	5	8	5	1	Chinese: Kuoyu*	PNB	b
8759	Haroi	0.02000	823	922	1,435	AON10b	20-LDBA	tonda cluster		30.00	276	0....	9	5	5	3	0		...	.
8760	Hermit Islander (Agomes)	0.00070	29	32	50	AON09b	35-BAAA-b	luf		95.00	31	0....	10	7	11	4	1		...	.
8761	Hewa (Umairof)	0.05956	2,452	2,745	4,273	AON10b	26-IBAA-a	proper hewa		80.00	2,196	0....	10	7	6	5	2	Hewa	P..	.
8762	Hinihon	0.03469	1,428	1,599	2,489	AON10b	22-GFAA-a	hinihon		80.00	1,279	0....	10	7	6	3	0		...	.
8763	Hiri Motu	0.11406	4,696	5,256	8,182	AON09b	34-GBCB-a	hiri-motu	9	95.00	4,993	1.su.	10	10	7	5	1	Hiri Motu*	PNB	b
8764	Hotei (Hotec)	0.08777	3,613	4,045	6,296	AON09b	34-BPAA-a	hote		80.00	3,236	0....	10	7	6	4	1	Hote	P..	.
8765	Hube (Kube, Mongi)	0.16203	6,670	7,467	11,624	AON10b	24-UAAA	mongi cluster		60.00	4,480	0....	10	5	5	4	2	Kube	...	.
8766	Hula	0.08100	3,335	3,733	5,811	AON09b	34-GBAC-a	hula		80.00	2,986	0....	10	7	7	5	1	Hula	PN.	.
8767	Huli (Tari, Huri)	1.89036	77,821	87,111	135,611	AON10b	24-LCAA-a	huli		95.00	82,755	1.su.	10	9	10	5	3	Huli	PN.	.
8768	Humene	0.02028	835	935	1,455	AON10b	23-DAAA-a	humene		90.00	841	0....	10	7	11	5	2		...	b
8769	Hunjara	0.16622	6,843	7,660	11,924	AON10b	23-ABDB-a	hunjara		90.00	6,894	0....	10	7	7	4	1		...	.
8770	Idi (Dimisi)	0.05444	2,241	2,509	3,905	AON10b	20-MAAA-a	idi		80.00	2,007	0....	10	8	7	5	3	Idi	...	b
8771	Igana	0.00360	148	166	258	AON10b	26-TDAC-a	igana		90.00	149	0....	10	7	11	3	0		...	.
8772	Igom	0.03412	1,405	1,572	2,448	AON10b	26-TBAA-b	igom 2		80.00	1,258	0....	10	7	6	3	0		...	.
8773	Igora (Kakabai)	0.03476	1,431	1,602	2,494	AON09b	34-FJAC-a	igora		85.00	1,362	0....	10	7	7	4	2		...	b
8774	Ikobi-Mena (Kopo-Monia)	0.02279	938	1,050	1,635	AON10b	20-VAAB	ikobi cluster		90.00	945	0....	10	7	11	5	2		...	.
8775	Ikundun (Anamgura)	0.03410	1,404	1,571	2,446	AON10b	22-AACA-a	ikundun		85.00	1,336	0....	10	7	7	4	1		...	.
8776	Imbinis	0.02000	823	922	1,435	AON10b	21-IAAB-a	imbinis		80.00	737	0....	10	7	7	5	2		...	.
8777	Imbongu (Imbonggo)	0.45571	18,760	21,000	32,692	AON10b	24-NAAB	umbu-ungu cluster		87.00	18,270	0.s..	10	7	6	5	1	Imbongu	PN.	.
8778	Imonda	0.00621	256	286	445	AON10b	21-HBAA-b	imonda		30.00	86	0....	9	5	8	0	0		pn.	.
8779	Ipiko (Ipikoi)	0.00701	289	323	503	AON10b	20-QAAA-a	ipiko		90.00	291	0....	10	7	11	4	1		...	.
8780	Ipili (Ipili-Payala)	0.24484	10,079	11,283	17,564	AON10b	24-LDAC-b	west ipili		85.00	9,590	0....	10	8	7	5	2	Ipili	P..	.
8781	Irumu (Upper Irumu)	0.03280	1,350	1,511	2,353	AON10b	24-SEBB-a	irumu		80.00	1,209	0....	10	7	7	4	1	Irumu	P..	.
8782	Isabi (Maruhia)	0.00883	364	407	633	AON10b	22-EDAA-a	isabi		90.00	366	0....	10	7	11	3	0		...	.
8783	Isan (Jopna, Bongiman)	0.18904	7,782	8,711	13,561	AON10b	24-SCBG-a	yupna		90.00	7,840	0....	10	7	7	4	1	Yupna*	P..	n
8784	Isebe	0.02879	1,185	1,327	2,065	AON10b	22-PDAB	isebe-bau cluster		80.00	1,061	0....	10	7	7	5	3		...	.
8785	Isi	0.02000	823	922	1,435	AON10b	21-IAAE-a	isi		80.00	737	0....	10	7	7	5	0		p..	.
8786	Itaem	0.02000	823	922	1,435	AON10b	24-NAAB	umbu-ungu cluster		30.00	276	0.s..	9	5	5	3	0	Imbongu	PN.	.
8787	Iteri (Yinibu)	0.00348	143	160	250	AON10b	25-WABB-a	iteri		30.00	48	0....	9	5	5	4	1	Iteri	P..	.
8788	Itutang	0.00694	286	320	498	AON10b	26-TDAA-a	itutang		35.00	112	0....	9	5	5	3	0		...	.
8789	Ivanga	0.02000	823	922	1,435	AON09b	35-EABC-a	ibanga		80.00	737	0....	10	7	7	5	1		...	.
8790	Ivori (Vori)	0.02523	1,039	1,163	1,810	AON10b	24-RAGA-a	tainae		40.00	465	0....	9	5	4	3	1		...	.
8791	Iwal	0.04051	1,668	1,867	2,906	AON09b	34-BNAA-a	iwal		80.00	1,493	0....	10	7	6	4	2	Iwal	PN.	.
8792	Iwam	0.05045	2,077	2,325	3,619	AON10b	27-JCAA-e	iwam		50.00	1,162	0....	10	5	5	5	1	Iwam*	PN.	.
8793	Jewish	0.01275	525	588	915	CMT35	52-ABAE-ic	papua-new-guinea-english		1.00	6	0B.uh	6	4	2	5	0		pnb	b
8794	Jilim	0.01290	531	594	925	AON10b	22-SEAA-a	jilim		90.00	535	0....	10	7	11	3	0		...	.
8795	Jimajima (Dima)	0.02188	901	1,008	1,570	AON10b	23-ICAA	jimajima cluster		90.00	907	0....	10	7	11	4	1		...	.
8796	Kabiano (Gabiano)	0.00853	351	393	612	AON10b	26-IABB-a	gabiano		40.00	157	0....	9	5	3	3	0		...	.
8797	Kaeti	0.14700	6,052	6,774	10,545	AON10b	24-KDCB-g	southeast kaeti		55.00	3,726	0....	10	5	5	3	0		...	.
8798	Kaiep	0.00762	314	351	547	AON09b	34-BBAB-a	kaiep		90.00	316	0....	10	7	11	3	0		...	.
8799	Kaikovu	0.02000	823	922	1,435	AON10b	23-KBAA	kanasi cluster		90.00	829	0....	10	7	11	4	1	Kanasi	PN.	b
8800	Kairak	0.02025	834	933	1,453	AON10b	27-RAAF-a	kairak		50.00	467	0....	10	6	5	3	0		...	.
8801	Kairi (Tumu, Gairi, Dumu)	0.02848	1,172	1,312	2,043	AON10b	20-WAAA-a	kairi		95.00	1,247	1....	10	7	11	5	1	Kairi*	P..	b
8802	Kairiru	0.11060	4,553	5,097	7,934	AON09b	34-BBAA-a	kairiru		85.00	4,332	0....	10	7	7	4	1		...	n
8803	Kaliai	0.04969	2,046	2,290	3,565	AON09b	34-BJCB-a	lusi		78.00	1,786	0....	10	7	7	3	3		...	.
8804	Kalokalo	0.02601	1,071	1,199	1,866	AON09b	34-FCHA-a	kalakalo		80.00	959	0....	10	7	7	4	1	Koluawa	...	.
8805	Kalou	0.02586	1,065	1,192	1,855	AON10b	26-EAAA-a	kalou		25.00	298	0....	9	5	5	1	0		...	.
8806	Kamano	1.74000	71,631	80,182	124,824	AON10b	24-ODAA-e	kamano	2	85.00	68,154	1.s..	10	8	7	5	1	Kamano-kafe	PN.	.
8807	Kamasa	0.00068	28	31	49	AON10b	24-RAEA-a	kamasa		90.00	28	0....	10	7	11	4	1		...	.
8808	Kamasau (Wand Tan)	0.02482	1,022	1,144	1,781	AON10b	27-LAEB-a	kamasau		80.00	915	0....	10	7	7	4	1	Kamasau	P..	.
8809	Kamba	0.03217	1,324	1,482	2,308	AON10b	22-PABB-a	wagi		90.00	1,334	0....	10	7	11	4	1		...	.
8810	Kambaira	0.00545	224	251	391	AON10b	24-PACC-a	kambaira		90.00	226	0....	10	7	11	4	1		...	n
8811	Kamberataro (Mannguar)	0.01855	764	855	1,331	AON10a	21-UAAA	kamberataro cluster		90.00	769	0....	10	7	11	4	1		...	.
8812	Kambot (Kambaramba)	0.18904	7,782	8,711	13,561	AON10b	26-PAAA-a	kambot		87.00	7,579	0....	10	7	6	4	1	Ap Ma	P..	.
8813	Kamnum	0.01366	562	629	980	AON10b	26-DBAA-a	kamnum		90.00	567	0....	10	7	11	4	1		...	.
8814	Kamura (Kamula)	0.01925	792	887	1,381	AON10b	24-KFBA-a	kamula		35.00	310	0....	9	5	6	4	2	Kamula	...	.
8815	Kandas	0.01896	781	874	1,360	AON09b	35-CFEA-a	kandas		90.00	786	0....	10	7	11	4	1		...	.
8816	Kaningra	0.00883	364	407	633	AON10b	26-KBAA-a	kaningra		90.00	366	0....	10	7	11	4	1		...	n
8817	Kanite	0.20182	8,308	9,300	14,478	AON10b	24-ODAA-d	kanite		80.00	7,440	1.s..	10	8	7	5	1	Kanite	PN.	.
8818	Kanum (Enkelembu)	0.00500	206	230	359	AON10a	20-LCAA	kanum cluster		30.00	69	0....	9	5	5	5	2		...	.
8819	Kapau (Kukukuku, Watut)	1.10957	45,678	51,131	79,598	AON10b	24-RAHA-d	hamtai		87.00	44,484	0....	10	8	4	5	3	Hamtai	PN.	.
8820	Kapriman (Karambit)	0.04022	1,656	1,853	2,885	AON10b	26-JFAA-a	proper kapriman		85.00	1,575	0....	10	7	7	5	1		...	.
8821	Kara (Lemakot, Lemusmus)	0.12109	4,985	5,580	8,687	AON09b	35-CBDA	kara cluster		80.00	4,464	0....	10	7	6	5	1	Kara	P..	.
8822	Karam (Kalam, Simbai)	0.37807	15,564	17,422	27,122	AON10b	24-MAAB-a	kalam		87.00	15,157	0....	10	8	7	5	1	Kalam	PN.	.
8823	Karangi	0.00512	211	236	367	AON10b	24-SDAB-a	weliki		90.00	212	0....	10	7	11	4	1		...	n
8824	Karawa	0.01232	507	568	884	AON10b	26-DCAA-a	karawa		35.00	199	0....	9	5	5	5	2		...	.
8825	Kare	0.01211	499	558	869	AON10b	22-OAAA-a	kare		90.00	502	0....	10	7	11	5	2		...	.
8826	Karkar (Yuri, Karkarrap)	0.02837	1,168	1,307	2,035	AON10b	22-KBAA-a	karkar		80.00	1,046	0.s..	10	7	6	4	2	Karkar-yuri	PN.	.
8827	Karore	0.01335	550	615	958	AON09b	35-GAAA-d	karore		80.00	492	0....	10	7	8	0	0		p..	.
8828	Karua (Xarua, Harua)	0.04112	1,693	1,895	2,950	AON09b	35-DBAA-b	harua		90.00	1,705	0....	10	7	11	4	2		pn.	n
8829	Kasua	0.01633	672	753	1,171	AON10b	24-KIIA-a	kasua		40.00	301	0....	9	5	3	4	2	Kasua	...	.
8830	Kate (Kai, Katedong)	0.20904	8,606	9,633	14,996	AON10b	23-BCAB-b	kate	5	90.00	8,670	0....	10	7	7	5	3	Kate	PNB	.
8831	Katiati	0.10363	4,266	4,775	7,434	AON10b	22-ADAA-a	katiati		80.00	3,820	0....	10	7	7	4	1	Mum	...	.
8832	Katinja	0.03857	1,588	1,777	2,767	AON10b	24-LDAA-a	katinja		35.00	622	0....	9	5	6	3	0		...	.
8833	Kaugel (Ubu Ugu)	0.62123	25,574	28,627	44,566	AON10b	24-NAAB-a	kaugel		83.00	23,761	0.s..	10	7	6	5	1	Umbu-ungu: Kala	PN.	.
8834	Kavwol (Kawol)	0.00700	288	323	502	AON10a	24-KEBA-a	kauwol		90.00	290	0....	10	7	11	4	1		...	.
8835	Kawacha	0.00102	42	47	73	AON10b	24-RADA-a	kawacha		90.00	42	0....	10	7	11	4	1		...	.
8836	Kayan (Kaian)	0.01015	418	468	728	AON10b	26-RAAC-a	kaian		90.00	421	0....	10	7	11	3	0		...	.
8837	Kela (Gela)	0.06951	2,862	3,203	4,987	AON09b	34-BMAA-a	kela		80.00	2,562	0....	10	7	7	4	1		...	.
8838	Kelana (Gitoa, Gitua)	0.01648	678	759	1,182	AON09b	34-BJAA	gitua cluster		90.00	683	0....	10	7	11	4	1		...	.
8839	Kenati (Kenathi)	0.02586	1,065	1,192	1,855	AON10b	24-QAAA-a	kenati		80.00	953	0....	10	7	6	5	1	Aziana*	P..	.
8840	Kenele	0.02774	1,142	1,278	1,990	AON10b	26-MCBA-a	kyenele		70.00	895	0....	10	7	6	3	1	Kianying Balang*	P..	.
8841	Keopara (Keapara, Hula)	0.60916	25,077	28,071	43,700	AON09b	34-GBAB-a	keopara		87.00	24,422	0....	10	7	7	5	1	Keapara*	P..	.

Continued opposite

Table 8-2 continued

EVANGELIZATION								EVANGELISM			ADDITIONAL DESCRIPTIVE DATA
Ref 1	*Da* 28	*C* 29	*CG%* 30	*r* 31	*E* 32	*U* 33	*W* 34	*e* 35	*R* 36	*T* 37	*Locations, civil divisions, literacy, religions, church history, denominations, dioceses, church growth, missions, agencies, ministries, movements* 38
8718	3	6	5.77	0	99.80	0.20	C	347.48	157	9	Milne Bay Province, northeast coast of Fergusson Island. Animists 20%. D=UCPNGSI,RCC,SDA. Syncretism strong. Dobu widely spoken.
8719	4	6	5.39	0	99.80	0.20	C	329.96	157	9	Madang Province, Bogia District. Animists 15%. D=RCC,ELCPNG,SDA,CC. M=PBT.
8720	1	6	3.05	0	99.90	0.10	C	407.34	91	10	Madang Province. Related languages: Yabong, Dumun, Saep. Animists 5%. D=ELCPNG.
8721	2	5	6.43	0	99.89	0.11	C	406.06	164	10	Western Highlands Province, Hagen District in upper Jimi headwaters. 18 villages. Few animists. D=83% RCC,17% ELCPNG. 1 school. M=SIL.
8722	0	6	5.47	0	99.75	0.25	C	276.48	177	8	Madang Province, west of Macin river. Animists 5%.
8723	0	7	2.40	0	99.90	0.10	C	400.77	78	10	East Sepik Province, near Watam. Language isolate. Animists 10%.
8724	2	6	5.56	0	99.80	0.20	C	341.64	155	9	Madang Province, Madang District, 45 villages. Forest, mountains. Animists 20%. D=RCC,ELCPNG. Third-generation Christians. M=SIL.
8725	2	5	5.29	0	99.80	0.20	C	329.96	154	9	Madang, Astrolabe Bay. Related languages: Bagupi, Matepi, Mosimo, Murupi, Rapting, Samosa, Silopi. Animists 15%. D=RCC(limited mission activity),ELCPNG.
8726	1	7	3.67	0	99.90	0.10	C	420.48	101	10	Milne Bay Province, between Taupota, Wedau, and East Cape. Bilingual in Wedau, Motu, Tawala. Animists 5%. D=Anglican Ch of PNG.
8727	1	7	3.32	0	99.90	0.10	C	410.62	96	10	West New Britain Province, southwest coast. Tropical forest, coral coast. Animists 5%. D=RCC.
8728	3	5	3.85	0	99.89	0.11	C	409.31	107	10	East Sepik Province, around west boundary of Maprik District; tropical forest, plains. 40 villages. Few animists. D=SSEC,RCC,New Apostolic Church. M=SIL,SSEM.
8729	3	6	4.31	0	99.80	0.20	C	344.56	125	9	Manus Province, south coast inland. Bilingual in Kurti and Ere. Animists 15%. D=RCC(New Life charismatics),SDA,Paliau Ch(New Way).
8730	0	6	4.87	0	99.80	0.20	C	315.36	151	9	Simbu Province. Related to Kuman, and all bilingual in it. Animists 20%.
8731	1	5	7.03	0	99.90	0.10	C	394.20	185	9	Madang Province, Bundi District, near Bundi. Mountainous area. Animists 2%. D=RCC.
8732	3	6	5.63	0	99.80	0.20	C	341.64	157	9	Western Province, eastern third of area between Fly Delta, estuary, and south coast. 15 dialects. Animists 15%. D=UCPNGSI,SDA,ECP. Motu and Kiwai used.
8733	3	5	8.30	1	99.89	0.11	C	415.80	201	10	Eastern Highlands Province, Okapa District, near Papua border. Few animists. D=ELCPNG,NTM,SDA. M=SIL.
8734	1	6	4.86	0	99.80	0.20	C	324.12	146	9	Milne Bay Province, Mount Simpson to coast at Naraka. Animists 15%. D=Anglican Ch of PNG.
8735	1	7	4.18	0	99.90	0.10	C	410.62	115	10	Madang Province. Animists 5%. D=ELCPNG.
8736	1	5	6.34	0	99.80	0.20	C	329.96	180	9	Madang Province, Ramu District. Related languages: Munit, Bemal. Tropical forest, mountains. Animists 2%. D=ELCPNG. Nominalism. M=SIL.
8737	1	7	4.76	0	99.90	0.10	C	423.76	124	10	Western Province, 3 villages. Animists 5%. D=United Church of PNGSI(strong). Little activity. Motu, Kiwai used.
8738	1	6	4.85	0	99.80	0.20	C	324.12	146	9	Sandaun Province, Namblo Census Division, northwest of Maimai. Isolated tribe; cargo cult area. Animists 15%. Some RCs, some Protestants. D=RCC.
8739	0	6	4.17	0	57.00	43.00	B	62.41	252	6	Western Province. Traditional religionists(animists) 20%. M=Pioneers Inc.
8740	1	5	7.01	1	99.75	0.25	C	301.12	201	9	Western Province, north bank of Fly river, Aramia river; 301 villages. Closest to Ari. Animists 5%. D=ECP. M=APCM/UFM(since 1931).
8741	2	6	9.22	1	99.91	0.09	C	435.11	215	10	Simbu Province, Gumine District. Close to Dom. Animists 1%. D=ELCPNG,RCC. M=SIL,SEBM.
8742	1	8	4.33	0	99.95	0.05	C	454.24	113	10	East Sepik Province, Bangapela village, Ramu river. Nearly extinct; people speak Banaro. D=RCC.
8743	2	6	2.98	1	99.80	0.20	C	344.56	94	9	Madang Province, Astrolabe Bay, 4 islands. Lingua franca. Animists 15%. D=ELCPNG,GLC. M=NGLM/LCMS.
8744	2	5	5.70	0	99.80	0.20	C	327.04	166	9	Central Province, east of Port Moresby and to coast. Close to Koita. Animists 15%. D=UCPNGSI,SDA.
8745	1	10	3.97	7	99.85	0.15	C	471.58	89	10	Traders from Greece. D=Greek Orthodox Ch(AD-Australia,E-All Oceania).
8746	1	5	7.00	0	99.88	0.12	C	395.07	180	9	Morobe Province, Lae District; also Oro Province. Animists 2%. D=ELCPNG. Revival spreading, due to 1975 publication of NT. M=SIL,PNGBTA.
8747	0	7	2.88	0	99.90	0.10	C	400.77	89	10	Madang Province, about 15 miles west of Seure. Animists 10%.
8748	0	6	3.63	0	99.90	0.10	C	397.48	106	9	Madang Province, west of Madang City. Related languages: Sihan, Amele, Isebe, Bau, Panim. Animists 5%.
8749	3	6	3.78	0	99.90	0.10	C	420.48	104	10	Milne Bay Province, several small islands. Hostile to foreigners. Few literates. Animists 10%. D=UCPNGSI,RCC,SDA; all weak. M=SIL.
8750	0	0	4.47	0	47.00	53.00	A	51.46	323	6	Western Province, Morehead District. Animists 70%.
8751	0	7	1.40	0	97.00	3.00	C	247.83	70	8	New Ireland Province. Nearly extinct. Animists 20%.
8752	0	6	3.67	0	99.80	0.20	C	309.52	123	9	Sandaun Province, Amanab District. Animists 17%.
8753	1	6	4.66	0	99.80	0.20	C	315.36	145	9	Morobe Province, Saruwaged range. Animists 20%. D=ELCPNG.
8754	1	6	4.46	0	99.90	0.10	C	407.34	122	10	Morobe Province, west of Ufim. Animists 10%. D=ELCPNG.
8755	1	6	2.36	0	99.90	0.10	C	407.34	76	10	Morobe Province, Busu river. Animists 10%. D=ELCPNG.
8756	1	5	5.63	0	99.80	0.20	C	332.88	161	9	Milne Bay Province, coast of Goodenough Bay. Some speakers of English. Tropical forest, mountains. Animists 15%. D=Anglican Ch of PNG. M=SIL.
8757	0	5	6.81	0	99.85	0.15	C	347.48	193	9	Simbu Province, Goroka District. Close to Siane. Animists 5%.
8758	1	10	4.90	7	71.00	29.00	B	25.91	214	5	Chinese merchants, traders. Buddhists/Chinese folk-religionists 80%, nonreligious 10%. D=RCC.
8759	0	6	3.37	0	54.00	46.00	B	59.13	225	6	Western Province. Tribal religionists(animists) 70%.
8760	1	8	3.49	0	99.95	0.05	C	454.24	95	10	Western Manus Province. Luf, Maron Islands. Nearly extinct. D=SDA.
8761	2	5	5.54	0	99.80	0.20	C	329.96	160	9	Enga, Southern Highlands, Enga, Sandaun Provinces; Lagaip River area; in bush north of Duna, Ipili. Primitive nomads. Animists 20%. D=Gutnius Lutheran Ch.
8762	0	6	4.97	0	99.80	0.20	C	312.44	155	9	Madang Province, Adelbert range, north central. Related language: Kowaki. Animists 20%.
8763	4	7	6.41	2	99.95	0.05	C	506.25	140	10	Central Province lingua franca, also Oro, Gulf, Milne Bay Provinces. Official language of UCPNG Papua Mainland Region. D=UCPNGSI,SDA,ACPNG,ECP.
8764	1	6	5.95	0	99.80	0.20	C	324.12	173	9	Morobe Province, Lee District, Francisco River area. Close to Yamap, Misim. Animists 15%. D=Ev Lutheran Ch of PNG. Nominalism. M=SIL.
8765	1	5	6.29	0	89.00	11.00	C	194.91	227	7	Morobe Province, Dindiu District, eastern headwaters of Mongi river. Mountains. Animists 5%. D=ELCPNG. M=Global Bible Translators (Korea),SIL.
8766	2	6	5.86	0	99.80	0.20	C	341.64	162	9	Central Province, Hood Peninsula. Animists 15%. D=UCPNGSI,SDA. M=LMS.
8767	6	5	9.44	1	99.95	0.05	C	478.51	209	10	Southern Highlands and Enga Provinces, around Tari. Major language of UCPNG Highlands Region. D=UCPNGSI,ECP,RCC,CB,SDA,and 4 others.
8768	2	7	4.53	0	99.90	0.10	C	430.33	117	10	Central Province, lower edge of Sogeri Plateau. Some Hiri Motu, Motu, English. Animists 5%. D=UCPNGSI,SDA.
8769	1	6	6.75	0	99.90	0.10	C	397.48	177	9	Oro Province, villages from Koroda to Waseda. Close to Orokaiva. Few animists. D=Anglican Ch of PNG. High educational standard.
8770	4	6	5.44	0	99.80	0.20	C	347.48	150	9	Western Province, northwest of Agob. Savannah, forest, swamp. Animists 10%. D=UCPNGSI,ECP,SDA,One Way. Slow work. Motu and Kiwai spoken. M=APCM.
8771	0	7	2.74	0	99.90	0.10	C	400.77	86	10	East Sepik Province. Related languages: Romkun, Breri, Kominimung, Akrukay, Itutang, Midsivindi. Animists 5%.
8772	0	6	4.95	0	99.80	0.20	C	312.44	154	9	Madang Province. Related languages: Andarum, Tangu, Tanguat. Animists 16%.
8773	2	6	5.04	0	99.85	0.15	C	375.40	138	9	Milne Bay Province, eastern tip of Papua, inland villages. Partially bilingual in Wedau, Motu. Animists 10%. D=Anglican Ch of PNG,SDA.
8774	2	6	4.65	0	99.90	0.10	C	417.19	123	10	Gulf Province, south of Kibirowi Island. Closest to Omati (Mini). Animists 5%. D=UCPNGSI,SDA.
8775	1	6	5.02	0	99.85	0.15	C	359.89	144	9	Madang Province. Tribal religionists(animists) 15%. D=RCC.
8776	2	6	4.39	0	99.80	0.20	C	329.96	132	9	Sandaun Province. Closest to Pagi. Animists 20%. D=RCC,SDA.
8777	0	5	7.80	1	99.87	0.13	C	390.58	198	9	Southern Highlands Province, Ialibu District. Animists 3%. M=SIL.
8778	0	0	4.56	0	50.00	50.00	B	54.75	309	6	Sandaun Province, Amanab District near Imonda airstrip. Animists 10%. D=ELCPNG.
8779	1	7	3.43	0	99.90	0.10	C	410.62	99	10	Gulf Province, 5 miles up Pie river beyond Baimuri, 2 villages. Forest, swamp. Semi-nomadic. Animists 10%. D=UCPNGSI.
8780	4	5	7.11	0	99.85	0.15	C	372.30	187	9	Enga Province around Porgera patrol post. Forest, mountains. Few animists. D=GLC(NGLM/LCMS),RCC,SDA,Apostolic Church. M=ACM,LCMS.
8781	1	6	4.91	0	99.80	0.20	C	327.04	146	9	Morobe Province. Mountains. Agriculturalists. Animists 20%. D=ELCPNG. M=SIL.
8782	0	6	3.67	0	99.90	0.10	C	397.48	107	9	Madang Province, Marcia river. Related languages: Biyom, Tauya, Faita. Animists 10%.
8783	1	6	6.89	0	99.90	0.10	C	400.77	179	10	Madang and Morobe Provinces. Related dialects or languages: Mebu, Gabutamon, Wandabong, Nokopo, Kewieng. D=Ev Lutheran Ch of PNG. M=SIL.
8784	3	6	4.77	0	99.80	0.20	C	338.72	138	9	Madang Province, Gogol River area. Related languages: Sihan, Gumalu, Amele, Bau, Panim. Animists 15%. D=ELCPNG,RCC,SDA.
8785	0	6	4.39	0	99.80	0.20	C	321.20	136	9	Sandaun Province. Closest to Kilmera, Ossima. Animists 20%.
8786	0	6	3.37	1	60.00	40.00	B	65.70	203	6	Western Province. Tribal religionists(animists) 70%.
8787	1	7	3.95	0	59.00	41.00	B	64.60	233	6	Sandaun Province, Left May river. Isolated area. Animists 70%. D=NTM.
8788	0	7	2.45	0	60.00	40.00	B	76.65	161	6	East Sepik Province, Guam river. Related languages: Romkun, Breri, Kominimung, Akrukay, Igana, Midsivindi. Animists 65%.
8789	1	6	4.39	0	99.80	0.20	C	324.12	135	9	West New Britain Province. Animists 20%. D=RCC.
8790	0	6	3.91	0	64.00	36.00	B	93.44	213	6	Gulf Province. 3 villages. Close to Angoya. Animists 60%. M=SIL.
8791	1	6	5.13	0	99.80	0.20	C	335.80	148	9	Morobe Province, Lae District, between Wau and Salamaua. Close to Yabem. Animists 15%. D=ELCPNG. M=SIL,PNGBTA.
8792	3	6	4.87	0	86.00	14.00	B	156.95	189	7	East Sepik Province, Ambunti District. Animists 20%. D=AoG,NTM,RCC. M=SIL.
8793	0	10	1.81	8	48.00	52.00	A	1.75	143	4	Small community of practicing Jews. In urban areas and towns.
8794	0	6	4.06	0	99.90	0.10	C	397.48	116	9	Madang Province, Mindjim river. Related languages: Kwato, Ogea, Usu, Duduela, Rerau, Yangulam. Animists 10%.
8795	1	6	4.61	0	99.90	0.10	C	407.34	126	10	Milne Bay Province, along coast east of Moi Bay. Animists 10%. D=Anglican Ch of PNG. Traditional magic strong, widespread syncretism.
8796	0	7	2.79	0	63.00	37.00	B	91.98	168	6	East Sepik Province, 4 hamlets. Few understand Tok Pisin. Tropical forest, mountains. Animists 60%.
8797	0	5	6.10	0	80.00	20.00	B	160.60	246	7	Western Province east of Fly river, and across into Irian Jaya (Indonesia). Animists 15%.
8798	0	7	3.51	0	99.90	0.10	C	400.77	103	10	East Sepik Province, along coast around Taul. Animists 10%.
8799	1	6	4.52	0	99.90	0.10	C	420.48	120	10	Madang Province, Evapu and Ramu rivers. Animists 5%. D=ELCPNG.
8800	0	6	3.92	0	75.00	25.00	B	136.87	182	7	East New Britain Province, Gazelle Peninsula. Most are bilingual in Uramat. Animists 50%.
8801	3	6	4.94	0	99.95	0.05	C	478.51	119	10	Gulf Province north of Kikori on Kikori, Sirebi, and Tiviri rivers; 7 villages. Scattered animists, 5%. D=UCPNGSI,SDA,Independents. Motu used by all. M=SIL.
8802	1	5	6.26	0	99.85	0.15	C	362.99	172	9	East Sepik Province, several coastal and island villages. Close to Kaiep. Highly bilingual in Tok Pisin. Animists 15%. D=RCC.
8803	3	7	5.32	0	99.78	0.22	C	321.71	155	9	West New Britain Province, northwest coast. Few animists. D=RCC,AoG,SDA.
8804	1	6	4.67	0	99.80	0.20	C	321.20	143	9	Milne Bay Province, northwest tip of Fergusson Island. Close to Iamalele. Animists 15%. D=UCPNGSI.
8805	0	6	3.45	0	47.00	53.00	A	42.88	264	6	Sandaun Province. Isolated. Animists 75%.
8806	5	6	3.59	1	99.85	0.15	C	394.01	101	9	Eastern Highlands Province, Kainantu and Henganofi Sub-Provinces, 100 villages. Forest, mountains. Few animists. D=ELCPNG,SEBC,ICFG,SA,SDA. M=SIL.
8807	1	9	3.39	0	99.90	0.10	C	417.19	96	10	Morobe Province. Nearly extinct. D=ELCPNG.
8808	1	6	4.62	0	99.80	0.20	C	324.12	140	9	East Sepik Province, Wewak District. 7 villages. Magic, spiritism, necromancy. Animists 20%. D=RCC. Many youths charismatic. M=SIL.
8809	1	6	5.02	0	99.90	0.10	C	410.62	133	10	Madang Province, just northwest of Madang City. All Lutherans: D=ELCPNG. Third-generation church life, much nominalism. M=PBT.
8810	1	7	3.17	0	99.90	0.10	C	417.19	91	10	Eastern Highlands Province, Kainantu District. Nearly extinct. Trilingual in Binumarien, Gadsup. D=ELCPNG.
8811	1	6	4.44	0	99.90	0.10	C	407.34	120	10	On border, Sandaun Province, Amanab District; most in Indonesia. Animists 10%. D=RCC only; no Protestants.
8812	1	5	6.86	0	99.87	0.13	C	371.53	186	9	Madang Province; also in Angoram District, East Sepik Province. Few animists. D=RCC. M=Pioneer Bible Translators.
8813	1	6	4.12	0	99.90	0.10	C	407.34	115	10	East Sepik Province. Related languages: Karawa, Bouye. Animists 10%. D=RCC.
8814	1	6	3.49	0	64.00	36.00	B	81.76	195	6	Western Province, Wawoi Falls area, Aramia river northwards. Closest to Pare. Animists 65%. D=ECP. M=APCM/UFM,SIL.
8815	1	6	4.46	0	99.90	0.10	C	407.34	122	10	New Ireland Province, southern. Animists 5%. D=UCPNGSI.
8816	1	6	3.67	0	99.90	0.10	C	413.91	103	10	East Sepik Province, Blackwater river south of Lake Kuvanmas. Bilingual in Tok Pisin. D=RCC. Well-established work. M=SVD.
8817	5	6	6.84	1	99.80	0.20	C	353.32	179	9	Eastern Highlands Province, Okapa District. Close to Keyagani, Inoke-Yate. Scattered animists. D=ELCPNG,SDA,SA,ICFG,Independents. M=SIL.
8818	2	6	4.33	0	60.00	40.00	B	65.70	243	6	Western Province, between Fly river and coast. Also in Irian Jaya (Indonesia). 4 primary schools. Animists 70%. D=ECP,UCPNGSI.
8819	4	5	3.45	1	99.87	0.13	C	396.93	99	9	Gulf Province, Kukipi District: Morobe Province. Few animists. D=ELCPNG,RCC,NTM,SDA. NT translation now not used.
8820	2	6	5.19	0	99.85	0.15	C	366.09	145	9	East Sepik Province, Blackwater river and Korosameri river. Animists 15%. D=RCC,NTM. Well-established work. M=SVD.
8821	3	6	6.29	0	99.80	0.20	C	332.88	177	9	New Ireland Province, northern, 10 villages. Tropical forest, coastal. Animists 1%. D=UCPNGSI,RCC,some SDA. M=SIL.
8822	4	5	7.60	0	99.87	0.13	C	396.93	190	9	Madang Province, Ramu District, also in Western Highlands Province, Hagen District, 40 villages. Related to Gants, Kobon. D=Anglican Ch of PNG,ELCPNG,SDA.
8823	1	6	3.10	0	99.90	0.10	C	407.34	92	10	Morobe Province(Timbe river). Bilinguals in Timbe. Animists 10%. D=ELCPNG.
8824	2	8	3.04	0	67.00	33.00	B	85.59	168	6	East Sepik Province. Related languages: Kamnum, Bouye. Animists 65%. D=ELCPNG,NTM.
8825	2	6	3.99	0	99.90	0.10	C	417.19	109	10	Madang Province. Animists 10%. D=ELCPNG,RCC.
8826	1	6	4.76	0	99.80	0.20	C	338.72	138	9	Sandaun Province, Amanab District. Language isolate. Animists 15%. D=CB. M=SIL,CMML. A few churches. Literacy work.
8827	0	0	3.97	0	99.00	1.00	C	289.08	139	8	West New Britain Province, Kandrian District. Animists 10%. D=ELCPNG.
8828	2	6	5.27	0	99.90	0.10	C	433.62	132	10	West New Britain Province. Bilingual in Bola. D=RCC:all are Catholics, with many nominal.
8829	1	7	3.46	0	67.00	33.00	B	97.82	185	6	Southern Highlands Province, east and south of Mount Bosavi. Animists 10%. D=ECP. M=APCM/UFM,SIL.
8830	3	7	2.89	0	99.90	0.10	C	450.04	79	10	Morobe Province, Finschhafen District. Major Lutheran language. 1927, Eemasang (Cleanup Movement) revival. D=ELCPNG,NTM,et alia. Weekly attenders 25%.
8831	1	6	6.13	0	99.80	0.20	C	324.12	178	9	Madang Province. Related language: Seleibi. Animists 20%. D=RCC.
8832	0	6	4.22	0	60.00	40.00	B	76.65	242	6	Enga Province, middle southern edge, beyond Kandep, round Rumbiplaya. Animists 10%.
8833	4	5	8.08	1	99.83	0.17	C	369.59	206	9	Western Highlands Province, Hagen District. Forest, mountains. 100 villages. Strong animism. Animists 5%. D=ELCPNG,RCC,SDA,SEBC. M=SIL.
8834	1	6	3.42	0	99.90	0.10	C	407.34	98	10	Western Province straddling Indonesia border. Closely related to Faiwol. Animists 5%. D=Baptist Ch.
8835	1	8	3.81	0	99.90	0.10	C	413.91	106	10	Morobe Province, east of Ampale. Nearly extinct. Bilingual in Yagwoia. D=ELCPNG.
8836	0	6	3.81	0	99.90	0.10	C	397.48	111	9	Madang Province, on coast north of Boroi. Animists 10%.
8837	1	5	5.70	0	99.80	0.20	C	321.20	169	9	Morobe Province, southern coast of Huon Gulf, Paiawa river; 10 villages. Coastal. Animists 20%. D=ELCPNG.
8838	1	7	4.31	0	99.90	0.10	C	410.62	118	10	Morobe Province, north coast of Huon Peninsula. Animists 10%. D=ELCPNG.
8839	2	6	4.66	0	99.80	0.20	C	327.04	140	9	Eastern Highlands Province, Womenara District, 3 villages. Mountainous. Animists 20%. D=ELCPNG,NTM. M=SIL.
8840	0	6	4.60	0	98.00	2.00	C	250.39	159	8	East Sepik Province, Giling village, Yuat river. Animists 30%. M=PBT.
8841	2	5	8.11	0	99.87	0.13	C	384.23	208	9	Central Province, Hood Peninsula. 8 dialects. Coastal. Few animists. D=UCPNGSI,SDA. High standard of education and income. M=LMS.

Continued overleaf

Table 8-2 continued

PEOPLE		POPULATION				IDENTITY CODE		LANGUAGE		CHURCH		MINISTRY						SCRIPTURE		
Ref 1	Ethnic name 2	P% 3	In 1995 4	In 2000 5	In 2025 6	Race 7	Language 8	Autoglossonym 9	S 10	AC 11	Members 12	Jayuh 13-17	d 18	wa 19	xc 20	mc 21	mi 22	Biblioglossonym 23	Pub 24-26	ss 27
8842	Kerewo (Kerewa-Goari)	0.08160	3,359	3,760	5,854	AON10b	20-PAEA	kerewo cluster		80.00	3,008	0....	10	7	7	4	1	Kerawa*	P..	.
8843	Kesawai (Namuya)	0.01697	699	782	1,217	AON10b	22-RDAA-a	kesawai		90.00	704	0....	10	7	11	3	0		...	.
8844	Keuro (Belepa)	0.14313	5,892	6,596	10,268	AON10b	20-TAAB	keuru cluster		55.00	3,628	0....	10	5	3	4	0		...	.
8845	Kewieng	0.02586	1,065	1,192	1,855	AON10b	24-SCBF-a	kewieng		80.00	953	0....	10	7	7	3	0		...	.
8846	Keyagana (Keigana)	0.38739	15,948	17,851	27,791	AON10b	24-ODAA-c	keyagana		83.00	14,817	1.s..	10	7	7	3	0	Keyagana	PN.	.
8847	Kibiri (Porome, Poromi)	0.03857	1,588	1,777	2,767	AON09b	25-YAAA	porome cluster		85.00	1,511	0....	10	7	7	4	1		...	b
8848	Kilmera	0.05937	2,444	2,736	4,259	AON10b	21-IAAE-c	kilmeri		80.00	2,189	0....	10	7	7	5	2	Kilmeri	P..	.
8849	Kinalakna	0.00747	308	344	536	AON10b	24-TCBA-a	kinalakna		90.00	310	0....	10	7	11	4	1		...	.
8850	Kire-Puire (Giri)	0.05548	2,284	2,557	3,980	AON10b	26-SAAA-a	kire		80.00	2,045	0.s..	10	7	6	5	1	Kire	P..	.
8851	Kiriwina (Vakuta, Kitava)	0.55499	22,847	25,575	39,814	AON09b	34-FDAA-b	kilivila		82.00	20,971	0..u.	10	8	7	5	3	Kiriwina*	PN.	.
8852	Kis	0.00757	312	349	543	AON09b	34-BBFA-a	kis		90.00	314	0....	10	7	11	4	1		...	.
8853	Kobon	0.15136	6,231	6,975	10,858	AON10b	24-MAAA-a	kobon		75.00	5,231	0....	10	7	7	4	1	Kobon	P..	.
8854	Koguman	0.02974	1,224	1,370	2,133	AON10b	22-HAAA-a	koguman		98.00	1,343	0....	10	7	12	4	1		...	.
8855	Koita	0.07922	3,261	3,651	5,683	AON10b	23-CABA-b	east koita		80.00	2,920	0....	10	7	7	4	1		...	b
8856	Koiwat	0.01669	687	769	1,197	AON10b	26-HEAB-a	koiwat		75.00	577	0....	10	7	6	3	0		...	.
8857	Kol (Kole, Kola)	0.10091	4,154	4,650	7,239	AON10b	27-PAAA	kol-sui cluster		95.00	4,418	0....	10	7	11	4	1	Kol	...	.
8858	Kolom	0.00659	271	304	473	AON10b	22-UEAA-a	kolom		90.00	273	0....	10	7	11	4	1		...	.
8859	Komba	0.41758	17,191	19,243	29,956	AON10b	24-TBCA	komba cluster		83.00	15,971	0....	10	8	7	5	1	Komba	PN.	.
8860	Kombio	0.08247	3,395	3,800	5,916	AON10b	27-JADA	kombio cluster		80.00	3,040	0....	10	7	7	5	2	Kombio	...	.
8861	Kominimung	0.01034	426	476	742	AON10b	26-TDBA-a	kominimung		90.00	429	0....	10	7	11	3	0		...	.
8862	Komutu	0.01741	717	802	1,249	AON10b	24-SDAD-a	komutu		90.00	722	0....	10	7	11	4	1		...	.
8863	Konai	0.01596	657	735	1,145	AON10b	24-KGBA-a	konai		40.00	294	0....	9	6	3	4	1	Konai	...	.
8864	Konomala (Muliama, Nokon)	0.02279	938	1,050	1,635	AON09b	35-CGAA-b	konomala		90.00	945	0....	10	7	11	4	1		...	.
8865	Kopar	0.00722	297	333	518	AON10b	27-EABA-a	kopar		90.00	299	0....	10	7	11	3	0		...	.
8866	Korak	0.00646	266	298	463	AON10b	22-KAAA-a	korak		90.00	268	0....	10	7	11	4	1		...	.
8867	Korape (Kwarafe, Mokorua)	0.16235	6,684	7,481	11,647	AON10b	23-ABJA-a	proper korafe		80.00	5,985	0....	10	7	7	5	1	Korafe	PN.	.
8868	Koro	0.01197	493	552	859	AON09b	35-BCAC-a	koro		70.00	386	0....	10	7	5	4	1		...	.
8869	Kosena	0.05401	2,223	2,489	3,875	AON10b	24-PABA-b	kosena		75.00	1,867	0....	10	7	7	3	1	Kosena	PN.	.
8870	Kosorong	0.03808	1,568	1,755	2,732	AON10b	24-TDBA-b	kosorong		25.00	439	0....	9	5	6	4	1		pn.	b
8871	Kovai	0.11352	4,673	5,231	8,144	AON10b	24-VAAA-a	kovai		80.00	4,185	0....	10	7	7	5	2	Kovai	P..	.
8872	Kove	0.16773	6,905	7,729	12,033	AON09b	34-BJCA-a	kove		80.00	6,183	0....	10	7	7	5	3		...	.
8873	Kowaki	0.00098	40	45	70	AON10b	22-GEAA-a	kowaki		95.00	43	0....	10	7	11	3	0		...	.
8874	Krisa	0.01017	419	469	730	AON10b	25-OBAA-a	krisa		90.00	422	0....	10	7	11	3	0		...	.
8875	Kukuya	0.04858	2,000	2,239	3,485	AON09b	34-FCJA-b	kukuya		80.00	1,791	0....	10	7	7	5	1		p..	b
8876	Kumai	0.10635	4,378	4,901	7,629	AON10b	24-NCAC-e	kumai		80.00	3,921	0.s..	10	7	6	4	1	Kumai	Pn.	.
8877	Kumalu	0.08950	3,684	4,124	6,421	AON09b	34-DABB-b	kumaru		70.00	2,887	0....	10	7	8	0	0		...	.
8878	Kumukio	0.01884	776	868	1,352	AON10b	24-TCAA-a	kumukio		90.00	781	0....	10	7	11	4	1		...	.
8879	Kuni	0.11441	4,710	5,272	8,208	AON09b	34-GCAA-a	kuni		80.00	4,218	0....	10	7	6	4	1		...	b
8880	Kunimaipa (Karuama)	0.27750	11,424	12,788	19,907	AON10b	23-BCAB	kunimaipa cluster		80.00	10,230	0....	10	8	7	5	1	Kunimaipa	PNB	.
8881	Kurada	0.03693	1,520	1,702	2,649	AON09b	34-FCTA	auhelawa cluster		80.00	1,361	0....	10	7	7	5	2	Auhelawa	P..	.
8882	Kuruti-Pare	0.07077	2,913	3,261	5,077	AON09b	35-BCAB-f	kurti		70.00	2,283	0....	10	8	5	5	1	Kurti	pn.	.
8883	Kwale (Tware, Uare)	0.05045	2,077	2,325	3,619	AON10b	23-DAAB-a	kwale		80.00	1,860	0....	10	7	7	5	1	Kwale	...	.
8884	Kware	0.01261	519	581	905	AON10b	24-KIGA-a	kware		40.00	232	0....	9	6	3	3	0	Kware	P..	.
8885	Kwasengen (West Wosera)	0.17983	7,403	8,287	12,901	AON10b	26-HCAA-a	kwasengen		70.00	5,801	0....	10	5	6	5	1	Ambulas: Wosera*	P..	.
8886	Kwato	0.02453	1,010	1,130	1,760	AON10b	22-SDAA-a	kwato		80.00	904	0....	10	7	7	4	1		...	.
8887	Kwomtari (Maragin)	0.02270	934	1,046	1,628	AON10b	25-PABA	kwomtari cluster		25.00	262	0....	9	5	6	4	2	Kwomtari	...	.
8888	Label	0.00500	206	230	359	AON09b	35-CFEB-a	label		90.00	207	0....	10	8	8	0	0		...	.
8889	Labu	0.04225	1,739	1,947	3,031	AON09b	34-BLBA	labu cluster		80.00	1,558	0....	10	7	6	4	1		...	.
8890	Lae (Lahe)	0.00034	14	16	24	AON09b	34-BLAB-c	lae		95.00	15	0....	10	7	11	3	0		...	.
8891	Laeko-Libuat	0.01836	756	846	1,317	AON10b	27-IAAA	laeko cluster		90.00	761	0....	10	7	11	4	1		...	.
8892	Laewomba (Wampar, Dagin)	0.13294	5,473	6,126	9,537	AON09b	34-CCAA-a	wampar		80.00	4,901	0....	10	7	7	4	1	Wampar	PN.	.
8893	Lamogai	0.12370	5,092	5,700	8,874	AON09b	35-EABA-a	lamogai		80.00	4,560	0....	10	7	7	5	2	Mulakaino*	P..	.
8894	Langam	0.00801	330	369	575	AON10b	26-NBAA-a	langam		40.00	148	0....	9	5	3	3	0		...	.
8895	Latep	0.00751	309	346	539	AON09b	34-DABA-g	latep		70.00	242	0....	10	7	7	4	1		pn.	.
8896	Latoma	0.00416	171	192	298	AON10b	26-JGAA-a	sumariup		30.00	58	0....	9	5	6	3	1		...	n
8897	Laua (Labu)	0.00003	1	1	2	AON10b	23-GBCA-a	laua		95.00	1	0....	10	7	11	3	0		...	b
8898	Lavatbura-Lamusong (Ugana	0.05166	2,127	2,381	3,706	AON09b	35-CEAA	lavatbura cluster		90.00	2,143	0....	10	7	11	5	2		...	.
8899	Lavongai	0.32665	13,447	15,053	23,433	AON09b	35-CBAA-a	tungag		89.00	13,397	0....	10	8	7	5	1	Tungag	P..	.
8900	Lele (Moanus, Sabon)	0.03993	1,644	1,840	2,864	AON09b	35-BCAB-g	lele		90.00	1,656	0....	10	8	11	5	2	Manus*	PN.	.
8901	Lembena	0.03727	1,534	1,717	2,674	AON10b	24-LDBA-a	lembena		10.00	172	0....	8	5	3	5	2	Lembena	...	.
8902	Lemio	0.00552	227	254	396	AON10b	22-UBAA-a	lemio		90.00	229	0....	10	7	11	5	2		...	.
8903	Lenkau	0.00768	316	354	551	AON09b	35-BDBA-a	lenkau		90.00	319	0....	10	8	11	5	1		...	.
8904	Lesing	0.02853	1,175	1,315	2,047	AON09b	35-FAAB	lesing-atui cluster		80.00	1,052	0....	10	7	7	5	3		...	.
8905	Levei-Ndrehet	0.04036	1,662	1,860	2,895	AON09b	35-BBBB-a	levei		80.00	1,488	0....	10	7	7	5	1	Khehek	...	.
8906	Lewada-Dewara	0.01424	586	656	1,022	AON10b	20-NAAA	lewada-dewara cluster		60.00	394	0....	10	7	7	4	0	Tirio	P..	.
8907	Lihir	0.17089	7,035	7,875	12,259	AON09b	35-CDBA-a	lihir		75.00	5,906	0....	10	7	7	4	2		...	.
8908	Likum	0.00351	144	162	252	AON09b	35-BBAA-a	likum		95.00	154	0....	10	7	6	4	1		...	p
8909	Lilau (Ngaimbom)	0.01416	583	653	1,016	AON10b	27-MAAB-a	lilau		90.00	587	0....	10	7	11	3	0		...	.
8910	Lindrou (Nyindrou)	0.08545	3,518	3,938	6,130	AON09b	35-BBBA	nyindrou cluster		80.00	3,150	0....	10	7	11	5	3	Lindrou*	P..	.
8911	Lohiki (Obi)	0.02270	934	1,046	1,628	AON10b	24-RAGB-a	angoya		80.00	837	0....	10	7	6	3	1	Angoya	...	.
8912	Loko	0.11354	4,674	5,232	8,145	AON09b	35-FAAC-a	gimi		70.00	3,662	0....	10	7	6	3	0	Gimi	p..	.
8913	Loniu	0.01613	664	743	1,157	AON09b	35-BABB-a	loniu		90.00	669	0....	10	7	11	5	1		...	n
8914	Lou	0.02484	1,023	1,145	1,782	AON09b	27-JABA	lou cluster		80.00	916	0....	10	8	7	5	2		...	.
8915	Lower Morehead (Peremka)	0.00755	311	348	542	AON10b	20-LDDA-a	proper peremka		30.00	104	0....	9	5	5	5	1		...	.
8916	Lugitama (Pahi, Riahoma)	0.01973	812	909	1,415	AON10b	26-EBAA-a	pahi		85.00	773	0..,.	10	7	7	5	1		...	.
8917	Lukep (Siasi, Siassi)	0.01915	788	882	1,374	AON09b	34-BFAA-a	lukep		80.00	706	0....	10	7	7	5	1	Lokep	P..	.
8918	Madak (Mandak, Katingan)	0.08545	3,518	3,938	6,130	AON10b	35-CEBA	madak cluster		80.00	3,150	0....	10	7	7	5	1	Madak	PN.	.
8919	Magori	0.00807	332	372	579	AON09b	34-GACA-a	magori		90.00	335	0....	10	7	11	4	1		...	n
8920	Mailu (Derebai, Ilai)	0.19443	8,004	8,960	13,948	AON10b	23-GBCB-d	mailu		85.00	7,616	0....	10	7	7	5	1	Magi*	PN.	b
8921	Maisin (Maisan)	0.07121	2,932	3,281	5,108	AON09b	34-EAAA-a	kosirava		80.00	2,625	0....	10	7	7	5	2		...	p
8922	Maiwa (Baiawa)	0.06307	2,596	2,906	4,525	AON10b	23-IBAA	maiwa cluster		80.00	2,325	0....	10	7	7	3	1	Maiwa	...	n
8923	Makarim	0.04051	1,668	1,867	2,906	AON10b	27-IBAA-b	makarim		35.00	653	0....	9	5	5	2	0		...	.
8924	Malala (Pai)	0.02425	998	1,117	1,740	AON10b	34-BFAA-bb	malala		70.00	782	0....	10	7	7	5	0	Mala	P..	.
8925	Malalamai	0.01196	492	551	858	AON09b	34-BGAA-a	malalamai		90.00	496	0....	10	7	11	4	1		...	.
8926	Malas	0.00694	286	320	498	AON10b	22-LBAA-a	malas		90.00	288	0....	10	7	11	4	1		...	.
8927	Malasanga	0.01097	452	506	787	AON10b	34-BFAB-b	malasanga		85.00	430	0....	10	7	7	5	0		...	.
8928	Male (Koliku)	0.01239	510	571	889	AON10b	22-TBAA-a	male		90.00	514	0....	10	7	11	3	0		...	.
8929	Maleu (Kaitarolea)	0.12614	5,193	5,813	9,049	AON09b	34-BKAB-a	maleu		80.00	4,650	0....	10	7	7	5	1	Maleu-kilenge	P..	.
8930	Malol (Sissano, Arop)	0.05627	2,316	2,593	4,037	AON09b	34-BAAB-c	malol.		90.00	2,334	0....	10	7	11	4	2		p..	.
8931	Mamaa	0.00676	278	312	485	AON10b	24-SFBA-a	mamaa		90.00	280	0....	10	7	11	4	1		...	.
8932	Mamusi	0.17089	7,035	7,875	12,259	AON09b	35-HABA-a	mamusi		85.00	6,694	0....	10	7	7	4	2	Mamusi	...	.
8933	Managalasi (Muaturaina)	0.15356	6,322	7,076	11,016	AON10b	23-CBBB	managalasi cluster		80.00	5,661	0....	10	7	7	4	1	Managalasi	PN.	.
8934	Manam	0.16398	6,751	7,556	11,764	AON09b	34-BBDA-a	manam		75.00	5,667	0....	10	7	6	4	1	Manam	PN.	.
8935	Manambu	0.06490	2,672	2,991	4,656	AON10b	26-HBAA-a	manambu		75.00	2,243	0....	10	7	7	5	1	Manambu	PN.	.
8936	Mandi	0.00511	210	235	367	AON10b	27-LAAA-a	mandi		90.00	212	0....	10	7	11	3	0		...	.
8937	Manem (Yeti, Wembi)	0.01271	523	586	912	AON10b	21-HAAA	manem cluster		30.00	176	0....	9	5	6	3	0		...	.
8938	Mangga Buang (Lagis)	0.08322	3,426	3,835	5,970	AON09b	34-DABD-a	mangga		80.00	3,068	0....	10	7	7	4	1	Buang: Mangga*	PN.	.
8939	Mape (East, West Mape)	0.17464	7,189	8,048	12,528	AON10b	24-UBEA	mape cluster		75.00	6,036	0....	10	7	7	4	1		...	b
8940	Mapena	0.01059	436	488	760	AON10b	23-IABA-a	mapena		90.00	439	0....	10	7	11	4	1		...	.
8941	Maralango	0.00584	240	269	419	AON09b	34-CEAB-a	maralango		85.00	229	0....	10	7	6	3	0		...	.
8942	Maraliinan (Middle Watut)	0.03674	1,512	1,693	2,636	AON09b	34-CEAA-b	maraliinan		90.00	1,524	0....	10	7	11	4	1		...	n
8943	Maramba	0.00946	389	436	679	AON10b	26-LAAA-a	maramba		40.00	174	0....	9	5	3	2	0		...	.
8944	Mari	0.00378	156	174	271	AON10b	26-JCAA-a	mari		90.00	157	0....	10	7	11	3	0		...	n
8945	Mari (Hop)	0.02177	896	1,003	1,562	AON09b	34-CAAA-a	mari		5.00	50	0....	7	4	3	4	1		...	n
8946	Maria (Manubara, Didigaru	0.02946	1,213	1,358	2,113	AON10b	23-FABA-e	maria		80.00	1,086	0....	10	7	6	5	2		...	.
8947	Maring (Yoadabe-Watoare)	0.21604	8,894	9,955	15,498	AON10b	24-NBAA	maring cluster		65.00	6,471	0....	10	5	6	4	2		P..	.
8948	Masegi (Masek, Mangseng)	0.05045	2,077	2,325	3,619	AON09b	35-GABA	mangseng cluster		80.00	1,860	0....	10	7	7	5	1	Mangsing	P..	n
8949	Mataru	0.02000	823	922	1,435	AON10b	22-PABB-a	wagi		90.00	829	0....	10	7	11	3	0		...	.
8950	Matepi	0.00751	309	346	539	AON10b	22-PCEA-a	matepi		95.00	329	0....	10	7	11	3	0		...	.
8951	Matukar	0.00691	284	318	496	AON09b	34-BCAC-a	matukar		95.00	303	0....	10	7	11	3	0		...	.
8952	Mawae	0.03218	1,325	1,483	2,309	AON10b	23-ABAD-a	mawae		80.00	1,186	0....	10	7	7	4	1		...	.
8953	Mawak	0.00098	40	45	70	AON10b	22-GDAA-a	mawak		95.00	43	0....	10	7	11	3	1		...	.
8954	Mawan	0.00848	349	391	608	AON10b	22-PCIA-a	mawan		90.00	352	0....	10	7	11	5	2		...	.
8955	Mayo (Mayo-Yessan)	0.03027	1,246	1,395	2,172	AON10b	26-ECBA-b	yessan-mayo		80.00	1,116	0....	10	7	7	5	2	Yessan-mayo*	PN.	.
8956	Mbula (Mangap)	0.06307	2,596	2,906	4,525	AON09b	34-BFBA-a	mbula		80.00	2,325	0....	10	7	7	4	1	Mbula	P..	.
8957	Mebu	0.01006	414	464	722	AON10b	24-SCAA-a	mebu		30.00	139	0....	9	5	5	3	0		...	.
8958	Medebur	0.01353	557	623	971	AON09b	34-BBEA-a	medebur		90.00	561	0....	10	7	11	5	2		...	.
8959	Medlpa (Melpa, Hagen)	3.27952	135,009	151,125	235,266	AON10b	24-NAAA-a	proper medlpa		87.50	132,234	1.s..	10	8	7	5	1	Melpa*	PN.	.
8960	Megiar	0.02709	1,115	1,248	1,943	AON09b	34-BCAB-a	megiar		75.00	936	0....	10	7	7	3	0		...	.
8961	Mehek (Indinogosima)	0.15655	6,445	7,214	11,231	AON10b	26-EBBA-a	mehek		75.00	5,411	0....	10	8	7	5	1		...	.
8962	Mekeo (Bush Mekeo, Kovio)	0.30272	12,462	13,950	21,717	AON09b	34-GEAA-a	mekeo		77.00	10,741	0....	10	8	7	5	3	Mekeo	P..	.
8963	Mekmek	0.03267	1,345	1,505	2,344	AON10b	26-MBAA-a	mekmek		10.00	151	0....	8	5	3	1	0		...	.
8964	Mena	0.01286	529	593	923	AON10b	20-VAAA-a	mena		70.00	415	0....	10	7	6	3	0		...	.
8965	Mengen (Poeng, Mio, Pau)	0.25799	10,621	11,889	18,508	AON09b	35-HACC	east mengen cluster		79.00	9,392	0....	10	7	7	3	1	Mengen	...	.

Continued opposite

Table 8-2 continued

EVANGELIZATION								EVANGELISM			ADDITIONAL DESCRIPTIVE DATA
Ref 1	D 28	aC 29	CG% 30	r 31	E 32	U 33	W 34	e 35	R 36	T 37	*Locations, civil divisions, literacy, religions, church history, denominations, dioceses, church growth, missions, agencies, ministries, movements* 38
8842	1	6	5.87	1	99.80	0.20	C	329.96	168	9	Gulf Province, west bank of Omati river; Goaribari Island. Animists 15%. D=UCPNGSI. M=LMS.
8843	0	6	4.35	0	99.90	0.10	C	397.48	123	9	Madang Province, Ramu river. Related languages: Sinsauru, Asas, Sausi, Dumpu. Animists 10%.
8844	0	6	6.07	0	80.00	20.00	B	160.60	245	7	Gulf Province, from mouth of Purari river eastward. Animists 10%.
8845	0	6	4.66	0	99.80	0.20	C	312.44	147	9	Madang Province, around Kewieng town, border with Morobe Province. Related languages: Mebu, Gabutamon, Wandabong, Nokopo, Yupna. Animists 20%.
8846	0	5	7.57	1	99.83	0.17	C	357.48	201	9	Eastern Highlands Province, Okapa and Henganofi Districts. Animists 2%.
8847	2	6	5.15	0	99.85	0.15	C	372.30	142	9	Gulf Province, near Aird Hills, Kikori river, 6 villages. Language isolate. Animists 15%. D=UCPNGSI, since 1912. Services in Motu lingua franca. M=PNGBTA.
8848	2	6	5.54	0	99.80	0.20	C	335.80	157	9	Sandaun Province, Vanimo District near Ossima; 14 villages. Close to Isi, Ossima languages. Animists 20%. D=RCC,SDA.
8849	1	6	3.49	0	99.90	0.10	C	407.34	101	10	Morobe Province. Animists 10%. D=ELCPNG.
8850	2	6	5.46	0	99.80	0.20	C	332.88	157	9	Madang Province, lower Ramu, around Garati village. Animists 15%. D=ELCPNG,RCC. M=PBT.
8851	3	5	7.95	0	99.82	0.18	C	362.15	204	9	Milne Bay Province, Trobriand Islands. Many schools. Animists 3%. Syncretism strong. D=UCPNGSI,RCC,SDA.
8852	1	6	3.51	0	99.90	0.10	C	407.34	101	10	East Sepik Province, southeast of Samap, inland from coast. Animists 5%. D=UCPNGSI.
8853	1	6	6.46	0	99.75	0.25	C	292.91	193	8	Madang Province, Middle Ramu District; Western Highlands Province on Kaironk river. Tropical forest, mountains. Few animists. D=Ch of the Nazarene. M=SIL.
8854	1	6	5.02	0	99.98	0.02	C	479.31	125	10	Madang Province. Related language: Abasakur. Entirely baptized Lutherans: D=ELCPNG.
8855	1	6	5.84	0	99.80	0.20	C	332.88	166	9	Central Province, around Port Moresby. Close to Grass Koiari. Bilingual in Motu, Hiri Motu. Animists 15%. D=UCPNGSI. M=CWM(LMS).
8856	0	6	4.14	0	99.75	0.25	C	276.48	141	8	East Sepik Province, Ambunti District. Animists 25%.
8857	1	6	6.28	0	99.95	0.05	C	450.77	155	10	East New Britain Province, Open Bay to waterfall; most live on south side of island. Tropical forest. D=RCC: all Catholics. M=SIL.
8858	1	7	3.36	0	99.90	0.10	C	410.62	97	10	Madang Province. Animists 10%. D=ELCPNG.
8859	3	6	2.81	0	99.83	0.17	C	369.59	87	9	Morobe Province, Kabwum District. Savannah, mountains. Few animists. D=ELCPNG(95% baptized,60% committed),SDA,40 youths in Church of Christ. M=SIL.
8860	2	6	5.88	0	99.80	0.20	C	332.88	167	9	East Sepik Province, Dreikikir District, Torricelli Mountains, 31 villages. Animists 20%. D=RCC,SSEC. M=SIL,SVD.
8861	0	6	3.83	0	99.90	0.10	C	397.48	111	9	East Sepik Province. Related languages: Romkun, Breri, Igana, Akrukay, Itutang, Midsivindi. Animists 10%.
8862	1	6	4.37	0	99.90	0.10	C	407.34	120	10	Morobe Province, lower Timbe River valley. Animists 5%. D=ELCPNG.
8863	0	6	3.44	0	64.00	36.00	B	93.44	193	6	Western Province, west side of Upper Strickland river. Closest to Kalamo, Agala. Animists 60%. M=Pioneers Inc.
8864	1	6	4.65	0	99.90	0.10	C	407.34	126	10	New Ireland Province, southeastern coast; 8 villages. People now speak Siar. Animists 5%. D=RCC.
8865	0	7	3.46	0	99.90	0.10	C	400.77	102	10	East Sepik Province, at mouth of Sepik river. Related language: Murik. Animists 10%.
8866	1	7	3.34	0	99.90	0.10	C	410.62	97	10	Madang Province. Traditional religionists(animists) 10%. D=RCC.
8867	2	5	6.60	0	99.80	0.20	C	338.72	181	9	Oro Province, near Baruga and Tufi. Tropical forest. 45 coastal villages. Fishermen. D=Anglican Ch of PNG,SDA(very few). M=SIL.
8868	1	6	3.72	0	98.00	2.00	C	250.39	134	8	Manus Province. Close language: Papitalai. Animists 30%. D=RCC.
8869	0	5	5.37	0	99.75	0.25	C	292.91	165	8	Eastern Highlands Province, Kainantu and Okapa Districts. Tropical forest, mountains. Agriculturalists. Animists 25%. M=SIL.
8870	1	6	3.85	0	59.00	41.00	B	53.83	228	6	Morobe, 5 villages in southeast Huon Peninsula. Evangelized by D=Ev Lutheran Ch of PNG. Nominalism. Several community schools. Church language: Kate.
8871	2	6	6.22	0	99.80	0.20	C	335.80	174	9	Morobe Province, Siassi District, Umboi/Rooke Island. Animists 20%. No cargo cults. D=90% Lutherans(ELCPNG),10% RCs.
8872	3	6	6.64	0	99.80	0.20	C	338.72	182	9	West New Britain Province, northwest coast. Close to Kaliai. Animists 20%. D=RCC,AoG,SDA.
8873	0	8	3.83	0	99.95	0.05	C	443.84	105	10	Madang Province, south of Sikor. Related languages: Mawak, Hinihon, Musar, Wanambre. Animists 5%.
8874	0	6	3.81	0	99.90	0.10	C	397.48	111	9	Sandaun Province, inland from Vanimo, near coast. Related languages: Rawo, Puari, Warapu. Animists 10%.
8875	2	6	5.32	0	99.80	0.20	C	341.64	150	9	Milne Bay Province, southwest tip of Fergusson Island. Lingua franca: Dobu (numerous bilinguals). Animists 20%. Syncretism strong. D=UCPNGSI,RCC. M=SIL.
8876	1	6	6.15	1	99.80	0.20	C	335.80	172	9	Simbu Province. Close to Kuman. Animists 20%. D=SDA.
8877	0	0	5.83	0	89.00	11.00	C	227.39	212	8	Morobe Province, Mumeng District. Tropical forest. Swidden agriculturalists. Animists 20%. D=ELCPNG.
8878	1	6	4.45	0	99.90	0.10	C	407.34	122	10	Morobe Province. Animists 10%. D=ELCPNG.
8879	1	6	6.23	0	99.80	0.20	C	329.96	177	9	Central Province, Kairuku and southwest Goilala Districts, south of Mekeo. Close to Motu. Animists 20%. D=RCC.
8880	3	5	7.18	0	99.80	0.20	C	362.08	182	9	Morobe and Central Provinces, northern Goilola District, Wau District. Tropical forest, mountains. Few animists. D=RCC,UCPNGSI,ELCPNG. M=SIL.
8881	2	6	5.04	0	99.80	0.20	C	335.80	146	9	Milne Bay Province, Normanby Island. Esaala District. Animists 20%. Syncretism strong. D=UCPNGSI,RCC. M=SIL,PNGBTA.
8882	3	6	5.58	0	99.70	0.30	C	268.27	174	8	Manus Province, north central coast. Animists 25%. D=RCC(New Life charismatics),SDA,Paliau Ch(New Way). M=PBT.
8883	2	6	5.36	0	99.80	0.20	C	329.96	156	9	Central Province, Rigo Inland district, coast south of Port Moresby, Kemp Welsh river. Animists 15%. D=UCPNGSI,SDA. M=SIL.
8884	0	6	3.19	0	63.00	37.00	B	91.98	185	6	Western Province, Southern Highlands Province, around Simo. Animists 60%.
8885	3	6	6.57	0	99.70	0.30	C	265.72	201	8	East Sepik Province, Pagwi District, 16 villages. Close to Ambulas. 3 community schools; difficult access. Animists 15%. D=SSEC,RCC,AoG. M=SIL.
8886	1	6	4.61	0	99.80	0.20	C	321.20	141	9	Madang Province. Related languages: Usu, Ogea, Duduela, Rerau, Jilim, Yangulam. Animists 20%. D=ELCPNG.
8887	1	6	3.32	0	54.00	46.00	B	49.27	223	6	Sandaun Province, Amanab District, north of Namia, 6 villages. Tropical forest. No schools. Animists 75%. D=Christian Brethren. M=CMML,SIL.
8888	0	0	3.08	0	99.90	0.10	C	354.78	105	9	New Ireland Province, on southwest coast. Nasko and Tampakar villages. Animists 5%. D=ELCPNG.
8889	1	6	5.18	0	99.80	0.20	C	321.20	156	9	Morobe Province, coast near mouth of Markham river. Culture declining. Animists 20%. D=ELCPNG.
8890	0	9	2.75	0	99.95	0.05	C	447.30	81	10	Morobe Province, Lower Wamped river. Nearly extinct.
8891	1	6	4.43	0	99.90	0.10	C	407.34	122	10	Sandaun Province, Torricelli Mountains, west of Mehek. Animists 10%. D=RCC.
8892	1	5	2.54	0	99.80	0.20	C	332.88	87	9	Morobe Province, lower Markham and Wamped rivers. Close to Azera. Few animists. D=ELCPNG.
8893	2	6	6.31	0	99.80	0.20	C	335.80	176	9	West New Britain Province, northwest interior. Related to Pulie-Rauto. Animists 15%. D=RCC,NTM.
8894	0	6	2.73	0	62.00	38.00	B	90.52	168	6	East Sepik Province, near Yuat river. Related languages: Mongol, Yaul. Animists 60%.
8895	1	6	3.24	0	99.70	0.30	C	263.16	115	8	Morobe Province. In Mumeng dialect chain. Animists 30%. D=ELCPNG.
8896	0	5	4.14	0	56.00	44.00	B	61.32	255	6	East Sepik Province, Angoram District, bordering Alamblak. Bilingual in Alamblak. Animists 70%. M=SM.
8897	0	8	0.00	0	99.95	0.05	C	454.24	22	10	Central Province, south coast around Laua town. Virtually extinct (1 speaker only, in 1987).
8898	2	6	5.51	0	99.90	0.10	C	420.48	141	10	New Ireland Province, central. Animists 5%. D=RCC,UCPNGSI.
8899	3	6	7.47	0	99.89	0.11	C	406.06	187	10	New Ireland Province, New Hanover, Tingwon, Umbukul Islands. Forest. D=RCC,UCPNGSI(using Tungak, Tok Pisin),SDA. Headquarters of Johnson cargo cult.
8900	4	4	5.24	0	99.90	0.10	C	430.33	132	10	Manus Island, Manus Province. Tropical forest, coastal. Fishermen. Animists 5%. D=MEC,RCC(New Life charismatics),SDA,Paliau Ch(New Way). M=MEM.
8901	3	6	2.89	0	38.00	62.00	A	13.87	286	5	Enga Province, northeast corner and Erem village. Relatively unevangelized. Many animists 40%. D=BUWH,ELCPNG,SDA. M=ABMS(Baptist),SIL.
8902	2	6	3.18	0	99.90	0.10	C	417.19	92	10	Madang Province, several villages on coast near Saidor. Animists 10%. D=ELCPNG,RCC.
8903	4	6	3.52	0	99.90	0.10	C	417.19	99	10	Manus Province, Rambutyo Is; 1 village only. All bilingual in Titan & Penchal. Animists 10%. D=Paliau Ch,RCC,MEC; 40% Evangelical, 10% Pentecostal. M=MEM.
8904	3	5	4.77	0	99.80	0.20	C	335.80	139	9	West New Britain Province, southwest coast. Tropical forest, coral coast. 3 primary schools. Animists 15%. D=RCC,ACPNG,SDA.
8905	1	6	5.13	0	99.80	0.20	C	327.04	152	9	Manus Province, Soparibeu District. Animists 20%. D=RCC. M=SIL.
8906	0	6	3.74	0	89.00	11.00	C	194.91	148	7	Western Province, southern bank of Fly estuary. Close to Aturu. Animists 40%.
8907	2	6	6.59	0	99.75	0.25	C	295.65	194	8	New Ireland Province, Lihir Island and 3 smaller islands. Scattered animists. D=UCPNGSI,RCC.
8908	1	7	2.77	0	99.95	0.05	C	436.90	84	10	Manus Province. All bilingual in Lindrou. Animists 5%. D=RCC.
8909	0	6	4.16	0	99.90	0.10	C	397.48	118	9	East Sepik Province, on coast south of Bogia. A few animists, 7%.
8910	3	6	5.92	0	99.80	0.20	C	353.32	158	9	Manus Province, 9 villages. Bilingual in Kurti. Tropical forest, coastal. Fishermen, hunters, agriculturalists. Animists 10%. D=MEC,RCC,SDA. M=MEM.
8911	0	6	4.53	0	99.80	0.20	C	312.44	143	9	Gulf Province, valleys between Nabo Range and Albert Mountains, Lohiki river. Agriculturalists. Animists 20%. M=SIL.
8912	0	6	6.08	0	98.00	2.00	C	250.39	200	8	West New Britain Province, southwest coast and inland, Johanna river to Anu river. Dialect chain with Moewehafen, Palik. Some animists.
8913	2	6	4.29	0	99.90	0.10	C	420.48	115	10	Manus Province, south coast of Los Negros Island, 2 villages. Bilingual in Lele, Papitalai. Close to Bipi. D=MEC,RCC. M=MEM(Liebenzell Mission).
8914	4	6	4.62	0	99.80	0.20	C	332.88	137	9	Manus Province, Lou Island. Bilingual in Baluan-Pam, Titan. Some Baha'is, animists 10%. D=RCC(40%),SDA(33%),20% Paliau/cargo cult,MEC. M=MEM,SIL.
8915	2	6	2.37	0	59.00	41.00	B	64.60	160	6	Western Province, extreme southwest. Related to Kanum, Aramba, Bothar, Rouku. Swamp, savannah. Animists 70%. D=ECP,UCPNGSI. M=UFM.
8916	2	6	4.44	0	99.85	0.15	C	362.99	129	9	Sandaun Province, extending north into Maimai Namblo Division. Related to Pasi, Kalou, Mehek, Yessan-Mayo. Animists 10%. D=RCC,CB. M=CMML.
8917	1	6	4.35	0	99.80	0.20	C	327.04	133	9	Morobe Province, Tolokiwa and north tip of Umboi Island. Close to Arop. Animists 15%. D=ELCPNG; some RCs.
8918	2	6	5.92	0	99.80	0.20	C	341.64	164	9	New Ireland Province. 5 dialects. Animists 15%. D=RCC,UCPNGSI. M=SIL.
8919	1	6	3.57	0	99.90	0.10	C	413.91	101	10	Central Province, eastern end of Table Bay. Trilingual in Gadaisu, Suau, Hiri Motu, Mailu. Animists 5%. D=UCPNGSI.
8920	2	5	6.86	0	99.85	0.15	C	384.71	175	9	Central Province, south coast, Gadaisu to Baramata, Table Bay, Toulon Island. Highly educated. Few animists. D=UCPNGSI,SDA. M=LMS.
8921	2	6	5.73	0	99.80	0.20	C	335.80	162	9	Oro Province along coast of Collingwood Bay and swamps of Kosirava. Bilingual in Ubir. Animists 15%. D=Anglican Ch of PNG,SDA.
8922	1	6	5.60	0	99.80	0.20	C	327.04	163	9	Milne Bay Province northern slopes and foothills. Animists 10%. D=Anglican Ch of PNG. Church language: Wedau. Traditional magic strong, syncretism.
8923	0	6	4.27	0	58.00	42.00	B	74.09	252	6	Sandaun Province. Many tribal religionists(animists)15%.
8924	0	5	4.46	0	99.00	1.00	C	252.94	153	8	Madang Province, Bogia District. Savannah, coastal mountains. Fishermen. Animists 30%.
8925	1	6	3.98	0	99.90	0.10	C	407.34	112	10	Madang Province, Rai coast east and west of Saidor and on Long Island; 2 villages. Animists 5%. D=ELCPNG.
8926	1	6	3.42	0	99.90	0.10	C	407.34	99	10	Madang Province near Tokain. Animists 10%. D=RCC.
8927	0	5	3.83	0	99.85	0.15	C	350.58	119	9	Morobe Province, north coast, 2 villages. Animists 15%.
8928	0	6	4.02	0	99.90	0.10	C	397.48	115	9	Madang Province, on coast south of Bom. Related to Bongu and Anjam. Animists 7%.
8929	2	6	6.33	0	99.80	0.20	C	332.88	178	9	West New Britain Province, Talasea District, western tip. Savannah, tropical forest, volcano. Few animists. D=Anglican Ch of PNG,RCC. M=SIL.
8930	1	6	5.60	0	99.90	0.10	C	417.19	144	10	Sandaun Province, 3 villages. D=RCC(all are RCs, since 1908). M=SIL,OFM.
8931	1	6	3.39	0	99.90	0.10	C	407.34	99	10	Morobe Province, 1 village. A few animists. D=ELCPNG.
8932	2	5	6.72	0	99.85	0.15	C	362.99	182	9	East New Britain Province, southeast coast. Inland villages, scattered village schools. Literates 25%(youth). Animists 2%. D=RCC(almost all are Catholics),NTM.
8933	1	6	6.54	0	99.80	0.20	C	335.80	181	9	Oro Province, Popondetta District, southeast of the Omie. 14 dialects. Scattered animists. D=Anglican Ch of PNG(strong). M=SIL.
8934	0	6	6.55	0	99.75	0.25	C	295.65	193	8	Mandang Province, Manam Island and on mainland. Related to Wogeo, Biem, Sepa, Medebur. Tropical forest. Animists 2%. M=SIL.
8935	2	6	5.56	0	99.75	0.25	C	306.60	162	9	East Sepik Province, Ambunti District. Strong animists, 25%. D=RCC(mainly),AoG(growing). New Testament not well used. M=SIL.
8936	0	7	3.10	0	99.90	0.10	C	400.77	94	10	East Sepik Province, on coast southeast of Wewak. Animists 10%.
8937	0	6	2.91	0	55.00	45.00	B	60.22	198	6	West Sepik Province, 1 village; also in Irian Jaya (Indonesia). Animists 70%.
8938	1	7	5.89	0	99.80	0.20	C	338.72	164	9	Morobe Province, mid-upper Snake River area, Mumeng District. 8 villages. Savannah, mountains. Animists 10%. D=ELCPNG. Nominalism pervasive. M=SIL.
8939	1	5	6.61	0	99.75	0.25	C	295.65	195	8	Morobe Province along Mape river. Close to Kate (lingua franca). Few animists. D=ELCPNG.
8940	1	6	3.85	0	99.90	0.10	C	407.34	109	10	Milne Bay Province, round Mt Gwoira. Close to Daga. Animists 5%. D=Anglican Ch of PNG.
8941	0	6	3.18	0	99.85	0.15	C	344.37	105	9	Morobe Province, lower Watut river. Animists 15%.
8942	1	6	5.15	0	99.90	0.10	C	417.19	134	10	Morobe Province, Mumeng District, lower Watut Valley, 7 villages. Animists 5%. D=ELCPNG. Church language: Yabim.
8943	0	6	2.90	0	61.00	39.00	B	89.06	178	6	East Sepik Province. Tribal religionists(animists) 60%.
8944	0	6	2.79	0	99.90	0.10	C	404.05	86	10	East Sepik Province, near Mari Lake and on Salumei river. Highly bilingual in Tok Pisin. Animists 10%.
8945	1	6	3.99	0	30.00	70.00	A	5.47	462	4	Madang Province, Markham headwaters. 4 villages. Bilingual in Tok Pisin. Animists 95%, very strong. D=ELCPNG; no mission outreach.
8946	2	6	4.80	0	99.80	0.20	C	329.96	142	9	Central Province, Marshall Lagoon area. Remote. 7 dialects. Close to Doromu language. Animists 15%. D=UCPNGSI,SDA.
8947	1	5	6.69	0	96.00	4.00	C	227.76	221	8	Western Highlands Province, Hagen District; a few in Madang Province; 18 villages. Forest, mountains. D=Anglican Ch of PNG. M=SIL,PNGBTA.
8948	3	6	5.36	0	99.80	0.20	C	341.64	151	9	West and East New Britain Provinces, northwest coast inland to southwest coast. Trilingual with Nakanai, Tok Pisin. Animists 15%. D=RCC,UCPNGSI,NTM. M=SIL.
8949	0	6	4.52	0	99.90	0.10	C	397.48	127	9	Madang Province. Language isolate. Animists 5%.
8950	0	6	3.56	0	99.95	0.05	C	436.90	101	10	Madang Province, west of Madang City. Related languages: 18, including Rapting, Wamas, Samosa, Murupi, Saruga, Nake. Animists 5%.
8951	0	6	3.47	0	99.95	0.05	C	436.90	99	10	Madang Province, on coast round Matuka 40 miles north of Madang City. Related to Gedaged. Coastal. Animists 5%.
8952	1	6	4.89	0	99.80	0.20	C	324.12	147	9	Morobe and Oro Provinces, Iema to Pema. Close to Zia language. Animists 20%. D=ELCPNG.
8953	0	8	3.83	0	99.95	0.05	C	447.30	104	10	Madang Province, Adelbert range, southwest of Mauwake. Related to Hinahon. Animists 5%. M=SIL.
8954	2	6	3.63	0	99.90	0.10	C	417.19	101	10	Madang Province, Gogol River area. Animists 10%. D=ELCPNG,RCC.
8955	2	6	4.83	0	99.80	0.20	C	344.56	137	9	East Sepik Province, Ambunti District; West Sepik Province east of Mehek. 10 villages. Fishermen. Animists 15%. D=AoG,RCC. M=SIL,LBT.
8956	1	6	5.60	0	99.80	0.20	C	327.04	163	9	Morobe Province, Sakar Island, eastern Umboi Island; 7 villages. D=ELCPNG. M=SIL. No cargo cults. Animists 20%.
8957	0	6	2.67	0	54.00	46.00	B	59.13	190	6	Madang Province, north of Finisterre range, 20 miles southwest of Saidor. Related languages: Yupna, Gabutamon, Wandabong, Nokopo, Kewieng. Animists 70%.
8958	2	6	4.11	0	99.90	0.10	C	417.19	112	10	Madang Province, coast just north of Sikor. Related to Wogeo, Biem, Sepa, Manam. Animists 5%. D=RCC,ELCPNG.
8959	4	5	4.58	1	99.88	0.12	C	410.39	120	10	Western Highlands Province, Hagen District; around Mt Hagen town. Few animists, 0.5%. D=Ev Lutheran Ch of PNG,RCC,SDA,&c. M=SIL.
8960	0	6	4.64	0	99.75	0.25	C	279.22	153	8	Madang Province, on coast opposite Karkar Island, midway between Karim and Matuka. Related to Gedaged. Animists 25%.
8961	4	6	6.50	0	99.75	0.25	C	298.38	190	8	Sandaun Province, Makru-Klaplei area, foothills, 9 large villages. Majority of children are in primary schools. D=RCC,SSEC,CB(rapid growth),SDA. M=CMML.
8962	2	6	7.23	0	99.77	0.23	C	320.39	199	9	Central Province, Kaiyuku District, inland; Gulf Province. High educational standard. Prestigious language. D=RCC,UCPNGSI. M=LMS,GBT,SIL.
8963	0	5	2.75	0	28.00	72.00	A	10.22	374	5	East Sepik Province. Related languages: Changriwa, Miyak, Biwat, Bun. Animists 40%. Relatively unevangelized.
8964	0	6	3.80	0	96.00	4.00	C	245.28	139	8	Gulf Province, Hawoi river. Animists 30%.
8965	3	5	7.08	0	99.79	0.21	C	317.18	203	9	East New Britain Province, Jacquinot Bay and inland, 20 villages. Forest, coastal. Fishermen. D=RCC,SDA(few),Jehovah's Witnesses(few). M=SIL.

Continued overleaf

Table 8-2 continued

PEOPLE		POPULATION				IDENTITY CODE		LANGUAGE		CHURCH		MINISTRY						SCRIPTURE		
Ref 1	Ethnic name 2	P% 3	In 1995 4	In 2000 5	In 2025 6	Race 7	Language 8	Autoglossonym 9	S 10	AC 11	Members 12	Jayuh 13-17	d 18	wa 19	xc 20	mc 21	mi 22	Biblioglossonym 23	Pub 24-26	ss 27
8966	Menya (Menye)	0.37841	15,578	17,438	27,146	AON10b	24-RAHB-a	menya		84.00	14,648	0....	10	8	7	5	1	Menya	P..	.
8967	Meramera (Ubili)	0.04857	1,999	2,238	3,484	AON09b	35-DAAA	melamela cluster		80.00	1,791	0....	10	7	7	5	1	Meramera	...	.
8968	Mian (Bush People)	0.05000	2,058	2,304	3,587	AON10b	24-NCBE-c	golin		40.00	922	0....	9	5	5	3	0	Golin	PN.	.
8969	Mianmin	0.06938	2,856	3,197	4,977	AON10b	24-KEBH-a	mian-min		85.00	2,718	0....	10	7	7	4	2	Mianmin	PN.	.
8970	Midsivindi	0.04385	1,805	2,021	3,146	AON10b	26-TDAB-a	midsivindi		80.00	1,617	0....	10	7	6	4	1		...	.
8971	Migabac	0.03538	1,456	1,630	2,538	AON10b	24-UBAA	migabac cluster		80.00	1,304	0....	10	7	7	3	0		...	b
8972	Mikarew (Ariawiai)	0.20650	8,501	9,516	14,814	AON10b	26-SACA-a	mikarew		76.00	7,232	0....	10	7	7	4	1	Aruamu	P..	.
8973	Minanibai (Pepeha)	0.00946	389	436	679	AON10b	20-RAAA-a	minanibai		90.00	392	0....	10	7	11	3	0		...	.
8974	Mindiri	0.00293	121	135	210	AON09b	34-BEAA-a	mindiri		95.00	128	0....	10	7	11	4	1		...	.
8975	Mineveha (Minavega)	0.03975	1,636	1,832	2,852	AON09b	34-FCJA-a	minaveha		80.00	1,465	0....	10	7	6	5	2	Minaveha	P..	.
8976	Minigir	0.01293	532	596	928	AON09d	36-BEAC-a	minigir		80.00	477	0....	10	7	8	0	0		...	.
8977	Miriam (Mer, Mir)	0.00600	247	276	430	AON10b	20-ODAA-a	meriam		85.00	235	0....	10	7	7	5	2	Miriam Mir*	P..	b
8978	Misim	0.00857	353	395	615	AON09b	34-BPAA-b	misim		90.00	355	0....	10	7	11	3	0		p..	.
8979	Misima-Paneati (Tokunu)	0.34788	14,321	16,031	24,956	AON09b	34-FEAB-b	misima	1	87.00	13,947	0.s..	10	7	9	4	1	Misima*	PN.	n
8980	Mitang (Nambi)	0.01401	577	646	1,005	AON10b	27-HBAA-a	mitang		90.00	581	0....	10	7	11	4	1		...	.
8981	Miu	0.01210	498	558	868	AON09b	35-GAAA-a	miu		80.00	446	0....	10	7	6	4	1	Miu	p..	.
8982	Miyak	0.01728	711	796	1,240	AON10b	26-MCAA-a	miyak		40.00	319	0....	9	6	3	3	0		...	.
8983	Moere	0.00177	73	82	127	AON10b	22-GCAA-a	moere		95.00	77	0....	10	7	11	3	0		...	.
8984	Moewehafen (Agerlep)	0.09326	3,839	4,298	6,690	AON09b	35-FAAC-c	ai-klep		80.00	3,438	0....	10	7	6	5	2		p..	.
8985	Moikodi (Doriri)	0.01801	741	830	1,292	AON10b	23-GACA-a	moikodi		90.00	747	0....	10	7	11	4	1	Moikodi	...	n
8986	Mok (Aria-Mouk)	0.01923	792	886	1,380	AON09b	35-EAAA-c	mouk		75.00	665	0....	10	7	6	5	2	Mouk-aria	...	.
8987	Mokerang (Los Negros)	0.00631	260	291	453	AON09b	35-BCAE-a	mokerang		80.00	233	0....	10	7	7	5	1		...	.
8988	Molima (Morima, Fagululu)	0.12583	5,180	5,798	9,027	AON09b	34-FCKD-a	morima		75.00	4,349	0....	10	7	7	5	2		...	b
8989	Momole (Momare)	0.01769	728	815	1,269	AON10b	24-UBBA-a	momare		85.00	693	0....	10	7	6	4	1		...	b
8990	Momolili (Mesem)	0.04541	1,869	2,093	3,258	AON10b	24-TAAA-a	mesem		25.00	523	0....	9	5	5	4	1	Mesem	...	b
8991	Mondropolon	0.00946	389	436	679	AON09b	35-BBCA-a	mondropolon		90.00	392	0....	10	7	11	4	1		...	.
8992	Mongol	0.01066	439	491	765	AON10b	26-NAAA-a	mongol		40.00	196	0....	9	6	3	3	0		...	.
8993	Monumbo	0.01447	596	667	1,038	AON10b	27-MAAA-a	monumbo		90.00	600	0....	10	7	11	3	0		...	.
8994	Morafa	0.02119	872	976	1,520	AON10b	24-SBBC-a	morafa		90.00	879	0....	10	7	11	4	1		...	.
8995	Morawa	0.02918	1,201	1,345	2,093	AON10b	23-GBBC-a	morawa		85.00	1,143	0....	10	7	7	4	1		...	b
8996	Morigi Islander (Dabura)	0.02596	1,069	1,196	1,862	AON10b	20-PADA-a	morigi		85.00	1,017	0....	10	7	7	3	0		...	.
8997	Moromiranga	0.01000	412	461	717	AON09b	34-BFAA-c	moromiranga		90.00	415	0....	10	7	11	5	2		p..	.
8998	Mosimo	0.00183	75	84	131	AON10b	22-PBAA-a	mosimo		90.00	76	0....	10	7	11	3	0		...	.
8999	Motu	0.46341	19,077	21,355	33,244	AON09b	34-GBCA-a	motu	2	96.00	20,500	0.su.	10	10	7	5	3	Motu	PNB	.
9000	Mountain Arapesh (Kavu)	0.29146	11,999	13,431	20,909	AON10b	27-JCAB	bukiyip cluster		89.00	11,954	0....	10	10	7	5	2	Bukiyip	PN.	.
9001	Mountain Koiari	0.06306	2,596	2,906	4,524	AON10b	23-CAAD-a	central koiali		80.00	2,325	0....	10	7	7	4	1	Koiali: Mountain*	PN.	.
9002	Mugil (Bunu, Saker)	0.10127	4,169	4,667	7,265	AON10b	22-NAAA-a	bargam		80.00	3,733	0....	10	9	7	4	1	Bargam	P..	.
9003	Mukawa (Are)	0.04758	1,959	2,193	3,413	AON09b	34-FCCA-b	are		80.00	1,754	0....	10	7	7	4	1	Mukawa*	PNB	n
9004	Mumeng	0.07543	3,105	3,476	5,411	AON09b	34-DABA-f	mumeng		70.00	2,433	0....	10	7	7	4	1		pn.	.
9005	Munit	0.01088	448	501	781	AON10b	22-PEAA-a	munit		90.00	451	0....	10	7	11	4	1		...	.
9006	Muniwara (Mambe, Tumaru)	0.03064	1,261	1,412	2,198	AON10b	27-LACA-a	muniwara		80.00	1,130	0....	10	7	6	3	0		...	.
9007	Munkip	0.00468	193	216	336	AON10b	24-SFFE-a	munkip		90.00	194	0....	10	7	11	4	2		...	b
9008	Murik (Nor)	0.05175	2,130	2,385	3,712	AON10b	27-EAAA-a	murik		80.00	1,908	0....	10	7	6	3	1		...	.
9009	Murisapa (Moresada)	0.00621	256	286	445	AON10b	22-AABA-a	moresada		90.00	258	0....	10	7	11	3	0		...	.
9010	Murupi	0.00949	391	437	681	AON10b	22-PBDA-a	murupi		90.00	394	0....	10	7	11	3	0		...	.
9011	Musak	0.01120	461	516	803	AON10b	22-DBAA-a	musak		90.00	465	0....	10	7	11	5	2		...	.
9012	Musan (Musian, Musa)	0.00237	98	109	170	AON10b	25-VBAA-a	musan		10.00	11	0....	8	5	3	1	0		...	.
9013	Musom	0.00734	302	338	527	AON09b	34-CCBB-a	musom		95.00	321	0....	10	7	11	4	1		...	.
9014	Muyuw (Murua, Yanaba)	0.11848	4,877	5,460	8,500	AON09b	34-FDAB-e	muyuw		80.00	4,368	0.s..	10	8	7	5	1	Muyuw	PN.	b
9015	Mwatebu	0.00656	270	302	471	AON09b	34-FCRA-a	mwatebu		90.00	272	0....	10	7	11	4	1		...	b
9016	Nabak (Naba)	0.39758	16,367	18,321	28,522	AON10b	24-TABA	nabak cluster		87.00	15,939	0....	10	7	7	4	1	Nabak	P..	.
9017	Nagatman (Nagatiman)	0.01514	623	698	1,086	AON10b	25-TAAA-a	yade		20.00	140	0....	9	5	3	4	2		...	.
9018	Naho (Nahu)	0.15136	6,231	6,975	10,858	AON10b	24-SABA	nahu cluster		75.00	5,231	0....	10	7	7	4	1	Nahu	...	.
9019	Nakama	0.03185	1,311	1,468	2,285	AON10b	24-SFFD	nakama cluster		80.00	1,174	0....	10	7	7	4	2		...	b
9020	Nake	0.00546	225	252	392	AON10b	22-PCCA-a	nake		90.00	226	0....	10	7	11	4	1		...	.
9021	Nali-Yiru	0.05528	2,276	2,547	3,966	AON09b	35-BCAA	nali cluster		80.00	2,038	0....	10	8	7	5	3	Nali	P..	n
9022	Nalik (Lugagon)	0.13986	5,758	6,445	10,033	AON09b	35-CBDB-a	nalik		80.00	5,156	0....	10	7	7	5	2		...	.
9023	Namau (Koriki, Eurika)	0.18904	7,782	8,711	13,561	AON10b	20-SAAA-b	iai		75.00	6,533	0.s..	10	7	7	5	1	Iai: Papua New Guinea	PN.	.
9024	Namie (Yellow River)	0.08829	3,635	4,069	6,334	AON10b	26-CAAA	namia cluster		80.00	3,255	0....	10	7	7	4	2	Namia	...	n
9025	Nane	0.00946	389	436	679	AON09b	35-BCAB-b	nane		80.00	349	0....	10	7	6	4	1		pn.	.
9026	Nankina	0.06307	2,596	2,906	4,525	AON10b	24-SCAB-a	nankina		90.00	2,616	0....	10	7	7	4	1	Nankina	P..	b
9027	Nara (Pokau)	0.24052	9,902	11,084	17,254	AON09b	34-GBFA-a	nara		85.00	9,421	0....	10	7	7	5	2		...	b
9028	Narak	0.12907	5,313	5,948	9,259	AON10b	24-NBBA-a	proper narak		85.00	5,056	0.s..	10	8	7	5	1	Narak	PN.	.
9029	Nauna	0.00456	188	210	327	AON09b	35-BDDA-a	nauna		90.00	189	0....	10	7	11	4	1		...	.
9030	Nawaru (Sirio)	0.00490	202	226	352	AON10b	23-GABA-a	nawaru		90.00	203	0....	10	7	11	5	2		...	n
9031	Nek	0.03918	1,613	1,805	2,811	AON10b	24-SFFB	nek cluster		80.00	1,444	0....	10	7	7	4	1	Nek	...	b
9032	Nekgini	0.01356	558	625	973	AON10b	24-SACA-a	nekgini		90.00	562	0....	10	7	11	4	1		...	.
9033	Neko	0.00993	409	458	712	AON10b	24-SACB-a	neko		90.00	412	0....	10	7	11	4	1		...	.
9034	Nembi	0.54010	22,234	24,889	38,746	AON10b	24-LBCA-a	south nembi		89.00	22,151	0....	10	7	6	4	1	Nembi	P..	.
9035	Nemeyam	0.02000	823	922	1,435	AON10b	24-KFAB	pa cluster		30.00	276	0.s..	9	5	5	3	0		P..	.
9036	Nenaya (Nengaya)	0.01075	443	495	771	AON09b	34-BHBA-a	nenaya		90.00	446	0....	10	7	11	4	1		...	.
9037	Neo-Melanesian Papuan	1.53563	63,218	70,764	110,163	AON09f	52-ABAI-c	tok-pisin-creole	65	85.00	60,149	3asuh	10	10	9	5	2	Tok Pisin	PNB	b
9038	Nete	0.03071	1,264	1,415	2,203	AON10b	24-LDAD-a	nete		90.00	1,274	0....	10	7	11	4	1	Nete	...	.
9039	Ngaing	0.07454	3,069	3,435	5,347	AON10b	24-SACC-a	ngaing		80.00	2,748	0....	10	7	6	5	2		...	.
9040	Ngala (Kara, Swagup)	0.00429	177	198	308	AON10b	26-HAAA-a	ngala		9.80	19	0....	7	5	3	4	1		...	.
9041	Ngalum	0.25237	10,389	11,630	18,105	AON10b	24-KEBJ	ngalum cluster		87.00	10,118	0....	10	7	6	5	1	Ngalum	PN.	.
9042	Ngariawan (Ngariwan)	0.01253	516	577	899	AON09b	34-CBBA-a	ngariawan		90.00	520	0....	10	7	11	3	0		...	.
9043	Nii	0.30272	12,462	13,950	21,717	AON10b	24-NCAA-a	nii		91.00	12,694	0....	10	7	7	5	1	Nii	PN.	.
9044	Nimi	0.04475	1,842	2,062	3,210	AON10b	24-SFEA-a	nimi		80.00	1,650	0....	10	7	6	4	1		...	.
9045	Nimo (Nakwi)	0.00862	355	397	618	AON10b	25-WACA-a	nimo		90.00	357	0....	10	7	11	4	1	Nimo	...	.
9046	Nimowa (Nimoa)	0.02971	1,223	1,369	2,131	AON09b	34-FFAC-a	nimowa		90.00	1,232	0....	10	7	11	4	1	Nimowa*	P..	n
9047	Ninggera	0.01017	419	469	730	AON10b	21-IAAF-a	ningera		40.00	187	0....	9	6	5	5	2		...	.
9048	Ninggerum (Kativa, Tedi)	0.11128	4,581	5,128	7,983	AON10a	24-KEAE-e	obgwo		56.00	2,872	0....	10	5	5	5	3	Ninggerum	...	.
9049	Ningil	0.01649	679	760	1,183	AON10b	27-HAFA-a	ningil		35.00	266	0....	9	5	5	3	0		...	.
9050	Ninigo (Seimat)	0.02601	1,071	1,199	1,866	AON09b	35-ABAA	seimat cluster		90.00	1,079	0....	10	7	11	5	2		...	.
9051	Nokopo	0.05263	2,167	2,425	3,776	AON10b	24-SCBE-a	nokopo		80.00	1,940	0....	10	7	6	3	0		...	.
9052	Nomad (Kalamo)	0.01300	535	599	933	AON10b	24-KGAA	kalamo cluster		70.00	419	0....	10	7	6	3	0	Kalamo	P..	.
9053	Nomane (Kiari)	0.14648	6,030	6,750	10,508	AON10b	24-NCCA	nomane cluster		80.00	5,400	0....	10	7	6	5	3		...	.
9054	Nomu	0.02754	1,134	1,269	1,976	AON10b	24-TCCA-a	nomu		80.00	1,015	0....	10	7	7	4	1		...	p
9055	North-Central Fore	0.32000	13,174	14,746	22,956	AON10b	24-OGAA-b	north fore		92.00	13,566	0....	10	9	7	5	1	Fore: North Central	PN.	.
9056	Northeast Kiwai (Gibaio)	0.12205	5,024	5,624	8,756	AON10b	20-PAFA-c	gibaio		80.00	4,499	0....	10	7	7	4	3		...	.
9057	Notsi	0.04036	1,662	1,860	2,895	AON09b	35-CCAA-a	notsi		80.00	1,488	0....	10	7	7	5	1	Notsi	P..	.
9058	Nuk	0.03270	1,346	1,507	2,346	AON10b	24-SFFC	nuk cluster		85.00	1,281	0....	10	7	7	4	2		...	b
9059	Numanggang	0.07761	3,195	3,576	5,568	AON10b	24-SFFA	numanggang cluster		80.00	2,861	0....	10	7	7	4	1	Numanggang	P..	b
9060	Oganibi	0.02000	823	922	1,435	AON10b	24-KFAB	pa cluster		30.00	276	0.s..	9	5	5	3	0		P..	.
9061	Okro	0.00631	260	291	453	AON09b	35-BCAB-d	okro		90.00	262	0....	10	7	11	3	0		pn.	.
9062	Oksapmin	0.20182	8,308	9,300	14,478	AON10b	21-VAAA-a	oksapmin		75.00	6,975	0....	10	7	6	5	2	Oksapmin	PN.	.
9063	Olo (Wapi, Wape)	0.32406	13,341	14,933	23,247	AON10b	27-HABA	olo cluster		90.00	13,440	0....	10	7	11	5	3	Olo	P..	.
9064	Omati	0.02805	1,155	1,293	2,012	AON10b	20-VABA-a	omati		80.00	1,034	0....	10	7	6	5	2		...	.
9065	Omo (Tigak)	0.15136	6,231	6,975	10,858	AON09b	35-CBBC-a	central tigak		80.00	5,580	0....	10	7	7	4	2	Tigak	P..	.
9066	Omwunra-Togura	0.05500	2,264	2,534	3,946	AON10b	24-PBAB-h	omwunra-toqura		88.00	2,230	0.s..	10	9	8	0	0	Tairora: Omwunra-toqura*	PN.	.
9067	Onabasulu	0.01485	611	684	1,065	AON10b	24-KIDA-a	onabasulu		35.00	240	0....	9	5	6	4	1	Onobasulu*	P..	.
9068	Onank (Northern Watut)	0.01323	545	610	949	AON09b	34-CACA-a	unank		90.00	549	0....	10	7	11	4	1		...	.
9069	Onjob (Onjab)	0.00505	208	233	362	AON10b	23-HAAA-a	onjab		90.00	209	0....	10	7	11	4	1		...	b
9070	Ono	0.13983	5,756	6,444	10,031	AON10b	24-TCEA	ono cluster		70.00	4,510	0....	10	7	7	5	1	Ono	PN.	.
9071	Ontenu	0.07122	2,932	3,282	5,109	AON10b	24-PACA-c	ontena		89.00	2,921	0....	10	9	8	0	0		pn.	.
9072	Opao	0.04489	1,848	2,069	3,220	AON10b	20-TAAC-a	opao		88.00	1,820	0....	10	8	8	0	0		...	.
9073	Orokaiva (Wasida, Periho)	0.71297	29,351	32,855	51,147	AON10b	23-ABDA	orokaiva cluster	1	93.00	30,555	0....	10	7	7	5	1	Orokaiva	PN.	.
9074	Orokolo (Keuru, Muro)	0.45582	18,765	21,005	32,700	AON10b	20-TAAA-a	orokolo		88.00	18,484	0.s..	10	7	7	5	1	Orokolo	PN.	.
9075	Osima	0.01000	412	461	717	AON10b	21-IAAE-b	ossima		80.00	369	0....	10	7	6	3	0		p..	p
9076	Osum	0.01306	538	602	937	AON10b	22-ACAA-a	osum		90.00	542	0....	10	7	11	4	1		...	.
9077	Ouma	0.00013	5	6	9	AON09b	34-GADA-a	ouma		95.00	6	0....	10	7	11	4	0		...	.
9078	Owiniga (Samo)	0.00740	305	341	531	AON10b	25-WADA-a	owiniga		35.00	119	0....	9	5	6	4	1	Owininga*	P..	.
9079	Pa (Pare, East Awin)	0.05401	2,223	2,489	3,875	AON10b	24-KFAB-a	pare		90.10	2,242	0.s..	10	7	11	4	1	Pa*	P..	.
9080	Pagi (Pagei)	0.05085	2,093	2,343	3,648	AON10b	21-IAAD-a	pagi		80.00	1,875	0....	10	7	7	5	1		...	p
9081	Pai (Pei)	0.00656	270	302	471	AON10b	22-FAAA	pay cluster		90.00	272	0....	10	7	11	4	0		...	.
9082	Paiwa (Manape)	0.04969	2,046	2,290	3,565	AON09b	34-FCDA	paiwa cluster		80.00	1,832	0....	10	7	7	4	1	Gapapaiwa	...	n
9083	Pak-Tong	0.03401	1,400	1,567	2,440	AON09b	35-BDEA	pak-tong cluster		80.00	1,254	0....	10	7	7	5	1		...	.
9084	Panaras (Kuot)	0.02848	1,172	1,312	2,043	AON10b	27-TAAA	kuot cluster		75.00	984	0....	10	7	7	4	2	Kuot	P..	.
9085	Panim	0.00479	197	221	344	AON10b	22-PDAA	panim cluster		90.00	199	0....	10	7	11	3	0		...	.
9086	Papi (Paupe)	0.00237	98	109	170	AON10b	27-AAAA-a	papi		40.00	44	0....	9	6	3	3	0		...	.
9087	Papitalai	0.01823	750	840	1,308	AON09b	35-BCAD-a	papitalai		90.00	756	0....	10	7	11	4	1		...	.
9088	Parawen	0.01353	557	623	971	AON10b	22-IBAA-a	parawen		90.00	561	0....	10	7	11	5	2		...	.
9089	Pasi (Besi, Warasai)	0.01490	613	687	1,069	AON10b	26-ECAA-a	pasi		95.00	652	0....	10	7	11	4	1		...	.

Continued opposite

Table 8-2 continued

EVANGELIZATION								EVANGELISM			ADDITIONAL DESCRIPTIVE DATA
Ref 1	D 28	aC 29	CG% 30	r 31	E 32	U 33	W 34	e 35	R 36	T 37	Locations, civil divisions, literacy, religions, church history, denominations, dioceses, church growth, missions, agencies, ministries, movements 38
8966	4	5	7.56	0	99.84	0.16	C	364.85	199	9	Morobe Province, Menyamya District, from Papua border north. Forest, savannah, mountains; 60 villages. D=ELCPNG,RCC,SDA,Independent Baptists. M=SIL.
8967	2	6	5.32	0	99.80	0.20	C	329.96	155	9	West New Britain Province, Bialla District, northwest coast. Animists 15%. D=RCC,UCPNGSI. M=SIL.
8968	0	5	4.63	1	68.00	32.00	B	99.28	230	6	Bush people in Nondipi village area in Simbu Province, Gumine District. Animists 20%.
8969	1	6	5.77	0	99.85	0.15	C	375.40	155	9	Sandaun Province, Telefomin District, upper August and upper May rivers, 4 villages. Animists 10%. D=BUWH(Baptists). M=SIL,ABMS.
8970	1	6	5.22	0	99.80	0.20	C	321.20	157	9	Madang Province. Animists(tribal religionists) 20%. D=RCC.
8971	0	6	4.99	0	99.80	0.20	C	324.12	150	9	Morobe Province, Masaweng River area, on Huon coast. Lingua franca: Kate. Animists 20%.
8972	1	5	6.81	0	99.76	0.24	C	296.81	202	8	Madang Province, west of Bogia. Scattered animists, 3%. D=RCC. M=PBT.
8973	0	6	3.74	0	99.90	0.10	C	397.48	109	9	Gulf Province, mouth of Omati river, Ikobi Kairi and Goaribari Census Districts. Animists 10%.
8974	1	7	2.58	0	99.95	0.05	C	450.77	77	10	Madang Province, along Rai coast west of Saidor, 1 village. Close to Biliau and Wab. D=ELCPNG.
8975	2	6	5.11	0	99.80	0.20	C	332.88	149	9	Milne Bay Province, southwest projection on Fergusson Island. Coastal; access by plane and boat. Animists 10%. D=UCPNGSI,RCC.
8976	0	0	3.94	0	98.00	2.00	C	286.16	122	8	East New Britain Province, Gazelle Peninsula, Lungalunga village on Atalkilikun Bay. Few animists. D=ELCPNG.
8977	2	5	3.21	0	99.85	0.15	C	375.40	97	9	Islands in Torres Strait. Most in Australia. Most speak Tok Pisin. Animists 10%. D=UCPNGSI,Anglican Ch of PNG. M=ABOM,LMS.
8978	0	6	3.63	0	99.90	0.10	C	400.77	106	10	Morobe Province, Francisco River area, Huon Gulf, around Misim town. Close to Yamap, Hote. Animists 10%.
8979	1	5	7.51	0	99.87	0.13	C	403.28	185	10	Milne Bay Province, Misima Island and others. 22 villages. Lingua franca. Many schools. Methodists arrived 1891. D=UCPNGSI(all workers Misiman). M=SIL.
8980	1	6	4.15	0	99.90	0.10	C	407.34	115	10	West Sepik Province, on Wagasu river. Animists 5%. D=Baluan Ch.
8981	2	6	3.87	0	99.80	0.20	C	324.12	122	9	West New Britain Province, southwest interior. Mountains. Related to Kaulong. Animists 10%. D=RCC,NTM. M=GR.
8982	0	6	3.52	0	62.00	38.00	B	90.52	203	6	East Sepik Province, Yuat river. Related languages: Changriwa, Mekmek, Biwat, Bun. Animists 60%.
8983	0	8	4.44	0	99.95	0.05	C	443.84	118	10	Madang Province, on coast near Dove point. Related languages: Mauwake, Bepour. Animists 5%.
8984	2	6	6.01	0	99.80	0.20	C	332.88	170	9	West New Britain Province, southwest coast and inland. Dialect chain. Animists 10%. D=Anglican Ch of PNG,RCC.
8985	1	6	4.41	0	99.90	0.10	C	413.91	119	10	Oro, slopes of Owen Stanleys around Mount Brown. Several dialects. Bilingual in Hiri Motu. Partially literate. Closest to Abie. Animists 5%. D=ACPNG.
8986	2	6	4.29	0	99.75	0.25	C	292.91	137	8	West New Britain Province, southeast to northwest coast. Animists 20%. D=RCC,NTM.
8987	2	6	3.20	0	99.80	0.20	C	327.04	104	9	Manus Province, north Los Negros Island, Ndrilo Island. Animists 15%. Almost all Roman Catholics (New Life charismatics). D=RCC,MEC. M=Manus Ev Mission.
8988	2	5	6.26	0	99.75	0.25	C	303.86	181	9	Milne Bay Province, south central Fergusson Island. Bilingual in Dobu. Few animists. Syncretism strong. D=UCPNGSI,RCC.
8989	1	6	4.33	0	99.85	0.15	C	362.99	126	9	Morobe Province, north of Masaweng river. Lingua franca: Kate. Animists 10%. D=ELCPNG.
8990	1	6	4.04	0	55.00	45.00	B	50.18	255	6	Morobe Province, Lae District, Boana area, 11 villages. Bilingual in Tok Pisin, Jabem or Kate in church. Forest, mountains. Cargo cult area.Animists 10%.
8991	1	6	3.74	0	99.90	0.10	C	407.34	106	10	Manus Province, north central coast. All Catholics. D=RCC. Most are bilingual in Kurti.
8992	0	6	3.02	0	62.00	38.00	B	90.52	181	6	East Sepik Province, near Yuat river. Related languages: Langam, Yaul. Animists 60%.
8993	0	6	4.18	0	99.90	0.10	C	397.48	119	9	Madang Province, on coast opposite Manam Island. Animists 10%.
8994	1	6	4.58	0	99.90	0.10	C	407.34	125	10	Madang Province, southeast of Saidor, 3 villages. Animists 5%. D=ELCPNG.
8995	1	6	4.85	0	99.85	0.15	C	369.19	136	9	Central Province, south coast around Cloudy Bay. 95% bilingual in Magi, Suau, Hiri Motu, English. Animists 15%. D=SDA.
8996	0	6	4.73	0	99.85	0.15	C	350.58	141	9	Gulf Province, Lower Turama Census Division, Turama river estuary. Animists 15%.
8997	2	7	3.80	0	99.90	0.10	C	423.76	103	10	Madang Province. 3 villages immediately east of Saidor. Animists 5%. D=ELCPNG,RCC.
8998	0	8	4.43	0	99.90	0.10	C	404.05	123	10	Madang Province, northwest of Madang City. Related languages: Rapting, Wamas, Samosa, Murupi, Saruga, and 13 others. Animists 10%.
8999	4	7	7.92	4	99.96	0.04	C	518.59	166	10	Central Province, in and around Port Moresby. Lingua franca. Major language of UCPNG Papua Mainland Region. D=UCPNGSI,SDA,SA,RCC.
9000	6	5	7.34	0	99.89	0.11	C	415.80	180	10	East Sepik Province, Torricelli Mountains, Maprik and Yangoru Districts. Tropical forest, mountains. D=RCC,AoG,SEBC,NAC,SDA,JWs. Materialism pervasive.
9001	1	6	5.60	0	99.80	0.20	C	335.80	159	9	Central Province, Port Moresby District, north of Koita. Tropical forest, mountains. Animists 15%. D=SDA. M=SIL.
9002	1	6	6.10	0	99.80	0.20	C	327.04	175	9	Madang Province, north coast opposite Karkar Island, 20 villages. Animism, syncretism. Animists 20%. Heavily missionized by RCs. D=RCC. M=SIL.
9003	1	6	5.30	0	99.80	0.20	C	359.16	142	9	Milne Bay, tip of Cape Vogel. Close to Paiwa. All Anglicans. Magic and syncretism very strong. Bible translation too old. D=ACPNG. Displaced as church language.
9004	1	6	3.24	0	99.70	0.30	C	265.72	114	8	Morobe Province, Mumeng District. Dialect chain. Tropical forest, mountains. Animists 20%. D=ELCPNG.
9005	1	6	3.88	0	99.90	0.10	C	407.34	109	10	Madang Province, west of Madang City, Trans-Gogol District. Related languages: Girawa, Bemal. Animists 5%. D=ELCPNG.
9006	0	6	4.84	0	99.80	0.20	C	312.44	151	9	East Sepik Province, 20 miles south-southeast of Wewak. Animists 20%.
9007	2	7	3.01	0	99.90	0.10	C	427.05	86	10	Morobe Province. Animists 5%. D=ELCPNG(Lutherans), using Tok Pisin and Kate.
9008	0	6	5.39	0	99.80	0.20	C	315.36	164	9	East Sepik Province, Angoram District, coast west of mouth of Sepik river. Related language: Kopar. Animists 20%. M=SIL.
9009	0	7	3.30	0	99.90	0.10	C	400.77	98	10	Madang Province, south of Bogia. Animists 10%.
9010	0	6	3.74	0	99.90	0.10	C	397.48	109	9	Madang Province, northwest of Madang City. Related languages: 18, including Rapting, Wamas, Samosa, Mosimo, Saruga, Nake. Animists 10%.
9011	2	6	3.91	0	99.90	0.10	C	417.19	107	10	Madang Province, east of Astrolabe Bay on Ramu river. Animists 5%. D=ELCPNG,RCC.
9012	0	6	2.43	0	29.00	71.00	A	10.58	331	5	Sandaun Province, east of Amto, 1 village. Frequent interaction with Amto. Animists 90%. Relatively unreached tribe.
9013	1	6	3.53	0	99.95	0.05	C	447.30	98	10	Morobe Province, Markham Valley, Huon Peninsula, Busu river. In Azera dialect chain. D=ELCPNG.
9014	2	6	6.27	0	99.80	0.20	C	353.32	166	9	Milne Bay Province, 30 villages on Woodlark Island. Bilingual in Dobu, Kiriwina, Misima. Tropical forest. Animists 15%. D=UCPNGSI,RCC. M=SIL.
9015	1	6	3.36	0	99.90	0.10	C	417.19	96	10	Milne Bay Province, 1 village on Normanby Island. Bilingual in Duau, Dobu. Few literates. Animists 5%. D=UCPNGSI.
9016	1	5	7.65	0	99.87	0.13	C	377.88	201	9	Morobe Province, Lae District, eastern headwaters of Busa river, 45 villages. Christians are Lutherans: D=ELCPNG. M=SIL.
9017	0	6	2.67	0	45.00	55.00	A	32.85	228	5	Sandaun Province, Amanab District, west of Namia, 6 villages. Hunter-gatherers. Animists 80%. M=CMML,SIL. Primitive, isolated, no vernacular work or education.
9018	1	6	6.46	0	99.75	0.25	C	290.17	195	8	Madang Province, bordering east of Rawa area. Scattered animists. D=ELCPNG. M=SIL.
9019	2	6	4.88	0	99.80	0.20	C	338.72	141	9	Morobe Province, 6 villages in rugged terrain. Mountains. Animists 15%. D=ELCPNG(Lutherans), using Tok Pisin and Kate.
9020	1	7	3.17	0	99.90	0.10	C	410.62	93	10	Madang Province, northwest of Madang City. Animists 5%. D=ELCPNG.
9021	2	6	5.46	0	99.80	0.20	C	344.56	152	9	Manus Province, southeast. Moderately bilingual in Lele. Animists 10%. Primarily D=Manus Evangelical Church; also RCC,SDA. M=MEM(Liebenzell Mission),SIL.
9022	2	6	6.44	0	99.80	0.20	C	332.88	181	9	New Ireland Province, north central. Tropical forest. Coastal. Animists 10%. D=RCC,UCPNGSI.
9023	2	5	6.70	0	99.75	0.25	C	306.60	190	9	Gulf Province, Purari river delta. Scattered animists left. D=RCC,UCPNGSI. M=LMS.
9024	2	5	5.96	0	99.80	0.20	C	332.88	169	9	Sandaun Province, 16 villages; one in East Sepik Province. Closest to Ak and Awun. Swamp, savannah. Animists 10%. D=Christian Brethren, using Tok Pisin.
9025	1	6	3.62	0	99.80	0.20	C	327.04	115	9	Manus Province, south central coast, west of Okro. Close to E language. Animists 10%. D=RCC.
9026	1	6	5.72	0	99.90	0.10	C	410.62	149	10	Madang Province, upper Nankina River valley, 8 villages. Forest, mountains. Bilingual in Kate, Tok Pisin. Animists 10%. D=ELCPNG. M=SIL.
9027	2	5	7.09	0	99.85	0.15	C	375.40	185	9	Central Province, between Kuni and Roro. Many also speak Motu, Hiri Motu. Few animists remaining. D=UCPNGSI,RCC.
9028	3	6	6.42	0	99.85	0.15	C	384.71	166	9	Western Highlands Province, Hagen District, Jimi headwaters. Close to Maring and Ganja. Forest, mountains. Animists 10%. Mainly D=RCC,Lutherans(ELCPNG).
9029	1	1	2.98	0	99.90	0.10	C	390.91	93	9	Manus Province, Nauna Island. 1 village. Bilingual in Titan. Animists 5%. Former RCs, now all in D=Paliau Church.
9030	2	6	3.06	0	99.90	0.10	C	423.76	88	10	Oro Province, around upper Musa River valley. Bilingual in Hiri Motu. Close to Yareba. Animists 5%. D=Anglican Ch of PNG,SDA.
9031	2	6	5.10	0	99.80	0.20	C	335.80	147	9	Morobe Province, 8 villages in rugged terrain north of Boana. Mountains. Animists 15%. D=ELCPNG(Lutherans), using Tok Pisin and Kate. M=SIL.
9032	1	6	4.11	0	99.90	0.10	C	407.34	114	10	Madang Province, west of Mot river. Coastal and foothills. One community school. Animists 10%. D=ELCPNG.
9033	1	6	3.79	0	99.90	0.10	C	407.34	107	10	Madang Province, coast near Biliau. Coastal, foothills. Animists 10%. D=ELCPNG.
9034	1	5	8.01	0	99.89	0.11	C	389.82	207	9	Western Highlands Province. Animists 2%. D=Christian Union Mission.
9035	0	6	3.37	0	56.00	44.00	B	61.32	217	6	Western Province. Tribal religionists(animists) 70%.
9036	1	6	3.87	0	99.90	0.10	C	407.34	109	10	Morobe Province, north coast of Huon Peninsula. Animists 10%. D=ELCPNG.
9037	4	10	3.23	5	99.85	0.15	C	474.68	58	10	National language (Tok Pisin, an English-based creole), also mother tongue of urban dwellers. D=ELCPNG,RCC,UCPNGSI,and 100 others. M=UBS, 120 others.
9038	1	6	4.97	0	99.90	0.10	C	410.62	132	10	Enga Province, East Sepik Province, adjoining Hewa area. Close to Bisorio. Animists 5%. D=GLC. M=NGLM/LCMS.
9039	2	6	5.78	0	99.80	0.20	C	329.96	166	9	Madang Province, foothills from coast to Finisterre Range, 11 villages. Community school. Animists 15%. D=ELCPNG,RCC.
9040	0	6	2.99	0	31.80	68.20	A	11.37	350	5	East Sepik Province, Ambunti District, 1 village. Animists 90%. Relatively unreached tribe; some contact by M=AoG.
9041	2	6	7.16	0	99.87	0.13	C	393.76	182	9	Sandaun Province. Majority in Irian Jaya (Indonesia). Animists 2%. D=ECP,RCC. M=UFM(from Indonesia).
9042	0	6	4.03	0	99.90	0.10	C	397.48	115	9	Morobe Province, around Wongat town. Animists 10%.
9043	3	5	7.41	0	99.91	0.09	C	428.47	180	10	Western Highlands Province, Hagen District. Forest, mountains. Scattered animists. D=ELCPNG,RCC,Ch of the Nazarene. M=SIL.
9044	1	6	5.24	0	99.80	0.20	C	321.20	157	9	Morobe Province, upper Erap river, south of Saruwaged Range. Mountains. Animists 15%. D=ELCPNG.
9045	1	6	3.64	0	99.90	0.10	C	407.34	104	10	East Sepik Province, southeast of Ama language area, 8 villages. Animists 10%. D=NTM.
9046	1	6	4.93	0	99.90	0.10	C	420.48	128	10	Milne Bay Province, Misima District, group of islands. Bilingual in Misima. Animists 10%. D=RCC. Some NT translation by RC priest.
9047	2	5	2.97	0	69.00	31.00	B	100.74	160	7	Sandaun Province, Vanimo District, east of Vanimo. Animists 60%. D=RCC,Christian Brethren. M=PNGBTA,CMML.
9048	2	5	5.82	0	88.00	12.00	B	179.87	212	7	Western Province, between Ok Birim and Ok Tedi rivers. 30% live in Irian Jaya(Indonesia). Many animists 14%. D=ECP,RCC. M=APCM/UFM,Pioneers Inc,SIL.
9049	0	6	3.34	0	59.00	41.00	B	75.37	205	6	Sandaun Province, south of Torricelli Mountains. Related languages: Olo, Yau, Yis, Valman. Animists 65%.
9050	2	6	4.79	0	99.90	0.10	C	420.48	125	10	Western Manus Province, Ninigo Islands. Animists 10%. D=SDA,RCC.
9051	0	6	5.41	0	99.80	0.20	C	312.44	166	9	Madang Province, around Taplen town. Related dialects or languages: Mebu, Gabutamon, Wandabong, Yupna, Kewieng. Animists 20%.
9052	0	6	3.81	0	97.00	3.00	C	247.83	138	8	Western Province, mostly at Wawoi Falls. Closest to Agala, Konai. Animists 30%.
9053	3	6	6.49	1	99.80	0.20	C	338.72	179	9	Simbu Province, Tua river. Few animists. D=ELCPNG,RCC,NTM.
9054	1	6	4.73	0	99.80	0.20	C	327.04	142	9	Morobe Province, northern coast, Huon Peninsula. Bilingual in Ono. Animists 15%. D=ELCPNG.
9055	6	5	2.64	0	99.92	0.08	C	436.54	78	10	Eastern Highlands Province, Okapa District. Scattered animists. D=ELCPNG,CHM,SDA,NTM,WM,UCPNGSI. M=SIL.
9056	1	5	6.30	0	99.80	0.20	C	327.04	180	9	Western Province. 4 dialects. Few animists. D=United Church of PNGSI; strong work. M=LMS,PNGBTA,SIL.
9057	2	6	5.13	0	99.80	0.20	C	332.88	149	9	New Ireland Province, east coast. Animists 10%. D=UCPNGSI,RCC. M=SIL.
9058	2	6	4.97	0	99.85	0.15	C	375.40	137	9	Morobe Province. Mountainous. Animists 10%. D=ELCPNG(Lutherans), using Tok Pisin and Kate.
9059	1	6	5.82	0	99.80	0.20	C	335.80	164	9	Morobe Province, 10 villages. Tropical forest, mountains. Animists 15%. D=ELCPNG. 60% also speak Tok Pisin, 60% Kate. M=SIL.
9060	0	6	3.37	0	56.00	44.00	B	61.32	217	6	Western Province. Tribal religionists(animists) 70%.
9061	0	7	3.32	0	99.90	0.10	C	410.62	96	10	Manus Province, south central coast, east of Nane. Coastal. Animists 10%.
9062	2	6	6.77	0	99.75	0.25	C	306.60	192	9	Sandaun Province, Telefomin District. Several dialects. Tropical forest, mountains. Few animists left. D=Baptist Ch,SDA. M=ABMS,SIL.
9063	2	5	7.47	0	99.90	0.10	C	427.05	180	10	Sandaun Province; 55 villages. Related languages: Yis, Yau, Ningil, Valman. Forest, mountains. D=Christian Brethren,RCC. Widespread nominalism. M=CMML.
9064	2	6	4.75	0	99.80	0.20	C	329.96	141	9	Gulf Province, 5 isolated villages on Omati river. One school. Animists 15%. D=SDA,UCPNGSI.
9065	1	6	6.53	0	99.80	0.20	C	329.96	184	9	New Ireland Province, northern; also western Djaul Island. Tropical forest, coastal. Few animists. D=UCPNGSI. M=Australian Methodists,SIL.
9066	0	0	5.56	0	99.88	0.12	C	359.74	162	9	Eastern Highlands Province, Kainantu and Obura districts. Hunters, agriculturalists. Animists 2%. D=ELCPNG.
9067	1	6	3.23	0	64.00	36.00	B	81.76	184	6	Southern Highlands Province midway between Mount Sisa and Mount Bosavi. Animists 65%. D=ECP. M=APCM/UFM.
9068	1	7	4.09	0	99.90	0.10	C	410.62	113	10	Morobe Province, Kaiapit area, Waffa Valley. Animists 10%. D=ELCPNG.
9069	1	7	3.09	0	99.90	0.10	C	420.48	89	10	Oro Province, 2 villages. Literate in English. Animists 5%. D=Anglican Ch of PNG.
9070	2	5	2.45	0	99.70	0.30	C	270.83	91	8	Morobe Province, Finschhafen District. Lingua franca. Forest, mountains. Few animists. D=ELCPNG(Lutheran),et alia. M=SIL.
9071	0	0	5.84	0	99.89	0.11	C	360.58	171	9	Eastern Highlands Province, Kainantu District. Related to Gadsup. Swidden agriculturalists. Animists 1%. D=ELCPNG.
9072	0	0	5.34	0	99.88	0.12	C	343.68	164	9	Gulf Province, near Orokolo and Keuru. Animists 2%. D=ELCPNG.
9073	2	5	8.36	1	99.93	0.07	C	444.68	197	10	Oro Province, Popondetta District, 200 villages. 12 dialects. Forest. Origin of major cargo cult Baigona. D=ACPNG,Christian Revival Crusade. M=SIL.
9074	3	5	7.81	1	99.88	0.12	C	411.13	190	10	Gulf Province, mouth of Purari river east to Bairu river. Coastal. Scattered animists. D=UCPNGSI,RCC,SDA. M=LMS.
9075	0	6	3.67	0	99.80	0.20	C	315.36	120	9	Sandaun Province, town of Osima. Closest to Kilmeri, Isi. Animists 20%.
9076	1	6	4.07	0	99.90	0.10	C	407.34	114	10	Madang Province. Animists 10%. D=RCC.
9077	0	10	1.81	0	99.95	0.05	C	454.24	60	10	Central Province, Table Bay, around Labu on south coast. Nearly extinct; only 4 speakers left (in 1981).
9078	1	7	2.51	0	65.00	35.00	B	83.03	151	6	East Sepik Province, southeast of Nimo language, 4 villages. Traditional culture. Animists 65%. D=NTM.
9079	1	6	5.56	0	99.90	0.10	C	417.98	143	10	Western Province. Animists 10%. D=ECP. M=APCM/UFM.
9080	3	6	5.37	0	99.80	0.20	C	335.80	153	9	Sandaun Province, Vanimo District, Bewani Sub-District, 5 villages. Related to Kilmeri and Ningera; close to Imbinis. Animists 10%. D=RCC,SDA,Christian Brethren.
9081	0	7	3.36	0	99.90	0.10	C	404.05	99	10	Sandaun Province, middle Sepik region, Hauna and Leonard Schultze river. Few speak Tok Pisin. Animists 5%. Nearly all are Christians.
9082	1	6	5.35	0	99.80	0.20	C	329.96	156	9	Milne Bay Province, south coast of Cape Vogel. Close to Boaniki. Church language: Wedau. Literates 10%. Animists 10%. D=Anglican Ch of PNG. Syncretism.SET
9083	2	6	4.95	0	99.80	0.20	C	329.96	146	9	Manus Province, Pak and Tong Islands. Animists 10%. D=SDA,Manus Evangelical Church. M=MEM(Liebenzell Mission).
9084	2	6	4.70	0	99.75	0.25	C	295.65	146	8	New Ireland Province, northwest coast, 9 villages. Animists 10%. D=UCPNGSI,RCC. M=Global Bible Translators(Korea),SIL.
9085	0	7	3.04	0	99.90	0.10	C	400.77	92	10	Madang Province; western outskirts of Madang urban area. Related languages: Gumalu, Sihan, Isebe, Bau, Amele. Animists 5%.
9086	0	7	3.86	0	63.00	37.00	B	91.98	214	6	Sandaun Province, Frieda river, 1 village. Literates 3%. Some bilinguals in Tok Pisin. Animists 60%.
9087	1	6	4.42	0	99.90	0.10	C	407.34	121	10	Manus Province, Los Negros Island. Bilingual in Loniu. Close to Koro. Shore-dwellers, fishermen, hunters, pig raisers. Animists 5%. D=RCC.
9088	2	6	4.11	0	99.90	0.10	C	417.19	112	10	Madang Province. Animists 5%. D=ELCPNG,RCC.
9089	1	6	4.27	0	99.95	0.05	C	447.30	113	10	Sandaun Province, Wan Wan Division. Close to Yessan-Mayo. D=SDA.

Continued overleaf

Table 8-2 continued

PEOPLE		POPULATION				IDENTITY CODE		LANGUAGE		CHURCH		MINISTRY						SCRIPTURE		
Ref 1	*Ethnic name* 2	*P%* 3	*In 1995* 4	*In 2000* 5	*In 2025* 6	*Race* 7	*Language* 8	*Autoglossonym* 9	*S* 10	*AC* 11	*Members* 12	*Jayuh* 13-17	*d* 18	*wa* 19	*xc* 20	*mc* 21	*mi* 22	*Biblioglossonym* 23	*Pub* 24-26	*ss* 27
9090	Pasismanua (Kowlong)	0.07568	3,116	3,487	5,429	AON09b	35-GAAA	pasismanua cluster		85.00	2,964	0....	10	7	6	5	1	Kaulong	P..	n
9091	Paswam (Mutum)	0.01484	611	684	1,065	AON10b	20-NABB-a	mutum		90.00	615	0....	10	7	11	4	1		...	.
9092	Patep	0.04591	1,890	2,116	3,293	AON09b	34-DABA-d	ptep		75.00	1,587	0....	10	7	7	4	1	Patep	PN.	.
9093	Patpatar (Gelik, Pala)	0.15136	6,231	6,975	10,858	AON09b	35-CFBA-c	patpatar		80.00	5,580	0....	10	7	7	5	1	Patpatar	P..	.
9094	Pawaia (Sira, Aurama)	0.10091	4,154	4,650	7,239	AON10b	20-ZAAC-a	pawaia		80.00	3,720	0....	10	7	7	5	2	Pawaia	...	.
9095	Pay (Banara, Dagoi, Hatz)	0.02425	998	1,117	1,740	AON10b	22-FAAA	pay cluster		10.00	112	0....	8	5	3	4	2		...	.
9096	Paynamar	0.00556	229	256	399	AON10b	22-BAAA-a	paynamar		90.00	231	0....	10	7	11	4	1		...	.
9097	Penchal	0.01689	695	778	1,212	AON09b	35-BCBA-f	rambutyo		90.00	700	0....	10	8	11	5	1		...	.
9098	Piame (Biami)	0.00315	130	145	226	AON10b	26-ICAA-a	piame		9.70	14	0....	7	5	3	1	0		...	.
9099	Pikiwa (Bainapi, Turumasa	0.01261	519	581	905	AON10b	24-KICA-a	bainapi		30.00	174	0....	9	5	5	3	0		...	.
9100	Pila (Suaru, Miani)	0.04051	1,668	1,867	2,906	AON10b	22-FABA	miani cluster		90.00	1,680	0....	10	7	11	4	2	Miani: South	P..	.
9101	Pinai (Pinaye)	0.01525	628	703	1,094	AON10b	24-MDAB-a	pinai		55.00	387	0....	10	5	6	4	1	Pinai	...	.
9102	Pitilu (Pityilu, Leipon)	0.02279	938	1,050	1,635	AON09b	35-BAEA-a	pitilu		90.00	945	0....	10	7	11	5	1		...	n
9103	Piu (Sanbiau)	0.00537	221	247	385	AON09b	34-DAAA-a	piu		95.00	235	0....	10	7	11	4	1		...	.
9104	Podopa (Polopa, Foraba)	0.08545	3,518	3,938	6,130	AON10b	20-YAAA	folopa cluster		70.00	2,756	0....	10	5	6	5	3	Podopa*	P..	.
9105	Pogaya (Bogaia)	0.00946	389	436	679	AON10b	24-KHAA-a	pogaya		40.00	174	0....	9	6	3	4	1		...	.
9106	Ponam	0.01473	606	679	1,057	AON09b	35-BADA-a	ponam		90.00	611	0....	10	7	11	4	1		...	.
9107	Pondoma (Anam)	0.01883	775	868	1,351	AON10b	22-ABAA-a	pondoma		90.00	781	0....	10	7	11	4	1		...	.
9108	Puari	0.01170	482	539	839	AON10b	25-OBCA-a	puari		90.00	485	0....	10	7	11	3	0		...	.
9109	Pulabu	0.00366	151	169	263	AON10b	22-UAAA-a	pulabu		35.00	59	0....	9	5	6	3	0		...	.
9110	Pulie (Roto, Rauto)	0.01861	766	858	1,335	AON09b	35-EABB	pulie-rauto cluster		85.00	729	0....	10	7	7	4	1		...	.
9111	Pyu	0.00355	146	164	255	AON10b	25-RAAA-a	pyu		25.00	41	0....	9	5	6	3	0		...	.
9112	Rabaul Creole German	0.00270	111	124	194	AON09f	52-ABCE-ca	unserdeutsch-new-britain		95.00	118	1c.uh	10	8	11	4	1		pnb	b
9113	Rapting	0.01047	431	482	751	AON10b	22-PBEA-a	rapting		95.00	458	0....	10	7	11	3	0		...	.
9114	Rawa (Erewa)	0.22510	9,267	10,373	16,148	AON10b	24-SABB	rawa cluster		87.00	9,024	0....	10	7	7	4	1	Rawa	PN.	.
9115	Rawo	0.01596	657	735	1,145	AON10b	25-OBBA-a	rawo		90.00	662	0....	10	7	11	3	0		...	.
9116	Rempin (Erempi)	0.01867	769	860	1,339	AON10b	22-PAAC-a	rempi		90.00	774	0....	10	7	11	4	1		...	.
9117	Rerau	0.00741	305	341	532	AON10b	22-SFAA-a	rerau		95.00	324	0....	10	7	11	3	0		...	.
9118	Rocky Peak (Yinibu, Iyo)	0.01020	420	470	732	AON10b	25-WABA-a	laro		9.92	47	0....	7	5	3	4	1		...	.
9119	Roinji	0.00716	295	330	514	AON09b	34-BHAA-b	roinji		90.00	297	0....	10	7	11	4	1		...	.
9120	Romkun	0.01227	505	565	880	AON10b	26-TDBC-a	romkun		90.00	509	0....	10	7	11	4	1		...	.
9121	Roro (Bereina)	0.29482	12,137	13,586	21,150	AON09b	34-GDAA	roro cluster		88.00	11,955	0....	10	7	7	5	3	Roro	P..	.
9122	Rossel Islander (Bou)	0.08675	3,571	3,998	6,223	AON10b	27-WAAA	yele cluster		80.00	3,198	0....	10	7	7	5	1	Rossel*	PN.	b
9123	Rouku (Upper Morehead)	0.01104	454	509	792	AON10b	20-LDCB-a	rouku		30.00	153	0....	9	5	5	5	1	Ara	...	.
9124	Saep	0.01842	758	849	1,321	AON10b	22-VBAA-a	saep		90.00	764	0....	10	7	11	4	1	Saep	...	.
9125	Sakam	0.01741	717	802	1,249	AON10b	24-SDBA-a	sakam		90.00	722	0....	10	7	11	4	1		...	.
9126	Saki (Turutap)	0.06751	2,779	3,111	4,843	AON10b	22-FACA	maia cluster		80.00	2,489	0....	10	7	6	5	2	Maia	P..	.
9127	Salakahadi (Ebadidi)	0.01549	638	714	1,111	AON09b	34-FCKC-a	ebadidi		75.00	535	0....	10	7	7	5	1	Molima	...	.
9128	Salt (Salt-Yui)	0.20498	8,438	9,446	14,705	AON10b	24-NCBG-a	salt-yui		75.00	7,084	0....	10	8	7	5	2	Salt-yui	PN.	.
9129	Samberigi (Sau)	0.09855	4,057	4,541	7,070	AON10b	24-LBAA-a	samberigi		85.00	3,860	0.s..	10	7	7	4	1	Samberigi	PN.	.
9130	Sambio (Tayek)	0.08152	3,356	3,757	5,848	AON09b	34-DABC-a	kapin		90.00	3,381	0....	10	7	11	4	1		...	n
9131	Samo (Supai)	0.09145	3,765	4,214	6,560	AON10b	24-KGAA-c	samo		85.00	3,582	0....	10	7	6	4	3	Samo-kubo	P..	.
9132	Samosa	0.00296	122	136	212	AON10b	22-PBCA-a	samosa		95.00	130	0....	10	7	11	3	0		...	.
9133	Sanio (Nakiai)	0.02031	836	936	1,457	AON10b	26-IAAA	sanio-hiowe cluster		30.00	281	0....	9	5	6	4	1	Saniyo-hiyowe	P..	.
9134	Saruga	0.00407	168	188	292	AON10b	22-PCAA-a	saruga		95.00	178	0....	10	7	11	3	0		...	.
9135	Sau Enga	0.56387	23,213	25,984	40,451	AON10b	24-LDAB-i	sau-enga		91.00	23,645	0.s..	10	7	7	5	3	Enga: Sau	PN.	.
9136	Sauk	0.02065	850	952	1,481	AON10b	24-SFDA-a	sauk		90.00	856	0....	10	7	11	4	1		...	.
9137	Sausi (Uya)	0.01561	643	719	1,120	AON10b	22-RBAA-a	sausi		35.00	252	0....	9	5	5	3	0		...	.
9138	Seim	0.18040	7,427	8,313	12,942	AON10b	26-FBAA-a	seim		70.00	5,819	0....	10	7	6	5	1		...	.
9139	Selepet	0.18402	7,576	8,480	13,201	AON10b	24-TBBA	selepet cluster		80.00	6,784	0....	10	8	7	5	1	Selepet	PN.	.
9140	Sene	0.00034	14	16	24	AON10b	24-UBCA-a	sene		90.00	14	0....	10	7	11	4	1		...	.
9141	Sengo	0.01113	458	513	798	AON10b	26-HFAB-a	sengo		90.00	462	0....	10	7	11	3	0		...	.
9142	Sengseng	0.01391	573	641	998	AON09b	35-GAAA-c	a-sengseng		90.00	577	0....	10	7	11	5	2	Asengseng*	P..	n
9143	Sepa	0.00845	348	389	606	AON09b	34-BBDB-a	sepa		90.00	350	0....	10	7	11	3	0		...	.
9144	Sepen	0.01350	556	622	968	AON10b	26-SABA-a	sepen		90.00	560	0....	10	7	11	3	0		...	.
9145	Sepik Iwam	0.06751	2,779	3,111	4,843	AON10b	27-JCAA-e	iwam		85.00	2,644	0....	10	7	6	5	1	Iwam*	PN.	.
9146	Sepik Plains (Sawos)	0.24965	10,277	11,504	17,909	AON10b	26-HEAA	sawos cluster		80.00	9,203	0....	10	7	7	5	2		...	.
9147	Sera (Ssia)	0.01362	561	628	977	AON09b	34-BAAA-a	sera		90.00	565	0....	10	7	11	3	0		...	.
9148	Serki (Upper Morehead)	0.01849	761	852	1,326	AON10b	20-LDCA-a	aramba		20.00	170	0....	9	5	6	4	1	Aramba	...	.
9149	Seta	0.00489	201	225	351	AON10b	24-KEBF-a	selta-min		30.00	68	0....	9	5	5	3	0		...	.
9150	Setaman	0.00631	260	291	453	AON10b	24-KEBF-a	selta-min		40.00	116	0....	9	5	3	3	0		...	.
9151	Seti	0.00356	147	164	255	AON10b	27-GBAB-a	seti		25.00	41	0....	9	5	5	3	0		...	.
9152	Sewa Bay (Duau Pwata)	0.05987	2,465	2,759	4,295	AON09b	34-FCPA-b	miadeba		80.00	2,207	0....	10	7	7	5	2		...	b
9153	Sialum	0.02191	902	1,010	1,572	AON10b	24-TCDA-a	sialum		90.00	909	0....	10	7	11	4	1		...	p
9154	Siane (Koreipa, Lambau)	0.67092	27,620	30,917	48,130	AON10b	24-OCAA	siane cluster		91.00	28,134	0.s..	10	7	7	5	1	Siane: Komogu	PN.	.
9155	Siar	0.04541	1,869	2,093	3,258	AON09b	35-CFFA	siar cluster		85.00	1,779	0....	10	7	7	5	1	Siar	...	b
9156	Siboma (Sipoma)	0.00922	380	425	661	AON09b	34-BOAA-a	siboma		95.00	404	0....	10	7	11	4	1		...	.
9157	Sihan	0.00990	408	456	710	AON10b	22-PDCA-a	sihan		90.00	411	0....	10	7	11	3	0		...	.
9158	Sileibi	0.00817	336	376	586	AON10b	22-ADBA-a	sileibi		99.00	373	0....	10	7	12	4	1		...	.
9159	Silopi	0.00442	182	204	317	AON10b	22-PCDA-a	silopi		95.00	193	0....	10	7	11	3	0		...	.
9160	Simbali	0.00945	389	435	678	AON10b	27-RAAB-a	simbali		70.00	305	0....	10	7	7	5	0		...	.
9161	Simbari (Chimbari)	0.08264	3,402	3,808	5,928	AON10b	24-RAAA-a	simbari		90.00	3,427	0....	10	8	11	5	1	Simbari	...	.
9162	Simog	0.01017	419	469	730	AON10b	21-HBBA-a	simog		90.00	422	0....	10	7	11	4	1		...	.
9163	Sinagen (Alu)	0.00656	270	302	471	AON10b	27-HAHB	sinagen cluster		90.00	272	0....	10	7	11	3	0		...	.
9164	Sinagoro	0.37841	15,578	17,438	27,146	AON09b	34-GBBA	south sinagoro cluster		89.00	15,520	0....	10	9	7	5	3	Sinaugoro	PN.	b
9165	Sinaki	0.01288	530	594	924	AON09b	34-FIAJ-b	sinaki		90.00	534	0....	10	7	11	4	1		...	n
9166	Sinasina	1.57928	65,015	72,776	113,294	AON10b	24-NCBF	sinasina cluster		89.00	64,770	0....	10	7	7	4	1	Sinasina	PN.	.
9167	Sinsauru	0.01501	618	692	1,077	AON10b	22-RAAA-a	proper sinsauru		90.00	623	0....	10	7	11	3	0		...	.
9168	Sio	0.09452	3,891	4,356	6,781	AON09b	34-BIAA-a	sio		85.00	3,702	0....	10	7	7	4	1	Sio	PN.	.
9169	Sirak	0.00495	204	228	355	AON09b	34-CCBA-a	nafi		95.00	217	0....	10	7	11	4	1		...	.
9170	Sirasira	0.01342	552	618	963	AON09b	34-CBCA-a	sarasira		90.00	557	0....	10	7	11	4	1		...	.
9171	Sisano (Sinama, Sinano)	0.13000	5,352	5,991	9,326	AON09b	34-BAAB-a	sissano		90.00	5,392	0....	10	7	11	4	1		p..	.
9172	Sisi-Bipi	0.03266	1,345	1,505	2,343	AON09b	35-BABA	sisi-bipi cluster		98.00	1,475	0....	10	7	12	4	1		...	.
9173	Sokorok (Maimai)	0.00898	370	414	644	AON10b	27-IDAA-a	siliput		90.00	372	0....	10	7	11	5	1		...	.
9174	Som	0.00300	124	138	215	AON10b	24-SDAA	som cluster		95.00	131	0....	10	7	11	4	1		...	.
9175	Sona (Kanasi, Dima)	0.05401	2,223	2,489	3,875	AON10b	23-KBAA	kanasi cluster		90.00	2,240	0....	10	7	11	5	1	Kanasi	PN.	b
9176	Songum	0.01028	423	474	737	AON10b	22-TDAA-a	songum		90.00	426	0....	10	7	11	3	0		...	.
9177	Sonia	0.00853	351	393	612	AON10b	24-KIEA-a	sonia		40.00	157	0....	9	6	3	3	0		...	.
9178	Sori-Harengan	0.01999	823	921	1,434	AON09b	35-BACA-a	harengan		90.00	829	0....	10	7	11	5	2		...	p
9179	South Fore (Pamusa)	0.11000	4,528	5,069	7,891	AON10b	24-OGAA-a	pamusa		80.00	4,055	0....	10	9	7	5	3	Fore: Pamusa	PN.	.
9180	South Kewa (Pole)	0.16203	6,670	7,467	11,624	AON10b	24-LBBA	south kewa cluster		85.00	6,347	0.s..	10	10	7	5	2		PN.	.
9181	South Mendi (Angal Heneng	0.53436	21,998	24,624	38,334	AON10b	24-LBCA	south angal cluster		88.00	21,669	0....	10	7	7	5	2	Angal Enen	P..	.
9182	South Watut (Dangal)	0.02529	1,041	1,165	1,814	AON09b	34-CEAC-a	dangal		90.00	1,049	0....	10	7	11	4	1		...	.
9183	Southern Arapesh (North)	0.20000	8,233	9,216	14,348	AON10b	27-JCAA-a	balif		77.00	7,097	0....	10	7	6	5	2	Muhian: Balif	PN.	.
9184	Southern Arapesh (South)	0.16000	6,587	7,373	11,478	AON10b	27-JCAA-c	filifita		91.00	6,709	0....	10	7	7	4	1	Muhian: Ilahita	Pn.	.
9185	Southern Kiwai	0.35979	14,812	16,580	25,811	AON10b	20-PAAD-a	kiwai		87.00	14,424	0....	10	8	7	5	2	Kiwai*	PN.	.
9186	Sowanda (Waina, Wina)	0.03071	1,264	1,415	2,203	AON10b	21-HDAA-b	punda-umeda		85.00	1,203	0....	10	7	6	5	1		...	.
9187	Sua	0.21029	8,657	9,690	15,086	AON10b	24-NCDA-e	sua		80.00	7,752	0....	10	7	7	5	2		pn.	.
9188	Suain	0.04317	1,777	1,989	3,097	AON09b	34-BACB-b	suain		85.00	1,691	0....	10	7	7	4	1		...	.
9189	Suau (Fife Bay)	0.21429	8,822	9,875	15,373	AON09b	34-FIAF-c	vehicular suau	1	89.00	8,789	0....	10	7	7	4	1	Suau	PN.	.
9190	Suena (Yarawe)	0.07754	3,192	3,573	5,563	AON10b	23-ABAA-a	suena		99.00	3,537	0....	10	7	10	5	1	Suena	PN.	.
9191	Suganga	0.02208	909	1,017	1,584	AON10b	24-KEBI-a	suganga		30.00	305	0....	9	5	6	4	1		...	.
9192	Suki	0.05401	2,223	2,489	3,875	AON10b	24-JAAA-a	suki		40.00	996	0....	9	6	6	5	2	Suki	PN.	b
9193	Sukurum	0.02555	1,052	1,177	1,833	AON09b	34-CBAA-a	sukurum		90.00	1,060	0....	10	7	11	4	1		...	.
9194	Sulka	0.06307	2,596	2,906	4,525	AON10b	27-QAAA	sulka cluster		90.00	2,616	0....	10	7	11	4	1	Sulka	P..	.
9195	Sumariup	0.00205	84	94	147	AON10b	26-JGAA-a	sumariup		95.00	90	0....	10	7	11	5	2		...	n
9196	Sumau (Garia)	0.07912	3,257	3,646	5,676	AON10b	22-QAAA-a	garia		30.00	1,094	0....	9	5	5	1	3	Sumau	...	.
9197	Suroi (Pasa)	0.01890	778	871	1,356	AON10b	22-UDAA-a	siroi		90.00	784	0....	10	7	11	4	1	Siroi	PN.	.
9198	Sursurunga	0.07568	3,116	3,487	5,429	AON09b	35-CHAA-a	samo		80.00	2,790	0....	10	7	7	4	1	Sursurunga	P..	.
9199	Tabar	0.07120	2,931	3,281	5,108	AON09b	35-CDAA	mandara cluster		80.00	2,625	0....	10	7	7	5	1	Mandara	...	.
9200	Tabriak (Karawari)	0.03992	1,643	1,840	2,864	AON10b	26-KAAA-b	karawari		85.00	1,564	0....	10	7	6	5	2		p..	n
9201	Taga	0.02000	823	922	1,435	AON10b	24-KIEA	sonia cluster		90.00	829	0....	10	7	11	4	1		...	.
9202	Tagula (Sud Est, Rambuso)	0.05401	2,223	2,489	3,875	AON09b	34-FGAA	tagula cluster		85.00	2,116	0....	10	7	7	5	1	Sudest	...	b
9203	Tai	0.02500	1,029	1,152	1,793	AON10b	24-MABA-a	tai		75.00	864	0....	10	7	6	4	1	Tay*	P..	.
9204	Tairora (Northern, South)	0.27298	11,238	12,579	19,583	AON10b	24-PBAB	tairora cluster	1	88.00	11,070	0.s..	10	7	7	5	1	Tairora	PN.	.
9205	Takia	0.32406	13,341	14,933	23,247	AON09b	34-BCAA	takia-megiar cluster		85.00	12,693	0....	10	7	7	5	1	Takia	P..	.
9206	Tami	0.04372	1,800	2,015	3,136	AON09b	34-BJBA-a	tami		80.00	1,612	0....	10	7	6	4	1	Tami	...	.
9207	Tanga (Tangga)	0.15788	6,499	7,275	11,326	AON09b	35-CIAA	tangga cluster		80.00	5,820	0....	10	7	7	5	2		...	.
9208	Tangu	0.07568	3,116	3,487	5,429	AON10b	26-TBBA-a	tanggu		80.00	2,790	0....	10	7	7	4	1	Tanggu	P..	.
9209	Tanguat	0.01596	657	735	1,145	AON10b	26-TCAA-a	tanguat		90.00	662	0....	10	7	11	3	0		...	.
9210	Tani (Miami)	0.07871	3,240	3,627	5,646	AON10b	22-FADA	maiani cluster		85.00	3,083	0....	10	7	7	4	2	Maiani	P..	.
9211	Tao-Suamato (Mahigi)	0.01577	649	727	1,131	AON10b	20-RCAA-a	tao-suamato		40.00	291	0....	9	6	5	4	1		...	.
9212	Tati (Raepa Tati)	0.00788	324	363	565	AON10b	20-UAAA-a	tate		95.00	345	0....	10	7	11	4	1		...	b
9213	Tauade	0.27750	11,424	12,788	19,907	AON10b	23-BDAA-a	tauade		88.00	11,253	0....	10	8	7	5	3		...	.

Continued opposite

Table 8-2 continued

EVANGELIZATION								EVANGELISM			ADDITIONAL DESCRIPTIVE DATA
Ref 1	*D 28*	*aC 29*	*CG% 30*	*r 31*	*E 32*	*U 33*	*W 34*	*e 35*	*R 36*	*T 37*	*Locations, civil divisions, literacy, religions, church history, denominations, dioceses, church growth, missions, agencies, ministries, movements 38*
9090	2	6	5.86	0	99.85	0.15	C	366.09	161	9	West New Britain Province, southwest hinterland. Dialect chain. Forest, mountains. Animists 10%. D=RCC,Anglican Ch of PNG. M=SIL.
9091	1	6	4.21	0	99.90	0.10	C	407.34	117	10	Western Province, southern bank and hinterland of Fly river. Animists 10%. D=ECP. M=APCM/UFM.
9092	1	5	5.20	0	99.75	0.25	C	298.38	158	8	Morobe Province, Mumeng District, 5 villages. Forest, mountains. Dialect chain. Animists 15%. D=Ev Lutheran Ch of PNG. Nominalism. M=SIL.
9093	2	6	6.53	0	99.80	0.20	C	332.88	183	9	New Ireland Province, south central. Few animists. D=RCC,UCPNGSI(Methodist). M=SIL.
9094	2	6	6.10	0	99.80	0.20	C	332.88	172	9	Simbu Province, Kundiawa District; Gulf Province, Purari river near Oroi. Animists 20%. D=NTM,SDA(major language Pawaia).
9095	1	5	2.45	0	34.00	66.00	A	12.41	284	5	Madang Province, east of Bogia. Savannah, forest, mountains, coastal. Fishermen. Relatively unevangelized tribe; some mission contact. Animists 90%. D=RCC. .
9096	1	7	3.19	0	99.90	0.10	C	410.62	93	10	Madang Province. Tribal religionists(animists) 10%. D=ELCPNG.
9097	5	6	4.34	0	99.90	0.10	C	417.19	117	10	Manus Province, Rambutyo Island. 3 dialects. Moderately bilingual in Titan. Animists 5%. D=Paliau Ch,RCC(few),MEC(few),SDA,Pentecostals. M=MEM.
9098	0	7	2.67	0	28.70	71.30	A	10.16	357	5	Sandaun Province, middle Sepik region, headwaters of Niksek and Walio rivers. Animists 90%. Y=1982. Relatively unevangelized tribe; some mission contact.
9099	0	6	2.90	0	54.00	46.00	B	59.13	201	6	Western Province. 3 villages, via Balimo. Animists 70%.
9100	1	6	5.26	0	99.90	0.10	C	417.19	137	10	Madang Province, inland, southeast of Bogia. Animists 10%. D=RCC. M=SIL,PNGBTA.
9101	1	6	3.72	0	84.00	16.00	B	168.63	156	7	Enga Province, some in Madang Province, either side of Yuat river. Closest to Haruai, Hagahai, Wapi. Animists 45%. D=BUWH(Baptists). M=ABMS.
9102	2	6	4.65	0	99.90	0.10	C	420.48	122	10	Manus Province, Lolo village, Hauwai, Ndrilo, and Pityilu Islands. All bilingual in Lele. Animists 5%. D=RCC,Manus Evangelical Ch. M=MEM.
9103	1	7	3.21	0	99.95	0.05	C	450.77	90	10	Morobe Province, 1 village. Virtually no animists left. D=ELCPNG.
9104	2	6	5.78	0	99.70	0.30	C	268.27	179	8	Gulf Province, Baimuru District, Kerabi Valley; Southern Highlands Province; 20 villages. Forests, mountains; hunter-gatherers. Animists10%. D=ECP,Wesleyan Ch.
9105	1	6	2.90	0	65.00	35.00	B	94.90	167	6	Western Province, with some in Southern Highlands Province. Animists 60%. D=CB. M=CMML.
9106	1	6	4.20	0	99.90	0.10	C	407.34	116	10	Manus Province, Ponam Island. Bilingual in Kurti. Close to Andra-Hus. Virtually no animists left. Entirely Catholics; D=RCC.
9107	1	6	4.45	0	99.90	0.10	C	407.34	122	10	Madang Province. Animists 10%. D=RCC.
9108	0	6	3.96	0	99.90	0.10	C	397.48	114	9	Sandaun Province, on coast round Puari town. Related languages: Rawo, Krisa, Warapu. Animists 10%.
9109	0	7	4.16	0	61.00	39.00	B	77.92	235	6	Madang Province. South of Astrolabe Bay coast, on Kabenau river. Related languages: Siroi, Arawum, Kolom, Lemio. Animists 65%.
9110	1	5	4.38	0	99.85	0.15	C	353.68	131	9	West New Britain Province, north of Waku town. Related to Lamogai. Animists 5%. D=RCC.
9111	0	6	3.78	0	50.00	50.00	B	45.62	266	6	Sandaun Province, just east of Irian Jaya (Indonesia) border. One village on October river. Animists 75%.
9112	1	8	2.50	1	99.95	0.05	C	495.85	48	10	Vunapopes (German Catholic dependants). In New Britain, also southeastern Queensland (Australia). All multilingual in German, English, Tok Pisin. Nearly extinct.
9113	0	6	3.90	0	99.95	0.05	C	436.90	108	10	Madang Province, northwest of Madang City. Related languages: 18, including Murupi, Wamas, Samosa, Mosimo. Virtually no animists left.
9114	1	5	7.04	0	99.87	0.13	C	384.23	184	9	Madang Province, Ramu District. Literates 6%. Tropical forest, mountains. Some animists remain. D=ELCPNG. M=SIL.
9115	0	6	4.28	0	99.90	0.10	C	397.48	121	9	Sandaun Province, on coast around Rawo town. Related languages: Krisa, Puari, Warapu. A few animists.
9116	1	6	4.44	0	99.90	0.10	C	407.34	122	10	Madang Province. Some animists, 2%. D=RCC.
9117	0	6	3.54	0	99.95	0.05	C	436.90	100	10	Madang Province, south of Astrolabe Bay, on Mindjim river. Related languages: Kwato, Ogea, Usu, Duduela, Jilim, Yangulam.
9118	1	5	3.93	0	31.92	68.08	A	11.55	429	5	Sandaun Province, Rocky Peak Mountains, 5 villages. Traditional culture. Animists 90%. Relatively unreached tribe. D=NTM. M=SIL.
9119	1	6	3.45	0	99.90	0.10	C	407.34	100	10	Madang and Morobe Provinces, north coast of Huon Peninsula, 2 villages. Animists 10%. D=ELCPNG.
9120	1	6	4.01	0	99.90	0.10	C	407.34	112	10	Madang Province. Animists 10%. D=RCC.
9121	2	5	7.34	0	99.88	0.12	C	398.28	186	9	Central Province, near Kairuku, Yule Island and mainland. 2 dialects; many schools. Animists 1%. D=RCC,UCPNGSI. M=LMS,Global Bible Translators(Korea),SIL.
9122	2	6	5.94	0	99.80	0.20	C	350.40	160	9	Milne Bay Province, Misima District, Rossel Island. 6 dialects. English used. Coastal. Mainly Catholics; D=RCC,UCPNGSI. M=SIL.
9123	2	6	2.77	0	59.00	41.00	B	64.60	178	6	Western Province, near Morehead. Related to Tonda, Kanum, Peremka, Aramba, Bothar. Swamp, savannah. 4 primary schools. Animists 40%. D=ECP,UCPNGSI.
9124	1	6	4.43	0	99.90	0.10	C	407.34	122	10	Madang Province, Gowar River area, Rai coast, 75 miles southeast of Madang City. Related language: Dumun. Animists 1%. D=ELCPNG.
9125	1	6	4.37	0	99.90	0.10	C	407.34	120	10	Morobe Province. Some animists, 1%. D=ELCPNG.
9126	2	6	5.67	0	99.80	0.20	C	332.88	162	9	Madang Province, mainland south of Manam Island. Animists 2%. D=ELCPNG,RCC. M=PNGBTA,SIL.
9127	0	6	4.06	0	99.75	0.25	C	287.43	134	8	Milne Bay Province, Esaala District, Fergusson Island. Few animists. M=SIL.
9128	3	5	6.78	1	99.75	0.25	C	312.07	189	9	Simbu Province, 10 villages. Close to Nondiri. Scattered animists. D=RCC,ELCPNG,SDA. M=SIL,SVD.
9129	1	6	6.14	0	99.85	0.15	C	375.40	163	9	Southern Highlands Province, Lake Kutubu District, east of Erave. Few animists, 2%. D=ECP. M=APCM/UFM.
9130	1	6	6.00	0	99.90	0.10	C	417.19	153	10	Morobe Province, Mumeng District, Bulolo District. 5 villages. Most bilingual in Tok Pisin(35% being literate in it). D=ELCPNG.
9131	1	6	6.06	0	99.85	0.15	C	366.09	166	9	Western Province, east of Strickland river, north and south of Nomad town. Animists 3%. D=ECP. M=APCM/UFM,Pioneers Inc,SIL.
9132	0	7	2.60	0	99.95	0.05	C	440.37	79	10	Madang Province, northwest of Madang City. Related languages: 18, including Murupi, Wamas, Rapting, Mosimo.
9133	1	6	3.39	0	59.00	41.00	B	64.60	207	6	East Sepik Province, Ambunti District, foothills of Wogamus River basin. Tropical forest. Hunter-gatherers. Semi-nomads. Animists 30%. D=AoG. M=SIL.
9134	0	7	2.92	0	99.95	0.05	C	440.37	86	10	Madang Province. Virtually no animists left; all Christians.
9135	3	5	8.08	1	99.91	0.09	C	441.76	189	10	Enga Province, Sali river, around Kompiam. Few animists left. D=GLC,RCC,ELCPNG.
9136	1	6	4.55	0	99.90	0.10	C	407.34	124	10	Morobe Province. No animists left. D=ELCPNG.
9137	0	6	3.28	0	59.00	41.00	B	75.37	202	6	Madang Province, on Ramu river. Related languages: Sinsauru, Asas, Kesawai, Dumpu. Scattered animists, 10%.
9138	0	5	6.57	0	99.00	1.00	C	252.94	211	8	Sandaun Province, east of Mehek. Closely related to Kwanga. Animists 3%. M=SIL.
9139	3	5	6.74	0	99.80	0.20	C	341.64	183	9	Morobe Province, Kabwum District, valleys of Pumune and Kiari rivers, 15 villages. D=Ev Lutheran Ch of PNG,SDA(few),Ch of Christ(few). M=SIL.
9140	1	10	2.67	0	99.90	0.10	C	420.48	80	10	Morobe Province. Nearly extinct. D=ELCPNG.
9141	0	6	3.91	0	99.90	0.10	C	397.48	113	9	East Sepik Province. Adults fluent in Iatmul. Few animists left.
9142	2	6	4.14	0	99.90	0.10	C	427.05	110	10	West New Britain Province, southwest interior. Some animists left. D=RCC,NTM.
9143	0	6	3.62	0	99.90	0.10	C	397.48	106	9	Madang Province, around Bogia town. Related to Wogeo, Biem, Manam, Medebur. No animists.
9144	0	6	4.11	0	99.90	0.10	C	397.48	117	9	Madang Province. Virtually no traditional religionists(animists) left.
9145	3	6	5.74	0	99.85	0.15	C	378.50	153	9	East Sepik Province, Ambunti District. Few animists. D=AoG,RCC,NTM. M=SIL.
9146	2	5	7.06	0	99.80	0.20	C	329.96	197	9	East Sepik Province, Maprik District, 16 villages. Close to Gaikundi. Few animists. D=RCC,AoG.
9147	0	6	4.12	0	99.90	0.10	C	397.48	118	9	Sandaun Province, around Serai town on coast. No animists remain.
9148	1	6	2.87	0	48.00	52.00	A	35.04	225	5	Western Province. Animists 80%. D=ECP. M=APCM/UFM.
9149	0	6	4.31	0	54.00	46.00	B	59.13	273	6	Sandaun Province, on Sand river. Animists 70%.
9150	0	6	2.48	0	62.00	38.00	B	90.52	157	6	Sandaun and Western Provinces, Victor Emanuel range. Animists 60%.
9151	0	7	3.78	0	50.00	50.00	B	45.62	266	6	Sandaun Province, Weni river. Animists 75%.
9152	2	6	5.55	0	99.80	0.20	C	341.64	155	9	Milne Bay Province, center of Normanby Island. Bilingual in Dobu. Animists 5%. Syncretism strong. D=UCPNGSI,RCC.
9153	1	6	4.61	0	99.90	0.10	C	410.62	125	10	Morobe Province. Bilingual in Ono. Few animists. D=ELCPNG.
9154	3	5	8.27	0	99.91	0.09	C	431.79	197	10	Eastern Highlands Province, Goroka District. Forest, mountains. Some animists left. D=ELCPNG,SDA,NTM. M=SIL.
9155	2	6	5.32	0	99.85	0.15	C	375.40	145	9	New Ireland Province, southern. English used in schools. Coastal. A handful of animists. D=RCC,UCPNGSI. M=SIL.
9156	1	7	3.77	0	99.95	0.05	C	450.77	102	10	Morobe Province, Lae District, 1 village on coast. Virtually no animists left. D=ELCPNG.
9157	0	6	3.79	0	99.90	0.10	C	397.48	110	9	Madang Province, southwest of Madang City. Related languages: Gumalu, Amele, Isebe, Bau, Panim. Few animists.
9158	1	6	3.69	0	99.99	0.01	C	484.20	97	10	Madang Province. Related language: Katiati. No animists left. Entirely baptized Lutherans. D=ELCPNG.
9159	0	6	3.00	0	99.95	0.05	C	436.90	89	10	Madang Province, northwest of Madang City. Related languages: 18, including Murupi, Wamas, Rapting, Mosimo. Entirely Christians.
9160	0	5	3.48	0	98.00	2.00	C	250.39	127	8	East New Britain Province, Gazelle Peninsula. Mountainous. Many bilinguals in Mali(Gaxtai). Animists 5%.
9161	3	6	6.01	0	99.90	0.10	C	420.48	152	10	Eastern Highlands Province, Marawaka District. Few animists. D=ELCPNG,SDA,NTM. M=SIL. Response to Christianity very slow.
9162	1	6	3.81	0	99.90	0.10	C	407.34	108	10	Sandaun Province, Amanab District. Animists 2%. D=RCC.
9163	0	6	3.36	0	99.90	0.10	C	397.48	100	9	Sandaun Province, Torricelli Mountains. Animists few and scattered widely.
9164	4	5	7.62	0	99.89	0.11	C	428.80	180	10	Central Province south of Kwikila, Rigo District. 17 dialects. Scattered animists, 4%. D=UCPNGSI,RCC,SDA,Salvation Army. Most speak Motu, Hiri Motu.
9165	1	6	4.06	0	99.90	0.10	C	413.91	112	10	Milne Bay Province, Gadaisu to Saubina. Animists 5%. D=UCPNGSI. Bilingual in Suau.
9166	1	5	3.31	1	99.89	0.11	C	406.06	96	10	Simbu Province. Close to Dom and Golin. Few animists left. D=NTM.
9167	0	6	4.22	0	99.90	0.10	C	397.48	120	9	Madang Province, near Dumpu. Related languages: Asas, Sausi, Kesawai, Dumpu. Virtually no animists left.
9168	1	6	6.09	0	99.85	0.15	C	372.30	163	9	Morobe Province, mainland near Sio Island. Agriculturalists. Animists 2%. D=ELCPNG. M=SIL.
9169	1	7	3.13	0	99.95	0.05	C	450.77	89	10	Morobe Province, Busu river. A few animists only. D=ELCPNG.
9170	1	6	4.10	0	99.90	0.10	C	407.34	114	10	Morobe Province, Leron river. Animists 5%. D=ELCPNG.
9171	1	6	6.49	0	99.90	0.10	C	413.91	164	10	Sandaun Province, Aitape District, around Sissano to Malol. Related languages: Sera, Tumleo, Ali, Suain. Forest, coastal. Fishermen. D=RCC. M=SIL.
9172	1	6	5.12	0	99.98	0.02	C	479.31	127	10	Manus Province, west coast, 3 villages, Bipi and Sisi Islands. Close to Loniu. No animists. Entirely Roman Catholics. D=RCC.
9173	2	6	3.68	0	99.90	0.10	C	413.91	103	10	Sandaun Province, Makru-Klaplei Division, Nuku District, 1 village. Animists 5%. D=RCC,Christian Brethren. M=CMML.
9174	1	7	2.61	0	99.95	0.05	C	450.77	78	10	Morobe Province. Tribal religionists(animists) 5%. D=ELCPNG.
9175	2	6	5.56	0	99.90	0.10	C	440.19	136	10	Milne Bay Province, both sides of river valleys from Mount Thomson. Animists 5%. D=Anglican Ch of PNG,UCPNGSI. Bilingual in Motu and some English. M=SIL.
9176	0	6	3.82	0	99.90	0.10	C	397.48	111	9	Madang Province, south of Bongu, south of Astrolabe Bay, on Kabenau river. Few animists.
9177	0	5	2.79	0	61.00	39.00	B	89.06	173	6	Western and Southern Highlands Provinces, 20 miles southwest of Bosavi. Animists 30%.
9178	2	6	4.52	0	99.90	0.10	C	420.48	120	10	Manus Province, Sori and Harengan Islands. Bilingual in Lindrou. Few animists. Mostly Catholics. D=RCC,SDA.
9179	5	6	2.12	0	99.80	0.20	C	350.40	73	9	Eastern Highlands Province, Okapa District. Animists 2%. D=ELCPNG,WM,SDA,NTM,CHM.
9180	8	6	6.67	0	99.85	0.15	C	387.81	170	9	Southern Highlands Province. Some animists. D=ECP,RCC,UCPNGSI,CU,BMC,ELCPNG,EBM,SDA. M=SIL,APCM/UFM.
9181	2	5	7.98	0	99.88	0.12	C	395.07	202	9	Southern Highlands Province, from Nembi Plateau to Lai Valley. Scattered animists. D=UCPNGSI,Christian Union Mission.
9182	1	6	4.76	0	99.90	0.10	C	410.62	128	10	Morobe Province, Lower Watut river. Few animists. D=ELCPNG.
9183	2	6	6.79	0	99.77	0.23	C	320.39	189	9	Half in West Sepik Province, half in East. 60 Muhian villages. Animists 3%. D=SSEC,RCC. M=SVD,SIL.
9184	2	6	6.73	0	99.91	0.09	C	418.50	170	10	East Sepik Province, Torricelli Mountains, east of Wom. Tropical forest. Agriculturalists. Some animists, 1%. D=SSEC,RCC. M=SIL.
9185	3	5	7.55	1	99.87	0.13	C	403.28	186	10	Western Province, Fly River Delta. 6 dialects. Animists 3%. D=United Church of PNGSI(strong),ECP,SDA. M=LMS,APCM/UFM.
9186	2	5	4.91	0	99.85	0.15	C	359.89	141	9	Sandaun Province, Amanab District, 6 villages. Also in Irian Jaya (Indonesia). Animists 3%. D=RCC,Christian Brethren. M=CMML.
9187	2	6	6.88	1	99.80	0.20	C	344.56	185	9	Simbu Province. Some tribal religionists(animists) remain, 2%. D=ELCPNG,RCC.
9188	1	6	5.26	0	99.85	0.15	C	359.89	150	9	Sandaun Province, coast around Ulau and Suain. Few animists. D=RCC.
9189	1	6	7.01	1	99.89	0.11	C	406.06	177	10	Milne Bay Province. Coastal lingua franca, 10 dialects. Many literates. Few animists. D=UCPNGSI. M=LMS.
9190	1	6	6.04	0	99.99	0.01	C	498.66	141	10	Morobe Province, Lae District, north of Yekora, 8 villages. D=99% baptized Lutherans(ELCPNG); a few Church of Christ. M=SIL.
9191	0	6	3.48	0	57.00	43.00	B	62.41	219	6	Sandaun Province, Amanab District. Closely related to Mianmin. Animists 35%. M=CMML.
9192	1	6	4.71	0	77.00	23.00	B	112.42	206	7	Western Province, Lake Suki. Nomadic headhunters till 1940s. English used in schools. Animists 10%. D=ECP. M=APCM/UFM,Brethren Mission. D=ECP.
9193	1	6	4.77	0	99.90	0.10	C	410.62	128	10	Morobe Province, Leron river. Few animists. D=ELCPNG.
9194	1	6	5.72	0	99.90	0.10	C	413.91	148	10	East New Britain Province, Wide Bay coast. Dialect chain. Several primary schools. Swamps. Scattered animists. D=RCC. M=SIL.
9195	2	8	4.60	0	99.95	0.05	C	471.58	114	10	East Sepik Province, Upper Wagupmeri river, 1 village. Bilingual in Tok Pisin, Alamblak. Few animists. D=NGGM,SEBC.
9196	3	5	4.81	0	58.00	42.00	B	63.51	278	6	Madang Province, between Ramu and Naru rivers. Related languages: Usino, Urigina, Danaru. Animists 20%. No missions, though. D=ELCPNG.
9197	1	6	4.46	0	99.90	0.10	C	420.48	118	10	Madang Province, Saidor Sub-Province. Related languages: Arawum, Pulabu, Kolom, Lemio. Animists 1%. D=ELCPNG. M=SIL.
9198	1	6	5.79	0	99.80	0.20	C	327.04	168	9	New Ireland Province, south central, Namatanai. Few animists. D=UCPNGSI. M=SIL.
9199	3	6	5.73	0	99.80	0.20	C	332.88	163	9	New Ireland Province, Simberi, Tatau, Tabar Islands. No animists. D=RCC,SDA,UCPNGSI. M=SIL.
9200	2	6	5.18	0	99.85	0.15	C	375.40	142	9	East Sepik Province, near Chambri. Highly bilingual in Tok Pisin. Few animists. D=RCC,SDA.
9201	1	6	4.52	0	99.90	0.10	C	407.34	124	10	Madang Province. Animists 1%. D=ELCPNG.
9202	2	6	5.50	0	99.85	0.15	C	375.40	149	9	Milne Bay Province, several islands. Lingua francas: Misima, English. Few literates. Animists 2%. Sorcery strong. D=RCC,UCPNGSI. M=SIL.
9203	0	5	4.56	0	99.75	0.25	C	281.96	150	8	Madang Province, southwest, Dundrom village. A few animists. M=PBT.
9204	2	5	2.66	0	99.88	0.12	C	404.71	81	10	Eastern Highlands Province, Kainantu District. Closely related to Binumarien, Kambaira. Animists 2%. D=ELCPNG,SDA. M=SIL.
9205	2	5	7.41	0	99.85	0.15	C	369.19	195	9	Madang Province, southern half of Karkar Island. Few animists. D=Ch of the Nazarene,ELCPNG. M=SIL.
9206	1	6	5.21	0	99.80	0.20	C	321.20	156	9	Morobe Province, Tami Islands and villages on mainland south of Finschhafen. Very few animists left. D=ELCPNG.
9207	2	6	6.57	0	99.80	0.20	C	332.88	184	9	New Ireland Province, Tanga Islands, Anir (Feni) Island, 3 villages on New Ireland. Some animists. D=RCC,UCPNGSI.
9208	1	6	5.79	0	99.80	0.20	C	327.04	168	9	Madang Province. Agriculturalists, hunter-gatherers. Animists 10%. D=RCC. M=SIL.
9209	0	6	4.28	0	99.90	0.10	C	397.48	121	9	Madang Province. Tribal religionists(animists) very few.
9210	1	6	5.90	0	99.85	0.15	C	366.09	162	9	Madang Province. Few animists. D=RCC. M=SIL,PNGBTA.
9211	1	6	3.43	0	67.00	33.00	B	97.82	184	6	Western Province, northeast corner, upper Bamu, Wawoi, and Guavi rivers, 11 villages. Accessible only by boat. Forests, swamp. Animists 30%. D=ECP. M=UFM.
9212	1	6	3.60	0	99.95	0.05	C	457.71	97	10	Gulf Province. 3 villages. All bilingual in Toaripi. D=UCPNGSI.
9213	3	5	7.28	0	99.88	0.12	C	398.28	185	9	Central Province, Goilala District toward northeast. Few animists. D=RCC,ELCPNG,SDA(few). This language is used in RC schools.

Continued overleaf

Table 8-2 continued

PEOPLE		POPULATION				IDENTITY CODE		LANGUAGE		CHURCH		MINISTRY						SCRIPTURE	
Ref 1	Ethnic name 2	P% 3	In 1995 4	In 2000 5	In 2025 6	Race 7	Language 8	Autoglossonym 9	S 10	AC 11	Members 12	Jayuh 13-17	d 18	wa 19	xc 20	mc 21	mi 22	Biblioglossonym 23	Pub ss 24-26 27
9214	Taulil-Butam	0.02537	1,044	1,169	1,820	AON10b	27-SAAA-a	taulil		95.00	1,111	0....	10	7	11	5	2		... b
9215	Taupota (Maivara)	0.10437	4,297	4,810	7,487	AON09b	34-FHAD-b	taupota		80.00	3,848	0....	10	9	7	5	1		... b
9216	Tauya (Inafosa)	0.01094	450	504	785	AON10b	22-EBAA-a	tauya		40.00	202	0....	9	6	5	3	0		... .
9217	Tavara (Tawala, Bohilai)	0.26288	10,822	12,114	18,858	AON09b	34-FHAB-c	tawala		90.00	10,903	0....	10	10	7	5	2	Tawala	PN. b
9218	Telefol (Feramin)	0.13418	5,524	6,183	9,626	AON10b	24-KEBG-b	telefol-min		70.00	4,328	0....	10	5	6	4	2	Telefol	PN. .
9219	Tembogia (Miyemu)	0.65508	26,968	30,187	46,994	AON10b	24-NAAB-e	tembogia		91.00	27,470	0.s..	10	7	7	3	1	Umbu-ungu: Tambul*	Pn. .
9220	Tench (Tenis)	0.00194	80	89	139	AON09b	35-CABA-a	tenis		95.00	85	0....	10	7	11	3	0		... .
9221	Terepu (Turupu, Terebu)	0.00473	195	218	339	AON09b	34-BBAB-b	terebu		40.00	87	0....	9	6	6	3	0		... .
9222	Tiang (Djaul)	0.03124	1,286	1,440	2,241	AON09b	35-CBCA-a	tiang		85.00	1,224	0....	10	7	7	4	1		... .
9223	Tifal (Tifalmin)	0.08073	3,323	3,720	5,791	AON10b	24-KEBB-a	tifal-min		30.00	1,116	0....	9	5	6	5	2	Tifal	P.. .
9224	Timbe	0.27750	11,424	12,788	19,907	AON10b	24-TBAA	timbe cluster		88.00	11,253	0....	10	8	7	5	1	Timbe	PN. .
9225	Tirio (Dudi)	0.02996	1,233	1,381	2,149	AON10b	20-NAAA	lewada-dewara cluster		30.00	414	0....	9	5	6	4	1	Tirio	P.. .
9226	Titan (Manus, Moanus)	0.10015	4,123	4,615	7,185	AON09b	35-BCBA-a	proper titan		80.00	3,692	0....	10	10	7	5	3		... .
9227	Toaripi (East Elema)	0.80645	33,199	37,162	57,853	AON10b	20-TBAB-b	moveave-toaripi		88.00	32,703	0....	10	7	7	5	1	Toaripi	PNB .
9228	Tobo	0.07226	2,975	3,330	5,184	AON10b	24-TDAA-a	tobo		25.00	832	0....	9	5	6	4	1		... .
9229	Tokano (Lower Asaro)	0.18428	7,586	8,492	13,220	AON10b	24-OBAC-a	tokano		76.00	6,454	0....	10	7	6	5	1	Tokano	P.. .
9230	Tolai (Kuanua, Gunantuna)	1.53885	63,350	70,912	110,394	AON09b	35-CFDA-a	kuanua	5	87.00	61,694	0.su.	10	8	7	5	3	Tinata-tuna*	PNB .
9231	Tomu (Tomu River)	0.00946	389	436	679	AON10b	24-KIFA-a	tomu		40.00	174	0....	9	6	3	3	0		... .
9232	Tonda (Indorodoro)	0.01892	779	872	1,357	AON10b	20-LDBA-a	tonda		45.00	392	0....	9	6	5	3	0		... .
9233	Torricelli (Lou)	0.03005	1,237	1,385	2,156	AON10b	27-JABA	lou cluster		85.00	1,177	0....	10	8	7	5	2		... .
9234	Tuam (Mutu)	0.05262	2,166	2,425	3,775	AON09b	34-BJBB-d	tuam		80.00	1,940	0....	10	7	7	5	2		... .
9235	Tubetube	0.05045	2,077	2,325	3,619	AON09b	34-FCUA-a	tube-tube		85.00	1,976	0....	10	7	7	4	1	Bwanabwana	P.. b
9236	Tulu (Levei-Tulu)	0.03658	1,506	1,686	2,624	AON09b	35-BBBB-d	tulu		85.00	1,433	0....	10	8	6	5	3		... .
9237	Tumie (Tumuip)	0.02150	885	991	1,542	AON09b	35-IAAA-a	tumoip		98.00	971	0....	10	7	12	4	1		... .
9238	Tumleo	0.02129	876	981	1,527	AON09b	34-BABA-a	tumleo		90.00	883	0....	10	7	11	3	0		... .
9239	Turaka	0.00110	45	51	79	AON10b	23-IACA-a	turaka		95.00	48	0....	10	7	11	3	0		... .
9240	Tuwari	0.00385	158	177	276	AON10b	27-CBAA	tuwari cluster		40.00	71	0....	9	6	4	3	0		... .
9241	USA White	0.11000	4,528	5,069	7,891	CEW19s	52-ABAC-s	general american		78.00	3,954	1Bsuh	10	9	12	0	0	English*	PNB b
9242	Uaripi	0.10170	4,187	4,686	7,296	AON10b	20-TBAA-a	uaripi		65.00	3,046	0....	10	5	5	5	2		... .
9243	Ubir	0.05085	2,093	2,343	3,648	AON09b	34-FBAA	ubir cluster		90.00	2,109	0....	10	7	11	4	1	Ubir	P.. .
9244	Ufim	0.01877	773	865	1,347	AON10b	24-SAAA-a	ufim		90.00	778	0....	10	7	11	4	1		... .
9245	Ukuriguma	0.00423	174	195	303	AON10b	22-IBBA-a	ukuriguma		40.00	78	0....	9	6	6	3	0		... .
9246	Ulingan (Mauwake, Mawake)	0.05401	2,223	2,489	3,875	AON10b	22-GAAA-a	mauwake		80.00	1,991	0....	10	7	7	5	1	Mauwake	P.. .
9247	Umeda	0.00762	314	351	547	AON10b	21-HDAA-b	punda-umeda		85.00	298	0....	10	7	7	5	1		... .
9248	Uramat (Auramot)	0.04793	1,973	2,209	3,438	AON10b	27-RAAD-a	uramat		80.00	1,767	0....	10	7	7	4	1	Ura	... .
9249	Urapmin	0.01310	539	604	940	AON10b	24-KEBC-a	urap-min		80.00	483	0....	10	7	6	4	1		... .
9250	Urat	0.15136	6,231	6,975	10,858	AON10b	27-HCAA	urat cluster		75.00	5,231	0....	10	7	7	4	1	Urat: Yehre	P.. .
9251	Uri Vehees (Urii)	0.06307	2,596	2,906	4,525	AON10b	24-SFAA	uri cluster		80.00	2,325	0....	10	7	7	4	1	Uri	PN. .
9252	Uriginau (Origanau)	0.04428	1,823	2,040	3,177	AON10b	22-QDAA-a	urigina		80.00	1,632	0....	10	7	6	4	1		... .
9253	Urim (Kalp)	0.08102	3,335	3,734	5,812	AON10b	27-KAAA-a	urim		85.00	3,173	0....	10	7	7	5	1	Urim	P.. .
9254	Urimo	0.02633	1,084	1,213	1,889	AON10b	27-LADA-a	proper urimo		45.00	546	0....	9	6	5	3	0		... .
9255	Usan (Wanuma)	0.03511	1,445	1,618	2,519	AON10b	22-IAAA-a	usan		85.00	1,375	0....	10	7	7	4	2	Usan	... .
9256	Usino	0.05140	2,116	2,369	3,687	AON10b	22-QBAA-a	usino		80.00	1,895	0....	10	7	6	4	1		... .
9257	Usu	0.00251	103	116	180	AON10b	22-SAAA-a	usu		95.00	110	0....	10	7	11	4	1		... .
9258	Usarufa	0.03085	1,270	1,422	2,213	AON10b	24-PABB-a	usarufa		85.00	1,208	0....	10	8	7	5	1	Usarufa	PN. .
9259	Utu	0.01839	757	847	1,319	AON10b	22-PCFA-a	utu		90.00	763	0....	10	7	11	4	1		... .
9260	Uvol	0.12899	5,310	5,944	9,253	AON09b	35-HAAA-a	lote		90.00	5,350	0....	10	7	11	4	1	Lote	P.. .
9261	Valman (Koroko)	0.02034	837	937	1,459	AON10b	27-HAIA-a	valman		45.00	422	0....	9	6	5	3	0		... .
9262	Vanambre	0.01542	635	711	1,106	AON10b	22-GHAA-a	wanambre		98.00	696	0....	10	7	12	4	1		... .
9263	Vanimo (Manimo)	0.03000	1,235	1,382	2,152	AON10b	25-OADA-a	vanimo		85.00	1,175	0....	10	7	5	5	2		... .
9264	Vehes	0.00341	140	157	245	AON09b	34-DABF-a	vehes		95.00	149	0....	10	7	11	4	1		... .
9265	Vitu (Witu)	0.22200	9,139	10,230	15,926	AON09b	35-DCAA-a	vitu		87.00	8,900	0....	10	7	7	5	1	Vitu	... .
9266	Vivigani (Iduna, Ufaufa)	0.17513	7,210	8,070	12,563	AON09b	34-FCFA	iduna cluster		80.00	6,456	0....	10	7	7	5	2	Iduna	PN. .
9267	Wab	0.00498	205	229	357	AON09b	24-SDAA-a	som		95.00	218	0....	10	7	11	3	0		... .
9268	Wabuda Kiwai	0.05085	2,093	2,343	3,648	AON10b	20-PABA-a	proper wabuda		90.00	2,109	0....	10	7	12	3	0		... .
9269	Wadaginamb	0.01722	709	794	1,235	AON10b	22-AAAA-a	wadaginam		90.00	714	0....	10	7	11	4	1		... .
9270	Waffa (Kami)	0.03413	1,405	1,573	2,448	AON10b	24-PBBA-a	waffa		85.00	1,337	0....	10	7	7	5	2	Waffa	PN. .
9271	Wagawaga (Deamuni, Daioi)	0.04601	1,894	2,120	3,301	AON09b	34-FIAA-a	kila-kilana		85.00	1,802	0....	10	8	7	5	3		... n
9272	Wagumi	0.02000	823	922	1,435	AON10b	20-LDBA	tonda cluster		45.00	415	0....	9	6	5	3	0		... .
9273	Wahgi (Banz-Nondugl)	1.66914	68,714	76,916	119,741	AON10b	24-NCAC	wahgi cluster		82.00	63,071	0.s..	10	10	7	5	2	Wahgi	PN. .
9274	Waia (Kenedibi, Hiwi)	0.04969	2,046	2,290	3,565	AON10b	20-MBAA-a	proper waia		40.00	916	0....	9	6	5	4	1	Tabo: Aramia	P.. .
9275	Waibuk (Wiyaw, Taman)	0.02701	1,112	1,245	1,938	AON10b	24-MCAA-b	mambar		40.00	498	0....	9	6	3	5	3		... n
9276	Waisara (Owenda, Waijara)	0.01101	453	507	790	AON10b	24-PCAA-a	owena		95.00	482	0....	10	7	11	5	2	Owenia	... .
9277	Walio	0.00448	184	206	321	AON10b	27-BBAA-a	walio		85.00	175	0....	10	7	3	3	0		... .
9278	Wamas	0.00473	195	218	339	AON10b	22-PBBA-a	wamas		95.00	207	0....	10	7	11	3	0		... .
9279	Wampur	0.00935	385	431	671	AON09b	34-CADA-a	wampur		95.00	409	0....	10	7	12	4	1		... .
9280	Wamsak (Womsak, Nihamber)	0.15255	6,280	7,030	10,944	AON10b	26-FBBA-a	wamsak		65.00	4,569	0....	10	6	5	3	0		... .
9281	Wanap	0.02484	1,023	1,145	1,782	AON10b	27-HBCA-a	wanap		40.00	458	0....	9	6	5	3	0		... .
9282	Wandabong	0.01630	671	751	1,169	AON10b	24-SCBD-a	wandabong		90.00	676	0....	10	7	6	3	0		... .
9283	Wantoat	0.29147	11,999	13,431	20,909	AON10b	24-SEAC-a	wantoat		80.00	10,745	0....	10	7	7	5	1	Wantoat	PN. .
9284	Wapi	0.03154	1,298	1,453	2,263	AON10b	27-HABA-b	wapi		10.00	145	0....	8	5	5	3	0	Wape	P.. .
9285	Warapu	0.05076	2,090	2,339	3,641	AON10b	25-OBDA-a	warapu		90.00	2,105	0....	10	7	11	3	0		... .
9286	Waris	0.05934	2,443	2,734	4,257	AON10b	21-HBAA-a	proper waris		30.00	820	0....	9	5	6	4	1	Waris	Pn. .
9287	Waruna	0.01514	623	698	1,086	AON10b	24-JBAA-a	waruna		40.00	279	0....	9	6	5	3	0		... n
9288	Washkuk (Kwoma)	0.09035	3,719	4,163	6,482	AON10b	26-FAAB-a	kwoma		85.00	3,539	0....	10	9	7	5	1	Washkuk*	PN. .
9289	Wasi (Peleata, Uase)	0.04793	1,973	2,209	3,438	AON09b	27-OAAA-a	pele		90.00	1,988	0....	10	7	11	5	1	Pele-ata	P.. .
9290	Waskia	0.32406	13,341	14,933	23,247	AON10b	22-KBAA	waskia cluster		85.00	12,693	0.s..	10	10	7	5	1	Waskia	PN. .
9291	Watakataui	0.00505	208	233	362	AON10b	26-JEAA-a	watakataui		95.00	221	1....	10	7	11	5	2	Waxe*	P.. n
9292	Wataluma	0.00750	309	346	538	AON09b	34-FCEA-a	wataluma		95.00	328	0....	10	7	11	3	0		... n
9293	Watam	0.01186	488	547	851	AON10b	26-RAAA-a	watam		90.00	492	0....	10	7	11	3	0		... .
9294	Watiwa (Watifa)	0.00823	339	379	590	AON10b	22-REAA-a	dumpu		90.00	341	0....	10	7	11	4	1		... n
9295	Wedau (Wedaun, Wedawan)	0.08504	3,501	3,919	6,101	AON09b	34-FHCA-b	wedau vehicular	1	80.00	3,135	0.s..	10	7	7	4	1	Wedau	PN. b
9296	Weli	0.14208	5,849	6,547	10,193	AON10b	23-BBAA	weri cluster		80.00	5,238	0....	10	7	7	4	1	Weri	PN. .
9297	Weliki	0.00512	211	236	367	AON10b	24-SDAB-a	weliki		95.00	224	0....	10	7	11	4	1		... n
9298	Were	0.01000	412	461	717	AON10b	20-OAAA	gidra-bituri cluster		90.00	415	0....	10	9	8	0	0		... .
9299	West Angal Heneng (Mendi)	1.00929	41,550	46,510	72,404	AON10b	24-LBCB	west angal cluster		89.00	41,393	0....	10	8	7	5	1	Angal Heneng	PN. .
9300	West Kewa (Pasuma)	0.76800	31,616	35,391	55,095	AON10b	24-LBBC-a	pasuma	1	85.00	30,082	0....	10	10	7	5	2		pn. .
9301	West Nakanai (Maututu)	0.40997	16,877	18,892	29,410	AON09b	35-DAAB	west nakanai cluster		88.00	16,625	0....	10	8	7	5	2	Nakanai	PN. .
9302	Wiaki	0.01769	728	815	1,269	AON10b	27-ICAA-a	wiaki		90.00	734	0....	10	7	11	4	1		... .
9303	Wiru	0.48225	19,853	22,223	34,596	AON10b	24-LAAA-a	wiru		84.00	18,667	0....	10	8	7	5	1	Wiru	PN. .
9304	Wogamusin	0.01161	478	535	833	AON10b	26-BCBA-a	wogamusin		10.00	54	0....	8	5	3	5	2		... n
9305	Wogeo	0.03901	1,606	1,798	2,798	AON09b	34-BBBA-a	vokeo		85.00	1,528	0....	10	7	7	3	0		... .
9306	Wom (Wam)	0.05944	2,447	2,739	4,264	AON10b	27-JAFA	wom cluster		80.00	2,191	0....	10	8	7	5	3		... .
9307	Wutung (Udung)	0.01293	532	596	928	AON10b	25-OACA-a	wutung		90.00	536	0....	10	7	11	3	0		... .
9308	Wuvulu-Aua (Aua-Viwulu)	0.03071	1,264	1,415	2,203	AON09b	35-AAAA-a	wuvulu		90.00	1,274	0....	10	7	11	5	2	Wuvulu-aua	... .
9309	Yabem (Jabem, Yabim)	0.07113	2,928	3,278	5,103	AON09b	34-BLAA-a	yabem	3	80.00	2,622	0....	10	7	7	5	1	Jabem*	PN. .
9310	Yaben	0.02214	911	1,020	1,588	AON10b	22-IABA	yaben cluster		95.00	969	0....	10	7	11	5	2		... .
9311	Yabio	0.00351	144	162	252	AON10b	27-CAAA-a	yabio		35.00	57	0....	9	5	4	3	0		... .
9312	Yabiyufa (Yaweyuha)	0.05050	2,079	2,327	3,623	AON10b	24-OCAC-a	yaweyuha		95.00	2,211	0....	10	8	11	5	2	Yaweyuha	PN. .
9313	Yabong	0.01528	629	704	1,096	AON10b	22-VDAA-a	yabong		95.00	669	0....	10	7	11	4	1		... .
9314	Yagaria (Kami)	0.48120	19,810	22,174	34,520	AON10b	24-ODAA-a	yagaria		90.00	19,957	1.s..	10	9	7	5	3	Yagaria: Kami-kuluka	PN. .
9315	Yagaria (Move)	0.16733	6,889	7,711	12,004	AON10b	24-ODAA-ab	move		80.00	6,169	1.s..	10	8	7	5	3	Yagaria: Move	Pn. .
9316	Yagawak	0.01552	639	715	1,113	AON10b	24-SEBA-b	kandumin		90.00	644	0....	10	7	11	4	1		... .
9317	Yagomi	0.00432	178	199	310	AON10b	24-SBBF-a	yagomi		95.00	189	0....	10	7	11	3	0		... .
9318	Yagwoia (Yeghuye)	0.24305	10,006	11,200	17,436	AON10b	24-RACA-a	yagwoia		88.00	9,856	0....	10	8	5	5	3		... .
9319	Yahang	0.04034	1,661	1,859	2,894	AON10b	27-IEAA-a	yahang		85.00	1,580	0....	10	7	7	4	1		... .
9320	Yakamul	0.06679	2,750	3,078	4,791	AON09b	34-BACA-c	yakamul		25.00	769	0....	9	5	5	3	0		... .
9321	Yalu (Jaloc)	0.02484	1,023	1,145	1,782	AON09b	34-CCBC-a	yalu		90.00	1,030	0....	10	7	11	4	1		... .
9322	Yamalele (Maiodom)	0.07561	3,113	3,484	5,424	AON09b	34-FCIA-a	yamalele		80.00	2,787	0....	10	7	7	4	1	Iamalele	PN. .
9323	Yamap	0.02171	894	1,000	1,557	AON09b	34-BPAB-a	yamap		85.00	850	0....	10	7	7	4	1		... .
9324	Yambes	0.02712	1,116	1,250	1,946	AON10b	27-JAEA	yambes cluster		25.00	312	0....	9	5	6	3	0		... .
9325	Yambiyambi	0.01387	571	639	995	AON10b	26-JDAA-a	bisis		50.00	320	0....	10	6	6	3	2		... n
9326	Yangulam	0.00568	234	262	407	AON10b	22-SGAA-a	yangulam		95.00	249	0....	10	7	11	3	0		... .
9327	Yanta (Towangara)	0.09505	3,913	4,380	6,819	AON09b	34-DABA-a	yanta		70.00	3,066	0....	10	7	6	4	1		pn. .
9328	Yapunda	0.00218	90	100	156	AON10b	27-HAJA-a	yapunda		30.00	30	0....	9	5	5	3	0		... .
9329	Yarawata	0.00309	127	142	222	AON10b	22-IBBB-a	yarawata		25.00	36	0....	9	5	6	3	0		... .
9330	Yareba (Middle Musa)	0.02365	974	1,090	1,697	AON10b	23-GABB-a	yareba		90.00	981	0....	10	8	11	5	1	Yareba	PN. n
9331	Yate	0.25425	10,467	11,716	18,239	AON10b	24-ODAA-b	inoke-yate		87.00	10,193	1.s..	10	8	7	5	1	Inoke*	PN. .
9332	Yau	0.00442	182	204	317	AON10b	27-HAAB-a	yau		25.00	51	0....	9	5	6	3	0		... .
9333	Yau (Sindamon, Uruwa)	0.04289	1,766	1,976	3,077	AON10b	24-SDAC	yau cluster		90.00	1,779	0....	10	7	11	4	1	Yau	P.. .
9334	Yauan	0.01485	611	684	1,065	AON10b	24-SDAC-b	yawan		40.00	274	0....	9	6	6	3	0		p.. .
9335	Yaugiba	0.03000	1,235	1,382	2,152	AON10b	27-LADA-b	yaugiba		25.00	346	0....	9	5	6	3	0		p.. .
9336	Yaul	0.02567	1,057	1,183	1,842	AON10b	26-NCAA-a	yaul		10.00	118	0....	8	5	3	1	0		... .
9337	Yawa	0.00967	398	446	694	AON10b	25-IAAA-h	mantembu		50.00	223	0....	10	7	6	4	0		p.. .

Continued opposite

Table 8-2 continued

EVANGELIZATION								EVANGELISM			ADDITIONAL DESCRIPTIVE DATA
Ref 1	*D* 28	*aC* 29	*CG%* 30	*r* 31	*E* 32	*U* 33	*W* 34	*e* 35	*R* 36	*T* 37	*Locations, civil divisions, literacy, religions, church history, denominations, dioceses, church growth, missions, agencies, ministries, movements* 38
9214	2	6	4.82	0	99.95	0.05	C	471.58	119	10	East New Britain Province, Gazelle Peninsula. Bilingual in Tolai. No animists left. D=RCC,UCPNGSI.
9215	4	6	6.13	0	99.80	0.20	C	341.64	169	9	Milne Bay Province, north to Taupota. Bilingual in English, Motu, Wedau, Tawala. D=Anglican Ch,UCPNGSI,RCC,Baptists. M=American Baptist Mission. S-chools.
9216	0	6	3.05	0	64.00	36.00	B	93.44	176	6	Madang Province, Inbrum and Tauya rivers. Related languages: Biyom, Isabi, Faita. Animists 50%.
9217	5	5	7.24	0	99.90	0.10	C	433.62	172	10	Milne Bay Province, Alotau Sub-Province, 50 villages. Bilingual in 5 languages. D=RCC,ACPNG,UCPNGSI,SDA,Kwato Church. W=70%. M=SIL,LMS.
9218	1	6	6.26	0	99.70	0.30	C	268.27	191	8	Sandaun Province. Telefomin District. Forest, mountains. Animists 10%. D=BUWH(Baptists). M=SIL,ABMS.
9219	0	5	8.24	1	99.91	0.09	C	415.18	204	10	Western Highlands Province, Hagen District, extending into Papua. Animists 2%. M=SIL.
9220	0	9	4.54	0	99.95	0.05	C	447.30	119	10	New Ireland Province, Tench Island. Highly bilingual in Emira-Mussau. No animists remaining.
9221	0	7	4.57	0	66.00	34.00	B	96.36	234	6	East Sepik Province, coast southeast of Taul. Animists 30%.
9222	1	6	4.92	0	99.85	0.15	C	359.89	141	9	New Ireland Province, eastern Djaul Island. Tropical forest, coastal. Agriculturalists. Few animists. D=UCPNGSI.
9223	1	5	4.83	0	61.00	39.00	B	66.79	265	6	Sandaun Province, Telefomin District, 10 villages. Tropical forest, mountains. Animists 10%. D=Baptist Union Western Highlands. Very nominal. M=SIL,ABMS.
9224	3	5	2.82	0	99.88	0.12	C	404.71	85	10	Morobe Province, Kabwum District, Timbe River valley. Forest, mountains. Agriculturalists. D=95% ELCPNG(nominal),SDA,Church of Christ. M=SIL.
9225	1	6	3.79	0	59.00	41.00	B	64.60	226	6	Western Province, southern bank and hinterland of Fly Estuary. Animists 40%. D=ECP. M=APCM/UFM.
9226	4	6	6.09	0	99.80	0.20	C	338.72	169	9	Manus Province, Mbuke, Mouk, Rambutyo Islands. Trading ring. Coastal. Animists 2%. D=60% Paliau Ch(Makasol cargo cult,ex RCC),RCC,NAC,MEC. M=MEM.
9227	2	5	8.43	1	99.88	0.12	C	423.98	197	10	Gulf Province, Cape Possession to Cape Cupola. Few animists. D=UCPNGSI,RCC. M=LMS.
9228	1	6	4.52	0	53.00	47.00	B	48.36	289	6	Morobe Province, upper Kuat River valley, south of Cromwell Range. 2 schools. Mountains. Animists 10%. D=ELCPNG. Nominalism.
9229	1	5	6.68	0	99.76	0.24	C	296.81	198	8	Eastern Highlands Province, Goroka District. Some animists left. D=ELCPNG. M=independents.
9230	3	5	4.21	1	99.87	0.13	C	425.51	108	10	East New Britain Province, Gazelle Peninsula. Lingua franca. 14 dialects. D=RCC,UCPNGSI(official language of New Guinea Islands Region),WC.
9231	0	6	2.90	0	62.00	38.00	B	90.52	175	6	Western Province, some in Southern Highlands Province, along Tomu river. Animists 30%.
9232	0	6	3.74	0	69.00	31.00	B	113.33	191	7	Western Province, near Morehead, west of Nambu language. Indorodoro town is center. Close to Aramba. Related to Rouku, Nambu, Bothar, Kanum. Animists 25%.
9233	3	5	4.88	0	99.85	0.15	C	369.19	137	9	East Sepik Province, Maprik District, also West Sepik Province, west of Kombio; 5 villages. D=RCC,SSEC,Christian Brethren. M=CMML,SSEM.
9234	2	6	5.41	0	99.80	0.20	C	332.88	156	9	Morobe Province, 5 villages on the 5 Siassi Islands south of Umboi Island. Some animists remain. D=Lutherans(ELCPNG),few RCs.
9235	1	6	5.43	0	99.85	0.15	C	372.30	148	9	Milne Bay Province, 4 islands. Difficult access. Lingua franca, church language. Bilingual in Dobu, Motu, Suau, Duau. D=UCPNGSI(Australian Methodist). M=SIL.
9236	3	6	5.09	0	99.85	0.15	C	372.30	141	9	Manus Province. Many speak Kurti. 3 dialects. Predominantly D=RCC, with some MEC(Evangelicals), some Paliau Ch(Makasol cargo cult).
9237	1	6	4.68	0	99.98	0.02	C	475.74	118	10	East New Britain Province, Wide Bay to Waterfall Bay and interior. All Catholics. D=RCC.
9238	0	6	4.58	0	99.90	0.10	C	397.48	128	9	Sandaun Province, Tumleo Island and coast around Aitape. Very few animists.
9239	0	8	3.95	0	99.95	0.05	C	443.84	107	10	Milne Bay Province, inland from Goodenough Bay, 5 miles southwest of Radarada and Ruaba. 10 related languages, including Daga, Bagoi, Galeva, Gwoiden.
9240	0	7	4.35	0	64.00	36.00	B	93.44	232	6	Sandaun Province, middle Sepik region, Schatteburg mountains, upper Walio (Leonard Schultze) river. No literates; Tok Pisin not understood. Animists 60%.
9241	0	0	6.16	8	99.78	0.22	C	361.56	152	9	North Americans, in business, education. Nonreligious 10%. D=RCC,BBC,SDA,etc.
9242	2	6	5.89	0	97.00	3.00	C	230.13	197	8	Gulf Province. Gulf of Papua, on coast west of Kerema. Animists 10%. D=UCPNGSI,RCC.
9243	2	6	5.50	0	99.90	0.10	C	417.19	142	10	Oro Province, coast of Collingwood Bay, Kwagila river. Spoken also by Maisin and Miniafia speakers. Animists 5%. D=Anglican Ch of PNG, et alia. M=PNGBTA.
9244	1	6	4.45	0	99.90	0.10	C	407.34	122	10	Morobe Province. Animists 10%. D=ELCPNG.
9245	0	7	4.45	0	66.00	34.00	B	96.36	229	6	Madang Province, near Kosilanta. Related languages: Wanuma, Yaben, Yarawata, Parawen, Bilakura. Animists 60%.
9246	2	6	5.44	0	99.80	0.20	C	332.88	156	9	Madang Province, west of Tokain, 17 villages. Related language: Moere. Few animists. D=RCC,Ev Lutheran Ch of PNG. M=SIL.
9247	2	6	3.45	0	99.85	0.15	C	362.99	106	9	Sandaun Province, Amanda District, south of Imonda. Animists 5%. D=RCC,Christian Brethren. M=CMML.
9248	0	6	5.31	0	99.80	0.20	C	321.20	159	9	East New Britain Province, Rabaul District, Gazelle Peninsula. Mountainous. Scattered animists. M=SIL.
9249	1	6	3.95	0	99.80	0.20	C	318.28	126	9	Sandaun Province, Telefomin District. Related to Tifal and Telefol. Animists 4%. D=Baptist Ch.
9250	1	6	6.46	0	99.75	0.25	C	292.91	193	8	East Sepik Province, Dreikikir District, southwest of Wom, south of Kombio. Many villages. Animists 3%. D=SSEC. M=SIL.
9251	1	6	5.60	0	99.80	0.20	C	335.80	159	9	Morobe Province, Boana District. Savannah, forest, mountains. Animists 3%. D=ELCPNG. M=SIL.
9252	1	6	5.23	0	99.80	0.20	C	321.20	157	9	Madang Province. 30 miles downstream. Related languages: Usino, Danaru, Sumau. Animists 5%. Cargo cult area. D=ELCPNG.
9253	2	6	5.93	0	99.85	0.15	C	369.19	161	9	East Sepik Province, Maprik District, southwest of Kombio, 13 villages. Few animists. D=SSEC,RCC(2 villages). M=SIL.
9254	0	6	4.08	0	69.00	31.00	B	113.33	205	7	East Sepik Province. Related language: Elepi. Animists 20%.
9255	1	6	5.05	0	99.85	0.15	C	362.99	143	9	Madang Province, Madang District. Related dialects or languages: Yarawata, Bilakura, Ukuriguma. Forest, mountains. 12 villages. D=ELCPNG(Lutherans).
9256	1	6	5.38	0	99.80	0.20	C	321.20	161	9	Madang Province. Related languages: Sumau, Urigina, Danaru. Few animists. D=ELCPNG.
9257	1	7	2.43	0	99.95	0.05	C	450.77	74	10	Madang Province, Trans-Gogol District. Related languages: Kwato, Ogea, Rarau, Jilim, Yangulam, Duduela. D=Ev Lutheran Ch of PNG. Nominalism pervasive.
9258	3	6	4.91	0	99.85	0.15	C	381.60	133	9	Eastern Highlands Province, Okapa District, 4 villages. Scattered animists. D=ELCPNG,SDA,Salvation Army. M=SIL.
9259	1	6	4.43	0	99.90	0.10	C	407.34	122	10	Madang Province. Virtually no animists left. D=ELCPNG.
9260	1	6	6.48	0	99.90	0.10	C	413.91	164	10	East New Britain Province, southeast coast and inland near Cape Dampier. No animists. D=RCC. M=SIL.
9261	0	6	3.81	0	69.00	31.00	B	113.33	194	7	Sandaun Province, on coast by Lemieng. Related languages: Olo, Yau, Ningil, Yis. Animists 20%.
9262	1	6	4.33	0	99.98	0.02	C	475.74	111	10	Madang Province. Entirely baptized Lutherans. D=ELCPNG.
9263	2	6	4.88	0	99.85	0.15	C	362.99	139	9	Sandaun Province, Vanimo District. A few in Irian Jaya (Indonesia). Many highly educated. Related language: Wutung. D=RCC,Christian Brethren.
9264	1	7	2.74	0	99.95	0.05	C	450.77	80	10	Morobe Province, one village near coast. Closest to Buang. No animists left. D=ELCPNG.
9265	2	7	7.03	0	99.87	0.13	C	384.23	183	9	West New Britain Province, Talasea District, Witu Islands off coast. Animists 1%. D=RCC,SDA. M=SIL.
9266	2	6	6.68	0	99.80	0.20	C	344.56	180	9	Milne Bay Province, 9 villages on north coast of Goodenough Island. Close to Bwaidoka. D=UCPNGSI(Methodist),RCC. W=70%. M=SSH,SIL.
9267	0	7	3.13	0	99.95	0.05	C	440.37	91	10	Madang Province, north coast of Huon Peninsula, 2 villages next to Saidor. Related to Mindiri, Biliau. Very few animists left.
9268	0	6	5.50	0·	99.90	0.10	C	404.05	146	10	Western Province, Wabuda Island. No animists remaining.
9269	1	6	4.36	0	99.90	0.10	C	407.34	120	10	Madang Province. Virtually no animists. D=RCC.
9270	2	6	5.02	0	99.85	0.15	C	381.60	136	9	Morobe Province, Kaiapit District, headwaters of Waffa river. Few animists. D=ELCPNG,SEBC. M=SIL,SEBM.
9271	3	6	·5.33	0	99.85	0.15	C	381.60	143	9	Milne Bay Province, south shore of Milne Bay. Bilingual in Suau, Hiri Motu, Tawala. Many schools. Scattered animists, 2%. D=UCPNGSI,RCC,SDA.
9272	0	6	3.80	0	69.00	31.00	B	113.33	193	7	Western Province. Traditional religionists(animists) 55%.
9273	4	5	3.71	1	99.82	0.18	C	368.13	106	9	Western Highlands Province, Minj District, also in Simbu Province. Few animists left. D=RCC,Ch of the Nazarene,GLC,SEBC. M=SIL,SEBM.
9274	1	6	4.62	0	68.00	32.00	B	99.28	229	6	Western Province, lower Aramia river, 8 villages. Animists 50%. D=ECP. M=APCM/UFM.
9275	3	6	3.99	0	72.00	28.00	B	105.12	193	7	Madang Province, Mid-Ramu (Simbai) District, west of Kobon. Isolated. Many speak Tok Pisin. Animists 60%. Relatively unevangelized. D=CON,ACPNG,CC.
9276	2	6	3.95	0	99.95	0.05	C	457.71	104	10	Eastern Highlands Province, Obura District. Few animists left. D=ELCPNG,NTM.
9277	0	6	2.90	0	99.85	0.15	C	335.07	101	9	Sandaun Province. Tok Pisin not understood. Few animists.
9278	0	7	3.08	0	99.95	0.05	C	440.37	90	10	Madang Province. 10 villages. No animists.
9279	1	6	3.78	0	99.95	0.05	C	450.77	102	10	Morobe Province, Wanton river. Closest to Mari. Animists 5%. D=ELCPNG.
9280	0	6	6.32	0	91.00	9.00	C	215.89	223	8	Sandaun Province, north of Middle Sepik river. Animists still strong, 10%.
9281	0	6	3.90	0	64.00	36.00	B	93.44	213	6	Sandaun Province, north of Mehek, northeast of Siliput. Related languages: Agi, Bragat. Animists 60%.
9282	0	6	4.30	0	99.90	0.10	C	381.06	127	9	Madang Province, mainland opposite Long Island, 10 miles inland from Gali and Roinji. Related dialects or languages: Yupna, Mebu, Gabutamon, Nokopo.
9283	2	5	2.93	0	99.80	0.20	C	341.64	94	9	Morobe Province, Lae District. Some animists left. D=ELCPNG(Lutheran),et alia. M=SIL.
9284	0	6	2.71	0	34.00	66.00	A	12.41	305	5	Enga Province, northeast corner. Closest to Pinai. Animists 10%. Relatively unevangelized.
9285	0	6	5.50	0	99.90	0.10	C	400.77	148	10	Sandaun Province, coast. Related languages: Krisa, Rawo, Puari. Few animists.
9286	1	6	4.51	0	61.00	39.00	B	66.79	251	6	Sandaun Province, Amanab District, west of Imonda. Also in Indonesia. Straddles border with Indonesia. Animists10%. D=RCC. M=SIL.
9287	0	6	3.38	0	66.00	34.00	B	96.36	185	6	Western Province, Aramia River area, Waruna village. Second language Gogodala. Animists 60%.
9288	5	6	6.04	0	99.85	0.15	C	381.60	158	9	East Sepik Province, Ambunti Sub-Province, along Sepik river; 12 villages. Some animists. D=SSEC,RCC,PIM,AoG,SDA. M=SIL.
9289	2	6	5.43	0	99.90	0.10	C	420.48	139	10	West New Britain Province, inland from Bongula Bay. No animists. D=UCPNGSI,RCC. M=SIL.
9290	4	5	7.41	0	99.85	0.15	C	384.71	187	9	Madang Province, Karkar Island, Madang District. Closest to Korak. Volcanic island, 30 villages. D=90% ELCPNG,10% RCC,some SDA,ICFG. M=SIL.
9291	2	7	3.14	0	99.95	0.05	C	475.04	84	10	East Sepik Province, middle Korosameri river, 1 village. Highly bilingual in Tok Pisin. Virtually no animists. D=NTM,RCC.
9292	2	7	3.55	0	99.95	0.05	C	468.11	94	10	Milne Bay Province, 2 hamlets north of Goodenough Island. Bilingual in Bwaidoga, Iduna. No animists left. D=RCC,UCPNGSI.
9293	0	6	3.97	0	99.90	0.10	C	397.48	114	9	Madang Province. Tribal religionists(animists) 5%.
9294	1	6	3.59	0	99.90	0.10	C	413.91	101	10	Madang Province, 2 villages. Related languages: Sinsauru, Asas, Sausi, Kesawai. All men bilingual in Tok Pisin. No animists. D=ELCPNG.
9295	1	6	5.92	0	99.80	0.20	C	347.48	161	9	Milne Bay Province, Kuvira Bay to Dogura. Lingua franca of northeast Papua. D=Anglican Ch of PNG. Official church language, now displacing Mukawa. M=NGM.
9296	1	6	6.46	0	99.80	0.20	C	335.80	179	9	Morobe Province, Wau District, headwaters Biaru, Waria, Ono rivers. D=ELCPNG. M=SIL.
9297	1	7	3.16	0	99.95	0.05	C	457.71	88	10	Morobe Province, south of Malasanga, lower Timbe River valley. Bilingual in Timbe. No animists left. D=ELCPNG.
9298	0	0	3.80	0	99.90	0.10	C	354.78	124	9	Western Province, Dewara village. Animists 5%. D=ELCPNG.
9299	2	5	3.79	0	99.89	0.11	C	409.31	106	10	Southern Highlands Province, center in Nembi Valley. Animists 1%. D=Apostolic Christian Ch (very rapid growth),UCPNGSI(Methodist). M=ACM.
9300	9	5	8.34	0	99.85	0.15	C	381.60	210	9	Southern Highlands Province, Kagua and Mendi Districts. Tropical forest, mountains. D=ECP,RCC,UCPNGSI,CU,BMC,ELCPNG,EBM,Wesleyan Ch,et alia.
9301	3	5	7.70	0	99.88	0.12	C	407.92	189	10	West New Britain Province, northwest coast, 42 villages. D=UCPNGSI(Wesleyans),RCC,JWs. M=SIL,Sacred Heart Mission(200 sisters).
9302	1	6	4.39	0	99.90	0.10	C	407.34	121	10	Sandaun province, north of Beli, Laeko-Libuat; south of Torricelli Mountains. No animists. D=RCC.
9303	3	5	7.82	0	99.84	0.16	C	374.05	200	9	Southern Highlands Province, Ialibu District. Few animists. D=ELCPNG,RCC,Wesleyan Ch. M=WCUSA.
9304	2	6	4.07	0	39.00	61.00	A	14.23	361	5	East Sepik Province, Ambunti District, 3 villages. Many Tok Pisin speakers. Relatively unreached tribe. Animists 30%. D=AoG,RCC.
9305	0	6	5.16	0	99.85	0.15	C	350.58	151	9	East Sepik Province, Vokeo Island, Schouten Islands. Related to Manam, Biem, Sepa, Medebur. Forest, coastal. Agriculturalists. Few animists.
9306	3	6	5.54	0	99.80	0.20	C	338.72	156	9	East Sepik Province, Maprik District, foothills of Torricelli Mountains, 12 villages. Cargo cult 5%. D=RCC,SSEC,20% New Apostolic Church.
9307	0	6	4.06	0	99.90	0.10	C	397.48	116	9	Sandaun Province, Vanimo District, north coast, border with Indonesia. Virtually no animists.
9308	2	6	4.97	0	99.90	0.10	C	420.48	129	10	Western Manus Province, 4 islands off Manus Island. No animists. D=SDA,RCC.
9309	2	6	3.32	0	99.80	0.20	C	341.64	103	9	Morobe Province, coast close to Bukauwa. Virtually no animists. D=ELCPNG,Anglican Ch of PNG. Church language for Lutherans. M=NGM.
9310	2	6	4.68	0	99.95	0.05	C	457.71	119	10	Madang Province. Related languages: Usan, Yarawata, Bilakura, Parawen, Ukuriguma. No animists left. Mostly baptized Lutherans. D=ELCPNG,some RCC.
9311	0	7	4.13	0	59.00	41.00	B	75.37	241	6	Sandaun Province, 10 miles east of Duranmin, 1 village. No animists remaining.
9312	4	6	5.55	0	99.95	0.05	C	478.51	131	10	Eastern Highlands Province, Goroka District, 20 villages. No animists left. D=ELCPNG,SDA,RCC,ICFG. 95% baptized. M=PNGBTA,SIL.
9313	1	6	4.29	0	99.95	0.05	C	447.30	114	10	Madang Province. No animists left. D=ELCPNG.
9314	4	5	7.89	1	99.90	0.10	C	436.90	185	10	Eastern Highlands Province, Goroka District. 8 dialects. Related to Move. Few animists left. D=ELCPNG,NTM,SDA,indigenous churches.
9315	3	6	6.64	1	99.80	0.20	C	356.24	173	9	Eastern Highlands Province, Goroka District. Related to Kami. Few animists. D=ELCPNG,NTM,SDA.
9316	1	6	4.25	0	99.90	0.10	C	407.34	118	10	Morobe Province. All Christian. D=ELCPNG.
9317	0	7	2.98	0	99.95	0.05	C	440.37	87	10	Madang Province, coast southeast of Seure. Related to Degenan, Asat, Dahating. Coastal. Very few animists left.
9318	4	5	7.14	0	99.88	0.12	C	388.65	186	9	Morobe, Gulf, and Eastern Highlands Provinces. Forest, mountains, agriculturalists. D=ELCPNG,GLC,SDA,Independent Baptists. High nominalism. M=LCA.
9319	1	6	5.19	0	99.85	0.15	C	359.89	148	9	Sandaun Province, west of Mehek. Not many animists remaining. D=RCC.
9320	0	6	4.44	0	49.00	51.00	A	44.71	308	6	Sandaun Province, coast between Paup and Yakamul, and Ali, Seleo, and Angel Islands. Scattered animists, 10%.
9321	1	6	4.74	0	99.90	0.10	C	410.62	127	10	Morobe Province, Huon Gulf, northwest of Lae. Closely related to Musom, Guwot, Sirak. No animists. D=ELCPNG.
9322	1	6	5.79	0	99.80	0.20	C	335.80	163	9	Milne Bay Province, Bwaidoka District, west Fergusson Island. Forest, mountains, coastal. Some bilingual in Bwaidoga and Dobu. Low literacy. D=UCPNGSI.
9323	1	6	4.54	0	99.85	0.15	C	356.78	134	9	Morobe Province, Francisco River area, Huon Gulf, round Bobadu town. Close to Hote and Misim. Animists 5%. D=ELCPNG.
9324	0	6	3.50	0	50.00	50.00	B	45.62	250	6	East Sepik Province, Maprik District, northwest of Wom, east of Kombio. 4 villages. Animists 25%.
9325	2	6	3.53	0	80.00	20.00	B	146.00	158	7	East Sepik Province, Hunstein Range, Ambunti District, next to Bahinemo. Tropical forest, mountains. Hunter-gatherers. Animists 50%. D=NTM,RCC.
9326	0	7	3.27	0	99.95	0.05	C	440.37	94	10	Madang Province on coast south of Madang City. Related languages: Kwato, Ogea, Usu, Duduela, Rerau, Jilim.
9327	1	6	5.89	0	99.70	0.30	C	263.16	185	8	Morobe Province. In Mumeng dialect chain. Animists 5%. D=ELCPNG.
9328	0	8	3.46	0	56.00	44.00	B	61.32	222	6	Sandaun Province, Torricelli Mountains on Om river. Animists 20%.
9329	0	6	3.65	0	50.00	50.00	B	45.62	259	6	Madang Province, near Kosilanta. Related languages: Wanuma, Yaben, Bilakura, Parawen, Ukuriguma. Animists 15%.
9330	2	6	4.69	0	99.90	0.10	C	433.62	120	10	Oro Province, Popondetta District. Bilingual in Hiri Motu. Sorcery widespread and on increase. D=Anglican Ch of PNG,SDA. M=SIL.
9331	3	5	7.17	1	99.87	0.13	C	406.46	176	10	Eastern Highlands Province, Okapa District. Few animists. D=ELCPNG,SDA,et alia. M=SIL.
9332	0	7	4.01	0	51.00	49.00	B	46.53	273	6	Sandaun Province, West Sepik. Torricelli mountains. Related languages: Olo, Yis, Ningil, Valman. Animists 25%.
9333	1	6	5.32	0	99.90	0.10	C	413.91	139	10	Morobe Province. 6 dialects (villages). Mountains. Agriculturalists. Few animists. D=ELCPNG. M=SIL.
9334	0	6	3.37	0	66.00	34.00	B	96.36	184	6	Sandaun Province. Tribal religionists(animists) 50%.
9335	0	6	3.61	0	50.00	50.00	B	45.62	256	6	East Sepik Province. Animists(traditional religionists) 25%.
9336	0	5	2.50	0	28.00	72.00	A	10.22	349	5	East Sepik Province, near Yuat river. Related languages: Langam, Mongol. Relatively unevangelized. Animists 40%.
9337	0	6	3.15	0	78.00	22.00	B	142.35	148	7	East Sepik Province, northwest of Hauna in Sepik Iwam area. Animists 10%.

Continued overleaf

Table 8-2 continued

Ref 1	Ethnic name 2	P% 3	In 1995 4	In 2000 5	In 2025 6	Race 7	Language 8	Autoglossonym 9	S 10	AC 11	Members 12	Jayuh 13-17	dwa xcmc mi 18 19 20 21 22	Biblioglossonym 23	Pub ss 24-26 27
9338	Yega	0.02838	1,168	1,308	2,036	AON10b	23-ABIA-a	west yega		80.00	1,046	0....	10 7 6 4 1		... .
9339	Yekora	0.02428	1,000	1,119	1,742	AON10b	23-ABAB	yekora cluster		90.00	1,007	0....	10 7 11 4 1		... n
9340	Yelogu (Kaunga)	0.00725	298	334	520	AON10b	26-HBAB-a	yelogu		25.00	84	0....	9 5 6 3 0		... .
9341	Yerakai	0.01230	506	567	882	AON10b	26-GAAA-a	yerakai		95.00	538	0....	10 7 11 4 1		... .
9342	Yey (Je)	0.02000	823	922	1,435	AON10a	20-LBAA	yei cluster		25.00	230	0....	9 5 5 3 0		... b
9343	Yil	0.07846	3,230	3,616	5,629	AON10b	27-HAEA-a	yil		80.00	2,892	0....	10 7 6 5 1		... .
9344	Yimas	0.01104	454	509	792	AON10b	27-DBAA-a	yimas		95.00	483	0....	10 7 11 4 1		... .
9345	Yis	0.01559	642	718	1,118	AON10b	27-HAAA-a	yis		25.00	180	0....	9 5 6 3 0		... .
9346	Yoidik	0.00839	345	387	602	AON10b	22-PAAB-a	yoidik		95.00	367	0....	10 7 11 4 1		... .
9347	Yongom	0.40508	16,676	18,667	29,060	AON10b	24-KEAB-a	yonggom		76.00	14,187	0.s..	10 6 6 4 2	Yongkom*	P.. .
9348	Yubanakor	0.11400	4,693	5,253	8,178	AON10b	26-FBCA-e	yubanakor		65.00	3,415	0....	10 8 8 0 0	Yubanakor	PN. .
9349	Zanofil	0.02000	823	922	1,435	AON10b	24-KEAB	yonggom cluster		30.00	276	0.s..	9 5 5 3 2		P.. .
9350	Zenag	0.06304	2,595	2,905	4,522	AON09b	34-DABA-e	zenang		70.00	2,033	0....	10 7 6 4 1		pn. .
9351	Ziya (Lower Waria, Tsia)	0.07568	3,116	3,487	5,429	AON10b	23-ABAC-a	zia		85.00	2,964	0....	10 7 7 5 2	Zia	PN. .
9352	other minor peoples	2.61166	107,515	120,349	187,355	...				40.00	48,140		9 7 5 5 0		
	Paraguay	**100.00000**	**4,828,478**	**5,496,453**	**9,355,207**					**94.13**	**5,173,602**				
9353	Anglo-Australian	0.04000	1,931	2,199	3,742	CEW19c	52-ABAC-x	general australian	4	67.00	1,473	1Bsuh	10 9 13 5 3		pnb b
9354	Ayore (Moro, Tsiracua)	0.06823	3,294	3,750	6,383	MIR39z	86-BAAA-b	morotoco		55.00	2,063	0....	10 6 6 5 3	Ayoreo	PN. .
9355	Bahia Negra Chamacoco	0.02626	1,268	1,443	2,457	MIR39z	86-BBAA-a	ebitoso		40.00	577	0....	10 6 6 4 1		p.. .
9356	Black	1.00000	48,285	54,965	93,552	NFB71a	51-AABB-ht	paraguayo		98.00	53,865	1B.uh	10 7 12 4 3		pnb .
9357	Bravo Chamacoco (Ishiro)	0.04094	1,977	2,250	3,830	MIR39z	86-BBAA-b	chamacoco-bravo		30.00	675	0....	9 5 6 4 2	Chamacoco	P.. .
9358	Brazilian Guarani	0.14113	6,814	7,757	13,203	MIR39e	82-AAIF-g	mbyá		65.00	5,042	1c...	10 8 9 5 3	Guarani: Brazil, Southern*	PNb b
9359	Brazilian Mestico	0.60000	28,971	32,979	56,131	CLN28	51-AABA-e	general português		95.00	31,330	2Bsuh	10 9 11 5 3	Portuguese	PNB b
9360	Chiripa (Ava Guarani)	0.15920	7,687	8,750	14,893	MIR39e	82-AAIF-da	chiripa		80.00	7,000	1c...	10 7 8 5 1	Chiripa	Pnb n
9361	Chulupe (Nivacle)	0.40937	19,766	22,501	38,297	MIR39e	86-ABBA	niwaclé cluster		40.00	9,000	0....	9 6 6 5 3	Nivacle*	PNB .
9362	Eastern Bolivian Guarani	0.04549	2,196	2,500	4,256	MIR39e	82-AAIF-cb	chiriguano		70.00	1,750	3a...	10 8 6 5 3	Guarayu*	PNb b
9363	Emok (Machicui)	0.01938	936	1,065	1,813	MIR39d	86-CAAA-c	maskoy		80.00	852	0....	10 7 8 4 1		pnb b
9364	German	3.15451	152,315	173,386	295,111	CEW19m	52-ABCF-a	nord-bayrisch-t.		85.00	147,378	0B.uh	10 9 11 5 0		pn. b
9365	Greek	0.04500	2,173	2,473	4,210	CEW20	56-AAAA-c	dhimotiki		95.00	2,350	2B.uh	10 9 11 5 1	Greek: Modern	PNB b
9366	Guana (Kaskiha)	0.01251	604	688	1,170	MIR39a	86-CAAA-a	cashquiha		60.00	413	0....	10 7 7 5 1		pnb n
9367	Guayaki (Guaiaqui)	0.01814	876	997	1,697	MIR39e	82-AAID-a	aché		2.00	20	0....	6 4 4 5 3	Ache	P.. n
9368	Half-Indian	1.70000	82,084	93,440	159,039	MIR39z	82-AAIC-b	guarani-ete		92.00	85,965	0....	10 9 11 5 3		... b
9369	Han Chinese	0.16000	7,726	8,794	14,968	MSY42a	79-AAAB-ba	kuo-yü		50.00	4,397	2Bsuh	10 6 8 3 0	Chinese: Kuoyu*	PNB b
9370	Italian	0.60000	28,971	32,979	56,131	CEW21e	51-AABQ-c	standard italiano		84.00	27,702	2B.uh	10 9 14 5 3	Italian	PNB b
9371	Japanese	0.23000	11,105	12,642	21,517	MSY45a	45-CAAA-a	koku-go		27.00	3,413	1B.uh	9 5 8 5 1	Japanese	PNB b
9372	Jewish	0.05230	2,525	2,875	4,893	CMT35	51-AABB-ht	paraguayo		0.11	3	1B.uh	5 4 6 3 0		pnb .
9373	Kaiwa (Caingua, Pan)	0.25017	12,079	13,750	23,404	MIR39e	82-AAIF-f	kaingwá		60.00	8,250	1c...	10 7 8 4 3	Kaiwa	PNb .
9374	Korean	0.02000	966	1,099	1,871	MSY46	45-AAAA-b	kukö		51.00	561	2A...	10 6 9 5 3	Korean	PNB b
9375	Latin American White	3.40000	164,168	186,879	318,077	CLT27	51-AABB-ht	paraguayo		97.20	181,647	1B.uh	10 9 13 5 3		pnb .
9376	Low German	1.22632	59,213	67,404	114,725	CEW19m	52-ABCC	north deutsch cluster		93.00	62,686	2A.uh	10 9 11 5 3	German: Low*	PNB b
9377	Maca (Maka)	0.02274	1,098	1,250	2,127	MIR39e	86-ABCA-b	eni-maca		30.00	375	0....	9 5 6 5 3	Maca	PN. .
9378	Manjuy (Chorote)	0.01137	549	625	1,064	MIR39e	86-ABAA-a	yofúaha		60.00	375	0....	10 7 6 5 2	Chorote*	P.. b
9379	Mascoian Mestizo	0.10000	4,828	5,496	9,355	CLN29	86-CAAB-a	mascoy-pidgin		80.00	4,397	0....	10 7 7 5 1		... b
9380	Mataco	0.04000	1,931	2,199	3,742	MIR39e	86-AAAA-b	vejoz		90.00	1,979	0.s..	10 8 11 5 1	Mataco*	PN. b
9381	Mestizo	2.00000	96,570	109,929	187,104	CLN29	51-AABB-ht	paraguayo	75	99.00	108,830	1B.uh	10 9 12 5 1		pnb .
9382	Northern Lengua	0.13787	6,657	7,578	12,898	MIR39e	86-CAAA-e	north lengua		85.00	6,441	0....	10 8 8 5 3	Lengua: Northern	PNB b
9383	Northern Lengua (Angaite)	0.09191	4,438	5,052	8,598	MIR39e	86-CAAA-e	north lengua		85.00	4,294	0....	10 8 8 5 3	Lengua: Northern	PNB b
9384	Paraguayan Mestizo	82.94313	4,004,891	4,558,930	7,759,502	MIR39e	82-AAIF-b	vehicular aba-ñeeme	98	95.50	4,353,778	1a...	10 10 11 5 4		pnb b
9385	Paraguayan Toba	0.05686	2,745	3,125	5,319	MIR39e	86-CAAA-c	maskoy		85.00	2,656	0....	10 7 11 5 1		pnb b
9386	Pilaga Toba	0.00430	208	236	402	MIR39e	86-EBAB-a	toba-pilagá		95.00	225	0.s..	10 8 11 5 2	Pilaga*	PNB b
9387	Polish (Pole)	0.04000	1,931	2,199	3,742	CEW22i	53-AAAC-c	polski		88.00	1,935	2A.uh	10 9 11 5 3	Polish	PNB b
9388	Portuguese	0.10000	4,828	5,496	9,355	CEW21g	51-AABA-e	general português	7	93.00	5,112	2Bsuh	10 9 14 5 2	Portuguese	PNB b
9389	Russian	0.01300	628	715	1,216	CEW22j	53-AAAE-d	russkiy		70.00	500	4B.uh	10 8 8 5 2	Russian	PNB b
9390	Sanapana (Saapa, Sanam)	0.06595	3,184	3,625	6,170	MIR39d	86-CAAA-b	sanapaná		95.00	3,444	0....	10 8 11 5 3	Sanapana	pnb .
9391	Sanapana Toba	0.04202	2,029	2,310	3,931	MIR39d	86-CAAA-b	sanapaná		95.00	2,194	0....	10 8 11 5 1	Sanapana	pnb .
9392	Southern Lengua	0.10504	5,072	5,773	9,827	MIR39e	86-CAAA-f	south lengua		87.00	5,023	0....	10 8 8 5 3	Lengua: Southern	Pnb .
9393	Tapiete (Guasurango)	0.04094	1,977	2,250	3,830	MIR39e	82-AAIF-cc	tapieté		80.00	1,800	1c...	10 7 6 5 2		pnb n
9394	Toba (Com, Toba Sur)	0.01592	769	875	1,489	MIR39d	86-EBAA	qom cluster		95.00	831	0.s..	10 8 11 5 3	Toba	PN. b
9395	USA White	0.05000	2,414	2,748	4,678	CEW19s	52-ABAC-s	general american		78.00	2,144	1Bsuh	10 10 12 0 0	English*	PNB b
9396	Ukrainian	0.60000	28,971	32,979	56,131	CEW22p	53-AAAE-b	ukrainskiy		76.00	25,064	3A.uh	10 9 8 5 2	Ukrainian	PNB b
9397	other minor peoples	0.10000	4,828	5,496	9,355	...				69.00	3,793		10 7 6 5 0		
	Peru	**100.00000**	**23,531,685**	**25,661,669**	**35,518,199**					**96.26**	**24,702,057**				
9398	Achual Jivaro	0.01836	4,320	4,711	6,521	MIR39d	84-EAAA-b	achuara		15.00	707	1....	8 5 7 5 3	Achual*	PN. .
9399	Aguaruna (Ahuajun)	0.14124	33,236	36,245	50,166	MIR39d	84-EAAB-a	awahun		7.00	2,537	0....	7 5 7 5 3	Aguaruna	PN. b
9400	Amahuaca (Ipitineri)	0.00210	494	539	746	MIR39d	84-NAFA-a	ama-huaca		5.00	27	0....	7 5 5 5 3	Amahuaca	P.. .
9401	Amarakaire	0.00096	226	246	341	MIR39a	85-GAAB-a	amaraca-eri		10.00	25	0....	8 5 5 5 2	Amarakaeri	PN. b
9402	Ambo-Pasco Quechua	0.28401	66,832	72,882	100,875	MIR39g	85-FAAF-d	ambo-pasco		95.00	69,238	1....	10 7 11 4 1	Quechua: S Rafael, Huaria*	P.. b
9403	Amuesha (Lorenzo, Yanesha	0.02969	6,987	7,619	10,545	MIR39a	81-BABA-a	yanesha		45.00	3,429	0....	9 6 7 5 3	Amuesha	PN. b
9404	Andoa (Shimigae)	0.00002	5	5	7	MIR39z	84-HABA-c	simicai		70.00	4	0....	10 7 4 4 1		pn. b
9405	Apurimac Quechua	1.13225	266,438	290,554	402,155	MIR39g	85-FAAF-ad	apurimac		99.00	287,649	1As..	10 9 10 5 3	Quechua: Apurimac*	PNB b
9406	Arabela (Chiripunu)	0.00141	332	362	501	MIR39d	84-HABA-a	chiripuno		60.00	217	0....	10 7 4 4 3	Arabela	PN. b
9407	Arequipa Quechua	0.11429	26,894	29,329	40,594	MIR39g	85-FAAF-ba	cotahuasi		99.00	29,035	1cs..	10 9 11 5 3	Quechua: La Union	PNB b
9408	Ashaninca Campa	0.09322	21,936	23,922	33,110	MIR39a	81-BBAA-b	asháni-nga		65.00	15,549	0....	10 9 7 5 3	Campa: Ashaninca*	PN. b
9409	Asheninca Campa (Perene)	0.06681	15,722	17,145	23,730	MIR39a	81-BBAA-a	ashéni-nga		60.00	10,287	0....	10 7 7 5 3		pn. b
9410	Ayacucho Quechua (Chanka)	5.31936	1,251,735	1,365,037	1,889,341	MIR39g	85-FAAH-ac	andahuaylas		99.00	1,351,386	1As..	10 10 10 5 3	Quechua: Ayacucho*	PNB b
9411	Bora	0.00706	1,661	1,812	2,508	MIR39d	84-DAAA-a	muinane-bora		20.00	362	0....	9 5 6 4 3	Bora	PN. .
9412	British	0.02260	5,318	5,800	8,027	CEW19i	52-ABAC-b	standard-english		78.00	4,524	3Bsuh	10 9 8 5 2		PNB b
9413	Cahuarano	0.00003	7	8	11	MIR39z	84-HBAA-d	cawarán		38.00	3	0....	9 5 4 4 1		p.. .
9414	Cajamarca Quechua	0.19774	46,532	50,743	70,234	MIR39g	85-FAAD-b	cajamarca		99.00	50,236	0....	10 9 12 5 1	Quechua: Cajamarca*	Pn. b
9415	Candoshi (Shapra)	0.01695	3,989	4,350	6,020	MIR39d	84-LAAA-a	candoshi		6.00	261	0....	7 5 6 4 3	Candoshi*	PN. .
9416	Capanahua (Kapanawa)	0.00240	565	616	852	MIR39d	84-NACB-a	capanahua		10.00	62	0....	8 5 5 4 2	Capanahua	PN. b
9417	Caquinte Campa	0.00141	332	362	501	MIR39a	81-BBAB-b	caquinte		30.00	109	0....	9 5 4 4 1	Caquinte	Pn. .
9418	Cashibo (Cacataibo)	0.00706	1,661	1,812	2,508	MIR39d	84-NAAA-a	cashi-bo		15.00	272	0....	8 5 6 5 3	Cashibo*	PN. b
9419	Cashinahua (Kaxinawa)	0.00495	1,165	1,270	1,758	MIR39d	84-NAFB-a	cashi-nahua		10.00	127	0....	8 5 6 5 3	Cashinahua	PN. .
9420	Central Aymara	3.00000	705,951	769,850	1,065,546	MIR39b	85-JABA-a	central aymara		98.00	754,453	2.s..	10 10 12 5 3	Aymara*	PNB b
9421	Chachapoyas Quechua	0.02581	6,074	6,623	9,167	MIR39g	85-FAAD-c	chachapoyas		99.00	6,557	0....	10 7 11 4 1		pn. .
9422	Chamicura (Chamicolos)	0.00081	191	208	288	MIR39a	81-BAAA-a	chamicuro		70.00	146	0....	10 7 6 4 1		... .
9423	Chayahuita (Chawi)	0.03390	7,977	8,699	12,041	MIR39a	84-FAAA-a	proper chayahuita		40.00	3,480	0....	9 6 6 5 3	Chayahuita	PN. .
9424	Chilean Mestizo	0.30000	70,595	76,985	106,555	CLN29	51-AABB-hr	chileno		95.00	73,136	1B.uh	10 9 11 5 3		pnb .
9425	Chinocholo (Mulato)	0.10000	23,532	25,662	35,518	NFB71b	51-AABB-hq	peruano		90.00	23,096	1B.uh	10 8 11 4 3		pnb b
9426	Chiquian Ancash Quechua	0.10923	25,704	28,030	38,797	MIR39g	85-FAAF-ab	chiquian		90.00	25,227	1....	10 7 11 4 1		p.. .
9427	Cocama	0.08322	19,583	21,356	29,558	MIR39e	82-AAHA-a	cocama		10.00	2,136	0....	8 5 6 4 3	Cocama*	P.. b
9428	Cocamilla	0.01000	2,353	2,566	3,552	MIR39e	82-AAHA-b	cocamilla		15.00	385	0....	8 5 6 4 3	Cocamilla	P.. b
9429	Cogapacori	0.00100	235	257	355	MIR39a	81-BBAB-e	cogapac-ori		50.00	128	0....	10 7 7 4 1		pn. .
9430	Conchucos Ancash Quechua	1.01047	237,781	259,303	358,901	MIR39g	85-FAAF-aa	conchucos		90.00	233,373	3....	10 7 11 4 1	Quechua: Conchucos, N*	P.. .
9431	Corongo Ancash Quechua	0.06819	16,046	17,499	24,220	MIR39g	85-FAAE-aa	corongo		85.00	14,874	1....	10 7 7 4 1		p.. .
9432	Cujareno (Inapari)	0.00039	92	100	139	MIR39d	81-BCAA-e	mashco-piro		2.00	2	0....	6 4 3 5 1		pn. .
9433	Culina (Madija)	0.00173	407	444	614	MIR39a	88-PAAM-a	madijá		20.00	89	0....	9 5 5 5 2	Culina	P.. .
9434	Cuzco Quechua	7.10463	1,671,839	1,823,167	2,523,437	MIR39g	85-FAAH-c	cuzco		97.00	1,768,472	3cs..	10 10 11 5 3	Quechua: Cuzco*	PNB b
9435	Detribalized Aymara	1.62580	382,578	417,207	577,455	MIR39b	51-AABB-hq	peruano		98.50	410,949	1B.uh	10 8 10 5 1		pnb b
9436	Detribalized Quechua	28.00000	6,588,872	7,185,267	9,945,096	MIR39g	51-AABB-hq	peruano		98.00	7,041,562	1B.uh	10 10 10 5 4		pnb b
9437	Ese Ejja (Huarayo)	0.00184	433	472	654	MIR39d	84-RAAA	ese-ejja cluster		40.00	189	0....	9 6 6 5 1	Ese Ejja	PN. b
9438	Esperanto	0.00000	0	0	0	CEW21z	51-AAAC-a	proper esperanto		80.00	0	0A...	10 8 2 5 0	Esperanto	PNB b
9439	German	0.02000	4,706	5,132	7,104	CEW19m	52-ABCE-a	standard hoch-deutsch		69.00	3,541	2B.uh	10 9 8 5 3	German*	PNB b
9440	Greek	0.02000	4,706	5,132	7,104	CEW20	56-AAAA-c	dhimotiki		99.00	5,081	2B.uh	10 9 10 5 1	Greek: Modern	PNB b
9441	Gypsy	0.03000	7,060	7,699	10,655	CNN25f	59-AFAA-a	rodi		70.00	5,389	0B.uh	10 8 8 5 3	Calo	PNB b
9442	Han Chinese	0.10000	23,532	25,662	35,518	MSY42a	51-AABB-hq	peruano		48.00	12,318	1B.uh	9 6 8 5 2		pnb b
9443	Han Chinese (Cantonese)	0.33877	79,718	86,934	120,325	MSY42a	79-AAAM-a	central yue	1	44.70	38,860	3A.uh	9 6 8 5 3	Chinese, Yue	PNB b
9444	Huachipaire (Wacipaire)	0.00121	285	311	430	MIR39a	85-GAAA-a	huachipa-eri		10.00	31	0....	8 5 5 5 1		... b
9445	Huallaga Huanuco Quechua	0.17477	41,126	44,849	62,075	MIR39g	85-FAAF-cd	huallaga		90.00	40,364	1....	10 7 11 4 1	Quechua, Huanuco, Hualla	P.. .
9446	Huamalies Huanuco Quechua	0.16603	39,070	42,606	58,971	MIR39g	85-FAAF-cb	humalies		90.00	38,345	1....	10 7 11 4 1	Quechua: Huanuco, Huam*	P.. .
9447	Huambiza	0.03637	8,558	9,333	12,918	MIR39d	84-EAAA-c	huambisa		5.00	467	1....	7 5 6 4 2	Huambisa	PN. b
9448	Huaylas Ancash Quechua	1.31083	308,460	336,381	465,583	MIR39g	85-FAAE-bc	huailas		90.00	302,743	3....	10 7 11 4 3	Quechua, Ancash, Huaylas	P.. .
9449	Injerto	0.04000	9,413	10,265	14,207	MSY43	51-AABB-hq	peruano		90.00	9,238	1B.uh	10 7 11 4 1		pnb b
9450	Iquito (Amacacore)	0.00074	174	190	263	MIR39d	84-HBAA-a	iquito		70.00	133	0....	10 7 6 4 2	Iquito	P.. b
9451	Isconahua	0.00032	75	82	114	MIR39d	84-NACA-f	isco-nahua		50.00	41	1....	10 6 6 4 1		pn. p
9452	Japanese	0.47600	112,011	122,150	169,067	MSY45a	45-CAAA-a	koku-go		50.80	62,052	1B.uh	10 6 8 4 2	Japanese	PNB b
9453	Jaqaru (Haqearu, Aru)	0.00965	2,271	2,476	3,428	MIR39b	85-JAAA-a	jaqaru		80.00	1,981	0....	10 7 6 4 1		... b
9454	Jauja Huancayo Quechua	0.30289	71,275	77,727	107,581	MIR39g	85-FAAF-ga	jauja		99.00	76,949	1....	10 9 12 5 3		p.. b
9455	Jebero (Xebero)	0.01710	4,024	4,388	6,074	MIR39z	84-FABA-a	shewélo		60.00	2,633	0....	10 7 6 4 2	Jebero	P.. b
9456	Jewish	0.03726	8,768	9,562	13,234	CMT35	51-AABB-hq	peruano		0.10	10	1B.uh	5 3 2 1 0		pnb b
9457	Jungle Quechua (Lamista)	0.08738	20,562	22,423	31,036	MIR39g	85-FAAD-d	lamista		70.00	15,696	0....	10 7 6 4 1	Quechua: San Martin*	PN. b

Continued opposite

Table 8-2 continued

EVANGELIZATION								EVANGELISM			ADDITIONAL DESCRIPTIVE DATA
Ref	*D*	*aC*	*CG%*	*r*	*E*	*U*	*W*	*e*	*R*	*T*	*Locations, civil divisions, literacy, religions, church history, denominations, dioceses, church growth, missions, agencies, ministries, movements*
1	*28*	*29*	*30*	*31*	*32*	*33*	*34*	*35*	*36*	*37*	*38*
9338	1	6	4.76	0	99.80	0.20	C	321.20	145	9	Oro Province, between Notu and Bareji. Virtually no animists. D=Anglican Ch of PNG.
9339	1	6	4.72	0	99.90	0.10	C	417.19	125	10	Morobe Province north of Zia. Bilingual in Suena or Zia. Close to Mawae. Few animists. D=ELCPNG.
9340	0	6	4.53	0	50.00	50.00	B	45.62	307	6	East Sepik Province, Ambunti District, 1 village. Animists 25%.
9341	1	6	4.07	0	99.95	0.05	C	447.30	109	10	East Sepik Province, Ambunti District, southeast. Nominally RC, but strong paganism within church. D=RCC. No current evangelism going on.
9342	0	6	3.19	0	49.00	51.00	A	44.71	234	6	Western Province, south between Fly river and coast, 1 village. Also in Indonesia. Animists 15%.
9343	2	6	5.83	0	99.80	0.20	C	327.04	169	9	Sandaun Province. Cargo cult area, with animists 10%. D=Christian Brethren,RCC. M=CMML.
9344	1	7	3.95	0	99.95	0.05	C	450.77	106	10	East Sepik Province, near Chambri, Arafundi river, middle Karawari river. Related language: Karawari. D=RCC. Little continuous work. M=SVD.
9345	0	6	2.93	0	50.00	50.00	B	45.62	219	6	Sandaun Province, Kernam town and north. Related languages: Olo, Yau, Ningil, Valman. Animists 25%.
9346	1	6	3.67	0	99.95	0.05	C	447.30	101	10	Madang Province. Virtually no animists. D=RCC.
9347	1	5	7.53	1	99.76	0.24	C	305.14	214	9	Western Province, along Fly and Tedi rivers and Murray river. Some in Irian Jaya. Close to South Kati and Ninggerum. Animists 4%. D=ECP. M=APCM/UFM,SIL.
9348	0	0	6.01	0	88.00	12.00	C	208.78	220	8	East Sepik Province, Maprik District. Swidden agriculturalists. Animists 10%. D=ELCPNG.
9349	2	6	3.37	1	61.00	39.00	B	66.79	199	6	Western Province. Tribal religionists(animists) 25%. D=RCC,Protestants.
9350	1	6	5.46	0	99.70	0.30	C	263.16	174	8	Morobe Province. In dialect chain with Mumeng, Patep, Latep. Few animists. D=ELCPNG.
9351	2	6	5.86	0	99.85	0.15	C	381.60	154	9	Morobe Province, Morobe District near mouth of Waria river, 16 villages. Closest to Yekora. Virtually no animists left. D=ELCPNG(99% baptized Lutherans).
9352	0	7	8.85		65.00	35.00	B	94.90	373	6	Over 340 other small ethnic groups and languages, many nearly extinct; Germans, Pacific Islanders, Indonesians, Koreans(PCK-H), Irianese refugees from.
Paraguay											
9353	2	10	2.24	8	99.67	0.33	C	335.03	60	9	Immigrants from Australia, residents. Nonreligious 20%. D=Anglican Ch/CASA(D-Paraguay),RCC. M=SAMS,SDB,SJ.
9354	1	8	2.24	0	97.00	3.00	B	194.72	92	7	Chaco and northern Alta Paraguay. A third live in Bolivia. Animists 45%. D=EUSA. M=NTM,SAM,OMI.
9355	1	7	2.24	0	73.00	27.00	B	106.58	122	7	Eastern Alto Paraguay. Hunter-gatherers, nomads. Limited bilingualism. Animists 60%. D=RCC. M=NTM.
9356	1	10	2.24	8	99.98	0.02	C	590.20	47	10	Descendants of former slaves. D=RCC(10 Dioceses). M=SVD,SDB,SJ,OFM.
9357	1	8	2.24	0	65.00	35.00	B	71.17	137	6	Northeastern Chaco region. Nomads, hunter-gatherers. Some Spanish and Guarani known. Animists 70%. D=RCC. M=OMI,NTM.
9358	4	10	1.98	4	99.65	0.35	C	298.93	57	8	Also in Brazil, Argentina. Hunter-gatherers. Animists 30%. D=RCC,COG,IHL,EPMC. M=SDB,SJ,OMI,CMML,ACNC,SIM,GEPM.
9359	2	10	2.24	8	99.95	0.05	C	596.41	47	10	Immigrants, residents from Brazil. D=RCC(10 Dioceses),ICAB. M=SDB,SJ,SVD,OFM.
9360	1	10	2.24	4	99.80	0.20	C	391.28	59	9	On eastern border with Brazil; 30% in Brazil. Close to Paraguayan Guarani. Animists 15%. D=RCC. M=GPIM.
9361	5	6	2.24	0	87.00	13.00	B	127.02	91	7	Chaco, Presidente Hayes Department. Animists 56%, many Baha'is. D=RCC,HM,AC/CASA,CJCLdS,IEMP. M=OMI,MBCNA,SAMS.
9362	3	10	2.24	4	99.70	0.30	C	332.15	61	9	Mainly in Argentina and Bolivia. Animists 26%, some Baha'is. D=RCC,CJCLdS,IEMP. M=OMI,MCC,GEPM.
9363	1	8	2.24	0	99.80	0.20	C	362.08	65	9	Near Asuncion. Toba mainly spoken, also Lengua. Fishermen, hunters. Animists 20%. D=RCC.
9364	0	10	8.43	8	99.85	0.15	C	456.06	178	10	Chaco, Eastern Paraguay. Links with Germans in many other Latin American countries, USA, Canada. Agriculturalists. Mostly Protestants.
9365	1	10	2.24	7	99.95	0.05	C	575.60	53	10	Immigrants from Greece. D=Greek Orthodox Ch(AD-N&S America).
9366	3	7	2.24	0	99.60	0.40	C	229.95	85	8	Boqueron, Salado river. Large villages. Hunters. Animists 40%. D=RCC,CJCLdS,IEMP. M=OMI.
9367	2	6	2.33	0	35.00	65.00	A	2.55	233	4	Hostile, scattered nomadic hunter-gatherers in southeast. Animists 98%. D=RCC,IHL. M=NTM,CMML,independents.
9368	6	10	3.65	4	99.92	0.08	C	493.62	87	10	Many Baha'is. D=AC/CASA,RCC,COG,CJCLdS,IEMP,EPMC. M=SDB,SJ,SVD,OMI,SAMS,ACMC.
9369	0	10	5.15	7	99.50	0.50	B	209.87	138	8	Long-time immigrants from Chinese diaspora. Buddhists/Chinese folk-religionists 50%.
9370	1	10	2.24	7	99.84	0.16	C	493.62	55	10	Immigrants from Italy. Strong Catholics. D=RCC(10 Dioceses). M=SDB,SJ,SVD,OMI,OFM.
9371	3	10	6.01	7	95.00	5.00	B	93.62	195	6	In Itapua and Alto Parana. Buddhists 50%, New-Religionists(Nichiren Shoshu) 23%. D=RCC(PN-Alto Parana),SDA,FMCP. M=SVD.
9372	0	10	1.10	8	49.11	50.89	A	0.19	100	3	Small communities of Spanish-speaking practicing Jews, mainly in Asuncion.
9373	2	8	2.24	1	99.60	0.40	C	240.90	72	8	Eastern boundary with Brazil. As many more in Brazil; some in Argentina. Animists 35%. D=RCC,Disciples of Christ. M=NTM,GEPM,SIL.
9374	2	10	4.11	6	99.51	0.49	B	223.38	108	8	Buddhists 30%, shamanists 19%. D=Korean United Evangelical Ch,RCC. M=OMI,Korea Methodist Ch,PCK-H,PCK-T.
9375	4	10	2.24	8	99.97	0.03	C	596.74	50	10	Argentinians and others. Spanish origin. D=RCC,IEMA,COG,IEV. M=SDB,SVD,SJ,SAMS,SIM.
9376	5	10	7.56	8	99.93	0.07	C	563.48	144	10	Mennonite Germans. Agriculturalists. D=IEMP,IERP,AoG,NAC,COG. M=MBCNA,MCNA,GCMC,SDB,SJ,AMACOG(Argentina).
9377	0	7	2.24	0	68.00	32.00	B	74.46	116	6	Southwest. Hunters, craftsmen. Animists 50%, many Baha'is, 20%. M=NTM,OMI,FMB,independents.
9378	1	8	2.24	0	97.00	3.00	C	212.43	81	8	Mostly in Argentina. Monolinguals. Animists 20%. D=Anglican Ch/CASA(D-Paraguay). M=LTIM,NTM.
9379	1	10	2.24	0	99.80	0.20	C	356.24	63	9	Mixed-race persons on reserve in eastern Chaco. Some use Guarani, Spanish. D=RCC.
9380	3	8	2.24	0	99.90	0.10	C	453.33	57	10	Mostly in Argentina. D=RCC,IEMP,CJCLdS. M=OMI.
9381	6	10	2.24	8	99.99	0.01	C	603.45	46	10	Chileans, Bolivians. Many Baha'is. D=RCC(10 Dioceses),IEMP,IERP,JWs,SDA,&c. M=SIM.
9382	4	8	2.24	0	99.85	0.15	C	425.04	58	10	Chaco. Semi-nomadic. Animists 5%. D=RCC,IEMP,HM,AC/CASA. M=MBCNA,OMI,SAMS,NTM.
9383	5	8	2.24	0	99.85	0.15	C	431.24	57	10	Enlit. In southeast Chaco. Animists 5%. D=RCC,IEMP,AC/CASA,HM,CJCLdS. M=NTM,MBCNA,OMI,GCMC,MCNA,SAMS.
9384	12	8	2.14	5	99.96	0.04	C	569.92	47	10	Avanee, Jopara. D=RCC(10 Dioceses),IEMP,HM,IERP,AC/CASA,IHL,JWs,CEBP,SA,COG,EPMC,AoG. M=SDB,SJ,SVD,OMI,OFM,FMB,NTMU,PMA(Philippines).
9385	1	8	2.24	0	99.85	0.15	C	418.83	58	10	Cabanatit, Machicui, Enenlhit, Quilyilhrayrom. In northeast center. Animists 5%. D=RCC.
9386	2	8	2.22	0	99.95	0.05	C	492.38	55	10	Most live in Argentina. D=RCC,several pentecostal bodies.
9387	2	10	2.24	6	99.88	0.12	C	513.92	38	10	Refugees from Poland. Nonreligious 10%. D=RCC(10 Dioceses),AoG. M=SDB,SVD,SJ.
9388	1	10	2.24	8	99.93	0.07	C	577.06	53	10	Immigrants from Portugal. D=RCC(10 Dioceses). M=SDB,SJ.
9389	2	10	2.23	7	99.70	0.30	C	360.25	43	9	Refugees from USSR. Nonreligious 25%. D=Russian Orthodox Ch Outside of Russia(D-Argentina),AoG.
9390	3	8	2.24	0	99.95	0.05	C	506.25	55	10	Chaco, north of Angaite. D=RCC,CJCLdS,IEMP. M=OMI,SAMS,MBCNA.
9391	3	8	2.24	0	99.95	0.05	C	499.32	56	10	Toba-speaking. D=RCC,CJCLdS,IEMP. M=OMI.
9392	5	8	2.24	0	99.87	0.13	C	428.69	58	10	Chaco. Semi-nomadic pastoralists and hunter-gatherers. Animists 13%. D=RCC,HM,CJCLdS,IEMP,AC. M=MBCNA,OMI,SAMS,NTM.
9393	2	8	2.24	1	99.80	0.20	C	376.68	61	9	Chaco, also in Argentina, Bolivia. Bilingual in Guarani, some also in Spanish. Animists 5%, many Baha'is. D=RCC,CJCLdS. M=OMI,MBCNA.
9394	3	8	2.24	0	99.95	0.05	C	499.32	56	10	Chaco. Mainly in Argentina. Shamanists 4%, some Baha'is. D=Mennonites,pentecostals,RCC.
9395	0	0	5.51	8	99.78	0.22	C	370.11	135	9	North Americans, in business, education. Nonreligious 10%. D=RCC,BBC,SDA,etc.
9396	2	10	6.76	6	99.76	0.24	C	405.00	149	10	Refugees from USSR since 1917, 1945. Nonreligious 20%. D=Ukrainian Orthodox Ch in USA,AoG.
9397	0	10	2.24		99.69	0.31	C	254.36	61	8	Uruguayans, Peruvians, Bolivians, Argentinians, Spaniards. Nonreligious/atheists 6%.
Peru											
9398	1	6	2.43	0	54.00	46.00	B	29.56	159	5	Amazon jungle. Also in Ecuador. 10% bilingual in Spanish. Animists 85%. D=RCC(VA-Iquitos). M=SIL,OSA,SWIM,SPM.
9399	2	6	2.71	0	49.00	51.00	A	12.52	191	5	Western upper Maranon River area. Hunter-gatherers. 65% bilingual in Spanish. Animists 93%. D=RCC(VA-San Francisco Javier, Jaen),CON. M=SIL,SJ,SWIM.
9400	2	6	1.70	0	38.00	62.00	A	6.93	173	4	Sepahua. Hunters. 20% bilingual in Spanish. Animists 95%. D=RCC(VA-Puerto Maldonado),SDA. M=OP,SIL,GR.
9401	2	7	3.27	0	50.00	50.00	B	18.25	234	5	Madre de Dios and Colorado rivers. 5 ethnic groups related. 80% bilingual in Spanish. Animists 90%. D=RCC(VA-Puerto Maldonado),SDA. M=OP,SIL.
9402	1	7	4.13	5	99.95	0.05	C	502.78	91	10	San Rafael-Huariaca Quechua. 35% monolinguals. D=RCC(VA-San Ramon). M=OFM.
9403	3	6	2.45	0	90.00	10.00	B	147.82	105	7	Central and eastern Pasco Department. 95% bilingual in Spanish. Animists 55%. D=RCC(VA-San Ramon),SDA,IEP. M=SIL,OFM,Reapers.
9404	1	10	1.40	0	99.70	0.30	C	281.05	60	8	Pastaza river. Bilingual in Spanish and Quechua. Nearly extinct. Animists 30%. D=RCC(VA-Yurimaguas). M=CP.
9405	7	6	2.20	5	99.99	0.01	C	589.00	49	10	Southwestern Ayacucho region. Dialect of Chanka. D=RCC(M-Ayacucho; christopagans 50%),SDA,SA,AoG,IEP,JWs,CJCLdS. M=EUSA,SDB,OFM,SJ,OP,EMBMC.
9406	1	7	1.93	0	99.60	0.40	C	219.00	72	8	Amazon jungle. Only 150 speakers left. 100% bilingual in Spanish. Animists 40%. D=RCC(VA-Iquitos,VA-San Jose). M=SIL,OSA,OFM.
9407	6	6	2.03	4	99.99	0.01	C	574.54	47	10	Arequipa Department. Many monolinguals. D=RCC(M-Arequipa),SA,SDA,IEP,JWs,CJCLdS. M=EUSA,OFM,SDB,SJ,OP,MMG,EMBMC,SIM,SIL.
9408	2	6	2.13	0	99.65	0.35	C	263.34	77	8	Agriculturalists, hunter-gatherers. 60% bilingual in Spanish. Animists 35%. D=RCC(M-Cuzco),SDA. M=OFM,SAM,SWIM,SPM,SIL.
9409	2	6	2.15	0	99.60	0.40	C	229.95	82	8	Tributaries of Ucayali river. 60% bilingual in Spanish. Animists 40%. D=RCC(VA-San Ramon),SDA. M=OFM,OSA,SIL.
9410	8	6	2.10	5	99.99	0.01	C	607.06	46	10	69% bilingual in Spanish. D=RCC(M-Ayacucho; superficial Catholicism, with christopagans 50%),SA,SDA,IEP,Presbyterian Ch,JWs,AoG,CJCLdS. M=EMBMC.
9411	1	6	3.31	0	57.00	43.00	B	41.61	193	6	Northeast Yaguasyacu. Also in Colombia. Animists 80%. D=RCC(VA-San Jose de Amazonas). M=OFM,SIL,Baptist Mission.
9412	5	10	1.93	8	99.78	0.22	C	424.20	57	10	Expatriates from Britain, in development. D=Anglican Ch/CASA(D-Peru),IEP,SDA,JWs,RCC. M=CMS,SAMS.
9413	1	10	1.10	0	72.00	28.00	B	99.86	80	6	Nanay river. Rain forest. Nearly extinct. Animists 62%. D=RCC(VA-Iquitos). M=OSA.
9414	6	6	1.99	4	99.99	0.01	C	549.25	48	10	Rural, agricultural, poor. 30% monolingual, 70% bilingual in Spanish. D=RCC(D-Cajamarca),SA,IEP,JWs,CJCLdS,SDA. M=SIL.
9415	1	6	3.42	0	41.00	59.00	A	8.97	275	4	13% bilingual in Spanish. Animists 94%. D=RCC(VA-Yurimaguas). M=SIL,AoG,SIM,CP,SPM.
9416	1	7	4.21	0	48.00	52.00	A	17.52	280	5	Tapiche-Buncuya rivers area. 100% bilingual in Spanish. Animists 90%. D=RCC(VA-Requena). M=SIL,OFM.
9417	1	6	2.94	0	62.00	38.00	B	67.89	174	6	Poyeni river area. 1% bilingual in Spanish, 15% bilingual in Machiguenga. Animists 70%. D=RCC(M-Cuzco). M=SIL.
9418	1	6	2.64	0	55.00	45.00	B	30.11	166	5	Aguaytia river area. 66% bilingual in Spanish. Animists 85%. D=RCC(VA-Pucallpa). M=SIL,SIM,PME,SAIM,SPM.
9419	2	6	2.68	0	48.00	52.00	A	17.52	193	5	Curanja and Purus rivers area. Also in Brazil. Animists 90%. D=RCC(VA-Puerto Maldonado),SDA. M=OP,SIL,MSP.
9420	5	6	2.13	4	99.98	0.02	C	583.05	36	10	Lake Titicaca area. Strong Adventist work. D=SDA,RCC(D-Puno,PN-Juli; christopagans 60%) ,AoG,IEINP(Tabernaclers),CJCLdS. M=MM,OFM,IMCP,UBS.
9421	1	6	2.17	4	99.99	0.01	C	520.34	54	10	Amazonas, Chachapoyas and Luya Provinces, Northern Peru. D=RCC(D-Chachapoyas).
9422	1	7	2.53	0	99.70	0.30	C	263.16	94	8	Pampa Hermosa. Tropical rain-forest. Almost no speakers left. D=RCC(VA-Iquitos). M=OSA.
9423	2	6	2.43	0	80.00	20.00	B	116.80	117	7	Paranapura river area. 40% bilingual in Spanish. Animists 60%. D=RCC(VA-Yurimaguas),SDA. M=SIL,RBMU,CP,SWIM,SPM.
9424	5	10	2.03	8	99.95	0.05	C	568.67	43	10	Migrants from Chile. D=RCC(10 Dioceses),SDA,IEP,JWs,COG. M=IMP,IEP(Chile),&c.
9425	1	10	2.28	8	99.90	0.10	C	512.46	51	10	Mixed-race Spanish-speaking Mulattos, in urban coastal areas. D=RCC. M=SDB,OFM,SJ,OP,FSC.
9426	1	6	1.48	4	99.90	0.10	C	443.47	44	10	Southeast Ancash Department. Rurals are monolingual. D=RCC.
9427	1	6	2.96	0	47.00	53.00	A	17.15	210	5	Few speakers left; 100% bilingual in Spanish. Animists 90%. D=RCC(VA-Iquitos,VA-Requena). M=SIL,ABWE,SAM,OFM,OSA.
9428	1	6	2.69	0	51.00	49.00	B	27.92	179	5	Very few speakers remain. Animists 85%. D=RCC(VA-Iquitos,VA-Requena). M=OFM,OSA,ABWE,SAM.
9429	2	6	2.69	0	87.00	13.00	B	158.77	116	7	Near Machiguenga; close but separate. Animists 50%. D=RCC,SDA. M=OP.
9430	1	6	2.28	4	99.90	0.10	C	450.04	59	10	East central Ancash Department. 70% monolinguals. D=RCC(christopagans 60%). M=SIL.
9431	1	6	2.55	4	99.85	0.15	C	390.91	70	9	Northern Ancash Department. Very different from other Quechua. Limited bilingualism. D=RCC.
9432	2	9	0.70	0	35.00	65.00	A	2.55	110	4	Manu Park, Madre de Dios. Highly nomadic. Animists 98%. D=RCC(VA-Puerto Maldonado),SDA. M=OP.
9433	2	7	3.45	0	55.00	45.00	B	40.15	222	6	Southeast, near Brazil. 22% bilingual in Spanish. Animists 80%. D=RCC(VA-Puerto Maldonado),SDA. M=OP,SIL.
9434	7	6	2.42	5	99.97	0.03	C	584.18	52	10	Ancient Inca capital. Rapid growth of Baha'is, now 2%. D=RCC(M-Cuzco; christopagans 60%),SA,EUSA,SDA,CJCLdS,IEP,JWs. M=SDB,SJ,MMG,EMBMC,SIM.
9435	3	10	2.11	8	99.99	0.01	C	602.20	35	10	Shanty dwellers, in urban slums. D=SDA,AoG,RCC(D-Puno,D-Tacna,PN-Juli). M=MM.
9436	4	10	1.87	8	99.98	0.02	C	611.66	41	10	Most urban slumdwellers. D=RCC,AIENE,IEP,AMEN. M=OFM,SDB,SJ,OP,OSA,CM,MM,CP,CSSR,CMF,FSC,PFM. T=CBN. R=AWR.
9437	2	7	2.38	0	81.00	19.00	B	118.26	104	7	Extreme poverty. 95% bilingual in Spanish. Animists 60%. D=RCC(VA-Puerto Maldonado),SDA. M=OP.
9438	0	10	0.00	5	99.80	0.20	C	391.28	0	9	Artificial (constructed) language, in 80 countries. Speakers in Peru: 9,500(none mother-tongue). Nonreligious 20%.
9439	6	10	2.42	8	99.69	0.31	C	357.62	69	9	Expatriates from Germany, citizens. D=RCC,IEP,NAC,SDA,JWs,German Evangelical Ch.
9440	1	10	2.08	7	99.99	0.01	C	610.68	50	10	Traders, farmers from Greece. D=Greek Orthodox Ch(AD-North & South America).
9441	2	10	2.23	8	99.70	0.30	C	327.04	70	9	Nomads. Travellers. Nonreligious 30%. D=RCC,Gypsy Evangelical Movement. M=GGMS,SDB,OFM.
9442	2	6	2.26	8	99.48	0.52	B	192.72	72	7	Folk Buddhists 50%. D=RCC,Chinese Christian Fellowship.
9443	2	6	2.02	8	99.45	0.55	B	183.87	65	7	Half live in Lima. Buddhists/folk-religionists 50%. D=RCC((M-Lima),Chinese Christian Fellowship. M=OFM,SDB,SJ,OP.
9444	2	7	3.49	0	45.00	55.00	A	16.42	273	5	Upper Madre de Dios river. Mashco. Extreme poverty. 50% bilingual in Spanish. Animists 90%. D=RCC(VA-Puerto Maldonado),SDA. M=OP.
9445	4	6	3.02	4	99.90	0.10	C	450.04	74	10	Northeast Huanuco Department. 65% monolinguals. D=RCC,AoG,EUSA,CMA. M=SIL.
9446	1	6	1.72	4	99.90	0.10	C	443.47	49	10	North central Huanuco Department. 55% monolinguals. D=RCC. M=SIL.
9447	1	6	3.25	0	43.00	57.00	A	7.84	252	4	Morona and Santiago rivers. 80% bilingual in Spanish. Hunter-gatherers. Animists 95%. D=RCC(VA-San Francisco Javier, Jaen). M=SJ,SIL.
9448	6	6	2.00	1	99.90	0.10	C	453.33	53	10	Central Ancash Department. Rurals are monolingual. D=RCC(D-Huaras; christopagans 60%),AoG,IEP,SA,JWs,CJCLdS. M=SIL,EMBMC,SIM.
9449	1	10	2.01	8	99.90	0.10	C	502.60	50	10	Mixed-race persons (Chinese/Japanese with Latin America Whites). Nonreligious 10%. D=RCC.
9450	1	7	2.62	0	99.70	0.30	C	275.94	84	8	Northern Nanay River area. 60% bilingual in Spanish. Animists 30%. D=RCC(VA-Iquitos,VA-San Jose). M=SIL,OFM.
9451	1	9	3.78	0	90.00	10.00	B	164.25	136	7	Callaria river. Bilingual in Shipibo. Animists 50%. D=RCC(VA-Pucallpa). M=PME.
9452	1	10	2.05	7	99.51	0.49	B	220.27	65	8	Buddhists/New-Religionists 45%(mass conversions to Soka Gakkai). D=RCC(M-Lima). M=SJ,YBBC(Japan).
9453	1	6	2.36	0	99.80	0.20	C	338.72	56	9	Tupe. Lima Department, Yauyos Province. 90% bilingual in Spanish. Animists 20%. D=RCC(PN-Yauyos).
9454	4	6	2.13	4	99.99	0.01	C	552.86	51	10	Central Junin Department. D=RCC(christopagans 50%),IEP,Pentecostal Ch of Jesus Christ,CJCLdS. M=SIL,SJ,OP,SDB,OFM.
9455	1	6	2.67	0	98.00	2.00	C	214.62	103	8	District of Jeberos. 60% bilingual in Spanish. Animists 40%. D=RCC(VA-Yurimaguas). M=SIL,CP.
9456	0	10	2.33	8	46.10	53.90	A	0.16	179	3	Communities of Spanish-speaking practicing Jews, mostly in Lima.
9457	1	6	2.13	5	99.70	0.30	C	296.38	67	8	Along Ucayali river. 90% bilingual in Spanish. Animists 30%. D=RCC(VA-Yurimaguas). M=CP.

Continued overleaf

Table 8-2 continued

PEOPLE		POPULATION				IDENTITY CODE		LANGUAGE		CHURCH		MINISTRY						SCRIPTURE		
Ref 1	Ethnic name 2	P% 3	In 1995 4	In 2000 5	In 2025 6	Race 7	Language 8	Autoglossonym 9	S 10	AC 11	Members 12	Jayuh 13-17	d 18	wa 19	xc 20	mc 21	mi 22	Biblioglossonym 23	Pub 24-26	ss 27
9458	Lambayeque Quechua	0.10471	24,640	26,870	37,191	MIR39g	85-FAAD-af	ferrañafe		99.00	26,602	0....	10	7	11	4	1	Quechua: Lambayeque*	Pn.	.
9459	Loreto-Ucayali Indian	0.01000	2,353	2,566	3,552	MIR39g	51-AABB-j	ucayaliano		90.00	2,310	1c.uh	10	7	11	5	1		pnb	.
9460	Lowland Quichua (Napo)	0.04520	10,636	11,599	16,054	MIR39g	85-FAAB-a	quixo		99.00	11,483	0....	10	7	12	4	2		Pn.	.
9461	Machiguenga (Manaries)	0.03955	9,307	10,149	14,047	MIR39a	81-BBAB-c	machigue-nga		60.00	6,090	0....	10	7	6	5	3	Machiguenga	PN.	.
9462	Manu Park Panoan (Nahua)	0.00102	240	262	362	MIR39d	84-NAEB-a	parque-nahua		1.00	3	0....	6	4	3	5	2	Yora	...	.
9463	Maranon Huanuco Quechua	0.06283	14,785	16,123	22,316	MIR39g	85-FAAF-ca	marañon		85.00	13,705	1....	10	7	7	4	1		p..	.
9464	Mayoruna (Maxirona)	0.00452	1,064	1,160	1,605	MIR39d	84-NBAA-a	proper matsés		5.00	58	0....	7	5	0	5	2	Matses	PN.	.
9465	Meneca Huitoto	0.00002	5	5	7	MIR39d	84-BABA	meneca cluster		65.00	3	0....	10	7	5	4	2	Huitoto: Minica*	PN.	b
9466	Morunahua (Foredafa)	0.00074	174	190	263	MIR39d	84-NAEC-a	moru-nahua		0.00	0	0....	0	1	0	0	1		...	.
9467	Muinane (Muinana)	0.00038	89	98	135	MIR39d	84-BABA-b	muinane-meneca		70.00	68	0....	10	7	5	4	2	Huitoto: Muinani*	PN.	b
9468	Muinane Huitoto	0.00045	106	115	160	MIR39d	84-BABA-a	nüpode		50.00	58	0....	10	7	5	4	1	Huitoto, Nipode	Pn.	n
9469	Mulatto	0.20000	47,063	51,323	71,036	NFB71b	51-AABB-hq	peruano		89.50	45,934	1B.uh	10	8	11	5	3		pnb	b
9470	Muniche (Otanave)	0.00001	2	3	4	MIR39d	88-OAAA-a	muniche		70.00	2	0....	10	7	5	4	1		...	.
9471	Murui Huitoto	0.00420	988	1,078	1,492	MIR39d	84-BAAA-b	central murui		85.00	916	0....	10	7	6	4	2	Huitoto: Murui*	PN.	b
9472	Nomatsiguenga Campa	0.02097	4,935	5,381	7,448	MIR39a	81-BBAB-a	no-matsigue-nga		60.00	3,229	0....	10	7	7	4	3	Campa: Nomatsiguenga*	PN.	b
9473	North Junin Quechua	0.28571	67,232	73,318	101,479	MIR39g	85-FAAF-f	junín-tarma		99.00	72,585	1....	10	9	12	5	3	Quechua: Junin*	P..	b
9474	North Lima Quechua	0.11241	26,452	28,846	39,926	MIR39g	85-FAAF-ba	cajatambo		99.00	28,558	1....	10	8	11	5	3		p..	b
9475	Norwegian	0.03000	7,060	7,699	10,655	CEW19p	52-AAAC-e	ny-norsk		95.00	7,314	0B.uh	10	9	14	5	3	Norwegian*	PNB	b
9476	Ocaina	0.00129	304	331	458	MIR39d	84-BAFA-a	proper ocaina		70.00	232	0....	10	7	6	5	2	Ocaina	P..	.
9477	Omagua-Yete (Ariana)	0.00035	82	90	124	MIR39e	80-AHAA-b	jianá-coto		70.00	63	0....	10	7	5	4	1		...	b
9478	Orejon (Koto)	0.00158	372	405	561	MIR39d	84-BAGA-a	orejûn		60.00	243	0....	10	7	6	4	2	Orejon	P..	b
9479	Pachitea Quechua	0.12529	29,483	32,152	44,501	MIR39g	85-FAAF-cg	panao		99.00	31,830	1....	10	8	11	5	3	Quechua, Huanuco, Panao	p..	.
9480	Pajonal Campa (Atsiri)	0.01485	3,494	3,811	5,274	MIR39a	81-BBAA-c	pajonal		50.00	1,905	0....	10	6	7	4	3	Campa: Pajonal*	Pn.	.
9481	Pasco-Yanahuanca Quechua	0.14643	34,457	37,576	52,009	MIR39g	85-FAAF-eb	yanahuanca		99.00	37,201	1....	10	8	12	5	3		p..	.
9482	Peruvian Black	0.50000	117,658	128,308	177,591	NFB71a	51-AABB-hq	peruano		98.00	125,742	1B.uh	10	10	12	5	3		pnb	b
9483	Peruvian Mestizo	31.93579	7,515,030	8,195,257	11,343,017	CLN29	51-AABB-hq	peruano	46	98.10	8,039,547	1B.uh	10	10	10	5	3		pnb	b
9484	Peruvian White	12.00000	2,823,802	3,079,400	4,262,184	CLT27	51-AABB-hq	peruano		95.28	2,934,053	1B.uh	10	10	11	5	4		pnb	b
9485	Piro (Simirinche)	0.01200	2,824	3,079	4,262	MIR39a	81-BCAA-a	piro		69.90	2,153	0....	10	7	6	4	3	Piro	PN.	.
9486	Pisabo (Pisahua)	0.00200	471	513	710	MIR39d	84-NABA-b	pisa-bo		0.00	0	0....	0	0	1	4	0		...	.
9487	Puno Quechua	0.10000	23,532	25,662	35,518	MIR39g	85-FAAH-cb	puno		91.00	23,352	1cs..	10	7	11	5	1		pnb	.
9488	Resigaro	0.00009	21	23	32	MIR39d	81-AIAA-a	resígaro		60.00	14	0....	10	7	4	4	1		...	b
9489	Russian	0.00500	1,177	1,283	1,776	CEW22j	53-AAAE-d	russkiy		64.00	821	4B.uh	10	8	8	4	1	Russian	PNB	b
9490	S Ana de Tusi Pasco Quechua	0.04370	10,283	11,214	15,521	MIR39g	85-FAAF-d	ambo-pasco		70.00	7,850	1....	10	7	8	0	0	Quechua: S Rafael, Huaria*	P..	b
9491	Secoya (Angotero)	0.00081	191	208	288	MIR39d	88-KAAA-bb	secoya		30.00	62	0....	9	5	6	4	1	Secoya	PN.	.
9492	Sharanahua	0.00261	614	670	927	MIR39d	84-NAFC-a	shara-nahua		70.00	469	0....	10	7	6	5	2	Sharanahua	PN.	b
9493	Shipibol (Xipibo)	0.08484	19,964	21,771	30,134	MIR39d	84-NACA-b	coni-bo		65.00	14,151	1....	10	7	6	5	3	Shipibo-conibo	PN.	b
9494	Sihuas Ancash Quechua	0.04546	10,698	11,666	16,147	MIR39g	85-FAAE-ab	sihuas		90.00	10,499	1....	10	7	11	5	1		p..	b
9495	Southern Aymara (Carangas	0.77500	182,371	198,878	275,266	MIR39b	85-JABA-ad	caranga		98.00	194,900	1.s..	10	9	12	5	3		pnb	b
9496	Southern Huancayo Quechua	0.32770	77,113	84,093	116,393	MIR39g	85-FAAF-g	huanca		99.00	83,252	1....	10	9	12	5	3	Quechua, Huanca, Huaylla	P..	b
9497	Southern Huanuco Quechua	0.28796	67,762	73,895	102,278	MIR39g	85-FAAF-ce	dos-de-mayo		86.00	63,550	1....	10	7	8	4	1		p..	b
9498	Southern Pastaza Quechua	0.01412	3,323	3,623	5,015	MIR39g	85-FAAB-c	south pastaza		70.00	2,536	0....	10	7	6	4	2	Quechua: Pastaza*	Pn.	.
9499	Taushiro	0.00012	28	31	43	MIR39z	84-JAAA-a	ite'tshi		60.00	18	0....	10	7	4	4	1		...	.
9500	Ticuna	0.02823	6,643	7,244	10,027	MIR39d	88-MAAA-a	ticuna		90.00	6,520	0....	10	7	11	4	2	Ticuna	PN.	.
9501	Tigre Quichua (Bobonaza)	0.01250	2,941	3,208	4,440	MIR39g	85-FAAB-bd	tigre		99.00	3,176	0....	10	7	12	4	1		pn.	.
9502	USA White	0.03000	7,060	7,699	10,655	CEW19s	52-ABAC-s	general american	8	77.00	5,928	1Bsuh	10	10	9	5	3	English*	PNB	b
9503	Urarina (Shimacu)	0.01554	3,657	3,988	5,520	MIR39d	84-GAAA-a	proper urarina		9.00	359	0....	7	5	6	4	1	Urarina	Pn.	.
9504	Yagua (Yava)	0.01977	4,652	5,073	7,022	MIR39d	84-IACA-a	nixamwi		15.00	761	0....	8	5	6	4	3	Yagua	PN.	.
9505	Yaminahua (Jaminawa)	0.00508	1,195	1,304	1,804	MIR39d	84-NAFD-a	yami-nahua		40.00	521	0....	9	5	6	5	2	Yaminahua	P..	b
9506	Yauyos Quechua	0.12891	30,335	33,080	45,787	MIR39g	85-FAAG	yauyos cluster		99.00	32,750	0....	10	8	12	5	3		...	b
9507	Zambo	0.10000	23,532	25,662	35,518	NFB71b	51-AABB-hq	peruano		90.00	23,096	1B.uh	10	7	11	4	3		pnb	b
9508	other minor peoples	0.20000	47,063	51,323	71,036	...				69.00	35,413		10	7	6	5	3			
	Philippines	**100.00000**	**68,354,054**	**75,966,500**	**108,251,048**					**87.67**	**66,600,061**									
9509	Abaknon Sama	0.02759	18,859	20,959	29,866	MSY44z	31-EAAA-a	abak-non		60.00	12,575	0....	10	7	6	5	2	Sama: Abaknon*	P..	.
9510	Aborlan Tagbanwa	0.01610	11,005	12,231	17,428	MSY44m	31-CJDB-a	aborlan-tagbanwa		3.00	367	0....	6	4	4	5	3	Tagbanwa	PN.	.
9511	Aburlin Negrito	0.01260	8,613	9,572	13,640	AUG05	31-CHCA-a	abenlen-agta		30.00	2,872	0....	9	5	5	2	1	Ayta, Abenlen	...	b
9512	Adasen Itneg (Tinguian)	0.00690	4,716	5,242	7,469	MSY44x	31-CCAB	adasen cluster		14.00	734	0....	8	5	6	4	1	Adasen	PN.	b
9513	Aeta Negrito (Zambal)	0.07400	50,582	56,215	80,106	AUG05	31-CHAB-b	botolan		4.00	2,249	0....	6	7	4	5	3	Sambal: Botolan*	PN.	.
9514	Agusan Manobo	0.08052	55,039	61,168	87,164	MSY44x	31-CKOE-a	agusan		4.00	2,447	0.s..	6	7	6	5	3	Manobo: Agusan*	P..	.
9515	Agutaynon	0.01234	8,435	9,374	13,358	MSY44m	31-CJCB-a	agutay-nen		60.00	5,625	0....	10	7	6	4	2	Agutaynen	P..	.
9516	Aklano (Aklan, Panay)	0.68578	468,758	520,963	742,364	MSY44q	31-CKGD-a	akla-non		90.00	468,867	2....	10	7	6	5	3	Aklanon	P..	.
9517	Alabat Is Dumagat (Agta)	0.00011	75	84	119	AUG05	31-CDCA-a	alabat-agta		5.00	4	0.s..	7	5	4	4	1		pn.	b
9518	Alangan	0.01017	6,952	7,726	11,009	MSY44x	31-CIBA-a	alangan		40.00	3,090	0....	9	8	5	5	2	Alangan	PN.	.
9519	Albay Bicolano (Buhi)	1.12769	770,822	856,667	1,220,736	AUG05	31-CKFB-a	buhi-non		97.00	830,967	1....	10	5	4	2	1	Bicolano, Albay	...	.
9520	Ambala Sambal (Agta)	0.00293	2,003	2,226	3,172	AUG05	31-CHFA-a	ambala-agta		10.00	223	0....	8	5	5	3	1	Ayta, Ambala	...	.
9521	Amerasian (Eurasian)	0.01500	10,253	11,395	16,238	MSY43	52-ABAD-a	south-asian-english		95.00	10,825	0B.uh	10	9	12	5	1		...	b
9522	Amganad Ifugao	0.05435	37,150	41,288	58,834	MSY44x	31-CEDA-a	amganad		4.00	1,652	0....	6	7	6	5	3	Ifugao: Amganad*	PN.	.
9523	Antipolo Ifugao	0.01035	7,075	7,863	11,204	MSY44x	31-CGAA-a	keley-i		7.00	550	0....	7	8	5	5	3	Ifugao: Antipolo*	PN.	.
9524	Antique Aeta	0.00133	909	1,010	1,440	AUG05	31-CKGC-b	hamtik-non		4.00	40	1c...	6	4	4	4	1		p..	b
9525	Arab	0.03000	20,506	22,790	32,475	CMT30	12-AACF-g	syro-mesopotamian		0.10	23	1Asuh	5	3	2	1	1		pnb	b
9526	Arta Negrito	0.00004	27	30	43	AUG05	31-AAAA-a	arta		30.00	9	0....	9	7	7	2	0		...	.
9527	Ata Manobo (Langilan)	0.03523	24,081	26,763	38,137	AUG05	31-CKOH-a	manobo-agta		4.00	1,071	0.s..	6	4	5	5	3	Manobo: Ata*	PN.	b
9528	Ati Negrito	0.00310	2,119	2,355	3,356	AUG05	31-CKGN	panay-ati cluster		5.00	118	0....	7	5	4	5	3		...	.
9529	Ayangan Ifugao (Batad)	0.07414	50,678	56,322	80,257	MSY44x	31-CEDB-b	batad		6.00	3,379	0....	7	5	5	5	3	Ifugao: Batad*	PN.	.
9530	Babuyan Islands Ivatan	0.00138	943	1,048	1,494	MSY44x	31-CABB-a	i-bat-an		60.00	629	0....	10	7	6	4	2	Ibatan	PN.	.
9531	Bajau (Sea Gypsy, Laut)	0.07000	47,848	53,177	75,776	MSY44z	31-PHCA	moken cluster		0.00	0	0....	0	3	0	0	0	Moken	P..	b
9532	Bajau Kagayan	0.03020	20,643	22,942	32,692	MSY44z	31-EACE-a	mapun		0.01	2	0....	3	3	3	1	2	Mapun*	PN.	.
9533	Balangao Bontoc	0.01541	10,533	11,706	16,681	MSY44x	31-CEBA-a	balangao		7.00	819	0....	7	5	6	5	2	Balangao	PN.	.
9534	Banaue Ifugao	0.01000	6,835	7,597	10,825	MSY44x	31-CEDA-c	banaue		8.00	608	0....	7	5	5	5	3	Ifugao: Banaue	Pn.	.
9535	Bantuanon (Banton, Asiq)	0.11792	80,603	89,580	127,650	MSY44x	31-CKGG-e	bantua-non		70.00	62,706	0....	10	7	6	5	3	Bantoanon	P..	b
9536	Basque	0.01000	6,835	7,597	10,825	CEW16	40-AAAA-a	general euskara		93.00	7,065	3....	10	9	14	5	1	Basque	PNB	b
9537	Bataan Sambal	0.00101	690	767	1,093	AUG05	31-CHEA-a	bataan-agta		5.00	38	0....	7	5	4	1	1		...	b
9538	Binokid Manobo (Bukidnon)	0.17242	117,856	130,981	186,646	MSY44x	31-CKOC-a	binukid-non		39.00	51,083	0....	9	8	6	5	3	Binukid	PN.	.
9539	Binongan Itneg (Tinguian)	0.01372	9,378	10,423	14,852	MSY44x	31-CEAA-a	binongan		16.00	1,668	0....	8	5	6	2	1	Tinguian*	P..	b
9540	Bolinao Sambal	0.09071	62,004	68,909	98,195	AUG05	31-CHAA-a	bolinao		50.00	34,455	0....	10	9	6	5	3	Bolinao	P..	b
9541	British	0.01500	10,253	11,395	16,238	CEW19i	52-ABAC-b	standard-english	65	78.00	8,888	3Bsuh	10	9	13	5	1		PNB	b
9542	Brooke's Point Palawano	0.00925	6,323	7,027	10,013	MSY44m	31-CJEC-a	southeast palawano		0.10	7	0....	5	3	4	1	3	Palawano, Southwest*	P..	.
9543	Buhid (Bukil, Batangan)	0.01252	8,558	9,511	13,553	MSY44x	31-CJAA-a	buhid		20.00	1,902	0....	9	6	6	5	3	Buhid	PN.	.
9544	Butbut Kalinga	0.00805	5,503	6,115	8,714	MSY44x	31-CEAB-a	butbut		6.00	367	0....	7	5	4	1	1	Kalinga, Butbut	p..	.
9545	Butuanon	0.64103	438,170	486,968	693,922	MSY44x	31-CKGQ-a	butuan-non		90.00	438,271	0.s..	10	7	6	4	1		pn.	b
9546	Caluyanhon	0.04026	27,519	30,584	43,582	MSY44x	31-CKGE-b	caluya-nun		70.00	21,409	0.s..	10	7	6	2	2	Caluyanun	PN.	.
9547	Capisano	1.04714	715,763	795,476	1,133,540	MSY44q	31-CKGM-a	capiz-non		95.00	755,702	0....	10	7	6	2	1		...	b
9548	Casiguran Dumagat (Agta)	0.00212	1,449	1,610	2,295	AUG05	31-CDBD-a	casiguran-agta		15.00	242	0....	8	5	4	5	2	Dumagat: Casiguran*	PN.	.
9549	Cataelano Mandaya	0.03932	26,877	29,870	42,564	MSY44x	31-CKND-b	cataelano		6.00	1,792	0....	7	5	4	1	1		pn.	n
9550	Central Bikol (Naga)	4.58716	3,135,510	3,484,705	4,965,649	MSY44x	31-CKDA-b	legaspi		98.50	3,432,434	1A.u.	10	10	10	5	3	Bicolano, Central	PNB	b
9551	Central Cagayan Dumagat	0.00100	684	760	1,083	AUG05	31-CDBB-a	cagayan-agta		8.00	61	0.s..	7	5	4	5	3	Agta: Cagayan, Central*	PN.	.
9552	Central Palawano	0.05000	34,177	37,983	54,126	MSY44m	31-CJEA-a	central palawano		5.00	1,899	0....	7	3	6	5	2	Palawano	PN.	.
9553	Central Sama	0.12000	82,025	91,160	129,901	MSY44z	31-EACB-a	siasi		0.01	9	1.s..	3	4	3	5	3	Sinama	PN.	.
9554	Central Subanen	0.16104	110,077	122,336	174,327	MSY44x	31-CKQC-a	sindangan		27.00	33,031	0....	9	5	4	5	3	Subanon: Sindangan*	PN.	.
9555	Central Tagbanwa	0.00363	2,481	2,758	3,930	MSY44m	31-CJDB-a	aborlan-tagbanwa		5.00	138	0....	7	5	6	1	0	Tagbanwa	PN.	.
9556	Chabakano Creole	0.56364	385,271	428,178	610,146	MPY53	51-AACB-a	chavacano		90.00	385,360	1c.u.	10	10	11	5	3	Chavacano	PNb	.
9557	Cinamiguin Manobo	0.14815	101,267	112,544	160,374	MSY44x	31-CKOB-a	kinamigin		40.00	45,018	0....	9	5	7	4	1		...	b
9558	Cotabato Manobo	0.02347	16,043	17,829	25,407	MSY44x	31-CKON-a	proper cotabato		2.00	357	0....	6	4	4	5	3	Manobo: Cotabato*	PN.	.
9559	Cuyonon (Cuyo)	0.17749	121,322	134,833	192,135	MSY44x	31-CKGB-a	kuyo-non		60.00	80,900	0....	10	7	6	5	2	Cuyono*	PN.	.
9560	Davaweno	0.29246	199,908	222,172	316,591	MSY44q	31-CKNC-a	west davawenyo		80.00	177,737	0....	10	7	8	5	1		...	b
9561	Dibabawon Manobo	0.02173	14,853	16,508	23,523	MSY44x	31-CKOF-a	dibaba-won		8.90	1,469	0....	7	8	6	5	3	Dibabawon*	PN.	.
9562	Dibagat-Kabugao Isneg	0.01543	10,547	11,722	16,703	MSY44x	31-CCAA-a	dibagat-kabugao		9.00	1,055	0....	7	7	5	5	2	Isnag: Apayao	PN.	.
9563	Ditaylin Dumagat (Alta)	0.00037	253	281	401	AUG05	31-BAAA-a	ditaylin		5.00	14	0....	7	5	4	4	1		...	.
9564	Eastern Cagayan Dumagat	0.00212	1,449	1,610	2,295	AUG05	31-CDBB-a	cagayan-agta		5.00	81	0.s..	7	5	4	5	3	Agta: Cagayan, Central*	PN.	.
9565	Eastern Tawbuid (Batangan	0.00950	6,494	7,217	10,284	MSY44x	31-CJAA	buhid-batangan cluster		50.00	3,608	0....	10	8	6	5	3	Tawbuid, Eastern	PN.	.
9566	Eastern/Southern Bontoc	0.01061	7,252	8,060	11,485	MSY44x	31-CECB	kadaklan-barlig cluster		8.00	645	0.s..	7	5	6	5	3	Bontoc: Eastern*	P..	.
9567	Filipino Mestizo	3.00000	2,050,622	2,278,995	3,247,531	MPY53	31-CKAA-a	proper tagalog		98.00	2,233,415	4Bs..	10	10	11	5	4	Tagalog	PNB	b
9568	Filipino-Chinese Mestizo	0.50000	341,770	379,833	541,255	MSY42a	31-CKAA-a	proper tagalog		94.00	357,043	4Bs..	10	8	10	4	1	Tagalog	PNB	b
9569	Gadang (Baliwon)	0.02700	18,456	20,511	29,228	MSY44x	31-CCCA	ga'dang cluster		5.00	1,026	0....	7	5	6	4	2	Ga'dang*	PN.	.
9570	Gaddang (Cagayan)	0.05581	38,148	42,397	60,415	MSY44x	31-CCCB	gaddang cluster		60.00	25,438	0....	10	7	6	5	3		...	.
9571	Giangan Bagobo (Gulanga)	0.03994	27,301	30,341	43,235	MSY44x	31-DBAA-a	giangan		7.00	2,124	0....	7	7	5	5	3		...	.
9572	Han Chinese (Cantonese)	0.01293	8,838	9,822	13,997	MSY42a	79-AAAM-a	central yue		85.00	8,349	3A.uh	10	7	8	4	1	Chinese, Yue	PNB	b
9573	Han Chinese (Mandarin)	0.00108	738	820	1,169	MSY42a	79-AAAB-ba	kuo-yü	4	80.00	656	2Bsuh	10	7	8	4	1	Chinese: Kuoyu*	PNB	b
9574	Han Chinese (Min Nan)	1.07373	733,938	815,675	1,162,324	MSY42a	79-AAAJ	min-nan cluster		89.90	733,292	2A..h	10	7	10	5	1	Chinese, Min Nan	PNB	b
9575	Han Chinese (Min Nan)	0.00138	943	1,048	1,494	MSY42a	79-AAAJ-ic	chaozhou		85.00	891	1A..h	10	7	8	4	1	Chinese, Min Nan	PNB	b
9576	Hanonoo	0.01721	11,764	13,074	18,630	MSY44x	31-CJBA-a	hanu-noo		4.00	523	0....	6	7	6	5	3	Hanunoo	PN.	.
9577	Higaonon Manobo	0.00884	6,042	6,715	9,569	MSY44x	31-CKOD-a	higao-non		10.00	672	0....	8	5	6	4	2	Higaonon	P..	.
9578	Hiligaynon (Visaya)	9.38864	6,417,516	7,132,221	10,163,301	MSY44q	31-CKGL-e	vehicular hiligay		97.90	6,982,445	2Asu.	10	10	10	5	3	Hiligaynon	PNB	b
9579	Ibanag	0.80112	547,598	608,583	867,221	MSY44x	31-CCBA	ibanag cluster		98.00	596,411	1....	10	7	7	4	3	Ibanag	PN.	b

Continued opposite

Table 8-2 continued

EVANGELIZATION								EVANGELISM			ADDITIONAL DESCRIPTIVE DATA
Ref	D	aC	CG%	r	E	U	W	e	R	T	Locations, civil divisions, literacy, religions, church history, denominations, dioceses, church growth, missions, agencies, ministries, movements
1	28	29	30	31	32	33	34	35	36	37	38
9458	1	6	2.16	4	99.99	0.01	C	523.95	54	10	Lambayeque Region, Incahuasi and Canaris Districts. D=RCC. M=SIL.
9459	1	10	2.84	1	99.90	0.10	C	466.47	68	10	In Loreto and Ucayali. Language divergent from standard Spanish. Many monolinguals. D=RCC.
9460	1	6	2.06	5	99.99	0.01	C	534.79	51	10	Napo River region. Also in Ecuador, Colombia. Tropical forest. D=RCC(VA-San Jose de Amazonas). M=OFM,RBMU.
9461	2	6	2.05	0	99.60	0.40	C	221.19	83	8	40% bilingual in Spanish. Animists 40%. D=RCC(VA-Puerto Maldonado),SDA. M=SIL,SIM,OP,SPM.
9462	2	7	1.10	0	30.00	70.00	A	1.09	164	4	Panagua river. Close to Yaminahua, Sharanahua. Animists 99%. D=RCC(VA-Puerto Maldonado),SDA. M=OP,SIL.
9463	1	6	2.09	4	99.85	0.15	C	390.91	60	9	Northwest Huanuco Department. 75% monolinguals. Animists 5%. D=RCC.
9464	2	7	4.14	0	36.00	64.00	A	6.57	368	4	Yaquerana. 3% bilingual in Spanish. Animists 95%. D=RCC(VA-San Jose de Amazonas),Association of Baptists of Brazil. M=SIL,OFM.
9465	1	7	1.10	0	99.65	0.35	C	241.99	48	8	Most live in Colombia. Tropical rain-forest. Animists 35%. D=RCC(VA-San Jose de Amazonas). M=OFM,SIL.
9466	1	3	0.00	0	9.00	91.00	A	0.00	0	1.03	Headwaters of Embira river. Also in Brazil. Hostile, no contact by 1990. Animists 100%. D=RCC(VA-San Ramon). M=OFM.
9467	1	7	2.64	0	99.70	0.30	C	278.49	84	8	Also in Colombia. Bilingual in Bora or Witotoan. Animists 30%. D=RCC(VA-San Jose de Amazonas). M=OFM,SIL.
9468	1	6	4.14	0	86.00	14.00	B	156.95	154	7	Bilingual in Meneca Huitoto or Murui Huitoto. Animists 50%. D=RCC.
9469	3	10	2.09	8	99.90	0.10	C	517.78	47	10	Mixed-race descendants of slaves. Nonreligious 10%. D=RCC,AoG,SDA. M=SDB,OFM,OP,SJ,FSC.
9470	1	10	0.70	0	99.70	0.30	C	268.27	37	8	Paranapura river. Tropical rain-forest. Nearly extinct. Animists 30%. D=RCC(VA-Yurimaguas). M=CP.
9471	2	7	1.90	0	99.85	0.15	C	394.01	56	9	Putumayo, Napo rivers. 99% bilingual in Spanish. Animists 15%. D=RCC(VA-San Jose de Amazonas),Baptist Ch. M=SIL,OFM.
9472	1	6	2.17	0	99.60	0.40	C	225.57	84	8	South central Junin. 95% bilingual in Spanish, 95% in Ashaninca Campa. Animists 40%. D=RCC(VA-San Ramon). M=OFM,SAM,SIL.
9473	4	6	2.03	5	99.99	0.01	C	556.47	48	10	Junin Department. 18% monolingual, 70% bilingual in Spanish. D=RCC(PN-Tarma; christopagans 50%),CJCLdS,EUSA,IEP. M=SJ,SDB,OFM,OP,FSC,Reapers,SIL.
9474	3	6	1.98	4	99.99	0.01	C	549.25	48	10	Northeast Lima Department. D=RCC(D-Huacho),AoG,CJCLdS.
9475	4	10	2.14	6	99.95	0.05	C	579.07	53	10	Expatriates from Norway, in development. D=IEP,SDA,AoG,Scandinavian Seamen's Church.
9476	2	7	2.85	0	99.70	0.30	C	273.38	91	8	Urban, rain forest around Putumayo river. A few in Colombia. Bilingual in Murui Huitoto, Bora, or Spanish. Animists 30%. D=RCC(VA-San Jose de Amazonas).
9477	1	7	4.23	0	99.70	0.30	C	268.27	127	8	Also in Brazil. Rain forest. All bilingual in Spanish or Cocama. Nearly extinct. Animists 30%. D=RCC(VA-Iquitos). M=OSA.
9478	1	7	2.76	0	98.00	2.00	C	214.62	97	8	Yanayacu river. Tropical rain forest. Bilingual in Spanish. Animists 40%. D=RCC(VA-San Jose de Amazonas). M=SIL,OFM.
9479	5	6	2.02	5	99.99	0.01	C	542.02	50	10	Rural, mountains, forest. 66% monolingual. D=RCC(D-Huanuco),SDA,SA,CJCLdS,IEP. M=EUSA,SDB,OFM,SJ,OP,Reapers,EMBMC,SIM,SIL.
9480	2	6	2.38	0	90.00	10.00	B	164.25	103	7	Asheninca. Central Gran Pajonal area. 21% bilingual in Spanish. Animists 50%. D=RCC,SDA. M=SPM,SAM,SIL.
9481	2	6	1.99	4	99.99	0.01	C	538.41	49	10	Cerro de Pasco Department. Rural; cultivation, produce. D=RCC(PN-Tarma),CJCLdS. M=SDB,OFM,OP,SJ.
9482	9	10	1.96	8	99.98	0.02	C	600.93	42	10	Descendants of slaves. Coastal, urban. D=RCC,AoG,SDA,JWs,IEP,CON,IPA,SA,UPC. M=SFM,EUSA,OFM,FMB.
9483	12	10	1.86	8	99.98	0.02	C	601.90	39	10	Mixed-race persons(Amerindian/White). D=RCC(41 Dioceses),AoG,SDA,IEP,IEINP,CON,CJCLdS,IPA,SA,MEM,JWs,&c. M=SDB,SJ,OFM,EUSA,SIM,WMPL.
9484	10	9	1.94	8	99.95	0.05	C	574.79	46	10	Descendants of conquistadores. D=RCC(41 Dioceses),SDA,AoG,IEP,UPC,CON,CJCLdS,IPA,JWs,&c. M=SDB,OFM,SJ,OP,OSA,CM,MM,CP,CSSR,SIM,FMB.
9485	2	7	2.32	0	99.70	0.30	C	282.94	82	8	East central Urubamba River area; also in Brazil. Amazon forest. Animists 30%. D=RCC(VA-Requena),SDA. M=OFM,SIL,SPM.
9486	0	2	0.00	0	11.00	89.00	A	0.00	0	1.03	Between Tapiche and Blanco rivers. Isolated, with no contact from outside. Unreached. Animists 100%.
9487	1	7	2.06	1	99.91	0.09	C	471.65	53	10	Puno Department and adjacent areas. D=RCC.
9488	1	10	2.67	0	97.00	3.00	C	212.43	95	8	Northeast. Tropical rainforest. Bilingual in Ocaina, Bora, Huitoto, Spanish. Nearly extinct. Animists 40%. D=RCC(VA-San Jose de Amazonas). M=OFM.
9489	1	10	2.34	7	99.64	0.36	C	308.35	49	9	Refugees since 1917 USSR. Nonreligious 30%. D=Russian Orthodox Ch(D-South America). M=OCA.
9490	0	0	6.89	5	99.00	1.00	C	252.94	210	8	Pasco Department, west of Huariaca. Animists 10%. D=RCC.
9491	1	6	3.49	0	65.00	35.00	B	71.17	177	6	Napo river; mainly in Ecuador. Animists 70%. D=RCC(VA-San Jose de Amazonas). M=OFM.
9492	2	6	2.28	0	99.70	0.30	C	286.16	73	8	Upper Purus river, also in Brazil. 93% bilingual in Spanish. Animists 30%. D=RCC(VA-Puerto Maldonado),SDA. M=OP,SIL.
9493	1	7	2.03	0	99.65	0.35	C	263.34	67	8	Northeast middle Ucayali River area. 90% bilingual in Spanish. Animists 35%. D=RCC(VA-Requena,VA-Iquitos,VA-Pucallpa). M=OSA,SIM,SIL,SAIM,PME,OFM.
9494	1	7	2.15	1	99.90	0.10	C	450.04	57	10	Ancash Department. A few animists or nonreligious. D=RCC.
9495	5	6	1.97	4	99.98	0.02	C	565.16	34	10	Mostly in Bolivia, Chile, Argentina. D=SDA,RCC(PN-Juli,D-Tacna; christopagans 60%),AoG,IEINP,CJCLdS. M=MM,OFM,IMCP.
9496	2	6	1.72	4	99.99	0.01	C	549.25	43	10	Southern Junin Department. D=RCC(M-Huancayo; christopagans 50%),CJCLdS. M=SDB,OFM,SJ,OP,FSC,EMBMC,SIL.
9497	1	6	2.05	4	99.86	0.14	C	411.20	57	10	Margos Chaulan Quechua. Huanuco Department. 27% monolinguals. Animists 14%. D=RCC. M=SIL.
9498	1	7	2.25	4	99.70	0.30	C	286.16	72	8	Northern jungle. 40% bilingual in Spanish. Animists 10%. D=RCC(VA-Yurimaguas). M=CP,SIL.
9499	1	10	2.93	0	94.00	6.00	C	205.86	115	8	Tigre river. 30% bilingual in Spanish or Bobonaza-Tigre Quechua. Nearly extinct. Animists 40%. D=RCC(VA-Iquitos). M=OSA.
9500	1	6	2.17	0	99.90	0.10	C	436.90	59	10	Most in Brazil and Colombia. Rain forest. Language isolate. Animists 10%. D=RCC(VA-San Jose de Amazonas). M=OFM,SIL.
9501	1	7	2.50	4	99.99	0.01	C	527.57	60	10	Alamos, Tigre river. Also in Ecuador. Tropical forest. D=RCC(VA-San Jose de Amazonas). M=OFM.
9502	8	10	3.09	8	99.77	0.23	C	415.95	74	10	Expatriates from USA, in development. D=SDA,IEP,JWs,CJCLdS,AoG,RCC,CCCC,CCS.
9503	1	6	2.42	0	41.00	59.00	A	13.46	209	5	Urarinas District. 40% bilingual in Spanish. Animists 91%. D=RCC(VA-Iquitos). M=SIL.
9504	1	6	2.39	0	51.00	49.00	B	27.92	166	5	Northeastern Amazon River region. From Iquitos to Brazil border. 15% bilingual in Spanish. Animists 85%. D=RCC(VA-San Jose de Amazonas). M=SIL,SIM,OFM.
9505	2	7	2.68	0	79.00	21.00	B	115.34	117	7	50% bilingual in Spanish. Animists 60%. D=RCC(VA-Puerto Maldonado),SDA. M=OP,SIL.
9506	3	6	2.07	4	99.99	0.01	C	545.63	50	10	Yauyos Province. Some 15 major dialects. Some monolinguals. D=RCC(PN-Yauyos),AoG,CJCLdS.
9507	1	10	2.28	8	99.90	0.10	C	512.46	51	10	Mixed-race persons(Amerindian/Blacks). D=RCC. M=SDB,OFM,OP,SJ,CSSR,FSC.
9508	0	7	2.01		99.69	0.31	C	256.88	54	8	Koreans (M=PCK-Haptong), Cholon, Spaniards, Costarricans, Arabs, other Europeans, other South Americans. Nonreligious 10%.
Philippines											
9509	2	7	3.46	1	99.60	0.40	C	219.00	109	8	Capul Island, Northwest Samar. The only christianized group among the Sama/Bajaw. Muslims 30%(Shafi Sunnis). D=RCC,UCCP. M=SIL,TAP.
9510	1	6	3.67	0	36.00	64.00	A	3.94	333	4	Central Palawan. Animists 87%, Muslims 10%(living along east and west coasts). D=RCC. M=SIL,NTM,PFM.
9511	1	5	5.82	0	61.00	39.00	B	66.79	306	6	Tarlac Province (Luzon): Maontoc, Labnay, Maamot, San Pedro, Dalayap, Pilyen. Some monolinguals. Animists 60%. D=RCC. M=SIL. M=SIL.
9512	1	6	4.39	0	51.00	49.00	B	26.06	272	5	Luzon, northeastern Abra Province. Bilingual in Ilocano. Animists 86%. D=RCC. M=NTM.
9513	1	6	5.56	0	38.00	62.00	A	5.54	473	4	Central Luzon, Zambales Province. Some bilinguals in Tagalog. Animists 96%. D=RCC. M=NTM,SIL,FIFCOP,TAP,BBFI,GEM,PMF,CMA.
9514	2	6	5.65	0	39.00	61.00	A	5.69	445	4	Agusan del Norte/Sur. Animists 96%. D=RCC,Free Methodist Ch. M=SIL,SPUM,TAP,NTM,Reality of Christ,CBFMS,UPM,FMB.
9515	1	6	2.08	0	95.00	5.00	C	208.05	80	8	Agutaya Island, 5 smaller islands, 3 towns, Palawan, also Mindoro and Manila. Some bilinguals in Cuyonon, Tagalog, English. Animists 10%. D=RCC. M=TAP,SIL.
9516	2	7	2.66	1	99.90	0.10	C	436.90	69	10	Aklan Province, northern Panay. Few animists. D=RCC,AoG. M=TAP,EBT,SIL. R=FEBC.
9517	1	6	1.40	0	39.00	61.00	A	7.11	169	4	East of Quezon Province, Luzon. Bilingual in Tagalog. Animists 95%. D=RCC. M=NTM.
9518	4	6	5.90	0	79.00	21.00	B	115.34	228	7	North central Mindoro. Animists 30%. D=RCC(VA-Calapan),TCA,UCCP,ICFG. M=OMF,ABCUSA.
9519	1	6	5.95	1	99.97	0.03	C	456.72	148	10	Western Albay Province, and Buhi, Camarines Sur, Luzon. Some bilinguals in Central Bicolano. Few animists. D=RCC. M=CIC.
9520	1	5	3.15	0	37.00	63.00	A	13.50	307	5	San Marcelino, Subic City, Olongapa, in Zambales (Luzon). Isolated. Animists 90%. D=RCC.
9521	1	10	7.24	8	99.95	0.05	C	533.99	143	10	Children of USA servicemen on US military bases. D=RCC.
9522	1	6	5.24	0	40.00	60.00	A	5.84	406	4	Ifugao Province, Luzon. Animists 96%. D=RCC. M=SIL,TAP,Send International,EPM,GEM,NELBF,WVI,FMB.
9523	3	6	4.09	0	44.00	56.00	A	11.24	297	5	Napayo, Kiangan Ifugao Province, Luzon. Animists 93%. D=RCC,UCCP,UCMP. M=SIL,NTM,EPM,GEM,NELBF.
9524	1	6	3.76	0	36.00	64.00	A	5.25	362	4	Luzon, Antique Province. Very bilingual. Negritos. Animists 96%. D=RCC. M=Oriental Missionary Crusade.
9525	0	10	3.19	7	46.10	53.90	A	0.16	231	3	Traders. Muslims 100%(mostly Sunnis). M=FMB.
9526	0	7	2.22	0	59.00	41.00	B	64.60	150	6	Quirino Province, 4 towns. Isolated. Some bilinguals. Animists 70%.
9527	2	6	4.78	0	41.00	59.00	A	5.98	386	4	Negritos. Northwest Davao. Animists 96%. D=RCC,ICFG. M=Things to Come Mission,OMF,SPUM,SIL,TAP,GBFMS,UPM.
9528	1	6	2.50	0	35.00	65.00	A	6.38	274	4	Panay Island, small groups in all provinces. Some bilinguals in Hiligaynon, Kinaray-a. Animists 95%. D=RCC. M=TAP,COGWMP,PMF.
9529	1	6	6.00	0	42.00	58.00	A	9.19	436	4	Ifugao Province, Luzon. Animists 94%. D=RCC. M=SIL,TAP,EPM,GEM,NELBF,SEND.
9530	1	6	4.23	0	97.00	3.00	C	212.43	139	8	Babuyan Island, north of Luzon. Animists 10%. D=RCC. M=SIL,TAP.
9531	0	5	0.00	0	11.00	89.00	A	0.00	0	1.04	Sulu Archipelago, Mindanao. Sama Dilaut, spoken widely throughout Sulu-Tawi-Tawi area. Nomadic boat-dwellers. Muslims 100%(Shafi Sunnis, lightly islamized).
9532	0	4	0.70	1	22.01	77.99	A	0.00	151	1.08	Cagayan de Sulu and Palawan Islands. Also in Sabah (Malaysia). Some bilinguals in Tausug. Muslims 100%. M=RCC,SIL.
9533	3	6	4.50	0	44.00	56.00	A	11.24	323	5	Eastern Bontoc Province, Luzon. Agriculturalists. Animists 73%. D=RCC,PEC,Balangao Bible Ch. M=SIL,TAP.
9534	1	6	4.19	0	42.00	58.00	A	12.26	318	5	Ifugao Province, Luzon. Dialect of Amganad Ifugao. Animists 92%. D=RCC. M=EPM,SIL,TAP,GEM,NELBF.
9535	2	7	9.14	0	99.70	0.30	C	288.71	238	8	Romblon Province, between Masbate and Mindoro. Bilingual in Tagalog. Forestry, fishermen. Animists 5%. D=Baptist Chs,RCC. M=SIL,TAP,GMF.
9536	1	10	2.27	4	99.93	0.07	C	539.72	56	10	Settlers originally from Spain. Strongly Catholic. Nonreligious/atheists 7%. D=RCC. M=SJ.
9537	1	6	3.70	0	32.00	68.00	A	5.84	402	4	Negritos. Mariveles, Bataan Province, Luzon. Bilingual in Tagalog. Animists 95%. D=RCC.
9538	6	6	8.91	0	81.00	19.00	B	115.30	324	7	North central Mindanao, southern Bukidnon, northeastern Cotabato, Agusan del Sur. Many animists, 31%. . D=RCC,FMCP,BBFP,SDA,Christian Advent Ch,RCC.
9539	1	6	5.25	0	49.00	51.00	A	28.61	332	5	Ba-ay Valley and Licuan Abra Province, Luzon. Bilingual in Ilocano. Animists 84%. D=RCC. M=SIL.
9540	3	6	8.49	0	93.00	7.00	B	169.72	280	7	West Pangasinan Province, Luzon. Literate in Ilocano, Tagalog. D=RCC,BBFP,Pentecostals. M=SIL,NTM,TAP,FIFCOP,PBS,Methodists.
9541	5	10	2.13	8	99.78	0.22	C	435.59	59	10	Expatriates from Britain, in development. Nonreligious/atheists 10%. D=PEC(Anglican),UMCP,UCCP,SDA,JWs. M=FMB.
9542	0	6	1.96	0	24.10	75.90	A	0.08	302	2	Southeastern Palawan. Lingua franca: Tausug. Muslims 70%(Shafi Sunnis; coastal; islamization continuing), pagans/animists 25%. M=SIL,TAP,OMC,CMML.
9543	4	6	5.39	0	61.00	39.00	B	44.53	273	6	Southern Mindoro. Animists 50%. D=RCC(VA-Calapan),TCA,UCCP,ICFG. M=OMF,GMF,ABCUSA.
9544	1	6	3.67	0	31.00	69.00	A	6.78	384	4	Luzon, Butbut, Tinglayan, Kalinga-Apayao Province. Animists 94%. D=RCC. M=TAP.
9545	1	6	2.74	0	99.90	0.10	C	430.33	72	10	Language of Butuan City and surroundings, Agusan del Norte Province, Mindanao. Bilingual in Cebuano. Many nominal Christians. Y=1580 (Jesuit mission station).
9546	1	6	2.90	0	99.70	0.30	C	275.94	91	8	Caluya Islands, Antique. D=RCC. M=SIL,TAP.
9547	1	6	2.72	0	99.95	0.05	C	450.77	72	10	Northeast Panay. Close to Hiligaynon. Bilingual in Tagalog, Hiligaynon. Few animists. D=RCC.
9548	1	6	3.24	0	49.00	51.00	A	26.82	237	5	East coast of Luzon, north Quezon Province. Negritos, hunter-gatherers. Animists 85%. D=RCC. M=NTM,SIL.
9549	1	6	5.33	0	36.00	64.00	A	7.88	457	4	Town of Cateel, Davao Oriental, Mindanao. Bilingual in Mansaka. Animists 94%. D=RCC. M=FMB.
9550	9	7	2.42	1	99.99	0.01	C	584.22	52	10	Southern Catanduanes, Northern Sorsogon, Albay, Camarines, Luzon; Naga City. D=RCC,PIC,INC,UCCP,UMCP,JWs,SDA,AoG,CON. M=DOFC,CIC,FMB,APM.
9551	2	6	4.20	0	44.00	56.00	A	12.84	324	5	Negritos. Northeast Luzon. Animists 92%. D=Ch of the Living God,GBCP. M=SIL,TAP,NTM.
9552	1	8	5.39	0	43.00	57.00	A	7.84	388	4	Central Palawan. Lingua franca: Tausug. Animists 85%, Muslims 10%(Shafi Sunnis). D=RCC. M=NTM,OMC.
9553	0	6	2.22	1	31.01	68.99	A	0.01	241	2	Sulu Province. Also Sabah(Malaysia). Dilaut-Bajao are still animists, 50%; Moros (Moors) are Muslims 50%(Shafi Sunnis). M=SIL,TAP,SPUM,CMA,UCCP.
9554	2	6	8.44	0	66.00	34.00	B	65.04	379	6	Eastern Zamboango Peninsula, Sulu Archipelago. Animists 70%, Muslims 2%(Shafi Sunnis). D=Baptist Ch,CAMACOP. M=SIL,TAP,CMA.
9555	0	6	2.66	0	33.00	67.00	A	6.02	279	4	Northern Palawan; 235 families. Close to Cuyonon. Animists 95%.
9556	4	10	2.39	1	99.90	0.10	C	482.89	59	10	Caviteno, Ternateno, &c. In 60 out of 66 Provinces. D=RCC,CAMACOP,UMCP,ICFG. M=SIL,SPUM,CMA,UPM.
9557	1	7	8.78	0	78.00	22.00	B	113.88	332	7	Camiguin Island, north of Mindanao. Bilingual in Cebuano. Animists 60%. D=Faith Baptist Ch. M=SPUM.
9558	0	6	3.64	0	34.00	66.00	A	2.48	348	4	South Cotabato, Mindanao. Includes small alleged primeval Tasaday tribe. Animists 98%. M=CMA,SIL,SPUM,TAP,PEE.
9559	1	6	2.42	0	99.60	0.40	C	219.00	85	8	Palawan coast, Cuyo Islands between Palawan and Panay. Close to Ratagnon. Lingua franca. Many animists. Strong Christians. D=RCC. M=ABWE,PBS.
9560	1	7	2.39	0	99.80	0.20	C	353.32	70	9	Davao Oriental, Davao del Sur, Mindanao; Davao City. Synthesis of Tagalog/Cebuano. D=RCC. SIL,Reality of Christ.
9561	5	6	5.12	0	47.90	52.10	A	15.56	332	5	Manguagan, Davao del Norte, Mindanao. Animists 91%. D=RCC,CAMACOP,Baptists,ICFG,SDA. M=SIL,OMF,FMB,CMA.
9562	4	6	4.77	0	46.00	54.00	A	15.11	325	5	Northern Apayao, Luzon. Animists 50%. D=RCC,Baptists,Pentecostals,UCCP. M=SIL,NTM.
9563	0	6	2.67	0	31.00	69.00	A	5.65	324	4	Northern Alta; Baler Negritos. Luzon, Quezon Province. Animists 95%. M=NTM.
9564	1	6	4.49	0	40.00	60.00	A	7.30	376	4	Northeast Luzon, from Divilacan Bay to Palaui Island. 11 dialects. Hunter-gatherers. Animists 95%. D=RCC. M=SIL,TAP,NTM,OMC.
9565	4	6	6.07	0	92.00	8.00	B	167.90	201	7	Central Mindoro. Alternate names: Eastern Tabuid, Tiron, Barangan, Binatangan. Animists 15%. D=RCC(VA-Calapan),TCA,UCCP,ICFG. M=GMF,ABCUSA,OMF.
9566	1	6	4.25	0	42.00	58.00	A	12.26	322	5	Central Mountain Province, Luzon. Animists 92%. D=Pentecostal Chs. M=ABWE,SIL,TAP,CICM.
9567	9	10	2.42	5	99.98	0.02	C	622.39	51	10	Mixed-race persons. D=RCC(65 Dioceses),PIC(30 Dioceses),INC,UCCP,UMCP,CDCC,SDA,JWs,AoG. M=SVD,SJ,SSC,OMI,CICM,DOFC,OP,EPM,FIFCOP,UECP.
9568	1	10	2.37	5	99.94	0.06	C	555.82	51	10	Mixed-race persons (Chinese/Filipino). Mainly urban. D=RCC.
9569	1	6	4.74	0	40.00	60.00	A	7.30	371	4	Paracelis, foothills, Mt Province, Luzon. Uplands. Related to Itawit. Animists 95%. D=RCC. M=TAP,SIL.
9570	1	6	8.16	0	97.00	3.00	C	212.43	250	8	Central Isabela; Bagabag, Solano; Bayombong in Nueva Vizcaya, Luzon. Animists 10%. D=Lutheran Ch. M=BBM,TAP,SIL,ILM,LCMS.
9571	4	7	5.50	0	42.00	58.00	A	10.73	403	5	Davao City, Mindanao; eastern slopes of Mt Apo. Animists 63%. D=PBM,CAMACOP,ICFG,UCCP. M=SPUM,CMA,JCETP,CBFMS,FMB.
9572	1	10	4.12	8	99.85	0.15	C	474.68	85	10	Originally from Guangdong. Buddhists/folk-religionists 15%. D=RCC.
9573	1	10	5.23	7	99.80	0.20	C	429.24	110	10	Chinese businessmen from Mainland China or diaspora. Folk Buddhists 20%. D=RCC.
9574	3	10	3.88	6	99.90	0.10	C	531.25	77	10	Chinese control 66% all sales of 67 biggest businesses. Folk Buddhists 10%. D=RCC(200,000 Chinese),UECP,GGC. M=FMB.
9575	1	10	-2.87	6	99.85	0.15	C	462.27	2	10	Chinese immigrants from South China coast. Folk Buddhists 15%. D=RCC.
9576	4	6	4.04	0	41.00	59.00	A	5.98	315	4	Southern Oriental Mindoro. South Mangyan group. Animists 96%. D=RCC(VA-Calapan),TCA,UCCP,ICFG. M=OMF,GMF,ABCUSA.
9577	1	7	4.30	0	43.00	57.00	A	15.69	317	5	Misamis Oriental, Mindanao. Related to Binukid. Some bilinguals in Cebuano. Animists 90%. D=RCC. M=NTM,SIL.
9578	9	6	2.59	5	99.98	0.02	C	596.39	54	10	Iloilo and Capiz Provinces, Panay, Visayas. Also USA. D=RCC,PIC,INC,UCCP,UMCP,SDA,JWs,AoG,BCP. M=PBS,LBI,DOFC,PMF,FMB. R=FEBC,AWR.
9579	2	6	3.23	0	99.98	0.02	C	515.08	74	10	Isabela and Cagayan Provinces, Luzon. Bilingual in Ilocano, Tagalog. Few animists. D=RCC,UMC. M=SIL,TAP,PBS,FMB.

Continued overleaf

Table 8-2 continued

PEOPLE		POPULATION				IDENTITY CODE		LANGUAGE		CHURCH		MINISTRY		SCRIPTURE	
Ref 1	*Ethnic name* 2	*P%* 3	*In 1995* 4	*In 2000* 5	*In 2025* 6	*Race* 7	*Language* 8	*Autoglossonym* 9	*S* 10	*AC* 11	*Members* 12	*Jayuh* 13-17	*dwa xcmc mi* 18 19 20 21 22	*Biblioglossonym* 23	*Pub ss* 24-26 27
9580	Igorot (Central Bontok)	0.05173	35,360	39,297	55,998	MSY44x	31-CECA-a	i-gorot		8.00	3,144	0....	7 7 6 5 3	Bontoc: Central*	PN. .
9581	Ilianen Manobo	0.02013	13,760	15,292	21,791	MSY44x	31-CKOL-a	ilia-nen		9.00	1,376	0.s..	7 7 5 5 2	Manobo: Ilianen*	PN. .
9582	Ilocano	11.11819	7,599,734	8,446,100	12,035,557	MSY44f	31-CBAA-b	vehicular ilocano		97.80	8,260,286	2A.u.	10 10 10 5 3	Ilokano*	PNB b
9583	Ilongot (Bukalot)	0.01438	9,829	10,924	15,567	MSY44x	31-CGBA-a	i-lon-got		3.00	328	0.s..	6 4 5 4 3	Ilongot	PN. .
9584	Indo-Pakistani	0.00400	2,734	3,039	4,330	CNN25g	59-AAFO-e	general hindi		1.00	30	3Asuh	6 4 2 4 1		pnb b
9585	Indonesian	0.05000	34,177	37,983	54,126	MSY44k	31-PHAA-c	bahasa-indonesia		2.00	760	4Asuh	6 4 8 5 1	Indonesian	PNB b
9586	Inibaloi (Nabaloi)	0.20616	140,919	156,613	223,170	MSY44x	31-CGAE-a	i-baloi		8.00	12,529	1....	7 5 5 4 3	Ibaloi	PN. .
9587	Inlaod Itneg	0.02000	13,671	15,193	21,650	MSY44x	31-CEAA-b	inlaod		15.00	2,279	0....	8 5 6 2 1		p.. b
9588	Insinai (Isnay)	0.01327	9,071	10,081	14,365	MSY44x	31-CFAA-a	i-sinai		60.00	6,048	0....	10 7 7 2 1		... b
9589	Iraya (Alag-bako)	0.01565	10,697	11,889	16,941	MSY44x	31-CIAA	iraya cluster		9.00	1,070	0....	7 7 6 5 2	Iraya	PN. b
9590	Iriga Bicolano	0.42288	289,056	321,247	457,772	MSY44x	31-CKFA-a	rinconada		70.00	224,873	0....	10 7 7 2 1		... b
9591	Isarog Agta	0.00186	1,271	1,413	2,013	MSY44x	31-CDBB-a	cagayan-agta		5.00	71	0.s..	7 5 3 1 0	Agta: Cagayan, Central*	PN. .
9592	Itawit (Tawit)	0.24799	169,511	188,389	268,452	MSY44x	31-CCBC-a	itawis		65.00	122,453	1....	10 7 7 5 2	Itawes*	PN. b
9593	Ivatan	0.06039	41,279	45,876	65,373	MSY44x	31-CABA	north ivatan cluster		68.00	31,196	0.s..	10 7 7 5 1	Ivatan	PN. .
9594	Iwaak	0.00431	2,946	3,274	4,666	MSY44x	31-CGAB-a	i-wak		4.00	131	0....	6 4 4 4 3		....
9595	Japanese	0.05000	34,177	37,983	54,126	MSY45a	45-CAAA-a	koku-go		2.00	760	1B.uh	6 4 8 4 2	Japanese	PNB b
9596	Jewish	0.00134	916	1,018	1,451	CMT35	31-CKAA-a	proper tagalog		0.25	3	4Bs..	5 3 3 1 0	Tagalog	PNB b
9597	Kaagan Kalagan	0.01208	8,257	9,177	13,077	MSY44x	31-CKNF-a	kagan		7.00	642	0.s..	7 5 6 5 3	Kalagan: Kagan*	P.. .
9598	Kagayanen (Cagayan)	0.05878	40,179	44,653	63,630	MSY44x	31-CKOA	kagayanen cluster		70.00	31,257	0.s..	10 7 7 2 2	Kagayanen	P.. .
9599	Kalagan	0.10345	70,712	78,587	111,986	MSY44x	31-CKNE	kalagan cluster		1.00	786	0.s..	6 4 2 0 2	Kalagan	P.. .
9600	Kalamian Tagbanwa (Baras)	0.01007	6,883	7,650	10,901	MSY44m	31-CJCA-b	kalamian-tagbanwa.		4.00	306	0....	6 4 2 5 3	Tagbanwa: Kalamian*	P.. .
9601	Kamayo	0.01000	6,835	7,597	10,825	MSY44x	31-CKNA	kamayo cluster		50.00	3,798	0....	10 7 5 2 1		... b
9602	Kankanaey (Kibungan)	0.23472	160,441	178,309	254,087	MSY44x	31-CECD	south kankanay cluster		39.00	69,540	1....	9 8 5 5 3	Kankanaey: Central	PN. .
9603	Karaga Mandaya (Mandayan)	0.00588	4,019	4,467	6,365	MSY44x	31-CKND-c	karaga		1.00	45	0....	6 4 2 1 0		pn. n
9604	Karaw	0.00224	1,531	1,702	2,425	MSY44x	31-CGAD-a	karao		8.00	136	0....	7 5 5 2 1	Karao	... .
9605	Karolanos	0.02000	13,671	15,193	21,650	MSY44q	31-CKLA-a	karolanos		40.00	6,077	0....	9 6 5 2 1		... b
9606	Kasiguranin	0.02349	16,056	17,845	25,428	MSY44x	31-CDBE-a	kasiguranin		60.00	10,707	0....	10 7 5 2 1		... b
9607	Kayapa Kallahan (Kalkali)	0.02586	17,676	19,645	27,994	MSY44x	31-CGAC-a	kayapa		6.00	1,179	0....	7 5 5 5 1	Ikalahan*	PN. .
9608	Kiangan Ifugao (Gilipanes)	0.05033	34,403	38,234	54,483	MSY44x	31-CEDC-a	kiangan		9.00	3,441	0....	7 7 6 5 3	Ifugao: Kiangan*	PN. .
9609	Kinaray-a (Antiqueno)	0.54767	374,355	416,046	592,859	MSY44q	31-CKGC	kinaray cluster		80.00	332,837	1a...	10 8 7 5 2	Kinaray-a	P.. b
9610	Korean	0.03000	20,506	22,790	32,475	MSY46	45-AAAA-b	kukŏ		35.00	7,976	2A...	9 8 9 5 3	Korean	PNB b
9611	Koronadal Bilaan	0.20130	137,597	152,921	217,909	MSY44x	31-DABB-a	koronadal		45.00	68,814	1.s..	9 7 6 5 3	Blaan: Koronadal*	PN. .
9612	Lapuyan Subanun	0.05433	37,137	41,273	58,813	MSY44x	31-CKQB-a	lapuyan		9.00	3,715	0....	7 6 6 5 3	Subanon: Margosatubig*	PN. .
9613	Looknon (Unhan)	0.11345	77,548	86,184	122,811	MSY44x	31-CKGF	inonhan cluster		70.00	60,329	0....	10 7 6 2 1	Inonhan	... b
9614	Low Malay Creole	1.50000	1,025,311	1,139,498	1,623,766	MSY44k	31-PHAA-d	malayu-pasar	3	0.01	114	1csuh	3 3 2 0 3	Malay: Low	PNb b
9615	Lower Tanudan Kalinga	0.01107	7,567	8,409	11,983	MSY44x	31-CEAB-h	lower tanudan		6.00	505	0....	7 5 4 4 2	Kalinga: Tanudan*	P.. .
9616	Lubuagan Kalinga	0.08052	55,039	61,168	87,164	MSY44x	31-CEAC-d	lubuagan		8.00	4,893	0....	7 5 4 4 2	Kalinga, Lubuagan	PN. .
9617	Mabaka Valley Kalinga	0.01000	6,835	7,597	10,825	MSY44x	31-CEAB-c	mabaka		6.00	456	0....	7 5 5 1 1		p.. p
9618	Madukayang Kalinga	0.00240	1,640	1,823	2,598	MSY44x	31-CEAB-d	madukayang		7.00	128	0....	7 5 4 1 1	Kalinga, Madukayang	p.. .
9619	Mag-anchi Sambal	0.00737	5,038	5,599	7,978	AUG05	31-CHDA-a	mag-anchi-agta		20.00	1,120	0....	9 5 4 2 1	Ayta: Mag-anchi*	P.. .
9620	Mag-indi Sambal	0.00439	3,001	3,335	4,752	AUG05	31-CHGA-a	mag-indi-agta		15.00	500	0....	8 5 4 1 1	Ayta, Mag-indi	... .
9621	Magahat (Ata-man)	0.01000	6,835	7,597	10,825	MSY44x	31-CKOH-a	manobo-agta		20.00	1,519	0.s..	9 5 5 2 1	Manobo: Ata*	PN. b
9622	Magindanaw (Ilanum)	1.56477	1,069,584	1,188,701	1,693,880	MSY44x	31-CKPB	magindanao cluster		0.05	594	2.s..	4 4 5 5 3	Magindanao*	P.. .
9623	Malay (Melaju)	0.20000	136,708	151,933	216,502	MSY44k	31-PHAA-b	bahasa-malaysia		0.02	30	1asuh	3 3 6 0 1	Malay	PNB b
9624	Malaynon	0.02096	14,327	15,923	22,689	MSY44q	31-CKGD-d	malay-non		60.00	9,554	1....	10 7 6 2 1		p.. .
9625	Mamanwa Negrito	0.00302	2,064	2,294	3,269	AUG05	31-CKMA-a	mamanwa		2.00	46	0....	6 4 3 5 3	Minamanwa*	PN. .
9626	Mansaka Mandaya	0.07635	52,188	58,000	82,650	MSY44x	31-CKND-d	mansaka		6.00	3,480	0....	7 5 3 5 3	Mansaka	PN. .
9627	Maranao (Lanao, Ranao)	1.41575	967,723	1,075,496	1,532,564	MSY44x	31-CKPA-a	ma-ranao		2.00	21,510	2.s..	6 4 3 5 2	Maranao	PN. .
9628	Masadiit Itneg	0.01293	8,838	9,822	13,997	MSY44x	31-CEAA-c	masadiit		17.00	1,670	0....	8 5 6 2 1		p.. b
9629	Masbateno	0.58854	402,291	447,093	637,101	MSY44x	31-CKGI-b	masbate--o	2	85.00	380,029	1....	10 7 7 4 2	Masbatenyo	PN. .
9630	Matig-Salug Manobo	0.04924	33,658	37,406	53,303	MSY44x	31-CKOI-a	matig-salug		3.00	1,122	0.s..	6 4 5 5 3	Manobo: Matig Salug*	P.. .
9631	Mayoyao Ifugao	0.02623	17,929	19,926	28,394	MSY44x	31-CEDB-d	mayoyao		5.00	996	0....	7 5 5 5 3	Ifugao: Mayoyao*	Pn. .
9632	Molbog	0.01000	6,835	7,597	10,825	MSY44x	31-CJEE-a	molbog		0.10	8	0....	5 4 2 3 3	Molbog	P.. b
9633	Mount Iraya Agta	0.00042	287	319	455	MSY44x	31-CKDB-b	iraya-agta		70.00	223	0....	10 7 6 2 1		... b
9634	Mount Iriga Agta	0.00318	2,174	2,416	3,442	AUG05	31-CKFC-a	iriga-agta		50.00	1,208	0....	10 6 5 2 1		....
9635	North Camarines Agta	0.00042	287	319	455	AUG05	31-CDCA-d	camarines-agta		30.00	96	0.s..	9 5 6 1 0		pn. .
9636	Northern Bikol Sorsogon	0.19969	136,496	151,698	216,167	MSY44x	31-CKGI-c	north sorsogon		80.00	121,358	1....	10 7 6 4 1		pn. b
9637	Northern Cagayan Negrito	0.00092	629	699	996	AUG05	31-CCBB-a	pamplona-agta		5.00	35	0.s..	7 5 4 5 3	Atta*	PN. .
9638	Northern Catanduanes Biko	0.15271	104,383	116,008	165,310	MSY44x	31-CKEA-a	pandan		70.00	81,206	0....	10 7 6 2 1		....
9639	Northern Kalinga	0.04458	30,472	33,866	48,258	MSY44x	31-CEAB-b	limos-liwan		15.00	5,080	0....	8 5 4 4 2	Kalinga: Limos*	P.. .
9640	Northern Sinama (Sibuku)	0.12078	82,558	91,752	130,746	MSY44z	31-EACA-a	balingingi		0.05	46	0.s..	4 4 2 5 3	Sama: Balangingi*	P.. .
9641	Obo Manobo (Kidapawan)	0.01814	12,399	13,780	19,637	MSY44x	31-CKOJ-a	obo		4.20	579	0....	6 4 5 4 2	Manobo: Obo*	P.. .
9642	Palawan Batak Negrito	0.00056	383	425	606	AUG05	31-CJDA-a	east batak		4.00	17	0....	6 4 4 4 2		....
9643	Pampango	3.12955	2,139,174	2,377,410	3,387,771	MSY44x	31-CHBA-b	vehicular pampangan		97.60	2,320,352	1a.u.	10 9 9 5 3	Pampango*	PNB .
9644	Pangasinese	2.33000	1,592,649	1,770,019	2,522,249	MSY44x	31-CGAF-a	pangasinan		97.30	1,722,229	1A.u.	10 9 9 5 3	Pangasinan	PNB .
9645	Pangutaran Sama	0.03448	23,568	26,193	37,325	MSY44x	31-EACC-a	panguturan		1.00	262	0.s..	6 4 2 5 3	Sama: Pangutaran*	PN. n
9646	Paranan	0.02013	13,760	15,292	21,791	AUG05	31-CDBA-a	paranan		70.00	10,704	0....	10 7 7 5 3	Paranan	P.. .
9647	Porohanon	0.03966	27,109	30,128	42,932	MSY44x	31-CKGO-a	poroha-non		75.00	22,596	0....	10 7 7 2 1		....
9648	Pudtol Atta	0.00094	643	714	1,018	AUG05	31-CCBB-b	pudtol-agta		4.00	29	0.s..	6 4 4 4 1		pn. .
9649	Rajah Kabungsuan Manobo	0.01000	6,835	7,597	10,825	MSY44x	31-CKOG-a	kabunsuwan		50.00	3,798	0....	10 6 5 2 1		....
9650	Remontado Agta	0.00334	2,283	2,537	3,616	AUG05	31-CHHA-a	sinauna		4.00	101	0....	6 4 4 1 1		... b
9651	Romblon	0.34485	235,719	261,970	373,304	MSY44x	31-CKGH-a	rombloma-non		88.00	230,534	1....	10 7 5 5 3	Romblomanon	....
9652	Sama Mapun (Jama Mapun)	0.03020	20,643	22,942	32,692	MSY44z	31-EACE-a	mapun		0.04	9	0....	3 4 3 5 3	Mapun*	PN. .
9653	Sangab Mandaya	0.01000	6,835	7,597	10,825	MSY44x	31-CKND-a	sangab		10.00	760	0....	8 5 5 1 1		pn. .
9654	Sangil (Sanggil)	0.01711	11,695	12,998	18,522	MSY44y	31-RBAD-j	sangil		1.00	130	1....	6 4 2 1 0	Sangil	Pn. .
9655	Sangirese (Sangihe)	0.11072	75,682	84,110	119,856	MSY44y	31-RBAD	sangir cluster		91.00	76,540	4....	10 7 11 4 2	Sangirese	PN. b
9656	Sarangani Bilaan	0.31295	213,914	237,737	338,772	MSY44x	31-DABB-b	sarangani-blaan		80.00	190,190	1.s..	10 5 6 5 3	Blaan: Sarangani*	PN. .
9657	Sarangani Manobo	0.06035	41,252	45,846	65,330	MSY44x	31-CKOO	sarangani cluster		50.00	22,923	0....	10 5 6 5 3	Manobo: Sarangani*	PN. .
9658	Sorsogon Ayta	0.00007	48	53	76	MSY44x	31-CKHA-a	sorsogon-agta		80.00	43	0....	10 7 7 1 1		....
9659	Southern Alta (Kabaloan)	0.00196	1,340	1,489	2,122	AUG05	31-CDCA	south dumagat cluster		4.00	60	0.s..	6 4 4 4 1	Dumagat: Kabulowan	PN. b
9660	Southern Atta	0.00096	656	729	1,039	AUG05	31-CCBD-b	faire-agta		4.00	29	0....	6 4 4 4 1		....
9661	Southern Bikol Sorsogon	0.43463	297,087	330,173	470,492	MSY44x	31-CKGJ-a	south sorsogon		80.00	264,139	0....	10 7 7 2 2		... b
9662	Southern Catanduanes Biko	0.17111	116,961	129,986	185,228	MSY44x	31-CKDC-a	virac		85.00	110,488	0....	10 7 8 2 1		... b
9663	Southern Itneg	0.02000	13,671	15,193	21,650	MSY44x	31-CEAA-d	south itneg		17.00	2,583	0....	8 5 6 2 1		p.. b
9664	Southern Kalinga	0.02416	16,514	18,354	26,153	MSY44x	31-CCCA-f	kalinga		8.00	1,468	0....	7 5 5 4 3	Kalinga: Southern*	PN. .
9665	Southern Sama	0.05173	35,360	39,297	55,998	MSY44z	31-EACB-e	si-butuq		0.01	4	1.s..	3 4 4 5 3	Sama: Southern*	Pn. n
9666	Southwest Palawano	0.05000	34,177	37,983	54,126	MSY44m	31-CJEC-a	southeast palawano		5.00	1,899	0....	7 5 5 4 2	Palawano, Southwest*	P.. .
9667	Spaniard	0.01121	7,662	8,516	12,135	CEW21k	51-AABB-c	general español	4	96.00	8,175	2B.uh	10 9 15 5 4	Spanish	PNB b
9668	Sulod	0.02898	19,809	22,015	31,371	MSY44x	31-CKIA-a	sulod-agta		3.00	660	0....	6 4 5 1 1		....
9669	Surigaonon	0.70000	478,478	531,766	757,757	MSY44x	31-CKGR-a	surigao-non		89.00	473,271	0....	10 8 7 5 3		... b
9670	Tadyawan (Tadianan)	0.00392	2,679	2,978	4,243	MSY44x	31-CICA-a	tadyawan		4.00	119	0....	6 7 5 5 2	Tadyawan	....
9671	Tagabawa Manobo (Bagobo)	0.06897	47,144	52,394	74,661	MSY44x	31-CKOM-a	tagabawa		20.00	10,479	0....	9 5 6 5 3	Tagabawa*	P.. .
9672	Tagakaulu Kalagan	0.08888	60,753	67,519	96,214	MSY44x	31-CKNG-a	tagakaulu		19.00	12,829	0....	8 4 5 5 3	Kalagan: Tagakaulu*	P.. .
9673	Tagalog (Pilipino)	20.46855	13,991,084	15,549,241	22,157,420	MSY44o	31-CKAA-a	proper tagalog	85	98.30	15,284,904	4Bs..	10 10 12 5 5	Tagalog	PNB b
9674	Tausug (Moro Joloano)	0.77528	529,935	588,953	839,249	MSY44x	31-CKGQ-d	vehicular tau-sug		0.10	589	0.s..	5 4 4 5 3	Tausug	PN. .
9675	Tiboli (Kiamba)	0.13794	94,288	104,788	149,321	MSY44x	31-DABA	tboli cluster		10.00	10,479	1.s..	8 7 4 5 3	Tboli	PN. .
9676	Tina Sambal (Zambal)	0.13085	89,441	99,402	141,646	AUG05	31-CHAB-a	tina		60.00	59,641	0....	10 8 6 5 3	Sambal: Tina*	Pn. .
9677	Tiruray (Teduray)	0.08068	55,148	61,290	87,337	MSY44x	31-DAAA-a	tiruray		20.00	12,258	0.s..	9 5 6 5 3	Tiruray	PN. .
9678	Tuboy Subanon	0.01814	12,399	13,780	19,637	MSY44x	31-CKQA	tuboy-salog cluster		2.00	276	0....	6 4 4 5 3		....
9679	USA White	0.15000	102,531	113,950	162,377	CEW19s	52-ABAC-s	general american		77.00	87,741	1Bsuh	10 9 12 5 2	English*	PNB b
9680	Umiray Dumagat (Agta)	0.01007	6,883	7,650	10,901	AUG05	31-CDCA-b	umiray-agta		8.00	612	0.s..	7 5 5 5 3	Dumagat: Umiray*	PN. b
9681	Upper Tanudan Kalinga	0.00469	3,206	3,563	5,077	MSY44x	31-CEAB-g	upper tanudan		7.00	249	0....	7 5 6 2 1		p.. .
9682	Villaviciosa Agta	0.02000	13,671	15,193	21,650	MSY44x	31-CCBB-c	villaviciosa-agta		8.00	1,215	0.s..	7 5 5 2 1		pn. .
9683	Visayan (Bisayan, Cebu)	19.00073	12,987,769	14,434,190	20,568,489	MSY44q	31-CKGP-a	vehicular cebuan		98.20	14,174,374	2Asu.	10 10 11 5 4	Cebuano	PNB .
9684	Waray-Waray (Binisaya)	4.69432	3,208,758	3,566,111	5,081,651	MSY44q	31-CKGK	waray-waray cluster		98.80	3,523,317	2a.u.	10 9 10 5 3	Samarenyo*	PNB .
9685	Western Bontok (Igorot)	0.12070	82,503	91,692	130,659	MSY44x	31-CECC	north kankanay cluster		21.00	19,255	0....	9 5 6 2 1	Kankanay, Northern	PN. .
9686	Western Bukidnon Manobo	0.02516	17,198	19,113	27,236	MSY44x	31-CKOH-a	manobo-agta		4.00	765	0.s..	6 5 6 5 3	Manobo: Ata*	PN. b
9687	Western Subanon	0.08052	55,039	61,168	87,164	MSY44x	31-CKQD	siocon cluster		25.00	15,292	0.s..	9 5 2 5 3	Subanon: Western*	PN. .
9688	Western Tawbuid	0.00900	6,152	6,837	9,743	MSY44x	31-CJAB-a	west tawbuid		50.00	3,418	0....	10 8 6 5 2	Tawbuid, Western	....
9689	Yakan (Yacan)	0.10610	72,524	80,600	114,854	MSY44z	31-EABA-a	yakan		0.10	81	0.s..	5 5 2 5 3	Yakan	PN. .
9690	Yogad	0.03289	22,482	24,985	35,604	MSY44x	31-CCDA-a	yogad		60.00	14,991	0....	10 7 6 4 2		... b
9691	other minor peoples	0.33944	232,021	257,861	367,447	...				60.00	154,716		10 7 6 3 0		
	Pitcairn Islands	**100.00000**	**47**	**47**	**47**					**91.49**	**43**				
9692	British	3.00000	1	1	1	CEW19i	52-ABAC-b	standard-english	100	50.00	1	3Bsuh	10 10 13 5 1		PNB b
9693	Pitcairner	94.00000	44	44	44	MPY53	52-ABAI-h	pitcairnese		93.00	41	1csuh	10 10 14 5 1		pnb b
9694	other minor peoples	3.00000	1	1	1	...				50.00	1		10 9 8 5 0		
	Poland	**100.00000**	**38,610,173**	**38,765,085**	**39,069,168**					**96.73**	**37,498,058**				
9695	Baltic Gypsy (Latvian)	0.08000	30,888	31,012	31,255	CNN25f	59-ACBA-ag	north vlach		70.00	21,708	1c...	10 7 8 5 2	Romani: Latvian	Pn. b
9696	British	0.01000	3,861	3,877	3,907	CEW19i	52-ABAC-b	standard-english		79.00	3,062	3Bsuh	10 9 3 5 3		PNB b
9697	Byelorussian	0.53800	207,723	208,556	210,192	CEW22c	53-AAAE-c	bielorusskiy		75.00	156,417	3A.uh	10 9 1 5 2	Byelorussian*	PNB b
9698	Carpathian Gypsy (Galicia	0.03000	11,583	11,630	11,721	CNN25f	59-ACBA-ag	north vlach		80.00	9,304	1c...	10 7 8 3 1	Romani: Latvian	Pn. b
9699	Esperanto	0.00010	39	39	39	CEW21z	51-AAAC-a	proper esperanto	2	70.00	27	0A...	10 9 6 5 0	Esperanto	PNB b

Continued opposite

Table 8-2 continued

EVANGELIZATION								EVANGELISM			ADDITIONAL DESCRIPTIVE DATA
Ref 1	*D* 28	*aC* 29	*CG%* 30	*r* 31	*E* 32	*U* 33	*W* 34	*e* 35	*R* 36	*T* 37	*Locations, civil divisions, literacy, religions, church history, denominations, dioceses, church growth, missions, agencies, ministries, movements* 38
9580	5	6	5.19	0	47.00	53.00	A	13.72	342	5	Central Mountain Province, Luzon. Animists 92%. D=RCC,ICFG,PEC,AFBCP,UCCP. M=ABWE,ECUSA,TAP,SIL,CO,PEM.
9581	4	6	5.05	0	47.00	53.00	A	15.44	334	5	Northern Cotabato, Mindanao. Animists 60%, Muslims(folk Islam) 30%. D=UCCP,Disciples of Christ,PBM,CC. M=SPUM,SIL.
9582	11	6	14.60	4	99.98	0.02	C	591.85	253	10	Northwestern Luzon. Also USA. Lingua franca. Some animists and nonreligious. Strong Christians. D=RCC,PIC,INC,UCCP,UMCP,CDCC,SDA,CC,JWs,AoG,&c.
9583	1	6	3.55	0	37.00	63.00	A	4.05	313	4	Eastern Nueva Vizcaya, Western Quirino, Luzon. 5 dialects. Animists 77%. D=RCC. M=NTM,NELBF,WVI,WOF.
9584	1	10	3.46	7	54.00	46.00	B	1.97	226	4	Traders, merchants. Hindus 50%(including Ananda Marga), Muslims 25%, Baha'is 24%. D=RCC.
9585	2	10	4.43	7	68.00	32.00	B	4.96	207	4	Migrants of Indonesian origin. Muslims 90%(Shafi Sunnis). D=RCC,CAMACOP. M=CMA-Indonesia.
9586	1	6	7.39	0	45.00	55.00	A	13.14	491	5	Central and southern Benguet Province, western Nueva Vizcaya Province, Luzon. Animists 92%. D=RCC. M=SIL,NTM,PMA,FMB.
9587	1	6	5.58	0	48.00	52.00	A	26.28	357	5	Northern Luzon, southwest of Binongan Itneg, northwest of Masadiit Itneg. Bilingual in Ilocano. Animists 70%. D=RCC.
9588	1	6	2.33	0	95.00	5.00	C	208.05	87	8	Luzon: Bambang, Dupax; Aritao, Nueva Vizcaya. Closest to Ilocano and Kiangan Ifugao. Bilingual in Ilocano. Animists 10%. D=RCC.
9589	4	6	4.78	0	50.00	50.00	B	16.42	299	5	Northern Mindoro Province. 6 dialects. Tagalog spoken in many homes. Animists 90%. D=RCC(VA-Calapan),TCA,UCCP,ICFG. M=OMF,GMF.
9590	1	6	2.40	1	99.70	0.30	C	273.38	79	8	Iriga City, Baao, Nabua, Bato, Camarines Sur, Luzon. Bilingual in Central Bicolano and Tagalog. Few animists. D=RCC.
9591	0	5	4.35	0	30.00	70.00	A	5.47	459	4	Luzon, Bicol Province, Mount Isarog east of Naga City. Language nearly extinct. Animists 95%.
9592	2	6	9.87	0	99.65	0.35	C	263.34	260	8	Southern Cagayan, Luzon. Bilingual in Ilocano. Animists 5%. D=Mangyan Tribal Ch Association,STEP.
9593	3	6	8.38	0	99.68	0.32	C	275.50	224	8	Basco, Batanes Islands. A thousand relocated on Mindanao. Animists 5%. D=RCC,Basco Baptist Ch,Itbayat Baptist Ch. M=SIL.
9594	3	6	2.61	0	34.00	66.00	A	4.96	265	4	In 7 villages, eastern Itogon, Benguet Province, Luzon. Mountain group, unacculturated. Related to Karao, Ibaloi. Animists 96%. D=Kalahan Parish,Baptists,UCCP.
9595	1	10	4.43	7	64.00	36.00	B	4.67	222	4	Buddhists 65%, New-Religionists 30%(Soka Gakkai/Nichiren Shoshu). D=RCC. M=UCCJ,FMB.
9596	0	10	1.10	5	52.25	47.75	B	0.47	94	3	Small communities of practicing Jews, with synagogue in Manila.
9597	2	6	4.25	0	42.00	58.00	A	10.73	322	5	Davao City, Mindanao. Related to Kalagan. Animists 93%. D=UPC,CAMACOP. M=CMA,SIL,LCMS,ABCUSA.
9598	1	6	3.62	0	99.70	0.30	C	270.83	111	8	Cagayan Island, between Negros and Palawan, and on Palawan's coast. Animists 10%. D=RCC. M=SIL,TAP.
9599	0	5	4.46	0	22.00	78.00	A	0.80	640	3	Along east and west shores of Davao Gulf in Davao del Sur and Davao Oriental. Muslims 99%. M=SIL,TAP.
9600	2	6	3.48	0	33.00	67.00	A	4.81	347	4	Coron Island, north of Palawan; northern Palawan, Busuanga, Baras. Animists 96%. D=UCCP,RCC. M=NTM,SIL,TAP,PFM.
9601	1	7	3.57	0	84.00	16.00	B	153.30	139	7	Surigao del Sur, Mindanao. Bilingual in Cebuano. Animists 10%. D=RCC.
9602	1	6	9.25	0	79.00	21.00	B	112.45	344	7	Northern Benguet Province, southwestern Mountain Province, Luzon. Animists 60%. D=RCC. D=RCC,PEC,LCP,WCP,SDA,Baptists,Pentecostals. M=NTM,TAP.
9603	0	6	3.88	0	25.00	75.00	A	0.91	500	3	Lamiyawan area, Davao Oriental, Mindanao. Bilingual in Mansaka. Animists 99%.
9604	1	7	2.64	0	35.00	65.00	A	10.22	260	5	Karao and Ekip, Bokod, Benguet Province, Luzon. Closest to Ibaloi. Animists 92%. 70% being bilinguals. D=RCC.
9605	1	7	2.33	0	73.00	27.00	B	106.58	113	7	Mid-central Negros. Some bilinguals in Cebuano and Hiligaynon. Animists 20%. D=RCC.
9606	1	7	2.42	0	95.00	5.00	C	208.05	89	8	Quezon Province, Luzon. Bilingual in Tagalog. Close to Paranan. Animists 10%. D=RCC.
9607	3	6	4.89	0	42.00	58.00	A	9.19	363	4	Western Nueva Vizcaya, northeastern Pangasinan, western Ifugao, Luzon. Animists 74%. D=LCP,Kalahan Parish,UCCP. M=NTM.
9608	3	6	3.87	0	48.00	52.00	A	15.76	260	5	Ifugao Province, Luzon. Animists 91%. D=RCC,UCCP,Pentecostals. M=SIL,TAP,NTM,EPM,GEM,NELBF,WVI,YWAM.
9609	4	6	2.48	0	99.80	0.20	C	365.00	69	9	Iloilo and Antique Provinces, western Panay. Few animists. D=RCC,ICFG,Baptists,UCCP. M=SIL,TAP.
9610	1	10	6.91	6	99.35	0.65	B	131.58	200	7	Immigrants from Korea. 65% are shamanists, Buddhists, or Confucians. D=PCK. M=WOM,WMDKAG,FMB.
9611	5	6	9.24	1	90.00	10.00	B	147.82	302	7	South Cotabato Province, Mindanao. Animists 15%. D=RCC,UCCP,AoG,CAMACOP,ICFG. M=SPUM,CMA,SIL,JCETP,ABCUSA,FMB.
9612	1	6	6.10	0	46.00	54.00	A	15.11	404	5	Eastern Zamboango del Sur, Mindanao. Animists 91%. D=RCC. M=CMA,SPUM,PBS,OMC,ABCUSA.
9613	1	6	4.20	0	99.70	0.30	C	268.27	127	8	Southern Tablas Island, Romblon Province. Bilingual in Hiligaynon. Few animists, 5%. D=RCC. M=TAP.
9614	0	5	2.46	5	35.01	64.99	A	0.01	247	2	Mixed-race persons. Port lingua franca from Sumatra to Philippines. Muslims 100%(Shafi Sunnis). M=MEP,CICM,CSSR.
9615	1	6	4.00	0	35.00	65.00	A	7.66	366	4	Luzon, southern Kalinga-Apayao Province. Animists 94%. D=RCC. M=TAP,SIL.
9616	1	6	6.39	0	38.00	62.00	A	11.09	510	5	Eastern Abra and Kalinga-Apayao Provinces. Headhunters in northern Luzon. Animists 92%. D=RCC. M=SIL,TAP.
9617	1	5	3.89	0	32.00	68.00	A	7.00	391	4	Luzon, southeastern Kalinga-Apayao Province. Bilingual in Limos Kalinga. Animists 94%. D=RCC.
9618	1	6	2.58	0	32.00	68.00	A	8.17	279	4	Southern Mountain Province, Luzon. Close to Limos. Animists 93%. D=RCC. M=TAP.
9619	1	5	4.83	0	48.00	52.00	A	35.04	333	5	East side of mountain, Botolan Sambal area, central Luzon. Animists 60%. D=RCC. M=SIL.
9620	1	5	3.99	0	39.00	61.00	A	21.35	351	5	In Florida Blanca, Porac, San Marcelino, Zambales, Luzon. Mountainous. Animists 65%. D=RCC. M=SIL.
9621	1	5	5.15	0	56.00	44.00	B	40.88	285	6	Southwestern Negros, Mt Arniyo near Bayawan. Bilingual in Cebuano or Hiligaynon. Animists 60%. D=RCC.
9622	4	7	4.17	2	37.05	62.95	A	0.06	359	2	Cotabato, Zamboango Provinces. Literates 20%. Muslims 100%(folk Islam; Shafi Sunnis). D=RCC,ICFG,CAMACOP,UCCP. M=SEND,SIL,SPUM,CMA,OMF.
9623	0	10	3.46	5	48.02	51.98	A	0.03	237	2	Migrants from Malaysia, Indonesia. Muslims 100%(Shafi Sunnis). M=TAP.
9624	1	7	3.46	1	95.00	5.00	C	208.05	119	8	Malay, northwest Aklan Province, lowland, Panay. Close to Aklanon. Animists 40%. D=RCC.
9625	1	6	3.90	0	34.00	66.00	A	2.48	395	4	Agusan del Norte and Surigao Provinces, Mindanao. Animists 98%. D=Santiago Pentecostal Ch. M=PMF,SIL,Charismatic Full Gospel Ministries,JCETP,GBFMS.
9626	5	6	6.03	0	42.00	58.00	A	9.19	438	4	Eastern Davao, Davao Oriental Provinces, Mindanao. Animists 94%. D=RCC,ICFG,UCCP,Baptists,CAMACOP. M=SPUM,SIL,CFGM.
9627	5	6	7.98	0	40.00	60.00	A	2.92	593	4	Lanao del Norte/Sur Provinces, Mindanao. Literates 20%. Moros (Moors), in armed revolt since 1972. Muslims 98%(folk Islam, Shafi Sunnis). D=RCC,UCCP,LCP.
9628	1	6	5.25	0	50.00	50.00	B	31.02	325	5	Sallapadan and Bucloc, Abra Province, Luzon. Bilingual in Ilocano. Animists 53%. D=RCC.
9629	3	6	2.53	1	99.85	0.15	C	400.22	68	10	Masbate Province, 3 islands. Related to Hiligaynon. Literates 70%. Few animists. D=Baptist Ch,UCCP,RCC. M=SIL,TAP.
9630	2	6	4.83	0	37.00	63.00	A	4.05	408	4	Davao del Norte, southeast Bukidnon, Mindanao. Animists 97%. D=RCC,PBM. M=OMF,CMA,ABWE,SIL,FMB.
9631	1	6	4.71	0	39.00	61.00	A	7.11	379	4	Ifugao Province, Luzon. Mountainous. Agriculturalists. Animists 95%. D=RCC. M=TAP,WVI,EPM,NELBF,GEM,SIL.
9632	0	6	2.10	0	27.10	72.90	A	0.09	281	2	Aboriginal population of Balabac Island, southern Palawan. Also in Malaysia. Most speak Tagalog. 100% syncretistic Muslims, since around 1770. M=SIL,NTM.
9633	1	6	3.15	0	99.70	0.30	C	263.16	102	8	Rugnot Negritos. Bicol Province, east of Lake Buhi, Luzon. 4 dialects. Close to Bicolano. Animists 5%. D=RCC.
9634	1	6	4.91	0	80.00	20.00	B	146.00	202	7	Negritos. Bicol Province, west of Lake Buhi, east of Iriga City, Luzon. Animists 30%. D=RCC.
9635	0	6	4.67	0	60.00	40.00	B	65.70	259	6	Luzon, Santa Elena and Labo, Camarines Norte. Animists 40%.
9636	1	6	2.54	1	99.80	0.20	C	356.24	72	9	Casiguran, Juban, Sorsogon Province, Luzon. Bilingual in Tagalog. Few animists, 3%. D=RCC. M=GMF.
9637	2	6	3.62	0	41.00	59.00	A	7.48	309	4	Northwestern Cagayan Province, Luzon. Close to North Ibanag. Animists 95%. D=RCC,Ch of Christ. M=SIL,TAP,SPUM,NELBF.
9638	1	6	2.40	1	99.70	0.30	C	263.16	82	8	Northern Catanduanes, east of Bicol, Luzon. Scattered animists, 5%. D=RCC. M=RBMU.
9639	1	6	6.43	0	46.00	54.00	A	25.18	424	5	Kalinga-Apayao Province, Luzon. Headhunters. Animists 85%. D=Wesleyan Ch of the Philippines. M=SIL,TAP.
9640	0	6	3.90	1	27.05	72.95	A	0.04	447	2	Sulu Archipelago. Also in Sabah (Malaysia). Coastal fishermen. Strong Muslims 100%(Shafi Sunnis). M=SIL,CMA,TAP,UCCP.
9641	1	6	4.14	0	33.20	66.80	A	5.09	398	4	Between Davao del Sur and North Cotabato, Mindanao. Animists 96%. D=CAMACOP. M=SIL,CMA.
9642	0	6	2.87	0	30.00	70.00	A	4.38	353	4	Babuyan Negritos. North central Palawan. Animists 96%. M=SIL,NTM.
9643	3	6	2.37	1	99.98	0.02	C	554.30	54	10	Pampanga Province, Tarlac and Bataan, Luzon. Many nominal Christians. D=RCC,UPC(strong Jesus-Only followings),UCCP. M=Door of Faith Ch,UMC,PBS.
9644	4	6	2.19	1	99.97	0.03	C	555.09	50	10	Pangasinan Province, Luzon. D=RCC,RCJCLdS,Christ Jesus' Holy Church, and many other Catholic schisms. M=FIFCOP,GEM,RSIM,SKM,FMB,UMC,PBS.
9645	3	6	3.32	1	38.00	62.00	A	1.38	288	4	West central Sulu, west of Jolo; also on Palawan. Moros(Moors). Bilinguals in Tausug. Literates 50%. Muslims 99%(Shafi Sunnis). D=CAMACOP,UCCP,Ev Ch.
9646	2	6	2.41	0	99.70	0.30	C	281.05	85	8	East coast, Isabela Province, Luzon. Isolated among hills, forests. Literates 55%. Animists 10%. D=UMCP,RCC. M=SIL,TAP,NTM.
9647	1	6	2.40	0	99.75	0.25	C	295.65	78	8	Camotes Islands. Some bilinguals in Cebuano. Close to Masbateno, Hiligaynon. Animists 5%. D=RCC.
9648	0	6	3.42	0	33.00	67.00	A	4.81	367	4	Negritos. Pudtol, Kalinga-Apayao Province, Luzon. Animists 96%. M=NELBF.
9649	1	6	6.12	0	80.00	20.00	B	146.00	233	7	Southern Surigao del Sur, Mindanao. Animists 45%, some Muslims. D=RCC.
9650	0	6	2.34	0	29.00	71.00	A	4.23	316	4	Luzon; Santa Inez, Rizal Province; Paimohuan, General Nakar, Quezon Province. Bilingual in Tagalog. Animists 76%. M=TCM.
9651	2	6	2.72	0	99.88	0.12	C	404.71	74	10	Romblon Province: Romblon and Sibuyan Islands, north of Panay. Few animists. D=RCC,SDA. M=SIL,TAP,GMF.
9652	0	6	2.22	1	29.04	70.96	A	0.04	258	2	Cagayan Sulu Island, also on Palawan and in Malaysia. Agriculturalists. Muslims 100%(Shafi Sunnis). M=RCC,CAMCOP,UCCP,SIL,TAP,CMA,SPUM.
9653	1	6	4.43	0	39.00	61.00	A	14.23	359	5	Head of Carraga river, Banlalaysan area, highland, Davao del Norte, Mindanao. Some bilinguals in Cebuano. Animists 90%. D=RCC.
9654	0	8	2.60	0	26.00	74.00	A	0.94	364	3	Sarangani and Balut Islands. Limited bilingualism in Cebuano. Muslims 99%(Shafi Sunnis).
9655	1	8	2.34	0	99.91	0.09	C	468.33	62	10	Balut, Sarangani Bay area. Majority in Indonesia (Sulawesi, Maluku). Animists 1% and Muslims 1%. D=RCC. M=SPUM,SIL.
9656	2	6	10.35	1	99.80	0.20	C	365.00	242	9	South Cotabato Province, Sarangani Peninsula, Mindanao. Animists 45%. D=UCCP,RCC. M=SIL,TAP,JCETP,ABCUSA,FMB,CMA.
9657	4	6	8.04	0	93.00	7.00	B	169.72	257	7	Southern, eastern Davao, Mindanao. Animists 50%. D=RCC,Full Gospel Ch,ICFG,CAMACOP. M=SPUM,FMB,CMA,SIL.
9658	1	6	3.83	0	99.80	0.20	C	321.20	112	9	Prieto Diaz, Sorsogon Province. Frequent intermarriage with other groups; language nearly extinct. D=RCC.
9659	0	6	4.18	0	34.00	66.00	A	4.96	417	4	Eastern Nueva Ecija, Sierra Madre, Quezoon Province. Second language: Tagalog. Animists 96%. M=NTM.
9660	0	6	3.42	0	29.00	71.00	A	4.23	418	4	Negritos. Near Faire-Rizal, Cagayan Province, Luzon. 136 families (1981). Animists 96%. M=NELBF.
9661	2	6	2.39	0	99.80	0.20	C	344.56	71	9	Southern Sorsogon Province, Luzon. Closely related to Waray-Waray. Bilingual in Tagalog, Central Bicolano, Masbateno. D=Baptist Ch,UCCP.
9662	2	7	2.39	0	99.85	0.15	C	384.71	68	9	Luzon, Southern Catanduanes, east of Bicol. Bilingual in Central Bicolano. Virac used for literature. D=RCC,Baptist Ch. M=RBMU.
9663	1	6	5.71	0	50.00	50.00	B	31.02	350	5	Southern Abra Province, Luzon. Bilingual in Ilocano or Northern Kankanay. Headhunters. Animists 63%. D=RCC.
9664	1	6	5.12	0	43.00	57.00	A	12.55	370	5	Southern Kalinga-Apayao Province, Luzon; 12 villages. Mountainous. Headhunters. Animists 92%. D=RCC. M=SIL,NTM,TAP,YWAM.
9665	0	5	1.40	1	32.01	67.99	A	0.01	163	2	Southern Sulu Archipelago. Also in Sabah (Malaysia). Bilinguals in Tausug. Muslims 100%(Shafi Sunnis). M=SIL,RBMU,UCCP.
9666	1	5	5.39	0	35.00	65.00	A	6.38	477	4	Southwest Palawan from Canipaan to Canduaga. Lingua franca: Tausug. Animists 85%, Muslims 10%(Shafi Sunnis). Coastal islamization continuing. D=RCC.
9667	1	10	-2.20	8	99.96	0.04	C	602.68	2	10	Settlers from Spain, and expatriates, mainly in Manila. D=RCC. M=SVD,SJ,SSC,CICM,OMI,OP,OFM,SDB,ORSA,MSC,CM,FSC,FMB.
9668	1	6	4.28	0	27.00	73.00	A	2.95	503	4	Tapaz (Capiz Province), Lambunao (Iloilo Province), Valderrama (Antique Province), Panay. Animists 77%. D=Baptist Chs.
9669	4	7	2.73	0	99.89	0.11	C	432.05	70	10	Surigao, Carrascal, Cantilan, Madrid, Larosa; Mindanao. Bilingual in Cebuano. D=RCC,INC,UCCP,PIC. M=SPUM,Reality of Christ,FMB.
9670	4	6	2.51	0	35.00	65.00	A	5.11	250	4	East central Mindoro. Many Stone-Age animists 96%. D=RCC(VA-Colapan),UCCP,ICFG,TCA. M=OMF,ABCUSA.
9671	2	6	7.20	0	58.00	42.00	B	42.34	372	6	Davao City, slopes of Mt Apo, Mindanao. Animists 80%. D=CAMACOP,RCC. M=SIL,TAP,CMA,SPUM.
9672	3	6	7.42	0	56.00	44.00	B	38.83	396	5	Southern Mindanao, south Cotabato. Animists 76%, Muslims 20%. D=AoG,Evangelical Pentecostal Ch,UCCP. M=SIL,TAP,SPUM,LCMS,ABCUSA,FMB,LBT.
9673	12	6	1.97	5	99.98	0.02	C	621.79	42	10	D=RCC(65 Dioceses),PIC(30 Dioceses),INC,UCCP,UMCP,CDCC,SDA,JWs,AoG,CC,LCP,&c. M=SVD,SJ,SSC,CICM,OMI,OP,DOFC,EPM,FIFCOP,GEM,UECP.
9674	0	7	4.16	0	33.10	66.90	A	0.12	401	3	Jolo, Sulu Archipelago. Also Malaysia, Kalimantan. Armed struggle. Muslims 100%(Shafi Sunnis, since AD 1100). M=RCC,SIL,CMA,SPUM,TAP.
9675	3	6	7.20	0	51.00	49.00	B	18.61	423	5	On Mindanao. Animists 90%. D=RCC,CAMACOP,ICFG. M=SIL,SPUM,CMA,PMF,GBFMS,ABCUSA,FMB.
9676	4	6	9.08	0	99.60	0.40	C	223.38	271	8	Northern Zambales Province, Luzon. Some bilinguals in Tagalog. Animists 10%. D=RCC,ABCLUM,UMCP,PBM. M=ABWE,GEM,PMF,TAP,SIL.
9677	3	6	7.37	0	63.00	37.00	B	45.99	350	6	Upi, Cotabato, Mindanao. Animists 80%. D=RCC,PEC,CAMACOP. M=SIL,SPUM,CMA,CBFMS.
9678	2	6	3.37	0	32.00	68.00	A	2.33	347	4	Zamboango del Norte, Misamis Occidental, Mindanao. Animists 98%. D=RCC,CAMACOP. M=WBT,CMA,OMC,ABCUSA,TAP.
9679	10	10	3.58	8	99.77	0.23	C	424.38	81	10	Expatriates from USA, in development. D=UCCP,UMCP,SDA,JWs,CJCLdS,AoG,CCS,RCC,PBC,&c. M=FMB,&c.
9680	1	6	4.20	0	47.00	53.00	A	13.72	303	5	Quezon Province, Luzon. Bilingual in Tagalog. Hunter-gatherers. Animists 92%. D=RCC. M=SIL,NTM,OMC.
9681	1	6	3.27	0	35.00	65.00	A	8.94	309	4	Luzon, southern Kalinga-Apayao Province. Animists 93%. D=RCC.
9682	1	6	4.92	0	39.00	61.00	A	11.38	393	5	Luzon, Abra Province. Animists 70%. D=RCC.
9683	11	6	2.28	2	99.98	0.02	C	588.54	49	10	Negros,Cebu; also USA. Strong Christians. D=RCC,PIC,INC,UCCP,UMCP,LCP,CDCC,SDA,JWs,AoG,&c. M=SVD,SJ,SSC,OFM,OP,AEM,CFCP,COGWMP,EPM.
9684	5	7	2.52	1	99.99	0.01	C	576.27	55	10	Northern and eastern Samar-Leyte. Lingua franca. D=RCC,UCCP,UMCP,FMCP,ICFG. M=PBS,DOFC,GMF. R=FEBC.
9685	2	6	7.86	0	57.00	43.00	B	43.69	411	6	Western Mountain Province, southeastern Ilocos Sur, Luzon. Animists 79%. D=PEC,RCC. M=SIL.
9686	4	6	4.43	0	42.00	58.00	A	6.13	333	4	Southern Bukidnon Province, Mindanao. Tropical forest, mountains. Animists 96%. D=RCC,SDA,INC,ABWE. M=SPUM,SIL,TAP,UPM.
9687	2	6	7.61	0	63.00	37.00	B	57.48	361	6	Zamboango Peninsula, Mindanao. Animists 30%, Muslims 45%(Shafi Sunnis, including the 17,000 Kalibugan). D=CAMACOP,UCCP. M=SIL,TAP,SPUM,CMA.
9688	3	6	6.01	0	87.00	13.00	B	158.77	211	7	Central Mindoro. Too diverse to use Eastern Tawbuid literature. Animists 15%. D=RCC,UCCP,ICFG. M=OMF,ABCUSA.
9689	6	6	4.49	1	34.10	65.90	A	0.12	402	3	On Basilan Island, western Mindanao. Also in Sabah (Malaysia). Literates 5%. Heavy fighting. Muslims 100%(Shafi Sunnis). D=RCC(PN-Isabela),PEC,ICFG.
9690	1	6	2.42	0	98.00	2.00	C	214.62	87	8	Echague, Isabela Province, Luzon. Literates 80%. Related to Ibanag and Gaddang. Highly bilingual in Ilocano. Animists 5%. D=LCP. M=LCMS,TAP.
9691	0	10	10.13		91.00	9.00	C	199.29	305	7	Germans (NAC), Cambodians, Laotians, Vietnamese, Thais, Pacific Islanders, other Asians, other Europeans. Buddhists 10%, nonreligious 10%.
Pitcairn Islands											
9692	1	10	-0.69	8	99.50	0.50	B	222.65	10	8	A few individuals of British origin. Nonreligious 50%. D=SDA(Central Pacific Union Mission).
9693	1	6	-1.26	8	99.93	0.07	C	522.75	2	10	Euronesians, formerly Anglicans until 1877, with congregation in Adamstown. Many have migrated to Norfolk Island, Fiji, Australia, NZ. D=SDA.
9694	0	10	-0.69		83.00	17.00	B	151.47	3	7	Occasional individuals of other nationalities. Nonreligious 50%.
Poland											
9695	3	0	0.47	1	99.70	0.30	C	288.71	36	8	Baltic Romany (Polska Folditka,Roma). Also in Lithuania, Siberia, Estonia, Podolia. Nomadic. Nonreligious 30%. D=RCC,UECG,GEM. M=GGMS,UBS.
9696	6	0	0.47	8	99.79	0.21	C	392.15	33	9	Expatriates from Britain, in business, commerce. D=MCPR,SDA,JWs,CJCLdS,CCCC,RCC.
9697	2	0	0.70	5	99.75	0.25	C	347.66	37	9	White Russians. Refugees, settlers since 1917. Mainly in Russia, also Canada, USA. Nonreligious 20%. D=Orthodox Ch of Poland(D-Bialystok & Gdansk),RCC.
9698	1	0	0.47	1	99.80	0.20	C	341.64	35	9	South Poland. Also Czechoslovakia, USA, Hungary, Romania, Russia. Nonreligious 20%. D=RCC.
9699	0	0	0.46	5	99.70	0.30	C	301.49	34	9	Artificial (constructed) language, in 80 countries. Speakers in Poland: 948,000(only 39 mother-tongue). Nonreligious 30%.

Continued overleaf

Table 8-2 continued

PEOPLE		POPULATION				IDENTITY CODE		LANGUAGE		CHURCH		MINISTRY						SCRIPTURE		
Ref 1	*Ethnic name* 2	*P%* 3	*In 1995* 4	*In 2000* 5	*In 2025* 6	*Race* 7	*Language* 8	*Autoglossonym* 9	*S* 10	*AC* 11	*Members* 12	*Jayuh* 13-17	*d* 18	*wa* 19	*xc* 20	*mc* 21	*mi* 22	*Biblioglossonym* 23	*Pub* 24-26	*ss* 27
9700	German (High German)	4.02000	1,552,129	1,558,356	1,570,581	CEW19m	52-ABCE-a	standard hoch-deutsch		91.00	1,418,104	2B.uh	10	9	3	5	3	German*	PNB	b
9701	Greek	0.30000	115,831	116,295	117,208	CEW20	56-AAAA-c	dhimotiki		95.00	110,480	2B.uh	10	9	11	5	2	Greek: Modern	PNB	b
9702	Jewish	0.00700	2,703	2,714	2,735	CMT35	52-ABCH	yiddish cluster		0.10	3	0B..h	5	3	3	1	0		PNB	b
9703	Jewish	0.00280	1,081	1,085	1,094	CMT35	53-AAAC-c	polski		0.20	2	2A.uh	5	4	2	4	1	Polish	PNB	b
9704	Karaite (Karaim)	0.00700	2,703	2,714	2,735	CMT35	44-AABB-h	karaim		0.00	0	1c.u.	0	3	3	0	0	Karaite*	PN.	b
9705	Kashubian (Cashubian)	0.39700	153,282	153,897	155,105	CEW22f	53-AAAC-b	kaszubi		90.00	138,508	1c.uh	10	9	2	5	3		pnb	b
9706	Lithuanian	0.03000	11,583	11,630	11,721	CEW15b	54-AAAA-a	standard lietuvishkai		87.00	10,118	3A.u.	10	9	2	5	1	Lithuanian	PNB	b
9707	Lovari Gypsy (Rom)	0.01300	5,019	5,039	5,079	CNN25f	59-ACBA-ag	north vlach		60.00	3,024	1c...	10	7	7	5	1	Romani: Latvian	Pn.	b
9708	Macedonian	0.02000	7,722	7,753	7,814	CEW22g	53-AAAH-a	makedonski		89.00	6,900	2a.uh	10	7	1	4	1	Macedonian*	PNB	b
9709	Polish (Pole, Silesian)	89.95950	34,733,519	34,872,877	35,146,428	CEW22i	53-AAAC-c	polski		97.65	34,053,364	2A.uh	10	10	12	5	2	Polish	PNB	b
9710	Polish Gypsy	0.10000	38,610	38,765	39,069	CNN25f	53-AAAC-c	polski		76.00	29,461	2A.uh	10	8	7	5	1	Polish	PNB	b
9711	Polish Rom Gypsy (Manush)	0.09200	35,521	35,664	35,944	CNN25f	59-ACBA-ag	north vlach		70.00	24,965	1c...	10	7	7	5	1	Romani: Latvian	Pn.	b
9712	Russian	0.20000	77,220	77,530	78,138	CEW22j	53-AAAE-d	russkiy		71.00	55,046	4B.uh	10	8	2	5	3	Russian	PNB	b
9713	Slovak	0.10000	38,610	38,765	39,069	CEW22m	53-AAAD-b	slovensky		89.00	34,501	1Asuh	10	9	2	5	3	Slovak	PNB	b
9714	Slovincian (Slovincz)	0.00060	232	233	234	CEW22f	53-AAAC-a	slovincki		89.00	207	1c.uh	10	8	2	4	3		pnb	b
9715	Tatar (Tartar)	0.00300	1,158	1,163	1,172	MSY41h	44-AABB-e	tatar		2.00	23	2c.u.	6	4	8	1	0	Tatar: Kazan	Pn.	b
9716	USA White	0.04000	15,444	15,506	15,628	CEW19s	52-ABAC-s	general american		78.00	12,095	1Bsuh	10	10	12	0	0	English*	PNB	b
9717	Ukrainian	4.00000	1,544,407	1,550,603	1,562,767	CEW22p	53-AAAE-b	ukrainskiy		89.98	1,395,233	3A.uh	10	9	3	5	2	Ukrainian	PNB	b
9718	other minor peoples	0.05000	19,305	19,383	19,535	...				80.00	15,506		10	7	8	3	0			
	Portugal	**100.00000**	**9,856,155**	**9,874,853**	**9,348,354**					**91.95**	**9,080,229**									
9719	Angolan Mestico	0.80000	78,849	78,999	74,787	NAN58	51-AABA-e	general português		90.00	71,099	2Bsuh	10	7	11	4	3	Portuguese	PNB	b
9720	Black Gypsy (Spanish Calo	0.05200	5,125	5,135	4,861	CNN25f	59-AFAA-a	rodi		90.00	4,621	0B.uh	10	9	11	5	2	Calo	P..	b
9721	Brazilian	1.10000	108,418	108,623	102,832	CLT26	51-AABA-h	general brasileiro		89.50	97,218	3csuh	10	9	12	5	3	Portuguese: Brazilian	PNB	b
9722	Brazilian Mestico	0.30000	29,568	29,625	28,045	CLN28	51-AABA-e	general português		92.00	27,255	2Bsuh	10	9	13	5	3	Portuguese	PNB	b
9723	British	0.09300	9,166	9,184	8,694	CEW19i	52-ABAC-b	standard-english	13	78.00	7,163	3Bsuh	10	9	13	5	3		PNB	b
9724	Caboverdian Mestico	0.35000	34,497	34,562	32,719	NAN58	51-AABA-e	general português		98.00	33,871	2Bsuh	10	8	12	5	3	Portuguese	PNB	b
9725	Esperanto	0.00000	0	0	0	CEW21z	51-AAAC-a	proper esperanto	1	60.00	0	0A...	10	8	2	5	0	Esperanto	PNB	b
9726	French	0.20000	19,712	19,750	18,697	CEW21b	51-AABI-d	general français	15	84.00	16,590	1B.uh	10	9	14	5	1	French	PNB	b
9727	Galician	0.15300	15,080	15,109	14,303	CEW21d	51-AABA-b	galego		95.20	14,383	1csuh	10	9	15	4	1	Galician	PNB	b
9728	German	0.10000	9,856	9,875	9,348	CEW19m	52-ABCE-a	standard hoch-deutsch		86.00	8,492	2B.uh	10	9	13	5	2	German*	PNB	b
9729	Goanese	0.20000	19,712	19,750	18,697	CNN25d	59-AAFU-o	konkani-gomantaki		95.00	18,762	3asu.	10	9	12	5	1	Konkani: Goan*	PNb	b
9730	Greek	0.01500	1,478	1,481	1,402	CEW20	56-AAAA-c	dhimotiki		95.00	1,407	2B.uh	10	9	11	5	1	Greek: Modern	PNB	b
9731	Han Chinese	0.01000	986	987	935	MSY42a	79-AAAB-ba	kuo-yü		9.00	89	2Bsuh	7	5	8	4	1	Chinese: Kuoyu*	PNB	b
9732	Han Chinese	0.90000	88,705	88,874	84,135	MSY42a	79-AAAM-a	central yue		16.00	14,220	3A.uh	8	6	8	5	0	Chinese, Yue	PNB	b
9733	Italian	0.20000	19,712	19,750	18,697	CEW21e	51-AABQ-c	standard italiano	2	83.00	16,392	2B.uh	10	9	9	5	3	Italian	PNB	b
9734	Jewish	0.00450	444	444	421	CMT35	51-AABA-e	general português		0.08	0	2Bsuh	4	4	5	1	0	Portuguese	PNB	b
9735	Kurdish (Kurd)	0.00150	148	148	140	CNT24c	58-AAAA-a	kurmanji		0.10	0	3c...	5	4	4	4	1	Kurdish: Kurmanji*	PN.	b
9736	Levantine Arab	0.20000	19,712	19,750	18,697	CMT30	12-AACF-f	syro-palestinian		69.00	13,627	1Asuh	10	8	8	4	1	Arabic: Lebanese*	Pnb	b
9737	Maghreb Arab	0.06000	5,914	5,925	5,609	CMT30	12-AACB-b	east maghrebi		0.20	12	2A.uh	5	4	6	1	0	Arabic: Algerian*	PNB	b
9738	Marrano (Crypto-Jew)	1.16000	114,331	114,548	108,441	CMT35	51-AABA-e	general português		90.00	103,093	2Bsuh	10	8	10	4	1	Portuguese	PNB	b
9739	Mirandesa	0.10000	9,856	9,875	9,348	CEW21g	51-AABC-b	mirandés		96.00	9,480	0c.uh	10	8	11	0	0		p..	.
9740	Mozambican Mestico	0.40000	39,425	39,499	37,393	NAN58	51-AABA-e	general português		90.00	35,549	2Bsuh	10	7	12	4	3	Portuguese	PNB	b
9741	Portuguese	91.85300	9,053,174	9,070,349	8,586,744	CEW21g	51-AABA-e	general português		93.30	8,462,635	2Bsuh	10	10	15	5	4	Portuguese	PNB	b
9742	Portuguese Gypsy	0.74700	73,625	73,765	69,832	CNN25f	51-AABA-e	general português		75.00	55,324	2Bsuh	10	9	8	5	3	Portuguese	PNB	b
9743	Spaniard	0.40000	39,425	39,499	37,393	CEW21k	51-AABB-c	general español	20	95.50	37,722	2B.uh	10	9	15	5	3	Spanish	PNB	b
9744	Timorese	0.03000	2,957	2,962	2,805	MSY44y	32-BCBA	uab-atoni-pah-meto cluster		90.00	2,666	0A...	10	8	12	4	1	Timor*	PN.	b
9745	USA White	0.20000	19,712	19,750	18,697	CEW19s	52-ABAC-s	general american		78.00	15,405	1Bsuh	10	10	12	0	0	English*	PNB	b
9746	Vlach Gypsy (Kalderash)	0.00600	591	592	561	CNN25f	59-ACBA-a	vlach-romani		70.00	415	1a...	10	8	6	5	1	Romani: Finnish*	PN.	b
9747	West African	0.16500	16,263	16,294	15,425	NAN58	51-AABA	português cluster		20.00	3,259	3Bsuh	9	7	9	0	0		PNB	b
9748	other minor peoples	0.20000	19,712	19,750	18,697	...				48.00	9,480		9	5	8	4	3			
	Puerto Rico	**100.00000**	**3,715,139**	**3,868,602**	**4,477,962**					**96.22**	**3,722,292**									
9749	Black	15.00000	557,271	580,290	671,694	NFB71a	51-AABB-hk	puertorriqueño		97.00	562,882	1B.uh	10	8	13	5	2		pnb	b
9750	Cuban White	0.20000	7,430	7,737	8,956	CLT27	51-AABB-hi	cubano		58.00	4,488	1B.uh	10	9	8	5	3		pnb	b
9751	East Indian	0.11000	4,087	4,255	4,926	CNN25g	59-AAFO-e	general hindi		15.00	638	3Asuh	8	5	7	4	1		pnb	b
9752	Han Chinese	0.02000	743	774	896	MSY42a	79-AAAG-a	literary hakka		30.00	232	1A...	9	5	8	4	1	Chinese: Hakka, Wukingfu*	PNB	b
9753	Han Chinese	0.02000	743	774	896	MSY42a	79-AAAM-a	central yue		35.00	271	3A.uh	9	5	8	4	1	Chinese, Yue	PNB	b
9754	Jewish	0.07300	2,712	2,824	3,269	CMT35	51-AABB-hk	puertorriqueño		1.00	28	1B.uh	6	4	6	3	0		pnb	b
9755	Levantine Arab	0.10000	3,715	3,869	4,478	CMT30	12-AACF-f	syro-palestinian		80.00	3,095	1Asuh	10	8	8	5	2	Arabic: Lebanese*	Pnb	b
9756	Mulatto	10.00000	371,514	386,860	447,796	NFB71b	51-AABB-hk	puertorriqueño		96.00	371,386	1B.uh	10	8	12	5	3		pnb	b
9757	Puerto Rican White	72.07700	2,677,761	2,788,372	3,227,581	CLT27	51-AABB-hk	puertorriqueño		97.10	2,707,509	1B.uh	10	10	13	5	3		pnb	b
9758	Spaniard	0.10000	3,715	3,869	4,478	CEW21k	51-AABB-c	general español		96.00	3,714	2B.uh	10	9	13	5	1	Spanish	PNB	b
9759	USA White	2.20000	81,733	85,109	98,515	CEW19s	52-ABAC-s	general american		77.00	65,534	1Bsuh	10	9	10	5	3	English*	PNB	b
9760	other minor peoples	0.10000	3,715	3,869	4,478	...				65.00	2,515		10	5	8	5	0			
	Qatar	**100.00000**	**547,987**	**599,065**	**778,537**					**9.95**	**59,633**									
9761	African Bantu	9.50000	52,059	56,911	73,961	NAB57j	12-AACF-p	zanji		4.00	2,276	1Asuh	6	4	2	1	0		pnb	b
9762	Armenian	0.30000	1,644	1,797	2,336	CEW14	57-AAAA-b	ashkharik		90.00	1,617	4A.u.	10	9	13	2	1	Armenian: Modern, Eastern	PNB	b
9763	British	1.10000	6,028	6,590	8,564	CEW19i	52-ABAC-b	standard-english		75.00	4,942	3Bsuh	10	9	13	5	3		PNB	b
9764	Egyptian Arab	2.00000	10,960	11,981	15,571	CMT30	12-AACF-a	masri		15.00	1,797	2Asuh	8	5	8	5	3	Arabic*	PNB	b
9765	Filipino	4.00000	21,919	23,963	31,141	MSY44o	31-CKAA-a	proper tagalog		95.00	22,764	4Bs..	10	9	12	0	0	Tagalog	PNB	b
9766	French	0.30000	1,644	1,797	2,336	CEW21b	51-AABI-d	general français		51.00	917	1B.uh	10	9	14	5	1	French	PNB	b
9767	German	0.20000	1,096	1,198	1,557	CEW19m	52-ABCE-a	standard hoch-deutsch		56.00	671	2B.uh	10	9	13	5	2	German*	PNB	b
9768	Lebanese Arab	10.40000	56,991	62,303	80,968	CMT30	12-AACF-f	syro-palestinian		10.00	6,230	1Asuh	8	5	8	4	1	Arabic: Lebanese*	Pnb	b
9769	Malayali	2.80000	15,344	16,774	21,799	CNN23b	49-EBEB-a	malayalam		25.00	4,193	2Asu.	9	9	10	5	3	Malayalam	PNB	b
9770	Palestinian Arab	13.40000	73,430	80,275	104,324	CMT30	12-AACF-f	syro-palestinian		5.00	4,014	1Asuh	7	5	7	5	2	Arabic: Lebanese*	Pnb	b
9771	Persian (Irani)	16.45000	90,144	98,546	128,069	CNT24f	58-AACC-c	standard farsi		0.04	39	1Asu.	3	3	1	0	1		PNB	b
9772	Qatari Arab	13.28000	72,773	79,556	103,390	CMT30	12-AACF-i	kuwayti-qatari		1.50	1,193	1Asuh	6	4	5	2	1		pnb	b
9773	Saudi Arab	2.00000	10,960	11,981	15,571	CMT30	12-AACF-k	central `anazi		0.30	36	4Asuh	5	3	3	0	0		pnb	b
9774	Singhalese	2.00000	10,960	11,981	15,571	CNN25q	59-ABBA	sinhala cluster		4.00	479	2asuh	6	6	7	0	0		PNB	b
9775	Southern Baluch	2.00000	10,960	11,981	15,571	CNT24b	58-AABA	balochi cluster		0.01	1	3.s..	3	3	5	0	0		P..	b
9776	Sudanese Arab	2.00000	10,960	11,981	15,571	CMT30	12-AACF-c	sudani		1.20	144	4Asuh	6	4	3	0	0	Arabic: Sudan	PNb	b
9777	Syrian Arab	9.40000	51,511	56,312	73,182	CMT30	12-AACF-f	syro-palestinian		7.00	3,942	1Asuh	7	5	7	4	1	Arabic: Lebanese*	Pnb	b
9778	Tamil	1.00000	5,480	5,991	7,785	CNN23c	49-EBEA-b	tamil		25.00	1,498	2Asu.	9	6	8	5	2	Tamil	PNB	b
9779	USA White	0.50000	2,740	2,995	3,893	CEW19s	52-ABAC-s	general american		70.00	2,097	1Bsuh	10	9	13	5	3	English*	PNB	b
9780	Urdu	6.37000	34,907	38,160	49,593	CNN25r	59-AAFO-d	standard urdu		0.01	4	2Asuh	3	3	6	0	1	Urdu	PNB	b
9781	other minor peoples	1.00000	5,480	5,991	7,785	...				13.00	779		8	4	3	4	0			
	Reunion	**100.00000**	**654,914**	**699,406**	**879,761**					**86.8**	**607,104**									
9782	Bantu	0.50000	3,275	3,497	4,399	NAB57j	51-AACC-m	réunioné		50.00	1,749	1cs..	10	6	6	4	1		pnb	b
9783	Esperanto	0.00000	0	0	0	CEW21z	51-AAAC-a	proper esperanto		50.00	0	0A...	10	8	2	5	0	Esperanto	PNB	b
9784	French (Metropolitan)	0.40000	2,620	2,798	3,519	CEW21b	51-AABI-d	general français	70	85.00	2,378	1B.uh	10	9	14	5	3	French	PNB	b
9785	Gujarati (Zarabe)	2.50000	16,373	17,485	21,994	CNN25e	59-AAFH-b	standard gujaraati		2.00	350	2A.u.	6	4	2	5	2	Gujarati	PNB	b
9786	Han Chinese	0.35600	2,331	2,490	3,132	MSY42a	79-AAAB-ba	kuo-yü	5	90.00	2,241	2Bsuh	10	8	11	5	1	Chinese: Kuoyu*	PNB	b
9787	Han Chinese (Cantonese)	1.60000	10,479	11,190	14,076	MSY42a	79-AAAM-a	central yue		95.00	10,631	3A.uh	10	9	12	5	1	Chinese, Yue	PNB	b
9788	Han Chinese (Hakka)	1.40000	9,169	9,792	12,317	MSY42a	79-AAAG-a	literary hakka		95.00	9,302	1A...	10	8	12	5	2	Chinese: Hakka, Wukingfu*	PNB	b
9789	Malagasy	1.40000	9,169	9,792	12,317	MSY44j	31-LDAA-aa	standard merina		49.00	4,798	1Asu.	9	6	8	5	1		pnb	b
9790	Punjabi	0.40000	2,620	2,798	3,519	CNN25n	59-AAFE-c	general panjabi		10.00	280	1Asu.	8	5	8	4	1		PNB	b
9791	Reunionese Creole	42.64400	279,282	298,255	375,165	NAN58	51-AACC-m	réunioné	97	96.13	286,712	1cs..	10	10	11	5	3		pnb	b
9792	Reunionese White	4.00000	26,197	27,976	35,190	CEW21b	51-AACC-m	réunioné		95.00	26,577	1cs..	10	9	12	5	1		pnb	b
9793	Reunionese White	21.60000	141,461	151,072	190,028	CEW21b	51-AABI-mt	français-de-réunion	70	93.60	141,403	1A.uh	10	10	11	5	1		pnb	.
9794	Swahili	2.90000	18,993	20,283	25,513	NAB57j	99-AUSM-b	standard ki-swahili		0.23	47	4Asu.	5	4	2	1	0	Kiswahili*	PNB	b
9795	Tamil	5.00000	32,746	34,970	43,988	CNN23c	49-EBEA-b	tamil		70.00	24,479	2Asu.	10	9	11	5	2	Tamil	PNB	b
9796	Tamil	15.00000	98,237	104,911	131,964	CNN23c	51-AACC-m	réunioné		91.00	95,469	1cs..	10	9	9	5	2		pnb	b
9797	Urdu	0.10000	655	699	880	CNN25r	59-AAFO-d	standard urdu		0.50	3	2Asuh	5	3	2	0	1	Urdu	PNB	b
9798	other minor peoples	0.20000	1,310	1,399	1,760	...				49.00	685		9	6	6	4	0			
	Romania	**100.00000**	**22,730,877**	**22,326,502**	**19,945,452**					**87.91**	**19,627,363**									
9799	Armenian	0.06000	13,639	13,396	11,967	CEW14	57-AAAA-b	ashkharik		80.00	10,717	4A.u.	10	9	13	5	1	Armenian: Modern, Eastern	PNB	b
9800	Balkan Gypsy	0.10000	22,731	22,327	19,945	CNN25f	59-ACBA-ba	ursari		20.00	4,465	1c...	9	5	7	2	0	Romani, Balkan	Pn.	.
9801	British	0.01500	3,410	3,349	2,992	CEW19i	52-ABAC-b	standard-english		78.00	2,612	3Bsuh	10	9	13	5	3		PNB	b
9802	Bulgar	0.05400	12,275	12,056	10,771	CEW22b	53-AAAH-b	bulgarski		68.00	8,198	2A.uh	10	9	8	5	1	Bulgarian	PNB	b
9803	Carpathian Gypsy	0.05000	11,365	11,163	9,973	CNN25f	59-ACBA-ag	north vlach		80.00	8,931	1c...	10	7	7	2	2	Romani: Latvian	Pn.	b
9804	Crimean Tatar (Tartar)	0.11100	25,231	24,782	22,139	MSY41h	44-AABA-c	crimea-tatar		0.10	25	1c.u.	5	3	2	0	0	Crimean Tatar*	PNb	b
9805	Croat	0.10000	22,731	22,327	19,945	CEW22d	53-AAAG-b	standard hrvatski		88.00	19,647	2Asuh	10	8	11	5	2	Croatian	PNB	b
9806	Czech	0.05900	13,411	13,173	11,768	CEW22e	53-AAAD-a	czesky		75.00	9,879	2Asuh	10	8	8	5	1	Czech	PNB	b
9807	Esperanto	0.00000	0	0	0	CEW21z	51-AAAC-a	proper esperanto		70.00	0	0A...	10	9	2	0	0	Esperanto	PNB	b
9808	French	0.02000	4,546	4,465	3,989	CEW21b	51-AABI-d	general français		84.00	3,751	1B.uh	10	9	14	5	2	French	PNB	b
9809	Gagauzi Turk	0.00500	1,137	1,116	997	MSY41d	44-AABA-b	gagauzi		72.00	804	1c.u.	10	8	8	4	1	Gagauz	Pnb	b
9810	German	0.10000	22,731	22,327	19,945	CEW19m	52-ABCE-a	standard hoch-deutsch		83.00	18,531	2B.uh	10	9	13	5	2	German*	PNB	b
9811	Hungarian (Szekely, Sicul	11.59000	2,634,509	2,587,642	2,311,678	MSW51g	41-BAAA-a	general magyar		88.00	2,277,125	2A.u.	10	9	9	5	2	Hungarian	PNB	b
9812	Jewish	0.01200	2,728	2,679	2,393	CMT35	52-ABCH	yiddish cluster		0.10	3	0B..h	5	3	2	0	0		PNB	b
9813	Jewish	0.03600	8,183	8,038	7,180	CMT35	51-AADC-a	limba româneasca		0.20	16	3A.u.	5	4	2	0	0	Romanian	PNB	b

Continued opposite

Table 8-2 continued

EVANGELIZATION								EVANGELISM			ADDITIONAL DESCRIPTIVE DATA
Ref 1	*D* 28	*aC* 29	*CG%* 30	*r* 31	*E* 32	*U* 33	*W* 34	*e* 35	*R* 36	*T* 37	*Locations, civil divisions, literacy, religions, church history, denominations, dioceses, church growth, missions, agencies, ministries, movements* 38
9700	5	0	0.95	8	99.91	0.09	C	501.54	38	10	Silesia and elsewhere. Settlers, citizens. Nonreligious 5%. D=ECACP(6 Dioceses),NAC,RCC,SDA,JWs. R=TWR(Monaco),HCJB,FEBC.
9701	2	0	3.17	7	99.95	0.05	C	551.33	72	10	Migrants from Greece, settlers, traders. Nonreligious 5%. D=Orthodox Ch of Poland,RCC.
9702	0	0	1.10	5	38.10	61.90	A	0.13	129	3	Remnants of 3.5 million Polish Jews in 1939 (3,350,000 murdered by Nazis).
9703	0	0	0.70	6	42.20	57.80	A	0.30	90	3	Remnants of assimilated Polish-speaking practicing Jews. M=RCC.
9704	0	0	0.00	1	16.00	84.00	A	0.00	0	1.09	Readers of the Scriptures (Religious Karaite Union). Non-Talmudic Jews(Turkic).
9705	1	0	0.47	1	99.90	0.10	C	423.76	31	10	Left bank, Lower Vistula, north center; Gdansk, Gdynia. D=RCC(D-Gdansk,D-Chelmno). Nonreligious 10%. M=SDB,OFM,OFMConv,SJ,SAC,OH.
9706	1	0	0.86	5	99.87	0.13	C	435.04	17	10	Settlers from Lithuania. Nonreligious 15%. Strong Catholics. D=RCC.
9707	3	0	0.45	1	99.60	0.40	C	219.00	41	8	Widely dispersed. Also in 25 countries. Nonreligious 30%, some Muslims. Nomadic caravan churches. D=RCC,UECG,GEM. M=GGMS.
9708	1	0	1.10	5	99.89	0.11	C	428.80	43	10	Migrant workers, settlers from Macedonia. Nonreligious 9%. D=Orthodox Ch of Poland.
9709	10	0	0.54	6	99.98	0.02	C	583.28	9	10	4 million settlers abroad. Nonreligious 1.5%,atheists 0.2%. D=RCC(25 Dioceses),Orthodox Ch of Poland(4 Dioceses),PNCC(3 Dioceses),OCMCP,UECG,MCPR
9710	3	0	0.47	6	99.76	0.24	C	363.39	31	9	Polish-speaking nomadic and settled Gypsies. Nonreligious 20%. D=RCC,UECG,GEM. M=GGMS.
9711	3	0	0.47	1	99.70	0.30	C	283.60	37	8	Nomads. Also in 10 European countries. Nonreligious 20%, some Muslims. D=RCC,UECG,GEM. M=GGMS.
9712	3	0	0.82	7	99.71	0.29	C	336.89	17	9	Settlers since 1917. Nonreligious 25%. D=OCP(D-Warsaw,D-Bialystok),ROC,Old Ritualist Ch(Priestless).
9713	5	0	0.62	6	99.89	0.11	C	467.78	33	10	Settlers from Slovakia. Nonreligious 10%. D=RCC,OCP,UECG,SDA,JWs.
9714	1	0	0.47	1	99.89	0.11	C	406.06	32	10	Dialect of Kashubian. Heavily Germanized. Nonreligious 10%. D=RCC. M=SDB,OFM,SJ.
9715	0	0	3.19	6	35.00	65.00	A	2.55	312	4	Refugees since 1917 from USSR. Muslims 88%(Hanafi Sunnis; 2 mosques, 6 communities),nonreligious 10%.
9716	0	0	7.36	8	99.78	0.22	C	372.95	173	9	North Americans, in business, education.Nonreligious 10%. D=RCC,BBC,SDA,etc.
9717	2	0	0.75	6	99.90	0.10	C	479.43	37	10	Settlers, refugees. Also in 10 countries. Nonreligious 9%. D=OCP(D-Warsaw,D-Bialystok,D-Lodz),RCC(Ukrainian-rite, also Latin-rite). R=HCJB,VERITAS,AWR.
9718	0	0	0.47		99.80	0.20	C	300.76	13	9	Czechs, Hungarians, Latvians, Serbs, Croats, Slovenes, other Europeans, other Asians. Nonreligious 10%.
Portugal											
9719	1	10	4.99	8	99.90	0.10	C	538.74	102	10	Mixed-race. Refugees from Angola. Animists and nonreligious 10%. D=RCC. M=SJ,OFM,SDB,FMB.
9720	2	10	0.60	8	99.90	0.10	C	499.32	29	10	Iberian Romani. Nonreligious 10%. Nomadic caravan churches. D=RCC,MECP(GEM). M=GGMS,Brazilian Bethel Department of World Missions.
9721	4	10	5.68	8	99.90	0.10	C	534.11	109	10	Immigrants from Brazil, as migrant workers or professionals. D=RCC,AoG,CCB,&c.
9722	3	10	3.39	8	99.92	0.08	C	574.21	66	10	Migrants from Brazil. Spiritists 8%. D=RCC,Congregacao Crista em Portugal,IEC.
9723	5	10	0.60	8	99.78	0.22	C	438.43	31	10	Expatriates from Britain, in business. Many retirees. Nonreligious 9%. D=Anglican Ch(D-Gibraltar),IEMP,SDA,JWs,IEPP.
9724	4	10	4.12	8	99.98	0.02	C	629.55	81	10	Refugees from Cape Verde Islands. D=RCC,CON(Nazarenes),SDA,JWs.
9725	0	10	0.00	5	99.60	0.40	C	247.47	0	8	Artificial (constructed) language, in 80 countries. Speakers in Portugal: 62,000(none mother-tongue). Nonreligious 20%.
9726	1	10	0.60	8	99.84	0.16	C	484.42	27	10	Expatriates from France, in business. Nonreligious 13%. D=RCC.
9727	2	10	1.03	1	99.95	0.05	C	553.18	33	10	Northern Provinces Entre-Minho-e-Douro and Trazoz-Montes. Vast majority in Galicia (Spain). D=RCC,5 others. M=about 20.
9728	2	10	0.60	8	99.86	0.14	C	505.37	30	10	Expatriates from Germany, in business. Many retirees. D=IELP,NAC.
9729	1	10	4.21	4	99.95	0.05	C	554.80	89	10	Immigrants from former Portuguese Goa(India). All Catholics. D=RCC.
9730	1	10	0.60	7	99.95	0.05	C	572.13	26	10	Traders from Greece, merchants. D=Greek Orthodox Ch(D-France).
9731	1	10	0.60	7	72.00	28.00	B	23.65	48	5	Long-time residents from China and diaspora. Folk Buddhists 90%. D=RCC.
9732	0	10	2.91	8	81.00	19.00	B	47.30	120	6	Huge immigration from Hong Kong and Macao, 1985. Buddhists/folk-religionists 84%.
9733	1	10	0.60	7	99.83	0.17	C	466.54	28	10	Expatriates from Italy, in business. Strong Catholics. D=RCC. M=SJ,OFM,SDB.
9734	0	10	0.00	8	53.08	46.92	B	0.15	0	3	Small communities of practicing Jews, with 3 synagogues.
9735	0	10	0.00	0	38.10	61.90	A	0.13	0	3	Laborers, refugees from Iraq, Iran, Turkey. Muslims 100%(Sunnis). M=network of agencies.
9736	1	10	7.48	8	99.69	0.31	C	332.44	170	9	Refugees from Lebanon, Syria, Iraq. Muslims 25%. D=RCC(Maronites).
9737	0	10	2.52	8	53.20	46.80	B	0.38	166	3	Migrant workers, immigrants from Morocco, Algeria, Tunisia. Muslims 99%.
9738	1	10	5.25	8	99.90	0.10	C	528.88	101	10	Anusim/Conversos/New Christians: baptized Catholics from 1497 onward who practice Judaism. D=RCC.
9739	0	0	7.09	1	99.96	0.04	C	430.99	181	10	Northeast, city of Miranda near border with Spain. Related to Asturian and Leones. Agriculturalists. D=RCC.
9740	1	10	0.60	8	99.90	0.10	C	542.02	28	10	Refugees from civil war in Mozambique. D=RCC. M=SJ,OFM,SDB,FMB.
9741	7	10	0.47	8	99.93	0.07	C	600.38	23	10	In 16 countries. D=RCC(20 Dioceses),AoG,JWs,IEI(Brethren),SDA,CBP,&c. M=SJ,OFM,CSSp,SDB,SMP,CMF,OSB,IMC,CMML,GST(Japan),WEC,BFM,FMB,UBS.
9742	2	10	0.67	8	99.75	0.25	C	396.93	32	9	Settled, and nomads. Nonreligious 10%. D=RCC,MECP(GEM). M=GGMS,GST(Japan),Brazilian Bethel Department of World Missions.
9743	1	10	0.60	8	99.96	0.04	C	604.77	24	10	Settlers, residents, from Spain. Strong Catholics. D=RCC(20 Dioceses). M=SJ,OFM,SDB.
9744	1	10	5.74	0	99.90	0.10	C	473.04	125	10	Refugees from East Timor since 1975-98 civil war. D=RCC. M=SJ.
9745	0	0	7.62	8	99.78	0.22	C	370.11	180	9	North Americans, in business, education. Nonreligious 10%. D=RCC,BBC,SDA,etc.
9746	2	10	0.60	6	99.70	0.30	C	311.71	37	9	In 25 countries. Nomadic caravan churches. Nonreligious 10%. D=RCC,MECP(GEM). M=GGMS.
9747	0	0	5.96	8	69.00	31.00	B	50.37	280	6	Immigrants from Guinea Bissau and other West African countries. Muslims 80%. D=RCC.
9748	0	10	0.67		82.00	18.00	B	143.66	22	7	Swiss, Belgians, Dutch(retirees et al), Koreans(M=BFMGAP), Japanese (M=GST), Africans, Macanese.
Puerto Rico											
9749	2	10	1.42	8	99.97	0.03	C	598.34	33	10	From Jamaica, Cuba, et alia. Afro-Caribbean spiritists 1%(Mayombe,Rastafarians). D=RCC,ECUSA. T=CBN. R=AWR.
9750	4	10	1.51	8	99.58	0.42	B	266.74	52	8	Exiles, refugees from Cuba since 1959. Nonreligious 40%. D=RCC,IDP,SDA,CBPR.
9751	1	10	4.24	7	75.00	25.00	B	41.06	191	6	Immigrants from India. Hindus 80%(including Neo-Hindu sects). D=RCC.
9752	1	10	3.56	7	93.00	7.00	B	101.83	124	7	Long-time residents from China and diaspora. Chinese folk-religionists/Buddhists 60%. D=RCC.
9753	1	10	3.72	8	99.35	0.65	B	129.02	119	7	Immigrants from Guangdong/Canton(China). Folk Buddhists 65%. D=RCC.
9754	0	10	3.39	8	54.00	46.00	B	1.97	207	4	Small community of practicing Jews, mainly in San Juan.
9755	2	10	5.90	8	99.80	0.20	C	426.32	124	10	From Lebanon, Syria, Palestine. Muslims 19%. D=Antiochian Orthodox Ch(P-Antioch),RCC(Maronites).
9756	4	10	1.41	8	99.96	0.04	C	592.17	33	10	Afro-Caribbean spiritists 1%(Mayombe,Rastafarians). D=RCC,ECUSA,SDA,CBPR.
9757	9	9	1.36	8	99.97	0.03	C	606.40	36	10	D=RCC(4 Dioceses),IDP(PCG),SDA,IMU,CBPR,IDC,JWs,UCPR,&c. M=UCMS,AoG,UMC,COG,ABHMS,ECUSA,&c. T=CBN. R=AWR.
9758	1	10	1.41	8	99.96	0.04	C	595.68	38	10	Long-time settlers from Spain. D=RCC.
9759	9	10	1.41	8	99.77	0.23	C	421.57	42	10	Expatriates from mainland USA, in business, development. D=IMU,SDA,RCC,JWs,CJCLdS,CCS,IDC,IDP,UCPR.
9760	0	10	1.78		99.00	1.00	C	234.87	49	8	Bengalis, Germans(NAC), Papiamentu(200 speakers), Negerhollands speakers(nearly extinct), other Caribbean Islanders, other North and South Americans.
Qatar											
9761	0	7	5.58	7	45.00	55.00	A	6.57	429	4	Former Black African slaves and their descendants, now Qataris. Muslims 96%(mostly Sunnis).
9762	1	10	5.33	6	99.90	0.10	C	522.31	102	10	Migrant workers from Lebanon, Armenia. Nonreligious 10%. D=Armenian Apostolic Ch.
9763	4	10	5.84	8	99.75	0.25	C	416.10	126	10	Expatriates from Britain, in business. D=Anglican Ch/ECJME(D-Cyprus & The Gulf),CB,CoS,CSI.
9764	3	9	6.60	8	82.00	18.00	B	44.89	244	6	Migrant workers from Egypt. Muslims 85%(Sunnis). D=Coptic Orthodox Ch(P-Alexandria),CEC,CCC.
9765	0	0	8.04	5	99.95	0.05	C	513.19	161	10	Immigrant workers from the Philippines, many as maids. Nonreligious 5%. D=RCC.
9766	1	10	4.62	8	99.51	0.49	B	230.82	124	8	Expatriates from France, in business, commerce. D=RCC.
9767	2	10	4.30	8	99.56	0.44	B	267.76	114	8	Expatriates from Germany, in business, finance, commerce, industry. Nonreligious 15%.D=ELC,RCC.
9768	1	7	6.29	8	68.00	32.00	B	24.82	282	5	Migrant workers, refugees from Lebanon. Muslims 82%(Sunnis,Alawis). D=RCC(Maronites).
9769	4	10	6.22	4	91.00	9.00	B	83.03	217	6	From Kerala(India) after 1970. Hindus 30%, Muslims 10%. D=RCC,OSCE,CSI,MTSC.
9770	2	7	7.90	8	64.00	36.00	B	11.68	368	5	Refugees, migrant workers. Muslims 92%(Shafi Sunnis,Alawis,Druzes). D=GOC,RCC.
9771	0	9	3.73	5	39.04	60.96	A	0.05	311	2	Refugees, migrants from Iran. Muslims 97%(Ithna-Asharis), Baha'is 1%. M=LB1.
9772	0	8	4.90	7	48.50	51.50	A	2.65	316	4	Eastern Colloquial Arabic. Muslims 98.5%(Sunnis, primarily Wahhabis, with some Shias). M=FI.
9773	0	8	3.65	7	43.30	56.70	A	0.47	275	3	Migrants. Eastern Colloquial Arabic. Muslims 99%(Sunnis: Wahhabi,Shafi,Maliki,Hanbali).
9774	0	0	3.94	6	43.00	57.00	A	6.27	288	4	Immigrant workers from Sri Lanka. Theravada Buddhists 95%.
9775	0	0	0.00	1	17.01	82.99	A	0.00	161	1.07	Immigrant workers from Pakistan. Muslims 100%.
9776	0	8	2.70	7	46.20	53.80	A	2.02	202	4	Migrants workers from Sudan. Muslims 98%(Maliki Sunnis).
9777	1	7	6.54	8	60.00	40.00	B	15.33	331	5	Migrant workers from Syria. Muslims 93%(Hanafi Sunnis, some Alawis). D=SOC.
9778	2	10	5.14	6	89.00	11.00	B	81.21	189	6	From South India, influx after 1970. Hindus 70%, Muslims 5%. D=RCC,CSI.
9779	4	10	5.21	8	99.70	0.30	C	370.47	115	9	Expatriates from USA, in business, oil. D=AC/ECJME,RCC,CB,CSI.
9780	0	9	1.40	5	49.01	50.99	A	0.01	136	2	From India, Pakistan; large influx from 1970. Muslims 99%(Hanafi Sunnis). M=LBI.
9781	0	8	5.18		36.00	64.00	A	17.08	394	5	Greeks, Pakistanis, Afghanis, Kuwaitis, Iraqis, other Europeans, other Asians. Muslims 60%, nonreligious/atheists 17%.
Reunion											
9782	1	10	3.78	8	99.50	0.50	B	195.27	134	7	East Africans, migrant workers, and descendants of Black African slaves. Muslims 50%. D=RCC. M=CSSp.
9783	0	10	0.00	5	99.50	0.50	B	189.80	0	7	Artificial(constructed) language, in 80 countries. Speakers in Reunion: 260(none mother-tongue). Muslims 20%.
9784	2	10	1.25	8	99.85	0.15	C	493.29	38	10	Military and civilian citizens of France. D=RCC,ERR. M=CSSp,FSC,ERF.
9785	2	10	4.57	6	58.00	42.00	B	4.23	264	4	Long-time immigrants from Gujarat(India) as laborers. Hindus 60%, Muslims 30%(Bohras,Momins), Jains 5%. D=RCC,AoG.
9786	3	10	4.37	7	99.90	0.10	C	538.74	84	10	Immigrants of Chinese origin. Buddhists/Chinese folk-religionists 10%. D=RCC,SDA,JWs. M=CSSp.
9787	4	10	3.30	8	99.95	0.05	C	592.94	63	10	Buddhists/Chinese folk-religionists 5%. Almost all are now Christians. D=RCC,SDA,AoG,JWs. M=CSSp.
9788	3	10	3.72	7	99.95	0.05	C	582.54	71	10	From mainland China. Folk Buddhists 5%. D=RCC,AoG,SDA. M=CSSp,FSC.
9789	2	10	2.32	4	99.49	0.51	B	193.15	91	7	Migrants, laborers from Madagascar. Animists 30%, Muslims 1%. D=RCC,AoG. M=CSSp.
9790	1	10	4.64	5	70.00	30.00	B	25.55	223	5	From India, Pakistan. Hindus 40%, Muslims 30%(Hanafi Sunnis), Sikhs 20%. D=RCC.
9791	4	10	1.90	8	99.96	0.04	C	565.36	51	10	Mulattos, Eurasians(French/Black/Asiatic). D=RCC(D-La Reunion),SDA,AoG,JWs. M=CSSp,FSC,FMB.
9792	2	10	1.36	8	99.95	0.05	C	558.26	40	10	Whites, speaking French Creole, also French. D=RCC,AoG. M=CSSp.
9793	3	10	3.07	8	99.94	0.06	C	545.25	70	10	Whites with French as mother tongue. D=RCC,SDA,AoG. M=CSSp.
9794	0	10	3.93	5	49.23	50.77	A	0.41	300	3	Bantu immigrant laborers from coastal East Africa. Muslims 100%(Shafi Sunnis).
9795	5	10	5.08	6	99.70	0.30	C	365.36	116	9	From South India. Hindus 30%. D=RCC,SDA,JWs,AoG,EER. M=CSSp,AEF.
9796	4	10	6.08	8	99.91	0.09	C	508.19	127	10	Originally from Tamil Nadu. Hindus 9%. D=RCC,SDA,AoG,EER. M=AEF,CSSp.
9797	0	10	1.10	5	48.50	51.50	A	0.88	120	3	From India, Pakistan. Muslims 99%(Hanafi Sunnis). M=CSSp.
9798	0	10	1.90		78.00	22.00	B	139.50	67	7	Malabaris(Malayalis), Mauritians, other Africans, other Asians. Muslims 20%, nonreligious 10%.
Romania											
9799	1	10	0.71	6	99.80	0.20	C	446.76	23	10	Resident from Armenia. Nonreligious/atheists 20%. Gregorians. D=Armenian Apostolic Ch(C-Echmiadzin: D-Bucharest).
9800	0	9	0.71	1	58.00	42.00	B	42.34	82	6	Black Sea region. In 10 countries. Muslims 70%(Hanafi Sunnis),nonreligious 10%.
9801	4	10	0.71	8	99.78	0.22	C	441.28	33	10	Expatriates from Britain, in business. D=Ch of England(D-Europe),CB,SDA,JWs.
9802	1	10	0.71	6	99.68	0.32	C	325.14	41	9	Palitiani (Bogomil). In Romanian Banat. Migrant workers. Nonreligious/atheists 32%. D=Bulgarian Orthodox Ch(P-Sofia).
9803	2	10	0.71	1	99.80	0.20	C	362.08	38	9	Gypsies, in Transylvania. Also in Poland, Hungary, Ukraine, Czechoslovakia, USA. Nonreligious 20%. D=ROC,RCC.
9804	0	9	0.74	1	32.10	67.90	A	0.11	131	3	Eastern Romania. Also in former USSR, China, Turkey, Bulgaria, USA. Muslims 100%(Hanafi Sunnis).
9805	1	10	0.71	6	99.88	0.12	C	504.28	31	10	Migrant laborers from Croatia. D=RCC(5 Dioceses). M=OFM,SJ.
9806	2	10	0.71	6	99.75	0.25	C	383.25	36	9	Emigres from Moravia. Nonreligious 20%. D=RCC(5 Dioceses), Moravian Ch. M=OFM.
9807	0	10	0.00	5	99.70	0.30	C	293.82	0	8	Artificial(constructed) language, in 80 countries. Speakers in Romania: 9,500(none mother-tongue). Nonreligious 30%.
9808	2	10	0.71	8	99.84	0.16	C	490.56	29	10	Expatriates from France, in business. Nonreligious 13%. D=RCC,RCR. M=OFM,SJ.
9809	1	10	0.71	1	99.72	0.28	C	317.98	34	9	Mainly in Ukraine, Moldavia, Kazakhstan, Bulgaria. Greek Orthodox converts from Ottoman Islam from 15th century on. Nonreligious 28%. D=GOC.
9810	2	10	0.71	8	99.83	0.17	C	475.63	32	10	German expatriates from Germany, speaking High German. In business, commerce, industry. Nonreligious 5%. D=ECAC,RCC.
9811	4	10	0.68	6	99.88	0.12	C	510.70	35	10	In Transylvania, Trans-Carpathian provinces. Nonreligious 9%. D=Reformed Ch of Romania,Unitarian Chs in Romania,RCC(3 Dioceses),ELSPC. M=OFM,SJ.
9812	0	10	1.10	5	46.10	53.90	A	0.16	106	3	Southeast Yiddish. Remnant of large Yiddish practicing Jewish community before World War II.
9813	0	10	2.81	6	47.20	52.80	A	0.34	203	3	Practicing Jews. Decline from 500,000 in 1939. 60 communities, 110 synagogues.

Continued overleaf

Table 8-2 continued

PEOPLE		POPULATION				IDENTITY CODE		LANGUAGE		CHURCH		MINISTRY						SCRIPTURE		
Ref	Ethnic name	P%	In 1995	In 2000	In 2025	Race	Language	Autoglossonym	S	AC	Members	Jayuh	d	wa	xc	mc	mi	Biblioglossonym	Pub	ss
1	2	3	4	5	6	7	8	9	10	11	12	13-17	18	19	20	21	22	23	24-26	27
9814	Kalderash Gypsy (Rom)	1.09500	248,903	244,475	218,403	CNN25f	59-ACBA-a	vlach-romani		55.00	134,461	1a...	10	7	8	5	3	Romani: Finnish*	PN.	b
9815	Moldavian	0.10000	22,731	22,327	19,945	CEW21f	51-AADC-ab	standard moldavia		87.00	19,424	1A.u.	10	10	11	5	1		pnb	b
9816	Nogay Tatar (Nogai)	0.04800	10,911	10,717	9,574	MSY41h	44-AABA-c	crimea-tatar		0.10	11	1c.u.	5	1	3	0	0	Crimean Tatar*	PNb	b
9817	Polish (Pole)	0.04400	10,002	9,824	8,776	CEW22i	53-AAAC-c	polski		88.00	8,645	2A.uh	10	9	11	5	2	Polish	PNB	b
9818	Pomak	0.10500	23,867	23,443	20,943	CEW22b	53-AAAH-b	bulgarski		0.00	0	2A.uh	0	2	2	0	0	Bulgarian	PNB	b
9819	Romanian	82.56300	18,767,294	18,433,430	16,467,564	CEW21i	51-AADC-a	limba românească		89.87	16,566,123	3A.u.	10	10	9	5	3	Romanian	PNB	b
9820	Romanian Gypsy (Bayash)	1.86500	423,931	416,389	371,983	CNN25f	51-AADC-a	limba românească		80.00	333,111	3A.u.	10	7	8	5	3	Romanian	PNB	b
9821	Rumelian Turk	0.65000	147,751	145,122	129,645	MSY41j	44-AABA-a	osmanli		0.03	44	1A.u.	3	3	2	0	0	Turkish	PNB	b
9822	Russian	0.20000	45,462	44,653	39,891	CEW22j	53-AAAE-d	russkiy		56.00	25,006	4B.uh	10	5	8	2	2	Russian	PNB	b
9823	Saxon (Transylvanian)	0.17000	38,642	37,955	33,907	CEW19m	52-ABCE-a	standard hoch-deutsch		88.00	33,400	2B.uh	10	9	11	5	2	German*	PNB	b
9824	Serb	0.30000	68,193	66,980	59,836	CEW22l	53-AAAG-a	standard srpski		83.00	55,593	1Asuh	10	8	8	4	1	Serbian*	PNB	b
9825	Slovak	0.14800	33,642	33,043	29,519	CEW22m	53-AAAD-b	slovensky		77.00	25,443	1Asuh	10	9	8	4	2	Slovak	PNB	b
9826	Ukrainian	0.30000	68,193	66,980	59,836	CEW22p	53-AAAE-b	ukrainskiy		72.00	48,225	3A.uh	10	8	11	5	2	Ukrainian	PNB	b
9827	other minor peoples	0.10000	22,731	22,327	19,945	...				59.00	13,173		10	7	8	5	0			
	Russia	**100.00000**	**148,096,501**	**146,933,847**	**137,932,932**					**56.91**	**83,618,351**									
9828	Abazinian	0.02243	33,218	32,957	30,938	CEW17a	42-AABA-b	abazin		3.00	989	0....	6	3	6	0	0	Abaza	p..	b
9829	Abkhazian (Apswa)	0.00492	7,286	7,229	6,786	CEW17a	44-AABA-a	osmanli		60.00	4,337	1A.u.	10	5	8	1	1	Turkish	PNB	b
9830	Afghani (Pathan)	0.00058	859	852	800	CNT24a	58-ABDA-a	pashto		0.00	0	1As..	0	1	6	0	0		pnb	b
9831	Agul (Aguly, Koshan)	0.01206	17,860	17,720	16,635	CEW17b	42-BCAA-p	agul		0.04	7	1....	3	1	0	0	0	Aghul	p..	.
9832	Ainu	0.00120	1,777	1,763	1,655	AUG01b	45-BAAA	sakhalin-aynu cluster		1.15	20	0....	6	2	3	0	0	Ainu	PN.	b
9833	Akhvakh (Axvax)	0.00402	5,953	5,907	5,545	CEW17b	42-BBAB-j	akhvakh		0.05	3	0....	4	1	0	0	0		...	p
9834	Albanian	0.00278	4,117	4,085	3,835	CEW13	55-AAAB-a	standard tosk		5.00	204	0A...	7	3	4	0	3	Albanian: Tosk*	PNB	b
9835	Aleut	0.00026	385	382	359	MRY40a	60-AABA-c	unalaska		66.00	252	0....	10	5	8	1	1	Aleut: Eastern	P..	b
9836	Alutor	0.00050	740	735	690	MSY48	43-CACA	koryak-alutor cluster		4.00	29	0....	6	4	7	0	1		...	.
9837	Andi (Qwannab)	0.00723	10,707	10,623	9,973	CEW17b	42-BBAB	andi cluster		0.05	5	0....	4	1	0	0	0	Andi	...	p
9838	Arab	0.00184	2,725	2,704	2,538	CMT30	12-AACI-c	arab-uzbeki		2.00	54	0....	6	3	3	0	0		...	b
9839	Archin (Archintsy)	0.00070	1,037	1,029	966	CEW17b	42-BCAB-a	archin		1.00	10	0....	6	1	3	0	0		...	p
9840	Armenian	0.48500	718,268	712,629	668,975	CEW14	57-AAAA-b	ashkharik		75.90	540,886	4A.u.	10	7	13	2	2	Armenian: Modern, Eastern	PNB	b
9841	Assyrian	0.00654	9,686	9,609	9,021	CMT31	12-AAAA-f	aisor		78.00	7,495	4cs..	10	7	8	2	2	Assyrian Neo-aramaic	PNB	b
9842	Avar (Dagestani, Batlux)	0.41100	608,677	603,898	566,904	CEW17b	42-BBAA-a	north avar		0.01	60	1....	3	2	2	0	1	Avar	P..	b
9843	Azerbaijani	0.22846	338,341	335,685	315,122	MSY41a	44-AABA-fa	north azeri		0.00	0	2c.u.	0	3	3	0	2	Azerbaijani*	PNB	b
9844	Balkar	0.05329	78,921	78,301	73,504	MSY41z	44-AABB-a	literary karachay-balkar		0.00	0	1c.u.	0	3	3	0	0	Karachay-balkar	PN.	.
9845	Bashkir (Bashkirian)	0.93600	1,386,183	1,375,301	1,291,052	MSY41b	44-AABB-g	bashqurt		7.20	99,022	1A.u.	7	5	7	0	2	Bashkir	Pn.	b
9846	Botlikh (Botlix)	0.00292	4,324	4,290	4,028	CEW17b	42-BBAB-b	botlikh		0.05	2	0....	4	1	3	0	0		...	p
9847	British	0.00300	4,443	4,408	4,138	CEW19i	52-ABAC-b	standard-english		78.00	3,438	3Bsuh	10	8	13	2	1		PNB	b
9848	Bulgar (Bulgarian)	0.02230	33,026	32,766	30,759	CEW22b	53-AAAH-b	bulgarski		72.00	23,592	2A.uh	10	6	8	1	1	Bulgarian	PNB	b
9849	Buryat (North Mongolian)	0.30800	456,137	452,556	424,833	MSY41y	44-BAAB-b	buryat		11.00	49,781	3A..h	8	4	7	0	3	Buryat*	PNB	b
9850	Byelorussian	0.66200	980,399	972,702	913,116	CEW22c	53-AAAE-c	bielorusskiy		70.00	680,891	3A.uh	10	7	10	4	3	Byelorussian*	PNB	b
9851	Caucasian Mountain Jew	0.00475	7,035	6,979	6,552	CMT35	58-AACG-b	judeo-tat		0.50	35	0....	5	3	2	1	1	Judeo-tat	P..	b
9852	Central Asian Jew	0.00096	1,422	1,411	1,324	CMT35	58-AACC-kb	bukharik		0.00	0	1csu.	0	1	2	0	0		pnb	b
9853	Central Circassian	0.03453	51,138	50,736	47,628	CEW17a	42-AAAA-b	cherkes		0.00	0	1a...	0	2	3	0	0		pn.	b
9854	Chamalin (Gadyri, Gakvari	0.00443	6,561	6,509	6,110	CEW17b	42-BBAB-i	gigatl		0.03	2	0....	3	4	3	0	0		...	.
9855	Chechen (Shishan, Kokhchi	0.61147	905,566	898,456	843,418	CEW17d	42-BAAA-b	chechen		0.00	0	0....	0	3	2	0	1	Chechen	P..	b
9856	Chukchi (Chukot)	0.01028	15,224	15,105	14,180	MSY48	43-CAAA-a	chukot		9.00	1,359	0....	7	3	7	1	1	Chukot	...	.
9857	Chulym (Melets Tatar)	0.00805	11,922	11,828	11,104	MSY41z	44-AABD-h	chulym		1.00	118	1c.u.	6	4	3	0	1		pnb	b
9858	Chuvash (Bolgar, Bulgar)	1.17200	1,735,691	1,722,065	1,616,574	MSY41c	44-AAAA-a	chuvash		35.00	602,723	2....	9	6	8	0	1	Chuvash	PN.	b
9859	Crimean Tatar	0.01447	21,430	21,261	19,959	MSY41h	44-AABA-c	crimea-tatar		0.01	2	1c.u.	3	3	2	0	1	Crimean Tatar*	PNb	b
9860	Croat	0.00033	489	485	455	CEW22d	53-AAAG-b	standard hrvatski		84.00	407	2Asuh	10	7	11	2	1	Croatian	PNB	b
9861	Cuban	0.00346	5,124	5,084	4,772	CLT27	66-BFBB	pipil cluster		41.00	2,084	0A.uh	9	7	8	0	1		...	b
9862	Czech (Bohemian)	0.00298	4,413	4,379	4,110	CEW22e	53-AAAD-a	czesky		76.00	3,328	2Asuh	10	8	8	2	1	Czech	PNB	b
9863	Dargin (Darghin, Dargwa)	0.24034	355,935	353,141	331,508	CEW17b	42-BBBB-a	dargwa		0.01	35	1....	3	3	2	0	1	Dargwa	P..	b
9864	Didoi (Dido, Tsezy)	0.00474	7,020	6,965	6,538	CEW17b	42-BBAC-a	didoi		0.00	0	0....	0	1	0	0	0		...	p
9865	Dolgan	0.00448	6,635	6,583	6,179	MSY41m	44-AABE-b	dolgan		70.00	4,608	1....	10	7	8	0	1	Dolgan	p..	.
9866	Dutch	0.00031	459	455	428	CEW19h	52-ABCA-a	algemeen-nederlands		67.00	305	2Bsuh	10	8	15	3	2	Dutch	PNB	b
9867	East Circassian	0.27400	405,784	402,599	377,936	CEW17a	42-AAAA-c	qaberdey		10.00	40,260	1c...	8	4	3	1	1	Kabardian	PN.	.
9868	Eskimo	0.00116	1,718	1,704	1,600	MRY40b	53-AAAE-d	russkiy		19.00	324	4B.uh	8	5	8	1	1	Russian	PNB	b
9869	Esperanto	0.00000	0	0	0	CEW21z	51-AAAC-a	proper esperanto		50.00	0	0A...	10	8	2	0	0	Esperanto	PNB	b
9870	Estonian	0.03155	46,724	46,358	43,518	MSW51a	41-AAAC-b	eesti		75.00	34,768	4A.u.	10	8	8	2	2	Estonian: Tallinn	PNB	b
9871	Even (Lamut, Ola)	0.01160	17,179	17,044	16,000	MSY41i	44-CAAA-a	even		4.00	682	0....	6	5	6	0	1	Even	P..	.
9872	Evenk (Tungus)	0.02076	30,745	30,503	28,635	MSY41i	44-CAAB-a	evenki		10.00	3,050	0....	8	3	7	0	1	Evenki	P..	b
9873	Finnish (Finn)	0.03204	47,450	47,078	44,194	MSW51b	41-AAAA-bb	vehicular suomi		86.00	40,487	1A.uh	10	8	12	3	2	Finnish	PNB	b
9874	French	0.00024	355	353	331	CEW21b	51-AABI-d	general français		80.00	282	1B.uh	10	8	14	1	1	French	PNB	b
9875	Gagauzi Turk	0.00684	10,130	10,050	9,435	MSY41d	44-AABA-b	gagauzi		92.00	9,246	1c.u.	10	7	8	1	1	Gagauz	Pnb	b
9876	Georgian	0.08889	131,643	130,609	122,609	CEW17c	42-CABB-a	kharthuli		40.00	52,244	2A.u.	9	6	8	2	2	Georgian	PNB	b
9877	Georgian Jew	0.00080	1,185	1,175	1,103	CMT35	42-CABB-a	kharthuli		0.00	0	2A.u.	0	1	2	0	0	Georgian	PNB	b
9878	German (Volga German)	0.53600	793,797	787,565	739,321	CEW19m	52-ABCE-a	standard hoch-deutsch	5	77.00	606,425	2B.uh	10	8	13	3	1	German*	PNB	b
9879	Gilyak (Nivkh)	0.00315	4,665	4,628	4,345	MSY48	43-BAAA	nivkh cluster		8.00	370	0....	7	4	7	0	1		...	b
9880	Ginukh (Hinux)	0.00016	237	235	221	CEW17b	42-BBAC-c	ginukh		0.00	0	0....	0	1	3	0	0		...	p
9881	Godoberi (Ghibditli)	0.00200	2,962	2,939	2,759	CEW17b	42-BBAB-c	ghodoberi		0.00	0	0....	0	2	2	0	0		...	p
9882	Greek (Romeos, Urum)	0.06237	92,368	91,643	86,029	CEW20	56-AAAA-c	dhimotiki		90.00	82,478	2B.uh	10	8	10	2	2	Greek: Modern	PNB	b
9883	Han Chinese	0.00500	7,405	7,347	6,897	MSY42a	53-AAAE-d	russkiy		1.00	73	4B.uh	6	3	3	0	0	Russian	PNB	b
9884	Han Chinese (Mandarin)	0.00353	5,228	5,187	4,869	MSY42a	79-AAAB-ba	kuo-yü		0.10	5	2Bsuh	5	1	3	0	0	Chinese: Kuoyu*	PNB	b
9885	High Mari (Cheremiss)	0.09518	140,958	139,852	131,285	MSW51h	41-AACA-a	cheremis		90.00	125,866	1....	10	8	11	2	1	Mari: High*	PN.	b
9886	Hungarian	0.00391	5,791	5,745	5,393	MSW51g	41-BAAA-a	general magyar		81.00	4,654	2A.u.	10	9	8	3	1	Hungarian	PNB	b
9887	Hunzib	0.00136	2,014	1,998	1,876	CEW17b	42-BBAC-e	hunzib		0.01	0	0....	3	4	4	0	0		...	.
9888	Indo-Pakistani	0.00036	533	529	497	CNN25g	59-AAFO-e	general hindi		1.00	5	3Asuh	6	2	8	0	0		pnb	b
9889	Ingrian (Luzh, Khava)	0.00848	12,559	12,460	11,697	MSW51c	41-AAAB-f	izhor		38.00	4,735	1....	9	6	8	0	1		p..	b
9890	Ingush (Galgai, Ingus)	0.17200	254,726	252,726	237,245	CEW17d	42-BAAA-a	ingush		0.01	25	0....	3	3	0	0	1	Ingush	p..	b
9891	Italian	0.00043	637	632	593	CEW21e	51-AABQ-c	standard italiano		84.00	531	2B.uh	10	9	15	2	1	Italian	PNB	b
9892	Itelmen	0.00026	385	382	359	MSY48	43-CBAA-a	itelmen		70.00	267	0....	10	7	8	1	1	Itelmen	...	b
9893	Japanese	0.00040	592	588	552	MSY45a	45-CAAA-a	koku-go		1.00	6	1B.uh	6	1	9	0	0	Japanese	PNB	b
9894	Jat (Jati, Jatu)	0.03300	48,872	48,488	45,518	CNN25h	12-AACJ-a	jakati		1.00	485	0....	6	1	3	0	0		...	.
9895	Jewish	0.26800	396,899	393,783	369,660	CMT35	52-ABCH-b	east yiddish		0.01	39	0A..h	3	4	6	0	0	Yiddish	PNB	b
9896	Jewish	0.85000	1,258,820	1,248,938	1,172,430	CMT35	53-AAAE-d	russkiy		0.05	624	4B.uh	4	3	6	0	0	Russian	PNB	b
9897	Kalmyk (Western Mongolian	0.11279	167,038	165,727	155,575	MSY41y	44-BAAB-d	kalmyk		0.02	33	2c..h	3	3	6	0	3	Mongolian: Kalmyk*	PNb	b
9898	Kapuchin (Bezhetin)	0.00200	2,962	2,939	2,759	CEW17b	42-BBAC-d	kapuchin		0.00	0	0....	0	1	3	0	0		...	p
9899	Karachay (Alan)	0.10225	151,429	150,240	141,036	MSY41z	44-AABB-a	literary karachay-balkar		0.00	0	1c.u.	0	3	3	0	2	Karachay-balkar	PN.	.
9900	Karaite (Karaim)	0.00046	681	676	634	MSY41z	44-AABB-h	karaim		0.00	0	1c.u.	0	2	3	0	0	Karaite*	PN.	b
9901	Karakalpak	0.00419	6,205	6,157	5,779	MSY41z	44-AABC-b	karakalpak		0.00	0	1c.u.	0	2	0	0	1	Karakalpak	Pn.	b
9902	Karatin (Karatai)	0.00482	7,138	7,082	6,648	CEW17b	42-BBAB-d	karatin		0.00	0	0....	0	1	0	0	0		...	p
9903	Karelian (Norgorod)	0.11640	172,384	171,031	160,554	MSW51c	41-AAAB-a	central karely		67.00	114,591	1....	10	6	10	0	3	Karelian	P..	b
9904	Kazakh	0.38700	573,133	568,634	533,800	MSY41e	44-AABC-c	kazakh		0.10	569	4A.u.	5	3	3	0	2	Kazakh	PN.	b
9905	Kerek	0.00001	15	15	14	MSY48	43-CABA-a	kerek		19.00	3	0....	8	3	8	1	0		...	.
9906	Khalka Mongol (Mongolian)	0.00144	2,133	2,116	1,986	MSY41f	44-BAAB-c	halh		0.05	1	3A..h	4	1	3	0	0	Mongolian: Khalka*	PNb	b
9907	Khanti (Ostyak, Ostiak)	0.01516	22,451	22,275	20,911	MSW51z	41-BBAA	khanty cluster		4.00	891	0....	6	4	6	0	1	Khanty	P..	b
9908	Khvarshin (Khwarshi)	0.00144	2,133	2,116	1,986	CEW17b	42-BBAC-b	khvarshi		0.00	0	0....	0	1	3	0	0		...	p
9909	Kildin Lapp	0.00070	1,037	1,029	966	MSW51e	41-AABB-d	kildin		60.00	617	0c...	10	6	5	0	3		p..	b
9910	Kirghiz	0.02839	42,045	41,715	39,159	MSY41g	44-AABC-d	kirghiz		0.00	0	2r.u.	0	3	3	0	2	Kirghiz	PN.	b
9911	Kola Lapp (Saami)	0.00080	1,185	1,175	1,103	MSW51e	41-AABB-a	skolt		90.00	1,058	0A...	10	7	11	0	2	Saami: Russian*	P..	b
9912	Komi-Permyat	0.10017	148,348	147,184	138,167	MSW51d	41-AAEA-b	permyat		40.00	58,873	3....	9	6	8	1	1	Komi: Permyak*	Pn.	b
9913	Komi-Yazva	0.00300	4,443	4,408	4,138	MSW51d	41-AAEA-ac	yazva		40.00	1,763	1....	9	6	8	1	1		pn.	b
9914	Komi-Zyrian	0.24075	356,542	353,743	332,074	MSW51d	41-AAEA-a	komi		33.00	116,735	2....	9	6	8	1	1	Komi: Zyryan*	PN.	b
9915	Korean	0.30000	444,290	440,802	413,799	MSY46	45-AAAA-b	kukö		20.00	88,160	2A...	9	6	11	3	1	Korean	PNB	b
9916	Koryak (Nymylan)	0.00608	9,004	8,934	8,386	MSY48	43-CACA-a	koryak		4.00	357	0....	6	3	6	0	0	Koryak	...	.
9917	Kumyk (Kumuk, Khasav)	0.19500	288,788	286,521	268,969	MSY41z	44-AABB-d	kumyk		0.01	29	1c.u.	3	2	5	0	0	Kumuk*	Pn.	b
9918	Kurdish	0.00321	4,754	4,717	4,428	CNT24c	53-AAAE-d	russkiy		0.10	5	4B.uh	5	3	3	0	2	Russian	PNB	b
9919	Kvanadin (Bagulal)	0.00443	6,561	6,509	6,110	CEW17b	42-BBAB-fa	kvanadin		0.00	0	0....	0	1	0	0	0		...	p
9920	Lak (Laki, Kumux)	0.07985	118,255	117,327	110,139	CEW17b	42-BBBA-a	lak		0.01	12	1....	3	3	0	0	0	Lak	P..	b
9921	Latvian (Lett)	0.03185	47,169	46,798	43,932	CEW15a	54-AABA-a	standard latviashu		89.00	41,651	3A.u.	10	8	11	2	3	Latvian	PNB	b
9922	Lezghian (Lezghi)	0.20100	297,674	295,337	277,245	CEW17b	42-BCAA-a	lezgin		0.01	30	1....	3	4	0	0	1	Lezgi	P..	b
9923	Lithuanian	0.04790	70,938	70,381	66,070	CEW15b	54-AAAA-a	standard lietuvishkai		84.00	59,120	3A.u.	10	8	11	2	3	Lithuanian	PNB	b
9924	Low German	0.08000	118,477	117,547	110,346	CEW19m	52-ABCC	north deutsch cluster		80.00	94,038	2A.uh	10	8	13	3	1	German: Low*	PNB	b
9925	Low Mari (Eastern Mari)	0.34264	507,438	503,454	472,613	MSW51h	41-AACA-b	mariy		90.00	453,109	2....	10	8	11	2	1	Mari: Low*	PN.	b
9926	Ludic (Karelian)	0.00400	5,924	5,877	5,517	MSW51c	41-AAAB-d	north lüdi		60.00	3,526	1....	10	6	8	1	0		p..	b
9927	Luli Gypsy	0.00600	8,886	8,816	8,276	CNN25f	59-ACAA-a	domari		10.00	882	0....	8	4	7	0	0		...	b
9928	Mansi (Vogul)	0.00563	8,338	8,272	7,766	MSW51z	41-BBBA	mansy cluster		4.00	331	0....	6	2	6	0	1	Mansi	P..	b
9929	Mari	0.04500	66,643	66,120	62,070	MSW51h	53-AAAE-d	russkiy		89.00	58,847	4B.uh	10	8	11	2	1	Russian	PNB	b
9930	Mingat	0.00290	4,295	4,261	4,000	MSY41y	44-BAAB-cf	mingat		0.10	4	1c..h	5	1	3	0	0		pnb	b
9931	Moldavian	0.11745	173,939	172,574	162,002	CEW21f	51-AADC-ab	standard moldavia		79.00	136,333	1A.u.	10	7	8	2	2		pnb	b
9932	Mordvin-Erzya	0.28856	427,347	423,992	398,019	MSW51i	41-AADA-a	erzya	1	64.90	275,171	2....	10	8	8	2	1	Mordvin: Erzya*	PN.	b
9933	Mordvin-Moksha	0.20407	302,221	299,848	281,480	MSW51i	41-AADA-b	moksha	1	66.00	197,900	1....	10	8	8	2	1	Mordvin: Moksha*	Pn.	b
9934	Mordvinian	0.17222	255,052	253,049	237,548	MSW51i	53-AAAE-d	russkiy		55.00	139,177	4B.uh	10	8	8	2	1	Russian	PNB	b
9935	Nanai (Gold, Hezhen)	0.00808	11,966	11,872	11,145	MSY41i	44-CAAE-a	gold		4.00	475	0....	6	3	6	0	1	Nanai	P..	.

Continued opposite

Table 8-2 continued

EVANGELIZATION								EVANGELISM			ADDITIONAL DESCRIPTIVE DATA
Ref 1	*D* 28	*aC* 29	*CG%* 30	*r* 31	*E* 32	*U* 33	*W* 34	*e* 35	*R* 36	*T* 37	*Locations, civil divisions, literacy, religions, church history, denominations, dioceses, church growth, missions, agencies, ministries, movements* 38
9814	2	9	0.71	6	99.55	0.45	B	226.84	42	8	Wallachian, Danubian. In 25 countries. Nonreligious 30%, Muslims 15%. Nomadic caravan communities. D=RCC,GEM/GEC. M=GGMS,OFM,SJ,IGP,LBI.
9815	5	10	0.71	6	99.87	0.13	C	485.85	31	10	Province of Moldavia & Suceava. Nonreligious 10%. D=ROC(AD-Iasi),Russian Orthodox Ch,RCC(D-Iasi),PCR,BUR. M=OFM.
9816	0	9	0.79	1	33.10	66.90	A	0.12	132	3	Muslims 100%(Sunnis). Descendants of Muslims of the Volga in Russia.
9817	1	10	0.71	6	99.88	0.12	C	507.49	12	10	Migrant laborers from Poland. Strong Catholics. D=RCC(5 Dioceses). Nonreligious 10%. M=OFM,SJ.
9818	0	9	0.00	6	41.00	59.00	A	0.00	0	1.12	Dialect of Bulgarian. Bulgarian Muslims 100%, converted from Orthodoxy under Ottoman rule.
9819	7	8	0.69	6	99.90	0.10	C	524.41	31	10	Also in Moldavia, Serbia, Bulgaria, Greece, Albania, USA, Canada, Israel, Australia. D=Romanian Orthodox Ch(12 Dioceses),RCC(5 Dioceses),BUR,PCR,CB,SDA.
9820	2	9	0.71	6	99.80	0.20	C	432.16	32	10	Bayash=Gypsies who have lost their Gypsy language. Nomads or settled. Nonreligious 15%, Muslims 5%. Caravan communities. D=RCC,GEM. M=GGMS,OFM,SJ.
9821	0	10	1.72	8	42.03	57.97	A	0.04	158	2	In Dobruja; along Danube in southeast Romania. Muslims 100%(Hanafi Sunnis).
9822	2	10	1.38	7	99.56	0.44	B	257.54	30	8	Emigres, military. Nonreligious/atheists 44%. D=Russian Orthodox Ch(P-Moscow),ORC(AD-Moscow).
9823	3	10	-1.82	8	99.88	0.12	C	526.76	2	10	Transylvania. German emigres. Massive emigration (1989-). D=Ev Ch of the Augsburg Confession,RCC(D-Timisoara),NAC. M=OFM,SJ.
9824	1	10	1.17	6	99.83	0.17	C	451.39	22	10	Migrant workers from Serbia. Nonreligious 10%, many Muslims. D=Serbian Orthodox Ch(D-Timisoara).
9825	1	10	0.71	6	99.77	0.23	C	404.71	35	10	Emigres from Slovakia. Mainly Catholics. Nonreligious 20%. D=RCC. M=OFM,SJ.
9826	2	10	1.26	6	99.72	0.28	C	381.06	46	9	Migrant workers, traders from former USSR. Nonreligious 24%. D=Ukrainian Orthodox Ch,RCC. M=OFM,SJ.
9827	0	9	0.71		93.00	7.00	B	200.27	21	8	Italians, Spaniards, Albanians, Arabs, USA Whites, Ruthenes(Carpathians, in D-Satu Mare). Nonreligious 5%, Muslims 5%.
Russia											
9828	0	9	1.10	0	32.00	68.00	A	3.50	180	4	In Cherkes AO, Dagestan. Also in Turkey, USA, Germany. 70% fluent in Russian. Being assimilated into Cherkess. Muslims 96%(Hanafi Sunnis).
9829	2	9	1.80	8	99.60	0.40	C	267.18	63	8	Black Sea coast, based in Abkhazia (Georgia). Also in Turkey. Muslims 23%(Sunnis), nonreligious 17%. D=Georgian Orthodox Ch,AUCECB. M=IBT.
9830	0	5	0.00	5	36.00	64.00	A	0.00	0	1.11	Refugees, migrant workers from Afghan war 1979-90. Muslims 100%(Hanafi Sunnis).
9831	0	8	1.96	0	17.04	82.96	A	0.02	476	2	Southern Dagestan. Language unwritten. Muslims 100%(Shafi Sunnis).
9832	0	10	2.33	0	28.15	71.85	A	1.18	227	4	On south Sakhalin Island and Kuril Islands. Majority in Japan. Language isolate. 19 dialects. Shamanists/animists 90%.
9833	0	8	1.10	0	17.05	82.95	A	0.03	337	2	Southern Dagestan. Unwritten. Avar used as literary language. Muslims 100%(Shafi Sunnis).
9834	3	8	3.06	6	55.00	45.00	B	10.03	179	5	From Albania. Also in Italy, Turkey, Canada, USA, Egypt. Nonreligious 50%, Muslims 25%(Hanafi Sunnis,some Shias), atheists 20%. D=RCC,SDA,JWs.
9835	1	10	0.66	0	99.66	0.34	C	252.94	38	8	Commander Islands. Under 20 speakers: most now speak only Russian. Nonreligious 30%. D=Russian Orthodox Ch.
9836	1	10	3.42	0	33.00	67.00	A	4.81	342	4	On northern Kamchatka peninsula, Koryak National Okrug. Reindeer breeders. Only 30% use the language. Shamanists 86%. D=ROC.
9837	0	8	1.62	0	17.05	82.95	A	0.03	421	2	Southern Dagestan. Unwritten. Avar used as literary language. Muslims 100%(Shafi Sunnis).
9838	0	8	4.07	0	26.00	74.00	A	1.89	503	4	Mostly in Central Asia. Bilinguals in Tajiki, Uzbeki. Muslims 98%(Sunnis, some Shias).
9839	0	10	0.92	0	25.00	75.00	A	0.91	210	3	In southern Dagestan. Unwritten language; Avar used as literary language. Muslims 100%(Shafi Sunnis).
9840	2	7	0.72	6	99.76	0.24	C	401.42	25	10	Gregorians. In 28 countries. Nonreligious 16%, atheists 8%. D=Armenian Apostolic Ch,RCC. T=IBRA.
9841	2	10	3.61	5	99.78	0.22	C	401.42	83	10	Eastern-Syriac-speaking Assyrians; in 15 countries. D=Ancient Ch of the East,ROC.
9842	0	8	4.18	0	20.01	79.99	A	0.00	709	1.07	In Dagestan. Lingua franca: Kunzakh (Avar northern dialect). Muslims 100%(Shafi Sunnis). M=IBT.
9843	1	8	0.00	1	34.00	66.00	A	0.00	0	1.12	From Azerbaijan. 73% monolinguals. Muslims 78%(54% Shias, 24% Hanafi Sunnis), nonreligious 20%. D=ROC. M=IBT,CSI.
9844	0	9	0.00	1	22.00	78.00	A	0.00	0	1.09	In Karachi-Cherkess AO, Kabardinian-Balkar ASSR. Some in USA. Superficially 100% Muslims(Hanafi Sunnis). Uprooted 1943-44.
9845	1	9	1.08	4	54.20	45.80	B	14.24	95	5	Bashkiria. 400,000 use Tatar as mother tongue. Muslims 70%(Hanafi Sunnis), nonreligious 20%. 2 dialects: Yurmatin(steppe), Kuvakan(forest). D=ROC(D-Ufa).
9846	0	9	0.70	0	21.05	78.95	A	0.03	221	2	Southern Dagestan. Unwritten language; Avar is used as literary language. Close to Andi. Muslims 100%(Shafi Sunnis).
9847	1	10	0.49	8	99.78	0.22	C	429.89	30	10	Expatriates from Britain, in commerce, industry, education, business. D=Anglican Ch(D-Europe).
9848	1	10	0.47	6	99.72	0.28	C	354.78	35	9	From Bulgaria. In 15 countries. Nonreligious 18%, atheists 10%. D=Bulgarian Orthodox Ch(P-Sofia). M=LBI.
9849	2	9	1.23	4	72.00	28.00	B	28.90	76	5	Buryat-Mongol ex-ASSR. Mahayana/Lamaist Buddhists 48%, nonreligious 30%, shamanists 10%. D=Russian Orthodox Ch(strong until 1917),Pentecostal Ch. M=IBT.
9850	3	8	0.17	5	99.70	0.30	C	357.70	23	9	White Russians. Mainly live in Belorussia. Nonreligious 25%. D=ROC,RCC,Old Ritualist Chs. R=FEBC,TWR.
9851	1	6	3.62	0	24.50	75.50	A	0.44	482	3	Dagestan; also in Azerbaijan, Gengia, Iran. Language: Judeo-Tati, Hebrew Tati. Ethnic name: Bik. Religious Jews. Emigration to USA and Israel.
9852	0	6	0.00	1	24.00	76.00	A	0.00	0	1.12	Bukharian. Centered on Bokhara (Uzbekistan). Also in Israel, USA.
9853	0	9	0.00	0	24.00	76.00	A	0.00	0	1.08	Kabardino-Cherkess. In Karachay-Cherkess AO, western north Caucasus foothills. Muslims 100%(Hanafi Sunnis).
9854	0	9	0.70	0	19.03	80.97	A	0.02	245	2	Southern Dagestan. Unwritten; literacy language Avar. Muslims 100%(Shafi Sunnis).
9855	0	8	0.00	0	19.00	81.00	A	0.00	0	1.05	Also in Kazakhstan, Georgia, Germany. Most religious Muslims in former USSR 63%(fervent Hanafi Sunnis, strongly Sufi), atheists 21%, nonreligious 16%. .
9856	1	9	5.03	0	40.00	60.00	A	13.14	393	5	Dzhukhur. Gorskie Evrei. Reindeer Chukchee 71%, Maritime Chukchee 20%. Chukot and Koryak National Okrug, Yakutia. Literary language. Shamanists 80%.
9857	1	9	2.50	1	36.00	64.00	A	1.31	251	4	Basin of Chulym river, north of Altay Mountains. Close to Shor. Second language: Russian. Shamanists 99%, with thin veneer of Christianity. D=ROC.
9858	1	8	0.82	0	77.00	23.00	B	98.36	58	6	In Chuvashia. 65% also speak Russian. Muslims 35%(Sunnis), nonreligious 30%. Traditionally Orthodox. D=Russian Orthodox Ch(D-Cheboksary & Chuvash).
9859	0	7	0.70	1	29.01	70.99	A	0.01	142	2	Mainly in Uzbekistan (after 1944 deportation from Crimea). Muslims 100%(Hanafi Sunnis). M=IBT.
9860	1	8	3.78	6	99.84	0.16	C	453.76	90	10	Refugees, migrant workers from Croatia civil war, 1990-92. Nonreligious 14%. D=RCC.
9861	1	9	5.48	8	90.00	10.00	B	134.68	193	7	Immigrants during Soviet-Cuban collaboration, 1960-90. Former military personnel. Nonreligious 50%. D=RCC.
9862	5	10	2.28	6	99.76	0.24	C	393.90	66	9	Immigrants, residents from Czechoslovakia. Also in USA, Canada, Poland, Israel, Austria. Nonreligious 20%. D=RCC,ROC,SDA,JWs,AUCECB. M=UBS.
9863	0	8	3.62	0	23.01	76.99	A	0.00	550	1.07	Southern Dagestan. Many dialects. Literary language: Akusha. 65% speak Russian. Muslims 100%(Shafi Sunnis, with a few Shias). M=IBT.
9864	0	8	0.00	0	13.00	87.00	A	0.00	0	1.03	Southern Dagestan. Unwritten. Literary language: Avar. Muslims 100%(Shafi Sunnis).
9865	1	10	0.85	1	99.70	0.30	C	275.94	44	8	Turkic. Near Arctic Ocean. Dolgano-Nenetski National Region. Not close to Yakut. Shamanists 30%. D=Russian Orthodox Ch.
9866	2	9	0.39	6	99.67	0.33	C	342.37	25	9	Expatriates from Netherlands in development, commerce. Nonreligious 30%. D=DRC,RCC.
9867	1	9	0.73	0	45.00	55.00	A	16.42	105	5	Upper Circassian, Kabardino-Cherkess. Kabardinia. Muslims 90%(Hanafi Sunnis). D=Armenian Apostolic Ch (in Mozdok, North Ossetia). M=IBT.
9868	1	10	3.65	7	79.00	21.00	B	54.78	154	6	Asiatic Eskimos, Siberian Eskimos who now speak Russian as mother tongue. Shamanists 80%. D=ROC.
9869	0	9	0.00	5	98.00	2.00	B	178.85	0	7	Artificial(constructed) language, in 80 countries. Speakers in Russia: 107,000(none mother-tongue). Nonreligious 50%.
9870	5	10	0.45	5	99.75	0.25	C	388.72	31	9	Most are bilingual in Russian. Nonreligious 20%. D=Russian Orthodox Ch,ELCE,RCC,MCE,AUCECB. M=UBS,LBI.
9871	1	9	4.31	0	32.00	68.00	A	4.67	438	4	In Yakutia and Kamchatka, scattered over Okhotsk Arctic coast. Literary language. 10 dialects. Close to Koryaks, Yukagirs, Yakuts. Shamanists 90%.
9872	1	10	5.89	0	46.00	54.00	A	16.79	398	5	Evenki National Okrug, Sakhalin Island. 28 dialects. Russian widely used. Shamanists 70%, Lamaists 15%, nonreligious 5%. D=Russian Orthodox Ch.
9873	2	10	0.57	5	99.86	0.14	C	486.54	28	10	Immigrants from Finland. Also in 10 countries. Most are bilingual in Russian. Nonreligious 13%. D=ELC,ROC.
9874	1	10	0.47	8	99.80	0.20	C	435.08	27	10	Expatriates from France, in development, medicine, commerce. Nonreligious 16%. D=RCC.
9875	1	10	0.83	1	99.92	0.08	C	466.76	32	10	Turkic Christians based on Kishinev (Moldavia). 77% speak Russian. Nonreligious 8%. D=95% ROC. M=IBT.
9876	2	9	0.13	4	99.40	0.60	B	147.46	4	7	Mostly in Georgia. Nonreligious/atheists 54%, Muslims 5%(Sunnis, Shias). D=GOC,AUCECB.
9877	0	9	0.00	4	38.00	62.00	A	0.00	0	1.11	Oriental and Ashkenazi Jews. Religious Jews. Substantial emigration to Israel. Nonreligious 10%.
9878	3	10	0.38	8	99.77	0.23	C	427.19	27	10	Nemtsy. In Altai, Kirgizia, Kazakhstan. Nonreligious 20%. D=German Evangelical Lutheran Ch,Old Mennonites,AUCECB. M=FMB. R=FEBC,HCJB,AWR.
9879	1	10	3.68	0	41.00	59.00	A	11.97	293	5	Sakhalin Oblast, lower Amur river. All bilingual in Russian. Fishermen, agriculturalists. Shamanists/animists 92%(bear-worship). D=ROC.
9880	0	10	0.00	0	18.00	82.00	A	0.00	0	1.04	Southern Dagestan. Unwritten language; Avar as literary language. Muslims 100%(Shafi Sunnis).
9881	0	7	0.00	0	14.00	86.00	A	0.00	0	1.04	Highland west central Dagestan. Unwritten. Close to Avar(literary language). Muslims 100%(Sunnis).
9882	1	10	0.63	7	99.90	0.10	C	522.31	28	10	19th-century immigrants from Greece, around Black Sea. Romeos retain Greek language; Urum retain Turkish. D=Greek Orthodox Ch/ROC. M=UBS,LBI.
9883	0	10	4.38	7	54.00	46.00	B	1.97	255	4	Chinese whose mother tongue has now changed to Russian. Buddhists/Chinese folk-religionists 70%, nonreligious 29%.
9884	0	10	1.62	7	51.10	48.90	B	0.18	122	3	Buddhists/folk-religionists 55%, nonreligious/atheists 45%.
9885	1	9	1.10	0	99.90	0.10	C	453.33	42	10	Mountain Cheremis. Mari, Bashkir. Agriculturalists, lumbermen. Traditionally Orthodox, but now Muslims 10%. D=Russian Orthodox Ch(D-Kazan).
9886	2	10	2.62	6	99.81	0.19	C	428.69	76	10	Immigrants, refugees from Hungary. Nonreligious 15%. D=RCC,RCCU. M=LBI.
9887	0	0	0.00	0	10.01	89.99	A	0.00	0	1.02	Southern Dagestan. Not a written language. Avar is the literary language. Related to Dido. Muslims 100%.
9888	0	8	1.62	7	52.00	48.00	B	1.89	138	4	Refugees, traders, merchants from India, Pakistan, Kashmir. Mostly Hindus 80%, Muslims 19%.
9889	1	10	6.35	0	77.00	23.00	B	106.79	262	7	Baltic area, Kingisepp, Lomonosov, Leningrad Oblast. Close to Karelian. Most no longer speak Ingrian but are becoming assimilated into Russian. Shamanists 60%.
9890	0	8	-3.69	0	20.01	79.99	A	0.00	14	1.05	Lamur, Kisti. Chechen, Ingush. All deported by Stalin 1944-57. Muslims 100%(fervent Hanafi Sunnis with 2,600 mosques). Many Christians till 1820. M=IBT.
9891	1	8	0.53	7	99.84	0.16	C	469.09	27	10	Expatriates in commerce, development, construction. Strong Catholics. D=RCC.
9892	1	10	-0.31	0	99.70	0.30	C	275.94	10	8	Southern Kamchatka Peninsula, Koryak National Okrug. All bilingual in Russian, and acculturated. Shamanists 30%. D=Russian Orthodox Ch.
9893	0	8	1.81	7	55.00	45.00	B	2.00	128	4	Expatriates from Japan in business, commerce. Buddhists 90%, nonreligious 9%.
9894	0	8	3.96	0	22.00	78.00	A	0.80	619	3	Nomadic non-Romany (pre-Romany) Gypsies. Also in Moldavia, Ukraine, Afghanistan. Related to Arabic, Bangaru. Muslims 99%.
9895	0	10	3.73	5	47.01	52.99	A	0.01	258	2	Decline from 5,260,000 Jews in 1900. Bilingual in Russian. Sizeable annual emigrations to Israel, USA. Nonreligious 20%.
9896	0	10	4.22	7	54.05	45.95	B	0.09	249	2	Unassimilated Russian-speaking practicing Jews. Fluctuating annual emigrations to Israel; massive by 1990. Nonreligious 40%. R=FEBC,HCJB,TWR,KNLS.
9897	0	8	3.56	1	38.02	61.98	A	0.02	312	2	Kalmuk, Kalmytz, Oirots, Dzhungarians. In Kalmykia. Also Germany, Taiwan, USA(NJ). Vicious persecutions 1929-1966. Buddhists 70%(Lamaists).
9898	0	9	0.00	0	17.00	83.00	A	0.00	0	1.04	Southern Dagestan. 4 dialects. Unwritten language; Avar is literary language. Muslims 100%(Sunnis).
9899	0	9	0.00	1	24.00	76.00	A	0.00	0	1.09	Karachai-Cherkess AO. Long history of oppression, deportation, genocide. Some fled to USA. Muslims 100%(Hanafi Sunnis). M=SIL,IBT.
9900	0	10	0.00	1	26.00	74.00	A	0.00	0	1.10	'Readers of the Scriptures'. Heretical Jewish sect rejecting Talmud. Almost russified. Nonreligious 20%.
9901	0	7	0.00	1	19.00	81.00	A	0.00	0	1.09	In Karakalpak, also Bukhara. All bilingual in Uzbek. Muslims 78%(Hanafi Sunnis), nonreligious/atheists 22%. M=IBT.
9902	0	8	0.00	0	13.00	87.00	A	0.00	0	1.03	Southern Dagestan. Unwritten language. Avar is used as literary language. Muslims 100%(Shafi Sunnis).
9903	3	9	0.66	0	99.67	0.33	C	276.34	40	8	Karelia, Kalinin, Leningrad, Murmansk Oblasts. Also in Finland. Bilingual in Russian. Nonreligious 30%. D=Russian Orthodox Ch,RCC,ELC.
9904	0	8	4.12	4	41.10	58.90	A	0.15	328	3	Muslims 60%(Hanafi Sunnis, with Sufi influence), nonreligious 30%, atheists 10%. M=ROC,CSI. R=FEBC.
9905	0	10	1.10	0	50.00	50.00	B	34.67	99	5	Cape Navarin, Kamchatka. Related to Chukchi. Almost extinct(3 speakers in 1991). Shamanists 81%.
9906	0	9	0.00	4	43.05	56.95	A	0.07	49	2	Central Mongolian. Buryatia; also in Kirghizia. Originally from Mongolia. Nonreligious 50%, shamanists 30%, atheists 16%, Lamaists 3%.
9907	1	9	2.10	0	35.00	65.00	A	5.11	243	4	Kanty-Mansy National Okrug; along Ob river. Russian in use. Shamanists/animists 96%. D=ROC.
9908	0	10	0.00	0	18.00	82.00	A	0.00	0	1.04	Avar. Southern Dagestan. Unwritten language; Avar used as literary language. Muslims 100%(Shafi Sunnis).
9909	3	9	3.07	1	99.60	0.40	C	219.00	112	8	Karelia, Kola Peninsula. An officially recognized literary language. Many bilinguals in Russian. Nonreligious 30%. D=ROC,RCC,ELC.
9910	0	7	0.00	4	30.00	70.00	A	0.00	0	1.10	Mainly in Kirghizia; also in China, Afghanistan, Turkey. Muslims 55%(Hanafi Sunnis), nonreligious 40%. M=IBT,CSI.
9911	2	10	1.29	4	99.90	0.10	C	469.75	44	10	Kola Peninsula. Many bilingual in Russian. Shamanists/animists 10%. D=ELC,ROC.
9912	1	9	0.98	0	84.00	16.00	B	122.64	65	7	South Komi, Komi-Permyak National Okrug, east of central Ural Mountains. Industry, agriculture. Animists/shamanists 40%, nonreligious 20%. D=ROC.
9913	1	10	0.98	0	82.00	18.00	B	119.72	66	7	Dialect of Komi-Zyrian. Shamanists 50%, nonreligious 10%. D=Russian Orthodox Ch.
9914	1	9	0.85	0	77.00	23.00	B	92.74	66	6	North Komi. South of Yurak, west of Vogul peoples. Pastoralists, hunters. Shamanists/animists 45%, nonreligious 22%. D=Russian Orth Ch(D-Arkhangelsk).
9915	3	10	9.51	6	89.00	11.00	B	64.97	312	6	45% now speak Russian only; Korean by over-50s only. Nonreligious 40%, shamanists 20%, Buddhists 15%, atheists 5%. D=Reformed Chs,KMC(Methodists).
9916	0	10	3.64	0	30.00	70.00	A	4.38	396	4	On northern Kamchatka, Koryak National Okrug. Literary language. Shamanists/animists 96%.
9917	0	9	3.42	1	29.01	70.99	A	0.01	399	2	In southern Dagestan; also Turkey, USA. Lingua franca. Agriculturalists. Many trilingual in Kumyk, Azeri, Russian. Muslims 100%(Shafi,Hanafi Sunnis).
9918	0	8	1.62	7	52.10	47.90	B	0.19	190	3	Scattered groups of russified Kurds across Transcaucasia. Muslims 80%(Shias,Yazidis), nonreligious 20%. M=CSI,and whole network of agencies.
9919	0	8	0.00	0	13.00	87.00	A	0.00	0	1.03	Southern Dagestan. Unwritten language; Avar used as literary language. Muslims 100%(Shafi Sunnis).
9920	0	8	2.52	0	20.01	79.99	A	0.00	482	1.06	In Caucasus, southern Dagestan. Widely scattered from Ukraine to Central Asia. 5 dialects. Lingua franca. Fluent in Russian, Azeri, Kumyk. Muslims 100%(Shafi).
9921	5	9	0.58	5	99.89	0.11	C	513.26	31	10	In 25 countries, primarily Latvia. Nonreligious 9%. D=ROC,ELCL,RCC,RCL,CB.
9922	0	8	3.46	0	21.01	78.99	A	0.00	582	1.06	In Dagestan; also Azerbaijan. Lingua franca. Muslims 100%(Shafi Sunnis). M=IBT.
9923	4	8	0.53	5	99.84	0.16	C	466.03	10	10	From Lithuania; in 19 countries. Nonreligious 15%. D=RCC,ELCL,ERCL,ROC.
9924	1	8	9.58	8	99.80	0.20	C	438.00	196	10	Across Russia to China border. Also in 11 other countries. 50% speak Russian as second language. D=ELC. M=EKD.
9925	1	9	2.93	0	99.90	0.10	C	456.61	77	10	Mari, Udmurtia. Traditionally Orthodox, but Muslims 5%, shamanists 5%. D=Russian Orthodox Ch(D-Kazan & Mari ASSR). M=IBT.
9926	0	7	0.28	0	96.00	4.00	C	210.24	37	8	In Karelia. Transitional between Olonetsian and northern central Veps. Nonreligious 40%.
9927	0	8	4.58	7	44.00	56.00	A	16.06	349	5	Nomadic Gypsies in Uzbekistan. Caucasus. Also Iran, Syria, Turkey, India, 6 others. Muslims 75%, nonreligious 15%.
9928	1	9	0.69	0	35.00	65.00	A	5.11	132	4	Between Urals and Ob river. Closest to Hungarian. Shamanists/animists 96%. D=ROC.
9929	1	9	0.75	7	99.89	0.11	C	516.51	30	10	Mari who have Russian now as mother tongue. Muslims 10%. D=Russian Orthodox Ch(D-Kazan & Mari). M=IBT.
9930	0	9	1.40	1	32.10	67.90	A	0.11	185	3	Ethnic group within Khalkha Mongol. Nonreligious 47%, atheists 25%, shamanists 25%, some Lamaists 3%.
9931	2	9	0.47	6	99.79	0.21	C	397.92	29	9	From Moldavia, Romania. Nonreligious 18%. D=Russian Orthodox Ch, Romanian Orthodox Ch.
9932	1	9	0.63	7	99.65	0.35	C	279.28	15	8	Northern Mordvin. Acculturated to Russian life, and a few to Tatar culture. Nonreligious 30%. Some pagans; traditional Orthodoxy. D=ROC.
9933	1	9	0.97	1	99.66	0.34	C	267.39	24	8	Southern Mordvin. Nonreligious 30%. Traditionally Orthodox. D=Russian Orthodox Ch(D-Penza & Saransk).
9934	1	9	0.73	7	99.55	0.45	B	244.91	16	8	Russian-speakers are increasing, but Mordvin-speakers declined sizeably from 1900 to 1990. Nonreligious 45%. D=ROC.
9935	1	9	2.80	0	32.00	68.00	A	4.67	308	4	Ussuri Valley, Amur Valley below Khabarovsk. Also in China. Shamanists 90%, Chinese religionists 6%. D=Russian Orthodox Ch.

Continued overleaf

Table 8-2 continued

PEOPLE		POPULATION				IDENTITY CODE		LANGUAGE		CHURCH		MINISTRY						SCRIPTURE	
Ref 1	Ethnic name 2	P% 3	In 1995 4	In 2000 5	In 2025 6	Race 7	Language 8	Autoglossonym 9	S 10	AC 11	Members 12	Jayuh 13-17	d 18	wa 19	xc 20	mc 21	mi 22	Biblioglossonym 23	Pub ss 24-26 27
9936	Naukan Eskimo	0.00030	444	441	414	MRY40b	60-ABAB-b	naukan		20.00	88	0c...	9	7	7	3	1		p.. .
9937	Negidal (Nizovsk)	0.00040	592	588	552	MSY41i	44-CAAC-a	negidal		1.00	6	0....	6	3	6	0	1		pn. .
9938	Nogay Tatar (Nogai)	0.05013	74,241	73,658	69,146	MSY41z	44-AABA-c	crimea-tatar		0.05	37	1c.u.	4	1	3	0	0	Crimean Tatar*	PNb b
9939	Northern Altai	0.02000	29,619	29,387	27,587	MSY41z	44-AABD-gd	teleut		35.00	10,285	1c.u.	9	6	7	1	1		pnb .
9940	Northern Kurdish (Kurd)	0.26000	385,051	382,028	358,626	CNT24c	58-AAAA-a	kurmanji		1.00	3,820	3c...	6	4	4	3	1	Kurdish: Kurmanji*	PN. b
9941	Northern Yukagir (Tundra)	0.00120	1,777	1,763	1,655	MSY48	44-DAAA-a	odul-tundra		8.00	141	0....	7	4	8	0	1	Yukaghir, Northern	... b
9942	Oirat (Western Mongul)	0.03216	47,628	47,254	44,359	MSY41y	44-BAAB-e	oyrat		0.10	47	1a..h	5	1	3	0	0	Mongolian: Inner*	PNb b
9943	Olonetsian (Livvikovian)	0.00972	14,395	14,282	13,407	MSW51c	41-AAAB-c	olonec		60.00	8,569	1....	10	6	8	1	3	Livvi	P.. b
9944	Orochi (Orichen, Tez)	0.00080	1,185	1,175	1,103	MSY41i	44-CAAD-b	oroch		7.00	82	0....	7	4	8	0	1		... .
9945	Orok	0.00030	444	441	414	MSY41i	44-CAAE-f	orok		1.00	4	0....	6	2	3	0	1		p.. .
9946	Ossetian (Ossete, Iron)	0.31500	466,504	462,842	434,489	CNT24e	58-ABBA	oseti cluster		44.00	203,650	2....	9	5	8	1	1	Ossete*	PN. b
9947	Ostyak Samoyed (Selkup)	0.00300	4,443	4,408	4,138	MSW51j	41-CABA-a	selkup		6.00	264	0....	7	4	7	0	1		... b
9948	Persian	0.00175	2,592	2,571	2,414	CNT24f	58-AACC-c	standard farsi		0.03	1	1Asu.	3	3	2	0	0		PNB b
9949	Polish	0.06434	95,285	94,537	88,746	CEW22i	53-AAAC-c	polski		90.00	85,084	2A.uh	10	8	11	2	3	Polish	PNB b
9950	Romanian	0.00408	6,042	5,995	5,628	CEW21i	51-AADC-a	limba românească		83.00	4,976	3A.u.	10	8	8	3	3	Romanian	PNB b
9951	Russian	80.17210	118,732,075	117,799,951	110,583,728	CEW22j	53-AAAE-d	russkiy	84	63.20	74,449,569	4B.uh	10	8	9	5	3	Russian	PNB b
9952	Russian Gypsy (Ruska Roma	0.01440	21,326	21,158	19,862	CNN25f	59-ACBA-ai	rusicqo		70.00	14,811	1c...	10	7	7	0	3		pn. .
9953	Russian Itelmen	0.00165	2,444	2,424	2,276	MSY48	53-AAAE-d	russkiy		75.00	1,818	4B.uh	10	7	8	1	1	Russian	PNB b
9954	Russian Lapp (Skolt)	0.00038	563	558	524	MSW51e	41-AABB-a	skolt	84	85.00	475	0A...	10	8	10	2	1	Saami: Russian*	P.. b
9955	Russian Samoyed (Selkup)	0.00140	2,073	2,057	1,931	MSW51j	53-AAAE-d	russkiy	84	9.00	185	4B.uh	7	3	7	1	1	Russian	PNB b
9956	Russianized Gypsy	0.20000	296,193	293,868	275,866	CNN25f	53-AAAE-d	russkiy	84	56.00	164,566	4B.uh	10	5	8	1	1	Russian	PNB b
9957	Rutul (Rutal, Mukhad)	0.01327	19,652	19,498	18,304	CEW17b	42-BCAA-c	rutul		0.03	6	1....	3	1	0	0	0	Rutul	p.. .
9958	Sayan Samoyed (Karagas)	0.00050	740	735	690	MSY41z	44-AABD-l	karagas		1.00	7	1c.u.	6	3	3	0	1		pnb b
9959	Serb	0.00107	1,585	1,572	1,476	CEW22l	53-AAAG-a	standard srpski		80.00	1,258	1Asuh	10	8	9	3	1	Serbian*	PNB b
9960	Shorian (Kuznets Tatar)	0.01100	16,291	16,163	15,173	MSY41z	44-AABD-i	ku-kizhi		70.00	11,314	1c.u.	10	7	8	2	1	Shor	pnb b
9961	Siberian Eskimo (Aiwanat)	0.00120	1,777	1,763	1,655	MRY40b	60-ABAB-aa	chaplin		18.00	317	0A...	8	4	8	0	0	Yupik, Central Siberian	P.. .
9962	Slovak	0.01000	14,810	14,693	13,793	CEW22m	53-AAAD-b	slovensky		78.00	11,461	1Asuh	10	8	8	4	1	Slovak	PNB b
9963	Southern Altai (Oirot, Tu	0.04721	69,916	69,367	65,118	MSY41z	44-AABD-gc	talangit		40.00	27,747	1c.u.	9	5	8	1	1		pnb .
9964	Southern Yukagir	0.00050	740	735	690	MSY48	44-DAAA-b	odul-kolyma		7.00	51	0....	7	4	7	0	1		... b
9965	Spaniard	0.00140	2,073	2,057	1,931	CEW21k	51-AABB-c	general español		96.00	1,975	2B.uh	10	9	15	2	1	Spanish	PNB b
9966	Tabasaran (Ghumghum)	0.06632	98,218	97,447	91,477	CEW17b	42-BCAA-d	tabarasan		0.00	0	2....	0	2	2	0	0	Tabassaran	P.. b
9967	Tajik	0.02599	38,490	38,188	35,849	CNT24g	58-AACC-j	tajiki		0.00	0	2asu.	0	3	3	0	0	Tajik*	PNB b
9968	Tat	0.01321	19,564	19,410	18,221	CNT24f	58-AACG-a	muslim-tat		20.00	3,882	0....	9	4	7	1	1	Tat*	P.. b
9969	Tatar (Kazan Tatar, Tura)	3.75597	5,562,460	5,518,791	5,180,720	MSY41h	44-AABB-e	tatar		3.00	165,564	2c.u.	6	4	8	0	2	Tatar: Kazan	Pn. b
9970	Tavgi Samoyed (Nganasan)	0.00086	1,274	1,264	1,186	MSW51j	41-CAAA-d	nganasan		7.00	88	0....	7	4	7	0	1		... .
9971	Ter Lapp	0.00038	563	558	524	MSW51e	41-AABB-d	kildin		60.00	335	0c...	10	7	8	2	2		p.. b
9972	Tindin (Tindi)	0.00460	6,812	6,759	6,345	CEW17b	42-BBAB-e	tindal		0.00	0	0....	0	1	0	0	0		... p
9973	Tsakhur (Caxur)	0.00442	6,546	6,494	6,097	CEW17b	42-BCAC-a	tsakhur		0.03	2	0....	3	3	0	0	0	Tsakhur	p.. p
9974	Turkish	0.00673	9,967	9,889	9,283	MSY41j	44-AABA-a	osmanli		0.00	0	1A.u.	0	3	2	0	0	Turkish	PNB b
9975	Turkmen	0.02703	40,030	39,716	37,283	MSY41k	44-AABA-e	turkmen		0.00	0	3c.u.	0	3	2	0	1	Turkmen	PNb b
9976	Tuvinian (Uriankhai)	0.14400	213,259	211,585	198,623	MSY41z	44-AABD-k	tuvin		1.50	3,174	2c.u.	6	3	7	0	3	Tuvin	Pnb b
9977	Udekhe	0.00129	1,910	1,895	1,779	MSY41i	44-CAAD-a	udihe		3.00	57	0....	6	3	6	2	0		... .
9978	Udin (Udi)	0.00075	1,111	1,102	1,034	CEW17b	42-BCAC-d	udin		90.00	992	0....	10	7	11	2	2	Udin	P.. b
9979	Udmurt (Votyak, Kalmez)	0.48500	718,268	712,629	668,975	MSW51k	41-AAEA-c	udmurt		54.00	384,820	2....	10	5	8	2	1	Udmurt	Pn. .
9980	Uighur	0.00175	2,592	2,571	2,414	MSY41z	44-AABD-d	east uyghur		0.00	0	1r.u.	0	3	2	0	1	Uighur*	PNB b
9981	Ukrainian	2.34500	3,472,863	3,445,599	3,234,527	CEW22p	53-AAAE-b	ukrainskiy		79.00	2,722,023	3A.uh	10	7	9	4	3	Ukrainian	PNB b
9982	Ulchi (Olcha, Nani)	0.00200	2,962	2,939	2,759	MSY41i	44-CAAE-e	olcha		3.00	88	0....	6	4	6	0	1		p.. b
9983	Uzbek	0.08631	127,822	126,819	119,050	MSY41l	44-AABD-a	central uzbek		0.00	0	1A.u.	0	3	6	1	3	Uzbek*	PNb b
9984	Vepsian	0.00826	12,233	12,137	11,393	MSW51z	41-AAAB-e	lüdi-s		70.00	8,496	1....	10	6	8	1	2	Vepsi	P.. b
9985	Vietnamese (Kinh)	0.03600	53,315	52,896	49,656	MSY52b	46-EBAA-ac	general viêt		9.00	4,761	1Asu.	7	5	9	0	1	Vietnamese	PNB b
9986	Vlach Gypsy (Rusurja)	0.00740	10,959	10,873	10,207	CNN25f	59-ACBA-a	vlach-romani		70.00	7,611	1a...	10	4	7	0	0	Romani: Finnish*	PN. b
9987	Vod (Votish, Vodian)	0.00002	30	29	28	MSW51a	41-AAAC-a	vaddya		70.00	21	1c.u.	10	5	8	0	0		pnb b
9988	West Circassian (Kjax)	0.08360	123,809	122,837	115,312	CEW17a	42-AAAA-b	cherkes		0.01	12	1a...	3	3	3	0	1		pn. b
9989	Western Aleut (Unangan)	0.00004	59	59	55	MRY40a	60-AABA-c	unalaska		64.00	38	0....	10	5	8	1	1	Aleut: Eastern	P.. b
9990	Western Baluch	0.00020	296	294	276	CNT24b	58-AABA-b	west balochi		0.01	0	3.s..	3	1	3	0	0	Baluchi: Western*	P.. .
9991	Yakut	0.30000	444,290	440,802	413,799	MSY41m	44-AABE-a	yakut		56.00	246,849	2....	10	5	8	1	1	Yakut	P.. b
9992	Yenisei Ostyak (Ket, Kett	0.00084	1,244	1,234	1,159	MSY48	43-AAAA-a	ostik		6.00	74	0....	7	3	6	0	1		... .
9993	Yenisei Samoyedic (Enets)	0.00040	592	588	552	MSW51j	41-CAAA-c	enets		4.00	24	0....	6	4	6	0	1	Enets	... .
9994	Yenisei Tatar (Khakassian	0.05339	79,069	78,448	73,642	MSY41z	44-AABD-j	khakas		70.00	54,914	1c.u.	10	7	8	2	2	Khakas	Pnb .
9995	Yurak Samoyed (Nenets)	0.02326	34,447	34,177	32,083	MSW51j	41-CAAA-a	nenets		4.00	1,367	0....	6	4	7	0	1	Nenets	... .
9996	other minor peoples	0.20000	296,193	293,868	275,866	...				45.00	132,240		9	7	7	5	0		
	Rwanda	**100.00000**	**5,258,565**	**7,733,127**	**12,426,835**					**81.94**	**6,336,822**								
9997	Arab	0.10000	5,259	7,733	12,427	CMT30	12-AACF-p	zanji	4	0.04	3	1Asuh	3	3	2	0	0		pnb b
9998	British	0.00500	263	387	621	CEW19i	52-ABAC-b	standard-english	5	79.00	305	3Bsuh	10	9	13	5	1		PNB b
9999	Fleming	0.03000	1,578	2,320	3,728	CEW19k	52-ABCA-g	oostvlaandersch		90.00	2,088	1Bsuh	10	9	15	5	3		pnb b
10000	French	0.03000	1,578	2,320	3,728	CEW21b	51-AABI-d	general français	40	87.00	2,018	1B.uh	10	9	14	5	3	French	PNB b
10001	Gujarati	0.30000	15,776	23,199	37,281	CNN25e	59-AAFH-b	standard gujaraati		0.60	139	2A.u.	5	4	2	4	1	Gujarati	PNB b
10002	Hima	0.10870	5,716	8,406	13,508	NAB57d	99-AUSE-fd	o-ro-hima		80.00	6,725	1cs.h	10	9	10	5	2		pnb b
10003	Hutu	87.28630	4,590,007	6,749,960	10,846,924	NAB57d	99-AUSD-f	i-ki-nya-rwanda	100	83.20	5,615,967	2Asu.	10	10	9	5	3	Kinyarwanda*	PNB b
10004	Lingala (Zairian)	1.00000	52,586	77,331	124,268	NAB57c	99-AUIF-b	vehicular lingala	6	75.00	57,998	4asu.	10	8	8	5	1	Lingala	PNB b
10005	Rundi	4.90000	257,670	378,923	608,915	NAB57d	99-AUSD-c	i-ki-ruundi	15	93.00	352,399	4csu.	10	9	11	5	3	Kirundi*	PNB b
10006	Swahili	0.14000	7,362	10,826	17,398	NAB57j	99-AUSM-b	standard ki-swahili	41	0.00	0	4Asu.	0	3	1	3	0	Kiswahili*	PNB b
10007	Tutsi	4.00000	210,343	309,325	497,073	NAB57d	99-AUSD-f	i-ki-nya-rwanda		88.80	274,681	2Asu.	10	10	11	5	4	Kinyarwanda*	PNB b
10008	Twa (Gesera) Pygmy	1.80000	94,654	139,196	223,683	BYG12	99-AUSD-f	i-ki-nya-rwanda		7.60	10,579	2Asu.	7	5	6	5	3	Kinyarwanda*	PNB b
10009	other minor peoples	0.30000	15,776	23,199	37,281	...				60.00	13,920		10	7	7	5	0		
	Sahara	**100.00000**	**247,759**	**293,357**	**469,946**					**0.17**	**488**								
10010	Arosien Bedouin	1.30000	3,221	3,814	6,109	CMT30	12-AACD-a	hassaaniyya		0.00	0	0a...	0	2	0	0	0		pn. b
10011	Delim Bedouin (Sahrawi)	41.09000	101,804	120,540	193,101	CMT30	12-AACD-a	hassaaniyya	100	0.04	48	0a...	3	1	0	0	0		pn. b
10012	French	0.01000	25	29	47	CEW21b	51-AABI-d	general français	3	70.00	21	1B.uh	10	9	14	4	1	French	PNB b
10013	Imragen	4.00000	9,910	11,734	18,798	CMT30	12-AACD-a	hassaaniyya		0.00	0	0a...	0	2	0	0	0		pn. b
10014	Izarguien	6.00000	14,866	17,601	28,197	CMT32g	12-AACD-a	hassaaniyya		0.00	0	0a...	0	1	0	0	0		pn. b
10015	Moor (White, Black)	9.00000	22,298	26,402	42,295	CMT32y	12-AACD-a	hassaaniyya		0.00	0	0a...	0	1	2	0	0		pn. b
10016	Moroccan Arab	1.50000	3,716	4,400	7,049	CMT30	12-AACB-a	west maghrebi		0.18	8	1A.uh	5	3	3	0	0		pnb b
10017	Regeibat	13.00000	32,209	38,136	61,093	CMT30	12-AACD-a	hassaaniyya		0.00	0	0a...	0	2	0	0	0		pn. b
10018	Spaniard	0.10000	248	293	470	CEW21k	51-AABB-f	español-sahariano	20	96.00	282	1B.uh	10	9	15	4	1		pnb b
10019	Tajakant Bedouin	1.00000	2,478	2,934	4,699	CMT30	12-AACD-a	hassaaniyya		0.00	0	0a...	0	3	0	0	0		pn. b
10020	Tekna Berber (Sahrawi)	20.00000	49,552	58,671	93,989	CMT32g	10-AAAC-a	ta-shelhit		0.04	23	4c...	3	2	1	0	0	Shilha: Southern*	Pn. b
10021	other minor peoples	3.00000	7,433	8,801	14,098	...				1.20	106		6	5	2	2	0		
	Saint Helena	**100.00000**	**6,035**	**6,293**	**7,756**					**84.73**	**5,332**								
10022	British	10.00000	604	629	776	CEW19i	52-ABAC-b	standard-english		75.00	472	3Bsuh	10	10	13	5	2		PNB b
10023	Eurafrican White	79.00000	4,768	4,971	6,127	NAN58	52-ABAC-tb	st.helena-english		87.50	4,350	1Bsuh	10	10	12	5	3		pnb .
10024	USA White	10.00000	604	629	776	CEW19s	52-ABAC-s	general american		74.00	466	1Bsuh	10	9	13	5	3	English*	PNB b
10025	other minor peoples	1.00000	60	63	78	...				70.00	44		10	7	6	5	0		
	Saint Kitts & Nevis	**100.00000**	**40,000**	**38,473**	**35,052**					**93.57**	**36,000**								
10026	British	1.00000	400	385	351	CEW19i	52-ABAC-b	standard-english		75.00	289	3Bsuh	10	9	13	5	1		PNB b
10027	East Indian	3.00000	1,200	1,154	1,052	CNN25g	59-AAFO-e	general hindi		35.00	404	3Asuh	9	5	6	5	3		pnb b
10028	French	0.10000	40	38	35	CEW21b	51-AABI-d	general français		84.00	32	1B.uh	10	9	14	5	1	French	PNB b
10029	Mulatto	5.00000	2,000	1,924	1,753	NFB68b	52-ABAF-s	kittitian-creole		92.40	1,777	1c..h	10	9	10	5	3		pn. .
10030	West Indian Black	90.40000	36,160	34,780	31,687	NFB68a	52-ABAF-s	kittitian-creole		95.90	33,354	1c..h	10	10	10	5	3		pn. .
10031	other minor peoples	0.50000	200	192	175	...				75.00	144		10	7	8	5	0		
	Saint Lucia	**100.00000**	**144,100**	**154,366**	**208,093**					**93.51**	**144,340**								
10032	Black	44.60000	64,269	68,847	92,809	NFB68a	51-AACC-d	dominiquais	98	95.90	66,024	1cs..	10	10	11	5	3		pnb .
10033	British	1.00000	1,441	1,544	2,081	CEW19i	52-ABAC-b	standard-english	65	75.00	1,158	3Bsuh	10	10	13	5	3		PNB b
10034	East Indian	3.00000	4,323	4,631	6,243	CNN25g	59-AAFO-e	general hindi		87.90	4,071	3Asuh	10	8	8	5	3		pnb b
10035	French	0.30000	432	463	624	CEW21b	51-AABI-d	general français	50	87.00	403	1B.uh	10	9	14	5	2	French	PNB b
10036	Mulatto	44.40000	63,980	68,539	92,393	NFB68b	51-AACC-d	dominiquais		95.00	65,112	1cs..	10	10	10	5	2		pnb .
10037	West Indian Black	5.00000	7,205	7,718	10,405	NFB68b	52-ABAF	carib-anglo-creol cluster	70	93.00	7,178	1a..h	10	9	11	5	3	West Carib Creole English	PN. b
10038	other minor peoples	1.70000	2,450	2,624	3,538	...				15.00	394		8	7	6	5	0		
	Saint Pierre & Miquelon	**100.00000**	**6,475**	**6,567**	**7,171**					**97.27**	**6,388**								
10039	Anglo-Canadian	3.76000	243	247	270	CEW19d	52-ABAC-r	general canadian		90.00	222	1Bsuh	10	8	11	5	2		pnb b
10040	French-Canadian	95.24000	6,167	6,254	6,830	CEW21b	51-AACC-c	guadeloupéan		97.90	6,123	1cs..	10	8	15	5	1	Creole French: Lesser Antill	Pnb b
10041	other minor peoples	1.00000	65	66	72	...				65.00	43		10	6	6	5	0		
	Saint Vincent & the Grenadines	**100.00000**	**109,949**	**113,954**	**130,781**					**68.84**	**78,441**								
10042	Black Carib	2.00000	2,199	2,279	2,616	MIR39c	80-ACAA-d	garifuna		70.10	1,598	4.s..	10	8	7	5	2	Garifuna	PN. b
10043	British	3.00000	3,298	3,419	3,923	CEW19i	52-ABAC-b	standard-english	81	75.00	2,564	3Bsuh	10	10	13	5	3		PNB b
10044	East Indian	5.50000	6,047	6,267	7,193	CNN25g	59-AAFO-e	general hindi		18.00	1,128	3Asuh	8	5	8	5	3		pnb b
10045	French	0.20000	220	228	262	CEW21b	51-AABI-d	general français	3	87.00	198	1B.uh	10	9	14	5	2	French	PNB b

Continued opposite

Table 8-2 continued

EVANGELIZATION								EVANGELISM			ADDITIONAL DESCRIPTIVE DATA
Ref 1	D 28	aC 29	CG% 30	r 31	E 32	U 33	W 34	e 35	R 36	T 37	Locations, civil divisions, literacy, religions, church history, denominations, dioceses, church growth, missions, agencies, ministries, movements 38
9936	1	8	4.58	1	56.00	44.00	B	40.88	263	6	Chukota region, Chukot Peninsula, Siberia. 65% do not speak Naukan. Shamanists 80%(whale and walrus festivals). D=ROC.
9937	1	10	1.81	0	32.00	68.00	A	1.16	223	4	One of 3 Tungusic peoples (others: Evenk, Even). Dialects: Nizovsk, Verkhovsk. Becoming rapidly assimilated by surrounding populations. Shamanists 99%.
9938	0	9	3.68	1	32.05	67.95	A	0.05	383	2	Central, Black, White Nogay. Mangkyt, Nogailar. Cherkes AO. Muslims of the Volga(100% Hanafi Sunnis; nominal, Islam disappearing by assimilation to Russian).
9939	1	7	7.18	1	75.00	25.00	B	95.81	292	6	Gorno-Altai AO mountains(Mongolia/China border). Shamanists/animists 65%. D=ROC.
9940	1	8	6.13	0	40.00	60.00	A	1.46	557	4	Long history of persecution, refugees, massacres. Muslims 99%(Sunnis, Shias). D=ROC. M=network of agencies.
9941	1	10	2.68	0	42.00	58.00	A	12.26	221	5	Yakutia and Kamchatka. Language isolate. Only 10% speak Yukaghir now. Literary language: Even. Shamanists/animists 92%. D=ROC.
9942	0	6	3.93	4	36.10	63.90	A	0.13	357	3	Sart-Kalmyk. Ethnic group within Khalkha Mongol. Lamaists 60%, nonreligious 20%, shamanists 15%, Sunni Muslims.
9943	3	7	0.28	0	99.60	0.40	C	223.38	34	8	Northeast of Lake Ladoga. Scattered across Karelia and adjacent Finland. Close to Karelian, Ludic, Veps. Most are bilingual in Russian. Nonreligious 35%.
9944	1	10	4.51	0	38.00	62.00	A	9.70	383	4	Eastern Siberia near Khabarovsk and Amur river. Shamanists/animists 92%, Buddhists 1%. D=ROC.
9945	1	10	1.40	0	27.00	73.00	A	0.98	223	3	Sakhalin Island, Poronajsk District. Also in Japan (Hokkaido). Shamanists/animists 98%. D=ROC.
9946	1	8	0.93	0	87.00	13.00	B	139.72	64	7	In Caucasus Mountains, North Ossetia. Also in Georgia, Syria, Turkey. Stock-breeders. Muslims 39%(Sunnis), nonreligious 16%. D=Russian Orthodox Ch.
9947	1	10	-0.30	0	39.00	61.00	A	8.54	56	4	Tom Oblast, Yamalo-Nenets Okrug, both sides of Taz river and Narym District. Shamanists 94%. D=ROC.
9948	0	8	0.00	5	41.03	58.97	A	0.04	47	2	From Iran. Farsi is mother tongue for 31%. Muslims 90%(Imami Shias), Baha'is 10%.
9949	4	10	0.61	6	99.90	0.10	C	528.88	10	10	From Poland, also western Ukraine. Strong Catholics. Nonreligious 9%. D=RCC,ROC,CEF,CWE(Pentecostals).
9950	3	10	0.56	6	99.83	0.17	C	457.45	30	10	Expatriates, settlers from Romania. Nonreligious 14%. D=Romanian Orthodox Ch,RCC,Russian Orthodox Ch.
9951	8	9	0.37	7	99.63	0.37	C	325.72	7	9	In 70 countries. Nonreligious 30%, atheists 5%. D=ROC(64 Dioceses),RCC(4 Dioceses),AUCECB,Old Ritualists,CEF,CCECB,SDA,IPKh. M=IBT,1,000 agencies.
9952	4	10	1.55	1	99.70	0.30	C	293.82	61	8	Romani-speaking Baltic Gypsies, including North Russian Gypsies, White Russian Gypsies; also Latvian, Estonian, and Polish Gypsies. Nonreligious 30%.
9953	1	10	5.34	7	99.75	0.25	C	385.98	117	9	On Kamchatka Peninsula. Itelmens who now use Russian as mother tongue. Shamanists/animists 15%, nonreligious 10%. D=Russian Orthodox Ch.
9954	1	10	1.23	4	99.85	0.15	C	421.94	45	10	Northern and western Kola Peninsula around Petsamo. Also in Finland. Many bilingual in Russian. Nonreligious 15%. D=Russian Orthodox Ch.
9955	1	10	2.96	7	70.00	30.00	B	22.99	159	5	Selkup who have abandoned mother tongue for Russian. Shamanists 50%, nonreligious 40%. D=ROC.
9956	1	10	1.73	7	99.56	0.44	B	251.41	61	8	Gypsies of all kinds who are now settled, acculturated, and have lost their original language. Nonreligious 40%. D=Russian Orthodox Ch.
9957	0	8	1.81	0	17.03	82.97	A	0.01	452	2	South Dagestan. Unwritten; Lezgin used as literary language. Muslims 100%(Shafi Sunnis).
9958	1	9	1.96	1	36.00	64.00	A	1.31	210	4	In south central Siberia. Close to Tuvinians. Rapid assimilation by Russians (89% speak Russian). Collective farmers. Shamanists 99%. D=ROC.
9959	1	8	4.95	6	99.80	0.20	C	417.56	95	10	Refugees, migrant workers from Serbia, especially during 1990-92 civil war in Yugoslavia. Nonreligious/atheists 20%. D=Serbian Orthodox Ch.
9960	1	8	7.28	1	99.70	0.30	C	298.93	189	8	Khakass AO and Gorno-Altai AO. In northern Altai mountains. Turkic(Blacksmith Tatars). Russian-speakers 91%. Shamanists 30%. D=Russian Orthodox Ch.
9961	0	10	3.52	4	58.00	42.00	B	38.10	204	5	Yupik Eskimo, Asiatic Eskimo. Eastern tip of Siberia; also Alaska (USA). Chukchi National Okrug, 17 villages. 6 dialects incl Chaplino, Naukan, Sirenik. Shamanists.
9962	1	8	7.30	6	99.78	0.22	C	404.27	163	10	Immigrants from Slovakia, in business, commerce. Nonreligious 20%. D=RCC.
9963	1	6	8.25	1	80.00	20.00	B	116.80	310	7	Gorno-Altai AO. Turkic. Lingua franca. Lamaist Buddhists 50%, Muslims 10%(Sunnis among the Teleuts). D=Russian Orthodox Ch. M=West Siberian Christian.
9964	1	9	4.01	0	39.00	61.00	A	9.96	331	4	Yakutia and Kamchatka Peninsula. Language isolate. All bilingual in Russian. Shamanists 93%. D=ROC.
9965	1	9	5.43	8	99.96	0.04	C	588.67	104	10	Expatriates from Spain, in business, commerce. Strong Catholics. D=RCC.
9966	0	8	0.00	0	17.00	83.00	A	0.00	0	1.06	Southern Dagestan. Muslims 100%(Shafi Sunnis).
9967	0	8	0.00	4	38.00	62.00	A	0.00	0	1.12	From Tajikistan, Uzbekistan, Kirghizia. Most are trilingual (with Uzbek, Russian). Muslims 90%(Hanafi Sunnis), nonreligious 10%.
9968	1	7	6.14	0	52.00	48.00	B	37.96	360	5	Original inhabitants of northern Azerbaijan. Shia Muslims 70%, Jewish 10%. D=Armenian Apostolic Ch.
9969	4	8	0.69	6	50.00	50.00	B	5.47	82	4	Dispersed over 30 Provinces; 70% bilingual in Russian. Muslims 81%(Hanafi Sunnis; 300 mosques, from 2,000 in 1917), nonreligious 15%. D=ROC(Kryashen).
9970	1	10	4.58	0	37.00	63.00	A	9.45	421	4	Taymur National Okrug, Siberia. Northernmost people in Russia. Unwritten language. Close to Nenets culture. Hunters of wild reindeer. Shamanists/animists 90%.
9971	2	10	1.80	1	99.60	0.40	C	227.76	74	8	In Karelia and Kola Peninsula. Many bilinguals in Russian. Nonreligious 35%. D=ROC,ELC.
9972	0	8	0.00	0	13.00	87.00	A	0.00	0	1.03	Western Dagestan. Unwritten language; Avar used as literary language. Muslims 100%(Sunnis).
9973	0	8	0.70	0	17.03	82.97	A	0.01	274	2	Southern Dagestan; also in Azerbaijan. Unwritten; Avar used as literary language. Muslims 100%(Shafi Sunnis).
9974	0	8	0.00	8	40.00	60.00	A	0.00	0	1.11	Across Central Asia. Muslims 98%(85% Hanafi Sunnis,15% Alawi Shias),nonreligious 2%.
9975	0	8	0.00	1	29.00	71.00	A	0.00	0	1.11	From Turkmenistan, Iran, Afghanistan, Uzbekistan, et alia. Devout Muslims 93%(Hanafi Sunnis), nonreligious 5%. M=IBT.
9976	0	8	5.93	1	42.50	57.50	A	2.32	434	4	Republic of Tuva(Tannu-Tuva). Tuba. Also in Mongolia, China. 20% urbanites. Literates 99%. 60% use Russian. Buddhists 33%(Lamaists), shamanists 30%.
9977	0	10	4.13	0	31.00	69.00	A	3.39	436	4	Extreme Far East. 7 dialects. Khor is literary language. Shamanists/animists 90%, with Chinese elements.
9978	2	9	1.10	0	99.90	0.10	C	440.19	43	10	Mainly in Georgia and Azerbaijan. Azerbaijani is used as literary language. Nonreligious 10%. D=Georgian Orthodox Ch, Armenian Apostolic Ch (Gregorian).
9979	1	7	0.77	0	94.00	6.00	B	185.27	52	7	Udmurtia, near Urals. Traditionally Orthodox, but still many pagans. Shamanists 45%, with Muslim elements. D=Russian Orthodox Ch(D-Izhevsk & Udmurtia).
9980	0	7	0.00	4	34.00	66.00	A	0.00	0	1.11	In 15 countries. Agriculturalists. Muslims 100%(Hanafi Sunnis, with heavy Sufi influence). M=IBT.
9981	7	8	0.27	6	99.79	0.21	C	432.52	27	10	In 15 countries. Nonreligious/atheists 20%. D=ROC(E-Ukraine),Ukrainian Catholic Ch,AUCECB,CEF,CCECB,JWs,SDA. R=FEBC,HCJB,VERITAS,AWR. T=IBRA.
9982	1	7	4.58	0	32.00	68.00	A	3.50	461	4	A Manchu people. Along Amur river, Ulch region. Lingua franca: Russian. Shamanists 97%, with Chinese elements. D=ROC.
9983	0	9	0.00	5	43.00	57.00	A	0.00	0	1.12	55% Russian-speaking. Literates 100%. Muslims 80%(Hanafi Sunnis), nonreligious/atheists 20%. M=ROC,AUCECB,CSI.
9984	2	7	0.35	0	99.70	0.30	C	281.05	34	8	Karelia, St Petersburg. Bilingual in Russian (now first language for 60%). Close to Karelian. Nonreligious 30%. D=Russian Orthodox Ch,RCC.
9985	1	8	6.36	6	65.00	35.00	B	21.35	304	5	Refugees, immigrants after 1960s-1975 Viet Nam war, now 32,000 skilled laborers stranded there. Mahayana Buddhists 54%, nonreligious 30%. D=RCC.
9986	0	8	6.86	6	99.70	0.30	C	293.82	188	8	In Ukraine, Moldavia, western Russia. In 25 countries. Ethnic groups: Sarvi, Voloxuja, Chache, Lovari. Muslims 20%, nonreligious 10%.
9987	0	10	0.41	1	99.70	0.30	C	288.71	38	8	Kingisepp area of St Petersburg. Close to Estonian. Nearly extinct. Nonreligious 30%.
9988	0	9	2.52	0	28.01	71.99	A	0.01	344	2	Adyghian, Lower Circassian. In Adygei AO and Cherkess AO. Also in 9 other countries. Muslims 100%(Hanafi Sunnis). M=IBT.
9989	1	10	0.59	0	99.64	0.36	C	240.60	37	8	Aleutian Islands. Mostly Christians. Shamanists/animists 35%. D=Russian Orthodox Ch.
9990	0	9	0.00	1	25.01	74.99	A	0.00	0	1.08	Mainly in Pakistan, Afghanistan, Turkmenistan, Iran. Muslims 100%(Hanafi Sunnis).
9991	1	9	2.59	2	99.56	0.44	B	204.40	96	8	Eastern Siberia, in Yakutia near Arctic Ocean. Lingua franca. 60% speak Russian. Nomadic hunters, reindeer-breeders. Shamanists 30%. Nominal Christians.
9992	1	10	4.40	0	35.00	65.00	A	7.66	399	4	Upper Yenisei Valley, east of Khanti and Mansi. Other related peoples are now extinct. Shamanists 94%. D=ROC.
9993	1	10	3.23	0	32.00	68.00	A	4.67	371	4	Taymur National Okrug, along Yenisei river. Nearly extinct. Shamanists 80%. D=ROC.
9994	1	8	1.26	1	99.70	0.30	C	293.82	49	8	Southern Siberia, around city of Abakan, Khakass AO. Also in China. 6 dialects. Converted to Christianity in 12th century, though a veneer overlaying shamanism.
9995	1	10	5.04	0	34.00	66.00	A	4.96	495	4	Northwest Siberia, tundra area, from Yenisei delta to Kola Peninsula. Literary language. Shamanists 95%. D=ROC.
9996	0	7	2.22		78.00	22.00	B	128.11	78	7	USA Whites, Austrians, Japanese, Hungarian Gypsies, Swedes, Italians, Dutch, other Asians, other Europeans. Nonreligious 20%, Buddhists 3%, Muslims 2%.
Rwanda											
9997	0	10	1.10	7	38.04	61.96	A	0.05	130	2	Traders, originally from East African Coast. Muslims 100%(Shafi Sunnis).
9998	5	10	3.48	8	99.79	0.21	C	429.64	85	10	Expatriates from Britain, in development. D=Anglican Ch/EAR,SDA,EPR,UEBR,JWs. M=RCMS.
9999	2	10	5.49	6	99.90	0.10	C	522.31	114	10	Expatriates from Belgium, in development, commerce. D=RCC,EPR. M=SJ,OP,FSC.
10000	3	10	5.45	8	99.87	0.13	C	511.25	109	10	Teachers, businessmen from France. Nonreligious 13%. D=RCC,SDA,JWs. M=SJ,SDB,OP.
10001	1	10	2.67	6	48.60	51.40	A	1.06	207	4	Indian traders. Hindus 50%, Muslims 49%, Baha'is. D=RCC.
10002	2	10	6.73	4	99.80	0.20	C	400.04	177	10	Aristocratic Hamitic pastoral nomads. Animists 20%. D=mainly Anglican Ch/EAR,some RCC. M=WF,RCMS/MAM.
10003	7	8	14.15	4	99.83	0.17	C	450.05	300	10	Small-stature Ruandese. Animists 8%, Muslims 8%(Shafi Sunnis). D=RCC(6 Dioceses),AC/EAR,SDA,ADEEP,EPR,UEBR,AEBR. M=WF,OSB,FSC,EFM,RCMS.
10004	2	10	9.05	5	99.75	0.25	C	380.51	207	9	Migrants, refugees from Zaire. Animists 5%. D=EJCSK,RCC. M=WF.
10005	3	10	11.04	4	99.93	0.07	C	539.72	226	10	Hutu and Ruandese refugees, settlers from Burundi in south. Animists 5%. D=RCC,Anglican Ch/EAR(2 Dioceses),ELMR. M=WF,OSB,SJ,SDB,OP,FMC,FSC.
10006	0	10	0.00	5	41.00	59.00	A	0.00	0	1.13	Traders from Kenya/Tanzania Coast. Muslims 100%(Shafi Sunnis).
10007	3	10	10.76	4	99.89	0.11	C	511.46	223	10	Tall-stature Ruandese. Animists 5%, Muslims 5%. D=RCC,Anglican Ch/EAR(many Revivalists),SDA. M=WF,SJ,OP,OSB,PEFA,BCMC,SFM,FSC,EFM,RCMS,FMB.
10008	2	10	7.21	4	63.60	36.40	B	17.64	358	5	Jungle-dwellers. Animists 92%. D=RCC,Anglican Ch/EAR. M=RCMS,WF,FSC,EFM,FMB.
10009	0	10	7.51		90.00	10.00	C	197.10	229	7	Greeks(GOC), Ugandans, Tanzanians, Sudanese; vast numbers of Hutu and Tutsi refugees from Burundi move in, others scatter to surrounding countries.
Sahara											
10010	0	5	0.00	7	23.00	77.00	A	0.00	0	1.06	Saharan Arabs. Nomads, tent-dwellers. Muslims 100%(Maliki Sunnis).
10011	0	4	3.95	7	25.04	74.96	A	0.03	509	2	Sahrawi(Saharan) Arabs and arabized Berbers. Tent-dwelling nomads, of several tribes. Vast number of refugees live temporarily in Algeria. Muslims 100%(Maliki).
10012	1	10	3.09	8	99.70	0.30	C	355.14	80	9	Expatriates from France, in business. Nonreligious/atheist 30%. D=RCC(PA-Sahara). M=OMI.
10013	0	6	0.00	7	24.00	76.00	A	0.00	0	1.07	Moorish fishing culture along Atlantic shores. 3 nomadic Bedouin tribes. Muslims 100%(Maliki Sunnis).
10014	0	5	0.00	7	23.00	77.00	A	0.00	0	1.06	Saharan Arabs. Muslims 100%(Maliki Sunnis).
10015	0	3	0.00	7	23.00	77.00	A	0.00	0	1.08	Sahrawi arabized Berbers. Many refugees in Mauritania, Algeria. Muslims 100%(Maliki Sunnis).
10016	0	6	2.10	7	40.18	59.82	A	0.26	191	3	Immigrants and invading military occupation. Muslims 100%(Maliki Sunnis).
10017	0	5	0.00	7	23.00	77.00	A	0.00	0	1.06	Saharan Arabs. 10 nomadic Bedouin tribes in interior. Muslims 100%(Maliki Sunnis).
10018	2	10	1.04	8	99.96	0.04	C	581.66	32	10	Expatriates from Spain, in development. Nonreligious 4%. D=RCC(PA-Sahara),SDA. M=OMI.
10019	0	5	0.00	7	23.00	77.00	A	0.00	0	1.06	Nomads and semi-nomads. Muslims 100%(Maliki Sunnis).
10020	0	6	3.19	4	26.04	73.96	A	0.03	423	2	Sahrawis. 8 nomadic Berber tribes and 45 factions, with over 20 more tribes in Morocco. Muslims 100%(Maliki Sunnis).
10021	0	5	2.39		16.20	83.80	A	0.71	404	3	Other aliens, expatriates; Algerian Arabs, other Arabs, other Berbers, some Europeans. Muslims 86%, nonreligious 10%.
Saint Helena											
10022	4	10	0.68	8	99.75	0.25	C	410.62	33	10	Expatriates from Britain, in administration, military. Nonreligious 12%. D=Anglican Ch/CPSA,SA,SDA,JWs. M=USPG,BUSA.
10023	6	9	0.56	8	99.88	0.12	C	499.82	29	10	St Helena White(British/Chinese/African/Malay/seamen). D=Anglican Ch(2 Dioceses),Baptist Ch,SA,JWs,SDA,RCC.
10024	5	10	0.60	8	99.74	0.26	C	399.74	28	9	Expatriates from USA, in development. Nonreligious 16%. D=JWs,SDA,SA,AC,RCC.
10025	0	10	0.74		99.70	0.30	C	258.05	20	8	Other Europeans, other Americans. Nonreligious 10%.
Saint Kitts & Nevis											
10026	0	10	3.42	8	99.75	0.25	C	396.93	86	9	Expatriates from Britain, in administration, development. Nonreligious 13%. D-Anglican Ch/CPWI(D-Antigua),MCCA,SA,CB,JWs. M=USPG.
10027	4	10	3.77	7	99.00	1.00	B	126.47	132	7	Traders from India, Pakistan. Hindus 50%, Muslims 10%, Baha'is 5%. D=RCC,SDA,JWs,AC/CPWI.
10028	1	10	3.53	8	99.84	0.16	C	478.29	79	10	Expatriates from France, in business, development. Nonreligious 16%. D=RCC(D-Saint John's). M=CSSR.
10029	10	10	5.32	8	99.92	0.08	C	510.61	109	10	Mixed-race persons(Black/White). D=AC/CPWI,MCCA,MC,RCC,Antioch Baptist Ch,CGP,SDA,CB,COG,JWs.
10030	8	7	8.45	8	99.96	0.04	C	535.20	163	10	Lesser Antillean Creole. Rastafarians and Afro-American spiritists 1%. D=AC,MCCA,Moravian Ch,RCC,WC,Antioch Baptist Ch,SDA,JWs.
10031	0	10	2.70		99.75	0.25	C	292.91	69	8	Jamaicans, other Caribbean Islanders, USA Whites and Blacks, other Europeans.
Saint Lucia											
10032	6	10	1.07	2	99.96	0.04	C	538.70	30	10	St Lucia Creole. Rastas, Afro-American spiritists 2%. D=RCC,AC/CPWI,SDA,ECWI,MCCA,Spiritual Baptist Chs. M=BMM,SFM,FMB,SIL.
10033	4	10	1.08	8	99.75	0.25	C	413.36	40	10	Expatriates from Britain, in development. Nonreligious 13%. D=Anglican Ch/CPWI(D-Windward Islands),MCCA,SDA,JWs.
10034	5	10	6.19	7	99.88	0.12	C	500.18	126	10	Traders from India, Pakistan. Former Hindus and Muslims. Many Baha'i, 8%s. D=80% RCC,AC/CPWI,SDA,MCCA,JWs.
10035	3	10	1.14	8	99.87	0.13	C	514.43	36	10	Expatriates from France, settlers. Nonreligious 13%. D=RCC(M-Castries),SDA,JWs. M=SFM,FMI.
10036	5	10	1.05	2	99.95	0.05	C	523.59	32	10	Mixed-race persons. Afro-American spiritists and Rastas(Rastafarians) 2%. D=RCC,AC/CPWI,SDA,ECWI,MCCA. M=FMB,SIL.
10037	3	10	1.08	8	99.93	0.07	C	532.93	31	10	Jamaicans and others, including recent converts to Rastafarianism, 2%. D=RCC,AC/CPWI,SDA.
10038	0	10	1.14		43.00	57.00	A	23.54	73	5	USA Whites, Lesser Antillean Creole French, other Caribbean Islanders, USA Blacks(UHCA). Hindus 54%, Musims 27% (Sunnis).
Saint Pierre & Miquelon											
10039	2	10	0.01	8	99.90	0.10	C	522.31	13	10	Settlers from Canada of English-speaking background. Nonreligious 10%. D=ACC,UCC.
10040	2	5	0.19	8	99.98	0.02	C	574.95	20	10	Settlers from Canada of French/Basque origin. D=RCC(VA-Iles S-P & M),a few Protestants. M=CSSp.
10041	0	10	0.39		96.00	4.00	C	227.76	11	8	French, other Canadians, Spaniards, North African Arabs (Muslims), and several others. Muslims 15%, Nonreligious10%.
Saint Vincent & the Grenadines											
10042	3	10	0.89	4	99.70	0.30	C	320.08	42	9	Original Amerindian inhabitants. 1995, many Baha'i converts, 10%. D=AC/CPWI,ECWI,RCC. M=MMS,FMB.
10043	6	10	0.84	8	99.75	0.25	C	416.10	36	10	Expatriates from Britain, in development. Nonreligious 13%. D=Anglican Ch/CPWI(D-Windward Islands),MCCA,RCC,SDA,CB,JWs.
10044	4	10	4.84	7	85.00	15.00	B	55.84	188	6	Traders, from India. Hindus 61%, Muslims 19%, many Baha'is. D=RCC,AC/CPWI,SDA,SA.
10045	0	10	0.89	8	99.87	0.13	C	508.08	32	10	Expatriates from France, in business. Nonreligious 13%. D-RCC(D-Bridgetown-Kingstown),SDA,JWs. M=SFM,FSC.

Continued overleaf

Table 8-2 continued

PEOPLE		POPULATION				IDENTITY CODE		LANGUAGE		CHURCH		MINISTRY						SCRIPTURE		
Ref 1	*Ethnic name* 2	*P%* 3	*In 1995* 4	*In 2000* 5	*In 2025* 6	*Race* 7	*Language* 8	*Autoglossonym* 9	*S* 10	*AC* 11	*Members* 12	*Jayuh* 13-17	*d* 18	*wa* 19	*xc* 20	*mc* 21	*mi* 22	*Biblioglossonym* 23	*Pub* 24-26	*ss* 27
10046	Latin American White	1.00000	1,099	1,140	1,308	CLT27	51-AABB-h	south americano		90.00	1,026	4B.uh	10	9	12	5	2		pnb	b
10047	Mestizo	1.00000	1,099	1,140	1,308	CLN29	51-AABB-h	south americano		95.00	1,083	4B.uh	10	9	11	5	2		pnb	b
10048	Mulatto	19.90000	21,880	22,677	26,025	NFB68b	52-ABAF-v	vincentian-creole		71.20	16,146	1c..h	10	10	8	5	3		pn.	.
10049	Portuguese	0.20000	220	228	262	CEW21g	51-AABA-e	general português		93.00	212	2Bsuh	10	9	15	4	2	Portuguese	PNB	b
10050	Spaniard	0.20000	220	228	262	CEW21k	51-AABB-c	general español		96.00	219	2B.uh	10	9	15	5	2	Spanish	PNB	b
10051	Syrian Arab	0.50000	550	570	654	CMT30	12-AACF-f	syro-palestinian		11.00	63	1Asuh	8	5	7	5	2	Arabic: Lebanese*	Pnb	b
10052	USA White	1.00000	1,099	1,140	1,308	CEW19s	52-ABAC-s	general american		74.00	843	1Bsuh	10	9	13	5	2	English*	PNB	b
10053	West Indian Black	65.10000	71,577	74,184	85,138	NFB68a	52-ABAF-v	vincentian-creole	96	71.50	53,042	1c..h	10	10	10	5	3		pn.	.
10054	other minor peoples	0.40000	440	456	523	...				70.00	319		10	7	7	5	0			
	Samoa	**100.00000**	**167,622**	**180,073**	**271,417**					**93.92**	**169,129**									
10055	Anglo-New Zealander	0.30000	503	540	814	CEW19e	52-ABAC-y	general new-zealand		76.00	411	1Bsuh	10	9	14	5	3		pnb	b
10056	British	0.30000	503	540	814	CEW19i	52-ABAC-b	standard-english		75.00	405	3Bsuh	10	9	13	5	3		PNB	b
10057	Euronesian (Part-Samoan)	10.10000	16,930	18,187	27,413	MPY53	52-ABAC-bv	standard oceanian-english		95.00	17,278	1Bsuh	10	10	16	5	2		pnb	b
10058	Han Chinese	0.10000	168	180	271	MSY42a	79-AAAB-ba	kuo-yü		70.00	126	2Bsuh	10	8	8	5	1	Chinese: Kuoyu*	PNB	b
10059	Maori	0.10000	168	180	271	MPY55b	39-CAQA-a	standard maori		90.20	162	0a.u.	10	9	12	5	3	Maori: New Zealand	PNB	b
10060	Samoan	88.10000	147,675	158,644	239,118	MPY55e	39-CAOA	samoa cluster		94.20	149,443	2a.u.	10	10	16	5	3	Samoan	PNB	b
10061	USA White	0.60000	1,006	1,080	1,629	CEW19s	52-ABAC-s	general american		74.00	800	1Bsuh	10	10	12	0	0	English*	PNB	b
10062	other minor peoples	0.40000	670	720	1,086	...				70.00	504		10	7	8	5	0			
	San Marino	**100.00000**	**24,882**	**26,514**	**32,392**					**89.68**	**23,778**									
10063	Esperanto	0.00000	0	0	0	CEW21z	51-AAAC-a	proper esperanto	1	70.00	0	0A...	10	8	9	5	0	Esperanto	PNB	b
10064	Italian	91.00000	22,643	24,128	29,477	CEW21e	51-AABQ-c	standard italiano		89.30	21,546	2B.uh	10	10	16	5	2	Italian	PNB	b
10065	Sanmarinese	8.90000	2,214	2,360	2,883	CEW21e	51-AABQ-c	standard italiano		94.00	2,218	2B.uh	10	10	15	5	3	Italian	PNB	b
10066	other minor peoples	0.10000	25	27	32	...				54.00	14		10	7	8	5	0			
	Sao Tome & Principe	**100.00000**	**132,531**	**146,775**	**217,146**					**90**	**132,103**									
10067	Angolar	7.62712	10,108	11,195	16,562	NAB57b	51-AACA-d	angolar	95	88.50	9,907	1a...	10	10	11	5	1		pnb	b
10068	Eurafrican Creole	0.10000	133	147	217	NAN58	52-ABAH	west-coast-creole- cluster		90.00	132	4.s.h	10	9	11	5	3		PN.	b
10069	Fang (Pahouin)	10.00000	13,253	14,678	21,715	NAB57c	99-AUCC-u	fang	15	86.00	12,623	1....	10	8	12	5	1	Fang: Gabon*	PNB	b
10070	Portuguese	1.90000	2,518	2,789	4,126	CEW21g	51-AABA-e	general português	80	93.00	2,594	2Bsuh	10	9	15	5	3	Portuguese	PNB	b
10071	Principense Mestico	3.38983	4,493	4,975	7,361	NAN58	51-AACA-c	sao-tomense-principense	70	93.10	4,632	1c...	10	10	13	5	1		pnb	.
10072	Saotomense Mestico	75.98305	100,701	111,524	164,994	NAN58	51-AACA-c	sao-tomense-principense	70	90.60	101,041	1c...	10	10	12	5	1		pnb	.
10073	other minor peoples	1.00000	1,325	1,468	2,171	...				80.00	1,174		10	7	8	5	0			
	Saudi Arabia	**100.00000**	**18,252,536**	**21,606,691**	**39,964,965**					**3.64**	**786,982**									
10074	Armenian	0.00500	913	1,080	1,998	CEW14	57-AAAA-b	ashkharik		87.00	940	4A.u.	10	9	13	5	1	Armenian: Modern, Eastern	PNB	b
10075	Bedouin Arab	3.90000	711,849	842,661	1,558,634	CMT30	12-AACD	badawi-sahara cluster		0.01	84	0a...	3	2	3	0	0		PN.	b
10076	Bengali	0.10000	18,253	21,607	39,965	CNN25b	59-AAFT-e	west bengali		0.40	86	1Asuh	5	4	8	4	1	Bengali: Musalmani*	PNB	b
10077	Black African (Bantu)	1.50000	273,788	324,100	599,474	NAB57j	99-AUSM-q	ki-unguja		15.00	48,615	1Asu.	8	1	2	0	0		pnb	b
10078	British	0.06900	12,594	14,909	27,576	CEW19i	52-ABAC-b	standard-english	7	74.00	11,032	3Bsuh	10	9	13	5	1		PNB	b
10079	Egyptian Arab	1.80000	328,546	388,920	719,369	CMT30	12-AACF-a	masri		18.00	70,006	2Asuh	8	5	8	5	3	Arabic*	PNB	b
10080	Filipino	1.00000	182,525	216,067	399,650	MSY44o	31-CKAA-a	proper tagalog		90.00	194,460	4Bs..	10	9	10	5	3	Tagalog	PNB	b
10081	French	0.10000	18,253	21,607	39,965	CEW21b	51-AABI-d	general français		80.00	17,285	1B.uh	10	9	11	4	1	French	PNB	b
10082	Greek	0.01000	1,825	2,161	3,996	CEW20	56-AAAA-c	dhimotiki		95.00	2,053	2B.uh	10	9	11	4	1	Greek: Modern	PNB	b
10083	Gulf Arab	3.00000	547,576	648,201	1,198,949	CMT30	12-AACF-i	kuwayti-qatari	12	5.20	33,706	1Asuh	7	4	3	1	1		pnb	b
10084	Han Chinese	0.40000	73,010	86,427	159,860	MSY42a	79-AAAB-ba	kuo-yü		6.00	5,186	2Bsuh	7	4	8	1	0	Chinese: Kuoyu*	PNB	b
10085	Harasi	0.07000	12,777	15,125	27,975	CMT30	12-ABAA-ba	harsusi		0.00	0	0....	0	1	0	0	0		p..	b
10086	Hindi	0.50000	91,263	108,033	199,825	CNN25g	59-AAFO-e	general hindi		1.00	1,080	3Asuh	6	4	7	5	3		pnb	b
10087	Hui	0.10000	18,253	21,607	39,965	MSY42b	79-AAAB-ba	kuo-yü		0.00	0	2Bsuh	0	1	1	0	0	Chinese: Kuoyu*	PNB	b
10088	Indonesian	0.30000	54,758	64,820	119,895	MSY44k	31-PHAA-c	bahasa-indonesia		0.20	130	4Asuh	5	4	2	0	0	Indonesian	PNB	b
10089	Italian	0.11000	20,078	23,767	43,961	CEW21e	51-AABQ-c	standard italiano		80.00	19,014	2B.uh	10	9	12	4	1	Italian	PNB	b
10090	Javanese	0.09000	16,427	19,446	35,968	MSY44g	31-PIAA-g	general jawa		2.40	467	2As.h	6	4	8	1	0	Javanese	PNB	b
10091	Jordanian Arab	1.10000	200,778	237,674	439,615	CMT30	12-AACF-f	syro-palestinian		9.00	21,391	1Asuh	7	5	7	5	2	Arabic: Lebanese*	Pnb	b
10092	Kabardian	0.08000	14,602	17,285	31,972	CEW17a	42-AAAA-ba	beslenej		2.00	346	1c...	6	4	3	0	0		pn.	b
10093	Korean	0.52000	94,913	112,355	207,818	MSY46	45-AAAA-b	kukö		40.00	44,942	2A...	9	6	12	5	1	Korean	PNB	b
10094	Lebanese Arab	1.00000	182,525	216,067	399,650	CMT30	12-AACF-f	syro-palestinian		45.00	97,230	1Asuh	9	7	9	5	2	Arabic: Lebanese*	Pnb	b
10095	Mahra (South Arabic)	0.12000	21,903	25,928	47,958	CMT30	12-ABAA-a	mahri		0.01	3	0....	3	1	0	0	0	Mehri	P..	b
10096	Malay	0.05000	9,126	10,803	19,982	MSY44k	31-PHAA-b	bahasa-malaysia		0.02	2	1asuh	3	1	2	0	0	Malay	PNB	b
10097	Omani Arab	0.40000	73,010	86,427	159,860	CMT30	12-AACF-l	omani		0.10	86	1Asuh	5	1	3	0	0		pnb	b
10098	Palestinian Arab	0.60000	109,515	129,640	239,790	CMT30	12-AACF-f	syro-palestinian		15.00	19,446	1Asuh	8	5	8	5	2	Arabic: Lebanese*	Pnb	b
10099	Persian	0.70000	127,768	151,247	279,755	CNT24f	58-AACC-c	standard farsi		0.04	60	1Asu.	3	3	2	0	0		PNB	b
10100	Punjabi	2.40000	438,061	518,561	959,159	CNN25n	59-AAFE-c	general panjabi		2.00	10,371	1Asu.	6	5	9	0	0		PNB	b
10101	Saudi Arab	74.19600	13,542,652	16,031,300	29,652,405	CMT30	12-AACF-k	central `anazi		0.47	75,347	4Asuh	5	4	5	3	3		pnb	b
10102	Shahara	0.19000	34,680	41,053	75,933	CMT30	12-ABAA-da	shehri		0.01	4	0....	3	1	0	0	0		p..	b
10103	Somali	0.21000	38,330	45,374	83,926	CMT33e	14-GAGA-a	af-soomaali		0.04	18	2A...	3	3	2	0	0	Somali	PNB	b
10104	Southern Baluch	0.05000	9,126	10,803	19,982	CNT24b	58-AABA-c	south balochi		0.02	2	1.s..	3	3	2	1	1	Balochi, Southern	P..	b
10105	Sudanese Arab	0.49000	89,437	105,873	195,828	CMT30	12-AACF-c	sudani		1.40	1,482	4Asuh	6	4	2	1	1	Arabic: Sudan	PNb	b
10106	Syrian Arab	0.51000	93,088	110,194	203,821	CMT30	12-AACF-f	syro-palestinian		10.00	11,019	1Asuh	8	5	8	4	1	Arabic: Lebanese*	Pnb	b
10107	Tamil	0.20000	36,505	43,213	79,930	CNN23c	49-EBEA-b	tamil		15.00	6,482	2Asu.	8	7	9	0	0	Tamil	PNB	b
10108	Turk	0.10000	18,253	21,607	39,965	MSY41j	44-AABA-a	osmanli		0.02	4	1A.u.	3	3	2	0	0	Turkish	PNB	b
10109	USA White	0.40000	73,010	86,427	159,860	CEW19s	52-ABAC-s	general american		74.00	63,956	1Bsuh	10	9	12	5	3	English*	PNB	b
10110	Urdu	2.23000	407,032	481,829	891,219	CNN25r	59-AAFO-d	standard urdu		0.02	96	2Asuh	3	4	2	1	1	Urdu	PNB	b
10111	Yemeni Arab	0.70000	127,768	151,247	279,755	CMT30	12-AACF-n	yemeni		0.20	302	1Asuh	5	2	3	0	1		pnb	b
10112	other minor peoples	0.70000	127,768	151,247	279,755	...				20.00	30,249		9	4	5	1	0			
	Senegal	**100.00000**	**8,330,109**	**9,481,161**	**16,742,579**					**4.93**	**467,291**									
10113	Arab	0.20000	16,660	18,962	33,485	CMT30	12-AACD-a	hassaaniyya	5	0.01	2	0a...	3	3	5	0	1		pn.	b
10114	Badyara (Badyaranke)	0.08629	7,188	8,181	14,447	NAB56c	90-IBAA-a	ba-jar		1.00	82	0....	6	4	4	5	2	Badyara	...	n
10115	Balanta (Belanda, Alante)	1.03677	86,364	98,298	173,582	NAB56c	90-GABA	north balanta cluster		6.00	5,898	0....	7	5	7	5	2	Frase*	P..	n
10116	Bambara (Bamanakan)	0.73012	60,820	69,224	122,241	NAB63a	00-AAAB-a	bamanan-kan	12	3.00	2,077	4As..	6	4	7	4	1	Bambara	PNB	b
10117	Bandial	0.06000	4,998	5,689	10,046	NAB56c	90-DADB-a	banjaal		5.00	284	0....	7	5	7	0	0		...	.
10118	Banyun (Banyuk, Elomay)	0.27479	22,890	26,053	46,007	NAB56c	90-HAAA	bainuk cluster		16.00	4,169	0....	8	5	6	5	3		...	.
10119	Bassari (Tenda Basari)	0.08629	7,188	8,181	14,447	NAB56c	90-JAAA-a	o-ni-yan		16.80	1,374	0....	8	5	6	5	2	Basari	PN.	.
10120	Bayot (Baiote)	0.06903	5,750	6,545	11,557	NAB56c	90-EAAA-a	bayot		4.00	262	0....	6	4	5	1	1		...	n
10121	Bedik (Budik, Tenda)	0.07168	5,971	6,796	12,001	NAB56c	90-JAAA-d	o-nik		1.00	68	0....	6	3	6	4	1	Budik	pn.	.
10122	Black Moor (Maure)	0.50000	41,651	47,406	83,713	CMT32y	12-AACD-a	hassaaniyya	8	0.00	0	0a...	0	3	5	0	2		pn.	b
10123	British	0.01000	833	948	1,674	CEW19i	52-ABAC-b	standard-english	5	78.00	740	3Bsuh	10	9	13	5	3		PNB	b
10124	Caboverdian Mestico	0.50000	41,651	47,406	83,713	NAN58	51-AACA-a	caboverdense		96.00	45,510	1c...	10	8	13	5	1	Crioulo, Upper Guinea	PNB	b
10125	Dialonke (Jalonka)	0.17257	14,375	16,362	28,893	NAB63c	00-AACA-b	yalunka		0.11	18	1....	5	4	2	4	1	Yalunka	PN.	.
10126	Diola (Jola, Joola)	2.78773	232,221	264,309	466,738	NAB56c	90-DAAA-a	proper foonyi		15.00	39,646	4....	8	5	9	5	3	Diola*	P..	b
10127	Diola-Kasa (Casa, Huluf)	0.39825	33,175	37,759	66,677	NAB56c	90-DAFB-a	kasa		6.00	2,266	0....	7	5	5	4	1	Jola-kasa	P..	.
10128	Eurafrican Creole	0.05000	4,165	4,741	8,371	NAN58	52-ABAH-b	krio	3	70.00	3,318	4.s.h	10	8	8	5	3	Krio	PN.	b
10129	Falor (Palor, Waro)	0.09425	7,851	8,936	15,780	NAB56c	90-CABA-a	palor		5.00	447	0....	7	5	5	3	1		...	.
10130	Felupe (Fulup)	0.01991	1,659	1,888	3,333	NAB56c	90-DAHA-a	ku-jamut-aay		3.00	57	0....	6	4	5	1	1		...	b
10131	French	1.27000	105,792	120,411	212,631	CEW21b	51-AABI-d	general français	50	74.00	89,104	1B.uh	10	9	14	5	3	French	PNB	b
10132	Fula Toro (Fula Jeeri)	4.64622	387,035	440,516	777,897	NAB56c	90-BAAA-b	futa-tooro		0.01	44	1cs..	3	3	2	5	3		pnb	.
10133	Fulakunda (Fula Cunda)	12.41205	1,033,937	1,176,806	2,078,097	NAB56c	90-BAAA-c	fula-kunda		0.01	118	1as..	3	3	4	5	3	Pulaar: Fulakunda	Pnb	b
10134	Futa Jalon (Futa Fula)	1.32749	110,581	125,861	222,256	NAB56c	90-BAAA-d	futa-jalon		0.01	13	2as..	3	3	3	5	3	Fula: Futa-jalon*	Pnb	.
10135	Ganja (Bandal)	0.05000	4,165	4,741	8,371	NAB56c	90-GAAA-a	ganja-blip		6.00	284	0....	7	5	5	5	2		...	n
10136	Gusilay	0.17000	14,161	16,118	28,462	NAB56c	90-DADA-a	gu-siil-aay		5.00	806	0....	7	5	5	1	1		...	b
10137	Her	0.11720	9,763	11,112	19,622	NAB56c	90-DAGA-a	ke-era-ku		3.00	333	0....	6	4	5	1	1	Kerak	...	.
10138	Hulon	0.01327	1,105	1,258	2,222	NAB56c	90-DAEA-a	ku-luun-aay		4.00	50	0....	6	4	5	1	1		...	.
10139	Jahanka (Diakhanke)	0.29072	24,217	27,564	48,674	NAB63h	00-AAAA-e	jakhanka-kango		0.00	0	1c...	0	2	2	0	0		pn.	p
10140	Karon	0.08871	7,390	8,411	14,852	NAB56c	90-DBAA-a	karoon		5.00	421	0....	7	5	6	1	1		...	n
10141	Kassanga (Haal)	0.00400	333	379	670	NAB56c	90-HBBA-a	haal		10.00	38	0....	8	5	6	1	2		...	.
10142	Khasonke	0.07965	6,635	7,552	13,335	NAB63h	00-AAAA-f	xasonka-xango		0.30	23	1c...	5	4	2	4	1	Kassonke	pn.	n
10143	Kobiana (Cobiana)	0.00300	250	284	502	NAB56c	90-HBAA-a	buy		10.00	28	0....	8	5	6	1	0		...	p
10144	Konyagi (Coniagui)	0.16400	13,661	15,549	27,458	NAB56c	90-JAAA-b	wa-meyny		50.00	7,775	0....	10	5	5	1	1	Wamei	pn.	.
10145	Kwatay	0.04646	3,870	4,405	7,779	NAB56c	90-DBCA-a	ku-waat-aay		5.00	220	0....	7	5	4	1	1	Kwatay	...	p
10146	Lala	0.03717	3,096	3,524	6,223	NAB56c	90-CAAA-a	lehar		10.00	352	0....	8	5	5	4	1		...	n
10147	Lebanese Arab	0.50000	41,651	47,406	83,713	CMT30	12-AACF-f	syro-palestinian		28.20	13,368	1Asuh	9	7	8	4	1	Arabic: Lebanese*	Pnb	b
10148	Malinke (Malinka)	3.78999	315,710	359,335	634,542	NAB63h	00-AAAA-a	mandinka-kango		0.50	1,797	4a...	5	4	5	5	3	Mandinka	PN.	b
10149	Mandinka (Mandingo, Sose)	5.91398	492,641	560,714	990,153	NAB63h	00-AAAA-a	mandinka-kango		0.10	561	4a...	5	4	5	5	2	Mandinka	PN.	b
10150	Mandyak (Manjaco)	0.93190	77,628	88,355	156,024	NAB56c	90-FAAA-a	proper mandyak		7.00	6,185	0....	7	4	7	5	3	Manjako*	P..	b
10151	Maninka	0.30000	24,990	28,443	50,228	NAB63h	00-AAAA-h	maninka-kan		0.30	85	3a...	5	4	5	1	2	Maninka*	PN.	b
10152	Mankanya (Mankanha)	0.25753	21,453	24,417	43,117	NAB56c	90-FACA-a	mankany		30.00	7,325	0....	9	5	7	4	3		...	n
10153	Mossi	0.30000	24,990	28,443	50,228	NAB56a	91-GGAA-a	moo-re		17.00	4,835	2A...	8	5	8	5	2	Moore	PNB	b
10154	Ndut	0.28143	23,443	26,683	47,119	NAB56c	90-CABA-b	ndut		33.00	8,805	0....	9	5	5	4	1	Ndut	...	n
10155	Northern Mlomp	0.04777	3,979	4,529	7,998	NAB56c	90-DACA-a	mlomp		3.00	136	0....	6	4	5	1	1		...	.
10156	Papel (Pepel)	0.05000	4,165	4,741	8,371	NAB56c	90-FABA-a	proper papel		23.00	1,090	0....	9	5	7	5	2	Papel	PN.	p
10157	Portuguese	0.02000	1,666	1,896	3,349	CEW21g	51-AABA-e	general português		92.00	1,745	2Bsuh	10	9	15	4	2	Portuguese	PNB	b
10158	Senegalese Creole/Mestico	0.47400	39,485	44,941	79,360	NAN58	51-AACA-b	guineense		70.00	31,458	4c...	10	7	11	5	2		PNB	b
10159	Serer-Non	0.28143	23,443	26,683	47,119	NAB56c	90-CAAB-a	non		15.00	4,002	0....	8	5	9	5	3	Noon	...	.

Continued opposite

Table 8-2 continued

Ref 1	D 28	aC 29	CG% 30	r 31	E 32	U 33	W 34	e 35	R 36	T 37	Locations, civil divisions, literacy, religions, church history, denominations, dioceses, church growth, missions, agencies, ministries, movements 38
EVANGELIZATION								EVANGELISM			ADDITIONAL DESCRIPTIVE DATA
10046	3	10	0.89	8	99.90	0.10	C	538.74	29	10	Migrants from Central and South America. D=RCC,SDA,PAoWI. M=SFM,FSC.
10047	4	10	0.89	8	99.95	0.05	C	582.54	23	10	Emigres from Latin American countries. D=RCC,AC/CPWI,SDA,PAoWI. M=SFM,FSC.
10048	7	10	0.67	8	99.71	0.29	C	338.36	29	9	Black/White persons. Nominal Christians 25%, Afro-American spiritists 2%, Baha'is 1%. D=AC/CPWI,Spiritual Baptist Chs,RCC,MCCA,CB,SDA,ECWI.
10049	1	10	0.88	8	99.93	0.07	C	573.67	31	10	Expatriates from Portugal, settlers. D=RCC(D-Bridgetown-Kingstown). M=SFM,FSC.
10050	3	10	0.89	8	99.96	0.04	C	609.69	29	10	From Spain, settlers. D=RCC,SDA,JWs. M=SFM,FSC.
10051	2	10	4.23	8	73.00	27.00	B	29.31	185	5	Emigres from Syria. Muslims 89%(Hanafi Sunnis, Alawi Shias). D=SOC,RCC.
10052	7	10	0.84	8	99.74	0.26	C	397.04	32	9	Expatriates from USA, in development, business. Nonreligious 16%. D=SDA,RCC,AC/CPWI,CGP,COG,CC,JWs. M=BMM,FMB.
10053	4	9	0.55	8	99.72	0.28	C	343.18	24	9	Nominal Christians 22%, Afro-American spiritists 2%, Baha'is 1%. D=AC/CPWI,Spiritual Baptists Chs,ECWI,RCC. M=USPG,SFM,MMS.
10054	0	10	0.89		99.70	0.30	C	260.61	24	8	Jamaicans(Rastafarians), other Caribbean Islanders, other Latin Americans, other Europeans. Afro-Caribbean religionists 13%.
Samoa											
10055	5	10	1.72	8	99.76	0.24	C	402.23	48	10	Expatriates from New Zealand in education, business. D=Anglican Ch/CPNZ(D-Polynesia),CCCS,MCS,SDA,JWs.
10056	5	10	1.66	8	99.75	0.25	C	407.88	52	10	Expatriates from Britain, in development. Nonreligious 13%. D=Anglican Ch/CPNZ(D-Polynesia),MCS,CCCS,SDA,JWs.
10057	6	10	1.72	8	99.95	0.05	C	579.07	41	10	Mixed-race part-Samoans. D=CCCS,MCS,RCC,CJCLdS,AC/CPNZ,SDA. M=SM,CWM.
10058	1	10	2.57	7	99.70	0.30	C	347.48	65	9	Originally from China. Buddhists and Chinese folk-religionists 20%. D=RCC.
10059	4	10	1.70	4	99.90	0.10	C	510.96	39	10	Maori emigres from New Zealand. D=Anglican Ch/CPNZ,RCC,CJCLdS,SDA.
10060	7	8	1.66	5	99.94	0.06	C	571.44	36	10	Baha'is 2%, rapidly growing. D=CCCS,RCC(D-Samoa & Tokelau),CJCLdS,MCS,AoG,SDA,UPC.
10061	0	0	4.48	8	99.74	0.26	C	332.22	120	9	Expatriates from the USA, mainly in business. Nonreligious 14%. D=CJCLdS.
10062	0	10	1.72		99.70	0.30	C	265.72	45	8	Tongans(MCS), other Pacific Islanders, other Europeans. Nonreligious 10%.
San Marino											
10063	0	10	0.00	5	99.70	0.30	C	334.70	0	9	Artificial(constructed) language, in 80 countries. Speakers in San Marino: 240(non mother-tongue).
10064	2	10	1.08	7	99.89	0.11	C	548.56	34	10	91% of all residents are aliens (non-citizens). Nonreligious and atheists 7%, some Baha'is. D=RCC,JWs. M=OFM,OSM.
10065	3	5	1.21	7	99.94	0.06	C	576.40	36	10	20,000 citizens live abroad. Republic has 12 Parishes. D=RCC(part of D-Montefeltro,D-Rimini),JWs,SDA. M=OFM,OFMCap,OFMConv,OSM.
10066	0	10	1.26		87.00	13.00	B	171.47	40	7	Other Europeans, other Levantines, other Asians. Muslims 20%, nonreligious 6%.
Sao Tome & Principe											
10067	4	9	3.66	8	99.89	0.11	C	495.84	91	10	Nominal Christians 9%, animists 2%. D=RCC(D-Sao Tome & Principe),Evangelical Ch,SDA,AoG. M=CMF.
10068	3	10	2.61	8	99.90	0.10	C	502.60	66	10	West African Black/White mixed-race persons, mainly in urban areas. D=RCC,EC,SDA.
10069	4	9	6.51	8	99.86	0.14	C	480.26	143	10	Bantu immigrants from mainland. Animists 10%. D=RCC,EC,SDA,AoG. M=CMF.
10070	4	10	1.56	8	99.93	0.07	C	587.24	41	10	Whites originally from Portugal. D=RCC(D-Sao Tome & Principe),EC,SDA,AoG.
10071	3	10	5.40	8	99.93	0.07	C	527.05	95	10	Principe Island's mixed-race African/Whites. D=RCC,EC,AoG. M=CMF.
10072	4	10	6.90	8	99.91	0.09	C	504.63	144	10	Sao Tome mixed-race African/Whites. D=RCC,EC,AoG,SDA. M=CMF.
10073	0	10	4.88		99.80	0.20	C	329.96	118	9	Other Bantu peoples, other Europeans, other West Africans. Nonreligious 6%, Muslims 4%.
Saudi Arabia											
10074	1	7	5.02	6	99.87	0.13	C	492.20	99	10	Immigrants, professionals from Armenia or diaspora. Gregorians. Nonreligious 10%. D=Armenian Apostolic Ch.
10075	0	5	4.53	7	30.01	69.99	A	0.01	478	2	Nomads, tent-dwellers. Muslims 100%(Sunnis: Sanusiyya(Sufi brotherhood)strong).
10076	1	7	4.56	6	56.40	43.60	B	0.82	288	3	Migrant workers from India, Bangladesh. Muslims 99%(Hanafi Sunnis). D=RCC(VA-Arabia).
10077	0	6	8.86	5	57.00	43.00	B	31.20	496	5	Long-time descendants of slaves, plus migrant laborers. Muslims 85%(Shafi Sunnis).
10078	1	8	7.26	8	99.74	0.26	C	394.34	158	9	Expatriates from Britain, in business. D=Anglican Ch/ECJME(D-Cyprus & The Gulf).
10079	4	7	9.65	8	87.00	13.00	B	57.15	326	6	Migrant workers from Egypt. Muslims 74%. D=COC,RCC/CCC,CEC,AoG.
10080	3	8	10.38	5	99.90	0.10	C	538.74	185	10	Migrant laborers from Philippines. Mostly Tagalog-speaking. Moros(Moors, Muslims)8% (Shafi Sunnis). D=RCC,PIC,UCCP.
10081	1	8	7.74	8	99.80	0.20	C	435.08	160	10	Expatriates from France, in oil, business. Nonreligious 16%. D=RCC(VA-Arabia). M=OFMCap.
10082	1	8	5.47	7	99.95	0.05	C	565.20	108	10	Expatriate traders, from Greece. D=Greek Orthodox Ch.
10083	1	7	8.46	7	54.20	45.80	B	10.28	463	5	Immigrants and migrants from all Gulf states, speaking North Arabian Colloquial Arabic. Muslims 95%(Sunnis,Wahhabis). D=RCC. R=FEBA,AWR.
10084	0	6	6.45	7	62.00	38.00	B	13.57	314	5	Workers from China. Buddhists/Chinese folk-religionists 84%, nonreligious 9%.
10085	0	3	0.00	0	11.00	89.00	A	0.00	0	1.04	Local South Arabic tribe. Related to Mahri, and becoming proficient in it. Muslims 100%.
10086	3	6	4.79	7	61.00	39.00	B	2.22	260	4	Migrant workers from India, Pakistan. Muslims 96%, Hindus 2%, some Baha'is. D=CSI,OSCE,RCC.
10087	0	5	0.00	7	39.00	61.00	A	0.00	0	1.13	Migrant laborers from China. Chinese Muslims 95%(Hanafi Sunnis), nonreligious 5%.
10088	0	8	2.60	7	49.20	50.80	A	0.35	184	3	Migrant workers from Indonesia. Muslims 95%.
10089	1	10	7.84	7	99.80	0.20	C	443.84	159	10	Expatriates from Italy, in business. Strong Catholics. D=RCC(VA-Arabia). M=OFMCap.
10090	0	6	3.92	5	54.40	45.60	B	4.76	240	4	Migrant workers from Java. Muslims 67%, New-Religionists 30%.
10091	2	6	7.53	8	68.00	32.00	B	22.33	332	5	Migrant workers from Jordan. Muslims 91%(Shafi Sunnis). D=RCC,GOC.
10092	0	5	3.61	0	28.00	72.00	A	2.04	451	4	Migrant laborers from Turkey, Russia. Muslims 90%(Hanafi Sunnis), nonreligious 8%.
10093	2	8	8.77	6	99.40	0.60	B	159.14	236	7	Migrant laborers (especially in construction) from Korea. Shamanists/Buddhists/New-Religionists 60%. D=PCK,&c. M=WOM.
10094	2	7	10.18	8	99.45	0.55	B	179.03	273	7	Refugees, traders, migrant workers from Lebanon. Muslims 45%, Nonreligious 10%. D=RCC(Maronites),GOC.
10095	0	3	1.10	0	11.01	88.99	A	0.00	448	1.05	Biljaf, Buatahari. Indigenous Arab tribes near Mahra, including Harasi. Muslims 100%(Sunnis).
10096	0	6	0.70	5	39.02	60.98	A	0.02	98	2	Migrant workers from Malaysia. Muslims 100%(Shafi Sunnis).
10097	0	5	4.56	7	37.10	62.90	A	0.13	388	3	Workers from Oman. Muslims 100%(Hinawis,Ibadi Kharijites,Ghafiris).
10098	2	7	7.76	8	77.00	23.00	B	42.15	301	6	Migrant workers. Muslims 79%(Shafi Sunnis,Alawi Shias,Druzes), some Baha'is. D=RCC,GOC.
10099	0	6	4.18	5	39.04	60.96	A	0.05	343	2	Workers from Iran. Muslims 98%(Imami Shias,Ithna-Asharis).
10100	0	3	7.19	5	47.00	53.00	A	3.43	480	4	Workers from northwest India. Sikhs 8%, Hindus 40%, Muslim 50%.
10101	1	5	9.34	7	54.47	45.53	B	0.93	505	3	Eastern Colloquial Arabic(Hijazi 35.8%, Najdi 17.9%, Gulf 11.9%). Muslims 99%(almost all Sunnis: Wahhabis at center, Shafiites west, Malikites in east); 1% Shias.
10102	0	4	1.40	0	15.01	84.99	A	0.00	383	1.05	Indigenous Arab tribes(Qara,Bajahama,Bait,Ash,Shaikin) in Dofar. Muslims 100%(Sunnis).
10103	0	6	2.93	5	40.04	59.96	A	0.05	327	2	Migrant laborers from Somalia. Muslims 100%(Shafi Sunnis).
10104	0	5	0.70	1	23.02	76.98	A	0.01	202	2	Long-time residents from Baluchistan. Muslims 100%(Sunnis). M=RSMT.
10105	1	6	5.13	7	47.40	52.60	A	2.42	337	4	Migrant laborers from Sudan. Muslims 98%(Maliki Sunnis). D=RCC.
10106	1	6	8.24	8	68.00	32.00	B	24.82	360	5	Migrant workers from Syria. Muslims 90%(Hanafi Sunnis,Alawi Shias). D=Syrian Orthodox Ch.
10107	0	4	6.69	6	67.00	33.00	B	36.68	314	5	Workers from south India. Hindus 70%, Muslims 13%(Hanafi Sunnis).
10108	0	6	1.40	8	41.02	58.98	A	0.03	141	2	Migrant laborers from Turkey. Muslims 100%(Hanafi Sunnis,some Shias or Alawis).
10109	5	10	9.16	8	99.74	0.26	C	402.44	185	10	Expatriates from USA, in oil, business. Nonreligious 17%. D=AC/ECJME,RCC,CC,CB,Unitarians.
10110	1	5	4.67	5	43.02	56.98	A	0.03	363	2	Traders, construction workers, from India, Pakistan. Muslims 100%(Hanafi Sunnis). D=house churches.
10111	0	5	3.47	7	41.20	58.80	A	0.30	277	3	Remnant of 2.5 million migrant laborers from Yemen deported in 1991. Muslims 100%(50% Zaydi Shias,40% Sunnis,5% Ismailis). M=CSI.
10112	0	8	8.34		45.00	55.00	A	32.85	508	5	Other Arabs, other Asians, other Levantines, other African, other Europeans, other Americans. Muslims 70%, nonreligious 9%.
Senegal											
10113	0	4	0.70	7	33.01	66.99	A	0.01	116	2	From Chad, Sahara, North Africa. Muslims 100%(Sunnis). M=WEC.
10114	0	2	4.51	0	24.00	76.00	A	0.87	698	3	South central. Primarily in Guinea Bissau, also Guinea. Part of Tenda cluster. Bilingual in Mandinka. Muslims 80%(Maliki Sunnis), animists 19%. M=WEC,NTM.
10115	3	6	6.59	0	41.00	59.00	A	8.97	547	4	Southwest corner. Most in Guinea Bissau; some in Cape Verde islands. Some bilingual in Crioulo. Animists 83%, Muslims 11%. D=RCC,AoG,SDA. M=NTM,WEC.
10116	1	8	5.48	4	58.00	42.00	B	6.35	349	4	East central. Majority in Mali, Ivory Coast, Gambia, Burkina Faso. Muslims 83%(Sunnis), animists 14%. D=RCC.
10117	0	0	3.40	0	21.00	79.00	A	3.83	652	4	Casamance River as northern boundary of group of villages. Related to Bandial. Muslims 70%, Animists 25%.
10118	1	6	6.22	0	49.00	51.00	A	28.61	437	5	Southwest corner; also in Guinea Bissau. Animists 84%. D=RCC. M=MSC,OSB,CSSp,WEC,NTM.
10119	2	6	5.05	0	53.80	46.20	B	32.99	339	5	Southeast. Majority in Guinea, also Gambia. High mortality rate. Animists 75%, Muslims 8%. D=RCC(D-Kaolack,PA-Tambacounda),AoG. M=MSC,CSSp.
10120	1	6	3.32	0	27.00	73.00	A	3.94	499	4	Southwest corner; also in Gambia, Guinea Bissau. Animists 95%. D=RCC.
10121	0	6	4.31	0	30.00	70.00	A	1.09	540	4	In southeast. Part of Tenda cluster (Bedik, Boin, Badyara, Bassari, Konyagi). Many Muslims 80%, some animists 19%. M=NTM.
10122	0	5	0.00	7	29.00	71.00	A	0.00	0	1.08	From Mauritania (business, laborers, refugees). Lower castes(slave descendants). Muslims 100%(Maliki Sunnis). M=WEC,CBFMS.
10123	5	10	2.60	8	99.78	0.22	C	435.59	67	10	Expatriates from Britain, in development. D=Anglican Ch/CPWA(D-Gambia & The Rio Pongas),MEAO,SDA,JWs,RCC.
10124	3	10	2.86	8	99.96	0.04	C	571.15	67	10	Emigres from Cape Verde islands. Also in Guinea Bissau, Gambia. D=RCC(M-Dakar),CON,AoG. M=WEC.
10125	0	3	2.93	1	24.11	75.89	A	0.09	564	2	In extreme southeast corner, also Guinea, Sierra Leone, Mali. Muslims 100%(Maliki Sunnis). M=NTM.
10126	2	6	3.23	0	58.00	42.00	B	31.75	228	5	Felupes. 15 subgroups. Muslims 54%(41% Sufi Qadiriyya, most converted from 1940-70), animists 30%. D=RCC,AoG. M=WEC,CSSp,FMB,SIL,NTM.
10127	1	6	5.57	0	35.00	65.00	A	7.66	561	4	Near Diola. Muslims 75%, animists 19%. D=RCC. M=WEC.
10128	3	10	5.98	8	99.70	0.30	C	334.70	148	9	Creoles from Gambia, Sierra Leone, Liberia. Mostly urban. Animists 20%, Muslims 10%. D=RCC,AoG,SDA.
10129	1	6	3.87	0	31.00	69.00	A	5.65	483	4	West central. Part of Cangin cluster. Some bilinguals in Safen and French. No schools in area. Muslims 70%, animists 25%. D=RCC.
10130	1	6	4.13	0	29.00	71.00	A	3.17	541	4	Extreme southern Senegal. Also many in Guinea Bissau. A few villages. Muslims 70%, animists 27%. D=RCC.
10131	4	10	3.16	8	99.74	0.26	C	410.55	75	10	Expatriates from France, in business, government. Nonreligious 23%. D=RCC(6 Dioceses),PCD,AoG,SDA. M=PEMS,MSC,CSSp,OSB,FMB.
10132	0	4	3.86	4	33.01	66.99	A	0.01	453	2	In northeast, mingled with Tukulor in Bunndu geopolitical Fula state. Muslims 99%(Maliki Sunnis). M=CRWM,WEC,ELC.
10133	0	5	2.50	4	39.01	60.99	A	0.01	288	2	In south, upper Casamance; also in Guinea. Firdu (Fulakanda) is a Fula geopolitical state. Muslims 99%(Maliki Sunnis). M=WEC,American Lutheran Ch,CSI.
10134	2	5	2.60	4	41.01	58.99	A	0.01	281	2	Fulani labor migrants from Guinea, in Casamance, Dakar, eastern Senegal. Muslims 100%(Maliki Sunnis). D=RCC,EEP. M=WEC,CSSp,CMA.
10135	1	6	3.40	4	40.00	60.00	A	8.76	343	4	Southwest. Bilingual in Mandinka. Animists 80%, Muslims 14%. D=RCC. M=WEC,NTM.
10136	1	6	4.49	0	32.00	68.00	A	5.84	521	4	Spoken only in village of Tionk Essil, north of Casamance river. Related to Diola. Muslims 70%, animists 25%. D=RCC.
10137	1	6	3.57	0	26.00	74.00	A	2.84	545	4	Southwestern corner of Senegal. Related to Diola. Second language: Jola-Kasa or Wolof. Muslims 70%, animists 27%. D=RCC.
10138	1	6	3.99	0	27.00	73.00	A	3.94	567	4	Brin village, southwest of Ziguinchor. Second languages: Wolof, Jola-Kasa, or Jola-Fogny. Muslims 71%, animists 25%. D=RCC.
10139	0	6	0.00	1	18.00	82.00	A	0.00	0	1.09	Gambia, Guinea Bissau. Originally Soninke clans, now speaking Mandinka. Many diviners. Muslims 100%(Maliki Sunnis, many clerics). Slavery practised.
10140	1	6	3.81	0	30.00	70.00	A	5.47	494	4	Southwest near Gambia border and coast; also in Gambia. Muslims 70%, animists 25%. D=RCC.
10141	1	6	3.70	0	37.00	63.00	A	13.50	392	5	Also in Guinea Bissau. Close to Banyun. Animists 90%. D=RCC. M=WEC,CSSp.
10142	0	4	3.19	1	25.30	74.70	A	0.27	565	3	Also in Mali and Gambia. Muslims 95%(Maliki Sunnis), animists 4%. M=UWM.
10143	0	6	3.39	0	35.00	65.00	A	12.77	391	5	Southwest corner. Also in Guinea Bissau. Bilingual in Mandyak. Animists 85%, Muslims 5%.
10144	1	6	6.88	0	81.00	19.00	B	147.82	287	7	In southeast; most in Guinea. Part of Tenda cluster. Nomads. Animists 30%, Muslims 20%. D=RCC. M=SIL.
10145	1	6	3.14	0	29.00	71.00	A	5.29	448	4	Villages along coast south of Casamance river. Related to Diola-Gusilay. Muslims 70%, animists 25%. D=RCC. M=WEC.
10146	1	6	3.63	0	40.00	60.00	A	14.60	358	5	West central Senegal. Second language: Wolof. Some bilinguals in Non, Ndut, French. Muslims 80%, animists 10%. D=RCC.
10147	1	10	7.46	8	90.20	9.80	B	92.84	248	6	Traders, merchants from Lebanon. Muslims 70%(Sunnis,Shias). D=RCC(Maronites).
10148	1	5	5.33	4	45.50	54.50	A	0.83	443	3	Eastern Senegal, also in Mali. Muslims 90%(Sunnis), animists 9%. D=RCC. M=NTM,UWM,FMB.
10149	0	5	4.11	4	44.10	55.90	A	0.16	381	3	In southeast. Also in Gambia, Sierra Leone. Muslims 95%(Sunnis), animists 5%. M=CMA,WEC(Gambia).
10150	1	6	6.64	0	41.00	59.00	A	10.47	551	5	Southwest. Most in Guinea Bissau; also Gambia, France, Cape Verde islands. Animists 85%, Muslims 5%. D=RCC(D-Saint-Louis). M=NTM,WEC,CSSp.
10151	0	5	4.54	5	39.30	60.70	A	0.43	458	3	In southeast Senegal, also in neighboring countries. Muslims 90%(Sunnis), animists 10%. M=CSSp,WEC.
10152	1	6	6.82	0	65.00	35.00	B	71.17	355	6	Scattered. Mainly in Guinea Bissau. Bilingual in Mandyak. Animists 70%. D=RCC. M=MSC,CSSp,OSB,SIL.
10153	2	6	6.38	4	76.00	24.00	B	47.15	279	6	Migrants, laborers from Burkina Faso. Animists 45%, Muslims 38%(Maliki Sunnis). D=RCC,AoG.
10154	1	5	7.02	0	64.00	36.00	B	77.08	369	6	West central. Second language: Wolof. Some bilinguals in Lehar, Safen, French. Muslims 40%, animists 27%. D=RCC.
10155	1	6	2.64	0	26.00	74.00	A	2.84	447	4	Mlomp village north of Casamance river. Related to Diola. Second language: Jola-Fogny, Wolof. Muslims 70%, animists 27%. D=RCC.
10156	1	7	4.80	0	62.00	38.00	B	52.04	283	6	In southwest. Majority in Guinea Bissau. Animists 72%, Muslims 5%. D=RCC. M=CSSp,WEC.
10157	1	10	2.20	8	99.92	0.08	C	564.14	53	10	Settlers originally from Portugal. D=RCC(5 Dioceses). M=MSC,OSB.
10158	2	10	4.04	8	99.70	0.30	C	352.59	102	9	Mixed-race, Eurafricans. Muslims 20%, animists 10%. D=RCC,CON. M=WEC,FMB.
10159	2	6	4.54	0	52.00	48.00	B	28.47	324	5	Surrounding Thies Phils and coast. Some bilinguals in Lehar and French. Fishermen, agriculturalists. Muslims 80%, animists 5%. D=RCC,AoG. M=CBFMS,FLM.

Continued overleaf

Table 8-2 continued

PEOPLE		POPULATION			IDENTITY CODE		LANGUAGE		CHURCH		MINISTRY		SCRIPTURE	
Ref Ethnic name 1 2	*P%* 3	*In 1995* 4	*In 2000* 5	*In 2025* 6	*Race* 7	*Language* 8	*Autoglossonym* 9	*S* 10	*AC* 11	*Members* 12	*Jayuh* 13-17	*d wa xc mc mi* 18 19 20 21 22	*Biblioglossonym* 23	*Pub ss* 24-26 27
10160 Serer-Safen (Safi)	0.46993	39,146	44,555	78,678	NAB56c	90-CAAC-a	safen		19.00	8,465	0....	8 5 8 4 1	Safen	... b
10161 Serer-Sine	11.25714	937,732	1,067,308	1,884,736	NAB56c	90-BBAA-a	sine		15.00	160,096	2....	8 5 9 5 3	Seereer*	PN. n
10162 Soninke (Serahuli, Azer)	1.85849	154,814	176,206	311,159	NAB63j	00-BAAA-a	proper soninke		0.02	35	3....	3 2 5 0 3	Soninke	... b
10163 Susu (Soso)	0.30000	24,990	28,443	50,228	NAB63k	00-AACA-a	soso		0.01	3	4....	3 3 2 1 0	Soso*	PN. n
10164 Syrian Arab	0.10000	8,330	9,481	16,743	CMT30	12-AACF-f	syro-palestinian		7.00	664	1Asuh	7 5 8 4 2	Arabic: Lebanese*	Pnb b
10165 Tukulor (Takarir)	8.78136	731,497	832,575	1,470,226	NAB56c	90-BAAA-a	haal-pulaar		0.00	0	2As..	0 3 3 1 3	Fula: Pulaar*	Pnb n
10166 White Moor (Bidan)	1.00000	83,301	94,812	167,426	CMT32y	12-AACD-a	hassaaniyya		0.00	0	0a...	0 3 5 1 2		pn. b
10167 Wolof	34.60301	2,882,468	3,280,767	5,793,436	NAB56c	90-AAAA-a	vehicular wolof	82	0.01	328	4.s..	3 5 7 5 4	Wolof: Senegal	PN. b
10168 Yalunka (Dialonke)	0.17257	14,375	16,362	28,893	NAB63l	00-AACA-b	yalunka		0.50	82	1....	5 4 4 5 1	Yalunka	PN. .
10169 Zenaga	0.02000	1,666	1,896	3,349	CMT32i	10-AAAA-a	znaga		0.01	0	0....	3 3 0 0 0		... b
10170 other minor peoples	0.42185	35,141	39,996	70,629	...				26.00	10,399		9 5 7 5 0		
Seychelles	**100.00000**	**73,437**	**77,435**	**97,962**					**92.72**	**71,796**				
10171 British	3.00000	2,203	2,323	2,939	CEW19i	52-ABAC-b	standard-english	75	74.00	1,719	3Bsuh	10 9 13 5 1		PNB b
10172 French	1.85600	1,363	1,437	1,818	CEW21b	51-AABI-d	general français	70	87.00	1,250	1B.uh	10 9 14 5 1	French	PNB b
10173 Gujarati	0.29800	219	231	292	CNN25e	59-AAFH-b	standard gujaraati		1.80	4	2A.u.	6 4 6 1 0	Gujarati	PNB b
10174 Han Chinese	0.53200	391	412	521	MSY42a	79-AAAB-ba	kuo-yü	1	90.00	371	2Bsuh	10 8 12 5 1	Chinese: Kuoyu*	PNB b
10175 Hindi	0.30000	220	232	294	CNN25g	59-AAFO-e	general hindi		4.11	10	3Asuh	6 4 6 3 0		pnb b
10176 Reunionese Creole	0.30000	220	232	294	NAN58	51-AACC-m	réunioné		95.00	221	1cs..	10 9 12 5 1		pnb b
10177 Seychellese Creole	93.21400	68,454	72,180	91,314	NAN58	51-AACC-k	seselwa	99	94.30	68,066	1cs..	10 10 12 5 2	Creole: Seychelles*	PNb b
10178 Swahili	0.10000	73	77	98	NAB57j	99-AUSM-b	standard ki-swahili		0.00	0	4Asu.	0 3 2 1 0	Kiswahili*	PNB b
10179 Tamil	0.20000	147	155	196	CNN23c	49-EBEA-b	tamil		60.00	93	2Asu.	10 7 10 5 3	Tamil	PNB b
10180 other minor peoples	0.20000	147	155	196	...				40.00	62		9 5 8 3 0		
Sierra Leone	**100.00000**	**4,188,087**	**4,854,383**	**8,085,454**					**10.52**	**510,498**				
10181 Bassa	0.11800	4,942	5,728	9,541	NAB59j	95-ABAB-a	central basoo		42.00	2,406	0....	9 6 8 5 3	Bassa: Liberia	PN. b
10182 Bom (Bum)	0.11700	4,900	5,680	9,460	NAB56c	94-BAAA-c	bom		5.00	284	0....	7 5 4 1 0		p.. .
10183 British	0.04000	1,675	1,942	3,234	CEW19i	52-ABAC-b	standard-english	36	74.00	1,437	3Bsuh	10 9 13 5 1		PNB b
10184 East Limba	0.01200	503	583	970	NAB56c	90-PAAC	south limba cluster		15.00	87	0....	8 7 6 5 3	Limba	PN. .
10185 Eurafrican	0.10000	4,188	4,854	8,085	NAN58	52-ABAH	west-coast-creole- cluster	20	90.00	4,369	4.s.h	10 8 11 5 3		PN. b
10186 French	0.00500	209	243	404	CEW21b	51-AABI-d	general français	3	84.00	204	1B.uh	10 9 14 5 3	French	PNB b
10187 Fula Jalon (Futa Jallon)	3.76800	157,807	182,913	304,660	NAB56c	90-BAAA-d	futa-jalon	5	0.02	37	2as..	3 4 1 4 3	Fula: Futa-jalon*	Pnb .
10188 Gola (Gula)	0.19100	7,999	9,272	15,443	NAB56c	94-BBAA	gola cluster		3.00	278	0....	6 4 4 4 1	Gola	... b
10189 Greek	0.01500	628	728	1,213	CEW20	56-AAAA-c	dhimotiki		95.00	692	2B.uh	10 9 11 5 1	Greek: Modern	PNB b
10190 Indo-Pakistani	0.19000	7,957	9,223	15,362	CNN25g	59-AAFO-e	general hindi		2.00	184	3Asuh	6 4 6 1 0		pnb b
10191 Kono (Konnoh)	4.22600	176,989	205,146	341,691	NAB64e	00-AAAE-a	central kono	6	12.00	24,618	1....	8 6 6 5 3	Kono	P.. .
10192 Krim (Kimi)	0.24100	10,093	11,699	19,486	NAB56c	94-BAAB-a	krim		10.00	1,170	0....	8 5 4 3 1		... b
10193 Krio (Creole)	11.00000	460,690	533,982	889,400	NAN58	52-ABAH-b	krio	34	36.00	192,234	4.s.h	9 10 10 5 3	Krio	PN. b
10194 Krio Fula	1.01400	42,467	49,223	81,987	NAB56c	90-BAAA-d	futa-jalon	2	0.06	30	2as..	4 4 0 4 2	Fula: Futa-jalon*	Pnb .
10195 Kru	0.19800	8,292	9,612	16,009	NAB59j	95-ABAE-g	central klao		75.00	7,209	0....	10 8 12 5 3	Kru*	PN. b
10196 Kuranko (Koranko)	5.54000	232,020	268,933	447,934	NAB63g	00-AAAD-c	wasamandu-kuranko	6	2.00	5,379	0....	6 4 4 5 3	Kuranko	PN. .
10197 Lebanese Arab	0.60000	25,129	29,126	48,513	CMT30	12-AACF-f	syro-palestinian	3	19.50	5,680	1Asuh	8 6 8 5 2	Arabic: Lebanese*	Pnb b
10198 Loko (Landogo)	2.84200	119,025	137,962	229,789	NAB64g	00-ABAA-b	loko	3	3.70	5,105	1....	6 6 7 5 3	Loko: Sierra Leone	PNb b
10199 Maninka (Mandingo)	2.22400	93,143	107,961	179,820	NAB63h	00-AAAA-a	mandinka-kango	5	2.00	2,159	4a...	6 4 6 2 0	Mandinka	PN. b
10200 Mende (Boumpe, Kossa)	26.00000	1,088,903	1,262,140	2,102,218	NAB64i	00-ABAA-c	mende	54	9.20	116,117	3....	7 7 7 5 3	Mende	PNB b
10201 Northern Bullom	0.17200	7,204	8,350	13,907	NAB56c	94-BAAA-a	bolom	6	5.00	417	0....	7 5 6 4 2	Bullom*	P.. .
10202 Northern Kissi	0.93900	39,326	45,583	75,922	NAB56c	94-BABA-a	north kisi		5.00	2,279	3....	7 5 5 1 1	Kisi: Northern*	PN. .
10203 Sherbro (Southern Bullom)	3.00300	125,768	145,777	242,806	NAB56c	94-BAAA-b	shebra	9	8.00	11,662	0....	7 5 7 4 2		p.. .
10204 Southern Kissi (Kisi)	1.88000	78,736	91,262	152,007	NAB56c	94-BABA-b	south kisi	3	10.50	9,583	1....	8 6 6 5 3	Kisi: Southern*	PN. .
10205 Susu (Soso)	2.51100	105,163	121,894	203,026	NAB63k	00-AACA-a	soso	5	0.01	12	4....	3 3 2 4 3	Soso*	PN. n
10206 Temne (Timne, Timmanee)	24.64000	1,031,945	1,196,120	1,992,256	NAB56c	94-AAAC-a	ka-themne	40	5.50	65,787	3....	7 6 7 5 3	Themne	PN. .
10207 Vai (Vey, Vy)	0.36400	15,245	17,670	29,431	NAB64k	00-AAAE-e	vai		0.10	18	4....	5 3 4 4 1	Vai	P.. .
10208 West Central Limba	7.07800	296,433	343,593	572,288	NAB56c	90-PAAC	south limba cluster	9	14.00	48,103	0....	8 7 8 5 3	Limba	PN. .
10209 Yalunka (Yalun Soso)	0.69200	28,982	33,592	55,951	NAB63l	00-AACA-b	yalunka	1	1.00	336	1....	6 4 4 5 1	Yalunka	PN. .
10210 Yoruba	0.08000	3,350	3,884	6,468	NAB59n	98-AAAA-a	standard yoruba		45.00	1,748	3asu.	9 7 9 5 3	Yoruba	PNB b
10211 other minor peoples	0.20000	8,376	9,709	16,171	...				9.00	874		7 7 6 5 0		
Singapore	**100.00000**	**3,320,694**	**3,566,614**	**4,167,756**					**11.3**	**402,933**				
10212 Anglicized Chinese	5.95300	197,681	212,321	248,107	MSY42a	52-ABAC	english-mainland cluster		25.00	53,080	3Bsuh	9 8 13 5 3		PNB b
10213 Anglicized Indian	1.40000	46,490	49,933	58,349	MSY43	52-ABAD-ba	singaporean-english		30.00	14,980	0B.uh	9 9 9 5 0		... b
10214 Anglicized Malay-Indonesi	0.50000	16,603	17,833	20,839	MSY43	52-ABAD-ba	singaporean-english		5.00	892	0B.uh	7 5 6 5 0		... b
10215 Anglo-Australian	0.05000	1,660	1,783	2,084	CEW19c	52-ABAC-x	general australian		67.00	1,195	1Bsuh	10 9 13 5 3		pnb b
10216 Anglo-New Zealander	0.05000	1,660	1,783	2,084	CEW19e	52-ABAC-y	general new-zealand		76.00	1,355	1Bsuh	10 9 14 5 3		pnb b
10217 Arab	0.20000	6,641	7,133	8,336	CMT30	12-AACF-a	masri		1.00	71	2Asuh	6 4 2 3 0	Arabic*	PNB b
10218 Armenian	0.01000	332	357	417	CEW14	57-AAAA-b	ashkharik		89.00	317	4A.u.	10 9 13 5 2	Armenian: Modern, Eastern	PNB b
10219 Batak	0.02000	664	713	834	MSY44b	31-PECA	south batak cluster		85.00	606	2.s..	10 9 11 5 3		PNB b
10220 Bengali	0.05100	1,694	1,819	2,126	CNN25b	59-AAFT-e	west bengali		1.00	18	1Asuh	6 4 8 5 2	Bengali: Musalmani*	PNB b
10221 British	0.50000	16,603	17,833	20,839	CEW19i	52-ABAC-b	standard-english	35	74.00	13,196	3Bsuh	10 9 13 5 1		PNB b
10222 Buginese (Bugis)	0.30000	9,962	10,700	12,503	MSY44c	31-QBBA	bugis cluster		1.00	107	2....	6 4 2 1 0	Bugis	PNB b
10223 Eurasian	1.00000	33,207	35,666	41,678	MSY43	52-ABAD-a	south-asian-english		62.00	22,113	0B.uh	10 8 11 5 2		... b
10224 Filipino	1.80000	59,772	64,199	75,020	MSY44o	31-CKAA-a	proper tagalog		88.00	56,495	4Bs..	10 10 12 0 0	Tagalog	PNB b
10225 German	0.03000	996	1,070	1,250	CEW19m	52-ABCE-a	standard hoch-deutsch		80.00	856	2B.uh	10 9 13 5 3	German*	PNB b
10226 Gujarati	0.06300	2,092	2,247	2,626	CNN25e	59-AAFH-b	standard gujaraati		1.00	22	2A.u.	6 4 8 3 0	Gujarati	PNB b
10227 Han Chinese (Cantonese)	8.49600	282,126	303,020	354,093	MSY42a	79-AAAM-a	central yue		8.50	25,757	3A.uh	7 10 12 5 2	Chinese, Yue	PNB b
10228 Han Chinese (Hainanese)	2.86000	94,972	102,005	119,198	MSY42a	79-AAAK-c	wanning		7.00	7,140	1a...	7 9 10 5 3		p.. b
10229 Han Chinese (Hakka)	2.66700	88,563	95,122	111,154	MSY42a	79-AAAG-a	literary hakka		9.50	9,037	1A...	7 8 10 5 3	Chinese: Hakka, Wukingfu*	PNB b
10230 Han Chinese (Mandarin)	7.77000	258,018	277,126	323,835	MSY42a	79-AAAB-ba	kuo-yü		8.00	22,170	2Bsuh	7 10 12 5 3	Chinese: Kuoyu*	PNB b
10231 Han Chinese (Min Nan)	17.83100	592,113	635,963	743,153	MSY42a	79-AAAJ-ic	chaozhou		8.80	55,965	1A..h	7 10 12 5 3	Chinese, Min Nan	PNB b
10232 Han Chinese (Min Pei)	0.96600	32,078	34,453	40,261	MSY42a	79-AAAH-a	min-bei		9.50	3,273	0A...	7 9 10 5 3	Chinese, Min Bei	PN. b
10233 Han Chinese (Teochew)	9.64100	320,148	343,857	401,813	MSY42a	79-AAAP-c	east miao-chinese		8.00	27,509	0A...	7 10 10 5 3	Chinese: Swatow*	PNB b
10234 Hindi	0.24100	8,003	8,596	10,044	CNN25g	59-AAFO-e	general hindi		0.50	43	3Asuh	5 4 8 4 3		pnb b
10235 Hui (Dungan)	0.38700	12,851	13,803	16,129	MSY42b	79-AAAB-ba	kuo-yü		0.00	0	2Bsuh	0 3 2 1 0	Chinese: Kuoyu*	PNB b
10236 Indonesian	1.00000	33,207	35,666	41,678	MSY44k	31-PHAA-c	bahasa-indonesia		0.05	18	4Asuh	4 4 2 4 2	Indonesian	PNB b
10237 Japanese	0.71600	23,776	25,537	29,841	MSY45a	45-CAAA-a	koku-go		1.60	409	1B.uh	6 4 3 5 2	Japanese	PNB b
10238 Javanese (Jawa)	0.83000	27,562	29,603	34,592	MSY44g	31-PIAA-g	general jawa		15.00	4,440	2As.h	8 5 8 5 3	Javanese	PNB b
10239 Jewish	0.02000	664	713	834	CMT35	52-ABAD-ba	singaporean-english		0.95	7	0B.uh	5 4 2 1 0		... b
10240 Kanarese	0.40000	13,283	14,266	16,671	CNN23a	49-EBAA-a	kannada		5.00	713	2Asu.	7 5 8 5 2	Kannada	PNB b
10241 Korean	0.20300	6,741	7,240	8,461	MSY46	45-AAAA-b	kukö		50.00	3,620	2A...	10 9 13 5 2	Korean	PNB b
10242 Low Malay Creole	1.00000	33,207	35,666	41,678	MSY44k	31-PHAA-d	malayu-pasar	20	0.01	4	1csuh	3 4 2 1 3	Malay: Low	PNb b
10243 Madurese (Boyanese)	0.55900	18,563	19,937	23,298	MSY44h	31-PHJA-a	west madura		3.00	598	1.s..	6 5 7 5 0	Madura	PNB b
10244 Malaccan Creole	0.45000	14,943	16,050	18,755	MSY43	51-AACA-ha	malaquense	2	75.00	12,037	1c...	10 8 10 4 2	Malaccan Creole Portuguese	Pnb b
10245 Malay	12.67500	420,898	452,068	528,263	MSY44k	31-PHAA-b	bahasa-malaysia		0.50	2,260	1asuh	5 4 6 5 3	Malay	PNB b
10246 Malayali	0.47600	15,807	16,977	19,839	CNN23b	49-EBEB-a	malayalam		30.00	5,093	2Asu.	9 7 10 5 3	Malayalam	PNB b
10247 Orang Seletar	0.02200	731	785	917	MSY44z	31-PHCA	moken cluster		8.00	63	0....	7 5 6 3 0	Moken	P.. b
10248 Palembangese	0.30000	9,962	10,700	12,503	MSY44k	31-PIAA-j	jawa-palembang		0.01	1	1cs.h	3 3 4 1 0		pnb b
10249 Peranakan (Straits Chinese)	11.50000	381,880	410,161	479,292	MSY42a	31-PHBB-a	paranakan		7.00	28,711	0A...	7 5 8 5 2		... b
10250 Punjabi	0.46000	15,275	16,406	19,172	CNN25n	59-AAFE-c	general panjabi		1.00	164	1Asu.	6 4 8 5 1		PNB b
10251 Riau Malay	0.30000	9,962	10,700	12,503	MSY44k	31-PHAB-e	malayu-riau		0.03	3	0....	3 4 2 4 3		... b
10252 Siamese (Thai)	1.07000	35,531	38,163	44,595	MSY49d	47-AAAB-d	central thai		2.00	763	3asuh	6 4 6 5 2	Thai*	PNB b
10253 Sindhi	0.17900	5,944	6,384	7,460	CNN25p	59-AAFF-a	standard sindhi		1.00	64	1as..	6 4 5 1 0	Sindhi	PNB b
10254 Sinhalese (Cingalese)	0.43000	14,279	15,336	17,921	CNN25q	59-ABBA-aa	standard sinhala		5.00	767	1asuh	7 5 8 4 3		pnb b
10255 Tamil	4.05900	134,787	144,769	169,169	CNN23c	49-EBEA-b	tamil		12.00	17,372	2Asu.	8 6 12 5 3	Tamil	PNB b
10256 Telugu	0.01500	498	535	625	CNN23d	49-DBAB-a	telugu		10.00	53	2Asu.	8 6 12 5 3	Telugu	PNB b
10257 USA White	0.15000	4,981	5,350	6,252	CEW19s	52-ABAC-s	general american		75.00	4,012	1Bsuh	10 9 13 5 2	English*	PNB b
10258 other minor peoples	0.40000	13,283	14,266	16,671	...				39.00	5,564		9 5 4 5 0		
Slovakia	**100.00000**	**5,354,652**	**5,387,191**	**5,392,691**					**80.27**	**4,324,184**				
10259 British	0.01000	535	539	539	CEW19i	52-ABAC	english-mainland cluster		79.00	426	3Bsuh	10 10 11 0 0		PNB b
10260 Byelorussian	0.20000	10,709	10,774	10,785	CEW22c	53-AAAE-c	bielorusskiy		70.00	7,542	3A.uh	10 8 8 0 0	Byelorussian*	PNB b
10261 Carpathian Gypsy	1.10000	58,901	59,259	59,320	CNN25f	59-ACBB-a	carpathian-romani		60.00	35,555	0....	10 8 8 0 0		p.. .
10262 Croat	0.02000	1,071	1,077	1,079	CEW22d	53-AAAG-b	standard hrvatski		91.00	980	2Asuh	10 9 10 0 0	Croatian	PNB b
10263 Czech (Bohemian)	1.10000	58,901	59,259	59,320	CEW22e	53-AAAD-a	czesky		65.00	38,518	2Asuh	10 8 10 0 0	Czech	PNB b
10264 Esperanto	0.00000	0	0	0	CEW21z	51-AAAC-a	proper esperanto		50.00	0	0A...	10 9 1 0 0	Esperanto	PNB b
10265 French	0.03000	1,606	1,616	1,618	CEW21b	51-AABI-d	general français		75.00	1,212	1B.uh	10 10 13 0 0	French	PNB b
10266 German	0.10000	5,355	5,387	5,393	CEW19m	52-ABCE-a	standard hoch-deutsch		70.00	3,771	2B.uh	10 10 10 0 0	German*	PNB b
10267 Hungarian	11.14000	596,508	600,133	600,746	MSW51g	41-BAAA-a	general magyar		60.00	360,080	2A.u.	10 10 11 0 0	Hungarian	PNB b
10268 Italian	0.01000	535	539	539	CEW21e	51-AABQ-c	standard italiano		86.00	463	2B.uh	10 10 14 0 0	Italian	PNB b
10269 Jewish	0.10000	5,355	5,387	5,393	CMT35	51-AABQ-c	standard italiano		0.50	27	2B.uh	5 5 5 0 0	Italian	PNB b
10270 Lovari Gypsy	0.01300	696	700	701	CNN25f	59-ACBA-a	vlach-romani		70.00	490	1a...	10 7 8 0 0	Romani: Finnish*	PN. b
10271 Polish	0.20000	10,709	10,774	10,785	CEW22i	53-AAAC-c	polski		90.00	9,697	2A.uh	10 10 11 0 0	Polish	PNB b
10272 Russian	0.50000	26,773	26,936	26,963	CEW22j	53-AAAE-d	russkiy		50.00	13,468	4B.uh	10 10 8 0 0	Russian	PNB b
10273 Ruthene (Ruthenian)	0.40000	21,419	21,549	21,571	CEW22k	53-AAAE-a	rusyn		90.00	19,394	1c.uh	10 9 10 0 0		pnb b
10274 Slovak	83.77700	4,485,967	4,513,227	4,517,835	CEW22m	53-AAAD-b	slovensky		83.80	3,782,084	1Asuh	10 10 9 0 0	Slovak	PNB b
10275 Slovak Gypsy	0.60000	32,128	32,323	32,356	CNN25f	53-AAAD-b	slovensky		75.00	24,242	1Asuh	10 8 8 0 0	Slovak	PNB b

Continued opposite

Table 8-2 continued

EVANGELIZATION								EVANGELISM			ADDITIONAL DESCRIPTIVE DATA
Ref 1	D 28	aC 29	CG% 30	r 31	E 32	U 33	W 34	e 35	R 36	T 37	Locations, civil divisions, literacy, religions, church history, denominations, dioceses, church growth, missions, agencies, ministries, movements 38
10160	1	6	3.61	0	54.00	46.00	B	37.44	264	5	Southwest of Thies, near ocean. Lingua franca. Some bilinguals in Wolof, Ndut, French. Muslims 70%, animists 14%. D=RCC. M=SIL.
10161	2	6	3.42	0	59.00	41.00	B	32.30	233	5	Also in Gambia. Muslims 72%, animists 8% (rapidly decreasing). D=RCC(3 Dioceses),AoG. M=CBFMS,FLM,MSC,CSSp,Team Expansion,ELCA,FMB. R=ELWA.
10162	0	5	3.62	0	22.02	77.98	A	0.01	688	2	Mainly in Mali, Burkina Faso, Ivory Coast, Mauritania, et alia. Muslims 63%(Sunnis, most in Sufi Tijaniyya and in Hamali sect), animists 37%. M=WEC,FI,et alia.
10163	0	5	1.10	4	26.01	73.99	A	0.00	343	1.10	Majority live in Guinea and Sierra Leone; also Guinea Bissau. Muslims 70%(Maliki Sunnis), animists 30%.
10164	2	10	4.28	8	67.00	33.00	B	17.11	204	5	Traders from Syria. Muslims 93%(89% Hanafi Sunnis,11% Alawi Shias). D=SOC,RCC.
10165	0	5	0.00	4	33.00	67.00	A	0.00	0	1.12	In 8 countries. Futankobe. A geopolitical state. Muslims 100%(Sunnis, with Sufi Tijaniyya). Witchcraft persists. M=FLM,ALM,WEC,SIL,ELC.
10166	0	5	0.00	7	30.00	70.00	A	0.00	0	1.09	From Mauritania (business, laborers, refugees). Muslims 100% (Maliki Sunnis, with Sufi Qadiriyya, Tijaniyya). M=CSSp,WEC.
10167	6	6	0.05	4	47.01	52.99	A	0.01	96	2	Emigration to France. Literates 30%. Muslims 99% (Maliki Sunnis: 60% Tijaniyya,30% Muridiyya,10% Qadiriyya). D=RCC,AoG,PCD,MBS,JWs,SDA. M=UWM.
10168	0	5	4.51	1	29.50	70.50	A	0.53	620	3	Also in Sierra Leone, Guinea, Mali. Close to Susu but only marginally intelligible. Strong Muslims 99%(Maliki Sunnis). M=NTM.
10169	0	5	0.00	0	14.01	85.99	A	0.00	0	1.04	Arabized Bedouins, mainly in Mauritania. Pastoralists. Muslims 100%(Sunnis).
10170	0	9	7.19		57.00	43.00	B	54.09	346	6	Malagasy, Ivorians, Nigerians, Ghanaians, Togolese, Beninois, other francophone African peoples, other Europeans. Muslims 59%, nonreligious 10%.
Seychelles											
10171	3	10	1.32	8	99.74	0.26	C	402.44	45	10	Expatriates from Britain, in development. Nonreligious 14%. D=Anglican Ch/CPIO(D-Seychelles),SDA,JWs. M=USPG.
10172	3	10	1.40	8	99.87	0.13	C	517.60	40	10	Expatriates from France, in business. Nonreligious 13%.D=RCC(D-Port Victoria),SDA,JWs. M=OFMCap.
10173	0	10	1.40	6	53.80	46.20	B	3.53	123	4	Traders from India. Hindus 80%, Muslims 8%, Baha'is 10%.
10174	2	10	3.49	7	99.90	0.10	C	535.45	70	10	Chinese folk-religionists 10%. D=RCC,AC/CPIO(D-Seychelles). M=OFMCap.
10175	0	10	2.33	7	58.11	41.89	B	8.71	157	4	Traders from India, originally imported as laborers. Hindus 95%.
10176	3	10	1.40	8	99.95	0.05	C	544.39	44	10	Emigres from Reunion Island. D=RCC,SDA,JWs. M=OFMCap.
10177	5	7	1.36	8	99.94	0.06	C	541.41	43	10	Mixed-race speakers of Seychelles Creole French (Kreol Seychellois). Fishermen. D=RCC(D-Port Victoria), Anglican Ch/CPIO,SDA,JWs,ICF. M=OFMCap,USPG.
10178	0	10	0.00	5	41.00	59.00	A	0.00	0	1.13	Bantu/Arab immigrant works from East African coast. Muslims 100%(Shafi Sunnis).
10179	3	10	4.64	6	99.60	0.40	C	286.89	118	8	Originally laborers from South India. Hindus 25%, Muslims 15%. D=RCC,AC/CPIO,SDA.
10180	0	10	1.43		70.00	30.00	B	102.20	56	7	Parsis, various Bantu, Arabs, other Asians, other Europeans. Muslims 30%, Zoroastrians 15%.
Sierra Leone											
10181	3	10	3.20	4	92.00	8.00	B	141.03	95	7	Emigres, labor migrants from Liberia, resident especially in Freetown. Animists 57%. D=SLBU,AICs,JWs.
10182	0	8	3.40	0	29.00	71.00	A	5.29	472	4	Along Bome river. Related to Bullom; now being absorbed into Mende. Animists 85%, some Muslims.
10183	3	10	-0.30	8	99.74	0.26	C	399.74	16	9	Expatriates from Britain, in development. Nonreligious 13%. D=SLC/CPWA(D-Sierra Leone),MCSL,JWs. M=CMS.
10184	3	10	4.57	4	61.00	39.00	B	33.39	277	5	North central. Very different to West Central Limba. Muslims 50%, animists 35%. D=AoG,RCC,SLC.
10185	4	10	2.87	8	99.90	0.10	C	505.89	71	10	Mixed-race persons, Black-Whites. Mostly in urban areas. D=RCC,SLC,JWs,AICs.
10186	3	10	1.44	8	99.84	0.16	C	490.56	41	10	Expatriates from France, in business. Nonreligious 13%. D=RCC(4 Dioceses),SDA,JWs. M=SX,CSSp,OH.
10187	0	5	3.68	4	36.02	63.98	A	0.02	402	2	In north. Mainly in Guinea. Nomadic Fulani. Muslims 95%(Maliki Sunnis). M=LCMS,LBT,CMA.
10188	1	6	3.38	1	32.00	68.00	A	3.50	426	4	Most now speak Mende. Mainly in Liberia. Recently islamized. Muslims 75%(Maliki Sunnis), animists 22%. D=SLC/CPWA.
10189	1	10	4.33	7	99.95	0.05	C	568.67	89	10	Long-time residents from Greece. Traders. D=Greek Orthodox Ch(D-Accra).
10190	0	10	2.96	7	53.00	47.00	B	3.86	205	4	Traders from India, Pakistan. Muslims 70%, Hindus 27%, some Baha'is.
10191	11	6	8.12	4	55.00	45.00	B	24.09	512	5	Northeast. Wealthy diamond-mining area. Animists 78%, Muslims 10%. D=UMC,RCC(D-Kenema),SDA,JWs,AoG,COTLA,GIOL,LC,NPC(Pentecostals),ELC,AICs.
10192	2	6	4.88	0	41.00	59.00	A	14.96	433	5	On coast. Many speak Sherbro and Mende. Animists 50%, Muslims 40%. D=SLC,UBC. M=CRC.
10193	13	9	1.88	8	99.00	1.00	B	130.08	82	7	Muslims 12%(Maliki Sunnis).35 Christian denominations: D=MCSL,SLC/CPWA,WAMC,AoG,CHC,SLBU,AMEC,JWs,CC,PAOW,BLM,COTLA,AICs. M=MMS,CMS.
10194	0	5	3.46	4	35.06	64.94	A	0.07	395	2	Modified form of Fula Jalon language. Muslims 90%(Maliki Sunnis), Animists 5%. M=LBT,independent missionaries.
10195	5	10	3.67	4	99.75	0.25	C	355.87	77	9	Labor migrants in Freetown. Majority live in Liberia. Animists 10%. D=AoG,RCC,JWs,WAMC,other AICs. M=SX,CSSp,OH.
10196	3	5	3.98	0	36.00	64.00	A	2.62	457	4	Northern Province. Also in Guinea. Literates 1%. Animists 68%, Muslims 30%(Maliki Sunnis). D=SLMC,RCC,SLC/CPWA. M=CMS,MCA,CRC,WC.
10197	2	10	6.55	8	79.50	20.50	B	56.58	250	6	Traders. Muslims 75%(Sunnis,Shias), nonreligious, Baha'is. D=RCC(Maronites),GOC(D-Accra).
10198	4	6	6.43	4	49.70	50.30	A	6.71	474	4	Also in Guinea. Animists 57%, Muslims 39%(Maliki Sunnis). D=AoG,RCC(D-Makeni),SLWC,NCs(pentecostals). M=SX,WC,BLM,NLCM,LBT,FMB,NBC,CM.
10199	0	5	5.52	4	41.00	59.00	A	2.99	505	4	Common Mandingo. Mostly in Senegal, Gambia, Guinea Bissau. Lingua franca. Muslims 50%(Maliki Sunnis), animists 48%.
10200	11	7	2.71	4	67.20	32.80	B	22.56	199	5	Also Liberia. Lingua franca. Animists 42%, Muslims 42%(Maliki Sunnis; 10,000 Ahmadis). D=UMC,MCSL,WAMC,SLC/CPWA,RCC,AICs,SDA,UBC,GIOL,JWs,AICs.
10201	1	6	3.80	0	35.00	65.00	A	6.38	423	4	Coast to Guinea border. Intermarried with Temne and Susu. Language almost extinct. Muslims 80%(Maliki Sunnis), animists 15%. D=SLC/CPWA. M=CMS,FMB.
10202	3	6	5.58	5	44.00	56.00	A	8.03	447	4	Mainly in Guinea. Animists 87%, Muslims 8%. Resistant to advance of Islam. D=RCC,AoG,Methodists. M=CMA. R=ELWA.
10203	4	7	3.96	0	44.00	56.00	A	12.84	346	5	Southern Province. Animists 52%, Muslims 40%(Maliki Sunnis). D=RCC,UMC,SLC/CPWA,UBC. M=LBT,FMB.
10204	6	6	7.11	1	51.50	48.50	B	19.73	463	5	Also in Liberia. Literates 3%. Animists 60%, Muslims 29%(Maliki Sunnis). D=AoG,UMC,MCSL,RCC,CMA,JWs. M=MMS,NLCM,CRC.
10205	0	4	2.52	4	31.01	68.99	A	0.01	414	2	Most in Guinea. Subsistence agriculture. Muslims 100%(Maliki Sunnis, since AD 1600). Syncretism. M=CMA,Missionary Church Association(MC),PBT.
10206	11	5	3.98	4	52.50	47.50	B	10.53	291	5	Literates 6%. Muslims 60%(Maliki Sunnis; 2,000 Ahmadis), animists 34%(Poro Secret Society). D=UMC,AoG,RCC,SLC/CPWA,SLMC,CGP,SLWC,UPC,SDA,AICs.
10207	1	6	2.93	1	30.10	69.90	A	0.11	396	3	Most in Liberia. Speak Mende; own Vai script. Mass conversion to Islam since 1930: Muslims 83%(Sunnis, some Ahmadis), animists 16%. D=SLC. M=LBT(Liberia).
10208	6	6	8.85	4	60.00	40.00	B	30.66	477	5	North central area, north of Makeni. Also in Guinea. Muslims 52%(conversion begun 1880), animists 34%. D=AoG,RCC(D-Makeni),SLC,SLWC,UPC,AICS.
10209	2	5	3.58	1	33.00	67.00	A	1.20	477	4	Also in Guinea. Subsistence agriculture. Literates 2%. Strong Muslims 99%(Maliki Sunnis); no pagans left since 1950. D=SLMC,RCC. M=MCA/MC.
10210	5	10	5.30	5	99.45	0.55	B	185.60	162	7	Immigrants, traders from Nigeria. Muslims 45%(Maliki Sunnis), animists 10%. D=COTLA,NBC,JWs,CAC,other AICs.
10211	0	10	1.46		36.00	64.00	A	11.82	111	5	Ghanaians, Senegalese, Ivorians, Hausa, other Nigerians, other Africans, other Europeans. Muslims 40%, Animists 20%, nonreligious 10%.
Singapore											
10212	7	7	5.74	8	99.25	0.75	B	93.07	172	6	Anglicized Han Chinese using English. Folk-religionists 52%, nonreligious 20%. D=RCC,MCS,PCS,AC,SDA,JWs,AoG. M=MEP,CSSR,CICM.
10213	0	9	5.14	8	85.00	15.00	B	93.07	191	6	English-speaking Indians(Hindi, Tamil, Telugu, Malayali, Kanarese). Hindus 52%, Muslim 15%.
10214	0	9	4.59	8	53.00	47.00	B	9.67	279	4	English-speaking Malays, Javanese, Madurese. Muslims 95%.
10215	6	10	2.33	8	99.67	0.33	C	337.47	62	9	From Australia; expatriates in business. Nonreligious 30%. D=Anglican Ch(D-Singapore),MCS,PCS,JWs,SDA,SA.
10216	5	10	2.45	8	99.76	0.24	C	410.55	61	10	New Zealand expatriates in business. Nonreligious 24%. D=PCS,MCS,Anglican Ch(D-Singapore),JWs,SA.
10217	0	8	4.35	8	53.00	47.00	B	1.93	261	4	Traders from whole spectrum of Arab countries. Most speak Malay. Muslims 99%(Shafi Sunnis).
10218	2	10	3.52	6	99.89	0.11	C	526.25	70	10	Long-time residents, since 1850. Nonreligious 10%. D=Armenian Apostolic Ch(Gregorians, under C-Echmiadzin),RCC.
10219	3	10	4.19	0	99.85	0.15	C	456.06	94	10	Migrants from Sumatra, in various professions. A few animists 5%, Muslims 5%. D=HKBP,HKI,GKPI.
10220	2	8	2.93	6	62.00	38.00	B	2.26	190	4	Immigrants, migrant workers (54% Bengali non-speakers). Primarily in Bangladesh, India, UAE. Hindus 75%, Muslims 23%(Hanafi Sunnis). D=CNI, RCC.
10221	6	10	1.13	8	99.74	0.26	C	405.15	42	10	Expatriates from Britain, in business. D=Anglican Ch(D-Singapore),MCS,PCS,SDA,JWs,SA. M=PCE.
10222	0	8	2.40	2	36.00	64.00	A	1.31	247	4	Labor migrants from Sulawesi(Indonesia). Muslims 95%(strict Shafi Sunnis, and Sufi orders), some Hindus 2%.
10223	6	10	4.39	8	99.62	0.38	C	278.34	116	8	Mixed-race persons, European/Asians. Mostly in urban areas. Nonreligious 15%, Muslims 5%. D=RCC,AC,MCS,PCS,SDA,AoG. M=MEP,CSSR.
10224	0	0	9.02	5	99.88	0.12	C	452.89	188	10	Immigrant workers from the Philippines, many as maids. D=RCC.
10225	4	10	5.28	8	99.80	0.20	C	458.44	112	10	Expatriates from Germany, in business. D=ELCMS,NAC,SDA,JWs.
10226	0	8	3.14	6	55.00	45.00	B	2.00	207	4	Traders, from Gujarat(India). Only 50% speak Gujarati. Hindus 90%, Muslims 9%.
10227	8	8	3.10	8	80.50	19.50	B	24.97	128	5	Mahayana Buddhists/Chinese folk-religionists 90%. D=RCC,MCS,AC,CBA,TJC,CC,MSBC,SA. M=FMB,MEP.
10228	4	8	3.56	0	57.00	43.00	B	14.56	202	5	Originally from Hainan Island(China). Folk Buddhists 92%. D=RCC,AC,MCS,AoG.
10229	4	7	5.03	7	75.50	24.50	B	26.18	206	5	From China, Malaysia. Buddhists/ folk-religionists 90%. D=RCC,AC,MCS,AoG.
10230	6	7	4.85	7	80.00	20.00	B	23.36	188	5	Language use increasing. 12% use English at home. Chinese folk-religionists 92%. D=RCC,AC,CC,AoG,SDA,SA.
10231	9	7	9.01	6	77.80	22.20	B	24.98	340	5	Hokkien(Fukienese, Southern Min) is major Chinese language in Singapore. From China, Malaysia. Folk Buddhists 89%. D=RCC,AC,MCS,ACS,AoG,TJC,CBA.
10232	2	7	3.58	6	66.50	33.50	B	23.05	174	5	From Fuchow area. Chinese folk-religionists 91%. D=RCC,AC. M=MEP,CSSR,CICM,OFM,SSCC,SJ.
10233	8	7	3.33	4	71.00	29.00	B	20.73	154	5	From Swatow coast. Folk Buddhists 79%, Chinese New-Religionists 10%(Tao Yuan, World Red Swastika Society). D=RCC,AC,MCS,PCS,AoG,TJC,SA,ABCUSA.
10234	0	8	3.83	7	57.50	42.50	B	1.04	230	4	Traders from India. Hindus 95%, Baha'is 5%. M=MEP,CSSR,SJ.
10235	0	7	0.00	7	43.00	57.00	A	0.00	0	1.14	100% Chinese Muslims(Hanafi Sunnis), originally from inland China.
10236	1	8	2.93	7	55.05	44.95	B	0.10	181	3	Immigrants from Indonesia. Muslims 99%(mostly Shafi Sunnis). D=RCC. M=MEP,CSSR.
10237	3	9	3.78	7	60.60	39.40	B	3.53	205	4	From Japan, in business, commerce, finance. Buddhists 50%, New-Religionists 30%(including Soka Gakkai), nonreligious 15%, Shintoists 3%. D=RCC,AC,PCS.
10238	3	9	6.29	5	80.00	20.00	B	43.80	245	6	30% bilinguals in Malay. Koranic Muslims 50%(Shafi Sunnis), Javanese mystical religionists 35%. D=RCC,PCS,MCS.
10239	0	10	1.96	8	39.95	60.05	A	1.38	182	4	Small community of practicing Jews, with 2 synagogues.
10240	5	10	4.36	5	69.00	31.00	B	12.59	213	5	Labor migrants from Karnataka, south India. Hindus 90%, Muslims 5%. D=RCC,AC,PCS,MCS,SDA. M=MEP,CSSR.
10241	2	10	6.07	6	99.50	0.50	B	224.47	149	8	Immigrants, migrant workers from South Korea, especially in construction industry. New-Religionists 30%, Buddhists 15%, Muslims 3%. D=PCK-T,&c.
10242	0	7	1.40	5	38.01	61.99	A	0.01	151	2	Many regional non-standard Malay dialects. Port lingua franca from Sumatra to Philippines. Muslims 100%(Sunnis). M=MEP,CSSR,CICM.
10243	0	7	4.18	1	48.00	52.00	A	5.25	287	4	Immigrants from Java (Indonesia). Only 6% now speak Madurese. Related to Javanese. Bilingual in Malay. Muslims 97%.
10244	1	10	7.35	8	99.75	0.25	C	366.82	167	9	Straits of Malacca (Melaka). Portuguese creole; lingua franca. Fishermen. Nonreligious 10%. D=RCC(Portuguese Parish under D-Macao). M=MEP,CSSR.
10245	3	9	5.57	5	57.50	42.50	B	1.04	299	4	National language. 85% literate. Muslims 99%(Shafi Sunnis). D=AC,HKBP,CBA. M=MEP,CSSR,OMF,AEF,FMB,FI,EFC,YWAM,Pioneers.
10246	5	10	3.11	4	99.00	1.00	B	108.40	114	7	Immigrants from Kerala, South India. Hindus 49%, Muslims 18%. D=RCC,OSCE,MTSC,IPCG,ACS.
10247	0	7	4.23	0	36.00	64.00	A	10.51	361	5	Aboriginal Malays. North coast of Singapore, also on opposite coast of Malaysia. Animists 92%.
10248	0	7	0.00	5	37.01	62.99	A	0.01	52	2	From Palembang city, south Sumatra. Strong Muslims 100% (Shafi Sunnis).
10249	2	8	8.29	7	60.00	40.00	B	15.33	408	5	Ethnic Babas number 12% of Singapore population, but all but 0.4% now speak Standard Malay. Chinese folk-religionists/Buddhists 70%, nonreligious 20%.
10250	2	9	3.20	5	60.00	40.00	B	2.19	194	4	Indians speaking Eastern Panjabi. Sikhs 95%(4 temples), Hindus 3%, Muslims 1%(Hanafi Sunnis). D=RCC,SA. M=FMB.
10251	1	9	1.10	5	31.03	68.97	A	0.03	159	2	Islands south of Singapore. Muslims 100%(Shafi Sunnis). D=RCC. M=MEP,CSSR,CICM.
10252	2	7	4.43	6	61.00	39.00	B	4.45	225	4	Migrants from Thailand. Also in UAE, USA. Theravada Buddhists 96%, Muslims 1%, Hindus, Baha'is. D=RCC,CCT.
10253	0	7	4.25	4	47.00	53.00	A	1.71	306	4	Migrant workers from India, Pakistan. Hindus 93%, Muslims 4%, Sikhs.
10254	1	10	4.44	6	63.00	37.00	B	11.49	218	5	Traders from Ceylon. Theravada Buddhists 95%. D=RCC. M=MEP,CSSR,CICM,OFM.
10255	4	9	4.55	6	84.00	16.00	B	36.79	181	5	Traders, from south India. Hindus 79%(including Ananda Marga sect), Muslims 8%. D=MCS,AC,CPC,ELCMS. M=CPM,TELC,SKM,MMS,UMC,MEP,CSSR,FMB.
10256	2	9	4.05	5	77.00	23.00	B	28.10	180	5	Labor migrants from South India. Also in UAE, Fiji. Hindus 84%, Muslims 5%, Baha'is. D=RCC,AC.
10257	9	10	5.25	8	99.75	0.25	C	407.88	113	10	Expatriates from USA, in business, commerce. D=AC,PCS,MCS,SDA,SA,JWs,CJCLdS,CCS,CC. M=CMS,FMB.
10258	0	10	4.10		68.00	32.00	B	96.79	165	6	Peoples from all over world: Europeans, Asians, Americans, Africans. Muslims 30%, Nonreligious 10%.
Slovakia											
10259	0	0	0.28	8	99.79	0.21	C	377.73	30	9	Expatriates from Britain, in business. Nonreligious 9%. D=Church of England.
10260	0	0	2.41	5	99.70	0.30	C	293.82	81	8	Emigres from Belorussia. Nonreligious 15%. D=Orthodox Church, RCC.
10261	0	0	0.38	0	84.00	16.00	C	183.96	46	7	Sarvike, or Ungrike. In Moravia, Bohemia, USA. Nonreligious 10%. D=RCC,nomadic caravan churches, many Jehovah's Witnesses.
10262	0	0	0.28	6	99.91	0.09	C	458.36	27	10	In 10 countries. Nonreligious 7%, atheists 2%. Strongly Catholic. D=RCC,COGY,COCC,CNOCC.
10263	0	0	0.28	6	99.65	0.35	C	270.46	34	8	Bohemia, Moravia, Silesia. Also Poland, Austria, &c. Nonreligious 20%, atheists 8%. D=Czechoslovak Hussite Ch,RCC,ECCB,CUA,OCCC,COB,SDA. M=UBS,LBI.
10264	0	0	0.00	5	84.00	16.00	B	153.30	0	7	Artificial (constructed) language, in 80 nations. Speakers in this country: 100,000(non mother-tongue). Nonreligious 30%, atheists 10%.
10265	0	0	0.28	8	99.75	0.25	C	347.66	27	9	Expatriates from France, in business, in schools. Nonreligious 20%, atheists 5%. D=RCC.
10266	0	0	0.28	8	99.70	0.30	C	306.60	32	9	Expatriates from Germany, in many professions. Nonreligious 15%, atheist 5%. D=EKD, RCC.
10267	0	0	0.32	6	99.60	0.40	C	236.52	43	8	Expatriates from Hungary in various professions. Nonreligious 20%, atheists 10%. D=RCC.
10268	0	0	0.28	7	99.86	0.14	C	433.18	25	10	Expatriates from Italy, in business, in schools. Nonreligious 10%, atheist 1%. D=RCC.
10269	0	0	3.35	7	38.50	61.50	A	0.70	288	3	Residual Jews left after emigration of 1,000 a year since 1950. Nonreligious 9%.
10270	0	0	0.28	6	99.70	0.30	C	270.83	34	8	Romungre. In Czech Republic; also in 25 other countries. Nonreligious 20%, atheists 10%. D=RCC,JWs.
10271	0	0	-0.84	6	99.90	0.10	C	453.33	2	10	Migrant workers, from Poland. Nonreligious 8%. D=RCC,PCCY. M=OFM,SJ,SDB,OP.
10272	0	0	2.47	7	99.50	0.50	B	182.50	68	7	Refugees and migrant workers from Russia, many since 1989. Nonreligious 30%, atheists 15%. D=Russian Orthodox Church.
10273	0	0	-1.32	6	99.90	0.10	C	423.76	2	10	Carpathians. Eastern Slavs/Ukrainians. Presov region. Also Ukraine, Romania, USA. Nonreligious 9%. D=RCC(D-Kosice, Slovak-rite D-Presov,OCC.
10274	0	0	0.14	6	99.84	0.16	C	403.13	26	10	Nonreligious 9%. D=Orthodox Ch of Czechoslovakia(4 Dioceses), RCC(5 Dioceses),SECAC,RCCS; D-Presov claimed by both RCC and OCC. M=LBI. R=HCJB.
10275	0	0	0.28	6	99.75	0.25	C	331.23	30	9	Slovak Romany. Related to Sinti Manush. Nonreligious 10%. D=nomadic caravan churches,RCC,Gypsy Evangelical Movement. M=GGMS.

Continued overleaf

Table 8-2 continued

PEOPLE						IDENTITY CODE		LANGUAGE		CHURCH		MINISTRY						SCRIPTURE		
Ref	Ethnic name	P%	In 1995	In 2000	In 2025	Race	Language	Autoglossonym	S	AC	Members	Jayuh	d	w	a	xcmc	mi	Biblioglossonym	Pub	ss
1	2	3	4	5	6	7	8	9	10	11	12	13-17	18	19	20	21	22	23	24-26	27
10276	Ukrainian	0.30000	16,064	16,162	16,178	CEW22p	53-AAAE-b	ukrainskiy		69.00	11,151	3A.uh 10	9	9	0	0		Ukrainian	PNB	b
10277	other minor peoples	0.40000	21,419	21,549	21,571					70.00	15,084	10	8	8	0	0				
	Slovenia	**100.00000**	**1,990,000**	**1,985,557**	**1,817,953**					**87.47**	**1,736,807**									
10278	Austrian	1.25000	24,875	24,819	22,724	CEW19f	52-ABCF-b	donau-bayrisch-t.		88.00	21,841	0B.uh 10	9	13	5	3			pn.	b
10279	Croat	4.93000	98,107	97,888	89,625	CEW22d	53-AAAG-b	standard hrvatski		87.90	86,044	2Asuh 10	9	11	5	3		Croatian	PNB	b
10280	Czech	0.20000	3,980	3,971	3,636	CEW22e	53-AAAD-a	czesky		74.00	2,939	2Asuh 10	9	8	5	3		Czech	PNB	b
10281	Friulian (Priulian)	0.10000	1,990	1,986	1,818	CEW21h	51-AABM	furlan cluster		83.00	1,648	0.... 10	9	13	5	1		Friulian	PN.	b
10282	German	0.97400	19,383	19,339	17,707	CEW19m	52-ABCE-a	standard hoch-deutsch		87.00	16,825	2B.uh 10	9	13	5	3		German*	PNB	b
10283	Hungarian	0.54000	10,746	10,722	9,817	MSW51g	41-BAAA-a	general magyar		76.00	8,149	2A.u. 10	9	10	5	3		Hungarian	PNB	b
10284	Italian	0.40000	7,960	7,942	7,272	CEW21e	51-AABQ-c	standard italiano		83.00	6,592	2B.uh 10	9	15	5	3		Italian	PNB	b
10285	Polish (Pole)	0.30000	5,970	5,957	5,454	CEW22i	53-AAAC-c	polski		88.00	5,242	2A.uh 10	9	9	5	3		Polish	PNB	b
10286	Serb	0.60000	11,940	11,913	10,908	CEW22l	53-AAAG-a	standard srpski		80.00	9,531	1Asuh 10	9	9	5	3		Serbian*	PNB	b
10287	Slovak	0.10000	1,990	1,986	1,818	CEW22d	53-AAAD-b	slovensky		77.00	1,529	1Asuh 10	9	8	5	3		Slovak	PNB	b
10288	Slovene	89.82600	1,787,537	1,783,546	1,632,994	CEW22n	53-AAAF-a	slovensko		87.80	1,565,954	1a..h 10	10	11	5	1		Slovenian*	PNB	b
10289	Slovene (Prekmurian)	0.13000	2,587	2,581	2,363	CEW22n	53-AAAF-b	slovensko		95.00	2,452	1a..h 10	9	11	5	2		Slovenian*	PNB	b
10290	Slovenian-Croatian Gypsy	0.20000	3,980	3,971	3,636	CNN25f	59-ACBB-bd	southeast sinti		75.00	2,978	0.... 10	7	8	5	1			p..	.
10291	Ukrainian	0.25000	4,975	4,964	4,545	CEW22p	53-AAAE-b	ukrainskiy		76.00	3,773	3A.uh 10	8	11	5	3		Ukrainian	PNB	b
10292	other minor peoples	0.20000	3,980	3,971	3,636	...				33.00	1,310	9	6	6	5	0				
	Solomon Islands	**100.00000**	**379,144**	**443,643**	**816,561**					**90.88**	**403,199**									
10293	Anuta	0.08798	334	390	718	MPY55z	39-CAFB-a	anuta		80.00	312	0.... 10	8	6	5	0			...	.
10294	Areare	4.03400	15,295	17,897	32,940	AON09d	38-GAEB-a	'are'are		95.00	17,002	0.... 10	7	9	5	1		Areare	P...	.
10295	Arosi (San Cristobal)	1.19658	4,537	5,309	9,771	AON09d	38-GBAA-a	arosi		86.00	4,565	0.s.. 10	8	7	4	1		Arosi	P...	.
10296	Asumbua	0.02381	90	106	194	AON09d	36-FABA-a	asumboa		80.00	85	0.... 10	8	6	4	1			...	n
10297	Babatana	2.13675	8,101	9,480	17,448	AON09d	36-CBAA-b	babatana vehicular		86.00	8,152	0.s.. 10	10	8	5	2		Babatana	PN.	.
10298	Baniata (Mbaniata)	0.38462	1,458	1,706	3,141	AON10d	27-XBAA-a	baniata		81.00	1,382	0.... 10	9	6	5	3			...	.
10299	Bareke-Vangunu	0.38500	1,460	1,708	3,144	AON09d	36-DBBA	vangunu cluster		80.00	1,366	0.... 10	8	6	5	3			...	.
10300	Bauro	1.19658	4,537	5,309	9,771	AON09d	38-GBBA-a	bauro		86.00	4,565	0.... 10	7	11	5	0		Bauro	P...	.
10301	Bilua (Mbilua)	2.23550	8,476	9,918	18,254	AON10d	27-XAAA	bilua cluster		89.40	8,866	0.... 10	9	12	5	1		Bilua	PN.	b
10302	Birao (Mbirau)	1.74250	6,607	7,730	14,229	AON09d	38-FACD-a	m-birao		88.00	6,803	0.... 10	7	12	5	2			...	.
10303	Blablanga	0.18750	711	832	1,531	AON09d	36-EBAC-a	blablanga		80.00	665	0.... 10	8	6	5	1			...	.
10304	British	0.80000	3,033	3,549	6,532	CEW19i	52-ABAC-b	standard-english		74.00	2,626	3Bsuh 10	9	13	5	3			PNB	b
10305	Bugoto (Mbughotu)	0.81197	3,079	3,602	6,630	AON09d	38-FAAA-a	m-bughotu		90.00	3,242	0.s.. 10	9	11	5	1		Bugotu*	PN.	b
10306	Buma	0.11300	428	501	923	AON09d	36-FBCA-a	teanu		80.00	401	0.... 10	7	7	4	5		Teanu	...	p
10307	Dorio	0.38462	1,458	1,706	3,141	AON09d	38-GAEA-a	dori'o		91.00	1,553	0.... 10	7	7	5	2			...	.
10308	Duke (Nduke)	0.64103	2,430	2,844	5,234	AON09d	36-FABA-a	n-duke		94.00	2,673	0.... 10	8	7	5	2			...	n
10309	Euronesian	3.10000	11,753	13,755	25,313	MPY53	52-ABAC-bv	standard oceanian-english		97.50	13,409	1Bsuh 10	10	12	5	3			pnb	b
10310	Fagani	0.12821	486	569	1,047	AON09d	38-GBAB-a	fagani		83.00	472	0.... 10	7	7	3	0			...	.
10311	Fataleka	1.40625	5,332	6,239	11,483	AON09d	38-GABA-e	fataleka		80.00	4,991	0.s.. 10	9	6	5	3			pn.	n
10312	Fijian	0.30000	1,137	1,331	2,450	AON08	39-BBAA-b	fiji		90.00	1,198	1.s.. 10	9	12	5	3		Fijian*	PNB	b
10313	Fiu	0.50000	1,896	2,218	4,083	AON09d	38-GABA-k	fiu		85.00	1,885	0.s.. 10	8	7	5	3		Fiu	Pn..	.
10314	Florida Islander (Nggela)	2.66150	10,091	11,808	21,733	AON09d	38-FABA-a	n-gela		97.00	11,453	0.... 10	7	12	5	1		Gela	PN.	.
10315	Gao	0.17188	652	763	1,404	AON09d	36-EBBB-a	gao		80.00	610	0.... 10	8	6	5	1			...	n
10316	Ghari (Tangarare)	2.63400	9,987	11,686	21,508	AON09d	38-FACA-a	ghari		98.00	11,452	0.... 10	8	12	5	2		Gari*	PN.	b
10317	Gilbertese (Kiribertese)	1.50000	5,687	6,655	12,248	MPY54a	38-GAAA-a	i-kiribati		88.00	5,856	3.s.. 10	9	12	5	2		Kiribati	PNB	b
10318	Gulaalaa (Kwai)	0.41152	1,560	1,826	3,360	AON09d	38-GABA-i	gula'alaa		79.00	1,442	0.... 10	7	6	4	1			pn.	.
10319	Han Chinese	0.66000	2,502	2,928	5,389	MSY42a	79-AAAB-ba	kuo-yü		41.90	1,227	2Bsuh 9	6	7	5	0		Chinese: Kuoyu*	PNB	b
10320	Hoava	0.25641	972	1,138	2,094	AON09d	36-DADA-a	hoava		80.00	910	0.... 10	7	6	4	1			...	n
10321	Kahua (Narihua)	1.38356	5,246	6,138	11,298	AON09d	38-GBCA-a	kahua		87.00	5,340	0.s.. 10	8	11	5	3		Kahua	PN.	b
10322	Kokota	0.06250	237	277	510	AON09d	36-EBAA-a	kokota		89.00	247	0.... 10	7	11	4	1			...	.
10323	Kumbokota	0.94850	3,596	4,208	7,745	AON09d	36-DAAA-a	ghanongga		90.00	3,787	0.... 10	7	6	4	0			...	.
10324	Kusaghe	0.52950	2,008	2,349	4,324	AON09d	36-DACA-a	kusaghe		91.00	2,138	0.... 10	7	11	4	1			...	.
10325	Kwaio	4.26214	16,160	18,909	34,803	AON09d	38-GADA-a	kwaio		94.00	17,774	0.s.. 10	8	8	5	2			...	n
10326	Kwaraae	8.00395	30,346	35,509	65,357	AON09d	38-GABA-j	kwara'ae		97.00	34,444	0.s.. 10	9	10	5	3		Kwara'ae*	PN.	b
10327	Lagu	0.00214	8	9	17	AON09d	36-EABA-a	laghu		85.00	8	0.... 10	7	6	3	0			...	.
10328	Langalanga	2.01646	7,645	8,946	16,466	AON09d	38-GACA-a	langalanga		84.00	7,515	0.... 10	7	6	5	1		Langalanga	...	.
10329	Lau (Ndai)	4.23868	16,071	18,805	34,611	AON09d	38-GABA-f	lau		90.00	16,924	0.s.. 10	7	7	5	2		Lau	PN.	.
10330	Lengo (Tasemboko)	2.69600	10,222	11,961	22,014	AON09d	38-FABB-a	lengo		95.00	11,363	0.... 10	7	11	5	3			...	.
10331	Longgu	0.32051	1,215	1,422	2,617	AON09d	38-GAAA-a	longgu		90.00	1,280	0.... 10	7	11	4	1		Lungga	...	n
10332	Lungga	0.55102	2,089	2,445	4,499	AON09d	36-DAAB-a	lungga		90.00	2,200	0.... 10	7	11	5	1			...	n
10333	Malango	0.87379	3,313	3,877	7,135	AON09d	38-FACC-a	malango		94.00	3,644	0.... 10	7	12	3	2			...	.
10334	Maringe (Hograno)	2.44900	9,285	10,865	19,998	AON09d	36-EBBA	cheke-holo cluster		95.00	10,322	0.... 10	9	11	5	1		Cheke Holo	PN.	b
10335	Marovo	2.28800	8,675	10,151	18,683	AON09d	36-DBAA	marovo cluster		96.00	9,745	0.... 10	9	12	5	2		Marovo	PNB	b
10336	Mono (Alu)	2.33600	8,857	10,364	19,075	AON09d	36-BHAA-a	mono		85.00	8,809	0.... 10	7	6	4	1		Mono	...	.
10337	Nanggu	0.11900	451	528	972	AON10d	27-ZBCA-a	nanggu		80.00	422	0.... 10	7	6	3	0			...	p
10338	Nembao	0.11111	421	493	907	AON09d	36-FAAA-a	amba		80.00	394	0.... 10	7	6	4	1			...	.
10339	Neo-Melanesian Papuan	1.30000	4,929	5,767	10,615	AON09f	52-ABAI-c	tok-pisin-creole		82.00	4,729	3asuh 10	9	8	5	2		Tok Pisin	PNB	b
10340	Ontong Java Islander	0.47009	1,782	2,086	3,839	MPY55z	39-CACD-a	luangiua		95.00	1,981	0.... 10	7	13	4	1		Ontong Java	P...	.
10341	Oroha (Oraha)	0.04274	162	190	349	AON09d	38-GAFA-a	oroha		70.00	133	0.... 10	7	7	3	2			...	.
10342	Pileni	0.43900	1,664	1,948	3,585	MPY55z	39-CAEA-c	pileni		91.00	1,772	0.... 10	7	11	4	1			...	n
10343	Reef Islander (Gnivo)	1.97950	7,505	8,782	16,164	AON10d	27-ZAAA-a	ayiwo		89.00	7,816	0.... 10	7	12	4	1		Ayiwo	...	.
10344	Rennellese (Mugaba)	0.87500	3,321	3,886	7,152	MPY55z	39-CADA-a	munggava		98.00	3,808	0.s.. 10	8	7	5	2		Rennell-bellona	PN.	.
10345	Ririo	0.09709	368	431	793	AON09d	36-CABA-a	ririo		86.00	370	0.... 10	7	11	3	2			...	.
10346	Roviana (Robiana)	2.68250	10,171	11,901	21,904	AON09d	36-DAEA-b	roviana vehicular		93.00	11,068	0.s.. 10	10	11	5	3		Roviana	PN.	b
10347	Russel Islander	0.29915	1,134	1,327	2,443	AON10d	27-XCAA-a	lavukaleve		90.00	1,194	0.... 10	7	11	4	1			...	.
10348	Saa (South Malaita)	1.67457	6,349	7,429	13,674	AON09d	38-GAGA-a	sa'a		78.00	5,795	0.... 10	8	7	5	1		Sa'a*	PN.	.
10349	Santa Cruz	1.25000	4,739	5,546	10,207	AON10d	27-ZBBA	nea cluster		98.00	5,435	0.s.. 10	7	12	4	1		Santa Cruz	P...	.
10350	Savo Islander (Savosavo)	0.57350	2,174	2,544	4,683	AON10d	27-XDAA-a	savo		91.00	2,315	0.... 10	7	11	5	2			...	.
10351	Sikayana	0.24150	916	1,071	1,972	MPY55z	39-CACE-a	sikaiana		90.00	964	0.... 10	7	11	5	1			...	.
10352	Simbo (Sibo)	0.83650	3,172	3,711	6,831	AON09d	36-DAAC-a	simbo		93.00	3,451	0.... 10	8	8	5	0			...	.
10353	Solomoni Creole	4.05336	15,368	17,982	33,098	MPY53	52-ABAI-bl	solomonic-creole	89	96.00	17,263	1csuh 10	10	12	5	1		Pijin: Solomon Islands	PNb	b
10354	Talise	2.55350	9,681	11,328	20,851	AON09d	38-FACB-d	talise		93.00	10,535	0.... 10	8	11	5	2			...	.
10355	Tanima	0.05952	226	264	486	AON09d	36-FBBA-a	tanema		80.00	211	0.... 10	8	9	4	1			...	p
10356	Tanimbili	0.04688	178	208	383	AON09d	36-FACA-a	nyisunggu		88.00	183	0.... 10	7	11	4	1			...	p
10357	Tavula (Vagua)	0.42735	1,620	1,896	3,490	AON09d	36-CAAA-a	vaghua		87.00	1,649	0.... 10	7	6	4	1			...	.
10358	Tikopia	0.92800	3,518	4,117	7,578	MPY55z	39-CAFA-a	tikopia		98.00	4,035	0.s.. 10	7	6	4	1		Tikopia	P...	.
10359	Toambaita (Maluu, Mwala)	7.07202	26,813	31,375	57,747	AON09d	38-GABA-a	to'abaita		98.00	30,747	0.s.. 10	8	12	5	1		To'abaita*	PN.	.
10360	Ugele	0.27778	1,053	1,232	2,268	AON09d	36-DAFA-a	ughele		80.00	986	0.... 10	8	6	4	1			...	.
10361	Ulawa	1.10321	4,183	4,894	9,008	AON09d	38-GAGA-c	ulawa		91.00	4,454	0.... 10	7	6	4	1		Ulawa	PN.	.
10362	Vanikoro	0.04762	181	211	389	AON09d	36-FBAA-a	vano		79.80	169	0.... 10	8	6	4	1			...	.
10363	Vanuatu Melanesian	2.00000	7,583	8,873	16,331	AON09c	52-ABAI-e	bislama		88.00	7,808	4ssuh 10	9	13	5	2		Bislama	PNB	b
10364	Varese	1.81818	6,894	8,066	14,847	AON09d	36-CAAB-b	varisi		88.00	7,098	0.... 10	7	12	4	1		Varisi	P...	.
10365	Vaturanga (Ndi)	0.48824	1,851	2,166	3,987	AON09d	38-FACA-e	n-di		85.00	1,841	0.s.. 10	7	7	5	2		Vaturanga	Pn.	.
10366	Zabana	0.42735	1,620	1,896	3,490	AON09d	36-EAAA-a	zabana		85.00	1,612	0.... 10	8	7	4	1		Zabana	...	n
10367	Zazao (Kilokaka)	0.05188	197	230	424	AON09d	36-EBAB-a	zazao		80.00	184	0.... 10	7	6	4	1			...	n
10368	other minor peoples	2.60000	9,858	11,535	21,231	...				70.00	8,074	10	7	6	5	0				
	Somalia	**100.00000**	**5,670,628**	**7,264,500**	**16,227,263**					**1.36**	**98,583**									
10369	Amhara	1.20000	68,048	87,174	194,727	CMT34a	12-ACBA-b	general amarinya	2	95.00	82,815	3Asuh 10	9	11	4	1		Amharic	PNB	b
10370	Arab	0.02000	1,134	1,453	3,245	CMT30	12-AACF-pd	south somalia		1.00	15	1Asuh 6	4	5	1	0			pnb	b
10371	Bajun (Shirazi)	0.10000	5,671	7,265	16,227	NAB57j	99-AUSM-d	ki-tikuu		0.07	5	1csu. 4	2	1	0	0			pnb	b
10372	Baluch	0.10000	5,671	7,265	16,227	CNT24b	58-AABC-c	south balochi		0.10	7	1.s.. 5	2	1	0	0		Balochi, Southern	P...	b
10373	Baraawe (Swahili)	0.50813	28,814	36,913	82,456	NAB57j	99-AUSM-c	ci-miini	6	0.00	0	1Asu. 0	3	2	1	0		Swahili	PNB	b
10374	Boni (Sanye, Waata)	0.00300	170	218	487	BYG11b	14-GAFA-a	aweera		1.00	2	0.... 6	2	0	0	0			...	.
10375	Boon	0.00100	57	73	162	BYG11b	14-GAGC-a	af-boon		1.00	0	0.... 0	1	0	0	0			...	.
10376	British	0.01000	567	726	1,623	CEW19i	52-ABAC-b	standard-english	14	70.00	509	3Bsuh 10	9	13	5	1			PNB	b
10377	Dabarre	0.44461	25,212	32,299	72,148	CMT33d	14-GAGA-a	af-tunni		0.00	0	1c... 0	1	0	0	0			pnb	.
10378	Danakil (Afar)	1.00000	56,706	72,645	162,273	CMT33z	14-AAAB-a	'afar-af		0.00	0	1.s.. 0	2	1	0	0		Afar	PN.	b
10379	French	0.01000	567	726	1,623	CEW21b	51-ABI-f	general français		84.00	610	1B.uh 10	9	14	5	1		French	PNB	b
10380	Garre	3.00000	170,119	217,935	486,818	CMT33e	14-GAGC-b	af-garre		0.00	0	0.... 0	2	0	0	0			pnb	.
10381	Gosha (Gobawein)	0.65000	36,859	47,219	105,477	NAB57j	99-AUSO-e	ki-mushu-ngulu		0.00	472	0c... 6	4	1	2	0			pnb	b
10382	Indo-Pakistani	0.10000	5,671	7,265	16,227	CNN25e	59-AAFH-D	standard gujaraati		0.19	14	2A.u. 5	4	3	1	0		Gujarati	PNB	b
10383	Italian	0.02000	1,134	1,453	3,245	CEW21e	51-AABQ-c	standard italiano	15	80.00	1,162	2B.uh 10	9	15	5	1		Italian	PNB	b
10384	Jiddu	0.50813	28,814	36,913	82,456	CMT33d	14-GAGA-c	af-tunni		0.00	0	1c... 0	1	0	0	0			pnb	.
10385	Juba Somali (Rahanwein)	9.53744	540,833	692,847	1,547,665	CMT33e	14-GAGA-k	af-maay		0.01	69	1c... 3	2	3	0	0			pnb	.
10386	Midgan (Ribi, Waribi)	0.10000	5,671	7,265	16,227	BYG11b	14-GAFA	aweera cluster		0.00	0	1c... 0	1	0	0	0			...	.
10387	Omani Arab	0.40000	22,683	29,058	64,909	CMT30	12-AACF-l	omani	35	0.10	29	1Asuh 5	2	2	0	0			pnb	b
10388	Sab (Digil, Bimal)	3.50000	198,472	254,258	567,954	CMT33e	14-GAGA-a	af-soomaali		2A... 5	2	1	0	0	0.00	0		Somali	PNB	b
10389	Sheegle (Shebelle)	0.36000	20,414	26,152	58,418	NAB57j	14-GAGA-a	af-soomaali		0.00	0	2A... 5	2	1	0	0		Somali	PNB	b
10390	Somali	74.31769	4,214,280	5,398,809	12,059,727	CMT33e	14-GAGA-a	af-soomaali	99	0.05	2,699	2A... 4	4	6	5	4		Somali	PNB	b
10391	Somali (Ogaden)	1.00000	56,706	72,645	162,273	CMT33e	14-GAGA-a	af-soomaali		0.01	7	2A... 4	4	1	0	0		Somali	PNB	b
10392	Southern Oromo	0.70000	39,694	50,851	113,591	CMT33b	14-FBAA-ha	proper borana		1.00	509	1As.. 6	4	3	0	0		Borana-oromo*	PNB	b
10393	Tulama (Shoa Galla)	0.10000	5,671	7,265	16,227	CMT33b	14-FBAA-ac	selale		90.00	6,538	1cs.. 10	9	11	5	2			pnb	.

Continued opposite

Table 8-2 continued

EVANGELIZATION								EVANGELISM			ADDITIONAL DESCRIPTIVE DATA
Ref 1	*D* 28	*aC* 29	*CG%* 30	*r* 31	*E* 32	*U* 33	*W* 34	*e* 35	*R* 36	*T* 37	*Locations, civil divisions, literacy, religions, church history, denominations, dioceses, church growth, missions, agencies, ministries, movements* 38
10276	0	0	2.89	6	99.69	0.31	C	294.66	96	8	Emigres from Ukraine, in business, commerce. Nonreligious 25%. D=ROC,RCC,SOC,PCCY.
10277	0	0	0.27		89.00	11.00	C	227.39	8	8	Other Europeans, some Arabs and Asians. Nonreligious 12%.
Slovenia											
10278	3	10	0.73	8	99.88	0.12	C	507.49	32	10	Emigres. Includes Bavarian-Austrian speakers. Nonreligious 10%, atheist 2%. D=RCC,ELCA,NAC. M=OFM,SJ,SDB,OP.
10279	8	8	0.73	6	99.88	0.12	C	516.22	31	10	Refugees from Republic of Croatia. In 10 countries. Nonreligious 9%. Strongly Catholic. D=RCC(19 Dioceses),COGY,COCC,CNOCC,PCCY,ECCBHV,RCCY,CAC.
10280	4	10	0.73	6	99.74	0.26	C	391.64	35	9	Emigres, from Czechoslovakia. Nonreligious 20%. D=RCC,Moravian Ch,CHC,Unitas Fratrum.
10281	1	10	0.73	0	99.83	0.17	C	408.98	35	10	Mainly in Italy, also Austria. Bilinguals. Nonreligious 15%. D=RCC.
10282	6	10	0.73	8	99.87	0.13	C	527.13	31	10	Expatriates from Germany, in business. Nonreligious 5%. D=RCC,ECCBHV,PCCY,NAC,SDA,JWs(UJWY).
10283	4	8	0.73	6	99.76	0.24	C	402.23	40	10	Emigres, refugees from Hungary. Nonreligious 19%. D=RCC(D-Subotica,AA-Banat),RCCY,ECS,CNC.
10284	1	10	0.73	7	99.83	0.17	C	484.72	30	10	Emigres, workers, settlers from Italy. Strong Catholics. D=RCC(D-Porec & Pula). M=OFM,SJ,SDB,OP.
10285	2	10	0.73	6	99.88	0.12	C	517.13	12	10	Migrant workers, from Poland. Nonreligious 10%, atheists 2%. D=RCC,PCCY. M=OFM,SJ,SDB,OP.
10286	6	8	0.73	6	99.80	0.20	C	435.08	13	10	From Republic of Serbia. In 18 countries. Nonreligious 11%, atheists 7%, many Muslims. D=Serbian OC(21 Dioceses),RCC(3 Dioceses),UBCY,ECS,OCCSV,PCCY.
10287	3	10	0.73	6	99.77	0.23	C	413.14	35	10	Emigres from Slovakia. Also in USA, Canada, 8 other countries. Nonreligious 20%, atheists 3%. D=RCC,SECC,Ch of United Brethren in Christ in Slovenia.
10288	5	8	0.64	6	99.88	0.12	C	505.70	28	10	Republic of Slovenia. Also in Croatia, Italy, Austria, USA, Canada, Hungary. D=RCC(4 Slovenian-speaking Dioceses),ECCS,OCCS,PCCY,CAC. M=UBS. R=TWR.
10289	1	10	0.73	6	99.95	0.05	C	568.67	29	10	Hungarian Slovenes, still numerous in Hungary. D=RCC. M=SJ,OFM.
10290	3	10	0.73	0	99.75	0.25	C	323.02	41	9	Slovenian-Croatian Romany. Related to Sinti Manush. Nonreligious 10%. D=nomadic caravan churches,RCC,Gypsy Evangelical Movement. M=GGMS.
10291	4	8	2.01	6	99.76	0.24	C	410.55	59	10	Emigres from Ukraine, in business, commerce. Nonreligious 20%. D=ROC,RCC,SOC,PCCY.
10292	0	8	0.73		62.00	38.00	B	74.67	32	6	Bosnians(Muslims), Jewish, Istro-Romanians, many other Europeans, Slavs. Muslims 30%, nonreligious 11%, Jews 3%, Baha'is 3%.
Solomon Islands											
10293	0	7	3.50	0	99.80	0.20	C	318.28	101	9	Anuta Island. Related to Tikopia. Traditional religionists(animists) 10%. Nominal Christians 10%.
10294	3	6	7.72	0	99.95	0.05	C	461.17	168	10	South Malaita Island. Tropical forest, mountains. Hunters, agriculturalists. Animists 3%. Nominal Christians 2%. D=RCC,COM,SSEC. M=SIL.
10295	1	6	3.36	0	99.86	0.14	C	373.54	87	9	Northwest Makira Island. Many dialects. Animists 4%. D=Ch of Melanesia.
10296	1	7	3.40	0	99.80	0.20	C	327.04	94	9	Temotu Province. Utupua Island, Asumbuo village. Tropical forest. Agriculturalists, fishermen. Bilingual in Amba, Nyisunggu, Pijin. Animists 5%. D=COM.
10297	2	6	3.36	0	99.86	0.14	C	404.93	81	10	East Choiseul Island. Main lingua franca of UCPNGSI. 5 dialects. Related to Ririo. Animists 2%. Nominal Christians 5%. D=UCPNGSI,RCC.
10298	3	6	3.30	0	99.81	0.19	C	348.86	87	9	South Rendova Island, Western Province. Bilingual in Roviana (decreasing). Animists 10%. D=UCPNGSI,SDA,CFC.
10299	3	6	3.28	0	99.80	0.20	C	335.80	89	9	North Vangunu Island (Bareke), southwest Vangunu Island (Vangunu), Western Province. Second language Marovo. Animists 6%. D=UCPNGSI,SDA,CFC.
10300	0	6	3.36	0	99.86	0.14	C	379.81	86	9	Central Makira (San Cristobal) Island. 3 groups: Bauro, Haununu, Rawo. Animists 4%.
10301	2	7	3.40	0	99.89	0.11	C	441.82	78	10	Vella Lavella Island, Western Province. Lingua franca. Animists 1%. D=UCPNGSI,SDA. M=SIL.
10302	2	7	3.38	0	99.88	0.12	C	411.13	82	10	Eastern Guadalcanal Island. Animists 2%. D=Ch of Melanesia,RCC.
10303	1	6	3.05	0	99.80	0.20	C	321.20	87	9	Santa Isabel Island, over 4 villages. Conversing in Maringe language. Animists 15%. Nominal Christians 5%. D=Ch of Melanesia.
10304	5	10	1.74	8	99.74	0.26	C	399.74	54	9	Expatriates from Britain, in development. Nonreligious 13%. D=Ch of Melanesia/CPM(4 Dioceses),RCC,UCPNGSI,SDA,JWs.
10305	1	6	2.92	0	99.90	0.10	C	440.19	69	10	Santa Isabel Island, southeast end, and on Furona Island off northwest coast. Lingua franca; COM church language. Animists 3%. D=Ch of Melanesia.
10306	1	8	5.02	0	99.80	0.20	C	329.96	132	9	Puma village, Vanikolo Island, Temotu Province. Second language: Pijin. Tropical forest, mountains, coast. Fishermen. Animists 3%. D=Ch of Melanesia. M=SIL.
10307	2	6	3.42	0	99.91	0.09	C	415.18	85	10	West central Malaita Island. Tropical forest, mountains, coast. Hunters, agriculturalists. Animists 5%. Nominal Christians 10%. D=RCC,SSEC.
10308	2	7	3.45	0	99.94	0.06	C	449.46	81	10	Kolombangara Island, Western Province. Bilingual in Roviana. Close to Lungga. Animists 4%. Nominal Christians 6%. D=Ch of Melanesia,SDA.
10309	6	10	3.64	8	99.98	0.02	C	588.97	74	10	Mixed-race persons, European/Austronesian. D=RCC,CPM/COM,SSEC,SDA,UCPNGSI,JWs. M=SM,OP,PFM.
10310	0	8	3.32	0	99.83	0.17	C	339.30	92	9	Northwest Makira Island. 3 dialects. Animists 17%.
10311	3	6	3.12	0	99.80	0.20	C	353.32	81	9	Malaita Island. Hunters in tropical forest, mountains. Dialect of Toabaita. Animists 6%. Nominal Christians 14%. D=COM,RCC,SSEC.
10312	5	10	1.70	4	99.90	0.10	C	505.89	38	10	Migrants from Fiji, mostly Methodists. D=UCPNGSI(SI Region),RCC,AoG,SDA,CPM/COM.
10313	3	7	3.04	0	99.85	0.15	C	390.91	76	9	On northwestern coast of Malaita Island. Close to Kwaraae. Animists 15%. D=COM,SSEC,RCC.
10314	1	7	7.30	0	99.97	0.03	C	495.67	151	10	Gela and Florida Islands, Guadalcanal (immigrants), and Savo Islands. Similar to Lengo. Subsistence agriculturalists, fishermen. Animists 1%. D=Ch of Melanesia.
10315	1	6	3.06	0	99.80	0.20	C	327.04	86	9	Central Isabel Island, from Tausese southeast to Floakora Point. Speakers also use Maringe and Bughotu. Animists 20%. D=Ch of Melanesia.
10316	2	7	3.49	0	99.98	0.02	C	525.81	73	10	Language also called West Guadalcanal. Lingua franca. 6 dialects. Animists 1%. D=RCC,Ch of Melanesia.
10317	2	10	6.58	4	99.88	0.12	C	488.22	130	10	Migrants from Kiribati. Also in Tuvalu, Fiji, Nauru, Vanuatu. D=RCC(2 Dioceses),GIPC.
10318	2	6	3.27	0	99.79	0.21	C	328.71	89	9	Kwai and Ngongosila Islands on east side of Kwaraae, Malaita. Fishermen, craftsmen. Animists 20%. D=SSEC,COM. M=SSEM.
10319	0	6	5.46	7	99.90	0.10	B	152.78	168	7	Residents, from China. Traders, merchants. Buddhists/Chinese folk-religionists 48%, nonreligious 10%.
10320	1	6	3.28	0	99.80	0.20	C	324.12	92	9	North Marovo Lagoon, New Georgia Island, Western Province. Bilingual in Roviana. Close to Kusaghe. Animists 10%. Nominal Christians 10%. D=CFC.
10321	3	7	3.37	0	99.87	0.13	C	431.86	77	10	South Makira Island. Lingua franca. 4 dialects, including Tawarafa. Animists 3%. D=SSEC,COM,RCC.
10322	1	10	3.26	0	99.89	0.11	C	412.56	80	10	Santa Isabel, 3 villages. Speakers also use Maringe and Zabana. Animists 5%. D=Ch of Melanesia.
10323	0	6	6.12	0	99.90	0.10	C	387.63	152	9	North Ranonga Island, Western Province. Related to Lungga and Simbo. Animists 5%.
10324	1	6	3.42	0	99.91	0.09	C	425.15	83	10	North New Georgia Island, Western Province. Close to and bilingual in Roviana. Animists 5%. D=CFC.
10325	2	7	3.42	0	99.94	0.06	C	452.89	80	10	Central Malaita Island. Hunters in tropical forest. Close to Kwaraae. Animists 10%, noticeably strong. Nominal Christians 5%. D=SSEC,RCC.
10326	3	7	3.69	0	99.97	0.03	C	516.91	78	10	Central Malaita Island. Extensive lingua franca. Mountains, forest, coast. Hunters, agriculturalists. Animists 1%. Nominal Christians 5%. D=SSEC,COM,RCC.
10327	0	10	2.10	0	99.85	0.15	C	356.78	61	9	Santa Isabel, villages of Baolo and Samasodu in Kia District. Nearly extinct.
10328	2	6	3.33	0	99.84	0.16	C	355.65	89	9	West central Malaita Island. Fishermen, craftsmen, on coast, coral reef. Animists 5%. Nominal Christians 14%. D=RCC,SSEC. M=SIL.
10329	3	6	3.40	0	99.90	0.10	C	430.33	80	10	Northeast Malaita Island. Coastal area, coral reef. Fishermen, craftsmen. Animists 5%. Nominal Christians 5%. D=COM,RCC,SDA. M=UBS,SIL.
10330	5	7	3.46	0	99.95	0.05	C	475.04	78	10	North and east central Guadalcanal Island. 4 dialects. D=RCC,COM,SSEC,UCPNGSI,SDA.
10331	1	7	3.40	0	99.90	0.10	C	413.91	84	10	East coast of Guadalcanal Island. Originally brought by settlers from Malaita. Animists 10%. D=Ch of Melanesia.
10332	2	6	2.06	0	99.90	0.10	C	423.76	53	10	Western Province, South Ranonga Island. Close to Duke. Declining use of Roviana. Animists 10%. D=UCPNGSI,SDA. M=SIL.
10333	2	6	3.45	0	99.94	0.06	C	449.46	81	10	Central Guadalcanal Island. Related to Ghari. Animists 6%. D=RCC,COM.
10334	1	7	3.43	0	99.95	0.05	C	485.45	76	10	Central Santa Isabel Island. Widespread lingua franca. Animists 3%. D=Ch of Melanesia.
10335	2	7	3.47	0	99.96	0.04	C	522.09	72	10	South New Georgia Island, Marovo Lagoon, Vangunu Island, Nggatokae Island, Western Province. Lingua franca. Animists 2%. D=SDA,UCPNGSI.
10336	2	7	4.56	0	99.85	0.15	C	369.19	115	9	Shortland Island, Treasury Island, Fauro Island. Animists 10%. D=RCC,UCPNGSI.
10337	0	7	3.26	0	99.80	0.20	C	315.36	94	9	Santa Cruz Island. Most bilingual in Santa Cruz language. Animists 15%.
10338	1	7	3.26	0	99.80	0.20	C	321.20	92	9	Temotu Province, Utupua Island, 3 villages. Tropical forest, mountains, coastal. Fishermen. Animists 17%. D=COM.
10339	2	10	3.31	5	99.82	0.18	C	430.99	63	10	Immigrants from Papua speaking Tok Pisin. Animists 1%, nonreligious 1%, nominal Christians 13%. D=RCC,COM.
10340	1	6	3.46	0	99.95	0.05	C	457.71	83	10	Ontong Java Atoll (Lord Howe Island), 160 miles north of Santa Isabel Island. Close to Sikaiana. D=Ch of Melanesia. M=SIL.
10341	2	6	3.15	0	99.70	0.30	C	263.16	96	8	South Malaita Island. Bilinguals in Saa. Animists 20%. Nominal Christians 10%. D=RCC,COM.
10342	1	7	3.41	0	99.91	0.09	C	421.83	85	10	Duff and Reed Islands: Matema, Taumako, Nupani, Nukapu, Pileni, Nifiloli. Animists 5%. D=Ch of Melanesia.
10343	1	7	3.39	0	99.89	0.11	C	409.31	83	10	Nifilole, Lomlom. Santa Cruz Islands, Eastern Solomons. Animists 1%. D=Ch of Melanesia. M=SIL.
10344	2	6	3.38	0	99.98	0.02	C	504.35	76	10	Rennell and Bellona Islands, Central Solomons. A few animists left. D=SSEC,SDA. M=SIL.
10345	2	7	3.33	0	99.86	0.14	C	382.95	85	9	Choiseul Island. Close to Babatana. Animists 14%. D=UCPNGSI,RCC.
10346	3	7	3.37	0	99.93	0.07	C	482.01	74	10	New Georgia, Roviana, Vonavona Lagoons. Lingua franca in Western Province, being replaced by Pijin. Animists 1%. Nominals 16%. D=UCPNGSI,SDA,CFC.
10347	1	6	3.40	0	99.90	0.10	C	410.62	84	10	Russell Islands, northwest of Guadalcanal, Central Solomons. Animists 10%. D=Ch of Melanesia.
10348	2	6	2.77	0	99.78	0.22	C	327.40	76	9	Ulawa, Three Sisters, South Malaita Islands. Hunters in mountains, tropical forests, coasts. Animists 10%, strong. Nominal Christians 12%. D=COM,SSEC. M=SIL.
10349	1	7	3.26	0	99.98	0.02	C	490.04	74	10	Santa Cruz Islands. 7 dialects. Fishermen. Few animists left. D=Ch of Melanesia. M=SIL.
10350	2	7	3.41	0	99.91	0.09	C	431.79	81	10	Savo Island, north of Guadalcanal, Central Solomons. Use of Savo declining among youth. Animists 9%. D=RCC,COM.
10351	1	7	3.40	0	99.90	0.10	C	410.62	86	10	Stewart Atoll, Central Solomons. Close to Luangiua (Ontong Java). Animists 10%. D=Ch of Melanesia.
10352	0	8	6.02	0	99.93	0.07	C	427.70	140	10	Simbo(Eddystone) Island, Western Province. Use of Roviana decreasing. Animists 5%. Nominal Christians 10%.
10353	6	10	4.92	4	99.96	0.04	C	550.12	100	10	Mixed-race and detribalized speakers of Solomons Pidgin, an English-based creole. Widespread lingua franca. Animists 2%. D=SSEC,RCC,COM,UCPNGSI,SDA.
10354	2	8	3.45	0	99.93	0.07	C	454.86	80	10	Guadalcanal Island, southeast to southwest coast. 6 dialects. Animists 2%. D=SSEC, et alia.
10355	1	8	3.33	0	99.80	0.20	C	335.80	90	9	Emua village, Vanikolo Island, Temotu Province. Highly bilingual in Pijin and Teanu. Forest, mountains, coast. Animists 10%. Nominal Christians 10%. D=COM.
10356	1	10	3.48	0	99.88	0.12	C	407.92	85	10	Tanimbili village, Utupua Island, Temotu. Mountains, tropical forest, coasts. Also speak Amba, Asumbuo, Pijin. Fishermen, agriculturalists. Animists 12%. D=COM.
10357	1	8	3.37	0	99.87	0.13	C	377.88	88	9	Tavula, Choiseul Island. Closely related to Varese. Animists 13%. D=RCC.
10358	2	7	3.40	0	99.98	0.02	C	468.58	82	10	Tikopia, Russell, Anuta Islands. Agriculturalists. Animists 1%. D=Ch of Melanesia,RCC. Gospel translated in 1976 but not published. M=SIL.
10359	3	7	3.37	0	99.98	0.02	C	515.08	72	10	North Malaita Island. Hunters in tropical forest, mountains. Agriculturalists. Animists 1%. D=SSEC,COM,SDA. M=SIL.
10360	1	7	3.28	0	99.80	0.20	C	327.04	91	9	North end of Rendova Island, Western Province. Bilingual in Roviana. Animists 18%. D=SDA.
10361	1	6	3.12	0	99.91	0.09	C	415.18	78	10	Ulawa Island, off South Malaita Island. Closely related to Saa. Animists 5%. Nominal Christians 12%. D=Ch of Melanesia.
10362	1	9	3.24	0	99.80	0.20	C	328.55	89	9	Lale and Lavaka villages, Vanikolo Island, Temotu Province. Bilingual in Pijin, Teanu. Tropical forest, mountains, coast. Agriculturalists, fishermen. Animists 10%.
10363	2	10	4.33	4	99.88	0.12	C	501.07	95	10	Immigrants from New Hebrides (Vanuatu). D=RCC,COM.
10364	1	7	3.57	0	99.88	0.12	C	404.71	87	10	Northeast Choiseul Island. 2 dialects. Closely related to Tavula. Animists 2%. D=RCC.
10365	2	7	2.86	0	99.85	0.15	C	384.71	73	9	West Guadalcanal (Ghari) language, Ndi dialect. Forest. Animists 15%. D=RCC,Ch of Melanesia.
10366	1	8	3.35	0	99.85	0.15	C	369.19	87	9	Santa Isabel Island, from Samasodu up to Kia village, Baolo village. Links with Roviana. Animists 10%. Nominal Christians 5%. D=Ch of Melanesia. M=SIL.
10367	1	10	3.32	0	99.80	0.20	C	329.96	91	9	Central Isabel Island, village of Kilokaka on Hograno coast. Speakers know Maringe and Zabana. Animists 15%. Nominal Christians 5%. D=Ch of Melanesia.
10368	0	10	6.92		99.00	1.00	C	252.94	192	8	Minor Melanesian peoples, also Indians, Japanese, Koreans, Indonesians, Filipinos, Australians. Baha'is 15%, Muslims 5%, Nonreligious 3%, Animists 1%.
Somalia											
10369	1	9	6.82	5	99.95	0.05	C	561.73	146	10	Refugees from Ethiopia. All Orthodox Christians. D=Ethiopian Orthodox Ch.
10370	0	1	2.75	7	39.00	61.00	A	1.42	242	4	Internationalized, educated Arabs, speaking Modern Standard Arabic. Muslims 99%.
10371	0	1	1.62	5	24.07	75.93	A	0.06	351	2	Fishermen on coast, especially Kismayu. Also in Kenya. Close to Swahili language and culture. Muslims 100%(Shafi Sunnis).
10372	0	1	1.96	1	16.10	83.90	A	0.05	504	2	Immigrants from Baluchistan. Muslims 100%(Sunnis).
10373	0	3	0.00	5	32.00	68.00	A	0.00	0	1.13	Migrants from Kenya, Tanzania. Mainly spoken in south. Muslims 100%(Shafi Sunnis).
10374	0	1	0.70	0	10.00	90.00	A	0.36	466	3	Nomadic hunter-gatherers in forests in south. Mainly in Kenya. Monolingual; some speak Somali. Muslims 70%, animists 29%.
10375	0	1	0.00	0	3.00	97.00	A	0.00	0	1.01	Jilib District, Middle Juba Region. Hunter-gatherers in scattered bush settlements. Shifting to Maay language. Nearly extinct. Muslims 100%.
10376	1	10	0.79	8	99.70	0.30	C	357.70	38	9	Expatriates from Britain, in relief, development, refugee work. Nonreligious 17%. D=Anglican Ch/ECJME(D-Egypt).
10377	0	1	0.00	1	12.00	88.00	A	0.00	0	1.07	Dhiinsoor District, May Region, Baraawe District. In Digil clan family. Muslims 100%.
10378	0	4	0.00	4	17.00	83.00	A	0.00	0	1.09	In northwest. Mainly in Eritrea, Ethiopia, and Djibouti. Nomadic. Muslims 100%(Sunnis).
10379	1	9	4.43	8	99.84	0.16	C	472.16	96	10	Expatriates from France, in relief, development. Nonreligious 13%. D=RCC(D-Mogadishu). M=OFM.
10380	0	2	0.00	0	4.00	96.00	A	0.00	0	1.02	Part of Hawiya clan family, dominating southern Somalia. Only 28% speak Garre, rest Maay or Somali. Muslims 100%.
10381	0	4	3.93	0	26.00	74.00	A	0.94	568	3	Remnants of former Bantu(Zigula, Kamba) 19th-century occupation of Juba valley. Acculturated to Sab. Muslims 90% (Shafi Sunnis), animists 9%.
10382	0	5	2.67	6	41.19	58.81	A	0.28	245	3	Development workers from India, Pakistan. Muslims 57%(Sunnis,with 1,000 Shias), Hindus 40%, Baha'is.
10383	1	10	1.59	7	99.80	0.20	C	426.32	49	10	Expatriates from Italy, in development, also some citizens. Language used in south. Nonreligious 13%. D=RCC(D-Mogadishu). M=OFM.
10384	0	1	0.00	1	12.00	88.00	A	0.00	0	1.07	Jiddu clan, in Middle Juba regions, lower Shabelle Bay. Muslims 100%.
10385	0	4	4.33	1	21.01	78.99	A	0.00	806	1.10	Gedo Region in south. West Somali. Unintelligible with Standard Somali. Muslims 100%(Shafi Sunnis).
10386	0	1	0.00	0	3.00	97.00	A	0.00	0	1.00	Endogamous caste of despised hunters, scattered among Somali tribes. Animists 70%, Muslims 30%.
10387	0	8	3.42	7	40.10	59.90	A	0.14	282	3	Migrants from Oman. Muslims 100%(Hinawis,Ibadi Kharijites,Ghafiris).
10388	0	4	0.00	5	28.00	72.00	A	0.00	0	1.09	Remnant Galla tribe now acculturated to Somali. Muslims 100%(Shafi Sunnis).
10389	0	1	0.00	5	25.00	75.00	A	0.00	0	1.08	Remnants of former Bantu occupation, now completely acculturated to Somali. Muslims 100%(Shafi Sunnis).
10390	2	4	5.76	5	50.05	49.95	B	0.09	417	2	5 tribal confederations. Muslims 100%(Shafis,Hanafis; Sufis,Ahmadis), 1,000 Baha'is. D=RCC,MCC. M=SIM,LBI,OFM,CRA,EMBMC,WC,Caritas,FMB,WVI,CSI,FI.
10391	0	4	1.96	5	34.01	65.99	A	0.01	307	2	Northern Common Somali. Large fluctuations of refugees to and from Ethiopia. Muslims 100% (Shafi Sunnis,Hanafis).
10392	0	4	4.01	5	41.00	59.00	A	1.49	395	4	Gedo Region in south. Related to Orma Galla of Kenya. Muslims 99%(Shafi Sunnis).
10393	2	9	6.70	5	99.90	0.10	C	479.61	161	10	Refugees from Ethiopia. Muslims 10% (Sunnis). D=Ethiopian Orthodox Ch,SDA.

Continued overleaf

Table 8-2 continued

PEOPLE		POPULATION				IDENTITY CODE		LANGUAGE		CHURCH		MINISTRY						SCRIPTURE		
Ref 1	Ethnic name 2	P% 3	In 1995 4	In 2000 5	In 2025 6	Race 7	Language 8	Autoglossonym 9	S 10	AC 11	Members 12	Jayuh 13-17	d 18	wa 19	xc 20	mc 21	mi 22	Biblioglossonym 23	Pub 24-26	ss 27
10394	Tunni	0.50000	28,353	36,323	81,136	CMT33e	14-GAGA-m	af-tunni		0.00	0	1c...	0	1	0	0	0		pnb	.
10395	USA White	0.01000	567	726	1,623	CEW19s	52-ABAC-s	general american		74.00	538	1Bsuh	10	9	8	5	1	English*	PNB	b
10396	Yemeni Arab	1.10000	62,377	79,910	178,500	CMT30	12-AACF-n	yemeni	35	0.05	40	1Asuh	4	3	1	1	1		pnb	b
10397	other minor peoples	0.70000	39,694	50,851	113,591	...				5.00	2,543		7	4	2	1	0			
	Somaliland	**100.00000**	**2,530,000**	**2,832,677**	**4,984,017**					**0.3**	**8,380**									
10398	Arab	0.06000	1,518	1,700	2,990	CMT30	12-AACF-pc	central somalia		1.00	17	1csuh	6	4	5	1	0		pnb	b
10399	British	0.01000	253	283	498	CEW19i	52-ABAC-b	standard-english		74.00	210	3Bsuh	10	9	13	5	1		PNB	b
10400	Danakil (Afar)	2.00000	50,600	56,654	99,680	CMT33z	14-AAAB-a	'afar-af		0.00	0	1.s..	0	2	1	0	0	Afar	PN.	b
10401	French	0.02000	506	567	997	CEW21b	51-AABI-d	general français		80.00	453	1B.uh	10	9	14	5	1	French	PNB	b
10402	Indo-Pakistani	0.20000	5,060	5,665	9,968	CNN25e	59-AAFH-b	standard gujaraati		0.20	11	2A.u.	5	4	3	1	0	Gujarati	PNB	b
10403	Omani Arab	0.80000	20,240	22,661	39,872	CMT30	12-AACF-l	omani		0.10	23	1Asuh	5	2	2	0	0		pnb	b
10404	Somali	89.71000	2,269,663	2,541,195	4,471,162	CMT33e	14-GAGA-a	af-soomaali		0.01	254	2A...	3	4	5	5	1	Somali	PNB	b
10405	Somali (Ogaden)	3.00000	75,900	84,980	149,521	CMT33e	14-GAGA-a	af-soomaali		0.01	8	2A...	3	2	3	0	0	Somali	PNB	b
10406	Tulama (Shoa Galla)	0.20000	5,060	5,665	9,968	CMT33b	14-FBAA-a	tulema		90.00	5,099	1cs..	10	9	11	5	3		pnb	b
10407	Yemeni Arab	3.00000	75,900	84,980	149,521	CMT30	12-AACF-n	yemeni		0.03	25	1Asuh	3	3	1	1	0		pnb	b
10408	other minor peoples	1.00000	25,300	28,327	49,840	...				8.05	2,280		7	4	2	1	0			
	South Africa	**100.00000**	**37,470,244**	**40,376,579**	**46,015,286**					**78.76**	**31,800,793**									
10409	Afrikaner	6.70000	2,510,506	2,705,231	3,083,024	CEW19a	52-ABCB-a	afrikaans	17	91.00	2,461,760	2B.uh	10	10	13	5	3	Afrikaans	PNB	b
10410	Arab	0.01000	3,747	4,038	4,602	CMT30	12-AACF-f	syro-palestinian		50.00	2,019	1Asuh	10	7	6	5	3	Arabic: Lebanese*	Pnb	b
10411	Birwa	0.02000	7,494	8,075	9,203	NAB57q	99-AUTE-aa	birwa		29.00	2,342	1csu.	9	5	6	2	3		pnb	b
10412	British	4.50000	1,686,161	1,816,946	2,070,688	CEW19i	52-ABAC-b	standard-english	63	71.00	1,290,032	3Bsuh	10	10	13	5	3		PNB	b
10413	Chewa (Western Nyanja)	0.40000	149,881	161,506	184,061	NAB57b	99-AUSX-ac	standard ci-cewa		60.70	98,034	1.su.	10	9	11	5	1	Chichewa	PNB	b
10414	Coloured (Cape Malay)	0.56000	209,833	226,109	257,686	NAN58	52-ABCB-a	afrikaans		70.00	158,276	2B.uh	10	7	11	5	1	Afrikaans	PNB	b
10415	Coloured (Eurafrican)	7.25000	2,716,593	2,927,302	3,336,108	NAN58	52-ABCB-a	afrikaans		91.60	2,681,409	2B.uh	10	9	12	5	3	Afrikaans	PNB	b
10416	Coloured (Eurafrican)	2.33000	873,057	940,774	1,072,156	NAN58	52-ABAC-u	south-british-african-english		94.00	884,328	1Bsuh	10	9	13	5	3		PNB	b
10417	Coloured Creole	0.07000	26,229	28,264	32,211	NAN58	52-ABCB-c	oorlans		80.00	22,611	1c.uh	10	8	10	5	0		pnb	.
10418	Detribalized Tswana	0.50000	187,351	201,883	230,076	NAB57q	99-AUTE-g	se-tswana	28	58.10	117,294	4Asu.	10	7	12	5	3	Tswana: Central*	PNB	b
10419	Detribalized urbanites	0.15000	56,205	60,565	69,023	NAN58	52-ABCB-g	fly taal		70.00	42,395	1c.uh	10	7	7	5	1		pnb	b
10420	Dutch	0.50000	187,351	201,883	230,076	CEW19h	52-ABCA-a	algemeen-nederlands		73.00	147,375	2Bsuh	10	9	15	5	3	Dutch	PNB	b
10421	Eastern Sotho (Khutswe)	1.00000	374,702	403,766	460,153	NAB57m	99-AUTE-c	khutswe		65.00	262,448	1csu.	10	9	12	5	3		pnb	b
10422	Esperanto	0.00000	0	0	0	CEW21z	51-AAAC-a	proper esperanto		50.00	0	0A...	10	8	10	5	0	Esperanto	PNB	b
10423	French	0.20000	74,940	80,753	92,031	CEW21b	51-AABI-d	general français		84.00	67,833	1B.uh	10	9	14	5	2	French	PNB	b
10424	German	0.93000	348,473	375,502	427,942	CEW19m	52-ABCE-a	standard hoch-deutsch		85.00	319,177	2B.uh	10	10	13	5	3	German*	PNB	b
10425	Gimsbok Nama (Bushman)	0.01000	3,747	4,038	4,602	BYG11c	08-AAAE-a	gemsbok-nama		60.00	2,423	0.s..	10	7	8	4	1		...	.
10426	Greek	0.20000	74,940	80,753	92,031	CEW20	56-AAAA-c	dhimotiki		92.00	74,293	2B.uh	10	9	11	5	1	Greek: Modern	PNB	b
10427	Griqua (Cape Hottentot)	0.00020	75	81	92	BYG11c	08-AAAD-a	q'xiri		70.00	57	0....	10	7	8	4	0		...	.
10428	Gujarati	0.35000	131,146	141,318	161,054	CNN25e	59-AAFH-b	standard gujaraati	1	2.30	3,250	2A.u.	6	4	6	5	1	Gujarati	PNB	b
10429	Han Chinese	0.00600	2,248	2,423	2,761	MSY42a	79-AAAB-ba	kuo-yü	1	26.70	647	2Bsuh	9	5	8	5	0	Chinese: Kuoyu*	PNB	b
10430	Han Chinese	0.01000	3,747	4,038	4,602	MSY42a	52-ABAC	english-mainland cluster		36.00	1,454	3Bsuh	9	5	8	5	2		PNB	b
10431	Han Chinese (Cantonese)	0.01200	4,496	4,845	5,522	MSY42a	79-AAAM-a	central yue		30.00	1,454	3A.uh	9	5	8	5	0	Chinese, Yue	PNB	b
10432	Han Chinese (Hakka)	0.01400	5,246	5,653	6,442	MSY42a	79-AAAG-a	literary hakka		25.00	1,413	1A...	9	5	8	5	0	Chinese: Hakka, Wukingfu*	PNB	b
10433	Hindi	0.80000	299,762	323,013	368,122	CNN25g	59-AAFO-e	general hindi	2	3.10	10,013	3Asuh	6	4	7	5	3		pnb	b
10434	Hurutshe Tswana	1.50000	562,054	605,649	690,229	NAB57q	99-AUTE-gg	hurutshe		40.00	242,259	1asu.	9	5	8	5	2		pnb	b
10435	Indian (English-speaking)	0.80000	299,762	323,013	368,122	CNN25z	52-ABAD-ap	south-african-asian-english		25.00	80,753	0c.uh	9	5	8	5	1		...	.
10436	Indo-Mauritian	0.10000	37,470	40,377	46,015	CNN25g	59-AAFO-k	bhojpuri-mauritius		5.00	2,019	1csuh	7	4	6	5	3	Bhojpuri	PNB	b
10437	Jewish	0.03000	11,241	12,113	13,805	CMT35	52-ABCH-a	west yiddish		0.10	12	0B..h	5	4	4	4	0	Yiddish	PNB	b
10438	Jewish	0.40000	149,881	161,506	184,061	CMT35	52-ABAC-u	south-british-african-english		0.30	485	1Bsuh	5	4	5	5	0		pnb	b
10439	Kgatla Tswana	0.70000	262,292	282,636	322,107	NAB57q	99-AUTE-gj	kgatla		38.00	107,402	1asu.	9	5	8	5	3		pnb	b
10440	Korana (Ora)	0.03000	11,241	12,113	13,805	BYG11d	08-AAAF	q'ora cluster		70.00	8,479	0....	10	7	7	4	0	Korana	PNB	.
10441	Kwena Tswana	0.10000	37,470	40,377	46,015	NAB57q	99-AUTE-ge	kwena		27.00	10,902	1asu.	9	5	7	5	2		pnb	b
10442	Lovedu (Lubedu)	0.50000	187,351	201,883	230,076	NAB57m	99-AUTE-a	khe-lobedu		24.00	48,452	1csu.	9	5	7	5	1		pnb	b
10443	Makua	0.03000	11,241	12,113	13,805	NAB57b	99-AUSY	makhua cluster		21.00	2,544	2.s..	9	5	5	5	3	Kimakhua	PNB	b
10444	Malete Tswana (Moletse)	0.10000	37,470	40,377	46,015	NAB57q	99-AUTE-gi	me-lete		28.00	11,305	1asu.	9	5	8	5	3		pnb	b
10445	Mine Kaffir	0.05000	18,735	20,188	23,008	NAB57i	99-AUTF-h	fanakolo	5	70.00	14,132	1csu.	10	7	8	5	1		pnb	b
10446	Nama Hottentot (Namaqua)	0.11628	43,570	46,950	53,507	BYG11c	08-AAAA-a	standard nama		95.00	44,602	1a...	10	9	11	5	2	Nama	PNB	b
10447	Nghuki	0.00100	375	404	460	BYG11d	09-CAAA-a	proper nc'hu-ki		40.00	162	0....	9	6	6	1	0		...	.
10448	Ngwaketse Tswana	0.30000	112,411	121,130	138,046	NAB57q	99-AUTE-gf	ngwaketse		27.00	32,705	1asu.	9	7	11	5	1		pnb	b
10449	Ngwato Tswana	0.10000	37,470	40,377	46,015	NAB57q	99-AUTE-gd	si-ngwato		30.00	12,113	1asu.	9	7	11	5	1		pnb	b
10450	Nusan (Ngamani, Auni)	0.00081	304	327	373	BYG11d	09-CAAH-a	nc'usa		0.00	0	0....	7	5	6	1	0		...	.
10451	Pedi (Northern Sotho)	7.19000	2,694,111	2,903,076	3,308,499	NAB57m	99-AUTE-d	se-pedi	26	91.20	2,647,605	2asu.	10	10	11	5	3	Sesotho: Northern	PNB	b
10452	Pondo	1.65000	618,259	666,214	759,252	NAB57i	99-AUTF-ai	mpondo		65.00	433,039	1csu.	10	7	8	5	2		pnb	b
10453	Portuguese	1.75045	655,898	706,772	805,475	CEW21g	51-AABA-e	general português		92.00	650,230	2Bsuh	10	9	15	5	2	Portuguese	PNB	b
10454	Rolong Tswana	1.00000	374,702	403,766	460,153	NAB57q	99-AUTE-gn	south se-rolong		48.00	193,808	1asu.	9	7	11	5	3	Setswana: Serolong	PNb	b
10455	Romanichal Gypsy	0.03000	11,241	12,113	13,805	CNN25f	59-AGAA-a	pogadi-chib		70.00	8,479	0....	10	7	8	4	3		...	b
10456	Ronga	0.20000	74,940	80,753	92,031	NAB57p	99-AUTD-d	shi-ronga	7	65.00	52,490	1.s..	10	8	10	5	1	Shironga*	PNB	b
10457	Seroa	0.00300	1,124	1,211	1,380	BYG11d	09-CBAC	seroa cluster		60.00	727	0....	10	7	6	1	3		...	.
10458	Shona	0.70000	262,292	282,636	322,107	NAB57l	99-AUTA-a	standard chi-shona		67.00	189,366	3csuh	10	6	10	3	1	Shona: Standard	PNB	b
10459	Sotho (Southern Sotho)	5.55586	2,081,794	2,243,266	2,556,545	NAB57m	99-AUTE-e	se-sotho	29	89.90	2,016,696	3asu.	10	10	11	5	3	Sesotho: Southern*	PNB	b
10460	Southern Ndebele (Ndzundz	2.02194	757,626	816,390	930,401	NAB57i	99-AUTF-i	south i-si-ndebele	8	69.00	563,309	1csu.	10	10	11	5	3	Isindebele: Southern	PNB	b
10461	Swazi (Tekela, Swati)	2.34293	877,902	945,995	1,078,106	NAB57i	99-AUTF-e	i-si-swati	9	71.00	671,656	2csu.	10	10	12	5	3	Siswati*	PNB	b
10462	Tamil	0.94340	353,494	380,913	434,108	CNN23c	49-EBEA-b	tamil	2	25.00	95,228	2Asu.	9	7	8	5	3	Tamil	PNB	b
10463	Telugu	0.20000	74,940	80,753	92,031	CNN23d	49-DBAB-a	telugu		15.00	12,113	2Asu.	8	7	8	5	3	Telugu	PNB	b
10464	Tembu	1.50000	562,054	605,649	690,229	NAB57i	99-AUTF-af	thembu		70.00	423,954	1csu.	10	8	11	5	2		pnb	b
10465	Tlhaping Tswana	0.70000	262,292	282,636	322,107	NAB57q	99-AUTE-gk	tlhaping		46.00	130,013	1asu.	9	10	11	5	2	Setswana: Setlhaping	PNB	b
10466	Tlharu Tswana	0.80000	299,762	323,013	368,122	NAB57q	99-AUTE-gl	thlware		50.00	161,506	1asu.	10	9	10	5	1		pnb	b
10467	Tlokwa Tswana	0.40000	149,881	161,506	184,061	NAB57q	99-AUTE-gh	northwest tlokwa		30.00	48,452	1asu.	9	9	10	5	2		pnb	b
10468	Tsonga (Shangaan)	3.41289	1,278,818	1,378,008	1,570,451	NAB57p	99-AUTD-c	shi-shangana	11	68.00	937,046	3.s..	10	10	12	5	3	Tsonga	PNB	b
10469	Tswa (Hlengwe)	0.05000	18,735	20,188	23,008	NAB57p	99-AUTD-a	shi-tswa		19.00	3,836	1.s..	8	5	6	5	2	Xitshwa*	PNB	b
10470	USA White	0.02000	7,494	8,075	9,203	CEW19s	52-ABAC-s	general american		78.00	6,299	1Bsuh	10	10	13	0	0	English*	PNB	b
10471	Urdu	0.51490	192,934	207,899	236,933	CNN25r	59-AAFO-d	standard urdu	1	1.80	3,742	2Asuh	6	4	6	3	0	Urdu	PNB	b
10472	Venda	1.93094	723,528	779,648	888,528	NAB57m	99-AUTB-a	chi-venda		21.40	166,845	4.su.	9	7	8	5	3	Tshivenda*	PNB	b
10473	Xam (Cape Bushman)	0.00030	112	121	138	BYG11d	09-EAAA-a	c'xam-t'ke		80.00	97	0....	10	7	6	5	3		...	.
10474	Xegwi (Khegwi)	0.00050	187	202	230	BYG11d	09-DAAA-a	l'xegwi		60.00	121	0....	10	7	6	1	0		...	.
10475	Xhosa	15.17052	5,684,431	6,125,337	6,980,758	NAB57i	99-AUTF-a	i-si-xhosa	27	87.40	5,353,545	2Asu.	10	10	13	5	3	Xhosa	PNB	b
10476	Zanzibari	0.00303	1,135	1,223	1,394	NAB57j	99-AUSM-q	ki-unguja		0.00	0	1Asu.	0	3	2	3	0		pnb	b
10477	Zulu	20.32905	7,617,345	8,208,175	9,354,470	NAB57i	99-AUTF-g	i-si-zulu	35	93.85	7,703,372	3asu.	10	10	13	5	3	Isizulu*	PNB	b
10478	other minor peoples	0.20000	74,940	80,753	92,031	...				70.00	56,527		10	7	7	5	0			
	South Korea	**100.00000**	**44,948,666**	**46,843,989**	**52,532,789**					**39.88**	**18,681,875**									
10479	Esperanto	0.00000	0	0	0	CEW21z	51-AAAC-a	proper esperanto		50.00	0	0A...	10	8	8	5	0	Esperanto	PNB	b
10480	Eurasian	0.02600	11,687	12,179	13,659	MSY43	52-ABAD-cd	korean-english		80.00	9,744	0B.uh	10	9	10	5	2		...	.
10481	French	0.01000	4,495	4,684	5,253	CEW21b	51-AABI-d	general français		84.00	3,935	1B.uh	10	9	14	5	2	French	PNB	b
10482	Han Chinese (Mandarin)	0.07500	33,711	35,133	39,400	MSY42a	79-AAAB-ba	kuo-yü	1	7.00	2,459	2Bsuh	7	5	11	5	3	Chinese: Kuoyu*	PNB	b
10483	Japanese	2.00000	898,973	936,880	1,050,656	MSY45a	45-CAAA-a	koku-go		3.00	28,106	1B.uh	6	4	9	5	2	Japanese	PNB	b
10484	Russian	0.00500	2,247	2,342	2,627	CEW22j	53-AAAE-d	russkiy		40.00	937	4B.uh	9	7	11	4	1	Russian	PNB	b
10485	South Korean	97.73700	43,931,478	45,783,910	51,343,972	MSY46	45-AAAA-bb	south onmun		40.60	18,588,267	1A...	9	8	13	5	1	Korean	PNB	.
10486	USA White	0.13700	61,580	64,176	71,970	CEW19s	52-ABAC-s	general american	11	74.00	47,490	1Bsuh	10	9	14	5	2	English*	PNB	b
10487	other minor peoples	0.01000	4,495	4,684	5,253	...				20.00	937		9	7	6	4	0			
	Spain	**100.00000**	**39,568,100**	**39,629,775**	**36,658,293**					**93.55**	**37,073,668**									
10488	Aragonese	5.00000	1,978,405	1,981,489	1,832,915	CEW21k	51-AABD-b	aragonés		95.00	1,882,414	0....	10	9	14	5	1	Aragonese	...	b
10489	Aranese Gascon	0.01500	5,935	5,944	5,499	CEW21z	51-AABF-f	aranés		90.00	5,350	0....	10	9	11	5	1	Gascon, Aranese	P..	b
10490	Asturian	1.25000	494,601	495,372	458,229	CEW21k	51-AABC-a	astur		90.00	445,835	0B.uh	10	9	13	5	1	Spanish: Asturian*	P..	b
10491	Basque	3.79000	1,499,631	1,501,968	1,389,349	CEW16	51-AABB-cg	vasco		95.00	1,426,870	1B.uh	10	10	15	5	3		pnb	b
10492	Basque (Eskualdunak)	1.70800	675,823	676,877	626,124	CEW16	40-AAAA-c	gipuzkera		93.00	629,495	1....	10	10	15	5	2	Basque: Guipuzcoan	PNB	b
10493	Black Gypsy (Spanish Calo	0.42000	166,186	166,445	153,965	CNN25f	59-AFAA-a	rodi		80.00	133,156	0B.uh	10	8	13	5	1	Calo	P..	b
10494	British	0.08000	31,654	31,704	29,327	CEW19i	52-ABAC-b	standard-english	7	78.00	24,729	3Bsuh	10	9	13	5	2		PNB	b
10495	Catalonian	28.00000	11,079,068	11,096,337	10,264,322	CEW21a	51-AABE-b	català		94.00	10,430,557	2a..h	10	10	16	5	3	Catalan-valencian-balear	PNB	b
10496	Cuban White	0.04300	17,014	17,041	15,763	CLT27	51-AABB-hi	cubano		75.00	12,781	1B.uh	10	8	8	4	1		pnb	b
10497	Esperanto	0.00000	0	0	0	CEW21z	51-AAAC-a	proper esperanto		70.00	0	0A...	10	8	8	5	0	Esperanto	PNB	b
10498	Extremaduran	2.75000	1,088,123	1,089,819	1,008,103	CEW21k	51-AABB-ck	estremadura		96.00	1,046,226	1c.uh	10	9	14	0	0		pnb	.
10499	Fala	0.02650	10,486	10,502	9,714	CEW21d	51-AABB-cc	galicia		95.00	9,977	1c.uh	10	8	12	0	0		pnb	.
10500	French	0.10000	39,568	39,630	36,658	CEW21b	51-AABI-d	general français	15	84.00	33,289	1B.uh	10	9	14	5	3	French	PNB	b
10501	Galician (Galega, Gallego	8.18700	3,239,440	3,244,490	3,001,214	CEW21d	51-AABA-b	galego		95.00	3,082,265	1csuh	10	9	15	5	1	Galician	PNB	b
10502	German	0.03000	11,870	11,889	10,997	CEW19m	52-ABCE-a	standard hoch-deutsch	1	86.00	10,224	2B.uh	10	9	13	5	3	German*	PNB	b
10503	Greek	0.00500	1,978	1,981	1,833	CEW20	56-AAAA-c	dhimotiki		90.00	1,783	2B.uh	10	9	11	5	1	Greek: Modern	PNB	b
10504	Han Chinese	0.06000	23,741	23,778	21,995	MSY42a	79-AAAB-ba	kuo-yü		30.00	7,133	2Bsuh	9	5	8	4	1	Chinese: Kuoyu*	PNB	b
10505	Italian	0.20000	79,136	79,260	73,317	CEW21e	51-AABQ-c	standard italiano	3	84.00	66,578	2B.uh	10	9	15	5	3	Italian	PNB	b
10506	Japanese	0.00500	1,978	1,981	1,833	MSY45a	45-CAAA-a	koku-go		3.00	59	1B.uh	6	4	3	1	1	Japanese	PNB	b
10507	Jewish	0.03200	12,662	12,682	11,731	CMT35	51-AABB-c	general español		0.30	38	2B.uh	5	4	5	1	1	Spanish	PNB	b
10508	Kurdish (Kurd)	0.00200	791	793	733	CNT24c	58-AAAA-a	kurmanji		0.00	0	3c...	0	4	2	4	1	Kurdish: Kurmanji*	PN.	b
10509	Latin American Mestizo	0.23000	91,007	91,148	84,314	CLN29	51-AABB-h	south americano		93.00	84,768	4B.uh	10	9	13	5	1		pnb	b

Continued opposite

Table 8-2 continued

Ref 1	D 28	aC 29	CG% 30	r 31	E 32	U 33	W 34	e 35	R 36	T 37	Locations, civil divisions, literacy, religions, church history, denominations, dioceses, church growth, missions, agencies, ministries, movements 38
			EVANGELIZATION					**EVANGELISM**			**ADDITIONAL DESCRIPTIVE DATA**
10394	0	1	0.00	1	12.00	88.00	A	0.00	0	1.07	Nomads in Lower Shabelle and Middle Juba Regions. Pastoralists. Muslims 100% (Sunnis).
10395	2	10	4.30	8	99.74	0.26	C	372.73	103	9	Expatriates from USA, in refugee work, relief, development. Nonreligious 15%. D=AC,RCC(D-Mogadishu). M=OFM.
10396	0	4	3.76	7	36.05	63.95	A	0.06	339	2	Eastern Colloquial Arabic. Refugees and migrant laborers from Yemen. Muslims 100%(50% Zaydis,40% Sunnis,5% Ismailis). M=OFM.
10397	0	6	5.69		20.00	80.00	A	3.65	780	4	Punjabis(Sikhs), Eritreans, Sudanese, Saudi Arabs, Gulf Arabs; around 830,000 refugees from Ethiopia have fled to or from Somalia. Muslims 91% (Sunnis).
Somaliland											
10398	0	1	2.87	7	35.00	65.00	A	1.27	279	4	Educated Arabs, speaking Modern Standard Arabic. Muslims 99%.
10399	1	10	3.09	8	99.74	0.26	C	388.94	81	9	Expatriates from Britain, in relief, development, refugee work. Nonreligious 18%. D=ECJME.
10400	0	4	0.00	4	20.00	80.00	A	0.00	0	1.09	In west. Mainly in Eritrea, Ethiopia, Djibouti. Nomads. Muslims 100%.
10401	1	9	3.89	8	99.80	0.20	C	429.24	91	10	Expatriates from France, in relief, development. Nonreligious 17%. D=RCC(D-Mogadishu). M=OFM.
10402	0	5	2.43	6	41.20	58.80	A	0.30	229	3	Development workers, traders, from India, Pakistan. Muslims 55%, Hindus 40%, Baha'is.
10403	0	8	3.19	7	40.10	59.90	A	0.14	266	3	Migrants from Oman. Muslims 100%(Hinawis,Ibadi Kharijites,Ghafiris).
10404	1	4	3.29	5	46.01	53.99	A	0.01	306	2	Tribal confederations: Muslims 100%(Shafi, Hanafis; Sufis,Ahmadis). D=RCC.R=FEBA,AWR.
10405	0	4	2.10	5	37.01	62.99	A	0.01	292	2	Northern Common Somali. Vast waves of refugees from and to Ethiopia, Somalia. Muslims 100%(Shafi Sunnis,Hanafis).
10406	3	9	6.43	5	99.90	0.10	C	496.03	151	10	Refugees from Ethiopia. Muslims 10%. D=Ethiopia Orthodox Ch,SDA,RCC.
10407	0	4	3.27	7	34.03	65.97	A	0.03	320	2	Eastern Colloquial Arabic. Migrant laborers, refugees from Yemen. Muslims 100%.(Zaydis,Sunnis,Ismailis).
10408	0	6	5.58		23.05	76.95	A	6.77	663	4	Eritreans, other Ethiopians, other Arabs, Sudanese, Italians, other Europeans, other Africans, other Asians. Muslims 88% (Sunnis, Shias).
South Africa											
10409	6	9	2.07	5	99.91	0.09	C	554.69	49	10	Boers, Whites of Dutch origin (60% of all Whites). Nonreligious 6%. D=NGK(General Synod DRC),NHK,GKSA,AFMSA,RCC,LRASA. M=OP,LM,FMB,USPG,LBI,&c.
10410	3	10	5.45	8	99.50	0.50	B	211.70	145	8	Traders, migrant workers. Muslims 50%. D=RCC(Maronites,&c),CPSA,COC.
10411	4	8	5.61	1	74.00	26.00	B	78.32	242	6	Also in Botswana and Zimbabwe. Related to Shona peoples. Animists 70%. D=DRCM,RCC,CPSA,AICs.
10412	9	10	2.16	8	99.71	0.29	C	388.72	60	9	40% of all Whites. Long-time settlers, farmers, professionals. D=CPSA(11 Dioceses),MCSA,PCSA,BUSA,UCCSA,CESA,RCC,SDA,JWs. M=OP,LM,FMB,USPG,&c.
10413	1	10	5.44	5	99.61	0.39	C	274.06	153	8	Migrant laborers from Malawi. Animists 20%, Muslims 19%. D=AICs.
10414	3	10	10.15	5	99.70	0.30	C	362.81	217	9	Some bilinguals in English. Muslims 21.7%(Shafi Sunnis since 1652 influx from Java; 75% in Cape Town area). D=DRMC,Moravian Ch,AFMSA. M=SIM.
10415	7	9	2.83	5	99.92	0.08	C	557.01	65	10	Muslims 7.4%(Sunnis). D=CA,DRMC,CPSA,MCSA,AFMSA,BBCZSA,RCC. M=OMI,SAC,OSB,OFM,FMB.
10416	8	10	1.64	8	99.94	0.06	C	569.54	45	10	Muslims 3%. D=RCC,CPSA,PCA,UCCSA,CPCSA,ELCSA,SDA,JWs. M=OMI,OSFS,CMM,OFM,SAC,FMB. R=local stations.
10417	0	10	2.34	1	99.80	0.20	C	379.60	73	9	Afrikaans-based creole, spoken by many small colonies of Blacks. Animists 10%, nonreligious 10%.
10418	4	10	1.69	5	99.58	0.42	B	278.01	55	8	Large numbers across urban north. Animists 10%, Muslims, Baha'is. Nominal Christians 30%. D=DRCA,RCC,SDA,JWs. M=OMI,CMM,FSC,FMB,USPG.
10419	1	10	8.71	1	99.70	0.30	C	311.71	220	9	Flaai taal. Afrikaans-based township creole since 1886. Animists 10%, Muslims 5%, nonreligious 5%. D=many AICs.
10420	4	10	1.85	6	99.73	0.27	C	407.66	49	10	Original settlers, farmers, business. Nonreligious 24%. D=NGK,NHK,AFMSA,RCC.
10421	5	7	5.02	2	99.65	0.35	C	294.19	132	8	Eastern Transvaal, north of Swaziland. Related to Pedi. Animists 20%. Nominal Christians 15%. D=ZCC,ELCSA,RCC,MCSA,many other AICs.
10422	0	10	0.00	5	99.50	0.50	B	204.40	0	8	Artificial(constructed) language, in 80 countries. Speakers in South Africa: 23,00(none mother-tongue).
10423	2	10	1.96	8	99.84	0.16	C	493.62	50	10	Settlers from France, in all walks of life. Nonreligious 13%. D=RCC(26 Dioceses),JWs.
10424	6	10	1.98	8	99.85	0.15	C	508.81	52	10	Settlers originally from Germany, expatriates in business, commerce, farming. Nonreligious 5%. D=ELCSA,NAC,UELCSA,ACAU,FELSSA,JWs.
10425	1	7	3.98	0	97.00	3.00	C	212.43	143	8	Central Khoisan. One of last remaining Bushman peoples, slowly dying out. Animists 10%. D=AICs.
10426	1	10	5.17	7	99.92	0.08	C	550.71	103	10	Settlers from Greece. Traders, merchants. Nonreligious 8%. D=Greek Orthodox Ch(2 Dioceses,under P-Alexandria).
10427	0	10	0.83	0	99.70	0.30	C	270.83	50	8	Central Khoisan. Long history with Christian missions. Now nearly extinct.
10428	4	10	5.95	6	63.30	36.70	B	5.31	301	4	In Natal, mostly around Durban. Traders, artisans, lawyers. Hindus 70%, Muslims 27%, Baha'is. D=CPSA,RCC,ICC,UPC. M=WVI.
10429	0	10	4.26	7	91.70	8.30	B	89.36	147	6	Long-time immigrants from China. Buddhist/folk-religionists/Confucianists 70%. Many churches and missions at work.
10430	2	10	5.11	8	99.36	0.64	B	141.91	146	7	Anglicized, English-speaking. Buddhists/Chinese folk-religionists 60%. D=CPSA,&c.
10431	0	10	5.11	8	96.00	4.00	B	105.12	164	7	Originally from Guangdong(China). Buddhists/folk-religionists 65%.
10432	0	10	5.08	7	88.00	12.00	B	80.30	178	6	Buddhists/folk-religionists 70%. Links with churches in China(Taiwan).
10433	4	10	7.15	7	68.10	31.90	B	7.70	328	4	Traders from India. Hindus 90%, Muslims 6%, Baha'is. D=CPSA,RCC,ICC,UPC. M=WVI,SAGM,FMB.
10434	2	6	2.84	5	97.00	3.00	B	141.62	106	7	Also in Botswana. Animists 20%, Muslims, Baha'is. Nominal Christians 40%. D=DRC,AICs. M=LM,FMB.
10435	7	10	4.28	8	76.00	24.00	B	69.35	191	6	Immigrant labor from India. Traders, artisans. Hindus 67%, Baha'is, Sikhs. D=FGCOGSA,BBCZSA,RCC,CON,ELCSA,UPC,ICC. M=FMB.
10436	3	10	5.45	6	66.00	34.00	B	12.04	268	5	Mauritians, originally from Bihar(India). Hindus 80%, Muslims 10%, Baha'is 5%. D=SDA,JWs,RCC.
10437	0	10	2.52	4	51.10	48.90	B	0.18	172	3	Recent immigrants from Europe. Practicing Jews, mostly in larger cities.
10438	0	10	3.96	8	54.30	45.70	B	0.59	235	3	Descendants of earlier immigrants. Some 500 prosperous middle-class communities of practicing Jews in Cape, Johannesburg.
10439	3	6	2.79	5	99.38	0.62	B	140.08	101	7	Also Botswana. Animists 20%, Baha'is 5%. Nominal Christians 30%. D=large number of AICs,DRCM,&c.
10440	0	6	6.98	0	99.70	0.30	C	286.16	195	8	Nomads in northwest. Only 50 Korana speakers remain; Nearly extinct. Animists 10%. Nominal Christians 20%.
10441	2	6	2.21	5	83.00	17.00	B	81.79	104	6	Also in Botswana. Animists 15%, Baha'is. Nominal Christians 45%. D=AICs,et alia.
10442	1	6	8.86	1	71.00	29.00	B	62.19	379	6	Transvaal. Ritual of Rain Queen. Dialect of Pedi. Close to Venda and (culturally) Shona. Animists 50%. Nominal Christians 26%. D=AICs.
10443	3	10	5.70	0	74.00	26.00	B	56.72	265	6	Labor immigrants from Mozambique. Animists 60%, Muslims 19%. D=RCC,AEC,JWs.
10444	3	8	2.77	5	89.00	11.00	B	90.95	114	6	Primarily in Botswana. Animists 15%, Baha'is. Nominal Christians 45%. D=AICs,DRC,RCC.
10445	1	10	7.52	1	99.70	0.30	C	314.26	191	9	Isipiki, Chilapalapa. Pidgin in mine compounds. also in Zambia. Vocabulary: 70% Zulu, 24% English, 6% Afrikaans. Animists 20%, Muslims 5%. D=AICs.
10446	4	6	4.46	4	99.95	0.05	C	554.80	95	10	From Namibia. D=Self-Supporting Rhenish Ch,AMEC,Independent Rhenish Mission of SA,UECN. M=RM,VEM.
10447	0	7	2.82	0	67.00	33.00	B	97.82	156	6	Southern Khoisan. Nearly extinct. Also in Namibia. Animists 10%.
10448	1	6	2.44	5	85.00	15.00	B	83.76	109	6	Mainly in Botswana. Animists 20%, Muslims 3%, Baha'is 3%, nonreligious 2%. Nominal Christians 45%. D=AICs.
10449	1	6	2.55	5	88.00	12.00	B	96.36	108	6	Primarily in Botswana. Urban migrants. Animists 29%, Muslims 1%. Nominal Christians 40%. D=AICs.
10450	0	7	3.42	0	34.00	66.00	A	11.16	356	5	Khoisan. Also in Namibia, Botswana. Dialects include Kakia, Katia, Vaalpens. Animists 91%.
10451	9	7	5.48	4	99.91	0.09	C	533.27	110	10	Transvaal. Close to Tswana. Animists 5%, Muslims, Baha'is. Many nominal Christians. D=Zion Christian Ch,ELCSA,RCC(M-Pretoria),MCSA,ACBCSA,IPA.
10452	2	6	3.64	5	99.65	0.35	C	284.70	107	8	Close to and dialect of Xhosa. Animists 15%. D=AICs,RCC(D-Umtata). M=CMM,FSC.
10453	2	10	2.76	8	99.92	0.08	C	577.57	60	10	Portuguese Whites, emigres from Angola, Mozambique. Nonreligious 7%. D=RCC,Igreja de Deus.
10454	5	6	3.03	5	99.48	0.52	B	194.47	98	7	North Rolong on Botswana border, South Rolong on Lesotho border. Animists 15%, Muslims, Baha'is. Nominal Christians 50%. D=AICs,DRC,CPSA,MCSA,RCC.
10455	3	10	3.71	0	99.70	0.30	C	288.71	115	8	Anglo-Romani Gypsies(Britain-originating). Nonreligious 30%. D=GEM,RCC,AICs.
10456	3	6	8.94	5	99.65	0.35	C	298.93	234	8	Mainly in Mozambique. Animists 10%, Muslims 4%, Baha'is 3%. D=RCC,Tsonga Presbyterian Ch,AICs. M=Swiss Mission.
10457	4	7	4.38	0	94.00	6.00	C	205.86	157	8	Khoisan. Also in Lesotho. 3 dialects. Animists 30%. D=RCC,DRC,CPSA,AICs.
10458	1	10	10.35	4	99.67	0.33	C	317.91	241	9	Labor migrants from Zimbabwe(Zezuru, Karanga, Manyika, Ndau). Animists 23%. D=AICs.
10459	11	6	3.86	5	99.90	0.10	C	527.96	82	10	Also in Lesotho. Animists 5%, Muslims, Baha'is. D=RCC,ELCSA,BPCSA,ACC,LEC,KMBM,AHZMSA,CAFCZ,NWACZ,CPSA,&c. M=OMI,CSSp,SCJ,OFM,LM.
10460	7	8	5.40	5	99.69	0.31	C	329.92	135	9	Transvaal Ndebele(Laka/Black Ndebele and Manala tribes). Close to Sotho. Animists 20%. D=RCC,NGKA,CPSA,ELCSA,AoG,many AICs,&c. M=OSB,FIFM.
10461	5	6	4.03	5	99.71	0.29	C	355.03	101	9	Also in Swaziland. Animists 25%. Y=1880. D=SJAFM,RCC(D-Umtata),SCCZSA,ZMCSA,very many other AICs. M=Christian Aid Mission,CMM,OSM,LM,&c.
10462	6	10	4.74	6	95.00	5.00	B	86.68	166	6	From South India. Traders, professionals. Hindus 60%, Muslims 10%, Baha'is 5%. D=FGCOGSA,RCC,IRCA,CPSA,UPC,ICC. M=OMI,FSC,WVI,SAGM,FMB.
10463	4	10	4.93	5	83.00	17.00	B	45.44	196	6	Immigrants from Andhra Pradesh(India). Traders. Hindus 65%, Muslims 15%, Baha'is 5%. D=CPSA,ICC,RCC,UPC. M=IRCA,FGCOGSA,WVI,FMB.
10464	4	6	3.42	5	99.70	0.30	C	329.59	95	9	Rich cultural history. A Xhosa dialect. Animists 25%. Y=1830. Nominal Christians 5%. D=National Tembu Ch,MCSA,RCC(D-Umtata), other AICs. M=CMM,FSC.
10465	2	6	2.99	5	99.46	0.54	B	177.97	101	7	North, near Botswana border. Animists 40%; many nominal Christians. Y=1821. D=Native Independent Congregational Ch, and 20 other AICs.
10466	1	6	3.07	5	99.50	0.50	B	197.10	101	7	Some in Botswana. Animists 25%. Nominal Christians widespread. D=many AICs.
10467	2	6	2.55	5	89.00	11.00	B	97.45	107	6	Mainly in Botswana. Animists 50%. Widespread nominal Christians. D=ELCSA,AICs.
10468	5	6	4.24	5	99.68	0.32	C	335.07	123	9	Includes 180,000 Shangaan refugees from Mozambique. Mainly Mozambique; also Swaziland, Zimbabwe. Animists 30%, Muslims, Baha'is. D=RCC,TPC,ZCACSA.
10469	2	8	4.46	4	74.00	26.00	B	51.31	233	6	Miners from Mozambique. Also in Zimbabwe. Nonreligious 17%, Animists 4%. D=United Methodist Ch(SE Conference),AICs.
10470	0	0	6.66	8	99.78	0.22	C	372.95	158	9	Expatriates from the USA, in business, education. Nonreligious 10%. D=CJCLdS.
10471	0	10	6.10	5	57.80	42.20	B	3.79	338	4	Traders in Transvaal. Natal coast, Durban, Johannesburg. Official language of South African Muslims. Most speak English. Muslims 97%(Sunnis).
10472	9	6	10.21	4	82.40	17.60	B	64.36	372	6	Transvaal. Also in Zimbabwe. Animists 65%. D=DRCA,AoG,CPSA,WC,RCC,ABC,CBCSA,ZCC,other AICs. M=Berlin Mission,MSC,FSC,BEA,Frontline Fellowship.
10473	3	8	4.68	0	99.80	0.20	C	347.48	131	9	Khoisan. Now almost extinct. D=RCC,CPSA,Moravian Ch.
10474	0	7	2.52	0	88.00	12.00	C	192.72	110	7	Southern Khoisan. Also in Namibia, Botswana, Zimbabwe. Language now virtually extinct.
10475	14	7	3.80	5	99.87	0.13	C	514.88	82	10	Southwest Cape; also in Transkei. Animists 6%, Muslims, Baha'is, Buddhists, Hindus. Y=1799(LMS). D=AAoG,CoC,ACC,AGC,AMEC,AFMSA,BPCSA,BUSA,RCC.
10476	0	10	0.00	5	39.00	61.00	A	0.00	0	1.13	Market gardeners in Chatsworth (Durban). East African Muslims who immigrated from 1873-85. In Durban; classed as 'Indians'. Muslims 100% (Shafi Sunnis).
10477	11	7	5.35	5	99.94	0.06	C	574.97	104	10	Animists 3%; Muslims(10,000 converts to Islam; 1982: Quran in Zulu), Baha'is, Buddhists, Hindus. D=Nazirite Baptist Ch,PCA,AAoG,ACongC,AGC,AMEC.
10478	0	8	9.02		99.70	0.30	C	260.61	242	8	Other Mozambicans(many Muslims), Malawians, other Black Africans, Asians, other Europeans. Animists 5%, nonreligious 6%, Muslims 3%, Baha'is.
South Korea											
10479	0	10	0.00	5	99.50	0.50	B	200.75	0	8	Artificial(constructed) language, in 80 countries. Speakers in South Korea: 76,000(none mother-tongue). Nonreligious 20%.
10480	2	10	7.36	8	99.80	0.20	C	402.96	162	10	Mixed race persons, Korean/Whites. Mainly in urban areas. Nonreligious 5%, Buddhists 5%. D=PCK,RCC(14 Dioceses).
10481	1	10	4.03	8	99.84	0.16	C	490.56	86	10	Expatriates from France, in commerce. Nonreligious 13%. D=RCC. M=WM,MEP,SSC,SJ,SDB,MSC,OSB,OFM.
10482	3	10	5.66	7	80.00	20.00	B	20.44	216	5	Trade, commerce. Chinese folk-religionists 90%. D=RCC,PCK,50 others including True Jesus Ch and 20 other Chinese indigenous denominations.
10483	2	10	8.26	7	70.00	30.00	B	7.66	353	4	Residents originating in Japan. Buddhists 57%, New-Religionists 24%, nonreligious 10%, Shintoists 3%. D=RCC,&c. M=FMB,&c. R=HCJB,AWR.
10484	1	10	0.91	7	99.40	0.60	B	160.60	23	7	Expatriates from Russia, in commerce. Nonreligious 50%. D=Greek Orthodox Ch(D-New Zealand).
10485	5	5	6.28	6	99.41	0.59	B	156.48	179	7	Shamanists 16%, Mahayana Buddhists 15%, New-Religionists 15%(260 religions), Confucianists 11%, 60,000 Muslims(Sunnis) since 1950. D=RCC,Olive Tree Ch.
10486	8	10	5.90	8	99.74	0.26	C	405.15	124	10	Expatriates from USA, in commerce, military. Nonreligious 9%. D=PCK,RCC,SDA,CCS,JWs,CJCLdS,AoG,CCCC. M=FMB,&c.
10487	0	10	4.64		49.00	51.00	A	35.77	259	5	Greeks(GOC), Germans(NAC), Taiwanese, Australians, Cantonese, Vietnamese, other Asians, Europeans. Buddhists 20%, nonreligious 19%, new religionists.
Spain											
10488	1	10	5.04	0	99.95	0.05	C	506.25	112	10	Northern region, Zaragoza. Strong vernacular culture. Nonreligious 5%. D=RCC.
10489	1	10	0.74	1	99.90	0.10	C	453.33	35	10	Arar Valley, in the Pyrenees mountains. Nonreligious 10%. D=RCC.
10490	1	10	4.58	8	99.90	0.10	C	505.89	98	10	Northern. Asturias Region in northwest, east of Galicia. Close to Leonese, and Castilian. Nonreligious 10%. D=RCC.
10491	3	10	0.75	8	99.95	0.05	C	596.41	28	10	Staunch Catholics. D=RCC(D-Bilbao,et alia),IEH,UEBE. M=SJ,SDB,OFM,CMF,OP,AoG,CAM.
10492	1	8	0.75	3	99.93	0.07	C	532.93	31	10	Euzkadi, Heuskara, Batua, Navarrese. Basque Provinces; also in France, Costa Rica, USA, Philippines, Australia. D=RCC(M-Pamplona & 4 Dioceses). M=SJ,FMB.
10493	3	8	0.75	8	99.80	0.20	C	420.48	34	10	Iberian Romani. Also in France, Portugal, Brazil, Latin America. D=nomadic caravan churches,IEF(MSG/GEM; mass charismatic movement),RCC. M=GGMS.
10494	2	10	0.75	8	99.78	0.22	C	438.43	34	10	Expatriates from Britain, in business, commerce. Nonreligious 9%. D=Ch of England(D-Gibraltar),IERE.
10495	7	8	0.72	4	99.94	0.06	C	583.27	26	10	Catalonia, Valencia Provinces. Also France, Andorra, Italy, USA. D=RCC(M-Tarragona & 8 Dioceses),JWs,IEH,UEBE,IEE,AHC,&c. M=SJ,SDB,OFM,CMF,OP,FMB.
10496	1	10	0.75	8	99.75	0.25	C	372.30	32	9	Refugees from Communist Cuba. Nonreligious/atheists 25%. D=RCC.
10497	0	10	0.00	5	99.70	0.30	C	332.15	0	9	Artificial(constructed) language, in 80 countries. Speakers in Spain: 123,000(none mother-tongue). Nonreligious 30%.
10498	0	0	12.25	1	99.96	0.04	C	473.04	267	10	Autonomous region of Extremadura. Educated speak Spanish. Most speakers over 30 years old. D=RCC.
10499	0	0	7.15	1	99.95	0.05	C	450.77	170	10	Northwest, Galicia Province, Extremadura. Nearly 100% literate. Related to Galician. D=RCC.
10500	1	10	0.75	8	99.84	0.16	C	493.62	29	10	Expatriates from France, in business. Nonreligious 13%. D=RCC. M=SJ,SDB,OFM,OP,FSC. M=FMB,&c.
10501	1	8	0.75	1	99.95	0.05	C	551.33	28	10	Northwest. Galicia Province. Some in Portugal. Many dialects. D=RCC(M-Santiago de Compostela & 4 Dioceses).
10502	4	10	0.75	8	99.86	0.14	C	517.93	31	10	Expatriates from Germany, in business. D=NAC,SDA,JWs,RCC. M=EKD,FMB,&c.
10503	1	10	0.82	7	99.90	0.10	C	528.88	31	10	Migrant workers from Greece. D=Spanish Greek Orthodox Ch(D-France).
10504	1	10	2.95	7	97.00	3.00	B	106.21	102	7	Long-time residents from China. Buddhists/Chinese folk-religionists 60%, nonreligious 10%. D=RCC.
10505	1	10	0.75	7	99.84	0.16	C	496.69	30	10	Expatriates from Italy. Staunch Catholics. D=RCC(20 Dioceses). M=SJ,OP,OFM,FSC.
10506	1	9	4.16	7	55.00	45.00	B	6.02	245	4	Residents from Japan, in commerce, finance. Buddhists 95%. D=RCC. M=Group of Supporters of Tezukas (Japan).
10507	0	10	0.75	8	55.30	44.70	B	0.60	71	3	7 communities of practicing Sefardic Jews. M=FMB.
10508	0	10	0.00	0	32.00	68.00	A	0.00	0	1.09	Refugees from Iraq, Iran, Turkey. Muslims 100%(Sunnis). M=network of agencies.
10509	1	10	0.75	8	99.93	0.07	C	553.30	22	10	Immigrants, refugees from 30 years of civil wars in Latin America. Nonreligious 7%. D=RCC.

Continued overleaf

Table 8-2 continued

PEOPLE		POPULATION				IDENTITY CODE		LANGUAGE		CHURCH		MINISTRY						SCRIPTURE		
Ref 1	Ethnic name 2	P% 3	In 1995 4	In 2000 5	In 2025 6	Race 7	Language 8	Autoglossonym 9	S 10	AC 11	Members 12	Jayuh 13-17	dwa xcmc mi 18	19	20	21	22	Biblioglossonym 23	Pub 24-26	ss 27
10510	Latin American White	0.10000	39,568	39,630	36,658	CLT27	51-AABB-h	south americano		90.00	35,667	4B.uh	10	9	14	5	1		pnb	b
10511	Levantine Arab	0.15000	59,352	59,445	54,987	CMT30	12-AACF-f	syro-palestinian		70.00	41,611	1Asuh	10	8	8	5	3	Arabic: Lebanese*	Pnb	b
10512	Maghrebi Arab	0.30000	118,704	118,889	109,975	CMT30	12-AACB-b	east maghrebi		0.21	250	2A.uh	5	4	4	1	1	Arabic: Algerian*	PNB	b
10513	Maghrebi Berber	0.16000	63,309	63,408	58,653	CMT32e	12-AACB-a	west maghrebi		0.10	63	1A.uh	5	4	3	3	0		pnb	b
10514	Marrano (Anusim)	0.59500	235,430	235,797	218,117	CMT35	51-AABB-c	general español		90.00	212,217	2B.uh	10	9	10	4	1	Spanish	PNB	b
10515	Portuguese	0.10000	39,568	39,630	36,658	CEW21g	51-AABA-e	general português		92.00	36,459	2Bsuh	10	9	15	5	1	Portuguese	PNB	b
10516	Russian	0.00200	791	793	733	CEW22j	53-AAAE-d	russkiy		75.00	594	4B.uh	10	8	8	4	1	Russian	PNB	b
10517	Spaniard	44.91000	17,770,034	17,797,732	16,463,239	CEW21k	51-AABB-c	general español		94.40	16,801,059	2B.uh	10	10	16	5	4	Spanish	PNB	b
10518	Spanish Gypsy (Gitano)	1.55000	613,306	614,262	568,204	CNN25f	59-AFAA-a	rodi		90.00	552,835	0B.uh	10	8	14	5	3	Calo	P..	b
10519	Spanish Jew	0.00200	791	793	733	CMT35	51-AAAB-d	djudezmo		0.13	1	0....	5	4	3	3	0	Spanish: Judaeo*	PNB	b
10520	USA White	0.06500	25,719	25,759	23,828	CEW19s	52-ABAC-s	general american		77.00	19,835	1Bsuh	10	9	13	5	2	English*	PNB	b
10521	Valencian	0.03000	11,870	11,889	10,997	CEW21k	51-AABE-d	valencià		96.00	11,413	1c..h	10	9	15	5	1		pnb	b
10522	Vlach Gypsy (Kalderash)	0.00250	989	991	916	CNN25f	59-ACBA-a	vlach-romani		79.98	792	1a...	10	8	11	5	1	Romani: Finnish*	PN.	b
10523	other minor peoples	0.10000	39,568	39,630	36,658	...				69.00	27,345		10	7	8	4	3			
	Spanish North Africa	**100.00000**	**128,491**	**130,000**	**140,000**					**80.25**	**104,324**									
10524	Maghrebi Arab	14.10000	18,117	18,330	19,740	CMT30	12-AACB-b	east maghrebi	30	0.20	37	2A.uh	5	4	7	4	2	Arabic: Algerian*	PNB	b
10525	Maghrebi Jewish	0.50000	642	650	700	CMT35	12-AACH-b	judeo-tunisian		0.05	0	0A...	4	3	2	0	0	Arabic: Judaeo-tunisian*	P..	b
10526	Riffian (Northern Shilha)	1.00000	1,285	1,300	1,400	CMT32e	10-AAAC-e	senhaja		0.20	3	1c...	5	3	6	0	0		pn.	b
10527	Spaniard (Andalusian)	84.20000	108,189	109,460	117,880	CEW21k	51-AABB-c	general español	99	95.20	104,206	2B.uh	10	10	12	5	3	Spanish	PNB	b
10528	other minor peoples	0.20000	257	260	280	...				30.00	78		9	5	7	1	0			
	Sri Lanka	**100.00000**	**17,919,983**	**18,827,054**	**23,546,757**					**9.32**	**1,755,118**									
10529	Arab	0.02000	3,584	3,765	4,709	CMT30	12-AACF-f	syro-palestinian		0.09	3	1Asuh	4	3	2	0	0	Arabic: Lebanese*	Pnb	b
10530	Bengali	0.10000	17,920	18,827	23,547	CNN25b	59-AAFT-e	west bengali		0.40	75	1Asuh	5	4	7	5	3	Bengali: Musalmani*	PNB	b
10531	British	0.05600	10,035	10,543	13,186	CEW19i	52-ABAC-b	standard-english	45	74.00	7,802	3Bsuh	10	9	13	5	3		PNB	b
10532	Burgher (Eurasian)	0.33700	60,390	63,447	79,353	CNN25z	52-ABAD-ag	sri-lankan-english		85.10	53,994	0B.uh	10	9	12	5	3		...	.
10533	Ceylon Moor	7.39000	1,324,287	1,391,319	1,740,105	CNN23c	49-EBEA-bn	north sri-lanka-tamil		0.00	0	1Asu.	0	2	2	3	3		pnb	b
10534	Ceylon Tamil	12.62000	2,261,502	2,375,974	2,971,601	CNN23c	49-EBEA-bn	north sri-lanka-tamil		33.00	784,071	1Asu.	9	7	12	5	2		pnb	b
10535	Han Chinese	0.01000	1,792	1,883	2,355	MSY42a	79-AAAB-ba	kuo-yü		4.00	75	2Bsuh	6	4	8	3	0	Chinese: Kuoyu*	PNB	b
10536	Hindi	0.20000	35,840	37,654	47,094	CNN25g	59-AAFO-e	general hindi		0.50	188	3Asuh	5	4	8	1	0		pnb	b
10537	Indian Moor	0.21300	38,170	40,102	50,155	CNN23c	49-EBEA-b	tamil		0.01	4	2Asu.	3	3	2	0	1	Tamil	PNB	b
10538	Indian Tamil	5.18000	928,255	975,241	1,219,722	CNN23c	49-EBEA-b	tamil		27.00	263,315	2Asu.	9	7	11	5	3	Tamil	PNB	b
10539	Indo-Portuguese Burgher	0.01800	3,226	3,389	4,238	CNN25z	51-AACA-g	indo-português	1	90.00	3,050	1c...	10	9	12	5	1	Indo-portuguese	PNb	b
10540	Japanese	0.02000	3,584	3,765	4,709	MSY45a	45-CAAA-a	koku-go		1.59	60	1B.uh	6	4	8	1	0	Japanese	PNB	b
10541	Malay Creole (Javar)	0.30600	54,835	57,611	72,053	MSY44k	51-AACA-h	malaio-português		0.02	12	1c...	3	4	2	5	3		Pnb	b
10542	Mappilla (Moplah)	0.02400	4,301	4,518	5,651	CNN23b	49-EBEB-a	malayalam		0.00	0	2Asu.	0	2	2	0	0	Malayalam	PNB	b
10543	Parsi	0.01200	2,150	2,259	2,826	CNN25m	58-AACC-a	parsi-i		0.00	0	1Asu.	0	3	3	0	0	Gujarati: Parsi	PNb	b
10544	Punjabi	0.50000	89,600	94,135	117,734	CNN25n	59-AAFE-c	general panjabi		0.50	471	1Asu.	5	4	3	1	0		PNB	b
10545	Sinhalese (Singhalese)	72.44200	12,981,594	13,638,694	17,057,742	CNN25q	59-ABBA-aa	standard sinhala		4.61	628,744	1asuh	6	7	8	5	4		pnb	b
10546	Telugu	0.30000	53,760	56,481	70,640	CNN23d	49-DBAB-a	telugu		8.00	4,518	2Asu.	7	5	8	5	3	Telugu	PNB	b
10547	USA White	0.02000	3,584	3,765	4,709	CEW19s	52-ABAC-s	general american		77.00	2,899	1Bsuh	10	9	13	5	3	English*	PNB	b
10548	Urdu	0.03000	5,376	5,648	7,064	CNN25r	59-AAFO-d	standard urdu		0.02	1	2Asuh	3	3	2	1	0	Urdu	PNB	b
10549	Veddah (Vedda, Beda)	0.00200	358	377	471	AUG07	59-ABBA-aa	standard sinhala		50.00	188	1asuh	10	7	6	1	0		pnb	b
10550	other minor peoples	0.20000	35,840	37,654	47,094	...				15.00	5,648		8	5	6	1	0			
	Sudan	**100.00000**	**26,617,234**	**29,489,719**	**46,264,179**					**16.53**	**4,874,383**									
10551	Acholi	0.15331	40,807	45,211	70,928	NAB62a	04-ACBA-b	acholi		89.00	40,238	4....	10	8	10	5	3	Acholi	PNB	b
10552	Afitti (Ditti, Unietti)	0.02129	5,667	6,278	9,850	NAB62m	05-GABA-d	dinik		0.00	0	0....	0	2	3	0	0		...	.
10553	Amhara	0.20000	53,234	58,979	92,528	CMT34a	12-ACBA-b	general amarinya		95.00	56,030	3Asuh	10	9	9	5	1	Amharic	PNB	b
10554	Amri	0.16424	43,716	48,434	75,984	CMT30	12-AACF-c	sudani		0.00	0	4Asuh	0	2	3	0	0	Arabic: Sudan	PNb	b
10555	Andang (Mima)	0.25726	68,475	75,865	119,019	NAB66d	05-CABA-a	simi-andang-ti		0.00	0	0....	0	3	0	0	0		...	b
10556	Anuak	0.20045	53,354	59,112	92,737	NAB62c	04-ABAB-a	adongo		12.50	7,389	0As..	8	5	8	5	2	Anuak	PN.	.
10557	Arab	3.00000	798,517	884,692	1,387,925	CMT30	12-AACF-c	sudani		6.00	53,081	4Asuh	7	5	9	2	3	Arabic: Sudan	PNb	b
10558	Arabized Burun	0.28000	74,528	82,571	129,540	NAB62y	12-AACF-c	sudani	58	0.01	8	4Asuh	3	2	3	0	0	Arabic: Sudan	PNb	b
10559	Arabized Dilling	0.15926	42,391	46,965	73,680	NAB62m	12-AACF-c	sudani		0.01	5	4Asuh	3	3	3	1	0	Arabic: Sudan	PNb	b
10560	Arabized Ghulfan	0.09462	25,185	27,903	43,775	NAB62m	12-AACF-c	sudani		0.00	0	4Asuh	0	3	3	1	0	Arabic: Sudan	PNb	b
10561	Arabized Kadaru	0.09469	25,204	27,924	43,808	NAB62m	12-AACF-c	sudani		0.00	0	4Asuh	0	3	3	0	0	Arabic: Sudan	PNb	b
10562	Arabized Kadugli (Miri)	0.46533	123,858	137,225	215,281	NAB66h	12-AACF-c	sudani		10.00	13,722	4Asuh	8	5	6	2	3	Arabic: Sudan	PNb	b
10563	Arabized Karko	0.05266	14,017	15,529	24,363	NAB62m	12-AACF-c	sudani		1.00	155	4Asuh	6	4	4	1	0	Arabic: Sudan	PNb	b
10564	Arabized Katla	0.02519	6,705	7,428	11,654	NAB66h	12-AACF-c	sudani		3.00	223	4Asuh	6	4	5	1	0	Arabic: Sudan	PNb	b
10565	Arabized Krongo	0.16694	44,435	49,230	77,233	NAB66h	12-AACF-c	sudani		2.00	985	4Asuh	6	4	6	4	1	Arabic: Sudan	PNb	b
10566	Arabized Lafofa	0.06340	16,875	18,696	29,331	NAB66h	12-AACF-c	sudani		2.00	374	4Asuh	6	4	5	1	0	Arabic: Sudan	PNb	b
10567	Arabized Mararit	0.21642	57,605	63,822	100,125	NAB66d	12-AACF-c	sudani		0.01	6	4Asuh	3	3	3	0	0	Arabic: Sudan	PNb	b
10568	Arabized Midob (Tidda)	0.18701	49,777	55,149	86,519	NAB62m	12-AACF-c	sudani		0.00	0	4Asuh	0	2	3	0	0	Arabic: Sudan	PNb	b
10569	Arabized Nyimang	0.13000	34,602	38,337	60,143	NAB62m	12-AACF-c	sudani		1.00	383	4Asuh	6	4	5	1	0	Arabic: Sudan	PNb	b
10570	Arabized Otoro	0.08486	22,587	25,025	39,260	NAB66h	12-AACF-c	sudani		37.70	9,434	4Asuh	9	6	9	2	1	Arabic: Sudan	PNb	b
10571	Arabized Shwai	0.05053	13,450	14,901	23,377	NAB66h	12-AACF-c	sudani		20.00	2,980	4Asuh	9	5	8	2	1	Arabic: Sudan	PNb	b
10572	Arabized Tagale (Taqali)	0.20639	54,935	60,864	95,485	NAB66h	12-AACF-c	sudani		0.01	6	4Asuh	3	3	4	0	0	Arabic: Sudan	PNb	b
10573	Arabized Talodi	0.06673	17,762	19,678	30,872	NAB66h	12-AACF-c	sudani		2.00	394	4Asuh	6	4	5	1	0	Arabic: Sudan	PNb	b
10574	Arabized Temein	0.08777	23,362	25,883	40,606	NAB62m	12-AACF-c	sudani		1.00	259	4Asuh	6	4	5	1	0	Arabic: Sudan	PNb	b
10575	Arabized Tira	0.27085	72,093	79,873	125,307	NAB66h	12-AACF-c	sudani		1.00	799	4Asuh	6	4	6	4	1	Arabic: Sudan	PNb	b
10576	Arabized Wali	0.10599	28,212	31,256	49,035	NAB62m	12-AACF-c	sudani		1.00	313	4Asuh	6	4	5	1	0	Arabic: Sudan	PNb	b
10577	Arabized Zaghawa	0.28566	76,035	84,240	132,158	NAB61	12-AACE-b	baggaari		0.00	0	0...h	0	2	3	0	0		pn.	b
10578	Armenian	0.00300	799	885	1,388	CEW14	57-AAAA-b	ashkharik		87.00	770	4A.u.	10	9	13	4	1	Armenian: Modern, Eastern	PNB	b
10579	Atwot	0.17495	46,567	51,592	80,939	NAB62n	04-AABB-a	thok-cieng		4.00	2,064	0....	6	4	6	2	0		...	.
10580	Avukaya	0.07614	20,266	22,453	35,226	NAB66g	03-BAAB-a	avokaya		60.00	13,472	0....	10	7	9	4	2	Avokaya	P..	b
10581	Awlad Hassan	0.26503	70,544	78,157	122,614	CMT30	12-AACF-c	sudani		0.02	16	4Asuh	3	3	3	0	0	Arabic: Sudan	PNb	b
10582	Awlad Mana	0.11348	30,205	33,465	52,501	NAB66d	02-CAAA-a	beri-aa		0.00	0	0....	0	2	0	0	0		...	b
10583	Bai	0.01749	4,655	5,158	8,092	NAB66z	93-ACBA-b	bai		10.00	516	0....	8	5	6	1	1		...	p
10584	Baka (Mbaka)	0.09383	24,975	27,670	43,410	NAB66e	03-ABAA-a	tara-baaka		60.00	16,602	0....	10	7	9	2	1	Baka	P..	b
10585	Banda	0.05016	13,351	14,792	23,206	NAB66b	93-ABAB-a	banda-ndele		60.00	8,875	0....	10	7	8	2	0	Banda, South Central	...	b
10586	Bari (Pojulu, Fajulu)	1.28329	341,576	378,439	593,704	NAB62e	04-BAAB-a	kutuk-na-bari	7	91.00	344,379	1.s..	10	8	12	5	3	Bari	PNB	.
10587	Batahin	0.53414	142,173	157,516	247,115	CMT30	12-AACE-b	baggaari		0.02	32	0...h	3	3	3	0	0		pn.	b
10588	Baya (Gbaya)	0.03000	7,985	8,847	13,879	NAB66c	93-AAAA-a	vehicular gbaya		27.00	2,389	0.s..	9	5	9	2	1	Gbaya: Gbea*	PNB	b
10589	Baygo	0.00483	1,286	1,424	2,235	NAB66d	12-AACF-c	sudani		0.00	0	4Asuh	0	3	0	0	0	Arabic: Sudan	PNb	b
10590	Bederia	1.99626	531,349	588,691	923,553	CMT30	12-AACE-b	baggaari		0.01	59	0...h	3	3	3	0	0		pn.	b
10591	Beja (Beni-Amer)	1.70000	452,493	501,325	786,491	CMT33z	13-AAAA-a	ti-bedaauye		0.01	50	0....	3	3	3	0	2		...	b
10592	Beja (Beni-Amer, Ababda)	3.07050	817,282	905,482	1,420,542	CMT33z	13-AAAA-a	ti-bedaauye	8	0.00	0	0....	0	3	3	0	2		...	b
10593	Belanda Bor	0.03891	10,357	11,474	18,001	NAB62y	04-ABCA-a	dhe-bor		10.00	1,147	0....	8	5	5	4	1	Belanda Bor	...	.
10594	Beli	0.03311	8,813	9,764	15,318	NAB66e	03-ADAA-a	jur-beli		30.00	2,929	0....	9	5	8	3	0	Jur Modo	P..	.
10595	Berti	0.68149	181,394	200,969	315,286	NAB61	02-CABA-a	berti		0.01	20	0....	3	2	3	0	0		...	.
10596	Bideyat (Beri)	0.02000	5,323	5,898	9,253	NAB61	02-CAAA-a	beri-aa		0.00	0	0....	0	2	0	0	0		...	b
10597	Birked (Bergid)	0.37612	100,113	110,917	174,009	NAB62m	05-FAEA-a	murgi		0.00	0	0....	0	2	0	0	0		...	.
10598	Bongo	0.03243	8,632	9,564	15,003	NAB66e	03-ABBA-a	bongo		45.00	4,304	0....	9	6	8	2	0		...	p
10599	Boya (Longarim, Narim)	0.03010	8,012	8,876	13,926	NAB62y	05-PAAA-a	doth-ki-larimo		25.00	2,219	0....	9	5	4	4	1		p..	.
10600	British	0.02000	5,323	5,898	9,253	CEW19i	52-ABAC-b	standard-english	11	78.00	4,600	3Bsuh	10	9	13	5	1		PNB	b
10601	Burun (Barun, Borun)	0.10540	28,055	31,082	48,762	NAB62z	04-AEAA-e	mabaan		0.00	0	0.s..	0	2	3	0	0	Mabaan	PN.	.
10602	Bviri (Belanda Viri)	0.11197	29,803	33,020	51,802	NAB66z	93-ACBA-a	b-viri		10.00	3,302	0....	8	5	7	4	2	Belanda Viri	...	.
10603	Central Dinka	0.10000	26,617	29,490	46,264	NAB62f	04-AAAD-bb	ciec		8.00	2,359	1....	7	5	12	2	3	Dinka: Ciec*	P..	.
10604	Central Koma (Komo)	0.05464	14,544	16,113	25,279	NAB62z	05-OBBA	koma cluster		5.00	806	0....	7	5	8	1	1		...	.
10605	Dair	0.00568	1,512	1,675	2,628	NAB62m	05-FACA-c	thaminyi-ni-be		0.00	0	0....	0	2	3	0	0		...	.
10606	Dar Fur Daju (Fininga)	0.46005	122,453	135,667	212,838	NAB66d	05-EAAC-b	fini		0.00	0	0....	0	3	0	0	0		...	.
10607	Dar Hamid	1.59700	425,077	470,951	738,839	CMT30	12-AACF-c	sudani		0.01	47	4Asuh	3	2	3	0	0	Arabic: Sudan	PNb	b
10608	Dar Sila Daju (Bokoruge)	0.16000	42,588	47,184	74,023	NAB66d	05-EAAB-a	bokor-u-ge		0.00	0	0....	0	3	3	0	0		...	b
10609	Dasenach (Reshiat)	0.01000	2,662	2,949	4,626	CMT33d	14-GACA-a	af-dasenach		5.00	147	0....	7	5	4	1	0	Daasanech	...	.
10610	Debri (Wei)	0.00462	1,230	1,362	2,137	NAB62m	05-FACA-e	debri		0.00	0	0....	0	3	3	0	0		...	.
10611	Didinga (Xaroxa,Toi)	0.32934	87,661	97,121	152,366	NAB62y	05-PAAA-b	doth-ki-didinga		10.00	9,712	0....	8	4	6	5	2	Didinga	P..	.
10612	Dilling (Delen)	0.02499	6,652	7,369	11,561	NAB62m	05-FACA-k	warki-m-be		0.10	7	0....	5	3	2	0	2		...	.
10613	Dongolese Nubian	0.73429	195,448	216,540	339,713	NAB62m	05-FABA-b	dongola	6	0.02	43	0....	3	3	3	0	0		p..	b
10614	Dongotono	0.02000	5,323	5,898	9,253	NAB62y	04-BBDA-a	ibalit-na-dongotono		30.00	1,769	0....	9	6	6	5	0		...	.
10615	Donyiro	0.03000	7,985	8,847	13,879	NAB62y	04-BDAA-c	aku-tuk-angi-nyangatom		5.00	442	0....	7	5	6	1	0		...	n
10616	Dubasiyin	0.22226	59,159	65,544	102,827	CMT30	12-AACE-b	baggaari		0.00	0	0...h	0	2	3	0	0		pn.	b
10617	Dukpu	0.02000	5,323	5,898	9,253	NAB66z	93-ABAF-d	dukpu		20.00	1,180	0....	9	5	7	2	0		...	.
10618	Eastern Nuer(Jikany Door)	3.24105	862,678	955,777	1,499,445	NAB62n	04-AABA-c	door-nyuong		21.00	200,713	4A...	9	5	8	5	2	Nuer: Eastern*	PN.	.
10619	Egyptian Arab	1.20000	319,407	353,877	555,170	CMT30	12-AACF-a	masri		19.00	67,237	2Asuh	8	5	11	5	2	Arabic*	PNB	b
10620	El Hugeirat	0.00568	1,512	1,675	2,628	NAB62m	12-AACD-a	hassaaniyya		0.00	0	0a...	0	3	2	0	0		pn.	b
10621	Eliri	0.01649	4,389	4,863	7,629	NAB66h	06-CAAD-a	nding		2.00	97	0....	6	4	3	0	0		...	.
10622	Erenga	0.16034	42,678	47,284	74,180	NAB66d	05-DAAA-g	erenga		0.00	0	0....	0	3	3	0	0		...	.
10623	Eurafrican	0.03000	7,985	8,847	13,879	NAN58	51-AACC-c	guadeloupéan	5	60.00	5,308	1cs..	10	7	13	5	1	Creole French: Lesser Antill	Pnb	b
10624	Falasha (Qimant, Kwara)	0.00500	1,331	1,474	2,313	CMT33a	14-BABA-c	kwara		10.00	147	0....	8	5	7	1	0	Kara: Falasha	P..	.
10625	Fedicca/Mohas Nubian	0.28957	77,076	85,393	133,967	NAB62m	05-FAAA	nobiin cluster	2	0.04	34	0....	3	3	3	0	0	Nobiin	P..	b
10626	Fertit	0.02561	6,817	7,552	11,848	NAB66z	12-AACE-b	baggaari		0.00	0	0...h	0	2	3	0	0		pn.	b
10627	Fezara	0.70000	186,321	206,428	323,849	CMT30	12-AACE-b	baggaari		0.01	21	0...h	3	3	3	0	0		pn.	b

Continued opposite

Table 8-2 continued

EVANGELIZATION								EVANGELISM			ADDITIONAL DESCRIPTIVE DATA
Ref 1	D 28	aC 29	CG% 30	r 31	E 32	U 33	W 34	e 35	R 36	T 37	Locations, civil divisions, literacy, religions, church history, denominations, dioceses, church growth, missions, agencies, ministries, movements 38
10510	1	10	0.75	8	99.90	0.10	C	528.88	27	10	Expatriates, immigrants, refugees from Central and South America. Nonreligious 10%. D=RCC.
10511	3	10	8.69	8	99.70	0.30	C	355.14	185	9	Refugees from Lebanon, Syria, Palestine, Jordan. Muslims 30%. D=RCC(Maronites),GOC,SOC.
10512	0	10	3.27	8	50.21	49.79	B	0.38	217	3	Migrant laborers from Morocco. Muslims 100% (Maliki Sunnis,some Ahmadis). M=OM.
10513	0	10	4.23	7	47.10	52.90	A	0.17	294	3	Arabized Berbers from Morocco. Immigrant laborers, professionals. Muslim 99%.
10514	1	10	0.75	8	99.90	0.10	C	519.03	25	10	New Christians, Conversos, Crypto-Jews. Descendants of Jews forcibly baptized from 1492 on. Nonreligious 10%. D=RCC.
10515	1	10	0.75	8	99.92	0.08	C	570.86	29	10	Emigres and residents from Portugal, in all professions. Nonreligious 7%. D=RCC. M=GST(Japan).
10516	1	10	0.72	7	99.75	0.25	C	391.46	14	9	Refugees from USSR since 1917. Nonreligious 20%. D=Spanish Greek Orthodox Ch(D-France).
10517	7	9	0.45	8	99.94	0.06	C	611.24	21	10	2,000 Baha'is, 1,000 Muslims. D=RCC(64 Dioceses),JWs,IEH,UEBE,IEE,SDA,FIEIDE. M=SJ,SDB,OFM,CMF,OP,SP,OFMCap,AA,OCD,SMI,FSC,PFM,CMML,.
10518	4	10	0.75	8	99.90	0.10	C	512.46	31	10	Massive Christian movement. D=nomadic caravan churches,IEF(MSG/GEM; mass charismatic movement)/Philadelphia Ch,RCC. M=GGMS,GST(Japan),FMB.
10519	0	10	0.00	8	46.13	53.87	A	0.21	41	3	Ladino is the main language of Sefardic Jewry. Many Jewish communities.
10520	5	10	2.61	8	99.77	0.23	C	427.19	63	10	Expatriates from USA, in business or military. Nonreligious 6%. D=CJCLdS,SDA,JWs,CCS,CC. M=FMB,&c.
10521	1	10	0.75	1	99.96	0.04	C	550.12	29	10	Valencia. Close to Catolan than to Castilian. D=RCC.
10522	2	10	0.72	6	99.80	0.20	C	402.80	35	10	Nomadic, semi-nomadic Gypsies. In 25 countries. Caravan churches. Nonreligious 9%. D=IEF(GEM/MSG),RCC. M=GGMS.
10523	0	10	0.75		99.69	0.31	C	266.96	19	8	Dutch, Belgians, Swiss(Reformed Chs of Barcelona), Koreans(M=BFMGAP), Filipinos, Quingui(non-Gypsy urban nomads). Nonreligious 23%, Buddhists 4%.
Spanish North Africa											
10524	1	10	2.54	8	61.20	38.80	B	0.44	145	3	Moroccan Arabs. Muslims 99%(Maliki Sunnis), Baha'is. D=RCC(D-Cadiz,D-Malaga). M=AA,OFMCap.
10525	0	10	0.00	7	36.05	63.95	A	0.06	0	2	Sefardis, in practicing Jewish communities in Ceuta and Melilla.
10526	0	10	1.10	1	34.20	65.80	A	0.25	155	3	Berbers from Northern Morocco. Muslims 97%(Maliki Sunnis), some Baha'is.
10527	5	7	1.64	8	99.95	0.05	C	591.41	41	10	In government, business. Some Baha'is. Nonreligious 4%. D=RCC(D-Cadiz,D-Malaga),UEBE,SDA,IDE,CC. M=AA,OFMCap,FSC,FMB.
10528	0	10	1.73		57.00	43.00	B	62.41	83	6	Other Arabs, other Berbers, other Africans, other Europeans. Muslims 60%, Nonreligious 10%.
Sri Lanka											
10529	0	7	1.10	8	39.09	60.91	A	0.12	126	3	First Muslim Arab traders arrived AD c750. Now from many Arab countries. Muslims 100%(Sunnis).
10530	3	9	4.41	6	60.40	39.60	B	0.88	262	3	Migrants from India. Hindus 75%, Muslims 23%(Hanafi Sunnis), many Baha'is. D=RCC,CNI,MCSA.
10531	5	10	0.14	8	99.74	0.26	C	402.44	24	10	Expatriates from Britain, in development. Nonreligious 13%. D=Ch of Ceylon(D-Colombo,D-Kurunagala),MCC,SLBU,SA,JWs.
10532	6	10	8.97	8	99.85	0.15	C	453.80	187	10	Dutch/Portuguese/Asian mixed-race persons. D=Ch of Ceylon,Presbytery of Ceylon(DRC),SA,RCC,SDA,JWs. M=CMS,SJ,OMI.
10533	0	7	0.00	6	38.00	62.00	A	0.00	0	1.13	Citizens. Muslims 100%(Shafi Sunnis,some Ahmadis). M=Ch of Ceylon,MCC,NLC,ICFG,SDA,JWs,SA,FI. R=FEBA,VERITAS,AWR.
10534	10	8	2.31	6	97.00	3.00	B	116.83	93	7	In north. Citizens. Hindus 60%(Shaivites), Muslims 5%(Hanafi Sunnis). D=RCC,SLBU,MCC,Ch of Ceylon,CSI,CPM,JWs,SA,UPC,SDA. M=JLEM,LBI. R=FEBA.
10535	0	8	4.41	7	60.00	40.00	B	8.76	231	4	Long-time settlers from China. Buddhists 50% (Mahayana and Theravada), Chinese folk-religionists 40%, nonreligious 6%.
10536	0	9	2.98	7	50.50	49.50	B	0.92	216	3	Traders from India. Hindus 95%, many Baha'is.
10537	0	7	1.40	6	41.01	58.99	A	0.01	160	2	Labbais. Much repatriation to India over several decades. Muslims 100%(Shafi Sunnis; some Shias, Bohras, also Ahmadis). M=FI.
10538	10	8	2.61	6	96.00	4.00	B	94.60	103	6	Treated as aliens. Hindus 65%(Shaivites), Muslims 5%(Hanafi Sunnis), Baha'is. D=RCC,CSI,ICFG,MCC,DRC,AoG,JWs,Ch of Ceylon,CPM,SDA. M=FFFM,OMI,SJ.
10539	2	10	1.28	1	99.90	0.10	C	469.75	44	10	Batticaloa District. Extinct in India. Mixed-race. All fluent in Tamil, some in English, some in Sinhalese. D=RCC(8 Dioceses),DRC. M=WMM.
10540	0	10	4.18	7	55.59	44.41	B	3.22	243	4	Settlers, expatriates from Japan, in commerce. Buddhists 57%, New-Religionists 24%, nonreligious 13%.
10541	6	7	2.52	8	41.02	58.98	A	0.03	215	2	Bilinguals in Tamil. In cities: Colombo, Kandy, Badulla, Hambantota. Muslims 100%(Shafi Sunnis). D=Ch of Ceylon,MCC,RCC,NLC,ICFG,SA.
10542	0	7	0.00	4	35.00	65.00	A	0.00	0	1.12	Indian Moors (Hindu-Arabs) who speak Malayalam. Muslims 100%(Shafi Sunnis).
10543	0	7	0.00	4	32.00	68.00	A	0.00	0	1.12	All Zoroastrians(Parsees), originally from India(Bombay) and Persia.
10544	0	9	3.93	5	44.50	55.50	A	0.81	307	3	Emigres from India, Pakistan. Sikhs 50%, Hindus 30%, Muslims 18%, Baha'is.
10545	9	7	0.85	6	59.61	40.39	B	10.03	66	5	Theravada Buddhists 94%(6,000 temples; 17,000 bhikkus(monks); 14,000 novices). D=RCC,SLBU,MCC,SA,Ch of Ceylon,JWs,SDA,DRC,CPM. M=FFFM,SJ,OMI.
10546	4	9	2.15	5	71.00	29.00	B	20.73	122	5	From South India. Hindus 84%(Shaivites), Muslims 5%, many Baha'is. D=AoG,JWs,RCC,SA.
10547	4	10	1.45	8	99.77	0.23	C	421.57	43	10	Expatriates from USA, in development. D=Ch of Ceylon(D-Colombo,D-Kurunagala),SDA,JWs,SA.
10548	0	9	-3.91	5	43.02	56.98	A	0.03	6	2	From North India, Pakistan. Muslims 100%(Hanafi Sunnis). Muslim foreign missions organized.
10549	0	8	2.98	6	95.00	5.00	B	173.37	115	7	Badulla, Polonnaruwa Districts. Aboriginals in Eastern mountains and forests. Veddah language rarely used. Animists 50%, few Buddhists.
10550	0	7	6.54		36.00	64.00	A	19.71	498	5	Germans (NAC,SLLCC), Malays, Indonesians, other Europeans, other Asians, Africans. Buddhists 78%, Nonreligious 5%.
Sudan											
10551	4	6	8.65	1	99.89	0.11	C	484.02	187	10	Opari District. Most in Uganda. Animists 10%. D=AIC,RCC,CER/Strivers,other small AICs. M=CMS,AIM,FSCJ,Norwegian Church Aid.
10552	0	5	0.00	0	11.00	89.00	A	0.00	0	1.03	Nuba Hills, eastern Jebel ed Dair. Main center, Sidra. Related to Nyimang. Muslims 100%(Maliki Sunnis).
10553	1	9	9.01	5	99.95	0.05	C	561.73	184	10	Refugees from Ethiopia. D=Ethiopian Orthodox Ch. M=SIM.
10554	0	4	0.00	7	34.00	66.00	A	0.00	0	1.13	Muslims 100%(Maliki Sunnis).
10555	0	2	0.00	0	5.00	95.00	A	0.00	0	1.03	Darfur and Kordofan Province. Also in Chad (Mimi). Muslims 100%(Sunnis). Teachers, craftsmen, traders.
10556	3	6	6.83	0	58.50	41.50	B	26.69	320	5	Upper Nile Province. Most now in Ethiopia. Animists 87%, Muslims 1%, highly resistant to Islam. D=RCC(D-Malakal),Sudanese Ch of Christ,ELC in Ethiopia.
10557	4	6	8.96	7	68.00	32.00	B	14.89	389	5	Literate Arabs, speaking Modern Standard Arabic, language used for education and official purposes (unintelligible to illiterate Sudanese Arabs). Muslims 89%.
10558	0	4	2.10	7	37.01	62.99	A	0.01	261	2	Northern Sudan, southeast of Renk. Arabic-speaking Burun. Muslims 100%(Sunnis).
10559	0	3	1.62	7	37.01	62.99	A	0.01	224	2	Around Dilling town, Kordofan Province. Muslims 100%(Sunnis).
10560	0	4	0.00	7	35.00	65.00	A	0.00	0	1.14	In Kordofan, south of Dilling town. Arabic-speaking Ghulfan. Muslims 100%(Sunnis).
10561	0	3	0.00	7	33.00	67.00	A	0.00	0	1.13	Nuba Mountains, Kadaru Hills. Arabic-speaking Kadaru. Muslims 100%(Sunnis).
10562	3	6	7.49	7	67.00	33.00	B	24.45	365	5	Kadugli village, south of Nuba Hills. Includes Miri people. Arabic-speaking Kadugli. Muslims 90%(Sunnis). D=RCC,PECS,CCNM.
10563	0	6	2.78	7	45.00	55.00	A	1.64	255	4	Karko Hills, Kordofan Province. Arabic-speaking Karko. Muslims 99%(Sunnis).
10564	0	6	3.15	7	48.00	52.00	A	5.25	261	4	Katla Hills, Nuba Hills, Kordofan Province. Arabic-speaking Katla. Muslims 97%(Sunnis).
10565	1	6	4.70	7	55.00	45.00	B	4.01	305	4	Krongo Hills, Kordofan Province. Arabic-speaking Krongo. Animists 70%, Muslims 28%(Sunnis). D=Sudanese Ch of Christ. M=SUM.
10566	0	6	3.69	7	47.00	53.00	A	3.43	298	4	Northern Sudan, central Eliri range, Kordofan Province. Arabic-speaking Lafofa. Muslims 98%(Sunnis).
10567	0	4	1.81	7	37.01	62.99	A	0.01	267	2	Abu Sharib. Arabic-speaking Mararit, near border with Chad. Muslims 100%(Sunnis).
10568	0	3	0.00	7	33.00	67.00	A	0.00	0	1.13	Darfur Province, Dar Meidob. Arabized Midob. 100% strict Muslims(Maliki Sunnis).
10569	0	6	3.71	7	47.00	53.00	A	1.71	298	4	Northern Sudan, northwest of Dilling. Arabic-speaking Nyimang. Muslims 99%(Sunnis).
10570	1	6	7.09	7	95.70	4.30	B	131.68	244	7	Otoro Hills, Kordofan Province. Arabic-speaking Otoro. Muslims 60%(Sunnis), Animists 2%. D=Ch of Christ in the Nuba Mountains(SCOC). M=SUM.
10571	1	7	5.86	7	76.00	24.00	B	55.48	263	6	Kordofan Province, villages in Shwai Hills. Arabic-speaking Shwai. Muslims 80%(Sunnis), some animists. D=SCOC.
10572	0	5	1.81	7	39.01	60.99	A	0.01	228	2	Nuba Hills, Tegali Range. Arabic-speaking Tegali. Muslims 100%(Sunnis).
10573	0	6	3.74	7	47.00	53.00	A	3.43	301	4	Nuba Hills, around Talodi town. Arabic-speaking Talodi. Muslims 95%(Sunnis), Animists 3%.
10574	0	6	3.31	7	46.00	54.00	A	1.67	281	4	Northern Sudan, Nuba Hills, Temein Hills southwest of Dilling. Arabic-speaking Temein. Muslims 99%(Sunnis).
10575	1	6	4.48	7	52.00	48.00	B	1.89	311	4	Northern Sudan, Nuba Hills near Otoro. Arabic-speaking Tira. Muslims 99%(Sunnis). D=SCOC. M=SUM.
10576	0	6	3.50	7	46.00	54.00	A	1.67	292	4	Northern Sudan, Wali Hills. Arabic-speaking Wali. Muslims 99%(Sunnis).
10577	0	4	0.00	7	21.00	79.00	A	0.00	0	1.08	Arabic-speaking Zaghawa. In Darfur; also in Chad and Libya. Muslims 95%(Sunnis), animists 5%.
10578	1	10	4.44	6	99.87	0.13	C	495.37	89	10	In North. In business. Gregorians. Nonreligious 11%. D=Armenian Apostolic Ch(D-Egypt).
10579	0	6	5.47	0	28.00	72.00	A	4.08	675	4	Lakes District. Nomads. Culturally similar to Dinka. Animists 95%.
10580	2	6	7.47	0	99.60	0.40	C	223.38	246	8	Western Equatorial Province; also in Zaire. Bilingual in Baka, Mundu, Zande. Animists 40%. D=RCC,PECS. M=SIL,FSCJ.
10581	0	4	2.81	7	37.02	62.98	A	0.02	260	2	Bedouin, tent-dwellers. Muslims 100%(Sunnis).
10582	0	2	0.00	0	5.00	95.00	A	0.00	0	1.03	Linked to Zaghawa in northwest Darfur. Muslims 75%, animists 25%.
10583	1	6	4.02	0	37.00	63.00	A	13.50	404	5	Southern Sudan, Western District, 2 villages north of Tembura. Bilingual in Ndogo. Animists 70%, Muslims 20%. D=RCC.
10584	1	6	7.70	0	98.00	2.00	C	214.62	255	8	Western Equatorial Province; a few in Zaire. Bilingual in Zande, Avokaya, Mundu. Animists 40%. D=PECS. M=SIL.
10585	0	7	7.02	0	93.00	7.00	C	203.67	261	8	Most in Central African Republic; use Pidgin Arabic as lingua franca. Many dialects. Animists 21%, Muslims 20%(Sunnis).
10586	3	7	11.01	0	99.91	0.09	C	491.58	230	10	Both banks of White Nile near Uganda border. Animists 9%. D=PECS(strong Anglican work, especially through East African Revival),RCC,a few small AICs.
10587	0	4	3.53	7	24.02	75.98	A	0.01	483	2	Baggara(Negroid Bedouins). Camel nomads occupying the island of Meroe. Muslims 100%(Maliki Sunnis).
10588	1	7	5.63	4	75.00	25.00	B	73.91	273	6	Immigrants from Central African Republic. Animists 53%, Muslims 20%. D=RCC.
10589	0	2	0.00	7	29.00	71.00	A	0.00	0	1.12	Southern Darfur. Baygo language now extinct. Muslims 100%(Maliki Sunnis).
10590	0	4	4.16	7	24.01	75.99	A	0.00	555	1.09	Baggara(mixed-race Negroid Bedouins). Semi-nomadic tent-dwellers in Kordofan. Muslims 100%(Maliki Sunnis).
10591	0	4	3.99	7	25.01	74.99	A	0.00	645	1.06	Languages: Arabic and Tigre. Beja are also found in Ethiopia, Egypt. Muslims 100%(Sunnis,mainly Khatmiyya Sufis). M=RSMT,CSI.
10592	0	4	0.00	7	19.00	81.00	A	0.00	0	1.05	Also in Eritrea. 3% urban, 97% pastoralist nomads. Tribes: Bisharin, Hadendowa, Amarar, Ababda, Beni Amer. Muslims 100%(weak Sunnis practicing folk Islam).
10593	1	6	4.86	0	39.00	61.00	A	14.23	442	5	South of Wau. Most are bilingual in Belanda Viri. Animists 85%, Muslims 5%. D=RCC. M=SIL.
10594	0	6	5.84	0	61.00	39.00	B	66.79	327	6	Southwest of Rumbek. Intermingled with Dinkas. Animists 60%.
10595	0	3	3.04	7	19.01	80.99	A	0.00	640	1.05	Saharan Negroes. In Darfur. Berti language now extinct. Muslims 100%(Maliki Sunnis; a few Sufis in Tijaniyya).
10596	0	2	0.00	0	5.00	95.00	A	0.00	0	1.03	Saharan Negroes. Majority in Chad. Related to Zaghawa. Nomadic camel-breeders. Muslims 100%(Maliki Sunnis).
10597	0	2	0.00	0	5.00	95.00	A	0.00	0	1.02	In North Darfur. Birgid language now extinct. Muslims 100%(Maliki Sunnis).
10598	0	6	6.25	0	75.00	25.00	B	123.18	281	7	Scattered pockets near Tambio. Now speak Mundu, Avukaya. Animists 45%, Muslims 10%(Sunnis).
10599	1	6	5.55	0	55.00	45.00	B	50.18	348	6	Boya Hills, north of the Didinga, Southern Sudan. Close to Murle, Didinga. Animists 75%. D=RCC.
10600	1	10	1.50	8	99.78	0.22	C	427.05	48	10	Expatriates from Britain, in development. Nonreligious 9%. D=PECS(4 Dioceses). M=CMS.
10601	0	4	0.00	0	15.00	85.00	A	0.00	0	1.06	Northern Sudan, south of Tabi tribe, southeast of Renk. Related to Maban. Muslims 100%(Sunnis).
10602	1	6	5.97	0	42.00	58.00	A	15.33	483	5	In southwest, around Raffili near Bor. Some bilinguals in Belanda Bor. Animists 90%. D=RCC(D-Wau). M=SIL,FSCJ.
10603	3	6	5.62	0	47.00	53.00	A	13.72	411	5	Southeast Bahr al Ghazal. Nomadic animists 92%, highly resistant to Islam. Strong churches. D=RCC,PECS,AICs.
10604	1	6	4.49	0	32.00	68.00	A	5.84	513	4	Northern Sudan, Daga river around Daga Post. Also in Ethiopia. Animists 95%. Resistant to Islam. D=CECS. M=SIM.
10605	0	4	0.00	0	10.00	90.00	A	0.00	0	1.03	Northern Sudan, Jebel Dair, Kordofan. Muslims 100%(Sunnis).
10606	0	2	0.00	0	5.00	95.00	A	0.00	0	1.02	Northeast of Nyala, Darfur Province. Muslims 100%(Maliki Sunnis).
10607	0	4	3.93	7	37.01	62.99	A	0.01	343	2	Tent-dwelling. Bedouin. Muslims 100%(Sunnis).
10608	0	4	0.00	0	10.00	90.00	A	0.00	0	1.04	Also in Chad, though most have immigrated into Sudan(Darfur Province). Muslims 100%(Maliki Sunnis).
10609	0	6	2.72	0	26.00	74.00	A	4.74	487	4	Also in Kenya. Animists 95%.
10610	0	3	0.00	0	9.00	91.00	A	0.00	0	1.03	Kordofan Province, Nuba Mountains. Muslims 100%(Sunnis).
10611	2	6	7.12	0	44.00	56.00	A	16.06	532	5	In Didinga Hills. Animists 90%, resistant to Islam and Christianity. D=AIC,RCC. M=Norwegian Church Aid,SIL.
10612	2	5	1.96	0	19.10	80.90	A	0.07	482	2	Northern Sudan, town of Dilling, Kordofan Province. Most Dilling no longer speak the language. Muslims 99%(Maliki Sunnis). D=PECS,RCC.
10613	0	5	3.83	0	18.02	81.98	A	0.01	795	2	Dongolawis. Ethnic consciousness rapidly increasing among adults. Muslims 100%(Sunnis).
10614	0	7	5.31	0	61.00	39.00	B	66.79	303	6	Eastern Equatoria Province, hills southeast of Torit. Close to Otuho language. Animists 70%.
10615	0	6	3.86	1	30.00	70.00	A	5.47	483	4	Also in Kenya, Ethiopia. Close to Turkana. Animists 95%.
10616	0	4	0.00	7	21.00	79.00	A	0.00	0	1.08	Bedouin, tent-dwellers. Muslims 100%(Sunnis).
10617	0	7	4.89	0	49.00	51.00	A	35.77	353	5	In south. Also in CAR. Related to Banda. Animists 60%, Muslims 20% (Sunnis).
10618	5	6	10.41	0	72.00	28.00	B	55.18	451	6	Nomadic animists 79%, highly resistant to Islam. D=RCC(D-Malakal),CCUN,COC,ECMY,CB. M=FSCJ,APM.
10619	4	8	4.24	8	90.00	10.00	B	62.41	150	6	Sudanese Arabs of Egyptian origin; and expatriates. Muslims 79%(Sunnis). D=COC,Injili Ch(ECS),RCC,GOC. M=PCUSA,FSCJ.
10620	0	3	0.00	7	22.00	78.00	A	0.00	0	1.08	El Hugeirat Hills, West Kordofan. Muslims 100%(Sunnis).
10621	0	6	4.68	0	20.00	80.00	A	1.46	837	4	Southern Eliri range, Northern Sudan. Muslims 98%(Maliki Sunnis).
10622	0	4	0.00	0	10.00	90.00	A	0.00	0	1.03	On border with Chad. Agriculture, animal husbandry. Muslims 100%(Sunnis).
10623	2	10	6.48	8	99.60	0.40	C	267.18	170	8	Mixed-race Europeans/Africans. Muslims 20%. D=RCC,PECS. M=FSCJ.
10624	0	8	2.72	0	38.00	62.00	A	13.87	333	5	Refugees from Ethiopia civil war. Mostly traditionally Jewish, though unable to join most Falashas in Israel.
10625	0	5	3.59	0	18.04	81.96	A	0.02	758	2	Strong Christian past until total extinction under Islam by AD 1499. Ethnic consciousness increasing among adults. Muslims 100%(Sunnis).
10626	0	4	0.00	7	21.00	79.00	A	0.00	0	1.08	Mixed-race Baggara(Negroid Bedouin). Former escaped Negro slaves in Dar Fertit region. Sedentary tillers. Muslims 100%(Sunnis).
10627	0	4	3.09	7	24.01	75.99	A	0.00	433	1.09	Baggara(Negroid Bedouins). In northern Kordofan. Cattle/camel/sheep nomads; tent-dwellers. Muslims 100%(Sunnis).

Continued overleaf

Table 8-2 continued

PEOPLE		POPULATION				IDENTITY CODE		LANGUAGE		CHURCH		MINISTRY						SCRIPTURE		
Ref 1	Ethnic name 2	P% 3	In 1995 4	In 2000 5	In 2025 6	Race 7	Language 8	Autoglossonym 9	S 10	AC 11	Members 12	Jayuh 13-17	d 18	wa 19	xc 20	mc 21	mi 22	Biblioglossonym 23	Pub 24-26	ss 27
10628	Fongoro (Gelege)	0.00495	1,318	1,460	2,290	NAB66z	03-AACB-a	gele		0.00	0	0....	0	3	2	0	0		...	.
10629	French	0.00300	799	885	1,388	CEW21b	51-AABI-a	historical français	2	84.00	743	1B.uh	10	9	14	5	1		pnb	b
10630	Fulani (Sudanese Fula)	0.45147	120,169	133,137	208,869	NAB56c	90-BAAA-s	fula-fellata		0.01	13	1cs..	3	3	3	0	0	Fulfulde, Adamawa	PNB	b
10631	Fungor (Kau, Nyaro)	0.01260	3,354	3,716	5,829	NAB66h	06-BBBA-a	kraw-ka-iro		0.00	0	0....	0	0	2	0	0		...	.
10632	Fur (Furawi)	2.43167	647,243	717,093	1,124,992	NAB66d	05-CAAA-a	bele-for		0.00	0	0....	0	3	4	0	3		...	b
10633	Gaaliin	6.69377	1,781,696	1,973,974	3,096,818	CMT30	12-AACF-c	sudani	77	7.40	146,074	4Asuh	7	4	10	5	1	Arabic: Sudan	PNb	b
10634	Gawamaa	2.06574	549,843	609,181	955,698	CMT30	12-AACE-b	baggaari		0.01	61	0...h	3	3	3	0	0		pn.	b
10635	Gberi (Gweri, Gbara)	0.00351	934	1,035	1,624	NAB66e	03-ACBA-a	mo'da		10.00	104	0....	8	5	4	1	0		...	.
10636	Ghulfan (Gulfan)	0.07551	20,099	22,268	34,934	NAB62m	05-FACA-d	wunci-m-be		0.00	0	0....	0	3	3	0	0		...	.
10637	Gimma	0.34262	91,196	101,038	158,510	CMT30	12-AACF-c	sudani		0.02	20	4Asuh	3	3	3	0	0	Arabic: Sudan	PNb	b
10638	Greek	0.03705	9,862	10,926	17,141	CEW20	56-AAAA-c	dhimotiki		95.00	10,380	2B.uh	10	9	10	5	2	Greek: Modern	PNB	b
10639	Guhayna	3.10408	826,220	915,384	1,436,077	CMT30	12-AACF-c	sudani		0.00	0	4Asuh	0	3	3	0	0	Arabic: Sudan	PNb	b
10640	Gule (Fung, Hameg)	0.06120	16,290	18,048	28,314	NAB62z	12-AACF-c	sudani		1.00	180	4Asuh	6	4	4	1	0	Arabic: Sudan	PNb	b
10641	Gulud	0.06649	17,698	19,608	30,761	NAB62m	12-AACF-c	sudani		0.50	98	4Asuh	5	4	3	0	0	Arabic: Sudan	PNb	b
10642	Gumuz (Debatsa, Deguba)	0.18333	48,797	54,064	84,816	NAB62z	05-LAAA-a	dakunza		0.01	5	0....	3	3	4	0	0	Gumuz	...	.
10643	Habbania (Baggara)	0.74049	197,098	218,368	342,582	CMT30	12-AACE-b	baggaari		0.01	22	0...h	3	3	3	0	0		pn.	b
10644	Hamar	0.90101	239,824	265,705	416,845	CMT30	12-AACE-b	baggaari		0.02	53	0...h	3	4	3	0	0		pn.	b
10645	Hasania	1.57514	419,259	464,504	728,726	CMT30	12-AACF-c	sudani		1.40	6,503	4Asuh	6	4	6	2	0	Arabic: Sudan	PNb	b
10646	Hausa Fulani (Fellata)	1.65955	441,726	489,397	767,777	NAB60a	19-HAAB-a	hausa		0.01	49	4Asu.	3	3	2	0	0	Hausa	PNB	b
10647	Hawawir	0.51370	136,733	151,489	237,659	CMT30	12-AACF-c	sudani		0.01	15	4Asuh	3	2	3	0	0	Arabic: Sudan	PNb	b
10648	Heiban Nuba	0.02071	5,512	6,107	9,581	NAB66h	06-BACB-a	dhu-nguna-dha-eebang		70.00	4,275	0As..	10	7	9	5	2	Nuba: Heiban*	PN.	.
10649	Homa	0.01000	2,662	2,949	4,626	NAB57c	93-BAAA-a	pa-zande		30.00	885	4As..	9	5	6	2	3	Pazande*	PNB	b
10650	Husseinat (Husaynat)	0.34055	90,645	100,427	157,553	CMT30	12-AACF-c	sudani		0.00	0	4Asuh	0	2	3	0	0	Arabic: Sudan	PNb	b
10651	Indo-Pakistani	0.02200	5,856	6,488	10,178	CNN25g	59-AAFO-e	general hindi		0.09	6	3Asuh	4	3	4	0	0		pnb	b
10652	Indri	0.00312	830	920	1,443	NAB66z	93-ACCA-b	indri		20.00	184	0....	9	5	6	0	0		...	b
10653	Ingessana (Tabi, Metabi)	0.10000	26,617	29,490	46,264	NAB62z	05-MBAA-a	kor-e-gaam		0.50	147	0....	5	3	3	1	1		...	.
10654	Italian	0.01000	2,662	2,949	4,626	CEW21e	51-AABQ-c	standard italiano		83.00	2,448	2B.uh	10	9	15	5	1	Italian	PNB	b
10655	Jewish	0.00009	24	27	42	CMT35	12-AACF-c	sudani		0.00	0	4Asuh	0	3	2	0	0	Arabic: Sudan	PNb	b
10656	Jumjum (Wadega)	0.16214	43,157	47,815	75,013	NAB62z	04-AEAA-c	jumjum		2.00	956	0.s..	6	4	5	4	1		pn.	.
10657	Jur Modo	0.07725	20,562	22,781	35,739	NAB62y	03-ADAA-a	jur-beli		10.00	2,278	0....	8	5	6	1	1	Jur Modo	P..	.
10658	Kababish	0.83072	221,115	244,977	384,326	CMT30	12-AACF-c	sudani		0.01	24	4Asuh	3	3	3	0	0	Arabic: Sudan	PNb	b
10659	Kadaru (Kodhin)	0.03975	10,580	11,722	18,390	NAB62m	05-FACA-b	kodin-ni-ai		0.00	0	0....	0	3	3	0	0		...	.
10660	Kadugli (Katcha)	0.26702	71,073	78,743	123,535	NAB66h	05-IAAA	dhalla-miri cluster		10.00	7,874	0....	8	5	8	5	1		...	.
10661	Kakwa (Sudan Kakwa)	0.22713	60,456	66,980	105,080	NAB62y	04-BAAC-a	kakwa		58.00	38,848	0....	10	7	10	5	2	Kakwa*	PNB	.
10662	Kaligi (Feroge)	0.04013	10,681	11,834	18,566	NAB66z	93-ACCB-b	kali-gi		20.00	2,367	0....	9	5	6	3	0		...	p
10663	Kaliko	0.03975	10,580	11,722	18,390	NAB66e	03-BAAD-a	keliko-madi		20.00	2,344	0....	9	5	7	3	1	Kaliko	...	.
10664	Kanga (Abu Sinun)	0.03266	8,693	9,631	15,110	NAB66h	05-IAAB-a	kufo		1.00	96	0....	6	4	4	1	0		...	.
10665	Kara (Yulu, Gula)	0.00475	1,264	1,401	2,198	NAB66z	93-AAAA-ko	kara		20.00	280	0.s..	9	5	8	1	0		pnb	b
10666	Karko (Garko)	0.06097	16,229	17,980	28,207	NAB62m	05-FACA-g	kithoniri-she		1.00	180	0....	6	4	3	0	0		...	.
10667	Katla (Akalak)	0.06670	17,754	19,670	30,858	NAB66h	06-AAAA	katla cluster		3.00	590	0....	6	4	5	0	0		...	.
10668	Kawahla	2.05735	547,610	606,707	951,816	CMT30	12-AACE-b	baggaari		0.01	61	0...h	3	3	3	0	0		pn.	b
10669	Keiga	0.02851	7,589	8,408	13,190	NAB66h	05-HABA-b	proper jirru		1.00	84	0....	6	4	4	1	0		...	.
10670	Keiga Jirru	0.00980	2,608	2,890	4,534	NAB62m	05-HABA-a	proper jirru		0.00	0	0....	0	2	3	0	0		...	.
10671	Kenuzi Nubian	0.10000	26,617	29,490	46,264	NAB62m	05-FABA-a	kenuz	6	0.08	24	0....	4	3	3	0	0	Nubian: Kunuzi*	P..	b
10672	Kenuzi-Dongolese Nubian	0.75946	202,147	223,963	351,358	NAB62m	12-AACF-ca	shayqiyya		0.01	22	1Asuh	3	3	3	1	0		pnb	b
10673	Kerarish	0.09530	25,366	28,104	44,090	CMT30	12-AACE-b	baggaari		0.00	0	0...h	0	2	3	0	0		pn.	b
10674	Kichepo (Shuri, Kacipo)	0.02432	6,473	7,172	11,251	NAB62y	05-PBAB-d	kacipo		10.00	717	0....	8	5	6	1	0	Suri	...	.
10675	Kimr (Gimr)	0.34282	91,249	101,097	158,603	NAB66d	12-AACF-c	sudani		0.01	10	4Asuh	3	3	4	1	0	Arabic: Sudan	PNb	b
10676	Kineenawi	0.05635	14,999	16,617	26,070	NAB66d	12-AACE	badawi-sahel cluster		0.00	0	0...h	0	3	3	0	0		PN.	b
10677	Koalib Nuba (Ngunduna)	0.20778	55,305	61,274	96,128	NAB66h	06-BACD-b	ngi-reere	3	50.00	30,637	0.s..	10	8	10	5	1	Nuba: Ngirere*	PN.	.
10678	Kreish (Kparla, Aja)	0.06918	18,414	20,401	32,006	NAB66e	03-AEAA	kpara cluster		14.00	2,856	0....	8	5	11	4	1		...	.
10679	Krongo Nuba	0.10182	27,102	30,026	47,106	NAB66h	05-IABA	krongo cluster		3.00	901	0....	6	4	6	4	1	Nuba: Krongo*	PN.	.
10680	Kuku	0.13344	35,518	39,351	61,735	NAB62e	04-BAAB-e	kutuk-na-kuku		60.00	23,611	1.s..	10	7	9	5	2		pnb	.
10681	Kunama	0.05000	13,309	14,745	23,132	NAB62h	05-KAAA-a	marda-kunama		21.00	3,096	0....	9	5	11	2	1	Kunama	PN.	.
10682	Kuraan	0.07751	20,631	22,857	35,859	NAB66z	12-AACE	badawi-sahel cluster		20.00	4,571	0...h	9	5	7	2	0		PN.	b
10683	Lafofa (Jebel)	0.02413	6,423	7,116	11,164	NAB66h	06-CBAA-a	kidie-lafofa		2.00	142	0....	6	4	5	0	0		...	.
10684	Lahawin	0.33871	90,155	99,885	156,701	CMT30	12-AACE-b	baggaari		0.00	0	0...h	0	2	3	0	0		pn.	b
10685	Langgo	0.08648	23,019	25,503	40,009	NAB62z	04-BBEA-a	north lango		5.00	1,275	0....	7	5	4	1	0		...	n
10686	Laro (Laru, Ngwullaro)	0.03544	9,433	10,451	16,396	NAB66h	06-BACB-c	yi-l-laaru		70.00	7,316	0cs..	10	7	8	2	0		pn.	.
10687	Liguri (Daju)	0.01400	3,726	4,129	6,477	NAB66d	05-EBAA-a	liguri		2.00	83	0....	6	4	4	0	0		...	.
10688	Lingala (Zairian)	0.10000	26,617	29,490	46,264	NAB57c	99-AUIF-b	vehicular lingala	4	70.00	20,643	4asu.	10	8	12	5	3	Lingala	PNB	b
10689	Logo (Logo Kuli)	0.02000	5,323	5,898	9,253	NAB66e	03-BAAC-a	logo-ti		56.00	3,303	0....	10	7	8	4	1	Logo	P..	.
10690	Logol (Lukha)	0.02512	6,686	7,408	11,622	NAB66h	06-BACC	logol cluster		30.00	2,222	0....	9	7	7	4	0		...	.
10691	Lokoja (Lowoi, Oirya)	0.12908	34,358	38,065	59,718	NAB62y	04-BBAA	koriuk cluster		20.00	7,613	0....	9	5	6	5	2		...	n
10692	Lopid	0.17794	47,363	52,474	82,322	NAB62y	04-BBCA-a	rori-ne-lopit		20.00	10,495	0....	9	7	7	5	0		...	.
10693	Lotuko (Latuka)	0.92802	247,013	273,670	429,341	NAB62y	04-BBBA-a	o-tuho	2	38.00	103,995	0....	9	7	9	5	3	Lotuho	PN.	.
10694	Lugbara	0.11353	30,219	33,480	52,524	NAB66g	03-BAAF-a	uru-leba-ti		20.00	6,696	1As..	9	5	9	5	2	Lugbara	PNB	.
10695	Lwo (Jur, Jur Luo, Giur)	0.27088	72,101	79,882	125,320	NAB62y	04-ABBC-a	dhe-lwo		28.00	22,367	0....	9	6	10	5	3	Luwo	P..	.
10696	Maalia	0.23842	63,461	70,309	110,303	CMT30	12-AACE-b	baggaari		0.01	7	0...h	3	2	3	0	0		pn.	b
10697	Maba (Borgu, Mabang)	0.05270	14,027	15,541	24,381	NAB66z	05-AAAA-a	bura-maba-ng	1	1.00	155	0....	6	4	6	2	0	Maba	...	b
10698	Mabaan (Meban)	0.16214	43,157	47,815	75,013	NAB62z	04-AEAA-e	mabaan	1	4.00	1,913	0.s..	6	5	7	2	2	Mabaan	PN.	.
10699	Madi (Pandikeri, Lokai)	0.09029	24,033	26,626	41,772	NAB66e	03-BAAI-a	moyo		83.00	22,100	1....	10	8	9	5	3	Madi	PN.	.
10700	Maghrib Arab	0.48010	127,789	141,580	222,114	CMT30	12-AACF-c	sudani		0.01	14	4Asuh	3	3	3	0	0	Arabic: Sudan	PNb	b
10701	Mahas Nubian	0.67168	178,783	198,077	310,747	NAB62m	12-AACF-ca	shayqiyya		0.01	20	1Asuh	3	2	3	0	0		pnb	b
10702	Mandala	0.06329	16,846	18,664	29,281	NAB62m	12-AACF-c	sudani		3.00	560	4Asuh	6	4	5	1	0	Arabic: Sudan	PNb	b
10703	Mangaya (Mongaiyat, Bug)	0.00173	460	510	800	NAB66z	93-ACCB-a	buga		20.00	102	0....	9	5	7	1	0		...	p
10704	Mararit (Abiyi, Ebiri)	0.07028	18,707	20,725	32,514	NAB66d	05-DABA-a	abiyi		0.00	0	0....	0	2	3	0	0		...	b
10705	Masalit	0.55896	148,780	164,836	258,598	NAB66z	05-AAAD-a	kaana-masala		0.01	16	0....	3	2	4	0	0	Masalit	...	b
10706	Mekan (Miekan, Tishena)	0.00500	1,331	1,474	2,313	NAB62y	05-PBAA-a	tuk-te-me'en-en		25.00	369	0....	9	5	7	1	2	Meen	...	.
10707	Mesakin (Masakin)	0.19062	50,738	56,213	88,189	NAB66h	06-CAAA-a	ngile		0.50	281	0....	5	4	4	0	0		...	.
10708	Messiria (Baggara)	1.26963	337,940	374,410	587,384	CMT30	12-AACE-b	baggaari		0.01	37	0...h	3	3	3	0	0		pn.	b
10709	Midob (Meidob, Tiddi)	0.14423	38,390	42,533	66,727	NAB62m	05-FADA-a	tid-n-aal		0.00	0	0....	0	3	0	0	0		...	.
10710	Molo	0.00042	112	124	194	NAB62z	03-ACAB-b	molo		1.00	1	0....	6	4	6	2	0		...	.
10711	Mondari (Shir)	0.37304	99,293	110,008	172,584	NAB62e	04-BAAB-a	kutuk-na-mundari		60.00	66,005	0....	10	5	9	2	2		...	.
10712	Mongallese Arab	0.08648	23,019	25,503	40,009	CMT30	12-AACG-b	juba	9	0.02	5	0....	3	3	4	1	3		...	.
10713	Moro Hills (Tacho)	0.02225	5,922	6,561	10,294	NAB66h	06-CAAB-a	acheron		2.00	131	0....	6	4	4	0	0		...	.
10714	Moro Nuba	0.63714	169,589	187,891	294,768	NAB66h	06-BAAA-a	dhi-morong		70.00	131,524	0As..	10	8	9	5	2	Nuba: Moro*	PN.	.
10715	Morokodo	0.01991	5,299	5,871	9,211	NAB66e	03-ACCA-a	morokodo		10.00	587	0....	8	5	5	1	0		...	n
10716	Moru (Miza, Balimba)	0.35114	93,464	103,550	162,452	NAB66g	03-BAAA-a	kala-moru		60.00	62,130	1.s..	10	8	9	5	3	Moru	PN.	.
10717	Mundu (Mondo)	0.11537	30,708	34,022	53,375	NAB66z	93-AEBA-b	mundu-shatt		20.00	6,804	0....	9	5	7	5	1	Mundu	P..	b
10718	Murle (Beir, Ajibba)	0.30098	80,113	88,758	139,246	NAB62y	05-PAAB-a	dod-murle		10.00	8,876	0....	8	4	6	5	3	Murle	PN.	.
10719	Narim (Longarim)	0.03010	8,012	8,876	13,926	NAB62y	05-PAAA-a	doth-ki-larimo		2.00	178	0....	6	4	6	1	0		p..	.
10720	Ndogo	0.07507	19,982	22,138	34,731	NAB66z	93-ACAB-a	ndogo		50.00	11,069	0....	10	6	9	4	1	Ndogo	P..	.
10721	Ngala	0.09193	24,469	27,110	42,531	NAB57c	99-AUIF-c	bangala-3		70.00	18,977	1csu.	10	7	8	5	1	Bangala	PNB	b
10722	Ngulgule (Begi, Beko)	0.00527	1,403	1,554	2,438	NAB66d	05-EAAC-e	nyool		1.00	16	0....	6	4	4	1	0		...	p
10723	Northeastern Dinka (Padan	1.40690	374,478	414,891	650,891	NAB62f	04-AAAA-a	padang		72.50	300,796	4A...	10	5	8	5	3	Dinka: Padang*	PN.	.
10724	Northwestern Dinka (Ruwen	0.35173	93,621	103,724	162,725	NAB62f	04-AAAB-a	ruweng		58.00	60,160	0....	10	5	9	5	0		...	.
10725	Nyamusa	0.03574	9,513	10,540	16,535	NAB66e	03-ACAB-b	molo		10.00	1,054	0....	8	5	5	1	0		...	.
10726	Nyimang (Nyima, Ama)	0.23570	62,737	69,507	109,045	NAB62m	05-GAAA-aa	i-nyimang		2.00	1,390	0....	6	4	11	4	1	Nyimang	P..	p
10727	Olubo (Oluboti)	0.05000	13,309	14,745	23,132	NAB66g	03-BAAL-a	olubo-ti		40.00	5,898	0....	9	6	8	2	2		...	b
10728	Otoro Nuba	0.05308	14,128	15,653	24,557	NAB66h	06-BACA-a	dhi-toro		48.70	7,623	0.s..	9	6	9	5	1	Nuba: Otoro*	PN.	.
10729	Pari (Lokoro)	0.12107	32,225	35,703	56,012	NAB62c	04-ABAC-a	lumi-pari		5.00	1,785	0....	7	5	5	5	2	Lokoro	...	.
10730	Rashaida	0.23440	62,391	69,124	108,443	CMT30	12-AACF-c	sudani		0.01	7	4Asuh	3	3	3	0	0	Arabic: Sudan	PNb	b
10731	Rizeiqat (Rizaykat)	0.85446	227,434	251,978	395,309	CMT30	12-AACE-b	baggaari		0.00	0	0...h	0	2	4	0	0		pn.	b
10732	Rufaa (Rufaiyin)	1.22191	325,239	360,338	565,307	CMT30	12-AACF-c	sudani		0.20	721	4Asuh	5	3	3	0	0	Arabic: Sudan	PNb	b
10733	Sara Gambai	0.02564	6,825	7,561	11,862	NAB66z	03-AAAE-a	ngambai		60.00	4,537	0.s..	10	6	8	3	2	Ngambai*	PNB	b
10734	Sebei	0.03771	10,037	11,121	17,446	NAB62m	12-AACF-c	sudani		3.00	334	4Asuh	6	4	3	1	0	Arabic: Sudan	PNb	b
10735	Selim (Baggara, Beni Seli	0.13033	34,690	38,434	60,296	CMT30	12-AACF-c	sudani		0.00	0	4Asuh	0	2	3	0	0	Arabic: Sudan	PNb	b
10736	Shaikia (Cheykye)	2.10525	560,359	620,832	973,977	CMT30	12-AACF-ca	shayqiyya		0.30	1,862	1Asuh	5	4	3	2	0		pnb	b
10737	Shatt	0.07079	18,842	20,876	32,750	NAB66d	93-AEBA-b	mundu-shatt		3.00	626	0....	6	4	5	3	0	Mundu	P..	b
10738	Sherifi	0.38710	103,035	114,155	179,089	CMT30	12-AACE-b	baggaari		0.01	11	0...h	3	3	3	0	0		pn.	b
10739	Shilluk	0.87785	233,659	258,875	406,130	NAB62o	04-ABAA	dho-colo cluster		45.00	116,494	4.s..	9	5	10	5	3	Shilluk	PN.	.
10740	Shita	0.00800	2,129	2,359	3,701	NAB62z	05-OBBB-a	opo-shiita		5.00	118	0....	7	5	5	1	1		...	b
10741	Shukria (Dubania)	0.56616	150,696	166,959	261,929	CMT30	12-AACE-f	shukri		0.30	501	0...h	5	4	3	0	0		pn.	.
10742	Shuweihat	0.20830	55,444	61,427	96,368	CMT30	12-AACE-b	baggaari		0.00	0	0...h	0	2	3	0	0		pn.	b
10743	Shwai (Shuway)	0.01429	3,804	4,214	6,611	NAB66h	06-BABA-b	ngurun-nga-lu-dumör		51.60	2,174	0....	10	6	11	2	1		...	.
10744	Sillok (Aka)	0.01000	2,662	2,949	4,626	NAB62z	05-MAAA-a	aka		10.00	295	0....	8	5	5	2	1		...	.
10745	Sinyar (Shamya)	0.02000	5,323	5,898	9,253	NAB66z	03-ACAA-a	taar-shamyan		0.00	0	0....	0	3	0	1	0		...	b
10746	Somali	0.00400	1,065	1,180	1,851	CMT33e	14-GAGA-a	af-soomaali		0.00	0	2A...	0	3	2	4	1	Somali	PNB	b
10747	South Central Dinka (Agar	1.11259	296,141	328,100	514,731	NAB62f	04-AAAD-bb	ciec		60.00	196,860	1....	10	5	9	5	2	Dinka: Ciec*	P..	.
10748	Southeastern Dinka (Bor)	1.20000	319,407	353,877	555,170	NAB62f	04-AAAE-aa	bor		72.00	254,791	1As..	10	5	9	5	2	Dinka: Bor*	PN.	.
10749	Sudanese Arab	12.15387	3,235,024	3,584,142	5,622,888	CMT30	12-AACF-c	sudani	58	10.30	369,167	4Asuh	8	4	7	4	3	Arabic: Sudan	PNb	b
10750	Sungor (Assagori, Shaale)	0.07295	19,417	21,513	33,750	NAB66d	05-DAAA-e	a-songor-i		0.00	0	0....	0	2	0	0	0		...	b
10751	Swahili	0.05000	13,309	14,745	23,132	NAB57j	99-AUSM-b	standard ki-swahili		0.00	0	4Asu.	0	2	2	0	0	Kiswahili*	PNB	b

Continued opposite

Table 8-2 continued

EVANGELIZATION								EVANGELISM			ADDITIONAL DESCRIPTIVE DATA
Ref 1	*D 28*	*aC 29*	*CG% 30*	*r 31*	*E 32*	*U 33*	*W 34*	*e 35*	*R 36*	*T 37*	*Locations, civil divisions, literacy, religions, church history, denominations, dioceses, church growth, missions, agencies, ministries, movements 38*
10628	0	2	0.00	0	7.00	93.00	A	0.00	0	1.03	Many small tribes. Muslims 100%(Sunnis).
10629	1	10	4.40	8	99.84	0.16	C	466.03	97	10	Expatriates in development. Nonreligious 13%. D=RCC(7 Dioceses). M=FSCJ.
10630	0	5	2.60	4	34.01	65.99	A	0.01	338	2	Adamawa Fulani, Fellata. From Kordofan Province across to Ethiopian border. Also speak Hausa, Songhai, Arabic. Muslims 100%(Maliki Sunnis).
10631	0	4	0.00	0	9.00	91.00	A	0.00	0	1.02	Nuba Hills, between Talodi and White Nile. All animists 100%, with Muslim encroachment.
10632	0	4	0.00	5	19.00	81.00	A	0.00	0	1.05	Darfur Province, with a few in Chad. Muslims 100%(Maliki Sunnis). M=CMS,ACROSS,both expelled in 1986.
10633	2	6	10.06	7	67.40	32.60	B	18.20	437	5	Baggara(Negroid Bedouins) along Nile in Nubia. Sedentary. Muslims 93%(Maliki Sunnis). D=RCC,PECS. A sudden rush of converts in the 1990s. M=FSCJ.
10634	0	4	4.20	7	24.01	75.99	A	0.00	559	1.09	Baggara Arabs(Negroid Bedouins). Tent-dwellers. Muslims 100%(Sunnis).
10635	0	6	2.37	0	32.00	68.00	A	11.68	325	5	On border of Lakes and Western Equatoria Provinces. Animists 70%, Muslims 20%.
10636	0	3	0.00	0	9.00	91.00	A	0.00	0	1.03	In Kordofan south of Dilling town. Muslims 100%(Sunnis).
10637	0	4	3.04	7	37.02	62.98	A	0.02	277	2	Baggara Arabs. Seminomadic tribe along White Nile. Muslims 100%(Sunnis).
10638	2	10	7.19	7	99.95	0.05	C	579.07	134	10	Greeks, Greek Cypriots. Traders. D=Greek Orthodox Ch(P-Alexandria: D-Nubia),RCC(Melkites).
10639	0	4	0.00	7	34.00	66.00	A	0.00	0	1.13	Arabs. Muslims 100%(Sunnis).
10640	0	6	2.93	7	45.00	55.00	A	1.64	270	4	Arabized Gule. North of Tabi tribe. Gule language (Hameg) now extinct. Muslims 99%(Sunnis).
10641	0	5	4.69	7	40.50	59.50	A	0.73	412	3	Arabized. Muslims 99%(Sunnis).
10642	0	4	1.62	0	14.01	85.99	A	0.00	610	1.04	Also in Ethiopia. Many animists 70%, Muslims 30%.
10643	0	4	3.14	7	25.01	74.99	A	0.00	421	1.09	Baggara Arabs(Negroid Bedouins). Pastoralists. Muslims 100%(Sunnis).
10644	0	4	4.05	7	24.02	75.98	A	0.01	542	2	In Dar Hamer, Kordofan. Baggara Arabs(Negroid Bedouins). Seminomadic camel nomads. Muslims 100%(Sunnis).
10645	0	6	6.69	7	49.40	50.60	A	2.52	410	4	Seminomadic Baggara Arab tribe on White Nile above Khartoum. Muslims 99%.
10646	0	5	3.97	5	40.01	59.99	A	0.01	354	2	Ethnic Fulani who no longer speak Fulfulde. Pockets across Sudan, up to Ethiopia border. Lingua franca. Muslims 100%(Maliki Sunnis).
10647	0	4	2.75	7	37.01	62.99	A	0.01	255	2	Muslims 100%(Sunnis). Baggara Arabs with slight Negro admixture. Camel nomads.
10648	2	6	6.25	0	99.70	0.30	C	301.49	178	9	Around Heiban town, Kordofan Province. Muslims 20%(Sunnis), animists 10%. D=SCOC(Ch of Christ in the Nuba Mountains),PECS. M=SUM,CMS.
10649	4	6	4.59	0	82.00	18.00	B	89.79	202	6	On border of Zaire and CAR. Homa language extinct in 1975. Animists 70%. D=RCC,PECS,AIC,SCOC.
10650	0	4	0.00	7	34.00	66.00	A	0.00	0	1.13	Baggara Arabs on White Nile. Seminomadic. Muslims 100%(Sunnis).
10651	0	9	1.81	7	45.09	54.91	A	0.14	171	3	Traders from India, Pakistan. Muslims 90%, some Hindus 9%, Baha'is.
10652	0	6	2.96	0	47.00	53.00	A	34.31	256	5	Southwest, around Raga. Bilingual in Arabic or Feroge. Many Muslims 60%, animists 20%.
10653	0	5	2.72	0	18.50	81.50	A	0.33	625	3	Some in Ethiopia. Animists 99%, resistant to Islam and Christianity. M=SIM.
10654	1	10	5.65	7	99.83	0.17	C	475.63	116	10	Expatriates from Italy, in development. D=RCC(7 Dioceses).
10655	0	10	0.00	7	42.00	58.00	A	0.00	0	1.13	Rapidly-diminishing community of practicing Sefardi Jews; emigrating to Israel.
10656	1	6	4.67	0	32.00	68.00	A	2.33	528	4	Northern Upper Nile Province. Animists 98%, resistant to Islam. D=CECS. M=SIM.
10657	0	6	5.58	0	37.00	63.00	A	13.50	519	5	Southern Sudan, around Mvolo and on Naam river. Animists 60%, Muslims 30%. M=SIL.
10658	0	4	3.23	7	37.01	62.99	A	0.01	291	2	Baggara Arabs with slight Negro element. Camel nomads. Muslims 100%(Sunnis).
10659	0	3	0.00	0	9.00	91.00	A	0.00	0	1.03	Nuba Mountains, Kadaru Hills. Mostly Muslims 95% (Sunnis), animists 5%.
10660	2	6	6.90	0	44.00	56.00	A	16.06	519	5	Kadugli village and others south of Nuba Hills. Animists 50%, Muslims 40%. D=RCC,PECS. M=CMS.
10661	4	7	8.62	1	99.58	0.42	B	234.98	248	8	Yei District. Also in Uganda, Zaire. Animists 40%. D=RCC,PECS,Episcopal Praisers(Revivalists ex PECS),a few other AICs. M=CMS,FSCJ.
10662	0	6	5.62	0	49.00	51.00	A	35.77	394	5	Western Bahr El Ghazal, 8 miles northeast of Raga. Many bilinguals in Sudanese Arabic. Muslims 60%(Sunnis), animists 20%.
10663	0	6	5.61	0	50.00	50.00	B	36.50	386	5	Yei District, also many in Zaire. Animists 80%. M=SIL.
10664	0	6	4.67	0	21.00	79.00	A	0.76	796	3	Northern Sudan, Miri Hills south of Nuba Hills area. Mostly Muslims 90%, a few animists 9%.
10665	0	6	3.39	1	56.00	44.00	B	40.88	236	6	Extreme western Bahr El Ghazal, Province; also in CAR. Many bilinguals in Kresh or Arabic. Muslims 50%, animists 30%.
10666	0	6	2.93	0	19.00	81.00	A	0.69	624	3	Karko Hills, Kordofan Province. Muslims 99%.
10667	0	6	4.16	0	23.00	77.00	A	2.51	666	4	Katla Hills, Nuba Hills, Kordofan Province. Muslims 97%.
10668	0	4	4.20	7	24.01	75.99	A	0.00	559	1.09	Baggara Arabs(Negroid Bedouins), in northern Kordofan. Cattle and sheep nomads. Muslims 100%(Sunnis).
10669	0	6	4.53	0	21.00	79.00	A	0.76	778	3	Jebel Demik, north of Miri, Kordofan Province. Muslims 95%.
10670	0	3	0.00	0	9.00	91.00	A	0.00	0	1.03	Teis-Umm-Danab. In Keiga Jirru west of Debri, Nuba Hills. Muslims 99%(Maliki Sunnis).
10671	0	5	3.23	0	19.08	80.92	A	0.05	665	2	Nile Nubians. Northern Province; also in Egypt. Ethnic consciousness increasing among adults. Muslims 100%(Sunnis, with active saints' cults).
10672	0	5	3.14	7	38.01	61.99	A	0.01	327	2	Arabic-speaking and arabized Nubians. Use of Nubian language disappearing. Muslims 100%(Sunnis).
10673	0	4	0.00	7	21.00	79.00	A	0.00	0	1.08	Arabized Nubian Baggara tribe of camel nomads, in Dongola region. Muslims 100%(Sunnis).
10674	0	6	4.37	0	34.00	66.00	A	12.41	467	5	Western Suri. Mainly in Ethiopia. Monolinguals. Animists 90%.
10675	0	4	2.33	7	39.01	60.99	A	0.01	290	2	Sandy land, few natural resources. Kimr language extinct. Muslims 100%(Sunnis).
10676	0	4	0.00	7	22.00	78.00	A	0.00	0	1.08	Sudanese Arab/Negro people. Muslims 100%(Sunnis).
10677	3	6	8.36	0	95.00	5.00	B	173.37	282	7	Nuba Mountains around Delami. Animists 30%, Muslims 20%(Sunnis). D=SCOC(Ch of Christ in the Nuba Mountains),RCC,PECS. M=SUM.
10678	1	6	5.82	0	49.00	51.00	A	25.03	405	5	Western Bahr El Ghazal Province. Muslims 85%(Sunnis). D=RCC. M=SIL.
10679	1	6	4.60	0	34.00	66.00	A	3.72	486	4	Krongo Hills. Animists 95%, Muslims 2%(Sunnis). D=SCOC(Sudanese Ch of Christ). M=SUM.
10680	4	7	8.08	0	99.60	0.40	C	238.71	239	8	Related to Bari. Animists 40%. D=PECS(strong Anglican work; East African Revival),RCC,Trumpeters(1957),other small AICs. M=CMS,FSCJ.
10681	3	6	5.90	0	61.00	39.00	B	46.75	328	6	Refugees from Eritrean civil war. Muslims 79%. Strong Catholics. D=RCC,ECE,LCE. M=OFMCap.
10682	0	6	6.32	7	60.00	40.00	B	43.80	354	6	Partially islamized tribe. Muslims 80%(Sunnis).
10683	0	6	2.69	0	22.00	78.00	A	1.60	513	4	Northern Sudan, central Eliri range, Kordofan. Muslims 95%(Sunnis), Animists 3%.
10684	0	4	0.00	7	21.00	79.00	A	0.00	0	1.08	Baggara Arabs(Negroid Bedouins). Blue Nile region. Seminomadic(sheep and goats). Muslims 100%(Sunnis).
10685	0	6	4.97	0	29.00	71.00	A	5.29	611	4	Torit District, southern Equatoria Province. Pastoralists. Bilingual in Lotuko. Animists 80%, Muslims 15%.
10686	0	6	6.82	0	99.70	0.30	C	268.27	215	8	Nuba Hills. Animists 20%, Muslims 10%(Sunnis).
10687	0	6	4.52	0	21.00	79.00	A	1.53	825	4	Nuba Hills, Liguri Hills. Animists 60%, Muslims 38%(Sunnis).
10688	3	10	7.93	5	99.70	0.30	C	360.25	183	9	Migrants from river Zaire area. Lingua franca. Animists 10%. Nominal Christians 20%. D=RCC,PECS,some AICs from Zaire.
10689	1	7	5.97	0	92.00	8.00	B	188.04	220	7	Yei District. Vast majority in Zaire. Animists 44%. D=RCC.
10690	0	7	5.55	0	61.00	39.00	B	66.79	314	6	Northern Sudan, east of Nuba Hills, between Talodi and White Nile. Close to Otoro. Animists 40%, Muslims 30%.
10691	2	6	6.86	0	56.00	44.00	B	40.88	406	6	Torit District, southern Equatoria Province. Bilingual in Lotuko. Animists 80%. D=RCC,AIC. M=AIM,FSCJ.
10692	0	7	7.20	0	53.00	47.00	B	38.69	446	5	Lopit Hills, northeast of Torit, Equatoria Province. Close to Otuho. Blacksmiths. Animists 75%, Muslims 5%.
10693	3	7	9.69	0	83.00	17.00	B	115.12	367	7	Torit District. Agriculturalists, pastoralists. Literates 10%. Animists 58%, Muslims 4%(Sunnis), but highly resistant to Islam. D=RCC,PECS,AIC. M=AIM,CMS,FSCJ.
10694	2	7	6.72	1	76.00	24.00	B	55.48	303	6	In extreme south, Uganda border. Also in Uganda, Zaire. Animists 70%, some Muslims 10%. D=RCC,PECS. M=FSCJ,CMS.
10695	2	6	8.02	0	69.00	31.00	B	70.51	375	6	Southern Sudan, north and southeast of Wau. Animists 70%. D=RCC(D-Wau),PECS. M=SIM,FSCJ,SIL.
10696	0	4	1.96	7	24.01	75.99	A	0.00	304	1.09	Baggara Arabs(Negroid Bedouins). Muslims 100%(Maliki Sunnis).
10697	0	6	2.78	0	24.00	76.00	A	0.87	481	3	Darfur Province. Primarily in Chad. Muslims 99%(Maliki Sunnis).
10698	1	6	5.39	0	37.00	63.00	A	5.40	510	4	Southern Burun. Also in Ethiopia. Animists 96%, resistant to Islam. D=CECS(15 Mabaan churches). M=SIM,APM. Rapid church growth, many baptisms.
10699	4	6	8.01	1	99.83	0.17	C	393.83	199	9	Equatoria Province. Majority in Uganda. Animists 15%, some Muslims. D=RCC,SDA,AIC,PECS. M=AIM,FSCJ,CMS,SIL.
10700	0	4	2.67	7	40.01	59.99	A	0.01	231	2	Arabs from North Africa(Morocco,Algeria,Tunisia). Muslims 100%(Sunnis).
10701	0	5	3.04	7	36.01	63.99	A	0.01	338	2	Use of Nubian language disappearing, now Arabic speaking. Muslims 100%(Sunnis).
10702	0	6	4.11	7	48.00	52.00	A	5.25	315	4	Nomadic Baggara of Negroid stock(escaped Negro slaves). Muslims 97%(Sunnis).
10703	0	6	2.35	0	47.00	53.00	A	34.31	220	5	In Western Bahr El Ghazal, near Raga. Many bilinguals in Kresh or Arabic. Muslims 70%, some animists 10%.
10704	0	4	0.00	0	11.00	89.00	A	0.00	0	1.04	Darfur Province, Dar Masalit. Agriculture, animal husbandry. Most are bilingual in Arabic. Muslims 100%(Sunnis).
10705	0	3	2.81	0	14.01	85.99	A	0.00	829	1.05	Darfur Province. Also in Chad. Most are bilingual in Arabic. Muslims 100%(Sunnis).
10706	2	6	3.67	0	55.00	45.00	B	50.18	254	6	Refugees from Ethopian civil war. Animists 60%, Muslims 15%. D=EOC,WLEC.
10707	0	6	3.39	0	18.50	81.50	A	0.33	714	3	Kordofan Province, Mesakin Hills. Primitive tribe, little contact with outside. Animists 99%.
10708	0	4	3.68	7	24.01	75.99	A	0.00	500	1.09	Baggara Arab tribe(Negroid Bedouins). Cattle nomads, in Dar el Homr region of Kordofan. Muslims 100%(Sunnis).
10709	0	2	0.00	0	5.00	95.00	A	0.00	0	1.02	Darfur Province, Dar Meidob. 100% strict Muslims(Maliki Sunnis).
10710	0	6	0.00	0	24.00	76.00	A	0.87	171	3	South of Blue Nile, at Jebel Malkan near Ethiopia border. Muslims 90%, Animists 9%.
10711	2	6	9.19	0	96.00	4.00	C	210.24	303	8	Southern Sudan, near the Bari. Nomadic pastoralists. Close to Bari, Nyangganwara, Ngyepu. Animists 40%. D=PECS,RCC.
10712	3	6	1.62	7	30.02	69.98	A	0.02	212	2	Sudanese Creole/Pidgin Arabic, Southern Sudan/Juba Arabic. Used in southern towns. Muslims 100%(Maliki Sunnis). D=RCC,AIC,PECS. M=SIM,AIM,MEM.
10713	0	6	2.61	0	21.00	79.00	A	1.53	527	4	Lumun, Torona. Northern Sudan, Moro Hills, Talodi. Several dialects are also place names. Muslims 90%, some animists 8%.
10714	2	6	9.95	0	99.70	0.30	C	304.04	262	9	Eastern Nuba Mountains, Kordofan Province. Muslims 20%, animists 10%. D=SCOC(Ch of Christ in the Nuba Mountains),PECS. M=SUM,CMS.
10715	0	6	4.16	0	35.00	65.00	A	12.77	438	5	Southern Sudan, between Amadi and Maridi. Bilingual in Moru. Animists 80%, Muslims 10%.
10716	4	7	9.13	0	99.60	0.40	C	236.52	275	8	Equatoria Province, Mundri District. Literates 40%. Animists 35%. D=PECS(strong Anglican work),RCC,Evangelical Revival Ch, small AICs. M=CMS,FSCJ,SIL.
10717	2	6	6.74	0	58.00	42.00	B	42.34	386	6	Western Equatoria Prov, around Yei and Maridi. Also in Zaire. Intermarriage with Avukaya, Baka. Bilingual in Avukaya, Baka, Zande. Animists 80%. D=PECS,RCC.
10718	2	6	7.02	0	48.00	52.00	A	17.52	482	5	Pibor District; some also in Ethiopia. Semi-nomadic pastoralists. Animists 90%, resistant to Islam. D=SCOC(Sudanese Ch of Christ),RCC. M=SIL,APM,FMB.
10719	0	6	2.92	0	25.00	75.00	A	1.82	477	4	Southern Sudan, Boya Hills, north of the Didinga. Close to Murle, Didinga. Animists 98%, resistant to Islam.
10720	1	6	7.26	0	87.00	13.00	B	158.77	274	7	Southern Sudan, Western District. Some in CAR. Animists 40%, some Muslims 10%. D=RCC(D-Wau). M=SIL.
10721	2	6	7.84	4	99.70	0.30	C	314.26	207	9	Migrants and immigrants originally from Zaire. Animists 30%. D=RCC,PECS. M=ECZ.
10722	0	6	2.81	0	22.00	78.00	A	0.80	574	3	Southern Sudan, on Sopo river. Bilingual in Arabic. Muslims 99%(Sunnis).
10723	5	6	10.86	0	99.73	0.27	C	332.10	268	9	White Nile Dinka. South from Renk on Nile. Nomadic animists 90%, Muslims 1%(Sunnis), but highly resistant to Islam. D=RCC(D-Rumbek),PECS,CCUN,JWs,SDA.
10724	0	6	9.09	0	93.00	7.00	B	196.88	310	7	North of Bahr el Ghazal river; southern Kordofan around Abyei. Animists 42%.
10725	0	6	4.77	0	34.00	66.00	A	12.41	500	5	Western Equatoria Province, northeast of Morokodo. Animists 80%, Muslims 10%.
10726	1	6	5.06	0	37.00	63.00	A	2.70	478	4	Northern Sudan, northwest of Dilling. Educated in Arabic. Muslims 95%(Sunnis), some animists. D=PECS.
10727	2	6	6.59	0	76.00	24.00	B	110.96	299	7	East of Equatoria Province. Some in Uganda. Many bilinguals in Bari. Animists 60%. D=PECS,RCC.
10728	2	6	6.86	0	89.70	10.30	B	159.44	253	7	Otoro Hills, Kordofan Province. Muslims 40%(Sunnis), animists 10%. D=SCOC(Ch of Christ in the Nuba Mountains),PECS. M=SUM.
10729	2	6	5.32	0	36.00	64.00	A	6.57	405	4	Southern Sudan, Upper Nile Province. A Nilotic people related to the Luo. Animists 95%. D=RCC,AIC.
10730	0	4	1.96	7	37.01	62.99	A	0.01	197	2	Sudanese Arabs with Negroid/Bedouin ancestry. Muslims 100%(Sunnis).
10731	0	5	0.00	7	23.00	77.00	A	0.00	0	1.08	Baggara Arabs(Negroid Bedouins). Pastoralists related to Habbania. Muslims 100%(Maliki Sunnis).
10732	0	6	4.37	7	41.20	58.80	A	0.30	337	3	Baggara Arabs(Negroid Bedouins). Blue Nile region. Seminomads(sheep and goats). Muslims 100%(Maliki Sunnis).
10733	2	9	6.31	2	99.60	0.40	C	243.09	191	8	Immigrants, migrants, or refugees from southern Chad. Muslims 25%, animists 15%. D=RCC,ACT.
10734	0	6	3.57	7	46.00	54.00	A	5.03	296	4	Sudanese Arabs with some Negroid ancestry. Muslims 97%(Sunnis).
10735	0	4	0.00	7	34.00	66.00	A	0.00	0	1.13	Baggara Arabs(strong Negroid ancestry). Pastoralists, cattle nomads along White Nile. Muslims 100%(Maliki Sunnis).
10736	0	4	5.37	7	38.30	61.70	A	0.41	434	3	Camel nomad Baggara Arabs ruling over Nubian serfs along Nile. Muslims 100%(Maliki Sunnis).
10737	0	6	4.22	0	27.00	73.00	A	2.95	611	4	Northern Sudan, Shatt Hills southwest of Kadugli. Close to Liguri, Dorfur Daju. Muslims 97%.
10738	0	4	2.43	7	24.01	75.99	A	0.00	357	1.09	Baggara Arabs(Negroid Bedouins). Nomadic tribe. Muslims 100%(Sunnis).
10739	3	6	9.82	0	95.00	5.00	B	156.03	324	7	Upper Nile Province. Nomadic animists 72%, highly resistant to Islam. D=RCC(D-Malakal),CECS,CCUN. M=PCUSA,Basel Mission,SIM,SIL.APM.
10740	1	6	2.50	0	29.00	71.00	A	5.29	378	4	Northern Sudan; also across border in Ethiopia. Related to Koma. Animists 95%. D=CECS. M=SIM.
10741	0	6	3.99	7	28.30	71.70	A	0.31	454	3	Baggara Arabs(Negroid Bedouins) on Atbara tributary of Nile. Camel nomads. Muslims 100%(Sunnis).
10742	0	4	0.00	7	21.00	79.00	A	0.00	0	1.08	Baggara Arabs, with some Negro ancestors. Tent-dwellers. Muslims 100%(Sunnis).
10743	1	7	5.53	0	87.60	12.40	B	164.98	218	7	Kordofan Province, villages in Shwai Hills. Muslims 30%(Sunnis), animists 18%. D=SCOC.
10744	0	6	3.44	0	35.00	65.00	A	12.77	387	5	Northern Sudan, Sillok Hills, west of Berta. Heavily arabized, also influenced by Berta. Muslims 70%, animists 20%. M=ECMY(Ethiopia).
10745	0	2	0.00	0	6.00	94.00	A	0.00	0	1.04	Pastoral nomads. Also in Chad. Named Zimirra by the Fur. Muslims 100%(lax Sunnis).
10746	0	5	0.00	5	37.00	63.00	A	0.00	0	1.11	Migrants from Somalia. Muslims 100%(Shafi Sunnis). M=FSCJ.
10747	2	6	10.39	0	99.60	0.40	C	221.19	321	8	West of White Nile to Rumbek. Nomadic animists 39%, Muslims 1%; highly resistant to Islam. D=RCC(D-Wau),PECS. M=SIM,SIL.
10748	3	6	10.68	0	99.72	0.28	C	323.24	270	9	East of White Nile, north of Bor. Nomadic animists 27%, Muslims 1% but highly resistant to Islam. D=RCC(D-Wau),PECS,CCUN. M=FSCJ,SIM.
10749	2	5	7.47	7	71.30	28.70	B	26.80	314	5	Northern Sudan primarily, also Ethiopia, Egypt, Chad, Djibouti. Lingua franca. Muslims 85%. D=RCC,COC. M=SIM,CMS,BA,MEM,FI. R=TWR.
10750	0	2	0.00	0	5.00	95.00	A	0.00	0	1.03	In Dar Masalit, on Chad border; mainly in Chad. Muslims 100%(Sunnis).
10751	0	6	0.00	5	35.00	65.00	A	0.00	0	1.12	Long-term residents, black Bantu slaves from Zanzibar. Muslims 100%(Shafi Sunnis).

Continued overleaf

Table 8-2 continued

PEOPLE		POPULATION				IDENTITY CODE		LANGUAGE		CHURCH		MINISTRY						SCRIPTURE		
Ref	*Ethnic name*	*P%*	*In 1995*	*In 2000*	*In 2025*	*Race*	*Language*	*Autoglossonym*	*S*	*AC*	*Members*	*Jayuh*	*d*	*wa*	*xc*	*mc*	*mi*	*Biblioglossonym*	*Pub*	*ss*
1	*2*	*3*	*4*	*5*	*6*	*7*	*8*	*9*	*10*	*11*	*12*	*13-17*	*18*	*19*	*20*	*21*	*22*	*23*	*24-26*	*27*
10752	Syrian Arab	0.20000	53,234	58,979	92,528	CMT30	12-AACF-f	syro-palestinian		8.00	4,718	1Asuh	7	5	8	4	1	Arabic: Lebanese*	Pnb	b
10753	Tagale (Taqalawin, Aquali	0.16778	44,658	49,478	77,622	NAB66h	06-DAAB-a	tegali		0.01	5	0....	3	3	4	0	0		...	.
10754	Tagbu (Togbo)	0.00500	1,331	1,474	2,313	NAB66a	93-ACAB-b	tagbu		40.20	593	0....	9	6	6	1	1		p..	.
10755	Tagoi (Moreb)	0.06521	17,357	19,230	30,169	NAB66h	06-DAAA-a	ngon-nga-ta-goi		1.00	192	0....	6	4	4	0	0		...	.
10756	Talodi (Ajomang)	0.00681	1,813	2,008	3,151	NAB66h	06-CAAC-c	ga-jomang		5.00	100	0....	7	5	4	1	0		...	.
10757	Tama (Tamongobo)	0.15000	39,926	44,235	69,396	NAB66d	05-DAAA-a	tamo-ngo'bo		0.01	4	0....	3	3	4	0	0		...	b
10758	Teda	0.02000	5,323	5,898	9,253	NAB61	02-BAAA	teda-daza cluster		0.00	0	0....	0	3	0	0	0	Daza*	...	b
10759	Temein	0.04719	12,561	13,916	21,832	NAB62m	05-HAAA	temein cluster		2.00	278	0....	6	4	4	0	0		...	.
10760	Tenet	0.01461	3,889	4,308	6,759	NAB62y	05-PAAC-a	tenet		2.00	86	0....	6	4	4	5	2	Tennet	...	p
10761	Thuri (Jo Thuri)	0.06377	16,974	18,806	29,503	NAB62y	04-ABBA-a	dhe-thuri		10.00	1,881	0....	8	5	7	4	1		...	n
10762	Tigrai	0.10000	26,617	29,490	46,264	CMT34b	12-ACAC-a	tigray		89.00	26,246	2As..	10	9	10	5	2	Tigrinya	PNB	b
10763	Tigre	0.04000	10,647	11,796	18,506	CMT34c	12-ACAB-aa	khasa		0.10	12	1B...	5	4	3	5	3		pnb	b
10764	Tima (Tamanik)	0.01063	2,829	3,135	4,918	NAB66h	06-AABA-a	tamanik-l-omuriki		1.00	31	0....	6	4	4	0	0		...	.
10765	Tingal (Kajaja)	0.04013	10,681	11,834	18,566	NAB66h	06-DAAB-c	tingal		0.01	1	0....	3	2	2	0	0		...	.
10766	Tira (Thiro)	0.06448	17,163	19,015	29,831	NAB66h	06-BAAB-a	ngarta-nga-tiro		3.00	570	0....	6	4	5	4	1	Tira	...	.
10767	Tirma	0.00486	1,294	1,433	2,248	NAB62y	05-PBAB-b	tirma		30.00	430	0....	9	5	6	4	1		...	.
10768	Toposa (Topotha)	0.47655	126,844	140,533	220,472	NAB62y	04-BDAA-b	akero-a-toposa		85.00	119,453	0....	10	7	10	5	3		...	.
10769	Tornasi (Kelo-Beni Sheko)	0.00770	2,050	2,271	3,562	NAB62z	05-MAAB	kelo-tornasi cluster		10.00	227	0....	8	5	4	1	0		...	.
10770	Tukam	0.04013	10,681	11,834	18,566	NAB66h	06-DAAB	tegali-kom cluster		0.01	1	0....	3	2	2	0	0		...	.
10771	Tulishi	0.05052	13,447	14,898	23,373	NAB66h	05-IAAC-a	thulishi		1.00	149	0....	6	4	4	0	0		...	.
10772	Tumma (Krongo Abdullah)	0.06280	16,716	18,520	29,054	NAB66h	05-IAAB-b	tumma-sangali		1.00	185	0....	6	4	4	0	0		...	.
10773	Tumtum	0.03249	8,648	9,581	15,031	NAB66h	05-IABB-a	tumtum		3.00	287	0....	6	4	5	0	1		...	.
10774	Tungur	0.55933	148,878	164,945	258,769	CMT30	12-AACE-b	baggaari		0.01	16	0...h	3	2	3	0	0		pn.	b
10775	Tunjur (Sokoro)	0.00400	1,065	1,180	1,851	NAB60b	05-CAAA-a	bele-for		0.01	0	0....	3	3	4	0	0		...	b
10776	Turkana	0.01000	2,662	2,949	4,626	NAB62r	04-BDAB-a	nga-turkana		2.00	59	1As..	6	4	5	5	3	Turkana	PN.	.
10777	Turum	0.00468	1,246	1,380	2,165	NAB66h	06-DAAB	tegali-kom cluster		0.00	0	0....	0	3	2	0	0		...	.
10778	Uduk (Kwanim Pa, Koma)	0.05350	14,240	15,777	24,751	NAB62z	05-OBAA-a	twam-pa		20.00	3,155	0....	9	5	11	4	1	Uduk	PN.	.
10779	Umm Heitan	0.05170	13,761	15,246	23,919	NAB66h	12-AACF-c	sudani		2.00	305	4Asuh	6	4	4	0	0	Arabic: Sudan	PNb	b
10780	Vidiri (Mvedere)	0.01000	2,662	2,949	4,626	NAB66b	93-ABAC-e	vidiri		20.00	590	0....	9	5	7	1	1		...	b
10781	Wada	0.02000	5,323	5,898	9,253	NAB66b	93-ABAG-e	wada		25.00	1,474	0....	9	5	7	1	1		...	.
10782	Wali (Walari)	0.00285	759	840	1,319	NAB62m	05-FACA-h	waliri-she		2.00	17	0....	6	4	4	0	0		...	.
10783	Wallega (Galla)	0.20000	53,234	58,979	92,528	CMT33b	14-FBAA-b	mecha		35.00	20,643	2cs..	9	6	9	2	2	Oromo: Western*	PNB	b
10784	Werni	0.01063	2,829	3,135	4,918	NAB66h	06-BBAA-a	guro-ra-warnang		0.01	0	0....	3	2	3	0	0		...	.
10785	West Central Banda (Golo)	0.01523	4,054	4,491	7,046	NAB66z	93-ABAI-d	golo		10.00	449	0....	8	5	6	1	0		...	p
10786	Western Dinka (Rek)	2.25734	600,841	665,683	1,044,340	NAB62f	04-AAAC-c	rek		68.00	452,665	0....	10	5	9	5	3		...	.
10787	Western Nuer	1.28176	341,169	377,987	592,996	NAB62n	04-AABA-d	dar-cieng	3	25.40	96,009	1A...	9	5	9	5	2	Nuer: Western	Pn.	.
10788	Wetawit (Berta, Barta)	0.11000	29,279	32,439	50,891	NAB62z	05-MAAB	kelo-tornasi cluster		18.00	5,839	0....	8	5	8	4	1		...	.
10789	Yazeed	0.90199	240,085	265,994	417,298	CMT30	12-AACF-c	sudani		0.01	27	4Asuh	3	2	3	0	0	Arabic: Sudan	PNb	b
10790	Yemeni Arab	0.05313	14,142	15,668	24,580	CMT30	12-AACF-n	yemeni		0.02	3	1Asuh	3	3	1	0	0		pnb	b
10791	Yerwa Kanuri	0.73200	194,838	215,865	338,654	NAB61	02-AAAA-b	yerwa		0.01	22	4....	3	3	1	0	0	Kanuri*	PN.	.
10792	Yulu (Youlou)	0.01297	3,452	3,825	6,000	NAB66z	03-AABA-d	yulu		10.00	382	0....	8	5	5	1	0		...	b
10793	Zaghawa	0.49515	131,795	146,018	229,077	NAB61	02-CAAA-a	beri-aa		0.00	0	0....	0	3	2	0	0		...	b
10794	Zande (Azande, Mbomu)	1.75571	467,321	517,754	812,265	NAB66a	93-BAAA-a	pa-zande		85.40	442,162	4As..	10	8	9	5	3	Pazande*	PNB	b
10795	other minor peoples	3.00000	798,517	884,692	1,387,925	...				75.80	670,596		10	5	4	4	0			
	Suriname	**100.00000**	**409,039**	**417,130**	**524,642**					**41.31**	**172,334**									
10796	Akuliyo (Wama, Wayaricuri	0.01200	49	50	63	MIR39c	80-AHAB-c	akuriyo		18.00	9	0....	8	5	5	5	1		pn.	n
10797	Apalai (Aparai)	0.09000	368	375	472	MIR39c	80-AGAA-a	apalaí		70.00	263	0....	10	7	8	3	2	Apalai	PN.	.
10798	Arawak (Lokono)	0.53900	2,205	2,248	2,828	MIR39a	81-ACBA	arawák cluster		91.00	2,046	0....	10	8	11	5	2	Arawak	P..	b
10799	Boni (Bush Negro)	0.25000	1,023	1,043	1,312	NFB68b	52-ABAG-h	aluku		80.00	834	1.s..	10	9	7	5	3		pn.	.
10800	British	0.20000	818	834	1,049	CEW19i	52-ABAC-b	standard-english		78.00	651	3Bsuh	10	9	13	5	3		PNB	b
10801	Caribbean Hindi	27.87400	114,016	116,271	146,239	CNN25g	59-AAFP-ec	sarnami-hindi		9.00	10,464	1c.u.	7	5	8	5	3		pn.	.
10802	Caribbean Javanese	12.79000	52,316	53,351	67,102	MSY44g	31-PIAA-k	jawa-surinam		28.00	14,938	1As.h	9	6	8	5	3	Javanese: Caribbean*	Pnb	b
10803	Coastal Carib (Galibi)	0.60400	2,471	2,519	3,169	MIR39c	80-ACAA-b	central carib		70.00	1,764	1.s..	10	9	8	5	3	Carib*	Pn.	b
10804	Dutch	0.27800	1,137	1,160	1,459	CEW19h	52-ABCA-a	algemeen-nederlands	25	76.00	881	2Bsuh	10	9	15	5	3	Dutch	PNB	b
10805	Dutch Jew	0.13000	532	542	682	CMT35	52-ABCA-a	algemeen-nederlands		0.14	1	2Bsuh	5	4	2	1	0	Dutch	PNB	b
10806	Guyanese	13.15800	53,821	54,886	69,032	NFB68b	52-ABAG-a	guyanese	17	60.50	33,206	1.s..	10	9	10	5	2		pn.	b
10807	Han Chinese (Cantonese)	1.22000	4,990	5,089	6,401	MSY42a	79-AAAM-a	central yue		71.00	3,613	3A.uh	10	7	8	4	2	Chinese, Yue	PNB	b
10808	Han Chinese (Hakka)	1.68000	6,872	7,008	8,814	MSY42a	79-AAAG-a	literary hakka		70.00	4,905	1A...	10	8	8	5	3	Chinese: Hakka, Wukingfu*	PNB	b
10809	Indonesian	3.00000	12,271	12,514	15,739	MSY44k	31-PHAA-c	bahasa-indonesia		4.00	501	4Asuh	6	4	6	3	0	Indonesian	PNB	b
10810	Kwinti Creole	0.09200	376	384	483	NFB68b	52-ABAG-f	kwinti		70.00	269	1.s..	10	7	8	3	3		pn.	.
10811	Laotian Hmong	0.40000	1,636	1,669	2,099	MSY47a	48-AAAA-b	hmong-njua		10.00	167	1A...	8	5	7	4	0	Hmong Njua	PN.	b
10812	Lebanese Arab	0.50000	2,045	2,086	2,623	CMT30	12-AACF-f	syro-palestinian		60.00	1,251	1Asuh	10	7	8	4	1	Arabic: Lebanese*	Pnb	b
10813	Matawari Creole	0.27700	1,133	1,155	1,453	NFB68b	52-ABAG-e	matawari		8.00	92	1.s..	7	5	6	5	2		pn.	.
10814	Mestizo (Mestico)	0.50000	2,045	2,086	2,623	CLN29	51-AABB-h	south americano		95.00	1,981	4B.uh	10	9	12	5	3		pnb	b
10815	Ndjuka (Djuka, Okanisi)	3.12000	12,762	13,014	16,369	NFB68b	52-ABAG-g	ndjuka		60.00	7,809	1.s..	10	9	7	5	3	Aukan*	Pn.	.
10816	Portuguese Jew	0.06000	245	250	315	CMT35	51-AABA-e	general português		0.00	0	2Bsuh	0	3	2	1	0	Portuguese	PNB	b
10817	Saramaccan Bush Negro	5.82700	23,835	24,306	30,571	NFB68b	52-ABAG-d	saramacca-tongo		60.00	14,584	1.s..	10	9	9	5	2	Saramaccan	PN.	.
10818	Surinamese Creole	26.21000	107,209	109,330	137,509	NFB67b	52-ABAG-c	sranan-tongo	85	65.00	71,064	4.s..	10	10	9	5	3	Sranan	PN.	b
10819	Syrian Arab	0.50000	2,045	2,086	2,623	CMT30	12-AACF-f	syro-palestinian		20.00	417	1Asuh	9	5	8	4	1	Arabic: Lebanese*	Pnb	b
10820	Trio	0.22200	908	926	1,165	MIR39c	80-AHAB-a	proper tiriyû		29.00	269	0....	9	5	6	5	3	Trio	PN.	.
10821	Warao (Warrau, Guarao)	0.10000	409	417	525	MIR39e	52-ABAG-a	guyanese		50.00	209	1.s..	10	6	6	5	1		pn.	b
10822	Wayana (Oyana, Upurui)	0.16700	683	697	876	MIR39c	80-AEDA-a	wayâna		9.00	63	0....	7	5	4	5	2	Wajana*	PN.	.
10823	other minor peoples	0.20000	818	834	1,049	...				10.00	83		8	5	6	5	0			
	Svalbard & Jan Mayen Islands	**100.00000**	**3,500**	**3,676**	**4,696**					**47.58**	**1,749**									
10824	Norwegian	41.90000	1,467	1,540	1,968	CEW19p	52-AAAC-e	ny-norsk	70	65.00	1,001	0B.uh	10	9	14	5	2	Norwegian*	PNB	b
10825	Russian	57.80000	2,023	2,125	2,714	CEW22j	53-AAAE-d	russkiy	80	35.00	744	4B.uh	9	5	10	5	1	Russian	PNB	b
10826	other minor peoples	0.30000	11	11	14	...			5	40.00	4		9	5	6	5	0			
	Swaziland	**100.00000**	**872,554**	**1,007,895**	**1,784,790**					**67.55**	**680,839**									
10827	Afrikaner	1.40000	12,216	14,111	24,987	CEW19a	52-ABCB-a	afrikaans	10	82.00	11,571	2B.uh	10	10	14	5	3	Afrikaans	PNB	b
10828	British	0.80000	6,980	8,063	14,278	CEW19i	52-ABAC-b	standard-english	60	79.00	6,370	3Bsuh	10	9	13	5	1		PNB	b
10829	Coloured (Eurafrican)	1.00000	8,726	10,079	17,848	NAN58	52-ABCB-a	afrikaans		64.90	6,541	2B.uh	10	9	12	5	3	Afrikaans	PNB	b
10830	Comorian	0.06400	558	645	1,142	NAB57j	99-AUSM-s	shi-ngazidya		3.00	19	1csu.	6	4	5	5	0	Comorian*	PNb	b
10831	Indo-Pakistani	0.76000	6,631	7,660	13,564	CNN25g	59-AAFO-e	general hindi		7.00	536	3Asuh	7	5	5	5	3		pnb	b
10832	Mine Kaffir	0.30000	2,618	3,024	5,354	NAB57i	99-AUTF-h	fanakolo	35	65.00	1,965	1csu.	10	9	8	5	2		pnb	b
10833	Nyasa (Western Nyanja)	0.60000	5,235	6,047	10,709	NAB57b	99-AUSX-af	ci-nyasa		63.11	3,816	1.su.	10	9	8	5	3		pnb	b
10834	Sotho (Southern Sotho)	0.50000	4,363	5,039	8,924	NAB57m	99-AUTE-e	se-sotho	30	64.90	3,271	3asu.	10	10	12	5	3	Sesotho: Southern*	PNB	b
10835	Swazi (Tekeza)	82.31000	718,199	829,598	1,469,061	NAB57i	99-AUTF-e	i-si-swati	99	67.13	556,909	2csu.	10	10	12	5	3	Siswati*	PNB	b
10836	Tsonga (Shangaan)	2.30000	20,069	23,182	41,050	NAB57p	99-AUTD-c	shi-shangana		71.80	16,644	3.s..	10	9	12	5	1	Tsonga	PNB	b
10837	Zulu	9.63000	84,027	97,060	171,875	NAB57i	99-AUTF-g	i-si-zulu	70	73.60	71,436	3asu.	10	10	14	5	2	Isizulu*	PNB	b
10838	other minor peoples	0.33600	2,932	3,387	5,997	...				52.00	1,761		10	7	8	5	0			
	Sweden	**100.00000**	**8,799,986**	**8,910,214**	**9,096,927**					**67.34**	**6,000,356**									
10839	Albanian	0.04600	4,048	4,099	4,185	CEW13	55-AAAB-a	standard tosk		25.00	1,025	0A...	9	6	9	0	0	Albanian: Tosk*	PNB	b
10840	Arctic Lapp (Ume)	0.01200	1,056	1,069	1,092	MSW51e	41-AABC-a	ume		90.00	962	0....	10	8	11	4	1		...	.
10841	Assyrian	0.11200	9,856	9,979	10,189	CMT31	12-AAAA-d	east syriac		88.00	8,782	1as..	10	9	10	5	2	Syriac: Ancient*	PNB	b
10842	Black Gypsy (Finnish Kalo	0.01800	1,584	1,604	1,637	CNN25f	59-AFAA-a	rodi		80.00	1,283	0B.uh	10	8	8	5	2	Calo	P..	b
10843	Bosniac (Muslmani)	1.30000	114,400	115,833	118,260	CEW22a	53-AAAG-a	standard srpski		0.05	58	1Asuh	4	5	5	4	2	Serbian*	PNB	b
10844	Brazilian	0.30000	26,400	26,731	27,291	CLT26	51-AABA-h	general brasileiro		90.00	24,058	3csuh	10	9	11	4	3	Portuguese: Brazilian	PNB	b
10845	British	0.12200	10,736	10,870	11,098	CEW19i	52-ABAC-b	standard-english	50	78.00	8,479	3Bsuh	10	9	13	5	3		PNB	b
10846	Chilean Mestizo	0.20000	17,600	17,820	18,194	CLN29	51-AABB-hr	chileno		89.00	15,860	1B.uh	10	9	11	4	3		pnb	.
10847	Croat	0.30000	26,400	26,731	27,291	CEW22d	53-AAAG-b	standard hrvatski	2	91.00	24,325	2Asuh	10	8	11	4	3	Croatian	PNB	b
10848	Czech	0.01200	1,056	1,069	1,092	CEW22e	53-AAAD-a	czesky		75.00	802	2Asuh	10	9	8	5	2	Czech	PNB	b
10849	Danish (Dane)	0.50000	44,000	44,551	45,485	CEW19g	52-AAAD-c	general dansk	100	94.00	41,878	2A.uh	10	9	11	5	3	Danish	PNB	b
10850	Dutch	0.50000	44,000	44,551	45,485	CEW19h	52-ABCA-a	algemeen-nederlands	2	76.00	33,859	2Bsuh	10	9	15	5	3	Dutch	PNB	b
10851	Esperanto	0.00000	0	0	0	CEW21z	51-AAAC-a	proper esperanto	4	50.00	0	0A...	10	9	10	5	0	Esperanto	PNB	b
10852	Estonian	0.69000	60,720	61,480	62,769	MSW51a	41-AAAC-b	eesti	1	77.00	47,340	4A.u.	10	9	8	5	2	Estonian: Tallinn	PNB	b
10853	Finnish (Finn)	3.59300	316,183	320,144	326,853	MSW51b	41-AAAA-bb	vehicular suomi	10	86.00	275,324	1A.uh	10	10	12	5	3	Finnish	PNB	b
10854	French	0.03000	2,640	2,673	2,729	CEW21b	51-AABI-d	general français	10	84.00	2,245	1B.uh	10	9	14	5	3	French	PNB	b
10855	German	0.60000	52,800	53,461	54,582	CEW19m	52-ABCE-a	standard hoch-deutsch	38	86.00	45,977	2B.uh	10	9	13	5	3	German*	PNB	b
10856	German Swiss	0.01000	880	891	910	CEW19m	52-ABCG-a	general schwytzer-tütsch	38	86.00	766	0B.uh	10	9	13	5	3	Schwyzerdutsch*	PN.	b
10857	Greek	0.60000	52,800	53,461	54,582	CEW20	56-AAAA-c	dhimotiki	1	95.00	50,788	2B.uh	10	8	11	4	1	Greek: Modern	PNB	b
10858	Hungarian	0.05000	4,400	4,455	4,548	MSW51g	41-BAAA-a	general magyar		75.00	3,341	2A.u.	10	8	8	5	3	Hungarian	PNB	b
10859	Ingrian	0.15000	13,200	13,365	13,645	MSW51z	41-AAAB-f	izhor		75.00	10,024	1....	10	8	9	5	2		p..	b
10860	Italian	0.20000	17,600	17,820	18,194	CEW21e	51-AABQ-c	standard italiano	2	83.00	14,791	2B.uh	10	9	15	5	3	Italian	PNB	b
10861	Jewish	0.22600	19,888	20,137	20,559	CMT35	52-AAAD-r	svea-svensk		0.30	60	1A.uh	5	4	6	4	1	Swedish	PNB	b
10862	Kurdish (Kurd)	0.11500	10,120	10,247	10,461	CNT24c	58-AAAA-a	kurmanji		1.00	102	3c...	6	5	5	5	1	Kurdish: Kurmanji*	PN.	b
10863	Latvian (Lettish)	0.07200	6,336	6,415	6,550	CEW15a	54-AABA-a	standard latviashu		98.90	6,345	3A.u.	10	9	12	5	1	Latvian	PNB	b
10864	Levantine Arab	0.20000	17,600	17,820	18,194	CMT30	12-AACF-f	syro-palestinian		45.00	8,019	1Asuh	9	6	7	5	2	Arabic: Lebanese*	Pnb	b
10865	Lovari Gypsy (Rom)	0.01200	1,056	1,069	1,092	CNN25f	59-ACBA-a	vlach-romani		80.00	855	1a...	10	7	8	5	1	Romani: Finnish*	PN.	b
10866	Lule Lapp (Same)	0.06000	5,280	5,346	5,458	MSW51e	41-AABA-b	lule		90.00	4,812	0....	10	8	11	5	0	Saami: Swedish*	PNB	b
10867	Northern Lapp (Ruija)	0.05000	4,400	4,455	4,548	MSW51e	41-AABA-a	ruija		90.00	4,010	0....	10	8	11	5	1	Saami: Norwegian*	PNB	b

Continued opposite

Table 8-2 continued

	EVANGELIZATION							EVANGELISM			ADDITIONAL DESCRIPTIVE DATA
Ref 1	D 28	aC 29	CG% 30	r 31	E 32	U 33	W 34	e 35	R 36	T 37	Locations, civil divisions, literacy, religions, church history, denominations, dioceses, church growth, missions, agencies, ministries, movements 38
10752	1	8	6.35	8	62.00	38.00	B	18.10	312	5	Traders originally from Syria. Muslims 89%(80% Hanafi Sunnis, 9% Alawis). D=SOC.
10753	0	5	1.62	0	15.01	84.99	A	0.00	557	1.04	A kingdom in the Nuba Hills, Tegali Range. Muslims 100%(Sunnis, with Sufi Qadiriyya order). Spirit possession widespread.
10754	0	9	4.17	0	70.20	29.80	B	103.00	234	7	Southern Sudan, also in CAR. Animists 40%, Muslims 20%. M=GR.
10755	0	6	3.00	0	20.00	80.00	A	0.73	607	3	Nuba Mountains, Kordofan Province. 3 dialects. Muslims 95%, some animists.
10756	0	6	2.33	0	26.00	74.00	A	4.74	396	4	Nuba Hills, round Talodi town. Muslims 90%(Sunnis), some animists 5%.
10757	0	4	1.40	0	15.01	84.99	A	0.00	584	1.05	On Chad border, also in Chad. Many know Arabic. Muslims 100%(Sunnis,with Tijaniyya gaining ground).
10758	0	2	0.00	0	5.00	95.00	A	0.00	0	1.03	Nomads. Also in Chad. Muslims 100%(Maliki Sunnis, with Sanusi influence).
10759	0	6	3.38	0	21.00	79.00	A	1.53	624	4	Northern Sudan, Nuba Hills, Temein Hills southwest of Dilling. Muslims 90%(Sunnis), some animists 8%.
10760	2	5	4.56	0	30.00	70.00	A	2.19	547	4	Equatoria Province, Lafit Hills north of Torit. Semi-nomadic pastoralists. Second language: Murle. Animists 98%. D=AIC,RCC.
10761	1	6	5.38	0	43.00	57.00	A	15.69	434	5	In south between Wau and Aweil. All speak Dinka; virtually absorbed into Dinka. Animists 90%. D=RCC.
10762	2	9	8.19	4	99.89	0.11	C	510.01	175	10	Refugees from northern Ethiopia. D=Ethiopian Orthodox Ch, Eritrean Ch in the Sudan. M=FEM,SIM.
10763	2	7	2.52	4	48.10	51.90	A	0.17	252	3	Refugees from Eritrea. Muslims 98%(Sunnis). D=Eritrean Ch in the Sudan, RCC. M=EOC,FEM,ECE,EFS.
10764	0	6	3.49	0	20.00	80.00	A	0.73	674	3	Northern Sudan, Nuba Hills, West Kordofan District. Muslims 98%(Sunnis), some animists 1%.
10765	0	5	0.00	0	13.01	86.99	A	0.00	301	1.04	Northern Sudan, Tegali Hills. Muslims 100%(Sunnis).
10766	1	6	4.13	0	29.00	71.00	A	3.17	525	4	Northern Sudan, Nuba Hills near Otoro. Muslims 90%(Sunnis), animists 7%. M=SCOC. M=SUM.
10767	1	6	3.83	0	60.00	40.00	B	65.70	240	6	Boma Plateau. Also in Ethiopia. Monolinguals. Animists 65%, Muslims 5%. Resistant to Islam. D=RCC.
10768	2	6	9.84	1	99.85	0.15	C	394.01	243	9	Also in Ethiopia. Semi-nomadic. Animists 10%, highly resistant to Islam. D=AIC,RCC. M=FSCJ,AIM,SIL.
10769	0	6	3.17	0	32.00	68.00	A	11.68	400	5	Tornasi Hills. Tornasi language now extinct, replaced by Berta. Muslims 80%, animists 10%.
10770	0	5	0.00	0	13.01	86.99	A	0.00	301	1.04	Northern Sudan, Tegali Hills. Muslims 100%(Maliki Sunnis).
10771	0	6	2.74	0	20.00	80.00	A	0.73	571	3	South of Nuba Hills, south of Katla and Tulishi. Several dialects. Animists, Muslims.
10772	0	6	2.96	0	20.00	80.00	A	0.73	601	3	Between Katla Range and Miri, Nuba Hills. Animists 95%, Muslims 2%.
10773	1	6	3.41	0	25.00	75.00	A	2.73	530	4	Near Talodi town, Nuba Hills. Close to Krongo. Animists 90%, some Muslims. D=PECS.
10774	0	4	2.81	7	24.01	75.99	A	0.00	401	1.09	Baggara Arabs(strong Negroid ancestry) in Darfur, Kanem, Wadai. Sedentary. Muslims 100%(Maliki Sunnis).
10775	0	4	0.00	5	20.01	79.99	A	0.00	0	1.06	Darfur Province. Former imperial glories. Mainly in Chad northeast of Melfi. Tunjur language virtually extinct. Bilinguals in Arabic. Zealous Muslims 100%(Malikites).
10776	3	6	4.16	0	44.00	56.00	A	3.21	352	4	Also in Kenya, Uganda. Animists 98%. D=RCC,PECS,AIC. M=FSCJ,CMS,AIM.
10777	0	4	0.00	0	9.00	91.00	A	0.00	0	1.03	Northern Sudan, Tegali Range. Muslims 100%.
10778	1	7	5.92	0	61.00	39.00	B	44.53	333	6	Blue Nile to Yabus river. Related to Koma(Ethiopia). Animists 80%, highly resistant to Islam. D=CECS. M=SIM.
10779	0	6	3.48	7	45.00	55.00	A	3.28	299	4	Arab tribe, Nuba Mountains. Muslims 95%(Sunnis), animists 3%.
10780	1	7	4.16	0	49.00	51.00	A	35.77	335	5	In south, also in Central African Republic. Related to Banda. Animists 50%, Muslims 30%. D=RCC.
10781	1	6	5.12	0	54.00	46.00	B	49.27	353	6	In south, also in CAR. Related to Banda. Animists 50%, Muslims 25%. D=RCC.
10782	0	6	2.87	0	21.00	79.00	A	1.53	557	4	Northern Sudan, Wali Hills. Muslims 90%(Maliki Sunnis), some animists 8%.
10783	2	8	7.93	5	91.00	9.00	B	116.25	296	7	Refugees from Ethiopia. Animists 45%, Muslims 20%(Shafi Sunnis). D=EOC,ECMY.
10784	0	4	0.00	0	13.01	86.99	A	0.00	0	1.04	Northern Sudan, on small isolated hills between Nuba Hills and White Nile. Closest to Kau(Ko). Animists 99%.
10785	0	6	3.88	0	35.00	65.00	A	12.77	416	5	In south between Wau and Mboro, and in Chad. Bilingual in Ndogo. Mostly animists 80%, Muslims 10% (Sunnis).
10786	4	6	11.32	0	99.68	0.32	C	270.53	321	8	Southwestern Dinka. Far west of White Nile. Nomadic animists 30%, Muslims 1%, but high resistance to Islam. D=RCC(D-Rumbek),PECS,SDA,JWs. M=FSCJ.
10787	5	6	9.60	0	73.40	26.60	B	68.04	412	6	Jikany Cien. In bend of White Nile. Nomadic pastoralists. Animists 75%, highly resistant to Islam. D=RCC(D-Malakal),CCUN,ELC in Ethiopia,ECMY,CB. M=APM.
10788	1	6	6.58	0	50.00	50.00	B	32.85	443	5	Northeast border. Also in Ethiopia. Agriculturalists in north. Animists 60%, Muslims 20%(Sunnis). D=ECMY(Ethiopia).
10789	0	4	3.35	7	37.01	62.99	A	0.01	300	2	Baggara Arab tribe with strong Negro ancestry. Camel nomads. Muslims 100%(Sunnis).
10790	0	6	1.10	7	36.02	63.98	A	0.02	137	2	Migrants, expatriates, refugees from Yemen wars. Muslims 98%(48% Zaydis,40% Sunnis,5% Ismailis, 5% others).
10791	0	5	3.14	4	24.01	75.99	A	0.00	518	1.08	Pockets on Blue Nile north of Ar-Rusayris. Outside, mainly in Niger, Nigeria, Chad, Cameroon. Muslims 100%(Maliki Sunnis).
10792	0	6	3.71	0	34.00	66.00	A	12.41	414	5	Western Bahr El Ghazal Province, Darfur; also in CAR. Many bilinguals in Kresh or Arabic. Muslims 85%(Sunnis), Animists 5%.
10793	0	4	0.00	0	9.00	91.00	A	0.00	0	1.04	Saharan Negroes. Northwest Darfur, Western Province. Also in Chad. Semi-nomadic, also settled cattle-raisers. Muslims 75%(Maliki Sunnis), animists 25%.
10794	4	6	11.29	0	99.85	0.15	C	456.34	246	10	Mostly in Zaire, also CAR. Animists 15%. D=RCC(D-Tombora),PECS(strong Anglican work; East Africa Revival),AIC,Sudan Church of Christ. M=AIM,CMS,FSCJ.
10795	0	6	11.75		99.76	0.24	C	278.88	319	8	Koreans(SIM,PCK); since 1980, 2 million southern Sudanese are displaced refugees, with 660,000 other refugees from Ethiopia, 120,000 from Chad.

Suriname

Ref	D	aC	CG%	r	E	U	W	e	R	T	
10796	1	9	2.22	0	56.00	44.00	B	36.79	158	5	Carib. Southeast jungle. Mostly bilinguals in Trio. Nearly extinct. Animists 80%. D=RCC. M=WT.
10797	1	6	1.72	0	99.70	0.30	C	275.94	69	8	Mainly in Brazil. Animists 30%. D=RCC. M=NTM,SIL.
10798	2	7	1.71	0	99.91	0.09	C	451.72	55	10	Near coast. Also in Guyana, French Guiana, Venezuela. 35% speak the language, rest use Sranan. Animists 9%. D=RCC,AC/CPWI.
10799	4	6	1.72	1	99.80	0.20	C	362.08	54	9	Maroons. Along border with French Guiana. Shamanists 20%. D=EBGS/MCS,ECWI,SA,WC. M=ZZG,DLM,WIM,IM,DTLM,PHC.
10800	5	10	1.71	0	99.78	0.22	C	438.43	51	10	Expatriates from Britain, in development. Nonreligious 9%. D=Anglican Ch/CPWI(D-Guyana),WC,SDA,SA,JWs.
10801	1	10	1.70	1	54.00	46.00	B	17.73	137	5	Caribbean Hindustani. Small farmers. Hindus 64%(2 branches: Arya Dewaker,Sanathan Dharm), Muslims 22%(mostly Sunnis), Baha'is 5%. D=EBGS.
10802	2	8	1.68	7	90.00	10.00	B	91.98	77	6	Small farmers. Muslims 41%(Shafi Sunnis), New-Religionists 31%, Baha'is 5%. D=ZZG,RCC. M=ZZG,Worldteam,FMB,SIL.
10803	5	6	1.72	1	99.70	0.30	C	296.38	64	8	Near coast. Bilinguals in Sranan. Shamanists 30%. D=RCC,ECWI,AoG,SDA,Baptists. M=CSSR,OMI,WIM,IM,SIL.
10804	5	10	1.72	6	99.76	0.24	C	427.19	46	10	Settlers, officials, expatriates from Holland, in business. Dutch spoken by 25% of country. Nonreligious/atheists 24%. D=DRC,EBGS,ELCS,OCC,RCC. M=WT,IM.
10805	0	10	0.00	6	50.14	49.86	B	0.25	38	3	Refugees from Brazil (1639 persecution). Practicing Jews.
10806	2	10	1.43	8	99.61	0.39	C	261.67	49	8	Some also in French Guiana. Afro-American spiritists 13%(Voodoo). D=RCC,AC/CPWI.
10807	1	10	5.39	8	99.71	0.29	C	362.81	118	9	1863, contract workers, now shopkeepers. Buddhists/folk-religionists 28%. D=RCC. M=CSSR,FMB.
10808	5	10	4.93	7	99.70	0.30	C	357.70	109	9	Labor immigrants from 1863. Buddhists/Chinese folk-religionists 30%. D=RCC,CPWI,EBGS,SDA,CMA. M=CSSR,OMI,FMB.
10809	0	10	3.99	7	63.00	37.00	B	9.19	204	4	Migrants, emigres from Indonesia. Muslims 65%(Shafi Sunnis), New-Religionists 30%, Baha'is.
10810	3	6	1.72	1	99.70	0.30	C	288.71	59	8	North central, on Coppename river. English-based creole. Animists 30%. D=RCC,CPWI,EBGS.
10811	0	5	2.86	4	52.00	48.00	B	18.98	188	5	Blue Meo. From Laos, also in Viet Nam, Thailand, China, USA, France. Animists 90%.
10812	1	10	4.95	8	99.60	0.40	C	269.37	126	8	Refugees from Lebanon. Muslims 30%(Sunnis,Shias), Baha'is 10%. D=RCC(Maronites).
10813	2	7	1.70	1	47.00	53.00	A	13.72	140	5	Along Saramacca river. English-based creole. Animists 90%. D=AC/CPWI,RCC.
10814	4	9	1.72	8	99.95	0.05	C	586.00	37	10	Emigres from Latin American countries. D=RCC,AC/CPWI,SDA,JWs.
10815	4	6	1.72	1	99.60	0.40	C	229.95	63	8	Shamanists 20%. D=RCC,EBGS,WC,Pentecostals. M=SIL,WIM,Independent Faith Mission,WT,WC.
10816	0	9	0.00	8	46.00	54.00	A	0.00	0	1.14	Refugees in 1639 from persecution in Brazil. Practicing Jews.
10817	4	7	1.64	1	99.60	0.40	C	238.71	59	8	Maroons. Along Saramacca river. Lexicon 20% African. Afro-American spiritists 15%. D=EBGS,ELCS,RCC(D-Paramaribo),SDA. M=SIL,Worldteam.
10818	6	10	1.62	5	99.65	0.35	C	296.56	48	8	Lingua franca of 80% of country. Afro-American spiritists 7%(Winti,Vodoun,Obeah). D=EBGS,ELCS,RCC,SDA,SA,JWs. M=Worldteam,FMB,SIL.
10819	1	10	3.80	8	81.00	19.00	B	59.13	152	6	Refugees from Syria. Muslims 79%(Hanafi Sunnis,some Alawi Shias), Baha'is. D=Syrian Orthodox Ch.
10820	2	7	1.72	0	69.00	31.00	B	73.03	108	6	South central villages. Some also in Brazil. Animists 70%. D=RCC,ECWI. M=UFM,WIM,WT.
10821	1	8	1.72	8	98.00	2.00	B	178.85	66	7	Near Guyana border; mainly in Venezuela. Language isolate. Animists 50%. D=RCC. M=BMM.
10822	2	7	1.76	0	44.00	56.00	A	14.45	172	5	Villages in southeastern Surinam. Animists/shamanists 90%. D=RCC,ECWI. M=WIM,WT.
10823	0	9	1.73		38.00	62.00	A	13.87	125	5	West Indian Blacks (AMEC,CPWI), Central Americans, other South Americans, other Europeans. Nonreligious 28%, Afro-Cariobbean religionists 20%.

Svalbard & Jan Mayen Islands

Ref	D	aC	CG%	r	E	U	W	e	R	T	
10824	2	5	1.05	6	99.65	0.35	C	315.54	44	9	Nonreligious 30%. D=Ch of Norway,RCC(VA-North Norway/Tromso).
10825	1	9	2.06	7	99.35	0.65	B	132.86	54	7	D=Russian Orthodox Ch(P-Moscow).
10826	0	10	1.40		70.00	30.00	B	102.20	55	7	Individuals from several Europeans countries. Nonreligious 60%.

Swaziland

Ref	D	aC	CG%	r	E	U	W	e	R	T	
10827	5	10	4.46	5	99.82	0.18	C	472.89	93	10	Expatriates from South Africa, in administration. Nonreligious 5%. D=NGK(General Synod DRC,Mother Ch),NHK,AFMSA,SDA,JWs.
10828	3	10	3.53	8	99.79	0.21	C	441.17	84	10	Expatriates from Britain, in business, development. Nonreligious 9%. D=Anglican Ch/CPSA(D-Swaziland),MCSA,JWs. M=USPG.
10829	4	10	5.46	5	99.65	0.35	C	319.55	133	9	Mixed-race persons. Animists 10%. D=RCC(D-Manzini),Evangelical Bible Ch,JWs,AICs. M=OSM,SDB,SM,TEAM.
10830	0	10	2.99	6	46.00	54.00	A	5.03	265	4	Migrant workers from Comoro Islands. Muslims 97%(Shafi Sunnis).
10831	3	10	4.06	7	68.00	32.00	B	17.37	204	5	Traders from India, Pakistan. Hindus 20%, Muslims 77%, many Baha'is 3%. D=RCC,FGCOGSA,JWs.
10832	4	10	5.42	1	99.65	0.35	C	282.32	149	8	Isipiki, Chilapalapa. Migrant miners speaking Xhosa-based pidgin. Animists 10%. D=RCC,CPSA,ELCSA,over 30 AICs. M=OSM,SDB.
10833	5	10	6.12	5	99.63	0.37	C	278.97	171	8	Migrant workers from Malawi. Nonreligious 16%, animists 6%. D=BSFC,RCC,CPSA,MCSA,many AICs.
10834	5	10	6.94	5	99.65	0.35	C	324.29	158	9	From Lesotho and South Africa. Animists 3%. D=over 200 AICs,RCC,CPSA,MCSA,&c.
10835	10	8	7.89	5	99.67	0.33	C	328.65	182	9	Also in South Africa. Animists 12%. Nominal Christians 20%. D=over 50 AICs,RCC,CCAHSCZ,MCSA,SCCZSA,ECS,CON,AEC,AoG,&c. M=SAGM/AEF,OSM,SDB.
10836	4	10	7.70	5	99.72	0.28	C	358.51	191	9	Migrants and refugees(recently up to 60,000) from Mozambique and South Africa. Animists 4%, Muslims, Baha'is. D=TPC,AICs,RCC,SDA,JWs. M=FMB.
10837	8	10	8.64	5	99.74	0.26	C	396.51	180	9	Migrants from KwaZulu(Zululand). Animists 9%. D=over 30 AICs,RCC,CPSA,MCSA,ECS,ELCSA,COG,&c. M=LBI,&c.
10838	0	10	5.31		85.00	15.00	B	161.33	171	7	Norwegians, East Africans, other Mozambicans, other Europeans. Nonreligious/atheists 20%.

Sweden

Ref	D	aC	CG%	r	E	U	W	e	R	T	
10839	0	0	4.74	6	68.00	32.00	B	62.05	212	6	Refugees and migrant workers from Albania, most in the 1990s. Nonreligious 40%, Muslims 25%, atheists 10%. D=Albanian Orthodox Church.
10840	1	9	0.55	2	99.90	0.10	C	433.62	32	10	Along Ume river, and south in Lycksele, Mala, and Sorsele. Also in Norway. D=Ch of Sweden.
10841	2	10	7.01	5	99.88	0.12	C	501.07	135	10	Refugees from Lebanon and Cyprus wars. Nonreligious 10%. D=Ancient Ch of the East(P-Tehran),RCC.
10842	3	10	0.55	8	99.80	0.20	C	402.96	31	10	Also in Finland.D=nomadic caravan churches,Ch of Sweden,GEM. M=GGMS,FBS.
10843	0	10	4.14	6	55.05	44.95	B	0.10	251	3	Refugees from Bosnia civil war, 1992. Muslims 90%. M=RCC,SLM.
10844	1	10	8.10	8	99.90	0.10	C	528.88	152	10	Mesticos. Portuguese-speaking migrants from Brazil. D=RCC. M=SJ,OFM,OP.
10845	7	10	1.23	9	99.78	0.22	C	441.28	42	10	Expatriates from Britain, in business. Nonreligious 9%. D=Ch of England(D-Europe),MCS,SA,BUS,SDA,JWs,CB.
10846	1	10	7.65	8	99.89	0.11	C	503.51	145	10	Spanish-speaking migrant workers from Chile; Mestizos. Nonreligious 11%. D=SJ,OFM,OP.
10847	1	10	5.45	8	99.91	0.09	C	531.44	112	10	Migrant workers from Croatia (ex-Yugoslavia). Nonreligious 8%. D=RCC(D-Stockholm). M=SJ,OP,OFM.
10848	1	10	0.55	8	99.75	0.25	C	388.72	32	9	Czech-speaking refugees from Moravia, Czechoslovakia. Nonreligious 9%. D=RCC. M=SJ,OFM.
10849	5	10	0.55	9	99.94	0.06	C	576.40	28	10	Expatriates from Denmark in business. Nonreligious 5%. D=Ch of Denmark,Ch of Sweden,MCS,SA,JWs.
10850	4	10	0.55	8	99.76	0.24	C	432.74	25	10	Expatriates from Holland, in industry, professions. Nonreligious 5%. D=DRC(NHK),GKN,GKV,RCC.
10851	0	10	0.00	5	99.50	0.50	B	204.40	0	8	Artificial(constructed) language, in 80 countries. Speakers in Sweden: 314,000(non mother-tongue). Nonreligious 50%.
10852	2	10	1.39	5	99.77	0.23	C	410.33	48	10	Refugees from USSR since 1939. Also in USA, Canada, UK, Finland, Australia. Nonreligious 10%. D=Estonian Orthodox Ch in Exile,Estonian ELC in Exile.
10853	3	10	0.55	8	99.86	0.14	C	499.10	27	10	Northeast coast. Migrant workers from Finland. D=Finnish Evangelical Lutheran Ch,Finnish Orthodox Ch,SDA.
10854	3	10	0.55	8	99.84	0.16	C	487.49	26	10	Expatriates from France, in business. D=RCC(D-Stockholm),French Reformed Ch,JWs.
10855	8	10	0.55	8	99.86	0.14	C	517.93	28	10	Expatriates from Germany, in business. Nonreligious 5%. D=EKD,RCC,Ch of Sweden,MCS,SA,SDA,JWs,NAC.
10856	3	10	0.55	8	99.86	0.14	C	477.12	30	10	Expatriates from Switzerland in business. Nonreligious 5%. D=SRC,EKD,NAC.
10857	1	10	2.29	7	99.95	0.05	C	575.60	54	10	Migrant workers from Greece. Merchants. D=Orthodox Ch in Sweden(D-Swedia & All Scandinavia).
10858	3	10	0.55	6	99.75	0.25	C	394.20	37	9	Refugees and migrant workers from Hungary. Nonreligious 19%. D=RCC,Hungarian Protestant Congregations(Reformed,Lutheran),JWs.
10859	2	10	0.55	9	99.75	0.25	C	339.45	34	9	Also in Russia. Only 1% (the elderly) speak Ingrian, the rest speak Finnish. Close to Karelian. Nonreligious 25%. D=GOC,Ch of Sweden.
10860	1	10	0.55	9	99.83	0.17	C	478.66	27	10	Expatriates from Italy, in business. D=RCC(D-Stockholm). M=SJ,OMI,OP,CP,SDB,OCD,OFM.
10861	0	10	4.18	6	55.30	44.70	B	0.60	241	3	Present since 1774. In 8 congregations of practicing Jews. Nonreligious 20%.
10862	0	10	2.35	0	43.00	57.00	A	1.57	277	4	Refugees from Turkey, Iraq, Iran. Some speak Sorani, some Zaza. Muslims 99%(Sunnis). M=whole network of agencies.
10863	1	10	0.55	9	99.90	0.01	C	606.09	29	10	Latgalians. Refugees from USSR after 1917, 1939. Others in USA, Australia, Canada, Germany, UK, NZ, Brazil, Venezuela. D=Latvian Ev Lutheran Ch in Exile.
10864	2	10	6.92	8	99.45	0.55	B	179.03	192	7	Refugees from Lebanon. Muslims 50%, Baha'is 5%. D=RCC(Maronites),OCS.
10865	2	9	0.55	6	99.80	0.20	C	391.28	32	9	Murga caravan communities. D=Ch of Sweden,GEM. M=GGMS.
10866	0	9	-0.66	2	99.90	0.10	C	476.32	6	10	Swedish Lapps. Lapland along Lule river in Gellivare and Jokkmokk; also in Norway. 50% no longer speak same language. Nonreligious 6%.
10867	1	9	0.55	9	99.90	0.10	C	473.04	29	10	Northern Lapps; in Karesuando and Jukkasjarvi. Mainly in Norway, also Finland. Nonreligious 7%. D=Ch of Sweden. M=SLM.

Continued overleaf

Table 8-2 continued

PEOPLE		POPULATION				IDENTITY CODE		LANGUAGE		CHURCH		MINISTRY						SCRIPTURE	
Ref 1	Ethnic name 2	P% 3	In 1995 4	In 2000 5	In 2025 6	Race 7	Language 8	Autoglossonym 9	S 10	AC 11	Members 12	Jayuh 13-17	d 18	wa 19	xc 20	mc 21	mi 22	Biblioglossonym 23	Pub ss 24-26 27
10868	Norwegian	0.60000	52,800	53,461	54,582	CEW19p	52-AAAC-e	ny-norsk	100	92.50	49,452	0B.uh	10	9	14	5	2	Norwegian*	PNB b
10869	Persian	0.40000	35,200	35,641	36,388	CNT24f	58-AACC-c	standard farsi		0.10	36	1Asu.	5	5	7	0	0		PNB b
10870	Pite Lapp	0.01200	1,056	1,069	1,092	MSW51e	41-AABA-c	pite		90.00	962	0....	10	8	11	5	1	Saami, Pite	PNB .
10871	Polish	0.07500	6,600	6,683	6,823	CEW22i	53-AAAC-c	polski		86.00	5,747	2A.uh	10	9	11	5	3	Polish	PNB b
10872	Romanian	0.10000	8,800	8,910	9,097	CEW21i	51-AADC-a	limba românească		80.00	7,128	3A.u.	10	8	8	4	1	Romanian	PNB b
10873	Russian	0.30000	26,400	26,731	27,291	CEW22j	53-AAAE-d	russkiy	2	65.00	17,375	4B.uh	10	8	9	5	2	Russian	PNB b
10874	Serb	0.60000	52,800	53,461	54,582	CEW22l	53-AAAG-a	standard srpski	2	85.00	45,442	1Asuh	10	8	8	4	1	Serbian*	PNB b
10875	Slovak	0.01200	1,056	1,069	1,092	CEW22m	53-AAAD-b	slovensky		77.00	823	1Asuh	10	8	8	4	3	Slovak	PNB b
10876	Slovene	0.06000	5,280	5,346	5,458	CEW22n	53-AAAF-a	slovensko		94.00	5,025	1a..h	10	9	9	4	2	Slovenian*	PNB b
10877	Somalian	0.14000	12,320	12,474	12,736	MSY44o	14-GAGA-a	af-soomaali		0.01	1	2A...	3	4	6	0	0	Somali	PNB b
10878	Southern Lapp	0.03000	2,640	2,673	2,729	MSW51e	41-AABC	south saame cluster		90.00	2,406	0....	10	8	11	5	1	Saami, Southern	... b
10879	Spaniard	0.05000	4,400	4,455	4,548	CEW21k	51-AABB-c	general español	2	95.00	4,232	2B.uh	10	9	15	5	2	Spanish	PNB b
10880	Swedish (Swede)	86.63500	7,623,868	7,719,364	7,881,123	CEW19q	52-AAAD-r	svea-svensk	100	67.20	5,187,413	1A.uh	10	10	13	5	2	Swedish	PNB b
10881	Swedish Gypsy	0.05000	4,400	4,455	4,548	CNN25f	52-AAAD-r	svea-svensk		70.00	3,119	1A.uh	10	7	8	5	1	Swedish	PNB b
10882	Swedish Traveller	0.01000	880	891	910	CNN25f	59-AGAA-ac	anglo-romani-africa		70.00	624	0....	10	7	8	4	0		... .
10883	Syrian Arab	0.10000	8,800	8,910	9,097	CMT30	12-AACF-f	syro-palestinian		21.00	1,871	1Asuh	9	5	8	4	2	Arabic: Lebanese*	Pnb b
10884	Syrian Aramaic	0.18000	15,840	16,038	16,374	CMT31	12-AAAA-e	sur-oyo		95.00	15,236	4as..	10	9	11	5	2	Syriac	PNB b
10885	Tibetan	0.01000	880	891	910	MSY50r	70-AAAA-c	utsang		1.00	9	0a...	6	4	6	1	0	Tibetan	PNB b
10886	Turk	0.25900	22,792	23,077	23,561	MSY41j	44-AABA-a	osmanli		0.50	115	1A.u.	5	4	6	1	0	Turkish	PNB b
10887	USA White	0.09000	7,920	8,019	8,187	CEW19s	52-ABAC-s	general american		77.00	6,175	1Bsuh	10	9	13	5	3	English*	PNB b
10888	Vlach Gypsy (Zigenare)	0.00600	528	535	546	CNN25f	59-ACBA-a	vlach-romani		80.00	428	1a...	10	8	8	5	3	Romani: Finnish*	PN. b
10889	other minor peoples	0.20100	17,688	17,910	18,285	...				59.00	10,567		10	7	8	4	3		
	Switzerland	**100.00000**	**7,142,904**	**7,385,708**	**7,586,992**					**87.27**	**6,445,545**								
10890	Arab	0.03700	2,643	2,733	2,807	CMT30	12-AACF-k	central `anazi		21.00	574	4Asuh	9	5	8	5	3		pnb b
10891	Bavarian Austrian	0.50000	35,715	36,929	37,935	CEW19f	52-ABCF-b	donau-bayrisch-t.		88.00	32,497	0B.uh	10	9	13	5	1		pn. b
10892	Bosniac (Muslmani)	1.55000	110,715	114,478	117,598	CEW22a	53-AAAG-a	standard srpski		0.05	57	1Asuh	4	7	8	5	0	Serbian*	PNB b
10893	British	0.50000	35,715	36,929	37,935	CEW19i	52-ABAC-b	standard-english	30	78.00	28,804	3Bsuh	10	9	13	5	3		PNB b
10894	Ceylon Tamil	0.45000	32,143	33,236	34,141	CNN23c	49-EBEA-bn	north sri-lanka-tamil		30.00	9,971	1Asu.	9	6	12	0	0		pnb b
10895	Croat	0.40000	28,572	29,543	30,348	CEW22d	53-AAAG-b	standard hrvatski		91.00	26,884	2Asuh	10	9	11	0	0	Croatian	PNB b
10896	Czech	0.20000	14,286	14,771	15,174	CEW22e	53-AAAD-a	czesky	1	73.00	10,783	2Asuh	10	8	8	5	2	Czech	PNB b
10897	Dutch	0.20000	14,286	14,771	15,174	CEW19h	52-ABCA-a	algemeen-nederlands	3	76.00	11,226	2Bsuh	10	9	15	5	1	Dutch	PNB b
10898	Esperanto	0.00000	0	0	0	CEW21z	51-AAAC-a	proper esperanto	1	60.00	0	0A...	10	9	8	5	0	Esperanto	PNB b
10899	Franco-Swiss	16.83000	1,202,151	1,243,015	1,276,891	CEW21b	51-AABI-f	français-suisse		84.83	1,054,449	1B.uh	10	10	14	5	3		pnb b
10900	French	0.70000	50,000	51,700	53,109	CEW21b	51-AABI-d	general français	66	84.00	43,428	1B.uh	10	9	14	5	3	French	PNB b
10901	French (Vaudois)	2.10000	150,001	155,100	159,327	CEW21b	51-AABJ-e	vaudois	3	88.00	136,488	0....	10	9	14	5	2	French: Vaudois, Ancient*	PN. b
10902	French Jew	0.10000	7,143	7,386	7,587	CMT35	51-AABI-a	historical français		0.30	22	1B.uh	5	4	4	5	0		pnb b
10903	German (High German)	1.60000	114,286	118,171	121,392	CEW19m	52-ABCF-a	nord-bayrisch-t.	85	87.00	102,809	0B.uh	10	9	13	5	3		pn. b
10904	German Jew	0.23000	16,429	16,987	17,450	CMT35	52-ABCE-a	standard hoch-deutsch		0.30	51	2B.uh	5	4	6	5	0	German*	PNB b
10905	German Swiss (Alemannic)	55.28000	3,948,597	4,082,819	4,194,089	CEW19m	52-ABCG-a	general schwytzer-tütsch	85	92.33	3,769,667	0B.uh	10	10	15	5	3	Schwyzerdutsch*	PN. b
10906	Greek	0.20000	14,286	14,771	15,174	CEW20	56-AAAA-c	dhimotiki		95.00	14,033	2B.uh	10	9	11	5	1	Greek: Modern	PNB b
10907	Han Chinese	0.02000	1,429	1,477	1,517	MSY42a	79-AAAB-ba	kuo-yü		25.00	369	2Bsuh	9	5	8	4	1	Chinese: Kuoyu*	PNB b
10908	Hungarian	0.20000	14,286	14,771	15,174	MSW51g	41-BAAA-a	general magyar		79.00	11,669	2A.u.	10	9	8	5	2	Hungarian	PNB b
10909	Italian	0.50000	35,715	36,929	37,935	CEW21e	51-AABQ-c	standard italiano	25	84.00	31,020	2B.uh	10	9	15	5	3	Italian	PNB b
10910	Italo-Swiss (Ticanese)	11.02000	787,148	813,905	836,087	CEW21e	51-AABO-b	ticinese		94.00	765,071	0B...	10	10	15	5	3		pn. b
10911	Japanese	0.07000	5,000	5,170	5,311	MSY45a	45-CAAA-a	koku-go		2.00	103	1B.uh	6	4	9	0	0	Japanese	PNB b
10912	Jewish	0.02000	1,429	1,477	1,517	CMT35	52-ABCH-a	west yiddish		0.07	1	0B..h	4	4	3	4	0	Yiddish	PNB b
10913	Kurdish (Kurd)	0.49000	35,000	36,190	37,176	CNT24c	58-AAAA-a	kurmanji		0.01	4	3c...	3	4	4	5	1	Kurdish: Kurmanji*	PN. b
10914	Portuguese	1.20000	85,715	88,628	91,044	CEW21g	51-AABA-e	general português	1	94.00	83,311	2Bsuh	10	9	15	5	3	Portuguese	PNB b
10915	Romanian	0.10000	7,143	7,386	7,587	CEW21i	51-AADC-a	limba românească		84.00	6,204	3A.u.	10	8	8	5	1	Romanian	PNB b
10916	Romansch (Engadine)	0.37000	26,429	27,327	28,072	CEW21h	51-AABK-a	sursilvan		91.60	25,032	0....	10	9	11	4	2	Romansch: Sursilvan	PNB b
10917	Romansch (Grishun)	0.30000	21,429	22,157	22,761	CEW21h	51-AABK-a	sursilvan		90.00	19,941	0....	10	9	11	4	2	Romansch: Sursilvan	PNB b
10918	Romansch (Ladin)	0.35000	25,000	25,850	26,554	CEW21h	51-AABK-a	sursilvan	3	91.00	23,523	0....	10	9	11	4	2	Romansch: Sursilvan	PNB b
10919	Russian	0.10000	7,143	7,386	7,587	CEW22j	53-AAAE-d	russkiy	1	67.00	4,948	4B.uh	10	8	9	5	2	Russian	PNB b
10920	Serb	0.95000	67,858	70,164	72,076	CEW22d	53-AAAF-a	slovensko		85.00	59,640	1a..h	10	9	8	0	0	Slovenian*	PNB b
10921	Sinte Gypsy (Rom)	0.04000	2,857	2,954	3,035	CNN25f	59-ACBB-b	sinti		80.00	2,363	0....	10	8	8	5	1	Romani: Sinti, Italian	P.. b
10922	Spaniard	2.00000	142,858	147,714	151,740	CEW21k	51-AABB-c	general español	5	96.00	141,806	2B.uh	10	9	15	5	2	Spanish	PNB b
10923	Swedish (Swede)	0.03000	2,143	2,216	2,276	CEW19q	52-AAAD-r	svea-svensk	1	73.00	1,617	1A.uh	10	9	13	5	1	Swedish	PNB b
10924	Swiss Gypsy	0.28000	20,000	20,680	21,244	CNN25f	52-ABCE-a	standard hoch-deutsch		70.00	14,476	2B.uh	10	8	8	5	1	German*	PNB b
10925	Tibetan	0.02000	1,429	1,477	1,517	MSY50r	70-AAAA-c	utsang		0.10	1	0a...	5	4	6	5	0	Tibetan	PNB b
10926	Turk	0.80000	57,143	59,086	60,696	MSY41j	44-AABA-a	osmanli		0.50	295	1A.u.	5	4	6	5	0	Turkish	PNB b
10927	USA White	0.06000	4,286	4,431	4,552	CEW19s	52-ABAC-s	general american		77.00	3,412	1Bsuh	10	9	13	5	3	English*	PNB b
10928	other minor peoples	0.20300	14,500	14,993	15,402	...				60.00	8,996		10	7	8	5	3		
	Syria	**100.00000**	**14,199,860**	**16,124,618**	**26,291,810**					**7.8**	**1,257,710**								
10929	Armenian	2.75800	391,632	444,717	725,128	CEW14	57-AAAA-b	ashkharik		88.00	391,351	4A.u.	10	9	13	5	3	Armenian: Modern, Eastern	PNB b
10930	Assyrian (Aisor)	0.30000	42,600	48,374	78,875	CMT31	12-AAAA-f	aisor		95.00	45,955	4cs..	10	8	11	5	2	Assyrian Neo-aramaic	PNB b
10931	Bedouin Arab	7.40000	1,050,790	1,193,222	1,945,594	CMT30	12-AACD-f	west egyptian		0.01	119	0c...	3	3	3	1	0	Arabic: Egyptian*	PN. .
10932	British	0.00500	710	806	1,315	CEW19i	52-ABAC-b	standard-english	65	70.00	564	3Bsuh	10	9	13	5	3		PNB b
10933	Bulgar	0.01000	1,420	1,612	2,629	CEW22b	53-AAAH-b	bulgarski		72.00	1,161	2A.uh	10	8	8	4	1	Bulgarian	PNB b
10934	Circassian	0.23100	32,802	37,248	60,734	CEW17a	42-AAAA-b	cherkes		0.20	74	1a...	5	3	2	1	1		pn. b
10935	French	0.06000	8,520	9,675	15,775	CEW21b	51-AABI-d	general français	35	75.00	7,256	1B.uh	10	9	14	5	3	French	PNB b
10936	German	0.01000	1,420	1,612	2,629	CEW19m	52-ABCE-a	standard hoch-deutsch	10	87.00	1,403	2B.uh	10	9	13	5	2	German*	PNB b
10937	Greek	0.03000	4,260	4,837	7,888	CEW20	56-AAAA-c	dhimotiki		95.00	4,596	2B.uh	10	9	11	5	2	Greek: Modern	PNB b
10938	Iraqi Arab	0.30000	42,600	48,374	78,875	CMT30	12-AACF-g	syro-mesopotamian		0.70	339	1Asuh	5	4	8	1	3		pnb b
10939	Jordanian Arab	0.20000	28,400	32,249	52,584	CMT30	12-AACF-f	syro-palestinian		4.90	1,580	1Asuh	6	5	6	2	3	Arabic: Lebanese*	Pnb b
10940	Lebanese Arab	0.50000	70,999	80,623	131,459	CMT30	12-AACF-f	syro-palestinian		51.00	41,118	1Asuh	10	7	8	5	1	Arabic: Lebanese*	Pnb b
10941	Ossetian (Allagir, Tagaur	0.30000	42,600	48,374	78,875	CNT24e	58-ABBA	oseti cluster		36.00	17,415	2....	9	6	7	5	2	Ossete*	PN. b
10942	Palestinian Arab	3.90000	553,795	628,860	1,025,381	CMT30	12-AACF-f	syro-palestinian		3.80	23,897	1Asuh	6	4	8	5	1	Arabic: Lebanese*	Pnb b
10943	Persian	0.10000	14,200	16,125	26,292	CNT24f	58-AACC-c	standard farsi		0.04	6	1Asu.	3	3	8	1	0		PNB b
10944	Portuguese	0.00500	710	806	1,315	CEW21g	51-AABA-e	general português		92.00	742	2Bsuh	10	9	15	5	3	Portuguese	PNB b
10945	Russian	0.01800	2,556	2,902	4,733	CEW22j	53-AAAE-d	russkiy	5	31.00	900	4B.uh	9	8	11	5	1	Russian	PNB b
10946	Spaniard	0.00500	710	806	1,315	CEW21k	51-AABB-c	general español		96.00	774	2B.uh	10	9	15	5	3	Spanish	PNB b
10947	Syrian Arab	74.90200	10,635,979	12,077,661	19,693,092	CMT30	12-AACF-f	syro-palestinian		5.60	676,349	1Asuh	7	8	8	5	2	Arabic: Lebanese*	Pnb b
10948	Syrian Aramaic (Eastern)	0.14000	19,880	22,574	36,809	CMT31	12-AAAA-e	sur-oyo		95.00	21,446	4as..	10	9	11	5	3	Syriac	PNB b
10949	Syrian Jew	0.03200	4,544	5,160	8,413	CMT35	12-AACF-f	syro-palestinian		0.10	5	1Asuh	5	3	2	0	0	Arabic: Lebanese*	Pnb b
10950	Turk	0.30000	42,600	48,374	78,875	MSY41j	44-AABA-a	osmanli		0.02	10	1A.u.	3	3	1	0	0	Turkish	PNB b
10951	Turkmen (Azerbaijani)	0.65800	93,435	106,100	173,000	MSY41k	44-AABA-f	azeri		0.02	21	2a.u.	3	3	1	0	0		PNB b
10952	USA White	0.01000	1,420	1,612	2,629	CEW19s	52-ABAC-s	general american		78.00	1,258	1Bsuh	10	10	12	0	0	English*	PNB b
10953	West Aramaic	0.08000	11,360	12,900	21,033	CMT31	12-AAAA-b	west neo-aramaic		40.00	5,160	1cs..	9	9	11	5	2	Aramaic: Ancient	PNb b
10954	Western Kurd (Kermanji)	7.33300	1,041,276	1,182,418	1,927,978	CNT24c	58-AAAA-a	kurmanji		0.13	1,537	3c...	5	4	2	1	3	Kurdish: Kurmanji*	PN. b
10955	Zott Gypsy (Nawar, Nuar)	0.21300	30,246	34,345	56,002	CNN25f	59-ACAA-a	domari		20.00	6,869	0....	9	5	6	5	3		... b
10956	other minor peoples	0.20000	28,400	32,249	52,584	...				18.00	5,805		8	5	3	1	0		
	Taiwan	**100.00000**	**21,561,000**	**22,401,000**	**25,730,000**					**5.27**	**1,179,743**								
10957	Ami (Amis, Pangtsah)	0.67659	145,880	151,563	174,087	AUG01a	30-KAAA-c	central amis	1	90.00	136,407	0....	10	9	11	5	3	Amis	PN. .
10958	Babusa	0.00100	216	224	257	AUG01a	30-CBCA-a	proper babuza		80.00	179	0....	10	8	10	5	1	Babuza	... .
10959	British	0.02000	4,312	4,480	5,146	CEW19i	52-ABAC-b	standard-english	19	78.00	3,495	3Bsuh	10	9	13	5	2		PNB b
10960	Bunun (Bunan, Bubukun)	0.18769	40,468	42,044	48,293	AUG01a	30-IAAA-d	central bunun		80.00	33,636	0....	10	8	8	4	1	Bunun	PN. .
10961	Drukai (Tsalisen, Rutkai)	0.03764	8,116	8,432	9,685	AUG01a	30-HAAA	rukai cluster		80.00	6,745	0....	10	8	8	4	1		... .
10962	Filipino	0.38000	81,932	85,124	97,774	MSY44o	31-CKAA-a	proper tagalog		80.00	68,099	4Bs..	10	10	12	5	1	Tagalog	PNB b
10963	Han Chinese (Hakka)	10.11588	2,181,085	2,266,058	2,602,816	MSY42a	79-AAAG-a	literary hakka	2	3.00	67,982	1A...	6	5	11	5	4	Chinese: Hakka, Wukingfu*	PNB b
10964	Han Chinese (Mandarin)	15.89000	3,426,043	3,559,519	4,088,497	MSY42a	79-AAAB-bc	proper pu-tong-hua	80	5.36	190,790	1Bsuh	7	5	12	5	3		pnb b
10965	Hui (Chinese Muslim)	0.24000	51,746	53,762	61,752	MSY42b	79-AAAB-ba	kuo-yü	80	0.00	0	2Bsuh	0	3	1	5	0	Chinese: Kuoyu*	PNB b
10966	Japanese	0.05000	10,781	11,201	12,865	MSY45a	45-CAAA-a	koku-go	68	3.00	336	1B.uh	6	5	2	5	2	Japanese	PNB b
10967	Jewish	0.00085	183	190	219	CMT35	79-AAAB-ba	kuo-yü		1.23	2	2Bsuh	6	4	2	5	0	Chinese: Kuoyu*	PNB b
10968	Kavalan (Kuwarawan)	0.00050	108	112	129	AUG01a	30-BDAA-a	kava-lan		80.00	90	0....	10	8	6	4	2		... .
10969	Khalka Mongol (Mongolian)	0.03000	6,468	6,720	7,719	MSY41f	44-BAAB-c	halh		0.02	1	3A..h	3	3	1	5	0	Mongolian: Khalka*	PNb b
10970	Korean	0.02900	6,253	6,496	7,462	MSY46	45-AAAA-b	kukö		40.00	2,599	2A...	9	7	9	5	2	Korean	PNB b
10971	Malay	0.05000	10,781	11,201	12,865	MSY44k	31-PHAA-b	bahasa-malaysia		0.02	2	1asuh	3	3	2	4	0	Malay	PNB b
10972	Nataoran Ami	0.01000	2,156	2,240	2,573	AUG01a	30-KBAB-a	sakizaya		80.00	1,792	0....	10	8	8	4	2		... .
10973	Paiwanese (Tamari)	0.29602	63,825	66,311	76,166	AUG01a	30-GAAA	paiwan cluster	1	80.00	53,049	0....	10	9	9	5	2	Paiwan	PN. .
10974	Pazeh (Kahabu)	0.00100	216	224	257	AUG01a	30-CBBA-a	pazeh		80.00	179	0....	10	8	6	4	2		... .
10975	Pyuma (Kadas, Tipun)	0.04642	10,009	10,399	11,944	AUG01a	30-JAAA-a	central pi-yuma		70.00	7,279	0....	10	8	8	4	2		... .
10976	Saiset (Seisirat)	0.01877	4,047	4,205	4,830	AUG01a	30-CAAA	saisiyat cluster		70.00	2,943	0....	10	8	8	4	1		... .
10977	Sediq (Taroko, Hogo)	0.14664	31,617	32,849	37,730	AUG01a	30-AABA-a	taroko		80.00	26,279	0....	10	8	8	4	1	Taroko	PN. .
10978	Taiwanese (Hoklo)	71.23622	15,359,241	15,957,626	18,329,079	MSY42a	79-AAAJ-ic	chaozhou	90	3.20	510,644	1A..h	6	8	9	4	4	Chinese, Min Nan	PNB b
10979	Tayal (Atayal)	0.24048	51,850	53,870	61,876	AUG01a	30-AAAA	sqoleq cluster	1	90.00	48,483	0....	10	5	9	5	3	Tayal*	PN. .
10980	Thao (Sau, Shao)	0.00163	351	365	419	AUG01a	30-DAAA	thao cluster		80.00	292	0....	10	8	6	4	2		... .
10981	Tibetan (Bhotia, Lhasa)	0.01000	2,156	2,240	2,573	MSY50r	70-AAAA-c	utsang		0.52	12	0a...	5	4	2	4	0	Tibetan	PNB b
10982	Tsou (Northern Tsuu, Tso)	0.02752	5,934	6,165	7,081	AUG01a	30-EAAA	tsou cluster		70.00	4,315	0....	10	8	8	4	1	Tsou	... .
10983	USA White	0.04000	8,624	8,960	10,292	CEW19s	52-ABAC-s	general american		77.00	6,900	1Bsuh	10	9	13	5	1	English*	PNB b
10984	Uighur	0.00090	194	202	232	MSY41z	44-AABD-d	east uyghur		0.00	0	1r.u.	0	3	3	1	0	Uighur*	PNB b
10985	Yami (Botel Tabago)	0.01525	3,288	3,416	3,924	MSY44x	31-CAAA-a	yami		80.00	2,733	0....	10	9	8	4	3	Yami	PN. .

Continued opposite

Table 8-2 continued

EVANGELIZATION								EVANGELISM			ADDITIONAL DESCRIPTIVE DATA
Ref 1	*D* 28	*aC* 29	*CG%* 30	*r* 31	*E* 32	*U* 33	*W* 34	*e* 35	*R* 36	*T* 37	*Locations, civil divisions, literacy, religions, church history, denominations, dioceses, church growth, missions, agencies, ministries, movements* 38
10868	2	10	0.55	6	99.93	0.07	C	562.14	27	10	Emigres, residents from Norway. Nonreligious 7%. D=Ch of Norway,Ch of Sweden.
10869	0	0	3.65	5	36.10	63.90	A	0.13	330	3	Refugees and migrant workers from Iran, most after 1980. Muslims 97%, Baha'is 3%.
10870	1	9	0.55	2	99.90	0.10	C	469.75	30	10	Lapland along Pite river in Arjeplog and Arvidsjaur. Also in Norway. Nonreligious 6%. D=Ch of Sweden.
10871	1	10	0.55	6	99.86	0.14	C	492.82	10	10	Refugees, migrant workers from Poland. D=RCC. M=SJ,OP,OMI,OFM.
10872	1	10	4.27	6	99.80	0.20	C	414.64	104	10	Migrant laborers from Romania. Nonreligious 15%. D=Romanian Orthodox Ch(P-Bucharest).
10873	2	10	2.88	7	99.65	0.35	C	329.77	57	9	Refugees since 1917 from USSR. Nonreligious 28%. D=Russian Orthodox Ch Outside of Russia(D-Western Europe),ROC(P-Moscow).
10874	1	10	5.61	6	99.85	0.15	C	459.17	104	10	Migrant laborers from Serbia. Some nonreligious 12%, atheists 3%, Muslims. D=Serbian Orthodox Ch(P-Belgrade).
10875	1	10	0.55	6	99.77	0.23	C	401.90	32	10	Refugees from Slovakia. Nonreligious 19%. D=RCC. M=SJ,OMI,OP.
10876	1	10	0.56	6	99.94	0.06	C	538.66	27	10	Migrant workers from Slovenia (ex-Yugoslavia). D=RCC. M=SJ,OMI.
10877	0	0	0.00	5	34.01	65.99	A	0.01	55	2	Refugees from Somalia in late 1980s and early 1990s. Muslims 100%.
10878	1	9	0.57	2	99.90	0.10	C	440.19	32	10	Jemtland, Herjedalen. Also in Norway. Nonreligious 6%. D=Ch of Sweden.
10879	1	10	2.29	8	99.95	0.05	C	586.00	52	10	Expatriates, migrant workers from Spain. D=RCC(D-Stockholm). M=SJ,OFM.
10880	9	7	0.09	6	99.67	0.33	C	341.43	2	9	Nonreligious 19.3%, atheists 13.5%. D=Ch of Sweden(13 Dioceses),PRMS,SMCC,SA,BUS,RCC,FELC,OMC,SAM. M=UFM,LBI.
10881	2	10	0.55	6	99.70	0.30	C	347.48	32	9	Nomadic caravan churches. Nonreligious 10%. D=Ch of Sweden,GEM. M=GGMS.
10882	0	9	0.55	0	99.70	0.30	C	268.27	41	8	Secret Gypsy language used by the Tattare. Related to Norwegian Traveller, Danish Traveller. Many nonreligious 14%.
10883	2	10	5.37	8	85.00	15.00	B	65.15	196	6	Migrant laborers from Syria. Muslims 75%(Hanafi Sunnis, Alawis). D=Syrian Orthodox Ch(Jacobites: P-Antioch),RCC.
10884	2	10	7.60	5	99.95	0.05	C	572.13	137	10	Western Syriac. Refugees from eastern Syria, southeast Turkey, northern Iraq. D=Syrian Orthodox Ch (Jacobites),RCC.
10885	0	10	2.22	4	46.00	54.00	A	1.67	232	4	Refugees from PR China after 1950. Lamaist Buddhists 99%. Active religious life.
10886	0	10	2.47	8	49.50	50.50	A	0.90	176	3	Migrant laborers from Turkey. Muslims 99%(Hanafi Sunnis).
10887	7	10	1.96	8	99.77	0.23	C	427.19	52	10	Expatriates from USA, in business. D=SDA,JWs,CJCLdS,CCS,CC,COG,CON.
10888	2	10	0.56	6	99.80	0.20	C	400.04	32	10	In 25 countries. Nomadic caravan communities. D=Ch of Sweden,GEM. M=GGMS,IGP,NBS.
10889	0	10	0.55		96.00	4.00	B	206.73	16	8	Lithuanians, Palestinians, Belorussians, Armenians, Indians, Koreans(M=PCK-T), Macedonians, Bulgarians, other Europeans, other Asians, Egyptians, Ethiopians.
Switzerland											
10890	5	10	4.13	7	89.00	11.00	B	68.21	149	6	Migrant laborers: Palestinians, Egyptians, Levantines, Syrians. Muslims 77%. D=RCC(Maronites),SOC,GOC,COC,CCC.
10891	1	10	0.80	8	99.88	0.12	C	494.64	34	10	Emigres from Austria, expatriates on business. Nonreligious 10%. D=RCC.
10892	0	10	4.13	6	57.05	42.95	B	0.10	242	3	Refugees from Bosnian civil war from 1991 on. Muslims 90%(Sunnis), Nonreligious 8%.
10893	4	10	2.31	8	99.78	0.22	C	444.13	61	10	Expatriates from Britain, in business. D=Ch of England(D-Gibraltar),Ch of Scotland,JWs,MCGB.
10894	0	0	7.15	6	73.00	27.00	B	79.93	306	6	Immigrant workers from Sri Lanka. Hindus 60%, Muslims 5%. D=RCC.
10895	0	0	8.22	6	99.91	0.09	C	468.33	181	10	Refugees from Croatia, most after 1990. Nonreligious 9%. D=RCC.
10896	2	10	0.80	6	99.73	0.27	C	381.02	37	9	Refugees from CSSR after 1945. Nonreligious 21%. D=RCC,FEPS.
10897	1	10	0.80	6	99.76	0.24	C	421.64	30	10	Expatriates from Holland, in business, industry. Nonreligious 20%. D=DRC/NHK.
10898	0	10	0.00	5	99.60	0.40	C	262.80	0	8	Artificial(constructed) language, in 80 countries. Speakers in Switzerland: 62,000(none mother-tongue). Nonreligious 40%.
10899	7	10	0.80	8	99.85	0.15	C	497.97	30	10	French-speaking Swiss. Nonreligious 13%. D=FEPS/SFPC(4 Cantonal Churches),RCC(8 Dioceses),Friends of Man,SA,JWs,AEEBF,SDA. R=TWR,HCJB.
10900	4	10	0.80	8	99.84	0.16	C	499.75	30	10	Expatriates from France, in business. Nonreligious 13%. D=RCC,FEPS,AEEBF,JWs. M=OFMCap,OSB,SJ,CSSR,WF,CSSp.
10901	2	10	0.80	8	99.88	0.12	C	488.22	32	10	Speakers of Vaudois, a Franco-Provencal dialect. Nonreligious 10%. D=SRC,RCC.
10902	0	10	3.14	8	52.30	47.70	B	0.57	201	3	Secular and religious Jews in 20 cities; practicing Judaism. Nonreligious 30%.
10903	7	10	0.80	8	99.87	0.13	C	498.55	34	10	Expatriates from Germany, in business. Main language in Swiss education. D=RCC,FEPS,NAC,SA,JWs,AELC,VAC.
10904	0	10	4.01	8	59.30	40.70	B	0.64	217	3	Secular and religious Jews, mostly urban in over 22 cities. Nonreligious 34%.
10905	10	10	0.54	8	99.92	0.08	C	560.54	28	10	Alemannic, with 70 dialects. D=RCC(8 Dioceses),FEPS/SFPC(14 Cantonal Churches),Friends of Man,NAC,SA,CCC(D-Bern),JWs,BUS,AELC,UMC.
10906	1	10	2.41	7	99.95	0.05	C	579.07	56	10	Migrant workers from Greece. Nonreligious 5%. D=Greek Orthodox Ch(D-Austria).
10907	1	10	3.67	7	91.00	9.00	B	83.03	130	6	Long-time residents from China and its diaspora. Buddhists/Chinese folk-religionists 74%. D=RCC.
10908	2	10	0.80	6	99.79	0.21	C	423.87	41	10	Refugees from Hungary after 1945. Nonreligious 18%. D=RCC,Hungarian Reformed Congregations.
10909	3	10	0.80	7	99.84	0.16	C	502.82	30	10	Expatriates from Italy, in business. D=RCC(8 Dioceses),ACELIS,CCNA/CCINE. M=OFMCap,OSB,SMB.
10910	3	10	0.92	7	99.94	0.06	C	566.11	32	10	Ticino Canton, Graubunden, 2 Districts south of St Moritz. Form of Italian used in homes. Citizens. D=RCC(8 Dioceses),CCNA/CCINE,ACELIS.
10911	0	0	2.36	7	44.00	56.00	A	3.21	194	4	Immigrants from Japan, most in business. Mahayana Buddhists 98%.
10912	0	10	0.00	4	49.07	50.93	A	0.12	39	3	Communities of practicing Jews, mostly in cities and urban areas. Nonreligious 10%.
10913	0	10	1.40	0	38.01	61.99	A	0.01	245	2	Laborers, refugees from Turkey, Iraq, Iran. 1,000 speak Sorani, 1,000 Zaza. Muslims 100%(Sunnis). M=whole network of agencies.
10914	1	10	2.74	8	99.94	0.06	C	596.99	59	10	Migrant workers from Portugal. Nonreligious 6%. D=RCC. M=OFMCap,OSB,SJ,CSSR.
10915	1	10	0.80	6	99.84	0.16	C	459.90	35	10	Refugees from Romania. Nonreligious 15%. D=Romanian Orthodox Ch(P-Bucharest).
10916	2	10	0.80	3	99.92	0.08	C	510.20	32	10	Rhaeto-Romance(Engadine). Upper Engadine dialect, in southeastern Switzerland. D=SRC,RCC.
10917	2	10	0.80	3	99.90	0.10	C	496.03	33	10	Rhaeto-Romance(Grishun). Lower Engadine. Borders of Switzerland with France, Austria, Italy; Graubunden (Grisons) Canton. D=RCC,SRC.
10918	2	10	0.80	3	99.91	0.09	C	504.86	32	10	Rhaeto-Romance(Ladin). Oberland dialect, throughout Oberland Valley(of the Upper Rhine). D=RCC,SRC.
10919	2	10	1.81	7	99.67	0.33	C	342.37	35	9	Refugees since 1917 from USSR. Nonreligious 27%, atheists 6%. D=ROC(P-Moscow),ROCOR(D-Western Europe).
10920	0	0	9.08	6	99.85	0.15	C	403.32	214	10	Refugees from Yugoslavia, most after 1989. Nonreligious 12%. D=Serbian Orthodox Church.
10921	2	10	0.80	0	99.80	0.20	C	356.24	41	9	Nomadic Gypsies in 10 countries. Caravan communities. D=RCC,GEM. M=GGMS.
10922	2	10	2.37	8	99.96	0.04	C	613.20	52	10	Expatriates from Spain, in business. D=RCC,Spanish-speaking Evangelical Churches.
10923	1	10	0.80	6	99.73	0.27	C	381.02	15	9	Expatriates from Sweden, in business. Nonreligious 19%. D=Ch of Sweden(AD-Uppsala).
10924	2	10	0.80	8	99.70	0.30	C	352.59	36	9	Settled, German-speaking Gypsies. Nomadic caravan churches. Nonreligious 10%. D=RCC,GEM. M=GGMS.
10925	0	10	0.00	4	48.10	51.90	A	0.17	95	3	Refugees from Communist China after 1950. In 12 countries. Lamaist Buddhists 95%; study centers, monasteries.
10926	0	10	3.44	8	53.50	46.50	B	0.97	213	3	Migrant laborers from Turkey. Muslims 99%(Hanafi Sunnis).
10927	6	10	0.80	8	99.77	0.23	C	427.19	31	10	Expatriates from USA, in business, commerce. D=RCC,CJCLdS,SDA,JWs,CCS,CC.
10928	0	10	0.80		97.00	3.00	C	212.43	23	8	Armenians(Gregorians), Ukrainians(UOC), Koreans(M=PCK-T), and other Asians, Africans, Europeans, Americans. Nonreligious 15%, Muslims 3%, Buddhists 2%.
Syria											
10929	3	10	2.04	6	99.88	0.12	C	529.98	44	10	Gregorians. Nonreligious 10%. D=Armenian Apostolic Ch(C-Cilicia),RCC(P-Cilicia: VP-Syria),UAECNE.
10930	2	10	1.51	5	99.95	0.05	C	572.13	36	10	1933 refugees from Iraq. D=Ancient Ch of the East(Nestorians: D-Hassake),RCC(Chaldeans: D-Halab).
10931	0	7	2.51	7	30.01	69.99	A	0.01	293	2	Nomads, tent-dwellers, across widely-scattered areas. Muslims 100%(Sunnis).
10932	3	10	4.11	8	99.70	0.30	C	373.03	99	9	Expatriates from Britain, in business. Nonreligious 18%. D=ECJME(D-Jerusalem),RCC,AoG.
10933	1	10	1.93	6	99.72	0.28	C	352.15	65	9	Expatriates military and civilian from Bulgaria. D=Bulgarian Orthodox Ch(P-Sofia).
10934	2	9	4.40	0	35.20	64.80	A	0.25	420	3	Urbanites. In 10 countries. Muslims 100%(Sunnis). D=GOC,Free Evangelical Ch. M=CMA.
10935	1	10	6.81	8	99.75	0.25	C	413.36	141	10	Expatriates from France, in business. Nonreligious 22%. D=RCC. M=OFM,SJ,CM,SDB,OFMCap,PFM.
10936	1	10	5.07	8	99.87	0.13	C	514.43	105	10	Expatriates from Germany, in business. D=RCC. M=SJ,OFM.
10937	2	10	2.20	7	99.95	0.05	C	582.54	52	10	Traders. D=Greek Orthodox Ch(P-Antioch: 6 Dioceses),RCC(Melkites: 5 Dioceses).
10938	3	6	1.87	7	53.70	46.30	B	1.37	131	4	Originally from Iraq. Refugees, migrant workers. Muslims 97%(60% Shias,37% Hanafi Sunnis). D=RCC,SOC,GOC.
10939	4	8	2.22	8	61.90	38.10	B	11.07	129	5	Migrant workers from Jordan. Muslims 95%(Shafi Sunnis,Alawis; Sufi influence strong). D=RCC,GOC,SDA,ECJME.
10940	1	7	2.08	8	99.51	0.49	B	210.35	67	8	Refugees from Lebanon's civil war. Muslims 45%(Sunnis,Alawis,Druzes). D=RCC(Maronites: 3 Dioceses).
10941	2	6	7.75	0	82.00	18.00	B	107.74	296	7	From Caucasus. Muslims 60%(Sunnis). D=GOC,ROC.
10942	3	8	1.30	8	64.80	35.20	B	8.98	85	4	Refugees. Muslims 93%(Shafi Sunnis, also Alawi Shias,Druzes). D=SOC,GOC,RCC. M=MEM.
10943	0	8	1.81	5	45.04	54.96	A	0.06	153	2	Refugees from Iran. Muslims 99%(Imami Shias/Ithna-Asharis), Baha'is, Parsis(Zoroastrians).
10944	1	10	4.40	8	99.92	0.08	C	570.86	87	10	Expatriates from Portugal, in development. Nonreligious 7%. D=RCC. M=SJ,OFM,CM,SDB.
10945	1	10	4.60	7	99.31	0.69	B	115.41	124	7	Military and advisors from Russia. Nonreligious/atheists 60%. D=GOC(P-Antioch).
10946	1	10	4.44	8	99.96	0.04	C	606.19	85	10	Expatriates from Spain in development. D=RCC. M=SJ,OFM,CM,SDB,PFM.
10947	3	6	1.26	8	66.60	33.40	B	13.61	81	5	Muslims 92%(82% Hanafi Sunnis,9% Alawis,Druzes,Ismailis,Yazidis). D=Syrian Orthodox Ch(Jacobites: 4 Dioceses),RCC(4 Dioceses),NECAC. M=MEM,FI.
10948	3	10	1.90	5	99.95	0.05	C	589.47	42	10	In Syria,Turkey, Sweden, Iraq, USA, Netherlands, Germany. D=SOC(Jacobites),Ancient Ch of the East(Nestorians: D-Hassake),RCC(P-Babilonia: D-Halab).
10949	0	10	-2.86	8	45.10	54.90	A	0.16	6	3	Arabic-speaking Sefardis. Practicing Jews, declining by emigration to Israel. Religious freedom. 22 synagogues.
10950	0	6	2.33	8	40.02	59.98	A	0.02	208	2	Long-time residents, immigrants from Turkey, recent expatriates. Muslims 100%(Hanafi Sunnis).
10951	0	6	3.09	1	33.02	66.98	A	0.02	323	2	Speakers of Azerbaijani, Turkish, Turkmen. Region of Homs and Hama. Devout Muslims 100%(Hanafi Sunnis, some Shias; Sufi orders).
10952	0	0	4.95	8	99.78	0.22	C	370.11	123	9	North Americans, in business, education. Nonreligious 10%. D=RCC,BBC,SDA,etc.
10953	2	8	2.05	1	96.00	4.00	B	140.16	78	7	3 villages near Damascus. Also in USA. Bilingual in Syrian Arabic. Peasants. Muslims 60%. D=RCC(Maronites),SOC.
10954	0	6	5.16	0	33.13	66.87	A	0.15	592	3	Northern Kurdish. In northern Syria; also 9 countries. Lingua franca. Bilinguals in Arabic. Muslims 100%(Sunnis, some Shias). M=CSI,WEC,and a large network.
10955	3	9	6.75	7	67.00	33.00	B	48.91	318	6	Arab Gypsies, Muslim Gypsies. Nomads. In 12 countries. Muslims 80%(Sunnis). D=GOC,SOC,RCC.
10956	0	8	1.43		39.00	61.00	A	25.62	100	5	Armenian Bosha Gypsies(Lomavren), other Arab peoples, other Levantines, other Europeans. Muslims 70%, Nonreligious 2%.
Taiwan											
10957	3	7	9.99	0	99.90	0.10	C	456.61	197	10	Plains and coast between Hualien and Taitung. Agriculturalists(rice). Matrilineal. Animists 10%. D=RCC(D-Hualien),Presbyterian Ch of Taiwan,many JWs.
10958	1	7	2.93	0	99.80	0.20	C	344.56	68	9	West central coast and inland, beyond Tatu and Choshui rivers. Nearly extinct; people sinicized. Animists 20%. D=PCT.
10959	4	9	4.24	8	99.78	0.22	C	435.59	97	10	Expatriates from UK, in education, development, business. English is studied by all school children. D=PCT,JWs,SDA,TEC(D-Taiwan). M=CMS,FMB.
10960	1	7	8.46	0	99.80	0.20	C	353.32	192	9	East central plain, south of the Taroko. Animists 20%. D=PCT. M=JJCC(Japan).
10961	1	6	6.73	0	99.80	0.20	C	335.80	160	9	South central mountains, west of the Pyuma; 14 villages. Written language. Animists 20%. D=PCT. M=BSROC.
10962	1	10	9.23	5	99.80	0.20	C	449.68	176	10	Legal and illegal immigrants from Philippines. Laborers, professionals. D=RCC.
10963	4	6	6.06	7	70.00	30.00	B	7.66	263	4	Buddhists/Folk-religionists 97%. D=PCT,AoG,RCC,Lutheran Brethren. M=BM,YWAM-Taiwan,FMB,Presbyterian Ch,Norwegian Lutheran,Swedish Holiness,EFCC.
10964	4	7	10.36	7	72.36	27.64	B	14.15	417	5	Mainlanders. In Taipei, 5 other cities. Folk-religionists 91%. D=Assembly Hall Chs,RCC,FMB,Taiwan Lutheran Ch. M=SCIUM,IBPFM,CMA(Hong Kong),HKOM.
10965	0	6	0.00	7	42.00	58.00	A	0.00	0	1.14	Refugees from mainland China in 17th century up to 1949. Muslims 100%(Hanafi Sunnis).
10966	2	6	-0.54	7	57.00	43.00	B	6.24	10	4	Lingua franca among Aborigines and some Chinese. Buddhists 97%(Mahayana, plus Soka Gakkai and other New-Religionists). D=RCC,SA. M=LBI,UBS.
10967	0	9	0.70	7	56.23	43.77	B	2.52	68	4	Small communities of Jews practicing Judaism.
10968	2	7	4.60	0	99.80	0.20	C	335.80	110	9	Northeast coast above Toucheng and inland. Nearly extinct; people sinicized. Animists 20%. D=PCT,RCC.
10969	0	6	0.00	4	39.02	60.98	A	0.02	54	2	Refugees, immigrants from Mongolia. Lamaist Buddhists(Tantrists) 94%.
10970	2	6	5.72	6	99.40	0.60	B	151.84	167	7	Immigrants from Korea. Shamanists 35%, Buddhists 15%. D=PCK-T,PCK-H. M=BFMGAP,FMB.
10971	0	7	0.70	5	41.02	58.98	A	0.03	94	2	Immigrants from Malaysia, Indonesia. Muslims 100%(Shafi Sunnis).
10972	2	7	5.33	0	99.80	0.20	C	344.56	124	9	Villages in Hualien area and north of Fenglin. Language on verge of extinction. Animists 20%. D=RCC,PCT.
10973	3	7	8.95	4	99.80	0.20	C	379.60	189	9	Southern, southeastern mountains. Animists 20%. D=RCC,Ch of the Nazarene,TEC(D-Taiwan). M=EPM,FMB.
10974	2	7	2.93	0	99.80	0.20	C	335.80	70	9	Near west coast north of 24 degrees N, east of Tayal, around Cholan. Sinicized; nearly extinct. Animists 20%. D=PCT,RCC.
10975	2	6	6.81	0	99.70	0.30	C	273.38	174	8	Along east coast south of Taitung and inland. Animists 30%. D=RCC,PCT. M=TEAM,Presbyterian Mission.
10976	1	6	5.85	0	99.70	0.30	C	268.27	153	8	Western mountains, west of the Tayal. Language unwritten. Animists 30%. D=Saisiat Churches. M=WEC.
10977	1	7	8.19	0	99.80	0.20	C	353.32	185	9	Central, eastern, and coastal; northern mountains, and coast south of Hualien. Animists 20%. D=CBA. M=CBFMS.
10978	4	6	4.54	6	67.20	32.80	B	7.84	212	4	Tainan, eastern region, coast. Popular-religionists 39%, Buddhists 28%. D=Assembly Hall Chs,RCC,TJC,DRC. M=SCIUM,CICM,OFM,MM,MEP,OP,SJ,SVD,LMS.
10979	2	7	8.86	0	99.90	0.10	C	446.76	179	10	Mountains in north, south of Ketagalan area. Animists 10%. D=PCT,RCC. M=CPM,WEC,FMB.
10980	2	7	3.43	0	99.80	0.20	C	335.80	82	9	Central; one village around Lake Suisha. People are now sinicized. Animists 20%. D=RCC,PCT.
10981	0	6	2.52	4	42.52	57.48	A	0.80	270	3	Originally refugees from Tibet after 1949. Lamaist Buddhists(Tantrists)100%.
10982	2	6	6.26	0	99.70	0.30	C	270.83	162	8	West central mountains southeast of Kagi around Mt. Ali. Animists 30%. D=PCT,Tsou Churches. M=Japan Jesus Christ Ch(Japan).
10983	2	9	3.99	8	99.77	0.23	C	415.95	91	10	Expatriates from USA, in business, commerce, education, government. Nonreligious 10%. D=PCT,RCC. M=FMB.
10984	0	3	0.00	4	31.00	69.00	A	0.00	0	1.12	Refugees from Mainland in 1949 exodus. Over 10,000 in 1950 with nearly all returning to Xinjiang. Muslims 100%(Sunnis, with heavy Sufi influence).
10985	3	7	5.77	0	99.80	0.20	C	362.08	143	9	On Orchid Island, Botel Tobago(Laanyu) Island, southeast coast. Animists 20%. D=RCC,PCT,BBFI. M=PCA,PCUSA,TEAM,independents.

Continued overleaf

Table 8-2 continued

PEOPLE		POPULATION				IDENTITY CODE		LANGUAGE		CHURCH		MINISTRY						SCRIPTURE		
Ref 1	*Ethnic name* 2	*P%* 3	*In 1995* 4	*In 2000* 5	*In 2025* 6	*Race* 7	*Language* 8	*Autoglossonym* 9	*S* 10	*AC* 11	*Members* 12	*Jayuh* 13-17	*d* 18	*wa* 19	*xc* 20	*mc* 21	*mi* 22	*Biblioglossonym* 23	*Pub* 24-26	*ss* 27
10986	other minor peoples	0.20000	43,122	44,802	51,460	...				10.00	4,480		8	7	2	4	0			
	Tajikistan	**100.00000**	**5,750,497**	**6,188,201**	**8,856,904**					**2.09**	**129,610**									
10987	Afghani (Western Pathan)	0.40000	23,002	24,753	35,428	CNT24a	58-ABDA-a	pashto		0.02	5	1As..	3	2	2	0	1		pnb	b
10988	Armenian	0.11096	6,381	6,866	9,828	CEW14	57-AAAA-b	ashkharik		70.00	4,806	4A.u.	10	7	12	2	1	Armenian: Modern, Eastern	PNB	b
10989	Azerbaijani	0.06983	4,016	4,321	6,185	MSY41a	44-AABA-fa	north azeri		0.00	0	2c.u.	0	3	3	0	2	Azerbaijani*	PNB	b
10990	Bashkir	0.13394	7,702	8,288	11,863	MSY41b	44-AABB-g	bashqurt		7.00	580	1A.u.	7	5	7	0	1	Bashkir	Pn.	b
10991	Bulgarian	0.02105	1,210	1,303	1,864	CEW22b	53-AAAH-b	bulgarski		72.00	938	2A.uh	10	6	8	1	1	Bulgarian	PNB	b
10992	Byelorussian	0.08000	4,600	4,951	7,086	CEW22c	53-AAAE-c	bielorusskiy		70.00	3,465	3A.uh	10	7	8	2	3	Byelorussian*	PNB	b
10993	Central Asian Gypsy	0.03520	2,024	2,178	3,118	CNN25f	58-AACC-j	tajiki		0.00	0	2asu.	0	3	2	0	0	Tajik*	PNB	b
10994	Central Asian Jew	0.09581	5,510	5,929	8,486	CMT35	58-AACC-kb	bukharik		0.00	0	1csu.	0	1	2	0	0		pnb	b
10995	Chuvash	0.04933	2,837	3,053	4,369	MSY41c	44-AAAA-a	chuvash		35.00	1,068	2....	9	6	8	0	1	Chuvash	PN.	b
10996	Crimean Tatar	0.14166	8,146	8,766	12,547	MSY41h	44-AABA-c	crimea-tatar		0.00	0	1c.u.	0	2	2	0	1	Crimean Tatar*	PNb	b
10997	Georgian	0.01917	1,102	1,186	1,698	CEW17c	42-CABB-a	kharthuli		40.00	475	2A.u.	9	6	8	2	1	Georgian	PNB	b
10998	German	0.04000	2,300	2,475	3,543	CEW19m	52-ABCE-a	standard hoch-deutsch		78.00	1,931	2B.uh	10	8	13	3	3	German*	PNB	b
10999	Greek	0.01159	666	717	1,027	CEW20	56-AAAA-c	dhimotiki		90.00	645	2B.uh	10	8	11	2	3	Greek: Modern	PNB	b
11000	Guhjali (Wakhi, Vakhan)	0.16400	9,431	10,149	14,525	CNT24z	58-ABDC	wakhi cluster		0.00	0	0....	0	1	0	0	0	Wakhi	...	b
11001	Jewish	0.05410	3,111	3,348	4,792	CMT35	52-ABCH	yiddish cluster		0.00	0	0B..h	0	4	6	0	0		PNB	b
11002	Kazakh	0.22338	12,845	13,823	19,785	MSY41e	44-AABC-c	kazakh		0.00	0	4A.u.	0	3	3	0	2	Kazakh	PN.	b
11003	Kirghiz	1.25343	72,078	77,565	111,015	MSY41g	44-AABC-d	kirghiz		0.00	0	2r.u.	0	3	3	0	3	Kirghiz	PN.	b
11004	Korean	0.26374	15,166	16,321	23,359	MSY46	45-AAAA-b	kukö		25.00	4,080	2A...	9	6	11	3	1	Korean	PNB	b
11005	Lak	0.02745	1,579	1,699	2,431	CEW17b	42-BBBA-a	lak		0.00	0	1....	0	3	0	0	0	Lak	P..	b
11006	Lithuanian	0.01043	600	645	924	CEW15b	54-AAAA-a	standard lietuvishkai		84.00	542	3A.u.	10	8	9	2	3	Lithuanian	PNB	b
11007	Mari	0.01190	684	736	1,054	MSW51h	41-AACA-b	mariy		90.00	663	2....	10	8	11	2	1	Mari: Low*	PN.	b
11008	Moldavian	0.01726	993	1,068	1,529	CEW21f	51-AADC-ab	standard moldavia		81.00	865	1A.u.	10	7	8	2	1		pnb	b
11009	Mordvinian	0.10837	6,232	6,706	9,598	MSW51i	41-AADA-b	moksha		65.00	4,359	1....	10	8	8	2	1	Mordvin: Moksha*	Pn.	b
11010	Northern Uzbek	23.52119	1,352,585	1,455,539	2,083,249	MSY41l	44-AABD-a	central uzbek		0.05	728	1A.u.	4	3	6	1	2	Uzbek*	PNb	b
11011	Ossete	0.15436	8,876	9,552	13,672	CNT24e	58-ABBA	oseti cluster		36.00	3,439	2....	9	5	8	1	1	Ossete*	PN.	b
11012	Parya	0.01964	1,129	1,215	1,739	CNT24z	59-AAAD-c	laghmani		0.00	0	0....	0	2	2	0	0		...	b
11013	Persian	1.20000	69,006	74,258	106,283	CNT24f	58-AACC-ca	west farsi		0.00	0	1asu.	0	3	2	0	0	Farsi, Western	PNB	b
11014	Polish	0.01406	809	870	1,245	CEW22i	53-AAAC-c	polski		89.00	774	2A.uh	10	8	11	2	3	Polish	PNB	b
11015	Russian	2.20000	126,511	136,140	194,852	CEW22j	53-AAAE-d	russkiy	84	60.00	81,684	4B.uh	10	7	9	3	3	Russian	PNB	b
11016	Sanglechi (Ishkashimi)	0.00982	565	608	870	CNT24z	58-ABDD-a	sanglechi		0.00	0	0....	0	1	3	0	0		...	b
11017	Shughni (Shugnan-Rushan)	0.78545	45,167	48,605	69,567	CNT24z	58-ABDE-a	shughni-bajuvi		0.00	0	0....	0	1	0	0	0	Shughni	...	b
11018	Tajik (Tadzhik)	66.18500	3,805,966	4,095,661	5,861,942	CNT24g	58-AACC-j	tajiki		0.03	1,229	2asu.	3	3	2	0	3	Tajik*	PNB	b
11019	Tatar	1.41829	81,559	87,767	125,617	MSY41h	44-AABB-e	tatar		1.50	1,316	2c.u.	6	4	8	0	2	Tatar: Kazan	Pn.	b
11020	Turkish (Turk)	0.01508	867	933	1,336	MSY41j	44-AABA-a	osmanli		0.00	0	1A.u.	0	3	2	0	0	Turkish	PNB	b
11021	Turkmen	0.40229	23,134	24,895	35,630	MSY41k	44-AABA-e	turkmen		0.00	0	3c.u.	0	3	2	0	2	Turkmen	PNb	b
11022	Udmurt	0.01247	717	772	1,104	MSW51k	41-AAEA-c	udmurt		55.00	424	2....	10	5	8	2	1	Udmurt	Pn.	.
11023	Uighur	0.01111	639	688	984	MSY41z	44-AABD-d	east uyghur		0.00	0	1r.u.	0	3	2	0	2	Uighur*	PNB	b
11024	Ukrainian	0.30000	17,251	18,565	26,571	CEW22p	53-AAAE-b	ukrainskiy		79.00	14,666	3A.uh	10	7	10	3	2	Ukrainian	PNB	b
11025	Yagnob (Yagnobi)	0.04124	2,372	2,552	3,653	CNT24g	58-ABCB-a	yaghnobi		0.00	0	0....	0	1	3	0	0		...	b
11026	Yazgul (Yazgulam)	0.06740	3,876	4,171	5,970	CNT24g	58-ABDF-a	yazghulami		0.00	0	0....	0	1	3	0	0	Yazgulyam	...	b
11027	other minor peoples	0.30000	17,251	18,565	26,571	...				5.00	928		7	5	0	0	0			
	Tanzania	**100.00000**	**29,925,404**	**33,517,014**	**57,918,322**					**46.91**	**15,722,780**									
11028	Aramanik	0.01507	4,510	5,051	8,728	BYG11b	04-CAAE-c	l-aramanik		2.00	101	0....	6	4	6	5	2		...	.
11029	Arusa Maasai (Arusha)	0.74278	222,280	248,958	430,206	NAB62k	04-BCAA-ak	arusha		25.00	62,239	1cs..	9	7	8	5	3		pnb	.
11030	Arusha	0.38795	116,096	130,029	224,694	NAB57e	99-AUNA-a	ki-arusha		80.00	104,023	0....	10	8	9	5	3		pn.	.
11031	Asa (Dorobo)	0.01683	5,036	5,641	9,748	BYG11b	15-ABBA-a	aasax		2.00	113	0....	6	4	5	5	2		...	.
11032	Bajun	0.03480	10,414	11,664	20,156	NAB57j	99-AUSM-d	ki-tikuu		0.01	1	1csu.	3	3	5	1	0		pnb	b
11033	Barabaig	0.58000	173,567	194,399	335,926	NAB62g	04-CACA-h	barba-ik		3.00	5,832	0....	6	4	7	5	2		...	.
11034	Baraguyu	0.12251	36,662	41,062	70,956	NAB62k	04-BCAA-a	enkutuk-oo-l-maasai		8.00	3,285	4As..	7	7	7	5	3	Maasai	PNB	b
11035	Bemba (Wemba)	0.11679	34,950	39,145	67,643	NAB57b	99-AURR-h	i-ci-bemba	4	85.00	33,273	4.su.	10	9	12	5	3	Chibemba*	PNB	b
11036	Bena	1.90098	568,876	637,152	1,101,016	NAB57o	99-AUSU-b	e-ki-bena		88.00	560,694	0....	10	9	8	5	3	Ekibena*	PN.	b
11037	Bende	0.08167	24,440	27,373	47,302	NAB57o	99-AUSC-a	bende		90.00	24,636	0....	10	8	10	4	1		...	b
11038	Bondei	0.32669	97,763	109,497	189,213	NAB57j	99-AUSO-b	ki-bondei		22.00	24,089	0c...	9	5	7	5	1	Kibondei*	Pnb	b
11039	British	0.14000	41,896	46,924	81,086	CEW19i	52-ABAC-b	standard-english	28	78.00	36,601	3Bsuh	10	9	13	5	3		PNB	b
11040	Burungi (Bulunge)	0.12659	37,883	42,429	73,319	CMT33z	15-AAAB-b	burunge		12.00	5,092	0....	8	5	5	5	1		...	.
11041	Chagga (Kirwa)	1.80000	538,657	603,306	1,042,530	NAB57e	99-AUNA-jc	ki-rwa		95.00	573,141	0....	10	9	13	5	3		pn.	b
11042	Chagga (Machame)	1.20000	359,105	402,204	695,020	NAB57e	99-AUNA-f	ki-mashami		95.00	382,094	0....	10	9	13	5	3	Chagga: Machame	PN.	b
11043	Coast Arab	0.71526	214,044	239,734	414,267	CMT30	12-AACF-p	zanji	3	0.01	24	1Asuh	3	3	4	1	0		pnb	b
11044	Comorian	0.03000	8,978	10,055	17,375	NAB57j	99-AUSM-s	shi-ngazidya		0.02	2	1csu.	3	3	1	0	0	Comorian*	PNb	b
11045	Cutchi Indian (Kohli)	0.10000	29,925	33,517	57,918	CNN25p	59-AAFF-j	kachchi		1.00	335	1cs..	6	3	4	1	0	Kachchi	Pnb	b
11046	Dabida Taita	0.04068	12,174	13,635	23,561	NAB57e	99-AUOA	dawida cluster		68.00	9,272	1....	10	7	12	5	0	Taita	PNB	b
11047	Digo	0.35936	107,540	120,447	208,135	NAB57j	99-AUSL-i	ki-digo		0.10	120	4....	5	4	7	5	2	Kidigo*	Pnb	b
11048	Doe	0.09801	29,330	32,850	56,766	NAB57j	99-AUSO-f	doe		20.00	6,570	0c...	9	5	6	5	2		pnb	b
11049	Eurafrican	0.02000	5,985	6,703	11,584	NAN58	52-ABAE-e	west-african-english		85.00	5,698	0B.uh	10	8	12	5	3		pnb	b
11050	Fipa (Fiba)	0.73518	220,006	246,410	425,804	NAB57o	99-AUSA-k	i-ci-fipa		90.00	221,769	1....	10	9	11	5	1	Ichifipa*	PNB	.
11051	French	0.00400	1,197	1,341	2,317	CEW21b	51-AABI-d	general français	1	84.00	1,126	1B.uh	10	9	14	5	3	French	PNB	b
11052	Ganda	0.10171	30,437	34,090	58,909	NAB57d	99-AUSE-r	o-lu-ganda	1	70.00	23,863	3Bs.h	10	8	13	5	3	Luganda*	PNB	b
11053	German	0.02000	5,985	6,703	11,584	CEW19m	52-ABCE-a	standard hoch-deutsch		87.00	5,832	2B.uh	10	9	13	5	3	German*	PNB	b
11054	Gisamjang	0.33000	98,754	110,606	191,130	NAB62g	04-CACA-g	gisam-jank		3.00	3,318	0....	6	4	5	5	1		...	.
11055	Gogo	4.41683	1,321,754	1,480,390	2,558,154	NAB57o	99-AUSO-p	ci-gogo	4	73.00	1,080,684	0a...	10	5	10	5	3	Chigogo*	PNB	b
11056	Goroa (Fiome)	0.12251	36,662	41,062	70,956	CMT33z	15-AAAA-b	goroa		27.50	11,292	0.s..	9	5	8	5	2		pn.	.
11057	Greek	0.05000	14,963	16,759	28,959	CEW20	56-AAAA-c	dhimotiki		95.00	15,921	2B.uh	10	9	10	5	1	Greek: Modern	PNB	b
11058	Gujarati	0.73111	218,788	245,046	423,447	CNN25e	59-AAFH-b	standard gujaraati		0.05	123	2A.u.	4	4	3	1	0	Gujarati	PNB	b
11059	Gusii	0.12324	36,880	41,306	71,379	NAB57d	99-AUKA-a	i-ki-gusii		78.00	32,219	3....	10	7	11	5	3	Ekegusii*	PNB	b
11060	Gweno	0.10000	29,925	33,517	57,918	NAB57e	99-AUNB-a	ki-gweno		80.00	26,814	0....	10	8	11	5	2		...	b
11061	Ha	2.86063	856,055	958,798	1,656,829	NAB57d	99-AUSD-b	i-ki-ha		65.50	628,013	1csu.	10	7	10	5	3	Giha*	Pnb	b
11062	Han Chinese	0.15100	45,187	50,611	87,457	MSY42a	79-AAAB-ba	kuo-yü		0.05	25	2Bsuh	4	4	2	1	1	Chinese: Kuoyu*	PNB	b
11063	Hangaza	0.61254	183,305	205,305	354,773	NAB57d	99-AUSD-e	ki-hangaza		70.00	143,714	1csu.	10	8	10	5	3	Kihangaza*	Pnb	b
11064	Haya (Ziba, Bumbira)	4.23146	1,266,282	1,418,259	2,450,791	NAB57d	99-AUSE-h	ru-haya	6	85.00	1,205,520	1as.h	10	10	10	5	3	Ruhaya*	PNb	b
11065	Hehe	2.60000	778,061	871,442	1,505,876	NAB57o	99-AUSU-a	e-ki-hehe		90.00	784,298	0....	10	9	8	5	3	Hehe	pn.	b
11066	Hima	0.02000	5,985	6,703	11,584	NAB57d	99-AUSE-fd	o-ro-hima		80.00	5,363	1cs.h	10	8	7	5	2		pnb	b
11067	Hindi	0.10000	29,925	33,517	57,918	CNN25g	59-AAFO-e	general hindi		0.10	34	3Asuh	5	4	4	1	0		pnb	b
11068	Holoholo (Kalanga)	0.01300	3,890	4,357	7,529	NAB57b	99-AUJE-d	ki-holoholo		80.00	3,486	0.s..	10	7	7	5	2	Holoholo	Pnb	b
11069	Hutu (Ruanda, Ruandese)	0.38956	116,577	130,569	225,627	NAB57d	99-AUSD-f	i-ki-nya-rwanda		70.00	91,398	2Asu.	10	9	8	5	2	Kinyarwanda*	PNB	b
11070	Hutu (Rundi)	0.94935	284,097	318,194	549,848	NAB57d	99-AUSD-c	i-ki-ruundi		70.00	222,736	4csu.	10	9	8	5	3	Kirundi*	PNB	b
11071	Ikizu	0.11434	34,217	38,323	66,224	NAB57d	99-AUSG-bh	i-ki-zu		35.00	13,413	0c...	9	6	7	5	1		pn.	b
11072	Ikoma (Nata, Isenyi)	0.06125	18,329	20,529	35,475	NAB57d	99-AUSG-bf	i-koma		65.00	13,344	0c...	10	7	8	5	2		pn.	b
11073	Iramba (Nyilamba, Iambi)	1.79680	537,700	602,234	1,040,676	NAB57o	99-AUSH-da	i-ki-ni-lyamba		34.00	204,759	0....	9	5	7	5	1	Kinilamba*	PN.	.
11074	Iraqw (Mbulu, Erokh, Asa)	1.38027	413,051	462,625	799,429	CMT33c	15-AAAA-a	iraqw		25.50	117,969	0.s..	9	5	8	5	3	Iraqw	PN.	.
11075	Isanzu	0.13231	39,594	44,346	76,632	NAB57o	99-AUSH-dc	i-sanzu		20.00	8,869	0....	9	5	7	5	3		pn.	b
11076	Jewish	0.00066	198	221	382	CMT35	99-AUSM-b	standard ki-swahili		0.74	2	4Asu.	5	4	2	1	0	Kiswahili*	PNB	b
11077	Jiji	0.04900	14,663	16,423	28,380	NAB57d	99-AUSD-b	i-ki-ha		37.00	6,077	1csu.	9	6	7	5	3	Giha*	Pnb	b
11078	Jita	0.88615	265,184	297,011	513,243	NAB57d	99-AUSE-l	e-ci-jita		45.20	134,249	1cs.h	9	7	7	5	3	Ecijita*	PNb	b
11079	Kaguru (Northern Sagara)	0.94015	281,344	315,110	544,519	NAB57o	99-AUSO-n	ci-kagulu		32.30	101,781	0c...	9	6	7	5	2	Chikaguru*	Pnb	b
11080	Kahe	0.01103	3,301	3,697	6,388	NAB57e	99-AUNA-n	ki-kahe		80.00	2,958	0....	10	8	11	5	2		pn.	.
11081	Kamba	0.20959	62,721	70,248	121,391	NAB57e	99-AUMA-i	ki-kamba		57.00	40,042	1cs..	10	8	12	5	3	Kikamba*	PNB	b
11082	Kami	1.28634	384,942	431,143	745,027	NAB57j	99-AUSO-k	ki-kami		2.00	8,623	0c...	6	4	6	5	2		pnb	b
11083	Kara (Regi)	0.35119	105,095	117,708	203,403	NAB57d	99-AUSE-m	ki-kara		14.50	17,068	1cs.h	8	5	7	4	1		pnb	b
11084	Karanga (Kalanga)	0.02363	7,071	7,920	13,686	NAB57l	99-AUTA-i	chi-kalanga		80.00	6,336	1csuh	10	8	12	5	1	Kalanga	Pnb	.
11085	Kerewe (Kerebe)	0.40836	122,203	136,870	236,515	NAB57d	99-AUSE-j	e-ci-kerebe		87.00	119,077	1cs.h	10	8	11	4	1	Kikerewe*	PNb	b
11086	Kikuyu	0.06987	20,909	23,418	40,468	NAB57e	99-AUMA-a	gi-gikuyu		69.00	16,159	3as..	10	9	14	5	3	Gigikuyu*	PNB	b
11087	Kimbu (Yanzi)	0.31852	95,318	106,758	184,481	NAB57o	99-AUSB-b	ki-kimbu		68.00	72,596	0....	10	7	8	5	2		...	b
11088	Kindiga (Tindiga, Hadza)	0.01507	4,510	5,051	8,728	BYG11b	07-CAAA-a	hadza		50.00	2,526	0....	10	8	7	5	2		...	b
11089	Kinga	0.78919	236,168	264,513	457,086	NAB57o	99-AUSU-f	e-ki-kinga		50.00	132,256	0....	10	6	7	4	2	Kikinga*	PN.	.
11090	Kisankasa (Dorobo)	0.01907	5,707	6,392	11,045	BYG11b	04-CAAE-d	kisankasa		3.00	192	0....	6	4	6	5	2		...	.
11091	Kisi	0.05309	15,887	17,794	30,749	NAB57o	99-AUSR-e	kisi		35.00	6,228	0....	9	5	8	4	2		pn.	.
11092	Konongo	0.20827	62,326	69,806	120,626	NAB57o	99-AUSH-cd	konongo		51.00	35,601	0....	10	6	8	5	0		pn.	.
11093	Kuria (Tende)	0.86981	260,294	291,534	503,779	NAB57d	99-AUSG-a	e-ke-koria		52.00	151,598	0a...	10	8	8	5	3	Igikuria*	PN.	b
11094	Kutu (Ziraha)	0.18376	54,991	61,591	106,431	NAB57j	99-AUSO-i	ki-kutu		20.00	12,318	0c...	9	5	7	4	0		pnb	b
11095	Kwavi	0.07933	23,740	26,589	45,947	NAB62k	04-BCAA-ao	kwavi		8.00	2,127	1cs..	7	5	6	4	1		pnb	b
11096	Kwaya	0.41653	124,648	139,608	241,247	NAB57d	99-AUSE-k	kwaya		35.00	48,863	1cs.h	9	6	7	5	1		pnb	b
11097	Kwere	0.40020	119,761	134,135	231,789	NAB57j	99-AUSO-h	ki-nghwele		19.90	26,693	0c...	8	5	8	4	1		pnb	b
11098	Lambya (Rambia)	0.16335	48,883	54,750	94,610	NAB57o	99-AUSA-e	i-ci-lambya		90.00	49,275	4....	10	7	11	4	1		pnb	b
11099	Luguru (Ruguru)	1.96632	588,429	659,052	1,138,860	NAB57j	99-AUSO-j	ci-lugulu		53.40	351,934	0c...	10	7	7	5	2		pnb	b
11100	Luhya	0.03308	9,899	11,087	19,159	NAB57d	99-AUSF-f	standard o-lu-luyia		88.00	9,757	1.s..	10	9	14	5	3	Oluluyia	PNB	b
11101	Lungu (Rungu)	0.13884	41,548	46,535	80,414	NAB57b	99-AUSA-j	mambwe-lungu		80.00	37,228	1....	10	8	7	5	1	Ichimambwe-ichilungu*	PNb	b
11102	Luo (Kavirondo)	0.84531	252,962	283,323	489,589	NAB62j	04-ACCA-b	dho-luo		92.00	260,657	2As..	10	9	14	5	3	Dholuo*	PNB	b
11103	Maasai (Masai)	0.63306	189,446	212,183	366,658	NAB62k	04-BCAA-a	enkutuk-oo-l-maasai		7.90	16,762	4As..	7	7	8	5	4	Maasai	PNB	b
11104	Machinga	0.14701	43,993	49,273	85,146	NAB57b	99-AUSQ-b	macinga		25.00	12,318	1.s..	9	5	7	4	1		pnb	b
11105	Makonde (Matambwe)	3.30983	990,480	1,109,356	1,916,998	NAB57b	99-AUSQ-d	ci-makonde		9.00	99,842	1.s..	7	5	8	5	3	Makonde	pnb	b

Continued opposite

Table 8-2 continued

EVANGELIZATION								EVANGELISM			ADDITIONAL DESCRIPTIVE DATA
Ref 1	D 28	aC 29	CG% 30	r 31	E 32	U 33	W 34	e 35	R 36	T 37	Locations, civil divisions, literacy, religions, church history, denominations, dioceses, church growth, missions, agencies, ministries, movements 38
10986	0	6	3.49		31.00	69.00	A	11.31	308	5	Dutch, Germans, Vietnamese, Indians, Cambodians, Laotians, Thais. Buddhists 49%, Muslims 20%, nonreligious 10%.
Tajikistan											
10987	0	8	1.62	5	38.02	61.98	A	0.02	277	2	Refugees, migrant workers from Afghanistan, Iran. Unintelligible to Eastern Pushto. Muslims 100%(Hanafi Sunnis). M=CSI.
10988	1	8	3.58	6	99.70	0.30	C	344.92	85	9	Gregorians, from Armenia. Nonreligious 20%, atheists 5%. D=Armenian Apostolic Ch.
10989	1	5	0.00	1	30.00	70.00	A	0.00	0	1.12	73% monolinguals. Muslims 80%(56% Shias,24% Hanafi Sunnis), nonreligious 20%. D=ROC. M=IBT,CSI.
10990	1	9	2.33	4	50.00	50.00	B	12.77	172	5	Many speak Tatar as mother tongue. Muslims 72%(Hanafi Sunnis), nonreligious 20%. D=Russian Orthodox Ch. M=CSI.
10991	1	10	4.65	6	99.72	0.28	C	346.89	122	9	Origins in Bulgaria. In 12 other countries. Nonreligious 18%, atheists 10%. D=Bulgarian Orthodox Ch. M=LBI.
10992	3	7	2.01	5	99.70	0.30	C	339.81	62	9	White Russians, from Belorussia. Nonreligious 25%. D=Russian Orthodox Ch,RCC,Old Ritualist Chs.
10993	0	7	0.00	4	32.00	68.00	A	0.00	0	1.12	Most are trilingual (with Uzbek, Russian, or Tajiki). Muslims 100%(Hanafi Sunnis).
10994	0	6	0.00	1	23.00	77.00	A	0.00	0	1.12	Judeo-Tadzhik, Bukharian. Centered on Bokhara (Uzbekistan). Also in Israel, USA. Close to Tajiki. Religious Jews 100%.
10995	1	9	3.87	0	76.00	24.00	B	97.09	168	6	Origins in Chuvashia (Russia). Muslims 35%(Sunnis), nonreligious 30%. D=ROC. M=IBT.
10996	0	7	0.00	1	25.00	75.00	A	0.00	0	1.11	Descendants of 13th-century Mongols. 1944 deported to Uzbek SSR. Muslims 100%(Hanafi Sunnis). M=IBT.
10997	1	9	2.16	4	96.00	4.00	B	140.16	62	7	Nonreligious/atheists 55%, Muslims 5%(Sunnis,Shias). D=Georgian Orthodox Ch.
10998	3	10	5.40	8	99.78	0.22	C	435.59	117	10	Also in Altai (Russia), Kirghizia. Nonreligious 20%. D=German ELC,Old Mennonites,AUCECB.
10999	2	10	2.49	7	99.90	0.10	C	522.31	60	10	Immigrants from Greece: Urum (Turkish-speaking). Nonreligious 10%. D=Greek Orthodox Ch,ROC. M=UBS,LEV,LBI.
11000	0	7	0.00	0	13.00	87.00	A	0.00	0	1.03	Pamir Mountains, Gorno-Badakhshan AO. Also Afghanistan, Pakistan, China. Tajiki is used as literary language. Muslims 100%(Ismaili Shias, since 11th century).
11001	0	9	0.00	5	43.00	57.00	A	0.00	0	1.10	Bilingual in Russian, Tajiki. Emigration to Israel, but also returns. Religious Jews 88%.
11002	0	7	0.00	4	34.00	66.00	A	0.00	0	1.10	Muslims 60%(Hanafi Sunnis, with Sufi influence), nonreligious 30%, atheists 10%. M=ROC,CSI.
11003	0	7	0.00	4	31.00	69.00	A	0.00	0	1.10	From Kirghizia. Also in China, Afghanistan, Turkey. Muslims 45%(Hanafi Sunnis), nonreligious 40%, atheists 10%, shamanists, Lamaists. M=IBT,CSI,WEC,FI.
11004	1	9	6.20	6	89.00	11.00	B	81.21	210	6	45% now speak Russian or Tajiki. Nonreligious 35%, shamanists 20%, Buddhists 15%, atheists 5%. D=KMC. M=CSI.
11005	0	6	0.00	0	11.00	89.00	A	0.00	0	1.05	From southern Dagestan (Russia). Lingua franca. Muslims 100%(Shafi Sunnis).
11006	3	7	4.07	5	99.84	0.16	C	447.63	76	10	Found in 24 countries. Strong Catholics. Nonreligious 10%. D=RCC,ERCL,ROC.
11007	1	7	5.55	0	99.90	0.10	C	440.19	134	10	Originally from Mari (Russia). Agriculturalists. Muslims 7%, many shamanists. D=ROC. M=IBT.
11008	1	7	4.56	6	99.81	0.19	C	393.21	115	9	From Bessarabia (Moldavia), Romania. Nonreligious 10%. D=Russian Orthodox Ch.
11009	1	7	6.07	1	99.65	0.35	C	251.48	157	8	From Mordvinia (Russia). Acculturated to Russian. Nonreligious 30%. D=ROC. M=IBT.
11010	4	7	4.38	5	46.05	53.95	A	0.08	302	2	100% literates. 55% speak Russian. Muslims 80%(Hanafi Sunnis), nonreligious/atheists 20%. D=ROC(D-Tashkent),AUCECB,CEF,SDA. M=CSI,FI. R=HCJB,FEBC.
11011	1	7	6.01	0	76.00	24.00	B	99.86	256	6	Mainly in Russia, Georgia; also in Syria, Turkey. Muslims 55%(Sunnis), nonreligious 9%. D=ROC.
11012	0	7	0.00	0	15.00	85.00	A	0.00	0	1.04	Hissar Valley. Also in Uzbekistan, Afghanistan. Bilingual in Tajiki. Collective farm workers. Muslims 99%(Sunnis).
11013	0	7	0.00	5	35.00	65.00	A	0.00	0	1.12	Farsi spoken as mother tongue by 31% of Persians. Muslims 99%(Ithna-Ashari Shias), Baha'is.
11014	4	8	4.44	6	99.89	0.11	C	503.51	78	10	From Poland. Strong Catholics. Nonreligious 9%.D=RCC,ROC,CEF,CWE.
11015	8	8	3.14	7	99.60	0.40	C	286.89	66	8	In 70 countries. Nonreligious 30%, atheists 10%. D=ROC,RCC,AUCECB,Old Ritualists,CEF,CCECB,SDA,IPKh.
11016	0	9	0.00	0	18.00	82.00	A	0.00	0	1.04	Shikoshumi, Zebaki. Part of Pamir peoples. Also in Afghanistan. Unwritten language. Bilingual in Tajiki (literary language). Muslims 100%(Ismaili Shias, since 1050).
11017	0	7	0.00	0	13.00	87.00	A	0.00	0	1.03	Pamir Mountains. Including Bartangi, Oroshor, Rushan, Shugnan. Unwritten language; Tajiki used as literary language. Pastoralists. Muslims 100%(Ismaili Shias).
11018	0	7	4.93	4	42.03	57.97	A	0.04	367	2	Also in Uzbekistan, Kirghizia. Most are trilingual (with Uzbek, Russian). Muslims 90%(Hanafi Sunnis,also some Shias), nonreligious 10%. M=CSI,IBT,OM,BF.
11019	0	8	5.00	6	43.50	56.50	A	2.38	365	4	Bilingual in Russian. Muslims 83%(Hanafi Sunnis), nonreligious 15%. M=CSI,ROC.
11020	0	6	0.00	8	37.00	63.00	A	0.00	0	1.11	Across Central Asia. Muslims 98%(83% Hanafi Sunnis,15% Alawi Shias), nonreligious 2%.
11021	0	7	0.00	1	28.00	72.00	A	0.00	0	1.11	In Iran, Afghanistan, Uzbekistan, et alia. Devout Muslims 95%(Hanafi Sunnis), nonreligious 5%. M=IBT,CSI.
11022	1	7	4.35	0	92.00	8.00	B	184.69	159	7	From Udmurtia (Russia). Strong shamanists/animists 40%, some Muslims. D=ROC.
11023	0	6	0.00	4	33.00	67.00	A	0.00	0	1.11	Also in Kirghizia, Uzbekistan. In 15 countries. Muslims 100%(Hanafi Sunnis, heavy Sufi influence). M=IBT,CSI.
11024	7	8	3.51	6	99.79	0.21	C	423.87	88	10	In 15 countries. Nonreligious/atheists 20%. D=ROCUOC(P-Kiev),(E-Ukraine),Ukrainian Catholic Ch,AUCECB,CEF,CCECB,JWs,SDA. M=FMB, 300 other agencies.
11025	0	9	0.00	0	18.00	82.00	A	0.00	0	1.04	Mountain valley in Tajikistan. Two dialects (Western, Eastern). Unwritten. Bilingual in Tajiki (as literary language). Muslims 100%(Sunnis,a few Ismailis).
11026	0	10	0.00	0	19.00	81.00	A	0.00	0	1.04	Pamiris. Gorno-Badakhshan AO. Unwritten. Bilingual in Tajiki (used as literary language). Muslims 100%(Ismaili Shias).
11027	0	0	4.63		11.00	89.00	A	2.00	1,153	4	Lezgin, Dargin, Kabardin, Central Asian Arabs, Hazara-Berberi(Tajikified Mongols). Muslism 83%, Nonreligious 10%, atheists 2%.
Tanzania											
11028	2	6	2.34	1	32.00	68.00	A	2.33	286	4	One of several Dorobo hunter-gatherer tribes. Animists 98%. D=RCC,ELCT.
11029	5	6	6.82	4	76.00	24.00	B	69.35	282	6	Near Arusha town in north. Dialect of Maasai. Related to Maasai, but agriculturalists. Animists 70%. D=RCC(D-Arusha),ELCT,AoG,SDA,BCT. M=AIM,LWF,CSSp.
11030	2	6	5.07	0	99.80	0.20	C	356.24	137	9	Near Arusha town. Bantu, unrelated to Maasai, related to Chagga. Animists 10%. D=RCC(D-Arusha),ELCT. M=LWF,CSSp,TAC,FMB.
11031	2	6	2.45	0	30.00	70.00	A	2.19	315	4	Hunter-gatherers, nomads. South of Chagga; dependent on Maasai. Language extinct. Animists 98%. D=RCC,ELCT.
11032	0	8	0.00	5	32.01	67.99	A	0.01	125	2	On Coast. Fishermen. Dialect of Swahili. Muslims 100%(Shafi Sunnis).
11033	4	5	6.58	0	34.00	66.00	A	3.72	611	4	Close to Taturu. Semi-nomadic pastoralists. Animists 97%. D=RCC,ELCT,PEFA,Elim Pentecostal Ch. M=Pallotines,EFGA.
11034	3	6	5.97	4	66.00	34.00	B	19.27	289	5	Related to Maasai, but separate ethnic group. Dialect of Maasai. Nomads ranging from Indian Ocean to Malawi. Animists 92%. D=RCC,ELCT,AoG.
11035	3	8	8.45	8	99.85	0.15	C	480.88	175	10	Mainly from Zambia; also in Zaire, Zimbabwe. Animists 5%. D=UCZ,RCC,AICs.
11036	2	6	11.55	0	99.88	0.12	C	427.19	268	10	Southwest central. Animists 10%. D=RCC(D-Iringa,D-Njombe),ELCT. M=IMC,OSB,BMW,TAC.
11037	1	6	8.12	0	99.90	0.10	C	423.76	203	10	Bilingual in Swahili. Animists 5%. D=RCC(D-Sumbawanga).
11038	2	7	5.41	0	67.00	33.00	B	53.80	281	6	Usambara Mountains. Bilingual in Swahili. Animists 20%, Muslims 58%(Shafi Sunnis). D=RCC(D-Tanga),CPT. M=USPG.
11039	6	10	4.73	8	99.78	0.22	C	438.43	105	10	Expatriates from Britain, in development. Nonreligious 9%. D=CPT(9 Dioceses),RCC,BCT,CB,SDA,JWs. M=CMS,SOMA,FMB.
11040	3	6	6.43	0	43.00	57.00	A	18.83	531	5	Central Province, Kondoa District. Animists 58%, Muslims 30%. D=RCC,PEFA,CPT. M=CMS.
11041	3	6	5.25	0	99.95	0.05	C	502.78	119	10	Northeast slopes of Mt Kilimanjaro. Animists 1%. D=RCC(D-Arusha,D-Moshi),ELCT,AIC. M=CSSp,TAC,FMB.
11042	2	6	5.25	0	99.95	0.05	C	502.78	119	10	Animists 1%. D=RCC(D-Arusha,D-Moshi),ELCT. M=TAC,CSSp,FMB.
11043	0	8	3.23	7	41.01	58.99	A	0.01	263	2	Original ruling class and slave traders at Coast. Muslims 100%(Shafi Sunnis).
11044	0	10	0.70	5	33.02	66.98	A	0.02	179	2	Migrant workers from Comoro Islands. Muslims 100%(Shafi Sunnis).
11045	0	7	3.57	1	34.00	66.00	A	1.24	368	4	Indian merchants in cities. Second language: English. Hindus 79%, Muslims 20%.
11046	0	8	5.45	0	99.68	0.32	C	297.84	148	8	From Kenya. Muslims 20%(Shafi Sunnis), animists 12%.
11047	4	7	2.52	0	44.10	55.90	A	0.16	247	3	Northeast coast around Tanga. Majority live in Kenya. Mijikenda. Muslims 99%(Shafi Sunnis). D=ELCT,CPT,RCC,Brethren. M=NLM,Canadian Brethren.
11048	2	7	6.70	0	64.00	36.00	B	46.72	349	6	Coastal Bantu. Bilingual in Swahili. Animists 30%, Muslims 50%. D=RCC,CPT.
11049	5	10	5.50	8	99.85	0.15	C	477.78	117	10	Mixed-race persons(Black/White). Mainly in urban areas. Muslims 5%. D=RCC,CPT,ELCT,SDA,JWs.
11050	6	6	5.01	0	99.90	0.10	C	463.18	126	10	West central. Animists 5%. D=RCC(M-Tabora,D-Sumbawanga),Moravian Ch,AMEC,JWs,CJC,some AICs. M=UBS.
11051	1	8	3.50	8	99.84	0.16	C	478.29	79	10	Expatriates from France, in development. Nonreligious 13%. D=RCC. M=WF,OSB,CSSp,OFMCap,IMC,MM,FSC,FICP.
11052	3	10	2.79	4	99.70	0.30	C	373.03	92	9	Migrants from Uganda. Muslims 20%(Shafi Sunnis), animists 10%. D=RCC(D-Bukoba),CPT,AICs.
11053	3	8	-0.87	8	99.87	0.13	C	511.25	5	10	Expatriates from Germany, in development. Nonreligious 5%. D=ELCT,NAC,RCC.
11054	2	6	5.98	0	31.00	69.00	A	3.39	617	4	Semi-nomadic tribe, south of the Iraqw. Pastoralists. Close to Barabaig; dialect of Taturu. Animists 97%. D=ELCT,RCC. M=LCA.
11055	5	8	4.87	0	99.73	0.27	C	357.04	129	9	Semi-nomadic. In Rift Valley. Animists 5%, Muslims 20%. D=RCC(D-Dodoma),CPT(D-Central Tanganyika),TAC,PCT,other AICs. M=CP,CMS,NKM,CAET,FMB.
11056	3	6	7.28	0	68.50	31.50	B	68.75	367	6	South of Lake Manyara, Kondoa Central Province, Mbulu District. Animists 63%. D=RCC(D-Mbulu),GFF,PAG. M=SAC,PAOC.
11057	1	10	5.52	7	99.95	0.05	C	568.67	109	10	Traders, and Cypriot refugees from Cyprus. Nonreligious 5%. D=African Greek Orthodox Ch(D-Eirenopolis).
11058	0	10	2.54	6	45.05	54.95	A	0.08	216	2	Traders from India. Hindu 90%, Muslims 10%.
11059	5	6	8.41	4	99.78	0.22	C	398.58	206	9	Migrants from Western Kenya. Animists 7%. D=RCC,PAG,SDA,LMC,other AICs.
11060	2	6	5.07	0	99.80	0.20	C	359.16	136	9	Around Mt Kilimanjaro. Close to Chagga. Animists 5%. D=RCC,ELCT.
11061	5	6	11.68	1	99.66	0.34	C	283.30	319	8	Northwest. Kigoma Province. Animists 21%, Muslims 21%. D=RCC(M-Tabora,D-Kigoma),PCSAT,CPT,CMC,other AICs. M=CMS,NKM,SFM,NPY,FFFM,FMB.
11062	0	10	3.27	7	49.05	50.95	A	0.09	219	2	Traders, merchants, originally from China. Buddhists/Chinese folk-religionists 90%, nonreligious 10%. M=FMB.
11063	5	6	10.05	1	99.70	0.30	C	314.26	271	9	Southwest of Bukoba. Animists 10%. D=RCC(D-Rulenge),CPT,PCSAT,SDA,ELCT. M=CMS,SFM,NPY,FFFM.
11064	4	6	7.62	1	99.85	0.15	C	449.86	184	10	Northwest, Bukoba area. Muslims 9%, animists 1%. D=RCC(D-Bukoba,D-Rulenge),ELCT,CHS,other AICs. M=CSM,VEM,TAC,FMB.
11065	3	6	5.21	0	99.90	0.10	C	443.47	135	10	Southeast central, north of Pogolo. Animists 5%. D=RCC(D-Dodoma),CPT,ELCT. M=CP,IMC,BMW,TAC.
11066	2	7	6.49	4	99.80	0.20	C	388.36	177	9	Aristocratic cattle-breeders, refugees from Rwanda and Burundi. Animists 2%. D=RCC,CPT.
11067	0	10	3.59	7	47.10	52.90	A	0.17	267	3	Traders from India. Hindus 90%, Muslims 10%.
11068	2	7	6.03	0	99.80	0.20	C	367.92	163	9	Horohoro. On shores of Lake Tanganyika. Majority in Zaire. Animists 5%. D=CPT,RCC.
11069	2	9	9.55	4	99.70	0.30	C	342.37	238	9	Refugees from genocide in Burundi and Rwanda. Animists 5%. D=RCC,AC.
11070	4	9	10.53	4	99.70	0.30	C	342.37	258	9	Refugees from genocide first in Burundi, then Rwanda. Animists 3%. D=RCC,AC,Mungu Mwema(God is Good), other AICs.
11071	3	6	7.47	1	78.00	22.00	B	99.64	336	6	East of Lake Victoria, on edge of Serengeti. Bilingual in Swahili. Animists 45%. D=ELCT,RCC,SDA. M=EMBMC.
11072	2	6	7.46	1	99.65	0.35	C	260.97	238	8	Near northwest border with Kenya. Bilingual in Swahili. Animists 5%. D=SDA,RCC.
11073	2	6	10.44	0	72.00	28.00	B	89.35	453	6	Ilamba. Northeast of Singida, north of the Nyaturu. Animists 30%, Muslims 35%(Shafi Sunnis). D=RCC(D-Singida),ELCT. M=TAC.
11074	4	6	9.83	0	68.50	31.50	B	63.75	457	6	Mbulu District, highlands south of Lake Eyasi. Animists 72%, Muslims 1%. D=RCC(D-Mbulu),ELCT,PEFA,COG. M=SAC,TAC,EFS,NLM.
11075	4	6	7.02	0	62.00	38.00	B	45.26	375	6	East and southeast of the Sukuma. Limited bilinguals in Swahili. Animists 75%. D=RCC,AIC,SDA,CPT.
11076	0	10	0.70	5	47.74	52.26	A	1.28	80	4	Small community of practicing Jews, mainly in Dar es Salaam.
11077	3	7	6.62	1	86.00	14.00	B	116.14	278	7	On northern shores of Lake Tanganyika, around Ujiji. Related to Ha and Vinza. Bilingual in Swahili. Muslims 30%, animists 23%. D=RCC,CPT,ELCT.
11078	4	6	9.97	1	97.20	2.80	B	160.36	340	7	Southeastern shore of Lake Victoria. Animists 50%. D=RCC(D-Musoma),CPT,AIC,TMC. M=CMS,AIM,EMBMC.
11079	2	6	4.36	0	77.30	22.70	B	91.13	206	6	East central, east of Dodoma. Bilingual in Swahili. Muslims 55%(Shafi Sunnis), animists 10%. D=CPT,RCC. M=CMS,BCMS.
11080	2	6	4.35	0	99.80	0.20	C	356.24	121	9	Northeastern slopes of Mt Kilimanjaro. Related to Chagga. Animists 4%. D=RCC,ELCT.
11081	5	9	3.57	4	99.57	0.43	B	255.90	102	8	Migrants from Kenya. Animists 20%, Muslims 2%, Baha'is 1%. D=CPT,AIC,RCC,JWs,ABC.
11082	2	6	6.99	0	42.00	58.00	A	3.06	551	4	Coastal; related to Zaramo, Doe, Ruguru. Muslims 95%(Shafi Sunnis), strong animists also 3%. D=ELCT,RCC.
11083	1	6	7.73	1	59.50	40.50	B	31.49	453	5	Southeastern shore of Lake Victoria. Many bilinguals in Swahili. Animists 83%. D=RCC(D-Mwanza).
11084	1	7	6.66	1	99.80	0.20	C	376.68	165	9	Shona-speaking migrants from Zimbabwe. Animists 5%. D=AACJM; mostly a large single Zimbabwean indigenous denomination moving north.
11085	1	6	9.84	1	99.87	0.13	C	441.39	235	10	Northwestern Ukerewe Island, Lake Victoria. Animists 5%. D=RCC(D-Mwanza).
11086	4	10	5.89	4	99.69	0.31	C	360.14	133	9	Migrants from Central Kenya. Animists 10%, Baha's 1%, Muslims 1%. D=CPT,AIC,RCC,AGOC.
11087	2	6	9.30	0	99.68	0.32	C	268.05	273	8	Central. Bilingual in Swahili. Semi-nomadic hunter-gatherers. Muslims 19%, animists 6%. D=Moravian Ch,RCC.
11088	2	8	5.69	0	90.00	10.00	B	164.25	204	7	South of Lake Eyasi. Nomadic hunter-gatherers. Only 200 Hatsa speakers remain. Animists 30%. D=ELCT,PCT.
11089	2	6	9.95	0	89.00	11.00	B	162.42	351	7	Livingston Mountains, shores of Lake Malawi. Animists 40%. D=RCC(D-Iringa),ELCT. M=IMC,FMB.
11090	2	7	3.00	1	34.00	66.00	A	3.72	322	4	Hunters in forests. Animists 97%. D=RCC,ELCT.
11091	2	7	6.65	0	73.00	27.00	B	93.25	304	6	On northeastern tip of Lake Nyasa/Malawi. Animists 54%.D=RCC,ELCT.
11092	0	6	8.52	0	87.00	13.00	B	161.95	314	7	West Central Tanganyika. South of the Nyamwezi. Agriculturalists. Some bilinguals in Swahili. Animists 29%.
11093	6	7	10.10	4	99.52	0.48	B	203.08	312	8	East of Lake Victoria; many in Kenya. Animists 27%. D=RCC(D-Musoma),PCSAT,PEFA,TMC,LMC,other AICs. M=SFM,NPY,EMBMC.
11094	0	6	7.38	0	60.00	40.00	B	43.80	404	6	South Morogodo and Kilosa Districts, E Region. 100 miles west of Dar-es-Salaam. Matrilineal. Close to Kami, Zaramo. Bilingual in Swahili. Muslims 80%(Shafites).
11095	2	7	5.51	4	54.00	46.00	B	15.76	330	5	In northeast. Related to Maasai people. Animists 92%. D=RCC,ELCT. M=FMB.
11096	4	6	8.87	1	84.00	16.00	B	107.31	358	7	Southeastern shore of Lake Victoria. Close to Jita. Animists 55%. D=RCC(D-Musoma),CPT,AIC,TMC. M=CMS.
11097	3	6	8.21	0	63.90	36.10	B	46.41	415	6	A few miles inland from Dar-es-Salaam. Bilingual in Swahili. Animists 17%, Muslims 63%(Shafi Sunnis). D=RCC(D-Morogoro),SDA,Pentecostals. M=FMB.
11098	1	6	5.20	0	99.90	0.10	C	459.90	130	10	In south. Also in Malawi. Animists 3%. D=RCC(D-Morogoro).
11099	2	6	11.04	0	99.40	0.60	B	193.74	345	7	Around Morogoro town, near coast. Muslims 43%(Shafi Sunnis), animists 3%. D=RCC(D-Morogoro),CPT. M=CMS,FMB.
11100	4	10	6.15	4	99.88	0.12	C	497.86	146	10	Migrants from Western Kenya. Baha'is 4%, Muslims 3%, animists 2%. D=RCC,CPT,AICN,CGEA.
11101	2	6	8.57	0	99.80	0.20	C	365.00	220	9	Southwest of Lake Rukwa. Very close to Mambwe language. Animists 9%. D=RCC(D-Sumbawanga),SDA. M=LMS.
11102	9	9	4.49	4	99.92	0.08	C	554.07	90	10	Mainly in Kenya. Animists 2%, Muslims 1%, Baha'is 1%. D=CPT,RCC(D-Musoma),AIC,AICN,CCA,MLA,NLC,TMC,many other AICs. M=EMBMC,CMS,CPK.
11103	9	6	6.03	4	68.90	31.10	B	19.86	280	5	Nomads in north. Half are in Kenya. Animists 86%. D=ELCT,RCC,PCSAT,CPT,COG,SDA,BCT,AIC,PCEA. M=TAC,AMI,CAET,AMEC(Zaire),MAI,WVI,FMB,LWF,AIM.
11104	1	6	7.38	1	69.00	31.00	B	62.96	351	6	Along coast, close to Mwera. Bilingual in Swahili. Muslims 73%(Shafi Sunnis), animists 2%. D=RCC.
11105	3	5	9.65	1	56.00	44.00	B	18.39	544	5	Also in Mozambique. Muslims 90%(Shafi Sunnis); pagan customs still widespread. D=RCC(D-Mtwara),CPT,Christian Brethren. M=CMML,USPG,SGT,FMB,SIM.

Continued overleaf

Table 8-2 continued

PEOPLE		POPULATION			IDENTITY CODE		LANGUAGE		CHURCH		MINISTRY		SCRIPTURE	
Ref Ethnic name	P%	In 1995	In 2000	In 2025	Race	Language	Autoglossonym	S	AC	Members	Jayuh dwa xcmc mi		Biblioglossonym	Pub ss
1 2	3	4	5	6	7	8	9	10	11	12	13-17 18 19 20 21 22		23	24-26 27
11106 Makua (Emeto, Medo)	1.33000	398,008	445,776	770,314	NAB57b	99-AUSY-a	e-meeto		53.00	236,261	2.s.. 10 6 8 5 3			pnb b
11107 Malila (Malilia)	0.21235	63,547	71,173	122,990	NAB57o	99-AUSA-f	i-shi-malila		10.00	7,117	1.... 8 5 7 5 2			pnb b
11108 Mambwe	0.25727	76,989	86,229	149,006	NAB57b	99-AUSA-j	mambwe-lungu		25.00	21,557	1.... 9 5 7 5 1		Ichimambwe-ichilungu*	PNb b
11109 Manda (Nyasa)	0.07351	21,998	24,638	42,576	NAB57o	99-AUSR-a	ci-manda		70.00	17,247	0.... 10 7 8 2 3		Chimanda*	PN. .
11110 Matengo	0.61254	183,305	205,305	354,773	NAB57o	99-AUSR-c	ci-matengo		44.80	91,977	0.... 10 7 8 4 3			pn. .
11111 Matumbi	0.50897	152,311	170,592	294,787	NAB57o	99-AUSP-c	ki-matumbi		15.50	26,442	0.... 8 5 7 4 1			... b
11112 Maviha (Mawia)	0.49617	148,481	166,301	287,373	NAB57o	99-AUSQ-e	ci-mabiha		7.00	11,641	1.s.. 7 5 5 5 2			pnb b
11113 Mbugu (Maa, VaMaa)	0.13068	39,107	43,800	75,688	CMT33z	15-ACAA-a	ma'a		10.00	4,380	0.... 8 5 6 2 1			... b
11114 Mbugwe	0.06534	19,553	21,900	37,844	NAB57o	99-AUSI-b	mbugwe		90.00	19,710	0.... 10 8 11 5 3			... b
11115 Mbunga	0.11843	35,441	39,694	68,593	NAB57o	99-AUST-b	mbunga		15.00	5,954	0.... 8 5 6 4 1			... b
11116 Mediak (Dorobo)	0.01500	4,489	5,028	8,688	BYG11b	04-CAAE-d	kisankasa		3.00	151	0.... 6 4 6 1 1			... .
11117 Meru (Rwo, South Meru)	0.36753	109,985	123,185	212,867	NAB57e	99-AUNA-b	ki-rwo		64.90	79,947	0.... 10 7 11 5 3		Kichaga: Kirwa*	PN. .
11118 Moshi Chagga (Moci)	1.65517	495,306	554,764	958,647	NAB57e	99-AUNA-m	ki-mochi		93.00	515,930	0.... 10 10 11 5 3		Kichaga: Mochi*	PN. b
11119 Mosiro (Wandorobo)	0.01500	4,489	5,028	8,688	BYG11b	04-CAAE-d	kisankasa		2.00	101	0.... 6 4 6 5 2			... .
11120 Mpoto (Nyasa)	0.13000	38,903	43,572	75,294	NAB57o	99-AUSR-a	ci-mpoto		70.00	30,500	0.... 10 7 10 2 3		Chimpoto*	Pn. .
11121 Mwanga (Nyamwanga)	0.35528	106,319	119,079	205,772	NAB57o	99-AUSA-a	i-cii-na-mwanga	1	60.00	71,448	1.... 10 7 7 4 1		Ichinamwanga*	PNB .
11122 Mwera (Mwela)	1.40885	421,604	472,204	815,982	NAB57o	99-AUSQ-a	ci-mwera		28.30	133,634	1.s.. 9 5 8 4 2			pnb b
11123 Ndali	0.61254	183,305	205,305	354,773	NAB57o	99-AUSV-b	i-ci-ndali		65.00	133,448	1.... 10 6 6 5 2			pnb b
11124 Ndamba	0.22460	67,212	75,279	130,085	NAB57o	99-AUST-a	ndamba		70.00	52,695	0.... 10 7 7 4 1			... b
11125 Ndendeule	0.32261	96,542	108,129	186,850	NAB57o	99-AUSA-f	ndendeule		15.00	16,219	0.... 8 5 6 2 0			pn. b
11126 Ndengereko	0.44920	134,425	150,558	260,169	NAB57j	99-AUSP-a	ki-ndengereko		2.00	3,011	0.... 6 4 5 5 2			... b
11127 Ndonde (Mawanda)	0.13476	40,327	45,168	78,051	NAB57j	99-AUSO-c	ci-ndonde		10.00	4,517	1.s.. 8 5 4 5 3			pnb b
11128 Nghwele	0.10000	29,925	33,517	57,918	NAB57j	99-AUSO-h	ki-nghwele		20.00	6,703	0c... 9 5 6 5 2			pnb b
11129 Ngindo	0.89840	268,850	301,117	520,338	NAB57o	99-AUST-b	ki-ngindo		33.00	99,369	0.... 9 5 7 4 1			pnb b
11130 Ngoni (Magwangara, Sutu)	0.69422	207,748	232,682	402,081	NAB57i	99-AUSX-c	south ci-ngoni		65.30	151,941	1.su. 10 6 12 5 3		Ngoni	Pnb b
11131 Nguruimi	0.13068	39,107	43,800	75,688	NAB57d	99-AUSG-bd	i-ki-ngurimi		60.00	26,280	0c... 10 7 8 5 1			pn. .
11132 Nguu (Nguru, Ngulu)	0.53904	161,310	180,670	312,203	NAB57j	99-AUSO-a	ki-ngulu		10.00	18,067	0c... 8 5 7 5 1			pnb b
11133 Nkole	0.03034	9,079	10,169	17,572	NAB57d	99-AUSE-f	o-ru-nya-nkore		47.00	4,779	3As.h 9 7 10 5 2		Runyankore*	PNB b
11134 Nyakyusa	2.75695	825,028	924,047	1,596,779	NAB57o	99-AUSV	nyakyusa-ngonde cluster	3	91.00	840,883	1.... 10 10 11 5 3		Nyakyusa-ngonde	PNB b
11135 Nyambo (Ragwe)	0.02859	8,556	9,583	16,559	NAB57d	99-AUSE-g	ru-nyambo		54.00	4,791	1cs.h 10 7 6 5 2			pnb n
11136 Nyamwezi (Nyanyembe)	3.59160	1,074,801	1,203,797	2,080,194	NAB57o	99-AUSH-a	ki-nyamwezi		29.50	355,120	0.... 9 7 10 5 3		Kinyamwezi*	PN. b
11137 Nyanja (Cewa, Chewa)	0.10000	29,925	33,517	57,918	NAB57b	99-AUSX-aa	standard ci-nyanja	2	85.00	28,489	1.su. 10 9 14 5 3		Nyanja	PNB b
11138 Nyiha (Nyasa Nyika, Nyixa	1.24959	373,945	418,825	723,742	NAB57o	99-AUSA-h	i-shi-nyiha		25.00	104,706	1.... 9 5 7 5 3		Shinyiha*	PNb b
11139 Ongamo (Ngasa)	0.01220	3,651	4,089	7,066	NAB62y	04-BCBA-a	ngasa		5.00	204	0.... 7 5 4 4 1			... b
11140 Pangwa	0.72280	216,301	242,261	418,634	NAB57o	99-AUSU-c	e-ki-pangwa		80.00	193,809	0.... 10 7 7 4 1			pn. b
11141 Pare (Asu)	1.28634	384,942	431,143	745,027	NAB57e	99-AUSJ-b	ci-athu		45.60	196,601	0.... 9 6 8 5 3		Chasu*	PN. b
11142 Pemba (Phemba)	0.00427	1,278	1,431	2,473	NAB57j	99-AUSO-a	pemba		0.30	4	1csu. 5 4 3 5 3			pnb b
11143 Pimbwe	0.11843	35,441	39,694	68,593	NAB57o	99-AUSA-m	i-ci-pimbwe		70.00	27,786	0.... 10 7 7 4 1			pnb b
11144 Pogoro (Pogolo)	0.75547	226,077	253,211	437,556	NAB57o	99-AUSS-a	ci-pogolu		72.70	184,084	0.... 10 7 7 5 1			pnb b
11145 Portuguese	0.00200	599	670	1,158	CEW21g	51-AABA-e	general português	1	92.00	617	2Bsuh 10 9 15 5 3		Portuguese	PNB b
11146 Punjabi	0.10000	29,925	33,517	57,918	CNN25n	59-AAFE-c	general panjabi		1.00	335	1Asu. 6 4 8 1 0			PNB b
11147 Qwadza (Kwadza)	0.01000	2,993	3,352	5,792	CMT33z	15-ABAA-a	kwadza		1.00	34	0.... 6 4 3 4 1			... .
11148 Rangi (Irangi, Langi)	1.12300	336,062	376,396	650,423	NAB57o	99-AUSI-a	ki-langi		26.90	101,251	0.... 9 5 7 5 3			... b
11149 Rufiji (Ruihi, Fiji)	0.81673	244,410	273,744	473,036	NAB57o	99-AUSP-b	ki-ruihi		5.00	13,687	0.... 7 5 6 5 2			... b
11150 Rungi	0.67780	202,834	227,178	392,570	NAB57o	99-AUSD	west nyanza cluster		40.00	90,871	4Asu. 9 5 7 5 2			PNB b
11151 Rungwa (Runga)	0.07351	21,998	24,638	42,576	NAB57o	99-AUSA-l	i-ci-rungwa		50.00	12,319	1.... 10 7 7 4 1			pnb b
11152 Safwa (Guruku, Songwe)	0.64521	193,082	216,255	373,695	NAB57o	99-AUSA-g	i-shi-safwa		11.80	25,518	1.... 8 5 8 5 3			pnb b
11153 Sagara (Southern Sagala)	0.32261	96,542	108,129	186,850	NAB57o	99-AUSO-m	ki-sagara		60.00	64,878	0c... 10 7 8 5 1			pnb b
11154 Sandawe (Sandwe)	0.28585	85,542	95,808	165,560	BYG11b	07-DAAA-a	sandawe		80.00	76,647	0.... 10 8 8 4 1		Sandawe	... .
11155 Sangu (Sango, Rori)	0.30627	91,653	102,653	177,386	NAB57o	99-AUSU-d	e-shi-sangu		36.30	37,263	0.... 9 6 7 4 1			pn. b
11156 Segeju (Dhaiso)	0.11843	35,441	39,694	68,593	NAB57j	99-AUMB-a	ki-daiso		0.02	8	0.... 3 4 3 4 2			pn. .
11157 Shambala (Sambaa)	1.98056	592,691	663,825	1,147,107	NAB57e	99-AUSO-a	ki-shambala		44.00	292,083	0c... 9 6 8 5 3		Kishambala*	PNb .
11158 Shashi (Sasi)	0.33486	100,208	112,235	193,945	NAB57d	99-AUSG-be	sizaki		60.00	67,341	0c... 10 7 7 5 1			pn. .
11159 Shirazi	1.44207	431,545	483,339	835,223	NAB57j	99-AUSM-q	ki-unguja		0.01	48	1Asu. 3 3 3 1 0			pnb b
11160 Soga	0.00762	2,280	2,554	4,413	NAB57d	99-AUSE-s	o-lu-soga		70.00	1,788	2cs.h 10 8 11 2 3		Lusoga*	Pnb b
11161 Somali	0.10000	29,925	33,517	57,918	CMT33e	14-GAGA-a	af-soomaali		0.02	7	2A... 3 3 2 1 0		Somali	PNB b
11162 Sonjo (Batemi)	0.06737	20,161	22,580	39,020	NAB57d	99-AULA-a	ba-temi		7.00	1,581	0.... 7 5 6 5 2			... .
11163 Suba	0.10000	29,925	33,517	57,918	NAB57d	04-ACCA-b	dho-luo		96.00	32,176	2As.. 10 8 11 5 3		Dholuo*	PNB b
11164 Suba	0.12251	36,662	41,062	70,956	NAB57d	99-AUSG-aa	suba		95.00	39,009	0c... 10 8 11 5 3		Suba	Pn. b
11165 Subi (Sinja, Shubi)	0.62480	186,974	209,414	361,874	NAB57d	99-AUSG-a	u-ru-shubi		80.00	167,531	1csu. 10 8 7 5 3			pnb .
11166 Sukuma	9.46465	2,832,335	3,172,268	5,481,766	NAB57o	99-AUSA-ke	e-ci-sukuma		36.00	1,142,017	1.... 9 5 8 5 3		Sukuma	PNB .
11167 Sumbwa	0.77997	233,409	261,423	451,746	NAB57o	99-AUSA-o	ki-sumbwa		26.00	67,970	0.... 9 5 7 4 1			pn. .
11168 Swahili (Mrima)	1.53529	459,442	514,583	889,214	NAB57j	99-AUSM-b	standard ki-swahili	84	0.01	51	4Asu. 3 3 3 1 3		Kiswahili*	PNB b
11169 Tatoga (Tatoga, Mangati)	0.50000	149,627	167,585	289,592	NAB62g	04-CACA	datog cluster		2.00	3,352	0.... 6 4 4 5 2		Datooga	.
11170 Taveta (Tubeta)	0.01000	2,993	3,352	5,792	NAB57j	99-AUSJ-a	ki-tuveta		65.00	2,179	0.... 10 7 8 5 1		Kitaveta*	PN. b
11171 Tongwe	0.08984	26,885	30,112	52,034	NAB57o	99-AUSC-b	ki-tongwe		80.00	24,089	0.... 10 8 8 5 2			... b
11172 Tumbatu	0.45670	136,669	153,072	264,513	NAB57j	99-AUSM-pa	ci-tumbatu		0.00	0	1csu. 0 3 3 1 2			pnb b
11173 Tumbuka	0.40000	119,702	134,068	231,673	NAB57b	99-AUSW-c	ci-tumbuka		85.00	113,958	3.... 10 9 12 5 3		Chitumbuka*	PNB b
11174 Turu (Nyaturu, Rimi, Limi)	1.90098	568,876	637,152	1,101,016	NAB57o	99-AUSH-e	ki-nya-turu		73.00	465,121	0.... 10 7 7 5 3		Nyaturu	Pn. .
11175 Tutsi (Tuzi)	0.50000	149,627	167,585	289,592	NAB57d	99-AUSD-f	i-ki-nya-rwanda		75.00	125,689	2Asu. 10 8 10 4 3		Kinyarwanda*	PNB b
11176 Twa (Gesera) Pygmy	0.01091	3,265	3,657	6,319	BYG12	99-AUSD-f	i-ki-nya-rwanda		8.00	293	2Asu. 7 5 5 4 2		Kinyarwanda*	PNB b
11177 Vidunda	0.13068	39,107	43,800	75,688	NAB57o	99-AUSD-l	ci-vidunda		60.00	26,280	0c... 10 7 8 5 2			pnb b
11178 Vinza	0.04084	12,222	13,688	23,654	NAB57o	99-AUSD-b	vinza		39.00	5,338	1csu. 9 6 7 5 3			pnb b
11179 Wanda (Wandia)	0.09801	29,330	32,850	56,766	NAB57o	99-AUSA-i	i-ci-wanda		20.00	6,570	1.... 9 5 7 5 2			pnb b
11180 Wanji	0.24502	73,323	82,123	141,911	NAB57o	99-AUSU-e	ki-wanji		30.00	24,637	0.... 9 5 7 5 3		Kivwanji*	Pn. .
11181 Wasi (Alawa, Alagwa)	0.04030	12,060	13,507	23,341	CMT33z	15-AAAB-a	wasi		12.00	1,621	0.... 8 5 5 5 3			... .
11182 Wungu (Bungu)	0.14701	43,993	49,273	85,146	NAB57o	99-AUSB-a	i-ki-bungu		70.00	34,491	0.... 10 7 8 2 1			... b
11183 Yao (Ajao, Ajawa)	1.47011	439,936	492,737	851,463	NAB57b	99-AUSQ-f	ci-yao		14.00	68,983	4.s.. 8 5 8 5 3		Chiyao*	PNB .
11184 Zanaki	0.25319	75,768	84,862	146,643	NAB57d	99-AUSG-b	zanaki-koma		60.00	50,917	0c... 10 7 8 4 1		Ikizanaki*	Pn. b
11185 Zanzibari (Hadimu)	0.01931	5,779	6,472	11,184	NAB57j	99-AUSM-pb	ki-hadimu		0.00	0	1csu. 0 3 3 1 3			... b
11186 Zaramo (Zalamo)	1.87030	559,695	626,869	1,083,246	NAB57j	99-AUSO-g	ki-zalamo	9	2.00	12,537	0c... 6 4 7 5 2		Kizaramo*	PNb b
11187 Zigwa (Zigula)	1.37210	410,606	459,887	794,697	NAB57j	99-AUSO-d	ki-zigula		10.00	45,989	0c... 8 5 8 5 2		Kizigula*	PNb .
11188 Zinza	0.56354	168,642	188,882	326,393	NAB57o	99-AUSE-i	e-ki-jinja		93.80	177,171	1cs.h 10 7 10 5 1		Kizinza*	pnb .
11189 Zoba (Joba)	0.01000	2,993	3,352	5,792	NAB57c	99-AUSD-h	ki-joba		75.00	2,514	1csu. 10 9 9 4 0			pnb p
11190 other minor peoples	0.38666	115,710	129,597	223,947	...				65.00	84,238	10 6 7 5 0			
Thailand	100.00000	58,610,315	61,399,249	72,716,978					2.19	1,345,167				
11191 Akha (Ikaw, Khako)	0.04764	27,922	29,251	34,642	MSY50z	77-BBAA-d	akha		9.00	2,633	1.... 7 7 8 5 3		Akha	PN. b
11192 Anglo-Australian	0.00300	1,758	1,842	2,182	CEW19c	52-ABAC-x	general australian		65.00	1,197	1Bsuh 10 9 13 5 3			pnb b
11193 Anglo-New Zealander	0.00100	586	614	727	CEW19e	52-ABAC-y	general new-zealand		75.00	460	1Bsuh 10 9 14 5 3			pnb b
11194 Bengali	0.10000	58,610	61,399	72,717	CNN25b	59-AAFT-e	west bengali		0.55	338	1Asuh 5 4 8 5 1		Bengali: Musalmani*	PNB b
11195 Bghai Karen (Kayin)	0.00302	1,770	1,854	2,196	MSY50g	78-AABC-a	bghai		21.00	389	0.... 9 5 6 5 2		Karen: Bghai*	P... .
11196 Bisu (Mbisu)	0.00188	1,102	1,154	1,367	MSY50g	77-BBBB-a	bisu		1.00	12	0.... 6 4 4 4 1			P... .
11197 Black Karen (Pao Karen)	0.00121	709	743	880	MSY50g	78-AAAA-a	pa'o		25.00	186	0.... 9 5 6 4 2		Pa'o*	PN. .
11198 Black Tai (Tai Dam)	0.03551	20,813	21,803	25,822	MSY49z	47-AAAD-a	tai-dam		4.00	872	0.... 6 4 4 4 3		Tai: Dam*	P.. b
11199 Blue/Green/Black Meo	0.06190	36,280	38,006	45,012	MSY47a	48-AAAA-bd	tak		12.00	4,561	1A.. 8 5 6 5 3			pnb .
11200 British	0.00800	4,689	4,912	5,817	CEW19i	52-ABAC-b	standard-english	12	74.00	3,635	3Bsuh 10 9 13 5 1			pnb b
11201 Burmese	0.10000	58,610	61,399	72,717	MSY50b	77-AABA-a	bama		0.20	123	4Asu. 6 4 6 5 3		Burmese	PNB b
11202 Central Khmer (Cambodian)	0.09000	52,749	55,259	65,445	AUG03b	46-FBAA-b	khmae		1.00	553	2A... 6 6 6 5 3		Khmer*	PNB b
11203 Central Thai (Siamese)	34.94044	20,478,702	21,453,168	25,407,632	MSY49d	47-AAAB-a	central thai	80	2.50	536,329	3asuh 6 10 7 5 4		Thai*	PNB b
11204 Chong (Shong)	0.00100	586	614	727	AUG03z	46-FCAB-a	chong		1.40	9	0.... 6 4 4 1 0			... .
11205 East Pua Pray	0.01000	5,861	6,140	7,272	AUG03z	46-DDCB-b	lua'		5.00	307	0.... 7 5 5 1 1		Lua	P... .
11206 Eastern/Northern Lawa	0.01313	7,696	8,062	9,548	AUG03z	46-DBAB-d	wiang-papao-lua		1.40	113	0.... 6 4 4 5 1		Lawa, Western	PN. n
11207 Eurasian	0.08000	46,888	49,119	58,174	MSY43	52-ABAD-a	south-asian-english		50.00	24,560	0B.uh 10 8 11 5 3			pnb b
11208 Flowery/Southern Lisu	0.02621	15,362	16,093	19,059	MSY50l	77-BACA-a	lisu		15.00	2,414	4rs.. 8 5 7 5 3		Lisu: Central*	PNB b
11209 French	0.00300	1,758	1,842	2,182	CEW21g	51-AABI-d	general français	5	84.00	1,547	1B.uh 10 9 14 5 3		French	PNB b
11210 Han Chinese (Cantonese)	8.23990	4,829,431	5,059,237	5,991,806	MSY42a	47-AAAB-d	central thai		0.72	36,427	3asuh 5 4 6 2 2		Thai*	PNB b
11211 Han Chinese (Cantonese)	0.05810	34,053	35,673	42,249	MSY42a	79-AAAB-a	central yue		10.00	3,567	3a.uh 8 5 8 5 2		Chinese, Yue	PNB b
11212 Han Chinese (Hainanese)	0.01400	8,205	8,596	10,180	MSY42a	79-AAAK-c	wanning		16.60	1,427	1a.. 8 5 6 5 2			p.. b
11213 Han Chinese (Hainanese)	0.01000	5,861	6,140	7,272	MSY42a	79-AAAL-a	shao-jiang		17.00	1,044	0A.. 8 5 8 5 3		Chinese: Cantonese	PNB b
11214 Han Chinese (Hakka)	0.11621	68,111	71,352	84,504	MSY42a	79-AAAG-a	literary hakka		14.30	10,203	1A.. 8 5 8 5 3		Chinese: Hakka, Wukingfu*	PNB b
11215 Han Chinese (Mandarin)	0.01160	6,799	7,122	8,435	MSY42a	79-AAAH-a	kuo-yü	11	10.00	712	2Bsuh 8 5 10 5 3		Chinese: Kuoyu*	PNB b
11216 Han Chinese (Min Nan)	2.13818	1,253,194	1,312,826	1,554,820	MSY42a	79-AAAJ-ic	chaozhou	20	8.10	106,339	1A..h 7 10 8 5 3		Chinese, Min Nan	PNB b
11217 Han Chinese (Min Pei)	0.02000	11,722	12,280	14,543	MSY42a	79-AAAI-ce	fuzhou		10.00	1,228	1A.. 8 5 8 2 0		Chinese: Foochow	PNB b
11218 Hkun (Khun)	0.01000	5,861	6,140	7,272	MSY49z	47-AAAA-ec	khyn		2.00	123	1.s.. 6 4 2 1 0		Khun	Pnb b
11219 Hui (Panthay)	0.01143	6,699	7,018	8,312	MSY42b	79-AAAB-ba	kuo-yü		0.00	0	2Bsuh 0 2 2 1 0		Chinese: Kuoyu*	PNB b
11220 Japanese	0.02000	11,722	12,280	14,543	MSY45a	45-CAAA-a	koku-go		1.60	196	0.... 8 5 8 5 2		Japanese	PNB b
11221 Jewish	0.00014	82	86	102	CMT35	47-AAAB-d	central thai		0.00	0	3asuh 0 3 1 1 0		Thai*	PNB b
11222 Kedah Malay	0.01000	5,861	6,140	7,272	MSY44k	31-PHAB-a	malayu-kedah		0.00	0	0.... 6 4 4 1 0			... b
11223 Kensiu Negrito (Semang)	0.00059	346	362	429	AUG05	46-GBAA-b	kensiu		5.00	18	0.... 7 5 4 4 1		Kensiu	... .
11224 Khamet (Lamet)	0.00021	123	129	153	AUG03z	46-DBCA	lamet-khamet cluster		5.00	6	0.... 6 4 4 5 3		Lamet	... .
11225 Khmu	0.04941	28,959	30,337	35,929	AUG03z	46-DDBA-a	kha-khmu		1.40	425	0.... 6 7 6 5 3		Khmu'	P... .
11226 Khon Doi (Wa, Bulang)	0.00212	1,243	1,302	1,542	AUG03z	46-DBAC-e	kontoi		5.00	65	0.... 7 5 6 1 0		Blang	... .
11227 Kintaq Negrito (Kenta)	0.00020	117	123	145	AUG05	46-GBAA-bh	kintaq-bong		4.90	6	0.... 6 4 3 1 0			... .

Continued opposite

Table 8-2 continued

EVANGELIZATION								EVANGELISM			ADDITIONAL DESCRIPTIVE DATA
Ref 1	*D 28*	*aC 29*	*CG% 30*	*r 31*	*E 32*	*U 33*	*W 34*	*e 35*	*R 36*	*T 37*	*Locations, civil divisions, literacy, religions, church history, denominations, dioceses, church growth, missions, agencies, ministries, movements 38*
11106	2	6	10.59	0	99.53	0.47	B	199.25	321	7	Majority in Mozambique. Muslims 42%(Shafi Sunnis), animists 3%. D=RCC(D-Mtwara),CPT. M=OSB,SGT,FMB,OSM,SDS,USPG.
11107	2	6	6.79	0	53.00	47.00	B	19.34	427	5	Central. Bilingual in Swahili. Animists 85%. D=RCC,Moravian Ch.
11108	2	6	3.14	0	70.00	30.00	B	63.87	180	6	Southwest of Lake Rukwa. Closely related to Lungu. Animists 65%. D=SDA,RCC. M=LMS.
11109	3	7	7.74	0	99.70	0.30	C	283.60	227	8	Northeast shore of Lake Nyasa/Malawi. Animists 10%. D=RCC,ANC,other AICs.
11110	1	6	9.56	0	79.80	20.20	B	130.48	378	7	Northeast Lake Nyasa; some in Malawi and Mozambique. Animists 50%. D=RCC(D-Njombe). M=OSB.
11111	1	6	8.20	0	49.50	50.50	A	28.00	535	5	Along Ruvuma river on Mozambique border. Bilingual in Swahili. Mostly nominal Muslims 78%, animists 6%. D=RCC.
11112	2	6	7.31	1	47.00	53.00	A	12.00	511	5	In south. Also in Mozambique. Closely related to Makonde. Muslims 90%(Shafi Sunnis). Strong paganism. D=RCC,CPT.
11113	2	6	6.27	0	41.00	59.00	A	14.96	546	5	In Usambara, Eastern Province, just north of Korogwe. Hybrid language(Bantu/Cushitic); language isolate. Close to Pare. Animists 20%, Muslims 70%.D=ELCT.
11114	4	6	7.88	0	99.90	0.10	C	443.47	190	10	All around Lake Manyara. Bilingual in Swahili. Animists 4%. D=RCC(D-Mbulu),ELCT,GFF,PAG. M=SAC,TAC,PAOC,NLC.
11115	1	6	6.60	0	47.00	53.00	A	25.73	470	5	Central southeast. Close to Ndamba, Pogolu. Bilingual in Swahili. Animists 80%. D=RCC(D-Mahenge).
11116	1	7	2.75	1	28.00	72.00	A	3.06	367	4	Hunters in forests. One of several isolated tribal groups. Animists 97%. D=RCC.
11117	2	6	5.82	0	99.65	0.35	C	260.33	171	8	Around Mt Meru in north. Animists 15%. D=ELCT,RCC. M=TAC,AMI,FMB.
11118	3	6	11.46	0	99.93	0.07	C	482.01	241	10	Northeast corner of Chagga area. Animists 1%. D=RCC(D-Arusha,D-Moshi),ELCT,AIC. M=CSSp,TAC,FMB.
11119	2	7	2.34	1	33.00	67.00	A	2.40	277	4	Hunters in forests. Isolated tribal group. Animists 98%. D=RCC,ELCT.
11120	3	6	8.35	0	99.70	0.30	C	283.60	242	8	Northern shores of Lake Nyasa/Malawi. Partly in Malawi, few in Mozambique. Animists 5%, Muslims 5%. D=RCC,ANC,other AICs.
11121	1	6	5.31	0	99.60	0.40	C	227.76	178	8	Southwest of Lake Rukwa. Majority in Zambia. Animists 30%, somewhat strong. D=RCC.
11122	1	6	9.97	1	74.30	25.70	B	76.74	422	6	Southeast, north of Makonde along coast. Muslims 70%(Shafi Sunnis), animists 2%. D=RCC(D-Mtwara). M=SDS,FMB.
11123	2	6	4.86	0	99.65	0.35	C	260.97	157	8	In south, west of Mbeya, close to Zambia/Malawi/Tanzania border point. Animists 25%. D=RCC(D-Mbeya),ELCT.
11124	1	6	8.95	0	99.70	0.30	C	270.83	269	8	Central southeast. Bilingual in Swahili. Animists 10%, some Muslims 5%. D=RCC(D-Mahenge).
11125	0	6	7.67	0	47.00	53.00	A	25.73	532	5	Northeast of Songea in south. Isolated from other languages. Animists 80%.
11126	2	6	5.87	0	34.00	66.00	A	2.48	591	4	Arabized tribe inland from coast south of Dar-es-Salaam. Mostly nominal Muslims 93%, animists 25%. D=RCC,ELCT.
11127	2	6	6.30	1	53.00	47.00	B	19.34	401	5	In southeast, north of Masasi. Related to Yao, Ngindo. Mostly nominal Muslims 80%, animists 10%. D=RCC(D-Nachingwea),CPT(D-Masasi). M=SDS,USPG,CR.
11128	2	6	6.72	0	63.00	37.00	B	45.99	356	6	Inland from coast north of Dar-es-Salaam. Bilingual in Swahili. Muslims 65%, animists 15%. D=RCC,CPT.
11129	1	6	9.64	0	68.00	32.00	B	81.90	447	6	East central, south of Rufiji river, south of Zaramo people. Bilingual in Swahili. Mostly nominal Muslims 63%, animists 2%. D=RCC.
11130	2	7	10.11	5	99.65	0.35	C	293.87	248	8	In south. Formerly Zulus from South Africa. Animists 20%. D=RCC(D-Njombe,D-Tanga),AICs. M=CMML,FCSM,OSB.
11131	2	6	8.19	1	99.60	0.40	C	221.19	279	8	East of Lake Victoria. Related to Zanaki, Kuria. Animists 15%. D=RCC,TMC. M=EMBMC.
11132	2	6	7.79	0	53.00	47.00	B	19.34	478	5	Inland from Zaramo. Animists 15%, Muslims 70%(Sunnis). Strong Christian missions. D=RCC(D-Morogoro),CPT. M=CMS.
11133	2	10	6.36	4	99.47	0.53	B	197.28	202	7	Migrants from Uganda. Animists 11%, Muslims 2%(Shafi Sunnis). D=CPT(strong East African Revivalists),RCC.
11134	9	6	7.14	0	99.91	0.09	C	488.26	160	10	In south; known as Ngonde in Malawi. Animists 3%, Muslims 1%. D=RCC(D-Mbeya),ELCT,PHC,Moravian Ch,BCT,ANC,LCGHC,ALC,several other AICs. M=BMW.
11135	2	6	5.53	1	97.00	3.00	B	177.02	216	7	In northwest. Bilingual in Haya. Animists 25%, Muslims 5%. D=RCC,ELCT.
11136	8	6	4.00	0	76.50	23.50	B	82.37	196	6	Hoe agriculturalists. Muslims 64%(Shafi Sunnis, since 1840), animists 1%. D=RCC(M-Tabora),Moravian Ch,SA,AIC,PCSAT,TAC,ANC,several other AICs.
11137	5	8	5.14	5	99.85	0.15	C	468.47	120	10	Primarily in Malawi, also Zambia, Zimbabwe, Mozambique. Lingua franca. Muslims 10%(Shafi Sunnis), animists 1%. Baha'is. D=RCC,CPT,SDA,many AICs,AoG.
11138	4	6	5.54	0	73.00	27.00	B	66.61	263	6	South and west of Lake Rukwa, on Zambia border. Also in Zambia, Malawi. Animists 70%. D=Moravian Ch,RCC,ANC,other AICs.
11139	1	6	3.06	0	33.00	67.00	A	6.02	373	4	Near Kenya border, on eastern slopes of Mt Kilimanjaro. Only 250 Ngasa-speakers left; language nearly extinct. Animists 95%. D=ELCT.
11140	1	6	10.38	0	99.80	0.20	C	347.48	273	9	Central south. Related to Bena, Kinga. Bilingual in Swahili. Animists 15%. D=RCC(D-Njombe). M=OSB.
11141	3	6	5.02	0	90.60	9.40	B	150.79	183	7	Monolinguals 5%, 63% bilingual in Swahili, 32% trilingual in Swahili and English. Muslims 30%(Sunnis), animists 23%. D=RCC(D-Moshi,D-Same),ELCT,AICs.
11142	3	8	1.40	5	45.30	54.70	A	0.49	173	3	Swahili speakers on Pemba Island. Muslims 99%(Shafi Sunnis). D=PYMF,RCC,CPT.
11143	1	6	8.25	0	99.70	0.30	C	288.71	235	8	Southwest, on northwest of Lake Rukwa. Bilingual in Swahili. Animists 20%. D=RCC.
11144	1	6	10.32	0	99.73	0.27	C	280.48	305	8	South of Rufiji river, around Mahenge town. Animists 10%, some Muslims 8%. D=RCC(D-Mahenge).
11145	1	10	2.14	8	99.92	0.08	C	564.14	52	10	Emigres from Mozambique. Nonreligious 7%. D=RCC. M=SJ,WF,OSB,CSSp.
11146	0	10	3.57	5	52.00	48.00	B	1.89	243	4	Traders from India. Hindus 60%, Sikhs 30%, Muslims 9%.
11147	1	10	3.59	0	28.00	72.00	A	1.02	537	4	Small Dorobo group living among the Gogo south of Kondoa. Animists 99%. D=CPT.
11148	2	6	9.66	0	62.90	37.10	B	61.75	484	6	Central: around and north of Kondoa. Muslims 70%(Shafi Sunnis), Animists 3%. D=RCC(D-Dodoma),PCSAT. M=CP,SFM,NPY.
11149	2	6	7.49	0	40.00	60.00	A	7.30	613	4	South bank of Rufiji river, near coast. Arabized. Bilingual in Swahili. Muslims 90%, animists 5%. D=RCC,ELCT.
11150	2	6	9.54	4	98.00	2.00	B	143.08	308	7	Central Bantu. Southeast shore of Lake Tanganyika. Animists 55%. D=RCC,ELCT.
11151	1	6	7.38	0	93.00	7.00	B	169.72	260	7	Related to Tongwe, north of Lake Rukwa. Bilingual in Swahili. Animists 30%. D=RCC.
11152	3	6	8.16	0	55.80	44.20	B	24.03	472	5	In south, around Mbeya town. Animists 78%. D=RCC(D-Mbeya),CPT,Moravian Ch.
11153	2	6	4.42	0	99.60	0.40	C	232.14	152	8	Southeast of the Gogo. Bilingual in Swahili. Muslims 40%(Shafi Sunnis). D=RCC(D-Morogoro),CPT. M=CMS.
11154	3	6	9.36	0	99.80	0.20	C	338.72	245	9	Kondoa District. Khoisan race. Hunters, agriculturalists. Monogamists. Muslims 14%, animists 1%. D=RCC(D-Dodoma),CPT,Pentecostals. M=CP.
11155	1	6	8.57	0	74.30	25.70	B	98.44	370	6	Northeast of Mbeya town. Bilingual in Swahili. Animists 53%. D=RCC(D-Iringa). M=IMC.
11156	1	7	2.10	0	25.02	74.98	A	0.01	390	2	On Coast, Tanga region. Arabized. Bilingual in Swahili. Related to Digo. Muslims 100%(Shafi Sunnis). D=CPT(D-Zanzibar & Tanga). M=CMS,USPG.
11157	5	6	5.41	0	90.00	10.00	B	144.54	196	7	Usambara Mountains. Muslims 50%(Shafi Sunnis), animists 6%. D=RCC(D-Tanga),ELCT,CPT,People on Strike, other AICs. M=USPG,BMS(Bethel),FMB.
11158	3	7	9.22	1	99.60	0.40	C	223.38	304	8	Near the Zanaki. Animists 20%. D=Mennonite Ch/TMC,LMC,other AICs. M=EMBMC.
11159	0	6	3.95	5	32.01	67.99	A	0.01	463	2	On Coast. Part of the whole Swahili/Arab culture. Muslims 100%(Shafi Sunnis).
11160	3	10	6.60	4	99.70	0.30	C	332.15	183	9	Migrants from Uganda. Muslims 15%(Shafi Sunnis), Animists 2%. D=CPT,RCC,AICs.
11161	0	9	1.96	5	42.02	57.98	A	0.03	248	2	Refugees, migrants laborers from Somalia. Muslims 100%(Shafi Sunnis).
11162	2	5	5.19	0	36.00	64.00	A	9.19	555	4	Small nomadic Bantu tribe, west of Lake Natron. Bilingual in Swahili. Animists 90%. D=RCC(D-Arusha),ELCT. M=CSSp,LWF.
11163	3	8	8.41	4	99.96	0.04	C	567.64	178	10	On Lake Victoria. Luo is now their mother tongue. All Christians. D=CPT,SDA,RCC.
11164	3	8	8.62	1	99.95	0.05	C	509.72	200	10	Majority live in Kenya. Bilingual in Swahili. All Christians. D=CPT,SDA,RCC.
11165	3	6	10.22	1	99.80	0.20	C	370.84	266	9	Northwest corner; close to the Hangaza north of Sumbwa. Animists 10%. D=RCC(D-Bukoba),ELCT,CPT.
11166	10	6	4.42	0	86.00	14.00	B	113.00	187	7	In north. Animists 33%, Muslims 30%(Shafi Sunnis). D=RCC(D-Mwanza,D-Shinyanga),AIC,SDA,CPT,BCT,PCSAT,CWC,KOAB,Polygamous Ch, other AICs.
11167	1	6	9.23	0	61.00	39.00	B	57.88	480	6	West of the Sukuma. Animists 53%, Muslims 19%(Shafi Sunnis). D=RCC(M-Tabora).
11168	1	10	4.01	5	47.01	52.99	A	0.01	319	2	Language of coastal peoples, also national official lingua franca. Muslims 100%(Shafi Sunnis). D=RCC. M=CTD,FIFM(Zimbabwe),EMBMC,FMB,UBS,LBI.
11169	3	6	5.99	0	31.00	69.00	A	2.26	618	4	South of the Iraqw. Semi-nomadic pastoralists. Animists 97%. D=ELCT,RCC,Pentecostal Ch. M=Christ Ambassadors Evangelistic Team,LCA.
11170	2	7	4.66	0	99.65	0.35	C	256.23	144	8	Southeast of Kilimanjaro; also in Kenya. Fluent in Swahili. Animists 10%, Muslims 15%(Shafi Sunnis). D=CPT,RCC. M=CMS.
11171	2	6	8.10	0	99.80	0.20	C	350.40	218	9	Near Lake Tanganyika, south of the Ha and Vinza. Bilingual in Swahili. Animists 10%. D=RCC,CPT.
11172	0	9	0.00	5	33.00	67.00	A	0.00	0	1.13	Swahili speakers on southern Pemba and northeastern Zanzibar Islands. Muslims 100%(Shafi Sunnis). M=CS,WVI.
11173	4	6	6.11	0	99.85	0.15	C	446.76	144	10	Majority in Malawi and Zambia. Animists 4%, some Baha'is. Mass movement church from Malawi. D=CCAP,UCZ,RCC,AICs.
11174	3	6	11.35	0	99.73	0.27	C	303.75	308	9	South of Singida. Animists 5%, Muslims 20%(Shafi Sunnis). Powerful women's secret society Imaa. D=RCC(D-Singida,D-Mbula),ELCT,PCT. M=SAC,TAC,ELCA.
11175	3	10	9.90	4	99.75	0.25	C	391.46	230	9	Refugees from 1962 and 1994 genocidal massacres in Rwanda. Animists 5%. D=RCC(D-Bukoba),CPT,ELCT.
11176	2	10	3.44	4	61.00	39.00	B	17.81	204	5	Refugees from genocide in Rwanda. Animists 87%. D=RCC(D-Bukoba),CPT.
11177	2	6	8.19	0	99.60	0.40	C	234.33	247	8	North of Rufiji river. Bilingual in Swahili. Muslims 38%, animists 2%. D=RCC,CPT.
11178	3	6	6.48	1	87.00	13.00	B	123.84	270	7	Around Ujiji on Lake Tanganyika. Bilingual in Swahili. Animists 10%, Muslims 40%. D=CPT,ELCT,RCC.
11179	2	6	6.70	0	64.00	36.00	B	46.72	349	6	South of Lake Rukwa. Close to the Safwa. Bilingual in Swahili. Animists 75%. D=RCC,CPT.
11180	3	6	8.12	0	70.00	30.00	B	76.65	375	6	In south, north of the related Kinga and Bena. Animists 65%. D=RCC,ELCT,CPT.
11181	3	6	5.22	0	45.00	55.00	A	19.71	434	5	Lake Eyasi area east of Kondoa. Related to Iraqw. Animists 88%. D=ELCT,RCC,PCSAT.
11182	1	6	8.49	0	99.70	0.30	C	268.27	260	8	Related to Kimbu, Sumbwa. Bilingual in Swahili. Animists 10%, Muslims 10%. D=RCC.
11183	3	5	5.67	4	69.00	31.00	B	35.25	283	5	Matrilineal. 30% of men absent as migrant laborers. Muslims 84%(Shafi Sunnis), animists 1%; syncretism rite. D=CPT,RCC,CB. M=CMML,USPG,SDS,SGT,SIM.
11184	1	7	8.91	1	99.60	0.40	C	225.57	293	8	Southeast shore of Lake Victoria. Bilingual in Swahili. Animists 20%. D=Mennonite Ch. M=EMBMC.
11185	0	10	0.00	5	35.00	65.00	A	0.00	0	1.13	Swahili speakers in and from Zanzibar. Muslims 100%(Shafi Sunnis). M=CS,WVI,FMB.
11186	2	7	7.39	0	46.00	54.00	A	3.35	527	4	Coastal area around Dar-es-Salaam. Arabized. Muslims 95%(Shafi Sunnis), but strong animists in practice. D=ELCT,RCC. M=TAC,LWF.
11187	3	7	4.58	0	57.00	43.00	B	20.80	290	5	Tanga and Coast Provinces. Bilingual in Swahili. Muslims 89%(Shafi Sunnis). D=ELCT,CPT,RCC. M=USPG,FMB.
11188	3	6	10.28	1	99.94	0.06	C	502.59	231	10	Southwest shore of Lake Victoria. Bilingual in Swahili. Animists 1%, Muslims 3%. D=RCC(D-Mwanza,D-Rulenge),SDA,AIC. M=AIM.
11189	2	7	5.68	1	99.75	0.25	C	333.97	161	9	Most live in Tanzania near Lake Tanganyika. Some in Zaire. Animists 10%. D=RCC,ELCT.
11190	0	8	9.46		95.00	5.00	C	225.38	273	8	USA Whites(CC,SDA,JWs), Sabaot, Goanese, Mozambicans, Bembe, and refugees from virtually all neighboring countries. Muslims 21%, nonreligious 7%.
Thailand											
11191	3	5	5.73	0	48.00	52.00	A	15.76	390	5	Chiang Mai, Maehongson, Chiang Rai Provinces. Most in China, Burma; also Laos, Viet Nam. Animists 50%, Buddhists 40%. D=RCC,OMF Akha Churches,CCT.
11192	3	10	3.09	8	99.65	0.35	C	317.91	79	9	Expatriates from Australia, in business, development. Nonreligious 24%. D=CCT,Anglican Ch,RCC.
11193	3	10	3.90	8	99.75	0.25	C	394.20	90	9	Expatriates from New Zealand, in development. Nonreligious 10%. D=Anglican Ch(D-Singapore),RCC,CCT.
11194	2	9	3.58	6	58.55	41.45	B	1.17	231	4	Immigrants from Bengal(India). Traders. Hindus 75%, Muslims 23%(Hanafi Sunnis). D=RCC,CCT. M=FMB.
11195	2	7	3.73	4	59.00	41.00	B	45.22	224	6	In extreme northwest, Maehongson; vast majority in Burma. Animists 79%. D=CCT,RCC. M=NTM,AO.
11196	0	7	2.52	1	26.00	74.00	A	0.94	381	3	Southwest Chiang Rai, North Lampang, 2 villages. Close to Mpi, Pyen, Phunoi. Averse to outsiders. Animists 99%. M=NTM.
11197	3	7	2.97	0	63.00	37.00	B	57.48	177	6	Maehongson Province. Vast majority in Burma. Animists 72%, some Baha'is. D=BBC,CCT,RCC. M=Shan States Home Mission Society,AO.
11198	1	6	4.57	4	35.00	65.00	A	5.11	405	4	Vast majority in Viet Nam; also USA, France, China, Laos. Refugee camps. Animists 95%. D=RCC. M=SIL,CSSR,MEP.
11199	1	6	6.31	4	57.00	43.00	B	24.96	337	5	Majority in Laos, others in USA, France, China, Viet Nam, Burma. Polytheists/animists 88%. D=Meo Church. M=OMF,CMO(Taiwan),NTM,AO.
11200	2	10	3.51	8	99.74	0.26	C	394.34	87	9	Expatriates from Britain, in development. Nonreligious 13%. D=Anglican Ch(D-Singapore),CCT. M=USPG.
11201	2	7	2.54	6	56.20	43.80	B	0.41	178	3	Immigrants, settlers, migrant workers from Burma. Theravada Buddhists 97%, Muslims 2%(Shafi Sunnis), many Baha'is. D=BBC,RCC.
11202	4	6	4.09	5	57.00	43.00	B	2.08	265	4	Eastern Thailand (in refugee camps), 14 villages. Most in Cambodia, Viet Nam, France, USA. Theravada Buddhists 92%, animists 3%, Baha'is 1%. D=RCC,TBCA.
11203	6	6	4.25	6	64.50	35.50	B	5.88	205	4	Theravada Buddhists 96%(180,000 monks),Muslims 1%(Shafi Sunnis), Hindus 0.2%, Baha'is. D=CCT,RCC,EGCT,UPCT,SDA,TBCA. M=OMF,LBI,CMA,UPCI.
11204	0	7	2.22	0	21.40	78.60	A	1.09	412	4	Chantaburi, Trat Province northwest of Par. Majority are scattered across Cambodia. Close to Somray. Animists 98%.
11205	0	7	3.48	0	29.00	71.00	A	5.29	423	4	East of Pua District in Nan Province, also on Laos border. Animists 95%. M=ACCM.
11206	2	7	2.45	0	34.40	65.60	A	1.75	275	4	Northern: Chiang Mai, Chiang Rai Provinces, one village. Bilingual in Northern Tai. Animists 78%, Buddhists 20%. D=RCC,GCT. M=NTM.
11207	2	10	7.18	8	99.50	0.50	B	198.92	201	7	Mixed-race persons, Asian/Americans. Mainly in urban areas. Buddhist 40%.D=CCT,RCC. M=CSSR,MEP,SDB,FSC.
11208	3	6	5.64	4	75.00	25.00	B	41.06	243	6	In 6 northern Provinces. Majority in China, Burma. Animists 80%, many Baha'is. D=Thai Lisu Christian Ch Fellowship,AoG,KBCT. M=OMF,CCT,ABCUSA,NTCM.
11209	1	10	5.17	8	99.84	0.16	C	484.42	107	10	Expatriates from France, in business, education. Nonreligious 13%. D=RCC. M=CSSR,MEP,SDB,FSC.
11210	7	6	0.65	6	55.72	44.28	B	1.46	64	4	Ethnic Chinese who are mother-tongue Thai speakers. Control 90% of all commercial assets, 50% capital of all banks. Folk Buddhists(Mahayana)/Confucianists.
11211	2	8	3.59	8	75.00	25.00	B	27.37	155	5	Immigrants originally from Guangdong(China). Mahayana Buddhists/Chinese folk-religionists 85%. D=RCC,CCT. M=FMB,SDB.
11212	3	9	5.32	0	64.60	35.40	B	39.14	253	5	From Hainan Islands, South China. Buddhists/folk-religionists 80%. D=RCC,AHC,CCT.
11213	2	9	4.99	7	78.00	22.00	B	48.39	198	6	Hoklo=Hainanese immigrants from South Fukien. Buddhists/folk-religionists 83%. D=RCC,CCT.
11214	5	8	6.38	7	79.30	20.70	B	41.39	243	6	Folk Buddhists 80%/Confucianists 5%. D=RCC,CCT,AHC,TJC,CB. M=SDB,FMB,FFFM(Finland).
11215	2	9	5.32	7	78.00	22.00	B	28.47	210	5	In Bangkok, provincial towns, Kra Peninsula. Mahayana Buddhists/Chinese folk-religionists 80%, nonreligious 10%. D=RCC,CCT. M=CEM,OMF,FFFM.
11216	7	7	9.72	6	71.10	28.90	B	21.02	400	5	Fukienese. Most speak Chaochow. Buddhists 40%, Chinese folk-religionists 40%, nonreligious 12%. D=RCC,AHC,CCT,TJC,CB,SDA,JWs. M=CEM(Hong Kong).
11217	0	8	4.74	6	64.00	36.00	B	23.36	231	5	Northern Min, from Northeastern Fukien(China). Buddhists 40%, Chinese folk-religionists 40%, nonreligious 10%.
11218	0	6	2.54	1	31.00	69.00	A	2.26	278	4	In Chiang Rai, Chiang Mai Provinces. Mainly in Burma. Close to Lu, Northern Tai. Buddhists 90%.
11219	0	5	0.00	7	39.00	61.00	A	0.00	0	1.14	Huizui. 100% Chinese Muslims(Hanafi Sunnis).
11220	1	8	3.02	7	60.60	39.40	B	3.53	170	4	Businessmen et alii. Buddhists 57%, New-Religionists 24%, nonreligious 13%. D=CCT. M=United Ch of Christ in Japan,NSKK.
11221	0	9	0.00	6	40.00	60.00	A	0.00	0	1.14	Small community of practicing Thai-speaking religious Jews.
11222	0	5	0.00	5	21.00	79.00	A	0.00	0	1.06	A few villages near Satun. Muslims 100%(Shafi Sunnis).
11223	0	7	2.93	0	30.00	70.00	A	5.47	359	4	Southern Yala Province, Phattaloong, Satun, Narathiwat Provinces. Most in Malaysia. Negrito Pygmies, nomads, small bands in tropical forest. Animists 95%.
11224	0	6	1.81	0	27.00	73.00	A	4.92	285	4	Lampang, Chiang Rai; mainly in northwest Laos (called Lamet), also USA. Animists 95%.
11225	5	5	3.82	4	36.40	63.60	A	1.86	363	4	Scattered throughout Thailand. Also in Laos, Viet Nam, China, France, USA. Animists 98%. D=RCC,EGCT,UPCT,CCT,SDA. M=CMA,PCUSA,UPCI,CC,SIL,NTM.
11226	0	6	4.26	0	27.00	73.00	A	4.92	534	4	Chiang Rai Province. Almost all in China; also Burma. Close to Wa. Hinayana Buddhists 95%.
11227	0	8	1.81	0	24.90	75.10	A	4.45	309	4	Kedah-Perak border area, southern Yala Province. Pygmy hunter-gatherers. Animists 95%.

Continued overleaf

Table 8-2 continued

PEOPLE		POPULATION				IDENTITY CODE		LANGUAGE		CHURCH		MINISTRY		SCRIPTURE	
Ref 1	*Ethnic name* 2	*P%* 3	*In 1995* 4	*In 2000* 5	*In 2025* 6	*Race* 7	*Language* 8	*Autoglossonym* 9	*S* 10	*AC* 11	*Members* 12	*Jayuh* 13-17	*d wa xc mc mi* 18 19 20 21 22	*Biblioglossonym* 23	*Pub ss* 24-26 27
11228	Korean	0.01000	5,861	6,140	7,272	MSY46	45-AAAA-b	kukö		40.00	2,456	2A...	9 8 12 5 3	Korean	PNB b
11229	Kui (Suei)	0.35410	207,539	217,415	257,491	AUG03z	46-FAAB-a	kuy		1.40	3,044	0....	6 4 5 5 3	Kuy	PN. .
11230	Lao Phuan	0.15723	92,153	96,538	114,333	MSY49z	47-AAAB-c	phuan		1.70	1,641	1csuh	6 4 4 1 2		pnb b
11231	Lu	0.13545	79,388	83,165	98,495	MSY49z	47-AAAA-g	tai-lü		0.50	416	1.s..	5 3 4 0 2	Lu	PNb .
11232	Malay (Malay Thai)	1.00000	586,103	613,992	727,170	MSY44k	47-AAAB-d	central thai		0.03	184	3asuh	3 4 1 4 3	Thai*	PNB b
11233	Malay (Melaju)	0.80000	468,883	491,194	581,736	MSY44k	31-PHAC-c	malayu-pattani		0.02	98	2.s..	3 4 1 4 3	Malay: Pattani*	PN. b
11234	Manbu (Mang)	0.00001	6	6	7	AUG03z	46-DEAA	mang cluster		20.00	1	0....	9 5 5 1 0		... .
11235	Mok (Amok)	0.00001	6	6	7	AUG03z	46-DBBA-d	pou-ma		2.00	0	0....	6 4 5 1 0		... b
11236	Moken (Sea Gypsy, Selung)	0.00400	2,344	2,456	2,909	MSY44z	31-PHCA	moken cluster		0.04	1	0....	3 4 1 5 1	Moken	P.. b
11237	Moklen	0.00296	1,735	1,817	2,152	MSY44z	31-PHCB-a	moklen		2.00	36	0....	6 4 4 1 1	Moklen	... .
11238	Mos Negrito	0.00030	176	184	218	AUG05	46-GBAA	north semang cluster		5.00	9	0....	7 5 5 1 0		... .
11239	Mpi	0.00419	2,456	2,573	3,047	MSY50z	77-BBBB-b	mpi		1.00	26	0....	6 4 4 4 1		... .
11240	Northeastern Tai (Isan)	26.48710	15,524,173	16,262,880	19,260,619	MSY49b	47-AAAC-a	isan		1.40	227,680	1cs..	6 7 6 5 4	Tai, Northeastern	PNB b
11241	Northern Khmer (Cambodian	1.77048	1,037,684	1,087,061	1,287,440	AUG03b	46-FBAA-c	north khmeer		0.10	1,087	1c...	5 5 6 5 3	Khmer, Northern	PNb .
11242	Northern Pwo Karen	0.00400	2,344	2,456	2,909	MSY50g	78-AAAB-f	pwo-phrae		12.00	295	1.su.	8 5 10 5 2	Karen, Northern Pwo	pnb .
11243	Northern Tai (Yuan, Phyap	10.59483	6,209,663	6,505,146	7,704,240	MSY49d	47-AAAB-a	yuan		0.90	58,546	1csuh	5 5 4 5 3	Tai, Northern	PNB b
11244	Nyahkur (Chaobon, Chao Bo	0.00560	3,282	3,438	4,072	AUG03c	46-GAAB-a	nyah-kur		0.70	24	0....	5 4 4 4 1	Nyahkur	... .
11245	Nyaw (Yo)	0.08976	52,609	55,112	65,271	MSY49b	47-AAAC-ad	yo		1.00	551	1cs..	6 4 6 4 1	Nyaw	pnb b
11246	Nyong	0.02000	11,722	12,280	14,543	MSY49z	47-AAAA	northwest tai cluster		1.00	123	3.s..	6 4 5 1 0		PNB b
11247	Padaung Karen	0.00400	2,344	2,456	2,909	MSY50g	78-AABD-a	pa-daung		20.00	491	0....	9 5 10 2 2		... .
11248	Pattani Malay (Thai Islam	1.87568	1,099,342	1,151,653	1,363,938	MSY44k	31-PHAC-c	malayu-pattani		0.02	230	2.s..	3 4 4 4 3	Malay: Pattani*	PN. b
11249	Phay (Pray)	0.05383	31,550	33,051	39,144	AUG03z	46-DDCB-a	kha-phai		1.00	331	0....	6 4 5 1 2	Phai	p.. .
11250	Pho Kanchanaburi Karen	0.12000	70,332	73,679	87,260	MSY50g	78-AAAB-e	pwo-kanchana-buri		15.00	11,052	1.su.	8 5 10 5 2	Karen, Pwo Kanchana Buri	pnb .
11251	Phunoi	0.02000	11,722	12,280	14,543	MSY50z	77-BBBA-a	phunoi		1.00	123	0....	6 4 4 1 0		... .
11252	Phuthai (Puthai)	0.10081	59,085	61,897	73,306	MSY49z	47-AAAB-d	central thai		0.60	371	3asuh	5 4 4 5 3	Thai*	PNB b
11253	Punjabi	0.03430	20,103	21,060	24,942	CNN25n	59-AAFE-c	general panjabi		1.00	211	1Asu.	6 4 8 4 1		PNB b
11254	Red Karen (Eastern Kayah)	0.15706	92,053	96,434	114,209	MSY50g	78-AABE-a	kayah		25.00	24,108	0....	9 5 10 4 2	Kayah, Western*	... p
11255	Red Meo	0.01000	5,861	6,140	7,272	MSY47a	48-AAAB-a	meo-do		10.00	614	0r...	8 5 7 4 2		... .
11256	Red/Black Lahu (Musso)	0.04637	27,178	28,471	33,719	MSY50i	77-BBAB-a	lahu		65.00	18,506	4a...	10 8 11 5 3	Lahu*	PNB b
11257	Saek (Sek)	0.02000	11,722	12,280	14,543	MSY49z	47-AAAF-ab	saek-thailand		0.20	25	0....	5 4 4 4 1		... b
11258	Sgaw Karen (Thai Paganyaw	0.56270	329,800	345,494	409,178	MSY50g	78-AABF-a	sgaw		32.00	110,558	3.s..	9 8 13 5 3	Sgaw Kayin*	PNB b
11259	Shan (Great Thai, Red Sha	0.09724	56,993	59,705	70,710	MSY49c	47-AAAA-e	shan		0.70	418	3.s..	5 7 7 5 3	Shan*	PNB b
11260	Silver Palaung (Taang)	0.00910	5,334	5,587	6,617	AUG03z	46-DCAA	palaung cluster		0.20	11	0r...	5 4 1 4 0	Palaung, Pale	... b
11261	Sinhalese	0.10000	58,610	61,399	72,717	CNN25q	59-ABBA-aa	standard sinhala		2.80	1,719	1asuh	6 4 8 5 3		pnb b
11262	So	0.09378	54,965	57,580	68,194	AUG03z	46-FAAA-c	mangkong		1.40	806	0.s..	6 4 4 4 1		pn. b
11263	So Tri	0.01088	6,377	6,680	7,912	AUG03z	46-FAAA-c	mangkong		1.40	94	0.s..	6 4 4 1 1		pn. b
11264	Southern Tai (Pak Thai)	7.86184	4,607,849	4,827,111	5,716,892	MSY49z	47-AAAB-f	pak-thai	13	1.00	48,271	1csuh	6 4 6 5 3		pnb b
11265	Talaing (Mon, Peguan)	0.17137	100,440	105,220	124,615	AUG03c	46-GAAA-e	talaing	1	0.70	737	1....	5 4 7 5 2		pnb .
11266	Tamil	0.20000	117,221	122,798	145,434	CNN23c	49-EBEA-b	tamil		10.50	12,894	2Asu.	8 5 11 4 3	Tamil	PNB b
11267	Thai Song (Lao Song)	0.05144	30,149	31,584	37,406	MSY49z	47-AAAB-d	central thai		2.00	632	3asuh	6 4 4 5 3	Thai*	PNB b
11268	Thin (Tin, Htin, Phay)	0.00719	4,214	4,415	5,228	AUG03z	46-DDCA-a	mal		5.00	221	0....	7 4 6 5 2	Mal	PN. .
11269	USA Black	0.00100	586	614	727	NFB68a	52-ABAE-a	talkin-black		78.00	479	0B.uh	10 9 13 5 3		pnb b
11270	USA White	0.01500	8,792	9,210	10,908	CEW19s	52-ABAC-s	general american		81.00	7,460	1Bsuh	10 9 13 5 3	English*	PNB b
11271	Ugong (Lawa)	0.00018	105	111	131	MSY50z	77-BDAA-a	ugong		1.00	1	0....	6 4 5 1 0		... b
11272	Urak Lawoi Aborigine	0.00593	3,476	3,641	4,312	AUG05	31-PHDA	urak-lawoi cluster		3.00	109	0.s..	6 4 5 4 1	Urak Lawoi'	P.. .
11273	Urdu	0.01000	5,861	6,140	7,272	CNN25r	59-AAFO-d	standard urdu		0.01	1	2Asuh	3 3 2 4 1	Urdu	PNB b
11274	Vietnamese	0.17000	99,638	104,379	123,619	MSY52b	46-EBAA-ac	general viêt		35.00	36,533	1Asu.	9 6 11 5 3	Vietnamese	PNB b
11275	Western (Cambodian) Cham	0.00700	4,103	4,298	5,090	MSY44z	31-MBBC-b	west cham		0.01	0	0.s..	3 4 5 0 0	Cham, Western	p.. b
11276	Western Bru (Baru)	0.03811	22,336	23,399	27,712	AUG03z	46-FAAA-eb	bru-thailand		2.00	468	0.s..	6 4 4 4 3	Bru, Western	pn. .
11277	Western Lawa (Lavua)	0.01500	8,792	9,210	10,908	AUG03z	46-DBAB-a	la-oor		14.00	1,289	0....	8 4 6 5 2	Lawa	PN. .
11278	White Karen (Pwo Karen)	0.12097	70,901	74,275	87,966	MSY50g	78-AAAB-ae	omkoi		15.00	11,141	1.su.	8 5 11 5 3	Karen, Pwo Omkoi	Pnb .
11279	White Meo (Meo Kao)	0.05158	30,231	31,670	37,507	MSY47a	48-AAAA-a	hmong-daw		15.00	4,750	2A...	8 5 10 5 3	Hmong Daw*	PN. .
11280	Yao (Highland Yao, Myen)	0.06019	35,278	36,956	43,768	MSY47b	48-ABAA-a	mien		0.80	296	0.s..	5 4 6 5 3	Mien	PN. b
11281	Yellow Lahu (Shi)	0.00600	3,517	3,684	4,363	MSY50i	77-BBAB-b	kutsung		20.00	737	1a...	9 5 11 4 3	Lahu Shi	pnb .
11282	Yeu	0.00300	1,758	1,842	2,182	AUG03z	46-FAAB	kuy-nyeu cluster		1.00	18	0....	6 4 4 4 0		PN. .
11283	Yoy	0.00898	5,263	5,514	6,530	MSY49z	47-AAAC-ad	yo		3.00	165	1cs..	6 4 7 4 1	Nyaw	pnb b
11284	Yumbri(Yellow Leaf)	0.00042	246	258	305	AUG03z	46-DDDA-a	mlabri		1.20	3	0....	6 4 4 4 1	Mlabri	... .
11285	other minor peoples	0.20000	117,221	122,798	145,434	...				9.00	11,052		7 4 6 4 3		
	Timor	**100.00000**	**813,906**	**884,541**	**1,184,977**					**92.18**	**815,393**				
11286	Adabe (Atauru, Ataura)	0.13700	1,115	1,212	1,623	AON10e	20-CBAA-a	adabe		60.00	727	0....	10 5 5 1 1		... .
11287	Dagoda (Fataluku)	3.42500	27,876	30,296	40,585	AON10e	20-EAAA-a	fataluku	7	90.00	27,266	0....	10 4 3 4 3		... .
11288	Eastern Tetum (Belu)	44.83560	364,920	396,589	531,292	AON09e	32-BCCA-f	east tetun	55	99.30	393,813	1....	10 9 11 5 3	Tetun	... b
11289	Euronesian (Eurasian)	0.30000	2,442	2,654	3,555	MPY53	51-AABA-e	general português		85.00	2,256	2Bsuh	10 8 12 5 2	Portuguese	PNB b
11290	Galoli (Edi, Baba)	6.85000	55,753	60,591	81,171	MSY44y	32-BCCG-d	galoli	1	95.00	57,562	0....	10 5 4 4 1		... .
11291	Habu	0.13700	1,115	1,212	1,623	AON10e	20-ACBA	kairui-midiki cluster		55.00	667	0....	10 6 6 1 1		... .
11292	Han Chinese	0.50000	4,070	4,423	5,925	MSY42a	79-AAAB-ba	kuo-yü	3	27.00	1,194	2Bsuh	9 5 11 4 2	Chinese: Kuoyu*	PNB b
11293	Idate	0.68490	5,574	6,058	8,116	MSY44y	32-BCCF-a	idate		60.00	3,635	0....	10 5 4 4 1		... .
11294	Indonesian	2.50000	20,348	22,114	29,624	MSY44k	31-PHAC-c	bahasa-indonesia	25	5.00	1,106	4Asuh	7 4 6 5 3	Indonesian	PNB b
11295	Javanese	1.50000	12,209	13,268	17,775	MSY44g	31-PIAA-g	general jawa	20	25.00	3,317	2As.h	9 5 8 6 2	Javanese	PNB b
11296	Kairui-Midik	0.27400	2,230	2,424	3,247	AON10e	20-ACBA-a	kairui		90.00	2,181	0....	10 7 10 4 2		... .
11297	Kemak	6.84930	55,747	60,585	81,163	MSY44y	32-BCCB-b	kemak	8	95.00	57,556	0....	10 4 4 4 2		... .
11298	Lakalei	0.68490	5,574	6,058	8,116	MSY44y	32-BCCE-a	lakalei		80.00	4,847	0....	10 5 6 1 1		... .
11299	Makasai (Macassai)	1.37000	11,151	12,118	16,234	AON10e	20-ACAA-a	proper makasai	14	70.00	8,483	0....	10 4 4 4 3		... .
11300	Makua	0.00690	56	61	82	AON10e	20-FAAA-a	maku'a		20.00	12	0....	9 4 5 1 1		... .
11301	Mambai (Damata)	10.95890	89,195	96,936	129,860	MSY44y	32-BCCD-d	mambai	17	98.00	94,997	0....	10 5 6 4 3		... .
11302	Naueti (Naumik)	0.13700	1,115	1,212	1,623	AON10e	32-BDAA	naueti cluster		70.00	848	0....	10 7 6 4 2		... .
11303	Portuguese	0.10000	814	885	1,185	CEW21g	51-AABA-e	general português	30	93.00	823	2Bsuh	10 9 15 5 2	Portuguese	PNB b
11304	Timorese (Vaikino)	7.00000	56,973	61,918	82,948	MSY44y	32-BCBA	uab-atoni-pah-meto cluster	45	98.00	60,680	0A...	10 10 13 5 2	Timor*	PN. b
11305	Tokode (Tukudede)	6.85000	55,753	60,591	81,171	MSY44y	32-BCCC-a	tukudede	10	95.00	57,562	0....	10 6 11 4 2		... .
11306	Waimaha (Waimoa)	0.41100	3,345	3,635	4,870	AON10e	32-CAAA-a	waima'a		80.00	2,908	0....	10 7 10 4 1		... .
11307	other minor peoples	4.48850	36,532	39,703	53,188	...				83.00	32,953		10 5 3 4 0		
	Togo	**100.00000**	**4,059,575**	**4,629,218**	**8,482,467**					**37.78**	**1,749,100**				
11308	Adele (Lolo)	0.28996	11,771	13,423	24,596	NAB59b	96-GAAA	adele cluster		21.00	2,819	0....	9 5 5 2 1	Adele	PN. .
11309	Adja (Aja)	3.03596	123,247	140,541	257,524	NAB59e	96-MAAE	aja cluster		30.00	42,162	0....	9 5 7 4 3		... b
11310	Akan	1.00000	40,596	46,292	84,825	NAB59a	96-FCCB-c	twi	8	30.00	13,888	4ssu.	9 6 12 5 3		PNB b
11311	Akebu (Kebu)	1.11721	45,354	51,718	94,767	NAB59b	96-IABA-a	ke-gberi-ke		25.00	12,930	0....	9 5 6 4 2		... b
11312	Akpe	0.09333	3,789	4,320	7,917	NAB59b	96-GABA-a	gi-seme		50.00	2,160	0....	10 7 8 5 1		... .
11313	Ana (Ife)	2.03129	82,462	94,033	172,304	NAB59n	98-AAAA-cg	west ede-ife		49.00	46,076	1csu.	9 7 11 5 3	Ife	Pnb b
11314	Anglo (Igo, Anlo, Ahlo)	0.17885	7,261	8,279	15,171	NAB59b	96-JBAA	igo-ahlo cluster		80.00	6,623	0....	10 7 7 2 1		... b
11315	Anyanga	0.19764	8,023	9,149	16,765	NAB59a	96-FDFB-a	a-nyanga		30.00	2,745	0....	9 5 6 2 1		... b
11316	Bago	0.16744	6,797	7,751	14,203	NAB56a	91-GFCB-d	bago		1.00	78	1c...	6 5 4 1 0		pn. .
11317	Bariba (Bargu)	0.30000	12,179	13,888	25,447	NAB56a	91-GIAA-a	baatonum		8.00	1,111	3....	7 5 5 5 3	Bariba	PNB .
11318	Basila (Anii, Baseca)	0.01921	780	889	1,629	NAB59b	96-GABB	anii cluster		60.00	534	0....	10 7 11 2 2		... .
11319	Bassari (Tobota, Ncham)	2.57394	104,491	119,153	218,334	NAB56a	91-GGDD-a	n-cam-m	2	15.00	17,873	0..u.	8 5 6 5 3	Ntcham	PN. .
11320	Benin-Togo Fulani	1.35922	55,179	62,921	115,295	NAB56c	90-BAAA-n	fula-sokoto		0.50	315	1cs..	5 4 4 4 1	Fulfulde	PNB b
11321	Bijobe (Soruba-Kuyobe)	0.04666	1,894	2,160	3,958	NAB56a	91-GHAA-a	mi-yobe		6.00	130	0....	7 5 6 4 1	Sola	... p
11322	Bimoba (Moba, Moab)	5.19901	211,058	240,674	441,004	NAB56a	91-GGDC-b	bi-moba	5	20.00	48,135	0..u.	9 5 7 5 3	Bimoba	PN. .
11323	British	0.00500	203	231	424	CEW19i	52-ABAC-b	standard-english	5	78.00	181	3Bsuh	10 9 13 5 3		PNB b
11324	Buem (Lelemi, Lefana)	0.10000	4,060	4,629	8,482	NAB59b	96-HAAA-a	le-lemi		90.00	4,166	0....	10 8 13 2 3	Lelemi	PN. .
11325	Busansi (Bisa)	0.08235	3,343	3,812	6,985	NAB63z	00-DFAA-a	bisa		15.00	572	1....	8 5 6 4 1	Bissa	P.. b
11326	Chakosi (Anufo, Tchokossi)	1.14741	46,580	53,116	97,329	NAB59z	96-FCAD-a	anu-fo		10.00	5,312	0....	8 7 10 5 3	Anufo	P.. .
11327	Chamba (Kasele, Akasele)	0.94153	38,222	43,585	79,865	NAB56a	91-GGDD-d	a-kasele-m		20.00	8,717	0..u.	9 5 7 4 1		pn. .
11328	Dagomba	0.15000	6,089	6,944	12,724	NAB56a	91-GGAC-e	dagba-ne		4.00	278	4....	6 4 4 1 3	Dagbani	PN. .
11329	Dompago (Logba)	0.30000	12,179	13,888	25,447	NAB56a	91-GFCB-e	lukpa		10.00	1,389	1c...	8 5 5 1 1	Lokpa*	PN. b
11330	Eurafrican	0.04000	1,624	1,852	3,393	NAN58	52-ABCE-a	standard hoch-deutsch		80.00	1,481	2B.uh	10 7 12 2 2	German*	PNB b
11331	Ewe (Ahoulan, Ehve)	22.24000	902,849	1,029,538	1,886,501	NAB59d	96-MAAA-a	standard ewe	56	76.70	789,656	4Asu.	10 10 11 5 4	Ewe	PNB b
11332	Fon (Dahomean, Fo)	0.99975	40,586	46,281	84,803	NAB59e	96-MAAG-a	standard fon		51.00	23,603	2as..	10 7 8 5 1	Fon*	PNB b
11333	French	0.07721	3,134	3,574	6,549	CEW21b	51-AABI-d	general français	35	84.00	3,002	1B.uh	10 9 14 5 3	French	PNB b
11334	Ga (Acra, Amina, Gain)	0.60000	24,357	27,775	50,895	NAB59f	96-LAAA-a	accra	3	65.50	18,193	1.s..	10 8 13 5 1	Ga*	PNB b
11335	Gangam (Ngangan, Dye)	0.91957	37,331	42,569	78,002	NAB56a	91-GGDB-a	mi-gangam		6.00	2,554	1c.u.	7 4 4 5 3	Ngangam	pnb p
11336	German	0.01000	406	463	848	CEW19m	52-ABCE-a	standard hoch-deutsch	1	86.00	398	2B.uh	10 9 13 5 2	German*	PNB b
11337	Gurma (Migulimancema)	3.39455	137,804	157,141	287,942	NAB56a	91-GGDA-b	central gulma-ncema		25.00	39,285	3.s..	9 5 6 5 3	Gourma*	PN. .
11338	Hausa	0.27034	10,975	12,515	22,932	NAB60a	19-HAAB-a	hausa	21	0.10	13	4Asu.	5 4 8 4 1	Hausa	PNB b
11339	Hwe (Ehoue)	0.11529	4,680	5,337	9,779	NAB59d	96-MAAE-c	hwe		50.00	2,669	0....	10 7 7 4 2		... .
11340	Kabre (Cabrai, Kabure)	13.42849	545,140	621,634	1,139,067	NAB56a	91-GFCB-a	kabiye	53	23.00	142,976	3a...	9 7 7 5 3	Kabiye	PN. .
11341	Kambole	0.54900	22,287	25,414	46,569	NAB59n	47-AAAA	northwest tai cluster		10.00	2,541	3.s..	8 5 6 5 0		PNB b
11342	Konkomba	1.37524	55,829	63,663	116,654	NAB56a	91-GGDB-g	le-kpekpam		15.00	9,549	2A.u.	8 5 6 5 3	Konkomba	PNB .
11343	Kotokoli (Tim, Temba)	5.60253	227,439	259,353	475,233	NAB56a	91-GFCC-a	tem		7.00	18,155	2..u.	7 5 6 4 2	Tem	... .
11344	Kpessi	0.08670	3,520	4,014	7,354	NAB64f	96-MAAB-a	kpesi		16.00	642	0....	8 5 6 5 3		... b
11345	Kposo (Akposo)	2.60500	105,752	120,591	220,968	NAB59b	96-JABA	i-kposo cluster		73.00	88,032	0....	10 8 11 5 3	Akposo	... b
11346	Kusaal (Kusasi)	0.20000	8,119	9,258	16,965	NAB56a	91-GGAC-a	kusaal		8.00	741	1....	7 5 6 1 3	Kusaal*	PN. .
11347	Lamba (Namba, Losso)	3.22262	130,825	149,182	273,358	NAB56a	91-GFCB-b	lama	3	17.00	25,361	1c...	8 5 6 5 3	Lama: Togo	PN. .

Continued opposite

Table 8-2 continued

EVANGELIZATION								EVANGELISM			ADDITIONAL DESCRIPTIVE DATA
Ref 1	D 28	aC 29	CG% 30	r 31	E 32	U 33	W 34	e 35	R 36	T 37	Locations, civil divisions, literacy, religions, church history, denominations, dioceses, church growth, missions, agencies, ministries, movements 38
11228	4	6	5.66	6	99.40	0.60	B	156.22	161	7	Immigrants, expatriates from South Korea. Buddhists 20%, New-Religionists 20%, Confucians 15%. D=PCK,RCC,OTC,UC.
11229	2	6	5.89	0	34.40	65.60	A	1.75	549	4	East central Thailand; also Cambodia, Laos. Animists 78%, Buddhists 20%. D=EGCT,UPCT. M=CMA,UPCI,SIL,FFFM,FMB.
11230	2	6	5.23	1	38.70	61.30	A	2.40	413	4	Uthai Thani, Phichit, Petchabun, et alia. Also in Laos. Closely related to Central Thai, Northern Tai, Lao. Theravada Buddhists 96%, Muslims 1%, many Baha'is.
11231	0	5	3.80	1	28.50	71.50	A	0.52	423	3	Throughout northern Thailand. Majority in China, Burma; also Laos, Viet Nam. Close to Khun. Forests. Fishermen. Animists 79%, Buddhists 20%. M=PCUSA,SIL.
11232	1	6	2.96	6	47.03	52.97	A	0.05	213	2	Thai-speaking Malays. Muslims 100%(Shafi Sunnis). Traditionalists. D=OMF Independent Chs. M=OMF,FI,OM.
11233	0	5	4.69	5	33.02	66.98	A	0.02	447	2	Villages in Ranong, south Thailand. Muslims 100%(Shafi Sunnis). Traditionalists. M=OMF(Korea,Singapore),CMA,OM,FI.
11234	0	5	0.00	0	42.00	58.00	A	30.66	65	5	Montagnards. One village in north. Almost all live in Viet Nam and China. Animists 80%.
11235	0	5	0.00	0	21.00	79.00	A	1.53	0	4	Northwest: east northeast of Chiang Mai, on Wang river. Angkuic. Nearly extinct. Animists 98%.
11236	2	5	0.00	0	20.04	79.96	A	0.02	70	2	West coast of south Thailand. Mainly in Burma. Boat-dwellers. Animists 80%, Muslims 20%. D=AC(D-Singapore),Christian Brethren. M=CMML.
11237	0	6	3.65	0	22.00	78.00	A	1.60	518	4	West coast of south Thailand; Phuket, Phangnga. Boat-dwellers. Animists 78%, Muslims 20%. M=Christian Brethren.
11238	0	5	2.22	0	25.00	75.00	A	4.56	353	4	Two areas in south. Also in Malaysia. Close to Kensiu. Animists 95%.
11239	0	7	3.31	5	30.00	70.00	A	1.09	403	4	Phrae, Phaya, 2 villages. Closely related to Bisu, Pyen, and Phunoi. Animists 99%. M=NTM.
11240	6	6	4.22	5	53.40	46.60	B	2.72	295	4	Lao. Sakorn Nakota, Nakorn Panom, Bangkok. Theravada Buddhists 98%, animists 1%. D=RCC,TFGC,EGCT,ECCT,UPCT,SDA. M=ECCA,NTM,CMA,UPCI.
11241	6	6	4.80	5	45.10	54.90	A	0.16	378	3	Northeast: Surin, Sisaket, Buriram, Korat Provinces. Refugee camps. Theravada Buddhists 95%, animists 3%. D=RCC,TBCA,EGCT,UPCT,CC,SDA. M=CMA
11242	2	6	3.44	1	55.00	45.00	B	24.09	226	5	North Central Thailand. Animists 88%. D=CCT,SDA.
11243	5	6	3.04	6	52.90	47.10	B	1.73	188	4	Khon Mung, Western Laotian. Across north. Also in Laos. Theravada Buddhists 98%, many Baha'is. D=CCT,RCC,EGCT,UPCT,SDA. M=CMA,UPCI,OMF,CSSR.
11244	0	6	3.23	0	22.70	77.30	A	0.58	571	3	Central: Korat, Petchabun, Chayaphum. Buddhists 90%, animists 9%. M=NTM.
11245	0	6	4.09	1	39.00	61.00	A	1.42	394	4	Sakorn Nakorn, Nong Khai, Panom. Closely related to Isan. Buddhists 90%, some animists 9%. M=NTM.
11246	0	5	2.54	4	40.00	60.00	A	1.46	215	4	Chiang Rai, Chiang Mai, Lamphun. Also in northern Burma. Second language: Northern Tai. Buddhists 98%.
11247	1	6	3.97	0	52.00	48.00	B	37.96	267	5	Maehongson Province. Most in Myanmar(Burma). Animists 60%, Buddhists 20%. D=RCC. M=BBC,AO.
11248	0	5	3.19	5	36.02	63.98	A	0.02	296	2	East coast below Songkhla. Muslims 100%(Shafi Sunnis). Traditionalists. Few speak Thai. M=OMF(Korea,Singapore),CMA,FI,OM. R=FEBC.
11249	0	5	3.56	0	23.00	77.00	A	0.84	543	3	Thung Chang District of Nan Province. Also in Laos. Animists 99%. M=NTM,GR.
11250	2	6	7.26	1	60.00	40.00	B	32.85	382	5	14 villages in Uthai Thani northwest of Bangkok. Animists 85%. D=CCT,SDA.
11251	0	5	2.54	0	19.00	81.00	A	0.69	525	3	Black Khoany, White Khoany. Also in Laos. Closely related to Bisu, Pyen, and Mpi. Animists 99%.
11252	1	6	3.68	6	50.60	49.40	B	1.10	232	4	Nakorn Panom, Ubon, Kalasin, Sakorn Nakorn. Also in Laos. Buddhists 90%, animists 9%. D=Gospel Ch of Thailand. M=NTM,OMF,CMA(Cambodia).
11253	1	9	3.10	5	56.00	44.00	B	2.04	203	4	Traders from Punjab(India), in and around Bangkok. Sikhs 90%, Hindus, Muslims. D=RCC. M=FMB.
11254	0	6	8.10	4	65.00	35.00	B	59.31	388	6	Maehongson Province. Majority in Myanmar(Burma). Related to Bwe, in dialect chain. Animists 75%. M=NTM,AO.
11255	2	6	4.20	4	48.00	52.00	A	17.52	280	5	Also in Viet Nam and China. Polytheists/animists 90%. D=RCC,Meo Ch. M=OMF,AO.
11256	3	5	7.81	4	99.65	0.35	C	303.68	191	9	From Burma and Laos. Animists 35%. D=BBC,RCC,CCT. M=ABFMS/ABCUSA,China Evangelistic Mission(Hong Kong),Mission Ministries,FMB,AO.
11257	0	6	3.27	0	25.20	74.80	A	0.18	421	3	In northeast Thailand, Nakorn Panom. Also in Laos. Second language: Lao. Buddhists 90%, some animists 10%. M=NTM.
11258	3	6	5.95	4	96.00	4.00	B	112.12	201	7	Tak, Maehongson, Chiang Mai, Chiang Rai. Animists 65%. D=BBC,RCC,CCT. M=WEC,OMF,ABFMS,MEP,LCMS,FMB,AO,FFFM.
11259	1	5	3.20	4	49.70	50.30	A	1.27	238	4	Maehongson, Myuang Haeng, et alia. Also in Burma, China. Theravada Buddhists 80%, animists 19%. D=BBC. M=OMF,Shan States HMS,FFFM.
11260	0	3	2.43	4	22.20	77.80	A	0.16	423	3	Most live in Myanmar, some in China. Buddhists 99%.
11261	3	9	5.28	6	60.80	39.20	B	6.21	264	4	From Ceylon: workers, immigrants, refugees, settlers. Theravada Buddhists 96%. D=RCC,CCT,JWs. M=CSSR,MEP,SDB,FSC.
11262	0	6	4.49	1	32.40	67.60	A	1.65	464	4	Both sides of Mekong river in northeast. Majority in Laos. Becoming bilingual in (and acculturated to) Lao. Close to Bru. Buddhists 70%, animists 28%. M=NTM.
11263	0	6	4.65	1	29.40	70.60	A	1.50	527	4	Sakorn Nakorn. Also in Laos. Bilingual in Northeastern Tai. Close to So. Not used by youth. Animists 98%. M=NTM.
11264	6	6	4.84	1	47.00	53.00	A	1.71	317	4	In 14 southern Provinces. Theravada Buddhists 66%, Muslims 33%. D=CCT,RCC,TFGC,EGCT,SDA,CB. M=OMF,SFM,PAOC,FFFM,CMA,CSSR,MEP,FMB.
11265	1	6	4.39	0	35.70	64.30	A	0.91	452	3	On Burma border, and around Bangkok. Most in Burma. Animists 79%, Buddhists 20%. D=BBC(Mon Baptist Churches Union). M=ABMU,FFFM.
11266	1	8	7.42	6	75.50	24.50	B	28.93	306	5	Traders from South India. Hindus 82%, Muslims 5%. D=RCC. M=CSSR,MEP,SDB,FMB.
11267	2	6	4.23	6	53.00	47.00	B	3.86	250	4	Kanchanaburi, Phetburi, et alia. Close to Tai Dam. Animists 98%. D=Petchaburi Ch,CCT. M=NTM,DC.
11268	2	6	3.14	0	39.00	61.00	A	7.11	291	4	East of Pua District and Chiang Kam, Nan. Also in Laos, USA. Animists 95%. D=CC/CCCC,Presbyterian Ch. M=NTM,ACCM.
11269	3	10	3.94	8	99.78	0.22	C	409.96	87	10	Expatriates from USA, in military. commerce. D=TFGC,JWs,SDA.
11270	7	9	5.71	8	99.81	0.19	C	452.34	118	10	Expatriates in military, education, development. Nonreligious 6%. D=CJCLdS,JWs,SDA,CCT,CCCC,CCS,AC.
11271	0	6	0.00	0	24.00	76.00	A	0.87	126	3	Kanchanaburi, Uthai Thani, Suphanaburi. All speak some variety of Thai. Buddhists 99%.
11272	1	6	2.42	0	30.00	70.00	A	3.28	312	4	Phuket and Langta Islands, west coast, south Thailand. Strand dwellers. Aboriginal Malays with unique Malay language. Animists 97%. D=Christian Brethren.
11273	1	8	0.00	5	47.01	52.99	A	0.01	60	2	In Bangkok, Mookherji area. Indians, Pakistanis, Bangladeshis. Traders, settlers, migrant workers. Muslims 100%(Hanafi Sunnis). D=RCC.
11274	4	6	8.55	6	98.00	2.00	B	125.19	263	7	Refugee camps. Mahayana Buddhists 40%, nonreligious 14%, Cao Daists 10%. D=RCC,TBCA,EGCT,UPCT. M=FMB,CMA,UPCI,CSSR.
11275	0	0	0.00	1	12.01	87.99	A	0.00	0	1.06	Refugees from Cambodia, most after 1975. Theravada Buddhists 95%, Animists 5%.
11276	0	5	3.92	1	31.00	69.00	A	2.26	435	4	Ubon, Sakorn Nakorn; 2 villages. Majority in Laos; also USA. Buddhists 70%, animists 28%. M=OMF,SIL,NTM.
11277	3	6	4.98	0	51.00	49.00	B	26.06	321	5	Mountain Lawa. Many villages in Chiang Mai, Maehongson Provinces; also in China. Animists 68%, Buddhists 18%. D=CCT,RCC,GCT. M=ABFMS,NTM.
11278	4	7	5.87	1	64.00	36.00	B	35.04	298	5	Phlong, Shu. Northwest. Mainly in Burma. Close to Pao. Animists 84%. D=CCT,Independent Chs,Baptist Ch,SDA. M=OMF,NTM,ABFMS,AO,Karen Baptist Conv.
11279	4	6	6.36	4	68.00	32.00	B	37.23	284	5	70,000 now in USA; others in Laos, Viet Nam, France, China. Includes Striped Mao. Animists 85%. D=RCC,SDA,Chinese Presbyterian Ch,Meo Ch. M=OMF.
11280	2	6	3.45	0	34.80	65.20	A	1.01	327	4	Chiang Mai, Chiang Rai, Phayao, Lampang. Also in China, Viet Nam, Laos, Taiwan, USA, France, Canada. Polytheists/animists 97%, many Baha'is. D=CCT.
11281	0	6	4.39	1	67.00	33.00	B	48.91	225	6	Most in Myanmar (Burma), China, Laos, USA. Thai refugee camps. Animists 80%. M=ABFMS,AO,CEM,FMB.
11282	0	6	2.93	0	27.00	73.00	A	0.98	399	3	Sisaket. Closely related to Kuy. Animists 80%, Buddhists 19%.
11283	0	6	2.84	1	42.00	58.00	A	4.59	224	4	Sakorn Nakorn. Also in Laos. Bilingual in Kaleung (Northeastern Tai). Animists 50%, Buddhists 47%. M=NTM.
11284	0	6	1.10	0	24.20	75.80	A	1.06	238	4	Laos border area: in 8 Provinces. No literates. Tropical forest. Nomads, agriculturalists. Animists 98%. M=NTM.
11285	0	6	7.26		35.00	65.00	A	11.49	568	5	Koreans(M=PCK-T), Telugu, Kanarese, Hindi, Malayalis, Javanese, Iban, Sindhi, Samtao, refugees. Muslims 38%, Buddhists 20%, Hindus 10%, nonreligious 10%.
Timor											
11286	1	6	4.38	0	84.00	16.00	C	183.96	175	7	Atauro Island, north of Dili. Animists 40%. D=RCC.
11287	1	6	5.04	0	99.90	0.10	C	390.91	139	9	Northeast Timor. Major language. Animists 10%. D=RCC. M=IMF,SJ,SDB,WEC.
11288	3	6	2.92	0	99.99	0.01	C	519.38	75	10	Central Timor. Main lingua franca. Many also in western Timor (in original Indonesia). Animists 0.5%. D=RCC(D-Dili),GMIT,AoG. M=SJ,SDB,IBS-1.
11289	2	10	3.17	8	99.85	0.15	C	477.78	71	10	Mixed-race persons, Portuguese/Austronesian. D=RCC,GMIT. M=SJ,SDB.
11290	1	6	2.47	0	99.95	0.05	C	426.50	74	10	North coast east of Dili. Animists 5%. D=RCC.
11291	1	6	4.29	0	80.00	20.00	B	160.60	181	7	Northeast of Idate language. Related to Waimaa, Kairui. Animists 40%. D=RCC.
11292	1	10	4.90	7	94.00	6.00	B	92.63	162	6	Buddhists/Chinese folk-religionists 70%, nonreligious 3%. D=RCC(D-Dili). M=SJ,SDB.
11293	1	6	6.07	0	87.00	13.00	C	190.53	218	7	Central Timor mountains. Closest to Lakalei, Galoli. Animists 40%. D=RCC.
11294	0	10	4.82	7	67.00	33.00	B	12.22	226	5	Military, administrators, settlers. Muslims 90%(Shafi Sunnis). M=SJ,SDB,GMIT.
11295	2	9	5.98	5	89.00	11.00	B	81.21	210	6	Immigrant settlers, farmers from Java. Folk-religionists 38%, Muslims 29%, Hindus 8%. D=RCC,GKJ.
11296	1	6	3.85	0	99.90	0.10	C	407.34	107	10	Two mountainous areas east of Laclubar. Related to Waimaa, Habu. Animists 5%. D=RCC. M=SJ,SDB.
11297	1	6	2.58	0	99.95	0.05	C	429.97	76	10	North central Timor. Closely related to Tetum, Mambai, Tukudede, Timorese. Animists 5%. D=RCC. M=SJ,SDB.
11298	1	6	4.68	0	99.80	0.20	C	309.52	143	9	Central Timor north of Same. Closely related to Idate, Tetum, Galoli. Animists 20%. D=RCC.
11299	1	6	6.98	0	99.00	1.00	C	252.94	221	8	Eastern end of Timor Island, west of Fataluku. Animists 30%. D=RCC(D-Dili). M=SJ,SDB,IMF,WEC.
11300	1	6	2.52	0	43.00	57.00	A	31.39	224	5	Northeast tip of Timor Island. Assimilated to Fataluku; nearly extinct. Animists 80%. D=RCC.
11301	1	6	2.80	0	99.98	0.02	C	465.01	77	10	Mountains of central Timor, around Ermera. Second lingua franca on Timor. Animists 95%. D=RCC. M=SDB,IMF,SJ,WEC.
11302	1	7	4.54	0	99.70	0.30	C	255.50	152	8	East Timor Island, west of Tiomar. Animists 20%. D=RCC. M=SJ,SDB.
11303	1	10	2.84	8	99.93	0.07	C	563.48	64	10	Settlers, some expatriates from Portugal. D=RCC(D-Dili). M=SDB,SJ.
11304	3	9	3.05	0	99.98	0.02	C	550.85	69	10	Originating in West Timor Island. 8 dialects. Animists 1%, very few Muslims. D=RCC(D-Dili),GMIT,AoG. M=SJ,SDB.
11305	1	6	2.70	0	99.95	0.05	C	454.24	74	10	North coast of Timor, west of Dili. Animists 5%. D=RCC. M=SJ,SDB.
11306	1	6	5.84	0	99.80	0.20	C	329.96	166	9	Southwest of Makassai language area. Related to Habu and Kairui. Animists 20%. D=RCC.
11307	0	6	8.44		99.83	0.17	C	315.06	222	9	Bunak, other Indonesian peoples and islanders. Muslims 10%, nonreligious 5%, animists 1%.
Togo											
11308	1	6	5.80	0	53.00	47.00	B	40.62	366	6	West central. Majority in Ghana. Animists 79%. D=ABT. M=FMB.
11309	2	6	8.70	4	70.00	30.00	B	76.65	410	6	Southeast. Mainly in Benin. Animists 50%, Muslims 20% (Maliki Sunnis). D=RCC,AoG. M=SMA,OFM,FSCJ,OM,FSC,FMB.
11310	3	8	7.50	4	95.00	5.00	B	104.02	250	7	Migrants from Ghana. Animists 23%, Muslims 44%. D=RCC,AC/CPWA,AICs.
11311	2	6	4.48	0	62.00	38.00	B	56.57	255	6	Wawa Prefecture; also in Ghana. Bilingual in Ewe. Animists 67%, some Muslims. D=90%RCC;AoG,EET.
11312	1	8	5.52	0	87.00	13.00	B	158.77	214	7	Main centers: Afem and Boussou(Giseme dialect), Balenka(Ananjubi dialect). Close ot Anii. Muslims 35%, animists 10%. D=RCC.
11313	4	7	6.30	5	99.49	0.51	B	187.79	201	7	Around Atakpame. Also in Benin. Animists 20%, Muslims 20%(Maliki Sunnis). D=RCC,ABT,AoG,AICs. M=NBC,SIL,FMB,SMA.
11314	2	6	6.71	0	99.80	0.20	C	335.80	190	9	Kloto Prefecture. Also in Ghana. Closely related to Akpe. Bilingual in Ewe. Animists 10%. D=EET,ARS. M=SIL.
11315	1	6	5.78	0	62.00	38.00	B	67.89	307	6	Central, west and south of Blitta. Bilingual in Ewe. Animists 70%. D=RCC.
11316	0	6	4.45	1	27.00	73.00	A	0.98	591	3	Centering on Bagou, Koussountou. Muslims 80%, animists 19%.
11317	4	6	4.82	4	58.00	42.00	B	16.93	292	5	Mainly in Benin; also Nigeria. Animists 51%, Muslims 41%(Maliki Sunnis). D=ECWA,AoG,MCT,RCC. M=MMS,SIM,EMS,FMB.
11318	2	6	4.06	0	96.00	4.00	C	210.24	152	8	Around Bassila. Great majority live in Benin. Closely related to Akpe. Muslims 20%, animists 10%. D=AICs,RCC.
11319	2	6	7.78	0	53.00	47.00	B	29.01	473	5	West central; many in Ghana. Animists 75%, Muslims 10%. D=RCC(D-Sokode),AoG. M=SMA,OFM,FSC,SIL,FMB.
11320	0	8	3.51	4	42.50	57.50	A	0.77	329	3	Nomads across West Africa. Muslims 99%(Maliki Sunnis), a few animists. M=SIM.
11321	1	6	2.60	0	35.00	65.00	A	7.66	311	4	Solla. Northeast of Kpagouda; also in Benin. Most are bilingual in Kabiye. Animists 93%. D=RCC. M=FMB.
11322	6	6	8.85	0	61.00	39.00	B	44.53	459	6	Also in Burkina Faso. Animists 80%. D=AoG,RCC(D-Dapango),Lutheran Ch,Apostolic Ch,Baptist Ch,New Apostolic Ch. M=SIL,OFM,SMA,LCMS,MOJ,FMB,ABWE.
11323	3	10	3.05	8	99.78	0.22	C	435.59	75	10	Expatriates from Britain, in development. Nonreligious 9%. D=Anglican Ch/CPWA,SDA,JWs.
11324	3	7	6.22	0	99.90	0.10	C	446.76	151	10	Mainly in Ghana. Animists 5%. D=RCC,EPC,Buem-Krachi Presbyterian Ch.
11325	1	6	4.13	3	52.00	48.00	B	28.47	318	5	Northwest corner. Vast majority in Burkina Faso. Also in Ghana, Ivory Coast. Many bilinguals in More (Mossi). Animists 35%, Muslims 50%. D=AoG.
11326	3	6	6.48	0	50.00	50.00	B	18.25	432	5	Northwest around Nzara; also in Ghana, Benin. Some read French or Arabic. Muslims 68%(Maliki Sunnis), animists 22%. D=EET,RCC,AoG. M=SMA,OFM,SIL.
11327	1	6	7.00	0	54.00	46.00	B	39.42	425	5	Central, near the Kotokoli. Men are bilingual in Tem. Muslims 50%, animists 30%; much syncretism. D=RCC.
11328	4	6	3.38	4	42.00	58.00	A	6.13	310	4	Vast majority in Ghana. Literates 2%. Muslims 60%, animists 36%. D=AoG,ECWA,SDA,RCC.
11329	2	6	5.06	2	45.00	55.00	A	16.42	392	5	Primarily in Benin. Animists 80%, Muslims 10%. D=EET,UEEB. M=SIM.
11330	2	10	5.12	8	99.80	0.20	C	432.16	115	10	Remnants from years of German colonization up to 1914. D=RCC,EPC.
11331	13	7	6.64	4	99.77	0.23	C	407.89	149	10	Animists 13%(with temples to Mawu). D=RCC,EET,ARS,ABT,AoG,ECC,C&S,SDA,EATB,DHCT,EPA,COTLA,many other AICs. M=NBC,ABWE,FMB,PEMS,UCC.
11332	1	7	8.08	4	99.51	0.49	B	197.31	255	7	Small minorities in south. Mainly in Benin. Animists 39%(fetishism still strong; fetish temples, priests). D=RCC.
11333	3	10	4.99	8	99.84	0.16	C	493.62	102	10	Expatriates from France, in development. D=RCC(4 Dioceses),EET,JWs.
11334	1	8	4.98	4	99.66	0.34	C	304.82	132	9	Akra Ga. Mainly in Ghana. Animists 23%, Muslims 1.5%(Sunnis,Ahmadis). Nominal Christians 10%. D=AICs.
11335	2	6	5.70	0	45.00	55.00	A	9.85	430	4	Around Mogou, Gando, Namoni. Most also speak Anufo, some French. Animists 94%. D=RCC,AoG. M=SIL,SMA,OFM,LCMS.
11336	2	10	-0.84	8	99.86	0.14	C	502.24	5	10	Expatriates from Germany, in development. Lengthy German colonial history in Togo. D=EET,RCC.
11337	2	6	8.63	4	73.00	27.00	B	66.61	375	6	Primarily in Burkina Faso; also Benin. Animists 22%, Muslims 53%. D=RCC(D-Dapango),AoG. M=OFM,SMA,LCMS.
11338	0	8	2.60	5	55.10	44.90	B	0.20	189	3	Traders. Hausa widely spoken in Togo. Muslims 100%(Maliki Sunnis). M=UBS.
11339	2	7	5.75	1	87.00	13.00	B	158.77	221	7	Southeast Togo, north of Tabligbo. Close to Ewe, Aja. Animists 30%. D=EPC,AICs.
11340	4	6	10.04	4	76.00	24.00	B	63.80	411	6	Also in Benin, Ghana. Animists 65%, Muslims 10%. D=EET,RCC(D-Dapango,D-Sokode),AoG,Pentecostals. M=PEMS,SIL,SIM,OFM,SMA,FSC,VEA(Ghana),MOJ.
11341	0	6	5.69	4	57.00	43.00	B	20.80	340	5	East central. Kambole town plus villages. Close of Ife. Muslims 80%, animists 10%.
11342	4	6	7.10	0	66.00	34.00	B	36.13	352	5	Primarily in northeast Ghana. Animists 40%, Muslims 45%. D=AoG,RCC,EET,AICs. M=SMA,OFM,FSC,WEC.
11343	2	5	7.79	0	39.00	61.00	A	9.96	644	4	Around Sokode. Also in Benin, Ghana. Muslims 88%(Maliki Sunnis), animists 5%. D=RCC,AoG. M=SMA,FMB.
11344	3	6	4.25	0	50.00	50.00	B	29.20	311	5	In south, around Kpetsi, Langanbou. Animists 84%. D=RCC,EET,ARS.
11345	5	6	6.77	0	99.73	0.27	C	317.07	185	9	West of Atakpame in south. Also some in Ghana. Bilingual in Ewe. Animists 7%. D=EET,AoG,RCC(D-Atakpame),JWs, some AICs. M=SMA,OFM,FMB.
11346	3	6	4.40	1	43.00	57.00	A	12.55	368	5	Northwest. Mainly in Ghana. Literates 2%. Animists 84%, Muslims 7.5 %. D=AoG,PCG,RCC.
11347	2	6	8.15	1	59.00	41.00	B	36.61	442	5	Region of Kande; also in Benin. Literates 20%. Animists 49%, Muslims 34%. D=AoG,RCC. M=SIL,SMA,OFM,LCMS,MOJ,FMB.

Continued overleaf

Table 8-2 continued

PEOPLE		POPULATION				IDENTITY CODE		LANGUAGE		CHURCH		MINISTRY						SCRIPTURE	
Ref	*Ethnic name*	*P%*	*In 1995*	*In 2000*	*In 2025*	*Race*	*Language*	*Autoglossonym*	*S*	*AC*	*Members*	*Jayuh*	*d wa xcmc mi*					*Biblioglossonym*	*Pub ss*
1	*2*	*3*	*4*	*5*	*6*	*7*	*8*	*9*	*10*	*11*	*12*	*13-17*	*18*	*19*	*20*	*21*	*22*	*23*	*24-26 27*
11348	Lebanese Arab	0.10000	4,060	4,629	8,482	CMT30	12-AACF-f	syro-palestinian	1	30.00	1,389	1Asuh	9	7	8	4	1	Arabic: Lebanese*	Pnb b
11349	Losso (Loso, Naoudem)	3.99671	162,249	185,016	339,020	NAB56a	91-GGCA-a	nawd-m		30.00	55,505	0....	9	5	7	4	3	Nawdm	P.. .
11350	Mahi	0.69448	28,193	32,149	58,909	NAB59e	96-MAAG-b	maxi		40.00	12,860	1cs..	9	7	6	4	1		pnb n
11351	Mamprusi	0.20000	8,119	9,258	16,965	NAB56a	91-GGAC-d	mampru-li		3.50	324	1....	6	4	6	4	3	Mampruli	Pn. .
11352	Mina (Ge, Popo, Guin)	5.66156	229,835	262,086	480,240	NAB59l	96-MAAD	gen cluster	13	70.20	183,984	0....	10	10	11	5	3	Mina*	PN. .
11353	Mossi	0.55387	22,485	25,640	46,982	NAB56a	91-GGAA-a	moo-re		26.00	6,666	2A...	9	7	11	5	3	Moore	PNB b
11354	Ntrubo (Ntribu)	0.13953	5,664	6,459	11,836	NAB59b	91-GFCB-c	delo		89.00	5,749	1c...	10	7	11	2	1	Delo	pn. .
11355	Somba (Tamberma, Soma)	0.54351	22,064	25,160	46,103	NAB56a	91-GGEC-b	di-tammari		17.00	4,277	0....	8	5	6	4	1	Ditamari*	PN. .
11356	Togolese Creole	0.05000	2,030	2,315	4,241	NAN58	52-ABAH-f	cameroonian-creole	10	74.00	1,713	4.s.h	10	7	12	2	2	Pidgin: Cameroon*	Pn. b
11357	Waama (Yoabu)	0.25510	10,356	11,809	21,639	NAB56a	91-GGEB-a	waa-ma		6.00	709	0....	7	5	6	1	2	Waama	PN. .
11358	Wachi (Watyi)	10.03294	407,295	464,447	851,041	NAB59e	96-MAAC-a	waci		15.00	69,667	0....	8	7	7	5	3		... .
11359	Yoruba (Anago, Nago)	1.50000	60,894	69,438	127,237	NAB59n	98-AAAA-a	standard yoruba	4	25.00	17,360	3asu.	9	7	14	5	3	Yoruba	PNB b
11360	other minor peoples	0.20000	8,119	9,258	16,965	...				20.00	1,852		9	5	6	4	0		
	Tokelau Islands	**100.00000**	**1,500**	**1,500**	**1,500**					**91.2**	**1,368**								
11361	Samoan	1.00000	15	15	15	MPY55e	39-CAOA	samoa cluster		85.00	13	2a.u.	10	10	15	5	1	Samoan	PNB b
11362	Tokelauan	97.00000	1,455	1,455	1,455	MPY55z	39-CAKC	tokelau cluster		91.50	1,331	0.s..	10	10	13	5	2		... b
11363	other minor peoples	2.00000	30	30	30	...				80.00	24		10	7	8	5	0		
	Tonga	**100.00000**	**97,162**	**98,546**	**105,126**					**91.01**	**89,688**								
11364	Anglo-Australian	0.30000	291	296	315	CEW19c	52-ABAC-x	general australian		67.00	198	1Bsuh	10	9	13	5	1		pnb b
11365	British	0.20000	194	197	210	CEW19i	52-ABAC-b	standard-english		79.00	156	3Bsuh	10	9	13	5	3		PNB b
11366	Euronesian (Eurasian)	0.70000	680	690	736	MPY53	52-ABAC-bv	standard oceanian-english		97.00	669	1Bsuh	10	8	14	5	3		pnb b
11367	Han Chinese	0.20000	194	197	210	MSY42a	79-AAAB-ba	kuo-yü		30.00	59	2Bsuh	9	8	12	5	2	Chinese: Kuoyu*	PNB b
11368	Maori	0.05000	49	49	53	MPY55b	39-CAQA-a	standard maori		67.00	33	0a.u.	10	8	13	5	2	Maori: New Zealand	PNB b
11369	Niuafoou	0.69000	670	680	725	MPY55g	39-CAMB-a	niuafo'ou		97.00	660	0....	10	9	12	5	1		... .
11370	Niuatoputapu	1.65000	1,603	1,626	1,735	MPY55g	39-CAPB	tonga cluster		96.00	1,561	4a...	10	9	12	5	2	Tongan	PNB b
11371	Niuean	0.03000	29	30	32	MPY55z	39-CAPA-a	niue		89.00	26	0.s..	10	8	11	4	1	Niuean	PNB b
11372	Tongan	95.18000	92,479	93,796	100,059	MPY55g	39-CAPB	tonga cluster		91.30	85,636	4a...	10	10	14	5	3	Tongan	PNB b
11373	other minor peoples	1.00000	972	985	1,051	...				70.00	690		10	7	8	4	0		
	Trinidad & Tobago	**100.00000**	**1,262,474**	**1,294,958**	**1,493,418**					**61.46**	**795,864**								
11374	British	0.50000	6,312	6,475	7,467	CEW19i	52-ABAC-b	standard-english	70	78.00	5,050	3Bsuh	10	9	13	5	3		PNB b
11375	Caribbean Hindi (Awadhi)	3.73800	47,191	48,406	55,824	CNN25g	59-AAFP-ea	trinidad	46	4.90	2,372	1c.u.	6	5	10	5	3		pn. b
11376	East Indian	34.94800	441,209	452,562	521,920	CNN25g	52-ABAD-ak	london-asian-english		24.00	108,615	0B.uh	9	6	7	5	1		... b
11377	French	0.30000	3,787	3,885	4,480	CEW21b	51-AABI-d	general français	5	84.00	3,263	1B.uh	10	9	14	5	3	French	PNB b
11378	French West Indian	0.70000	8,837	9,065	10,454	NFB69a	51-AACC-e	martiniquais	10	90.00	8,158	1As..	10	9	10	5	2		pnb b
11379	German	0.20000	2,525	2,590	2,987	CEW19m	52-ABCE-a	standard hoch-deutsch		88.00	2,279	2B.uh	10	9	13	5	3	German*	PNB b
11380	Han Chinese (Cantonese)	1.50000	18,937	19,424	22,401	MSY42a	79-AAAM-a	central yue	4	70.00	13,597	3A.uh	10	7	9	4	1	Chinese, Yue	PNB b
11381	Han Chinese (Hakka)	1.61400	20,376	20,901	24,104	MSY42a	79-AAAG-a	literary hakka	2	65.00	13,585	1A...	10	7	9	4	1	Chinese: Hakka, Wukingfu*	PNB b
11382	Jewish	0.04700	593	609	702	CMT35	52-ABAD-al	trinidadian-asian-english		0.60	4	0B.uh	5	4	2	1	0		... b
11383	Portuguese	0.20000	2,525	2,590	2,987	CEW21g	51-AABA-e	general português		93.00	2,409	2Bsuh	10	9	15	5	3	Portuguese	PNB b
11384	Spaniard	0.30000	3,787	3,885	4,480	CEW21k	51-AABB-c	general español	5	96.00	3,729	2B.uh	10	9	15	5	2	Spanish	PNB b
11385	Syro-Lebanese Arab	0.20000	2,525	2,590	2,987	CMT30	12-AACF-f	syro-palestinian		61.00	1,580	1Asuh	10	7	8	5	3	Arabic: Lebanese*	Pnb b
11386	Trinidad Black	39.20000	494,890	507,624	585,420	NFB68a	52-ABAF-y	trinidadian-ex-creole	85	88.80	450,770	1c..h	10	10	14	5	2	Lesser Antill Creole French	Pn. .
11387	Trinidad Mulatto	16.30000	205,783	211,078	243,427	NFB68b	52-ABAF-y	trinidadian-ex-creole		84.40	178,150	1c..h	10	10	11	5	3	Lesser Antill Creole French	Pn. .
11388	USA White	0.20000	2,525	2,590	2,987	CEW19s	52-ABAC-s	general american		77.00	1,994	1Bsuh	10	9	13	5	3	English*	PNB b
11389	other minor peoples	0.05300	669	686	792	...				45.00	309		9	6	8	5	0		
	Tunisia	**100.00000**	**8,943,050**	**9,585,611**	**12,843,081**					**0.53**	**50,502**								
11390	Algerian Arab	2.40000	214,633	230,055	308,234	CMT30	12-AACB-b	east maghrebi		0.15	345	2A.uh	5	4	7	5	2	Arabic: Algerian*	PNB b
11391	Arad Bedouin	0.49000	43,821	46,969	62,931	CMT30	12-AACD	badawi-sahara cluster		0.01	5	0a...	3	2	0	0	0		PN. b
11392	British	0.00130	116	125	167	CEW19i	52-ABAC-b	standard-english	7	74.00	92	3Bsuh	10	9	13	5	1		PNB b
11393	Byelorussian	0.00100	89	96	128	CEW22c	53-AAAE-c	bielorusskiy		77.00	74	3A.uh	10	8	11	4	1	Byelorussian*	PNB b
11394	Duwinna Berber	0.04300	3,846	4,122	5,523	CMT32z	10-AAAC-rd	chnini		0.00	0	1c...	0	2	3	0	0		pn. .
11395	French	0.16000	14,309	15,337	20,549	CEW21b	51-AABI-d	general français	38	82.00	12,576	1B.uh	10	9	14	5	2	French	PNB b
11396	Gafsa Bedouin	0.33000	29,512	31,633	42,382	CMT30	12-AACD	badawi-sahara cluster		0.02	6	0a...	3	2	0	0	0		PN. b
11397	Greek	0.00300	268	288	385	CEW20	56-AAAA-c	dhimotiki		95.00	273	2B.uh	10	9	11	5	1	Greek: Modern	PNB b
11398	Hamama Bedouin	3.50000	313,007	335,496	449,508	CMT30	12-AACD	badawi-sahara cluster		0.01	34	0a...	3	2	6	0	0		PN. b
11399	Italian	0.05000	4,472	4,793	6,422	CEW21e	51-AABQ-c	standard italiano	4	84.00	4,026	2B.uh	10	9	15	5	2	Italian	PNB b
11400	Jerba (Gerba)	1.17000	104,634	112,152	150,264	CMT32z	10-AAAC-s	jerba		0.01	11	1c...	3	3	2	1	0		pn. b
11401	Jerid Bedouin (Djerid)	0.88000	78,699	84,353	113,019	CMT30	12-AACD	badawi-sahara cluster		0.02	17	0a...	3	2	0	0	0		PN. b
11402	Levantine Arab	2.00000	178,861	191,712	256,862	CMT30	12-AACF-f	syro-palestinian		9.15	17,542	1Asuh	7	7	8	5	2	Arabic: Lebanese*	Pnb b
11403	Maghreb Jewish	0.04000	3,577	3,834	5,137	CMT35	12-AACH-b	judeo-tunisian		0.11	4	0A...	5	3	2	1	1	Arabic: Judaeo-tunisian*	P.. b
11404	Maltese	0.03000	2,683	2,876	3,853	CMT36	12-AACC-a	maltiya		90.00	2,588	0a.u.	10	9	16	4	2	Maltese	PNB b
11405	Matmata	0.09000	8,049	8,627	11,559	CMT32z	10-AAAC-s	jerba		0.00	0	1c...	0	2	0	0	0		pn. b
11406	Sahel Bedouin	21.40000	1,913,813	2,051,321	2,748,419	CMT30	12-AACD-a	hassaaniyya		0.01	205	0a...	3	3	3	0	0		pn. b
11407	Sened	0.05700	5,098	5,464	7,321	CMT32z	10-AAAC-s	jerba		0.00	0	1c...	0	2	0	0	0		pn. b
11408	Tamezret	0.03370	3,014	3,230	4,328	CMT32z	10-AAAC-s	jerba		0.00	0	1c...	0	2	0	0	0		pn. b
11409	Taoujjout	0.01000	894	959	1,284	CMT32z	10-AAAC-s	jerba		0.00	0	1c...	0	2	0	0	0		pn. b
11410	Tmagourt	0.05000	4,472	4,793	6,422	CMT32z	10-AAAC-s	jerba		0.00	0	1c...	0	2	0	0	0		pn. b
11411	Tunisian Arab	67.15200	6,005,437	6,436,929	8,624,386	CMT30	12-AACB-b	east maghrebi	100	0.18	11,586	2A.uh	5	4	5	2	3	Arabic: Algerian*	PNB b
11412	USA White	0.00200	179	192	257	CEW19s	52-ABAC-s	general american		78.00	150	1Bsuh	10	9	13	5	3	English*	PNB b
11413	Zawa (Zaoua)	0.00600	537	575	771	CMT32z	10-AAAC-ra	zrawa		0.00	0	1c...	0	2	0	0	0		pn. b
11414	other minor peoples	0.10100	9,032	9,681	12,972	...				10.00	968		8	5	2	4	0		
	Turkey	**100.00000**	**61,275,605**	**66,590,940**	**87,869,200**					**0.56**	**373,157**								
11415	Abazinian	0.01614	9,890	10,748	14,182	CEW17a	42-AABA-b	abazin		0.10	11	0....	5	3	5	0	0	Abaza	p.. b
11416	Abkhazian (Abxazo, Ubyx)	0.05872	35,981	39,102	51,597	CEW17a	44-AABA-a	osmanli		0.01	4	1A.u.	3	3	2	0	0	Turkish	PNB b
11417	Alevica Kurdish (Kirmandz	0.25000	153,189	166,477	219,673	CNT24c	58-AAAA-b	kurmanjiki		0.03	50	1A...	3	3	2	0	0	Kirmanjki	pn. .
11418	Armenian (Ermeni)	0.15752	96,521	104,894	138,412	CEW14	57-AAAA-b	ashkharik		71.00	74,475	4A.u.	10	9	12	5	3	Armenian: Modern, Eastern	PNB b
11419	Assyrian (Eastern Syriac)	0.05476	33,555	36,465	48,117	CMT31	12-AAAA-f	aisor		87.00	31,725	4cs..	10	9	11	5	2	Assyrian Neo-aramaic	PNB b
11420	Azerbaijani	1.03005	631,169	685,920	905,097	MSY41a	44-AABA-fb	south azeri		0.00	0	1a.u.	0	3	3	0	1	Azerbaijani, South	pnb b
11421	Balkan Gagauz Turk	0.51806	317,444	344,981	455,215	MSY41d	44-AABA-b	gagauzi		0.00	0	1c.u.	0	3	2	0	0	Gagauz	Pnb b
11422	Balkan Rom Gypsy	0.09002	55,160	59,945	79,100	CNN25f	59-ACBA-bc	arlija		5.00	2,997	1A...	7	5	8	3	0	Romani: Arlija	Pn. .
11423	Bosniac (Musselmani)	0.13727	84,113	91,409	120,618	CEW22a	53-AAAG-a	standard srpski		0.03	27	1Asuh	3	3	1	0	1	Serbian*	PNB b
11424	British	0.00500	3,064	3,330	4,393	CEW19i	52-ABAC-b	standard-english	9	74.00	2,464	3Bsuh	10	9	13	5	1		PNB b
11425	Bulgar	0.10000	61,276	66,591	87,869	CEW22b	53-AAAH	bulgarski cluster		65.00	43,284	2A.uh	10	8	8	5	2		PNB b
11426	Chechen (Shishan)	0.01000	6,128	6,659	8,787	CEW17d	42-BAAA-b	chechen		0.00	0	0....	0	3	2	0	0	Chechen	P.. b
11427	Circassian	0.41732	255,715	277,897	366,696	CEW17a	42-AAAA-b	cherkes		0.01	28	1a...	3	3	2	1	0		pn. b
11428	Crimean Tatar	7.00000	4,289,292	4,661,366	6,150,844	MSY41h	44-AABA-a	osmanli		0.01	466	1A.u.	3	3	2	1	0	Turkish	PNB b
11429	Crimean Tatar	0.20000	122,551	133,182	175,738	MSY41h	44-AABA-c	crimea-tatar		0.00	0	1c.u.	0	2	2	0	0	Crimean Tatar*	PNb b
11430	Dimili Kurd (Southern Zaza)	1.71954	1,053,659	1,145,058	1,510,946	CNT24c	58-AAAB-a	dimli		0.00	0	0....	0	2	3	0	2	Dimli	... .
11431	Dutch	0.00400	2,451	2,664	3,515	CEW19h	52-ABCA-a	algemeen-nederlands		72.00	1,918	2Bsuh	10	9	15	5	2	Dutch	PNB b
11432	East Circassian (Kabardian)	0.40000	245,102	266,364	351,477	CEW17a	42-AAAA-c	qaberdey		1.00	2,664	1c...	6	4	4	1	0	Kabardian	PN. .
11433	French	0.00750	4,596	4,994	6,590	CEW21b	51-AABI-d	general français		84.00	4,195	1B.uh	10	9	14	5	3	French	PNB b
11434	German	0.01000	6,128	6,659	8,787	CEW19m	52-ABCE-a	standard hoch-deutsch	2	80.00	5,327	2B.uh	10	9	13	5	2	German*	PNB b
11435	Greek	0.01424	8,726	9,483	12,513	CEW20	56-AAAA-c	dhimotiki		70.00	6,638	2B.uh	10	9	10	5	3	Greek: Modern	PNB b
11436	Han Chinese	0.06812	41,741	45,362	59,856	MSY42a	79-AAAB-ba	kuo-yü		2.10	953	2Bsuh	6	4	8	1	0	Chinese: Kuoyu*	PNB b
11437	Herki Kurd	0.05000	30,638	33,295	43,935	CNT24c	58-AAAA-ae	herki		0.20	67	1c...	5	2	5	0	1		pn. b
11438	Hungarian	0.01000	6,128	6,659	8,787	MSW51g	41-BAAA-a	general magyar		77.00	5,128	2A.u.	10	9	8	5	3	Hungarian	PNB b
11439	Italian	0.01100	6,740	7,325	9,666	CEW21e	51-AABQ-c	standard italiano		83.00	6,080	2B.uh	10	9	15	5	3	Italian	PNB b
11440	Jewish	0.01300	7,966	8,657	11,423	CMT35	44-AABA-a	osmanli		0.10	9	1A.u.	5	3	3	0	0	Turkish	PNB b
11441	Kara-Kalpak	0.10000	61,276	66,591	87,869	MSY41z	44-AABC-b	karakalpak		0.00	0	1c.u.	0	2	0	0	0	Karakalpak	Pn. b
11442	Kazakh (Qazaqi)	0.00200	1,226	1,332	1,757	MSY41e	44-AABC-c	kazakh		0.04	1	4A.u.	3	3	1	1	3	Kazakh	PN. b
11443	Kirghiz	0.00243	1,489	1,618	2,135	MSY41g	44-AABC-d	kirghiz		0.00	0	2r.u.	0	3	3	1	2	Kirghiz	PN. b
11444	Kumyk (Khaidak)	0.00200	1,226	1,332	1,757	MSY41y	44-AABB-d	kumyk		0.00	0	1c.u.	0	3	2	0	0	Kumuk*	Pn. b
11445	Levantine Arab	1.82276	1,116,907	1,213,793	1,601,645	CMT30	12-AACF-f	syro-palestinian		1.50	18,207	1Asuh	6	5	8	5	3	Arabic: Lebanese*	Pnb b
11446	Middle East Gypsy	0.04269	26,159	28,428	37,511	CNN25f	59-ACAA-a	domari		1.00	284	0....	6	4	5	0	0		... b
11447	Mingrelian (Laz, Zan)	0.20703	126,859	137,863	181,916	CEW17c	42-CAAB	laz cluster		2.00	2,757	0....	6	4	6	1	0		... b
11448	Northern Kurd (Kermanji)	8.89879	5,452,787	5,925,788	7,819,296	CNT24c	58-AAAA-a	kurmanji	22	0.01	593	3c...	3	4	4	2	3	Kurdish: Kurmanji*	PN. b
11449	Ossetian (Western Ossete)	0.05000	30,638	33,295	43,935	CNT24e	58-ABBA	oseti cluster		10.00	3,330	2....	8	5	6	4	1	Ossete*	PN. b
11450	Pathan	0.08000	49,020	53,273	70,295	CNT24a	58-ABDA-a	pashto		0.01	5	1As..	3	3	5	0	0		pnb b
11451	Persian	0.84000	514,715	559,364	738,101	CNT24f	58-AACC-c	standard farsi		0.03	168	1Asu.	3	3	1	0	1		PNB b
11452	Pomak Bulgar	0.45304	277,603	301,684	398,083	CEW22b	53-AAAH-b	bulgarski		6.00	18,101	2A.uh	7	5	6	0	0	Bulgarian	PNB b
11453	Romanian	0.03000	18,383	19,977	26,361	CEW21i	51-AADC-a	limba românească		75.00	14,983	3A.u.	10	8	8	5	1	Romanian	PNB b
11454	Russian	0.03000	18,383	19,977	26,361	CEW22j	53-AAAE-d	russkiy		51.00	10,188	4B.uh	10	8	8	5	1	Russian	PNB b
11455	Serb	0.05000	30,638	33,295	43,935	CEW22l	53-AAAG-a	standard srpski		66.00	21,975	1Asuh	10	8	8	5	1	Serbian*	PNB b
11456	Shikaki Kurd (Kurdish)	0.03000	18,383	19,977	26,361	CNT24c	58-AAAA-af	shikaki		0.00	0	1c...	0	2	0	0	1		pn. b
11457	Southern Uzbek	0.00423	2,592	2,817	3,717	MSY41l	44-AABD-b	south uzbek		0.10	3	1c.u.	5	3	4	1	1		pnb b
11458	Spanish Jew (Hakitia)	0.01800	11,030	11,986	15,816	CMT35	51-AAAB-dd	djudezmo-türkiye		0.00	0	0....	0	3	1	0	0		pnb b
11459	Syrian Aramaic (Turoyo)	0.04300	26,349	28,634	37,784	CMT31	12-AAAA-e	sur-oyo		83.00	23,766	4as..	10	9	10	5	3	Syriac	PNB b
11460	Tatar (Tartar)	0.03497	21,428	23,287	30,728	MSY41h	44-AABB-e	tatar		1.00	233	2c.u.	6	4	3	0	0	Tatar: Kazan	Pn. b
11461	Tosk Albanian	0.13727	84,113	91,409	120,618	CEW13	55-AAAB-j	tosk-anatolia		10.00	9,141	0c...	8	5	6	1	0		pnb b

Continued opposite

Table 8-2 continued

EVANGELIZATION								EVANGELISM			ADDITIONAL DESCRIPTIVE DATA
Ref 1	*D* 28	*aC* 29	*CG%* 30	*r* 31	*E* 32	*U* 33	*W* 34	*e* 35	*R* 36	*T* 37	*Locations, civil divisions, literacy, religions, church history, denominations, dioceses, church growth, missions, agencies, ministries, movements* 38
11348	1	10	5.06	8	91.00	9.00	B	99.64	173	6	Traders from Lebanon. Muslims 70%(Sunnis,Shias). D=RCC(Maronites).
11349	3	6	9.00	0	68.00	32.00	B	74.46	418	6	Doufelgou Prefecture. Animists 75%. D=RCC,EET,AoG. M=OFM,SMA,FSCJ,SIL,FMB.
11350	1	6	7.42	2	83.00	17.00	B	121.18	304	7	Majority live in Benin. Close to Fon. Animists 60%. D=EPMB.
11351	3	6	3.54	1	39.50	60.50	A	5.04	341	4	Vast majority in Ghana. Animists 80%, Muslims 15%(Sunnis,Ahmadis). D=AoG,MCG,SDA.
11352	7	8	6.76	2	99.70	0.30	C	310.55	182	9	On Coast, also into Benin. Animists 6%. D=EPMT,RCC(M-Loma),ECC,C&S,COTLA,AoG,other AICs. M=MMS,SMA,OFM,FMB,UMC.
11353	2	10	6.72	4	91.00	9.00	B	86.35	244	6	Labor migrants. Many monolinguals. Animists 27%, Muslims 45%(Maliki Sunnis). D=AoG,RCC. M=SMA,OFM,FSC,FMB.
11354	3	6	6.94	1	99.89	0.11	C	428.80	171	10	Primarily in Ghana. Animists 4%, Muslims 1%. D=ARS,EPC,RCC. M=SIL.
11355	1	6	6.25	0	51.00	49.00	B	31.64	409	5	East of Kante. No literacy. Muslims 60%(Maliki Sunnis), animists 23%. D=RCC. M=SIL.
11356	2	10	2.71	8	99.74	0.26	C	359.23	78	9	Variant of English/Pidgin/Wescos &c. Mixed-race persons. Animists 10%. D=RCC,AICs.
11357	2	6	4.35	2	39.00	61.00	A	8.54	402	4	Northeast Togo. Mainly in Benin. Animists 70%, Muslims 24%. D=AoG,RCC.
11358	7	7	6.16	4	57.00	43.00	B	31.20	382	5	Main centers Vogan, Tabligbo; also in Benin. Animists 65%, Muslims 20% (Maliki Sunnis). D=RCC,EET,COTLA,EPMT,AoG,ABT, AICs. M=NBC,FMB,SMA,OFM.
11359	6	7	7.74	5	96.00	4.00	B	87.60	261	6	Muslims 44%(Maliki Sunnis,many Ahmadis), animists 12%. Nominal Christians 18%. D=RCC,ECC,CAC,ABT,COTLA,many other AICs. M=NBC,FMB,SMA.
11360	0	9	5.36		48.00	52.00	A	35.04	306	5	Gun, Fante(MDCC), Wudu, other West African peoples, other Europeans. Muslims 40%, Animists 25%, Nonreligious 5%.
Tokelau Islands											
11361	1	10	0.62	5	99.85	0.15	C	474.68	20	10	Samoan migrants, expatriates. D=Congregational Christian Ch in Samoa; this is the major church on Tokelau.
11362	2	6	0.40	5	99.92	0.08	C	472.57	18	10	Some Portuguese ancestry. 68% in North Island, New Zealand; also Hawaii. Bilingual in Samoan, English. Baha'is 5%. D=CCCS,RCC. M=SM,LMS/CWM.
11363	0	10	3.23		99.80	0.20	C	327.04	79	9	New Zealanders, other Pacific Islanders, other Asians, Europeans.
Tonga											
11364	5	10	1.61	8	99.67	0.33	C	327.69	49	9	Expatriates from Australia, in business, development. Nonreligious 23%. D=FWCT,RCC,AC,SDA,JWs. M=SM.
11365	3	10	1.60	8	99.79	0.21	C	444.05	49	10	Expatriates from Britain, in development, education. D=Anglican Ch/CPNZ(D-Polynesia),FWCT,JWs.
11366	5	10	1.96	8	99.97	0.03	C	591.26	45	10	Mixed-race persons, European/Asian/Austronesian. D=RCC,FWCT,CJCLdS,AC,SDA.
11367	2	10	4.16	7	99.30	0.70	B	111.69	129	7	From China and its diaspora. Traders. Buddhists/Chinese folk-religionists 60%, nonreligious 10%. D=RCC,SDA.
11368	2	10	1.56	4	99.67	0.33	C	322.80	43	9	Migrants from New Zealand. Traditional religionists/animists 10%. Many nominal Christians. D=AC/CPNZ,CJCLdS.
11369	3	10	1.60	0	99.97	0.03	C	499.21	41	10	On Niuafo'ou and Eua Islands. D=FWCT,CJCLdS,RCC. M=SM.
11370	2	10	1.60	5	99.96	0.04	C	585.16	35	10	On Niuatoputapu Island. Related to Tongan language. D=FWCT,CJCLdS.
11371	1	10	1.48	5	99.89	0.11	C	480.77	37	10	Migrants from Niue Island. D=FWCT.
11372	7	6	1.50	5	99.91	0.09	C	544.18	34	10	Also in NZ, Fiji, American Samoa. Baha'is 7%. D=FWCT/MCT,CJCLdS(rapidly expanding),RCC(D-Tonga),Free Ch of Tonga,Ch of Tonga,SDA,JWs. M=SM,AoG.
11373	0	10	4.33		99.70	0.30	C	258.05	117	8	Indians (Hindus), other Pacific Islanders, other Asians, other Europeans. Hindus 10%.
Trinidad & Tobago											
11374	4	10	1.57	8	99.78	0.22	C	441.28	48	10	Expatriates from Britain, in development. Nonreligious 9%. D=Anglican Ch/CPWI(D-Trinidad & Tobago),MCCA,SDA,JWs.
11375	4	10	1.57	1	54.90	45.10	B	9.81	128	4	Indo-Pakistanis. 70% literates. Hindus 68%(Sanatanists), Muslims 22%(Sunnis,Ahmadis), Baha'is 5%. D=RCC,AC/CPWI,PAOWI,PCTG. M=Worldteam,OP,OSB.
11376	3	9	5.53	8	81.00	19.00	B	70.95	221	6	Indo-Pakistanis, assimilated. Hindus 58%, Muslims 17%(Sunnis),Baha'is. D=RCC,AC,PAOWI. M=FMB.
11377	1	10	1.57	8	99.84	0.16	C	490.56	44	10	Expatriates from France, in development. Nonreligious 13%. D=RCC(M-Port of Spain). M=OP,CSSp,OSB.
11378	3	10	1.57	8	99.90	0.10	C	522.31	48	10	Trinidad Creole French (Patois, Trinidadien). Black/French Creoles. D=RCC,SDA,JWs. M=CSSp,Worldteam(WIM).
11379	3	10	1.57	8	99.88	0.12	C	533.19	45	10	Expatriates from Germany, in business, development. Nonreligious 11%. D=RCC,PCTG,JWs.
11380	1	10	7.48	8	99.70	0.30	C	357.70	159	9	Long-term residents from China and its diaspora. Buddhists/Chinese folk-religionists 20%, nonreligious 10%. D=RCC. M=FMB.
11381	1	10	7.48	7	99.65	0.35	C	313.17	169	9	Mainland China Hakka origins. Buddhists/folk-religionists 25%, nonreligious 10%. D=RCC.
11382	0	10	1.40	8	39.60	60.40	A	0.86	145	3	Small community of practicing Jews in capital.
11383	1	10	1.57	8	99.93	0.07	C	583.85	41	10	Citizens, settlers from Portugal. Nonreligious 7%. D=RCC(M-Port of Spain). M=OP,CSSp,OSB.
11384	1	10	1.57	8	99.96	0.04	C	606.19	39	10	Long-time residents dating back to the Conquest. D=RCC(M-Port of Spain). M=OP,OSB.
11385	3	10	5.19	8	99.61	0.39	C	287.21	125	8	Refugees from Lebanon, Syria. Muslims 30%(Sunnis,Alawis,Druzes), Baha'is. D=RCC(Maronites),SOC,GOC.
11386	7	10	1.22	8	99.89	0.11	C	495.25	33	10	Afro-Caribbean spiritists 1%(Shango,Obeah,Rastas), Baha'is. D=RCC,AC/CPWI,PAOWI,PCTG,SDA,MCCA,JWs. M=FMB,&c.
11387	10	10	1.30	8	99.84	0.16	C	451.00	38	10	Most now use English. Low(Afro-Caribbean) spiritists 6%. D=RCC,AC/CPWI,PAOWI,EOC,AMEC,PCTG,JWs,MCCA,BUTT,10 NWICs.
11388	8	10	0.86	8	99.77	0.23	C	427.19	32	10	Expatriates from USA, in business, development. Nonreligious 6%. D=PCTG,PAOWI,JWs,SDA,MCCA,CCS,CGP,COG.
11389	0	10	1.57		77.00	23.00	B	126.47	56	7	Arawak Indians(remnants), Greeks, Urdu (official language of Trinidad's Muslims), Nigerians(COTLA), USA Blacks(BWCOLJCWW). Muslims 15%, Nonreligious.
Tunisia											
11390	2	5	3.60	8	58.15	41.85	B	0.31	203	3	Immigrant, expatriates, workers from Algeria. Muslims 99%(Maliki Sunnis). D=RCC,many radio believers. M=WF,FSC.
11391	0	3	1.62	7	25.01	74.99	A	0.00	254	1.08	Nomads, tent-dwellers, including Attia, Gumrage, and 4 other southern tribes. Muslims 100%(Sunnis).
11392	4	10	1.83	8	99.74	0.26	C	399.74	55	9	Expatriates from Britain, in business. Nonreligious 10%. D=ECJME(D-Egypt),MCNA,SDA,JWs. M=UMC.
11393	1	10	4.40	5	99.77	0.23	C	404.71	103	10	Refugees from USSR from 1917. Nonreligious 20%. D=Byelorussian Autocephalous Orthodox Ch.
11394	0	0	0.00	1	12.00	88.00	A	0.00	0	1.06	In the South in isolated villages near Jerba. Duwinna spoken only in the home. Muslims (Sunnis) 100%.
11395	4	10	-2.21	8	99.82	0.18	C	478.88	2	10	Expatriates from France, in business. Nonreligious 13%. D=RCC(PN-Tunis),SDA,ERF,JWs. M=WF,FSC.
11396	0	3	1.81	7	25.02	74.98	A	0.01	275	2	Nomadic tent-dwelling Bedouins in central Tunisia, including sedentary inhabitants of 3 oases: El Ksar, Gafsa, Lala. Muslims 100%(Sunnis).
11397	1	10	3.36	7	99.95	0.05	C	572.13	72	10	From Greece. In trade, commerce. D=Greek Orthodox Ch(D-Carthage).
11398	0	5	3.59	7	33.01	66.99	A	0.01	356	2	Nomads, tent-dwellers of the interior steppe region, including 8 tribes. Muslims 100%(Sunnis).
11399	1	10	0.97	7	99.84	0.16	C	490.56	34	10	Major fluctuations in numbers, since 1900. Expatriates from Italy. D=RCC. M=WF,FSC.
11400	0	5	2.43	1	24.01	75.99	A	0.00	357	1.11	Berbers on Djerba Island. Sedentary cultivators. Muslims 100%(Ibadis/Kharijites/Seceders).
11401	0	3	2.87	7	25.02	74.98	A	0.01	391	2	Nomads, including sedentary inhabitants of 6 southern oases, and Nefzawa tribe. Muslims 100%(Sunnis).
11402	2	6	7.76	8	69.15	30.85	B	23.09	335	5	Refugees from Lebanon. Muslims 88%(Sunnis,Alawis,Druzes), Baha'is. D=RCC(Maronites),GOC.
11403	0	7	1.40	7	36.11	63.89	A	0.14	159	3	Judeo-Tunisian Arabic. Rapid emigration from 57,840 in 1956 to 9,000 by 1980. Most remaining now speak French. Practicing Jews. M=CMJ.
11404	1	10	0.74	5	99.90	0.10	C	522.31	27	10	Migrant workers from Malta. D=RCC(PN-Tunis). M=WF,FSC.
11405	0	3	0.00	1	16.00	84.00	A	0.00	0	1.08	Berbers. Small remnant tribe in Tabaga Mountains in south. Muslims 100%(Sunnis).
11406	0	5	3.07	7	29.01	70.99	A	0.01	356	2	Nomads, agriculturalists, including 3 sedentary tribes and 50 towns and villages. Muslims 99%(Maliki Sunnis).
11407	0	3	0.00	1	16.00	84.00	A	0.00	0	1.08	Berbers around Sened town in mid-Tunisia mountains. Muslims 100%(Sunnis).
11408	0	2	0.00	1	15.00	85.00	A	0.00	0	1.08	Tamezret village, near Zeraoua, south of Gabes. Muslims 100%(Sunnis).
11409	0	2	0.00	1	15.00	85.00	A	0.00	0	1.08	Berbers in southern Tunisia, Taoujjout village, near Tamezret. Muslims 100%(Sunnis).
11410	0	3	0.00	1	16.00	84.00	A	0.00	0	1.08	Berbers. Tmagourt village near Sered. Muslims 100%(Sunnis).
11411	5	4	7.31	8	56.18	43.82	B	0.36	391	3	Western Colloquial Arabic. Muslims 99%(Maliki Sunnis, with 40,000 Ibadis). D=RCC(PN-Tunis),ECJME,MCNA,SDA,ERF. M=NAM,ICI,GMU,CSI,FI,FMB,OM,MEM.
11412	5	10	2.75	8	99.78	0.22	C	432.74	66	10	Expatriates from USA, in business. D=MCNA,SDA,JWs,RCC,ECJME.
11413	0	2	0.00	1	15.00	85.00	A	0.00	0	1.08	Berbers. Zeraoua village, near Tamezret. Muslims 100%(Sunnis).
11414	0	6	4.68		30.00	70.00	A	10.95	427	5	Egyptian Arabs, Turks, Moroccans, Palestinians, other Asians, other Europeans. Muslims 79%, nonreligious 10%.
Turkey											
11415	0	5	2.43	0	23.10	76.90	A	0.08	407	2	Also in Dagestan (Russia), a few in Germany. Bilingual in Turkish. Muslims 99%(Hanafi Sunnis).
11416	0	1	1.40	8	36.01	63.99	A	0.01	183	2	Villages in Bolu and Sakarya Prov. 96% bilingual in Turkish. Agriculturalists. Muslims 100%(Sunnis, who left Georgia in 1864, leaving Orthodox Abkhazians there).
11417	0	1	3.99	0	19.03	80.97	A	0.02	862	2	Centered around town of Tunceli. Also in Germany. 90% monolinguals (distant variety of Kurdish), but numerous bilinguals in Turkish. Muslims 99%(mostly Alawi).
11418	3	6	-2.90	6	99.71	0.29	C	370.58	2	9	Remnant after 1915 genocide. In Istanbul. 96% bilingual in Turkish. Nonreligious 20%, Muslims 5%. D=Armenian Apost Ch(P-Constantinople),RCC(AD-Istanbul).
11419	2	7	8.40	5	99.87	0.13	C	479.50	165	10	Mardin, Istanbul. Also Iraq, Iran, Israel, Cyprus, Syria, USA. Nonreligious 10%. D=Ancient Ch of the East(Nestorians: P-Tehran),RCC(Chaldeans: AD Diarbekir).
11420	0	8	0.00	1	30.00	70.00	A	0.00	0	1.11	In Kars Province. Mainly in Iran, Russia, Iraq; also in Syria, Afghanistan. Turkish used as literary language. Muslims 99%(Shias,Hanafi Sunnis). M=CSI. R=FEBA.
11421	0	1	0.00	1	18.00	82.00	A	0.00	0	1.10	Surguch, Macedonian Gagauz, Gerlovo Turks, Tozluk Turks, Kyzylbash, Karamanli. Yuruk dialect (Konyar). Muslims 99%.
11422	0	7	5.87	6	50.00	50.00	B	9.12	378	4	Cingane, Karachi. Speak Arlija (Balkan Romany) and Domari (Middle Eastern Romany). In 15 countries. Muslims 95%(Sunnis).
11423	0	5	3.35	6	40.03	59.97	A	0.04	291	2	Scattered in western Turkey. 33% have Serbo-Croatian as mother tongue. In 14 countries. 95% bilingual in Turkish. Ethnic Muslims 100%(all Sunnis). M=LBI.
11424	1	10	1.12	8	99.74	0.26	C	397.04	42	9	Expatriates from Britain, in business. Nonreligious 13%. D=Ch of England(D-Gibraltar).
11425	3	10	1.17	6	99.65	0.35	C	320.28	49	9	Bulgaria origin. Nonreligious 32%. D=Bulgarian Orthodox Ch(P-Sofia),RCC,BCC. M=CCCI,LBI.
11426	0	6	0.00	0	16.00	84.00	A	0.00	0	1.05	From Chechnya homeland in Russian Caucasus. Strong Hanafi Sunnis: Muslims 83%, Nonreligious 17% .
11427	0	1	3.39	0	22.01	77.99	A	0.00	547	1.09	In many Provinces in Anatolia. Also Israel, Syria, Jordan, Iraq, USA, Germany, Yugoslavia, Saudi Arabia, Greece. 94% bilingual in Turkish. Muslims 100%.
11428	0	5	3.92	8	38.01	61.99	A	0.01	340	2	Acculturated and mostly assimilated to Turkish life. Muslims 100%(Hanafi Sunnis). R=TWR,IBRA.
11429	0	5	0.00	1	20.00	80.00	A	0.00	0	1.11	Ankara Province, Polatli District; several villages. Also in Romania, Bulgaria, USA. Still retaining mother tongue and Tatar identity. Muslims 100%(Hanafi Sunnis).
11430	0	3	0.00	0	12.00	88.00	A	0.00	0	1.03	East central, mainly in Elazig, Bingol, and Diyarbakir Provinces. Related to, but distinct from Kurdish. Muslims 99%(Alawi Shias, a few Sunnis). M=CSI.
11431	2	10	5.40	6	99.72	0.28	C	391.57	115	9	Expatriates from Holland, in business. D=Dutch Chapel, in Netherlands embassy.
11432	0	5	1.56	0	28.00	72.00	A	1.02	251	4	Most around Kayseri. Also in former USSR, USA, Saudi Arabia. Close to Adyghe. Muslims 99%(Sunnis).
11433	1	10	0.53	8	99.84	0.16	C	490.56	26	10	Expatriates from France, in business. Nonreligious 13%. D=RCC(8 Dioceses). M=OFMCap,CM,FSC.
11434	2	10	0.99	8	99.80	0.20	C	455.52	37	10	Expatriates from Germany, in business. Nonreligious 11%. D=German Protestant Ch(Istanbul,Izmir,Ankara),NAC.
11435	3	10	-5.30	7	99.70	0.30	C	367.92	2	9	Remnants after continuous emigration. In Istanbul. Nonreligious 10%. D=Ecumenical Patriarchate of Constantinople(5 Dioceses),RCC(Byzantine: EA-Istanbul).
11436	0	8	4.66	7	58.10	41.90	B	4.45	250	4	Long-time immigrants from China; in business. Buddhists 55%, Chinese folk-religionists 35%, nonreligious 8%.
11437	0	4	4.29	0	26.20	73.80	A	0.19	658	3	Also in Iran, Iraq. Dialect of Kurmanji. Muslims 100%(Sunnis). M=CSI.
11438	1	10	1.34	6	99.77	0.23	C	404.71	52	10	Emigres from Hungary. Nonreligious 19%. D=RCC. M=OFMCap,CM,FSC.
11439	1	10	1.36	7	99.83	0.17	C	475.63	41	10	Expatriates from Italy, in business. Strong Catholics. D=RCC(8 Dioceses). M=OFMCap,CM,FSC.
11440	0	10	2.22	8	48.10	51.90	A	0.17	166	3	Sefardi Jews, declining by emigration to Israel from 38,267 in 1965.
11441	0	5	0.00	1	16.00	84.00	A	0.00	0	1.09	In mountains of eastern Turkey. Also in former USSR, Afghanistan. Muslims 100%(Hanafi Sunnis).
11442	0	5	0.00	4	36.04	63.96	A	0.05	61	2	Salihli town in Manisa Province, also Istanbul; Kayseri Province. Refugees from Afghanistan; also in Germany. Muslims 99%. M=FOT,WEC,CSI.
11443	0	7	0.00	4	31.00	69.00	A	0.00	0	1.11	In Van and Kars Provinces. Also in former USSR, China, Afghanistan. Refugees. Muslims 99%(Sunnis). M=FOT,CSI.
11444	0	5	0.00	1	19.00	81.00	A	0.00	0	1.10	A few villages. Vast majority in Volga area (Russia), some in USA. Lingua franca. Muslims 100%(Shafi, Hanafi Sunnis).
11445	3	5	-1.44	8	61.50	38.50	B	3.36	4	4	Syrians, Iraqis, Lebanese, Egyptians. Muslims 92%(Sunnis,Shias). D=GOC(P-Antioch: D-Tarsus),RCC(Melkites: VP-Turkey),SOC(P-Antioch: D-Midyat, D-Mardin).
11446	0	5	3.40	7	28.00	72.00	A	1.02	434	4	Mainly in western Turkey. Also in Iran, Iraq, Syria, Libya, Egypt, Israel, ex-USSR, Afghanistan, India. Muslims 99%.
11447	0	5	1.56	0	28.00	72.00	A	2.04	153	4	Many towns in northeast. Also in former USSR, Germany. Fishermen. 95% bilingual in Turkish. Muslims 98%(Shafi Sunnis).
11448	2	4	4.17	0	30.01	69.99	A	0.01	563	2	Kurmanji speakers. In 25 Provinces and 20 countries. Literates 28%. Muslims 95%(Shafi Sunnis,some Alawi Shias in Cilicia,some Yezidis),nonreligious 5%.
11449	1	5	5.98	0	46.00	54.00	A	16.79	422	5	Also in Russia, Georgia, Germany. Muslims 90%(Sunnis). D=Russian Orthodox Ch.
11450	0	0	1.62	5	29.01	70.99	A	0.01	363	2	Immigrants from Pakistan and Afghanistan from civil war. Muslims 100% (Sunnis).
11451	0	6	2.86	5	39.03	60.97	A	0.04	250	2	Emigres from Iran; many in Istanbul. Muslims 98%(Imami Shias/Ithna-Asharis), Baha'is 2%. M=FI.
11452	0	8	7.79	6	59.00	41.00	B	12.92	419	5	In Edirne and western provinces. 93% bilinguals in Turkish. Sunni Muslims 94%(early Bulgarian converts from Orthodoxy,also arrivals and deportees since 1950).
11453	1	10	1.37	6	99.75	0.25	C	388.72	48	9	Emigres, migrants from Romania. Nonreligious 16%. D=Romanian Orthodox Ch(P-Bucharest).
11454	1	10	0.92	7	99.51	0.49	B	227.10	21	8	Emigres from Russia. Nonreligious 35%, atheists 14%. D=Russian Orthodox Ch(P-Moscow).
11455	1	10	1.17	6	99.66	0.34	C	320.39	24	9	Migrants, emigres from Serbia. Nonreligious 28%. D=Serbian Orthodox Ch(P-Belgrade). M=LBI.
11456	0	1	0.00	0	13.00	87.00	A	0.00	0	1.06	A variant of Kurdish, understandable to Kurmanji. Also in Iraq and Iran. Muslims 100%(Sunnis). M=CSI.
11457	0	5	1.10	5	35.10	64.90	A	0.12	141	3	Hatay, Gaziantep, and Urfa Provinces. Refugees from Afghanistan. Also in Pakistan, Germany. Muslims 99%(Sunnis). M=FOT.
11458	0	10	0.00	8	32.00	68.00	A	0.00	0	1.08	Judeo-Spanish, Judezmo, Haketia. Practicing Sefardi Jews mainly in Istanbul, Izmir. Also in Israel. Bilingual in Turkish.
11459	3	9	1.42	5	99.83	0.17	C	463.51	38	10	Western Syriac language. In southeast. Also in 8 other countries. D=Syrian Orthodox Ch(Jacobites: P-Antioch,2 Dioceses),RCC(EP Turkey),Ancient Ch of the East.
11460	0	5	3.20	6	33.00	67.00	A	1.20	332	4	In Istanbul. Also in Russia, Romania, Bulgaria, China, Finland, Afghanistan, USA. Muslims 99%(Hanafi Sunnis).
11461	0	9	0.86	6	55.00	45.00	B	20.07	69	5	Scattered in western Turkey. 96% bilingual in Turkish. Muslims 70%(63% Sunnis,7% Shias), nonreligious 20%.

Continued overleaf

Table 8-2 continued

PEOPLE		POPULATION				IDENTITY CODE		LANGUAGE		CHURCH		MINISTRY						SCRIPTURE		
Ref 1	Ethnic name 2	P% 3	In 1995 4	In 2000 5	In 2025 6	Race 7	Language 8	Autoglossonym 9	S 10	AC 11	Members 12	Jayuh 13-17	d 18	wa 19	xc 20	mc 21	mi 22	Biblioglossonym 23	Pub 24-26	ss 27
11462	Turk	64.56168	39,560,560	42,992,230	56,729,832	MSY41j	44-AABA-a	osmanli	98	0.09	38,693	1A.u.	4	4	5	2	3	Turkish	PNB	b
11463	Turkish Gypsy (Cingane)	0.75000	459,567	499,432	659,019	CNN25f	44-AABA-a	osmanli		0.10	499	1A.u.	5	2	2	0	0	Turkish	PNB	b
11464	Turkish Kurd	8.00000	4,902,048	5,327,275	7,029,536	CNT24c	44-AABA-a	osmanli		0.01	533	1A.u.	3	4	2	5	3	Turkish	PNB	b
11465	Turkmen (Turkoman)	0.00197	1,207	1,312	1,731	MSY41k	44-AABA-e	turkmen		0.00	0	3c.u.	0	2	0	0	2	Turkmen	PNB	b
11466	USA White	0.02000	12,255	13,318	17,574	CEW19s	52-ABAC-s	general american		67.00	8,923	1Bsuh	10	9	13	5	3	English*	PNB	b
11467	Uighur	0.00110	674	733	967	MSY41z	44-AABD-d	east uyghur		0.00	0	1r.u.	0	3	2	0	2	Uighur*	PNB	b
11468	Urdu	0.03000	18,383	19,977	26,361	CNN25r	59-AAFO-d	standard urdu		0.01	2	2Asuh	3	3	2	1	0	Urdu	PNB	b
11469	Western Georgian	0.20478	125,480	136,365	179,939	CEW17c	42-CABA-a	imeruli		4.06	5,536	0A...	6	4	6	4	1		...	b
11470	Yoruk (Anatolian Gagauzi)	1.00000	612,756	665,909	878,692	MSY41j	44-AABA-a	osmanli		0.01	67	1A.u.	3	3	0	0	0	Turkish	PNB	b
11471	other minor peoples	0.20000	122,551	133,182	175,738	...				5.00	6,659		7	4	2	4	3			
	Turkmenistan	**100.00000**	**4,077,855**	**4,459,293**	**6,286,522**					**2.22**	**98,884**									
11472	Afghani	0.03565	1,454	1,590	2,241	CNT24a	58-ABDA-a	pashto		0.00	0	1As..	0	1	6	0	0		pnb	b
11473	Armenian	0.80354	32,767	35,832	50,515	CEW14	57-AAAA-b	ashkharik		67.70	24,258	4A.u.	10	7	11	2	2	Armenian: Modern, Eastern	PNB	b
11474	Avar	0.01485	606	662	934	CEW17b	42-BBAA-a	north avar		0.01	0	1....	3	3	2	0	1	Avar	P..	b
11475	Azerbaijani	0.94714	38,623	42,236	59,542	MSY41a	44-AABA-fa	north azeri		0.00	0	2c.u.	0	3	3	0	2	Azerbaijani*	PNB	b
11476	Bashkir	0.13280	5,415	5,922	8,349	MSY41b	44-AABB-g	bashqurt		7.00	415	1A.u.	7	5	7	0	1	Bashkir	Pn.	b
11477	Bulgarian	0.02583	1,053	1,152	1,624	CEW22b	53-AAAH-b	bulgarski		72.00	829	2A.uh	10	6	8	1	1	Bulgarian	PNB	b
11478	Byelorussian	0.16173	6,595	7,212	10,167	CEW22c	53-AAAE-c	bielorusskiy		60.00	4,327	3A.uh	10	7	8	2	3	Byelorussian*	PNB	b
11479	Chechen	0.01439	587	642	905	CEW17d	42-BAAA-b	chechen		0.00	0	0....	0	3	2	0	1	Chechen	P..	b
11480	Chuvash	0.06475	2,640	2,887	4,071	MSY41c	44-AAAA-a	chuvash		35.00	1,011	2....	9	6	8	0	1	Chuvash	PN.	b
11481	Dargin	0.04616	1,882	2,058	2,902	CEW17b	42-BBBB-a	dargwa		0.01	0	1....	3	3	2	0	1	Dargwa	P..	b
11482	Georgian	0.02725	1,111	1,215	1,713	CEW17c	42-CABB-a	kharthuli		40.00	486	2A.u.	9	6	8	2	1	Georgian	PNB	b
11483	German	0.10587	4,317	4,721	6,656	CEW19m	52-ABCE-a	standard hoch-deutsch		76.00	3,588	2B.uh	10	8	13	3	2	German*	PNB	b
11484	Greek	0.01263	515	563	794	CEW20	56-AAAA-c	dhimotiki		90.00	507	2B.uh	10	8	11	2	2	Greek: Modern	PNB	b
11485	Jewish	0.07031	2,867	3,135	4,420	CMT35	52-ABCH	yiddish cluster		0.00	0	0B..h	0	4	6	0	0		PNB	b
11486	Karakalpak	0.08692	3,544	3,876	5,464	MSY41z	44-AABC-b	karakalpak		0.00	0	1c.u.	0	3	0	0	1	Karakalpak	Pn.	b
11487	Kazakh	2.51245	102,454	112,038	157,946	MSY41e	44-AABC-c	kazakh		0.00	0	4A.u.	0	3	3	0	1	Kazakh	PN.	b
11488	Kirghiz	0.01800	734	803	1,132	MSY41g	44-AABC-d	kirghiz		0.00	0	2r.u.	0	3	3	0	1	Kirghiz	PN.	b
11489	Korean	0.08085	3,297	3,605	5,083	MSY46	45-AAAA-b	kukö		20.00	721	2A...	9	6	12	3	1	Korean	PNB	b
11490	Kurdish	0.12453	5,078	5,553	7,829	CNT24c	58-AAAA-a	kurmanji		0.00	0	3c...	0	3	3	0	0	Kurdish: Kurmanji*	PN.	b
11491	Lak	0.06929	2,826	3,090	4,356	CEW17b	42-BBBA-a	lak		0.00	0	1....	0	3	0	0	0	Lak	P..	b
11492	Latvian (Lett)	0.01587	647	708	998	CEW15a	54-AABA-a	standard latviashu		89.00	630	3A.u.	10	8	11	2	3	Latvian	PNB	b
11493	Lezgin	0.29594	12,068	13,197	18,604	CEW17b	42-BCAA-a	lezgin		0.00	0	1....	0	4	0	0	1	Lezgi	P..	b
11494	Lithuanian	0.01019	416	454	641	CEW15b	54-AAAA-a	standard lietuvishkai		91.00	414	3A.u.	10	8	11	2	3	Lithuanian	PNB	b
11495	Mari (Cheremis)	0.01436	586	640	903	MSW51h	41-AACA-b	mariy		90.00	576	2....	10	8	11	2	1	Mari: Low*	PN.	b
11496	Moldavian	0.07000	2,854	3,122	4,401	CEW21f	51-AADC-ab	standard moldavia		84.00	2,622	1A.u.	10	7	8	2	1		pnb	b
11497	Mordvinian	0.07290	2,973	3,251	4,583	MSW51i	41-AADA-a	erzya		65.00	2,113	2....	10	8	8	1	1	Mordvin: Erzya*	PN.	b
11498	Ossete	0.06722	2,741	2,998	4,226	CNT24e	58-ABBA	oseti cluster		36.00	1,079	2....	9	5	8	1	1	Ossete*	PN.	b
11499	Persian (Iranian)	0.21679	8,840	9,667	13,629	CNT24f	58-AACC-c	standard farsi		0.03	3	1Asu.	3	3	2	0	0		PNB	b
11500	Polish	0.01760	718	785	1,106	CEW22i	53-AAAC-c	polski		88.00	691	2A.uh	10	8	11	3	3	Polish	PNB	b
11501	Russian	3.00000	122,336	133,779	188,596	CEW22j	53-AAAE-d	russkiy	84	28.00	37,458	4B.uh	9	7	9	3	3	Russian	PNB	b
11502	Tajik	0.08939	3,645	3,986	5,620	CNT24g	58-AACC-j	tajiki		0.00	0	2asu.	0	3	3	0	1	Tajik*	PNB	b
11503	Tatar	1.11405	45,429	49,679	70,035	MSY41h	44-AABB-e	tatar		1.50	745	2c.u.	6	4	8	0	1	Tatar: Kazan	Pn.	b
11504	Turkmen (Trukhmeny)	79.21264	3,230,177	3,532,324	4,979,720	MSY41k	44-AABA-e	turkmen		0.01	353	3c.u.	3	3	2	0	3	Turkmen	PNb	b
11505	Uighur	0.03713	1,514	1,656	2,334	MSY41z	44-AABD-d	east uyghur		0.00	0	1r.u.	0	3	2	0	1	Uighur*	PNB	b
11506	Ukrainian	0.50000	20,389	22,296	31,433	CEW22p	53-AAAE-b	ukrainskiy		70.00	15,608	3A.uh	10	7	10	3	3	Ukrainian	PNB	b
11507	Uzbek	9.00819	367,341	401,702	566,302	MSY41l	44-AABD-a	central uzbek		0.00	0	1A.u.	0	3	6	1	3	Uzbek*	PNB	b
11508	Western Baluch	0.80279	32,737	35,799	50,468	CNT24b	58-AABA-b	west balochi		0.01	4	3.s..	3	1	3	0	0	Baluchi: Western*	P..	.
11509	other minor peoples	0.10000	4,078	4,459	6,287	...				10.00	446		8	5	8	0	0			
	Turks & Caicos Islands	**100.00000**	**14,008**	**16,760**	**33,769**					**79.13**	**13,262**									
11510	Black	77.00000	10,786	12,905	26,002	NFB68a	52-ABAF-o	turks-caicos-creole		80.00	10,324	1c..h	10	10	12	5	3		pn.	.
11511	British	1.20000	168	201	405	CEW19i	52-ABAC-b	standard-english	99	74.00	149	3Bsuh	10	9	13	5	3		PNB	b
11512	Mulatto	17.30000	2,423	2,899	5,842	NFB68b	52-ABAF	carib-anglo-creol cluster		78.00	2,262	1a..h	10	10	11	5	1	West Carib Creole English	PN.	b
11513	USA White	4.30000	602	721	1,452	CEW19s	52-ABAC-s	general american		70.00	504	1Bsuh	10	9	13	5	3	English*	PNB	b
11514	other minor peoples	0.20000	28	34	68	...				69.73	23		10	7	8	5	0			
	Tuvalu	**100.00000**	**10,242**	**11,719**	**20,674**					**83.16**	**9,746**									
11515	British	0.50000	51	59	103	CEW19i	52-ABAC-b	standard-english		71.00	42	3Bsuh	10	9	13	5	2		PNB	b
11516	Euronesian	1.00000	102	117	207	MPY53	52-ABAC-bv	standard oceanian-english		80.00	94	1Bsuh	10	9	12	5	3		pnb	b
11517	Han Chinese	0.40000	41	47	83	MSY42a	79-AAAB-ba	kuo-yü		70.00	33	2Bsuh	10	8	12	5	2	Chinese: Kuoyu*	PNB	b
11518	Kiribertese (Gilbertese)	1.00000	102	117	207	MPY54a	38-DAAA-a	i-kiribati		94.00	110	3.s..	10	9	13	5	3	Kiribati	PNB	b
11519	Samoan	0.40000	41	47	83	MPY55e	39-CAOA	samoa cluster	85	95.00	45	2a.u.	10	9	15	5	3	Samoan	PNB	b
11520	Tuvaluan (Ellice Islander	96.30000	9,863	11,285	19,909	MPY55z	39-CAKB-a	funafuti		83.20	9,389	0....	10	10	13	5	3	Tuvaluan	PNB	b
11521	other minor peoples	0.40000	41	47	83	...				70.00	33		10	7	7	5	0			
	Uganda	**100.00000**	**18,934,896**	**21,778,450**	**44,435,310**					**86.99**	**18,944,171**									
11522	Acholi (Shuli)	4.01618	760,460	874,662	1,784,602	NAB62a	04-ACBA-b	acholi		94.90	830,054	4....	10	10	13	5	2	Acholi	PNB	b
11523	Alur (Lur, Luri)	2.10630	398,826	458,719	935,941	NAB62b	04-ACAA-a	dho-aluur	3	92.90	426,150	0.s..	10	10	12	5	3	Alur	PNB	.
11524	Amba (Hamba, Bulebule)	0.33840	64,076	73,698	150,369	NAB57c	99-ASHA-b	ku-amba		39.30	28,963	0....	9	5	8	2	2		p..	.
11525	Arab	0.03000	5,680	6,534	13,331	CMT30	12-AACF-f	syro-palestinian	3	0.00	0	1Asuh	0	3	8	3	0	Arabic: Lebanese*	Pnb	b
11526	Bakedi	1.00000	189,349	217,785	444,353	NAB62q	04-BDAE-a	a-teso		91.00	198,184	3.s..	10	10	11	5	1	Ateso*	PNB	b
11527	Bari (Kuku, Fajulu)	0.50000	94,674	108,892	222,177	NAB62e	04-BAAB-a	kutuk-na-bari	2	78.00	84,936	1.s..	10	9	12	5	1	Bari	PNB	.
11528	British	0.09000	17,041	19,601	39,992	CEW19i	52-ABAC-b	standard-english	37	74.00	14,504	3Bsuh	10	9	13	5	3		PNB	b
11529	Bwisi (Talinga)	0.28753	54,444	62,620	127,765	NAB57d	99-AUSD-t	talinga-bwisi		70.00	43,834	1csu.	10	9	10	5	0	Talinga-bwisi	pnb	b
11530	Chiga (Kiga)	7.48300	1,416,898	1,629,681	3,325,094	NAB57d	99-AUSE-fc	o-lu-ciga		96.90	1,579,161	1cs.h	10	10	11	5	3		pnb	b
11531	Cuban White	0.02000	3,787	4,356	8,887	CLT27	51-AABB-hi	cubano		20.00	871	1B.uh	9	5	8	1	1		pnb	b
11532	French	0.00300	568	653	1,333	CEW21b	51-AABI-d	general français	1	83.98	549	1B.uh	10	9	14	5	3	French	PNB	b
11533	Ganda	13.82793	2,618,304	3,011,509	6,144,484	NAB57d	99-AUSE-r	o-lu-ganda	39	71.60	2,156,240	3Bs.h	10	10	12	5	3	Luganda*	PNB	b
11534	Goanese	0.10000	18,935	21,778	44,435	CNN25d	59-AAFU-o	konkani-gomantaki		95.00	20,690	3asu.	10	9	13	5	3	Konkani: Goan*	PNB	b
11535	Gujarati	0.91686	173,606	199,678	407,410	CNN25e	59-AAFH-b	standard gujaraati		0.05	100	2A.u.	4	4	2	3	0	Gujarati	PNB	b
11536	Gungu	0.13444	25,456	29,279	59,739	NAB57d	99-AUSE-a	ru-gungu		80.00	23,423	1cs.h	10	9	8	5	2		pnb	b
11537	Gwere	1.48219	280,651	322,798	658,616	NAB57d	99-AUSE-w	o-lu-gwere		93.00	300,202	1cs.h	10	9	7	5	3	Gwere	pnb	.
11538	Haya	0.60000	113,609	130,671	266,612	NAB57d	99-AUSE-h	ru-haya		87.63	114,507	1as.h	10	8	13	5	3	Ruhaya*	PNB	b
11539	High Lugbara (Terego/Arua)	1.40318	265,691	305,591	623,507	NAB66g	03-BAAF-a	uru-leba-ti		89.00	271,976	1As..	10	8	10	5	3	Lugbara	PNB	.
11540	Hima	0.75000	142,012	163,338	333,265	NAB57d	99-AUSE-fd	o-ro-hima		98.00	160,072	1cs.h	10	9	10	5	1		pnb	b
11541	Jie	0.34700	65,704	75,571	154,191	NAB62y	04-BDAD-b	south jiye		74.00	55,923	0....	10	9	8	5	2		pn.	.
11542	Kakwa (Bari Kakwa)	0.46503	88,053	101,276	206,638	NAB62y	04-BAAC-a	kakwa	7	66.90	67,754	0....	10	7	11	5	2	Kakwa*	PNB	.
11543	Kamba	0.02000	3,787	4,356	8,887	NAB57e	99-AUMA-i	ki-kamba		60.00	2,613	1cs..	10	9	13	5	3	Kikamba*	PNB	b
11544	Karamojong (Dodoth, Jie)	1.79427	339,743	390,764	797,289	NAB62y	04-BDAD-c	a-karimojong		69.90	273,144	0....	10	6	8	5	2	Karimojong*	PN.	.
11545	Kikuyu	0.30000	56,805	65,335	133,306	NAB57e	99-AUMA-a	gi-gikuyu		68.00	44,428	3as..	10	9	14	5	3	Gigikuyu*	PNB	b
11546	Kongo	0.01000	1,893	2,178	4,444	NAB57b	99-AURG-f	central ki-koongo		80.00	1,742	4as..	10	9	14	5	3	Kongo	PNB	b
11547	Konjo	1.94523	368,327	423,641	864,369	NAB57d	99-AUSD-r	o-ru-konzo		87.80	371,957	1csu.	10	7	7	5	3	Lhukonzo*	Pnb	b
11548	Kumam (Akokolemu)	0.60570	114,689	131,912	269,145	NAB62q	04-ACBB-a	kumam		76.00	100,253	0....	10	6	8	5	3		...	.
11549	Kupsabiny (Sebei, Mbai)	0.58192	110,186	126,733	258,578	NAB62y	04-CAAC-a	ku-p-sabiny	1	89.50	113,426	1....	10	9	8	5	1	Kupsapiny*	PN.	b
11550	Lango (Langi)	5.25000	994,082	1,143,369	2,332,854	NAB62i	04-ACBA-f	leb-lango		93.70	1,071,336	1....	10	6	10	5	3	Lango	PNB	b
11551	Lendu (Badha, Baledha)	0.10000	18,935	21,778	44,435	NAB66g	03-BADA-b	bale-dha		60.00	13,067	0.s..	10	7	7	4	1	Lendu	PN.	.
11552	Lingala (Zairian)	0.05000	9,467	10,889	22,218	NAB57c	99-AUIF-b	vehicular lingala	2	70.00	7,622	4asu.	10	9	12	5	3	Lingala	PNB	b
11553	Low Lugbara (Aringa)	3.66700	694,343	798,616	1,629,443	NAB66g	03-BAAE-a	andre-leba-ti		91.80	733,129	1....	10	7	7	5	3		...	b
11554	Luhya (Kabras, Nyala)	0.90000	170,414	196,006	399,918	NAB57d	99-AUSF-g	o-lu-wanga		93.80	183,854	2.s..	10	9	14	5	3	Oluhanga	PNb	b
11555	Luhya (Nyore)	1.23100	233,089	268,093	546,999	NAB57d	99-AUSF-d	o-lu-nyore		96.00	257,369	1.s..	10	9	14	5	3	Lunyore*	PNb	b
11556	Luo	0.50000	94,674	108,892	222,177	NAB62j	04-ACCA-b	dho-luo		93.00	101,270	2As..	10	9	14	5	3	Dholuo*	PNB	b
11557	Madi (South Madi)	1.04000	196,923	226,496	462,127	NAB66e	03-BAAI-a	moyo		90.80	205,658	1....	10	10	8	5	3	Madi	PN.	.
11558	Mangbetu (Makere)	0.19818	37,525	43,161	88,062	NAB66g	03-BABA-a	na-mangbetu-ti		55.00	23,738	0....	10	7	7	5	3	Mangbetu	...	b
11559	Masaba (Gisu, Gishu)	4.04000	764,970	879,849	1,795,187	NAB57d	99-AUSF-a	u-lu-masaba		82.00	721,476	3.s..	10	7	8	5	3	Lumasaaba*	PNb	.
11560	Mbuti (Twa) Pygmy	0.00400	757	871	1,777	BYG12	99-ASHA-a	ki-bira		5.00	44	0....	7	5	5	5	2	Kibira*	P..	.
11561	Mening	0.02000	3,787	4,356	8,887	NAB62q	04-BDAC-d	mening		20.00	871	0....	9	7	6	3	2		...	.
11562	Moru	0.04000	7,574	8,711	17,774	NAB66g	03-BAAA-a	kala-moru		60.00	5,227	1.s..	10	7	10	5	2	Moru	PN.	.
11563	Nande (Nandi)	0.05000	9,467	10,889	22,218	NAB57d	99-AUSD-q	e-ki-nande		95.00	10,345	4csu.	10	9	11	4	1	Kinandi*	PNB	b
11564	Nkole (Nkore)	8.80664	1,667,528	1,917,950	3,913,258	NAB57d	99-AUSE-f	o-ru-nya-nkore		96.90	1,858,493	3As.h	10	10	10	5	3	Runyankore*	PNB	b
11565	Nubian (Sudanese)	0.07900	14,959	17,205	35,104	NAB62b	12-AACG-c	ki-nubi	2	0.01	2	0....	3	3	2	1	0		...	b
11566	Nyangiya	0.04000	7,574	8,711	17,774	BYG11b	07-BBAA-a	nyang'i		20.00	1,742	0....	9	7	7	5	0		...	b
11567	Nyoro	2.66400	504,426	580,178	1,183,757	NAB57d	99-AUSE-c	nyoro-toro		88.90	515,778	4cs.h	10	10	11	5	3	Runyoro-rutooro*	PNB	b
11568	Okebu (Kebu, Ndo)	0.97000	183,668	211,251	431,023	NAB66g	03-BACC-a	ke'bu-tu		65.70	138,792	0....	10	7	7	5	3	Kebu*	PN.	.
11569	Olubo (Oluboti)	0.00500	947	1,089	2,222	NAB66e	03-BAAL-a	olubo-ti		50.00	544	0....	10	7	7	5	2		...	b
11570	Padhola (Dama)	1.58620	300,345	345,450	704,833	NAB62j	04-ACCA-a	dho-p-adhola	2	94.00	324,723	4cs..	10	8	12	5	3	Dhopadhola*	Pnb	b
11571	Pokot (Western Suk)	0.30612	57,964	66,668	136,025	NAB62p	04-CAAA-a	ngal-ap-pokot		48.00	32,001	0.s..	9	9	7	5	3	Pokoot	PN.	.
11572	Rundi Hutu	1.83372	347,213	399,356	814,819	NAB57d	99-AUSD-c	i-ki-ruundi		93.00	371,401	4csu.	10	9	11	5	3	Kirundi*	PNB	b
11573	Ruruli	0.36575	69,254	79,655	162,522	NAB57d	99-AUSE-b	o-ru-ruli		80.00	63,724	1cs.h	10	9	8	5	3		pnb	.
11574	Rwandese Hutu	5.40900	1,024,189	1,177,996	2,403,506	NAB57d	99-AUSD-f	i-ki-nya-rwanda		96.30	1,134,410	2Asu.	10	9	10	5	2	Kinyarwanda*	PNB	b
11575	Saamia (Gwe)	1.21000	229,112	263,519	537,667	NAB57d	99-AUSF-e	o-lu-saamia		95.00	250,343	1.s..	10	9	11	5	3	Saamia	Pnb	b
11576	Soga (Kenyi)	7.37000	1,395,502	1,605,072	3,274,882	NAB57d	99-AUSE-s	o-lu-soga		83.90	1,346,655	2cs.h	10	10	9	5	3	Lusoga*	Pnb	b
11577	Swahili	0.01000	1,893	2,178	4,444	NAB57j	99-AUSM-b	standard ki-swahili	35	4.97	108	4Asu.	6	5	2	5	1	Kiswahili*	PNB	b

Continued opposite

Table 8-2 continued

EVANGELIZATION								EVANGELISM			ADDITIONAL DESCRIPTIVE DATA
Ref 1	D 28	aC 29	CG% 30	r 31	E 32	U 33	W 34	e 35	R 36	T 37	Locations, civil divisions, literacy, religions, church history, denominations, dioceses, church growth, missions, agencies, ministries, movements 38
11462	7	5	8.61	8	54.09	45.91	B	0.17	472	3	84% Anatolian, 16% Rumelian. Muslims 98%(83% Hanafi Sunnis,15% Alawi Shias). D=Turkish Orthodox Ch,JWs,RCC,AAC,AEC,SOC,GOC;each few converts.
11463	0	6	3.99	8	43.10	56.90	A	0.15	319	3	Scattered especially across western Turkey. Most also speak Domari (Romani). Muslims 100%.
11464	2	4	4.06	8	49.01	50.99	A	0.01	339	2	Kurds who now use Turkish as mother tongue. Muslims 100%(Shafi Sunnis). D=Syrian Evangelical Church,RCC. M=FOT,OM,PI,CSI,WEC. T=CTV. R=TWR,IBRA.
11465	0	4	0.00	1	24.00	76.00	A	0.00	0	1.10	Tokat Province. Refugees from Afghanistan. Also in former USSR, Iran, Pakistan, USA, Germany. Devout Muslims 100%(Hanafi Sunnis). M=CSI,AFM.
11466	5	10	4.27	8	99.67	0.33	C	347.26	100	9	Expatriates from USA, on business and at military bases. Nonreligious 16%. D=CC,CCCC,SDA,JWs,CJCLdS.
11467	0	5	0.00	4	33.00	67.00	A	0.00	0	1.11	In Kayseri city, also in Istanbul. Many in ex-USSR, Afghanistan, Mongolia, Pakistan, Iran, Taiwan. Muslims 99% (Sunnis). M=FOT,CSI.
11468	0	8	0.70	5	44.01	55.99	A	0.01	44	2	Immigrants from Pakistan. Religious lingua franca. Muslims 100%(Sunnis).
11469	1	6	6.52	4	45.06	54.94	A	6.67	396	4	Western dialect of Georgian. 95% bilingual in Turkish. Muslims 95%(Sunnis). D=Georgian Orthodox Ch.
11470	0	4	4.29	8	34.01	65.99	A	0.01	403	2	Southeastern Turkey. Nomadic herders, livestock exporters (to Iraq); in 88 tribes. Muslims 99%(Hanafi Sunnis). R=TWR,IBRA.
11471	0	5	6.72		27.00	73.00	A	4.92	682	4	Including Karaites(non-Talmudic Jews), Koreans(M=PCK-H), other Asians,Europeans, other Arabs. Muslims 64% (Sunnis, Shias), Buddhists 10%, Shamanists 8%.
Turkmenistan											
11472	0	5	0.00	5	34.00	66.00	A	0.00	0	1.11	Migrant workers, refugees from 1979-90 Afghanistan war. Muslims 100%(Hanafi Sunnis).
11473	2	6	4.02	6	99.68	0.32	C	327.90	95	9	Gregorians. Also in 27 more countries. Nonreligious 24%, atheists 8%. D=Armenian Apostolic Ch,RCC.
11474	0	6	0.00	0	17.01	82.99	A	0.00	0	1.07	From Dagestan (Russia). Muslims 100%(Shafi Sunnis). M=IBT.
11475	1	5	0.00	1	29.00	71.00	A	0.00	0	1.12	Monolinguals 73%. Muslims 77%(53% Shias,24% Hanafi Sunnis), nonreligious 20%. D=ROC. M=IBT,CSI.
11476	1	9	4.17	4	49.00	51.00	A	12.52	278	5	Many speak Tatar as mother tongue. Muslims 72%(Hanafi Sunnis), nonreligious 21%. D=ROC.
11477	1	10	4.52	6	99.72	0.28	C	346.89	119	9	From Bulgaria; in 12 other countries. Nonreligious 18%, atheists 10%. D=Bulgarian Orthodox Ch. M=LBI.
11478	3	7	3.48	5	99.60	0.40	C	269.37	100	8	White Russians, from Belorussia. Nonreligious 30%, atheists 10%. D=ROC,RCC,Old Ritualist Chs.
11479	0	8	0.00	0	17.00	83.00	A	0.00	0	1.05	Nokhchuo. From Chechen, Ingush (Russia). Highly religious Muslims 63%(fervent Hanafi Sunnis), atheists 21%, nonreligious 16%. M=IBT.
11480	1	9	4.17	0	76.00	24.00	B	97.09	179	6	From Chuvashia (Russia). Muslims 35%(Sunnis), nonreligious 30%. D=ROC. M=IBT.
11481	0	6	0.00	0	17.01	82.99	A	0.00	0	1.07	From southern Dagestan (Russia). Muslims 100%(Shafi Sunnis). M=IBT.
11482	1	7	2.86	4	93.00	7.00	B	135.78	84	7	Nonreligious/atheists 55%, Muslims 5%(Sunnis, Shias). D=Georgian Orthodox Ch.
11483	2	7	6.06	8	99.76	0.24	C	405.00	135	10	Also found in Volga, Altai(Russia), Kazakhstan, Kirghizia. Nonreligious 20%. D=GELC,AUCECB.
11484	2	10	2.17	7	99.90	0.10	C	519.03	55	10	Greek-speaking immigrants, also merchants from Greece (Turkish-speaking). Nonreligious 10%. D=GOC,ROC. M=UBS,LBI.
11485	0	7	0.00	5	41.00	59.00	A	0.00	0	1.10	Religious Jews; bilingual in Russian, Turkmenian. Sizeable numbers have emigrated to Israel. Nonreligious 10%.
11486	0	7	0.00	1	18.00	82.00	A	0.00	0	1.09	In Kara Kalpak (Uzbekistan), from Aral Sea south. Fishermen. Muslims 78%(Hanafi Sunnis), nonreligious/atheists 22%. M=IBT.
11487	0	7	0.00	4	32.00	68.00	A	0.00	0	1.10	Muslims 60%(Hanafi Sunnis, with Sufi influence), nonreligious 30%, atheists 10%. M=ROC.
11488	0	8	0.00	4	29.00	71.00	A	0.00	0	1.10	Mainly in Kirghizia. Also in China, Afghanistan, Turkey. Nomadic pastoralists. 29% speak Russian. Muslims 45%(Hanafi Sunnis), nonreligious 40%, atheists 15%.
11489	1	9	4.37	6	84.00	16.00	B	61.32	162	6	45% monolinguals in Russian. Nonreligious 40%, shamanists 20%, Buddhists 15%, atheists 5%. D=KMC. M=CSI.
11490	0	6	0.00	0	22.00	78.00	A	0.00	0	1.08	Scattered groups across Central Asia and in cities. Muslims 80%(Shias,Yazidis), nonreligious 20%.
11491	0	6	0.00	0	14.00	86.00	A	0.00	0	1.05	From southern Dagestan (Russia). Lingua franca. Trilingual. Muslims 100%(Shafi Sunnis).
11492	5	8	4.23	5	99.89	0.11	C	500.26	97	10	In 25 countries. Nonreligious 9%. D=Russian Orthodox Ch,ELCL,RCC,RCL,CB.
11493	0	7	0.00	0	16.00	84.00	A	0.00	0	1.05	Also in south Dagestan (Russia). 50% understand Russian. Lingua franca. Muslims 100%(Shafi Sunnis). M=IBT.
11494	3	8	3.79	5	99.91	0.09	C	518.15	67	10	Found in 24 countries. Strong Catholics. Nonreligious 9%. D=RCC,ERCL,ROC.
11495	1	6	5.40	0	99.90	0.10	C	436.90	132	10	Originally in Mari, Bashkiria (Russia). Agriculturalists. Muslims 7%, many shamanists. D=ROC, M=IBT.
11496	1	7	5.73	6	99.84	0.16	C	420.04	135	10	From Bessarabia, Romania, Bulgaria. Traditionally Orthodox. Nonreligious 14%. D=Russian Orthodox Ch.
11497	1	7	4.77	7	99.65	0.35	C	268.09	116	8	From northern Mordvinia (Russia). Nonreligious 30%. Acculturated to Russian. D=Russian Orthodox Ch.
11498	1	5	3.68	0	73.00	27.00	B	95.92	179	6	From south Ossetian AO(Georgia). Stock-breeders. Muslims 40%(Sunnis), nonreligious 24%. D=ROC.
11499	0	5	1.10	5	36.03	63.97	A	0.03	137	2	Farsi spoken as mother tongue by 14%. Muslims 90%(Imami Shias), Baha'is 10%.
11500	4	7	4.33	6	99.88	0.12	C	494.64	77	10	Poles from Poland, Ukraine. Nonreligious 9%. D=RCC,ROC,CEF,CWE(Polish Pentecostals).
11501	8	7	2.51	7	96.00	4.00	B	98.11	72	6	In 70 countries. Nonreligious 56%, atheists 14%. D=ROC,RCC,AUCECB,Old Ritualists,CEF,CCECB,SDA,IPKh.
11502	0	6	0.00	4	36.00	64.00	A	0.00	0	1.12	Most are multilingual(in Uzbek, Turkmen, Russian). Muslims 90%(Hanafi Sunnis,some Shias), nonreligious 10%. M=CSI.
11503	1	7	4.41	6	41.50	58.50	A	2.27	344	4	70% bilingual in Russian or Turkmen. Muslims 81%(Hanafi Sunnis), nonreligious 15%. D=ROC.
11504	0	6	3.63	1	30.01	69.99	A	0.01	404	2	Kara Kum Desert. Also in Uzbekistan, Iran, Afghanistan, Turkey, Pakistan, USA, Germany. Devout Muslims 95%(Hanafi Sunnis, with Sufi Naqshbandiyya).
11505	0	6	0.00	4	31.00	69.00	A	0.00	0	1.11	Also in Kirghizia, Uzbekistan, China and 12 other countries. Settled agriculturalists. Muslims 100%(Hanafi Sunnis, with heavy Sufi influence). M=IBT.
11506	7	8	3.40	6	99.70	0.30	C	355.14	91	9	In 15 countries. Nonreligious/atheists 30%. D=ROC(E-Ukraine),Ukrainian Catholic Ch,AUCECB,CEF,CCECB,JWs,SDA.
11507	0	9	0.00	5	42.00	58.00	A	0.00	0	1.12	55% Russian-speaking. Literates 100%. Muslims 80%(Hanafi Sunnis), nonreligious/atheists 20%. M=ROC,AUCECB,CSI.
11508	0	9	1.40	1	24.01	75.99	A	0.00	274	1.08	Near Merv. From Afghanistan, Iran, Pakistan. Muslims 100%(Hanafi Sunnis).
11509	0	7	2.92		32.00	68.00	A	11.68	250	5	Udmurts, Gagauzis, Kumyks, Tabasaran, other Asians, other Europeans. Muslims 77%, Nonreligious 8%, Buddhists 2%.
Turks & Caicos Islands											
11510	7	9	0.95	8	99.80	0.20	C	411.72	31	10	Citizens. Afro-Caribbean religionists 2%, Baha'is 1%. D=Jamaica Baptist Union,MCCA,Anglican Ch/CPWI,NTCOG,CGP,SDA,JWs.
11511	5	10	1.69	8	99.74	0.26	C	402.44	52	10	Expatriates from Britain in government, education. Nonreligious 13%. D=Anglican Ch/CPWI(D-Nassau & The Bahamas),MCCA,CB,SDA,JWs.
11512	8	10	0.97	8	99.78	0.22	C	398.58	33	9	Citizens, of mixed race. Afro-Caribbean religionists 6%. D=JBU,MCCA,AC/CPWI,NTCOG,CGP,Spiritual Baptist Chs,JWs,SDA. M=OCD.
11513	7	10	1.55	8	99.70	0.30	C	365.36	47	9	Expatriates from USA, in development. Nonreligious 14%. D=JBU,NTCOG,CGP,RCC,SDA,JWs,BBFI.
11514	0	10	3.19		99.70	0.30	C	258.91	86	8	USA Blacks(CoGiC), other Caribbean Islanders, other Europeans, Latin Americans. Nonreligious 7%.
Tuvalu											
11515	2	10	-3.34	8	99.71	0.29	C	375.76	2	9	Expatriates from Britain, in development. Nonreligious 15%. D=Tuvalu Ch,SDA.
11516	3	10	4.65	8	99.80	0.20	C	435.08	100	10	Mixed-race persons, European/Asian/Austronesian. D=RCC,TC,SDA.
11517	2	10	3.56	7	99.70	0.30	C	367.92	80	9	Traders. A few Buddhists. Most are Christians. Buddhists 30%. D=TC,RCC.
11518	4	10	2.43	4	99.94	0.06	C	559.25	51	10	From Kiribati; also in Fiji, Solomons, Nauru, Vanuatu. Baha'is 6%. D=GIPC,TC,RCC(D-Tarawa,Nauru & Funafuti),SDA.
11519	4	10	3.88	5	99.95	0.05	C	582.54	72	10	Baha'is 3%, expanding. First missionaries and pastors. Y=1861. D=CCCS,RCC,SDA,TC.
11520	3	6	2.04	5	99.83	0.17	C	443.98	48	10	Before 1978 called Ellice Islanders. Also in Nauru, NZ, Fiji. Literates 90%. Baha'is 5%(growing). D=99% Tuvalu Ch,RCC,SDA. M=CWM(LMS),UBS,APM.
11521	0	10	3.56		99.70	0.30	C	260.61	96	8	Other Pacific Islanders, other Europeans, other Asians. Baha'is 15%.
Uganda											
11522	4	8	4.49	1	99.95	0.05	C	543.47	105	10	Also in Sudan. Animists 3%. D=RCC(D-Gulu),CU(D-Northern Uganda),CER,other AICs. M=CMS,Good News Foundation.
11523	4	7	11.25	5	99.93	0.07	C	515.07	230	10	In West Nile. Majority in Zaire. Animists 4%. D=RCC(D-Arua),CU(D-Madi & West Nile),CER,other AICs. M=FSCJ,AIM,TCC,GNF.
11524	2	7	8.30	4	77.30	22.70	B	110.88	346	7	Ruwenzori Kibira. South of Lake Albert; also in Zaire. Close to Bila, Komo, Bera. Animists 55%. D=RCC,CU.
11525	0	10	0.00	8	46.00	54.00	A	0.00	0	1.14	Sudanese, Coastal, Palestinian. Traders, military, mercenaries. Muslims 100%(Sunnis,some Shias).
11526	3	9	4.41	1	99.91	0.09	C	501.54	104	10	In Bukedi. Part of Teso people. Muslims 8%. D=CU(D-Bukedi),RCC,SA. M=CMS.
11527	3	8	9.47	0	99.78	0.22	C	375.80	226	9	Strong Christian tribe mainly from Southern Sudan; some also in Zaire. Lingua franca. Animists 10%. D=CU,RCC,AICs(Trumpeters). M=CMS.
11528	5	10	7.55	8	99.74	0.26	C	402.44	160	10	Expatriates from Britain, in development. Nonreligious 13%. D=CU,PCEA,RCC,SDA,JWs.
11529	0	8	7.25	1	99.70	0.30	C	301.49	217	9	Near Kilembe; also in Zaire. Bilingual in Nyoro-Toro. Animists 10%.
11530	2	8	12.72	1	99.97	0.03	C	544.32	264	10	Ankole Province. Animists 3%. D=RCC(D-Kabale,D-Mbarara),CU(D-Kigezi). M=RCMS,CMS,ANMBTC,GMU,TCC,GNF.
11531	1	10	4.57	8	75.00	25.00	B	54.75	198	6	Military advisers, reduced after 1978. Nonreligious 60%, atheists 20%. D=RCC.
11532	1	10	4.09	8	99.84	0.16	C	478.12	89	10	Expatriates from France, in development. Nonreligious 13%. D=RCC(12 Dioceses). M=FSCJ,MHM,CSC,FICP,SC.
11533	7	7	3.89	4	99.72	0.28	C	375.28	114	9	Muslims 20%(Shafi Sunnis,2,000 Ahmadis), animists 3%. Y=1877. D=RCC(2 Dioceses),Ch of Uganda(3 Dioceses),Gospel Ch,AGOC,SDA,PEFA,other AICs.
11534	1	10	7.93	4	99.95	0.05	C	558.26	152	10	Indians from Goa(India). Hindus 3%. D=RCC(M-Kampala). M=FSCJ,MHM,CSC.
11535	0	10	2.33	6	45.05	54.95	A	0.08	203	2	Successors of large Asian commercial community before 1972 expulsion and later partial return. Bilingual in Hindi. Hindus 87%, Muslims 12%.
11536	2	8	8.07	1	99.80	0.20	C	385.44	211	9	Northeast shore of Lake Albert. Bilingual in Nyoro-Toro. Animists 3%, Muslims 5%. D=RCC,CU.
11537	2	8	5.11	1	99.93	0.07	C	482.01	139	10	Close to Ganda and Soga. Animists 4%. D=Ch of Uganda,RCC. M=CMS,FBCB(Burma),TCC.
11538	3	8	9.80	1	99.88	0.12	C	472.19	221	10	Mainly in Tanzania. Animists 3%. D=RCC(D-Masaka),CU,AICs.
11539	3	7	10.75	1	99.89	0.11	C	480.77	230	10	In West Nile; also in Zaire. Animists 5%, Muslims 5%, Baha'is 1%. D=RCC(D-Arua),CU(D-Madi & West Nile),AICs(Trumpeters). M=FSCJ,AIM,FBCB(Burma),TCC.
11540	2	8	10.16	4	99.98	0.02	C	550.85	218	10	Aristocratic Hamitic pastoral nomads, cattle/hides/skins exporters. Animists 1%. D=70% Ch of Uganda,RCC. M=CMS.
11541	2	6	9.01	1	99.74	0.26	C	307.91	251	9	Animists 20%. D=RCC(D-Moroto),CU(D-Karamoja). M=FSCJ,BCMS.
11542	3	7	9.22	1	99.67	0.33	C	290.33	245	8	Northwest, in West Nile District. Close to Pojulu, Bari, Kuku. Animists 17%, Muslims 13%. D=RCC(D-Arua),CU(D-Madi & West Nile),AICs. M=AIM,FSCJ.
11543	4	10	5.72	4	99.60	0.40	C	269.37	150	8	Immigrants from Eastern Kenya. Animists 10%. D=African Brotherhood Ch(Uganda Pastorate),RCC,CU,other AICs.
11544	5	6	10.76	1	99.70	0.30	C	285.49	298	8	Karamoja District. Cattle-rustling gangs armed with submachine-guns. Animists 29%. D=RCC(D-Moroto),Ch of Uganda(D-Karamoja),PAG,PEFA,SDA. M=FSCJ.
11545	4	10	5.36	4	99.68	0.32	C	349.96	124	9	Immigrants from Central Kenya. Animists 5%. D=RCC,CU,PCEA,numerous AICs.
11546	4	10	4.25	5	99.80	0.20	C	449.68	102	10	Migrants from Zaire. Animists 2%. D=RCC,EJCSK,ECZ,other AICs.
11547	4	7	11.10	1	99.88	0.12	C	431.99	268	10	On Ruwenzori mountains. Animists 11%. D=RCC,SDA,BCU,CU. M=FMB,CMS,Fundamental Baptists Ch of Burma,CBFMS.
11548	4	8	9.65	1	99.76	0.24	C	324.55	256	9	South of Lake Kwania, Western Teso District. Related to Dinka(Sudan). Animists 20%. D=CU,RCC,PEFA,PAG.
11549	2	7	9.79	1	99.90	0.10	C	429.57	234	10	North of Mbale, Sebei Province. On Mount Elgon. Related to Sabaot (Kenya). Animists 9%. D=CU(D-Mbale),RCC(D-Tororo). M=BCMS.
11550	5	8	12.28	1	99.94	0.06	C	518.82	249	10	North of Lake Kyoga, Lango Province. Animists 3%. D=RCC(D-Lira),Ch of Uganda(D-Lango),AGOC(D-Eirenopolis),LMC,other AICs. M=CMS,FMB,AIM.
11551	1	10	7.44	1	99.60	0.40	C	223.38	245	8	Majority in Zaire, across Lake Albert. Animists 17%. D=CU.
11552	4	10	4.86	5	99.70	0.30	C	360.25	123	9	Migrants from river Zaire. Animists 3%. D=RCC,EJCSK,CU,AICs.
11553	3	6	11.85	0	99.92	0.08	C	444.97	279	10	Northwest corner, north of Lake Albert. Close to Madi. Animists 6%. D=CU,RCC,AICs.
11554	8	9	3.89	1	99.94	0.06	C	529.98	106	10	Immigrants from Western Kenya. Bilingual in Luganda. Animists 2%, Muslims 2%. D=CU,RCC,AICN,SDA,PAG,CGEA,EAYM,many AICs. M=MHM,FBCB(Burma).
11555	7	9	10.69	1	99.96	0.04	C	546.62	225	10	Another 50% live in Bunyore(Kenya). Bilingual in Luganda. Baha'is 1%, animists 1%, Muslims 1%. D=CU,RCC,SDA,AICN,PAG,CGEA,many AICs. M=MHM,CMS.
11556	5	10	3.94	4	99.93	0.07	C	563.48	80	10	Traders, immigrants from Western Kenya. Animists 3%. D=CU,RCC(D-Tororo),Ch of Christ in Africa(D-Tororo),MLA,other AICs. M=CMS,GMU,FMB.
11557	4	7	10.44	1	99.91	0.09	C	450.06	239	10	Northwest, near Nimule. Also in Sudan. Animists 4%, some Muslims. D=RCC,CU,SDA,AICs(Trumpeters). M=AIM,CMS,FSCJ,FBCB(Burma).
11558	3	7	8.08	0	93.00	7.00	B	186.69	288	7	Northwest, on Zaire border. Primarily in Zaire. Animists 30%. D=RCC,CU,AoG.
11559	7	7	4.68	1	99.82	0.18	C	398.06	140	9	Around Mount Elgon. Animists 10%(Dini ya Msambwa/Religion of the Ancestors), Baha'is 2%, Muslims 5%. D=RCC(D-Tororo),CU(D-Mbale),BCU,PAG,PEFA,AICs.
11560	2	10	3.86	1	39.00	61.00	A	7.11	348	4	Pygmies in equatorial rain forest along Zaire border. Animists 95%. D=CU(D-Ruwenzori),RCC. M=CMS,CBFMS.
11561	2	6	4.57	0	49.00	51.00	A	35.77	328	5	On Sudan border. Related to Karamojong and Teso. Animists 80%. D=CU,RCC.
11562	2	8	6.46	0	99.60	0.40	C	229.95	213	8	In northwest. Animists 5%. Strongly Christian tribe from Southern Sudan. D=CU(East African Revival),RCC. M=CMS,FSCJ.
11563	1	8	5.42	1	99.95	0.05	C	516.65	138	10	Migrants from Zaire. Animists 5%. D=RCC.
11564	5	10	4.72	4	99.97	0.03	C	597.37	111	10	Animists 1% (Cult of Bagyendnawa Royal Drum), Muslims 2%(Shafi Sunnis, since 1887). D=RCC(D-Mbarara),CU(D-Ankole; East African Revival),SDA,KOAB,AICs.
11565	0	10	0.70	1	18.01	81.99	A	0.00	335	1.07	In West Nile District, Arua and other cities. Descendants of Arabic-speaking colonial armies and soldiers. Muslims 100%(Maliki Sunnis).
11566	0	8	5.30	0	54.00	46.00	B	39.42	320	5	Teso Province. Spoken only by 100 elderly; youth speak Dodoth. Hunters. Animists 80%.
11567	3	8	4.20	4	99.89	0.11	C	505.87	111	10	Bunyoro Province, south of Lake Albert. Muslims 5%, Animists 2%. D=RCC(D-Hoima),CU(D-Bunyoro-Kitara),SDA. M=CMS,ANMBTC,GMU,TCC.
11568	3	10	10.01	0	99.66	0.34	C	265.46	290	8	Northwest, around Mahigi. Mainly in Zaire. Blacksmiths. Animists 23%. D=RCC,CU,AICs.
11569	2	7	4.08	0	87.00	13.00	B	158.77	174	7	Most are in Sudan. Many bilinguals in Bari. Animists 15%. D=CU,RCC.
11570	2	8	10.95	4	99.94	0.06	C	535.23	208	10	Jopadhola. Eastern, Mbale District. Animists 5%. D=RCC,CU. M=CMS,FMB,UBS.
11571	4	7	8.41	0	90.00	10.00	B	157.68	302	7	East central; mainly in Kenya. Semi-nomadic. Animists 51%. D=RCC,CU,IAC,AICs. M=BCMS,FSCJ,AIM,UBS.
11572	4	10	11.10	4	99.93	0.07	C	543.12	226	10	Refugees from 1962-94 genocide in Burundi. Animists 3%. D=RCC(M-Kampala),CU,other Protestant bodies,some AICs.
11573	3	8	7.35	1	99.80	0.20	C	382.52	198	9	East of Nyoro, a similar language. Animists 7%, some Muslims. D=RCC,CU,SDA.
11574	2	10	12.34	4	99.96	0.04	C	573.99	242	10	Refugees from 1962-1994 genocide in Rwanda, Burundi. Animists 1%. D=RCC,CU. M=CMS,CBFMS.
11575	2	8	4.47	1	99.95	0.05	C	516.65	121	10	Mainly in Kenya. Bilingual in Luganda. Animists 2%, Baha'is 1%, Muslims 2%. D=RCC(D-Jinja),CU(D-Busoga). M=MHM,CMS,FMB.
11576	9	9	4.57	4	99.84	0.16	C	443.73	126	10	Southeast. Animists 1%, Muslims 15%(Shafi Sunnis, expanding slowly; Ahmadiyya active). D=RCC(D-Jinja),CU(D-Busoga),PAG,PEFA,BCU,SA,KOAB,AOC,AICs.
11577	2	10	2.41	5	58.97	41.03	B	10.69	180	5	Traders, from Coast. Muslims 93%(Shafi Sunnis), Baha'is 2%. D=CU,RCC. M=CMS.

Continued overleaf

Table 8-2 continued

PEOPLE		POPULATION				IDENTITY CODE		LANGUAGE		CHURCH		MINISTRY						SCRIPTURE		
Ref	*Ethnic name*	*P%*	*In 1995*	*In 2000*	*In 2025*	*Race*	*Language*	*Autoglossonym*	*S*	*AC*	*Members*	*Jayuh*	*d*	*wa*	*xc*	*mc*	*mi*	*Biblioglossonym*	*Pub*	*ss*
1	2	3	4	5	6	7	8	9	10	11	12	13-17	18	19	20	21	22	23	24-26	27
11578	Tepeth (Tepes, So)	0.04808	9,104	10,471	21,364	NAB62y	07-BBBA-a	soo		60.00	6,283	0....	10	7	6	5	2		...	.
11579	Teso (Iteso)	5.37500	1,017,751	1,170,592	2,388,398	NAB62q	04-BDAE-a	a-teso		98.80	1,156,545	3.s..	10	9	10	5	3	Ateso*	PNB	b
11580	Teuso (Ik, Ngulak)	0.01980	3,749	4,312	8,798	BYG11b	07-BAAA-a	ik		95.00	4,097	0....	10	8	11	5	1		...	n
11581	Toposa	0.11000	20,828	23,956	48,879	NAB62y	04-BDAA-b	akero-a-toposa		70.00	16,769	0....	10	8	10	5	2		...	.
11582	Toro	2.62000	496,094	570,595	1,164,205	NAB57d	99-AUSE-cc	o-ru-tooro		93.00	530,654	1cs.h	10	10	11	5	3		pnb	b
11583	Tutsi (Ruanda)	2.40000	454,438	522,683	1,066,447	NAB57d	99-AUSD-f	i-ki-nya-rwanda		95.40	498,639	2Asu.	10	9	10	5	2	Kinyarwanda*	PNB	b
11584	other minor peoples	0.52335	99,096	113,978	232,552	...				63.00	71,806		10	6	7	5	0			
	Ukraine	**100.00000**	**51,431,546**	**50,455,980**	**45,687,963**					**82.59**	**41,669,099**									
11585	Abkhazian	0.00192	987	969	877	CEW17a	44-AABA-a	osmanli		20.00	194	1A.u.	9	5	8	1	1	Turkish	PNB	b
11586	Albanian	0.00967	4,973	4,879	4,418	CEW13	55-AAAB-i	tosk-ukraine		4.00	195	0A...	6	4	8	1	3		pnb	b
11587	Arab	0.00241	1,240	1,216	1,101	CMT30	12-AACI-c	arab-uzbeki		10.00	122	0....	8	3	3	0	0		...	b
11588	Armenian	0.10534	54,178	53,150	48,128	CEW14	57-AAAA-b	ashkharik		70.00	37,205	4A.u.	10	7	13	2	2	Armenian: Modern, Eastern	PNB	b
11589	Assyrian	0.00536	2,757	2,704	2,449	CMT31	12-AAAA-f	aisor		87.00	2,353	4cs..	10	6	10	2	2	Assyrian Neo-aramaic	PNB	b
11590	Avar	0.00520	2,674	2,624	2,376	CEW17b	42-BBAA-a	north avar		0.02	1	1....	3	3	2	0	1	Avar	P..	b
11591	Azerbaijani	0.07184	36,948	36,248	32,822	MSY41a	44-AABA-fa	north azeri		0.00	0	2c.u.	0	3	3	0	2	Azerbaijani*	PNB	b
11592	Balkan Gypsy	1.36049	699,721	686,449	621,580	CNN25f	59-ACBA-b	balkan-romani		10.00	68,645	1A...	8	4	6	0	1		Pn.	b
11593	Bashkir	0.01439	7,401	7,261	6,574	MSY41b	44-AABB-g	bashqurt		7.00	508	1A.u.	7	5	7	0	1	Bashkir	Pn.	b
11594	Bulgar (Bulgarian)	0.45440	233,705	229,272	207,606	CEW22b	53-AAAH-b	bulgarski		72.00	165,076	2A.uh	10	6	8	1	1	Bulgarian	PNB	b
11595	Buryat	0.00165	849	833	754	MSY41y	44-BAAB-b	buryat		10.00	83	3A..h	8	4	7	0	1	Buryat*	PNB	b
11596	Byelorussian	0.85525	439,868	431,525	390,746	CEW22c	53-AAAE-c	bielorusskiy		65.00	280,491	3A.uh	10	7	8	4	3	Byelorussian*	PNB	b
11597	Carpathian Gypsy	0.00389	2,001	1,963	1,777	CNN25f	59-ACBA-ag	north vlach		80.00	1,570	1c...	10	7	7	0	2	Romani: Latvian	Pn.	b
11598	Chechen	0.00358	1,841	1,806	1,636	CEW17d	42-BAAA-b	chechen		0.00	0	0....	0	3	2	0	1	Chechen	P..	b
11599	Chuvash	0.03964	20,387	20,001	18,111	MSY41c	44-AAAA-a	chuvash		35.00	7,000	2....	9	6	8	0	1	Chuvash	PN.	b
11600	Crimean Jew (Krymchak)	0.00132	679	666	603	CMT35	44-AABA-c	crimea-tatar		0.00	0	1c.u.	0	1	1	0	0	Crimean Tatar*	PNb	b
11601	Crimean Tatar	0.09097	46,787	45,900	41,562	MSY41h	44-AABA-c	crimea-tatar		0.00	0	1c.u.	0	3	2	0	1	Crimean Tatar*	PNB	b
11602	Croat	0.00200	1,029	1,009	914	CEW22d	53-AAAG-b	standard hrvatski		84.00	848	2Asuh	10	7	9	2	1	Croatian	PNB	b
11603	Czech (Bohemian)	0.04060	20,881	20,485	18,549	CEW22e	53-AAAD-a	czesky		75.00	15,364	2Asuh	10	8	8	3	1	Czech	PNB	b
11604	Dargin	0.00301	1,548	1,519	1,375	CEW17b	42-BBBB-a	dargwa		0.04	1	1....	3	3	2	0	1	Dargwa	P..	b
11605	East Circassian	0.00186	957	938	850	CEW17a	42-AAAA-c	qaberdey		10.00	94	1c...	8	4	3	1	1	Kabardian	PN.	.
11606	Estonian	0.00818	4,207	4,127	3,737	MSW51a	41-AAAC-b	eesti		67.00	2,765	4A.u.	10	8	8	2	2	Estonian: Tallinn	PNB	b
11607	Finnish	0.00211	1,085	1,065	964	MSW51b	41-AAAA-bb	vehicular suomi		87.00	926	1A.uh	10	8	12	3	2	Finnish	PNB	b
11608	Gagauzi Turk	0.06213	31,954	31,348	28,386	MSY41d	44-AABA-b	gagauzi		72.00	22,571	1c.u.	10	7	8	1	1	Gagauz	Pnb	b
11609	Georgian	0.04575	23,530	23,084	20,902	CEW17c	42-CABB-a	kharthuli		40.00	9,233	2A.u.	9	6	8	2	1	Georgian	PNB	b
11610	German	0.07356	37,833	37,115	33,608	CEW19m	52-ABCE-a	standard hoch-deutsch		77.00	28,579	2B.uh	10	8	13	3	2	German*	PNB	b
11611	Greek (Romeos, Urum)	0.19162	98,553	96,684	87,547	CEW20	56-AAAA-c	dhimotiki		90.00	87,015	2B.uh	10	8	11	2	1	Greek: Modern	PNB	b
11612	Han Chinese	0.00132	679	666	603	MSY42a	79-AAAB-ba	kuo-yü		1.00	7	2Bsuh	6	1	3	0	0	Chinese: Kuoyu*	PNB	b
11613	Hungarian	0.36274	186,563	183,024	165,729	MSW51g	41-BAAA-a	general magyar		76.00	139,098	2A.u.	10	9	9	3	1	Hungarian	PNB	b
11614	Jat (Jati, Jatu)	0.05901	30,350	29,774	26,960	CNN25h	12-AACJ-a	jakati		1.00	298	0....	6	1	3	0	0		...	.
11615	Jewish	0.64578	332,135	325,835	295,044	CMT35	52-ABCH-b	east yiddish		0.03	98	0A..h	3	4	6	0	0	Yiddish	PNB	b
11616	Kalmyk	0.00123	633	621	562	MSY41y	44-BAAB-d	kalmyk		1.00	6	2c..h	6	3	6	0	0	Mongolian: Kalmyk*	PNb	b
11617	Karaite (Karaim)	0.00273	1,404	1,377	1,247	MSY41z	44-AABB-h	karaim		0.00	0	1c.u.	0	2	3	0	0	Karaite*	PN.	b
11618	Karelian	0.00442	2,273	2,230	2,019	MSW51c	41-AAAB-a	central karely		66.00	1,472	1....	10	6	8	0	3	Karelian	P..	b
11619	Kazakh	0.02042	10,502	10,303	9,329	MSY41e	44-AABC-c	kazakh		0.00	0	4A.u.	0	3	3	0	2	Kazakh	PNB	b
11620	Kirghiz	0.00446	2,294	2,250	2,038	MSY41g	44-AABC-d	kirghiz		0.00	0	2r.u.	0	3	3	0	2	Kirghiz	PN.	b
11621	Komi-Permyat	0.00417	2,145	2,104	1,905	MSW51d	41-AAEA-b	permyat		40.00	842	3....	9	6	8	1	1	Komi: Permyak*	Pn.	b
11622	Komi-Zyrian	0.00769	3,955	3,880	3,513	MSW51d	41-AAEA-a	komi		33.00	1,280	2....	9	6	8	1	1	Komi: Zyryan*	PN.	b
11623	Korean	0.01685	8,666	8,502	7,698	MSY46	45-AAAA-b	kukö		20.00	1,700	2A...	9	6	8	3	1	Korean	PNB	b
11624	Kumyk	0.00169	869	853	772	MSY41z	44-AABB-d	kumyk		0.01	0	1c.u.	3	2	5	0	0	Kumuk*	Pn.	b
11625	Lak	0.00201	1,034	1,014	918	CEW17b	42-BBBA-a	lak		0.00	0	1....	0	3	0	0	0	Lak	P..	b
11626	Latvian	0.01388	7,139	7,003	6,341	CEW15a	54-AABA-a	standard latviashu		89.00	6,233	3A.u.	10	8	11	2	3	Latvian	PNB	b
11627	Lezghian	0.00935	4,809	4,718	4,272	CEW17b	42-BCAC	south lezgin cluster		0.01	0	0....	3	4	0	0	1		P..	b
11628	Lithuanian	0.02192	11,274	11,060	10,015	CEW15b	54-AAAA-a	standard lietuvishkai		91.00	10,065	3A.u.	10	8	11	2	3	Lithuanian	PNB	b
11629	Mari (Cheremis)	0.01432	7,365	7,225	6,543	MSW51h	41-AACA-b	mariy		90.00	6,503	2....	10	8	11	2	1	Mari: Low*	PN.	b
11630	Moldavian	0.63073	324,394	318,241	288,168	CEW21f	51-AADC-ab	standard moldavia		80.00	254,593	1A.u.	10	7	8	2	2		pnb	b
11631	Mordvinian	0.03757	19,323	18,956	17,165	MSW51i	41-AADA-a	erzya		61.00	11,563	2....	10	8	9	2	1	Mordvin: Erzya*	PN.	b
11632	Ossetian (Ossete, Iron)	0.01233	6,342	6,221	5,633	CNT24e	58-ABBA	oseti cluster		46.00	2,862	2....	9	5	8	1	1	Ossete*	PN.	b
11633	Polish (Pole)	2.30000	1,182,926	1,160,488	1,050,823	CEW22i	53-AAAC-c	polski		88.00	1,021,229	2A.uh	10	8	11	2	1	Polish	PNB	b
11634	Romanian	0.30000	154,295	151,368	137,064	CEW21i	51-AADC-a	limba românească		80.00	121,094	3A.u.	10	8	9	3	3	Romanian	PNB	b
11635	Russian	20.07023	10,322,430	10,126,631	9,169,679	CEW22j	53-AAAE-d	russkiy	84	72.00	7,291,174	4B.uh	10	8	9	4	3	Russian	PNB	b
11636	Ruthene (Ruthenian)	1.13000	581,176	570,153	516,274	CEW22k	53-AAAE-a	rusyn		90.20	514,278	1c.uh	10	7	11	4	3		pnb	b
11637	Serb	0.00500	2,572	2,523	2,284	CEW22l	53-AAAG-a	standard srpski		78.00	1,968	1Asuh	10	8	9	3	1	Serbian*	PNB	b
11638	Slovak	0.01544	7,941	7,790	7,054	CEW22m	53-AAAD-b	slovensky		78.00	6,077	1Asuh	10	8	8	4	3	Slovak	PNB	b
11639	Spaniard	0.00142	730	716	649	CEW21k	51-AABB-c	general español		96.00	688	2B.uh	10	9	15	2	1	Spanish	PNB	b
11640	Tabasaran	0.00181	931	913	827	CEW17b	42-BCAA-d	tabarasan		0.00	0	2....	0	2	2	0	0	Tabassaran	P..	b
11641	Tajik	0.00864	4,444	4,359	3,947	CNT24g	58-AACC-j	tajiki		0.00	0	2asu.	0	3	3	0	1	Tajik*	PNB	b
11642	Tatar	0.16885	86,842	85,195	77,144	MSY41h	44-AABB-e	tatar		1.50	1,278	2c.u.	6	4	8	0	1	Tatar: Kazan	PNb	b
11643	Turkmen	0.00661	3,400	3,335	3,020	MSY41k	44-AABA-e	turkmen		0.00	0	3c.u.	0	3	2	0	1	Turkmen	PNB	b
11644	Udmurt	0.01668	8,579	8,416	7,621	MSW51k	41-AAEA-c	udmurt		55.00	4,629	2....	10	5	8	2	0	Udmurt	Pn.	.
11645	Ukrainian	70.48050	36,249,211	35,561,627	32,201,105	CEW22p	53-AAAE-b	ukrainskiy		88.60	31,507,602	3A.uh	10	7	10	4	2	Ukrainian	PNB	b
11646	Uzbek	0.03952	20,326	19,940	18,056	MSY41l	44-AABD-a	central uzbek		0.00	0	1A.u.	0	3	6	1	2	Uzbek*	PNb	b
11647	Vlach Gypsy (Rusurja)	0.02000	10,286	10,091	9,138	CNN25f	59-ACBA-a	vlach-romani		70.00	7,064	1a...	10	4	7	0	1	Romani: Finnish*	PN.	b
11648	West Circassian (Kjax)	0.00134	689	676	612	CEW17a	42-AAAA-a	adyghe		0.10	1	2a...	5	3	3	0	1	Adyghe	PN.	.
11649	Yakut	0.00120	617	605	548	MSY41m	44-AABE-a	yakut		56.00	339	2....	10	5	8	1	1	Yakut	P..	b
11650	other minor peoples	0.10000	51,432	50,456	45,688	...				48.00	24,219		9	7	7	5	0			
	United Arab Emirates	**100.00000**	**2,209,731**	**2,441,436**	**3,283,949**					**10.76**	**262,744**									
11651	Bengali	2.99000	66,071	72,999	98,190	CNN25b	59-AAFT-e	west bengali		1.00	730	1Asuh	6	4	4	0	0	Bengali: Musalmani*	PNB	b
11652	Black African	0.30000	6,629	7,324	9,852	NAB57j	99-AUSM-q	ki-unguja		0.07	5	1Asu.	4	3	1	0	0		pnb	b
11653	British	0.80000	17,678	19,531	26,272	CEW19i	52-ABAC-b	standard-english		66.00	12,891	3Bsuh	10	9	13	5	3		PNB	b
11654	Central Thai (Siamese)	0.21400	4,729	5,225	7,028	MSY49d	47-AAAB-d	central thai		2.00	104	3asuh	6	4	8	1	0	Thai*	PNB	b
11655	Dutch	0.04300	950	1,050	1,412	CEW19h	52-ABCA-a	algemeen-nederlands		70.00	735	2Bsuh	10	9	13	0	0	Dutch	PNB	b
11656	Eastern Pathan	5.12800	113,315	125,197	168,401	CNT24a	58-ABDA-c	pakhto		1.00	1,252	1as..	6	4	5	0	0	Pashto*	PNB	b
11657	Egyptian Arab	6.20000	137,003	151,369	203,605	CMT30	12-AACF-a	masri		20.00	30,274	2Asuh	9	7	8	5	3	Arabic*	PNB	b
11658	Filipino (Pilipino)	3.36400	74,335	82,130	110,472	MSY44o	31-CKAA-a	proper tagalog		90.00	73,917	4Bs..	10	9	11	5	1	Tagalog	PNB	b
11659	French	0.28500	6,298	6,958	9,359	CEW21b	51-AABI-d	general français		76.00	5,288	1B.uh	10	9	14	5	1	French	PNB	b
11660	German	0.10000	2,210	2,441	3,284	CEW19m	52-ABCE-a	standard hoch-deutsch		80.00	1,953	2B.uh	10	9	13	5	3	German*	PNB	b
11661	Gulf Arab (Emirian)	12.21500	269,919	298,221	401,134	CMT30	12-AACF-i	kuwayti-qatari		1.20	3,579	1Asuh	6	4	6	5	3		pnb	b
11662	Gulf Bedouin	9.40000	207,715	229,495	308,691	CMT30	12-AACD	badawi-sahara cluster		0.02	46	0a...	3	2	3	0	0		PN.	b
11663	Indo-Pakistani	1.00000	22,097	24,414	32,839	CNN25g	59-AAFO-e	general hindi		4.00	977	3Asuh	6	4	8	5	3		PNB	b
11664	Iraqi Arab	0.48200	10,651	11,768	15,829	CMT30	12-AACF-g	syro-mesopotamian		0.80	94	1Asuh	5	4	3	5	2		pnb	b
11665	Japanese	0.20000	4,419	4,883	6,568	MSY45a	45-CAAA-a	koku-go		2.00	98	1B.uh	6	4	3	5	0	Japanese	PNB	b
11666	Jordanian Arab	3.44100	76,037	84,010	113,001	CMT30	12-AACF-f	syro-palestinian		6.00	5,041	1Asuh	7	5	8	5	2	Arabic: Lebanese*	PNb	b
11667	Lebanese Arab	1.72100	38,029	42,017	56,517	CMT30	12-AACF-f	syro-palestinian		30.00	12,605	1Asuh	9	7	8	5	2	Arabic: Lebanese*	PNb	b
11668	Malay	0.29900	6,607	7,300	9,819	MSY44k	31-PHAB-b	bahasa-malaysia		0.50	36	1asuh	5	3	5	0	0	Malay	PNB	b
11669	Malayali	7.07300	156,294	172,683	232,274	CNN23b	49-EBEB-a	malayalam		34.00	58,712	2Asu.	9	7	10	5	3	Malayalam	PNB	b
11670	Omani Arab	4.11000	90,820	100,343	134,970	CMT30	12-AACF-l	omani		0.10	100	1Asuh	5	3	2	0	1		pnb	b
11671	Palestinian Arab	3.30000	72,921	80,567	108,370	CMT30	12-AACF-f	syro-palestinian		10.00	8,057	1Asuh	8	5	8	5	3	Arabic: Lebanese*	Pnb	b
11672	Persian	5.00200	110,531	122,121	164,263	CNT24f	58-AACC-ca	west farsi		0.10	122	1asu.	5	3	2	0	0	Farsi, Western	PNB	b
11673	Punjabi	3.00000	66,292	73,243	98,518	CNN25n	59-AAFE-c	general panjabi		2.00	1,465	1Asu.	6	4	8	5	0		PNB	b
11674	Saudi Arab	4.00000	88,389	97,657	131,358	CMT30	12-AACF-k	central `anazi		0.09	88	4Asuh	4	3	2	0	2		pnb	b
11675	Shihuh	0.40000	8,839	9,766	13,136	CMT30	12-AACF-kq	shihu		0.10	10	1csuh	5	2	3	0	0		pnb	b
11676	Sindhi	1.50000	33,146	36,622	49,259	CNN25p	59-AAFF-a	standard sindhi		10.00	3,662	1as..	8	4	2	1	0	Sindhi	PNB	b
11677	Sinhalese	1.78200	39,377	43,506	58,520	CNN25q	59-ABBA-aa	standard sinhala		10.00	4,351	1asuh	8	5	7	5	0		PNB	b
11678	Somali (Issa)	1.78100	39,355	43,482	58,487	CMT33e	14-GAGA-a	af-soomaali		0.04	17	2A...	3	3	2	0	0	Somali	PNB	b
11679	Southern Baluch	7.12800	157,510	174,026	234,080	CNT24b	58-AABA-ce	balochi-émigré		0.02	35	1.s..	3	3	1	0	1		p..	b
11680	Sudanese Arab	1.00000	22,097	24,414	32,839	CMT30	12-AACF-c	sudani		1.00	244	4Asuh	6	4	2	1	0	Arabic: Sudan	PNb	b
11681	Syrian Arab	1.37600	30,406	33,594	45,187	CMT30	12-AACF-f	syro-palestinian		9.00	3,023	1Asuh	7	5	8	4	1	Arabic: Lebanese*	PNb	b
11682	Telugu	3.80000	83,970	92,775	124,790	CNN23d	49-DBAB-a	telugu		10.00	9,277	2Asu.	8	7	11	0	0	Telugu	PNB	b
11683	Turk	0.04000	884	977	1,314	MSY41j	44-AABA-a	osmanli		0.00	0	1A.u.	0	1	1	0	0	Turkish	PNB	b
11684	USA White	1.20000	26,517	29,297	39,407	CEW19s	52-ABAC-s	general american		74.00	21,680	1Bsuh	10	9	13	5	3	English*	PNB	b
11685	Urdu	0.30000	6,629	7,324	9,852	CNN25r	59-AAFO-d	standard urdu		0.07	5	2Asuh	4	3	2	0	0	Urdu	PNB	b
11686	Western Pathan (Afghani)	2.00000	44,195	48,829	65,679	CNT24a	58-ABDA-a	pashto		0.10	49	1As..	5	3	4	0	0		pnb	b
11687	Yemeni Arab	0.82600	18,252	20,166	27,125	CMT30	12-AACF-n	yemeni		0.05	10	1Asuh	4	3	2	0	0		pnb	b
11688	Zott Gypsy (Nawar)	0.70000	15,468	17,090	22,988	CNN25f	12-AACF-i	kuwayti-qatari		0.09	15	1Asuh	4	2	0	0	0		pnb	b
11689	other minor peoples	1.50000	33,146	36,622	49,259	...				6.00	2,197		7	4	2	3	5			
	United States of America (USA)	**100.00000**	**267,019,845**	**278,357,141**	**325,572,586**					**68.91**	**191,827,633**									
11690	Abnaki-Penobscot	0.00040	1,068	1,113	1,302	MIR38a	62-AEAC	abenaki cluster		91.30	1,017	0....	10	9	11	5	0	Abenaqui*	P..	b
11691	Achumawi (Pitt River)	0.00034	908	946	1,107	MIR38a	63-TCBA-a	achumawi		78.00	738	0....	10	9	3	5	0		...	b
11692	Afghani Pathan	0.01559	41,628	43,396	50,757	CNT24a	58-ABDA-a	pashto		2.00	868	1As..	6	4	5	5	0		pnb	b
11693	African American (Black)	3.00000	8,010,595	8,350,714	9,767,178	NFB68a	52-ABAE-a	talkin-black		79.00	6,597,064	0B.uh	10	10	12	5	4		pnb	b
11694	Afro-Seminole Creole	0.05000	133,510	139,179	162,786	NFB68b	52-ABAF-c	afro-seminole-creole		90.00	125,261	1c..h	10	9	11	5	1		pn.	.
11695	Ahtena (Copper River)	0.00027	721	752	879	MIR38a	63-GCAB	shuswap cluster		80.00	601	0....	10	7	7	5	0		...	b

Continued opposite

Table 8-2 continued

Ref 1	D 28	aC 29	CG% 30	r 31	E 32	U 33	W 34	e 35	R 36	T 37	Locations, civil divisions, literacy, religions, church history, denominations, dioceses, church growth, missions, agencies, ministries, movements 38
EVANGELIZATION								EVANGELISM			ADDITIONAL DESCRIPTIVE DATA
11578	2	7	6.66	0	94.00	6.00	C	205.86	236	8	Isolated semi-nomads on Mt Moroto, Karamoja District. Animists 40%. D=RCC,Ch of Uganda.
11579	7	8	12.37	1	99.99	0.01	C	576.27	234	10	Teso Province. Also in Kenya. Animists 1%. Y=1912. D=RCC(D-Tororo),CU(D-Mbale,D-Soroti),PAG,PEFA,BCU,KOAB,other AICs. M=CMS,FMB,UBS.
11580	2	7	6.20	0	99.95	0.05	C	468.11	146	10	Northeast Karamoja. Isolated. Bilingual in Karamojong. Animists 5%. D=Ch of Uganda,RCC. M=FSCJ(Verona Fathers).
11581	2	8	7.71	1	99.70	0.30	C	283.60	226	8	Northwest corner. Also in Sudan, Kenya. Animists 10%. D=RCC(D-Moroto),CU(D-Karamoja). M=FSCJ,BCMS.
11582	7	8	4.28	1	99.93	0.07	C	509.17	117	10	Toro Province. Muslims 5%(slowly increasing), animists 1%. D=RCC(D-Fort Portal),CU(D-Ruwenzori),PEFA,UPF,SDA,MM,other AICs. M=CSC,SFM,FFFM,CMS.
11583	2	10	11.42	4	99.95	0.05	C	562.01	230	10	On southwestern border with Rwanda; also in Zaire, Burundi, Tanzania. Refugees from 1962-72 and 1994 genocide in Rwanda. D=RCC(M-Kampala,D-Masaka).
11584	0	9	9.29		93.00	7.00	C	213.85	274	8	Greeks(AGOC), African Jews(Bayudaya), USA Whites, Sudanese, Shona(AACJM), and refugees from all neighbouring countries. Muslims 10%, Animists 10%.
Ukraine											
11585	2	10	2.74	8	81.00	19.00	B	59.13	127	6	Mainly in Abkhazia (Georgia), also Turkey. Nonreligious 40%, Muslims 23%(Sunnis), atheists 17%. D=Georgian Orthodox Ch,AUCECB. M=IBT.
11586	3	7	3.01	6	56.00	44.00	B	8.17	173	4	From Albania, refugees, migrants. Nonreligious 50%, Muslims 25%(Hanafi Sunnis), atheists 21%. D=RCC,SDA,JWs.
11587	0	8	2.53	0	36.00	64.00	A	13.14	246	5	Mostly from Central Asia. Bilinguals in Tajiki, Uzbeki. Muslims 89%(Sunnis, some Shias).
11588	2	6	3.18	6	99.70	0.30	C	352.59	75	9	Gregorians. In 28 countries. Nonreligious 20%, atheists 8%. D=Armenian Apostolic Ch,RCC.
11589	2	10	5.61	5	99.87	0.13	C	482.67	113	10	Eastern-Syriac-speaking Assyrians, in 12 countries. Nonreligious 12%. D=Ancient Ch of the East,ROC.
11590	0	8	0.00	0	20.02	79.98	A	0.01	137	2	From Dagestan (Russia). Lingua franca. Muslims 100%(Shafi Sunnis). M=IBT.
11591	1	8	0.00	1	31.00	69.00	A	0.00	0	1.12	Residents, laborers. 73% monolinguals. Muslims 78%(54% Shias,24% Hanafi Sunnis), nonreligious 20%. D=ROC. M=IBT,CSI.
11592	1	8	0.54	6	55.00	45.00	B	20.07	78	5	Crimean Peninsula. In 15 countries. Many speak Ukrainian or Moldavian as mother tongue. Ethnic groups: Ursari, Karamitika, Roma. Muslims 90%. D=ROC.
11593	1	9	4.01	4	51.00	49.00	B	13.03	258	5	From Bashkiria (Russia). 20% use Tatar as mother tongue. Muslims 72%(Hanafi Sunnis), nonreligious 20%. D=ROC.
11594	1	10	0.54	6	99.72	0.28	C	354.78	36	9	Expatriates, migrants from Bulgaria. Nonreligious 18%, atheists 10%. D=Bulgarian Orthodox Ch. M=LBI.
11595	1	9	4.52	4	63.00	37.00	B	22.99	230	5	From Buryat Mongol (Russia). Lamaist Buddhists 50%, shamanists 20%, nonreligious 20%. D=ROC. M=IBT.
11596	3	8	1.50	5	99.65	0.35	C	315.54	52	9	White Russians, mainly in Belorussia. Nonreligious 30%. D=ROC,RCC,Old Ritualist Chs.
11597	2	10	0.54	1	99.80	0.20	C	356.24	35	9	Ungrike Roma. In Ukraine, Transcarpathia. Dialects in East Hungary, Czechoslovakia, south Poland, Galicia, Romania, USA. Shamanists/animists 20%. D=RCC.
11598	0	8	0.00	0	19.00	81.00	A	0.00	0	1.05	From Chechen, Ingush (Russia). Most religious Muslims in ex-USSR 63%(fervent Hanafi Sunnis), atheists 21%, nonreligious 16%. M=IBT.
11599	1	8	0.54	0	76.00	24.00	B	97.09	48	6	In Chuvashia (Russia). 65% also speak Russian. Muslims 35%(Sunnis), nonreligious 30%. D=ROC.
11600	0	9	0.00	1	26.00	74.00	A	0.00	0	1.11	Tatarized religious Jews; nearly exterminated by Nazis in World War II.
11601	0	7	0.00	1	26.00	74.00	A	0.00	0	1.11	Descendants of 13th-century Mongols. 1944 deported to Uzbek SSR. Literary. Muslims 100%(Hanafi Sunnis). M=IBT.
11602	1	8	0.54	6	99.84	0.16	C	447.63	30	10	Migrant workers from Croatia. In 15 other countries. Nonreligious 15%. D=RCC.
11603	5	10	0.54	6	99.75	0.25	C	391.46	32	9	Immigrants, residents from Czechoslovakia. Nonreligious 20%. D=RCC,ROC,SDA,JWs,AUCECB. M=UBS.
11604	0	8	0.00	0	20.04	79.96	A	0.02	137	2	From southern Dagestan (Russia). 65% speak Russian. Muslims 100%(Shafi Sunnis). M=IBT.
11605	1	9	4.65	0	43.00	57.00	A	15.69	360	5	Upper Circassian, from Kabardinia (Russia). Muslims 88%(Hanafi Sunnis). D=Armenian Apostolic Ch.
11606	3	10	0.54	5	99.67	0.33	C	325.25	35	9	Most speak Ukrainian, Russian. Nonreligious 29%. D=ROC,RCC,AUCECB. M=UBS,LBI.
11607	2	10	0.54	5	99.87	0.13	C	489.02	28	10	Immigrants from Finland. Most are bilingual in Ukrainian, Russian. Nonreligious 10%. D=ELC,ROC.
11608	1	10	5.36	1	99.72	0.28	C	315.36	141	9	Also in Moldavia, Kazakhstan. Center: Kishinev. Russian-speakers 77%. Nonreligious 25%. D=95% Russian Orthodox Ch(D-Kishinev & Moldavia). M=IBT.
11609	1	9	0.54	4	98.00	2.00	B	143.08	15	7	From Georgia. Nonreligious/atheists 55%, Muslims 5%(Sunnis,Shias). D=Georgian Orthodox Ch.
11610	2	10	0.54	8	99.77	0.23	C	427.19	30	10	Long-time residents from Volga or Germany, Kazakhstan, Kirghizia. Nonreligious 20%. D=GELC,AUCECB.
11611	1	10	2.13	7	99.90	0.10	C	522.31	54	10	19th-century immigrants from Greece to Crimea. Romeos retain Greek language; Urum retain Turkish. Nonreligious 10%. D=Greek Orthodox Ch/ROC.
11612	0	10	1.96	7	53.00	47.00	B	1.93	135	4	Long-time immigrants, residents. Traders. Mainly Buddhists/folk-religionists 50%, nonreligious/atheists 45%.
11613	2	10	1.24	6	99.76	0.24	C	393.90	51	9	Immigrants, refugees from Hungary. Nonreligious 19%. D=RCC,Reformed Ch in Carpatho-Ukraine. M=LBI.
11614	0	8	3.45	0	22.00	78.00	A	0.80	555	3	Nomadic non-Romany (Pre-romany) Gypsies. Also in Moldavia, Russian Asia, Afghanistan. Related to Arabic, Bangaru. Muslims 99%.
11615	0	10	4.69	5	47.03	52.97	A	0.05	313	2	Religious Jews. Declining annually due to emigration to Israel (but with many returning later). Nonreligious 30%.
11616	0	8	1.81	1	37.00	63.00	A	1.35	191	4	Dzhungarians, from Kalmykia on Volga (Russia). Buddhists 69%(Lamaists), nonreligious 29%.
11617	0	10	0.00	1	26.00	74.00	A	0.00	0	1.10	In Crimea (city of Galiche), Egypt, Israel, Turkey, USA, Poland, Russia, and Lithuania. 'Readers of the Scriptures'. Heretical Jewish sect rejecting Talmud.
11618	3	9	2.27	0	99.66	0.34	C	262.58	82	8	From Karelia (Russia), also Finland. Bilingual in Russian, Ukrainian. Nonreligious 30%. D=ROC,RCC,ELC.
11619	0	8	0.00	4	36.00	64.00	A	0.00	0	1.10	Labor migrants. Muslims 60%(Hanafi Sunnis, with Sufi influence), nonreligious 30%, atheists 10%. M=ROC,CSI.
11620	0	8	0.00	4	32.00	68.00	A	0.00	0	1.10	Mainly based in Kirghizia; some from China, Afghanistan, Turkey. Muslims 45%(Hanafi Sunnis), nonreligious 45%, atheists 10%. M=IBT,CSI.
11621	1	9	2.27	0	82.00	18.00	B	119.72	109	7	From South Komi (Russia), near Ural Mountains. Animists/shamanists 40%, nonreligious 20%. D=Russian Orthodox Ch.
11622	1	9	3.43	0	76.00	24.00	B	91.54	160	6	From North Komi (Russia). Pastoralists, hunters. Animists/shamanists 46%, nonreligious 21%. D=Russian Orthodox Ch.
11623	2	10	5.27	6	84.00	16.00	B	61.32	192	6	Immigrants from Korea. 45% speak Russian, Ukrainian. Nonreligious 40%, shamanists 20%, Buddhists 15%, atheists 5%. D=Methodist Ch, Reformed Ch. M=CSI.
11624	0	9	0.00	1	29.01	70.99	A	0.01	0	2	From southern Dagestan (Russia), also Turkey. Many are trilingual. Muslims 100%(Shafi,Hanafi Sunnis).
11625	0	8	0.00	0	17.00	83.00	A	0.00	0	1.05	Widely scattered from Ukraine to Central Asia. Lingua franca. Fluent in 3 languages. Muslims 100%(Shafi Sunnis).
11626	5	9	0.54	5	99.89	0.11	C	510.01	31	10	Found in 25 countries, mainly Latvia. Nonreligious 9%. D=ROC,ELCL,RCC,RCL,CB.
11627	0	8	0.00	0	20.01	79.99	A	0.00	0	1.05	From Dagestan (Russia). Lingua franca. Muslims 100%(Shafi Sunnis). M=IBT.
11628	4	8	0.54	5	99.91	0.09	C	528.11	9	10	Mainly from Lithuania. Nonreligious 8%. D=RCC,ELCL,ERCL,ROC.
11629	1	9	0.54	0	99.90	0.10	C	453.33	31	10	Traditionally Orthodox, from Mari (Russia). Muslims 5%, shamanists 5%. D=ROC. M=IBT.
11630	2	9	0.54	6	99.80	0.20	C	405.88	30	10	Immigrants, transients from Moldavia, Romania. Nonreligious 15%. D=Russian Orthodox Ch, Romanian Orthodox Ch.
11631	1	9	0.54	7	99.61	0.39	C	256.04	13	8	Russian-speakers mainly. Nonreligious 35%. D=Russian Orthodox Ch.
11632	1	8	0.54	0	88.00	12.00	B	147.75	51	7	From Caucasus Mountains, North Ossetia (Russia). Muslims 39%(Sunnis), nonreligious 15%. D=ROC.
11633	4	10	1.25	6	99.88	0.12	C	507.49	22	10	Poles in Western Ukraine. 29% speak Polish as mother tongue. Nonreligious 9%. D=RCC(3 Dioceses),ROC,CEF,Polish Pentecostal Movement/CWE. M=UBS.
11634	3	10	2.38	6	99.80	0.20	C	438.00	64	10	Settlers from Romania. Nonreligious 15%. D=Romanian Orthodox Ch,RCC,Russian Orthodox Ch.
11635	8	9	0.66	7	99.72	0.28	C	386.31	12	9	In 70 countries. Nonreligious 20%, atheists 8%. D=ROC,RCC,AUCECB,Old Ritualists,CEF,CCECB,SDA,IPKh. R=FEBC,HCJB,TWR,KNLS,VERTIAS,local stations.
11636	3	9	0.54	6	99.90	0.10	C	504.38	10	10	Carpathians. Eastern Slavs/Ukrainians. Transcarpathian Oblast, Ukraine. Also in Czechoslovakia, USA, Romania. D=RCC(Ruthenian rite: D-Mukachevo),ROC.
11637	1	8	0.54	6	99.78	0.22	C	401.42	10	10	Migrant workers from Serbia. Also in 16 countries. Nonreligious 15%, some Muslims 5%. D=Serbian Orthodox Ch.
11638	4	10	0.54	6	99.78	0.22	C	418.50	31	10	Immigrants from Slovakia. Also in USA, Yugoslavia, Canada. Nonreligious 19%. D=ROC,RCC,RCCS,SECAC.
11639	1	9	0.54	8	99.96	0.04	C	585.16	24	10	Expatriates from Spain, in business, commerce. Strong Catholics. Nonreligious 4%. D=RCC.
11640	0	8	0.00	0	20.00	80.00	A	0.00	0	1.06	From southern Dagestan. Muslims 100%(Shafi Sunnis).
11641	0	8	0.00	4	39.00	61.00	A	0.00	0	1.12	Labor migrants from Tajikistan, Uzbekistan, Afghanistan. Trilingual. Muslims 90%(Hanafi Sunnis), nonreligious 10%. M=CSI.
11642	1	8	4.97	6	44.50	55.50	A	2.43	355	4	Across Ukraine and Russia. 70% bilingual in Russian. Muslims 83%(Hanafi Sunnis), nonreligious 15%. D=ROC.
11643	0	8	0.00	1	29.00	71.00	A	0.00	0	1.11	From Turkmenistan, Iran, Afghanistan. Devout Muslims 95%(Hanafi Sunnis), nonreligious 5%. M=IBT.
11644	0	7	1.92	0	92.00	8.00	B	184.69	87	7	Orginally from Udmurtia (Russia, near Urals). Traditionally Orthodox. Shamanists 45%, with Muslim elements.
11645	9	8	0.38	6	99.89	0.11	C	519.36	27	10	In 20 countries. Nonreligious/atheists 11%. D=UOC/ROC(E-Ukraine; 27 million),Ukrainian Catholic Ch(4 million; illegal 1945-90),UAOC,OB,AUCECB,CEF,CCECB.
11646	0	9	0.00	5	42.00	58.00	A	0.00	0	1.12	Russian spoken by 55%. Literates 100%. Muslims 80%(Hanafi Sunnis), nonreligious/atheists 20%. M=ROC,CSI.
11647	1	8	0.54	6	99.70	0.30	C	298.93	37	8	Also in Moldavia, western Russia. In 25 countries. Ethnic groups: Sarvi, Voloxuja, Chache, Lovari. Muslims 20%, nonreligious 10%. D=Ukrainian Orthodox Ch.
11648	0	0	0.00	0	23.10	76.90	A	0.08	119	2	Lower Circassian. In 10 countries. Muslims 97%(Hanafi Sunnis), nonreligious 2%. M=IBT.
11649	1	0	1.49	2	89.00	11.00	B	181.91	74	7	From Yakut (Russia). 60% speak Russian. Nomadic. Shamanists 30%. Nominal Christians with shamanist survivals, 14%. D=ROC.
11650	0	0	8.10		74.00	26.00	B	129.64	300	7	Other Europeans, other Asians, other Levantines, other Scandinavians, other Eurasians. Nonreligious 20%, Muslims 10%.
United Arab Emirates											
11651	0	6	4.38	6	47.00	53.00	A	1.71	335	4	Workers from Bangladesh and India. Muslims 78%(Hanafi Sunnis), Hindus 15%, Baha'is.
11652	0	8	1.62	5	37.07	62.93	A	0.09	228	2	Blacks from Zanzibar and East Africa (originally as slaves). 59% still retain Swahili as mother tongue; 41% use only now Arabic. Muslims 100%(Shafi Sunnis).
11653	3	9	7.06	8	99.66	0.34	C	344.48	157	9	Expatriates from Britain, in business. Nonreligious 14%. D=Anglican Ch(D-Cyprus & The Gulf),CB,JWs.
11654	0	7	2.37	6	55.00	45.00	B	4.01	147	4	Laborers from Thailand, Singapore. Theravada Buddhists 98%.
11655	0	0	4.39	6	99.70	0.30	C	309.15	119	9	Expatriates from the Netherlands, in business. Nonreligious 15%. D=RCC, NHK.
11656	0	7	4.95	5	45.00	55.00	A	1.64	437	4	Pakistani (Eastern) Pashtu. Workers from Pakistan: laborers, drivers. Literary dialect: Yusufzai. Muslims 98%(Sunnis).
11657	4	9	9.10	8	92.00	8.00	B	67.16	292	6	Workers, professionals from Egypt. Muslims 80%(Shafi Sunnis). D=Coptic Orthodox Ch,RCC,CEC,CB.
11658	1	10	9.32	5	99.90	0.10	C	535.45	168	10	Laborers from Philippines: hotel workers, nurses, housemaids, store clerks, technicians. Muslims 10%. D=RCC,INC,PIC,PEC,UCCP. M=CBFMS.
11659	2	9	6.47	8	99.76	0.24	C	416.10	136	10	Expatriates from France: business executives, oil company employees, agricultural consultants, et alii. Nonreligious 17%. D=RCC(VA-Arabia),JWs. M=OFMCap.
11660	4	9	5.42	8	99.80	0.20	C	458.44	114	10	Expatriates from Germany, in commerce. Nonreligious 11%. D=RCC,EAM,CB,JWs.
11661	3	9	6.06	7	61.20	38.80	B	2.68	303	4	Citizens, ruling elite; 50% sedentary, 50% nomads. Muslims 98%(Sunnis of various schools,some Shias). D=RCC,AC,EAM. M=OFMCap,FI,MEM.
11662	0	7	3.90	7	32.02	67.98	A	0.02	394	2	Citizen nomads, tent-dwellers. Muslims 100%(Sunnis).
11663	4	9	4.69	7	67.00	33.00	B	9.78	233	4	Migrant workers, traders. Hindus 60%, Muslims 36%. D=RCC,AC,CB,IPC.
11664	2	9	2.98	7	53.80	46.20	B	1.57	187	4	Migrant workers from Iraq. Muslims 99%(60% Shias,39% Hanafi Sunnis). D=RCC,AC/ECJME.
11665	0	9	4.69	7	56.00	44.00	B	4.08	266	4	Expatriates from Japan. Buddhists 58%, New-Religionists 25%, nonreligious 14%.
11666	2	9	5.99	8	68.00	32.00	B	14.89	270	5	Workers from Jordan. Muslims 94%(Shafi Sunnis,Alawis). D=RCC,GOC.
11667	2	9	8.15	8	95.00	5.00	B	104.02	255	7	Refugees from Lebanon. Muslims 67%(Sunnis,Shias), Nonreligious 2%. D=RCC(Maronites),GOC.
11668	0	9	3.65	5	47.50	52.50	A	0.86	251	3	Workers from Malaysia, Singapore, Indonesia, Brunei. Muslims 98%(Shafi Sunnis).
11669	5	9	9.07	4	99.34	0.66	B	127.82	268	7	Migrant workers from South India: medical doctors, engineers, laborers. Hindus 46%, Muslims 19%, Baha'is. D=RCC,OSCE,MTSC,CSI,IPC.
11670	0	8	2.33	7	43.10	56.90	A	0.15	193	3	Migrants from Oman. Muslims 100%(Hinawis,Ibadi Kharijites,Ghafiris). M=CSI.
11671	3	9	7.30	8	75.00	25.00	B	27.37	292	5	Refugees, migrant workers. Muslims 85%(Shafi Sunnis,Alawi Shias,Druzes). Nonreligious/atheists 5%. D=RCC,Greek Orthodox Ch,JWs.
11672	0	8	2.53	5	42.10	57.90	A	0.15	210	3	Western Farsi. Also in Iran, Iraq, Bahrain, Oman, Qatar, former USSR, USA, Canada. Merchants, traders. Muslims 60%(Imami Shias), Baha'is 40%.
11673	0	9	5.11	5	59.00	41.00	B	4.30	286	4	Migrant workers from Pakistan, India. Muslims 79%, Hindus 10%, Sikhs 8%, Baha'is.
11674	0	9	4.58	7	47.09	52.91	A	0.15	307	3	Muslims 100%(Shafi, Maliki,and Hanbali Sunnis). M=CSI,FI.
11675	0	7	2.33	1	32.10	67.90	A	0.11	259	3	Cave-dwellers. Unwritten language, related to Arabic. Some literates in Arabic. Muslims 100%.
11676	0	9	6.08	4	58.00	42.00	B	21.17	334	5	Migrants from Pakistan. Muslims 89%(Hanafi Sunnis), Baha'is.
11677	0	9	6.26	6	62.00	38.00	B	22.63	302	5	Housemaids, cleaners, laborers, professionals from Sri Lanka. Theravada Buddhists 90%.
11678	0	9	2.87	5	40.04	59.96	A	0.05	323	2	Migrant laborers from Somalia, Djibouti, Ethiopia, Kenya, Yemen. Muslims 100%(Shafi and Hanafi Sunnis).
11679	0	8	3.62	1	21.02	78.98	A	0.01	602	2	Long-time residents, originally from Baluchistan (Pakistan); also in Oman, Iran. Muslims 100%(Sunnis). M=FI.
11680	0	9	3.25	7	47.00	53.00	A	1.71	230	4	Migrant laborers from Sudan. Muslims 99%(mostly Maliki Sunnis).
11681	1	9	6.85	8	68.00	32.00	B	22.33	304	5	Migrants from Syria. Muslims 90%(81% Hanafi Sunnis,8% Alawis,1% Druzes). D=Syrian Orthodox Ch.
11682	0	0	7.07	5	55.00	45.00	B	20.07	402	5	Migrant workers from India. Hindus 80%, Muslims 8%. D=CSI.
11683	0	0	0.00	8	27.00	73.00	A	0.00	0	1.09	Migrant workers from Turkey. Muslims 100%.
11684	5	9	7.98	8	99.74	0.26	C	402.44	163	10	Expatriates from USA, in commerce, oil industry. Nonreligious 12%. D=AC/ECJME,RCC,EAM,CB,JWs.
11685	0	9	1.62	5	45.07	54.93	A	0.11	161	3	Migrant workers from Pakistan, India, Afghanistan, Oman, Qatar, Fiji, Bahrain, South Africa, Germany, Thailand, Mauritius. Muslims 100%(Hanafi Sunnis).
11686	0	7	3.97	5	38.10	61.90	A	0.13	445	3	Workers from Afghanistan, and refugees; also in Iran. Language is unintelligible with Eastern Pashtu. Drivers, shopkeepers, laborers. Muslims 99%(Sunnis).
11687	0	8	2.33	7	38.05	61.95	A	0.06	218	2	Migrant workers from Yemen. Muslims 100%(50% Zaydis,40% Sunnis,5% Ismailis, 5% others).
11688	0	7	2.75	7	35.09	64.91	A	0.11	295	3	Arab Gypsy, Muslim Gypsy. Nomads. Muslims 100%(Sunnis).
11689	0	9	5.54		33.00	67.00	A	7.22	460	4	Koreans(M=PCK-Tonghap), Tunisians, Algerians, Moroccans, Libyans, other Arabs, other Levantines, Turks, Indonesians, Chinese, other Asians, Dutch, Italians.
United States of America (USA)											
11690	0	10	1.31	0	99.91	0.09	C	454.21	44	10	Near Bangor, Maine (Penobscot). The Abnaki are in Canada. Language nearly extinct; elderly speakers only. 99% use English only.
11691	0	10	1.30	0	99.78	0.22	C	321.71	53	9	Northeast California. Language nearly extinct. 99% use English only. Animists 5%.
11692	0	9	4.56	5	49.00	51.00	A	3.57	379	4	Refugees, workers from Afghanistan. Muslims 98%(Hanafi Sunnis).
11693	11	10	1.19	8	99.79	0.21	C	435.40	33	10	Muslims 3%. D=CoGiC,CoGiCI,AMEC,AMEZC,CMEC,AOHCOG,COLJCAF,CC,EOC,JWs,and many others. T=CBN,TBN,LESEA. R=1,000 local stations.
11694	1	10	1.31	1	99.90	0.10	C	463.18	39	10	English-based creole in Texas, Oklahoma; also in Mexico. Similar to Sea Islands Creole, Bahamas Creole. D=NACNA.
11695	0	10	1.31	0	99.80	0.20	C	347.48	51	9	South central Alaska, Copper river and adjacent areas. Speakers middle-aged. Only 33% use the language.

Continued overleaf

Table 8-2 continued

PEOPLE		POPULATION				IDENTITY CODE		LANGUAGE		CHURCH		MINISTRY						SCRIPTURE		
Ref 1	Ethnic name 2	P% 3	In 1995 4	In 2000 5	In 2025 6	Race 7	Language 8	Autoglossonym 9	S 10	AC 11	Members 12	Jayuh 13-17	d 18	wa 19	xc 20	mc 21	mi 22	Biblioglossonym 23	Pub 24-26	ss 27
11696	Alabama	0.00024	641	668	781	MIR38a	65-FBAA-b	alabama		80.00	534	0....	10	8	7	5	1		...	b
11697	Amerasian	0.00624	16,662	17,369	20,316	MSY43	52-ABAD-a	south-asian-english		85.00	14,764	0B.uh	10	9	9	5	3		...	b
11698	American Part-Indian	3.50136	9,349,326	9,746,286	11,399,468	MIR38b	52-ABAC-s	general american		75.00	7,309,714	1Bsuh	10	8	8	5	3	English*	PNB	b
11699	Anglo-Australian	0.02500	66,755	69,589	81,393	CEW19c	52-ABAC-x	general australian		64.00	44,537	1Bsuh	10	9	12	5	3		pnb	b
11700	Anglo-Canadian	0.40000	1,068,079	1,113,429	1,302,290	CEW19d	52-ABAC-r	general canadian		68.00	757,131	1Bsuh	10	9	13	5	3		pnb	b
11701	Anglo-Romani Gypsy (Rom)	0.04012	107,128	111,677	130,620	CNN25f	59-AGAA-ab	anglo-romani-america		80.00	89,342	0....	10	10	8	5	1		...	b
11702	Arapaho	0.00226	6,035	6,291	7,358	MIR38a	62-ABAB	hinana'eina cluster		90.00	5,662	0....	10	9	11	5	1	Arapahoe	P..	b
11703	Arikara	0.00045	1,202	1,253	1,465	MIR38a	64-BAAA-a	arikara		94.90	1,189	0....	10	9	11	5	0		...	.
11704	Armenian	0.12388	330,784	344,829	403,319	CEW14	57-AAAA-b	ashkharik		90.00	310,346	4A.u.	10	10	13	5	3	Armenian: Modern, Eastern	PNB	b
11705	Armenian	0.18000	480,636	501,043	586,031	CEW14	52-ABAC-s	general american		90.00	450,939	1Bsuh	10	10	13	5	3	English*	PNB	b
11706	Assiniboin	0.00070	1,869	1,948	2,279	MIR38a	64-AACA-a	assiniboine		96.10	1,873	0....	10	8	11	4	1		pnb	b
11707	Assyrian	0.02081	55,567	57,926	67,752	CMT31	12-AAAA-d	east syriac		90.00	52,134	1as..	10	10	11	5	3	Syriac: Ancient*	PNB	b
11708	Atsugewi	0.00009	240	251	293	MIR38a	63-TCBB-a	atsugewi		20.00	50	0....	9	5	2	3	0		...	.
11709	Austrian	0.34771	928,455	967,876	1,132,048	CEW19f	52-ABCF-b	donau-bayrisch-t.		83.00	803,337	0B.uh	10	9	13	5	3		pn.	b
11710	Bahamian	0.00848	22,643	23,605	27,609	NFB68a	52-ABAF-n	bahamian-creole		84.00	19,828	1a..h	10	8	8	5	3		pn.	b
11711	Basque	0.02475	66,087	68,893	80,579	CEW16	40-AAAA-a	general euskara		94.00	64,760	3....	10	9	15	5	2	Basque	PNB	b
11712	Bengali	0.05100	136,180	141,962	166,042	CNN25b	59-AAFT-e	west bengali		1.00	1,420	1Asuh	6	5	9	5	3	Bengali: Musalmani*	PNB	b
11713	Bering Eskimo (Siorarmiut	0.00045	1,202	1,253	1,465	MRY40b	60-ABAB-ab	saint-lawrence		86.00	1,077	0c...	10	8	8	5	1	Eskimo: Yupik, St Lawrence	P..	.
11714	Black Creole (Gullah)	0.05682	151,721	158,163	184,990	NFB68b	52-ABAF-a	sea-island-creole		85.00	134,438	1c..h	10	9	8	5	1	Gullah*	Pn.	b
11715	Black Jew	0.01600	42,723	44,537	52,092	NFB68a	52-ABAE-a	talkin-black		15.00	6,681	0B.uh	8	5	5	5	2		pnb	b
11716	Black Tai (Thai Den)	0.00130	3,471	3,619	4,232	MSY49z	47-AAAD-a	tai-dam		5.00	181	0....	7	5	8	5	2	Tai: Dam*	P..	b
11717	Blackfoot (Siksika, Blood	0.00240	6,408	6,681	7,814	MIR38a	62-AAAA-a	sikasi-ka		82.00	5,478	0a...	10	7	8	4	1	Blackfoot	P..	b
11718	Bolivian Mestizo	0.05000	133,510	139,179	162,786	CLN29	51-AABB-hs	boliviano		98.00	136,395	1B.uh	10	7	12	4	1		pnb	b
11719	British	0.40000	1,068,079	1,113,429	1,302,290	CEW19i	52-ABAC-b	standard-english	100	66.00	734,863	3Bsuh	10	10	13	5	3		PNB	b
11720	Bulgar	0.05000	133,510	139,179	162,786	CEW22b	53-AAAH-b	bulgarski		76.00	105,776	2A.uh	10	9	8	5	3	Bulgarian	PNB	b
11721	Burmese	0.00348	9,292	9,687	11,330	MSY50b	77-AABA-a	bama		3.00	291	4Asu.	6	4	8	5	0	Burmese	PNB	b
11722	Byelorussian	0.02500	66,755	69,589	81,393	CEW22c	53-AAAE-c	bielorusskiy		66.00	45,929	3A.uh	10	9	9	5	3	Byelorussian*	PNB	b
11723	Caboverdian Mestico/Brava	0.02041	54,499	56,813	66,449	NAN58	51-AACA-a	caboverdense		98.00	55,676	1c...	10	7	13	4	1	Crioulo, Upper Guinea	PNB	b
11724	Caddo	0.00081	2,163	2,255	2,637	MIR38a	64-BBAA-a	caddo		90.00	2,029	0....	10	8	11	4	1		...	b
11725	Cahuilla	0.00036	961	1,002	1,172	MIR37z	66-BCCB-a	kavia		80.80	810	0....	10	7	4	3	0		...	b
11726	Cajun (Arcadian, Cajan)	0.40747	1,088,026	1,134,222	1,326,611	CEW21c	51-AABH-o	acadjin		82.00	930,062	0c.uh	10	9	12	5	1		p..	b
11727	Cambodian (Khmer)	0.07546	201,493	210,048	245,677	AUG03b	46-FBAA-b	khmae		5.00	10,502	2A...	7	5	8	5	3	Khmer*	PNB	b
11728	Catawba	0.00023	614	640	749	MIR38a	64-ABAA-a	catawba		95.70	613	0....	10	7	11	3	0		...	b
11729	Cayuga	0.00040	1,068	1,113	1,302	MIR38a	64-CAAD-b	cayuga		91.90	1,023	0....	10	8	11	3	0		p..	b
11730	Central American Mestizo	0.20000	534,040	556,714	651,145	CLN29	51-AABB-h	south americano		90.00	501,043	4B.uh	10	10	13	5	3		pnb	b
11731	Chehalis	0.00009	240	251	293	MIR38a	63-GBAB-a	west chehalis		78.00	195	0....	10	7	3	3	0		...	b
11732	Cherokee	0.02900	77,436	80,724	94,416	MIR38a	64-CABA	tsalagi cluster		72.00	58,121	0....	10	7	8	4	1	Cherokee	PN.	b
11733	Cheyenne	0.00200	5,340	5,567	6,511	MIR38a	62-ACAA	cheyenne cluster		80.00	4,454	0....	10	8	6	4	1	Cheyenne	PN.	b
11734	Chinook (Lower Chinook)	0.00014	374	390	456	MIR38a	63-JAAB-b	clatsop		20.00	78	0....	9	5	2	3	0		...	b
11735	Chinook Creole	0.00005	134	139	163	MIR38b	63-JAAC-a	chinook-wawa		90.00	125	0....	10	8	11	3	0	Chinook*	P..	b
11736	Choctaw-Chickasaw	0.01027	27,423	28,587	33,436	MIR38a	65-FAAA-a	choctaw		95.00	27,158	0....	10	9	11	4	2	Choctaw	PN.	.
11737	Clallam	0.00001	27	28	33	MIR38a	63-GAAF	saanich-clallam cluster		60.00	17	0....	10	6	6	5	0		...	b
11738	Cocopa	0.00023	614	640	749	MIR38a	63-VDCA-a	cocopa		90.00	576	0....	10	8	11	4	2	Cocopa	P..	.
11739	Coeur d'Alene	0.00036	961	1,002	1,172	MIR38a	63-GCBC-a	skitsamish		96.00	962	0....	10	7	11	3	0		...	b
11740	Columbia River Sahaptin	0.00005	134	139	163	MIR38a	63-IAAA-d	umatilla		89.00	124	0....	10	7	11	3	0		p..	b
11741	Columbia-Wenatchi	0.00023	614	640	749	MIR38a	63-GCCA	wenatchi-columbia cluster		80.00	512	0....	10	7	3	3	0		...	b
11742	Comanche	0.00273	7,290	7,599	8,888	MIR37a	66-BABD-a	comanche		94.00	7,143	0....	10	8	12	4	1	Comanche	P..	b
11743	Coos (Hanis)	0.00011	294	306	358	MIR38a	63-MAAA-a	coos		10.00	31	0....	8	7	2	3	0		...	b
11744	Corsican	0.04000	106,808	111,343	130,229	CEW21z	51-AABP-b	central corsu		77.00	85,734	0....	10	8	8	4	1	Italian: Corsican*	P..	b
11745	Creek (Seminole)	0.00909	24,272	25,303	29,595	MIR38a	65-FBBB	muskogee cluster		80.00	20,242	0....	10	10	8	5	3	Muskogee	PN.	b
11746	Croat	0.21884	584,346	609,157	712,483	CEW22d	53-AAAG-b	standard hrvatski		81.00	493,417	2Asuh	10	9	11	4	1	Croatian	PNB	b
11747	Crow	0.00288	7,690	8,017	9,376	MIR38a	64-AAAB-a	absaroka		90.00	7,215	0a...	10	9	11	4	1	Crow	P..	.
11748	Cuban White	0.40000	1,068,079	1,113,429	1,302,290	CLT27	51-AABB-hi	cubano		79.90	889,629	1B.uh	10	9	9	5	1		pnb	b
11749	Cupeno	0.00008	214	223	260	MIR37z	66-BCCA-a	kupa		78.00	174	0....	10	7	3	3	0		...	b
11750	Czech	0.52125	1,391,841	1,450,937	1,697,047	CEW22e	53-AAAD-a	czesky	1	70.00	1,015,656	2Asuh	10	9	13	5	3	Czech	PNB	b
11751	Dakota (Sioux)	0.00800	21,362	22,269	26,046	MIR38a	64-AACA-e	east dakota		72.00	16,033	0....	10	8	8	4	3	Dakota	PNB	b
11752	Danish (Dane)	0.65726	1,755,015	1,829,530	2,139,858	CEW19g	52-AAAD-c	general dansk		79.70	1,458,136	2A.uh	10	9	13	5	1	Danish	PNB	b
11753	Delaware (Lenni-Lenape)	0.00070	1,869	1,948	2,279	MIR38a	62-AEBB-a	munsee		89.30	1,740	0....	10	7	11	3	0	Delaware*	P..	b
11754	Detribalized Amerindian	0.13434	358,714	373,945	437,374	MIR38y	52-ABAC-s	general american		73.00	272,980	1Bsuh	10	8	11	5	1	English*	PNB	b
11755	Diegueno	0.00004	107	111	130	MIR38a	63-VDCA-b	diegueño		80.00	89	0....	10	7	6	3	0		p..	b
11756	Dominican	0.20333	542,931	565,984	661,987	NFB71b	51-AACC-d	dominiquais		96.00	543,344	1cs..	10	8	13	5	3		pnb	.
11757	Dutch	0.50000	1,335,099	1,391,786	1,627,863	CEW19h	52-ABCA-a	algemeen-nederlands	1	64.50	897,702	2Bsuh	10	9	15	5	3	Dutch	PNB	b
11758	Eastern Aleut	0.00090	2,403	2,505	2,930	MRY40a	60-AABA-c	unalaska		80.00	2,004	0....	10	8	7	5	2	Aleut: Eastern	P..	b
11759	Eastern Kanjobal (Conob)	0.02500	66,755	69,589	81,393	MIR37b	68-ADAC-b	east kanjobal		85.00	59,151	0....	10	7	7	4	1	K'anjobal*	PNB	.
11760	Eastern Keres Pueblo	0.00250	6,675	6,959	8,139	MIR38a	63-XAAB	east keres cluster		90.00	6,263	0....	10	8	11	4	1	Keres: Eastern*	P..	.
11761	Eastern Ojibwa (Chippewa)	0.02100	56,074	58,455	68,370	MIR38a	62-ADAF-a	east ojibwa		75.00	43,841	0....	10	8	8	4	1	Ojibwa, Eastern	Pn.	b
11762	Egyptian Arab	0.08300	221,626	231,036	270,225	CMT30	12-AACF-a	masri		50.00	115,518	2Asuh	10	8	8	5	3	Arabic*	PNB	b
11763	English Gypsy	0.40000	1,068,079	1,113,429	1,302,290	CNN25f	52-ABAC-b	standard-english		80.00	890,743	3Bsuh	10	9	8	5	1		PNB	b
11764	Eskimo	0.00690	18,424	19,207	22,465	MRY40b	52-ABAC-s	general american		86.00	16,518	1Bsuh	10	10	8	5	3	English*	PNB	b
11765	Eskimo Creole	0.00100	2,670	2,784	3,256	MRY40b	60-ABBC-b	copper		88.00	2,450	1....	10	8	11	5	3	Eskimo: Copper*	PNb	b
11766	Esperanto	0.00000	0	0	0	CEW21z	51-AAAC-a	proper esperanto		70.00	0	0A...	10	9	2	0	0	Esperanto	PNB	b
11767	Estonian	0.01076	28,731	29,951	35,032	MSW51a	41-AAAC-b	eesti		72.00	21,565	4A.u.	10	10	8	5	2	Estonian: Tallinn	PNB	b
11768	Eurasian	0.00570	15,220	15,866	18,558	MSY43	52-ABAD-a	south-asian-english		90.00	14,280	0B.uh	10	9	13	5	3		...	b
11769	Eyak	0.00001	27	28	33	MIR38a	61-AAAA-a	eyak		10.00	3	0....	8	5	2	3	0		...	b
11770	Fall Indian (Atsina)	0.00055	1,469	1,531	1,791	MIR38a	62-ABAA-a	hitowunena		78.20	1,197	0....	10	7	3	3	0		...	b
11771	Fijian	0.00300	8,011	8,351	9,767	AON08	39-BBAA-b	fiji		84.00	7,015	1.s..	10	10	10	5	3	Fijian*	PNB	b
11772	Filipino	1.17000	3,124,132	3,256,779	3,809,199	MSY44o	31-CKAA-a	proper tagalog		92.00	2,996,236	4Bs..	10	10	13	5	3	Tagalog	PNB	b
11773	Finnish (Finn)	0.26492	707,389	737,424	862,507	MSW51b	41-AAAA-bb	vehicular suomi		86.00	634,184	1A.uh	10	10	12	5	3	Finnish	PNB	b
11774	Flathead-Kalispel	0.00136	3,631	3,786	4,428	MIR38a	63-GCBB-a	flathead		80.00	3,029	0....	10	8	6	4	1		...	b
11775	Flemish	0.00569	15,193	15,839	18,525	CEW19k	52-ABCA-g	oostvlaandersch		90.00	14,255	1Bsuh	10	9	15	5	2		pnb	b
11776	French	0.90000	2,403,179	2,505,214	2,930,153	CEW21b	51-AABI-d	general français	13	70.00	1,753,650	1B.uh	10	10	14	5	3	French	PNB	b
11777	French Cree (Mitchif)	0.00200	5,340	5,567	6,511	MIR38a	62-ADBA-a	mitchif		96.00	5,344	0....	10	9	13	4	1		...	b
11778	French-Canadian	0.87135	2,326,677	2,425,465	2,836,877	CEW21c	51-AABI-ib	français-du-canada		68.00	1,649,316	1B.uh	10	9	15	5	1		pnb	b
11779	Frisian (Western Frisian)	0.01500	40,053	41,754	48,836	CEW19l	52-ABBA-a	west-frysk		72.00	30,063	0....	10	10	11	5	3		pnb	b
11780	German	2.50000	6,675,496	6,958,929	8,139,315	CEW19m	52-ABCE-a	standard hoch-deutsch	14	61.00	4,244,946	2B.uh	10	10	15	5	4	German*	PNB	b
11781	Gheg Albanian	0.04000	106,808	111,343	130,229	CEW13	55-AAAA-b	northwest gheg		58.00	64,579	1a.u.	10	7	8	5	1	Albanian: Gheg*	PN.	b
11782	Greek	0.44645	1,192,110	1,242,725	1,453,519	CEW20	56-AAAA-c	dhimotiki	1	85.00	1,056,317	2B.uh	10	10	11	5	3	Greek: Modern	PNB	b
11783	Greek Cypriot	0.00285	7,610	7,933	9,279	CEW20	56-AAAA-c	dhimotiki		90.00	7,140	2B.uh	10	9	11	5	1	Greek: Modern	PNB	b
11784	Guamanian	0.01756	46,889	48,880	57,171	MSY44d	31-UAAA-d	guam-chamorro		99.00	48,391	1.s..	10	10	13	5	3	Chamorro	P..	b
11785	Guyanese	0.03284	87,689	91,412	106,918	NFB68b	52-ABAG-a	guyanese		85.00	77,701	1.s..	10	9	8	5	2		pn.	b
11786	Haida	0.00045	1,202	1,253	1,465	MIR38a	63-BAAB-a	skidegate		92.90	1,164	0....	10	8	11	4	1	Haida	P..	b
11787	Haitian Black	0.31000	827,762	862,907	1,009,275	NFB69a	51-AACC-b	haitien		89.00	767,987	3As..	10	9	12	5	1	Haitian*	PNB	b
11788	Han (Moosehide, Dawson)	0.00010	267	278	326	MIR38a	61-BAEB-a	han		91.30	254	0....	10	8	11	3	0		pnb	b
11789	Han Chinese	0.03000	80,106	83,507	97,672	MSY42a	52-ABAC	english-mainland cluster		33.90	28,309	3Bsuh	9	5	13	5	3		PNB	b
11790	Han Chinese (Cantonese)	0.16000	427,232	445,371	520,916	MSY42a	79-AAAM-a	central yue		23.00	102,435	3A.uh	9	5	13	5	1	Chinese, Yue	PNB	b
11791	Han Chinese (Fukienese)	0.10000	267,020	278,357	325,573	MSY42a	79-AAAJ-ic	chaozhou		21.00	58,455	1A..h	9	5	13	5	2	Chinese, Min Nan	PNB	b
11792	Han Chinese (Mandarin)	0.30000	801,060	835,071	976,718	MSY42a	79-AAAB-ba	kuo-yü		20.00	167,014	2Bsuh	9	5	13	5	1	Chinese: Kuoyu*	PNB	b
11793	Hawaiian (Hawaii)	0.00100	2,670	2,784	3,256	MPY55a	39-CAQE-b	hawai'i		72.30	2,013	0....	10	6	8	5	1	Hawaiian	PNB	b
11794	Hawaiian American	0.08500	226,967	236,604	276,737	MPY55a	52-ABAC-sd	hawaiian-american		90.00	212,943	1Bsuh	10	10	11	5	3		pnb	.
11795	Hawaiian Creole	0.10000	267,020	278,357	325,573	MPY53	52-ABAI-g	hawaiian-creole		90.00	250,521	1csuh	10	9	11	5	1	Hawaii Creole English	pnb	b
11796	Hidatsa	0.00050	1,335	1,392	1,628	MIR38a	64-AAAA-a	hidatsa		80.00	1,113	0....	10	8	5	4	1		...	b
11797	Hocak (Winnebago)	0.00227	6,061	6,319	7,390	MIR38a	64-AACD	winnebago cluster		90.00	5,687	0....	10	9	12	4	1	Winnebago*	P..	b
11798	Holikachuk	0.00007	187	195	228	MIR38a	61-BABA-b	holikachuk		78.00	152	0c...	10	7	3	3	0		p..	b
11799	Hopi (Hopitu-Shinumu)	0.00295	7,877	8,212	9,604	MIR37z	66-BDAA-a	hopi		85.00	6,980	0....	10	10	10	5	1	Hopi	PN.	.
11800	Houma (Half-Choctaw)	0.00146	3,898	4,064	4,753	MIR38b	52-ABAC-s	general american		90.00	3,658	1Bsuh	10	8	11	4	1	English*	PNB	b
11801	Hungarian	0.63620	1,698,780	1,770,908	2,071,293	MSW51g	41-BAAA-a	general magyar	1	77.70	1,375,996	2A.u.	10	10	13	5	3	Hungarian	PNB	b
11802	Hupa	0.00050	1,335	1,392	1,628	MIR38a	61-BCBA-a	hupa		91.50	1,273	0....	10	8	11	3	0		...	b
11803	Hutterite (Tyrolese)	0.00207	5,527	5,762	6,739	CEW19f	52-ABCF-i	tirolisch-t.		90.00	5,186	0c.uh	10	9	12	4	1		pn.	b
11804	Icelander	0.01630	43,524	45,372	53,068	CEW19n	52-AAAB-a	íslensk		95.00	43,104	0..uh	10	10	13	5	3	Icelandic	PNB	b
11805	Ilocano	0.20000	534,040	556,714	651,145	MSY44f	31-CBAA-b	vehicular ilocano		89.00	495,476	2A.u.	10	10	13	5	3	Ilokano*	PNB	b
11806	Indo-Pakistani	0.50000	1,335,099	1,391,786	1,627,863	CNN25g	59-AAFO-b	historical hindi	1	15.00	208,768	1Asuh	8	5	8	2	3	Hindi: Sarnami*	PNB	b
11807	Ingalik	0.00014	374	390	456	MIR38a	61-BABA-a	degexit'an		80.40	313	0c...	10	7	3	3	0		p..	b
11808	Iowa	0.00041	1,095	1,141	1,335	MIR38a	64-AACC-c	iowa		80.30	916	0....	10	7	3	3	0		...	b
11809	Iraqi Arab	0.15200	405,870	423,103	494,870	CMT30	12-AACF-g	syro-mesopotamian		8.00	33,848	1Asuh	7	5	5	5	2		pnb	b
11810	Iraqi Arab	0.00933	24,913	25,971	30,376	CMT30	12-AACF-g	syro-mesopotamian		3.00	779	1Asuh	6	5	8	5	1		pnb	b
11811	Irish	1.00000	2,670,198	2,783,571	3,255,726	CEW18b	52-ABAE-i	oceanian-english		69.90	1,945,716	0B.uh	10	10	16	5	2		pnb	b
11812	Irish Traveller (Gypsy)	0.00012	320	334	391	CNN25f	50-ACAA-a	west sheldruu		85.00	284	0....	10	9	15	5	1		...	b
11813	Israeli Jew	0.05000	133,510	139,179	162,786	CMT35	12-AABA-b	ivrit-x.	1	0.20	278	2B.uh	5	4	5	5	0	Hebrew	PNB	b
11814	Italian	2.00000	5,340,397	5,567,143	6,511,452	CEW21e	51-AABQ-c	standard italiano	6	74.80	4,164,223	2B.uh	10	10	15	5	3	Italian	PNB	b
11815	Jamaican	0.17491	467,044	486,874	569,459	NFB68a	52-ABAF-m	jamaican-creole		80.00	389,500	1c..h	10	9	9	5	3	West Carib Creole English	pn.	b
11816	Japanese	0.40394	1,078,600	1,124,396	1,315,118	MSY45a	45-CAAA-a	koku-go	1	23.00	258,611	1B.uh	9	5	8	5	3	Japanese	PNB	b
11817	Japanese Creole	0.05000	133,510	139,179	162,786	MSY43	45-CAAA-a	koku-go		40.00	55,671	1B.uh	9	6	2	3	1	Japanese	PNB	b
11818	Jemez	0.00065	1,736	1,809	2,116	MIR37z	66-ABAA-a	jemez		95.00	1,719	0....	10	8	11	5	1		...	.
11819	Jewish	1.91500	5,113,430	5,330,539	6,234,715	CMT35	52-ABAC-s	general american		2.70	143,925	1Bsuh	6	4	8	5	2	English*	PNB	b

Continued opposite

Table 8-2 continued

EVANGELIZATION								EVANGELISM			ADDITIONAL DESCRIPTIVE DATA
Ref 1	*D 28*	*aC 29*	*CG% 30*	*r 31*	*E 32*	*U 33*	*W 34*	*e 35*	*R 36*	*T 37*	*Locations, civil divisions, literacy, religions, church history, denominations, dioceses, church growth, missions, agencies, ministries, movements 38*
11696	1	10	1.31	0	99.80	0.20	C	353.32	50	9	Reservation in Texas, Louisiana. Still spoken by 70%. Bilingual in English. D=Native American Ch of North America.
11697	4	10	6.36	8	99.85	0.15	C	449.86	135	10	Mixed-race persons(Indochinese/Americans). Urbanites. D=UMC,PCUSA,AoG,RCC.
11698	5	10	1.18	8	99.75	0.25	C	402.41	35	10	Mixed-race persons, Amerindian/Whites. Huge numbers have Amerindian ancestry and claim it. D=RCC,UMC,SBC,AoG,&c. T=CNB,TBN,LESEA.
11699	6	8	1.31	8	99.64	0.36	C	310.68	43	9	Immigrants from Australia. Nonreligious 15%. D=ECUSA,UMC,UCC,PCUSA,AoG,RCC.
11700	4	10	1.21	8	99.68	0.32	C	354.92	38	9	Citizens, expatriates from Canada, in all walks of life. Nonreligious 8%. D=RCC,UCC,ACC,PAOC.T=CBN,TBN,LESEA,25+ other networks. R=1,000 local stations.
11701	3	10	1.31	0	99.80	0.20	C	367.92	51	9	Also in UK, Australia. Language is English with heavy Romani lexical borrowings. Nomadic caravan churches. D=RCC,UMC,Gypsy Evang Movement. M=GGMS.
11702	1	10	1.31	0	99.90	0.10	C	450.04	44	10	Wyoming, Wind River Reservation. Spoken by 30%(middle-aged or older). D=Native American Ch of North America.
11703	0	10	1.31	0	99.95	0.05	C	467.27	45	10	North Dakota, Fort Berthold Reservation. Spoken by 20%(middle-aged or older). Closely related to Pawnees.
11704	4	10	1.43	6	99.90	0.10	C	548.59	33	10	Gregorians, refugees after 1915 genocide. D=ACNA(2 Dioceses),AACA(C-Cilicia),AEUC,AESB.
11705	4	10	1.84	8	99.90	0.10	C	555.16	40	10	Refugees after 1915 genocide, now English-speaking. Nonreligious 10%. D=ACNA(2 Dioceses),AACA(C-Cilicia),AEUC,AESB.
11706	1	10	1.31	0	99.96	0.04	C	515.97	41	10	Montana, and Canada. Spoken by only 5%(older). Closely related to Stoney. English used widely. D=Native American Ch of North America.
11707	5	10	3.82	5	99.90	0.10	C	532.17	76	10	Refugees since 1915. D=Assyrian Ch of the East(Nestorians: P-Tehran),RCC(Chaldeans),AEC,ACCSA,AAAC.
11708	0	10	1.28	0	48.00	52.00	A	35.04	124	5	Northeast California. Language nearly extinct. A few animists left. Nonreligious 30%.
11709	5	10	1.80	8	99.83	0.17	C	463.51	52	10	Immigrants, from Austria. Nonreligious 10%. D=RCC,ELCA,NAC,NABGC,WELS. R=HCJB.
11710	4	10	3.95	8	99.84	0.16	C	447.63	86	10	Workers from Bahamas. Afro-American spiritists 3%. D=ECUSA,UMC,UCC,PCUSA.
11711	1	10	1.43	4	99.94	0.06	C	559.25	41	10	Immigrants from Spain. Strong Catholics. D=RCC. M=SJ,OFM.
11712	5	10	5.08	6	68.00	32.00	B	2.48	259	4	Immigrants from Bangladesh and West Bengal(India). Muslims 65%(Hanafi Sunnis), Hindus 34%. D=RCC,ABC,SBC,ABWE,AoG.
11713	4	9	1.31	4	99.86	0.14	C	417.48	43	10	St Lawrence Island, Alaska. Also in Russia. Spoken by 82%. D=ECUSA,OCA,SDA,PCUSA. M=SIL.
11714	2	10	1.31	8	99.85	0.15	C	446.76	38	10	Sea Islands Creole (English-based). Coastal region and Sea Islands of Georgia coast. Monolinguals 8%, bilinguals in English 92%. D=NBCUSA,&c. M=SIL.
11715	2	10	3.07	8	72.00	28.00	B	39.42	140	5	Jewish (85% (Black Hebrews(Orthodox Jews), Black Israelites, USA Blacks in White synagogues). D=Ch of God & Saints of Christ, Ch of God(Black Jews).
11716	2	10	2.94	4	48.00	52.00	A	8.76	202	4	Refugees from North Viet Nam(along Red and Black rivers). Animists 90%. D=RCC,CMA.
11717	1	10	1.31	0	99.82	0.18	C	386.09	47	9	Montana (Blackfoot Reservation), and Canada. Lingua franca, still spoken by 60%. Animists 5%. D=Native American Ch of North America.
11718	1	10	2.09	8	99.98	0.02	C	583.05	44	10	Immigrants, refugees from Bolivia; laborers, seasonal workers. D=RCC. M=GMU.
11719	8	10	1.13	8	99.66	0.34	C	346.89	43	9	Recent immigrants from UK. Another 50 million are Americans of British descent. D=ECUSA(92 Dioceses),SBC,UMC,PCUSA,RCC,ORCC,CB,COGBIO. T=CBN.
11720	3	10	1.31	6	99.76	0.24	C	407.77	47	10	Refugees from Bulgaria. Nonreligious 22%. D=Bulgarian Eastern Orthodox Ch(3 Dioceses),BODA,OCA.
11721	0	9	3.43	6	63.00	37.00	B	6.89	197	4	Immigrants from Burma. Theravada Buddhists 94%, Muslims 2%(Shafi Sunnis), many Baha'is.
11722	4	10	2.94	5	99.66	0.34	C	332.44	78	9	Refugees from White Russia. Nonreligious 30%. D=Byelorussian Autocephalic Orthodox Ch,RCC,COC(E-Americas),OCA.
11723	1	10	3.91	8	99.98	0.02	C	583.05	84	10	Immigrants from Cape Verde Islands, living in southeastern New England. D=RCC.
11724	1	10	1.31	0	99.90	0.10	C	443.47	45	10	Western Oklahoma, Caddo County. Still spoken by 16% (middle-aged or older). D=Native American Ch of North America.
11725	0	10	1.31	0	99.81	0.19	C	338.56	50	9	Southern California. Still spoken by 6% (middle-aged or older). Bilinguals in English.
11726	1	10	1.21	2	99.82	0.18	C	401.06	41	10	Southern Louisiana, west of Mississippi. Bilinguals in English, many also in Standard French. Swamps. Fishermen. D=RCC.
11727	2	10	7.20	5	68.00	32.00	B	12.41	347	5	Refugees from Indochina since 1960. Large numbers in Long Beach, CA. Theravada Buddhists 86%, animists 5%. D=Christian Ch,KEC. M=CMA,YWAM,CCCI.
11728	0	10	1.31	0	99.96	0.04	C	477.50	44	10	Northern South Carolina, near Rock Hill. Language nearly extinct (under 10 speakers).
11729	0	10	1.31	0	99.92	0.08	C	452.50	45	10	Western New York (Cattaraugus Reservation), northeastern Oklahoma. Also in Canada. Few speakers left.
11730	3	10	2.65	8	99.90	0.10	C	548.59	53	10	Mainly political refugees from Nicaragua(200,000), Guatemala, Honduras, El Salvador. D=RCC,ABC,UMC. T=CBN,LESEA. R=1,000 local stations,AWR.
11731	0	10	1.29	0	99.78	0.22	C	316.01	54	9	Upper Chehalis. Washington State, south of Puget Sound. Under 10 speakers left.
11732	1	10	1.31	0	99.72	0.28	C	312.73	51	9	Eastern and northeastern Oklahoma, also Cherokee Reservation, Great Smokey Mountains. Spoken by 20%. Tribal religionists 10%. D=Native American CNA.
11733	1	10	1.31	0	99.80	0.20	C	362.08	49	9	Southeastern Montana, Northern Cheyenne Reservation. Spoken by 40% (adults). D=Native American Ch of North America. M=SIL.
11734	0	10	1.32	0	51.00	49.00	B	37.23	119	5	Oregon, Washington, Lower Columbia river. Language extinct, replaced now by English. Shamanists 60%.
11735	0	10	1.31	0	99.90	0.10	C	433.62	42	10	Former Pacific Coast lingua franca from Oregon to Alaska (USA), Canada). Under 100 speakers (over 50 years old).
11736	1	10	1.31	0	99.95	0.05	C	495.85	42	10	Southeast Oklahoma, east central Mississippi. Spoken by 48% (older persons). D=Native American Ch of North America. M=SIL,independents.
11737	0	9	1.23	0	97.00	3.00	C	212.43	60	8	Washington, northeastern Olympic Peninsula. All speakers elderly. Nearly extinct.
11738	1	9	1.31	0	99.90	0.10	C	433.62	46	10	Arizona (Lower Colorado river); mainly in Mexico (Baja California). Spoken by 90%. D=NACNA. M=SIL,independents.
11739	0	10	1.31	0	99.96	0.04	C	480.04	44	10	Northern Idaho, Coeur d'Alene Reservation. Language nearly extinct; under 20 speakers.
11740	0	10	1.30	0	99.89	0.11	C	425.55	46	10	Oregon, Umatilla Reservation. Spoken by 41% (middle-aged or older).
11741	0	10	1.31	0	99.80	0.20	C	329.96	54	9	North central Washington State, Colville Reservation. Spoken by 30% (middle-aged or older).
11742	1	10	1.31	0	99.94	0.06	C	483.77	40	10	Western Oklahoma. Spoken by only 8% (middle-aged or older). Closely related to Shoshoni. D=NACNA. M=SIL.
11743	0	10	1.36	0	40.00	60.00	A	14.60	155	5	Southern Oregon coast. Language virtually extinct. Nonreligious 20%.
11744	1	10	1.31	4	99.77	0.23	C	351.31	51	9	Immigrants from Corsica (France). Also in Canada, Puerto Rico, Venezuela, Cuba, Bolivia, Uruguay. Nonreligious 10%. D=RCC.
11745	7	10	1.31	0	99.80	0.20	C	385.44	46	9	East central Oklahoma, Alabama, Florida. Spoken by 50% (including most adults). D=NACNA,RCC,ECUSA,Creek Independent Indian Baptist Chs,Seminole IIC.
11746	1	10	1.21	6	99.81	0.19	C	437.56	42	10	Refugees from Croatia, since 1940 and especially 1990s Yugoslavia civil war. Nonreligious 9%. D=RCC.
11747	1	8	1.31	0	99.90	0.10	C	443.47	45	10	Southern Montana. Spoken by 78%. Close to Hidatsa. D=Native American Ch of North America. M=SIL.
11748	1	10	4.33	8	99.80	0.20	C	425.49	97	10	Mostly refugees from Cuba since 1959. Concentrated in Florida. Nonreligious 10%. D=RCC. T=CBN. R=local stations,AWR. T=LESEA.
11749	0	10	1.30	0	99.78	0.22	C	316.01	52	9	Southern California. Language nearly extinct; spoken only by 5% (all elderly).
11750	4	10	2.26	6	99.70	0.30	C	378.14	63	9	Refugees from 1968 crisis, and subsequent Communist persecution. Nonreligious 21%. D=RCC,Moravian Ch,Czechoslovak Hussite Ch,Unitas Fratrum.
11751	4	10	1.31	0	99.72	0.28	C	331.12	48	9	Nebraska, Dakotas, Minnesota, Montana. Also in Canada. Speakers 82%, but declining. D=Native American Ch of North America,RCC,ECUSA,ELCA.
11752	2	10	1.19	6	99.80	0.20	C	447.12	42	10	Expatriates from Denmark. Nonreligious 10%, some Muslims. D=ELCA,EFCA. M=Ch of Denmark.
11753	0	10	1.31	0	99.89	0.11	C	431.22	46	10	Northeast, west central Oklahoma, northern New Jersey. Also in Canada. Language nearly extinct; under 50 elderly speakers.
11754	1	10	2.98	8	99.73	0.27	C	381.02	57	9	Part-Indians, or uprooted. Mainly in urban areas. Nonreligious 10%. D=NACNA.
11755	0	8	1.32	0	99.80	0.20	C	335.80	53	9	Southern California. Also Baja California (Mexico). Bilingual in English. Spoken by 50%.
11756	3	10	3.45	2	99.96	0.04	C	550.12	71	10	Immigrants from Dominica in Caribbean. Afro-Caribbean spiritists 4%. D=RCC,ECUSA,UMC.
11757	8	10	1.31	6	99.65	0.35	C	340.18	41	9	Recent immigrants from Holland. Another 5 million are Americans of Dutch descent. Nonreligious 20%. D=PCUSA,RCC,CMC,CRC,RCA,NRC,RCUS,True DRC.
11758	2	10	1.31	0	99.80	0.20	C	365.00	46	9	Aleutian Islands. Also in Russia. Still spoken by 25% (most over 40 years). D=Orthodox Ch in America,NACNA.
11759	1	10	1.31	0	99.85	0.15	C	415.73	43	10	Mayan Indian refugees from Guatemala. Santa Eulalia Kanjobal. D=RCC. M=CAM.
11760	1	9	1.31	0	99.90	0.10	C	433.62	46	10	North central New Mexico. 5 dialects. Spoken by 80%. D=Native American Ch of North America. M=SIL.
11761	2	10	2.06	0	99.75	0.25	C	333.97	66	9	Michigan. A few in Canada. Spoken by 32%. D=Native American Ch of North America,ECUSA. M=NCEM.
11762	5	9	5.52	8	99.50	0.50	B	224.47	139	8	Immigrants from Egypt. Muslims 50%(Shafi, Maliki, Hanafi Sunnis). D=Coptic Orthodox Ch(P-Alexandria),RCC(CCC),CEC,AoG,CB.
11763	4	10	1.31	8	99.80	0.20	C	440.92	42	10	Nomadic caravan churches. Nonreligious 10%. D=RCC,UMC,AoG,Gypsy Evangelical Movement. M=GGMS. T=CBN,TBN,LESEA. R=1,000+ stations.
11764	3	8	1.31	8	99.86	0.14	C	486.54	37	10	Alaska. Eskimos who no longer use original mother tongue, but only English. D=ECUSA,OCA,NACNA.
11765	3	10	1.31	8	99.88	0.12	C	485.01	38	10	Alaska. Eskimos and mixed-race persons using creole. D=ECUSA,NACNA,OCA.
11766	0	10	0.00	5	99.70	0.30	C	304.04	0	9	Artificial(constructed) language, in 80 countries. Speakers in USA: 154,000(none mother-tongue). Nonreligious 10%.
11767	2	10	5.67	5	99.72	0.28	C	370.54	133	9	Refugees from USSR after 1939. Nonreligious 25%. D=Estonian Evangelical Lutheran Ch,EOC in Exile.
11768	4	10	6.85	8	99.90	0.10	C	505.89	136	10	Mixed-race persons from 15 Asia countries. Urbanites. Buddhists 3%, Muslims 2%. D=RCC,UMC,ECUSA,PCUSA.
11769	0	10	1.10	0	40.00	60.00	A	14.60	137	5	Mouth of Copper river, Alaska. Language nearly extinct. Nonreligious 40%.
11770	0	10	1.31	0	99.78	0.22	C	320.25	54	9	Fort Belknap Reservation, Milk river, north central Montana. Nearly extinct; under 10 speakers left.
11771	4	10	4.20	4	99.84	0.16	C	456.83	86	10	Immigrants from Fiji. All Christians. D=UMC,AoG,RCC,SDA.
11772	13	10	8.00	5	99.92	0.08	C	580.93	137	10	From Philippines. 1.5 million in New York, 200,000 in Chicago. D=RCC,PIC,INC,CDCC,SDA,JWs,AoG,COLJCAF,FGMH,AOFB,ECUSA,UMC,SBC. M=SVD,SJ.
11773	5	10	1.31	5	99.86	0.14	C	499.10	40	10	Immigrants from Finland. Nonreligious 13%. D=Finnish Orthodox Ch,ELCA,LCMS,AELC,ALCA.
11774	1	10	1.31	0	99.80	0.20	C	350.40	50	9	Northeast Washington State, Kalispel Reservation; Flathead Reservation, northwest Montana. Spoken by 26%. D=NACNA.
11775	2	10	1.31	6	99.90	0.10	C	535.45	41	10	Immigrants from Flanders(Belgium). Nonreligious 6%. D=RCC,GKB.
11776	6	10	1.10	8	99.70	0.30	C	383.25	38	9	Immigrants from France. Another 8 million are Americans of French descent. Nonreligious 15%. D=RCC(166 Dioceses),PCUSA,RCA,JWs,Amis de l'Homme.
11777	1	10	1.31	3	99.96	0.04	C	501.07	42	10	Cree Part-Indians. North Dakota, Turtle Mountain Reservation. Also in Canada, scattered. Cree-French creole. D=Native American Ch of North America.
11778	1	10	1.21	8	99.68	0.32	C	349.96	39	9	Citizens, expatriates of Quebec, and Canada. Nonreligious 18%. D=RCC. R=AWR.
11779	3	10	1.31	0	99.72	0.28	C	339.01	52	9	Immigrants from Holland, and Germany. Nonreligious 10%. D=RCC,ELCA,PCUSA.
11780	13	10	1.06	8	99.61	0.39	C	322.84	42	9	Recent immigrants from Germany. Another 53 million are Americans of German descent. Nonreligious 20%. D=ELCA,LCMS,NAC,JWs,COB,AELC,LCR,ACCA.
11781	2	10	9.17	6	99.58	0.42	B	247.68	227	8	Refugees from Albania. Sunni Muslims 30%, nonreligious 10%. D=Albanian Orthodox AD in America,AODA. M=OCA.
11782	7	10	1.19	7	99.85	0.15	C	502.60	37	10	D=Greek Orthodox AD of N&S America,RCC(Melkites: EA-Boston),AOCADNY,AGOC,GEC,HOCA,OCGOC.
11783	1	10	3.95	7	99.90	0.10	C	519.03	85	10	From Greece. Trade, commerce. Largely urban. Nonreligious 10%. D=GOC(AD-North & South America). Many charismatics.
11784	5	10	1.31	5	99.99	0.01	C	578.16	29	10	From Guam and Northern Mariana Islands. Strong Christians. D=RCC,SDA,JWs,CJCLdS,AoG.
11785	2	10	1.95	8	99.85	0.15	C	446.76	51	10	From Guyana. Afro-American spiritists(voodoo) 15%. D=RCC,ECUSA.
11786	1	10	1.31	0	99.93	0.07	C	470.98	44	10	Southern tip of Alaska panhandle; also in Canada (British Columbia). Language isolate. Mother-tongue speakers 15%, all old. D=NACNA.
11787	5	10	6.47	4	99.89	0.11	C	516.51	132	10	Refugees from Haiti. 500,000 in Brooklyn, New York, 70,000 in Chicago; Miami. Afro-American spiritists 5%, many Baha'is. D=RCC(90% Spiritist Catholics),ABC.
11788	0	10	1.31	0	99.91	0.09	C	460.87	44	10	Yukon river, Alaska-Canada border. Spoken by 20%, all elderly. Language nearly extinct.
11789	3	10	2.84	8	99.34	0.66	B	140.93	84	7	Americanized Chinese. Buddhists/folk-religionists 34%, nonreligious 20%. D=RCC,TJC,AHC.
11790	3	10	2.59	8	99.00	1.00	B	83.11	90	6	Mostly in Manhattan, NYC. Mahayana Buddhists/Chinese folk-religionists 61%, nonreligious 15%. D=RCC,AHC,TJC. M=HKOM.
11791	2	10	3.45	6	94.00	6.00	B	72.05	120	6	Mahayana Buddhists/folk-religionists 64%, nonreligious 10%. D=RCC,AHC.
11792	2	10	3.45	7	95.00	5.00	B	69.35	118	6	Long-time residents from China and diaspora. Buddhists/folk-religionists 57%, nonreligious 20%. D=RCC,AHC. M=HKOM.
11793	2	10	1.31	0	99.72	0.28	C	333.29	40	9	2% mother-tongue speakers, 9% pure Hawaiian, rest Half-Hawaiian. All bilingual in Hawaiian Pidgin. Many traditional religionists (reverted from Christianity) 20%.
11794	3	10	1.31	8	99.90	0.10	C	525.60	31	10	Hawaiians with English as mother tongue. Traditional religionists 10%. D=UCC,RCC,&c.
11795	2	10	1.31	8	99.90	0.10	C	509.17	37	10	English-based creole. 70% bilingual in English. Buddhists 5%, traditional religionists 5%. D=RCC,&c. M=SIL.
11796	1	10	1.31	0	99.80	0.20	C	347.48	51	9	Fort Berthold Reservation, North Dakota. Close to Crow. Spoken by 12%. D=NACNA.
11797	1	10	1.67	0	99.90	0.10	C	450.04	51	10	Central Wisconsin (scattered locations), eastern Nebraska (Winnebago Reservation). Spoken by 42% including most adults. Animists 5%.D=Native Ch of North A.
11798	0	10	1.29	0	99.78	0.22	C	321.71	53	9	Lower Yukon river, Alaska. Language nearly extinct; spoken by 15% (middle-aged or older).
11799	5	9	1.31	0	99.85	0.15	C	409.53	44	10	Several villages in northeast Arizona. Spoken by 77%. Animists 2%. D=NACNA,AoG,First Mesa Baptist Ch,Hopi Independent Indian Chs,Mennonite Chs. M=SIL.
11800	1	10	1.31	8	99.90	0.10	C	528.88	34	10	Half-Indian. Southeast Oklahoma, Mississippi. D=NACNA.
11801	5	10	1.18	6	99.78	0.22	C	435.90	46	10	Refugees from Hungary after 1956 crisis. Nonreligious 10%. D=RCC,PCUSA,UCC,Hungarian Reformed Ch in America,Hungarian Orthodox Greek Catholic Ch.
11802	0	10	1.31	0	99.92	0.08	C	445.85	45	10	Hoopa Valley Reservation, northwest California. Language nearly extinct; spoken by only 4%, all elderly.
11803	1	10	1.31	1	99.90	0.10	C	463.18	47	10	30 colonies in South and North Dakota, Montana; Washington, Minnesota: 116 in Canada. Dialect of Upper German. Bilingual. D=Hutterites. Strict communal living.
11804	3	10	3.25	2	99.95	0.05	C	554.80	68	10	Immigrants from Iceland. Non-Christians 4%. D=National Ch of Iceland,ELCA,LCMS.
11805	8	10	1.31	4	99.89	0.11	C	526.25	34	10	Immigrants from Philippines. Strong Christians. D=RCC,PIC,INC,UMC,UCC,PCUSA,SDA,JWs.
11806	4	10	6.03	6	81.00	19.00	B	44.34	238	6	Refugees from India, Pakistan. Shopkeepers, laborers. Hindus 60%(including 60 neo-Hindu sects), Muslims 15%, Baha'is 10%. D=RCC,UMC,PCUSA,SBC.
11807	0	10	1.31	0	99.80	0.20	C	338.65	52	9	Alaska, area of lower Yukon river, inland from Eskimo. Spoken by 33% (middle-aged or older).
11808	0	10	1.31	0	99.80	0.20	C	332.07	53	9	North central Oklahoma, northeast Kansas. Language nearly extinct; spoken only by 2% (elderly).
11809	2	10	8.47	7	68.00	32.00	B	19.85	369	5	Refugees, labor migrants, immigrants from Iraq. Muslims 90% (54% Shias, 35% Hanafi Sunnis, 1% others). D=RCC,ACE.
11810	1	9	4.45	7	60.00	40.00	B	6.57	235	4	Migrant workers from Iraq. Muslims 97%(68% Shias, 29% Hanafi Sunnis). D=RCC.
11811	2	10	1.26	8	99.70	0.30	C	362.03	42	9	Recent immigrants from Ireland. Another 37 million are Americans of Irish Catholic descent. D=RCC(21 million in USA are of Irish origin),Cooneyites. T=CBN,TBN.
11812	3	10	1.30	8	99.85	0.15	C	437.45	45	10	Nomadic caravan churches. D=RCC,AoG,Gypsy Evangelical Movement. M=GGMS.
11813	0	10	3.38	5	55.20	44.80	B	0.40	202	3	Secularized Jews. Sabras. Residents, immigrants from Israel. Nominally Jewish. Nonreligious 2%.
11814	5	10	1.24	7	99.75	0.25	C	425.36	39	10	Recent immigrants from Italy. Another 10 million are Americans of Italian descent. Nonreligious 10%. D=RCC(166 Dioceses),CCNA,NAORCC,ORCAC,Waldensians.
11815	3	10	4.20	8	99.80	0.20	C	408.80	89	10	Immigrants from Jamaica. Afro-American spiritists 10%. D=ABCUSA,SBC,indigenous chs.
11816	3	10	3.25	7	94.00	6.00	B	78.91	117	6	Mahayana Buddhists 25%, New-Religionists 35%(NSA), nonreligious 12%, Shintoists 5%. D=RCC,UMC,AoG. M=UCCJ,EFDC,JAM,JLCA,SEND. R=HCJB.
11817	1	10	5.80	7	96.00	4.00	B	140.16	188	7	Pre-World War II immigrants of Japanese origin, and mixed-race persons. Buddhists 60%. D=RCC.
11818	5	8	1.31	0	99.95	0.05	C	478.51	42	10	North central New Mexico. Spoken by 90%. Tribal religionists 5%. D=NACNA,AoG,Presbyterians,RCC,SBC. M=SIL.
11819	0	10	5.15	8	68.70	31.30	B	6.77	233	4	Mainly Ashkenazis. Practicing Jews: 28% Orthodox, 42% Conservative, 30% Reform. Nonreligious 5%. Christians: in 30 denominations, with many Messianic Jews.

Continued overleaf

Table 8-2 continued

PEOPLE		POPULATION				IDENTITY CODE		LANGUAGE		CHURCH		MINISTRY						SCRIPTURE		
Ref 1	Ethnic name 2	P% 3	In 1995 4	In 2000 5	In 2025 6	Race 7	Language 8	Autoglossonym 9	S 10	AC 11	Members 12	Jayuh 13-17	d 18	wa 19	xc 20	mc 21	mi 22	Biblioglossonym 23	Pub 24-26	ss 27
11820	Jewish (Judeo-German)	0.20000	534,040	556,714	651,145	CMT35	52-ABCH-a	west yiddish		1.00	5,567	0B..h	6	4	7	5	2	Yiddish	PNB	b
11821	Jicarilla Apache	0.00090	2,403	2,505	2,930	MIR38a	61-BDAA-b	west apache		72.00	1,804	1as..	10	7	6	4	1	Apache: Western*	PNb	b
11822	Jordanian Arab	0.00831	22,189	23,131	27,055	CMT30	12-AACF-fe	'ammani		30.00	6,939	1csuh	9	8	8	5	3		pnb	.
11823	Kalderash Gypsy (Rom)	0.08000	213,616	222,686	260,458	CNN25f	59-ACBA-a	vlach-romani		90.00	200,417	1a...	10	9	11	5	1	Romani: Finnish*	PN.	b
11824	Kalmyk	0.00030	801	835	977	MSY41y	44-BAAB-d	kalmyk		3.00	25	2c..h	6	4	4	1	0	Mongolian: Kalmyk*	PNb	b
11825	Kansa	0.00010	267	278	326	MIR38a	64-AACB-e	kansa		78.00	217	0....	10	7	3	3	0		...	b
11826	Karok	0.00162	4,326	4,509	5,274	MIR38a	63-TAAA-a	karok		80.30	3,621	0....	10	7	3	3	0		...	b
11827	Kato	0.00004	107	111	130	MIR38a	61-BCBC-d	kato		78.00	87	0....	10	7	5	3	0		...	b
11828	Kawaiisu	0.00007	187	195	228	MIR37z	66-BACA-a	kawaiisu		79.00	154	0....	10	7	3	3	0		...	b
11829	Kickapoo	0.00068	1,816	1,893	2,214	MIR38a	62-ADCB-b	kikapoo		90.00	1,704	0....	10	7	12	4	1	Kikapoo	p..	.
11830	Kiowa	0.00273	7,290	7,599	8,888	MIR37z	66-ABBA-a	kiowa		85.00	6,459	0....	10	7	5	4	1		...	b
11831	Kiowa Apache	0.00045	1,202	1,253	1,465	MIR38a	61-BDAA-b	west apache		73.90	926	1as..	10	7	3	3	0	Apache: Western*	PNb	b
11832	Klamath-Modoc	0.00091	2,430	2,533	2,963	MIR38a	63-NAAA-a	klamath		90.00	2,280	0....	10	7	11	4	1		...	b
11833	Koasati (Coushatta)	0.00018	481	501	586	MIR38a	65-FBAA-a	koasati		60.00	301	0....	10	6	6	5	0		...	b
11834	Kodiak Aleut (Alutiiq)	0.00136	3,631	3,786	4,428	MRY40a	60-ABAD-b	kodiak		86.00	3,256	0....	10	10	6	5	2	Eskimo: Yupik, Pacific Gulf*	P..	b
11835	Korean	0.72070	1,924,412	2,006,120	2,346,402	MSY46	45-AAAA-b	kukö		62.00	1,243,794	2A...	10	10	14	5	3	Korean	PNB	b
11836	Koyukon	0.00100	2,670	2,784	3,256	MIR38a	61-BABA-c	koyukon		80.00	2,227	0a...	10	7	7	4	1	Koyukon	P..	b
11837	Kurdish (Kurd)	0.01600	42,723	44,537	52,092	CNT24c	58-AAAA-a	kurmanji		1.00	445	3c...	6	4	4	5	1	Kurdish: Kurmanji*	PN.	b
11838	Kutchin (Gwichin)	0.00060	1,602	1,670	1,953	MIR38a	61-BAEB-b	gwich'in		96.00	1,603	0....	10	7	12	4	1	Gwichin: Western	PNB	b
11839	Kutenai	0.00015	401	418	488	MIR38a	63-HAAA	kutenai cluster		92.00	384	0....	10	7	11	3	0		...	b
11840	Lakota	0.00400	10,681	11,134	13,023	MIR38a	64-AACA-d	lakota		80.00	8,907	0....	10	7	8	3	3		pnb	b
11841	Lao (Laotian Tai)	0.05908	157,755	164,453	192,348	MSY49b	47-AAAC-b	lao		4.00	6,578	2As..	6	5	8	5	1	Lao	PNB	b
11842	Latvian (Lett)	0.04034	107,716	112,289	131,336	CEW15a	54-AABA-a	standard latviashu		90.00	101,060	3A.u.	10	10	12	5	1	Latvian	PNB	b
11843	Levantine Arab	1.00000	2,670,198	2,783,571	3,255,726	CMT30	12-AACF-f	syro-palestinian	2	67.00	1,864,993	1Asuh	10	10	8	5	3	Arabic: Lebanese*	Pnb	b
11844	Lipan Apache	0.00005	134	139	163	MIR38a	61-BDAA-b	west apache		78.00	109	1as..	10	7	3	3	0	Apache: Western*	PNb	b
11845	Lithuanian	0.32643	871,633	908,641	1,062,767	CEW15b	54-AAAA-a	standard lietuvishkai		89.90	816,868	3A.u.	10	10	12	5	3	Lithuanian	PNB	b
11846	Louisiana Creole French	0.68182	1,820,595	1,897,895	2,219,819	NFB69b	51-AACC-a	louisianais	1	85.00	1,613,210	1cs..	10	7	13	3	0		pnb	b
11847	Lovari Gypsy (Lowara)	0.00220	5,874	6,124	7,163	CNN25f	59-ACBA-a	vlach-romani		80.00	4,899	1a...	10	8	7	5	1	Romani: Finnish*	PN.	b
11848	Low German	0.00450	12,016	12,526	14,651	CEW19m	52-ABCC	north deutsch cluster		81.00	10,146	2A.uh	10	10	13	5	3	German: Low*	PNB	b
11849	Lower Cowlitz	0.00008	214	223	260	MIR38a	63-GBBB-a	cowlitz		60.00	134	0....	10	6	6	5	0		...	b
11850	Luiseno	0.00068	1,816	1,893	2,214	MIR37z	66-BCDA-a	luiseño		80.30	1,520	0....	10	7	3	3	0		...	b
11851	Lumbee	0.01364	36,422	37,968	44,408	MIR38a	62-AECB-b	lumbee		60.00	22,781	0....	10	6	4	3	0		...	b
11852	Luxemburger	0.01973	52,683	54,920	64,235	CEW19o	52-ABCD-b	letzebürgesch-t.		87.00	47,780	0a.uh	10	9	13	5	1	Luxembourgeois	...	b
11853	Macedonian	0.00819	21,869	22,797	26,664	CEW22G	53-AAAH-a	makedonski		91.00	20,746	2a.uh	10	8	11	5	2	Macedonian*	PNB	b
11854	Maidu	0.00009	240	251	293	MIR38a	63-SBAA	maidu-nishinam cluster		78.00	195	0....	10	7	3	3	0		...	b
11855	Makah	0.00027	721	752	879	MIR38a	63-EABB-a	makah		90.00	676	0....	10	7	11	3	0		...	b
11856	Malay	0.00300	8,011	8,351	9,767	MSY44k	31-PHAA-b	bahasa-malaysia		0.50	42	1asuh	5	4	3	5	3	Malay	PNB	b
11857	Malayali	0.02300	61,415	64,022	74,882	CNN23b	49-EBEB-a	malayalam		50.00	32,011	2Asu.	10	8	8	5	3	Malayalam	PNB	b
11858	Maltese	0.01592	42,510	44,314	51,831	CMT36	12-AACC-a	maltiya		95.00	42,099	0a.u.	10	9	16	5	1	Maltese	PNB	b
11859	Mandan	0.00017	454	473	553	MIR38a	64-AABA-a	mandan		91.30	432	0....	10	7	11	3	0		...	b
11860	Maricopa	0.00018	481	501	586	MIR38a	63-VDBA-c	maricopa		84.80	425	0....	10	7	2	3	0		...	b
11861	Massachusett (Wampanoag)	0.00055	1,469	1,531	1,791	MIR38a	62-AEBA-a	massachu-set		20.00	306	0....	9	6	2	3	0	Massachusetts*	PNB	b
11862	Menomini	0.00159	4,246	4,426	5,177	MIR38a	62-ADCA-a	menomini		95.70	4,236	0....	10	7	11	3	0		...	b
11863	Mescalero Apache	0.00090	2,403	2,505	2,930	MIR38a	61-BDAB-b	mescalero-chiricahua		72.00	1,804	0....	10	10	6	5	3		...	.
11864	Mexican Creole (Tirilone)	0.05000	133,510	139,179	162,786	CLN29	59-AEAA-a	caló	1	90.00	125,261	0....	10	8	11	5	1		...	b
11865	Mexican Mestizo	3.45000	9,212,185	9,603,321	11,232,254	CLN29	51-AABB-ha	mexicano		87.40	8,393,303	1B.uh	10	10	13	5	1		pnb	b
11866	Miami	0.00091	2,430	2,533	2,963	MIR38a	62-ADCC	miami-peoria cluster		20.00	507	0....	9	6	2	3	0		...	b
11867	Micmac	0.00100	2,670	2,784	3,256	MIR38a	62-AEAA-b	southeast micmac		85.00	2,366	0....	10	7	8	3	0	Micmac	PN.	b
11868	Mikasuki Seminole	0.00055	1,469	1,531	1,791	MIR38a	65-FBBA-a	mikasuki		80.00	1,225	0s...	10	8	6	5	1	Mikasuki	P..	b
11869	Miwok	0.00014	374	390	456	MIR38a	63-SDAA-b	lake-miwok		78.00	304	0....	10	7	3	3	0		...	b
11870	Mohave (Mojave)	0.00068	1,816	1,893	2,214	MIR38a	63-VDBA-a	mohave		90.00	1,704	0....	10	8	11	5	3		...	b
11871	Mohawk	0.00073	1,949	2,032	2,377	MIR38a	64-CAAC-a	mohawk		92.00	1,869	0....	10	7	12	4	2	Mohawk	P..	b
11872	Mongolian	0.00141	3,765	3,925	4,591	MSY41f	44-BAAB-c	halh		1.00	39	3A..h	6	4	4	5	0	Mongolian: Khalka*	PNb	b
11873	Mono	0.00009	240	251	293	MIR37z	66-BAAA-a	mono		78.00	195	0....	10	7	3	3	0		...	b
11874	Moroccan Arabized Berber	0.00768	20,507	21,378	25,004	CMT32a	12-AACB-a	west maghrebi		1.00	214	1A.uh	6	4	5	3	1		pnb	b
11875	Nanticoke	0.00018	481	501	586	MIR38a	62-AEBB-c	nanticoke		10.00	50	0....	8	5	2	3	0		p..	b
11876	Narraganset (Mohegan)	0.00064	1,709	1,781	2,084	MIR38a	62-AEBA-k	montauk		10.00	178	0....	8	5	2	5	1		pnb	b
11877	Navaho	0.08770	234,176	244,119	285,527	MIR38a	61-BDAA-a	navaho		72.00	175,766	4As..	10	10	8	5	2	Navajo*	PNB	.
11878	Nepalese	0.00101	2,697	2,811	3,288	CNN25k	59-AAFD-b	nepali		2.00	56	2Asu.	6	4	7	5	3	Nepali	PNB	b
11879	Nez Perce	0.00068	1,816	1,893	2,214	MIR38a	63-IAAA-a	nez-percé		90.00	1,704	0....	10	7	11	4	1	Nez Perce	P..	b
11880	Nooksack	0.00016	427	445	521	MIR38a	63-GAAG-a	nooksack		91.30	407	0....	10	7	11	3	0		...	b
11881	North Alaskan Eskimo	0.00195	5,207	5,428	6,349	MRY40b	60-ABBB-b	kobuk		86.00	4,668	0....	10	10	13	5	2		pn.	b
11882	Northeast Sahaptin	0.00032	854	891	1,042	MIR38a	63-IAAA-c	walla-walla		80.40	716	0....	10	7	2	3	0		p..	b
11883	Northern Paiute	0.00164	4,379	4,565	5,339	MIR37z	66-BAAB	north paiute cluster		90.00	4,109	0A...	10	9	11	5	1	Paiute: Northern*	PN.	b
11884	Northern Tiwa (Picuris)	0.00051	1,362	1,420	1,660	MIR37z	66-AAAA	north tiwa cluster		80.00	1,136	1A...	10	7	6	4	2	Tiwa: Northern*	P..	.
11885	Northwest Alaskan Eskimo	0.00325	8,678	9,047	10,581	MRY40b	60-ABBA-a	qawiaraq		86.00	7,780	0....	10	10	10	5	1	Inuktitut, Nw Inupiat	P..	b
11886	Norwegian	1.55579	4,154,268	4,330,653	5,065,226	CEW19p	52-AAAC-e	ny-norsk	1	86.00	3,724,361	0B.uh	10	9	16	5	3	Norwegian*	PNB	b
11887	Oirat (Western Mongul)	0.00054	1,442	1,503	1,758	MSY41y	44-BAAB-e	oyrat		5.00	75	1a..h	7	5	4	3	0	Mongolian: Inner*	PNb	b
11888	Okanagon	0.00070	1,869	1,948	2,279	MIR38a	63-GCBA-b	shwoy-el-pi		92.00	1,793	0....	10	7	11	4	1		...	b
11889	Okinawan	0.00428	11,428	11,914	13,935	MSY45b	45-CACA-i	luchu		4.00	477	0....	6	5	9	5	3	Japanese: Luchu*	P..	b
11890	Omaha (Dhegiha)	0.00114	3,044	3,173	3,712	MIR38a	64-AACB-a	omaha		90.00	2,856	0....	10	7	11	4	1		...	b
11891	Oneida	0.00100	2,670	2,784	3,256	MIR38a	64-CAAC-b	oneida		93.00	2,589	0....	10	7	11	3	0	Oneida	P..	b
11892	Onondaga	0.00038	1,015	1,058	1,237	MIR38a	64-CAAD-c	onondaga		89.40	946	0....	10	7	11	3	0		p..	b
11893	Osage	0.00104	2,777	2,895	3,386	MIR38a	64-AACB-c	osage		92.30	2,672	0....	10	7	11	3	0	Osage	...	b
11894	Otoe (Chiwere)	0.00058	1,549	1,614	1,888	MIR38a	64-AACC-a	oto		89.70	1,448	0....	10	7	11	3	0		...	b
11895	Palestinian Arab	0.01931	51,562	53,751	62,868	CMT30	12-AACF-f	syro-palestinian		30.00	16,125	1Asuh	9	5	8	5	3	Arabic: Lebanese*	Pnb	b
11896	Part-Indian (Half-Indian)	0.10000	267,020	278,357	325,573	MIR38b	52-ABAF	carib-anglo-creol cluster		90.00	250,521	1a..h	10	7	12	4	1	West Carib Creole English	PN.	b
11897	Passamaquoddy (Malecite)	0.00060	1,602	1,670	1,953	MIR38a	62-AEAB	maliseet cluster		96.00	1,603	0....	10	7	11	4	1	Maliseet*	P..	b
11898	Pawnee	0.00091	2,430	2,533	2,963	MIR38a	64-BAAB-a	proper pawnee		90.20	2,285	0....	10	7	12	4	1		...	b
11899	Pennsylvania Dutch	0.12297	328,354	342,296	400,357	CEW19m	52-ABCF-t	pennsylvanisch-dietsch		88.00	301,220	0c.uh	10	10	14	5	1	German: Pennsylvania*	PN.	b
11900	Persian	0.09470	252,868	263,604	308,317	CNT24f	58-AACC-c	standard farsi		20.00	52,721	1Asu.	9	6	6	5	1		PNB	b
11901	Polish (Pole)	1.20000	3,204,238	3,340,286	3,906,871	CEW22i	53-AAAC-c	polski	3	78.00	2,605,423	2A.uh	10	10	14	5	3	Polish	PNB	b
11902	Polynesian	0.00436	11,642	12,136	14,195	MPY55z	52-ABAC-bv	standard oceanian-english		96.00	11,651	1Bsuh	10	9	12	5	3		pnb	b
11903	Pomo	0.00045	1,202	1,253	1,465	MIR38a	63-VAAA-d	kashaya		80.30	1,006	0....	10	7	4	3	0		...	b
11904	Ponca	0.00083	2,216	2,310	2,702	MIR38a	64-AACB-b	ponca		89.70	2,072	0....	10	7	11	3	0		...	b
11905	Portuguese	0.46373	1,238,251	1,290,826	1,509,778	CEW21g	51-AABA-e	general português		88.00	1,135,927	2Bsuh	10	9	15	5	1	Portuguese	PNB	b
11906	Potawatomi	0.00150	4,005	4,175	4,884	MIR38a	62-ADAE-a	potawatomi		91.10	3,804	0....	10	7	11	4	1	Pottawotomi*	P..	b
11907	Powhatan	0.00136	3,631	3,786	4,428	MIR38a	62-AECA-a	powhatan		10.00	379	0....	8	5	2	3	0		...	b
11908	Puerto Rican White	0.78619	2,099,283	2,188,416	2,559,619	CLT27	51-AABB-hk	puertorriqueño		91.00	1,991,459	1B.uh	10	10	13	5	3		pnb	b
11909	Puget Sound Salish	0.00080	2,136	2,227	2,605	MIR38a	63-GABA	lushootseed cluster		60.00	1,336	0....	10	6	7	5	0		...	b
11910	Punjabi	0.14000	373,828	389,700	455,802	CNN25n	59-AAFE-c	general panjabi		10.00	38,970	1Asu.	8	5	6	3	0		PNB	b
11911	Quapaw (Arkansas, Hegiha)	0.00091	2,430	2,533	2,963	MIR38a	64-AACB-d	quapaw		10.00	253	0....	8	5	2	3	0		...	b
11912	Quechan (Kechan)	0.00068	1,816	1,893	2,214	MIR38a	63-VDBA-b	quechan		90.00	1,704	0....	10	7	11	4	1		...	b
11913	Quileute	0.00014	374	390	456	MIR38a	63-FAAA-a	quileute		91.00	355	0....	10	7	11	3	0		...	b
11914	Quinault (Lower Chehalis)	0.00068	1,816	1,893	2,214	MIR38a	63-GBAA-a	quinault		91.30	1,728	0....	10	7	11	3	0		...	b
11915	Romanian	0.14698	392,466	409,129	478,527	CEW21i	51-AADC-a	limba românească		83.00	339,577	3A.u.	10	9	8	5	2	Romanian	PNB	b
11916	Romanichal Gypsy	0.05000	133,510	139,179	162,786	CNN25f	52-ABAC-s	general american		80.00	111,343	1Bsuh	10	10	8	5	1	English*	PNB	b
11917	Russian	1.18732	3,170,380	3,304,990	3,865,588	CEW22j	53-AAAE-d	russkiy		67.00	2,214,343	4B.uh	10	10	12	5	3	Russian	PNB	b
11918	Ruthene (Ruthenian, Rusin	0.20000	534,040	556,714	651,145	CEW22k	53-AAAE-a	rusyn		80.00	445,371	1c.uh	10	10	9	5	3		pnb	b
11919	Samoan	0.02228	59,492	62,018	72,538	MPY55e	39-CAOA	samoa cluster		86.00	53,335	2a.u.	10	10	15	5	1	Samoan	PNB	b
11920	Saudi Arab	0.00180	4,806	5,010	5,860	CMT30	12-AACF-k	central `anazi		0.04	2	4Asuh	3	4	4	5	0		pnb	b
11921	Sauk-Fox	0.00114	3,044	3,173	3,712	MIR38a	62-ADCB-a	mesquaki		90.00	2,856	0....	10	7	11	4	1	Mesquakie	P..	b
11922	Scottish Traveller(Gypsy)	0.00010	267	278	326	CNN25f	50-ACAA-b	north sheldruu		80.00	223	0....	10	8	6	5	1		...	b
11923	Seneca	0.00200	5,340	5,567	6,511	MIR38a	64-CAAD-a	seneca		89.70	4,994	0....	10	8	12	5	3	Seneca	P..	b
11924	Serb (Serbian)	0.06000	160,212	167,014	195,344	CEW22l	53-AAAG-a	standard srpski		84.00	140,292	1Asuh	10	9	9	5	2	Serbian*	PNB	b
11925	Shasta (Sastean)	0.00001	27	28	33	MIR38a	63-TCAA-a	shasta		78.00	22	0....	10	7	3	3	0		...	b
11926	Shawnee	0.00091	2,430	2,533	2,963	MIR38a	62-ADDA-a	east shawnee		90.00	2,280	0....	10	7	11	4	1	Shawnee	P..	b
11927	Shoshoni	0.00318	8,491	8,852	10,353	MIR37z	66-BABB	shoshoni cluster		85.00	7,524	0a...	10	7	6	4	1	Shoshone*	P..	b
11928	Skagit	0.00016	427	445	521	MIR38a	63-GABA-a	skagit		79.00	352	0....	10	7	2	3	0		...	b
11929	Slovak	0.75707	2,021,527	2,107,358	2,464,812	CEW22m	53-AAAD-b	slovensky		70.00	1,475,151	1Asuh	10	10	11	5	3	Slovak	PNB	b
11930	Slovene	0.05003	133,590	139,262	162,884	CEW22n	53-AAAF-a	slovensko		95.00	132,299	1a..h	10	10	12	5	1	Slovenian*	PNB	b
11931	Snohomish	0.00036	961	1,002	1,172	MIR38a	63-GABA-b	snohomish		78.00	782	0....	10	7	2	3	0		...	b
11932	Somali	0.00029	774	807	944	CMT33e	14-GAGA-a	af-soomaali		0.00	0	2A...	0	4	4	5	0	Somali	PNB	b
11933	South Alaska Eskimo	0.00120	3,204	3,340	3,907	MRY40b	60-ABAD-b	kodiak		85.00	2,839	0....	10	8	8	5	0	Eskimo: Yupik, Pacific Gulf*	P..	b
11934	South American Mestizo	1.30000	3,471,258	3,618,643	4,232,444	CLN29	51-AABB-k	chicano		84.00	3,039,660	1B.uh	10	10	13	5	1		pnb	b
11935	Southern Paiute (Ute)	0.00227	6,061	6,319	7,390	MIR37z	66-BACB-c	ute		90.00	5,687	0....	10	8	11	4	1		...	b
11936	Southern Puget Salish	0.00091	2,430	2,533	2,963	MIR38a	63-GABB	lushootseedsth cluster		81.00	2,052	0....	10	7	3	3	0		...	b
11937	Southern Tiwa	0.00108	2,884	3,006	3,516	MIR37z	66-AAAB	south tiwa cluster		80.00	2,405	0A...	10	7	6	4	1	Tiwa: Southern*	P..	.
11938	Spaniard	0.14512	387,499	403,952	472,471	CEW21k	51-AABB-c	general español	22	96.00	387,794	2B.uh	10	10	15	5	1	Spanish	PNB	b
11939	Spanish Jew	0.00500	13,351	13,918	16,279	CMT35	51-AAAB-a	ladino		1.00	139	0....	6	4	4	3	0		pnb	b
11940	Spokane	0.00045	1,202	1,253	1,465	MIR38a	63-GCBB-d	spokane		80.00	1,002	0....	10	7	3	3	0		...	b
11941	Straits Salish (Saanich)	0.00060	1,602	1,670	1,953	MIR38a	63-GAAF	saanich-clallam cluster		91.30	1,525	0....	10	7	12	3	0		...	b
11942	Swedish (Swede)	1.88206	5,025,474	5,238,848	6,127,471	CEW19q	52-AAAD-r	svea-svensk		65.00	3,405,251	1A.uh	10	10	15	5	3	Swedish	PNB	b
11943	Syrian Arab	0.05211	139,144	145,052	169,656	CMT30	12-AACF-f	syro-palestinian		15.00	21,758	1Asuh	8	5	8	5	1	Arabic: Lebanese*	Pnb	b

Continued opposite

Table 8-2 continued

EVANGELIZATION								EVANGELISM			ADDITIONAL DESCRIPTIVE DATA
Ref	*D*	*aC*	*CG%*	*r*	*E*	*U*	*W*	*e*	*R*	*T*	*Locations, civil divisions, literacy, religions, church history, denominations, dioceses, church growth, missions, agencies, ministries, movements*
1	*28*	*29*	*30*	*31*	*32*	*33*	*34*	*35*	*36*	*37*	*38*
11820	2	10	3.91	4	62.00	38.00	B	2.26	203	4	Ashkenazis. High Jewish practice. D=Hebrew-Christian communities, Union of Messianic Jewish Congregations. M=ABMJ,JFJ.
11821	1	9	1.31	1	99.72	0.28	C	320.61	50	9	Northern New Mexico, area of Dulce. Language spoken by 75% (young adults prefer English). Animists 3%. D=Native American Ch of North America.
11822	3	10	6.76	7	89.00	11.00	B	97.45	230	6	Workers from Jordan. Muslims 70%(Shafi Sunnis, Alawis). D=GOC,RCC,ECUSA.
11823	4	10	1.31	6	99.90	0.10	C	496.03	42	10	Nomadic caravan churches. D=RCC,AoG,UMC,Gypsy Evangelical Movement. M=GGMS.
11824	0	10	1.28	1	40.00	60.00	A	4.38	140	4	Tartars from former USSR, from Volga region. Buddhists 97%.
11825	0	10	1.31	0	99.78	0.22	C	316.01	55	9	North central Oklahoma. Language virtually extinct; no speakers known. Related to Omaha, Osage, Ponca, Quapaw.
11826	0	10	1.31	0	99.80	0.20	C	335.00	53	9	Northwest California, banks of Klamath river. Spoken by only 2% (middle-aged or over).
11827	0	10	1.30	0	99.78	0.22	C	321.71	53	9	Northwest California, Laytonville Reservation. Language nearly extinct; under 10 elderly speakers.
11828	0	10	1.31	0	99.79	0.21	C	322.95	52	9	South central California. Language nearly extinct; under 10 elderly speakers.
11829	1	10	1.31	0	99.90	0.10	C	440.19	45	10	Northeastern Kansas, central Oklahoma. Also in Mexico. Spoken by 80%. Animists 3%. D=Native American Ch of North America.
11830	1	10	1.31	0	99.85	0.15	C	384.71	47	9	West central Oklahoma. Spoken by under 13% (middle-aged or older). D=Native American Ch of North America.
11831	0	10	1.31	1	99.74	0.26	C	326.11	50	9	Western Oklahoma, Caddo County. Language nearly extinct (spoken by 1%).
11832	1	10	1.31	0	99.90	0.10	C	443.47	45	10	South central Oregon. Speakers only 7% (middle-aged or older). D=Native American Ch of North America.
11833	0	9	1.31	0	97.00	3.00	C	212.43	62	8	Koasati Reservation, Louisiana; also Texas, Oregon. Church language. Animists 6%, Nonreligious 4%.
11834	2	8	1.31	5	99.86	0.14	C	417.48	43	10	Alaska Peninsula, Kodiak Island. Spoken by 33%. Animists 4%. D=OCA,NACNA.
11835	5	10	11.56	6	99.62	0.38	C	316.82	238	9	Immigrants from Korea. Buddhists/shamanists 20%, New-Religionists 10%. . D=KPC,KMC,SBC,AoG,Unification Ch of America(HSAUWC).
11836	1	10	1.31	0	99.80	0.20	C	367.92	48	9	Alaska, Koyukuk and middle Yukon rivers. Spoken by 31% (middle-aged or older). Animists 3%. D=NACNA. M=SIL.
11837	0	10	3.87	0	42.00	58.00	A	1.53	383	4	Refugees from Iraq, Iran, Turkey. 9,600 speak Sorani. Muslims 99%(Sunnis). M=a whole network of agencies and local churches.
11838	1	10	1.31	0	99.96	0.04	C	522.09	41	10	Northeastern Alaska on Yukon river. Also in Canada. Spoken by 57%. English use increasing. D=NACNA. M=SIL.
11839	0	10	1.31	0	99.92	0.08	C	446.61	46	10	Northern Idaho, Flathead Reservation, Montana. Also in Canada. Spoken by 30% (elderly).
11840	3	10	1.31	0	99.80	0.20	C	382.52	46	9	Northern Nebraska, southern Minnesota, Dakotas, northeast Montana. Also in Canada. Spoken by 30%. D=RCC,ECUSA,ELCA.
11841	3	10	6.70	5	65.00	35.00	B	9.49	347	4	Refugees from Laos. Theravada Buddhists 60%, animists 33%, nonreligious 3%. D=RCC,SBC,GCL. M=CMA.
11842	1	10	5.28	5	99.90	0.10	C	525.60	111	10	Refugees from USSR since 1939. Nonreligious/atheists 10%. D=Latvian Evangelical Lutheran Ch in Exile.
11843	6	10	6.07	8	99.67	0.33	C	335.03	135	9	Refugees from Middle East. Muslims 15%, Baha'is. D=RCC(Maronites: D-Brooklyn),SOC,GOC,AOAD-Toledo,AOCADNY,ACCSA. M=GMU,UPM,SEND.
11844	0	10	1.30	1	99.78	0.22	C	355.87	48	9	New Mexico, Mescalero Reservation. Nearly extinct; spoken by under 10%.
11845	4	10	5.76	5	99.90	0.10	C	537.81	96	10	Refugees from USSR after 1939. Nonreligious 10%. D=RCC,Lithuanian National Catholic Ch in America, NAORCC,LRC in Exile.
11846	0	10	1.25	8	99.85	0.15	C	459.17	38	10	Louisiana: St Martinville, Breaux Bridge, Cecilia; east Texas. Spoken by 2.6%. Bilingual in English, some monolinguals.
11847	4	10	1.31	6	99.80	0.20	C	397.12	47	9	Travelling Gypsies. Nonreligious 10%. D=nomadic caravan churches,RCC,UMC,Gypsy Evangelical Movement. M=GGMS.
11848	8	10	1.31	8	99.81	0.19	C	461.21	43	10	Mennonite Germans. Kansas, Oklahoma; also in Canada, Mexico, 10 other countries. Literates 95%. Nonreligious 10%. D=ELCA,LCMS,AELC,NAC,COB,JWs.
11849	0	9	1.32	0	97.00	3.00	C	212.43	63	8	Southwestern Washington. Only 2 speakers left(in 1990).
11850	0	10	1.31	0	99.80	0.20	C	335.00	51	9	Southern California. Spoken by 6% (middle-aged or older).
11851	0	10	1.31	0	96.00	4.00	C	210.24	63	8	Carolinas, Maryland. Language extinct: no speakers left out of 36,000 ethnic group. Racially mixed, but still a distinct group. Tribal religionists 40%.
11852	1	10	1.31	8	99.87	0.13	C	469.97	44	10	Luxemburgers now residents in USA. Professionals. Nonreligious 12%. D=RCC.
11853	2	10	3.50	5	99.91	0.09	C	524.79	61	10	Immigrants from former Yugoslavia. Nonreligious 8%. D=Macedonian Orthodox Ch, Serbian Orthodox Ch.
11854	0	10	1.29	0	99.78	0.22	C	316.01	54	9	California, western foothills of northern Sierras. Speakers under 10% (elderly).Language nearly extinct.
11855	0	10	1.30	0	99.90	0.10	C	430.33	46	10	Washington State, northern tip of Olympic Peninsula. Spoken by 33% (middle-aged or older).
11856	3	10	1.35	5	54.50	45.50	B	0.99	103	3	Immigrants from Malaysia. Muslims 99%(Shafi Sunnis, also proselytic Dakwah). D=SBC,RCC,ECUSA.
11857	6	10	5.59	4	99.50	0.50	B	217.17	152	8	From Kerala (India). Hindus 35%, Muslims 10%, Baha'is 5%. D=OSCE,MTSC,IPC,RCC,ECUSA,AoG.
11858	1	10	2.26	5	99.95	0.05	C	572.13	51	10	Immigrants from Malta, in professions. All Catholics. D=RCC(large % charismatics).
11859	0	10	1.31	0	99.91	0.09	C	440.88	46	10	North Dakota, Fort Berthold Reservation. Language nearly extinct; under 6 elderly speakers.
11860	0	10	1.31	0	99.85	0.15	C	361.51	52	9	Arizona, related to Pima on Gila River and Salt River Reservations near Phoenix. Spoken by 37% (middle-aged or older).
11861	0	10	1.30	1	62.00	38.00	B	45.26	97	6	Southeast Massachusetts. Language extinct; members of ethnic group; 1,200 speak English only. Nonreligious 20%.
11862	0	10	1.31	0	99.96	0.04	C	480.99	44	10	Northeast Wisconsin. Language nearly extinct; under 50 speakers (elderly).
11863	4	8	1.31	0	99.72	0.28	C	294.33	54	8	New Mexico. Spoken by 80%. D=Native American Ch of NA,St Joseph's Indian Reform Ch,Apache Pentecostal Ch,Apache Independent Ch.
11864	1	10	1.31	8	99.90	0.10	C	466.47	36	10	Mixed-race persons of Mexican origin, with Amerindian ancestry. D=RCC.
11865	8	10	3.15	8	99.87	0.13	C	502.12	64	10	Expatriates, recent immigrants(legal and illegal), residents, many USA citizens. D=RCC(166 Dioceses),PCUSA,ECUSA,AoG,AAFJC,LACCC,LWC,GEB. M=GMU.
11866	0	10	1.31	8	59.00	41.00	B	43.07	103	6	Northeast Oklahoma, north central Indiana. Language extinct; no speakers out of the 2,000 ethnic group. Tribal religionists 70%.
11867	0	10	1.31	0	99.85	0.15	C	397.12	47	9	Mainly in Boston, some in New York City. Large majority resides in Canada (Quebec).
11868	3	9	1.31	0	99.80	0.20	C	365.00	48	9	Southern Florida. Spoken by 83%; some monolinguals. Animists 4%. D=Native American Ch of NA,Miccosukee Independent Indian Ch,SBC. M=SIL.
11869	0	10	1.31	0	99.78	0.22	C	316.01	55	9	California. 4 dialects. Language nearly extinct; under 10 speakers.
11870	3	10	1.31	0	99.90	0.10	C	459.90	43	10	California-Arizona border, Fort Mohave and Colorado River Reservations. Spoken by 46% (and most adults). D=NACNA,Mohave Mission Ch,ABCUSA.
11871	2	10	1.31	0	99.92	0.08	C	473.47	43	10	Northern New York, St Regis Reservation. Also in Canada. Spoken by 30% (middle-aged, older). D=Native American Ch of North America,RCC.
11872	0	5	3.73	4	45.00	55.00	A	1.64	274	4	Refugees from Mongolia. Nonreligious 40%, shamanists 30%, Lamaist Buddhist 19%, atheist 10%.
11873	0	10	1.29	0	99.78	0.22	C	316.01	52	9	East central California. Language nearly extinct; under 20 speakers left (elderly). Related to Northern Pointe.
11874	1	10	3.11	7	53.00	47.00	B	1.93	197	4	Labor migrants from Morocco, often via France. Muslims 99%(Maliki Sunnis). D=RCC.
11875	0	10	1.28	0	41.00	59.00	A	14.96	146	5	Southern Delaware. Language extinct; no speakers left in ethnic group of 400. Nonreligious 30%, animists 10%.
11876	1	10	1.30	8	58.00	42.00	B	21.17	104	5	Connecticut, NY. Language extinct; no speaker in 1,500 ethnic group. Animists 20%, Nonreligious 10%. D=Narraganset Indian Ch (oldest AIC in USA).
11877	9	8	1.40	1	99.72	0.28	C	354.78	47	9	Northeast Arizona, Utah, New Mexico. Spoken by 74%. Tribal religionists 9%, nonreligious 5%. D=Navajo Native American Ch,NACNA,CCC,ELCA,ECUSA,PCUSA.
11878	4	5	4.11	4	59.00	41.00	B	4.30	251	4	Immigrants from Nepal and India. Hindus 98%. D=RCC,ECUSA,SBC,ABCUSA.
11879	1	10	1.31	0	99.90	0.10	C	446.76	45	10	Northern Idaho. Spoken by 33% (middle-aged or older). D=NACNA. M=APM.
11880	0	10	1.31	0	99.91	0.09	C	440.88	46	10	Northwest corner of Washington State. Language nearly extinct; no speakers out of 350 ethnic group.
11881	3	8	1.31	4	99.86	0.14	C	436.32	42	10	West Arctic Eskimo. Norton Sound, Alaska to MacKenzie delta region, Canada. Spoken by 67% (adults). D=ECUSA,OCA,NACNA. M=SIL,Presbyterian Mission.
11882	0	10	1.31	0	99.80	0.20	C	332.78	53	9	Oregon, Umatilla Reservation. Spoken by 14% (middle-aged or older).
11883	5	10	1.31	0	99.90	0.10	C	482.89	39	10	Northern Nevada, also Oregon, California, Idaho. 20 Reservations. Spoken by 50% of members of tribe. Related to Mono. D=NACNA,PCUSA,AoG,ECUSA,UMC.
11884	1	9	1.31	0	99.80	0.20	C	362.08	47	9	North central New Mexico, Taos. Spoken by 90%. Animists 5%. D=Native American Ch of North America. M=Lutheran Bible Translators,SIL.
11885	3	8	1.31	4	99.86	0.14	C	426.90	43	10	Northwest Alaska, Kobuk and Noatak rivers, Seward Penisula. Spoken by 50%. Animists 2%. D=ECUSA,OCA,NACNA. M=SIL.
11886	5	10	1.23	6	99.86	0.14	C	517.93	38	10	Citizens, expatriates from Norway, recent immigrants. D=ELCA,EFCA,AFLC,CLBA,ELS.
11887	0	10	1.33	4	53.00	47.00	B	9.67	109	4	Refugees from Siberia. Ethnic group within Khalka Mongolian. Lamaist Buddhists 60%, nonreligious 20%, shamanists 14%, Muslims.
11888	1	10	1.31	0	99.92	0.08	C	460.04	44	10	Washington State, Colville Reservation. Also in Canada. Spoken by 16% (middle-aged or older). D=NACNA.
11889	3	5	1.31	0	40.00	60.00	A	5.84	140	4	Workers, immigrants from Okinawa Island(Japan). Buddhists 96%. D=ECUSA,RCC,UCC.
11890	1	10	1.31	0	99.90	0.10	C	433.62	46	10	Eastern Nebraska, Omaha Reservation. Spoken by 60% (including most adults). D=Native American Ch of North America.
11891	0	10	1.31	0	99.93	0.07	C	461.65	45	10	Central New York, eastern Wisconsin. Some in Canada. Spoken by under 3% (middle-aged or older).
11892	0	10	1.55	0	99.89	0.11	C	428.77	51	10	Central New York south of Syracuse. Also in Canada. Spoken by 6% (middle-aged or older).
11893	0	10	1.31	0	99.92	0.08	C	452.45	45	10	North central Oklahoma. Language nearly extinct; under 25 elderly speakers (1% of ethnic group). Closely related to Omaha, Kansa.
11894	0	10	1.30	0	99.90	0.10	C	431.19	46	10	North central Oklahoma. Language nearly extinct; under 50 speakers (3% of ethnic group).
11895	3	9	5.19	8	97.00	3.00	B	106.21	166	7	Refugees from Palestine, migrant workers. Muslims 64%(54% Shafi Sunnis, 5% Alawi Shias, 5% Druzes). D=RCC,GOC,JWs.
11896	1	10	1.31	8	99.90	0.10	C	499.32	36	10	Mixed-race persons, especially found in urban areas. D=Native American Ch of North America.
11897	1	10	1.31	0	99.96	0.04	C	497.56	43	10	Maine, and Canada. Spoken by 50% (middle-aged or older). D=NACNA.
11898	1	10	1.31	0	99.90	0.10	C	448.41	44	10	North central Oklahoma. Spoken by 10%. Close to Arikara. D=NACNA.
11899	3	10	1.31	1	99.88	0.12	C	468.95	46	10	Pennsylvania, Ohio, Indiana, 5 other States. Also Canada. Rhenish Low German. First language for 35%. D=83% Old Order Amish,16% Old Order Mennonites.
11900	1	10	8.95	5	82.00	18.00	B	59.86	322	6	Refugees from Iran after 1979 revolution. Muslims 50%(Imami Shias), Zoroastrians 20%, Baha'is 8%. D=AoG.
11901	6	10	1.21	6	99.78	0.22	C	444.13	21	10	Recent refugees from Poland. Nonreligious 13%. D=RCC(166 Dioceses),PNCCA,PMC,OCA,NAORCC,SCUSA.
11902	4	9	1.31	8	99.96	0.04	C	592.17	30	10	Immigrants from many Polynesian cultures. D=RCC,UMC,UCC,ABCUSA.
11903	0	10	1.31	0	99.80	0.20	C	337.93	53	9	Northern California, Clear Lake area. 7 dialects. Spoken by under 10%. Language nearly extinct.
11904	0	10	1.31	0	99.90	0.10	C	431.19	46	10	North central Oklahoma. Language nearly extinct. Closely related to Kansa, Omaha. Spoken by under 1% (all elderly).
11905	1	10	1.25	8	99.88	0.12	C	536.40	37	10	Citizens, expatriates from Portugal. D=RCC. R=AWR.
11906	1	10	1.31	0	99.91	0.09	C	455.87	44	10	Southern Michigan, northern Wisconsin. Also in Canada. Spoken by 6% (middle-aged or older). D=NACNA.
11907	0	10	1.31	0	40.00	60.00	A	14.60	151	5	Scattered in eastern Virginia. Language extinct. no speakers out of 3,000 ethnic population. Animists 25%, Nonreligious 10%.
11908	7	10	1.25	8	99.91	0.09	C	551.36	35	10	From Puerto Rico. D=RCC(166 Dioceses),ECUSA,SCC,Defenders of the Faith,LACCC,ACC,Damascus Christian Ch. T=CBN. R=HA,AWR. T=LESEA.
11909	0	8	1.31	0	98.00	2.00	C	214.62	62	8	110 elderly speakers(in 1990) in Northern and Southern Puget Sound Salish. Nearly extinct.
11910	0	10	8.62	5	67.00	33.00	B	24.45	395	5	Mainly from India, Punjab State. Sikhs 60%, Hindus 30%, Muslims.
11911	0	10	1.31	0	40.00	60.00	A	14.60	151	5	Northeast corner of Oklahoma. Language nearly extinct. Closely related to Kansa, Omaha. Nonreligious 20%.
11912	1	10	1.31	0	99.90	0.10	C	443.47	45	10	Southeast corner of California. Closely related to Maricopa, Mohave. Spoken by 33% (middle-aged or older). D=NACNA.
11913	0	10	1.31	0	99.91	0.09	C	438.43	46	10	Washington State, Olympic Peninsula. Language nearly extinct; under 10 speakers.
11914	0	10	1.31	0	99.91	0.09	C	444.21	45	10	Washington State, Pacific side of Olympic Peninsula. Language nearly extinct; under 10 speakers.
11915	2	10	1.31	6	99.83	0.17	C	460.48	44	10	Refugees from Romania since 1917; 1951-1980, 49,800 more. Nonreligious 16%. D=Romanian Orthodox E-America(OCA),ROME.
11916	5	10	1.31	8	99.80	0.20	C	435.08	43	10	Anglo-Romani Gypsies from Britain. Nonreligious 10%. D=nomadic caravan churches,RCC,UMC,AoG,Gypsy Evangelical Movement. M=GGMS.
11917	9	10	2.04	7	99.67	0.33	C	359.48	38	9	Refugees from USSR since 1917. Many speak only English now. Nonreligious 20%. D=Orthodox Ch in America(7 Dioceses),ROC,ROCOR,ORCP,EMBC,AOCC.
11918	4	10	1.31	6	99.80	0.20	C	417.56	25	10	Refugees from Carpathia under USSR. Nonreligious 19%. D=RCC(3 Ruthenian-rite Dioceses),OCA,American Carpatho-Russian OGCC,UOCUSA.
11919	1	10	1.31	5	99.86	0.14	C	492.82	32	10	Immigrants from Samoa. Mainly Congregationalists. D=UCC.
11920	0	9	0.70	7	51.04	48.96	B	0.07	75	2	Technical personnel, students, from Saudi Arabia. Muslims 99%(Shafi,Wahhabi, Maliki,and Hanbali Sunnis).
11921	1	10	1.31	0	99.90	0.10	C	446.76	45	10	Iowa, Oklahoma, Kansas-Nebraska border. Spoken by 32% (middle-aged or elderly). Animists 5%. D=NACNA. M=SIL.
11922	4	10	1.30	1	99.80	0.20	C	359.16	52	9	D=nomadic caravan communities,RCC,UMC,Gypsy Evangelical Movement. M=GGMS.
11923	3	10	1.31	0	99.90	0.10	C	463.93	43	10	New York, Allegheny Reservations; Oklahoma. Canada. Spoken by 2%. D=RCC,also oldest ongoing prophet movement in world, begun 1800: Handsome Lake.
11924	2	10	2.06	6	99.84	0.16	C	472.16	37	10	Refugees from Yugoslavia civil war, 1990 on. Nonreligious 15%. D=Serbian Orthodox Ch in USA & Canada(3 Dioceses),SOD.
11925	0	10	1.31	0	99.78	0.22	C	316.01	55	9	Northern California. Language nearly extinct; under 5 speakers.
11926	1	10	1.30	0	99.90	0.10	C	446.76	44	10	Central and northeastern Oklahoma. Spoken by 10% (middle-aged, elderly). D=NACNA.
11927	1	10	1.31	0	99.85	0.15	C	403.32	44	10	California, Nevada, Wyoming, Utah, Idaho. Spoken by 42%. Closely related to Comanche. Animists 5%. D=Native American Ch of North America. M=independents.
11928	0	10	1.32	0	99.79	0.21	C	320.06	55	9	Washington State, east side of Puget Sound. Spoken by 28% (middle-aged and older). Animists 5%.
11929	3	10	1.18	6	99.70	0.30	C	370.47	44	9	Refugees from Slovakia. Nonreligious 20%. D=RCC(166 Dioceses),Slovak National Catholic Ch in America,SELC(LCMS).
11930	1	10	1.31	6	99.95	0.05	C	572.13	38	10	Refugees from Slovenia (Yugoslavia) until 1992 independence. D=RCC.
11931	0	10	1.30	0	99.78	0.22	C	313.17	55	9	Northwestern Washington State. Tulalip Reservation. Nearly extinct; under 20 elderly speakers.
11932	0	10	0.00	5	48.00	52.00	A	0.00	0	1.11	Refugees from Somalia. In Washington DC, especially as taxi drivers. Muslims 100%(Shafi,Hanafi Sunnis).
11933	0	9	1.31	5	99.85	0.15	C	406.42	44	10	Alaska Peninsula, Kodiak Island. English as second language. Only 600 elderly speakers(20%) left. Animists 4%.
11934	1	10	2.38	8	99.84	0.16	C	466.03	53	10	Mixed-race Spanish-speaking Amerindian/Whites, from most South American countries. D=RCC. T=CBN. R=HA,AWR. T=LESEA.
11935	2	10	1.31	0	99.90	0.10	C	446.76	43	10	Colorado, Utah, Arizona, Nevada, California. Spoken by 50% (adults). D=Native American Ch of North America,ABCUSA. M=SIL.
11936	0	10	1.31	0	99.81	0.19	C	339.99	53	9	Washington State, southern end of Puget Sound. Language nearly extinct; spoken by under 2% (elderly).
11937	1	9	1.31	0	99.80	0.20	C	356.24	47	9	New Mexico, around Albuquerque. Spoken by 83% (adults, elderly). Animists 7%. D=Native American Ch of North America. M=SIL.
11938	1	10	1.31	8	99.96	0.04	C	606.19	35	10	Citizens, expatriates from Spain, descendants of first colonizers in North America. D=RCC.
11939	0	10	1.31	1	38.00	62.00	A	1.38	144	4	Dzhudezmo, Spanyol. Sefardi Jews from Spain and North Africa, Mostly practicing Jews.
11940	0	10	1.30	0	99.80	0.20	C	332.88	53	9	Northeast Washington State. Spoken by 10% only (all middle-aged or older).
11941	0	10	1.31	0	99.91	0.09	C	447.54	45	10	Washington State, southeastern tip of Vancouver Island. Also many in Canada. Spoken by under 1% (elderly).
11942	5	10	1.16	6	99.65	0.35	C	339.26	22	9	Recent immigrants. Swedish Pietist origins. Nonreligious 22%. D=ELCA,ECCA,EFCA,BGC,IAoG.
11943	1	9	6.50	8	77.00	23.00	B	42.15	256	6	Immigrants from Syria. Muslims 85%(77% Hanafi Sunnis,4% Alawis,4% Druzes).D=SOC.

Continued overleaf

Table 8-2 continued

PEOPLE		POPULATION				IDENTITY CODE		LANGUAGE		CHURCH		MINISTRY						SCRIPTURE		
Ref 1	Ethnic name 2	P% 3	In 1995 4	In 2000 5	In 2025 6	Race 7	Language 8	Autoglossonym 9	S 10	AC 11	Members 12	Jayuh 13-17	d 18	wa 19	xc 20	mc 21	mi 22	Biblioglossonym 23	Pub 24-26	ss 27
11944	Tanaina	0.00041	1,095	1,141	1,335	MIR38a	61-BAAA	tanaina cluster		80.00	913	0....	10	7	4	4	1		...	b
11945	Tanana	0.00016	427	445	521	MIR38a	61-BAEA-e	nabesna		81.00	361	0....	10	7	3	3	0	Tanana: Upper*	P..	b
11946	Tenino (Warm Springs)	0.00045	1,202	1,253	1,465	MIR38a	63-IAAA-g	tenino		80.00	1,002	0....	10	7	3	4	1		p..	b
11947	Tewa	0.00105	2,804	2,923	3,419	MIR37z	66-AABA	tewa cluster		80.00	2,338	0....	10	7	6	4	1		...	.
11948	Thai	0.04508	120,373	125,483	146,768	MSY49d	47-AAAB-d	central thai		2.00	2,510	3asuh	6	4	8	4	2	Thai*	PNB	b
11949	Tho (Tai Tho, Tay)	0.00020	534	557	651	MSY49a	47-AAAE-ae	tai-tho		3.00	17	0....	6	4	4	3	1	Tho*	P..	.
11950	Tlingit (Thlinget)	0.00300	8,011	8,351	9,767	MIR38a	63-AAAA-a	north tlingit		92.00	7,683	0....	10	8	12	4	1	Tlingit	P..	b
11951	Tongan	0.00644	17,196	17,926	20,967	MPY55g	39-CAPB	tonga cluster		97.00	17,388	4a...	10	10	14	5	2	Tongan	PNB	b
11952	Tonkawa	0.00004	107	111	130	MIR38a	65-AHAA-a	tonkawa		10.00	11	0....	8	5	2	3	0		...	b
11953	Tosk Albanian	0.00700	18,691	19,485	22,790	CEW13	55-AAAB-a	standard tosk		55.00	10,717	0A...	10	8	8	5	2	Albanian: Tosk*	PNB	b
11954	Trinidadian	0.03067	81,895	85,372	99,853	NFB68a	52-ABAF-y	trinidadian-ex-creole		92.00	78,542	1c..h	10	10	13	5	3	Lesser Antill Creole French	Pn.	.
11955	Tsimshian (Zimshian)	0.00080	2,136	2,227	2,605	MIR38a	63-CAAA-b	southeast tsimshian		94.00	2,093	0....	10	7	12	4	1	Tsimshian: Coastal	P..	b
11956	Tubatulabal	0.00002	53	56	65	MIR37z	66-BBAA-a	tubatulabal		79.00	44	0....	10	7	2	3	0		...	b
11957	Tunica	0.00007	187	195	228	MIR38a	65-EAAA-a	tunica		10.00	19	0....	8	5	2	3	0		...	b
11958	Turk	0.03371	90,012	93,834	109,751	MSY41j	44-AABA-a	osmanli		3.00	2,815	1A.u.	6	4	6	4	1	Turkish	PNB	b
11959	Tuscarora	0.00020	534	557	651	MIR38a	64-CAAE-b	tuscarora		91.30	508	0....	10	7	11	3	0		...	b
11960	Twana (Skokomish)	0.00016	427	445	521	MIR38a	63-GABC-b	skokomish		78.30	349	0....	10	7	2	3	0		...	b
11961	USA Black (Afro-American)	8.70000	23,230,727	24,217,071	28,324,815	NFB68a	52-ABAE-a	talkin-black		74.00	17,920,633	0B.uh	10	10	12	5	3		pnb	b
11962	USA Mestizo (Chicano)	3.35000	8,945,165	9,324,964	10,906,682	CLN29	51-AABB-k	chicano		82.80	7,721,070	1B.uh	10	10	14	5	2		pnb	b
11963	USA White	41.44081	110,655,187	115,353,454	134,919,917	CEW19s	52-ABAC-s	general american		65.40	75,441,159	1Bsuh	10	10	16	5	4	English*	PNB	b
11964	Ukrainian	0.29786	795,345	829,115	969,751	CEW22p	53-AAAE-b	ukrainskiy		85.00	704,747	3A.uh	10	10	13	5	3	Ukrainian	PNB	b
11965	Upper Chinook	0.00034	908	946	1,107	MIR38a	63-JAAA	east chinook cluster		78.30	741	0....	10	7	2	3	0		...	b
11966	Upper Colorado Yuman	0.00068	1,816	1,893	2,214	MIR38a	63-VDAA	walapai-yavapai cluster		80.00	1,514	0....	10	8	6	5	2	Havasupai-walapai-yavapai	P..	b
11967	Upper Kuskokwim (Ingalik)	0.00007	187	195	228	MIR38a	61-BAEA-a	kolchan		80.00	156	0....	10	7	3	3	0		p..	.
11968	Upper Piman (Papago-Pima)	0.00909	24,272	25,303	29,595	MIR37z	66-BEAA	pima-papago cluster		90.00	22,772	0A...	10	9	11	5	1	Papago-pima	PN.	b
11969	Upper Tanana (Tanacross)	0.00021	561	585	684	MIR38a	61-BAEA-e	nabesna		80.00	468	0....	10	7	5	4	1	Tanana: Upper*	P..	b
11970	Urdu	0.05000	133,510	139,179	162,786	CNN25r	59-AAFO-d	standard urdu		0.10	139	2Asuh	5	4	4	1	0	Urdu	PNB	b
11971	Uzbek	0.00800	21,362	22,269	26,046	MSY41l	44-AABD-a	central uzbek		0.10	22	1A.u.	5	4	4	1	0	Uzbek*	PNb	b
11972	Vietnamese	0.41544	1,109,307	1,156,407	1,352,559	MSY52b	46-EBAA-ac	general viêt		20.00	231,281	1Asu.	9	6	9	5	2	Vietnamese	PNB	b
11973	Vlach Gypsy	0.41078	1,096,864	1,143,435	1,337,387	CNN25f	59-ACBA-av	vlach-america		90.00	1,029,092	1c...	10	8	11	4	1		pn.	.
11974	Wappo	0.00002	53	56	65	MIR38a	63-RAAA	wappo cluster		10.00	6	0....	8	5	2	3	0		...	b
11975	Washo	0.00045	1,202	1,253	1,465	MIR38a	63-UAAA-a	washo		80.30	1,006	0....	10	7	3	5	0		...	b
11976	Welsh	0.81778	2,183,635	2,276,349	2,662,467	CEW18d	50-ABAA-bc	cymraeg-safonol		78.50	1,786,934	2A.uh	10	10	15	5	3	Welsh	PNB	b
11977	West Alaskan Eskimo	0.00773	20,641	21,517	25,167	MRY40b	60-ABAC-a	yukon-kuskokwim		86.00	18,505	0...h	10	10	13	5	3	Eskimo: Yupik, Central*	PN.	b
11978	West Indian Black	0.05000	133,510	139,179	162,786	NFB68a	52-ABAE-c	caribbean-english		90.00	125,261	0B.uh	10	9	13	5	1		pnb	b
11979	Western Apache (Coyotero)	0.00543	14,499	15,115	17,679	MIR38a	61-BDAA-b	west apache		80.00	12,092	1as..	10	9	7	4	1	Apache: Western*	PNB	b
11980	Western Cree	0.01000	26,702	27,836	32,557	MIR38a	62-ADAA-a	plains-cree		93.00	25,887	1.s..	10	9	12	4	1	Cree: Saskatchewan, North*	PNB	b
11981	Western Keres Pueblo	0.00258	6,889	7,182	8,400	MIR38a	63-XAAA-a	acoma		90.00	6,463	0....	10	9	11	4	1	Keres, Western	P..	.
11982	Western Ojibwa (Chippewa)	0.02000	53,404	55,671	65,115	MIR38a	62-ADAF-c	southwest ojibwa		94.00	52,331	0....	10	9	12	4	3	Ojibway*	PN.	b
11983	White Meo (Hmu, Miao)	0.03411	91,080	94,948	111,053	MSY47a	48-AAAA-a	hmong-daw		35.00	33,232	2A...	9	6	6	5	1	Hmong Daw*	PN.	.
11984	White Tai (Thai Trang)	0.00400	10,681	11,134	13,023	MSY49z	47-AAAD-b	tai-kao		8.00	891	0....	7	5	4	3	1	Tai: White*	P..	.
11985	Wichita	0.00034	908	946	1,107	MIR38a	64-BACA-a	wichita		89.40	846	0....	10	7	12	3	0		...	b
11986	Wintu	0.00043	1,148	1,197	1,400	MIR38a	63-SAAA-a	proper wintu		78.30	937	0....	10	7	2	3	0		...	b
11987	Wiyot	0.00005	134	139	163	MIR38a	63-PAAA-a	wiyot		20.00	28	0....	9	5	2	3	0		...	b
11988	Wyandot (Huron)	0.00050	1,335	1,392	1,628	MIR38a	64-CAAB-a	wyandot		10.00	139	0....	8	5	2	3	0		...	b
11989	Yakima (Northwest Sahapti	0.00364	9,720	10,132	11,851	MIR38a	63-IAAA-e	yakima		90.00	9,119	0....	10	10	11	5	3		p..	b
11990	Yaqui	0.00241	6,435	6,708	7,846	MIR37z	66-BEDA-a	yaqui		95.00	6,373	1....	10	10	11	5	2	Yaqui	PN.	b
11991	Yemeni Arab	0.00161	4,299	4,482	5,242	CMT30	12-AACF-n	yemeni		0.20	9	1Asuh	5	3	3	5	0		pnb	b
11992	Yokuts (Chuckchansi)	0.00023	614	640	749	MIR38a	63-SCAA-a	yokuts		78.30	501	0....	10	7	2	3	0		...	b
11993	Yuchi	0.00068	1,816	1,893	2,214	MIR38a	65-GAAA-a	yuchi		80.90	1,531	0....	10	7	3	3	0		...	b
11994	Yurok	0.00186	4,967	5,177	6,056	MIR38a	63-OAAA-a	yurok		91.30	4,727	0....	10	7	11	3	0		...	b
11995	Zuni Pueblo	0.00260	6,943	7,237	8,465	MIR38a	63-WAAA-a	zuñi		92.00	6,658	0....	10	10	11	5	1	Zuni	P..	.
11996	other minor peoples	0.10000	267,020	278,357	325,573	...				50.00	139,179		10	7	8	5	0			
Uruguay		**100.00000**	**3,218,187**	**3,337,058**	**3,906,674**					**64.78**	**2,161,731**									
11997	Amerindian	0.01000	322	334	391	MIR39z	51-AABB-hu	uruguayo		80.00	267	1B.uh	10	7	2	4	1		pnb	b
11998	Argentinian White	0.90000	28,964	30,034	35,160	CLT27	51-AABB-hv	argentino		86.00	25,829	1B.uh	10	9	11	5	1		pnb	b
11999	Armenian	0.03400	1,094	1,135	1,328	CEW14	57-AAAA-b	ashkharik		79.00	896	4A.u.	10	9	13	5	1	Armenian: Modern, Eastern	PNB	b
12000	Assyrian	0.10000	3,218	3,337	3,907	CMT31	12-AAAA-d	east syriac		95.00	3,170	1as..	10	8	11	5	2	Syriac: Ancient*	PNB	b
12001	Basque	0.30000	9,655	10,011	11,720	CEW16	40-AAAA-a	general euskara		91.00	9,110	3....	10	9	15	5	1	Basque	PNB	b
12002	Black	0.30000	9,655	10,011	11,720	NFB71a	51-AABB-hu	uruguayo		91.00	9,110	1B.uh	10	8	11	5	3		pnb	b
12003	Brazilian Mulato	0.30000	9,655	10,011	11,720	NFB70b	51-AABA-e	general português		94.00	9,411	2Bsuh	10	9	13	5	3	Portuguese	PNB	b
12004	Brazilian White	0.60000	19,309	20,022	23,440	CLT26	51-AABA-e	general português		94.00	18,821	2Bsuh	10	9	12	5	2	Portuguese	PNB	b
12005	Bulgar	0.05000	1,609	1,669	1,953	CEW22b	53-AAAH-b	bulgarski		71.00	1,185	2A.uh	10	8	8	4	1	Bulgarian	PNB	b
12006	Chilean Mestizo	0.10000	3,218	3,337	3,907	CLN29	51-AABB-hr	chileno		89.00	2,970	1B.uh	10	9	12	5	3		pnb	.
12007	Croat	0.10000	3,218	3,337	3,907	CEW22d	53-AAAG-b	standard hrvatski		88.00	2,937	2Asuh	10	9	11	5	1	Croatian	PNB	b
12008	Czech	0.15000	4,827	5,006	5,860	CEW22e	53-AAAD-a	czesky		76.00	3,804	2Asuh	10	9	8	5	2	Czech	PNB	b
12009	French	0.60000	19,309	20,022	23,440	CEW21b	51-AABI-d	general français	6	74.00	14,817	1B.uh	10	9	14	5	2	French	PNB	b
12010	Galician	1.20000	38,618	40,045	46,880	CEW21d	51-AABA-b	galego		76.00	30,434	1csuh	10	8	15	4	1	Galician	PNB	b
12011	German	0.90000	28,964	30,034	35,160	CEW19m	52-ABCE-a	standard hoch-deutsch		86.00	25,829	2B.uh	10	9	13	5	2	German*	PNB	b
12012	Greek	0.40000	12,873	13,348	15,627	CEW20	56-AAAA-c	dhimotiki		91.00	12,147	2B.uh	10	9	11	4	1	Greek: Modern	PNB	b
12013	Han Chinese	0.00480	154	160	188	MSY42a	79-AAAB-ba	kuo-yü	1	50.00	80	2Bsuh	10	7	8	5	1	Chinese: Kuoyu*	PNB	b
12014	Hungarian	0.03000	965	1,001	1,172	MSW51g	41-BAAA-a	general magyar		78.00	781	2A.u.	10	9	8	5	3	Hungarian	PNB	b
12015	Italian	2.60000	83,673	86,764	101,574	CEW21e	51-AABQ-c	standard italiano		80.00	69,411	2B.uh	10	9	15	5	3	Italian	PNB	b
12016	Jewish	1.75000	56,318	58,399	68,367	CMT35	51-AABB-hu	uruguayo		0.10	58	1B.uh	5	4	2	1	0		pnb	b
12017	Mulatto	1.70000	54,709	56,730	66,413	NFB71b	51-AABB-hu	uruguayo		83.00	47,086	1B.uh	10	9	12	5	3		pnb	b
12018	Platine Italian	0.20000	6,436	6,674	7,813	CEW21e	51-AABB-ia	cocoliche		83.00	5,540	1B.uh	10	10	15	5	3		pnb	b
12019	Polish	0.10000	3,218	3,337	3,907	CEW22i	53-AAAC-c	polski		88.00	2,937	2A.uh	10	9	11	5	2	Polish	PNB	b
12020	Russian	0.40000	12,873	13,348	15,627	CEW22j	53-AAAE-d	russkiy		75.00	10,011	4B.uh	10	9	12	5	2	Russian	PNB	b
12021	Serb	0.15000	4,827	5,006	5,860	CEW22l	53-AAAG-a	standard srpski		80.00	4,004	1Asuh	10	8	8	5	1	Serbian*	PNB	b
12022	Slovak	0.10000	3,218	3,337	3,907	CEW22m	53-AAAD-b	slovensky		77.00	2,570	1Asuh	10	9	8	5	1	Slovak	PNB	b
12023	Spaniard	0.90000	28,964	30,034	35,160	CEW21k	51-AABB-hu	uruguayo		91.00	27,331	1B.uh	10	10	15	5	1		pnb	b
12024	USA White	0.06000	1,931	2,002	2,344	CEW19s	52-ABAC-s	general american	9	67.00	1,341	1Bsuh	10	9	13	5	1	English*	PNB	b
12025	Ukrainian	0.06000	1,931	2,002	2,344	CEW22p	53-AAAE-b	ukrainskiy		76.00	1,522	3A.uh	10	9	12	5	1	Ukrainian	PNB	b
12026	Uruguayan Mestizo	3.00000	96,546	100,112	117,200	CLN29	51-AABB-hu	uruguayo		62.00	62,069	1B.uh	10	10	12	5	2		pnb	b
12027	Uruguayan White	82.80120	2,664,697	2,763,124	3,234,773	CLT27	51-AABB-hu	uruguayo		63.50	1,754,584	1B.uh	10	10	12	5	2		pnb	b
12028	other minor peoples	0.10000	3,218	3,337	3,907	...				50.00	1,669		10	7	6	5	0			
Uzbekistan		**100.00000**	**22,480,286**	**24,317,851**	**33,354,778**					**1.62**	**394,334**									
12029	Afghani Pathan	0.00835	1,877	2,031	2,785	CNT24a	58-ABDA-a	pashto		0.00	0	1As..	0	3	6	0	0		pnb	b
12030	Armenian	0.24511	55,101	59,605	81,756	CEW14	57-AAAA-b	ashkharik		75.00	44,704	4A.u.	10	7	11	2	2	Armenian: Modern, Eastern	PNB	b
12031	Avar	0.00387	870	941	1,291	CEW17b	42-BBAA-a	north avar		0.00	0	1....	0	3	2	0	1	Avar	P..	b
12032	Azerbaijani	0.22418	50,396	54,516	74,775	MSY41a	44-AABA-fa	north azeri		0.00	0	2c.u.	0	3	3	0	2	Azerbaijani*	PNB	b
12033	Balkar	0.00246	553	598	821	MSY41z	44-AABB-a	literary karachay-balkar		0.00	0	1c.u.	0	3	3	0	0	Karachay-balkar	PN.	.
12034	Bashkir	0.17552	39,457	42,683	58,544	MSY41b	44-AABB-g	bashqurt		7.00	2,988	1A.u.	7	5	7	0	1	Bashkir	Pn.	b
12035	Bulgarian	0.01093	2,457	2,658	3,646	CEW22b	53-AAAH-b	bulgarski		72.00	1,914	2A.uh	10	6	8	1	1	Bulgarian	PNB	b
12036	Buryat	0.00321	722	781	1,071	MSY41y	44-BAAB-b	buryat		5.00	39	3A..h	7	4	7	0	1	Buryat*	PNB	b
12037	Byelorussian	0.07855	17,658	19,102	26,200	CEW22c	53-AAAE-c	bielorusskiy		50.00	9,551	3A.uh	10	7	8	4	3	Byelorussian*	PNB	b
12038	Central Asian Arab	0.01416	3,183	3,443	4,723	CMT30	12-AACI-c	arab-uzbeki		2.00	69	0....	6	3	3	0	0		...	b
12039	Central Asian Gypsy	0.04300	9,667	10,457	14,343	CNN25f	58-AACC-j	tajiki		0.01	1	2asu.	3	1	0	0	0	Tajik*	PNB	b
12040	Central Asian Jew	0.04377	9,840	10,644	14,599	CMT35	58-AACC-kb	bukharik		0.02	2	1csu.	3	1	2	0	0		pnb	b
12041	Central Circassian	0.00107	241	260	357	CEW17a	42-AAAA-b	cherkes		0.00	0	1a...	0	2	3	0	0		pn.	b
12042	Chechen	0.00508	1,142	1,235	1,694	CEW17d	42-BAAA-b	chechen		0.00	0	0....	0	3	2	0	1	Chechen	P..	b
12043	Chuvash	0.05085	11,431	12,366	16,961	MSY41c	44-AAAA-a	chuvash		35.00	4,328	2....	9	6	8	0	1	Chuvash	PN.	b
12044	Crimean Tatar	0.95291	214,217	231,727	317,841	MSY41h	44-AABA-c	crimea-tatar		0.00	0	1c.u.	0	3	2	0	1	Crimean Tatar*	PNB	b
12045	Dargin (Darghin)	0.01025	2,304	2,493	3,419	CEW17b	42-BBBB-a	dargwa		0.00	0	1c.u.	0	3	2	0	1	Dargwa	P..	b
12046	Dungan (Hui, Huizui)	0.00683	1,535	1,661	2,278	MSY42b	79-AAAB-l	hui-zu		0.00	0	1Asuh	0	1	3	0	0		pnb	b
12047	East Circassian	0.00458	1,030	1,114	1,528	CEW17a	42-AAAA-c	qaberdey		10.00	111	1c...	8	4	3	1	1	Kabardian	PN.	.
12048	Estonian	0.00431	969	1,048	1,438	MSW51a	41-AAAC-b	eesti		75.00	786	4A.u.	10	8	8	2	2	Estonian: Tallinn	PNB	b
12049	Georgian	0.02375	5,339	5,775	7,922	CEW17c	42-CABB-a	kharthuli		40.00	2,310	2A.u.	9	6	8	2	1	Georgian	PNB	b
12050	German (Volga German)	0.05000	11,240	12,159	16,677	CEW19m	52-ABCE-a	standard hoch-deutsch		76.00	9,241	2B.uh	10	8	13	3	3	German*	PNB	b
12051	Greek	0.03277	7,367	7,969	10,930	CEW20	56-AAAA-c	dhimotiki		90.00	7,172	2B.uh	10	8	10	2	2	Greek: Modern	PNB	b
12052	Han Chinese	0.00412	926	1,002	1,374	MSY42a	79-AAAB-ba	kuo-yü		1.00	10	2Bsuh	6	1	3	0	0	Chinese: Kuoyu*	PNB	b
12053	Hungarian	0.00107	241	260	357	MSW51g	41-BAAA-a	general magyar		65.00	169	2A.u.	10	9	10	3	1	Hungarian	PNB	b
12054	Indo-Pakistani	0.00382	859	929	1,274	CNN25g	59-AAFO-e	general hindi		1.00	9	3Asuh	6	2	8	0	1		pnb	b
12055	Ingush	0.00239	537	581	797	CEW17d	42-BAAA-a	ingush		0.00	0	0....	0	3	0	0	1	Ingush	p..	b
12056	Jewish	0.18477	41,537	44,932	61,630	CMT35	52-ABCH	yiddish cluster		0.02	9	0B..h	3	4	6	0	0		PNB	b
12057	Judeo-Crimean Tatar	0.00200	450	486	667	CMT35	44-AABA-d	judeo-crimean-tatar		0.00	0	1c.u.	0	1	3	0	0		pnb	b
12058	Kalmyk	0.00261	587	635	871	MSY41y	44-BAAB-d	kalmyk		1.00	6	2c..h	6	3	6	0	0	Mongolian: Kalmyk*	PNb	b
12059	Karachai (Alan)	0.00166	373	404	554	MSY41z	44-AABB-a	literary karachay-balkar		0.00	0	1c.u.	0	2	3	0	1	Karachay-balkar	PN.	.
12060	Karakalpak (Black Hat)	2.07913	467,394	505,600	693,489	MSY41z	44-AABC-b	karakalpak		0.01	51	1c.u.	3	3	0	0	1	Karakalpak	Pn.	b
12061	Kazakh	4.07988	917,169	992,139	1,360,835	MSY41e	44-AABC-c	kazakh		0.00	0	1c.u.	0	3	0	0	2	Kazakh	PN.	b
12062	Khemshin (Kemshili)	0.00500	1,124	1,216	1,668	CEW14	57-AAAA-b	ashkharik		10.00	122	4A.u.	8	3	6	0	0	Armenian: Modern, Eastern	PNB	b
12063	Kirghiz	0.88292	198,483	214,707	294,496	MSY41g	44-AABC-d	kirghiz		0.00	0	2r.u.	0	3	3	0	2	Kirghiz	PN.	b

Continued opposite

Table 8-2 continued

EVANGELIZATION								EVANGELISM			ADDITIONAL DESCRIPTIVE DATA
Ref 1	*D* 28	*aC* 29	*CG%* 30	*r* 31	*E* 32	*U* 33	*W* 34	*e* 35	*R* 36	*T* 37	*Locations, civil divisions, literacy, religions, church history, denominations, dioceses, church growth, missions, agencies, ministries, movements* 38
11944	1	10	1.31	0	99.80	0.20	C	341.64	52	9	Southern Alaska, Cook Inlet and adjacent area. Spoken by 27% (middle-aged or elderly). Animists 5%. D=NACNA.
11945	0	10	1.31	0	99.81	0.19	C	339.99	53	9	Central Alaska, lower and middle Tanana river. Spoken by 27% (middle-aged, or older).
11946	1	10	1.31	0	99.80	0.20	C	344.56	51	9	Oregon, Warm Springs Reservation. Spoken by 20% (middle-aged or older). D=NACNA.
11947	1	10	5.61	0	99.80	0.20	C	341.64	150	9	North of Santa Fe, New Mexico, also Arizona. Spoken by 66% (mainly adults and elderly). 7 dialects. Animists 5%. D=Native American Ch of North America.
11948	2	10	1.31	6	63.00	37.00	B	4.59	82	4	Refugees from Thailand. Theravada Buddhists 95%, Muslims 1%, Hindus, Baha'is. D=Thai Outreach Chs,&c.
11949	1	10	1.23	4	37.00	63.00	A	4.05	139	4	Refugees from northeastern Viet Nam near China border. Polytheists 95%. D=RCC. M=CMA.
11950	1	10	1.31	0	99.92	0.08	C	466.76	44	10	Alaska panhandle, also Canada. Language isolate. Spoken by 21% (middle-aged or older). Fishermen, foresters. Animists 2%. D=Native American Ch of NA.
11951	2	10	1.31	5	99.97	0.03	C	608.96	29	10	Immigrants from Tonga. Mainly Methodists. D=UMC,ECUSA.
11952	0	10	1.31	0	40.00	60.00	A	14.60	151	5	North central Oklahoma. Language extinct; no fluent speakers left out of ethnic group of 100. Nonreligious 20%.
11953	2	10	7.23	6	99.55	0.45	B	244.91	174	8	Refugees from south Albania. Muslims 30% (Sunnis), nonreligious 10%. D=AOC,RCC.
11954	4	10	2.91	8	99.92	0.08	C	523.84	62	10	Migrants from Trinidad & Tobago. Afro-American spiritists 3%, Baha'is. D=RCC,ECUSA,AoG,indigenous chs.
11955	3	10	1.31	0	99.94	0.06	C	490.63	42	10	Alaska, tip of panhandle. Also in Canada. Spoken by half of ethnic group (middle-aged, elderly). Animists 2%. D=NACNA,ECUSA,ACC. M=CMS.
11956	0	10	1.31	0	99.79	0.21	C	320.06	52	9	Southern California. Language nearly extinct; under 6 elderly speakers.
11957	0	10	1.34	0	40.00	60.00	A	14.60	153	5	Central Louisiana. Language extinct; no speakers left out of ethnic group of over 150. Nonreligious 10%.
11958	1	10	5.80	8	59.00	41.00	B	6.46	302	4	Immigrants from Turkey. Muslims 92%. D=Turkish Orthodox Ch in America(P-Istanbul).
11959	0	10	1.30	0	99.91	0.09	C	440.88	46	10	Tuscarora Reservation, near Niagara Falls, New York. Also in Canada. Language nearly extinct; spoken by only 3% (elderly).
11960	0	10	1.31	0	99.78	0.22	C	315.23	55	9	Washington State, east of Puget Sound. Nearly extinct; spoken by only 2% (elderly).
11961	9	10	0.98	8	99.74	0.26	C	397.04	30	9	African Americans. Muslims 5%(Nation of Islam, and American Muslim Mission), Sunnis Muslims 2%, Baha'is 1%. D=NBCUSA,NBCA,CoGiC,NPBC,AMEC,SDA.
11962	2	10	1.23	8	99.83	0.17	C	473.88	31	10	Citizens of Latin American mixed-race origins(Amerindian/Whites). D=RCC,many Pentecostals bodies. T=CBN. R=AWR. T=LESEA.
11963	12	10	1.10	8	99.65	0.35	C	356.63	37	9	Nonreligious 11%. Christians: Protestants 71%, 17% RCs, 6% marginal. D=RCC,SBC,UMC,CJCLdS,JWs,ELCA,CC,PCUSA,ECUSA,UCC, & 1,300 others.
11964	10	10	1.31	6	99.85	0.15	C	502.60	42	10	Refugees from former USSR since 1917. Nonreligious 14%. D=UOCUSA(3 Dioceses),RCC(3 Ukrainian-rite Dioceses),OCA,UOCA,HUAOCE,MBCNA,AOCC.
11965	0	10	1.31	0	99.78	0.22	C	315.23	55	9	North central Oregon and Washington States. Nearly extinct; under 10 speakers.
11966	2	8	1.31	0	99.80	0.20	C	356.24	50	9	Central and northwest Arizona. Spoken by 80%. Animists 5%. D=NACNA,Havasupai Bible Ch. M=United Indian Mission,SIL.
11967	0	10	1.32	0	99.80	0.20	C	324.12	55	9	McGrath Ingalik. Spoken by 90%. Central Alaska, upper Kuskokwim river. Animists 5%.
11968	7	9	1.31	0	99.90	0.10	C	473.04	40	10	South central Arizona. Also in Mexico. Spoken by 75%. Animists 5%. D=NACNA,SBC,PCUSA,RCC,AoG,CON,Pima Independent Ch. M=SIL.
11969	1	9	1.30	0	99.80	0.20	C	335.80	52	9	East central Alaska, also Canada. Spoken by 80% including most adults. Animists 4%.D=NACNA. M=SIL.
11970	0	10	2.67	5	50.10	49.90	B	0.18	202	3	Migrants from India, Pakistan. Muslims 100%(Hanafi Sunnis).
11971	0	10	3.14	5	44.10	55.90	A	0.16	239	3	In New York City; refugees from Afghanistan, USSR. Muslims 78%(Hanafi Sunnis), nonreligious 20%.
11972	7	10	10.57	6	89.00	11.00	B	64.97	352	6	Refugees since 1960 from Viet Nam. Mahayana Buddhists 52%, nonreligious 13%, New-Religionists 12%, Bahai's 1%. D=SBC,PCUSA,ABCUSA,UMC,ELCA.
11973	1	10	1.31	1	99.90	0.10	C	459.90	46	10	Pacific northwest, Los Angeles, Texas, Chicago, Virginia. Also in 25 countries. D=OCA(Russian Orthodox).
11974	0	10	1.10	0	40.00	60.00	A	14.60	137	5	California, north of San Francisco bay area. No speakers in ethnic group; language extinct. Nonreligious 10%.
11975	0	10	1.31	0	99.80	0.20	C	340.86	52	9	On Nevada-California border, southeast of Lake Tahoe. Spoken by 10% (middle-aged or older). Animists 5%.
11976	6	10	1.19	5	99.79	0.21	C	448.41	38	10	Settlers from Wales over last hundred years. Nonreligious 11%.D=UCC,AoG,SDA,UMC,PCUSA,ECUSA.
11977	4	7	1.31	4	99.86	0.14	C	455.15	40	10	Central Yupik. Alaska, Nunivak Island. Spoken by 88%. Bilingual. Animists 4%. D=ECUSA,Orthodox Ch in America,NACNA,Moravian Ch.
11978	3	10	1.31	8	99.90	0.10	C	528.88	33	10	From St Vincent, Grenada, St Kitts, USVI,and many other islands. Afro-American spiritists 5%(many Rastafarians). D=CPWI,RCC,UMC. D=SBC,NBC,EOC,COFB.
11979	1	8	1.31	1	99.80	0.20	C	382.52	46	9	East central Arizona, several Reservations. Language spoken by 92%. Animists 5%, Nonreligious 5%.D=Native American Ch of North America. M=SIL.
11980	1	7	1.31	4	99.93	0.07	C	509.17	40	10	North central Montana; majority in Canada. Spoken by 66%. Animists 3%. D=Native American Ch of North America.
11981	1	10	1.31	0	99.90	0.10	C	436.90	46	10	North central New Mexico. Spoken by 56%. D=Native American Ch of North America. M=SIL.
11982	4	10	2.17	0	99.94	0.06	C	500.92	58	10	From Lake Superior to North Dakota, Montana. Also in Canada. Spoken by 58% (middle-aged or older). Animists 2%. D=NACN,ECUSA,CMA.
11983	1	10	8.45	4	88.00	12.00	B	112.42	285	7	Striped Meo refugees from North Viet Nam, northwestern Tonkin Province. Polytheists 65%. D=RCC. M=CLA.
11984	1	10	4.59	4	43.00	57.00	A	12.55	331	5	Refugees from North Viet Nam, along Red, Black rivers. Animists 55%, Buddhists 35%. D=RCC.
11985	0	10	1.31	0	99.89	0.11	C	428.77	46	10	West central Oklahoma. Spoken by only 6% (middle-aged or older).
11986	0	10	1.31	0	99.78	0.22	C	315.23	55	9	California, Clear Lake and Colusa area and northward. Nearly extinct; under 20 speakers.
11987	0	10	1.26	0	51.00	49.00	B	37.23	116	5	Northwest California. Extinct since 1962; no speakers left in ethnic group of over 100. Nonreligious 10%.
11988	0	10	1.31	0	40.00	60.00	A	14.60	151	5	Northeast Oklahoma. Also in Canada. Extinct, no speakers although large ethnic group remains. Nonreligious 15%.
11989	3	10	1.31	0	99.90	0.10	C	463.18	43	10	South central Washington State(Yakima Valley), northern California. Spoken by 37%. Animists 4%. D=RCC,Indian Shaker Ch(begun 1883),NACNA.
11990	2	7	1.31	0	99.95	0.05	C	492.38	41	10	Arizona (Tucson, Phoenix areas); majority in Mexico. Animists 4%. D=Native American Ch of NA,Yaqui Church.
11991	0	6	2.22	7	46.20	53.80	A	0.33	173	3	Refugees from Yemen wars. Muslims 100%(50% Zaydis, 40% Sunnis, 5% Ismailis, 5% others).
11992	0	10	1.31	0	99.78	0.22	C	315.23	55	9	California, southern San Joaquin Valley and Sierra foothills. Nearly extinct; under 10 speakers.
11993	0	10	1.31	0	99.81	0.19	C	339.28	53	9	East central Oklahoma, among Creek people. Language isolate. Spoken by 3% only (middle-aged or older). Nonreligious 21%.
11994	0	10	1.31	0	99.91	0.09	C	444.21	45	10	Northwest California. Language nearly extinct, with under 10 speakers in ethnic groups of around 5,000.
11995	4	8	1.31	0	99.92	0.08	C	456.68	45	10	New Mexico, south of Gallup. Language isolate. Spoken by 91%. Animists 6%. D=NACNA,CRC,RCC,SBC. M=SIL.
11996	0	10	1.41		85.00	15.00	B	155.12	45	7	Swiss, Karaite Jews, Parsis, Shona(AACJM), Tamil(CPM), Yoruba(COTLA), Congo(EJCSK). Nonreligious 11%, Hindus 5%, Muslims 5%.
Uruguay											
11997	1	10	1.31	8	99.80	0.20	C	388.36	48	9	Scattered members of former Amerindian tribes, mainly in urban areas. Nonreligious 15%. D=RCC.
11998	7	10	1.30	8	99.86	0.14	C	489.68	38	10	Emigres, expatriates in business. Nonreligious 10%. D=RCC,MCCA,JWs,SDA,UPCI,ECC,NTMU. M=FMB.
11999	3	10	4.60	6	99.79	0.21	C	438.29	94	10	Refugees from 1915 genocide. Nonreligious 18%. D=Armenian Apostolic Ch(Gregorians: C-Echmiadzin),RCC,AEC. M=AMAA.
12000	2	10	5.93	5	99.95	0.05	C	568.67	110	10	Refugees from Middle East. D=Ancient Ch of the East,RCC.
12001	1	10	4.62	4	99.91	0.09	C	524.79	97	10	Strong Catholics, from Spain. D=RCC. M=SJ.
12002	6	10	1.30	8	99.91	0.09	C	528.11	33	10	Afro-American spiritists 7%(Umbanda). D=RCC,ECUSA,MCCA,SDA,JWs,ECC.
12003	4	10	1.30	8	99.94	0.06	C	593.56	43	10	Mixed-race persons(Black/White). Migrants. D=RCC,SA,SDA,JWs.
12004	7	10	1.30	8	99.94	0.06	C	590.13	34	10	Expatriates from Brazil, in business. D=RCC,AoG,WC,FWBC,JWs,SDA,NTMU. M=NAFWB,FMB.
12005	1	10	3.93	6	99.71	0.29	C	352.44	104	9	Refugees from Bulgaria. Nonreligious 25%. D=Bulgarian Orthodox Ch(P-Sofia).
12006	6	10	1.30	8	99.89	0.11	C	513.26	32	10	Immigrants from Chile. D=Evangelical Pentecostal Ch of Chile,RCC,SA,SDA,JWs,UPCI.
12007	1	10	5.85	6	99.88	0.12	C	507.49	120	10	Refugees from former Yugoslavia. Nonreligious 10%. D=RCC.
12008	2	10	4.56	6	99.76	0.24	C	402.23	108	10	Refugees from CSSR after 1940. Nonreligious 20%. D=RCC,Moravian Ch.
12009	1	10	2.67	8	99.74	0.26	C	405.15	67	10	Expatriates from France, in business. Nonreligious 23%. D=RCC. M=SJ,OFM.
12010	1	10	1.30	1	99.76	0.24	C	388.36	43	9	Expatriates from western Spain. Nonreligious 20%. D=RCC. M=SJ.
12011	8	10	3.22	8	99.86	0.14	C	514.79	73	10	Expatriates from Germany. D=RCC,IEM(Mennonite),IERP,IM,NAC,SDA,JWs,ECC. M=MBCNA,GCMC.
12012	1	10	3.66	7	99.91	0.09	C	538.08	78	10	Immigrants from Greece, Cyprus. In trade, commerce. D=Greek Orthodox Ch(AD-N&S America).
12013	1	10	4.48	7	99.50	0.50	B	215.35	119	8	Long-time immigrants from China. Buddhists/Chinese folk-religionists 40%, nonreligious 10%. D=RCC.
12014	4	10	1.30	6	99.78	0.22	C	415.66	50	10	Refugees from Hungary after 1945, 1956. Nonreligious 15%. D=Hungarian Reformed Ch of Uruguay,SDA,JWs,RCC.
12015	6	10	1.77	7	99.80	0.20	C	467.20	47	10	Immigrants from Italy. Nonreligious 9%. D=RCC,Waldensian Ch,JWs,AoG,SDA,UPCI. M=OFM,SJ,TE.
12016	0	10	4.14	8	46.10	53.90	A	0.16	287	3	Annual immigration of practicing Jews from Russia, Germany, Eastern Europe, Middle East. Nonreligious 30%.
12017	5	10	1.30	8	99.83	0.17	C	472.60	33	10	Mixed-race Uruguayans. Afro-American spiritists 7%(Umbanda), Nonreligious 10%. D=RCC,MCCA,AoG,SDA,JWs.
12018	6	10	1.30	8	99.83	0.17	C	478.66	40	10	Settlers with own culture in River Plate area. Nonreligious 10%. D=RCC,WC,JWs,AoG,SDA,UPCI.
12019	3	10	1.30	6	99.88	0.12	C	513.92	22	10	Refugees from Poland. Nonreligious 9%. D=RCC,IEM(Mennonite),IM. M=MBCNA,GCMC.
12020	5	10	4.11	7	99.75	0.25	C	418.83	74	10	Refugees from USSR since 1917. Nonreligious 23%. D=Russian Orthodox Ch(P-Moscow),ROCOR(D-Argentina),IM,IEM(Mennonite),Novy Izrail. M=MBCNA,GCMC.
12021	1	10	3.77	6	99.80	0.20	C	426.32	71	10	Refugees from Serbia. Nonreligious 17%. D=Serbian Orthodox Ch(P-Belgrade).
12022	1	10	3.25	6	99.77	0.23	C	401.90	84	10	Refugees from Slovakia. Nonreligious 20%. D=RCC.
12023	1	10	1.62	8	99.91	0.09	C	531.44	43	10	Emigres from Spain, and long-time Uruguay citizens. D=RCC. M=FMB.
12024	7	10	1.34	8	99.67	0.33	C	342.37	44	9	Expatriates from USA, in business. Nonreligious 16%. D=CJCLdS,SDA,JWs,ECUSA/CASA(D-Argentina),ECC,LCA,CCS. M=FMB.
12025	1	10	5.15	6	99.76	0.24	C	407.77	118	10	Refugees from USSR after 1917. Nonreligious 20%. D=Ukrainian Autocephalous Orthodox Ch. M=UOCUSA.
12026	8	10	1.30	8	99.62	0.38	C	296.45	39	8	Mixed-race persons(White/Amerindians). Nonreligious 30%, Baha'is. D=RCC,WC(IEV),AoG,SA,SDA,JWs,ICFG,CON. M=Team Expansion,FMB.
12027	9	7	1.27	8	99.64	0.36	C	302.46	45	9	Nonreligious 29%, atheists 7%, Baha'is. D=RCC,AoG,Waldensian Ch,JWs,IEMU,CEBU,AC,COG,Avante(Brazil). M=TE,FMB. R=AWR. T=LESEA.
12028	0	10	5.25		82.00	18.00	B	149.65	175	7	USA Blacks(NBCUSA), British, Portuguese, other Latin Americans, other Europeans, other Asians. Nonreligious 15%, Muslims 15%.
Uzbekistan											
12029	0	5	0.00	5	34.00	66.00	A	0.00	0	1.10	Migrant workers, refugees from 1979-90 Afghanistan war. Muslims 100%(Hanafi Sunnis).
12030	2	7	4.73	6	99.75	0.25	C	385.98	104	9	Gregorians. Also in 27 more countries. Nonreligious 20%. D=Armenian Apostolic Ch, RCC.
12031	0	7	0.00	0	15.00	85.00	A	0.00	0	1.06	From Dagestan (Russia). Muslims 100%(Shafi Sunnis). M=IBT.
12032	1	7	0.00	1	31.00	69.00	A	0.00	0	1.12	Monolinguals 73%. Muslims 77%(53% Shias,24% Hanafi Sunnis), nonreligious 20%. D=ROC. M=IBT,CSI.
12033	0	7	0.00	1	19.00	81.00	A	0.00	0	1.09	Mainly in Russia. Superficially 100% Muslims(Hanafi Sunnis).
12034	1	8	4.82	4	49.00	51.00	A	12.52	314	5	Many speak Tatar as mother tongue. Muslims 72%(Hanafi Sunnis), nonreligious 20%. D=ROC. M=CSI.
12035	1	10	5.39	6	99.72	0.28	C	349.52	136	9	Workers, residents from Bulgaria. Nonreligious 18%, atheists 10%. D=Bulgarian Orthodox Ch. M=LBI.
12036	1	9	3.73	4	59.00	41.00	B	10.76	209	5	From Buryat-Mongol (Russia). Lamaist Buddhists 55%, nonreligious 30%, shamanists 10%. D=ROC. M=IBT.
12037	3	8	3.85	5	99.50	0.50	B	211.70	115	8	White Russians, mainly in Belorussia. Nonreligious 44%. D=ROC,RCC,Old Ritualist Chs.
12038	0	8	4.33	0	25.00	75.00	A	1.82	551	4	Mostly in Central Asia. Bilinguals in Tajiki, Uzbeki. Muslims 98%(Sunnis, some Shias).
12039	0	6	0.00	4	34.01	65.99	A	0.01	83	2	Nomads, roving bands continually on the move. Bilingual in Uzbek. Muslims 100%(Hanafi Sunnis).
12040	0	6	0.70	1	26.02	73.98	A	0.01	146	2	Judaeo-Tadzhik, Bukharian. Centered on city Bokhara. Also Israel, USA. Close to Tajiki. Religious Jews. Nonreligious 10%.
12041	0	7	0.00	0	21.00	79.00	A	0.00	0	1.08	Workers from Karachay-Cherkess AO (Russia). Muslims 100%(Hanafi Sunnis).
12042	0	7	0.00	0	16.00	84.00	A	0.00	0	1.05	From Chechen, Ingush (Russia). Most religious Muslims in ex-USSR 63% (fervent Hanafi Sunnis), atheists 21%, nonreligious 16%. M=IBT.
12043	1	8	6.64	0	75.00	25.00	B	95.81	272	6	From Chuvashia (Russia). 65% speak Russian. Muslims 35%(Sunnis), nonreligious/atheists 30%. D=ROC. M=IBT.
12044	0	7	0.00	1	24.00	76.00	A	0.00	0	1.11	Descendants of 13th-century Mongols. 1944 deported to Uzbek SSR. Literary. Muslims 100%(Hanafi Sunnis). M=IBT.
12045	0	8	0.00	0	16.00	84.00	A	0.00	0	1.06	From southern Dagestan (Russia). 65% speak Russian. Muslims 100%(Shafi Sunnis, with a few Shias). M=IBT.
12046	0	9	0.00	7	37.00	63.00	A	0.00	0	1.13	Dzhunyan, Tungan. Also in Kazakhstan, Kirghizia. Nomads. 100% Chinese Muslims(strict Hanafi Sunnis); migrated here in 1867 from northwest China.
12047	1	9	2.44	0	42.00	58.00	A	15.33	224	5	Upper Circassian. Muslims 90%(Hanafi Sunnis). D=Armenian Apostolic Ch.
12048	5	8	4.46	5	99.75	0.25	C	375.03	113	9	Most are bilingual in Russian. Nonreligious 20%. D=Russian Orthodox Ch,ELCE,RCC,MCE,AUCECB. M=UBS,LBI.
12049	1	9	4.86	4	97.00	3.00	B	141.62	137	7	Based in Georgia. Nonreligious/atheists 54%, Muslims 5%(Sunnis,Shias). D=Georgian Orthodox Ch.
12050	3	10	7.07	8	99.76	0.24	C	418.87	149	10	In Altai, Kirgizia, Kazakhstan. Nonreligious 20%. D=German Evangelical Lutheran Ch,Old Mennonites,AUCECB.
12051	2	10	2.50	7	99.90	0.10	C	519.03	60	10	Residents, merchants from Greece. Nonreligious 10%. D=Greek Orthodox Ch,ROC. M=UBS,LBI.
12052	0	10	2.33	7	51.00	49.00	B	1.86	160	4	Residents originally from China. Buddhists/folk-religionists 54%, nonreligious 40%, athiests 5%.
12053	2	9	2.87	6	99.65	0.35	C	303.68	91	9	Immigrants, refugees from Hungary. Nonreligious 25%. D=RCC,RCCU. M=LBI.
12054	0	8	2.22	7	51.00	49.00	B	1.86	173	4	Traders, merchants, refugees from India, Pakistan, Kashmir. Mostly Hindus 70%, Muslims 29%. M=IBT.
12055	0	8	0.00	0	13.00	87.00	A	0.00	0	1.04	Originally from Chechen, Ingush (Russia). Muslims 100%(fervent Hanafi Sunnis). M=IBT.
12056	0	10	2.22	5	47.02	52.98	A	0.03	170	2	Religious Jews. Declining by emigration to Israel. Bilingual in Russian.
12057	0	7	0.00	1	24.00	76.00	A	0.00	0	1.11	Judeo-Crimean Turkish. Most in Uzbekistan, also Georgia, Kazakhstan. Older speakers only. Religious Jews.
12058	0	8	1.81	1	36.00	64.00	A	1.31	196	4	Dzhungarians, from Kalmykia on Volga (Russia). Buddhists(Lamaists) 70%, nonreligious 29%.
12059	0	9	0.00	1	22.00	78.00	A	0.00	0	1.09	From Karachai-Cherkess AO. Muslims 100%(Hanafi Sunnis). M=SIL.
12060	0	7	4.01	1	22.01	77.99	A	0.00	599	1.10	In Karakalpak from Aral Sea south. Fishermen. 30% urban. Muslims 78%(Hanafi Sunnis with Sufism, Dervishes strong), nonreligious/atheists 22%. M=IBT.
12061	0	8	0.00	4	34.00	66.00	A	0.00	0	1.10	Migrants, residents from Kazakhstan. Muslims 60%(Hanafi Sunnis, with Sufi influence), nonreligious 30%, atheists 10%. M=ROC,CSI. R=FEBC,TWR.
12062	0	8	4.20	6	62.00	38.00	B	22.63	212	5	Armenians converted to Sunni Islam by Ottoman Turks in 1750s. Deported to Uzbek SSR in 1944 with Meskhetian Turks. Bilingual in Turkish. Muslims 90%(Hanafi).
12063	0	7	0.00	4	29.00	71.00	A	0.00	0	1.10	Mainly from Kirghizia, some from Afghanistan. Muslims 55%(Hanafi Sunnis), nonreligious 40%. M=IBT,CSI.

Continued overleaf

Table 8-2 continued

PEOPLE		POPULATION				IDENTITY CODE		LANGUAGE		CHURCH		MINISTRY						SCRIPTURE		
Ref 1	Ethnic name 2	P% 3	In 1995 4	In 2000 5	In 2025 6	Race 7	Language 8	Autoglossonym 9	S 10	AC 11	Members 12	Jayuh 13-17	d 18	wa 19	xc 20	mc 21	mi 22	Biblioglossonym 23	Pub 24-26	ss 27
12064	Komi	0.00324	728	788	1,081	MSW51d	41-AAEA-b	permyat		40.00	315	3....	9	6	8	1	1	Komi: Permyak*	Pn.	b
12065	Korean	0.92448	207,826	224,814	308,358	MSY46	45-AAAA-b	kukö		20.00	44,963	2A...	9	6	12	3	1	Korean	PNB	b
12066	Kumyk	0.00360	809	875	1,201	MSY41z	44-AABB-d	kumyk		0.00	0	1c.u.	0	2	5	0	0	Kumuk*	Pn.	b
12067	Kurdish	0.00928	2,086	2,257	3,095	CNT24c	58-AAAA-a	kurmanji		0.00	0	3c...	0	3	3	0	0	Kurdish: Kurmanji*	PN.	b
12068	Lak	0.01417	3,185	3,446	4,726	CEW17b	42-BBBA-a	lak		0.00	0	1....	0	3	0	0	0	Lak	P..	b
12069	Latvian	0.00571	1,284	1,389	1,905	CEW15a	54-AABA-a	standard latviashu		82.00	1,139	3A.u.	10	8	11	2	3	Latvian	PNB	b
12070	Lezghian	0.01550	3,484	3,769	5,170	CEW17b	42-BCAA-a	lezgin		0.01	0	1....	3	4	0	0	1	Lezgi	P..	b
12071	Lithuanian	0.00822	1,848	1,999	2,742	CEW15b	54-AAAA-a	standard lietuvishkai		90.00	1,799	3A.u.	10	8	12	2	3	Lithuanian	PNB	b
12072	Luli Gypsy	0.04000	8,992	9,727	13,342	CNN25f	59-ACAA-a	domari		25.00	2,432	0....	9	4	7	0	0		...	b
12073	Mari (Cheremis)	0.01496	3,363	3,638	4,990	MSW51h	41-AACA-b	mariy		80.00	2,910	2....	10	8	11	2	1	Mari: Low*	PN.	b
12074	Meskhetian Turk	0.53661	120,631	130,492	178,985	MSY41j	44-AABA-a	osmanli		0.00	0	1A.u.	0	3	2	0	0	Turkish	PNB	b
12075	Moldavian	0.03006	6,758	7,310	10,026	CEW21f	51-AADC-ab	standard moldavia		80.00	5,848	1A.u.	10	7	8	2	2		pnb	b
12076	Mordvinian	0.06014	13,520	14,625	20,060	MSW51i	41-AADA-b	moksha		60.00	8,775	1....	10	8	8	1	1	Mordvin: Moksha*	Pn.	b
12077	Northern Uzbek	78.23232	17,586,849	19,024,419	26,094,217	MSY41l	44-AABD-a	central uzbek		0.10	19,024	1A.u.	5	3	5	1	3	Uzbek*	PNb	b
12078	Ossete	0.02939	6,607	7,147	9,803	CNT24e	58-ABBA	oseti cluster		45.00	3,216	2....	9	5	8	1	1	Ossete*	PN.	b
12079	Persian	0.12508	28,118	30,417	41,720	CNT24f	58-AACC-c	standard farsi		0.04	12	1Asu.	3	3	2	0	0		PNB	b
12080	Polish	0.01518	3,413	3,691	5,063	CEW22i	53-AAAC-c	polski		87.00	3,212	2A.uh	10	8	11	3	3	Polish	PNB	b
12081	Russian	2.50000	562,007	607,946	833,869	CEW22j	53-AAAE-d	russkiy	84	30.00	182,384	4B.uh	9	7	10	3	3	Russian	PNB	b
12082	Shorian	0.00143	321	348	477	MSY41z	44-AABD-i	ku-kizhi		70.00	243	1c.u.	10	7	8	2	1	Shor	pnb	b
12083	Tabasaran	0.00231	519	562	770	CEW17b	42-BCAA-d	tabarasan		0.00	0	2....	0	2	2	0	0	Tabassaran	P..	b
12084	Tajik (Tadzhik)	4.71255	1,059,395	1,145,991	1,571,861	CNT24g	58-AACC-j	tajiki		0.00	0	2asu.	0	3	3	0	1	Tajik*	PNB	b
12085	Tatar	2.36157	530,888	574,283	787,696	MSY41h	44-AABB-e	tatar		1.00	5,743	2c.u.	6	4	8	0	0	Tatar: Kazan	Pn.	b
12086	Turkmen	0.61372	137,966	149,244	204,705	MSY41k	44-AABA-e	turkmen		0.03	45	3c.u.	3	3	2	0	2	Turkmen	PNb	b
12087	Udmurt	0.01245	2,799	3,028	4,153	MSW51k	41-AAEA-c	udmurt		55.00	1,665	2....	10	5	8	2	1	Udmurt	Pn.	.
12088	Uighur (Kashgar Turki)	0.18052	40,581	43,899	60,212	MSY41z	44-AABD-d	east uyghur		0.00	0	1r.u.	0	3	2	0	2	Uighur*	PNB	b
12089	Ukrainian	0.20000	44,961	48,636	66,710	CEW22p	53-AAAE-b	ukrainskiy		50.00	24,318	3A.uh	10	7	12	3	3	Ukrainian	PNB	b
12090	Vietnamese	0.00118	265	287	394	MSY52b	46-EBAA-ac	general viêt		7.00	20	1Asu.	7	5	9	0	1	Vietnamese	PNB	b
12091	Yenisei Tatar (Khakassian	0.00145	326	353	484	MSY41z	44-AABD-j	khakas		70.00	247	1c.u.	10	7	8	2	1	Khakas	Pnb	.
12092	other minor peoples	0.10000	22,480	24,318	33,355	...				10.00	2,432		8	3	6	0	0			
	Vanuatu	**100.00000**	**168,835**	**190,417**	**319,146**					**89.31**	**170,052**									
12093	Ahamb	0.39773	672	757	1,269	AON09c	38-HANG-a	axamb		90.00	682	0....	10	8	11	5	2	Ahamb*	P..	.
12094	Amblong	0.11364	192	216	363	AON09c	38-HALI-h	amblong		60.00	130	0....	10	6	3	5	2		p..	.
12095	Aneityumese (Aneiteum)	0.45455	767	866	1,451	AON09c	37-ACAA	aneityum cluster		85.10	737	0....	10	8	12	4	1	Aneityum	PNB	.
12096	Aore	0.00079	1	2	3	AON09c	38-HALN-b	aore		10.00	0	0....	8	5	2	5	2		pn.	.
12097	Araki	0.07955	134	151	254	AON09c	38-HALK-a	araki		70.50	107	0....	10	8	3	4	1		...	.
12098	Atchin	1.04167	1,759	1,984	3,324	AON09c	38-HAMF-a	atchin		70.00	1,388	0....	10	9	6	5	1		p..	.
12099	Aulua Bay	0.22727	384	433	725	AON09c	38-HANC-a	aulua		80.00	346	0....	10	8	4	5	2	Aulua	P..	.
12100	Baetora (Nasawa)	0.40909	691	779	1,306	AON09c	38-HAGC-a	baetora		90.00	701	0.s..	10	10	11	5	3		...	.
12101	Baiap (South Ambrym)	0.45455	767	866	1,451	AON09c	38-HAJC-a	dakaka		90.00	779	0....	10	10	10	5	3		...	.
12102	Baki	0.16393	277	312	523	AON09c	38-HAPC-a	baki		80.00	250	0....	10	9	6	4	1	Baki	P..	.
12103	Bierebo	0.34091	576	649	1,088	AON09c	38-HAPB-a	bierebo		80.00	519	0....	10	9	6	4	1		...	p
12104	Bieri (Bieria, Epi)	0.13934	235	265	445	AON09c	38-HAPE-a	bieria		80.00	212	0....	10	9	3	4	1	Bieria	P..	p
12105	Big Nambas	1.36364	2,302	2,597	4,352	AON09c	38-HCAA-a	'big-nambas'		80.00	2,077	0....	10	6	4	5	3	Big Nambas*	PN.	.
12106	Bislama Creole	3.70410	6,254	7,053	11,821	AON09f	52-ABAI-e	bislama	92	97.00	6,842	4ssuh	10	10	13	5	2	Bislama	PNB	b
12107	British	0.56438	953	1,075	1,801	CEW19i	52-ABAC-b	standard-english		84.00	903	3Bsuh	10	10	13	5	3		PNB	b
12108	Butmas-Tur	0.39773	672	757	1,269	AON09c	38-HBBB-a	butmas-tur		50.00	379	0....	10	6	6	5	2		...	.
12109	Central Maewo	0.28689	484	546	916	AON09c	38-HAGB-b	tanoriki		90.10	492	0....	10	10	11	5	3	Maewo, Central	P..	.
12110	Central Raga (Bwatnapni)	3.40909	5,756	6,491	10,880	AON09c	38-HAIB	apma cluster		95.00	6,167	0.s..	10	10	12	5	2	Apma	PN.	.
12111	Craig Cove (Fali)	0.45455	767	866	1,451	AON09c	38-HAJB	lonwolwol cluster		90.00	779	0....	10	10	11	5	3	Lonwolwol	P..	.
12112	Detribalized Vanuatuan	15.92406	26,885	30,322	50,821	MPY53	52-ABAI-e	bislama		96.00	29,109	4ssuh	10	10	11	5	3	Bislama	PNB	b
12113	Dixon Reef	0.03937	66	75	126	AON09c	38-HCBD-a	'dixon-reef'		57.00	43	0....	10	7	3	5	2		...	.
12114	East Ambae (Omba, Aoba)	3.06748	5,179	5,841	9,790	AON09c	38-HAHB-d	lambahi		91.00	5,315	0.s..	10	10	11	5	3	Lombaha*	P..	.
12115	Eastern Efate	0.34279	579	653	1,094	AON09c	38-HAQD-a	eton		90.00	587	0....	10	9	8	0	0		...	.
12116	Emae (Mae)	0.16393	277	312	523	MPY55z	39-CAGA-a	emae		80.00	250	0....	10	9	6	4	1		...	.
12117	Erromangan (Sie)	0.68182	1,151	1,298	2,176	AON09c	37-AABA-d	sie		90.00	1,168	0....	10	9	12	4	1	Eromanga*	PN.	.
12118	Fijian	0.27559	465	525	880	AON08	39-BBAA-b	fiji		90.00	472	1.s..	10	10	13	5	3	Fijian*	PNB	b
12119	Fortsenal	0.11364	192	216	363	AON09c	38-HALI-c	fortsenal		45.00	97	0....	9	6	3	5	2		p..	p
12120	French	1.02000	1,722	1,942	3,255	CEW21b	51-AABI-d	general français		84.00	1,631	1B.uh	10	10	14	5	1	French	PNB	b
12121	Gilbertese (Kiribertese)	0.29134	492	555	930	MPY54a	38-DAAA-a	i-kiribati		90.00	499	3.s..	10	9	13	5	2	Kiribati	PNB	b
12122	Han Chinese	0.20000	338	381	638	MSY42a	79-AAAB-ba	kuo-yü		70.00	267	2Bsuh	10	9	8	4	1	Chinese: Kuoyu*	PNB	b
12123	Koro	0.07955	134	151	254	AON09c	39-BBAC-a	koro		96.00	145	0....	10	10	11	4	1		...	.
12124	Kwamera Tannese	1.62338	2,741	3,091	5,181	AON09c	37-ABDA	kwamera cluster		79.00	2,442	0....	10	6	7	5	3	Kwamera	PN.	.
12125	Lakon	0.22727	384	433	725	AON09c	38-HAEB-a	lakona		90.00	389	0....	10	9	11	4	1	Nume	...	b
12126	Lamenu (varmali)	0.50000	844	952	1,596	AON09c	38-HAPA	lewo-mate cluster		90.00	857	0....	10	9	11	4	1	Lamenu	P..	.
12127	Lametin	0.11364	192	216	363	AON09c	38-HALH-a	lametin		45.00	97	0....	9	6	3	5	2		...	.
12128	Larevat	0.11360	192	216	363	AON09c	38-HCAC-a	larevat		80.00	173	0....	10	9	3	5	2		...	.
12129	Lenakel Tannese	4.36242	7,365	8,307	13,922	AON09c	37-ABBA-a	lenakel		79.00	6,562	0....	10	6	7	5	3	Lenakel	P..	.
12130	Lewo	0.51370	867	978	1,639	AON09c	38-HAPA-a	lewo	2	90.00	880	0....	10	8	11	4	1	Lewo: Varmali	P..	.
12131	Lingarak (Bushman's Bay)	0.15909	269	303	508	AON09c	38-HCAE-a	lingarak		70.00	212	0....	10	9	3	5	2		...	.
12132	Litzlitz-Visele	0.25000	422	476	798	AON09c	38-HCAD	litzlitz-visele cluster		80.00	381	0....	10	8	4	5	2		...	.
12133	Lorediakarkar	0.05682	96	108	181	AON09c	38-HBBA-a	lorediakarkar		40.00	43	0....	9	6	3	5	2		...	.
12134	Mae	0.56818	959	1,082	1,813	AON09c	38-HAMD	mae cluster		85.00	920	0....	10	9	6	5	2		...	.
12135	Mafea	0.04098	69	78	131	AON09c	38-HALM-a	mafea		70.00	55	0....	10	8	3	5	2		...	.
12136	Maii (Mafilau)	0.08197	138	156	262	AON09c	38-HAPD-a	maii		90.00	140	0....	10	8	11	4	1		...	.
12137	Makura (Namakuran)	2.15910	3,645	4,111	6,891	AON09c	38-HAQA-d	na-makura		93.00	3,824	0....	10	10	6	5	1		...	.
12138	Malmariv	0.11364	192	216	363	AON09c	38-HALG-a	malmariv		40.00	87	0....	9	6	3	5	2		...	.
12139	Malo (Ataripoe)	1.22951	2,076	2,341	3,924	AON09c	38-HALN-c	avunatari		94.00	2,201	0....	10	10	11	5	3	Malo	PN.	.
12140	Malua Bay (Middle Nambas)	0.22727	384	433	725	AON09c	38-HAMA-a	'malua-bay'		60.00	260	0....	10	7	4	5	2		...	.
12141	Maragus	0.01176	20	22	38	AON09c	38-HCAB-a	maragus		75.00	17	0....	10	8	3	5	2		...	.
12142	Marino (Big Bay)	0.13636	230	260	435	AON09c	38-HAGA-a	marino		90.00	234	0....	10	10	11	5	3		...	.
12143	Maskelyne Islander	0.75949	1,282	1,446	2,424	AON09c	38-HANF-a	kuliviu		96.00	1,388	0....	10	9	11	5	1	Maskelynes	P..	.
12144	Mele-Fila	1.70940	2,886	3,255	5,455	MPY55z	39-CAHA-a	mele		95.00	3,092	0.s..	10	10	11	5	1	Mele-fila	...	n
12145	Merelava-Merig	0.89404	1,509	1,702	2,853	AON09c	38-HAFA-b	merlav		95.00	1,617	0.s..	10	9	11	4	1		...	.
12146	Mewun	0.28689	484	546	916	AON09c	38-HCCA-a	labo		80.00	437	0....	10	9	6	4	2	Meaun*	P..	.
12147	Moruas (Vetumboso)	0.11364	192	216	363	AON09c	38-HALI-a	morouas		40.00	87	0....	9	6	3	5	2		p..	.
12148	Mosin	0.32787	554	624	1,046	AON09c	38-HADB-c	mosina		90.00	562	0....	10	9	11	5	1	Mosina	...	.
12149	Mota	0.34091	576	649	1,088	AON09c	38-HACB	mota cluster		95.00	617	0.s..	10	9	12	5	1	Mota	PNB	.
12150	Motalava (Motlav)	0.96591	1,631	1,839	3,083	AON09c	38-HACA	motlav cluster		96.00	1,766	0.s..	10	8	11	5	1		...	.
12151	Mpotovoro	0.13636	230	260	435	AON09c	38-HAMC-a	mpotovoro		61.00	158	0....	10	8	4	5	2		...	.
12152	Napuanmen Tannese	2.34899	3,966	4,473	7,497	AON09c	37-ABAB-a	waesisi		88.00	3,936	0....	10	5	7	3	3	Weasisi*	PN.	.
12153	Narango	0.13115	221	250	419	AON09c	38-HALI-i	narango		60.00	150	0....	10	7	3	5	2		p..	.
12154	Nasarian	0.01515	26	29	48	AON09c	38-HCBA-a	nasarian		38.00	11	0....	9	5	4	5	2		...	.
12155	Navut	0.39773	672	757	1,269	AON09c	38-HALG-b	navut		40.00	303	0....	9	6	3	5	2		...	.
12156	New Caledonian	1.00000	1,688	1,904	3,191	AON09a	51-AABI-c	standard français		85.00	1,619	4B.uh	10	9	12	5	2	French	PNB	b
12157	Nokuku (Nogugu)	0.13115	221	250	419	AON09c	38-HALB-a	nokuku		90.00	225	0....	10	8	11	5	2	Nogugu*	P..	.
12158	North Ambrym Islands	2.15909	3,645	4,111	6,891	AON09c	38-HAJA-b	magam		85.00	3,495	0....	10	10	6	5	1		...	.
12159	North Efate Ngunese	2.27273	3,837	4,328	7,253	AON09c	38-HAQB-a	n-guna		90.00	3,895	0....	10	10	11	5	1	Ngunese	PNB	.
12160	North Raga (Lamalanga)	4.29448	7,251	8,177	13,706	AON09c	38-HAIA-a	hano		96.00	7,850	0.s..	10	10	11	5	3	Raga*	P..	.
12161	North Tannese	1.34228	2,266	2,556	4,284	AON09c	37-ABAA	tanna-imafin cluster		84.00	2,147	0....	10	5	7	5	1	Tanna: North*	P..	.
12162	Northern Torres Islander	0.09091	153	173	290	AON09c	38-HAAA-a	hiw		95.00	164	0....	10	9	12	4	1	Hiw	P..	.
12163	Onua (Bush Onua)	0.34768	587	662	1,110	AON09c	38-HANA-a	unua		70.00	463	0....	10	7	6	5	2	Unua	P..	.
12164	Orierh	0.20000	338	381	638	AON09c	38-HAOA-c	orierh		80.00	305	0.s..	10	8	6	5	2		p..	.
12165	Paama (Pauma)	3.97727	6,715	7,573	12,693	AON09c	38-HAKA	paama-lopevi cluster		97.00	7,346	0....	10	10	12	4	2	Paama	PN.	.
12166	Pangkumu Bay	0.28409	480	541	907	AON09c	38-HANB-a	rerep		90.00	487	0....	10	9	11	5	2	Pangkumu*	P..	.
12167	Piamatsina	0.12295	208	234	392	AON09c	38-HALC-b	piamatsina		45.00	105	0....	9	6	5	5	2		...	.
12168	Polonombauk	0.17045	288	325	544	AON09c	38-HBBC-a	polonombauk		70.00	227	0....	10	8	4	5	2		...	.
12169	Port Sandwich	0.56818	959	1,082	1,813	AON09c	38-HANE-a	port sandwich		80.00	866	0....	10	8	6	5	1		...	.
12170	Port Vato	0.56820	959	1,082	1,813	AON09c	38-HAJD-a	'port-vato'		80.00	866	0....	10	9	6	5	1	Port Vato	P..	.
12171	Repanbitip	0.06818	115	130	218	AON09c	38-HCBB-a	repanbitip		70.00	91	0....	10	8	3	5	2		...	.
12172	Roria	0.11360	192	216	363	AON09c	38-HALI-b	roria		40.00	87	0....	9	6	3	5	2		p..	.
12173	Sa (South Raga)	1.36368	2,302	2,597	4,352	AON09c	38-HAIE	sa cluster		97.00	2,519	0....	10	9	11	5	1		...	.
12174	Sakau (Hog Harbour)	1.13636	1,919	2,164	3,627	AON09c	38-HBAA-a	sakao		98.00	2,121	0....	10	9	11	5	1	Sakau*	P..	.
12175	Samoan	0.10000	169	190	319	MPY55e	39-CAOA	samoa cluster		91.00	173	2a.u.	10	9	15	4	1	Samoan	PNB	b
12176	Seke	0.22727	384	433	725	AON09c	38-HAID-a	seke		90.00	389	0....	10	10	11	5	3		...	.
12177	Shark Bay	0.17045	288	325	544	AON09c	38-HBBA-b	'shark-bay'		60.00	195	0....	10	9	4	5	2		...	.
12178	Small Nambas (Mbotgote)	0.23106	390	440	737	AON09c	38-HCBC-a	letemboi		30.00	132	0....	9	5	5	5	2		...	.
12179	Southeast Ambrym	1.36364	2,302	2,597	4,352	AON09c	38-HAJE	southeast ambrym cluster	4	89.00	2,311	0....	10	10	6	5	1	Ambrym, Southeast	P..	.
12180	Southern Efate (Erakor)	2.84091	4,796	5,410	9,067	AON09c	38-HAQC-a	fate		94.00	5,085	0....	10	10	12	5	2	Efate*	PNB	.
12181	Southern Torres Islander	0.23864	403	454	762	AON09c	38-HAAB	loh-toga cluster		95.00	432	0....	10	9	12	4	1	Torres Island*	P..	.
12182	Southwest Bay (Sinesip)	0.20492	346	390	654	AON09c	38-HAOA-f	sinesip		90.00	351	0.s..	10	9	11	5	2	Sinesip*	P..	.
12183	Southwest Tannese	1.70455	2,878	3,246	5,440	AON09c	37-ABCA-b	nowai		88.00	2,856	0....	10	6	6	5	1		...	.
12184	Sowa	0.02353	40	45	75	AON09c	38-HAIC-a	sowa		90.00	40	0....	10	10	11	5	3		...	.
12185	Tahitian	0.20000	338	381	638	MPY55f	39-CAQH-b	vehicular tahiti		95.00	362	0....	10	8	12	5	2	Tahitian	PNB	b

Continued opposite

Table 8-2 continued

EVANGELIZATION								EVANGELISM			ADDITIONAL DESCRIPTIVE DATA
Ref 1	*D* 28	*aC* 29	*CG%* 30	*r* 31	*E* 32	*U* 33	*W* 34	*e* 35	*R* 36	*T* 37	*Locations, civil divisions, literacy, religions, church history, denominations, dioceses, church growth, missions, agencies, ministries, movements* 38
12064	1	9	3.51	0	81.00	19.00	B	118.26	153	7	From Komi (Russia), near Ural Mountains. Animists/shamanists 40%, nonreligious 20%. D=Russian Orthodox Ch.
12065	1	10	8.77	6	86.00	14.00	B	62.78	299	6	Long-time residents, from Korea. Bilingual. Nonreligious 40%, shamanists 20%, Buddhists 15%, atheists 5%. D=Reformed Chs. M=CSI.
12066	0	9	0.00	1	25.00	75.00	A	0.00	0	1.10	Originally from southern Dagestan (Russia), also Turkey. Many are trilingual. Muslims 100%(Shafi, Hanafi Sunnis).
12067	0	6	0.00	0	22.00	78.00	A	0.00	0	1.08	Refugees, migrants from Kurdistan. Muslims 100%(Shias,Yazidis,some Sunnis).
12068	0	8	0.00	0	15.00	85.00	A	0.00	0	1.05	From southern Dagestan (Russia). Trilingual. Muslims 100%(Shafi Sunnis).
12069	5	8	4.85	5	99.82	0.18	C	442.96	112	10	In 25 countries, mainly Latvia. Nonreligious 15%. D=ROC,ELCL,RCC,RCL,CB.
12070	0	7	0.00	0	19.01	80.99	A	0.00	0	1.06	Also in south Dagestan (Russia). 50% understand Russian. Muslims 100%(Shafi Sunnis). M=IBT.
12071	3	8	5.33	5	99.90	0.10	C	515.74	93	10	Found in 24 countries. Strong Catholics. Nonreligious 9%. D=RCC,ERCL,ROC.
12072	0	8	2.64	7	60.00	40.00	B	54.75	168	6	Nomadic Gypsies in Uzbekistan, Caucasus; also Iran, Syria, Turkey, India, 6 other countries. Muslims 75%.
12073	1	6	4.96	0	99.80	0.20	C	362.08	132	9	Traditionally Orthodox, from Mari (Russia). Muslims 5%, shamanists 5%, Nonreligious 10%. D=ROC. M=IBT.
12074	0	7	0.00	8	37.00	63.00	A	0.00	0	1.11	Muslim peoples from Georgia deported in 1944 to Uzbek SSR. 46% also speak Russian. Most religious of all Central Asians. Georgian Muslims 100%(Hanafi).
12075	2	7	6.58	6	99.80	0.20	C	394.20	154	9	Immigrants, refugees from Moldavia, Romania. Nonreligious 17%. D=Russian Orthodox Ch, Romanian Orthodox Ch.
12076	1	7	5.71	1	99.60	0.40	C	219.00	156	8	Russian-speakers mainly. Nonreligious 35%. D=Russian Orthodox Ch.
12077	4	7	7.84	5	49.10	50.90	A	0.17	477	3	Descendants of Golden Horde. 100% literates. 55% speak Russian. Muslims 80%(Hanafi Sunnis), nonreligious/atheists 20%. D=ROC,AUCECB,CEF,SDA. M=10.
12078	1	5	5.21	0	83.00	17.00	B	136.32	208	7	Mainly from Russia and Georgia; also Syria, Turkey. Muslims 40%(Sunnis), nonreligious 15%. D=ROC.
12079	0	5	2.52	5	36.04	63.96	A	0.05	245	2	Farsi is mother tongue for 31%. Muslims 88%(Imami Shias), Baha'is 2%, Zoroastrians 10%.
12080	4	7	5.94	6	99.87	0.13	C	489.02	106	10	From Poland, migrants, workers. D=RCC,ROC,CEF,CWE.
12081	8	7	2.42	7	99.30	0.70	B	109.50	66	7	In 70 countries. Nonreligious 50%, atheists 20%. D=ROC,RCC,AUCECB,Old Ritualists,CEF,CCECB,SDA,IPKh. R=FEBC,HCJB,TWR,KNLS,VERITAS.
12082	1	7	2.64	1	99.70	0.30	C	288.71	83	8	From Khakass AO (Russia). In northern Altai mountains. 91% speak Russian. Shamanists 30%. D=Russian Orthodox Ch.
12083	0	8	0.00	0	18.00	82.00	A	0.00	0	1.06	From southern Dagestan (Russia). Muslims 100%(Shafi Sunnis).
12084	0	6	0.00	4	36.00	64.00	A	0.00	0	1.12	Mainly in Tajikistan; also some in Kirghizia, Afghanistan. Most are trilingual (with Uzbek, Russian). Muslims 90%(Hanafi Sunnis,also some Shias), nonreligious 10%.
12085	0	7	3.82	6	40.00	60.00	A	1.46	316	4	From Tatarstan (Russia). Bilingual in Russian. Muslims 80%(Hanafi Sunnis), nonreligious 16%. R=IBRA.
12086	0	6	3.88	1	29.03	70.97	A	0.03	442	2	In Afghanistan, Iran, as well as Turkmenistan. Devout Muslims 95%(Hanafi Sunnis), nonreligious 5%. M=IBT,CSI.
12087	1	7	4.29	0	93.00	7.00	B	186.69	156	7	From Udmurtia (Russia). Strong shamanists/animists 40%, some Muslims. D=ROC.
12088	0	6	0.00	4	32.00	68.00	A	0.00	0	1.11	Also in Kazakhstan, Kirghizia. In 15 countries. Settled agriculturalists. Muslims 100%(Hanafi Sunnis, with heavy Sufi influence). M=IBT,CSI.
12089	7	8	3.27	6	99.50	0.50	B	220.82	101	8	In 15 countries. Nonreligious/atheists 50%. D=ROC(E-Ukraine),Ukrainian Catholic Ch,AUCECB,CEF,CCECB,JWs,SDA.
12090	1	6	3.04	6	58.00	42.00	B	14.81	184	5	Refugees, immigrants stranded after 1960s-75 Viet Nam war. Mahayana Buddhists 61%, nonreligious 30%. D=RCC.
12091	1	8	3.16	1	99.70	0.30	C	283.60	98	8	Originally from southern Siberia, around Abakan city. De facto shamanists 30%. D=Russian Orthodox Ch.
12092	0	8	4.07		32.00	68.00	A	11.68	348	5	Czechs, Krimchaks, Romanians, Finns, Yakuts, Gagauz, Koryaks, Assyrians, Agul, Nogai, Abkhazi, Italians, Turks. Muslims 27%, nonreligious 20%, Shamanists.
Vanuatu											
12093	2	7	4.31	0	99.90	0.10	C	427.05	114	10	South Malekula Island. D=Presbyterian Ch of Vanuatu,RCC(D-Port Vila).
12094	2	6	2.60	0	91.00	9.00	C	199.29	111	7	South Santo Island. Closely related to Narango and Morouas. Animists('Custom') 40%. D=PCV,RCC.
12095	1	7	4.39	0	99.85	0.15	C	410.32	114	10	Aneityum Island. Bible translated in 1879. Baha'is 5%. D=PCV. M=LMS.
12096	2	10	0.00	0	44.00	56.00	A	16.06	0	5	Mafea Island, East Santo. Closely related to Malo and Tutuba. Nearly extinct. Traditionally, Animists 80%. D=SDA,PCV.
12097	1	7	2.40	0	98.50	1.50	C	253.46	97	8	Araki Island, South Santo. Animists 30%. D=PCV.
12098	4	7	1.96	0	99.70	0.30	C	270.83	79	8	Atchin Island, northeast Malekula area. Animists 10%. D=SDA,RCC(D-Port Vila),Free Ch(FPC),PCV. M=SM.
12099	2	7	3.61	0	99.80	0.20	C	329.96	114	9	East Malekula. Animists 20%. D=PCV,RCC(D-Port Vila).
12100	3	7	4.34	0	99.90	0.10	C	433.62	113	10	Maewo Island. D=PCV,CCV,Ch of Melanesia(D-Vanuatu).
12101	3	7	4.45	0	99.90	0.10	C	427.05	117	10	South Ambrym. Several dialects. D=PCV,RCC(D-Port Vila),SDA.
12102	2	7	3.27	0	99.80	0.20	C	329.96	106	9	West Epi Island. D=PCV,AoG. M=SIL.
12103	1	7	4.03	0	99.80	0.20	C	327.04	126	9	West Epi Island. Close to Lewo. Many bilingual in Baki. D=PCV.
12104	1	7	3.10	0	99.80	0.20	C	321.20	105	9	Southwest Epi Island. Bilingual in Baki. D=PCV.
12105	3	6	5.48	0	99.80	0.20	C	344.56	153	9	Northwest Malekula Island. Animists 10%, Baha'is 10%. D=PCV,RCC,Presbyterian Reformed Ch.
12106	4	10	1.94	4	99.97	0.03	C	591.26	32	10	Bichelamer. Lingua franca of commerce, press. English-based creole (official language). Baha'is 3%. D=PCV,RCC,Ch of Melanesia,JWs. M=SM,UBS.
12107	3	10	1.11	8	99.84	0.16	C	484.42	39	10	Expatriates from Britain, in development. D=Ch of Melanesia(D-Vanuatu),JWs,SDA.
12108	2	6	3.70	0	83.00	17.00	B	151.47	158	7	East central Santo Island. Animists 50%. D=PCV,RCC.
12109	3	7	3.97	0	99.90	0.10	C	434.43	105	10	Aurora (Maewo) Island. D=PCV,CCV,Ch of Melanesia(D-Vanuatu).
12110	4	7	1.84	0	99.95	0.05	C	492.38	57	10	Central Pentecost(Raga) Island. Baha'is 5%. D=PCV,CCV,RCC(D-Port Vila),Ch of Melanesia(D-Vanuatu). M=SM,UBS.
12111	4	7	4.45	0	99.90	0.10	C	433.62	115	10	West Ambrym, and Maat village, Efate Island. D=PCV,SDA,AoG,RCC(D-Port Vila).
12112	3	10	2.57	4	99.96	0.04	C	581.66	56	10	Numbers of urbanized and deculturated persons abandoning traditional customs. D=PCV,RCC,COM.
12113	2	7	3.83	0	88.00	12.00	B	183.08	154	7	Southwest Malekula Island. Animists 13%. D=PCV,RCC.
12114	6	7	1.68	0	99.91	0.09	C	448.40	56	10	North East Aoban. Lepers (Ambae,Aobo,Oba) Island. 15 dialects. Baha'is 5%. D=AC(ACANZ),CCV,PCV,RCC,COM,SDA.
12115	0	0	4.16	0	99.90	0.10	C	358.06	132	9	Southeastern Efete Island at Eton, Pang Pang, and other villages. Related to Lelepa. D=PCV,SDA,AoG,RCC.
12116	1	7	3.27	0	99.80	0.20	C	324.12	94	9	Emae, Three Hills Island. 2 villages on Sesake Island. D=PCV.
12117	1	7	4.88	0	99.90	0.10	C	433.62	124	10	Erromanga Island. 4 dialects. Bahas'i 5%. D=PCV.
12118	3	10	3.93	4	99.90	0.10	C	509.17	77	10	Migrant workers from Fiji Islands. D=Methodist Ch in Fiji,RCC,CPNZ.
12119	2	6	4.68	0	76.00	24.00	B	124.83	208	7	Central Santo Island. Closely related to Akei. Animists 55%. D=PCV,RCC.
12120	3	10	0.49	8	99.84	0.16	C	484.42	25	10	Expatriates from France, in development. Nonreligious 13%. D=RCC(D-Port Vila),FPC,JWs. M=SM.
12121	2	10	3.99	4	99.90	0.10	C	509.17	82	10	Migrants from Kiribati nation. D=GIPC,RCC.
12122	1	10	3.34	7	99.70	0.30	C	344.92	81	9	Refugees from Viet Nam. Buddhists/Chinese folk-religionists 30%. D=RCC.
12123	1	7	2.71	0	99.96	0.04	C	462.52	79	10	Gaua Island (Banks Islands), 2 villages. All Anglicans. D=Ch of Melanesia (D-Vanuatu).
12124	3	8	5.65	0	99.79	0.21	C	351.78	152	9	Southeast Tanna. 2 main dialects. Animists (followers of Custom) 15%, Bah'is 6%. D=PCV,RCC,SDA.
12125	1	8	3.73	0	99.90	0.10	C	427.05	102	10	Gaua, Moa Islands (Banks Islands). English mostly used now. All Anglicans. D=Ch of Melanesia(D-Vanuatu).
12126	1	7	4.55	0	99.90	0.10	C	417.19	122	10	Northwest of Epi Island, on Lamenu Island, Varmali region. D=PCV. M=SIL.
12127	2	6	4.68	0	74.00	26.00	B	121.54	214	7	Central Santo Island, north of Morouas. Animists 55%. D=PCV,RCC.
12128	2	7	2.89	0	99.80	0.20	C	324.12	98	9	Central Malekula Island. A few animists left. D=PCV,RCC.
12129	5	8	2.13	0	99.79	0.21	C	343.13	74	9	West central Tanna, 10 dialects. Animists (followers of Custom) 12%. D=PCV,RCC,SDA,AoG,CC.
12130	2	7	4.58	0	99.90	0.10	C	420.48	122	10	Eastern Epi Island. D=PCV,SDA. M=SIL.
12131	2	7	3.10	0	99.70	0.30	C	258.05	114	8	Malekula Island. Some animists remain 10%. D=PCV,RCC.
12132	2	7	3.71	0	99.80	0.20	C	327.04	118	9	Malekula Island. Animists few in number. D=PCV,RCC.
12133	2	6	3.83	0	69.00	31.00	B	100.74	196	7	Central east coast, Santo Island. Closely related to Shark Bay language. Animists 60%. D=PCV,RCC.
12134	2	6	4.63	0	99.85	0.15	C	366.09	133	9	Malekula Island. Close to Small Nambas. D=PCV,RCC(D-Port Vila).
12135	2	7	4.09	0	99.70	0.30	C	258.05	141	8	East Santo, Mafea Island. Animists 30%. D=PCV,RCC.
12136	1	7	2.67	0	99.90	0.10	C	413.91	82	10	Mafilau village, west Epi. D=PCV.
12137	4	7	6.13	0	99.93	0.07	C	434.49	155	10	North Efate, Tongoa, Tongariki. Emwae Islands. Baha'is 7%. D=SDA,PCV,AoG,RCC. M=SM.
12138	2	6	4.57	0	69.00	31.00	B	100.74	225	7	North central Santo Island. Closely related to Navut. Animists 60%. D=PCV,RCC.
12139	4	6	5.54	0	99.94	0.06	C	476.90	131	10	Malo Island, other small islands. Closely related to Aore, Tutuba. Baha'is 6%. D=Ch of Melanesia(D-Vanuatu),CCV,PCV,ACANZ.
12140	2	7	3.31	0	92.00	8.00	C	201.48	131	8	Espiegle Bay. Northwest coast of Malekula Island. Several dialects. Animists 10%. D=PCV,RCC.
12141	2	6	2.87	0	99.75	0.25	C	287.43	104	8	Central north Malekula Island. Nearly extinct. D=PCV,RCC.
12142	3	6	3.20	0	99.90	0.10	C	427.05	91	10	North Maewo. D=PCV,CCV,Ch of Melanesia(D-Vanuatu).
12143	2	6	5.06	0	99.96	0.04	C	473.04	125	10	South Malekula Island, Maskelyne Islets. Baha'is 4%. D=PCV,RCC. M=SM.
12144	4	7	5.90	0	99.95	0.05	C	478.51	127	10	Mele village on Efate Island, 500 on Fila. Also in Solomon Islands. Bilinguals in South Efate. Baha'is 5%. D=PCV,SDA,AoG,RCC(D-Port Vila). M=SM.
12145	1	7	5.22	0	99.95	0.05	C	461.17	130	10	Mere Lava and Merig Islands (Banks Group). Predominantly Anglicans. Baha'is 5%. D=Ch of Melanesia(D-Vanuatu).
12146	2	7	3.85	0	99.80	0.20	C	332.88	119	9	Southwest Bay, Malekula. Hunters, fishermen, agriculturalists. Animists 20%, strong. D=PCV,RCC.
12147	2	6	4.57	0	70.00	30.00	B	102.20	222	7	Central Santo Island. Several dialects. Animists 60%. D=PCV,RCC.
12148	1	7	4.11	0	99.90	0.10	C	417.19	112	10	Vanua Lava (Banks Group). Predominantly Anglicans. D=Ch of Melanesia(D-Vanuatu).
12149	1	7	4.21	0	99.95	0.05	C	499.32	101	10	Sugarloaf (Mota) Island. Banks Group. Formerly a lingua franca. Anglicans. D=Ch of Melanesia(D-Vanuatu). M=SIL.
12150	1	7	5.31	0	99.96	0.04	C	473.04	130	10	Saddle (Mota Lava) Island. Banks Group. Anglicans. Baha'is 4%. D=Ch of Melanesia(D-Vanuatu).
12151	2	7	2.80	0	93.00	7.00	C	207.06	115	8	North tip of Malekula Island. Animists 5%. D=PCV,RCC.
12152	4	8	6.16	0	99.88	0.12	C	414.34	154	10	East coast of Tanna Island. Animists(followers of Custom) 5%, Baha'is 6%. D=PCV,RCC,SDA,AoG.
12153	2	8	2.75	0	93.00	7.00	C	203.67	113	8	South Santo Island. Several dialects. Closely related to Amblong and Morouas. Animists 40%. D=PCV,RCC.
12154	2	6	2.43	0	68.00	32.00	B	94.31	142	6	Southwest coast of Malekula. Nearly extinct. Animists 60%. D=PCV,RCC.
12155	2	6	3.47	0	69.00	31.00	B	100.74	181	7	West central Santo Island. Closely related to Malmariv. Animists 60%. D=PCV,RCC.
12156	2	10	5.22	8	99.85	0.15	C	496.40	105	10	Migrants from New Caledonia. Baha'is 10%. D=RCC,Free Church(French Protestant Ch).
12157	2	8	3.16	0	99.90	0.10	C	430.33	89	10	Northwest Santo Island. Still a remnant of animists, 3%. D=PCV,RCC.
12158	2	7	6.03	0	99.85	0.15	C	369.19	164	9	North Ambrym Island. Strong animists 10%, Baha'is 5%. D=PCV,RCC(D-Port Vila). M=SM.
12159	4	7	6.15	0	99.90	0.10	C	459.90	142	10	Northern 25% of Efate Island, several smaller islands. Baha'is 8%. D=PCV,SDA,AoG,RCC. M=SM.
12160	4	7	2.08	0	99.96	0.04	C	490.56	62	10	Bwatvenua. North Pentecost and southern Maewo Islands. Lingua franca, trade language. D=PCV,CCV,RCC(D-Port Vila),Ch of Melanesia(D-Vanuatu).
12161	4	8	5.52	0	99.84	0.16	C	374.05	149	9	North Tanna Island. Agriculturalists. Animists(followers of Custom) 6%, Baha'is 6%. D=PCV,RCC,SDA,AoG. M=SIL.
12162	1	8	2.84	0	99.95	0.05	C	464.64	81	10	Torres Islands. Exclusively Anglicans. D=Ch of Melanesia(D-Vanuatu).
12163	2	7	3.91	0	99.70	0.30	C	268.27	131	8	East Malekula Island. Several dialects. Animists 10%. D=PCV,RCC.
12164	2	7	3.48	0	99.80	0.20	C	338.72	108	9	South Malekula Island. Dialect of Malfaxal. D=PCV,RCC.
12165	2	6	2.01	0	99.97	0.03	C	495.67	61	10	Paama, one village on east Epi, large group in Vila. Close to Southeast Ambrym language. D=PCV,COM.
12166	2	7	3.96	0	99.90	0.10	C	427.05	107	10	East Malekula Island. D=PCV,RCC.
12167	2	8	2.38	0	78.00	22.00	B	128.11	122	7	Northwest Santo Island. Close to Vunapu. Animists 55%. D=PCV,RCC.
12168	2	7	3.17	0	99.70	0.30	C	260.61	115	8	Southeast Santo Island. Animists 30%. D=PCV,RCC.
12169	2	8	4.56	0	99.80	0.20	C	332.88	136	9	Southeast Malekula Island. Several dialects. D=PCV,RCC. M=SM.
12170	2	7	4.56	0	99.80	0.20	C	332.88	136	9	Southwest Ambrym Island. D=PCV,RCC. M=SM.
12171	2	7	4.61	0	99.70	0.30	C	258.05	155	8	East Malekula Island. Animists 10%. D=PCV,RCC.
12172	2	6	4.57	0	70.00	30.00	B	102.20	222	7	Central Santo Island. Animists 60%. D=PCV,RCC.
12173	4	7	5.68	0	99.97	0.03	C	485.04	136	10	South Raga Island. D=PCV,CCV,RCC,Ch of Melanesia. M=SM.
12174	2	8	5.50	0	99.98	0.02	C	497.20	130	10	Northeast Santo Island. Agriculturalists, pig-raisers. A few animists left. D=PCV,RCC. M=SM.
12175	1	10	2.89	5	99.91	0.09	C	521.47	60	10	Migrants from Samoa. Strong Protestants. D=CCCS.
12176	4	7	3.73	0	99.90	0.10	C	430.33	101	10	Central Raga Island. D=PCV,CCV,RCC,Ch of Melanesia(D-Vanuatu).
12177	2	7	3.01	0	92.00	8.00	C	201.48	122	8	East Santo Island, on Litaro (Pilot) Island, also nearby coast. Close to Lorediakarkar. Animists 40%. D=PCV,RCC.
12178	2	6	2.61	0	61.00	39.00	B	66.79	167	6	South interior of Malekula Island. Animists 70%. Hunters, fishermen, agriculturalists. D=PCV,RCC.
12179	2	7	5.59	0	99.89	0.11	C	402.81	148	10	Southeast Ambrym Island. Linked with Paama. Strong animists 5%. D=PCV,RCC. M=SM.
12180	4	7	1.64	0	99.94	0.06	C	500.92	51	10	South Ngunese. Southern 75% of Efate Island, including capital of Port Vila. 2 main dialects. Baha'is 5%. D=PCV,SDA,AoG,RCC. M=SM,SIL.
12181	1	10	3.84	0	99.95	0.05	C	471.58	100	10	Torres Islands. Exclusively Anglicans. D=Ch of Melanesia(D-Vanuatu).
12182	2	7	3.62	0	99.90	0.10	C	430.33	99	10	Southwest Malekula Island. Hunters, fishermen, agriculturalists. D=PCV,RCC.
12183	3	7	5.82	0	99.88	0.12	C	395.07	154	9	Southwest Tanna Island. Animists(followers of Custom) 3%, Baha'is 5%. D=PCV,RCC,SDA. M=SM.
12184	4	7	3.76	0	99.90	0.10	C	430.33	102	10	Central Raga Island. Nearly extinct. D=PCV,CCV,RCC,Ch of Melanesia.
12185	2	10	3.65	5	99.95	0.05	C	530.52	74	10	Migrants from French Polynesia. In urban areas. D=EEPF,RCC.

Continued overleaf

Table 8-2 continued

PEOPLE		POPULATION				IDENTITY CODE		LANGUAGE		CHURCH		MINISTRY						SCRIPTURE		
Ref 1	Ethnic name 2	P% 3	In 1995 4	In 2000 5	In 2025 6	Race 7	Language 8	Autoglossonym 9	S 10	AC 11	Members 12	Jayuh 13-17	d 18	wa 19	xc 20	mc 21	mi 22	Biblioglossonym 23	Pub 24-26	ss 27
12186	Tambotalo	0.04098	69	78	131	AON09c	38-HALL-a	tambotalo		81.00	63	0....	10	7	3	5	2		...	.
12187	Tangoa	0.28409	480	541	907	AON09c	38-HALJ-a	tangoa		89.00	481	0....	10	9	11	4	1	Tangoan	P..	.
12188	Tarasag	0.34091	576	649	1,088	AON09c	38-HAEB-a	lakona		90.00	584	0....	10	9	11	4	1	Nume	...	b
12189	Tasiko (Lewo)	0.15000	253	286	479	AON09c	38-HAPA-c	tasiko		91.00	260	0....	10	9	12	4	1	Tasiko	P..	.
12190	Tasiriki	0.53279	900	1,015	1,700	AON09c	38-HALI-e	tasiriki		80.00	812	0....	10	9	6	5	1	Tasiriki	P..	.
12191	Tasmate	0.11400	192	217	364	AON09c	38-HALD	tasmate cluster		90.00	195	0....	10	8	11	5	2		...	.
12192	Tembimbe-Katbol (Tisvel)	0.34091	576	649	1,088	AON09c	38-HCAH-b	katbol		70.00	454	0....	10	8	6	5	2		...	.
12193	Teqel (Lehali)	0.11364	192	216	363	AON09c	38-HABA-a	lehali		80.00	173	0....	10	9	4	4	1		...	.
12194	Tolomako-Jereviu	0.34091	576	649	1,088	AON09c	38-HALE-a	tolomako		90.00	584	0....	10	9	11	5	3	Tolomako	P..	.
12195	Toman Islander (Malvaxal)	0.45455	767	866	1,451	AON09c	38-HAOA-a	malfaxal		60.00	519	0.s..	10	9	6	5	1	Malfaxal	P..	.
12196	Tongan	0.10000	169	190	319	MPY55g	39-CAPB	tonga cluster		89.00	169	4a...	10	9	12	5	3	Tongan	PNB	b
12197	Tutuba	0.11360	192	216	363	AON09c	38-HALN-a	tutuba		90.00	195	0....	10	10	11	5	3		pn.	.
12198	Ura	0.00962	16	18	31	AON09c	37-AAAA-a	ura		70.00	13	0....	10	9	3	4	1		...	.
12199	Ureparapara	0.06818	115	130	218	AON09c	38-HABB-a	lehalurup		95.00	123	0....	10	9	12	4	1		...	.
12200	Uripiv (Uri, Tautu)	4.02685	6,799	7,668	12,852	AON09c	38-HAMF-d	uripiv		97.00	7,438	0....	10	10	11	5	2	Uripiv-wala-rano-atchin	P..	.
12201	Valpay (Valpei-Hukua)	0.22727	384	433	725	AON09c	38-HALA	valpei-hukua cluster		90.00	389	0....	10	9	11	5	2		...	.
12202	Vao	1.02273	1,727	1,947	3,264	AON09c	38-HAME-a	vao		89.00	1,733	0....	10	6	6	5	3		...	.
12203	Varsu (Lewo)	0.51370	867	978	1,639	AON09c	38-HAPA-b	varsu		75.00	734	0....	10	7	6	3	0		p..	.
12204	Vartavo (Banan Bay)	0.39773	672	757	1,269	AON09c	38-HAND-a	burmbar		70.00	530	0....	10	8	6	5	2		...	.
12205	Vatrata (Vanua Lava)	0.45455	767	866	1,451	AON09c	38-HADA-a	vatrata		80.00	692	0....	10	8	6	4	1		...	.
12206	Vietnamese (Kinh)	0.45480	768	866	1,451	MSY52b	46-EBAA-ac	general viêt		60.00	520	1Asu.	10	7	8	4	1	Vietnamese	PNB	b
12207	Vinmavis (Lambumbu)	0.15909	269	303	508	AON09c	38-HCAF-a	vinmavis		70.00	212	0....	10	8	3	5	2		...	.
12208	Vunapu	0.28409	480	541	907	AON09c	38-HALC-a	vunapu		90.00	487	0....	10	8	11	5	2		...	.
12209	Wailapa	0.08197	138	156	262	AON09c	38-HALI-f	wailapa		70.00	109	0....	10	7	6	3	0		p..	p
12210	Wallisian (East Uvean)	0.39370	665	750	1,256	MPY55i	39-CALA	uvean cluster		90.00	675	0....	10	8	12	4	1	Wallisian	P..	b
12211	West Ambae (Duindui)	3.40909	5,756	6,491	10,880	AON09c	38-HAHA-a	nduindui		97.00	6,297	0.s..	10	10	11	5	3	Ambae: West*	PN.	.
12212	West Futunan (Erronan)	0.49180	830	936	1,570	MPY55z	39-CAIA	west futuna cluster		80.00	749	0....	10	8	6	4	2	Futuna-aniwa	PN.	.
12213	Wetamut	0.07955	134	151	254	AON09c	38-HAED-a	wetamut		90.00	136	0....	10	9	11	4	1		...	.
12214	Wusi-Kerepua	0.16346	276	311	522	AON09c	38-HALF	wusi-kerepua cluster		95.00	296	0....	10	9	11	5	2		...	.
12215	other minor peoples	0.20000	338	381	638	...				67.00	255		10	7	6	4	0			
	Venezuela	**100.00000**	**21,844,481**	**24,169,722**	**34,775,110**					**94.07**	**22,735,837**									
12216	Achagua	0.00040	87	97	139	MIR39e	81-AFAA-a	achagua		70.00	68	0....	10	7	5	4	1	Achagua	...	b
12217	Akawaio (Kapon)	0.00080	175	193	278	MIR39c	80-AFAC-a	acawayo		75.00	145	0....	10	8	7	4	1	Acawaio*	Pn.	.
12218	Arab	0.46000	100,485	111,181	159,966	CMT30	12-AACF-f	syro-palestinian		47.00	52,255	1Asuh	9	7	8	5	3	Arabic: Lebanese*	Pnb	b
12219	Arawak	0.00300	655	725	1,043	MIR39a	81-ACBA	arawák cluster		92.00	667	0....	10	9	11	4	1	Arawak	P..	b
12220	Armenian	0.00400	874	967	1,391	CEW14	57-AAAA-b	ashkharik		90.00	870	4A.u.	10	9	13	5	1	Armenian: Modern, Eastern	PNB	b
12221	Arutani (Auaque, Uruak)	0.00022	48	53	77	MIR39d	88-CBAA-a	arutani		30.00	16	0....	9	5	4	4	1		...	p
12222	Baniwa	0.00321	701	776	1,116	MIR39a	81-AGBB-c	south baniwa		70.20	545	0....	10	8	6	4	1	Baniua*	PN.	.
12223	Bare (Barawana)	0.00188	411	454	654	MIR39a	81-AHAB	baré cluster		20.00	91	0....	9	5	4	3	1		...	b
12224	Bari (Motilon)	0.00566	1,236	1,368	1,968	MIR39a	83-EHAA-a	barí		70.00	958	0....	10	8	6	4	1	Motilon	...	.
12225	Basque	0.02000	4,369	4,834	6,955	CEW16	40-AAAA-a	general euskara		92.00	4,447	3....	10	9	15	5	2	Basque	PNB	b
12226	British	0.02000	4,369	4,834	6,955	CEW19i	52-ABAC-b	standard-english	7	78.00	3,770	3Bsuh	10	9	13	5	2		PNB	b
12227	Carib (Galibi, Kalinya)	0.03214	7,021	7,768	11,177	MIR39c	80-ACAA-b	central carib		60.00	4,661	1.s..	10	8	8	4	1	Carib*	Pn.	b
12228	Carib Motilon (Yukpa)	0.00700	1,529	1,692	2,434	MIR39c	80-AAAA	yucpa cluster		75.00	1,269	0....	10	8	6	4	1	Yukpa	...	.
12229	Catalonian	0.02000	4,369	4,834	6,955	CEW21a	51-AABE-b	català		95.00	4,592	2a..h	10	9	15	5	2	Catalan-valencian-balear	PNB	b
12230	Central Tunebo	0.00200	437	483	696	MIR39e	83-EFAB-a	central tunebo		40.00	193	0....	9	5	5	4	1	Tunebo*	PN.	.
12231	Colombian White	0.70000	152,911	169,188	243,426	CLT27	51-AABB-ho	colombiano		95.00	160,729	1B.uh	10	9	13	5	1		pnb	b
12232	Cuban White	0.30000	65,533	72,509	104,325	CLT27	51-AABB-hi	cubano		40.00	29,004	1B.uh	9	6	8	5	3		pnb	b
12233	Cuiba	0.00297	649	718	1,033	MIR39d	88-GAAB-a	proper cuiba		5.00	36	0....	7	4	3	4	1	Cuiba	PN.	.
12234	Curipaco	0.00198	433	479	689	MIR39a	81-AGBA-a	kúrrim		60.00	287	0....	10	7	6	4	2	Curripaco	PN.	.
12235	Esperanto	0.00000	0	0	0	CEW21z	51-AAAC-a	proper esperanto		70.00	0	0A...	10	7	8	4	0	Esperanto	PNB	b
12236	French	0.03000	6,553	7,251	10,433	CEW21b	51-AABI-d	general français	2	84.00	6,091	1B.uh	10	9	14	5	3	French	PNB	b
12237	German	0.03000	6,553	7,251	10,433	CEW19m	52-ABCE-a	standard hoch-deutsch		86.00	6,236	2B.uh	10	9	13	5	1	German*	PNB	b
12238	Greek	0.02200	4,806	5,317	7,651	CEW20	56-AAAA-c	dhimotiki		90.00	4,786	2B.uh	10	9	11	5	1	Greek: Modern	PNB	b
12239	Guajibo (Guahibo, Quivo)	0.03145	6,870	7,601	10,937	MIR39d	88-GAAA-a	proper guahibo		85.00	6,461	0....	10	9	7	5	2	Guajibo*	PN.	b
12240	Guajiro (Arahuaco)	0.77822	169,998	188,094	270,627	MIR39a	81-ACAA-a	wayúu		30.00	56,428	0....	9	5	8	5	3	Guajiro*	P..	.
12241	Guarequena (Arequena)	0.00226	494	546	786	MIR39a	81-AFEA-a	walékhena		60.00	328	0....	10	9	6	4	1		...	b
12242	Han Chinese (Cantonese)	0.11200	24,466	27,070	38,948	MSY42a	79-AAAM-a	central yue	1	25.00	6,768	3A.uh	9	5	8	5	2	Chinese, Yue	PNB	b
12243	Han Chinese (Mandarin)	0.10000	21,844	24,170	34,775	MSY42a	79-AAAB-ba	kuo-yü	2	30.00	7,251	2Bsuh	9	5	8	5	2	Chinese: Kuoyu*	PNB	b
12244	Italian	1.30000	283,978	314,206	452,076	CEW21e	51-AABQ-c	standard italiano		83.00	260,791	2B.uh	10	9	15	5	3	Italian	PNB	b
12245	Jamaican Black	0.01000	2,184	2,417	3,478	NFB68a	52-ABAF-m	jamaican-creole		69.00	1,668	1c..h	10	6	10	5	3	West Carib Creole English	pn.	b
12246	Japreria (Yapreria)	0.00063	138	152	219	MIR39c	80-AAAB-a	yapreria		40.00	61	0....	9	5	5	4	1		...	.
12247	Jewish	0.19815	43,285	47,892	68,907	CMT35	51-AABB-hn	venezolano		0.10	48	1B.uh	5	4	2	1	0		pnb	b
12248	Macushi (Macuxi)	0.00438	957	1,059	1,523	MIR39c	80-AFAA-a	macushi		40.00	423	0....	9	6	6	5	2	Makuchi*	PN.	b
12249	Mandahuaca (Bare)	0.01686	3,683	4,075	5,863	MIR39a	81-AFEB-a	mandahuaca		80.00	3,260	0....	10	9	5	4	1		...	.
12250	Mapoyo (Mopoi)	0.00088	192	213	306	MIR39c	80-AEAA-a	mapoyo		40.00	85	0....	9	6	3	4	1		...	b
12251	Maquiritari (Maiongong)	0.03628	7,925	8,769	12,616	MIR39c	80-AEBA-a	proper maquiritari		80.00	7,015	0....	10	9	6	5	3	Maquiritare*	PN.	.
12252	Mutu	0.00097	212	234	337	MIR39c	83-LAAB-a	mutús		30.00	70	0....	9	8	3	4	1		...	b
12253	Ninam	0.00056	122	135	195	MIR39d	88-DAAA	ninam cluster		70.00	95	0....	10	7	6	4	1	Ninam	P..	b
12254	Panare (Eye)	0.00675	1,475	1,631	2,347	MIR39c	80-ADAA-a	e'nyapa		50.00	816	0....	10	8	6	5	1	Panare	P..	.
12255	Paraujano	0.03400	7,427	8,218	11,824	MIR39a	81-ACAB	anyu cluster		80.60	6,623	0....	10	8	6	4	1		...	b
12256	Patamona (Patamuna)	0.00100	218	242	348	MIR39c	80-AFAC-c	patamona		70.00	169	0....	10	7	6	4	1	Patamuna*	PN.	.
12257	Pemon (Pemong, Arecuna)	0.02726	5,955	6,589	9,480	MIR39c	80-AFAB-a	are-cuna		60.00	3,953	0....	10	7	6	5	2	Pemon	P..	.
12258	Piapoco	0.00078	170	189	271	MIR39a	81-AFAC-a	tsase		50.00	94	0....	10	7	6	4	1	Piapoco	PN.	.
12259	Piaroa	0.06568	14,347	15,875	22,840	MIR39d	88-FAAA-a	proper piaroa		20.00	3,175	0....	9	5	5	5	3	Piaroa	PN.	b
12260	Polish	0.03000	6,553	7,251	10,433	CEW22i	53-AAAC-c	polski		88.00	6,381	2A.uh	10	9	11	5	3	Polish	PNB	b
12261	Portuguese	0.40000	87,378	96,679	139,100	CEW21g	51-AABA-e	general português		92.00	88,945	2Bsuh	10	9	15	5	3	Portuguese	PNB	b
12262	Puinave	0.00189	413	457	657	MIR39d	88-HAAA-b	east puinave		60.00	274	0....	10	7	6	4	1	Puinave	PN.	.
12263	Romanian	0.00560	1,223	1,354	1,947	CEW21i	51-AADC-a	limba româneasca		81.00	1,096	3A.u.	10	8	8	4	1	Romanian	PNB	b
12264	Russian	0.01690	3,692	4,085	5,877	CEW22j	53-AAAE-d	russkiy		50.00	2,042	4B.uh	10	8	8	5	1	Russian	PNB	b
12265	Saliba	0.00125	273	302	435	MIR39d	88-FAAB-a	sáliba		56.00	169	0....	10	7	6	4	1	Saliba	...	b
12266	Sanuma (Xamatari)	0.01908	4,168	4,612	6,635	MIR39d	88-DABA	sanumá cluster		25.00	1,153	0....	9	5	4	5	3	Sanuma	...	.
12267	Sape (Kariana)	0.00058	127	140	202	MIR39d	88-CAAA-a	sapé		70.00	98	0....	10	8	6	3	1	Sape	...	b
12268	Sikiana	0.00300	655	725	1,043	MIR39c	80-AHBA-a	sikiâna		60.00	435	0....	10	7	6	2	1		...	b
12269	Spaniard	0.30000	65,533	72,509	104,325	CEW21k	51-AABB-hn	venezolano		96.00	69,609	1B.uh	10	10	15	5	1		pnb	b
12270	Spanish Creole (Pidgin)	0.50000	109,222	120,849	173,876	NFB71b	51-AACB-d	criollo-de-bobures		86.00	103,930	1c.u.	10	8	12	5	3		pnb	.
12271	Tabajari (Tabare)	0.01000	2,184	2,417	3,478	MIR39c	80-ACAA-ab	tabajari		60.00	1,450	1.s..	10	7	6	3	1		pn.	.
12272	Tupi-Guarani	0.01107	2,418	2,676	3,850	MIR39z	82-AAIG-a	nhengatu		69.00	1,846	0....	10	9	6	5	1	Nyengato*	PN.	b
12273	Turkish	0.10000	21,844	24,170	34,775	MSY41j	44-AABA-a	osmanli		0.00	0	1A.u.	0	3	2	0	0	Turkish	PNB	b
12274	USA White	0.08000	17,476	19,336	27,820	CEW19s	52-ABAC-s	general american		77.00	14,889	1Bsuh	10	9	8	5	3	English*	PNB	b
12275	Ukrainian	0.03400	7,427	8,218	11,824	CEW22p	53-AAAE-b	ukrainskiy		62.00	5,095	3A.uh	10	8	9	5	1	Ukrainian	PNB	b
12276	Venezuelan Black	10.00000	2,184,448	2,416,972	3,477,511	NFB71a	51-AABB-hn	venezolano		86.00	2,078,596	1B.uh	10	10	10	5	1		pnb	b
12277	Venezuelan Mestizo	63.66661	13,907,641	15,388,043	22,140,134	CLN29	51-AABB-hn	venezolano		98.00	15,080,282	1B.uh	10	10	11	5	2		pnb	b
12278	Venezuelan White	20.00625	4,370,261	4,835,455	6,957,195	CLT27	51-AABB-hn	venezolano		94.88	4,587,880	1B.uh	10	10	12	5	3		pnb	b
12279	Warao (Warrau)	0.08607	18,802	20,803	29,931	MIR39e	83-PAAA-a	proper guarao		20.00	4,161	0....	9	5	5	5	3	Warao	PN.	.
12280	Yabarana (Yauarana)	0.00045	98	109	156	MIR39c	80-AEAB-a	proper yabarana		25.00	27	0....	9	5	5	4	1		...	b
12281	Yanomam (Zamatali, Guaica)	0.06500	14,199	15,710	22,604	MIR39d	88-DACA-a	west yanomamö		15.00	2,357	1....	8	5	4	5	2	Guaica	Pn.	.
12282	Yaruro (Pume)	0.01405	3,069	3,396	4,886	MIR39d	83-KAAA-a	pume		10.00	340	0....	8	5	4	5	3	Yaruro	...	.
12283	Yuana (Yuwana, Waruwaru)	0.00283	618	684	984	MIR39d	88-EAAA	hotí cluster		3.00	21	0....	6	4	4	4	1	Yuwana	...	.
12284	Zambo	0.05000	10,922	12,085	17,388	NFB71b	51-AABB-hn	venezolano		70.00	8,459	1B.uh	10	8	8	5	3		pnb	b
12285	other minor peoples	0.20000	43,689	48,339	69,550	...				60.00	29,004		10	7	3	3	0			
	Viet Nam	**100.00000**	**73,865,716**	**79,831,650**	**108,037,101**					**8.23**	**6,567,922**									
12286	Akha (Kaw)	0.00400	2,955	3,193	4,321	MSY50i	77-BBAA-d	akha		5.00	160	1....	7	4	7	3	1	Akha	PN.	b
12287	Arem	0.00080	591	639	864	AUG03z	46-EABA-d	arem		1.00	6	0....	6	4	4	0	0		...	.
12288	Bahnar (Bonom, Kontum)	0.18515	136,762	147,808	200,031	AUG03z	46-FACB-d	bahnar		21.00	31,040	0.s..	9	5	7	5	3	Bahnar	PN.	.
12289	Black Tai (Thai Den)	0.80799	596,828	645,032	872,929	MSY49z	47-AAAD-a	tai-dam		4.40	28,381	0....	6	5	7	5	3	Tai: Dam*	P..	b
12290	Blue Meo (Green Miao)	0.01000	7,387	7,983	10,804	MSY47a	48-AAAA-bd	tak		5.00	399	1A...	7	5	7	4	1		pn.	.
12291	Brau (Laveh)	0.00700	5,171	5,588	7,563	AUG03z	46-FADC-a	brao		1.00	56	0....	6	4	4	1	0	Brao	...	b
12292	British	0.00200	1,477	1,597	2,161	CEW19i	52-ABAC-b	standard-english	4	78.00	1,245	3Bsuh	10	9	13	5	2		PNB	b
12293	Cacgia Roglai (Ra-Glai)	0.00436	3,221	3,481	4,710	MSY44z	31-MBBA-a	cacgia-roglai		29.00	1,009	0....	9	5	6	2	1		...	.
12294	Center Khmer (Cambodian)	1.21705	898,983	971,591	1,314,866	AUG03b	46-FBAA-b	khmae		0.10	972	2A...	5	4	8	5	2	Khmer*	PNB	b
12295	Central Mnong (Pnong)	0.11000	81,252	87,815	118,841	AUG03z	46-FAEA-a	pnong		26.00	22,832	0.s..	9	6	7	5	2		p..	.
12296	Chinese Nung (Cantonese)	0.83251	614,939	664,606	899,420	MSY42a	79-AAAM-a	central yue		3.00	19,938	3A.uh	6	4	8	4	1	Chinese, Yue	PNB	b
12297	Chrau (Tamun, Ro)	0.02200	16,250	17,563	23,768	AUG03z	46-FAEC-b	chrau		26.00	4,566	0.s..	9	5	7	5	3	Chrau	PN.	.
12298	Chru (Seyu)	0.03812	28,158	30,432	41,184	MSY44z	31-MBBB-d	chru		29.00	8,825	0....	9	6	7	4	1	Chru	P..	.
12299	Cua (Kol, Bong Miew)	0.02723	20,114	21,738	29,419	AUG03z	46-FACA-e	cua		20.00	4,348	0....	9	6	6	5	3	Cua	P..	.
12300	Eastern Bru (Galler)	0.08505	62,823	67,897	91,886	AUG03z	46-FAAA-f	west bru		45.00	30,554	0.s..	9	7	7	5	3	Bru*	PN.	.
12301	Eastern Cham	0.05248	38,765	41,896	56,698	MSY44z	31-MBBC-a	east cham		10.00	4,190	0.s..	8	5	7	5	2	Cham: Eastern*	P..	.
12302	Eastern Mnong	0.08732	64,500	69,709	94,338	AUG03z	46-FAEA-c	east mnong		25.00	17,427	0.s..	9	5	6	5	2	Mnong, Eastern	P..	.
12303	Eurasian	0.50000	369,329	399,158	540,186	MSY43	51-AABI-d	general français		89.00	355,251	1B.uh	10	9	12	5	3	French	PNB	b
12304	Flowery Meo (Miao Hwa)	0.22000	162,505	175,630	237,682	MSY47a	48-AAAA-b	hmong-njua		11.00	19,319	1A...	8	5	7	2	1	Hmong Njua	PN.	b
12305	Franco-Annamite	0.01000	7,387	7,983	10,804	MSY43	51-AACC-p	tay boi	2	38.00	3,034	1cs..	9	6	6	4	1		pnb	.

Continued opposite

Table 8-2 continued

EVANGELIZATION								EVANGELISM			ADDITIONAL DESCRIPTIVE DATA
Ref 1	*D* 28	*aC* 29	*CG%* 30	*r* 31	*E* 32	*U* 33	*W* 34	*e* 35	*R* 36	*T* 37	*Locations, civil divisions, literacy, religions, church history, denominations, dioceses, church growth, missions, agencies, ministries, movements* 38
12186	2	7	4.23	0	99.81	0.19	C	331.12	130	9	Southeast Santo Island, Tambotalo village. Animists 19%. D=PCV,RCC.
12187	1	7	3.95	0	99.89	0.11	C	409.31	110	10	Tangoa Island, off south Santo. D=PCV. M=Canadian Presbyterian Mission.
12188	1	7	4.15	0	99.90	0.10	C	413.91	114	10	Gaua Island (Banks Group). Predominantly Anglicans. D=Ch of Melanesia(D-Vanuatu).
12189	1	7	3.31	0	99.91	0.09	C	428.47	94	10	A dialect of Lewo, Southeast Epi Island. D=PCV.
12190	2	7	4.50	0	99.80	0.20	C	332.88	135	9	Southwest Santo Island. Close to Fortsenal. Animists 10%. D=PCV,RCC. M=SM.
12191	2	8	3.01	0	99.90	0.10	C	427.05	87	10	West Santo Island. Animists 10%. D=PCV,RCC.
12192	2	6	3.89	0	99.70	0.30	C	263.16	133	8	Central Malekula Island. Animists 10%. D=PCV,RCC.
12193	1	7	2.89	0	99.80	0.20	C	318.28	100	9	Ureparapara Island (Banks Islands). Close to Lehalurup. Anglicans. D=Ch of Melanesia(D-Vanuatu).
12194	3	8	4.15	0	99.90	0.10	C	436.90	108	10	Big Bay, Santo Island. Animists 2%. D=PCV,RCC,COM.
12195	2	7	4.03	0	95.00	5.00	C	208.05	148	8	Toman Island, off south Malekula Island. Animists 10%. D=PCV,RCC. M=independents.
12196	3	10	2.87	5	99.89	0.11	C	519.76	58	10	Migrants from Tonga. Strong Methodists. D=FWCT,CJCLdS,RCC.
12197	3	7	3.01	0	99.90	0.10	C	440.19	84	10	Tutuba Island, south Santo. Close to Aore and Malo. Animists 5%. D=CCV,PCV,RCC.
12198	1	9	2.60	0	99.70	0.30	C	255.50	101	8	North Erromanga Island. Nearly extinct. D=PCV.
12199	1	7	2.54	0	99.95	0.05	C	457.71	76	10	Ureparapara Island (Banks Islands). Close to Lehali. All Anglicans. D=Ch of Melanesia(D-Vanuatu).
12200	3	6	2.03	0	99.97	0.03	C	488.58	62	10	Northeast Malekula and nearby Islands. Dialect chain. Catholics strong. D=RCC,PCV,SDA. M=SM,SIL.
12201	2	8	3.73	0	99.90	0.10	C	427.05	102	10	Northwest Santo Island. Animists 5%. D=PCV,RCC.
12202	3	6	2.18	0	99.89	0.11	C	406.06	72	10	Vao Island, north Malekula. Agriculturalists, fishermen, pig-raisers. Animists 5%, rest predominantly Catholics. D=RCC,PCV,SDA.
12203	0	7	4.39	0	99.75	0.25	C	284.70	145	8	Epi Island, Varsu, Varmali regions. Some animists remain, 5%.
12204	2	7	4.05	0	99.70	0.30	C	265.72	136	8	Southeast Malekula Island. D=PCV,RCC.
12205	1	9	4.33	0	99.80	0.20	C	329.96	132	9	Vanua Lava Island. Extinct dialects: Leon, Sasar, Pak. D=Ch of Melanesia.
12206	1	10	4.03	6	99.60	0.40	C	264.99	111	8	Immigrants, refugees from Viet Nam. Tonkinese (North Vietnamese). Buddhists 40%, some Cao Daists. D=RCC.
12207	2	7	3.10	0	99.70	0.30	C	258.05	114	8	Central west Malekula Island. Animists 10%. D=PCV,RCC.
12208	2	8	3.96	0	99.90	0.10	C	427.05	107	10	Northwest Santo Island. Close to Piamatsina. Animists 5%. D=PCV,RCC.
12209	0	7	2.42	0	99.70	0.30	C	255.50	96	8	Southwest Santo Island. Dialect chain from Akei to Penantsiro. Animists 10%.
12210	1	10	4.30	4	99.90	0.10	C	443.47	98	10	Migrant workers from Uvea Island(Wallis & Futuna). D=RCC.
12211	4	7	1.86	0	99.97	0.03	C	509.83	56	10	West Ambae (Lepers, Aoba, Oba) Island. Many dialects. D=CCV,PCV,Ch of Melanesia(D-Vanuatu),ACANZ.
12212	1	7	4.41	0	99.80	0.20	C	338.72	116	9	Futuna and Aniwa Islands, east of Tanna. Fishermen, agriculturalists. Strong residual animists 20% (Aniwa 62% in 1967). D=PCV. M=LMS,FCSM.
12213	1	7	2.64	0	99.90	0.10	C	413.91	81	10	Gaua Island (Banks Group), 2 villages. Anglicans. D=Ch of Melanesia(D-Vanuatu).
12214	2	8	3.45	0	99.95	0.05	C	468.11	92	10	West Santo Island. Animists 5%. D=PCV,RCC.
12215	0	8	3.29		93.00	7.00	C	227.43	97	8	Other Pacific Islanders, Melanesians, Micronesians, Polynesians, other Europeans, other Asians. Nonreligious 10%.
Venezuela											
12216	1	7	4.31	0	99.70	0.30	C	260.61	133	8	Lake Maracaibo region and other areas. Mainly in Colombia. Animists 30%. D=RCC.
12217	2	8	2.71	0	99.75	0.25	C	312.07	89	9	In Bolivar State. Mainly in Guyana, also Brazil. Animists 25%. D=RCC,AC/CPWI. M=SDB.
12218	3	7	8.94	8	99.47	0.53	B	192.13	236	7	Immigrants, migrants, refugees: Palestinian, Syrian, Lebanese, Levantine. Muslims 50%. D=RCC(Maronites),GOC,SOC.
12219	1	8	2.31	0	99.92	0.08	C	443.25	69	10	Coastal area near Guyana, Delta Amacuro. Mainly in Guyana, Surinam, French Guiana. Animists 8%. D=RCC.
12220	1	8	4.57	6	99.90	0.10	C	522.31	89	10	Refugees from USSR, Middle East since 1910. Nonreligious 10%. D=Armenian Apostolic Ch(Gregorians).
12221	1	6	2.81	0	60.00	40.00	B	65.70	160	6	Headwaters of Paraqua, Bolivar State. Also in Brazil. Bilingual in Ninam. Nearly extinct. Animists 60%. D=RCC.
12222	1	7	2.30	0	99.70	0.30	C	274.67	84	8	Along Colombian border; mainly in Brazil. Related to Curripaco. Animists 30%. D=RCC. M=NTM.
12223	1	5	4.61	0	50.00	50.00	B	36.50	307	5	Amazonas. On Colombian border in southwest. 50% speak the language; all bilingual in Spanish. Animists 80%. D=RCC.
12224	1	6	2.31	0	99.70	0.30	C	260.61	89	8	Zulia State. Also in Colombia. Warlike jungle tribe in tropical forest. Animists 30%. D=RCC(VA-Machiques). M=OFMCap.
12225	2	10	2.31	4	99.92	0.08	C	540.63	56	10	Settlers from Spain. D=RCC,AoG. M=SJ,OP.
12226	2	10	2.31	8	99.78	0.22	C	435.59	62	10	Expatriates from Britain, in development, business. D=Ch of Province of West Indies(D-Venezuela),JWs.
12227	1	7	2.31	1	99.60	0.40	C	229.95	87	8	Northeast of Orinoco. Also in Surinam, Guyana, French Guiana, Brazil. No monolinguals. Animists 30%, Baha'is 10%. D=RCC.
12228	1	7	4.96	0	99.75	0.25	C	298.38	150	8	Northern Motilon. Sierra de Perija, Cesar Region, Zulia State. Also in Colombia. Animists 25%. D=RCC. M=OFMCap.
12229	2	10	3.36	4	99.95	0.05	C	582.54	69	10	Settlers, expatriate Spaniards from Catalonia. D=RCC,AoG.
12230	1	6	3.00	0	74.00	26.00	B	108.04	135	7	Apure State. Mostly in Colombia. Animists 60%. D=RCC. M=OP.
12231	3	10	2.29	8	99.95	0.05	C	568.67	53	10	Persons of Spanish White descent, from Colombia. D=RCC,AoG,UPCI. M=FMB.
12232	4	10	2.31	8	99.40	0.60	B	153.30	83	7	Refugees from Cuba. Nonreligious 40%. D=RCC,CNBV,AoG,UPCI.
12233	1	5	3.65	0	34.00	66.00	A	6.20	351	4	Mainly in Colombia. Monolingual nomadic bands of hunter-gatherers. Animists 95%. D=RCC.
12234	1	6	2.75	0	97.00	3.00	C	212.43	106	8	Mainly in Colombia. Animists 40%. D=RCC. M=FMB,WEC.
12235	0	10	0.00	5	99.70	0.30	C	329.59	0	9	Artificial(constructed) language, in 80 countries. Speakers in Venezuela: 13,000(none mother-tongue). Nonreligious 20%.
12236	4	10	2.31	8	99.84	0.16	C	496.69	56	10	Expatriates from France, in development. Nonreligious 13%. D=RCC,JWs,AoG,SDA.
12237	7	10	2.31	8	99.86	0.14	C	499.10	59	10	Expatriates from Germany, in business, development. D=CLV,NAC,ILV,AoG,SDA,JWs,RCC. M=LCMS.
12238	1	10	2.31	7	99.90	0.10	C	528.88	56	10	Immigrants from Greece. Nonreligious 10%. D=Greek Orthodox Ch(AD-North & South America).
12239	3	6	2.31	0	99.85	0.15	C	394.01	65	9	Mainly in Colombia. Orinoco river. Animists 15%. D=RCC,AoG,OVICE. M=TEAM,FMB.
12240	2	6	3.11	0	70.00	30.00	B	76.65	161	6	Most live in Colombia. Western Zulia State. Animists 50%, Baha'is 20%. D=RCC(VA-Machiques),AoG. M=OFMCap,FMB,TEAM.
12241	1	8	2.32	0	97.00	3.00	C	212.43	94	8	San Miguel river. Also in Brazil. All bilingual in Spanish. Animists 40%. D=RCC.
12242	2	10	6.73	8	95.00	5.00	B	86.68	213	6	Large number of wealthy businessmen. Buddhists/Chinese folk-religionists 70%. D=RCC,AoG.
12243	2	10	6.81	7	99.30	0.70	B	109.50	204	7	Ongoing large-scale immigration from Singapore et alia. Buddhists/folk-religionists 65%. D=RCC,AoG.
12244	4	10	3.74	7	99.83	0.17	C	484.72	81	10	Expatriates from Italy, in business. D=RCC,UPCI,AoG,CCNA.
12245	3	10	2.31	8	99.69	0.31	C	324.88	62	9	Migrant workers from Jamaica. Afro-American spiritists 20%(Rastas,Shango), Baha'is 10%. D=CPWI(D-Venezuela),JBU,RCC.
12246	1	6	4.20	0	70.00	30.00	B	102.20	204	7	Northern region of Sierra de Perija, Zulia State. Animists 60%. D=RCC.
12247	0	10	3.95	8	46.10	53.90	A	0.16	276	3	Practicing Jews: Sefardis in west(Coro area) and east; and Ashkenazis from Eastern Europe after 1945.
12248	3	6	3.54	0	82.00	18.00	B	119.72	152	7	Mainly in Brazil, Guyana. Eastern border area. English as second language. Animists 60%. D=RCC,Hallelujah Ch,AC/CPWI. M=UFM,BMM.
12249	1	7	2.67	0	99.80	0.20	C	329.96	89	9	Amazonas, east of the Bare, Colombian border at southwest. Animists 20%. D=RCC.
12250	1	5	4.54	0	70.00	30.00	B	102.20	217	7	Suapure river. Nearly extinct: only 2 speakers of mother tongue. Animists 60%. D=RCC.
12251	1	8	2.64	0	99.80	0.20	C	356.24	82	9	Bolivar State, near Brazil border. Literates 15%. Animists 20%. D=RCC(VA-Puerto Ayacucho). M=ORM,NTM,SDB,FMB.
12252	1	6	4.34	0	61.00	39.00	B	66.79	240	6	Town of Mutus, Barinas State. Civilized, prosperous farmers. Bilingual in Spanish. Syncretism. Animists 60%, Baha'is 10%. D=RCC.
12253	1	8	4.66	0	99.70	0.30	C	275.94	136	8	Bolivar State. All bilingual in Spanish and/or Arecuna. Animists 30%. D=RCC.
12254	1	6	3.26	0	84.00	16.00	B	153.30	139	7	Over 20 villages, Bolivar State. Nearly all monolingual. Animists 50%. D=RCC. M=NTM.
12255	1	9	2.47	0	99.81	0.19	C	351.85	79	9	Zulia State. 20 speakers left (rest use Spanish). Animists 19%. D=RCC(VA-Machiques). M=OFMCap.
12256	1	7	3.24	0	99.70	0.30	C	273.38	109	8	Mainly in Guyana. Animists 30%. D=RCC.
12257	2	6	3.01	0	97.00	3.00	C	212.43	114	8	Bolivar State. Mostly monolinguals. Animists 40%. D=RCC(VA-Caroni),SDA AoG. M=OFMCap,independents.
12258	1	6	4.65	0	86.00	14.00	B	156.95	180	7	Mostly in Colombia. Along Orinoco river. Animists 50%. D=RCC. M=FMB.
12259	1	5	3.30	0	60.00	40.00	B	43.80	183	6	South bank of Orinoco. 50% bilingual. Animists 80%. D=RCC(VA-Puerto Ayacucho). M=NTM,SDB,FMB.
12260	1	10	2.31	6	99.88	0.12	C	510.70	40	10	Refugees, settlers from Poland. Nonreligious 10%. D=RCC. M=SJ,SDB,OP.
12261	3	10	2.31	8	99.92	0.08	C	584.29	52	10	Settlers from Portugal, Brazil. D=RCC,AoG,UPCI. M=SJ,OP,SDB.
12262	1	6	2.76	0	96.00	4.00	C	210.24	99	8	In Amazonas. Mainly in Colombia. Animists 40%. D=RCC.
12263	1	10	2.76	6	99.81	0.19	C	431.64	73	10	Refugees from Romania. Nonreligious 15%. D=Romanian Orthodox Ch. M=ROME(USA).
12264	2	9	2.97	7	99.50	0.50	B	219.00	68	8	Refugees from USSR since 1917. Nonreligious/atheists 50%. D=Russian Orthodox Ch(P-Moscow),ROCOR. M=OCA.
12265	1	7	2.87	0	92.00	8.00	B	188.04	106	7	Cedono Department. Mostly in Colombia. Very acculturated. Animists 44%. D=RCC.
12266	2	6	2.61	0	59.00	41.00	B	53.83	154	6	Nearly all monolinguals. Animists 75%. D=RCC,AIELV(EFCA)/OVICE. M=TEAM,ORM,independents.
12267	1	8	4.69	0	99.70	0.30	C	270.83	147	8	Some also in Brazil. Most intermarried with Arecuna, Pemon, Arutani, Ninam. Animists 30%. D=RCC. M=BMM.
12268	1	8	3.50	0	95.00	5.00	C	208.05	130	8	Mostly in Brazil. Nearly extinct. Animists 40%. D=RCC. M=ORM.
12269	3	10	2.31	8	99.96	0.04	C	585.16	53	10	White settlers originally from Spain. D=RCC,AoG,UPCI. M=FMB.
12270	4	10	2.31	8	99.86	0.14	C	470.85	53	10	Mixed-race persons. Afro-American spiritists 5%, Baha'is 4%. D=RCC,AoG,UPCI,JWs.
12271	1	7	3.47	1	99.00	1.00	C	216.81	124	8	Dialect of Carib. Animists 40%. D=RCC.
12272	1	10	5.36	0	99.69	0.31	C	287.10	153	8	Yeral. Modern Tupi, a creolized Tupi lingua franca. Mainly in Brazil. Animists 20%, Baha'is. D=RCC. M=NTM.
12273	0	0	0.00	8	28.00	72.00	A	0.00	0	1.09	Immigrant workers from Turkey. Muslims 99%.
12274	9	10	2.44	8	99.77	0.23	C	415.95	62	10	Expatriates from USA, in development, business. D=RCC,SDA,JWs,AoG,CJCLdS,ICFG,CCS,COG,CGP.
12275	1	10	6.43	6	99.62	0.38	C	294.19	161	8	Refugees from USSR. Nonreligious 30%. D=Ukrainian Orthodox Ch in the USA.
12276	2	10	2.31	8	99.86	0.14	C	477.12	52	10	Afro-American spiritists 10%(Shango, Maria Lionza), Baha'is 4%. D=RCC,AoG. M=FMB. T=CBN. R=AWR.
12277	10	10	2.33	8	99.98	0.02	C	597.35	47	10	Amerindian/Whites. D=RCC(Spiritist Catholics, christo-pagans widespread),INVA,AoG,JWs,CB,SDA,ASIGEO,UPCI,CNBV,ICAV/ICAB. M=WEC,FMB. T=CBN.
12278	5	10	2.31	8	99.95	0.05	C	574.46	52	10	Spanish descent. D=RCC(26 Dioceses),AoG,JWs,UPCI,VEPU. M=SDB,SJ,OP,OFMCap,FSC,FMB. T=CBN. R=AWR.
12279	1	5	3.44	0	57.00	43.00	B	41.61	196	6	Delta of Orinoco. Also in Guyana and Surinam. Language isolate. Animists 80%. D=RCC(VA-Tucupita). M=BMM,OFMCap,BLL.
12280	1	5	3.35	0	57.00	43.00	B	52.01	210	6	North central Amazonas. Nearly extinct, 64 speakers in 1975. Animists 75%. D=RCC.
12281	1	6	4.13	0	50.00	50.00	B	27.37	265	5	Orinoco-Mavaca area. Also in Brazil. Animists 85%. D=RCC. M=NTM,SDB.
12282	1	5	3.59	0	40.00	60.00	A	14.60	294	5	Orinoco, Apure rivers. Language isolate. Animists 90%. D=RCC. M=TEAM,OP,Evangelical Service Mission,NTM.
12283	1	5	3.09	0	28.00	72.00	A	3.06	371	4	North, central, south Venezuela. Animists 97%. D=RCC. M=NTM.
12284	3	10	2.31	8	99.70	0.30	C	344.92	59	9	Amerindian/Negro. Afro-Amerindian spiritists 25%(Maria Lionza, Shango), Baha'is 5%. D=RCC,AoG,JWs.
12285	0	6	8.30		84.00	16.00	C	183.96	271	7	Caribbean Islanders(West Indian Blacks), Brazilians, Mexicans, Central Americans, other Americans, other Europeans. Afro-Caribbean spiritists 7%.
Viet Nam											
12286	1	5	2.81	0	38.00	62.00	A	6.93	282	4	Northwest border with Laos. Animists 70%, Buddhists 25%. D=RCC.
12287	0	6	1.81	0	18.00	82.00	A	0.65	428	3	East central Viet Nam, both sides of Laos border, northeast of Phuc Trach. Also in Laos. Animists 99%.
12288	3	5	8.37	4	65.00	35.00	B	49.82	395	6	Montagnards. Southeastern Gia Lai-Cong Tum Province. Also in USA. Animists 79%. D=RCC,ECVN,SDA. M=UWM,CMA,SIL.
12289	3	5	8.28	4	41.40	58.60	A	6.64	588	4	Most in North Viet Nam along Red and Black rivers; a few in Thailand, 3,000 in USA, others in France, Laos, China. Animists 95%. D=RCC,ECVN,SDA. M=CMA.
12290	0	5	3.76	4	43.00	57.00	A	7.84	284	4	In north, border with Laos; northwestern Tonkin Province. Most in Laos; also Thailand, USA, France, China. Polytheists 89%, Animists 5%. M=OMF.
12291	0	6	4.11	0	22.00	78.00	A	0.80	636	3	Cambodia-Laos border. Many in Cambodia; a few in USA, France. Many bilinguals. Animists 98%.
12292	2	10	4.94	8	99.78	0.22	C	427.05	111	10	Expatriates from Britain, in aid, development. Nonreligious 9%. D=Anglican Ch(D-Singapore),ECVN.
12293	1	7	4.72	4	61.00	39.00	B	64.56	235	6	Thuan Hai Province, on coast northeast of Phan Rang. Animists 71%. D=RCC.
12294	3	6	4.41	5	52.10	47.90	B	0.19	307	3	Mekong Delta. Also in Cambodia, Thailand, France, USA. Some 25,000 refugees from Cambodia. Theravada Buddhists 87%(20,000 monks), nonreligious 9%.
12295	3	5	8.04	4	66.00	34.00	B	62.63	375	6	Montagnards. Southwest of Rade area, mainly in Song Be and western Dac Lac Province. Also in Cambodia. Animists 74%. D=RCC,ECVN,SDA. M=UWM,CMA.
12296	1	10	7.89	8	65.00	35.00	B	7.11	360	4	Han Chinese (Tay Nung, Lowland Nung) from Canton as laborers/soldiers in 1930s. Folk-religionists/Buddhists 80%, nonreligious 17%. D=RCC. R=AWR.
12297	2	5	6.32	4	68.00	32.00	B	64.53	295	6	Dong Nai Province; also Tayninh, Binhlong Provinces. Montagnards. M=SIL. Animists 74%. D=RCC,ECVN. M=CMA,UWM,SIL.
12298	1	6	7.02	4	64.00	36.00	B	67.74	322	6	Lam Dong Province. Closely related to Cham. 25% bilingual in Vietnamese. Animists 70%. D=ECVN. M=CMA.
12299	2	6	6.26	4	58.00	42.00	B	42.34	343	6	Gia Lai-Cong Tum Province. Animists 80%. D=RCC,ECVN. M=CMA,UWM,SIL,WEC.
12300	3	6	8.36	4	90.00	10.00	B	147.82	285	7	Montagnards. Thien Province. Related to Khua, Mangkong, Leun. Animists 55%. D=RCC,ECVN,SDA. M=UWM,CMA,SIL.
12301	2	6	6.22	4	48.00	52.00	A	17.52	384	5	Known as Khmer Islam. Phan Rang, Phan Ri areas. Literates 60%. Muslims(Cham Paks) 50%, Brahmanist Hindus(Cham Jats) 40%. D=RCC,ECVN. M=CMA,SIL.
12302	2	5	7.75	4	63.00	37.00	B	57.48	381	6	Montagnards. Southeast of Rade area, Darlac and Tuyonduc Provinces. Also in USA. Animists 75%. D=RCC,ECVN. M=CMA,UWM.
12303	4	7	1.99	8	99.89	0.11	C	519.76	48	10	Mixed-race USA/Indochinese, left after USA war. Nonreligious 10%. D=RCC(24 Dioceses),ECVN,SDA,VNIM. M=SOC,OSB,SJ,OFM,OP,CMA,UWM.
12304	1	6	7.86	4	53.00	47.00	B	21.28	443	5	Flowered Meo. Northwestern Tonkin Province. Also in China, Laos. Polytheists 88%. D=RCC.
12305	1	10	3.03	8	88.00	12.00	B	122.05	119	7	Mixed-race French/Vietnamese since days of French occupation. Vietnamese Pidgin French. Buddhists 60%. D=RCC.

Continued overleaf

Table 8-2 continued

PEOPLE		POPULATION				IDENTITY CODE		LANGUAGE		CHURCH		MINISTRY						SCRIPTURE		
Ref 1	Ethnic name 2	P% 3	In 1995 4	In 2000 5	In 2025 6	Race 7	Language 8	Autoglossonym 9	S 10	AC 11	Members 12	Jayuh 13-17	d 18	wa 19	xc 20	mc 21	mi 22	Biblioglossonym 23	Pub 24-26	ss 27
12306	French	0.00600	4,432	4,790	6,482	CEW21b	51-AABI-d	general français	12	84.00	4,024	1B.uh	10	9	14	5	3	French	PNB	b
12307	Halang	0.02178	16,088	17,387	23,530	AUG03z	46-FACA-c	halang		26.00	4,521	0....	9	5	6	5	3	Halang	P..	.
12308	Halang Doan	0.00200	1,477	1,597	2,161	AUG03z	46-FACA-g	doan		20.00	319	0....	9	5	5	3	0		p..	.
12309	Han Chinese	1.60000	1,181,851	1,277,306	1,728,594	MSY42a	46-EBAA-ac	general viêt		2.10	26,823	1Asu.	6	4	8	4	1	Vietnamese	PNB	b
12310	Han Chinese (Mandarin)	0.90000	664,791	718,485	972,334	MSY42a	79-AAAB-ba	kuo-yü	30	2.00	14,370	2Bsuh	6	4	8	4	1	Chinese: Kuoyu*	PNB	b
12311	Hani	0.05187	38,314	41,409	56,039	MSY50i	77-BBAA	hani cluster		5.00	2,070	1....	7	5	6	2	0		PN.	b
12312	Haroi (Bahnar Cham)	0.04626	34,170	36,930	49,978	MSY44z	31-MBAB-a	haroi		28.00	10,340	0....	9	5	7	2	2		...	.
12313	Highland Nung (Tai Nung)	1.00377	741,442	801,326	1,084,444	MSY49d	47-AAAE-b	tai-nung		1.00	8,013	0....	6	4	4	0	1	Nung	P..	b
12314	Highland Yao (Myen)	0.40243	297,258	321,267	434,774	MSY47b	48-ABAA-b	iu-mien		0.80	2,570	0.s..	5	4	6	5	2	Iu Mien	PN.	b
12315	Hre (Davak, Creq)	0.18191	134,369	145,222	196,530	AUG03z	46-FACA-k	hre		26.00	37,758	0....	9	5	7	2	1	Hre	P..	.
12316	Hung (Cuoi)	0.00182	1,344	1,453	1,966	AUG03z	46-EADA-a	hung		2.00	29	0....	6	4	4	0	0		...	.
12317	I (Yi, Lolo)	0.00961	7,098	7,672	10,382	MSY50i	77-BADA-a	nasö		0.19	15	1....	5	4	2	0	0	Nosu*	PN.	.
12318	Indonesian	0.00500	3,693	3,992	5,402	MSY44k	31-PHAA-c	bahasa-indonesia		2.00	80	4Asuh	6	4	2	5	2	Indonesian	PNB	b
12319	Japanese	0.01000	7,387	7,983	10,804	MSY45a	45-CAAA-a	koku-go		2.20	176	1B.uh	6	4	2	5	3	Japanese	PNB	b
12320	Jarai (Djarai)	0.42622	314,830	340,258	460,476	MSY44z	31-MBAA	jarai cluster		88.00	299,427	0....	10	7	7	2	1	Jorai*	PN.	b
12321	Jeh (Die, Yeh, Gie)	0.02178	16,088	17,387	23,530	AUG03z	46-FACA-b	jeh		85.00	14,779	0....	10	6	8	4	3	Jeh	P..	p
12322	Katu (Attouat, Thap)	0.04000	29,546	31,933	43,215	AUG03z	46-FABF-b	katu		29.00	9,260	0....	9	5	7	2	3	Katu	PN.	.
12323	Katua	0.00546	4,033	4,359	5,899	AUG03z	46-FACA-f	katua		20.00	872	0....	9	5	7	2	1		p..	.
12324	Kayong (Katang)	0.00364	2,689	2,906	3,933	AUG03z	46-FACA-d	kayong		25.00	726	0....	9	5	7	2	0		p..	.
12325	Kelao (Ilao, Thu)	0.01140	8,421	9,101	12,316	MSY47a	47-BDAA-a	gelo		10.00	910	0....	8	5	6	2	0	Gelao	P..	.
12326	Khang (Teng, Tayhay)	0.00654	4,831	5,221	7,066	AUG03z	47-AAAD-g	tai-khang		20.00	1,044	0....	9	5	6	2	0		p..	.
12327	Khao	0.01819	13,436	14,521	19,652	AUG03z	46-DDAA-b	khao		5.00	726	0....	7	5	5	0	0		...	.
12328	Khmu	0.06526	48,205	52,098	70,505	AUG03z	46-DDBA-a	kha-khmu		10.00	5,210	0....	8	5	6	2	0	Khmu'	P..	.
12329	Khua	0.00300	2,216	2,395	3,241	AUG03z	46-FAAA-d	khua		1.00	24	0.s..	6	4	4	0	0		pn.	.
12330	Koho (Sre)	0.21782	160,894	173,889	235,326	AUG03z	46-FAEB-a	koho		72.00	125,200	0....	10	7	7	5	1	Koho	PN.	.
12331	Laha	0.00274	2,024	2,187	2,960	MSY49z	47-BBBA-b	laha		0.50	11	0....	5	4	4	0	0		...	.
12332	Lahu (Musso)	0.00400	2,955	3,193	4,321	MSY50i	77-BBAB-a	lahu		30.00	958	4a...	9	7	9	2	1	Lahu*	PNB	b
12333	Lao (Laotian Tai)	0.20000	147,731	159,663	216,074	MSY49b	47-AAAC-b	lao		1.40	2,235	2As..	6	4	6	5	1	Lao	PNB	b
12334	Laqua	0.00910	6,722	7,265	9,831	MSY49z	47-BBBA-a	laqua		5.00	363	0....	7	5	3	0	0		...	.
12335	Lowland Yao (Lanten)	0.01000	7,387	7,983	10,804	MSY47b	48-ABAA-e	mun		1.00	80	0.s..	6	4	4	0	0		pn.	.
12336	Lu (Pa-I, Tai Lu)	0.00870	6,426	6,945	9,399	MSY49z	47-AAAA-g	tai-lü		4.50	313	1.s..	6	5	4	0	1	Lu	PNb	.
12337	Maaq (Ma)	0.05133	37,915	40,978	55,455	AUG03z	46-FAEB-ad	maa' ma		50.00	20,489	0....	10	6	6	3	1		pn.	.
12338	Makong	0.00300	2,216	2,395	3,241	AUG03z	46-FAAA-c	mangkong		0.20	5	0.s..	5	4	5	1	0		pn.	b
12339	Man Cao Lan	0.12581	92,930	100,436	135,921	MSY49d	47-AAAE-ab	man-cao-lan		1.00	1,004	0....	6	4	5	0	0		p..	.
12340	Mang (Chaman, Manbu)	0.00337	2,489	2,690	3,641	AUG03z	46-DEAA	mang cluster		25.00	673	0....	9	5	6	0	0		...	.
12341	May	0.00100	739	798	1,080	AUG03z	46-EABA-b	may		3.00	24	0....	6	4	4	0	0		...	.
12342	Monom (Bonom)	0.01089	8,044	8,694	11,765	AUG03z	46-FACA-jc	monom		20.00	1,739	0....	9	5	6	2	0		p..	.
12343	Muong (Thang, Wang)	1.39526	1,030,619	1,113,859	1,507,398	MSY52a	46-EAAA-a	muong		5.30	59,035	0as..	7	5	7	0	1	Muong	P..	.
12344	Nguon	0.00100	739	798	1,080	AUG03z	46-EAAA-b	nguùn		3.00	24	0cs..	6	4	4	0	0		p..	.
12345	Nhang (Giang, Dioi)	0.04593	33,927	36,667	49,621	MSY49z	47-AAAF-c	nhang		4.50	1,650	0....	6	4	6	0	0		...	.
12346	Northern Roglai (Radlai)	0.04548	33,594	36,307	49,135	MSY44z	31-MBBB	roglai-chru cluster		28.00	10,166	0....	9	5	7	0	2	Roglai*	P..	.
12347	Pa Hung (Meo Lai)	0.00300	2,216	2,395	3,241	MSY47b	48-AAAF-b	pa-heng		3.00	72	0....	6	5	6	2	0		...	.
12348	Pacoh (River Van Kieu)	0.01300	9,603	10,378	14,045	AUG03z	46-FABE-a	pa-cùh		26.00	2,698	0....	9	5	6	1	1	Pacoh	P..	.
12349	Phunoi	0.00200	1,477	1,597	2,161	MSY50i	77-AAAA-a	hpon		2.00	32	0....	6	4	6	0	0		...	.
12350	Phuong (Phuang)	0.01089	8,044	8,694	11,765	AUG03z	46-FABE-b	phuùng		10.00	869	0....	8	5	5	0	0		p..	.
12351	Phuthai (Phu Thai)	0.21030	155,340	167,886	227,202	MSY49z	47-AAAB-d	central thai		4.50	7,555	3asuh	6	4	6	0	1	Thai*	PNB	b
12352	Pula (Lati, Akhu, Lachi)	0.01179	8,709	9,412	12,738	MSY47a	47-BCAA-a	lati		11.00	1,035	0....	8	5	3	0	0		...	.
12353	Puok (Kha Puhoc)	0.01669	12,328	13,324	18,031	AUG03z	46-DDEA-a	kha-puok		26.00	3,464	0....	9	5	6	0	0		...	.
12354	Puyi (Buyi)	0.00221	1,632	1,764	2,388	MSY49a	47-AAAH-a	bu-yi		2.00	35	0....	6	4	4	0	0	Bouyei	...	b
12355	Red Meo (Meo Do)	0.20000	147,731	159,663	216,074	MSY47a	48-AAAB-a	meo-do		12.00	19,160	0r...	8	5	7	0	1		...	.
12356	Red Tai (Thai Deng)	0.16160	119,367	129,008	174,588	MSY49z	47-AAAD-c	tai-deng		4.50	5,805	0....	6	4	6	1	1		p..	.
12357	Rengao (Western Rengao)	0.03267	24,132	26,081	35,296	AUG03z	46-FACA-h	rengao		25.00	6,520	0....	9	5	6	0	1	Rengao	P..	.
12358	Rhade (Kpa, Raday)	0.21829	161,241	174,265	235,834	MSY44z	31-MBAC	rhade cluster		60.00	104,559	0....	10	7	7	5	1	Rade	PN.	.
12359	Romam	0.00100	739	798	1,080	AUG03z	46-FACB	bahnaric-central cluster		5.00	40	0.s..	7	5	6	2	1		PN.	b
12360	Ruc	0.00030	222	239	324	MSY52z	46-EABA-a	ruc		3.00	7	0....	6	5	4	1	0		...	.
12361	Russian	0.01000	7,387	7,983	10,804	CEW22j	53-AAAE-d	russkiy		31.00	2,475	4B.uh	9	6	12	2	0	Russian	PNB	b
12362	Sach	0.00182	1,344	1,453	1,966	MSY52z	46-EABA-c	sach		3.00	44	0....	6	5	4	1	0		...	.
12363	Sedang (Roteang, Hadang)	0.08713	64,359	69,557	94,133	AUG03z	46-FACA-i	sedang		26.00	18,085	0....	9	5	7	0	1		p..	.
12364	Sila	0.00200	1,477	1,597	2,161	MSY50i	77-BBCA-a	sila		10.00	160	0....	8	6	7	2	0		...	.
12365	So (So Phong)	0.00300	2,216	2,395	3,241	AUG03z	46-FAAA-c	mangkong		0.20	5	0.s..	5	4	4	4	0		pn.	b
12366	Southern Mnong	0.08700	64,263	69,454	93,992	AUG03z	46-FAEA-d	south mnong		25.00	17,363	0.s..	9	5	6	0	1		p..	.
12367	Southern Roglai	0.03638	26,872	29,043	39,304	MSY44z	31-MBBB-b	south roglai		30.00	8,713	0....	9	5	7	2	1		p..	.
12368	Stieng (Rangah)	0.10455	77,227	83,464	112,953	AUG03z	46-FAEC-a	stieng		45.00	37,559	0.s..	9	6	7	2	2	Stieng	Pn.	.
12369	Takua (Langya)	0.01634	12,070	13,044	17,653	AUG03z	46-FACA-a	takua		25.00	3,261	0....	9	5	6	2	0		p..	.
12370	Tamil	0.01000	7,387	7,983	10,804	CNN23c	49-EBEA-b	tamil		10.00	798	2Asu.	8	5	7	5	3	Tamil	PNB	b
12371	Tay Hat (O Du, Odu)	0.00033	244	263	357	AUG03z	46-DDBA-c	hat		25.00	66	0....	9	5	6	2	0		p..	.
12372	Tay Pong (Poong, Phong)	0.00200	1,477	1,597	2,161	AUG03z	46-EAAA-e	kha-pong		2.00	32	0cs..	6	4	4	0	0		p..	.
12373	Tho (Keo, Mon)	0.07816	57,733	62,396	84,442	AUG03z	47-AAAE-ae	tai-tho		2.00	1,248	0....	6	5	6	0	0	Tho*	P..	.
12374	Tho (Tai Tho, Tay)	1.47989	1,093,131	1,181,421	1,598,830	MSY49a	47-AAAE-ae	tai-tho	1	1.00	11,814	0....	6	4	6	0	2	Tho*	P..	.
12375	Todrah (Sedang Didrah)	0.01170	8,642	9,340	12,640	AUG03z	46-FACA-j	todrah		26.00	2,428	0....	9	5	6	2	0		p..	.
12376	Tri (So Trii)	0.01000	7,387	7,983	10,804	AUG03z	46-FAAA-c	mangkong		0.10	8	0.s..	5	4	4	0	0		pn.	b
12377	Trieng	0.04000	29,546	31,933	43,215	AUG03z	46-FADA	laven cluster		27.00	8,622	0....	9	5	7	2	0		...	.
12378	Tsun-Lao	0.05000	36,933	39,916	54,019	MSY49d	47-AAAE-aa	ts'un-lao		1.00	399	0....	6	4	5	0	1		p..	.
12379	Upper Ta-Oy (Kantua)	0.02500	18,466	19,958	27,009	AUG03z	46-FABB-a	ta'-oih		2.00	399	0....	6	4	5	0	1	Taoih, Upper	...	.
12380	Vietnamese (Kinh)	85.00295	62,788,038	67,859,258	91,834,723	MSY52b	46-EBAA-ac	general viêt		7.40	5,021,585	1Asu.	7	5	12	5	3	Vietnamese	PNB	b
12381	Western (Cambodian) Cham	0.02998	22,145	23,934	32,390	MSY44z	31-MBBC-b	west cham		0.02	5	0.s..	3	4	3	5	3	Cham, Western	p..	b
12382	White Lati (Lachi)	0.00240	1,773	1,916	2,593	MSY47a	47-BCAA-b	lipupo		10.00	192	0....	8	5	6	2	0		...	.
12383	White Meo (Meo Trang/Kao)	0.30000	221,597	239,495	324,111	MSY47a	48-AAAA-a	hmong-daw		18.00	43,109	2A...	8	5	7	4	1	Hmong Daw*	PN.	.
12384	White Tai (Thai Trang)	0.32320	238,734	258,016	349,176	MSY49z	47-AAAD-b	tai-kao		5.00	12,901	0....	7	5	7	4	1	Tai: White*	P..	.
12385	other minor peoples	0.20000	147,731	159,663	216,074	...				2.00	3,193		6	4	6	4	0			
	US Virgin Islands	**100.00000**	**97,000**	**92,954**	**83,559**					**92.69**	**86,159**									
12386	Black	61.17000	59,335	56,860	51,113	NFB68a	52-ABAF-p	virgin-islands-creole		98.60	56,064	1c..h	10	10	12	5	4		pn.	.
12387	British	1.00000	970	930	836	CEW19i	52-ABAC-b	standard-english		74.00	688	3Bsuh	10	9	13	5	3		PNB	b
12388	East Indian	0.70000	679	651	585	CNN25g	59-AAFO-e	general hindi		15.00	98	3Asuh	8	5	7	5	0		pnb	b
12389	French	0.50000	485	465	418	CEW21b	51-AABI-d	general français		80.00	372	1B.uh	10	9	14	5	1	French	PNB	b
12390	French Creole	9.00000	8,730	8,366	7,520	NFB69b	51-AACC-g	trinidadien		93.00	7,780	1cs..	10	9	13	5	1		pnb	.
12391	Jewish	0.33000	320	307	276	CMT35	52-ABAE-ch	american-virgin-islands-english		0.85 3	0B.uh	5		4	2	5	0	pnb	b	
12392	Puerto Rican White	12.00000	11,640	11,154	10,027	CLT27	51-AABB-hk	puertorriqueño		94.00	10,485	1B.uh	10	9	13	5	3		pnb	b
12393	USA White	15.00000	14,550	13,943	12,534	CEW19s	52-ABAC-s	general american		75.00	10,457	1Bsuh	10	10	13	5	3	English*	PNB	b
12394	other minor peoples	0.30000	291	279	251	...				76.00	212		10	8	8	5	0			
	Wallis & Futuna Islands	**100.00000**	**14,088**	**14,517**	**17,500**					**96.58**	**14,021**									
12395	East Futunan	31.90000	4,494	4,631	5,583	MPY55z	39-CAMA-a	east futuna		97.00	4,492	0....	10	10	12	4	2	Futuna, East	...	.
12396	French	0.90000	127	131	158	CEW21b	51-AABI-d	general français		86.50	113	1B.uh	10	9	14	5	1	French	PNB	b
12397	Wallisian (East Uvean)	66.50000	9,369	9,654	11,638	MPY55i	39-CALA	uvean cluster		96.80	9,345	0....	10	10	13	4	2	Wallisian	P..	b
12398	other minor peoples	0.70000	99	102	123	...				70.00	71		10	7	8	5	0			
	Yemen	**100.00000**	**15,021,738**	**18,112,066**	**38,985,203**					**0.17**	**30,655**									
12399	Arabized Black	1.10000	165,239	199,233	428,837	NAB57j	12-AACF-p	zanji		0.10	199	1Asuh	5	3	2	0	3		pnb	b
12400	British	0.00300	451	543	1,170	CEW19i	52-ABAC-b	standard-english		74.00	402	3Bsuh	10	9	13	5	1		PNB	b
12401	Cuban White	0.10000	15,022	18,112	38,985	CLT27	51-AABB-hi	cubano		20.00	3,622	1B.uh	9	4	8	1	1		pnb	b
12402	Egyptian Arab	0.33000	49,572	59,770	128,651	CMT30	12-AACF-a	masri		7.00	4,184	2Asuh	7	5	8	2	1	Arabic*	PNB	b
12403	German	0.02500	3,755	4,528	9,746	CEW19m	52-ABCE-a	standard hoch-deutsch		72.00	3,260	2B.uh	10	9	13	5	1	German*	PNB	b
12404	Gulf Arab	0.06900	10,365	12,497	26,900	CMT30	12-AACF-i	kuwayti-qatari		0.50	62	1Asuh	5	4	7	0	0		pnb	b
12405	Indo-Pakistani	1.00000	150,217	181,121	389,852	CNN25g	59-AAFO-e	general hindi		1.00	1,811	3Asuh	6	4	8	1	1		pnb	b
12406	Italian	0.00200	300	362	780	CEW21e	51-AABQ-c	standard italiano		83.00	301	2B.uh	10	9	15	5	3	Italian	PNB	b
12407	Jewish	0.00600	901	1,087	2,339	CMT35	12-AACF-n	yemeni		0.00	0	1Asuh	0	1	2	0	0		pnb	b
12408	Lebanese Arab	0.15000	22,533	27,168	58,478	CMT30	12-AACF-f	syro-palestinian		20.00	5,434	1Asuh	9	8	9	5	2	Arabic: Lebanese*	Pnb	b
12409	Mahra (Mehri, Mahri)	0.38500	57,834	69,731	150,093	CMT30	12-ABAA-a	mahri		0.01	7	0....	3	1	0	0	0	Mehri	P..	b
12410	Malay	0.20000	30,043	36,224	77,970	MSY44k	31-PHAA-b	bahasa-malaysia		0.02	7	1asuh	3	2	2	0	0	Malay	PNB	b
12411	Omani Arab	0.70000	105,152	126,784	272,896	CMT30	12-AACF-l	omani		0.10	127	1Asuh	5	2	3	0	0		pnb	b
12412	Palestinian Arab	0.10000	15,022	18,112	38,985	CMT30	12-AACF-f	syro-palestinian		4.00	724	1Asuh	6	4	8	1	3	Arabic: Lebanese*	Pnb	b
12413	Persian	0.15000	22,533	27,168	58,478	CNT24f	58-AACC-c	standard farsi		0.09	24	1Asu.	4	3	3	0	0		PNB	b
12414	Russian	0.07000	10,515	12,678	27,290	CEW22j	53-AAAE-d	russkiy		20.00	2,536	4B.uh	9	5	11	4	1	Russian	PNB	b
12415	Socotran (Sokotri)	0.61900	92,985	112,114	241,318	CMT30	12-ABBA-a	sqatri		0.30	336	0....	5	1	3	0	0	Sokotri*	P..	.
12416	Somali	3.70000	555,804	670,146	1,442,453	CMT33e	14-GAGA-a	af-soomaali		0.04	268	2A...	3	3	3	0	1	Somali	PNB	b
12417	Sudanese Arab	1.70000	255,370	307,905	662,748	CMT30	12-AACF-c	sudani		0.10	308	4Asuh	5	4	8	4	1	Arabic: Sudan	PNb	b
12418	USA White	0.03000	4,507	5,434	11,696	CEW19s	52-ABAC-s	general american		67.00	3,641	1Bsuh	10	9	13	5	3	English*	PNB	b
12419	Yemeni Arab	89.38000	13,426,429	16,188,565	34,844,974	CMT30	12-AACF-n	yemeni		0.02	3,238	1Asuh	3	4	5	4	3		pnb	b
12420	other minor peoples	0.18100	27,189	32,783	70,563	...				0.50	164		5	4	0	3	0			
	Yugoslavia	**100.00000**	**10,566,804**	**10,640,150**	**10,844,276**					**64.71**	**6,885,557**									
12421	Arab	0.18755	19,818	19,956	20,338	CMT30	12-AACF-b	sa`idi		5.00	998	1Asuh	7	5	6	5	2		pnb	b

Continued opposite

Table 8-2 continued

EVANGELIZATION								EVANGELISM			ADDITIONAL DESCRIPTIVE DATA
Ref *1*	*D* *28*	*aC* *29*	*CG%* *30*	*r* *31*	*E* *32*	*U* *33*	*W* *34*	*e* *35*	*R* *36*	*T* *37*	*Locations, civil divisions, literacy, religions, church history, denominations, dioceses, church growth, missions, agencies, ministries, movements* *38*
12306	5	10	-0.31	8	99.84	0.16	C	487.49	12	10	Expatriates from France, in aid, development. Nonreligious 13%. D=RCC,ERF,ECVN,SDA,JWs.
12307	2	6	6.30	4	64.00	36.00	B	60.73	313	6	Montagnards. Gia Lai-Cong Tum Province. Also in Laos. Animists 74%; strong. D=RCC,ECVN. M=SIL,CMA,UWM.
12308	0	8	3.52	4	51.00	49.00	B	37.23	243	5	Montagnards. Northeastern Dac Lac Province. Also in Laos. Animists 80%.
12309	1	10	1.78	6	60.10	39.90	B	4.60	111	4	Partially assimilated Chinese. Folk Buddhists 75%, nonreligious 18%. D=RCC. R=FEBC,HA,AWR.
12310	1	10	2.71	7	64.00	36.00	B	4.67	144	4	Chinese folk-religionists/Buddhists 70%, nonreligious 15%, atheists 12%. D=RCC. R=KNLS,FEBC,TWR,HA,AWR.
12311	0	5	5.48	0	32.00	68.00	A	5.84	563	4	Lai Chau Lao Kay and Yen Bay in North Viet Nam. Majority in China; also Burma, Laos. Polytheists 85% (ancestor worship), many Buddhists 10%.
12312	2	5	7.19	4	62.00	38.00	B	63.36	340	6	Phu Yen, Binh Dinh, Phu Bon Provinces. Animists 70%. D=RCC,ECVN.
12313	0	5	6.91	1	21.00	79.00	A	0.76	977	3	Lang Son and Bac Giang area. Mixed with Chinese Nung. Also in China, Laos. Closely related to Tho and Southern Zhuang. Polytheists 98%(ancestor worship).
12314	1	6	5.71	0	35.80	64.20	A	1.04	491	4	Scattered across northern Tonkin; Banmethuot. Most in China; Laos, Thailand, USA, France. Many speak Chinese. Polytheists 99%. D=RCC. M=OMF,ACCM.
12315	0	5	8.59	4	58.00	42.00	B	55.04	453	6	Montagnards. Gia Lai-Cong Tum Province. Closest to Sedang. Animists 74%. M=WEC.
12316	0	5	3.42	0	18.00	82.00	A	1.31	673	4	In north, along Laos border. Closely related: Pong-2, Tum. Animists 95%.
12317	0	6	2.75	0	19.19	80.81	A	0.13	550	3	Immigrants, refugees from PR China. Polytheists/animists 100%.
12318	2	10	4.48	7	60.00	40.00	B	4.38	237	4	Migrant workers, settlers from Indonesia. Muslims 98%(mostly Shafi Sunnis). D=RCC,ECVN.
12319	3	10	2.91	7	59.20	40.80	B	4.75	169	4	Settlers, businessmen from Japan. Mahayana Buddhists 56%, New-Religionists 23%, nonreligious/atheists 13%. D=RCC,ECVN,SDA.
12320	1	5	10.86	4	99.88	0.12	C	401.50	249	10	Montagnards. Gia Lai-Cong Tum and Dac Lac Provinces. Some in USA. 10 dialects. Animists 12%. D=ECVN. M=CMA.
12321	2	7	7.57	4	99.85	0.15	C	394.01	185	9	Montagnards. Quang Nam-Da Nang and Gia Lai-Cong Tum Provinces. Also in Laos. Animists 15%. D=RCC,ECVN. M=SIL,OMF,WEC.
12322	2	6	7.07	4	68.00	32.00	B	71.97	325	6	Montagnards. Quang Nam-Da Nang Province. Also in Laos. Animists 71%. D=RCC,ECVN. M=SIL,CMA,WEC.
12323	0	6	4.57	1	48.00	52.00	A	35.04	318	5	Montagnards. South Viet Nam, around Mang Bu, west of Kayong language area. Animists 80%. M=SIL.
12324	0	6	4.38	1	52.00	48.00	B	47.45	283	6	Montagnards, in remote mountains of Gia Lai-Cong Tum Province. Fierce fighters. Animists 75%.
12325	0	5	4.61	0	33.00	67.00	A	12.04	441	5	In north. Mainly live in China. Agriculturalists. Polytheists/animists 90%.
12326	0	8	4.76	1	49.00	51.00	A	35.77	322	5	Montagnards. Scattered through northwest Tai Provinces, and in western Nghean Province, North Viet Nam. Related to Puoc. Animists 80%.
12327	0	5	4.38	0	23.00	77.00	A	4.19	641	4	Northwest, near Ma river, north of Pa Ma. Related to Bit in Laos. Animists 95%.
12328	0	5	6.46	4	38.00	62.00	A	13.87	538	5	Mostly in Laos, Thailand, China, Burma, France, USA. Animists 90%.
12329	0	6	3.23	1	23.00	77.00	A	0.84	504	3	West central; southeast of Giap Tam. Also in Laos. Related to Bru, Mangkong, Leun. Animists 99%.
12330	2	6	9.89	4	99.72	0.28	C	299.59	262	8	Montagnards. Lam Dong, Dong Nai, Thuan Hai Provinces. Also USA. Animists 17%. D=RCC,ECVN(since 1934). M=CMA.
12331	0	5	2.43	0	15.50	84.50	A	0.28	536	3	Northwest Viet Nam, Ha Tuyen Province. Polytheists 99%.
12332	1	5	4.67	4	83.00	17.00	B	90.88	190	6	Vast majority in China; others in Myanmar, Thailand, Laos. Animists 60%, Mahayana Buddhists 10%. D=Lahu Ch.
12333	2	6	4.73	5	55.40	44.60	B	2.83	309	4	Migrants, refugees, settlers from Laos. Theravada Buddhists 56%, tribal religionists 33%, nonreligious 8%. D=RCC,ECVN. M=CSI.
12334	0	8	3.66	0	24.00	76.00	A	4.38	486	4	On Viet Nam/Yunnan/Kwangsi border (Viet Nam and China). Animists 95%.
12335	0	6	4.48	0	22.00	78.00	A	0.80	645	3	Also in Laos, China. Polytheists 89%, many Buddhists 10%.
12336	0	7	3.50	1	33.50	66.50	A	5.50	335	4	North Viet Nam in Binh Lu area. Mainly in China and Burma; also in Thailand, Laos. Many literates. Polytheists 75%, Buddhists 20%. M=APM.
12337	1	6	7.92	1	84.00	16.00	B	153.30	291	7	Widespread, across Lam Dong, Dong Nai, and Thuan Hai Provinces. Related to Koho. Animists 50%. D=RCC.
12338	0	5	1.62	1	22.20	77.80	A	0.16	323	3	Binh Tri Thien Province. Most in Laos. Related to Bru, Khua. Animists 99%.
12339	0	5	4.72	1	21.00	79.00	A	0.76	692	3	Moncay Province, North Viet Nam/China border. Also in China. Polytheists 99%.
12340	0	7	4.30	0	48.00	52.00	A	43.80	303	6	Montagnards. Lai Chau Province, North Viet Nam. Also in China. Animists 75%.
12341	0	6	3.23	0	20.00	80.00	A	2.19	580	4	East central, both sides of Viet Nam/Laos border, east of Phuc Trach, southeast of Arem. Animists 97%.
12342	0	6	5.29	1	47.00	53.00	A	34.31	367	5	Montagnards. Eastern Gia Lai-Cong Tum Province. Animists 80%.
12343	1	6	9.07	4	40.30	59.70	A	7.79	671	4	Mostly in mountains of north central Viet Nam; also near Banmethuot in south. Animists 94%. D=RCC. M=SIL. R=FEBC.
12344	0	6	3.23	1	24.00	76.00	A	2.62	483	4	East central, south of Bai Dinh. Also in Laos. Closest to Muong. Animists 97%.
12345	0	6	5.24	0	24.50	75.50	A	4.02	653	4	Northwestern Viet Nam and a few in South. Also in China (southern Yunnan), Laos, France. Related to Zhuang, Zhongjia. Animists 95%(strong ancestor worship).
12346	1	5	7.17	4	60.00	40.00	B	61.32	351	6	Montagnards. In mountains west and south of Nhatrang, and some near Dalat. Animists 72%. D=ECVN. M=SIL,CMA.
12347	0	6	4.37	0	24.00	76.00	A	2.62	579	4	Ha Tuyen Province. Close to Western Hmong(Flowery Meo). Polytheists 97%.
12348	1	6	5.76	0	53.00	47.00	B	50.29	349	6	Montagnards. Thien Province; also in Laos. Animists 74%. D=RCC. M=SIL.
12349	0	0	3.53	0	14.00	86.00	A	1.02	906	4	Lai Chau Province, Muong Te District. Some in Thailand. Official ethnic group. Animists 98%. D=RCC.
12350	0	6	4.57	0	31.00	69.00	A	11.31	492	5	Southeast of Pacoh language. Animists 90%.
12351	0	7	6.85	6	50.50	49.50	B	8.29	404	4	North Viet Nam. Majority in Laos; some in Thailand. Agriculturalists. Animists 95%. M=SIL.
12352	0	7	4.75	0	31.00	69.00	A	12.44	482	5	West of Ha Giang in upper Riviere Claire Valley on China border. Also in Yunnan (China). Polytheists/animists 89%.
12353	0	6	6.02	0	49.00	51.00	A	46.50	393	6	Montagnards. Lai Chau, Moc Chau, Phu Yen, Yen Chau Provinces (North Viet Nam). Also in Laos. Related to Khang. Animists 74%.
12354	0	6	3.62	0	19.00	81.00	A	1.38	616	4	Vast majority live in China. Polytheists 89%, Taoists 9%.
12355	1	6	7.85	4	45.00	55.00	A	19.71	521	5	Northwest Tonkin Province. Also in China, Thailand. Polytheists 88%. D=RCC.
12356	1	6	6.57	1	29.50	70.50	A	4.84	666	4	Central north Viet Nam and Laos in the area of Thanh Hoa Province. Some in USA. Animists 95%. D=RCC.
12357	1	6	6.69	4	55.00	45.00	B	50.18	383	6	Montagnards. Gia Lai-Cong Tum Province, between Sedang and Bahnar peoples. Animists 75%. D=RCC. M=SIL.
12358	2	5	9.70	4	99.60	0.40	C	221.19	277	8	Montagnards. Dac Lac, Phu Khanh Provinces (Banmethuot). Also in USA, Cambodia. Animists 39%. D=RCC,ECVN(since 1934). M=CMA.
12359	1	5	3.76	4	37.00	63.00	A	6.75	352	4	On Viet Nam-Cambodia border. An official ethnic community. Animists 95%. D=RCC.
12360	0	6	1.96	0	21.00	79.00	A	2.30	360	4	Binh Tri Thien Province, Laos border area. Animists 97%.
12361	0	10	5.67	7	93.00	7.00	B	105.23	167	7	Military advisers, some civilians. Nonreligious 49%, atheists 20%.
12362	0	6	3.86	0	21.00	79.00	A	2.30	608	4	Binh Tri Thien Province near Laos border and Chiang river. Animists 97%.
12363	1	5	7.79	4	57.00	43.00	B	54.09	423	6	Montagnards. Gia Lai-Cong Tum Province. Closest to Hre. Animists 74%. D=RCC. M=SIL.
12364	0	5	2.81	0	33.00	67.00	A	12.04	325	5	Lai Chau Province. An official ethnic community. Animists 90%.
12365	0	6	1.62	1	25.20	74.80	A	0.18	285	3	Binh Tri Thien Province. Mainly in Laos and Thailand. Buddhists 70%, animists 30%.
12366	2	6	7.74	4	58.00	42.00	B	52.92	413	6	Montagnards. Mostly in Quang Duc Province north of Stieng language area. Animists 75%. D=ECVN,RCC. M=CMA.
12367	2	5	7.00	4	63.00	37.00	B	68.98	327	6	Montagnards. Thuan Hai Province, and a few in Tuyen Duc, South Viet Nam. Closely related to Chru, Northern Raglai. Animists 70%. D=RCC,ECVN. M=CMA.
12368	2	6	8.58	4	84.00	16.00	B	137.97	312	7	Montagnards. Song Be Province. Also in Cambodia. Animists 55%. D=ECVN,RCC. M=SIL,CMA.
12369	0	6	5.96	1	52.00	48.00	B	47.45	367	6	Montagnards. Quang Nam-Da Nang Province. Closest to Cua and Kayong. Animists 75%.
12370	3	6	4.48	6	69.00	31.00	B	25.18	218	5	In all large towns. Migrants, settlers, laborers from South India, Sri Lanka. Most have returned to India. Merchants. Hindus 84%, Muslims 5%. D=RCC,ECVN,SDA.
12371	0	7	4.28	1	52.00	48.00	B	47.45	278	6	Montagnards. Western Nghe An Province in North Viet Nam. Animists 75%.
12372	0	5	3.53	1	22.00	78.00	A	1.60	564	4	Northwest central, Neun river, southeast of Sam Thong. Also in Laos. Animists 98%.
12373	0	0	4.95	4	20.00	80.00	A	1.46	815	4	Western Nghe and Thanh Hoa provinces. Animists 98%. D=RCC.
12374	2	6	7.33	4	31.00	69.00	A	1.13	705	4	Northeastern Viet Nam near China border; Tung Nghia and Song Mao in south. Also in China, Laos, USA, France. Close to Nung, Zhuang. Polytheists 99%.
12375	0	7	5.65	1	54.00	46.00	B	51.24	337	6	Montagnards. Northwest of Kontum from Kon Hring to Kon Braih. Animists 74%.
12376	0	6	2.10	1	21.10	78.90	A	0.07	403	2	Binh Tri Thien Province. Close to So. Montagnards. Animists 99%.
12377	0	6	6.99	0	53.00	47.00	B	52.23	413	6	Montagnards. Northwest of Dak Rotah in western Quang Tin Province; also in Laos. Animists 73%.
12378	1	6	3.76	1	23.00	77.00	A	0.84	517	3	Lai Chau Province, northwestern Viet Nam. Buddhists 50%, animists 49%. D=RCC.
12379	1	6	3.76	0	22.00	78.00	A	1.60	593	4	East of A Tuc. Also in Laos, and California (USA). Monolinguals 70%. Montagnards. Animists 98%. D=RCC.
12380	4	6	1.81	6	69.40	30.60	B	18.74	105	5	In 18 countries. Literates 65%. Mahayana Buddhists 54%, nonreligious 15%, New-Religionists 13%(CDMC), atheists 8%, Baha'is 1%. D=RCC(24 Dioceses).
12381	0	5	1.62	1	23.02	76.98	A	0.01	254	2	Cambodian Cham. Khmer Islam. Near Chau Doc and Tay Ninh, also Saigon. Majority in Cambodia; 8 other countries. Muslims 50%(Shafi), Brahmanist Hindus 50%.
12382	0	5	3.00	0	32.00	68.00	A	11.68	317	5	North Viet Nam, Ha Tuyen Province, south of Maguan, Manbang, Manmei. Polytheists 90%.
12383	1	6	8.73	4	63.00	37.00	B	41.39	410	6	Striped Meo. Northwestern Tonkin Province, North Viet Nam. Also in Laos, France, China. Polytheists 80%. D=RCC. M=OMF(Thailand).
12384	1	6	7.43	4	39.00	61.00	A	7.11	564	4	North Viet Nam along Red, Black rivers. Also in Laos, China, France, USA. Animists 60%, Buddhists 35%. D=RCC. M=SIL.
12385	0	8	5.94		24.00	76.00	A	1.75	678	4	Malays, Thai, Filipinos(INC,RCC,PIC), other Asia peoples. Buddhists 56%, Muslims 30%, Nonreligious 10%, atheists 2%.
US Virgin Islands											
12386	11	10	1.05	8	99.99	0.01	C	585.18	28	10	Citizens. D=RCC,ECUSA,Moravian Ch,CGP,MCCA,LCA,SA,SDA,AMEC,AMEZC,UPC.
12387	6	10	1.05	8	99.74	0.26	C	402.44	40	10	Expatriates from Britain, in development. Nonreligious 16%. D=ECUSA(D-Virgin Islands),MCCA,SA,SDA,JWs,CB.
12388	0	10	4.69	7	73.00	27.00	B	39.96	214	5	Traders from India. Hindus 60%, Muslims 15%, Baha'is 10%.
12389	1	10	0.85	8	99.80	0.20	C	443.84	33	10	Expatriates from France, in development. Nonreligious 20%. D=RCC(D-Saint Thomas). M=CSSR.
12390	1	10	1.18	8	99.93	0.07	C	522.75	35	10	From Guadeloupe, Martinique. In urban areas. D=RCC.
12391	0	10	1.10	8	48.85	51.15	A	1.51	100	4	Small community of practicing Jews.
12392	9	10	1.15	8	99.94	0.06	C	572.97	33	10	Migrants from Puerto Rico. D=RCC,ECUSA,MCCA,Damascus Christian Ch,UMC,UPC,WC,LCA,BIM.
12393	7	10	1.08	8	99.75	0.25	C	410.62	36	10	Residents from USA, in development, education, administration. Nonreligious 11%. D=ECUSA,RCC,MCCA,LCA,CGP,BIM,UPC.
12394	0	10	3.10		99.76	0.24	C	299.59	79	8	USA Blacks(AMEC,AMEZC,CoGiC), Papiamento-speaking Antilleans (200), Negerholland speakers (nearly extinct), other Caribbean Islanders, other Europeans.
Wallis & Futuna Islands											
12395	1	10	2.23	2	99.97	0.03	C	492.13	54	10	On Futuna Island, Alofi. 3,000 migrant workers live in New Caledonia; also Vanuatu, Fiji. Agriculturalists, fishermen. Animists 2%. D=RCC(D-Wallis & Futuna).
12396	1	10	1.97	8	99.87	0.13	C	481.48	53	10	Expatriates from France, in administration, business. Nonreligious 13.5%. D=RCC(D-Wallis & Futuna). M=SM.
12397	1	9	2.27	4	99.97	0.03	C	501.00	54	10	12,000 migrant workers live in New Caledonia. Animists 1%. Almost all Catholics, some Baha'is. D=RCC(D-Wallis & Futuna). M=SM,PFM.
12398	0	10	4.35		99.00	1.00	C	252.94	120	8	Other Europeans, Samoans, Pacific Islanders.
Yemen											
12399	1	6	3.04	7	43.10	56.90	A	0.15	286	3	Black (Bantu) Africans, former slaves. Muslims 100%(Shafi Sunnis). D=RCC. M=WF,OFMCap,MC.
12400	1	10	-2.11	8	99.74	0.26	C	391.64	2	9	Expatriates from Britain, in business, development. Nonreligious 9%. D=Anglican Ch/ECJME(D-Cyprus & The Gulf). M=CMS.
12401	1	6	6.07	8	74.00	26.00	B	54.02	257	6	Military and advisors from Cuba. Nonreligious 55%, atheists 25%. D=RCC.
12402	3	6	2.95	8	67.00	33.00	B	17.11	149	5	Migrant workers from Egypt. Muslims 91%(Shafi Sunnis,some Ahmadis). D=COC,CCC,CEC. M=WF.
12403	1	6	5.96	8	99.72	0.28	C	370.54	138	9	Expatriates from Germany, in development. Nonreligious 15%. D=RCC(VA-Arabia).
12404	0	0	4.21	7	34.50	65.50	A	0.63	390	3	Immigrants from other Gulf countries. Muslims 100%.
12405	1	6	1.28	7	53.00	47.00	B	1.93	118	4	Traders from India, Pakistan. Hindus 69%, Muslims 30%(Sunnis,Shias). D=RCC.
12406	1	10	3.46	7	99.83	0.17	C	469.57	79	10	Expatriates from Italy, in development. D=RCC(VA-Arabia). M=OFMCap,WF,MC.
12407	0	6	0.00	7	34.00	66.00	A	0.00	0	1.13	Remnants of over 60,000 North Yemeni Jews and 6,000 South Yemeni Jews in 1948, most emigrating to Israel.
12408	2	6	2.70	8	81.00	19.00	B	59.13	115	6	Refugees from Lebanon. Muslims 74%(Sunnis,Shias,Druzes), Nonreligious 5%. D=RCC(Maronites),GOC.
12409	0	4	1.96	0	11.01	88.99	A	0.00	662	1.05	Mahrah State. Also in Saudi Arabia. South Arabic. Indigenous Arab tribes near Mahra. Muslims 100%(Sunnis).
12410	0	6	1.96	5	38.02	61.98	A	0.02	192	2	Migrant workers from Malaysia. Muslims 100%(Shafi Sunnis).
12411	0	6	2.57	7	37.10	62.90	A	0.13	242	3	Migrants from Oman. Muslims 100%(Hinawis,Ibadi Kharijites,Ghafiris).
12412	4	6	4.38	8	58.00	42.00	B	8.46	240	4	Migrant workers from Palestine and diaspora. Muslims 93%(Shafi Sunnis,Druzes,Alawis,Ahmadis). D=GOC,RCC,ECJME,CB. Numerous Christian school teachers.
12413	0	4	3.23	5	38.09	61.91	A	0.12	283	3	Refugees from Iran. Muslims 96%(Imami Shias or Ithna-Asharis), Baha'is 4%.
12414	1	6	5.69	7	86.00	14.00	B	62.78	181	6	Military advisors. Nonreligious 60%, atheists 20%. D=Russian Orthodox Ch.
12415	0	3	3.58	0	15.30	84.70	A	0.16	766	3	Socotra Island. Muslims 99%(Zaydis,Sunnis,Ismailis).
12416	0	4	3.34	5	39.04	60.96	A	0.05	364	2	Migrant workers from Somalia. Muslims 100%(Shafi Sunnis,Hanafis). M=RSMT. R=AWR.
12417	1	6	3.49	7	55.10	44.90	B	0.20	208	3	Migrants from Sudan. Muslims 100%(Maliki Sunnis). D=RCC(VA-Arabia).
12418	3	10	6.07	8	99.67	0.33	C	344.81	135	9	Expatriates from USA, in business, development. Nonreligious 16%. D=Baptist Ch,RCC,ECJME.
12419	1	4	5.95	7	47.02	52.98	A	0.03	388	2	Eastern Colloquial Arabic. Muslims 100%(50% Zaydis,40% Shafi Sunnis,5% Ismailis;, 5% Ahmadis). D=RCC(VA-Arabia). M=OFMCap,RSMT,CRS,FMB,WF,MC.
12420	0	8	2.84		15.50	84.50	A	0.28	502	3	Saudi Arabs, Bedouin, Iraqi Arabs, Levantine Arabs, other Europeans, Eritreans, Ethiopians, Filipinos. 89% Muslim (48% Shafi Sunnis, 30% Wahhabis).
Yugoslavia											
12421	2	9	4.71	7	63.00	37.00	B	11.49	235	5	Migrant workers from North Africa, Levant, Arabia. Muslims 90%(Sunnis,Shias). D=RCC,GOC.

Continued overleaf

Table 8-2 continued

PEOPLE		POPULATION				IDENTITY CODE		LANGUAGE		CHURCH		MINISTRY						SCRIPTURE		
Ref 1	Ethnic name 2	P% 3	In 1995 4	In 2000 5	In 2025 6	Race 7	Language 8	Autoglossonym 9	S 10	AC 11	Members 12	Jayuh 13-17	d 18	wa 19	xc 20	mc 21	mi 22	Biblioglossonym 23	Pub 24-26	ss 27
12422	Aromanian (Aromunen)	0.09378	9,910	9,978	10,170	CEW21i	51-AADB-a	limba armâneasc-a		84.00	8,382	0a...	10	9	8	5	3	Romanian: Macedonian*	P..	b
12423	Balkan Gypsy (Arliski)	0.46889	49,547	49,891	50,848	CNN25f	59-ACBA-bc	arlija		20.00	9,978	1A...	9	5	8	5	1	Romani: Arlija	Pn.	.
12424	Balkan Gypsy (Dzambazi)	0.18755	19,818	19,956	20,338	CNN25f	59-ACBA-bf	dzambazi		30.00	5,987	1c...	9	5	8	5	1		pn.	b
12425	Bosniac (Muslimani)	1.75237	185,170	186,455	190,032	CEW22a	53-AAAG-a	standard srpski		0.03	56	1Asuh	3	4	5	5	3	Serbian*	PNB	b
12426	British	0.04689	4,955	4,989	5,085	CEW19i	52-ABAC-b	standard-english		78.00	3,892	3Bsuh	10	9	13	5	3		PNB	b
12427	Bulgar	0.56267	59,456	59,869	61,017	CEW22b	53-AAAH-b	bulgarski		68.00	40,711	2A.uh	10	8	8	5	2	Bulgarian	PNB	b
12428	Circassian	0.01876	1,982	1,996	2,034	CEW17a	42-AAAA-a	adyghe		0.01	0	2a...	3	1	3	0	0	Adyghe	PN.	.
12429	Croat	3.07766	325,210	327,468	333,750	CEW22d	53-AAAG-b	standard hrvatski		90.90	297,668	2Asuh	10	9	11	5	2	Croatian	PNB	b
12430	Esperanto	0.00000	0	0	0	CEW21z	51-AAAC-a	proper esperanto		80.00	0	0A...	10	8	9	5	0	Esperanto	PNB	b
12431	French	0.05627	5,946	5,987	6,102	CEW21b	51-AABI-d	general français		84.00	5,029	1B.uh	10	9	14	5	3	French	PNB	b
12432	German	0.28133	29,728	29,934	30,508	CEW19m	52-ABCE-a	standard hoch-deutsch		87.00	26,043	2B.uh	10	9	13	5	3	German*	PNB	b
12433	Greek	0.09378	9,910	9,978	10,170	CEW20	56-AAAA-c	dhimotiki		95.00	9,479	2B.uh	10	9	10	5	3	Greek: Modern	PNB	b
12434	Hungarian	4.25754	449,886	453,009	461,699	MSW51g	41-BAAA-a	general magyar		81.00	366,937	2A.u.	10	9	10	5	1	Hungarian	PNB	b
12435	Istro-Romanian	0.01876	1,982	1,996	2,034	CEW21z	51-AADA	istro-roman cluster		90.00	1,796	0....	10	9	11	5	3		...	.
12436	Italian	0.19377	20,475	20,617	21,013	CEW21e	51-AABQ-c	standard italiano		86.00	17,731	2B.uh	10	9	15	5	3	Italian	PNB	b
12437	Jewish	0.02827	2,987	3,008	3,066	CMT35	53-AAAG-a	standard srpski		0.20	6	1Asuh	5	3	3	1	0	Serbian*	PNB	b
12438	Kalderash Gypsy (Rom)	0.00657	694	699	712	CNN25f	59-ACBA-a	vlach-romani		70.00	489	1a...	10	8	6	5	1	Romani: Finnish*	PN.	b
12439	Kosovar (Gheg Albanian)	17.06569	1,803,298	1,815,815	1,850,651	CEW13	55-AAAA-c	kosove		21.60	392,216	2c.u.	9	5	5	2	3		pn.	b
12440	Macedonian	0.46889	49,547	49,891	50,848	CEW22g	53-AAAH-a	makedonski		94.50	47,147	2a.uh	10	9	12	5	3	Macedonian*	PNB	b
12441	Meglenite (Vlasi)	0.00937	990	997	1,016	CEW21i	51-AADC-a	limba româneasca		84.00	837	3A.u.	10	9	8	5	1	Romanian	PNB	b
12442	Montenegrin	4.31020	455,450	458,612	467,410	CEW22h	53-AAAG-a	standard srpski		66.70	305,894	1Asuh	10	10	11	5	2	Serbian*	PNB	b
12443	Romanian	0.75023	79,275	79,826	81,357	CEW21i	51-AADC-a	limba româneasca		84.00	67,054	3A.u.	10	8	8	4	2	Romanian	PNB	b
12444	Rumelian Turk	0.56267	59,456	59,869	61,017	MSY41j	44-AABA-a	osmanli		0.02	12	1A.u.	3	3	3	0	0	Turkish	PNB	b
12445	Russian	0.46889	49,547	49,891	50,848	CEW22j	53-AAAE-d	russkiy		61.00	30,433	4B.uh	10	8	11	4	3	Russian	PNB	b
12446	Ruthene (Ruthenian, Rusyn	0.28133	29,728	29,934	30,508	CEW22k	53-AAAD-bn	saris		91.00	27,240	1csuh	10	9	11	5	1		pnb	b
12447	Serb	62.06199	6,557,969	6,603,489	6,730,173	CEW221	53-AAAG-a	standard srpski		76.40	5,045,065	1Asuh	10	10	10	5	2	Serbian*	PNB	b
12448	Serbian Rom Gypsy	0.31885	33,692	33,926	34,577	CNN25f	59-ACBA-b	balkan-romani		65.00	22,052	1A...	10	8	8	5	1		Pn.	b
12449	Sinti Gypsy (Manush)	0.00937	990	997	1,016	CNN25f	59-ACBB-bd	southeast sinti		70.00	698	0....	10	8	6	5	1		p..	.
12450	Slovak	0.93778	99,093	99,781	101,695	CEW22m	53-AAAD-b	slovensky		83.00	82,818	1Asuh	10	9	8	5	3	Slovak	PNB	b
12451	Turk	0.46889	49,547	49,891	50,848	MSY41j	44-AABA-a	osmanli		1.00	499	1A.u.	6	3	2	1	0	Turkish	PNB	b
12452	USA White	0.02000	2,113	2,128	2,169	CEW19s	52-ABAC-s	general american		72.00	1,532	1Bsuh	10	10	12	0	0	English*	PNB	b
12453	Ukrainian	0.02813	2,972	2,993	3,050	CEW22p	53-AAAE-b	ukrainskiy		76.00	2,275	3A.uh	10	8	11	5	3	Ukrainian	PNB	b
12454	Vlach Gypsy (Gurbeti)	0.37420	39,541	39,815	40,579	CNN25f	59-ACBA-ak	kalderash-machvanicqo		70.00	27,871	1c...	10	8	8	5	1		pn.	.
12455	other minor peoples	0.53111	56,121	56,511	57,595	...				65.00	36,732		10	7	7	5	0			
	Zambia	**100.00000**	**8,193,351**	**9,168,700**	**15,616,246**					**76.91**	**7,052,076**									
12456	Afrikaner	0.40000	32,773	36,675	62,465	CEW19a	52-ABCB-a	afrikaans	3	90.00	33,007	2B.uh	10	10	14	5	1	Afrikaans	PNB	b
12457	Ambo	0.02478	2,030	2,272	3,870	NAB57b	99-AURR-u	ambo		88.00	1,999	1.su.	10	9	6	3	0		pnb	b
12458	Arab	0.01500	1,229	1,375	2,342	CMT30	12-AACF-f	syro-palestinian		10.00	138	1Asuh	8	5	5	5	3	Arabic: Lebanese*	Pnb	b
12459	Aushi (Northern Bemba)	2.21088	181,145	202,709	345,256	NAB57b	99-AURR-q	i-c-aushi		89.00	180,411	1.su.	10	10	10	5	3		pnb	b
12460	Bemba	19.28781	1,580,318	1,768,441	3,012,032	NAB57b	99-AURR-h	i-ci-bemba	56	90.00	1,591,597	4.su.	10	10	11	5	4	Chibemba*	PNB	b
12461	Bisa (Biza, Wiza)	1.61115	132,007	147,722	251,601	NAB57b	99-AURR-n	i-ci-biisa	4	93.00	137,381	1.su.	10	10	7	5	3	Chibiza-chilala*	PNb	.
12462	British	1.01554	83,207	93,112	158,589	CEW19i	52-ABAC-b	standard-english	40	78.00	72,627	3Bsuh	10	9	13	5	1		PNB	b
12463	Buka-Khwe (Hukwe)	0.00200	164	183	312	BYG11d	08-AABE-j	tcaiti-khoe		8.15	15	0....	7	5	3	3	0		p..	.
12464	Bwile	0.30373	24,886	27,848	47,431	NAB57b	99-AURR-f	ki-bwile		90.00	25,063	1.su.	10	8	7	3	0		pnb	b
12465	Central Shona	0.09000	7,374	8,252	14,055	NAB571	99-AUTA-a	standard chi-shona		64.00	5,281	3csuh	10	8	10	5	3	Shona: Standard	PNB	b
12466	Chewa	2.89000	236,788	264,975	451,310	NAB57b	99-AUSX-ac	standard ci-cewa		77.00	204,031	1.su.	10	10	12	5	3	Chichewa	PNB	b
12467	Chokwe (Tshokwe, Djok)	0.60689	49,725	55,644	94,773	NAB57b	99-AURP-f	ki-cokwe	1	50.00	27,822	0....	10	5	7	5	3	Chokwe	PNB	.
12468	Cishinga (Chisinga)	0.41359	33,887	37,921	64,587	NAB57b	99-AURR-k	ci-shinga		70.00	26,545	1.su.	10	9	7	5	3		pnb	.
12469	Eurafrican (Coloured)	0.09313	7,630	8,539	14,543	NAN58	99-AURR-hd	chikabanga		90.00	7,685	1.su.	10	10	12	5	3		pnb	b
12470	French	0.03000	2,458	2,751	4,685	CEW21b	51-AABI-d	general français	5	84.00	2,311	1B.uh	10	9	14	5	2	French	PNB	b
12471	Greek	0.10000	8,193	9,169	15,616	CEW20	56-AAAA-c	dhimotiki		95.00	8,710	2B.uh	10	9	10	5	1	Greek: Modern	PNB	b
12472	Gujarati	0.17126	14,032	15,702	26,744	CNN25e	59-AAFH-b	standard gujaraati		1.00	157	2A.u.	6	4	5	4	1	Gujarati	PNB	b
12473	Han Chinese	0.20000	16,387	18,337	31,232	MSY42a	79-AAAB-bc	proper pu-tong-hua		3.00	550	1Bsuh	6	4	8	4	1		pnb	b
12474	Ila (Shukulumbwe)	0.84031	68,850	77,046	131,225	NAB57g	99-AURS-c	ci-ila	2	60.00	46,227	1..u.	10	8	7	5	3	Chiila*	PNb	.
12475	Imilangu (Mdundulu)	0.14515	11,893	13,308	22,667	NAB57g	99-AURN-j	i-milangu		70.00	9,316	1cs..	10	7	7	2	0		pnb	.
12476	Italian	0.05000	4,097	4,584	7,808	CEW21e	51-AABQ-c	standard italiano		83.00	3,805	2B.uh	10	9	15	5	3	Italian	PNB	b
12477	Iwa	0.35849	29,372	32,869	55,983	NAB57o	99-AUSA-c	i-wa		75.00	24,652	1....	10	8	7	4	3		pnb	.
12478	Jewish	0.01362	1,116	1,249	2,127	CMT35	52-ABAE-fg	zambian-english		0.33	4	0B.uh	5	4	2	3	0		pnb	b
12479	Kabende	0.69219	56,714	63,465	108,094	NAB57b	99-AURR-r	kabende		90.00	57,118	1.su.	10	9	7	2	2		pnb	b
12480	Kaonde (Luba Kawonde)	2.70768	221,850	248,259	422,838	NAB57b	99-AURQ-z	ci-kaonde	7	88.00	218,468	2Asu.	10	10	7	5	3	Kikaonde*	PNB	.
12481	Kunda	0.41577	34,065	38,121	64,928	NAB57b	99-AUSX-e	south ci-kunda		47.00	17,917	1.su.	9	5	7	5	2	Kunda	Pnb	.
12482	Kwandi	0.29546	24,208	27,090	46,140	NAB57g	99-AURN-b	kwandi		46.00	12,461	1cs..	9	5	7	3	0		pnb	.
12483	Kwanga	0.71544	58,619	65,597	111,725	NAB57g	99-AURQ-nb	kwanga		52.00	34,110	1csu.	10	5	7	2	0		pnb	.
12484	Kwengo (Black Bushman)	0.00120	98	110	187	BYG11d	08-AABF-hc	kwengo		10.00	11	1....	8	5	4	4	1		...	.
12485	Lala	2.42452	198,649	222,297	378,619	NAB57b	99-AURR-t	i-ci-lala	4	91.00	202,290	1.su.	10	8	11	5	3	Lala-bisa	PNb	.
12486	Lamba (Lima)	2.33420	191,249	214,016	364,514	NAB57b	99-AURR-o	i-ci-lamba	2	90.00	192,614	1.su.	10	10	12	5	3	Ichilamba*	PNB	.
12487	Lenje (Mukuni)	1.86736	152,999	171,213	291,612	NAB57g	99-AURS-a	lenje	2	68.00	116,425	1..u.	10	9	7	5	2	Chilenje*	PNb	.
12488	Leya	0.11579	9,487	10,616	18,082	NAB57g	99-AURS-e	leya		40.00	4,247	1..u.	9	6	7	5	0		pnb	.
12489	Lima	0.28737	23,545	26,348	44,876	NAB57b	99-AURR-v	vu-lima		90.00	23,713	1.su.	10	8	7	3	0		pnb	b
12490	Lozi (Rotse, Tozvi)	5.22861	428,398	479,396	816,513	NAB57g	99-AUTE-f	si-lozi	17	76.30	365,779	3asu.	10	10	12	5	3	Silozi*	PNB	b
12491	Luano	0.07238	5,930	6,636	11,303	NAB57b	99-AURR-x	luano		70.00	4,645	1.su.	10	7	7	2	1		pnb	.
12492	Luapula Lunda	0.78678	64,464	72,137	122,866	NAB57b	99-AURR-j	ngoma		89.00	64,202	1.su.	10	10	7	5	3		pnb	.
12493	Luchazi (Ponda)	0.74694	61,199	68,485	116,644	NAB57b	99-AURP-i	ci-lucazi	1	75.00	51,364	0....	10	10	7	5	3	Chiluchazi*	PNB	.
12494	Lukolwe	0.70000	57,353	64,181	109,314	NAB57g	99-AURO-ba	lukolwe		60.00	38,509	0....	10	7	7	4	1		pn.	.
12495	Lungu (Rungu)	1.34751	110,406	123,549	210,430	NAB57b	99-AUSA-j	mambwe-lungu	2	83.00	102,546	1....	10	10	7	5	1	Ichimambwe-ichilungu*	PNb	b
12496	Luyana (Lui, Rouyi)	1.02705	84,150	94,167	160,387	NAB57n	99-AURN-a	e-si-luyana	4	76.00	71,567	1as..	10	7	7	2	1		pnb	.
12497	Lwena (Luvale)	2.24083	183,599	205,455	349,934	NAB57b	99-AURP-h	lwena-luvale	8	55.00	113,000	0....	10	7	7	5	3	Chiluvale*	PNB	.
12498	Makoma	0.31024	25,419	28,445	48,448	NAB57g	99-AURN-h	makoma		40.00	11,378	1cs..	9	5	7	2	2		pnb	b
12499	Mambwe	1.60324	131,359	146,996	250,366	NAB57b	99-AUSA-j	mambwe-lungu	2	45.00	66,148	1....	9	5	7	5	1	Ichimambwe-ichilungu*	PNb	b
12500	Mashi Bushman	0.00500	410	458	781	BYG11d	99-AUSD-k	a-ma-shi		10.00	46	4csu.	8	5	4	1	0	Mashi*	PNB	.
12501	Masi (Mashi)	0.50968	41,760	46,731	79,593	NAB57g	99-AURN-n	ca-mashi		37.00	17,290	1cs..	9	5	7	2	0		pnb	.
12502	Mbowe	0.06598	5,406	6,050	10,304	NAB57g	99-AURN-d	e-si-mbowe		43.00	2,601	1cs..	9	5	6	2	1		pnb	.
12503	Mbukushu (Gova, Kusso)	0.30000	24,580	27,506	46,849	NAB57g	99-AURN-p	south thi-mbukushu		87.00	23,930	1cs..	10	10	9	5	2	Thimbukushu*	PNb	.
12504	Mbunda (Mbuunda)	1.40052	114,750	128,409	218,709	NAB57b	99-AURP-j	ci-mbunda	2	48.00	61,637	0....	9	5	7	5	1	Chimbunda*	PNb	.
12505	Mine Kaffir	0.05000	4,097	4,584	7,808	NAB57i	99-AUTF-h	fanakolo	3	79.00	3,622	1csu.	10	10	7	5	3		pnb	b
12506	Mukulu	0.16477	13,500	15,107	25,731	NAB57b	99-AURR-l	mukululu		87.00	13,143	1.su.	10	8	7	2	0		pnb	.
12507	Mwanga (Nyamwanga)	1.86736	152,999	171,213	291,612	NAB57o	99-AUSA-a	i-cii-na-mwanga	6	82.00	140,394	1....	10	7	7	4	1	Ichinamwanga*	PNB	.
12508	Mwenyi	0.14254	11,679	13,069	22,259	NAB57g	99-AURN-g	mwenyi		45.00	5,881	1cs..	9	5	7	2	2		pnb	.
12509	Ndebele	0.05630	4,613	5,162	8,792	NAB57i	99-AUTF-k	north i-si-ndebele		53.00	2,736	1Asu.	10	10	8	5	3	Isindebele	PNB	b
12510	Ndembu Lunda (Humba,Kusa)	2.42757	198,899	222,577	379,095	NAB57b	99-AURP-ka	east ndembu	5	81.00	180,287	0....	10	10	12	5	3	Chilunda: Chindembu*	PNB	.
12511	Ng'umbo	1.03926	85,150	95,287	162,293	NAB57b	99-AURR-m	ngumbo		95.00	90,522	1.su.	10	8	7	5	3		pnb	.
12512	Ngoni (Mpezeni)	3.77335	309,164	345,967	589,256	NAB57i	99-AUSX-c	south ci-ngoni		78.00	269,854	1.su.	10	10	11	5	3	Ngoni	Pnb	b
12513	Nkoya (Lambya, Mbwera)	0.74028	60,654	67,874	115,604	NAB57g	99-AURO-a	shi-nkoya	2	55.00	37,331	0....	10	6	7	4	1	Shinkoya*	PN.	.
12514	Northern Shona (Korekore)	0.19671	16,117	18,036	30,719	NAB571	99-AUTA-b	chi-korekore	2	56.00	10,100	1csuh	10	8	7	5	3		pnb	b
12515	Nsenga (Senga)	5.08245	416,423	465,995	793,688	NAB57b	99-AUSX-f	ci-nsenga	5	59.00	274,937	1.su.	10	9	12	5	3	Chinsenga*	PNb	.
12516	Nyengo	0.24876	20,382	22,808	38,847	NAB57g	99-AURN-i	nyengo		53.00	12,088	1cs..	10	5	7	2	2		pnb	.
12517	Nyiha (Nyasa Nyika)	0.10000	8,193	9,169	15,616	NAB57o	99-AUSA-h	i-shi-nyiha		37.00	3,392	1....	9	5	7	4	1	Shinyiha*	PNb	b
12518	Plateau Tonga	4.85294	397,618	444,952	757,847	NAB57b	99-AURS-da	north tonga		82.00	364,860	1..u.	10	10	7	5	3		pnb	b
12519	Portuguese	0.02000	1,639	1,834	3,123	CEW21g	51-AABA-e	general português	1	93.00	1,705	2Bsuh	10	9	15	5	2	Portuguese	PNB	b
12520	Sala	0.28010	22,950	25,682	43,741	NAB57g	99-AURS-cg	west sala		45.00	11,557	1..u.	9	5	7	5	2		pnb	.
12521	Senga	0.49509	40,564	45,393	77,314	NAB57b	99-AUSW-a	senga		71.00	32,229	1....	10	9	7	5	2		pnb	b
12522	Serb	0.02000	1,639	1,834	3,123	CEW221	53-AAAG-a	standard srpski		83.00	1,522	1Asuh	10	8	8	5	1	Serbian*	PNB	b
12523	Shasha (Mashasha)	0.04351	3,565	3,989	6,795	NAB57g	99-AURO-bc	ma-shasha		55.00	2,194	0....	10	5	6	4	1		pn.	n
12524	Shila (Sila)	0.12752	10,448	11,692	19,914	NAB57b	99-AURR-g	ki-shila		86.00	10,055	1.su.	10	9	7	5	3		pnb	.
12525	Simaa (Liyuwa)	1.02705	84,150	94,167	160,387	NAB57g	99-AURN-k	simaa		47.00	44,259	1cs..	9	5	7	2	3		pnb	b
12526	Soli	0.74694	61,199	68,485	116,644	NAB57g	99-AURS-b	soli	1	58.00	39,721	1..u.	10	6	7	5	1	Soli	pnb	.
12527	Subia	0.13477	11,042	12,357	21,046	NAB57g	99-AURS-f	ci-ikuhane		47.00	5,808	1..u.	9	5	7	5	3		pnb	.
12528	Swahili	0.18280	14,977	16,760	28,546	NAB57j	99-AUSM-b	standard ki-swahili	3	0.02	3	4Asu.	3	3	1	1	0	Kiswahili*	PNB	b
12529	Swaka	0.65140	53,371	59,725	101,724	NAB57b	99-AURR-w	i-ci-swaka		82.00	48,974	1.su.	10	7	7	5	3		pnb	.
12530	Tabwa (Rungu)	0.64936	53,204	59,538	101,406	NAB57b	99-AURR-e	i-ci-taabwa		61.00	36,318	1.su.	10	7	7	5	3		pnb	.
12531	Tambo (Tembo)	0.17490	14,330	16,036	27,313	NAB57o	99-AUSA-d	tambo		58.00	9,301	1....	10	7	7	5	2		pnb	.
12532	Toka (Southern Tonga)	0.17638	14,451	16,172	27,544	NAB57g	99-AURS-de	toka		47.00	7,601	1..u.	9	5	7	2	1		pnb	.
12533	Totela	0.32483	26,614	29,783	50,726	NAB57g	99-AURS-h	e-ci-totela		43.00	12,807	1..u.	9	5	7	2	0		pnb	.
12534	Tumbuka	4.27962	350,644	392,386	668,316	NAB57b	99-AUSW-c	ci-tumbuka	7	82.30	322,933	3....	10	10	12	5	3	Chitumbuka*	PNB	b
12535	Unga	0.34496	28,264	31,628	53,870	NAB57b	99-AURR-s	unga-twa		93.00	29,414	1.su.	10	10	7	5	3		pnb	.
12536	Western Nyanja	3.94665	323,363	361,856	616,319	NAB57b	99-AUSX-aa	standard ci-nyanja	42	78.00	282,248	1.su.	10	10	11	5	3	Nyanja	PNB	b
12537	Xegwi (Twa, Nkqeshe)	0.00160	131	147	250	BYG11d	09-DAAA-a	l'xegwi		20.00	29	0....	9	5	5	1	0		...	.
12538	Yauma	0.05000	4,097	4,584	7,808	NAB57g	99-AURP-jb	yauma		76.00	3,484	0....	10	7	7	2	0	Yauma	Pnb	.
12539	Yombe	0.02529	2,072	2,319	3,949	NAB57b	99-AUSW-b	yombe		87.00	2,017	1....	10	10	6	5	3		pnb	.
12540	Zambezi Tonga	6.27987	514,532	575,782	980,680	NAB57g	99-AURS-d	west ci-tonga	23	77.50	446,231	4..u.	10	10	11	5	3	Chitonga*	PNB	b
12541	other minor peoples	0.20000	16,387	18,337	31,232	...				50.00	9,169		10	5	7	5	0			

Continued opposite

Table 8-2 continued

Ref 1	D 28	aC 29	CG% 30	r 31	E 32	U 33	W 34	e 35	R 36	T 37	Locations, civil divisions, literacy, religions, church history, denominations, dioceses, church growth, missions, agencies, ministries, movements 38
EVANGELIZATION								EVANGELISM			ADDITIONAL DESCRIPTIVE DATA
12422	3	10	1.01	6	99.84	0.16	C	426.17	42	10	Armini. In Macedonia, southern Yugoslavia. Also in northern Greece, Bulgaria. Nonreligious 15%. D=ROC,MOC,RCC.
12423	2	8	1.01	6	73.00	27.00	B	53.29	77	6	Jerlides. Tinners Romani. In 15 countries. Muslims 80%(Hanafi Sunnis). D=RCC,Gypsy Evangelical Movement. M=GGMS.
12424	2	10	1.01	1	76.00	24.00	B	83.22	74	6	Close to Balkan Romany (Arliski). Muslims 70%(Hanafi Sunnis). D=RCC,Gypsy Evangelical Movement. M=GGMS.
12425	4	8	1.74	6	57.03	42.97	B	0.06	127	2	All are ethnic Muslims(45% of inhabitants of Bosnia), all Hanafi Sunnis. D=RCC,SOC,OCCBH,CAC.
12426	5	10	1.01	8	99.78	0.22	C	441.28	38	10	Expatriates from Britain in Business. D=Ch of England(D-Gibraltar),MCY,SDA,SA,JWs.
12427	2	10	1.01	6	99.68	0.32	C	340.03	45	9	Workers, settlers from Bulgaria. Dmitrovgrad and Bosiljgrad Districts. Nonreligious 29%. D=Bulgarian Orthodox Ch(P-Sofia),RCC(in Banat).
12428	0	9	0.00	0	29.01	70.99	A	0.01	0	2	Adyghian, Lower Circassian. A few villages. Mainly in former USSR; also Turkey, Israel, Jordan, Syria, Iraq, Germany, USA. Almost all Muslims 100%.
12429	8	8	1.09	6	99.91	0.09	C	540.47	37	10	In 10 countries. Nonreligious 6%, atheists 3%. Strongly Catholic. D=RCC(19 Dioceses),COGY,COCC,CNOCC,PCCY,ECCBHV,RCCY,CAC. M=FMB,UBS.
12430	0	8	0.00	5	99.80	0.20	C	405.88	0	10	Artificial(constructed) language, in 80 countries. Speakers in Serbia: 210,000(none mother-tongue).
12431	3	10	1.01	8	99.84	0.16	C	496.69	34	10	Expatriates from France, in business. D=RCC,SDA,JWs. M=OFM,SJ,SDB,OP,OFMConv.
12432	6	10	1.01	8	99.87	0.13	C	527.13	35	10	Expatriates from Germany, in business, commerce. D=RCC,ECCBHV,PCCY,NAC,SDA,JWs(UJWY).
12433	4	10	1.01	7	99.95	0.05	C	586.00	32	10	Emigres from Greece. Trades. D=SOC,MOC,AOC,RCC(Byzantine-rite: D-Krizevci),GOC.
12434	4	8	1.01	6	99.81	0.19	C	440.51	44	10	Emigres, refugees from Hungary. In Vojvodina. Nonreligious 15%. D=RCC(D-Subotica,AA-Banat),RCCY,ECS,CNC. M=FMB.
12435	3	10	1.01	0	99.90	0.10	C	450.04	40	10	From Istria, western Croatian peninsula. Related to Romanian. D=Romanian OC,SOC,RCC.
12436	1	10	1.07	7	99.86	0.14	C	514.79	35	10	Emigres, workers, settlers from Italy. Strong Catholics. D=RCC(D-Porec & Pula). M=OFM,SJ,SDB,OP.
12437	0	10	1.81	6	49.20	50.80	A	0.35	139	3	Decline from 80,000 in 1925 due to mass murders by Nazis. High percent practicing Jews.
12438	2	10	1.02	6	99.70	0.30	C	314.26	46	9	Nomads. Muslims 30%(Hanafi Sunnis). D=RCC,Gypsy Evangelical Movement. M=GGMS.
12439	3	8	0.98	6	71.60	28.40	B	56.44	58	6	Kosovo-Metohija (Kosmet). 1990 revolt, military crackdown. Muslims 65%(Hanafi Sunnis), nonreligious 12%. D=Albanian Orth Ch,RCC(D-Skopje-Prizren),UBCY.
12440	6	9	1.01	5	99.95	0.05	C	574.30	32	10	Macedonian Republic. In 8 countries. 3 dialects. Nonreligious 4%. D=Macedonian Orthodox Ch(5 Dioceses),RCC(D-Skopje-Prizren),SOC(D-Skopje),MCY,UBCY.
12441	1	10	1.01	6	99.84	0.16	C	447.63	40	10	Megleno-Romanian, from Meglen region (Greece). Nonreligious 15%. D=Greek Orthodox Ch.
12442	2	8	0.67	6	99.67	0.33	C	332.80	35	9	D=Serbian Orthodox Ch(M-Montenegro & Coastland),RCC(D-Kotor,AD-Bar).
12443	2	9	1.01	6	99.84	0.16	C	462.96	39	10	Citizens, migrant workers. Nonreligious 15%. D=Romanian Orthodox Ch(P-Bucharest),PCCY.
12444	0	10	2.52	8	46.02	53.98	A	0.03	192	2	In Kosovo; also in Macedonia and 20 other countries. Muslims 100%(Hanafi Sunnis).
12445	3	10	5.18	7	99.61	0.39	C	307.25	103	9	Emigres. Nonreligious 30%, atheists 9%. D=Russian Orthodox Ch(P-Moscow),RCC,PCCY.
12446	1	10	1.01	6	99.91	0.09	C	508.19	18	10	Language spoken is not Rusyn but Eastern Slovak, Sarish dialect. D=RCC.
12447	6	8	0.72	6	99.76	0.24	C	411.04	13	10	In 18 countries. Nonreligious 11%, atheists 7%, many Muslims. D=Serbian Orthodox Ch(21 Dioceses),RCC(3 Dioceses),UBCY,ECS,OCCSV,PCCY. M=FMB,UBS.
12448	3	8	1.01	6	99.65	0.35	C	287.07	46	8	Closely related to Sinti Manush. Muslims 20%(Hanafi Sunnis), animists and nonreligious. D=RCC,SOC,GEM. M=GGMS.
12449	2	10	1.01	0	99.70	0.30	C	278.49	51	8	Sasitka Roma. In 15 countries. Nomads. Nonreligious 25%. D=RCC,Gypsy Evangelical Movement. M=GGMS.
12450	4	10	1.05	6	99.83	0.17	C	466.54	39	10	Emigres from Slovakia (also in 12 other countries). Official regional status in Vojvodina. Nonreligious 15%. D=Orthodox Ch,SOC,RCC,RCCS.
12451	0	9	3.99	8	49.00	51.00	A	1.78	263	4	Long-time residents, mainly in Kosovo. Muslims 99%(Hanafi Sunnis).
12452	0	0	5.16	8	99.72	0.28	C	325.87	134	9	North Americans, in business, education. Nonreligious 16%. D=RCC,BBC,SDA,etc.
12453	4	8	2.91	6	99.76	0.24	C	410.55	76	10	Emigres from Ukraine. Nonreligious 20%. D=ROC,RCC,SOC,PCCY.
12454	3	10	1.71	6	99.70	0.30	C	316.82	61	9	Serbo-Bosnians (Machvano), Southern Vlach. 20 countries. Mostly sedentarized, many assimilated. Muslims 30%(Hanafi Sunnis). D=Serbian Orthodox,RCC,GEM.
12455	0	9	1.22		98.00	2.00	C	232.50	34	8	Austrians,Czechs, Polish, Tent Gypsies, other Europeans, other Slavs.
Zambia											
12456	7	10	6.29	5	99.90	0.10	C	538.74	120	10	Whites from South Africa. Nonreligious 5%. D=DRC(NGK),NHK,GK(CRC),AFMSA,JWs,RCZ,SDA. M=LBI.
12457	0	8	5.44	1	99.88	0.12	C	417.56	145	10	On border with Mozambique. Dialect of Lala-Bisa. Animists 10%.
12458	4	7	2.66	8	68.00	32.00	B	24.82	135	5	Traders. Syrian Arabs, Palestinians, Coastal Arabs. Muslims 90% (Sunnis , Shias). D=Syrian Orthodox Ch,GOC,RCC,OSCE.
12459	4	8	10.30	4	99.89	0.11	C	477.53	219	10	Northern Province. Also in Zaire, Tanzania, Zimbabwe. Lingua franca. Animists 8%. D=RCC(D-Mansa),JWs,SDA,AICs.
12460	13	7	9.40	8	99.90	0.10	C	532.17	184	10	Many Baha'is 4%. D=RCC,UCZ,JWs,NAC,SDA,AMEC,ANC,BCZ,CC,ECZ,ACZ,CCSH,many other AICs. M=CMML,WF,OFMConv,USPG,NAC(Burma),AMEC(Zaire).
12461	5	7	10.00	1	99.93	0.07	C	482.01	221	10	East, northeast. Many Baha'is, 5%. D=RCC(M-Kasama,D-Mbala),JWs,SDA,Lumpa Ch,other AICs. M=WF,SJ,SC.
12462	4	10	6.43	8	99.78	0.22	C	435.59	136	10	Expatriates from Britain, in development. Nonreligious 9%. D=Anglican Ch in Zambia/CPCA(3 Dioceses),SDA,UCZ,JWs. M=USPG.
12463	0	7	2.75	0	32.15	67.85	A	9.56	320	4	River Bushmen. Mainly in Botswana, also Angola. Almost all animists 92%.
12464	0	7	7.24	3	99.90	0.10	C	443.47	177	10	On both sides of northern border with Zaire. Northern Province. Dialect of Bemba. Animists 2%, Baha'is 3%.
12465	4	10	6.47	4	99.64	0.36	C	306.01	158	9	In Mumbwa, Central Province. Immigrants and settlers from Zimbabwe. Animists 26%. D=AACJM,IMC,RCC,other AICs.
12466	7	9	9.52	5	99.77	0.23	C	401.90	210	10	Animists 15%, many Baha'is 5%. D=RCC,JWs,NAC,ACZ/CPCA,LCCA,RCZ,many AICs. M=SJ,WELS,USPG,BCZ,FMB,LBI.
12467	7	6	6.61	2	99.50	0.50	B	184.32	219	7	Northwestern Province, east of the Mbunda. Also in Angola, Zaire, with many as refugees in Zambia. Animists 40%. D=CB,RCC,Mennonites,BiCC,IBA,JWs,AICs.
12468	3	7	8.20	1	99.70	0.30	C	301.49	224	9	Northern Province, north of Lake Bangweulu. Animists 20%. D=RCC,JWs,SDA.
12469	6	10	7.61	8	99.90	0.10	C	509.17	154	10	Mixed-race, Mulatto. Language a mixture of Bemba and English, now a lingua franca (unpopular because of White origin). Baha'is 5%. D=RCC,ACZ,JWs,SDA,SA.
12470	2	10	5.97	8	99.84	0.16	C	487.49	120	10	Expatriates from France, in business, development. Nonreligious 13%. D=RCC(9 Dioceses),UCZ. M=SJ,WF.
12471	1	10	7.00	7	99.95	0.05	C	568.67	133	10	From Greece, in traders, commerce. D=Greek Orthodox Ch(P-Alexandria: AD-Zimbabwe).
12472	1	10	2.79	6	56.00	44.00	B	2.04	186	4	Settlers, traders from India. Originally Hindus 74%, Muslims 15%, Baha'is 10%. D=RCC.
12473	1	10	4.09	7	60.00	40.00	B	6.57	216	4	Technicians from PR China. Nonreligious 50%, atheists 30%, Buddhists 17%. D=RCC.
12474	5	7	8.81	2	99.60	0.40	C	238.71	267	8	Central and Southern Provinces, west of the Sala. Animists 25%, Baha'is 5%. D=UCZ,RCC,JWs,LCCA,SDA. M=WELS,CLM,VMHSWE.
12475	0	7	7.08	4	99.70	0.30	C	288.71	215	8	Western Province. Dialect of Simaa. Animists 19%.
12476	1	10	4.27	7	99.83	0.17	C	481.69	91	10	Expatriates in development, business, commerce. D=RCC(9 Dioceses). M=SJ,OFMCap,SC,WF.
12477	3	7	6.32	0	99.75	0.25	C	331.23	176	9	Eastern part of Northern Province, west of northern end of Lake Malawi. Animists 20%. D=RCC,ANC,other AICs.
12478	0	10	1.40	8	46.33	53.67	A	0.55	124	3	Small communities of practicing Jews in cities.
12479	2	7	7.25	3	99.90	0.10	C	453.33	173	10	Dialect of Bemba. Northern Province. Baha'is 3%, Animists 2%. D=RCC,AICs.
12480	6	8	10.51	4	99.88	0.12	C	481.80	219	10	Northwest and Central Provinces; also in Zaire. Animists 10%. D=Evangelical Ch in Zambia,RCC(D-Solwezi),JWs,SDA,BCZ,CC. M=OFMConv,AEF,CLM,CTD.
12481	3	7	7.78	1	93.00	7.00	B	159.54	272	7	Eastern Province, near Zambia/Malawi/Mozambique border. Animists 50%. D=UCZ,SDA,RCC. M=CSM,FMB.
12482	0	7	7.39	4	90.00	10.00	B	151.11	280	7	Western Province. North of Senanga town. Animists 50%.
12483	0	7	8.47	4	95.00	5.00	B	180.31	296	7	In extreme west of Western Province. Animists 45%.
12484	1	10	2.43	0	42.00	58.00	A	15.33	224	5	Bushmen in west, also in Angola. Animists 90%. D=RCC.
12485	9	8	7.93	1	99.91	0.09	C	481.61	177	10	North, Central, Eastern Provinces; also in Zaire. Baha'is 4%, few animists. D=UCZ,ACZ(D-Central Zambia),JWs,RCC,NAC,SDA,BCZ,Watchtower, other AICs.
12486	8	8	10.37	1	99.90	0.10	C	486.18	219	10	Copperbelt. Animists 1%, Baha'is 5%. D=RCC(D-Ndola),BCZ,LBC,CAC,ECZ,JWs,SDA,other AICs. M=FMB,SBM,OFMConv,BUO,CTD,VMHSWE.
12487	5	8	9.81	1	99.68	0.32	C	287.91	274	8	Central Province, Lukanga Swamp area. Animists 29%. D=RCC,JWs,SDA,CAC,other AICs. M=AMEC(Zaire),VMHSWE.
12488	0	7	6.24	2	80.00	20.00	B	116.80	275	7	Dialect of Tonga (Lakeside Tonga) west of Lake Malawi. Animists 50%.
12489	0	7	8.08	1	99.90	0.10	C	436.90	197	10	Dialect of Lamba. Southwest of Ndola. Baha'is 3%, Animists 2%.
12490	7	8	7.01	5	99.76	0.24	C	401.86	167	10	Barotseland; also in Zimbabwe. Muslims 16%, Baha'is, Nzila healing movement. D=NAC,UCZ,JWs,RCC(D-Livingstone,D-Monze),CON,CC,a few AICs. M=PEMS.
12491	1	7	6.33	1	99.70	0.30	C	281.05	194	8	Southeast of Ndola. Animists 20%. D=RCC.
12492	5	7	7.24	3	99.89	0.11	C	451.54	171	10	Northern Province, south of Lake Mweru. Animists 5%. D=RCC(D-Mansa),JWs,Independent Watchtower,SDA,other AICs.
12493	5	6	8.92	2	99.75	0.25	C	344.92	226	9	West central Northwestern Province. Also in Angola. Animists 20%. D=ECZ,RCC,JWs,ACZ,SDA. M=AEF,WF,AFHGC.
12494	1	7	8.61	0	98.00	2.00	C	214.62	291	8	Dialect of Nkoya. Mankoya area, Western and Southern Provinces. Animists 35%. D=ECZ. M=AEF.
12495	4	7	9.68	0	99.83	0.17	C	390.80	237	9	In northeast of Northern Province; also in Tanzania. Animists 15%. D=RCC(M-Kasama),UCZ,SDA,AICs. M=LMS/CWM.
12496	1	6	9.28	4	99.76	0.24	C	343.97	247	9	Western Province, Eastern Lozi-Luyana area. Also Angola, Namibia, Botswana. Animists 20%. D=RCC.
12497	11	6	7.47	4	99.55	0.45	B	218.81	224	8	Northwestern and Western Provinces. Mainly in Angola, also in Zaire. Animists 40%. D=CB,AMEC,CAC,IBA,JWs,SDA,5% RCC(D-Livingstone),CC,AAC,EEA,AICs.
12498	2	7	7.29	1	87.00	13.00	B	127.02	286	7	Western Province. Dialect of Simaa. Animists 50%. D=RCC,AICs.
12499	5	7	6.52	0	90.00	10.00	B	147.82	243	7	Northeastern Northern Province. Also in Tanzania. Animists 50%. D=UCZ,SDA,RCC,JWs,AICs. M=LMS/CWM.
12500	0	9	3.90	1	51.00	49.00	B	18.61	263	5	Nomadic Bushmen among Bantu Masi, in Western Province. Animists 90%.
12501	0	6	7.74	4	79.00	21.00	B	106.69	331	7	Southwest part of Western Province. Nomadic. Strong animists 60%.
12502	1	7	5.72	4	86.00	14.00	B	134.97	240	7	Western Province. Animists 55%. D=RCC.
12503	2	10	8.09	4	99.87	0.13	C	457.27	188	10	In west. Also in Namibia, Angola, Botswana. Animists 10%. D=RCC,AC/CPCA.
12504	4	7	9.12	1	93.00	7.00	B	162.93	312	7	Northern Barotseland; also in Angola. Animists 50%. D=AEC/Evangelical Ch in Zambia,RCC,JWs,AICs. M=AEF.
12505	5	10	6.07	1	99.79	0.21	C	374.85	150	9	Mine laborers from South Africa, speaking Isipiki or Isilololo (a Xhosa-based pidgin). Lingua franca. Animists 20%. D=Zulu AICs,JWs,RCC,SDA,SA. M=WF,SJ,OFM.
12506	0	7	7.25	3	99.87	0.13	C	406.46	186	10	Northern Province, west of Lake Bangweulu. Animists 10%.
12507	1	7	7.90	0	99.82	0.18	C	383.10	200	9	Eastern part of Northern Province. Also in Tanzania. Animists 10%. D=RCC. M=ORGM.
12508	2	7	6.58	1	88.00	12.00	B	144.54	261	7	Western Province. Dialect of Simaa. Animists 50%. D=RCC,AICs.
12509	4	10	8.24	5	99.53	0.47	B	232.14	212	8	Immigrants, migrants, refugees from Zimbabwe. Related to Zulu. Animists 40%. D=RCC,AGC,AACJM,JWs.
12510	6	8	10.30	2	99.81	0.19	C	410.95	232	10	Northwestern Province, Copperbelt; also in Zaire, Angola. Animists 10%, Baha'is. D=RCC(D-Mansa,D-Solwezi),JWs,NAC,SDA,ECZ,AICs. M=OFMConv,SJ,CTD.
12511	3	7	6.57	3	99.95	0.05	C	502.78	152	10	Dialect of Bemba. Northern Province. D=RCC(D-Mansa),JWs,SDA.
12512	5	7	7.84	5	99.78	0.22	C	390.03	178	9	Close to Nsenga. Animists 13%, Baha'is. D=RCC(D-Chipata,D-Ndola),JWs,NAC,Zionists,many other AICs. M=OFMConv,WF,FMB.
12513	3	7	8.57	0	96.00	4.00	B	192.72	296	7	Mankoya area, Western and Southern Provinces. Many dialects. Animists 40%. D=Evangelical Ch in Zambia/AEC,UCZ,ECZ. M=AEF.
12514	6	10	7.16	4	99.56	0.44	B	235.06	197	8	Central Province. From Zimbabwe, also Mozambique. Main Shona dialect in Zambia. Animists 40%. D=AACJM,AGC,IMC,SDA,JWs,other AICs.
12515	7	7	10.76	1	99.59	0.41	B	243.34	296	8	East and Central Provinces. Animists 30%, Baha'is. D=RCC(D-Chipata),ACZ/CPCA(D-Lusaka),JWs,NAC,SDA,Zionists,other AICs. M=USPG,BUO,ORGM,FMB.
12516	2	6	7.36	1	97.00	3.00	B	187.64	259	7	Western Province. Dialect of Simaa. Animists 45%. D=RCC,AICs.
12517	1	7	6.24	0	78.00	22.00	B	105.33	270	7	Northern Province, on Tanzania border; majority in Tanzania, some in Malawi. Animists 60%. D=RCC.
12518	12	7	11.08	2	99.82	0.18	C	401.06	256	10	Predominant across south. Animists 10%. D=RCC,JWs,WHM,ACZ/CPCA(D-Lusaka),SDA,BiCC,CON,CC,SA,LCCA,WMCF,other AICs. M=BUO,CC,ORGM.
12519	1	10	4.45	8	99.93	0.07	C	577.06	88	10	Refugees from Mozambique wars, expatriates. Nonreligious 7%. D=RCC. M=SJ,SC.
12520	5	6	7.31	2	90.00	10.00	B	147.82	277	7	Southern part of Central Province. Animists 50%. D=Apostolic Ch in Zambia,AFM,LCCA,UCZ,JWs. M=AFMSA,UMC.
12521	5	7	7.72	0	99.71	0.29	C	310.98	210	9	On Malawi border west of Lake Malawi. Dialect of Tumbuka. Animists 25%. D=RCC,LVSC,JWs,SDA,AICs. M=VMHSWE,FMB.
12522	1	10	5.15	6	99.83	0.17	C	448.36	95	10	Expatriates from Yugoslavia. Nonreligious 15%. D=Serbian Orthodox Ch(P-Belgrade).
12523	1	7	5.54	0	93.00	7.00	B	186.69	216	7	Dialect of Nkoya. Mankoya area, Western and Southern Provinces. Animists 40%. D=ECZ. M=AEF.
12524	3	7	7.16	3	99.86	0.14	C	426.90	174	10	On both sides of Lake Mweru, including in Zaire. Animists 9%, Muslims 1%. D=RCC,JWs,SDA.
12525	3	7	8.76	5	99.47	0.53	B	171.55	289	7	Western Province, western Lozi-Luyana area. Animists 50%. D=RCC,UCZ,AICs.
12526	3	7	8.64	1	99.58	0.42	B	218.05	278	8	Central Province, east of Lusaka. Animists 40%. D=RCC,JWs,DRC. M=FMB.
12527	4	6	6.57	4	94.00	6.00	B	161.25	244	7	Southwest corner of Zambia. Animists 50%. D=JWs,UCZ,ACZ,10% RCC. M=OFMCap,SJ,WF.
12528	0	10	1.10	5	45.02	54.98	A	0.03	156	2	East Africans originating on Coast. Traders. Muslims 100%(Shafi Sunnis).
12529	3	7	8.87	1	99.82	0.18	C	389.09	218	9	South of Ndola. Animists 15%. D=RCC,JWs,SDA.
12530	6	6	7.60	3	99.61	0.39	C	244.91	226	8	Extreme northern part of Zambia. Also in Zaire. Animists 36%, Muslims 1%. D=RCC,JWs,SDA,NAC,Lumpa Ch,other AICs.
12531	2	7	6.79	0	99.58	0.42	B	215.93	222	8	Eastern part of Northern Province, west of northern end of Lake Malawi. Animists 40%. D=RCC,JWs.
12532	4	7	6.86	2	88.00	12.00	B	150.96	270	7	Dialect of West Chitonga (Valley Tonga, Zambezi Tonga), on southern border with Zimbabwe. Animists 50%. D=RCC,CCAP,WMCF,other AICs. M=FMB.
12533	0	7	7.42	2	81.00	19.00	B	127.13	312	7	Southwest corner of Zambia. Animists 55%.
12534	9	6	10.94	0	99.82	0.18	C	427.46	239	10	Also in Malawi, Tanzania. Animists 12%, some Baha'is. D=UCZ,CCAP,JWs,RCC,IW,NAC,SA,SDA,many other AICs. M=CCAP(Malawi),BUO,VMHSWE,FMB.
12535	3	7	8.31	3	99.93	0.07	C	485.41	187	10	Dialect of Bemba, Northern Province. Baha'is 3%, Animists 2%. D=RCC,JWs,SDA. M=WF,SJ,OFM,SC.
12536	7	9	8.84	5	99.78	0.22	C	407.12	197	10	Animists 12%, many Baha'is. D=RCC(M-Lusaka,D-Chipata,D-Monze),JWs,NAC,RCZ,ACZ/CPCA(D-Lusaka),LCCA,many AICs. M=SJ,USPG,WELS,BCZ,BUO.
12537	0	9	3.42	0	47.00	53.00	A	34.31	258	5	Remnants of Bushmen, almost extinct. Animists 80%.
12538	0	6	6.03	1	99.76	0.24	C	310.68	192	9	Southwest corner, Kwando River area. Also in Angola. Animists 20%.
12539	3	7	7.16	0	99.87	0.13	C	419.16	179	10	Dialect of Tumbuka, west of northern end of Lake Malawi. Animists 10%. D=RCC,JWs,SDA. M=WF,OFM,SC,SJ.
12540	12	7	11.30	4	99.78	0.22	C	403.09	252	10	Valley Tonga. Animists 20%. D=RCC(D-Monze),JWs,CC,ACZ,UCZ,BiCC,IPHC,NAC,SA,SDA,WMCF,other AICs. M=SJ,UBS,PM.
12541	0	8	7.06		80.00	20.00	B	146.00	242	7	Malawians, Zairians, Mozambican refugees, Zulu(AICs), USA Whites(CJCLdS,WCOG,JWs), Germans(NAC), Malayalis(OSCE), Koreans, Hindi, Urdu, Angolans.

Continued overleaf

Table 8-2 continued

PEOPLE		POPULATION			IDENTITY CODE		LANGUAGE		CHURCH		MINISTRY	SCRIPTURE	
Ref 1 Ethnic name 2	P% 3	In 1995 4	In 2000 5	In 2025 6	Race 7	Language 8	Autoglossonym 9	S 10	AC 11	Members 12	Jayuh dwa xcmc mi 13-17 18 19 20 21 22	Biblioglossonym 23	Pub ss 24-26 27
Zimbabwe	100.00000	10,871,122	11,669,029	15,092,435					59.28	6,917,364			
12542 Afrikaner	0.26808	29,143	31,282	40,460	CEW19a	52-ABCB-a	afrikaans		87.00	27,216	2B.uh 10 10 14 5 3	Afrikaans	PNB b
12543 Bemba	0.20000	21,742	23,338	30,185	NAB57b	99-AURR-h	i-ci-bemba		85.00	19,837	4.su. 10 9 13 5 3	Chibemba*	PNB b
12544 Birwa	0.10000	10,871	11,669	15,092	NAB57q	99-AUTE-aa	birwa		30.00	3,501	1csu. 9 5 7 2 0		pnb b
12545 British	3.50000	380,489	408,416	528,235	CEW19i	52-ABAC-b	standard-english	55	82.00	334,901	3Bsuh 10 10 13 5 2		PNB b
12546 Central Shona	22.03944	2,395,934	2,571,789	3,326,288	NAB571	99-AUTA-a	standard chi-shona	82	60.00	1,543,073	3csuh 10 10 10 5 3	Shona: Standard	PNB b
12547 Chewa (Western Nyanja)	4.92759	535,684	575,002	743,693	NAB57b	99-AUSX-ac	standard ci-cewa		52.00	299,001	1.su. 10 9 11 5 2	Chichewa	PNB b
12548 Eurafrican (Coloured)	0.50000	54,356	58,345	75,462	NAN58	52-ABAE-fh	zimbabwean-english		95.00	55,428	0B.uh 10 9 13 4 1	English	PNB b
12549 Greek	0.10000	10,871	11,669	15,092	CEW20	56-AAAA-c	dhimotiki		95.00	11,086	2B.uh 10 9 10 5 1	Greek: Modern	PNB b
12550 Gujarati	0.17692	19,233	20,645	26,702	CNN25e	59-AAFH-b	standard gujaraati		11.00	2,271	2A.u. 8 5 3 9 3	Gujarati	PNB b
12551 Han Chinese	0.01000	1,087	1,167	1,509	MSY42a	79-AAAB-ba	kuo-yü		2.00	23	2Bsuh 6 4 8 4 0	Chinese: Kuoyu*	PNB b
12552 Hiechware (Kwe-Etshori)	0.02847	3,095	3,322	4,297	BYG11d	08-AABD	central tshu cluster		12.00	399	0.... 8 5 5 5 2		... .
12553 Jewish	0.09740	10,588	11,366	14,700	CMT35	52-ABAE-fh	zimbabwean-english		0.20	23	0B.uh 5 4 2 1 0	English	PNB b
12554 Kalanga (Kalana)	1.68493	183,171	196,615	254,297	NAB571	99-AUTA-i	chi-kalanga	2	60.00	117,969	1csuh 10 10 10 5 2	Kalanga	Pnb .
12555 Karanga (Shona, Rozwi)	14.72300	1,600,555	1,718,031	2,222,059	NAB571	99-AUTA-f	chi-karanga	19	66.00	1,133,901	1asuh 10 10 11 5 3	Chishona: Chikaranga	PNb b
12556 Korekore (Northern Shona)	2.81840	306,392	328,880	425,365	NAB571	99-AUTA-b	chi-korekore		61.00	200,617	1csuh 10 10 12 5 3		pnb b
12557 Kunda	1.15000	125,018	134,194	173,563	NAB57b	99-AUSX-e	south ci-kunda		35.00	46,968	1.su. 9 6 7 5 1	Kunda	Pnb .
12558 Lozi (Rozi, Rotse)	1.12000	121,757	130,693	169,035	NAB57g	99-AUTE-f	si-lozi		83.00	108,475	3asu. 10 9 13 5 3	Silozi*	PNB b
12559 Makua (Makhua)	0.10000	10,871	11,669	15,092	NAB57b	99-AUSY-a	e-meeto		28.00	3,267	2.s.. 9 5 7 5 3		pnb b
12560 Manyika (Shona, Hungwe)	6.81703	741,088	795,481	1,028,856	NAB571	99-AUTA-e	central chi-manyika	10	60.00	477,289	1csuh 10 10 12 5 3	Chishona: Chimanyika*	PNb b
12561 Maratha	0.04000	4,348	4,668	6,037	CNN25j	59-AAFU-m	deshi-marathi		1.00	47	2Asu. 6 4 2 3 0	Marathi*	PNB b
12562 Nambya (Nanzva)	0.70866	77,039	82,694	106,954	NAB571	99-AUTA-j	chi-nambya		35.00	28,943	1csuh 9 6 7 5 2	Chinambya*	Pnb .
12563 Ndau (Southeast Shona)	3.55872	386,873	415,268	537,098	NAB571	99-AUTA-g	chi-ndau	4	30.00	124,580	1csuh 9 8 11 5 3	Chindau*	PNB b
12564 Ndebele (Tabele)	13.02000	1,415,420	1,519,308	1,965,035	NAB57i	99-AUTF-k	north i-si-ndebele	30	57.80	878,160	1Asu. 10 10 12 5 3	Isindebele	PNB b
12565 Nsenga	0.31507	34,252	36,766	47,552	NAB57b	99-AUSX-f	ci-nsenga		56.00	20,589	1.su. 10 8 11 5 3	Chinsenga*	PNb .
12566 Nyungwe	0.20000	21,742	23,338	30,185	NAB57b	99-AUSX-h	ci-nyungwe		35.00	8,168	1.su. 9 6 10 5 3	Chinyungwi*	Pnb .
12567 Pedi (Northern Sotho)	1.10000	119,582	128,359	166,017	NAB57m	99-AUTE-d	se-pedi		40.80	52,371	2asu. 9 8 13 5 3	Sesotho: Northern	PNB b
12568 Portuguese	0.10000	10,871	11,669	15,092	CEW21g	51-AABA-e	general português	9	92.00	10,736	2Bsuh 10 9 15 5 1	Portuguese	PNB b
12569 Sena	0.90000	97,840	105,021	135,832	NAB57b	99-AUSX-i	ci-sena		62.00	65,113	1.su. 10 8 7 5 2	Chisena*	PNb .
12570 Swazi	0.50000	54,356	58,345	75,462	NAB57f	99-AUTF-e	i-si-swati	5	66.00	38,508	2csu. 10 9 14 5 3	Siswati*	PNB b
12571 Tawana Tswana	0.20000	21,742	23,338	30,185	NAB57q	99-AUTE-gc	tawana		28.00	6,535	1asu. 9 5 10 5 3		pnb b
12572 Tawara (Tavara, Barwe)	0.40000	43,484	46,676	60,370	NAB571	99-AUTA-bd	tavara		39.00	18,204	1csuh 9 9 12 5 3		pnb b
12573 Tsonga (Shangaan)	0.03300	3,587	3,851	4,981	NAB57p	99-AUTD-c	shi-shangana		68.00	2,619	3.s.. 10 9 13 5 3	Tsonga	PNB b
12574 Tswa (Hlengwe)	1.20000	130,453	140,028	181,109	NAB57p	99-AUTD-a	shi-tswa		19.00	26,605	1.s.. 8 5 8 5 3	Xitshwa*	PNB b
12575 Tswana	0.57436	62,439	67,022	86,685	NAB57g	99-AUTE-g	se-tswana		79.40	53,216	4Asu. 10 9 13 5 1	Tswana: Central*	PNB b
12576 Tumbuka	0.10000	10,871	11,669	15,092	NAB57b	99-AUSW-c	ci-tumbuka		90.00	10,502	3..... 10 9 12 5 3	Chitumbuka*	PNB b
12577 Venda	0.98051	106,592	114,416	147,983	NAB57m	99-AUTB-a	chi-venda		31.00	35,469	4..su. 9 6 10 5 2	Tshivenda*	PNB b
12578 Xhosa	0.20000	21,742	23,338	30,185	NAB57f	99-AUTF-a	i-si-xhosa	5	60.80	14,190	2Asu. 10 9 14 5 3	Xhosa	PNB b
12579 Yao	0.40000	43,484	46,676	60,370	NAB57g	99-AUSQ-f	ci-yao		21.00	9,802	4.s.. 9 5 8 5 2	Chiyao*	PNB .
12580 Zambezi Tonga (Leya, We)	1.17926	128,199	137,608	177,979	NAB57g	99-AURS-d	west ci-tonga	2	41.00	56,419	4..u. 9 6 11 5 3	Chitonga*	PNB b
12581 Zezuru	12.72916	1,383,803	1,485,369	1,921,140	NAB571	99-AUTA-c	chi-zezuru	29	66.80	992,227	1csuh 10 10 12 5 3	Chishona: Chizezuru	PNb b
12582 Zulu	1.00000	108,711	116,690	150,924	NAB57i	99-AUTF-g	i-si-zulu	15	55.80	65,113	3asu. 10 9 14 5 3	Isizulu*	PNB b
12583 other minor peoples	0.20000	21,742	23,338	30,185	...				60.00	14,003	10 7 7 4 0		

Table 8-2 concluded

	EVANGELIZATION							EVANGELISM			ADDITIONAL DESCRIPTIVE DATA
Ref 1	D 28	aC 29	CG% 30	r 31	E 32	U 33	W 34	e 35	R 36	T 37	Locations, civil divisions, literacy, religions, church history, denominations, dioceses, church growth, missions, agencies, ministries, movements 38
Zimbabwe											
12542	6	10	3.68	5	99.87	0.13	C	517.60	77	10	Whites from South Africa. Nonreligious 10%. D=DRC(NGK),NHK,GK,AFMSA,JWs,UAFC.
12543	8	10	7.89	8	99.85	0.15	C	493.29	161	10	Immigrants from Zambia. Lingua franca. Many Baha'is 5%, few animists left. D=RCC,ACZ/CPCA,MCZ,JWs,NAC,SDA,AMEC,AICs.
12544	0	6	6.03	1	67.00	33.00	B	73.36	285	6	Bantu people related to Shona, living where Botswana/Zimbabwe/South Africa borders meet. Animists 60%.
12545	7	10	4.29	8	99.82	0.18	C	472.89	94	10	Farmers, settlers, expatriates from Britain in development. D=Anglican Ch in Zimbabwe/CPCA(2 Dioceses),SDA,JWs,AOCZ,PCSA,BUCA,UAFC. M=USPG.
12546	11	6	6.22	4	99.60	0.40	C	275.94	159	8	Main Shona dialect. Animists 33%. D=RCC,SA,ACZ/CPCA,AACJM,JWs,AFMSA,GGCZ,SDA,FGC,DRC,many other AICs. M=USPG,FMB,LBI. R=FEBA,TWR.
12547	7	7	10.86	5	99.52	0.48	B	216.37	296	8	Mainly in Malawi, Zambia; also Tanzania. Animists 30%, many Baha'is. D=RCC,JWs,ACZ/CPCA,RCZ,LCCA,SOG,many other AICs. M=FMB-SBC.
12548	1	10	6.76	8	99.95	0.05	C	565.20	132	10	Mixed-race, White/Black. Muslims 3%(Shafi Sunnis), Baha'is 2%. D=RCC. M=FMB-SBC.
12549	1	10	4.87	7	99.95	0.05	C	572.13	97	10	Settlers and traders from Greece, Egypt, Cyprus. D=Greek Orthodox Ch(P-Alexandria: AD-Zimbabwe). M=FMB-SBC.
12550	0	10	5.58	6	69.00	31.00	B	27.70	262	5	Traders from India. Hindus 63%, Muslims 16%, Baha'is 10%. M=RCC,ACZ,BCZ,DRC,MCZ,TEAM.
12551	0	10	3.19	7	62.00	38.00	B	4.52	170	4	Traders. Buddhists/folk-religionists 70%, nonreligious 28%.
12552	2	9	3.76	0	46.00	54.00	A	20.14	284	5	Primarily in Botswana. Nomadic Bushmen. Animists 88%. D=RCC,BiCC.
12553	0	10	3.19	8	48.20	51.80	A	0.35	221	3	First pioneers 1869. Practicing Jewish communities (Ashkenazi,Sefardi) in Bulawayo, Gatooma, Harare, Que Que.
12554	4	9	5.80	1	99.60	0.40	C	249.66	166	8	Western Shona. Southwest of Bulawayo; also in Botswana. Animists 30%, Baha'is. D=RCC(D-Bulawayo),ACZ,SDA,AICs. M=LMS/CWM,CMM.
12555	13	6	6.05	4	99.66	0.34	C	315.57	150	9	Southernmost Shona. Animists 30%. D=RCC(D-Gwelo),DRC,ACZ,ZCC,ELCZ(2 Dioceses),FEC,FMC,SDA,SOG,ZAC,CCNZ,SA,many other AICs. M=SMB,SJ,CMM.
12556	9	6	10.41	4	99.61	0.39	C	269.40	261	8	Northernmost Shona people. Many in Mozambique. Animists 30%. D=RCC,ACZ,DRC,ECZ,SA,SDA,ACI,MCC,many other AICs. M=TEAM,LBI,SJ,CMM,SMB.
12557	2	6	8.82	1	78.00	22.00	B	99.64	361	6	Across northern border; mainly in Mozambique, also Zambia. Animists 45%. D=SDA,RCC. M=WWM.
12558	5	10	9.74	5	99.83	0.17	C	466.54	205	10	From western Zambia. Muslims 16%, animists 1%. D=NAC,RCC,UCCSA,JWs,AICs.
12559	3	10	5.96	0	78.00	22.00	B	79.71	261	6	Mainly in Mozambique, also Tanzania. Animists 49%, Muslims 18%(Shafi Sunnis), Baha'is 5%. D=RCC,AEC,JWs.
12560	10	7	6.03	4	99.60	0.40	C	267.18	160	8	Manicaland Province northeast of Umtali; also in Mozambique. Animists 30%. D=AACJM,RCC(D-Umtali),SA,MCZ,MCC,UMC,ACZ,IAC,SDA,many other AICs.
12561	0	10	3.93	4	49.00	51.00	A	1.78	276	4	Traders from India. Hindus 83%, Muslims 10%, Baha'is 6%.
12562	7	8	8.30	1	84.00	16.00	B	107.31	307	7	In extreme northwest corner. Animists 45%. D=RCC(D-Wankie),MCZ,UMC,AICs,WC,SA,SDA. M=DM,SMI.
12563	10	6	9.89	4	92.00	8.00	B	100.74	327	7	Also in Mozambique, with many as refugees in Zimbabwe. Animists 50%. D=RCC,AACJM,UCCZ,AEC,ACC,ACZ,SA,SDA,UBCZ,many other AICs. M=AEF,SJ.
12564	17	6	10.07	5	99.58	0.42	B	267.51	240	8	Animists 36%. D=RCC(D-Bulawayo,D-Gwelo,D-Wankie),AOC,ACZ,CCNZ,ELCZ,AMCZ,BCZ,BiCC,CMCCA,UCCSA,SDA,JWs,DRC,CCCC,MCZ,SOG,&c. M=SMB.
12565	6	7	7.93	1	99.56	0.44	B	222.79	236	8	Also in Zambia, Mozambique. Animists 24%, Baha'is 4%. D=RCC,ACZ/CPCA,JWs,NAC,SDA,AICs.
12566	3	6	6.94	1	83.00	17.00	B	106.03	277	7	Northeast corner. Mainly in Mozambique. Animists 55%. D=RCC,ICFG,AICs.
12567	7	10	8.94	4	99.41	0.59	B	166.49	243	7	Workers, migrants from Transvaal(South Africa). Animists 35%, Baha'is, Muslims. D=ZCC,ELCZ,RCC,MCZ,JWs,SDA,many other AICs.
12568	1	10	3.87	8	99.92	0.08	C	567.50	79	10	Refugee settlers from Mozambique wars. D=RCC(5 Dioceses). M=FMB-SBC.
12569	2	6	9.18	1	99.62	0.38	C	244.40	270	8	In east of country; primarily in Mozambique. Animists 17%, Muslims 1%. D=RCC,AICs.
12570	3	10	8.61	5	99.66	0.34	C	330.03	193	9	Migrants, immigrants from Swaziland. Animists 12%. Nominal Christians 22%. D=over 50 AICs,RCC,MCZ.
12571	3	10	4.80	5	88.00	12.00	B	89.93	178	6	Bantu tribe from northwest Botswana. Animists 40%. Many nominal Christians 32%. D=many AICs,UCCSA,ELCZ.
12572	8	6	7.80	4	98.00	2.00	B	139.50	249	7	Across northeast border. Also in Mozambique. Animists 41%. D=RCC,AACJM,MCZ,UMC,ACZ,SA,SDA,many other AICs.
12573	4	6	5.73	5	99.68	0.32	C	325.14	158	9	Mainly in South Africa and Mozambique. Many Shangaan refugees from Mozambique. Animists 5%, Muslims, Baha'is. D=TPC,FPCS,RCC,AICs.
12574	6	6	8.21	4	73.00	27.00	B	50.62	376	6	Many Tswa also in Mozambique. Animists 60%. D=RCC,UCCSA,ACZ/CPCA,FMC,PAG,AICs.
12575	3	9	5.59	5	99.79	0.21	C	441.67	117	10	Primarily in Botswana, South Africa, Namibia. Animists 20%. D=UCCSA,ELCZ,over 30 AICs. M=LMS/CWM.
12576	8	10	7.20	0	99.90	0.10	C	505.89	154	10	Mainly in Malawi and Zambia. Animists 9%, some Baha'is. D=UCCSA,CCAP,JWs,RCC,NAC,SA,SDA,AICs.
12577	10	7	8.52	4	90.00	10.00	B	101.83	289	7	In south. Primarily in South Africa. Animists 58%. D=DRCA,AoG,RCC,ELCZ,AFGC,ACZ,ZCC,ABC,CBCSA,other AICs. M=VMHSWE(Zambia),FMB-SBC.
12578	5	10	5.81	9	99.61	0.39	C	301.36	138	9	Immigrants, migrants from South Africa. Animists 20%, Muslims, Baha'is, Hindus. D=AAoG,AFMSA,CoC,RCC,many other AICs.
12579	2	10	7.13	4	80.00	20.00	B	61.32	294	6	Primarily in Mozambique, Malawi, Tanzania. Muslims 77%(Shafi Sunnis), Animists 2%. D=ACZ/CPCA,RCC.
12580	6	7	9.02	4	99.41	0.59	B	151.14	294	7	Valley Tonga. Animists 37%. D=Church of Christ,BCZ,RCC,UMC,Pentecostals,AICs. M=Back to God Crusade,VMHSWE(Zambia),FMB-SBC.
12581	11	6	7.57	4	99.67	0.33	C	314.04	184	9	Animists 28%. D=RCC(M-Harare/Salisbury,D-Gwelo,D-Wankie),AACJM,ACZ/CPCA,SDA,SA,DRC,BCZ,MCZ,UMC,CMCCA,AICs. M=SMB,SJ,SMI,MMS,BGC,ZCC.
12582	6	10	9.18	5	99.56	0.44	B	266.40	214	8	Primarily in South Africa. Animists 16%, Muslims 10%, many Baha'is. D=AoG(Back to God),NBC,PCA,RCC,CPSA,vast numbers of AICs.
12583	0	8	5.80		90.00	10.00	C	197.10	177	7	Germans(NAC), USA Whites(CJCLdS,CCS,JWs), Ethiopians(Amhara, Oromo), Mauritians, Namibians, Fanagolo speakers. Nonreligious 10%, Baha'is, Muslims.

Part 9

LINGUAMETRICS

Demographics, ministries, and scriptures via
13,500 language profiles

*I saw another angel. This one was flying across the sky and had the eternal good news to
announce to the people of every race, tribe, language, and nation on Earth.*
—Revelation 14:6, Contemporary English Version

All real science rests on classification.
—Comparative philologist F. Max Müller, father of the history of religion, 1860

Part 9 describes the world of the church's measurable language ministries—Scripture translation and distribution, literacy planning, Christian literature, Christian publishing, books and periodicals, broadcasting and telecasting, audiovisual approaches, ministries to the blind, the deaf, and to nonliterates. These activities are described and analyzed by means of a new global classification of 13,500 distinct and different languages, evolved for this survey. It arranges languages by their linguistic proximity to or distance from all other languages. This enables measurement of any 2 languages' degree of mutual intelligibility or mutual intercomprehension. It thus demonstrates and charts the influence of Christian literature and other ministries far beyond the initial language of use or translation to large numbers of related languages.

Demographics, ministries, and scriptures via 13,500 language profiles

1. A WORLD LANGUAGE CLASSIFICATION

A large part of the Christian mission in the world centers on understanding and utilizing the vast world of languages. From Apostolic days the church pioneered translation and the uses of mother tongues, vernaculars, and lingua francas in the proclamation and spread of the gospel.

Many observers of the language scene have realized for a long time that the church today has not been fully aware of this vast world. For this reason the first section of this Part 9 develops a global survey and taxonomy of languages, their demography, and their relation to race, ethnicity, cultures, religions, and statistical enumeration.

Classifying the world of language and its users

The next few pages summarize the schema worked out over 25 years by linguist David Dalby in his 2000 publication *The Linguasphere: register of the world's languages and speech communities* (Linguasphere Press, Wales: Contributing Editors David B. Barrett, Michael Mann). Readers interested in the sources used, assumptions made, and methodology employed should study this seminal publication. Its application here to the world of Christian language ministries is based on the 1997 abbreviated version which uses the same codes except in a handful of cases. Full-length versions with all dialects and alternate names are available on electronic media.

This Part 9 thus sets out a new and original classification of all the world's living languages. It does this by assigning to each language a unique 7-character code, and to each of its dialects an 8-character code, such as 01-AAAA-aa. By means of this code the reader can then search or navigate through large areas of data describing geography, linguistics, demography, Christian resources, translations of the Scriptures, agencies at work, ministries, and the like. By comparing the codes of any 2 languages the reader can immediately discover how close or how distant they are to or from each other.

Although the basic system is relatively easy to grasp, there are many useful implications to assist readers working with 2 or more languages or wanting to locate, explore, or investigate particular groupings. For this reason the next few pages develop a variety of tables that explain the classification and its codes from different starting-points.

Table 9-1. Shorthand terms for comprehension levels.

Within...		All share a minimum of...	Which means intercomprehension is...
1		*2*	*3*
a	MACROZONE	0%	zero
	GLOSSOZONE	5%	negligible
	GLOSSOSET	30%	acquirable
	GLOSSOCHAIN	50%	potential
	GLOSSONET	70%	partial
	GLOSSOCLUSTER	80%	general
	language	85%	adequate
	dialect	90%	mutual

Eight groupings of speechforms

The 7 characters of each language's code, or the 8 for each of its dialects, represent distinct varieties or levels of groupings of their related speech forms. These are as set out in Table 9-1.

Getting the idea through single adjectives (Table 9-1)

A way of understanding this schema therefore is to draw up the simplified table which we can verbalize as follows: 'Within 1 (a particular level or category, in the first column), all speech forms share a mini-

mum of 2 (second column, %), which means that the poorest intercomprehension between any 2 of them is a minimum of 3 (third column).'

Starting near the bottom of the table, the term **language** is here defined as a speech form in which all its related component or subsidiary speech forms such as dialects share with the language 85% or more of basic vocabulary of human experience. This thus gives their speakers adequate intercomprehension—they can all understand each other at least adequately. Moving down in the table, within a **dialect** all speech forms then share 90% or more, providing mutual intercomprehension.

Moving up in the table, a language and any other related languages which share 80% or more of basic vocabulary are here defined as forming a GLOSSO-CLUSTER. They share general intercomprehension. If several of these exist sharing 70% or more, this forms a GLOSSONET, sharing partial intercomprehension. Several related glossonets may then make up a GLOSSOCHAIN, sharing 50% or more and having potential intercomprehension. Several of these may make up a GLOSSOSET (30%). And lastly to complete this schema there are 2 top levels, GLOSSOZONE and MACROZONE, with virtually no intercomprehension but essential to complete this worldwide classification of all languages and speechforms.

Identifying 8 levels by codes

The 8 levels of speech forms can now be coded by assigning a character to each level. The result is both a unique classification, and also an organic or independent one. This is set out in Table 9-2.

Forming a speech form's glossocode

The 8 levels described above result in 8 characters which together form what we here term a glossocode, as with 01-AAAA-aa as mentioned above. This code can be seen to form a proximity scale. It will now be divided into 3 smaller scales. The first scale is composed of the first 2 characters, always one digit each; they describe the first 2 lines of Table 9-1's and 9-2's list. The second scale consists of 4 capital letters, describing the next 4 lines of that table. The third scale closes with 2 lowercase letters. The makeup of these scales needs now to be explained in detail.

LANGUAGE PROXIMITY SCALES

The main entity listed in this classification is a lan-

Table 9-2. Recognizing partial or abbreviated codes in the World Language Classification.

Partial codes in this classification all start from the left end. They have the following meanings:

a 1-character code by itself	=	a **MACROZONE**
a 2-character code by itself	=	a **GLOSSOZONE**
a 3-character code by itself	=	a **GLOSSOSET**
a 4-character code by itself	=	a **GLOSSOCHAIN**
a 5-character code by itself	=	a **GLOSSONET**
a 6-character code by itself	=	a **GLOSSOCLUSTER**
a 7-character code by itself	=	a **language**
a 8-character code by itself	=	a **dialect**
name in capitals, any code	=	anglicized cover-name
name in lowercase	=	reference-name (autoglossonym) with affix (prefix or suffix) where used, added in medium type
in medium type with capital	=	anglicized name where different from foregoing, or geographic or personal name
name in lowercase medium (only in full *LinguaMetrics*)	=	dialect or alternate name/names

guage, being defined as the mother tongue of a distinct, uniform speech community with its own identity. Each language is characterized here by a 7-character computer code or language code or language proximity scale (scale of linguistic proximity), which locates the language in its relationships with other living languages. Likewise, each dialect is described by an 8-character code. This proximity scale is divided into 3 indexes or scales: first a wider scale, which is a 2-digit reference grid situating the language within the wider world; second a closeness scale, which is a 4-letter lexical similarity index, grouping each language by its closeness to other related languages; and third a comprehension scale, which is a 2-letter intelligibility index, classifying speech forms into languages (defined as speech forms each of which needs, requires, or already has its own separate literature and broadcasting) and dialects (defined as speech forms each of which is sufficiently interintelligible with its parent language and with sister dialects to not need or require separate literature or broadcasting).

The first 2 of these scales present cover names in anglicized form, where such exist. The third scale presents each language's or dialect's own autoglossonym—what it calls itself.

The 3 indexes or scales can be elaborated on as follows, in words and in tables.

1. WIDER SCALE
(a 2-digit reference grid)

This first scale or grid situates the language within the wider world. It is a schematic grid dividing the world's languages for arbitrary convenience into 100 linguistic or geolinguistic zones.

Table 9-3. The world of languages divided into 10 macrozones.

This digit provides the first character of the 8-character proximity scale.

Code	Name	Code	Name
0	AFRICAN	1	AFRO-ASIAN
2	AUSTRALASIAN	3	AUSTRONESIAN
4	EURASIAN	5	INDO-EUROPEAN
6	NORTH AMERICAN	7	SINO-TIBETAN
8	SOUTH AMERICAN	9	TRANSAFRICAN

First character (Table 9-3)

The initial digit divides the entire world into 10 primary reference zones that we here call **macrozones**, which are major areas of linguistic affinity or continental reference. The digit thus assigns the language to one of the 10 macrozones shown below. Further, we recognize 2 types of macrozone (though we leave them uncoded, excluded from the coding system): of either geographic or linguistic character, and for which we coin respectively the terms geozone and phylozone. Firstly, a macrozone can be a geozone, defined here as one of the world's 5 geographical continents (continental land-masses), regarded as geolinguistic regions or continental language regions covering the 2,000 or so languages in the world which do not belong to the 5 recognized major language phyla or families. These geozones are shown in the lefthand column of Table 9-3 coded by an even digit 0, 2, 4, 6, 8. Alternatively, a macrozone can be a phylozone (one of the world's 5 recognized major language phyla or families, which contain over 70% of the world's distinct languages). These phylozones are shown in the righthand column of Table 9-3 coded by an odd digit 1, 3, 5, 7, or 9. These even and odd digits have been allocated in sequences which are

Graphic 9-1. Closeness or distance in relationships between any 2 or more languages on Earth, AD 2000.

The diagram sets out a schema illustrating the World Language Classification. Every language has a unique 7-character code, enabling immediate estimates to be made of its proximity to any other languages. Thus if 2 languages share the first six characters of the code, they belong to the same cluster or outer language. This means they share over

80% basic vocabulary of common human experience, differing only in under 20% of vocabulary.

The diagram illustrates this by zeroing in on one small but highly significant part of the world of languages—the Central Indic network in northern India.

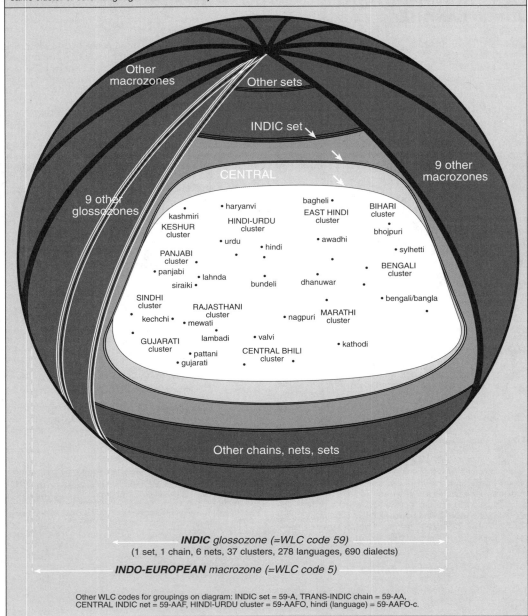

INDIC glossozone (=WLC code 59)
(1 set, 1 chain, 6 nets, 37 clusters, 278 languages, 690 dialects)

INDO-EUROPEAN macrozone (=WLC code 5)

Other WLC codes for groupings on diagram: INDIC set = 59-A, TRANS-INDIC chain = 59-AA, CENTRAL INDIC net = 59-AAF, HINDI-URDU cluster = 59-AAFO, hindi (language) = 59-AAFO-c.

both alphabetic and logical at the same time.

To recapitulate: The first character of each language code (or proximity scale) indicates either the geographic position of the language within one of 5 continents or geozones = initial even digit; or its linguistic position within one of the 5 major language phyla or phylozones = initial odd digit. The titles we use are as follows.

(a) The 5 geozones are arranged to be both alphabetical and also logical, i.e. geographically anticlockwise they cover the world. (b) Phylozones 1, 3, and 5 each represent an intercontinental phylum. (c) The 5 phylozones are named using the current universally-recognized family names except for Trans-African, which stands for the old widely-used Niger-Congo family, minus the Mande languages of the Niger basin and the Kordofanian languages.

Second character (Table 9-4)
The second digit divides each macrozone into 10 subordinate reference zones called **glossozones**, 10 to each macrozone. These are defined and constructed in order to fit, as closely as possible, the linguistic and geolinguistic realities of each macrozone. Each glos-

sozone can be either geographic or linguistic in character. Again, we coin 2 more non-coded terms and call each glossozone respectively either a topozone (a local geographic or geolinguistic area, having only geographic significance, covering 2 or more geographically adjacent sets of languages), or a glossozone (a discrete linguistic grouping, having linguistic significance, covering one or more related sets of languages).

In conjunction with the first digit, the second digit therefore assigns the language to one of 100 glossozones, coded 00 to 99, each covering one or more sets of languages. In practice, virtually all glossozones have linguistic meaning, being sub-families of related languages; in general, it is found that each glossozone's constituent languages share something like 5% of basic vocabulary in common. The rest of the glossozones are topozones (or geomicrozones); each's constituent languages may share no vocabulary at all, or some may share over 10%.

The names of the 100 glossozones are set out in full in Table 9-4. Each set of 10 is there arranged not in alphabetical order but in geolinguistic order, that is in the order which best corresponds to linguistic real-

ity, keeping glossozones of related sets together and observing, as far as convenient, the sequences of west to east and north to south.

Defining the 10 levels used in this classification (Table 9-5)
In addition to the above 2 levels of macrozone and glossozone, the classification utilizes 9 other levels. Before describing these in detail, it would be useful at this point to briefly outline the whole 11 levels and how they relate to each other. This is set out in Table 9-5. This table is given as a general guide to understanding a complex situation. It attempts to present the world situation and then to present and define 10 levels or categories or subdivisions or groupings of relationships among the world's languages. Of these, the 8 shown in boldface type are the major levels or categories used and coded in this classification, and a minor subcategory is added at the end to assist in understanding the classification. The percentages shown should be interpreted only as indicators of

Table 9-4. Ten macrozones and 100 glossozones covering the whole world.

This table sets out the first 2 digits of the 8-character proximity scale.

Macrozones. The 10 macrozones are set out below in large bold capitals. The left-hand pair of columns below, codes plus names, list the 5 macrozones which are geographic (also here termed and explained as geozones). The right-hand pair of columns, codes plus names, list the 5 macrozones which are linguistic (also here termed and explained as phylozones).

Glossozones. All the 2-digit codes represent 100 glossozones. The 9 followed by an asterisk (*) may be called 'open glossozones' in which their unity may not be external. Sets included within such a glossozone will normally, but not necessarily exclusively, be more closely related among themselves than any one of them will be with a set in another glossozone.

0 AFRICAN	1 AFRO-ASIAN
00 Mandic	10 Tamazic
01 Songhaic	11 Coptic
02 Saharic	12 Semitic
03 Sudanic	13 Bejic
04 Nilotic	14 Mid-Cushitic
05 Nilo-Sahelic*	15 Para-Cushitic
06 Kordofanic	16 Omotic
07 Riftic*	17 East Chadic
08 Nama-Tshuic	18 Biumandaric
09 Kalaharic*	19 West Chadic

2 AUSTRALASIAN	3 AUSTRONESIAN
20 West Irianic	30 Formosic
21 North Irianic	31 Hesperonesic
22 Madangic	32 Mesonesic
23 South Irianic	33 Halyamapenic
24 Transirianic	34 Neoguineic
25 West Papuasic	35 Neobritannic
26 Sepic	36 Solomonic
27 East Papuic	37 Neocaledonic
28 Darwinic*	38 West Pacific
29 Pama-Nyungic	39 Transpacific

4 EURASIAN	5 INDO-EUROPEAN
40 Euskaric	50 Celtic
41 Uralic	51 Romanic
42 Caucasic	52 Germanic
43 Siberic	53 Slavonic
44 Transasiatic	54 Baltic
45 East Asiatic	55 Albanic
46 South Asiatic	56 Hellenic
47 Daic	57 Armenic
48 Mienic	58 Iranic*
49 Dravidic	59 Indic

6 NORTH AMERICAN	7 SINO-TIBETAN
60 Arctic	70 Bodic
61 Athabaskic	71 Himalayic
62 Algonkic	72 Garic
63 North Pacific	73 Kukic
64 Iroquo-Dakotic	74 Miric
65 Circumgolfic	75 Kachinic
66 Aztecotanic	76 Rungic*
67 Oto-Mangic	77 Lolo-Burmic
68 Mayanic	78 Karenic
69 Mesomeric	79 Sinitic

8 SOUTH AMERICAN	9 TRANSAFRICAN
80 Caribic	90 Atlantic*
81 Arawakic	91 Voltaic*
82 Tupic	92 Adamawic
83 Interoceanic	93 Ubangic
84 Pre-Andinic	94 Melic
85 Andinic	95 Kru-Grebic
86 Chaconic	96 West Akanic
87 Matogrossic	97 Deltic
88 Amazonic	98 Benuic*
89 Bahianic	99 Bantuic

Table 9-5.   Meaning of proximity scale by 10 levels or groupings of languages, 8 being coded.

Column 1: Examples of typical values of the coded components of the proximity scale (from 1-8 characters horizontally, representing 8 coded types of groupings vertically).
Column 2: Our 8 basic levels or categories of classification used in the scale, all coded, shown in boldface type, with 4 other subsidiary levels or categories which are uncoded or only partially coded, shown in medium type. The 6 levels in capital letters are the classification's anglicized cover names for groupings and families of languages.
Column 3: A statement about how much common basic vocabulary (%) is shared by any 2 of each level's major components; the percentage shows the minimum threshold.
Column 4: Validity or value of lexical relationships.
Column 5: A single adjective expressing degree of lexical similarity shared by all components within each level, or minimum shared by any 2 components.
Column 6: A single adjective expressing degree of intercomprehension (interintelligibility) shared by all components within each level, or minimum shared by any 2 components.

Code	Level or category	Within this level-- (minimum threshold for % vocabulary shared)	Lexical relationships shared across this level	Lexical similarity shared by all within this level	Intercomprehension shared by all within this level
column 1	2	3	4	5	6
-	World	Any 2 macrozones share 0%	None measurable	zero	zero
0	**MACROZONE**	Any 2 glossozones share under 5%	Little quantifiable	nil	zero
01	**GLOSSOZONE**	Any 2 glossosets share 5% or more	Somewhat quantifiable	minimal	negligible
01-A	**GLOSSOSET**	Any 2 glossochains share 30% or more	Apparent to native speakers	occasional	acquirable
01-AA	**GLOSSOCHAIN**	Any 2 glossonets share 50% or more	Facilitate learning	partial	potential
01-AAA	**GLOSSONET**	Any 2 glossoclusters share 70% or more	Obvious to all	general	partial
01-AAAA	**GLOSSOCLUSTER**	Any 2 languages share 80% or more	Facilitate communication	sequential	general
01-AAAA-a	**language**	Any 2 dialects share 85% or more	Functional understanding	similar	adequate
01-AAAA-aa	**dialect**	Any 2 voices share 90% or more	Close understanding	close	mutual
-	variety	Any 2 idioms share 95% or more	Very similar	full	high
-	voice	One speaker, 100%	Identical speech forms	identical	complete

general order of magnitude, claiming accuracy perhaps only to plus or minus 10%.

The description of scales can now continue with an examination of the second of the 3 scales.

2. CLOSENESS SCALE
(a 4-capital lexical similarity index)

This second scale or index describes relationships and groups the language by its closeness to other languages. Comprehension and intelligibility between languages cannot be measured solely by lexical closeness, grammar, pronunciation, and discourse markers; but they can be measured by tested or reported intelligibility and systematic and careful linguistic comparison, including direct testing as well as lexicostatistics (comparison of word lists) and other pointers to the language's closest known lexical relationships).

The 4 levels represented by the next 4 capital letters of the code are shown in detail in Table 9-5 and also on the Quick-Reference Schema in Table 9-11. The full names for these 4 levels throughout the classification form its structure, consisting of 9,843 **cover names**, which are always given there as anglicized and capitalized names followed in every case by one word describing its level—glossoset, glossochain, glossonet, glossocluster—always appearing there in lowercase (noncapitalized) letters.

Third character (first capital letter)
This first letter assigns the language to a **glossoset,** defined as a grouping of languages each of which shares at least around one third (30%) of their basic vocabulary of common human experience, as measured by the use of phonologically related forms with the same meanings, using wherever possible Swadesh's 200-item comparative wordlist. Glossosets can be identified in the classification by (a) the abbreviated term 'set' after each's capitalized cover-name and (b) each's 3-character code.

Fourth character (second capital letter)
In cases where a glossoset is very complex, it may be divided among 2 or more subdivisions, each called a **glossochain**, a linked grouping or groupings within a glossoset. A glossochain shares within its component languages at least 50% of their basic vocabulary of common human experience. Glossochains can be identified in the classification by (a) the abbreviated term 'chain' after each's capitalized cover-name and (b) each's 4-character code.

Three varieties of glossochain are shown in the classification, all coded by a single capital as fourth character:
1. a chain (or, chain proper, being a multinet chain linking 2 or more nets);
2. a minimal chain, and
3. a monochain (absence of chain).

Fifth character (third capital letter)
This third letter assigns the language to a **glossonet** (implying a network of words and meanings). A glossonet is defined as a grouping of languages each of which shares at least around two-thirds (70%) of their basic vocabulary of common human experience. Glossonets can be identified in the classification by (a) the abbreviated term 'net' after each's capitalized cover-name and (b) each's 5-character code.

Sixth character (fourth capital letter)
In cases where a glossonet is very complex, this letter divides it into 2 or more subdivisions, each called a **glossocluster** (or outer language, or wider language, broad language, or tongue) which is a grouping of languages each of which shares at least around 80% or more of their basic vocabulary of common human experience. Glossoclusters can be identified in the classification by (a) the abbreviated term 'cluster' after each's capitalized cover-name and (b) each's 6-character code.

Three varieties of glossocluster are shown in the classification, all coded by a single capital as the sixth character:
1. a cluster (or cluster proper, being a multilingual cluster linking 2 or more languages);
2. a monolanguage cluster (an internal cluster of idioms or dialects within a single language); and
3. a minimal monolanguage cluster (a language or grouping with a marked absence of clusters of any sort).

An additional clarifying definition is that it may be helpful to regard our level 'glossocluster' as 'broad language', and our level 'language' as 'narrow language'. A typical glossocluster would consist of several narrow languages including any literary languages and any colloquial or popular or vehicular (or even ecclesiastical) languages.

3. COMPREHENSION SCALE
(a 2-miniscule intelligibility index)

The third scale or index deals with the internal relationships between a language and its dialects. This final part of the proximity code has 2 miniscules (lowercase letters, a-z). It describes which speech forms are languages eligible for their own literature and broadcasting, and which speech forms are dialects interintelligible enough not to be eligible for their own literature and broadcasting. Obviously other considerations, sociocultural and not purely linguistic, come into the evolution of such eligibility, but it forms a useful and usable approximation to reality.

Again, these 2 levels are shown in detail in Tables 9-5 and 9-11.

Seventh character (first lowercase letter)
This letter, a miniscule (lowercase), identifies the individual **language** (recognized and named as such by its speakers), which usually does not share more than 85% or more of basic vocabulary (of common human experience) with other languages. It is defined as needing, requiring, or having its own separate literature and broadcasting.

Languages can be identified in the classification's listing by (a) being in lowercase type and (b) each's 7-character code.

Eighth character (second lowercase letter)

This final letter, a miniscule, identifies a **dialect** sufficiently close to its parent language and sister dialects to not need or justify separate literature or broadcasting. A dialect is defined here as a speech form whose component varieties and idioms (if any) share 90% or more of basic vocabulary. Dialects can be identified in the classification's listing by each's 8-character code (these being listed here only on CD).

The ordering and listing here of glossosets within glossozones, of glossochains within glossosets, of glossonets within glossochains, of glossoclusters within glossonets, of languages within glossoclusters, and of dialects within languages, are not alphabetical but geolinguistic (approximating to linguistic reality). Codes are then applied at the left of the listing in strict alphabetical sequence.

Example:
LANGUAGE CODE = 2 digits + 4 capitals + 2 small letters
    Illustration: 52-AAAD-ra

macrozone = Indo-European phylozone
  glossozone = Germanic zone
    glossoset = Germanic set
      glossochain = Nordic chain
        glossonet = Nordic net
          glossocluster = Nordic East cluster
            language = svea-svensk (Swedish)
              dialect = halsinglandsk

Lexicostatistics as one of several guides
As mentioned above, to establish degrees of intelligibility, and lack of intelligibility, between languages needs empirical testing followed by systematic and careful linguistic comparison. Lexical similarity or lexicostatistics normally only measures a small sample of the total vocabulary, and for this reason should be treated with caution. Nevertheless, they are valuable as an indicator in the absence of more detailed testing, and are certainly a better guide than nothing at all. Table 9-5 sets out their meaning in the present classification.

In dealing with relationships between languages, it is often possible to measure how much basic vocabulary 2 languages share in common. Lexicostatistics takes a scientific approach by using a standard word list (Swadesh's 200-word list, or a similar one). The result for 2 languages is expressed as a percentage of words thus shared. In the present analysis, these percentages as we define them have a broader meaning than merely sharing basic vocabulary. They cover vocabulary, but also to some degree phonology (accent, pronunciation), grammar (morphology and/or syntax), discourse structure. They measure: closeness, intercomprehension, interintelligibility, similarity. For ease of reference, however, we usually abbreviate the meaning of the percentages to shared vocabulary, although we fully recognize the limitations of lexicostatistics as a measure of closeness of languages.

To sum up, these 8 levels measure degrees of proximity or closeness between speech forms. The percentage ranges of each level represent approximate areas of magnitude and symbolize the cumulative effects of similarities which are not only lexical but also

Table 9-6. Implications of percentages of closeness.

90%-95%	Two speech forms sharing this much vocabulary are sometimes called idioms; they understand each other mutually and more than adequately; they differ one from another principally in terms of pronunciation or "accent".
85%-90%	Functional or adequate intercomprehension exists between the 2 speech forms for communication, conversation, or use of literature.
80%-85%	Relationship between 2 languages sharing these amounts facilitate communication and provide general intercomprehension.
70%-80%	Partial or general interintelligibility or intercomprehension, often functional, exists between the 2 languages or idioms, or can be readily acquired, and this is obvious to all.
50%-70%	Languages are close enough to facilitate acquisition of them as additional languages.
30%-50%	Relationships between 2 languages or other speech forms are apparent to their speakers, and indicate that knowledge of the other is acquirable as a second language.
5%-30%	Lexical relationships, though still somewhat quantifiable, become less obvious to speakers and less useful for acquisition.
1%-5%	Lexical calculations become less quantifiable and less reliable, and grammatical relationships become relatively more important for classification.

grammatical, morphological, syntactic, and phonological.

It needs to be understood that all such resulting percentages should be treated as approximate, giving only the general order of magnitude of the relationship rather than exact figures fully valid for comparative purposes. Moreover, for many languages, no such tests or detailed calculations have yet been conducted. In these cases, estimates have been utilized here.

Understanding 8 percentage levels (Table 9-6)
Before presenting the classification in detail, some observations can be made about different levels of this numerical relationship, as follows. Table 9-6 shows on the left a percentage range within this concept of 'closeness', as measured by common basic vocabulary shared by 2 speech forms; on the right, some explanatory comments.

Using proximity codes to estimate intercomprehension (Table 9-5, -6, -7)
Yet another way of understanding this schema, or of presenting and verbalizing our classification with its proximity scales, is as follows. Any 2 or more languages or speech forms or aggregates thereof which share proximity codes or parts of codes (as shown in first column of Table 9-7), also share basic vocabulary within a clear percentage range (given in the second column), as a result of which they are classified as being within the same level or category (in the third column).

Table 9-7. Moving from codes shared to intercomprehension.

If languages share these code characters	*they also share this vocabulary*	*and they all become assigned to this level..*
No first character	0%	The World
First character only	0-5%	a MACROZONE
First 2 characters only	5-30%	a GLOSSOZONE
First 3 characters only	30-50%	a GLOSSOSET
First 4 characters only	50-70%	a GLOSSOCHAIN
First 5 characters only	70-80%	a GLOSSONET
First 6 characters only	80-85%	a GLOSSOCLUSTER
First 7 characters only	85-90%	a **language**
All 8 characters	90-100%	a dialect

Comparing 2 speech forms
The justification for Table 9-7 needs interpretation and explanation. This is done by greatly expanding words into detailed statements, and this is set out in Table 9-8.

Summarizing this whole schema of coding (Table 9-8)
The briefest way, and probably the easiest way, to comprehend the classification and codes is to arrange the schema in 8 vertical blocks corresponding to the 8 characters of the proximity code, with closeness ranged vertically from 0% at the bottom to 100% at the top. This is set out in Table 9-8. Thus, for example, a glossoset consists of languages which share at least 30% basic vocabulary; some glossosets consist each of a single glossonet only, and some of a single language within that glossonet, whereupon obviously intercomprehension in the glossoset is 100%.

Spacing and rules (Tables 9-9 and 9-11)
The presence of thin rules (lines) and/or linespaces across the page at any point throughout the classification indicates a break or end in intercomprehension between adjacent nets, or sets, or microzones, or macrozones, above and below the rule or linespace. All blocs of languages listed together without rules or linespaces can therefore be regarded as generally similar lexically, and as partially or generally interintelligible or intercomprehensible, i.e. as each a single language cluster whose languages share at least 80% basic vocabulary.

A full linespace without a rule normally signals the beginning of a new cluster whose constituent languages share at least 80% basic vocabulary. Two languages separated by one such linespace share only from 80% or more basic vocabulary.

Rules plus linespaces signal the ends of occasional lexical similarity and of any interintelligible blocks of languages, and the beginnings of unrelated new parts of the classification.

The whole combination of rules and linespaces therefore conveys the following meanings.

Setting out the various levels on paper (Table 9-9)
These levels of classification enable the user to divide up lengthy listings of thousands of languages into understandable and manageable blocs, and to display them for immediate understanding as follows:

a. Languages within a glossocluster (which share over 80% vocabulary) are shown listed on adjacent lines with no blank lines or linespaces between them; their 7-character codes are given on the left, their names on the right. This type of listing is the major one in the whole classification, and the reader should familiarize himself or herself with its 'solid' appearance and its position on the page so that it can be identified at once. Around this listing, to its left or (occasionally) within it, are various groupings of languages using cover-names in capital letters.
b. GLOSSOCLUSTERS (groupings of related languages) are likewise shown on adjacent lines but separated from each other by one linespace.
c. GLOSSONETS (larger groupings of geoclusters) are shown as separate blocs separated from each other by one line.
d. GLOSSOCHAINS (chained or linked or related glossonets) are shown separated from each other by 2 rules.
e. GLOSSOSETS (larger groupings of glossochains) are shown separated from each other by 3 rules close together.
f. GLOSSOZONES (groupings of glossosets) are shown separated from each other by 4 rules close together.
g. MACROZONES (groupings of glossozones) are shown separated from each other by 5 rules close together.

This layout is shown in Tables 9-9 and 9-11.

FEATURES OF THE CLASSIFICATION

The following are a series of notes, explanations, and technical comments on the features of the actual classification itself in the book version *Linguasphere* with its long lists of names of cover-names, languages, and other speechforms.

Cover-names of 6 kinds
Cover-names are anglicized names in use for our major levels or categories. They are always shown throughout the classification in capital letters. Cover-names are always shown preceded by a code which classifies the 6 basic levels or categories or groups of languages: *macrozones, glossozones, glossosets, glossochains, glossonets, glossoclusters*. These 6 basic categories are globally applicable and so are found regularly and consistently throughout the classification in all parts of the world. They are basic to the whole classification with its system for totalling or subtotalling the various statistical categories of macrozones, glossozones, glossosets, glossochains, glossonets, glossoclusters, languages, and dialects. They follow regular rules of coding and each's code describes it and its place in the classification.

Types of language names
After each 7-character code on the left, the relevant language names on its line on the right are presented (in the *Linguasphere* book) in the following standardized order, using parentheses, square brackets, periods, colons, commas, boldface, italics, or medium type. Note that all names of languages and dialects are shown with lowercase initial letter, this being the universal practice by the speakers themselves (except for English, and all anglicized names). The dozen or so various distinct elements of each entry are as follows:

reference name, being one or both of 2 elements: (1) anglicized name with initial capital(s); and/or (2) autoglossonym, consisting of root-name in medium type, plus affixes if any in medium type (then in parentheses phonetic representation in italics, anglicized name(s) if any, lowercase names as used in French, German, Spanish, Russian or other major literature; other alternate names or close names or versions): after a colon, dialects, varieties and regional variants (and their anglicized and alternate names in parentheses); [Notes on bridges, continua, extended units, or relations with other codes]; Location of language in particular countries, provinces, regions, islands, etc.

Table 9-8. Comparing the closeness or proximity of 2 or more languages or other speech forms.

To find out the comparative closeness of (or distance between) any 2 speech forms, write the 2 codes one under the other, then begin at the left and see how far to the right the characters are the same, then count them (how many of the 8 code characters in sequence from the left are the same for both). The following 9 conclusions can then be drawn, arranged firstly in ascending order of closeness, then the same 9 in descending order.

In ascending order of intercomprehension or closeness:
- 2 speech forms which have different first characters share no vocabulary (and share zero intercomprehension).
- 2 speech forms which share only the first character share under 5% vocabulary (zero intercomprehension).
- 2 speech forms which share only the first 2 characters share 5-30% vocabulary (negligible intercomprehension).
- 2 speech forms which share only the first 3 characters share 30-50% vocabulary (and acquirable intercomprehension).
- 2 speech forms which share only the first 4 characters share 50-70% vocabulary (potential intercomprehension).
- 2 speech forms which share only the first 5 characters share 70-80% vocabulary (partial intercomprehension).
- 2 speech forms which share only the first 6 characters share 80-85% vocabulary (general intercomprehension).
- 2 speech forms which share only the first 7 characters share over 85% vocabulary (adequate intercomprehension).
- Any 2 speech forms which share the same 8-character code share over 90% vocabulary (mutual intercomprehension).

In descending order of intercomprehension or closeness:
- Any 2 speech forms which share the same 8-character code share over 90% basic vocabulary (mutual intercomprehension).
- 2 speech forms which share only the first 7 characters share over 85% vocabulary (adequate intercomprehension).
- 2 speech forms which share only the first 6 characters share 80-85% vocabulary (general intercomprehension).
- 2 speech forms which share only the first 5 characters share 70-80% vocabulary (partial intercomprehension).
- 2 speech forms which share only the first 4 characters share 50-70% vocabulary (potential intercomprehension).
- 2 speech forms which share only the first 3 characters share 30-50% vocabulary (acquirable intercomprehension).
- 2 speech forms which share only the first 2 characters share 5-30% vocabulary (negligible intercomprehension).
- Two speech forms which share only the first character share under 5% vocabulary (and zero intercomprehension).
- Two speech forms which have different first characters share no vocabulary apart from the occasional loanword (and share zero intercomprehension).

Table 9-9. Intercomprehension between languages set out by rules and linespaces.

The degree of interintelligibility between nearby languages is set out systematically by the following sequence of rules and line-spaces:

macrozone

zone

set

chain

net

CLUSTER
language

Example:

German: **deutsch** (alemão, allemand, nemetski, tedesco, tudesco): hochdeutsch (Standard German, High (Upper) German) [for Regional German see 52-ABCF]; Location Germany, Austria.

Note that alternate names are usually given within parentheses (round brackets). Any lists of such alternate names within parentheses, which are all equivalent, are shown separated by commas. By contrast, names of subdialects are given (on the CD) outside of any parentheses. Any lists of such subdialects, shown outside parentheses, describe different dialectal variants which are dissimilar or nonequivalent or nonidentical even though also shown separated by commas.

Reference-names

These need additional explanation. In this classification every language is given its own reference-name, specifically for use in large-scale comparative contexts. This is the first name on the line after each idiom's code, where unhyphenated. Usually, this is also the root-name—the shortest form of the language's own name for itself. Reference-names are shown in 2 forms: (1) if it is an anglicized name, it is shown in medium type with initial capital letter(s), or (2) if a reference-name is also the autoglossonym, or part of an autoglossonym, it is also shown in medium type. A complication is that small numbers of unrelated languages in different glossozones use identical root-names, and so, to avoid confusion in such cases we add a numeral (-1, -2, -3, etc.). This becomes part of this usage of the reference-name.

Autoglossonyms

In many cases, such as with the great majority of Bantu language and dialects, affixes (prefixes or suffixes) meaning 'the language of' are widely used attached to root reference-names. Each such longer name, shown hyphenated in this classification, is the speech form's autoglossonym—the name used by speakers themselves to identify their own language. This is given for every language and dialect except where unknown.

Some reference-names as just explained have numerals appended (-1, -2, -3, etc.). To get any particular language's actual autoglossonym as used by its speakers, one should of course remove this number.

Occurrence of homonyms

Homonyms or duplicate language-names are of 2 sorts: (1) those which result from the splitting of a language into 2 or more languages or dialects, or from the splitting of an ethnic group between 2 or more languages, both of which cases refer to different applications of the same name, related but distinct; and (2) those which result from the coincidental use of a similar name in different parts of the world. Homonyms of type (1) are found in the same set or in the same country and are shown in this classification followed by an arabic numeral, thus: malinke-1, malinke-2, etc. Homonyms of type (2) are relatively rare and are not differentiated in situ, but the reader is alerted to their existence in the indexes at the end of the *Linguasphere* volume.

Order of names

Language names are listed and set out vertically, not in alphabetical order, but in the manner which best

represents linguistic reality, including chains of interintelligible languages where they exist, and/or geographic sequences. Cover-names of macrozones, glossozones, glossosets, glossochains, glossonets and glossoclusters are all given in capital letters. Those for macrozones happen to be coded in alphabetical order and so are listed throughout in this alphabetical order. Other cover-names, however, are listed not in alphabetical order but in a geolinguistic (lines of relationship) order or geographic order (west to east, north to south) corresponding to linguistic reality.

Chains and extended nets

Linguistic reality often consists of long chains of related language nets or languages in which adjacent nets or languages are lexically much closer to each other than those at the beginning of the chain are to those at the end. These realities are shown by the order of listing in the right-hand column, amplified by adjacent textual remarks in square brackets, but the requirements of coding mean that such chains are then subdivided into nets and languages/idioms as defined and presented here. These chains do not always or necessarily run in any single direction such as north to south. Sometimes, as with the Great Bantu Chain, chains may start off in one direction only to double back on themselves to near their point of origin. Sometimes, therefore, a more useful analogy than 'chain' is 'chain-link' or a 'chain-link fence', since the links run in all directions, weaker in some directions and stronger in others.

Transitional nets and linked nets

These 2 technical usages should be noted: (1) a 'transitional net' is a net which is seen to be located between 2 sets or subsets (such as 2 streams of Bantu languages) with relationships to both; and (2) a net is said to be 'linked with' one or more adjacent or nearby nets, as listed, when it shares with them a high degree of intercomprehension placed at over 65% of basic vocabulary in common.

Use of hyphens

Many names of languages in this classification contain one, 2 or even very occasionally 3 hyphens within the letters of the name itself (excluding at this point consideration of hyphen plus number, which is dealt with in the paragraph 'Occurrence of homonyms' above). A single hyphen usually separates the root-name from an affix (prefix or suffix) meaning 'the language of..'. Two hyphens usually delineate 2 levels of prefix (i.e. prefix and preprefix), with essentially the same meaning. Usual practice among language speakers, linguists, governments, churches, Bible societies et alia is to write these names with an initial capital and without hyphens. Usual practice also is to include affixes in some circles, but to omit them in others. All this makes it difficult or impossible for persons not familiar with the languages to identify them, to use the literature concerning them, or to find them in indexes. Our final recommendation to all users therefore after spending many years on this problem is (1) to follow existing practice and omit all hyphens when writing names for limited local contexts, but (2) to retain all hyphens when using numerous names in large geographical contexts (countries, continents, the world). For large-scale comparative use of language names, our recommendation is (3) to omit both hyphens and affixes, and to use root-names as reference-names, but at the same time to provide nearby at least a single listing of equivalents (full hyphenated names with root-name of each, and vice versa).

Dialects

Dialects of languages, including regional variants, are presented in *Linguasphere* and in the CD version in 2 distinct and different ways. (1) If they are sufficiently distinct from their parent language to warrant being regarded as separate languages/idioms (because of sharing less than 90% vocabulary), they are given a separate line each and a separate 8-character code each. In cases where their status is dialectal, this is shown by their names in medium type, since their associated autoglossonym is usually the parent language's autoglossonym, already given above either on its own line or often on that of the language net's or cluster's name. (2) If not sufficiently distinct from their parent language (because of sharing over 95%), they are simply listed after the same code as the parent language and after a colon (:) following it. Note that lists of dialects are never placed within paren-

theses and are shown separated by commas but all refer to different nonidentical dialectal variants. (Alternate names, by contrast, are shown within parentheses, separated by commas). Note also again that all carryover lines are indented 2 or more spaces to indicate continuation from the previous line.

Country names and geographical names

The countries and localities in which nets and languages are mainly or primarily located are given (in the electronic database version) after the italicized word Location; if several countries are listed, this is the order in which languages/idioms below it are shown. If component idioms are spoken in a different country or countries, this fact is noted on their own lines after their words Location ('also in... '). By this means, the dominant location or countries of every idiom can be seen by the reader.

This geographical locating is not done for every idiom or net, in the printed version of the classification: it is only done where necessary for clarification, or advisable to avoid confusion. However, in the computerized version of the classification, every idiom has a variable in which location is stated exactly (country, province, island, etc.) both (a) in words and through online maps.

All other country names or place names or geographical names used in the classification, but which do not follow a word Location, are adjectives describing differing varieties of languages/idioms or dialects/varieties and do not refer simply or primarily to places where a particular idiom or dialect is spoken.

Standard or literary languages

Many languages have a recognized standard form or version, often referred to as the literary language or the literary or written version of the language. In this classification, a clear distinction is made between 2 types of standard language:

(a) those standard languages which have been created as a compromise (e.g. Standard Italian, Standard Shona), which are listed as idioms in their own right, and which (at least initially) are spoken by no one as a natural mother tongue; in all these, the word 'Standard' is always shown preceding the idiom's name; and

(b) those already existing idioms which have been chosen as standards for a unit, or part of a unit, in which case they are listed with 'standard' following the idiom's name (e.g. Acoli Standard, West Dinka Standard).

Comments in situ

Additional short explanatory comments are given [in square brackets, thus] at a number of points in the listings. These pinpoint bridge languages, which provide a bridge between 2 adjacent nets; chains or continua or linked languages or nets or sets which although not linked by sufficient basic vocabulary in common (30% minimum) to be shown related on these definitions are nevertheless somewhat related (e.g. with 25% in common); the presence of extended nets; relations to other codes; and lower-limits nets or sets in each of which basic shared vocabulary is at its lowest limit on the definition and which is therefore a candidate for further subdivision into 2 nets or sets.

Further conventions employed

1. Quotes are placed around a language name in use or recorded in the literature but to be discouraged because of racist or other pejorative or unscientific connotations. Quotes around numbers, e.g. 'A25', refer to names in other existing clas-

Table 9-10. World totals of languages and cover-names.

10	language MACROZONES,
100	language GLOSSOZONES,
684	language GLOSSOSETS,
1,403	language GLOSSOCHAINS,
2,684	language GLOSSONETS,
4,962	language GLOSSOCLUSTERS,
13,511	**languages** with some 10,000 distinct and different autoglossonyms,
30,000	dialects, and
50,000	speech-form names of all kinds, including alternates.

Table 9-11.   Quick-reference schema explaining the World Language Classification.

CODES (PROXIMITY SCALES AND NAMES)

Levels and codes
The 8 pairs of lines on the left below stand for the 8 main or usual or standard worldwide categories or levels or meanings or codes. The resulting proximity scale is then composed of 3 shorter more focused scales (named below in bold italic capitals at left margin) which are shown separated by 2 hyphens for ease of use (as with telephone numbers). Together they make up an 8-character code or proximity scale for a language or for any dialects.

Meaning
Note that the one, 2, 3, 4 or 5 rules (or one linespace) across the page shown below introduce new categories as explained on previous pages and represent differing barriers defining varying levels of lexical closeness or distance (implying varying degrees of intelligibility or intercomprehension or the absence of them). The %s represent *minimum threshold* figures for closeness (shared vocabulary, etc.).

WIDER SCALE or reference grid (2 digits): First character (0-9) *Example of code:* 0	=	**LANGUAGE MACROZONE** (geozone or phylozone; each is a grouping sharing little or no basic vocabulary apart from handfuls of loan words, i.e. with zero, nil, or nonexistent intercomprehension)
Second character (0-9) *Example of code:* 01	=	**LANGUAGE GLOSSOZONE** (topozone or glossozone; abbreviated to 'zone'; each is a grouping sharing limited basic vocabulary (a minimum of 5%), i.e. with negligible, minimal, marginal, scant, slight, or limited intercomprehension).
CLOSENESS SCALE or similarity index (next 4 capital letters): Third character (A-Z, uppercase) = *Example of code:* 01-A		**GLOSSOSET** (abbreviated to 'set'; a grouping sharing over 30% basic vocabulary, i.e. acquirable intercomprehension); note that a glossoset may sometimes have within it a chain of languages, or an extended unit, i.e. chain of units where there is closer relationship between adjacent members than there is between beginning and end.
Fourth character (A-Z, uppercase) = *Example of code:* 01-AA		**GLOSSOCHAIN** (or chain or chains, or group or groups of linked units: it signifies a subdivision of a large or very extensive glossoset; it is a grouping sharing over 50% basic vocabulary, i.e.potential moderate, or consecutive intercomprehension).
Fifth character (A-Z, uppercase) = *Example of code:* 01-AAA		**GLOSSONET** (abbreviated to 'net'; a grouping sharing over 70% basic vocabulary, i.e. partial intercomprehension); usually divisible into a number of glossoclusters, which are listed next, and which can be identified by the single linespace before each's name (and the term 'cluster' after its name).
Sixth character (A-Z, uppercase) = *Example of code:* 01-AAAA		**GLOSSOCLUSTER** (or outer language, or broad language, or wider language, or tongue, or a cluster of languages; abbreviated to 'cluster'; a grouping of related languages sharing over 80% basic vocabulary, i.e. sharing general intercomprehension); 3 varieties are listed (but not separately coded): *cluster* (of languages; multilingual, i.e. with 2 or more languages), *monolanguage cluster* (internal cluster of idioms, within a single language), *minimal monolanguage cluster* (marked absence of clustering).
COMPREHENSION SCALE, or intelligibility index (last 2 letters): Seventh character (a-z,lowercase) = *Example of code:* 01-AAAA-a		**language** (or inner language, or narrow language; a speech form or grouping of speech forms widely recognized by people and observers as a "language", based on political reality, ethnic or social affiliation, or literary history, or availability of literature or scriptures, et alia; usually a grouping of interintelligible speech forms here termed dialects and/or idioms sharing over 85% basic vocabulary and which are mutually intelligible to each other, i.e. with adequate intercomprehension. This reference name for a language is always shown in lowercase type, and is given in 2 forms: in most cases (a) as the **autoglossonym**, with in medium type separated by hyphen any affix (prefix or suffix meaning "the language of") where used; or, in cases where an autoglossonym does not appear to be in use, or where it is not known, (b) as an anglicized name given in boldface lowercase type but with initial capital(s). Any alternate or variant names then follow in parentheses (given on CD version only).
Eighth character (a-z, lowercase) = *Example of code:* 01-AAAA-aa		**dialect** (a sequence or grouping of varieties or subdialects or idioms, sharing over 90% basic vocabulary, i.e. sharing mutual intercomprehension); shown only on CD version.
Uncoded	=	variety, subdialect, or idiom (a speech form identified and recognized as distinct by speakers, sharing (variety) more than 95% or (idiom) more than 99% or (voice) 100% vocabulary with other adjacent varieties or idioms).

vergent dialects, sufficiently distinct to justify separate codes, it is often cited for the first of these only and can be assumed to cover any or all items following on succeeding lines as anglicized names.

Language totals
The total number of distinct languages in any net, or set, or microzone, or macrozone, or in the whole world, is defined here as equal to the total number of different 7-character proximity codes shown. Thus to find the total of languages in the Indo-European macrozone, simply total its distinct or different 7-character codes (which each terminate in a lowercase letter): this particular total comes to 300.

World totals
The grand total of languages for the whole world, defined in this way, comes to 13,511. This can be expanded. Our classification yields the global totals as shown in Table 9-10.

LAYOUT OF THE CLASSIFICATION

Languages and their groupings are listed in the classification after their respective codes. The following listing summarizes the various usages and features of this listing.

Typefaces
Throughout this classification, type styles and formats have the following standardized meanings:
- The first name on each line, immediately after its code on the left, is this classification's standard, definitive reference-name. This may be the anglicized form (with initial capital letter) in cases where such a form is widely known and used. If no anglicized form is in use, the reference-name is the autoglossonym, always shown here in lowercase type.
- All names in CAPITALS are anglicized cover-names for the first 6 levels: MACROZONE, ZONE, SET, CHAIN, NET, CLUSTER. In English text usage outside the classification, they should be written with an initial capital followed by lowercase letters ('Afro-Asiatic', 'Indo-European', etc.).
- The great majority of names in the classification are the standard reference-names, often anglicized, for **languages**, and dialects. Languages (or 'narrow languages') may be instantly recognized by (a) each always having a 7-character code, (b) always being shown in lowercase letters, and (c) always forming the main vertically-aligned listing of names, the great majority of which are autoglossonyms shown in lowercase type.
- All names in lowercase are **autoglossonyms** (each being a people's own name for their own language), except dialects. These are always the first version of the reference name; they may be followed by any anglicized reference name for the language.

sifications in widespread use, in this case Guthrie's widely-quoted numbers for Bantu languages.
2. The recommended reference-name for each language is the root-name shown in medium type which is often part of the autoglossonym (people's own name for their language), and is the first name cited and printed in lowercase type, but with affixes (prefixes or suffixes) if any (usually translating 'the language of..') in medium type. The recommended reference-name is thus the autoglossonym minus any affix. For comparative purposes, the root-name alone by itself would serve better than the autoglossonym. Even then, affixes should be retained with reference-names in cases where they serve to distinguish 2 otherwise identical language names. Where no autoglossonym is given first, the first name shown (which is in medium type) can be regarded as the recommended reference-name, and its autoglossonym is that shown for the net or cluster as a whole.

3. Although many languages use different prefixes to distinguish between the name of a language and the name of its speakers (e.g. the Baganda (people) of Uganda speak the language luganda), for other languages the practice is not so clearcut but is mixed. Since normally-used nomenclature is being recorded here, a number of people-names are included because, although not correctly language-names, they are used by adjacent peoples as language-names (this is frequently the case with Bantu names). Many other languages make no distinction but use the same name for both (e.g. the English speak English).
4. Initial capitals are used only to distinguish anglicized names (which are always given in medium type) or geographic (including directional) names, e.g. North Kono (always given in medium type). If no anglicized name is given, then normal anglicized usage can be assumed to be the same as the autoglossonym but with first letter capitalized and hyphens removed.
5. Where an autoglossonym covers a range of di-

2. COMPILING THE LINGUAMETRIC DATABASE

Utilizing this classification, data were now added covering all of the church's worldwide ministries that focus on languages. These cover: Scripture translation and distribution, Christian publishing, Christian literature, books and periodicals, broadcasting and telecasting, audiovisual approaches, ministries to the blind, the deaf, the handicapped, with special reference to children of all ages and also to nonliterates. Of particular interest is Table 9-12, Names for God in 900 languages.

This extensive database is available on CDs related to David Dalby's *Linguasphere: register of the world's languages and speech communities*, including the forthcoming CD, *World Christian database*. It is partially re-produced here as Table 9-13 which lists all 13,511 languages of the world (but not dialects) together with many of the ministries listed above.

Of many new discoveries that flow from this material, one of the most significant is the relationship between languages with direct ministries (e.g. the Zulu Bible, or the 'Jesus' Film in Hindi) and their thousands of closely related languages. This can be stated in single-sentence form: Every language (also termed 'inner language' or 'narrow language') listed here benefits directly from language ministries in any other language shown as within the same language cluster (also termed 'outer language' or 'broad language'). Thus at the end of Table 9-13 it can be seen that a number of languages around Zulu, and within its cluster, in practice have access to the Scriptures. Though termed here 'indirect access', it is nevertheless adequate access. This analysis terms this further here by stating that a language has access to, or understands or uses, a *near-Bible*. This role of near-scriptures—near-Bible, near-New Testament, near-gospel, near-selection, near-'Jesus' Film, near-audio scripture, near-Braille scripture, near-signed scripture, near-broadcast, et alia—clearly revolutionizes the extent to which Gutenberg's original vision in inventing printing with movable type (to see the Holy Scriptures disseminated and available to all the peoples of the world) is being realized today.

CODEBOOK FOR LINGUAMETRICS TABLE 9-13

The 280 pages that follow set out the 13,500 distinct and separate languages spoken during the 20th century. Data for each language occupies one single line across one page only. Note that the unit 'a language' is a single entity independent of any country or countries it is spoken in. By contrast, the unit 'a people' refers to one ethnocultural ethnolinguistic people residing in one particular country; spread over 10 countries, it would count as 10 peoples.

Extinct languages
Note that some 1,000 languages spoken in the 20th century are now extinct. This is demonstrated by the firm '0', zero, in the population columns 5 and 6. Some 400 others are either nearly extinct (dying, with under 10 speakers), or endangered (under 100), or moribund (under 1,000).

Little-known languages
Note also that numerous languages have a blank space in those 2 columns, meaning that no population figure is assigned to them. At this stage in the evolution of this complex database, their populations (mostly unknown or relatively unknown in the literature because as yet unstudied by linguists or anthropologists) are combined with other better-studied and better-known languages within their language cluster. In many cases, also, their situation is one of duplication—their 'speakers' can also be said to be at the same time speakers of other closely-related near-languages.

For full understanding of the origins, compilation from 1975-1999, and rationale for this Linguasphere/World Language Classification's categories and codes, consult the definitive publication by David Dalby, *Linguasphere*. The version employed here is a slightly earlier published version differing only in the codes assigned to a few languages.

Column and codes
The following brief listing will enable the reader to use the lengthy compilation of data for 13,511 languages that follows. For more explanation, consult Part 3 "Codebook".

Note that most languages have several alternate names or spellings; these, together with several thousand dialects, are not given here but are published in Dalby's *Linguasphere*, and on related CDs.

Note also that although almost all reference names here are written out in full, a number as part of their name end with a capital letter, or occasionally a lowercase one, and period, with the following meanings:

A	= proper	P	= peripheral
C	= Central	N	= North
E	= East	S	= South
F	= formalized, revived	T	= traditional
G	= generalized, standard	U	= urban
H	= historical	V	= vehicular
M	= Middle	W	= West

Names for Scripture languages
Column 12 in this table records each language's biblioglossonym, if any exists. This is the official or formal name given as the language's name in connection with its translation of the Christian Scriptures. Usually, it is an anglicized name ('French', 'German', 'Zulu', etc) but in many cases it is named by the speakers themselves who term it in their own language ('français', 'deutsch', 'isiZulu', etc).

The 2 major Scripture translation agencies—United Bible Societies (UBS), and Wycliffe Bible Translators/Summer Institute of Linguistics (WBT/SIL)—often have confusingly different language names for the same autoglossonym (own language). Sometimes it is simply a small difference in spelling, but often it is a completely different name: WBT utilizes anglicized names while UBS uses many vernacular names. In the majority of cases, this database shows the UBS name.

The disadvantage of this difference is that the 2 biblioglossonyms in such cases are incompatible from the standpoint of each other's computers, databases, and hence search capability. Even if the difference is a single letter, ordinary programs will not note that these refer to the identical language.

This distinction is recorded in column 12 by means of an asterisk (*) attached to a biblioglossonym. *Its presence* means: either (a) in addition to this biblioglossonym, there is at least one other biblioglossonym (usually that used by WBT/SIL) not given on this printout; or (b) 2 or more biblioglossonyms are or have been used by one of the 2 agencies; or (c) in addition to the main biblioglossonym shown, one or more of this language's dialects have their own translations (not recorded here) and thus their own distinct biblioglossonyms.

Likewise, the *absence* of an asterisk means either (a) the 2 agencies use an identical biblioglossonym for the language under consideration, or (b) only one agency knows of or uses a biblioglossonym at this point.

Meanings of columns in Table 9-13
Column
  1. Language code

REFERENCE NAME
  2. Cover-name (in capitals)
     Autoglossonym (own name for language)
  3. Countries where significantly spoken or used
  4. Peoples using this language as mother tongue

MOTHER-TONGUE (NATIVE) SPEAKERS
  5. In AD 2000
  6. In AD 2025 (assuming current trends)

MEDIA
  7. Countries broadcasting Christian programs in this language:
Code Meaning
  0 No broadcasts
  1 Local only or in same-cluster language
  2 National, within this country
  3 External broadcasts from this country
  4 International, from one foreign country
  5 Plurinational, from 2–4 countries
  6 Multinational, from 5–9 countries
  7 Multicontinental, from 10-20 countries
  8 Global broadcasts from 20 or more countries

CHURCH among language's native speakers
  8. Affiliated Christians (AC), % of population
  9. Evangelization, E (% of population evangelized)
  10. Worlds A/B/C: location of most speakers

SCRIPTURES
  11. Scripture Translation Status (a scale 0-92): see details at end of Part 1.
  12. Biblioglossonym (official name of Scripture translation, if published or under way); sometimes the anglicized name is preferred by speakers, sometimes the autoglossonym)
     Note meaning of any asterisk after a biblioglossonym (see detailed explanation above): an asterisk * means: one or more additional biblioglossonyms for this autoglossonym (language reference name) exist
     No asterisk means: biblioglossonym is the only one in use for this autoglossonym

PRINT SCRIPTURES
  13-15. Scriptures in print (...=none, P..=gospel only, PN.=New Testament, PNB=whole Bible, pnb=near-Bible)
  16. Portion/gospel activity (year of first publication and year of latest, if any)
  17. New Testament activity (year of first publication and year of latest, if any)
  18. Bible activity (year of first publication and year of latest, if any)

AVAILABILITY OF AUDIOVISUALS
  19. 'Jesus' Film year first published
  20. 'Jesus' Film availability, viewership:
Code Meaning
  0 not available in mother tongue or its cluster of languages
  1 Available in mother tongue (if under 10% of all speakers) or in its cluster
  2 Available, viewers 10–50%
  3 Available, viewers 51–100%
  4 Vast impact in mother tongue (viewers>100%)

     Next 4 lines 21–24: a dot in any of these 4 columns means: Nothing available
  21. Audio scriptures available:

Code Item		Value	Meaning
•	nothing	0	No audio scriptures available
c	materials	1	Audio materials available only in same-cluster language
s	selection	1	Selections/teaching/music purchasable on cassette
r	radio	2	Radio audio selections hearable
a	portion	3	Audio gospels purchasable
A	Testament	4	Audio NT purchasable
B	Bible	5	Audio whole Bible purchasable

  22. New Reader Scriptures available = y
  23. Braille scriptures available = u
  24. Signed scriptures available = h

DIALECTS
  25. Reference number: indicating a language's total of *dialects* (not listed here but named only on CD); subtract any language's reference number from the next reference number shown, minus 1 (e.g. 00-AAAA-a mandinka-kango has minus 7 plus 12 minus 1 = 4 dialects).

Table 9-12. Names for God in 900 languages.

This index is in 2 parts. The first index (1) is an alphabetical listing of names for God used in translations of the Scriptures in some 900 languages based originally on a listing prepared by the British and Foreign Bible Society, each followed by the name or names of all languages using the name. Names which are normally in non-roman script are here transliterated into roman characters. The second index (2) is the same but arranged alphabetically by language. Orthographies used in these 2 listings differ in places from those adopted in the classification set out here in Table 9-13. For full identification and details of languages, see the *Book of a thousand tongues* (revised edition) (London: United Bible Societies, 1972) and its current electronic update.

(1) Names for God followed (after comma) by languages

Aabi, Gio
Abece, Ibembe
Abradu,
  Nuba
  Nyimang
Ade, Mer
Aê Diê, Radé
Agwatana,
  Bassa
  Kwomu
Ahi, Paama
Ahogbre, Eggon
Aitu, Rotuma
Akôtesieti, Lifu
Akua, Hawaiian
Akuj,
  Karamajong
  Turkana
Ala,
  Kambera
  Koalib
  Krongo
  Nirere
  Nuba
  Wajewa
Alatalla,
  Dayak
  Manyan
Alauna, Masana
Alhou,
  Naga
  Sema
Alla,
  Bambara
  Eggon
  Kuranko
  Madurese
  Maltese
  Mandingo
  Maninka
  Soso
  Yalunka
Allach,
  Gagauzi
  Turkish
Allah,
  Algerian Arabic
  Arabic
  Balantian
  Bentuni
  Bisaya
  Eggon
  Fulani
  Goulei
  Hausa
  Indonesian
  Javanese
  Judeo-Arabic
  Kabba Laka
  Kabyle
  Kazan
  Kumuk
  Macina
  Madjingai
  Malay
  Mbai
  Murut
  Ngambai
  Nogai
  Palestinian Arabic
  Pashto
  Sara
  Sasak
  Shilha
  Sundanese
  Syriac
  Transcaucasian
  Turkish
Allah Taala,
  Land Dayak
  Sea Dayak
Allaha,
  Fula
  Futa-Jalon
  Macina
Allahi,
  Egyptian Arabic
  Tunisian Arabic
Allahu,
  Hebrew
  Moorish
Alla-taâla,
  Bugis
  Macassar
Altjira, Aranda
Ama, Habbe
Anatumi, Kyaka
Andriamanitra, Malagasy
Anna, Kunama

Anôtô, Jabim
Anut,
  Amele
  Graged
Anutu,
  Adzera
  Kate
  Kuman
  Melpa
  Sinasina
Anyambe, Benga
Anyambie,
  Galwa
  Kele
  Omyene
Anyambye, Omyene
Anyame, Fang
Aôndo, Tiv
Apajul, Aguaruna
Apistotokiua, Blackfoot
Arnam, Mikir
Asapavan, Anal
Asdulaz, Armenian
Asila, Dakkarkari
Atemit, Diola
Atua,
  Aneityum
  Aniwa
  Aulua
  Baki
  Bieria
  Efate
  Ellice Islander
  Epi
  Gilbertese
  Kwamera
  Malekula
  Maori
  Marquesan
  Nguna
  Niuean
  Nogugu
  Pangkumu
  Rarotongan
  Samoan
  Santo
  Tahitian
  Tanna
  Uripiv
Aualari, Orokolo
Augad,
  Mabuiag
  Saibai
Ayeba, Ljo
A-pa Li Bol,
  Asho
  Chin
Ba, Iregwe
Balî, Gouro
Banara,
  Bambatana
  Vella Lavella
Bao, Houailou
Bari, Ogoni
Bhagawan,
  Bhili
  Chhattisgarhi
  Gurmukhi
  Punjabi
  Sundhi
  Valvi
Bhagwan, Kurku
Bhogana,
  Bhili
Dehwali
Bhogawan, Bhili
Blei, Khasi
Bog,
  Bulgarian
  Byelorussian
  Croatian
  Hungaro
  Macedonian
  Polish
  Russian
  Serbian
  Slavonic
  Slovenian
  Wendish
  White Russian
Bôh, Slovak
Boi ogoda, Mailu
Bok Kei-Dei, Bahnar
Bon Dié, Dominican
Bondié, Mauritius Creole
Bondiu, Carib
Borgan,
  Kalmuk

Mongolian
Borhan, Mongolian
Bozymy, Ukrainian
Buh, Czech
Chido,
  Jukun
  Wukari
Chihowa, Choctaw
Chineke, Ibo
Chios, Igorot
Chiuta, Tonga
Ciong-Di,
  Chinese
  Kienning
Ciuta, Tumbuka
Cuku, Ibo
Dagwi, Burum
Dagwonom, Jarawa
De,
  Epi
  Lewo
  Tasiko
Debata,
  Angkola-Mandailing
  Batak
  Toba Batak
Deews, Latvian
Deis, Romansh
Del i Luma,
  German Romany
  Romany
Demenu, Bobo
Dén-did,
  Dinka
  Kyec
Deos, Indo-Portuguese
Deovel,
  Finnish Romany
  Romany
Déu, Catalan
Deus,
  Brazilian
  Latin
  Portuguese
  Romansch
  Sardinian
Devac, Konkani
Devadu, Telugu
Devam, Malayalam
Devan,
  Konkani
  Tamil
Devaru,
  Badaga
  Kannada
Devel,
  German Romany
  Latvian Romany
  Moravian Romany
  Romany
Dever, Tulu
Deviyanwahansay,
  Sinhalese
Devlehée,
  Romany
  Yugoslav Romany
Devléskere, Romany
Devudu,
  Gondi
  Koi
Dévuni,
  Gondi
  Koi
Dewa,
  Marathi
  Pali
Dia, Gaelic
Día, Irish
Dieu,
  French
  Provençal
  Romansh
Dievas, Lithuanian
Dievs, Latvian
Diewas, Samogit
Diews, Lithuanian
Dio,
  Corsican
  Esperanto
  Italian
Dios,
  Ancash
  Ayacucho
  Aymara
  Bicol
  Cakchiquel
  Cebuano

  Cuzco
  Huanuco
  Ibanag
  Ilocano
  Judeo-Spanish
  Junín
  Lengua
  Mataco
  Mexican
  Pampangan
  Panayan
  Pangasinan
  Quechua
  Quiché
  Samareño
  Shipibo
  Spanish
  Toba
  Visayan
Diou, Vaudois
Dioz, Maya
Dirava,
  Motu
  Police Motu
Diws, Latgalian
Diyos, Tagalog
Dkon-mchhog, Tibetan
Dkon-mjog, Ladakhi
Dok, Kim
Doue, Breton
Droué, Ponérihouen
Duata, Sangir
Duc Chua Troi,
  Vietnamese
Duc Chua Pha, Tho
Dumnedelu, Macedonian
Dumnezeu, Rumanian
Duw, Welsh
Eaubada,
  Bwaidoga
  Dobu
  Kiriwina
  Suau
  Tavara
  Tubetube
Edeke, Teso
Efile Mukulu,
  Kalebwe
  Luba
  Songi
Efozu, Avikam
Elo,
  Nuba
  Otoro
Eloba, Nama
Elohim,
  Hebrew
  Moorish
Eloi, Namau
engai, Maasai
Eso, Kabre
Foy, Bullom
Gaddel, Sora
Gado, Negro-English
Gala, Loma
Gedepo, Bassa
Gnallaeh,
  Nancowry
  Nicobarese
God,
  Afrikaans
  Ahamb
  Anganiwei
  Arosi
  Bamu
  Binandere
  Bislama
  Bugotu
  Dutch
  English
  Epi
  Fanting
  Fiu
  Flemish
  Frisian
  Gogodala
  Guadalcanar
  Gunwingu
  Kiwai
  Kuliviu
  Kunini
  Kusaiean
  Kwagutl
  Kwara'ae
  Lau
  Lewo
Ilahey, Somali

Mabuiag
Malekula
Malo
Malu
Marovo
Moskito
Mota
Mukawa
Mwala
Navajo
Neo-Melanesian
Notu
Nunggubuyu
Opa
Orokaiva
Pitjantjatjara
Raga
Rennellese
Saa
Santo
Suki
Tangoa
Tasiko
Tasiriki
Tawarafa
Ubir
Ulawa
Wedau
Worrora
Yahgan
Goda, Dieri
Godebo, Foe
Godim, Eskimo (Western Arctic)
Godimli, Eskimo (Copper)
Godku, Gupapuynu
Gosanyith, Malto
Gospod,
  Perm
  Zyryan
Got,
  Yapese
  Yiddish
Gotega, Gawigh
Goteme, Kewa
Gott,
  German
  Nauruan
Goyakalu, Piro
Gud,
  Danish
  Icelandic
  Norwegian
  Swedish
Gûdib,
  Eskimo
  Labrador Eskimo
Guisha, Lahu
Gusune, Bariba
Gûtip,
  Eskimo
  Greenlandic
Gvray Gvsvng, Rawang
G'mert'man, Georgian
G't'n, Georgian
Hadayun, Khasi
Hananim, Korean
Hatalla,
  Dayak
  Ngaju
Hera,
  Naga
  Zeme
Hinegbau, Igbira
Hollum, Latuka
Hudha, Balochi
Hunavan, Teop
Hven, Mbum
Hyalatamwa, Higi
Hyel, Bura
Ibmel,
  Lapp
  Norwegian Lapp
Iddio, Italian
Iddiou, Piedmontese
Iehova,
  Goaribari
  Kiwai
  Panaieti
Igziabiheir,
  Amharic
  Tigrinya
Iju, Margi
Ikkegon,
  Kunuzi
  Nubian

Imana,
  Ha
  Hangaza
  Ruanda
  Rundi
Immlja,
  Lapp
  Russian Lapp
Inallah, Shilha
Inan, Yergum
Inmar, Votiak
Iricouei, Dyerma
Iruva,
  Chagga
  Machame
Isawr, Riang
Ishal,
  Achik
  Garo
Ishor,
  Abor Miri
  Diamasa
Ishôra, Boro
Ishwar,
  Assamese
  Bagheli
  Bengali
  Bhatneri
  Bhojpuri
  Bihari
  Bikaneri
  Chhindwara
  Dogri
  Gonda
  Gujarati
  Harauti
  Hindi
  Ho
  Jaunsari
  Kanauji
  Kanauri
  Kashmiri
  Kharia
  Kumaoni
  Magahi
  Malvi
  Mandla
  Manipuri
  Marwari
  Nagpuria
  Nepali
  Palpa
  Panjabi
  Parsi
  Rabha
  Sanskrit
Isol, Garo
Isor, Santali
Issur,
  Garhwati
  Tehri
Isten, Hungarian
Izuwa, Taveta
Jainkoak,
  Basque
  Labourdin
Jañahary, Tsimihety
Jaungoicoac,
  Basque
  Guipuzcoan
Jee, Manx
Jehoba, Kipsigis
Jehova,
  Manus Islander
  Nandi
Jehovah,
  Nandi-Kipsigis
  Narrinyeri
Jen, Zyryan
Jihova,
  Konyak
  Mao
  Naga
Jihova-a,
  Angami
  Naga
Jincouac,
  Basque
  Souletin
Jing-ming,
  Chinese
  Ningpo
Jiwheyewhe, Gu
Joo, Murle
Jueng, Maban
Juma,
  Buryat
  Mongolian

Jumahlto, Livonian
Jumal,
    Estonian
    Finnish
    Karelian
    Reval
Jumala, Finnish
Jummal,
    Dorpat
    Estonian
    Setu
Jupmel, Swedish Lapp
Jwok, Shilluk

Kabeshyampungu,
    Kalanga
    Luba
Kalaga, Lega
Kalo,
    Heiban
    Nuba
Kalou,
    Fijian
    Patpatar
Kalunga,
    Kuanyama
    Luimbe
    Ndonga
    Nyembe
Kami, Japanese
Kamisama, Bunun
Kanu, Limba
Karai Kasang,
    Atsi
    Kachin
Karunga, Kwangali
Katonda,
    Ganda
    Haya
Kavangi,
    Naga
    Phom
Kawas, Ami
Khaien, Chuvash
Khazopa, Lakher
Khoda,
    Bengali
    Kurdish
    Kurmanji
    Musalmani
Khong, Uvea
Khozai,
    Bashkir
    Turkish
Khuda,
    Balti
    Brahui
    Dakhini
    Gurezi
    Hindko
    Kachchhi
    Kashgar
    Kashmiri
    Kazan
    Kermanshahi
    Kirgiz
    Kurdish
    Lahnda
    Mukri
    Persian
    Shina
    Sindhi
    Tamil
    Turkish
    Urdu
    Uzbek
Khudadin, Kirgiz
Khudai, Kirgiz
Khutzau, Ossete
Khwedê,
    Kurdish
    Kurmanji
Kibumba, Soga
Kinerehingan, Dusun
Kinikhawma,
    Chin
    Khumi Awa
Kinorohingan,
    Dusun
    Ranau
Kishemanito, Chippewa
Kon-chhog,
    Bunan
    Lahuli
Kon-chok,
    Lahuli
    Tinan
Kot,
    Mortlock
    Tanna
Kuma, Nanjeri
Kumno, Lele
Kunzi, Bua
Kurmam,
    Jukun
    Kona
Kuru,
    Rukuba
    Temne

Kwama, Tula
Kwoth, Nuer
Kyaik, Mon
Kayala,
    Ngonde
    Nyakyusa

Lago, Dida
Lesa,
    Bemba
    Kaonde
    Lamba
    Luba
    Mukuni
Leza,
    Ila
    Inamwanga
    Kiluba
    Lungu
    Mambwe
    Tonga
Loba, Duala
Lowalangi, Nias
Lu, Moru
Lubah,
    Doba
    Mbai
Lubanga,
    Acholi
    Lango
    Lwo

Madaru, Maré
Manetualain, Rotti
Masing, Mundang
Mawu,
    Adangme
    Ewe
    Popo
Maxam, Tera
Mbongo, Ngbandi
Mbori, Azande
Messiner, Tamahaq
Miyeh, Akha
Mluku, Makua
Mlungu,
    Dabida
    Mpoto
    Nsenga
    Nyanja
    Sagalla
    Taita
    Yao
    Zigula
Mngari, Ndau
Mngu, Swahili
Modimo,
    Pedi
    Sotho
    Tlhaping
    Tswana
Mudzimu, Venda
Mûhghai,
    Chang
    Naga
Mukuru, Herero
Mulimu, Lozi
Mulungu,
    Giriama
    Gogo
    Kaguru
    Mambwe
    Manda
    Nyamwezi
    Nyanja
    Nyiha
    Nyika
    Rabai
    Sena
    Shambala
    Sukuma
Mulunguo,
    Nyika
    Ribé
Muento, Cree
Mungu,
    Alur
    Bira
    Fuliro
    Hunde
    Iraqw
    Kebu
    Kele
    Lendu
    Mashi
    Ngwana
    Pere
    Swahili
    Zanaki
Munguni, Lugbara
Murungu,
    Asu
    Meru
Muungu,
    Bondei
    Nyaturu-Rimi
    Pokomo
Mwali, Nambya
Mwari,
    Manyika

Shona
Naawuni, Dagbane
Nagha Tgha, Beaver
Naibata, Simalungun
    Batak
Nan, Sura
Nara, Duke of York
    Islander
Nawen, Buli
Ncembi,
    Inkongo
    Kuba
Ndjambi, Okela
Ndzimu, Kalaña
Nen, Angas
Ngai,
    Kamba
    Kikuyu
    Tharaka
Ngaor, Angal Heneng
Ngewo, Mende
Ngodehanda, Huli
Nguluvi, Bena
Ngünemapun,
    Mapudungu
Nhialic,
    Bor
    Dinka
Nialic,
    Chich
    Dinka
Niio, Iroquois
Nikskam, Micmac
Njambe,
    Lingala
    Ngombe
Njambi,
    Luchazi
    Mbunda
Njambyé,
    Kele
    Ongom
Nkulukumba, Chopi
Nkulunkulu,
    Ndebele
    Zulu
Nobu, Eromanga
Nom, Jaba
Norin,
    Fiadidja
    Nubian
Noohtsi, Slave
Nsembi, Nzebi
Nukskam, Maliseet
Nuleso,
    Bari
    Kukua
Nun,
    Bari
    Kakwa
Nungungulu,
    Inhambane Tonga
    Tonga
    Tswa
Nyam, Adjukru
Nyambe,
    Bassa
    Bobangi
    Cameroon Bassa
    Ntomba
Nyambi, Nkoya
Nyamiapbili, Agni
Nyamuanga, Jita
Nyamuhanga,
    Konjo
    Nande
Nyanka, Ebrie
Nyankopon, Fante
Nyanmien, Baule
Nyasaye,
    Gusii
    Hanga
    Luo
Nyesoa,
    Grebo
    Kru
Nyinyi, Bamum
Nyonmo, Ga
Nzakomba,
    Elekeu
    Mongo
    Nkundu
Nzambe,
    Bungili
    Ikota
    Logo
    Ngala
    Ngbaka
    Nkutu
Nzambi,
    Fioti
    Gimbunda
    Kituba
    Kiyaka
    Kongo
    Kwese
    Luba
    Lulua
    Lumbu
    Mbundu

Ndembu
Pende
Sakata
Suku
Nzambi Mawezi, Holo
Nzame,
    Fang
    Ogowe
Nzapa,
    Banu
    Baya
    Gbea
    Sango
Nzembi, Nzebi
Nzua, Ilamba
Nzyambi, Yaka

Obana, Lango
Oco,
    Agatu
    Idoma
Oeë Ala, Mori
Oesif Neno, Timorese
Oghene,
    Isoko
    Urhobo
Ohonga, Guhu-Sumane
Oiseleburua, Ora
Ojo, Igala
Olorun, Yoruba
Onyankopon,
    Akwapim
    Ashanti
    Twi
Oqmasi, Gahuku
Osanobua, Edo
Otienu, Gourma
Otua, Tongan
Ouone,
    Karre
    Pana
Owo, Aladian
Owoico, Idoma
Owuso, Arago
O'i Adai, Jorai

Pachia,
    Chin
    Zotung
Pai,
    Chin
    Ngawn
Palagu,
    Hula
    Keapara
Parameshwar,
    Betul
    Bihari
    Garhwali
    Gondi
    Gurmukhi
    Hindustani
    Kulu
    Nagpuria
    Oriya
    Panjabi
    Srinagria
Parameswar,
    Mundari
    Oriya
Parameswarah, Sanskrit
Paramushreela,
    Khondi
    Kuvi
Parmeswar,
    Lahuli
    Manchad
Pasian,
    Chin
    Tiddim
Pathenin,
    Chin
    Kom
    Thado-Kuki
Pathian,
    Bawm
    Chin
    Falam
    Lushai
    Paite
    Simte
    Vaiphei
Pathien,
    Chin
    Gangte
    Haka
Pathienin,
    Biete
    Hmar
Pay-yah-thē-kin,
    Burmese
Paz,
    Ersa
    Mordoff
Pa-ra-pyin-zowk, Pa-o
Pêku Thekatong, Makuchi
Penu,
    Khondi
    Kui
Perendia,

Albanian
Gheg
Tosk
Phra, Singpho
Phtha, Coptic
Pô Longi, Chru
Poeang Matoea, Ta'e
Poee Ala, Kulawi
Potsona,
    Lotha
    Naga
Prajow, Siamese
Progru, Kanakura
Pwa, Bachama
P'ra Pinsau, Shan

Rabuna, Coptic
Rab, Coptic
Rabbi, Kabyle
Rabbi Kulu, Shilha
Rabi, Tigre
Raguanghrui,
    Naga
    Nruanghmei
Ramwa,
    Moro
    Nuba
Rebbi, Kabyle
Rua,
    Chagga
    Mochi
Ruata,
    Sangir
    Siaow
Ruba, Madi
Ruhanga,
    Kiga
    Nkore
    Nyoro
Rûm, Lepcha

Saghalie Tyee, Chinook
Saka-Ntanga, Salampasu
Sâng-di, Chungchia
Säthaw, Mro
Schkais,
    Moksha
    Mordoff
    Mordva
Sedibi, Abor Miri
Shang-ti,
    Chihli
    Chinese
    Kiaotung
    Mandarin
    Wenli
Shanung-itlagadas, Haida
Shashe,
    Gbari
    Yamma Paiko
Shekwohi,
    Gbari
    Gyengyen
Shen,
    Chinese
    Shanghai
Sheûng-Tai,
    Cantonese
    Chinese
Shido,
    Donga
    Jukun
Shiong-Doi,
    Chinese
    Kienyang
Shong-ti,
    Chinese
    Hakka
    Tingchow
    Wukingfu
Siag-di,
    Chinese
    Hainanese
Siang-ti,
    Chinese
    Swatow
Sibu, Bribri
Sidja,
    Shan
    Yunnanese
Sikwembu, Tsonga
Sikwembu Nkulukumba,
    Ronga
Sîong-Dá,
    Chinese
    Foochow
Siong-te,
    Amoy
    Chinese
Sirama, Roro
Siyeh, Wa
So,
    Baya
    Mbere
Sõ,
    Baya
    Kalla
Soko, Nupe
Son-ti,
    Chinese

Hakka
Suandaran, Tsamba
Suku, Umbundu
Sunahan, Petats
Sunggigüle,
    Naga
    Rengma
Supe, Nguna
Swami, Toda

Taikamanoea, Mentawei
Tamasa, Roviana
Tameuh,
    Chin
    Khumi
Tanara,
    Turkish
    Yakut
Tanbei, Ganawuri
Tanutanu, Siwai
Tapa, Zomi
Teatua, Futunan
Tev,
    Car
    Nicobarese
Tevanudaiya, Tamil
Thedä, Mawken
Theos, Greek
Thixo, Xhosa
Tingranpui,
    Mzieme
    Naga
Tixo, Xhosa
Toepoe, Kaili
Tororut,
    Ng'ala
    Pokot
Toruimuinne, Vogul
Torym, Ostiak
Tsau Pra, Riang-Lang
Tsen, Chawi
Tsineke, Ibo
Tsingrang,
    Naga
    Sangtam
Tsosa, Gofa
Tsuku,
    Ibo
    Isuama
Tsungremi,
    Ao
    Naga
Tswashe,
    Gbari
    Yamma Gayegi
Tuhan, Indonesian
Tumpa,
    Guaraní
    Izoceno
Tüpâ Nandeyára,
    Guaraní
Tupan, Tupi

Ualare, Toaripi
Ugatameja, Kapauku
Ukepenuopfu,
    Angami
    Naga
umLimi, Sotho
Undebél,
    Romany
    Spanish Romany
Unguve, Kinga
Usula, Kamberri

Varivarana.
    Naga
    Tangkhul
Vittekwichanchyo,
    Tukudh

Wacinaci, Arawak
Wagayo, Galla
Wagayon, Galla
Wain, Galla
Wakantanka, Dakota
Wala, Mano
Waqa, Boran
Waqake,
    Galla
    Shoa
Wedenga, Karanga
Wennam, Moré
Were, Gisu
Wonyingi, Ijo
Wuhgin,
    Lenakel
    Tanna
Xu, Xu
Xwedê,
    Kurdish
    Kurmanji

Yakomba, Ngandu
Yala, Guerze
Yalla, Wolof
Yalli, Afaraf
Yam, Tangale
Yamba,
    Waja

Wurkum	Hog Harbour	Bghai Karen	Zambe, Bulu	Wenchow
Yang Tom Trô, Koho	Santo	Karen	Zambi, Chokwe	Zo, Atche
Yataa, Kono	Yehovah, Mowk	Pwo Karen	Zhikle, Matakam	Zông-ti,
Yau. Mandingo	Yumui, Cheremiss	Sgaw Karen	Zie-ti,	Chinese
Yehova,	Ywa,		Chinese	Taichow

(2) Languages followed (after comma) by names for God.

Abor Miri,
   Ishor
   Sedibi
Achik, Ishal
Acholi, Lubanga
Adangme, Mawu
Adjukru, Nyam
Adzera, Anutu
Afaraf, Yalli
Afrikaans, God
Agatu, Oco
Agni, Nyamiapbili
Aguaruna, Apajuí
Ahamb, God
Ainu, Kamui
Akha, Miyeh
Akwapim, Onyankopon
Aladian, Owo
Albanian, Perendia
Algerian Arabic, Allah
Alur, Mungu
Amela, Anut
Amharic, Igziabiheir
Ami, Kawas
Amoy, Siong-te
Anal, Asapaven
Ancash, Dios
Aneityum, Atua
Angal Heneng, Ngaor
Angami,
   Jihova-a
   Ukepenuopfu
Anganiwei, God
Angas, Nen
Angkola Mandailing,
   Debata
Aniwa, Atua
Ao, Tsüngremi
Arabic, Allah
Arago, Owuso
Aranda, Altjira
Arawak, Wacinaci
Armenian, Asdulaz
Arosi, God
Ashanti, Onyankopon
Asho, A-pa Li Boi
Assamese, Ishwar
Asu, Murungu
Atche, Zo
Atsi, Karai Kasang
Aulua, Atua
Avikam, Efozu
Ayacucho, Dios
Aymara, Dios
Azande, Mbori

Bachama, Pwa
Badaga, Devaru
Bagheli, Ishwar
Bahnar, Bok Kei-Dei
Baki, Atua
Balantian, Allah
Balochi, Hudha
Balti, Khuda
Bambara, Alla
Bambatana, Banara
Bamu, God
Bamum, Nyinyi
Banu, Nzapa
Bari,
   Nuleso
   Nun
Bariba, Gusune
Bashkir, Khozai
Basque,
   Jainkoak
   Jaungoicoac
   Jincouac
Bassa,
   Agwatana
   Gedepo
   Nyambe
Batak, Debata
Baule, Nyanmien
Bawm, Pathian
Baya,
   Nzapa
   So
   Sö
Beaver, Nagha Tgha
Bemba, Lesa
Bena, Nguluvi
Benga, Anyambe
Bengali,
   Ishwar
   Khoda
Bentuni, Allah
Betul, Parameshwar
Bghai Karen, Ywa

Bhatneri, Ishwar
Bhili,
   Bhagawan
   Bhogana
   Bhogawan
Bhojpuri, Ishwar
Bicol, Dios
Bieria, Atua
Biete, Pathenin
Bihari,
   Ishwar
   Parameshwar
Bikaneri, Ishwar
Binandere, God
Bira, Mungu
Bisaya, Allah
Bislama, God
Blackfoot, Apistotokiua
Bobangi, Nyembe
Bobo, Demenu
Bondei, Muungu
Bor, Nhialic
Boran, Waqa
Boro, Ishôra
Brahui, Khuda
Brazilian, Deus
Breton, Doue
Bribri, Sibu
Bua, Kunzi
Bugis, Alla-taâla
Bugotu, God
Bulgarian, Bog
Buli, Nawan
Bullom, Foy
Bulu, Zambe
Bunan, Kon-chhog
Bungili, Nzambe
Bunun, Kamisama
Bura, Hyel
Burmese, Pay-yah-thë-kin
Burum, Dagwi
Buryat, Juma
Bwaidoga, Eaubada
Byelorussian, Bog

Cakchiquel, Dios
Cameroon Bassa,
   Nyambe
Cantonese, Sheûng-Tai
Car, Tev
Carib, Bondiu
Catalan, Déu
Cebuano, Dios
Chagga,
   Iruva
   Rua
Chang, Mühghai
Chawi, Tsen
Cheremiss, Yumui
Chhattisgarhi, Bhagawan
Chhindwara, Ishwar
Chich, Nialic
Chihli, Shang-ti
Chin,
   A-pa Li Boi
   Kinikhawma
   Pachia
   Pai
   Pasian
   Pathenin
   Pathian
   Pathien
   Tameuh
Chinese,
   Ciong-Di
   Jing-ming
   Shang-ti
   Shen
   Sheûng-Tai
   Shiong-Doi
   Shong-ti
   Siag-di
   Siang-ti
   Siong-te
   Siông-Dá
   Son-ti
   Zie-ti
   Zông-ti
Chinook, Saghalie Tyee
Chippewa, Kishemanito
Chockaw, Chihowa
Chokwe, Zambi
Chopi, Nkulukumba
Chru, Pô Longi
Chungchia, Sǎng-di
Chuvash, Khaien
Coptic,
   Phtha
   Rab

Rabuna
Corsican, Dio
Cree, Muneto
Croatian, Bog
Cuzco, Dios
Czech, Buh

Dabida, Mlungu
Dagbane, Naawuni
Dakhini, Khuda
Dakkarkari, Asila
Dakota, Wakantanka
Danish, Gud
Dayak,
   Atatalla
   Hatalla
Dehwali, Bhogana
Dida, Lago
Dien, Goda
Dimasa. Ishor
Dinka,
   Dën-did
   Nhialic
   Nialic
Diola, Atemit
Doba, Lubah
Dobu, Eaubada
Dogri, Ishwar
Dominican, Bon Dié
Donga, Shido
Dorpat, Jummal
Duala, Loba
Duke of York Islander,
   Nara
Dusun,
   Kinerehingan
   Kinorohingan
Dutch, God
Dyerma, Iricouei

Ebrie, Nyanka
Edo, Osanobua
Efate, Atua
Eggon,
   Ahogbre
   Alla
   Allah
Egyptian Arabic, Allahi
Elekeu, Nzakomba
Ellice Islander, Atua
English, God
Epi,
   Atua
   De
   God
Eromanga, Nobu
Ersa, Paz
Eskimo,
   Gûdib
   Gûtip
Eskimo (Copper),
   Godimli
Eskimo (Western Arctic),
   Godim
Esperanto, Dio
Estonian,
   Jumal
   Jummal
Ewe, Mawu

Falam, Pathian
Fang,
   Ányame
   Nzame
Fante, Nyankopon
Fanting, God
Fiadidya, Norin
Fijian, Kalou
Finnish,
   Jumal
   Jummal
Finnish Romany, Doevel
Fioti, Nzambi
Fiu, God
Flemish, God
Foe, Godebo
Foochow, Siông-Dá
French, Dieu
Frisian, God
Fula, Allah
Fulani, Allah
Fuliro, Mungu
Futa-Jalon, Allaha
Futunan, Teatua

Ga, Nyonmo
Gaelic, Dia
Gagauzi, Allach
Gahuku, Oqmasi

Galla,
   Wagayo
   Wagayon
   Wain
   Waqake
Galwa, Anyambie
Ganawuri, Tanbei
Ganda, Katonda
Gangte, Pathien
Garhwali,
   Issur
   Parameshwar
Garo,
   Ishal
   Isol
Gawigh, Gotega
Gbari
   Shashe
   Shekwohi
   Tswashe
Gbea, Nzapa
Georgian,
   G'mert'man
   G't'n
German, Gott
German Romany,
   Del i Luma
   Devel
Gheg, Perendia
Gilbertese, Atua
Gimbunda, Nzambi
Gio, Aabi
Giriama, Mulungu
Gisu, Were
Goaribari, Iehova
Gofa, Tsoso
Gogo, Mulungu
Gogodala, God
Gonda, Ishwar
Gondi,
   Devudu
   Dévuni
   Parameshwar
Goulei, Allah
Gourma, Otienu
Guoro, Balî
Graged, Anut
Grebo, Nyesoa
Greek, Theos
Greenlandic, Gûtip
Gu, Jiwheyewhe
Guadalcanar, God
Guaraní,
   Tumpa
   Tûpá Nandeyâra
Guerze, Yala
Guhu-Samane, Ohanga
Guipuzcoan,
   Jaungoicoac
Gujarati, Ishwar
Gunwingu, God
Gupapuynu, Godku
Gurezi, Khuda
Gurmukhi,
   Bhagawan
   Parameshwar
Gusii, Nyasaye
Gyengyen, Shekwohi

Ha, Imana
Habbe, Ama
Haida, Shanungitlagadas
Hainanese, Siag-di
Haka, Pathien
Hakka,
   Shong-ti
   Son-ti
Hanga, Nyasaye
Hangaza, Imana
Harauti, Ishwar
Hausa, Allah
Hawaiian, Akua
Haya, Katonda
Hebrew,
   Allahu
   Elohim
Heiban, Kalo
Herero, Mukuru
Higi, Hyalatamwa
Hindi, Ishwar
Hindko, Khuda
Hindustani, Parameshwar
Hmar, Pathienin
Ho, Iswar
Hog Harbour, Yehova
Holo, Nzambi Mawezi
Houailou, Bao
Huanuco, Dios
Hula, Palagu

Huli, Ngodehanda
Hunde, Mungu
Hungarian, Isten
Hungaro, Bog

Ibanag, Dios
Ibembe, Abece
Ibo,
   Cuku
   Tsineke
   Tsuku
Ibo (Union), Chineke
Icelandic, Gud
Idoma,
   Oco
   Owoico
Igala, Ojo
Igbira, Hinegbau
Igorot, Chios
Ijo,
   Ayeba
   Wonyingi
Ikota, Nzambe
Ila, Leza
Ilamba, Nzua
Ilocano, Dios
Inamwanga, Leza
Indonesian,
   Allah
   Tuhan
Indo-Portuguese, Deos
Inhambane Tonga,
   Nungungula
Inkongo, Ncembi
Iraqw, Mungu
Iregwe, Ba
Irish, Día
Iroquois, Niio
Isoko, Oghene
Isuama, Tsuku
Italian,
   Dio
   Iddio
Izoceno, Tumpa

Jaba, Nom
Jabim, Anôtô
Japanese, Kami
Jarawa, Dagwonom
Jaunsari, Ishwar
Javanese, Allah
Jita, Nyamuanga
Joria, O'i Adai
Judeo-Arabic, Allah
Judeo-Spanish, Dios
Jukun,
   Chido
   Kurmam
   Shido
Junin, Dios

Kabba Laka, Allah
Kabre, Eso
Kabyle,
   Allha
   Rabbi
   Rebbi
Kachchhi, Khuda
Kachin, Karai Kasang
Kaguru, Mulungu
Kaili, Toepoe
Kakwa, Nun
Kalaña, Ndzimu
Kalanga,
   Kabeshyampungu
Kalebwe, Ehle Makulu
Kalla, Sö
Kalmuk, Borgan
Kamba, Ngai
Kambera, Ala
Kamberi, Usula
Kanakura, Progru
Kanauji, Ishwar
Kanauri, Ishwar
Kannada, Devaru
Kaonde, Lesa
Kapauku, Ugatameja
Karamajong, Akuj
Karanga, Wedenga
Karelian, Jumal
Karen, Ywa
Karre, Ouone
Kashgar, Khuda
Kashmiri,
   Ishwar
   Khuda
Kate, Anutu
Kazan,
   Allah

Khuda
Keapara, Palagu
Kebu, Mungu
Kele,
   Anyambie
   Mungo
   Njambyé
Kermanshahi, Khuda
Kewa, Goteme
Kharia, Ishwar
Khasi,
   Blei
   Hayayun
Khondi,
   Paramushreela
   Penu
Khumi, Tameuh
Khumi Awa, Kinikhawma
Kiaotung, Shang-ti
Kienning, Ciong-Di
Kienyang, Shiong-Doi
Kiga, Ruhanga
Kikuyu, Ngai
Kiluba, Leza
Kim, Dok
Kinga, Unguluve
Kipsigis, Jehova
Kirghiz,
   Khuda,
   Khudadin
   Khudai
Kiriwina, Eaubada
Kituba, Nzambi
Kiwai,
   God
   Iehova
Kiyaka, Nzambi
Koalib, Ala
Koho, Yang Tom Trô
Koi,
   Devudu
   Dévuni
Kom, Pathenin
Kona, Kurmam
Kongo, Nzambi
Konjo, Nyamuhanga
Konkani,
   Devac
   Devan
Kono, Yataa
Konyak, Jihova
Korean, Hananim
Krongo, Ala
Kru, Nyesoa
Kuanyama, Kalunga
Kuba, Ncembi
Kui, Penu
Kukua, Nuleso
Kulawi, Poee Ala
Kuliviu, God
Kulu, Parameshwar
Kuman, Anutu
Kumaoni, Ishwar
Kumuk, Allah
Kunama, Anna
Kunini, God
Kunuzi, Ikkegon
Kuranko, Alla
Kurdish,
   Khoda
   Khuda
   Khwedê
   Xwedê
Kurku, Bhagwan
Kurmanji,
   Khoda
   Khwedê
   Xwedê
Kusaiean, God
Kuvi, Paramushreela
Kwagutl, God
Kwamera, Atua
Kwangali, Karunga
Kwara'ae, God
Kwese, Nzambi
Kwomu, Agwatana
Kyaka, Anatumi
Kyec, Dén-did

Labourdin, Jainkoak
Labrador Eskimo, Gûdib
Ladakhi, Dkon-mjog
Lahnda, Khuda
Lahu, Guisha
Lahuli,
   Kon-chhog
   Kon-chok
   Parameswar
Lakher, Khazopa

Lamba, Lesa
Land Dayak, Allah Taala
Lango,
  Lubanga
  Obana
Lapp,
  Ibmel
  Immlja
Latgalian, Diws
Latin, Deus
Latuka, Hollum·
Latvian,
  Deews
  Dievs
Latvian Romany, Devel
Lau, God
Lega, Kalaga
Lele, Kumno
Lenakil, Wuhgin
Lendu, Mungu
Lengua, Dios
Lepcha, Rum
Lewo,
  De
  God
Lifu, Okötesieti
Limba, Kanu
Lingala, Njambe
Lithuanian,
  Dievas
  Diews
Livonian, Jumahlto
Logo, Nzambe
Loma, Gala
Lotho, Potsona
Lozi, Mulimu
Luba,
  Efile Mukulu
  Kabeshyampungu
  Lesa
  Nzambi
Luchazi, Njambi
Lugbara, Munguni
Luimbe, Kalunga
Lulua, Nzambi
Lumbu, Nzambi
Lunda, Nzambi
Lungu, Lesa
Luo, Nyasaye
Lushai, Pathian
Lwo, Lubanga

Maasai, engai
Maban, Jueng
Mabuiag,
  Augad
  God
Macassar, Alla-taâla
Macedonian,
  Bog
  Dumnedelu
Machame, Iruva
Machina,
  Allah
  Allaha
Madi, Ruba
Madjingai, Allah
Madurese, Alla
Magahi, Ishwar
Mailu, Boi ogada
Makua, Mluku
Makuchi,
  Pêku
  Thekatong
Malagasy,
  Andriamanitra
Malay, Allah
Malayalam, Devam
Malekula,
  Atua
  God
Maliseet, Nukskam
Malo, God
Maltese, Alla
Malto, Gosanyith
Malu, God
Malvi, Ishwar
Mambwe,
  Leza
  Mulungu
Manchad, Parmeswar
Manda, Mulungu
Mandarin, Shang-ti
Mandingo
  Alla
  Yau
Mandla, Ishwar
Maninka, Alla
Manipuri, Ishwar
Mano, Wala
Manus Islander,

Jehova
Manyan, Alatalla
Manyika, Mwari
Manx, Jee
Mao, Jihova
Maori, Atua
Mapudungun,
  Ngünemapun
Marathi, Dewa
Maré Madaru
Margi, Iju
Marova, God
Marquesan, Atua
Marwari, Ishwar
Masana, Alauna
Mashi, Mungu
Mataco, Dios
Matakam, Zhikle
Mauritius Creole,
  Bondié
Mawken, Thedä
Maya, Dioz
Mbai,
  Allah
  Lubah
Mbere, So
Mbum, Hven
Mbunda, Njambi
Mbundu, Nzambi
Melpa, Anutu
Mende, Ngewo
Mentawei, Taikamanoea
Mer, Ade
Meru, Murungu
Mexican, Dios
Micmac, Nikskam
Mikir, Arnam
Mochi, Rua
Mohawk, Yehovah
Moksha, Schkais
Mon, Kyaik
Mongo, Nzakomba
Mongolian,
  Borgan
  Borhan
  Juma
Moorish,
  Allahu
  Elohim
Moravian Romany,
  Devel
Mordoff,
  Paz
  Schkais
Mordva, Schkais
Moré, Wennam
Mori, Oeë Ala
Moro, Ramwa
Mortlock, Kot
Moru, Lu
Moskito, God
Mota, God
Motu, Dirava
Mpoto, Mlungu
Mro, Säthaw
Mukawa, God
Mukri, Khuda
Mukuni, Lesa
Mundang, Masing
Mundari, Parmeswar
Murle, Joo
Murut, Allah
Musalmani, Khoda
Mwala, God
Mzieme, Tingrangpui

Naga,
  Alhou
  Hera
  Jihova
  Jihova-a
  Kavangi
  Mühghai
  Potsona
  Raguanghrui
  Sunggigüle
  Tingrangpui
  Tsingrang
  Tsüngremi
  Ukepenuopfu
  Varivarana
Nagpuria,
  Ishwar
  Parameshwar
Nama, Eloba
Namau, Eloi
Nambya, Mwali
Nancowry, Gnallaeh
Nande, Nyamuhanga
Nandi, Jehova
Nandi-Kipsigis, Jehovah

Nanjeri,
  Kuma
  Kurna
Narrinyeri, Jehovah
Nauruan, Gott
Navajo, God
Ndau, Mngari
Ndebele, Nkulunkulu
Ndembu, Nzambi
Ndonga, Kalunga
Negro English, Gado
Neo-Melanesian, God
Nepali, Ishwar
Ngaju, Hatalla
Ngala, Nzambe
Ngambai, Allah
Ngandu, Yakomba
Ngawn, Pai
Ngbaka, Nzambe
Ngbandi, Mbongo
Ngombe, Njambe
Ngonde, Kyala
Nguna,
  Atua
  Supe
Ngwana, Mungu
Ng'ala, Tororut
Nkore, Ruhanga
Nkoya, Nyambi
Nkundu, Nzakomba
Nkutu, Nzambe
Nias, Lowalangi
Nicobarese,
  Gnallaeh
  Tev
Ningpo, Jing-ming
Nirere, Ala
Niuean, Atua
Nogai, Allah
Nogugu, Atua
Norwegian, Gud
Norwegian Lapp, Ibmel
Notu, God
Nruanghmei,
  Raguanghrui
Nsenga, Mlungu
Ntomba, Nyambe
Nuba,
  Abradu
  Ala
  Elo
  Kalo
  Ramwa
Nubian,
  Ikkegon
  Norin
Nuer, Kwoth
Nunggubuyu, God
Nupe, Soko
Nyakyusa, Kyala
Nyamwezi, Mulungu
Nyanja,
  Mlungu
  Mulungu
Nyaturu-Rimi, Muungu
Nyemba, Kalunga
Nyiha, Mulungu
Nyika,
  Mulungu
  Mulungu
Nyimang, Abradu
Nyoro, Ruhanga
Nzebi,
  Nsembi
  Nzembi

Ogoni, Bari
Ogowe, Nzame
Okele, Ndjambi
Omyene,
  Anyambie
  Anyambye
Ongom, Njambyé
Opa, God
Ora, Oiseleburua
Orokaiva, God
Orokolo, Aualeri
Ossete, Khutzau
Ostiak, Torym
Otoro, Elo

Paama, Ahi
Paite, Pathian
Palestinian Arabic, Allah
Pali, Dewa
Palpa, Ishwar
Pampanyan, Dios
Pana, Ouone

Panareti, Iehova
Panayan, Dios
Pangasinan, Dios
Pangkumu, Atua
Panjabi,
  Ishwar
  Parameshwar
Parsi, Ishwar
Pashto, Allah
Patpatar, Kalou
Pa-O, Pa-ra-pyin-zowk
Pedi, Modimo
Pende, Nzambi
Pere, Mungu
Perm, Gospod
Persian, Khuda
Petats, Sunahan
Phom, Kavangi
Piedmontese, Iddiou
Piro, Goyakalu
Pitjantjatjara, God
Pokomo, Muungu
Pokot, Tororut
Police Motu, Dirava
Polish, Bog
Ponérihouen, Droué
Popo, Mawu
Portuguese, Deus
Provençal, Dieu
Punjabi, Bhagawan
Pwo Karen, Ywa

Quechua, Dios
Quiché, Dios

Rabai, Mulungu
Rabha, Ishwar
Radé, Aê Diê
Raga. God
Ranau, Kinorohingan
Rarotonga, Atua
Rawang, Gvray Gvsvng
Rengma, Sunggigüle
Rennellese, God
Reval, Jumal
Riang-Isawr
Riang-Lang, Tsau Pra
Ribé, Mulungua
Romansch,
  Deis
  Deus
  Dieu
Romany,
  Del i Luma
  Deovel
  Devel
  Devlehée
  Devléskere
  Undebél
Ronga, Sikwembu
  Nkulukumba
Roro, Sirama
Rotti, Manetualain
Rotuma, Aitu
Roviana, Tamasa
Ruanda, Imana
Rukuba, Kuru
Rumanian, Dumnezeu
Rundi, Imana
Russian, Bog
Russian Lapp, Immlja

Saa, God
Sagalla, Mlungu
Saibai, Augad
Sakata, Nzambi
Salampasu, Saka-Ntanga
Samareño, Dios
Samoan, Atua
Samogit, Diewas
Sanghir, Duata
Sangir, Ruata
Sango, Nzapa
Sangtam, Tsingrang
Sanskrit,
  Ishwar
  Parameswarah
Santali, Isor
Santo,
  Atua
  God
  Yehova
Sara, Allah
Sardinian, Deus
Sasak, Allah
Sea Dayak, Allah Taala
Sema, Alhou
Sena, Mulungu
Serbian, Bog
Setu, Jummal
Sgaw Karen, Ywa

Shambala, Mulungu
Shan,
  P'ra Pinsau
  Sidja
Shanghai, Shen
Shilha,
  Allah
  Inallah
  Rabbi Kulu
Shilluk, Jwok
Shina, Khuda
Shipibo, Dios
Shoa, Waqake
Shona, Mwari
Siamese, Prajow
Siaow, Ruata
Simalungun Batak,
  Naibata
Simte, Pathian
Sinasina, Anutu
Sindhi,
  Bhagawan
  Khuda
Singpho, Phra
Sinhalese,
  Deviyanwahansay
Siwai, Tanutanu
Slave, Noohtsi
Slavonic, Bog
Slovak, Bôh
Slovenian, Bog
Soga, Kibumba
Somali, Ilahey
Songi, Efile Mukulu
Sora, Gaddeh
Soso, Alla
Sotha, Modimo
Sotho, umLimu
Souletin, Jincouac
Spanish, Dios
Spanish Romany,
  Undebél
Srinagria, Parameshwar
Suau, Eaubada
Suki, God
Suku, Nzambi
Sukuma, Mulungu
Sundanese, Allah
Sura, Nan
Swahili,
  Mngu
  Mungu
Swatow, Siang-ti
Swedish, Gud
Swedish Lapp, Jupmel
Syriac, Allah

Tagalog, Diyos
Tahitian, Atua
Taichow, Zông-ti
Taita, Mlungu
Tamahaq, Messiner
Tamil,
  Devan
  Khuda
  Tevanudaiya
Tangali, Yam
Tangkhul, Varivarana
Tangoa, God
Tanna,
  Atua
  Kot
  Wuhgin
Tasiko,
  De
  God
Tasiriki, God
Tavara, Eaubada
Taveta, Izuwa
Tawarafa, God
Ta'e, Poeang Matoea
Tehri, Issur
Telugu, Devadu
Temne, Kuru
Teop, Hunavan
Tera, Maxam
Teso, Edeke
Thado-Kuki, Pathenin
Tharaka, Ngai
Tho, Duc Chua Pha
Tibetan, Dkon-mchhog
Tiddim, Pasian
Tigre, Rabi
Tigrinya, Igziabiheir
Timorese, Oesif Neno
Tinan, Kon-chok
Tingchow, Shong-ti
Tiv, Aôndo
Tlhaping, Modimo
Toaripi, Ualare
Toba, Dios

Toba Batak, Debata
Toda, Swami
Tonga,
  Chiuta
  Leza
  Nungungulu
Tongan, Otua
Tosk, Perendia
Transcaucasian, Allah
Tsamba, Suandaran
Tsimihety, Jañahary
Tsonga, Sikwembu
Tswa, Nungungulu
Tswana, Modimo
Tubetube, Devadu
Tukudh,
  Vittekwichanchyo
Tula, Kwama
Tulu, Dever
Tumbuka, Ciuta
Tunisian Arabic, Allahi
Tupi, Tupan
Turkana, Akuj
Turkish,
  Allach
  Allah
  Khozai
  Khuda
  Tanara
Twi, Onyankopon

Ubir, God
Ukrainian, Bozymy
Ulawa, God
Umbundu, Suku
Urdu, Khuda
Urhobo, Oghene
Uripiv, Atua
Uvea, Khong
Uzbek, Khuda

Vaiphei, Pathian
Valvi, Bhagawan
Vaudois, Diou
Vella Lavella, Banara
Venda, Mudzimu
Vietnamese,
  Duc Chua Troi
Visayan, Dios
Vogul, Toruimunne
Votiak, Inmar

Wa, Siyeh
Waja, Yamba
Wajewa, Ala
Wedau, God
Welsh, Duw
Wenchow, Zie-ti
Wendish, Bog
Wenli, Shang-ti
White Russian, Bog
Wolof, Yalla
Worrora, God
Wukingfu, Shong-ti
Wukum, Yamba
Wukuri, Chido

Xhosa,
  Thixo
  Tixo
Xu, Xu

Yahgan, God
Yaka, Nzyambi
Yakut, Tanara
Yalunka, Alla
Yamma Gayegi, Tswashe
Yamma Paiko, Shashe
Yao, Mlungu
Yapese, Got
Yergum, Inan
Yiddish, Got
Yoruba, Olorun
Yugoslav Romany,
  Devlehée
Yunnanese, Sidja

Zanaki, Mungu
Zeme, Hera
Zigula, Mlungu
Zomi, Tapa
Zotung, Pachia
Zulu, Nkulunkulu
Zyryan,
  Gospod
  Jen

Table 9-13. The globe's 13,500 distinct and different languages, with speakers, Christians, scriptures, audiovisual ministries.

Code 1	REFERENCE NAME / Autoglossonym 2	Coun 3	Peo 4	Mother-tongue speakers in 2000 5	in 2025 6	Media radio 7	AC% 8	E% 9	Wld 10	Tr 11	Biblioglossonym 12	Print 13-15	P-activity 16	N-activity 17	B-activity 18	J-year 19	Jayuh 20-24	Ref 25
0	**AFRICAN macrozone**	37	557	69,440,731	120,922,018		31.68	63	B	68		PNB					4Asu.	1
00	**MANDIC zone**	18	136	22,935,471	40,401,572		6.03	50	B	68		PNB					4As..	2
00-A	**NORTHWEST MANDE set**	15	82	17,416,271	30,479,615		3.96	51	B	68		PNB					4As..	3
00-AA	MANDING chain	15	72	14,477,858	25,196,933		1.55	49	A	61		PNB					4As..	4
00-AAA	**MANDEKAN net**	15	59	13,131,504	22,926,335		1.69	50	A	61		PNB					4As..	5
00-AAAA	WEST MANDEKAN cluster	13	25	5,548,959	9,305,278		0.49	44	A	42		PN.					4a...	6
00-AAAA-a	mandinka-kango	7	8	1,746,145	3,002,540	4	0.48	44	A	42	Mandinka	PN.	1837-1966	1989		1992	4a...	7
00-AAAA-b	sijanka-kango	1	1	59,080	61,662	4	2.00	48	A	42		pn.					1c...	12
00-AAAA-c	maninka-xanwo	1	1	92,081	154,870	1	0.50	22	A	42		pn.					1c...	13
00-AAAA-d	kalanke-kango	1	1	2,611	4,302	1	0.00	22	A	42		pn.					1c...	14
00-AAAA-e	jakhanka-kango	1	1	27,564	48,674	1	0.00	18	A	42		pn.					1c...	15
00-AAAA-f	xasonka-xango	3	3	150,665	284,305	1	2.56	37	A	42	Kassonke	pn.					1c...	16
00-AAAA-g	kakolo-qango	1	1	25,405	48,160	4	1.00	38	A	42		pn.					1c...	17
00-AAAA-h	maninka-kan	7	8	3,440,117	5,690,735	5	0.38	45	A	42	Maninka*	PN.	1931-1964	1932-1966		1989	3a...	18
00-AAAB	EAST MANDEKAN cluster	12	21	6,536,498	11,753,300		1.99	56	B	61		PNB					4As..	22
00-AAAB-a	bamanan-kan	10	10	4,366,464	7,990,122	4	2.54	63	B	61	Bambara	PNB	1923-1942	1933-1995	1961-1987	1983	4As..	23
00-AAAB-b	manenka-kan					1				61		pnb					1cs..	32
00-AAAB-c	mikifore-kan					1				61		pnb					1cs..	37
00-AAAB-d	manya-kan	1	1	53,851	112,988	5	0.03	39	A	61		pnb					1cs..	38
00-AAAB-e	wasulunka-kan	1	1	740,441	1,403,622	4	2.00	45	A	61		pnb					1cs..	39
00-AAAB-f	konyanka-kan	2	2	147,933	235,100	4	0.10	33	A	61		pnb					1cs..	40
00-AAAB-g	tenenga-kan					1				61		pnb					1cs..	41
00-AAAB-h	mauka-kan	1	1	187,780	296,483	1	1.00	41	A	61		pnb					1cs..	42
00-AAAB-i	koroka-kan					1				61		pnb					1cs..	43
00-AAAB-j	baralaka-finanga					1				61		pnb					1cs..	44
00-AAAB-k	sienkoka-kan					1				61		pnb					1cs..	47
00-AAAB-l	wojeneka-kan					1				61		pnb					1cs..	48
00-AAAB-m	gbelebanka-foloka					1				61		pnb					1cs..	49
00-AAAB-n	boduguka-kan					1				61		pnb					1cs..	52
00-AAAB-o	tuduguka-kan					1				61		pnb					1cs..	53
00-AAAB-p	vanduguka-kan					1				61		pnb					1cs..	54
00-AAAB-q	nowoloka-kan					1				61		pnb					1cs..	55
00-AAAB-r	karanjanka-kan					1				61		pnb					1cs..	56
00-AAAB-s	woroduguka-kan					1				61		pnb					1cs..	57
00-AAAB-t	kanika-kan					1				61		pnb					1cs..	61
00-AAAB-u	nigbi-kan					1				61		pnb					1cs..	62
00-AAAB-v	sagaka-kan					1				61		pnb					1cs..	63
00-AAAB-w	koro-kan					1				61		pnb					1cs..	64
00-AAAB-x	koyaga-kan					1				61		pnb					1cs..	67
00-AAAB-y	siaka-kan					1				61		pnb					1cs..	68
00-AAAB-z	jula-kan	4	6	1,040,029	1,714,985	4	0.22	42	A	61	Jula	PNb	1992	1993-1994			1cs..	69
00-AAAC	MARKA cluster	2	3	272,781	532,515		11.53	44	A	20		. . .					0....	77
00-AAAC-a	bolon-kan	1	1	14,230	27,801	1	3.00	27	A	20		. . .					0....	78
00-AAAC-b	da-fin-kan					1				20		. . .					0....	81
00-AAAC-c	maraka-jalan-kan	2	2	258,551	504,714	2	12.00	45	A	20	Marka	. . .					0....	84
00-AAAC-d	meeka-kan					1				20		. . .					0....	85
00-AAAD	KURANKO cluster	2	3	415,721	694,815		1.53	32	A	51		PN.					0....	86
00-AAAD-a	falanko-kuranko	1	1	77,634	130,572	0	1.00	25	A	51		pn.					0....	87
00-AAAD-b	muso-kuranko					0				51		pn.					0....	88
00-AAAD-c	wasamandu-kuranko	2	2	338,087	564,243	0	1.65	33	A	51	Kuranko	PN.	1899-1911	1972			0....	98
00-AAAE	VAI-KONO cluster	5	6	356,601	638,582		7.52	45	A	35		P..					4....	99
00-AAAE-a	Central kono	4	4	232,770	386,410	4	11.20	53	B	35	Kono	P..	1919-1993				1....	100
00-AAAE-b	North kono					1				35		p..					1....	105
00-AAAE-c	kono-P.					1				35		p..					1....	109
00-AAAE-d	dama			0	0	1	0.00	0		35		p..					1....	116
00-AAAE-e	vai	2	2	123,831	252,172	1	0.61	31	A	35	Vai	P..	1995			1993	4....	117
00-AAAF	JELKUNA cluster	1	1	944	1,845		2.97	24	A	6		. . .					0....	118
00-AAAF-a	jelkuna	1	1	944	1,845	0	2.97	24	A	6		. . .					0....	119
00-AAB	**LIGBI-NUMU net**	2	2	19,051	33,592		0.28	23	A	4		. . .					0....	120
00-AABA	LIGBI-NUMU cluster	2	2	19,051	33,592		0.28	23	A	4		. . .					0....	121
00-AABA-a	ligbi	2	2	19,051	33,592	0	0.28	23	A	4		. . .					0....	122
00-AABA-b	hwela					0				4		. . .					0....	128
00-AABA-c	numu					0				4		. . .					0....	129
00-AAC	**SOSO-YALUNKA net**	6	11	1,327,303	2,237,006		0.19	37	A	41		PN.					4....	130
00-AACA	SOSO-YALUNKA cluster	6	11	1,327,303	2,237,006		0.19	37	A	41		PN.					4....	131
00-AACA-a	soso	5	6	1,065,843	1,792,660	4	0.19	41	A	41	Soso*	PN.	1869-1963	1884-1988		1994	4....	132
00-AACA-b	yalunka	4	5	261,460	444,346	1	0.18	21	A	41	Yalunka	PN.	1907	1976			1....	133
00-AB	SOUTHWEST MANDE chain	3	10	2,938,413	5,282,682		15.85	65	B	68		PNB					3....	137
00-ABA	**SOUTHWEST MANDE net**	3	10	2,938,413	5,282,682		15.85	65	B	68		PNB					3....	138
00-ABAA	LOKO-MENDE cluster	3	6	1,606,671	2,724,116		8.53	63	B	68		PNB					3....	139
00-ABAA-a	bandi	2	2	178,744	335,583	1	6.18	44	A	68	Bandi	Pnb	1954-1995				1....	140
00-ABAA-b	loko	2	2	142,420	237,287	4	3.65	49	A	68	Loko: Sierra Leone	PNb		1983			1....	143
00-ABAA-c	mende	2	2	1,285,507	2,151,246	4	9.40	67	B	68	Mende	PNB	1867-1954	1956	1959	1985	3....	154
00-ABAB	LOMA-TOMA cluster	2	2	348,350	655,894		10.60	54	B	42		PN.					0....	160
00-ABAB-a	loma	1	1	168,198	352,901	3	15.00	61	B	42	Loma	PN.	1949-1967	1971			0....	161
00-ABAB-b	toma	1	1	180,152	302,993	1	6.50	47	A	42	Toma	PN.	1961	1981			0....	167
00-ABAC	KPELLE cluster	2	2	983,392	1,902,672		29.67	72	B	42		PN.					2....	168
00-ABAC-a	kpele	1	1	597,530	1,253,700	1	25.00	69	B	42	Kpelle*	PN.	1922-1964	1967			1....	169
00-ABAC-b	kpelese	1	1	385,862	648,972	1	36.90	77	B	42	Kpelee*	Pn.	1945-1969			1997	2....	170
00-B	**SONINKE-BOZO set**	9	17	1,601,693	2,934,483		0.03	19	A	32		. . .					3....	171
00-BA	SONINKE chain	9	12	1,460,214	2,666,148		0.03	19	A	32		. . .					3....	172
00-BAA	**SONINKE net**	9	12	1,460,214	2,666,148		0.03	19	A	32		. . .					3....	173
00-BAAA	SONINKE cluster	9	12	1,460,214	2,666,148		0.03	19	A	32		. . .					3....	174
00-BAAA-a	Proper soninke	9	9	1,435,752	2,625,567	0	0.02	19	A	32	Soninke	. . .				1988	1....	175
00-BAAA-b	azayr	3	3	24,462	40,581	0	0.26	19	A	32		. . .					1....	176
00-BAAA-c	girganke			0	0	0	0.00	0		32		. . .					1....	177
00-BAAA-d	kinbakka					0				32		. . .					1....	178
00-BAAA-e	xenqenna					0				32		. . .					1....	179
00-BB	BOZO chain	2	5	141,479	268,335		0.02	15	A	20		. . .					0....	180
00-BBA	**TIEMA net**	1	1	2,954	5,601		0.10	14	A	4		. . .					0....	181

Continued opposite

Table 9-13 continued

Code 1	REFERENCE NAME / Autoglossonym 2	Coun 3	Peo 4	Mother-tongue speakers in 2000 5	in 2025 6	Media radio 7	CHURCH AC% 8	E% 9	Wld 10	Tr 11	Biblioglossonym 12	SCRIPTURES Print 13-15	P-activity 16	N-activity 17	B-activity 18	J-year 19	Jayuh 20-24	Ref 25
00-BBAA	TIEMA cluster	1	1	2,954	5,601		0.10	14	A	4		. . .					0	182
00-BBAA-a	tiema-ciewe	1	1	2,954	5,601	0	0.10	14	A	4							0	183
00-BBB	**SOROGAMA net**	1	1	118,164	223,998		0.02	15	A	20		. . .					0	184
00-BBBA	SOROGAMA cluster	1	1	118,164	223,998		0.02	15	A	20	Boso, Sorogama	. . .					0	185
00-BBBA-a	kotya-xo					0				20		. . .					0	186
00-BBBA-b	pondori					0				20		. . .					0	187
00-BBBA-c	korondugu					0				20		. . .					0	190
00-BBBA-d	debo					0				20		. . .					0	193
00-BBC	**TIEYA net**	2	2	9,127	17,441		0.08	13	A	20		. . .					0	194
00-BBCA	TIEYA cluster	2	2	9,127	17,441		0.08	13	A	20		. . .					0	195
00-BBCA-a	tieya-xo	2	2	9,127	17,441	0	0.08	13	A	20							0	196
00-BBD	**HAINYA net**	1	1	11,234	21,295		0.00	13	A	20		. . .					0	197
00-BBDA	HAINYA cluster	1	1	11,234	21,295		0.00	13	A	20		. . .					0	198
00-BBDA-a	hainya-xo	1	1	11,234	21,295	0	0.00	13	A	20							0	199
00-C	**SEMBLA-JUNG set**	2	5	53,554	103,808		10.15	37	A	12		. . .					0	200
00-CA	SEMBLA-JUNG chain	2	5	53,554	103,808		10.15	37	A	12		. . .					0	201
00-CAA	**SEMBLA net**	2	2	23,034	44,806		20.98	55	B	2		. . .					0	202
00-CAAA	SENKU cluster	2	2	23,034	44,806		20.98	55	B	2		. . .					0	203
00-CAAA-a	senku	2	2	23,034	44,806	2	20.98	55	B	2		. . .					0	204
00-CAB	**JUNG net**	2	3	30,520	59,002		1.98	24	A	12		. . .					0	208
00-CABA	JUNG cluster	2	3	30,520	59,002		1.98	24	A	12		. . .					0	209
00-CABA-a	kpango	2	3	30,520	59,002	0	1.98	24	A	12	Jowulu	. . .					0	210
00-CABA-b	jungo					0				12	Dzuungoo	. . .					0	211
00-CABA-c	jung-oma					0				12		. . .					0	212
00-CABA-d	bakaridugu					0				12		. . .					0	215
00-CABA-e	jo-wulu					0				12		. . .					0	218
00-D	**EAST MANDE set**	11	32	3,863,953	6,883,666		17.77	58	B	61		PNB					4 . s . .	219
00-DA	MAN chain	2	2	234,826	474,861		4.36	42	A	41		PN .					0	220
00-DAA	**MAN net**	2	2	234,826	474,861		4.36	42	A	41		PN .					0	221
00-DAAA	MAN cluster	2	2	234,826	474,861		4.36	42	A	41		PN .					0	222
00-DAAA-a	man-wi	2	2	234,826	474,861	1	4.36	42	A	41	Mano	PN .	1946-1987	1978			0	223
00-DB	DAN chain	3	5	1,251,783	2,106,743		22.43	68	B	41		PN .					3	226
00-DBA	**DAN net**	3	5	1,251,783	2,106,743		22.43	68	B	41		PN .					3	227
00-DBAA	TURA-DAN cluster	3	5	1,251,783	2,106,743		22.43	68	B	41	Gio	PN .	1943	1981			3	228
00-DBAA-a	dan	3	4	1,209,034	2,039,248	2	22.58	68	B	41	Dan*	PN .	1981	1981-1993		1997	3	229
00-DBAA-b	ween	1	1	42,749	67,495	1	18.00	56	B	41	Toura	PN .	1972	1979-1986			1	234
00-DC	GOLO-YAURE chain	2	3	406,480	643,612		19.28	71	B	61		PNB					4	240
00-DCA	**GOLO net**	2	2	377,297	597,536		19.22	72	B	61		PNB					4	241
00-DCAA	GOLO cluster	2	2	377,297	597,536		19.22	72	B	61		PNB					4	242
00-DCAA-a	golo	2	2	377,297	597,536	2	19.22	72	B	61	Gouro*	PNB	1951-1961	1956-1968	1979	1997	4	243
00-DCB	**YAURE net**	1	1	29,183	46,076		20.00	57	B	22		P . .					0	244
00-DCBA	YOWELE cluster	1	1	29,183	46,076		20.00	57	B	22		P . .					0	245
00-DCBA-a	yowele	1	1	29,183	46,076	0	20.00	57	B	22	Yaoure	P . .	1992-1993				0	246
00-DD	BEN-GBAN chain	1	2	59,510	93,959		7.78	38	A	35		P . .					0	252
00-DDA	**GBAN net**	1	1	40,634	64,157		10.00	44	A	35		P . .					0	253
00-DDAA	GBAN cluster	1	1	40,634	64,157		10.00	44	A	35		P . .					0	254
00-DDAA-a	gba	1	1	40,634	64,157	0	10.00	44	A	35	Gban*	P . .	1970				0	255
00-DDB	**BEN net**	1	1	18,876	29,802		3.00	25	A	2		. . .					0	260
00-DDBA	BEN cluster	1	1	18,876	29,802		3.00	25	A	2		. . .					0	261
00-DDBA-a	beng	1	1	18,876	29,802	0	3.00	25	A	2		. . .					0	262
00-DE	NWA-MWA chain	1	2	42,223	66,664		15.90	50	A	22		P . .					0	263
00-DEA	**MWA net**	1	1	17,795	28,096		24.00	58	B	22		P . .					0	264
00-DEAA	MWA cluster	1	1	17,795	28,096		24.00	58	B	22		P . .					0	265
00-DEAA-a	mwa	1	1	17,795	28,096	0	24.00	58	B	22	Mwan*	P . .	1995				0	266
00-DEB	**NWA net**	1	1	24,428	38,568		10.00	44	A	0		. . .					0	267
00-DEBA	NWA cluster	1	1	24,428	38,568		10.00	44	A	0		. . .					0	268
00-DEBA-a	wan	1	1	24,428	38,568	0	10.00	44	A	0		. . .					0	269
00-DF	BISA chain	4	4	696,690	1,310,150		16.40	56	B	22		P . .					1	272
00-DFA	**BISA net**	4	4	696,690	1,310,150		16.40	56	B	22		P . .					1	273
00-DFAA	BISA cluster	4	4	696,690	1,310,150		16.40	56	B	22		P . .					1	274
00-DFAA-a	bisa	4	4	696,690	1,310,150	3	16.40	56	B	22	Bissa	P . .	1996				1	275
00-DG	BUSA-SANE chain	5	10	800,862	1,469,420		13.63	44	A	61		PNB					0	278
00-DGA	**SANE net**	1	1	509,645	944,962		11.68	42	A	51		PN .					0	279
00-DGAA	GOE cluster	1	1	309,645	604,962		16.00	53	B	51	Samo	PN .	1964-1991	1995			0	280
00-DGAA-a	tougan					1				51		pn .					0	281
00-DGAA-b	louta					1				51		pn .					0	282
00-DGAA-c	zoumou					1				51		pn .					0	283
00-DGAA-d	maya					1				51		pn .					0	284
00-DGAB	MAKAA cluster	1	1	200,000	340,000		5.00	24	A	0		. . .					0	285
00-DGAB-a	makaa	1	1	200,000	340,000	0	5.00	24	A	0		. . .					0	286
00-DGB	**DUUN net**	2	2	83,909	159,130		0.02	24	A	20		. . .					0	289
00-DGBA	DUUN cluster	2	2	83,909	159,130		0.02	24	A	20		. . .					0	290
00-DGBA-a	duun	2	2	83,909	159,130	0	0.02	24	A	20		. . .					0	291
00-DGC	**JO net**	1	1	3,000	5,100		5.00	24	A	0		. . .					0	294
00-DGCA	JO cluster	1	1	3,000	5,100		5.00	24	A	0		. . .					0	295
00-DGCA-a	jowulu	1	1	3,000	5,100	0	5.00	24	A	0		. . .					0	296

Continued overleaf

Table 9-13 continued

Code 1	REFERENCE NAME 2 / Autoglossonym	Coun 3	Peo 4	Mother-tongue speakers in 2000 5	in 2025 6	Media radio 7	CHURCH AC% 8	E% 9	Wld 10	Tr 11	Biblioglossonym 12	SCRIPTURES Print 13-15	P–activity 16	N–activity 17	B–activity 18	J-year 19	Jayuh 20-24	Ref 25
00-DGD	**BUSA net**	3	7	204,308	360,228		24.19	59	B	61		PNB					0....	297
00-DGDA	BUSA-BOKO cluster	3	4	191,707	339,340		25.78	62	B	61	Busa	PNB					0....	298
00-DGDA-a	boko	2	2	65,746	117,923	1	46.43	67	B	61	Boko	PNB		1984	1992		0....	299
00-DGDA-b	wawa					1				61		pnb					0....	300
00-DGDA-c	bokobaru					1				61	Bokobaru	Pnb	1972-1994				0....	301
00-DGDB	SHANGA-TYENGA cluster	2	3	12,601	20,888		0.02	14	A	5		...					0....	305
00-DGDB-a	shanga	2	3	12,601	20,888	0	0.02	14	A	5		...					0....	306
00-DGDB-b	tyenga					0				5		...					0....	307
00-DH	BOBO-FING chain	3	4	371,579	718,257		22.19	57	B	51		PN.					0.s..	308
00-DHA	**BOBO-FING net**	3	4	371,579	718,257		22.19	57	B	51		PN.					0.s..	309
00-DHAA	BOBO-FING cluster	3	4	371,579	718,257		22.19	57	B	51	Bobo: Madare	PN.	1965	1981			0.s..	310
00-DHAA-a	zara-dan	1	1	13,079	25,553	0	0.00	19	A	51	Bobo Madare, Southern	PN.	1965	1981			0.s..	311
00-DHAA-b	benge					0				51		pn.					0.s..	312
00-DHAA-c	sogokiri					0				51		pn.					0.s..	313
00-DHAA-d	sya	1	1	322,547	630,170	0	25.00	61	B	51		pn.					0.s..	314
00-DHAA-e	vore					0				51		pn.					0.s..	315
01	**SONGHAIC zone**	8	18	4,665,290	9,118,823		0.27	36	A	61		PNB					2..u.	316
01-A	**SONGHAY-SAHAQ set**	8	18	4,665,290	9,118,823		0.27	36	A	61		PNB					2..u.	317
01-AA	SONGHAY-SAHAQ chain	8	18	4,665,290	9,118,823		0.27	36	A	61		PNB					2..u.	318
01-AAA	**SONGHAY-ZARMA net**	7	16	4,626,106	9,045,689		0.27	36	A	61		PNB					2..u.	319
01-AAAA	SONGHAY-KINE cluster	6	7	1,628,466	3,095,383		0.33	29	A	41	Songhai*	PN.	1928	1936-1976			0....	320
01-AAAA-a	jene-kine					0				41		pn.					0....	321
01-AAAA-b	kaado					0				41		pn.					0....	326
01-AAAA-c	hombori-kine	1	1	3,450	6,740	0	0.00	14	A	41		pn.					0....	327
01-AAAA-d	gao-kine					0				41		pn.					0....	331
01-AAAB	DENDI-ZARMA cluster	6	9	2,967,640	5,899,306		0.23	40	A	61		PNB					2..u.	336
01-AAAB-a	dendi	4	4	105,242	199,104	4	5.12	32	A	61	Dendi	PNb		1994			1..u.	337
01-AAAB-b	zarma	5	5	2,862,398	5,700,202	1	0.05	41	A	61	Zarma	PNB	1934	1954	1990	1996	2..u.	341
01-AAAC	TIHISIT cluster	1	1	30,000	51,000		1.00	16	A	0		...					0....	344
01-AAAC-a	tihisit	1	1	30,000	51,000	0	1.00	16	A	0		...					0....	345
01-AAB	**SAHAQ-BELBALI net**	2	2	39,184	73,134		0.00	9	A	12		...					0....	348
01-AABA	DAKSAHAQ cluster	1	1	36,421	69,042		0.00	9	A	12		...					0....	349
01-AABA-a	daksahaq	1	1	36,421	69,042	0	0.00	9	A	12	Tadaksahak	...					0....	350
01-AABB	BELBALI cluster	1	1	2,763	4,092		0.00	8	A	0		...					0....	353
01-AABB-a	koranje	1	1	2,763	4,092	0	0.00	8	A	0		...					0....	354
02	**SAHARIC zone**	6	28	6,137,999	10,411,376		0.01	30	A	41		PN.					4....	355
02-A	**KANURI-KANEMBU set**	5	12	5,089,225	8,592,097		0.01	34	A	41		PN.					4....	356
02-AA	KANURI-KANEMBU chain	5	12	5,089,225	8,592,097		0.01	34	A	41		PN.					4....	357
02-AAA	**KANURI-KANEMBU net**	5	12	5,089,225	8,592,097		0.01	34	A	41		PN.					4....	358
02-AAAA	KANURI cluster	5	9	4,989,014	8,407,568		0.01	35	A	41		PN.					4....	359
02-AAAA-a	manga	2	2	940,019	1,691,526	1	0.00	24	A	41		pn.					1....	360
02-AAAA-b	yerwa	5	6	4,026,807	6,675,708	4	0.01	37	A	41	Kanuri*	PN.	1949	1995		1983	4....	361
02-AAAA-c	kwayyamo					1				41		pn.					1....	374
02-AAAA-d	mavar					1				41		pn.					1....	375
02-AAAB	KANEMBU cluster	3	3	100,211	184,529		0.01	18	A	12		...					0....	376
02-AAAB-a	kanembu	3	3	100,211	184,529	0	0.01	18	A	12	Kanembu	...					0....	377
02-B	**TUBU set**	5	8	573,255	1,044,735		0.00	9	A	20		...					0....	381
02-BA	TUBU chain	5	8	573,255	1,044,735		0.00	9	A	20		...					0....	382
02-BAA	**TEDA-DAZA net**	5	8	573,255	1,044,735		0.00	9	A	20		...					0....	383
02-BAAA	TEDA-DAZA cluster	5	8	573,255	1,044,735		0.00	9	A	20	Daza*	...					0....	384
02-BAAA-a	tuda-ga	2	2	69,685	117,487	0	0.01	11	A	20		...					0....	385
02-BAAA-b	daza-ga	3	4	443,914	810,303	0	0.00	7	A	20		...					0....	390
02-C	**ZAGHAWA-BERTI set**	4	8	475,519	774,544		0.01	13	A	20		...					0....	395
02-CA	ZAGHAWA-BERTI chain	4	8	475,519	774,544		0.01	13	A	20		...					0....	396
02-CAA	**ZAGHAWA net**	4	7	274,550	459,258		0.00	8	A	20		...					0....	397
02-CAAA	ZAGHAWA cluster	4	7	274,550	459,258		0.00	8	A	20		...					0....	398
02-CAAA-a	beri-aa	4	7	274,550	459,258	0	0.00	8	A	20		...					0....	399
02-CAAA-b	beli					0				20		...					0....	403
02-CAB	**BERTI net**	1	1	200,969	315,286		0.01	19	A	20		...					0....	408
02-CABA	BERTI cluster	1	1	200,969	315,286		0.01	19	A	20		...					0....	409
02-CABA-a	berti	1	1	200,969	315,286	7	0.01	19	A	20		...					0....	410
03	**SUDANIC zone**	7	94	8,124,081	15,736,712		68.88	90	C	68		PNB					1As..	411
03-A	**BONGO-BAGIRMI set**	6	58	2,545,119	4,535,118		34.25	73	B	68		PNB					0.s..	412
03-AA	SARA-BAGIRMI chain	6	47	2,384,301	4,275,283		35.12	74	B	68		PNB					0.s..	413
03-AAA	**BAGIRMI net**	5	36	2,305,889	4,136,525		35.72	76	B	68		PNB					0.s..	414
03-AAAA	BARMA cluster	2	2	66,587	120,572		0.01	21	A	12		...					0....	415
03-AAAA-a	tar-barma	2	2	66,587	120,572	0	0.01	21	A	12	Bagirmi	...					0....	416
03-AAAA-b	beraku					0				12		...					0....	420
03-AAAB	KUKA-KODOI cluster	1	3	295,905	537,904		0.00	9	A	2		...					0....	423
03-AAAB-a	kuka	1	1	97,588	177,398	0	0.00	8	A	2		...					0....	424
03-AAAB-b	bilala	1	1	173,928	316,171	0	0.00	9	A	2		...					0....	428
03-AAAB-c	kodoi	1	1	24,389	44,335	0	0.03	12	A	2		...					0....	429
03-AAAC	KENGA cluster	1	2	40,989	74,511		0.30	20	A	12		...					0....	430
03-AAAC-a	tar-cenge	1	1	38,189	69,421	0	0.30	20	A	12	Kenga	...					0....	431
03-AAAC-b	tar-binama					0				12		...					0....	432
03-AAAC-c	tar-bolongo					0				12		...					0....	433
03-AAAC-d	tar-murba					0				12		...					0....	434
03-AAAC-e	tar-jaie	1	1	2,800	5,090	0	0.29	11	A	12		...					0....	435

Continued opposite

Table 9-13 continued

Code 1	REFERENCE NAME / Autoglossonym 2	Coun 3	Peo 4	Mother-tongue speakers in 2000 5	in 2025 6	Media radio 7	AC% 8	E% 9	Wld 10	Tr 11	Biblioglossonym 12	Print 13-15	P–activity 16	N–activity 17	B–activity 18	J-year 19	Jayuh 20-24	Ref 25
03-AAAD	DISA cluster	1	1	2,000	3,400		0.00	14	A	4		. . .					0.....	436
03-AAAD-a	disa	1	1	2,000	3,400	0	0.00	14	A	4		. . .					0.....	437
03-AAAE	SARA cluster	5	18	1,728,327	3,103,281		43.26	91	B	68		PNB					0.s..	438
03-AAAE-a	ngambai	3	3	774,887	1,406,234	2	32.61	87	B	68	Ngambai*	PNB	1936-1990	1954-1968	1993		0.s..	439
03-AAAE-b	murum					1				68		pnb					0.s..	440
03-AAAE-c	gor					1				68		pnb					0.s..	441
03-AAAE-d	dagba-goré	1	1	42,575	67,171	1	30.00	58	B	68		pnb					0.s..	442
03-AAAE-e	mbai-doba	1	1	76,723	139,469	1	50.00	89	B	68	Mbai: Doba*	PNB	1932-1968	1943	1980		0.s..	443
03-AAAE-f	laka	3	3	80,820	146,114	1	20.80	60	B	68	Kabba-laka*	PNb	1948-1950	1960			0.s..	446
03-AAAE-g	mbai					1				68		pnb					0.s..	450
03-AAAE-h	mbai-kan	4	4	186,453	335,255	4	67.39	100	C	68	Mbai: Moissala	PNB	1932	1943	1980		0.s..	451
03-AAAE-i	dagba-batangafo					1				68		pnb					0.s..	452
03-AAAE-j	majingai	2	2	298,633	527,236	1	50.45	99	B	68	Sara-majingai	PNb	1950	1972-1986			0.s..	453
03-AAAE-k	nar					1				68		pnb					0.s..	454
03-AAAE-l	sara-no					1				68		pnb					0.s..	455
03-AAAE-m	peni					1				68		pnb					0.s..	456
03-AAAE-n	bejondo					1				68		pnb					0.s..	457
03-AAAE-o	gulai	1	1	207,844	377,822	1	55.00	100	B	68	Goulei*	Pnb	1956				0.s..	458
03-AAAE-p	gula					1				68		pnb					0.s..	462
03-AAAE-q	ngam	2	2	55,070	95,584	1	60.00	100	C	68	Ngam	pnb					0.s..	463
03-AAAF	KABA cluster	2	6	121,095	215,629		53.52	85	B	41	Kaba*	PN.					0.....	464
03-AAAF-a	tar-kaba					0				41		pn.					0.....	465
03-AAAF-b	dunjo					0				41		pn.					0.....	468
03-AAAF-c	demi					0				41		pn.					0.....	471
03-AAAF-d	sime					0				41		pn.					0.....	472
03-AAAF-e	mara					0				41		pn.					0.....	473
03-AAAF-f	kuruwer					0				41		pn.					0.....	474
03-AAAF-g	bumayga					0				41		pn.					0.....	475
03-AAAF-h	boho					0				41		pn.					0.....	476
03-AAAF-i	jaha					0				41		pn.					0.....	477
03-AAAF-j	ndoko					0				41		pn.					0.....	478
03-AAAF-k	kurumi					0				41		pn.					0.....	479
03-AAAF-l	kulfa					0				41		pn.					0.....	480
03-AAAF-m	male					0				41		pn.					0.....	481
03-AAAF-n	soko					0				41		pn.					0.....	482
03-AAAF-o	na	1	1	44,555	80,993	0	60.00	91	C	41	Kaba Na	PN.		1988			0.....	483
03-AAAF-p	dana					0				41		pn.					0.....	484
03-AAAF-q	banga					0				41		pn.					0.....	485
03-AAAF-r	tye					0				41		pn.					0.....	486
03-AAAF-s	jinge					0				41		pn.					0.....	487
03-AAAF-t	joko					0				41		pn.					0.....	488
03-AAAF-u	so					0				41		pn.					0.....	489
03-AAAF-v	suka					0				41		pn.					0.....	490
03-AAAF-w	hor					0				41		pn.					0.....	491
03-AAAG	VALE cluster	2	5	50,986	81,228		21.77	49	A	5		. . .					0.....	492
03-AAAG-a	ruto	1	1	2,518	4,577	0	29.98	47	A	5		. . .					0.....	493
03-AAAG-b	vale	2	2	6,513	10,459	0	30.00	56	B	5		. . .					0.....	494
03-AAAG-c	vale-dagba									5		. . .					0.....	495
03-AAAG-d	nduka	1	1	18,094	28,547	0	20.00	44	A	5		. . .					0.....	496
03-AAAG-e	tana	1	1	23,861	37,645	0	20.00	52	B	5		. . .					0.....	497
03-AAAG-f	tele					0				5		. . .					0.....	498
03-AAB	**KARA net**	4	7	57,874	103,257		23.51	50	A	4		. . .					0.....	499
03-AABA	KARA cluster	4	7	57,874	103,257		23.51	50	A	4		. . .					0.....	500
03-AABA-a	mamun-gula	2	3	24,796	41,752	0	11.30	31	A	4		. . .					0.....	501
03-AABA-b	kara					0				4		. . .					0.....	502
03-AABA-c	furu	2	2	24,996	48,789	0	36.59	70	B	4		. . .					0.....	505
03-AABA-d	yulu	2	2	8,082	12,716	0	20.53	49	A	4		. . .					0.....	506
03-AABA-e	binga									4		. . .					0.....	510
03-AAC	**SINYAR-GELE net**	2	4	20,538	35,501		0.00	8	A	2		. . .					0.....	513
03-AACA	SINYAR cluster	2	2	17,853	30,984		0.00	8	A	2		. . .					0.....	514
03-AACA-a	taar-shamyan	2	2	17,853	30,984	0	0.00	8	A	2		. . .					0.....	515
03-AACB	GELE cluster	2	2	2,685	4,517		0.00	7	A	0		. . .					0.....	516
03-AACB-a	gele	2	2	2,685	4,517	0	0.00	7	A	0		. . .					0.....	517
03-AB	BONGO-BAKA chain	2	3	39,352	62,709		57.59	93	B	22		P..					0.....	518
03-ABA	**BAKA net**	2	2	29,788	47,706		61.64	98	C	22		P..					0.....	519
03-ABAA	BAKA cluster	2	2	29,788	47,706		61.64	98	C	22		P..					0.....	520
03-ABAA-a	tara-baaka	2	2	29,788	47,706	0	61.64	98	C	22	Baka	P..	1990				0.....	521
03-ABB	**BONGO net**	1	1	9,564	15,003		45.00	75	B	4		. . .					0.....	522
03-ABBA	BONGO cluster	1	1	9,564	15,003		45.00	75	B	4		. . .					0.....	523
03-ABBA-a	Bongo	1	1	9,564	15,003	0	45.00	75	B	4		. . .					0.....	524
03-ABBA-b	bungo					0				4		. . .					0.....	527
03-AC	MOROKODO-MODO chain	1	4	47,570	78,564		5.31	25	A	9		. . .					0.....	528
03-ACA	**MODO-MOLO net**	1	2	40,664	67,729		4.51	23	A	9		. . .					0.....	529
03-ACAA	MODO cluster	1	1	30,000	51,000		2.59	19	A	9		. . .					0.....	530
03-ACAA-a	jur-modo					0				9		. . .					0.....	531
03-ACAA-b	lori					0				9		. . .					0.....	534
03-ACAA-c	wira					0				9		. . .					0.....	535
03-ACAA-d	mittu			0	0	0	0.00	0		9		. . .					0.....	536
03-ACAB	NYAMUSA-MOLO cluster	1	2	10,664	16,729		9.89	34	A	4		. . .					0.....	537
03-ACAB-a	nyamusa					0				4		. . .					0.....	538
03-ACAB-b	molo	1	2	10,664	16,729	0	9.89	34	A	4		. . .					0.....	539
03-ACB	**GBERI net**	1	1	1,035	1,624		10.05	32	A	4		. . .					0.....	540
03-ACBA	GBERI cluster	1	1	1,035	1,624		10.05	32	A	4		. . .					0.....	541
03-ACBA-a	mo'da	1	1	1,035	1,624	0	10.05	32	A	4		. . .					0.....	542
03-ACC	**MOROKODO net**	1	1	5,871	9,211		10.00	35	A	2		. . .					0.....	543
03-ACCA	MOROKODO cluster	1	1	5,871	9,211		10.00	35	A	2		. . .					0.....	544
03-ACCA-a	morokodo	1	1	5,871	9,211	0	10.00	35	A	2		. . .					0.....	545
03-ACCA-b	biti					0				2		. . .					0.....	546
03-ACCA-c	mädu					0				2		. . .					0.....	547
03-AD	BELI chain	1	2	32,545	51,057		16.00	44	A	22		P..					0.....	548
03-ADA	**BELI net**	1	2	32,545	51,057		16.00	44	A	22		P..					0.....	549
03-ADAA	JUR-BELI cluster	1	2	32,545	51,057		16.00	44	A	22		P..					0.....	550
03-ADAA-a	jur-beli	1	2	32,545	51,057	0	16.00	44	A	22	Jur Modo	P..	1986-1993				0.....	551
03-ADAA-b	wulu					0				22		p..					0.....	552
03-ADAA-c	bahri-girinti					0				22		p..					0.....	553
03-ADAA-d	sopi					0				22		p..					0.....	554
03-AE	KRESH chain	2	2	41,351	67,505		9.67	37	A	4		. . .					0.....	555
03-AEA	**KRESH net**	2	2	41,351	67,505		9.67	37	A	4		. . .					0.....	556

Continued overleaf

Table 9-13 continued

Code 1	REFERENCE NAME Autoglossonym 2	Coun 3	Peo 4	Mother-tongue speakers in 2000 5	in 2025 6	Media radio 7	CHURCH AC% 8	E% 9	Wld 10	Tr 11	Biblioglossonym 12	SCRIPTURES Print 13-15	P-activity 16	N-activity 17	B-activity 18	J-year 19	Jayuh 20-24	Ref 25
03-AEAA	KPARA cluster	2	2	21,351	33,505		14.05	49	A	4		...					0....	557
03-AEAA-a	dongo					0				4		...					0....	558
03-AEAA-b	naka					0				4		...					0....	559
03-AEAA-c	gbaya-ngbongbo					0				4		...					0....	560
03-AEAA-d	gbaya-ndogo					0				4		...					0....	561
03-AEAA-e	gbaya-gboko					0				4		...					0....	562
03-AEAA-f	gbaya-dara					0				4		...					0....	563
03-AEAA-g	aja					0				4		...					0....	564
03-AEAB	WORO cluster	1	1	20,000	34,000		5.00	24	A	0		...					0....	565
03-AEAB-a	orlo	1	1	20,000	34,000	0	5.00	24	A	0		...					0....	566
03-B	**MORU-MANGBETU set**	3	36	5,578,962	11,201,594		84.67	98	C	62		PNB					1As..	567
03-BA	MORU-MADI chain	3	36	5,578,962	11,201,594		84.67	98	C	62		PNB					1As..	568
03-BAA	**MORU-MADI net**	3	19	2,509,602	4,971,778		83.39	97	C	62		PNB					1As..	569
03-BAAA	MORU cluster	3	3	122,592	201,184		60.00	100	C	41		PN.					1.s..	570
03-BAAA-a	kala-moru	3	3	122,592	201,184	0	60.00	100	C	41	Moru	PN.	1928-1963	1951-1996			1.s..	571
03-BAAA-b	andri					0				41		pn.					1.s..	576
03-BAAA-c	bälibä					0				41		pn.					1.s..	577
03-BAAA-d	kala-ägi					0				41		pn.					1.s..	578
03-BAAA-e	wadi-ti					0				41		pn.					1.s..	579
03-BAAB	AVUKAYA cluster	2	2	59,939	111,270		63.13	100	C	22		P..					0....	580
03-BAAB-a	avokaya	2	2	59,939	111,270	0	63.13	100	C	22	Avokaya	P..	1986-1990				0....	581
03-BAAB-b	odzila-ti					0				22		p..					0....	582
03-BAAB-c	ajiga-ti					0				22		p..					0....	583
03-BAAC	LOGO cluster	2	2	320,773	648,017		90.36	100	C	24		P..					0....	584
03-BAAC-a	logo-ti	2	2	320,773	648,017	0	90.36	100	C	24	Logo	P..	1924-1927				0....	585
03-BAAC-b	bäri-ti					0				24		p..					0....	594
03-BAAD	KELIKO cluster	2	3	82,194	161,351		57.44	86	B	12	Omi	...					0....	595
03-BAAD-a	keliko-madi	2	3	82,194	161,351	0	57.44	86	B	12	Kaliko	...					0....	596
03-BAAD-b	kaliko					0				12		...					0....	599
03-BAAE	ANDRELEBA cluster	1	1	798,616	1,629,443		91.80	100	C	32		...					1....	602
03-BAAE-a	andre-leba-ti	1	1	798,616	1,629,443	0	91.80	100	C	32		...				1981	1....	603
03-BAAE-b	kulu-ti					0				32		...					1....	606
03-BAAF	URULEBA cluster	3	3	699,878	1,407,972		86.73	99	C	62		PNB					1As..	607
03-BAAF-a	uru-leba-ti	3	3	699,878	1,407,972	1	86.73	99	C	62	Lugbara	PNB	1922-1964	1936-1978	1966	1981	1As..	608
03-BAAG	MADI-OKOLLO cluster	1	1	20,000	34,000		30.00	65	B	4		...					0....	617
03-BAAG-a	okollo	1	1	20,000	34,000	0	30.00	65	B	4		...					0....	618
03-BAAH	MADI-OGOKO cluster	1	1	30,000	51,000		30.00	65	B	0		...					0....	619
03-BAAH-a	ogoko	1	1	30,000	51,000	0	30.00	65	B	0		...					0....	620
03-BAAI	MADI-MOYO cluster	3	3	304,776	608,687		89.14	100	C	41		PN.					1....	621
03-BAAI-a	moyo	3	3	304,776	608,687	1	89.14	100	C	41	Madi	PN.	1935-1938	1977			1....	622
03-BAAJ	MADI-OYUWI cluster	1	1	30,000	51,000		20.00	50	B	0		...					0....	623
03-BAAJ-a	oyuwi	1	1	30,000	51,000	0	20.00	50	B	0		...					0....	624
03-BAAK	NORTHEAST MADI cluster	1	1	25,000	42,500		20.00	50	B	0		...					0....	625
03-BAAK-a	lokai					0				0		...					0....	626
03-BAAK-b	pandikeri					0				0		...					0....	627
03-BAAK-c	burulo					0				0		...					0....	628
03-BAAL	MADI-OLUBO cluster	2	2	15,834	25,354		40.68	77	B	2		...					0....	629
03-BAAL-a	olubo-ti	2	2	15,834	25,354	0	40.68	77	B	2		...					0....	630
03-BAB	**MANGBETU-MANGBELE net**	2	5	1,060,336	2,151,529		90.46	99	C	20		...					0....	631
03-BABA	MANGBETU-MANGBELE cluster	2	5	1,060,336	2,151,529		90.46	99	C	20		...					0....	632
03-BABA-a	na-mangbetu-ti	2	2	1,009,147	2,047,684	0	92.33	100	C	20	Mangbetu	...					0....	633
03-BABA-b	na-meje-ti					0				20		...					0....	634
03-BABA-c	na-makere-ti					0				20		...					0....	639
03-BABA-d	na-ma-popoi-ti					0				20		...					0....	640
03-BABA-e	na-aberu-ti					0				20		...					0....	641
03-BABA-f	na-mabisanga					0				20		...					0....	642
03-BABA-g	mangbele	1	1	10,331	20,958	0	60.00	92	C	20		...					0....	643
03-BABA-h	na-majuu					0				20		...					0....	646
03-BABA-i	odya-lombi-to	1	1	15,031	30,493	0	55.00	90	B	20		...					0....	647
03-BABA-j	asua-ti	1	1	25,827	52,394	0	50.00	82	B	20		...					0....	648
03-BAC	**MANGBUTU-EFE net**	2	8	1,076,350	2,185,985		80.12	98	C	41		PN.					0....	649
03-BACA	MAMVU-EFE cluster	1	5	213,818	433,758		50.53	90	B	24		P..					0....	650
03-BACA-a	amengi	1	1	28,126	57,057	0	55.00	94	B	24		p..					0....	651
03-BACA-b	mamvu	1	1	84,383	171,181	0	55.00	94	B	24	Mamvu	P..	1931				0....	654
03-BACA-c	ba-lese					0				24		p..					0....	662
03-BACA-d	lese-otsodu	1	2	96,144	195,041	0	46.94	87	B	24	Lese	p..					0....	663
03-BACA-e	mvu'ba	1	1	5,165	10,479	0	20.00	54	B	24		p..					0....	669
03-BACA-f	efe-e					0				24		p..					0....	672
03-BACB	MANGBUTU cluster	1	1	21,096	42,795		50.00	87	B	4		...					0....	673
03-BACB-a	mangbutu-li	1	1	21,096	42,795	0	50.00	87	B	4		...					0....	674
03-BACB-b	awimeri					0				4		...					0....	678
03-BACB-c	angwe					0				4		...					0....	679
03-BACB-d	makutana					0				4		...					0....	680
03-BACB-e	andinai					0				4		...					0....	681
03-BACB-f	bamodo					0				4		...					0....	682
03-BACC	NDO cluster	2	2	841,436	1,709,432		88.39	100	C	41		PN.					0....	683
03-BACC-a	ke'bu-tu	2	2	841,436	1,709,432	0	88.39	100	C	41	Kebu*	PN.	1964	1994			0....	684
03-BACC-b	avari-tu					0				41		pn.					0....	685
03-BACC-c	membi					0				41		pn.					0....	686
03-BAD	**LENDU net**	2	4	932,674	1,892,302		86.82	99	C	41		PN.					0.s..	687
03-BADA	NORTH LENDU cluster	2	2	877,342	1,780,053		89.26	100	C	41		PN.					0.s..	688
03-BADA-a	jo-dha					1				41							0.s..	689
03-BADA-b	bale-dha	2	2	877,342	1,780,053	1	89.26	100	C	41	Lendu	PN.	1926-1985	1936-1989			0.s..	690
03-BADA-c	go-dha					1				41		pn.					0.s..	691
03-BADA-d	ta-dha					1				41		pn.					0.s..	692
03-BADA-e	pi-dha					1				41		pn.					0.s..	693
03-BADA-f	ke-dha					1				41		pn.					0.s..	694
03-BADA-g	ddra-lo					1				41		pn.					0.s..	695
03-BADA-h	njaw-lo					1				41		pn.					0.s..	696
03-BADB	SOUTH LENDU cluster	1	2	55,332	112,249		48.13	83	B	4		...					0....	697
03-BADB-a	n-dru-na	1	1	10,331	20,958	0	40.00	72	B	4		...					0....	698
03-BADB-b	ma-bendi	1	1	45,001	91,291	0	50.00	86	B	4		...					0....	703
04	**NILOTIC zone**	6	98	20,810,161	34,390,731		68.16	91	C	63		PNB					4As..	704
04-A	**WEST NILOTIC set**	6	35	12,322,484	20,474,698		75.52	94	C	62		PNB					4As..	705

Continued opposite

Table 9-13 continued

Code 1	REFERENCE NAME / Autoglossonym 2	Coun 3	Peo 4	Mother-tongue speakers in 2000 5	in 2025 6	Media radio 7	AC% 8	E% 9	Wld 10	Tr 11	Biblioglossonym 12	Print 13-15	P-activity 16	N-activity 17	B-activity 18	J-year 19	Jayuh 20-24	Ref 25
04-AA	DINKA-NUER chain	2	11	3,460,550	5,478,405		45.52	84	B	43		PN.					4As..	706
04-AAA	**DINKA net**	1	6	1,895,765	2,974,121		66.87	98	C	43		PN.					4As..	707
04-AAAA	NORTHEAST JIANG cluster	1	1	414,891	650,891		72.50	100	C	42		PN.					4A...	708
04-AAAA-a	padang	1	1	414,891	650,891	0	72.50	100	C	42	Dinka: Padang*	PN.	1926-1943	1952		1990	4A...	709
04-AAAA-b	ngok									42		pn.					1c...	713
04-AAAA-c	thoi-luac					0				42		pn.					1c...	714
04-AAAA-d	rut					0				42		pn.					1c...	717
04-AAAB	NORTH JIANG cluster	1	1	103,724	162,725		58.00	93	B	4		...					0....	718
04-AAAB-a	ruweng	1	1	103,724	162,725	0	58.00	93	B	4		...					0....	719
04-AAAC	WEST JIANG cluster	1	1	665,683	1,044,340		68.00	100	C	0		...					0....	726
04-AAAC-a	malual-tuic					0				0		...					0....	727
04-AAAC-b	palioupiny					0				0		...					0....	731
04-AAAC-c	rek	1	1	665,683	1,044,340	0	68.00	100	C	0		...					0....	736
04-AAAD	SOUTH JIANG cluster	1	2	357,590	560,995		55.71	95	B	32	Dinka, Southwestern	P..					1....	745
04-AAAD-a	gok					0				32		p..					1....	746
04-AAAD-b	agar-ciec	1	2	357,590	560,995		55.71	95	B	32		P..				1996	1....	747
04-AAAD-c	aliap					0				32		p..					1....	750
04-AAAE	EAST JIANG cluster	1	1	353,877	555,170		72.00	100	C	43		PN.					1As..	753
04-AAAE-a	bor-twi	1	1	353,877	555,170	0	72.00	100	C	43	Dinka, Southeastern	PN.	1915-1936	1940			1As..	754
04-AAAE-b	nyarueng-ghol					0				43		pn.					1cs..	758
04-AAB	**NUER-ATWOT net**	2	5	1,564,785	2,504,284		19.67	67	B	42		PN.					4A...	761
04-AABA	NAATH cluster	2	4	1,513,193	2,423,345		20.20	69	B	42		PN.					4A...	762
04-AABA-a	thiang					0				42		pn.					1c...	763
04-AABA-b	gawaar					0				42		pn.					1c...	769
04-AABA-c	door-nyuong	1	1	955,777	1,499,445		21.00	72	B	42	Nuer: Eastern*	PN.	1968	1968		1991	4A...	770
04-AABA-d	dar-cieng	2	3	557,416	923,900		18.83	63	B	42	Nuer: Western	Pn.	1935				1A...	773
04-AABA-e	jagei					0				42		pn.					1c...	776
04-AABA-f	leek-laak					0				42		pn.					1c...	777
04-AABA-g	bul					0				42		pn.					1c...	780
04-AABA-h	West jikany					0				42		pn.					1c...	781
04-AABA-i	lou					0				42		pn.					1c...	782
04-AABA-j	East jikany					0				42		pn.					1c...	783
04-AABB	ATUOT cluster	1	1	51,592	80,939		4.00	28	A	4		...					0....	784
04-AABB-a	thok-cieng	1	1	51,592	80,939	0	4.00	28	A	4		...					0....	785
04-AB	NORTH LWO chain	2	7	498,942	791,982		30.59	75	B	42		PN.					4As..	788
04-ABA	**COLO-ANYWAA net**	2	4	385,780	614,058		32.82	79	B	42		PN.					4As..	789
04-ABAA	DHO-COLO cluster	1	1	258,875	406,130		45.00	95	B	41	Shilluk	PN.	1911-1961	1977		1996	4.s..	790
04-ABAA-a	North colo					0				41		pn.					1.s..	791
04-ABAA-b	colo-sobat					0				41		pn.					1.s..	792
04-ABAB	DHO-ANYWAA cluster	2	2	91,202	151,916		9.16	52	B	42		PN.					0As..	793
04-ABAB-a	adongo	2	2	91,202	151,916	0	9.16	52	B	42	Anuak	PN.	1956-1993	1962-1965			0As..	794
04-ABAB-b	ciro					0				42		pn.					0cs..	795
04-ABAB-c	lul					0				42		pn.					0cs..	796
04-ABAB-d	openo					0				42		pn.					0cs..	797
04-ABAC	PARI cluster	1	1	35,703	56,012		5.00	36	A	12		...					0....	798
04-ABAC-a	lumi-pari	1	1	35,703	56,012	0	5.00	36	A	12	Lokoro	...					0....	799
04-ABB	**LWO-THURI net**	1	2	101,688	159,923		24.44	64	B	22		P..					0....	800
04-ABBA	SOUTH THURI-COLO cluster	1	1	18,806	29,503		10.00	43	A	5		...					0....	801
04-ABBA-a	dhe-thuri	1	1	18,806	29,503	0	10.00	43	A	5		...					0....	802
04-ABBA-b	dhe-bodho					0				5		...					0....	803
04-ABBA-c	dhe-colo					0				5		...					0....	804
04-ABBB	MANANGEER cluster	1	1	3,000	5,100		20.00	50	B	0		...					0....	805
04-ABBB-a	manangeer	1	1	3,000	5,100	0	20.00	50	B	0		...					0....	806
04-ABBC	LWO cluster	1	1	79,882	125,320		28.00	69	B	22		P..					0....	807
04-ABBC-a	dhe-lwo	1	1	79,882	125,320	0	28.00	69	B	22	Luwo	P..	1954-1995				0....	808
04-ABC	**BOR net**	1	1	11,474	18,001		10.00	39	A	12		...					0....	809
04-ABCA	BOR cluster	1	1	11,474	18,001		10.00	39	A	12		...					0....	810
04-ABCA-a	dhe-bor	1	1	11,474	18,001	0	10.00	39	A	12	Belanda Bor	...					0....	811
04-AC	SOUTH LWO chain	5	13	8,210,427	13,961,162		92.24	100	C	62		PNB					4As..	812
04-ACA	**DHO-ALUR net**	2	2	1,161,902	2,362,436		93.57	100	C	62		PNB					0.s..	813
04-ACAA	ALUUR cluster	2	2	1,161,902	2,362,436		93.57	100	C	62		PNB					0.s..	814
04-ACAA-a	dho-aluur	2	2	1,161,902	2,362,436	5	93.57	100	C	62	Alur	PNB	1921-1985	1933-1979	1936-1955		0.s..	815
04-ACB	**ACHOLI net**	2	4	2,195,154	4,457,529		93.02	100	C	61		PNB					4....	820
04-ACBA	ACHOLI-LANGO cluster	2	3	2,063,242	4,188,384		94.11	100	C	61		PNB					4....	821
04-ACBA-a	Standard acholi-lango					1				61		pnb					1....	822
04-ACBA-b	acholi	2	2	919,873	1,855,530	1	94.61	100	C	61	Acholi	PNB	1905-1962	1933	1986		4....	823
04-ACBA-c	log-me-labwor					1				61		pnb					1....	826
04-ACBA-d	dho-pa-lwo					1				61		pnb					1....	827
04-ACBA-e	nyakwai					1				61		pnb					1....	828
04-ACBA-f	leb-lango	1	1	1,143,369	2,332,854	1	93.70	100	C	61	Lango	PNB	1967	1974	1979		1....	829
04-ACBB	KUMAM cluster	1	1	131,912	269,145		76.00	100	C	20		...					0....	830
04-ACBB-a	kumam	1	1	131,912	269,145	1	76.00	100	C	20		...					0....	831
04-ACC	**LUO net**	3	7	4,853,371	7,141,197		91.57	100	C	61		PNB					4As..	832
04-ACCA	LUO-PADHOLA cluster	3	7	4,853,371	7,141,197		91.57	100	C	61		PNB					4As..	833
04-ACCA-a	dho-p-adhola	2	2	375,530	746,589	4	93.28	100	C	61	Dhopadhola*	Pnb	1977-1979			1995	4cs..	834
04-ACCA-b	dho-luo	3	5	4,477,841	6,394,608	4	91.43	100	C	61	Dholuo*	PNB	1911-1964	1926	1953-1977	1983	2As..	835
04-AD	NORTH BURUN chain	1	1	23,000	39,100		4.61	23	A	2		...					0....	836
04-ADA	**NORTH BURUN net**	1	1	23,000	39,100		4.61	23	A	2		...					0....	837
04-ADAA	RAGREIG cluster	1	1	3,000	5,100		2.00	18	A	0		...					0....	838
04-ADAA-a	ragreig	1	1	3,000	5,100	0	2.00	18	A	0		...					0....	839
04-ADAB	BARUN cluster	1	1	20,000	34,000		5.00	24	A	2		...					0....	840
04-ADAB-a	mughaja					0				2		...					0....	841
04-ADAB-b	abuldugu					0				2		...					0....	842
04-ADAB-c	mufwa					0				2		...					0....	843
04-ADAB-d	tarak					0				2		...					0....	844
04-ADAB-e	maiak					0				2		...					0....	845
04-AE	SOUTH BURUN chain	2	4	129,565	204,049		2.32	30	A	41		PN.					0.s..	846
04-AEA	**SOUTH BURUN net**	2	4	129,565	204,049		2.32	30	A	41		PN.					0.s..	847

Continued overleaf

Table 9-13 continued

Code 1	REFERENCE NAME / Autoglossonym 2	Coun 3	Peo 4	Mother-tongue speakers in 2000 5	in 2025 6	Media radio 7	CHURCH AC% 8	E% 9	Wld 10	Tr 11	Biblioglossonym 12	SCRIPTURES Print 13-15	P-activity 16	N-activity 17	B-activity 18	J-year 19	Jayuh 20-24	Ref 25
04-AEAA	MABAAN cluster	2	4	129,565	204,049		2.32	30	A	41		PN.					0.s..	848
04-AEAA-a	gerawi					0				41		pn.					0.s..	849
04-AEAA-b	begu					0				41		pn.					0.s..	850
04-AEAA-c	jumjum	1	1	47,815	75,013	0	2.00	32	A	41		pn.					0.s..	851
04-AEAA-d	wadega					0				41		pn.					0.s..	854
04-AEAA-e	mabaan	2	3	81,750	129,036	0	2.51	28	A	41	Mabaan	PN.	1947	1988			0.s..	855
04-B	**EAST NILOTIC set**	6	42	5,442,834	9,395,278		60.30	90	C	62		PNB					4As..	856
04-BA	BARIC chain	3	9	878,517	1,511,167		76.78	99	C	61		PNB					1.s..	857
04-BAA	**BARI-KAKWA net**	3	9	878,517	1,511,167		76.78	99	C	61		PNB					1.s..	858
04-BAAA	MUNDARI cluster	1	1	110,008	172,584		60.00	96	C	4		...					0....	859
04-BAAA-a	kutuk-na-mundari	1	1	110,008	172,584	0	60.00	96	C	4		...					0....	860
04-BAAB	BARI cluster	3	4	542,178	909,052		85.17	100	C	61		PNB					1.s..	861
04-BAAB-a	kutuk-na-bari	3	3	502,827	847,317	0	87.14	100	C	61	Bari	PNB	1927-1964	1954	1979		1.s..	862
04-BAAB-b	nyangbara					0				61		pnb					1.s..	863
04-BAAB-c	pojulu					0				61		pnb					1.s..	866
04-BAAB-d	nyepu					0				61		pnb					1.s..	869
04-BAAB-e	kutuk-na-kuku	1	1	39,351	61,735	0	60.00	100	C	61		pnb					1.s..	870
04-BAAB-f	ligo					0				61		pnb					1.s..	871
04-BAAC	KAKWA cluster	3	4	226,331	429,531		64.83	100	C	61		PNB					0....	872
04-BAAC-a	kakwa	3	4	226,331	429,531	1	64.83	100	C	61	Kakwa*	PNB	1930-1967	1974	1983		0....	873
04-BB	LOTUHO-NAPORE chain	1	5	405,610	637,643		31.35	72	B	42		PN.					0....	877
04-BBA	**KORIUK net**	1	1	48,065	76,718		20.00	55	B	5		...					0....	878
04-BBAA	KORIUK cluster	1	1	38,065	59,718		20.00	56	B	5		...					0....	879
04-BBAA-a	o-ghutuk-no-khoriuk					0				5		...					0....	880
04-BBAB	GHORIUK cluster	1	1	10,000	17,000		20.00	50	B	0		...					0....	884
04-BBAB-a	netuk-on-o-ghoriuk	1	1	10,000	17,000	0	20.00	50	B	0		...					0....	885
04-BBB	**LOTUHO net**	1	1	273,670	429,341		38.00	83	B	42		PN.					0....	886
04-BBBA	LOTUHO cluster	1	1	273,670	429,341		38.00	83	B	42		PN.					0....	887
04-BBBA-a	o-tuho	1	1	273,670	429,341	0	38.00	83	B	42	Lotuho	PN.	1954	1969			0....	888
04-BBBA-b	lowudo					0				42		pn.					0....	889
04-BBBA-c	logotok					0				42		pn.					0....	890
04-BBC	**LAFIT net**	1	1	52,474	82,322		20.00	53	B	4		...					0....	891
04-BBCA	LAFIT cluster	1	1	52,474	82,322		20.00	53	B	4		...					0....	892
04-BBCA-a	rori-ne-lopit	1	1	52,474	82,322	0	20.00	53	B	4		...					0....	893
04-BBCA-b	lomya					0				4		...					0....	894
04-BBD	**DONGOTONO net**	1	1	5,898	9,253		29.99	61	B	4		...					0....	895
04-BBDA	DONGOTONO cluster	1	1	5,898	9,253		29.99	61	B	4		...					0....	896
04-BBDA-a	ibalit-na-dongotono	1	1	5,898	9,253	0	29.99	61	B	4		...					0....	897
04-BBDA-b	lorwama					0				4		...					0....	898
04-BBDA-c	lokathan					0				4		...					0....	899
04-BBE	**LOGIRI net**	1	1	25,503	40,009		5.00	29	A	4		...					0....	900
04-BBEA	LOGIRI cluster	1	1	25,503	40,009		5.00	29	A	4		...					0....	901
04-BBEA-a	North lango	1	1	25,503	40,009	0	5.00	29	A	4		...					0....	902
04-BBEA-b	logiri-lolibai					0				4		...					0....	905
04-BBEA-c	logir					0				4		...					0....	908
04-BC	MAA-ONGAMO chain	2	13	1,427,089	2,162,126		26.84	82	B	61		PNB					4As..	909
04-BCA	**MAA net**	2	12	1,423,000	2,155,060		26.90	82	B	61		PNB					4As..	910
04-BCAA	MAASAI cluster	2	7	1,225,306	1,880,631		29.19	87	B	61		PNB					4As..	911
04-BCAA-a	enkutuk-oo-l-maasai	2	7	1,225,306	1,880,631	4	29.19	87	B	61	Maasai	PNB	1905-1961	1923-1967	1991	1981	4As..	912
04-BCAB	SAMPUR-CHAMUS cluster	1	5	197,694	274,429		12.69	52	B	20		...					0....	929
04-BCAB-a	sampur	1	4	179,646	249,375	1	12.76	52	B	20		...					0....	930
04-BCAB-b	chamus	1	1	18,048	25,054	1	12.00	52	B	20		...					0....	931
04-BCB	**ONGAMO net**	1	1	4,089	7,066		4.99	33	A	6		...					0....	932
04-BCBA	NGASA cluster	1	1	4,089	7,066		4.99	33	A	6		...					0....	933
04-BCBA-a	ngasa	1	1	4,089	7,066	0	4.99	33	A	6		...					0....	934
04-BD	TESO-TURKANA chain	4	15	2,731,618	5,084,342		76.78	93	C	62		PNB					3As..	935
04-BDA	**TESO-TURKANA net**	4	15	2,731,618	5,084,342		76.78	93	C	62		PNB					3As..	936
04-BDAA	TOPOSA cluster	4	6	230,918	388,598		65.56	85	C	20		...					0....	937
04-BDAA-a	North jiye					1				20		...					0....	938
04-BDAA-b	akero-a-toposa	3	3	182,727	302,985	1	81.54	100	C	20		...					0....	939
04-BDAA-c	aku-tuk-angi-nyangatom	3	3	48,191	85,613	1	5.00	31	A	20		...					0....	942
04-BDAA-d	puma					1				20		...					0....	943
04-BDAB	TURKANA cluster	3	3	402,018	570,006		18.81	64	B	41		PN.					1As..	944
04-BDAB-a	nga-turkana	3	3	402,018	570,006	0	18.81	64	B	41	Turkana	PN.	1972-1994	1986		1981	1As..	945
04-BDAC	SOUTH LOTUHO cluster	1	1	4,356	8,887		20.00	49	A	2		...					0....	948
04-BDAC-a	ketebo					0				2		...					0....	949
04-BDAC-b	o-rom					0				2		...					0....	950
04-BDAC-c	pore					0				2		...					0....	951
04-BDAC-d	mening	1	1	4,356	8,887	0	20.00	49	A	2		...					0....	952
04-BDAD	KARIMOJONG cluster	1	2	466,335	951,480		70.56	100	C	41		PN.					0....	953
04-BDAD-a	i-dodotho					1				41		pn.					0....	954
04-BDAD-b	South jiye	1	1	75,571	154,191	1	74.00	100	C	41		pn.					0....	955
04-BDAD-c	a-karimojong	1	1	390,764	797,289	1	69.90	100	C	41	Karimojong*	PN.	1932-1967	1974-1996			0....	956
04-BDAE	TESO cluster	2	3	1,627,991	3,165,371		94.62	100	C	62		PNB					3.s..	957
04-BDAE-a	a-teso	2	3	1,627,991	3,165,371	1	94.62	100	C	62	Ateso*	PNB	1910-1960	1930-1966	1961	1982	3.s..	958
04-BDAE-b	tesyo					1				62		pnb					1.s..	961
04-C	**SOUTH NILOTIC set**	3	21	3,044,843	4,520,755		52.43	83	B	63		PNB					4As..	964
04-CA	SOUTH NILOTIC chain	3	21	3,044,843	4,520,755		52.43	83	B	63		PNB					4As..	965
04-CAA	**KALENJIN net**	3	17	2,572,163	3,703,982		61.58	93	C	63		PNB					4As..	966
04-CAAA	POKOT cluster	2	2	357,100	539,187		21.57	64	B	41		PN.					0.s..	967
04-CAAA-a	ngal-ap-pokot	2	2	357,100	539,187	0	21.57	64	B	41	Pokoot	PN.	1936-1991	1967-1996			0.s..	968
04-CAAA-b	ngi-kadama					0				41		pn.					0.s..	971
04-CAAB	MARAKWET cluster	1	2	100,529	139,549		43.82	89	B	12		...					0....	972
04-CAAB-a	markwet					1				12		...					0....	973
04-CAAB-b	endo	1	1	63,169	87,688	1	44.30	89	B	12	Endo	...					0....	976
04-CAAB-c	sambirir					1				12		...					0....	977

Continued opposite

Table 9-13 continued

Code 1	REFERENCE NAME / Autoglossonym 2	Coun 3	Peo 4	Mother-tongue speakers in 2000 5	in 2025 6	Media radio 7	AC% 8	E% 9	Wld 10	Tr 11	Biblioglossonym 12	Print 13-15	P–activity 16	N–activity 17	B–activity 18	J-year 19	Jayuh 20-24	Ref 25
04-CAAB-d	talai					1				12		...					0....	978
04-CAAB-e	North tugen					1				12							0....	979
04-CAAC	SABINY cluster	2	2	284,050	476,958		82.85	100	C	41		PN.					1....	980
04-CAAC-a	ku-p-sabiny	2	2	284,050	476,958	1	82.85	100	C	41	Kupsapiny*	PN.	1975-1993	1996			1....	981
04-CAAC-b	mbai					1				41		pn.					1....	982
04-CAAC-c	ki-p-sorai					1				41		pn.					1....	983
04-CAAC-d	pok					1				41		pn.					1....	984
04-CAAC-e	nga-lek-ap-I-kony					1				41		pn.					1....	985
04-CAAC-f	ngoma					1				41		pn.					1....	986
04-CAAD	NANDI-KIPSIGIS cluster	1	6	1,772,813	2,460,927		69.15	100	C	63		PNB					4As..	987
04-CAAD-a	Standard kalenjin	1	1	30,080	41,756	1	53.70	100	B	63	Kalenjin	PNB	1958	1968	1969	1985	4As..	988
04-CAAD-b	kalenjin-tugen	1	1	200,639	278,517	1	56.20	100	B	63	Kalenjin	PNB	1912-1966	1933-1968	1939-1969		1cs..	989
04-CAAD-c	keyyo	1	1	200,588	278,446	1	68.40	100	C	63		pnb					1cs..	990
04-CAAD-d	ngalek-ap-naandi	1	1	473,793	657,694	1	74.30	100	C	63	Nandi	PNB	1926	1933	1939		1cs..	991
04-CAAD-e	terik	1	1	15,040	20,878	1	50.00	100	B	63		pnb					1cs..	994
04-CAAD-f	ngalek-ap-kipsigiis	1	1	852,673	1,183,636	1	70.40	100	C	63	Kipsigis	PNb	1912	1953			1cs..	995
04-CAAD-g	cherangany					1				63		pnb					1cs..	996
04-CAAE	OKIEK cluster	2	5	57,671	87,361		2.83	38	A	5		...					0....	997
04-CAAE-a	sogoo					1				5		...					0....	998
04-CAAE-b	suiei					1				5		...					0....	999
04-CAAE-c	l-aramanik	1	1	5,051	8,728	1	2.00	32	A	5		...					0....	1000
04-CAAE-d	kisankasa	1	3	16,448	28,421	1	2.70	32	A	5		...					0....	1001
04-CAAE-e	mediak					1				5		...					0....	1002
04-CAAE-f	mosiro					1				5		...					0....	1003
04-CAB	**SAWASKA net**	1	1	90	125		4.44	30	A	5		...					0....	1004
04-CABA	OMOTIK cluster	1	1	90	125		4.44	30	A	5		...					1005
04-CABA-a	omotik	1	1	90	125	0	4.44	30	A	5		...					0....	1006
04-CAC	**DATOG net**	1	3	472,590	816,648		2.65	32	A	20		...					0....	1007
04-CACA	DATOG cluster	1	3	472,590	816,648		2.65	32	A	20	Datooga	...					0....	1008
04-CACA-a	kangara					0				20		...					0....	1009
04-CACA-b	bura-dik					0				20		...					0....	1010
04-CACA-c	roti-genk					0				20		...					0....	1011
04-CACA-d	bianjit					0				20		...					0....	1012
04-CACA-e	darora-jek					0				20		...					0....	1013
04-CACA-f	bajut					0				20		...					0....	1014
04-CACA-g	gisam-jank	1	1	110,606	191,130	0	3.00	31	A	20		...					0....	1015
04-CACA-h	barba-ik	1	1	194,399	335,926	0	3.00	34	A	20		...					0....	1016
04-CACA-i	isim-jeg					0				20		...					0....	1017
04-CACA-j	daragwa-jek					0				20		...					0....	1018
04-CACA-k	reimo-jik					0				20		...					0....	1019
04-CACA-l	manga-t'k					0				20		...					0....	1020
04-CACA-m	ghumbi-ek					0				20		...					0....	1021
04-CACA-n	bisiyed					0				20		...					0....	1022
05	**NILO-SAHELIC zone**	7	99	5,726,792	9,250,044		5.56	25	A	43		PN.					0....	1023
05-A	**MABAN set**	3	13	973,718	1,708,336		9.82	30	A	20		...					0....	1024
05-AA	MABA-RUNGA chain	3	13	973,718	1,708,336		9.82	30	A	20		...					0....	1025
05-AAA	**MABA-RUNGA net**	3	13	953,718	1,674,336		10.01	30	A	20		...					0....	1026
05-AAAA	MABA cluster	2	4	182,667	328,186		0.12	15	A	20		...					0....	1027
05-AAAA-a	bura-maba-ng	2	2	173,212	310,998	0	0.13	16	A	20	Maba	...					0....	1028
05-AAAA-b	kodoi					0				20		...					0....	1036
05-AAAA-c	uled-jemaa					0				20		...					0....	1037
05-AAAA-d	kujinga					0				20		...					0....	1038
05-AAAA-e	kondongo					0				20		...					0....	1039
05-AAAA-f	keshmere					0				20		...					0....	1040
05-AAAA-g	ab-sharin					0				20		...					0....	1041
05-AAAB	MARFA cluster	1	1	247,579	450,054		5.00	32	A	20		...					0....	1042
05-AAAB-a	marfa	1	1	247,579	450,054	0	5.00	32	A	20		...					0....	1043
05-AAAC	KARANGA cluster	1	1	120,935	219,839		50.00	80	B	20		...					0....	1046
05-AAAC-a	karanga	1	1	120,935	219,839	0	50.00	80	B	20		...					0....	1047
05-AAAC-b	mooyo					0				20		...					0....	1048
05-AAAC-c	faala					0				20		...					0....	1049
05-AAAC-d	baxa					0				20		...					0....	1050
05-AAAC-e	konyare					0				20		...					0....	1051
05-AAAD	MASALIT cluster	3	4	317,617	527,382		7.05	24	A	20		...					0....	1052
05-AAAD-a	kaana-masala	3	4	317,617	527,382	0	7.05	24	A	20	Masalit	...					0....	1053
05-AAAE	RUNGA cluster	2	2	50,226	85,807		0.00	11	A	2		...					0....	1057
05-AAAE-a	runga	2	2	50,226	85,807	0	0.00	11	A	2		...					0....	1058
05-AAAE-b	aykindang					0				2		...					0....	1059
05-AAAE-c	runga-ndele					0				2		...					0....	1060
05-AAAF	KIBEET cluster	1	1	34,694	63,068		0.00	9	A	2		...					0....	1061
05-AAAF-a	muro					0				2		...					0....	1062
05-AAAF-b	dagel					0				2		...					0....	1063
05-AAAF-c	kaben-tang					0				2		...					0....	1064
05-AAB	**MIGE net**	1	1	20,000	34,000		1.00	16	A	0		...					0....	1065
05-AABA	MIGE cluster	1	1	20,000	34,000		1.00	16	A	0		...					0....	1066
05-AABA-a	mige	1	1	20,000	34,000	0	1.00	16	A	0		...					0....	1067
05-B	**MIMI set**	1	1	79,864	145,179		0.10	18	A	2		...					0....	1068
05-BA	MIMI chain	1	1	79,864	145,179		0.10	18	A	2		...					0....	1069
05-BAA	**MIMI net**	1	1	79,864	145,179		0.10	18	A	2		...					0....	1070
05-BAAA	MIMI cluster	1	1	79,864	145,179		0.10	18	A	2		...					0....	1071
05-BAAA-a	mimi	1	1	79,864	145,179	0	0.10	18	A	2		...					0....	1072
05-C	**FUR set**	3	7	926,757	1,497,092		6.57	25	A	4		...					0....	1073
05-CA	FUR chain	3	7	926,757	1,497,092		6.57	25	A	4		...					0....	1074
05-CAA	**FUR net**	3	5	811,043	1,305,635		7.51	28	A	2		...					0....	1075
05-CAAA	FOR cluster	3	5	811,043	1,305,635		7.51	28	A	2		...					0....	1076
05-CAAA-a	bele-for	3	4	809,445	1,302,731	5	7.53	28	A	2		...					0....	1077
05-CAB	**ANDANG net**	2	2	115,714	191,457		0.00	6	A	4		...					0....	1078
05-CABA	ANDANG cluster	2	2	115,714	191,457		0.00	6	A	4		...					0....	1079
05-CABA-a	simi-andang-ti	2	2	115,714	191,457	0	0.00	6	A	4		...					0....	1080

Continued overleaf

Table 9-13 continued

Code 1	REFERENCE NAME / Autoglossonym 2	Coun 3	Peo 4	Mother-tongue speakers in 2000 5	in 2025 6	Media radio 7	AC% 8	E% 9	Wld 10	Tr 11	Biblioglossonym 12	Print 13-15	P-activity 16	N-activity 17	B-activity 18	J-year 19	Jayuh 20-24	Ref 25
05-D	**TAMA-MARARIT set**	2	8	353,047	608,471		0.00	11	A	20		...					0....	1083
05-DA	TAMA-MARARIT chain	2	8	353,047	608,471		0.00	11	A	20		...					0....	1084
05-DAA	**TAMA-SUNGOR net**	2	5	223,145	377,493		0.00	10	A	20		...					0....	1085
05-DAAA	TAMA-SUNGOR cluster	2	5	223,145	377,493		0.00	10	A	20		...					0....	1086
05-DAAA-a	tamo-ngo'bo	2	2	124,433	215,182	0	0.00	11	A	20		...					0....	1087
05-DAAA-b	jabaal					0				20		...					0....	1088
05-DAAA-c	haura					0				20		...					0....	1089
05-DAAA-d	shale					0				20		...					0....	1090
05-DAAA-e	a-songor-i	2	2	51,428	88,131	0	0.00	8	A	20		...					0....	1091
05-DAAA-f	bognak					0				20		...					0....	1095
05-DAAA-g	erenga	1	1	47,284	74,180		0.00	10	A	20		...					0....	1096
05-DAB	**MARARIT net**	2	3	129,902	230,978		0.00	12	A	20		...					0....	1097
05-DABA	MARARIT cluster	2	3	129,902	230,978		0.00	12	A	20		...					0....	1098
05-DABA-a	abiyi	2	2	74,684	130,602	0	0.01	15	A	20		...					0....	1099
05-DABA-b	abu-sharib	1	1	55,218	100,376	0	0.00	9	A	20		...					0....	1100
05-E	**DAJU set**	2	6	322,231	535,278		0.22	9	A	20		...					0....	1101
05-EA	SAARONG-BEKE chain	2	5	288,102	477,801		0.01	8	A	20		...					0....	1102
05-EAA	**SAARONG-BEKE net**	2	5	288,102	477,801		0.01	8	A	20		...					0....	1103
05-EAAA	SAARONG cluster	1	1	29,406	53,454		0.00	10	A	12		...					0....	1104
05-EAAA-a	saarong-ge	1	1	29,406	53,454	0	0.00	10	A	12	Daju, Dar Daju	...					0....	1105
05-EAAB	BOKORUGE cluster	2	2	121,475	209,071		0.00	10	A	2		...					0....	1106
05-EAAB-a	bokor-u-ge	2	2	121,475	209,071	0	0.00	10	A	2		...					0....	1107
05-EAAC	FINI-BAYGO cluster	1	2	137,221	215,276		0.01	5	A	20		...					0....	1110
05-EAAC-a	zalingei					0				20		...					0....	1111
05-EAAC-b	fini	1	1	135,667	212,838	0	0.00	5	A	20		...					0....	1112
05-EAAC-c	baygo					0				20		...					0....	1113
05-EAAC-d	lagowa					0				20		...					0....	1114
05-EAAC-e	nyool	1	1	1,554	2,438	0	1.03	22	A	20		...					0....	1115
05-EB	LIGURI-SHATT chain	1	1	34,129	57,477		2.00	18	A	4		...					0....	1118
05-EBA	**LIGURI net**	1	1	4,129	6,477		2.01	21	A	4		...					0....	1119
05-EBAA	LIGURI cluster	1	1	4,129	6,477		2.01	21	A	4		...					0....	1120
05-EBAA-a	liguri	1	1	4,129	6,477	0	2.01	21	A	4		...					0....	1121
05-EBAA-b	saburi					0				4		...					0....	1122
05-EBAA-c	tallau					0				4		...					0....	1123
05-EBB	**SHATT net**	1	1	30,000	51,000		2.00	18	A	0		...					0....	1124
05-EBBA	IKIJANING cluster	1	1	30,000	51,000		2.00	18	A	0		...					0....	1125
05-EBBA-a	ikijaning	1	1	30,000	51,000	0	2.00	18	A	0		...					0....	1126
05-F	**NUBIAN set**	2	14	1,780,543	2,580,934		0.03	17	A	24		P..					0....	1130
05-FA	NUBIAN chain	2	14	1,780,543	2,580,934		0.03	17	A	24		P..					0....	1131
05-FAA	**NUBIAN net**	2	2	427,741	612,044		0.04	19	A	24		P..					0....	1132
05-FAAA	NOBIIN cluster	2	2	427,741	612,044		0.04	19	A	24	Nobiin	P..	1860-1899				0....	1133
05-FAAA-a	fiadidja					0				24	Nubian: Fiadidja	P..	1860				0....	1134
05-FAAA-b	mahas					0				24		p..					0....	1135
05-FAB	**KENUZ-DONGOLA net**	2	3	1,136,136	1,628,978		0.01	19	A	24		P..					0....	1136
05-FABA	KENUZ-DONGOLA cluster	2	3	1,136,136	1,628,978		0.01	19	A	24		P..					0....	1137
05-FABA-a	kenuz	1	1	29,490	46,264	0	0.08	19	A	24	Nubian: Kunuzi*	P..	1912				0....	1138
05-FABA-b	dongola	1	1	216,540	339,713	0	0.02	18	A	24		p..					0....	1139
05-FAC	**SOUTH NUBIAN net**	1	7	63,216	99,176		0.32	13	A	4		...					0....	1140
05-FACA	SOUTH NUBIAN cluster	1	7	63,216	99,176		0.32	13	A	4		...					0....	1141
05-FACA-a	hagarat					0				4		...					0....	1142
05-FACA-b	kodin-ni-ai	1	1	11,722	18,390	0	0.00	9	A	4		...					0....	1143
05-FACA-c	thaminyi-ni-be	1	1	1,675	2,628	0	0.00	10	A	4		...					0....	1144
05-FACA-d	wunci-m-be	1	1	22,268	34,934	0	0.00	9	A	4		...					0....	1145
05-FACA-e	debri	1	1	1,362	2,137	0	0.00	9	A	4		...					0....	1148
05-FACA-f	kadero					0				4		...					0....	1149
05-FACA-g	kithoniri-she	1	1	17,980	28,207	0	1.00	19	A	4		...					0....	1150
05-FACA-h	waliri-she	1	1	840	1,319	0	2.02	21	A	4		...					0....	1151
05-FACA-i	ginuk					0				4		...					0....	1152
05-FACA-j	tabaq					0				4		...					0....	1153
05-FACA-k	warki-m-be	1	1	7,369	11,561	0	0.09	19	A	4		...					0....	1154
05-FAD	**MIDOB net**	1	1	42,533	66,727		0.00	5	A	4		...					0....	1155
05-FADA	MIDOB cluster	1	1	42,533	66,727		0.00	5	A	4		...					0....	1156
05-FADA-a	tid-n-aal	1	1	42,533	66,727	0	0.00	5	A	4		...					0....	1157
05-FAE	**BIRGID net**	1	1	110,917	174,009		0.00	5	A	0		...					0....	1160
05-FAEA	BIRGID cluster	1	1	110,917	174,009		0.00	5	A	0		...					0....	1161
05-FAEA-a	murgi	1	1	110,917	174,009	0	0.00	5	A	0		...					0....	1162
05-FAF	**HARAZA net**									0		...					0....	1163
05-FAFA	HARAZA cluster			0	0		0.00	0		0		...					0....	1164
05-FAFA-a	haraza			0	0	0	0.00	0		0		...					0....	1165
05-G	**NYIMANG-AFITTI set**	1	2	75,785	118,895		1.83	35	A	24		P..					0....	1166
05-GA	NYIMANG-AFITTI chain	1	2	75,785	118,895		1.83	35	A	24		P..					0....	1167
05-GAA	**NYIMANG net**	1	1	69,507	109,045		2.00	37	A	24		P..					0....	1168
05-GAAA	AMA cluster	1	1	69,507	109,045		2.00	37	A	24		P..					0....	1169
05-GAAA-a	ama	1	1	69,507	109,045	0	2.00	37	A	24	Ama	P..	1950				0....	1170
05-GAB	**AFITTI-DITTI net**	1	1	6,278	9,850		0.00	11	A	4		...					0....	1173
05-GABA	AFITTI-DITTI cluster	1	1	6,278	9,850		0.00	11	A	4		...					0....	1174
05-GABA-a	afitti					0				4		...					0....	1175
05-GABA-b	ditti					0				4		...					0....	1176
05-GABA-c	unietti					0				4		...					0....	1177
05-GABA-d	dinik	1	1	6,278	9,850	0	0.00	11	A	4		...					0....	1178
05-H	**TEMEIN set**	1	3	25,214	39,556		1.44	20	A	4		...					0....	1179

Continued opposite

Table 9-13 continued

Code 1	REFERENCE NAME / Autoglossonym 2	Coun 3	Peo 4	Mother-tongue speakers in 2000 / in 2025 5 / 6	Media radio 7	AC% 8	E% 9	Wld 10	Tr 11	Biblioglossonym 12	Print 13-15	P-activity 16	N-activity 17	B-activity 18	J-year 19	Jayuh 20-24	Ref 25
05-HA	TEMEIN chain	1	3	25,214 / 39,556		1.44	20	A	4		...					0....	1180
05-HAA	**TEMEIN net**	1	1	13,916 / 21,832		2.00	21	A	4		...					0....	1181
05-HAAA	TEMEIN cluster	1	1	13,916 / 21,832		2.00	21	A	4		...					0....	1182
05-HAAA-a	longot-na-ronge				0				4		...					0....	1183
05-HAB	**JIRRU net**	1	2	11,298 / 17,724		0.74	18	A	4		...					0....	1184
05-HABA	JIRRU cluster	1	2	11,298 / 17,724		0.74	18	A	4		...					0....	1185
05-HABA-a	Proper jirru	1	2	11,298 / 17,724	0	0.74	18	A	4		...					0....	1186
05-HABA-b	tesei				0				4		...					0....	1187
05-HABA-c	umm-danab				0				4		...					0....	1188
05-I	**KADUGLI-AIGANG set**	1	6	163,399 / 256,609		5.87	35	A	42		PN.					0....	1189
05-IA	KADUGLI-KRONGO chain	1	6	161,399 / 253,209		5.88	35	A	42		PN.					0....	1190
05-IAA	**KADUGLI-KANGA net**	1	4	121,792 / 191,072		6.82	36	A	20		...					0....	1191
05-IAAA	DHALLA-MIRI cluster	1	1	78,743 / 123,535		10.00	44	A	20		...					0....	1192
05-IAAA-a	thoma-ma-miri				0				20		...					0....	1193
05-IAAA-b	thoma-ma-dhalla				0				20		...					0....	1194
05-IAAA-c	thoma-ma-dholubi				0				20		...					0....	1195
05-IAAB	KANGA-TUMMA cluster	1	2	28,151 / 44,164		1.00	20	A	4		...					0....	1196
05-IAAB-a	kufo	1	1	9,631 / 15,110	0	1.00	21	A	4		...					0....	1197
05-IAAB-b	tumma-sangali	1	1	18,520 / 29,054	0	1.00	20	A	4		...					0....	1202
05-IAAC	MUDO cluster	1	1	14,898 / 23,373		1.00	20	A	4		...					0....	1207
05-IAAC-a	thulishi	1	1	14,898 / 23,373	0	1.00	20	A	4		...					0....	1208
05-IAAC-b	kamdang				0				4		...					0....	1209
05-IAAC-c	turuj				0				4		...					0....	1210
05-IAB	**KRONGO-TUMTUM net**	1	2	39,607 / 62,137		3.00	32	A	42		PN.					0....	1211
05-IABA	KRONGO cluster	1	1	30,026 / 47,106		3.00	34	A	42	Nuba: Krongo*	PN.	1934-1943	1963			0....	1212
05-IABA-a	kadho-mo-di				0				42		pn.					0....	1213
05-IABB	TUMTUM-TALASA cluster	1	1	9,581 / 15,031		3.00	25	A	4		...					0....	1217
05-IABB-a	tumtum	1	1	9,581 / 15,031	0	3.00	25	A	4		...					0....	1218
05-IABB-b	talasa				0				4		...					0....	1219
05-IABB-c	karondi				0				4		...					0....	1220
05-IB	AIGANG chain	1	1	2,000 / 3,400		5.00	24	A	0		...					0....	1221
05-IBA	**AIGANG net**	1	1	2,000 / 3,400		5.00	24	A	0		...					0....	1222
05-IBAA	AIGANG cluster	1	1	2,000 / 3,400		5.00	24	A	0		...					0....	1223
05-IBAA-a	sani-m-aigang				0				0		...					0....	1224
05-IBAA-b	sani-mo-rofik				0				0		...					0....	1229
05-J	**NARA set**	1	1	72,516 / 125,819		5.00	28	A	2		...					0....	1230
05-JA	NARA chain	1	1	72,516 / 125,819		5.00	28	A	2		...					0....	1231
05-JAA	**NARA net**	1	1	72,516 / 125,819		5.00	28	A	2		...					0....	1232
05-JAAA	NARA cluster	1	1	72,516 / 125,819		5.00	28	A	2		...					0....	1233
05-JAAA-a	higir				0				2		...					0....	1234
05-JAAA-b	mogareb				0				2		...					0....	1235
05-JAAA-c	koyta				0				2		...					0....	1236
05-JAAA-d	santora				0				2		...					0....	1237
05-K	**KUNAMA-ILIT set**	3	3	228,942 / 400,135		20.09	56	B	43		PN.					0....	1238
05-KA	KUNAMA-ILIT chain	3	3	228,942 / 400,135		20.09	56	B	43		PN.					0....	1239
05-KAA	**KUNAMA-ILIT net**	3	3	228,942 / 400,135		20.09	56	B	43		PN.					0....	1240
05-KAAA	KUNAMA cluster	3	3	225,942 / 395,035		20.29	57	B	43		PN.					0....	1241
05-KAAA-a	marda-kunama	3	3	225,942 / 395,035	0	20.29	57	B	43	Kunama	PN.	1906-1970	1927			0....	1242
05-KAAA-b	aimara				0				43		pn.					0....	1243
05-KAAA-c	sokodasa				0				43		pn.					0....	1244
05-KAAA-d	tiika				0				43		pn.					0....	1245
05-KAAA-e	setiit				0				43		pn.					0....	1246
05-KAAA-f	berka				0				43		pn.					0....	1247
05-KAAA-g	bitaama				0				43		pn.					0....	1248
05-KAAB	ILIT cluster	1	1	3,000 / 5,100		5.00	24	A	0		...					0....	1249
05-KAAB-a	ilit	1	1	3,000 / 5,100	0	5.00	24	A	0		...					0....	1250
05-L	**GUMUZ set**	2	2	128,066 / 221,290		5.78	27	A	20		...					0....	1251
05-LA	GUMUZ chain	2	2	128,066 / 221,290		5.78	27	A	20		...					0....	1252
05-LAA	**GUMUZ net**	2	2	128,066 / 221,290		5.78	27	A	20		...					0....	1253
05-LAAA	BAGA-TSE cluster	2	2	128,066 / 221,290		5.78	27	A	20		...					0....	1254
05-LAAA-a	dakunza	2	2	128,066 / 221,290	0	5.78	27	A	20	Gumuz	...					0....	1255
05-LAAA-b	sai				0				20		...					0....	1256
05-LAAA-c	sese				0				20		...					0....	1257
05-LAAA-d	disoha				0				20		...					0....	1258
05-LAAA-e	dekoka				0				20		...					0....	1259
05-LAAA-f	dewiya				0				20		...					0....	1260
05-LAAA-g	kukwaya				0				20		...					0....	1261
05-LAAA-h	gombo				0				20		...					0....	1262
05-LAAA-i	jemhwa				0				20		...					0....	1263
05-LAAA-j	modea				0				20		...					0....	1264
05-M	**SILLOK-TABI set**	2	5	69,952 / 110,468		9.47	34	A	9		...					0....	1265
05-MA	SILLOK chain	1	3	37,959 / 59,589		17.03	48	A	9		...					0....	1266
05-MAA	**SILLOK net**	1	3	37,959 / 59,589		17.03	48	A	9		...					0....	1267
05-MAAA	AKA cluster	1	1	2,949 / 4,626		10.00	35	A	5		...					0....	1268
05-MAAA-a	aka	1	1	2,949 / 4,626	0	10.00	35	A	5		...					0....	1269
05-MAAB	KELO-TORNASI cluster	1	2	34,710 / 54,453		17.48	49	A	9		...					0....	1270
05-MAAB-a	keelo			0 / 0	0	0.00	0		9		...					0....	1271
05-MAAB-b	beni-sheko			0 / 0	0	0.00	0		9		...					0....	1272
05-MAAB-c	tornasi			0 / 0	0	0.00	0		9		...					0....	1273
05-MAAC	MOLO cluster	1	1	300 / 510		34.00	70	B	0		...					0....	1274
05-MAAC-a	molo	1	1	300 / 510	0	34.00	70	B	0		...					0....	1275
05-MB	TABI chain	2	2	31,993 / 50,879		0.50	18	A	2		...					0....	1276

Continued overleaf

Table 9-13 continued

Code 1	REFERENCE NAME / Autoglossonym 2	Coun 3	Peo 4	Mother-tongue speakers in 2000 5	in 2025 6	Media radio 7	CHURCH AC% 8	E% 9	Wld 10	Tr 11	Biblioglossonym 12	SCRIPTURES Print 13-15	P-activity 16	N-activity 17	B-activity 18	J-year 19	Jayuh 20-24	Ref 25
05-MBA	**TABI net**	2	2	31,993	50,879		0.50	18	A	2		. . .					0	1277
05-MBAA	GAAM cluster	2	2	31,993	50,879		0.50	18	A	2		. . .					0	1278
05-MBAA-a	kor-e-gaam	2	2	31,993	50,879	0	0.50	18	A	2		. . .					0	1279
05-N	**BERTA set**	1	3	60,907	112,325		12.13	38	A	5		. . .					0	1288
05-NA	BERTA chain	1	3	60,907	112,325		12.13	38	A	5		. . .					0	1289
05-NAA	**BERTA net**	1	3	60,907	112,325		12.13	38	A	5		. . .					0	1290
05-NAAA	BERTHU cluster	1	1	54,406	100,336		10.00	36	A	2		. . .					0	1291
05-NAAA-a	ndu-berthu	1	1	54,406	100,336	0	10.00	36	A	2		. . .					0	1292
05-NAAB	GAMILA cluster	1	1	4,680	8,631		30.00	60	B	0		. . .					0	1299
05-NAAB-a	gamila	1	1	4,680	8,631	0	30.00	60	B	0		. . .					0	1300
05-NAAC	GOBATO cluster	1	1	1,821	3,358		29.98	56	B	5		. . .					0	1301
05-NAAC-a	gobato	1	1	1,821	3,358	0	29.98	56	B	5		. . .					0	1302
05-O	**KOMAN set**	2	7	78,144	134,682		8.38	36	A	42		PN .					0	1303
05-OA	GULE chain									0		. . .					0	1304
05-OAA	**GULE net**									0		. . .					0	1305
05-OAAA	ANEJ cluster			0	0		0.00	0		0		. . .					0	1306
05-OAAA-a	anej			0	0	0	0.00	0		0		. . .					0	1307
05-OB	UDUK-KOMA chain	2	7	78,144	134,682		8.38	36	A	42		PN .					0	1308
05-OBA	**UDUK net**	1	1	15,777	24,751		20.00	61	B	42		PN .					0	1309
05-OBAA	TWAM-PA cluster	1	1	15,777	24,751		20.00	61	B	42		PN .					0	1310
05-OBAA-a	twam-pa	1	1	15,777	24,751	0	20.00	61	B	42	Uduk	PN .	1947-1966	1963			0	1311
05-OBB	**KOMA net**	2	6	62,367	109,931		5.44	29	A	4		. . .					0	1314
05-OBBA	KOMA cluster	2	4	54,590	96,238		5.00	28	A	2		. . .					0	1315
05-OBBA-a	twa-kwama					0				2		. . .					0	1316
05-OBBA-b	ta-komo					0				2		. . .					0	1317
05-OBBA-c	madiin	1	3	38,477	70,959	0	5.00	27	A	2		. . .					0	1320
05-OBBB	SHITA cluster	2	2	7,777	13,693		8.49	33	A	4		. . .					0	1321
05-OBBB-a	opo-shiita	2	2	7,777	13,693	0	8.49	33	A	4		. . .					0	1322
05-OBBB-b	buldiit					0				4		. . .					0	1323
05-OBBB-c	kusgilo					0				4		. . .					0	1324
05-P	**SURMAN set**	2	18	387,707	654,975		18.44	51	B	41		PN .					0	1325
05-PA	DIDINGA-ZILMAMU chain	2	8	225,664	358,910		10.08	44	A	41		PN .					0	1326
05-PAA	**DIDINGA-MURLE net**	2	6	217,230	343,357		9.83	44	A	41		PN .					0	1327
05-PAAA	DIDINGA-LARIMO cluster	1	3	114,873	180,218		10.54	43	A	22		P . .					0	1328
05-PAAA-a	doth-ki-larimo	1	2	17,752	27,852	0	13.50	40	A	22		p . .					0	1329
05-PAAA-b	doth-ki-didinga	1	1	97,121	152,366	0	10.00	44	A	22	Didinga	P . .	1994				0	1330
05-PAAB	MURLE cluster	2	2	98,049	156,380		9.34	46	A	41		PN .					0	1333
05-PAAB-a	dod-murle	2	2	98,049	156,380	0	9.34	46	A	41	Murle	PN .	1969-1985	1996			0	1334
05-PAAC	TENET cluster	1	1	4,308	6,759		2.00	30	A	12		. . .					0	1339
05-PAAC-a	tenet	1	1	4,308	6,759	0	2.00	30	A	12	Tennet	. . .					0	1340
05-PAB	**ZILMAMU net**	1	2	8,434	15,553		16.48	44	A	0		. . .					0	1341
05-PABA	ZILMAMU cluster	1	2	8,434	15,553		16.48	44	A	0		. . .					0	1342
05-PABA-a	zelmamu					0				0		. . .					0	1343
05-PABA-b	bale	1	1	3,873	7,142	0	30.00	62	B	0		. . .					0	1344
05-PB	SURMA-MEKAN chain	2	7	126,481	230,481		30.44	61	B	12		. . .					0	1345
05-PBA	**SURMA-MEKAN net**	2	7	126,481	230,481		30.44	61	B	12		. . .					0	1346
05-PBAA	MEKAN cluster	2	2	63,188	116,126		34.77	66	B	12		. . .					0	1347
05-PBAA-a	tuk-te-me'en-en	2	2	63,188	116,126	0	34.77	66	B	12	Meen	. . .					0	1348
05-PBAB	SURMA cluster	2	5	63,293	114,355		26.12	55	B	12		. . .					0	1351
05-PBAB-a	mursi	1	1	6,788	12,519	0	15.00	43	A	12	Mursi	. . .					0	1352
05-PBAB-b	tirma	2	2	35,525	65,120	0	30.00	60	B	12		. . .					0	1353
05-PBAB-c	tug-a-suri					0				12		. . .					0	1354
05-PBAB-d	kacipo	2	2	20,980	36,716	0	23.16	52	B	12	Suri	. . .					0	1355
05-PC	KWEGU chain	1	1	763	1,408		9.96	33	A	6		. . .					0	1356
05-PCA	**KWEGU net**	1	1	763	1,408		9.96	33	A	6		. . .					0	1357
05-PCAA	KWEGU cluster	1	1	763	1,408		9.96	33	A	6		. . .					0	1358
05-PCAA-a	toko-kwegoi	1	1	763	1,408	0	9.96	33	A	6		. . .					0	1359
05-PCAA-b	yidinich					0				6		. . .					0	1360
05-PCAA-c	muguji-apo					0				6		. . .					0	1361
05-PD	MAJANG chain	1	1	33,779	62,295		30.00	58	B	12		. . .					0	1362
05-PDA	**MAJANG net**	1	1	33,779	62,295		30.00	58	B	12		. . .					0	1363
05-PDAA	MAJANG cluster	1	1	33,779	62,295		30.00	58	B	12		. . .					0	1364
05-PDAA-a	ato-majang	1	1	33,779	62,295	0	30.00	58	B	12	Majang	. . .					0	1365
05-PE	SHABO chain	1	1	1,020	1,881		5.00	29	A	5		. . .					0	1366
05-PEA	**SHABO net**	1	1	1,020	1,881		5.00	29	A	5		. . .					0	1367
05-PEAA	SHABO cluster	1	1	1,020	1,881		5.00	29	A	5		. . .					0	1368
05-PEAA-a	shabo	1	1	1,020	1,881	0	5.00	29	A	5		. . .					0	1369
06	**KORDOFANIC zone**	1	22	512,186	803,532		36.69	63	B	42		PN .					0As . .	1370
06-A	**KATLA-TIMA set**	1	2	22,805	35,776		2.72	23	A	4		. . .					0	1371
06-AA	KATLA-TIMA chain	1	2	22,805	35,776		2.72	23	A	4		. . .					0	1372
06-AAA	**KATLA net**	1	1	19,670	30,858		3.00	23	A	2		. . .					0	1373
06-AAAA	KATLA cluster	1	1	19,670	30,858		3.00	23	A	2		. . .					1374
06-AAAA-a	betel-gali-a-kalak					0				2		. . .					0	1375
06-AAB	**TIMA net**	1	1	3,135	4,918		0.99	20	A	4		. . .					0	1380

Continued opposite

Table 9-13 continued

Code 1	REFERENCE NAME / Autoglossonym 2	Coun 3	Peo 4	Mother-tongue speakers in 2000 5	in 2025 6	Media radio 7	CHURCH AC% 8	E% 9	Wld 10	Tr 11	Biblioglossonym 12	SCRIPTURES Print 13-15	P-activity 16	N-activity 17	B-activity 18	J-year 19	Jayuh 20-24	Ref 25
06-AABA	OMURIKI cluster	1	1	3,135	4,918		0.99	20	A	4		. . .					0....	1381
06-AABA-a	tamanik-l-omuriki	1	1	3,135	4,918	0	0.99	20	A	4		. . .					0....	1382
06-B	**HEIBAN set**	1	10	318,864	500,241		58.44	91	B	42		PN.					0As..	1383
06-BA	WEST HEIBAN-CENTRAL chain	1	8	312,013	489,494		59.72	93	B	42		PN.					0As..	1384
06-BAA	**WEST HEIBAN net**	1	2	206,906	324,599		63.84	93	C	41		PN.					0As..	1385
06-BAAA	MORONG cluster	1	1	187,891	294,768		70.00	100	C	41		PN.					0As..	1386
06-BAAA-a	dhi-morong	1	1	187,891	294,768	0	70.00	100	C	41	Nuba: Moro*	PN.	1951-1989	1965-1994			0As..	1387
06-BAAB	TIRO cluster	1	1	19,015	29,831		3.00	29	A	12		. . .					0....	1393
06-BAAB-a	ngarta-nga-tiro	1	1	19,015	29,831	0	3.00	29	A	12	Tira	. . .					0....	1394
06-BAB	**SHIRUMBA net**	1	1	4,214	6,611		51.59	88	B	4		. . .					0....	1399
06-BABA	SHIRUMBA cluster	1	1	4,214	6,611		51.59	88	B	4		. . .					0....	1400
06-BABA-a	nguron-ngadi-ngi-shirumba					0				4		. . .					0....	1401
06-BABA-b	ngurun-nga-lu-dumör	1	1	4,214	6,611	0	51.59	88	B	4		. . .					0....	1402
06-BABA-c	sheibun					0				4		. . .					0....	1403
06-BABA-d	ndano					0				4		. . .					0....	1404
06-BAC	**HEIBAN-CENTRAL net**	1	5	100,893	158,284		51.61	92	B	42		PN.					0As..	1405
06-BACA	OTORO cluster	1	1	15,653	24,557		48.70	90	B	42		PN.					0.s..	1406
06-BACA-a	dhi-toro	1	1	15,653	24,557	0	48.70	90	B	42	Nuba: Otoro*	PN.		1966			0.s..	1407
06-BACA-b	dhi-jama					0				42		pn.					0.s..	1408
06-BACA-c	dhu-gwujur					0				42		pn.					0.s..	1409
06-BACA-d	dhu-kwara					0				42		pn.					0.s..	1410
06-BACA-e	dhu-gurila					0				42		pn.					0.s..	1411
06-BACA-f	dho-rombe					0				42		pn.					0.s..	1412
06-BACA-g	dha-garro					0				42		pn.					0.s..	1413
06-BACA-h	dhõ-görindi					0				42		pn.					0.s..	1414
06-BACB	EEBANG-LAARU cluster	1	2	16,558	25,977		70.00	100	C	42		PN.					0As..	1415
06-BACB-a	dhu-nguna-dha-eebang	1	1	6,107	9,581	0	70.00	100	C	42	Nuba: Heiban*	PN.	1931-1955	1966			0As..	1416
06-BACB-b	dhu-gun-dha-dhi-l-abla-a					0				42		pn.					0cs..	1417
06-BACB-c	yi-l-laaru	1	1	10,451	16,396	0	70.00	100	C	42		pn.					0cs..	1418
06-BACB-d	igwormany					0				42		pn.					0cs..	1419
06-BACC	LOGOL cluster	1	1	7,408	11,622		29.99	61	B	4		. . .					0....	1420
06-BACC-a	tha-logol-i					0				4		. . .					0....	1421
06-BACD	KOALIB cluster	1	1	61,274	96,128		50.00	95	B	41		PN.					0.s..	1422
06-BACD-a	ngu-qwurang					0				41		pn.					0.s..	1423
06-BACD-b	ngi-reere	1	1	61,274	96,128	0	50.00	95	B	41	Nuba: Ngirere*	PN.	1937-1989	1967-1994			0.s..	1424
06-BACD-c	ngu-nduna					0				41		pn.					0.s..	1425
06-BACD-d	ngi-nyukwur					0				41		pn.					0.s..	1426
06-BB	EAST HEIBAN chain	1	2	6,851	10,747		0.00	11	A	4		. . .					0....	1429
06-BBA	**WARNANG net**	1	1	3,135	4,918		0.00	13	A	4		. . .					0....	1430
06-BBAA	WARNANG cluster	1	1	3,135	4,918		0.00	13	A	4		. . .					0....	1431
06-BBAA-a	guro-ra-warnang	1	1	3,135	4,918	0	0.00	13	A	4		. . .					0....	1432
06-BBB	**FUNGOR-KO net**	1	1	3,716	5,829		0.00	9	A	4		. . .					1433
06-BBBA	FUNGOR-KO cluster	1	1	3,716	5,829		0.00	9	A	4		. . .					0....	1434
06-BBBA-a	kraw-ka-iro	1	1	3,716	5,829	0	0.00	9	A	4		. . .					0....	1435
06-BBBA-b	nyaro					0				4		. . .					0....	1436
06-BBBA-c	fungor					0				4		. . .					0....	1437
06-C	**TALODI-TEGEM set**	1	5	76,761	120,427		0.98	19	A	9		. . .					0....	1438
06-CA	TALODI-MASAKIN chain	1	4	69,645	109,263		0.87	19	A	9		. . .					0....	1439
06-CAA	**TALODI-MASAKIN net**	1	4	69,645	109,263		0.87	19	A	9		. . .					0....	1440
06-CAAA	MASAKIN cluster	1	1	56,213	88,189		0.50	18	A	4		. . .					0....	1441
06-CAAA-a	ngile	1	1	56,213	88,189	0	0.50	18	A	4		. . .					0....	1442
06-CAAA-b	dengebu					0				4		. . .					0....	1447
06-CAAB	MORO cluster	1	1	6,561	10,294		2.00	21	A	9		. . .					0....	1448
06-CAAB-a	acheron	1	1	6,561	10,294	0	2.00	21	A	9		. . .					0....	1449
06-CAAB-b	lumun					0				9		. . .					0....	1450
06-CAAB-c	tacho					0				9		. . .					0....	1451
06-CAAB-d	torona					0				9		. . .					0....	1452
06-CAAC	TALODI cluster	1	1	2,008	3,151		4.98	26	A	4		. . .					0....	1453
06-CAAC-a	talodi					0				4		. . .					0....	1454
06-CAAC-b	tasomi									4		. . .					0....	1455
06-CAAC-c	ga-jomang	1	1	2,008	3,151	0	4.98	26	A	4		. . .					0....	1456
06-CAAD	ELIRI cluster	1	1	4,863	7,629		1.99	20	A	4		. . .					0....	1457
06-CAAD-a	nding	1	1	4,863	7,629	0	1.99	20	A	4		. . .					0....	1458
06-CB	LAFOFA chain	1	1	7,116	11,164		2.00	22	A	4		. . .					0....	1459
06-CBA	**LAFOFA net**	1	1	7,116	11,164		2.00	22	A	4		. . .					0....	1460
06-CBAA	LAFOFA-TEGEM cluster	1	1	7,116	11,164		2.00	22	A	4		. . .					0....	1461
06-CBAA-a	kidie-lafofa	1	1	7,116	11,164	0	2.00	22	A	4		. . .					0....	1462
06-CBAA-b	amira					0				4		. . .					0....	1465
06-CBAA-c	tegem					0				4		. . .					0....	1466
06-D	**RASHAD set**	1	5	93,756	147,088		0.21	15	A	3		. . .					0....	1467
06-DA	RASHAD chain	1	5	93,756	147,088		0.21	15	A	3		. . .					0....	1468
06-DAA	**TEGALI-TAGOI net**	1	5	93,756	147,088		0.21	15	A	3		. . .					0....	1469
06-DAAA	TAGOI-TUMALE cluster	1	1	19,230	30,169		1.00	20	A	3		. . .					0....	1470
06-DAAA-a	ngon-nga-ta-goi	1	1	19,230	30,169	0	1.00	20	A	3		. . .					0....	1471
06-DAAA-b	orig					0				3		. . .					0....	1472
06-DAAA-c	tu-male					0				3		. . .					0....	1473
06-DAAA-d	moreb					0				3		. . .					0....	1474
06-DAAA-e	tagogen					0				3		. . .					0....	1475
06-DAAA-f	wadelka					0				3		. . .					0....	1476
06-DAAB	TEGALI-KOM cluster	1	4	74,526	116,919		0.01	14	A	3		. . .					0....	1477
06-DAAB-a	tegali	1	1	49,478	77,622	0	0.01	15	A	3		. . .					0....	1478
06-DAAB-b	nge-kom					0				3		. . .					0....	1479
06-DAAB-c	tingal	1	1	11,834	18,566		0.01	13	A	3		. . .					0....	1480
07	**RIFTIC zone**	4	7	125,343	223,639		73.42	96	C	20		. . .					0....	1482
07-A	**BIRALE set**	1	1	88	162		4.55	26	A	8		. . .					0....	1483

Continued overleaf

Table 9-13 continued

Code 1	REFERENCE NAME / Autoglossonym 2	Coun 3	Peo 4	Mother-tongue speakers in 2000 5	in 2025 6	Media radio 7	CHURCH AC% 8	E% 9	Wld 10	Tr 11	Biblioglossonym 12	SCRIPTURES Print 13-15	P-activity 16	N-activity 17	B-activity 18	J-year 19	Jayuh 20-24	Ref 25
07-AA	BIRALE chain	1	1	88	162		4.55	26	A	8		...					0....	1484
07-AAA	BIRALE net	1	1	88	162		4.55	26	A	8		...					0....	1485
07-AAAA	ONGOTA cluster	1	1	88	162		4.55	26	A	8		...					0....	1486
07-AAAA-a	ifa-'ongota	1	1	88	162	0	4.55	26	A	8		...					0....	1487
07-B	KULIAK set	2	4	24,396	49,189		52.65	81	B	6		...					0....	1488
07-BA	TEUSO chain	2	2	5,214	10,051		92.42	100	C	2		...					0....	1489
07-BAA	TEUSO net	2	2	5,214	10,051		92.42	100	C	2		...					0....	1490
07-BAAA	IK cluster	2	2	5,214	10,051		92.42	100	C	2		...					0....	1491
07-BAAA-a	ik	2	2	5,214	10,051	0	92.42	100	C	2		...					0....	1492
07-BB	NGANGEA-SO chain	1	2	19,182	39,138		41.84	76	B	6		...					0....	1493
07-BBA	NGANGEA net	1	1	8,711	17,774		20.00	54	B	6		...					0....	1494
07-BBAA	NYANGI cluster	1	1	8,711	17,774		20.00	54	B	6		...					0....	1495
07-BBAA-a	nyang'i	1	1	8,711	17,774	0	20.00	54	B	6		...					0....	1496
07-BBB	SO net	1	1	10,471	21,364		60.00	94	C	2		...					0....	1497
07-BBBA	SO cluster	1	1	10,471	21,364		60.00	94	C	2		...					0....	1498
07-BBBA-a	soo	1	1	10,471	21,364	0	60.00	94	C	2		...					0....	1499
07-BBC	NORTH DOROBO net									0		...					0....	1500
07-BBCA	NORTH DOROBO cluster	0	0	0	0		0.00	0	0	0		...					0....	1501
07-BBCA-a	dorobo-karamoja	0	0	0	0	0	0.00	0	0	0		...					0....	1502
07-C	HADZA set	1	1	5,051	8,728		50.01	90	B	4		...					0....	1503
07-CA	HADZA chain	1	1	5,051	8,728		50.01	90	B	4		...					0....	1504
07-CAA	HADZA net	1	1	5,051	8,728		50.01	90	B	4		...					0....	1505
07-CAAA	HADZA cluster	1	1	5,051	8,728		50.01	90	B	4		...					0....	1506
07-CAAA-a	hadza	1	1	5,051	8,728	0	50.01	90	B	4		...					0....	1507
07-D	SANDAWE set	1	1	95,808	165,560		80.00	100	C	20		...					0....	1511
07-DA	SANDAWE chain	1	1	95,808	165,560		80.00	100	C	20		...					0....	1512
07-DAA	SANDAWE net	1	1	95,808	165,560		80.00	100	C	20		...					0....	1513
07-DAAA	SANDAWE cluster	1	1	95,808	165,560		80.00	100	C	20		...					0....	1514
07-DAAA-a	sandawe	1	1	95,808	165,560	0	80.00	100	C	20	Sandawe	...					0....	1515
08	NAMA-TSHUIC zone	6	31	342,117	487,144		63.86	80	C	63		PNB					4as..	1516
08-A	KHOISAN-CENTRAL set	6	30	314,520	433,343		67.71	83	C	63		PNB					4as..	1517
08-AA	KHOI chain	6	28	288,765	398,076		72.84	87	C	63		PNB					4as..	1518
08-AAA	NAMA net	3	7	234,830	310,387		86.45	97	C	63		PNB					1as..	1519
08-AAAA	KXHWE-KOVAB cluster	3	4	201,598	262,988		92.93	100	C	62		PNB					1a....	1520
08-AAAA-a	Standard nama	3	3	123,934	157,796	4	94.76	100	C	62	Nama	PNB 1831-1984	1866-1909	1966		1989	1a....	1521
08-AAAA-b	Vehicular nama					1				62		pnb					1c...	1522
08-AAAA-c	q'ami-nt'u					1				62		pnb					1c...	1523
08-AAAA-d	q'xara-kai-kxoe					1				62		pnb					1c...	1524
08-AAAA-e	kxaro-q'oa					1				62		pnb					1c...	1525
08-AAAA-f	l'ghapope					1				62		pnb					1c...	1526
08-AAAA-g	kai-l'xau					1				62		pnb					1c...	1527
08-AAAA-h	l'o-kai					1				62		pnb					1c...	1528
08-AAAA-i	l'xau-c'goa					1				62		pnb					1c...	1529
08-AAAA-j	t'ao-ni					1				62		pnb					1c...	1530
08-AAAA-k	mun-l'i					1				62		pnb					1c...	1531
08-AAAA-l	t'ama					1				62		pnb					1c...	1532
08-AAAA-m	c'hai-c'xaua					1				62		pnb					1c...	1533
08-AAAA-n	c'xope-si					1				62		pnb					1c...	1534
08-AAAA-o	l'aixa-l'ae					1				62		pnb					1c...	1535
08-AAAA-p	kai-l'xaua					1				62		pnb					1c...	1536
08-AAAA-q	East damara	1	1	77,664	105,192	3	90.00	100	C	62		pnb					1a....	1537
08-AAAB	T'AU-KXOE cluster	1	1	15,000	25,500		30.00	65	B	0		...					0....	1538
08-AAAB-a	ao-kupu					0				0		...					0....	1539
08-AAAB-b	tauna-tama					0				0		...					0....	1540
08-AAAB-c	q'oe-t'ga					0				0		...					0....	1541
08-AAAC	AI-L'AE cluster	2	1	2,000	3,400		10.00	33	A	0		...					0....	1542
08-AAAC-a	t'nam-l'ae					0				0		...					0....	1543
08-AAAC-b	c'oo-xoo					0				0		...					0....	1544
08-AAAC-c	q'ao					0				0		...					0....	1545
08-AAAC-d	c'hoa					0				0		...					0....	1546
08-AAAD	Q'XIRI cluster	1	1	81	92		70.37	100	C	8		...					0....	1547
08-AAAD-a	q'xiri	1	1	81	92	0	70.37	100	C	8		...					0....	1548
08-AAAE	GEMSBOK-NAMA cluster	1	1	4,038	4,602		60.00	97	C	0		...					0.s..	1549
08-AAAE-a	gemsbok-nama	1	1	4,038	4,602	0	60.00	97	C	0		...					0.s..	1550
08-AAAF	Q'ORA cluster	1	1	12,113	13,805		70.00	100	C	63	Korana	PNB			1933		0....	1551
08-AAAF-a	t'nuu-l'ae			0	0	0	0.00	0		63		pnb					0....	1552
08-AAAF-b	c'hoa-l'ae			0	0	0	0.00	0		63		pnb					0....	1553
08-AAAF-c	kx'am-l'oa			0	0	0	0.00	0		63		pnb					0....	1554
08-AAAF-d	l'are-maa-l'ae			0	0	0	0.00	0		63		pnb					0....	1555
08-AAAF-e	kai-q'ora			0	0	0	0.00	0		63		pnb					0....	1556
08-AAB	TSHU net	5	21	53,935	87,689		13.59	41	A	32		P..					4....	1557
08-AABA	NHARO cluster	2	2	5,327	7,315		8.00	31	A	12	Naro	...					0....	1558
08-AABA-a	l'ai-khoe					0				12		...					0....	1559
08-AABA-b	c'am-kwe					0				12		...					0....	1560
08-AABA-c	ts'auru-khoe					0				12		...					0....	1561
08-AABA-d	q'ave-khoe					0				12		...					0....	1562
08-AABA-e	q'gin-khoe					0				12		...					0....	1563
08-AABA-f	q'ko-khoe					0				12		...					0....	1564
08-AABB	TS'AO-NC`HAI cluster	1	2	3,326	4,596		7.79	30	A	0		...					0....	1565
08-AABB-a	ts'ao-khoe	1	1	2,596	3,587	0	8.01	30	A	0		...					0....	1566
08-AABB-b	nc'hai					0				0		...					0....	1567
08-AABB-c	nc'hai-tse	1	1	730	1,009	0	6.99	29	A	0		...					0....	1568
08-AABC	L'GANA cluster	1	2	2,595	3,587		13.10	37	A	4		...					0....	1569

Continued opposite

Table 9-13 continued

Code 1	REFERENCE NAME / Autoglossonym 2	Coun 3	Peo 4	in 2000 5	in 2025 6	Media radio 7	AC% 8	E% 9	Wld 10	Tr 11	Biblioglossonym 12	Print 13-15	P-activity 16	N-activity 17	B-activity 18	J-year 19	Jayuh 20-24	Ref 25
08-AABC-a	k'ere-khoe					0				4		. . .					0	1570
08-AABC-b	l'gaa-khoe					0				4		. . .					0	1571
08-AABC-c	dom-khoe					0				4		. . .					0	1572
08-AABC-d	du-kwe					0				4		. . .					0	1573
08-AABC-e	nyive-kxo					0				4		. . .					0	1574
08-AABC-f	t'heva-khoe					0				4		. . .					0	1575
08-AABC-g	gl'ana-khoe	1	1	973	1,345	0	9.97	33	A	4		. . .					0	1576
08-AABC-h	c'wi-khoe	1	1	1,622	2,242		14.98	40	A	4		. . .					0	1577
08-AABC-i	mo-lepolole					0				4		. . .					0	1578
08-AABD	CENTRAL TSHU cluster	2	2	4,620	6,090		12.58	45	A	4		. . .					0	1579
08-AABD-a	l'gulu					0				4		. . .					0	1580
08-AABD-b	l'golo					0				4		. . .					0	1581
08-AABD-c	l'goro-khwe					0				4		. . .					0	1582
08-AABD-d	ganadi					0				4		. . .					0	1583
08-AABD-e	kwe-e-tsho-ri					0				4		. . .					0	1584
08-AABD-f	tshwa					0				4		. . .					0	1585
08-AABD-g	c'hai-tsho-ri	1	1	1,298	1,793		14.02	41	A	4		. . .					0	1586
08-AABD-h	l'gabake-tsho-ri					0				4		. . .					0	1587
08-AABD-i	mohisa					0				4		. . .					0	1588
08-AABD-j	kovee-n-tsho-ri					0				4		. . .					0	1589
08-AABE	SHUA cluster	3	6	9,090	15,126		10.23	33	A	23	Shua	P . .	1978				0	1590
08-AABE-a	nl`oo-khoe					0				23		p . .					0	1591
08-AABE-b	ts'ixa-khoe					0				23		p . .					0	1592
08-AABE-c	bore-khoe					0				23		p . .					0	1593
08-AABE-d	shua-khoe	1	1	1,249	1,726		14.97	41	A	23		p . .					0	1594
08-AABE-e	l'aiye					0				23		p . .					0	1595
08-AABE-f	danisa	1	1	162	224		6.79	30	A	23		p . .					0	1596
08-AABE-g	tshuma-khoe	1	1	4,413	8,604	0	9.99	32	A	23	Kung: Tsumkwe*	P . .	1974				0	1597
08-AABE-h	l'oree-khoe					0				23		p . .					0	1598
08-AABE-i	c'haise									23		p . .					0	1599
08-AABE-j	tcaiti-khoe	1	1	183	312		8.20	32	A	23		p . .					0	1600
08-AABE-k	hura					0				23		p . .					0	1601
08-AABE-l	deti-khoe	1	1	2,596	3,587	0	8.01	31	A	23		p . .					0	1602
08-AABF	NORTH TSHU cluster	4	7	28,977	50,975		16.54	47	A	32		. . .					4	1603
08-AABF-a	handa-khoe	1	1	3,277	4,529	0	10.01	37	A	32		. . .					1	1604
08-AABF-b	gali-kwe					0				32		. . .					1	1605
08-AABF-c	goe-kwe					0				32		. . .					1	1606
08-AABF-d	gari-kwe					0				32		. . .					1	1607
08-AABF-e	l`kani-kxoe	3	3	24,119	44,232	0	18.02	49	A	32		. . .				1990	4	1608
08-AABF-f	boga-kxoe	1	1	1,298	1,793	0	8.01	31	A	32		. . .					1	1609
08-AABF-g	buma-kxoe					0				32		. . .					1	1610
08-AABF-h	x~u-kxoe	1	1	110	187	0	10.00	42	A	32		. . .					1	1611
08-AB	HAINUM chain	2	2	25,755	35,267		10.25	43	A	4		. . .					0	1617
08-ABA	HAINUM net	2	2	25,755	35,267		10.25	43	A	4		. . .					0	1618
08-ABAA	HEIKOM-KEDI cluster	2	2	25,755	35,267		10.25	43	A	4		. . .					0	1619
08-ABAA-a	hai-nl'um	1	1	25,111	34,012	0	10.00	43	A	4		. . .					0	1620
08-ABAA-b	kedi	1	1	644	1,255	0	20.03	48	A	4		. . .					0	1621
08-ABAA-c	cwaga					0				4		. . .					0	1622
08-ABAA-d	strandläufer					0				4		. . .					0	1623
08-B	KWADI set	1	1	27,597	53,801		20.00	48	* A	4		. . .					0	1624
08-BA	KWADI chain	1	1	27,597	53,801		20.00	48	A	4		. . .					0	1625
08-BAA	KWADI net	1	1	27,597	53,801		20.00	48	A	4		. . .					0	1626
08-BAAA	KWADI cluster	1	1	27,597	53,801		20.00	48	A	4		. . .					0	1627
08-BAAA-a	kwise	1	1	27,597	53,801	0	20.00	48	A	4		. . .					0	1628
08-BAAA-b	zorotua					0				4		. . .					0	1629
09	KALAHARIC zone	6	24	61,291	98,445		15.07	41	A	22		P . .					0 . s . .	1630
09-A	KUNG set	3	12	46,086	75,987		15.16	42	A	22		P . .					0 . s . .	1631
09-AA	NORTH Q'XUNG chain	1	1	2,189	4,268		20.01	43	A	4		. . .					0	1632
09-AAA	NORTH Q'XUNG net	1	1	2,189	4,268		20.01	43	A	4		. . .					0	1633
09-AAAA	Q'O-Q'XUNG cluster	1	1	2,189	4,268		20.01	43	A	4		. . .					0	1634
09-AAAA-a	maligo	1	1	2,189	4,268	0	20.01	43	A	4		. . .					0	1635
09-AAAA-b	Central q'o-q'xung					0				4		. . .					0	1636
09-AAAA-c	South q'o-q'xung					0				4		. . .					0	1637
09-AB	WEST KUNG chain	3	11	43,897	71,719		14.92	42	A	22		P . .					0 . s . .	1638
09-ABA	EKOKA-Q'XUNG net	3	6	27,937	46,734		16.64	45	A	22		P . .					0 . s . .	1639
09-ABAA	XUNG-UKUAMBI cluster	3	6	24,437	40,784		16.96	45	A	22		P . .					0 . s . .	1640
09-ABAA-a	uukualuthi	3	6	24,437	40,784	0	16.96	45	A	22	Kung: Ekoka*	P . .	1980				0 . s . .	1641
09-ABAA-b	ukuambi					0				22		p . .					0 . s . .	1642
09-ABAB	XUNG-HEIKUM cluster	2	1	1,500	2,550		20.00	50	B	0		. . .					0	1643
09-ABAB-a	heil'um					0				0		. . .					0	1644
09-ABAB-b	heikum					0				0		. . .					0	1645
09-ABAC	XUNG-CHU cluster	2	1	500	850		10.00	33	A	0		. . .					0	1646
09-ABAC-a	chu	1	1	500	850	0	10.00	33	A	0		. . .					0	1647
09-ABAD	NORTH XUNG-KUNG cluster	2	1	800	1,360		10.00	33	A	0		. . .					0	1648
09-ABAD-a	l'kung					0				0		. . .					0	1649
09-ABAD-b	l'kung-2					0				0		. . .					0	1650
09-ABAE	XUNG-KU cluster	1	1	100	170		15.00	42	A	0		. . .					0	1651
09-ABAE-a	l'ku					0				0		. . .					0	1652
09-ABAE-b	l'ku-2					0				0		. . .					0	1653
09-ABAF	SOUTH XUNG-KUNG cluster	1	1	600	1,020		10.00	34	A	0		. . .					0	1654
09-ABAF-a	l'kung-3			0	0	0	0.00	0		0		. . .					0	1655
09-ABAF-b	l'kung-4					0				0		. . .					0	1656
09-ABB	A-KHOE net	3	3	10,331	17,205		10.72	36	A	22		P . .					0 . s . .	1657
09-ABBA	L'KHAU-L'EN cluster	3	1	1,000	1,700		10.00	33	A	0		. . .					0	1658
09-ABBA-a	l'khau-l'en	1	1	1,000	1,700	0	10.00	33	A	0		. . .					0	1659
09-ABBB	AU-KWE cluster	3	3	7,331	12,105		11.01	37	A	22		P . .					0 . s . .	1660
09-ABBB-a	au-kwe	3	3	7,331	12,105	0	11.01	37	A	22	Akhoe	P . .	1975-1980				0 . s . .	1661
09-ABBB-b	au-kwe-2					0				22		p . .					0 . s . .	1662
09-ABBB-c	au-kwe-3					0				22		p . .					0 . s . .	1663
09-ABBC	AU-SAN cluster	3	1	2,000	3,400		10.00	33	A	0		. . .					0	1664
09-ABBC-a	au-san	1	1	2,000	3,400	0	10.00	33	A	0		. . .					0	1665
09-ABBD	NO-GAU cluster									0		. . .					0	1666
09-ABBD-a	no-gau					0				0		. . .					0	1667

Continued overleaf

Table 9-13 continued

Code 1	REFERENCE NAME / Autoglossonym 2	Coun 3	Peo 4	Mother-tongue speakers in 2000 5	in 2025 6	Media radio 7	AC% 8	E% 9	Wld 10	Tr 11	Biblioglossonym 12	Print 13-15	P-activity 16	N-activity 17	B-activity 18	J-year 19	Jayuh 20-24	Ref 25
09-ABC	**EAST KUNG net**	1	2	5,629	7,780		14.05	38	A	4		. . .					0	1668
09-ABCA	ZHU cluster	1	1	4,867	6,726		15.00	39	A	0		. . .					0	1669
09-ABCA-a	zhu-hoa	1	1	4,867	6,726	0	15.00	39	A	0		. . .					0	1670
09-ABCA-b	zhu-oase					0				0		. . .					0	1671
09-ABCB	EAST HUA cluster	1	1	762	1,054		8.01	30	A	4		. . .					0	1672
09-ABCB-a	hoa	1	1	762	1,054	0	8.01	30	A	4		. . .					0	1673
09-B	**TA'A set**	2	2	7,117	11,598		7.26	29	A	2		. . .					0	1674
09-BA	XONG chain	2	2	7,117	11,598		7.26	29	A	2		. . .					0	1675
09-BAA	**EAST XONG net**	1	1	4,100	6,970		7.17	28	A	2		. . .					0	1676
09-BAAA	C'HUA-WANI cluster	1	1	2,000	3,400		7.00	28	A	0		. . .					0	1677
09-BAAA-a	c'hua-p'wani	1	1	2,000	3,400	0	7.00	28	A	0		. . .					0	1678
09-BAAB	Q'XONY cluster	1	1	300	510		8.00	30	A	0		. . .					0	1679
09-BAAB-a	q'xony	1	1	300	510	0	8.00	30	A	0		. . .					0	1680
09-BAAC	P'KHA cluster	1	1	500	850		7.00	28	A	0		. . .					0	1681
09-BAAC-a	p'kha	1	1	500	850	0	7.00	28	A	0		. . .					0	1682
09-BAAD	TSHA-SI cluster	1	1	500	850		6.00	26	A	0		. . .					0	1683
09-BAAD-a	tsha-si	1	1	500	850	0	6.00	26	A	0		. . .					0	1684
09-BAAE	TYORO cluster	1	1	300	510		5.00	24	A	0		. . .					0	1685
09-BAAE-a	tyoro	1	1	300	510	0	5.00	24	A	0		. . .					0	1686
09-BAAF	NAH cluster	1	1	100	170		10.00	33	A	0		. . .					0	1687
09-BAAF-a	l'nah	1	1	100	170	0	10.00	33	A	0		. . .					0	1688
09-BAAG	HA cluster	1	1	100	170		10.00	33	A	0		. . .					0	1689
09-BAAG-a	p'ha	1	1	100	170	0	10.00	33	A	0		. . .					0	1690
09-BAAH	L'NGAMANI cluster	1	1	200	340		10.00	34	A	2		. . .					0	1691
09-BAAH-a	l'ngamani	1	1	200	340	0	10.00	34	A	2		. . .					0	1692
09-BAAI	C'GWI cluster	1	1	100	170		10.00	33	A	0		. . .					0	1693
09-BAAI-a	c'gwi	1	1	100	170	0	10.00	33	A	0		. . .					0	1694
09-BAB	**WEST Q'XONG net**	2	2	3,017	4,628		7.39	30	A	0		. . .					0	1695
09-BABA	Q'XONY-2 cluster	1	1	100	170		5.00	24	A	0		. . .					0	1696
09-BABA-a	q'xony-2	1	1	100	170	0	5.00	24	A	0		. . .					0	1697
09-BABB	Q'GAO-KXA cluster	1	1	100	170		5.00	24	A	0		. . .					0	1698
09-BABB-a	q'gao-kx'a	1	1	100	170	0	5.00	24	A	0		. . .					0	1699
09-BABC	Q'KONG cluster	1	1	100	170		5.00	24	A	0		. . .					0	1700
09-BABC-a	q'kong	1	1	100	170	0	5.00	24	A	0		. . .					0	1701
09-BABD	NC'U-L'EN cluster	2	2	1,517	2,078		9.16	34	A	0		. . .					0	1702
09-BABD-a	nc'u-l'en	2	2	1,517	2,078	0	9.16	34	A	0		. . .					0	1703
09-BABE	NC'U-SAN cluster	1	1	100	170		6.00	26	A	0		. . .					0	1704
09-BABE-a	nc'u-san	1	1	100	170	0	6.00	26	A	0		. . .					0	1705
09-BABF	NC'U-MDE cluster	1	1	100	170		5.00	24	A	0		. . .					0	1706
09-BABF-a	nc'u-mde	1	1	100	170	0	5.00	24	A	0		. . .					0	1707
09-BABG	NL'AHNSA cluster	1	1	300	510		5.00	24	A	0		. . .					0	1708
09-BABG-a	tuu-nl'ahnsa	1	1	300	510	0	5.00	24	A	0		. . .					0	1709
09-BABG-b	lala					0				0		. . .					0	1710
09-BABG-c	owa					0				0		. . .					0	1711
09-BABG-d	l'naheh					0				0		. . .					0	1712
09-BABH	L'GUI cluster	1	1	100	170		7.00	28	A	0		. . .					0	1713
09-BABH-a	l'gui	1	1	100	170	0	7.00	28	A	0		. . .					0	1714
09-BABI	Q'AMA cluster	1	1	100	170		6.00	26	A	0		. . .					0	1715
09-BABI-a	q'ama	1	1	100	170	0	6.00	26	A	0		. . .					0	1716
09-BABJ	Q'OHJU cluster	1	1	100	170		6.00	26	A	0		. . .					0	1717
09-BABJ-a	q'ohju	1	1	100	170	0	6.00	26	A	0		. . .					0	1718
09-BABK	QUNKA-TE cluster	1	1	100	170		5.00	24	A	0		. . .					0	1719
09-BABK-a	unka-te	1	1	100	170	0	5.00	24	A	0		. . .					0	1720
09-BABL	L'OAL'EI cluster	1	1	100	170		7.00	28	A	0		. . .					0	1721
09-BABL-a	l'oal'ei	1	1	100	170	0	7.00	28	A	0		. . .					0	1722
09-BABM	KIC'HAZI-KAKIA cluster	1	1	100	170		6.00	26	A	0		. . .					0	1723
09-BABM-a	kic'hazi					0				0		. . .					0	1724
09-BABM-b	kakia					0				0		. . .					0	1725
09-BABN	T'ATIA cluster	1	1	100	170		6.00	26	A	0		. . .					0	1726
09-BABN-a	t'atia	1	1	100	170	0	6.00	26	A	0		. . .					0	1727
09-C	**Q'WI set**	4	7	7,618	10,242		19.51	47	A	9		. . .					0	1728
09-CA	NC'HU-C'AUNI chain	3	5	6,299	8,687		11.02	37	A	2		. . .					0	1729
09-CAA	**NC'HU-C'AUNI net**	3	5	6,299	8,687		11.02	37	A	0		. . .					0	1730
09-CAAA	NC'HU cluster	1	1	404	460		40.10	67	B	0		. . .					0	1731
09-CAAA-a	Proper nc'hu-ki	1	1	404	460	0	40.10	67	B	0		. . .					0	1732
09-CAAB	T'KHOMANI cluster	1	1	100	170		7.00	28	A	0		. . .					0	1733
09-CAAB-a	t'khomani	1	1	100	170	0	7.00	28	A	0		. . .					0	1734
09-CAAC	L'KHAU cluster	1	1	100	170		5.00	24	A	0		. . .					0	1735
09-CAAC-a	l'khau	1	1	100	170	0	5.00	24	A	0		. . .					0	1736
09-CAAD	NL' cluster	1	1	100	170		5.00	24	A	0		. . .					0	1737
09-CAAD-a	nl'-t'ke	1	1	100	170	0	5.00	24	A	0		. . .					0	1738
09-CAAE	C'AUNI cluster	1	1	100	170		7.00	28	A	0		. . .					0	1739
09-CAAE-a	c'auni	1	1	100	170	0	7.00	28	A	0		. . .					0	1740
09-CAAF	KIC'HASI cluster	1	1	100	170		7.00	28	A	0		. . .					0	1741
09-CAAF-a	kic'hasi	1	1	100	170	0	7.00	28	A	0		. . .					0	1742
09-CAAG	T'KAURURE cluster	1	1	100	170		8.00	30	A	0		. . .					0	1743
09-CAAG-a	t'kaurure-nl`ai	1	1	100	170	0	8.00	30	A	0		. . .					0	1744
09-CAAH	NC'USA cluster	3	4	5,295	7,207		9.31	36	A	0		. . .					0	1745
09-CAAH-a	nc'usa	3	4	5,295	7,207	0	9.31	36	A	0		. . .					0	1746
09-CAB	**VASEKELA net**									2		. . .					0	1747

Continued opposite

Table 9-13 continued

Code 1	REFERENCE NAME / Autoglossonym 2	Coun 3	Peo 4	Mother-tongue speakers in 2000 5	in 2025 6	Media radio 7	CHURCH AC% 8	E% 9	Wld 10	Tr 11	Biblioglossonym 12	SCRIPTURES Print 13-15	P-activity 16	N-activity 17	B-activity 18	J-year 19	Jayuh 20-24	Ref 25
09-CABA	VASEKELA cluster									2		...					0....	1748
09-CABA-a	vasekela					0				2		...					0....	1749
09-CB	SEROA chain	2	2	1,319	1,555		60.05	94	C	9		...					0....	1750
09-CBA	**SEROA net**	2	2	1,319	1,555		60.05	94	C	9		...					0....	1751
09-CBAA	Q'ANQ'E cluster			0	0		0.00	0		0		...					0....	1752
09-CBAA-a	q`anq`e			0	0	0	0.00	0		0		...					0....	1753
09-CBAB	L'KUL'E cluster			0	0		0.00	0		0		...					0....	1754
09-CBAB-a	l'kul'e			0	0	0	0.00	0		0		...					0....	1755
09-CBAC	SEROA cluster	2	2	1,319	1,555		60.05	94	C	9		...					0....	1756
09-CBAC-a	seroa			0	0	0	0.00	0		9		...					0....	1757
09-CBAD	QACHA'S-NECK cluster			0	0		0.00	0		0		...					0....	1758
09-CBAD-a	qacha's-neck			0	0	0	0.00	0		0		...					0....	1759
09-CBAE	MALUTI cluster									0		...					0....	1760
09-CBAE-a	maluti					0				0		...					0....	1761
09-CBAF	BOSHOF cluster									0		...					0....	1762
09-CBAF-a	boshof					0				0		...					0....	1763
09-D	**XEGWI set**	2	2	349	480		42.98	71	B	9		...					0....	1764
09-DA	XEGWI chain	2	2	349	480		42.98	71	B	9		...					0....	1765
09-DAA	**XEGWI net**	2	2	349	480		42.98	71	B	9		...					0....	1766
09-DAAA	L'XEGWI-L'XOGWI cluster	2	2	349	480		42.98	71	B	9		...					0....	1767
09-DAAA-a	l'xegwi	2	2	349	480	0	42.98	71	B	9		...					0....	1768
09-DAAA-b	l'xogwi			0	0	0	0.00	0		9		...					0....	1769
09-E	**C'XAM set**	1	1	121	138		80.17	100	C	9		...					0....	1770
09-EA	C'XAM chain	1	1	121	138		80.17	100	C	9		...					0....	1771
09-EAA	**C'XAM net**	1	1	121	138		80.17	100	C	9		...					0....	1772
09-EAAA	C'XAM cluster	1	1	121	138		80.17	100	C	9		...					0....	1773
09-EAAA-a	c'xam-t'ke	1	1	121	138	0	80.17	100	C	9		...					0....	1774
09-EAAB	KATKOP cluster			0	0		0.00	0		0		...					0....	1775
09-EAAB-a	katkop			0	0	0	0.00	0		0		...					0....	1776
09-EAAC	STRONTBERGEN cluster									0		...					0....	1777
09-EAAC-a	strontbergen			0	0	0	0.00	0		0		...					0....	1778
1	**AFROASIAN macrozone**	135	1044	390,489,529	634,065,878		14.30	63	B	82		PNB					4Bsuh	1779
10	**TAMAZIC zone**	17	76	19,733,756	28,825,249		0.29	33	A	42		PN.					4A...	1780
10-A	**TAMAZIC set**	17	76	19,733,756	28,825,249		0.29	33	A	42		PN.					4A...	1781
10-AA	TAMAZIC chain	17	76	19,733,756	28,825,249		0.29	33	A	42		PN.					4A...	1782
10-AAA	**TAMAZIC net**	17	76	19,733,756	28,825,249		0.29	33	A	42		PN.					4A...	1783
10-AAAA	ZNAGA cluster	3	6	40,029	71,459		0.01	12	A	4		...					0....	1784
10-AAAA-a	znaga	2	3	37,935	67,696	0	0.01	12	A	4		...					0....	1785
10-AAAA-b	nimadi	2	2	492	903	0	0.00	4	A	4		...					0....	1786
10-AAAB	TAMASHEQ cluster	8	16	2,983,069	5,463,207		0.01	19	A	41		PN.					3....	1787
10-AAAB-a	ta-mahaq	6	8	232,609	379,103	0	0.02	17	A	41	Tamahaq: Hoggar*	Pn.	1934-1985	1990			1....	1788
10-AAAB-b	ta-majeq	3	8	2,750,460	5,084,104	0	0.01	19	A	41	Tamajeq, Tahoua	Pn.	1979-1985			1996	3....	1795
10-AAAC	NORTH TAMAZIGH cluster	10	50	16,658,527	23,215,767		0.34	36	A	42		PN.					4A...	1802
10-AAAC-a	ta-shelhit	3	6	4,549,316	6,323,142	4	0.11	32	A	42	Shilha: Southern*	Pn.	1906-1925			1993	4c...	1803
10-AAAC-b	ta-mazight	3	8	3,917,170	5,441,187	4	0.07	33	A	42	Shilha: Central*	Pn.	1919-1981			1997	1a...	1810
10-AAAC-c	judeo-tamazigh	2	2	3,972	5,389	1	0.00	17	A	42		pn.					1c...	1816
10-AAAC-d	ghomara	1	1	56,442	77,060	1	0.01	20	A	42		pn.					1c...	1819
10-AAAC-e	senhaja	2	2	119,459	124,724	1	0.10	38	A	42		pn.					1c...	1820
10-AAAC-f	ta-rift	2	2	2,252,477	3,145,359	4	0.12	39	A	42	Shilha: Northern*	Pn.	1887-1890			1991	1A...	1821
10-AAAC-g	menasser-metmata	1	1	15,736	23,305	1	0.00	11	A	42		pn.					1c...	1836
10-AAAC-h	tha-qabaylith	4	5	2,710,890	3,677,890	4	1.65	52	B	42	Kabyle: Greater	Pn.	1885-1990	1901-1958		1989	1a...	1837
10-AAAC-i	East tha-qabaylith	1	1	776,365	1,149,836	4	0.20	44	A	42	Kabyle: Lesser	Pn.	1954				1a...	1840
10-AAAC-j	shawiya	3	3	1,845,815	2,653,943	1	0.01	24	A	42	Chaouia	Pn.	1950				1c...	1841
10-AAAC-k	tugurt	1	1	6,757	10,007	1	0.01	19	A	42		pn.					1c...	1851
10-AAAC-l	wargla-ngusa	1	1	5,630	8,339	1	0.02	19	A	42		pn.					1c...	1855
10-AAAC-m	mzab	1	1	78,848	116,778	1	0.01	21	A	42		pn.					1c...	1858
10-AAAC-n	gurara	1	1	22,030	32,627	1	0.01	19	A	42		pn.					1c...	1863
10-AAAC-o	tuat	1	1	22,030	32,627	1	0.01	16	A	42		pn.					1c...	1866
10-AAAC-p	tidikelt	1	2	25,873	38,318	1	0.02	14	A	42		pn.					1c...	1869
10-AAAC-q	sened					1				42		pn.					1c...	1872
10-AAAC-r	tamezret	1	2	4,697	6,294	1	0.00	12	A	42		pn.					1c...	1875
10-AAAC-s	jerba	2	7	168,853	233,059	1	0.01	22	A	42		pn.					1c...	1881
10-AAAC-t	zuara					1				42		pn.					1c...	1882
10-AAAC-u	nefusi	1	1	44,838	69,174	1	0.00	20	A	42		pn.					1c...	1883
10-AAAC-v	ghudamis	1	1	4,988	7,696	1	0.04	18	A	42		pn.					1c...	1887
10-AAAD	EAST TAMAZIGH cluster	2	4	52,131	74,816		0.01	9	A	4		...					0....	1890
10-AAAD-a	sokna	1	1	5,773	8,906	0	0.05	13	A	4		...					0....	1891
10-AAAD-b	wajili	1	2	8,015	12,365	0	0.04	13	A	4		...					0....	1892
10-AAAD-c	siwa	1	1	38,343	53,545	0	0.00	7	A	4		...					0....	1893
11	**COPTIC zone**	1	2	7,189	10,040		99.01	100	C	46		PN.					0....	1894
11-A	**EGYPTIAN set**	1	2	7,189	10,040		99.01	100	C	46		PN.					0....	1895
11-AA	EGYPTIAN chain	1	2	7,189	10,040		99.01	100	C	46		PN.					0....	1896
11-AAA	**EGYPTIAN net**	1	2	7,189	10,040		99.01	100	C	46		PN.					0....	1897
11-AAAA	COPTIC cluster	1	2	7,189	10,040		99.01	100	C	46	Coptic: Sahidic	PN.		1924			0....	1898
11-AAAA-a	bohayric	1	1	6,847	9,562	2	98.99	100	C	46	Coptic: Bohairic	PN.		1716-1924			0....	1899
12	**SEMITIC zone**	133	556	279,933,025	442,567,385		15.34	65	B	71		PNB					4Bsuh	1902
12-A	**SEMITIC set**	133	556	279,933,025	442,567,385		15.34	65	B	71		PNB					4Bsuh	1903
12-AA	ABRAMIC chain	133	517	250,986,487	389,525,753		8.03	61	B	71		PNB					4Bsuh	1904

Continued overleaf

Table 9-13 continued

Code 1	REFERENCE NAME / Autoglossonym 2	Coun 3	Peo 4	in 2000 5	in 2025 6	Media radio 7	AC% 8	E% 9	Wld 10	Tr 11	Biblioglossonym 12	Print 13-15	P-activity 16	N-activity 17	B-activity 18	J-year 19	Jayuh 20-24	Ref 25
12-AAA	**ARAMAIC net**	22	35	934,680	1,460,159		87.16	97	C	67		PNB					4as..	1905
12-AAAA	ARAMAIC cluster	22	35	934,680	1,460,159		87.16	97	C	67		PNB					4as..	1906
12-AAAA-a	Religious samaritan					1				67	Samaritan	PNB	1632-1965		1853		1cs..	1907
12-AAAA-b	West neo-aramaic	3	3	32,902	49,012	1	61.89	98	C	67	Aramaic: Ancient	PNb	1482	1517			1cs..	1908
12-AAAA-c	West syriac									67		pnb					1cs..	1909
12-AAAA-d	East syriac	10	10	127,506	155,790	5	89.24	100	C	67	Syriac: Ancient*	PNB	1840-1983	1846-1920	1852-1891		1as..	1910
12-AAAA-e	sur-oyo	5	5	90,736	113,966	5	90.09	100	C	67	Syriac	PNB	1625-1904	1555-1920	1645-1891	1995	4as..	1911
12-AAAA-f	aisor	11	11	205,780	310,505	5	90.72	100	C	67	Assyrian Neo-aramaic	PNB	1840-1993	1846-1864	1852-1911	1995	4cs..	1914
12-AAAA-g	kald-oyo	1	3	436,871	775,156	5	94.23	100	A	67	Chaldean: Modern*	Pnb	1993			1997	3cs..	1920
12-AAAA-h	kurdit	2	2	32,084	43,450	1	0.00	25	A	67		pnb					1cs..	1931
12-AAAA-i	hartevan									67		pnb					1cs..	1934
12-AAAA-j	nasoraye	1	1	8,801	12,280	1	5.00	35	A	67		pnb					1cs..	1935
12-AAB	**HEBRAIC net**	6	6	1,741,410	2,445,492		0.65	58	B	63		PNB					2B.uh	1938
12-AABA	IVRIT cluster	6	6	1,741,410	2,445,492		0.65	58	B	63		PNB					2B.uh	1939
12-AABA-a	Religious ivrit					1				63		pnb					1c.uh	1940
12-AABA-b	ivrit-X.	6	6	1,741,410	2,445,492	5	0.65	58	B	63	Hebrew	PNB	1477-1790	1487-1986	1599-1877	1990	2B.uh	1941
12-AAC	**ARABIC net**	129	476	248,310,397	385,620,102		7.78	61	B	71		PNB					4Asuh	1946
12-AACA	STANDARD ARABIC cluster	4	4	15,820	17,913		20.59	41	A	0		...					0.su.	1947
12-AACA-a	Religious al-`arabiyya					0				0		...					0.su.	1948
12-AACA-b	Literary al-`arabiyya					0				0		...					0.su.	1949
12-AACB	MAGHREBI cluster	22	50	49,873,508	69,758,656		0.61	55	B	62		PNB					2A.uh	1953
12-AACB-a	West maghrebi	11	13	17,567,113	23,656,563	7	0.23	48	A	62		pnb					1A.uh	1954
12-AACB-b	East maghrebi	18	34	31,989,657	45,620,952	8	0.83	59	B	62	Arabic: Algerian*	PNB	1872-1973	1932-1965	1963		2A.uh	1962
12-AACC	MALTIYA cluster	7	8	562,811	627,734		95.07	100	C	61		PNB					0a.u.	1971
12-AACC-a	maltiya	7	8	562,811	627,734	5	95.07	100	C	61	Maltese	PNB	1822-1872	1847-1959	1932-1984		0a.u.	1972
12-AACD	BADAWI-SAHARA cluster	21	64	16,947,173	25,777,436		0.01	27	A	43		PN.					0a...	1975
12-AACD-a	hassaaniyya	11	32	11,602,633	17,601,395	7	0.01	27	A	43		pn.					0a...	1976
12-AACD-b	ma`qili					1				43		pn.					0c...	1980
12-AACD-c	hilaali					1				43		pn.					0c...	1981
12-AACD-d	sulaymi					1				43		pn.					0c...	1982
12-AACD-e	fezzani					1				43		pn.					0c...	1985
12-AACD-f	West egyptian	2	2	2,562,616	3,857,903	7	0.00	23	A	43	Arabic: Egyptian*	PN.	1905-1991	1932			0c...	1986
12-AACE	BADAWI-SAHEL cluster	6	23	5,910,168	9,658,342		0.10	27	A	42	Arabic: Chad	PN.					0...h	1993
12-AACE-a	shuwa	5	5	1,705,638	3,056,456	7	0.02	33	A	42	Arabic: Chad	PN.	1964	1967			0...h	1994
12-AACE-b	baggaari	2	20	3,998,097	6,278,028	7	0.01	24	A	42		pn.					0...h	2001
12-AACE-c	South kordofani					1				42		pn.					0...h	2006
12-AACE-d	North kordofani					1				42		pn.					0...h	2013
12-AACE-e	guhayna					1				42		pn.					0...h	2018
12-AACE-f	shukri	1	1	166,959	261,929	7	0.30	28	A	42		pn.					0...h	2019
12-AACF	MASHRIQI cluster	111	299	174,354,694	278,962,052		10.60	67	B	71		PNB					4Asuh	2020
12-AACF-a	masri	23	31	65,696,200	92,252,751	8	15.86	81	B	71	Arabic*	PNB	1516-1985	1616-1991	1671-1991	1994	2Asuh	2021
12-AACF-b	sa`idi	3	3	77,990	78,615	7	8.49	64	B	71		pnb					1Asuh	2030
12-AACF-c	sudani	9	55	16,498,744	25,470,774	7	4.04	56	B	71	Arabic: Sudan	PNb	1927			1991	4Asuh	2034
12-AACF-d	badawi-masri					1				71		pnb					1csuh	2044
12-AACF-e	hijaazi					1				71		pnb					1csuh	2048
12-AACF-f	syro-palestinian	80	128	34,259,297	52,676,387	8	20.67	76	B	71	Arabic: Lebanese*	Pnb	1940-1973				1Asuh	2061
12-AACF-g	syro-mesopotamian	15	18	16,698,031	29,212,566	7	0.62	53	B	71		pnb				1998	1asuh	2084
12-AACF-h	Northeast `anazi	2	3	2,282,960	3,190,557	7	0.20	38	A	71		pnb					1asuh	2109
12-AACF-i	kuwayti-Qatari	7	10	2,129,836	3,375,432	7	4.36	59	B	71		pnb					1Asuh	2117
12-AACF-j	North `anazi	3	3	1,254,526	2,180,865	1	0.02	23	A	71		pnb					1csuh	2126
12-AACF-k	Central `anazi	9	10	16,195,129	29,888,651	7	0.47	54	B	71		pnb				1980	4Asuh	2137
12-AACF-l	Omani	9	9	1,684,619	3,398,111	7	0.75	48	A	71		pnb					1Asuh	2159
12-AACF-m	Omani-bedawi					1				71		pnb					1csuh	2165
12-AACF-n	yemeni	16	17	16,934,426	36,098,448	7	0.02	47	A	71		pnb					1Asuh	2168
12-AACF-o	perso-arabic					7				71		pnb					1csuh	2194
12-AACF-p	zanji	12	12	642,936	1,138,895	7	1.06	44	A	71		pnb					1Asuh	2195
12-AACG	ARABO-CREOLE cluster	6	7	90,893	154,188		0.01	21	A	8		...					0....	2203
12-AACG-a	babaliya	1	1	5,012	9,111	1	0.00	10	A	8		...					0....	2204
12-AACG-b	juba	1	1	25,503	40,009	7	0.02	30	A	8		...					0....	2205
12-AACG-c	ki-nubi	2	2	33,918	58,304	1	0.01	20	A	8		...					0....	2206
12-AACG-d	turku	3	3	26,460	46,764	7	0.00	16	A	8		...					0....	2209
12-AACG-e	bimbashi					1				8		...					0....	2210
12-AACH	JUDEO-ARABIC cluster	7	9	298,908	404,320		0.00	25	A	24		P..					0A...	2211
12-AACH-a	judeo-moroccan					1				24		P..					0c...	2212
12-AACH-b	judeo-tunisian	3	3	13,191	17,612	7	0.03	32	A	24	Arabic: Judaeo-tunisian*	P..	1897-1937				0A...	2216
12-AACH-c	yudi	4	5	285,546	386,404	8	0.00	24	A	24		p..					0c...	2217
12-AACH-d	yahudi	1	1	171	304	7	0.00	24	A	24		p..					0c...	2218
12-AACI	JUGARI cluster	3	3	7,363	8,362		3.33	27	A	0		...					0....	2219
12-AACI-a	arab-balkhi					0				0		...					0....	2220
12-AACI-b	arab-tajiki					0				0		...					0....	2221
12-AACI-c	arab-uzbeki	3	3	7,363	8,362	0	3.33	27	A	0		...					0....	2222
12-AACJ	JAKATI cluster	4	4	249,059	251,099		0.99	23	A	20		...					0....	2223
12-AACJ-a	jakati	4	4	249,059	251,099	0	0.99	23	A	20		...					0....	2224
12-AB	MESOSEMITIC chain	4	8	361,345	739,522		0.10	14	A	24		P..					0....	2225
12-ABA	**MAHRI-SHEHRI net**	4	7	249,231	498,204		0.01	13	A	24		P..					0....	2226
12-ABAA	MAHRI-SHEHRI cluster	4	7	249,231	498,204		0.01	13	A	24		P..					0....	2227
12-ABAA-a	mahri	4	4	161,281	327,397	0	0.01	13	A	24	Mehri	P..	1902				0....	2228
12-ABAA-b	arsusi	1	1	15,125	27,975	0	0.00	11	A	24		p..					0....	2232
12-ABAA-c	bautahari					0				24		p..					0....	2235
12-ABAA-d	jibbali	2	2	72,825	142,832	0	0.01	15	A	24		p..					0....	2236
12-ABAA-e	habyot					0				24		p..					0....	2243
12-ABB	**SOCOTRAN net**	1	1	112,114	241,318		0.30	15	A	24		P..					0....	2244
12-ABBA	SQATRI cluster	1	1	112,114	241,318		0.30	15	A	24		P..					0....	2245
12-ABBA-a	sqatri	1	1	112,114	241,318	0	0.30	15	A	24	Sokotri*	P..	1902				0....	2246
12-AC	ETHIOSEMITIC chain	10	31	28,585,193	52,302,110		79.74	97	C	71		PNB					3Bsuh	2249
12-ACA	**NORTH ETHIOSEMITIC net**	7	12	6,242,219	11,133,055		66.93	94	C	66		PNB					2Bs..	2250
12-ACAA	GE`EZ cluster	1	1	626	1,154		98.88	100	C	66		PNB					0....	2251
12-ACAA-a	Historical ge`ez					0				66		pnb					0....	2252
12-ACAA-b	Literary ge`ez	1	1	626	1,154	0	98.88	100	C	66		PNB					0....	2253
12-ACAB	TIGRE cluster	4	5	775,659	1,334,689		5.15	56	B	61		PNB					1B...	2258
12-ACAB-a	tigre	4	5	775,659	1,334,689	4	5.15	56	B	61	Tigre	PNB	1889-1981	1902-1931	1988		1B...	2259
12-ACAC	TIGRAY cluster	6	6	5,465,934	9,797,212		75.69	99	C	62		PNB					2As..	2266
12-ACAC-a	tigray	6	6	5,465,934	9,797,212	4	75.69	99	C	62	Tigrinya	PNB	1866	1909-1991	1956	1988	2As..	2267
12-ACB	**AMHARIC net**	8	10	19,977,138	36,849,243		88.65	100	C	71		PNB					3Asuh	2270
12-ACBA	AMARINYA cluster	8	10	19,977,138	36,849,243		88.65	100	C	71		PNB					3Asuh	2271
12-ACBA-a	Standard amarinya					1				71		pnb					1csuh	2272
12-ACBA-b	General amarinya	8	9	19,932,579	36,767,068	5	88.83	100	C	71	Amharic	PNB	1824-1988	1829-1988	1840-1988	1984	3Asuh	2273
12-ACBA-c	argobbinya	1	1	44,559	82,175	1	10.00	44	A	71		pnb					1csuh	2285

Continued opposite

Table 9-13 continued

Code 1	REFERENCE NAME / Autoglossonym 2	Coun 3	Peo 4	in 2000 5	in 2025 6	Media radio 7	AC% 8	E% 9	Wld 10	Tr 11	Biblioglossonym 12	Print 13-15	P-activity 16	N-activity 17	B-activity 18	J-year 19	Jayuh 20-24	Ref 25
12-ACC	**HARARI-SILTI net**	1	4	666,779	1,229,672		42.20	76	B	22		P..					0.s..	2288
12-ACCA	HARARI cluster	1	1	40,073	73,902		0.00	25	A	20		...					0.s..	2289
12-ACCA-a	ge-sinan	1	1	40,073	73,902	0	0.00	25	A	20		...					0.s..	2290
12-ACCB	EAST GURAGE cluster	1	3	626,706	1,155,770		44.90	80	B	22		P..					0.s..	2291
12-ACCB-a	zway	1	1	5,712	10,534	0	44.99	78	B	22		p..					0.s..	2292
12-ACCB-b	walane					0				22		p..					0.s..	2293
12-ACCB-c	silti	1	1	608,481	1,122,160	0	45.00	80	B	22	Gurage, East	P..	1981				0.s..	2294
12-ACCB-d	mesmes	1	1	12,513	23,076	0	40.00	70	B	22		p..					0.s..	2298
12-ACD	**GAFAT net**									25		P..					0....	2299
12-ACDA	GAFAT cluster			0	0		0.00	0		25		P..					0....	2300
12-ACDA-a	gafat			0	0	0	0.00	0		25	Gafat	P..	1945				0....	2301
12-ACE	**GURAGE net**	1	5	1,699,057	3,090,140		36.75	77	B	51		PN.					3.s..	2302
12-ACEA	NORTH GURAGE cluster	1	1	300,000	510,000		5.00	24	A	0		...					0....	2303
12-ACEA-a	soddo					0				0		...					0....	2304
12-ACEA-b	gogot					0				0		...					2307
12-ACEA-c	kistane					0				0		...					0....	2310
12-ACEA-d	muxir					0				0		...					0....	2311
12-ACEB	CENTRAL GURAGE cluster	1	4	1,349,005	2,487,834		43.69	88	B	51		PN.					3.s..	2312
12-ACEB-a	misqan					1				51		pn.					1.s..	2313
12-ACEB-b	gura	1	2	941,701	1,736,685	5	42.86	89	B	51		PN.					1.s..	2314
12-ACEB-c	innamor	1	2	407,304	751,149	1	45.61	87	B	51		PN.					3.s..	2320
12-ACEB-d	geto					1				51		pn.					1.s..	2324
12-ACEC	SOUTHWEST GURAGE cluster	1	1	50,052	92,306		40.00	73	B	0		...					0....	2325
12-ACEC-a	Indiagegn	1	1	50,052	92,306	0	40.00	73	B	0		...					0....	2326
13	**BEJIC zone**	5	7	2,513,771	4,144,868		0.01	22	A	0		...					0....	2327
13-A	**BEJA set**	5	7	2,513,771	4,144,868		0.01	22	A	0		...					0....	2328
13-AA	BEJA chain	5	7	2,513,771	4,144,868		0.01	22	A	0		...					0....	2329
13-AAA	**BEJA net**	5	7	2,513,771	4,144,868		0.01	22	A	0		...					0....	2330
13-AAAA	BEDAUYE cluster	5	7	2,513,771	4,144,868		0.01	22	A	0		...					0....	2331
13-AAAA-a	ti-bedaauye	5	7	2,513,771	4,144,868	7	0.01	22	A	0		...					0....	2332
14	**MID CUSHITIC zone**	18	114	43,004,230	81,159,474		18.65	66	B	61		PNB					3As..	2339
14-A	**SAHO-AFAR set**	5	7	1,455,686	2,602,530		0.90	30	A	41		PN.					1.s..	2340
14-AA	SAHO-AFAR chain	5	7	1,455,686	2,602,530		0.90	30	A	41		PN.					1.s..	2341
14-AAA	**SAHO-AFAR net**	5	7	1,455,686	2,602,530		0.90	30	A	41		PN.					1.s..	2342
14-AAAA	SAHO cluster	2	2	258,659	458,927		5.00	30	A	20		...					0....	2343
14-AAAA-a	saho	2	2	258,659	458,927	0	5.00	30	A	20		...					0....	2344
14-AAAB	AFAR cluster	5	5	1,197,027	2,143,603		0.01	30	A	41		PN.					1.s..	2349
14-AAAB-a	'afar-af	5	5	1,197,027	2,143,603	4	0.01	30	A	41	Afar	PN.	1975-1986	1994			1.s..	2350
14-B	**AGAW set**	4	11	386,877	669,483		39.07	72	B	24		P..					0....	2355
14-BA	AGAW-NC. chain	3	7	233,839	422,512		43.12	77	B	24		P..					0....	2356
14-BAA	**NORTH AGAW net**	1	1	76,323	132,425		30.00	64	B	22		P..					0....	2357
14-BAAA	BILIN cluster	1	1	76,323	132,425		30.00	64	B	22		P..					0....	2358
14-BAAA-a	bilin	1	1	76,323	132,425	0	30.00	64	B	22	Bogos*	P..	1882-1984				0....	2359
14-BAB	**WEST AGAW net**	2	3	40,764	74,773		41.65	77	B	24		P..					0....	2362
14-BABA	KEMANT cluster	2	3	40,764	74,773		41.65	77	B	24	Agaw, Western	P..	1885				0....	2363
14-BABA-a	kemantenay	1	1	33,034	60,922	0	50.00	88	B	24		p..					0....	2364
14-BABA-b	dembiya	1	1	6,256	11,538	0	5.00	31	A	24		p..					0....	2367
14-BABA-c	kwara	1	1	1,474	2,313	0	9.97	38	A	24	Kara: Falasha	P..	1885				0....	2368
14-BAC	**EAST AGAW net**	1	3	116,752	215,314		52.21	85	B	2		...					0....	2371
14-BACA	XAMTA-XAMIR cluster	1	3	116,752	215,314		52.21	85	B	2		...					0....	2372
14-BACA-a	xamtanga	1	1	90,913	167,662	0	50.00	83	B	2		...					0....	2373
14-BACA-b	xamta	1	1	13,326	24,576	0	60.00	91	C	2		...					0....	2374
14-BACA-c	xamir	1	1	12,513	23,076	0	60.00	93	C	2		...					0....	2375
14-BACA-d	abergelle-agaw			0	0	0	0.00	0		2		...					0....	2378
14-BB	SOUTH AGAW chain	2	4	153,038	246,971		32.88	63	B	20		...					0....	2379
14-BBA	**SOUTH AGAW net**	2	4	153,038	246,971		32.88	63	B	20		...					0....	2380
14-BBAA	AWNGI cluster	2	4	153,038	246,971		32.88	63	B	20		...					0....	2381
14-BBAA-a	awngi	2	3	146,782	235,433	0	32.15	63	B	20		...					0....	2382
14-BBAA-b	kunfel	1	1	6,256	11,538	0	50.00	83	B	20		...					0....	2387
14-C	**SIDAMO-BURJI set**	2	9	5,987,066	11,031,743		40.12	82	B	41		PN.					3.s..	2388
14-CA	SIDAMO-HADIYA chain	1	7	5,872,344	10,829,775		40.19	83	B	41		PN.					3.s..	2389
14-CAA	**HADIYYA-LIBIDO net**	1	2	1,499,849	2,766,020		27.61	68	B	41		PN.					3.s..	2390
14-CAAA	HADIYYA-LIBIDO cluster	1	2	1,499,849	2,766,020		27.61	68	B	41		PN.					3.s..	2391
14-CAAA-a	hadiyya	1	1	1,376,427	2,538,406	0	30.00	72	B	41	Hadiyya	PN.	1935	1992-1993			3.s..	2392
14-CAAA-b	libido	1	1	123,422	227,614	0	1.00	27	A	41		pn.					1.s..	2396
14-CAB	**KEMBATA-ALABA net**	1	3	1,629,026	3,004,250		60.69	100	C	41		PN.					1.s..	2399
14-CABA	KEMBATA-ALABA cluster	1	3	1,629,026	3,004,250		60.69	100	C	41		PN.					1.s..	2400
14-CABA-a	timbara-qebena	1	1	6,256	11,538	0	75.00	100	C	41		pn.					1.s..	2401
14-CABA-b	kembata	1	1	1,520,326	2,803,785	0	60.00	100	C	41	Kambaata	PN.	1979-1990	1992			1.s..	2404
14-CABA-c	alaba	1	1	102,444	188,927	0	70.00	100	C	41	Alaba	pn.					1.s..	2405
14-CAC	**SIDAMO net**	1	1	1,917,613	3,536,461		37.00	83	B	41		PN.					2.s..	2406
14-CACA	SIDAMO cluster	1	1	1,917,613	3,536,461		37.00	83	B	41		PN.					2.s..	2407
14-CACA-a	sidaamo-'afo	1	1	1,917,613	3,536,461	4	37.00	83	B	41	Sidamo	PN.	1933	1990		1998	2.s..	2408
14-CAD	**DERASA net**	1	1	825,856	1,523,044		30.00	74	B	41		PN.					2....	2412
14-CADA	DERASA cluster	1	1	825,856	1,523,044		30.00	74	B	41		PN.					2....	2413
14-CADA-a	gede-inke-afa'o	1	1	825,856	1,523,044	0	30.00	74	B	41	Gedeo	PN.	1980	1986-1987			2....	2414
14-CB	BURJI chain	2	2	114,722	201,968		36.33	71	B	41		PN.					0....	2417

Continued overleaf

Table 9-13 continued

Code 1	REFERENCE NAME 2 / Autoglossonym	Coun 3	Peo 4	Mother-tongue speakers in 2000 5	in 2025 6	Media radio 7	CHURCH AC% 8	E% 9	Wld 10	Tr 11	Biblioglossonym 12	SCRIPTURES Print 13-15	P–activity 16	N–activity 17	B–activity 18	J-year 19	Jayuh 20-24	Ref 25
14-CBA	**BURJI net**	2	2	114,722	201,968		36.33	71	B	41		PN.					0....	2418
14-CBAA	DAASHE cluster	2	2	114,722	201,968		36.33	71	B	41		PN.					0....	2419
14-CBAA-a	daashe	2	2	114,722	201,968	0	36.33	71	B	41		PN.					0....	2420
14-D	**WERIZE-TSAMAI set**	1	9	158,672	292,620		6.65	31	A	20		...					1....	2424
14-DA	WERIZE-TSAMAI chain	1	9	158,672	292,620		6.65	31	A	20		...					1....	2425
14-DAA	**WERIZE-TSAMAI net**	1	9	158,672	292,620		6.65	31	A	20		...					1....	2426
14-DAAA	WERIZE cluster	1	8	144,726	266,901		3.44	27	A	20		...					1....	2427
14-DAAA-a	go-waze					0				20		...					1....	2428
14-DAAA-b	go-beze	1	1	44,421	81,921	0	2.00	22	A	20		...					1....	2429
14-DAAA-c	harso	1	1	4,974	9,173	0	3.00	26	A	20		...					1....	2433
14-DAAA-d	go-lango	1	1	4,142	7,638	0	14.99	42	A	20		...					1....	2434
14-DAAA-e	go-rose	1	1	3,454	6,369	0	20.01	48	A	20		...					1....	2435
14-DAAA-f	dihina	1	1	3,729	6,877	0	2.01	24	A	20		...					1....	2436
14-DAAA-g	gaba	1	1	3,109	5,734	0	10.00	35	A	20		...					1....	2437
14-DAAA-h	gergere	1	1	3,454	6,369	0	20.01	48	A	20		...					1....	2438
14-DAAA-i	ko-kawwate	1	1	77,443	142,820	0	2.00	27	A	20		...					1....	2439
14-DAAB	TSAMAY cluster	1	1	13,946	25,719		40.00	69	B	4		...					0....	2442
14-DAAB-a	go-tsamakula	1	1	13,946	25,719		40.00	69	B	4		...					0....	2443
14-E	**MUKOGODO set**	1	1	60	84		11.67	38	A	8		...					0....	2446
14-EA	MUKOGODO chain	1	1	60	84		11.67	38	A	8		...					0....	2447
14-EAA	**MUKOGODO net**	1	1	60	84		11.67	38	A	8		...					0....	2448
14-EAAA	YAAKU cluster	1	1	60	84		11.67	38	A	8		...					0....	2449
14-EAAA-a	yaaku	1	1	60	84	0	11.67	38	A	8		...					0....	2450
14-F	**OROMO-SHAMO set**	6	34	20,979,510	38,489,189		25.90	80	B	61		PNB					2As..	2451
14-FA	SHAMO-LACUSTRINE chain	2	5	264,779	486,934		21.99	54	B	35		P..					0.s..	2452
14-FAA	**SHAMO-LACUSTRINE net**	2	5	264,779	486,934		21.99	54	B	35		P..					0.s..	2453
14-FAAA	SHAMO cluster	2	5	264,779	486,934		21.99	54	B	35		P..					0.s..	2454
14-FAAA-a	mosiya	1	1	6,813	12,565	0	70.00	100	C	35		p..					0.s..	2455
14-FAAA-b	kap-dirashat	1	1	7,746	14,284	0	50.00	83	B	35		p..					0.s..	2456
14-FAAA-c	mashile	1	1	5,931	10,938	0	12.00	41	A	35		p..					0.s..	2457
14-FAAA-d	gato					0				35		p..					0.s..	2458
14-FAAA-e	turo					0				35		p..					0.s..	2459
14-FAAA-f	afa-karatti	2	2	244,289	449,147	0	20.00	52	B	35	Komso	P..	1996				0.s..	2460
14-FB	OROMO chain	6	29	20,714,731	38,002,255		25.95	80	B	61		PNB					2As..	2461
14-FBA	**OROMO net**	6	29	20,714,731	38,002,255		25.95	80	B	61		PNB					2As..	2462
14-FBAA	OROMO cluster	6	29	20,714,731	38,002,255		25.95	80	B	61		PNB					2As..	2463
14-FBAA-a	tulema	4	5	4,714,154	8,695,023	5	40.10	96	B	61		pnb					1cs..	2464
14-FBAA-b	mecha	2	2	3,562,612	6,553,925	5	35.00	94	B	61	Oromo: Western*	PNB	1981	1876-1979	1899-1994	1997	2cs..	2468
14-FBAA-c	raya	1	2	125,130	230,764	5	0.01	31	A	61		pnb					1cs..	2471
14-FBAA-d	wello	1	1	199,670	368,230	5	10.00	59	B	61		pnb					1cs..	2472
14-FBAA-e	qottu	1	1	3,253,374	5,999,869	5	25.00	74	B	61	Oromo: Eastern*	PNb	1870	1875			1cs..	2473
14-FBAA-f	arusi	1	1	1,814,381	3,346,081	5	3.00	52	B	61	Oromo: Central	Pnb	1841			1986	2cs..	2480
14-FBAA-g	guji	1	1	462,767	853,435	5	10.00	56	B	61		pnb					1cs..	2481
14-FBAA-h	borena	2	7	411,259	613,890	5	4.90	51	B	61		PNB					1As..	2484
14-FBAA-i	orma	1	4	88,202	122,437	5	1.76	37	A	61	Orma	pnb					1cs..	2492
14-G	**OMO-TANA set**	16	43	14,036,359	28,073,825		0.07	43	A	61		PNB					2A...	2496
14-GA	OMO-TANA chain	16	43	14,036,359	28,073,825		0.07	43	A	61		PNB					2A...	2497
14-GAA	**ABAYA-LACUSTRINE net**	1	1	1,145	2,111		2.01	29	A	4		...					0....	2498
14-GAAA	BAISO cluster	1	1	1,145	2,111		2.01	29	A	4		...					0....	2499
14-GAAA-a	bayso	1	1	1,145	2,111	0	2.01	29	A	4		...					0....	2500
14-GAB	**STEFANIE LACUSTRINE net**	1	1	4,649	8,573		2.00	21	A	5		...					0....	2501
14-GABA	ARBORE cluster	1	1	4,649	8,573		2.00	21	A	5		...					0....	2502
14-GABA-a	oho-arbore	1	1	4,649	8,573	0	2.00	21	A	5		...					0....	2503
14-GAC	**RUDOLF LACUSTRINE net**	3	3	47,386	84,516		5.00	29	A	12		...					0....	2504
14-GACA	DASENACH cluster	3	3	47,386	84,516		5.00	29	A	12		...					0....	2505
14-GACA-a	af-dasenach	3	3	47,386	84,516	0	5.00	29	A	12	Daasanech	...					0....	2506
14-GAD	**ELMOLO net**	1	1	12	17		8.33	50	B	8		...					0....	2515
14-GADA	GURU-PAWA cluster	1	1	12	17		8.33	50	B	8		...					0....	2516
14-GADA-a	guru-pawa	1	1	12	17	0	8.33	50	B	8		...					0....	2517
14-GAE	**RENDILLE net**	1	1	34,210	47,489		5.00	37	A	32		P..					1....	2518
14-GAEA	RENDILLE cluster	1	1	34,210	47,489		5.00	37	A	32		P..					1....	2519
14-GAEA-a	afi-rendille	1	1	34,210	47,489	1	5.00	37	A	32	Rendille	P..	1993			1985	1....	2520
14-GAF	**AWEERA net**	2	3	11,333	22,059		0.19	9	A	2		...					0....	2524
14-GAFA	AWEERA cluster	2	3	11,333	22,059		0.19	9	A	2		...					0....	2525
14-GAFA-a	aweera	2	2	4,068	5,832	0	0.52	20	A	2		...					0....	2526
14-GAG	**SOMALI net**	16	33	13,937,624	27,909,060		0.04	43	A	61		PNB					2A...	2529
14-GAGA	SOOMAALI cluster	16	31	13,689,616	27,371,080		0.04	44	A	61		PNB					2A...	2530
14-GAGA-a	af-soomaali	16	26	12,882,661	25,575,775	5	0.04	45	A	61	Somali	PNB	1915-1935	1972-1976	1979	1981	2A...	2531
14-GAGA-b	af-ciise					1				61		pnb					1c...	2534
14-GAGA-c	af-geedabuursi					1				61		pnb					1c...	2535
14-GAGA-d	af-isaaq					1				61		pnb					1c...	2536
14-GAGA-e	North af-hawiyya					1				61		pnb					1c...	2537
14-GAGA-f	af-daarood					1				61		pnb					1c...	2538
14-GAGA-g	af-digil					1				61		pnb					1c...	2544
14-GAGA-h	Southeast af-ajuran	1	1	8,573	11,900	5	1.00	41	A	61		pnb					1c...	2545
14-GAGA-i	af-benaadir					1				61		pnb					1c...	2546
14-GAGA-j	af-ashraaf					1				61		pnb					1c...	2550
14-GAGA-k	af-maay	1	1	692,847	1,547,665	1	0.01	21	A	61		pnb					1c...	2551
14-GAGA-l	af-helledi					1				61		pnb					1c...	2552
14-GAGA-m	af-tunni	1	3	105,535	235,740	1	0.00	12	A	61		pnb					1c...	2553
14-GAGA-n	af-jiddu					1				61		pnb					1c...	2554
14-GAGB	DABARE-IROLE cluster	1	1	30,000	51,000		0.02	14	A	4		...					0....	2555
14-GAGB-a	af-dabarre					0				4		...					0....	2556
14-GAGB-b	af-iroole					0				4		...					0....	2557
14-GAGC	GARRE-BOON cluster	1	2	218,008	486,980		0.00	4	A	8		...					0....	2558

Continued opposite

Table 9-13 continued

Code 1	REFERENCE NAME / Autoglossonym 2	Coun 3	Peo 4	Mother-tongue speakers in 2000 5	in 2025 6	Media radio 7	CHURCH AC% 8	E% 9	Wld 10	Tr 11	Biblioglossonym 12	SCRIPTURES Print 13-15	P-activity 16	N-activity 17	B-activity 18	J-year 19	Jayuh 20-24	Ref 25
14-GAGC-a	af-boon	1	1	73	162	0	0.00	3	A	8		. . .					0	2559
14-GAGC-b	af-garre	1	1	217,935	486,818	0	0.00	4	A	8		. . .					0	2560
15	**PARA-CUSHITIC zone**	2	8	616,597	1,064,077		22.79	63	B	41		PN .					0 . s . .	2561
15-A	**SOUTH RIFT set**	1	7	612,416	1,058,273		22.94	64	B	41		PN .					0 . s . .	2562
15-AA	IRAQW-BURUNGE chain	1	4	559,623	967,045		24.30	66	B	41		PN .					0 . s . .	2563
15-AAA	**IRAQW-BURUNGE net**	1	4	559,623	967,045		24.30	66	B	41		PN .					0 . s . .	2564
15-AAAA	IRAQW-GOROWA cluster	1	2	503,687	870,385		25.66	68	B	41		PN .					0 . s . .	2565
15-AAAA-a	iraqw	1	1	462,625	799,429	0	25.50	68	B	41	Iraqw	PN .	1957	1977			0 . s . .	2566
15-AAAA-b	goroa	1	1	41,062	70,956	0	27.50	68	B	41		pn .					0 . s . .	2567
15-AAAB	BURUNGE-ALAGWA cluster	1	2	55,936	96,660		12.00	43	A	3		. . .					0	2568
15-AAAB-a	wasi	1	1	13,507	23,341	0	12.00	45	A	3		. . .					0	2569
15-AAAB-b	burunge	1	1	42,429	73,319	0	12.00	43	A	3		. . .					0	2570
15-AB	KWADZA-ASA chain	1	2	8,993	15,540		1.63	29	A	9		. . .					0	2571
15-ABA	**KWADZA net**	1	1	3,352	5,792		1.01	28	A	4		. . .					0	2572
15-ABAA	KWADZA cluster	1	1	3,352	5,792		1.01	28	A	4		. . .					0	2573
15-ABAA-a	kwadza	1	1	3,352	5,792	0	1.01	28	A	4		. . .					0	2574
15-ABB	**ASAX net**	1	1	5,641	9,748		2.00	30	A	9		. . .					0	2575
15-ABBA	ASAX cluster	1	1	5,641	9,748		2.00	30	A	9		. . .					0	2576
15-ABBA-a	aasax	1	1	5,641	9,748	0	2.00	30	A	9		. . .					0	2577
15-AC	MBUGU chain	1	1	43,800	75,688		10.00	41	A	4		. . .					0	2578
15-ACA	**MBUGU net**	1	1	43,800	75,688		10.00	41	A	4		. . .					2579
15-ACAA	MA'A cluster	1	1	43,800	75,688		10.00	41	A	4		. . .					0	2580
15-ACAA-a	ma'a	1	1	43,800	75,688	0	10.00	41	A	4		. . .					0	2581
15-B	**TANA-COASTAL set**	1	1	4,181	5,804		0.12	24	A	5		. . .					0	2582
15-BA	TANA-COASTAL chain	1	1	4,181	5,804		0.12	24	A	5		. . .					0	2583
15-BAA	**DAHALO net**	1	1	4,181	5,804		0.12	24	A	5		. . .					0	2584
15-BAAA	DAHALO cluster	1	1	4,181	5,804		0.12	24	A	5		. . .					0	2585
15-BAAA-a	guo-garimani	1	1	4,181	5,804	0	0.12	24	A	5		. . .					0	2586
16	**OMOTIC zone**	1	35	5,600,309	10,324,707		40.55	78	B	41		PN .					2 . s . .	2589
16-A	**SOUTH OMOTIC set**	1	4	169,135	311,485		16.38	47	A	12		. . .					0	2590
16-AA	SOUTH OMOTIC chain	1	4	169,135	311,485		16.38	47	A	12		. . .					0	2591
16-AAA	**HAMAR-BANA net**	1	2	31,320	57,760		3.78	24	A	12		. . .					0	2592
16-AAAA	HAMAR-BANA cluster	1	2	31,320	57,760		3.78	24	A	12		. . .					0	2593
16-AAAA-a	hamar-apo	1	1	30,156	55,614	0	2.00	22	A	12	Hamer-banna	. . .					0	2594
16-AAAA-b	bana-apo					0				12		. . .					0	2595
16-AAAA-c	karo	1	1	1,164	2,146	0	50.00	77	B	12		. . .					0	2596
16-AAAA-d	bashada-apo					0				12		. . .					0	2597
16-AAB	**ARI net**	1	1	134,499	247,610		19.67	53	B	12		. . .					0	2598
16-AABA	AARI-SHANGAMA cluster	1	1	131,499	242,510		20.00	54	B	12	Aari	. . .					0	2599
16-AABA-a	aari					0				12		. . .					0	2600
16-AABA-b	gozza					0				12		. . .					0	2601
16-AABA-c	biyo					0				12		. . .					0	2602
16-AABA-d	laydo					0				12		. . .					0	2603
16-AABA-e	seyki					0				12		. . .					0	2604
16-AABA-f	shangama					0				12		. . .					0	2605
16-AABA-g	sido					0				12		. . .					0	2606
16-AABA-h	wubahamer					0				12		. . .					0	2607
16-AABA-i	zeddo					0				12		. . .					0	2608
16-AABB	GALILA cluster	1	1	3,000	5,100		5.00	24	A	0		. . .					0	2609
16-AABB-a	galila	1	1	3,000	5,100	0	5.00	24	A	0		. . .					0	2610
16-AAC	**DIM net**	1	1	3,316	6,115		1.99	22	A	2		. . .					0	2611
16-AACA	DIM cluster	1	1	3,316	6,115		1.99	22	A	2		. . .					0	2612
16-AACA-a	dim-'ap	1	1	3,316	6,115	0	1.99	22	A	2		. . .					0	2613
16-B	**OMETO-GONGA set**	1	23	5,317,555	9,803,689		41.25	79	B	41		PN .					2 . s . .	2614
16-BA	OMETO chain	1	15	4,207,269	7,758,983		41.42	80	B	41		PN .					2 . s . .	2615
16-BAA	**CHARA net**	1	1	20,371	37,568		40.00	69	B	4		. . .					0	2616
16-BAAA	CHARA cluster	1	1	20,371	37,568		40.00	69	B	4		. . .					0	2617
16-BAAA-a	chara	1	1	20,371	37,568	0	40.00	69	B	4		. . .					0	2618
16-BAB	**ZAYSE-ZERGULLA net**	1	1	30,976	57,126		2.00	24	A	2		. . .					0	2619
16-BABA	ZAYSE-ZERGULLA cluster	1	1	30,976	57,126		2.00	24	A	2		. . .					0	2620
16-BABA-a	zayse	1	1	30,976	57,126	0	2.00	24	A	2		. . .					0	2621
16-BABA-b	zergulla					0				2		. . .					0	2622
16-BAC	**KOYRA-GIDICHO net**	1	1	40,360	74,375		30.00	64	B	12		. . .					0	2623
16-BACA	KOORE cluster	1	1	39,960	73,695		30.00	64	B	12		. . .					0	2624
16-BACA-a	koore-nuuna	1	1	39,960	73,695	0	30.00	64	B	12	Koorete	. . .					0	2625
16-BACB	GIDICHO cluster	1	1	400	680		30.00	65	B	0		. . .					0	2626
16-BACB-a	gidicho	1	1	400	680	0	30.00	65	B	0		. . .					0	2627
16-BAD	**KACHAMA net**	1	1	776	1,431		39.95	69	B	0		. . .					0	2628
16-BADA	KACHAMA cluster	1	1	776	1,431		39.95	69	B	0		. . .					0	2629
16-BADA-a	kachama	1	1	776	1,431	0	39.95	69	B	0		. . .					0	2630
16-BAE	**GANJULE net**	1	1	63	115		9.52	37	A	5		. . .					0	2631
16-BAEA	GANJULE cluster	1	1	63	115		9.52	37	A	5		. . .					0	2632
16-BAEA-a	ganjule	1	1	63	115	0	9.52	37	A	5		. . .					0	2633
16-BAF	**OMETO-CENTRAL net**	1	7	3,836,578	7,075,413		40.13	81	B	41		PN .					2 . s . .	2634
16-BAFA	WELAITTA cluster	1	3	2,888,526	5,327,017		44.98	89	B	41		PN .					2 . s . .	2635

Continued overleaf

Table 9-13 continued

Code 1	REFERENCE NAME / Autoglossonym 2	Coun 3	Peo 4	Mother-tongue speakers in 2000 5	in 2025 6	Media radio 7	CHURCH AC% 8	E% 9	Wld 10	Tr 11	Biblioglossonym 12	Print 13-15	P-activity 16	N-activity 17	B-activity 18	J-year 19	Jayuh 20-24	Ref 25
16-BAFA-a	welaitta	1	1	2,877,984	5,307,576	0	45.00	89	B	41	Wolayta*	PN.	1934-1943	1981		1998	2.s..	2636
16-BAFA-b	dache	1	1	5,318	9,807	0	50.00	84	B	41		pn.					1.s..	2639
16-BAFA-c	dorze	1	1	5,224	9,634	0	30.00	63	B	41		pn.					1.s..	2640
16-BAFB	GEMU-GOFA cluster	1	2	745,573	1,374,985		18.74	47	A	24		P..					0....	2641
16-BAFB-a	gemu-dona	1	1	559,787	1,032,358	0	15.00	43	A	24		p..					0....	2642
16-BAFB-b	gofa	1	1	185,786	342,627	0	30.00	61	B	24	Gofa	P..	1934				0....	2643
16-BAFC	KULO-KONTA cluster	1	1	196,648	362,657		50.00	82	B	0		...					0....	2644
16-BAFC-a	kulo-kale	1	1	196,648	362,657	0	50.00	82	B	0		...					0....	2645
16-BAFC-b	kunta					0				0		...					0....	2650
16-BAFD	OYDA cluster	1	1	5,831	10,754		39.99	74	B	4		...					0....	2651
16-BAFD-a	oyda	1	1	5,831	10,754	0	39.99	74	B	4		...					0....	2652
16-BAG	**MALE net**	1	2	113,637	209,569		44.00	64	B	12		...					0....	2653
16-BAGA	MALE cluster	1	2	113,637	209,569		44.00	64	B	12		...					0....	2654
16-BAGA-a	male	1	2	113,637	209,569	0	44.00	64	B	12	Male	...					0....	2655
16-BAH	**BASKETO net**	1	1	164,508	303,386		80.00	100	C	20		...					0....	2656
16-BAHA	BASKETO cluster	1	1	164,508	303,386		80.00	100	C	20		...					0....	2657
16-BAHA-a	basketo	1	1	164,508	303,386	0	80.00	100	C	20		...					0....	2658
16-BB	GIMIRA chain	1	1	118,740	216,096		30.00	66	B	41		PN.					0....	2662
16-BBA	**GIMIRA net**	1	1	118,740	216,096		30.00	66	B	41		PN.					0....	2663
16-BBAA	BENCH cluster	1	1	98,740	182,096		30.00	66	B	41	Gimira*	PN.		1990			0...	2664
16-BBAA-a	bench-non					0				41		pn.					0....	2665
16-BBAA-b	mieru					0				41		pn.					0....	2666
16-BBAB	SHE cluster	1	1	20,000	34,000		30.00	65	B	0		...					0....	2667
16-BBAB-a	siiz-dod					0				0		...					0....	2668
16-BBAB-b	kaba					0				0		...					0....	2669
16-BC	YEMSA chain	1	1	603,213	1,112,445		50.00	85	B	12		...					0....	2670
16-BCA	**YEMSA-FUGA net**	1	1	603,213	1,112,445		50.00	85	B	12		...					0....	2671
16-BCAA	YEMSA-FUGA cluster	1	1	603,213	1,112,445		50.00	85	B	12		...					0....	2672
16-BCAA-a	yemsa	1	1	603,213	1,112,445	0	50.00	85	B	12	Yemsa	...					0....	2673
16-BCAA-b	fuga					0				12		...					0....	2674
16-BD	GONGA chain	1	6	388,333	716,165		29.26	62	B	22		P..					0....	2675
16-BDA	**SOUTH GONGA net**	1	2	368,845	680,224		30.00	63	B	22		P..					0....	2676
16-BDAA	SOUTH GONGA cluster	1	2	368,845	680,224		30.00	63	B	22		P..					0....	2677
16-BDAA-a	kafaa	1	1	260,426	480,278	0	30.00	63	B	22	Kafa*	P..	1934-1986				0....	2678
16-BDAA-b	mocha	1	1	108,419	199,946	0	30.00	62	B	22		p..					0....	2682
16-BDAA-c	bosha			0	0	0	0.00	0		22		p..					0....	2683
16-BDB	**GONGA-CENTRAL net**	1	1	1,270	2,342		5.04	32	A	6		...					0....	2684
16-BDBA	CENTRAL GONGA cluster	1	1	1,270	2,342		5.04	32	A	6		...					0....	2685
16-BDBA-a	afan-mao	1	1	1,270	2,342	0	5.04	32	A	6		...					0....	2686
16-BDC	**NORTH GONGA net**	1	2	11,962	22,061		21.69	47	A	5		...					0....	2687
16-BDCA	NORTH GONGA cluster	1	2	11,962	22,061		21.69	47	A	5		...					0....	2688
16-BDCA-a	boro	1	1	5,706	10,523	0	39.99	68	B	5		...					0....	2689
16-BDCA-b	guba	1	1	6,256	11,538	0	5.00	27	A	5		...					0....	2690
16-BDCA-c	naga					0				5		...					0....	2691
16-BDCA-d	amuru					0				5		...					0....	2692
16-BDD	**GONGA-WAMBERA net**	1	1	6,256	11,538		5.00	29	A	0		...					0....	2693
16-BDDA	WAMBERA cluster	1	1	6,256	11,538		5.00	29	A	0		...					0....	2694
16-BDDA-a	wambera	1	1	6,256	11,538	0	5.00	29	A	0		...					0....	2695
16-C	**DIZI-SHEKO set**	1	3	91,576	168,884		49.13	79	B	4		...					0....	2696
16-CA	DIZI-SHEKO chain	1	3	91,576	168,884		49.13	79	B	4		...					0....	2697
16-CAA	**DIZI net**	1	1	27,879	51,414		70.00	100	C	2		...					0....	2698
16-CAAA	DIZI cluster	1	1	27,879	51,414		70.00	100	C	2		...					0....	2699
16-CAAA-a	dizi-nuu	1	1	27,879	51,414	0	70.00	100	C	2		...					0....	2700
16-CAB	**NAO net**	1	1	19,007	35,053		40.00	68	B	4		...					0....	2706
16-CABA	NA'O cluster	1	1	19,007	35,053		40.00	68	B	4		...					0....	2707
16-CABA-a	na'o	1	1	19,007	35,053	0	40.00	68	B	4		...					0....	2708
16-CAC	**SHEKO-DORSA net**	1	1	44,690	82,417		40.00	70	B	2		...					0....	2709
16-CACA	SHEKO-DORSA cluster	1	1	44,690	82,417		40.00	70	B	2		...					0....	2710
16-CACA-a	sheko					0				2		...					0....	2711
16-CACA-b	bulla					0				2		...					0....	2712
16-CACA-c	dorsha	1	1	44,690	82,417	0	40.00	70	B	2		...					0....	2713
16-D	**BAMBESHI-DIDESSA set**	1	2	8,979	16,557		31.56	61	B	4		...					0....	2714
16-DA	NORTH MAO chain	1	2	8,979	16,557		31.56	61	B	4		...					0....	2715
16-DAA	**DIDESSA net**	1	1	1,233	2,273		9.98	38	A	0		...					0....	2716
16-DAAA	DIDESSA cluster	1	1	1,233	2,273		9.98	38	A	0		...					0....	2717
16-DAAA-a	didessa	1	1	1,233	2,273	0	9.98	38	A	0		...					0....	2718
16-DAB	**BAMBESHI net**	1	1	7,746	14,284		35.00	65	B	4		...					0....	2719
16-DABA	BAMBESHI cluster	1	1	7,746	14,284		35.00	65	B	4		...					0....	2720
16-DABA-a	mao-koole	1	1	7,746	14,284	0	35.00	65	B	4		...					0....	2721
16-E	**HOZO-SEZO set**	1	2	6,808	12,554		22.49	44	A	2		...					0....	2724
16-EA	HOZO-SEZO chain	1	2	6,808	12,554		22.49	44	A	2		...					0....	2725
16-EAA	**HOZO-SEZO net**	1	2	6,808	12,554		22.49	44	A	2		...					0....	2726
16-EAAA	HOZO-SEZO cluster	1	2	6,808	12,554		22.49	44	A	2		...					0....	2727
16-EAAA-a	hozo-wandi	1	1	3,404	6,277	0	9.99	37	A	2		...					0....	2728
16-EAAA-b	sezo-wangi	1	1	3,404	6,277	0	34.99	52	B	2		...					0....	2729
16-F	**GANZA set**	1	1	6,256	11,538		10.01	36	A	8		...					0....	2730
16-FA	GANZA chain	1	1	6,256	11,538		10.01	36	A	8		...					0....	2731

Continued opposite

Table 9-13 continued

Code 1	REFERENCE NAME / Autoglossonym 2	Coun 3	Peo 4	Mother-tongue speakers in 2000 5	in 2025 6	Media radio 7	CHURCH AC% 8	E% 9	Wld 10	Tr 11	Biblioglossonym 12	SCRIPTURES Print P-activity 13-15 16	N-activity 17	B-activity 18	J-year 19	Jayuh 20-24	Ref 25
16-FAA	**GANZA net**	1	1	6,256	11,538		10.01	36	A	8		. . .				0. . . .	2732
16-FAAA	GANZA cluster	1	1	6,256	11,538		10.01	36	A	8		. . .				0. . . .	2733
16-FAAA-a	ganza	1	1	6,256	11,538	0	10.01	36	A	8		. . .				0. . . .	2734
17	**EAST CHADIC zone**	3	51	1,726,563	3,087,156		28.15	61	B	82		PNB				0.s..	2737
17-A	**MUBI-DANGLA set**	2	11	258,076	468,127		11.74	31	A	12		. . .				0. . . .	2738
17-AA	MUBI-BIRGIT chain	1	5	140,860	256,060		17.88	44	A	4		. . .				0. . . .	2739
17-AAA	**MASMAJE net**	1	1	32,750	59,534		20.00	47	A	4		. . .				0. . . .	2740
17-AAAA	MASMAJE cluster	1	1	32,750	59,534		20.00	47	A	4		. . .				0. . . .	2741
17-AAAA-a	masmaje	1	1	32,750	59,534	0	20.00	47	A	4		. . .				0. . . .	2742
17-AAB	**MUBI net**	1	1	73,843	134,234		25.00	56	B	2		. . .				0. . . .	2743
17-AABA	MUBI cluster	1	1	73,843	134,234		25.00	56	B	2		. . .				0. . . .	2744
17-AABA-a	mubi	1	1	73,843	134,234	0	25.00	56	B	2		. . .				0. . . .	2745
17-AAC	**KAJAKSE net**	1	1	15,973	29,036		1.00	15	A	4		. . .				0. . . .	2746
17-AACA	KAJAGISE cluster	1	1	15,973	29,036		1.00	15	A	4		. . .				0. . . .	2747
17-AACA-a	kajagise	1	1	15,973	29,036	0	1.00	15	A	4		. . .				0. . . .	2748
17-AAD	**BIRGIT net**	1	1	10,089	18,341		0.10	19	A	4		. . .				0. . . .	2749
17-AADA	BIRGIT cluster	1	1	10,089	18,341		0.10	19	A	4		. . .				0. . . .	2750
17-AADA-a	birgit	1	1	10,089	18,341	0	0.10	19	A	4		. . .				0. . . .	2751
17-AAE	**TORAM net**	1	1	8,205	14,915		0.10	14	A	4		. . .				0. . . .	2752
17-AAEA	TORAM cluster	1	1	8,205	14,915		0.10	14	A	4		. . .				0. . . .	2753
17-AAEA-a	toram	1	1	8,205	14,915	0	0.10	14	A	4		. . .				0. . . .	2754
17-AB	DANGLA-BIDIYO chain	2	6	117,216	212,067		4.36	16	A	12		. . .				0. . . .	2755
17-ABA	**SOUTH JONKOR net**	1	1	3,000	5,100		1.00	16	A	4		. . .				0. . . .	2756
17-ABAA	SOUTH JONKOR cluster	1	1	3,000	5,100		1.00	16	A	4		. . .				0. . . .	2757
17-ABAA-a	South jonkor	1	1	3,000	5,100	0	1.00	16	A	4		. . .				0. . . .	2758
17-ABB	**MOGUM net**	2	2	15,324	27,670		31.81	55	B	2		. . .				0. . . .	2759
17-ABBA	MOGUM cluster	2	2	15,324	27,670		31.81	55	B	2		. . .				0. . . .	2760
17-ABBA-a	kofa	2	2	15,324	27,670	0	31.81	55	B	2		. . .				0. . . .	2761
17-ABBA-b	East mogum					0				2		. . .				0. . . .	2762
17-ABBA-c	West mogum					0				2		. . .				0. . . .	2763
17-ABC	**JEGU net**	1	1	2,000	3,400		10.00	33	A	0		. . .				0. . . .	2764
17-ABCA	JEGU cluster	1	1	2,000	3,400		10.00	33	A	0		. . .				0. . . .	2765
17-ABCA-a	jegu					0				0		. . .				0. . . .	2766
17-ABD	**BIDIYO-WAANA net**	1	1	23,388	42,516		0.00	9	A	2		. . .				0. . . .	2767
17-ABDA	BIDIYO-WAANA cluster	1	1	23,388	42,516		0.00	9	A	2		. . .				0. . . .	2768
17-ABDA-a	bidiyo	1	1	23,388	42,516	0	0.00	9	A	2		. . .				0. . . .	2769
17-ABDA-b	waana					0				2		. . .				0. . . .	2772
17-ABE	**NORTH JONKOR net**	1	1	30,768	55,932		0.00	9	A	12		. . .				0. . . .	2776
17-ABEA	NORTH JONKOR cluster	1	1	30,768	55,932		0.00	9	A	12		. . .				0. . . .	2777
17-ABEA-a	migaama	1	1	30,768	55,932	0	0.00	9	A	12	Migaama	. . .				0. . . .	2778
17-ABEA-b	gamiya					0				12		. . .				0. . . .	2779
17-ABEA-c	doga					0				12		. . .				0. . . .	2780
17-ABF	**DANGLA net**	1	1	36,371	65,879		0.01	9	A	12		. . .				0. . . .	2781
17-ABFA	EAST DANGLA cluster	1	1	34,371	62,479		0.00	9	A	12		. . .				0. . . .	2782
17-ABFA-a	dangla-korlongo	1	1	34,371	62,479	0	0.00	9	A	12	Dangaleat	. . .				0. . . .	2783
17-ABFA-b	Central dangla					0				12		. . .				0. . . .	2788
17-ABFB	WEST DANGLA cluster	1	1	2,000	3,400		0.10	14	A	0		. . .				0. . . .	2793
17-ABFB-a	West dangla	1	1	2,000	3,400	0	0.10	14	A	0		. . .				0. . . .	2794
17-ABG	**MAHWA net**	1	1	6,365	11,570		0.02	8	A	2		. . .				0. . . .	2799
17-ABGA	MAHWA cluster	1	1	6,365	11,570		0.02	8	A	2		. . .				0. . . .	2800
17-ABGA-a	mahwa	1	1	6,365	11,570	0	0.02	8	A	2		. . .				0. . . .	2801
17-B	**MOKULU set**	1	2	18,080	32,864		0.11	10	A	12		. . .				0. . . .	2802
17-BA	MOKULU chain	1	2	18,080	32,864		0.11	10	A	12		. . .				0. . . .	2803
17-BAA	**MOKULU net**	1	2	18,080	32,864		0.11	10	A	12		. . .				0. . . .	2804
17-BAAA	MOKULU cluster	1	2	18,080	32,864		0.11	10	A	12	Mokulu	. . .				0. . . .	2805
17-BAAA-a	mokilko	1	1	16,170	29,393	0	0.00	9	A	12		. . .				0. . . .	2806
17-BAAA-b	seginki					0				12		. . .				0. . . .	2807
17-BAAA-c	doliki					0				12		. . .				0. . . .	2808
17-BAAA-d	moriko					0				12		. . .				0. . . .	2809
17-BAAA-e	mezimko					0				12		. . .				0. . . .	2810
17-BAAA-f	gugiko					0				12		. . .				0. . . .	2811
17-C	**SOKORO-BAREIN set**	1	3	14,740	26,793		2.10	16	A	12		. . .				0. . . .	2812
17-CA	SOKORO-BAREIN chain	1	3	14,740	26,793		2.10	16	A	12		. . .				0. . . .	2813
17-CAA	**BAREIN net**	1	1	5,219	9,487		0.00	10	A	3		. . .				0. . . .	2814
17-CAAA	BAREIN cluster	1	1	5,219	9,487		0.00	10	A	3		. . .				0. . . .	2815
17-CAAA-a	barein	1	1	5,219	9,487	0	0.00	10	A	3		. . .				0. . . .	2816
17-CAB	**SOKORO net**	1	1	6,187	11,246		4.99	23	A	12		. . .				0. . . .	2817
17-CABA	SOKORO cluster	1	1	6,187	11,246		4.99	23	A	12	Sokoro	. . .				0. . . .	2818
17-CABA-a	sokoro					0				12		. . .				0. . . .	2819
17-CABA-b	bedanga					0				12		. . .				0. . . .	2820
17-CAC	**SABA net**	1	1	3,334	6,060		0.00	11	A	3		. . .				0. . . .	2821
17-CACA	SABA cluster	1	1	3,334	6,060		0.00	11	A	3		. . .				0. . . .	2822
17-CACA-a	saba	1	1	3,334	6,060	0	0.00	11	A	3		. . .				0. . . .	2823
17-D	**SOMRAI-MILTU set**	3	18	359,964	632,184		37.92	71	B	61		PNB				0. . . .	2824
17-DA	SARWA chain	2	2	2,788	5,013		1.00	23	A	4		. . .				0. . . .	2825

Continued overleaf

Table 9-13 continued

Code 1	REFERENCE NAME / Autoglossonym 2	Coun 3	Peo 4	Mother-tongue speakers in 2000 5	in 2025 6	Media radio 7	CHURCH AC% 8	E% 9	Wld 10	Tr 11	Biblioglossonym 12	SCRIPTURES Print 13-15	P-activity 16	N-activity 17	B-activity 18	J-year 19	Jayuh 20-24	Ref 25
17-DAA	**SARWA net**	2	2	2,788	5,013		1.00	23	A	4		...					0....	2826
17-DAAA	SARWA cluster	2	2	2,788	5,013		1.00	23	A	4		...					0....	2827
17-DAAA-a	sarwa	2	2	2,788	5,013	0	1.00	23	A	4		...					0....	2828
17-DB	BUSO chain	1	1	103	186		30.10	52	B	8		...					0....	2829
17-DBA	**BUSO net**	1	1	103	186		30.10	52	B	8		...					0....	2830
17-DBAA	BUSO cluster	1	1	103	186		30.10	52	B	8		...					0....	2831
17-DBAA-a	buso	1	1	103	186	0	30.10	52	B	8		...					0....	2832
17-DC	GADANG chain	1	1	4,710	8,562		0.00	9	A	2		...					0....	2833
17-DCA	**GADANG net**	1	1	4,710	8,562		0.00	9	A	2		...					0....	2834
17-DCAA	GADANG cluster	1	1	4,710	8,562		0.00	9	A	2		...					0....	2835
17-DCAA-a	gadang	1	1	4,710	8,562	0	0.00	9	A	2		...					0....	2836
17-DD	MILTU chain	1	1	345	627		2.03	24	A	5		...					0....	2837
17-DDA	**MILTU net**	1	1	345	627		2.03	24	A	5		...					0....	2838
17-DDAA	MILTU cluster	1	1	345	627		2.03	24	A	5		...					0....	2839
17-DDAA-a	miltu	1	1	345	627	0	2.03	24	A	5		...					0....	2840
17-DE	NDAM-TUMAK chain	1	3	42,788	77,780		22.60	52	B	41		PN.					0....	2841
17-DEA	**NDAM net**	1	1	8,760	15,923		0.10	17	A	12		...					0....	2842
17-DEAA	NDAM cluster	1	1	8,760	15,923		0.10	17	A	12	Ndam	...					0....	2843
17-DEAA-a	dik-ndam					0				12		...					0....	2844
17-DEAA-b	ndam-ndam					0				12		...					0....	2845
17-DEB	**MAWER-MIRE net**	1	1	1,887	3,430		1.01	19	A	4		...					0....	2846
17-DEBA	MAWER-MIRE cluster	1	1	1,887	3,430		1.01	19	A	4		...					0....	2847
17-DEBA-a	mawer					0				4		...					0....	2848
17-DEBA-b	mire	1	1	1,887	3,430	0	1.01	19	A	4		...					0....	2849
17-DEC	**TUMAK net**	1	1	32,141	58,427		30.00	63	B	41		PN.					0....	2850
17-DECA	TUMAK cluster	1	1	32,141	58,427		30.00	63	B	41		PN.					0....	2851
17-DECA-a	tumak	1	1	32,141	58,427	0	30.00	63	B	41	Tumak	PN.		1988			0....	2852
17-DF	SOMRAI chain	2	2	71,506	115,081		30.00	61	B	12		...					0....	2853
17-DFA	**SOMRAI net**	2	2	71,506	115,081		30.00	61	B	12		...					0....	2854
17-DFAA	SOMRAI cluster	2	2	71,506	115,081		30.00	61	B	12		...					0....	2855
17-DFAA-a	somrai	2	2	71,506	115,081	0	30.00	61	B	12	Somrai	...					0....	2856
17-DG	GABRI-KIMRE chain	2	5	107,704	189,710		30.56	60	B	41		PN.					0....	2857
17-DGA	**KIMRE net**	1	1	20,212	36,741		20.00	46	A	12		...					0....	2858
17-DGAA	KIMRE cluster	1	1	20,212	36,741		20.00	46	A	12		...					0....	2859
17-DGAA-a	kimruwa	1	1	20,212	36,741	0	20.00	46	A	12	Kimre	...					0....	2860
17-DGAA-b	bordo					0				12		...					0....	2861
17-DGAA-c	tchere-aiba					0				12		...					0....	2862
17-DGB	**GABRI-TOBANGA net**	2	3	64,725	111,583		37.57	69	B	41		PN.					0....	2863
17-DGBA	GABRI cluster	2	3	64,725	111,583		37.57	69	B	12	Gabri	...					0....	2864
17-DGBA-a	moonde					0				12		...					0....	2865
17-DGBA-b	dormo					0				12		...					0....	2866
17-DGBA-c	darbe					0				12		...					0....	2867
17-DGBB	TOBANGA cluster									41		PN.					0....	2868
17-DGBB-a	tobanga					0				41	Tobanga	PN.	1975	1978			0....	2869
17-DGC	**KABALAI net**	1	1	22,767	41,386		20.00	47	A	4		...					0....	2870
17-DGCA	KABALAI cluster	1	1	22,767	41,386		20.00	47	A	4		...					0....	2871
17-DGCA-a	kabalai	1	1	22,767	41,386	0	20.00	47	A	4		...					0....	2872
17-DH	NANCERE chain	1	1	91,157	165,707		60.00	100	B	61		PNB					0....	2873
17-DHA	**NANCERE net**	1	1	91,157	165,707		60.00	100	B	61		PNB					0....	2874
17-DHAA	NANCERE cluster	1	1	91,157	165,707		60.00	100	B	61		PNB					0....	2875
17-DHAA-a	nancere	1	1	91,157	165,707	0	60.00	100	B	61	Nangjere*	PNB	1947-1949	1956	1986		0....	2876
17-DI	LELE chain	2	2	38,863	69,518		45.60	81	B	41		PN.					0....	2877
17-DIA	**LELE net**	2	2	38,863	69,518		45.60	81	B	41		PN.					0....	2878
17-DIAA	LELE cluster	2	2	38,863	69,518		45.60	81	B	41		PN.					0....	2879
17-DIAA-a	lele	2	2	38,863	69,518	0	45.60	81	B	41	Lele	PN.	1962-1985	1991			0....	2880
17-E	**KWANG-KERA set**	2	3	85,296	154,605		32.51	65	B	35		P..					0....	2881
17-EA	KWANG chain	1	1	21,391	38,886		40.00	68	B	12		...					0....	2882
17-EAA	**KWANG net**	1	1	21,391	38,886		40.00	68	B	12		...					0....	2883
17-EAAA	KWANG cluster	1	1	21,391	38,886		40.00	68	B	12		...					0....	2884
17-EAAA-a	kwang	1	1	21,391	38,886	0	40.00	68	B	12	Kwang	...					0....	2885
17-EAAA-b	ngam					0				12	Ngam	...					0....	2886
17-EAAA-c	tchagin					0				12		...					0....	2890
17-EAAA-d	mobu					0				12		...					0....	2891
17-EB	KERA chain	2	2	63,905	115,719		30.00	64	B	35		P..					0....	2892
17-EBA	**KERA net**	2	2	63,905	115,719		30.00	64	B	35		P..					0....	2893
17-EBAA	KERA cluster	2	2	63,905	115,719		30.00	64	B	35		P..					0....	2894
17-EBAA-a	kera	2	2	63,905	115,719	0	30.00	64	B	35	Kera	P..	1988-1995				0....	2895
17-F	**MASA set**	2	12	852,256	1,529,108		30.12	68	B	82		PNB					0.s..	2896
17-FA	MASA chain	2	12	852,256	1,529,108		30.12	68	B	82		PNB					0.s..	2897
17-FAA	**MASA net**	2	7	735,821	1,319,578		27.48	65	B	82		PNB					0....	2898
17-FAAA	MASA cluster	2	3	396,866	705,506		23.41	60	B	42		PN.					0....	2899
17-FAAA-a	yagwa	1	1	256,282	449,949	0	20.00	57	B	42	Masana	PN.	1934-1985	1950-1955			0....	2900
17-FAAA-b	domo					0				42		pn.					0....	2901
17-FAAA-c	walya					0				42		pn.					0....	2902
17-FAAA-d	bugudum					0				42		pn.					0....	2903
17-FAAA-e	viri					0				42		pn.					0....	2904
17-FAAA-f	gizay					0				42		pn.					0....	2905

Continued opposite

Table 9-13 continued

Code 1	REFERENCE NAME / Autoglossonym 2	Coun 3	Peo 4	Mother-tongue speakers in 2000 5	in 2025 6	Media radio 7	CHURCH AC% 8	E% 9	Wld 10	Tr 11	Biblioglossonym 12	SCRIPTURES Print 13-15	P–activity 16	N–activity 17	B–activity 18	J-year 19	Jayuh 20-24	Ref 25
17-FAAA-g	bongor	1	1	138,875	252,450		30.00	66	B	42		pn.					0....	2906
17-FAAA-h	tura					0				42		pn.					0....	2907
17-FAAA-i	gumay					0				42		pn.					0....	2908
17-FAAA-j	ham					0				42		pn.					0....	2909
17-FAAA-k	may-mbara	1	1	1,709	3,107	0	0.18	20	A	42		pn.					0....	2910
17-FAAB	**ZUMAYA cluster**	1	1	60	106		20.00	47	A	8		...					0....	2911
17-FAAB-a	zumaya	1	1	60	106	0	20.00	47	A	8		...					0....	2912
17-FAAC	**MOSI cluster**	2	2	178,589	322,793		43.33	78	B	41		PN.					0....	2913
17-FAAC-a	mosi	2	2	178,589	322,793	0	43.33	78	B	41	Musey	PN.	1967-1986	1995-1996			0....	2914
17-FAAD	**MARBA cluster**	1	1	158,306	287,773		20.00	64	B	82		PNB					0....	2919
17-FAAD-a	marba	1	1	158,306	287,773	0	20.00	64	B	82	Azumeina*	PNB	1967-1986	1978	1996		0....	2920
17-FAAE	**MONOGOY cluster**	1	1	2,000	3,400		10.00	33	A	4		...					0....	2921
17-FAAE-a	monogoy	1	1	2,000	3,400	0	10.00	33	A	4		...					0....	2922
17-FAB	**ZIME net**	2	5	116,435	209,530		46.82	83	B	41		PN.					0.s..	2923
17-FABA	**MESME cluster**	1	1	15,000	25,500		65.00	96	C	0		...					0....	2924
17-FABA-a	mesme	1	1	15,000	25,500	0	65.00	96	C	0		...					0....	2925
17-FABA-b	bero					0				0		...					0....	2926
17-FABA-c	zamre					0				0		...					0....	2927
17-FABB	**ZIME cluster**	2	5	101,435	184,030		44.13	81	B	41	Zime*	PN.	1983-1991	1995-1996			0.s..	2928
17-FABB-a	pala-wa					0				41		pn.					0.s..	2929
17-FABB-b	sorga					0				41		pn.					0.s..	2930
17-FABB-c	ngete	1	1	13,140	23,886	0	10.00	43	A	41	Ngete	pn.					0.s..	2931
17-FABB-d	ngoy					0				41		pn.					0.s..	2932
17-FABB-e	batna					0				41		pn.					0.s..	2933
17-FABB-f	herd'e	1	1	30,604	55,632	0	50.00	90	B	41	Kado*	PN.		1980			0.s..	2934
17-FABB-g	cimiang					0				41		pn.					0.s..	2935
17-FABB-h	taari					0				41		pn.					0.s..	2936
17-FABB-i	peve	2	2	32,079	57,953	0	35.84	74	B	41	Peve	PN.	1983	1986			0.s..	2937
17-G	**GIDAR-LAM set**	2	2	138,151	243,475		25.00	63	B	41		PN.					0.s..	2938
17-GA	GIDAR-LAM chain	2	2	138,151	243,475		25.00	63	B	41		PN.					0.s..	2939
17-GAA	**GIDAR-LAM net**	2	2	138,151	243,475		25.00	63	B	41		PN.					0.s..	2940
17-GAAA	**GIDAR-LAM cluster**	2	2	138,151	243,475		25.00	63	B	41		PN.					0.s..	2941
17-GAAA-a	gidar	2	2	138,151	243,475	0	25.00	63	B	41	Guidar*	PN.	1973-1978	1986			0.s..	2942
17-GAAA-b	lam					0				41		pn.					0.s..	2943
18	**BIUMANDARIC zone**	4	103	4,566,039	7,717,157		23.02	57	B	61		PNB					4.s..	2944
18-A	**MUSGU-MBARA set**	2	2	154,576	273,700		19.99	55	B	46		PN.					0....	2945
18-AA	MUSGU-MBARA chain	2	2	154,576	273,700		19.99	55	B	46		PN.					0....	2946
18-AAA	**MUSGU-MULWI net**	2	2	154,276	273,190		20.00	56	B	46		PN.					0....	2947
18-AAAA	**MUSGU-MULWI cluster**	2	2	154,276	273,190		20.00	56	B	46		PN.					0....	2948
18-AAAA-a	muzuk					0				46		pn.					0....	2949
18-AAAA-b	mpus					0				46		pn.					0....	2950
18-AAAA-c	beege					0				46		pn.					0....	2951
18-AAAA-d	mulwi	1	1	37,490	68,150	0	20.00	54	A	46		pn.					0....	2952
18-AAAA-e	muskum	1	1	116,786	205,040	0	20.00	56	B	46	Mousgoum*	PN.		1964			0....	2953
18-AAAA-f	gwai					0				46		pn.					0....	2954
18-AAAA-g	ngilemong					0				46		pn.					0....	2955
18-AAAA-h	maniling					0				46		pn.					0....	2956
18-AAAA-i	abi					0				46		pn.					0....	2957
18-AAAA-j	luggong					0				46		pn.					0....	2958
18-AAB	**MBARA net**	1	1	300	510		15.00	42	A	0		...					0....	2959
18-AABA	**MBARA cluster**	1	1	300	510		15.00	42	A	0		...					2960
18-AABA-a	mbara	1	1	300	510	0	15.00	42	A	0		...					0....	2961
18-B	**KOTOKO-MIDA set**	4	22	351,557	622,494		9.40	30	A	12		...					0....	2962
18-BA	MIDA chain	1	2	12,294	21,584		10.00	34	A	4		...					0....	2963
18-BAA	**MIDA net**	1	2	12,294	21,584		10.00	34	A	4		...					0....	2964
18-BAAA	**MAJERA-HWALEM cluster**	1	1	7,769	13,639		10.00	34	A	4		...					0....	2965
18-BAAA-a	majera	1	1	7,769	13,639	0	10.00	34	A	4		...					0....	2966
18-BAAA-b	kajire-d'ulo					0				4		...					0....	2967
18-BAAA-c	hwalem					0				4		...					0....	2968
18-BAAB	**JINA cluster**	1	1	4,525	7,945		10.01	34	A	4		...					0....	2969
18-BAAB-a	jina	1	1	4,525	7,945	0	10.01	34	A	4		...					0....	2970
18-BAAB-b	sarassara					0				4		...					0....	2971
18-BAAB-c	tchide					0				4		...					0....	2972
18-BAAB-d	muxule					0				4		...					0....	2973
18-BAAB-e	mae					0				4		...					0....	2974
18-BB	KOTOKO chain	4	20	339,263	600,910		9.37	30	A	12		...					0....	2975
18-BBA	**KOTOKO net**	3	16	264,690	464,880		12.01	33	A	5		...					0....	2976
18-BBAA	**SOUTH KOTOKO cluster**	3	8	110,625	194,180		4.54	21	A	3		...					0....	2977
18-BBAA-a	lagwan	3	4	80,003	138,702	0	5.89	25	A	3		...					0....	2978
18-BBAA-b	mser	2	2	4,547	8,079	0	6.71	33	A	3		...					0....	2982
18-BBAB	**CENTRAL KOTOKO cluster**	3	7	152,069	267,424		17.56	41	A	5		...					0....	2989
18-BBAB-a	maslam	2	2	15,650	27,962	0	1.05	19	A	5		...					0....	2990
18-BBAB-b	afade	2	2	36,316	61,335	0	1.72	21	A	5		...					0....	2993
18-BBAB-c	malgbe	2	2	98,595	175,479	0	25.52	52	B	5		...					0....	2994
18-BBAB-d	mpade	1	1	1,508	2,648	0	50.00	82	B	5		...					0....	2999
18-BBAC	**JILBE cluster**	1	1	1,996	3,276		3.01	18	A	4		...					0....	3005
18-BBAC-a	jilbe	1	1	1,996	3,276	0	3.01	18	A	4		...					0....	3006
18-BBB	**BUDUMA net**	4	4	74,573	136,030		0.02	19	A	12		...					0....	3007
18-BBBA	**BUDUMA cluster**	4	4	74,573	136,030		0.02	19	A	12		...					0....	3008
18-BBBA-a	yidena	4	4	74,573	136,030	0	0.02	19	A	12	Buduma	...					0....	3009
18-BBBA-b	kakaa					0				12		...					0....	3010
18-C	**WANDALA-LAAMANG set**	2	17	453,983	766,895		8.98	38	A	41		PN.					0....	3011
18-CA	WANDALA-GLAVDA chain	2	9	275,813	470,028		6.97	36	A	41		PN.					0....	3012
18-CAA	**WANDALA net**	2	4	115,407	195,740		2.00	31	A	41		PN.					0....	3013
18-CAAA	**WANDALA cluster**	2	4	115,407	195,740		2.00	31	A	41		PN.					0....	3014

Continued overleaf

Table 9-13 continued

Code 1	REFERENCE NAME / Autoglossonym 2	Coun 3	Peo 4	Mother-tongue speakers in 2000 5	in 2025 6	Media radio 7	CHURCH AC% 8	E% 9	Wld 10	Tr 11	Biblioglossonym 12	Print 13-15	P-activity 16	N-activity 17	B-activity 18	J-year 19	Jayuh 20-24	Ref 25
18-CAAA-a	gamargu	1	1	20,250	33,240	0	2.00	34	A	41		pn.					0....	3015
18-CAAA-b	masfeima					0				41		pn.					0....	3016
18-CAAA-c	jampalam					0				41		pn.					0....	3017
18-CAAA-d	zlogba					0				41		pn.					0....	3018
18-CAAA-e	mazagwa					0				41		pn.					0....	3019
18-CAAA-f	gwanje					0				41		pn.					0....	3020
18-CAAA-g	kirawa	1	1	18,833	30,916	0	2.00	31	A	41		pn.					0....	3021
18-CAAA-h	kamburwama					0				41		pn.					0....	3022
18-CAAA-i	mora					0				41		pn.					0....	3023
18-CAAA-j	Vehicular wandala	2	2	76,324	131,584	0	2.00	30	A	41	Mandara*	PN.	1967	1988			0....	3024
18-CAB	**GLAVDA-GUDUF net**	2	5	160,406	274,288		10.55	39	A	41		PN.					0....	3025
18-CABA	PAREKWA cluster	1	1	36,139	63,449		10.00	41	A	41		PN.					0....	3026
18-CABA-a	parekwa	1	1	36,139	63,449	0	10.00	41	A	41	Podoko*	PN.	1981	1992			0....	3027
18-CABA-b	kudala					0				41		pn.					0....	3028
18-CABB	GLAVDA cluster	2	2	32,507	53,888		9.14	43	A	23		P..					0....	3029
18-CABB-a	gelvaxda-xa	2	2	32,507	53,888	0	9.14	43	A	23	Glavda	P..	1967				0....	3030
18-CABB-b	ngoshe					0				23		p..					0....	3031
18-CABB-c	vale					0				23		p..					0....	3032
18-CABB-d	bokwa					0				23		p..					0....	3033
18-CABC	GUDUF cluster	2	2	91,760	156,951		11.26	37	A	23		P..					0....	3034
18-CABC-a	kudupa-xa	2	2	91,760	156,951	0	11.26	37	A	23	Guduf	P..	1966				0....	3035
18-CABC-b	yaghwatada-xa					0				23		p..					0....	3036
18-CABC-c	chikide					0				23		p..					0....	3037
18-CABC-d	nakatsa					0				23		p..					0....	3038
18-CB	LAAMANG chain	2	8	178,170	296,867		12.09	41	A	41		PN.					0....	3039
18-CBA	**LAAMANG-LOWLAND net**	1	1	67,361	112,037		10.00	35	A	0		...					0....	3040
18-CBAA	NORTH LAAMANG cluster	1	1	25,000	42,500		10.00	33	A	0		...					0....	3041
18-CBAA-a	zaladava					0				0		...					0....	3042
18-CBAA-b	dzuba					0				0		...					0....	3043
18-CBAA-c	leghva					0				0		...					0....	3044
18-CBAA-d	gwozo					0				0		...					0....	3045
18-CBAA-e	wakane					0				0		...					0....	3046
18-CBAB	CENTRAL LAAMANG cluster	1	1	42,361	69,537		10.00	36	A	0		...					0....	3047
18-CBAB-a	dlige					0				0		...					0....	3048
18-CBAB-b	hi'dkala					0				0		...					0....	3049
18-CBAB-c	waga					0				0		...					0....	3050
18-CBB	**LAAMANG-HIGHLAND net**	2	6	87,616	146,757		8.95	42	A	41		PN.					0....	3051
18-CBBA	DGHWEDE cluster	2	6	87,616	146,757		8.95	42	A	41		PN.					0....	3052
18-CBBA-a	zeghvana	2	2	44,542	73,462	0	10.00	46	A	41	Dghwede	PN.	1976	1980			0....	3053
18-CBBA-b	turu-xedi	2	2	24,705	42,253	0	10.00	40	A	41	Hedi	pn.					0....	3054
18-CBBA-c	vizik					0				41		pn.					0....	3057
18-CBBA-d	vemgo					0				41		pn.					0....	3058
18-CBBA-e	mabas	2	2	18,369	31,042	0	5.00	34	A	41		pn.					0....	3059
18-CBC	**GVOKO net**	1	1	23,193	38,073		30.00	57	B	4		...					0....	3060
18-CBCA	GVOKO cluster	1	1	23,193	38,073		30.00	57	B	4		...					0....	3061
18-CBCA-a	gvoko					0				4		...					0....	3062
18-CBCA-b	ngweshe	1	1	23,193	38,073	0	30.00	57	B	4		...					0....	3063
18-D	**SUKUR set**	1	1	16,135	26,486		10.00	39	A	4		...					0....	3064
18-DA	SUKUR chain	1	1	16,135	26,486		10.00	39	A	4		...					0....	3065
18-DAA	**SUKUR net**	1	1	16,135	26,486		10.00	39	A	4		...					0....	3066
18-DAAA	SUKUR cluster	1	1	16,135	26,486		10.00	39	A	4		...					0....	3067
18-DAAA-a	sukur	1	1	16,135	26,486	0	10.00	39	A	4		...					0....	3068
18-E	**MATAKAM-MADA set**	2	21	897,416	1,572,968		5.55	39	A	61		PNB					1.s..	3069
18-EA	PELASLA-MADA chain	1	13	212,597	373,254		5.71	34	A	41		PN.					0....	3070
18-EAA	**PELASLA-MBUKO net**	1	2	23,479	41,223		7.36	34	A	12		...					0....	3071
18-EAAA	PELASLA-MBREME cluster	1	1	12,401	21,773		5.00	33	A	2		...					0....	3072
18-EAAA-a	pelasla-gwendele	1	1	12,401	21,773	0	5.00	33	A	2		...					0....	3073
18-EAAA-b	ndreme					0				2		...					0....	3077
18-EAAA-c	vame-mbreme					0				2		...					0....	3078
18-EAAA-d	demwa					0				2		...					0....	3082
18-EAAA-e	hurza					0				2		...					0....	3083
18-EAAB	MBUKO cluster	1	1	11,078	19,450		10.00	36	A	12		...					0....	3084
18-EAAB-a	mbuko	1	1	11,078	19,450	0	10.00	36	A	12	Mbuko	...					0....	3085
18-EAB	**MATAL-BALDA net**	1	2	44,848	78,738		7.98	39	A	41		PN.					0....	3086
18-EABA	MATAL-BALDA cluster	1	2	44,848	78,738		7.98	39	A	41		PN.					0....	3087
18-EABA-a	matal	1	1	29,763	52,254	0	10.00	43	A	41	Matal	PN.		1989			0....	3088
18-EABA-b	balda	1	1	15,085	26,484	0	4.00	30	A	41		pn.					0....	3089
18-EAC	**MADA-WUZLAM net**	1	4	80,796	141,854		3.82	30	A	22		P..					0....	3090
18-EACA	WUZLAM cluster	1	1	17,361	30,481		4.00	29	A	12		...					0....	3091
18-EACA-a	wuzlam	1	1	17,361	30,481	0	4.00	29	A	12	Wuzlam	...					0....	3092
18-EACB	MUYANG cluster	1	1	24,803	43,546		3.00	27	A	2		...					0....	3093
18-EACB-a	muyang	1	1	24,803	43,546	0	3.00	27	A	2		...					0....	3094
18-EACC	MADA cluster	1	1	28,109	49,351		4.00	34	A	22		P..					0....	3095
18-EACC-a	mada	1	1	28,109	49,351	0	4.00	34	A	22	Mada: Cameroon	P..	1989				0....	3096
18-EACD	MOLKWO cluster	1	1	10,523	18,476		5.00	30	A	2		...					0....	3097
18-EACD-a	melokwo	1	1	10,523	18,476	0	5.00	30	A	2		...					0....	3098
18-EACD-b	mikiri					0				2		...					0....	3099
18-EAD	**ZULGWA-MEREY net**	1	5	63,474	111,439		5.90	35	A	41		PN.					0....	3100
18-EADA	ZULGWA-MINEO cluster	1	1	29,763	52,254		4.00	34	A	41		PN.					0....	3101
18-EADA-a	zulgwa	1	1	29,763	52,254	0	4.00	34	A	41	Zulgo*	PN.	1983	1988			0....	3102
18-EADA-b	mineo					0				41		pn.					0....	3103
18-EADA-c	mukuno					0				41		pn.					0....	3104
18-EADB	MEREY cluster	1	1	16,535	29,030		10.00	40	A	22		P..					0....	3105
18-EADB-a	merey	1	1	16,535	29,030	0	10.00	40	A	22	Merey	P..	1986				0....	3106
18-EADC	DUGWOR cluster	1	1	3,017	5,297		10.01	37	A	4		...					0....	3107
18-EADC-a	dugwor	1	1	3,017	5,297	0	10.01	37	A	4		...					0....	3108
18-EADD	GEMZEK cluster	1	1	11,142	19,561		4.00	32	A	5		...					0....	3109
18-EADD-a	gemzek	1	1	11,142	19,561	0	4.00	32	A	5		...					0....	3110

Continued opposite

Table 9-13 continued

Code 1	REFERENCE NAME / Autoglossonym 2	Coun 3	Peo 4	Mother-tongue speakers in 2000 5	in 2025 6	Media radio 7	CHURCH AC% 8	E% 9	Wld 10	Tr 11	Biblioglossonym 12	SCRIPTURES Print 13-15	P-activity 16	N-activity 17	B-activity 18	J-year 19	Jayuh 20-24	Ref 25
18-EADE	GADUWA cluster	1	1	3,017	5,297		5.00	31	A	4		. . .					0....	3111
18-EADE-a	gaduwa	1	1	3,017	5,297	0	5.00	31	A	4							0....	3112
18-EB	MOFU-GIZIGA chain	1	4	246,313	432,446		6.03	36	A	42		PN.					0.s..	3113
18-EBA	**GIZIGA net**	1	2	110,548	194,086		7.29	38	A	41		PN.					0.s..	3114
18-EBAA	NORTH GIZIGA cluster	1	1	36,595	64,249		20.00	53	B	22	Giziga	P..	1986				0....	3115
18-EBAA-a	mi-marva					0				22		p..					0....	3116
18-EBAA-b	mi-dogba					0				22		p..					0....	3117
18-EBAB	SOUTH GIZIGA cluster	1	1	73,953	129,837		1.00	30	A	41		PN.					0.s..	3118
18-EBAB-a	mi-muturwa	1	1	73,953	129,837	0	1.00	30	A	41	Giziga, South	PN.	1988	1996			0.s..	3119
18-EBAB-b	mi-mijivin					0				41		pn.					0.s..	3120
18-EBAB-c	rum					0				41		pn.					0.s..	3121
18-EBAB-d	lulu					0				41		pn.					0.s..	3122
18-EBB	**MOFU net**	1	2	135,765	238,360		5.00	35	A	42		PN.					0....	3123
18-EBBA	NORTH MOFU cluster	1	1	60,340	105,938		5.00	36	A	42		PN.					0....	3124
18-EBBA-a	durum					0				42		pn.					0....	3125
18-EBBA-b	duvangar	1	1	60,340	105,938	0	5.00	36	A	42	Mofu, North	PN.		1975			0....	3126
18-EBBA-c	wazang					0				42		pn.					0....	3127
18-EBBB	SOUTH MOFU cluster	1	1	75,425	132,422		5.00	35	A	22		P..					0....	3128
18-EBBB-a	gudur	1	1	75,425	132,422	0	5.00	35	A	22	Mofu-gudur*	P..	1985-1995				0....	3129
18-EBBB-b	mokong					0				22		p..					0....	3130
18-EBBB-c	masagal					0				22		p..					0....	3131
18-EBBB-d	zidim					0				22		p..					0....	3132
18-EBBB-e	njeleng					0				22		p..					0....	3133
18-EBBB-f	dimeo					0				22		p..					0....	3134
18-EBBB-g	gudal					0				22		p..					0....	3135
18-EC	MAFA chain	2	4	438,506	767,268		5.20	44	A	61		PNB					1.s..	3136
18-ECA	**MAFA net**	2	2	416,119	728,074		4.00	43	A	61		PNB					1.s..	3137
18-ECAA	WEST MAFA cluster	2	1	25,000	42,500		4.00	22	A	0		. . .					0....	3138
18-ECAA-a	magumaz					0				0		. . .					0....	3139
18-ECAA-b	mavumay					0				0		. . .					0....	3140
18-ECAB	CENTRAL MAFA cluster	2	2	381,119	668,574		4.00	45	A	61	Mofa*	PNB	1958-1961	1965	1978-1989		1.s..	3141
18-ECAB-a	uzal					0				61		pnb					1.s..	3142
18-ECAB-b	koza					0				61		pnb					1.s..	3143
18-ECAB-c	mokala					0				61		pnb					1.s..	3144
18-ECAB-d	ldamtsai					0				61		pnb					1.s..	3145
18-ECAC	EAST MAFA cluster	1	1	10,000	17,000		4.00	22	A	0		. . .					0....	3146
18-ECAC-a	sulede					0				0		. . .					0....	3147
18-ECAC-b	rua					0				0		. . .					0....	3148
18-ECB	**MEFELE-BULA net**	1	1	14,380	25,136		9.30	33	A	4		. . .					0....	3149
18-ECBA	BULA cluster	1	1	2,000	3,400		5.00	24	A	0		. . .					0....	3150
18-ECBA-a	bula					0				0		. . .					0....	3151
18-ECBB	MEFELE-SIRAK cluster	1	1	12,380	21,736		10.00	34	A	4		. . .					0....	3152
18-ECBB-a	mefele	1	1	12,380	21,736	0	10.00	34	A	4		. . .					0....	3153
18-ECBB-b	sirak					0				4		. . .					0....	3154
18-ECBB-c	muhura					0				4		. . .					0....	3155
18-ECBB-d	shugule					0				4		. . .					0....	3156
18-ECC	**CUVOK net**	1	1	8,007	14,058		60.00	93	B	3		. . .					0....	3157
18-ECCA	CUVOK cluster	1	1	8,007	14,058		60.00	93	B	3		. . .					0....	3158
18-ECCA-a	cuvok	1	1	8,007	14,058	0	60.00	93	B	3		. . .					0....	3159
18-F	**DABA-HINA set**	1	5	118,435	207,935		6.21	38	A	41		PN.					0....	3160
18-FA	BUWAL-GAVAR chain	1	2	14,196	24,925		4.00	29	A	3		. . .					0....	3161
18-FAA	**BUWAL net**	1	1	8,007	14,058		4.00	28	A	3		. . .					0....	3162
18-FAAA	BUWAL cluster	1	1	8,007	14,058		4.00	28	A	3		. . .					0....	3163
18-FAAA-a	ma-buwal	1	1	8,007	14,058	0	4.00	28	A	3		. . .					0....	3164
18-FAB	**GAVAR-GADALA net**	1	1	6,189	10,867		4.01	30	A	3		. . .					0....	3165
18-FABA	GAVAR-GADALA cluster	1	1	6,189	10,867		4.01	30	A	3		. . .					0....	3166
18-FABA-a	gavar	1	1	6,189	10,867	0	4.01	30	A	3		. . .					0....	3167
18-FABA-b	kortchi					0				3		. . .					0....	3168
18-FABA-c	gadala					0				3		. . .					0....	3169
18-FB	DABA-HINA chain	1	3	104,239	183,010		6.51	40	A	41		PN.					0....	3170
18-FBA	**DABA-HINA net**	1	3	104,239	183,010		6.51	40	A	41		PN.					0....	3171
18-FBAA	MBEDAM cluster	1	1	2,263	3,973		49.98	81	B	4		. . .					0....	3172
18-FBAA-a	mbedam	1	1	2,263	3,973	0	49.98	81	B	4		. . .					0....	3173
18-FBAB	HINA cluster	1	1	11,142	19,561		10.00	37	A	2		. . .					0....	3174
18-FBAB-a	besleri	1	1	11,142	19,561	0	10.00	37	A	2		. . .					0....	3175
18-FBAB-b	jingjing					0				2		. . .					0....	3176
18-FBAB-c	gamdugun					0				2		. . .					0....	3177
18-FBAC	DABA cluster	1	1	90,834	159,476		5.00	39	A	41		PN.					0....	3178
18-FBAC-a	daba	1	1	90,834	159,476	0	5.00	39	A	41	Daba	PN.	1984	1992			0....	3179
18-FBAC-b	nive					0				41		pn.					0....	3180
18-FBAC-c	pologozom					0				41		pn.					0....	3181
18-FBAC-d	mazagway					0				41		pn.					0....	3182
18-FBAC-e	kpala					0				41		pn.					0....	3183
18-G	**BURA-HIGI set**	2	17	1,740,873	2,869,972		36.01	76	B	45		PN.					4.s..	3184
18-GA	HIGI chain	2	9	567,092	943,171		29.14	69	B	42		PN.					0.s..	3185
18-GAA	**HIGI net**	2	9	567,092	943,171		29.14	69	B	42		PN.					0.s..	3186
18-GAAA	KAMWE cluster	2	2	333,572	548,259		39.46	82	B	42	Kamwe	PN.	1972	1975			0....	3187
18-GAAA-a	nkafa					0				42		pn.					0....	3188
18-GAAA-b	baza-dakwa					0				42		pn.					0....	3189
18-GAAA-c	sina					0				42		pn.					0....	3192
18-GAAA-d	futu					0				42		pn.					0....	3193
18-GAAA-e	tili-pte					0				42		pn.					0....	3194
18-GAAA-f	modi					0				42		pn.					0....	3195
18-GAAA-g	humsi					0				42		pn.					0....	3196
18-GAAB	KAPSIKI cluster	2	4	108,354	187,124		26.26	61	B	41		PN.					0.s..	3197
18-GAAB-a	psikye	1	1	81,101	142,388	0	25.00	61	B	41	Kapsiki*	PN.		1988			0.s..	3198
18-GAAB-b	zlenge					0				41		pn.					0.s..	3201
18-GAAB-c	wula	1	1	12,266	20,135	0	30.00	64	B	41		pn.					0.s..	3202

Continued overleaf

Table 9-13 continued

Code 1	REFERENCE NAME / Autoglossonym 2	Coun 3	Peo 4	Mother-tongue speakers in 2000 5	in 2025 6	Media radio 7	CHURCH AC% 8	E% 9	Wld 10	Tr 11	Biblioglossonym 12	SCRIPTURES Print 13-15	P-activity 16	N-activity 17	B-activity 18	J-year 19	Jayuh 20-24	Ref 25
18-GAAC	HYA-ZA cluster	1	1	1,508	2,648		10.01	36	A	4		...					0....	3203
18-GAAC-a	ghye					0				4		...					0....	3204
18-GAAC-b	za					0				4		...					0....	3205
18-GAAC-c	hya					0				4		...					0....	3206
18-GAAD	BANA cluster	2	2	123,658	205,140		4.07	39	A	12	Bana	...					0....	3207
18-GAAD-a	thlukufu					0				12		...					0....	3208
18-GAAD-b	bwagira					0				12		...					0....	3209
18-GAAD-c	gamboura					0				12		...					0....	3210
18-GAAD-d	gili					0				12		...					0....	3211
18-GAAD-e	kiria-fali					0				12		...					0....	3212
18-GAAD-f	mijilu-fali					0				12		...					0....	3213
18-GB	BURA-MARGI chain	1	8	1,173,781	1,926,801		39.33	79	B	45		PN.					4.s..	3214
18-GBA	**MARGI-HUBA net**	1	4	610,329	1,001,875		58.15	98	B	45		PN.					1....	3215
18-GBAA	HUBA cluster	1	1	191,066	313,641		60.00	99	B	22	Kilba*	P..	1976				0....	3216
18-GBAA-a	hong					0				22		p..					0....	3217
18-GBAA-b	gashala					0				22		p..					0....	3218
18-GBAA-c	gaya					0				22		p..					0....	3219
18-GBAA-d	luwa					0				22		p..					0....	3220
18-GBAB	SOUTH MARGI cluster	1	1	139,383	228,801		58.00	95	B	4		...					0....	3221
18-GBAB-a	wamdiu					0				4		...					0....	3222
18-GBAB-b	hildi					0				4		...					0....	3223
18-GBAC	CENTRAL MARGI cluster	1	2	279,880	459,433		56.97	100	B	45	Margi*	PN.	1940-1961	1987			1....	3224
18-GBAC-a	Lower marghi					0				45		pn.					1....	3225
18-GBAC-b	Upper margi					0				45		pn.					1....	3230
18-GBB	**BURA-PUTAI net**	1	4	563,452	924,926		18.93	58	B	41		PN.					4.s..	3233
18-GBBA	CIBAK cluster	1	1	105,920	173,871		10.00	44	A	2		...					0....	3234
18-GBBA-a	cibak	1	1	105,920	173,871	0	10.00	44	A	2		...					0....	3235
18-GBBB	NGWAHYI cluster	1	1	5,575	9,152		5.00	28	A	4		...					0....	3236
18-GBBB-a	ngwahyi	1	1	5,575	9,152	0	5.00	28	A	4		...					0....	3237
18-GBBC	PUTAI cluster									0		...					0....	3238
18-GBBC-a	putai					0				0		...					0....	3239
18-GBBD	BURA cluster	1	2	451,957	741,903		21.20	62	B	41		PN.					4.s..	3240
18-GBBD-a	bura-pabir	1	2	451,957	741,903	0	21.20	62	B	41	Bura*	PN.	1925-1937	1937-1987		1992	4.s..	3241
18-GBBD-b	hyil-hawul					0				41		pn.					1.s..	3245
18-GBBD-c	pela					0				41		pn.					1.s..	3246
18-H	**TERA-GANDA set**	1	4	245,900	404,822		33.26	64	B	24		P..					0....	3247
18-HA	TERA-JARA chain	1	2	143,832	236,104		37.40	70	B	24		P..					0....	3248
18-HAA	**TERA net**	1	1	98,538	161,753		50.00	86	B	24		P..					0....	3249
18-HAAA	TERA cluster	1	1	98,538	161,753		50.00	86	B	24	Tera	P..	1930				0....	3250
18-HAAA-a	nyimatli					0				24	Nyemathi	P..	1930				0....	3251
18-HAAA-b	pidlimdi					0				24		p..					0....	3252
18-HAB	**JARA net**	1	1	45,294	74,351	.	10.00	36	A	4		...					0....	3253
18-HABA	JARA cluster	1	1	45,294	74,351		10.00	36	A	4		...					0....	3254
18-HABA-a	jara	1	1	45,294	74,351	0	10.00	36	A	4		...					0....	3255
18-HB	GANDA-HWANA chain	1	2	102,068	168,718		27.42	56	B	4		...					0....	3256
18-HBA	**GANDA net**	1	1	66,944	111,060		36.56	65	B	4		...					0....	3257
18-HBAA	GA'ANDA-GABIN cluster	1	1	46,944	77,060		50.00	83	B	4		...					0....	3258
18-HBAA-a	ga'anda	1	1	46,944	77,060		50.00	83	B	4		...					0....	3259
18-HBAA-b	gabin					0				4		...					0....	3260
18-HBAB	BOGA cluster	1	1	20,000	34,000		5.00	24	A	4		...					0....	3261
18-HBAB-a	boga	1	1	20,000	34,000	0	5.00	24	A	4		...					0....	3262
18-HBB	**HWANA net**	1	1	35,124	57,658		10.00	39	A	2		...					0....	3263
18-HBBA	TUFTERA cluster	1	1	35,124	57,658		10.00	39	A	2		...					0....	3264
18-HBBA-a	tuftera	1	1	35,124	57,658	0	10.00	39	A	2		...					0....	3265
18-I	**BATA-GUDU set**	2	14	587,164	971,885		30.51	63	B	24		P..					0....	3266
18-IA	GUDU chain	1	1	5,285	8,676		2.01	23	A	4		...					0....	3267
18-IAA	**GUDU net**	1	1	5,285	8,676		2.01	23	A	4		...					0....	3268
18-IAAA	GUDU cluster	1	1	5,285	8,676		2.01	23	A	4		...					0....	3269
18-IAAA-a	gudu	1	1	5,285	8,676		2.01	23	A	4		...					0....	3270
18-IAAA-b	kumbi					0				4		...					0....	3271
18-IB	BATA-GUDE chain	2	13	581,879	963,209		30.77	63	B	24		P..					0....	3272
18-IBA	**GUDE-BWAGIRA net**	2	8	150,003	251,670		30.53	65	B	22		P..					0....	3273
18-IBAA	GUDE-BWAGIRA cluster	2	8	150,003	251,670		30.53	65	B	22		P..					0....	3274
18-IBAA-a	bwagira					0				22		p..					0....	3275
18-IBAA-b	chede	1	1	1,508	2,648	0	3.98	28	A	22		p..					0....	3276
18-IBAA-c	cheke					0				22		p..					0....	3277
18-IBAA-d	gude	2	2	126,100	211,559	0	34.79	71	B	22	Gude	P..	1974-1995				0....	3278
18-IBAA-e	jimjimen	2	2	6,489	11,312	0	10.08	38	A	22		p..					0....	3279
18-IBAA-f	mapodi					0				22		p..					0....	3280
18-IBAA-g	mubi					0				22		p..					0....	3281
18-IBAA-h	mucella					0				22		p..					0....	3282
18-IBAA-i	mudaye					0				22		p..					0....	3283
18-IBAA-j	ngwaba	1	1	10,571	17,352	0	10.00	37	A	22		p..					0....	3284
18-IBAA-k	sharwan					0				22		p..					0....	3285
18-IBAA-l	terki					0				22		p..					0....	3286
18-IBAA-m	tsuvan					0				22		p..					0....	3287
18-IBAA-n	vin	1	1	4,984	8,182	0	3.01	24	A	22		p..					0....	3288
18-IBAA-o	ziziliveken	1	1	351	617	0	3.13	26	A	22		p..					0....	3289
18-IBB	**NZANYI-KOBOCHI net**	2	2	96,314	159,786		10.00	39	A	2		...					0....	3290
18-IBBA	NZANYI-KOBOCHI cluster	2	2	96,314	159,786		10.00	39	A	2		...					0....	3291
18-IBBA-a	nzanyi	2	2	96,314	159,786	0	10.00	39	A	2		...					0....	3292
18-IBBA-b	kobochi					0				2		...					0....	3293
18-IBBA-c	paka					0				2		...					0....	3294
18-IBBA-d	holma					0				2		...					0....	3295
18-IBC	**BATA net**	2	3	335,562	551,753		36.84	70	B	24		P..					0....	3296
18-IBCA	BATA cluster	2	3	335,562	551,753		36.84	70	B	24		P..					0....	3297
18-IBCA-a	gbwata	2	2	171,793	282,920	0	10.00	41	A	24		p..					0....	3298
18-IBCA-b	jirai					0				24		p..					0....	3302

Continued opposite

Table 9-13 continued

Code 1	REFERENCE NAME Autoglossonym 2	Coun 3	Peo 4	Mother-tongue speakers in 2000 5	in 2025 6	Media radio 7	CHURCH AC% 8	E% 9	Wld 10	Tr 11	Biblioglossonym 12	SCRIPTURES Print 13-15	P-activity 16	N-activity 17	B-activity 18	J-year 19	Jayuh 20-24	Ref 25
18-IBCA-c	kobotachi					0				24		p..					0....	3303
18-IBCA-d	malabu					0				24		p..					0....	3304
18-IBCA-e	ndeewe					0				24		p..					0....	3305
18-IBCA-f	wadi					0				24		p..					0....	3306
18-IBCA-g	zumu					0				24		p..					0....	3307
18-IBCA-h	bacama	1	1	163,769	268,833	0	65.00	100	C	24	Bacama	P.. 1915					0....	3308
19	**WEST CHADIC zone**	18	92	32,788,050	55,165,765		2.56	59	B	61		PNB					4Asu.	3311
19-A	**TANGALE-KANAKURU set**	1	8	273,468	448,909		52.96	89	B	42		PN.					4....	3312
19-AA	KANAKURU chain	1	2	45,160	74,132		42.22	73	B	24		P..					0....	3313
19-AAA	**KANAKURU net**	1	2	45,160	74,132		42.22	73	B	24		P..					0....	3314
19-AAAA	DERA cluster	1	2	45,160	74,132		42.22	73	B	24	Dera	P.. 1937					0....	3315
19-AAAA-a	kiri					0				24		p..					0....	3316
19-AAAA-b	gasi	1	1	10,036	16,474	0	15.00	45	A	24		p..					0....	3317
19-AB	TANGALE chain	1	1	175,600	288,253		60.00	100	C	42		PN.					4....	3318
19-ABA	**TANGALE net**	1	1	175,600	288,253		60.00	100	C	42		PN.					4....	3319
19-ABAA	TANGALE cluster	1	1	175,600	288,253		60.00	100	C	42		PN.					4....	3320
19-ABAA-a	tangle	1	1	175,600	288,253	0	60.00	100	C	42	Tangle*	PN. 1920-1929	1932-1963				4....	3321
19-ABAA-b	biliri					0				42		pn.					1....	3322
19-ABAA-c	kaltungo					0				42		pn.					1....	3323
19-ABAA-d	shongom					0				42		pn.					1....	3324
19-AC	PERO chain	1	3	46,375	76,127		42.65	73	B	24		P..					0....	3325
19-ACA	**PERO net**	1	3	46,375	76,127		42.65	73	B	24		P..					0....	3326
19-ACAA	PEERO-CHONGE cluster	1	2	40,922	67,176		44.33	75	B	24		P..					0....	3327
19-ACAA-a	peero	1	1	35,124	57,658	0	50.00	82	B	24	Pero	P.. 1936-1938					0....	3328
19-ACAA-b	chonge	1	1	5,798	9,518	0	10.00	34	A	24		p..					0....	3329
19-ACAB	AMBANDI cluster	1	1	5,453	8,951		30.00	57	B	24		P..					0....	3330
19-ACAB-a	ambandi	1	1	5,453	8,951	0	30.00	57	B	24	Piya	P.. 1950					0....	3331
19-AD	KUPTO chain	1	1	2,988	4,906		10.01	33	A	4		...					0....	3332
19-ADA	**KUPTO net**	1	1	2,988	4,906		10.01	33	A	4		...					0....	3333
19-ADAA	KUPTO cluster	1	1	2,988	4,906		10.01	33	A	4		...					0....	3334
19-ADAA-a	kupto	1	1	2,988	4,906	0	10.01	33	A	4		...					0....	3335
19-AE	KWAMI chain	1	1	3,345	5,491		10.01	33	A	4		...					0....	3336
19-AEA	**KWAMI net**	1	1	3,345	5,491		10.01	33	A	4		...					0....	3337
19-AEAA	KWAAMI cluster	1	1	3,345	5,491		10.01	33	A	4		...					0....	3338
19-AEAA-a	kwaami	1	1	3,345	5,491	0	10.01	33	A	4		...					0....	3339
19-B	**BOLE-DENO set**	1	9	291,301	478,301		13.12	44	A	4		...					0....	3340
19-BA	BOLE-NGAMO chain	1	3	192,095	315,449		16.27	51	B	4		...					0....	3341
19-BAA	**MAHA net**	1	1	10,582	17,371		10.00	33	A	4		...					0....	3342
19-BAAA	MAAKA cluster	1	1	10,582	17,371		10.00	33	A	4		...					0....	3343
19-BAAA-a	maaka	1	1	10,582	17,371	0	10.00	33	A	4		...					0....	3344
19-BAB	**BOLE net**	1	1	117,966	193,763		19.68	54	B	4		...					0....	3345
19-BABA	BARA-PIKA cluster	1	1	115,966	190,363		20.00	55	B	4		...					0....	3346
19-BABA-a	bara	1	1	115,966	190,363	0	20.00	55	B	4		...					0....	3347
19-BABA-b	am-pika					0				4		...					0....	3348
19-BABB	BELE cluster	1	1	2,000	3,400		1.00	16	A	4		...					0....	3349
19-BABB-a	bele	1	1	2,000	3,400	0	1.00	16	A	4		...					0....	3350
19-BAC	**NGAMO net**	1	1	63,547	104,315		11.00	47	A	4		...					0....	3351
19-BACA	NGAMO cluster	1	1	63,547	104,315		11.00	47	A	4		...					0....	3352
19-BACA-a	ngamo	1	1	63,547	104,315	0	11.00	47	A	4		...					0....	3353
19-BB	GERA-DENO chain	1	6	99,206	162,852		7.02	31	A	4		...					0....	3354
19-BBA	**KIRIFI net**	1	1	25,033	41,093		10.00	37	A	4		...					0....	3355
19-BBAA	GIIWO cluster	1	1	25,033	41,093		10.00	37	A	4		...					0....	3356
19-BBAA-a	giiwo	1	1	25,033	41,093	0	10.00	37	A	4		...					0....	3357
19-BBB	**KUBI net**	1	1	1,583	2,599		9.98	34	A	4		...					0....	3358
19-BBBA	KUBI cluster	1	1	1,583	2,599		9.98	34	A	4		...					0....	3359
19-BBBA-a	kubi	1	1	1,583	2,599	0	9.98	34	A	4		...					0....	3360
19-BBC	**DENO net**	1	1	17,562	28,829		10.00	35	A	4		...					0....	3361
19-BBCA	DENO cluster	1	1	17,562	28,829		10.00	35	A	4		...					0....	3362
19-BBCA-a	North deno					0				4		...					0....	3363
19-BBCA-b	South deno					0				4		...					0....	3364
19-BBD	**GALAMBU net**	1	1	21,175	34,760		10.00	35	A	4		...					0....	3365
19-BBDA	GALAMBU cluster	1	1	21,175	34,760		10.00	35	A	4		...					0....	3366
19-BBDA-a	galambu	1	1	21,175	34,760	0	10.00	35	A	4		...					0....	3367
19-BBE	**GERA net**	1	1	25,011	41,056		1.00	22	A	4		...					0....	3368
19-BBEA	GERA cluster	1	1	25,011	41,056		1.00	22	A	4		...					0....	3369
19-BBEA-a	gera	1	1	25,011	41,056	0	1.00	22	A	4		...					0....	3370
19-BBF	**GERUMA net**	1	1	8,842	14,515		2.00	23	A	4		...					0....	3371
19-BBFA	GERUMA cluster	1	1	8,842	14,515		2.00	23	A	4		...					0....	3372
19-BBFA-a	geruma-bauchi					0				4		...					0....	3373
19-BBFA-b	geruma-darazo	1	1	8,842	14,515	0	2.00	23	A	4		...					0....	3374
19-C	**KAREKARE set**	1	1	89,818	147,440		10.00	46	A	20		...					0....	3375
19-CA	KAREKARE chain	1	1	89,818	147,440		10.00	46	A	20		...					0....	3376
19-CAA	**KAREKARE net**	1	1	89,818	147,440		10.00	46	A	20		...					0....	3377
19-CAAA	KERE-KERE cluster	1	1	89,818	147,440		10.00	46	A	20		...					0....	3378
19-CAAA-a	jalalum					0				20		...					0....	3379
19-CAAA-b	pakaro					0				20		...					0....	3380

Continued overleaf

Table 9-13 continued

Code 1	REFERENCE NAME / Autoglossonym 2	Coun 3	Peo 4	Mother-tongue speakers in 2000 5	in 2025 6	Media radio 7	CHURCH AC% 8	E% 9	Wld 10	Tr 11	Biblioglossonym 12	SCRIPTURES Print 13-15	P–activity 16	N–activity 17	B–activity 18	J-year 19	Jayuh 20-24	Ref 25
19-CAAA-c	ngwajum					0				20		...					0....	3381
19-D	**BADE-NGIZIM set**	1	12	518,161	850,697		1.96	27	A	20		...					0....	3382
19-DA	BADE-NGIZIM chain	1	3	360,700	592,101		1.19	25	A	20		...					0....	3383
19-DAA	**NGIZIM net**	1	1	84,733	139,093		5.00	35	A	4		...					0....	3384
19-DAAA	NGIZIM cluster	1	1	84,733	139,093		5.00	35	A	4		...					0....	3385
19-DAAA-a	ngezem	1	1	84,733	139,093	0	5.00	35	A	4		...					0....	3386
19-DAB	**BADE net**	1	1	264,816	434,704		0.02	22	A	20		...					0....	3387
19-DABA	BADE cluster	1	1	264,816	434,704		0.02	22	A	20		...					0....	3388
19-DABA-a	gashua					0				20		...					0....	3389
19-DABA-b	mazgarwa					0				20		...					0....	3390
19-DABA-c	bade-kado	1	1	264,816	434,704	0	0.02	22	A	20		...					0....	3391
19-DABA-d	magwaram					0				20		...					0....	3392
19-DAC	**DUWAI net**	1	1	11,151	18,304		0.05	18	A	4		...					0....	3393
19-DACA	DUWAI cluster	1	1	11,151	18,304		0.05	18	A	4		...					0....	3394
19-DACA-a	duwai	1	1	11,151	18,304	0	0.05	18	A	4		...					0....	3395
19-DAD	**AUYOKAWA net**									9		...					0....	3396
19-DADA	AUYOKAWA cluster			0	0		0.00	0		9		...					0....	3397
19-DADA-a	auyokawa			0	0	0	0.00	0		9		...					0....	3398
19-DAE	**SHIRAWA net**									0		...					0....	3399
19-DAEA	SHIRAWA cluster			0	0		0.00	0		0		...					0....	3400
19-DAEA-a	shirawa			0	0	0	0.00	0		0		...					0....	3401
19-DAF	**MOBER net**									0		...					0....	3402
19-DAFA	MOBER cluster			0	0		0.00	0		0		...					0....	3403
19-DAFA-a	mober			0	0	0	0.00	0		0		...					0....	3404
19-DB	WARJI-DIRI chain	1	9	157,461	258,596		3.71	31	A	20		...					0....	3405
19-DBA	**WARJI net**	1	1	103,656	170,155		2.00	30	A	20		...					0....	3406
19-DBAA	SERZA-KWAY cluster	1	1	103,656	170,155		2.00	30	A	20		...					0....	3407
19-DBAA-a	serza-kway	1	1	103,656	170,155	0	2.00	30	A	20		...					0....	3408
19-DBB	**SIRI net**	1	1	3,167	5,198		19.99	44	A	4		...					0....	3409
19-DBBA	SIRI cluster	1	1	3,167	5,198		19.99	44	A	4		...					0....	3410
19-DBBA-a	North siri					0				4		...					0....	3411
19-DBBA-b	South siri					0				4		...					0....	3412
19-DBC	**DIRI-CIWOGAI net**	1	2	9,935	16,309		10.01	36	A	4		...					0....	3413
19-DBCA	DIRI cluster	1	1	7,047	11,568		10.00	34	A	4		...					0....	3414
19-DBCA-a	West diri					0				4		...					0....	3415
19-DBCA-b	East diri					0				4		...					0....	3416
19-DBCB	CIWOOGAI cluster	1	1	2,888	4,741		10.01	40	A	0		...					0....	3417
19-DBCB-a	ciwoogai	1	1	2,888	4,741	0	10.01	40	A	0		...					0....	3418
19-DBD	**AFA net**	1	1	14,808	24,308		5.00	36	A	3		...					0....	3419
19-DBDA	FUUCAKA cluster	1	1	14,808	24,308		5.00	36	A	3		...					0....	3420
19-DBDA-a	fuucaka	1	1	14,808	24,308	0	5.00	36	A	3		...					0....	3421
19-DBE	**MIYA net**	1	1	9,779	16,053		3.00	32	A	4		...					0....	3422
19-DBEA	MIYA cluster	1	1	9,779	16,053		3.00	32	A	4		...					0....	3423
19-DBEA-a	gala					0				4		...					0....	3424
19-DBEA-b	faishang					0				4		...					0....	3425
19-DBEA-c	fursum					0				4		...					0....	3426
19-DBEA-d	demshin					0				4		...					0....	3427
19-DBEA-e	federe					0				4		...					0....	3428
19-DBF	**KARIYA net**	1	1	5,040	8,273		10.00	33	A	4		...					0....	3429
19-DBFA	VINAHE cluster	1	1	5,040	8,273		10.00	33	A	4		...					0....	3430
19-DBFA-a	vinahe	1	1	5,040	8,273	0	10.00	33	A	4		...					0....	3431
19-DBG	**MBURKU net**	1	1	6,255	10,269		2.00	23	A	4		...					0....	3432
19-DBGA	VERAN cluster	1	1	6,255	10,269		2.00	23	A	4		...					0....	3433
19-DBGA-a	veran	1	1	6,255	10,269	0	2.00	23	A	4		...					0....	3434
19-DBH	**JIMBIN net**	1	1	2,821	4,631		10.00	33	A	4		...					0....	3435
19-DBHA	ZUMBUN cluster	1	1	2,821	4,631		10.00	33	A	4		...					0....	3436
19-DBHA-a	zumbun	1	1	2,821	4,631	0	10.00	33	A	4		...					0....	3437
19-DBI	**AJANCI net**	1	1	2,000	3,400		10.00	33	A	0		...					0....	3438
19-DBIA	AJANCI cluster	1	1	2,000	3,400		10.00	33	A	0		...					0....	3439
19-DBIA-a	ajanci	1	1	2,000	3,400	0	10.00	33	A	0		...					0....	3440
19-E	**SOUTH BAUCHI set**	1	14	270,043	445,158		13.94	43	A	23		P..					0....	3441
19-EA	WEST JIMI chain	1	1	300	510		10.00	33	A	0		...					0....	3442
19-EAA	**WEST JIMI net**	1	1	300	510		10.00	33	A	0		...					0....	3443
19-EAAA	WEST JIMI cluster	1	1	300	510		10.00	33	A	0		...					0....	3444
19-EAAA-a	jimi					0	.			0		...					0....	3445
19-EAAA-b	zumo					0				0		...					0....	3446
19-EB	GURUNTUM-TALA chain	1	5	20,071	32,949		5.92	33	A	4		...					0....	3447
19-EBA	**GURUNTUM-MBARU net**	1	1	17,919	29,415		5.00	32	A	4		...					0....	3448
19-EBAA	GURUNTUM-MBAARU cluster	1	1	17,919	29,415		5.00	32	A	4		...					0....	3449
19-EBAA-a	guruntum					0				4		...					0....	3450
19-EBAA-b	mbaaru					0				4		...					0....	3451
19-EBB	**JU net**	1	1	948	1,556		4.96	28	A	4		...					0....	3452
19-EBBA	JU cluster	1	1	948	1,556		4.96	28	A	4		...					0....	3453
19-EBBA-a	ju	1	1	948	1,556	0	4.96	28	A	4		...					0....	3454
19-EBC	**ZANGWAL net**	1	1	100	165		30.00	58	B	4		...					0....	3455
19-EBCA	ZANGWAL cluster	1	1	100	165		30.00	58	B	4		...					0....	3456
19-EBCA-a	zangwal					0				4		...					0....	3457

Continued opposite

Table 9-13 continued

Code 1	REFERENCE NAME 2 / Autoglossonym	Coun 3	Peo 4	Mother-tongue speakers in 2000 5	in 2025 6	Media radio 7	CHURCH AC% 8	E% 9	Wld 10	Tr 11	Biblioglossonym 12	SCRIPTURES Print 13-15	P-activity 16	N-activity 17	B-activity 18	J-year 19	Jayuh 20-24	Ref 25
19-EBD	**TALA net**	1	1	1,048	1,721		20.04	46	A	4		...					0....	3458
19-EBDA	TALA cluster	1	1	1,048	1,721		20.04	46	A	4		...					0....	3459
19-EBDA-a	tala	1	1	1,048	1,721	0	20.04	46	A	4		...					0....	3460
19-EBE	**LURI net**	1	1	56	92		10.71	36	A	4		...					0....	3461
19-EBEA	LURI cluster	1	1	56	92		10.71	36	A	4		...					0....	3462
19-EBEA-a	luri	1	1	56	92	0	10.71	36	A	4		...					0....	3463
19-EC	GEJI-POLCI chain	1	2	32,747	54,703		9.72	35	A	4		...					0....	3464
19-ECA	**GEJI net**	1	1	9,984	16,682		3.21	26	A	4		...					0....	3465
19-ECAA	GEJI cluster	1	1	4,984	8,182		3.01	31	A	4		...					0....	3466
19-ECAA-a	geji	1	1	4,984	8,182	0	3.01	31	A	4		...					0....	3467
19-ECAB	BOLU-MAGONG cluster	1	1	3,000	5,100		3.00	20	A	0		...					0....	3468
19-ECAB-a	bolu					0				0		...					0....	3469
19-ECAB-b	magong					0				0		...					0....	3470
19-ECAB-c	pelu					0				0		...					0....	3471
19-ECAC	ZARANDA-BUU cluster	1	1	2,000	3,400		4.00	22	A	0		...					0....	3472
19-ECAC-a	zaranda					0				0		...					0....	3473
19-ECAC-b	buu					0				0		...					0....	3474
19-ECB	**PELCI-ZUL net**	1	1	22,763	38,021		12.58	39	A	4		...					0....	3475
19-ECBA	PELCI cluster	1	1	11,563	18,981		15.00	45	A	4		...					0....	3476
19-ECBA-a	pelci	1	1	11,563	18,981	0	15.00	45	A	4		...					0....	3477
19-ECBB	ZUL cluster	1	1	2,000	3,400		10.00	33	A	0		...					0....	3478
19-ECBB-a	zul	1	1	2,000	3,400	0	10.00	33	A	0		...					0....	3479
19-ECBC	BARAM cluster	1	1	2,200	3,740		15.00	42	A	0		...					0....	3480
19-ECBC-a	m-barmi					0				0		...					0....	3481
19-ECBC-b	m-baram					0				0		...					0....	3482
19-ECBD	DIIR cluster	1	1	3,500	5,950		10.00	33	A	0		...					0....	3483
19-ECBD-a	diir					0				0		...					0....	3484
19-ECBD-b	dra					0				0		...					0....	3485
19-ECBE	BULI cluster	1	1	1,500	2,550		10.00	33	A	0		...					0....	3486
19-ECBE-a	buli					0				0		...					0....	3487
19-ECBF	LANGAS-LUNDUR cluster	1	1	2,000	3,400		5.00	24	A	0		...					0....	3488
19-ECBF-a	langas					0				0		...					0....	3489
19-ECBF-b	nyamzax					0				0		...					0....	3490
19-ECBF-c	lundur					0				0		...					0....	3491
19-ED	BARAWA chain	1	4	125,567	207,030		19.19	49	A	4		...					0....	3492
19-EDA	**DASS net**	1	2	23,147	38,570		2.53	22	A	4		...					0....	3493
19-EDAA	ZUMBUL-BOODLA cluster	1	1	10,002	16,419		2.00	23	A	4		...					0....	3494
19-EDAA-a	zumbul	1	1	10,002	16,419	0	2.00	23	A	4		...					0....	3495
19-EDAA-b	boodla					0				4		...					0....	3496
19-EDAB	DOT cluster	1	1	4,000	6,800		2.00	18	A	0		...					0....	3497
19-EDAB-a	dot					0				0		...					0....	3498
19-EDAC	WANDI cluster	1	1	300	510		1.00	16	A	0		...					0....	3499
19-EDAC-a	wandi					0				0		...					0....	3500
19-EDAD	LUKSHI cluster	1	1	2,000	3,400		2.00	18	A	0		...					0....	3501
19-EDAD-a	lukshi					0				0		...					0....	3502
19-EDAE	DURR-BARAZA cluster	1	1	1,500	2,550		1.00	16	A	0		...					0....	3503
19-EDAE-a	durr					0				0		...					0....	3504
19-EDAE-b	baraza					0				0		...					0....	3505
19-EDAF	ZEEM-TULAI cluster	1	1	3,345	5,491		4.99	27	A	4		...					0....	3506
19-EDAF-a	zeem					0				4		...					0....	3507
19-EDAF-b	tulai					0				4		...					0....	3508
19-EDAG	DANSHE-CHAARI cluster	1	1	2,000	3,400		4.00	22	A	0		...					0....	3509
19-EDAG-a	danshe					0				0		...					0....	3510
19-EDAG-b	chaari					0				0		...					0....	3511
19-EDB	**ZARI-ZAKSHI net**	1	1	11,920	19,743		8.41	31	A	4		...					0....	3512
19-EDBA	ZAKSHI cluster	1	1	1,000	1,700		3.00	20	A	0		...					0....	3513
19-EDBA-a	zakshi	1	1	1,000	1,700	0	3.00	20	A	0		...					0....	3514
19-EDBB	ZARI-KOPTI cluster	1	1	8,920	14,643		10.00	34	A	4		...					0....	3515
19-EDBB-a	zari	1	1	8,920	14,643	0	10.00	34	A	4		...					0....	3516
19-EDBB-b	kopti					0				4		...					0....	3517
19-EDBB-c	kwapm					0				4		...					0....	3518
19-EDBC	BOTO cluster	1	1	2,000	3,400		4.00	22	A	0		...					0....	3519
19-EDBC-a	boto	1	1	2,000	3,400	0	4.00	22	A	0		...					0....	3520
19-EDC	**SAYA-SIGIDI net**	1	1	90,500	148,717		24.88	58	B	2		...					0....	3521
19-EDCA	SAYA cluster	1	1	87,800	144,127		25.00	58	B	2		...					0....	3522
19-EDCA-a	saya					0				2		...					0....	3523
19-EDCB	SIGIDI cluster	1	1	200	340		20.00	51	B	0		...					0....	3524
19-EDCB-a	sigidi	1	1	200	340	0	20.00	51	B	0		...					0....	3525
19-EDCC	ZAAR cluster	1	1	2,500	4,250		21.00	52	B	0		...					0....	3526
19-EDCC-a	vikzar					0				0		...					0....	3527
19-EDCC-b	kal					0				0		...					0....	3528
19-EDCC-c	gambar-leere					0				0		...					0....	3529
19-EDCC-d	lusa					0				0		...					0....	3530
19-EE	BOGHOM-MANGAS chain	1	3	91,358	149,966		10.00	41	A	23		P..					0....	3531
19-EEA	**BOGHOM-MANGAS net**	1	3	91,358	149,966		10.00	41	A	23		P..					0....	3532
19-EEAA	KIR-BALA cluster	1	1	3,223	5,290		9.99	34	A	4		...					0....	3533
19-EEAA-a	kir					0				4		...					0....	3534
19-EEAA-b	bala					0				4		...					0....	3535
19-EEAB	MANGAS cluster	1	1	335	549		9.85	34	A	4		...					0....	3536
19-EEAB-a	mangas	1	1	335	549	0	9.85	34	A	4		...					0....	3537
19-EEAC	BOGHOM cluster	1	1	87,800	144,127		10.00	41	A	23		P..					0....	3538
19-EEAC-a	boghom	1	1	87,800	144,127	0	10.00	41	A	23	Boghom	P.. 1955					0....	3539
19-F	**ANGAS-YIWOM set**	1	12	1,052,841	1,728,274		37.49	66	B	41		PN.					4....	3540
19-FA	YIWOM chain	1	1	14,050	23,063		30.00	56	B	4		...					0....	3541

Continued overleaf

Table 9-13 continued

Code 1	REFERENCE NAME / Autoglossonym 2	Coun 3	Peo 4	Mother-tongue speakers in 2000 5	in 2025 6	Media radio 7	AC% 8	E% 9	Wld 10	Tr 11	Biblioglossonym 12	Print 13-15	P–activity 16	N–activity 17	B–activity 18	J-year 19	Jayuh 20-24	Ref 25
19-FAA	**YIWOM net**	1	1	14,050	23,063		30.00	56	B	4		. . .					0. . . .	3542
19-FAAA	YIWOM cluster	1	1	14,050	23,063		30.00	56	B	4		. . .					0. . . .	3543
19-FAAA-a	yiwom	1	1	14,050	23,063	0	30.00	56	B	4		. . .					0. . . .	3544
19-FB	ANGAS-GOEMAI chain	1	11	1,038,791	1,705,211		37.59	66	B	41		PN.					4. . . .	3545
19-FBA	**ANGAS net**	1	1	175,600	288,253		60.00	100	C	41		PN.					0. . . .	3546
19-FBAA	ANGAS cluster	1	1	175,600	288,253		60.00	100	C	41	Angas	PN.	1916-1928	1977-1979			0. . . .	3547
19-FBAA-a	Upper ngas					0				41		pn.					0. . . .	3548
19-FBAA-b	Lower ngas					0				41		pn.					0. . . .	3552
19-FBB	**SURA-KOFYAR net**	1	3	511,211	839,171		51.65	78	B	41		PN.					4. . . .	3555
19-FBBA	MWAGHAVUL cluster	1	1	317,781	521,649		77.00	100	C	41		PN.					4. . . .	3556
19-FBBA-a	mwaghavul					0				41	Mwaghavul	PN.	1915-1966	1991-1995		1988	4. . . .	3557
19-FBBA-b	mapun					0				41		pn.					1. . . .	3558
19-FBBA-c	panyam					0				41		pn.					1. . . .	3559
19-FBBA-d	cakfem					0				41		pn.					1. . . .	3560
19-FBBA-e	mushere					0				41		pn.					1. . . .	3561
19-FBBB	KOFYAR-GWORAM cluster	1	1	176,503	289,736		10.00	43	A	2		. . .					0. . . .	3562
19-FBBB-a	kofyar					0				2		. . .					0. . . .	3563
19-FBBB-b	kwagallak					0				2		. . .					0. . . .	3564
19-FBBB-c	dimmuk					0				2		. . .					0. . . .	3565
19-FBBB-d	mirriam					0				2		. . .					0. . . .	3566
19-FBBB-e	bwol					0				2		. . .					0. . . .	3567
19-FBBB-f	gworam					0				2		. . .					0. . . .	3568
19-FBBB-g	jipal					0				2		. . .					0. . . .	3569
19-FBBC	JORTO cluster	1	1	16,927	27,786		10.00	35	A	4		. . .					0. . . .	3570
19-FBBC-a	jorto	1	1	16,927	27,786	0	10.00	35	A	4		. . .					0. . . .	3571
19-FBC	**CHIP net**	1	1	6,791	11,147		10.00	34	A	4		. . .					0. . . .	3572
19-FBCA	CHIP cluster	1	1	6,791	11,147		10.00	34	A	4		. . .					0. . . .	3573
19-FBCA-a	mi-ship	1	1	6,791	11,147	0	10.00	34	A	4		. . .					0. . . .	3574
19-FBCA-b	doka									4		. . .					0. . . .	3575
19-FBD	**GOEMAI net**	1	1	278,765	457,603		0.03	27	A	2		. . .					0. . . .	3576
19-FBDA	GOEMAI cluster	1	1	278,765	457,603		0.03	27	A	2		. . .					0. . . .	3577
19-FBDA-a	goemai	1	1	278,765	457,603	0	0.03	27	A	2		. . .					0. . . .	3578
19-FBE	**TAL-MONTOL net**	1	4	60,849	99,885		30.64	56	B	4		. . .					0. . . .	3579
19-FBEA	TAL-KWABZAK cluster	1	1	17,562	28,829		30.00	57	B	4		. . .					0. . . .	3580
19-FBEA-a	tal					0				4		. . .					0. . . .	3581
19-FBEA-b	kwabzak					0				4		. . .					0. . . .	3582
19-FBEB	PYAPUN cluster	1	2	20,830	34,192		31.87	53	B	4		. . .					0. . . .	3583
19-FBEB-a	pyapun	1	2	20,830	34,192	0	31.87	53	B	4		. . .					0. . . .	3584
19-FBEC	MONTOL-BALTAP cluster	1	1	22,457	36,864		30.00	57	B	4		. . .					0. . . .	3585
19-FBEC-a	montol	1	1	22,457	36,864	0	30.00	57	B	4		. . .					0. . . .	3586
19-FBEC-b	baltap					0				4		. . .					0. . . .	3587
19-FBEC-c	lalin					0				4		. . .					0. . . .	3588
19-FBF	**KOENOEM net**	1	1	5,575	9,152		30.01	56	B	4		. . .					0. . . .	3589
19-FBFA	KOENOEM cluster	1	1	5,575	9,152		30.01	56	B	4		. . .					0. . . .	3590
19-FBFA-a	koenoem	1	1	5,575	9,152	0	30.01	56	B	4		. . .					0. . . .	3591
19-G	**RON-FYER set**	1	9	375,753	616,814		44.20	76	B	23		P . .					0. . . .	3592
19-GA	FYER chain	1	2	8,675	14,241		16.08	41	A	4		. . .					0. . . .	3593
19-GAA	**FYER net**	1	2	8,675	14,241		16.08	41	A	4		. . .					0. . . .	3594
19-GAAA	FYEER-TAMBAS cluster	1	2	8,675	14,241		16.08	41	A	4		. . .					0. . . .	3595
19-GAAA-a	fyeer	1	1	3,401	5,583	0	10.00	33	A	4		. . .					0. . . .	3596
19-GAAA-b	tambas					0				4		. . .					0. . . .	3597
19-GB	RON-SHA chain	1	7	367,078	602,573		44.86	76	B	23		P . .					0. . . .	3598
19-GBA	**RON-SHA net**	1	7	367,078	602,573		44.86	76	B	23		P . .					0. . . .	3599
19-GBAA	RON cluster	1	3	341,811	561,095		44.98	77	B	23		P . .					0. . . .	3600
19-GBAA-a	daffo-batura	1	1	11,151	18,304	0	5.00	28	A	23		p . .					0. . . .	3601
19-GBAA-b	nafunia					0				23		p . .					0. . . .	3604
19-GBAA-c	shagawu					0				23		p . .					0. . . .	3605
19-GBAA-d	maleni	1	1	22,647	37,176	0	10.00	44	A	23	Shagawu	P . .	1963				0. . . .	3606
19-GBAA-e	mangar					0				23		p . .					0. . . .	3607
19-GBAA-f	monguna					0				23		p . .					0. . . .	3608
19-GBAA-g	bokkos	1	1	308,013	505,615	0	49.00	81	B	23	Ron	p . .					0. . . .	3609
19-GBAB	SHA cluster	1	2	8,374	13,747		30.68	58	B	4		. . .					0. . . .	3612
19-GBAB-a	sha	1	1	569	934	0	39.89	67	B	4		. . .					0. . . .	3613
19-GBAB-b	mundat	1	1	7,805	12,813	0	30.01	57	B	4		. . .					0. . . .	3614
19-GBAC	KARFA cluster	1	1	903	1,483		39.98	65	B	4		. . .					0. . . .	3615
19-GBAC-a	karfa	1	1	903	1,483	0	39.98	65	B	4		. . .					0. . . .	3616
19-GBAD	KULERE cluster	1	1	15,990	26,248		50.00	79	B	4		. . .					0. . . .	3617
19-GBAD-a	richa					0				4		. . .					0. . . .	3618
19-GBAD-b	ambul					0				4		. . .					0. . . .	3619
19-GBAD-c	tof					0				4		. . .					0. . . .	3620
19-GBAD-d	korom-boye					0				4		. . .					0. . . .	3621
19-H	**HAUSA-GWANDARA set**	18	27	29,916,665	50,450,172		0.13	60	B	61		PNB					4Asu.	3622
19-HA	HAUSA-GWANDARA chain	18	27	29,916,665	50,450,172		0.13	60	B	61		PNB					4Asu.	3623
19-HAA	**HAUSA-GWANDARA net**	18	27	29,916,665	50,450,172		0.13	60	B	61		PNB					4Asu.	3624
19-HAAA	GWANDARA cluster	1	1	52,675	86,469		2.00	33	A	2		. . .					0. . . .	3625
19-HAAA-a	karshi					0	*			2		. . .					0. . . .	3626
19-HAAA-b	kyankyara	1	1	52,675	86,469	0	2.00	33	A	2		. . .					0. . . .	3627
19-HAAA-c	toni					0				2		. . .					0. . . .	3628
19-HAAA-d	koro					0				2		. . .					0. . . .	3629
19-HAAA-e	gitata									2		. . .					0. . . .	3630
19-HAAA-f	nimbia					0				2		. . .					0. . . .	3631
19-HAAB	HAUSA cluster	18	26	29,863,990	50,363,703		0.13	60	B	61		PNB					4Asu.	3632
19-HAAB-a	hausa	18	26	29,863,990	50,363,703	5	0.13	60	B	61	Hausa	PNB	1857-1988	1880-1993	1932-1980	1981	4Asu.	3633
19-HAAB-b	barikanchi					1				61		pnb					1csu.	3639
2 AUSTRALASIAN macrozone		7	958	5,284,757	7,783,572		73.91	92	C	61		PNB					1asu.	3640

Continued opposite

Table 9-13 continued

Code 1	REFERENCE NAME / Autoglossonym 2	Coun 3	Peo 4	Mother-tongue speakers in 2000 5	in 2025 6	Media radio 7	CHURCH AC% 8	E% 9	Wld 10	Tr 11	Biblioglossonym 12	SCRIPTURES Print 13-15	P-activity 16	N-activity 17	B-activity 18	J-year 19	Jayuh 20-24	Ref 25
20	**WEST IRIANIC zone**	4	92	540,169	757,888		56.08	79	B	61		PNB					1.s..	3641
20-A	**ALOR-MAKASAI set**	2	13	123,207	159,629		41.07	67	B	20		. . .					0....	3642
20-AA	PANTAR chain	1	4	35,739	46,075		10.08	33	A	4		. . .					0....	3643
20-AAA	**LAMMA net**	1	1	12,323	15,887		8.00	28	A	4		. . .					0....	3644
20-AAAA	LAMMA cluster	1	1	12,323	15,887		8.00	28	A	4		. . .					0....	3645
20-AAAA-a	kalondama					0				4		. . .					0....	3646
20-AAAA-b	tubal					0				4		. . .					0....	3647
20-AAAA-c	biangwala					0				4		. . .					0....	3648
20-AAB	**TEWA net**	1	1	6,893	8,887		15.00	39	A	0		. . .					0....	3649
20-AABA	TEWA cluster	1	1	6,893	8,887		15.00	39	A	0		. . .					0....	3650
20-AABA-a	deing					0				0		. . .					0....	3651
20-AABA-b	madar					0				0		. . .					0....	3652
20-AABA-c	lebang					0				0		. . .					0....	3653
20-AAC	**NEDEBANG net**	1	1	1,379	1,777		5.00	27	A	4		. . .					0....	3654
20-AACA	NEDEBANG cluster	1	1	1,379	1,777		5.00	27	A	4		. . .					0....	3655
20-AACA-a	nedebang	1	1	1,379	1,777	0	5.00	27	A	4		. . .					0....	3656
20-AAD	**BLAGAR net**	1	1	15,144	19,524		10.00	34	A	4		. . .					0....	3657
20-AADA	BLAGAR cluster	1	1	15,144	19,524		10.00	34	A	4		. . .					0....	3658
20-AADA-a	bakalang					0				4		. . .					0....	3659
20-AADA-b	retta-ternate					0				4		. . .					0....	3660
20-AADA-c	limarahing					0				4		. . .					0....	3661
20-AADA-d	apuri					0				4		. . .					0....	3662
20-AADA-e	retta-pura					0				4		. . .					0....	3663
20-AADA-f	tereweng					0				4		. . .					0....	3664
20-AB	ALOR chain	1	6	71,714	92,450		49.74	78	B	4		. . .					0....	3665
20-ABA	**KELON net**	1	1	13,766	17,746		53.00	80	B	4		. . .					0....	3666
20-ABAA	KELON cluster	1	1	13,766	17,746		53.00	80	B	4		. . .					0....	3667
20-ABAA-a	panggar					0				4		. . .					0....	3668
20-ABAA-b	probur					0				4		. . .					0....	3669
20-ABAA-c	halerman					0				4		. . .					0....	3670
20-ABAA-d	gendok					0				4		. . .					0....	3671
20-ABB	**KAFOA net**	1	1	1,379	1,777		39.96	63.	B	4		. . .					0....	3672
20-ABBA	KAFOA cluster	1	1	1,379	1,777		39.96	63	B	4		. . .					0....	3673
20-ABBA-a	kafoa	1	1	1,379	1,777	0	39.96	63	B	4		. . .					0....	3674
20-ABC	**KUI net**	1	1	4,242	5,469		54.01	81	B	4		. . .					0....	3675
20-ABCA	KUI cluster	1	1	4,242	5,469		54.01	81	B	4		. . .					0....	3676
20-ABCA-a	Proper kui	1	1	4,242	5,469	0	54.01	81	B	4		. . .					0....	3677
20-ABCA-b	kiramang					0				4		. . .					0....	3680
20-ABD	**ABUI net**	1	1	22,038	28,411		43.00	73	B	4		. . .					0....	3681
20-ABDA	ABUI cluster	1	1	22,038	28,411		43.00	73	B	4		. . .					0....	3682
20-ABDA-a	kobola	1	1	22,038	28,411	0	43.00	73	B	4		. . .					0....	3683
20-ABDA-b	atimelang					0				4		. . .					0....	3684
20-ABDA-c	alakaman									4		. . .					0....	3685
20-ABE	**KABOLA net**	1	1	13,766	17,746		53.00	80	B	4		. . .					0....	3686
20-ABEA	KABOLA cluster	1	1	13,766	17,746		53.00	80	B	4		. . .					0....	3687
20-ABEA-a	hamap					0				4		. . .					0....	3688
20-ABEA-b	pintumbang					0				4		. . .					0....	3689
20-ABEA-c	aimoli					0				4		. . .					0....	3690
20-ABF	**WOISIKA net**	1	1	16,523	21,301		53.00	80	B	4		. . .					0....	3691
20-ABFA	WOISIKA cluster	1	1	16,523	21,301		53.00	80	B	4		. . .					0....	3692
20-ABFA-a	lembur					0				4		. . .					0....	3693
20-ABFA-b	kamot					0				4		. . .					0....	3694
20-ABFA-c	kamana					0				4		. . .					0....	3695
20-ABFA-d	petimpui					0				4		. . .					0....	3696
20-ABFA-e	kamengmi					0				4		. . .					0....	3697
20-ABFA-f	ateita					0				4		. . .					0....	3698
20-ABFA-g	apui					0				4		. . .					0....	3699
20-ABFA-h	silaipui					0				4		. . .					0....	3700
20-ABFA-i	langkuru-kolomano					0				4		. . .					0....	3701
20-ABFA-j	pido					0				4		. . .					0....	3702
20-AC	MAKASAI chain	1	3	15,754	21,104		71.92	98	C	20		. . .					0....	3703
20-ACA	**MAKASAI net**	1	1	12,118	16,234		70.00	99	C	20		. . .					0....	3704
20-ACAA	MAKASAI cluster	1	1	12,118	16,234		70.00	99	C	20		. . .					0....	3705
20-ACAA-a	Proper makasai	1	1	12,118	16,234	0	70.00	99	C	20		. . .					0....	3706
20-ACAA-b	maklere									20		. . .					0....	3709
20-ACB	**KAIRUI-MIDIKI net**	1	2	3,636	4,870		78.33	93	C	4		. . .					0....	3710
20-ACBA	KAIRUI-MIDIKI cluster	1	2	3,636	4,870		78.33	93	C	4		. . .					0....	3711
20-ACBA-a	kairui	1	1	2,424	3,247	0	89.98	100	C	4		. . .					0....	3712
20-ACBA-b	midiki					0				4		. . .					0....	3713
20-B	**TANGLAPUI set**	1	1	16,523	21,301		45.00	72	B	3		. . .					0....	3714
20-BA	TANGLAPUI chain	1	1	16,523	21,301		45.00	72	B	3		. . .					0....	3715
20-BAA	**TANGLAPUI net**	1	1	16,523	21,301		45.00	72	B	3		. . .					0....	3716
20-BAAA	TANGLAPUI cluster	1	1	16,523	21,301		45.00	72	B	3		. . .					0....	3717
20-BAAA-a	tanglapui	1	1	16,523	21,301	0	45.00	72	B	3		. . .					0....	3718
20-C	**KOLANA set**	2	2	59,860	77,230		54.12	89	B	4		. . .					0....	3719
20-CA	KOLANA chain	1	1	58,648	75,607		54.00	89	B	4		. . .					0....	3720
20-CAA	**KOLANA net**	1	1	58,648	75,607		54.00	89	B	4		. . .					0....	3721
20-CAAA	KOLANA cluster	1	1	58,648	75,607		54.00	89	B	4		. . .					0....	3722
20-CAAA-a	kolana	1	1	58,648	75,607	0	54.00	89	B	4		. . .					0....	3723
20-CB	ADABE chain	1	1	1,212	1,623		59.98	84	B	4		. . .					0....	3727
20-CBA	**ADABE net**	1	1	1,212	1,623		59.98	84	B	4		. . .					0....	3728

Continued overleaf

Table 9-13 continued

Code 1	REFERENCE NAME / Autoglossonym 2	Coun 3	Peo 4	Mother-tongue speakers in 2000 5	in 2025 6	Media radio 7	CHURCH AC% 8	E% 9	Wld 10	Tr 11	Biblioglossonym 12	Print 13-15	P-activity 16	N-activity 17	B-activity 18	J-year 19	Jayuh 20-24	Ref 25
20-CBAA	ADABE cluster	1	1	1,212	1,623		59.98	84	B	4		. . .					0	3729
20-CBAA-a	adabe	1	1	1,212	1,623	0	59.98	84	B	4		. . .					0	3730
20-D	**BUNAK set**	1	1	74,810	96,443		5.00	28	A	3		. . .					0	3731
20-DA	BUNAK chain	1	1	74,810	96,443		5.00	28	A	3		. . .					0	3732
20-DAA	**BUNAK net**	1	1	74,810	96,443		5.00	28	A	3		. . .					0	3733
20-DAAA	BUNAK cluster	1	1	74,810	96,443		5.00	28	A	3		. . .					0	3734
20-DAAA-a	bunak	1	1	74,810	96,443	0	5.00	28	A	3		. . .					0	3735
20-E	**FATALUKU set**	1	1	30,296	40,585		90.00	100	C	3		. . .					0	3736
20-EA	FATALUKU chain	1	1	30,296	40,585		90.00	100	C	3		. . .					0	3737
20-EAA	**FATALUKU net**	1	1	30,296	40,585		90.00	100	C	3		. . .					0	3738
20-EAAA	FATALUKU cluster	1	1	30,296	40,585		90.00	100	C	3		. . .					0	3739
20-EAAA-a	fataluku	1	1	30,296	40,585	0	90.00	100	C	3		. . .					0	3740
20-F	**MAKUA set**	1	1	61	82		19.67	43	A	0		. . .					0	3741
20-FA	MAKUA chain	1	1	61	82		19.67	43	A	0		. . .					0	3742
20-FAA	**MAKUA net**	1	1	61	82		19.67	43	A	0		. . .					0	3743
20-FAAA	MAKU'A cluster	1	1	61	82		19.67	43	A	0		. . .					0	3744
20-FAAA-a	maku'a	1	1	61	82	0	19.67	43	A	0		. . .					0	3745
20-G	**OIRATA set**	1	1	1,506	1,941		52.99	83	B	3		. . .					0	3746
20-GA	OIRATA chain	1	1	1,506	1,941		52.99	83	B	3		. . .					0	3747
20-GAA	**OIRATA net**	1	1	1,506	1,941		52.99	83	B	3		. . .					0	3748
20-GAAA	OIRATA cluster	1	1	1,506	1,941		52.99	83	B	3		. . .					0	3749
20-GAAA-a	oirata	1	1	1,506	1,941	0	52.99	83	B	3		. . .					0	3750
20-H	**MACCLUER- DURIANKERE set**	1	9	28,249	40,610		61.41	90	C	4		. . .					0	3751
20-HA	DURIANKERE chain	1	1	127	164		65.35	91	C	4		. . .					0	3752
20-HAA	**DURIANKERE net**	1	1	127	164		65.35	91	C	4		. . .					0	3753
20-HAAA	DURIANKERE cluster	1	1	127	164		65.35	91	C	4		. . .					0	3754
20-HAAA-a	duriankere	1	1	127	164	0	65.35	91	C	4		. . .					0	3755
20-HB	MIRAGA chain	1	2	7,736	12,028		63.70	93	C	4		. . .					0	3756
20-HBA	**MIRAGA net**	1	2	7,736	12,028		63.70	93	C	4		. . .					0	3757
20-HBAA	INANWATAN cluster	1	1	1,951	2,516		64.99	91	C	0		. . .					0	3758
20-HBAA-a	inanwatan	1	1	1,951	2,516	0	64.99	91	C	0		. . .					0	3759
20-HBAB	PURAGI cluster	1	1	785	1,012		64.97	91	C	4		. . .					0	3760
20-HBAB-a	puragi	1	1	785	1,012	0	64.97	91	C	4		. . .					0	3761
20-HBAC	YAMAREMA cluster	1	1	2,000	3,400		60.00	93	C	0		. . .					0	3762
20-HBAC-a	yamarema	1	1	2,000	3,400	0	60.00	93	C	0		. . .					0	3763
20-HBAD	SAGA cluster	1	1	3,000	5,100		65.00	96	C	0		. . .					0	3764
20-HBAD-a	saga	1	1	3,000	5,100	0	65.00	96	C	0		. . .					0	3765
20-HC	TAROF-KASUWERI chain	1	3	15,569	21,796		59.41	88	B	4		. . .					0	3766
20-HCA	**KASUWERI-UDAGAGA net**	1	2	11,275	16,179		62.99	92	C	4		. . .					0	3767
20-HCAA	KASUWERI cluster	1	2	7,275	9,379		62.91	91	C	4		. . .					0	3768
20-HCAA-a	kasuweri	1	2	7,275	9,379	0	62.91	91	C	4		. . .					0	3769
20-HCAB	NEGERI-BESAR cluster	1	1	1,500	2,550		60.00	93	C	0		. . .					0	3770
20-HCAB-a	negeri-besar	1	1	1,500	2,550	0	60.00	93	C	0		. . .					0	3771
20-HCAC	UDAGAGA cluster	1	1	2,500	4,250		65.00	96	C	0		. . .					0	3772
20-HCAC-a	udagaga	1	1	2,500	4,250	0	65.00	96	C	0		. . .					0	3773
20-HCB	**TAROF net**	1	1	4,294	5,617		50.00	78	B	3		. . .					0	3774
20-HCBA	TAROF cluster	1	1	4,094	5,277		50.00	78	B	3		. . .					0	3775
20-HCBA-a	tarof	1	1	4,094	5,277	0	50.00	78	B	3		. . .					0	3776
20-HCBA-b	tambani					0				3		. . .					0	3777
20-HCBB	MIGORI cluster	1	1	200	340		50.00	87	B	0		. . .					0	3778
20-HCBB-a	migori	1	1	200	340	0	50.00	87	B	0		. . .					0	3779
20-HD	AMBERAI-KEMBERANO chain	1	3	4,817	6,622		64.13	91	C	3		. . .					0	3780
20-HDA	**ARANDAI net**	1	2	2,272	3,053		64.70	91	C	3		. . .					0	3781
20-HDAA	TOMU cluster	1	1	300	510		50.00	86	B	0		. . .					0	3782
20-HDAA-a	tomu	1	1	300	510	0	50.00	86	B	0		. . .					0	3783
20-HDAB	ARANDAI cluster	1	2	1,972	2,543		66.94	91	C	3		. . .					0	3784
20-HDAB-a	arandai	1	1	1,230	1,586	0	65.04	92	C	3		. . .					0	3785
20-HDB	**KEMBERANO-BARAU net**	1	1	2,545	3,569		63.61	92	C	3		. . .					0	3786
20-HDBA	KEMBERANO cluster	1	1	1,845	2,379		64.99	91	C	3		. . .					0	3787
20-HDBA-a	kemberano	1	1	1,845	2,379	0	64.99	91	C	3		. . .					0	3788
20-HDBB	WERIAGAR cluster	1	1	400	680		60.00	93	C	0		. . .					0	3789
20-HDBB-a	weriagar	1	1	400	680	0	60.00	93	C	0		. . .					0	3790
20-HDBC	BARAU cluster	1	1	300	510		60.00	93	C	0		. . .					0	3791
20-HDBC-a	barau	1	1	300	510	0	60.00	93	C	0		. . .					0	3792
20-I	**OGIT set**	1	2	1,145	1,477		62.62	89	C	4		. . .					0	3793
20-IA	OGIT chain	1	2	1,145	1,477		62.62	89	C	4		. . .					0	3794
20-IAA	**OGIT net**	1	2	1,145	1,477		62.62	89	C	4		. . .					0	3795
20-IAAA	KONDA cluster	1	1	594	766		64.98	91	C	4		. . .					0	3796
20-IAAA-a	konda	1	1	594	766	0	64.98	91	C	4		. . .					0	3797
20-IAAB	YAHADIAN cluster	1	1	551	711		60.07	86	C	4		. . .					0	3798
20-IAAB-a	mugim	1	1	551	711	0	60.07	86	C	4		. . .					0	3799

Continued opposite

Table 9-13 continued

Code 1	REFERENCE NAME / Autoglossonym 2	Coun 3	Peo 4	Mother-tongue speakers in 2000 5	in 2025 6	Media radio 7	CHURCH AC% 8	E% 9	Wld 10	Tr 11	Biblioglossonym 12	SCRIPTURES Print 13-15	P-activity 16	N-activity 17	B-activity 18	J-year 19	Jayuh 20-24	Ref 25
20-IAAB-b	nerigo	1	1	551	711	0	60.07	86	C	4		...					0....	3800
20-IAAB-c	kampong-baru					0				4		...					0....	3801
20-J	**KOLOPOM set**	1	3	6,024	7,766		65.55	92	C	4		...					0....	3802
20-JA	RIANTANA chain	1	1	1,654	2,133		64.99	92	C	4		...					0....	3803
20-JAA	**RIANTANA net**	1	1	1,654	2,133		64.99	92	C	4		...					0....	3804
20-JAAA	RIANTANA cluster	1	1	1,654	2,133		64.99	92	C	4		...					0....	3805
20-JAAA-a	riantana	1	1	1,654	2,133	0	64.99	92	C	4		...					0....	3806
20-JB	KIMAGHAMA chain	1	1	3,691	4,758		65.00	92	C	4		...					0....	3807
20-JBA	**KIMAGHAMA net**	1	1	3,691	4,758		65.00	92	C	4		...					0....	3808
20-JBAA	KIMAGHAMA cluster	1	1	3,691	4,758		65.00	92	C	4		...					0....	3809
20-JBAA-a	Northeast kimaghama					0				4		...					0....	3810
20-JBAA-b	Southwest kimaghama					0				4		...					0....	3811
20-JC	NDOM chain	1	1	679	875		69.96	96	C	4		...					0....	3812
20-JCA	**NDOM net**	1	1	679	875		69.96	96	C	4		...					0....	3813
20-JCAA	NDOM cluster	1	1	679	875		69.96	96	C	4		...					0....	3814
20-JCAA-a	ndom	1	1	679	875	0	69.96	96	C	4		...					0....	3815
20-K	**BULAKA set**	1	2	742	957		65.09	92	C	4		...					0....	3816
20-KA	BULAKA chain	1	2	742	957		65.09	92	C	4		...					0....	3817
20-KAA	**YELMEK net**	1	1	594	766		64.98	92	C	4		...					0....	3818
20-KAAA	YELMEK cluster	1	1	594	766		64.98	92	C	4		...					0....	3819
20-KAAA-a	North yelmek					0				4		...					0....	3820
20-KAAA-b	South yelmek					0				4		...					0....	3821
20-KAB	**MAKLEW net**	1	1	148	191		65.54	93	C	4		...					0....	3822
20-KABA	MAKLEW cluster	1	1	148	191		65.54	93	C	4		...					0....	3823
20-KABA-a	maklew	1	1	148	191	0	65.54	93	C	4		...					0....	3824
20-L	**NAMBU-YEI set**	2	17	11,830	17,892		49.52	74	B	23		P..					0....	3825
20-LA	MORAORI chain	1	1	64	82		59.38	91	B	4		...					0....	3826
20-LAA	**MORAORI net**	1	1	64	82		59.38	91	B	4		...					0....	3827
20-LAAA	MORAORI cluster	1	1	64	82		59.38	91	B	4		...					0....	3828
20-LAAA-a	moraori	1	1	64	82	0	59.38	91	B	4		...					0....	3829
20-LB	YEI chain	2	2	1,558	2,255		39.28	66	B	4		...					0....	3830
20-LBA	**YEI net**	2	2	1,558	2,255		39.28	66	B	4		...					0....	3831
20-LBAA	YEI cluster	2	2	1,558	2,255		39.28	66	B	4		...					0....	3832
20-LBAA-a	North yei					0				4		...					0....	3833
20-LBAA-b	South yei					0				4		...					0....	3834
20-LC	KANUM chain	2	2	803	1,097		54.92	83	B	2		...					0....	3835
20-LCA	**KANUM net**	2	2	803	1,097		54.92	83	B	2		...					0....	3836
20-LCAA	KANUM cluster	2	2	803	1,097		54.92	83	B	2		...					0....	3837
20-LCAA-a	North kanum					0				2		...					0....	3838
20-LCAA-b	Central kanum					0				2		...					0....	3839
20-LCAA-c	South kanum					0				2		...					0....	3840
20-LD	TONDA-MOREHEAD chain	2	10	6,493	9,879		37.39	63	B	12		...					0....	3841
20-LDA	**BOTHAR net**	2	2	954	1,259		61.11	88	C	3		...					0....	3842
20-LDAA	BOTHAR cluster	2	2	954	1,259		61.11	88	C	3		...					0....	3843
20-LDAA-a	bothar	2	2	954	1,259	0	61.11	88	C	3		...					0....	3844
20-LDB	**TONDA net**	1	4	2,978	4,634		39.02	62	B	3		...					0....	3845
20-LDBA	TONDA cluster	1	4	2,978	4,634		39.02	62	B	3		...					0....	3846
20-LDBA-a	tonda	1	1	872	1,357	0	44.95	69	B	3		...					0....	3847
20-LDC	**ROUKU net**	1	3	2,213	3,444		26.16	54	B	12		...					0....	3848
20-LDCA	ARAMBA cluster	1	2	1,704	2,652		25.00	53	B	12		...					0....	3849
20-LDCA-a	aramba	1	2	1,704	2,652	0	25.00	53	B	12	Aramba	...					0....	3850
20-LDCB	ROUKU cluster	1	1	509	792		30.06	59	B	12		...					0....	3851
20-LDCB-a	rouku	1	1	509	792	0	30.06	59	B	12	Ara	...					0....	3852
20-LDD	**PEREMKA net**	1	1	348	542		29.89	59	B	2		...					0....	3853
20-LDDA	PEREMKA cluster	1	1	348	542		29.89	59	B	2		...					0....	3854
20-LDDA-a	Proper peremka	1	1	348	542	0	29.89	59	B	2		...					0....	3855
20-LDDA-b	gambadi					0				2		...					0....	3856
20-LDDA-c	semariji					0				2		...					0....	3857
20-LE	NAMBU chain	1	2	2,912	4,579		80.32	100	C	23		P..					0....	3858
20-LEA	**NAMBU net**	1	1	2,809	4,419		79.99	100	C	23		P..					0....	3859
20-LEAA	NAMBU cluster	1	1	2,489	3,875		79.99	100	C	23		P..					0....	3860
20-LEAA-a	nambu	1	1	2,489	3,875	0	79.99	100	C	23	Arufe*	P..	1974				0....	3861
20-LEAB	IAUGA cluster	1	1	20	34		80.00	100	C	0		...					0....	3862
20-LEAB-a	iauga	1	1	20	34	0	80.00	100	C	0		...					0....	3863
20-LEAC	TAIS cluster	1	1	300	510		80.00	100	C	4		...					0....	3864
20-LEAC-a	tais	1	1	300	510	0	80.00	100	C	4		...					0....	3865
20-LEB	**DORRO net**	1	1	103	160		89.32	100	C	4		...					0....	3866
20-LEBA	DORRO cluster	1	1	103	160		89.32	100	C	4		...					0....	3867
20-LEBA-a	dorro	1	1	103	160	0	89.32	100	C	4		...					0....	3868
20-M	**PAHOTURI-WAIA set**	1	3	9,189	14,304		70.03	92	C	33		P..					0....	3869
20-MA	PAHOTURI chain	1	2	6,899	10,739		80.00	100	C	12		...					0....	3870
20-MAA	**IDI-AGÖB net**	1	2	6,899	10,739		80.00	100	C	12		...					0....	3871
20-MAAA	IDI cluster	1	1	2,509	3,905		79.99	100	C	12		...					0....	3872

Continued overleaf

Table 9-13 continued

Code 1	REFERENCE NAME / Autoglossonym 2	Coun 3	Peo 4	in 2000 5	in 2025 6	Media radio 7	AC% 8	E% 9	Wld 10	Tr 11	Biblioglossonym 12	Print 13-15	P–activity 16	N–activity 17	B–activity 18	J-year 19	Jayuh 20-24	Ref 25
20-MAAA-a	idi	1	1	2,509	3,905	0	79.99	100	C	12	Idi	. . .					0	3873
20-MAAB	AGÖB cluster	1	1	4,390	6,834		80.00	100	C	2		. . .					0	3874
20-MAAB-a	agöb	1	1	4,390	6,834	0	80.00	100	C	2		. . .					0	3875
20-MAAB-b	buji					0				2		. . .					0	3876
20-MB	WAIA chain	1	1	2,290	3,565		40.00	68	B	33		P . .					0	3877
20-MBA	**WAIA net**	1	1	2,290	3,565		40.00	68	B	33		P . .					0	3878
20-MBAA	WAIA cluster	1	1	2,290	3,565		40.00	68	B	33		P . .					0	3879
20-MBAA-a	Proper waia	1	1	2,290	3,565	0	40.00	68	B	33	Tabo: Aramia	P . .	1992-1995				0	3880
20-MBAA-b	kenedibi					0				33		p . .					0	3881
20-N	**TIRIO set**	1	5	5,806	9,324		72.32	89	C	23		P . .					0	3882
20-NA	TIRIO chain	1	5	5,806	9,324		72.32	89	C	23		P . .					0	3883
20-NAA	**LEWADA-ATURU net**	1	4	3,122	4,859		57.14	80	B	23		P . .					0	3884
20-NAAA	LEWADA-DEWARA cluster	1	3	2,801	4,360		53.37	77	B	23	Tirio	P . .	1975				0	3885
20-NAAA-a	lewada					0				23		p . .					0	3886
20-NAAA-b	balamula					0				23		p . .					0	3887
20-NAAA-c	dewala					0				23		p . .					0	3888
20-NAAB	ATURU cluster	1	1	321	499		90.03	100	C	4		. . .					0	3889
20-NAAB-a	aturu	1	1	321	499	0	90.03	100	C	4		. . .					0	3890
20-NAB	**TIRIO-MUTUM net**	1	1	2,684	4,465		89.98	99	C	23		P . .					0	3891
20-NABA	TIRIO cluster	1	1	2,000	3,400		90.00	99	C	23		P . .					0	3892
20-NABA-a	tirio	1	1	2,000	3,400	0	90.00	99	C	23	Dudi	P . .	1975				0	3893
20-NABB	MUTUM cluster	1	1	684	1,065		89.91	100	C	4		. . .					0	3894
20-NABB-a	mutum	1	1	684	1,065	0	89.91	100	C	4		. . .					0	3895
20-O	**GIDGA-GIZRA set**	2	6	12,066	19,270		81.29	100	C	41		PN .					0	3896
20-OA	GIDRA chain	1	2	5,451	8,772		80.85	100	C	12		. . .					0	3897
20-OAA	**GIDRA net**	1	2	5,451	8,772		80.85	100	C	12		. . .					0	3898
20-OAAA	GIDRA-BITURI cluster	1	1	461	717		90.02	100	C	0		. . .					0	3899
20-OAAA-a	guiam					0				0		. . .					0	3900
20-OAAA-b	yuta					0				0		. . .					0	3901
20-OAAA-c	rual					0				0		. . .					0	3902
20-OAAA-d	kapal					0				0		. . .					0	3903
20-OAAB	GIDRA-WIPIM cluster	1	1	2,000	3,400		80.00	100	C	0		. . .					0	3904
20-OAAB-a	wipim					0				0		. . .					0	3905
20-OAAB-b	podari					0				0		. . .					0	3906
20-OAAB-c	zim					0				0		. . .					0	3907
20-OAAB-d	wonie					0				0		. . .					0	3908
20-OAAB-e	iamega					0				0		. . .					0	3909
20-OAAB-f	gamaewe					0				0		. . .					0	3910
20-OAAC	GIDRA-DONGORI cluster	1	1	2,990	4,655		80.00	100	C	12	Gidra	. . .					0	3911
20-OAAC-a	ume					0				12		. . .					0	3912
20-OAAC-b	kuru					0				12		. . .					0	3913
20-OAAC-c	dongori					0				12		. . .					0	3914
20-OAAC-d	abam					0				12		. . .					0	3915
20-OAAC-e	peawa					0				12		. . .					0	3916
20-OB	BINE chain	1	1	4,489	7,275		80.00	100	C	41		PN .					0	3917
20-OBA	**BINE net**	1	1	4,489	7,275		80.00	100	C	41		PN .					0	3918
20-OBAA	NORTHEAST BINE cluster	1	1	2,489	3,875		79.99	100	C	41	Bine	PN .	1934-1982	1993			0	3919
20-OBAA-a	sogal					0				41		pn .					0	3920
20-OBAA-b	boze-giringarede					0				41		pn .					0	3921
20-OBAA-c	kunini					0				41		pn .					0	3922
20-OBAB	SOUTHWEST BINE cluster	1	1	2,000	3,400		80.00	100	C	0		. . .					0	3923
20-OBAB-a	masingle					0				0		. . .					0	3924
20-OBAB-b	tati					0				0		. . .					0	3925
20-OBAB-c	irupi-drageli					0				0		. . .					0	3926
20-OBAB-d	sebe					0				0		. . .					0	3927
20-OC	GIZRA chain	1	1	1,463	2,320		89.95	100	C	12		. . .					0	3928
20-OCA	**GIZRA net**	1	1	1,463	2,320		89.95	100	C	12		. . .					0	3929
20-OCAA	WEST GIZRA cluster	1	1	1,163	1,810		89.94	100	C	12	Gizra	. . .					0	3930
20-OCAA-a	kupere					0				12		. . .					0	3931
20-OCAA-b	togo					0				12		. . .					0	3932
20-OCAB	EAST GIZRA cluster	1	1	300	510		90.00	99	C	0		. . .					0	3933
20-OCAB-a	waidoro	1	1	300	510	0	90.00	99	C	0		. . .					0	3934
20-OD	MERIAM chain	2	2	663	903		74.51	100	C	24		P . .					0	3935
20-ODA	**MERIAM net**	2	2	663	903		74.51	100	C	24		P . .					0	3936
20-ODAA	MERIAM cluster	2	2	663	903		74.51	100	C	24		P . .					0	3937
20-ODAA-a	meriam	2	2	663	903	0	74.51	100	C	24	Miriam Mir*	P . .	1879-1902				0	3938
20-P	**KIWAIAN set**	1	6	42,710	67,623		86.30	100	C	44		PN .					0	3939
20-PA	KIWAIAN chain	1	6	42,710	67,623		86.30	100	C	44		PN .					0	3940
20-PAA	**SOUTH KIWAI net**	1	1	21,880	34,821		86.26	100	C	44		PN .					0	3941
20-PAAA	DOUMORI cluster	1	1	300	510		80.00	100	C	0		. . .					0	3942
20-PAAA-a	Proper doumori					0				0		. . .					0	3943
20-PAAA-b	wasua					0				0		. . .					0	3944
20-PAAB	SEWERIMABU cluster	1	1	2,000	3,400		80.00	100	C	0		. . .					0	3945
20-PAAB-a	sewerimabu					0				0		. . .					0	3946
20-PAAB-b	panama					0				0		. . .					0	3947
20-PAAC	DARU cluster	1	1	3,000	5,100		87.00	99	C	0		. . .					0	3948
20-PAAC-a	daru	1	1	3,000	5,100	0	87.00	99	C	0		. . .					0	3949
20-PAAD	KIWAI cluster	1	1	16,580	25,811		87.00	100	C	44		PN .					0	3950
20-PAAD-a	kiwai	1	1	16,580	25,811	1	87.00	100	C	44	Kiwai*	PN .	1911-1927	1960			0	3951
20-PAB	**WABUDA net**	1	1	2,343	3,648		90.01	100	C	2		. . .					0	3952
20-PABA	WABUDA cluster	1	1	2,343	3,648		90.01	100	C	2		. . .					0	3953
20-PABA-a	Proper wabuda	1	1	2,343	3,648	0	90.01	100	C	2		. . .					0	3954
20-PABA-b	sagero					0				2		. . .					0	3955

Continued opposite

Table 9-13 continued

Code 1	REFERENCE NAME / Autoglossonym 2	Coun 3	Peo 4	Mother-tongue speakers in 2000 5	in 2025 6	Media radio 7	AC% 8	E% 9	Wld 10	Tr 11	Biblioglossonym 12	Print 13-15	P-activity 16	N-activity 17	B-activity 18	J-year 19	Jayuh 20-24	Ref 25
20-PABA-c	dibiri					0				2		...					0....	3956
20-PAC	**BAMU net**	1	1	7,607	12,172		93.49	100	C	23		P..					0....	3957
20-PACA	WAKAU cluster	1	1	5,307	8,262		95.01	100	C	23		P..					0....	3958
20-PACA-a	wakau	1	1	5,307	8,262	0	95.01	100	C	23	Bamu	P..	1952				0....	3959
20-PACB	PIRUPIRU cluster	1	1	300	510		90.00	99	C	0		...					0....	3960
20-PACB-a	pirupiru	1	1	300	510	0	90.00	99	C	0		...					0....	3961
20-PACC	SISIAME cluster	1	1	2,000	3,400		90.00	99	C	0		...					0....	3962
20-PACC-a	sisiame	1	1	2,000	3,400	0	90.00	99	C	0		...					0....	3963
20-PAD	**MORIGI net**	1	1	1,196	1,862		85.03	100	C	2		...					0....	3964
20-PADA	MORIGI cluster	1	1	1,196	1,862		85.03	100	C	2		...					0....	3965
20-PADA-a	morigi	1	1	1,196	1,862	0	85.03	100	C	2		...					0....	3966
20-PAE	**KEREWO net**	1	1	3,760	5,854		80.00	100	C	24		P..					0....	3967
20-PAEA	KEREWO cluster	1	1	3,760	5,854		80.00	100	C	24	Kerawa*	P..	1926-1941				0....	3968
20-PAEA-a	kikori					1				24		p..					0....	3969
20-PAEA-b	ururumba					1				24		p..					0....	3970
20-PAEA-c	gibario					1				24		p..					0....	3971
20-PAF	**GIBAIO-ARIGIBI net**	1	1	5,924	9,266		80.00	100	C	0		...					0....	3972
20-PAFA	GIBAIO-URAMA cluster	1	1	5,624	8,756		80.00	100	C	0		...					0....	3973
20-PAFA-a	urama					0				0		...					0....	3974
20-PAFA-b	kope					0				0		...					0....	3975
20-PAFA-c	gibaio	1	1	5,624	8,756	0	80.00	100	C	0		...					0....	3976
20-PAFB	ARIGIBI cluster	1	1	300	510		80.00	100	C	0		...					0....	3977
20-PAFB-a	arigibi	1	1	300	510	0	80.00	100	C	0		...					0....	3978
20-Q	**IPIKO set**	1	1	323	503		90.09	100	C	2		...					0....	3979
20-QA	IPIKO chain	1	1	323	503		90.09	100	C	2		...					0....	3980
20-QAA	**IPIKO net**	1	1	323	503		90.09	100	C	2		...					0....	3981
20-QAAA	IPIKO cluster	1	1	323	503		90.09	100	C	2		...					0....	3982
20-QAAA-a	ipiko	1	1	323	503	0	90.09	100	C	2		...					0....	3983
20-R	**MINANIBAIAN set**	1	2	1,163	1,810		58.73	79	B	9		...					0....	3984
20-RA	MINANIBAI chain	1	1	436	679		89.91	100	C	2		...					0....	3985
20-RAA	**MINANIBAI net**	1	1	436	679		89.91	100	C	2		...					0....	3986
20-RAAA	MINANIBAI cluster	1	1	436	679		89.91	100	C	2		...					0....	3987
20-RAAA-a	minanibai	1	1	436	679	0	89.91	100	C	2		...					0....	3988
20-RB	MAHIGI chain									0		...					0....	3989
20-RBA	**MAHIGI net**									0		...					0....	3990
20-RBAA	MAHIGI cluster			0	0		0.00	0		0		...					0....	3991
20-RBAA-a	mahigi			0	0	0	0.00	0		0		...					0....	3992
20-RC	TAO-SUAMATO chain	1	1	727	1,131		40.03	67	B	2		...					0....	3993
20-RCA	**TAO-SUAMATO net**	1	1	727	1,131		40.03	67	B	2		...					0....	3994
20-RCAA	TAO-SUAMATO cluster	1	1	727	1,131		40.03	67	B	2		...					0....	3995
20-RCAA-a	tao-suamato	1	1	727	1,131	0	40.03	67	B	2		...					0....	3996
20-RD	KARAMI chain									9		...					0....	3997
20-RDA	**KARAMI net**									9		...					0....	3998
20-RDAA	KARAMI cluster			0	0		0.00	0		9		...					0....	3999
20-RDAA-a	karami			0	0	0	0.00	0		9		...					0....	4000
20-S	**PURARI set**	1	1	8,711	13,561		75.00	100	C	43		PN.					0.s..	4001
20-SA	PURARI chain	1	1	8,711	13,561		75.00	100	C	43		PN.					0.s..	4002
20-SAA	**PURARI net**	1	1	8,711	13,561		75.00	100	C	43		PN.					0.s..	4003
20-SAAA	PURARI cluster	1	1	8,711	13,561		75.00	100	C	43		PN.					0.s..	4004
20-SAAA-a	Proper purari					0				43	Purari	PN.	1910-1967	1920			0.s..	4005
20-SAAA-b	iai	1	1	8,711	13,561	0	75.00	100	C	43	Iai: Papua New Guinea	PN.	1910	1920			0.s..	4006
20-T	**ELEMAN set**	1	5	71,518	111,337		83.45	98	C	61		PNB					0.s..	4007
20-TA	VAILALA chain	1	3	29,670	46,188		80.66	95	C	44		PN.					0.s..	4008
20-TAA	**VAILALA net**	1	3	29,670	46,188		80.66	95	C	44		PN.					0.s..	4009
20-TAAA	OROKOLO cluster	1	1	21,005	32,700		88.00	100	C	44		PN.					0.s..	4010
20-TAAA-a	orokolo	1	1	21,005	32,700	1	88.00	100	C	44	Orokolo	PN.	1926-1951	1963			0.s..	4011
20-TAAA-b	muru					1				44		pn.					0.s..	4012
20-TAAB	KEURU cluster	1	1	6,596	10,268		55.00	80	B	4		...					0....	4013
20-TAAB-a	aheave					0				4		...					0....	4014
20-TAAB-b	haura-haela					0				4		...					0....	4015
20-TAAB-c	hae-haela					0				4		...					0....	4016
20-TAAC	OPAO cluster	1	1	2,069	3,220		87.97	100	C	4		...					0....	4017
20-TAAC-a	opao	1	1	2,069	3,220	0	87.97	100	C	4		...					0....	4018
20-TB	LAKEKAMU chain	1	2	41,848	65,149		85.43	100	C	61		PNB					0....	4019
20-TBA	**LAKEKAMU net**	1	2	41,848	65,149		85.43	100	C	61		PNB					0....	4020
20-TBAA	UARIPI cluster	1	1	4,686	7,296		65.00	97	C	4		...					0....	4021
20-TBAA-a	uaripi	1	1	4,686	7,296	0	65.00	97	C	4		...					0....	4022
20-TBAB	TOARIPI cluster	1	1	37,162	57,853		88.00	100	C	61		PNB					0....	4023
20-TBAB-a	melaripi-kaipi					1				61		pnb					0....	4024
20-TBAB-b	moveave-toaripi	1	1	37,162	57,853	1	88.00	100	C	61	Toaripi	PNB	1902-1968	1914-1960	1983		0....	4027
20-TBAB-c	moripi-iokea					1				61		pnb					0....	4030
20-TBAB-d	sepoe					1				61		pnb					0....	4033
20-U	**TATE set**	1	1	363	565		95.04	100	C	2		...					0....	4034
20-UA	TATE chain	1	1	363	565		95.04	100	C	2		...					0....	4035

Continued overleaf

Table 9-13 continued

Code 1	REFERENCE NAME / Autoglossonym 2	Coun 3	Peo 4	Mother-tongue speakers in 2000 5	in 2025 6	Media radio 7	AC% 8	CHURCH E% 9	Wld 10	Tr 11	Biblioglossonym 12	SCRIPTURES Print 13-15	P-activity 16	N-activity 17	B-activity 18	J-year 19	Jayuh 20-24	Ref 25
20-UAA	**TATE net**	1	1	363	565		95.04	100	C	2		...					0....	4036
20-UAAA	TATE cluster	1	1	363	565		95.04	100	C	2		...					0....	4037
20-UAAA-a	tate	1	1	363	565	0	95.04	100	C	2		...					0....	4038
20-V	**IKOBI-OMATI set**	1	3	2,936	4,570		81.54	99	C	2		...					0....	4039
20-VA	IKOBI-OMATI chain	1	3	2,936	4,570		81.54	99	C	2		...					0....	4040
20-VAA	**IKOBI-MENA net**	1	2	1,643	2,558		82.78	98	C	2		...					0....	4041
20-VAAA	MENA cluster	1	1	593	923		69.98	96	C	0		...					0....	4042
20-VAAA-a	mena	1	1	593	923	0	69.98	96	C	0		...					0....	4043
20-VAAB	IKOBI cluster	1	1	1,050	1,635		90.00	100	C	2		...					0....	4044
20-VAAB-a	pimuru					0				2		...					0....	4045
20-VAAB-b	gorau					0				2		...					0....	4046
20-VAAB-c	utabi					0				2		...					0....	4047
20-VAB	**OMATI net**	1	1	1,293	2,012		79.97	100	C	2		...					0....	4048
20-VABA	OMATI cluster	1	1	1,293	2,012		79.97	100	C	2		...					0....	4049
20-VABA-a	omati	1	1	1,293	2,012	0	79.97	100	C	2		...					0....	4050
20-W	**KAIRI set**	1	1	1,312	2,043		95.05	100	C	32		P..					1....	4051
20-WA	KAIRI chain	1	1	1,312	2,043		95.05	100	C	32		P..					1....	4052
20-WAA	**KAIRI net**	1	1	1,312	2,043		95.05	100	C	32		P..					1....	4053
20-WAAA	KAIRI cluster	1	1	1,312	2,043		95.05	100	C	32		P..					1....	4054
20-WAAA-a	kairi	1	1	1,312	2,043	0	95.05	100	C	32	Kairi*	P..	1965			1995	1....	4055
20-X	**EAST KUTUBUAN set**	1	2	4,617	7,188		61.71	94	C	41		PN.					0....	4056
20-XA	EAST KUTUBUAN chain	1	2	4,617	7,188		61.71	94	C	41		PN.					0....	4057
20-XAA	**EAST KUTUBUAN net**	1	2	4,617	7,188		61.71	94	C	41		PN.					0....	4058
20-XAAA	FOI cluster	1	1	4,181	6,509		65.01	98	C	41	Foe*	PN.	1961-1968	1978			0....	4059
20-XAAA-a	kutubu					0				41		pn.					0....	4060
20-XAAA-b	igi					0				41		pn.					0....	4061
20-XAAA-c	kafa					0				41		pn.					0....	4062
20-XAAB	FIWAGA cluster	1	1	436	679		30.05	55	B	4		...					0....	4063
20-XAAB-a	fiwaga					0				4		...					0....	4064
20-Y	**TEBERAN set**	1	2	16,052	24,988		85.09	100	C	41		PN.					0....	4065
20-YA	FOLOPA chain	1	1	3,938	6,130		69.98	100	C	22		P..					0....	4066
20-YAA	**FOLOPA net**	1	1	3,938	6,130		69.98	100	C	22		P..					0....	4067
20-YAAA	FOLOPA cluster	1	1	3,938	6,130		69.98	100	C	22	Podopa*	P..	1978-1989				0....	4068
20-YAAA-a	keba-wopasali					0				22		p..					0....	4069
20-YAAA-b	waraga					0				22		p..					0....	4072
20-YAAA-c	pupitau					0				22		p..					0....	4073
20-YAAA-d	sopese					0				22		p..					0....	4074
20-YAAA-e	suri					0				22		p..					0....	4075
20-YAAA-f	boro					0				22		p..					0....	4076
20-YAAA-g	siligi					0				22		p..					0....	4077
20-YAAA-h	diauwereke					0				22		p..					0....	4078
20-YAAA-i	omo					0				22		p..					0....	4079
20-YAAA-j	tebera					0				22		p..					0....	4080
20-YAAA-k	bara					0				22		p..					0....	4081
20-YAAA-l	trabedesare					0				22		p..					0....	4082
20-YAAA-m	aurei					0				22		p..					0....	4083
20-YAAA-n	ro					0				22		p..					0....	4084
20-YAAA-o	sesa					0				22		p..					0....	4085
20-YB	DADIBI chain	1	1	12,114	18,858		90.00	100	C	41		PN.					0....	4086
20-YBA	**DADIBI net**	1	1	12,114	18,858		90.00	100	C	41		PN.					0....	4087
20-YBAA	DADIBI cluster	1	1	12,114	18,858		90.00	100	C	41	Dadibi	PN.	1976-1981	1987			0....	4088
20-YBAA-a	erave					1				41	Erave	PN.	1975-1990	1993			0....	4089
20-YBAA-b	mikaru					1				41		pn.					0....	4090
20-YBAA-c	elu					1				41		pn.					0....	4091
20-Z	**PAWAIAN set**	1	1	9,150	14,889		80.00	100	C	12		...					0....	4092
20-ZA	PAWAIAN chain	1	1	9,150	14,889		80.00	100	C	12		...					0....	4093
20-ZAA	**PAWAIAN net**	1	1	9,150	14,889		80.00	100	C	12		...					0....	4094
20-ZAAA	HAURUHA cluster	1	1	2,000	3,400		80.00	100	C	0		...					0....	4095
20-ZAAA-a	hauruha	1	1	2,000	3,400	0	80.00	100	C	0		...					0....	4096
20-ZAAB	AURAMA cluster	1	1	2,500	4,250		80.00	100	C	0		...					0....	4097
20-ZAAB-a	West pawaian					0				0		...					0....	4098
20-ZAAB-b	Central pawaian					0				0		...					0....	4099
20-ZAAC	PAWAIA cluster	1	1	4,650	7,239		80.00	100	C	12		...					0....	4100
20-ZAAC-a	pawaia	1	1	4,650	7,239	0	80.00	100	C	12	Pawaia	...					0....	4101
21	**NORTH IRIANIC zone**	2	86	197,538	267,586		44.96	68	B	44		PN.					0....	4102
21-A	**WEST MEERVLAKTE set**	1	5	3,978	5,334		76.80	96	C	12		...					0....	4103
21-AA	KIRIKIRI-FAYU chain	1	2	784	1,012		65.18	95	C	12		...					0....	4104
21-AAA	**FAYU net**	1	1	445	574		65.17	95	C	12		...					0....	4105
21-AAAA	FAYU cluster	1	1	445	574		65.17	95	C	12		...					0....	4106
21-AAAA-a	fayu	1	1	445	574	0	65.17	95	C	12	Fayu	...					0....	4107
21-AAB	**KIRIKIRI net**	1	1	339	438		65.19	94	C	12		...					0....	4108
21-AABA	KIRIKIRI cluster	1	1	339	438		65.19	94	C	12		...					0....	4109
21-AABA-a	kirikiri	1	1	339	438	0	65.19	94	C	12	Kirikiri	...					0....	4110
21-AB	TAUSE chain	1	1	382	492		50.00	78	B	2		...					0....	4111
21-ABA	**TAUSE net**	1	1	382	492		50.00	78	B	2		...					0....	4112
21-ABAA	TAUSE cluster	1	1	382	492		50.00	78	B	2		...					0....	4113
21-ABAA-a	tause	1	1	382	492	0	50.00	78	B	2		...					0....	4114

Continued opposite

Table 9-13 continued

Code 1	REFERENCE NAME / Autoglossonym 2	Coun 3	Peo 4	Mother-tongue speakers in 2000 5	in 2025 6	Media radio 7	CHURCH AC% 8	E% 9	Wld 10	Tr 11	Biblioglossonym 12	Print 13-15	P-activity 16	N-activity 17	B-activity 18	J-year 19	Jayuh 20-24	Ref 25
21-AC	TURU-EDOPI chain	1	2	2,812	3,830		83.68	98	C	12		. . .					0	4115
21-ACA	**EDOPI net**	1	1	1,061	1,367		64.94	97	C	12		. . .					0	4116
21-ACAA	EDOPI cluster	1	1	1,061	1,367		64.94	97	C	12		. . .					0	4117
21-ACAA-a	edopi	1	1	1,061	1,367	0	64.94	97	C	12	Edopi	. . .					0	4118
21-ACB	**TURU-IAU net**	1	1	1,751	2,463		95.03	99	C	0		. . .					0	4119
21-ACBA	POI cluster	1	1	300	510		95.00	98	C	0		. . .					0	4120
21-ACBA-a	poi	1	1	300	510	0	95.00	98	C	0		. . .					0	4121
21-ACBB	TURU-NO cluster	1	1	200	340		95.00	98	C	0		. . .					0	4122
21-ACBB-a	turu-no	1	1	200	340	0	95.00	98	C	0		. . .					0	4123
21-ACBC	IAU cluster	1	1	1,251	1,613		95.04	100	C	0		. . .					0	4124
21-ACBC-a	bareri					0				0		. . .					0	4125
21-ACBC-b	fauwi					0				0		. . .					0	4126
21-ACBC-c	urundi					0				0		. . .					0	4127
21-B	**CENTRAL MEERVLAKTE set**	1	9	3,987	5,141		63.71	94	C	22		P . .					0	4128
21-BA	BARUA-WARI chain	1	8	3,457	4,457		63.55	94	C	22		P . .					0	4129
21-BAA	**BARUA net**	1	1	530	684		65.09	96	C	22		P . .					0	4130
21-BAAA	BARUA cluster	1	1	530	684		65.09	96	C	22	Obokuitai	P . .	1994				0	4131
21-BAAA-a	barua					0				22		p . .					0	4132
21-BAAA-b	eri-tai	1	1	530	684	0	65.09	96	C	22		p . .					0	4133
21-BAB	**OBOGWI net**	1	1	127	164		63.78	93	C	2		. . .					0	4134
21-BABA	OBOGWI cluster	1	1	127	164		63.78	93	C	2		. . .					0	4135
21-BABA-a	obogwi-tai	1	1	127	164	0	63.78	93	C	2		. . .					0	4136
21-BABA-b	biri-tai					0				2		. . .					0	4137
21-BAC	**TAOGWE net**	1	1	42	55		59.52	88	B	8		. . .					0	4138
21-BACA	TAOGWE cluster	1	1	42	55		59.52	88	B	8		. . .					0	4139
21-BACA-a	taogwe	1	1	42	55	0	59.52	88	B	8		. . .					0	4140
21-BAD	**DUVLE net**	1	1	933	1,203		65.06	96	C	12		. . .					0	4141
21-BADA	DUVLE cluster	1	1	933	1,203		65.06	96	C	12	Duvle	. . .					0	4142
21-BADA-a	West duvle					0				12		. . .					0	4143
21-BADA-b	East duvle					0				12		. . .					0	4144
21-BAE	**TOLI net**	1	1	361	465		64.82	93	C	2		. . .					0	4145
21-BAEA	TOLI cluster	1	1	361	465		64.82	93	C	2		. . .					0	4146
21-BAEA-a	toli-tai	1	1	361	465	0	64.82	93	C	2		. . .					0	4147
21-BAF	**KAIY net**	1	1	276	355		63.77	95	C	2		. . .					0	4148
21-BAFA	KAIY cluster	1	1	276	355		63.77	95	C	2		. . .					0	4149
21-BAFA-a	kaiy	1	1	276	355	0	63.77	95	C	2		. . .					0	4150
21-BAG	**SIKARI net**	1	1	870	1,121		60.00	91	C	12		. . .					0	4151
21-BAGA	SIKARI cluster	1	1	870	1,121		60.00	91	C	12		. . .					0	4152
21-BAGA-a	sikari-tai	1	1	870	1,121	0	60.00	91	C	12	Sikaritai	. . .					0	4153
21-BAH	**WARI net**	1	1	318	410		65.09	95	C	2		. . .					0	4154
21-BAHA	WARI cluster	1	1	318	410		65.09	95	C	2		. . .					0	4155
21-BAHA-a	wari-tai	1	1	318	410	0	65.09	95	C	2		. . .					0	4156
21-BB	PAPASENA chain	1	1	530	684		64.72	91	C	2		. . .					0	4157
21-BBA	**PAPASENA net**	1	1	530	684		64.72	91	C	2		. . .					0	4158
21-BBAA	PAPASENA cluster	1	1	530	684		64.72	91	C	2		. . .					0	4159
21-BBAA-a	papasena	1	1	530	684	0	64.72	91	C	2		. . .					0	4160
21-C	**EAST MEERVLAKTE set**	1	3	657	847		64.84	92	C	4		. . .					0	4161
21-CA	TAWORTA-FOAU chain	1	3	657	847		64.84	92	C	4		. . .					0	4162
21-CAA	**TAWORTA-DABRA net**	1	2	296	382		64.86	92	C	4		. . .					0	4163
21-CAAA	TAWORTA cluster	1	1	148	191		65.54	90	C	4		. . .					0	4164
21-CAAA-a	taworta	1	1	148	191	0	65.54	90	C	4		. . .					0	4165
21-CAAB	DABRA cluster	1	1	148	191		64.19	93	C	4		. . .					0	4166
21-CAAB-a	dabra	1	1	148	191	0	64.19	93	C	4		. . .					0	4167
21-CAB	**FOAU net**	1	1	361	465		64.82	93	C	4		. . .					0	4168
21-CABA	FOAU cluster	1	1	361	465		64.82	93	C	4		. . .					0	4169
21-CABA-a	foau	1	1	361	465	0	64.82	93	C	4		. . .					0	4170
21-D	**TOR set**	1	11	5,924	7,658		65.07	93	C	41		PN .					0	4171
21-DA	BERIK chain	1	2	1,930	2,488		65.03	96	C	41		PN .					0	4172
21-DAA	**BERIK net**	1	2	1,930	2,488		65.03	96	C	41		PN .					0	4173
21-DAAA	BERIK cluster	1	2	1,930	2,488		65.03	96	C	41		PN .					0	4174
21-DAAA-a	daranto					0				41		pn .					0	4175
21-DAAA-b	guamer					0				41		pn .					0	4176
21-DAAA-c	waf					0				41		pn .					0	4177
21-DAAA-d	bew					0				41		pn .					0	4178
21-DAAA-e	berik	1	1	1,294	1,668	0	64.99	100	C	41	Berik	PN .	1979-1986	1993			0	4179
21-DAAA-f	safrontani					0				41		pn .					0	4180
21-DAAA-g	sewan					0				41		pn .					0	4181
21-DB	MANDER chain	1	2	63	82		66.67	94	C	8		. . .					0	4182
21-DBA	**MANDER net**	1	2	63	82		66.67	94	C	8		. . .					0	4183
21-DBAA	MANDER cluster	1	2	63	82		66.67	94	C	8		. . .					0	4184
21-DBAA-a	mander	1	2	63	82	0	66.67	94	C	8		. . .					0	4185
21-DC	TOR-BU chain	1	1	198	276		66.67	92	C	8		. . .					0	4186
21-DCA	**FOYA net**	1	1	50	85		70.00	98	C	8		. . .					0	4187
21-DCAA	FOYA cluster	1	1	50	85		70.00	98	C	8		. . .					0	4188
21-DCAA-a	foya	1	1	50	85	0	70.00	98	Wld	8		. . .					0	4189

Continued overleaf

Table 9-13 continued

Code 1	REFERENCE NAME / Autoglossonym 2	Coun 3	Peo 4	Mother-tongue speakers in 2000 5	in 2025 6	Media radio 7	CHURCH AC% 8	E% 9	Wld 10	Tr 11	Biblioglossonym 12	SCRIPTURES Print 13-15	P-activity 16	N-activity 17	B-activity 18	J-year 19	Jayuh 20-24	Ref 25
21-DCB	**BONERIF net**	1	1	148	191		65.54	90	C	8		...					0....	4190
21-DCBA	BONERIF cluster	1	1	148	191		65.54	90	C	8		...					0....	4191
21-DCBA-a	bonerif	1	1	148	191	0	65.54	90	C	8		...					0....	4192
21-DD	KWESTEN chain	1	1	2,460	3,172		65.00	92	C	2		...					0....	4193
21-DDA	**KWESTEN net**	1	1	2,460	3,172		65.00	92	C	2		...					0....	4194
21-DDAA	KWESTEN cluster	1	1	2,460	3,172		65.00	92	C	2		...					0....	4195
21-DDAA-a	takar					0				2		...					0....	4196
21-DDAA-b	holmhaven					0				2		...					0....	4197
21-DDAA-c	mafenter					0				2		...					0....	4198
21-DDAA-d	arare					0				2		...					0....	4199
21-DDAA-e	omte					0				2		...					0....	4200
21-DE	KEDER-DABE chain	1	2	891	1,148		65.10	91	C	4		...					0....	4201
21-DEA	**DABE net**	1	1	212	273		65.09	91	C	4		...					0....	4202
21-DEAA	DABE cluster	1	1	212	273		65.09	91	C	4		...					0....	4203
21-DEAA-a	dabe	1	1	212	273	0	65.09	91	C	4		...					0....	4204
21-DEB	**KEDER net**	1	1	679	875		65.10	91	C	4		...					0....	4205
21-DEBA	KEDER cluster	1	1	679	875		65.10	91	C	4		...					0....	4206
21-DEBA-a	keder	1	1	679	875	0	65.10	91	C	4		...					0....	4207
21-DF	ITIK chain	1	1	148	191		65.54	91	C	4		...					0....	4208
21-DFA	**ITIK net**	1	1	148	191		65.54	91	C	4		...					0....	4209
21-DFAA	ITIK cluster	1	1	148	191		65.54	91	C	4		...					0....	4210
21-DFAA-a	itik-tor	1	1	148	191	0	65.54	91	C	4		...					0....	4211
21-DFAA-b	Proper itik					0				4		...					0....	4212
21-DG	WARES chain	1	1	170	219		64.12	90	C	4		...					0....	4213
21-DGA	**WARES net**	1	1	170	219		64.12	90	C	4		...					0....	4214
21-DGAA	WARES cluster	1	1	170	219		64.12	90	C	4		...					0....	4215
21-DGAA-a	wares	1	1	170	219	0	64.12	90	C	4		...					0....	4216
21-DH	MAREMGI chain	1	1	64	82		64.06	94	C	4		...					0....	4217
21-DHA	**MAREMGI net**	1	1	64	82		64.06	94	C	4		...					0....	4218
21-DHAA	MAREMGI cluster	1	1	64	82		64.06	94	C	4		...					0....	4219
21-DHAA-a	maremgi	1	1	64	82	0	64.06	94	C	4		...					0....	4220
21-E	**MAWES set**	1	1	1,082	1,395		69.96	96	C	4		...					0....	4221
21-EA	MAWES chain	1	1	1,082	1,395		69.96	96	C	4		...					0....	4222
21-EAA	**MAWES net**	1	1	1,082	1,395		69.96	96	C	4		...					0....	4223
21-EAAA	MAWES cluster	1	1	1,082	1,395		69.96	96	C	4		...					0....	4224
21-EAAA-a	West mawes					0				4		...					0....	4225
21-EAAA-b	East mawes					0				4		...					0....	4226
21-F	**ORYA set**	1	1	2,036	2,625		65.03	95	C	22		P..					0....	4227
21-FA	ORYA chain	1	1	2,036	2,625		65.03	95	C	22		P..					0....	4228
21-FAA	**ORYA net**	1	1	2,036	2,625		65.03	95	C	22		P..					0....	4229
21-FAAA	ORYA cluster	1	1	2,036	2,625		65.03	95	C	22	Orya	P..	1987-1995				0....	4230
21-FAAA-a	barat					0				22		p..					0....	4231
21-FAAA-b	timur					0				22		p..					0....	4232
21-FAAA-c	yapsi					0				22		p..					0....	4233
21-G	**TAIKAT-AWYI set**	1	2	1,464	1,887		65.78	92	C	4		...					0....	4234
21-GA	AWYI chain	1	1	594	766		63.97	91	C	4		...					0....	4235
21-GAA	**AWYI net**	1	1	594	766		63.97	91	C	4		...					0....	4236
21-GAAA	AWYI cluster	1	1	594	766		63.97	91	C	4		...					0....	4237
21-GAAA-a	awyi	1	1	594	766	0	63.97	91	C	4		...					0....	4238
21-GB	TAIKAT chain	1	1	870	1,121		67.01	93	C	2		...					0....	4239
21-GBA	**TAIKAT net**	1	1	870	1,121		67.01	93	C	2		...					0....	4240
21-GBAA	TAIKAT cluster	1	1	870	1,121		67.01	93	C	2		...					0....	4241
21-GBAA-a	taikat	1	1	870	1,121	0	67.01	93	C	2		...					0....	4242
21-H	**WARIS-MANEM set**	2	14	25,380	37,753		66.58	92	C	41		PN.					0....	4243
21-HA	MANEM chain	2	2	1,180	1,678		45.08	71	B	2		...					0....	4244
21-HAA	**MANEM net**	2	2	1,180	1,678		45.08	71	B	2		...					0....	4245
21-HAAA	MANEM cluster	2	2	1,180	1,678		45.08	71	B	2		...					0....	4246
21-HAAA-a	wembi					0				2		...					0....	4247
21-HAAA-b	yeti					0				2		...					0....	4248
21-HAAA-c	skofro					0				2		...					0....	4249
21-HAAA-d	skotiau					0				2		...					0....	4250
21-HB	WARIS chain	2	6	12,022	18,387		60.11	87	C	41		PN.					0....	4251
21-HBA	**WARIS net**	2	5	11,553	17,657		58.89	86	B	41		PN.					0....	4252
21-HBAA	WARIS cluster	2	3	4,250	6,288		38.68	69	B	41	Waris	PN.	1987	1996			0....	4253
21-HBAA-a	Proper waris	2	2	3,964	5,843	0	39.30	70	B	41	Waris	Pn.	1987				0....	4254
21-HBAA-b	imonda	1	1	286	445	0	30.07	50	B	41		pn.					0....	4255
21-HBAB	DAONDA cluster	1	2	7,303	11,369		70.66	96	C	4		...					0....	4256
21-HBAB-a	daonda	1	1	234	364	0	90.17	100	C	4		...					0....	4257
21-HBB	**SIMOG net**	1	1	469	730		89.98	100	C	4		...					0....	4258
21-HBBA	SIMOG cluster	1	1	469	730		89.98	100	C	4		...					0....	4259
21-HBBA-a	simog	1	1	469	730	0	89.98	100	C	4		...					0....	4260
21-HC	SENGGI chain	1	1	170	219		65.88	99	C	4		...					0....	4261
21-HCA	**SENGGI net**	1	1	170	219		65.88	99	C	4		...					0....	4262
21-HCAA	SENGGI cluster	1	1	170	219		65.88	99	C	4								4263

Continued opposite

Table 9-13 continued

Code 1	REFERENCE NAME / Autoglossonym 2	Coun 3	Peo 4	Mother-tongue speakers in 2000 5	in 2025 6	Media radio 7	CHURCH AC% 8	E% 9	Wld 10	Tr 11	Biblioglossonym 12	Print 13-15	P-activity 16	N-activity 17	B-activity 18	J-year 19	Jayuh 20-24	Ref 25
21-HCAA-a	senggi	1	1	170	219	0	65.88	99	C	4		. . .					0	4264
21-HD	SOWANDA chain	2	3	1,978	3,023		83.92	100	C	2		. . .					0	4265
21-HDA	**SOWANDA net**	2	3	1,978	3,023		83.92	100	C	2		. . .					0	4266
21-HDAA	SOWANDA cluster	2	3	1,978	3,023		83.92	100	C	2		. . .					0	4267
21-HDAA-a	Proper sowanda	1	1	212	273	0	75.00	100	C	2		. . .					0	4268
21-HDAA-b	punda-umeda	1	2	1,766	2,750	0	84.99	100	C	2		. . .					0	4269
21-HE	AMANAB chain	2	2	10,030	14,446		73.47	99	C	12		. . .					0	4270
21-HEA	**AMANAB net**	2	2	10,030	14,446		73.47	99	C	12		. . .					0	4271
21-HEAA	AMANAB cluster	2	2	10,030	14,446		73.47	99	C	12	Amanab	. . .					0	4272
21-HEAA-a	West amanab					0				12		. . .					0	4273
21-HEAA-b	East amanab					0				12		. . .					0	4274
21-I	**BEWANI set**	1	7	8,309	12,976		77.55	98	C	24		P . .					0	4275
21-IA	BEWANI chain	1	7	8,309	12,976		77.55	98	C	24		P . .					0	4276
21-IAA	**BEWANI net**	1	7	8,309	12,976		77.55	98	C	24		P . .					0	4277
21-IAAA	UMEDA cluster	1	1	300	510		75.00	99	C	0		. . .					0	4278
21-IAAA-a	umeda	1	1	300	510	0	75.00	99	C	0		. . .					0	4279
21-IAAB	IMBINIS cluster	1	1	922	1,435		79.93	100	C	0		. . .					0	4280
21-IAAB-a	imbinis	1	1	922	1,435	0	79.93	100	C	0		. . .					0	4281
21-IAAC	AINBAI cluster	1	1	156	242		80.13	100	C	4		. . .					0	4282
21-IAAC-a	ainbai	1	1	156	242	0	80.13	100	C	4		. . .					0	4283
21-IAAD	PAGI cluster	1	1	2,343	3,648		80.03	100	C	2		. . .					0	4284
21-IAAD-a	pagi	1	1	2,343	3,648	0	80.03	100	C	2		. . .					0	4285
21-IAAE	KILMERI-ISI cluster	1	3	4,119	6,411		80.00	100	C	24		P . .					0	4286
21-IAAE-a	isi	1	1	922	1,435	0	79.93	100	C	24		p . .					0	4287
21-IAAE-b	ossima	1	1	461	717	0	80.04	100	C	24		p . .					0	4288
21-IAAE-c	kilmeri	1	1	2,736	4,259	0	80.01	100	C	24	Kilmeri	P . .	1880				0	4289
21-IAAF	NINGERA cluster	1	1	469	730		39.87	69	B	2		. . .					0	4290
21-IAAF-a	ningera	1	1	469	730	0	39.87	69	B	2		. . .					0	4291
21-J	**NIMBORAN-KEMTUIK set**	1	6	17,542	22,614		50.03	79	B	22		P . .					0	4292
21-JA	NIMBORAN-KEMTUIK chain	1	6	17,542	22,614		50.03	79	B	22		P . .					0	4293
21-JAA	**NIMBORAN net**	1	1	4,306	5,551		65.00	98	C	22		P . .					0	4294
21-JAAA	NIMBORAN cluster	1	1	4,306	5,551		65.00	98	C	22		P . .					0	4295
21-JAAA-a	nimboran	1	1	4,306	5,551	0	65.00	98	C	22	Nimboran	P . .	1982-1985				0	4296
21-JAB	**KWANSU-BONGGRANG net**	1	1	530	684		65.09	95	C	2		. . .					0	4297
21-JABA	KWANSU-BONGGRANG cluster	1	1	530	684		65.09	95	C	2		. . .					0	4298
21-JABA-a	kwansu					0				2		. . .					0	4299
21-JABA-b	bonggrang					0				2		. . .					0	4300
21-JAC	**KEMTUIK-GRESI net**	1	2	6,152	7,930		17.49	48	A	22		P . .					0	4301
21-JACA	GRESI cluster	1	1	3,076	3,965		19.99	50	B	2		. . .					0	4302
21-JACA-a	gresi	1	1	3,076	3,965	0	19.99	50	B	2		. . .					0	4303
21-JACB	KEMTUIK cluster	1	1	3,076	3,965		14.99	46	A	22		P . .					0	4304
21-JACB-a	kemtuik	1	1	3,076	3,965	0	14.99	46	A	22	Kemtuik	P . .	1980				0	4305
21-JAD	**MEKWEI net**	1	2	6,554	8,449		69.53	94	C	4		. . .					0	4306
21-JADA	MEKWEI cluster	1	2	6,554	8,449		69.53	94	C	4		. . .					0	4307
21-JADA-a	mekwei	1	2	6,554	8,449	0	69.53	94	C	4		. . .					0	4308
21-K	**MORWAP set**	1	2	784	1,012		66.45	93	C	4		. . .					0	4309
21-KA	MORWAP chain	1	2	784	1,012		66.45	93	C	4		. . .					0	4310
21-KAA	**MORWAP net**	1	2	784	1,012		66.45	93	C	4		. . .					0	4311
21-KAAA	MORWAP cluster	1	2	784	1,012		66.45	93	C	4		. . .					0	4312
21-KAAA-a	morwap	1	2	784	1,012	0	66.45	93	C	4		. . .					0	4313
21-L	**SAUSE set**	1	1	318	410		70.13	97	C	2		. . .					0	4314
21-LA	SAUSE chain	1	1	318	410		70.13	97	C	2		. . .					0	4315
21-LAA	**SAUSE net**	1	1	318	410		70.13	97	C	2		. . .					0	4316
21-LAAA	SAUSE cluster	1	1	318	410		70.13	97	C	2		. . .					0	4317
21-LAAA-a	sause	1	1	318	410	0	70.13	97	C	2		. . .					0	4318
21-M	**KAPORI set**	1	1	85	109		65.88	94	C	2		. . .					0	4319
21-MA	KAPORI chain	1	1	85	109		65.88	94	C	2		. . .					0	4320
21-MAA	**KAPORI net**	1	1	85	109		65.88	94	C	2		. . .					0	4321
21-MAAA	KAPORI cluster	1	1	85	109		65.88	94	C	2		. . .					0	4322
21-MAAA-a	kapori	1	1	85	109	0	65.88	94	C	2		. . .					0	4323
21-N	**KAURE set**	1	4	60,282	77,712		1.77	15	A	22		P . .					0	4324
21-NA	KAURE chain	1	4	60,282	77,712		1.77	15	A	22		P . .					0	4325
21-NAA	**KAURE net**	1	4	60,282	77,712		1.77	15	A	22		P . .					0	4326
21-NAAA	NARAU cluster	1	1	891	1,148		64.98	87	C	4		. . .					0	4327
21-NAAA-a	narau	1	1	891	1,148	0	64.98	87	C	4		. . .					0	4328
21-NAAB	KAURE cluster	1	3	59,391	76,564		0.82	14	A	22		P . .					0	4329
21-NAAB-a	kaure	1	2	59,115	76,209	0	0.51	14	A	22	Kaure	P . .	1990				0	4330
21-NAAB-b	kosadle	1	1	276	355	0	65.94	93	C	22		p . .					0	4331
21-O	**MOLOF set**	1	1	297	383		59.93	88	B	4		. . .					0	4332
21-OA	MOLOF chain	1	1	297	383		59.93	88	B	4		. . .					0	4333
21-OAA	**MOLOF net**	1	1	297	383		59.93	88	B	4		. . .					0	4334

Continued overleaf

Table 9-13 continued

Code 1	REFERENCE NAME / Autoglossonym 2	Coun 3	Peo 4	Mother-tongue speakers in 2000 5	in 2025 6	Media radio 7	CHURCH AC% 8	E% 9	Wld 10	Tr 11	Biblioglossonym 12	SCRIPTURES Print 13-15	P-activity 16	N-activity 17	B-activity 18	J-year 19	Jayuh 20-24	Ref 25
21-OAAA	MOLOF cluster	1	1	297	383		59.93	88	B	4		...					0....	4335
21-OAAA-a	molof	1	1	297	383	0	59.93	88	B	4		...					0....	4336
21-P	**USKU set**	1	1	170	219		65.88	99	C	4		...					0....	4337
21-PA	USKU chain	1	1	170	219		65.88	99	C	4		...					0....	4338
21-PAA	**USKU net**	1	1	170	219		65.88	99	C	4		...					0....	4339
21-PAAA	USKU cluster	1	1	170	219		65.88	99	C	4		...					0....	4340
21-PAAA-a	usku	1	1	170	219	0	65.88	99	C	4		...					0....	4341
21-Q	**TOFAMNA set**	1	1	170	219		64.71	89	C	4		...					0....	4342
21-QA	TOFAMNA chain	1	1	170	219		64.71	89	C	4		...					0....	4343
21-QAA	**TOFAMNA net**	1	1	170	219		64.71	89	C	4		...					0....	4344
21-QAAA	TOFAMNA cluster	1	1	170	219		64.71	89	C	4		...					0....	4345
21-QAAA-a	tofamna	1	1	170	219	0	64.71	89	C	4		...					0....	4346
21-R	**MEK set**	1	8	50,106	66,855		60.68	93	C	44		PN.					0....	4347
21-RA	WEST MEK chain	1	7	36,043	47,288		59.00	91	B	44		PN.					0....	4348
21-RAA	**KOSAREK-NIPSAN net**	1	4	17,350	22,368		64.57	98	C	44		PN.					0....	4349
21-RAAA	KOSAREK cluster	1	1	2,524	3,254		63.99	97	C	33	Yale: Kosarek*	P..	1992				0....	4350
21-RAAA-a	wanam					0				33		p..					0....	4351
21-RAAA-b	in-lom					0				33		p..					0....	4352
21-RAAB	GILIKA cluster	1	1	976	1,258		59.94	88	B	0		...					0....	4353
21-RAAB-a	gilika	1	1	976	1,258	0	59.94	88	B	0		...					0....	4354
21-RAAC	NIPSAN cluster	1	1	2,757	3,555		65.00	100	C	44		PN.					0....	4355
21-RAAC-a	yali-pass					0				44	Yali, Pass Valley	PN.		1977			0....	4356
21-RAAC-b	landikma					0				44		pn.					0....	4357
21-RAAC-c	apahapsili					0				44		pn.					0....	4358
21-RAAD	HMANGGONA cluster	1	1	11,093	14,301		65.00	99	C	12		...					0....	4359
21-RAAD-a	hmanggona	1	1	11,093	14,301	0	65.00	99	C	12	Nalca	...					0....	4360
21-RAB	**KORUPUN-SELA net**	1	1	10,442	14,283		45.00	75	B	22		P..					0....	4361
21-RABA	KORUPUN cluster	1	1	8,442	10,883		45.00	73	B	22		P..					0....	4362
21-RABA-a	korupun	1	1	8,442	10,883	0	45.00	73	B	22	Kimyal*	P..	1980-1986				0....	4363
21-RABA-b	dagi					0				22		p..					0....	4364
21-RABA-c	sisibna					0				22		p..					0....	4365
21-RABA-d	deibula					0				22		p..					0....	4366
21-RABB	SELA cluster	1	1	2,000	3,400		45.00	82	B	0		...					0....	4367
21-RABB-a	Northwest sela					0				0		...					0....	4368
21-RABB-b	Southeast sela					0				0		...					0....	4369
21-RAC	**UNA net**	1	2	8,251	10,637		65.00	97	C	12		...					0....	4370
21-RACA	UNA cluster	1	1	4,560	5,879		65.00	98	C	12		...					0....	4371
21-RACA-a	una	1	1	4,560	5,879	0	65.00	98	C	12	Una	...					0....	4372
21-RACB	EIPO cluster	1	1	3,691	4,758		65.00	95	C	2		...					0....	4373
21-RACB-a	fa-mek					0				2		...					0....	4374
21-RACB-b	keririmna					0				2		...					0....	4375
21-RACB-c	eipo-mek	1	1	3,691	4,758	0	65.00	95	C	2		...					0....	4376
21-RB	EAST MEK chain	1	1	14,063	19,567		65.00	97	C	22		P..					0....	4377
21-RBA	**EAST MEK net**	1	1	14,063	19,567		65.00	97	C	22		P..					0....	4378
21-RBAA	SIRKAI cluster	1	1	1,500	2,550		65.00	96	C	0		...					0....	4379
21-RBAA-a	sirkai	1	1	1,500	2,550	0	65.00	96	C	0		...					0....	4380
21-RBAB	KETENGBAN cluster	1	1	10,563	13,617		65.00	98	C	22	Ketengban	P..	1985-1995				0....	4381
21-RBAB-a	limeri					0				22		p..					0....	4382
21-RBAB-b	tanime					0				22		p..					0....	4383
21-RBAB-c	bima					0				22		p..					0....	4384
21-RBAB-d	kanume					0				22		p..					0....	4385
21-RBAB-e	teli					0				22		p..					0....	4386
21-RBAB-f	kirome					0				22		p..					0....	4387
21-RBAB-g	bame					0				22		p..					0....	4388
21-RBAB-h	ok-bab					0				22		p..					0....	4389
21-RBAB-i	larye					0				22		p..					0....	4390
21-RBAC	KINOME cluster	1	1	2,000	3,400		65.00	96	C	0		...					0....	4391
21-RBAC-a	kinome	1	1	2,000	3,400	0	65.00	96	C	0		...					0....	4392
21-S	**WEST PAUWASI set**	1	2	361	465		64.54	94	C	4		...					0....	4393
21-SA	WEST PAUWASI chain	1	2	361	465		64.54	94	C	4		...					0....	4394
21-SAA	**DUBU net**	1	1	191	246		64.92	95	C	4		...					0....	4395
21-SAAA	DUBU cluster	1	1	191	246		64.92	95	C	4		...					0....	4396
21-SAAA-a	dubu	1	1	191	246	0	64.92	95	C	4		...					0....	4397
21-SAB	**TOWEI net**	1	1	170	219		64.12	93	C	4		...					0....	4398
21-SABA	TOWEI cluster	1	1	170	219		64.12	93	C	4		...					0....	4399
21-SABA-a	towei	1	1	170	219	0	64.12	93	C	4		...					0....	4400
21-T	**EAST PAUWASI set**	1	2	1,633	2,105		64.97	91	C	4		...					0....	4401
21-TA	EAST PAUWASI chain	1	2	1,633	2,105		64.97	91	C	4		...					0....	4402
21-TAA	**YAFI net**	1	1	276	355		64.86	96	C	4		...					0....	4403
21-TAAA	YAFI cluster	1	1	276	355		64.86	96	C	4		...					0....	4404
21-TAAA-a	yafi	1	1	276	355	0	64.86	96	C	4		...					0....	4405
21-TAB	**EMUMU net**	1	1	1,357	1,750		65.00	90	C	4		...					0....	4406
21-TABA	EMUMU cluster	1	1	1,357	1,750		65.00	90	C	4		...					0....	4407
21-TABA-a	emumu	1	1	1,357	1,750	0	65.00	90	C	4		...					0....	4408
21-U	**SENAGI set**	2	3	3,673	5,389		77.29	97	C	22		P..					0....	4409
21-UA	SENAGI chain	2	3	3,673	5,389		77.29	97	C	22		P..					0....	4410
21-UAA	**KAMBERATARO net**	2	2	2,085	2,917		75.25	95	C	2		...					0....	4411

Continued opposite

Table 9-13 continued

Code 1	REFERENCE NAME / Autoglossonym 2	Coun 3	Peo 4	Mother-tongue speakers in 2000 5	in 2025 6	Media radio 7	AC% 8	E% 9	Wld 10	Tr 11	Biblioglossonym 12	Print 13-15	P-activity 16	N-activity 17	B-activity 18	J-year 19	Jayuh 20-24	Ref 25
21-UAAA	KAMBERATARO cluster	2	2	2,085	2,917		75.25	95	C	2		. . .					0	4412
21-UAAA-a	North kamberataro					0				2		. . .					0	4413
21-UAAA-b	South kamberataro					0				2		. . .					0	4414
21-UAAA-c	mengau					0				2		. . .					0	4415
21-UAAA-d	lihen					0				2		. . .					0	4416
21-UAAA-e	duka-ekor					0				2		. . .					0	4417
21-UAB	**ANGOR net**	1	1	1,588	2,472		79.97	100	C	22		P . .					0	4418
21-UABA	ANGOR cluster	1	1	1,588	2,472		79.97	100	C	22	Anggor*	P . .	1973-1992				0	4419
21-UABA-a	nai					0				22	Nai	p . .					0	4420
21-UABA-b	monga					0				22		p . .					0	4421
21-UABA-c	samanai					0				22		p . .					0	4422
21-V	**OKSAPMIN set**	1	1	9,300	14,478		75.00	100	C	41		PN .					0	4423
21-VA	OKSAPMIN chain	1	1	9,300	14,478		75.00	100	C	41		PN .					0	4424
21-VAA	**OKSAPMIN net**	1	1	9,300	14,478		75.00	100	C	41		PN .					0	4425
21-VAAA	OKSAPMIN cluster	1	1	9,300	14,478		75.00	100	C	41		PN .					0	4426
21-VAAA-a	oksapmin	1	1	9,300	14,478	0	75.00	100	C	41	Oksapmin	PN .	1976-1977	1992			0	4427
22	**MADANGIC zone**	1	106	120,006	186,821		81.73	97	C	42		PN .					0 . s . .	4428
22-A	**JOSEPHSTAAL set**	1	7	9,272	14,434		84.38	100	C	12		. . .					0	4429
22-AA	MORESADA chain	1	3	2,651	4,126		87.06	100	C	4		. . .					0	4430
22-AAA	**WADAGINAM net**	1	1	794	1,235		89.92	100	C	4		. . .					0	4431
22-AAAA	WADAGINAM cluster	1	1	794	1,235		89.92	100	C	4		. . .					0	4432
22-AAAA-a	wadaginam	1	1	794	1,235	0	89.92	100	C	4		. . .					0	4433
22-AAB	**MORESADA net**	1	1	286	445		90.21	100	C	4		. . .					0	4434
22-AABA	MORESADA cluster	1	1	286	445		90.21	100	C	4		. . .					0	4435
22-AABA-a	moresada	1	1	286	445	0	90.21	100	C	4		. . .					0	4436
22-AAC	**IKUNDUN net**	1	1	1,571	2,446		85.04	100	C	2		. . .					0	4437
22-AACA	IKUNDUN cluster	1	1	1,571	2,446		85.04	100	C	2		. . .					0	4438
22-AACA-a	ikundun	1	1	1,571	2,446	0	85.04	100	C	2		. . .					0	4439
22-AB	PONDOMA chain	1	1	868	1,351		89.98	100	C	5		. . .					0	4440
22-ABA	**PONDOMA net**	1	1	868	1,351		89.98	100	C	5		. . .					0	4441
22-ABAA	PONDOMA cluster	1	1	868	1,351		89.98	100	C	5		. . .					0	4442
22-ABAA-a	pondoma	1	1	868	1,351	0	89.98	100	C	5		. . .					0	4443
22-AC	OSUM chain	1	1	602	937		90.03	100	C	2		. . .					0	4444
22-ACA	**OSUM net**	1	1	602	937		90.03	100	C	2		. . .					0	4445
22-ACAA	OSUM cluster	1	1	602	937		90.03	100	C	2		. . .					0	4446
22-ACAA-a	osum	1	1	602	937	0	90.03	100	C	2		. . .					0	4447
22-AD	SIKAN chain	1	2	5,151	8,020		81.40	100	C	12		. . .					0	4448
22-ADA	**KATIATI net**	1	1	4,775	7,434		80.00	100	C	12		. . .					0	4449
22-ADAA	KATIATI cluster	1	1	4,775	7,434		80.00	100	C	12		. . .					0	4450
22-ADAA-a	katiati	1	1	4,775	7,434	0	80.00	100	C	12	Mum	. . .					0	4451
22-ADB	**SILEIBI net**	1	1	376	586		99.20	100	C	4		. . .					0	4452
22-ADBA	SILEIBI cluster	1	1	376	586		99.20	100	C	4		. . .					0	4453
22-ADBA-a	sileibi	1	1	376	586	0	99.20	100	C	4		. . .					0	4454
22-B	**PAYNAMAR set**	1	1	256	399		90.23	100	C	4		. . .					0	4455
22-BA	PAYNAMAR chain	1	1	256	399		90.23	100	C	4		. . .					0	4456
22-BAA	**PAYNAMAR net**	1	1	256	399		90.23	100	C	4		. . .					0	4457
22-BAAA	PAYNAMAR cluster	1	1	256	399		90.23	100	C	4		. . .					0	4458
22-BAAA-a'	paynamar	1	1	256	399	0	90.23	100	C	4		. . .					0	4459
22-C	**ATAN set**	1	2	2,419	3,766		80.61	100	C	12		. . .					0	4460
22-CA	ATAN chain	1	2	2,419	3,766		80.61	100	C	12		. . .					0	4461
22-CAA	**ANGAUA net**	1	1	2,325	3,619		80.00	100	C	12		. . .					0	4462
22-CAAA	NENT cluster	1	1	2,325	3,619		80.00	100	C	12		. . .					0	4463
22-CAAA-a	nent	1	1	2,325	3,619	0	80.00	100	C	12	Nend	. . .					0	4464
22-CAB	**ATEMBLE net**	1	1	94	147		95.74	100	C	4		. . .					0	4465
22-CABA	ATEMBLE cluster	1	1	94	147		95.74	100	C	4		. . .					0	4466
22-CABA-a	atemble	1	1	94	147	0	95.74	100	C	4		. . .					0	4467
22-D	**EMUAN set**	1	2	1,246	1,939		84.19	100	C	35		P . .					0	4468
22-DA	APAL chain	1	1	730	1,136		80.00	100	C	35		P . .					0	4469
22-DAA	**APAL net**	1	1	730	1,136		80.00	100	C	35		P . .					0	4470
22-DAAA	APAL cluster	1	1	730	1,136		80.00	100	C	35	Apali	P . .	1992-1993				0	4471
22-DAAA-a	North apal					0				35		p . .					0	4472
22-DAAA-b	South apal					0				35		p . .					0	4473
22-DB	MUSAK chain	1	1	516	803		90.12	100	C	4		. . .					0	4474
22-DBA	**MUSAK net**	1	1	516	803		90.12	100	C	4		. . .					0	4475
22-DBAA	MUSAK cluster	1	1	516	803		90.12	100	C	4		. . .					0	4476
22-DBAA-a	musak	1	1	516	803	0	90.12	100	C	4		. . .					0	4477
22-E	**BRAHMAN set**	1	4	1,545	2,404		73.98	88	C	4		. . .					0	4478
22-EA	FAITA chain	1	1	83	129		95.18	100	C	4		. . .					0	4479
22-EAA	**FAITA net**	1	1	83	129		95.18	100	C	4		. . .					0	4480
22-EAAA	FAITA cluster	1	1	83	129		95.18	100	C	4		. . .					0	4481

Continued overleaf

Table 9-13 continued

Code 1	REFERENCE NAME / Autoglossonym 2	Coun 3	Peo 4	Mother-tongue speakers in 2000 5	in 2025 6	Media radio 7	AC% 8	E% 9	Wld 10	Tr 11	Biblioglossonym 12	Print 13-15	P-activity 16	N-activity 17	B-activity 18	J-year 19	Jayuh 20-24	Ref 25
22-EAAA-a	faita	1	1	83	129	0	95.18	100	C	4		. . .					0	4482
22-EB	TAUYA chain	1	1	504	785		40.08	64	B	4		. . .					0	4483
22-EBA	**TAUYA net**	1	1	504	785		40.08	64	B	4		. . .					0	4484
22-EBAA	TAUYA cluster	1	1	504	785		40.08	64	B	4		. . .					0	4485
22-EBAA-a	tauya	1	1	504	785	0	40.08	64	B	4		. . .					0	4486
22-EC	BIYOM chain	1	1	551	857		90.02	100	C	4		. . .					0	4487
22-ECA	**BIYOM net**	1	1	551	857		90.02	100	C	4		. . .					0	4488
22-ECAA	BIYOM cluster	1	1	551	857		90.02	100	C	4		. . .					0	4489
22-ECAA-a	biyom	1	1	551	857	0	90.02	100	C	4		. . .					0	4490
22-ED	ISABI chain	1	1	407	633		89.93	100	C	4		. . .					0	4491
22-EDA	**ISABI net**	1	1	407	633		89.93	100	C	4		. . .					0	4492
22-EDAA	ISABI cluster	1	1	407	633		89.93	100	C	4		. . .					0	4493
22-EDAA-a	isabi	1	1	407	633	0	89.93	100	C	4		. . .					0	4494
22-F	**KAUKOMBARAN set**	1	5	10,024	15,606		76.18	93	C	22		P . .					0	4495
22-FA	KAUKOMBARAN chain	1	5	10,024	15,606		76.18	93	C	22		P . .					0	4496
22-FAA	**PAY net**	1	2	1,419	2,211		27.06	48	A	2		. . .					0	4497
22-FAAA	PAY cluster	1	2	1,419	2,211		27.06	48	A	2		. . .					0	4498
22-FAAA-a	dagoi					0				2		. . .					0	4499
22-FAAA-b	hatzfeldthaven					0				2		. . .					0	4500
22-FAAA-c	malala					0				2		. . .					0	4501
22-FAB	**PILA net**	1	1	1,867	2,906		89.98	100	C	22		P . .					0	4502
22-FABA	MIANI cluster	1	1	1,867	2,906		89.98	100	C	22	Miani: South	P . .	1982-1988				0	4503
22-FABA-a	bonaputa-mopu					0				22		p . .					0	4504
22-FABA-b	suaru					0				22		p . .					0	4505
22-FAC	**SAKI net**	1	1	3,111	4,843		80.01	100	C	22		P . .					0	4506
22-FACA	MAIA cluster	1	1	3,111	4,843		80.01	100	C	22	Maia	P . .	1988				0	4507
22-FACA-a	turatapa					0				22		p . .					0	4508
22-FACA-b	yakiba					0				22		p . .					0	4509
22-FACA-c	mugumat-saki					0				22		p . .					0	4510
22-FAD	**TANI net**	1	1	3,627	5,646		85.00	100	C	22		P . .					0	4511
22-FADA	MAIANI cluster	1	1	3,627	5,646		85.00	100	C	22	Maiani	P . .	1982-1988				0	4512
22-FADA-a	mugumat-tani					0				22		p . .					0	4513
22-FADA-b	wagimuda					0				22		p . .					0	4514
22-G	**KUMILAN-TIBORAN set**	1	8	6,048	9,413		84.38	100	C	22		P . .					0	4515
22-GA	MAUWAKE chain	1	1	2,489	3,875		79.99	100	C	22		P . .					0	4516
22-GAA	**MAUWAKE net**	1	1	2,489	3,875		79.99	100	C	22		P . .					0	4517
22-GAAA	MAUWAKE cluster	1	1	2,489	3,875		79.99	100	C	22		P . .					0	4518
22-GAAA-a	mauwake	1	1	2,489	3,875	0	79.99	100	C	22	Mauwake	P . .	1991				0	4519
22-GB	BEPOUR chain	1	1	83	129		95.18	100	C	4		. . .					0	4520
22-GBA	**BEPOUR. net**	1	1	83	129		95.18	100	C	4		. . .					0	4521
22-GBAA	BEPOUR cluster	1	1	83	129		95.18	100	C	4		. . .					0	4522
22-GBAA-a	bepour	1	1	83	129	0	95.18	100	C	4		. . .					0	4523
22-GC	MOERE chain	1	1	82	127		93.90	100	C	4		. . .					0	4524
22-GCA	**MOERE net**	1	1	82	127		93.90	100	C	4		. . .					0	4525
22-GCAA	MOERE cluster	1	1	82	127		93.90	100	C	4		. . .					0	4526
22-GCAA-a	moere	1	1	82	127	0	93.90	100	C	4		. . .					0	4527
22-GD	MAWAK chain	1	1	45	70		95.56	100	C	4		. . .					0	4528
22-GDA	**MAWAK net**	1	1	45	70		95.56	100	C	4		. . .					0	4529
22-GDAA	MAWAK cluster	1	1	45	70		95.56	100	C	4		. . .					0	4530
22-GDAA-a	mawak	1	1	45	70	0	95.56	100	C	4		. . .					0	4531
22-GE	KOWAKI chain	1	1	45	70		95.56	100	C	4		. . .					0	4532
22-GEA	**KOWAKI net**	1	1	45	70		95.56	100	C	4		. . .					0	4533
22-GEAA	KOWAKI cluster	1	1	45	70		95.56	100	C	4		. . .					0	4534
22-GEAA-a	kowaki	1	1	45	70	0	95.56	100	C	4		. . .					0	4535
22-GF	HINIHON chain	1	1	1,599	2,489		79.99	100	C	2		. . .					0	4536
22-GFA	**HINIHON net**	1	1	1,599	2,489		79.99	100	C	2		. . .					0	4537
22-GFAA	HINIHON cluster	1	1	1,599	2,489		79.99	100	C	2		. . .					0	4538
22-GFAA-a	hinihon	1	1	1,599	2,489	0	79.99	100	C	2		. . .					0	4539
22-GG	MUSAR chain	1	1	994	1,547		90.04	100	C	2		. . .					0	4540
22-GGA	**MUSAR net**	1	1	994	1,547		90.04	100	C	2		. . .					0	4541
22-GGAA	MUSAR cluster	1	1	994	1,547		90.04	100	C	2		. . .					0	4542
22-GGAA-a	musar	1	1	994	1,547	0	90.04	100	C	2		. . .					0	4543
22-GH	WANAMBRE chain	1	1	711	1,106		97.89	100	C	2		. . .					0	4544
22-GHA	**WANAMBRE net**	1	1	711	1,106		97.89	100	C	2		. . .					0	4545
22-GHAA	WANAMBRE cluster	1	1	711	1,106		97.89	100	C	2		. . .					0	4546
22-GHAA-a	wanambre	1	1	711	1,106	0	97.89	100	C	2		. . .					0	4547
22-H	**OMOSAN set**	1	2	2,476	3,855		89.98	100	C	4		. . .					0	4548
22-HA	OMOSAN chain	1	2	2,476	3,855		89.98	100	C	4		. . .					0	4549
22-HAA	**KOGUMAN net**	1	1	1,370	2,133		98.03	100	C	4		. . .					0	4550
22-HAAA	KOGUMAN cluster	1	1	1,370	2,133		98.03	100	C	4		. . .					0	4551
22-HAAA-a	koguman	1	1	1,370	2,133	0	98.03	100	C	4		. . .					0	4552
22-HAB	**ABASAKUR net**	1	1	1,106	1,722		80.02	100	C	4		. . .					0	4553

Continued opposite

Table 9-13 continued

Code 1	REFERENCE NAME Autoglossonym 2	Coun 3	Peo 4	Mother-tongue speakers in 2000 5	in 2025 6	Media radio 7	CHURCH AC% 8	E% 9	Wld 10	Tr 11	Biblioglossonym 12	SCRIPTURES Print 13-15	P-activity 16	N-activity 17	B-activity 18	J-year 19	Jayuh 20-24	Ref 25
22-HABA	ABASAKUR cluster	1	1	1,106	1,722		80.02	100	C	4		. . .					0	4554
22-HABA-a	abasakur	1	1	1,106	1,722	0	80.02	100	C	4		. . .					0	4555
22-I	**NUMAGENAN set**	1	6	3,647	5,680		84.07	96	C	12		. . .					0	4556
22-IA	USAN-YABEN chain	1	2	2,638	4,107		88.86	100	C	12		. . .					0	4557
22-IAA	**USAN net**	1	1	1,618	2,519		84.98	100	C	12		. . .					0	4558
22-IAAA	USAN cluster	1	1	1,618	2,519		84.98	100	C	12		. . .					0	4559
22-IAAA-a	usan	1	1	1,618	2,519	0	84.98	100	C	12	Usan	. . .					0	4560
22-IAB	**YABEN net**	1	1	1,020	1,588		95.00	100	C	4		. . .					0	4561
22-IABA	YABEN cluster	1	1	1,020	1,588		95.00	100	C	4		. . .					0	4562
22-IABA-a	Southwest yaben					0				4		. . .					0	4563
22-IABA-b	Northeast yaben					0				4		. . .					0	4564
22-IB	PARAWEN-UKURIGAMA chain	1	3	960	1,496		70.31	86	C	4		. . .					0	4565
22-IBA	**PARAWEN net**	1	1	623	971		90.05	100	C	4		. . .					0	4566
22-IBAA	PARAWEN cluster	1	1	623	971		90.05	100	C	4		. . .					0	4567
22-IBAA-a	parawen	1	1	623	971	0	90.05	100	C	4		. . .					0	4568
22-IBB	**UKURIGUMA-YARAWATA net**	1	2	337	525		33.83	59	B	4		. . .					0	4569
22-IBBA	UKURIGUMA cluster	1	1	195	303		40.00	66	B	4		. . .					0	4570
22-IBBA-a	ukuriguma	1	1	195	303	0	40.00	66	B	4		. . .					0	4571
22-IBBB	YARAWATA cluster	1	1	142	222		25.35	50	B	4		. . .					0	4572
22-IBBB-a	yarawata	1	1	142	222	0	25.35	50	B	4		. . .					0	4573
22-IC	BILAKURA chain	1	1	49	77		95.92	100	C	8		. . .					0	4574
22-ICA	**BILAKURA net**	1	1	49	77		95.92	100	C	8		. . .					0	4575
22-ICAA	BILAKURA cluster	1	1	49	77		95.92	100	C	8		. . .					0	4576
22-ICAA-a	bilakura	1	1	49	77	0	95.92	100	C	8		. . .					0	4577
22-J	**AMAIMON set**	1	1	532	828		90.04	100	C	4		. . .					0	4578
22-JA	AMAIMON chain	1	1	532	828		90.04	100	C	4		. . .					0	4579
22-JAA	**AMAIMON net**	1	1	532	828		90.04	100	C	4		. . .					0	4580
22-JAAA	AMAIMON cluster	1	1	532	828		90.04	100	C	4		. . .					0	4581
22-JAAA-a	amaimon	1	1	532	828	0	90.04	100	C	4		. . .					0	4582
22-K	**KOWAN set**	1	3	16,538	25,745		84.70	100	C	41		PN .					0 . s . .	4583
22-KA	KORAK chain	1	1	298	463		89.93	100	C	4		. . .					0	4584
22-KAA	**KORAK net**	1	1	298	463		89.93	100	C	4		. . .					0	4585
22-KAAA	KORAK cluster	1	1	298	463		89.93	100	C	4		. . .					0	4586
22-KAAA-a	korak	1	1	298	463	0	89.93	100	C	4		. . .					0	4587
22-KB	WASKIA chain	1	2	16,240	25,282		84.60	100	C	41		PN .					0 . s . .	4588
22-KBA	**WASKIA net**	1	2	16,240	25,282		84.60	100	C	41		PN .					0 . s . .	4589
22-KBAA	WASKIA cluster	1	2	16,240	25,282		84.60	100	C	41	Waskia	PN .	1978	1985			0 . s . .	4590
22-KBAA-a	karkar	1	1	1,307	2,035	0	80.03	100	C	41	Karkar-yuri	PN .	1990	1994			0 . s . .	4591
22-KBAA-b	tokain					0				41		pn .					0 . s . .	4592
22-L	**MABUAN set**	1	2	1,171	1,823		90.01	100	C	4		. . .					0	4593
22-LA	BUNABUN chain	1	1	851	1,325		90.01	100	C	4		. . .					0	4594
22-LAA	**BUNABUN net**	1	1	851	1,325		90.01	100	C	4		. . .					0	4595
22-LAAA	BUNABUN cluster	1	1	851	1,325		90.01	100	C	4		. . .					0	4596
22-LAAA-a	bunabun	1	1	851	1,325	0	90.01	100	C	4		. . .					0	4597
22-LB	MABUAN chain	1	1	320	498		90.00	100	C	4		. . .					0	4598
22-LBA	**MALAS net**	1	1	320	498		90.00	100	C	4		. . .					0	4599
22-LBAA	MALAS cluster	1	1	320	498		90.00	100	C	4		. . .					0	4600
22-LBAA-a	malas	1	1	320	498	0	90.00	100	C	4		. . .					0	4601
22-M	**DIMIR set**	1	1	2,173	3,383		80.03	100	C	6		. . .					0	4602
22-MA	DIMIR chain	1	1	2,173	3,383		80.03	100	C	6		. . .					0	4603
22-MAA	**DIMIR net**	1	1	2,173	3,383		80.03	100	C	6		. . .					0	4604
22-MAAA	DIMIR cluster	1	1	2,173	3,383		80.03	100	C	6		. . .					0	4605
22-MAAA-a	dimir	1	1	2,173	3,383	0	80.03	100	C	6		. . .					0	4606
22-N	**MUGIL set**	1	1	4,667	7,265		79.99	100	C	22		P . .					0	4607
22-NA	MUGIL chain	1	1	4,667	7,265		79.99	100	C	22		P . .					0	4608
22-NAA	**MUGIL net**	1	1	4,667	7,265		79.99	100	C	22		P . .					0	4609
22-NAAA	BARGAM cluster	1	1	4,667	7,265		79.99	100	C	22		P . .					0	4610
22-NAAA-a	bargam	1	1	4,667	7,265	0	79.99	100	C	22	Bargam	P . .	1989-1991				0	4611
22-O	**KARE set**	1	1	558	869		89.96	100	C	4		. . .					0	4612
22-OA	KARE chain	1	1	558	869		89.96	100	C	4		. . .					0	4613
22-OAA	**KARE net**	1	1	558	869		89.96	100	C	4		. . .					0	4614
22-OAAA	KARE cluster	1	1	558	869		89.96	100	C	4		. . .					0	4615
22-OAAA-a	kare	1	1	558	869	0	89.96	100	C	4		. . .					0	4616
22-P	**MABUSO set**	1	30	34,409	53,568		84.08	98	C	41		PN .					0	4617
22-PA	KAMBA-GARUS chain	1	7	10,533	16,398		83.64	100	C	41		PN .					0	4618
22-PAA	**GARUS-REMPI net**	1	3	3,422	5,327		84.19	100	C	4		. . .					0	4619
22-PAAA	GARUS cluster	1	1	2,175	3,386		80.00	100	C	2		. . .					0	4620

Continued overleaf

Table 9-13 continued

Code 1	REFERENCE NAME 2 / Autoglossonym	Coun 3	Peo 4	Mother-tongue speakers in 2000 5	in 2025 6	Media radio 7	CHURCH AC% 8	E% 9	Wld 10	Tr 11	Biblioglossonym 12	Print 13-15	P-activity 16	N-activity 17	B-activity 18	J-year 19	Jayuh 20-24	Ref 25
22-PAAA-a	garus	1	1	2,175	3,386	0	80.00	100	C	2		...					0	4621
22-PAAB	YOIDIK cluster	1	1	387	602		94.83	100	C	4		...					0	4622
22-PAAB-a	yoidik	1	1	387	602	0	94.83	100	C	4		...					0	4623
22-PAAC	REMPI cluster	1	1	860	1,339		90.00	100	C	4		...					0	4624
22-PAAC-a	rempi	1	1	860	1,339	0	90.00	100	C	4		...					0	4625
22-PAB	GARUH-KAMBA net	1	4	7,111	11,071		83.38	100	C	41		PN.					0	4626
22-PABA	GARUH cluster	1	1	2,790	4,343		80.00	100	C	41		PN.					0	4627
22-PABA-a	22-PABA-a	1	1	2,790	4,343	0	80.00	100	C	41	Nobanob	PN.	1984	1992			0	4628
22-PABB	KAMBA cluster	1	3	4,321	6,728		85.56	100	C	3		...					0	4629
22-PABB-a	wagi	1	3	4,321	6,728	0	85.56	100	C	3		...					0	4630
22-PB	MURUPI-WAMAS chain	1	5	1,357	2,114		93.22	100	C	4		...					0	4631
22-PBA	MOSIMO net	1	1	84	131		90.48	100	C	4		...					0	4632
22-PBAA	MOSIMO cluster	1	1	84	131		90.48	100	C	4		...					0	4633
22-PBAA-a	mosimo	1	1	84	131	0	90.48	100	C	4		...					0	4634
22-PBB	WAMAS net	1	1	218	339		94.95	100	C	4		...					0	4635
22-PBBA	WAMAS cluster	1	1	218	339		94.95	100	C	4		...					0	4636
22-PBBA-a	wamas	1	1	218	339	0	94.95	100	C	4		...					0	4637
22-PBC	SAMOSA net	1	1	136	212		95.59	100	C	4		...					0	4638
22-PBCA	SAMOSA cluster	1	1	136	212		95.59	100	C	4		...					0	4639
22-PBCA-a	samosa	1	1	136	212	0	95.59	100	C	4		...					0	4640
22-PBD	MURUPI net	1	1	437	681		90.16	100	C	4		...					0	4641
22-PBDA	MURUPI cluster	1	1	437	681		90.16	100	C	4		...					0	4642
22-PBDA-a	murupi	1	1	437	681	0	90.16	100	C	4		...					0	4643
22-PBE	RAPTING net	1	1	482	751		95.02	100	C	4		...					0	4644
22-PBEA	RAPTING cluster	1	1	482	751		95.02	100	C	4		...					0	4645
22-PBEA-a	rapting	1	1	482	751	0	95.02	100	C	4		...					0	4646
22-PC	SARUGA-UTU chain	1	9	3,278	5,102		89.29	100	C	4		...					0	4647
22-PCA	SARUGA net	1	1	188	292		94.68	100	C	4		...					0	4648
22-PCAA	SARUGA cluster	1	1	188	292		94.68	100	C	4		...					0	4649
22-PCAA-a	saruga	1	1	188	292	0	94.68	100	C	4		...					0	4650
22-PCB	BAGUPI net	1	1	84	131		95.24	100	C	4		...					0	4651
22-PCBA	BAGUPI cluster	1	1	84	131		95.24	100	C	4		...					0	4652
22-PCBA-a	bagupi	1	1	84	131	0	95.24	100	C	4		...					0	4653
22-PCC	NAKE net	1	1	252	392		89.68	100	C	4		...					0	4654
22-PCCA	NAKE cluster	1	1	252	392		89.68	100	C	4		...					0	4655
22-PCCA-a	nake	1	1	252	392	0	89.68	100	C	4		...					0	4656
22-PCD	SILOPI net	1	1	204	317		94.61	100	C	4		...					0	4657
22-PCDA	SILOPI cluster	1	1	204	317		94.61	100	C	4		...					0	4658
22-PCDA-a	silopi	1	1	204	317	0	94.61	100	C	4		...					0	4659
22-PCE	MATEPI net	1	1	346	539		95.09	100	C	4		...					0	4660
22-PCEA	MATEPI cluster	1	1	346	539		95.09	100	C	4		...					0	4661
22-PCEA-a	matepi	1	1	346	539	0	95.09	100	C	4		...					0	4662
22-PCF	UTU net	1	1	847	1,319		90.08	100	C	4		...					0	4663
22-PCFA	UTU cluster	1	1	847	1,319		90.08	100	C	4		...					0	4664
22-PCFA-a	utu	1	1	847	1,319	0	90.08	100	C	4		...					0	4665
22-PCG	GAL net	1	1	325	506		90.15	100	C	4		...					0	4666
22-PCGA	GAL cluster	1	1	325	506		90.15	100	C	4		...					0	4667
22-PCGA-a	gal	1	1	325	506	0	90.15	100	C	4		...					0	4668
22-PCH	BAIMAK net	1	1	641	998		80.03	100	C	4		...					0	4669
22-PCHA	BAIMAK cluster	1	1	641	998		80.03	100	C	4		...					0	4670
22-PCHA-a	baimak	1	1	641	998	0	80.03	100	C	4		...					0	4671
22-PCI	MAWAN net	1	1	391	608		90.03	100	C	4		...					0	4672
22-PCIA	MAWAN cluster	1	1	391	608		90.03	100	C	4		...					0	4673
22-PCIA-a	mawan	1	1	391	608	0	90.03	100	C	4		...					0	4674
22-PD	GUM chain	1	6	12,052	18,761		89.10	100	C	41		PN.					0	4675
22-PDA	ISEBE-AMELE net	1	3	4,606	7,170		80.46	100	C	4		...					0	4676
22-PDAA	PANIM cluster	1	1	221	344		90.05	100	C	4		...					0	4677
22-PDAA-a	pan					0				4		...					0	4678
22-PDAB	ISEBE-BAU cluster	1	2	4,385	6,826		79.98	100	C	4		...					0	4679
22-PDAB-a	isebe					0	79.99	100	C	4		...					0	4680
22-PDAB-b	bau	1	1	3,058	4,761	0				4		...					0	4681
22-PDB	GUMALU net	1	1	394	613		90.10	100	C	4		...					0	4682
22-PDBA	GUMALU cluster	1	1	394	613		90.10	100	C	4		...					0	4683
22-PDBA-a	gumalu	1	1	394	613	0	90.10	100	C	4		...					0	4684
22-PDC	SIHAN net	1	1	456	710		90.13	100	C	4		...					0	4685
22-PDCA	SIHAN cluster	1	1	456	710		90.13	100	C	4		...					0	4686
22-PDCA-a	sihan	1	1	456	710	0	90.13	100	C	4		...					0	4687
22-PDD	AMELE net	1	1	6,596	10,268		95.00	100	C	41		PN.					0	4688
22-PDDA	AMELE cluster	1	1	6,596	10,268		95.00	100	C	41		PN.					0	4689
22-PDDA-a	amele	1	1	6,596	10,268	0	95.00	100	C	41	Amele	PN.	1952-1989	1996			0	4690
22-PE	KOKON chain	1	3	7,189	11,193		72.22	92	C	41		PN.					0	4691
22-PEA	MUNIT net	1	1	501	781		90.02	100	C	4		...					0	4692
22-PEAA	MUNIT cluster	1	1	501	781		90.02	100	C	4		...					0	4693
22-PEAA-a	munit	1	1	501	781	0	90.02	100	C	4		...					0	4694
22-PEB	BEMAL net	1	1	871	1,356		9.99	33	A	4		...					0	4695

Continued opposite

Table 9-13 continued

Code 1	REFERENCE NAME / Autoglossonym 2	Coun 3	Peo 4	in 2000 5	in 2025 6	Media radio 7	AC% 8	E% 9	Wld 10	Tr 11	Biblioglossonym 12	Print 13-15	P-activity 16	N-activity 17	B-activity 18	J-year 19	Jayuh 20-24	Ref 25
22-PEBA	BEMAL cluster	1	1	871	1,356		9.99	33	A	4		...					0....	4696
22-PEBA-a	bemal	1	1	871	1,356	0	9.99	33	A	4		...					0....	4697
22-PEC	**GIRAWA net**	1	1	5,817	9,056		80.01	100	C	41		PN.					0....	4698
22-PECA	GIRAWA cluster	1	1	5,817	9,056		80.01	100	C	41		PN.					0....	4699
22-PECA-a	girawa	1	1	5,817	9,056	0	80.01	100	C	41	Girawa	PN.	1987	1994			0....	4700
22-Q	**PEKA set**	1	4	8,222	12,800		58.04	81	B	12		...					0....	4701
22-QA	GARIA chain	1	1	3,646	5,676		30.01	58	B	12		...					0....	4702
22-QAA	**GARIA net**	1	1	3,646	5,676		30.01	58	B	12		...					0....	4703
22-QAAA	GARIA cluster	1	1	3,646	5,676		30.01	58	B	12		...					0....	4704
22-QAAA-a	garia	1	1	3,646	5,676	0	30.01	58	B	12	Sumau	...					0....	4705
22-QB	USINO chain	1	1	2,369	3,687		79.99	100	C	4		...					0....	4706
22-QBA	**USINO net**	1	1	2,369	3,687		79.99	100	C	4		...					0....	4707
22-QBAA	USINO cluster	1	1	2,369	3,687		79.99	100	C	4		...					0....	4708
22-QBAA-a	usino	1	1	2,369	3,687	0	79.99	100	C	4		...					0....	4709
22-QC	DANARU chain	1	1	167	260		90.42	100	C	4		...					0....	4710
22-QCA	**DANARU net**	1	1	167	260		90.42	100	C	4		...					0....	4711
22-QCAA	DANARU cluster	1	1	167	260		90.42	100	C	4		...					0....	4712
22-QCAA-a	danaru	1	1	167	260	0	90.42	100	C	4		...					0....	4713
22-QD	URIGINA chain	1	1	2,040	3,177		80.00	100	C	2		...					0....	4714
22-QDA	**URIGINA net**	1	1	2,040	3,177		80.00	100	C	2		...					0....	4715
22-QDAA	URIGINA cluster	1	1	2,040	3,177		80.00	100	C	2		...					0....	4716
22-QDAA-a	urigina	1	1	2,040	3,177	0	80.00	100	C	2		...					0....	4717
22-R	**EVAPIA set**	1	5	3,056	4,757		77.06	90	C	4		...					0....	4718
22-RA	SINSAURU chain	1	1	692	1,077		90.03	100	C	2		...					0....	4719
22-RAA	**SINSAURU net**	1	1	692	1,077		90.03	100	C	2		...					0....	4720
22-RAAA	SINSAURU cluster	1	1	692	1,077		90.03	100	C	2		...					0....	4721
22-RAAA-a	Proper sinsauru	1	1	692	1,077	0	90.03	100	C	2		...					0....	4722
22-RAAA-b	saipa					0				2		...					0....	4723
22-RB	SAUSI chain	1	1	719	1,120		35.05	59	B	4		...					0....	4724
22-RBA	**SAUSI net**	1	1	719	1,120		35.05	59	B	4		...					0....	4725
22-RBAA	SAUSI cluster	1	1	719	1,120		35.05	59	B	4		...					0....	4726
22-RBAA-a	sausi	1	1	719	1,120	0	35.05	59	B	4		...					0....	4727
22-RC	ASAS chain	1	1	484	753		89.88	100	C	4		...					0....	4728
22-RCA	**ASAS net**	1	1	484	753		89.88	100	C	4		...					0....	4729
22-RCAA	ASAS cluster	1	1	484	753		89.88	100	C	4		...					0....	4730
22-RCAA-a	asas	1	1	484	753	0	89.88	100	C	4		...					0....	4731
22-RD	KESAWAI chain	1	1	782	1,217		90.03	100	C	4		...					0....	4732
22-RDA	**KESAWAI net**	1	1	782	1,217		90.03	100	C	4		...					0....	4733
22-RDAA	KESAWAI cluster	1	1	782	1,217		90.03	100	C	4		...					0....	4734
22-RDAA-a	kesawai	1	1	782	1,217	0	90.03	100	C	4		...					0....	4735
22-RE	DUMPU chain	1	1	379	590		89.97	100	C	4		...					0....	4736
22-REA	**DUMPU net**	1	1	379	590		89.97	100	C	4		...					0....	4737
22-REAA	DUMPU cluster	1	1	379	590		89.97	100	C	4		...					0....	4738
22-REAA-a	dumpu	1	1	379	590	0	89.97	100	C	4		...					0....	4739
22-S	**NURU set**	1	7	3,911	6,089		88.03	100	C	22		P..					0....	4740
22-SA	USU chain	1	1	116	180		94.83	100	C	0		...					0....	4741
22-SAA	**USU net**	1	1	116	180		94.83	100	C	0		...					0....	4742
22-SAAA	USU cluster	1	1	116	180		94.83	100	C	0		...					0....	4743
22-SAAA-a	usu	1	1	116	180	0	94.83	100	C	0		...					0....	4744
22-SB	OGEA chain	1	1	786	1,224		90.08	100	C	22		P..					0....	4745
22-SBA	**OGEA net**	1	1	786	1,224		90.08	100	C	22		P..					0....	4746
22-SBAA	OGEA cluster	1	1	786	1,224		90.08	100	C	22		P..					0....	4747
22-SBAA-a	ogea	1	1	786	1,224	0	90.08	100	C	22	Ogea	P..	1981				0....	4748
22-SC	DUDUELA chain	1	1	682	1,061		89.88	100	C	4		...					0....	4749
22-SCA	**DUDUELA net**	1	1	682	1,061		89.88	100	C	4		...					0....	4750
22-SCAA	DUDUELA cluster	1	1	682	1,061		89.88	100	C	4		...					0....	4751
22-SCAA-a	duduela	1	1	682	1,061	0	89.88	100	C	4		...					0....	4752
22-SD	KWATO chain	1	1	1,130	1,760		80.00	100	C	2		...					0....	4753
22-SDA	**KWATO net**	1	1	1,130	1,760		80.00	100	C	2		...					0....	4754
22-SDAA	KWATO cluster	1	1	1,130	1,760		80.00	100	C	2		...					0....	4755
22-SDAA-a	kwato	1	1	1,130	1,760	0	80.00	100	C	2		...					0....	4756
22-SE	JILIM chain	1	1	594	925		90.07	100	C	4		...					0....	4757
22-SEA	**JILIM net**	1	1	594	925		90.07	100	C	4		...					0....	4758
22-SEAA	JILIM cluster	1	1	594	925		90.07	100	C	4		...					0....	4759
22-SEAA-a	jilim	1	1	594	925	0	90.07	100	C	4		...					0....	4760
22-SF	RERAU chain	1	1	341	532		95.01	100	C	4		...					0....	4761
22-SFA	**RERAU net**	1	1	341	532		95.01	100	C	4		...					0....	4762
22-SFAA	RERAU cluster	1	1	341	532		95.01	100	C	4		...					0....	4763
22-SFAA-a	rerau	1	1	341	532	0	95.01	100	C	4		...					0....	4764
22-SG	YANGULAM chain	1	1	262	407		95.04	100	C	4		...					0....	4765

Continued overleaf

Table 9-13 continued

Code 1	REFERENCE NAME Autoglossonym 2	Coun 3	Peo 4	Mother-tongue speakers in 2000 5	in 2025 6	Media radio 7	CHURCH AC% 8	E% 9	Wld 10	Tr 11	Biblioglossonym 12	SCRIPTURES Print P-activity 13-15 16	N-activity 17	B-activity 18	J-year 19	Jayuh 20-24	Ref 25
22-SGA	**YANGULAM net**	1	1	262	407		95.04	100	C	4		. . .				0	4766
22-SGAA	YANGULAM cluster	1	1	262	407		95.04	100	C	4		. . .				0	4767
22-SGAA-a	yangulam	1	1	262	407	0	95.04	100	C	4		. . .				0	4768
22-T	**MINDJIM set**	1	4	3,416	5,317		85.10	100	C	22		P . .				0	4769
22-TA	ANJAM chain	1	1	1,662	2,587		79.96	100	C	22		P . .				0	4770
22-TAA	**ANJAM net**	1	1	1,662	2,587		79.96	100	C	22		P . .				0	4771
22-TAAA	ANJAM cluster	1	1	1,662	2,587		79.96	100	C	22		P . .				0	4772
22-TAAA-a	anjam	1	1	1,662	2,587	0	79.96	100	C	22	Anjam	P . . 1987				0	4773
22-TB	MALE chain	1	1	571	889		90.02	100	C	4		. . .				0	4774
22-TBA	**MALE net**	1	1	571	889		90.02	100	C	4		. . .				0	4775
22-TBAA	MALE cluster	1	1	571	889		90.02	100	C	4		. . .				0	4776
22-TBAA-a	male	1	1	571	889	0	90.02	100	C	4		. . .				0	4777
22-TC	BONGU chain	1	1	709	1,104		89.99	100	C	3		. . .				0	4778
22-TCA	**BONGU net**	1	1	709	1,104		89.99	100	C	3		. . .				0	4779
22-TCAA	BONGU cluster	1	1	709	1,104		89.99	100	C	3		. . .				0	4780
22-TCAA-a	bongu	1	1	709	1,104	0	89.99	100	C	3		. . .				0	4781
22-TD	SONGUM chain	1	1	474	737		89.87	100	C	4		. . .				0	4782
22-TDA	**SONGUM net**	1	1	474	737		89.87	100	C	4		. . .				0	4783
22-TDAA	SONGUM cluster	1	1	474	737		89.87	100	C	4		. . .				0	4784
22-TDAA-a	songum	1	1	474	737	0	89.87	100	C	4		. . .				0	4785
22-U	**KABENAU set**	1	5	1,707	2,658		84.53	96	C	42		PN .				0	4786
22-UA	PULABU chain	1	1	169	263		34.91	61	B	4		. . .				0	4787
22-UAA	**PULABU net**	1	1	169	263		34.91	61	B	4		. . .				0	4788
22-UAAA	PULABU cluster	1	1	169	263		34.91	61	B	4		. . .				0	4789
22-UAAA-a	pulabu	1	1	169	263	0	34.91	61	B	4		. . .				0	4790
22-UAAA-b	kadda					0				4		. . .				0	4791
22-UB	LEMIO chain	1	1	254	396		90.16	100	C	4		. . .				0	4792
22-UBA	**LEMIO net**	1	1	254	396		90.16	100	C	4		. . .				0	4793
22-UBAA	LEMIO cluster	1	1	254	396		90.16	100	C	4		. . .				0	4794
22-UBAA-a	lemio	1	1	254	396	0	90.16	100	C	4		. . .				0	4795
22-UBAA-b	gurumbu									4		. . .				0	4796
22-UC	ARAWUM chain	1	1	109	170		89.91	100	C	4		. . .				0	4797
22-UCA	**ARAWUM net**	1	1	109	170		89.91	100	C	4		. . .				0	4798
22-UCAA	ARAWUM cluster	1	1	109	170		89.91	100	C	4		. . .				0	4799
22-UCAA-a	arawum	1	1	109	170	0	89.91	100	C	4		. . .				0	4800
22-UD	SIROI chain	1	1	871	1,356		90.01	100	C	42		PN .				0	4801
22-UDA	**SIROI net**	1	1	871	1,356		90.01	100	C	42		PN .				0	4802
22-UDAA	SIROI cluster	1	1	871	1,356		90.01	100	C	42		PN .				0	4803
22-UDAA-a	siroi	1	1	871	1,356	0	90.01	100	C	42	Siroi	PN . 1971-1986 1975				0	4804
22-UDAA-b	pasa					0				42		pn .				0	4805
22-UDAA-c	komisanga					0				42		pn .				0	4806
22-UE	KOLOM chain	1	1	304	473		89.80	100	C	4		. . .				0	4807
22-UEA	**KOLOM net**	1	1	304	473		89.80	100	C	4		. . .				0	4808
22-UEAA	KOLOM cluster	1	1	304	473		89.80	100	C	4		. . .				0	4809
22-UEAA-a	kolom	1	1	304	473	0	89.80	100	C	4		. . .				0	4810
22-V	**YAGANON set**	1	4	1,838	2,861		92.11	100	C	12		. . .				0	4811
22-VA	DUMUN chain	1	1	61	95		95.08	100	C	4		. . .				0	4812
22-VAA	**DUMUN net**	1	1	61	95		95.08	100	C	4		. . .				0	4813
22-VAAA	DUMUN cluster	1	1	61	95		95.08	100	C	4		. . .				0	4814
22-VAAA-a	dumun	1	1	61	95	0	95.08	100	C	4		. . .				0	4815
22-VB	SAEP chain	1	1	849	1,321		89.99	100	C	12		. . .				0	4816
22-VBA	**SAEP net**	1	1	849	1,321		89.99	100	C	12		. . .				0	4817
22-VBAA	SAEP cluster	1	1	849	1,321		89.99	100	C	12		. . .				0	4818
22-VBAA-a	saep	1	1	849	1,321	0	89.99	100	C	12	Saep	. . .				0	4819
22-VC	GANGLAU chain	1	1	224	349		90.18	100	C	4		. . .				0	4820
22-VCA	**GANGLAU net**	1	1	224	349		90.18	100	C	4		. . .				0	4821
22-VCAA	GANGLAU cluster	1	1	224	349		90.18	100	C	4		. . .				0	4822
22-VCAA-a	ganglau	1	1	224	349	0	90.18	100	C	4		. . .				0	4823
22-VD	YABONG chain	1	1	704	1,096		95.03	100	C	4		. . .				0	4824
22-VDA	**YABONG net**	1	1	704	1,096		95.03	100	C	4		. . .				0	4825
22-VDAA	YABONG cluster	1	1	704	1,096		95.03	100	C	4		. . .				0	4826
22-VDAA-a	yabong	1	1	704	1,096	0	95.03	100	C	4		. . .				0	4827
22-W	**WASEMBO set**	1	1	875	1,362		90.06	100	C	4		. . .				0	4828
22-WA	WASEMBO chain	1	1	875	1,362		90.06	100	C	4		. . .				0	4829
22-WAA	**WASEMBO net**	1	1	875	1,362		90.06	100	C	4		. . .				0	4830
22-WAAA	WASEMBO cluster	1	1	875	1,362		90.06	100	C	4		. . .				0	4831
22-WAAA-a	wasembo	1	1	875	1,362	0	90.06	100	C	4		. . .				0	4832
23	**SOUTH IRIANIC zone**	2	54	246,567	385,113		84.93	99	C	61		PNB				0 . s . .	4833
23-A	**BINANDEREAN-GUHU set**	1	16	100,819	156,953		88.16	100	C	41		PN .				0	4834

Continued opposite

Table 9-13 continued

Code 1	REFERENCE NAME / Autoglossonym 2	Coun 3	Peo 4	Mother-tongue speakers in 2000 5	in 2025 6	Media radio 7	AC% 8	E% 9	Wld 10	Tr 11	Biblioglossonym 12	Print 13-15	P-activity 16	N-activity 17	B-activity 18	J-year 19	Jayuh 20-24	Ref 25
23-AA	GUHU-SAMANE chain	1	1	9,891	15,398		88.00	100	C	41		PN.					0....	4835
23-AAA	**GUHU-SAMANE net**	1	1	9,891	15,398		88.00	100	C	41		PN.					0....	4836
23-AAAA	GUHU-SAMANE cluster	1	1	9,891	15,398		88.00	100	C	41	Guhu-samane	PN.	1966-1983	1975-1983			0....	4837
23-AAAA-a	waria-M.					0				41		pn.					0....	4838
23-AAAA-b	sekare					0				41		pn.					0....	4839
23-AAAA-c	paiawa					0				41		pn.					0....	4840
23-AAAA-d	eipa					0				41		pn.					0....	4841
23-AB	BINANDEREAN chain	1	15	90,928	141,555		88.18	100	C	41		PN.					0....	4842
23-ABA	**SUENA-ZIA net**	1	4	9,662	15,043		89.98	100	C	41		PN.					0....	4843
23-ABAA	SUENA cluster	1	1	3,573	5,563		98.99	100	C	41		PN.					0....	4844
23-ABAA-a	suena	1	1	3,573	5,563	0	98.99	100	C	41	Suena	PN.	1972	1978			0....	4845
23-ABAB	YEKORA cluster	1	1	1,119	1,742		89.99	100	C	0		...					0....	4846
23-ABAB-a	East yekora					0				0		...					0....	4847
23-ABAB-b	West yekora					0				0		...					0....	4848
23-ABAC	ZIA cluster	1	1	3,487	5,429		85.00	100	C	41		PN.					0....	4849
23-ABAC-a	zia	1	1	3,487	5,429	0	85.00	100	C	41	Zia	PN.	1978	1982			0....	4850
23-ABAD	MAWAE cluster	1	1	1,483	2,309		79.97	100	C	0		...					0....	4851
23-ABAD-a	mawae	1	1	1,483	2,309	0	79.97	100	C	0		...					0....	4852
23-ABB	**BINANDERE-AMBASI net**	1	2	8,608	13,400		77.02	100	C	24		P..					0....	4853
23-ABBA	BINANDERE cluster	1	1	6,864	10,685		75.00	100	C	24		P..					0....	4854
23-ABBA-a	binandere	1	1	6,864	10,685	0	75.00	100	C	24	Binandere	P..	1912-1949				0....	4855
23-ABBB	AMBASI cluster	1	1	1,744	2,715		84.98	100	C	0		...					0....	4856
23-ABBB-a	ambasi	1	1	1,744	2,715	0	84.98	100	C	0		...					0....	4857
23-ABBB-b	killerton					0				0		...					0....	4858
23-ABC	**AEKA net**	1	1	2,906	4,525		85.00	100	C	0		...					0....	4859
23-ABCA	AEKA cluster	1	1	2,906	4,525		85.00	100	C	0		...					0....	4860
23-ABCA-a	aeka	1	1	2,906	4,525	0	85.00	100	C	0		...					0....	4861
23-ABD	**OROKAIVA-HUNJARA net**	1	2	40,515	63,071		92.43	100	C	41		PN.					0....	4862
23-ABDA	OROKAIVA cluster	1	1	32,855	51,147		93.00	100	C	41	Orokaiva	PN.	1956	1988			0....	4863
23-ABDA-a	wasida					1				41		pn.					0....	4864
23-ABDA-b	jegasi-saruhu					1				41		pn.					0....	4865
23-ABDA-c	periho					1				41		pn.					0....	4866
23-ABDA-d	kombu-sangara					1				41		pn.					0....	4867
23-ABDA-e	sairope					1				41		pn.					0....	4868
23-ABDA-f	kendata					1				41		pn.					0....	4869
23-ABDA-g	jegarata-kakendetta					1				41		pn.					0....	4870
23-ABDA-h	sohe					1				41		pn.					0....	4871
23-ABDA-i	popondetta					1				41		pn.					0....	4872
23-ABDA-j	doboduru					1				41		pn.					0....	4873
23-ABDB	HUNJARA cluster	1	1	7,660	11,924		90.00	100	C	0		...					0....	4874
23-ABDB-a	hunjara	1	1	7,660	11,924	0	90.00	100	C	0		...					0....	4875
23-ABE	**EWAGE-NOTU net**	1	1	16,914	26,331		89.00	100	C	41		PN.					0....	4876
23-ABEA	EWAGE-NOTU cluster	1	1	16,914	26,331		89.00	100	C	41		PN.					0....	4877
23-ABEA-a	ewage-notu	1	1	16,914	26,331	1	89.00	100	C	41	Ewage-notu	PN.	1930-1952	1987			0....	4878
23-ABF	**GAINA net**	1	1	1,406	2,189		80.01	100	C	4		...					0....	4881
23-ABFA	GAINA cluster	1	1	1,406	2,189		80.01	100	C	4		...					0....	4882
23-ABFA-a	bareji					0				4		...					0....	4883
23-ABFA-b	gaina	1	1	1,406	2,189	0	80.01	100	C	4		...					0....	4884
23-ABG	**BARUGA net**	1	1	1,955	3,044		80.00	100	C	12		...					0....	4885
23-ABGA	BARUGA cluster	1	1	1,955	3,044		80.00	100	C	12		...					0....	4886
23-ABGA-a	songadi-karisoa	1	1	1,955	3,044	0	80.00	100	C	12	Baruga	...					0....	4887
23-ABGA-b	tugari					0				12		...					0....	4890
23-ABGA-c	gombara					0				12		...					0....	4891
23-ABGA-d	kinjaki					0				12		...					0....	4892
23-ABGA-e	kakasa					0				12		...					0....	4893
23-ABGA-f	embessa					0				12		...					0....	4894
23-ABGA-g	gugumu					0				12		...					0....	4895
23-ABGA-h	totore					0				12		...					0....	4896
23-ABH	**DOGORO net**	1	1	173	269		94.80	100	C	0		...					0....	4897
23-ABHA	DOGORO cluster	1	1	173	269		94.80	100	C	0		...					0....	4898
23-ABHA-a	dogoro	1	1	173	269	0	94.80	100	C	0		...					0....	4899
23-ABI	**GONA net**	1	1	1,308	2,036		79.97	100	C	0		...					0....	4900
23-ABIA	GONA cluster	1	1	1,308	2,036		79.97	100	C	0		...					0....	4901
23-ABIA-a	West yega	1	1	1,308	2,036	0	79.97	100	C	0		...					0....	4902
23-ABIA-b	okeina					0				0		...					0....	4903
23-ABJ	**KORAFE net**	1	1	7,481	11,647		80.00	100	C	41		PN.					0....	4904
23-ABJA	KORAFE cluster	1	1	7,481	11,647		80.00	100	C	41		PN.					0....	4905
23-ABJA-a	Proper korafe	1	1	7,481	11,647	0	80.00	100	C	41	Korafe	PN.	1975	1984			0....	4906
23-ABJA-b	mokorua					0				41		pn.					0....	4907
23-B	**GOILALAN set**	1	6	65,995	103,024		86.44	100	C	61		PNB					0.s..	4908
23-BA	BIANGAI chain	1	1	1,628	2,534		79.98	100	C	41		PN.					0....	4909
23-BAA	**BIANGAI net**	1	1	1,628	2,534		79.98	100	C	41		PN.					0....	4910
23-BAAA	BIANGAI cluster	1	1	1,628	2,534		79.98	100	C	41	Biangai	PN.	1973	1985			0....	4911
23-BAAA-a	ngowiye					0				41		pn.					0....	4912
23-BAAA-b	yongolei					0				41		pn.					0....	4913
23-BB	WERI chain	1	1	6,547	10,193		80.01	100	C	41		PN.					0....	4914
23-BBA	**WERI net**	1	1	6,547	10,193		80.01	100	C	41		PN.					0....	4915
23-BBAA	WERI cluster	1	1	6,547	10,193		80.01	100	C	41	Weri	PN.	1966	1984			0....	4916
23-BBAA-a	sim					0				41		pn.					0....	4917
23-BBAA-b	biaru-waria					0				41		pn.					0....	4918
23-BBAA-c	ono					0				41		pn.					0....	4921
23-BC	KUNIMAIPA-GAJILI chain	1	2	24,421	38,303		83.94	100	C	61		PNB					0....	4922
23-BCA	**KUNIMAIPA-GAJILI net**	1	2	24,421	38,303		83.94	100	C	61		PNB					0....	4923
23-BCAA	GAJILI cluster	1	1	2,000	3,400		80.00	100	C	0		...					0....	4924

Continued overleaf

Table 9-13 continued

Code 1	REFERENCE NAME 2 / Autoglossonym	Coun 3	Peo 4	in 2000 5	in 2025 6	Media radio 7	AC% 8	E% 9	Wld 10	Tr 11	Biblioglossonym 12	Print 13-15	P-activity 16	N-activity 17	B-activity 18	J-year 19	Jayuh 20-24	Ref 25
23-BCAA-a	gajila	1	1	2,000	3,400	0	80.00	100	C	0		...					0....	4925
23-BCAB	KUNIMAIPA cluster	1	2	22,421	34,903		84.30	100	C	61	Kunimaipa	PNB	1979-1980	1989-1990			0....	4926
23-BCAB-a	karuama					0				61		pnb					0....	4927
23-BCAB-b	kate	1	1	9,633	14,996	0	90.00	100	C	61	Kate	PNB	1919-1965	1938-1965	1978		0....	4928
23-BD	TAUADE chain	1	1	12,788	19,907		88.00	100	C	3		...					0....	4929
23-BDA	**TAUADE net**	1	1	12,788	19,907		88.00	100	C	3		...					0....	4930
23-BDAA	TAUADE cluster	1	1	12,788	19,907		88.00	100	C	3		...					0....	4931
23-BDAA-a	tauade	1	1	12,788	19,907	0	88.00	100	C	3		...					0....	4932
23-BE	FUYUGE chain	1	1	20,611	32,087		91.00	100	C	22		P..					0.s..	4933
23-BEA	**FUYUGE net**	1	1	20,611	32,087		91.00	100	C	22		P..					0.s..	4934
23-BEAA	FUYUGE cluster	1	1	20,611	32,087		91.00	100	C	22	Fuyuge	P..	1994				0.s..	4935
23-BEAA-a	auga					0				22		p..					0.s..	4936
23-BEAA-b	dilava					0				22		p..					0.s..	4937
23-BEAA-c	ononge					0				22		p..					0.s..	4938
23-BEAA-d	chirima					0				22		p..					0.s..	4939
23-C	**KOIARIAN set**	1	6	34,836	55,879		80.00	100	C	42		PN.					0....	4940
23-CA	KOIALI-KOIARI chain	1	3	21,263	34,749		80.00	100	C	41		PN.					0....	4941
23-CAA	**KOIALI net**	1	1	14,406	24,074		80.00	100	C	41		PN.					0....	4942
23-CAAA	KOIALI-E cluster	1	1	3,000	5,100		80.00	100	C	0		...					0....	4943
23-CAAA-a	awoma					0				0		...					0....	4944
23-CAAA-b	kovio					0				0		...					0....	4945
23-CAAB	NORTH KOIALI cluster	1	1	2,000	3,400		80.00	100	C	0		...					0....	4946
23-CAAB-a	North koiali	1	1	2,000	3,400	0	80.00	100	C	0		...					0....	4947
23-CAAC	WEST KOIALI cluster	1	1	4,000	6,800		80.00	100	C	0		...					0....	4948
23-CAAC-a	West koiali	1	1	4,000	6,800	0	80.00	100	C	0		...					0....	4949
23-CAAD	CENTRAL KOIALI cluster	1	1	2,906	4,524		80.01	100	C	41		PN.					0....	4950
23-CAAD-a	Central koiali	1	1	2,906	4,524	0	80.01	100	C	41	Koiali: Mountain*	PN.	1974	1981			0....	4951
23-CAAE	SOUTH KOIALI cluster	1	1	2,500	4,250		80.00	100	C	0		...					0....	4952
23-CAAE-a	varagadi					0				0		...					0....	4953
23-CAAE-b	uberi					0				0		...					0....	4954
23-CAAE-c	moroka					0				0		...					0....	4955
23-CAAE-d	herei					0				0		...					0....	4956
23-CAAE-e	eava					0				0		...					0....	4957
23-CAB	**KOIARI-KOITA net**	1	2	6,857	10,675		79.99	100	C	2		...					0....	4958
23-CABA	KOITA cluster	1	1	3,651	5,683		79.98	100	C	2		...					0....	4959
23-CABA-a	West koita					0				2		...					0....	4960
23-CABA-b	East koita	1	1	3,651	5,683	0	79.98	100	C	2		...					0....	4961
23-CABB	KOIARI cluster	1	1	3,206	4,992		80.01	100	C	2		...					0....	4962
23-CABB-a	West koiari					0				2		...					0....	4963
23-CABB-b	East koiari	1	1	3,206	4,992	0	80.01	100	C	2		...					0....	4964
23-CB	BARAI-MANAGALASI chain	1	3	13,573	21,130		80.00	100	C	42		PN.					0....	4965
23-CBA	**BARAI net**	1	1	5,128	7,983		79.99	100	C	41		PN.					0....	4966
23-CBAA	BARAI cluster	1	1	5,128	7,983		79.99	100	C	41		PN.					0....	4967
23-CBAA-a	nigubaiba					0				41		pn.					0....	4968
23-CBAA-b	barai	1	1	5,128	7,983	0	79.99	100	C	41	Barai	PN.	1973-1980	1994			0....	4969
23-CBAA-c	pitoni					0				41		pn.					0....	4970
23-CBAA-d	tabu					0				41		pn.					0....	4971
23-CBAA-e	laroni					0				41		pn.					0....	4972
23-CBAA-f	manoa					0				41		pn.					0....	4973
23-CBAA-g	mogoni					0				41		pn.					0....	4974
23-CBAA-h	umwate					0				41		pn.					0....	4975
23-CBAA-i	u_a					0				41		pn.					0....	4976
23-CBAA-j	kokora					0				41		pn.					0....	4977
23-CBAA-k	pirimi					0				41		pn.					0....	4978
23-CBAA-l	emo					0				41		pn.					0....	4979
23-CBAA-m	seramina	0	0			0	0.00	0		41		pn.					0....	4980
23-CBAA-n	uala	0	0			0	0.00	0		41		pn.					0....	4981
23-CBB	**MANAGALASI-ÖMIE net**	1	2	8,445	13,147		80.00	100	C	42		PN.					0....	4982
23-CBBA	ÖMIE cluster	1	1	1,369	2,131		79.99	100	C	41		PN.					0....	4983
23-CBBA-a	zuwadza					0				41		pn.					0....	4984
23-CBBA-b	asapa	1	1	1,369	2,131	0	79.99	100	C	41	Omie	PN.	1987	1991			0....	4985
23-CBBA-c	gora-bomahouji					0				41		pn.					0....	4986
23-CBBB	MANAGALASI cluster	1	1	7,076	11,016		80.00	100	C	42	Managalasi	PN.	1966-1968	1975			0....	4987
23-CBBB-a	nami					0				42		pn.					0....	4988
23-CBBB-b	mesari					0				42		pn.					0....	4989
23-CBBB-c	averi					0				42		pn.					0....	4990
23-CBBB-d	minjori					0				42		pn.					0....	4991
23-CBBB-e	numba					0				42		pn.					0....	4992
23-CBBB-f	akabara					0				42		pn.					0....	4993
23-CBBB-g	wakue					0				42		pn.					0....	4994
23-CBBB-h	karira					0				42		pn.					0....	4995
23-CBBB-i	jimuni					0				42		pn.					0....	4996
23-CBBB-j	oko					0				42		pn.					0....	4997
23-CBBB-k	afore					0				42		pn.					0....	4998
23-CBBB-l	muaturaina					0				42		pn.					0....	4999
23-CBBB-m	chimona					0				42		pn.					0....	5000
23-CBBB-n	dea					0				42		pn.					0....	5001
23-D	**KWALEAN set**	1	2	3,260	5,074		82.85	100	C	12		...					0....	5002
23-DA	KWALEAN chain	1	2	3,260	5,074		82.85	100	C	12		...					0....	5003
23-DAA	**KWALEAN net**	1	2	3,260	5,074		82.85	100	C	12		...					0....	5004
23-DAAA	HUMENE cluster	1	1	935	1,455		89.95	100	C	2		...					0....	5005
23-DAAA-a	humene	1	1	935	1,455	0	89.95	100	C	2		...					0....	5006
23-DAAA-b	lagume					0				2		...					0....	5007
23-DAAB	KWALE cluster	1	1	2,325	3,619		80.00	100	C	12		...					0....	5008
23-DAAB-a	kwale	1	1	2,325	3,619	0	80.00	100	C	12	Kwale	...					0....	5009
23-DAAB-b	garia					0				12		...					0....	5010
23-E	**MULAHA set**									9		...					0....	5011
23-EA	MULAHA chain									9		...					0....	5012
23-EAA	**MULAHA net**									9		...					0....	5013

Continued opposite

Table 9-13 continued

Code 1	REFERENCE NAME Autoglossonym 2	Coun 3	Peo 4	Mother-tongue speakers in 2000 5	in 2025 6	Media radio 7	CHURCH AC% 8	E% 9	Wld 10	Tr 11	Biblioglossonym 12	SCRIPTURES Print 13-15	P-activity 16	N-activity 17	B-activity 18	J-year 19	Jayuh 20-24	Ref 25
23-EAAA	MULAHA cluster			0	0		0.00	0		9		...					0....	5014
23-EAAA-a	mulaha			0	0	0	0.00	0		9		...					0....	5015
23-EAAA-b	iaibu			0	0	0	0.00	0		9		...					0....	5016
23-F	**MANUBARAN set**	2	3	5,415	7,720		45.24	66	B	2		...					0....	5017
23-FA	MANUBARAN chain	2	3	5,415	7,720		45.24	66	B	2		...					0....	5018
23-FAA	**DOROMU net**	1	1	1,406	2,189		80.01	100	C	2		...					0....	5019
23-FAAA	DOROMU cluster	1	1	1,406	2,189		80.01	100	C	2		...					0....	5020
23-FAAA-a	kokila					0				2		...					0....	5021
23-FAAA-b	doromu	1	1	1,406	2,189	0	80.01	100	C	2		...					0....	5022
23-FAAA-c	koriko					0				2		...					0....	5023
23-FAB	**MARIA net**	2	2	4,009	5,531		33.05	54	B	2		...					0....	5024
23-FABA	MARIA cluster	2	2	4,009	5,531		33.05	54	B	2		...					0....	5025
23-FABA-a	didigaru					0				2		...					0....	5026
23-FABA-b	oibu					0				2		...					0....	5027
23-FABA-c	gebi	1	1	2,651	3,418	0	9.02	30	A	2		...					0....	5028
23-FABA-d	amota					0				2		...					0....	5029
23-FABA-e	maria	1	1	1,358	2,113	0	79.97	100	C	2		...					0....	5030
23-FABA-f	imila					0				2		...					0....	5031
23-FABA-g	uderi					0				2		...					0....	5032
23-G	**YAREBAN-MAILUAN set**	1	11	16,741	26,105		85.58	100	C	42		PN.					0....	5033
23-GA	YAREBAN chain	1	5	3,375	5,255		87.73	100	C	42		PN.					0....	5034
23-GAA	**BARIJI net**	1	1	456	710		90.13	100	C	4		...					0....	5035
23-GAAA	BARIJI cluster	1	1	456	710		90.13	100	C	4		...					0....	5036
23-GAAA-a	bariji	1	1	456	710	0	90.13	100	C	4		...					0....	5037
23-GAB	**YAREBA-NAWARU net**	1	2	1,316	2,049		89.97	100	C	42		PN.					0....	5038
23-GABA	NAWARU cluster	1	1	226	352		89.82	100	C	6		...					0....	5039
23-GABA-a	nawaru	1	1	226	352	0	89.82	100	C	6		...					0....	5040
23-GABB	YAREBA cluster	1	1	1,090	1,697		90.00	100	C	42		PN.					0....	5041
23-GABB-a	yareba	1	1	1,090	1,697	0	90.00	100	C	42	Yareba	PN.	1966	1973			0....	5042
23-GAC	**ABIA-MOIKODI net**	1	2	1,603	2,496		85.22	100	C	41		PN.					0....	5043
23-GACA	MOIKODI cluster	1	1	830	1,292		90.00	100	C	12		...					0....	5044
23-GACA-a	moikodi	1	1	830	1,292	0	90.00	100	C	12	Moikodi	...					0....	5045
23-GACB	ANEME-WAKE cluster	1	1	773	1,204		80.08	100	C	41	Aneme Wake	PN.		1988			0....	5046
23-GACB-a	jari					0				41		pn.					0....	5047
23-GACB-b	auwaka					0				41		pn.					0....	5048
23-GACB-c	doma					0				41		pn.					0....	5049
23-GACB-d	buniabura					0				41		pn.					0....	5050
23-GACB-e	mori					0				41		pn.					0....	5051
23-GB	MAILUAN chain	1	6	13,366	20,850		85.04	100	C	41		PN.					0....	5052
23-GBA	**BAUWAKI-DOMU net**	1	2	1,568	2,441		90.05	100	C	6		...					0....	5053
23-GBAA	BAUWAKI cluster	1	1	621	966		90.02	100	C	4		...					0....	5054
23-GBAA-a	North ba-vake					0				4		...					0....	5055
23-GBAA-b	South ba-vake					0				4		...					0....	5056
23-GBAB	DOMU cluster	1	1	947	1,475		90.07	100	C	6		...					0....	5057
23-GBAB-a	domu	1	1	947	1,475	0	90.07	100	C	6		...					0....	5058
23-GBB	**NEME-MORAWA net**	1	2	2,837	4,459		82.38	100	C	6		...					0....	5059
23-GBBA	NEME-DA'A cluster	1	1	1,192	1,856		80.03	100	C	5		...					0....	5060
23-GBBA-a	neme-da'a	1	1	1,192	1,856	0	80.03	100	C	5		...					0....	5061
23-GBBB	MA-DA'A cluster	1	1	300	510		80.00	100	C	0		...					0....	5062
23-GBBB-a	doma 2					0				0		...					0....	5063
23-GBBB-b	sigili					0				0		...					0....	5064
23-GBBB-c	apaeva					0				0		...					0....	5065
23-GBBC	MORAWA cluster	1	1	1,345	2,093		84.98	100	C	6		...					0....	5066
23-GBBC-a	morawa	1	1	1,345	2,093	0	84.98	100	C	6		...					0....	5067
23-GBC	**MAGI-LAUA net**	1	2	8,961	13,950		85.00	100	C	41		PN.					0....	5068
23-GBCA	LAUA cluster	1	1	1	2		100.00	100	C	8		...					0....	5069
23-GBCA-a	laua	1	1	1	2	0	100.00	100	C	8		...					0....	5070
23-GBCB	MAGI cluster	1	1	8,960	13,948		85.00	100	C	41		PN.					0....	5071
23-GBCB-a	domara					0				41		pn.					0....	5072
23-GBCB-b	darava					0				41		pn.					0....	5073
23-GBCB-c	asiaoro					0				41		pn.					0....	5074
23-GBCB-d	mailu	1	1	8,960	13,948	0	85.00	100	C	41	Magi*	PN.	1907-1920	1936-1979			0....	5075
23-GBCB-e	derebai					0				41		pn.					0....	5076
23-GBCB-f	borebo					0				41		pn.					0....	5077
23-GBCB-g	geagea					0				41		pn.					0....	5078
23-GBCB-h	ilai					0				41		pn.					0....	5079
23-GBCB-i	baibara					0				41		pn.					0....	5080
23-H	**ONJOB set**	1	1	233	362		89.70	100	C	2		...					0....	5081
23-HA	ONJOB chain	1	1	233	362		89.70	100	C	2		...					0....	5082
23-HAA	**ONJOB net**	1	1	233	362		89.70	100	C	2		...					0....	5083
23-HAAA	ONJOB cluster	1	1	233	362		89.70	100	C	2		...					0....	5084
23-HAAA-a	onjab	1	1	233	362	0	89.70	100	C	2		...					0....	5085
23-I	**DAGA-MAIWA set**	1	5	11,428	17,792		81.37	100	C	42		PN.					0....	5086
23-IA	DAGA-MAPENA chain	1	3	7,514	11,697		80.74	100	C	42		PN.					0....	5087
23-IAA	**DAGA net**	1	1	6,975	10,858		80.00	100	C	42		PN.					0....	5088
23-IAAA	DAGA cluster	1	1	6,975	10,858		80.00	100	C	42	Daga	PN.	1970	1974			0....	5089
23-IAAA-a	bonua					0				42		pn.					0....	5090
23-IAAA-b	tavanei					0				42		pn.					0....	5091
23-IAAA-c	ulumanu					0				42		pn.					0....	5092
23-IAAA-d	Upper ruaba					0				42		pn.					0....	5093
23-IAB	**MAPENA net**	1	1	488	760		89.96	100	C	4		...					0....	5094
23-IABA	MAPENA cluster	1	1	488	760		89.96	100	C	4		...					0....	5095
23-IABA-a	mapena	1	1	488	760	0	89.96	100	C	4		...					0....	5096

Continued overleaf

Table 9-13 continued

Code 1	REFERENCE NAME / Autoglossonym 2	Coun 3	Peo 4	Mother-tongue speakers in 2000 5	in 2025 6	Media radio 7	CHURCH AC% 8	E% 9	Wld 10	Tr 11	Biblioglossonym 12	Print 13-15	P-activity 16	N-activity 17	B-activity 18	J-year 19	Jayuh 20-24	Ref 25
23-IAC	**TURAKA net**	1	1	51	79		94.12	100	C	4		. . .					0	5097
23-IACA	TURAKA cluster	1	1	51	79		94.12	100	C	4		. . .					0	5098
23-IACA-a	turaka	1	1	51	79	0	94.12	100	C	4		. . .					0	5099
23-IB	MAIWA chain	1	1	2,906	4,525		80.01	100	C	12		. . .					0	5100
23-IBA	**MAIWA net**	1	1	2,906	4,525		80.01	100	C	12		. . .					0	5101
23-IBAA	MAIWA cluster	1	1	2,906	4,525		80.01	100	C	12	Maiwa	. . .					0	5102
23-IBAA-a	biniguni					0				12		. . .					0	5103
23-IBAA-b	wapon					0				12		. . .					0	5104
23-IBAA-c	South maiwa					0				12		. . .					0	5105
23-IBAA-d	pumani					0				12		. . .					0	5106
23-IBAA-e	baiawa					0				12		. . .					0	5107
23-IC	JIMAJIMA chain	1	1	1,008	1,570		89.98	100	C	2		. . .					0	5108
23-ICA	**JIMAJIMA net**	1	1	1,008	1,570		89.98	100	C	2		. . .					0	5109
23-ICAA	JIMAJIMA cluster	1	1	1,008	1,570		89.98	100	C	2		. . .					0	5110
23-ICAA-a	buburida					0				2		. . .					0	5111
23-ICAA-b	ruaba					0				2		. . .					0	5112
23-J	**GWEDENA set**	1	1	2,987	4,649		79.98	100	C	41		PN.					0	5113
23-JA	GWEDENA chain	1	1	2,987	4,649		79.98	100	C	41		PN.					0	5114
23-JAA	**GWEDENA net**	1	1	2,987	4,649		79.98	100	C	41		PN.					0	5115
23-JAAA	UMANAKAINA cluster	1	1	2,987	4,649		79.98	100	C	41		PN.					0	5116
23-JAAA-a	North umanakaina	1	1	2,987	4,649	0	79.98	100	C	41	Umanakaina	PN.	1987-1994	1995			0	5117
23-JAAA-b	ugu					0				41		pn.					0	5118
23-K	**GINUMAN-KANASI set**	1	3	4,853	7,555		87.02	100	C	41		PN.					0	5119
23-KA	GINUMAN chain	1	1	1,442	2,245		80.03	100	C	2		. . .					0	5120
23-KAA	**GINUMAN net**	1	1	1,442	2,245		80.03	100	C	2		. . .					0	5121
23-KAAA	GINUMAN cluster	1	1	1,442	2,245		80.03	100	C	2		. . .					0	5122
23-KAAA-a	ginuman	1	1	1,442	2,245	0	80.03	100	C	2		. . .					0	5123
23-KB	KANASI chain	1	2	3,411	5,310		89.97	100	C	41		PN.					0	5124
23-KBA	**KANASI net**	1	2	3,411	5,310		89.97	100	C	41		PN.					0	5125
23-KBAA	KANASI cluster	1	2	3,411	5,310		89.97	100	C	41	Kanasi	PN.	1992-1993	1996			0	5126
23-KBAA-a	Northwest kanasi					0				41		pn.					0	5127
23-KBAA-b	Northeast kanasi					0				41		pn.					0	5128
23-KBAA-c	Southeast kanasi					0				41		pn.					0	5129
23-KBAA-d	Southwest kanasi					0				41		pn.					0	5130
24	**TRANSIRIANIC zone**	2	284	3,001,807	4,475,821		81.96	98	C	57		PN.					1.su.	5131
24-A	**MOR set**	1	1	40	68		70.00	98	C	0		. . .					0	5132
24-AA	MOR chain	1	1	40	68		70.00	98	C	0		. . .					0	5133
24-AAA	**MOR net**	1	1	40	68		70.00	98	C	0		. . .					0	5134
24-AAAA	MOR cluster	1	1	40	68		70.00	98	C	0		. . .					0	5135
24-AAAA-a	mor	1	1	40	68	0	70.00	98	C	0		. . .					0	5136
24-B	**WEST BOMBERAI set**	1	3	8,420	10,856		65.00	92	C	4		. . .					0	5137
24-BA	KARAS chain	1	1	297	383		64.98	92	C	4		. . .					0	5138
24-BAA	**KARAS net**	1	1	297	383		64.98	92	C	4		. . .					0	5139
24-BAAA	KARAS cluster	1	1	297	383		64.98	92	C	4		. . .					0	5140
24-BAAA-a	karas	1	1	297	383	0	64.98	92	C	4		. . .					0	5141
24-BB	BAHAM-IHA chain	1	2	8,123	10,473		65.00	92	C	4		. . .					0	5142
24-BBA	**BAHAM-IHA net**	1	2	8,123	10,473		65.00	92	C	4		. . .					0	5143
24-BBAA	IHA cluster	1	1	6,766	8,723		65.00	92	C	2		. . .					0	5144
24-BBAA-a	iha					0				2		. . .					0	5145
24-BBAA-b	kapaur	1	1	6,766	8,723	0	65.00	92	C	2		. . .					0	5146
24-BBAB	BAHAM cluster	1	1	1,357	1,750		65.00	91	C	4		. . .					0	5147
24-BBAB-a	baham	1	1	1,357	1,750	0	65.00	91	C	4		. . .					0	5148
24-C	**MAIRASI-TANAMERAH set**	1	3	9,836	14,734		63.87	96	C	22		P. .					0	5149
24-CA	TANAMERAH chain	1	1	2,000	3,400		60.00	93	C	0		. . .					0	5150
24-CAA	**TANAMERAH net**	1	1	2,000	3,400		60.00	93	C	0		. . .					0	5151
24-CAAA	WEST TANAMERAH cluster	1	1	2,000	3,400		60.00	93	C	0		. . .					0	5152
24-CAAA-a	West tanamerah					0				0		. . .					0	5153
24-CB	MAIRASI chain	1	3	7,836	11,334		64.85	96	C	22		P. .					0	5154
24-CBA	**MAIRASI net**	1	3	7,836	11,334		64.85	96	C	22		P. .					0	5155
24-CBAA	CENTRAL MAIRASI cluster	1	1	3,000	5,100		65.00	96	C	0		. . .					0	5156
24-CBAA-a	mairasi-aturasa.					0				0		. . .					0	5157
24-CBAA-b	faranjao					0				0		. . .					0	5158
24-CBAA-c	kaniran					0				0		. . .					0	5159
24-CBAB	MAIRASI-E cluster	1	1	3,479	4,484		64.99	99	C	22		P. .					0	5160
24-CBAB-a	East mairasi	1	1	3,479	4,484	0	64.99	99	C	22	Mairasi	P. .	1986-1987				0	5161
24-CBAC	MER cluster	1	1	233	301		60.09	85	C	3		. . .					0	5162
24-CBAC-a	mer	1	1	233	301	0	60.09	85	C	3		. . .					0	5163
24-CBAD	SEMIMI cluster	1	1	1,124	1,449		65.04	91	C	4		. . .					0	5164
24-CBAD-a	semimi	1	1	1,124	1,449	0	65.04	91	C	4		. . .					0	5165
24-D	**WISSEL-KEMANDOGA set**	1	5	154,946	199,750		91.82	99	C	57		PN.					0	5166
24-DA	EKARI-MO chain	1	4	133,650	172,296		90.83	99	C	57		PN.					0	5167
24-DAA	**EKARI net**	1	4	133,650	172,296		90.83	99	C	57		PN.					0	5168

Continued opposite

Table 9-13 continued

Code 1	REFERENCE NAME / Autoglossonym 2	Coun 3	Peo 4	Mother-tongue speakers in 2000 5	in 2025 6	Media radio 7	AC% 8	E% 9	Wld 10	Tr 11	Biblioglossonym 12	Print 13-15	P–activity 16	N–activity 17	B–activity 18	J-year 19	Jayuh 20-24	Ref 25
24-DAAA	EKARI cluster	1	2	127,689	164,612		92.93	100	C	41		PN.					0....	5169
24-DAAA-a	ekari	1	1	127,413	164,257	0	93.00	100	C	41	Ekari	PN.	1955-1959	1963-1985			0....	5170
24-DAAA-b	simori					0				41		pn.					0....	5176
24-DAAA-c	yabi					0				41		pn.					0....	5177
24-DAAA-d	mapiya-kegata					0				41		pn.					0....	5178
24-DAAB	WODA-MO cluster	1	1	5,600	7,219		45.00	78	B	57		PN.					0....	5181
24-DAAB-a	wola-ni	1	1	5,600	7,219	0	45.00	78	B	57	Wolani	PN.	1984	1995			0....	5182
24-DAAB-b	mo-ni					0				57	Moni	PN.	1976	1990			0....	5183
24-DAAB-c	awembak					0				57		pn.					0....	5187
24-DAAC	AUYE cluster	1	1	361	465		59.83	89	B	12		...					0....	5188
24-DAAC-a	auye	1	1	361	465	0	59.83	89	B	12	Auye	...					0....	5189
24-DB	DAMAL chain	1	1	21,296	27,454		98.00	100	C	41		PN.					0....	5190
24-DBA	DAMAL net	1	1	21,296	27,454		98.00	100	C	41		PN.					0....	5191
24-DBAA	DAMAL cluster	1	1	21,296	27,454		98.00	100	C	41	Damal	PN.	1973-1992	1988			0....	5192
24-DBAA-a	uhundu-ni					0				41		pn.					0....	5193
24-DBAA-b	amung-me					0				41		pn.					0....	5194
24-DBAA-c	enggipilu					0				41		pn.					0....	5195
24-E	DEM set	1	1	1,230	1,586		65.04	96	C	2		...					0....	5196
24-EA	DEM chain	1	1	1,230	1,586		65.04	96	C	2		...					0....	5197
24-EAA	DEM net	1	1	1,230	1,586		65.04	96	C	2		...					0....	5198
24-EAAA	DEM cluster	1	1	1,230	1,586		65.04	96	C	2		...					0....	5199
24-EAAA-a	dem	1	1	1,230	1,586	0	65.04	96	C	2		...					0....	5200
24-F	DANI-KWERBA set	1	21	377,677	486,891		76.48	96	C	57		PN.					0....	5201
24-FA	DANI-NGALIK chain	1	13	370,296	477,374		77.19	96	C	57		PN.					0....	5202
24-FAA	WANO net	1	1	4,009	5,168		30.01	66	B	22		P..					0....	5203
24-FAAA	WANO cluster	1	1	4,009	5,168		30.01	66	B	22		P..					0....	5204
24-FAAA-a	wano	1	1	4,009	5,168	0	30.01	66	B	22	Wano	P..	1989				0....	5205
24-FAB	DANI net	1	5	309,591	399,115		81.89	99	C	41		PN.					0....	5206
24-FABA	WEST DANI cluster	1	1	199,190	256,789		85.00	100	C	41	Dani: Western*	PN.	1966-1994	1981-1992			0....	5207
24-FABA-a	'pyramid'-dani					0				41		pn.					0....	5208
24-FABA-b	bokondini-dani					0				41		pn.					0....	5209
24-FABA-c	'swart-valley'-dani					0				41		pn.					0....	5210
24-FABA-d	North balim					0				41		pn.					0....	5211
24-FABA-e	yamo					0				41		pn.					0....	5212
24-FABA-f	sinak					0				41		pn.					0....	5213
24-FABA-g	ilaga					0				41		pn.					0....	5214
24-FABB	DANI-TULEM cluster	1	1	57,545	74,185		80.00	100	C	41	Dani, Mid Grand Valley	PN.	1995	1990			0....	5215
24-FABB-a	tulem	1	1	57,545	74,185	0	80.00	100	C	41		PN.					0....	5216
24-FABC	DANI-WAMENA cluster	1	2	48,784	62,891		72.83	94	C	41	Dani: Lower Grand Valley*	PN.	1970	1988-1994			0....	5217
24-FABC-a	wodo					0				41		pn.					0....	5218
24-FABC-b	kimbin					0				41		pn.					0....	5219
24-FABC-c	Upper bele					0				41		pn.					0....	5220
24-FABC-d	Lower bele					0				41		pn.					0....	5221
24-FABC-e	aikhe					0				41		pn.					0....	5222
24-FABC-f	Upper pyramid					0				41		pn.					0....	5223
24-FABC-g	hitigima	1	2	48,784	62,891		72.83	94	C	41		pn.					0....	5224
24-FABD	HUPLA cluster	1	1	4,072	5,250		65.00	100	C	41		PN.					0....	5225
24-FABD-a	hupla	1	1	4,072	5,250	0	65.00	100	C	41	Hupla	PN.		1994			0....	5226
24-FABD-b	soba					0				41		pn.					0....	5227
24-FAC	NGGEM-WALAK net	1	2	4,688	6,043		60.20	94	C	22		P..					0....	5228
24-FACA	NGGEM cluster	1	1	3,415	4,402		64.01	98	C	22		P..					0....	5229
24-FACA-a	nggem	1	1	3,415	4,402	0	64.01	98	C	22	Nggem	P..	1982				0....	5230
24-FACB	WALAK cluster	1	1	1,273	1,641		49.96	85	B	2		...					0....	5231
24-FACB-a	walak	1	1	1,273	1,641	0	49.96	85	B	2		...					0....	5232
24-FAD	NGALIK-NDUGA net	1	5	52,008	67,048		54.41	84	B	57		PN.					0....	5238
24-FADA	NDUGA cluster	1	1	12,748	16,434		85.00	100	C	41	Nduga	PN.	1971	1984			0....	5239
24-FADA-a	pesechem-nduga					0				41		pn.					0....	5240
24-FADA-b	sinak-nduga					0				41		pn.					0....	5241
24-FADA-c	hitadipa-nduga					0				41		pn.					0....	5242
24-FADB	SILIMO cluster	1	1	6,151	7,930		25.00	66	B	41		PN.					0....	5243
24-FADB-a	silimo	1	1	6,151	7,930	0	25.00	66	B	41	Silimo	PN.		1992			0....	5244
24-FADB-b	samenage					0				41		pn.					0....	5245
24-FADC	NINIA cluster	1	1	10,181	13,125		35.00	72	B	57		PN.					0....	5246
24-FADC-a	ninia	1	1	10,181	13,125	0	35.00	72	B	57	Yali, Ninia	PN.	1976	1993			0....	5247
24-FADD	ANGGURUK cluster	1	2	22,928	29,559		53.92	86	B	51		PN.					0....	5248
24-FADD-a	angguruk	1	1	16,947	21,848	0	50.00	85	B	51	Yali: Angguruk*	PN.	1976	1988			0....	5249
24-FB	KWERBA chain	1	6	4,645	5,989		26.09	54	B	22		P..					0....	5250
24-FBA	KWERBA net	1	6	4,645	5,989		26.09	54	B	22		P..					0....	5251
24-FBAA	AIRORAN cluster	1	1	551	711		64.97	93	C	2		...					0....	5252
24-FBAA-a	airoran	1	1	551	711	0	64.97	93	C	2		...					0....	5253
24-FBAB	BAGUSA cluster	1	1	361	465		9.97	32	A	2		...					0....	5254
24-FBAB-a	bagusa	1	1	361	465	0	9.97	32	A	2		...					0....	5255
24-FBAC	NOPUK cluster	1	1	318	410		10.06	29	A	4		...					0....	5256
24-FBAC-a	nopuk	1	1	318	410	0	10.06	29	A	4		...					0....	5257
24-FBAD	SASAWA cluster	1	1	297	383		65.99	95	C	0		...					0....	5258
24-FBAD-a	sasawa	1	1	297	383	0	65.99	95	C	0		...					0....	5259
24-FBAE	KAUWERAWEC cluster	1	1	488	629		39.96	64	B	2		...					0....	5260
24-FBAE-a	kauwerawec	1	1	488	629	0	39.96	64	B	2		...					0....	5261
24-FBAF	KWERBA cluster	1	1	2,630	3,391		15.02	45	A	22		P..					0....	5262
24-FBAF-a	Proper kwerba	1	1	2,630	3,391	0	15.02	45	A	22	Kwerba	P..	1986-1991				0....	5263
24-FBAF-b	kaowerawedj					0				22		p..					0....	5264
24-FBAF-c	airmati					0				22		p..					0....	5265
24-FBAF-d	koassa					0				22		p..					0....	5266
24-FBAF-e	kamboi-ramboi					0				22		p..					0....	5267
24-FBAF-f	nogukwabai					0				22		p..					0....	5268
24-FBAF-g	naibedj					0				22		p..					0....	5269
24-FBAF-h	tekutameso					0				22		p..					0....	5270
24-FBAF-i	serikenam					0				22		p..					0....	5271

Continued overleaf

Table 9-13 continued

Code 1	REFERENCE NAME / Autoglossonym 2	Coun 3	Peo 4	MT speakers in 2000 (5)	in 2025 (6)	Media radio 7	AC% 8	E% 9	Wld 10	Tr 11	Biblioglossonym 12	Print 13-15	P-activity 16	N-activity 17	B-activity 18	J-year 19	Jayuh 20-24	Ref 25
24-FC	SAMAROKENA chain	1	1	530	684		65.09	92	C	2		...					0....	5272
24-FCA	**SAMAROKENA net**	1	1	530	684		65.09	92	C	2		...					0....	5273
24-FCAA	SAMAROKENA cluster	1	1	530	684		65.09	92	C	2		...					0....	5274
24-FCAA-a	Proper samarkena	1	1	530	684	0	65.09	92	C	2		...					0....	5275
24-FCAA-b	karfasia					0				2		...					0....	5276
24-FCAA-c	tamaya					0				2		...					0....	5277
24-FCAA-d	maseb					0				2		...					0....	5278
24-FD	ISIRAWA chain	1	1	2,206	2,844		64.91	96	C	22		P..					0....	5279
24-FDA	**ISIRAWA net**	1	1	2,206	2,844		64.91	96	C	22		P..					0....	5280
24-FDAA	ISIRAWA cluster	1	1	2,206	2,844		64.91	96	C	22	Isirawa	P..	1977-1992				0....	5281
24-FDAA-a	West isirawa					0				22		p..					0....	5282
24-FDAA-b	East isirawa					0				22		p..					0....	5283
24-G	**SENTANI-DEMTA set**	1	5	40,618	52,364		29.34	65	B	22		P..					0....	5284
24-GA	DEMTA chain	1	1	1,315	1,695		65.02	96	C	4		...					0....	5285
24-GAA	**DEMTA net**	1	1	1,315	1,695		65.02	96	C	4		...					0....	5286
24-GAAA	DEMTA cluster	1	1	1,315	1,695		65.02	96	C	4		...					0....	5287
24-GAAA-a	demta	1	1	1,315	1,695	0	65.02	96	C	4		...					0....	5288
24-GAAA-b	muris					0				4		...					0....	5289
24-GB	TABLA chain	1	2	5,048	6,508		60.74	91	C	22		P..					0....	5290
24-GBA	**TABLA net**	1	2	5,048	6,508		60.74	91	C	22		P..					0....	5291
24-GBAA	TABLA cluster	1	2	5,048	6,508		60.74	91	C	22	Tabla	P..	1986				0....	5292
24-GBAA-a	yokari					0				22		p..					0....	5293
24-GBAA-b	tepera	1	1	4,306	5,551	0	59.99	91	B	22	Tabla	P..	1986				0....	5294
24-GBAA-c	tawona					0				22		p..					0....	5295
24-GBAA-d	yewena-yongsu					0				22		p..					0....	5296
24-GC	SENTANI chain	1	1	31,710	40,880		20.00	58	B	22		P..					0....	5297
24-GCA	**SENTANI net**	1	1	31,710	40,880		20.00	58	B	22		P..					0....	5298
24-GCAA	BUYAKA cluster	1	1	31,710	40,880		20.00	58	B	22		P..					0....	5299
24-GCAA-a	West sentani					0				22		p..					0....	5300
24-GCAA-b	Central sentani	1	1	31,710	40,880	0	20.00	58	B	22	Sentani	P..	1984-1992				0....	5301
24-GCAA-c	East sentani					0				22		p..					0....	5302
24-GD	NAFRI chain	1	1	2,545	3,281		64.99	92	C	4		...					0....	5303
24-GDA	**NAFRI net**	1	1	2,545	3,281		64.99	92	C	4		...					0....	5304
24-GDAA	NAFRI cluster	1	1	2,545	3,281		64.99	92	C	4		...					0....	5305
24-GDAA-a	nafri	1	1	2,545	3,281	0	64.99	92	C	4		...					0....	5306
24-H	**KAYAGARI set**	1	3	16,587	21,383		36.99	64	B	4		...					0....	5307
24-HA	KAYAGARI chain	1	3	16,587	21,383		36.99	64	B	4		...					0....	5308
24-HAA	**KAUGAT net**	1	1	1,230	1,586		65.04	97	C	4		...					0....	5309
24-HAAA	ATOHWAIM cluster	1	1	1,230	1,586		65.04	97	C	4		...					0....	5310
24-HAAA-a	North atohwaim					0				4		...					0....	5311
24-HAAA-b	South atohwaim					0				4		...					0....	5312
24-HAB	**KAYGIR-TAMAGARIO net**	1	2	15,357	19,797		34.74	62	B	4		...					0....	5313
24-HABA	KAYGIR cluster	1	1	11,051	14,246		21.00	48	A	2		...					0....	5314
24-HABA-a	kaygir	1	1	11,051	14,246	0	21.00	48	A	2		...					0....	5315
24-HABB	TAMAGARIO cluster	1	1	4,306	5,551		70.00	97	C	4		...					0....	5316
24-HABB-a	tamaraw					0				4		...					0....	5317
24-HABB-b	buru					0				4		...					0....	5318
24-HABB-c	wagow					0				4		...					0....	5319
24-HABB-d	yogo					0				4		...					0....	5320
24-I	**MARIND-YAQAY set**	2	5	26,437	35,382		52.60	86	B	41		PN.					0....	5321
24-IA	YAQAY-WARKAY chain	1	2	12,684	16,352		49.72	84	B	2		...					0....	5322
24-IAA	**WARKAY net**	1	1	361	465		39.89	69	B	2		...					0....	5323
24-IAAA	WARKAY-BIPIM cluster	1	1	361	465		39.89	69	B	2		...					0....	5324
24-IAAA-a	warkay-bipim	1	1	361	465	0	39.89	69	B	2		...					0....	5325
24-IAB	**YAQAY net**	1	1	12,323	15,887		50.00	84	B	2		...					0....	5326
24-IABA	YAQAY cluster	1	1	12,323	15,887		50.00	84	B	2		...					0....	5327
24-IABA-a	yaqay	1	1	12,323	15,887	0	50.00	84	B	2		...					0....	5328
24-IABA-b	oba-miwamön					0				2		...					0....	5329
24-IABA-c	nambeomön-mabur					0				2		...					0....	5330
24-IABA-d	bapai					0				2		...					0....	5331
24-IABA-e	Lower mapi					0				2		...					0....	5332
24-IABA-f	sohur					0				2		...					0....	5333
24-IB	BIAN chain	1	2	9,969	12,852		64.86	97	C	4		...					0....	5334
24-IBA	**BIAN net**	1	2	9,969	12,852		64.86	97	C	4		...					0....	5335
24-IBAA	LOWER MARIND cluster	1	1	8,633	11,129		64.99	98	C	4		...					0....	5336
24-IBAA-a	Lower bian					0				4		...					0....	5337
24-IBAA-b	atih					0				4		...					0....	5338
24-IBAA-c	okaba					0				4		...					0....	5339
24-IBAA-d	merauke					0				4		...					0....	5340
24-IBAA-e	kumbe					0				4		...					0....	5341
24-IBAB	UPPER MARIND cluster	1	1	1,336	1,723		64.00	90	C	4		...					0....	5342
24-IBAB-a	Upper marind					0				4		...					0....	5343
24-IC	BOAZI-ZIMAKANI chain	1	1	3,784	6,178		29.99	64	B	41		PN.					0....	5344
24-ICA	**BOAZI-ZIMAKANI net**	1	1	3,784	6,178		29.99	64	B	41		PN.					0....	5345
24-ICAA	BOAZI cluster	2	1	2,000	3,400		30.00	65	B	2		...					0....	5346
24-ICAA-a	North boazi					0				2		...					0....	5347
24-ICAA-b	South boazi					0				2		...					0....	5348
24-ICAA-c	kuni					0				2		...					0....	5349
24-ICAB	ZIMAKANI cluster	1	1	1,784	2,778		29.99	62	B	41		PN.					0....	5350
24-ICAB-a	Proper zimakani	1	1	1,784	2,778	0	29.99	62	B	41	Zimakani	PN.	1958-1961	1989			0....	5351
24-ICAB-b	bagwa					0				41		pn.					0....	5352

Continued opposite

Table 9-13 continued

Code 1	REFERENCE NAME / Autoglossonym 2	Coun 3	Peo 4	Mother-tongue speakers in 2000 5	in 2025 6	Media radio 7	AC% 8	E% 9	Wld 10	Tr 11	Biblioglossonym 12	Print 13-15	P-activity 16	N-activity 17	B-activity 18	J-year 19	Jayuh 20-24	Ref 25
24-ICAB-c	dea					0				41		pn.					0....	5353
24-J	**GOGODALA-SUKI set**	1	4	16,458	25,620		63.73	91	C	41		PN.					0.s..	5354
24-JA	SUKI chain	1	1	2,489	3,875		40.02	77	B	41		PN.					0....	5355
24-JAA	**SUKI net**	1	1	2,489	3,875		40.02	77	B	41		PN.					0....	5356
24-JAAA	SUKI cluster	1	1	2,489	3,875		40.02	77	B	41		PN.					0....	5357
24-JAAA-a	suki	1	1	2,489	3,875	0	40.02	77	B	41	Suki	PN.	1952-1956	1982			0....	5358
24-JB	GOGODALA-WARUNA chain	1	3	13,969	21,745		67.95	93	C	41		PN.					0.s..	5359
24-JBA	**WARUNA net**	1	1	698	1,086		39.97	66	B	0		...					0....	5360
24-JBAA	WARUNA cluster	1	1	698	1,086		39.97	66	B	0		...					0....	5361
24-JBAA-a	waruna	1	1	698	1,086	0	39.97	66	B	0		...					0....	5362
24-JBB	**ARI net**	1	1	1,646	2,562		30.01	59	B	5		...					0....	5363
24-JBBA	ARI cluster	1	1	1,646	2,562		30.01	59	B	5		...					0....	5364
24-JBBA-a	ari	1	1	1,646	2,562	0	30.01	59	B	5		...					0....	5365
24-JBC	**GOGODALA net**	1	1	11,625	18,097		75.00	100	C	41		PN.					0.s..	5368
24-JBCA	GOGODALA cluster	1	1	11,625	18,097		75.00	100	C	41		PN.					0.s..	5369
24-JBCA-a	gogodala	1	1	11,625	18,097	1	75.00	100	C	41	Gogodala	PN.	1942-1988	1981			0.s..	5370
24-JBCA-b	adiba					1				41		pn.					0.s..	5371
24-K	**SOUTH CENTRAL IRIANIC. set**	2	75	278,833	395,943		68.11	94	C	41		PN.					0.s..	5372
24-KA	ASMAT-ASIENARA chain	1	10	50,060	64,661		69.61	99	C	41		PN.					0....	5373
24-KAA	**ASIENARA-IRIA net**	1	2	2,736	3,528		65.02	93	C	2		...					0....	5374
24-KAAA	ASIENARA cluster	1	1	1,018	1,313		65.03	92	C	2		...					0....	5375
24-KAAA-a	North asienara					0				2		...					0....	5376
24-KAAA-b	South asienara					0				2		...					0....	5377
24-KAAB	IRIA cluster	1	1	1,718	2,215		65.02	93	C	2		...					0....	5378
24-KAAB-a	West iria					0				2		...					0....	5379
24-KAAB-b	Central iria					0				2		...					0....	5380
24-KAAB-c	East iria					0				2		...					0....	5381
24-KAB	**ASMAT-KAMORO net**	1	8	47,324	61,133		69.87	99	C	41		PN.					0....	5382
24-KABA	KAMORO cluster	1	1	9,863	12,715		65.00	100	C	4		...					0....	5383
24-KABA-a	oba					0				4		...					0....	5384
24-KABA-b	umari					0				4		...					0....	5385
24-KABA-c	tarya					0				4		...					0....	5386
24-KABA-d	Central kamoro	1	1	9,863	12,715	0	65.00	100	C	4		...					0....	5387
24-KABA-e	kamora					0				4		...					0....	5390
24-KABA-f	wania					0				4		...					0....	5391
24-KABA-g	Upper wania					0				4		...					0....	5392
24-KABA-h	mukamuga					0				4		...					0....	5393
24-KABA-i	nefarpi					0				4		...					0....	5394
24-KABB	SEMPAN cluster	1	1	1,230	1,586		60.00	90	C	4		...					0....	5395
24-KABB-a	Proper sempan	1	1	1,230	1,586	0	60.00	90	C	4		...					0....	5396
24-KABB-b	nararapi					0				4		...					0....	5397
24-KABC	NORTH ASMAT cluster	1	1	300	510		80.00	100	C	4		...					0....	5398
24-KABC-a	Upper tiemaro					0				4		...					0....	5399
24-KABC-b	Lower tiemaro					0				4		...					0....	5400
24-KABD	CENTRAL ASMAT cluster	1	2	12,875	16,598		80.00	100	C	41	Asmat, Central	PN.	1966-1976	1985			0....	5401
24-KABD-a	kawenak					0				41		pn.					0....	5402
24-KABD-b	keenok	1	1	1,124	1,449	0	79.98	100	C	41		pn.					0....	5407
24-KABD-c	keenakap					0				41		pn.					0....	5410
24-KABD-d	sokoni					0				41		pn.					0....	5411
24-KABD-e	sirow					0				41		pn.					0....	5412
24-KABD-f	ayam					0				41	Asmat: Ajam	PN.	1966	1985			0....	5413
24-KABD-g	angadi					0				41		pn.					0....	5414
24-KABD-h	kajakaja					0				41		pn.					0....	5415
24-KABE	CITAK-TAMNIM cluster	1	1	318	410		60.06	88	C	22		P..					0....	5416
24-KABE-a	citak-tamnim	1	1	318	410	0	60.06	88	C	22	Citak	P..	1979				0....	5417
24-KABF	CITAK-ASMAT cluster	1	1	10,202	13,153		55.00	100	B	41	Citak	PN.	1979-1989	1995			0....	5422
24-KABF-a	senggo					0				41		pn.					0....	5423
24-KABF-b	komasma					0				41		pn.					0....	5424
24-KABF-c	jinak					0				41		pn.					0....	5425
24-KABF-d	bubis					0				41		pn.					0....	5426
24-KABF-e	esaun					0				41		pn.					0....	5427
24-KABF-f	pirabanak					0				41		pn.					0....	5428
24-KABF-g	vakam					0				41		pn.					0....	5429
24-KABG	CASUARINA-ASMAT cluster	1	1	10,266	13,235		80.00	100	C	12	Asmat, Casuarina Coast	...					0....	5430
24-KABG-a	batia					0				12		...					0....	5431
24-KABG-b	sapan					0				12		...					0....	5432
24-KABH	YAOSAKOR-ASMAT cluster	1	1	2,270	2,926		60.00	95	C	41		PN.					0....	5433
24-KABH-a	yaosakor-asmat	1	1	2,270	2,926	0	60.00	95	C	41	Asmat, Yaosakor	PN.		1995			0....	5434
24-KB	SOMAHAI chain	1	1	3,330	4,293		63.99	99	C	22		P..					0....	5435
24-KBA	**SOMAHAI net**	1	1	3,330	4,293		63.99	99	C	22		P..					0....	5436
24-KBAA	SOMAHAI cluster	1	1	3,330	4,293		63.99	99	C	22		P..					0....	5437
24-KBAA-a	momuna	1	1	3,330	4,293	0	63.99	99	C	22	Momuna	P..	1985-1987				0....	5438
24-KC	MOMBUM-KONERAW chain	1	4	1,315	1,695		49.51	70	B	4		...					0....	5439
24-KCA	**MOMBUM net**	1	1	318	410		61.95	90	C	4		...					0....	5440
24-KCAA	MOMBUM cluster	1	1	318	410		61.95	90	C	4		...					5441
24-KCAA-a	mombum	1	1	318	410	0	61.95	90	C	4		...					0....	5442
24-KCB	**KONERAW net**	1	3	997	1,285		45.54	64	B	4		...					0....	5443
24-KCBA	KONERAW cluster	1	3	997	1,285		45.54	64	B	4		...					0....	5444
24-KCBA-a	koneraw	1	1	445	574	0	62.02	89	C	4		...					0....	5445
24-KD	AWYU-SAWI chain	2	14	77,180	105,583		64.67	95	C	41		PN.					0....	5446
24-KDA	**SAWI net**	1	1	3,860	4,977		85.00	100	C	41		PN.					0....	5447
24-KDAA	SAWI cluster	1	1	3,860	4,977		85.00	100	C	41		PN.					0....	5448
24-KDAA-a	sawi	1	1	3,860	4,977	0	85.00	100	C	41	Sawi	PN.	1994	1973-1994			0....	5449
24-KDB	**AWYU net**	1	8	49,725	68,377		64.30	96	C	12		...					0....	5452

Continued overleaf

Table 9-13 continued

Code 1	REFERENCE NAME / Autoglossonym 2	Coun 3	Peo 4	Mother-tongue speakers in 2000 5	in 2025 6	Media radio 7	CHURCH AC% 8	E% 9	Wld 10	Tr 11	Biblioglossonym 12	Print 13-15	P–activity 16	N–activity 17	B–activity 18	J-year 19	Jayuh 20-24	Ref 25
24-KDBA	AIRO-SUMAGAXE cluster	1	1	2,000	3,400		70.00	98	C	0		. . .					0	5453
24-KDBA-a	North airo-sumagaxe									0		. . .					0	5454
24-KDBA-b	Central airo-sumagaxe					0				0		. . .					0	5455
24-KDBA-c	South airo-sumagaxe					0				0		. . .					0	5456
24-KDBB	PISA cluster	1	1	764	984		70.03	98	C	4		. . .					0	5457
24-KDBB-a	kampung	1	1	764	984	0	70.03	98	C	4		. . .					0	5458
24-KDBB-b	wildeman					0				4		. . .					0	5459
24-KDBC	KOROWAI-KAEME cluster	1	1	2,460	3,172		60.00	91	C	4		. . .					0	5460
24-KDBC-a	korowai	1	1	2,460	3,172	0	60.00	91	C	4		. . .					0	5461
24-KDBC-b	kaeme									4		. . .					0	5462
24-KDBD	SIAGHA-YENIMU cluster	1	1	3,691	4,758		65.00	94	C	4		. . .					0	5463
24-KDBD-a	yenimu					0				4		. . .					0	5464
24-KDBD-b	siagha					0				4		. . .					0	5465
24-KDBE	UPPER MAPI cluster	1	1	3,000	5,100		60.00	93	C	0		. . .					0	5466
24-KDBE-a	Upper mapi	1	1	3,000	5,100	0	60.00	93	C	0		. . .					0	5467
24-KDBF	EDERAH cluster	1	1	400	680		65.00	96	C	0		. . .					0	5468
24-KDBF-a	ederah	1	1	400	680	0	65.00	96	C	0		. . .					0	5469
24-KDBG	WEST KIA cluster	1	1	2,000	3,400		60.00	93	C	0		. . .					0	5470
24-KDBG-a	West kia	1	1	2,000	3,400	0	60.00	93	C	0		. . .					0	5471
24-KDBH	AWYU cluster	1	4	31,859	41,072		64.73	98	C	12	Awyu, Nohon	. . .					0	5472
24-KDBH-a	dyair	1	1	3,691	4,758	0	65.00	95	C	12		. . .					0	5473
24-KDBH-b	yair					0				12		. . .					0	5474
24-KDBH-c	nohon	1	1	22,165	28,575	0	65.00	100	C	12		. . .					0	5475
24-KDBH-d	miaro	1	1	4,306	5,551	0	65.00	94	C	12	Awyu, Miaro	. . .					0	5476
24-KDBH-e	avio					0				12		. . .					0	5477
24-KDBI	UPPER DIGUL cluster	1	1	3,000	5,100		65.00	96	C	0		. . .					0	5478
24-KDBI-a	Upper digul	1	1	3,000	5,100	0	65.00	96	C	0		. . .					0	5479
24-KDBJ	KOTOGüT cluster	1	1	551	711		60.07	89	C	4		. . .					0	5480
24-KDBJ-a	kotogüt	1	1	551	711	0	60.07	89	C	4		. . .					0	5481
24-KDBJ-b	tsokwambo					0				4		. . .					0	5482
24-KDC	**DUMUT net**	2	5	23,595	32,229		62.13	92	C	12		. . .					0	5483
24-KDCA	WANGGOM cluster	1	2	6,024	7,766		64.99	98	C	0		. . .					0	5484
24-KDCA-a	wanggom	1	2	6,024	7,766	0	64.99	98	C	0		. . .					0	5485
24-KDCB	KAETI-WAMBON cluster	2	3	17,571	24,463		61.15	90	C	12		. . .					0	5486
24-KDCB-a	North wambon					0				12		. . .					0	5487
24-KDCB-b	South wambon					0				12		. . .					0	5488
24-KDCB-c	rungwayap									12		. . .					0	5489
24-KDCB-d	kambon	1	1	7,106	9,160	0	65.00	96	C	12		. . .					0	5490
24-KDCB-e	South kaeti					0				12		. . .					0	5491
24-KDCB-f	mandobo					0				12	Mandobo	. . .					0	5492
24-KDCB-g	Southeast kaeti	1	1	6,774	10,545	0	55.00	80	B	12		. . .					0	5493
24-KE	OK chain	2	22	93,662	136,758		69.21	95	C	41		PN.					0.s..	5494
24-KEA	**MUYU net**	2	9	45,800	65,658		66.93	94	C	22		P. .					0.s..	5495
24-KEAA	SOUTH KATI cluster									4		. . .					0	5496
24-KEAA-a	metomka					0				4		. . .					0	5497
24-KEAA-b	kowan					0				4		. . .					0	5498
24-KEAB	YONGGOM cluster	2	4	23,088	35,007		71.96	97	C	22		P. .					0.s..	5499
24-KEAB-a	yonggom	2	2	21,127	32,232	1	74.14	99	C	22	Yongkom*	P. .	1965-1988				0.s..	5500
24-KEAC	NORTH KATI cluster	1	2	14,784	19,059		63.34	93	C	4		. . .					0	5501
24-KEAC-a	niinati					0				4		. . .					0	5502
24-KEAC-b	kanggewot					0				4		. . .					0	5503
24-KEAC-c	tumutu					0				4		. . .					0	5504
24-KEAC-d	sibil					0				4		. . .					0	5505
24-KEAD	IWUR cluster	1	1	1,230	1,586		65.04	90	C	4		. . .					0	5506
24-KEAD-a	iwur	1	1	1,230	1,586	0	65.04	90	C	4		. . .					0	5507
24-KEAE	NINGGERUM cluster	2	2	6,698	10,006		57.88	89	B	12		. . .					0	5508
24-KEAE-a	ninggerum	1	1	1,570	2,023	0	64.01	91	C	12	Ninggerum	. . .					0	5509
24-KEAE-b	kasuwa					0				12		. . .					0	5510
24-KEAE-c	daupka					0				12		. . .					0	5511
24-KEAE-d	kativa					0				12		. . .					0	5512
24-KEAE-e	obgwo	1	1	5,128	7,983	0	56.01	88	B	12	Ninggerum	. . .					0	5513
24-KEAE-f	tedi					0				12		. . .					0	5514
24-KEB	**UPPER OK net**	2	13	47,862	71,100		71.39	95	C	41		PN.					0	5515
24-KEBA	KAUWOL cluster	2	2	747	1,049		75.77	95	C	2		. . .					0	5516
24-KEBA-a	kauwol	2	2	747	1,049	0	75.77	95	C	2		. . .					0	5517
24-KEBB	TIFAL cluster	1	1	3,720	5,791		30.00	61	B	22		P. .					0	5518
24-KEBB-a	tifal-min	1	1	3,720	5,791	0	30.00	61	B	22	Tifal	P. .	1969-1979				0	5519
24-KEBB-b	busil-min					0				22		p. .					0	5520
24-KEBB-c	wopkei-min					0				22		P. .					0	5521
24-KEBB-d	atbal-min									22		P. .					0	5522
24-KEBC	URAP cluster	1	1	604	940		79.97	100	C	4		. . .					0	5523
24-KEBC-a	urap-min	1	1	604	940	0	79.97	100	C	4		. . .					0	5524
24-KEBD	FAIWOL cluster	1	1	5,600	8,718		80.00	100	C	41		PN.					0	5525
24-KEBD-a	faiwol-min	1	1	5,600	8,718	0	80.00	100	C	41	Faiwol	PN.	1980-1990	1995			0	5526
24-KEBD-b	unkia					0				41		pn.					0	5527
24-KEBE	BI cluster	1	1	2,325	3,619		80.00	100	C	12		. . .					0	5528
24-KEBE-a	bi-min	1	1	2,325	3,619	0	80.00	100	C	12	Bimin	. . .					0	5529
24-KEBE-b	kwei-min					0				12		. . .					0	5530
24-KEBF	SELTA cluster	1	2	516	804		35.66	59	B	4		. . .					0	5531
24-KEBF-a	selta-min	1	2	516	804	0	35.66	59	B	4		. . .					0	5532
24-KEBG	TELEFOL cluster	1	1	6,183	9,626		70.00	100	C	41		PN.					0	5533
24-KEBG-a	fera-min					0				41		pn.					0	5534
24-KEBG-b	telefol-min	1	1	6,183	9,626	0	70.00	100	C	41	Telefol	PN.	1966-1969	1988			0	5535
24-KEBH	MIAN cluster	1	1	3,197	4,977		85.02	100	C	41	Mian	PN.	1975-1977	1986			0	5536
24-KEBH-a	mian-min	1	1	3,197	4,977	0	85.02	100	C	41	Mianmin	PN.	1974	1986			0	5537
24-KEBH-b	august-min					0				41		pn.					0	5538
24-KEBH-c	usage					0				41		pn.					0	5539
24-KEBI	SUGANGA cluster	1	1	1,017	1,584		29.99	57	B	4		. . .					0	5540
24-KEBI-a	suganga	1	1	1,017	1,584	0	29.99	57	B	4		. . .					0	5541
24-KEBJ	NGALUM cluster	2	2	23,953	33,992		75.68	100	C	41	Ngalum	PN.	1974-1991	1992			0	5542
24-KEBJ-a	apmi-sibil					0				41		pn.					0	5543
24-KEBJ-b	Central ngalum					0				41		pn.					0	5544
24-KEBJ-c	South ngalum					0				41		pn.					0	5545

Continued opposite

Table 9-13 continued

Code 1	REFERENCE NAME / Autoglossonym 2	Coun 3	Peo 4	Mother-tongue speakers in 2000 5	in 2025 6	Media radio 7	AC% 8	E% 9	Wld 10	Tr 11	Biblioglossonym 12	Print 13-15	P-activity 16	N-activity 17	B-activity 18	J-year 19	Jayuh 20-24	Ref 25
24-KF	AWIN-KAMULA chain	1	5	15,175	23,624		79.50	92	C	41		PN.					0.s..	5546
24-KFA	**AWIN-PA net**	1	4	14,288	22,243		82.26	94	C	41		PN.					0.s..	5547
24-KFAA	AWIN cluster	1	1	9,955	15,498		90.01	100	C	41	Aekyom	PN.	1958-1964	1987			0.s..	5548
24-KFAA-a	North awin					0				41		pn.					0.s..	5549
24-KFAA-b	South awin					0				41		pn.					0.s..	5550
24-KFAA-c	East awin					0				41		pn.					0.s..	5551
24-KFAB	PA cluster	1	3	4,333	6,745		64.48	81	C	35		P..					0.s..	5552
24-KFAB-a	pare	1	1	2,489	3,875	0	90.08	100	C	35	Pa*	P..	1978-1980				0.s..	5553
24-KFB	**KAMULA net**	1	1	887	1,381		34.95	64	B	12		...					0....	5554
24-KFBA	KAMULA cluster	1	1	887	1,381		34.95	64	B	12		...					0....	5555
24-KFBA-a	kamula	1	1	887	1,381	0	34.95	64	B	12	Kamula	...					0....	5556
24-KG	EAST STRICKLAND chain	1	5	7,966	12,402		63.56	84	C	22		P..					0....	5557
24-KGA	**KUBO net**	1	3	6,795	10,578		67.62	87	C	22		P..					0....	5558
24-KGAA	KALAMO cluster	1	3	6,795	10,578		67.62	87	C	22	Kalamo	P..					0....	5559
24-KGAA-a	bibo					0				22		p..					0....	5560
24-KGAA-b	honibo					0				22		p..					0....	5561
24-KGAA-c	samo	1	1	4,214	6,560	0	85.00	100	C	22	Samo-kubo	P..	1980				0....	5562
24-KGAA-d	kubo					0				22		p..					0....	5563
24-KGAA-e	oiba					0				22		p..					0....	5564
24-KGAA-f	gobasi	1	1	1,982	3,085	0	29.97	57	B	22		p..					0....	5565
24-KGB	**KONAI net**	1	1	735	1,145		40.00	64	B	12		...					0....	5566
24-KGBA	KONAI cluster	1	1	735	1,145		40.00	64	B	12		...					0....	5567
24-KGBA-a	konai	1	1	735	1,145	0	40.00	64	B	12	Konai	...					0....	5568
24-KGC	**AGALA net**	1	1	436	679		39.91	64	B	4		...					0....	5569
24-KGCA	AGALA cluster	1	1	436	679		39.91	64	B	4		...					0....	5570
24-KGCA-a	agala	1	1	436	679	0	39.91	64	B	4		...					0....	5571
24-KH	DUNA-POGAYA chain	1	2	13,224	20,586		87.38	99	C	41		PN.					0....	5572
24-KHA	**POGAYA net**	1	2	13,224	20,586		87.38	99	C	41		PN.					0....	5573
24-KHAA	POGAYA cluster	1	1	436	679		39.91	65	B	2		...					0....	5574
24-KHAA-a	pogaya	1	1	436	679	0	39.91	65	B	2		...					0....	5575
24-KHAB	DUNA cluster	1	1	12,788	19,907		89.00	100	C	41		PN.					0....	5576
24-KHAB-a	duna	1	1	12,788	19,907	0	89.00	100	C	41	Duna	PN.	1968	1976			0....	5577
24-KI	BOSAVI chain	1	11	15,177	23,626		54.91	81	B	41		PN.					0.s..	5578
24-KIA	**BEAMI net**	1	1	6,103	9,502		70.00	100	C	41		PN.					0....	5579
24-KIAA	BEAMI cluster	1	1	6,103	9,502		70.00	100	C	41	Bedamuni*	PN.	1977	1991			0....	5580
24-KIAA-a	North beami					0				41		pn.					0....	5581
24-KIAA-b	komo_o					0				41		pn.					0....	5582
24-KIB	**ETORO net**	1	1	1,134	1,765		64.99	92	C	12		...					0....	5583
24-KIBA	ETORO cluster	1	1	1,134	1,765		64.99	92	C	12		...					0....	5584
24-KIBA-a	etoro	1	1	1,134	1,765	0	64.99	92	C	12	Edolo	...					0....	5585
24-KIC	**BAINAPI net**	1	1	581	905		29.95	54	B	2		...					0....	5586
24-KICA	BAINAPI cluster	1	1	581	905		29.95	54	B	2		...					0....	5587
24-KICA-a	bainapi	1	1	581	905	0	29.95	54	B	2		...					0....	5588
24-KID	**ONABASULU net**	1	1	684	1,065		35.09	64	B	33		P..					0....	5589
24-KIDA	ONABASULU cluster	1	1	684	1,065		35.09	64	B	33		P..					0....	5590
24-KIDA-a	onabasulu	1	1	684	1,065	0	35.09	64	B	33	Onobasulu*	P..	1996				0....	5591
24-KIE	**SONIA net**	1	2	1,315	2,047		74.98	88	C	4		...					0....	5592
24-KIEA	SONIA cluster	1	2	1,315	2,047		74.98	88	C	4		...					0....	5593
24-KIEA-a	sonia	1	1	393	612	0	39.95	61	B	4		...					0....	5594
24-KIF	**TOMU net**	1	1	436	679		39.91	62	B	0		...					0....	5595
24-KIFA	TOMU cluster	1	1	436	679		39.91	62	B	0		...					0....	5596
24-KIFA-a	tomu	1	1	436	679	0	39.91	62	B	0		...					0....	5597
24-KIG	**KWARE net**	1	2	1,308	2,036		23.32	47	A	22		P..					0....	5598
24-KIGA	KWARE cluster	1	2	1,308	2,036		23.32	47	A	22		P..					0....	5599
24-KIGA-a	kware	1	1	581	905	0	39.93	63	B	22	Kware	P..	1994				0....	5600
24-KIGA-b	aimele	1	1	727	1,131	0	10.04	35	A	22		p..					0....	5601
24-KIH	**KALULI net**	1	1	2,863	4,456		39.99	67	B	12		...					0.s..	5602
24-KIHA	KALULI cluster	1	1	2,863	4,456		39.99	67	B	12		...					0.s..	5603
24-KIHA-a	kaluli	1	1	2,863	4,456	0	39.99	67	B	12	Kaluli	...					0.s..	5604
24-KII	**KASUA net**	1	1	753	1,171		39.97	67	B	12		...					0....	5605
24-KIIA	KASUA cluster	1	1	753	1,171		39.97	67	B	12		...					0....	5606
24-KIIA-a	kasua	1	1	753	1,171	0	39.97	67	B	12	Kasua	...					0....	5607
24-KJ	WEST KUTUBUAN chain	1	1	1,744	2,715		29.99	60	B	41		PN.					0....	5608
24-KJA	**FASU net**	1	1	1,744	2,715		29.99	60	B	41		PN.					0....	5609
24-KJAA	FASU cluster	1	1	1,744	2,715		29.99	60	B	41		PN.					0....	5610
24-KJAA-a	namome					0				41		pn.					0....	5611
24-KJAA-b	Proper fasu	1	1	1,744	2,715	0	29.99	60	B	41	Fasu	PN.	1964	1976-1995			0....	5612
24-KJAA-c	some					0				41		pn.					0....	5613
24-KJAA-d	kaibu					0				41		pn.					0....	5614
24-L	**ANGAL-ENGA set**	1	19	597,547	930,237		88.19	100	C	51		PN.					1.su.	5615
24-LA	WIRU chain	1	1	22,223	34,596		84.00	100	C	41		PN.					0....	5616
24-LAA	**WIRU net**	1	1	22,223	34,596		84.00	100	C	41		PN.					0....	5617
24-LAAA	WIRU cluster	1	1	22,223	34,596		84.00	100	C	41		PN.					0....	5618
24-LAAA-a	wiru	1	1	22,223	34,596	0	84.00	100	C	41	Wiru	PN.	1967-1968	1990			0....	5619
24-LB	ANGAL-KEWA chain	1	8	197,408	307,315		88.18	100	C	42		PN.					0.s..	5620
24-LBA	**SAMBERIGI net**	1	1	4,541	7,070		85.00	100	C	41		PN.					0.s..	5621
24-LBAA	SAMBERIGI cluster	1	1	4,541	7,070		85.00	100	C	41		PN.					0.s..	5622

Continued overleaf

Table 9-13 continued

Code 1	REFERENCE NAME / Autoglossonym 2	Coun 3	Peo 4	in 2000 5	in 2025 6	Media radio 7	AC% 8	E% 9	Wld 10	Tr 11	Biblioglossonym 12	Print 13-15	P-activity 16	N-activity 17	B-activity 18	J-year 19	Jayuh 20-24	Ref 25
24-LBAA-a	samberigi	1	1	4,541	7,070	0	85.00	100	C	41	Samberigi	PN.	1970-1993	1993			0.s..	5623
24-LBB	**KEWA net**	1	3	78,240	121,800		87.71	100	C	42		PN.					0.s..	5624
24-LBBA	SOUTH KEWA cluster	1	1	7,467	11,624		85.00	100	C	41		PN.					0.s..	5625
24-LBBA-a	Southeast kewa					0				41		pn.					0.s..	5626
24-LBBA-b	pole (Erave)					0				41	Pole	PN.	1975	1993			0.s..	5627
24-LBBB	EAST KEWA cluster	1	1	35,382	55,081		91.00	100	C	22		P..					0....	5628
24-LBBB-a	East kewa	1	1	35,382	55,081	0	91.00	100	C	22	Kewa: East*	P..	1967-1988				0....	5629
24-LBBC	WEST KEWA cluster	1	1	35,391	55,095		85.00	100	C	42		PN.					0....	5630
24-LBBC-a	pasuma	1	1	35,391	55,095	0	85.00	100	C	42		pn.					0....	5631
24-LBBC-b	Northwest kewa					0				42	Kewa: West*	PN.		1973			0....	5632
24-LBC	**ANGAL net**	1	4	114,627	178,445		88.62	100	C	41		PN.					0.s..	5633
24-LBCA	SOUTH ANGAL cluster	1	2	49,513	77,080		88.50	100	C	35	Angal Enen	P..	1968-1996				0....	5634
24-LBCA-a	South nembi	1	1	24,889	38,746	0	89.00	100	C	35	Nembi	P..	1979				0....	5635
24-LBCA-b	megi					0				35		p..					0....	5636
24-LBCB	WEST ANGAL cluster	1	1	46,510	72,404		89.00	100	C	41	Angal Heneng	PN.	1967	1978			0....	5637
24-LBCB-a	augu					0				41		pn.					0....	5638
24-LBCB-b	nipa					0				41		pn.					0....	5639
24-LBCB-c	waola					0				41		pn.					0....	5640
24-LBCC	NORTH ANGAL cluster	1	1	18,604	28,961		88.00	100	C	35		P..					0.s..	5641
24-LBCC-a	mendi	1	1	18,604	28,961	1	88.00	100	C	35	Mendi*	P..	1990				0.s..	5642
24-LC	HULI chain	1	1	87,111	135,611		95.00	100	C	51		PN.					1.su.	5643
24-LCA	**HULI net**	1	1	87,111	135,611		95.00	100	C	51		PN.					1.su.	5644
24-LCAA	HULI cluster	1	1	87,111	135,611		95.00	100	C	51		PN.					1.su.	5645
24-LCAA-a	huli	1	1	87,111	135,611	1	95.00	100	C	51	Huli	PN.	1965-1991	1983		1995	1.su.	5646
24-LD	ENGA-LEMBENA chain	1	9	290,805	452,715		86.47	99	C	42		PN.					0.s..	5649
24-LDA	**ENGA-IPILI net**	1	8	289,088	450,041		86.92	100	C	42		PN.					0.s..	5650
24-LDAA	KATINJA cluster	1	1	1,777	2,767		35.00	60	B	0		...					0....	5651
24-LDAA-a	katinja	1	1	1,777	2,767	0	35.00	60	B	0		...					0....	5652
24-LDAB	ENGA cluster	1	3	274,116	426,734		87.38	100	C	42		PN.					0.s..	5653
24-LDAB-b	laiagam					1				42		pn.					0.s..	5654
24-LDAB-c	tayato					1				42		pn.					0.s..	5655
24-LDAB-d	maramuni					1				42		pn.					0.s..	5656
24-LDAB-e	yandapo					1				42		pn.					0.s..	5657
24-LDAB-f	mae	1	1	225,799	351,516	1	87.00	100	C	42	Enga	PN.	1965	1979-1988			0.s..	5659
24-LDAB-g	kaina					1				42		pn.					0.s..	5660
24-LDAB-h	layapo					1				42		pn.					0.s..	5661
24-LDAB-i	sau-enga	1	1	25,984	40,451	1	91.00	100	C	42	Enga: Sau	PN.	1970	1979			0.s..	5662
24-LDAB-j	kapona					1				42		pn.					0.s..	5667
24-LDAB-k	kyaka	1	1	22,333	34,767	1	87.00	100	C	42	Enga: Kyaka*	PN.	1961-1987	1973			0.s..	5668
24-LDAC	IPILI cluster	1	1	11,283	17,564		85.00	100	C	22		P..					0....	5671
24-LDAC-a	tipinini					0				22		p..					0....	5672
24-LDAC-b	West ipili	1	1	11,283	17,564	0	85.00	100	C	22	Ipili	P..	1978				0....	5673
24-LDAD	NETE cluster	1	1	1,415	2,203		90.04	100	C	12		...					0....	5674
24-LDAD-a	nete	1	1	1,415	2,203	0	90.04	100	C	12	Nete	...					0....	5675
24-LDAE	BISORIO-INIAI cluster	1	2	497	773		56.14	81	B	41		PN.					0....	5676
24-LDAE-a	East pikaru	1	1	145	226	0	10.34	35	A	41		pn.					0....	5677
24-LDAE-b	bisorio	1	1	352	547	0	75.00	100	C	41	Bisorio	PN.	1984	1993			0....	5678
24-LDAE-c	gadio					0				41		pn.					0....	5679
24-LDAE-d	iniai					0				41		pn.					0....	5680
24-LDB	**LEMBENA net**	1	1	1,717	2,674		10.02	38	A	12		...					0....	5681
24-LDBA	LEMBENA cluster	1	1	1,717	2,674		10.02	38	A	12		...					0....	5682
24-LDBA-a	lembena	1	1	1,717	2,674	0	10.02	38	A	12	Lembena	...					0....	5683
24-LDBA-b	yariba					0				12		...					0....	5684
24-LDBA-c	maibi					0				12		...					0....	5685
24-M	**KALAM-ARAMO set**	1	7	35,171	55,396		76.31	97	C	41		PN.					0.s..	5686
24-MA	KALAM-KOBON chain	1	3	25,549	39,773		83.18	100	C	41		PN.					0....	5687
24-MAA	**KALAM-KOBON net**	1	2	24,397	37,980		83.57	100	C	41		PN.					0....	5688
24-MAAA	KOBON cluster	1	1	6,975	10,858		75.00	100	C	22		P..					0....	5689
24-MAAA-a	kobon	1	1	6,975	10,858	0	75.00	100	C	22	Kobon	P..	1988				0....	5690
24-MAAB	KALAM cluster	1	1	17,422	27,122		87.00	100	C	41		PN.					0....	5691
24-MAAB-a	kalam	1	1	17,422	27,122	0	87.00	100	C	41	Kalam	PN.	1982-1986	1992			0....	5692
24-MAB	**TAI net**	1	1	1,152	1,793		75.00	100	C	35		P..					0....	5693
24-MABA	TAI cluster	1	1	1,152	1,793		75.00	100	C	35		P..					0....	5694
24-MABA-a	tai	1	1	1,152	1,793	0	75.00	100	C	35	Tay*	P..	1995				0....	5695
24-MB	GANTS chain	1	1	2,738	4,262		74.98	100	C	4		...					0....	5696
24-MBA	**GANTS net**	1	1	2,738	4,262		74.98	100	C	4		...					0....	5697
24-MBAA	GANTS cluster	1	1	2,738	4,262		74.98	100	C	4		...					0....	5698
24-MBAA-a	gants	1	1	2,738	4,262	0	74.98	100	C	4		...					0....	5699
24-MC	WAIBUK chain	1	1	1,245	1,938		40.00	72	B	2		...					0....	5700
24-MCA	**WAIBUK net**	1	1	1,245	1,938		40.00	72	B	2		...					0....	5701
24-MCAA	HARUAI cluster	1	1	1,245	1,938		40.00	72	B	2		...					0....	5702
24-MCAA-a	hamil					0				2		...					0....	5703
24-MCAA-b	mambar	1	1	1,245	1,938	0	40.00	72	B	2		...					0....	5704
24-MCAA-c	arama					0				2		...					0....	5705
24-MD	ARAMO-PINAI chain	1	2	5,639	9,423		53.84	87	B	12		...					0....	5706
24-MDA	**ARAMO-PINAI net**	1	2	5,639	9,423		53.84	87	B	12		...					0....	5707
24-MDAA	ARAMO cluster	1	1	436	679		39.91	64	B	0		...					0....	5708
24-MDAA-a	hagahai	1	1	436	679	0	39.91	64	B	0		...					0....	5709
24-MDAB	PINAI cluster	1	1	703	1,094		55.05	84	B	12		...					0....	5710
24-MDAB-a	pinai	1	1	703	1,094	0	55.05	84	B	12	Pinai	...					0....	5711
24-MDAC	WAPI cluster	1	1	2,000	3,400		55.00	90	B	0		...					0....	5715
24-MDAC-a	wapi	1	1	2,000	3,400	0	55.00	90	B	0		...					0....	5716
24-MDAD	EREM cluster	1	1	2,500	4,250		55.00	90	B	0		...					0....	5717

Continued opposite

Table 9-13 continued

Code 1	REFERENCE NAME / Autoglossonym 2	Coun 3	Peo 4	Mother-tongue speakers in 2000 5	in 2025 6	Media radio 7	AC% 8	E% 9	Wld 10	Tr 11	Biblioglossonym 12	Print 13-15	P-activity 16	N-activity 17	B-activity 18	J-year 19	Jayuh 20-24	Ref 25
24-MDAD-a	erem	1	1	2,500	4,250	0	55.00	90	B	0		. . .					0....	5718
24-N	**CHIMBU-JIMI set**	1	21	689,873	1,077,551		86.88	100	C	42		PN.					1.s..	5719
24-NA	HAGEN chain	1	5	231,861	360,953		87.13	100	C	41		PN.					1.s..	5720
24-NAA	**HAGEN net**	1	5	231,861	360,953		87.13	100	C	41		PN.					1.s..	5721
24-NAAA	MEDLPA cluster	1	1	151,125	235,266		87.50	100	C	41		PN.					1.s..	5722
24-NAAA-a	Proper medlpa	1	1	151,125	235,266	1	87.50	100	C	41	Melpa*	PN.	1956-1991	1965-1996		1995	1.s..	5723
24-NAAA-b	tembagla					1				41		pn.					1.s..	5724
24-NAAB	UMBU-UNGU cluster	1	4	80,736	125,687		86.43	99	C	41	Imbongu	PN.	1990				0.s..	5725
24-NAAB-a	kaugel	1	1	28,627	44,566	1	83.00	100	C	41	Umbu-ungu: Kala	PN.	1967-1990	1995			0.s..	5726
24-NAAB-b	kala					1				41		pn.					0.s..	5727
24-NAAB-c	penge					1				41	Umbu-ungu: No-penge	PN.	1987	1995			0.s..	5728
24-NAAB-d	andelale					1				41		pn.					0.s..	5729
24-NAAB-e	tembogia	1	1	30,187	46,994	1	91.00	100	C	41	Umbu-ungu: Tambul*	PN.	1967-1990				0.s..	5730
24-NAAB-f	miyemu					1				41		pn.					0.s..	5731
24-NAAB-g	mara-gomu					1				41	Kaugel: Mara-gomu	Pn.	1990				0.s..	5732
24-NAAB-h	ialibu-awa					1				41		pn.					0.s..	5733
24-NB	JIMI chain	1	3	21,628	33,670		76.85	98	C	41		PN.					0.s..	5734
24-NBA	**MARING net**	1	1	9,955	15,498		65.00	96	C	22		P..					0....	5735
24-NBAA	MARING cluster	1	1	9,955	15,498		65.00	96	C	22		P..					0....	5736
24-NBAA-a	Central maring					0				22	Maring	P..	1974-1979				0....	5737
24-NBAA-b	East maring					0				22		p..					0....	5738
24-NBAA-c	timbunki					0				22		p..					0....	5739
24-NBAA-d	tsuwenki					0				22		p..					0....	5740
24-NBAA-e	karamba					0				22		p..					0....	5741
24-NBAA-f	kambegl					0				22		p..					0....	5742
24-NBB	**NARAK-GANDJA net**	1	2	11,673	18,172		86.96	100	C	41		PN.					0.s..	5743
24-NBBA	NARAK cluster	1	2	11,673	18,172		86.96	100	C	41		PN.					0.s..	5744
24-NBBA-a	Proper narak	1	1	5,948	9,259	0	85.00	100	C	41	Narak	PN.	1975-1994	1981			0.s..	5745
24-NBBA-b	kandawo	1	1	5,725	8,913	0	89.00	100	C	41	Kandawo	Pn.	1989				0.s..	5746
24-NC	CHIMBU-WAHGI chain	1	13	436,384	682,928		87.24	100	C	42		PN.					0.s..	5747
24-NCA	**WAHGI net**	1	3	115,767	183,087		84.55	100	C	41		PN.					0.s..	5748
24-NCAA	NII cluster	1	1	13,950	21,717		91.00	100	C	41		PN.					0....	5749
24-NCAA-a	nii	1	1	13,950	21,717	0	91.00	100	C	41	Nii	PN.	1971	1980			0....	5750
24-NCAB	WEST NEMBI cluster	1	1	20,000	34,000		91.00	99	C	0		. . .					0....	5751
24-NCAB-a	West nembi	1	1	20,000	34,000	0	91.00	99	C	0		. . .					0....	5752
24-NCAC	WAHGI cluster	1	2	81,817	127,370		81.88	100	C	41	Wahgi	PN.	1966-1979	1989			0.s..	5753
24-NCAC-a	banz-nondugl					1				41		pn.					0.s..	5754
24-NCAC-b	pukamigl-andegabu					1				41		pn.					0.s..	5755
24-NCAC-c	kunjip					1				41		pn.					0.s..	5756
24-NCAC-d	kambia					1				41		pn.					0.s..	5757
24-NCAC-e	kumai	1	1	4,901	7,629	1	80.00	100	C	41	Kumai	Pn.	1934				0.s..	5758
24-NCAC-f	North wahgi					1				41		pn.					0.s..	5759
24-NCB	**CHIMBU net**	1	7	270,597	421,972		88.49	100	C	42		PN.					0....	5760
24-NCBA	KUMAN cluster	1	1	91,610	142,615		89.00	100	C	35		P..					0....	5761
24-NCBA-a	kuman	1	1	91,610	142,615	1	89.00	100	C	35	Kuman	P..	1968-1995				0....	5762
24-NCBB	ERA cluster	1	1	3,000	5,100		80.00	100	C	0		. . .					0....	5763
24-NCBB-a	era	1	1	3,000	5,100	0	80.00	100	C	0		. . .					0....	5764
24-NCBC	NAGANE cluster	1	1	1,453	2,263		80.04	100	C	0		. . .					0....	5765
24-NCBC-a	nagane	1	1	1,453	2,263	0	80.04	100	C	0		. . .					0....	5766
24-NCBD	DOM cluster	1	1	13,741	21,392		91.00	100	C	12		. . .					0....	5767
24-NCBD-a	dom	1	1	13,741	21,392	1	91.00	100	C	12	Dom	. . .					0....	5768
24-NCBE	GOLIN-MARIGL cluster	1	2	76,571	119,203		89.47	99	C	41		PN.					0....	5769
24-NCBE-a	yuri					1				41		pn.					0....	5770
24-NCBE-b	East kia					1				41		pn.					0....	5771
24-NCBE-c	golin	1	2	76,571	119,203	1	89.47	99	C	41	Golin	PN.	1969-1970	1980			0....	5774
24-NCBE-d	keri					1				41		pn.					0....	5775
24-NCBE-e	marigl					1				41		pn.					0....	5776
24-NCBF	SINASINA cluster	1	1	72,776	113,294		89.00	100	C	42	Sinasina	PN.	1967-1980	1975			0....	5777
24-NCBF-a	tabare					1				42		pn.					0....	5778
24-NCBF-b	guna					1				42		pn.					0....	5779
24-NCBG	SALT-YUI cluster	1	1	9,446	14,705		74.99	100	C	41		PN.					0....	5780
24-NCBG-a	salt-yui	1	1	9,446	14,705	1	74.99	100	C	41	Salt-yui	PN.	1967	1978			0....	5781
24-NCBH	NONDIRI cluster	1	1	2,000	3,400		75.00	99	C	0		. . .					0....	5782
24-NCBH-a	nondiri	1	1	2,000	3,400	0	75.00	99	C	0		. . .					0....	5783
24-NCC	**NOMANE net**	1	1	6,750	10,508		80.00	100	C	2		. . .					0....	5784
24-NCCA	NOMANE cluster	1	1	6,750	10,508		80.00	100	C	2		. . .					5785
24-NCCA-a	West nomane					1				2		. . .					0....	5786
24-NCCA-b	East nomane					1				2		. . .					0....	5787
24-NCD	**CHUAVE net**	1	2	43,270	67,361		87.76	100	C	41		PN.					0....	5788
24-NCDA	CHUAVE cluster	1	2	43,270	67,361		87.76	100	C	41		PN.					5789
24-NCDA-a	chuave	1	1	33,580	52,275	1	90.00	100	C	41	Chuave	PN.	1973-1987	1992-1994			0....	5790
24-NCDA-b	elimbari					1				41	Elimbari	Pn.	1987				0....	5791
24-NCDA-c	gomia					1				41		pn.					0....	5792
24-NCDA-d	kebai					1				41		pn.					0....	5793
24-NCDA-e	sua	1	1	9,690	15,086	1	80.00	100	C	41		pn.					0....	5794
24-O	**KAMANO-GAHUKU set**	1	18	352,105	548,144		87.47	100	C	42		PN.					1.s..	5795
24-OA	GENDE chain	1	1	9,955	15,498		90.01	100	C	12		. . .					0....	5796
24-OAA	**GENDE net**	1	1	9,955	15,498		90.01	100	C	12		. . .					0....	5797
24-OAAA	GENDE cluster	1	1	9,955	15,498		90.01	100	C	12		. . .					5798
24-OAAA-a	gende	1	1	9,955	15,498	0	90.01	100	C	12	Gende	. . .					0....	5799
24-OB	GAHUKU-BENABENA chain	1	4	98,748	153,728		88.93	100	C	41		PN.					0.s..	5800
24-OBA	**GAHUKU-ASARO net**	1	3	69,226	107,769		88.89	100	C	41		PN.					0.s..	5801
24-OBAA	ASARO cluster	1	1	37,333	58,119		88.00	100	C	41		PN.					5802
24-OBAA-a	dano	1	1	37,333	58,119	0	88.00	100	C	41	Dano	PN.	1969-1994	1989			0....	5803
24-OBAA-b	lunube-mado					0				41		pn.					0....	5804
24-OBAA-c	bohena					0				41		pn.					0....	5805
24-OBAA-d	amaizuho					0				41		pn.					0....	5806

Continued overleaf

Table 9-13 continued

Code 1	REFERENCE NAME / Autoglossonym 2	Coun 3	Peo 4	Mother-tongue speakers in 2000 5	in 2025 6	Media radio 7	AC% 8	E% 9	Wld 10	Tr 11	Biblioglossonym 12	Print 13-15	P–activity 16	N–activity 17	B–activity 18	J-year 19	Jayuh 20-24	Ref 25
24-OBAA-e	kongi					0				41		pn.					0....	5807
24-OBAB	GAHUKU cluster	1	1	23,401	36,430		95.00	100	C	41		PN.					0.s..	5808
24-OBAB-a	alekano	1	1	23,401	36,430	1	95.00	100	C	41	Alekano	PN.	1963-1968	1973-1986			0.s..	5809
24-OBAC	TOKANO cluster	1	1	8,492	13,220		76.00	100	C	22		P..					0....	5810
24-OBAC-a	tokano	1	1	8,492	13,220	0	76.00	100	C	22	Tokano	P..	1979				0....	5811
24-OBAC-b	Lower asaro					0				22		p..					0....	5812
24-OBAC-c	zuhuzuho					0				22		p..					0....	5813
24-OBB	BENABENA net	1	1	29,522	45,959		89.00	100	C	41		PN.					0....	5814
24-OBBA	BENABENA cluster	1	1	29,522	45,959		89.00	100	C	41		PN.					0....	5815
24-OBBA-a	benabena	1	1	29,522	45,959	0	89.00	100	C	41	Bena-bena*	PN.	1969	1982-1983			0....	5816
24-OC	SIANE chain	1	3	41,791	65,058		90.00	100	C	41		PN.					0.s..	5817
24-OCA	SIANE net	1	3	41,791	65,058		90.00	100	C	41		PN.					0.s..	5818
24-OCAA	SIANE cluster	1	1	30,917	48,130		91.00	100	C	41	Siane: Komogu	PN.	1964-1977	1991			0.s..	5819
24-OCAA-a	koreipa					0				41		pn.					0.s..	5820
24-OCAA-b	lambau					0				41		pn.					0.s..	5821
24-OCAA-c	komonggu					0				41		pn.					0.s..	5822
24-OCAA-d	West ono					0				41		pn.					0.s..	5823
24-OCAB	HAKOA cluster	1	1	8,547	13,305		85.00	100	C	0		...					0....	5824
24-OCAB-a	hakoa	1	1	8,547	13,305	0	85.00	100	C	0		...					0....	5825
24-OCAC	YAWEYUHA cluster	1	1	2,327	3,623		95.02	100	C	41		PN.					0....	5826
24-OCAC-a	yaweyuha	1	1	2,327	3,623	0	95.02	100	C	41	Yaweyuha	PN.		1982			0....	5827
24-OD	KAMANO-YAGARIA chain	1	6	148,934	231,856		85.09	100	C	41		PN.					1.s..	5828
24-ODA	KAMANO-YAGARIA net	1	6	148,934	231,856		85.09	100	C	41		PN.					1.s..	5829
24-ODAA	YAGARIA-KAMANO cluster	1	6	148,934	231,856		85.09	100	C	41		PN.					1.s..	5830
24-ODAA-a	yagaria	1	2	29,885	46,524	1	87.42	100	C	41	Yagaria: Kami-kuluka	PN.	1969-1977	1977			1.s..	5831
24-ODAA-b	inoke-yate	1	1	11,716	18,239	1	87.00	100	C	41	Inoke*	PN.	1968-1987	1992			1.s..	5840
24-ODAA-c	keyagana	1	1	17,851	27,791	1	83.00	100	C	41	Keyagana	PN.	1969	1996			1.s..	5843
24-ODAA-d	kanite	1	1	9,300	14,478	1	80.00	100	C	41	Kanite	PN.	1965-1968	1980			1.s..	5844
24-ODAA-e	kamano	1	1	80,182	124,824	1	85.00	100	C	41	Kamano-kafe	PN.	1967	1977-1982		1992	1.s..	5845
24-OE	ABAGA chain	1	1	218	339		89.91	100	C	8		...					0....	5848
24-OEA	ABAGA net	1	1	218	339		89.91	100	C	8		...					0....	5849
24-OEAA	ABAGA cluster	1	1	218	339		89.91	100	C	8		...					0....	5850
24-OEAA-a	abaga	1	1	218	339	0	89.91	100	C	8		...					0....	5851
24-OF	GIMI chain	1	1	32,644	50,818		89.00	100	C	41		PN.					0....	5852
24-OFA	GIMI net	1	1	32,644	50,818		89.00	100	C	41		PN.					0....	5853
24-OFAA	GIMI cluster	1	1	32,644	50,818		89.00	100	C	41	Gimi	PN.	1974-1985	1994			0....	5854
24-OFAA-a	West gimi					1				41		pn.					0....	5855
24-OFAA-b	East gimi					1				41		pn.					0....	5856
24-OG	FORE chain	1	2	19,815	30,847		88.93	100	C	42		PN.					0....	5857
24-OGA	FORE net	1	2	19,815	30,847		88.93	100	C	42		PN.					0....	5858
24-OGAA	FORE cluster	1	2	19,815	30,847		88.93	100	C	42		PN.					0....	5859
24-OGAA-a	pamusa	1	1	5,069	7,891	0	80.00	100	C	42	Fore: Pamusa	PN.	1966	1970			0....	5860
24-OGAA-b	North fore	1	1	14,746	22,956	0	92.00	100	C	42	Fore: North Central	PN.	1966-1969	1970-1974			0....	5861
24-P	GADSUP-TAIRORA set	1	13	68,336	106,384		85.96	100	C	42		PN.					0.s..	5864
24-PA	GADSUP-AUYANA chain	1	8	50,692	78,915		85.26	99	C	42		PN.					0....	5865
24-PAA	AWA net	1	1	2,600	4,047		60.00	92	C	42		PN.					0....	5866
24-PAAA	AWA cluster	1	1	2,600	4,047		60.00	92	C	42	Awa	PN.	1964	1974			0....	5867
24-PAAA-a	tauna					0				42		pn.					0....	5868
24-PAAA-b	ilakia					0				42		pn.					0....	5869
24-PAAA-c	South awa					0				42		pn.					0....	5870
24-PAAA-d	Northeast awa					0				42		pn.					0....	5871
24-PAB	AWIYAANA-USARUFA net	1	3	15,021	23,384		82.60	100	C	41		PN.					0....	5872
24-PABA	AWIYAANA cluster	1	2	13,599	21,171		82.36	100	C	41		PN.					0....	5873
24-PABA-a	awiyaana	1	1	11,110	17,296	0	84.01	100	C	41	Awiyaana	PN.	1980	1984			0....	5874
24-PABA-b	kosena	1	1	2,489	3,875	0	75.01	100	C	41	Kosena	PN.	1973	1980			0....	5875
24-PABB	USARUFA cluster	1	1	1,422	2,213		84.95	100	C	41		PN.					0....	5876
24-PABB-a	usarufa	1	1	1,422	2,213	0	84.95	100	C	41	Usarufa	PN.	1969	1980			0....	5877
24-PAC	GADSUP-AGARABI net	1	4	33,071	51,484		88.45	100	C	41		PN.					0....	5878
24-PACA	GADSUP cluster	1	2	14,220	22,137		89.00	100	C	41		PN.					0....	5879
24-PACA-a	gadsup	1	1	10,938	17,028	0	89.00	100	C	41	Gadsup	PN.	1968	1981			0....	5880
24-PACA-b	oyana					0				41		pn.					0....	5881
24-PACA-c	ontena	1	1	3,282	5,109		89.00	100	C	41		pn.					0....	5882
24-PACB	AGARABI cluster	1	1	18,600	28,956		88.00	100	C	23		P..					0....	5883
24-PACB-a	agarabi	1	1	18,600	28,956	0	88.00	100	C	23	Agarabi	P..	1970				0....	5884
24-PACC	KAMBAIRA cluster	1	1	251	391		90.04	100	C	5		...					0....	5885
24-PACC-a	kambaira	1	1	251	391	0	90.04	100	C	5		...					0....	5886
24-PB	TAIRORA-WAFFA chain	1	4	17,137	26,679		87.78	100	C	41		PN.					0.s..	5887
24-PBA	TAIRORA-BINUMARIEN net	1	3	15,564	24,231		88.06	100	C	41		PN.					0.s..	5888
24-PBAA	BINUMARIEN cluster	1	1	451	702		90.02	100	C	41		PN.					0....	5889
24-PBAA-a	binumarien	1	1	451	702	0	90.02	100	C	41	Binumarien	PN.	1968	1983			0....	5890
24-PBAB	TAIRORA cluster	1	2	15,113	23,529		88.00	100	C	41	Tairora	PN.	1967-1982	1979			0.s..	5891
24-PBAB-a	arua					0				41		pn.					0.s..	5892
24-PBAB-b	obura					0				41		pn.					0.s..	5893
24-PBAB-c	suwaira					0				41		pn.					0.s..	5894
24-PBAB-d	North tairora					0				41		pn.					0.s..	5895
24-PBAB-e	Central tairora					0				41		pn.					0.s..	5896
24-PBAB-f	South tairora					0				41		pn.					0.s..	5897
24-PBAB-g	pinata					0				41		pn.					0.s..	5898
24-PBAB-h	omwunra-toqura	1	1	2,534	3,946	0	88.00	100	C	41	Tairora: Omwunra-toqura*	PN.	1982	1994			0.s..	5899
24-PBB	WAFFA net	1	1	1,573	2,448		85.00	100	C	41		PN.					0....	5900
24-PBBA	WAFFA cluster	1	1	1,573	2,448		85.00	100	C	41		PN.					0....	5901
24-PBBA-a	waffa	1	1	1,573	2,448	0	85.00	100	C	41	Waffa	PN.	1969	1975-1988			0....	5902
24-PC	OWENA chain	1	1	507	790		95.07	100	C	12		...					0....	5903

Continued opposite

Table 9-13 continued

Code 1	REFERENCE NAME / Autoglossonym 2	Coun 3	Peo 4	Mother-tongue speakers in 2000 5	in 2025 6	Media radio 7	CHURCH AC% 8	E% 9	Wld 10	Tr 11	Biblioglossonym 12	SCRIPTURES Print 13-15	P–activity 16	N–activity 17	B–activity 18	J-year 19	Jayuh 20-24	Ref 25
24-PCA	**OWENA net**	1	1	507	790		95.07	100	C	12		. . .					0	5904
24-PCAA	OWENA cluster	1	1	507	790		95.07	100	C	12		. . .					0	5905
24-PCAA-a	owena	1	1	507	790	0	95.07	100	C	12	Owenia	. . .					0	5906
24-Q	**KENATI set**	1	1	1,192	1,855		79.95	100	C	22		P . .					0	5907
24-QA	KENATI chain	1	1	1,192	1,855		79.95	100	C	22		P . .					0	5908
24-QAA	**KENATI net**	1	1	1,192	1,855		79.95	100	C	22		P . .					0	5909
24-QAAA	KENATI cluster	1	1	1,192	1,855		79.95	100	C	22		P . .					0	5910
24-QAAA-a	kenati	1	1	1,192	1,855	0	79.95	100	C	22	Aziana*	P . .	1989				0	5911
24-R	**ANGAN set**	1	12	104,115	162,510		83.92	99	C	42		PN .					0	5912
24-RA	SIMBARI-KAPAU chain	1	11	102,700	160,307		84.04	99	C	42		PN .					0	5913
24-RAA	**SIMBARI-BARUYA net**	1	2	12,087	18,816		87.94	100	C	41		PN .					0	5914
24-RAAA	SIMBARI cluster	1	1	3,808	5,928		89.99	100	C	12		. . .					0	5915
24-RAAA-a	simbari	1	1	3,808	5,928	0	89.99	100	C	12	Simbari	. . .					0	5916
24-RAAB	BARUYA cluster	1	1	8,279	12,888		86.99	100	C	41		PN .					0	5917
24-RAAB-a	wantakia					0				41		pn .					0	5918
24-RAAB-b	baruya	1	1	8,279	12,888	0	86.99	100	C	41	Baruya	PN .	1973-1980	1992			0	5919
24-RAAB-c	gulicha					0				41		pn .					0	5920
24-RAAB-d	usirampia					0				41		pn .					0	5921
24-RAB	**AMPEELI-WOJOKESO net**	1	1	6,566	10,651		74.99	99	C	41		PN .					0	5922
24-RABA	AMPEELI cluster	1	1	3,566	5,551		74.99	100	C	41	Ampeeli*	PN .	1971-1977	1988-1989			0	5923
24-RABA-a	simiso					0				41		pn .					0	5924
24-RABA-b	yayoponjo					0				41		pn .					0	5925
24-RABA-c	folimaso					0				41		pn .					0	5926
24-RABA-d	aiewomba					0				41		pn .					0	5927
24-RABB	WOJOKESO cluster	1	1	3,000	5,100		75.00	99	C	0		. . .					0	5928
24-RABB-a	wojokeso	1	1	3,000	5,100	0	75.00	99	C	0		. . .					0	5929
24-RAC	**YAGWOIA net**	1	1	11,200	17,436		88.00	100	C	3		. . .					0	5930
24-RACA	YAGWOIA cluster	1	1	11,200	17,436		88.00	100	C	3		. . .					0	5931
24-RACA-a	yagwoia	1	1	11,200	17,436	0	88.00	100	C	3		. . .					0	5932
24-RAD	**KAWACHA net**	1	1	47	73		89.36	100	C	8		. . .					0	5933
24-RADA	KAWACHA cluster	1	1	47	73		89.36	100	C	8		. . .					0	5934
24-RADA-a	kawacha	1	1	47	73	0	89.36	100	C	8		. . .					0	5935
24-RAE	**KAMASA net**	1	1	31	49		90.32	100	C	8		. . .					0	5936
24-RAEA	KAMASA cluster	1	1	31	49		90.32	100	C	8		. . .					0	5937
24-RAEA-a	kamasa	1	1	31	49	0	90.32	100	C	8		. . .					0	5938
24-RAF	**ANKAVE net**	1	1	1,991	3,100		19.99	52	B	41		PN .					0	5939
24-RAFA	ANKAVE cluster	1	1	1,991	3,100		19.99	52	B	41	Ankave	PN .	1986-1992	1991			0	5940
24-RAFA-a	sawuve					0				41		pn .					0	5941
24-RAFA-b	wiyagwa					0				41		pn .					0	5942
24-RAFA-c	wunavai					0				41		pn .					0	5943
24-RAFA-d	miyatnu					0				41		pn .					0	5944
24-RAFA-e	ankai					0				41		pn .					0	5945
24-RAFA-f	bu'u					0				41		pn .					0	5946
24-RAG	**TAINAE-ANGOYA net**	1	2	2,209	3,438		58.94	81	B	12		. . .					0	5947
24-RAGA	TAINAE cluster	1	1	1,163	1,810		39.98	64	B	3		. . .					0	5948
24-RAGA-a	tainae	1	1	1,163	1,810	0	39.98	64	B	3		. . .					0	5949
24-RAGB	ANGOYA cluster	1	1	1,046	1,628		80.02	100	C	12		. . .					0	5950
24-RAGB-a	angoya	1	1	1,046	1,628	0	80.02	100	C	12	Angoya	. . .					0	5951
24-RAH	**HAMTAI-MENYA net**	1	2	68,569	106,744		86.24	100	C	42		PN .					0	5952
24-RAHA	HAMTAI cluster	1	1	51,131	79,598		87.00	100	C	42		PN .					0	5953
24-RAHA-a	wenta					1				42		pn .					0	5954
24-RAHA-b	howi					1				42		pn .					0	5955
24-RAHA-c	pmasa'a					1				42		pn .					0	5956
24-RAHA-d	hamtai	1	1	51,131	79,598	1	87.00	100	C	42	Hamtai	PN .	1963	1974			0	5957
24-RAHA-e	kaintiba					1				42		pn .					0	5958
24-RAHB	MENYA cluster	1	1	17,438	27,146		84.00	100	C	22		P . .					0	5959
24-RAHB-a	menya	1	1	17,438	27,146	0	84.00	100	C	22	Menya	P . .	1994-1995				0	5960
24-RB	ANGAATIHA chain	1	1	1,415	2,203		74.98	100	C	22		P . .					0	5961
24-RBA	**ANGAATIHA net**	1	1	1,415	2,203		74.98	100	C	22		P . .					0	5962
24-RBAA	ANGAATIHA cluster	1	1	1,415	2,203		74.98	100	C	22		P . .					0	5963
24-RBAA-a	angaatiha	1	1	1,415	2,203	0	74.98	100	C	22	Angaatihe*	P . .	1976-1980				0	5964
24-S	**FINISTERRE set**	1	48	88,903	138,504		82.51	99	C	42		PN .					0	5965
24-SA	GUSAP-MOT chain	1	7	23,401	36,427		82.72	100	C	41		PN .					0	5966
24-SAA	**UFIM net**	1	1	865	1,347		89.94	100	C	4		. . .					0	5967
24-SAAA	UFIM cluster	1	1	865	1,347		89.94	100	C	4		. . .					0	5968
24-SAAA-a	ufim	1	1	865	1,347	0	89.94	100	C	4		. . .					0	5969
24-SAB	**NAHU-RAWA net**	1	2	17,348	27,006		82.17	100	C	41		PN .					0	5970
24-SABA	NAHU cluster	1	1	6,975	10,858		75.00	100	C	12	Nahu	. . .					0	5971
24-SABA-a	Southwest nahu					0				12		. . .					0	5972
24-SABA-b	Northeast nahu					0				12		. . .					0	5973
24-SABB	RAWA cluster	1	1	10,373	16,148		87.00	100	C	41	Rawa	PN .	1978	1992			0	5974
24-SABB-a	East rawa					0				41		pn .					0	5975
24-SABB-b	South rawa					0				41		pn .					0	5976
24-SABB-c	North rawa					0				41		pn .					0	5977
24-SAC	**NGAING-NEKGINI net**	1	3	4,518	7,032		82.38	100	C	4		. . .					0	5978
24-SACA	NEKGINI cluster	1	1	625	973		89.92	100	C	4		. . .					0	5979
24-SACA-a	nekgini	1	1	625	973	0	89.92	100	C	4		. . .					0	5980
24-SACB	NEKO cluster	1	1	458	712		89.96	100	C	2		. . .					0	5981
24-SACB-a	neko	1	1	458	712	0	89.96	100	C	2		. . .					0	5982
24-SACC	NGAING cluster	1	1	3,435	5,347		80.00	100	C	2		. . .					0	5983

Continued overleaf

Table 9-13 continued

Code 1	REFERENCE NAME / Autoglossonym 2	Coun 3	Peo 4	Mother-tongue speakers in 2000 5	in 2025 6	Media radio 7	AC% 8	E% 9	Wld 10	Tr 11	Biblioglossonym 12	Print 13-15	P-activity 16	N-activity 17	B-activity 18	J-year 19	Jayuh 20-24	Ref 25
24-SACC-a	ngaing	1	1	3,435	5,347	0	80.00	100	C	2		. . .					0	5984
24-SAD	**GIRA net**	1	1	670	1,042		90.00	100	C	4		. . .					0	5985
24-SADA	GIRA cluster	1	1	670	1,042		90.00	100	C	4		. . .					0	5986
24-SADA-a	gira	1	1	670	1,042	0	90.00	100	C	4		. . .					0	5987
24-SB	WARUP-DAHATING chain	1	8	5,299	8,249		85.05	100	C	22		P . .					0	5988
24-SBA	**DAHATING net**	1	1	1,375	2,140		69.96	100	C	22		P . .					0	5989
24-SBAA	DAHATING cluster	1	1	1,375	2,140		69.96	100	C	22		P . .					0	5990
24-SBAA-a	dahating	1	1	1,375	2,140	0	69.96	100	C	22	Dahating*	P . .	1992-1993				0	5991
24-SBB	**WARUP net**	1	7	3,924	6,109		90.34	100	C	6		. . .					0	5992
24-SBBA	BULGEBI cluster	1	1	76	118		94.74	100	C	4		. . .					0	5993
24-SBBA-a	bulgebi	1	1	76	118	0	94.74	100	C	4		. . .					0	5994
24-SBBB	GUIARAK cluster	1	1	190	296		90.00	100	C	4		. . .					0	5995
24-SBBB-a	guiarak	1	1	190	296	0	90.00	100	C	4		. . .					0	5996
24-SBBC	MORAFA cluster	1	1	976	1,520		90.06	100	C	2		. . .					0	5997
24-SBBC-a	morafa	1	1	976	1,520	0	90.06	100	C	2		. . .					0	5998
24-SBBD	FORAK cluster	1	1	237	369		89.87	100	C	6		. . .					0	5999
24-SBBD-a	forak	1	1	237	369	0	89.87	100	C	6		. . .					0	6000
24-SBBE	DEGENAN cluster	1	1	612	953		90.03	100	C	4		. . .					0	6001
24-SBBE-a	degenan	1	1	612	953	0	90.03	100	C	4		. . .					0	6002
24-SBBF	YAGOMI cluster	1	1	199	310		94.97	100	C	4		. . .					0	6003
24-SBBF-a	yagomi	1	1	199	310	0	94.97	100	C	4		. . .					0	6004
24-SBBG	ASAT cluster	1	1	1,634	2,543		89.96	100	C	2		. . .					0	6005
24-SBBG-a	asat	1	1	1,634	2,543	0	89.96	100	C	2		. . .					0	6006
24-SC	YUPNA-NANKINA chain	1	9	19,954	31,123		85.69	98	C	22		P . .					0	6007
24-SCA	**NANKINA-MEBU net**	1	2	3,370	5,247		81.75	94	C	22		P . .					0	6008
24-SCAA	MEBU cluster	1	1	464	722		29.96	54	B	4		. . .					0	6009
24-SCAA-a	mebu	1	1	464	722	0	29.96	54	B	4		. . .					0	6010
24-SCAB	NANKINA cluster	1	1	2,906	4,525		90.02	100	C	22		P . .					0	6011
24-SCAB-a	nankina	1	1	2,906	4,525	0	90.02	100	C	22	Nankina	P . .	1990				0	6012
24-SCB	**YUPNA net**	1	7	16,584	25,876		86.49	99	C	22		P . .					0	6013
24-SCBA	GABUTAMON cluster	1	1	439	683		39.86	62	B	4		. . .					0	6014
24-SCBA-a	gabutamon	1	1	439	683	0	39.86	62	B	4		. . .					0	6015
24-SCBB	DOMUNG cluster	1	1	2,452	3,818		90.01	100	C	4		. . .					0	6016
24-SCBB-a	domung	1	1	2,452	3,818	0	90.01	100	C	4		. . .					0	6017
24-SCBC	BONKIMAN cluster	1	1	400	680		90.00	99	C	0		. . .					0	6018
24-SCBC-a	bonkiman	1	1	400	680	0	90.00	99	C	0		. . .					0	6019
24-SCBD	WANDABONG cluster	1	1	751	1,169		90.01	100	C	0		. . .					0	6020
24-SCBD-a	wandabong	1	1	751	1,169	0	90.01	100	C	0		. . .					0	6021
24-SCBE	NOKOPO cluster	1	1	2,425	3,776		80.00	100	C	0		. . .					0	6022
24-SCBE-a	nokopo	1	1	2,425	3,776	0	80.00	100	C	0		. . .					0	6023
24-SCBF	KEWIENG cluster	1	1	1,192	1,855		79.95	100	C	0		. . .					0	6024
24-SCBF-a	kewieng	1	1	1,192	1,855	0	79.95	100	C	0		. . .					0	6025
24-SCBG	YUPNA cluster	1	2	8,925	13,895		90.01	100	C	22		P . .					0	6026
24-SCBG-a	yupna	1	2	8,925	13,895	0	90.01	100	C	22	Yupna*	P . .	1979-1993				0	6027
24-SD	URUWA chain	1	8	5,103	7,946		83.91	95	C	22		P . .					0	6028
24-SDA	**SOM-YAU net**	1	7	4,301	6,697		82.77	95	C	22		P . .					0	6029
24-SDAA	SOM cluster	1	2	367	572		95.10	100	C	4		. . .					0	6030
24-SDAA-a	som	1	1	229	357	0	95.20	100	C	4		. . .					0	6031
24-SDAB	WELIKI cluster	1	2	472	734		92.37	100	C	6		. . .					0	6032
24-SDAB-a	weliki	1	2	472	734	0	92.37	100	C	6		. . .					0	6033
24-SDAC	YAU cluster	1	2	2,660	4,142		77.18	91	C	22	Yau	P . .	1991-1994				0	6034
24-SDAC-a	worin					0				22		p . .					0	6035
24-SDAC-b	yawan	1	1	684	1,065	0	40.06	66	B	22		p . .					0	6036
24-SDAC-c	kotet					0				22		p . .					0	6037
24-SDAC-d	mitmit					0				22		p . .					0	6038
24-SDAC-e	mup					0				22		p . .					0	6039
24-SDAC-f	sindamon					0				22		p . .					0	6040
24-SDAD	KOMUTU cluster	1	1	802	1,249		90.02	100	C	4		. . .					0	6041
24-SDAD-a	komutu	1	1	802	1,249	0	90.02	100	C	4		. . .					0	6042
24-SDB	**SAKAM net**	1	1	802	1,249		90.02	100	C	4		. . .					0	6043
24-SDBA	SAKAM cluster	1	1	802	1,249		90.02	100	C	4		. . .					0	6044
24-SDBA-a	sakam	1	1	802	1,249	0	90.02	100	C	4		. . .					0	6045
24-SDBA-b	kamdarang					0				4		. . .					0	6046
24-SE	WANTOAT-IRUMU chain	1	5	18,418	28,717		80.57	100	C	42		PN .					0	6047
24-SEA	**WANTOAT net**	1	2	15,574	24,289		79.81	100	C	42		PN .					0	6048
24-SEAA	AWARA cluster	1	1	1,843	2,870		80.03	99	C	12		. . .					0	6049
24-SEAA-a	awara	1	1	1,843	2,870	0	80.03	99	C	12	Awara	. . .					0	6050
24-SEAB	LERON cluster	1	1	300	510		70.00	98	C	0		. . .					0	6051
24-SEAB-a	leron	1	1	300	510	0	70.00	98	C	0		. . .					0	6052
24-SEAC	WANTOAT cluster	1	1	13,431	20,909		80.00	100	C	42		PN .					0	6053
24-SEAC-a	wantoat	1	1	13,431	20,909	0	80.00	100	C	42	Wantoat	PN .	1973	1975			0	6054
24-SEAC-b	wapu					0				42		pn .					0	6055
24-SEB	**IRUMU net**	1	3	2,844	4,428		84.70	100	C	22		P . .					0	6056
24-SEBA	BAM cluster	1	2	1,333	2,075		90.02	100	C	0		. . .					0	6057
24-SEBA-a	bam	1	1	618	962	0	89.97	100	C	0		. . .					0	6058
24-SEBA-b	kandumin	1	1	715	1,113	0	90.07	100	C	0		. . .					0	6059
24-SEBA-c	yagawak					0				0		. . .					0	6060
24-SEBB	IRUMU cluster	1	1	1,511	2,353		80.01	100	C	22		P . .					0	6061
24-SEBB-a	irumu	1	1	1,511	2,353	0	80.01	100	C	22	Irumu	P . .	1988				0	6062
24-SF	ERAP chain	1	11	16,728	26,042		79.34	98	C	41		PN .					0	6063
24-SFA	**URI net**	1	1	2,906	4,525		80.01	100	C	41		PN .					0	6064

Continued opposite

Table 9-13 continued

Code 1	REFERENCE NAME / Autoglossonym 2	Coun 3	Peo 4	Mother-tongue speakers in 2000 5	in 2025 6	Media radio 7	CHURCH AC% 8	E% 9	Wld 10	Tr 11	Biblioglossonym 12	SCRIPTURES Print 13-15	P-activity 16	N-activity 17	B-activity 18	J-year 19	Jayuh 20-24	Ref 25
24-SFAA	URI cluster	1	1	2,906	4,525		80.01	100	C	41	Uri	PN.	1974	1984			0....	6065
24-SFAA-a	West urii					0				41		pn.					0....	6066
24-SFAA-b	East urii					0				41		pn.					0....	6067
24-SFB	**FINUNGWA-MAMAA net**	1	2	1,050	1,634		51.24	72	B	4		...					0....	6068
24-SFBA	MAMAA cluster	1	1	312	485		89.74	100	C	4		...					0....	6069
24-SFBA-a	mamaa	1	1	312	485	0	89.74	100	C	4		...					0....	6070
24-SFBB	FINUNGWA cluster	1	1	738	1,149		34.96	60	B	4		...					0....	6071
24-SFBB-a	finungwa	1	1	738	1,149	0	34.96	60	B	4		...					0....	6072
24-SFC	**GUSAN net**	1	1	1,186	1,846		80.02	100	C	4		...					0....	6073
24-SFCA	GUSAN cluster	1	1	1,186	1,846		80.02	100	C	4		...					0....	6074
24-SFCA-a	gusan	1	1	1,186	1,846	0	80.02	100	C	4		...					0....	6075
24-SFD	**SAUK net**	1	1	952	1,481		89.92	100	C	4		...					0....	6076
24-SFDA	SAUK cluster	1	1	952	1,481		89.92	100	C	4		...					0....	6077
24-SFDA-a	sauk	1	1	952	1,481	0	89.92	100	C	4		...					0....	6078
24-SFE	**NIMI net**	1	1	2,062	3,210		80.02	100	C	2		...					0....	6079
24-SFEA	NIMI cluster	1	1	2,062	3,210		80.02	100	C	2		...					0....	6080
24-SFEA-a	nimi	1	1	2,062	3,210	0	80.02	100	C	2		...					0....	6081
24-SFF	**NUMANGANG-NUK net**	1	5	8,572	13,346		81.12	100	C	22		P..					0....	6082
24-SFFA	NUMANGGANG cluster	1	1	3,576	5,568		80.01	100	C	22	Numanggang	P..	1984-1994				0....	6083
24-SFFA-a	sugu					0				22		p..					0....	6084
24-SFFA-b	ngain					0				22		p..					0....	6085
24-SFFB	NEK cluster	1	1	1,805	2,811		80.00	100	C	12	Nek	...					0....	6086
24-SFFB-a	West nek					0				12		...					0....	6087
24-SFFB-b	East nek					0				12		...					0....	6088
24-SFFC	NUK cluster	1	1	1,507	2,346		85.00	100	C	2		...					0....	6089
24-SFFC-a	North nuk					0				2		...					0....	6090
24-SFFC-b	South nuk					0				2		...					0....	6091
24-SFFD	NAKAMA cluster	1	1	1,468	2,285		79.97	100	C	2		...					0....	6092
24-SFFD-a	North nakama									2		...					0....	6093
24-SFFD-b	South nakama					0				2		...					0....	6094
24-SFFE	MUNKIP cluster	1	1	216	336		89.81	100	C	4		...					0....	6095
24-SFFE-a	munkip	1	1	216	336	0	89.81	100	C	4		...					0....	6096
24-T	**WEST HUON set**	1	13	84,463	131,487		77.23	96	C	41		PN.					0....	6097
24-TA	MESEM-NABAK chain	1	2	20,414	31,780		80.64	95	C	22		P..					0....	6098
24-TAA	**MESEM net**	1	1	2,093	3,258		24.99	55	B	12		...					0....	6099
24-TAAA	MESEM cluster	1	1	2,093	3,258		24.99	55	B	12		...					0....	6100
24-TAAA-a	mesem	1	1	2,093	3,258	0	24.99	55	B	12	Mesem	...					0....	6101
24-TAB	**NABAK net**	1	1	18,321	28,522		87.00	100	C	22		P..					0....	6102
24-TABA	NABAK cluster	1	1	18,321	28,522		87.00	100	C	22	Nabak	P..	1977-1987				0....	6103
24-TABA-a	Southeast nabak					0				22		p..					0....	6104
24-TABA-b	Northwest nabak					0				22		p..					0....	6105
24-TB	TIMBE-KOMBA chain	1	3	40,511	63,064		83.95	100	C	41		PN.					0....	6106
24-TBA	**TIMBE net**	1	1	12,788	19,907		88.00	100	C	41		PN.					0....	6107
24-TBAA	TIMBE cluster	1	1	12,788	19,907		88.00	100	C	41	Timbe	PN.	1978-1986	1987			0....	6108
24-TBAA-a	South timbe					0				41		pn.					0....	6109
24-TBAA-b	West Central timbe.					0				41		pn.					0....	6110
24-TBAA-c	East timbe					0				41		pn.					0....	6113
24-TBB	**SELEPET net**	1	1	8,480	13,201		80.00	100	C	41		PN.					0....	6114
24-TBBA	SELEPET cluster	1	1	8,480	13,201		80.00	100	C	41	Selepet	PN.	1975	1986			0....	6115
24-TBBA-a	South selepet					0				41		pn.					0....	6116
24-TBBA-b	North selepet					0				41		pn.					0....	6117
24-TBC	**KOMBA net**	1	1	19,243	29,956		83.00	100	C	41		PN.					0....	6120
24-TBCA	KOMBA cluster	1	1	19,243	29,956		83.00	100	C	41	Komba	PN.	1974	1980			0....	6121
24-TBCA-a	East komba					0				41		pn.					0....	6122
24-TBCA-b	Central komba					0				41		pn.					0....	6123
24-TBCA-c	West Central komba.					0				41		pn.					0....	6124
24-TBCA-d	West komba					0				41		pn.					0....	6125
24-TBCA-e	Southwest komba					0				41		pn.					0....	6126
24-TC	NOMU-ONO chain	1	5	9,935	15,467		75.74	100	C	41		PN.					0....	6127
24-TCA	**KUMUKIO net**	1	1	868	1,352		89.98	100	C	4		...					0....	6128
24-TCAA	KUMUKIO cluster	1	1	868	1,352		89.98	100	C	4		...					0....	6129
24-TCAA-a	kumukio	1	1	868	1,352	0	89.98	100	C	4		...					0....	6130
24-TCB	**KINALAKNA net**	1	1	344	536		90.12	100	C	4		...					0....	6131
24-TCBA	KINALAKNA cluster	1	1	344	536		90.12	100	C	4		...					0....	6132
24-TCBA-a	kinalakna	1	1	344	536	0	90.12	100	C	4		...					0....	6133
24-TCC	**NOMU net**	1	1	1,269	1,976		79.98	100	C	4		...					0....	6134
24-TCCA	NOMU cluster	1	1	1,269	1,976		79.98	100	C	4		...					0....	6135
24-TCCA-a	nomu	1	1	1,269	1,976	0	79.98	100	C	4		...					0....	6136
24-TCD	**SIALUM net**	1	1	1,010	1,572		90.00	100	C	4		...					0....	6137
24-TCDA	SIALUM cluster	1	1	1,010	1,572		90.00	100	C	4		...					0....	6138
24-TCDA-a	sialum	1	1	1,010	1,572	0	90.00	100	C	4		...					0....	6139
24-TCE	**ONO net**	1	1	6,444	10,031		69.99	100	C	41		PN.					0....	6140
24-TCEA	ONO cluster	1	1	6,444	10,031		69.99	100	C	41	Ono	PN.	1980	1991			0....	6141
24-TCEA-a	ziwe					0				41		pn.					0....	6142
24-TCEA-b	amugen					0				41		pn.					0....	6143
24-TD	TOBO-MINDIK chain	1	3	13,603	21,176		53.17	83	B	41		PN.					0....	6144
24-TDA	**TOBO net**	1	1	3,330	5,184		24.98	53	B	2		...					0....	6145
24-TDAA	TOBO cluster	1	1	3,330	5,184		24.98	53	B	2		...					0....	6146
24-TDAA-a	tobo	1	1	3,330	5,184	0	24.98	53	B	2		...					0....	6147
24-TDB	**BURUM-MINDIK net**	1	2	10,273	15,992		62.31	93	C	41		PN.					0....	6148

Continued overleaf

Table 9-13 continued

Code 1	REFERENCE NAME / *Autoglossonym* 2	Coun 3	Peo 4	Mother-tongue speakers in 2000 5	in 2025 6	Media radio 7	AC% 8	E% 9	Wld 10	Tr 11	Biblioglossonym 12	Print 13-15	P–activity 16	N–activity 17	B–activity 18	J-year 19	Jayuh 20-24	Ref 25
24-TDBA	BURUM-MINDIK cluster	1	2	10,273	15,992		62.31	93	C	41	Burum-mindik	PN.	1984-1992	1996			0....	6149
24-TDBA-a	siawari					0				41		pn.					0....	6150
24-TDBA-b	kosorong	1	1	1,755	2,732	0	25.01	59	B	41		pn.					0....	6151
24-TDBA-c	somba					0				41		pn.					0....	6152
24-U	**EAST HUON set**	1	6	43,789	71,032		75.77	98	C	22		P..					0....	6153
24-UA	MONGI chain	1	1	7,467	11,624		60.00	89	B	12		...					0....	6154
24-UAA	**MONGI net**	1	1	7,467	11,624		60.00	89	B	12		...					0....	6155
24-UAAA	MONGI cluster	1	1	7,467	11,624		60.00	89	B	12	Kube	...					0....	6156
24-UAAA-a	kurungtufu					0				12		...					0....	6157
24-UAAA-b	yoangen					0				12		...					0....	6158
24-UB	MASAWENG-MAPE chain	1	5	36,322	59,408		79.01	100	C	22		P..					0....	6159
24-UBA	**MIGABAC net**	1	1	1,630	2,538		80.00	100	C	4		...					0....	6160
24-UBAA	MIGABAC cluster	1	1	1,630	2,538		80.00	100	C	4		...					0....	6161
24-UBAA-a	North migabac					0				4		...					0....	6162
24-UBAA-b	South migabac					0				4		...					0....	6163
24-UBB	**MOMARE net**	1	1	815	1,269		85.03	100	C	4		...					0....	6164
24-UBBA	MOMARE cluster	1	1	815	1,269		85.03	100	C	4		...					0....	6165
24-UBBA-a	momare	1	1	815	1,269	0	85.03	100	C	4		...					0....	6166
24-UBC	**SENE net**	1	1	16	24		87.50	100	C	8		...					0....	6167
24-UBCA	SENE cluster	1	1	16	24		87.50	100	C	8		...					0....	6168
24-UBCA-a	sene	1	1	16	24	0	87.50	100	C	8		...					0....	6169
24-UBD	**DEDUA net**	1	1	5,813	9,049		79.99	100	C	22		P..					0....	6170
24-UBDA	DEDUA cluster	1	1	5,813	9,049		79.99	100	C	22	Dedua	P..	1990				0....	6171
24-UBDA-a	North dedua					0				22		p..					0....	6172
24-UBDA-b	South dedua					0				22		p..					0....	6173
24-UBE	**MAPE net**	1	1	8,048	12,528		75.00	100	C	4		...					0....	6174
24-UBEA	MAPE cluster	1	1	8,048	12,528		75.00	100	C	4		...					0....	6175
24-UBEA-a	naga					0				4		...					0....	6176
24-UBEA-b	East mape					0				4		...					0....	6177
24-UBEA-c	West mape					0				4		...					0....	6178
24-UBEA-d	nigac					0				4		...					0....	6179
24-UBEA-e	fukac					0				4		...					0....	6180
24-UBF	**KATE net**	1	1	20,000	34,000		80.00	100	C	0		...					0....	6181
24-UBFA	KATE cluster	1	1	20,000	34,000		80.00	100	C	0		...					0....	6182
24-UBFA-a	wana					0				0		...					0....	6183
24-UBFA-b	magobineng			0	0	0	0.00	0		0		...					0....	6184
24-UBFA-c	wamora					0				0		...					0....	6185
24-UBFA-d	wemo					0				0		...					0....	6186
24-UBFA-e	parec			0	0	0	0.00	0		0		...					0....	6187
24-V	**KOVAI set**	1	1	5,231	8,144		80.00	100	C	22		P..					0....	6188
24-VA	KOVAI chain	1	1	5,231	8,144		80.00	100	C	22		P..					0....	6189
24-VAA	**KOVAI net**	1	1	5,231	8,144		80.00	100	C	22		P..					0....	6190
24-VAAA	KOVAI cluster	1	1	5,231	8,144		80.00	100	C	22		P..					0....	6191
24-VAAA-a	kovai	1	1	5,231	8,144	0	80.00	100	C	22	Kovai	P..	1993				0....	6192
25	**WEST PAPUASIC zone**	2	81	458,957	599,776		37.14	68	B	41		PN.					0.s..	6193
25-A	**NORTH HALMAHERA set**	1	16	290,713	374,781		24.82	58	B	41		PN.					0.s..	6194
25-AA	TOBELO-SAHO chain	1	13	179,145	230,951		36.47	74	B	41		PN.					0.s..	6195
25-AAA	**TOBELO-TUGETIL net**	1	2	30,310	39,075		47.07	89	B	41		PN.					0.s..	6196
25-AAAA	TOBELO cluster	1	1	27,722	35,739		51.00	94	B	41	Tobelo	PN.		1993			0.s..	6197
25-AAAA-a	boëng					0				41		pn.					0.s..	6198
25-AAAA-b	heleworuru					0				41		pn.					0.s..	6199
25-AAAA-c	dodinga					0				41		pn.					0.s..	6200
25-AAAB	TUGUTIL cluster	1	1	2,588	3,336		4.98	33	A	12	Tugutil	...					0....	6201
25-AAAB-a	Proper tugutil					0				12		...					0....	6202
25-AAAB-b	teluk-lili					0				12		...					0....	6203
25-AAAB-c	kusuri					0				12		...					0....	6204
25-AAB	**GALELA-LOLODA net**	1	3	110,741	142,765		28.04	65	B	24		P..					0....	6205
25-AABA	GALELA cluster	1	1	90,930	117,225		28.00	66	B	22	Galela	P..	1990-1991				0....	6206
25-AABA-a	kadai					0				22		p..					0....	6207
25-AABA-b	kadina					0				22		p..					0....	6208
25-AABA-c	morotai					0				22		p..					0....	6209
25-AABA-d	sopi					0				22		p..					0....	6210
25-AABB	LODA cluster	1	1	17,541	22,614		28.00	63	B	24		P..					0....	6211
25-AABB-a	loda	1	1	17,541	22,614	0	28.00	63	B	24	Loloda	P..	1915				0....	6212
25-AABB-b	bakun					0				24		p..					0....	6213
25-AABC	LABA cluster	1	1	2,270	2,926		30.00	62	B	4		...					0....	6214
25-AABC-a	laba	1	1	2,270	2,926	0	30.00	62	B	4		...					0....	6215
25-AAC	**TOBARU net**	1	1	16,947	21,848		68.00	100	C	12		...					0....	6216
25-AACA	TOBARU cluster	1	1	16,947	21,848		68.00	100	C	12	Tabaru	...					0....	6217
25-AACA-a	nyeku					0				12		...					0....	6218
25-AACA-b	adu					0				12		...					0....	6219
25-AAD	**SAHU net**	1	4	14,784	19,059		45.56	79	B	12		...					0....	6220
25-AADA	SAHU cluster	1	1	9,142	11,785		60.00	95	B	12	Sahu	...					0....	6221
25-AADA-a	pa'disua					0				12		...					0....	6222
25-AADA-b	tala'ai					0				12		...					0....	6223
25-AADB	IBU cluster	1	3	5,642	7,274		22.17	54	B	8		...					0....	6224
25-AADB-a	Proper ibu	1	1	170	219	0	27.65	64	B	8		...					0....	6225
25-AADB-b	waioli	1	1	3,648	4,703	0	28.02	62	B	8		...					0....	6226
25-AADB-c	gamkonora	1	1	1,824	2,352	0	9.98	36	A	8		...					0....	6227
25-AAE	**KAO-PAGU net**	1	3	6,363	8,204		27.47	61	B	2		...					0....	6228
25-AAEA	MODOLE cluster	1	1	2,651	3,418		27.99	61	B	2		...					0....	6229
25-AAEA-a	North modole					0				2		...					0....	6230

Continued opposite

Table 9-13 continued

Code 1	REFERENCE NAME / Autoglossonym 2	Coun 3	Peo 4	Mother-tongue speakers in 2000 5	in 2025 6	Media radio 7	CHURCH AC% 8	E% 9	Wld 10	Tr 11	Biblioglossonym 12	SCRIPTURES Print 13-15	P-activity 16	N-activity 17	B-activity 18	J-year 19	Jayuh 20-24	Ref 25
25-AAEA-b	South modole					0				2		. . .					0	6231
25-AAEB	PAGU cluster	1	1	3,309	4,266		26.99	61	B	2		. . .					0	6232
25-AAEB-a	isam					0				2		. . .					0	6233
25-AAEB-b	Proper pagu	1	1	3,309	4,266	0	26.99	61	B	2		. . .					0	6234
25-AAEB-c	toliwiku					0				2		. . .					0	6235
25-AAEC	KAO cluster	1	1	403	520		28.04	61	B	4		. . .					0	6236
25-AAEC-a	kao	1	1	403	520	0	28.04	61	B	4		. . .					0	6237
25-AB	WEST MAKIAN chain	1	1	17,944	23,133		28.00	62	B	2		. . .					0	6238
25-ABA	**WEST MAKIAN net**	1	1	17,944	23,133		28.00	62	B	2		. . .					0	6239
25-ABAA	WEST MAKIAN cluster	1	1	17,944	23,133		28.00	62	B	2		. . .					0	6240
25-ABAA-a	West makian	1	1	17,944	23,133	0	28.00	62	B	2		. . .					0	6241
25-AC	TERNATE-TIDORE chain	1	2	93,624	120,697		1.92	28	A	12		. . .					0	6242
25-ACA	**TERNATE-TIDORE net**	1	2	93,624	120,697		1.92	28	A	12		. . .					0	6243
25-ACAA	TERNATE cluster	1	1	57,820	74,540		0.01	26	A	2		. . .					0	6244
25-ACAA-a	Proper ternate					0				2		. . .					0	6245
25-ACAA-b	Vehicular ternate	1	1	57,820	74,540	0	0.01	26	A	2		. . .					0	6246
25-ACAB	TIDORE cluster	1	1	35,804	46,157		5.00	32	A	12		. . .					0	6247
25-ACAB-a	mareku					0				12		. . .					0	6248
25-ACAB-b	soasiu					0				12		. . .					0	6249
25-ACAB-c	Vehicular tidore	1	1	35,804	46,157	0	5.00	32	A	12	Tidore	. . .					0	6250
25-B	**MOI-TEHIT set**	1	5	20,033	27,056		63.23	94	C	12		. . .					0	6251
25-BA	SEGET chain	1	1	1,442	1,859		65.05	91	C	4		. . .					0	6252
25-BAA	**SEGET net**	1	1	1,442	1,859		65.05	91	C	4		. . .					0	6253
25-BAAA	SEGET cluster	1	1	1,442	1,859		65.05	91	C	4		. . .					0	6254
25-BAAA-a	seget	1	1	1,442	1,859	0	65.05	91	C	4		. . .					0	6255
25-BB	MOI chain	1	1	3,000	5,100		60.00	93	C	0		. . .					0	6256
25-BBA	**MOI net**	1	1	3,000	5,100		60.00	93	C	0		. . .					0	6257
25-BBAA	MOI cluster	1	1	3,000	5,100		60.00	93	C	0		. . .					0	6258
25-BBAA-a	waipu					0				0		. . .					0	6259
25-BBAA-b	mosana					0				0		. . .					0	6260
25-BBAA-c	East moi					0				0		. . .					0	6261
25-BC	MORAID chain	1	1	1,188	1,531		64.98	91	C	2		. . .					0	6262
25-BCA	**MORAID net**	1	1	1,188	1,531		64.98	91	C	2		. . .					0	6263
25-BCAA	MORAID cluster	1	1	1,188	1,531		64.98	91	C	2		. . .					0	6264
25-BCAA-a	moraid	1	1	1,188	1,531	0	64.98	91	C	2		. . .					0	6265
25-BD	KALABRA-TEHIT chain	1	3	14,403	18,566		63.58	95	C	12		. . .					0	6266
25-BDA	**KALABRA net**	1	1	3,288	4,238		65.09	92	C	4		. . .					0	6267
25-BDAA	KALABRA cluster	1	1	3,288	4,238		65.09	92	C	4		. . .					0	6268
25-BDAA-a	kalabra	1	1	3,288	4,238	0	65.09	92	C	4		. . .					0	6269
25-BDB	**TEHIT net**	1	1	9,736	12,551		65.00	98	C	12		. . .					0	6270
25-BDBA	TEHIT cluster	1	1	9,736	12,551		65.00	98	C	12		. . .					0	6271
25-BDBA-a	tehit	1	1	9,736	12,551	0	65.00	98	C	12	Tehit	. . .					0	6272
25-BDC	**KUWANI net**	1	1	1,379	1,777		49.96	78	B	4		. . .					0	6273
25-BDCA	KUWANI cluster	1	1	1,379	1,777		49.96	78	B	4		. . .					0	6274
25-BDCA-a	kuwani	1	1	1,379	1,777	0	49.96	78	B	4		. . .					0	6275
25-C	**ABUN set**	1	1	3,563	4,594		65.00	96	C	22		P . .					0	6276
25-CA	ABUN chain	1	1	3,563	4,594		65.00	96	C	22		P . .					0	6277
25-CAA	**ABUN net**	1	1	3,563	4,594		65.00	96	C	22		P . .					0	6278
25-CAAA	ABUN cluster	1	1	3,563	4,594		65.00	96	C	22		P . .					0	6279
25-CAAA-a	abun-tat					0				22		p . .					0	6280
25-CAAA-b	abun-ji					0				22		p . .					0	6281
25-CAAA-c	abun-je	1	1	3,563	4,594	0	65.00	96	C	22	Abun	P . .	1991-1995				0	6282
25-D	**AMARU set**	1	2	32,792	42,274		15.44	45	A	22		P . .					0	6283
25-DA	AMARU chain	1	2	32,792	42,274		15.44	45	A	22		P . .					0	6284
25-DAA	**AMARU net**	1	2	32,792	42,274		15.44	45	A	22		P . .					0	6285
25-DAAA	KARON-DORI cluster	1	1	6,151	7,930		65.00	92	C	4		. . .					0	6286
25-DAAA-a	mai-yach	1	1	6,151	7,930	0	65.00	92	C	4		. . .					0	6287
25-DAAB	BRAT cluster	1	1	26,641	34,344		4.00	34	A	22	Mai Brat	P . .	1990-1994				0	6288
25-DAAB-a	mai-brat					0				22		p . .					0	6289
25-DAAB-b	mai-sawiet					0				22		p . .					0	6290
25-DAAB-c	mai-yah					0				22		p . .					0	6291
25-DAAB-d	mai-maka					0				22		p . .					0	6292
25-DAAB-e	mai-te					0				22		p . .					0	6293
25-DAAB-f	mai-sefa					0				22		p . .					0	6294
25-E	**MPUR set**	1	1	7,742	9,981		65.00	93	C	12		. . .					0	6295
25-EA	MPUR chain	1	1	7,742	9,981		65.00	93	C	12		. . .					0	6296
25-EAA	**MPUR net**	1	1	7,742	9,981		65.00	93	C	12		. . .					0	6297
25-EAAA	MPUR cluster	1	1	7,742	9,981		65.00	93	C	12		. . .					0	6298
25-EAAA-a	mpur	1	1	7,742	9,981	0	65.00	93	C	12	Mpur	. . .					0	6299
25-F	**BORAI-HATTAM set**	1	2	18,920	24,391		65.00	99	C	41		PN .					0	6300
25-FA	BORAI-HATTAM chain	1	2	18,920	24,391		65.00	99	C	41		PN .					0	6301
25-FAA	**BORAI-HATTAM net**	1	2	18,920	24,391		65.00	99	C	41		PN .					0	6302
25-FAAA	HATAM cluster	1	1	17,690	22,805		65.00	100	C	41		PN .					0	6303
25-FAAA-a	hatam	1	1	17,690	22,805	0	65.00	100	C	41	Hatam	PN .		1993			0	6304
25-FAAA-b	moire					0				41		pn .					0	6305

Continued overleaf

Table 9-13 continued

Code 1	REFERENCE NAME / Autoglossonym 2	Coun 3	Peo 4	Mother-tongue speakers in 2000 5	in 2025 6	Media radio 7	AC% 8	E% 9	Wld 10	Tr 11	Biblioglossonym 12	Print 13-15	P-activity 16	N-activity 17	B-activity 18	J-year 19	Jayuh 20-24	Ref 25
25-FAAB	BORAI cluster	1	1	1,230	1,586		65.04	91	C	0		...					0....	6306
25-FAAB-a	borai	1	1	1,230	1,586	0	65.04	91	C	0		...					0....	6307
25-G	**MEAH-MANTION set**	1	3	41,998	54,142		81.98	100	C	41		PN.					0....	6308
25-GA	MEAH chain	1	3	41,998	54,142		81.98	100	C	41		PN.					0....	6309
25-GAA	**MEAH net**	1	2	27,214	35,083		80.34	100	C	22		P..					0....	6310
25-GAAA	MEAH cluster	1	1	18,772	24,200		85.00	100	C	22		P..					0....	6311
25-GAAA-a	meah	1	1	18,772	24,200	0	85.00	100	C	22	Meah*	P..	1990-1995				0....	6312
25-GAAB	MOSKONA cluster	1	1	8,442	10,883		70.00	100	C	12		...					0....	6313
25-GAAB-a	moskona	1	1	8,442	10,883	0	70.00	100	C	12	Moskona	...					0....	6314
25-GAB	**MANTION net**	1	1	14,784	19,059		85.00	100	C	41		PN.					0....	6315
25-GABA	MANTION cluster	1	1	14,784	19,059		85.00	100	C	41		PN.					0....	6316
25-GABA-a	manikion	1	1	14,784	19,059	0	85.00	100	C	41	Manikion	PN.	1965-1969	1996			0....	6317
25-GABA-b	Proper mantion					0				41		pn.					0....	6318
25-GABA-c	sough					0				41		pn.					0....	6319
25-H	**AWERA set**	1	3	403	519		71.22	93	C	8		...					0....	6320
25-HA	AWERA chain	1	3	403	519		71.22	93	C	8		...					0....	6321
25-HAA	**AWERA net**	1	3	403	519		71.22	93	C	8		...					0....	6322
25-HAAA	AWERA cluster	1	1	127	164		55.12	83	B	3		...					0....	6323
25-HAAA-a	awera	1	1	127	164	0	55.12	83	B	3		...					0....	6324
25-HAAB	RASAWA cluster	1	1	255	328		80.00	100	C	3		...					0....	6325
25-HAAB-a	rasawa	1	1	255	328	0	80.00	100	C	3		...					0....	6326
25-HAAC	SAPONI cluster	1	1	21	27		61.90	81	C	8		...					0....	6327
25-HAAC-a	saponi	1	1	21	27	0	61.90	81	C	8		...					0....	6328
25-I	**YAWA set**	2	3	8,166	10,648		64.19	98	C	33		P..					0....	6329
25-IA	YAWA chain	2	3	8,166	10,648		64.19	98	C	33		P..					0....	6330
25-IAA	**YAWA net**	2	3	8,166	10,648		64.19	98	C	33		P..					0....	6331
25-IAAA	YAWA cluster	2	3	8,166	10,648		64.19	98	C	33	Iau	P..	1985-1993				0....	6332
25-IAAA-a	yawa-kiriow					0				33		p..					0....	6333
25-IAAA-b	yawa-yobi					0				33		p..					0....	6334
25-IAAA-c	yawa-maninon					0				33	Yawa	P..	1989-1990				0....	6335
25-IAAA-d	ariepi					0				33		p..					0....	6336
25-IAAA-e	tatui					0				33		p..					0....	6337
25-IAAA-f	sarawandori					0				33		p..					0....	6338
25-IAAA-g	mariadei					0				33		p..					0....	6339
25-IAAA-h	mantembu	1	1	446	694	0	50.00	78	B	33		p..					0....	6340
25-IAAA-i	tarau					0				33		p..					0....	6341
25-IAAA-j	tutu					0				33		p..					0....	6342
25-IAAA-k	kabuaena					0				33		p..					0....	6343
25-IAAA-l	yapanani-borai					0				33		p..					0....	6344
25-IAAA-m	konti-unai					0				33		p..					0....	6345
25-IAAA-n	wadapi-darat					0				33		p..					0....	6346
25-IAAA-o	saweru	1	1	339	438	0	65.19	86	C	33		p..					0....	6347
25-J	**TUNGGARE-BAPU set**	1	13	9,479	12,223		59.23	89	B	22		P..					0....	6348
25-JA	TUNGGARE-BAUZI chain	1	2	2,248	2,899		64.77	95	C	22		P..					0....	6349
25-JAA	**TUNGGARE net**	1	2	2,248	2,899		64.77	95	C	22		P..					0....	6350
25-JAAA	TUNGGARE cluster	1	1	551	711		64.07	96	C	4		...					0....	6351
25-JAAA-a	tunggare	1	1	551	711	0	64.07	96	C	4		...					0....	6352
25-JAAB	BAUZI cluster	1	1	1,697	2,188		65.00	95	C	22		P..					0....	6353
25-JAAB-a	bauzi	1	1	1,697	2,188	0	65.00	95	C	22	Bauzi	P..	1983-1994				0....	6354
25-JB	DEMISA-BURATE chain	1	4	826	1,066		51.21	77	B	8		...					0....	6357
25-JBA	**DEMISA net**	1	1	551	711		60.07	86	C	2		...					0....	6358
25-JBAA	DEMISA cluster	1	1	551	711		60.07	86	C	2		...					0....	6359
25-JBAA-a	Proper demisa					0				2		...					0....	6360
25-JBAA-b	Vehicular demisa	1	1	551	711	0	60.07	86	C	2		...					0....	6361
25-JBB	**BURATE net**	1	1	127	164		10.24	35	A	2		...					0....	6362
25-JBBA	BURATE cluster	1	1	127	164		10.24	35	A	2		...					0....	6363
25-JBBA-a	burate	1	1	127	164	0	10.24	35	A	2		...					0....	6364
25-JBC	**TEFARO net**	1	1	127	164		50.39	77	B	3		...					0....	6365
25-JBCA	TEFARO cluster	1	1	127	164		50.39	77	B	3		...					0....	6366
25-JBCA-a	tefaro	1	1	127	164	0	50.39	77	B	3		...					0....	6367
25-JBD	**WORIA net**	1	1	21	27		71.43	95	C	8		...					0....	6368
25-JBDA	WORIA cluster	1	1	21	27		71.43	95	C	8		...					0....	6369
25-JBDA-a	woria	1	1	21	27	0	71.43	95	C	8		...					0....	6370
25-JC	BARAPASI-NISA chain	1	6	4,199	5,414		54.80	86	B	12		...					0....	6371
25-JCA	**KOFEI net**	1	1	127	164		65.35	89	C	2		...					0....	6372
25-JCAA	KOFEI cluster	1	1	127	164		65.35	89	C	2		...					0....	6373
25-JCAA-a	kofei	1	1	127	164	0	65.35	89	C	2		...					0....	6374
25-JCB	**SAURI net**	1	1	127	164		65.35	91	C	2		...					0....	6375
25-JCBA	SAURI cluster	1	1	127	164		65.35	91	C	2		...					0....	6376
25-JCBA-a	sauri	1	1	127	164	0	65.35	91	C	2		...					0....	6377
25-JCC	**BARAPASI net**	1	2	2,906	3,746		50.00	82	B	12		...					0....	6378
25-JCCA	BARAPASI cluster	1	2	2,906	3,746		50.00	82	B	12		...					0....	6379
25-JCCA-a	barapasi	1	1	2,673	3,445	0	49.98	83	B	12	Barapasi	...					0....	6380
25-JCD	**NISA net**	1	2	1,039	1,340		65.64	93	C	2		...					0....	6381
25-JCDA	NISA cluster	1	2	1,039	1,340		65.64	93	C	2		...					0....	6382
25-JCDA-a	Proper nisa	1	1	615	793	0	66.02	95	C	2		...					0....	6383
25-JCDA-b	bonefa	1	1	424	547	0	65.09	91	C	2		...					0....	6384
25-JD	BAPU chain	1	1	2,206	2,844		65.00	94	C	4		...					0....	6385

Continued opposite

Table 9-13 continued

Code 1	REFERENCE NAME / Autoglossonym 2	Coun 3	Peo 4	Mother-tongue speakers in 2000 5	in 2025 6	Media radio 7	AC% 8	E% 9	Wld 10	Tr 11	Biblioglossonym 12	Print 13-15	P-activity 16	N-activity 17	B-activity 18	J-year 19	Jayuh 20-24	Ref 25
25-JDA	**BAPU net**	1	1	2,206	2,844		65.00	94	C	4		...					0....	6386
25-JDAA	BAPU cluster	1	1	2,206	2,844		65.00	94	C	4		...					0....	6387
25-JDAA-a	bapu	1	1	2,206	2,844	0	65.00	94	C	4		...					0....	6388
25-K	**WAREMBORI set**	1	1	400	680		50.00	86	B	0		...					0....	6389
25-KA	WAREMBORI chain	1	1	400	680		50.00	86	B	0		...					0....	6390
25-KAA	**WAREMBORI net**	1	1	400	680		50.00	86	B	0		...					0....	6391
25-KAAA	WAREMBORI cluster	1	1	400	680		50.00	86	B	0		...					0....	6392
25-KAAA-a	warembori	1	1	400	680	0	50.00	86	B	0		...					0....	6393
25-L	**PAUWI set**	1	1	148	191		50.00	77	B	4		...					0....	6394
25-LA	PAUWI chain	1	1	148	191		50.00	77	B	4		...					0....	6395
25-LAA	**PAUWI net**	1	1	148	191		50.00	77	B	4		...					0....	6396
25-LAAA	PAUWI cluster	1	1	148	191		50.00	77	B	4		...					0....	6397
25-LAAA-a	pauwi	1	1	148	191	0	50.00	77	B	4		...					0....	6398
25-M	**BURMESO set**	1	1	255	328		60.00	91	C	4		...					0....	6399
25-MA	BURMESO chain	1	1	255	328		60.00	91	C	4		...					0....	6400
25-MAA	**BURMESO net**	1	1	255	328		60.00	91	C	4		...					0....	6401
25-MAAA	BURMESO cluster	1	1	255	328		60.00	91	C	4		...					0....	6402
25-MAAA-a	burmeso	1	1	255	328	0	60.00	91	C	4		...					0....	6403
25-N	**MASSEP set**	1	1	64	82		59.38	89	B	4		...					0....	6404
25-NA	MASSEP chain	1	1	64	82		59.38	89	B	4		...					0....	6405
25-NAA	**MASSEP net**	1	1	64	82		59.38	89	B	4		...					0....	6406
25-NAAA	MASSEP cluster	1	1	64	82		59.38	89	B	4		...					0....	6407
25-NAAA-a	massep	1	1	64	82	0	59.38	89	B	4		...					0....	6408
25-O	**SKO set**	2	9	7,417	11,184		86.65	99	C	4		...					0....	6409
25-OA	VANIMO-SANGKE chain	2	5	3,335	4,829		82.55	98	C	4		...					0....	6410
25-OAA	**SANGKE net**	1	1	212	273		65.09	93	C	4		...					0....	6411
25-OAAA	SANGKE cluster	1	1	212	273		65.09	93	C	4		...					0....	6412
25-OAAA-a	sangke	1	1	212	273	0	65.09	93	C	4		...					0....	6413
25-OAB	**TUMAWO net**	1	1	509	656		65.03	92	C	4		...					0....	6414
25-OABA	TUMAWO cluster	1	1	509	656		65.03	92	C	4		...					0....	6415
25-OABA-a	tumawo	1	1	509	656	0	65.03	92	C	4		...					0....	6416
25-OAC	**WUTUNG net**	1	1	596	928		89.93	100	C	4		...					0....	6417
25-OACA	WUTUNG cluster	1	1	596	928		89.93	100	C	4		...					0....	6418
25-OACA-a	wutung	1	1	596	928	0	89.93	100	C	4		...					0....	6419
25-OAD	**VANIMO net**	2	2	2,018	2,972		86.62	100	C	2		...					0....	6420
25-OADA	VANIMO cluster	2	2	2,018	2,972		86.62	100	C	2		...					0....	6421
25-OADA-a	vanimo	2	2	2,018	2,972	0	86.62	100	C	2		...					0....	6422
25-OB	KRISA-WARAPU chain	1	4	4,082	6,355		90.00	100	C	4		...					0....	6423
25-OBA	**KRISA net**	1	1	469	730		89.98	100	C	2		...					0....	6424
25-OBAA	KRISA cluster	1	1	469	730		89.98	100	C	2		...					0....	6425
25-OBAA-a	krisa	1	1	469	730	0	89.98	100	C	2		...					0....	6426
25-OBB	**RAWO net**	1	1	735	1,145		90.07	100	C	4		...					0....	6427
25-OBBA	RAWO cluster	1	1	735	1,145		90.07	100	C	4		...					0....	6428
25-OBBA-a	rawo	1	1	735	1,145	0	90.07	100	C	4		...					0....	6429
25-OBC	**PUARI net**	1	1	539	839		89.98	100	C	4		...					0....	6430
25-OBCA	PUARI cluster	1	1	539	839		89.98	100	C	4		...					0....	6431
25-OBCA-a	puari	1	1	539	839	0	89.98	100	C	4		...					0....	6432
25-OBD	**WARAPU net**	1	1	2,339	3,641		90.00	100	C	4		...					0....	6433
25-OBDA	WARAPU cluster	1	1	2,339	3,641		90.00	100	C	4		...					0....	6434
25-OBDA-a	warapu	1	1	2,339	3,641	0	90.00	100	C	4		...					0....	6435
25-P	**KWOMTARI-FAS set**	1	4	6,135	9,550		48.00	74	B	12		...					0....	6436
25-PA	KWOMTARI-FAS chain	1	4	6,135	9,550		48.00	74	B	12		...					0....	6437
25-PAA	**FAS net**	1	2	4,628	7,205		50.00	76	B	2		...					0....	6438
25-PAAA	FAS cluster	1	2	4,628	7,205		50.00	76	B	2		...					0....	6439
25-PAAA-a	fas	1	2	4,628	7,205	0	50.00	76	B	2		...					0....	6440
25-PAB	**KWOMTARI net**	1	1	1,046	1,628		25.05	54	B	12		...					0....	6441
25-PABA	KWOMTARI cluster	1	1	1,046	1,628		25.05	54	B	12	Kwomtari	...					0....	6442
25-PABA-a	West Central kwomtari.					0				12		...					0....	6443
25-PABA-b	ekos					0				12		...					0....	6444
25-PAC	**GURIASO net**	1	1	461	717		80.04	100	C	2		...					0....	6445
25-PACA	GURIASO cluster	1	1	461	717		80.04	100	C	2		...					0....	6446
25-PACA-a	guriaso	1	1	461	717	0	80.04	100	C	2		...					0....	6447
25-Q	**BAIBAI-NAI set**	1	2	1,092	1,699		68.32	84	C	4		...					0....	6448
25-QA	BAIBAI-NAI chain	1	2	1,092	1,699		68.32	84	C	4		...					0....	6449
25-QAA	**BAIBAI net**	1	1	394	613		29.95	55	B	4		...					0....	6450
25-QAAA	BAIBAI cluster	1	1	394	613		29.95	55	B	4		...					0....	6451
25-QAAA-a	baibai	1	1	394	613	0	29.95	55	B	4		...					0....	6452
25-QAB	**NAI net**	1	1	698	1,086		89.97	100	C	0		...					0....	6453

Continued overleaf

Table 9-13 continued

Code 1	REFERENCE NAME / Autoglossonym 2	Coun 3	Peo 4	Mother-tongue speakers in 2000 5	in 2025 6	Media radio 7	CHURCH AC% 8	E% 9	Wld 10	Tr 11	Biblioglossonym 12	SCRIPTURES Print 13-15	P-activity 16	N-activity 17	B-activity 18	J-year 19	Jayuh 20-24	Ref 25
25-QABA	NAI cluster	1	1	698	1,086		89.97	100	C	0		. . .					0	6454
25-QABA-a	nai	1	1	698	1,086	0	89.97	100	C	0							0	6455
25-R	**PYU set**	2	2	249	364		38.55	63	B	4		. . .					0	6456
25-RA	PYU chain	2	2	249	364		38.55	63	B	4		. . .					0	6457
25-RAA	**PYU net**	2	2	249	364		38.55	63	B	4		. . .					0	6458
25-RAAA	PYU cluster	2	2	249	364		38.55	63	B	4		. . .					0	6459
25-RAAA-a	pyu	2	2	249	364	0	38.55	63	B	4		. . .					0	6460
25-S	**YURI set**	1	1	3,000	5,100		50.00	86	B	0		. . .					0	6461
25-SA	YURI chain	1	1	3,000	5,100		50.00	86	B	0		. . .					0	6462
25-SAA	**YURI net**	1	1	3,000	5,100		50.00	86	B	0		. . .					0	6463
25-SAAA	YURI cluster	2	1	3,000	5,100		50.00	86	B	0		. . .					0	6464
25-SAAA-a	North Central yuri.					0				0		. . .					0	6465
25-SAAA-b	auia-tarauwi					0				0		. . .					0	6466
25-SAAA-c	usari					0				0		. . .					0	6467
25-T	**YADE set**	1	1	698	1,086		20.06	45	A	0		. . .					0	6468
25-TA	YADE chain	1	1	698	1,086		20.06	45	A	0		. . .					0	6469
25-TAA	**YADE net**	1	1	698	1,086		20.06	45	A	0		. . .					0	6470
25-TAAA	YADE cluster	1	1	698	1,086		20.06	45	A	0		. . .					0	6471
25-TAAA-a	yade	1	1	698	1,086	0	20.06	45	A	0		. . .					0	6472
25-U	**BUSA set**	1	1	446	694		19.96	46	A	2		. . .					0	6473
25-UA	BUSA chain	1	1	446	694		19.96	46	A	2		. . .					0	6474
25-UAA	**BUSA net**	1	1	446	694		19.96	46	A	2		. . .					0	6475
25-UAAA	BUSA cluster	1	1	446	694		19.96	46	A	2		. . .					0	6476
25-UAAA-a	busa	1	1	446	694	0	19.96	46	A	2		. . .					0	6477
25-V	**AMTO-MUSAN set**	1	2	443	690		17.61	40	A	4		. . .					0	6478
25-VA	AMTO chain	1	1	334	520		20.06	44	A	4		. . .					0	6479
25-VAA	**AMTO net**	1	1	334	520		20.06	44	A	4		. . .					0	6480
25-VAAA	AMTO cluster	1	1	334	520		20.06	44	A	4		. . .					0	6481
25-VAAA-a	amto	1	1	334	520	0	20.06	44	A	4		. . .					0	6482
25-VB	MUSAN chain	1	1	109	170		10.09	29	A	4		. . .					0	6483
25-VBA	**MUSAN net**	1	1	109	170		10.09	29	A	4		. . .					0	6484
25-VBAA	MUSAN cluster	1	1	109	170		10.09	29	A	4		. . .					0	6485
25-VBAA-a	musan	1	1	109	170	0	10.09	29	A	4		. . .					0	6486
25-W	**ARAI set**	1	6	2,563	4,035		36.29	62	B	41		PN.					0	6487
25-WA	AMA chain	1	6	2,563	4,035		36.29	62	B	41		PN.					0	6488
25-WAA	**AMA net**	1	1	596	928		30.03	64	B	41		PN.					0	6489
25-WAAA	AMA cluster	1	1	596	928		30.03	64	B	41		PN.					0	6490
25-WAAA-a	ama	1	1	596	928	0	30.03	64	B	41	Ama	PN.	1981-1991	1990			0	6491
25-WAB	**LARO-BO net**	1	3	929	1,448		13.46	36	A	22		P . .					0	6492
25-WABA	LARO cluster	1	1	470	732		10.00	32	A	4		. . .					0	6493
25-WABA-a	laro	1	1	470	732	0	10.00	32	A	4		. . .					0	6494
25-WABB	ITERI cluster	1	1	160	250		30.00	59	B	22		P . .					0	6495
25-WABB-a	iteri	1	1	160	250	0	30.00	59	B	22	Iteri	P . .	1988				0	6496
25-WABC	BO cluster	1	1	299	466		10.03	29	A	4		. . .					0	6497
25-WABC-a	bo	1	1	299	466	0	10.03	29	A	4		. . .					0	6498
25-WAC	**NIMO net**	1	1	697	1,128		72.74	94	C	12		. . .					0	6499
25-WACA	NIMO cluster	1	1	397	618		89.92	100	C	12		. . .					0	6500
25-WACA-a	nimo	1	1	397	618	0	89.92	100	C	12	Nimo	. . .					0	6501
25-WACB	NAKWI cluster	1	1	300	510		50.00	86	B	4		. . .					0	6502
25-WACB-a	nakwi	1	1	300	510	0	50.00	86	B	4		. . .					0	6503
25-WAD	**OWINIGA net**	1	1	341	531		34.90	65	B	22		P . .					0	6504
25-WADA	OWINIGA cluster	1	1	341	531		34.90	65	B	22		P . .					0	6505
25-WADA-a	owiniga	1	1	341	531	0	34.90	65	B	22	Owininga*	P . .	1991				0	6506
25-X	**BIBASA set**	1	1	461	717		90.02	100	C	0		. . .					0	6507
25-XA	BIBASA chain	1	1	461	717		90.02	100	C	0		. . .					0	6508
25-XAA	**BIBASA net**	1	1	461	717		90.02	100	C	0		. . .					0	6509
25-XAAA	BIBASA cluster	1	1	461	717		90.02	100	C	0		. . .					0	6510
25-XAAA-a	bibasa	1	1	461	717	0	90.02	100	C	0		. . .					0	6511
25-Y	**POROME set**	1	1	1,777	2,767		85.03	100	C	0		. . .					0	6512
25-YA	POROME chain	1	1	1,777	2,767		85.03	100	C	0		. . .					0	6513
25-YAA	**POROME net**	1	1	1,777	2,767		85.03	100	C	0		. . .					0	6514
25-YAAA	POROME cluster	1	1	1,777	2,767		85.03	100	C	0		. . .					0	6515
25-YAAA-a	Proper porome					0				0		. . .					0	6516
25-YAAA-b	kibiri					0				0		. . .					0	6517
26	**SEPIC zone**	2	93	357,893	564,626		79.75	96	C	42		PN.					1 . s . .	6518
26-A	BIKSI set	2	3	1,046	1,412		65.01	91	C	4		. . .					0	6519
26-AA	BIKSI chain	2	3	1,046	1,412		65.01	91	C	4		. . .					0	6520

Continued opposite

Table 9-13 continued

Code 1	REFERENCE NAME / Autoglossonym 2	Coun 3	Peo 4	Mother-tongue speakers in 2000 5	in 2025 6	Media radio 7	CHURCH AC% 8	E% 9	Wld 10	Tr 11	Biblioglossonym 12	SCRIPTURES Print 13-15	P-activity 16	N-activity 17	B-activity 18	J-year 19	Jayuh 20-24	Ref 25
26-AAA	**BIKSI net**	2	3	1,046	1,412		65.01	91	C	4		. . .					0	6521
26-AAAA	BIKSI cluster	2	3	1,046	1,412	0	65.01	91	C	4		. . .					0	6522
26-AAAA-a	biksi	2	2	537	756	0	64.99	89	C	4		. . .					0	6523
26-AAAA-b	kimki	1	1	509	656	0	65.03	92	C	4		. . .					0	6524
26-B	**UPPER SEPIK set**	2	5	13,961	21,980		71.00	94	C	22		P . .					0 . s . .	6525
26-BA	ABAU chain	2	2	8,090	12,196		80.51	99	C	22		P . .					0 . s . .	6526
26-BAA	**ABAU net**	2	2	8,090	12,196		80.51	99	C	22		P . .					0 . s . .	6527
26-BAAA	ABAU cluster	2	2	8,090	12,196		80.51	99	C	22		P . .					0 . s . .	6528
26-BAAA-a	abau	2	2	8,090	12,196	0	80.51	99	C	22	Abau	P . .	1990				0 . s . .	6529
26-BB	IWAM-AMAL chain	1	1	5,064	8,528		65.54	93	C	4		. . .					0	6530
26-BBA	**IWAM net**	1	1	4,500	7,650		70.00	98	C	0		. . .					0	6531
26-BBAA	WEST IWAM cluster	1	1	2,000	3,400		70.00	98	C	0		. . .					0	6532
26-BBAA-a	West iwam	1	1	2,000	3,400	0	70.00	98	C	0		. . .					0	6533
26-BBAB	EAST IWAM cluster	1	1	2,500	4,250		70.00	98	C	0		. . .					0	6534
26-BBAB-a	East iwam	1	1	2,500	4,250	0	70.00	98	C	0		. . .					0	6535
26-BBB	**AMAL net**	1	1	564	878		29.96	56	B	4		. . .					0	6536
26-BBBA	AMAL cluster	1	1	564	878		29.96	56	B	4		. . .					0	6537
26-BBBA-a	amal	1	1	564	878	0	29.96	56	B	4		. . .					0	6538
26-BBBA-b	alai					0				4		. . .					0	6539
26-BC	CHENAP-WOGAMUSIN chain	1	2	807	1,256		10.04	36	A	2		. . .					0	6540
26-BCA	**CHENAP net**	1	1	272	423		9.93	31	A	2		. . .					0	6541
26-BCAA	CHENAP cluster	1	1	272	423		9.93	31	A	2		. . .					0	6542
26-BCAA-a	chenap	1	1	272	423	0	9.93	31	A	2		. . .					0	6543
26-BCB	**WOGAMUSIN net**	1	1	535	833		10.09	39	A	2		. . .					0	6544
26-BCBA	WOGAMUSIN cluster	1	1	535	833		10.09	39	A	2		. . .					0	6545
26-BCBA-a	wogamusin	1	1	535	833	0	10.09	39	A	2		. . .					0	6546
26-C	**YELLOW-RIVER set**	1	3	4,748	7,391		72.83	93	C	12		. . .					0	6547
26-CA	NAMIA chain	1	1	4,069	6,334		80.00	100	C	12		. . .					0	6548
26-CAA	**NAMIA net**	1	1	4,069	6,334		80.00	100	C	12		. . .					0	6549
26-CAAA	NAMIA cluster	1	1	4,069	6,334		80.00	100	C	12	Namia	. . .					0	6550
26-CAAA-a	ailuaki					0				12		. . .					0	6551
26-CAAA-b	amani					0				12		. . .					0	6552
26-CAAA-c	wiari					0				12		. . .					0	6553
26-CAAA-d	lawo					0				12		. . .					0	6554
26-CB	AK chain	1	1	121	188		29.75	57	B	4		. . .					0	6555
26-CBA	**AK net**	1	1	121	188		29.75	57	B	4		. . .					0	6556
26-CBAA	AK cluster	1	1	121	188		29.75	57	B	4		. . .					0	6557
26-CBAA-a	ak	1	1	121	188	0	29.75	57	B	4		. . .					0	6558
26-CC	AWUN chain	1	1	558	869		29.93	55	B	4		. . .					0	6559
26-CCA	**AWUN net**	1	1	558	869		29.93	55	B	4		. . .					0	6560
26-CCAA	AWUN cluster	1	1	558	869		29.93	55	B	4		. . .					0	6561
26-CCAA-a	awun	1	1	558	869	0	29.93	55	B	4		. . .					0	6562
26-D	**RAM set**	1	3	2,178	3,391		48.67	70	B	12		. . .					0	6563
26-DA	BOUYE chain	1	1	981	1,527		29.97	53	B	12		. . .					0	6564
26-DAA	**BOUYE net**	1	1	981	1,527		29.97	53	B	12		. . .					0	6565
26-DAAA	BOUYE cluster	1	1	981	1,527		29.97	53	B	12		. . .					0	6566
26-DAAA-a	bouye	1	1	981	1,527	0	29.97	53	B	12	Pouye	. . .					0	6567
26-DB	KAMNUM chain	1	1	629	980		90.14	100	C	3		. . .					0	6568
26-DBA	**KAMNUM net**	1	1	629	980		90.14	100	C	3		. . .					0	6569
26-DBAA	KAMNUM cluster	1	1	629	980		90.14	100	C	3		. . .					0	6570
26-DBAA-a	kamnum	1	1	629	980	0	90.14	100	C	3		. . .					0	6571
26-DC	KARAWA chain	1	1	568	884		35.04	67	B	4		. . .					0	6572
26-DCA	**KARAWA net**	1	1	568	884		35.04	67	B	4		. . .					0	6573
26-DCAA	KARAWA cluster	1	1	568	884		35.04	67	B	4		. . .					0	6574
26-DCAA-a	karawa	1	1	568	884	0	35.04	67	B	4		. . .					0	6575
26-E	**TAMA set**	1	5	11,397	17,742		72.39	94	C	41		PN .					0	6576
26-EA	KALOU chain	1	1	1,192	1,855		25.00	47	A	2		. . .					0	6577
26-EAA	**KALOU net**	1	1	1,192	1,855		25.00	47	A	2		. . .					0	6578
26-EAAA	KALOU cluster	1	1	1,192	1,855		25.00	47	A	2		. . .					0	6579
26-EAAA-a	kalou	1	1	1,192	1,855	0	25.00	47	A	2		. . .					0	6580
26-EB	PAHI-MEHEK chain	1	2	8,123	12,646		76.13	100	C	2		. . .					0	6581
26-EBA	**PAHI net**	1	1	909	1,415		85.04	100	C	2		. . .					0	6582
26-EBAA	PAHI cluster	1	1	909	1,415		85.04	100	C	2		. . .					0	6583
26-EBAA-a	pahi	1	1	909	1,415	0	85.04	100	C	2		. . .					0	6584
26-EBB	**MEHEK net**	1	1	7,214	11,231		75.01	100	C	2		. . .					0	6585
26-EBBA	MEHEK cluster	1	1	7,214	11,231		75.01	100	C	2		. . .					0	6586
26-EBBA-a	mehek	1	1	7,214	11,231	0	75.01	100	C	2		. . .					0	6587
26-EC	MAYO-PASI chain	1	2	2,082	3,241		84.92	100	C	41		PN .					0	6588
26-ECA	**PASI net**	1	1	687	1,069		94.91	100	C	4		. . .					0	6589
26-ECAA	PASI cluster	1	1	687	1,069		94.91	100	C	4		. . .					0	6590
26-ECAA-a	pasi	1	1	687	1,069	0	94.91	100	C	4		. . .					0	6591

Continued overleaf

Table 9-13 continued

Code 1	REFERENCE NAME / Autoglossonym 2	Coun 3	Peo 4	Mother-tongue speakers in 2000 5	in 2025 6	Media radio 7	CHURCH AC% 8	E% 9	Wld 10	Tr 11	Biblioglossonym 12	SCRIPTURES Print 13-15	P-activity 16	N-activity 17	B-activity 18	J-year 19	Jayuh 20-24	Ref 25
26-ECB	**MAYO net**	1	1	1,395	2,172		80.00	100	C	41		PN.					0	6592
26-ECBA	MAYO cluster	1	1	1,395	2,172		80.00	100	C	41		PN.					0	6593
26-ECBA-a	yaw					0				41		pn.					0	6594
26-ECBA-b	yessan-mayo	1	1	1,395	2,172	0	80.00	100	C	41	Yessan-mayo*	PN.	1993	1980-1996			0	6595
26-F	**KWANGA-KWOMA set**	1	6	31,686	49,759		68.84	94	C	42		PN.					0	6596
26-FA	KWOMA chain	1	1	7,163	11,582		74.54	97	C	42		PN.					0	6597
26-FAA	**KWOMA-NUKUMA net**	1	1	7,163	11,582		74.54	97	C	42		PN.					0	6598
26-FAAA	NUKUMA cluster	1	1	3,000	5,100		60.00	93	C	0		...					0	6599
26-FAAA-a	nukuma	1	1	3,000	5,100	0	60.00	93	C	0		...					0	6600
26-FAAB	KWOMA cluster	1	1	4,163	6,482		85.01	100	C	42		PN.					0	6601
26-FAAB-a	kwoma	1	1	4,163	6,482	0	85.01	100	C	42	Washkuk*	PN.	1963-1968	1974-1975			0	6602
26-FB	KWANGA chain	1	5	24,523	38,177		67.18	93	C	41		PN.					0	6603
26-FBA	**SEIM net**	1	1	8,313	12,942		70.00	99	C	0		...					0	6604
26-FBAA	SEIM cluster	1	1	8,313	12,942		70.00	99	C	0		...					0	6605
26-FBAA-a	seim	1	1	8,313	12,942	0	70.00	99	C	0		...					0	6606
26-FBB	**WAMSAK net**	1	1	7,030	10,944		64.99	91	C	2		...					0	6607
26-FBBA	WAMSAK cluster	1	1	7,030	10,944		64.99	91	C	2		...					0	6608
26-FBBA-a	wamsak	1	1	7,030	10,944	0	64.99	91	C	2		...					0	6609
26-FBC	**KWANGA net**	1	3	9,180	14,291		66.30	88	C	41		PN.					0	6610
26-FBCA	KWANGA cluster	1	3	9,180	14,291		66.30	88	C	41	Kwanga	PN.	1982				0	6611
26-FBCA-a	bongos	1	1	3,435	5,347	0	65.01	87	C	41		pn.					0	6612
26-FBCA-b	tau					0				41		pn.					0	6613
26-FBCA-c	apos					0				41		pn.					0	6614
26-FBCA-d	bongomaisi					0				41		pn.					0	6615
26-FBCA-e	yubanakor	1	1	5,253	8,178	0	65.01	88	C	41	Yubanakor	PN.	1982	1991			0	6616
26-G	**YERAKAI set**	1	1	567	882		94.89	100	C	4		...					0	6617
26-GA	YERAKAI chain	1	1	567	882		94.89	100	C	4		...					0	6618
26-GAA	**YERAKAI net**	1	1	567	882		94.89	100	C	4		...					0	6619
26-GAAA	YERAKAI cluster	1	1	567	882		94.89	100	C	4		...					0	6620
26-GAAA-a	yerakai	1	1	567	882	0	94.89	100	C	4		...					0	6621
26-H	NDU set	1	13	210,514	334,481		86.68	100	C	42		PN.					0	6622
26-HA	NGALA chain	1	1	198	308		9.60	32	A	4		...					0	6623
26-HAA	**NGALA net**	1	1	198	308		9.60	32	A	4		...					0	6624
26-HAAA	NGALA cluster	1	1	198	308		9.60	32	A	4		...					0	6625
26-HAAA-a	ngala	1	1	198	308	0	9.60	32	A	4		...					0	6626
26-HB	MANAMBU-YELOGU chain	1	2	3,325	5,176		69.98	95	C	41		PN.					0	6627
26-HBA	**MANAMBU net**	1	2	3,325	5,176		69.98	95	C	41		PN.					0	6628
26-HBAA	MANAMBU cluster	1	1	2,991	4,656		74.99	100	C	41		PN.					0	6629
26-HBAA-a	manambu	1	1	2,991	4,656	0	74.99	100	C	41	Manambu	PN.	1972	1979			0	6630
26-HBAB	YELOGU cluster	1	1	334	520		25.15	50	B	4		...					0	6631
26-HBAB-a	yelogu	1	1	334	520	0	25.15	50	B	4		...					0	6632
26-HC	KWASENGEN chain	1	3	79,055	123,070		88.85	100	C	41		PN.					0	6633
26-HCA	**KWASENGEN net**	1	1	8,287	12,901		70.00	100	C	22		P..					0	6634
26-HCAA	KWASENGEN cluster	1	1	8,287	12,901		70.00	100	C	22		P..					0	6635
26-HCAA-a	kwasengen	1	1	8,287	12,901	0	70.00	100	C	22	Ambulas: Wosera*	P..	1978				0	6636
26-HCB	**AMBULAS net**	1	2	70,768	110,169		91.06	100	C	41		PN.					0	6637
26-HCBA	AMBULAS cluster	1	2	70,768	110,169		91.06	100	C	41	Ambulas	PN.	1989-1992	1983			0	6638
26-HCBA-a	East wosera					0				41		pn.					0	6639
26-HCBA-b	maprik	1	1	19,618	30,541	0	86.00	100	C	41	Ambulas: Maprik	PN.	1974	1983			0	6640
26-HCBA-c	wingei					0				41	Ambulas: Wingei	Pn.	1989				0	6641
26-HD	BOIKIN-MUNJI chain	1	1	98,359	159,883		86.03	100	C	22		P..					0	6642
26-HDA	**BOIKIN-MUNJI net**	1	1	98,359	159,883		86.03	100	C	22		P..					0	6643
26-HDAA	KUBALIA cluster	1	1	3,000	5,100		80.00	100	C	0		...					0	6644
26-HDAA-a	rabundogum					0				0		...					0	6645
26-HDAA-b	yumungu					0				0		...					0	6646
26-HDAB	KUNAI cluster	1	1	200	340		70.00	98	C	0		...					0	6647
26-HDAB-a	kunai	1	1	200	340	0	70.00	98	C	0		...					0	6648
26-HDAC	YANGORU cluster	1	1	15,000	25,500		80.00	100	C	0		...					0	6649
26-HDAC-a	kwolyik					0				0		...					0	6650
26-HDAC-b	mambuk					0				0		...					0	6651
26-HDAC-c	kworabri					0				0		...					0	6652
26-HDAC-d	ambukanja					0				0		...					0	6653
26-HDAC-e	soli					0				0		...					0	6654
26-HDAD	MUNJI cluster	1	1	2,000	3,400		80.00	100	C	0		...					0	6655
26-HDAD-a	niagombi					0				0		...					0	6656
26-HDAD-b	nyakandogun					0				0		...					0	6657
26-HDAE	NAGUM cluster	1	1	25,000	42,500		85.00	100	C	0		...					0	6658
26-HDAE-a	mundjiharanji					0				0		...					0	6659
26-HDAE-b	tuanumbu					0				0		...					0	6660
26-HDAE-c	passam					0				0		...					0	6661
26-HDAF	BOIKIN cluster	1	1	51,159	79,643		89.00	100	C	22	Boiken: Yangoru*	P..	1971-1979				0	6662
26-HDAF-a	karawop					1				22		p..					0	6663
26-HDAF-b	salimbua					1				22		P..					0	6664
26-HDAG	WEST MUSHU cluster	1	1	2,000	3,400		85.00	100	C	0		...					0	6665
26-HDAG-a	West mushu	1	1	2,000	3,400	0	85.00	100	C	0		...					0	6666
26-HE	SAWOS chain	1	4	13,725	21,367		80.07	100	C	22		P..					0	6667
26-HEA	**SAWOS-GAIKUNDI net**	1	4	13,725	21,367		80.07	100	C	22		P..					0	6668
26-HEAA	SAWOS cluster	1	1	11,504	17,909		80.00	100	C	2		...					0	6669
26-HEAA-a	Central sawos					0				2		...					0	6670

Continued opposite

Table 9-13 continued

Code 1	REFERENCE NAME / Autoglossonym 2	Coun 3	Peo 4	Mother-tongue speakers in 2000 5	in 2025 6	Media radio 7	AC% 8	E% 9	Wld 10	Tr 11	Biblioglossonym 12	Print 13-15	P-activity 16	N-activity 17	B-activity 18	J-year 19	Jayuh 20-24	Ref 25
26-HEAA-b	East sawos					0				2		. . .					0	6671
26-HEAA-c	chimbian					0				2		. . .					0	6672
26-HEAB	KOIWAT cluster	1	1	769	1,197		75.03	100	C	4		. . .					0	6673
26-HEAB-a	koiwat	1	1	769	1,197	0	75.03	100	C	4		. . .					0	6674
26-HEAC	BURUI cluster	1	1	256	399		75.00	100	C	4		. . .					0	6675
26-HEAC-a	burui	1	1	256	399	0	75.00	100	C	4		. . .					0	6676
26-HEAD	GAIKUNDI cluster	1	1	1,196	1,862		85.03	100	C	22		P . .					0	6677
26-HEAD-a	gaikundi	1	1	1,196	1,862	0	85.03	100	C	22	Gaikundi	P . .	1978				0	6678
26-HF	IATMUL chain	1	2	15,852	24,677		90.00	100	C	42		PN .					0	6679
26-HFA	IATMUL net	1	2	15,852	24,677		90.00	100	C	42		PN .					0	6680
26-HFAA	IATMUL cluster	1	1	15,339	23,879		90.00	100	C	42	Ngepma Kwundi*	PN .	1965	1975			0	6681
26-HFAA-a	palimbei					0				42		pn .					0	6682
26-HFAA-b	nyaura					0				42		pn .					0	6683
26-HFAA-c	West nyaura					0				42		pn .					0	6684
26-HFAB	SENGO cluster	1	1	513	798		90.06	100	C	4		. . .					0	6685
26-HFAB-a	sengo	1	1	513	798	0	90.06	100	C	4		. . .					0	6686
26-I	SANIO-HEWA set	1	4	5,019	7,928		62.92	86	C	22		P . .					0	6687
26-IA	SANIO-NIKSEK chain	1	2	1,629	2,579		39.78	67	B	22		P . .					0	6688
26-IAA	SANIO-HIOWE net	1	1	936	1,457		30.02	59	B	22		P . .					0	6689
26-IAAA	SANIO-HIOWE cluster	1	1	936	1,457		30.02	59	B	22	Saniyo-hiyowe	P . .	1983-1984				0	6690
26-IAAA-a	sanio					0				22		p . .					0	6691
26-IAAA-b	hiowe					0				22		p . .					0	6692
26-IAAA-c	makabuky					0				22		p . .					0	6693
26-IAAA-d	nakiai					0				22		p . .					0	6694
26-IAB	NIKSEK net	1	1	693	1,122		52.96	78	B	2		. . .					0	6695
26-IABA	PAKA cluster	1	1	300	510		70.00	98	C	0		. . .					0	6696
26-IABA-a	Proper paka					0				0		. . .					0	6697
26-IABA-b	setiali					0				0		. . .					0	6698
26-IABB	GABIANO cluster	1	1	393	612		39.95	63	B	2		. . .					0	6699
26-IABB-a	gabiano	1	1	393	612	0	39.95	63	B	2		. . .					0	6700
26-IB	HEWA chain	1	1	2,745	4,273		80.00	100	C	22		P . .					0	6701
26-IBA	HEWA net	1	1	2,745	4,273		80.00	100	C	22		P . .					0	6702
26-IBAA	HEWA cluster	1	1	2,745	4,273		80.00	100	C	22		P . .					0	6703
26-IBAA-a	Proper hewa	1	1	2,745	4,273	0	80.00	100	C	22	Hewa	P . .	1985				0	6704
26-IBAA-b	yoliapi					0				22		p . .					0	6705
26-IBAA-c	umairof					0				22		p . .					0	6706
26-IBAA-d	morubanmin					0				22		p . .					0	6707
26-IBAA-e	kiane					0				22		p . .					0	6708
26-IBAA-f	mongolipa					0				22		p . .					0	6709
26-IBAA-g	pauia					0				22		p . .					0	6710
26-IC	PIAME chain	1	1	145	226		9.66	29	A	2		. . .					0	6711
26-ICA	PIAME net	1	1	145	226		9.66	29	A	2		. . .					0	6712
26-ICAA	PIAME cluster	1	1	145	226		9.66	29	A	2		. . .					0	6713
26-ICAA-a	piame	1	1	145	226	0	9.66	29	A	2		. . .					0	6714
26-ID	BIKARU chain	1	1	500	850		60.00	93	C	0		. . .					0	6715
26-IDA	BIKARU net	1	1	500	850		60.00	93	C	0		. . .					0	6716
26-IDAA	BIKARU cluster	1	1	500	850		60.00	93	C	0		. . .					0	6717
26-IDAA-a	bikaru	1	1	500	850	0	60.00	93	C	0		. . .					0	6718
26-J	BAHINEMO-KAPRIMAN set	1	9	4,687	7,297		73.57	91	C	32		P . .					1	6719
26-JA	BITARA chain	1	1	353	550		94.90	100	C	4		. . .					0	6720
26-JAA	BITARA net	1	1	353	550		94.90	100	C	4		. . .					0	6721
26-JAAA	BITARA cluster	1	1	353	550		94.90	100	C	4		. . .					0	6722
26-JAAA-a	bitara	1	1	353	550	0	94.90	100	C	4		. . .					0	6723
26-JAAA-b	apowasi					0				4		. . .					0	6724
26-JB	BAHINEMO chain	1	1	465	724		89.89	100	C	22		P . .					0	6725
26-JBA	BAHINEMO net	1	1	465	724		89.89	100	C	22		P . .					0	6726
26-JBAA	BAHINEMO cluster	1	1	465	724		89.89	100	C	22		P . .					0	6727
26-JBAA-a	bahinemo	1	1	465	724	0	89.89	100	C	22	Bahinemo	P . .	1973-1983				0	6728
26-JC	MARI chain	1	1	174	271		90.23	100	C	4		. . .					0	6729
26-JCA	MARI net	1	1	174	271		90.23	100	C	4		. . .					0	6730
26-JCAA	MARI cluster	1	1	174	271		90.23	100	C	4		. . .					0	6731
26-JCAA-a	mari	1	1	174	271	0	90.23	100	C	4		. . .					0	6732
26-JD	BISIS chain	1	2	1,323	2,060		44.90	73	B	4		. . .					0	6733
26-JDA	BISIS net	1	2	1,323	2,060		44.90	73	B	4		. . .					0	6734
26-JDAA	BISIS cluster	1	2	1,323	2,060		44.90	73	B	4		. . .					0	6735
26-JDAA-a	bisis	1	2	1,323	2,060	0	44.90	73	B	4		. . .					0	6736
26-JE	WATAKATAUI chain	1	1	233	362		94.85	100	C	32		P . .					1	6737
26-JEA	WATAKATAUI net	1	1	233	362		94.85	100	C	32		P . .					1	6738
26-JEAA	WATAKATAUI cluster	1	1	233	362		94.85	100	C	32		P . .					1	6739
26-JEAA-a	watakataui	1	1	233	362	0	94.85	100	C	32	Waxe*	P . .	1991			1987	1	6740
26-JF	KAPRIMAN chain	1	1	1,853	2,885		85.00	100	C	4		. . .					0	6741
26-JFA	KAPRIMAN net	1	1	1,853	2,885		85.00	100	C	4		. . .					0	6742
26-JFAA	KAPRIMAN cluster	1	1	1,853	2,885		85.00	100	C	4		. . .					0	6743
26-JFAA-a	Proper kapriman	1	1	1,853	2,885	0	85.00	100	C	4		. . .					0	6744
26-JFAA-b	karambit					0				4		. . .					0	6745
26-JG	SUMARIUP chain	1	2	286	445		51.75	71	B	6		. . .					0	6746
26-JGA	SUMARIUP net	1	2	286	445		51.75	71	B	6		. . . .						6747

Continued overleaf

Table 9-13 continued

Code 1	REFERENCE NAME / Autoglossonym 2	Coun 3	Peo 4	Mother-tongue speakers in 2000 5	in 2025 6	Media radio 7	AC% 8	E% 9	Wld 10	Tr 11	Biblioglossonym 12	Print 13-15	P-activity 16	N-activity 17	B-activity 18	J-year 19	Jayuh 20-24	Ref 25
26-JGAA	SUMARIUP cluster	1	2	286	445		51.75	71	B	6		...					0....	6748
26-JGAA-a	sumariup	1	2	286	445	0	51.75	71	B	6		...					0....	6749
26-K	**ALAMBLAK-KANINGRA set**	1	3	4,114	6,403		60.53	83	C	22		P..					0....	6750
26-KA	ALAMBLAK chain	1	2	3,707	5,770		57.30	81	B	22		P..					0....	6751
26-KAA	**ALAMBLAK net**	1	2	3,707	5,770		57.30	81	B	22		P..					0....	6752
26-KAAA	ALAMBLAK cluster	1	2	3,707	5,770		57.30	81	B	22	Alamblak	P..	1974-1987				0....	6753
26-KAAA-a	kuvenmas					0				22		p..					0....	6754
26-KAAA-b	karawari	1	1	1,840	2,864	0	85.00	100	C	22		p..					0....	6755
26-KB	KANINGRA chain	1	1	407	633		89.93	100	C	4		...					0....	6756
26-KBA	**KANINGRA net**	1	1	407	633		89.93	100	C	4		...					0....	6757
26-KBAA	KANINGRA cluster	1	1	407	633		89.93	100	C	4		...					0....	6758
26-KBAA-a	kaningra	1	1	407	633	0	89.93	100	C	4		...					0....	6759
26-L	**MARAMBA set**	1	1	436	679		39.91	61	B	4		...					0....	6760
26-LA	MARAMBA chain	1	1	436	679		39.91	61	B	4		...					0....	6761
26-LAA	**MARAMBA net**	1	1	436	679		39.91	61	B	4		...					0....	6762
26-LAAA	MARAMBA cluster	1	1	436	679		39.91	61	B	4		...					0....	6763
26-LAAA-a	maramba	1	1	436	679	0	39.91	61	B	4		...					0....	6764
26-M	**MEKMEK-BIWAT set**	1	6	7,391	11,509		45.72	68	B	22		P..					0....	6765
26-MA	CHANGRIWA chain	1	1	723	1,126		30.01	53	B	4		...					0....	6766
26-MAA	**CHANGRIWA net**	1	1	723	1,126		30.01	53	B	4		...					0....	6767
26-MAAA	CHANGRIWA cluster	1	1	723	1,126		30.01	53	B	4		...					0....	6768
26-MAAA-a	changriwa	1	1	723	1,126	0	30.01	53	B	4		...					0....	6769
26-MB	MEKMEK chain	1	1	1,505	2,344		10.03	28	A	4		...					0....	6770
26-MBA	**MEKMEK net**	1	1	1,505	2,344		10.03	28	A	4		...					0....	6771
26-MBAA	MEKMEK cluster	1	1	1,505	2,344		10.03	28	A	4		...					0....	6772
26-MBAA-a	mekmek	1	1	1,505	2,344	0	10.03	28	A	4		...					0....	6773
26-MC	MIYAK-BIWAT chain	1	4	5,163	8,039		58.32	81	B	22		P..					0....	6774
26-MCA	**MIYAK net**	1	1	796	1,240		40.08	62	B	0		...					0....	6775
26-MCAA	MIYAK cluster	1	1	796	1,240		40.08	62	B	0		...					0....	6776
26-MCAA-a	miyak	1	1	796	1,240	0	40.08	62	B	0		...					0....	6777
26-MCB	**KYENELE net**	1	1	1,278	1,990		70.03	98	C	22		P..					0....	6778
26-MCBA	KYENELE cluster	1	1	1,278	1,990		70.03	98	C	22		P..					0....	6779
26-MCBA-a	kyenele	1	1	1,278	1,990	0	70.03	98	C	22	Kianying Balang*	P..	1993-1994				0....	6780
26-MCC	**BIWAT-BUN net**	1	2	3,089	4,809		58.17	79	B	5		...					0....	6781
26-MCCA	BUN cluster	1	1	282	439		40.07	61	B	5		...					0....	6782
26-MCCA-a	bun	1	1	282	439	0	40.07	61	B	5		...					0....	6783
26-MCCB	BIWAT cluster	1	1	2,807	4,370		59.99	81	B	2		...					0....	6784
26-MCCB-a	biwat	1	1	2,807	4,370	0	59.99	81	B	2		...					0....	6785
26-N	**MONGOL-LANGAM set**	1	3	2,043	3,182		22.61	42	A	4		...					0....	6786
26-NA	MONGOL chain	1	1	491	765		39.92	62	B	4		...					0....	6787
26-NAA	**MONGOL net**	1	1	491	765		39.92	62	B	4		...					0....	6788
26-NAAA	MONGOL cluster	1	1	491	765		39.92	62	B	4		...					0....	6789
26-NAAA-a	mongol	1	1	491	765	0	39.92	62	B	4		...					0....	6790
26-NB	LANGAM chain	1	1	369	575		40.11	62	B	4		...					0....	6791
26-NBA	**LANGAM net**	1	1	369	575		40.11	62	B	4		...					0....	6792
26-NBAA	LANGAM cluster	1	1	369	575		40.11	62	B	4		...					0....	6793
26-NBAA-a	langam	1	1	369	575	0	40.11	62	B	4		...					0....	6794
26-NC	YAUL chain	1	1	1,183	1,842		9.97	28	A	4		...					0....	6795
26-NCA	**YAUL net**	1	1	1,183	1,842		9.97	28	A	4		...					0....	6796
26-NCAA	YAUL cluster	1	1	1,183	1,842		9.97	28	A	4		...					0....	6797
26-NCAA-a	yaul	1	1	1,183	1,842	0	9.97	28	A	4		...					0....	6798
26-O	**ARAFUNDI set**	1	1	1,565	2,509		26.01	51	B	4		...					0....	6799
26-OA	ARAFUNDI chain	1	1	1,565	2,509		26.01	51	B	4		...					0....	6800
26-OAA	**ALFENDIO net**	1	1	1,065	1,659		10.05	31	A	4		...					0....	6801
26-OAAA	ALFENDIO cluster	1	1	1,065	1,659		10.05	31	A	4		...					0....	6802
26-OAAA-a	alfendio	1	1	1,065	1,659	0	10.05	31	A	4		...					0....	6803
26-OAB	**MEAKAMBUT net**	1	1	500	850		60.00	93	C	0		...					0....	6804
26-OABA	MEAKAMBUT cluster	1	1	500	850		60.00	93	C	0		...					0....	6805
26-OABA-a	meakambut	1	1	500	850	0	60.00	93	C	0		...					0....	6806
26-P	**PORAPORA set**	1	4	13,498	21,069		84.46	100	C	23		P..					0....	6807
26-PA	BOTIN chain	1	1	8,711	13,561		87.00	100	C	22		P..					0....	6808
26-PAA	**BOTIN net**	1	1	8,711	13,561		87.00	100	C	22		P..					0....	6809
26-PAAA	BOTIN cluster	1	1	8,711	13,561		87.00	100	C	22		P..					0....	6810
26-PAAA-a	kambot	1	1	8,711	13,561	0	87.00	100	C	22	Ap Ma	P..	1994				0....	6811
26-PAAA-b	kambaramba					0				22		p..					0....	6812
26-PB	AION-ABU chain	1	2	4,714	7,395		79.61	99	C	23		P..					0....	6813
26-PBA	**AION-ABU net**	1	2	4,714	7,395		79.61	99	C	23		P..					0....	6814
26-PBAA	AION cluster	1	1	1,246	1,939		84.99	100	C	4		...					0....	6815
26-PBAA-a	aion	1	1	1,246	1,939	0	84.99	100	C	4		...					0....	6816

Continued opposite

Table 9-13 continued

Code 1	REFERENCE NAME / Autoglossonym 2	Coun 3	Peo 4	Mother-tongue speakers in 2000 5	in 2025 6	Media radio 7	CHURCH AC% 8	E% 9	Wld 10	Tr 11	Biblioglossonym 12	Print 13-15	P-activity 16	N-activity 17	B-activity 18	J-year 19	Jayuh 20-24	Ref 25
26-PBAB	LEMBUM cluster	1	1	400	680		60.00	93	C	0		. . .					0	6817
26-PBAB-a	lembum	1	1	400	680	0	60.00	93	C	0		. . .					0	6818
26-PBAC	ABU cluster	1	1	3,068	4,776		79.99	100	C	23		P . .					0	6819
26-PBAC-a	Proper abu	1	1	3,068	4,776	0	79.99	100	C	23	Abu	P . .	1969				0	6820
26-PBAC-b	adjora					0				23		p . .					0	6821
26-PBAC-c	azao					0				23		p . .					0	6822
26-PC	GOROVU chain	1	1	73	113		94.52	100	C	8		. . .					0	6823
26-PCA	GOROVU net	1	1	73	113		94.52	100	C	8		. . .					0	6824
26-PCAA	GOROVU cluster	1	1	73	113		94.52	100	C	8		. . .					0	6825
26-PCAA-a	gorovu	1	1	73	113	0	94.52	100	C	8		. . .					0	6826
26-Q	BANARO set	1	1	2,887	4,495		80.01	100	C	12		. . .					0	6827
26-QA	BANARO chain	1	1	2,887	4,495		80.01	100	C	12		. . .					0	6828
26-QAA	BANARO net	1	1	2,887	4,495		80.01	100	C	12		. . .					0	6829
26-QAAA	BANARO cluster	1	1	2,887	4,495		80.01	100	C	12		. . .					0	6830
26-QAAA-a	banaro	1	1	2,887	4,495	0	80.01	100	C	12	Banaro	. . .					0	6831
26-R	OTTILIEN set	1	5	5,597	8,713		83.54	100	C	12		. . .					0	6832
26-RA	WATAM-BOREI chain	1	3	3,394	5,283		82.97	100	C	12		. . .					0	6833
26-RAA	WATAM-BOREI net	1	3	3,394	5,283		82.97	100	C	12		. . .					0	6834
26-RAAA	WATAM cluster	1	1	547	851		89.95	100	C	4		. . .					0	6835
26-RAAA-a	watam	1	1	547	851	0	89.95	100	C	4		. . .					0	6836
26-RAAB	BOREI cluster	1	1	2,379	3,704		79.99	100	C	12	Borei	. . .					0	6837
26-RAAB-a	boroi					0				12		. . .					0	6838
26-RAAB-b	borewar					0				12		. . .					0	6839
26-RAAB-c	botbot					0				12		. . .					0	6840
26-RAAB-d	gamei					0				12		. . .					0	6841
26-RAAC	KAIAN cluster	1	1	468	728		89.96	100	C	0		. . .					0	6842
26-RAAC-a	kaian	1	1	468	728	0	89.96	100	C	0		. . .					0	6843
26-RB	BOSMAN-AWAR chain	1	2	2,203	3,430		84.43	100	C	4		. . .					0	6844
26-RBA	BOSMAN net	1	1	1,225	1,908		80.00	100	C	4		. . .					0	6845
26-RBAA	BOSMAN cluster	1	1	1,225	1,908		80.00	100	C	4		. . .					0	6846
26-RBAA-a	bosman	1	1	1,225	1,908	0	80.00	100	C	4		. . .					0	6847
26-RBB	AWAR net	1	1	978	1,522		89.98	100	C	4		. . .					0	6848
26-RBBA	AWAR cluster	1	1	978	1,522		89.98	100	C	4		. . .					0	6849
26-RBBA-a	Proper awar					0				4		. . .					0	6850
26-RBBA-b	nubia	1	1	978	1,522	0	89.98	100	C	4		. . .					0	6851
26-S	MISEGIAN set	1	3	12,695	19,762		77.49	100	C	35		P . .					0 . s . .	6852
26-SA	MISEGIAN chain	1	3	12,695	19,762		77.49	100	C	35		P . .					0 . s . .	6853
26-SAA	KIRE net	1	1	2,557	3,980		79.98	100	C	35		P . .					0 . s . .	6854
26-SAAA	KIRE cluster	1	1	2,557	3,980		79.98	100	C	35		P . .					0 . s . .	6855
26-SAAA-a	kire	1	1	2,557	3,980	0	79.98	100	C	35	Kire	P . .	1992-1993				0 . s . .	6856
26-SAB	SEPEN net	1	1	622	968		90.03	100	C	4		. . .					0	6857
26-SABA	SEPEN cluster	1	1	622	968		90.03	100	C	4		. . .					0	6858
26-SABA-a	sepen	1	1	622	968	0	90.03	100	C	4		. . .					0	6859
26-SAC	MIKAREW net	1	1	9,516	14,814		76.00	100	C	35		P . .					0	6860
26-SACA	MIKAREW cluster	1	1	9,516	14,814		76.00	100	C	35		P . .					0	6861
26-SACA-a	mikarew	1	1	9,516	14,814	0	76.00	100	C	35	Aruamu	P . .	1995				0	6862
26-T	GOAM set	1	11	12,600	19,619		80.64	99	C	22		P . .					0	6863
26-TA	ANDARUM chain	1	1	1,575	2,452		80.00	100	C	4		. . .					0	6864
26-TAA	ANDARUM net	1	1	1,575	2,452		80.00	100	C	4		. . .					0	6865
26-TAAA	ANDARUM cluster	1	1	1,575	2,452		80.00	100	C	4		. . .					0	6866
26-TAAA-a	andarum	1	1	1,575	2,452	0	80.00	100	C	4		. . .					0	6867
26-TB	IGOM-TANGGU chain	1	2	5,059	7,877		80.02	100	C	22		P . .					0	6868
26-TBA	IGOM net	1	1	1,572	2,448		80.03	100	C	4		. . .					0	6869
26-TBAA	IGOM cluster	1	1	1,572	2,448		80.03	100	C	4		. . .					0	6870
26-TBAA-a	igom 1					0				4		. . .					0	6871
26-TBAA-b	igom 2	1	1	1,572	2,448	0	80.03	100	C	4		. . .					0	6872
26-TBB	TANGGU net	1	1	3,487	5,429		80.01	100	C	22		P . .					0	6873
26-TBBA	TANGGU cluster	1	1	3,487	5,429		80.01	100	C	22		P . .					0	6874
26-TBBA-a	tanggu	1	1	3,487	5,429	0	80.01	100	C	22	Tanggu	P . .	1993				0	6875
26-TC	TANGUAT chain	1	1	735	1,145		90.07	100	C	4		. . .					0	6876
26-TCA	TANGUAT net	1	1	735	1,145		90.07	100	C	4		. . .					0	6877
26-TCAA	TANGUAT cluster	1	1	735	1,145		90.07	100	C	4		. . .					0	6878
26-TCAA-a	tanguat	1	1	735	1,145	0	90.07	100	C	4		. . .					0	6879
26-TD	TAMOLAN chain	1	7	5,231	8,145		80.12	97	C	4		. . .					0	6880
26-TDA	MIDSIVINDI-ITUTANG net	1	3	2,507	3,902		74.91	95	C	4		. . .					0	6881
26-TDAA	ITUTANG cluster	1	1	320	498		35.00	60	B	4		. . .					0	6882
26-TDAA-a	itutang	1	1	320	498	0	35.00	60	B	4		. . .					0	6883
26-TDAB	MIDSIVINDI cluster	1	1	2,021	3,146		80.01	100	C	2		. . .					0	6884
26-TDAB-a	midsivindi	1	1	2,021	3,146	0	80.01	100	C	2		. . .					0	6885
26-TDAC	IGANA cluster	1	1	166	258		89.76	100	C	4		. . .					0	6886
26-TDAC-a	igana	1	1	166	258	0	89.76	100	C	4		. . .					0	6887
26-TDB	ROMKUN-BRERI net	1	3	2,447	3,811		84.31	100	C	4		. . .					0	6888
26-TDBA	KOMINIMUNG cluster	1	1	476	742		90.13	100	C	4		. . .					0	6889
26-TDBA-a	kominimung	1	1	476	742	0	90.13	100	C	4		. . .					0	6890

Continued overleaf

Table 9-13 continued

Code 1	REFERENCE NAME / Autoglossonym 2	Coun 3	Peo 4	in 2000 5	in 2025 6	Media radio 7	AC% 8	E% 9	Wld 10	Tr 11	Biblioglossonym 12	Print 13-15	P-activity 16	N-activity 17	B-activity 18	J-year 19	Jayuh 20-24	Ref 25
26-TDBB	BRERI cluster	1	1	1,406	2,189		80.01	100	C	3							0....	6891
26-TDBB-a	breri	1	1	1,406	2,189	0	80.01	100	C	3		...					0....	6892
26-TDBC	ROMKUN cluster	1	1	565	880		90.09	100	C	4							0....	6893
26-TDBC-a	romkun	1	1	565	880	0	90.09	100	C	4		...					0....	6894
26-TDC	**AKRUKAY net**	1	1	277	432		90.25	100	C	4		...					0....	6895
26-TDCA	AKRUKAY cluster	1	1	277	432		90.25	100	C	4							0....	6896
26-TDCA-a	akrukay	1	1	277	432	0	90.25	100	C	4		...					0....	6897
26-U	**RAO set**	1	1	7,192	11,197		50.00	78	B	35		P..					0.s..	6898
26-UA	RAO chain	1	1	7,192	11,197		50.00	78	B	35		P..					0.s..	6899
26-UAA	**RAO net**	1	1	7,192	11,197		50.00	78	B	35		P..					0.s..	6900
26-UAAA	RAO cluster	1	1	7,192	11,197		50.00	78	B	35		P..					0.s..	6901
26-UAAA-a	rao	1	1	7,192	11,197	0	50.00	78	B	35	Rao	P..	1991-1995				0.s..	6902
26-V	**AIAN set**	1	2	2,072	3,226		84.75	100	C	4		...					0....	6903
26-VA	AIAN chain	1	2	2,072	3,226		84.75	100	C	4		...					0....	6904
26-VAA	**ANOR net**	1	1	981	1,527		90.01	100	C	4		...					0....	6905
26-VAAA	ANOR cluster	1	1	981	1,527		90.01	100	C	4							0....	6906
26-VAAA-a	anor	1	1	981	1,527	0	90.01	100	C	4		...					0....	6907
26-VAB	**AIOME net**	1	1	1,091	1,699		80.02	100	C	2		...					0....	6908
26-VABA	AIOME cluster	1	1	1,091	1,699		80.02	100	C	2							0....	6909
26-VABA-a	aiome	1	1	1,091	1,699	0	80.02	100	C	2		...					0....	6910
27	**EAST PAPUIC zone**	4	98	304,176	473,289		84.35	97	C	41		PN.					0.s..	6911
27-A	**PAPI-SUARMIN set**	1	2	397	618		36.52	63	B	2		...					0....	6912
27-AA	PAPI chain	1	1	109	170		40.37	63	B	2		...					0....	6913
27-AAA	**PAPI net**	1	1	109	170		40.37	63	B	2		...					0....	6914
27-AAAA	PAPI cluster	1	1	109	170		40.37	63	B	2							0....	6915
27-AAAA-a	papi	1	1	109	170	0	40.37	63	B	2		...					0....	6916
27-AB	SUARMIN chain	1	1	288	448		35.07	63	B	2		...					0....	6917
27-ABA	**SUARMIN net**	1	1	288	448		35.07	63	B	2		...					0....	6918
27-ABAA	SUARMIN cluster	1	1	288	448		35.07	63	B	2							0....	6919
27-ABAA-a	suarmin	1	1	288	448	0	35.07	63	B	2		...					0....	6920
27-B	**WALIO-PEI set**	1	1	706	1,171		67.28	95	C	2		...					0....	6921
27-BA	PEI chain	1	1	500	850		60.00	93	C	0		...					0....	6922
27-BAA	**PEI net**	1	1	500	850		60.00	93	C	0		...					0....	6923
27-BAAA	PEI cluster	1	1	500	850		60.00	93	C	0							0....	6924
27-BAAA-a	pei	1	1	500	850	0	60.00	93	C	0		...					0....	6925
27-BB	WALIO chain	1	1	206	321		84.95	100	C	2		...					0....	6926
27-BBA	**WALIO net**	1	1	206	321		84.95	100	C	2		...					0....	6927
27-BBAA	WALIO cluster	1	1	206	321		84.95	100	C	2							0....	6928
27-BBAA-a	walio	1	1	206	321	0	84.95	100	C	2		...					0....	6929
27-C	**YABIO-TUWARI set**	1	2	339	528		37.76	62	B	4		...					0....	6930
27-CA	YABIO chain	1	1	162	252		35.19	59	B	4		...					0....	6931
27-CAA	**YABIO net**	1	1	162	252		35.19	59	B	4		...					0....	6932
27-CAAA	YABIO cluster	1	1	162	252		35.19	59	B	4							0....	6933
27-CAAA-a	yabio	1	1	162	252	0	35.19	59	B	4		...					0....	6934
27-CB	TUWARI chain	1	1	177	276		40.11	64	B	2		...					0....	6935
27-CBA	**TUWARI net**	1	1	177	276		40.11	64	B	2		...					0....	6936
27-CBAA	TUWARI cluster	1	1	177	276		40.11	64	B	2		...					0....	6937
27-CBAA-a	North tuwari					0				2		...					0....	6938
27-CBAA-b	South tuwari					0				2		...					0....	6939
27-D	**PONDO-CHAMBRI set**	1	3	13,495	21,295		77.36	90	C	4		...					0....	6940
27-DA	CHAMBRI chain	1	1	1,976	3,077		10.02	37	A	4		...					0....	6941
27-DAA	**CHAMBRI net**	1	1	1,976	3,077		10.02	37	A	4		...					0....	6942
27-DAAA	CHAMBRI cluster	1	1	1,976	3,077		10.02	37	A	4							0....	6943
27-DAAA-a	chambri	1	1	1,976	3,077	0	10.02	37	A	4		...					0....	6944
27-DB	YIMAS-TABRIAK chain	1	1	2,509	4,192		67.08	95	C	4		...					0....	6945
27-DBA	**YIMAS net**	1	1	509	792		94.89	100	C	4		...					0....	6946
27-DBAA	YIMAS cluster	1	1	509	792		94.89	100	C	4							0....	6947
27-DBAA-a	yimas	1	1	509	792	0	94.89	100	C	4		...					0....	6948
27-DBB	**TABRIAK net**	1	1	2,000	3,400		60.00	93	C	0		...					0....	6949
27-DBBA	TABRIAK cluster	1	1	2,000	3,400		60.00	93	C	0							0....	6950
27-DBBA-a	tabriak	1	1	2,000	3,400	0	60.00	93	C	0		...					0....	6951
27-DC	ANGORAM chain	1	1	9,010	14,026		94.99	100	C	4		...					0....	6952
27-DCA	**ANGORAM net**	1	1	9,010	14,026		94.99	100	C	4		...					0....	6953
27-DCAA	ANGORAM cluster	1	1	9,010	14,026		94.99	100	C	4							0....	6954
27-DCAA-a	angoram	1	1	9,010	14,026	0	94.99	100	C	4		...					0....	6955
27-E	**NOR set**	2	3	4,484	6,689		51.18	74	B	4		...					0....	6956
27-EA	MURIK-KOPAR chain	2	3	4,484	6,689		51.18	74	B	4		...					0....	6957

Continued opposite

Table 9-13 continued

Code 1	REFERENCE NAME / Autoglossonym 2	Coun 3	Peo 4	in 2000 5	in 2025 6	Media radio 7	AC% 8	E% 9	Wld 10	Tr 11	Biblioglossonym 12	Print 13-15	P-activity 16	N-activity 17	B-activity 18	J-year 19	Jayuh 20-24	Ref 25
27-EAA	**MURIK net**	2	2	4,151	6,171		48.08	72	B	4		...						0....	6958
27-EAAA	MURIK cluster	2	2	4,151	6,171		48.08	72	B	4		...						0....	6959
27-EAAA-a	murik	2	2	4,151	6,171	0	48.08	72	B	4		...						0....	6960
27-EAB	**KOPAR net**	1	1	333	518		89.79	100	C	4		...						0....	6961
27-EABA	KOPAR cluster	1	1	333	518		89.79	100	C	4		...						0....	6962
27-EABA-a	kopar	1	1	333	518	0	89.79	100	C	4		...						0....	6963
27-F	**GAPUN set**	1	1	119	185		89.92	100	C	4		...						0....	6964
27-FA	GAPUN chain	1	1	119	185		89.92	100	C	4		...						0....	6965
27-FAA	**GAPUN net**	1	1	119	185		89.92	100	C	4		...						0....	6966
27-FAAA	GAPUN cluster	1	1	119	185		89.92	100	C	4		...						0....	6967
27-FAAA-a	gapun	1	1	119	185	0	89.92	100	C	4		...						0....	6968
27-G	**AUNALEI-SETA set**	1	2	3,870	6,096		75.09	97	C	4		...						0....	6969
27-GA	AUNALEI chain	1	1	3,206	4,991		80.01	100	C	3		...						0....	6970
27-GAA	**AUNALEI net**	1	1	3,206	4,991		80.01	100	C	3		...						0....	6971
27-GAAA	AUNALEI cluster	1	1	3,206	4,991		80.01	100	C	3		...						0....	6972
27-GAAA-a	aunalei	1	1	3,206	4,991	0	80.01	100	C	3		...						0....	6973
27-GB	SETA-SETI chain	1	1	664	1,105		51.36	83	B	4		...						0....	6974
27-GBA	**SETA-SETI net**	1	1	664	1,105		51.36	83	B	4		...						0....	6975
27-GBAA	SETA cluster	1	1	500	850		60.00	93	C	0		...						0....	6976
27-GBAA-a	seta	1	1	500	850	0	60.00	93	C	0		...						0....	6977
27-GBAB	SETI cluster	1	1	164	255		25.00	50	B	4		...						0....	6978
27-GBAB-a	seti	1	1	164	255	0	25.00	50	B	4		...						0....	6979
27-H	**WAPEI-PALEI set**	1	21	47,996	74,718		77.47	95	C	41		PN.						0....	6980
27-HA	WAPEI chain	1	13	35,693	55,567		78.09	94	C	41		PN.						0....	6981
27-HAA	**YIS-YAU net**	1	2	922	1,435		25.05	50	B	2		...						0....	6982
27-HAAA	YIS cluster	1	1	718	1,118		25.07	50	B	2		...						0....	6983
27-HAAA-a	yis	1	1	718	1,118	0	25.07	50	B	2		...						0....	6984
27-HAAB	YAU cluster	1	1	204	317		25.00	51	B	2		...						0....	6985
27-HAAB-a	yau	1	1	204	317	0	25.00	51	B	2		...						0....	6986
27-HAB	**OLO net**	1	2	16,386	25,510		82.91	94	C	22		P..						0....	6987
27-HABA	OLO cluster	1	2	16,386	25,510	0	82.91	94	C	22	Olo	P..	1969-1989				0....	6988
27-HABA-a	payi					0				22		p..						0....	6989
27-HABA-b	wapi	1	1	1,453	2,263	0	9.98	34	A	22	Wape	P..	1989				0....	6990
27-HAC	**ELKEI net**	1	1	2,084	3,245		70.01	100	C	2		...						0....	6991
27-HACA	ELKEI cluster	1	1	2,084	3,245		70.01	100	C	2		...						0....	6992
27-HACA-a	elkei	1	1	2,084	3,245	0	70.01	100	C	2		...						0....	6993
27-HAD	**AU net**	1	1	5,813	9,049		89.99	100	C	41		PN.						0....	6994
27-HADA	AU cluster	1	1	5,813	9,049		89.99	100	C	41		PN.						0....	6995
27-HADA-a	au	1	1	5,813	9,049	0	89.99	100	C	41	Au	PN.	1971-1972	1982			0....	6996
27-HAE	**YIL net**	1	1	3,616	5,629		79.98	100	C	2		...						0....	6997
27-HAEA	YIL cluster	1	1	3,616	5,629		79.98	100	C	2		...						0....	6998
27-HAEA-a	yil	1	1	3,616	5,629	0	79.98	100	C	2		...						0....	6999
27-HAF	**NINGIL net**	1	1	760	1,183		35.00	59	B	4		...						0....	7000
27-HAFA	NINGIL cluster	1	1	760	1,183		35.00	59	B	4		...						0....	7001
27-HAFA-a	ningil	1	1	760	1,183	0	35.00	59	B	4		...						0....	7002
27-HAG	**GNAU net**	1	1	1,424	2,217		80.06	100	C	4		...						0....	7003
27-HAGA	GNAU cluster	1	1	1,424	2,217		80.06	100	C	4		...						0....	7004
27-HAGA-a	gnau	1	1	1,424	2,217	0	80.06	100	C	4		...						0....	7005
27-HAH	**GALU net**	1	2	3,651	5,684		71.65	100	C	4		...						0....	7006
27-HAHA	DIA cluster	1	1	3,349	5,213		69.99	100	C	2		...						0....	7007
27-HAHA-a	dia	1	1	3,349	5,213	0	69.99	100	C	2		...						0....	7008
27-HAHB	SINAGEN cluster	1	1	302	471		90.07	100	C	4		...						0....	7009
27-HAHB-a	sinagen	1	1	302	471	0				4		...						0....	7010
27-HAI	**VALMAN net**	1	1	937	1,459		45.04	69	B	4		...						0....	7011
27-HAIA	VALMAN cluster	1	1	937	1,459		45.04	69	B	4		...						0....	7012
27-HAIA-a	valman	1	1	937	1,459	0	45.04	69	B	4		...						0....	7013
27-HAJ	**YAPUNDA net**	1	1	100	156		30.00	56	B	4		...						0....	7014
27-HAJA	YAPUNDA cluster	1	1	100	156		30.00	56	B	4		...						0....	7015
27-HAJA-a	yapunda	1	1	100	156	0	30.00	56	B	4		...						0....	7016
27-HB	PALEI chain	1	7	5,328	8,293		76.58	92	C	4		...						0....	7017
27-HBA	**MITANG net**	1	1	646	1,005		89.94	100	C	2		...						0....	7018
27-HBAA	MITANG cluster	1	1	646	1,005		89.94	100	C	2		...						0....	7019
27-HBAA-a	mitang	1	1	646	1,005	0	89.94	100	C	2		...						0....	7020
27-HBB	**AGI net**	1	1	820	1,276		80.00	100	C	4		...						0....	7021
27-HBBA	AGI cluster	1	1	820	1,276		80.00	100	C	4		...						0....	7022
27-HBBA-a	agi	1	1	820	1,276	0	80.00	100	C	4		...						0....	7023
27-HBC	**WANAP net**	1	1	1,145	1,782		40.00	64	B	2		...						0....	7024
27-HBCA	WANAP cluster	1	1	1,145	1,782		40.00	64	B	2		...						0....	7025
27-HBCA-a	wanap	1	1	1,145	1,782	0	40.00	64	B	2		...						0....	7026
27-HBD	**AIKU net**	1	1	1,190	1,853		85.04	100	C	4		...						0....	7027
27-HBDA	AIKU cluster	1	1	1,190	1,853		85.04	100	C	4		...						0....	7028
27-HBDA-a	aiku	1	1	1,190	1,853	0	85.04	100	C	4		...						0....	7029

Continued overleaf

Table 9-13 continued

Code 1	REFERENCE NAME / Autoglossonym 2	Coun 3	Peo 4	Mother-tongue speakers in 2000 5	in 2025 6	Media radio 7	CHURCH AC% 8	E% 9	Wld 10	Tr 11	Biblioglossonym 12	SCRIPTURES Print 13-15	P–activity 16	N–activity 17	B–activity 18	J-year 19	Jayuh 20-24	Ref 25
27-HBE	**ARUOP net**	1	1	858	1,336		89.98	100	C	2		. . .					0	7030
27-HBEA	ARUOP cluster	1	1	858	1,336		89.98	100	C	2		. . .					0	7031
27-HBEA-a	aruop	1	1	858	1,336	0	89.98	100	C	2		. . .					0	7032
27-HBF	**BRAGAT net**	1	1	487	758		89.94	100	C	4		. . .					0	7033
27-HBFA	BRAGAT cluster	1	1	487	758		89.94	100	C	4		. . .					0	7034
27-HBFA-a	bragat	1	1	487	758	0	89.94	100	C	4		. . .					0	7035
27-HBG	**ALATIL net**	1	1	182	283		89.56	100	C	4		. . .					0	7036
27-HBGA	ALATIL cluster	1	1	182	283		89.56	100	C	4		. . .					0	7037
27-HBGA-a	alatil	1	1	182	283	0	89.56	100	C	4		. . .					0	7038
27-HC	URAT chain	1	1	6,975	10,858		75.00	100	C	22		P . .					0	7039
27-HCA	**URAT net**	1	1	6,975	10,858		75.00	100	C	22		P . .					0	7040
27-HCAA	URAT cluster	1	1	6,975	10,858		75.00	100	C	22	Urat: Yehre	P . .	1993				0	7041
27-HCAA-a	Central urat					0				22		p . .					0	7042
27-HCAA-b	East urat					0				22		p . .					0	7043
27-HCAA-c	South urat					0				22		p . .					0	7044
27-I	**MAIMAI-BELI set**	1	7	10,296	16,027		74.74	92	C	4		. . .					0	7045
27-IA	LAEKO chain	1	1	846	1,317		89.95	100	C	2		. . .					0	7046
27-IAA	**LAEKO net**	1	1	846	1,317		89.95	100	C	2		. . .					0	7047
27-IAAA	LAEKO cluster	1	1	846	1,317		89.95	100	C	2		. . .					0	7048
27-IAAA-a	laeko					0				2		. . .					0	7049
27-IB	BELI chain	1	2	4,069	6,334		59.33	81	B	3		. . .					0	7052
27-IBA	**BELI net**	1	2	4,069	6,334		59.33	81	B	3		. . .					0	7053
27-IBAA	BELI cluster	1	2	4,069	6,334		59.33	81	B	3		. . .					0	7054
27-IBAA-a	beli	1	1	2,202	3,428	0	79.97	100	C	3		. . .					0	7055
27-IBAA-b	makarim	1	1	1,867	2,906	0	34.98	58	B	3		. . .					0	7056
27-IC	WIAKI chain	1	1	815	1,269		90.06	100	C	4		. . .					0	7057
27-ICA	**WIAKI net**	1	1	815	1,269		90.06	100	C	4		. . .					0	7058
27-ICAA	WIAKI cluster	1	1	815	1,269		90.06	100	C	4		. . .					0	7059
27-ICAA-a	wiaki	1	1	815	1,269	0	90.06	100	C	4		. . .					0	7060
27-ID	NORTH MAIMAI chain	1	1	414	644		89.86	100	C	2		. . .					0	7061
27-IDA	**SILIPUT net**	1	1	414	644		89.86	100	C	2		. . .					0	7062
27-IDAA	SILIPUT cluster	1	1	414	644		89.86	100	C	2		. . .					0	7063
27-IDAA-a	siliput	1	1	414	644	0	89.86	100	C	2		. . .					0	7064
27-IE	RURUHIP chain	1	2	4,152	6,463		82.23	100	C	2		. . .					0	7065
27-IEA	**YAHANG net**	1	1	1,859	2,894		84.99	100	C	2		. . .					0	7066
27-IEAA	YAHANG cluster	1	1	1,859	2,894		84.99	100	C	2		. . .					0	7067
27-IEAA-a	yahang	1	1	1,859	2,894	0	84.99	100	C	2		. . .					0	7068
27-IEB	**ARINUA net**	1	1	2,293	3,569		79.98	100	C	2		. . .					0	7069
27-IEBA	ARINUA cluster	1	1	2,293	3,569		79.98	100	C	2		. . .					0	7070
27-IEBA-a	arinua					0				2		. . .					0	7071
27-IEBA-b	lolopani					0				2		. . .					0	7072
27-IEBA-c	heyo	1	1	2,293	3,569	0	79.98	100	C	2		. . .					0	7073
27-J	**KOMBIO-ARAPESH set**	1	13	54,820	85,772		81.33	98	C	41		PN .					0	7074
27-JA	KOMBIO chain	1	7	11,784	18,345		75.99	95	C	12		. . .					0	7075
27-JAA	**ARUEK net**	1	1	892	1,389		90.02	100	C	4		. . .					0	7076
27-JAAA	ARUEK cluster	1	1	892	1,389		90.02	100	C	4		. . .					0	7077
27-JAAA-a	aruek	1	1	892	1,389	0	90.02	100	C	4		. . .					0	7078
27-JAB	**LOU net**	1	2	2,530	3,938		82.73	100	C	3		. . .					0	7079
27-JABA	LOU cluster	1	2	2,530	3,938		82.73	100	C	3		. . .					0	7080
27-JABA-a	West lou					0				3		. . .					0	7081
27-JABA-b	East lou					0				3		. . .					0	7082
27-JAC	**EITIEP net**	1	1	573	892		90.05	100	C	4		. . .					0	7083
27-JACA	EITIEP cluster	1	1	573	892		90.05	100	C	4		. . .					0	7084
27-JACA-a	eitiep	1	1	573	892	0	90.05	100	·C	4		. . .					0	7085
27-JAD	**KOMBIO net**	1	1	3,800	5,916		80.00	100	C	12		. . .					0	7086
27-JADA	KOMBIO cluster	1	1	3,800	5,916		80.00	100	C	12	Kombio	. . .					0	7087
27-JADA-a	North kombio					0				12		. . .					0	7088
27-JADA-b	Central kombio					0				12		. . .					0	7089
27-JADA-c	South kombio					0				12		. . .					0	7090
27-JAE	**YAMBES net**	1	1	1,250	1,946		24.96	50	B	3		. . .					0	7091
27-JAEA	YAMBES cluster	1	1	1,250	1,946		24.96	50	B	3		. . .					0	7092
27-JAEA-a	West yambes					0				3		. . .					0	7093
27-JAEA-b	East yambes					0				3		. . .					0	7094
27-JAF	**WOM net**	1	1	2,739	4,264		79.99	100	C	2		. . .					0	7095
27-JAFA	WOM cluster	1	1	2,739	4,264		79.99	100	C	2		. . .					0	7096
27-JAFA-a	North wom					0				2		. . .					0	7097
27-JAFA-b	South wom					0				2		. . .					0	7098
27-JB	BUMBITA chain	1	1	3,000	5,100		80.00	100	C	0		. . .					0	7099
27-JBA	**BUMBITA net**	1	1	3,000	5,100		80.00	100	C	0		. . .					0	7100
27-JBAA	BUMBITA cluster	1	1	3,000	5,100		80.00	100	C	0		. . .					0	7101
27-JBAA-a	bonahoi					0				0		. . .					0	7102
27-JBAA-b	urita					0				0		. . .					0	7103
27-JBAA-c	timingir					0				0		. . .					0	7104
27-JC	ARAPESH chain	1	6	40,036	62,327		83.00	99	C	41		PN .					0	7105
27-JCA	**ARAPESH net**	1	6	40,036	62,327		83.00	99	C	41		PN .					0	7106
27-JCAA	MUHIANG cluster	1	5	26,605	41,418		79.97	99	C	41	Mufian	PN .	1978-1981	1988			0	7107

Continued opposite

Table 9-13 continued

Code 1	REFERENCE NAME / Autoglossonym 2	Coun 3	Peo 4	Mother-tongue speakers in 2000 5	in 2025 6	Media radio 7	AC% 8	E% 9	Wld 10	Tr 11	Biblioglossonym 12	Print 13-15	P-activity 16	N-activity 17	B-activity 18	J-year 19	Jayuh 20-24	Ref 25
27-JCAA-a	balif	1	1	9,216	14,348	0	77.01	100	C	41	Muhian: Balif	PN.	1978	1988			0....	7108
27-JCAA-b	supari					0				41		pn.					0....	7109
27-JCAA-c	filifita	1	1	7,373	11,478	0	90.99	100	C	41	Muhian: Ilahita	Pn.	1978				0....	7110
27-JCAA-d	balanga					0				41		pn.					0....	7111
27-JCAA-e	iwam	1	2	5,436	8,462	0	70.01	94	C	41	Iwam*	PN.	1991	1989			0....	7112
27-JCAA-f	womsak					0				41		pn.					0....	7113
27-JCAA-g	walihiga					0				41		pn.					0....	7114
27-JCAA-h	nagipeim					0				41		pn.					0....	7115
27-JCAB	BUKIYIP cluster	1	1	13,431	20,909		89.00	100	C	41	Bukiyip	PN.	1976-1990	1994			0....	7116
27-JCAB-a	South bukiyip					0				41		pn.					0....	7117
27-JCAB-b	North bukiyip					0				41		pn.					0....	7118
27-K	**URIM set**	1	1	3,734	5,812		84.98	100	C	22		P..					0....	7119
27-KA	URIM chain	1	1	3,734	5,812		84.98	100	C	22		P..					0....	7120
27-KAA	**URIM net**	1	1	3,734	5,812		84.98	100	C	22		P..					0....	7121
27-KAAA	URIM cluster	1	1	3,734	5,812		84.98	100	C	22		P..					0....	7122
27-KAAA-a	urim	1	1	3,734	5,812	0	84.98	100	C	22	Urim	P..	1981-1992				0....	7123
27-L	**MARIENBERG set**	1	8	12,050	18,962		65.50	87	C	22		P..					0....	7124
27-LA	MANDI-KAMASAU chain	1	7	11,192	17,626		68.22	90	C	22		P..					0....	7125
27-LAA	**MANDI net**	1	1	235	367		90.21	100	C	4		...					0....	7126
27-LAAA	MANDI cluster	1	1	235	367		90.21	100	C	4		...					0....	7127
27-LAAA-a	mandi	1	1	235	367	0	90.21	100	C	4		...					0....	7128
27-LAB	**BUNGAIN net**	1	1	4,189	6,522		80.00	100	C	5		...					0....	7129
27-LABA	BUNGAIN cluster	1	1	4,189	6,522		80.00	100	C	5		...					0....	7130
27-LABA-a	bungain	1	1	4,189	6,522	0	80.00	100	C	5		...					0....	7131
27-LAC	**MUNIWARA net**	1	1	1,412	2,198		80.03	100	C	4		...					0....	7132
27-LACA	MUNIWARA cluster	1	1	1,412	2,198		80.03	100	C	4		...					0....	7133
27-LACA-a	muniwara	1	1	1,412	2,198	0	80.03	100	C	4		...					0....	7134
27-LAD	**URIMO net**	1	2	2,595	4,041		34.37	59	B	2		...					0....	7135
27-LADA	URIMO cluster	1	2	2,595	4,041		34.37	59	B	2		...					0....	7136
27-LADA-a	Proper urimo	1	1	1,213	1,889	0	45.01	69	B	2		...					0....	7137
27-LADA-b	yaugiba	1	1	1,382	2,152	0	25.04	50	B	2		...					0....	7138
27-LAE	**KAMASAU net**	1	1	2,544	4,161		72.92	98	C	22		P..					0....	7139
27-LAEA	PARUWA-KENYARI cluster	1	1	500	850		70.00	98	C	0		...					0....	7140
27-LAEA-a	paruwa					0				0		...					0....	7141
27-LAEA-b	kenyari					0				0		...					0....	7142
27-LAEB	KAMASAU-TRING cluster	1	1	1,144	1,781		79.98	100	C	22		P..					0....	7143
27-LAEB-a	kamasau	1	1	1,144	1,781	0	79.98	100	C	22	Kamasau	P..	1985-1992				0....	7144
27-LAEB-b	tring					0				22		pn.					0....	7145
27-LAEB-c	wau					0				22		pn.					0....	7146
27-LAEC	YIBAB cluster	1	1	400	680		60.00	93	C	0		...					0....	7147
27-LAEC-a	yibab	1	1	400	680	0	60.00	93	C	0		...					0....	7148
27-LAED	WANDOMI cluster	1	1	500	850		70.00	98	C	0		...					0....	7149
27-LAED-a	wandomi	1	1	500	850	0	70.00	98	C	0		...					0....	7150
27-LAF	**ELEPI net**	1	1	217	337		89.86	100	C	4		...					0....	7151
27-LAFA	ELEPI cluster	1	1	217	337		89.86	100	C	4		...					0....	7152
27-LAFA-a	elepi	1	1	217	337	0	89.86	100	C	4		...					0....	7153
27-LB	BUNA chain	1	1	858	1,336		30.07	53	B	3		...					0....	7154
27-LBA	**BUNA net**	1	1	858	1,336		30.07	53	B	3		...					0....	7155
27-LBAA	BUNA cluster	1	1	858	1,336		30.07	53	B	3		...					0....	7156
27-LBAA-a	North buna					0				3		...					0....	7157
27-LBAA-b	South buna					0				3		...					0....	7158
27-LBAA-c	masan					0				3		...					0....	7159
27-M	**MONUMBO set**	1	2	1,320	2,054		89.92	100	C	4		...					0....	7160
27-MA	MONUMBO chain	1	2	1,320	2,054		89.92	100	C	4		...					0....	7161
27-MAA	**MONUMBO net**	1	2	1,320	2,054		89.92	100	C	4		...					0....	7162
27-MAAA	MONUMBO cluster	1	1	667	1,038		89.96	100	C	4		...					0....	7163
27-MAAA-a	monumbo	1	1	667	1,038	0	89.96	100	C	4		...					0....	7164
27-MAAB	LILAU cluster	1	1	653	1,016		89.89	100	C	4		...					0....	7165
27-MAAB-a	lilau	1	1	653	1,016	0	89.89	100	C	4		...					0....	7166
27-N	**ANEM set**	1	1	639	995		89.98	100	C	4		...					0....	7167
27-NA	ANEM chain	1	1	639	995		89.98	100	C	4		...					0....	7168
27-NAA	**ANEM net**	1	1	639	995		89.98	100	C	4		...					0....	7169
27-NAAA	ANEM cluster	1	1	639	995		89.98	100	C	4		...					0....	7170
27-NAAA-a	anem	1	1	639	995	0	89.98	100	C	4		...					0....	7171
27-O	**WASI set**	1	1	2,209	3,438		90.00	100	C	22		P..					0....	7172
27-OA	WASI chain	1	1	2,209	3,438		90.00	100	C	22		P..					0....	7173
27-OAA	**WASI net**	1	1	2,209	3,438		90.00	100	C	22		P..					0....	7174
27-OAAA	WASI cluster	1	1	2,209	3,438		90.00	100	C	22		P..					0....	7175
27-OAAA-a	pele	1	1	2,209	3,438	0	90.00	100	C	22	Pele-ata	P..	1992				0....	7176
27-OAAA-b	ata					0				22		pn.					0....	7177
27-P	**KOL set**	1	1	4,650	7,239		95.01	100	C	12		...					0....	7178
27-PA	KOL chain	1	1	4,650	7,239		95.01	100	C	12		...					0....	7179
27-PAA	**KOL net**	1	1	4,650	7,239		95.01	100	C	12		...					0....	7180
27-PAAA	KOL-SUI cluster	1	1	4,650	7,239		95.01	100	C	12	Kol	...					0....	7181
27-PAAA-a	sui					0				12		...					0....	7182
27-PAAA-b	kol					0				12		...					0....	7183

Continued overleaf

Table 9-13 continued

Code 1	REFERENCE NAME / Autoglossonym 2	Coun 3	Peo 4	Mother-tongue speakers in 2000 5	in 2025 6	Media radio 7	CHURCH AC% 8	E% 9	Wld 10	Tr 11	Biblioglossonym 12	Print 13-15	P-activity 16	N-activity 17	B-activity 18	J-year 19	Jayuh 20-24	Ref 25
27-Q	**SULKA set**	1	1	2,906	4,525		90.02	100	C	22		P..					0....	7184
27-QA	SULKA chain	1	1	2,906	4,525		90.02	100	C	22		P..					0....	7185
27-QAA	**SULKA net**	1	1	2,906	4,525		90.02	100	C	22		P..					0....	7186
27-QAAA	SULKA cluster	1	1	2,906	4,525		90.02	100	C	22	Sulka	P..	1989				0....	7187
27-QAAA-a	kanakadran					0				22		p..					0....	7188
27-QAAA-b	nambling					0				22		p..					0....	7189
27-R	**BAINING set**	1	5	14,267	22,218		82.72	98	C	41		PN.					0....	7190
27-RA	BAINING chain	1	5	14,267	22,218		82.72	98	C	41		PN.					0....	7191
27-RAA	**BAINING net**	1	5	14,267	22,218		82.72	98	C	41		PN.					0....	7192
27-RAAA	MAKOLKOL cluster	2	1	50	85		80.00	100	C	8		...					0....	7193
27-RAAA-a	makolkol	2	1	50	85	0	80.00	100	C	8		...					0....	7194
27-RAAB	SIMBALI cluster	1	1	435	678		70.11	98	C	4		...					0....	7195
27-RAAB-a	simbali	1	1	435	678	0	70.11	98	C	4		...					0....	7196
27-RAAC	QAQET cluster	1		7,902	12,302		89.00	100	C	41	Baining: Qaqet*	PN.	1976-1987	1996			0....	7197
27-RAAC-a	South qaqet					0				41		pn.					0....	7198
27-RAAC-b	North qaqet					0				41		pn.					0....	7199
27-RAAD	URAMAT cluster	1	1	2,209	3,438		79.99	100	C	12		...					0....	7200
27-RAAD-a	uramat	1	1	2,209	3,438		79.99	100	C	12	Ura	...					0....	7201
27-RAAE	MALI-GAKTAI cluster	1	1	2,738	4,262		79.99	100	C	0		...					0....	7202
27-RAAE-a	mali	1	1	2,738	4,262	0	79.99	100	C	0		...					0....	7203
27-RAAE-b	gaktai									0		...					0....	7204
27-RAAF	KAIRAK cluster	1	1	933	1,453		50.05	75	B	4		...					0....	7205
27-RAAF-a	kairak	1	1	933	1,453	0	50.05	75	B	4		...					0....	7206
27-S	**TAULIL-BUTAM set**	1	1	1,169	1,820		95.04	100	C	5		...					0....	7207
27-SA	TAULIL-BUTAM chain	1	1	1,169	1,820		95.04	100	C	5		...					0....	7208
27-SAA	**TAULIL-BUTAM net**	1	1	1,169	1,820		95.04	100	C	5		...					0....	7209
27-SAAA	TAULIL cluster	1	1	1,169	1,820		95.04	100	C	5		...					0....	7210
27-SAAA-a	taulil	1	1	1,169	1,820	0	95.04	100	C	5		...					0....	7211
27-SAAB	BUTAM cluster			0	0		0.00	0		0		...					0....	7212
27-SAAB-a	butam			0	0	0	0.00	0		0		...					0....	7213
27-T	**KUOT set**	1	1	1,312	2,043		75.00	100	C	22		P..					0....	7214
27-TA	KUOT chain	1	1	1,312	2,043		75.00	100	C	22		P..					0....	7215
27-TAA	**KUOT net**	1	1	1,312	2,043		75.00	100	C	22		P..					0....	7216
27-TAAA	KUOT cluster	1	1	1,312	2,043		75.00	100	C	22	Kuot	P..	1994				0....	7217
27-TAAA-a	kul					0				22		p..					0....	7218
27-TAAA-b	naiyama					0				22		p..					0....	7219
27-TAAA-c	letatan					0				22		p..					0....	7220
27-U	**WEST BOUGAINVILLE set**	1	4	12,201	17,586		94.38	100	C	41		PN.					0....	7221
27-UA	KUNUA chain	1	1	2,779	4,005		90.00	100	C	12		...					0....	7222
27-UAA	**KUNUA net**	1	1	2,779	4,005		90.00	100	C	12		...					0....	7223
27-UAAA	KUNUA cluster	1	1	2,779	4,005		90.00	100	C	12		...					0....	7224
27-UAAA-a	kunua	1	1	2,779	4,005	0	90.00	100	C	12	Kunua	...					0....	7225
27-UB	KERIAKA chain	1	1	1,445	2,083		89.97	100	C	2		...					0....	7226
27-UBA	**KERIAKA net**	1	1	1,445	2,083		89.97	100	C	2		...					0....	7227
27-UBAA	KERIAKA cluster	1	1	1,445	2,083		89.97	100	C	2		...					0....	7228
27-UBAA-a	keriaka	1	1	1,445	2,083	0	89.97	100	C	2		...					0....	7229
27-UC	ROTOKAS chain	1	1	6,244	9,000		98.00	100	C	41		PN.					0....	7230
27-UCA	**ROTOKAS net**	1	1	6,244	9,000		98.00	100	C	41		PN.					0....	7231
27-UCAA	ROTOKAS cluster	1	1	6,244	9,000		98.00	100	C	41	Rotokas	PN.	1969	1982			0....	7232
27-UCAA-a	pipipaia					0				41		pn.					0....	7233
27-UCAA-b	aita					0				41		pn.					0....	7234
27-UCAA-c	atsilima					0				41		pn.					0....	7235
27-UD	EIVO chain	1	1	1,733	2,498		92.04	100	C	4		...					0....	7236
27-UDA	**EIVO net**	1	1	1,733	2,498		92.04	100	C	4		...					0....	7237
27-UDAA	EIVO cluster	1	1	1,733	2,498		92.04	100	C	4		...					0....	7238
27-UDAA-a	eivo	1	1	1,733	2,498	0	92.04	100	C	4		...					0....	7239
27-V	**EAST BOUGAINVILLE set**	1	9	74,848	108,011		95.30	100	C	41		PN.					0.s..	7240
27-VA	NASIOI-NAGOVISI chain	1	6	32,976	47,659		94.31	100	C	41		PN.					0.s..	7241
27-VAA	**NASIOI-SIMEKU net**	1	2	19,751	28,467		95.12	100	C	41		PN.					0.s..	7242
27-VAAA	SIMEKU cluster	1	1	4,367	6,294		85.00	100	C	2		...					0....	7243
27-VAAA-a	mainoki					0				2		...					0....	7244
27-VAAA-b	koopei					0				2		...					0....	7245
27-VAAB	NASIOI cluster	1	1	15,384	22,173		98.00	100	C	41		PN.					0.s..	7246
27-VAAB-a	Proper nasioi	1	1	15,384	22,173	0	98.00	100	C	41	Nasioi*	PN.	1970-1980	1994			0.s..	7247
27-VAAB-b	kongara					0				41		pn.					0.s..	7248
27-VAAB-c	orami					0				41		pn.					0.s..	7249
27-VAAB-d	pakia-sideronsi					0				41		pn.					0.s..	7250
27-VAB	**OUNE net**	1	1	97	140		79.38	100	C	2		...					0....	7251
27-VABA	OUNE cluster	1	1	97	140		79.38	100	C	2		...					0....	7252
27-VABA-a	oune	1	1	97	140	0	79.38	100	C	2		...					0....	7253
27-VABA-b	dapera									2		...					0....	7254
27-VAC	**LANTANAI net**	1	1	357	515		80.11	100	C	4		...					0....	7255
27-VACA	LANTANAI cluster	1	1	357	515		80.11	100	C	4		...					0....	7256
27-VACA-a	lantanai	1	1	357	515	0	80.11	100	C	4		...					0....	7257

Continued opposite

Table 9-13 continued

27 EAST PAPUIC 333

Code 1	REFERENCE NAME / Autoglossonym 2	Coun 3	Peo 4	Mother-tongue speakers in 2000 5	in 2025 6	Media radio 7	CHURCH AC% 8	E% 9	Wld 10	Tr 11	Biblioglossonym 12	SCRIPTURES Print 13-15	P–activity 16	N–activity 17	B–activity 18	J-year 19	Jayuh 20-24	Ref 25
27-VAD	**KOROMIRA net**	1	1	2,287	3,426		77.83	99	C	2		. . .					0	7258
27-VADA	KOROMIRA cluster	1	1	1,787	2,576		80.02	100	C	2		. . .					0	7259
27-VADA-a	koromira	1	1	1,787	2,576	0	80.02	100	C	2		. . .					0	7260
27-VADB	KOIANU cluster	1	1	500	850		70.00	98	C	0		. . .					0	7261
27-VADB-a	koianu	1	1	500	850	0	70.00	98	C	0		. . .					0	7262
27-VAE	**NAGOVISI net**	1	1	10,484	15,111		97.00	100	C	22		P . .					0	7263
27-VAEA	NAGOVISI cluster	1	1	10,484	15,111		97.00	100	C	22		P . .					0	7264
27-VAEA-a	nagovisi	1	1	10,484	15,111	0	97.00	100	C	22	Nagovisi	P . .	1984				0	7265
27-VB	SIWAI chain	1	1	10,153	14,634		96.49	100	C	41		PN .					0	7266
27-VBA	**SIWAI net**	1	1	10,153	14,634		96.49	100	C	41		PN .					0	7267
27-VBAA	SIWAI cluster	1	1	10,153	14,634		96.49	100	C	41		PN .					0	7268
27-VBAA-a	Proper siwai	1	1	10,153	14,634	0	96.49	100	C	41	Motuna*	PN .	1952-1968	1977			0	7269
27-VBAA-b	baitsi					0				41		pn .					0	7270
27-VC	BUIN-UISAI chain	1	2	31,719	45,718		95.94	100	C	22		P . .					0	7271
27-VCA	**UISAI net**	1	1	2,739	3,948		90.00	100	C	22		P . .					0	7272
27-VCAA	UISAI cluster	1	1	2,739	3,948		90.00	100	C	22		P . .					0	7273
27-VCAA-a	uisai	1	1	2,739	3,948	0	90.00	100	C	22	Uisai	P . .	1986				0	7274
27-VCB	**BUIN net**	1	1	28,980	41,770		96.50	100	C	22		P . .					0	7275
27-VCBA	BUIN cluster	1	1	28,980	41,770		96.50	100	C	22		P . .					0	7276
27-VCBA-a	Proper buin	1	1	28,980	41,770	0	96.50	100	C	22	Buin	P . .	1973-1978				0	7277
27-VCBA-b	rugara					0				22		p . .					0	7278
27-VCBA-c	telei					0				22		p . .					0	7279
27-W	**YELE set**	1	1	3,998	6,223		79.99	100	C	41		PN .					0	7280
27-WA	YELE chain	1	1	3,998	6,223		79.99	100	C	41		PN .					0	7281
27-WAA	**YELE net**	1	1	3,998	6,223		79.99	100	C	41		PN .					0	7282
27-WAAA	YELE cluster	1	1	3,998	6,223		79.99	100	C	41	Rossel*	PN .	1982-1985	1987			0	7283
27-WAAA-a	daminyu					0				41		pn .					0	7284
27-WAAA-b	bou					0				41		pn .					0	7285
27-WAAA-c	wulanga					0				41		pn .					0	7286
27-WAAA-d	jinjo					0				41		pn .					0	7287
27-WAAA-e	abaletti					0				41		pn .					0	7288
27-WAAA-f	jaru					0				41		pn .					0	7289
27-X	**CENTRAL SOLOMONS set**	1	4	15,495	28,521		88.78	100	C	41		PN .					0	7290
27-XA	BILUA chain	1	1	9,918	18,254		89.39	100	C	41		PN .					0	7291
27-XAA	**BILUA net**	1	1	9,918	18,254		89.39	100	C	41		PN .					0	7292
27-XAAA	BILUA cluster	1	1	9,918	18,254		89.39	100	C	41	Bilua	PN .	1919-1992	1995			0	7293
27-XAAA-a	vella lavella					0				41		pn .					0	7294
27-XAAA-b	mbava					0				41		pn .					0	7295
27-XAAA-c	Northeast gizo					0				41		pn .					0	7296
27-XB	BANIATA chain	1	1	1,706	3,141		81.01	100	C	2		. . .					0	7297
27-XBA	**BANIATA net**	1	1	1,706	3,141		81.01	100	C	2		. . .					0	7298
27-XBAA	BANIATA cluster	1	1	1,706	3,141		81.01	100	C	2		. . .					0	7299
27-XBAA-a	baniata	1	1	1,706	3,141	0	81.01	100	C	2		. . .					0	7300
27-XC	LAVUKALEVE chain	1	1	1,327	2,443		89.98	100	C	2		. . .					0	7301
27-XCA	**LAVUKALEVE net**	1	1	1,327	2,443		89.98	100	C	2		. . .					0	7302
27-XCAA	LAVUKALEVE cluster	1	1	1,327	2,443		89.98	100	C	2		. . .					0	7303
27-XCAA-a	lavukaleve	1	1	1,327	2,443	0	89.98	100	C	2		. . .					0	7304
27-XD	SAVO chain	1	1	2,544	4,683		91.00	100	C	2		. . .					0	7305
27-XDA	**SAVO net**	1	1	2,544	4,683		91.00	100	C	2		. . .					0	7306
27-XDAA	SAVO cluster	1	1	2,544	4,683		91.00	100	C	2		. . .					0	7307
27-XDAA-a	savo	1	1	2,544	4,683	0	91.00	100	C	2		. . .					0	7308
27-Y	**KAZUKURU set**									9		. . .					0	7309
27-YA	KAZUKURU chain									9		. . .					0	7310
27-YAA	**KAZUKURU net**									9		. . .					0	7311
27-YAAA	KAZUKURU cluster			0	0		0.00	0		9		. . .					0	7312
27-YAAA-a	Proper kazukuru			0	0	0	0.00	0		9		. . .					0	7313
27-YAAA-b	dororo			0	0	0	0.00	0		9		. . .					0	7314
27-YAAA-c	guliguli			0	0	0	0.00	0		9		. . .					0	7315
27-Z	**AYIWO-SANTA CRUZ set**	1	3	16,856	30,743		89.42	100	C	35		P . .					0 . s . .	7316
27-ZA	AYIWO chain	1	1	8,782	16,164		89.00	100	C	12		. . .					0	7317
27-ZAA	**AYIWO net**	1	1	8,782	16,164		89.00	100	C	12		. . .					0	7318
27-ZAAA	AYIWO cluster	1	1	8,782	16,164		89.00	100	C	12		. . .					0	7319
27-ZAAA-a	ayiwo	1	1	8,782	16,164	0	89.00	100	C	12	Ayiwo	. . .					0	7320
27-ZB	SANTA CRUZ chain	1	2	8,074	14,579		89.88	99	C	35		P . .					0 . s . .	7321
27-ZBA	**LONDAI net**	1	1	2,000	3,400		70.00	98	C	0		. . .					0	7322
27-ZBAA	LöNDäl cluster	1	1	2,000	3,400		70.00	98	C	0		. . .					0	7323
27-ZBAA-a	löndäi	1	1	2,000	3,400	0	70.00	98	C	0		. . .					0	7324
27-ZBB	**NEA net**	1	1	5,546	10,207		98.00	100	C	35		P . .					0 . s . .	7325
27-ZBBA	NEA cluster	1	1	5,546	10,207		98.00	100	C	35	Santa Cruz	P . .	1985-1991				0 . s . .	7326
27-ZBBA-a	natügu					0				35		p . .					0 . s . .	7327
27-ZBBA-b	nendö					0				35		p . .					0 . s . .	7328
27-ZBBA-c	ndeni					0				35		p . .					0 . s . .	7329
27-ZBBA-d	te-motu					0				35		p . .					0 . s . .	7330
27-ZBBA-e	nemboi					0				35		p . .					0 . s . .	7331
27-ZBBA-f	nooli					0				35		p . .					0 . s . .	7332
27-ZBBA-g	lvova					0				35		p . .					0 . s . .	7333
27-ZBBA-h	mbanua					0				35		p . .					0 . s . .	7334

Continued overleaf

Table 9-13 continued

Code 1	REFERENCE NAME Autoglossonym 2	Coun 3	Peo 4	Mother-tongue speakers in 2000 5	in 2025 6	Media radio 7	CHURCH AC% 8	E% 9	Wld 10	Tr 11	Biblioglossonym 12	SCRIPTURES Print 13-15	P-activity 16	N-activity 17	B-activity 18	J-year 19	Jayuh 20-24	Ref 25
27-ZBC	**NANGGU** net	1	1	528	972		79.92	100	C	4		. . .					0	7335
27-ZBCA	NANGGU cluster	1	1	528	972		79.92	100	C	4		. . .					0	7336
27-ZBCA-a	nanggu	1	1	528	972	0	79.92	100	C	4		. . .					0	7337
28	**DARWINIC zone**	1	19	9,875	12,986		60.13	89	C	41		PN.					0 . s . .	7338
28-A	**NYULNYULAN** set	1	1	480	816		75.00	99	C	9		. . .					0	7339
28-AA	NYULNYULAN chain	1	1	480	816		75.00	99	C	9		. . .					0	7340
28-AAA	**YAWURU** net	1	1	40	68		75.00	100	C	9		. . .					0	7341
28-AAAA	YAWURU cluster	1	1	40	68		75.00	100	C	9		. . .					0	7342
28-AAAA-a	yawuru	1	1	40	68	0	75.00	100	C	9		. . .					0	7343
28-AAB	**NYULNYUL-DYUGUN** net	1	1	390	663		75.13	99	C	8		. . .					0	7344
28-AABA	DYUGUN cluster	1	1	20	34		75.00	100	C	8		. . .					0	7345
28-AABA-a	dyugun	1	1	20	34	0	75.00	100	C	8		. . .					0	7346
28-AABB	DYABERDYABER cluster									8		. . .					0	7347
28-AABB-a	dyaberdyaber					0				8		. . .					0	7348
28-AABC	NYULNYUL cluster	1	1	20	34		75.00	100	C	8		. . .					0	7349
28-AABC-a	nyulnyul	1	1	20	34	0	75.00	100	C	8		. . .					0	7350
28-AABD	BAADI cluster	1	1	300	510		75.00	99	C	0		. . .					0	7351
28-AABD-a	Proper baadi					0				0		. . .					0	7352
28-AABD-b	lombadina					0				0		. . .					0	7353
28-AABE	DJAWI cluster	1	1	30	51		76.67	100	C	8		. . .					0	7354
28-AABE-a	djawi	1	1	30	51	0	76.67	100	C	8		. . .					0	7355
28-AABF	NIMANBUR cluster	1	1	20	34		75.00	100	C	8		. . .					0	7356
28-AABF-a	nimanbur	1	1	20	34	0	75.00	100	C	8		. . .					0	7357
28-AAC	**WARWA** net	1	1	30	51		76.67	100	C	0		. . .					0	7358
28-AACA	WARWA cluster	1	1	30	51		76.67	100	C	0		. . .					0	7359
28-AACA-a	warwa					0				0		. . .					0	7360
28-AAD	**NYIGINA** net	1	1	20	34		70.00	100	C	6		. . .					0	7361
28-AADA	NYIGINA cluster	1	1	20	34		70.00	100	C	6		. . .					0	7362
28-AADA-a	nyigina	1	1	20	34	0	70.00	100	C	6		. . .					0	7363
28-B	**BUNABAN** set	1	1	30	51		70.00	100	C	6		. . .					0	7364
28-BA	BUNABAN chain	1	1	30	51		70.00	100	C	6		. . .					0 . s . .	7365
28-BAA	**BUNABAN** net	1	1	30	51		70.00	100	C	6		. . .					0	7366
28-BAAA	GOONIYANDI cluster	1	1	10	17		70.00	100	C	6		. . .					0	7367
28-BAAA-a	gooniyandi	1	1	10	17	0	70.00	100	C	6		. . .					0	7368
28-BAAB	BUNABA cluster	1	1	20	34		70.00	100	C	6		. . .					0	7369
28-BAAB-a	bunaba	1	1	20	34	0	70.00	100	C	6		. . .					0	7370
28-C	**WORORAN** set	1	3	512	783		68.55	96	C	24		P . .					0	7371
28-CA	WORORAN chain	1	3	512	783		68.55	96	C	24		P . .					0	7372
28-CAA	**WORORA-NGARINYIN** net	1	1	223	368		74.44	99	C	24		P . .					0	7373
28-CAAA	WORORA cluster	1	1	23	28		69.57	100	C	24		P . .					0	7374
28-CAAA-a	worora	1	1	23	28	0	69.57	100	C	24	Worora	P . .	1930-1943				0	7375
28-CAAB	UNGGUMI cluster	1	1	200	340		75.00	99	C	0		. . .					0	7376
28-CAAB-a	unggumi	1	1	200	340	0	75.00	99	C	0		. . .					0	7377
28-CAB	**WUNAMBAL-MIWA** net	1	1	117	171		60.68	89	C	8		. . .					0	7378
28-CABA	WUNAMBAL cluster	1	1	20	34		75.00	100	C	8		. . .					0	7379
28-CABA-a	wunambal	1	1	20	34	0	75.00	100	C	8		. . .					0	7380
28-CABB	GAMBERA cluster	1	1	30	51		76.67	100	C	8		. . .					0	7381
28-CABB-a	gambera	1	1	30	51	0	76.67	100	C	8		. . .					0	7382
28-CABC	KUNAN cluster	1	1	57	69		43.86	77	B	0		. . .					0	7383
28-CABC-a	kunan	1	1	57	69	0	43.86	77	B	0		. . .					0	7384
28-CABD	MIWA cluster	1	1	10	17		80.00	100	C	8		. . .					0	7385
28-CABD-a	miwa	1	1	10	17	0	80.00	100	C	8		. . .					0	7386
28-CAC	**NGARINYIN-WILAWILA** net	1	1	172	244		66.28	97	C	12		. . .					0	7387
28-CACA	WILAWILA cluster	1	1	20	34		75.00	100	C	8		. . .					0	7388
28-CACA-a	wilawila	1	1	20	34	0	75.00	100	C	8		. . .					0	7389
28-CACB	WOLYAMIDI cluster	1	1	30	51		76.67	100	C	0		. . .					0	7390
28-CACB-a	wolyamidi	1	1	30	51	0	76.67	100	C	0		. . .					0	7391
28-CACC	NGARINYIN cluster	1	1	102	125		59.80	94	B	12		. . .					0	7392
28-CACC-a	ngarinyin	1	1	102	125	0	59.80	94	B	12	Ngarinyin	. . .					0	7393
28-CACD	GUWIDJ cluster	1	1	20	34		75.00	100	C	0		. . .					0	7394
28-CACD-a	guwidj	1	1	20	34	0	75.00	100	C	0		. . .					0	7395
28-D	**DJERAGAN** set	1	2	578	726		18.69	50	A	22		P . .					0	7396
28-DA	DJERAGAN chain	1	2	578	726		18.69	50	A	22		P . .					0	7397
28-DAA	**KITJA-GULUWARIN** net	1	1	143	184		48.25	79	B	22		P . .					0	7398
28-DAAA	KITJA cluster	1	1	123	150		44.72	76	B	22		P . .					0	7399
28-DAAA-a	Proper kitja	1	1	123	150	0	44.72	76	B	22	Kitja	P . .	1978				0	7400
28-DAAA-b	lungga					0				22		p . .					0	7401
28-DAAB	GULUWARIN cluster	1	1	20	34		70.00	100	C	0		. . .					0	7402
28-DAAB-a	guluwarin					0				0		. . .					0	7403
28-DAB	**MIRIWUNG** net	1	1	435	542		8.97	40	A	8		. . .					0	7404
28-DABA	MIRIWUNG cluster	1	1	415	508		6.02	37	A	8		. . .					0	7405
28-DABA-a	miriwung	1	1	415	508	0	6.02	37	A	8		. . .					0	7406
28-DABB	GADJERAWANG cluster	1	1	20	34		70.00	100	C	8		. . .					0	7407
28-DABB-a	gadjerawang	1	1	20	34	0	70.00	100	C	8		. . .					0	7408

Continued opposite

Table 9-13 continued

Code 1	REFERENCE NAME / Autoglossonym 2	Coun 3	Peo 4	Mother-tongue speakers in 2000 5	in 2025 6	Media radio 7	CHURCH AC% 8	E% 9	Wld 10	Tr 11	Biblioglossonym 12	SCRIPTURES Print 13-15	P-activity 16	N-activity 17	B-activity 18	J-year 19	Jayuh 20-24	Ref 25
28-E	**DJAMINDJUNGAN set**	1	1	50	85		70.00	98	C	8		. . .					0	7409
28-EA	DJAMINDJUNGAN chain	1	1	50	85		70.00	98	C	8		. . .					0	7410
28-EAA	**DJAMINDJUNGAN net**	1	1	50	85		70.00	98	C	8		. . .					0	7411
28-EAAA	DJAMINDJUNG cluster	1	1	30	51		70.00	97	C	6		. . .					0	7412
28-EAAA-a	djamindjung					0				6		. . .					0	7413
28-EAAA-b	ngaliwuru	1	1	30	51	0	70.00	97	C	6		. . .					0	7414
28-EAAB	NUNGALI cluster	1	1	20	34		70.00	100	C	8		. . .					0	7415
28-EAAB-a	nungali	1	1	20	34	0	70.00	100	C	8		. . .					0	7416
28-F	**DALY RIVER set**	1	2	1,579	2,037		67.38	94	C	22		P . .					0 . s . .	7417
28-FA	MURRINH-PATHA chain	1	1	1,054	1,294		75.05	100	C	22		P . .					0 . s . .	7418
28-FAA	**MURRINH-PATHA net**	1	1	1,044	1,277		75.00	100	C	22		P . .					0 . s . .	7419
28-FAAA	MURRINH-PATHA cluster	1	1	1,044	1,277		75.00	100	C	22		P . .					0 . s . .	7420
28-FAAA-a	Proper murrinh-patha	1	1	1,044	1,277	0	75.00	100	C	22	Murrinh-patha	P . .	1982				0 . s . .	7421
28-FAAA-b	murrinh-kura					0				22		p . .					0 . s . .	7422
28-FAAA-c	murrinh-diminin					0				22		p . .					0 . s . .	7423
28-FAB	**GARAMA net**	1	1	10	17		80.00	100	C	0		. . .					0	7424
28-FABA	GARAMA cluster	1	1	10	17		80.00	100	C	0		. . .					0	7425
28-FABA-a	garama	1	1	10	17	0	80.00	100	C	0		. . .					0	7426
28-FB	MANINDJI-WAGAYDY chain	1	1	170	289		70.00	99	C	8		. . .					0	7427
28-FBA	**MANINDJI net**	1	1	150	255		70.00	99	C	8		. . .					0	7428
28-FBAA	MARI-MANINDJI cluster	1	1	20	34		70.00	100	C	8		. . .					0	7429
28-FBAA-a	mari-manindji	1	1	20	34	0	70.00	100	C	8		. . .					0	7430
28-FBAB	MARI-THIEL cluster	1	1	20	34		70.00	100	C	8		. . .					0	7431
28-FBAB-a	Proper mari-thiel	1	1	20	34		70.00	100	C	8		. . .					0	7432
28-FBAB-b	nganygit					0				8		. . .					0	7433
28-FBAB-c	mare-ammu					0				8		. . .					0	7434
28-FBAC	MAGA-DIGE cluster	1	1	30	51		70.00	97	C	8		. . .					0	7435
28-FBAC-a	maga-dige	1	1	30	51	0	70.00	97	C	8		. . .					0	7436
28-FBAD	MARI-DJABIN cluster	1	1	20	34		70.00	100	C	6		. . .					0	7437
28-FBAD-a	mari-djabin	1	1	20	34	0	70.00	100	C	6		. . .					0	7438
28-FBAE	MARI-NGARR cluster	1	1	30	51		70.00	97	C	8		. . .					0	7439
28-FBAE-a	mari-ngarr					0				8		. . .					0	7440
28-FBAE-b	mara-nunggu					0				8		. . .					0	7441
28-FBAF	MARI-DAN cluster	1	1	20	34		70.00	100	C	8		. . .					0	7442
28-FBAF-a	mari-dan	1	1	20	34	0	70.00	100	C	8		. . .					0	7443
28-FBAG	MARI-YEDI cluster	1	1	10	17		70.00	100	C	8		. . .					0	7444
28-FBAG-a	mari-yedi	1	1	10	17	0	70.00	100	C	8		. . .					0	7445
28-FBB	**WAGAYDY net**	1	1	20	34		70.00	100	C	8		. . .					0	7446
28-FBBA	WADJIGINY cluster	1	1	20	34		70.00	100	C	8		. . .					0	7447
28-FBBA-a	wadjiginy					0				8		. . .					0	7448
28-FBBA-b	kuwama					0				8		. . .					0	7449
28-FBBA-c	ami					0				8		. . .					0	7450
28-FBBA-d	manda					0				8		. . .					0	7451
28-FBBB	GIYUG cluster			0	0		0.00	0		8		. . .					0	7452
28-FBBB-a	giyug			0	0	0	0.00	0		8		. . .					0	7453
28-FC	MOIL chain	1	1	315	386		40.00	71	B	6		. . .					0	7454
28-FCA	**MOIL net**	1	1	315	386		40.00	71	B	6		. . .					0	7455
28-FCAA	NANGI cluster	1	1	315	386		40.00	71	B	6		. . .					0	7456
28-FCAA-a	nangio-meri					0				6		. . .					0	7457
28-FCAA-b	nangi-kurrunggurr	1	1	315	386	0	40.00	71	B	6		. . .					0	7458
28-FCAA-c	tye-meri					0				6		. . .					0	7459
28-FD	MALAG-MADNGELE chain	1	1	40	68		70.00	100	C	8		. . .					0	7460
28-FDA	**MALAG-MADNGELE net**	1	1	40	68		70.00	100	C	8		. . .					0	7461
28-FDAA	MADNGELE cluster	1	1	20	34		70.00	100	C	8		. . .					0	7462
28-FDAA-a	madngele					0				8		. . .					0	7463
28-FDAA-b	yunggor			0	0	0	0.00	0		8		. . .					0	7464
28-FDAA-c	kamu					0				8		. . .					0	7465
28-FDAB	MALAG-MALAG cluster	1	1	20	34		70.00	100	C	8		. . .					0	7466
28-FDAB-a	Proper malag-malag					0				8		. . .					0	7467
28-FDAB-b	tyaraity					0				8		. . .					0	7468
28-G	**KUNGARAGANY set**									9		. . .					0	7469
28-GA	KUNGARAGANY chain									9		. . .					0	7470
28-GAA	**KUNGARAGANY net**									9		. . .					0	7471
28-GAAA	KUNGARAKANY cluster			0	0		0.00	0		9		. . .					0	7472
28-GAAA-a	kungarakany			0	0	0	0.00	0		9		. . .					0	7473
28-H	**LARAGIA-WULNA set**	1	1	30	51		70.00	100	C	8		. . .					0	7474
28-HA	WULNA chain	1	1	10	17		70.00	100	C	8		. . .					0	7475
28-HAA	**WULNA net**	1	1	10	17		70.00	100	C	8		. . .					0	7476
28-HAAA	WULNA cluster	1	1	10	17		70.00	100	C	8		. . .					0	7477
28-HAAA-a	wulna	1	1	10	17	0	70.00	100	C	8		. . .					0	7478
28-HB	LARAGIA chain	1	1	20	34		70.00	100	C	8		. . .					0	7479
28-HBA	**LARAGIA net**	1	1	20	34		70.00	100	C	8		. . .					0	7480
28-HBAA	LARAGIA cluster	1	1	20	34		70.00	100	C	8		. . .					0	7481
28-HBAA-a	laragia	1	1	20	34	0	70.00	100	C	8		. . .					0	7482
28-I	**TIWI set**	1	1	1,846	2,258		75.03	100	C	22		P . .					0	7483
28-IA	TIWI chain	1	1	1,846	2,258		75.03	100	C	22		P . .					0	7484

Continued overleaf

Table 9-13 continued

Code 1	REFERENCE NAME 2 / Autoglossonym	Coun 3	Peo 4	Mother-tongue speakers in 2000 5	in 2025 6	Media radio 7	AC% 8	E% 9	Wld 10	Tr 11	Biblioglossonym 12	Print 13-15	P–activity 16	N–activity 17	B–activity 18	J-year 19	Jayuh 20-24	Ref 25
28-IAA	**TIWI net**	1	1	1,846	2,258		75.03	100	C	22		P..					0....	7485
28-IAAA	NGIU cluster	1	1	1,846	2,258		75.03	100	C	22		P..					0....	7486
28-IAAA-a	ngiu	1	1	1,846	2,258	0	75.03	100	C	22	Tiwi	P..	1979-1985				0....	7487
28-J	**ADELAIDE RIVERS set**	1	1	120	204		70.00	99	C	8		...					0....	7488
28-JA	ADELAIDE RIVERS chain	1	1	120	204		70.00	99	C	8		...					0....	7489
28-JAA	**LIMILNGAN net**	1	1	40	68		70.00	100	C	8		...					0....	7490
28-JAAA	LIMILNGAN cluster	1	1	20	34		70.00	100	C	8		...					0....	7491
28-JAAA-a	limilngan					0				8		...					0....	7492
28-JAAB	BUNEIDJA cluster	1	1	20	34		70.00	100	C	0		...					0....	7493
28-JAAB-a	buneidja	1	1	20	34	0	70.00	100	C	0		...					0....	7494
28-JAB	**UMBUGARLA net**	1	1	20	34		70.00	100	C	8		...					0....	7495
28-JABA	UMBUGARLA cluster	1	1	20	34		70.00	100	C	8		...					0....	7496
28-JABA-a	umbugarla	1	1	20	34	0	70.00	100	C	8		...					0....	7497
28-JAC	**NGURMBUR net**	1	1	30	51		70.00	97	C	8		...					0....	7498
28-JACA	NGURMBUR cluster	1	1	30	51		70.00	97	C	8		...					0....	7499
28-JACA-a	ngurmbur	1	1	30	51	0	70.00	97	C	8		...					0....	7500
28-JAD	**BUGUNIDJA net**	1	1	10	17		70.00	100	C	0		...					0....	7501
28-JADA	BUGUNIDJA cluster	1	1	10	17		70.00	100	C	0		...					0....	7502
28-JADA-a	bugunidja	1	1	10	17	0	70.00	100	C	0		...					0....	7503
28-JAE	**NGARDUK net**	1	1	20	34		70.00	100	C	0		...					0....	7504
28-JAEA	NGARDUK cluster	1	1	20	34		70.00	100	C	0		...					0....	7505
28-JAEA-a	ngarduk	1	1	20	34	0	70.00	100	C	0		...					0....	7506
28-K	**GAGADU set**									8		...					0....	7507
28-KA	GAGADU chain									8		...					0....	7508
28-KAA	**GAGADU net**									8		...					0....	7509
28-KAAA	GAGADU cluster			0	0		0.00	0		8		...					0....	7510
28-KAAA-a	gagadu			0	0	0	0.00	0		8		...					0....	7511
28-L	**MANGERRIAN set**	1	1	50	85		70.00	98	C	8		...					0....	7512
28-LA	MANGERRIAN chain	1	1	50	85		70.00	98	C	8		...					0....	7513
28-LAA	**MANGERRIAN net**	1	1	50	85		70.00	98	C	8		...					0....	7514
28-LAAA	URNINGANGG-ERE cluster	1	1	20	34		70.00	100	C	8		...					0....	7515
28-LAAA-a	urningangg					0				8		...					0....	7516
28-LAAA-b	erre					0				8		...					0....	7517
28-LAAB	MANGERR cluster	1	1	30	51		70.00	97	C	8		...					0....	7518
28-LAAB-a	mangerr	1	1	30	51	0	70.00	97	C	8		...					0....	7519
28-M	**IWAIDJAN set**	1	2	516	655		42.25	74	B	23		P..					0.s..	7520
28-MA	AMARAG chain	1	1	30	51		70.00	97	C	8		...					0....	7521
28-MAA	**AMARAG net**	1	1	30	51		70.00	97	C	8		...					0....	7522
28-MAAA	AMARAG cluster	1	1	30	51		70.00	97	C	8		...					0....	7523
28-MAAA-a	amarag	1	1	30	51	0	70.00	97	C	8		...					0....	7524
28-MB	IWAIDJA-MAUNG chain	1	2	466	570		40.13	72	B	23		P..					0.s..	7525
28-MBA	**MAUNG net**	1	1	245	300		70.20	100	C	23		P..					0.s..	7526
28-MBAA	MAUNG cluster	1	1	245	300		70.20	100	C	23		P..					0.s..	7527
28-MBAA-a	maung	1	1	245	300	0	70.20	100	C	23	Maung	P..	1960				0.s..	7528
28-MBB	**IWAIDJA net**	1	1	221	270		6.79	41	A	6		...					0....	7529
28-MBBA	IWAIDJA-GARIG cluster	1	1	221	270		6.79	41	A	6		...					0....	7530
28-MBBA-a	iwaidja	1	1	221	270	0	6.79	41	A	6		...					0....	7531
28-MBBA-b	oidbi					0				6		...					0....	7532
28-MBBA-c	bijnalumbo					0				6		...					0....	7533
28-MBBA-d	garig					0				6		...					0....	7534
28-MC	MARGU chain	1	1	20	34		50.00	85	B	8		...					0....	7535
28-MCA	**MARGU net**	1	1	20	34		50.00	85	B	8		...					0....	7536
28-MCAA	MARGU cluster	1	1	20	34		50.00	85	B	8		...					0....	7537
28-MCAA-a	margu	1	1	20	34	0	50.00	85	B	8		...					0....	7538
28-N	**BURARRAN set**	1	2	714	898		46.22	81	B	41		PN.					0.s..	7539
28-NA	GUNAVIDJI chain	1	1	111	136		50.45	81	B	4		...					0....	7540
28-NAA	**GUNAVIDJI net**	1	1	111	136		50.45	81	B	4		...					0....	7541
28-NAAA	DJEEBBANA cluster	1	1	111	136		50.45	81	B	4		...					0....	7542
28-NAAA-a	djeebbana	1	1	111	136	0	50.45	81	B	4		...					0....	7543
28-NB	NAKARA chain	1	1	30	51		50.00	87	B	6		...					0....	7544
28-NBA	**NAKARA net**	1	1	30	51		50.00	87	B	6		...					0....	7545
28-NBAA	NAKARA cluster	1	1	30	51		50.00	87	B	6		...					0....	7546
28-NBAA-a	nakara	1	1	30	51	0	50.00	87	B	6		...					0....	7547
28-NC	GUJINGALIA chain	1	1	573	711		45.20	81	B	41		PN.					0.s..	7548
28-NCA	**GUJINGALIA net**	1	1	553	677		45.03	81	B	41		PN.					0.s..	7549
28-NCAA	GU-JINGALIA cluster	1	1	553	677		45.03	81	B	41		PN.					0.s..	7550
28-NCAA-a	burarra	1	1	553	677	0	45.03	81	B	41	Burarra	PN.	1972-1980	1991			0.s..	7551
28-NCAA-b	gu-naidbe					0				41		pn.					0.s..	7552
28-NCAA-c	gu-djalavia									41		pn.					0.s..	7553
28-NCB	**GURAGONE net**	1	1	20	34		50.00	85	B	6		...					0....	7554
28-NCBA	GURAGONE cluster	1	1	20	34		50.00	85	B	6		...					0....	7555
28-NCBA-a	gu-ragone	1	1	20	34	7	50.00	85	B	6		...					0....	7556

Continued opposite

Table 9-13 continued

Code 1	REFERENCE NAME Autoglossonym 2	Coun 3	Peo 4	Mother-tongue speakers in 2000 5	in 2025 6	Media radio 7	CHURCH AC% 8	E% 9	Wld 10	Tr 11	Biblioglossonym 12	SCRIPTURES Print 13-15	P-activity 16	N-activity 17	B-activity 18	J-year 19	Jayuh 20-24	Ref 25
28-O	**GUNWINGGUAN set**	1	4	1,593	2,063		54.87	86	B	22		P..					0.s..	7557
28-OA	WARAY chain	1	1	20	34		50.00	85	B	8		...					0....	7558
28-OAA	**WARAY net**	1	1	20	34		50.00	85	B	8		...					0....	7559
28-OAAA	WARAY cluster	1	1	20	34		50.00	85	B	8		...					0....	7560
28-OAAA-a	waray	1	1	20	34	0	50.00	85	B	8		...					0....	7561
28-OB	WAGEMAN chain	1	1	70	119		50.00	86	B	8		...					0....	7562
28-OBA	**WAGEMAN net**	1	1	20	34		50.00	85	B	6		...					0....	7563
28-OBAA	WAGE-MAN cluster	1	1	20	34		50.00	85	B	6		...					0....	7564
28-OBAA-a	wage-man	1	1	20	34	0	50.00	85'	B	6		...					0....	7565
28-OBB	**YANGMAN-DAGOMAN net**	1	1	30	51		50.00	87	B	8		...					0....	7566
28-OBBA	NOLGIN cluster	1	1	30	51		50.00	87	B	8		...					0....	7567
28-OBBA-a	dago-man					0				8		...					0....	7568
28-OBBA-b	yang-man					0				8		...					0....	7569
28-OBC	**WARDAMAN net**	1	1	20	34		50.00	85	B	6		...					0....	7570
28-OBCA	WARDA-MAN cluster	1	1	20	34		50.00	85	B	6		...					0....	7571
28-OBCA-a	warda-man	1	1	20	34	0	50.00	85	B	6		...					0....	7572
28-OC	JAWAN chain	1	1	10	17		50.00	90	B	6		...					0....	7573
28-OCA	**JAWAN net**	1	1	10	17		50.00	90	B	6		...					0....	7574
28-OCAA	JAWAN cluster	1	1	10	17		50.00	90	B	6		...					0....	7575
28-OCAA-a	jawan	1	1	10	17	0	50.00	90	B	6		...					0....	7576
28-OD	GUNWINGGU chain	1	2	808	1,022		52.10	82	B	22		P..					0.s..	7577
28-ODA	**BI net**	1	1	205	260		6.83	35	A	6		...					0....	7578
28-ODAA	BOUN cluster	1	1	20	34		5.00	30	A	0		...					0....	7579
28-ODAA-a	boun	1	1	20	34	0	5.00	30	A	0		...					0....	7580
28-ODAB	NGALK-BUN cluster	1	1	185	226		7.03	35	A	6		...					0....	7581
28-ODAB-a	ngalk-bun	1	1	185	226	0	7.03	35	A	6		...					0....	7582
28-ODAB-b	dala-bon					0				6		...					0....	7583
28-ODAB-c	ngala-gan					0				6		...					0....	7584
28-ODAB-d	gundang-bon					0				6		...					0....	7585
28-ODB	**GUNWINGGU net**	1	1	553	677		69.98	100	C	22		P..					0.s..	7586
28-ODBA	GUNWINGGU cluster	1	1	553	677		69.98	100	C	22	Kunwinjku*	P..	1942-1993				0.s..	7587
28-ODBA-a	gumadir					0				22		p..					0.s..	7588
28-ODBA-b	muralid-ban					0				22		p..					0.s..	7589
28-ODBA-c	gunei					0				22		p..					0.s..	7590
28-ODBA-d	gundjeipme					0				22		p..					0.s..	7591
28-ODBA-e	maiali					0				22		p..					0.s..	7592
28-ODC	**KUNBARLANG net**	1	1	50	85		40.00	76	B	6		...					0....	7593
28-ODCA	KUNBARLANG cluster	1	1	50	85		40.00	76	B	6		...					0....	7594
28-ODCA-a	kunbarlang	1	1	50	85	0	40.00	76	B	6		...					0....	7595
28-OE	REMBARUNGA chain	1	1	185	226		40.00	76	B	6		...					0....	7596
28-OEA	**REMBARUNGA net**	1	1	185	226		40.00	76	B	6		...					0....	7597
28-OEAA	REMBARUNGA cluster	1	1	185	226		40.00	76	B	6		...					0....	7598
28-OEAA-a	rembarunga	1	1	185	226	0	40.00	76	B	6		...					0....	7599
28-OF	MANGARAYI chain	1	1	40	68		40.00	78	B	6		...					0....	7600
28-OFA	**MANGARAYI net**	1	1	40	68		40.00	78	B	6		...					0....	7601
28-OFAA	MANGARAYI cluster	1	1	40	68		40.00	78	B	6		...					0....	7602
28-OFAA-a	mangarayi	1	1	40	68	0	40.00	78	B	6		...					0....	7603
28-OG	NGANDI chain	1	1	30	51		40.00	77	B	9		...					0....	7604
28-OGA	**NGANDI net**	1	1	30	51		40.00	77	B	9		...					0....	7605
28-OGAA	NGANDI cluster	1	1	30	51		40.00	77	B	9		...					0....	7606
28-OGAA-a	ngandi	1	1	30	51	0	40.00	77	B	9		...					0....	7607
28-OH	NUNGGUBUYU chain	1	1	430	526		70.00	100	C	22		P..					0....	7608
28-OHA	**NUNGGUBUYU net**	1	1	430	526		70.00	100	C	22		P..					0....	7609
28-OHAA	NUNGGUBUYU cluster	1	1	430	526		70.00	100	C	22		P..					0....	7610
28-OHAA-a	nunggubuyu	1	1	430	526	0	70.00	100	C	22	Nunggubuyu	P..	1946-1993				0....	7611
28-P	**ANINDILYAKWA set**	1	1	1,231	1,506		70.02	100	C	22		P..					0.s..	7612
28-PA	ANINDILYAKWA chain	1	1	1,231	1,506		70.02	100	C	22		P..					0.s..	7613
28-PAA	**ANINDILYAKWA net**	1	1	1,231	1,506		70.02	100	C	22		P..					0.s..	7614
28-PAAA	ANINDILYAKWA cluster	1	1	1,231	1,506		70.02	100	C	22		P..					0.s..	7615
28-PAAA-a	anindilyakwa	1	1	1,231	1,506	0	70.02	100	C	22	Anindilyakwa	P..	1976-1993				0.s..	7616
28-Q	**ALAWA set**	1	1	100	170		56.00	85	B	9		...					0....	7617
28-QA	ALAWA chain	1	1	50	85		36.00	72	B	8		...					0....	7618
28-QAA	**ALAWA net**	1	1	50	85		36.00	72	B	8		...					0....	7619
28-QAAA	ALAWA cluster	1	1	50	85		36.00	72	B	8		...					0....	7620
28-QAAA-a	alawa	1	1	50	85	0	36.00	72	B	8		...					0....	7621
28-QB	MARAN chain	1	1	50	85		76.00	98	C	9		...					0....	7622
28-QBA	**WANDARANG net**									9		...					0....	7623
28-QBAA	WANDARANG cluster			0	0		0.00	0		9		...					0....	7624
28-QBAA-a	wandarang			0	0	0	0.00	0		9		...					0....	7625
28-QBB	**GARIYIMAR net**	1	1	50	85		76.00	98	C	8		...					0....	7626
28-QBBA	GARIYIMAR cluster	1	1	50	85		76.00	98	C	8		...					0....	7627
28-QBBA-a	mara					0				8		...					0....	7628
28-QBBA-b	jugul					0				8		...					0....	7629

Continued overleaf

Table 9-13 continued

Code 1	REFERENCE NAME / Autoglossonym 2	Coun 3	Peo 4	Mother-tongue speakers in 2000 5	in 2025 6	Media radio 7	CHURCH AC% 8	E% 9	Wld 10	Tr 11	Biblioglossonym 12	SCRIPTURES Print 13-15	P-activity 16	N-activity 17	B-activity 18	J-year 19	Jayuh 20-24	Ref 25
28-R	**YANYUWA set**	1	1	111	136		15.32	50	B	22		P..					0....	7630
28-RA	YANYUWA chain	1	1	111	136		15.32	50	B	22		P..					0....	7631
28-RAA	**YANYUWA net**	1	1	111	136		15.32	50	B	22		P..					0....	7632
28-RAAA	YANYUWA cluster	1	1	111	136		15.32	50	B	22		P..					0....	7633
28-RAAA-a	yanyuwa	1	1	111	136	0	15.32	50	B	22	Yanyuwa	P..	1980				0....	7634
28-S	**JINGILI-WAMBAYA set**	1	1	110	187		24.55	55	B	8		...					0....	7635
28-SA	JINGILI chain	1	1	30	51		36.67	70	B	0		...					0....	7636
28-SAA	**JINGILI net**	1	1	30	51		36.67	70	B	0		...					0....	7637
28-SAAA	JINGILI cluster	1	1	30	51		36.67	70	B	0		...					0....	7638
28-SAAA-a	jingili	1	1	30	51	0	36.67	70	B	0		...					0....	7639
28-SB	WAMBAYA-NGARNDJI chain	1	1	80	136		20.00	50	B	8		...					0....	7640
28-SBA	**NGARNDJI net**	1	1	50	85		20.00	50	B	8		...					0....	7641
28-SBAA	NGARNDJI cluster	1	1	50	85		20.00	50	B	8		...					0....	7642
28-SBAA-a	ngarndji	1	1	50	85	0	20.00	50	B	8		...					0....	7643
28-SBB	**WAMBAYAN net**	1	1	30	51		20.00	50	B	8		...					0....	7644
28-SBBA	WAMBAYA-GUDANDJI cluster	1	1	30	51		20.00	50	B	8		...					0....	7645
28-SBBA-a	wambaya					0				8		...					0....	7646
28-SBBA-b	binbinga					0				8		...					0....	7647
28-SBBA-c	gudandji					0				8		...					0....	7648
28-T	**GARAWAN set**	1	1	225	275		40.00	75	B	22		P..					0....	7649
28-TA	GARAWAN chain	1	1	225	275		40.00	75	B	22		P..					0....	7650
28-TAA	**GARAWAN net**	1	1	225	275		40.00	75	B	22		P..					0....	7651
28-TAAA	GARAWA-WANJI cluster	1	1	225	275		40.00	75	B	22	Garawa	P..	1983				0....	7652
28-TAAA-a	garawa					0				22		p..					0....	7653
28-TAAA-b	wanji					0				22		p..					0....	7654
28-U	**MINGIN set**									0		...					0....	7655
28-UA	MINGIN chain									0		...					0....	7656
28-UAA	**MINGIN net**									0		...					0....	7657
28-UAAA	MINGIN cluster			0	0		0.00	0		0		...					0....	7658
28-UAAA-a	mingin			0	0	0	0.00	0		0		...					0....	7659
29	**PAMA-NYUNGIC zone**	2	45	47,769	59,666		59.24	88	B	51		PN.					0as..	7660
29-A	**YUULNGU set**	1	10	4,221	5,208		40.13	74	B	41		PN.					0.s..	7661
29-AA	YUULNGU chain	1	10	4,221	5,208		40.13	74	B	41		PN.					0.s..	7662
29-AAA	**JINBA-GANALBWINGU net**	1	1	30	51		30.00	63	B	6		...					0....	7663
29-AAAA	JINBA-GANALBWINGU cluster	1	1	30	51		30.00	63	B	6		...					0....	7664
29-AAAA-a	jinba					0				6		...					0....	7665
29-AAAA-b	ganal-bingu					0				6		...					0....	7668
29-AAAA-c	dabi					0				6		...					0....	7669
29-AAAA-d	mandjal-pingu					0				6		...					0....	7670
29-AAB	**JINANG net**	1	1	312	381		11.86	42	A	22		P..					0....	7671
29-AABA	JINANG cluster	1	1	312	381		11.86	42	A	22		P..					0....	7672
29-AABA-a	jinang	1	1	312	381	0	11.86	42	A	22	Djinang	P..	1985-1987				0....	7673
29-AABA-b	jadiwitjibi					0				22		p..					0....	7676
29-AABA-c	wulaki					0				22		p..					0....	7677
29-AABA-d	balurbi					0				22		p..					0....	7678
29-AABA-e	murrungun					0				22		p..					0....	7679
29-AABA-f	manyarring					0				22		p..					0....	7680
29-AAC	**JARNANGO net**	1	1	10	17		50.00	90	B	8		...					0....	7681
29-AACA	JARNANGO cluster	1	1	10	17		50.00	90	B	8		...					0....	7682
29-AACA-a	jarnango					0				8		...					0....	7683
29-AACA-b	garmalangga					0				8		...					0....	7684
29-AACA-c	gurjindi					0				8		...					0....	7685
29-AAD	**DHANGU-JANGU net**	1	3	1,150	1,430		48.52	79	B	22		P..					0....	7686
29-AADA	DHANGU cluster	1	3	1,100	1,345		48.45	78	B	22	Dhangu'mi	P..	1977				0....	7687
29-AADA-a	galpu	1	1	430	526	0	14.88	45	A	22		p..					0....	7688
29-AADA-b	wan'guri	1	1	240	293	0	70.00	100	C	22	Wangurri	P..	1977				0....	7689
29-AADA-c	ngaymil					0				22		p..					0....	7690
29-AADA-d	golumala					0				22		p..					0....	7691
29-AADB	NGATANG-THUNDAMI cluster	1	1	30	51		50.00	87	B	0		...					0....	7692
29-AADB-a	rirratjingu					0				0		...					0....	7693
29-AADB-b	lamami					0				0		...					0....	7694
29-AADC	JANGU cluster	1	1	20	34		50.00	85	B	0		...					0....	7695
29-AADC-a	warramiri					0				0		...					0....	7696
29-AADC-b	mandatja					0				0		...					0....	7697
29-AAE	**DHUWALA-DHUWAL net**	1	4	2,104	2,576		41.87	78	B	41		PN.					0.s..	7698
29-AAEA	DHUWALA cluster	1	2	936	1,146		46.47	81	B	41		PN.					0.s..	7699
29-AAEA-a	gupa-puyngu	1	1	566	693	0	65.02	100	C	41	Gupapuyngu	Pn.	1967				0.s..	7700
29-AAEA-b	wubulkarra			0	0	0	0.00	0		41		pn.					0.s..	7705
29-AAEA-c	gumatj	1	1	370	453	0	18.11	53	B	41	Gumatj	PN.	1977-1979	1985			0.s..	7706
29-AAEA-d	madarrpa					0				41		pn.					0.s..	7710
29-AAEB	DHUWAL-JAMBARR cluster	1	2	1,168	1,430		38.18	75	B	22		P..					0.s..	7711
29-AAEB-a	jambarr-puyngu	1	1	553	677	0	24.95	59	B	22	Djambarrpuyngu	P..	1977-1993				0.s..	7712
29-AAEB-b	marrangu					0				22		p..					0.s..	7717
29-AAEB-c	datiwuy					0				22		p..					0.s..	7718
29-AAEB-d	dhuwal					0				22		p..					0.s..	7719
29-AAF	**DAYI net**	1	1	245	300		15.10	47	A	8		...					0....	7724
29-AAFA	DAYI cluster	1	1	245	300		15.10	47	A	8		...					0....	7725
29-AAFA-a	dhalwangu	1	1	245	300	0	15.10	47	A	8		...					0....	7726
29-AAFA-b	djarrwark					0				8		....					0....	7727

Continued opposite

Table 9-13 continued

Code 1	REFERENCE NAME / Autoglossonym 2	Coun 3	Peo 4	Mother-tongue speakers in 2000 5	in 2025 6	Media radio 7	AC% 8	E% 9	Wld 10	Tr 11	Biblioglossonym 12	Print 13-15	P-activity 16	N-activity 17	B-activity 18	J-year 19	Jayuh 20-24	Ref 25
29-AAG	**DHIYAKUY net**	1	1	370	453		45.14	77	B	4		...					0....	7728
29-AAGA	DHIYAKUY cluster	1	1	370	453		45.14	77	B	4		...					0....	7729
29-AAGA-a	ritarungo	1	1	370	453	0	45.14	77	B	4		...					0....	7730
29-AAGA-b	wagelak					0				4		...					0....	7731
29-AAGA-c	manggurra					0				4		...					0....	7732
29-B	**SOUTHWEST AUSTRALIAN set**	2	18	27,265	34,310		62.67	88	C	51		PN.					0as..	7733
29-BA	NGARGA chain	1	1	3,417	4,208		70.03	100	C	35		P..					0....	7734
29-BAA	**NGARGA net**	1	1	3,417	4,208		70.03	100	C	35		P..					0....	7735
29-BAAA	WARL-PIRI cluster	1	1	3,357	4,106		70.00	100	C	35		P..					0....	7736
29-BAAA-a	warl-piri	1	1	3,357	4,106	0	70.00	100	C	35	Warlpiri	P..	1985-1993				0....	7737
29-BAAB	WARL-MANPA cluster	1	1	30	51		70.00	97	C	6		...					0....	7738
29-BAAB-a	warl-manpa	1	1	30	51	0	70.00	97	C	6		...					0....	7739
29-BAAC	NGARDI cluster	1	1	20	34		70.00	100	C	0		...					0....	7740
29-BAAC-a	ngardi	1	1	20	34	0	70.00	100	C	0		...					0....	7741
29-BAAD	NORTH NGALIA cluster	1	1	10	17		80.00	100	C	0		...					0....	7742
29-BAAD-a	North ngalia	1	1	10	17	0	80.00	100	C	0		...					0....	7743
29-BB	NGUMBIN chain	1	3	2,107	2,795		44.90	77	B	22		P..					0a...	7744
29-BBA	**MUDBURA net**	1	1	30	51		70.00	97	C	6		...					0....	7745
29-BBAA	MUDBURA cluster	1	1	30	51		70.00	97	C	6		...					0....	7746
29-BBAA-a	mudbura	1	1	30	51	0	70.00	97	C	6		...					0....	7747
29-BBB	**NGARINMAN-BILINARA net**	1	1	240	307		16.67	42	A	6		...					0....	7748
29-BBBA	NGARINMAN cluster	1	1	210	256		16.19	41	A	6		...					0....	7749
29-BBBA-a	ngarinman					0				6		...					0....	7750
29-BBBB	BILINARA cluster	1	1	30	51		20.00	50	B	0		...					0....	7751
29-BBBB-a	North bilinara					0				0		...					0....	7752
29-BBBB-b	South bilinara					0				0		...					0....	7753
29-BBC	**GURINJI-MALNGIN net**	1	1	400	680		27.50	61	B	22		P..					0....	7754
29-BBCA	GURINJI cluster	1	1	300	510		30.00	65	B	22		P..					0....	7755
29-BBCA-a	gurinji	1	1	300	510	0	30.00	65	B	22	Gurindji*	P..	1981-1986				0....	7756
29-BBCB	MALNGIN cluster	1	1	100	170		20.00	50	B	0		...					0....	7757
29-BBCB-a	malngin	1	1	100	170	0	20.00	50	B	0		...					0....	7758
29-BBD	**JARU net**	1	1	317	388		14.83	44	A	12		...					0....	7759
29-BBDA	JARU cluster	1	1	317	388		14.83	44	A	12		...					0....	7760
29-BBDA-a	jaru	1	1	317	388	0	14.83	44	A	12	Jaru	...					0....	7761
29-BBDA-b	nyininy					0				12		...					0....	7762
29-BBE	**WALMAJARRI net**	1	1	1,120	1,369		65.00	100	C	22		P..					0a...	7763
29-BBEA	WAL-MAJARRI cluster	1	1	1,120	1,369		65.00	100	C	22		P..					0a...	7764
29-BBEA-a	wal-majarri	1	1	1,120	1,369	0	65.00	100	C	22	Walmajarri	P..	1978-1985				0a...	7765
29-BBEA-b	juwarliny					0				22		p..					0c...	7766
29-BC	MARNGU chain	1	1	624	787		71.31	97	C	12		...					0....	7767
29-BCA	**MARNGU net**	1	1	624	787		71.31	97	C	12		...					0....	7768
29-BCAA	MANGALA cluster	1	1	20	34		30.00	65	B	8		...					0....	7769
29-BCAA-a	mangala	1	1	20	34	0	30.00	65	B	8		...					0....	7770
29-BCAB	KARAJERI cluster	1	1	30	51		30.00	63	B	0		...					0....	7771
29-BCAB-a	karajeri	1	1	30	51	0	30.00	63	B	0		...					0....	7772
29-BCAC	NYANGUMARTA cluster	1	1	574	702		74.91	100	C	12		...					0....	7773
29-BCAC-a	nyangumarta	1	1	574	702	0	74.91	100	C	12	Nyangumarta	...					0....	7774
29-BD	NGAYARDA-KANYARA chain	1	1	1,278	1,821		36.62	69	B	9		...					0....	7775
29-BDA	**EAST NGAYARDA net**	1	1	100	170		30.00	64	B	8		...					0....	7776
29-BDAA	NGARLA cluster	1	1	20	34		30.00	65	B	8		...					0....	7777
29-BDAA-a	ngarla	1	1	20	34	0	30.00	65	B	8		...					0....	7778
29-BDAB	NYAMAL cluster	1	1	30	51		30.00	63	B	6		...					0....	7779
29-BDAB-a	nyamal	1	1	30	51	0	30.00	63	B	6		...					0....	7780
29-BDAC	PANYTYIMA cluster	1	1	30	51		30.00	63	B	6		...					0....	7781
29-BDAC-a	panytyima	1	1	30	51	0	30.00	63	B	6		...					0as..	7782
29-BDAD	NGARLA-WANGGA cluster	1	1	20	34		30.00	65	B	0		...					0....	7783
29-BDAD-a	ngarla-wangga	1	1	20	34	0	30.00	65	B	0		...					0....	7784
29-BDB	**WEST NGAYARDA net**	1	1	80	136		40.00	76	B	9		...					0....	7785
29-BDBA	KARIYARRA cluster			0	0		0.00	0		9		...					0....	7786
29-BDBA-a	kariyarra			0	0	0	0.00	0		9		...					0....	7787
29-BDBB	NGARLUMA cluster	1	1	30	51		40.00	77	B	6		...					0....	7788
29-BDBB-a	ngarluma	1	1	30	51	0	40.00	77	B	6		...					0....	7789
29-BDBC	MARTUYHUNIRA cluster	1	1	30	51		40.00	77	B	8		...					0....	7790
29-BDBC-a	martuyhunira	1	1	30	51	0	40.00	77	B	8		...					0....	7791
29-BDBD	NHUWALA cluster	1	1	20	34		40.00	75	B	8		...					0....	7792
29-BDBD-a	nhuwala	1	1	20	34	0	40.00	75	B	8		...					0....	7793
29-BDC	**CENTRAL NGAYARDA net**	1	1	808	1,022		39.48	71	B	9		...					0....	7794
29-BDCA	YINDJIBARNDI cluster	1	1	738	903		39.97	71	B	6		...					0....	7795
29-BDCA-a	yindjibarndi	1	1	738	903	0	39.97	71	B	6		...					0....	7796
29-BDCB	KURRAMA cluster	1	1	30	51		40.00	77	B	6		...					0....	7797
29-BDCB-a	kurrama	1	1	30	51	0	40.00	77	B	6		...					0....	7798
29-BDCC	TJURRURU cluster			0	0		0.00	0		9		...					0....	7799
29-BDCC-a	tjurruru			0	0	0	0.00	0		9		...					0....	7800
29-BDCD	YINHAWANGGA cluster	1	1	40	68		30.00	65	B	0		...					0....	7801
29-BDCD-a	yinha-wangga	1	1	40	68	0	30.00	65	B	0		...					0....	7802
29-BDD	**KANYARA net**	1	1	150	255		30.00	64	B	8		...					0....	7803
29-BDDA	DHALANDJI cluster	1	1	40	68		30.00	65	B	6		...					0....	7804
29-BDDA-a	dhalandji	1	1	40	68	0	30.00	65	B	6		...					0....	7805

Continued overleaf

Table 9-13 continued

Code 1	REFERENCE NAME 2 / Autoglossonym	Coun 3	Peo 4	Mother-tongue speakers in 2000 5	in 2025 6	Media radio 7	CHURCH AC% 8	E% 9	Wld 10	Tr 11	Biblioglossonym 12	Print 13-15	P-activity 16	N-activity 17	B-activity 18	J-year 19	Jayuh 20-24	Ref 25
29-BDDB	BAYUNGU cluster	1	1	30	51		30.00	63	B	8		. . .					0	7806
29-BDDB-a	bayungu	1	1	30	51	0	30.00	63	B	8		. . .					0	7807
29-BDDC	BURDUNA cluster	1	1	20	34		30.00	65	B	8		. . .					0	7808
29-BDDC-a	burduna	1	1	20	34	0	30.00	65	B	8		. . .					0	7809
29-BDDD	DHARGARI cluster	1	1	30	51		30.00	63	B	8		. . .					0	7810
29-BDDD-a	dhargari	1	1	30	51	0	30.00	63	B	8		. . .					0	7811
29-BDDE	PINIGURA cluster	1	1	30	51		30.00	63	B	8		. . .					0	7812
29-BDDE-a	pinigura	1	1	30	51	0	30.00	63	B	8		. . .					0	7813
29-BDE	**MANTHARTHA net**	1	1	140	238		30.00	64	B	0		. . .					0	7814
29-BDEA	THARGARI cluster	1	1	50	85		30.00	64	B	0		. . .					0	7815
29-BDEA-a	thargari	1	1	50	85	0	30.00	64	B	0		. . .					0	7816
29-BDEB	THIINMA cluster	1	1	40	68		30.00	65	B	0		. . .					0	7817
29-BDEB-a	thiin-ma	1	1	40	68	0	30.00	65	B	0		. . .					0	7818
29-BDEC	JIWARLI cluster	1	1	50	85		30.00	64	B	0		. . .					0	7819
29-BDEC-a	jiwarli	1	1	50	85	0	30.00	64	B	0		. . .					0	7820
29-BDED	WARI-WONGA cluster			0	0		0.00	0		0		. . .					0	7821
29-BDED-a	wari-wonga			0	0	0	0.00	0		0		. . .					0	7822
29-BE	KARDU chain	1	1	50	85		30.00	64	B	9		. . .					0	7823
29-BEA	**KARDU net**	1	1	50	85		30.00	64	B	9		. . .					0	7824
29-BEAA	SHARK-BAY cluster	1	1	50	85		30.00	64	B	9		. . .					0	7825
29-BEAA-a	maya			0	0	0	0.00	0		9		. . .					0	7826
29-BEAA-b	yinggarda					0				9		. . .					0	7827
29-BEAA-c	malgana					0				9		. . .					0	7828
29-BEAA-d	buluguda			0	0	0	0.00	0		9		. . .					0	7829
29-BEAA-e	tamala			0	0	0				9		. . .					0	7830
29-BEAB	MURCHISON cluster			0	0		0.00	0		0		. . .					0	7831
29-BEAB-a	watjandi			0	0	0	0.00	0		0		. . .					0	7832
29-BEAB-b	nhanda			0	0	0	0.00	0		0		. . .					0	7833
29-BEAB-c	bulinya			0	0	0	0.00	0		0		. . .					0	7834
29-BF	NYUNGAR-WATJARI chain	1	3	11,594	14,200		77.06	97	C	9		. . .					0	7835
29-BFA	**WATJARI-BADIMAY net**	1	2	481	589		13.31	44	A	6		. . .					0	7836
29-BFAA	WATJARI-BADIMAY cluster	1	2	481	589		13.31	44	A	6		. . .					0	7837
29-BFAA-a	watjari	1	1	370	453	0	5.14	35	A	6		. . .					0	7838
29-BFAA-b	wirdi-may			0	0	0	0.00	0		6		. . .					0	7839
29-BFAA-c	badi-may	1	1	111	136	0	40.54	73	B	6		. . .					0	7840
29-BFB	**NYUNGAR net**	1	1	11,073	13,543		80.00	100	C	9		. . .					0	7841
29-BFBA	NYUNGA cluster	1	1	11,073	13,543		80.00	100	C	9		. . .					0	7842
29-BFBA-a	pipel-man			0	0	0	0.00	0		9		. . .					0	7843
29-BFBA-b	nanakarti			0	0	0	0.00	0		9		. . .					0	7844
29-BFBA-c	watjan-may			0	0	0	0.00	0		9		. . .					0	7845
29-BFBA-d	tjapan-may			0	0	0	0.00	0		9		. . .					0	7846
29-BFBA-e	karla-may			0	0	0	0.00	0		9		. . .					0	7847
29-BFBA-f	ngatju-may			0	0	0	0.00	0		9		. . .					0	7848
29-BFBA-g	kwetj-man			0	0	0	0.00	0		9		. . .					0	7849
29-BFBA-h	mirnong			0	0	0	0.00	0		9		. . .					0	7850
29-BFBA-i	kaniyang			0	0	0	0.00	0		9		. . .					0	7851
29-BFC	**MIRNING-KALARKO net**	1	1	40	68		30.00	65	B	9		. . .					0	7852
29-BFCA	KALARKO-WUDJARI cluster	1	1	40	68		30.00	65	B	9		. . .					0	7853
29-BFCA-a	kalarko			0	0	0	0.00	0		9		. . .					0	7854
29-BFCA-b	ngadjun-maya					0				9		. . .					0	7855
29-BFCA-c	wudjari			0	0	0	0.00	0		9		. . .					0	7856
29-BFCB	MIRNING cluster			0	0		0.00	0		0		. . .					0	7857
29-BFCB-a	mirning			0	0	0	0.00	0		0		. . .					0	7858
29-BG	WATI chain	2	9	8,155	10,346		47.49	76	B	51		PN.					0.s..	7859
29-BGA	**CENTRAL WATI net**	1	5	3,560	4,378		70.79	95	C	51		PN.					0.s..	7860
29-BGAA	MURUNITJA cluster			0	0		0.00	0		0		. . .					0	7861
29-BGAA-a	murunitja			0	0	0	0.00	0		0		. . .					0	7862
29-BGAB	PINTIINI-WANGGAYI cluster	1	1	368	450		70.11	100	C	4		. . .					0	7863
29-BGAB-a	pintiini	1	1	368	450	0	70.11	100	C	4		. . .					0	7864
29-BGAB-b	wanggayi			0	0	0	0.00	0		4		. . .					0	7865
29-BGAC	MARDU cluster			0	0		0.00	0		0		. . .					0	7866
29-BGAC-a	mardu-djara			0	0	0	0.00	0		0		. . .					0	7867
29-BGAD	NGURLU cluster			0	0		0.00	0		0		. . .					0	7868
29-BGAD-a	ngurlu			0	0	0	0.00	0		0		. . .					0	7869
29-BGAE	GUWARA cluster			0	0		0.00	0		0		. . .					0	7870
29-BGAE-a	guwara			0	0	0	0.00	0		0		. . .					0	7871
29-BGAF	PINIRI cluster	1	1	50	85		40.00	76	B	0		. . .					0	7872
29-BGAF-a	piniri-tjara	1	1	50	85	0	40.00	76	B	0		. . .					0	7873
29-BGAG	BUDI cluster			0	0		0.00	0		0		. . .					0	7874
29-BGAG-a	budi-djara			0	0	0	0.00	0		0		. . .					0	7875
29-BGAH	NGANA cluster	1	1	935	1,143		60.00	98	C	51		PN.					0.s..	7876
29-BGAH-a	giya-djara			0	0	0	0.00	0		51		pn.					0.s..	7877
29-BGAH-b	nana-djara			0	0	0	0.00	0		51		pn.					0.s..	7878
29-BGAH-c	ngaadja-djara			0	0	0	0.00	0		51		pn.					0.s..	7879
29-BGAH-d	ngaanya-tjara	1	1	935	1,143	0	60.00	98	C	51	Ngaanyatjarra	PN.	1976-1986	1991			0.s..	7880
29-BGAH-e	djalga-djara			0	0	0	0.00	0		51		pn.					0.s..	7881
29-BGAH-f	mandjindja-djara			0	0	0	0.00	0		51		pn.					0.s..	7882
29-BGAH-g	nyanganya-tjara					0				51		pn.					0.s..	7883
29-BGAI	SOUTH NGALIA cluster			0	0		0.00	0		0		. . .					0	7884
29-BGAI-a	South ngalia			0	0	0	0.00	0		0		. . .					0	7885
29-BGAI-b	nakako			0	0	0	0.00	0		0		. . .					0	7886
29-BGAJ	YANKUNTA cluster	1	1	300	367		50.00	83	B	6		. . .					0	7887
29-BGAJ-a	yankunta-tjara	1	1	300	367	0	50.00	83	B	6		. . .					0	7888
29-BGAJ-b	kulbandja-tjarra			0	0	0	0.00	0		6		. . .					0	7889
29-BGAJ-c	wirdjara-gandja			0	0	0	0.00	0		6		. . .					0	7890
29-BGAK	PITJANTJA cluster	1	2	1,907	2,333		80.28	95	C	33		P..					0.s..	7891
29-BGAK-a	pitjantja-tjara	1	1	1,537	1,880	1	89.98	100	C	33	Pitjantjatjara	P..	1949-1995				0.s..	7892
29-BGAK-b	Vehicular pitjantja					1				33		p..					0.s..	7893
29-BGAK-c	kukatja	1	1	370	453	1	40.00	73	B	33		p..					0.s..	7894
29-BGAL	YUMU cluster			0	0		0.00	0		0		. . . .					0	7895

Continued opposite

Table 9-13 continued

Code 1	REFERENCE NAME / Autoglossonym 2	Coun 3	Peo 4	Mother-tongue speakers in 2000 5	in 2025 6	Media radio 7	CHURCH AC% 8	E% 9	Wld 10	Tr 11	Biblioglossonym 12	Print 13-15	P-activity 16	N-activity 17	B-activity 18	J-year 19	Jayuh 20-24	Ref 25
29-BGAL-a	yumu			0	0	0	0.00	0		0		...					0....	7896
29-BGB	**BIDUNGU net**									0		...					0....	7897
29-BGBA	BIDUNGU cluster			0	0		0.00	0		0		...					0....	7898
29-BGBA-a	bidungu			0	0	0	0.00	0		0		...					0....	7899
29-BGC	**NIJADALI net**	1	1	40	68		30.00	65	B	8		...					0....	7900
29-BGCA	NIJADALI cluster	1	1	40	68		30.00	65	B	8		...					0....	7901
29-BGCA-a	nijadali					0				8		...					0....	7902
29-BGCA-b	balygu					0				8		...					0....	7903
29-BGCA-c	jauna			0	0		0.00	0		8		...					0....	7904
29-BGD	**WANMAN net**									6		...					0....	7905
29-BGDA	WANMAN cluster									6		...					0....	7906
29-BGDA-a	wanman					0				6		...					0....	7907
29-BGE	**MARTU net**	2	3	3,169	4,015		18.62	47	A	33		P..					0....	7908
29-BGEA	MARTU cluster	2	3	3,169	4,015		18.62	47	A	33	Martu Wangka	P..	1994				0....	7909
29-BGEA-a	manyjily-jara					0				33		p..					0....	7910
29-BGEA-b	kartu-jarra					0				33		p..					0....	7911
29-BGEA-c	pudi-tara			0	0	0	0.00	0		33		p..					0....	7912
29-BGEA-d	wangka-junga					0				33		p..					0....	7913
29-BGEA-e	nanga-tara			0	0	0	0.00	0		33		p..					0....	7914
29-BGEA-f	ilda-wongga			0	0	0	0.00	0		33		p..					0....	7915
29-BGF	**GUGADJA net**	1	1	300	510		40.00	77	B	0		...					0....	7916
29-BGFA	GUGADJA cluster	1	1	300	510		40.00	77	B	0		...					0....	7917
29-BGFA-a	gugadja-wati	1	1	300	510	0	40.00	77	B	0		...					0....	7918
29-BGG	**PINTUPI-LURITJA net**	1	1	986	1,205		59.94	100	B	41		PN.					0.s..	7919
29-BGGA	PINTUPI-LURITJA cluster	1	1	986	1,205		59.94	100	B	41		PN.					0.s..	7920
29-BGGA-a	pintupi	1	1	986	1,205	0	59.94	100	B	41	Pintupi-luritja	PN.	1972-1977	1981			0.s..	7921
29-BGGA-b	luritja					0				41		pn.					0.s..	7922
29-BGH	**ANTAKARINYA net**	1	1	30	51		40.00	77	B	6		...					0....	7923
29-BGHA	ANTAKARINYA cluster	1	1	30	51		40.00	77	B	6		...					0....	7924
29-BGHA-a	antakarinya	1	1	30	51	0	40.00	77	B	6		...					0....	7925
29-BGI	**KOKATA net**	1	1	40	68		40.00	78	B	8		...					0....	7926
29-BGIA	KOKATA cluster	1	1	40	68		40.00	78	B	8		...					0....	7927
29-BGIA-a	kokata	1	1	40	68	0	40.00	78	B	8		...					0....	7928
29-BGJ	**WIRANGU net**	1	1	30	51		40.00	77	B	8		...					0....	7929
29-BGJA	WIRANGU cluster	1	1	30	51		40.00	77	B	8		...					0....	7930
29-BGJA-a	wirangu	1	1	30	51	0	40.00	77	B	8		...					0....	7931
29-BH	YURA chain	1	1	40	68		30.00	65	B	9		...					0....	7932
29-BHA	**GUYANI-BANGGARLA net**	1	1	40	68		30.00	65	B	9		...					0....	7933
29-BHAA	GUYANI cluster			0	0		0.00	0		0		...					0....	7934
29-BHAA-a	guyani			0	0	0	0.00	0		0		...					0....	7935
29-BHAB	ADYNYAMATHANHA cluster	1	1	40	68		30.00	65	B	6		...					0....	7936
29-BHAB-a	adynyamathanha					0				6		...					0....	7937
29-BHAB-b	wailpi					0				6		...					0....	7938
29-BHAC	BANGGARLA cluster			0	0		0.00	0		9		...					0....	7939
29-BHAC-a	banggarla			0	0	0	0.00	0		9		...					0....	7940
29-BHAD	NAWU cluster			0	0		0.00	0		0		...					0....	7941
29-BHAD-a	nawu			0	0	0	0.00	0		0		...					0....	7942
29-BHB	**NUGUNU-NGADJURI net**									8		...					0....	7943
29-BHBA	NUGUNU cluster			0	0		0.00	0		8		...					0....	7944
29-BHBA-a	nugunu			0	0	0	0.00	0		8		...					0....	7945
29-BHBB	NGADJURI cluster			0	0		0.00	0		0		...					7946
29-BHBB-a	ngadjuri			0	0	0	0.00	0		0		...					20-24		7947
29-BHC	**NARUNGGA net**									8		...					0....	7948
29-BHCA	NARUNGGA cluster			0	0		0.00	0		8		...					0....	7949
29-BHCA-a	Proper narungga			0	0	0	0.00	0		8		...					0....	7950
29-BHCA-b	adjabdurah			0	0	0	0.00	0		8		...					0....	7951
29-BHCA-c	turra			0	0	0	0.00	0		8		...					0....	7952
29-C	**KARNIC set**	1	1	80	136		40.00	76	B	46		PN.					0....	7953
29-CA	ARABANIC-PALKU chain	1	1	30	51		40.00	77	B	8		...					0....	7954
29-CAA	**ARABANIC net**	1	1	30	51		40.00	77	B	8		...					0....	7955
29-CAAA	ARABANA-NGURU cluster	1	1	30	51		40.00	77	B	8		...					0....	7956
29-CAAA-a	wang-arabana					0				8		...					0....	7957
29-CAAA-b	wonga-djaga			0	0	0	0.00	0		8		...					0....	7958
29-CAAA-c	wangga-nguru					0				8		...					0....	7959
29-CAB	**PALKU net**									8		...					0....	7960
29-CABA	PALKU cluster									8		...					0....	7961
29-CABA-a	wangga-mala			0	0	0	0.00	0		8		...					0....	7962
29-CABA-b	lhanima			0	0	0	0.00	0		8		...					0....	7963
29-CABA-c	gunggalanya			0	0	0	0.00	0		8		...					0....	7964
29-CABA-d	yurla-yurlanya			0	0	0	0.00	0		8		...					0....	7965
29-CABA-e	rangwa			0	0	0	0.00	0		8		...					0....	7966
29-CABA-f	bidha-bidha			0	0	0	0.00	0		8		...					0....	7967
29-CABA-g	ringu-ringu			0	0	0	0.00	0		8		...					0....	7968
29-CABA-h	ragaya			0	0	0	0.00	0		8		...					0....	7969
29-CABA-i	ngurlubulu			0	0	0	0.00	0		8		...					0....	7970
29-CABA-j	garanya			0	0	0	0.00	0		8		...					0....	7971
29-CABA-k	mayawarli			0	0	0	0.00	0		8		...					0....	7972
29-CB	DIERI-GARUWALI chain									46		PN.					0....	7973
29-CBA	**GARUWALI-MIDHAGA net**									0		...					0....	7974
29-CBAA	MIDHAGA cluster			0	0		0.00	0		0		...					0....	7975
29-CBAA-a	Proper midhaga			0	0	0	0.00	0		0		...					0....	7976
29-CBAA-b	marrula			0	0	0	0.00	0		0		...					7977
29-CBAB	GARUWALI cluster			0	0		0.00	0		0		...					0....	7978
29-CBAB-a	garuwali			0	0	0	0.00	0		0		...					0....	7979

Continued overleaf

Table 9-13 continued

Code 1	REFERENCE NAME / Autoglossonym 2	Coun 3	Peo 4	Mother-tongue speakers in 2000 5	in 2025 6	Media radio 7	CHURCH AC% 8	E% 9	Wld 10	Tr 11	Biblioglossonym 12	Print 13-15	P-activity 16	N-activity 17	B-activity 18	J-year 19	Jayuh 20-24	Ref 25
29-CBB	**DIERIC net**									46		PN.					0....	7980
29-CBBA	YARLUYANDI cluster			0	0		0.00	0		0		...					0....	7981
29-CBBA-a	yarluyandi			0	0	0	0.00	0		0		...					0....	7982
29-CBBB	NGAMINI cluster			0	0		0.00	0		8		...					0....	7983
29-CBBB-a	ngamini			0	0	0	0.00	0		8		...					0....	7984
29-CBBC	YAWARA-YANDRU cluster			0	0		0.00	0		8		...					0....	7985
29-CBBC-a	yawara-warga			0	0	0	0.00	0		8		...					0....	7986
29-CBBC-b	yandru-wandha			0	0	0	0.00	0		8		...					0....	7987
29-CBBD	DIERI-DIRARI cluster									46		PN.					0....	7988
29-CBBD-a	dieri			0	0	0	0.00	0		46	Dieri	PN.		1897			0....	7989
29-CBBD-b	dirari			0	0	0	0.00	0		46		pn.					0....	7990
29-CBBE	BILADABA cluster			0	0		0.00	0		8		...					0....	7991
29-CBBE-a	biladaba			0	0	0	0.00	0		8		...					0....	7992
29-CC	NGURA chain	1	1	50	85		40.00	76	B	8		...					0....	7993
29-CCA	**NGURA net**	1	1	50	85		40.00	76	B	8		...					0....	7994
29-CCAA	NGURA cluster	1	1	50	85		40.00	76	B	8		...					0....	7995
29-CCAA-a	ngurawarla			0	0	0	0.00	0		8		...					0....	7996
29-CCAA-b	garandala			0	0	0	0.00	0		8		...					0....	7997
29-CCAA-c	yarumarra			0	0	0	0.00	0		8		...					0....	7998
29-CCAA-d	wongkumara					0				8		...					0....	7999
29-CCAA-e	punthamara			0	0	0	0.00	0		8		...					0....	8000
29-CCAA-f	kalali			0	0	0	0.00	0		8		...					0....	8001
29-CCAA-g	badjiri			0	0	0	0.00	0		8		...					0....	8002
29-CCAA-h	dhiraila			0	0	0	0.00	0		8		...					0....	8003
29-CCAA-i	bidjara			0	0	0	0.00	0		8		...					0....	8004
29-CCAA-j	mambangura			0	0	0	0.00	0		8		...					0....	8005
29-CCAA-k	mingbari			0	0	0	0.00	0		8		...					0....	8006
29-CD	YARLI chain									0		...					0....	8007
29-CDA	**YARLI net**									0		...					0....	8008
29-CDAA	YARLI cluster			0	0		0.00	0		0		...					0....	8009
29-CDAA-a	wadigali			0	0	0	0.00	0		0		...					0....	8010
29-CDAA-b	malyangaba			0	0	0	0.00	0		0		...					0....	8011
29-CDAA-c	yardliwarra			0	0	0	0.00	0		0		...					0....	8012
29-D	**MURUWARI set**									8		...					0....	8013
29-DA	MURUWARI chain									8		...					0....	8014
29-DAA	**MURUWARI net**									8		...					0....	8015
29-DAAA	MURUWARI cluster			0	0		0.00	0		8		...					0....	8016
29-DAAA-a	gunga-guri			0	0	0	0.00	0		8		...					0....	8017
29-DAAA-b	gunda-guri			0	0	0	0.00	0		8		...					0....	8018
29-DAAA-c	buru-guri			0	0	0	0.00	0		8		...					0....	8019
29-DAAA-d	dhindundu			0	0	0	0.00	0		8		...					0....	8020
29-DAAA-e	nundu-guri			0	0	0	0.00	0		8		...					0....	8021
29-E	**BAAGANDJI set**	1	1	40	68		40.00	78	B	8		...					0....	8022
29-EA	BAAGANDJI chain	1	1	40	68		40.00	78	B	8		...					0....	8023
29-EAA	**BANDJI-BAARUNDJI net**	1	1	40	68		40.00	78	B	8		...					0....	8024
29-EAAA	BANDJI-BAARUNDJI cluster			0	0		0.00	0		8		...					0....	8025
29-EAAA-a	bandji-gali			0	0	0	0.00	0		8		...					0....	8026
29-EAAA-b	wanyu-barlgu			0	0	0	0.00	0		8		...					0....	8027
29-EAAA-c	na-barlgu			0	0	0	0.00	0		8		...					0....	8028
29-EAAA-d	baarundji			0	0	0	0.00	0		8		...					0....	8029
29-EAAA-e	gurnu			0	0	0	0.00	0		8		...					0....	8030
29-EAAB	SOUTH BAAGANDJI cluster	1	1	40	68		40.00	78	B	0		...					0....	8031
29-EAAB-a	baagandji					0				0		...					0....	8032
29-EAAB-b	wilja-kali			0	0	0	0.00	0		0		...					0....	8033
29-EAAB-c	wiljali			0	0	0	0.00	0		0		...					0....	8034
29-EAB	**MARAWARA net**									0		...					0....	8035
29-EABA	MARAWARA cluster			0	0		0.00	0		0		...					0....	8036
29-EABA-a	marawara			0	0	0	0.00	0		0		...					0....	8037
29-F	**NGARINYERI-YITHAYITHA set**									0		...					0....	8038
29-FA	NGARINYERI chain									0		...					0....	8039
29-FAA	**NGARINYERI-YITHAYITHA net**									0		...					0....	8040
29-FAAA	YITHA-YITHA cluster			0	0		0.00	0		0		...					0....	8041
29-FAAA-a	yitha-yitha			0	0	0	0.00	0		0		...					0....	8042
29-FAAB	KERAMIN cluster			0	0		0.00	0		0		...					0....	8043
29-FAAB-a	keramin			0	0	0	0.00	0		0		...					0....	8044
29-FAAC	YUYU cluster			0	0		0.00	0		0		...					0....	8045
29-FAAC-a	ngintait			0	0	0	0.00	0		0		...					0....	8046
29-FAAC-b	erawirung			0	0	0	0.00	0		0		...					0....	8047
29-FAAC-c	ngawait			0	0	0	0.00	0		0		...					0....	8048
29-FAAC-d	ngarkat			0	0	0	0.00	0		0		...					0....	8049
29-FAAD	NGAYAWUNG cluster			0	0		0.00	0		0		...					0....	8050
29-FAAD-a	ngayawung			0	0	0	0.00	0		0		...					0....	8051
29-FAAD-b	ngangurugu			0	0	0	0.00	0		0		...					0....	8052
29-FAAE	PERAMANGK cluster			0	0		0.00	0		0		...					0....	8053
29-FAAE-a	peramangk			0	0	0	0.00	0		0		...					0....	8054
29-FAAF	NGARINYERI cluster			0	0		0.00	0		0		...					0....	8055
29-FAAF-a	raminyeri			0	0	0	0.00	0		0		...					0....	8056
29-FAAF-b	warki			0	0	0	0.00	0		0		...					0....	8057
29-FAAF-c	portawulun			0	0	0	0.00	0		0		...					0....	8058
29-FAAF-d	yaraldi			0	0	0	0.00	0		0		...					0....	8059
29-FAAF-e	tanganalun			0	0	0	0.00	0		0		...					0....	8060
29-FAAF-f	meintaangk			0	0	0	0.00	0		0		...					0....	8061
29-G	**KULINIC set**									0		...					0....	8062
29-GA	BUNGANDIDJIC chain									0		...					0....	8063
29-GAA	**BUNGANDIDJ net**									0		...					0....	8064

Continued opposite

Table 9-13 continued

Code 1	REFERENCE NAME Autoglossonym 2	Coun 3	Peo 4	Mother-tongue speakers in 2000 5	in 2025 6	Media radio 7	CHURCH AC% 8	E% 9	Wld 10	Tr 11	Biblioglossonym 12	SCRIPTURES Print 13-15	P-activity 16	N-activity 17	B-activity 18	J-year 19	Jayuh 20-24	Ref 25
29-GAAA	BUNGANDIDJ cluster			0	0		0.00	0		0		. . .					0. . . .	8065
29-GAAA-a	bungandidj			0	0	0	0.00	0		0		. . .					0. . . .	8066
29-GAB	**WUURONG net**									0		. . .					0. . . .	8067
29-GABA	WUURONG cluster			0	0		0.00	0		0		. . .					0. . . .	8068
29-GABA-a	chaap-wuurong			0	0	0	0.00	0		0		. . .					0. . . .	8069
29-GABA-b	kii-wuurong			0	0	0	0.00	0		0		. . .					0. . . .	8070
29-GABA-c	kuurn-kopan-noot			0	0	0	0.00	0		0		. . .					0. . . .	8071
29-GABA-d	peek-whurrong			0	0	0	0.00	0		0		. . .					0. . . .	8072
29-GABA-e	kirrae-wuurong			0	0	0	0.00	0		0		. . .					0. . . .	8073
29-GB	WEMBAWEMBA chain									0		. . .					0. . . .	8074
29-GBA	**WEMBAWEMBA net**									0		. . .					0. . . .	8075
29-GBAA	WEMBAWEMBA cluster			0	0		0.00	0		0		. . .					0. . . .	8076
29-GBAA-a	nari-nari			0	0	0	0.00	0		0		. . .					0. . . .	8077
29-GBAA-b	latji-latji			0	0	0	0.00	0		0		. . .					0. . . .	8078
29-GBAA-c	yari-yari			0	0	0	0.00	0		0		. . .					0. . . .	8079
29-GBAA-d	wati-wati			0	0	0	0.00	0		0		. . .					0. . . .	8080
29-GBAA-e	wemba-wemba			0	0	0	0.00	0		0		. . .					0. . . .	8081
29-GBAA-f	bara-parapa			0	0	0	0.00	0		0		. . .					0. . . .	8082
29-GBAA-g	yuga-pulk			0	0	0	0.00	0		0		. . .					0. . . .	8083
29-GBAA-h	warka-warka			0	0	0	0.00	0		0		. . .					0. . . .	8084
29-GBAA-i	wotjobaluk			0	0	0	0.00	0		0		. . .					0. . . .	8085
29-GBAA-j	yaadwa			0	0	0	0.00	0		0		. . .					0. . . .	8086
29-GBAA-k	yaara			0	0	0	0.00	0		0		. . .					0. . . .	8087
29-GC	KOLAKNGAT chain									0		. . .					0. . . .	8088
29-GCA	**KOLAKNGAT net**									0		. . .					0. . . .	8089
29-GCAA	KOLAKNGAT cluster			0	0		0.00	0		0		. . .					0. . . .	8090
29-GCAA-a	kolakngat			0	0	0	0.00	0		0		. . .					0. . . .	8091
29-GCAB	WATHAWURUNG cluster			0	0		0.00	0		0		. . .					0. . . .	8092
29-GCAB-a	watha-wurung			0	0	0	0.00	0		0		. . .					0. . . .	8093
29-GCAC	WUYWURRONG cluster			0	0		0.00	0		0		. . .					0. . . .	8094
29-GCAC-a	bun-wurung			0	0	0	0.00	0		0		. . .					0. . . .	8095
29-GCAC-b	Proper wuy-wurrung			0	0	0	0.00	0		0		. . .					0. . . .	8096
29-GCAC-c	thaga-wurung			0	0	0	0.00	0		0		. . .					0. . . .	8097
29-H	**GANAY set**									0		. . .					0. . . .	8098
29-HA	GANAY chain									0		. . .					0. . . .	8099
29-HAA	**GANAY net**									0		. . .					8100
29-HAAA	MUK-THANG cluster			0	0		0.00	0		0		. . .					0. . . .	8101
29-HAAA-a	nulit			0	0	0	0.00	0		0		. . .					0. . . .	8102
29-HAAA-b	Proper muk-thang			0	0	0	0.00	0		0		. . .					0. . . .	8106
29-HAAA-c	thang-quai			0	0	0	0.00	0		0		. . .					0. . . .	8107
29-HAAA-d	bidhawal			0	0	0	0.00	0		0		. . .					0. . . .	8108
29-I	**DHUDOROA set**									0		. . .					0. . . .	8109
29-IA	DHUDOROA chain									0		. . .					0. . . .	8110
29-IAA	**DHUDOROA net**									0		. . .					0. . . .	8111
29-IAAA	DHUDOROA cluster			0	0		0.00	0		0		. . .					0. . . .	8112
29-IAAA-a	dhudoroa			0	0	0	0.00	0		0		. . .					0. . . .	8113
29-J	**PALLANGAN-MIDDANG set**									0		. . .					0. . . .	8114
29-JA	PALLANGAN-MIDDANG chain									0		. . .					0. . . .	8115
29-JAA	**PALLANGAN-MIDDANG net**									0		. . .					0. . . .	8116
29-JAAA	PALLANGAN-MIDDANG cluster			0	0		0.00	0		0		. . .					0. . . .	8117
29-JAAA-a	pallangan-middang			0	0	0	0.00	0		0		. . .					0. . . .	8118
29-K	**YOTAYOTIC set**									0		. . .					0. . . .	8119
29-KA	YOTAYOTIC chain									0		. . .					0. . . .	8120
29-KAA	**YOTAYOTIC net**									0		. . .					0. . . .	8121
29-KAAA	YOTA-YOTA cluster			0	0		0.00	0		0		. . .					0. . . .	8122
29-KAAA-a	yota-yota			0	0	0	0.00	0		0		. . .					0. . . .	8123
29-KAAB	YABULA-YABULA cluster			0	0		0.00	0		0		. . .					0. . . .	8124
29-KAAB-a	yabula-yabula			0	0	0	0.00	0		0		. . .					0. . . .	8125
29-L	**WIRADHURIC set**									9		. . .					0. . . .	8126
29-LA	WIRADHURIC chain									9		. . .					0. . . .	8127
29-LAA	**WIRADHURI net**									8		. . .					0. . . .	8128
29-LAAA	WIRADHURI cluster			0	0		0.00	0		8		. . .					0. . . .	8129
29-LAAA-a	wiradhuri			0	0	0	0.00	0		8		. . .					0. . . .	8130
29-LAB	**WAYILWAN-NGIYAMBAA net**									8		. . .					0. . . .	8131
29-LABA	WAYILWAN-NGIYAMBAA cluster			0	0		0.00	0		8		. . .					0. . . .	8132
29-LABA-a	wangaaybuwan			0	0	0	0.00	0		8		. . .					0. . . .	8133
29-LABA-b	ngiyambaa			0	0	0	0.00	0		8		. . .					0. . . .	8134
29-LABA-c	wayilwan			0	0	0	0.00	0		8		. . .					0. . . .	8135
29-LAC	**KAMILAROI net**									9		. . .					0. . . .	8136
29-LACA	KAMILAROI cluster			0	0		0.00	0		9		. . .					0. . . .	8137
29-LACA-a	guyinba-raay			0	0	0	0.00	0		9		. . .					0. . . .	8138
29-LACA-b	South gamila-raay			0	0	0	0.00	0		9		. . .					0. . . .	8139
29-LACA-c	North gamila-raay			0	0	0	0.00	0		9		. . .					0. . . .	8140
29-LACA-d	yuwaala-raay			0	0	0	0.00	0		9		. . .					0. . . .	8141
29-LACA-e	yuwaali-yaay			0	0	0	0.00	0		9		. . .					0. . . .	8142
29-LACA-f	gawamba-raay			0	0	0	0.00	0		9		. . .					0. . . .	8143
29-LACA-g	wiriya-raay			0	0	0	0.00	0		9		. . .					0. . . .	8144
29-M	**YUIN-KURIC set**									25		P. .					0. . . .	8145
29-MA	NGARIGO-NGUNAWAL chain									0		. . .					0. . . .	8146
29-MAA	**NGARIGO-NGUNAWAL net**						.			0		. . .					0. . . .	8147

Continued overleaf

Table 9-13 continued

Code 1	REFERENCE NAME / Autoglossonym 2	Coun 3	Peo 4	Mother-tongue speakers in 2000 5	in 2025 6	Media radio 7	CHURCH AC% 8	E% 9	Wld 10	Tr 11	Biblioglossonym 12	SCRIPTURES Print 13-15	P-activity 16	N-activity 17	B-activity 18	J-year 19	Jayuh 20-24	Ref 25
29-MAAA	NGARIGO cluster			0	0		0.00	0		0		...					0....	8148
29-MAAA-a	South ngarigo			0	0	0	0.00	0		0		...					0....	8149
29-MAAA-b	walgalu			0	0	0	0.00	0		0		...					0....	8150
29-MAAA-c	North ngarigo			0	0	0	0.00	0		0		...					0....	8151
29-MAAB	NGUNAWAL cluster			0	0		0.00	0		0		...					0....	8152
29-MAAB-a	ngunawal			0	0	0	0.00	0		0		...					0....	8153
29-MB	THAWA chain									0		...					0....	8154
29-MBA	**THAWA net**									0		...					0....	8155
29-MBAA	THAWA cluster			0	0		0.00	0		0		...					0....	8156
29-MBAA-a	thawa			0	0	0	0.00	0		0		...					0....	8157
29-MC	DYRRINGANY-DHURGA chain									9		...					0....	8158
29-MCA	**DYRRINGANY net**									0		...					0....	8159
29-MCAA	DYRRINGANY cluster			0	0		0.00	0		0		...					0....	8160
29-MCAA-a	dyrringany			0	0	0	0.00	0		0		...					0....	8161
29-MCB	**DHURGA net**									9		...					0....	8162
29-MCBA	DHURGA cluster			0	0		0.00	0		9		...					0....	8163
29-MCBA-a	dhurga			0	0	0	0.00	0		9		...					0....	8164
29-MD	THURAWAL chain									9		...					0....	8165
29-MDA	**THURAWAL net**									9		...					0....	8166
29-MDAA	THURAWAL cluster			0	0		0.00	0		9		...					0....	8167
29-MDAA-a	Proper thurawal			0	0	0	0.00	0		9		...					0....	8168
29-MDAA-b	wadiwadi			0	0	0	0.00	0		9		...					0....	8169
29-ME	GUNDUNGURA chain									0		...					0....	8170
29-MEA	**GUNDUNGURA net**									0		...					0....	8171
29-MEAA	GUNDUNGURA cluster			0	0		0.00	0		0		...					0....	8172
29-MEAA-a	gundungura			0	0	0	0.00	0		0		...					0....	8173
29-MF	SYDNEY chain									0		...					0....	8174
29-MFA	**SYDNEY net**									0		...					0....	8175
29-MFAA	DHARUK cluster			0	0		0.00	0		0		...					0....	8176
29-MFAA-a	iyora			0	0	0	0.00	0		0		...					0....	8177
29-MFAA-b	guringgai			0	0	0	0.00	0		0		...					0....	8178
29-MFAA-c	dharuk			0	0	0	0.00	0		0		...					0....	8179
29-MFB	**DARKINYUNG net**									0		...					0....	8180
29-MFBA	DARKINYUNG cluster			0	0		0.00	0		0		...					0....	8181
29-MFBA-a	darkinyung			0	0	0	0.00	0		0		...					0....	8182
29-MG	KURI chain									25		P..					0....	8183
29-MGA	**AWABAKAL net**									25		P..					0....	8184
29-MGAA	AWABAKAL cluster			0	0		0.00	0		25		P..					0....	8185
29-MGAA-a	awabakal			0	0	0	0.00	0		25	Awabakal	P.. 1891					0....	8186
29-MGB	**GADANG net**									9		...					0....	8187
29-MGBA	WORIMI cluster			0	0		0.00	0		9		...					0....	8188
29-MGBA-a	worimi			0	0	0	0.00	0		9		...					0....	8189
29-MGC	**DYANGADI net**									8		...					0....	8190
29-MGCA	DYANGADI cluster			0	0		0.00	0		8		...					0....	8191
29-MGCA-a	ngagu			0	0	0	0.00	0		8		...					0....	8192
29-MGCA-b	ngambaa			0	0	0	0.00	0		8		...					0....	8193
29-MGCA-c	Proper dyangadi			0	0	0	0.00	0		8		...					0....	8194
29-MGD	**NGAYAYWANA net**									9		...					0....	8195
29-MGDA	NGANYAYWANA cluster			0	0		0.00	0		9		...					0....	8196
29-MGDA-a	nganyaywana			0	0	0	0.00	0		9		...					0....	8197
29-MGE	**YUGAMBAL net**									9		...					0....	8198
29-MGEA	YUGAMBAL cluster			0	0		0.00	0		9		...					0....	8199
29-MGEA-a	yugambal			0	0	0	0.00	0		9		...					0....	8200
29-N	**GUMBAYNGGIRIC set**									0		...					0....	8201
29-NA	GUMBAYNGGIR chain									0		...					0....	8202
29-NAA	**GUMBAYNGGIR net**									0		...					8203
29-NAAA	GUMBAYNGGIR cluster			0	0		0.00	0		0		...					0....	8204
29-NAAA-a	gumbaynggir			0	0	0	0.00	0		0		...					0....	8205
29-NB	YAYGIR chain									0		...					0....	8206
29-NBA	**YAYGIR net**									0		...					0....	8207
29-NBAA	YAYGIR cluster									0		...					0....	8208
29-NBAA-a	yaygir			0	0	0	0.00	0		0		...					0....	8209
29-O	**BANDJALANG set**									6		...					0....	8210
29-OA	BANDJALANG chain									6		...					0....	8211
29-OAA	**BANDJALANG net**									6		...					0....	8212
29-OAAA	BANDJALANG cluster			0	0		0.00	0		6		...					0....	8213
29-OAAA-a	bandjalang			0	0	0	0.00	0		6		...					0....	8214
29-OAAA-b	biriin			0	0	0	0.00	0		6		...					0....	8217
29-OAAA-c	waalu-bal			0	0	0	0.00	0		6		...					0....	8218
29-OAAA-d	wudje-bal			0	0	0	0.00	0		6		...					0....	8219
29-OAAA-e	dingga-bal			0	0	0	0.00	0		6		...					0....	8220
29-OAAA-f	gida-bal			0	0	0	0.00	0		6		...					0....	8221
29-OAAA-g	gali-bal			0	0	0	0.00	0		6		...					0....	8222
29-OAAA-h	wiya-bal			0	0	0	0.00	0		6		...					0....	8223
29-OAAA-i	ngaraang-bal			0	0	0	0.00	0		6		...					0....	8224
29-OAAA-j	yugum-bal			0	0	0	0.00	0		6		...					0....	8225
29-P	**DURUBULIC set**									0		...					0....	8226

Continued opposite

Table 9-13 continued

Code 1	REFERENCE NAME / Autoglossonym 2	Coun 3	Peo 4	Mother-tongue speakers in 2000 5	in 2025 6	Media radio 7	CHURCH AC% 8	E% 9	Wld 10	Tr 11	Biblioglossonym 12	SCRIPTURES Print 13-15	P-activity 16	N-activity 17	B-activity 18	J-year 19	Jayuh 20-24	Ref 25
29-PA	DURUBULIC chain									0		...					0....	8227
29-PAA	**YAGARA net**									0		...					0....	8228
29-PAAA	YAGARA cluster			0	0		0.00	0		0		...					0....	8229
29-PAAA-a	yagara-bal			0	0	0	0.00	0		0		...					0....	8230
29-PAB	**DJENDJE net**									0		...					0....	8231
29-PABA	DJENDJE cluster			0	0		0.00	0		0		...					0....	8232
29-PABA-a	djende-wal			0	0	0	0.00	0		0		...					0....	8233
29-PABA-b	nunun-bal			0	0	0	0.00	0		0		...					0....	8234
29-PAC	**GOWAR net**									0		...					0....	8235
29-PACA	GOWAR cluster			0	0		0.00	0		0		...					0....	8236
29-PACA-a	gowar			0	0	0	0.00	0		0		...					0....	8237
29-Q	**WAKA-KABIC set**									9		...					0....	8238
29-QA	MIYAN chain									9		...					0....	8239
29-QAA	**MURINGAM-BARUNGGAM net**									0		...					0....	8240
29-QAAA	MURINGAM-BARUNGGAM cluster			0	0		0.00	0		0		...					0....	8241
29-QAAA-a	muringam			0	0	0	0.00	0		0		...					0....	8242
29-QAAA-b	barunggam			0	0	0	0.00	0		0		...					0....	8243
29-QAB	**GAYABARA net**									0		...					0....	8244
29-QABA	GAYABARA cluster									0		...					0....	8245
29-QABA-a	gayabara					0				0		...					0....	8246
29-QAC	**WULIWULI-WAGA net**									9		...					0....	8247
29-QACA	WAGA cluster			0	0		0.00	0		0		...					0....	8248
29-QACA-a	ngundanbi			0	0	0	0.00	0		0		...					0....	8249
29-QACA-b	ngalbu			0	0	0	0.00	0		0		...					0....	8250
29-QACA-c	dungibara			0	0	0	0.00	0		0		...					0....	8251
29-QACA-d	duungidjawu			0	0	0	0.00	0		0		...					0....	8252
29-QACA-e	dalla			0	0	0	0.00	0		0		...					0....	8253
29-QACA-f	garumga			0	0	0	0.00	0		0		...					0....	8254
29-QACA-g	ngundanbbi			0	0	0	0.00	0		0		...					0....	8255
29-QACA-h	waga-waga			0	0	0	0.00	0		0		...					0....	8256
29-QACB	WULIWULI cluster			0	0		0.00	0		9		...					0....	8257
29-QACB-a	wuli-wuli			0	0	0	0.00	0		9		...					0....	8258
29-QB	THAN chain									0		...					0....	8259
29-QBA	**GABI net**									0		...					0....	8260
29-QBAA	GABI cluster			0	0		0.00	0		0		...					0....	8261
29-QBAA-a	gabi-gabi			0	0	0	0.00	0		0		...					0....	8262
29-QBAA-b	badjala			0	0	0	0.00	0		0		...					0....	8263
29-QBB	**GURENG net**									0		...					0....	8264
29-QBBA	DARIBALANG cluster			0	0		0.00	0		0		...					0....	8265
29-QBBA-a	Proper daribalang			0	0	0	0.00	0		0		...					0....	8266
29-QBBA-b	gureng-gureng			0	0	0	0.00	0		0		...					0....	8267
29-QBBB	GUWENG cluster			0	0		0.00	0		0		...					0....	8268
29-QBBB-a	guweng			0	0	0	0.00	0		0		...					0....	8269
29-QC	KINGKEL chain									9		...					0....	8270
29-QCA	**BAYALI-KOINJMAL net**									9		...					0....	8271
29-QCAA	BAYALI cluster			0	0		0.00	0		9		...					0....	8272
29-QCAA-a	bayali			0	0	0	0.00	0		9		...					0....	8273
29-QCAB	DARAMBAL cluster			0	0		0.00	0		0		...					0....	8274
29-QCAB-a	daram-bal			0	0	0	0.00	0		0		...					0....	8275
29-QCAC	KOINJMAL cluster			0	0		0.00	0		0		...					0....	8276
29-QCAC-a	koinjmal			0	0	0	0.00	0		0		...					0....	8277
29-R	**PAMA-MARIC set**	1	10	8,657	10,717		59.50	93	B	41		PN.					0.s..	8278
29-RA	MARIC chain	1	1	30	51		40.00	77	B	9		...					0....	8279
29-RAA	**MARI net**	1	1	30	51		40.00	77	B	9		...					0....	8280
29-RAAA	SOUTHWEST MARI cluster	1	1	30	51		40.00	77	B	8		...					0....	8281
29-RAAA-a	mandandanyi			0	0	0	0.00	0		8		...					0....	8282
29-RAAA-b	guwamu			0	0	0	0.00	0		8		...					0....	8283
29-RAAA-c	gunya			0	0	0	0.00	0		8		...					0....	8284
29-RAAA-d	margany			0	0	0	0.00	0		8		...					0....	8285
29-RAAA-e	nguri			0	0	0	0.00	0		8		...					0....	8286
29-RAAA-f	bidyara					0				8		...					0....	8287
29-RAAA-g	wadjalang			0	0	0	0.00	0		8		...					0....	8288
29-RAAA-h	wadjabangay			0	0	0	0.00	0		8		...					0....	8289
29-RAAB	NORTHEAST MARIE cluster			0	0		0.00	0		9		...					0....	8290
29-RAAB-a	yiman			0	0	0	0.00	0		9		...					0....	8291
29-RAAB-b	gungabula			0	0	0	0.00	0		9		...					0....	8292
29-RAAB-c	garingbal			0	0	0	0.00	0		9		...					0....	8293
29-RAAB-d	wadjigu			0	0	0	0.00	0		9		...					0....	8294
29-RAAB-e	gangulu			0	0	0	0.00	0		9		...					0....	8295
29-RAAB-f	gayiri			0	0	0	0.00	0		9		...					0....	8296
29-RAAB-g	gabalbara			0	0	0	0.00	0		9		...					0....	8297
29-RAAB-h	barna			0	0	0	0.00	0		9		...					0....	8298
29-RAAB-i	wangan			0	0	0	0.00	0		9		...					0....	8299
29-RAAB-j	yambina			0	0	0	0.00	0		9		...					0....	8300
29-RAAB-k	baradha			0	0	0	0.00	0		9		...					0....	8301
29-RAAB-l	yuwibara			0	0	0	0.00	0		9		...					0....	8302
29-RAAB-m	giya			0	0	0	0.00	0		9		...					0....	8303
29-RAAB-n	wiri			0	0	0	0.00	0		9		...					0....	8304
29-RAAB-o	yangga			0	0	0	0.00	0		9		...					0....	8305
29-RAAB-p	miyan			0	0	0	0.00	0		9		...					0....	8306
29-RAAB-q	biri			0	0	0	0.00	0		9		...					0....	8307
29-RAAC	NORTHWEST MARIW cluster			0	0		0.00	0		0		...					0....	8308
29-RAAC-a	yagalingu			0	0	0	0.00	0		0		...					0....	8309
29-RAAC-b	yiningay			0	0	0	0.00	0		0		...					0....	8310
29-RAAC-c	yilba			0	0	0	0.00	0		0		...					0....	8311
29-RAAD	NORTH MARI cluster			0	0		0.00	0		8		...					0....	8312
29-RAAD-a	gudjala			0	0	0	0.00	0		8		...					0....	8313
29-RAAD-b	gugu-badhun			0	0	0	0.00	0		8		...					0....	8314

Continued overleaf

Table 9-13 continued

Code 1	REFERENCE NAME / Autoglossonym 2	Coun 3	Peo 4	Mother-tongue speakers in 2000 / 5	in 2025 / 6	Media radio 7	CHURCH AC% 8	E% 9	Wld 10	Tr 11	Biblioglossonym 12	SCRIPTURES Print 13-15	P-activity 16	N-activity 17	B-activity 18	J-year 19	Jayuh 20-24	Ref 25
29-RAAD-c	warungu			0	0	0	0.00	0		8		...					0....	8315
29-RAB	**KAPU net**									0		...					0....	8316
29-RABA	BIRRIA cluster			0	0		0.00	0		0		...					0....	8317
29-RABA-a	birria			0	0	0	0.00	0		0		...					0....	8318
29-RABB	GUNGA cluster			0	0		0.00	0		0		...					0....	8319
29-RABB-a	gungadudji			0	0	0	0.00	0		0		...					0....	8320
29-RABB-b	gulumali			0	0	0	0.00	0		0		...					0....	8321
29-RABB-c	gunggari			0	0	0	0.00	0		0		...					0....	8322
29-RAC	**YIRANDHALI net**									0		...					0....	8323
29-RACA	YIRANDHALI cluster			0	0		0.00	0		0		...					0....	8324
29-RACA-a	yirandhali			0	0	0	0.00	0		0		...					0....	8325
29-RAD	**GUWA net**									0		...					0....	8326
29-RADA	GUWA cluster			0	0		0.00	0		0		...					0....	8327
29-RADA-a	guwa			0	0	0	0.00	0		0		...					0....	8328
29-RAE	**YANDA net**									0		...					0....	8329
29-RAEA	YANDA cluster			0	0		0.00	0		0		...					0....	8330
29-RAEA-a	yanda			0	0	0	0.00	0		0		...					0....	8331
29-RB	NYAWAYGIC chain									8		...					0....	8332
29-RBA	**NYAWAYGIC net**									8		...					0....	8333
29-RBAA	YURU cluster			0	0		0.00	0		0		...					0....	8334
29-RBAA-a	yuru			0	0	0	0.00	0		0		...					0....	8335
29-RBAB	BINDAL cluster			0	0		0.00	0		0		...					0....	8336
29-RBAB-a	bindal			0	0	0	0.00	0		0		...					0....	8337
29-RBAC	WULGURU-KABA cluster			0	0		0.00	0		0		...					0....	8338
29-RBAC-a	wulguru-kaba			0	0	0	0.00	0		0		...					0....	8339
29-RBAD	NYAWAYGI cluster			0	0		0.00	0		8		...					0....	8340
29-RBAD-a	nyawaygi			0	0	0	0.00	0		8		...					0....	8341
29-RC	DYIRBALIC-YIDINIC chain	1	1	40	68		40.00	78	B	8		...					0....	8342
29-RCA	**DYIRBALIC net**	1	1	40	68		40.00	78	B	8		...					0....	8343
29-RCAA	WARRGAMAY cluster			0	0		0.00	0		8		...					0....	8344
29-RCAA-a	biyay			0	0	0	0.00	0		8		...					0....	8345
29-RCAA-b	warrga-may			0	0	0	0.00	0		8		...					0....	8346
29-RCAB	BANDYIN cluster			0	0		0.00	0		0		...					0....	8347
29-RCAB-a	bandyin			0	0	0	0.00	0		0		...					0....	8348
29-RCAC	DYIRBAL cluster	1	1	40	68		40.00	78	B	8		...					0....	8349
29-RCAC-a	girra-may					0				8		...					0....	8350
29-RCAC-b	walmal-barra			0	0	0	0.00	0		8		...					0....	8351
29-RCAC-c	dyiru			0	0	0	0.00	0		8		...					0....	8352
29-RCAC-d	guln-gay			0	0	0	0.00	0		8		...					0....	8353
29-RCAC-e	dyabun-barra			0	0	0	0.00	0		8		...					0....	8354
29-RCAC-f	dyirri-barra			0	0	0	0.00	0		8		...					0....	8355
29-RCAC-g	dulgu-barra			0	0	0	0.00	0		8		...					0....	8356
29-RCAC-h	wari-barra			0	0	0	0.00	0		8		...					0....	8357
29-RCAC-i	ngadyan			0	0	0	0.00	0		8		...					0....	8358
29-RCAC-j	gambil-barra					0				8		...					0....	8359
29-RCB	**YIDINIC net**									8		...					0....	8360
29-RCBA	YIDINY cluster			0	0		0.00	0		8		...					0....	8361
29-RCBA-a	wanyurr			0	0	0	0.00	0		8		...					0....	8362
29-RCBA-b	mad-yay			0	0	0	0.00	0		8		...					0....	8363
29-RCBA-c	Proper yidiny			0	0	0	0.00	0		8		...					0....	8364
29-RCBA-d	gung-gay			0	0	0	0.00	0		8		...					0....	8365
29-RCBB	DYAABU-GAY cluster			0	0		0.00	0		8		...					0....	8366
29-RCBB-a	yir-gay			0	0	0	0.00	0		8		...					0....	8367
29-RCBB-b	bul-way			0	0	0	0.00	0		8		...					0....	8368
29-RCBB-c	gulay			0	0	0	0.00	0		8		...					0....	8369
29-RCBB-d	Proper dyaabu-gay			0	0	0	0.00	0		8		...					0....	8370
29-RCBB-e	njakali			0	0	0	0.00	0		8		...					0....	8371
29-RD	YALANDIC chain	1	2	826	1,011		46.61	80	B	41		PN.					0....	8372
29-RDA	**YALANDIC net**	1	2	826	1,011		46.61	80	B	41		PN.					0....	8373
29-RDAA	MULURIDYI cluster			0	0		0.00	0		8		...					0....	8374
29-RDAA-a	muluridyi			0	0	0	0.00	0		8		...					0....	8375
29-RDAB	DJANGUN cluster			0	0		0.00	0		8		...					0....	8376
29-RDAB-a	djangun			0	0	0	0.00	0		8		...					0....	8377
29-RDAC	GUGU-YALANDYI cluster	1	1	379	464		19.00	56	B	41		PN.					0....	8378
29-RDAC-a	gugu-yalandyi	1	1	379	464	0	19.00	56	B	41	Kuku-yalanji	PN.	1967	1985			0....	8379
29-RDAD	GUUGUU-YIMIDHIRR cluster	1	1	447	547		70.02	100	C	24	Guguyimidjir	P..	1940				0....	8380
29-RDAD-a	West guuguu-yimidhirr					0				24		p..					0....	8381
29-RDAD-b	East guuguu-yimidhirr					0				24		p..					0....	8382
29-RE	BARROW-POINT chain									0		...					0....	8383
29-REA	**BARROW-POINT net**									0		...					0....	8384
29-REAA	BARROW-POINT cluster			0	0		0.00	0		0		...					0....	8385
29-REAA-a	'barrow-point'			0	0	0	0.00	0		0		...					0....	8386
29-RF	FLINDERS-ISLAND chain									0		...					0....	8387
29-RFA	**FLINDERS-ISLAND net**									0		...					0....	8388
29-RFAA	WALMBARIA cluster			0	0		0.00	0		0		...					0....	8389
29-RFAA-a	walmbaria			0	0	0	0.00	0		0		...					0....	8390
29-RFAA-b	mug-ngambaram			0	0	0	0.00	0		0		...					0....	8391
29-RG	MABUIAGIC chain	1	2	5,993	7,329		66.31	100	C	41		PN.					0....	8392
29-RGA	**MABUIAGIC net**	1	2	5,993	7,329		66.31	100	C	41		PN.					0....	8393
29-RGAA	KALA-YAGAW-YA cluster	1	2	5,993	7,329		66.31	100	C	41		PN.					0....	8394
29-RGAA-a	boigu					0				41		pn.					0....	8395
29-RGAA-b	dauan					0				41		pn.					0....	8396
29-RGAA-c	saibai	1	1	2,077	2,540	0	65.05	100	C	41	Mabuiag: Saibai	Pn.	1884				0....	8397
29-RGAA-d	mabuiag	1	1	3,916	4,789	0	66.98	100	C	41	Kala Lagaw Ya	PN.	1884-1900	1994			0....	8398
29-RGAA-e	muralag					0				41		pn.					0....	8402
29-RGAA-f	kaurareg					0				41		pn.					0....	8403

Continued opposite

Table 9-13 continued

Code 1	REFERENCE NAME / Autoglossonym 2	Coun 3	Peo 4	Mother-tongue speakers in 2000 5	in 2025 6	Media radio 7	CHURCH AC% 8	E% 9	Wld 10	Tr 11	Biblioglossonym 12	Print 13-15	P-activity 16	N-activity 17	B-activity 18	J-year 19	Jayuh 20-24	Ref 25
29-RGAA-g	muri					0				41		pn.					0....	8404
29-RGAA-h	yam					0				41		pn.					0....	8405
29-RGAA-i	tutu					0				41		pn.					0....	8406
29-RGAA-j	masig					0				41		pn.					0....	8407
29-RH	PAMA chain	1	6	1,768	2,258		43.21	76	B	41		PN.					0.s..	8408
29-RHA	CAPE-YORK net									8		. . .					0....	8409
29-RHAA	YUMUKU-ANGKAMU cluster			0	0		0.00	0		8		. . .					0....	8410
29-RHAA-a	yumuku-ntyi			0	0	0	0.00	0		8		. . .					0....	8411
29-RHAA-b	atampaya			0	0	0	0.00	0		8		. . .					0....	8412
29-RHAA-c	angkamu-thi			0	0	0	0.00	0		8		. . .					0....	8413
29-RHAA-d	apukwe			0	0	0	0.00	0		8		. . .					0....	8414
29-RHAA-e	utyangikwa-thia			0	0		0.00	0		8		. . .					0....	8415
29-RHAB	YARAY-WUDHA cluster			0	0		0.00	0		0		. . .					0....	8416
29-RHAB-a	yaray-tyana			0	0	0	0.00	0		0		. . .					0....	8417
29-RHAB-b	mutya-nthi			0	0	0	0.00	0		0		. . .					0....	8418
29-RHAB-c	wudha-dhi			0	0	0	0.00	0		0		. . .					0....	8419
29-RHAC	URA-TJUNGU cluster			0	0		0.00	0		8		. . .					0....	8420
29-RHAC-a	ura-dhi			0	0	0	0.00	0		8		. . .					0....	8421
29-RHAC-b	tjungu-ndji			0	0	0	0.00	0		8		. . .					0....	8422
29-RHAD	MPALI-LU cluster			0	0		0.00	0		0		. . .					0....	8423
29-RHAD-a	mpali-tyanh			0	0	0	0.00	0		0		. . .					0....	8424
29-RHAD-b	lu-thigh			0	0	0	0.00	0		0		. . .					0....	8425
29-RHAE	AWNG-YUP cluster			0	0		0.00	0		0		. . .					0....	8426
29-RHAE-a	awng-thim			0	0	0	0.00	0		0		. . .					0....	8427
29-RHAE-b	anda'-angeti			0	0	0	0.00	0		0		. . .					0....	8428
29-RHAE-c	tjan-ngayth			0	0	0	0.00	0		0		. . .					0....	8429
29-RHAE-d	mam-ngayt			0	0	0	0.00	0		0		. . .					0....	8430
29-RHAE-e	ntra'-angith			0	0	0	0.00	0		0		. . .					0....	8431
29-RHAE-f	winda-winda			0	0	0	0.00	0		0		. . .					0....	8432
29-RHAE-g	yup-ngayth			0	0	0	0.00	0		0		. . .					0....	8433
29-RHAF	AL-LIN cluster			0	0		0.00	0		8		. . .					0....	8434
29-RHAF-a	daini-guid			0	0	0	0.00	0		8		. . .					0....	8435
29-RHAF-b	al-ngith			0	0	0	0.00	0		8		. . .					0....	8436
29-RHAF-c	ngkoth			0	0	0	0.00	0		8		. . .					0....	8437
29-RHAF-d	trotj			0	0	0	0.00	0		8		. . .					0....	8438
29-RHAF-e	ladam-ngid			0	0	0	0.00	0		8		. . .					0....	8439
29-RHAF-f	lin-ngithigh			0	0	0	0.00	0		8		. . .					0....	8440
29-RHAG	YIN cluster			0	0		0.00	0		0		. . .					0....	8441
29-RHAG-a	yin-wum			0	0	0	0.00	0		0		. . .					0....	8442
29-RHAH	ARITIN-NTRA cluster			0	0		0.00	0		0		. . .					0....	8443
29-RHAH-a	aritin-ngithigh			0	0	0	0.00	0		0		. . .					0....	8444
29-RHAH-b	ntra-ngith			0	0	0	0.00	0		0		. . .					0....	8445
29-RHAI	MBIY cluster			0	0		0.00	0		0		. . .					0....	8446
29-RHAI-a	mbiy-wom			0	0	0	0.00	0		0		. . .					0....	8447
29-RHB	YA'U-KANJU net	1	1	276	410		44.57	80	B	8		. . .					0....	8448
29-RHBA	YA'U cluster	1	1	126	155		50.00	84	B	6		. . .					0....	8449
29-RHBA-a	kuuku-ya'u	1	1	126	155	0	50.00	84	B	6		. . .					0....	8450
29-RHBB	KANJU cluster	1	1	50	85		40.00	76	B	8		. . .					0....	8451
29-RHBB-a	iju					0				8		. . .					0....	8452
29-RHBB-b	i'o					0				8		. . .					0....	8453
29-RHBB-c	j'aalo					0				8		. . .					0....	8454
29-RHBB-d	wija-mo					0				8		. . .					0....	8455
29-RHBB-e	kokino					0				8		. . .					0....	8456
29-RHBB-f	ndhyrl					0				8		. . .					0....	8457
29-RHBC	UMPILA cluster	1	1	100	170		40.00	77	B	6		. . .					0....	8458
29-RHBC-a	umpila					0				6		. . .					0....	8459
29-RHBC-b	djandjanagu					0				6		. . .					0....	8460
29-RHC	LAMALAMA net									8		. . .					0....	8461
29-RHCA	GANGANDA cluster			0	0		0.00	0		8		. . .					0....	8462
29-RHCA-a	umbindha-mu			0·	0	0	0.00	0		8		. . .					0....	8463
29-RHCA-b	umbuyga-mu			0	0	0	0.00	0		8		. . .					0....	8464
29-RHCB	WURANGUNG cluster									8		. . .					0....	8465
29-RHCB-a	angandjan			0	0	0	0.00	0		8		. . .					0....	8466
29-RHCB-b	arlga			0	0	0	0.00	0		8		. . .					0....	8467
29-RHCB-c	m-bariman			0	0	0	0.00	0		8		. . .					0....	8468
29-RHCB-d	gudhinma			0	0	0	0.00	0		8		. . .					0....	8469
29-RHCB-e	jadeneni			0	0	0	0.00	0		8		. . .					0....	8470
29-RHCB-f	owynggan			0	0	0	0.00	0		8		. . .					0....	8471
29-RHCB-g	taipan			0	0	0	0.00	0		8		. . .					0....	8472
29-RHCC	BINDAGA cluster			0	0		0.00	0		0		. . .					0....	8473
29-RHCC-a	mbambyl-mu			0	0	0	0.00	0		0		. . .					0....	8474
29-RHCC-b	mudu-mui			0	0	0	0.00	0		0		. . .					0....	8475
29-RHCC-c	njegudi			0	0	0	0.00	0		0		. . .					0....	8476
29-RHCC-d	lamula-mu			0	0	0	0.00	0		0		. . .					0....	8477
29-RHCC-e	gugu-warra			0	0	0	0.00	0		0		. . .					0....	8478
29-RHD	RARMUL net									8		. . .					0....	8479
29-RHDA	RARMUL cluster			0	0		0.00	0		8		. . .					0....	8480
29-RHDA-a	koko-rarmul			0	0	0	0.00	0		8		. . .					0....	8481
29-RHDA-b	thaypan			0	0	0	0.00	0		8		. . .					0....	8482
29-RHDA-c	jawan			0	0	0	0.00	0		8		. . .					0....	8483
29-RHDA-d	aghu-laia			0	0	0	0.00	0		8		. . .					0....	8484
29-RHDA-e	aghu-tharnggala			0	0	0	0.00	0		8		. . .					0....	8485
29-RHE	MUNGKAN-KUNJEN net	1	5	1,492	1,848		42.96	75	B	41		PN.					0.s..	8486
29-RHEA	MUNGKAN-TAYOR cluster	1	4	1,110	1,357		38.47	69	B	41		PN.					0.s..	8487
29-RHEA-a	wik-mungkan	1	1	404	494	0	70.05	100	C	41	Wik-mungkan	PN.	1969-1981	1985			0.s..	8488
29-RHEA-b	wik-ompoma			0	0	0	0.00	0		41		pn.					0.s..	8489
29-RHEA-c	wik-keyangan			0	0	0	0.00	0		41		pn.					0.s..	8490
29-RHEA-d	wik-alkan	1	1	110	134	0	9.09	39	A	41		pn.					0.s..	8491
29-RHEA-e	wik-ngathana					0				41		pn.					0.s..	8492
29-RHEA-f	kuku-ugbanh			0	0	0	0.00	0		41		pn.					0.s..	8493
29-RHEA-g	kuku-muminh					0				41		pn.					0.s..	8494
29-RHEA-h	kuku-uwanh					0				41		pn.					0.s..	8495
29-RHEA-i	kuku-mu'inh			0	0	0	0.00	0		41		pn.					0.s..	8496
29-RHEA-j	kuku-mangk			0	0	0	0.00	0		41		pn.					0.s..	8497
29-RHEA-k	wik-ngatara	1	1	160	196	0	70.00	100	C	41		pn.					0.s..	8498
29-RHEA-l	wik-epa			0	0	0	0.00	0		41		pn.					0.s..	8499
29-RHEA-m	wik-me'anha					0				41		pn.					0.s..	8500
29-RHEA-n	wik-ngadanja					0				41		pn.					0.s..	8501
29-RHEA-o	kuku-yak					0				41		pn.					0.s..	8502
29-RHEA-p	wik-ngenchera					0				41		pn.					0.s..	8503
29-RHEA-q	koko-tayor	1	1	436	533	0	5.05	36	A	41	Thayore	Pn.	1981				0.s..	8504

Continued overleaf

Table 9-13 continued

Code 1	REFERENCE NAME Autoglossonym 2	Coun 3	Peo 4	Mother-tongue speakers in 2000 5	in 2025 6	Media radio 7	CHURCH AC% 8	E% 9	Wld 10	Tr 11	Biblioglossonym 12	SCRIPTURES Print 13-15	P-activity 16	N-activity 17	B-activity 18	J-year 19	Jayuh 20-24	Ref 25
29-RHEA-r	behran					0				41		pn.					0.s..	8505
29-RHEA-s	wik-iiyanh					0				41		pn.					0.s..	8506
29-RHEA-t	koka-ayabadhu			0	0	0	0.00	0		41		pn.					0.s..	8507
29-RHEA-u	pakanha			0	0	0	0.00	0		41		pn.					0.s..	8508
29-RHEB	YORONT cluster	1	1	10	17		30.00	60	B	8		...					0....	8509
29-RHEB-a	yir-yoront					0				8		...					0....	8510
29-RHEB-b	yir-thangedl					0				8		...					0....	8511
29-RHEB-c	yir-tutiym					0				8		...					0....	8512
29-RHEB-d	North koko-mindjen					0				8		...					0....	8513
29-RHEB-e	yir-mel					0				8		...					0....	8514
29-RHEC	BERA cluster	1	1	10	17		30.00	60	B	6		...					0....	8515
29-RHEC-a	gugu-bera					0				6		...					0....	8516
29-RHEC-b	anavilla					0				6		...					0....	8517
29-RHEC-c	badedj					0				6		...					0....	8518
29-RHEC-d	ninggora					0				6		...					0....	8519
29-RHEC-e	wab					0				6		...					0....	8520
29-RHEC-f	kwanthar					0				6		...					0....	8521
29-RHED	KUNJEN cluster	1	1	332	406		59.94	100	B	23		P..					0....	8522
29-RHED-a	oy-kangand					0				23		p..					0....	8523
29-RHED-b	ow-oilkulla					0				23		p..					0....	8524
29-RHED-c	o-kaurang			0	0	0	0.00	0		23		p..					0....	8525
29-RHED-d	gogo-mini					0				23		p..					0....	8526
29-RHED-e	o-kunjen	1	1	332	406	0	59.94	100	B	23	Kunjen	P..	1967				0....	8527
29-RHEE	GURDJAR cluster	1	1	30	51		30.00	63	B	8		...					0....	8528
29-RHEE-a	areba			0	0	0	0.00	0		8		...					0....	8529
29-RHEE-b	gurdjar					0				8		...					0....	8530
29-RHEE-c	kunggara			0	0		0.00	0		8		...					0....	8531
29-RHEE-d	kuthant			0	0		0.00	0		8		...					0....	8532
29-RHF	**WAMIN-BABARAM net**									9		...					0....	8533
29-RHFA	WAMIN-DAGALAG cluster			0	0		0.00	0		9		...					0....	8534
29-RHFA-a	walangama			0	0	0	0.00	0		9		...					0....	8535
29-RHFA-b	ag-wamin			0	0	0	0.00	0		9		...					0....	8536
29-RHFA-c	dagalag			0	0	0	0.00	0		9		...					0....	8537
29-RHFB	BABARAM cluster			0	0		0.00	0		0		...					0....	8538
29-RHFB-a	m-babaram			0	0	0	0.00	0		0		...					0....	8539
29-RHFB-b	n-gaygungu			0	0	0	0.00	0		0		...					0....	8540
29-RHFC	BARA cluster			0	0		0.00	0		8		...					0....	8541
29-RHFC-a	m-bara			0	0	0	0.00	0		8		...					0....	8542
29-RHG	**GUGADJ-MAYABIC net**									8		...					0....	8543
29-RHGA	GUGADJ cluster			0	0		0.00	0		8		...					0....	8544
29-RHGA-a	gugadj			0	0	0	0.00	0		8		...					0....	8545
29-RHGB	MAYABIC cluster			0	0		0.00	0		8		...					0....	8546
29-RHGB-a	maya-guduna			0	0	0	0.00	0		8		...					0....	8547
29-RHGB-b	maya-gulan			0	0	0	0.00	0		8		...					0....	8548
29-RHGB-c	ngawun			0	0	0	0.00	0		8		...					0....	8549
29-RHGB-d	maya-bi			0	0	0	0.00	0		8		...					0....	8550
29-RHGB-e	mayi-yapi			0	0	0	0.00	0		8		...					0....	8551
29-RHGB-f	mayi-dhagurdi			0	0	0	0.00	0		8		...					0....	8552
29-RHGB-g	wunumara			0	0	0	0.00	0		8		...					0....	8553
29-S	**GALIBAMU set**									0		...					0....	8554
29-SA	GALIBAMU chain									0		...					0....	8555
29-SAA	**GALIBAMU net**									0		...					0....	8556
29-SAAA	GALIBAMU cluster			0	0		0.00	0		0		...					0....	8557
29-SAAA-a	galibamu			0	0	0	0.00	0		0		...					0....	8558
29-SAAA-b	kukatji			0	0	0	0.00	0		0		...					0....	8559
29-T	**TANGIC set**	1	1	100	170		35.00	70	B	8		...					0....	8560
29-TA	TANGIC chain	1	1	100	170		35.00	70	B	8		...					0....	8561
29-TAA	**TANGIC net**	1	1	100	170		35.00	70	B	8		...					0....	8562
29-TAAA	GAYARDILT cluster	1	1	50	85		30.00	64	B	6		...					0....	8563
29-TAAA-a	gayardilt	1	1	50	85	0	30.00	64	B	6		...					0....	8564
29-TAAB	LARDIL cluster	1	1	50	85		40.00	76	B	8		...					0....	8565
29-TAAB-a	lardil					0				8		...					0....	8566
29-TAAB-b	daamin					0				8		...					0....	8567
29-TAAC	JAKULA cluster			0	0		0.00	0		8		...					0....	8568
29-TAAC-a	ganggalida			0	0	0	0.00	0		8		...					0....	8569
29-TAAC-b	nyangga			0	0	0	0.00	0		8		...					0....	8570
29-U	**GALGADUNIC set**									9		...					0....	8571
29-UA	GALGADUNIC chain									9		...					0....	8572
29-UAA	**KALKUTUNG net**									9		...					0....	8573
29-UAAA	KALKUTUNG cluster			0	0		0.00	0		9		...					0....	8574
29-UAAA-a	kalkutung			0	0	0	0.00	0		9		...				.	0....	8575
29-UAB	**YALARNNGA net**									9		...					0....	8576
29-UABA	YALARNNGA cluster			0	0		0.00	0		9		...					0....	8577
29-UABA-a	yalarnnga			0	0	0	0.00	0		9		...					0....	8578
29-V	**WAGAYA-WARLUWARIC set**									8		...					0....	8579
29-VA	WARLUWARIC chain									8		...					0....	8580
29-VAA	**WARLUWARIC net**									8		...					0....	8581
29-VAAA	WARLUWARA cluster			0	0		0.00	0		8		...					0....	8582
29-VAAA-a	warluwara			0	0	0	0.00	0		8		...					0....	8583
29-VAAB	WURGABUNGA cluster			0	0		0.00	0		0		...					0....	8584
29-VAAB-a	wurgabunga			0	0	0	0.00	0		0		...					0....	8585
29-VAAC	NGUBURINDI cluster			0	0		0.00	0		0		...					0....	8586
29-VAAC-a	nguburindi			0	0	0	0.00	0		0		...					0....	8587
29-VAAD	YINDJILANDJI cluster			0	0		0.00	0		8		...					0....	8588
29-VAAD-a	yindjilandji			0	0	0	0.00	0		8		...					0....	8589

Continued opposite

Table 9-13 continued

Code 1	REFERENCE NAME / Autoglossonym 2	Coun 3	Peo 4	Mother-tongue speakers in 2000 5	in 2025 6	Media radio 7	CHURCH AC% 8	E% 9	Wld 10	Tr 11	Biblioglossonym 12	SCRIPTURES Print 13-15	P-activity 16	N-activity 17	B-activity 18	J-year 19	Jayuh 20-24	Ref 25
29-VB	WAGAYA chain									8		...					0....	8590
29-VBA	**WAGAYA net**									8		...					0....	8591
29-VBAA	WAGAYA cluster			0	0		0.00	0		8		...					0....	8592
29-VBAA-a	wagaya			0	0	0	0.00	0		8		...					0....	8593
29-W	**WARUMUNGU set**	1	1	245	300		8.98	38	A	6		...					0....	8594
29-WA	WARUMUNGU chain	1	1	245	300		8.98	38	A	6		...					0....	8595
29-WAA	**WARUMUNGU net**	1	1	245	300		8.98	38	A	6		...					0....	8596
29-WAAA	WARUMUNGU cluster	1	1	245	300		8.98	38	A	6		...					0....	8597
29-WAAA-a	warumungu	1	1	245	300	0	8.98	38	A	6		...					0....	8598
29-X	**ARANDIC set**	1	6	7,161	8,757		59.53	93	B	42		PN.					0....	8599
29-XA	ARTUYA chain	1	1	245	300		44.90	78	B	6		...					0....	8600
29-XAA	**ARTUYA net**	1	1	245	300		44.90	78	B	6		...					0....	8601
29-XAAA	GAIDIDJ cluster	1	1	245	300		44.90	78	B	6		...					0....	8602
29-XAAA-a	gaididj	1	1	245	300	0	44.90	78	B	6		...					0....	8603
29-XB	URTWA chain	1	5	6,916	8,457		60.05	94	C	42		PN.					0....	8604
29-XBA	**ARANDA net**	1	4	5,264	6,437		60.07	92	C	42		PN.					0....	8605
29-XBAA	ANMATJIRRA cluster	1	1	984	1,203		70.02	100	C	4		...					0....	8606
29-XBAA-a	anmatjirra	1	1	984	1,203	0	70.02	100	C	4		...					0....	8607
29-XBAB	ARANDA cluster	1	2	3,013	3,685		52.64	87	B	42		PN.					0....	8608
29-XBAB-a	West aranda	1	2	3,013	3,685	0	52.64	87	B	42	Aranda*	PN.	1925-1928	1956			0....	8609
29-XBAB-b	akerre					0				42		pn.					0....	8610
29-XBAB-c	pirdima			0	0	0	0.00	0		42		pn.					0....	8611
29-XBAC	ARRERNTE cluster	1	1	1,267	1,549		70.01	100	C	12		...					0....	8612
29-XBAC-a	arrernte	1	1	1,267	1,549	0	70.01	100	C	12	Arrernte, Eastern	...					0....	8613
29-XBB	**ALYAWARRA net**	1	1	1,652	2,020		59.99	97	B	22		P..					0....	8614
29-XBBA	ALYAWARRA cluster	1	1	1,652	2,020		59.99	97	B	22		P..					0....	8615
29-XBBA-a	alyawarra	1	1	1,652	2,020	0	59.99	97	B	22	Alyawarr	P..	1996				0....	8616
29-XBC	**ANDAGEREBINHA net**									8		...					0....	8617
29-XBCA	ANDEGEREBINHA cluster			0	0		0.00	0		8		...					0....	8618
29-XBCA-a	andegerebinha			0	0	0	0.00	0		8		...					0....	8619
29-XBCA-b	yuruwinga			0	0	0	0.00	0		8		...					0....	8620
3	**AUSTRONESIAN macrozone**	68	1513	324,516,272	438,771,202		33.13	71	B	82		PNB					4Bsuh	8621
30	**FORMOSIC zone**	2	15	412,586	490,641		84.94	100	C	57		PN.					0....	8622
30-A	**ATAYALIC set**	1	2	116,719	150,606		87.19	100	C	57		PN.					0....	8623
30-AA	ATAYALIC chain	1	2	116,719	150,606		87.19	100	C	57		PN.					0....	8624
30-AAA	**ATAYAL net**	1	1	83,870	112,876		90.00	100	C	57		PN.					0....	8625
30-AAAA	SQOLEQ cluster	1	1	53,870	61,876		90.00	100	C	57	Tayal*	PN.	1964	1974			0....	8626
30-AAAA-a	bonotsek					0				57		pn.					0....	8627
30-AAAA-b	chin-wan					0				57		pn.					0....	8628
30-AAAA-c	shabogala					0				57		pn.					0....	8629
30-AAAA-d	takonan					0				57		pn.					0....	8630
30-AAAA-e	tangao					0				57		pn.					0....	8631
30-AAAA-f	yukan					0				57		pn.					0....	8632
30-AAAB	TSOLE cluster	1	1	30,000	51,000		90.00	99	C	0		...					0....	8633
30-AAAB-a	mana-wyan					0				0		...					0....	8634
30-AAAB-b	mayrinax					0				0		...					0....	8635
30-AAAB-c	pa'kuali'					0				0		...					0....	8636
30-AAAB-d	sikikun					0				0		...					0....	8637
30-AAB	**SEDEQ net**	1	1	32,849	37,730		80.00	100	C	41		PN.					0....	8638
30-AABA	SEDEQ cluster	1	1	32,849	37,730		80.00	100	C	41		PN.					0....	8639
30-AABA-a	taroko	1	1	32,849	37,730	0	80.00	100	C	41	Taroko	PN.	1956-1960	1963-1981			0....	8640
30-AABA-b	bu-hwan					0				41		pn.					0....	8641
30-AABA-c	che-whan					0				41		pn.					0....	8642
30-AABA-d	hogo					0				41		pn.					0....	8643
30-AABA-e	iboho					0				41		pn.					0....	8644
30-AABA-f	paran					0				41		pn.					0....	8645
30-AABA-g	sazek					0				41		pn.					0....	8646
30-B	**BASAY-KAVA set**	1	1	112	129		80.36	100	C	9		...					0....	8647
30-BA	BASAY chain									9		...					0....	8648
30-BAA	**BASAY net**									9		...					0....	8649
30-BAAA	BASAY cluster			0	0		0.00	0		9		...					0....	8650
30-BAAA-a	kawanu-wan			0	0	0	0.00	0		9		...					0....	8651
30-BAAA-b	trobia-wan			0	0	0	0.00	0		9		...					0....	8652
30-BAAA-c	linaw-quaqual			0	0	0	0.00	0		9		...					0....	8653
30-BB	KATANGA chain									0		...					0....	8654
30-BBA	**KATANGA net**									0		...					0....	8655
30-BBAA	KATANGA cluster			0	0		0.00	0		0		...					0....	8656
30-BBAA-a	katanga-lan			0	0	0	0.00	0		0		...					0....	8657
30-BBAA-b	lui-lang			0	0	0	0.00	0		0		...					0....	8658
30-BC	KULUN chain									9		...					0....	8659
30-BCA	**KULUN net**									9		...					0....	8660
30-BCAA	KULUN cluster			0	0		0.00	0		9		...					0....	8661
30-BCAA-a	kulun			0	0	0	0.00	0		9		...					0....	8662
30-BD	KAVA chain	1	1	112	129		80.36	100	C	8		...					0....	8663
30-BDA	**KAVA net**	1	1	112	129		80.36	100	C	8		...					0....	8664

Continued overleaf

Table 9-13 continued

Code 1	REFERENCE NAME / Autoglossonym 2	Coun 3	Peo 4	Mother-tongue speakers in 2000 5	in 2025 6	Media radio 7	CHURCH AC% 8	E% 9	Wld 10	Tr 11	Biblioglossonym 12	SCRIPTURES Print 13-15	P-activity 16	N-activity 17	B-activity 18	J-year 19	Jayuh 20-24	Ref 25
30-BDAA	KAVA cluster	1	1	112	129		80.36	100	C	8		. . .					0	8665
30-BDAA-a	kava-lan	1	1	112	129	0	80.36	100	C	8		. . .					0	8666
30-BDAA-b	kareo-wan					0				8		. . .					0	8667
30-BDAA-c	shek-wan					0				8		. . .					0	8668
30-C	**SAISIYAT-BABUZA set**	1	3	4,653	5,344		70.94	100	C	9		. . .					0	8669
30-CA	SAISIYAT chain	1	1	4,205	4,830		69.99	100	C	4		. . .					0	8670
30-CAA	**SAISIYAT net**	1	1	4,205	4,830		69.99	100	C	4		. . .					0	8671
30-CAAA	SAISIYAT cluster	1	1	4,205	4,830		69.99	100	C	4		. . .					0	8672
30-CAAA-a	taai					0				4		. . .					0	8673
30-CAAA-b	tungho					0				4		. . .					0	8674
30-CB	TAOKAS-BABUZA chain	1	2	448	514		79.91	100	C	9		. . .					0	8675
30-CBA	**TAOKAS net**									9		. . .					0	8676
30-CBAA	TAOKAS cluster			0	0		0.00	0		9		. . .					0	8677
30-CBAA-a	taokas			0	0	0	0.00	0		9		. . .					0	8678
30-CBB	**PAZEH-KAZEBU net**	1	1	224	257		79.91	100	C	8		. . .					0	8679
30-CBBA	PAZEH-KAZEBU cluster	1	1	224	257		79.91	100	C	8		. . .					0	8680
30-CBBA-a	pazeh	1	1	224	257	0	79.91	100	C	8		. . .					0	8681
30-CBBA-b	kahabu			0	0	0	0.00	0		8		. . .					0	8682
30-CBBA-c	lek-whan			0	0	0	0.00	0		8		. . .					0	8683
30-CBBA-d	sek-hwan			0	0	0	0.00	0		8		. . .					0	8684
30-CBC	**BABUZA net**	1	1	224	257		79.91	100	C	8		. . .					0	8685
30-CBCA	BABUZA cluster	1	1	224	257		79.91	100	C	8		. . .					0	8686
30-CBCA-a	Proper babuza	1	1	224	257	0	79.91	100	C	8	Babuza	. . .					0	8687
30-CBCA-b	favor-lang			0	0	0	0.00	0		8		. . .					0	8688
30-CBCA-c	jabor-lang			0	0	0	0.00	0		8		. . .					0	8689
30-CC	PAPORA chain									9		. . .					0	8690
30-CCA	**PAPORA net**									9		. . .					0	8691
30-CCAA	PAPORA cluster			0	0		0.00	0		9		. . .					0	8692
30-CCAA-a	Proper papora			0	0	0	0.00	0		9		. . .					0	8693
30-CCAA-b	hinapavosa			0	0	0	0.00	0		9		. . .					0	8694
30-D	**THAO set**	1	1	365	419		80.00	100	C	8		. . .					0	8695
30-DA	THAO chain	1	1	365	419		80.00	100	C	8		. . .					0	8696
30-DAA	**THAO net**	1	1	365	419		80.00	100	C	8		. . .					0	8697
30-DAAA	THAO cluster	1	1	365	419		80.00	100	C	8		. . .					0	8698
30-DAAA-a	brawbraw					0				8		. . .					0	8699
30-DAAA-b	shtafari					0				8		. . .					0	8700
30-DAAA-c	tsui-whan					0				8		. . .					0	8701
30-E	**TSOUIC set**	1	1	6,465	7,591		69.06	99	C	12		. . .					0	8702
30-EA	TSOUIC chain	1	1	6,465	7,591		69.06	99	C	12		. . .					0	8703
30-EAA	**NORTH TSOU net**	1	1	6,165	7,081		69.99	100	C	12		. . .					0	8704
30-EAAA	TSOU cluster	1	1	6,165	7,081		69.99	100	C	12	Tsou	. . .					0	8705
30-EAAA-a	duhtu					0				12		. . .					0	8706
30-EAAA-b	tapangu					0				12		. . .					0	8707
30-EAAA-c	tfuea					0				12		. . .					0	8708
30-EAAA-d	imutsu			0	0	0	0.00	0		12		. . .					0	8709
30-EAB	**SOUTH TSOU net**	1	1	300	510		50.00	86	B	8		. . .					0	8710
30-EABA	KANABU-SAAROA cluster	1	1	300	510		50.00	86	B	8		. . .					0	8711
30-EABA-a	kana-kanabu					0				8		. . .					0	8712
30-EABA-b	sek-hwan-2					0				8		. . .					0	8715
30-EABA-c	saaroa					0				8		. . .					0	8716
30-F	**HOANYA-SIRAYA set**									9		. . .					0	8720
30-FA	HOANYA-SIRAYA chain									9		. . .					0	8721
30-FAA	**HOANYA-SIRAYA net**									9		. . .					0	8722
30-FAAA	HOANYA cluster			0	0		0.00	0		9		. . .					0	8723
30-FAAA-a	Proper hoanya			0	0	0	0.00	0		9		. . .					0	8724
30-FAAA-b	lloa			0	0	0	0.00	0		9		. . .					0	8725
30-FAAA-c	arikun			0	0	0	0.00	0		9		. . .					0	8726
30-FAAA-d	baksa			0	0	0	0.00	0		9		. . .					0	8727
30-FAAA-e	kongana			0	0	0	0.00	0		9		. . .					0	8728
30-FAAB	SIRAYA cluster			0	0		0.00	0		0		. . .					0	8729
30-FAAB-a	pepo-hwan			0	0	0	0.00	0		0		. . .					0	8730
30-FAAB-b	taivoan			0	0	0	0.00	0		0		. . .					0	8731
30-FAAB-c	sinkan			0	0	0	0.00	0		0		. . .					0	8732
30-FAAB-d	lamai			0	0	0	0.00	0		0		. . .					0	8733
30-FAAB-e	longkiau			0	0	0	0.00	0		0		. . .					0	8734
30-FAAB-f	pongsoia-dolatok			0	0	0	0.00	0		0		. . .					0	8735
30-FAAB-g	makatao			0	0	0	0.00	0		0		. . .					0	8736
30-FAAB-h	liuchiu			0	0	0	0.00	0		0		. . .					0	8737
30-G	**PAIWAN set**	1	1	66,311	76,166		80.00	100	C	41		PN .					0	8738
30-GA	PAIWAN chain	1	1	66,311	76,166		80.00	100	C	41		PN .					0	8739
30-GAA	**PAIWAN net**	1	1	66,311	76,166		80.00	100	C	41		PN .					0	8740
30-GAAA	PAIWAN cluster	1	1	66,311	76,166		80.00	100	C	41	Paiwan	PN .	1959-1993	1973-1993			0	8741
30-GAAA-a	shimo-paiwan					1				41		pn .					0	8742
30-GAAA-b	kale-whan					1				41		pn .					0	8743
30-GAAA-c	kapiangan					1				41		pn .					0	8744
30-GAAA-d	katsausan					1				41		pn .					0	8745
30-GAAA-e	lilisha					1				41		pn .					0	8746
30-GAAA-f	samobi					1				41		pn .					0	8747
30-GAAA-g	samohai					1				41		pn .					0	8748
30-GAAA-h	saprek					1				41		pn .					0	8749
30-GAAA-i	tamari					1				41		pn .					0	8750
30-GAAA-j	butanglu					1				41		pn .					0	8751
30-GAAA-k	stimul					1				41		pn .					0	8752
30-GAAA-l	kachirai					1				41		pn .					0	8753
30-GAAA-m	kunanau					1				41		pn .					0	8754
30-GAAA-n	naibun					1				41		pn .					0	8755

Continued opposite

Table 9-13 continued

Code 1	REFERENCE NAME 2 / Autoglossonym	Coun 3	Peo 4	Mother-tongue speakers in 2000 5	in 2025 6	Media radio 7	AC% 8	E% 9	Wld 10	Tr 11	Biblioglossonym 12	Print 13-15	P-activity 16	N-activity 17	B-activity 18	J-year 19	Jayuh 20-24	Ref 25
30-GAAA-o	raisha					1				41		pn.					0....	8756
30-GAAA-p	tachaban					1				41		pn.					0....	8757
30-H	**RUKAI set**	1	1	8,432	9,685		79.99	100	C	12		...					0....	8758
30-HA	RUKAI chain	1	1	8,432	9,685		79.99	100	C	12		...					0....	8759
30-HAA	**RUKAI net**	1	1	8,432	9,685		79.99	100	C	12		...					0....	8760
30-HAAA	RUKAI cluster	1	1	8,432	9,685		79.99	100	C	12		...					0....	8761
30-HAAA-a	Proper rukai					0				12	Rukai	...					0....	8762
30-HAAA-b	rukai-paiwan					0				12		...					0....	8765
30-HAAA-c	taloma					0				12		...					0....	8766
30-HAAA-d	budai					0				12		...					0....	8767
30-HAAA-e	labuan					0				12		...					0....	8768
30-HAAA-f	tanan					0				12		...					0....	8769
30-HAAA-g	maga					0				12		...					0....	8770
30-HAAA-h	tona					0				12		...					0....	8771
30-HAAA-i	mantau-ran					0				12		...					0....	8772
30-I	**BUNUN set**	1	1	42,044	48,293		80.00	100	C	57		PN.					0....	8773
30-IA	BUNUN chain	1	1	42,044	48,293		80.00	100	C	57		PN.					0....	8774
30-IAA	**BUNUN net**	1	1	42,044	48,293		80.00	100	C	57		PN.					0....	8775
30-IAAA	BUNUN cluster	1	1	42,044	48,293		80.00	100	C	57		PN.					0....	8776
30-IAAA-a	tako-pulan			0	0	0	0.00	0		57		pn.					0....	8777
30-IAAA-b	si-bukun					0				57		pn.					0....	8778
30-IAAA-c	North bunun					0				57		pn.					0....	8779
30-IAAA-d	Central bunun	1	1	42,044	48,293	0	80.00	100	C	57	Bunun	PN.	1951-1962	1973			0....	8782
30-IAAA-e	randai					0				57		pn.					0....	8785
30-IAAA-f	tondai					0				57		pn.					0....	8786
30-J	**PIYUMA set**	1	1	10,399	11,944		70.00	100	C	2		...					0....	8787
30-JA	PIYUMA chain	1	1	10,399	11,944		70.00	100	C	2		...					0....	8788
30-JAA	**PIYUMA net**	1	1	10,399	11,944		70.00	100	C	2		...					0....	8789
30-JAAA	PIYUMA cluster	1	1	10,399	11,944		70.00	100	C	2		...					0....	8790
30-JAAA-a	Central pi-yuma	1	1	10,399	11,944	0	70.00	100	C	2		...					0....	8791
30-JAAA-b	pi-yuma-paiwan					0				2		...					0....	8792
30-JAAA-c	pi-nan					0				2		...					0....	8793
30-JAAA-d	pi-lam					0				2		...					0....	8794
30-JAAA-e	pi-mamba					0				2		...					0....	8795
30-JAAA-f	panapanayan					0				2		...					0....	8796
30-JAAA-g	tipun					0				2		...					0....	8797
30-K	**AMIS set**	2	3	157,086	180,464		89.02	100	C	41		PN.					0....	8798
30-KA	AMIS chain	2	2	154,846	177,891		89.15	100	C	41		PN.					0....	8799
30-KAA	**CENTRAL AMIS net**	2	2	154,846	177,891		89.15	100	C	41		PN.					0....	8800
30-KAAA	AMIS cluster	2	2	154,846	177,891		89.15	100	C	41		PN.					0....	8801
30-KAAA-a	South amis					0				41		pn.					0....	8802
30-KAAA-b	chengkung-kwangshan					0				41		pn.					0....	8806
30-KAAA-c	Central amis	1	1	151,563	174,087	0	90.00	100	C	41	Amis	PN.	1957-1981	1972-1981			0....	8809
30-KAAA-d	tavalong-vataan					0				41		pn.					0....	8812
30-KAAA-e	nanshi-amis	1	1	3,283	3,804	0	49.98	87	B	41		pn.					0....	8815
30-KB	NATAORAN-SAKIZAYA chain	1	1	2,240	2,573		80.00	100	C	4		...					0....	8816
30-KBA	**NATAORAN-SAKIZAYA net**	1	1	2,240	2,573		80.00	100	C	4		...					0....	8817
30-KBAA	NATAORAN cluster									4		...					0....	8818
30-KBAA-a	nataoran					0				4		...					0....	8819
30-KBAB	SAKIZAYA cluster	1	1	2,240	2,573		80.00	100	C	0		...					0....	8820
30-KBAB-a	sakizaya	1	1	2,240	2,573	0	80.00	100	C	0		...					0....	8821
31	**HESPERONESIC zone**	49	751	314,332,471	424,716,199		31.99	71	B	72		PNB					4Bsuh	8822
31-A	**ARTA set**	1	1	30	43		30.00	60	B	6		...					0....	8823
31-AA	ARTA chain	1	1	30	43		30.00	60	B	6		...					0....	8824
31-AAA	**ARTA net**	1	1	30	43		30.00	60	B	6		...					0....	8825
31-AAAA	ARTA cluster	1	1	30	43		30.00	60	B	6		...					0....	8826
31-AAAA-a	arta	1	1	30	43	0	30.00	60	B	6		...					0....	8827
31-B	**ALTA set**	1	1	3,281	5,501		5.00	25	A	23		P..					0....	8828
31-BA	NORTH ALTA chain	1	1	281	401		4.98	31	A	4		...					0....	8829
31-BAA	**DITAYLIN net**	1	1	281	401		4.98	31	A	4		...					0....	8830
31-BAAA	DITAYLIN cluster	1	1	281	401		4.98	31	A	4		...					0....	8831
31-BAAA-a	ditaylin	1	1	281	401	0	4.98	31	A	4		...					0....	8832
31-BB	SOUTH ALTA chain	1	1	3,000	5,100		5.00	24	A	23		P..					0....	8833
31-BBA	**KABALUWEN net**	1	1	3,000	5,100		5.00	24	A	23		P..					0....	8834
31-BBAA	KABALUWEN cluster	1	1	3,000	5,100		5.00	24	A	23	Alta, Southern	P..	1970				0....	8835
31-BBAA-a	san-miguel					0				23		p..					0....	8836
31-BBAA-b	bulacan					0				23		p..					0....	8837
31-C	**MACRO-PHILIPPINE set**	24	179	77,129,455	109,025,050		90.05	96	C	71		PNB					4Bsu.	8838
31-CA	BASHIIC chain	2	3	50,340	70,791		68.65	100	C	41		PN.					0.s..	8839
31-CAA	**YAMI net**	1	1	3,416	3,924		80.01	100	C	41		PN.					0....	8840
31-CAAA	YAMI cluster	1	1	3,416	3,924		80.01	100	C	41		PN.					0....	8841
31-CAAA-a	yami	1	1	3,416	3,924	0	80.01	100	C	41	Yami	PN.	1970-1990	1994			0....	8842
31-CAAA-b	imurut					0				41		pn.					0....	8843
31-CAB	**IVATAN net**	1	2	46,924	66,867		67.82	100	C	41		PN.					0.s..	8844
31-CABA	NORTH IVATAN cluster	1	1	45,876	65,373		68.00	100	C	41	Ivatan	PN.	1960	1984			0.s..	8845
31-CABA-a	itbayat					0				41		pn.					0.s..	8846
31-CABA-b	bat-an					0				41		pn.					0.s..	8847

Continued overleaf

Table 9-13 continued

Code 1	REFERENCE NAME / Autoglossonym 2	Coun 3	Peo 4	Mother-tongue speakers in 2000 5	in 2025 6	Media radio 7	AC% 8	E% 9	Wld 10	Tr 11	Biblioglossonym 12	Print 13-15	P–activity 16	N–activity 17	B–activity 18	J-year 19	Jayuh 20-24	Ref 25
31-CABB	SOUTH IVATAN cluster	1	1	1,048	1,494		60.02	97	C	41		PN.					0....	8848
31-CABB-a	i-bat-an	1	1	1,048	1,494	0	60.02	97	C	41	Ibatan	PN.	1981-1986	1996			0....	8849
31-CB	ILOCANO chain	3	3	9,024,596	12,716,294		97.26	100	C	61		PNB					2A.u.	8850
31-CBA	**ILOCANO net**	3	3	9,024,596	12,716,294		97.26	100	C	61		PNB					2A.u.	8851
31-CBAA	ILOCANO cluster	3	3	9,024,596	12,716,294		97.26	100	C	61		PNB					2A.u.	8852
31-CBAA-a	Proper ilocano					1				61		pnb					1c.u.	8853
31-CBAA-b	Vehicular ilocano	3	3	9,024,596	12,716,294	4	97.26	100	C	61	Ilokano*	PNB	1899-1965	1903-1906	1909-1996	1980	2A.u.	8854
31-CC	IBANAGIC chain	1	12	937,518	1,335,948		81.59	95	C	41		PN.					1.s..	8855
31-CCA	**ISNAG-ADASEN net**	1	2	16,964	24,172		10.55	48	A	41		PN.					0....	8856
31-CCAA	ISNAG cluster	1	1	11,722	16,703		9.00	46	A	41		PN.					0....	8857
31-CCAA-a	dibagat-kabugao	1	1	11,722	16,703	0	9.00	46	A	41	Isnag: Apayao	PN.	1961	1980			0....	8858
31-CCAA-b	bayag					0				41		pn.					0....	8859
31-CCAA-c	calanasan					0				41		pn.					0....	8860
31-CCAA-d	karagawan					0				41		pn.					0....	8861
31-CCAA-e	talifugu-ripang					0				41		pn.					0....	8862
31-CCAB	ADASEN cluster	1	1	5,242	7,469		14.00	51	B	41	Adasen	PN.		1990			0....	8863
31-CCAB-a	West adasen					0				41		pn.					0....	8864
31-CCAB-b	East adasen					0				41		pn.					0....	8865
31-CCB	**IBANAG-ITAWIT net**	1	6	814,307	1,160,376		88.44	99	C	41		PN.					1.s..	8866
31-CCBA	IBANAG cluster	1	1	608,583	867,221		98.00	100	C	41	Ibanag	PN.	1907-1989	1911-1989		1998	1....	8867
31-CCBA-a	North ibanag					0				41		pn.					1....	8868
31-CCBA-b	South ibanag					0				41		pn.					1....	8869
31-CCBB	IBANAG-AGTA cluster	1	3	16,606	23,664		7.70	39	A	41		PN.					0.s..	8870
31-CCBB-a	pamplona-agta	1	1	699	996	0	5.01	41	A	41	Atta*	PN.	1969-1980	1996			0.s..	8871
31-CCBB-b	pudtol-agta	1	1	714	1,018	0	4.06	33	A	41		pn.					0.s..	8872
31-CCBB-c	villaviciosa-agta	1	1	15,193	21,650	0	8.00	39	A	41		pn.					0.s..	8873
31-CCBC	ITAWIT cluster	1	1	188,389	268,452		65.00	100	C	41		PN.					1....	8874
31-CCBC-a	itawis	1	1	188,389	268,452	0	65.00	100	C	41	Itawes*	PN.	1978-1981	1992		1998	1....	8875
31-CCBD	ITAWIT-AGTA cluster	1	1	729	1,039		3.98	29	A	4		...					0....	8876
31-CCBD-a	malaweg					0				4		...					0....	8877
31-CCBD-b	faire-agta	1	1	729	1,039	0	3.98	29	A	4		...					0....	8878
31-CCC	**GA'DANG net**	1	3	81,262	115,796		34.37	70	B	41		PN.					0....	8879
31-CCCA	GA'DANG cluster	1	2	38,865	55,381		6.42	41	A	41	Ga'dang*	PN.	1976-1981				0....	8880
31-CCCA-a	baliwon					0				41		pn.					0....	8881
31-CCCA-b	ginabwal					0				41		pn.					0....	8882
31-CCCA-c	iraya-2					0				41		pn.					0....	8883
31-CCCA-d	masablang					0				41		pn.					0....	8884
31-CCCA-e	katalangan					0				41		pn.					0....	8885
31-CCCA-f	kalinga	1	1	18,354	26,153	0	8.00	43	A	41	Kalinga: Southern*	PN.	1977	1986			0....	8886
31-CCCA-g	maddukayang					0				41		pn.					0....	8887
31-CCCB	GADDANG cluster	1	1	42,397	60,415		60.00	97	B	4		...					0....	8888
31-CCCB-a	cagayan					0				4		...					0....	8889
31-CCCB-b	Southeast gaddang					0				4		...					0....	8890
31-CCD	**YOGAD net**	1	1	24,985	35,604		60.00	98	C	5		...					0....	8891
31-CCDA	YOGAD cluster	1	1	24,985	35,604		60.00	98	C	5		...					0....	8892
31-CCDA-a	yogad	1	1	24,985	35,604	0	60.00	98	C	5		...					0....	8893
31-CD	DUMAGAT chain	1	10	78,072	119,502		32.84	62	B	45		PN.					0.s..	8894
31-CDA	**DUPANINAN-AGTA net**	1	1	30,000	51,000		10.00	33	A	22		P..					0....	8895
31-CDAA	DUPANINAN-AGTA cluster	1	1	30,000	51,000		10.00	33	A	22	Agta: Dupaninan*	P..	1986				0....	8896
31-CDAA-a	palaui-agta					0				22		p..					0....	8897
31-CDAA-b	yaga					0				22		p..					0....	8898
31-CDAA-c	tanglagan					0				22		p..					0....	8899
31-CDAA-d	santa-ana-gonzaga					0				22		p..					0....	8900
31-CDAA-e	barongagunay					0				22		p..					0....	8901
31-CDAA-f	camonayan					0				22		p..					0....	8902
31-CDAA-g	valley-cove					0				22		p..					0....	8903
31-CDAA-h	bolos					0				22		p..					0....	8904
31-CDAA-i	pe-a-blanca					0				22		p..					0....	8905
31-CDAA-j	roso					0				22		p..					0....	8906
31-CDAA-k	santa-margarita					0				22		p..					0....	8907
31-CDB	**CENTRAL DUMAGAT net**	1	6	38,530	54,905		56.75	89	B	45		PN.					0.s..	8908
31-CDBA	PARANAN cluster	1	1	15,292	21,791		70.00	100	C	22		P..					0....	8909
31-CDBA-a	paranan	1	1	15,292	21,791	0	70.00	100	C	22	Paranan	P..	1988				0....	8910
31-CDBA-b	palanan-agta					0				22		P..					0....	8911
31-CDBB	CAGAYAN-AGTA cluster	1	3	3,783	5,391		5.63	37	A	45		PN.					0.s..	8912
31-CDBB-a	cagayan-agta	1	3	3,783	5,391	0	5.63	37	A	45	Agta: Cagayan, Central*	PN.	1962-1980	1992			0.s..	8913
31-CDBC	DICAMAY-AGTA cluster			0	0		0.00	0		9		...					0....	8914
31-CDBC-a	dicamay-agta			0	0	0	0.00	0		9		...					0....	8915
31-CDBD	CASIGURAN-AGTA cluster	1	1	1,610	2,295		15.03	49	A	41		PN.					0....	8916
31-CDBD-a	casiguran-agta	1	1	1,610	2,295	0	15.03	49	A	41	Dumagat: Casiguran*	PN.	1967	1979			0....	8917
31-CDBE	KASIGURANIN cluster	1	1	17,845	25,428		60.00	95	C	4		...					0....	8918
31-CDBE-a	kasiguranin	1	1	17,845	25,428	0	60.00	95	C	4		...					0....	8919
31-CDC	**SOUTH DUMAGAT net**	1	4	9,542	13,597		8.09	45	A	41		PN.					0.s..	8920
31-CDCA	SOUTH DUMAGAT cluster	1	4	9,542	13,597		8.09	45	A	41	Dumagat: Kabulowan	PN.	1970				0.s..	8921
31-CDCA-a	alabat-agta	1	1	84	119	0	4.76	39	A	41		pn.					0.s..	8922
31-CDCA-b	umiray-agta	1	1	7,650	10,901	0	8.00	47	A	41	Dumagat: Umiray*	PN.	1968	1977			0.s..	8923
31-CDCA-c	anglat-agta					0				41		pn.					0.s..	8924
31-CDCA-d	camarines-agta	1	1	319	455	0	30.09	60	B	41		pn.					0.s..	8925
31-CE	CENTRAL CORDILLERAN chain	1	21	695,603	999,471		18.60	54	B	41		PN.					1.s..	8926
31-CEA	**KALINGA-ITNEG net**	1	11	203,172	297,768		12.74	43	A	23		P..					0....	8927
31-CEAA	ITNEG cluster	1	4	50,631	72,149		16.20	49	A	23		P..					0....	8928
31-CEAA-a	binongan	1	1	10,423	14,852	0	16.00	49	A	23	Tinguian*	P..	1967				0....	8929
31-CEAA-b	inlaod	1	1	15,193	21,650	0	15.00	48	A	23		p..					0....	8930
31-CEAA-c	masadiit	1	1	9,822	13,997	0	17.00	50	B	23		p..					0....	8931
31-CEAA-d	South itneg	1	1	15,193	21,650	0	17.00	50	B	23		P..					0....	8932
31-CEAB	NORTH KALINGA cluster	1	6	61,373	87,455		11.06	40	A	22		P..					0....	8933
31-CEAB-a	butbut	1	1	6,115	8,714	0	6.00	31	A	22	Kalinga, Butbut	P..					0....	8934
31-CEAB-b	limos-liwan	1	1	33,866	48,258	0	15.00	46	A	22	Kalinga: Limos*	P..	1977-1985				0....	8935
31-CEAB-c	mabaka	1	1	7,597	10,825	0	6.00	32	A	22		p..					0....	8936
31-CEAB-d	madukayang	1	1	1,823	2,598	0	7.02	32	A	22	Kalinga, Madukayang	p..					0....	8937
31-CEAB-e	mangali					0				22		p..					0....	8938
31-CEAB-f	pangul					0				22		p..					0....	8939

Continued opposite

Table 9-13 continued

Code 1	REFERENCE NAME / Autoglossonym 2	Coun 3	Peo 4	Mother-tongue speakers in 2000 5	in 2025 6	Media radio 7	CHURCH AC% 8	E% 9	Wld 10	Tr 11	Biblioglossonym 12	SCRIPTURES Print 13-15	P-activity 16	N-activity 17	B-activity 18	J-year 19	Jayuh 20-24	Ref 25
31-CEAB-g	Upper tanudan	1	1	3,563	5,077	0	6.99	35	A	22		p..					0....	8940
31-CEAB-h	Lower tanudan	1	1	8,409	11,983		6.01	35	A	22	Kalinga: Tanudan*	P..	1980				0....	8941
31-CEAC	CENTRAL KALINGA cluster	1	1	61,168	87,164		8.00	38	A	23		P..					0....	8942
31-CEAC-a	guinaang					0				23	Kalinga: Guinaang	P..	1970				0....	8943
31-CEAC-b	balbalasang					0				23		p..					0....	8944
31-CEAC-c	banao					0				23		p..					0....	8945
31-CEAC-d	lubuagan	1	1	61,168	87,164		8.00	38	A	23	Kalinga, Lubuagan	P..	1970-1984				0....	8946
31-CEAC-e	ableg-salegseg					0				23		p..					0....	8947
31-CEAD	SOUTH KALINGA cluster	1	1	30,000	51,000		20.00	50	B	0		...					0....	8948
31-CEAD-a	mallango					0				0		...					0....	8949
31-CEAD-b	sumadel					0				0		...					0....	8950
31-CEAD-c	tinglayan					0				0		...					0....	8951
31-CEAD-d	bangad					0				0		...					0....	8952
31-CEB	**BALANGAO net**	1	1	11,706	16,681		7.00	44	A	41		PN.					0....	8953
31-CEBA	BALANGAO cluster	1	1	11,706	16,681		7.00	44	A	41		PN.					0....	8954
31-CEBA-a	balangao	1	1	11,706	16,681	0	7.00	44	A	41	Balangao	PN.	1966	1982			0....	8955
31-CEC	**IGOROT-KANKANAY net**	1	4	317,358	452,229		29.17	68	B	41		PN.					1.s..	8956
31-CECA	IGOROT cluster	1	1	39,297	55,998		8.00	47	A	41		PN.					0....	8957
31-CECA-a	i-gorot	1	1	39,297	55,998	0	8.00	47	A	41	Bontoc: Central*	PN.	1908-1992	1992			0....	8958
31-CECA-b	sadanga					0				41		pn.					0....	8959
31-CECA-c	bayyu					0				41		pn.					0....	8960
31-CECB	KADAKLAN-BARLIG cluster	1	1	8,060	11,485		8.00	42	A	22	Bontoc: Eastern*	P..	1977-1986				0.s..	8961
31-CECB-a	lias					0				22		p..					0.s..	8962
31-CECB-b	barlig					0				22		p..					0.s..	8963
31-CECB-c	kadaklan					0				22		p..					0.s'..	8964
31-CECC	NORTH KANKANAY cluster	1	1	91,692	130,659		21.00	57	B	41	Kankanay, Northern	PN.	1967-1980	1984			0....	8965
31-CECC-a	Proper kankanay					0				41		pn.					0....	8966
31-CECC-b	kankanay-itneg					0				41	Kankanay: Northern	PN.	1967	1984			0....	8967
31-CECD	SOUTH KANKANAY cluster	1	1	178,309	254,087		39.00	79	B	41	Kankanaey: Central	PN.	1960-1986	1990		1999	1....	8968
31-CECD-a	mankayan-buguias					0				41		pn.					1....	8969
31-CECD-b	kapangan					0				41		pn.					1....	8970
31-CECD-c	bakun-kibungan					0				41		pn.					1....	8971
31-CECD-d	guinzadan					0				41		pn.					1....	8972
31-CED	**IFUGAO net**	1	5	163,367	232,793		6.17	43	A	41		PN.					0....	8973
31-CEDA	AMGANAD-BANAUE cluster	1	2	48,885	69,659		4.62	40	A	41		PN.					0....	8974
31-CEDA-a	amganad	1	1	41,288	58,834	0	4.00	40	A	41	Ifugao: Amganad*	PN.	1962-1987	1980-1987			0....	8975
31-CEDA-b	burnay					0				41		pn.					0....	8976
31-CEDA-c	banaue	1	1	7,597	10,825	0	8.00	42	A	41	Ifugao: Banaue	Pn.	1962				0....	8977
31-CEDB	BATAD-MAYOYAO cluster	1	2	76,248	108,651		5.74	41	A	41		PN.					0....	8978
31-CEDB-a	ayangan					0				41		pn.					0....	8979
31-CEDB-b	batad	1	1	56,322	80,257	0	6.00	42	A	41	Ifugao: Batad*	PN.	1962-1965	1977			0....	8980
31-CEDB-c	ducligan					0				41		pn.					0....	8981
31-CEDB-d	mayoyao	1	1	19,926	28,394	0	5.00	39	A	41	Ifugao: Mayoyao*	Pn.	1993-1994				0....	8982
31-CEDC	TUWALI cluster	1	1	38,234	54,483		9.00	48	A	41		PN.					0....	8983
31-CEDC-a	kiangan	1	1	38,234	54,483	0	9.00	48	A	41	Ifugao: Kiangan*	PN.	1915-1993	1991			0....	8984
31-CEDC-b	hapao					0				41		pn.					0....	8985
31-CEDC-c	hungduan					0				41		pn.					0....	8986
31-CEDC-d	lagawe					0				41		pn.					0....	8987
31-CF	ISINAI chain	1	1	10,081	14,365		59.99	95	B	4		...					0....	8988
31-CFA	**ISINAI net**	1	1	10,081	14,365		59.99	95	B	4		...					0....	8989
31-CFAA	ISINAI cluster	1	1	10,081	14,365		59.99	95	B	4		...					0....	8990
31-CFAA-a	i-sinai	1	1	10,081	14,365	0	59.99	95	B	4		...					0....	8991
31-CG	KALAHAN-PANGASINAN chain	1	7	1,970,040	2,807,275		88.17	94	C	61		PNB					1Asu.	8992
31-CGA	**KALAHAN-IBALOI net**	1	6	1,959,116	2,791,708		88.65	95	C	61		PNB					1A.u.	8993
31-CGAA	KELEYI cluster	1	1	7,863	11,204		6.99	44	A	41		PN.					0....	8994
31-CGAA-a	keley-i	1	1	7,863	11,204	0	6.99	44	A	41	Ifugao: Antipolo*	PN.	1970-1993	1975-1980			0....	8995
31-CGAA-b	bayninan					0				41		pn.					0....	8996
31-CGAB	IWAK cluster	1	1	3,274	4,666		4.00	34	A	5		...					0....	8997
31-CGAB-a	i-wak	1	1	3,274	4,666	0	4.00	34	A	5		...					0....	8998
31-CGAC	KALAHAN cluster	1	1	19,645	27,994		6.00	42	A	41		PN.					0....	8999
31-CGAC-a	kayapa	1	1	19,645	27,994	0	6.00	42	A	41	Ikalahan*	PN.	1970-1984	1983			0....	9000
31-CGAC-b	tinoc					0				41		pn.					0....	9001
31-CGAD	KARAO cluster	1	1	1,702	2,425		7.99	35	A	12		...					0....	9002
31-CGAD-a	karao	1	1	1,702	2,425	0	7.99	35	A	12	Karao	...					0....	9003
31-CGAD-b	ekip					0				12		...					0....	9004
31-CGAE	IBALOI cluster	1	1	156,613	223,170		8.00	45	A	41		PN.					1....	9005
31-CGAE-a	i-baloi	1	1	156,613	223,170	0	8.00	45	A	41	Ibaloi	PN.	1965	1978			1....	9006
31-CGAE-b	daklan					0				41		pn.					1....	9007
31-CGAE-c	kabayan					0				41		pn.					1....	9008
31-CGAE-d	bokod					0				41		pn.					1....	9009
31-CGAF	PANGASINAN cluster	1	1	1,770,019	2,522,249		97.30	100	C	61		PNB					1A.u.	9010
31-CGAF-a	pangasinan	1	1	1,770,019	2,522,249	1	97.30	100	C	61	Pangasinan	PNB	1887-1964	1908-1924	1915-1983	1990	1A.u.	9011
31-CGB	**ILONGOT net**	1	1	10,924	15,567		3.00	37	A	41		PN.					0.s..	9012
31-CGBA	ILONGOT cluster	1	1	10,924	15,567		3.00	37	A	41		PN.					0.s..	9013
31-CGBA-a	i-lon-got	1	1	10,924	15,567	0	3.00	37	A	41	Ilongot	PN.	1964-1965	1982			0.s..	9014
31-CGBA-b	abaka					0				41		pn.					0.s..	9015
31-CGBA-c	e-gon-got					0				41		pn.					0.s..	9016
31-CGBA-d	i-balao					0				41		pn.					0.s..	9017
31-CGBA-e	i-talon					0				41		pn.					0.s..	9018
31-CGBA-f	i-yon-gut					0				41		pn.					0.s..	9019
31-CH	SAMBALIC-PAMPANGAN chain	1	10	2,625,972	3,741,969		92.22	98	C	61		PNB					1a.u.	9020
31-CHA	**SAMBALIC net**	1	3	224,526	319,947		42.91	82	B	41		PN.					0....	9021
31-CHAA	BOLINAO cluster	1	1	68,909	98,195		50.00	93	B	22		P..					0....	9022
31-CHAA-a	bolinao	1	1	68,909	98,195	0	50.00	93	B	22	Bolinao	P..	1963-1984				0....	9023
31-CHAB	TINA-BOTOLAN cluster	1	2	155,617	221,752		39.77	77	B	41		PN.					0....	9024
31-CHAB-a	tina	1	1	99,402	141,646	0	60.00	100	B	41	Sambal: Tina*	Pn.	1938-1979				0....	9025
31-CHAB-b	botolan	1	1	56,215	80,106	0	4.00	38	A	41	Sambal: Botolan*	PN.	1966-1974	1982			0....	9026
31-CHB	**PAMPANGAN net**	1	1	2,377,410	3,387,771		97.60	100	C	61		PNB					1a.u.	9027
31-CHBA	PAMPANGAN cluster	1	1	2,377,410	3,387,771		97.60	100	C	61		PNB					1a.u.	9028
31-CHBA-a	ka-pampangan					1				61		pnb					1c.u.	9029
31-CHBA-b	Vehicular pampangan	1	1	2,377,410	3,387,771	1	97.60	100	C	61	Pampango*	PNB	1901-1985	1908-1985	1915-1994	1990	1a.u.	9030

Continued overleaf

Table 9-13 continued

Code 1	REFERENCE NAME / Autoglossonym 2	Coun 3	Peo 4	Mother-tongue speakers in 2000 — 5	in 2025 — 6	Media radio 7	CHURCH AC% 8	E% 9	Wld 10	Tr 11	Biblioglossonym 12	Print 13-15	P-activity 16	N-activity 17	B-activity 18	J-year 19	Jayuh 20-24	Ref 25
31-CHC	**ABENLEN-AGTA net**	1	1	9,572	13,640		30.00	61	B	12		. . .					0	9031
31-CHCA	ABENLEN-AGTA cluster	1	1	9,572	13,640		30.00	61	B	12		. . .					0	9032
31-CHCA-a	abenlen-agta	1	1	9,572	13,640	0	30.00	61	B	12	Ayta, Abenlen	. . .					0	9033
31-CHD	**MAG-ANCHI-AGTA net**	1	1	5,599	7,978		20.00	48	A	22		P . .					0	9034
31-CHDA	MAG-ANCHI-AGTA cluster	1	1	5,599	7,978		20.00	48	A	22		P . .					0	9035
31-CHDA-a	mag-anchi-agta	1	1	5,599	7,978	0	20.00	48	A	22	Ayta: Mag-anchi*	P . .	1995				0	9036
31-CHE	**BATAAN-AGTA net**	1	1	767	1,093		4.95	32	A	4		. . .					0	9037
31-CHEA	BATAAN-AGTA cluster	1	1	767	1,093		4.95	32	A	4		. . .					0	9038
31-CHEA-a	bataan-agta	1	1	767	1,093	0	4.95	32	A	4		. . .					0	9039
31-CHF	**AMBALA-AGTA net**	1	1	2,226	3,172		10.02	37	A	12		. . .					0	9040
31-CHFA	AMBALA-AGTA cluster	1	1	2,226	3,172		10.02	37	A	12		. . .					0	9041
31-CHFA-a	ambala-agta	1	1	2,226	3,172	0	10.02	37	A	12	Ayta, Ambala	. . .					0	9042
31-CHG	**MAG-INDI-AGTA net**	1	1	3,335	4,752		14.99	39	A	12		. . .					0	9043
31-CHGA	MAG-INDI-AGTA cluster	1	1	3,335	4,752		14.99	39	A	12		. . .					0	9044
31-CHGA-a	mag-indi-agta	1	1	3,335	4,752	0	14.99	39	A	12	Ayta, Mag-indi	. . .					0	9045
31-CHH	**SINAUNA net**	1	1	2,537	3,616		3.98	29	A	4		. . .					0	9046
31-CHHA	SINAUNA cluster	1	1	2,537	3,616		3.98	29	A	4		. . .					0	9047
31-CHHA-a	sinauna	1	1	2,537	3,616	0	3.98	29	A	4		. . .					0	9048
31-CI	NORTH MINDORO chain	1	3	22,693	32,363		18.87	58	B	41		PN .					0	9049
31-CIA	**IRAYA net**	1	1	11,889	16,941		9.00	50	B	41		PN .					0	9050
31-CIAA	IRAYA cluster	1	1	11,889	16,941		9.00	50	B	41	Iraya	PN .	1966-1981	1991			0	9051
31-CIAA-a	abra-de-ilog					0				41		pn .					0	9052
31-CIAA-b	alag-bako					0				41		pn .					0	9053
31-CIAA-c	pagbahan					0				41		pn .					0	9054
31-CIAA-d	palauan-calavite					0				41		pn .					0	9055
31-CIAA-e	pambuhan					0				41		pn .					0	9056
31-CIAA-f	santa-cruz					0				41		pn .					0	9057
31-CIB	**ALANGAN net**	1	1	7,726	11,009		39.99	79	B	41		PN .					0	9058
31-CIBA	ALANGAN cluster	1	1	7,726	11,009		39.99	79	B	41	Alangan	PN .	1962-1981	1989			0	9059
31-CIBA-a	alangan	1	1	7,726	11,009	0	39.99	79	B	41		PN .					0	9060
31-CIC	**TADYAWAN net**	1	1	3,078	4,413		4.00	35	A	12		. . .					0	9061
31-CICA	TADYAWAN cluster	1	1	2,978	4,243		4.00	35	A	12		. . .					0	9062
31-CICA-a	tadyawan	1	1	2,978	4,243	0	4.00	35	A	12	Tadyawan	. . .					0	9063
31-CICB	PULA cluster	1	1	100	170		4.00	22	A	0		. . .					0	9064
31-CICB-a	balaban					0				0		. . .					0	9065
31-CJ	MANGYAN-PALAYAN chain	2	15	170,579	244,871		11.97	45	A	42		PN .					0	9066
31-CJA	**BUHID-TAWBUID net**	1	3	23,565	33,580		37.89	78	B	41		PN .					0	9067
31-CJAA	BUHID-BATANGAN cluster	1	2	16,728	23,837		32.94	74	B	41	Tawbuid, Eastern	PN .	1980	1995			0	9068
31-CJAA-a	buhid	1	1	9,511	13,553	0	20.00	61	B	41	Buhid	PN .	1981	1988			0	9069
31-CJAA-b	bukil					0				41		pn .					0	9070
31-CJAA-c	baribi					0				41		pn .					0	9071
31-CJAA-d	batag-non					0				41		pn .					0	9072
31-CJAA-e	batangan					0				41		pn .					0	9073
31-CJAA-f	tiron					0				41		pn .					0	9074
31-CJAA-g	suri					0				41		pn .					0	9075
31-CJAB	WEST TAWBUID cluster	1	1	6,837	9,743		49.99	87	B	12		. . .					0	9076
31-CJAB-a	West tawbuid	1	1	6,837	9,743	0	49.99	87	B	12	Tawbuid, Western	. . .					0	9077
31-CJB	**HANUNOO net**	1	1	13,074	18,630		4.00	41	A	41		PN .					0	9078
31-CJBA	HANUNOO cluster	1	1	13,074	18,630		4.00	41	A	41		PN .					0	9079
31-CJBA-a	hanu-noo	1	1	13,074	18,630	0	4.00	41	A	41	Hanunoo	PN .	1963-1981	1985			0	9080
31-CJBA-b	gubat-non					0				41		pn .					0	9081
31-CJBA-c	sorsogo-non					0				41		pn .					0	9082
31-CJBA-d	binli					0				41		pn .					0	9083
31-CJBA-e	kagankan					0				41		pn .					0	9084
31-CJBA-f	waigan					0				41		pn .					0	9085
31-CJBA-g	wawan					0				41		pn .					0	9086
31-CJBA-h	bulalakaw-non					0				41		pn .					0	9087
31-CJC	**KALAMIAN net**	1	2	17,024	24,259		34.84	67	B	22		P . .					0	9088
31-CJCA	KALAMIA cluster	1	1	7,650	10,901		4.00	33	A	22		P . .					0	9089
31-CJCA-a	kalamia-nen					0				22		P . .					0	9090
31-CJCA-b	kalamian-tagbanwa.	1	1	7,650	10,901	0	4.00	33	A	22	Tagbanwa: Kalamian*	P . .	1968-1991				0	9091
31-CJCA-c	baras					0				22		p . .					0	9092
31-CJCB	AGUTAYA cluster	1	1	9,374	13,358		60.01	95	C	22		P . .					0	9093
31-CJCB-a	agutay-nen	1	1	9,374	13,358	0	60.01	95	C	22	Agutaynen	P . .	1989-1993				0	9094
31-CJD	**BATAK-ABORLAN net**	1	3	15,414	21,964		3.39	35	A	41		PN .					0	9095
31-CJDA	EAST BATAK cluster	1	1	425	606		4.00	30	A	0		. . .					0	9096
31-CJDA-a	East batak	1	1	425	606	0	4.00	30	A	0		. . .					0	9097
31-CJDB	NORTH CENTRAL TAGBANWA. cluster	1		2	14,989	21,358	3.37	35	A	41		PN .					0	9098
31-CJDB-a	aborlan-tagbanwa	1	2	14,989	21,358	0	3.37	35	A	41	Tagbanwa	PN .	1968-1986	1992			0	9099
31-CJDB-b	tandula-non					0				41		pn .					0	9100
31-CJDB-c	silanga-non					0				41		pn .					0	9101
31-CJE	**PALAWANO net**	2	6	101,502	146,438		4.45	36	A	42		PN .					0	9102
31-CJEA	CENTRAL PALAWANO cluster	1	1	37,983	54,126		5.00	43	A	42		PN .					0	9103
31-CJEA-a	Central palawano	1	1	37,983	54,126	0	5.00	43	A	42	Palawano	PN .	1959	1964			0	9104
31-CJEB	SOUTHWEST PALAWANO cluster	1	1	4,000	6,800		5.00	24	A	0		. . .					0	9105
31-CJEB-a	Southwest palawano	1	1	4,000	6,800	0	5.00	24	A	0		. . .					0	9106
31-CJEC	SOUTHEAST PALAWANO cluster	1	2	45,010	64,139		4.23	33	A	22		P . .					0	9107
31-CJEC-a	Southeast palawano	1	2	45,010	64,139	0	4.23	33	A	22	Palawano, Southwest*	P . .	1992				0	9108
31-CJED	BUGSUK cluster	1	1	3,000	5,100		5.00	24	A	0		. . .					0	9109
31-CJED-a	bugsuk	1	1	3,000	5,100	0	5.00	24	A	0		. . .					0	9110
31-CJEE	MOLBOG cluster	2	2	9,821	13,922		0.10	25	A	22		P . .					0	9111
31-CJEE-a	molbog	2	2	9,821	13,922	0	0.10	25	A	22	Molbog	P . .	1977				0	9112
31-CJEF	BONGGI cluster	1	1	1,688	2,351		21.03	57	B	33		P . .					0	9113
31-CJEF-a	bonggi	1	1	1,688	2,351	0	21.03	57	B	33	Bonggi	P . .	1992				0	9114

Continued opposite

Table 9-13 continued

Code 1	REFERENCE NAME Autoglossonym 2	Coun 3	Peo 4	Mother-tongue speakers in 2000 5	in 2025 6	Media radio 7	CHURCH AC% 8	E% 9	Wld 10	Tr 11	Biblioglossonym 12	SCRIPTURES Print 13-15	P-activity 16	N-activity 17	B-activity 18	J-year 19	Jayuh 20-24	Ref 25
31-CK	TRANSPHILIPPINE chain	24	94	61,543,961	86,942,201		90.23	96	C	71		PNB					4Bsu.	9115
31-CKA	**TAGALOG net**	24	28	22,509,335	31,263,306		97.05	100	C	71		PNB					4Bs.	9116
31-CKAA	TAGALOG cluster	24	28	22,509,335	31,263,306		97.05	100	C	71		PNB					4Bs.	9117
31-CKAA-a	Proper tagalog	24	28	22,509,335	31,263,306	5	97.05	100	C	71	Tagalog	PNB	1898-1959	1902-1977	1905-1995	1980	4Bs.	9118
31-CKAA-b	lubang					1				71		pnb					1cs..	9122
31-CKAA-c	marinduque					1				71		pnb					1cs..	9123
31-CKAA-d	batangas					1				71		pnb					1cs..	9124
31-CKAA-e	bulacan-2					1				71		pnb					1cs..	9125
31-CKAA-f	bataan					1				71		pnb					1cs..	9126
31-CKAA-g	tanay-paete					1				71		pnb					1cs..	9127
31-CKAA-h	tayabas					1				71		pnb					1cs..	9128
31-CKB	**TAYABAS-AGTA net**									9		...					0....	9129
31-CKBA	TAYABAS-AGTA cluster			0	0		0.00	0		9		...					0....	9130
31-CKBA-a	tayabas-agta			0	0	0	0.00	0		9		...					0....	9131
31-CKC	**KATABAGA-AGTA net**									0		...					0....	9132
31-CKCA	KATABAGA-AGTA cluster			0	0		0.00	0		0		...					0....	9133
31-CKCA-a	katabaga-agta			0	0	0	0.00	0		0		...					0....	9134
31-CKD	**CENTRAL BIKOL net**	1	3	3,615,010	5,151,332		98.01	100	C	63		PNB					1A.u.	9135
31-CKDA	BICOL cluster	1	1	3,484,705	4,965,649		98.50	100	C	63		PNB					1A.u.	9136
31-CKDA-a	naga					1				63		pnb					1c.u.	9137
31-CKDA-b	legaspi	1	1	3,484,705	4,965,649	1	98.50	100	C	63	Bicolano, Central	PNB	1898-1987	1909-1987	1915-1992		1A.u.	9138
31-CKDA-c	Vehicular bicol					1				63	Bikol	PNB	1898	1909	1914	1990	1c.u.	9139
31-CKDB	BICOL-AGTA cluster	1	1	319	455		69.91	100	C	4		...					0....	9140
31-CKDB-a	isarog-agta					0				4		...					0....	9141
31-CKDB-b	iraya-agta	1	1	319	455	0	69.91	100	C	4		...					0....	9142
31-CKDC	VIRAC cluster	1	1	129,986	185,228		85.00	100	C	0		...					0....	9143
31-CKDC-a	virac	1	1	129,986	185,228	0	85.00	100	C	0		...					0....	9144
31-CKE	**NORTH BIKOL net**	1	1	116,008	165,310		70.00	100	C	0		...					0....	9145
31-CKEA	PANDAN cluster	1	1	116,008	165,310		70.00	100	C	0		...					0....	9146
31-CKEA-a	pandan	1	1	116,008	165,310	1	70.00	100	C	0		...					0....	9147
31-CKF	**SOUTH BIKOL net**	1	3	1,180,330	1,681,950		89.56	100	C	32		...					1....	9148
31-CKFA	RINCONADA cluster	1	1	321,247	457,772		70.00	100	C	0		...					0....	9149
31-CKFA-a	rinconada	1	1	321,247	457,772	1	70.00	100	C	0		...					0....	9150
31-CKFB	BUHI-DARAGA cluster	1	1	856,667	1,220,736		97.00	100	C	32		...					1....	9151
31-CKFB-a	buhi-non	1	1	856,667	1,220,736	1	97.00	100	C	32	Bicolano, Albay	...				1990	1....	9152
31-CKFB-b	oas					1				32		...					1....	9153
31-CKFB-c	daraga					1				32		...					1....	9154
31-CKFB-d	libon					1				32		...					1....	9155
31-CKFC	IRIGA cluster	1	1	2,416	3,442		50.00	80	B	4		...					0....	9156
31-CKFC-a	iriga-agta	1	1	2,416	3,442	0	50.00	80	B	4		...					0....	9157
31-CKG	**BISAYAN net**	3	23	30,240,282	43,084,135		93.93	98	C	71		PNB					2Asu.	9158
31-CKGA	DATAG cluster	1	1	50	85		10.00	34	A	4		...					0....	9159
31-CKGA-a	datag-non					0				4		...					0....	9160
31-CKGA-b	Santa-teresa					0				4		...					0....	9161
31-CKGB	KUYO cluster	1	1	134,833	192,135		60.00	100	C	41		PN.					0....	9162
31-CKGB-a	kuyo-non	1	1	134,833	192,135	0	60.00	100	C	41	Cuyono*	PN.	1939-1966	1982			0....	9163
31-CKGC	KINARAY cluster	1	2	417,056	594,299		79.82	100	C	22	Kinaray-a	P..	1982-1985				1a...	9164
31-CKGC-a	pandan-2					0				22		p..					1c...	9165
31-CKGC-b	hamtik-non	1	1	1,010	1,440	0	3.96	36	A	22		p..					1c...	9166
31-CKGC-c	hamtik-ati					0				22		p..					1c...	9167
31-CKGC-d	anini-y					0				22		p..					1c...	9168
31-CKGC-e	pototan					0				22		p..					1c...	9169
31-CKGC-f	lambunao					0				22		p..					1c...	9170
31-CKGC-g	miag-ao					0				22		p..					1c...	9171
31-CKGC-h	guimaras					0				22		p..					1c...	9172
31-CKGD	AKLAN cluster	1	2	536,886	765,053		89.11	100	C	32		P..					2....	9173
31-CKGD-a	akla-non	1	1	520,963	742,364	1	90.00	100	C	32	Aklanon	P..	1988-1993			1996	2....	9174
31-CKGD-b	buruanga					1				32		p..					1....	9175
31-CKGD-c	alcan					1				32		p..					1....	9176
31-CKGD-d	malay-non	1	1	15,923	22,689	1	60.00	95	C	32		p..					1....	9177
31-CKGE	SEMIRARA cluster	1	1	30,584	43,582		70.00	100	C	41		PN.					0.s..	9178
31-CKGE-a	semirara					0				41		pn.					0.s..	9179
31-CKGE-b	caluya-nun	1	1	30,584	43,582	0	70.00	100	C	41	Caluyanun	PN.	1981	1990			0.s..	9180
31-CKGE-c	sibay					0				41		pn.					0.s..	9181
31-CKGF	INONHAN cluster	1	1	86,184	122,811		70.00	100	C	20	Inonhan	...					0....	9182
31-CKGF-a	looc-non					0				20		...					0....	9183
31-CKGF-b	dispohol-non					0				20		...					0....	9184
31-CKGF-c	alcantara-non					0				20		...					0....	9185
31-CKGG	BANTUA-ODIONGAN cluster	1	1	89,580	127,650		70.00	100	C	22		P..					0....	9186
31-CKGG-a	odio-gan-non					0				22		p..					0....	9187
31-CKGG-b	sibale-non					0				22		p..					0....	9188
31-CKGG-c	calatrava-non					0				22		p..					0....	9189
31-CKGG-d	simara-non					0				22		p..					0....	9190
31-CKGG-e	bantua-non	1	1	89,580	127,650	0	70.00	100	C	22	Bantoanon	P..	1992				0....	9191
31-CKGH	ROMBLON cluster	1	1	261,970	373,304		88.00	100	C	20		...					1....	9192
31-CKGH-a	rombloma-non	1	1	261,970	373,304	0	88.00	100	C	20	Romblomanon	...					1....	9193
31-CKGH-b	sibuyan					0				20		...					1....	9194
31-CKGH-c	basiq					0				20		...					1....	9195
31-CKGI	MASBATE cluster	1	2	598,791	853,268		83.73	100	C	41		PN.					1....	9196
31-CKGI-a	burias					1				41		pn.					1....	9197
31-CKGI-b	masbate—o	1	1	447,093	637,101	1	85.00	100	C	41	Masbatenyo	PN.	1972-1991	1993			1....	9198
31-CKGI-c	North sorsogon	1	1	151,698	216,167	1	80.00	100	C	41		pn.					1....	9199
31-CKGJ	WARAY cluster	1	1	330,173	470,492		80.00	100	C	6		...					0....	9200
31-CKGJ-a	South sorsogon	1	1	330,173	470,492	0	80.00	100	C	6		...					0....	9201
31-CKGK	WARAY-WARAY cluster	1	1	3,566,111	5,081,651		98.80	100	C	61	Samarenyo*	PNB	1908-1962	1928	1937-1984	1990	2a.u.	9202
31-CKGK-a	North samaran					1				61		pnb					1c.u.	9203
31-CKGK-b	South samaran					1				61		pnb					1c.u.	9204
31-CKGK-c	leyte					1				61		pnb					1c.u.	9205
31-CKGK-d	homo-nhon					1				61		pnb					1c.u.	9206
31-CKGL	HILIGAY cluster	1	1	7,132,221	10,163,301		97.90	100	C	71		PNB					2Asu.	9207
31-CKGL-a	panay					1				71		pnb					1csu.	9208
31-CKGL-b	bantayan					1				71		pnb					1csu.	9209
31-CKGL-c	bacolod					1				71		pnb					1csu.	9210
31-CKGL-d	kawayan					1				71		pnb					1csu.	9211

Continued overleaf

Table 9-13 continued

Code 1	REFERENCE NAME Autoglossonym 2	Coun 3	Peo 4	Mother-tongue speakers in 2000 5	in 2025 6	Media radio 7	CHURCH AC% 8	E% 9	Wld 10	Tr 11	Biblioglossonym 12	Print 13-15	P-activity 16	N-activity 17	B-activity 18	J-year 19	Jayuh 20-24	Ref 25
31-CKGL-e	Vehicular hiligay	1	1	7,132,221	10,163,301	5	97.90	100	C	71	Hiligaynon	PNB	1900-1953	1903-1960	1912-1982	1990	2Asu.	9212
31-CKGM	CAPIZ cluster	1	1	795,476	1,133,540		95.00	100	C	4		...					0....	9213
31-CKGM-a	capiz-non	1	1	795,476	1,133,540	0	95.00	100	C	4		...					0....	9214
31-CKGN	PANAY-ATI cluster	1	1	2,355	3,356		5.01	35	A	6		...					0....	9215
31-CKGN-a	barotac					0				6		...					0....	9216
31-CKGN-b	malay-ati					0				6		...					0....	9217
31-CKGO	POROHA cluster	1	1	30,128	42,932		75.00	100	C	4		...					0....	9218
31-CKGO-a	poroha-non	1	1	30,128	42,932	0	75.00	100	C	4		...					0....	9219
31-CKGP	CEBUAN cluster	1	1	14,434,190	20,568,489		98.20	100	C	71		PNB					2Asu.	9220
31-CKGP-a	Vehicular cebuan	1	1	14,434,190	20,568,489	2	98.20	100	C	71	Cebuano	PNB	1902-1956	1908-1988	1917-1981	1980	2Asu.	9221
31-CKGP-b	cebuan-negros					1				71		pnb					1csu.	9222
31-CKGP-c	cebuan-no					1				71		pnb					1csu.	9223
31-CKGP-d	cebuan-masbate					1				71		pnb					1csu.	9224
31-CKGP-e	cebuan-leyte					1				71		pnb					1csu.	9225
31-CKGP-f	bohol-a-no					1				71		pnb					1csu.	9226
31-CKGP-g	cebuan-siquijor					1				71		pnb					1csu.	9227
31-CKGP-h	North visayan					1				71		pnb					1csu.	9228
31-CKGP-i	South visayan					1				71		pnb					1csu.	9229
31-CKGQ	BUTUAN-TAUSUG cluster	3	4	1,261,928	1,790,430		34.85	58	B	41		PN.					0.s..	9230
31-CKGQ-a	butuan-non	1	1	486,968	693,922	0	90.00	100	C	41		pn.					0.s..	9231
31-CKGQ-b	moro-joloan-no					0				41		pn.					0.s..	9232
31-CKGQ-c	suluk					0				41		pn.					0.s..	9233
31-CKGQ-d	Vehicular tau-sug	3	3	774,960	1,096,508	0	0.20	31	A	41	Tausug	PN.	1918-1993	1985			0.s..	9234
31-CKGR	SURIGAO cluster	1	1	531,766	757,757		89.00	100	C	5		...					0....	9235
31-CKGR-a	surigao-non	1	1	531,766	757,757	0	89.00	100	C	5		...					0....	9236
31-CKGR-b	cantilan					0				5		...					0....	9237
31-CKGR-c	jaun-jaun					0				5		...					0....	9238
31-CKGR-d	naturalis					0				5		...					0....	9239
31-CKGR-e	dinagat					0				5		...					0....	9240
31-CKGR-f	siargo					0				5		...					0....	9241
31-CKH	**SORSOGON-AGTA net**	1	1	53	76		81.13	100	C	8		...					0....	9242
31-CKHA	SORSOGON-AGTA cluster	1	1	53	76		81.13	100	C	8		...					0....	9243
31-CKHA-a	sorsogon-agta	1	1	53	76	0	81.13	100	C	8		...					0....	9244
31-CKI	**SULOD-AGTA net**	1	1	22,015	31,371		3.00	27	A	4		...					0....	9245
31-CKIA	SULOD-AGTA cluster	1	1	22,015	31,371		3.00	27	A	4		...					0....	9246
31-CKIA-a	sulod-agta	1	1	22,015	31,371	0	3.00	27	A	4		...					0....	9247
31-CKJ	**MAGAHAT-AGTA net**	1	1	30	51		6.67	23	A	0		...					0....	9248
31-CKJA	MAGAHAT-AGTA cluster	1	1	30	51		6.67	23	A	0		...					0....	9249
31-CKJA-a	magahat -agta	1	1	30	51	0	6.67	23	A	0		...					0....	9250
31-CKK	**NEGROS-AGTA net**	1	1	20	34		5.00	25	A	0		...					0....	9251
31-CKKA	NEGROS-AGTA cluster	1	1	20	34		5.00	25	A	0		...					0....	9252
31-CKKA-a	negros-agta	1	1	20	34	0	5.00	25	A	0		...					0....	9253
31-CKL	**KAROLANOS net**	1	1	15,193	21,650		40.00	73	B	4		...					0....	9254
31-CKLA	KAROLANOS cluster	1	1	15,193	21,650		40.00	73	B	4		...					0....	9255
31-CKLA-a	karolanos	1	1	15,193	21,650	0	40.00	73	B	4		...					0....	9256
31-CKM	**MAMANWA net**	1	1	2,294	3,269		2.01	34	A	41		PN.					0....	9257
31-CKMA	MAMANWA cluster	1	1	2,294	3,269		2.01	34	A	41		PN.					0....	9258
31-CKMA-a	mamanwa	1	1	2,294	3,269	0	2.01	34	A	41	Minamanwa*	PN.	1966-1967	1982			0....	9259
31-CKN	**MANSAKAN net**	1	9	684,986	1,031,097		49.91	76	B	42		PN.					0.s..	9260
31-CKNA	KAMAYO cluster	1	1	7,597	10,825		49.99	84	B	4		...					0....	9261
31-CKNA-a	North kamayo					0				4		...					0....	9262
31-CKNA-b	South kamayo					0				4		...					0....	9263
31-CKNB	EAST DAVAWENYO cluster	1	1	200,000	340,000		70.00	98	C	0		...					0....	9264
31-CKNB-a	East davawenyo	1	1	200,000	340,000	0	70.00	98	C	0		...					0....	9265
31-CKNC	WEST DAVAWENYO cluster	1	1	222,172	316,591		80.00	100	C	20		...					0....	9266
31-CKNC-a	West davawenyo	1	1	222,172	316,591	0	80.00	100	C	20		...					0....	9267
31-CKND	MANDAYA cluster	1	4	99,934	142,404		6.08	39	A	42		PN.					0....	9268
31-CKND-a	sangab	1	1	7,597	10,825	0	10.00	39	A	42		pn.					0....	9269
31-CKND-b	cataelano	1	1	29,870	42,564	0	6.00	36	A	42		pn.					0....	9270
31-CKND-c	karaga	1	1	4,467	6,365	0	1.01	25	A	42		pn.					0....	9271
31-CKND-d	mansaka	1	1	58,000	82,650	0	6.00	42	A	42	Mansaka	PN.	1959-1968	1975			0....	9272
31-CKNE	KALAGAN cluster	1	1	78,587	111,986		1.00	22	A	22	Kalagan	P..	1989				0.s..	9273
31-CKNE-a	i-samal					0				22		p..					0.s..	9274
31-CKNE-b	piso					0				22		p..					0.s..	9275
31-CKNE-c	tumuaong					0				22		p..					0.s..	9276
31-CKNE-d	lactan					0				22		p..					0.s..	9277
31-CKNF	KAGAN cluster	1	1	9,177	13,077		7.00	42	A	22	Kalagan: Kagan*	P..					0.s..	9278
31-CKNF-a	kagan	1	1	9,177	13,077	0	7.00	42	A	22		P..	1980				0.s..	9279
31-CKNG	TAGAKAULU cluster	1	1	67,519	96,214		19.00	56	B	22		P..					0....	9280
31-CKNG-a	tagakaulu	1	1	67,519	96,214	0	19.00	56	B	22	Kalagan: Tagakaulu*	P..	1964-1981				0....	9281
31-CKO	**MANOBO net**	1	16	646,186	929,058		27.41	64	B	45		PN.					0.s..	9282
31-CKOA	KAGAYANEN cluster	1	1	44,653	63,630		70.00	100	C	22	Kagayanen	P..	1983				0.s..	9283
31-CKOA-a	cagayanen					0				22		p..					0.s..	9284
31-CKOB	KINAMIGIN cluster	1	1	112,544	160,374		40.00	78	B	4		...					0....	9285
31-CKOB-a	kinamigin	1	1	112,544	160,374	0	40.00	78	B	4		...					0....	9286
31-CKOC	BINUKID cluster	1	1	130,981	186,646		39.00	81	B	41		PN.					0....	9287
31-CKOC-a	binukid-non	1	1	130,981	186,646	0	39.00	81	B	41	Binukid	PN.	1956-1979	1986			0....	9288
31-CKOD	HIGAO cluster	1	1	6,715	9,569		10.01	43	A	22		P..					0....	9289
31-CKOD-a	higao-non	1	1	6,715	9,569	0	10.01	43	A	22	Higaonon	P..	1987				0....	9290
31-CKOE	AGUSAN cluster	1	1	61,168	87,164		4.00	39	A	22		P..					0.s..	9291
31-CKOE-a	agusan	1	1	61,168	87,164	0	4.00	39	A	22	Manobo: Agusan*	P..	1962-1992				0.s..	9292
31-CKOE-b	omayam-non					0				22		p..					0.s..	9293
31-CKOE-c	adga-wan					0				22		p..					0.s..	9294
31-CKOE-d	banua-non					0				22		p..					0.s..	9295
31-CKOE-e	sagunto					0				22		p..					0.s..	9296
31-CKOF	DIBABA cluster	1	1	16,508	23,523		8.90	48	A	41		PN.					0....	9297
31-CKOF-a	dibaba-won	1	1	16,508	23,523	0	8.90	48	A	41	Dibabawon*	PN.	1967	1978			0....	9298
31-CKOF-b	manguagan					0				41		pn.					0....	9299
31-CKOG	KABUNSUWAN cluster	1	1	7,597	10,825		49.99	80	B	4		...					0....	9300
31-CKOG-a	kabunsuwan	1	1	7,597	10,825	0	49.99	80	B	4		...					0....	9301

Continued opposite

Table 9-13 continued

Code 1	REFERENCE NAME Autoglossonym 2	Coun 3	Peo 4	Mother-tongue speakers in 2000 5	in 2025 6	Media radio 7	CHURCH AC% 8	E% 9	Wld 10	Tr 11	Biblioglossonym 12	SCRIPTURES Print 13-15	P–activity 16	N–activity 17	B–activity 18	J-year 19	Jayuh 20-24	Ref 25
31-CKOH	MANOBO-AGTA cluster	1	3	53,473	76,198		6.27	43	A	45		PN.					0.s..	9302
31-CKOH-a	manobo-agta	1	3	53,473	76,198	0	6.27	43	A	45	Manobo: Ata*	PN.	1959-1981	1978			0.s..	9303
31-CKOI	MATIG-SALUG cluster	1	1	37,406	53,303		3.00	37	A	23		P..					0.s..	9304
31-CKOI-a	matig-salug	1	1	37,406	53,303	0	3.00	37	A	23	Manobo: Matig Salug*	P..	1972-1987				0.s..	9305
31-CKOI-b	kulamanen					0				23		p..					0.s..	9306
31-CKOI-c	tigwa					0				23	Manobo: Tigwa	P..	1972				0.s..	9307
31-CKOI-d	tala ingod					0				23		p..					0.s..	9308
31-CKOI-e	langilan					0				23		p..					0.s..	9309
31-CKOJ	OBO cluster	1	1	13,780	19,637		4.20	33	A	22		P..					0....	9310
31-CKOJ-a	obo	1	1	13,780	19,637	0	4.20	33	A	22	Manobo: Obo*	P..	1941-1993				0....	9311
31-CKOK	PULANGI cluster	1	1	30,000	51,000		4.00	22	A	0		...					0....	9312
31-CKOK-a	ilentun-gen					0				0		...					0....	9313
31-CKOK-b	kiriyente-ken					0				0		...					0....	9314
31-CKOK-c	Proper pulangi-yen					0				0		...					0....	9315
31-CKOL	ILIANEN cluster	1	1	15,292	21,791		9.00	47	A	41		PN.					0.s..	9316
31-CKOL-a	ilia-nen	1	1	15,292	21,791	0	9.00	47	A	41	Manobo: Ilianen*	PN.	1961-1981	1989			0.s..	9317
31-CKOL-b	livunga-nen					0				41		pn.					0.s..	9318
31-CKOL-c	puleni-yan					0				41		pn.					0.s..	9319
31-CKOM	TAGABAWA cluster	1	1	52,394	74,661		20.00	58	B	22		P..					0....	9320
31-CKOM-a	tagabawa	1	1	52,394	74,661	0	20.00	58	B	22	Tagabawa*	P..	1952-1992				0....	9321
31-CKON	COTABATO cluster	1	1	17,829	25,407		2.00	34	A	41		PN.					0....	9322
31-CKON-a	Proper cotabato	1	1	17,829	25,407	0	2.00	34	A	41	Manobo: Cotabato*	PN.	1964-1979	1988			0....	9323
31-CKON-b	tasaday					0				41		pn.					0....	9324
31-CKON-c	blit					0				41		pn.					0....	9325
31-CKOO	SARANGANI cluster	1	1	45,846	65,330		50.00	93	B	41	Manobo: Sarangani*	PN.	1967-1985	1982			0....	9326
31-CKOO-a	Southwest sarangani					0				41		pn.					0....	9327
31-CKOO-b	Northeast sarangani					0				41		pn.					0....	9328
31-CKP	**DANAO net**	2	3	2,273,662	3,239,621		0.97	38	A	44		PN.					2.s..	9329
31-CKPA	MARANAO-ILA cluster	2	2	1,084,961	1,545,741		1.98	40	A	44	Maranao	PN.	1937-1967	1981			2.s..	9330
31-CKPA-a	ma-ranao	2	2	1,084,961	1,545,741	0	1.98	40	A	44	Maranao	PN.	1937-1967	1981		1989	2.s..	9331
31-CKPA-b	sabah-ila-nun					0				44		pn.					1.s..	9332
31-CKPA-c	mindanao-ila-non					0				44		pn.					1.s..	9333
31-CKPA-d	isebanga-nen					0				44		pn.					1.s..	9334
31-CKPB	MAGINDANAO cluster	1	1	1,188,701	1,693,880	1	0.05	37	A	32	Magindanao*	P..	1946-1995			1996	2.s..	9335
31-CKPB-a	laya					1				32		p..					1.s..	9336
31-CKPB-b	ilud					1				32		p..					1.s..	9337
31-CKPB-c	biwangan					1				32		p..					1.s..	9338
31-CKPB-d	sibugay					1				32		p..					1.s..	9339
31-CKPB-e	tagakawa-nan					1				32		p..					1.s..	9340
31-CKQ	**SUBANON net**	1	4	238,557	339,941		21.93	60	B	41		PN.					0.s..	9341
31-CKQA	TUBOY-SALOG cluster	1	1	13,780	19,637		2.00	32	A	12		...					0....	9342
31-CKQA-a	tuboy					0				12	Subanen, Northern	...					0....	9343
31-CKQA-b	dapitan					0				12		...					0....	9344
31-CKQA-c	salog					0				12		...					0....	9345
31-CKQA-d	dikayu					0				12		...					0....	9346
31-CKQB	LAPUYAN cluster	1	1	41,273	58,813		9.00	46	A	41		PN.					0....	9347
31-CKQB-a	lapuyan	1	1	41,273	58,813	0	9.00	46	A	41	Subanon: Margosatubig*	PN.	1939-1967	1982			0....	9348
31-CKQC	SINDANGAN cluster	1	1	122,336	174,327		27.00	66	B	41		PN.					0....	9349
31-CKQC-a	sindangan	1	1	122,336	174,327	0	27.00	66	B	41	Subanon: Sindangan*	PN.	1973-1983	1992			0....	9350
31-CKQC-b	East kolibugan					0				41		pn.					0....	9351
31-CKQD	SIOCON cluster	1	1	61,168	87,164		25.00	63	B	41	Subanon: Western*	PN.	1971-1974	1996			0.s..	9352
31-CKQD-a	siocon					0				41		pn.					0.s..	9353
31-CKQD-b	Central kolibugan					0				41		pn.					0.s..	9354
31-CKQD-c	West kolibugan					0				41		pn.					0.s..	9355
31-D	**SOUTH MINDANAO set**	1	5	587,077	836,574		48.35	82	B	41		PN.					1.s..	9356
31-DA	TIRURAY-BILIC chain	1	4	556,736	793,339		50.61	84	B	41		PN.					1.s..	9357
31-DAA	**TIRURAY net**	1	1	61,290	87,337		20.00	63	B	41		PN.					0.s..	9358
31-DAAA	TIRURAY cluster	1	1	61,290	87,337		20.00	63	B	41		PN.					0.s..	9359
31-DAAA-a	tiruray	1	1	61,290	87,337	0	20.00	63	B	41	Tiruray	PN.	1955	1983			0.s..	9360
31-DAB	**BILIC net**	1	3	495,446	706,002		54.39	86	B	41		PN.					1.s..	9361
31-DABA	TBOLI cluster	1	1	104,788	149,321		10.00	51	B	41	Tboli	PN.	1963-1992	1979-1992			1.s..	9362
31-DABA-a	sinalon					0				41		pn.					1.s..	9363
31-DABA-b	kiamba					0				41		pn.					1.s..	9364
31-DABA-c	ubu					0				41		pn.					1.s..	9365
31-DABB	BLAAN cluster	1	2	390,658	556,681		66.30	96	C	41		PN.					1.s..	9366
31-DABB-a	koronadal	1	1	152,921	217,909	1	45.00	90	B	41	Blaan: Koronadal*	PN.	1955-1986	1995-1996		1999	1.s..	9367
31-DABB-b	sarangani-blaan	1	1	237,737	338,772	1	80.00	100	C	41	Blaan: Sarangani*	PN.	1968	1981			1.s..	9368
31-DB	BAGOBO chain	1	1	30,341	43,235		7.00	42	A	2		...					0....	9369
31-DBA	**BAGOBO net**	1	1	30,341	43,235		7.00	42	A	2		...					0....	9370
31-DBAA	GIANGAN cluster	1	1	30,341	43,235		7.00	42	A	2		...					0....	9371
31-DBAA-a	giangan	1	1	30,341	43,235	0	7.00	42	A	2		...					0....	9372
31-E	**SAMA-YAKAN set**	4	16	633,760	903,033		2.12	28	A	41		PN.					1.s..	9373
31-EA	SAMA-YAKAN chain	4	16	633,760	903,033		2.12	28	A	41		PN.					1.s..	9374
31-EAA	**ABAK net**	1	1	20,959	29,866		60.00	100	B	22		P..					0....	9375
31-EAAA	ABAK cluster	1	1	20,959	29,866		60.00	100	B	22		P..					0....	9376
31-EAAA-a	abak-non	1	1	20,959	29,866	1	60.00	100	B	22	Sama: Abaknon*	P..	1981-1982				0....	9377
31-EAB	**YAKAN net**	2	2	91,399	129,889		0.10	33	A	41		PN.					0.s..	9378
31-EABA	YAKAN cluster	2	2	91,399	129,889		0.10	33	A	41		PN.					0.s..	9379
31-EABA-a	yakan	2	2	91,399	129,889	1	0.10	33	A	41	Yakan	PN.	1959-1966	1984			0.s..	9380
31-EAC	**SAMA-BAJAW net**	4	13	521,402	743,278		0.15	24	A	41		PN.					1.s..	9381
31-EACA	BALANGINGI cluster	2	2	143,652	203,002		0.04	23	A	22		P..					0.s..	9382
31-EACA-a	balingingi	2	2	143,652	203,002	1	0.04	23	A	22	Sama: Balangingi*	P..	1981-1983				0.s..	9383
31-EACA-b	si-buguey					1				22		p..					0.s..	9384
31-EACA-c	lutangan					1				22		p..					0.s..	9385
31-EACA-d	si-buco					1				22		p..					0.s..	9386
31-EACA-e	daongdung									22		p..					0.s..	9387
31-EACA-f	kabinga'an					1				22		p..					0.s..	9388
31-EACB	SOUTH SAMA cluster	3	5	202,847	286,638		0.01	28	A	41		PN.					1.s..	9389

Continued overleaf

Table 9-13 continued

Code 1	REFERENCE NAME / Autoglossonym 2	Coun 3	Peo 4	Mother-tongue speakers in 2000 5	in 2025 6	Media radio 7	AC% 8	E% 9	Wld 10	Tr 11	Biblioglossonym 12	Print 13-15	P-activity 16	N-activity 17	B-activity 18	J-year 19	Jayuh 20-24	Ref 25
31-EACB-a	siasi	2	2	135,648	191,838	1	0.01	28	A	41	Sinama	PN.	1966	1987		1999	1.s..	9390
31-EACB-b	di-laut					1				41		pn.					1.s..	9391
31-EACB-c	ubian					1				41		pn.					1.s..	9392
31-EACB-d	si-munul					1				41		pn.					1.s..	9393
31-EACB-e	si-butuq	2	2	66,775	94,253	1	0.01	27	A	41	Sama: Southern*	Pn.	1979-1981				1.s..	9394
31-EACB-f	tandu-bas					1				41		pn.					1.s..	9395
31-EACB-g	east-coast-sama					1				41		pn.					1.s..	9396
31-EACB-h	pala'au					1				41		pn.					1.s..	9406
31-EACB-i	kajoa					1				41		pn.					1.s..	9407
31-EACB-j	bacan-bajaw					1				41		pn.					1.s..	9408
31-EACB-k	obi-bajaw					1				41		pn.					1.s..	9409
31-EACB-l	sula-mu					1				41		pn.					1.s..	9410
31-EACB-m	poso-bajaw					1				41		pn.					1.s..	9411
31-EACB-n	butung-bajaw					1				41		pn.					1.s..	9412
31-EACB-o	kabaena-bajaw					1				41		pn.					1.s..	9416
31-EACC	PANGUTARAN cluster	1	1	51,193	79,825		1.00	27	A	41		PN.					0.s..	9417
31-EACC-a	panguturan	1	1	26,193	37,325	1	1.00	38	A	41	Sama: Pangutaran*	PN.	1979-1986	1994			0.s..	9418
31-EACC-b	lapara					1				41		pn.					0.s..	9419
31-EACD	WEST-COAST-BAJAU cluster	2	2	73,377	102,235		0.25	16	A	0		...					0....	9420
31-EACD-a	sandakan-bajau					0				0		...					0....	9421
31-EACD-b	jembongan					0				0		...					0....	9422
31-EACD-c	banggi					0				0		...					0....	9423
31-EACD-d	pitas-bajau	1	1	61,632	85,804	0	0.30	15	A	0		...					0....	9424
31-EACD-e	Northwest bajau-Borneo					0				0		...					0....	9425
31-EACE	MAPUN cluster	2	3	50,333	71,578		0.02	25	A	41		PN.					0....	9430
31-EACE-a	mapun	2	3	50,333	71,578	1	0.02	25	A	41	Mapun*	PN.	1966-1985	1987			0....	9431
31-F	**IDAAN set**	1	1	8,244	11,477		20.00	57	B	22		P..					0.s..	9432
31-FA	IDAAN chain	1	1	8,244	11,477		20.00	57	B	22		P..					0.s..	9433
31-FAA	**IDAAN net**	1	1	8,244	11,477		20.00	57	B	22		P..					0.s..	9434
31-FAAA	IDAAN cluster	1	1	8,244	11,477		20.00	57	B	22		P..					0.s..	9435
31-FAAA-a	ida'an	1	1	8,244	11,477	0	20.00	57	B	22	Idaan	P..	1987				0.s..	9436
31-FAAA-b	bagahak					0				22		p..					0.s..	9437
31-FAAA-c	subpan					0				22		p..					0.s..	9438
31-G	**NORTHEAST BORNEO set**	3	61	989,571	1,366,820		32.26	68	B	61		PNB					4.s..	9439
31-GA	PAITANIC chain	1	6	49,117	69,765		30.64	64	B	33		P..					0.s..	9440
31-GAA	**PAITANIC net**	1	6	49,117	69,765		30.64	64	B	33		P..					0.s..	9441
31-GAAA	ABAI-SUNGAI cluster	1	1	300	510		20.00	50	B	0		...					0....	9442
31-GAAA-a	abai-sungai	1	1	300	510	0	20.00	50	B	0		...					0....	9443
31-GAAB	TAMBANUA cluster	1	2	29,000	40,373		24.90	55	B	33	Tombonuwo	P..	1987-1992				0.s..	9444
31-GAAB-a	Central tambanua					0				33		p..					0.s..	9445
31-GAAB-b	West tambanua					0				33		p..					0.s..	9446
31-GAAB-c	North tambanua					0				33		p..					0.s..	9447
31-GAAB-d	lingkabau-sugut	1	1	4,734	6,590	0	50.00	82	B	33		p..						9448
31-GAAC	LINGKABAU cluster	1	1	4,000	6,800		50.00	86	B	0		...					0....	9449
31-GAAC-a	lingkabau	1	1	4,000	6,800	0	50.00	86	B	0		...					0....	9450
31-GAAD	LANAS-LOBU cluster	1	1	3,937	5,481		19.99	52	B	4		...					0....	9451
31-GAAD-a	lobu					0				4		...					0....	9452
31-GAAD-b	rumanau-alab					0				4		...					0....	9453
31-GAAE	TAMPIAS-LOBU cluster	1	1	2,591	3,608		19.99	57	B	6		...					0....	9454
31-GAAE-a	tampias-lobu	1	1	2,591	3,608	0	19.99	57	B	6		...					0....	9455
31-GAAF	SEGAMA cluster	1	1	200	340		20.00	51	B	0		...					0....	9456
31-GAAF-a	segama	1	1	200	340	0	20.00	51	B	0		...					0....	9457
31-GAAG	UPPER KINABATANGAN cluster	1	1	7,866	10,950		50.00	92	B	22	Kinabatangan, Upper	P..	1984-1993				0.s..	9458
31-GAAG-a	kalabuan	1	1	7,866	10,950	0	50.00	92	B	22		p..					0.s..	9459
31-GAAG-b	makiang					0				22		p..					0.s..	9460
31-GAAG-c	sinarupa					0				22		p..					0.s..	9461
31-GAAH	SINABU cluster	1	1	1,223	1,703		39.98	75	B	11		...					0.s..	9462
31-GAAH-a	sinabu	1	1	1,223	1,703	0	39.98	75	B	11		...					0.s..	9463
31-GB	DUSUNIC chain	3	35	802,865	1,108,656		32.40	69	B	61		PNB					4.s..	9464
31-GBA	**KADAZAN-DUSUN net**	3	30	655,590	901,336		38.38	78	B	61		PNB					4.s..	9465
31-GBAA	DUMPAS cluster	1	1	1,079	1,502		8.99	36	A	5		...					0....	9466
31-GBAA-a	dumpas	1	1	1,079	1,502	0	8.99	36	A	5		...					0....	9467
31-GBAB	RUNGUS cluster	1	1	18,200	25,338		60.00	100	C	41		PN.					0.s..	9468
31-GBAB-a	rungus	1	1	18,200	25,338	0	60.00	100	C	41	Momogun*	PN.	1961-1966	1981			0.s..	9469
31-GBAB-b	nulu					0				41		pn.					0.s..	9470
31-GBAB-c	gonsomon					0				41		pn.					0.s..	9471
31-GBAC	KIMARAGANG cluster	1	1	13,447	18,720		50.00	89	B	12	Kimaragang	...					0.s..	9472
31-GBAC-a	tandek					0				12		...					0.s..	9473
31-GBAC-b	pitas-kimaragang					0				12		...					0.s..	9474
31-GBAC-c	sandayo					0				12		...					0.s..	9475
31-GBAD	SONSOGON cluster	1	1	2,945	4,100		10.02	40	A	0		...					0....	9476
31-GBAD-a	marudu-sonsogon	1	1	2,945	4,100	0	10.02	40	A	0		...					0....	9477
31-GBAD-b	pitas-sonsogon					0				0		...					0....	9478
31-GBAE	TINAGAS-TALANTANG cluster	1	3	15,336	21,349		35.35	68	B	6		...					0....	9479
31-GBAE-a	marudu-tinagas	1	1	1,800	2,505	0	20.00	47	A	6		...					0....	9480
31-GBAE-b	tanggal					0				6		...					0....	9481
31-GBAE-c	Tilau-llau					0				6		...					0....	9482
31-GBAE-d	talantang	1	1	1,297	1,805	0	59.98	90	B	6		...					0....	9483
31-GBAF	TEBILUNG cluster	1	1	2,945	4,100		40.00	68	B	2		...					0....	9484
31-GBAF-a	tebilung	1	1	2,945	4,100	0	40.00	68	B	2		...					0....	9485
31-GBAG	TEMPASUK cluster	1	1	9,465	13,177		29.99	67	B	0		...					0....	9486
31-GBAG-a	tempasuk	1	1	9,465	13,177	0	29.99	67	B	0		...					0....	9487
31-GBAH	LOTUD cluster	1	1	2,000	3,400		30.00	65	B	0		...					0....	9488
31-GBAH-a	lotud	1	1	2,000	3,400	0	30.00	65	B	0		...					0....	9489
31-GBAI	CENTRAL DUSUN cluster	1	1	170,474	237,336		50.00	100	B	61		PNB				1989	4.s..	9490
31-GBAI-a	sinulihan					0				61		pnb					1.s..	9491
31-GBAI-b	kadazan					0				61		pnb					1.s..	9492
31-GBAI-c	tagaro					0				61		pnb					1.s..	9493
31-GBAI-d	kiundu					0				61		pnb					1.s..	9494
31-GBAI-e	pahu'					0				61		pnb					1.s..	9495
31-GBAI-f	sokid					0				61		pnb					1.s..	9496
31-GBAI-g	bundu					0				61	Dusun: Bundu	Pnb	1959				1.s..	9497
31-GBAI-h	ulu-yuaran					0				61		pnb					1.s..	9498

Continued opposite

Table 9-13 continued

Code 1	REFERENCE NAME / Autoglossonym 2	Coun 3	Peo 4	Mother-tongue speakers in 2000 5	in 2025 6	Media radio 7	AC% 8	E% 9	Wld 10	Tr 11	Biblioglossonym 12	Print 13-15	P-activity 16	N-activity 17	B-activity 18	J-year 19	Jayuh 20-24	Ref 25
31-GBAI-i	luba					0				61		pnb					1.s..	9499
31-GBAI-j	menggatal					0				61		pnb					1.s..	9500
31-GBAI-k	ranau	1	1	170,474	237,336	0	50.00	100	B	61	Dusun, Central	PNB	1956-1984	1971-1975	1990		1.s..	9501
31-GBAI-l	beaufort					0				61		pnb					1.s..	9502
31-GBAJ	EAST KADAZAN cluster	2	4	41,184	56,486		34.35	71	B	41		PN.					0.s..	9503
31-GBAJ-a	labuk-kadazan	1	1	20,607	28,689	0	55.00	99	B	41	Kadazan: Labuk-kinabatan*	PN.	1976-1984	1995-1996			0.s..	9504
31-GBAJ-b	mangkaak									41		pn.					0.s..	9505
31-GBAJ-c	sukang					0				41		pn.					0.s..	9506
31-GBAJ-d	sogilitan					0				41		pn.					0.s..	9507
31-GBAJ-e	tompulung					0				41		pn.					0.s..	9508
31-GBAJ-f	kinabatangan-sungai	2	3	20,577	27,797		13.68	43	A	41		pn.					0.s..	9509
31-GBAJ-g	orang-sungai					0				41		pn.					0.s..	9510
31-GBAJ-h	tindakon-sungai					0				41		pn.					0.s..	9511
31-GBAK	MINOKOK cluster	1	1	3,000	5,100		20.00	50	B	0		...					0....	9512
31-GBAK-a	minokok	1	1	3,000	5,100	0	20.00	50	B	0		...					0....	9513
31-GBAL	TAMBUNAN cluster	3	11	270,375	364,353		31.75	67	B	61		PNB					0....	9514
31-GBAL-a	tambunan					0				61		pnb					0....	9515
31-GBAL-b	monsok-dusun	3	11	270,375	364,353	0	31.75	67	B	61	Dusun: Ranau*	PNB	1956-1992	1971	1990		0....	9516
31-GBAM	KUIJAU cluster	1	1	7,919	11,025		25.00	62	B	5		...					0....	9517
31-GBAM-a	kuijau	1	1	7,919	11,025		25.00	62	B	5		...					0....	9518
31-GBAM-b	minansut					0				5		...					0....	9519
31-GBAM-c	menindal					0				5		...					0....	9520
31-GBAN	GANAQ cluster	1	1	2,881	4,010		19.99	57	B	5		...					0....	9521
31-GBAN-a	ganaq	1	1	2,881	4,010	0	19.99	57	B	5		...					0....	9522
31-GBAO	WEST KADAZAN cluster	1	1	84,392	117,491		40.00	79	B	22	Kadazan, Coastal	P..	1986				0....	9523
31-GBAO-a	putatan					0				22		p..					0....	9524
31-GBAO-b	penampang					0				22		p..					0....	9525
31-GBAO-c	papar-kadazan					0				22		p..					0....	9526
31-GBAO-d	membakut-kadazan					0				22		p..					0....	9527
31-GBAP	KLIAS cluster	1	1	1,473	2,050		24.98	53	B	4		...					0....	9528
31-GBAP-a	klias	1	1	1,473	2,050	0	24.98	53	B	4		...					0....	9529
31-GBAQ	NORTH BISAYA cluster	1	1	8,475	11,799		12.00	42	A	13		...					0....	9530
31-GBAQ-a	tatanaq	1	1	8,475	11,799	0	12.00	42	A	13	Tatana	...					0....	9531
31-GBAQ-b	North bisaya					0				13		...					0....	9532
31-GBB	**BISAYA net**	3	5	147,275	207,320		5.80	31	A	24		P..					0....	9533
31-GBBA	CENTRAL BISAYA cluster	1	1	15,840	22,053		1.00	28	A	0		...					0....	9534
31-GBBA-a	Central bisaya	1	1	15,840	22,053	0	1.00	28	A	0		...					0....	9535
31-GBBB	SOUTH BISAYA cluster	3	4	101,435	134,267		4.72	30	A	24		P..					0....	9536
31-GBBB-a	Lower bisaya					0				24		p..					0....	9537
31-GBBB-b	bisaya-M.					0				24		p..					0....	9538
31-GBBB-c	Upper bisaya					0				24	Bisaya*	P..	1938				0....	9539
31-GBBC	LIMBANG-TUTONG cluster	2	1	30,000	51,000		12.00	37	A	0		...					0....	9540
31-GBBC-a	limbang					0				0		...					0....	9541
31-GC	MURUTIC chain	2	20	137,589	188,399		32.04	62	B	41		PN.					0.s..	9542
31-GCA	**MURUT net**	2	12	84,995	117,663		42.45	77	B	41		PN.					0.s..	9543
31-GCAA	BEAUFORT-MURUT cluster	1	1	2,233	3,109		9.99	34	A	0		...					0....	9544
31-GCAA-a	bintaq					0				0		...					0....	9545
31-GCAA-b	bukow					0				0		...					0....	9546
31-GCAA-c	sandiwar					0				0		...					0....	9547
31-GCAA-d	dabugus					0				0		...					0....	9548
31-GCAB	TIMUGON-MURUT cluster	1	1	12,112	16,862		10.00	35	A	35	Timugon Murut	P..	1986-1990				0.s..	9549
31-GCAB-a	kapagalan					0				35		p..					0.s..	9550
31-GCAB-b	poros					0				35		p..					0.s..	9551
31-GCAB-c	South timugon					0				35		p..					0.s..	9552
31-GCAC	KENINGAU-MURUT cluster	1	2	8,593	11,963		50.01	90	B	4		...					0....	9553
31-GCAC-a	nabay					0				4		...					9554
31-GCAC-b	tambual					0				4		...					9555
31-GCAC-c	apin-kuijau					0				4		...					9556
31-GCAC-d	dusun-murut	1	1	1,584	2,205		50.00	85	B	4		...					0....	9557
31-GCAD	PALUAN-MURUT cluster	1	2	7,507	10,452		7.25	34	A	6		...					0....	9558
31-GCAD-a	paluan	1	1	5,594	7,789	0	8.01	36	A	6		...					0....	9559
31-GCAD-b	dalit-murut					0				6		...					0....	9560
31-GCAD-c	sook-murut					0				6		...					0....	9561
31-GCAD-d	takapan					0				6		...					0....	9562
31-GCAD-e	makaheeliga					0				6		...					0....	9563
31-GCAD-f	pandewan	1	1	1,913	2,663	0	5.02	30	A	6		...					0....	9564
31-GCAE	TAGAL-MURUT cluster	2	2	48,567	67,363		57.97	97	B	41		PN.					0.s..	9565
31-GCAE-a	tumaniq					0				41		pn.					0.s..	9566
31-GCAE-b	sumambuq	1	1	2,460	3,172	0	20.00	50	B	41		pn.					0.s..	9567
31-GCAE-c	maligan					0				41		pn.					0.s..	9568
31-GCAE-d	tagal	1	1	46,107	64,191	0	60.00	100	B	41	Murut: Tagal*	PN.	1960-1990	1984-1991			0.s..	9569
31-GCAE-e	bol					0				41		pn.					0.s..	9570
31-GCAE-f	rundum					0				41		pn.					0.s..	9571
31-GCAE-g	tolokoson					0				41		pn.					0.s..	9572
31-GCAE-h	pentjangan					0				41		pn.					0.s..	9573
31-GCAE-i	sapulut					0				41		pn.					0.s..	9574
31-GCAE-j	lagunan					0				41		pn.					0.s..	9575
31-GCAE-k	kalimantan-kuijau					0				41		pn.					0.s..	9576
31-GCAE-l	tengara 1					0				41		pn.					0.s..	9577
31-GCAE-m	tenom					0				41		pn.					0.s..	9578
31-GCAE-n	alumbis					0				41		pn.					0.s..	9579
31-GCAE-o	salalir					0				41		pn.					0.s..	9580
31-GCAE-p	taw					0				41		pn.					0.s..	9581
31-GCAF	OKOLOD-MURUT cluster	2	2	4,973	6,574		29.52	58	B	12		...					0.s..	9582
31-GCAF-a	okolod	2	2	4,973	6,574	0	29.52	58	B	12	Okolod	...					0.s..	9583
31-GCAG	SELUNGAI-MURUT cluster	2	2	1,010	1,340		18.12	43	A	2		...					0....	9584
31-GCAG-a	selungai murut	2	2	1,010	1,340	0	18.12	43	A	2		...					0....	9585
31-GCB	**TIDONG net**	2	8	52,594	70,736		15.22	38	A	12		...					0....	9586
31-GCBA	BAUKAN cluster	1	2	3,199	4,453		25.38	52	B	12		...					0....	9587
31-GCBA-a	baukan	1	1	2,767	3,852	0	19.99	47	A	12	Baukan	...					0....	9588
31-GCBA-b	kokoroton murut					0				12		...					0....	9589
31-GCBA-c	tengara	1	1	432	601	0	59.95	86	B	12		...					0....	9590
31-GCBB	SEMBAKUNG cluster	2	4	13,361	18,273		12.37	36	A	11		...					0....	9591
31-GCBB-a	sembakung	2	2	9,855	13,393	0	13.22	38	A	11		...					0....	9592
31-GCBB-b	tinggalan					0				11		...					0....	9593
31-GCBB-c	serudung	1	1	1,275	1,774	0	9.96	34	A	11		...					0....	9594
31-GCBB-d	kalabakan	1	1	2,231	3,106	0	10.00	33	A	11		...					0....	9595
31-GCBC	SOUTH TIDONG cluster	2	2	36,034	48,010		15.38	38	A	2		...					0....	9596
31-GCBC-a	tawau					0				2		...					0....	9597

Continued overleaf

Table 9-13 continued

Code 1	REFERENCE NAME Autoglossonym 2	Coun 3	Peo 4	Mother-tongue speakers in 2000 5	in 2025 6	Media radio 7	CHURCH AC% 8	E% 9	Wld 10	Tr 11	Biblioglossonym 12	SCRIPTURES Print 13-15	P-activity 16	N-activity 17	B-activity 18	J-year 19	Jayuh 20-24	Ref 25
31-GCBC-b	tidong	2	2	36,034	48,010	0	15.38	38	A	2		...					0....	9598
31-GCBC-c	nonukan					0				2		...					0....	9599
31-GCBC-d	penchangan					0				2		...					0....	9600
31-GCBC-e	sedalir					0				2		...					0....	9601
31-GCBC-f	sibuku					0				2		...					0....	9602
31-GCBC-g	sesayap					0				2		...					0....	9603
31-GCBC-h	tarakan					0				2		...					0....	9604
31-H	**APO-DUAT set**	3	8	59,883	81,305		31.52	76	B	61		PNB					0.s..	9605
31-HA	APO-DUAT chain	3	8	59,883	81,305		31.52	76	B	61		PNB					0.s..	9606
31-HAA	**APO-DUAT net**	3	8	59,883	81,305		31.52	76	B	61		PNB					0.s..	9607
31-HAAA	PUTOH cluster	1	1	4,000	6,800		20.00	50	B	4		...					0....	9608
31-HAAA-a	putoh					0				4		...					0....	9609
31-HAAA-b	pa-kembaloh					0				4		...					0....	9610
31-HAAA-c	abai					0				4		...					0....	9611
31-HAAB	LENGILU cluster	1	1	21	27		19.05	48	A	8		...					0....	9612
31-HAAB-a	lengilu	1	1	21	27	0	19.05	48	A	8		...					0....	9613
31-HAAC	LUN-DAYE cluster	3	3	52,154	69,468		31.99	78	B	61		PNB					0.s..	9614
31-HAAC-a	kawang-menadong					0				61		pnb					0.s..	9615
31-HAAC-b	lawas					0				61		pnb					0.s..	9616
31-HAAC-c	trusan					0				61		pnb					0.s..	9617
31-HAAC-d	long-sukang					0				61		pnb					0.s..	9618
31-HAAC-e	long-semado					0				61		pnb					0.s..	9619
31-HAAC-f	adang					0				61		pnb					0.s..	9620
31-HAAC-g	Upper limbang					0				61		pnb					0.s..	9621
31-HAAC-h	tabun					0				61		pnb					0.s..	9622
31-HAAC-i	treng					0				61		pnb					0.s..	9623
31-HAAC-j	balait					0				61		pnb					0.s..	9624
31-HAAC-k	ba-kelalan					0				61		pnb					0.s..	9625
31-HAAC-l	padas					0				61		pnb					0.s..	9626
31-HAAC-m	long-pa-sia					0				61		pnb					0.s..	9627
31-HAAC-n	papadi					0				61		pnb					0.s..	9628
31-HAAC-o	lun-bawang	3	3	52,154	69,468	0	31.99	78	B	61	Lun Bawang*	PNB	1947	1962	1982		0.s..	9629
31-HAAD	SA'BAN cluster	2	2	1,960	2,642		17.19	46	A	23		P..					0....	9630
31-HAAD-a	sa'ban	2	2	1,960	2,642	0	17.19	46	A	23	Saban	P..	1969				0....	9631
31-HAAE	KELABIT cluster	2	2	1,748	2,368		60.01	92	C	23	Kelabit	P..	1965				0....	9632
31-HAAE-a	long-napir					0				23		p..					0....	9633
31-HAAE-b	long-seidan					0				23		p..					0....	9634
31-HAAE-c	long-lellang					0				23		p..					0....	9635
31-HAAE-d	long-bangaq					0				23		p..					0....	9636
31-HAAE-e	brung					0				23		p..					0....	9637
31-HAAE-f	libbung					0				23		p..					0....	9638
31-HAAE-g	lepu-potong					0				23		p..					0....	9639
31-HAAE-h	bario					0				23		p..					0....	9640
31-I	**TRANS-BORNEO set**	3	25	163,712	227,722		17.14	46	A	9		...					0....	9641
31-IA	WEST TRANS-BORNEO chain	3	22	130,239	184,446		9.05	38	A	9		...					0....	9642
31-IAA	**KIPUT-BERAWAN net**	2	8	56,491	78,848		11.05	40	A	4		...					0....	9643
31-IAAA	TUTONG-MARITIME cluster	2	3	45,661	63,752		13.09	44	A	4		...					0....	9644
31-IAAA-a	tutong-maritime	1	1	8,497	11,887	0	5.00	34	A	4		...					0....	9645
31-IAAB	KIPUT cluster	2	2	5,294	7,388		0.15	21	A	4		...					0....	9646
31-IAAB-a	long-kiput	2	2	5,294	7,388	0	0.15	21	A	4		...					0....	9647
31-IAAB-b	balait-jati					0				4		...					0....	9648
31-IAAB-c	lemiting					0				4		...					0....	9649
31-IAAC	BERAWAN cluster	1	1	1,372	1,911		5.03	28	A	4		...					0....	9650
31-IAAC-a	West berawan					0				4		...					0....	9651
31-IAAC-b	long-pata					0				4		...					0....	9652
31-IAAC-c	batu-baleh					0				4		...					0....	9653
31-IAAC-d	long-terawan					0				4		...					0....	9654
31-IAAC-e	long-jegan					0				4		...					0....	9655
31-IAAD	LELAK cluster	1	1	347	483		0.00	11	A	4		...					0....	9656
31-IAAD-a	lelak	1	1	347	483	0	0.00	11	A	4		...					0....	9657
31-IAAD-b	dali									4		...					0....	9658
31-IAAE	NAROM-MIRI cluster	1	1	3,817	5,314		5.00	29	A	4		...					0....	9659
31-IAAE-a	narom	1	1	3,817	5,314	1	5.00	29	A	4		...					0....	9660
31-IAAE-b	miri					1				4		...					0....	9661
31-IAB	**BINTULU net**	1	1	6,627	9,226		10.00	34	A	3		...					0....	9662
31-IABA	BINTULU cluster	1	1	6,627	9,226		10.00	34	A	3		...					0....	9663
31-IABA-a	bintulu	1	1	6,627	9,226	0	10.00	34	A	3		...					0....	9664
31-IAC	**LAHANAN-BUKITAN net**	2	7	3,687	5,074		29.16	54	B	4		...					0....	9665
31-IACA	KAJAMAN-SEKAPAN cluster	1	2	1,973	2,747		28.99	57	B	3		...					0....	9666
31-IACA-a	sekapan					0				3		...					0....	9667
31-IACA-b	kajaman					0				3		...					0....	9668
31-IACB	LAHANAN cluster	1	1	552	768		0.00	9	A	3		...					0....	9669
31-IACB-a	lahanan	1	1	552	768	0	0.00	9	A	3		...					0....	9670
31-IACC	BUKITAN-PUNAN cluster	2	4	1,162	1,559		43.29	71	B	4		...					0....	9671
31-IACC-a	bukitan	2	2	862	1,141	0	56.61	85	B	4		...					0....	9672
31-IACC-b	sian	1	1	111	155	0	5.41	27	A	4		...					0....	9673
31-IACC-c	West punan-batu					0				4		...					0....	9674
31-IACC-d	Northwest ukit									4		...					0....	9675
31-IACC-e	Southeast punan-ukit	1	1	189	263	0	4.76	35	A	4		...					0....	9676
31-IACC-f	punan-busang					0				4		...					0....	9677
31-IAD	**MELANAU net**	1	5	62,724	90,310		5.95	36	A	9		...					0....	9678
31-IADA	BALINGIAN cluster	1	1	4,000	6,800		5.00	24	A	0		...					0....	9679
31-IADA-a	balingian	1	1	4,000	6,800	0	5.00	24	A	0		...					0....	9680
31-IADB	MUKAH-OYA cluster	1	1	39,944	55,610		5.00	39	A	2		...					0....	9681
31-IADB-a	mukah					0				2		...					0....	9682
31-IADB-b	oya					0				2		...					0....	9683
31-IADB-c	dalat	1	1	39,944	55,610	0	5.00	39	A	2		...					0....	9684
31-IADC	DARO-MATU cluster	1	1	11,990	16,692		10.00	36	A	4		...					0....	9685
31-IADC-a	matu					0				4		...					0....	9686
31-IADC-b	daro					0				4		...					0....	9687
31-IADD	BRUIT cluster	1	1	3,000	5,100		5.00	24	A	0		...					0....	9688
31-IADD-a	bruit	1	1	3,000	5,100	0	5.00	24	A	0		...					0....	9689
31-IADE	SARIKEI cluster	1	1	2,000	3,400		5.00	24	A	0		...					0....	9690
31-IADE-a	sarikei	1	1	2,000	3,400	0	5.00	24	A	0		...					0....	9691

Continued opposite

Table 9-13 continued

Code 1	REFERENCE NAME / Autoglossonym 2	Coun 3	Peo 4	Mother-tongue speakers in 2000 5	in 2025 6	Media radio 7	AC% 8	E% 9	Wld 10	Tr 11	Biblioglossonym 12	Print 13-15	P-activity 16	N-activity 17	B-activity 18	J-year 19	Jayuh 20-24	Ref 25
31-IADF	SIBU cluster	1	1	663	923		4.98	30	A	4		...					0....	9692
31-IADF-a	West sibu					0				4		...					0....	9693
31-IADF-b	North sibu					0				4		...					0....	9694
31-IADG	KANOWIT cluster	1	1	269	375		4.83	35	A	4		...					0....	9695
31-IADG-a	kanowit	1	1	269	375	0	4.83	35	A	4		...					0....	9696
31-IADH	TANJONG cluster	1	1	158	220		5.06	28	A	4		...					0....	9697
31-IADH-a	tanjong	1	1	158	220	0	5.06	28	A	4		...					0....	9698
31-IADI	SERU cluster			0	0		0.00	0		9		...					0....	9699
31-IADI-a	seru			0	0	0	0.00	0		9		...					0....	9700
31-IADJ	SEGAHAN cluster	1	1	200	340		5.00	24	A	0		...					0....	9701
31-IADJ-a	segahan	1	1	200	340	0	5.00	24	A	0		...					0....	9702
31-IADK	PREHAN cluster	1	1	300	510		5.00	24	A	0		...					0....	9703
31-IADK-a	prehan	1	1	300	510	0	5.00	24	A	0		...					0....	9704
31-IADL	SITENG cluster	1	1	200	340		5.00	24	A	0		...					0....	9705
31-IADL-a	siteng	1	1	200	340	0	5.00	24	A	0		...					0....	9706
31-IAE	**PUNAN-BAH-BIAU net**	1	1	710	988		10.00	40	A	4		...					0....	9707
31-IAEA	PUNAN-BAH-BIAU cluster	1	1	710	988		10.00	40	A	4		...					0....	9708
31-IAEA-a	punan-bah					0				4		...					0....	9709
31-IAEA-b	punan-biau					0				4		...					0....	9710
31-IB	EAST TRANS-BORNEO chain	1	3	33,473	43,276		48.62	77	B	4		....					0....	9711
31-IBA	**SAJAU-BASAP net**	1	3	33,473	43,276		48.62	77	B	4		...					0....	9712
31-IBAA	PUNAN-MERAP cluster	1	1	300	510		25.00	58	B	0		...					0....	9713
31-IBAA-a	punan-merap	1	1	300	510	0	25.00	58	B	0		...					0....	9714
31-IBAB	BURUSU cluster	1	1	8,251	10,637		30.00	63	B	4		...					0....	9715
31-IBAB-a	burusu	1	1	8,251	10,637	0	30.00	63	B	4		...					0....	9716
31-IBAC	SAJAU-PUNAN cluster	1	1	8,272	10,664		25.00	51	B	4		...					0....	9717
31-IBAC-a	sajau-basap	1	1	8,272	10,664		25.00	51	B	4		...					0....	9718
31-IBAC-b	punan-sajau					0				4		...					0....	9719
31-IBAC-c	punan-basap 1					0				4		...					0....	9720
31-IBAC-d	East punan-batu					0				4		...					0....	9721
31-IBAD	BASAP cluster	1	1	16,650	21,465		70.00	98	C	4		...					0....	9722
31-IBAD-a	jembayan					0				4		...					0....	9723
31-IBAD-b	bulungan	1	1	16,650	21,465	0	70.00	98	C	4		...					0....	9724
31-IBAD-c	berau					0				4		...					0....	9725
31-IBAD-d	dumaring					0				4		...					0....	9726
31-IBAD-e	binatang					0				4		...					0....	9727
31-IBAD-f	karangan					0				4		...					0....	9728
31-J	**KAYAN-KENYAH set**	3	35	122,139	165,048		25.66	51	B	61		PNB					0.s..	9729
31-JA	PUNAN-NIBONG chain	1	1	4,000	6,800		10.00	33	A	44		PN.					0.s..	9730
31-JAA	**PUNAN-NIBONG net**	1	1	4,000	6,800		10.00	33	A	44		PN.					0.s..	9731
31-JAAA	PUNAN-NIBONG cluster	1	1	4,000	6,800		10.00	33	A	44		PN.					0.s..	9732
31-JAAA-a	punan-nibong	1	1	4,000	6,800	0	10.00	33	A	44	Punan-nibong	PN.	1958-1967	1974			0.s..	9733
31-JAAA-b	bok-punan					0				44		pn.					0.s..	9734
31-JAAA-c	punan-silat					0				44		pn.					0.s..	9735
31-JAAA-d	punan-gang					0				44		pn.					0.s..	9736
31-JAAA-e	punan-lusong					0				44		pn.					0.s..	9737
31-JAAA-f	punan-apo					0				44		pn.					0.s..	9738
31-JAAA-g	sipeng					0				44		pn.					0.s..	9739
31-JAAA-h	punan-lanying					0				44		pn.					0.s..	9740
31-JAAA-i	jelalong-punan					0				44		pn.					0.s..	9741
31-JB	KAYAN chain	3	19	65,440	87,641		9.19	34	A	61		PNB					0....	9742
31-JBA	**WEST KAYAN net**	3	9	25,410	33,775		15.00	42	A	61		PNB					0....	9743
31-JBAA	BARAM-KAYAN cluster	2	2	4,977	6,940		43.20	83	B	61	Kayan, Baram	PNB	1956-1965	1970	1990		0....	9744
31-JBAA-a	long-atip					0				61		pnb					0....	9745
31-JBAA-b	uma-bawang					0				61		pnb					0....	9746
31-JBAA-c	long-akah					0				61		pnb					0....	9747
31-JBAB	REJANG-KAYAN cluster	1	1	4,780	6,655		15.00	46	A	4		...					0....	9748
31-JBAB-a	ma'-aging	1	1	4,780	6,655	0	15.00	46	A	4		...					0....	9749
31-JBAB-b	long-badan					0				4		...					0....	9750
31-JBAB-c	uma-daro					0				4		...					0....	9751
31-JBAB-d	long-kehobo					0				4		...					0....	9752
31-JBAB-e	uma-juman					0				4		...					0....	9753
31-JBAB-f	long-murun					0				4		...					0....	9754
31-JBAB-g	long-geng					0				4		...					0....	9755
31-JBAB-h	kemena					0				4		...					0....	9756
31-JBAB-i	lisum					0				4		...					0....	9757
31-JBAC	LAKAN-KAYAN cluster	1	1	2,757	3,555		1.49	22	A	4		...					0....	9758
31-JBAC-a	uma-lakan	1	1	2,757	3,555	0	1.49	22	A	4		...					0....	9759
31-JBAC-b	kayaniyut-kayan					0				4		...					0....	9760
31-JBAD	WAHAU-KAYAN cluster	1	1	679	875		5.01	25	A	4		...					0....	9761
31-JBAD-a	wahau-kayan	1	1	679	875	0	5.01	25	A	4		...					0....	9762
31-JBAE	MENDALAM-KAYAN cluster	1	1	2,057	2,652		1.99	21	A	4		...					0....	9763
31-JBAE-a	mendalam-kayan	1	1	2,057	2,652	0	1.99	21	A	4		...					0....	9764
31-JBAF	MAHAKAM-KAYAN cluster	1	1	1,612	2,078		0.99	21	A	4		...					0....	9765
31-JBAF-a	mahakam-kayan	1	1	1,612	2,078	0	0.99	21	A	4		...					0....	9766
31-JBAG	BUSANG-KAYAN cluster	1	1	4,136	5,332		8.99	35	A	4		...					0....	9767
31-JBAG-a	mahakam-busang					0				4		...					0....	9768
31-JBAG-b	belayan					0				4		...					0....	9769
31-JBAG-c	long-bleh					0				4		...					0....	9770
31-JBAH	CENTRAL BAHAU cluster	1	1	4,412	5,688		10.00	32	A	4		...					0....	9771
31-JBAH-a	Central bahau	1	1	4,412	5,688	0	10.00	32	A	4		...					0....	9772
31-JBB	**MURIK-KAYAN net**	1	1	5,000	8,500		10.00	33	A	3		...					0....	9773
31-JBBA	MURIK-KAYAN cluster	1	1	5,000	8,500		10.00	33	A	3		...					0....	9774
31-JBBA-a	long-hubung					0				3		...					0....	9775
31-JBBA-b	long-banyuq					0				3		...					0....	9776
31-JBBA-c	long-semiang					0				3		...					0....	9777
31-JBC	**MODANG-KAYAN net**	1	2	23,819	30,708		5.00	28	A	4		...					0....	9778
31-JBCA	SEGAI cluster	1	1	2,757	3,555		5.01	27	A	4		...					0....	9779
31-JBCA-a	kelai					0				4		...					0....	9780
31-JBCA-b	punan-kelai-2					0				4		...					0....	9781
31-JBCA-c	punan-segah					0				4		...					0....	9782

Continued overleaf

Table 9-13 continued

Code 1	REFERENCE NAME / Autoglossonym 2	Coun 3	Peo 4	in 2000 5	in 2025 6	Media radio 7	AC% 8	E% 9	Wld 10	Tr 11	Biblioglossonym 12	Print 13-15	P-activity 16	N-activity 17	B-activity 18	J-year 19	Jayuh 20-24	Ref 25
31-JBCA-d	bolongan					0				4		...					0....	9783
31-JBCB	MODANG cluster	1	1	21,062	27,153		5.00	28	A	4		...					0....	9784
31-JBCB-a	long-wai	1	1	21,062	27,153		5.00	28	A	4		...					0....	9785
31-JBCB-b	long-glat					0				4		...					0....	9786
31-JBCB-c	long-bento'					0				4		...					0....	9787
31-JBCB-d	benehes					0				4		...					0....	9788
31-JBCB-e	nahes-liah-bing					0				4		...					0....	9789
31-JBD	**BUNGAN-AOHENG net**	1	8	11,211	14,658		4.58	27	A	12		...					0....	9790
31-JBDA	BUKAT cluster	1	1	551	711		2.00	21	A	4		...					0....	9791
31-JBDA-a	bukat	1	1	551	711	0	2.00	21	A	4		...					0....	9792
31-JBDB	HOVONGAN cluster	1	1	1,124	1,449		4.98	32	A	12		...					0....	9793
31-JBDB-a	hovongan	1	1	1,124	1,449	0	4.98	32	A	12	Hovongan	...					0....	9794
31-JBDB-b	semukung-uheng					0				12		...					0....	9795
31-JBDC	KEREHO-UHENG cluster	1	5	5,409	6,972		6.73	31	A	4		...					0....	9796
31-JBDC-a	kereho-uheng	1	5	5,409	6,972	0	6.73	31	A	4		...					0....	9797
31-JBDD	AOHENG cluster	1	1	3,627	4,676		2.01	22	A	4		...					0....	9798
31-JBDD-a	aoheng	1	1	3,627	4,676	0	2.01	22	A	4		...					0....	9799
31-JBDE	PUNAN-MERAH cluster	1	1	300	510		2.00	18	A	4		...					0....	9800
31-JBDE-a	punan-merah	1	1	300	510	0	2.00	18	A	4		...					0....	9801
31-JBDF	PUNAN-APUT cluster	1	1	200	340		2.00	18	A	0		...					0....	9802
31-JBDF-a	punan-aput	1	1	200	340	0	2.00	18	A	0		...					0....	9803
31-JC	**KENYAHIC chain**	3	16	52,699	70,607		47.29	74	B	61		PNB					0.s..	9804
31-JCA	**PUNAN-TUBU net**	1	1	2,757	3,555		3.99	25	A	0		...					0....	9805
31-JCAA	PUNAN-TUBU cluster	1	1	2,757	3,555		3.99	25	A	0		...					0....	9806
31-JCAA-a	punan-tubu	1	1	2,757	3,555	0	3.99	25	A	0		...					0....	9807
31-JCB	**SEBOB net**	1	1	2,749	3,834		14.91	46	A	2		...					0....	9808
31-JCBA	SEBOB-KENYAH cluster	1	1	2,729	3,800		14.99	46	A	2		...					0....	9809
31-JCBA-a	tinjar-sibop					0				2		...					0....	9810
31-JCBA-b	lirong					0				2		...					0....	9811
31-JCBA-c	long-pokun					0				2		...					0....	9812
31-JCBA-d	long-atun					0				2		...					0....	9813
31-JCBA-e	long-ekang					0				2		...					0....	9814
31-JCBA-f	long-luyang					0				2		...					0....	9815
31-JCBB	BAH-MALEI cluster	1	1	20	34		5.00	25	A	0		...					0....	9816
31-JCBB-a	bah-malei	1	1	20	34	0	5.00	25	A	0		...					0....	9817
31-JCC	**KENYAH net**	3	14	47,193	63,218		51.71	78	B	61		PNB					0.s..	9818
31-JCCA	TUTOH-KENYAH cluster	1	1	300	510		5.00	24	A	0		...					0....	9819
31-JCCA-a	long-wat					0				0		...					0....	9820
31-JCCA-b	long-labid					0				0		...					0....	9821
31-JCCA-c	lugat					0				0		...					0....	9822
31-JCCB	MADANG cluster	1	1	2,224	3,097		60.03	99	C	41	Madang	PN.	1957	1978			0....	9823
31-JCCB-a	madang	1	1	2,224	3,097	0	60.03	99	C	41	Kenya: Lepo'tau	PN.	1956	1978			0....	9824
31-JCCB-b	malang					0				41		pn.					0....	9825
31-JCCC	WEST KENYAH cluster	1	2	13,758	19,154		17.17	52	B	42		PN.					0....	9826
31-JCCC-a	long-bangan					0				42		pn.					0....	9827
31-JCCC-b	kemena-penan					0				42		pn.					0....	9828
31-JCCC-c	kakus-penan	1	1	11,785	16,407	0	10.00	44	A	42	Penan	PN.	1958	1974			0....	9829
31-JCCC-d	uma-bakah					0				42		pn.					0....	9830
31-JCCC-e	lunan	1	1	1,973	2,747	0	60.01	99	C	42		pn.					0....	9831
31-JCCC-f	lepu-anau					0				42		pn.					0....	9832
31-JCCC-g	lepu-pohun					0				42		pn.					0....	9833
31-JCCC-h	lepu-pun					0				42		pn.					0....	9834
31-JCCC-i	lepu-sawa					0				42		pn.					0....	9835
31-JCCD	BARAM-KENYAH cluster	2	2	2,860	3,917		75.59	97	C	4		...					0....	9836
31-JCCD-a	long-anap					0				4		...					0....	9837
31-JCCD-b	long-jeeh					0				4		...					0....	9838
31-JCCD-c	long-moh					0				4		...					0....	9839
31-JCCD-d	nyamok					0				4		...					0....	9840
31-JCCD-e	long-lamai					0				4		...					0....	9841
31-JCCE	BAHAU-KENYAH cluster	1	1	2,057	2,652		10.01	37	A	4		...					0....	9842
31-JCCE-a	long-atau					0				4		...					0....	9843
31-JCCE-b	long-bena					0				4		...					0....	9844
31-JCCE-c	long-puyungan					0				4		...					0....	9845
31-JCCE-d	punan-benalui					0				4		...					0....	9846
31-JCCF	KAYAN-KENYAH cluster	1	1	8,251	10,637		94.99	100	C	41		PN.					0.s..	9847
31-JCCF-a	Lower kayan-kenyah					0				41	Kenyah, Kayan River	PN.	1956-1957	1978			0.s..	9848
31-JCCF-b	punan-penjalin					0				41		pn.					0.s..	9849
31-JCCF-c	long-bia	1	1	8,251	10,637	0	94.99	100	C	41		pn.					0.s..	9850
31-JCCF-d	punan-ban					0				41		pn.					0.s..	9851
31-JCCF-e	kayaniyut-kenyah					0				41		pn.					0.s..	9852
31-JCCF-f	long-nawan					0				41		pn.					0.s..	9853
31-JCCF-g	long-kelawit					0				41		pn.					0.s..	9854
31-JCCG	MAHAKAM-KENYAH cluster	1	1	9,630	12,414		70.00	100	C	4		...					0....	9855
31-JCCG-a	mahakam	1	1	9,630	12,414		70.00	100	C	4		...					0....	9856
31-JCCG-b	boh					0				4		...					0....	9857
31-JCCH	KELINYAU-KENYAH cluster	1	1	1,654	2,133		70.01	100	C	4		...					0.s..	9858
31-JCCH-a	uma-bem					0				4		...				*	0.s..	9859
31-JCCH-b	uma-tau					0				4		...					0.s..	9860
31-JCCH-c	lepo'-kulit					0				4		...					0.s..	9861
31-JCCH-d	uma-jalam					0				4		...					0.s..	9862
31-JCCI	WAHAU-KENYAH cluster	1	1	1,379	1,777		59.97	87	B	4		...					0....	9863
31-JCCI-a	wahau	1	1	1,379	1,777	0	59.97	87	B	4		...					0....	9864
31-JCCI-b	uma-timai					0				4		...					0....	9865
31-JCCJ	BAKUNG-KENYAH cluster	3	4	5,080	6,927		34.63	65	B	61		PNB					0....	9866
31-JCCJ-a	boh-bakung					0				61		pnb					0....	9867
31-JCCJ-b	punan-oho'					0				61		pnb					0....	9868
31-JCCJ-c	oga-bakung					0				61		pnb					0....	9869
31-JCCJ-d	kayan-bakung					0				61	Kayan	PNB	1956	1970	1990		0....	9870
31-JCCJ-e	punan-poh					0				61		pnb					0....	9871
31-K	**LAND-DAYAK set**	2	22	774,112	1,020,336		28.18	62	B	47		PN.					0As..	9872
31-KA	LAND-DAYAK chain	2	22	774,112	1,020,336		28.18	62	B	47		PN.					0As..	9873
31-KAA	**LAND-DAYAK net**	2	22	774,112	1,020,336		28.18	62	B	47		PN.					0As..	9874
31-KAAA	SILAKAU cluster	2	2	143,674	185,837		2.29	26	A	0		...					0....	9875
31-KAAA-a	silakau	2	2	143,674	185,837	0	2.29	26	A	0		...					0....	9876

Continued opposite

Table 9-13 continued

Code 1	REFERENCE NAME / Autoglossonym 2	Coun 3	Peo 4	Mother-tongue speakers in 2000 5	in 2025 6	Media radio 7	CHURCH AC% 8	E% 9	Wld 10	Tr 11	Biblioglossonym 12	SCRIPTURES Print 13-15	P-activity 16	N-activity 17	B-activity 18	J-year 19	Jayuh 20-24	Ref 25
31-KAAB	LARA cluster	2	2	19,616	26,458		10.00	41	A	2							0....	9877
31-KAAB-a	lara	2	2	19,616	26,458	0	10.00	41	A	2		...					0....	9878
31-KAAC	JAGOI-TRINGUS cluster	1	2	30,526	42,498		17.82	48	A	12							0A...	9879
31-KAAC-a	jagoi	1	1	29,974	41,730		18.00	48	A	12	Jagoi	...					0A...	9880
31-KAAC-b	grogo					0				12		...					0c...	9881
31-KAAC-c	sentenggau					0				12		...					0c...	9882
31-KAAC-d	gumbang					0				12		...					0c...	9883
31-KAAC-e	serambau					0				12		...					0c...	9884
31-KAAC-f	empawa					0				12		...					0c...	9885
31-KAAC-g	suti					0				12		...					0c...	9886
31-KAAC-h	taup					0				12		...					0c...	9887
31-KAAC-i	assem					0				12		...					0c...	9888
31-KAAC-j	tengoh					0				12		...					0c...	9889
31-KAAC-k	dongay					0				12		...					0c...	9890
31-KAAC-l	krokong					0				12		...					0c...	9891
31-KAAC-m	tringus	1	1	552	768	0	7.97	30	A	12		...					0c...	9892
31-KAAD	SINGGI cluster	1	1	7,572	10,542		10.00	33	A	0							0....	9893
31-KAAD-a	singgi	1	1	7,572	10,542	0	10.00	33	A	0		...					0....	9894
31-KAAE	BIATAH-SERIAN cluster	2	5	150,737	208,111		43.96	89	B	47		PN.					0As..	9895
31-KAAE-a	bi-atah	2	2	29,727	40,513	4	40.58	87	B	47	Biatah	PN.	1887-1912	1963			0As..	9896
31-KAAE-b	lundu					1				47		pn.					0cs..	9897
31-KAAE-c	bi-deyu	1	1	79,160	110,207	4	50.00	98	B	47	Bideyu*	PN.	1887-1935	1963			0cs..	9898
31-KAAE-d	sadong	2	2	41,850	57,391	1	34.95	74	B	47	Bukar Sadong	pn.					0cs..	9899
31-KAAE-e	tebakang					1				47		pn.					0cs..	9900
31-KAAF	BIKUAP cluster	1	1	2,000	3,400		40.00	77	B	0							0....	9901
31-KAAF-a	bi-kuap					0				0		...					0....	9902
31-KAAF-b	be-ta					0				0		...					0....	9903
31-KAAG	MURANG-PUNAN cluster	1	1	3,000	5,100		40.00	77	B	0							0....	9904
31-KAAG-a	murang-punan					0				0		...					0....	9905
31-KAAG-b	penyabung-punan					0				0		...					0....	9906
31-KAAG-c	busang					0				0		...					0....	9907
31-KAAG-d	djuloi					0				0		...					0....	9908
31-KAAH	BEKATI cluster	1	1	4,921	6,344		20.00	53	B	22		P..					0.s..	9909
31-KAAH-a	be-kati	1	1	4,921	6,344	0	20.00	53	B	22	Bakatiq*	P..	1986				0.s..	9910
31-KAAI	BENYADU cluster	1	2	72,604	93,599		19.24	54	B	23		P..					0....	9911
31-KAAI-a	be-nyadu	1	1	61,511	79,298	0	20.00	57	B	23		p..					0....	9912
31-KAAI-b	ba-lantiang	1	1	11,093	14,301	0	15.00	39	A	23	Nyadu	P..	1952				0....	9913
31-KAAJ	KEMBAYAN cluster	1	1	61,957	79,872		40.00	79	B	4							0....	9914
31-KAAJ-a	kembayan	1	1	61,957	79,872	4	40.00	79	B	4		...					0....	9915
31-KAAK	RIBUN cluster	1	1	63,632	82,033		40.00	74	B	4							0....	9916
31-KAAK-a	ribun	1	1	63,632	82,033	0	40.00	74	B	4		...					0....	9917
31-KAAL	DJONGKANG cluster	1	1	63,632	82,033		40.00	76	B	4							0....	9918
31-KAAL-a	djongkang	1	1	63,632	82,033	0	40.00	76	B	4		...					0....	9919
31-KAAM	SANGGAU cluster	1	1	63,632	82,033		40.00	74	B	4							0....	9920
31-KAAM-a	sanggau	1	1	63,632	82,033	0	40.00	74	B	4		...					0....	9921
31-KAAN	SEMANDANG cluster	1	1	41,297	53,239		40.00	77	B	22		P..					0....	9922
31-KAAN-a	semandang	1	1	41,297	53,239	0	40.00	77	B	22	Semandang	P..	1982				0....	9923
31-KAAN-b	gerai					0				22		p..					0....	9924
31-KAAN-c	be-ginci					0				22		p..					0....	9925
31-KAAN-d	bi-hak					0				22		p..					0....	9926
31-KAAO	SARA cluster	1	1	6,363	8,203		30.00	58	B	12							0....	9927
31-KAAO-a	sara	1	1	6,363	8,203	0	30.00	58	B	12	Sara	...					0....	9928
31-KAAP	AHE cluster	1	1	36,949	47,634		10.00	37	A	12							0....	9929
31-KAAP-a	ahe	1	1	36,949	47,634	0	10.00	37	A	12	Ahe	...					0....	9930
31-KAAQ	SAU cluster	1	1	2,000	3,400		10.00	33	A	0							0....	9931
31-KAAQ-a	sau					0				0		...					0....	9932
31-KAAQ-b	bi-ratak					0				0		...					0....	9933
31-L	**BARITO-MALAGASY set**	8	58	16,553,677	29,413,413		47.43	83	B	72		PNB					2Asu.	9934
31-LA	WEST BARITO chain	1	6	716,126	923,289		34.30	66	B	72		PNB					0.s..	9935
31-LAA	**NORTHWEST BARITO net**	1	2	192,963	248,844		0.71	26	A	20							0.s..	9936
31-LAAA	DOHOI cluster	1	1	110,147	141,998		0.50	31	A	20							0.s..	9937
31-LAAA-a	ot-balawan					0				20		...					0.s..	9938
31-LAAA-b	ot-banu'u					0				20		...					0.s..	9939
31-LAAA-c	ot-olang					0				20		...					0.s..	9940
31-LAAA-d	ot-tuhup					0				20		...					0.s..	9941
31-LAAA-e	sarawai					0				20		...					0.s..	9942
31-LAAA-f	ot-danum	1	1	110,147	141,998	0	0.50	31	A	20	Dohoi	...					0.s..	9943
31-LAAA-g	ulu-ai'					0				20		...					0.s..	9944
31-LAAB	PUNAN-RATAH cluster	1	1	200	340		1.00	16	A	0							0....	9945
31-LAAB-a	punan-ratah	1	1	200	340	0	1.00	16	A	0		...					0....	9946
31-LAAC	SIANG cluster	1	1	82,616	106,506		1.00	21	A	20							0....	9947
31-LAAC-a	ot-siang	1	1	82,616	106,506	0	1.00	21	A	20		...					0....	9948
31-LAAC-b	Southeast ot-murung					0				20		...					0....	9949
31-LAB	**SOUTHWEST BARITO net**	1	4	523,163	674,445		46.69	81	B	72		PNB					0.s..	9950
31-LABA	KATINGAN cluster	1	1	61,935	79,845		30.00	57	B	4							0....	9951
31-LABA-a	katingan	1	1	61,935	79,845	0	30.00	57	B	4		...					0....	9952
31-LABB	NGAJU cluster	1	1	344,208	443,742		60.00	100	C	72		PNB					0.s..	9953
31-LABB-a	kapuas					0				72		pnb					0.s..	9954
31-LABB-b	Vehicular ngaju	1	1	344,208	443,742	0	60.00	100	C	72	Dayak: Ngaju*	PNB	1905	1846-1996	1858-1955		0.s..	9955
31-LABB-c	pulopetak					0				72		pnb					0.s..	9956
31-LABB-d	ba'amang					0				72		pnb					0.s..	9957
31-LABB-e	oloh-mantangai					0				72		pnb					0.s..	9958
31-LABC	KAHAYAN cluster	1	1	61,957	79,872		30.00	55	B	4							0....	9959
31-LABC-a	kahayan	1	1	61,957	79,872	0	30.00	55	B	4		...					0....	9960
31-LABD	BAKUMPAI cluster	1	1	55,063	70,986		1.00	21	A	4							0....	9961
31-LABD-a	bakumpai	1	1	55,063	70,986	0	1.00	21	A	4		...					0....	9962
31-LABD-b	oloh-mengkatip					0				4		...					0....	9963
31-LB	EAST BARITO chain	2	6	320,023	412,921		28.55	60	B	41		PN.					0.s..	9964
31-LBA	**SOUTHEAST BARITO net**	2	4	154,727	199,828		29.68	64	B	41		PN.					0.s..	9965
31-LBAA	MAANYAN-SAMIHIM cluster	2	3	127,195	164,335		29.61	66	B	41		PN.					0.s..	9966
31-LBAA-a	dusun-malang					0				41		pn.					0.s..	9967
31-LBAA-b	dusun-witu					0				41		pn.					0.s..	9968
31-LBAA-c	paku	1	1	27,532	35,493	0	30.00	61	B	41		pn.					0.s..	9969
31-LBAA-d	ma'anyan	2	2	99,663	128,842	0	29.51	68	B	41	Dayak: Maanyan*	PN.	1950	1996			0.s..	9970

Continued overleaf

Table 9-13 continued

Code 1	REFERENCE NAME / Autoglossonym 2	Coun 3	Peo 4	Mother-tongue speakers in 2000 5	in 2025 6	Media radio 7	AC% 8	E% 9	Wld 10	Tr 11	Biblioglossonym 12	Print 13-15	P-activity 16	N-activity 17	B-activity 18	J-year 19	Jayuh 20-24	Ref 25
31-LBAA-e	dusun-balangan					0				41		pn.					0.s..	9971
31-LBAA-f	samihim					0				41		pn.					0.s..	9972
31-LBAB	DUSUN-DEYAH cluster	1	1	27,532	35,493		30.00	56	B	4		...					0....	9973
31-LBAB-a	dusun deyah	1	1	27,532	35,493	0	30.00	56	B	4		...					0....	9974
31-LBB	**NORTHEAST BARITO net**	1	2	165,296	213,093		27.50	55	B	20		...					0.s..	9975
31-LBBA	LAWANGAN-TABOYAN cluster	1	2	165,296	213,093		27.50	55	B	20		...					0.s..	9976
31-LBBA-a	benua					0				20		...					0.s..	9977
31-LBBA-b	North benua					0				20		...					0.s..	9978
31-LBBA-c	South benua					0				20		...					0.s..	9979
31-LBBA-d	bantian					0				20		...					0.s..	9980
31-LBBA-e	North bantian					0				20		...					9981
31-LBBA-f	South bantian					0				20		...					0.s..	9982
31-LBBA-g	tabuyan	1	1	27,553	35,520	0	15.00	40	A	20		...					0.s..	9983
31-LBBA-h	bawu					0				20		...					0.s..	9984
31-LBBA-i	lawangan					0				20		...					0.s..	9985
31-LBBA-j	pasir					0				20		...					0.s..	9986
31-LBBA-k	ajuh					0				20		...					0.s..	9987
31-LBBA-l	bakoi					0				20		...					0.s..	9988
31-LBBA-m	banuwang					0				20		...					0.s..	9989
31-LBBA-n	kali					0				20		...					0.s..	9990
31-LBBA-o	karau					0				20		...					0.s..	9991
31-LBBA-p	lawa					0				20		...					0.s..	9992
31-LBBA-q	lolang					0				20		...					0.s..	9993
31-LBBA-r	mantararen					0				20		...					0.s..	9994
31-LBBA-s	njumit					0				20		...					0.s..	9995
31-LBBA-t	purai					0				20		...					0.s..	9996
31-LBBA-u	purung					0				20		...					0.s..	9997
31-LBBA-v	tuwang					0				20		...					0.s..	9998
31-LC	BARITO-MAHAKAM chain	1	2	110,147	141,998		35.00	66	B	12		...					0.s..	9999
31-LCA	**BARITO-MAHAKAM net**	1	2	110,147	141,998		35.00	66	B	12		...					0.s..	10000
31-LCAA	TUNJUNG cluster	1	1	68,850	88,759		20.00	51	B	12	Tunjung	...					0.s..	10001
31-LCAA-a	tengah					0				12		...					0.s..	10002
31-LCAA-b	linggang					0				12		...					0.s..	10003
31-LCAA-c	londong					0				12		...					0.s..	10004
31-LCAA-d	pahu					0				12		...					0.s..	10005
31-LCAB	AMPANANG cluster	1	1	41,297	53,239		60.00	92	B	4		...					0....	10006
31-LCAB-a	ampanang	1	1	41,297	53,239	0	60.00	92	B	4		...					0....	10007
31-LD	MALAGASY chain	6	44	15,407,381	27,935,205		48.52	84	B	63		PNB					2Asu.	10008
31-LDA	**MALAGASY net**	6	44	15,407,381	27,935,205		48.52	84	B	63		PNB					2Asu.	10009
31-LDAA	CENTRAL MALAGASY cluster	4	24	9,549,434	17,295,808		61.09	91	C	63	Malagasy	PNB	1828-1987	1830-1990	1835-1938		2Asu.	10010
31-LDAA-a	merina	4	5	3,891,494	7,016,200	4	82.43	100	C	63	Malagasy	PNB	1828	1830	1835	1982	2Asu.	10011
31-LDAA-b	sihanaka	1	1	362,626	658,836	4	26.70	79	B	63		pnb					1Asu.	10015
31-LDAA-c	North betsimisaraka	1	2	2,140,017	3,888,082	4	25.00	79	B	63		pnb					1Asu.	10016
31-LDAA-d	South betsimisaraka					1				63		pnb					1csu.	10017
31-LDAA-e	bezanuzanu	1	2	178,978	325,175	4	27.44	77	B	63		pnb					1Asu.	10018
31-LDAA-f	vorimo	1	1	16,962	30,817	4	18.00	61	B	63		pnb					1Asu.	10021
31-LDAA-g	taimanambondro	1	1	43,999	79,940	4	24.00	72	B	63		pnb					1Asu.	10022
31-LDAA-h	tanala	1	1	630,495	1,145,513	4	20.10	73	B	63		pnb					1Asu.	10023
31-LDAA-i	sahafatra	1	1	101,708	184,788	4	30.00	77	B	63		pnb					1Asu.	10026
31-LDAA-j	betsileo	1	1	1,807,792	3,284,479	4	91.80	100	C	63		pnb					1Asu.	10027
31-LDAB	SOUTHEAST MALAGASY cluster	1	8	2,170,435	3,943,346		33.73	75	B	0		...					0A.u.	10028
31-LDAB-a	an-tambahoaka	1	1	58,092	105,544	4	15.00	54	B	0		...					0A.u.	10029
31-LDAB-b	an-taimoro	1	1	561,452	1,020,071	4	43.90	87	B	0		...					0A.u.	10030
31-LDAB-c	zafisoro	1	1	67,912	123,385	4	14.00	49	A	0		...					0A.u.	10031
31-LDAB-d	zalisere					1				0		...					0c.u.	10032
31-LDAB-e	an-taifasy	1	1	104,753	190,320	4	14.20	54	B	0		...					0A.u.	10033
31-LDAB-f	an-taisaka	1	1	943,431	1,714,070	4	25.90	67	B	0		...					0A.u.	10034
31-LDAB-g	an-tanosy	1	3	434,795	789,956	4	47.86	89	B	0		...					0A.u.	10035
31-LDAC	SOUTHWEST MALAGASY cluster	1	3	1,477,750	2,684,844		29.12	71	B	3		...					0A.u.	10036
31-LDAC-a	an-tandroy	1	1	701,436	1,274,401	4	19.80	61	B	3		...					0A.u.	10037
31-LDAC-b	mahafale	1	1	239,939	435,932	4	24.90	66	B	3		...					0A.u.	10038
31-LDAC-c	tanalana					1				3		...					0c.u.	10039
31-LDAC-d	onilahy-tanosy					1				3		...					0c.u.	10042
31-LDAC-e	vezu					1				3		...					0c.u.	10043
31-LDAC-f	masikoro					1				3		...					0c.u.	10044
31-LDAC-g	bara-mikaty	1	1	536,375	974,511	4	43.20	86	B	3		...					0c.u.	10045
31-LDAC-h	East bara					1				3		...					0c.u.	10046
31-LDAD	WEST MALAGASY cluster	3	7	951,341	1,728,354		31.68	79	B	20		...					0A.u.	10047
31-LDAD-a	sakalava-menabe					1				20		...					0c.u.	10048
31-LDAD-b	sakalava-ambongo					1				20		...					0c.u.	10049
31-LDAD-c	sakalava-boina					1				20		...					0c.u.	10050
31-LDAD-d	an-talaotsy					1				20		...					0c.u.	10051
31-LDAE	NORTHWEST MALAGASY cluster	1	1	1,117,467	2,030,266		14.00	65	B	24		P..					0A.u.	10052
31-LDAE-a	sambiranu					1				24		p..					0c.u.	10053
31-LDAE-b	nosy-be					1				24		p..					0c.u.	10054
31-LDAE-c	tsimihety	1	1	1,117,467	2,030,266	4	14.00	65	B	24	Malagasy: Tsimihety*	P..	1924				0A.u.	10055
31-LDAF	NORTH MALAGASY cluster	1	1	110,954	201,587		13.40	56	B	3		...					0A...	10056
31-LDAF-a	an-tankarana	1	1	110,954	201,587	4	13.40	56	B	3		...					0A...	10057
31-LDAF-b	sambirano					1				3		...					0c...	10058
31-LDAG	MALAGASY-MAYOTTE cluster	1	1	30,000	51,000		20.00	50	B	63	Malagasy	PNB	1828-1987	1830-1990	1835-1938		0....	10059
31-LDAG-a	ki-boshy					0				63		pnb					0....	10060
31-LDAG-b	an-talaotra					0				63		pnb					0....	10061
31-M	**CHAMIC set**	6	17	1,062,621	1,483,346		42.82	67	B	42		PN.					0.s..	10062
31-MA	NORTH CHAMIC chain	1	1	5,050	5,852		0.10	15	A	4		...					0....	10063
31-MAA	**HUIHUI net**	1	1	5,050	5,852		0.10	15	A	4		...					0....	10064
31-MAAA	UTSAT cluster	1	1	5,050	5,852		0.10	15	A	4		...					0....	10065
31-MAAA-a	utsat	1	1	5,050	5,852	0	0.10	15	A	4		...					0....	10066
31-MB	SOUTH CHAMIC chain	5	16	1,057,571	1,477,494		43.02	67	B	42		PN.					0.s..	10067
31-MBA	**CHAMIC-PLATEAU net**	2	5	593,891	809,088		71.06	94	C	42		PN.					0....	10068
31-MBAA	JARAI cluster	2	2	371,528	506,750		81.44	96	C	42	Jorai*	PN.	1950-1963	1974			0....	10069
31-MBAA-a	hodrung					1				42		pn.					0....	10070
31-MBAA-b	golar					1				42		pn.					0....	10071
31-MBAA-c	jhue					1				42		pn.					0....	10072
31-MBAA-d	arap					1				42		pn.					0....	10073
31-MBAA-e	habau					1				42		pn.					0....	10074
31-MBAA-f	to-buan					1				42		pn.					0....	10075
31-MBAA-g	sesan					1				42		pn.					0....	10076
31-MBAA-h	chuty					1				42		pn.					0....	10077
31-MBAA-i	plei-kly					1				42		pn.					0....	10078

Continued opposite

Table 9-13 continued

Code 1	REFERENCE NAME / Autoglossonym 2	Coun 3	Peo 4	Mother-tongue speakers in 2000 5	in 2025 6	Media radio 7	AC% 8	E% 9	Wld 10	Tr 11	Biblioglossonym 12	Print 13-15	P-activity 16	N-activity 17	B-activity 18	J-year 19	Jayuh 20-24	Ref 25
31-MBAB	HAROI cluster	1	1	36,930	49,978		28.00	62	B	2		. . .					0	10079
31-MBAB-a	haroi	1	1	36,930	49,978	4	28.00	62	B	2							0	10080
31-MBAC	RHADE cluster	2	2	185,433	252,360		58.86	98	B	42	Rade	PN.	1937-1966	1964			0	10081
31-MBAC-a	rde-kpa					1				42		pn.					0	10082
31-MBAC-b	South krung					1				42		pn.					0	10083
31-MBAC-c	bih					1				42		pn.					0	10084
31-MBAC-d	ndhur					1				42		pn.					0	10085
31-MBAC-e	a-dham					1				42		pn.					0	10086
31-MBAC-f	blo					1				42		pn.					0	10087
31-MBAC-g	kodrao					1				42		pn.					0	10088
31-MBB	**COASTAL-CHAMIC net**	5	11	463,680	668,406		7.11	32	A	23		P . .					0 . s . .	10089
31-MBBA	CACGIA-ROGLAI cluster	1	1	3,481	4,710		28.99	61	B	2		. . .					0	10090
31-MBBA-a	cacgia-roglai	1	1	3,481	4,710	4	28.99	61	B	2							0	10091
31-MBBB	ROGLAI-CHRU cluster	1	3	95,782	129,623		28.92	62	B	23	Roglai*	P . .	1966-1973				0	10092
31-MBBB-a	noang					1				23		p . .					0	10093
31-MBBB-b	South roglai	1	1	29,043	39,304	4	30.00	63	B	23		p . .					0	10094
31-MBBB-c	rai					1				23		p . .					0	10095
31-MBBB-d	chru	1	1	30,432	41,184	4	29.00	64	B	23	Chru	P . .	1955				0	10096
31-MBBC	CHAM cluster	5	7	364,417	534,073		1.17	23	A	23		P . .					0 . s . .	10097
31-MBBC-a	East cham	2	2	42,119	57,029	4	10.00	48	A	23	Cham: Eastern*	P . .	1973				0 . s . .	10098
31-MBBC-b	West cham	5	5	322,298	477,044	1	0.02	20	A	23	Cham, Western	p . .					0 . s . .	10099
31-N	**ACEH set**	1	1	3,388,925	4,368,894		0.01	35	A	41		PN.					2A . . .	10100
31-NA	ACEH chain	1	1	3,388,925	4,368,894		0.01	35	A	41		PN.					2A . . .	10101
31-NAA	**ACEH net**	1	1	3,388,925	4,368,894		0.01	35	A	41		PN.					2A . . .	10102
31-NAAA	ACEH cluster	1	1	3,388,925	4,368,894		0.01	35	A	41	Aceh	PN.	1973	1996		1996	2A . . .	10103
31-NAAA-a	banda					1				41		pn.					1c . . .	10104
31-NAAA-b	baruh					1				41		pn.					1c . . .	10105
31-NAAA-c	bueng					1				41		pn.					1c . . .	10106
31-NAAA-d	daja					1				41		pn.					1c . . .	10107
31-NAAA-e	pase					1				41		pn.					1c . . .	10108
31-NAAA-f	tunong					1				41		pn.					1c . . .	10109
31-NAAA-g	pidie					1				41		pn.					1c . . .	10110
31-O	**ENGGANO set**	1	1	1,379	1,777		74.98	100	C	4		. . .					0	10111
31-OA	ENGGANO chain	1	1	1,379	1,777		74.98	100	C	4		. . .					0	10112
31-OAA	**ENGGANO net**	1	1	1,379	1,777		74.98	100	C	4		. . .					0	10113
31-OAAA	ENGGANO cluster	1	1	1,379	1,777		74.98	100	C	4		. . .					0	10114
31-OAAA-a	enggano	1	1	1,379	1,777	0	74.98	100	C	4		. . .					0	10115
31-P	**CENTRAL SUNDIC set**	32	183	198,290,915	256,836,689		9.60	62	B	72		PNB					4Asuh	10116
31-PA	EMBALOH chain	2	3	29,379	37,697		8.99	34	A	12		. . .					0	10117
31-PAA	**EMBALOH net**	2	3	29,379	37,697		8.99	34	A	12		. . .					0	10118
31-PAAA	EMBALOH cluster	2	3	29,379	37,697		8.99	34	A	12		. . .					0	10119
31-PAAA-a	embaloh	1	2	17,520	22,586	0	11.00	39	A	12	Embaloh*	. . .					0	10120
31-PAAA-b	taman	1	1	11,859	15,111	0	6.00	27	A	12		. . .					0	10121
31-PAAA-c	palin					0				12		. . .					0	10125
31-PAAA-d	lauk					0				12		. . .					0	10126
31-PAAA-e	leboyan					0				12		. . .					0	10127
31-PAAA-f	kalis					0				12		. . .					0	10128
31-PB	GAYO chain	1	1	211,132	272,184		0.01	14	A	20		. . .					0	10129
31-PBA	**GAYO net**	1	1	211,132	272,184		0.01	14	A	20		. . .					0	10130
31-PBAA	GAYO cluster	1	1	211,132	272,184		0.01	14	A	20		. . .					0	10131
31-PBAA-a	dorot					0				20		. . .					0	10132
31-PBAA-b	bobasan					0				20		. . .					0	10133
31-PBAA-c	serbodjadi					0				20		. . .					0	10134
31-PBAA-d	tampur					0				20		. . .					0	10135
31-PC	NIAS-SIMEULUE chain	2	5	748,266	964,648		60.25	85	C	72		PNB					0 . s . .	10136
31-PCA	**NIAS-SIMEULUE net**	2	5	748,266	964,648		60.25	85	C	72		PNB					0 . s . .	10137
31-PCAA	SIMEULUE cluster	1	1	137,679	177,491		1.00	23	A	20		. . .					0	10138
31-PCAA-a	West simeulue					0				20		. . .					0	10139
31-PCAA-b	East simeulue					0				20		. . .					0	10140
31-PCAA-c	babi					0				20		. . .					0	10141
31-PCAA-d	banjak					0				20		. . .					0	10142
31-PCAB	SICHULE cluster	1	1	24,647	31,774		50.00	79	B	4		. . .					0	10143
31-PCAB-a	sichule	1	1	24,647	31,774	0	50.00	79	B	4		. . .					0	10144
31-PCAB-b	lekon					0				4		. . .					0	10145
31-PCAB-c	tapah					0				4		. . .					0	10146
31-PCAC	NIAS cluster	2	3	585,940	755,383		74.60	100	C	72	Nias	PNB	1874-1937	1892	1911-1995		0 . s . .	10147
31-PCAC-a	Northwest nias					0				72		pnb					0 . s . .	10148
31-PCAC-b	Southeast nias					0				72		pnb					0 . s . .	10149
31-PCAC-c	batu	2	2	22,922	29,558	0	64.81	99	C	72	Batu	Pnb	1937				0 . s . .	10150
31-PD	MENTAWAI chain	1	1	58,648	75,607		80.00	100	C	41		PN.					0 . s . .	10151
31-PDA	**MENTAWAI net**	1	1	58,648	75,607		80.00	100	C	41		PN.					0 . s . .	10152
31-PDAA	MENTAWAI cluster	1	1	58,648	75,607		80.00	100	C	41	Mentawai	PN.	1911-1955	1987-1996			0 . s . .	10153
31-PDAA-a	North siberut					0				41		pn.					0 . s . .	10154
31-PDAA-b	simalegi					0				41		pn.					0 . s . .	10155
31-PDAA-c	South siberut					0				41		pn.					0 . s . .	10156
31-PDAA-d	sipura					0				41		pn.					0 . s . .	10157
31-PDAA-e	pagai					0				41		pn.					0 . s . .	10158
31-PDAA-f	sakalagan					0				41		pn.					0 . s . .	10159
31-PDAA-g	silabu					0				41		pn.					0 . s . .	10160
31-PDAA-h	taikaku					0				41		pn.					0 . s . .	10161
31-PDAA-i	saumanganja					0				41		pn.					0 . s . .	10162
31-PE	BATAK chain	2	11	7,882,984	10,162,408		60.42	91	C	72		PNB					4 . s . .	10163
31-PEA	**NORTH BATAK net**	1	4	2,404,406	3,099,685		62.57	96	C	71		PNB					4 . s . .	10164
31-PEAA	ALAS-KLUET cluster	1	1	93,836	120,971		0.01	19	A	20		. . .					0	10165
31-PEAA-a	West kluet					0				20		. . .					0	10166
31-PEAA-b	East kluet					0				20		. . .					0	10167
31-PEAA-c	alas					0				20		. . .					0	10168
31-PEAB	KARO cluster	1	1	739,109	952,836		60.00	100	C	71		PNB					4	10169
31-PEAB-a	karo	1	1	739,109	952,836	0	60.00	100	C	71	Batak: Karo*	PNB	1910-1951	1928-1979	1987-1995	1994	4	10170

Continued overleaf

Table 9-13 continued

Code 1	REFERENCE NAME / Autoglossonym 2	Coun 3	Peo 4	Mother-tongue speakers in 2000 5	in 2025 6	Media radio 7	CHURCH AC% 8	E% 9	Wld 10	Tr 11	Biblioglossonym 12	Print 13-15	P–activity 16	N–activity 17	B–activity 18	J-year 19	Jayuh 20-24	Ref 25
31-PEAC	PAKPAK-DAIRI cluster	1	2	1,571,461	2,025,878		67.51	100	C	61		PNB					1.s..	10171
31-PEAC-a	dairi	1	1	1,529,040	1,971,190	0	68.00	100	C	61	Batak Dairi	PNB		1983	1995	1999	1.s..	10172
31-PEAC-b	pakpak	1	1	42,421	54,688	0	50.00	95	B	61	Pakpak Dairi	PNb		1983			1.s..	10173
31-PEAC-c	singkil					0				61		pnb					1.s..	10174
31-PEB	**SIMALUNGUN net**	1	1	1,196,795	1,542,870		50.00	99	B	72		PNB					0.s..	10175
31-PEBA	SIMALUNGUN cluster	1	1	1,196,795	1,542,870		50.00	99	B	72		PNB					0.s..	10176
31-PEBA-a	simalungun	1	1	1,196,795	1,542,870	0	50.00	99	B	72	Batak: Simalungun*	PNB	1939	1953	1976		0.s..	10177
31-PEC	**SOUTH BATAK net**	2	5	4,281,719	5,519,771		62.12	85	C	72		PNB					2.s..	10178
31-PECA	SOUTH BATAK cluster	2	5	4,281,719	5,519,771		62.12	85	C	72		PNB					2.s..	10179
31-PECA-a	toba	1	2	2,887,927	3,723,024	0	86.47	100	C	72	Batak: Toba*	PNB	1859-1885	1878-1885	1894-1989	1996	2.s..	10180
31-PECA-b	mandailing	1	1	469,182	604,854	0	5.00	44	A	72		pnb					1.s..	10181
31-PECA-c	angkola	1	1	923,897	1,191,059	0	15.00	61	B	72	Batak: Angkola*	PNB	1872-1972	1879-1902	1991		1.s..	10182
31-PED	**LOM net**	1	1	64	82		9.38	30	A	4		. . .					0....	10183
31-PEDA	LOM cluster	1	1	64	82		9.38	30	A	4		. . .					0....	10184
31-PEDA-a	lom	1	1	64	82	0	9.38	30	A	4		. . .					0....	10185
31-PF	LAMPUNGIC chain	1	9	5,815,898	7,703,086		0.01	17	A	20		. . .					2....	10186
31-PFA	**ABUNG net**	1	1	1,264,499	1,835,567		0.01	16	A	20		. . .					0....	10187
31-PFAA	ABUNG cluster	1	1	764,499	985,567		0.01	18	A	20		. . .					0....	10188
31-PFAA-a	abung					0				20		. . .					0....	10189
31-PFAB	KOTABUMI cluster	1	1	200,000	340,000		0.01	14	A	0		. . .					0....	10190
31-PFAB-a	kotabumi	1	1	200,000	340,000	0	0.01	14	A	0		. . .					0....	10191
31-PFAC	MENGGALA cluster	1	1	300,000	510,000		0.01	14	A	0		. . .					0....	10192
31-PFAC-a	menggala	1	1	300,000	510,000	0	0.01	14	A	0		. . .					0....	10193
31-PFB	**LAMPUNG-KOMERING net**	1	8	4,551,399	5,867,519		0.01	17	A	20		. . .					2....	10194
31-PFBA	KOMERING cluster	1	2	1,172,932	1,512,107		0.01	19	A	20		. . .					2....	10195
31-PFBA-a	komering	1	1	821,046	1,058,467	0	0.02	21	A	20	Komering	. . .					2....	10196
31-PFBA-b	ogan	1	1	351,886	453,640	0	0.00	13	A	20		. . .					1....	10197
31-PFBB	SUNGKAI cluster	1	1	6,363	8,203		1.01	25	A	4		. . .					0....	10198
31-PFBB-a	sungkai	1	1	6,363	8,203	0	1.01	25	A	4		. . .					0....	10199
31-PFBC	LAMPUNG cluster	1	1	2,065,184	2,662,369		0.00	16	A	20		. . .					0....	10200
31-PFBC-a	lampung	1	1	2,065,184	2,662,369	0	0.00	16	A	20	Lampung	. . .					0....	10201
31-PFBD	PUBIAN cluster	1	1	610,869	787,513		0.01	18	A	20		. . .					0....	10202
31-PFBD-a	pubian					0				20		. . .					0....	10203
31-PFBE	PESISIR cluster	1	2	664,362	856,475		0.02	16	A	20		. . .					0....	10204
31-PFBE-a	kota-agung	1	1	52,772	68,032	0	0.10	19	A	20		. . .					0....	10205
31-PFBE-b	way-lima					0				20		. . .					0....	10206
31-PFBE-c	telukbetung					0				20		. . .					0....	10207
31-PFBE-d	talang-padang					0				20		. . .					0....	10208
31-PFBE-e	kalianda					0				20		. . .					0....	10209
31-PFBF	KRUI cluster	1	1	31,689	40,852		0.05	17	A	4		. . .					0....	10210
31-PFBF-a	krui	1	1	31,689	40,852	0	0.05	17	A	4		. . .					0....	10211
31-PG	REJANG chain	1	1	1,376,789	1,774,913		0.01	20	A	20		. . .					0....	10212
31-PGA	**REJANG net**	1	1	1,376,789	1,774,913		0.01	20	A	20		. . .					0....	10213
31-PGAA	REJANG cluster	1	1	1,376,789	1,774,913		0.01	20	A	20		. . .					0....	10214
31-PGAA-a	lebong					0				20		. . .					0....	10215
31-PGAA-b	musai					0				20		. . .					0....	10216
31-PGAA-c	lai					0				20		. . .					0....	10217
31-PGAA-d	bekulau					0				20		. . .					0....	10218
31-PGAA-e	bele-tebo					0				20		. . .					0....	10219
31-PH	MALAYIC chain	29	127	95,803,483	124,442,237		6.87	58	B	71		PNB					4Asuh	10220
31-PHA	**MALAYU net**	29	88	66,079,190	86,013,905		5.19	58	B	71		PNB					4Asuh	10221
31-PHAA	BAHASA-MALAYU cluster	26	45	55,521,017	72,513,544		5.17	64	B	71		PNB					4Asuh	10222
31-PHAA-a	malayu-riau-johor					1				71		pnb					1csuh	10223
31-PHAA-b	bahasa-malaysia	22	22	11,644,305	15,763,758	5	0.44	52	B	71	Malay	PNB	1629-1932	1668-1938	1733-1993	1992	1asuh	10224
31-PHAA-c	bahasa-indonesia	10	16	41,103,319	53,012,387	7	6.86	69	B	71	Indonesian	PNB	1955-1968	1968-1978	1974-1985	1980	4Asuh	10225
31-PHAA-d	malayu-pasar	5	5	2,772,120	3,735,758	5	0.01	34	A	71	Malay: Low	PNb	1815	1835			1csuh	10226
31-PHAA-e	gorap	1	1	1,103	1,422	1	1.00	31	A	71		pnb					1csuh	10227
31-PHAB	CENTRAL MALAYU cluster	4	4	2,269,311	2,932,759		0.01	28	A	20		. . .					0....	10228
31-PHAB-a	malayu-kedah	1	1	6,140	7,272	5	0.00	21	A	20		. . .					0....	10229
31-PHAB-b	malayu-johor					1				20		. . .					0....	10230
31-PHAB-c	malayu-negeri-sembilan					1				20		. . .					0....	10231
31-PHAB-d	deli					1				20		. . .					0....	10232
31-PHAB-e	malayu-riau	3	3	2,263,171	2,925,487	5	0.01	28	A	20		. . .					0....	10233
31-PHAB-f	malayu-lingga					1				20		. . .					0....	10234
31-PHAC	NORTH MALAYU cluster	1	2	1,642,847	1,945,674		0.02	35	A	51		PN.					2.s..	10235
31-PHAC-a	malayu-trengganu					1				51		pn.					1.s..	10236
31-PHAC-b	malayu-kelantan					1				51		pn.					1.s..	10237
31-PHAC-c	malayu-pattani	1	2	1,642,847	1,945,674	5	0.02	35	A	51	Malay: Pattani*	PN.	1981	1981		1996	2.s..	10238
31-PHAD	SOUTHWEST MALAYU cluster	1	14	2,216,864	2,857,906		0.57	24	A	41		PN.					0....	10239
31-PHAD-a	kerinci					1				41		pn.					0....	10240
31-PHAD-b	lematang	1	1	175,943	226,820	1	0.10	23	A	41		pn.					0....	10241
31-PHAD-c	rawas	1	1	175,943	226,820	1	0.01	20	A	41		pn.					0....	10244
31-PHAD-d	musi	1	1	175,943	226,820	1	0.00	17	A	41		pn.					0....	10245
31-PHAD-e	sekayu	1	1	469,182	604,854	1	0.01	15	A	41		pn.					0....	10248
31-PHAD-f	sindang-kelingi	1	1	58,648	75,607	1	0.10	25	A	41		pn.					0....	10249
31-PHAD-g	enim	1	1	82,107	105,849	1	1.00	25	A	41		pn.					0....	10250
31-PHAD-h	palembang					1				41		pn.					0....	10251
31-PHAD-i	ogan-2					1				41		pn.					0....	10252
31-PHAD-j	belide					1				41		pn.					0....	10253
31-PHAD-k	penesak	1	1	23,459	30,243	1	1.00	28	A	41		pn.					0....	10254
31-PHAD-l	kayu-agung					1				41		pn.					0....	10255
31-PHAD-m	lengkayap					1				41		pn.					0....	10256
31-PHAD-n	aji					1				41		pn.					0....	10257
31-PHAD-o	daya					1				41		pn.					0....	10258
31-PHAD-p	ranau					1				41		pn.					0....	10259
31-PHAD-q	semendo	1	1	123,150	158,760	5	0.02	30	A	41		pn.					0....	10260
31-PHAD-r	pasemah	1	1	469,182	604,854	5	0.06	31	A	41		pn.					0....	10263
31-PHAD-s	lintang	1	1	82,107	105,849	1	0.50	21	A	41		pn.					0....	10264
31-PHAD-t	lembak	1	1	58,648	75,607	1	0.00	18	A	41		pn.					0....	10265
31-PHAD-u	bengkulu	1	1	64,502	83,154	5	0.03	26	A	41		pn.					0....	10268
31-PHAD-v	serawai	1	1	175,943	226,820	5	6.00	47	A	41	Serawai	PN.	1990	1995			0....	10269
31-PHAD-w	mulak					1				41		pn.					0....	10270
31-PHAD-x	bangka					1				41		pn.					0....	10271
31-PHAD-y	belitung					1				41		pn.					0....	10272
31-PHAD-z	suku-batin	1	1	82,107	105,849	1	0.00	18	A	41		pn.					0....	10273
31-PHAE	MALAYU-TIOMAN cluster	1	1	40,000	68,000		0.04	14	A	0		. . .					0....	10274

Continued opposite

Table 9-13 continued

Code 1	REFERENCE NAME / Autoglossonym 2	Coun 3	Peo 4	Mother-tongue speakers in 2000 / 5	in 2025 / 6	Media radio 7	AC% 8	E% 9	Wld 10	Tr 11	Biblioglossonym 12	Print 13-15	P-activity 16	N-activity 17	B-activity 18	J-year 19	Jayuh 20-24	Ref 25
31-PHAE-a	tioman	1	1	40,000	68,000	0	0.04	14	A	0		...					0....	10275
31-PHAF	MALAYU-BORNEO cluster	3	11	3,955,375	5,146,981		6.96	26	A	20		...					0....	10276
31-PHAF-a	brunei-kedayan	2	2	209,900	293,220	0	4.81	38	A	20		...					0....	10277
31-PHAF-b	malayu-sarawak					0				20		...					0....	10281
31-PHAF-c	selako-kendayan	1	3	965,576	1,244,791	0	26.46	58	B	20		...					0....	10282
31-PHAF-d	banjar	2	3	2,357,084	3,063,890	0	0.00	13	A	20		...					0....	10300
31-PHAF-e	pasir-malay-2					0				20		...					0....	10310
31-PHAF-f	kutai	1	1	289,230	372,866	0	0.10	15	A	20		...					0....	10311
31-PHAF-g	kota-bangun	1	1	110,190	142,053	0	1.00	19	A	20		...					0....	10315
31-PHAF-h	bakumpai-malay					0				20		...					0....	10316
31-PHAF-i	merau					0				20		...					0....	10317
31-PHAF-j	labu	1	1	23,395	30,161	0	35.00	69	B	20		...					0....	10318
31-PHAG	MALAYU-SULAWESI cluster	1	1	106,054	136,721		0.01	24	A	4		...					0....	10319
31-PHAG-a	malayu-makassar					1				4		...					0....	10320
31-PHAG-b	malayu-manado	1	1	106,054	136,721	5	0.01	24	A	4		...					0....	10321
31-PHAH	NORTH MALAYU-MALUKU cluster	1	2	3,669	4,731		29.08	57	B	4		...					0....	10322
31-PHAH-a	malayu-ternate	1	1	848	1,094	5	10.02	39	A	4		...					0....	10323
31-PHAH-b	malayu-bacan	1	1	2,821	3,637	1	34.81	63	B	4		...					0....	10324
31-PHAI	SOUTH MALAYU-MALUKU cluster	2	2	288,763	359,993		91.59	100	C	43		PN.					0....	10325
31-PHAI-a	malayu-ambon	2	2	288,763	359,993	5	91.59	100	C	43	Malay, Ambonese	PN.		1877-1883			0....	10326
31-PHAJ	MALAYU-TENGGARA cluster	1	2	23,332	30,079		29.72	52	B	0		...					0....	10327
31-PHAJ-a	malayu-larantuka	1	1	14,848	19,141	0	1.00	24	A	0		...					0....	10328
31-PHAJ-b	basa-kupang	1	1	8,484	10,938	0	80.00	100	C	0		...					0....	10329
31-PHAK	MALAYU-IRIAN cluster	1	1	4,000	6,800		0.05	14	A	0		...					0....	10330
31-PHAK-a	malayu-irian	1	1	4,000	6,800	0	0.05	14	A	0		...					0....	10331
31-PHAL	MALAYU-KOKOS cluster	5	5	7,958	10,717		5.18	36	A	3		...					0a...	10332
31-PHAL-a	kokos-keeling					1				3		...					0c...	10333
31-PHAL-b	kokos-christmas	1	1	548	659	5	0.18	34	A	3		...					0a...	10334
31-PHAL-c	kokos-sabah	3	3	6,137	8,417	5	5.65	35	A	3		...					0c...	10335
31-PHB	**MALAYO-CREOLE net**	3	5	9,399,005	12,119,104		29.64	83	B	43		PN.					0A...	10336
31-PHBA	BABA-MALAY cluster	1	1	106,054	136,721		6.00	53	B	43		PN.					0....	10337
31-PHBA-a	baba-malay	1	1	106,054	136,721	5	6.00	53	B	43	Malay: Baba	PN.	1891	1913			0....	10338
31-PHBB	PERANAKAN cluster	3	3	6,253,448	8,035,193		40.65	96	B	0		...					0A...	10341
31-PHBB-a	paranakan	3	3	6,253,448	8,035,193	7	40.65	96	B	0		...					0A...	10342
31-PHBC	BETAWI cluster	1	1	2,969,503	3,828,190		8.00	57	B	20		...					0A...	10343
31-PHBC-a	bahasa-betawi	1	1	2,969,503	3,828,190	5	8.00	57	B	20		...					0A...	10344
31-PHBD	CHITI cluster	1	1	30,000	51,000		0.05	14	A	0		...					0....	10348
31-PHBD-a	chiti	1	1	30,000	51,000	0	0.05	14	A	0		...					0....	10349
31-PHBE	MALAYU-SRI-LANKA cluster	1	1	40,000	68,000		0.03	14	A	0		...					0....	10350
31-PHBE-a	Literary malayu-sri-lanka					0				0		...					0....	10351
31-PHBE-b	Urban malayu-sri-lanka					0				0		...					0....	10352
31-PHC	**MOKEN-MOKLEN net**	5	8	144,040	192,265		1.41	17	A	35		P..					0....	10353
31-PHCA	MOKEN cluster	5	7	142,223	190,113		1.40	17	A	35	Moken	P..	1913				0....	10354
31-PHCA-a	moken	1	1	74,810	96,443	0	0.03	17	A	35	Salong	P..	1913				0....	10355
31-PHCB	MOKLEN cluster	1	1	1,817	2,152		1.98	22	A	12		...					0....	10360
31-PHCB-a	moklen	1	1	1,817	2,152	0	1.98	22	A	12	Moklen	...					0....	10361
31-PHD	**URAK-LAWOI net**	1	1	3,641	4,312		2.99	30	A	35		P..					0.s..	10362
31-PHDA	URAK-LAWOI cluster	1	1	3,641	4,312		2.99	30	A	35	Urak Lawoi'	P..	1976				0.s..	10363
31-PHDA-a	North urak-lawoi			0	0	0				35		p..					0.s..	10364
31-PHDA-b	South urak-lawoi			0	0	0	0.00	0		35		p..					0.s..	10365
31-PHE	**DUANO net**	1	1	3,032	4,221		0.99	21	A	4		...					0....	10366
31-PHEA	DUANO cluster	1	1	3,032	4,221		0.99	21	A	4		...					0....	10367
31-PHEA-a	duano'	1	1	3,032	4,221	0	0.99	21	A	4		...					0....	10368
31-PHF	**TEMUAN-SELETAR net**	1	4	31,307	43,663		3.52	26	A	4		...					0....	10369
31-PHFA	TEMUAN cluster	1	1	14,690	20,452		6.00	30	A	4		...					0....	10370
31-PHFA-a	temuan	1	1	14,690	20,452	0	6.00	30	A	4		...					0....	10371
31-PHFA-b	beduanda					0				4		...					0....	10372
31-PHFA-c	belanda					0				4		...					0....	10373
31-PHFA-d	berembun					0				4		...					0....	10374
31-PHFA-e	besisi					0				4		...					0....	10375
31-PHFA-f	kenaboi			0	0	0	0.00	0		4		...					0....	10376
31-PHFA-g	mantra					0				4		...					0....	10377
31-PHFA-h	temuan					0				4		...					0....	10378
31-PHFA-i	udai					0				4		...					0....	10379
31-PHFB	ORANG-HULU cluster	1	3	16,367	22,786		1.28	23	A	4		...					0....	10380
31-PHFB-a	orang-hulu	1	3	16,367	22,786	0	1.28	23	A	4		...					0....	10381
31-PHFC	ORANG-KANAQ cluster	1	1	50	85		6.00	24	A	0		...					0....	10382
31-PHFC-a	orang-kanaq	1	1	50	85	0	6.00	24	A	0		...					0....	10383
31-PHFD	ORANG-SELETAR cluster	2	1	200	340		5.00	24	A	0		...					0....	10384
31-PHFD-a	orang-seletar	1	1	200	340	0	5.00	24	A	0		...					0....	10385
31-PHG	**MINANGKABAU net**	2	4	5,890,417	7,642,505		0.02	35	A	41		PN.					2....	10386
31-PHGA	MINANG cluster	2	4	5,890,417	7,642,505		0.02	35	A	41	Minangkabau	PN.	1980-1990	1995		1993	2....	10387
31-PHGA-a	West minang					1				41		pn.					1....	10388
31-PHGA-b	North minang					1				41		pn.					1....	10395
31-PHGA-c	Central minang					1				41		pn.					1....	10396
31-PHGA-d	South minang					1				41		pn.					1....	10402
31-PHGA-e	muko-muko	1	1	35,189	45,364	1	0.10	24	A	41		pn.					1....	10406
31-PHGA-f	pekal	1	1	35,189	45,364	1	0.10	24	A	41		pn.					1....	10407
31-PHGA-g	agam					1				41		pn.					1....	10408
31-PHGA-h	tanah					1				41		pn.					1....	10409
31-PHGA-i	minangkabau-negeri-sembilan	1	1	473,278	658,903	1	0.02	22	A	41		pn.					1....	10410
31-PHH	**LUBU-KUBU net**	1	4	1,343,255	1,731,681		0.02	17	A	20		...					0....	10411
31-PHHA	LUBU cluster	1	2	393,183	506,879		0.00	11	A	20		...					0....	10412
31-PHHA-a	ulu					0				20		...					0....	10413
31-PHHA-b	mamaq					0				20		...					0....	10414
31-PHHA-c	akit					0				20		...					0....	10415
31-PHHA-d	talang					0				20		...					0....	10416
31-PHHA-e	sakei									20		...					0....	10417
31-PHHB	KUBU cluster	1	2	950,072	1,224,802		0.02	19	A	20		...					0....	10418
31-PHHB-a	lalang					1				20		...					0....	10419
31-PHHB-b	bajat					1				20		...					0....	10420
31-PHHB-c	ulu-lako					1				20		...					0....	10421
31-PHHB-d	tungkal					1				20		...					0....	10422
31-PHHB-e	tungkal-ilir					1				20		...					0....	10423

Continued overleaf

Table 9-13 continued

Code 1	REFERENCE NAME / Autoglossonym 2	Coun 3	Peo 4	Mother-tongue speakers in 2000 5	in 2025 6	Media radio 7	CHURCH AC% 8	E% 9	Wld 10	Tr 11	Biblioglossonym 12	SCRIPTURES Print 13-15	P-activity 16	N-activity 17	B-activity 18	J-year 19	Jayuh 20-24	Ref 25
31-PHHB-f	dawas					1				20		. . .					0.....	10424
31-PHHB-g	supat					1				20		. . .					0.....	10425
31-PHHB-h	djamb	1	1	938,342	1,209,681	5	0.00	19	A	20		. . .					0.....	10426
31-PHHB-i	ridan					1				20		. . .					0.....	10427
31-PHHB-j	kubu-nomad					1				20		. . .					0.....	10428
31-PHI	**MALAYIC-DAYAK net**	3	8	771,964	1,045,535		42.86	93	B	71		PNB					3As..	10429
31-PHIA	IBAN-SARAWAK cluster	3	6	501,209	696,486		40.28	95	B	71	Iban	PNB	1864-1968	1933-1952	1988	1991	3.s..	10430
31-PHIA-a	batang-lupar	1	1	17,257	24,142	1	20.00	69	B	71		pnb					1.s..	10431
31-PHIA-b	bugau					1				71		pnb					1.s..	10432
31-PHIA-c	balau	1	1	7,888	10,981	1	29.99	70	B	71		pnb					1.s..	10433
31-PHIA-d	milikin	1	1	6,311	8,786	1	20.00	56	B	71		pnb					1.s..	10434
31-PHIA-e	sibuyau	1	1	14,198	19,767	1	5.00	39	A	71		pnb					1.s..	10435
31-PHIA-f	kantu'					1				71		pnb					1.s..	10436
31-PHIA-g	desa					1				71		pnb					1.s..	10437
31-PHIA-h	dali					1				71		pnb					1.s..	10438
31-PHIA-i	lemanak					1				71		pnb					1.s..	10439
31-PHIA-j	ulu-al					1				71		pnb					1.s..	10440
31-PHIA-k	undup					1				71		pnb					1.s..	10441
31-PHIA-l	sekarang					1				71		pnb					1.s..	10442
31-PHIA-m	dau					1				71		pnb					1.s..	10443
31-PHIB	IBAN-KETUNGAU cluster	1	1	248,632	320,529		51.00	94	B	0		. . .					0A....	10444
31-PHIB-a	air-tabun					0				0		. . .					0c....	10445
31-PHIB-b	sigarau					0				0		. . .					0c....	10446
31-PHIB-c	sekalau					0				0		. . .					0c....	10447
31-PHIB-d	sekapat					0				0		. . .					0c....	10448
31-PHIB-e	bugau					0				0		. . .					0c....	10449
31-PHIB-f	banjur					0				0		. . .					0c....	10450
31-PHIB-g	sebaru'					0				0		. . .					0c....	10451
31-PHIB-h	demam					0				0		. . .					0c....	10452
31-PHIB-i	maung					0				0		. . .					0c....	10453
31-PHIC	IBAN-SEBERUANG cluster	1	1	22,123	28,520		10.00	28	A	12	Seberuang	. . .					0.....	10454
31-PHIC-a	iban-seberuang					0				12		. . .					0.....	10455
31-PHJ	**MADURA net**	2	4	12,137,632	15,645,046		0.20	49	A	61		PNB					1.s..	10456
31-PHJA	MADURA cluster	2	3	12,116,421	15,617,702		0.21	49	A	61	Madurese*	PNB	1890-1964		1994	1992	1.s..	10457
31-PHJA-a	West madura	2	2	26,300	31,501	1	2.52	43	A	61	Madura	PNB	1890-1964		1994		1.s..	10458
31-PHJA-b	Central madura					1				61		pnb					1.s..	10461
31-PHJA-c	East madura					1				61		pnb					1.s..	10462
31-PHJA-d	pasuruan-besuki					1				61		pnb					1.s..	10465
31-PHJB	KANGEAN cluster	1	1	21,211	27,344		0.10	19	A	3		. . .					0.....	10468
31-PHJB-a	kangean	1	1	21,211	27,344	0	0.10	19	A	3		. . .					0.....	10469
31-PI	JAVANESE chain	13	19	56,840,245	73,341,928		12.53	78	B	68		PNB					2As.h	10470
31-PIA	**JAVANESE net**	13	19	56,840,245	73,341,928		12.53	78	B	68		PNB					2As.h	10471
31-PIAA	JAWA cluster	13	18	56,255,889	72,588,595		12.65	78	B	68		PNB					2As.h	10472
31-PIAA-a	tembung-kawi					1				68		pnb					1cs.h	10473
31-PIAA-b	jawa-halus					1				68		pnb					1cs.h	10474
31-PIAA-c	jawa-pegon					1				68		pnb					1cs.h	10475
31-PIAA-d	basa-kedatan					1				68		pnb					1cs.h	10476
31-PIAA-e	basa-krama					1				68		pnb					1cs.h	10477
31-PIAA-f	basa-madya					1				68		pnb					1cs.h	10480
31-PIAA-g	General jawa	10	11	55,104,197	71,106,869	5	12.86	79	B	68	Javanese	PNB	1954	1829-1981	1854-1994	1990	2As.h	10481
31-PIAA-h	banten					1				68		pnb					1cs.h	10494
31-PIAA-i	osing	1	1	481,887	621,233	1	2.00	37	A	68		pnb					1cs.h	10495
31-PIAA-j	jawa-palembang	2	2	597,177	768,570	5	0.01	41	A	68		pnb					1cs.h	10496
31-PIAA-k	jawa-surinam	3	3	63,057	79,155	7	26.95	88	B	68	Javanese: Caribbean*	Pnb	1985-1992				1As.h	10497
31-PIAA-l	jawa-nouméa	1	1	9,571	12,768	5	15.00	76	B	68		pnb					1As.h	10498
31-PIAB	TENGGER cluster	1	1	584,356	753,333		1.00	39	A	20		. . .					0.....	10499
31-PIAB-a	tengger	1	1	584,356	753,333	5	1.00	39	A	20		. . .					0.....	10500
31-PJ	SUNDANESE chain	1	2	22,499,439	29,005,564		0.08	55	B	61		PNB					1A...	10501
31-PJA	**SUNDA net**	1	2	22,499,439	29,005,564		0.08	55	B	61		PNB					1A...	10502
31-PJAA	SUNDA cluster	1	1	22,493,585	28,998,017		0.08	55	B	61		PNB					1A...	10503
31-PJAA-a	Central sunda	1	1	22,493,585	28,998,017	4	0.08	55	B	61	Sundanese	PNB	1854-1895	1877-1978	1891-1991	1991	1A...	10504
31-PJAA-b	West sunda					1				61		pnb					1c...	10505
31-PJAA-c	North sunda					1				61		pnb					1c...	10506
31-PJAA-d	East Central sunda.					1				61		pnb					1c...	10507
31-PJAA-e	Southeast sunda					1				61		pnb					1c...	10508
31-PJAA-f	Northeast sunda					1				61		pnb					1c...	10509
31-PJAB	BADUI cluster	1	1	5,854	7,547		1.01	25	A	4		. . .					0.....	10510
31-PJAB-a	badui	1	1	5,854	7,547	0	1.01	25	A	4		. . .					0.....	10511
31-PK	BALI-SASAK chain	2	4	7,024,652	9,056,417		0.64	38	A	61		PNB					1.....	10512
31-PKA	**BALI-SASAK net**	2	4	7,024,652	9,056,417		0.64	38	A	61		PNB					1.....	10513
31-PKAA	BALI cluster	2	2	4,209,605	5,427,348		1.05	46	A	61		pnb					1.....	10514
31-PKAA-a	bali	2	2	4,209,605	5,427,348	2	1.05	46	A	61		pnb				1992	1.....	10515
31-PKAA-b	Urban bali					1				61		pnb					1.....	10524
31-PKAA-c	bali-aga					1				61	Bali	PNB	1910-1957	1978-1989	1990		1.....	10528
31-PKAA-d	nusa-penida					1				61		pnb					1.....	10532
31-PKAB	SASAK cluster	1	1	2,463,161	3,175,429		0.02	26	A	41	Sasak	PN.	1948	1996		1997	1.....	10533
31-PKAB-a	kuto-kute					1				41		pn.					1.....	10534
31-PKAB-b	ngeto-ngete					1				41		pn.					1.....	10535
31-PKAB-c	meno-mene					1				41		pn.					1.....	10536
31-PKAB-d	ngeno-ngene					1				41		pn.					1.....	10537
31-PKAB-e	mriak-mriku					1				41		pn.					1.....	10538
31-PKAC	SUMBAWA cluster	1	1	351,886	453,640		0.01	19	A	20		. . .					0.....	10539
31-PKAC-a	sumbawa	1	1	351,886	453,640	0	0.01	19	A	20		. . .					0.....	10540
31-Q	**SULAWESI set**	3	115	13,338,277	17,317,827		13.09	49	A	72		PNB					2As..	10541
31-QA	MUNA-BUTON chain	2	18	656,603	847,848		3.25	25	A	22		P..					0.....	10542
31-QAA	**TUKANG-BONERATE net**	1	4	284,181	366,358		6.14	33	A	20		. . .					0.....	10543
31-QAAA	BONERATE cluster	1	1	11,581	14,930		0.05	16	A	2		. . .					0.....	10544
31-QAAA-a	bonerate	1	1	11,581	14,930	0	0.05	16	A	2		. . .					0.....	10545
31-QAAA-b	karompa					0				2		. . .					0.....	10546
31-QAAB	SOUTH TUKANG-BESI cluster	1	1	139,545	179,898		5.00	33	A	20		. . .					0.....	10547
31-QAAB-a	binongko					0				20		. . .					0.....	10548
31-QAAB-b	tomea					0				20		. . .					0.....	10549
31-QAAC	NORTH TUKANG-BESI cluster	1	2	133,055	171,530		7.87	35	A	4		. . .					0.....	10550
31-QAAC-a	kaledupa	1	1	4,242	5,469	0	4.01	26	A	4		. . .					0.....	10551
31-QAAC-b	wanci					0				4		. . .					0.....	10552
31-QAB	**KALAOTOA-LAIYOLO net**	1	2	1,909	2,461		1.68	23	A	4		. . .					0.....	10553

Continued opposite

Table 9-13 continued

Code 1	REFERENCE NAME / Autoglossonym 2	Coun 3	Peo 4	Mother-tongue speakers in 2000 5	in 2025 6	Media radio 7	AC% 8	E% 9	Wld 10	Tr 11	Biblioglossonym 12	Print 13-15	P-activity 16	N-activity 17	B-activity 18	J-year 19	Jayuh 20-24	Ref 25
31-QABA	KALAOTOA cluster	1	1	615	793		0.98	21	A	4		...					0....	10554
31-QABA-a	kalastoa	1	1	615	793	0	0.98	21	A	4		...					0....	10555
31-QABB	LAIYOLO cluster	1	1	1,294	1,668		2.01	24	A	2		...					0....	10556
31-QABB-a	barang-barang					0				2		...					0....	10557
31-QABB-b	laiyolo	1	1	1,294	1,668	0	2.01	24	A	2		...					0....	10558
31-QAC	**SOUTH BUTON net**	1	1	18,475	23,817		4.00	23	A	2		...					0....	10559
31-QACA	SOUTH BUTON cluster	1	1	18,475	23,817		4.00	23	A	2		...					0....	10560
31-QACA-a	kaesabu					0				2		...					0....	10561
31-QACA-b	sampolawa					0				2		...					0....	10562
31-QACA-c	wabula					0				2		...					0....	10563
31-QACA-d	masiri					0				2		...					0....	10570
31-QAD	**LASALIMU net**	1	1	2,863	3,691		9.99	35	A	4		...					0....	10571
31-QADA	LASALIMU cluster	1	1	2,863	3,691		9.99	35	A	4		...					0....	10572
31-QADA-a	lasalimu	1	1	2,863	3,691	0	9.99	35	A	4		...					0....	10573
31-QAE	**WOLIO net**	2	2	47,877	63,097		0.01	14	A	2		...					0....	10574
31-QAEA	WOLIO cluster	2	2	47,877	63,097		0.01	14	A	2		...					0....	10575
31-QAEA-a	wolio	2	2	47,877	63,097	0	0.01	14	A	2		...					0....	10576
31-QAF	**KAMARU net**	1	1	2,863	3,691		4.02	26	A	4		...					0....	10577
31-QAFA	KAMARU cluster	1	1	2,863	3,691		4.02	26	A	4		...					0....	10578
31-QAFA-a	kamaru	1	1	2,863	3,691	0	4.02	26	A	4		...					0....	10579
31-QAG	**WOTU net**	1	1	6,151	7,930		0.10	13	A	2		...					0....	10580
31-QAGA	WOTU cluster	1	1	6,151	7,930		0.10	13	A	2		...					0....	10581
31-QAGA-a	wotu	1	1	6,151	7,930	0	0.10	13	A	2		...					0....	10582
31-QAH	**MUNA net**	1	6	292,284	376,803		0.92	19	A	22		P..					0....	10583
31-QAHA	BUSOA cluster	1	1	573	738		2.97	25	A	4		...					0....	10584
31-QAHA-a	busoa	1	1	573	738	0	2.97	25	A	4		...					0....	10585
31-QAHB	LIABUKU cluster	1	1	1,124	1,449		0.27	19	A	4		...					0....	10586
31-QAHB-a	liabuku	1	1	1,124	1,449	0	0.27	19	A	4		...					0....	10587
31-QAHC	KAIMBULAWA cluster	1	1	1,697	2,188		0.47	21	A	4		...					0....	10588
31-QAHC-a	kaimbulawa	1	1	1,697	2,188	0	0.47	21	A	4		...					0....	10589
31-QAHC-b	lantoi					0				4		...					0....	10590
31-QAHC-c	kambe-kambero					0				4		...					0....	10591
31-QAHD	MUNA cluster	1	1	266,258	343,252		1.00	20	A	22	Muna	P..	1993				0....	10592
31-QAHD-a	gumas					0				22	Muna: Southern	P..	1993				0....	10593
31-QAHD-b	North muna					0				22		p..					0....	10608
31-QAHD-c	siompu					0				22		p..					0....	10615
31-QAHD-d	tiworo					0				22		p..					0....	10616
31-QAHE	PANCANA cluster	1	1	21,508	27,727		0.01	12	A	2		...					0....	10617
31-QAHE-a	kapontori					0				2		...					0....	10618
31-QAHE-b	kalende					0				2		...					0....	10619
31-QAHE-c	labuandiri					0				2		...					0....	10620
31-QAHF	KIOKO cluster	1	1	1,124	1,449		0.09	15	A	4		...					0....	10621
31-QAHF-a	kioko	1	1	1,124	1,449	0	0.09	15	A	4		...					0....	10622
31-QAHF-b	kambowa					0				4		...					0....	10623
31-QB	SOUTH SULAWESI chain	3	34	8,569,656	11,111,458		7.48	46	A	72		PNB					2As..	10624
31-QBA	**MAKASSAR-KONJO net**	1	5	2,337,255	3,013,113		0.73	40	A	61		PNB					2.s..	10625
31-QBAA	SALAYAR cluster	1	1	119,120	153,565		3.00	33	A	20		...					0....	10626
31-QBAA-a	salayar	1	1	119,120	153,565	0	3.00	33	A	20		...					0....	10627
31-QBAA-b	tanahjampea					0				20		...					0....	10628
31-QBAB	BENTONG cluster	1	1	30,798	39,704		3.00	26	A	4		...					0....	10629
31-QBAB-a	bentong	1	1	30,798	39,704	0	3.00	26	A	4		...					0....	10630
31-QBAC	MAKASSAR cluster	1	1	1,876,684	2,419,361		0.20	42	A	61	Macassar*	PNB	1864-1875	1888	1900-1995	1997	2.s..	10631
31-QBAC-a	gowa					1				61		pnb					1.s..	10632
31-QBAC-b	lakiung					1				61		pnb					1.s..	10633
31-QBAC-c	maros-pangkep					1				61		pnb					1.s..	10637
31-QBAC-d	turatea					1				61		pnb					1.s..	10638
31-QBAD	SOUTH KONJO cluster	1	1	141,200	182,030		0.20	24	A	20		...					0....	10639
31-QBAD-a	konjo-pesisir					0				20		...					0....	10640
31-QBAD-b	tana-toa					0				20		...					0....	10641
31-QBAD-c	banta-eng					0				20		...					0....	10642
31-QBAE	NORTHWEST KONJO cluster	1	1	169,453	218,453		5.00	35	A	20		...					0....	10643
31-QBAE-a	konjo-pegunungan	1	1	169,453	218,453	0	5.00	35	A	20		...					0....	10644
31-QBB	**BUGIS net**	3	3	3,950,506	5,156,601		1.00	47	A	72		PNB					2....	10645
31-QBBA	BUGIS cluster	3	3	3,950,506	5,156,601		1.00	47	A	72	Bugis	PNB	1863-1994	1888	1900-1995	1994	2....	10646
31-QBBA-a	enna					1				72		pnb					1....	10647
31-QBBA-b	bone					1				72		pnb					1....	10651
31-QBBA-c	soppeng					1				72		pnb					1....	10655
31-QBBA-d	barru					1				72		pnb					1....	10658
31-QBBA-e	sawitto					1				72		pnb					1....	10663
31-QBBA-f	sidrap					1				72		pnb					1....	10666
31-QBBA-g	wajo					1				72		pnb					1....	10670
31-QBBA-h	luwu'					1				72		pnb					1....	10671
31-QBBA-i	pasangkayu					1				72		pnb					1....	10676
31-QBBA-j	pangkep					1				72		pnb					1....	10677
31-QBBA-k	camba					1				72		pnb					1....	10678
31-QBC	**CAMPALAGIAN net**	1	1	36,949	47,634		1.00	20	A	2		...					0....	10679
31-QBCA	CAMPALAGIAN cluster	1	1	36,949	47,634		1.00	20	A	2		...					0....	10680
31-QBCA-a	campalagian	1	1	36,949	47,634	0	1.00	20	A	2		...					0....	10681
31-QBCA-b	buku					0				2		...					0....	10682
31-QBD	**MASENREMPULU net**	1	5	292,899	377,597		1.64	22	A	20		...					0....	10683
31-QBDA	MAIWA cluster	1	1	57,545	74,185		1.00	23	A	4		...					0....	10684
31-QBDA-a	maiwa	1	1	57,545	74,185	0	1.00	23	A	4		...					0....	10685
31-QBDB	ENREKANG cluster	1	2	122,662	158,132		1.66	24	A	20		...					0....	10686
31-QBDB-a	enrekang	1	1	56,484	72,818	0	0.10	20	A	20		...					0....	10687
31-QBDB-b	ranga					0				20		...					0....	10688
31-QBDB-c	pattinjo	1	1	66,178	85,314		3.00	27	A	20		...					0....	10689
31-QBDC	DURI cluster	1	1	107,326	138,362		2.00	20	A	20		...					0....	10693
31-QBDC-a	duri	1	1	107,326	138,362	0	2.00	20	A	20	Duri	...					0....	10694
31-QBDC-b	cakke					0				20		...					0....	10695
31-QBDC-c	kalosi					0				20		...					0....	10696

Continued overleaf

Table 9-13 continued

Code 1	REFERENCE NAME Autoglossonym 2	Coun 3	Peo 4	Mother-tongue speakers in 2000 5	in 2025 6	Media radio 7	CHURCH AC% 8	E% 9	Wld 10	Tr 11	Biblioglossonym 12	SCRIPTURES Print 13-15	P–activity 16	N–activity 17	B–activity 18	J-year 19	Jayuh 20-24	Ref 25
31-QBDD	MALIMPUNG cluster	1	1	5,366	6,918		1.01	25	A	4		. . .					0	10697
31-QBDD-a	malimpung					0				4		. . .					0	10698
31-QBE	**TORAJA-MAMASA net**	1	9	1,528,045	1,969,903		35.24	62	B	61		PNB					0A . . .	10699
31-QBEA	TOALA-PALILI cluster	1	1	39,707	51,188		0.90	29	A	3		. . .					0	10700
31-QBEA-a	toala'			39,707	51,188	0	0.90	29	A	3		. . .					0	10701
31-QBEA-b	toware					0				3		. . .					0	10702
31-QBEA-c	sangangalla'					0				3		. . .					0	10703
31-QBEA-d	sillanan-gandangbatu					0				3		. . .					0	10704
31-QBEA-e	palili'					0				3		. . .					0	10705
31-QBEB	TAE cluster	1	3	741,168	955,488		6.96	31	A	2		. . .					0	10706
31-QBEB-a	to-rongkong	1	1	277,246	357,416	0	10.00	38	A	2		. . .					0	10707
31-QBEB-b	Northeast luwu	1	1	424,215	546,884		0.01	21	A	2		. . .					0	10712
31-QBEB-c	bua					0				2		. . .					0	10713
31-QBEC	TALONDO cluster	1	1	615	793		70.08	100	C	4		. . .					0	10714
31-QBEC-a	talondo'	1	1	615	793	0	70.08	100	C	4		. . .					0	10715
31-QBEC-b	pedasi					0				4		. . .					0	10716
31-QBED	TORAJA-SADAN cluster	1	1	575,490	741,903	1	65.00	100	C	61		PNB					0	10717
31-QBED-a	makale					1				61		pnb					0	10718
31-QBED-b	tallulembangna					1				61		pnb					0	10719
31-QBED-c	rantepao					1				61		pnb					0	10720
31-QBED-d	kesu'					1				61		pnb					0	10721
31-QBED-e	toraja-barat	1	1	575,490	741,903	2	65.00	100	C	61	Toraja*	PNB	1933-1948	1951-1989	1960-1995		0	10722
31-QBEE	MANGKI cluster	1	1	13,554	17,473		70.00	100	C	2		. . .					0	10723
31-QBEE-a	kalumpang	1	1	13,554	17,473	0	70.00	100	C	2		. . .					0	10724
31-QBEE-b	karataun			0	0	0	0.00	0		2		. . .					0	10725
31-QBEE-c	mablei			0	0	0	0.00	0		2		. . .					0	10726
31-QBEE-d	mangki			0	0	0	0.00	0		2		. . .					0	10727
31-QBEE-e	bone hau			0	0	0	0.00	0		2		. . .					0	10728
31-QBEF	MAMASA cluster	1	2	157,511	203,058		65.11	79	C	22		P . .					0A . . .	10729
31-QBEF-a	pattae'	1	1	44,543	57,423	0	2.00	27	A	22		p . .					0c . . .	10730
31-QBEF-b	Central mamasa	1	1	112,968	145,635	0	90.00	100	C	22	Mamasa	P . .	1995				0A . . .	10735
31-QBEF-c	North mamasa					0				22		p . .					0c . . .	10736
31-QBF	**MANDAR net**	1	1	253,511	326,818		7.00	32	A	20		. . .					0	10737
31-QBFA	MANDAR cluster	1	1	253,511	326,818		7.00	32	A	20		. . .					0	10738
31-QBFA-a	balanipa					0				20		. . .					0	10739
31-QBFA-b	majene					0				20		. . .					0	10742
31-QBG	**PITU-ARALLE net**	1	5	92,859	119,713		12.36	36	A	22		P . .					0	10747
31-QBGA	ARALLE-TABULAHAN cluster	1	3	28,464	36,696		26.04	53	B	12	Aralle-tabulahan	. . .					0	10748
31-QBGA-a	aralle					0				12		. . .					0	10749
31-QBGA-b	dakka	1	1	1,845	2,379	0	4.99	29	A	12		. . .					0	10752
31-QBGA-c	pannei	1	1	11,093	14,301	0	3.00	26	A	12		. . .					0	10753
31-QBGB	PITU-ULUNNA-SALU cluster	1	1	27,107	34,946		15.00	45	A	22		P . .					0	10756
31-QBGB-a	bumal					0				22		P . .					0	10757
31-QBGB-b	bambam					0				22	Bambam	P . .	1994-1995				0	10758
31-QBGB-c	mehala'an					0				22		p . .					0	10759
31-QBGB-d	West rantebulahan					0				22		p . .					0	10760
31-QBGB-e	pattae					0				22		p . .					0	10761
31-QBGB-f	matangnga					0				22		p . .					0	10762
31-QBGB-g	issilita'					0				22		p . .					0	10763
31-QBGB-h	salu-mukanam					0				22		p . .					0	10764
31-QBGB-i	pakkau					0				22		p . .					0	10765
31-QBGC	ULUMANDA cluster	1	1	37,288	48,071		0.01	16	A	2		. . .					0	10766
31-QBGC-a	sondoang					0				2		. . .					0	10767
31-QBGC-b	tappalang					0				2		. . .					0	10768
31-QBGC-c	botteng					0				2		. . .					0	10769
31-QBH	**MAMUJU net**	1	1	67,768	87,365		6.00	32	A	20		. . .					0	10770
31-QBHA	MAMUJU cluster	1	1	67,768	87,365		6.00	32	A	20		. . .					0	10771
31-QBHA-a	mamuju	1	1	67,768	87,365	0	6.00	32	A	20		. . .					0	10772
31-QBHA-b	sumare-rangas					0				20		. . .					0	10773
31-QBHA-c	padang					0				20		. . .					0	10774
31-QBHA-d	sinyonyoi					0				20		. . .					0	10775
31-QBI	**TONGKOU-PANASUAN net**	1	2	1,146	1,476		74.17	94	C	4		. . .					0	10776
31-QBIA	TONGKOU cluster	1	1	85	109		2.35	24	A	4		. . .					0	10777
31-QBIA-a	tongkou	1	1	85	109	0	2.35	24	A	4		. . .					0	10778
31-QBIB	PANASUAN cluster	1	1	1,061	1,367		79.92	100	C	2		. . .					0	10779
31-QBIB-a	to-panasuan	1	1	1,061	1,367	0	79.92	100	C	2		. . .					0	10780
31-QBJ	**SEKO net**	1	2	8,718	11,238		80.00	100	C	12		. . .					0	10781
31-QBJA	SEKO-TENGAH cluster	1	1	2,673	3,445		79.99	100	C	2		. . .					0	10782
31-QBJA-a	tengah					0				2		. . .					0	10783
31-QBJA-b	pewanean					0				2		. . .					0	10784
31-QBJB	SEKO-PADANG cluster	1	1	6,045	7,793		80.00	100	C	12	Seko Padang	. . .					0	10785
31-QBJB-a	sua-to-padang					0				12		. . .					0	10786
31-QBJB-b	lodang					0				12		. . .					0	10787
31-QBJB-c	hono'					0				12		. . .					0	10788
31-QC	LEMOLANG chain	1	1	1,994	2,570		5.02	29	A	2		. . .					0	10789
31-QCA	**LEMOLANG net**	1	1	1,994	2,570		5.02	29	A	2		. . .					0	10790
31-QCAA	LEMOLANG cluster	1	1	1,994	2,570		5.02	29	A	2		. . .					0	10791
31-QCAA-a	sassa-salassa					0				2		. . .					0	10792
31-QCAA-b	baebunta					0				2		. . .					0	10793
31-QD	BUNGKU-MORI chain	1	17	563,234	736,295		3.40	28	A	44		PN .					0	10794
31-QDA	**MORONENE-TOKOTU'A net**	1	1	55,019	79,145		0.01	17	A	20		. . .					0	10795
31-QDAA	TOKOTU'A cluster	1	1	20,000	34,000		0.01	14	A	0		. . .					0	10796
31-QDAA-a	tokotu'-a					0				0		. . .					0	10797
31-QDAB	WITAEA cluster	1	1	35,019	45,145		0.01	18	A	20		. . .					0	10798
31-QDAB-a	moronene	1	1	35,019	45,145	0	0.01	18	A	20	Moronene	. . .					0	10799
31-QDAB-b	poleang					0				20		. . .					0	10800
31-QDAB-c	rumbia					0				20		. . .					0	10801
31-QDB	**KULISUSU-KORONI net**	1	3	24,817	31,993		0.98	23	A	4		. . .					0	10802
31-QDBA	TALOKI cluster	1	1	530	684		0.00	14	A	4		. . .					0	10803
31-QDBA-a	maligano					0				4		. . .					0	10804
31-QDBA-b	wakalambe					0				4		. . .					0	10805
31-QDBB	KULISUSU cluster	1	1	23,714	30,571		1.00	23	A	4		. . .					0	10806
31-QDBB-a	kulisusu	1	1	23,714	30,571	0	1.00	23	A	4		. . .					0	10807

Continued opposite

Table 9-13 continued

Code 1	REFERENCE NAME / Autoglossonym 2	Coun 3	Peo 4	Mother-tongue speakers in 2000 5	in 2025 6	Media radio 7	CHURCH AC% 8	E% 9	Wld 10	Tr 11	Biblioglossonym 12	SCRIPTURES Print 13-15	P-activity 16	N-activity 17	B-activity 18	J-year 19	Jayuh 20-24	Ref 25
31-QDBB-b	bonegunu					0				4		...					0	10808
31-QDBC	KORONI cluster	1	1	573	738		1.05	24	A	3		...					0	10809
31-QDBC-a	koroni	1	1	573	738	0	1.05	24	A	3		...					0	10810
31-QDC	**BUNGKU-WAWONII net**	1	3	58,163	76,831		0.92	20	A	4		...					0	10811
31-QDCA	WAWONII cluster	1	1	24,859	32,047		1.00	22	A	4		...					0	10812
31-QDCA-a	wawonii	1	1	24,859	32,047	0	1.00	22	A	4		...					0	10813
31-QDCA-b	menui					0				4		...					0	10814
31-QDCB	TORETE cluster	1	1	4,000	6,800		0.00	14	A	0		...					0	10815
31-QDCB-a	to-rete					0				0		...					0	10816
31-QDCB-b	South watu			0	0	0	0.00	0		0		...					0	10817
31-QDCC	TULAMBATU cluster	1	1	5,727	7,383		4.99	30	A	0		...					0	10818
31-QDCC-a	tu-lambatu	1	1	5,727	7,383	0	4.99	30	A	0		...					0	10819
31-QDCC-b	landawe					0				0		...					0	10820
31-QDCD	WATU cluster			0	0		0.00	0		0		...					0	10821
31-QDCD-a	watu			0	0	0	0.00	0		0		...					0	10822
31-QDCE	WAIA cluster	1	1	200	340		0.00	14	A	0		...					0	10823
31-QDCE-a	waia	1	1	200	340	0	0.00	14	A	0		...					0	10824
31-QDCF	BUNGKU cluster	1	1	23,077	29,751		0.01	17	A	2		...					0	10825
31-QDCF-a	bungku	1	1	23,077	29,751	0	0.01	17	A	2		...					0	10826
31-QDCG	ROUTA cluster	1	1	300	510		0.00	14	A	0		...					0	10827
31-QDCG-a	epe-routa	1	1	300	510	0	0.00	14	A	0		...					0	10828
31-QDD	**TOLAKI-MEKONGGA net**	1	5	385,317	496,864		1.73	27	A	20		...					0	10829
31-QDDA	MEKONGGA cluster	1	1	56,484	72,818		6.00	30	A	0		...					0	10830
31-QDDA-a	konio					0				0		...					0	10831
31-QDDA-b	tamboki					0				0		...					0	10832
31-QDDA-c	norio					0				0		...					0	10833
31-QDDA-d	laiwui					0				0		...					0	10834
31-QDDB	RAHAMBUU cluster	1	1	5,642	7,274		0.99	21	A	4		...					0	10835
31-QDDB-a	rahambuu	1	1	5,642	7,274	0	0.99	21	A	4		...					0	10836
31-QDDB-b	to-wiaoe					0				4		...					0	10837
31-QDDC	KODEOHA cluster	1	1	1,697	2,188		1.00	24	A	3		...					0	10838
31-QDDC-a	kodeoha	1	1	1,697	2,188	0	1.00	24	A	3		...					0	10839
31-QDDD	TOLAKI cluster	1	1	320,791	413,554		1.00	27	A	20	Tolaki	...					0	10840
31-QDDD-a	konawe					0				20		...					0	10841
31-QDDD-b	kendari					0				20		...					0	10842
31-QDDE	ASERA-WIWIRANO cluster	1	1	300	510		1.00	16	A	0		...					0	10843
31-QDDE-a	asera					0				0		...					0	10844
31-QDDE-b	labea'-u					0				0		...					0	10845
31-QDDE-c	wiwi-rano					0				0		...					0	10846
31-QDDF	WARU cluster	1	1	403	520		0.00	19	A	4		...					0	10847
31-QDDF-a	waru	1	1	403	520	0	0.00	19	A	4		...					0	10848
31-QDDF-b	lalomerui					0				4		...					0	10849
31-QDE	**BAHONSUAI-TOMADINO net**	1	2	912	1,176		0.99	20	A	4		...					0	10850
31-QDEA	BAHONSUAI cluster	1	1	233	301		0.86	21	A	4		...					0	10851
31-QDEA-a	bahonsuai	1	1	233	301	0	0.86	21	A	4		...					0	10852
31-QDEB	TOMADINO cluster	1	1	679	875		1.03	20	A	4		...					0	10853
31-QDEB-a	tomadino	1	1	679	875	0	1.03	20	A	4		...					0	10854
31-QDF	**MORI net**	1	3	39,006	50,286		29.95	61	B	44		PN.					0	10855
31-QDFA	PADOE cluster	1	1	6,787	8,750		70.00	100	C	2		...					0	10856
31-QDFA-a	padoe	1	1	6,787	8,750	0	70.00	100	C	2		...					0	10857
31-QDFA-b	alalao					0				2		...					0	10858
31-QDFB	MORI-ATAS cluster	1	1	16,099	20,754		3.00	36	A	44		PN.					0	10859
31-QDFB-a	mori-atas	1	1	16,099	20,754	0	3.00	36	A	44	Mori*	PN.	1938-1941	1948			0	10860
31-QDFB-b	aikoa					0				44		pn.					0	10861
31-QDFC	MORI-BAWAH cluster	1	1	16,120	20,782		40.00	70	B	4		...					0	10862
31-QDFC-a	tambe'e					0				4		...					0	10863
31-QDFC-b	nahina					0				4		...					0	10864
31-QDFC-c	petasia					0				4		...					0	10865
31-QDFC-d	soroako					0				4		...					0	10866
31-QDFC-e	karonsie					0				4		...					0	10867
31-QE	KAILI-PAMONA chain	1	16	774,508	1,045,715		58.39	90	B	41		PN.					0	10868
31-QEA	**PAMONA net**	1	3	291,007	422,402		76.46	99	C	41		PN.					0	10869
31-QEAA	SOUTHEAST PAMONA cluster	1	1	1,167	1,504		0.09	11	A	4		...					0	10870
31-QEAA-a	to-mbelala	1	1	1,167	1,504	0	0.09	11	A	4		...					0	10871
31-QEAA-b	sinohoan					0				4		...					0	10872
31-QEAA-c	batui					0				4		...					0	10875
31-QEAB	SOUTHWEST PAMONA cluster	1	1	30,000	51,000		70.00	98	C	0		...					0	10876
31-QEAB-a	laiwonu					0				0		...					0	10877
31-QEAB-b	pu'u-mbotu					0				0		...					0	10878
31-QEAC	CENTRAL PAMONA cluster	1	2	174,840	225,398		80.65	100	C	41		PN.					0	10879
31-QEAC-a	to-bau	1	1	152,017	195,976	0	80.00	100	C	41	Pamona	PN.	1913-1926	1933-1992			0	10880
31-QEAC-b	to-kondindi					0				41		pn.					0	10881
31-QEAC-c	to-pada					0				41		pn.					0	10882
31-QEAC-d	to-moni	1	1	22,823	29,422	0	85.00	100	C	41		pn.					0	10883
31-QEAC-e	rapangkaka					0				41		pn.					0	10884
31-QEAD	WEST PAMONA cluster	1	1	35,000	59,500		70.00	98	C	0		...					0	10885
31-QEAD-a	pusangke					0				0		...					0	10886
31-QEAD-b	kajumorangka					0				0		...					0	10887
31-QEAD-c	to-kasiala					0				0		...					0	10888
31-QEAD-d	burangas					0				0		...					0	10889
31-QEAE	NORTH PAMONA cluster	1	1	20,000	34,000		75.00	99	C	0		...					0	10890
31-QEAE-a	to-potaa					0				0		...					0	10891
31-QEAE-b	lalaeo					0				0		...					0	10892
31-QEAF	NORTHEAST PAMONA cluster	1	1	30,000	51,000		70.00	98	C	0		...					0	10893
31-QEAF-a	ampana					0				0		...					0	10894
31-QEAF-b	togian					0				0		...					0	10895
31-QEB	**RAMPI-NAPU net**	1	5	30,141	38,856		62.47	90	C	22		P..					0	10896
31-QEBA	RAMPI cluster	1	1	8,930	11,512		84.99	100	C	2		...					0	10897
31-QEBA-a	leboni	1	1	8,930	11,512	0	84.99	100	C	2		...					0	10898
31-QEBA-b	rampi					0				2		...					0	10899
31-QEBA-c	lambu					0				2		...					0	10900

Continued overleaf

Table 9-13 continued

Code 1	REFERENCE NAME / Autoglossonym 2	Coun 3	Peo 4	Mother-tongue speakers in 2000 5	in 2025 6	Media radio 7	CHURCH AC% 8	E% 9	Wld 10	Tr 11	Biblioglossonym 12	SCRIPTURES Print 13-15	P-activity 16	N-activity 17	B-activity 18	J-year 19	Jayuh 20-24	Ref 25
31-QEBA-d	rato					0				2		. . .					0. . . .	10901
31-QEBA-e	ha'uwa					0				2		. . .					0. . . .	10902
31-QEBB	TOBADA cluster	1	1	11,305	14,574		60.00	93	C	2		. . .					0. . . .	10903
31-QEBB-a	to-bada'	1	1	11,305	14,574	0	60.00	93	C	2		. . .					0. . . .	10904
31-QEBB-b	ako					0				2		. . .					0. . . .	10905
31-QEBB-c	hanggira			0	0	0	0.00	0		2		. . .					0. . . .	10906
31-QEBC	NAPU-BEHOA cluster	1	2	9,036	11,649		45.00	79	B	22		P. .					0. . . .	10907
31-QEBC-a	besoa	1	1	3,394	4,375	0	44.99	79	B	22	Besoa	p. .					0. . . .	10908
31-QEBC-b	napu	1	1	5,642	7,274	0	45.00	79	B	22	Napu	P. .	1995				0. . . .	10909
31-QEBD	SEDOA cluster	1	1	870	1,121		44.94	74	B	4		. . .					0. . . .	10910
31-QEBD-a	sedoa	1	1	870	1,121	0	44.94	74	B	4		. . .					0. . . .	10911
31-QEC	**LINDU net**	1	1	2,312	2,981		55.02	87	B	2		. . .					0. . . .	10912
31-QECA	LINDU cluster	1	1	2,312	2,981		55.02	87	B	2		. . .					0. . . .	10913
31-QECA-a	lindu	1	1	2,312	2,981	0	55.02	87	B	2		. . .					0. . . .	10914
31-QECA-b	linduan					0				2		. . .					0. . . .	10915
31-QED	**UMA-SARUDU net**	1	2	27,808	35,849		43.38	80	B	41		PN.					0. . . .	10916
31-QEDA	UMA cluster	1	1	23,205	29,915		50.00	89	B	41		PN.					0. . . .	10917
31-QEDA-a	uma	1	1	23,205	29,915	0	50.00	89	B	41	Uma	PN.	1984-1989	1996			0. . . .	10918
31-QEDA-b	banahu					0				41		pn.					0. . . .	10919
31-QEDA-c	kantewu					0				41		pn.					0. . . .	10920
31-QEDA-d	peana					0				41		pn.					0. . . .	10921
31-QEDA-e	to-le'e					0				41		pn.					0. . . .	10922
31-QEDA-f	winantu-gimpu					0				41		pn.					0. . . .	10923
31-QEDA-g	to-baku					0				41		pn.					0. . . .	10924
31-QEDA-h	bana					0				41		pn.					0. . . .	10925
31-QEDB	SARUDU cluster	1	1	4,603	5,934		9.99	36	A	2		. . .					0. . . .	10926
31-QEDB-a	sarudu	1	1	4,603	5,934	0	9.99	36	A	2		. . .					0. . . .	10927
31-QEDB-b	nunu'					0				2		. . .					0. . . .	10928
31-QEDB-c	kulu					0				2		. . .					0. . . .	10929
31-QEE	**TOPOIYO net**	1	1	2,397	3,090		0.08	20	A	3		. . .					0. . . .	10930
31-QEEA	TO-POIYO cluster	1	1	2,397	3,090		0.08	20	A	3		. . .					0. . . .	10931
31-QEEA-a	to-poiyo	1	1	2,397	3,090	0	0.08	20	A	3		. . .					0. . . .	10932
31-QEF	**KAILI net**	1	4	420,843	542,537		46.94	85	B	24		P. .					0. . . .	10933
31-QEFA	SOUTHWEST KAILI cluster	1	1	297	383		1.01	24	A	22		P. .					0. . . .	10934
31-QEFA-a	bara	1	1	297	383	0	1.01	24	A	22		p. .					0. . . .	10935
31-QEFA-b	inde					0				22		p. .					0. . . .	10936
31-QEFA-c	unde					0				22		p. .					0. . . .	10937
31-QEFA-d	da'a					0				22	Da'a*	P. .	1985-1988				0. . . .	10938
31-QEFB	NORTHEAST KAILI cluster	1	3	420,546	542,154		46.97	85	B	24		P. .					0. . . .	10939
31-QEFB-a	moma	1	1	7,000	9,024	0	80.00	100	C	24	Kulawi*	P. .	1939				0. . . .	10940
31-QEFB-b	ledo	1	2	413,546	533,130	0	46.41	85	B	24	Ledo*	P. .	1939				0. . . .	10941
31-QEFB-c	ija					0				24		p. .					0. . . .	10946
31-QEFB-d	tara					0				24		p. .					0. . . .	10950
31-QEFB-e	rai					0				24		p. .					0. . . .	10954
31-QEFB-f	doi					0				24		p. .					0. . . .	10957
31-QEFB-g	ado					0				24		p. .					0. . . .	10958
31-QEFB-h	edo					0				24		p. .					0. . . .	10959
31-QEFB-i	tado-2					0				24		p. .					0. . . .	10960
31-QEFB-j	raio					0				24		p. .					0. . . .	10961
31-QEFB-k	taa					0				24		p. .					0. . . .	10962
31-QF	BALAESAN chain	1	1	5,727	7,383		0.05	16	A	4		. . .					0. . . .	10963
31-QFA	**BALAESAN net**	1	1	5,727	7,383		0.05	16	A	4		. . .					0. . . .	10964
31-QFAA	BALAESAN cluster	1	1	5,727	7,383		0.05	16	A	4		. . .					0. . . .	10965
31-QFAA-a	balaesan	1	1	5,727	7,383	0	0.05	16	A	4		. . .					0. . . .	10966
31-QG	TOMINI-BUOL chain	1	12	281,528	362,939		1.02	25	A	20		. . .					0. . . .	10967
31-QGA	**TOMINI net**	1	11	193,567	249,543		1.47	25	A	20		. . .					0. . . .	10968
31-QGAA	TAJE cluster	1	1	551	711		0.00	17	A	4		. . .					0. . . .	10969
31-QGAA-a	taje	1	1	551	711	0	0.00	17	A	4		. . .					0. . . .	10970
31-QGAB	LAUJE cluster	1	2	98,290	126,713		0.49	26	A	20	Lauje	. . .					0. . . .	10971
31-QGAB-a	ampibabo					0				20		. . .					0. . . .	10972
31-QGAB-b	tinombo					0				20		. . .					0. . . .	10973
31-QGAB-c	tomini	1	1	47,448	61,169	0	1.00	32	A	20		. . .					0. . . .	10974
31-QGAC	TAJIO cluster	1	1	20,341	26,223		1.00	20	A	4		. . .					0. . . .	10975
31-QGAC-a	tajio	1	1	20,341	26,223	0	1.00	20	A	4		. . .					0. . . .	10976
31-QGAD	DAMPAL cluster	1	1	106	137		10.38	34	A	8		. . .					0. . . .	10977
31-QGAD-a	dampal	1	1	106	137	0	10.38	34	A	8		. . .					0. . . .	10978
31-QGAE	DAMPELASA-TOLITOLI cluster	1	6	74,279	95,759		2.90	26	A	12		. . .					0. . . .	10979
31-QGAE-a	dampelasa					0				12		. . .					0. . . .	10980
31-QGAE-b	pendau	1	1	3,945	5,086	0	0.99	21	A	12	Pendau	. . .					0. . . .	10981
31-QGAE-c	tolitoli	1	1	31,625	40,770	0	0.06	26	A	12		. . .					0. . . .	10982
31-QGAE-d	dondo	1	1	16,947	21,848	0	2.00	25	A	12		. . .					0. . . .	10983
31-QGAE-e	bolano	1	2	7,084	9,133	0	24.70	50	B	12		. . .					0. . . .	10984
31-QGB	**BUOL net**	1	1	87,961	113,396		0.02	23	A	20		. . .					0. . . .	10985
31-QGBA	BUOL cluster	1	1	87,961	113,396		0.02	23	A	20		. . .					0. . . .	10986
31-QGBA-a	buol	1	1	87,961	113,396	0	0.02	23	A	20		. . .					0. . . .	10987
31-QH	SALUAN-BALANTAK chain	1	4	138,420	178,448		43.46	81	B	41		PN.					0. . . .	10988
31-QHA	**SALUAN net**	1	2	108,259	139,565		50.00	90	B	41		PN.					0. . . .	10989
31-QHAA	SELUANG-LOINANG cluster	1	1	106,117	136,803		50.00	90	B	41		PN.					0. . . .	10990
31-QHAA-a	seluang					0				41	Saluan, Coastal	PN.		1996			0. . . .	10991
31-QHAA-b	loinang	1	1	106,117	136,803	0	50.00	90	B	41		pn.					0. . . .	10992
31-QHAA-c	madi					0				41		pn.					0. . . .	10993
31-QHAB	KAHUMAMAHON cluster	1	1	2,142	2,762		50.00	80	B	12		. . .					0. . . .	10994
31-QHAB-a	kahumamahon	1	1	2,142	2,762	0	50.00	80	B	12	Saluan, Kahumamahon	. . .					0. . . .	10995
31-QHB	**ANDIO net**	1	1	1,930	2,488		19.48	48	A	2		. . .					0. . . .	10996
31-QHBA	ANDIO cluster	1	1	1,930	2,488		19.48	48	A	2		. . .					0. . . .	10997
31-QHBA-a	andio'o	1	1	1,930	2,488	0	19.48	48	A	2		. . .					0. . . .	10998
31-QHBA-b	imbao'o					0				2		. . .					0. . . .	10999
31-QHC	**BALANTAK net**	1	1	28,231	36,395		20.00	51	B	22		P. .					11000
31-QHCA	BALANTAK cluster	1	1	28,231	36,395		20.00	51	B	22		P. .					0. . . .	11001
31-QHCA-a	balantak	1	1	28,231	36,395	0	20.00	51	B	22	Balantak	P. .	1991				0. . . .	11002
31-QHCA-b	kosian					0				22		p. .					0. . . .	11003

Continued opposite

Table 9-13 continued

Code 1	REFERENCE NAME / Autoglossonym 2	Coun 3	Peo 4	Mother-tongue speakers in 2000 / 5	in 2025 / 6	Media radio 7	CHURCH AC% 8	E% 9	Wld 10	Tr 11	Biblioglossonym 12	SCRIPTURES Print 13-15	P-activity 16	N-activity 17	B-activity 18	J-year 19	Jayuh 20-24	Ref 25
31-QI	BANGGAI chain	1	1	107,348	138,389		1.00	30	A	41		PN.					0....	11004
31-QIA	**BANGGAI net**	1	1	107,348	138,389		1.00	30	A	41		PN.					0....	11005
31-QIAA	BANGGAI cluster	1	1	107,348	138,389		1.00	30	A	41	Banggai	PN.		1993			0....	11006
31-QIAA-a	East banggai					0				41		pn.					0....	11007
31-QIAA-b	West banggai					0				41		pn.					0....	11008
31-QJ	MONGONDOW-GORONTALO chain	1	11	2,239,259	2,886,782		24.49	62	B	41		PN.					1....	11009
31-QJA	**GORONTALO-KAIDIPANG net**	1	8	1,177,365	1,517,822		1.67	37	A	41		PN.					1....	11010
31-QJAA	GORONTALO cluster	1	3	1,076,847	1,388,238		1.38	38	A	41		PN.					1....	11011
31-QJAA-a	kwandang	1	1	10,605	13,672	0	1.00	21	A	41		pn.					1....	11012
31-QJAA-b	marisa					0				41		pn.					1....	11013
31-QJAA-c	tilamuta					0				41		pn.					1....	11014
31-QJAA-d	limboto	1	1	10,605	13,672	0	0.05	19	A	41		pn.					1....	11015
31-QJAA-e	East gorontalo	1	1	1,055,637	1,360,894	0	1.40	38	A	41	Gorontalo	PN.	1993	1996		1996	1....	11016
31-QJAB	KAIDIPANG-ATINGGOLA cluster	1	4	86,752	111,838		5.48	29	A	4		...					0....	11017
31-QJAB-a	atinggola	1	1	20,659	26,633	0	7.00	31	A	4		...					0....	11018
31-QJAB-b	West kaidipang					0				4		...					0....	11019
31-QJAB-c	bolaang-itang									4		...					0....	11020
31-QJAB-d	bintauna	1	1	8,251	10,637	0	1.01	21	A	4		...					0....	11021
31-QJAB-e	bolango-uki	1	1	27,553	35,520	0	4.00	27	A	4		...					0....	11022
31-QJAC	SUWAWA-BUNDA cluster	1	1	13,766	17,746		0.03	16	A	4		...					0....	11023
31-QJAC-a	suwawa	1	1	13,766	17,746	0	0.03	16	A	4		...					0....	11024
31-QJAC-b	bunda					0				4		...					0....	11025
31-QJB	**MONGONDOW-PONOSAKAN net**	1	3	1,061,894	1,368,960		49.78	90	B	24		P..					0....	11026
31-QJBA	LOLAK cluster	1	1	2,121	2,734		10.00	35	A	4		...					0....	11027
31-QJBA-a	lolak	1	1	2,121	2,734	0	10.00	35	A	4		...					0....	11028
31-QJBB	MONGONDOW cluster	1	1	1,055,637	1,360,894		50.00	90	B	24		P..					0....	11029
31-QJBB-a	bola'ang-mongondow	1	1	1,055,637	1,360,894	0	50.00	90	B	24	Bolaang-mongondow*	P..	1932-1939				0....	11030
31-QJBB-b	lolayan					0				24		p..					0....	11031
31-QJBB-c	dumoga					0				24		p..					0....	11032
31-QJBB-d	pasi					0				24		p..					0....	11033
31-QJBB-e	minahassa					0				24		p..					0....	11034
31-QJBC	PONOSAKAN cluster	1	1	4,136	5,332		14.99	42	A	4		...					0....	11035
31-QJBC-a	ponosakan	1	1	4,136	5,332	0	14.99	42	A	4		...					0....	11036
31-R	**SANGIR-MINAHASAN set**	2	13	1,039,650	1,353,473		90.71	98	C	57		PN.					4.s..	11037
31-RA	MINAHASAN chain	1	5	519,621	669,879		93.87	100	C	24		P..					0.s..	11038
31-RAA	**TONTEMBOAN net**	1	1	172,655	222,582		95.00	100	C	24		P..					0....	11039
31-RAAA	TONTEMBOAN cluster	1	1	172,655	222,582		95.00	100	C	24		P..					0....	11040
31-RAAA-a	ton-paso					0				24		p..					0....	11041
31-RAAA-b	ton-temboan	1	1	172,655	222,582	0	95.00	100	C	24	Tontemboan	P..	1852				0....	11042
31-RAAA-c	sonder					0				24		p..					0....	11043
31-RAAA-d	langoan					0				24		p..					0....	11044
31-RAB	**TONSAWANG net**	1	1	27,532	35,493		95.00	100	C	4		...					0....	11045
31-RABA	TONSAWANG cluster	1	1	27,532	35,493		95.00	100	C	4		...					0....	11046
31-RABA-a	ton-sawang	1	1	27,532	35,493	0	95.00	100	C	4		...					0....	11047
31-RAC	**TONDANO-TONSEA net**	1	3	319,434	411,804		93.16	100	C	24		P..					0.s..	11048
31-RACA	TONDANO cluster	1	1	126,671	163,300		96.00	100	C	20		...					0....	11049
31-RACA-a	remboken					0				20		...					0....	11050
31-RACA-b	ka'kas	1	1	126,671	163,300	0	96.00	100	C	20	Tondano	...					0....	11051
31-RACB	TOMBULU cluster	1	1	82,616	106,506		93.00	100	C	24		P..					0....	11052
31-RACB-a	ton-bulu	1	1	82,616	106,506	0	93.00	100	C	24	Tombulu	P..	1933				0....	11053
31-RACB-b	minahasa					0				24		p..					0....	11054
31-RACB-c	taratara					0				24		p..					0....	11055
31-RACB-d	tomohon					0				24		p..					0....	11056
31-RACC	TONSEA cluster	1	1	110,147	141,998		90.00	100	C	20		...					0.s..	11057
31-RACC-a	kalabat-atas	1	1	110,147	141,998	0	90.00	100	C	20		...					0.s..	11058
31-RACC-b	maumbi					0				20		...					0.s..	11059
31-RACC-c	airmadidi					0				20		...					0.s..	11060
31-RACC-d	likupang					0				20		...					0.s..	11061
31-RACC-e	kauditan					0				20		...					0.s..	11062
31-RB	SANGIRIC chain	2	8	520,029	683,594		87.55	96	C	57		PN.					4....	11063
31-RBA	**SANGIRIC net**	2	8	520,029	683,594		87.55	96	C	57		PN.					4....	11064
31-RBAA	RATAHAN cluster	1	1	35,189	45,364		95.00	100	C	12		...					0....	11065
31-RBAA-a	ratahan	1	1	35,189	45,364	0	95.00	100	C	12	Ratahan	...					0....	11066
31-RBAA-b	bentenan					0				12		...					0....	11067
31-RBAA-c	pasan					0				12		...					0....	11068
31-RBAB	BANTIK cluster	1	1	15,144	19,524		30.00	62	B	4		...					0....	11069
31-RBAB-a	bantik	1	1	15,144	19,524	0	30.00	62	B	4		...					0....	11070
31-RBAC	TAHULANDANG cluster	1	1	13,766	17,746		15.00	48	A	0		...					0....	11071
31-RBAC-a	bangka					0				0		...					0....	11072
31-RBAC-b	lembeh					0				0		...					0....	11073
31-RBAC-c	tahulandang	1	1	13,766	17,746	0	15.00	48	A	0		...					0....	11074
31-RBAD	SANGIR cluster	2	4	373,314	494,454		91.32	97	C	57	Sangirese	PN.	1875-1980	1883-1994		1998	4....	11075
31-RBAD-a	siau	1	1	61,511	79,298	0	91.00	100	C	57	Sangirese: Siau	PN.	1875	1883			1....	11076
31-RBAD-b	karikitang					0				57		pn.					1....	11077
31-RBAD-c	tamako					0				57		pn.					1....	11078
31-RBAD-d	manganitu					0				57		pn.					1....	11079
31-RBAD-e	tahuna					0				57		pn.					1....	11080
31-RBAD-f	kandar					0				57		pn.					1....	11081
31-RBAD-g	North tabukang					0				57		pn.					1....	11082
31-RBAD-h	Central tabukang					0				57		pn.					1....	11083
31-RBAD-i	tabukang-S					0				57		pn.					1....	11084
31-RBAD-j	sangil	1	1	12,998	18,522	0	1.00	26	A	57	Sangil	Pn.	1979				1....	11085
31-RBAE	TALAUD cluster	1	1	82,616	106,506		90.00	100	C	41	Talaud	PN.		1993			0....	11086
31-RBAE-a	kaburuang					0				41		pn.					0....	11087
31-RBAE-b	lirang					0				41		pn.					0....	11088
31-RBAE-c	South karakelong					0				41		pn.					0....	11089
31-RBAE-d	beo					0				41		pn.					0....	11090
31-RBAE-e	awit					0				41		pn.					0....	11091
31-RBAE-f	dapalan					0				41		pn.					0....	11092
31-RBAE-g	arangka'a					0				41		pn.					0....	11093
31-RBAE-h	essang					0				41		pn.					0....	11094
31-RBAE-i	maingas					0				41		pn.					0....	11095

Continued overleaf

Table 9-13 continued

Code 1	REFERENCE NAME / Autoglossonym 2	Coun 3	Peo 4	Mother-tongue speakers in 2000 5	in 2025 6	Media radio 7	CHURCH AC% 8	E% 9	Wld 10	Tr 11	Biblioglossonym 12	SCRIPTURES Print 13-15	P-activity 16	N-activity 17	B-activity 18	J-year 19	Jayuh 20-24	Ref 25
31-S	**PALAUAN set**	3	3	22,942	41,586		96.03	100	C	51		PN.					1.s..	11096
31-SA	PALAUAN chain	3	3	22,942	41,586		96.03	100	C	51		PN.					1.s..	11097
31-SAA	**PALAUAN net**	3	3	22,942	41,586		96.03	100	C	51		PN.					1.s..	11098
31-SAAA	PALAU cluster	3	3	22,942	41,586		96.03	100	C	51		PN.					1.s..	11099
31-SAAA-a	palau	3	3	22,942	41,586	5	96.03	100	C	51	Palauan	PN.	1942-1985	1964-1996		1986	1.s..	11100
31-T	**YAPESE set**	1	1	12,581	20,099		77.50	100	C	51		PN.					0.s..	11101
31-TA	YAPESE chain	1	1	12,581	20,099		77.50	100	C	51		PN.					0.s..	11102
31-TAA	**YAPESE net**	1	1	12,581	20,099		77.50	100	C	51		PN.					0.s..	11103
31-TAAA	YAP cluster	1	1	12,581	20,099		77.50	100	C	51		PN.					0.s..	11104
31-TAAA-a	yap	1	1	12,581	20,099	2	77.50	100	C	51	Yapese	PN.		1973			0.s..	11105
31-U	**CHAMORRO set**	4	5	150,240	236,186		98.07	100	C	35		P..					1.s..	11106
31-UA	CHAMORRO chain	4	5	150,240	236,186		98.07	100	C	35		P..					1.s..	11107
31-UAA	**CHAMORRO net**	4	5	150,240	236,186		98.07	100	C	35		P..					1.s..	11108
31-UAAA	CHAMORRO cluster	4	5	150,240	236,186		98.07	100	C	35		P..					1.s..	11109
31-UAAA-a	saipan	1	1	3,323	5,309	2	95.00	100	C	35		p..					1.s..	11110
31-UAAA-b	tinian					1				35		p..					1.s..	11111
31-UAAA-c	rota					1				35		p..					1.s..	11112
31-UAAA-d	guam-chamorro	4	4	146,917	230,877	5	98.14	100	C	35	Chamorro	P..	1908-1992			1989	1.s..	11113
32	**MESONESIC zone**	3	141	5,887,742	7,762,274		55.85	73	B	61		PNB					4As..	11114
32-A	**BIMA-SUMBA set**	1	20	2,439,355	3,208,416		27.32	50	A	61		PNB					4.s..	11115
32-AA	BIMA-SUMBA chain	1	20	2,439,355	3,208,416		27.32	50	A	61		PNB					4.s..	11116
32-AAA	**BIMA net**	1	2	587,177	756,969		0.01	21	A	20		...					0....	11117
32-AAAA	BIMA cluster	1	2	587,177	756,969		0.01	21	A	20		...					0....	11118
32-AAAA-a	sanggar					0				20		...					0....	11119
32-AAAA-b	bima	1	1	586,477	756,067	0	0.01	21	A	20	Bima	...					0....	11120
32-AAAA-c	kolo					0				20		...					0....	11121
32-AAAA-d	toloweri					0				20		...					0....	11122
32-AAAA-e	komodo	1	1	700	902	0	1.00	16	A	20		...					0....	11123
32-AAB	**KODI-MBUKAMBERO net**	1	1	49,273	63,521		9.00	38	A	12		...					0.s..	11124
32-AABA	KODI-MBUKAMBERO cluster	1	1	49,273	63,521		9.00	38	A	12		...					0.s..	11125
32-AABA-a	kodi-bokol	1	1	49,273	63,521	0	9.00	38	A	12	Kodi	...					0.s..	11126
32-AABA-b	kodi-bangedo					0				12		...					0.s..	11127
32-AABA-c	mbukambero					0				12		...					0.s..	11128
32-AAC	**WEYEWA net**	1	5	178,998	230,758		19.05	48	A	42		PN.					4.s..	11129
32-AACA	WEYEWA-LAMBOYA cluster	1	1	103,254	133,112		0.02	30	A	42		PN.					4.s..	11130
32-AACA-a	weyewa	1	1	103,254	133,112	0	0.02	30	A	42	Wewewa*	PN.	1949-1954	1970		1997	1.s..	11131
32-AACA-b	laura					0				42		pn.					1.s..	11132
32-AACA-c	tana-righu					0				42		pn.					1.s..	11133
32-AACA-d	lauli					0				42		pn.					1.s..	11134
32-AACB	LAMBOYA cluster	1	1	20,659	26,633		45.00	72	B	3		...					0....	11135
32-AACB-a	lamboya	1	1	20,659	26,633	0	45.00	72	B	3		...					0....	11136
32-AACB-b	nggaura					0				3		...					0....	11137
32-AACC	WANUKAKA cluster	1	1	13,766	17,746		45.00	73	B	3		...					0....	11138
32-AACC-a	wanukaka	1	1	13,766	17,746	0	45.00	73	B	3		...					0....	11139
32-AACC-b	rua									3		...					0....	11140
32-AACD	ANAKALANGU cluster	1	1	19,281	24,856		45.00	74	B	3		...					0....	11141
32-AACD-a	anakalangu	1	1	19,281	24,856	0	45.00	74	B	3		...					0....	11142
32-AACD-b	lolina					0				3		...					0....	11143
32-AACD-c	massokarera					0				3		...					0....	11144
32-AACE	MAMBORU cluster	1	1	22,038	28,411		45.00	73	B	3		...					0....	11145
32-AACE-a	mamboru	1	1	22,038	28,411	0	45.00	73	B	3		...					0....	11146
32-AAD	**SUMBA-SAWU net**	1	3	354,495	457,004		64.38	81	C	61		PNB					4.s..	11147
32-AADA	SUMBA cluster	1	1	234,591	302,427		91.00	100	C	61	Sumba	PNB	1949-1993	1961	1995	1995	4.s..	11148
32-AADA-a	uma-ratu-nggai					0				61		pnb					1.s..	11149
32-AADA-b	lewa					0				61		pnb					1.s..	11150
32-AADA-c	kanatang					0				61		pnb					1.s..	11151
32-AADA-d	North kambera					0				61	Kambera	PNb	1949	1961		1995	4.s..	11152
32-AADA-e	melolo					0				61		pnb					1.s..	11153
32-AADA-f	mangili -waijelo					0				61		pnb					1.s..	11154
32-AADA-g	South sumba					0				61		pnb					1.s..	11155
32-AADB	SAWU cluster	1	1	115,089	148,370		9.00	41	A	35	Sawunese*	P..	1976				1.s..	11156
32-AADB-a	raijua					0				35		p..					1.s..	11157
32-AADB-b	mesara					0				35		p..					1.s..	11158
32-AADB-c	liae					0				35		p..					1.s..	11159
32-AADB-d	seba					0				35		p..					1.s..	11160
32-AADB-e	timu					1				35		p..					1.s..	11161
32-AADC	NDAO cluster	1	1	4,815	6,207		91.01	100	C	3		...					0....	11162
32-AADC-a	ndao	1	1	4,815	6,207	0	91.01	100	C	3		...					0....	11163
32-AAE	**MANGGARAI-NGADA net**	1	5	852,070	1,162,140		13.28	36	A	20		...					0....	11164
32-AAEA	MANGGARAI cluster	1	1	586,477	756,067		4.00	29	A	20		...					0....	11165
32-AAEA-a	West manggarai					0				20		...					0....	11166
32-AAEA-b	Central manggaraiW.					0				20		...					0....	11167
32-AAEA-c	Central manggarai					0				20		...					0....	11168
32-AAEA-d	East Central manggarai.					0				20		...					0....	11169
32-AAEA-e	East manggarai					0				20		...					0....	11170
32-AAEB	REMBONG cluster	1	1	40,000	68,000		4.00	22	A	0		...					0....	11171
32-AAEB-a	rembong					0				0		...					0....	11172
32-AAEB-b	wangka									0		...					0....	11173
32-AAEB-c	namu					0				0		...					0....	11174
32-AAEC	RIUNG cluster	1	1	19,281	24,856		15.00	44	A	3		...					0....	11175
32-AAEC-a	riung	1	1	19,281	24,856	0	15.00	44	A	3		...					0....	11176
32-AAED	WAE-RANA cluster	1	1	40,000	68,000		10.00	33	A	4		...					0....	11177
32-AAED-a	wae-rana	1	1	40,000	68,000	0	10.00	33	A	4		...					0....	11178
32-AAEE	RONGGA cluster	1	1	30,000	51,000		10.00	33	A	4		...					0....	11179
32-AAEE-a	rongga	1	1	30,000	51,000	0	10.00	33	A	4		...					0....	11180

Continued opposite

Table 9-13 continued

Code 1	REFERENCE NAME / Autoglossonym 2	Coun 3	Peo 4	Mother-tongue speakers in 2000 5	in 2025 6	Media radio 7	CHURCH AC% 8	E% 9	Wld 10	Tr 11	Biblioglossonym 12	Print 13-15	P-activity 16	N-activity 17	B-activity 18	J-year 19	Jayuh 20-24	Ref 25
32-AAEF	KEPO cluster	1	1	10,605	13,672		10.00	32	A	4		. . .					0....	11181
32-AAEF-a	kepo	1	1	10,605	13,672	0	10.00	32	A	4		. . .					0....	11182
32-AAEG	RAJONG cluster	1	1	45,000	76,500		10.00	33	A	4		. . .					0....	11183
32-AAEG-a	rajong	1	1	45,000	76,500	0	10.00	33	A	4		. . .					0....	11184
32-AAEH	NGADA cluster	1	2	80,707	104,045		90.00	100	C	20		. . .					0....	11185
32-AAEH-a	bajava	1	1	69,826	90,017	0	90.00	100	C	20		. . .					0....	11186
32-AAEH-b	soa	1	1	10,881	14,028	0	90.00	100	C	20		. . .					0....	11187
32-AAEH-c	Central ngada					0				20		. . .					0....	11188
32-AAEH-d	Southwest ngada									20		. . .					0....	11189
32-AAEH-e	Southeast ngada					0				20		. . .					0....	11190
32-AAF	**ENDE-PALUE net**	1	4	417,342	538,024		68.65	94	C	20		. . .					0....	11191
32-AAFA	ENDE-LIO cluster	1	4	417,342	538,024		68.65	94	C	20		. . .					0....	11192
32-AAFA-a	nage					0				20		. . .					0....	11193
32-AAFA-b	keo	1	1	114,326	147,385		70.00	98	C	20		. . .					0....	11194
32-AAFA-c	nga'o					0				20		. . .					0....	11195
32-AAFA-d	ende	1	1	119,819	154,467	0	50.00	82	B	20		. . .					0....	11196
32-AAFA-e	lio	1	1	179,061	230,840	0	80.00	100	C	20		. . .					0....	11197
32-AAFA-f	palu'e	1	1	4,136	5,332	0	80.00	100	C	20		. . .					0....	11198
32-B	**TIMOR-FLORES set**	3	43	2,780,400	3,689,069		87.93	99	C	44		PN.					4A...	11199
32-BA	FLORES-LEMBATA chain	1	3	774,109	1,065,744		73.99	98	C	20		. . .					0....	11200
32-BAA	**SIKKA net**	1	1	201,417	259,661		91.00	100	C	20		. . .					0....	11201
32-BAAA	SIKKA cluster	1	1	201,417	259,661		91.00	100	C	20		. . .					0....	11202
32-BAAA-a	sara-krow	1	1	201,417	259,661	0	91.00	100	C	20		. . .					0....	11203
32-BAAA-b	sikka-natar					0				20		. . .					0....	11204
32-BAAA-c	tana-ai					0				20		. . .					0....	11205
32-BAB	**LAMAHOLOT-KEDANG net**	1	2	572,692	806,083		68.00	97	C	20		. . .					0....	11206
32-BABA	WEST LAMAHOLOT cluster	1	1	30,000	51,000		60.00	93	C	0		. . .					0....	11207
32-BABA-a	pukaunu					0				0		. . .					0....	11208
32-BABA-b	muhang					0				0		. . .					0....	11209
32-BABB	CENTRAL LAMAHOLOTW. cluster									0		. . .						11210
32-BABB-a	lewotobi					0				0		. . .					0....	11211
32-BABB-b	lewolaga					0				0		. . .					0....	11212
32-BABB-c	ile-mandiri					0				0		. . .					0....	11213
32-BABB-d	tanjung-bunga					0				0		. . .					0....	11214
32-BABC	WEST SOLOR cluster	1	1	40,000	68,000		60.00	93	C	0		. . .					0....	11215
32-BABC-a	bari					0				0		. . .					0....	11216
32-BABC-b	eon					0				0		. . .					0....	11217
32-BABC-c	laän					0				0		. . .					0....	11218
32-BABD	TAKS cluster	1	1	383,616	502,762		71.37	99	C	20		. . .					0....	11219
32-BABD-a	takä	1	1	363,616	468,762	0	72.00	100	C	20		. . .					0....	11220
32-BABE	EAST SOLOR cluster	1	1	30,000	51,000		70.00	98	C	0		. . .					0....	11221
32-BABE-a	belang					0				0		. . .					0....	11222
32-BABE-b	kluang					0				0		. . .					0....	11223
32-BABE-c	lamatukan					0				0		. . .					0....	11224
32-BABE-d	lerek					0				0		. . .					0....	11225
32-BABE-e	lodobelolon					0				0		. . .					0....	11226
32-BABF	ADONARA cluster	1	1	15,000	25,500		70.00	98	C	0		. . .					0....	11227
32-BABF-a	adonara	1	1	15,000	25,500	0	70.00	98	C	0		. . .					0....	11228
32-BABG	EAST LAMAHOLOT cluster	1	1	30,000	51,000		70.00	98	C	0		. . .					0....	11229
32-BABG-a	lomblen					0				0		. . .					0....	11230
32-BABG-b	alor					0				0		. . .					0....	11231
32-BABH	KEDANG cluster	1	1	44,076	56,821		48.00	77	B	4		. . .					0....	11232
32-BABH-a	kedang	1	1	44,076	56,821	0	48.00	77	B	4		. . .					0....	11233
32-BB	HELONG chain	1	1	6,342	8,176		50.00	85	B	3		. . .					0....	11234
32-BBA	**HELONG net**	1	1	6,342	8,176		50.00	85	B	3		. . .					0....	11235
32-BBAA	HELONG cluster	1	1	6,342	8,176		50.00	85	B	3		. . .					0....	11236
32-BBAA-a	helong	1	1	6,342	8,176	0	50.00	85	B	3		. . .					0....	11237
32-BC	TIMORIC chain	3	38	1,998,737	2,613,526		93.46	99	C	44		PN.					4A...	11238
32-BCA	**ROTI net**	1	1	176,240	227,203		80.00	100	C	35		P..					0....	11239
32-BCAA	ROTI cluster	1	1	176,240	227,203		80.00	100	C	35	Roti*	P..	1895				0....	11240
32-BCAA-a	oenale-delha					0				35		p..					0....	11241
32-BCAA-b	thie					0				35		p..					0....	11244
32-BCAA-c	dengka-lelain					0				35		p..					0....	11245
32-BCAA-d	baa-loleh					0				35		p..					0....	11248
32-BCAA-e	termanu-keka					0				35		p..					0....	11251
32-BCAA-f	bokai					0				35		p..					0....	11256
32-BCAA-g	bilba-lelenuk					0				35		p..					0....	11257
32-BCAA-h	korbaffo					0				35		p..					0....	11261
32-BCAA-i	landu-oepao					0				35		p..					0....	11262
32-BCB	**ATONI net**	3	3	960,143	1,239,898		95.18	100	C	44		PN.					0A...	11266
32-BCBA	UAB-ATONI-PAH-METO cluster	3	3	960,143	1,239,898		95.18	100	C	44	Timor*	PN.	1941-1966	1948-1984			0A...	11267
32-BCBA-a	amarasi					0				44		pn.					0c...	11268
32-BCBA-b	amfoan-amabi					0				44		pn.					0c...	11271
32-BCBA-c	amanuban-amanatun					0				44		pn.					0c...	11275
32-BCBA-d	mollo-miomafo					0				44		pn.					0c...	11278
32-BCBA-e	ambenu					0				44		pn.					0c...	11281
32-BCBA-f	biboki-insana					0				44		pn.					0c...	11282
32-BCBA-g	kusa-manlea					0				44		pn.					0c...	11285
32-BCC	**CENTRAL TIMOR net**	2	10	779,399	1,039,481		96.61	100	C	20		. . .					4....	11288
32-BCCA	TETUN cluster	2	2	481,432	640,669		97.84	100	C	20		. . .					4....	11289
32-BCCA-a	West tetun	1	1	84,843	109,377	0	91.00	100	C	20		. . .					1....	11290
32-BCCA-b	tasi-feto					0				20		. . .					1....	11291
32-BCCA-c	tasi-mane					0				20		. . .					1....	11292
32-BCCA-d	terik					0				20		. . .					1....	11293
32-BCCA-e	soibada					0				20		. . .					1....	11294
32-BCCA-f	East tetun	1	1	396,589	531,292	0	99.30	100	C	20	Tetun	. . .					1....	11295
32-BCCA-g	dili-tetun					0				20	Tetun Dili	. . .					1....	11296
32-BCCB	KEMAK cluster	2	2	66,948	89,366		94.53	100	C	4		. . .					0....	11297
32-BCCB-a	nogo					0				4		. . .					0....	11298
32-BCCB-b	kemak	2	2	66,948	89,366	0	94.53	100	C	4		. . .					0....	11299
32-BCCC	TUKUDEDE cluster	1	1	60,591	81,171		95.00	100	C	3		. . .					0....	11300
32-BCCC-a	tukudede	1	1	60,591	81,171	0	95.00	100	C	3		. . .					0....	11301
32-BCCC-b	keha					0				3		. . .					0....	11302

Continued overleaf

Table 9-13 continued

Code 1	REFERENCE NAME / Autoglossonym 2	Coun 3	Peo 4	Mother-tongue speakers in 2000 5	in 2025 6	Media radio 7	AC% 8	E% 9	Wld 10	Tr 11	Biblioglossonym 12	Print 13-15	P-activity 16	N-activity 17	B-activity 18	J-year 19	Jayuh 20-24	Ref 25
32-BCCD	MAMBAI cluster	1	1	96,936	129,860		98.00	100	C	20		...					0....	11303
32-BCCD-a	damata					0				20		...					0....	11304
32-BCCD-b	lolei					0				20		...					0....	11305
32-BCCD-c	manua					0				20		...					0....	11306
32-BCCD-d	mambai	1	1	96,936	129,860	0	98.00	100	C	20		...					0....	11307
32-BCCE	LAKALEI cluster	1	1	6,058	8,116		80.01	100	C	4		...					0....	11308
32-BCCE-a	lakalei	1	1	6,058	8,116	0	80.01	100	C	4		...					0....	11309
32-BCCF	IDATE cluster	1	1	6,058	8,116		60.00	87	C	4		...					0....	11310
32-BCCF-a	idate	1	1	6,058	8,116	0	60.00	87	C	4		...					0....	11311
32-BCCG	GALOLI cluster	1	1	60,591	81,171		95.00	100	C	3		...					0....	11312
32-BCCG-a	na-nahek					0				3		...					0....	11313
32-BCCG-b	edi					0				3		...					0....	11314
32-BCCG-c	dadua					0				3		...					0....	11315
32-BCCG-d	galoli	1	1	60,591	81,171	0	95.00	100	C	3		...					0....	11316
32-BCCG-e	baba					0				3		...					0....	11317
32-BCCG-f	hahak					0				3		...					0....	11318
32-BCCH	TALUR cluster	1	1	785	1,012		9.94	38	A	4		...					0....	11319
32-BCCH-a	talur					0				4		...					0....	11320
32-BCCH-b	ilwaki	1	1	785	1,012	0	9.94	38	A	4		...					0....	11321
32-BCCH-c	ilputih					0				4		...					0....	11322
32-BCCH-d	galoleng					0				4		...					0....	11323
32-BCCH-e	lir-talo					0				4		...					0....	11324
32-BCCH-f	ilmedu					0				4		...					0....	11325
32-BCD	**WETAR net**	1	6	11,963	15,422		9.07	34	A	12		...					0....	11326
32-BCDA	APUTAI cluster	1	1	4,242	5,469		6.01	31	A	0		...					0....	11327
32-BCDA-a	lurang					0				0		...					0....	11328
32-BCDA-b	welemur	1	1	4,242	5,469	0	6.01	31	A	0		...					0....	11329
32-BCDB	ILIUN cluster	1	2	5,854	7,547		7.94	31	A	4		...					0....	11330
32-BCDB-a	iliun	1	1	1,612	2,078	0	13.03	39	A	4		...					0....	11331
32-BCDB-b	ilmaumau					0				4		...					0....	11332
32-BCDB-c	erai	1	1	4,242	5,469	0	6.01	28	A	4		...					0....	11333
32-BCDB-d	hahutau					0				4		...					0....	11334
32-BCDB-e	limera					0				4		...					0....	11335
32-BCDB-f	jeh			0	0	0	0.00	0		4		...					0....	11336
32-BCDB-g	juru			0	0	0	0.00	0		4		...					0....	11337
32-BCDC	PERAI cluster									4		...					0....	11338
32-BCDC-a	perai					0				4		...					0....	11339
32-BCDD	TUGUN cluster	1	3	1,867	2,406		19.55	47	A	12		...					0....	11340
32-BCDD-a	tugun	1	1	1,379	1,777	0	20.01	48	A	12	Tugun	...					0....	11341
32-BCDD-b	tutunohan	1	2	488	629	0	18.24	44	A	12		...					0....	11342
32-BCDD-c	mahuan					0				12		...					0....	11343
32-BCDD-d	arwala					0				12		...					0....	11344
32-BCE	**KISAR-MASELA net**	1	11	58,032	74,814		87.95	99	C	22		P..					0....	11345
32-BCEA	KISAR cluster	1	1	21,465	27,672		91.00	100	C	22		P..					0....	11346
32-BCEA-a	meher	1	1	21,465	27,672	0	91.00	100	C	22	Kisar	P..	1995-1996				0....	11347
32-BCEB	ROMA cluster	1	1	1,930	2,488		60.00	92	C	2		...					0....	11348
32-BCEB-a	roma	1	1	1,930	2,488	0	60.00	92	C	2		...					0....	11349
32-BCEC	LETRI-LGONA cluster	1	2	29,504	38,035		90.73	100	C	22		P..					0....	11350
32-BCEC-a	leti	1	1	8,039	10,363	0	90.00	100	C	22		p..					0....	11351
32-BCEC-b	moa					0				22		p..					0....	11352
32-BCEC-c	lakor					0				22		p..					0....	11353
32-BCEC-d	luang	1	1	21,465	27,672	0	91.00	100	C	22	Luang	P..	1995				0....	11354
32-BCEC-e	sermata					0				22		p..					0....	11355
32-BCEC-f	Central wetan-babar					0				22		P..					0....	11356
32-BCED	IMROING cluster	1	1	530	684		60.00	89	C	4		...					0....	11360
32-BCED-a	imroing	1	1	530	684	0	60.00	89	C	4		...					0....	11361
32-BCEE	SOUTH MASELA-BABAR cluster	1	5	4,136	5,333		69.80	94	C	4		...					0....	11362
32-BCEE-a	tela-masboar	1	1	1,209	1,559	0	50.04	83	B	4		...					0....	11363
32-BCEE-b	emplawas	1	1	297	383	0	59.93	89	B	4		...					0....	11364
32-BCEE-c	wakpapapi					0				4		...					0....	11365
32-BCEE-d	East masela	1	1	721	930	0	80.03	100	C	4		...					0....	11366
32-BCEE-e	Central masela					0				4		...					0....	11367
32-BCEE-f	West masela	1	1	1,188	1,531	0	79.97	100	C	4		...					0....	11368
32-BCEF	SERILI cluster	1	1	467	602		79.87	100	C	4		...					0....	11369
32-BCEF-a	serili	1	1	467	602	0	79.87	100	C	4		...					0....	11370
32-BCF	**DAI-DAWERA net**	1	2	2,863	3,692		70.00	100	C	4		...					0....	11371
32-BCFA	DAI cluster	1	1	1,103	1,422		69.99	100	C	2		...					0....	11372
32-BCFA-a	dai	1	1	1,103	1,422	0	69.99	100	C	2		...					0....	11373
32-BCFB	DAWERA-DAWELOOR cluster	1	1	1,760	2,270		70.00	100	C	4		...					0....	11374
32-BCFB-a	dawera					0				4		...					0....	11375
32-BCFB-b	daweloor					0				4		...					0....	11376
32-BCFB-c	East babar					0				4		...					0....	11377
32-BCG	**DAMAR net**	1	2	4,200	5,414		59.98	90	B	2		...					0....	11378
32-BCGA	WEST DAMAR cluster	1	1	976	1,258		59.94	89	B	2		...					0....	11379
32-BCGA-a	West damar	1	1	976	1,258	0	59.94	89	B	2		...					0....	11380
32-BCGB	EAST DAMAR cluster	1	1	3,224	4,156		59.99	90	B	2		...					0....	11381
32-BCGB-a	East damar	1	1	3,224	4,156	0	59.99	90	B	2		...					0....	11382
32-BCH	**SERUA-TEUN net**	1	3	5,897	7,602		60.00	90	B	4		...					0....	11383
32-BCHA	TEUN cluster	1	1	1,379	1,777		59.97	89	B	3		...					0....	11384
32-BCHA-a	teun	1	1	1,379	1,777	0	59.97	89	B	3		...					0....	11385
32-BCHB	NILA-SERUA cluster	1	2	4,518	5,825		60.00	90	C	4		...					0....	11386
32-BCHB-a	nila	1	1	2,206	2,844	0	60.02	90	C	4		...					0....	11387
32-BCHB-b	serua	1	1	2,312	2,981	0	59.99	90	B	4		...					0....	11388
32-BD	NAUETI chain	1	1	1,212	1,623		69.97	100	C	4		...					0....	11389
32-BDA	**NAUETI net**	1	1	1,212	1,623		69.97	100	C	4		...					0....	11390
32-BDAA	NAUETI cluster	1	1	1,212	1,623		69.97	100	C	4		...					0....	11391
32-BDAA-a	naumik					0				4		...					0....	11392
32-BDAA-b	oso-moko					0				4		...					0....	11393
32-C	**WAIMAHA-HABU set**	1	1	5,635	8,270		76.45	99	C	4		...					0....	11394
32-CA	WAIMAHA-HABU chain	1	1	5,635	8,270		76.45	99	C	4		...					0....	11395
32-CAA	**WAIMAHA net**	1	1	3,635	4,870		80.00	100	C	4		...					0....	11396

Continued opposite

Table 9-13 continued

Code 1	REFERENCE NAME / Autoglossonym 2	Coun 3	Peo 4	Mother-tongue speakers in 2000 5	in 2025 6	Media radio 7	CHURCH AC% 8	E% 9	Wld 10	Tr 11	Biblioglossonym 12	Print 13-15	P-activity 16	N-activity 17	B-activity 18	J-year 19	Jayuh 20-24	Ref 25
32-CAAA	WAIMA'A cluster	1	1	3,635	4,870		80.00	100	C	4		. . .					0	11397
32-CAAA-a	waima'a	1	1	3,635	4,870	0	80.00	100	C	4		. . .					0	11398
32-CAB	**HABU net**	1	1	2,000	3,400		70.00	98	C	4		. . .					0	11399
32-CABA	HABU cluster	1	1	2,000	3,400		70.00	98	C	4		. . .					0	11400
32-CABA-a	habu	1	1	2,000	3,400	0	70.00	98	C	4		. . .					0	11401
32-D	**SERAM-TANIMBAR set**	1	67	560,118	724,720		28.37	54	B	22		P . .					0	11402
32-DA	SELARU chain	1	1	9,375	12,086		91.00	100	C	12		. . .					0	11403
32-DAA	**SELARU net**	1	1	9,375	12,086		91.00	100	C	12		. . .					0	11404
32-DAAA	SELARU cluster	1	1	9,375	12,086		91.00	100	C	12		. . .					0	11405
32-DAAA-a	selaru	1	1	9,375	12,086	0	91.00	100	C	12	Selaru	. . .					0	11406
32-DB	SELUWASAN chain	1	1	3,988	5,141		79.99	100	C	2		. . .					0	11410
32-DBA	**SELUWASAN net**	1	1	3,988	5,141		79.99	100	C	2		. . .					0	11411
32-DBAA	SELUWASAN cluster	1	1	3,988	5,141		79.99	100	C	2		. . .					0	11412
32-DBAA-a	seluwasan	1	1	3,988	5,141	0	79.99	100	C	2		. . .					0	11413
32-DBAA-b	makatian					0				2		. . .					0	11414
32-DC	YAMDENA chain	1	1	42,358	54,606		91.00	100	C	12		. . .					0	11415
32-DCA	**YAMDENA net**	1	1	42,358	54,606		91.00	100	C	12		. . .					0	11416
32-DCAA	YAMDENA cluster	1	1	42,358	54,606		91.00	100	C	12	Yamdena	. . .					0	11417
32-DCAA-a	South yamdena					0				12		. . .					0	11418
32-DCAA-b	North yamdena					0				12		. . .					0	11422
32-DD	KEI-FORDATA chain	1	4	157,213	202,682		7.61	38	A	22		P . .					0	11425
32-DDA	**FORDATA net**	1	1	53,683	69,215		20.00	53	B	22		P . .					0	11426
32-DDAA	SERA cluster	1	1	20	34		20.00	50	B	0		. . .					0	11427
32-DDAA-a	sera	1	1	20	34	0	20.00	50	B	0		. . .					0	11428
32-DDAB	LARAT-FORDATA cluster	1	1	53,663	69,181		20.00	53	B	22		P . .					0	11429
32-DDAB-a	larat					0				22		p . .					0	11430
32-DDAB-b	North fordata	1	1	53,663	69,181	0	20.00	53	B	22	Fordata	P . .	1996				0	11431
32-DDAB-c	molu-maru					0				22		p . .					0	11432
32-DDB	**KEI net**	1	1	98,991	127,615		1.00	31	A	20		. . .					0	11433
32-DDBA	KEI cluster	1	1	98,991	127,615		1.00	31	A	20		. . .					0	11434
32-DDBA-a	kei-besar					0				20		. . .					0	11435
32-DDBA-b	kei-kecil					0				20		. . .					0	11436
32-DDBA-c	kei-tanimbar	1	1	98,991	127,615	0	1.00	31	A	20	Kei	. . .					0	11437
32-DDBA-d	ta'am					0				20		. . .					0	11438
32-DDBA-e	tayando					0				20		. . .					0	11439
32-DDC	**KUR-TEOR net**	1	2	4,539	5,852		5.09	30	A	4		. . .					0	11440
32-DDCA	KUR cluster	1	1	3,182	4,102		2.99	26	A	2		. . .					0	11441
32-DDCA-a	kur	1	1	3,182	4,102	0	2.99	26	A	2		. . .					0	11442
32-DDCA-b	kaimeer					0				2		. . .					0	11443
32-DDCB	TEOR cluster	1	1	1,357	1,750		10.02	40	A	4		. . .					0	11444
32-DDCB-a	gaur kristen	1	1	1,357	1,750	0	10.02	40	A	4		. . .					0	11445
32-DDCB-b	ut					0				4		. . .					0	11446
32-DE	ARU chain	1	14	49,696	64,069		44.77	74	B	22		P . .					0	11447
32-DEA	**WEST ARU net**	1	5	22,016	28,384		58.74	89	B	12		. . .					0	11448
32-DEAA	KAREY cluster	1	1	1,018	1,313		49.02	76	B	3		. . .					0	11449
32-DEAA-a	karey	1	1	1,018	1,313	0	49.02	76	B	3		. . .					0	11450
32-DEAB	EAST TARANGAN cluster	1	1	4,666	6,016		54.99	84	B	3		. . .					0	11451
32-DEAB-a	East tarangan	1	1	4,666	6,016	0	54.99	84	B	3		. . .					0	11452
32-DEAC	WEST TARANGAN cluster	1	1	7,975	10,281		60.00	92	C	12	Tarangan, West	. . .					0	11453
32-DEAC-a	coast-tarangan					0				12		. . .					0	11454
32-DEAC-b	river-tarangan					0				12		. . .					0	11455
32-DEAC-c	plains-tarangan					0				12		. . .					0	11456
32-DEAC-d	Northwest tarangan					0				12		. . .					0	11457
32-DEAD	LORANG cluster	1	1	339	438		79.94	100	C	4		. . .					0	11458
32-DEAD-a	lorang	1	1	339	438	0	79.94	100	C	4		. . .					0	11459
32-DEAE	MANOBAI cluster	1	1	8,018	10,336		60.00	89	C	2		. . .					0	11460
32-DEAE-a	manobai	1	1	8,018	10,336	0	60.00	89	C	2		. . .					0	11461
32-DEB	**EAST ARU net**	1	6	18,072	23,298		43.20	72	B	22		P . .					0	11462
32-DEBA	BARAKAI cluster	1	1	4,603	5,934		14.99	42	A	2		. . .					0	11463
32-DEBA-a	barakai	1	1	4,603	5,934	0	14.99	42	A	2		. . .					0	11464
32-DEBA-b	mesiang					0				2		. . .					0	11465
32-DEBB	DOBEL cluster	1	1	7,509	9,680		70.00	100	C	22	Dobel	P . .	1991				0	11466
32-DEBB-a	Central dobel					0				22		p . .					0	11467
32-DEBB-b	Southeast dobel					0				22		p . .					0	11468
32-DEBB-c	Northeast dobel					0				22		p . .					0	11469
32-DEBC	KOBA cluster	1	1	551	711		40.11	68	B	2		. . .					0	11470
32-DEBC-a	koba	1	1	551	711	0	40.11	68	B	2		. . .					0	11471
32-DEBD	LOLA cluster	1	1	891	1,148		5.95	30	A	3		. . .					0	11472
32-DEBD-a	lola	1	1	891	1,148	0	5.95	30	A	3		. . .					0	11473
32-DEBD-b	warabal					0				3		. . .					0	11474
32-DEBD-c	jambuair					0				3		. . .					0	11475
32-DEBE	MARIRI cluster	1	1	403	520		5.96	31	A	4		. . .					0	11476
32-DEBE-a	mariri	1	1	403	520	0	5.96	31	A	4		. . .					0	11477
32-DEBF	BATULEY cluster	1	1	4,115	5,305		38.01	67	B	2		. . .					0	11478
32-DEBF-a	batuley	1	1	4,115	5,305	0	38.01	67	B	2		. . .					0	11479
32-DEC	**UJIR-KOLA net**	1	3	9,608	12,387		15.70	43	A	12		. . .					0	11482
32-DECA	UJIR cluster	1	1	1,039	1,340		7.03	32	A	2		. . .					0	11483
32-DECA-a	ujir	1	1	1,039	1,340	0	7.03	32	A	2		. . .					0	11484
32-DECB	KOLA cluster	1	2	8,569	11,047		16.75	45	A	12		. . .					0	11485
32-DECB-a	warilau					0				12		. . .					0	11486
32-DECB-b	kola	1	1	8,251	10,637	0	17.00	45	A	12	Kola	. . .					0	11487
32-DECB-c	kulaha					0				12		. . .					0	11488
32-DECB-d	kompane	1	1	318	410	0	10.06	36	A	12		. . .					0	11489
32-DECB-e	marlasi					0				12		. . .					0	11490
32-DECB-f	wadakan					0				12		. . .					0	11491

Continued overleaf

Table 9-13 continued

Code 1	REFERENCE NAME Autoglossonym 2	Coun 3	Peo 4	Mother-tongue speakers in 2000 5	in 2025 6	Media radio 7	CHURCH AC% 8	E% 9	Wld 10	Tr 11	Biblioglossonym 12	SCRIPTURES Print 13-15	P-activity 16	N-activity 17	B-activity 18	J-year 19	Jayuh 20-24	Ref 25
32-DF	BANDA-WATUBELA chain	1	5	55,615	71,697		9.40	36	A	4		. . .					0. . . .	11492
32-DFA	**BANDA net**	1	1	3,691	4,758		10.00	36	A	2		. . .					0. . . .	11493
32-DFAA	BANDA cluster	1	1	3,691	4,758		10.00	36	A	2		. . .					0. . . .	11494
32-DFAA-a	banda			0	0	0	0.00	0		2		. . .					0. . . .	11495
32-DFAA-b	banda-eli	1	1	3,691	4,758	0	10.00	36	A	2		. . .					0. . . .	11496
32-DFAA-c	banda-elat					0				2		. . .					0. . . .	11497
32-DFB	**WATUBELA net**	1	1	4,603	5,934		30.00	59	B	3		. . .					0. . . .	11498
32-DFBA	WATUBELA cluster	1	1	4,603	5,934		30.00	59	B	3		. . .					0. . . .	11499
32-DFBA-a	kasiui					0				3		. . .					0. . . .	11500
32-DFBA-b	watubela	1	1	4,603	5,934	0	30.00	59	B	3		. . .					0. . . .	11501
32-DFBA-c	tamher-timur					0				3		. . .					0. . . .	11502
32-DFBA-d	sulmelang					0				3		. . .					0. . . .	11503
32-DFBA-e	wesi					0				3		. . .					0. . . .	11504
32-DFBA-f	matabello					0				3		. . .					0. . . .	11505
32-DFC	**GESER-BATI net**	1	3	47,321	61,005		7.35	33	A	4		. . .					0. . . .	11506
32-DFCA	GESER-GORAM cluster	1	2	43,206	55,700		8.00	35	A	2		. . .					0. . . .	11507
32-DFCA-a	goram-laut					0				2		. . .					0. . . .	11508
32-DFCA-b	mina-mina gorong					0				2		. . .					0. . . .	11509
32-DFCA-c	kelimuri	1	1	85	109	0	8.24	32	A	2		. . .					0. . . .	11510
32-DFCA-d	geser	1	1	43,121	55,591	0	8.00	35	A	2		. . .					0. . . .	11511
32-DFCA-e	seran-laut					0				2		. . .					0. . . .	11512
32-DFCB	BATI cluster	1	1	4,115	5,305		0.51	17	A	4		. . .					0. . . .	11513
32-DFCB-a	bati	1	1	4,115	5,305	0	0.51	17	A	4		. . .					0. . . .	11514
32-DFCB-b	gah					0				4		. . .					0. . . .	11515
32-DG	SERAM chain	1	41	241,873	314,439		28.61	55	B	22		P. .					0. . . .	11516
32-DGA	**MASIWANG net**	1	1	1,167	1,504		91.00	100	C	3		. . .					0. . . .	11517
32-DGAA	MASIWANG cluster	1	1	1,167	1,504		91.00	100	C	3		. . .					0. . . .	11518
32-DGAA-a	masiwang	1	1	1,167	1,504	0	91.00	100	C	3		. . .					0. . . .	11519
32-DGB	**BOBOT net**	1	1	6,151	7,930		30.00	59	B	2		. . .					0. . . .	11520
32-DGBA	BOBOT cluster	1	1	6,151	7,930		30.00	59	B	2		. . .					0. . . .	11521
32-DGBA-a	bobot	1	1	6,151	7,930	0	30.00	59	B	2		. . .					0. . . .	11522
32-DGC	**SALAS net**	1	1	64	82		50.00	84	B	4		. . .					0. . . .	11523
32-DGCA	SALAS cluster	1	1	64	82		50.00	84	B	4		. . .					0. . . .	11524
32-DGCA-a	salas	1	1	64	82	0	50.00	84	B	4		. . .					0. . . .	11525
32-DGD	**BENGGOI net**	1	2	424	547		11.79	38	A	4		. . .					0. . . .	11526
32-DGDA	BENGGOI cluster	1	2	424	547		11.79	38	A	4		. . .					0. . . .	11527
32-DGDA-a	lesa					0				4		. . .					0. . . .	11528
32-DGDA-b	benggoi	1	1	403	520	0	11.91	38	A	4		. . .					0. . . .	11529
32-DGDA-c	balakeo					0				4		. . .					0. . . .	11530
32-DGDA-d	kobi					0				4		. . .					0. . . .	11531
32-DGDA-e	hoti	1	1	21	27	0	9.52	33	A	4		. . .					0. . . .	11532
32-DGE	**LIANA net**	1	2	7,763	10,008		34.48	61	B	12		. . .					0. . . .	11533
32-DGEA	LIANA-KOBI cluster	1	2	7,763	10,008		34.48	61	B	12		. . .					0. . . .	11534
32-DGEA-a	liana	1	1	3,521	4,539	0	70.01	99	C	12	Liana-seti	. . .					0. . . .	11535
32-DGEA-b	wahakaim	1	1	4,242	5,469	0	5.00	30	A	12		. . .					0. . . .	11536
32-DGEA-c	kobi					0				12		. . .					0. . . .	11537
32-DGEA-d	teula					0				12		. . .					0. . . .	11538
32-DGEA-e	'seti'					0				12		. . .					0. . . .	11539
32-DGF	**SEPA-TELUTI net**	1	3	27,786	35,822		16.18	44	A	2		. . .					0. . . .	11540
32-DGFA	TELUTI cluster	1	2	24,732	31,884		16.95	45	A	2		. . .					0. . . .	11541
32-DGFA-a	laha-serani	1	1	4,794	6,180	0	50.00	85	B	2		. . .					0. . . .	11542
32-DGFA-b	tehoru-haya	1	1	19,938	25,704	0	9.00	35	A	2		. . .					0. . . .	11543
32-DGFB	SEPA cluster	1	1	3,054	3,938		9.99	35	A	4		. . .					0. . . .	11544
32-DGFB-a	tamilouw					0				4		. . .					0. . . .	11545
32-DGFB-b	sepa	1	1	3,054	3,938	0	9.99	35	A	4		. . .					0. . . .	11546
32-DGG	**MANUSELA-HUAULU net**	1	3	12,812	16,516		9.73	39	A	12		. . .					0. . . .	11547
32-DGGA	MANUSELA cluster	1	2	12,451	16,051		9.96	39	A	4		. . .					0. . . .	11548
32-DGGA-a	South manusela					0				4		. . .					0. . . .	11549
32-DGGA-b	kanikeh					0				4		. . .					0. . . .	11550
32-DGGA-c	hatuolu					0				4		. . .					0. . . .	11551
32-DGGA-d	maneo					0				4		. . .					0. . . .	11552
32-DGGA-e	maneoratu					0				4		. . .					0. . . .	11553
32-DGGB	HUAULU cluster	1	1	361	465		1.94	26	A	12		. . .					0. . . .	11554
32-DGGB-a	huaulu	1	1	361	465	0	1.94	26	A	12	Huaulu	. . .					0. . . .	11555
32-DGH	**NUAULU net**	1	1	1,891	2,561		7.99	34	A	22		P. .					0. . . .	11556
32-DGHA	NORTH NUAULU cluster	1	1	300	510		8.00	30	A	0		. . .					0. . . .	11557
32-DGHA-a	North nuaulu	1	1	300	510	0	8.00	30	A	0		. . .					0. . . .	11558
32-DGHB	SOUTH NUAULU cluster	1	1	1,591	2,051		7.98	35	A	22		P. .					0. . . .	11559
32-DGHB-a	South nuaulu	1	1	1,591	2,051	0	7.98	35	A	22	Nuaulu*	P. .	1991-1995				0. . . .	11560
32-DGI	**SALEMAN net**	1	1	5,621	7,246		4.00	28	A	2		. . .					0. . . .	11561
32-DGIA	SALEMAN cluster	1	1	5,621	7,246		4.00	28	A	2		. . .					0. . . .	11562
32-DGIA-a	wahai					0				2		. . .					0. . . .	11563
32-DGIA-b	pasanea					0				2		. . .					0. . . .	11564
32-DGIA-c	sawai					0				2		. . .					0. . . .	11565
32-DGIA-d	besi					0				2		. . .					0. . . .	11566
32-DGIA-e	saleman	1	1	5,621	7,246	0	4.00	28	A	2		. . .					0. . . .	11567
32-DGJ	**ATAMANU net**	1	1	912	1,176		6.03	30	A	12		. . .					0. . . .	11568
32-DGJA	YALAHATAN-HARURU cluster	1	1	912	1,176		6.03	30	A	12	Yalahatan	. . .					0. . . .	11569
32-DGJA-a	yalahatan					0				12		. . .					0. . . .	11570
32-DGJA-b	haruru					0				12		. . .					0. . . .	11571
32-DGK	**WEMALE net**	1	2	11,242	14,492		79.99	100	C	2		. . .					0. . . .	11572
32-DGKA	SOUTH WEMALE cluster	1	1	4,582	5,906		79.99	100	C	2		. . .					0. . . .	11573
32-DGKA-a	tala	1	1	4,582	5,906	0	79.99	100	C	2		. . .					0. . . .	11574
32-DGKA-b	honitetu					0				2		. . .					0. . . .	11575
32-DGKA-c	uwenpantai					0				2		. . .					0. . . .	11576
32-DGKB	NORTH WEMALE cluster	1	1	6,660	8,586		80.00	100	C	2		. . .					0. . . .	11577
32-DGKB-a	kasieh					0				2		. . .					0. . . .	11578
32-DGKB-b	horale					0				2		. . .					0. . . .	11579

Continued opposite

Table 9-13 continued

Code 1	REFERENCE NAME / Autoglossonym 2	Coun 3	Peo 4	Mother-tongue speakers in 2000 5	in 2025 6	Media radio 7	CHURCH AC% 8	E% 9	Wld 10	Tr 11	Biblioglossonym 12	SCRIPTURES Print 13-15	P–activity 16	N–activity 17	B–activity 18	J-year 19	Jayuh 20-24	Ref 25
32-DGL	**NORTHWEST SERAM net**	1	5	6,786	8,750		19.60	45	A	8		. . .					0	11580
32-DGLA	LOUN cluster	1	1	42	55		40.48	67	B	8		. . .					0	11581
32-DGLA-a	loun	1	1	42	55	0	40.48	67	B	8		. . .					0	11582
32-DGLB	HULUNG cluster	1	1	21	27		80.95	100	C	8		. . .					0	11583
32-DGLB-a	hulung	1	1	21	27	0	80.95	100	C	8		. . .					0	11584
32-DGLC	HORURU cluster	1	1	4,242	5,469		7.00	31	A	4		. . .					0	11585
32-DGLC-a	horuru	1	1	4,242	5,469	0	7.00	31	A	4		. . .					0	11586
32-DGLD	LISABATA-NUNIALI cluster	1	1	2,460	3,172		40.00	68	B	2		. . .					0	11587
32-DGLD-a	lisabata-timur					0				2		. . .					0	11588
32-DGLD-b	nuniali					0				2		. . .					0	11589
32-DGLD-c	sukaraja					0				2		. . .					0	11590
32-DGLD-d	kawa					0				2		. . .					0	11591
32-DGLE	NAKAELA cluster	1	1	21	27		71.43	100	C	8		. . .					0	11592
32-DGLE-a	naka'ela	1	1	21	27	0	71.43	100	C	8		. . .					0	11593
32-DGM	**ALUNE net**	1	1	17,244	22,231		80.00	100	C	22		P . .					0	11594
32-DGMA	ALUNE cluster	1	1	17,244	22,231		80.00	100	C	22	Alune	P . .	1991				0	11595
32-DGMA-a	North alune					0				22		P . .					0	11596
32-DGMA-b	Central aluneW.					0				22		p . .					0	11600
32-DGMA-c	Central aluneE.					0				22		p . .					0	11605
32-DGMA-d	South alune					0				22		p . .					0	11609
32-DGMA-e	Southwest alune					0				22		p . .					0	11613
32-DGN	**LAHA net**									2		. . .					0	11614
32-DGNA	LAHA cluster									2		. . .					0	11615
32-DGNA-a	laha					0				2		. . .					0	11616
32-DGO	**PIRU BAY net**	1	17	139,010	180,474		23.81	51	B	8		. . .					0	11617
32-DGOA	AMAHAI cluster	1	1	64	82		39.06	69	B	8		. . .					0	11618
32-DGOA-a	amahai	1	1	64	82	0	39.06	69	B	8		. . .					0	11619
32-DGOA-b	makariki					0				8		. . .					0	11620
32-DGOA-c	rutah					0				8		. . .					0	11621
32-DGOA-d	soahuku					0				8		. . .					0	11622
32-DGOB	PAULOHI cluster	1	1	64	82		90.63	100	C	8		. . .					0	11623
32-DGOB-a	paulohi-solahua	1	1	64	82	0	90.63	100	C	8		. . .					0	11624
32-DGOC	ELPAPUTIH cluster	1	1	424	547		9.91	36	A	4		. . .					0	11625
32-DGOC-a	elpaputih	1	1	424	547	0	9.91	36	A	4		. . .					0	11626
32-DGOD	LATU cluster	1	1	2,948	3,801		4.00	26	A	4		. . .					0	11627
32-DGOD-a	latu	1	1	2,948	3,801	0	4.00	26	A	4		. . .					0	11628
32-DGOE	IHA-SAPARUA cluster	1	2	18,093	23,324		4.68	28	A	2		. . .					0	11629
32-DGOE-a	kulur-saparua					0				2		. . .					0	11630
32-DGOE-b	iha-saparaua	1	1	6,109	7,875		6.01	31	A	2		. . .					0	11631
32-DGOE-c	siri-sori					0				2		. . .					0	11632
32-DGOF	IHA-SERAM cluster	1	1	3,000	5,100		4.00	22	A	0		. . .					0	11633
32-DGOF-a	kulur-seram					0				0		. . .					0	11634
32-DGOF-b	iha-seram					0				0		. . .					0	11635
32-DGOF-c	hualoy					0				0		. . .					0	11636
32-DGOF-d	tomalehu					0				0		. . .					0	11637
32-DGOG	NUSALAUT cluster	1	1	50	85		4.00	22	A	0		. . .					0	11638
32-DGOG-a	nusa-laut					0				0		. . .					0	11639
32-DGOH	HARUKU cluster	1	1	21,359	27,536		4.00	27	A	3		. . .					0	11640
32-DGOH-a	hulaliu	1	1	21,359	27,536	0	4.00	27	A	3		. . .					0	11641
32-DGOH-b	pelauw					0				3		. . .					0	11642
32-DGOH-c	kailolo					0				3		. . .					0	11643
32-DGOH-d	rohomoni					0				3		. . .					0	11644
32-DGOI	KAMARIAN cluster	1	1	21	27		4.76	33	A	8		. . .					0	11645
32-DGOI-a	kamarian	1	1	21	27	0	4.76	33	A	8		. . .					0	11646
32-DGOJ	KAIBOBO cluster	1	1	658	848		79.94	100	C	4		. . .					0	11647
32-DGOJ-a	kaibobo	1	1	658	848	0	79.94	100	C	4		. . .					0	11648
32-DGOJ-b	hatusua					0				4		. . .					0	11649
32-DGOK	PIRU cluster	1	1	21	27		80.95	100	C	8		. . .					0	11650
32-DGOK-a	piru	1	1	21	27	0	80.95	100	C	8		. . .					0	11651
32-DGOL	LUHU cluster	1	1	8,612	11,102		6.00	35	A	2		. . .					0	11652
32-DGOL-a	luhu	1	1	8,612	11,102	0	6.00	35	A	2		. . .					0	11653
32-DGOL-b	kelang					0				2		. . .					0	11654
32-DGOM	BATU-MERAH cluster	1	1	40	68		5.00	25	A	0		. . .					0	11655
32-DGOM-a	batu-merah	1	1	40	68	0	5.00	25	A	0		. . .					0	11656
32-DGON	TULEHU cluster	1	1	23,205	29,915		30.00	59	B	3		. . .					0	11657
32-DGON-a	tulehu	1	1	23,205	29,915	0	30.00	59	B	3		. . .					0	11658
32-DGON-b	liang					0				3		. . .					0	11659
32-DGON-c	tengah-tengah					0				3		. . .					0	11660
32-DGON-d	tial					0				3		. . .					0	11661
32-DGOO	HITU cluster	1	1	19,662	25,348		40.00	70	B	2		. . .					0	11662
32-DGOO-a	wakal					0				2		. . .					0	11663
32-DGOO-b	morela					0				2		. . .					0	11664
32-DGOO-c	mamala					0				2		. . .					0	11665
32-DGOO-d	hitu	1	1	19,662	25,348	0	40.00	70	B	2		. . .					0	11666
32-DGOP	SEIT-KAITETU cluster	1	1	12,536	16,160		50.00	82	B	4		. . .					0	11667
32-DGOP-a	hila					0				4		. . .					0	11668
32-DGOP-b	seit					0				4		. . .					0	11669
32-DGOP-c	kaitetu					0				4		. . .					0	11670
32-DGOQ	ASILULU cluster	1	1	10,796	13,918		8.00	34	A	2		. . .					0	11671
32-DGOQ-a	asilulu					0				2		. . .					0	11672
32-DGOQ-b	asilulu vehicular	1	1	10,796	13,918		8.00	34	A	2		. . .					0	11673
32-DGOQ-c	ureng					0				2		. . .					0	11674
32-DGOQ-d	negeri-lima					0				2		. . .					0	11675
32-DGOR	LARIKE-WAKASIHU cluster	1	1	15,463	19,934		51.00	83	B	2		. . .					0	11676
32-DGOR-a	allang					0				2		. . .					0	11677
32-DGOR-b	uraur-urusana					0				2		. . .					0	11678
32-DGOR-c	wakasihu					0				2		. . .					0	11679
32-DGOR-d	larike					0				2		. . .					0	11680
32-DGOR-e	lai					0				2		. . .					0	11681
32-DGOS	MANIPA cluster	1	1	1,994	2,570		6.02	28	A	3		. . .					0	11682
32-DGOS-a	manipa	1	1	1,994	2,570	0	6.02	28	A	3		. . .					0	11683
32-DGP	**BOANO net**	1	1	3,000	5,100		5.00	24	A	0		. . .					0	11684
32-DGPA	BOANO cluster	1	1	3,000	5,100		5.00	24	A	0		. . .					0	11685

Continued overleaf

Table 9-13 continued

Code 1	REFERENCE NAME Autoglossonym 2	Coun 3	Peo 4	Mother-tongue speakers in 2000 5	in 2025 6	Media radio 7	CHURCH AC% 8	E% 9	Wid 10	Tr 11	Biblioglossonym 12	SCRIPTURES Print P-activity 13-15	16	N-activity 17	B-activity 18	J-year 19	Jayuh 20-24	Ref 25
32-DGPA-a	North boano					0				0		. . .					0	11686
32-DGPA-b	South boana			0	0	0	0.00	0		0		. . .					0	11687
32-E	**BURU-SULA set**	1	10	102,234	131,799		13.61	39	A	22		P . .					0	11688
32-EA	BURU-SULA set / AMBELAU chain	1	1	6,681	8,613		20.00	50	B	2		. . .					0	11689
32-EAA	**AMBELAU net**	1	1	6,681	8,613		20.00	50	B	2		. . .					0	11690
32-EAAA	AMBELAU cluster	1	1	6,681	8,613		20.00	50	B	2		. . .					0	11691
32-EAAA-a	ambelau	1	1	6,681	8,613	0	20.00	50	B	2		. . .					0	11692
32-EAAA-b	wae-tawa					0				2		. . .					0	11693
32-EB	BURU chain	1	5	56,759	73,173		14.66	44	A	22		P . .					0	11694
32-EBA	**KAYELI net**	1	2	954	1,230		8.81	34	A	9		. . .					0	11695
32-EBAA	KAYELI cluster	1	2	954	1,230		8.81	34	A	8		. . .					0	11696
32-EBAA-a	kayeli	1	1	933	1,203	0	9.00	34	A	8		. . .					0	11697
32-EBAA-b	leliali	1	1	21	27	0	0.00	24	A	8		. . .					0	11698
32-EBAA-c	lumaete			0	0	0	0.00	0		8		. . .					0	11699
32-EBAB	MOKSELA cluster			0	0		0.00	0		9		. . .					0	11700
32-EBAB-a	moksela			0	0	0	0.00	0		9		. . .					0	11701
32-EBB	**BURU net**	1	3	55,805	71,943		14.76	44	A	22		P . .					0	11702
32-EBBA	BURU cluster	1	1	38,688	49,876		12.00	42	A	22		P . .					0	11703
32-EBBA-a	masarete					0				22		p . .					0	11704
32-EBBA-b	wae-sama					0				22		p . .					0	11705
32-EBBA-c	Central buru	1	1	38,688	49,876	0	12.00	42	A	22	Buru	P . .	1904-1991				0	11706
32-EBBA-d	li-emteban					0				22		p . .					0	11707
32-EBBB	LISELA cluster	1	2	17,117	22,067		21.00	49	A	4		. . .					0	11708
32-EBBB-a	li-sela	1	1	3,139	4,047	0	69.99	100	C	4		. . .					0	11709
32-EBBB-b	tagalisa					0				4		. . .					0	11710
32-EBBB-c	li-enyorot					0				4		. . .					0	11711
32-EBBB-d	wayapo					0				4		. . .					0	11712
32-EBC	**HUKUMINA net**									8		. . .					0	11713
32-EBCA	HUKUMINA cluster			0	0		0.00	0		8		. . .					0	11714
32-EBCA-a	hukumina			0	0	0	0.00	0		8		. . .					0	11715
32-EBD	**PALUMATA net**									9		. . .					0	11716
32-EBDA	PALUMATA cluster			0	0		0.00	0		9		. . .					0	11717
32-EBDA-a	palumata			0	0	0	0.00	0		9		. . .					0	11718
32-EC	SULA-MANGOLE chain	1	2	33,746	43,505		1.77	21	A	3		. . .					0	11719
32-ECA	**SULA net**	1	1	26,471	34,126		0.06	18	A	2		. . .					0	11720
32-ECAA	SULA cluster	1	1	26,471	34,126		0.06	18	A	2		. . .					0	11721
32-ECAA-a	facei					0				2		. . .					0	11722
32-ECAA-b	falahu					0				2		. . .					0	11723
32-ECAA-c	fagudu					0				2		. . .					0	11724
32-ECB	**SULABESI-MANGOLE net**	1	1	7,275	9,379		8.00	33	A	3		. . .					0	11725
32-ECBA	MANGOLE cluster	1	1	7,275	9,379		8.00	33	A	3		. . .					0	11726
32-ECBA-a	Sulabesi					0				3		. . .					0	11727
32-ECBA-b	mangole					0				3		. . .					0	11728
32-ED	TALIABU-KADAI chain	1	2	5,048	6,508		72.42	93	C	12		. . .					0	11729
32-EDA	**TALIABU-KADAI net**	1	2	5,048	6,508		72.42	93	C	12		. . .					0	11730
32-EDAA	KADAI cluster	1	1	530	684		7.92	34	A	4		. . .					0	11731
32-EDAA-a	East kadai					0				4		. . .					0	11732
32-EDAA-b	West kadai					0				4		. . .					0	11733
32-EDAB	TALIABU cluster	1	1	4,518	5,824		79.99	100	C	12		. . .					0	11734
32-EDAB-a	taliabu	1	1	4,518	5,824	0	79.99	100	C	12	Taliabu	. . .					0	11735
33	**HALYAMAPENIC zone**	1	48	197,652	260,063		52.76	74	B	41		PN .					0 . s . .	11739
33-A	**MALUKU-IRIAN set**	1	48	197,652	260,063		52.76	74	B	41		PN .					0 . s . .	11740
33-AA	SOUTH HALMAHERA chain	1	7	71,111	93,318		15.26	46	A	22		P . .					0	11741
33-AAA	**MAKIAN-GIMAN net**	1	2	30,395	39,185		17.44	50	A	3		. . .					0	11742
33-AAAA	EAST MAKIAN cluster	1	1	26,471	34,126		20.00	54	B	2		. . .					0	11743
33-AAAA-a	kayoa					0				2		. . .					0	11744
33-AAAA-b	East makian	1	1	26,471	34,126	0	20.00	54	B	2		. . .					0	11745
33-AAAB	GIMAN cluster	1	1	3,924	5,059		0.18	20	A	3		. . .					0	11746
33-AAAB-a	gane	1	1	3,924	5,059	0	0.18	20	A	3		. . .					0	11747
33-AAAB-b	Northwest giman					0				3		. . .					0	11748
33-AAAB-c	South giman					0				3		. . .					0	11749
33-AAB	**SAWAI net**	1	5	40,716	54,133		13.64	43	A	22		P . .					0	11750
33-AABA	SAWAI cluster	1	2	16,990	21,903		12.17	45	A	22		P . .					0	11751
33-AABA-a	weda	1	1	2,906	3,746	0	13.01	40	A	22		p . .					0	11752
33-AABA-b	sawai	1	1	14,084	18,157	0	12.00	46	A	22	Sawai	P . .	1994				0	11753
33-AABA-c	kobe					0				22		p . .					0	11754
33-AABB	PATANI cluster	1	1	10,584	13,645		12.00	39	A	2		. . .					0	11755
33-AABB-a	patani	1	1	10,584	13,645	0	12.00	39	A	2		. . .					0	11756
33-AABC	MABA-BICOLI cluster	1	1	6,618	8,531		16.00	44	A	3		. . .					0	11757
33-AABC-a	maba	1	1	6,618	8,531	0	16.00	44	A	3		. . .					0	11758
33-AABC-b	bitjoli					0				3		. . .					0	11759
33-AABC-c	ingli					0				3		. . .					0	11760
33-AABD	BULI-WAYAMLI cluster	1	1	6,524	10,054		17.73	44	A	2		. . .					0	11761
33-AABD-a	buli	1	1	2,524	3,254	0	29.99	60	B	2		. . .					0	11762
33-AABD-b	wayamli					0				2		. . .					0	11763
33-AB	RAJA-AMPAT chain	1	8	7,771	11,252		43.55	66	B	4		. . .					0	11764
33-ABA	**GEBE net**	1	1	3,000	5,100		20.00	50	B	3		. . .					0	11765
33-ABAA	GEBE cluster	1	1	3,000	5,100		20.00	50	B	3		. . .					0	11766
33-ABAA-a	umera					0				3		. . .					0	11767
33-ABAA-b	yu					0				3		. . .					0	11768
33-ABB	**MAYA-KAWE net**	1	6	3,859	4,976		67.30	83	C	4		. . .					0	11769

Continued opposite

Table 9-13 continued

Code 1	REFERENCE NAME / *Autoglossonym* 2	Coun 3	Peo 4	Mother-tongue speakers in 2000 5	in 2025 6	Media radio 7	CHURCH AC% 8	E% 9	Wld 10	Tr 11	Biblioglossonym 12	SCRIPTURES Print 13-15	P-activity 16	N-activity 17	B-activity 18	J-year 19	Jayuh 20-24	Ref 25
33-ABBA	LAGANYAN cluster	1	1	318	410		16.04	40	A	4		. . .					0. . . .	11770
33-ABBA-a	Northwest laganyan					0				4		. . .					0. . . .	11771
33-ABBA-b	Southeast laganyan					0				4		. . .					0. . . .	11772
33-ABBB	KAWE cluster	1	1	445	574		15.06	39	A	2		. . .					0. . . .	11773
33-ABBB-a	kawe	1	1	445	574	0	15.06	39	A	2		. . .					0. . . .	11774
33-ABBB-b	selpele					0				2		. . .					0. . . .	11775
33-ABBB-c	gam					0				2		. . .					0. . . .	11776
33-ABBC	MAYA cluster	1	4	3,096	3,992		80.07	94	C	4		. . .					0. . . .	11777
33-ABBC-a	waigeo					0				4		. . .					0. . . .	11778
33-ABBC-b	amber					0				4		. . .					0. . . .	11779
33-ABBC-c	saonek					0				4		. . .					0. . . .	11780
33-ABBC-d	kawit					0				4		. . .					0. . . .	11781
33-ABBC-e	banlol					0				4		. . .					0. . . .	11782
33-ABBC-f	batanta					0				4		. . .					0. . . .	11783
33-ABBC-g	samate									4		. . .					0. . . .	11784
33-ABBC-h	palamul	1	1	276	355	0	50.00	77	B	4		. . .					0. . . .	11785
33-ABBC-i	maden	1	1	551	711	0	50.09	78	B	4		. . .					0. . . .	11786
33-ABC	**MATBAT net**	1	1	615	793		11.06	35	A	4		. . .					0. . . .	11787
33-ABCA	MATBAT cluster	1	1	615	793		11.06	35	A	4		. . .					0. . . .	11788
33-ABCA-a	matbat	1	1	615	793	0	11.06	35	A	4		. . .					0. . . .	11789
33-ABD	**AS net**	1	1	297	383		40.07	68	B	4		. . .					0. . . .	11790
33-ABDA	AS cluster	1	1	297	383		40.07	68	B	4		. . .					0. . . .	11791
33-ABDA-a	as	1	1	297	383	0	40.07	68	B	4		. . .					0. . . .	11792
33-AC	BOMBERAI chain	1	7	3,777	4,867		38.95	61	B	4		. . .					0. . . .	11793
33-ACA	**ONIN-EROKWANUS net**	1	5	2,610	3,363		40.77	61	B	4		. . .					0. . . .	11794
33-ACAA	ONIN cluster	1	1	870	1,121		14.94	38	A	2		. . .					0. . . .	11795
33-ACAA-a	nikuda					0				2		. . .					0. . . .	11796
33-ACAA-b	ogar					0				2		. . .					0. . . .	11797
33-ACAA-c	patipi					0				2		. . .					0. . . .	11798
33-ACAA-d	sepa					0				2		. . .					0. . . .	11799
33-ACAB	SEKAR cluster	1	1	679	875		91.02	100	C	4		. . .					0. . . .	11800
33-ACAB-a	sekar	1	1	679	875	0	91.02	100	C	4		. . .					0. . . .	11801
33-ACAC	ARGUNI cluster	1	1	297	383		15.15	39	A	4		. . .					0. . . .	11802
33-ACAC-a	arguni	1	1	297	383	0	15.15	39	A	4		. . .					0. . . .	11803
33-ACAD	BEDOANAS cluster	1	1	382	492		59.95	88	B	4		. . .					0. . . .	11804
33-ACAD-a	bedoanas	1	1	382	492	0	59.95	88	B	4		. . .					0. . . .	11805
33-ACAE	EROKWANAS cluster	1	1	382	492		10.99	35	A	4		. . .					0. . . .	11806
33-ACAE-a	erokwanas	1	1	382	492	0	10.99	35	A	4		. . .					0. . . .	11807
33-ACB	**URUANGNRIN net**	1	1	382	492		45.03	74	B	4		. . .					0. . . .	11808
33-ACBA	URUANGNIRIN cluster	1	1	382	492		45.03	74	B	4		. . .					0. . . .	11809
33-ACBA-a	uruangnirin	1	1	382	492	0	45.03	74	B	4		. . .					0. . . .	11810
33-ACBA-b	faur					0				4		. . .					0. . . .	11811
33-ACC	**KOIWAI net**	1	1	785	1,012		29.94	56	B	2		. . .					0. . . .	11812
33-ACCA	KOIWAI cluster	1	1	785	1,012		29.94	56	B	2		. . .					0. . . .	11813
33-ACCA-a	koiwai	1	1	785	1,012	0	29.94	56	B	2		. . .					0. . . .	11814
33-ACCA-b	namatote-kayumerah					0				2		. . .					0. . . .	11815
33-ACCA-c	kilmala-karawatu					0				2		. . .					0. . . .	11819
33-ACCA-d	adi					0				2		. . .					0. . . .	11822
33-AD	TELUK-CENDRAWASIH chain	1	26	114,993	150,626		77.02	92	C	41		PN.					0.s..	11823
33-ADA	**KUWAI net**	1	2	5,600	7,219		57.25	87	B	22		P. .					0. . . .	11824
33-ADAA	IRARUTU cluster	1	1	4,921	6,344		61.00	91	C	22	Irarutu	P. .	1992				0. . . .	11825
33-ADAA-a	funiara					0				22		p. .					0. . . .	11826
33-ADAA-b	aroba					0				22		p. .					0. . . .	11827
33-ADAA-c	yaru					0				22		p. .					0. . . .	11828
33-ADAA-d	tugrama					0				22		p. .					0. . . .	11829
33-ADAA-e	tomage					0				22		p. .					0. . . .	11830
33-ADAA-f	werafuta					0				22		p. .					0. . . .	11831
33-ADAA-g	warmnu					0				22		p. .					0. . . .	11832
33-ADAA-h	kaitero					0				22		p. .					0. . . .	11833
33-ADAA-i	kasira					0				22		p. .					0. . . .	11834
33-ADAB	NABI-MODAN cluster	1	1	679	875		30.04	54	B	4		. . .					0. . . .	11835
33-ADAB-a	modan					0				4		. . .					0. . . .	11836
33-ADAB-b	nabi	1	1	679	875		30.04	54	B	4		. . .					0. . . .	11837
33-ADB	**BIAKIC net**	1	4	58,669	75,634		87.69	98	C	41		PN.					0.s..	11838
33-ADBA	BIAK-NUMFOR cluster	1	2	57,184	73,720		89.48	99	C	41	Biak	PN.	1870-1980	1990			0.s..	11839
33-ADBA-a	numfor					0				41		pn.					0.s..	11840
33-ADBA-b	baki-numfor-E					0				41		pn.					0.s..	11850
33-ADBB	MEOS-WAR cluster	1	1	276	355		35.14	59	B	4		. . .					0. . . .	11876
33-ADBB-a	meos-war	1	1	276	355	0	35.14	59	B	4		. . .					0. . . .	11877
33-ADBC	ROON cluster	1	1	1,209	1,559		14.97	38	A	4		. . .					0. . . .	11878
33-ADBC-a	roon	1	1	1,209	1,559	0	14.97	38	A	4		. . .					0. . . .	11879
33-ADC	**WAROPEN-YAPEN net**	1	12	36,628	49,396		63.69	85	C	22		P. .					0. . . .	11880
33-ADCA	WANDAMEN cluster	1	2	6,024	7,765		84.91	95	C	22		P. .					0. . . .	11881
33-ADCA-a	bintuni					0				22		p. .					0. . . .	11882
33-ADCA-b	wandamen	1	2	6,024	7,765		84.91	95	C	22	Wandamen	P. .	1937-1994				0. . . .	11883
33-ADCA-c	windesi					0				22		p. .					0. . . .	11884
33-ADCA-d	wasior					0				22		p. .					0. . . .	11885
33-ADCA-e	wamesa					0				22		p. .					0. . . .	11886
33-ADCA-f	ambumi					0				22		p. .					0. . . .	11887
33-ADCB	DUSNER cluster	1	1	21	27		33.33	62	B	8		. . .					0. . . .	11888
33-ADCB-a	dusner	1	1	21	27	0	33.33	62	B	8		. . .					0. . . .	11889
33-ADCC	ANSUS cluster	1	1	5,663	7,301		91.01	100	C	4		. . .					0. . . .	11890
33-ADCC-a	ansus	1	1	5,663	7,301	0	91.01	100	C	4		. . .					0. . . .	11891
33-ADCD	WOI cluster	1	1	1,612	2,078		91.00	100	C	4		. . .					0. . . .	11892
33-ADCD-a	woi	1	1	1,612	2,078	0	91.00	100	C	4		. . .					0. . . .	11893
33-ADCE	POM cluster	1	1	2,460	3,172		91.02	100	C	4		. . .					0. . . .	11894
33-ADCE-a	pom	1	1	2,460	3,172	0	91.02	100	C	4		. . .					0. . . .	11895
33-ADCE-b	jobi					0				4		. . .					0. . . .	11896
33-ADCF	AIBONDENI cluster	1	1	300	510		90.00	99	C	0		. . .					0. . . .	11897
33-ADCF-a	aibondeni	1	1	300	510	0	90.00	99	C	0		. . .					0. . . .	11898
33-ADCG	PAPUMA cluster	1	1	806	1,039		90.94	100	C	4		. . . .					0. . . .	11899

Continued overleaf

Table 9-13 continued

Code 1	REFERENCE NAME / Autoglossonym 2	Coun 3	Peo 4	Mother-tongue speakers in 2000 5	in 2025 6	Media radio 7	CHURCH AC% 8	E% 9	Wld 10	Tr 11	Biblioglossonym 12	SCRIPTURES Print 13-15	P-activity 16	N-activity 17	B-activity 18	J-year 19	Jayuh 20-24	Ref 25
33-ADCG-a	papuma	1	1	806	1,039	0	90.94	100	C	4		...					0....	11900
33-ADCH	MARAU-MUNGGUI cluster	1	3	3,924	5,059		53.70	71	B	4		...					0....	11901
33-ADCH-a	marau	1	1	2,100	2,707	0	91.00	100	C	4		...					0....	11902
33-ADCH-b	warabori	1	1	742	957	0	11.86	36	A	4		...					0....	11903
33-ADCH-c	natabui					0				4		...					0....	11904
33-ADCH-d	munggui	1	1	1,082	1,395	0	9.98	38	A	4		...					0....	11905
33-ADCH-e	morui					0				4		...					0....	11906
33-ADCI	BUSAMI cluster	1	1	764	984		15.05	44	A	4		...					0....	11907
33-ADCI-a	kaonda					0				4		...					0....	11908
33-ADCI-b	sasawa-2	1	1	764	984	0	15.05	44	A	4		...					0....	11909
33-ADCI-c	kamanap					0				4		...					0....	11910
33-ADCJ	ARUI cluster	1	1	5,000	8,500		40.00	77	B	4		...					0....	11911
33-ADCJ-a	arui					0				4		...					0....	11912
33-ADCJ-b	serui					0				4		...					0....	11913
33-ADCJ-c	nau					0				4		...					0....	11914
33-ADCK	AMBAI-MENAWI cluster	1	1	10,054	12,961		41.00	74	B	22		P..					0....	11915
33-ADCK-a	ambai	1	1	10,054	12,961	0	41.00	74	B	22	Ambai	P..	1994				0....	11916
33-ADCK-b	manawi					0				22		p..					0....	11917
33-ADCK-c	wadapi					0				22		p..					0....	11918
33-ADCK-d	randawaya					0				22		p..					0....	11919
33-ADCK-e	sumberbaba					0				22		p..					0....	11920
33-ADD	WABO-KURUDU net	1	2	4,242	5,469		69.26	87	C	4		...					0....	11921
33-ADDA	WABO cluster	1	1	1,845	2,379		41.03	70	B	4		...					0....	11922
33-ADDA-a	wabo					0				4		...					0....	11923
33-ADDA-b	woriasi					0				4		...					0....	11924
33-ADDA-c	nusari					0				4		...					0....	11925
33-ADDB	KURUDU-KAIPURI cluster	1	1	2,397	3,090		90.99	100	C	2		...					0....	11926
33-ADDB-a	kurudu					0				2		...					0....	11927
33-ADDB-b	kaipuri					0				2		...					0....	11928
33-ADE	WAROPEN-MOOR net	1	3	8,336	10,746		82.51	94	C	12		...					0....	11929
33-ADEA	WAROPEN cluster	1	3	8,336	10,746		82.51	94	C	12		...					0....	11930
33-ADEA-a	aropen	1	1	7,381	9,516	0	91.00	100	C	12	Waropen	...					0....	11931
33-ADEA-b	napan					0				12		...					0....	11932
33-ADEA-c	kai					0				12		...					0....	11933
33-ADEA-d	wonti					0				12		...					0....	11934
33-ADEA-e	mo'or	1	2	955	1,230	0	16.86	44	A	12		...					0....	11935
33-ADEA-f	maransabadi					0				12		...					0....	11936
33-ADEA-g	Southwest yapen					0				12		...					0....	11937
33-ADF	TANDIA net	1	1	500	850		90.00	99	C	8		...					0....	11938
33-ADFA	TANDIA cluster	1	1	500	850		90.00	99	C	8		...					0....	11939
33-ADFA-a	tandia					0				8		...					0....	11940
33-ADG	YERETUAR net	1	1	361	465		60.94	89	C	4		...					0....	11941
33-ADGA	YERETUAR cluster	1	1	361	465		60.94	89	C	4		...					0....	11942
33-ADGA-a	yeretuar	1	1	361	465	0	60.94	89	C	4		...					0....	11943
33-ADGA-b	goni					0				4		...					0....	11944
33-ADGA-c	umar					0				4		...					0....	11945
33-ADH	YAUR net	1	1	509	656		11.98	36	A	4		...					0....	11946
33-ADHA	YAUR cluster	1	1	509	656		11.98	36	A	4		...					0....	11947
33-ADHA-a	yaur	1	1	509	656	0	11.98	36	A	4		...					0....	11948
33-ADI	IRESIM net	1	1	148	191		25.00	50	B	4		...					0....	11949
33-ADIA	IRESIM cluster	1	1	148	191		25.00	50	B	4		...					0....	11950
33-ADIA-a	iresim	1	1	148	191	0	25.00	50	B	4		...					0....	11951
34	NEOGUINEIC zone	2	148	642,383	1,015,193		83.44	99	C	63		PNB					1.su.	11952
34-A	SOBEI-YOTAFA set	1	11	11,113	14,328		82.09	94	C	4		...					0....	11953
34-AA	SOBEI-YOTAFA chain	1	11	11,113	14,328		82.09	94	C	4		...					0....	11954
34-AAA	SOBEI-TARPIA net	1	7	5,196	6,699		84.22	96	C	4		...					0....	11955
34-AAAA	SOBEI cluster	1	5	3,690	4,758		81.44	95	C	4		...					0....	11956
34-AAAA-a	sarmi					0				4		...					0....	11957
34-AAAA-b	liki					0				4		...					0....	11958
34-AAAA-c	niroemoar					0				4		...					0....	11959
34-AAAA-d	wakde	1	1	551	711	0	70.05	91	C	4		...					0....	11960
34-AAAA-e	masimasi	1	1	318	410	0	70.13	90	C	4		...					0....	11961
34-AAAA-f	yamna	1	1	339	438	0	60.18	81	C	4		...					0....	11962
34-AAAA-g	podena					0				4		...					0....	11963
34-AAAA-h	yarsun	1	1	212	273	0	59.91	81	B	4		...					0....	11964
34-AAAA-i	anus					0				4		...					0....	11965
34-AAAA-j	biga					0				4		...					0....	11966
34-AAAB	BONGGO cluster	1	1	679	875		91.02	100	C	4		...					0....	11967
34-AAAB-a	bonggo	1	1	679	875	0	91.02	100	C	4		...					0....	11968
34-AAAB-b	armopa					0				4		...					0....	11969
34-AAAC	TARPIA cluster	1	1	827	1,066		91.05	100	C	4		...					0....	11970
34-AAAC-a	sufrai					0				4		...					0....	11971
34-AAAC-b	tarpia	1	1	827	1,066	0	91.05	100	C	4		...					0....	11972
34-AAAC-c	kaptiau					0				4		...					0....	11973
34-AAB	ORMU-YOTAFA net	1	4	5,917	7,629		80.23	92	C	4		...					0....	11974
34-AABA	ORMU cluster	1	1	636	820		14.94	41	A	4		...					0....	11975
34-AABA-a	ormu-besar					0				4		...					0....	11976
34-AABA-b	ormu-kecil					0				4		...					0....	11977
34-AABB	YOTAFA cluster	1	3	5,281	6,809		88.09	98	C	4		...					0....	11978
34-AABB-a	tobati	1	1	3,839	4,949	0	91.01	100	C	4		...					0....	11979
34-AABB-b	kayubatu					0				4		...					0....	11980
34-AABB-c	kayupulau	1	1	848	1,094	0	91.04	100	C	4		...					0....	11981
34-B	SIASSI set	1	51	128,357	199,936		81.67	98	C	42		PN.					0....	11982
34-BA	SERA-ALI chain	1	6	15,260	23,755		76.24	90	C	22		P..					0....	11983
34-BAA	SERA-SISSANO net	1	3	9,212	14,340		90.00	100	C	22		P..					0....	11984
34-BAAA	SERA cluster	1	1	628	977		89.97	100	C	4		...					0....	11985
34-BAAA-a	sera	1	1	628	977	0	89.97	100	C	4		...					0....	11986
34-BAAB	SISSANO cluster	1	2	8,584	13,363		90.00	100	C	22		P..					0....	11987
34-BAAB-a	sissano	1	1	5,991	9,326	0	90.00	100	C	22		p..					0....	11988

Continued opposite

Table 9-13 continued

Code 1	Reference Name / Autoglossonym 2	Coun 3	Peo 4	Mother-tongue speakers in 2000 5	in 2025 6	Media radio 7	CHURCH AC% 8	E% 9	Wld 10	Tr 11	Biblioglossonym 12	SCRIPTURES Print 13-15	P-activity 16	N-activity 17	B-activity 18	J-year 19	Jayuh 20-24	Ref 25
34-BAAB-b	West arop					0	90.01	100	C	22	Arop*	P . .	1988-1994				0	11989
34-BAAB-c	malol.	1	1	2,593	4,037	0				22		p . .					0	11990
34-BAAB-d	teles					0				22		p . .					0	11991
34-BAB	**TUMLEO net**	1	1	981	1,527		90.01	100	C	4		. . .					0	11992
34-BABA	TUMLEO cluster	1	1	981	1,527		90.01	100	C	4		. . .					0	11993
34-BABA-a	tumleo	1	1	981	1,527	0	90.01	100	C	4		. . .					0	11994
34-BABA-b	raiyu-yakoi					0				4		. . .					0	11995
34-BAC	**ALI-ULAU net**	1	2	5,067	7,888		48.55	69	B	4		. . .					0	11996
34-BACA	ALI-YAKAMUL cluster	1	1	3,078	4,791		24.98	49	A	4		. . .					0	11997
34-BACA-a	ali-seleo					0				4		. . .					0	11998
34-BACA-b	West ali					0				4		. . .					0	11999
34-BACA-c	yakamul	1	1	3,078	4,791	0	24.98	49	A	4		. . .					0	12000
34-BACB	ULAU-SUAIN cluster	1	1	1,989	3,097		85.02	100	C	2		. . .					0	12001
34-BACB-a	ulau					0				2		. . .					0	12002
34-BACB-b	suain	1	1	1,989	3,097	0	85.02	100	C	2		. . .					0	12003
34-BB	KAIRIRU-MANAM chain	1	9	18,495	28,793		80.84	99	C	41		PN .					0	12004
34-BBA	**KAIRIRU-KAIEP net**	1	3	5,666	8,820		83.57	99	C	5		. . .					0	12005
34-BBAA	KAIRIRU cluster	1	1	5,097	7,934		84.99	100	C	4		. . .					0	12006
34-BBAA-a	kairiru	1	1	5,097	7,934	0	84.99	100	C	4		. . .					0	12007
34-BBAA-b	yuo					0				4		. . .					0	12008
34-BBAA-c	karesau					0				4		. . .					0	12009
34-BBAA-d	mushu					0				4		. . .					0	12010
34-BBAA-e	karawop					0				4		. . .					0	12011
34-BBAB	KAIEP-TEREBU cluster	1	2	569	886		70.83	87	C	5		. . .					0	12012
34-BBAB-a	kaiep	1	1	351	547	0	90.03	100	C	5		. . .					0	12013
34-BBAB-b	terebu	1	1	218	339	0	39.91	66	B	5		. . .					0	12014
34-BBB	**WOGEO net**	1	1	1,798	2,798		84.98	100	C	4		. . .					0	12015
34-BBBA	WOGEO cluster	1	1	1,798	2,798		84.98	100	C	4		. . .					0	12016
34-BBBA-a	vokeo	1	1	1,798	2,798	0	84.98	100	C	4		. . .					0	12017
34-BBBA-b	koil									4		. . .					0	12018
34-BBC	**BIEM net**	1	1	2,114	3,291		85.00	100	C	4		. . .					0	12019
34-BBCA	BIEM cluster	1	1	2,114	3,291		85.00	100	C	4		. . .					0	12020
34-BBCA-a	viai					0				4		. . .					0	12021
34-BBCA-b	blupblup					0				4		. . .					0	12022
34-BBCA-c	kadovar					0				4		. . .					0	12023
34-BBCA-d	biem	1	1	2,114	3,291	0	85.00	100	C	4		. . .					0	12024
34-BBD	**MANAM-SEPA net**	1	2	7,945	12,370		75.73	100	C	41		PN .					0	12025
34-BBDA	MANAM cluster	1	1	7,556	11,764		75.00	100	C	41		PN .					0	12026
34-BBDA-a	manam	1	1	7,556	11,764	0	75.00	100	C	41	Manam	PN .	1988	1996			0	12027
34-BBDA-b	wanami					0				41		pn .					0	12028
34-BBDB	SEPA cluster	1	1	389	606		89.97	100	C	4		. . .					0	12029
34-BBDB-a	sepa	1	1	389	606	0	89.97	100	C	4		. . .					0	12030
34-BBE	**MEDEBUR net**	1	1	623	971		90.05	100	C	4		. . .					0	12031
34-BBEA	MEDEBUR cluster	1	1	623	971		90.05	100	C	4		. . .					0	12032
34-BBEA-a	medebur	1	1	623	971	0	90.05	100	C	4		. . .					0	12033
34-BBF	**KIS net**	1	1	349	543		89.97	100	C	4		. . .					0	12034
34-BBFA	KIS cluster	1	1	349	543		89.97	100	C	4		. . .					0	12035
34-BBFA-a	kis	1	1	349	543	0	89.97	100	C	4		. . .					0	12036
34-BC	BELAN chain	1	5	22,240	34,625		83.53	100	C	42		PN .					0	12037
34-BCA	**TAKIA-BILBIL net**	1	5	22,240	34,625		83.53	100	C	42		PN .					0	12038
34-BCAA	TAKIA-MEGIAR cluster	1	1	14,933	23,247		85.00	100	C	22	Takia	P . .	1979-1987				0	12039
34-BCAA-a	takia-karkar					0				22		p . .					0	12040
34-BCAA-b	takia-bagabag					0				22		p . .					0	12041
34-BCAB	MEGIAR cluster	1	1	1,248	1,943		75.00	100	C	4		. . .					0	12042
34-BCAB-a	megiar	1	1	1,248	1,943	0	75.00	100	C	4		. . .					0	12043
34-BCAB-b	serang					0				4		. . .					0	12044
34-BCAC	MATUKAR cluster	1	1	318	496		95.28	100	C	4		. . .					0	12045
34-BCAC-a	matukar	1	1	318	496	0	95.28	100	C	4		. . .					0	12046
34-BCAD	GEDAGED cluster	1	1	4,724	7,355		80.00	100	C	42		PN .					0	12047
34-BCAD-a	gedaged	1	1	4,724	7,355	1	80.00	100	C	42	Bel*	PN .	1925-1935	1960			0	12048
34-BCAD-b	siar					1				42		pn .					0	12049
34-BCAD-c	mitebog					1				42		pn .					0	12050
34-BCAD-d	rio					1				42		pn .					0	12051
34-BCAD-e	sek					1				42		pn .					0	12052
34-BCAD-f	panitibun					1				42		pn .					0	12053
34-BCAE	BILBIL cluster	1	1	1,017	1,584		85.05	100	C	4		. . .					0	12054
34-BCAE-a	bilbil	1	1	1,017	1,584	0	85.05	100	C	4		. . .					0	12055
34-BCAE-b	yabob					0				4		. . .					0	12056
34-BD	HAM chain	1	1	2,173	3,382		60.01	90	C	12		. . .					0	12057
34-BDA	**HAM net**	1	1	2,173	3,382		60.01	90	C	12		. . .					0	12058
34-BDAA	HAM cluster	1	1	2,173	3,382		60.01	90	C	12		. . .					0	12059
34-BDAA-a	ham					0				12		. . .					0	12060
34-BDAA-b	dami	1	1	2,173	3,382	0	60.01	90	C	12	Dami	. . .					0	12061
34-BE	MINDIRI-BILIAU chain	1	2	1,249	1,987		90.47	100	C	22		P . .					0	12062
34-BEA	**MINDIRI net**	1	1	135	210		94.81	100	C	4		. . .					0	12063
34-BEAA	MINDIRI cluster	1	1	135	210		94.81	100	C	4		. . .					0	12064
34-BEAA-a	mindiri	1	1	135	210	0	94.81	100	C	4		. . .					0	12065
34-BEB	**BILIAU-WAB net**	1	1	1,114	1,777		89.95	100	C	22		P . .					0	12066
34-BEBA	BILIAU cluster	1	1	814	1,267		89.93	100	C	22		P . .					0	12067
34-BEBA-a	biliau	1	1	814	1,267	0	89.93	100	C	22	Awad Bing	P . .	1992				0	12068
34-BEBA-b	sengam					0				22		p . .					0	12069
34-BEBA-c	yamai					0				22		p . .					0	12070
34-BEBA-d	swit					0				22		p . .					0	12071
34-BEBA-e	galek					0				22		p . .					0	12072
34-BEBA-f	telyat					0				22		p . .					0	12073
34-BEBA-g	teterai									22		p . .					0	12074
34-BEBB	WAB cluster	1	1	300	510		90.00	99	C	4		. . .					0	12075
34-BEBB-a	wab									4		. . .					0	12076

Continued overleaf

Table 9-13 continued

Code 1	REFERENCE NAME / Autoglossonym 2	Coun 3	Peo 4	Mother-tongue speakers in 2000 5	in 2025 6	Media radio 7	CHURCH AC% 8	E% 9	Wld 10	Tr 11	Biblioglossonym 12	Print 13-15	P-activity 16	N-activity 17	B-activity 18	J-year 19	Jayuh 20-24	Ref 25
34-BEBB-b	saui					0				4		. . .					0	12077
34-BEBB-c	som					0				4		. . .					0	12078
34-BF	LUKEP-MANGAP chain	1	7	8,953	13,938		80.14	100	C	22		P . .					0	12079
34-BFA	**LUKEP-MALASANGA net**	1	6	6,047	9,413		80.21	100	C	22		P . .					0	12080
34-BFAA	LUKEP-AROP cluster	1	4	5,018	7,812		78.70	100	C	22		P . .					0	12081
34-BFAA-a	lukep	1	1	882	1,374	0	80.05	100	C	22	Lokep	P . .	1993				0	12082
34-BFAA-b	arop-malala	1	2	3,675	5,721	0	76.95	100	C	22	Arop-lokep	P . .	1990-1993				0	12085
34-BFAA-c	moromiranga	1	1	461	717	0	90.02	100	C	22		p . .					0	12089
34-BFAA-d	pono					0				22		p . .					0	12090
34-BFAB	MALASANGA cluster	1	1	506	787		84.98	100	C	4		. . .					0	12091
34-BFAB-a	singorokai					0				4		. . .					0	12092
34-BFAB-b	malasanga	1	1	506	787	0	84.98	100	C	4		. . .					0	12093
34-BFAC	BARIM cluster	1	1	523	814		90.06	100	C	2		. . .					0	12094
34-BFAC-a	barim	1	1	523	814	0	90.06	100	C	2		. . .					0	12095
34-BFB	**MANGAP net**	1	1	2,906	4,525		80.01	100	C	22		P . .					0	12096
34-BFBA	MANGAP cluster	1	1	2,906	4,525		80.01	100	C	22		P . .					0	12097
34-BFBA-a	mbula	1	1	2,906	4,525	0	80.01	100	C	22	Mbula	P . .	1989-1990				0	12098
34-BFBA-b	kaimanga					0				22		p . .					0	12099
34-BFBA-c	gauru					0				22		p . .					0	12100
34-BG	MALALAMAI chain	1	1	551	858		90.02	100	C	4		. . .					0	12101
34-BGA	**MALALAMAI net**	1	1	551	858		90.02	100	C	4		. . .					0	12102
34-BGAA	MALALAMAI cluster	1	1	551	858		90.02	100	C	4		. . .					0	12103
34-BGAA-a	malalamai	1	1	551	858	0	90.02	100	C	4		. . .					0	12104
34-BGAA-b	bonga					0				4		. . .					0	12105
34-BH	ROINJI-NENAYA chain	1	2	825	1,285		90.06	100	C	4		. . .					0	12106
34-BHA	**ROINJI net**	1	1	330	514		90.00	100	C	4		. . .					0	12107
34-BHAA	ROINJI cluster	1	1	330	514		90.00	100	C	4		. . .					0	12108
34-BHAA-a	gali					0				4		. . .					0	12109
34-BHAA-b	roinji	1	1	330	514	0	90.00	100	C	4		. . .					0	12110
34-BHB	**NENAYA net**	1	1	495	771		90.10	100	C	4		. . .					0	12111
34-BHBA	NENAYA cluster	1	1	495	771		90.10	100	C	4		. . .					0	12112
34-BHBA-a	nenaya	1	1	495	771	0	90.10	100	C	4		. . .					0	12113
34-BI	SIO chain	1	1	4,356	6,781		84.99	100	C	41		PN .					0	12114
34-BIA	**SIO net**	1	1	4,356	6,781		84.99	100	C	41		PN .					0	12115
34-BIAA	SIO cluster	1	1	4,356	6,781		84.99	100	C	41		PN .					0	12116
34-BIAA-a	sio	1	1	4,356	6,781	0	84.99	100	C	41	Sio	PN .	1988	1995-1996			0	12117
34-BJ	BARIAI-MUTU chain	1	6	16,520	25,718		80.18	100	C	12		. . .					0	12118
34-BJA	**GITUA net**	1	1	759	1,182		89.99	100	C	4		. . .					0	12119
34-BJAA	GITUA cluster	1	1	759	1,182		89.99	100	C	4		. . .					0	12120
34-BJAA-a	gitua					0				4		. . .					0	12121
34-BJAA-b	kelana					0				4		. . .					0	12122
34-BJB	**TAMI-MUTU net**	1	2	4,440	6,911		80.00	100	C	12		. . .					0	12123
34-BJBA	TAMI cluster	1	1	2,015	3,136		80.00	100	C	12		. . .					0	12124
34-BJBA-a	tami	1	1	2,015	3,136	0	80.00	100	C	12	Tami	. . .					0	12125
34-BJBA-b	busiga					0				12		. . .					0	12126
34-BJBA-c	bua					0				12		. . .					0	12127
34-BJBB	TUAM-MUTU cluster	1	1	2,425	3,775		80.00	100	C	2		. . .					0	12128
34-BJBB-a	mutu-umboi					0				2		. . .					0	12129
34-BJBB-b	mutu-malau					0				2		. . .					0	12130
34-BJBB-c	malai					0				2		. . .					0	12131
34-BJBB-d	tuam	1	1	2,425	3,775	0	80.00	100	C	2		. . .					0	12132
34-BJBB-e	mandok					0				2		. . .					0	12133
34-BJC	**KOVE-BARIAI net**	1	3	11,321	17,625		79.60	100	C	12		. . .					0	12134
34-BJCA	KOVE cluster	1	1	7,729	12,033		80.00	100	C	2		. . .					0	12135
34-BJCA-a	kove	1	1	7,729	12,033	0	80.00	100	C	2		. . .					0	12136
34-BJCA-b	tamuniai					0				2		. . .					0	12137
34-BJCB	LUSI cluster	1	1	2,290	3,565		77.99	100	C	2		. . .					0	12138
34-BJCB-a	lusi	1	1	2,290	3,565	0	77.99	100	C	2		. . .					0	12139
34-BJCB-b	kaliai					0				2		. . .					0	12140
34-BJCB-c	kombe					0				2		. . .					0	12141
34-BJCC	BARIAI cluster	1	1	1,302	2,027		80.03	100	C	12		. . .					0	12142
34-BJCC-a	bariai	1	1	1,302	2,027	0	80.03	100	C	12	Bariai	. . .					0	12143
34-BJCC-b	kabana					0				12		. . .					0	12144
34-BJCC-c	sahe					0				12		. . .					0	12145
34-BK	MALEU-KILENGE chain	1	1	6,313	9,899		79.99	100	C	22		P . .					0	12146
34-BKA	**MAHEU-KILENGE net**	1	1	6,313	9,899		79.99	100	C	22		P . .					0	12147
34-BKAA	KILENGE cluster	1	1	500	850		80.00	100	C	0		. . .					0	12148
34-BKAA-a	kilenge	1	1	500	850	0	80.00	100	C	0		. . .					0	12149
34-BKAB	MALEU cluster	1	1	5,813	9,049		79.99	100	C	22		P . .					0	12150
34-BKAB-a	maleu	1	1	5,813	9,049	0	79.99	100	C	22	Maleu-kilenge	P . .	1990				0	12151
34-BKAB-b	idne					0				22		p . .					0	12152
34-BL	YABEM-LABU chain	1	4	20,487	31,893		87.45	100	C	42		PN .					0	12153
34-BLA	**YABEM-BUKAUA net**	1	3	18,540	28,862		88.23	100	C	42		PN .					0	12154
34-BLAA	YABEM cluster	1	1	3,278	5,103		79.99	100	C	42		PN .					0	12155
34-BLAA-a	yabem	1	1	3,278	5,103	0	79.99	100	C	42	Jabem*	PN .	1908-1980	1924-1974			0	12156
34-BLAB	BUKAUA cluster	1	2	15,262	23,759		90.00	100	C	12		. . .					0	12157
34-BLAB-a	bukaua	1	1	15,246	23,735	0	90.00	100	C	12	Bugawac	. . .					0	12158
34-BLAB-b	yalu					0				12		. . .					0	12159
34-BLAB-c	lae	1	1	16	24	0	93.75	100	C	12		. . .					0	12160
34-BLB	**LABU net**	1	1	1,947	3,031		80.02	100	C	6		. . .					0	12161
34-BLBA	LABU cluster	1	1	1,947	3,031		80.02	100	C	6		. . .					0	12162
34-BLBA-a	labu-butu					0				6		. . .					0	12163
34-BLBA-b	labu-miti					0				6		. . .					0	12164
34-BLBA-c	labu-tali					0				6		. . .					0	12165
34-BM	KELA chain	1	1	3,203	4,987		79.99	100	C	2		. . .					0	12166

Continued opposite

Table 9-13 continued

Code 1	REFERENCE NAME / Autoglossonym 2	Coun 3	Peo 4	Mother-tongue speakers in 2000 5	in 2025 6	Media radio 7	AC% 8	E% 9	Wld 10	Tr 11	Biblioglossonym 12	Print 13-15	P-activity 16	N-activity 17	B-activity 18	J-year 19	Jayuh 20-24	Ref 25
34-BMA	**KELA net**	1	1	3,203	4,987		79.99	100	C	2		. . .					0	12167
34-BMAA	KELA cluster	1	1	3,203	4,987		79.99	100	C	2		. . .					0	12168
34-BMAA-a	kela	1	1	3,203	4,987	0	79.99	100	C	2		. . .					0	12169
34-BN	IWAL chain	1	1	1,867	2,906		79.97	100	C	41		PN.					0	12170
34-BNA	**IWAL net**	1	1	1,867	2,906		79.97	100	C	41		PN.					0	12171
34-BNAA	IWAL cluster	1	1	1,867	2,906		79.97	100	C	41		PN.					0	12172
34-BNAA-a	iwal	1	1	1,867	2,906	0	79.97	100	C	41	Iwal	PN.	1975	1984			0	12173
34-BO	SIBOMA chain	1	1	425	661		95.06	100	C	4		. . .					0	12174
34-BOA	**SIBOMA net**	1	1	425	661		95.06	100	C	4		. . .					0	12175
34-BOAA	SIBOMA cluster	1	1	425	661		95.06	100	C	4		. . .					0	12176
34-BOAA-a	siboma	1	1	425	661	0	95.06	100	C	4		. . .					0	12177
34-BP	HOTE-YAMAP chain	1	3	5,440	8,468		81.64	100	C	22		P. .					0	12178
34-BPA	**HOTE-YAMAP net**	1	3	5,440	8,468		81.64	100	C	22		P. .					0	12179
34-BPAA	HOTE cluster	1	2	4,440	6,911		80.88	100	C	22		P. .					0	12180
34-BPAA-a	hote	1	1	4,045	6,296	0	80.00	100	C	22	Hote	P. .	1988				0	12181
34-BPAA-b	misim	1	1	395	615	0	89.87	100	C	22		p. .					0	12182
34-BPAB	YAMAP cluster	1	1	1,000	1,557		85.00	100	C	4		. . .					0	12183
34-BPAB-a	yamap	1	1	1,000	1,557	0	85.00	100	C	4		. . .					0	12184
34-C	**MARKHAM-BULOLO set**	1	15	71,680	115,889		83.83	99	C	41		PN.					0	12185
34-CA	ADZERA-WAMPUR chain	1	4	57,773	94,235		83.37	99	C	41		PN.					0	12186
34-CAA	**MARI net**	1	1	1,003	1,562		4.99	30	A	4		. . .					0	12187
34-CAAA	MARI cluster	1	1	1,003	1,562		4.99	30	A	4		. . .					0	12188
34-CAAA-a	mari	1	1	1,003	1,562	0	4.99	30	A	4		. . .					0	12189
34-CAAA-b	hop					0				4		. . .					0	12190
34-CAB	**ADZERA net**	1	1	55,729	91,053		84.62	100	C	41		PN.					0	12191
34-CABA	YARUS-AMARI cluster	1	1	30,000	51,000		80.00	100	C	0		. . .					0	12192
34-CABA-a	amari					0				0		. . .					0	12193
34-CABA-b	ngarowapum					0				0		. . .					0	12194
34-CABA-c	yarus					0				0		. . .					0	12195
34-CABB	CENTRAL ADZERA cluster	1	1	25,729	40,053		90.00	100	C	41	Adzera	PN.	1968	1976			0	12196
34-CABB-a	tsumim					0				41		pn.					0	12197
34-CABB-b	adzrac					0				41		pn.					0	12198
34-CABB-c	ongac					0				41		pn.					0	12199
34-CABB-d	guruf					0				41		pn.					0	12200
34-CAC	**UNANK net**	1	1	610	949		90.00	100	C	4		. . .					0	12201
34-CACA	UNANK cluster	1	1	610	949		90.00	100	C	4		. . .					0	12202
34-CACA-a	unank	1	1	610	949	0	90.00	100	C	4		. . .					0	12203
34-CAD	**WAMPUR net**	1	1	431	671		94.90	100	C	4		. . .					0	12204
34-CADA	WAMPUR cluster	1	1	431	671		94.90	100	C	4		. . .					0	12205
34-CADA-a	wampur	1	1	431	671	0	94.90	100	C	4		. . .					0	12206
34-CB	SUKURUM-SIRASIRA chain	1	3	2,372	3,695		90.09	100	C	0		. . .					0	12207
34-CBA	**SUKURUM net**	1	1	1,177	1,833		90.06	100	C	0		. . .					0	12208
34-CBAA	SUKURUM cluster	1	1	1,177	1,833		90.06	100	C	0		. . .					0	12209
34-CBAA-a	sukurum	1	1	1,177	1,833	0	90.06	100	C	0		. . .					0	12210
34-CBB	**NGARIAWAN net**	1	1	577	899		90.12	100	C	0		. . .					0	12211
34-CBBA	NGARIAWAN cluster	1	1	577	899		90.12	100	C	0		. . .					0	12212
34-CBBA-a	ngariawan	1	1	577	899	0	90.12	100	C	0		. . .					0	12213
34-CBC	**SARASIRA net**	1	1	618	963		90.13	100	C	0		. . .					0	12214
34-CBCA	SARASIRA cluster	1	1	618	963		90.13	100	C	0		. . .					0	12215
34-CBCA-a	sarasira	1	1	618	963	0	90.13	100	C	0		. . .					0	12216
34-CC	WAMPAR-NAFI chain	1	4	7,837	12,201		82.54	100	C	41		PN.					0	12217
34-CCA	**WAMPAR-DAGIN net**	1	1	6,126	9,537		80.00	100	C	41		PN.					0	12218
34-CCAA	WAMPAR-DAGIN cluster	1	1	6,126	9,537		80.00	100	C	41		PN.					0	12219
34-CCAA-a	wampar	1	1	6,126	9,537	0	80.00	100	C	41	Wampar	PN.	1973	1984			0	12220
34-CCAA-b	dagin					0				41		pn.					0	12221
34-CCB	**NAFI-MUSOM net**	1	3	1,711	2,664		91.64	100	C	4		. . .					0	12222
34-CCBA	NAFI cluster	1	1	228	355		95.18	100	C	4		. . .					0	12223
34-CCBA-a	nafi	1	1	228	355	0	95.18	100	C	4		. . .					0	12224
34-CCBB	MUSOM cluster	1	1	338	527		94.97	100	C	4		. . .					0	12225
34-CCBB-a	musom	1	1	338	527	0	94.97	100	C	4		. . .					0	12226
34-CCBC	YALU cluster	1	1	1,145	1,782		89.96	100	C	4		. . .					0	12227
34-CCBC-a	yalu	1	1	1,145	1,782	0	89.96	100	C	4		. . .					0	12228
34-CD	GUWOT chain	1	1	571	889		90.02	100	C	4		. . .					0	12229
34-CDA	**GUWOT net**	1	1	571	889		90.02	100	C	4		. . .					0	12230
34-CDAA	GUWOT cluster	1	1	571	889		90.02	100	C	4		. . .					0	12231
34-CDAA-a	guwot	1	1	571	889	0	90.02	100	C	4		. . .					0	12232
34-CDAA-b	duwet					0				4		. . .					0	12233
34-CDAA-c	waing					0				4		. . .					0	12234
34-CE	WATUT chain	1	3	3,127	4,869		89.61	100	C	4		. . .					0	12235
34-CEA	**WATUT net**	1	3	3,127	4,869		89.61	100	C	4		. . .					0	12236
34-CEAA	SILISILI cluster	1	1	1,693	2,636		90.02	100	C	0		. . .					0	12237
34-CEAA-a	silisili					0				0		. . .					0	12238
34-CEAA-b	maraliinan	1	1	1,693	2,636	0	90.02	100	C	0		. . .					0	12239
34-CEAA-c	bubwaf					0				0		. . .					0	12240
34-CEAA-d	dunguntung					0				0		. . .					0	12241
34-CEAB	MARALANGO cluster	1	1	269	419		85.13	100	C	2		. . .					0	12242
34-CEAB-a	maralango	1	1	269	419		85.13	100	C	2		. . .					0	12243
34-CEAC	DANGAL cluster	1	1	1,165	1,814		90.04	100	C	4		. . .					0	12244
34-CEAC-a	dangal	1	1	1,165	1,814	0	90.04	100	C	4		. . .					0	12245

Continued overleaf

Table 9-13 continued

Code 1	REFERENCE NAME / Autoglossonym 2	Coun 3	Peo 4	Mother-tongue speakers in 2000 5	in 2025 6	Media radio 7	CHURCH AC% 8	E% 9	Wld 10	Tr 11	Biblioglossonym 12	Print 13-15	P-activity 16	N-activity 17	B-activity 18	J-year 19	Jayuh 20-24	Ref 25
34-D	**BUANG-PIU set**	1	13	38,758	60,624		79.39	98	C	41		PN.					0....	12246
34-DA	BUANG-PIU chain	1	13	38,758	60,624		79.39	98	C	41		PN.					0....	12247
34-DAA	**PIU net**	1	1	247	385		95.14	100	C	4		...					0....	12248
34-DAAA	PIU cluster	1	1	247	385		95.14	100	C	4		...					0....	12249
34-DAAA-a	piu	1	1	247	385	0	95.14	100	C	4		...					0....	12250
34-DAAA-b	sanbiau					0				4		...					0....	12251
34-DAAA-c	lanzog					0				4		...					0....	12252
34-DAAA-d	kuruko					0				4		...					0....	12253
34-DAB	**BUANG-MUMENG net**	1	12	38,511	60,239		79.29	98	C	41		PN.					0....	12254
34-DABA	MUMENG cluster	1	6	13,443	20,927		70.78	100	C	41		PN.					0....	12255
34-DABA-a	yanta	1	1	4,380	6,819	0	70.00	100	C	41		pn.					0....	12256
34-DABA-b	towangara					0				41		pn.					0....	12257
34-DABA-c	gorakor					0				41		pn.					0....	12258
34-DABA-d	ptep	1	1	2,116	3,293	0	75.00	100	C	41	Patep	PN.	1975-1981	1986			0....	12259
34-DABA-e	zenang	1	1	2,905	4,522	0	69.98	100	C	41		pn.					0....	12260
34-DABA-f	mumeng	1	1	3,476	5,411	0	69.99	100	C	41		pn.					0....	12261
34-DABA-g	latep	1	1	346	539	0	69.94	100	C	41		pn.					0....	12262
34-DABA-h	dengalu	1	1	220	343	0	70.00	100	C	41		pn.					0....	12263
34-DABB	DAMBI-KUMARU cluster	1	2	4,835	7,528		70.01	89	C	4		...					0....	12264
34-DABB-a	dambi	1	1	711	1,107	0	70.04	89	C	4		...					0....	12265
34-DABB-b	kumaru	1	1	4,124	6,421	0	70.00	89	C	4		...					0....	12266
34-DABC	KAPIN cluster	1	1	3,757	5,848		89.99	100	C	2		...					0....	12267
34-DABC-a	kapin	1	1	3,757	5,848	0	89.99	100	C	2		...					0....	12268
34-DABC-b	sambio					0				2		...					0....	12269
34-DABC-c	taiak					0				2		...					0....	12270
34-DABC-d	katumene					0				2		...					0....	12271
34-DABC-e	garawa					0				2		...					0....	12272
34-DABD	BUANG cluster	1	2	14,319	22,291		87.32	100	C	41		PN.					0....	12273
34-DABD-a	mangga	1	1	3,835	5,970	0	80.00	100	C	41	Buang: Mangga*	PN.	1972	1981			0....	12274
34-DABD-b	lagis					0				41		pn.					0....	12275
34-DABD-c	kwasang					0				41		pn.					0....	12276
34-DABD-d	mapos	1	1	10,484	16,321	0	90.00	100	C	41	Buang: Central*	PN.	1971	1978			0....	12277
34-DABD-e	wagau					0				41		pn.					0....	12278
34-DABD-f	buweyeu					0				41		pn.					0....	12279
34-DABD-g	wins					0				41		pn.					0....	12280
34-DABD-h	chimbuluk					0				41		pn.					0....	12281
34-DABD-i	papakene					0				41		pn.					0....	12282
34-DABE	MAMBUMP cluster	1	1	2,000	3,400		80.00	100	C	0		...					0....	12283
34-DABE-a	mambump	1	1	2,000	3,400	0	80.00	100	C	0		...					0....	12284
34-DABF	VEHES cluster	1	1	157	245		94.90	100	C	4		...					0....	12285
34-DABF-a	vehes	1	1	157	245	0	94.90	100	C	4		...					0....	12286
34-E	**MAISIN set**	1	1	6,281	10,208		80.00	100	C	2		...					0....	12287
34-EA	MAISIN chain	1	1	6,281	10,208		80.00	100	C	2		...					0....	12288
34-EAA	**MAISIN net**	1	1	6,281	10,208		80.00	100	C	2		...					0....	12289
34-EAAA	KOSIRAVA cluster	1	1	3,281	5,108		80.01	100	C	2		...					0....	12290
34-EAAA-a	kosirava	1	1	3,281	5,108	0	80.01	100	C	2		...					0....	12291
34-EAAB	UIAKU cluster	1	1	3,000	5,100		80.00	100	C	0		...					0....	12292
34-EAAB-a	North uiaku					0				0		...					0....	12293
34-EAAB-b	South uiaku					0				0		...					0....	12294
34-F	**VITAZ-LOUISIADE set**	1	43	210,835	334,201		82.98	100	C	63		PNB					0.su.	12295
34-FA	MINIAFIA-ARIFAMA chain	1	1	3,469	5,400		79.99	100	C	22		P..					0....	12296
34-FAA	**MINIAFIA-ARIFAMA net**	1	1	3,469	5,400		79.99	100	C	22		P..					0....	12297
34-FAAA	MINIAFIA-ARIFAMA cluster	1	1	3,469	5,400		79.99	100	C	22	Miniafia*	P..	1990-1991				0....	12298
34-FAAA-a	berubona					0				22		p..					0....	12299
34-FAAA-b	gebara					0				22		p..					0....	12300
34-FAAA-c	leaga					0				22		p..					0....	12301
34-FB	UBIR chain	1	1	2,343	3,648		90.01	100	C	24		P..					0....	12302
34-FBA	**UBIR net**	1	1	2,343	3,648		90.01	100	C	24		P..					0....	12303
34-FBAA	UBIR cluster	1	1	2,343	3,648		90.01	100	C	24	Ubir	P..	1950				0....	12304
34-FBAA-a	wanigela					0				24		p..					0....	12305
34-FBAA-b	kwagila					0				24		p..					0....	12306
34-FC	ARE-DUAU chain	1	25	91,945	146,027		82.54	100	C	63		PNB					0..u.	12307
34-FCA	**DOGA net**	1	1	342	532		90.06	100	C	4		...					0....	12308
34-FCAA	DOGA cluster	1	1	342	532		90.06	100	C	4		...					0....	12309
34-FCAA-a	magabara					0				4		...					0....	12310
34-FCAA-b	doga	1	1	342	532	0	90.06	100	C	4		...					0....	12311
34-FCB	**ANUKI net**	1	1	788	1,226		89.97	100	C	4		...					0....	12312
34-FCBA	ANUKI cluster	1	1	788	1,226		89.97	100	C	4		...					0....	12313
34-FCBA-a	gabo-bora	1	1	788	1,226	0	89.97	100	C	4		...					0....	12314
34-FCC	**ARE net**	1	1	2,193	3,413		79.98	100	C	63		PNB					0....	12315
34-FCCA	ARE cluster	1	1	2,193	3,413		79.98	100	C	63		PNB					0....	12316
34-FCCA-a	mukawa					0				63		pnb					0....	12317
34-FCCA-b	are	1	1	2,193	3,413	0	79.98	100	C	63	Mukawa*	PNB	1904-1912	1921	1925		0....	12318
34-FCD	**PAIWA-BOINAKI net**	1	2	8,097	13,035		76.30	99	C	12		...					0....	12319
34-FCDA	PAIWA cluster	1	1	2,290	3,565		80.00	100	C	12	Gapapaiwa	...					0....	12320
34-FCDA-a	East gapa-paiwa					0				12		...					0....	12321
34-FCDA-b	West gapa-paiwa					0				12		...					0....	12322
34-FCDB	BOIANAKI cluster	1	1	2,807	4,370		80.01	100	C	5		...					0....	12323
34-FCDB-a	boianaki	1	1	2,807	4,370	0	80.01	100	C	5		...					0....	12324
34-FCDB-b	galavi					0				5		...					0....	12325
34-FCDC	VIDIA cluster	1	1	3,000	5,100		70.00	98	C	0		...					0....	12326
34-FCDC-a	vidia					0				0		...					0....	12327
34-FCE	**WATALUMA net**	1	1	346	538		94.80	100	C	2		...					0....	12328
34-FCEA	WATALUMA cluster	1	1	346	538		94.80	100	C	2		...					0....	12329
34-FCEA-a	wataluma	1	1	346	538	0	94.80	100	C	2		...					0....	12330

Continued opposite

Table 9-13 continued

Code 1	REFERENCE NAME / Autoglossonym 2	Coun 3	Peo 4	Mother-tongue speakers in 2000 5	in 2025 6	Media radio 7	CHURCH AC% 8	E% 9	Wld 10	Tr 11	Biblioglossonym 12	SCRIPTURES Print 13-15	P–activity 16	N–activity 17	B–activity 18	J-year 19	Jayuh 20-24	Ref 25
34-FCF	**IDUNA-BWAIDOKA net**	1	2	14,940	23,258		86.90	100	C	41		PN.					0....	12331
34-FCFA	IDUNA cluster	1	1	8,070	12,563		80.00	100	C	41	Iduna	PN.	1973	1983			0....	12332
34-FCFA-a	waibula					0				41		pn.					0....	12333
34-FCFA-b	ufaufa					0				41		pn.					0....	12334
34-FCFA-c	idakamenai					0				41		pn.					0....	12335
34-FCFA-d	vivigana					0				41		pn.					0....	12336
34-FCFA-e	ufufu					0				41		pn.					0....	12341
34-FCFA-f	kalauna					0				41		pn.					0....	12342
34-FCFA-g	belebele					0				41		pn.					0....	12343
34-FCFA-h	goiala					0				41		pn.					0....	12344
34-FCFB	BWAIDOKA cluster	1	1	6,870	10,695		95.01	100	C	35	Bwaidoka	P..	1934-1994				0....	12345
34-FCFB-a	bwaidoka	1	1	6,870	10,695	0	95.01	100	C	35		P..					0....	12346
34-FCFB-b	mataita					0				35		p..					0....	12347
34-FCFB-c	kilia					0				35		p..					0....	12348
34-FCFB-d	lauwela					0				35		p..					0....	12349
34-FCFB-e	wagifa					0				35		p..					0....	12350
34-FCG	**DIODIO net**	1	1	2,184	3,400		79.99	100	C	2		...					0....	12351
34-FCGA	DIODIO cluster	1	1	2,184	3,400		79.99	100	C	2		...					0....	12352
34-FCGA-a	awale					0				2		...					0....	12353
34-FCGA-b	diodio-molata	1	1	2,184	3,400	0	79.99	100	C	2		...					0....	12354
34-FCGA-c	utalo					0				2		...					0....	12357
34-FCGA-d	iauiaula					0				2		...					0....	12358
34-FCH	**KALOKALO net**	1	1	1,199	1,866		79.98	100	C	12		...					0....	12359
34-FCHA	KALAKALO cluster	1	1	1,199	1,866		79.98	100	C	12		...					0....	12360
34-FCHA-a	kalakalo	1	1	1,199	1,866	0	79.98	100	C	12	Koluawa	...					0....	12361
34-FCI	**YAMALELE-MAIODOM net**	1	1	5,484	8,824		80.00	100	C	41		PN.					0....	12362
34-FCIA	YAMALELE cluster	1	1	3,484	5,424		79.99	100	C	41		PN.					0....	12363
34-FCIA-a	yamalele	1	1	3,484	5,424	0	79.99	100	C	41	Iamalele	PN.	1976	1984			0....	12364
34-FCIA-b	masimasi					0				41		pn.					0....	12369
34-FCIB	MAIODOM cluster	1	1	2,000	3,400		80.00	100	C	0		...					0....	12370
34-FCIB-a	maiodom	1	1	2,000	3,400	0	80.00	100	C	0		...					0....	12371
34-FCJ	**MINAVEHA net**	1	2	4,071	6,337		79.98	100	C	22		P..					0....	12372
34-FCJA	MINAVEHEHA cluster	1	2	4,071	6,337		79.98	100	C	22		P..					0....	12373
34-FCJA-a	minaveha	1	1	1,832	2,852	0	79.97	100	C	22	Minaveha	P..	1993-1995				0....	12374
34-FCJA-b	kukuya	1	1	2,239	3,485	0	79.99	100	C	22		p..					0....	12375
34-FCK	**MORIMA-FAGULULU net**	1	2	7,012	10,988		75.36	100	C	12		...					0....	12376
34-FCKA	FAGULULU cluster	1	1	200	340		80.00	100	C	0		...					0....	12377
34-FCKA-a	fagululu	1	1	200	340	0	80.00	100	C	0		...					0....	12378
34-FCKB	TUTUBELA cluster	1	1	300	510		80.00	100	C	0		...					0....	12379
34-FCKB-a	tutubela	1	1	300	510	0	80.00	100	C	0		...					0....	12380
34-FCKC	EBADIDI cluster	1	1	714	1,111		74.93	100	C	12		...					0....	12381
34-FCKC-a	ebadidi	1	1	714	1,111	0	74.93	100	C	12	Molima	...					0....	12382
34-FCKD	MORIMA cluster	1	1	5,798	9,027		75.01	100	C	0		...					0....	12383
34-FCKD-a	morima	1	1	5,798	9,027	0	75.01	100	C	0		...					0....	12384
34-FCL	**BOSILEWA net**	1	1	637	991		89.95	100	C	6		...					0....	12385
34-FCLA	BOSILEWA cluster	1	1	637	991		89.95	100	C	6		...					0....	12386
34-FCLA-a	bosilewa	1	1	637	991	0	89.95	100	C	6		...					0....	12387
34-FCM	**GUMASI net**	1	1	455	708		89.89	100	C	22		P..					0....	12388
34-FCMA	GUMASI cluster	1	1	455	708		89.89	100	C	22		P..					0....	12389
34-FCMA-a	gumasi	1	1	455	708	0	89.89	100	C	22	Gumawana	P..	1992				0....	12390
34-FCN	**GALEYA-GAMETA net**	1	1	7,414	12,115		74.60	99	C	2		...					0....	12391
34-FCNA	GAMETA cluster	1	1	4,000	6,800		70.00	98	C	0		...					0....	12392
34-FCNA-a	wadalei					0				0		...					0....	12393
34-FCNA-b	gameta					0				0		...					0....	12394
34-FCNA-c	urua					0				0		...					0....	12395
34-FCNA-d	basima					0				0		...					0....	12396
34-FCNB	GALEYA cluster	1	1	3,414	5,315		79.99	100	C	2		...					0....	12397
34-FCNB-a	sebutuia					0				2		...					0....	12398
34-FCNB-b	garea	1	1	3,414	5,315	0	79.99	100	C	2		...					0....	12399
34-FCO	**DOBU-LOBODA net**	1	1	14,955	23,998		89.99	100	C	63		PNB					0..u.	12400
34-FCOA	DOBU cluster	1	1	9,955	15,498		95.01	100	C	63	Dobu	PNB	1894-1919	1908-1986	1926		0..u.	12401
34-FCOA-a	galubwa					1				63		pnb					0..u.	12402
34-FCOA-b	tewara					1				63		pnb					0..u.	12403
34-FCOA-c	sanaroa					1				63		pnb					0..u.	12404
34-FCOA-d	ubuia					1				63		pnb					0..u.	12405
34-FCOA-e	edugaura					1				63		pnb					0..u.	12406
34-FCOA-f	sisiana-ubuia					1				63		pnb					0..u.	12407
34-FCOB	LOBODA cluster	1	1	5,000	8,500		80.00	100	C	0		...					0....	12408
34-FCOB-a	loboda					0				0		...					0....	12409
34-FCOB-b	dawada-siausi					0				0		...					0....	12410
34-FCP	**SEWA net**	1	2	8,313	13,113		84.99	100	C	2		...					0....	12411
34-FCPA	DUAU-PWATA cluster	1	2	7,113	11,073		86.11	100	C	2		...					0....	12412
34-FCPA-a	duau-pwata	1	1	4,354	6,778	0	89.99	100	C	2		...					0....	12413
34-FCPA-b	miadeba	1	1	2,759	4,295	0	79.99	100	C	2		...					0....	12414
34-FCPA-c	bwakera					0				2		...					0....	12415
34-FCPB	SIBONAI cluster	1	1	300	510		70.00	98	C	0		...					0....	12416
34-FCPB-a	sibonai	1	1	300	510	0	70.00	98	C	0		...					0....	12417
34-FCPC	MAIABARE cluster	1	1	200	340		70.00	98	C	0		...					0....	12418
34-FCPC-a	maiabare	1	1	200	340	0	70.00	98	C	0		...					0....	12419
34-FCPD	DARUBIA cluster	1	1	400	680		80.00	100	C	0		...					0....	12420
34-FCPD-a	darubia	1	1	400	680	0	80.00	100	C	0		...					0....	12421
34-FCPE	SEWATAITAI cluster	1	1	300	510		90.00	99	C	0		...					0....	12422
34-FCPE-a	sewataitai	1	1	300	510	0	90.00	99	C	0		...					0....	12423
34-FCQ	**BUNAMA-SAWATUPWA net**	1	1	4,986	7,806		80.00	100	C	41		PN.					0....	12424
34-FCQA	SAWATUPWA cluster	1	1	300	510		80.00	100	C	0		...					0....	12425
34-FCQA-a	sawatupwa	1	1	300	510	0	80.00	100	C	0		...					0....	12426
34-FCQB	BUNAMA cluster	1	1	4,686	7,296		80.00	100	C	41		PN.					0....	12427
34-FCQB-a	bunama	1	1	4,686	7,296	0	80.00	100	C	41	Bunama	PN.	1978-1986	1991			0....	12428
34-FCQB-b	barabara					0				41		pn.					0....	12429

Continued overleaf

Table 9-13 continued

Code 1	REFERENCE NAME / Autoglossonym 2	Coun 3	Peo 4	Mother-tongue speakers in 2000 5	in 2025 6	Media radio 7	CHURCH AC% 8	E% 9	Wld 10	Tr 11	Biblioglossonym 12	Print 13-15	P-activity 16	N-activity 17	B-activity 18	J-year 19	Jayuh 20-24	Ref 25
34-FCR	**MWATEBU net**	1	1	302	471		90.07	100	C	6		. . .					0	12430
34-FCRA	MWATEBU cluster	1	1	302	471		90.07	100	C	6		. . .					0	12431
34-FCRA-a	mwatebu	1	1	302	471	0	90.07	100	C	6		. . .					0	12432
34-FCS	**DUAU net**	1	1	4,200	7,140		80.00	100	C	0		. . .					0	12433
34-FCSA	DUAU cluster	1	1	4,000	6,800		80.00	100	C	0		. . .					0	12434
34-FCSA-a	lomitawa					0				0		. . .					0	12435
34-FCSA-b	sigasiga					0				0		. . .					0	12436
34-FCSA-c	sipupu					0				0		. . .					0	12437
34-FCSA-d	meudana					0				0		. . .					0	12438
34-FCSA-e	weyoko					0				0		. . .					0	12439
34-FCSA-f	kerorogea					0				0		. . .					0	12440
34-FCSA-g	mwalukwasia					0				0		. . .					0	12441
34-FCSA-h	somwadina					0				0		. . .					0	12442
34-FCSA-i	biawa					0				0		. . .					0	12443
34-FCSA-j	guleguleu					0				0		. . .					0	12444
34-FCSA-k	kumarahu					0				0		. . .					0	12445
34-FCSA-l	sawabwala					0				0		. . .					0	12446
34-FCSA-m	urada					0				0		. . .					0	12447
34-FCSB	KASIKASI cluster	1	1	200	340		80.00	100	C	0		. . .					0	12448
34-FCSB-a	kasikasi	1	1	200	340	0	80.00	100	C	0		. . .					0	12449
34-FCT	**AUHELAWA net**	1	1	1,702	2,649		79.96	100	C	35		P . .					0	12450
34-FCTA	AUHELAWA cluster	1	1	1,702	2,649		79.96	100	C	35	Auhelawa	P . .	1986-1993				0	12451
34-FCTA-a	kurada					0				35		p . .					0	12452
34-FCTA-b	naukata					0				35		p . .					0	12453
34-FCU	**TUBE-TUBE net**	1	1	2,325	3,619		84.99	100	C	22		P . .					0	12454
34-FCUA	TUBE-TUBE cluster	1	1	2,325	3,619		84.99	100	C	22		P . .					0	12455
34-FCUA-a	tube-tube	1	1	2,325	3,619	0	84.99	100	C	22	Bwanabwana	P . .	1928-1994				0	12456
34-FCUA-b	wari					0				22		p . .					0	12457
34-FCUA-c	kitai					0				22		p . .					0	12458
34-FD	KILIVILA-BUDIBUD chain	1	3	31,344	48,795		81.73	100	C	51		PN .					0 . su .	12459
34-FDA	**KILIVILA-MUYUW net**	1	2	31,035	48,314		81.65	100	C	51		PN .					0 . su .	12460
34-FDAA	KILIVILA cluster	1	1	25,575	39,814		82.00	100	C	51		PN .					0 . . u .	12461
34-FDAA-a	lusancay					0				51		pn .					0 . . u .	12462
34-FDAA-b	kilivila	1	1	25,575	39,814	0	82.00	100	C	51	Kiriwina*	PN .	1908-1995	1985			0 . . u .	12463
34-FDAA-c	sinaketa					0				51		pn .					0 . . u .	12464
34-FDAA-d	vakuta					0				51		pn .					0 . . u .	12465
34-FDAB	MUYUW-KITAVA cluster	1	1	5,460	8,500		80.00	100	C	41		PN .					0 . s . .	12466
34-FDAB-a	kitava					0				41		pn .					0 . s . .	12467
34-FDAB-b	iwa					0				41		pn .					0 . s . .	12468
34-FDAB-c	lougwaw					0				41		pn .					0 . s . .	12469
34-FDAB-d	yanaba					0				41		pn .					0 . s . .	12470
34-FDAB-e	muyuw	1	1	5,460	8,500	0	80.00	100	C	41	Muyuw	PN .	1970	1976-1996			0 . s . .	12471
34-FDB	**BUDIBUD net**	1	1	309	481		89.97	100	C	4		. . .					0	12475
34-FDBA	BUDIBUD cluster	1	1	309	481		89.97	100	C	4		. . .					0	12476
34-FDBA-a	budibud	1	1	309	481	0	89.97	100	C	4		. . .					0	12477
34-FE	MISIMA-TEWATEWA chain	1	1	21,031	33,456		85.34	100	C	43		PN .					0 . s . .	12478
34-FEA	**MISIMA-TEWATEWA net**	1	1	21,031	33,456		85.34	100	C	43		PN .					0 . s . .	12479
34-FEAA	TEWATEWA cluster	1	1	5,000	8,500		80.00	100	C	0		. . .					0	12480
34-FEAA-a	bowagis					0				0		. . .					0	12481
34-FEAA-b	alcester					0				0		. . .					0	12482
34-FEAA-c	ole					0				0		. . .					0	12483
34-FEAA-d	tewatewa					0				0		. . .					0	12484
34-FEAB	MISIMA-PANAYATI cluster	1	1	16,031	24,956		87.00	100	C	43		PN .					0 . s . .	12485
34-FEAB-a	panayati					0				43		pn .					0 . s . .	12486
34-FEAB-b	misima	1	1	16,031	24,956	0	87.00	100	C	43	Misima*	PN .	1894-1993	1947			0 . s . .	12487
34-FEAB-c	nasikwabw					0				43		pn .					0 . s . .	12488
34-FEAB-d	tokunu					0				43		pn .					0 . s . .	12489
34-FF	NIMOWA chain	1	1	2,469	4,001		85.54	100	C	22		P . .					0	12490
34-FFA	**NIMOWA net**	1	1	2,469	4,001		85.54	100	C	22		P . .					0	12491
34-FFAA	PANA-WINA cluster	1	1	600	1,020		80.00	100	C	0		. . .					0	12492
34-FFAA-a	pana-wina					0				0		. . .					0	12493
34-FFAA-b	sabari					0				0		. . .					0	12494
34-FFAB	PANA-TINANAI cluster	1	1	200	340		80.00	100	C	0		. . .					0	12495
34-FFAB-a	pana-tinanai	1	1	200	340	0	80.00	100	C	0		. . .					0	12496
34-FFAC	NIMOWA cluster	1	1	1,369	2,131		89.99	100	C	22		P . .					0	12497
34-FFAC-a	nimowa	1	1	1,369	2,131	0	89.99	100	C	22	Nimowa*	P . .	1979-1984				0	12498
34-FFAD	WEST NIMOWA cluster	1	1	300	510		80.00	100	C	0		. . .					0	12499
34-FFAD-a	West nimowa	1	1	300	510	0	80.00	100	C	0		. . .					0	12500
34-FG	TAGULA chain	1	1	2,489	3,875		85.01	100	C	12		. . .					0	12501
34-FGA	**TAGULA net**	1	1	2,489	3,875		85.01	100	C	12		. . .					0	12502
34-FGAA	TAGULA cluster	1	1	2,489	3,875		85.01	100	C	12	Sudest	. . .					0	12503
34-FGAA-a	madaua					0				12		. . .					0	12504
34-FGAA-b	nine-hills					0				12		. . .					0	12505
34-FGAA-c	pamela					0				12		. . .					0	12506
34-FGAA-d	rambuso					0				12		. . .					0	12507
34-FGAA-e	rewa					0				12		. . .					0	12508
34-FGAA-f	griffin point					0				12		. . .					0	12509
34-FGAA-g	East tagula					0				12		. . .					0	12510
34-FH	TAWALA-WEDAU chain	1	4	28,353	45,154		82.30	99	C	41		PN .					0 . s . .	12511
34-FHA	**TAWALA-TAUPOTA net**	1	2	24,024	38,415		82.55	99	C	41		PN .					0	12512
34-FHAA	BASILAKI-SIDEIA cluster	1	1	4,000	6,800		70.00	98	C	0		. . .					0	12513
34-FHAA-a	bohilai					0				0		. . .					0	12514
34-FHAA-b	sideya					0				0		. . .					0	12515
34-FHAB	TAWALA cluster	1	1	12,114	18,858		90.00	100	C	41		PN .					0	12516
34-FHAB-a	kehelala					0				41		pn .					0	12517
34-FHAB-b	divinai					0				41		pn .					0	12518
34-FHAB-c	tawala	1	1	12,114	18,858	0	90.00	100	C	41	Tawala	PN .	1898-1980	1985			0	12519
34-FHAB-d	labe					0				41		pn .					0	12520
34-FHAB-e	huhuna					0				41		pn .					0	12521
34-FHAB-f	lelehudi					0				41		pn .					0	12522
34-FHAB-g	yaleba					0				41		pn .					0	12523
34-FHAC	AWAIAMA cluster	1	1	2,000	3,400		70.00	98	C	0		. . .					0	12524

Continued opposite

Table 9-13 continued

Code 1	REFERENCE NAME / Autoglossonym 2	Coun 3	Peo 4	Mother-tongue speakers in 2000 — 5	in 2025 — 6	Media radio 7	AC% 8	E% 9	Wld 10	Tr 11	Biblioglossonym 12	Print 13-15	P–activity 16	N–activity 17	B–activity 18	J-year 19	Jayuh 20-24	Ref 25
34-FHAC-a	awayama	1	1	2,000	3,400	0	70.00	98	C	0		...					0....	12525
34-FHAD	TAUPOTA cluster	1	1	4,810	7,487		80.00	100	C	6		...					0....	12526
34-FHAD-a	yanianini					0				6							0....	12527
34-FHAD-b	taupota	1	1	4,810	7,487	0	80.00	100	C	6		...					0....	12528
34-FHAE	WAIEMA cluster	1	1	200	340		80.00	100	C	0		...					0....	12529
34-FHAE-a	waiema	1	1	200	340	0	80.00	100	C	0		...					0....	12530
34-FHAF	LAVIAM cluster	1	1	200	340		80.00	100	C	0		...					0....	12531
34-FHAF-a	laviam	1	1	200	340	0	80.00	100	C	0		...					0....	12532
34-FHAG	MAIVARA cluster	1	1	300	510		80.00	100	C	0		...					0....	12533
34-FHAG-a	maivara	1	1	300	510	0	80.00	100	C	0		...					0....	12534
34-FHAH	NAURA cluster	1	1	400	680		80.00	100	C	0		...					0....	12535
34-FHAH-a	naura	1	1	400	680	0	80.00	100	C	0		...					0....	12536
34-FHB	**GARUWAHI net**	1	1	410	638		90.00	100	C	6		...					0....	12537
34-FHBA	GARUWAHI cluster	1	1	410	638		90.00	100	C	6		...					0....	12538
34-FHBA-a	garuwahi	1	1	410	638	0	90.00	100	C	6		...					0....	12539
34-FHC	**WEDAU net**	1	1	3,919	6,101		79.99	100	C	41		PN.					0.s..	12540
34-FHCA	WEDAU cluster	1	1	3,919	6,101		79.99	100	C	41		PN.					0.s..	12541
34-FHCA-a	wedau					0				41		pn.					0.s..	12542
34-FHCA-b	wedau vehicular	1	1	3,919	6,101	0	79.99	100	C	41	Wedau	PN.	1897-1983	1927-1980			0.s..	12543
34-FHCA-c	topura					0				41		pn.					0.s..	12544
34-FHCA-d	yapoa					0				41		pn.					0.s..	12545
34-FI	SUAU-BUHUTU chain	1	4	21,427	34,345		84.92	100	C	51		PN.					0....	12546
34-FIA	**SUAU-BUHUTU net**	1	4	21,427	34,345		84.92	100	C	51		PN.					0....	12547
34-FIAA	WAGA-WAGA cluster	1	1	2,120	3,301		85.00	100	C	4		...					0....	12548
34-FIAA-a	kila-kilana	1	1	2,120	3,301	0	85.00	100	C	4		...					0....	12549
34-FIAA-b	gamadougou					0				4		...					0....	12550
34-FIAA-c	waga-waga					0				4		...					0....	12551
34-FIAA-d	waga-gatu					0				4		...					0....	12552
34-FIAA-e	noabune					0				4		...					0....	12553
34-FIAA-f	goilawalika					0				4		...					0....	12554
34-FIAB	SARIBA cluster	1	1	5,000	8,500		80.00	100	C	0		...					0....	12555
34-FIAB-a	sariba					0				0		...					0....	12556
34-FIAB-b	samarai					0				0		...					0....	12557
34-FIAB-c	doini					0				0		...					0....	12558
34-FIAC	LOGEA cluster	1	1	400	680		80.00	100	C	0		...					0....	12559
34-FIAC-a	logea	1	1	400	680	0	80.00	100	C	0		...					0....	12560
34-FIAD	DAIO-MUNI cluster	1	1	200	340		80.00	100	C	0		...					0....	12561
34-FIAD-a	daio-muni	1	1	200	340	0	80.00	100	C	0		...					0....	12562
34-FIAE	BONARUA cluster	1	1	300	510		80.00	100	C	0		...					0....	12563
34-FIAE-a	guaugurina					0				0		...					0....	12564
34-FIAE-b	bonarua					0				0		...					0....	12565
34-FIAF	SUAU cluster	1	1	9,875	15,373		89.00	100	C	51		PN.					0....	12566
34-FIAF-a	modewa					1				51		pn.					0....	12567
34-FIAF-b	suau					1				51		pn.					0....	12568
34-FIAF-c	Vehicular suau	1	1	9,875	15,373	1	89.00	100	C	51	Suau	PN.	1885-1926	1956-1962			0....	12569
34-FIAF-d	baibesika					1				51		pn.					0....	12570
34-FIAG	DAUI cluster	1	1	300	510		80.00	100	C	0		...					0....	12571
34-FIAG-a	daui	1	1	300	510	0	80.00	100	C	0		...					0....	12572
34-FIAH	DAHUNI cluster	1	1	300	510		80.00	100	C	0		...					0....	12573
34-FIAH-a	dahuni	1	1	300	510	0	80.00	100	C	0		...					0....	12574
34-FIAI	BONA-BONA cluster	1	1	100	170		80.00	100	C	0		...					0....	12575
34-FIAI-a	bona-bona	1	1	100	170	0	80.00	100	C	0		...					0....	12576
34-FIAJ	SINAKI cluster	1	1	594	924		89.90	100	C	0		...					0....	12577
34-FIAJ-a	gaidasu					0				0		...					0....	12578
34-FIAJ-b	sinaki	1	1	594	924	0	89.90	100	C	0		...					0....	12579
34-FIAK	LEILEIAFA cluster	1	1	300	510		80.00	100	C	0		...					0....	12580
34-FIAK-a	leileiafa	1	1	300	510	0	80.00	100	C	0		...					0....	12581
34-FIAL	BUHUTU cluster	1	1	1,938	3,017		80.03	100	C	12		...					0....	12582
34-FIAL-a	buhutu	1	1	1,938	3,017	0	80.03	100	C	12	Buhutu	...					0....	12583
34-FIAL-b	yaleba					0				12		...					0....	12584
34-FIAL-c	siasada					0				12		...					0....	12585
34-FJ	IGORA-DAWAWA chain	1	2	5,965	9,500		81.34	100	C	22		P..					0....	12586
34-FJA	**IGORA net**	1	1	2,102	3,344		83.82	100	C	2		...					0....	12587
34-FJAA	POVA cluster	1	1	300	510		80.00	100	C	0		...					0....	12588
34-FJAA-a	pova	1	1	300	510	0	80.00	100	C	0		...					0....	12589
34-FJAB	KAKABAI cluster	1	1	200	340		80.00	100	C	0		...					0....	12590
34-FJAB-a	kakabai	1	1	200	340	0	80.00	100	C	0		...					0....	12591
34-FJAC	IGORA cluster	1	1	1,602	2,494		85.02	100	C	2		...					0....	12592
34-FJAC-a	igora	1	1	1,602	2,494	0	85.02	100	C	2		...					0....	12593
34-FJB	**DAWAWA net**	1	1	3,863	6,156		79.99	100	C	22		P..					0....	12594
34-FJBA	MANUBADA cluster	1	1	2,863	4,456		79.99	100	C	22		P..					0....	12595
34-FJBA-a	manubada	1	1	2,863	4,456	0	79.99	100	C	22	Dawawa	P..	1991-1992				0....	12596
34-FJBB	DIDIA cluster	1	1	1,000	1,700		80.00	100	C	0		...					0....	12597
34-FJBB-a	didia	1	1	1,000	1,700	0	80.00	100	C	0		...					0....	12598
34-G	**MOTO-MEKEO set**	1	14	175,359	280,007		86.23	100	C	62		PNB					1.su.	12599
34-GA	OUMA-BINA chain	1	2	378	588		90.21	100	C	9		...					0....	12600
34-GAA	**BINA net**									9		...					0....	12601
34-GAAA	BINA cluster			0	0		0.00	0		9		...					0....	12602
34-GAAA-a	bina			0	0	0	0.00	0		9		...					0....	12603
34-GAB	**YOBA net**									9		...					0....	12604
34-GABA	YOBA cluster			0	0		0.00	0		9		...					0....	12605
34-GABA-a	yoba			0	0	0	0.00	0		9		...					0....	12606
34-GAC	**MAGORI net**	1	1	372	579		90.05	100	C	6		...					0....	12607
34-GACA	MAGORI cluster	1	1	372	579		90.05	100	C	6		...					0....	12608

Continued overleaf

Table 9-13 continued

Code 1	REFERENCE NAME / Autoglossonym 2	Coun 3	Peo 4	Mother-tongue speakers in 2000 5	in 2025 6	Media radio 7	CHURCH AC% 8	E% 9	Wld 10	Tr 11	Biblioglossonym 12	SCRIPTURES Print 13-15	P–activity 16	N–activity 17	B–activity 18	J-year 19	Jayuh 20-24	Ref 25
34-GACA-a	magori	1	1	372	579	0	90.05	100	C	6		. . .					0	12609
34-GAD	**OUMA net**	1	1	6	9		100.00	100	C	9		. . .					0	12610
34-GADA	OUMA cluster	1	1	6	9		100.00	100	C	9		. . .					0	12611
34-GADA-a	ouma	1	1	6	9	0	100.00	100	C	9		. . .					0	12612
34-GB	MOTU-SINAGORO chain	1	8	115,664	183,639		88.25	100	C	62		PNB					1 . su .	12613
34-GBA	**HULA-AROMA net**	1	2	51,804	83,511		85.72	100	C	44		PN .					0	12614
34-GBAA	AROMA cluster	1	1	20,000	34,000		85.00	100	C	0		. . .					0	12615
34-GBAA-a	lalaura					0				0		. . .					0	12616
34-GBAA-b	kapari					0				0		. . .					0	12617
34-GBAA-c	wanigela					0				0		. . .					0	12618
34-GBAA-d	maopa					0				0		. . .					0	12619
34-GBAA-e	aroma					0				0		. . .					0	12620
34-GBAB	KEOPARA cluster	1	1	28,071	43,700		87.00	100	C	24		P . .					0	12621
34-GBAB-a	keopara	1	1	28,071	43,700	0	87.00	100	C	24	Keapara*	P . .	1892-1905				0	12622
34-GBAB-b	kalo									24		p . .					0	12623
34-GBAB-c	babaga					0				24		p . .					0	12624
34-GBAC	HULA cluster	1	1	3,733	5,811		79.99	100	C	44		PN .					0	12625
34-GBAC-a	hula	1	1	3,733	5,811	0	79.99	100	C	44	Hula	PN .	1949	1954			0	12626
34-GBB	**SINAGORO net**	1	1	22,438	35,646		88.11	100	C	41		PN .					0	12627
34-GBBA	SOUTH SINAGORO cluster	1	1	17,438	27,146		89.00	100	C	41	Sinauguro	PN .	1991	1995			0	12628
34-GBBA-a	alepa					0				41		pn .					0	12629
34-GBBA-b	omene					0				41		pn .					0	12630
34-GBBA-c	kwaibo					0				41		pn .					0	12631
34-GBBA-d	babagarupu					0				41		pn .					0	12632
34-GBBA-e	alomarupu					0				41		pn .					0	12633
34-GBBA-f	kemabolo					0				41		pn .					0	12634
34-GBBA-g	balawaia					0				41		pn .					0	12635
34-GBBA-h	gabone					0				41		pn .					0	12636
34-GBBA-i	ikolu					0				41		pn .					0	12637
34-GBBA-j	saroa					0				41		pn .					0	12638
34-GBBA-k	kwaibida					0				41		pn .					0	12639
34-GBBB	NORTH SINAGORO cluster	1	1	2,000	3,400		85.00	100	C	0		. . .					0	12640
34-GBBB-a	tubulamo					0				0		. . .					0	12641
34-GBBB-b	gomore					0				0		. . .					0	12642
34-GBBB-c	karekadobu					0				0		. . .					0	12643
34-GBBB-d	taboro					0				0		. . .					0	12644
34-GBBB-e	boku					0				0		. . .					0	12645
34-GBBB-f	wiga					0				0		. . .					0	12646
34-GBBB-g	buaga					0				0		. . .					0	12647
34-GBBB-h	ikega					0				0		. . .					0	12648
34-GBBB-i	kubuli					0				0		. . .					0	12649
34-GBBC	EAST SINAGORO cluster	1	1	3,000	5,100		85.00	100	C	0		. . .					0	12650
34-GBBC-a	vora					0				0		. . .					0	12651
34-GBBC-b	maipiko					0				0		. . .					0	12652
34-GBBC-c	oruone					0				0		. . .					0	12653
34-GBC	**MOTU-HIRI-MOTU net**	1	2	26,611	41,426		95.80	100	C	62		PNB					1 . su .	12654
34-GBCA	MOTU cluster	1	1	21,355	33,244		96.00	100	C	62		PNB					0 . su .	12655
34-GBCA-a	motu	1	1	21,355	33,244	4	96.00	100	C	62	Motu	PNB	1882-1964	1891-1964	1973		0 . su .	12656
34-GBCB	HIRI-MOTU cluster	1	1	5,256	8,182		95.00	100	C	61		PNB					1 . su .	12668
34-GBCB-a	hiri-motu	1	1	5,256	8,182	2	95.00	100	C	61	Hiri Motu*	PNB	1964	1982	1994	1997	1 . su .	12669
34-GBCB-b	West hiri-motu					1				61		pnb					1 . su .	12670
34-GBD	**DOURA net**	1	1	1,163	1,810		79.97	100	C	4		. . .					0	12671
34-GBDA	DOURA cluster	1	1	1,163	1,810		79.97	100	C	4		. . .					0	12672
34-GBDA-a	doura	1	1	1,163	1,810	0	79.97	100	C	4		. . .					0	12673
34-GBE	**KABADI net**	1	1	2,564	3,992		79.99	100	C	2		. . .					0	12674
34-GBEA	KABADI cluster	1	1	2,564	3,992		79.99	100	C	2		. . .					0	12675
34-GBEA-a	kabadi	1	1	2,564	3,992	0	79.99	100	C	2		. . .					0	12676
34-GBF	**NARA net**	1	1	11,084	17,254		85.00	100	C	6		. . .					0	12677
34-GBFA	NARA cluster	1	1	11,084	17,254		85.00	100	C	6		. . .					0	12678
34-GBFA-a	nara	1	1	11,084	17,254	0	85.00	100	C	6		. . .					0	12679
34-GBFA-b	pokau					0				6		. . .					0	12680
34-GC	KUNI chain	1	2	7,781	12,113		75.17	98	C	0		. . .					0	12681
34-GCA	**KUNI net**	1	2	7,781	12,113		75.17	98	C	0		. . .					0	12682
34-GCAA	KUNI cluster	1	2	7,781	12,113		75.17	98	C	0		. . .					0	12683
34-GCAA-a	kuni	1	2	7,781	12,113	0	75.17	98	C	0		. . .					0	12684
34-GD	RORO-WAIMA chain	1	1	28,586	46,650		86.42	100	C	22		P . .					0	12685
34-GDA	**RORO-WAIMA net**	1	1	28,586	46,650		86.42	100	C	22		P . .					0	12686
34-GDAA	RORO cluster	1	1	13,586	21,150		87.99	100	C	22	Roro	P . .	1947-1995				0	12687
34-GDAA-a	yule-delena					0				22		p . .					0	12688
34-GDAA-b	bioto					0				22		p . .					0	12691
34-GDAB	WAIMA cluster	1	1	15,000	25,500		85.00	100	C	12		. . .					0	12692
34-GDAB-a	bereina					0				12		. . .					0	12693
34-GDAB-b	kevori					0				12		. . .					0	12694
34-GE	MEKEO-KOVIO chain	1	1	22,950	37,017		79.48	100	C	22		P . .					0	12695
34-GEA	**MEKEO-KOVIO net**	1	1	22,950	37,017		79.48	100	C	22		P . .					0	12696
34-GEAA	MEKEO cluster	1	1	13,950	21,717		77.00	100	C	22		P . .					0	12697
34-GEAA-a	mekeo	1	1	13,950	21,717	0	77.00	100	C	22	Mekeo	P . .	1992				0	12698
34-GEAB	WEST MEKEO cluster	1	1	4,000	6,800		85.00	100	C	0		. . .					0	12699
34-GEAB-a	West mekeo	1	1	4,000	6,800	0	85.00	100	C	0		. . .					0	12700
34-GEAC	AMOAMO cluster	1	1	2,000	3,400		85.00	100	C	0		. . .					0	12701
34-GEAC-a	amoamo	1	1	2,000	3,400	0	85.00	100	C	0		. . .					0	12702
34-GEAD	KOVIO cluster	1	1	3,000	5,100		80.00	100	C	0		. . .					0	12703
34-GEAD-a	kovio	1	1	3,000	5,100	0	80.00	100	C	0		. . .					0	12704
35	**NEOBRITANNIC zone**	2	89	480,988	762,132		86.62	100	C	61		PNB					0 . suh	12705
35-A	**WUVULU-NINIGO set**	1	2	2,614	4,069		90.02	100	C	12		. . .					0	12706
35-AA	WUVULU-AUA chain	1	1	1,415	2,203		90.04	100	C	12		. . .					0	12707

Continued opposite

Table 9-13 continued

Code 1	REFERENCE NAME / Autoglossonym 2	Coun 3	Peo 4	Mother-tongue speakers in 2000 5	in 2025 6	Media radio 7	CHURCH AC% 8	E% 9	Wld 10	Tr 11	Biblioglossonym 12	SCRIPTURES Print 13-15	P-activity 16	N-activity 17	B-activity 18	J-year 19	Jayuh 20-24	Ref 25
35-AAA	**WUVULU-AUA** net	1	1	1,415	2,203		90.04	100	C	12		...					0....	12708
35-AAAA	WUVULU-AUA cluster	1	1	1,415	2,203		90.04	100	C	12		...					0....	12709
35-AAAA-a	wuvulu	1	1	1,415	2,203	0	90.04	100	C	12	Wuvulu-aua	...					0....	12710
35-AAAA-b	aua					0				12		...					0....	12711
35-AB	NINIGO-KANIET chain	1	1	1,199	1,866		89.99	100	C	2		...					0....	12712
35-ABA	**NINIGO** net	1	1	1,199	1,866		89.99	100	C	2		...					0....	12713
35-ABAA	SEIMAT cluster	1	1	1,199	1,866		89.99	100	C	2		...					0....	12714
35-ABAA-a	sumasuma					0				2		...					0....	12715
35-ABAA-b	mai					0				2		...					0....	12716
35-ABAA-c	ahu					0				2		...					0....	12717
35-ABAA-d	liot					0				2		...					0....	12718
35-ABB	KANIET net									0		...					0....	12719
35-ABBA	KANIET-THILENIUS cluster			0	0		0.00	0		0		...					0....	12720
35-ABBA-a	kaniet-thilenius			0	0	0	0.00	0		0		...					0....	12721
35-ABBB	KANIET-SMYTHE cluster			0	0		0.00	0		0		...					0....	12722
35-ABBB-a	kaniet-smythe			0	0	0	0.00	0		0		...					0....	12723
35-B	**MANUS set**	1	31	38,627	60,206		82.17	100	C	44		PN.					0....	12724
35-BA	NORTHWEST MANUS chain	1	7	6,239	9,713		89.87	100	C	9		...					0....	12725
35-BAA	**HERMIT** net	1	1	32	50		96.88	100	C	9		...					0....	12726
35-BAAA	AGOMES cluster	1	1	32	50		96.88	100	C	9		...					0....	12727
35-BAAA-a	maron					0				9		...					0....	12728
35-BAAA-b	luf	1	1	32	50	0	96.88	100	C	9		...					0....	12729
35-BAB	**SISI-LONIU** net	1	2	2,248	3,500		95.37	100	C	4		...					0....	12730
35-BABA	SISI-BIPI cluster	1	1	1,505	2,343		98.01	100	C	4		...					0....	12731
35-BABA-a	sisi					0				4		...					0....	12732
35-BABA-b	bipi					0				4		...					0....	12733
35-BABB	LONIU cluster	1	1	743	1,157		90.04	100	C	2		...					0....	12734
35-BABB-a	loniu	1	1	743	1,157	0	90.04	100	C	2		...					0....	12735
35-BABB-b	ndroku					0				2		...					0....	12736
35-BAC	**SORI-HARENGAN** net	1	1	921	1,434		90.01	100	C	4		...					0....	12737
35-BACA	SORI-HARENGAN cluster	1	1	921	1,434		90.01	100	C	4		...					0....	12738
35-BACA-a	harengan	1	1	921	1,434	0	90.01	100	C	4		...					0....	12739
35-BACA-b	Northwest sori					0				4		...					0....	12740
35-BACA-c	Southeast sori					0				4		...					0....	12741
35-BAD	**PONAM-ANDRA** net	1	2	1,988	3,094		83.40	100	C	4		...					0....	12742
35-BADA	PONAM cluster	1	1	679	1,057		89.99	100	C	4		...					0....	12743
35-BADA-a	ponam	1	1	679	1,057	0	89.99	100	C	4		...					0....	12744
35-BADB	ANDRA-HUS cluster	1	1	1,309	2,037		79.98	100	C	4		...					0....	12745
35-BADB-a	andra					0				4		...					0....	12746
35-BADB-b	hus					0				4		...					0....	12747
35-BAE	**LEIPON** net	1	1	1,050	1,635		90.00	100	C	4		...					0....	12748
35-BAEA	LEIPON cluster	1	1	1,050	1,635		90.00	100	C	4		...					0....	12749
35-BAEA-a	pitilu	1	1	1,050	1,635	0	90.00	100	C	4		...					0....	12750
35-BAEA-b	ndrilo					0				4		...					0....	12751
35-BAEA-c	hauwei					0				4		...					0....	12752
35-BB	WEST MANUS chain	1	6	10,064	15,665		83.47	100	C	22		P..					0....	12753
35-BBA	**LIKUM** net	1	1	162	252		95.06	100	C	4		...					0....	12754
35-BBAA	LIKUM cluster	1	1	162	252		95.06	100	C	4		...					0....	12755
35-BBAA-a	likum	1	1	162	252	0	95.06	100	C	4		...					0....	12756
35-BBB	**NYINDROU-LEVEI** net	1	4	9,466	14,734		82.97	100	C	22		P..					0....	12757
35-BBBA	NYINDROU cluster	1	1	3,938	6,130		79.99	100	C	22	Lindrou*	P..	1984-1994				0....	12758
35-BBBA-a	salien					0				22		p..					0....	12759
35-BBBA-b	nyada					0				22		P..					0....	12760
35-BBBB	LEVEI-BOHUAI cluster	1	3	5,528	8,604		85.09	100	C	12		...					0....	12761
35-BBBB-a	levei	1	1	1,860	2,895	0	80.00	100	C	12	Khehek	...					0....	12762
35-BBBB-b	ndrehet					0				12		...					0....	12763
35-BBBB-c	bucho					0				12		...					0....	12764
35-BBBB-d	tulu	1	1	1,686	2,624	0	84.99	100	C	12		...					0....	12765
35-BBBB-e	bohuai	1	1	1,982	3,085	0	89.96	100	C	12		...					0....	12766
35-BBBB-f	keli					0				12		...					0....	12767
35-BBBB-g	pelipowai					0				12		...					0....	12768
35-BBC	**MONDROPOLON** net	1	1	436	679		89.91	100	C	4		...					0....	12769
35-BBCA	MONDROPOLON cluster	1	1	436	679		89.91	100	C	4		...					0....	12770
35-BBCA-a	mondropolon	1	1	436	679	0	89.91	100	C	4		...					0....	12771
35-BC	EAST MANUS chain	1	14	18,278	28,457		78.99	100	C	44		PN.					0....	12772
35-BCA	**ERE-PAPITALAI** net	1	12	12,885	20,060		77.96	100	C	44		PN.					0....	12773
35-BCAA	NALI cluster	1	1	2,547	3,966		80.02	100	C	22	Nali	P..	1991				0....	12774
35-BCAA-a	nali					0				22		p..					0....	12775
35-BCAA-b	yiru					0				22		p..					0....	12776
35-BCAA-c	lauis					0				22		p..					0....	12777
35-BCAB	ERE-LELE cluster	1	8	8,655	13,474		76.63	100	C	44		PN.					0....	12778
35-BCAB-a	ere	1	1	1,607	2,502	0	70.01	100	C	44		pn.					0....	12779
35-BCAB-b	nane	1	1	436	679	0	80.05	100	C	44		pn.					0....	12780
35-BCAB-c	e	1	1	73	113	0	94.52	100	C	44		pn.					0....	12781
35-BCAB-d	okro	1	1	291	453	0	90.03	100	C	44		pn.					0....	12782
35-BCAB-e	kele	1	1	849	1,322	0	79.98	100	C	44		pn.					0....	12783
35-BCAB-f	kurti	1	1	3,261	5,077	0	70.01	100	C	44	Kurti	pn.					0....	12784
35-BCAB-g	lele	1	1	1,840	2,864	0	90.00	100	C	44	Manus*	PN.	1921	1956			0....	12785
35-BCAB-h	elu	1	1	298	464	0	70.13	100	C	44		pn.					0....	12786
35-BCAB-i	sabon					0				44		pn.					0....	12787
35-BCAB-j	ndroson					0				44		pn.					0....	12788
35-BCAC	KORO cluster	1	1	552	859		69.93	98	C	4		...					0....	12789
35-BCAC-a	koro	1	1	552	859	0	69.93	98	C	4		...					0....	12790
35-BCAD	PAPITALAI cluster	1	1	840	1,308		90.00	100	C	4		...					0....	12791
35-BCAD-a	papitalai	1	1	840	1,308	0	90.00	100	C	4		...					0....	12792
35-BCAD-b	naringel					0				4		...					0....	12793
35-BCAE	MOKERANG cluster	1	1	291	453		80.07	100	C	4		...					0....	12794

Continued overleaf

Table 9-13 continued

Code 1	REFERENCE NAME / Autoglossonym 2	Coun 3	Peo 4	Mother-tongue speakers in 2000 5	in 2025 6	Media radio 7	CHURCH AC% 8	E% 9	Wld 10	Tr 11	Biblioglossonym 12	SCRIPTURES Print 13-15	P–activity 16	N–activity 17	B–activity 18	J-year 19	Jayuh 20-24	Ref 25
35-BCAE-a	mokerang	1	1	291	453	0	80.07	100	C	4		...					0....	12795
35-BCB	**TITAN net**	1	2	5,393	8,397		81.44	100	C	4		...					0....	12796
35-BCBA	TITAN cluster	1	2	5,393	8,397		81.44	100	C	4		...					0....	12797
35-BCBA-a	Proper titan	1	1	4,615	7,185	0	80.00	100	C	4		...					0....	12798
35-BCBA-b	loisa					0				4		...					0....	12799
35-BCBA-c	m'bunai					0				4		...					0....	12800
35-BCBA-d	ndrowa					0				4		...					0....	12801
35-BCBA-e	horno					0				4		...					0....	12802
35-BCBA-f	rambutyo	1	1	778	1,212	0	89.97	100	C	4		...					0....	12803
35-BD	SOUTHEAST MANUS chain	1	4	4,046	6,371		81.41	100	C	6		...					0....	12804
35-BDA	**BALUAN-LOU net**	1	1	1,715	2,713		80.00	100	C	3		...					0....	12805
35-BDAA	BALUAN-PAM cluster	1	1	1,415	2,203		80.00	100	C	3		...					0....	12806
35-BDAA-a	baluan					0				3		...					0....	12807
35-BDAA-b	pam					0				3		...					0....	12808
35-BDAB	LOU cluster	1	1	300	510		80.00	100	C	0		...					0....	12809
35-BDAB-a	lou					0				0		...					0....	12810
35-BDAB-b	rei					0				0		...					0....	12811
35-BDB	**LENKAU net**	1	1	354	551		90.11	100	C	6		...					0....	12812
35-BDBA	LENKAU cluster	1	1	354	551		90.11	100	C	6		...					0....	12813
35-BDBA-a	lenkau	1	1	354	551	0	90.11	100	C	6		...					0....	12814
35-BDC	**PENCHAL net**	1	1	200	340		80.00	100	C	0		...					0....	12815
35-BDCA	PENCHAL cluster	1	1	200	340		80.00	100	C	0		...					0....	12816
35-BDCA-a	penchal	1	1	200	340	0	80.00	100	C	0		...					0....	12817
35-BDD	**NAUNA net**	1	1	210	327		90.00	100	C	6		...					0....	12818
35-BDDA	NAUNA cluster	1	1	210	327		90.00	100	C	6		...					0....	12819
35-BDDA-a	nauna	1	1	210	327	0	90.00	100	C	6		...					0....	12820
35-BDE	**PAK-TONG net**	1	1	1,567	2,440		80.03	100	C	2		...					0....	12821
35-BDEA	PAK-TONG cluster	1	1	1,567	2,440		80.03	100	C	2		...					0....	12822
35-BDEA-a	pak					0				2		...					0....	12823
35-BDEA-b	tong					0				2		...					0....	12824
35-C	**TUNGAG-TOLAI set**	1	24	178,598	279,365		84.86	100	C	61		PNB					0.su.	12825
35-CA	SAINT-MATTHIAS chain	1	2	5,603	8,723		90.09	100	C	12		...					0....	12826
35-CAA	**EMIRA-MUSSAU net**	1	1	5,514	8,584		90.01	100	C	12		...					0....	12827
35-CAAA	EMIRA-MUSSAU cluster	1	1	5,514	8,584		90.01	100	C	12		...					0....	12828
35-CAAA-a	mussau	1	1	5,514	8,584	0	90.01	100	C	12	Mussau-emira	...					0....	12829
35-CAAA-b	emira					0				12		...					0....	12830
35-CAB	**TENIS net**	1	1	89	139		95.51	100	C	5		...					0....	12831
35-CABA	TENIS cluster	1	1	89	139		95.51	100	C	5		...					0....	12832
35-CABA-a	tenis	1	1	89	139	0	95.51	100	C	5		...					0....	12833
35-CB	TUNGAG-MALIK chain	1	5	42,493	67,152		83.95	100	C	23		P..					0....	12834
35-CBA	**TUNGAG net**	1	1	15,053	23,433		89.00	100	C	22		P..					0....	12835
35-CBAA	TUNGAG cluster	1	1	15,053	23,433		89.00	100	C	22		P..					0....	12836
35-CBAA-a	tungag	1	1	15,053	23,433	0	89.00	100	C	22	Tungag	P..	1989				0....	12837
35-CBAA-b	lavongai					0				22		p..					0....	12838
35-CBAA-c	dang					0				22		p..					0....	12839
35-CBB	**TIGAK net**	1	1	13,975	22,758		81.79	100	C	23		P..					0....	12840
35-CBBA	WEST TIGAK cluster	2	1	3,000	5,100		85.00	100	C	0		...					0....	12841
35-CBBA-a	east-island					0				0		...					0....	12842
35-CBBA-b	bangatang					0				0		...					0....	12843
35-CBBA-c	selapiu					0				0		...					0....	12844
35-CBBA-d	baudisson					0				0		...					0....	12845
35-CBBB	SOUTH TIGAK cluster	2	1	2,000	3,400		85.00	100	C	0		...					0....	12846
35-CBBB-a	kaut					0				0		...					0....	12847
35-CBBB-b	dyaul					0				0		...					0....	12848
35-CBBC	CENTRAL TIGAK cluster	1	1	6,975	10,858		80.00	100	C	23		P..					0....	12849
35-CBBC-a	Central tigak	1	1	6,975	10,858	0	80.00	100	C	23	Tigak	P..	1912-1972				0....	12850
35-CBBD	EAST TIGAK cluster	2	1	2,000	3,400		80.00	100	C	0		...					0....	12851
35-CBBD-a	East tigak	1	1	2,000	3,400	0	80.00	100	C	0		...					0....	12852
35-CBC	**TIANG net**	1	1	1,440	2,241		85.00	100	C	4		...					0....	12853
35-CBCA	TIANG cluster	1	1	1,440	2,241		85.00	100	C	4		...					0....	12854
35-CBCA-a	tiang	1	1	1,440	2,241	0	85.00	100	C	4		...					0....	12855
35-CBD	**KARA-NALIK net**	1	2	12,025	18,720		80.00	100	C	22		P..					0....	12856
35-CBDA	KARA cluster	1	1	5,580	8,687		80.00	100	C	22	Kara	P..	1982-1986				0....	12857
35-CBDA-a	West kara					0				22		p..					0....	12858
35-CBDA-b	East kara					0				22		p..					0....	12859
35-CBDB	NALIK cluster	1	1	6,445	10,033		80.00	100	C	4		...					0....	12860
35-CBDB-a	nalik	1	1	6,445	10,033	0	80.00	100	C	4		...					0....	12861
35-CC	NOTSI chain	1	1	1,860	2,895		80.00	100	C	22		P..					0....	12862
35-CCA	**NOTSI net**	1	1	1,860	2,895		80.00	100	C	22		P..					0....	12863
35-CCAA	NOTSI cluster	1	1	1,860	2,895		80.00	100	C	22		P..					0....	12864
35-CCAA-a	notsi	1	1	1,860	2,895	0	80.00	100	C	22	Notsi	P..	1995				0....	12865
35-CD	TABAR-LIHIR chain	1	2	11,156	17,367		76.47	100	C	12		...					0....	12866
35-CDA	**TABAR net**	1	1	3,281	5,108		80.01	100	C	12		...					0....	12867
35-CDAA	MANDARA cluster	1	1	3,281	5,108		80.01	100	C	12	Mandara	...					0....	12868
35-CDAA-a	simberi					0				12		...					0....	12869
35-CDAA-b	tatau					0				12		...					0....	12870
35-CDAA-c	tabar					0				12		...					0....	12871
35-CDB	**LIHIR net**	1	1	7,875	12,259		75.00	100	C	2		...					0....	12872
35-CDBA	LIHIR cluster	1	1	7,875	12,259		75.00	100	C	2		...					0....	12873
35-CDBA-a	lihir	1	1	7,875	12,259	0	75.00	100	C	2		...					0....	12874
35-CDBA-b	masahet					0				2		...					0....	12875
35-CDBA-c	mahur					0				2		...					0....	12876

Continued opposite

Table 9-13 continued

Code 1	REFERENCE NAME / Autoglossonym 2	Coun 3	Peo 4	Mother-tongue speakers in 2000 5	in 2025 6	Media radio 7	AC% 8	E% 9	Wld 10	Tr 11	Biblioglossonym 12	Print 13-15	P-activity 16	N-activity 17	B-activity 18	J-year 19	Jayuh 20-24	Ref 25
35-CE	MADAK-LAVATBURA chain	1	2	6,319	9,836		83.76	100	C	41		PN.					0....	12877
35-CEA	**LAVATBURA-LAMUSONG net**	1	1	2,381	3,706		90.00	100	C	4		. . .					0....	12878
35-CEAA	LAVATBURA cluster	1	1	2,381	3,706		90.00	100	C	4		. . .					0....	12879
35-CEAA-a	lamusong					0				4		. . .					0....	12880
35-CEAA-b	lavatbura					0				4		. . .					0....	12881
35-CEAA-c	kontu					0				4		. . .					0....	12882
35-CEAA-d	ugana					0				4		. . .					0....	12883
35-CEB	**MADAK net**	1	1	3,938	6,130		79.99	100	C	41		PN.					0....	12884
35-CEBA	MADAK cluster	1	1	3,938	6,130		79.99	100	C	41	Madak	PN.	1982-1992	1995			0....	12885
35-CEBA-a	malom					0				41		pn.					0....	12886
35-CEBA-b	katingan					0				41		pn.					0....	12887
35-CEBA-c	lelet					0				41		pn.					0....	12888
35-CEBA-d	danu					0				41		pn.					0....	12889
35-CEBA-e	mesi					0				41		pn.					0....	12890
35-CF	PATPATAR-KUANUA chain	1	9	97,055	151,092		86.68	100	C	61		PNB					0.su.	12891
35-CFA	**BAROK net**	1	1	2,960	4,608		80.00	100	C	24		P. .					0....	12892
35-CFAA	BAROK cluster	1	1	2,960	4,608		80.00	100	C	24		P. .					0....	12893
35-CFAA-a	barok	1	1	2,960	4,608	0	80.00	100	C	24	Barok	P. .	1929				0....	12894
35-CFAA-b	usen					0				24		p. .					0....	12895
35-CFAA-c	komalu					0				24		p. .					0....	12896
35-CFAA-d	kanapit					0				24		p. .					0....	12897
35-CFAA-e	kulubi					0				24		p. .					0....	12898
35-CFB	**PATPATAR net**	1	1	6,975	10,858		80.00	100	C	22		P. .					0....	12899
35-CFBA	PATPATAR cluster	1	1	6,975	10,858		80.00	100	C	22		P. .					0....	12900
35-CFBA-a	pala					0				22		p. .					0....	12901
35-CFBA-b	sokirik					0				22		p. .					0....	12902
35-CFBA-c	patpatar	1	1	6,975	10,858	0	80.00	100	C	22	Patpatar	P. .	1921-1992				0....	12903
35-CFBA-d	gelik					0				22		p. .					0....	12904
35-CFC	**RAMUAINA net**	1	1	10,702	16,660		90.00	100	C	22		P. .					0....	12905
35-CFCA	RAMUAINA cluster	1	1	10,702	16,660		90.00	100	C	22	Ramoaaina	P. .	1882-1992				0....	12906
35-CFCA-a	makada					0				22		p. .					0....	12907
35-CFCA-b	molot					0				22		p. .					0....	12908
35-CFCA-c	utam					0				22		p. .					0....	12909
35-CFCA-d	mandan					0				22		p. .					0....	12910
35-CFCA-e	kabotirai					0				22		p. .					0....	12911
35-CFCA-f	ulu					0				22		p. .					0....	12912
35-CFCA-g	mioko					0				22		p. .					0....	12913
35-CFCA-h	kerawara					0				22		p. .					0....	12914
35-CFD	**TOLAI net**	1	2	73,216	113,981		87.10	100	C	61		PNB					0.su.	12915
35-CFDA	KUANUA cluster	1	1	70,912	110,394		87.00	100	C	61		PNB					0.su.	12916
35-CFDA-a	kuanua	1	1	70,912	110,394	1	87.00	100	C	61	Tinata-tuna*	PNB	1885-1931	1901-1962	1983		0.su.	12917
35-CFDA-b	tolai vehicular					1				61		pnb					0.su.	12933
35-CFDB	BILUR cluster	1	1	2,304	3,587		90.02	100	C	4		. . .					0....	12934
35-CFDB-a	bilur	1	1	2,304	3,587	0	90.02	100	C	4		. . .					0....	12935
35-CFE	**KANDAS-LABEL net**	1	2	1,104	1,719		89.95	100	C	4		. . .					0....	12936
35-CFEA	KANDAS cluster	1	1	874	1,360		89.93	100	C	4		. . .					0....	12937
35-CFEA-a	kandas	1	1	874	1,360	0	89.93	100	C	4		. . .					0....	12938
35-CFEB	LABEL cluster	1	1	230	359		90.00	100	C	4		. . .					0....	12939
35-CFEB-a	label	1	1	230	359	0	90.00	100	C	4		. . .					0....	12940
35-CFF	**SIAR net**	1	1	2,093	3,258		85.00	100	C	12		. . .					0....	12941
35-CFFA	SIAR cluster	1	1	2,093	3,258		85.00	100	C	12	Siar	. . .					0....	12942
35-CFFA-a	lambon					0				12		. . .					0....	12943
35-CFFA-b	bakum					0				12		. . .					0....	12944
35-CFG	**GURAMALUM net**	1	1	5	8		80.00	100	C	8		. . .					0....	12945
35-CFGA	GURAMALUM cluster	1	1	5	8		80.00	100	C	8		. . .					0....	12946
35-CFGA-a	guramalum	1	1	5	8	0	80.00	100	C	8		. . .					0....	12947
35-CG	KONOMALA chain	1	1	1,050	1,635		90.00	100	C	5		. . .					0....	12948
35-CGA	**KONOMALA net**	1	1	1,050	1,635		90.00	100	C	5		. . .					0....	12949
35-CGAA	KONOMALA cluster	1	1	1,050	1,635		90.00	100	C	5		. . .					0....	12950
35-CGAA-a	laket					0				5		. . .					0....	12951
35-CGAA-b	konomala	1	1	1,050	1,635	0	90.00	100	C	5		. . .					0....	12952
35-CH	SURSURUNGA chain	1	1	3,487	5,429		80.01	100	C	22		P. .					0....	12953
35-CHA	**SURSURUNGA net**	1	1	3,487	5,429		80.01	100	C	22		P. .					0....	12954
35-CHAA	SURSURUNGA cluster	1	1	3,487	5,429		80.01	100	C	22		P. .					0....	12955
35-CHAA-a	samo	1	1	3,487	5,429	0	80.01	100	C	22	Sursurunga	P. .	1979-1987				0....	12956
35-CHAA-b	suralil					0				22		p. .					0....	12957
35-CI	TANGGA-ANIR chain	1	1	9,575	15,236		80.00	100	C	2		. . .					0....	12958
35-CIA	**TANGGA net**	1	1	9,575	15,236		80.00	100	C	2		. . .					0....	12959
35-CIAA	TANGGA cluster	1	1	7,275	11,326		80.00	100	C	2		. . .					0....	12960
35-CIAA-a	boang					0				2		. . .					0....	12961
35-CIAA-b	malendok					0				2		. . .					0....	12962
35-CIAB	MAKET cluster	2	1	300	510		80.00	100	C	0		. . .					0....	12963
35-CIAB-a	maket	1	1	300	510	0	80.00	100	C	0		. . .					0....	12964
35-CIAC	ANIR cluster	2	1	2,000	3,400		80.00	100	C	0		. . .					0....	12965
35-CIAC-a	ambitle					0				0		. . .					0....	12966
35-CIAC-b	babase					0				0		. . .					0....	12967
35-D	**KIMBE set**	1	7	53,715	83,621		86.32	100	C	43		PN.					0...h	12968
35-DA	NAKANAI chain	1	2	21,130	32,894		87.16	100	C	41		PN.					0....	12969
35-DAA	**MELAMELA net**	1	2	21,130	32,894		87.16	100	C	41		PN.					0....	12970
35-DAAA	MELAMELA cluster	1	1	2,238	3,484		80.03	100	C	12	Meramera	. . .					0....	12971
35-DAAA-a	East melamela					0				12		. . .					0....	12972
35-DAAA-b	ubili					0				12		. . .					0....	12973
35-DAAA-c	lolobau					0				12		. . .					0....	12974
35-DAAB	WEST NAKANAI cluster	1	1	18,892	29,410		88.00	100	C	41	Nakanai	PN.	1974	1983			0....	12975
35-DAAB-a	maututu					0				41		pn.					0....	12976

Continued overleaf

Table 9-13 continued

Code 1	REFERENCE NAME / Autoglossonym 2	Coun 3	Peo 4	Mother-tongue speakers in 2000 5	in 2025 6	Media radio 7	CHURCH AC% 8	E% 9	Wld 10	Tr 11	Biblioglossonym 12	Print 13-15	P-activity 16	N-activity 17	B-activity 18	J-year 19	Jayuh 20-24	Ref 25
35-DAAB-b	vere					0				41		pn.					0....	12977
35-DAAB-c	losa					0				41		pn.					0....	12978
35-DAAB-d	ubae					0				41		pn.					0....	12979
35-DAAB-e	bileki					0				41		pn.					0....	12980
35-DB	WILLAUMEZ chain	1	3	13,377	20,824		82.01	100	C	43		PN.					0....	12981
35-DBA	BOLA-XARUA net	1	2	12,576	19,577		81.50	100	C	43		PN.					0....	12982
35-DBAA	BOLA-XARUA cluster	1	2	12,576	19,577		81.50	100	C	43		PN.					0....	12983
35-DBAA-a	bola	1	1	10,681	16,627	0	80.00	100	C	43	Bola	PN.		1934			0....	12984
35-DBAA-b	harua	1	1	1,895	2,950	0	89.97	100	C	43		pn.					0....	12985
35-DBB	BULU net	1	1	801	1,247		90.01	100	C	2		...					0....	12986
35-DBBA	BULU cluster	1	1	801	1,247		90.01	100	C	2		...					0....	12987
35-DBBA-a	bulu	1	1	801	1,247	0	90.01	100	C	2		...					0....	12988
35-DC	BALI-VITU chain	1	2	19,208	29,903		88.40	100	C	12		...					0...h	12989
35-DCA	BALI-VITU net	1	2	19,208	29,903		88.40	100	C	12		...					0...h	12990
35-DCAA	VITU cluster	1	1	10,230	15,926		87.00	100	C	12		...					0....	12991
35-DCAA-a	vitu	1	1	10,230	15,926	0	87.00	100	C	12	Vitu	...					0....	12992
35-DCAA-b	mundua					0				12		...					0....	12993
35-DCAB	BALI cluster	1	1	8,978	13,977		90.00	100	C	2		...					0...h	12994
35-DCAB-a	bali	1	1	8,978	13,977	0	90.00	100	C	2		...					0...h	12995
35-E	LAMOGAI-MOK set	1	5	10,065	15,669		79.98	100	C	22		P..					0....	12996
35-EA	LAMOGAI-MOK chain	1	5	10,065	15,669		79.98	100	C	22		P..					0....	12997
35-EAA	AMARA net	1	2	2,585	4,025		78.30	100	C	12		...					0....	12998
35-EAAA	AMARA cluster	1	2	2,585	4,025		78.30	100	C	12		...					0....	12999
35-EAAA-a	longa					0				12		...					0....	13000
35-EAAA-b	idne					0				12		...					0....	13001
35-EAAA-c	mouk	1	1	886	1,380	0	75.06	100	C	12	Mouk-aria	...					0....	13002
35-EAAA-d	aria					0				12		...					0....	13003
35-EAAA-e	bibling					0				12		...					0....	13004
35-EAAA-f	tourai					0				12		...					0....	13005
35-EAB	LAMOGAI-RAUTO net	1	3	7,480	11,644		80.56	100	C	22		P..					0....	13006
35-EABA	LAMOGAI cluster	1	1	5,700	8,874		80.00	100	C	22		P..					0....	13007
35-EABA-a	lamogai	1	1	5,700	8,874	0	80.00	100	C	22	Mulakaino*	P..		1991			0....	13008
35-EABB	PULIE-RAUTO cluster	1	1	858	1,335		84.97	100	C	0		...					0....	13009
35-EABB-a	rauto					0				0		...					0....	13010
35-EABB-b	pulie					0				0		...					0....	13011
35-EABC	IBANGA cluster	1	1	922	1,435		79.93	100	C	0		...					0....	13012
35-EABC-a	ibanga	1	1	922	1,435	0	79.93	100	C	0		...					0....	13013
35-F	ARAWE-GASMATA set	2	9	151,994	247,419		91.19	100	C	22		P..					0....	13014
35-FA	ARAWE-GASMATA chain	2	9	151,994	247,419		91.19	100	C	22		P..					0....	13015
35-FAA	ARAWE-GASMATA net	2	9	151,994	247,419		91.19	100	C	22		P..					0....	13016
35-FAAA	SOLONG cluster	1	1	3,197	4,977		80.01	100	C	12		...					0....	13017
35-FAAA-a	pililo					0				12		...					0....	13018
35-FAAA-b	sauren					0				12		...					0....	13019
35-FAAA-c	kambun					0				12		...					0....	13020
35-FAAA-d	a-kolet					0				12		...					0....	13021
35-FAAA-e	a-rawe	1	1	3,197	4,977		80.01	100	C	12	Solong	...					0....	13022
35-FAAB	LESING-ATUI cluster	1	1	1,315	2,047		80.00	100	C	4		...					0....	13023
35-FAAB-a	lesing					0				4		...					0....	13024
35-FAAB-b	a-tui					0				4		...					0....	13025
35-FAAC	MOEVEHAFEN cluster	2	5	138,895	227,028		91.63	100	C	22		P..					0....	13026
35-FAAC-a	gimi	1	1	5,232	8,145	0	69.99	98	C	22	Gimi	p..					0....	13027
35-FAAC-b	loko	1	1	127,418	209,161	0	93.00	100	C	22	Loko: Papua New Guinea	P..		1992			0....	13028
35-FAAC-c	ai-klep	1	1	4,298	6,690	0	79.99	100	C	22		P..					0....	13029
35-FAAC-d	a-palik	1	1	597	930	0	76.05	100	C	22		p..					0....	13030
35-FAAC-e	a-yuwet					0				22		p..					0....	13031
35-FAAC-f	a-kolet	1	1	1,350	2,102	0	90.00	100	C	22		p..					0....	13032
35-FAAD	GASMATA cluster	1	1	292	454		90.07	100	C	4		...					0....	13033
35-FAAD-a	gasmata	1	1	292	454	0	90.07	100	C	4		...					0....	13034
35-FAAE	AVAU cluster	1	1	8,295	12,913		89.99	100	C	4		...					0....	13035
35-FAAE-a	a-vau	1	1	8,295	12,913	0	89.99	100	C	4		...					0....	13036
35-G	WHITEMAN set	1	7	10,676	16,621		85.83	100	C	22		P..					0....	13037
35-GA	WHITEMAN chain	1	7	10,676	16,621		85.83	100	C	22		P..					0....	13038
35-GAA	PASISMANUA-KAPORE net	1	6	8,351	13,002		87.45	100	C	22		P..					0....	13039
35-GAAA	PASISMANUA cluster	1	5	6,865	10,688		86.89	100	C	22	Kaulong	P..		1992			0....	13040
35-GAAA-a	miu	1	1	558	868	0	79.93	100	C	22	Miu	p..					0....	13041
35-GAAA-b	West kaulong					0				22		p..					0....	13042
35-GAAA-c	a-sengseng	1	1	641	998	0	90.02	100	C	22	Asengseng*	P..		1992			0....	13043
35-GAAA-d	karore	1	1	615	958	0	80.00	99	C	22		p..					0....	13044
35-GAAA-e	psokhok	1	1	1,564	2,435	0	95.01	100	C	22		p..					0....	13045
35-GAAA-f	ai-gon					0				22		p..					0....	13046
35-GAAA-g	bao					0				22		p..					0....	13047
35-GAAA-h	East kaulong					0				22		p..					0....	13048
35-GAAA-i	getmata					0				22		p..					0....	13049
35-GAAB	KAPORE-BEBELI cluster	1	1	1,486	2,314		90.04	100	C	4		...					0....	13050
35-GAAB-a	bebeli					0				4		...					0....	13051
35-GAAB-b	benaule					0				4		...					0....	13052
35-GAAB-c	kapore					0				4		...					0....	13053
35-GAB	MANGSENG net	1	1	2,325	3,619		80.00	100	C	22		P..					0....	13054
35-GABA	MANGSENG cluster	1	1	2,325	3,619		80.00	100	C	22	Mangsing	P..		1991			0....	13055
35-GABA-a	aiwit					0				22		p..					0....	13056
35-GABA-b	roko					0				22		p..					0....	13057
35-GABA-c	sampantabil					0				22		p..					0....	13058
35-GABA-d	mirapu					0				22		p..					0....	13059
35-GABA-e	kukula					0				22		p..					0....	13060
35-H	MENGEN-MAMUSI set	1	3	33,708	53,620		82.58	100	C	22		P..					0....	13061
35-HA	MENGEN-MAMUSI chain	1	3	33,708	53,620		82.58	100	C	22		P..					0....	13062

Continued opposite

Table 9-13 continued

Code 1	REFERENCE NAME Autoglossonym 2	Coun 3	Peo 4	Mother-tongue speakers in 2000 5	in 2025 6	Media radio 7	CHURCH AC% 8	E% 9	Wld 10	Tr 11	Biblioglossonym 12	SCRIPTURES Print 13-15	P-activity 16	N-activity 17	B-activity 18	J-year 19	Jayuh 20-24	Ref 25
35-HAA	**UVOL net**	1	1	5,944	9,253		90.01	100	C	22		P..					0....	13063
35-HAAA	UVOL cluster	1	1	5,944	9,253		90.01	100	C	22		P..					0....	13064
35-HAAA-a	lote	1	1	5,944	9,253	0	90.01	100	C	22	Lote	P..	1993				0....	13065
35-HAAA-b	uvol					0				22		p..					0....	13066
35-HAB	**MAMUSI-KAKUNA net**	1	1	10,875	17,359		83.62	100	C	12		...					0....	13067
35-HABA	MAMUSI-MELKOI cluster	1	1	7,875	12,259		85.00	100	C	12		...					0....	13068
35-HABA-a	mamusi	1	1	7,875	12,259	0	85.00	100	C	12	Mamusi	...					0....	13069
35-HABB	MELKOI-KAKUNA cluster	2	1	3,000	5,100		80.00	100	C	0		...					0....	13070
35-HABB-a	melkoi					0				0		...					0....	13071
35-HABB-b	kakuna					0				0		...					0....	13072
35-HAC	**MENGEN net**	1	1	*16,889	27,008		79.29	100	C	12		...					0....	13073
35-HACA	SOUTH MENGEN cluster	2	1	2,000	3,400		80.00	100	C	0		...					0....	13074
35-HACA-a	maeng					0				0		...					0....	13075
35-HACA-b	poeng					0				0		...					0....	13076
35-HACA-c	malmal					0				0		...					0....	13077
35-HACB	NORTH MENGEN cluster	2	1	3,000	5,100		80.00	100	C	0		...					0....	13078
35-HACB-a	mio					0				0		...					0....	13079
35-HACB-b	pau					0				0		...					0....	13080
35-HACB-c	longeinga					0				0		...					0....	13081
35-HACC	EAST MENGEN cluster	1	1	11,889	18,508		79.00	100	C	12	Mengen	...					0....	13082
35-HACC-a	korapun-sampun					0				12		...					0....	13083
35-I	**TUMOIP set**	1	1	991	1,542		97.98	100	C	2		...					0....	13084
35-IA	TUMOIP chain	1	1	991	1,542		97.98	100	C	2		...					0....	13085
35-IAA	**TUMOIP net**	1	1	991	1,542		97.98	100	C	2		...					0....	13086
35-IAAA	TUMOIP cluster	1	1	991	1,542		97.98	100	C	2		...					0....	13087
35-IAAA-a	tumoip	1	1	991	1,542	0	97.98	100	C	2		...					0....	13088
36	**SOLOMONIC zone**	3	43	167,178	277,812		92.44	100	C	62		PNB					0.s..	13089
36-A	**NEHAN set**	1	1	7,940	11,444		98.00	100	C	12		...					0....	13090
36-AA	NEHAN chain	1	1	7,940	11,444		98.00	100	C	12		...					0....	13091
36-AAA	**NEHAN net**	1	1	7,940	11,444		98.00	100	C	12		...					0....	13092
36-AAAA	NEHAN cluster	1	1	7,940	11,444		98.00	100	C	12	Nehan	...					0....	13093
36-AAAA-a	nissan					0				12		...					0....	13094
36-AAAA-b	piripel					0				12		...					0....	13095
36-B	**BOUGAINVILLE set**	3	15	79,023	119,008		94.25	100	C	41		PN.					0....	13096
36-BA	HALIA-SOLOS chain	1	4	47,772	69,759		96.27	100	C	41		PN.					0....	13097
36-BAA	**HALIA net**	1	2	39,229	57,447		96.46	100	C	41		PN.					0....	13098
36-BAAA	EAST BUKA cluster	1	2	35,729	51,497		96.60	100	C	41		PN.					0....	13099
36-BAAA-a	hanahan	1	1	28,583	41,198	0	96.50	100	C	41	Halia	PN.	1970-1976	1978			0....	13100
36-BAAA-b	haku	1	1	7,146	10,299	0	96.99	100	C	41		pn.					0....	13101
36-BAAA-c	tulon					0				41	Tulun	Pn.	1976				0....	13102
36-BAAA-d	tasi					0				41		pn.					0....	13103
36-BAAA-e	lontes					0				41		pn.					0....	13104
36-BAAB	SELAU cluster	1	1	2,000	3,400		95.00	98	C	0		...					0....	13105
36-BAAB-a	selau	1	1	2,000	3,400	0	95.00	98	C	0		...					0....	13106
36-BAAC	KILINAILAU cluster	1	1	1,500	2,550		95.00	98	C	0		...					0....	13107
36-BAAC-a	kilinailau					0				0		...					0....	13108
36-BAB	**SOLOS net**	1	1	5,143	7,412		94.98	100	C	2		...					0....	13109
36-BABA	SOLOS cluster	1	1	5,143	7,412		94.98	100	C	2		...					0....	13110
36-BABA-a	solos	1	1	5,143	7,412	0	94.98	100	C	2		...					0....	13111
36-BAC	**PETATS-HITAU net**	1	1	3,400	4,900		96.00	100	C	22		P..					0....	13112
36-BACA	PETATS-HITAU cluster	1	1	3,400	4,900		96.00	100	C	22		P..					0....	13113
36-BACA-a	petats	1	1	3,400	4,900	0	96.00	100	C	22	Petats	P..	1934-1978				0....	13114
36-BACA-b	sumoun					0				22		p..					0....	13115
36-BACA-c	matsungan					0				22		p..					0....	13116
36-BACA-d	hitau-pororan					0				22		p..					0....	13117
36-BB	SAPOSA chain	1	1	1,445	2,083		97.02	100	C	22		P..					0....	13118
36-BBA	**SAPOSA net**	1	1	1,445	2,083		97.02	100	C	22		P..					0....	13119
36-BBAA	SAPOSA cluster	1	1	1,445	2,083		97.02	100	C	22		P..					0....	13120
36-BBAA-a	fa-saposa	1	1	1,445	2,083	0	97.02	100	C	22	Saposa	P..	1985-1987				0....	13121
36-BBAA-b	taiof					0				22		p..					0....	13122
36-BC	HAHON-TEOP chain	1	3	14,181	20,439		95.37	100	C	23		P..					0....	13123
36-BCA	**HAHON net**	1	1	2,382	3,433		91.02	100	C	4		...					0....	13124
36-BCAA	HAHON cluster	1	1	2,382	3,433		91.02	100	C	4		...					0....	13125
36-BCAA-a	hahon	1	1	2,382	3,433	0	91.02	100	C	4		...					0....	13126
36-BCAA-b	kurur					0				4		...					0....	13127
36-BCAA-c	ratsua					0				4		...					0....	13128
36-BCAA-d	aravia					0				4		...					0....	13129
36-BCB	**TIMPUTZ net**	1	1	4,407	6,351		94.99	100	C	23		P..					0....	13130
36-BCBA	TIMPUTZ cluster	1	1	4,407	6,351		94.99	100	C	23		P..					0....	13131
36-BCBA-a	vasuii					0				23	Vasui	P..	1975				0....	13132
36-BCBA-b	pokpapa					0				23		p..					0....	13133
36-BCBA-c	orig					0				23		p..					0....	13134
36-BCBA-d	dios					0				23		p..					0....	13135
36-BCBA-e	chundawan					0				23		p..					0....	13136
36-BCBA-f	vaadoo					0				23		p..					0....	13137
36-BCC	**TEOP net**	1	1	7,392	10,655		97.00	100	C	23		P..					0....	13138
36-BCCA	TEOP cluster	1	1	7,392	10,655		97.00	100	C	23		P..					0....	13139
36-BCCA-a	teop	1	1	7,392	10,655	0	97.00	100	C	23	Teop	P..	1958-1966				0....	13140
36-BCCA-b	wainanana					0				23		p..					0....	13141
36-BCCA-c	losiara					0				23		p..					0....	13142
36-BCCA-d	taunita					0				23		p..					0....	13143
36-BCCA-e	melilup					0				23		p..					0....	13144
36-BCCA-f	petspets					0				23		p..					0....	13145

Continued overleaf

Table 9-13 continued

Code 1	REFERENCE NAME / Autoglossonym 2	Coun 3	Peo 4	Mother-tongue speakers in 2000 5	in 2025 6	Media radio 7	AC% 8	E% 9	Wld 10	Tr 11	Biblioglossonym 12	Print 13-15	P–activity 16	N–activity 17	B–activity 18	J-year 19	Jayuh 20-24	Ref 25
36-BD	PAPAPANA chain	1	1	240	346		90.00	100	C	5		. . .					0	13146
36-BDA	**PAPAPANA net**	1	1	240	346		90.00	100	C	5		. . .					0	13147
36-BDAA	PAPAPANA cluster	1	1	240	346		90.00	100	C	5		. . .					0	13148
36-BDAA-a	papapana	1	1	240	346	0	90.00	100	C	5		. . .					0	13149
36-BE	PIVA-BANONI chain	2	3	3,663	5,349		88.40	100	C	5		. . .					0	13150
36-BEA	**PIVA-BANONI net**	2	3	3,663	5,349		88.40	100	C	5		. . .					0	13151
36-BEAA	PIVA cluster	1	1	883	1,273		90.03	100	C	5		. . .					0	13152
36-BEAA-a	amun					0				5		. . .					0	13153
36-BEAA-b	nagarige	1	1	883	1,273	0	90.03	100	C	5		. . .					0	13154
36-BEAB	BANONI cluster	1	1	2,184	3,148		90.02	100	C	4		. . .					0	13155
36-BEAB-a	banoni	1	1	2,184	3,148	0	90.02	100	C	4		. . .					0	13156
36-BEAB-b	tsunari					0				4		. . .					0	13157
36-BEAC	MINIGIR cluster	1	1	596	928		80.03	98	C	4		. . .					0	13158
36-BEAC-a	minigir	1	1	596	928	0	80.03	98	C	4		. . .					0	13159
36-BF	TORAU chain	1	1	1,350	1,946		96.00	100	C	4		. . .					0	13160
36-BFA	**TORAU net**	1	1	1,350	1,946		96.00	100	C	4		. . .					0	13161
36-BFAA	TORAU cluster	1	1	1,350	1,946		96.00	100	C	4		. . .					0	13162
36-BFAA-a	torau	1	1	1,350	1,946	0	96.00	100	C	4		. . .					0	13163
36-BFAA-b	rorovana					0				4		. . .					0	13164
36-BG	URUAVA chain	1	1	8	11		75.00	100	C	9		. . .					0	13165
36-BGA	**URUAVA net**	1	1	8	11		75.00	100	C	9		. . .					0	13166
36-BGAA	URUAVA cluster	1	1	8	11		75.00	100	C	9		. . .					0	13167
36-BGAA-a	uruava	1	1	8	11	0	75.00	100	C	9		. . .					0	13168
36-BH	MONO-ALU chain	1	1	10,364	19,075		85.00	100	C	12		. . .					0	13169
36-BHA	**MONO-ALU net**	1	1	10,364	19,075		85.00	100	C	12		. . .					0	13170
36-BHAA	MONO-ALU cluster	1	1	10,364	19,075		85.00	100	C	12		. . .					0	13171
36-BHAA-a	mono	1	1	10,364	19,075	0	85.00	100	C	12	Mono	. . .					0	13172
36-BHAA-b	alu					0				12		. . .					0	13173
36-BHAA-c	fauro					0				12		. . .					0	13174
36-C	**CHOISEUL set**	1	4	21,873	39,978		86.27	100	C	57		PN.					0 . s . .	13175
36-CA	NORTHWEST CHOISEUL chain	1	3	10,393	19,130		87.72	100	C	35		P . .					0	13176
36-CAA	**VAGHUA-VARISI net**	1	2	9,962	18,337		87.80	100	C	35		P . .					0	13177
36-CAAA	VAGHUA cluster	1	1	1,896	3,490		86.97	100	C	4		. . .					0	13178
36-CAAA-a	vaghua	1	1	1,896	3,490	0	86.97	100	C	4		. . .					0	13179
36-CAAB	VARISI cluster	1	1	8,066	14,847		88.00	100	C	35		P . .					0	13180
36-CAAB-a	ghone					0				35		p . .					0	13181
36-CAAB-b	varisi	1	1	8,066	14,847	0	88.00	100	C	35	Varisi	P . .	1995				0	13182
36-CAB	**RIRIO net**	1	1	431	793		85.85	100	C	4		. . .					0	13183
36-CABA	RIRIO cluster	1	1	431	793		85.85	100	C	4		. . .					0	13184
36-CABA-a	ririo	1	1	431	793	0	85.85	100	C	4		. . .					0	13185
36-CB	CENTRAL CHOISEULE chain	1	1	11,480	20,848		84.95	100	C	57		PN.					0 . s . .	13186
36-CBA	**BABATANA net**	1	1	11,480	20,848		84.95	100	C	57		PN.					0 . s . .	13187
36-CBAA	BABATANA cluster	1	1	9,480	17,448		85.99	100	C	57		PN.					0 . s . .	13188
36-CBAA-a	babatana					0				57		pn.					0 . s . .	13189
36-CBAA-b	babatana vehicular	1	1	9,480	17,448		85.99	100	C	57	Babatana	PN.	1927-1960	1960-1984			0 . s . .	13190
36-CBAA-c	katazi					0				57		pn.					0 . s . .	13191
36-CBAA-d	sengan					0				57		pn.					0 . s . .	13192
36-CBAA-e	kuboro					0				57		pn.					0 . s . .	13193
36-CBAA-f	lömaumbi					0				57		pn.					0 . s . .	13194
36-CBAA-g	avasö					0				57		pn.					0 . s . .	13195
36-CBAB	KIRUNGGELA cluster	1	1	2,000	3,400		80.00	100	C	0		. . .					0	13196
36-CBAB-a	kirunggela					0				0		. . .					0	13197
36-D	**NEW GEORGIA set**	1	10	41,687	76,726		91.93	100	C	62		PNB					0 . s . .	13198
36-DA	ROVIANA chain	1	8	29,828	54,899		91.23	100	C	57		PN.					0 . s . .	13199
36-DAA	**LUNGGA-GHANONGGA net**	1	3	10,364	19,075		91.07	100	C	12		. . .					0	13200
36-DAAA	GHANONGGA cluster	1	1	4,208	7,745		90.00	100	C	3		. . .					0	13201
36-DAAA-a	ghanongga	1	1	4,208	7,745	0	90.00	100	C	3		. . .					0	13202
36-DAAA-b	kubokota					0				3		. . .					0	13203
36-DAAB	LUNGGA cluster	1	1	2,445	4,499		89.98	100	C	12		. . .					0	13204
36-DAAB-a	lungga	1	1	2,445	4,499	0	89.98	100	C	12	Lungga	. . .					0	13205
36-DAAC	SIMBO cluster	1	1	3,711	6,831		92.99	100	C	3		. . .					0	13206
36-DAAC-a	simbo	1	1	3,711	6,831	0	92.99	100	C	3		. . .					0	13207
36-DAAC-b	madegugusu					0				3		. . .					0	13208
36-DAB	**NDUKE net**	1	1	2,844	5,234		93.99	100	C	4		. . .					0	13209
36-DABA	NDUKE cluster	1	1	2,844	5,234		93.99	100	C	4		. . .					0	13210
36-DABA-a	n-duke	1	1	2,844	5,234	0	93.99	100	C	4		. . .					0	13211
36-DAC	**KUSAGHE net**	1	1	2,349	4,324		91.02	100	C	6		. . .					0	13212
36-DACA	KUSAGHE cluster	1	1	2,349	4,324		91.02	100	C	6		. . .					0	13213
36-DACA-a	kusaghe	1	1	2,349	4,324	0	91.02	100	C	6		. . .					0	13214
36-DAD	**HOAVA net**	1	1	1,138	2,094		79.96	100	C	6		. . .					0	13215
36-DADA	HOAVA cluster	1	1	1,138	2,094		79.96	100	C	6		. . .					0	13216
36-DADA-a	hoava	1	1	1,138	2,094	0	79.96	100	C	6		. . .					0	13217
36-DAE	**ROVIANA net**	1	1	11,901	21,904		93.00	100	C	57		PN.					0 . s . .	13218
36-DAEA	ROVIANA cluster	1	1	11,901	21,904		93.00	100	C	57		PN.					0 . s . .	13219
36-DAEA-a	roviana					0				57		pn.					0 . s . .	13220
36-DAEA-b	roviana vehicular	1	1	11,901	21,904	0	93.00	100	C	57	Roviana	PN.	1916-1990	1953-1995			0 . s . .	13221
36-DAF	**UGHELE net**	1	1	1,232	2,268		80.03	100	C	6		. . .					0	13222
36-DAFA	UGHELE cluster	1	1	1,232	2,268		80.03	100	C	6		. . .					0	13223

Continued opposite

Table 9-13 continued

Code 1	REFERENCE NAME / Autoglossonym 2	Coun 3	Peo 4	Mother-tongue speakers in 2000 5	in 2025 6	Media radio 7	CHURCH AC% 8	E% 9	Wld 10	Tr 11	Biblioglossonym 12	Print 13-15	P-activity 16	N-activity 17	B-activity 18	J-year 19	Jayuh 20-24	Ref 25
36-DAFA-a	ughele	1	1	1,232	2,268	0	80.03	100	C	6		. . .					0	13224
36-DB	MAROVO chain	1	2	11,859	21,827		93.69	100	C	62		PNB					0	13225
36-DBA	**MAROVO net**	1	1	10,151	18,683		96.00	100	C	62		PNB					0	13226
36-DBAA	MAROVO cluster	1	1	10,151	18,683		96.00	100	C	62	Marovo	PNB	1931	1941	1956		0	13227
36-DBAA-a	West marovo					0				62		pnb					0	13228
36-DBAA-b	East marovo					0				62		pnb					0	13229
36-DBB	**VANGUNU net**	1	1	1,708	3,144		79.98	100	C	4		. . .					0	13230
36-DBBA	VANGUNU cluster	1	1	1,708	3,144		79.98	100	C	4		. . .					0	13231
36-DBBA-a	vangunu					0				4		. . .					0	13232
36-DBBA-b	m-bareke					0				4		. . .					0	13233
36-E	**ISABEL set**	1	7	14,872	27,374		91.77	100	C	51		PN.					0	13234
36-EA	WEST ISABEL chain	1	2	1,905	3,507		85.04	100	C	12		. . .					0	13235
36-EAA	**ZABANA net**	1	1	1,896	3,490		85.02	100	C	12		. . .					0	13236
36-EAAA	ZABANA cluster	1	1	1,896	3,490		85.02	100	C	12		. . .					0	13237
36-EAAA-a	zabana	1	1	1,896	3,490	0	85.02	100	C	12	Zabana	. . .					0	13238
36-EAB	**LAGHU net**	1	1	9	17		88.89	100	C	8		. . .					0	13239
36-EABA	LAGHU cluster	1	1	9	17		88.89	100	C	8		. . .					0	13240
36-EABA-a	laghu	1	1	9	17	0	88.89	100	C	8		. . .					0	13241
36-EB	EAST ISABEL chain	1	5	12,967	23,867		92.76	100	C	51		PN.					0	13242
36-EBA	**KOKOTA-ZAZAO net**	1	3	1,339	2,465		81.85	100	C	6		. . .					0	13243
36-EBAA	KOKOTA cluster	1	1	277	510		89.17	100	C	6		. . .					0	13244
36-EBAA-a	kokota	1	1	277	510	0	89.17	100	C	6		. . .					0	13245
36-EBAB	ZAZAO cluster	1	1	230	424		80.00	100	C	6		. . .					0	13246
36-EBAB-a	zazao	1	1	230	424	0	80.00	100	C	6		. . .					0	13247
36-EBAC	BLABLANGA cluster	1	1	832	1,531		79.93	100	C	6		. . .					0	13248
36-EBAC-a	blablanga	1	1	832	1,531	0	79.93	100	C	6		. . .					0	13249
36-EBAC-b	gema					0				6		. . .					0	13250
36-EBAC-c	goi					0				6		. . .					0	13251
36-EBB	**HOLO-GAO net**	1	2	11,628	21,402		94.01	100	C	51		PN.					0	13252
36-EBBA	CHEKE-HOLO cluster	1	1	10,865	19,998		95.00	100	C	51	Cheke Holo	PN.	1992	1993			0	13253
36-EBBA-a	maringe					0				51		pn.					0	13254
36-EBBA-b	hograno					0				51		pn.					0	13255
36-EBBA-c	a'ara					0				51		pn.					0	13256
36-EBBA-d	kubonitu					0				51		pn.					0	13257
36-EBBB	GAO cluster	1	1	763	1,404		79.95	100	C	4		. . .					0	13258
36-EBBB-a	gao	1	1	763	1,404	0	79.95	100	C	4		. . .					0	13259
36-F	**SANTA CRUZ set**	1	6	1,783	3,282		80.93	100	C	12		. . .					0	13260
36-FA	UTUPUA chain	1	3	807	1,484		82.03	100	C	4		. . .					0	13261
36-FAA	**AMBA net**	1	1	493	907		79.92	100	C	2		. . .					0	13262
36-FAAA	AMBA cluster	1	1	493	907		79.92	100	C	2		. . .					0	13263
36-FAAA-a	amba	1	1	493	907	0	79.92	100	C	2		. . .					0	13264
36-FAB	**ASUMBOA net**	1	1	106	194		80.19	100	C	4		. . .					0	13265
36-FABA	ASUMBOA cluster	1	1	106	194		80.19	100	C	4		. . .					0	13266
36-FABA-a	asumboa	1	1	106	194	0	80.19	100	C	4		. . .					0	13267
36-FAC	**NYISUNGGU net**	1	1	208	383		87.98	100	C	4		. . .					0	13268
36-FACA	NYISUNGGU cluster	1	1	208	383		87.98	100	C	4		. . .					0	13269
36-FACA-a	nyisunggu	1	1	208	383	0	87.98	100	Wld	4		. . .					0	13270
36-FB	VANIKORO chain	1	3	976	1,798		80.02	100	C	12		. . .					0	13271
36-FBA	**VANO net**	1	1	211	389		80.09	100	C	9		. . .					0	13272
36-FBAA	VANO cluster	1	1	211	389		80.09	100	C	9		. . .					0	13273
36-FBAA-a	vano	1	1	211	389	0	80.09	100	C	9		. . .					0	13274
36-FBB	**TANEMA net**	1	1	264	486		79.92	100	C	9		. . .					0	13275
36-FBBA	TANEMA cluster	1	1	264	486		79.92	100	C	9		. . .					0	13276
36-FBBA-a	tanema	1	1	264	486	0	79.92	100	C	9		. . .					0	13277
36-FBC	**TEANU net**	1	1	501	923		80.04	100	C	12		. . .					0	13278
36-FBCA	TEANU cluster	1	1	501	923		80.04	100	C	12		. . .					0	13279
36-FBCA-a	teanu	1	1	501	923	0	80.04	100	C	12	Teanu	. . .					0	13280
37	**NEOCALEDONIC zone**	2	40	104,799	148,801		88.06	100	C	63		PNB					0	13281
37-A	**SOUTH VANUATU set**	1	8	23,855	39,982		83.26	100	C	63		PNB					0	13282
37-AA	ERROMANGA-URA chain	1	2	1,316	2,207		89.74	100	C	44		PN.					0	13283
37-AAA	**URA net**	1	1	18	31		72.22	100	C	8		. . .					0	13284
37-AAAA	URA cluster	1	1	18	31		72.22	100	C	8		. . .					0	13285
37-AAAA-a	ura	1	1	18	31	0	72.22	100	C	8		. . .					0	13286
37-AAB	**ERROMANGA net**	1	1	1,298	2,176		89.98	100	C	44		PN.					0	13287
37-AABA	ERROMANGA cluster	1	1	1,298	2,176		89.98	100	C	44		PN.					0	13288
37-AABA-a	yoku					0				44		pn.					0	13289
37-AABA-b	ifo					0				44		pn.					0	13290
37-AABA-c	potnariven					0				44		pn.					0	13291
37-AABA-d	sie	1	1	1,298	2,176	0	89.98	100	C	44	Eromanga*	PN.	1864-1914	1909			0	13292
37-AB	TANNA chain	1	5	21,673	36,324		82.79	100	C	44		PN.					0	13293
37-ABA	**NORTH TANNA net**	1	2	7,029	11,781		86.54	100	C	44		PN.					0	13294
37-ABAA	TANNA-IMAFIN cluster	1	1	2,556	4,284		84.00	100	C	22	Tanna: North*	P. .	1990				0	13295
37-ABAA-a	East tanna					0				22		p. .					0	13296
37-ABAA-b	West tanna					0				22		p. .					0	13297
37-ABAA-c	imafin					0				22		p. . .					0	13298

Continued overleaf

Table 9-13 continued

Code 1	REFERENCE NAME / Autoglossonym 2	Coun 3	Peo 4	Mother-tongue speakers in 2000 5	in 2025 6	Media radio 7	CHURCH AC% 8	E% 9	Wld 10	Tr 11	Biblioglossonym 12	SCRIPTURES Print 13-15	P–activity 16	N–activity 17	B–activity 18	J-year 19	Jayuh 20-24	Ref 25
37-ABAB	NAPUANMEN cluster	1	1	4,473	7,497		87.99	100	C	44		PN.					0....	13299
37-ABAB-a	waesisi	1	1	4,473	7,497	0	87.99	100	C	44	Weasisi*	PN.	1895-1909	1924			0....	13300
37-ABAB-b	lometimeti					0				44		pn.					0....	13301
37-ABB	**LENAKEL net**	1	1	8,307	13,922		78.99	100	C	24		P..					0....	13302
37-ABBA	LENAKEL cluster	1	1	8,307	13,922		78.99	100	C	24		P..					0....	13303
37-ABBA-a	lenakel	1	1	8,307	13,922	0	78.99	100	C	24	Lenakel	P..	1900-1902				0....	13304
37-ABBA-b	loanatit					0				24		p..					0....	13305
37-ABBA-c	nerauya					0				24		p..					0....	13306
37-ABBA-d	itonga					0				24		p..					0....	13307
37-ABBA-e	ikyoo					0				24		p..					0....	13308
37-ABC	**SOUTHWEST TANNA net**	1	1	3,246	5,440		87.99	100	C	4		...					0....	13309
37-ABCA	SOUTHWEST TANNA cluster	1	1	3,246	5,440		87.99	100	C	4		...					0....	13310
37-ABCA-a	nvhal					0				4		...					0....	13311
37-ABCA-b	nowai	1	1	3,246	5,440	0	87.99	100	C	4		...					0....	13312
37-ABD	**KWAMERA net**	1	1	3,091	5,181		79.00	100	C	44		PN.					0....	13313
37-ABDA	KWAMERA cluster	1	1	3,091	5,181		79.00	100	C	44	Kwamera	PN.	1878-1883	1890			0....	13314
37-ABDA-a	North kwamera					0				44		pn.					0....	13315
37-ABDA-b	South kwamera					0				44		pn.					0....	13316
37-AC	ANEITYUM chain	1	1	866	1,451		85.10	100	C	63		PNB					0....	13317
37-ACA	**ANEITYUM net**	1	1	866	1,451		85.10	100	C	63		PNB					0....	13318
37-ACAA	ANEITYUM cluster	1	1	866	1,451		85.10	100	C	63	Aneityum	PNB	1853-1865	1863	1879		0....	13319
37-ACAA-a	North aneityum					0				63		pnb					0....	13320
37-ACAA-b	South aneityum					0				63		pnb					0....	13321
37-B	**NORTH KANAK set**	1	17	24,905	33,222		90.87	100	C	24		P..					0....	13322
37-BA	BELEP-YUAGA chain	1	4	6,813	9,088		91.40	100	C	2		...					0....	13323
37-BAA	**BELEP-KUMAK net**	1	4	6,813	9,088		91.40	100	C	2		...					0....	13324
37-BAAA	BELEP-NYALAYU cluster	1	1	1,862	2,484		80.02	100	C	2		...					0....	13325
37-BAAA-a	belep					0				2		...					0....	13326
37-BAAA-b	n-yaalayu	1	1	1,862	2,484	0	80.02	100	C	2		...					0....	13327
37-BAAB	KUMAK-NENEMA cluster	1	1	1,327	1,770		96.01	100	C	2		...					0....	13328
37-BAAB-a	nenema					0				2		...					0....	13329
37-BAAB-b	fwa-kumak	1	1	1,327	1,770	0	96.01	100	C	2		...					0....	13330
37-BAAC	YUAGA cluster	1	1	2,517	3,358		98.01	100	C	2		...					0....	13331
37-BAAC-a	juanga					0				2		...					0....	13332
37-BAAC-b	Central yuaga					0				2		...					0....	13333
37-BAAC-c	thuanga					0				2		...					0....	13334
37-BAAD	CAAC cluster	1	1	1,107	1,476		89.97	100	C	2		...					0....	13335
37-BAAD-a	pwebo					0				2		...					0....	13336
37-BAAD-b	caawac					0				2		...					0....	13337
37-BB	JAWE-HMWAVEKE chain	1	11	6,284	8,382		92.98	100	C	12		...					0....	13338
37-BBA	**JAWE-NEMI net**	1	4	3,853	5,139		93.15	100	C	4		...					0....	13339
37-BBAA	JAWE cluster	1	1	1,342	1,790		95.01	100	C	4		...					0....	13340
37-BBAA-a	Lower jawe					0				4		...					0....	13341
37-BBAA-b	jawe-M.					0				4		...					0....	13342
37-BBAA-c	Upper jawe					0				4		...					0....	13343
37-BBAB	NEMI cluster	1	1	886	1,182		96.95	100	C	4		...					0....	13344
37-BBAB-a	North nemi					0				4		...					0....	13345
37-BBAB-b	coulna					0				4		...					0....	13346
37-BBAB-c	ouango					0				4		...					0....	13347
37-BBAB-d	kavatch					0				4		...					0....	13348
37-BBAB-e	South nemi					0				4		...					0....	13349
37-BBAC	FWAI cluster	1	1	1,477	1,970		89.98	100	C	4		...					0....	13350
37-BBAC-a	fwai	1	1	1,477	1,970	0	89.98	100	C	4		...					0....	13351
37-BBAD	PIJE cluster	1	1	148	197		85.14	100	C	4		...					0....	13352
37-BBAD-a	pije	1	1	148	197	0	85.14	100	C	4		...					0....	13353
37-BBB	**PWAPWA net**	1	1	193	257		90.16	100	C	4		...					0....	13354
37-BBBA	PWAPWA cluster	1	1	193	257		90.16	100	C	4		...					0....	13355
37-BBBA-a	pwapwa	1	1	193	257	0	90.16	100	C	4		...					0....	13356
37-BBC	**PWAAMEI net**	1	1	539	719		96.10	100	C	4		...					0....	13357
37-BBCA	PWAAMEI cluster	1	1	539	719		96.10	100	C	4		...					0....	13358
37-BBCA-a	Lower pwaamei					0				4		...					0....	13359
37-BBCA-b	pwaamei-naaka					0				4		...					0....	13360
37-BBCA-c	pwaamei-yaak					0				4		...					0....	13361
37-BBD	**HMWAVEKE-BWATOO net**	1	5	1,699	2,267		91.94	100	C	12		...					0....	13362
37-BBDA	HMWAVEKE cluster	1	4	1,252	1,670		92.57	100	C	12		...					0....	13363
37-BBDA-a	vamale	1	1	220	294	0	91.36	100	C	12		...					0....	13364
37-BBDA-b	hmwaveke	1	1	441	588	0	95.01	100	C	12	Hmwaveke	...					0....	13365
37-BBDA-c	voh-kone					0				12		...					0....	13366
37-BBDA-d	haveke	1	1	443	591	0	90.07	100	C	12		...					0....	13367
37-BBDA-e	haeke	1	1	148	197	0	94.59	100	C	12		...					0....	13368
37-BBDB	WAAMWANG cluster			0	0		0.00	0		9		...					0....	13369
37-BBDB-a	waamwang			0	0	0	0.00	0		9		...					0....	13370
37-BBDC	BWATOO cluster	1	1	447	597		90.16	100	C	4		...					0....	13371
37-BBDC-a	bwatoo	1	1	447	597	0	90.16	100	C	4		...					0....	13372
37-BC	CENTRAL KANAK chain	1	2	11,808	15,752		89.44	100	C	24		P..					0....	13373
37-BCA	**CEMUHI net**	1	1	3,690	4,922		96.99	100	C	12		...					0....	13374
37-BCAA	CEMUHI cluster	1	1	3,690	4,922		96.99	100	C	12	Cemuhi	...					0....	13375
37-BCAA-a	u					0				12		...					0....	13376
37-BCAA-b	tié					0				12		...					0....	13377
37-BCAA-c	béko					0				12		...					0....	13378
37-BCAA-d	wagap					0				12		...					0....	13379
37-BCAA-e	tiparama					0				12		...					0....	13380
37-BCAA-f	South cemuhi					0				12		...					0....	13381
37-BCB	**PAICI net**	1	1	8,118	10,830		86.01	100	C	24		P..					0....	13382
37-BCBA	PAICI cluster	1	1	8,118	10,830		86.01	100	C	24		P..					0....	13383
37-BCBA-a	ponerihouen	1	1	8,118	10,830	0	86.01	100	C	24	Ponerihouen*	P..	1910				0....	13384
37-BCBA-b	West paici					0				24		p..					0....	13385

Continued opposite

Table 9-13 continued

Code 1	REFERENCE NAME / Autoglossonym 2	Coun 3	Peo 4	Mother-tongue speakers in 2000 5	in 2025 6	Media radio 7	CHURCH AC% 8	E% 9	Wld 10	Tr 11	Biblioglossonym 12	Print 13-15	P-activity 16	N-activity 17	B-activity 18	J-year 19	Jayuh 20-24	Ref 25
37-C	**SOUTH KANAK** set	1	12	24,977	34,160		92.11	100	C	51		PN.					0....	13386
37-CA	SOUTH CENTRAL KANAK. chain	1	10	17,953	23,949		91.59	100	C	51		PN.					0....	13387
37-CAA	**WAILIC net**	1	5	10,008	13,351		88.53	100	C	51		PN.					0....	13388
37-CAAA	ARHÖ cluster	1	1	811	1,082		90.01	100	C	4		...					0....	13389
37-CAAA-a	arhö	1	1	811	1,082	0	90.01	100	C	4		...					0....	13390
37-CAAB	ARHA cluster	1	1	415	554		90.12	100	C	4		...					0....	13391
37-CAAB-a	arha	1	1	415	554	0	90.12	100	C	4		...					0....	13392
37-CAAC	AJIE cluster	1	1	7,380	9,845		87.99	100	C	51		PN.					0....	13393
37-CAAC-a	monéo					0				51		pn.					0....	13394
37-CAAC-b	wailu	1	1	7,380	9,845	0	87.99	100	C	51	Houailou*	PN.	1903-1972	1922			0....	13395
37-CAAC-c	Upper wailu					0				51		pn.					0....	13396
37-CAAC-d	kouaoua					0				51		pn.					0....	13397
37-CAAC-e	West ajie					0				51		pn.					0....	13398
37-CAAD	OROWE cluster	1	1	1,107	1,476		89.97	100	C	12		...					0....	13399
37-CAAD-a	orowe	1	1	1,107	1,476	0	89.97	100	C	12	Orowe	...					0....	13400
37-CAAE	NEKU cluster	1	1	295	394		90.17	100	C	5		...					0....	13401
37-CAAE-a	neku	1	1	295	394	0	90.17	100	C	5		...					0....	13402
37-CAB	**ZIRE-TIRI net**	1	3	1,376	1,836		90.12	100	C	9		...					0....	13403
37-CABA	ZIRE cluster	1	1	45	60		93.33	100	C	9		...					0....	13404
37-CABA-a	zire	1	1	45	60	0	93.33	100	C	9		...					0....	13405
37-CABB	TIRI cluster	1	2	1,331	1,776		90.01	100	C	4		...					0....	13406
37-CABB-a	ha-tiri	1	1	886	1,182	0	89.95	100	C	4		...					0....	13407
37-CABB-b	ha-mea	1	1	445	594	0	90.11	100	C	4		...					0....	13408
37-CABB-c	tiri-mea					0				4		...					0....	13409
37-CABB-d	South tiri					0				4		...					0....	13410
37-CAC	**XARACUU-XARAGURE net**	1	2	6,569	8,762		96.57	100	C	4		...					0....	13411
37-CACA	XARACUU cluster	1	1	5,167	6,892		97.00	100	C	3		...					0....	13412
37-CACA-a	kanala					0				3		...					0....	13413
37-CACA-b	nakety					0				3		...					0....	13414
37-CACA-c	ouroué					0				3		...					0....	13415
37-CACA-d	xaracuu-C	1	1	5,167	6,892	0	97.00	100	C	3		...					0....	13416
37-CACA-e	Southwest xaracuu					0				3		...					0....	13417
37-CACA-f	Southeast xaracuu					0				3		...					0....	13418
37-CACB	XARAGURE cluster	1	1	1,402	1,870		95.01	100	C	4		...					0....	13419
37-CACB-a	thio					0				4		...					0....	13420
37-CACB-b	borindi					0				4		...					0....	13421
37-CACB-c	Southwest xaragure					0				4		...					0....	13422
37-CB	DUBEA-NUMEE chain	1	2	7,024	10,211		93.44	100	C	4		...					0....	13423
37-CBA	**DUBEA-NUMEE net**	1	2	7,024	10,211		93.44	100	C	4		...					0....	13424
37-CBAA	DUBEA cluster	1	1	2,068	2,758		93.96	100	C	4		...					0....	13425
37-CBAA-a	West naa-dubea					0				4		...					0....	13426
37-CBAA-b	East naa-dubea					0				4		...					0....	13427
37-CBAB	NUMEE cluster	1	1	2,000	3,400		90.00	99	C	0		...					0....	13428
37-CBAB-a	West naa-numee					0				0		...					0....	13429
37-CBAB-b	tuauru					0				0		...					0....	13430
37-CBAB-c	goro					0				0		...					0....	13431
37-CBAC	WEE cluster	1	1	300	510		90.00	99	C	0		...					0....	13432
37-CBAC-a	naa-wee	1	1	300	510	0	90.00	99	C	0		...					0....	13433
37-CBAD	KWENYII cluster	1	1	2,656	3,543		96.01	100	C	4		...					0....	13434
37-CBAD-a	naa-kwenyii	1	1	2,656	3,543	0	96.01	100	C	4		...					0....	13435
37-D	**LOYAUTE** set	1	3	31,062	41,437		86.25	100	C	63		PNB					0....	13436
37-DA	LOYAUTE chain	1	3	31,062	41,437		86.25	100	C	63		PNB					0....	13437
37-DAA	**IAAI net**	1	1	3,247	4,331		96.98	100	C	63		PNB					0....	13438
37-DAAA	IAAI cluster	1	1	3,247	4,331		96.98	100	C	63		PNB					0....	13439
37-DAAA-a	iaai	1	1	3,247	4,331	0	96.98	100	C	63	Iai: New Caledonia*	PNB	1868-1891	1878	1901		0....	13440
37-DAB	**DEHU net**	1	1	18,886	25,194		85.00	100	C	63		PNB					0....	13441
37-DABA	DEHU cluster	1	1	18,886	25,194		85.00	100	C	63	Dehu	PNB	1859-1877	1868-1968	1890		0....	13442
37-DABA-a	wet					0				63		pnb					0....	13443
37-DABA-b	lössi					0				63		pnb					0....	13444
37-DABA-c	miny					0				63		pnb					0....	13445
37-DAC	**NENGONE net**	1	1	8,929	11,912		85.00	100	C	63		PNB					0....	13446
37-DACA	NENGONE cluster	1	1	8,929	11,912		85.00	100	C	63		PNB					0....	13447
37-DACA-a	maré	1	1	8,929	11,912	0	85.00	100	C	63	Mare*	PNB	1855-1897	1864-1970	1903		0....	13448
37-DACA-b	pene-iwatenu					0				63		pnb					0....	13449
37-DACA-c	pene-egesho					0				63		pnb					0....	13450
38	**WEST PACIFIC zone**	11	151	611,588	1,061,290		92.51	100	C	72		PNB					3.s..	13451
38-A	**PONAPEIC-TRUKIC set**	4	17	91,040	154,426		95.65	100	C	67		PNB					1.s..	13452
38-AA	MACRO-TRUKIC chain	4	17	91,040	154,426		95.65	100	C	67		PNB					1.s..	13453
38-AAA	**MAPIA net**									9		...					0....	13454
38-AAAA	MAPIA cluster			0	0		0.00	0		9		...					0....	13455
38-AAAA-a	mapia					0				9		...					0....	13456
38-AAB	**TRUKIC net**	4	13	57,723	101,203		95.63	100	C	67		PNB					1.s..	13457
38-AABA	SONSOROL cluster	1	1	971	1,661		90.01	100	C	4		...					0....	13458
38-AABA-a	sonsorol					0				4		...					0....	13459
38-AABB	ULITHI cluster	2	2	4,252	6,712		96.45	100	C	57		PN.					0.s..	13460
38-AABB-a	ulithi	2	2	4,252	6,712	2	96.45	100	C	57	Ulithian	PN.		1995			0.s..	13461
38-AABC	WOLEAI cluster	3	3	3,736	8,449		97.59	100	C	2		...					0....	13462
38-AABC-a	woleai	3	3	3,736	8,449	0	97.59	100	C	2		...					0....	13463
38-AABD	SATAWAL-SAIPAN cluster	2	2	4,777	14,112		97.09	100	C	2		...					0....	13464
38-AABD-a	satawal	1	1	546	872	1	89.93	100	C	2		...					0....	13465
38-AABD-b	saipan	1	1	4,231	13,240	2	98.01	100	C	2		...					0....	13466
38-AABD-c	tanapag					1				2		...					0....	13467

Continued overleaf

Table 9-13 continued

Code 1	REFERENCE NAME / Autoglossonym 2	Coun 3	Peo 4	Mother-tongue speakers in 2000 5	in 2025 6	Media radio 7	CHURCH AC% 8	E% 9	Wld 10	Tr 11	Biblioglossonym 12	Print 13-15	P-activity 16	N-activity 17	B-activity 18	J-year 19	Jayuh 20-24	Ref 25
38-AABE	PULUWAT cluster	1	1	1,531	2,446		92.03	100	C	2		...					0....	13470
38-AABE-a	puluwat	1	1	1,531	2,446	0	92.03	100	C	2		...					0....	13471
38-AABF	NAMONUITO cluster	1	1	1,056	1,688		90.06	100	C	2		...					0....	13472
38-AABF-a	namonuito	1	1	1,056	1,688	0	90.06	100	C	2		...					0....	13473
38-AABG	PAAFANG cluster	1	1	1,484	2,370		91.98	100	C	4		...					0....	13474
38-AABG-a	paafang	1	1	1,484	2,370	0	91.98	100	C	4		...					0....	13475
38-AABH	TRUK cluster	1	1	33,269	53,147		95.50	100	C	67		PNB					1.s..	13476
38-AABH-a	Central truk					1				67		pnb				1990	1.s..	13477
38-AABH-b	Vehicular truk	1	1	33,269	53,147	2	95.50	100	C	67	Trukese*	PNB	1892-1962	1957-1984	1989-1996	1990	1.s..	13478
38-AABH-c	truk-E					1				67		pnb					1.s..	13479
38-AABH-d	fayichuk					1				67		pnb					1.s..	13480
38-AABI	MORTLOCK cluster	1	1	6,647	10,618		96.99	100	C	43	Mortlock*	PN.	1880-1882	1883			0....	13481
38-AABI-a	lukeisel					0				43		pn.					0....	13482
38-AABI-b	South mortlock					0				43		pn.					0....	13483
38-AAC	**PONAPEIC net**	1	4	33,317	53,223		95.68	100	C	61		PNB					0....	13484
38-AACA	PONAPE cluster	1	2	30,219	48,275		96.16	100	C	61	Pohnpeian*	PNB	1862-1935	1886-1977	1994		0....	13485
38-AACA-a	North ponape					1				61		pnb					0....	13486
38-AACA-b	kiti					1				61		pnb					0....	13487
38-AACA-c	ngatik	1	1	665	1,062	1	89.92	100	C	61		pnb					0....	13488
38-AACB	MOKIL cluster	1	1	1,389	2,218		91.00	100	C	3		...					0....	13489
38-AACB-a	mokil	1	1	1,389	2,218	0	91.00	100	C	3		...					0....	13490
38-AACC	PINGELAP cluster	1	1	1,709	2,730		90.99	100	C	3		...					0....	13491
38-AACC-a	pingelap	1	1	1,709	2,730	0	90.99	100	C	3		...					0....	13492
38-B	**KUSAIEAN set**	2	2	6,287	10,038		95.91	100	C	72		PNB					0....	13493
38-BA	KUSAIEAN chain	2	2	6,287	10,038		95.91	100	C	72		PNB					0....	13494
38-BAA	**KUSAIEAN net**	2	2	6,287	10,038		95.91	100	C	72		PNB					0....	13495
38-BAAA	KUSAIE cluster	2	2	6,287	10,038		95.91	100	C	72	Kusaien*	PNB	1863-1876		1928		0....	13496
38-BAAA-a	malen-utwe					1				72		pnb					0....	13497
38-BAAA-b	lelu-tafunsak					1				72		pnb					0....	13498
38-C	**MARSHALLESE set**	2	2	56,950	112,703		95.10	100	C	71		PNB					0.s..	13499
38-CA	MARSHALLESE chain	2	2	56,950	112,703		95.10	100	C	71		PNB					0.s..	13500
38-CAA	**MARSHALLESE net**	2	2	56,950	112,703		95.10	100	C	71		PNB					0.s..	13501
38-CAAA	RäLIK-RATAK cluster	2	2	56,950	112,703		95.10	100	C	71	Marshallese	PNB	1863-1983	1885-1977	1982		0.s..	13502
38-CAAA-a	rälik					1				71		pnb					0.s..	13503
38-CAAA-b	ratak					1				71		pnb					0.s..	13504
38-D	**KIRIBATI set**	6	6	96,545	140,847		92.66	100	C	72		PNB					3.s..	13505
38-DA	KIRIBATI chain	6	6	96,545	140,847		92.66	100	C	72		PNB					3.s..	13506
38-DAA	**KIRIBATI net**	6	6	96,545	140,847		92.66	100	C	72		PNB					3.s..	13507
38-DAAA	KIRIBATI cluster	6	6	96,545	140,847		92.66	100	C	72		PNB					3.s..	13508
38-DAAA-a	i-kiribati	6	6	96,545	140,847	4	92.66	100	C	72	Kiribati	PNB	1864-1895	1873-1996	1893-1954	1980	3.s..	13509
38-DAAA-b	butaritari					1				72		pnb					1.s..	13510
38-DAAA-c	banaban					1				72		pnb					1.s..	13511
38-DAAA-d	nui					1				72		pnb					1.s..	13512
38-E	**NAURUAN set**	1	1	5,529	8,554		80.50	100	C	63		PNB					0.s..	13513
38-EA	NAURUAN chain	1	1	5,529	8,554		80.50	100	C	63		PNB					0.s..	13514
38-EAA	**NAURUAN net**	1	1	5,529	8,554		80.50	100	C	63		PNB					0.s..	13515
38-EAAA	NAURU cluster	1	1	5,529	8,554		80.50	100	C	63		PNB					0.s..	13516
38-EAAA-a	nauru	1	1	5,529	8,554	2	80.50	100	C	63	Nauru*	PNB	1902-1906	1907	1918		0.s..	13517
38-F	**GELA-GUADALCANAL set**	1	8	64,158	118,087		94.04	100	C	43		PN.					0.s..	13518
38-FA	GELA-GUADALCANAL chain	1	8	64,158	118,087		94.04	100	C	43		PN.					0.s..	13519
38-FAA	**BUGHOTU net**	1	1	3,602	6,630		90.01	100	C	43		PN.					0.s..	13520
38-FAAA	BUGHOTU cluster	1	1	3,602	6,630		90.01	100	C	43		PN.					0.s..	13521
38-FAAA-a	m-bughotu	1	1	3,602	6,630	0	90.01	100	C	43	Bugotu*	PN.	1885-1923	1914-1934			0.s..	13522
38-FAAA-b	hageulu					0				43		pn.					0.s..	13523
38-FAAA-c	vulava					0				43		pn.					0.s..	13524
38-FAB	**GELA-LENGO net**	1	2	23,769	43,747		95.99	100	C	43		PN.					0....	13525
38-FABA	GELA cluster	1	1	11,808	21,733		96.99	100	C	43		PN.					0....	13526
38-FABA-a	n-gela	1	1	11,808	21,733	0	96.99	100	C	43	Gela	PN.	1879-1971	1923			0....	13527
38-FABB	LENGO cluster	1	1	11,961	22,014		95.00	100	C	2		...					0....	13528
38-FABB-a	lengo	1	1	11,961	22,014	0	95.00	100	C	2		...					0....	13529
38-FABB-b	ruavatu					0				2		...					0....	13530
38-FABB-c	tasemboko					0				2		...					0....	13531
38-FABB-d	aola					0				2		...					0....	13532
38-FABB-e	aripao					0				2		...					0....	13533
38-FABB-f	ghaimuta					0				2		...					0....	13534
38-FAC	**GUADALCANAL net**	1	5	36,787	67,710		93.17	100	C	41		PN.					0.s..	13535
38-FACA	GHARI cluster	1	2	13,852	25,495		95.96	100	C	41		PN.					0.s..	13536
38-FACA-a	ghari	1	1	11,686	21,508	0	98.00	100	C	41	Gari*	PN.	1905-1985	1989			0.s..	13537
38-FACA-b	tan-garare					0				41		pn.					0.s..	13538
38-FACA-c	n-gae					0				41		pn.					0.s..	13539
38-FACA-d	n-geri					0				41		pn.					0.s..	13540
38-FACA-e	n-di			2,166	3,987	0	85.00	100	C	41	Vaturanga	Pn.	1905				0.s..	13541
38-FACA-f	n-ginia					0				41		pn.					0.s..	13542
38-FACB	TALISE-TOLO cluster	1	1	11,328	20,851		93.00	100	C	4		...					0....	13543
38-FACB-a	poleo					0				4		...					0....	13544
38-FACB-b	ina-kono					0				4		...					0....	13545
38-FACB-c	malagheti					0				4		...					0....	13546
38-FACB-d	talise	1	1	11,328	20,851	0	93.00	100	C	4		...					0....	13547
38-FACB-e	tolo					0				4		...					0....	13548
38-FACB-f	moli					0				4		...					0....	13549
38-FACC	MALANGO cluster	1	1	3,877	7,135		93.99	100	C	3		...					0....	13550
38-FACC-a	malango	1	1	3,877	7,135	0	93.99	100	C	3		...					0....	13551
38-FACD	BIRAO cluster	1	1	7,730	14,229		88.01	100	C	2		...					0....	13552

Continued opposite

Table 9-13 continued

Code 1	REFERENCE NAME / Autoglossonym 2	Coun 3	Peo 4	Mother-tongue speakers in 2000 5	in 2025 6	Media radio 7	CHURCH AC% 8	E% 9	Wld 10	Tr 11	Biblioglossonym 12	Print 13-15	P-activity 16	N-activity 17	B-activity 18	J-year 19	Jayuh 20-24	Ref 25
38-FACD-a	m-birao	1	1	7,730	14,229	0	88.01	100	C	2		...					0....	13553
38-G	**MALAITA-MAKIRA set**	1	18	174,690	321,526		92.10	100	C	48		PN.					0.s.	13554
38-GA	MALAITA chain	1	14	157,365	289,639		92.74	100	C	48		PN.					0.s.	13555
38-GAA	**LONGGU net**	1	1	1,422	2,617		90.01	100	C	4		...					0....	13556
38-GAAA	LONGGU cluster	1	1	1,422	2,617		90.01	100	C	4		...					0....	13557
38-GAAA-a	longgu	1	1	1,422	2,617	0	90.01	100	C	4		...					0....	13558
38-GAB	**NORTH MALAITA net**	1	6	95,972	176,641		94.23	100	C	48		PN.					0.s.	13559
38-GABA	TO'ABAITA-KWARA'AE cluster	1	6	95,972	176,641		94.23	100	C	48		PN.					0.s.	13560
38-GABA-a	to'abaita	1	1	31,375	57,747		98.00	100	C	48	To'abaita*	PN.	1914-1951	1923			0.s.	13561
38-GABA-b	malu'u					0				48		pn.					0.s.	13562
38-GABA-c	m-baelelea					0				48		pn.					0.s.	13563
38-GABA-d	m-baegu					0				48		pn.					0.s.	13564
38-GABA-e	fataleka	1	1	6,239	11,483	0	80.00	100	C	48		pn.					0.s.	13565
38-GABA-f	lau	1	1	18,805	34,611	0	90.00	100	C	48	Lau	PN.	1905-1918	1929-1992			0.s.	13566
38-GABA-g	suafa					0				48		pn.					0.s.	13567
38-GABA-h	dai					0				48		pn.					0.s.	13568
38-GABA-i	gula'alaa	1	1	1,826	3,360	0	78.97	100	C	48		pn.					0.s.	13569
38-GABA-j	kwara'ae	1	1	35,509	65,357	0	97.00	100	C	48	Kwara'ae*	PN.	1909-1938	1961			0.s.	13570
38-GABA-k	fiu	1	1	2,218	4,083	0	84.99	100	C	48	Fiu	Pn.	1909				0.s.	13571
38-GAC	**LANGALANGA net**	1	1	8,946	16,466		84.00	100	C	12		...					0....	13572
38-GACA	LANGALANGA cluster	1	1	8,946	16,466		84.00	100	C	12		...					0....	13573
38-GACA-a	langalanga	1	1	8,946	16,466	0	84.00	100	C	12	Langalanga	...					0....	13574
38-GAD	**KWAIO net**	1	1	18,909	34,803		94.00	100	C	2		...					0.s.	13575
38-GADA	KWAIO cluster	1	1	18,909	34,803		94.00	100	C	2		...					0.s.	13576
38-GADA-a	kwaio	1	1	18,909	34,803	0	94.00	100	C	2		...					0.s.	13577
38-GAE	**DORI'O-'ARE'ARE net**	1	2	19,603	36,081		94.65	100	C	35		P..					0....	13578
38-GAEA	DORI'O cluster	1	1	1,706	3,141		91.03	100	C	4		...					0....	13579
38-GAEA-a	dori'o	1	1	1,706	3,141	0	91.03	100	C	4		...					0....	13580
38-GAEA-b	kwarekwareo					0				4		...					0....	13581
38-GAEB	'ARE'ARE cluster	1	1	17,897	32,940		95.00	100	C	35		P..					0....	13582
38-GAEB-a	'are'are	1	1	17,897	32,940	0	95.00	100	C	35	Areare	P..	1957				0....	13583
38-GAEB-b	marau					0				35		p..					0....	13584
38-GAF	**OROHA net**	1	1	190	349		70.00	99	C	4		...					0....	13585
38-GAFA	OROHA cluster	1	1	190	349		70.00	99	C	4		...					0....	13586
38-GAFA-a	oroha	1	1	190	349	0	70.00	99	C	4		...					0....	13587
38-GAG	**SOUTH MALAITA net**	1	2	12,323	22,682		83.17	100	C	48		PN.					0....	13588
38-GAGA	SOUTH MALAITA cluster	1	2	12,323	22,682		83.17	100	C	48		PN.					0....	13589
38-GAGA-a	sa'a	1	1	7,429	13,674	0	78.01	100	C	48	Sa'a*	PN.	1896-1995	1910-1927			0....	13590
38-GAGA-b	apae'aa					0				48		pn.					0....	13591
38-GAGA-c	ulawa	1	1	4,894	9,008	0	91.01	100	C	48	Ulawa	PN.	1896	1911			0....	13592
38-GAGA-d	ugi					0				48		pn.					0....	13593
38-GB	MAKIRA chain	1	4	17,325	31,887		86.25	100	C	41		PN.					0.s.	13594
38-GBA	**AROSI-FAGANI net**	1	2	5,878	10,818		85.69	100	C	35		P..					0.s.	13595
38-GBAA	AROSI cluster	1	1	5,309	9,771		85.99	100	C	35		P..					0.s.	13596
38-GBAA-a	arosi	1	1	5,309	9,771	0	85.99	100	C	35	Arosi	P..	1905-1921				0.s.	13597
38-GBAA-b	wango					0				35	Wango	P..	1905				0.s.	13598
38-GBAB	FAGANI cluster	1	1	569	1,047		82.95	100	C	4		...					0....	13599
38-GBAB-a	fagani	1	1	569	1,047	0	82.95	100	C	4		...					0....	13600
38-GBAB-b	rihu'a					0				4		...					0....	13601
38-GBAB-c	agufi					0				4		...					0....	13602
38-GBB	**BAURO net**	1	1	5,309	9,771		85.99	100	C	24		P..					0....	13603
38-GBBA	BAURO cluster	1	1	5,309	9,771		85.99	100	C	24		P..					0....	13604
38-GBBA-a	bauro	1	1	5,309	9,771	0	85.99	100	C	24	Bauro	P..	1922				0....	13605
38-GBBA-b	haununu					0				24		p..					0....	13606
38-GBBA-c	rawo					0				24		p..					0....	13607
38-GBBA-d	marmaregho					0				24		p..					0....	13608
38-GBC	**KAHUA net**	1	1	6,138	11,298		87.00	100	C	41		PN.					0.s.	13609
38-GBCA	KAHUA cluster	1	1	6,138	11,298		87.00	100	C	41		PN.					0.s.	13610
38-GBCA-a	kahua	1	1	6,138	11,298	0	87.00	100	C	41	Kahua	PN.	1927	1986			0.s.	13611
38-GBCA-b	tawarafa					0				41		pn.					0.s.	13612
38-GBCA-c	owa-raha					0				41	Santa Ana	pn.					0.s.	13613
38-GBCA-d	owa-riki					0				41		pn.					0.s.	13614
38-H	**TRANS-VANUATU set**	1	97	116,389	195,109		88.80	99	C	63		PNB					0.s.	13615
38-HA	NORTHEAST VANUATU chain	1	80	106,724	178,904		89.93	99	C	63		PNB					0.s.	13616
38-HAA	**TORRES net**	1	2	627	1,052		95.06	100	C	24		P..					0....	13617
38-HAAA	HIW cluster	1	1	173	290		94.80	100	C	24		P..					0....	13618
38-HAAA-a	hiw	1	1	173	290	0	94.80	100	C	24	Hiw	P..	1894-1900				0....	13619
38-HAAB	LOH-TOGA cluster	1	1	454	762		95.15	100	C	24	Torres Island*	P..	1894-1900				0....	13620
38-HAAB-a	tegua					0				24		p..					0....	13621
38-HAAB-b	loh					0				24		p..					0....	13622
38-HAAB-c	toga					0				24		p..					0....	13623
38-HAB	**LEHALI-LEHALURUP net**	1	2	346	581		85.55	100	C	4		...					0....	13624
38-HABA	LEHALI cluster	1	1	216	363		80.09	100	C	4		...					0....	13625
38-HABA-a	lehali	1	1	216	363	0	80.09	100	C	4		...					0....	13626
38-HABA-b	teqel					0				4		...					0....	13627
38-HABB	LEHALURUP cluster	1	1	130	218		94.62	100	C	4		...					0....	13628
38-HABB-a	lehalurup	1	1	130	218	0	94.62	100	C	4		...					0....	13629
38-HAC	**MOTLAV-MOTA net**	1	2	2,488	4,171		95.78	100	C	63		PNB					0.s.	13630
38-HACA	MOTLAV cluster	1	1	1,839	3,083		96.03	100	C	4		...					0.s.	13631
38-HACA-a	volow					0				4		...					0.s.	13632
38-HACA-b	beklag					0				4		...					0.s.	13633
38-HACA-c	totoglag					0				4		...					0.s.	13634
38-HACA-d	bun					0				4		...					0.s.	13635
38-HACB	MOTA cluster	1	1	649	1,088		95.07	100	C	63	Mota	PNB	1864-1902	1885-1931	1912		0.s.	13636
38-HACB-a	West mota					0				63		pnb					0.s.	13637
38-HACB-b	East mota					0				63		pnb					0.s.	13638

Continued overleaf

Table 9-13 continued

Code 1	REFERENCE NAME / Autoglossonym 2	Coun 3	Peo 4	Mother-tongue speakers in 2000 5	in 2025 6	Media radio 7	CHURCH AC% 8	E% 9	Wld 10	Tr 11	Biblioglossonym 12	Print 13-15	P–activity 16	N–activity 17	B–activity 18	J-year 19	Jayuh 20-24	Ref 25
38-HAD	**VATRATA-MOSINA net**	1	2	1,490	2,497		84.16	100	C	12		...					0....	13639
38-HADA	VATRATA cluster	1	1	866	1,451		79.91	100	C	4		...					0....	13640
38-HADA-a	vatrata	1	1	866	1,451	0	79.91	100	C	4		...					0....	13641
38-HADA-b	leon			0	0	0	0.00	0		4		...					0....	13642
38-HADA-c	pak			0	0	0	0.00	0		4		...					0....	13643
38-HADA-d	sasar			0	0	0	0.00	0		4		...					0....	13644
38-HADB	MOSINA cluster	1	1	624	1,046		90.06	100	C	12		...					0....	13645
38-HADB-a	vetumboso					0				12		...					0....	13646
38-HADB-b	vuras					0				12		...					0....	13647
38-HADB-c	mosina	1	1	624	1,046	0	90.06	100	C	12	Mosina	...					0....	13648
38-HAE	**GAUA net**	1	3	1,733	2,917		89.96	100	C	12		...					0.s..	13649
38-HAEA	NUME cluster	1	1	300	510		90.00	99	C	0		...					0.s..	13650
38-HAEA-a	nume					0				0		...					0.s..	13651
38-HAEA-b	tarasag					0				0		...					0.s..	13652
38-HAEB	LAKONA cluster	1	2	1,082	1,813		89.93	100	C	12		...					0....	13653
38-HAEB-a	lakona	1	2	1,082	1,813	0	89.93	100	C	12	Nume	...					0....	13654
38-HAEB-b	gog					0				12		...					0....	13655
38-HAEC	KORO cluster	1	1	200	340		90.00	99	C	0		...					0....	13656
38-HAEC-a	koro	1	1	200	340	0	90.00	99	C	0		...					0....	13657
38-HAED	WETAMUT cluster	1	1	151	254		90.07	100	C	4		...					0....	13658
38-HAED-a	wetamut	1	1	151	254	0	90.07	100	C	4		...					0....	13659
38-HAF	**MERLAV-MWERIG net**	1	1	1,702	2,853		95.01	100	C	4		...					0.s..	13660
38-HAFA	MERLAV-MWERIG cluster	1	1	1,702	2,853		95.01	100	C	4		...					0.s..	13661
38-HAFA-a	mwerig					0				4		...					0.s..	13662
38-HAFA-b	merlav	1	1	1,702	2,853	0	95.01	100	C	4		...					0.s..	13663
38-HAFA-c	matliwag					0				4		...					0.s..	13664
38-HAG	**MAEWO net**	1	3	1,585	2,657		90.03	100	C	24		P..					0.s..	13665
38-HAGA	MARINO cluster	1	1	260	435		90.00	100	C	4		...					0....	13666
38-HAGA-a	marino	1	1	260	435	0	90.00	100	C	4		...					0....	13667
38-HAGB	CENTRAL MAEWO cluster	1	1	546	916		90.11	100	C	24		P..					0....	13668
38-HAGB-a	lotora					0				24		p..					0....	13669
38-HAGB-b	tanoriki	1	1	546	916	0	90.11	100	C	24	Maewo, Central	P..	1906				0....	13670
38-HAGB-c	peterara					0				24		p..					0....	13671
38-HAGB-d	arata					0				24		p..					0....	13672
38-HAGB-e	bangoro					0				24		p..					0....	13673
38-HAGC	BAETORA cluster	1	1	779	1,306		89.99	100	C	4		...					0.s..	13674
38-HAGC-a	baetora	1	1	779	1,306	0	89.99	100	C	4		...					0.s..	13675
38-HAGC-b	nasawa					0				4		...					0.s..	13676
38-HAGC-c	talise					0				4		...					0.s..	13677
38-HAGC-d	narovorovo					0				4		...					0.s..	13678
38-HAH	**AMBAE net**	1	2	12,332	20,670		94.16	100	C	41		PN.					0.s..	13679
38-HAHA	WEST AMBAE cluster	1	1	6,491	10,880		97.01	100	C	41		PN.					0.s..	13680
38-HAHA-a	nduindui	1	1	6,491	10,880	0	97.01	100	C	41	Ambae: West*	PN.	1916	1984			0.s..	13681
38-HAHA-b	opa					0				41		pn.					0.s..	13682
38-HAHA-c	walaha					0				41		pn.					0.s..	13683
38-HAHB	EAST AMBAE cluster	1	1	5,841	9,790		90.99	100	C	35		P..					0.s..	13684
38-HAHB-a	omba					0				35		p..					0.s..	13685
38-HAHB-b	walurigi					0				35		p..					0.s..	13686
38-HAHB-c	tavalavola					0				35		p..					0.s..	13687
38-HAHB-d	lambahi	1	1	5,841	9,790	0	90.99	100	C	35	Lombaha*	P..	1971-1986				0.s..	13688
38-HAHB-e	longana					0				35		p..					0.s..	13689
38-HAHB-f	lolopwepwe					0				35		p..					0.s..	13690
38-HAHB-g	lolokaro					0				35		p..					0.s..	13691
38-HAHB-h	lolsiwoi					0				35		p..					0.s..	13692
38-HAI	**RAGA-SA net**	1	5	17,743	29,738		95.62	100	C	57		PN.					0.s..	13693
38-HAIA	HANO cluster	1	1	8,177	13,706		96.00	100	C	35		P..					0.s..	13694
38-HAIA-a	hano	1	1	8,177	13,706	0	96.00	100	C	35	Raga*	P..	1908-1989				0.s..	13695
38-HAIA-b	lamalanga					0				35		p..					0.s..	13696
38-HAIA-c	vunmarama					0				35		p..					0.s..	13697
38-HAIA-d	qatvenua					0				35		p..					0.s..	13698
38-HAIB	APMA cluster	1	1	6,491	10,880		95.01	100	C	57	Apma	PN.	1977	1996			0.s..	13699
38-HAIB-a	suro-bo					0				57		pn.					0.s..	13700
38-HAIB-b	suro-marani					0				57		pn.					0.s..	13701
38-HAIB-c	bwatnapi					0				57		pn.					0.s..	13702
38-HAIB-d	loltong					0				57		pn.					0.s..	13703
38-HAIB-e	melsisi					0				57		pn.					0.s..	13704
38-HAIC	SOWA cluster	1	1	45	75		88.89	100	C	8		...					0....	13705
38-HAIC-a	sowa	1	1	45	75	0	88.89	100	C	8		...					0....	13706
38-HAID	SEKE cluster	1	1	433	725		89.84	100	C	4		...					0....	13707
38-HAID-a	seke	1	1	433	725	0	89.84	100	C	4		...					0....	13708
38-HAIE	SA cluster	1	1	2,597	4,352		97.00	100	C	4		...					0....	13709
38-HAIE-a	ponorwal					0				4		...					0....	13710
38-HAIE-b	lolatavola					0				4		...					0....	13711
38-HAIE-c	ninebulo					0				4		...					0....	13712
38-HAIE-d	Northeast sa					0				4		...					0....	13713
38-HAIE-e	Southeast sa					0				4		...					0....	13714
38-HAIE-f	Southwest sa					0				4		...					0....	13715
38-HAIE-g	South sa					0				4		...					0....	13716
38-HAJ	**AMBRYM net**	1	5	9,522	15,958		86.43	100	C	24		P..					0....	13717
38-HAJA	NORTH AMBRYM cluster	1	1	4,111	6,891		85.02	100	C	2		...					0....	13718
38-HAJA-a	olal					0				2		...					0....	13719
38-HAJA-b	magam	1	1	4,111	6,891	0	85.02	100	C	2		...					0....	13720
38-HAJB	LONWOLWOL cluster	1	1	866	1,451		89.95	100	C	24	Lonwolwol	P..	1899-1949				0....	13721
38-HAJB-a	fali					0				24		p..					0....	13722
38-HAJB-b	fanting					0				24		p..					0....	13723
38-HAJC	DAKAKA cluster	1	1	866	1,451		89.95	100	C	4		...					0....	13724
38-HAJC-a	dakaka	1	1	866	1,451	0	89.95	100	C	4		...					0....	13725
38-HAJC-b	baiap					0				4		...					0....	13726
38-HAJC-c	sesivi					0				4		...					0....	13727
38-HAJD	PORT-VATO cluster	1	1	1,082	1,813		80.04	100	C	24		P..					0....	13728
38-HAJD-a	'port-vato'	1	1	1,082	1,813	0	80.04	100	C	24	Port Vato	P..	1899				0....	13729
38-HAJE	SOUTHEAST AMBRYM cluster	1	1	2,597	4,352		88.99	100	C	24	Ambrym, Southeast	P..	1949				0....	13730
38-HAJE-a	endu					0				24		p..					0....	13731
38-HAJE-b	toak					0				24		p..					0....	13732
38-HAJE-c	penapo					0				24		p..					0....	13733
38-HAJE-d	taviak					0				24		p..					0....	13734

Continued opposite

Table 9-13 continued

Code 1	REFERENCE NAME / Autoglossonym 2	Coun 3	Peo 4	Mother-tongue speakers in 2000 5	in 2025 6	Media radio 7	CHURCH AC% 8	E% 9	Wld 10	Tr 11	Biblioglossonym 12	SCRIPTURES Print 13-15	P-activity 16	N-activity 17	B-activity 18	J-year 19	Jayuh 20-24	Ref 25
38-HAK	**PAAMA-LOPEVI net**	1	1	7,573	12,693		97.00	100	C	43		PN.					0....	13735
38-HAKA	PAAMA-LOPEVI cluster	1	1	7,573	12,693		97.00	100	C	43	Paama	PN.	1907-1921	1944			0....	13736
38-HAKA-a	North paama					0				43		pn.					0....	13737
38-HAKA-b	South paama					0				43		pn.					0....	13738
38-HAKA-c	lopevi					0				43		pn.					0....	13739
38-HAL	**WEST SANTO net**	1	24	9,516	15,958		77.15	93	C	42		PN.					0....	13740
38-HALA	VALPEI-HUKUA cluster	1	1	433	725		89.84	100	C	4		...					0....	13741
38-HALA-a	valpei					0				4		...					0....	13742
38-HALA-b	hukua					0				4		...					0....	13743
38-HALB	NOKUKU cluster	1	1	250	419		90.00	100	C	24		P..					0....	13744
38-HALB-a	nokuku					0	90.00	100	C	24	Nogugu*	P..	1901-1918				0....	13745
38-HALC	VUNAPU-PIAMATSINA cluster	1	2	775	1,299		76.39	93	C	4		...					0....	13746
38-HALC-a	vunapu	1	1	541	907	0	90.02	100	C	4		...					0....	13747
38-HALC-b	piamatsina	1	1	234	392	0	44.87	78	B	4		...					0....	13748
38-HALD	TASMATE cluster	1	1	217	364		89.86	100	C	4		...					0....	13749
38-HALD-a	North tasmate					0				4		...					0....	13750
38-HALD-b	South tasmate					0				4		...					0....	13751
38-HALE	TOLOMAKO-JEREVIU cluster	1	1	649	1,088		89.98	100	C	24		P..					0....	13752
38-HALE-a	tolomako	1	1	649	1,088	0	89.98	100	C	24	Tolomako	P..	1904-1909				0....	13753
38-HALE-b	jereviu					0				24		p..					0....	13754
38-HALE-c	marina					0				24		p..					0....	13755
38-HALF	WUSI-KEREPUA cluster	1	1	311	522		95.18	100	C	4		...					0....	13756
38-HALF-a	wusi					0				4		...					0....	13757
38-HALF-b	kerepua					0				4		...					0....	13758
38-HALG	MALMARIV-NAVUT cluster	1	2	973	1,632		40.08	69	B	4		...					0....	13759
38-HALG-a	malmariv	1	1	216	363	0	40.28	69	B	4		...					0....	13760
38-HALG-b	navut	1	1	757	1,269	0	40.03	69	B	4		...					0....	13761
38-HALH	LAMETIN cluster	1	1	216	363		44.91	74	B	4		...					0....	13762
38-HALH-a	lametin	1	1	216	363	0	44.91	74	B	4		...					0....	13763
38-HALI	MOROUAS-AKEI cluster	1	7	2,285	3,833		64.42	90	C	24		P..					0....	13764
38-HALI-a	morouas	1	1	216	363	0	40.28	70	B	24		p..					0....	13765
38-HALI-b	roria	1	1	216	363	0	40.28	70	B	24		p..					0....	13766
38-HALI-c	fortsenal	1	1	216	363	0	44.91	76	B	24		p..					0....	13767
38-HALI-d	akei					0				24	Akei	P..	1909-1924				0....	13768
38-HALI-e	tasiriki	1	1	1,015	1,700	0	80.00	100	C	24	Tasiriki	P..	1909				0....	13769
38-HALI-f	wailapa	1	1	156	262	0	69.87	100	C	24		p..					0....	13770
38-HALI-g	penantsiro					0				24		p..					0....	13771
38-HALI-h	amblong	1	1	216	363	0	60.19	91	C	24		p..					0....	13772
38-HALI-i	narango	1	1	250	419	0	60.00	93	C	24		p..					0....	13773
38-HALJ	TANGOA cluster	1	1	541	907		88.91	100	C	24		P..					0....	13774
38-HALJ-a	tangoa	1	1	541	907	0	88.91	100	C	24	Tangoan	P..	1892-1923				0....	13775
38-HALK	ARAKI cluster	1	1	151	254		70.86	99	C	4		...					0....	13776
38-HALK-a	araki	1	1	151	254	0	70.86	99	C	4		...					0....	13777
38-HALL	TAMBOTALO cluster	1	1	78	131		80.77	100	C	4		...					0....	13778
38-HALL-a	tambotalo	1	1	78	131	0	80.77	100	C	4		...					0....	13779
38-HALM	MAFEA-AIS cluster	1	1	78	131		70.51	100	C	4		...					0....	13780
38-HALM-a	mafea	1	1	78	131	0	70.51	100	C	4		...					0....	13781
38-HALM-b	ais					0				4		...					0....	13782
38-HALN	MALO-TUTUBA cluster	1	3	2,559	4,290		93.63	100	C	42		PN.					0....	13783
38-HALN-a	tutuba	1	1	216	363	0	90.28	100	C	42		pn.					0....	13784
38-HALN-b	aore	1	1	2	3	0	0.00	50	B	42		pn.					0....	13785
38-HALN-c	avunatari	1	1	2,341	3,924	0	94.02	100	C	42	Malo	PN.	1892-1954	1954			0....	13786
38-HALN-d	ataripoe					0				42		pn.					0....	13787
38-HAM	**NORTHEAST MALEKULA net**	1	6	13,674	22,923		88.98	100	C	22		P..					0....	13788
38-HAMA	MALUA cluster	1	1	433	725		60.05	92	C	4		...					0....	13789
38-HAMA-a	'malua-bay'	1	1	433	725	0	60.05	92	C	4		...					0....	13790
38-HAMB	VOVO cluster	1	1	300	510		90.00	99	C	0		...					0....	13791
38-HAMB-a	vovo	1	1	300	510	0	90.00	99	C	0		...					0....	13792
38-HAMC	MPOTOVORO cluster	1	1	260	435		60.77	93	C	4		...					0....	13793
38-HAMC-a	mpotovoro	1	1	260	435	0	60.77	93	C	4		...					0....	13794
38-HAMD	MAE cluster	1	1	1,082	1,813		85.03	100	C	4		...					0....	13795
38-HAMD-a	mae					0				4		...					0....	13796
38-HAMD-b	North 'small-nambas'					0				4		...					0....	13797
38-HAME	VAO cluster	1	1	1,947	3,264		89.01	100	C	4		...					0....	13798
38-HAME-a	vao	1	1	1,947	3,264	0	89.01	100	C	4		...					0....	13799
38-HAMF	URIPIV-ATCHIN cluster	1	2	9,652	16,176		91.44	100	C	22		P..					0....	13800
38-HAMF-a	atchin	1	1	1,984	3,324	0	69.96	100	C	22		p..					0....	13801
38-HAMF-b	wala					0				22		p..					0....	13802
38-HAMF-c	rano					0				22		p..					0....	13803
38-HAMF-d	uripiv	1	1	7,668	12,852	0	97.00	100	C	22	Uripiv-wala-rano-atchin	P..	1893-1989				0....	13804
38-HAMF-e	tautu					0				22		p..					0....	13805
38-HAMF-f	uri					0				22		p..					0....	13806
38-HAN	**SOUTHEAST MALEKULA net**	1	7	5,678	9,517		83.87	100	C	24		P..					0....	13807
38-HANA	UNUA cluster	1	1	662	1,110		69.94	100	C	24		P..					0....	13808
38-HANA-a	unua	1	1	662	1,110	0	69.94	100	C	24	Unua	P..	1892-1913				0....	13809
38-HANA-b	'bush'-unua					0				24		p..					0....	13810
38-HANB	REREP-TISMAN cluster	1	1	541	907		90.02	100	C	24		P..					0....	13811
38-HANB-a	rerep	1	1	541	907	0	90.02	100	C	24	Pangkumu*	P..	1892-1913				0....	13812
38-HANB-b	tisman					0				24		p..					0....	13813
38-HANC	AULUA-ONESSO cluster	1	1	433	725		79.91	100	C	24		P..					0....	13814
38-HANC-a	aulua	1	1	433	725	0	79.91	100	C	24	Aulua	P..	1894-1925				0....	13815
38-HANC-b	onesso					0				24		p..					0....	13816
38-HANC-c	boinelang					0				24		p..					0....	13817
38-HAND	BURMBAR-VARTAVO cluster	1	1	757	1,269		70.01	100	C	4		...					0....	13818
38-HAND-a	burmbar	1	1	757	1,269	0	70.01	100	C	4		...					0....	13819
38-HAND-b	vartavo					0				4		...					0....	13820
38-HANE	LAMAP cluster	1	1	1,082	1,813		80.04	100	C	4		...					0....	13821
38-HANE-a	Port Sandwich	1	1	1,082	1,813	0	80.04	100	C	4		...					0....	13822
38-HANF	KULIVIU cluster	1	1	1,446	2,424		95.99	100	C	24		P..					0....	13823
38-HANF-a	kuliviu	1	1	1,446	2,424	0	95.99	100	C	24	Maskelynes	P..	1906				0....	13824
38-HANG	AXAMB cluster	1	1	757	1,269		90.09	100	C	24		P..					0....	13825
38-HANG-a	axamb	1	1	757	1,269	0	90.09	100	C	24	Ahamb*	P..	1935				0....	13826

Continued overleaf

Table 9-13 continued

Code 1	REFERENCE NAME / Autoglossonym 2	Coun 3	Peo 4	Mother-tongue speakers in 2000 5	in 2025 6	Media radio 7	CHURCH AC% 8	E% 9	Wld 10	Tr 11	Biblioglossonym 12	Print 13-15	P-activity 16	N-activity 17	B-activity 18	J-year 19	Jayuh 20-24	Ref 25
38-HAO	**SOUTHWEST MALEKULA net**	1	3	1,637	2,743		71.78	97	C	24		P..					0.s..	13827
38-HAOA	MALFAXAL-SENIANG cluster	1	3	1,637	2,743		71.78	97	C	24		P..					0.s..	13828
38-HAOA-a	malfaxal	1	1	866	1,451	0	59.93	95	B	24	Malfaxal	P..	1919				0.s..	13829
38-HAOA-b	ataripoe					0				24		p..					0.s..	13830
38-HAOA-c	orierh	1	1	381	638	0	80.05	100	C	24		p..					0.s..	13831
38-HAOA-d	nakahai					0				24	Na'ahai	p..	1919				0.s..	13832
38-HAOA-e	taman					0				24		p..					0.s..	13833
38-HAOA-f	sinesip	1	1	390	654	0	90.00	100	C	24	Sinesip*	P..	1905				0.s..	13834
38-HAOA-g	seniang					0				24		p..					0.s..	13835
38-HAP	**EPI net**	1	8	4,576	7,671		84.18	100	C	24		P..					0....	13836
38-HAPA	LEWO-MATE cluster	1	4	3,194	5,353		85.50	100	C	24	Lamenu	P..	1987				0....	13837
38-HAPA-a	lewo	1	1	978	1,639	0	89.98	100	C	24	Lewo: Varmali	P..	1892-1990				0....	13838
38-HAPA-b	varsu	1	1	978	1,639	0	75.05	100	C	24		p..					0....	13839
38-HAPA-c	tasiko	1	1	286	479	0	90.91	100	C	24	Tasiko	P..	1892				0....	13840
38-HAPA-d	mate					0				24		p..					0....	13841
38-HAPA-e	nul					0				24		p..					0....	13842
38-HAPA-f	filakara					0				24		p..					0....	13843
38-HAPB	BIEREBO-TAVIO cluster	1	1	649	1,088		79.97	100	C	5		...					0....	13844
38-HAPB-a	bierebo	1	1	649	1,088	0	79.97	100	C	5		...					0....	13845
38-HAPB-b	bonkovia					0				5		...					0....	13846
38-HAPB-c	yevali					0				5		...					0....	13847
38-HAPB-d	tavio					0				5		...					0....	13848
38-HAPC	BAKI cluster	1	1	312	523		80.13	100	C	22		P..					0....	13849
38-HAPC-a	baki	1	1	312	523	0	80.13	100	C	22	Baki	P..	1886-1987				0....	13850
38-HAPD	MAII cluster	1	1	156	262		89.74	100	C	4		...					0....	13851
38-HAPD-a	maii	1	1	156	262	0	89.74	100	C	4		...					0....	13852
38-HAPE	BIERIA cluster	1	1	265	445		80.00	100	C	24		P..					0....	13853
38-HAPE-a	bieria	1	1	265	445	0	80.00	100	C	24	Bieria	P..	1898				0....	13854
38-HAQ	**EMWAE-EFATE net**	1	4	14,502	24,305		92.34	100	C	63		PNB					0....	13855
38-HAQA	NAMAKURAN cluster	1	1	4,111	6,891		93.02	100	C	4		...					0....	13856
38-HAQA-a	tongoa					0				4		...					0....	13857
38-HAQA-b	tongariki					0				4		...					0....	13858
38-HAQA-c	buninga					0				4		...					0....	13859
38-HAQA-d	na-makura	1	1	4,111	6,891	0	93.02	100	C	4		...					0....	13860
38-HAQA-e	mataso					0				4		...					0....	13861
38-HAQB	NORTH EFATE cluster	1	1	4,328	7,253		90.00	100	C	63	Efate, North	PNB	1875-1892	1912	1972		0....	13862
38-HAQB-a	n-guna	1	1	4,328	7,253	0	90.00	100	C	63	Ngunese	PNB	1875	1908	1912		0....	13863
38-HAQB-b	lelepa					0				63	Lelepa	Pnb	1877-1883				0....	13864
38-HAQB-c	sesake					0				63		pnb					0....	13865
38-HAQB-d	emau					0				63		pnb					0....	13866
38-HAQB-e	paunangis					0				63		pnb					0....	13867
38-HAQB-f	livara					0				63		pnb					0....	13868
38-HAQC	SOUTH EFATE cluster	1	1	5,410	9,067		93.99	100	C	63		PNB					0....	13869
38-HAQC-a	fate	1	1	5,410	9,067	0	93.99	100	C	63	Efate*	PNB	1866-1880	1889-1930	1908		0....	13870
38-HAQC-b	erakor					0				63		pnb					0....	13871
38-HAQD	EAST EFATE cluster	1	1	653	1,094		89.89	100	C	4		...					0....	13872
38-HAQD-a	eton	1	1	653	1,094	0	89.89	100	C	4		...					0....	13873
38-HAQD-b	epwau					0				4		...					0....	13874
38-HB	EAST SANTO chain	1	5	3,679	6,165		80.59	95	C	24		P..					0....	13875
38-HBA	**NORTHEAST SANTO net**	1	1	2,164	3,627		98.01	100	C	24		P..					0....	13876
38-HBAA	SAKAO-LIVARA cluster	1	1	2,164	3,627		98.01	100	C	24		P..					0....	13877
38-HBAA-a	sakao	1	1	2,164	3,627	0	98.01	100	C	24	Sakau*	P..	1905-1949				0....	13878
38-HBAA-b	hog-harbour					0				24		p..					0....	13879
38-HBAA-c	livara			0	0	0	0.00	0		24		p..					0....	13880
38-HBB	**SOUTHEAST SANTO net**	1	4	1,515	2,538		55.71	88	B	4		...					0....	13881
38-HBBA	LOREDIAKARKAR-LITARO cluster	1	2	433	725		54.97	86	B	4		...					0....	13882
38-HBBA-a	lorediakarkar	1	1	108	181	0	39.81	69	B	4		...					0....	13883
38-HBBA-b	'shark-bay'	1	1	325	544	0	60.00	92	C	4		...					0....	13884
38-HBBA-c	litaro					0				4		...					0....	13885
38-HBBB	BUTMAS-TUR cluster	1	1	757	1,269		50.07	83	B	4		...					0....	13886
38-HBBB-a	butmas-tur	1	1	757	1,269	0	50.07	83	B	4		...					0....	13887
38-HBBC	POLONOMBAUK cluster	1	1	325	544		69.85	100	C	4		...					0....	13888
38-HBBC-a	polonombauk	1	1	325	544	0	69.85	100	C	4		...					0....	13889
38-HC	MALEKULA-INNER chain	1	12	5,986	10,040		73.84	97	C	41		PN.					0....	13890
38-HCA	**NAMBAS-KATBOL net**	1	7	4,766	7,995		77.76	100	C	41		PN.					0....	13891
38-HCAA	NORTH NAMBAS cluster	1	1	2,597	4,352		79.98	100	C	41		PN.					0....	13892
38-HCAA-a	'big-nambas'	1	1	2,597	4,352	0	79.98	100	C	41	Big Nambas*	PN.		1986			0....	13893
38-HCAB	MARAGUS cluster	1	1	22	38		77.27	100	C	8		...					0....	13894
38-HCAB-a	maragus	1	1	22	38	0	77.27	100	C	8		...					0....	13895
38-HCAC	LAREVAT cluster	1	1	216	363		80.09	100	C	4		...					0....	13896
38-HCAC-a	larevat	1	1	216	363	0	80.09	100	C	4		...					0....	13897
38-HCAD	LITZLITZ-VISELE cluster	1	1	476	798		80.04	100	C	4		...					0....	13898
38-HCAD-a	litzlitz					0				4		...					0....	13899
38-HCAD-b	visele					0				4		...					0....	13900
38-HCAE	LINGARAK cluster	1	1	303	508		69.97	100	C	4		...					0....	13901
38-HCAE-a	lingarak	1	1	303	508	0	69.97	100	C	4		...					0....	13902
38-HCAF	VINMAVIS-WINIV cluster	1	1	303	508		69.97	100	C	4		...					0....	13903
38-HCAF-a	vinmavis	1	1	303	508	0	69.97	100	C	4		...					0....	13904
38-HCAF-b	winiv					0				4		...					0....	13905
38-HCAG	TISVEL cluster	1	1	200	340		90.00	99	C	0		...					0....	13906
38-HCAG-a	tisvel	1	1	200	340	0	90.00	99	C	0		...					0....	13907
38-HCAH	TEMBIMBE-KATBOL cluster	1	1	649	1,088		69.95	100	C	4		...					0....	13908
38-HCAH-a	tembimbe					0				4		...					0....	13909
38-HCAH-b	katbol	1	1	649	1,088	0	69.95	100	C	4		...					0....	13910
38-HCAH-c	taremp					0				4		...					0....	13911
38-HCB	**SOUTH NAMBAS net**	1	4	674	1,129		41.10	72	B	8		...					0....	13912
38-HCBA	NASARIAN cluster	1	1	29	48		37.93	69	B	8		...					0....	13913
38-HCBA-a	nasarian	1	1	29	48	0	37.93	69	B	8		...					0....	13914
38-HCBB	REPANBITIP cluster	1	1	130	218		70.00	100	C	4		...					0....	13915
38-HCBB-a	repanbitip	1	1	130	218	0	70.00	100	C	4		...					0....	13916
38-HCBC	LETEMBOI cluster	1	1	440	737		30.00	61	B	4		...					0....	13917

Continued opposite

Table 9-13 continued

Code 1	REFERENCE NAME 2 / Autoglossonym	Coun 3	Peo 4	Mother-tongue speakers in 2000 5	in 2025 6	Media radio 7	AC% 8	E% 9	Wld 10	Tr 11	Biblioglossonym 12	Print 13-15	P-activity 16	N-activity 17	B-activity 18	J-year 19	Jayuh 20-24	Ref 25
38-HCBC-a	letemboi	1	1	440	737	0	30.00	61	B	4		...					0....	13918
38-HCBD	DIXON-REEF cluster	1	1	75	126		57.33	88	B	4		...					0....	13919
38-HCBD-a	'dixon-reef'	1	1	75	126	0	57.33	88	B	4		...					0....	13920
38-HCC	**LABO net**	1	1	546	916		80.04	100	C	24		P..					0....	13921
38-HCCA	LABO cluster	1	1	546	916		80.04	100	C	24		P..					0....	13922
38-HCCA-a	labo	1	1	546	916	0	80.04	100	C	24	Meaun*	P..	1905				0....	13923
39	**TRANSPACIFIC zone**	21	87	1,678,885	2,276,797		85.97	100	C	82		PNB					4asu.	13924
39-A	**ROTUMAN set**	1	1	9,476	12,808		93.00	100	C	82		PNB					0....	13925
39-AA	ROTUMAN chain	1	1	9,476	12,808		93.00	100	C	82		PNB					0....	13926
39-AAA	**ROTUMAN net**	1	1	9,476	12,808		93.00	100	C	82		PNB					0....	13927
39-AAAA	ROTUMAN cluster	1	1	9,476	12,808		93.00	100	C	82		PNB					0....	13928
39-AAAA-a	rotuman	1	1	9,476	12,808	0	93.00	100	C	82	Rotuman	PNB	1867-1928	1870-1930	1996		0....	13929
39-B	**FIJIAN set**	5	12	457,869	656,916		94.04	100	C	70		PNB					1.s..	13930
39-BA	WEST FIJIAN chain	1	2	75,223	108,640		95.70	100	C	4		...					0....	13931
39-BAA	**NADROGA-WAYA net**	1	1	73,589	106,432		95.83	100	C	0		...					0....	13932
39-BAAA	WAYA-MAGODRO cluster	1	1	20,000	34,000		90.00	99	C	0		...					0....	13933
39-BAAA-a	waya					0				0		...					0....	13934
39-BAAA-b	nakoroboya					0				0		...					0....	13935
39-BAAA-c	noikoro					0				0		...					0....	13936
39-BAAA-d	magodro					0				0		...					0....	13937
39-BAAB	NADROGA cluster	1	1	53,589	72,432		98.00	100	C	0		...					0....	13938
39-BAAB-a	nadroga	1	1	53,589	72,432	0	98.00	100	C	0		...					0....	13939
39-BAAB-b	tubaniwai					0				0		...					0....	13940
39-BAAB-c	baravi					0				0		...					0....	13941
39-BAB	**NAMOSI-SERUA net**	1	1	1,634	2,208		89.96	100	C	4		...					0....	13942
39-BABA	NAMOSI-SERUA cluster	1	1	1,634	2,208		89.96	100	C	4		...					0....	13943
39-BABA-a	namosi					0				4		...					0....	13944
39-BABA-b	naitasiri					0				4		...					0....	13945
39-BABA-c	serua					0				4		...					0....	13946
39-BABA-d	batiwai					0				4		...					0....	13947
39-BABA-e	tubai					0				4		...					0....	13948
39-BABA-f	nalea					0				4		...					0....	13949
39-BB	EAST FIJI chain	5	10	382,646	548,276		93.71	100	C	70		PNB					1.s..	13950
39-BBA	**EAST FIJI net**	5	10	382,646	548,276		93.71	100	C	70		PNB					1.s..	13951
39-BBAA	SOUTH VITI-LEVU cluster	5	5	254,741	343,193		96.03	100	C	70		PNB					1.s..	13952
39-BBAA-a	bau					1				70		pnb					1.s..	13953
39-BBAA-b	fiji	5	5	254,741	343,193	4	96.03	100	C	70	Fijian*	PNB	1839-1968	1847-1987	1864-1996		1.s..	13954
39-BBAA-c	naimasimasi					1				70		pnb					1.s..	13955
39-BBAA-d	nadrau					1				70		pnb					1.s..	13956
39-BBAA-e	waidina					1				70		pnb					1.s..	13957
39-BBAA-f	lutu					1				70		pnb					1.s..	13958
39-BBAB	NORTH VITI-LEVU cluster	1	1	25,000	42,500		80.00	100	C	0		...					0....	13959
39-BBAB-a	tokaimalo					0				0		...					0....	13960
39-BBAB-b	namena					0				0		...					0....	13961
39-BBAB-c	lovoni					0				0		...					0....	13962
39-BBAC	LOMAIVITI cluster	2	2	1,785	2,462		90.48	100	C	4		...					0....	13963
39-BBAC-a	koro	1	1	151	254	0	96.03	100	C	4		...					0....	13964
39-BBAC-b	makogai					0				4		...					0....	13965
39-BBAC-c	levuka					0				4		...					0....	13966
39-BBAC-d	ovalau					0				4		...					0....	13967
39-BBAC-e	batiki					0				4		...					0....	13968
39-BBAC-f	nairai					0				4		...					0....	13969
39-BBAC-g	gau					0				4		...					0....	13970
39-BBAD	KADAVU cluster	1	1	12,744	17,225		93.00	100	C	0		...					0....	13971
39-BBAD-a	tavuki					0				0		...					0....	13972
39-BBAD-b	nabukelevu					0				0		...					0....	13973
39-BBAD-c	ono					0				0		...					0....	13974
39-BBAE	LAU cluster	1	1	20,390	27,559		95.00	100	C	4		...					0.s..	13975
39-BBAE-a	matuku									4		...					0.s..	13976
39-BBAE-b	totoya					0				4		...					0.s..	13977
39-BBAE-c	naitaba					0				4		...					0.s..	13978
39-BBAE-d	moala					0				4		...					0.s..	13979
39-BBAE-e	yacata					0				4		...					0.s..	13980
39-BBAE-f	vanua-balavu					0				4		...					0.s..	13981
39-BBAE-g	mago					0				4		...					0.s..	13982
39-BBAE-h	tuvuca					0				4		...					0.s..	13983
39-BBAE-i	cicia					0				4		...					0.s..	13984
39-BBAE-j	nayau					0				4		...					0.s..	13985
39-BBAE-k	lakeba					0				4		...					0.s..	13986
39-BBAE-l	vanua-vatu					0				4		...					0.s..	13987
39-BBAE-m	oneata					0				4		...					0.s..	13988
39-BBAE-n	moce					0				4		...					0.s..	13989
39-BBAE-o	namuka					0				4		...					0.s..	13990
39-BBAE-p	kabara					0				4		...					0.s..	13991
39-BBAE-q	fulanga					0				4		...					0.s..	13992
39-BBAE-r	ongea					0				4		...					0.s..	13993
39-BBAE-s	vatoa					0				4		...					0.s..	13994
39-BBAE-t	ono-i-lau					0				4		...					0.s..	13995
39-BBAE-u	tuvana-i-ra					0				4		...					0.s..	13996
39-BBAE-v	tuvana-i-colo					0				4		...					0.s..	13997
39-BBAF	WEST VANUA-LEVU cluster	1	1	30,000	51,000		90.00	99	C	0		...					0....	13998
39-BBAF-a	West navatu					0				0		...					0....	13999
39-BBAF-b	solevu					0				0		...					0....	14000
39-BBAF-c	bua					0				0		...					0....	14001
39-BBAF-d	navakasiga					0				0		...					0....	14002
39-BBAG	CENTRAL VANUA cluster	1	1	10,000	17,000		90.00	99	C	0		...					0....	14003
39-BBAG-a	baravi					0				0		...					0....	14004
39-BBAG-b	seaqaqa					0				0		...					0....	14005
39-BBAG-c	savusavu					0				0		...					0....	14006
39-BBAG-d	nabalebale					0				0		...					0....	14007
39-BBAH	SOUTHEAST VANUA cluster	1	1	15,000	25,500		90.00	99	C	0		...					0....	14008
39-BBAH-a	Central navatu					0				0		...					0....	14009
39-BBAH-b	tunuloa					0				0		...					0....	14010
39-BBAH-c	naweni					0				0		...					0....	14011
39-BBAH-d	baumaa					0				0		...					0....	14012

Continued overleaf

Table 9-13 continued

Code 1	REFERENCE NAME / Autoglossonym 2	Coun 3	Peo 4	Mother-tongue speakers in 2000 5	in 2025 6	Media radio 7	CHURCH AC% 8	E% 9	Wld 10	Tr 11	Biblioglossonym 12	SCRIPTURES Print 13-15	P–activity 16	N–activity 17	B–activity 18	J-year 19	Jayuh 20-24	Ref 25
39-BBAI	NORTHEAST VANUA cluster	1	1	10,000	17,000		90.00	99	C	0		...					0....	14013
39-BBAI-a	labasa					0				0		...					0....	14014
39-BBAI-b	dogotuki					0				0		...					0....	14015
39-BBAI-c	saqan					0				0		...					0....	14016
39-BBAI-d	koroalau					0				0		...					0....	14017
39-BBAJ	GONE-DAU cluster	1	1	686	927		80.03	100	C	4		...					0....	14018
39-BBAJ-a	gone					0				4		...					0....	14019
39-BBAJ-b	dau					0				4		...					0....	14020
39-BBAK	TAVEUNI cluster	1	1	2,000	3,400		90.00	99	C	0		...					0....	14021
39-BBAK-a	taveuni	1	1	2,000	3,400	0	90.00	99	C	0		...					0....	14022
39-BBAL	OKOBIA cluster	1	1	300	510		90.00	99	C	0		...					0....	14023
39-BBAL-a	okobia	1	1	300	510	0	90.00	99	C	0		...					0....	14024
39-C	**POLYNESIAN set**	21	74	1,211,540	1,607,073		82.87	100	C	72		PNB					4asu.	14025
39-CA	POLYNESIAN chain	21	74	1,211,540	1,607,073		82.87	100	C	72		PNB					4asu.	14026
39-CAA	**NUKUORO net**	1	1	724	1,157		90.06	100	C	51		PN.					0.s..	14027
39-CAAA	NUKUORO cluster	1	1	724	1,157		90.06	100	C	51		PN.					0.s..	14028
39-CAAA-a	nukuoro	1	1	724	1,157	0	90.06	100	C	51	Nukuoro	PN.	1921-1949	1986			0.s..	14029
39-CAB	**KAPINGAMARANGI net**	1	1	2,860	4,570		92.03	100	C	2		...					0....	14030
39-CABA	KAPINGAMARANGI cluster	1	1	2,860	4,570		92.03	100	C	2		...					0....	14031
39-CABA-a	kapingamarangi	1	1	2,860	4,570	2	92.03	100	C	2		...					0....	14032
39-CAC	**NUGURIA-SIKIANA net**	2	5	4,095	7,165		89.43	98	C	35		P..					0....	14033
39-CACA	NUGURIA cluster	1	1	289	417		93.08	100	C	3		...					0....	14034
39-CACA-a	nuguria	1	1	289	417	0	93.08	100	C	3		...					0....	14035
39-CACB	TAKUU cluster	1	1	361	521		60.11	78	C	3		...					0....	14036
39-CACB-a	takuu	1	1	361	521	0	60.11	78	C	3		...					0....	14037
39-CACC	NUKUMANU cluster	1	1	288	416		80.21	100	C	2		...					0....	14038
39-CACC-a	nukumanu	1	1	288	416	0	80.21	100	C	2		...					0....	14039
39-CACD	ONTONG-JAVA cluster	1	1	2,086	3,839		94.97	100	C	35		P..					0....	14040
39-CACD-a	luangiua	1	1	2,086	3,839	0	94.97	100	C	35	Ontong Java	P..	1992				0....	14041
39-CACD-b	pelau					0				35		p..					0....	14042
39-CACE	SIKIANA cluster	1	1	1,071	1,972		90.01	100	C	2		...					0....	14043
39-CACE-a	sikaiana	1	1	1,071	1,972	0	90.01	100	C	2		...					0....	14044
39-CAD	**MUNGGAVA-MUNGIKI net**	1	1	3,886	7,152		97.99	100	C	51		PN.					0.s..	14045
39-CADA	MUNGGAVA-MUNGIKI cluster	1	1	3,886	7,152		97.99	100	C	51		PN.					0.s..	14046
39-CADA-a	munggava	1	1	3,886	7,152	0	97.99	100	C	51	Rennell-bellona	PN.	1942-1987	1994			0.s..	14047
39-CADA-b	mungiki					0				51		pn.					0.s..	14048
39-CAE	**PILENIC net**	1	1	2,148	3,925		89.94	100	C	2		...					0....	14049
39-CAEA	AUA-NUPANI cluster	1	1	1,948	3,585		90.97	100	C	2		...					0....	14050
39-CAEA-a	nupani					0				2		...					0....	14051
39-CAEA-b	nukapu					0				2		...					0....	14052
39-CAEA-c	pileni	1	1	1,948	3,585	0	90.97	100	C	2		...					0....	14053
39-CAEA-d	aua					0				2		...					0....	14054
39-CAEB	TAUMAKO-MATEMA cluster	1	1	200	340		80.00	100	C	0		...					0....	14055
39-CAEB-a	matema					0				0		...					0....	14056
39-CAEB-b	taumako					0				0		...					0....	14057
39-CAF	**TIKOPIA net**	1	2	4,507	8,296		96.45	100	C	22		P..					0....	14058
39-CAFA	TIKOPIA cluster	1	1	4,117	7,578		98.01	100	C	22		P..					0....	14059
39-CAFA-a	tikopia	1	1	4,117	7,578	0	98.01	100	C	22	Tikopia	P..	1989				0....	14060
39-CAFB	ANUTA-FATAKA cluster	1	1	390	718		80.00	100	C	4		...					0....	14061
39-CAFB-a	anuta	1	1	390	718	0	80.00	100	C	4		...					0....	14062
39-CAFB-b	fataka					0				4		...					0....	14063
39-CAG	**EMAE net**	1	1	312	523		80.13	100	C	4		...					0....	14064
39-CAGA	EMAE cluster	1	1	312	523		80.13	100	C	4		...					0....	14065
39-CAGA-a	emae	1	1	312	523	0	80.13	100	C	4		...					0....	14066
39-CAH	**MELE-FILA net**	1	1	3,555	5,965		93.73	100	C	12		...					0.s..	14067
39-CAHA	MELE cluster	1	1	3,255	5,455		94.99	100	C	12		...					0.s..	14068
39-CAHA-a	mele	1	1	3,255	5,455	0	94.99	100	C	12	Mele-fila	...					0.s..	14069
39-CAHB	FILA cluster	1	1	300	510		80.00	100	C	0		...					0....	14070
39-CAHB-a	fila	1	1	300	510	0	80.00	100	C	0		...					0....	14071
39-CAI	**FUTUNAN net**	1	1	1,136	1,910		80.02	100	C	44		PN.					0....	14072
39-CAIA	WEST FUTUNA cluster	1	1	936	1,570		80.02	100	C	44	Futuna-aniwa	PN.	1869-1923	1898			0....	14073
39-CAIA-a	West futuna					0				44	Futunian	Pn.	1869				0....	14074
39-CAIB	ANIWA cluster	1	1	200	340		80.00	100	C	43		PN.					0....	14075
39-CAIB-a	aniwa	1	1	200	340	0	80.00	100	C	43	Aniwa	PN.	1877	1898			0....	14076
39-CAJ	**FAGA-UVEA net**	1	1	2,761	3,683		96.99	100	C	4		...					0....	14077
39-CAJA	FAGA-UVEA cluster	1	1	2,761	3,683		96.99	100	C	4		...					0....	14078
39-CAJA-a	faga-uvea	1	1	2,761	3,683	0	96.99	100	C	4		...					0....	14079
39-CAK	**TUVALU-TOKELAU net**	7	8	38,396	62,879		82.17	100	C	72		PNB					0.s..	14080
39-CAKA	NORTH TUVALU cluster	1	1	20,000	34,000		80.00	100	C	0		...					0.s..	14081
39-CAKA-a	nanumanga					0				0		...					0.s..	14082
39-CAKA-b	nanumea					0				0		...					0.s..	14083
39-CAKA-c	niutao					0				0		...					0.s..	14084
39-CAKB	SOUTH TUVALU cluster	5	5	13,599	23,140		85.13	100	C	72		PNB					0....	14085
39-CAKB-a	funafuti	5	5	13,599	23,140	5	85.13	100	C	72	Tuvaluan	PNB	1969	1977	1987		0....	14086
39-CAKB-b	vaitupu					1				72		pnb					0....	14087
39-CAKB-c	nukulaila					1				72		pnb					0....	14088
39-CAKB-d	nukufetau					1				72		pnb					0....	14089
39-CAKC	TOKELAU cluster	3	3	4,797	5,739		82.84	100	C	14		...					0.s..	14090
39-CAKC-a	atafu					1				14		...					0.s..	14091
39-CAKC-b	nukunono					1				14		...					0.s..	14092
39-CAKC-c	fakaofo					1				14		...					0.s..	14093
39-CAKC-d	olosega					1				14		...					0.s..	14094
39-CAL	**TONGAN-UVEAN net**	4	4	24,981	32,354		91.63	100	C	23		P..					0....	14095
39-CALA	UVEAN cluster	4	4	24,981	32,354		91.63	100	C	23	Wallisian	P..	1971				0....	14096

Continued opposite

Table 9-13 continued

Code 1	REFERENCE NAME / Autoglossonym 2	Coun 3	Peo 4	Mother-tongue speakers in 2000 5	in 2025 6	Media radio 7	AC% 8	E% 9	Wld 10	Tr 11	Biblioglossonym 12	Print 13-15	P-activity 16	N-activity 17	B-activity 18	J-year 19	Jayuh 20-24	Ref 25
39-CALA-a	uvea					1				23		p..					0....	14097
39-CALA-b	uvea-vanuatu					1				23		p..					0....	14098
39-CALA-c	uvea-grande-terre					1				23		p..					0....	14099
39-CAM	**FUTUNA-NIUAFO'OU net**	3	3	9,427	11,798		93.94	100	C	12		...					0....	14100
39-CAMA	EAST FUTUNA cluster	2	2	8,747	11,073		93.70	100	C	12		...					0....	14101
39-CAMA-a	East futuna	2	2	8,747	11,073	2	93.70	100	C	12	Futuna, East	...					0....	14102
39-CAMA-b	East futuna Grande Terre					1				12		...					0....	14103
39-CAMA-c	alofi					1				12		...					0....	14104
39-CAMB	NIUAFO'OU cluster	1	1	680	725		97.06	100	C	4		...					0....	14105
39-CAMB-a	niuafo'ou	1	1	680	725	0	97.06	100	C	4		...					0....	14106
39-CAN	**PUKAPUKA net**	3	3	2,738	3,571		81.63	100	C	4		...					0....	14107
39-CANA	PUKAPUKA cluster	3	3	2,738	3,571		81.63	100	C	4		...					0....	14108
39-CANA-a	pukapuka	3	3	2,738	3,571	0	81.63	100	C	4		...					0....	14109
39-CAO	**SAMOAN net**	8	8	354,319	522,818		90.53	100	C	62		PNB					2a.u.	14110
39-CAOA	SAMOA cluster	8	8	354,319	522,818		90.53	100	C	62	Samoan	PNB	1836-1847	1846-1982	1855-1970	1980	2a.u.	14111
39-CAOA-a	West samoa					1				62		pnb					1c.u.	14112
39-CAOA-b	East samoa					1				62		pnb					1c.u.	14115
39-CAP	**TONGIC net**	8	11	149,108	166,662		92.76	100	C	72		PNB					4as..	14116
39-CAPA	NIUE cluster	4	4	12,788	14,760		89.62	100	C	68		PNB					0.s..	14117
39-CAPA-a	niue	4	4	12,788	14,760	5	89.62	100	C	68	Niuean	PNB	1861-1873	1866	1904		0.s..	14118
39-CAPB	TONGA cluster	6	7	136,320	151,902		93.06	100	C	72	Tongan	PNB	1844	1849-1992	1862-1966	1980	4a...	14119
39-CAPB-a	tonga-niuatoputapu					1				72		pnb					1c...	14120
39-CAPB-b	vava'u					1				72		pnb					1c...	14121
39-CAPB-c	ha'apai					1				72		pnb					1c...	14122
39-CAPB-d	tongatapu					1				72		pnb					1c...	14123
39-CAQ	**TAHITIC-MARQUESIC net**	9	21	603,195	758,286		75.07	100	C	71		PNB					0a.u.	14124
39-CAQA	MAORI cluster	4	4	401,292	488,012		67.32	100	C	62		PNB					0a.u.	14125
39-CAQA-a	Standard maori	4	4	401,292	488,012	4	67.32	100	C	62	Maori: New Zealand	PNB	1833-1862	1837-1862	1858-1952		0a.u.	14126
39-CAQA-b	West maori					1				62		pnb					0c.u.	14127
39-CAQA-c	Central maori					1				62		pnb					0c.u.	14131
39-CAQA-d	East maori					1				62		pnb					0c.u.	14135
39-CAQA-e	South maori					1				62		pnb					0c.u.	14140
39-CAQA-f	moriori			0	0	1	0.00	0		62		pnb					0c.uh.	14141
39-CAQB	RAROTONGAN cluster	3	3	41,931	51,221		88.56	100	C	67		PNB					0....	14142
39-CAQB-a	rarotonga	3	3	41,931	51,221	5	88.56	100	C	67	Maori: Cook Island*	PNB	1828-1981	1836	1851-1888		0....	14143
39-CAQB-b	mangaia					1				67		pnb					0....	14144
39-CAQB-c	mauke					1				67		pnb					0....	14145
39-CAQB-d	aitutaki					1				67		pnb					0....	14146
39-CAQB-e	atiu					1				67		pnb					0....	14147
39-CAQB-f	mitiaro					1				67		pnb					0....	14148
39-CAQC	RAKAHANGA cluster	2	2	5,804	7,055		89.20	100	C	4		...					0....	14149
39-CAQC-a	rakahanga					0				4		...					0....	14150
39-CAQC-b	manihiki					0				4		...					0....	14151
39-CAQD	TONGAREVA cluster	1	1	644	783		90.06	100	C	6		...					0....	14152
39-CAQD-a	tongareva	1	1	644	783	5	90.06	100	C	6		...					0....	14153
39-CAQE	HAWAI'I cluster	1	1	2,784	3,256		72.31	100	C	63		PNB					0....	14154
39-CAQE-a	ni'hau					0				63		pnb					0....	14155
39-CAQE-b	hawai'i	1	1	2,784	3,256	0	72.31	100	C	63	Hawaiian	PNB	1828-1976	1832-1836	1838-1839		0....	14156
39-CAQF	NORTH MARQUESAN cluster	1	1	5,188	7,160		85.00	100	C	41	Marquesan, North	PN.	1880-1995	1995			0....	14157
39-CAQF-a	hatutu					0				41		pn.					0....	14158
39-CAQF-b	nuku-hiva					0				41		pn.					0....	14159
39-CAQF-c	ua-huka					0				41		pn.					0....	14160
39-CAQF-d	ua-pou					0				41		pn.					0....	14161
39-CAQG	SOUTH MARQUESAN cluster	1	1	3,206	4,425		84.00	100	C	24	Marquesan, South	P..	1858-1905				0....	14162
39-CAQG-a	hiva-oa					0				24		p..					0....	14163
39-CAQG-b	tahuta					0				24		p..					0....	14164
39-CAQG-c	fatu-hiva					0				24		p..					0....	14165
39-CAQH	TAHITIAN cluster	4	4	107,499	147,958		94.31	100	C	71		PNB					0....	14166
39-CAQH-a	tahiti					1				71		pnb					0....	14167
39-CAQH-b	Vehicular tahiti	4	4	107,499	147,958	5	94.31	100	C	71	Tahitian	PNB	1818-1861	1829-1988	1838-1913		0....	14168
39-CAQI	PA'UMOTU cluster	1	1	19,912	27,483		84.00	100	C	4		...					0....	14178
39-CAQI-a	mihiroa					0				4		...					0....	14179
39-CAQI-b	vahitu					0				4		...					0....	14180
39-CAQI-c	napuka					0				4		...					0....	14181
39-CAQI-d	fangatau					0				4		...					0....	14182
39-CAQI-e	reao					0				4		...					0....	14183
39-CAQI-f	marangai					0				4		...					0....	14184
39-CAQI-g	tapuhoe					0				4		...					0....	14185
39-CAQI-h	parata					0				4		...					0....	14186
39-CAQJ	MORUROA cluster	1	1	1,000	1,700		80.00	100	C	0		...					0....	14187
39-CAQJ-a	moruroa	1	1	1,000	1,700	0	80.00	100	C	0		...					0....	14188
39-CAQK	TUBUAI-RURUTU cluster	1	1	11,048	15,249		84.00	100	C	4		...					0....	14189
39-CAQK-a	tubuai-rurutu	1	1	11,048	15,249	5	84.00	100	C	4		...					0....	14190
39-CAQL	MANGAREVA cluster	1	1	2,210	3,050		82.99	100	C	24		P..					0....	14191
39-CAQL-a	mangareva	1	1	2,210	3,050	0	82.99	100	C	24	Mangareva	P..	1908				0....	14192
39-CAQM	RAPA cluster	1	1	677	934		93.06	100	C	4		...					0....	14193
39-CAQM-a	rapa	1	1	677	934	0	93.06	100	C	4		...					0....	14194
39-CAR	**RAPANUI net**	1	1	3,392	4,359		69.99	100	C	12		...					0....	14195
39-CARA	RAPANUI cluster	1	1	3,392	4,359		69.99	100	C	12		...					0....	14196
39-CARA-a	rapanui	1	1	3,392	4,359	0	69.99	100	C	12	Rapa Nui	...					0....	14197
4	**EURASIAN macrozone**	125	1295	851,028,025	1,036,948,223		12.19	66	B	82		PNB					4Bsuh	14198
40	**EUSKARIC zone**	13	13	953,056	940,719		92.62	100	C	63		PNB					3....	14199
40-A	**EUSKARA set**	13	13	953,056	940,719		92.62	100	C	63		PNB					3....	14200
40-AA	EUSKARA chain	13	13	953,056	940,719		92.62	100	C	63		PNB					3....	14201
40-AAA	**EUSKARA net**	13	13	953,056	940,719		92.62	100	C	63		PNB					3....	14202
40-AAAA	EUSKARA cluster	13	13	953,056	940,719		92.62	100	C	63		PNB					3....	14203
40-AAAA-a	General euskara	10	10	170,564	203,152	4	93.84	100	C	63	Basque	PNB	1982	1571-1988	1855-1994	1993	3....	14204

Continued overleaf

Table 9-13 continued

Code 1	REFERENCE NAME / Autoglossonym 2	Coun 3	Peo 4	Mother-tongue speakers in 2000 5	in 2025 6	Media radio 7	CHURCH AC% 8	E% 9	Wld 10	Tr 11	Biblioglossonym 12	SCRIPTURES Print 13-15	P-activity 16	N-activity 17	B-activity 18	J-year 19	Jayuh 20-24	Ref 25
40-AAAA-b	bizkaiera					1				63	Basque: Biscayan	Pnb	1857				1....	14205
40-AAAA-c	gipuzkera	2	2	681,980	632,662	3	93.00	100	C	63	Basque: Guipuzcoan	PNB	1838	1931	1958		1....	14212
40-AAAA-d	Northwest nafarrera					1				63	Basque: Navarrese Spanish	Pnb	1857				1....	14217
40-AAAA-e	South nafarrera					1				63	Basque: Navarrese South Hi	Pnb	1868				1....	14221
40-AAAA-f	East euskara					1				63		pnb					1....	14226
40-AAAA-g	North Central nafarrera.					1				63		pnb					1....	14227
40-AAAA-h	nafarrera-NE					1				63	Basque: Navarrese E Low	Pnb	1856				1....	14232
40-AAAA-i	lapurtera	1	1	100,512	104,905	4	88.00	100	C	63	Basque: Labourdin*	PNB	1856	1571	1856-1865		1....	14238
40-AAAA-j	zuberoera					1				63	Basque: Souletin*	Pnb	1856-1888				1....	14243
40-AAAA-k	euskara-amerika					1				63		pnb					1....	14247
40-AAAA-l	euskara-idaho					1				63		pnb					1....	14253
41	**URALIC zone**	39	142	25,626,625	24,541,552		81.42	99	C	68		PNB					4A.uh	14254
41-A	FINNIC set	24	107	10,172,510	10,067,067		76.86	98	C	68		PNB					4A.uh	14255
41-AA	FINNIC chain	24	107	10,172,510	10,067,067		76.86	98	C	68		PNB					4A.uh	14256
41-AAA	**BALTO-FINNIC net**	19	48	7,397,529	7,433,140		82.08	100	C	61		PNB					4A.uh	14257
41-AAAA	SUOMI cluster	11	13	6,023,648	6,219,304		88.86	100	C	61		PNB					1A.uh	14258
41-AAAA-a	Historical suomi					1				61		pnb					1c.uh	14259
41-AAAA-b	General suomi	11	13	6,023,648	6,219,304	5	88.86	100	C	61		PNB				1985	1A.uh	14260
41-AAAA-c	Southwest suomi					1				61		pnb					1c.uh	14264
41-AAAA-d	North suomi					1				61		pnb					1c.uh	14272
41-AAAA-e	East Central suomi.					1				61		pnb					1c.uh	14279
41-AAAA-f	suomi-värmland					1				61		pnb					1c.uh	14285
41-AAAA-g	Southeast suomi					1				61		pnb					1c.uh	14286
41-AAAB	KARELY-LüDI cluster	7	13	283,436	270,582		67.12	99	C	35		P..					1....	14289
41-AAAB-a	Central karely	6	6	219,287	208,979	0	68.59	100	C	35	Karelian	P..	1820-1996				1....	14290
41-AAAB-b	South karely					0				35		p..					1....	14294
41-AAAB-c	olonec	2	2	19,458	18,661	0	63.99	100	C	35	Livvi	P..	1992-1995				1....	14301
41-AAAB-d	North lüdi	1	1	5,877	5,517	0	60.00	96	B	35		p..					1....	14308
41-AAAB-e	lüdi-S	1	1	12,137	11,393	0	70.00	100	C	35	Vepsi	P..	1992-1996				1....	14312
41-AAAB-f	izhor	3	3	26,677	26,032	0	57.56	89	B	35		p..					1....	14316
41-AAAC	EESTI-VADDYA cluster	18	22	1,090,445	943,254		48.52	99	B	61		PNB					4A.u.	14321
41-AAAC-a	vaddya	1	1	29	28	1	72.41	100	C	61		pnb					1c.u.	14322
41-AAAC-b	eesti	18	20	1,089,096	942,142	5	48.49	99	B	61	Estonian: Tallinn	PNB	1991	1686-1989	1739-1995	1984	4A.u.	14325
41-AAAC-c	liiv	1	1	1,320	1,084	1	70.00	100	C	61	Livonian: Eastern	PNb	1863-1937	1942			1c.u.	14333
41-AAB	**SAAME net**	4	17	37,538	39,016		91.05	100	C	68		PNB					0A...	14337
41-AABA	NORTHWEST SAAME cluster	3	7	25,975	27,284		93.80	100	C	68		PNB					0....	14338
41-AABA-a	ruija	3	3	17,285	18,280	2	95.16	100	C	68	Saami: Norwegian*	PNB	1838-1993	1840-1874	1895		0....	14339
41-AABA-b	lule	2	2	6,506	6,709	2	91.44	100	C	68	Saami: Swedish*	PNB	1648	1755-1903	1811		0....	14343
41-AABA-c	pite	2	2	2,184	2,295	2	90.02	100	C	68	Saami, Pite	PNB	1648-1881	1755	1811		0....	14346
41-AABB	EAST SAAME cluster	2	6	4,252	4,062		78.17	100	C	24		P..					0A...	14349
41-AABB-a	skolt	2	3	2,251	2,152	4	88.80	100	C	24	Saami: Russian*	P..	1878-1988				0A...	14350
41-AABB-b	anar	1	1	414	420	1	90.10	100	C	24	Saami: Inari*	P..	1903-1980				0c...	14354
41-AABB-c	ter					1				24		p..					0c...	14356
41-AABB-d	kildin	1	2	1,587	1,490	1	59.99	100	B	24		p..					0c...	14357
41-AABC	SOUTH SAAME cluster	2	4	7,311	7,670		88.78	100	C	12	Saami, Southern	...					0....	14358
41-AABC-a	ume	2	2	1,961	2,054	2	85.47	100	C	12		...					0....	14359
41-AABC-b	almoch					1				12		...					0....	14362
41-AAC	**MARI net**	8	9	668,905	631,699		89.95	100	C	43		PN.					2....	14365
41-AACA	MARI cluster	8	9	668,905	631,699		89.95	100	C	43		PN.					2....	14366
41-AACA-a	cheremis	3	3	141,189	132,480	0	90.00	100	C	43	Mari: High*	PN.	1821-1895	1824			1....	14367
41-AACA-b	mariy	6	6	527,716	499,219	0	89.93	100	C	43	Mari: Low*	PN.	1870-1995	1986		1994	2....	14373
41-AAD	**MORDVIN net**	14	15	808,556	775,739		65.13	100	C	43		PN.					2....	14380
41-AADA	MORDVIN cluster	14	15	808,556	775,739		65.13	100	C	43		PN.					2....	14381
41-AADA-a	erzya	10	10	482,063	457,994	7	64.75	100	C	43	Mordvin: Erzya*	PN.	1821-1996	1824		1991	2....	14382
41-AADA-b	moksha	5	5	326,493	317,745	1	65.69	100	C	43	Mordvin: Moksha*	Pn.	1879-1996				1....	14389
41-AAE	**PERMIC net**	10	18	1,259,982	1,187,473		46.32	88	B	41		PN.					3....	14391
41-AAEA	PERMIC cluster	10	18	1,259,982	1,187,473		46.32	88	B	41		PN.					3....	14392
41-AAEA-a	komi	3	4	363,154	340,865	0	33.17	77	B	41	Komi: Zyryan*	PN.	1823-1995	1979		1996	3....	14393
41-AAEA-b	permyat	5	5	153,274	144,533	0	40.00	84	B	41	Komi: Permyak*	Pn.	1866-1882			1996	3....	14398
41-AAEA-c	udmurt	9	9	743,554	702,075	0	54.04	94	B	41	Udmurt	Pn.	1847-1995			1994	2....	14404
41-B	**UGRIC set**	26	31	15,413,678	14,436,526		84.63	99	C	61		PNB					2A.u.	14408
41-BA	MAGYAR chain	26	29	15,383,131	14,407,849		84.79	99	C	61		PNB					2A.u.	14409
41-BAA	**MAGYAR net**	26	29	15,383,131	14,407,849		84.79	99	C	61		PNB					2A.u.	14410
41-BAAA	MAGYAR cluster	26	29	15,383,131	14,407,849		84.79	99	C	61		PNB					2A.u.	14411
41-BAAA-a	General magyar	26	29	15,383,131	14,407,849	6	84.79	99	C	61	Hungarian	PNB	1533-1988	1541-1952	1590-1991	1984	2A.u.	14412
41-BAAA-b	palóc					1				61		pnb					1c.u.	14428
41-BAAA-c	magyar-északkeleti					1				61		pnb					1c.u.	14433
41-BAAA-d	mez sÁgi					1				61		pnb					1c.u.	14438
41-BAAA-e	székely					1				61		pnb					1c.u.	14441
41-BAAA-f	csángó					1				61		pnb					1c.u.	14442
41-BB	EAST UGRIC chain	1	2	30,547	28,677		4.00	35	A	24		P..					0....	14443
41-BBA	**OSTYAK net**	1	1	22,275	20,911		4.00	35	A	24		P..					0....	14444
41-BBAA	KHANTY cluster	1	1	22,275	20,911		4.00	35	A	24	Khanty	P..	1868				0....	14445
41-BBAA-a	North khanty					0				24		p..					0....	14446
41-BBAA-b	East khanty					0				24		p..					0....	14449
41-BBAA-c	Southwest khanty					0				24		P..					0....	14452
41-BBAA-d	vach					0				24		p..					0....	14453
41-BBB	**MANSY net**	1	1	8,272	7,766		4.00	35	A	24		P..					0....	14454
41-BBBA	MANSY cluster	1	1	8,272	7,766		4.00	35	A	24	Mansi	P..	1868-1882				0....	14455
41-BBBA-a	sosyvin					0				24		p..					0....	14456
41-BBBA-b	lozyvin					0				24		p..					0....	14457
41-BBBA-c	kondin					0				24		p..					0....	14460
41-BBBA-d	tavdin					0				24		p..					0....	14461
41-C	**SAMOYED set**	1	4	40,437	37,959		4.31	35	A	12		...					0....	14462
41-CA	SAMOYED chain	1	4	40,437	37,959		4.31	35	A	12		...					0....	14463
41-CAA	**NORTH SAMOYED net**	1	3	36,029	33,821		4.11	34	A	12		...					0....	14464
41-CAAA	NORTH SAMOYED cluster	1	3	36,029	33,821		4.11	34	A	12		...					0....	14465
41-CAAA-a	nenets	1	1	34,177	32,083	0	4.00	34	A	12	Nenets	...					0....	14466
41-CAAA-b	pan-hasawa					0				12		...					0....	14479
41-CAAA-c	enets	1	1	588	552	0	4.08	32	A	12	Enets	...					0....	14481

Continued opposite

Table 9-13 continued

Code 1	REFERENCE NAME / Autoglossonym 2	Coun 3	Peo 4	Mother-tongue speakers in 2000 5	in 2025 6	Media radio 7	CHURCH AC% 8	E% 9	Wld 10	Tr 11	Biblioglossonym 12	SCRIPTURES Print 13-15	P-activity 16	N-activity 17	B-activity 18	J-year 19	Jayuh 20-24	Ref 25
41-CAAA-d	nganasan	1	1	1,264	1,186	0	6.96	37	A	12							0....	14484
41-CAB	**SOUTH SAMOYED net**	1	1	4,408	4,138		5.99	39	A	8		...					0....	14487
41-CABA	SELKUP cluster	1	1	4,408	4,138		5.99	39	A	8		...					0....	14488
41-CABA-a	selkup	1	1	4,408	4,708	0	5.99	39	A	8		...					0....	14489
41-CABA-b	kamas			0	0	0	0.00	0		8		...					0....	14495
42	**CAUCASIC zone**	26	118	8,449,113	8,901,613		28.36	53	B	63		PNB					2A.u.	14498
42-A	**CAUCASIAN-NW set**	12	19	1,335,867	1,600,683		3.34	32	A	41		PN.					2a...	14499
42-AA	CAUCASIAN-NW chain	12	19	1,335,867	1,600,683		3.34	32	A	41		PN.					2a...	14500
42-AAA	**CIRCASSIAN net**	12	17	1,292,162	1,555,563		3.38	33	A	41		PN.					2a...	14501
42-AAAA	CIRCASSIAN cluster	12	17	1,292,162	1,555,563		3.38	33	A	41		PN.					2a...	14502
42-AAAA-a	adyghe	3	3	4,785	4,708	0	0.02	29	A	41	Adyghe	PN.	1977	1991-1992		1994	2a...	14503
42-AAAA-b	cherkes	9	10	616,362	819,064	0	0.08	26	A	41		pn.					1a...	14510
42-AAAA-c	qaberdey	4	4	671,015	731,791	0	6.43	38	A	41	Kabardian	PN.	1991	1993		1993	1c...	14516
42-AAB	**ABKHAZ-ABAZIN net**	2	2	43,705	45,120		2.29	30	A	35		P..					0....	14524
42-AABA	ABKHAZ-ABAZIN cluster	2	2	43,705	45,120		2.29	30	A	35		P..					0....	14525
42-AABA-a	abkhaz					0				35	Abkhazian	P..	1912-1981				0....	14526
42-AABA-b	abazin	2	2	43,705	45,120		2.29	30	A	35	Abaza	p..					0....	14532
42-AAC	**UBYKH net**									8		...					0....	14538
42-AACA	UBYKH cluster			0	0		0.00	0		8		...					0....	14539
42-AACA-a	ubykh			0	0	0	0.00	0		8		...					0....	14540
42-B	**NORTHEAST CAUCASIAN set**	13	73	3,164,540	3,085,045		0.16	20	A	35		P..					2....	14543
42-BA	VEJNAKH chain	10	15	1,243,028	1,186,729		0.00	19	A	22		P..					0....	14544
42-BAA	**CHECHEN-INGUSH net**	10	14	1,239,799	1,183,363		0.00	19	A	22		P..					0....	14545
42-BAAA	CHECHEN-INGUSH cluster	10	14	1,239,799	1,183,363		0.00	19	A	22		P..					0....	14546
42-BAAA-a	ingush	4	4	273,581	260,295	0	0.01	20	A	22	Ingush	p..					0....	14547
42-BAAA-b	chechen	10	10	966,218	923,068	0	0.00	19	A	22	Chechen	P..	1986-1995				0....	14548
42-BAB	**BATS net**	1	1	3,229	3,366		0.06	20	A	2		...					0....	14557
42-BABA	BATS cluster	1	1	3,229	3,366		0.06	20	A	2		...					0....	14558
42-BABA-a	bats	1	1	3,229	3,366	0	0.06	20	A	2		...					0....	14559
42-BB	DAGESTAN chain	10	35	1,222,123	1,170,221		0.01	21	A	35		P..					1....	14560
42-BBA	**AVAR-ANDI- DIDO net**	8	21	729,258	699,877		0.01	20	A	35		P..					1....	14561
42-BBAA	AVAR cluster	8	8	664,387	638,979		0.01	20	A	35	Avar	P..	1979-1996				1....	14562
42-BBAA-a	North avar	8	8	664,387	638,979	0	0.01	20	A	35	Avar	P..	1979-1996				1....	14563
42-BBAA-b	Central avar					0				35		p..				1997	1....	14568
42-BBAA-c	South avar					0				35		p..					1....	14574
42-BBAB	ANDI cluster	1	8	50,618	47,518		0.02	16	A	12	Andi	...					0....	14581
42-BBAB-a	qwannab					0				12		...					0....	14582
42-BBAB-b	botlikh	1	1	4,290	4,028	0	0.05	21	A	12		...					0....	14589
42-BBAB-c	ghodoberi	1	1	2,939	2,759	0	0.00	14	A	12		...					0....	14592
42-BBAB-d	karatin	1	1	7,082	6,648	0	0.00	13	A	12		...					0....	14593
42-BBAB-e	tindal	1	1	6,759	6,345	0	0.00	13	A	12		...					0....	14597
42-BBAB-f	bagvalal	1	1	6,509	6,110	0	0.00	13	A	12		...					0....	14598
42-BBAB-g	gadyri					0				12		...					0....	14601
42-BBAB-h	gakvari					0				12		...					0....	14604
42-BBAB-i	gigatl	1	1	6,509	6,110	0	0.03	19	A	12		...					0....	14609
42-BBAB-j	akhvakh	1	1	5,907	5,545	0	0.05	17	A	12		...					0....	14610
42-BBAC	DIDO cluster	1	5	14,253	13,380		0.00	14	A	12		...					0....	14614
42-BBAC-a	didoi	1	1	6,965	6,538	0	0.00	13	A	12		...					0....	14615
42-BBAC-b	khvarshi	1	1	2,116	1,986	0	0.00	18	A	12		...					0....	14619
42-BBAC-c	ginukh	1	1	235	221	0	0.00	18	A	12		...					0....	14622
42-BBAC-d	kapuchin	1	1	2,939	2,759	0	0.00	17	A	12		...					0....	14623
42-BBAC-e	hunzib	1	1	1,998	1,876	0	0.00	10	A	12		...					0....	14627
42-BBB	**LAK-DARGWA net**	9	14	492,865	470,344		0.01	22	A	35		P..					1....	14630
42-BBBA	LAK cluster	6	6	127,837	124,104		0.01	20	A	35	Lak	P..	1996				1....	14631
42-BBBA-a	lak	6	6	127,837	124,104	0	0.01	20	A	35	Lak	P..	1996				1....	14632
42-BBBB	DARGWA cluster	8	8	365,028	346,240		0.01	23	A	35	Dargwa	P..	1996				1....	14639
42-BBBB-a	dargwa	8	8	365,028	346,240	0	0.01	23	A	35	Dargwa	P..	1996				1....	14640
42-BC	LEZGIAN chain	9	23	699,389	728,095		0.72	20	A	35		P..					2....	14652
42-BCA	**LEZGIAN net**	9	22	697,455	725,744		0.72	20	A	35		P..					2....	14653
42-BCAA	NORTH LEZGIN cluster	6	10	451,430	432,795		0.01	20	A	35		P..					2....	14654
42-BCAA-a	lezgin	5	5	315,290	304,782	0	0.01	21	A	35	Lezgi	P..	1990-1996			1996	1....	14655
42-BCAA-b	agul	1	1	17,720	16,635	0	0.04	17	A	35	Aghul	p..					1....	14664
42-BCAA-c	rutul	1	1	19,498	18,304	0	0.03	17	A	35	Rutul	p..					1....	14669
42-BCAA-d	tabarasan	3	3	98,922	93,074	0	0.00	17	A	35	Tabassaran	P..	1996			1997	2....	14674
42-BCAB	ARCHIN cluster	1	1	1,029	966		0.97	25	A	2		...					0....	14678
42-BCAB-a	archin	1	1	1,029	966	0	0.97	25	A	2		...					0....	14679
42-BCAC	SOUTH LEZGIN cluster	5	11	244,996	291,983		2.03	21	A	24		P..					0....	14680
42-BCAC-a	tsakhur	2	2	21,164	23,932	0	0.03	16	A	24	Tsakhur	p..					0....	14681
42-BCAC-b	budukh	1	1	5,413	6,581	0	0.09	21	A	24		p..					0....	14686
42-BCAC-c	kryz	1	1	7,806	9,490	0	0.00	16	A	24		p..					0....	14689
42-BCAC-d	udin	3	3	5,485	6,348	0	90.01	100	C	24	Udin	P..	1902				0....	14695
42-BCB	**KHINALUGI net**	1	1	1,934	2,351		0.00	15	A	4		...					0....	14698
42-BCBA	KHINALUGI cluster	1	1	1,934	2,351		0.00	15	A	4		...					0....	14699
42-BCBA-a	khinalugh	1	1	1,934	2,351	0	0.00	15	A	4		...					0....	14700
42-C	**KARTVELIAN set**	19	26	3,948,706	4,215,885		59.43	86	B	63		PNB					2A.u.	14701
42-CA	ZAN-GRUZIN chain	19	25	3,890,649	4,142,215		59.42	86	B	63		PNB					2A.u.	14702
42-CAA	**ZAN net**	2	3	591,330	654,604		1.23	32	A	20		...					0....	14703
42-CAAA	MEGREL cluster	1	1	451,601	470,743		1.00	33	A	20		...					0....	14704
42-CAAA-a	megrel	1	1	451,601	470,743	0	1.00	33	A	20		...					0....	14705
42-CAAB	LAZ cluster	2	2	139,729	183,861		1.99	28	A	4		...					0....	14708
42-CAAB-a	West laz					0				4		...					0....	14709
42-CAAB-b	East laz	1	1	1,866	1,945	0	1.02	32	A	4		...					0....	14712

Continued overleaf

Table 9-13 continued

Code 1	REFERENCE NAME / Autoglossonym 2	Coun 3	Peo 4	Mother-tongue speakers in 2000 5	in 2025 6	Media radio 7	CHURCH AC% 8	E% 9	Wld 10	Tr 11	Biblioglossonym 12	SCRIPTURES Print 13-15	P-activity 16	N-activity 17	B-activity 18	J-year 19	Jayuh 20-24	Ref 25
42-CAB	**GEORGIAN net**	19	22	3,299,319	3,487,611		69.85	96	C	63		PNB					2A.u.	14715
42-CABA	WEST GEORGIAN cluster	1	1	136,365	179,939		4.06	45	A	0		...					0A...	14716
42-CABA-a	imeruli	1	1	136,365	179,939	4	4.06	45	A	0		...					0A...	14717
42-CABA-b	rachuli					1				0		...					0c...	14720
42-CABA-c	lechkhum					1				0		...					0c...	14721
42-CABA-d	guruli					1				0		...					0c...	14722
42-CABA-e	adzhar					1				0		...					0c...	14723
42-CABB	EAST GEORGIAN cluster	18	21	3,162,954	3,307,672		72.68	98	C	63		PNB					2A.u.	14724
42-CABB-a	kharthuli	17	19	3,099,083	3,225,373	4	74.18	99	C	63	Georgian	PNB	1709-1982	1709-1993	1743-1989	1989	2A.u.	14725
42-CABB-b	ferejdan					1				63							1c.u.	14736
42-CABB-c	judeo-georgian	2	2	63,871	82,299	4	0.09	37	A	63		pnb					1A.u.	14737
42-CB	SVAN chain	1	1	58,057	73,670		60.00	97	B	2		...					0....	14738
42-CBA	**SVAN net**	1	1	58,057	73,670		60.00	97	B	2		...					0....	14739
42-CBAA	SVANURI cluster	1	1	38,057	39,670		60.00	99	B	2		...					0....	14740
42-CBAA-a	svanuri	1	1	38,057	39,670	0	60.00	99	B	2		...					0....	14741
42-CBAB	LASHKH-LENTEKH cluster	1	1	20,000	34,000		60.00	93	C	0		...					0....	14744
42-CBAB-a	lashkh					0				0		...					0....	14745
42-CBAB-b	lentekh					0				0		...					0....	14746
43	**SIBERIC zone**	1	7	31,033	29,133		7.92	38	A	12		...					0....	14747
43-A	**KET set**	1	1	1,234	1,159		6.00	35	A	4		...					0....	14748
43-AA	KET chain	1	1	1,234	1,159		6.00	35	A	4		...					0....	14749
43-AAA	**YENISEI-OSTYAK net**	1	1	1,234	1,159		6.00	35	A	4		...					0....	14750
43-AAAA	YENISEI-OSTYAK cluster	1	1	1,234	1,159		6.00	35	A	4		...					0....	14751
43-AAAA-a	ostik	1	1	1,234	1,159	0	6.00	35	A	4		...					0....	14752
43-B	**GILYAK set**	1	1	4,628	4,345		7.99	41	A	4		...					0....	14753
43-BA	GILYAK chain	1	1	4,628	4,345		7.99	41	A	4		...					0....	14754
43-BAA	**NIVKH net**	1	1	4,628	4,345		7.99	41	A	4		...					0....	14755
43-BAAA	NIVKH cluster	1	1	4,628	4,345		7.99	41	A	4		...					0....	14756
43-BAAA-a	amur-nivkh					0				4		...					0....	14757
43-BAAA-b	sakhalin-nivkh					0				4		...					0....	14758
43-C	**CHUKCHI-KAMCHATKAN set**	1	5	25,171	23,629		8.01	37	A	12		...					0....	14759
43-CA	CHUKCHI-KORYAK chain	1	4	24,789	23,270		7.05	36	A	12		...					0....	14760
43-CAA	**CHUKCHI net**	1	1	15,105	14,180		9.00	40	A	12		...					0....	14761
43-CAAA	CHUKOT cluster	1	1	15,105	14,180		9.00	40	A	12		...					0....	14762
43-CAAA-a	chukot	1	1	15,105	14,180	0	9.00	40	A	12	Chukot	...					0....	14763
43-CAB	**NAVARIN net**	1	1	15	14		20.00	53	B	8		...					0....	14773
43-CABA	KEREK cluster	1	1	15	14		20.00	53	B	8		...					0....	14774
43-CABA-a	kerek	1	1	15	14	0	20.00	53	B	8		...					0....	14775
43-CAC	**KORYAK-ALUTOR net**	1	2	9,669	9,076		3.99	30	A	12		...					0....	14778
43-CACA	KORYAK-ALUTOR cluster	1	2	9,669	9,076		3.99	30	A	12		...					0....	14779
43-CACA-a	koryak	1	1	8,934	8,386	0	4.00	30	A	12	Koryak	...					0....	14780
43-CACA-b	alutor					0				12		...					0....	14787
43-CB	KAMCHADAL chain	1	1	382	359		69.90	100	C	12		...					0....	14791
43-CBA	**KAMCHADAL net**	1	1	382	359		69.90	100	C	12		...					0....	14792
43-CBAA	ITELMEN cluster	1	1	382	359		69.90	100	C	12		...					0....	14793
43-CBAA-a	itelmen	1	1	382	359	0	69.90	100	C	12	Itelmen	...					0....	14794
44	**TRANSASIATIC zone**	61	322	156,921,579	200,748,803		1.12	44	A	72		PNB					4A.uh	14799
44-A	**TURKIC set**	60	269	148,836,333	190,980,897		1.13	44	A	72		PNB					4A.u.	14800
44-AA	TURKIC chain	60	269	148,836,333	190,980,897		1.13	44	A	72		PNB					4A.u.	14801
44-AAA	**BULGAR TURKIC net**	12	12	1,792,286	1,693,997		35.00	77	B	51		PN.					2....	14802
44-AAAA	CHUVASH cluster	12	12	1,792,286	1,693,997		35.00	77	B	51		PN.					2....	14803
44-AAAA-a	chuvash	12	12	1,792,286	1,693,997	0	35.00	77	B	51	Chuvash	PN.	1820-1996	1904-1911		1991	2....	14804
44-AAB	**SOUTHWEST TURKIC net**	60	257	147,044,047	189,286,900		0.71	44	A	72		PNB					4A.u.	14808
44-AABA	OGHUZ cluster	55	117	87,669,302	115,428,560		0.43	45	A	72		PNB					3A.u.	14809
44-AABA-a	osmanli	47	60	59,476,231	76,873,573	8	0.34	52	B	72	Turkish	PNB	1782-1985	1819-1991	1827-1941	1983	1A.u.	14810
44-AABA-b	gagauzi	7	7	583,530	695,520	1	29.99	51	B	72	Gagauz	Pnb	1927-1996				1c.u.	14827
44-AABA-c	crimea-tatar	10	13	564,326	683,289	1	0.01	25	A	72	Crimean Tatar*	PNb	1659-1996	1825			1c.u.	14831
44-AABA-d	judeo-crimean-tatar	1	1	486	667	1	0.00	24	A	72		pnb					1c.u.	14837
44-AABA-e	turkmen	12	12	5,398,497	7,898,232	1	0.01	27	A	72	Turkmen	PNb	1880-1994	1994		1991	3c.u.	14838
44-AABA-f	azeri	21	22	20,657,868	27,898,249	1	0.01	29	A	72	Azerbaijan*	PNB	1842-1891	1878-1995	1891		2a.u.	14851
44-AABA-g	teimurtash					1				72		pnb					1c.u.	14878
44-AABA-h	salchuq					1				72		pnb					1c.u.	14879
44-AABA-i	khalaj	1	1	40,533	56,555	1	0.00	16	A	72		pnb					1c.u.	14880
44-AABA-j	qashqai	1	1	947,831	1,322,475	1	0.00	17	A	72		pnb					1c.u.	14881
44-AABB	NORTHWEST TURKIC cluster	21	50	8,845,441	8,748,620		3.27	48	A	43		PN.					2A.u.	14882
44-AABB-a	Literary karachay-balkar	5	9	240,420	228,863	1	0.00	23	A	43	Karachay-balkar	PN.	1978-1995	1994			1c.u.	14883
44-AABB-b	karachay					1				43		pn.					1c.u.	14884
44-AABB-c	balkar					1				43		pn.					1c.u.	14885
44-AABB-d	kumyk	5	5	291,267	274,538	1	0.01	29	A	43	Kumuk*	Pn.	1888-1996			1993	1c.u.	14886
44-AABB-e	tatar	21	21	6,819,156	6,809,108	6	2.67	48	A	43	Tatar: Kazan	Pn.	1864-1995			1997	1c.u.	14893
44-AABB-f	baraba					1				43		pn.				1991	1c.u.	14909
44-AABB-g	bashqurt	11	11	1,487,996	1,429,796	4	7.18	54	B	43	Bashkir	Pn.	1899-1995			1991	1A.u.	14910
44-AABB-h	karaim	4	4	6,602	6,315	1	0.00	22	A	43	Karaite*	PN.	1819-1889	1842			1c.u.	14915
44-AABC	CENTRAL TURKIC cluster	20	37	15,763,619	18,411,444		0.02	38	A	43		PN.					4A.u.	14924
44-AABC-a	noghai	1	1	2,056	1,756	1	0.10	26	A	43	Nogay*	PN.	1659-1996	1666			1c.u.	14925
44-AABC-b	karakalpak	7	7	627,060	856,404	1	0.01	20	A	43	Karakalpak	Pn.	1996				1c.u.	14931
44-AABC-c	kazakh	19	19	11,811,949	13,256,644	4	0.03	41	A	43	Kazakh	PN.	1818-1989	1820-1910		1990	4A.u.	14936
44-AABC-d	kirghiz	10	10	3,322,554	4,296,640	4	0.02	32	A	43	Kirghiz	PN.	1982-1987	1991		1991	2r.u.	14942
44-AABD	EAST TURKIC cluster	23	50	34,317,695	46,277,750		0.38	43	A	63		PNB					2A.u.	14946
44-AABD-a	Central uzbek	19	19	22,854,002	31,240,417	5	0.09	47	A	63	Uzbek*	PNb	1891-1992	1992-1995		1990	1A.u.	14947
44-AABD-b	South uzbek	3	3	2,467,143	4,691,502	5	0.01	25	A	63		pnb					1c.u.	14956
44-AABD-c	West uyghur					1				63		pnb					1c.u.	14957

Continued opposite

Table 9-13 continued

Code 1	REFERENCE NAME / Autoglossonym 2	Coun 3	Peo 4	Mother-tongue speakers in 2000 5	in 2025 6	Media radio 7	CHURCH AC% 8	E% 9	Wld 10	Tr 11	Biblioglossonym 12	Print 13-15	P-activity 16	N-activity 17	B-activity 18	J-year 19	Jayuh 20-24	Ref 25
44-AABD-d	East uyghur	13	14	8,430,864	9,773,969	4	0.00	34	A	63	Uighur*	PNB	1898-1995	1914-1939	1950		1993 1r.u.	14960
44-AABD-e	salar	1	1	97,722	113,231	1	0.01	20	A	63		pnb					1c.u.	14977
44-AABD-f	West yugur	1	1	13,636	15,800	1	0.01	19	A	63		pnb					1c.u.	14978
44-AABD-g	altay-kizhi	1	2	98,754	92,705	1	38.51	79	B	63	Altai*	Pnb	1894-1910				1c.u.	14979
44-AABD-h	chulym	1	1	11,828	11,104	1	1.00	36	A	63		pnb					1c.u.	14984
44-AABD-i	ku-kizhi	2	2	16,511	15,650	1	70.00	100	C	63	Shor	pnb					1c.u.	14988
44-AABD-j	khakas	3	3	79,937	75,443	1	69.43	45	C	63	Khakas	Pnb	1995				1c.u.	14992
44-AABD-k	tuvin	3	3	246,563	247,239	1	1.43	41	A	63	Tuvin	Pnb	1995				1c.u.	15000
44-AABD-l	karagas	1	1	735	690	1	0.95	36	A	63		pnb				1996	2c.u.	15007
44-AABD-m	turkmen-tibet					1				63		pnb					1c.u.	15008
44-AABE	NORTHEAST TURKIC cluster	2	3	447,990	420,526		56.21	100	B	32		P..					2....	15009
44-AABE-a	yakut	2	2	441,407	414,347	2	56.00	100	B	32	Yakut	P..	1858-1995			1996	2....	15010
44-AABE-b	dolgan	1	1	6,583	6,179	1	70.00	100	C	32	Dolgan	p..					1....	15028
44-B	**MONGOL set**	10	38	7,779,079	9,427,609		1.05	41	A	68		PNB					3A..h	15031
44-BA	MONGOL chain	10	38	7,779,079	9,427,609		1.05	41	A	68		PNB					3A..h	15032
44-BAA	**MONGOLIAN net**	10	38	7,779,079	9,427,609		1.05	41	A	68		PNB					3A..h	15033
44-BAAA	MOGHOLI cluster	1	1	4,544	8,987		0.00	6	A	8		...					0....	15034
44-BAAA-a	mogholi	1	1	4,544	8,987	0	0.00	6	A	8		...					0....	15035
44-BAAB	MONGHOL cluster	9	31	6,987,204	8,506,337		1.16	45	A	68		PNB					3A..h	15037
44-BAAB-a	Historical monghol					1				68		pnb					1c..h	15038
44-BAAB-b	buryat	5	5	607,718	621,374	4	8.46	65	B	68	Buryat*	PNB	1819-1995	1840-1846	1846	1994	3A..h	15039
44-BAAB-c	halh	7	13	1,986,639	2,749,474	4	1.11	44	A	68	Mongolian: Khalka*	PNb	1979-1991	1990		1991	3A..h	15053
44-BAAB-d	kalmyk	7	7	571,223	683,202	1	0.09	34	A	68	Mongolian: Kalmyk*	PNb	1815-1887	1827-1894		1995	2c..h	15069
44-BAAB-e	oyrat	4	6	3,821,624	4,452,287	4	0.19	43	A	68	Mongolian: Inner*	PNb	1815-1995	1827-1952			1a..h	15073
44-BAAC	DAUR cluster	1	1	135,094	156,534		0.01	10	A	20		...					1....	15079
44-BAAC-a	daur	1	1	135,094	156,534	0	0.01	10	A	20		...					1....	15080
44-BAAD	TU cluster	1	2	215,392	249,576		0.03	13	A	20		...					0....	15084
44-BAAD-a	tu	1	2	215,392	249,576	0	0.03	13	A	20		...					0....	15085
44-BAAE	DONGXIANG-BONAN cluster	1	3	436,845	506,175		0.05	11	A	20		...					0....	15099
44-BAAE-a	dongxiang	1	1	416,391	482,475	0	0.05	11	A	20		...					0....	15100
44-BAAE-b	bonan	1	1	13,636	15,800	0	0.03	11	A	20		...					0....	15108
44-BAAE-c	shira-yugur	1	1	6,818	7,900	0	0.10	13	A	20		...					0....	15109
44-C	**TUNGUSIC set**	3	13	303,669	337,952		1.67	24	A	43		PN.					0....	15110
44-CA	TUNGUSIC chain	3	13	303,669	337,952		1.67	24	A	43		PN.					0....	15111
44-CAA	**TUNGUS net**	3	13	303,669	337,952		1.67	24	A	43		PN.					0....	15112
44-CAAA	EVEN cluster	1	1	17,044	16,000		4.00	32	A	24		P..					0....	15113
44-CAAA-a	even	1	1	17,044	16,000	0	4.00	32	A	24	Even	P..	1880				0....	15114
44-CAAB	EVENKI-SOLON cluster	3	4	70,504	75,690		5.11	33	A	24		P..					0....	15126
44-CAAB-a	evenki	3	3	62,802	66,766	0	5.37	35	A	24	Evenki	P..	1880				0....	15127
44-CAAB-b	solon					0				24		p..					0....	15153
44-CAAB-c	manegir					0				24		p..					0....	15154
44-CAAB-d	oroqen	1	1	7,702	8,924	0	3.00	23	A	24		p..					0....	15155
44-CAAC	MANCHU cluster	2	2	193,128	223,649		0.02	19	A	43		PN.					0....	15156
44-CAAC-a	negidal	1	1	588	552	0	1.02	32	A	43		pn.					0....	15157
44-CAAC-b	manchu	1	1	192,540	223,097	0	0.02	19	A	43	Manchu	PN.	1822	1835			0....	15160
44-CAAC-c	ju-chen			0	0	0	0.00	0		43		pn.					0....	15166
44-CAAD	UDIHE-OROCH cluster	1	2	3,070	2,882		4.53	34	A	8		...					0....	15167
44-CAAD-a	udihe	1	1	1,895	1,779	0	3.01	31	A	8		...					0....	15168
44-CAAD-b	oroch	1	1	1,175	1,103	0	6.98	38	A	8		...					0....	15176
44-CAAE	NANAI cluster	2	4	19,923	19,731		2.97	28	A	24		P..					0....	15181
44-CAAE-a	gold	1	1	11,872	11,145	0	4.00	32	A	24	Nanai	P..	1884				0....	15182
44-CAAE-b	akani					0				24		p..					0....	15188
44-CAAE-c	birar					0				24		p..					0....	15189
44-CAAE-d	kile					0				24		p..					0....	15190
44-CAAE-e	olcha	2	2	7,610	8,172	0	1.47	21	A	24		p..					0....	15191
44-CAAE-f	orok	1	1	441	414	0	0.91	27	A	24		p..					0....	15192
44-CAAE-g	samagir					0				24		p..					0....	15193
44-D	**YUKAGHIR set**	1	2	2,498	2,345		7.69	41	A	12		...					0....	15194
44-DA	YUKAGHIR chain	1	2	2,498	2,345		7.69	41	A	12		...					0....	15195
44-DAA	**ODUL net**	1	2	2,498	2,345		7.69	41	A	12		...					0....	15196
44-DAAA	ODUL cluster	1	2	2,498	2,345		7.69	41	A	12		...					0....	15197
44-DAAA-a	odul-tundra	1	1	1,763	1,655	0	8.00	42	A	12	Yukaghir, Northern	...					0....	15198
44-DAAA-b	odul-kolyma	1	1	735	690	0	6.94	39	A	12		...					0....	15199
45	**EAST ASIATIC zone**	54	97	206,387,843	213,869,830		12.36	73	B	61		PNB					2B.uh	15200
45-A	**KOREAN set**	35	36	75,967,890	87,960,718		27.78	83	B	61		PNB					2A...	15201
45-AA	KOREAN chain	35	36	75,967,890	87,960,718		27.78	83	B	61		PNB					2A...	15202
45-AAA	**CHOSEN net**	35	36	75,967,890	87,960,718		27.78	83	B	61		PNB					2A...	15203
45-AAAA	CHAOXIAN cluster	35	36	75,664,890	87,445,618		27.88	83	B	61		PNB					2A...	15204
45-AAAA-a	Historical chaoxian					1				61		pnb					1c...	15205
45-AAAA-b	kukŏ	35	36	75,664,890	87,445,618	6	27.88	83	B	61	Korean	PNB	1882-1961	1887-1983	1911-1993	1980	2A...	15206
45-AAAA-c	keijogo					1				61		pnb					1c...	15210
45-AAAA-d	West Central chaoxian.					1				61		pnb					1c...	15213
45-AAAA-e	East Central chaoxian.					1				61		pnb					1c...	15219
45-AAAA-f	cholla-do					1				61		pnb					1c...	15222
45-AAAA-g	p'yong'an-do					1				61		pnb					1c...	15225
45-AAAB	EAST KOREAN cluster	2	1	300,000	510,000		1.00	16	A	0		...					0....	15229
45-AAAB-a	hamgyong-do					0				0		...					0....	15230
45-AAAB-b	kyongsang-do					0				0		...					0....	15233
45-AAAC	CHEHU cluster	1	1	3,000	5,100		35.00	71	B	0		...					0....	15236
45-AAAC-a	chehu					0				0		...					0....	15237
45-B	**AINU set**	3	3	22,777	22,922		16.78	50	A	46		PN.					0A...	15238
45-BA	AINU chain	3	3	22,777	22,922		16.78	50	A	46		PN.					0A...	15239
45-BAA	**AYNU net**	3	3	22,777	22,922		16.78	50	A	46		PN.					0A...	15240
45-BAAA	SAKHALIN-AYNU cluster	2	2	7,571	8,384		0.26	19	A	46	Ainu	PN.	1889-1896	1897			0....	15241
45-BAAA-a	sakhalin-aynu			0	0	0	0.00	0	A	46		pn.					0....	15242
45-BAAA-b	taraika			0	0	0	0.00	0		46		pn.					0....	15249

Continued overleaf

Table 9-13 continued

Code 1	REFERENCE NAME / Autoglossonym 2	Coun 3	Peo 4	Mother-tongue speakers in 2000 5	in 2025 6	Media radio 7	CHURCH AC% 8	E% 9	Wld 10	Tr 11	Biblioglossonym 12	SCRIPTURES Print 13-15	P-activity 16	N-activity 17	B-activity 18	J-year 19	Jayuh 20-24	Ref 25
45-BAAB	HOKKAIDOO-AYNU cluster	1	1	15,206	14,538		25.00	65	B	45	Ainu	PN.	1889-1896	1897			0A...	15250
45-BAAB-a	ezo			0	0	0	0.00	0		45		pn.					0c...	15251
45-BAAB-b	yukar			0	0	0	0.00	0		45		pn.					0c...	15258
45-BAAC	KURILE cluster			0	0		0.00	0		0		...					0....	15259
45-BAAC-a	shikotan			0	0	0	0.00	0		0		...					0....	15260
45-C	**JAPANESE set**	38	58	130,397,176	125,886,190		3.38	67	B	61		PNB					1B.uh	15261
45-CA	JAPANESE chain	38	58	130,397,176	125,886,190		3.38	67	B	61		PNB					1B.uh	15262
45-CAA	**JAPANESE-CENTRAL net**	38	45	128,986,605	124,530,216		3.39	68	B	61		PNB					1B.uh	15263
45-CAAA	NIHON-GO cluster	38	45	128,986,605	124,530,216		3.39	68	B	61		PNB					1B.uh	15264
45-CAAA-a	koku-go	38	45	128,986,605	124,530,216	7	3.39	68	B	61	Japanese	PNB	1837-1992	1879-1993	1883-1987	1982	1c.uh	15265
45-CAAA-b	kyootuu-go					1				61		pnb					1c.uh	15268
45-CAAA-c	shitamachi-kotoba					1				61		pnb					1c.uh	15282
45-CAAA-d	kantoo					1				61		pnb					1c.uh	15283
45-CAAA-e	toohoku					1				61		pnb					1c.uh	15287
45-CAAA-f	kansai					1				61		pnb					1c.uh	15292
45-CAAA-g	kyuushuu					1				61		pnb					1c.uh	15312
45-CAAA-h	satsuma					1				61		pnb					1c.uh	15317
45-CAB	**IZU net**	1	1	5,000	8,500		1.00	16	A	0		...					0....	15318
45-CABA	HACHIJOO-JIMA cluster	1	1	3,000	5,100		1.00	16	A	0		...					0....	15319
45-CABA-a	hachijoo-jima	1	1	3,000	5,100	0	1.00	16	A	0		...					0....	15320
45-CABB	KO-JIMA cluster	1	1	2,000	3,400		1.00	16	A	0		...					0....	15321
45-CABB-a	ko-jima	1	1	2,000	3,400	0	1.00	16	A	0		...					0....	15322
45-CAC	**NANTO net**	3	13	1,405,571	1,347,474		2.90	41	A	24		P..					0....	15323
45-CACA	AMAMI-OKINAWA cluster	3	10	1,288,348	1,235,398		2.94	41	A	24		P..					0....	15324
45-CACA-a	kikai-shima	1	1	13,026	12,454	0	2.50	34	A	24		p..					0....	15325
45-CACA-b	North amami	1	1	75,813	72,484	0	2.40	37	A	24		p..					0....	15326
45-CACA-c	South amami	1	1	16,587	15,859	0	2.50	37	A	24		p..					0....	15329
45-CACA-d	toku-no-shima	1	1	38,394	36,708	0	3.00	36	A	24		p..					0....	15334
45-CACA-e	oki-no-erabu-shima	1	1	18,310	17,506	0	2.80	33	A	24		p..					0....	15337
45-CACA-f	yoron-jima	1	1	7,565	7,233	0	2.80	33	A	24		p..					0....	15340
45-CACA-g	iheya-jima					0				24		p..					0....	15341
45-CACA-h	kunigami	1	1	123,673	118,242	0	2.80	37	A	24		p..					0....	15345
45-CACA-i	luchu	3	3	994,980	954,912	0	3.01	43	A	24	Japanese: Luchu*	P..	1855-1858				0....	15357
45-CACA-j	South okinawa-mainland					0				24		p..					0....	15383
45-CACA-k	West okinawa-islands					0				24		p..					0....	15389
45-CACA-l	East okinawa islands					0				24		p..					0....	15394
45-CACB	SAKISHIMA-SHOTO cluster	1	3	117,223	112,076		2.40	40	A	6		...					0....	15400
45-CACB-a	miyako	1	1	67,450	64,488	7	2.70	45	A	6		...					0....	15401
45-CACB-b	yaeyama	1	1	47,492	45,407	1	2.00	34	A	6		...					0....	15408
45-CACB-c	yonaguni	1	1	2,281	2,181	1	2.02	32	A	6		...					0....	15417
46	**SOUTH ASIATIC zone**	31	284	105,161,730	142,554,225		7.97	65	B	82		PNB					4Asu.	15418
46-A	**BURUSHASKI set**	2	2	102,204	169,795		0.03	18	A	20		...					0....	15419
46-AA	BURUSHASKI chain	2	2	102,204	169,795		0.03	18	A	20		...					0....	15420
46-AAA	**BURUSHASKI net**	2	2	102,204	169,795		0.03	18	A	20		...					0....	15421
46-AAAA	BURUSHASKI cluster	2	2	102,204	169,795		0.03	18	A	20		...					0....	15422
46-AAAA-a	Proper burushaski	2	2	102,204	169,795	0	0.03	18	A	20	Burushaski	...					0....	15423
46-AAAA-b	Southwest burushaski					0				20		...					0....	15426
46-B	**NIHALI set**	1	1	6,285	8,249		9.99	34	A	3		...					0....	15428
46-BA	NIHALI chain	1	1	6,285	8,249		9.99	34	A	3		...					0....	15429
46-BAA	**KALTO-NIHALI net**	1	1	6,285	8,249		9.99	34	A	3		...					0....	15430
46-BAAA	KALTO-NIHALI cluster	1	1	6,285	8,249		9.99	34	A	3		...					0....	15431
46-BAAA-a	kalto	1	1	6,285	8,249	0	9.99	34	A	3		...					0....	15432
46-C	**MUNDA set**	4	36	11,838,466	15,598,614		9.51	60	B	63		PNB					3as..	15435
46-CA	NORTH MUNDA chain	4	28	11,143,376	14,684,976		7.50	59	B	63		PNB					3as..	15436
46-CAA	**MUNDA-NW net**	1	2	541,600	710,858		10.00	45	A	22		P..					0....	15437
46-CAAA	KORKU cluster	1	2	541,600	710,858		10.00	45	A	22	Korku	P..	1900-1981				0....	15438
46-CAAA-a	bouriya					0				22		p..					0....	15439
46-CAAA-b	bondoy-bopchi	1	1	39,026	51,222	0	10.00	39	A	22		p..					0....	15440
46-CAB	**NORTHEAST MUNDA net**	4	26	10,601,776	13,974,118		7.37	60	B	63		PNB					3as..	15445
46-CABA	KHERWARI cluster	4	26	10,601,776	13,974,118		7.37	60	B	63		PNB					3as..	15446
46-CABA-a	santali	4	7	6,845,086	9,039,256	4	3.65	61	B	63	Santali	PNB	1868-1989	1887-1962	1914-1994	1988	2as..	15447
46-CABA-b	karmali	1	1	168,166	220,721	1	1.00	32	A	63		pnb					1cs..	15452
46-CABA-c	turi	1	1	6,082	7,983	1	10.00	48	A	63		pnb					1cs..	15453
46-CABA-d	mundari	3	3	1,644,118	2,161,167	1	26.11	78	B	63	Mundari	PNB	1876-1965	1895-1996	1910-1932	1990	3cs..	15457
46-CABA-e	ho	2	2	1,133,916	1,488,409	1	0.55	40	A	63	Ho	PNb	1915-1987	1991-1996			1cs..	15462
46-CABA-f	bhumij	1	1	72,781	95,526	1	0.51	29	A	63		pnb					1cs..	15465
46-CABA-g	korwa	1	2	106,637	139,963	1	0.27	25	A	63	Majhi	pnb					1cs..	15470
46-CABA-h	asuri-birjia	1	2	12,873	16,896	1	14.88	49	A	63		pnb					1cs..	15474
46-CABA-i	koda-khaira	1	2	217,532	285,515	1	9.70	46	A	63		pnb					1cs..	15478
46-CABA-j	birhor	1	1	2,331	3,060	1	0.04	24	A	63		pnb					1cs..	15485
46-CABA-k	koraku					1				63		pnb					1cs..	15489
46-CABA-l	agariya	1	1	21,794	28,605	1	0.04	26	A	63		pnb					1cs..	15491
46-CABA-m	kol	1	1	116,774	153,268	* 1	60.00	100	B	63		pnb					1cs..	15492
46-CB	SOUTH MUNDA chain	2	8	695,090	913,638		41.65	76	B	61		PNB					0.s..	15493
46-CBA	**MUNDA-CENTRAL net**	2	3	339,497	446,916		65.24	93	C	23		P..					0....	15494
46-CBAA	KHARIA cluster	2	2	312,027	410,861		70.98	100	C	23		P..					0....	15495
46-CBAA-a	kharia	2	2	312,027	410,861	0	70.98	100	C	23	Kharia	P..	1951				0....	15496
46-CBAB	JUANG cluster	1	1	27,470	36,055		0.01	13	A	4		...					0....	15500
46-CBAB-a	juang	1	1	27,470	36,055	0	0.01	13	A	4		...					0....	15501
46-CBB	**KORAPUT net**	1	5	355,593	466,722		19.13	60	B	61		PNB					0.s..	15503
46-CBBA	SORA-PARENGI cluster	1	2	307,039	402,993		22.11	60	B	61		PNB					0.s..	15504
46-CBBA-a	sora	1	1	302,173	396,607	0	22.47	67	B	61	Sora	PNB	1939-1985	1965	1992		0.s..	15505
46-CBBA-b	juray					0				61		pnb					0.s..	15509
46-CBBA-c	parengi	1	1	4,866	6,386	0	0.00	22	A	61		pnb					0.s..	15510
46-CBBB	GUTOB-REMO cluster	1	2	44,398	58,274		0.25	18	A	12		...					0....	15511
46-CBBB-a	gutob	1	1	40,445	53,085	0	0.20	17	A	12	Gadaba	...					0....	15512

Continued opposite

Table 9-13 continued

Code 1	REFERENCE NAME / Autoglossonym 2	Coun 3	Peo 4	Mother-tongue speakers in 2000 5	in 2025 6	Media radio 7	AC% 8	E% 9	Wld 10	Tr 11	Biblioglossonym 12	Print 13-15	P-activity 16	N-activity 17	B-activity 18	J-year 19	Jayuh 20-24	Ref 25
46-CBBB-b	remo	1	1	3,953	5,189	0	0.81	23	A	12		...					0....	15515
46-CBBC	GTA cluster	1	1	4,156	5,455		0.05	16	A	4		...					0....	15516
46-CBBC-a	gta'	1	1	4,156	5,455	0	0.05	16	A	4		...					0....	15517
46-D	**NORTH MON-KHMER set**	7	62	4,373,283	5,886,082		22.88	63	B	72		PNB					4as..	15520
46-DA	MON-KHMER chain	2	3	1,215,511	1,610,257		48.39	99	B	72		PNB					2as..	15521
46-DAA	**KHASI net**	2	3	1,215,511	1,610,257		48.39	99	B	72		PNB					2as..	15522
46-DAAA	KHASI cluster	2	3	1,215,511	1,610,257		48.39	99	B	72		PNB					2as..	15523
46-DAAA-a	khasi-war	2	2	1,117,389	1,481,470	4	48.51	99	B	72	Khasi	PNB	1816-1891	1831-1991	1891	1997	2as..	15524
46-DAAA-b	pnar	1	1	98,122	128,787	8	47.00	99	B	72		pnb					1as..	15532
46-DAAA-c	amwi					1				72		pnb					1cs..	15533
46-DB	WEST PALAUNGIC chain	4	23	1,803,098	2,237,687		18.94	56	B	51		PN.					4....	15534
46-DBA	**WAIC net**	3	11	1,744,712	2,148,278		19.51	57	B	51		PN.					4....	15535
46-DBAA	WA cluster	2	4	1,509,845	1,870,917		22.15	62	B	43		PN.					4....	15536
46-DBAA-a	wa	2	2	677,067	855,041	4	11.48	56	B	43	Wa	PN.	1934	1938		1994	4....	15537
46-DBAA-b	son					1				43		pn.					1....	15541
46-DBAA-c	en					1				43		pn.					1....	15542
46-DBAA-d	la					1				43		pn.					1....	15543
46-DBAA-e	parauk	2	2	832,778	1,015,876	1	30.82	67	B	43	Parauk	PN.	1934-1935	1938			1....	15544
46-DBAB	LAWA cluster	2	3	100,853	117,302		3.05	28	A	51	Lawa, Western	PN.	1961-1967	1972			0....	15548
46-DBAB-a	la-oor	1	1	9,210	10,908	0	14.00	51	B	51	Lawa	PN.	1961	1971			0....	15549
46-DBAB-b	Literary lawa					0				51		pn.					0....	15550
46-DBAB-c	lawa-yunnan					0				51		pn.					0....	15551
46-DBAB-d	wiang-papao-lua	1	1	8,062	9,548	0	1.40	34	A	51	Lawa, Western	PN.	1961-1967	1972			0....	15552
46-DBAB-e	phalo					0				51		pn.					0....	15553
46-DBAB-f	phang					0				51		pn.					0....	15554
46-DBAC	BULANG cluster	3	4	134,014	160,059		2.23	21	A	12	Blang	...					0....	15555
46-DBAC-a	samtau	1	1	9,122	11,624	0	5.00	27	A	12		...					0....	15556
46-DBAC-b	phang					0				12		...					0....	15557
46-DBAC-c	kem-degne					0				12		...					0....	15558
46-DBAC-d	k'ala					0				12		...					0....	15559
46-DBAC-e	kontoi	1	1	1,302	1,542	0	4.99	27	A	12	Blang	...					0....	15560
46-DBAC-f	puman					0				12		...					0....	15561
46-DBB	**ANGKUIC net**	4	9	32,993	44,371		2.10	21	A	8		...					0....	15562
46-DBBA	ANGKU cluster	4	9	29,993	39,271		2.21	22	A	8		...					0....	15563
46-DBBA-a	kiorr	1	1	9,122	11,624	0	1.00	21	A	8		...					0....	15564
46-DBBA-b	angku					0				8		...					0....	15565
46-DBBA-c	a-mok					0				8		...					0....	15566
46-DBBA-d	pou-ma	4	6	18,472	24,867	0	2.93	22	A	8		...					0....	15567
46-DBBA-e	hu	1	1	1,263	1,463	0	1.98	21	A	8		...					0....	15568
46-DBBA-f	man-met	1	1	1,136	1,317	0	0.53	18	A	8		...					0....	15569
46-DBBB	TAI-LOI cluster	3	1	3,000	5,100		1.00	16	A	0		...					0....	15570
46-DBBB-a	tai-loi					0				0		...					0....	15571
46-DBBB-b	doi					0				0		...					0....	15572
46-DBBB-c	monglwe					0				0		...					0....	15573
46-DBC	**LAMET-KHAMET net**	2	3	25,393	45,038		1.02	19	A	12		...					0....	15574
46-DBCA	LAMET-KHAMET cluster	2	3	25,393	45,038		1.02	19	A	12	Lamet	...					0....	15575
46-DBCA-a	con	1	1	3,566	6,335	0	1.01	20	A	12		...					0....	15576
46-DBCA-b	lamet					0				12		...					0....	15577
46-DBCA-c	khamet					0				12		...					0....	15580
46-DC	EAST PALAUNGIC chain	3	12	472,207	597,914		2.71	28	A	24		P..					0r...	15581
46-DCA	**PALAUNG net**	3	12	472,207	597,914		2.71	28	A	24		P..					0r...	15582
46-DCAA	PALAUNG cluster	3	8	403,904	511,244		1.10	26	A	20	Palaung, Pale	...					0r...	15583
46-DCAA-a	pale					1				20		...					0c...	15584
46-DCAA-b	shwe	1	1	193,765	246,907	1	1.00	27	A	20		...					0c...	15588
46-DCAA-c	da'ang					1				20		...					0c...	15591
46-DCAA-d	rumai	1	1	2,020	2,341	1	0.00	12	A	20		...					0c...	15592
46-DCAA-e	manton					1				20		...					0c...	15595
46-DCAA-f	nam-hsan					1				20		...					0c...	15596
46-DCAB	RIANG-LANG cluster	2	3	55,910	70,879		3.86	28	A	24		P..					0....	15597
46-DCAB-a	riang-lang	2	2	49,789	63,079	0	1.87	24	A	24	Riang Lang	P..	1950				0....	15598
46-DCAB-b	yinchia	1	1	6,121	7,800	0	20.00	56	B	24		p..					0....	15601
46-DCAC	DANAU cluster	1	1	12,393	15,791		50.00	93	B	4		...					0....	15602
46-DCAC-a	danau	1	1	12,393	15,791	6	50.00	93	B	4		...					0....	15603
46-DD	KHMUIC chain	5	21	879,013	1,435,698		6.53	44	A	41		PN.					0....	15604
46-DDA	**BIT-KHAO net**	3	3	17,338	24,345		4.35	22	A	4		...					0....	15605
46-DDAA	BIT-KHAO cluster	3	3	17,338	24,345		4.35	22	A	4		...					0....	15606
46-DDAA-a	kha-bit	2	2	2,817	4,693	0	0.99	18	A	4		...					0....	15607
46-DDAA-b	khao	1	1	14,521	19,652	0	5.00	23	A	4		...					0....	15611
46-DDB	**KHMU net**	5	9	771,439	1,282,888		6.54	45	A	24		P..					0....	15612
46-DDBA	KHMU cluster	5	9	771,439	1,282,888		6.54	45	A	24		P..					0....	15613
46-DDBA-a	kha-khmu	5	5	764,474	1,271,249	4	6.57	46	A	24	Khmu'	P..	1918				0....	15614
46-DDBA-b	khuen	1	1	5,433	9,653	1	0.99	21	A	24	Khuen	p..					0....	15622
46-DDBA-c	hat	2	2	522	816	1	15.13	36	A	24		p..					0....	15623
46-DDBA-d	phsin					1				24		p..					0....	15624
46-DDC	**MAL-PRAY net**	2	5	70,166	98,832		2.37	28	A	41		PN.					0....	15625
46-DDCA	MAL cluster	2	2	25,542	42,763		2.52	32	A	41		PN.					0....	15626
46-DDCA-a	mal	2	2	25,542	42,763	0	2.52	32	A	41	Mal	PN.	1983	1994			0....	15627
46-DDCB	PRAY cluster	2	3	44,624	56,069		2.28	25	A	22		P..					0....	15630
46-DDCB-a	kha-phai	2	2	38,484	48,797	0	1.85	24	A	22	Phai	p..					0....	15631
46-DDCB-b	lua'	1	1	6,140	7,272	0	5.00	29	A	22	Lua	P..	1984				0....	15634
46-DDCB-c	pray					0				22		p..					0....	15637
46-DDD	**MLABRI-YUMBRI net**	2	2	475	691		1.05	24	A	12		...					0....	15640
46-DDDA	MLABRI cluster	2	2	475	691		1.05	24	A	12		...					0....	15641
46-DDDA-a	mlabri	2	2	475	691	0	1.05	24	A	12	Mlabri	...					0....	15642
46-DDDB	YUMBRI cluster			0	0		0.00	0		0		...					0....	15643
46-DDDB-a	yumbri			0	0	0	0.00	0		0		...					0....	15644
46-DDE	**PUOK-KHANG net**	2	2	19,595	28,942		23.37	48	A	2		...					0....	15645
46-DDEA	PUOK cluster	2	2	16,595	23,842		21.27	43	A	2		...					0....	15646
46-DDEA-a	kha-puok	2	2	16,595	23,842	0	21.27	43	A	2		...					0....	15647
46-DDEA-b	phong					0				2		...					0....	15652

Continued overleaf

Table 9-13 continued

Code 1	REFERENCE NAME / Autoglossonym 2	Coun 3	Peo 4	in 2000 5	in 2025 6	Media radio 7	AC% 8	E% 9	Wld 10	Tr 11	Biblioglossonym 12	Print 13-15	P-activity 16	N-activity 17	B-activity 18	J-year 19	Jayuh 20-24	Ref 25
46-DDEB	KHANG cluster	3	1	3,000	5,100		35.00	71	B	0		...					0....	15654
46-DDEB-a	khang					0				0		...					0....	15655
46-DE	MANGIC chain	3	3	3,454	4,526		19.63	41	A	2		...					0....	15659
46-DEA	**MANG net**	3	3	3,454	4,526		19.63	41	A	2		...					0....	15660
46-DEAA	MANG cluster	3	3	3,454	4,526		19.63	41	A	2		...					0....	15661
46-DEAA-a	mang-u					0				2		...					0....	15662
46-E	**VIETIC set**	22	45	73,221,874	98,635,574		7.75	69	B	82		PNB					1Asu.	15666
46-EA	MUONG-CUOI chain	2	21	1,164,478	1,594,375		5.18	40	A	23		P..					0as..	15667
46-EAA	**MUONG-BO net**	2	10	1,154,699	1,578,942		5.21	40	A	23		P..					0as..	15668
46-EAAA	MUONG-BO cluster	2	10	1,154,699	1,578,942		5.21	40	A	23		P..					0as..	15669
46-EAAA-a	muong	2	2	1,117,662	1,514,155	4	5.30	40	A	23	Muong	P..	1963				0as..	15670
46-EAAA-b	nguôn	2	2	2,156	3,493	1	4.27	28	A	23		p..					0cs..	15675
46-EAAA-c	kha-tong-luang	1	1	36	64	1	2.78	25	A	23	Luang	P..	1995				0cs..	15678
46-EAAA-d	bo					1				23		p..					0cs..	15679
46-EAAA-e	kha-pong	2	4	31,535	55,350	1	2.44	24	A	23		p..					0cs..	15682
46-EAB	**CHUT net**	2	7	5,846	9,060		2.45	21	A	4		...					0....	15683
46-EABA	CHUT cluster	2	7	5,846	9,060		2.45	21	A	4		...					0....	15684
46-EABA-a	ruc	2	2	1,108	1,868	0	4.51	24	A	4		...					0....	15685
46-EABA-b	may	2	2	1,885	3,011	0	1.86	20	A	4		...					0....	15686
46-EABA-c	sach	1	1	1,453	1,966	0	3.03	21	A	4		...					0....	15689
46-EABA-d	arem	2	2	1,400	2,215	0	1.00	19	A	4		...					0....	15690
46-EAC	**PAKATAN net**	1	2	1,654	2,940		2.06	20	A	4		...					0....	15693
46-EACA	PAKATAN cluster	1	2	1,654	2,940		2.06	20	A	4		...					0....	15694
46-EACA-a	thavung	1	1	827	1,470	0	2.06	20	A	4		...					0....	15695
46-EACA-b	phon-sung					0				4		...					0....	15696
46-EACA-c	pakatan					0				4		...					0....	15697
46-EAD	**CUOI net**	2	2	2,279	3,433		2.02	18	A	4		...					0....	15698
46-EADA	CUôI cluster	2	2	2,279	3,433		2.02	18	A	4		...					0....	15699
46-EADA-a	hung	1	1	1,453	1,966	0	2.00	18	A	4		...					0....	15700
46-EADA-b	poong					0				4		...					0....	15701
46-EADA-c	tum	1	1	826	1,467	0	2.06	19	A	4		...					0....	15702
46-EADA-d	uy-lô					0				4		...					0....	15703
46-EADA-e	không-khêng					0				4		...					0....	15704
46-EB	VIETNAMESE chain	22	23	72,046,664	97,028,764		7.79	70	B	82		PNB					1Asu.	15705
46-EBA	**VIETNAMESE net**	22	23	72,046,664	97,028,764		7.79	70	B	82		PNB					1Asu.	15706
46-EBAA	VIêT cluster	22	23	72,046,664	97,028,764		7.79	70	B	82		PNB					1Asu.	15707
46-EBAA-a	viêt	22	23	72,046,664	97,028,764	6	7.79	70	B	82		PNB					1Asu.	15708
46-EC	LAI chain	1	1	10,732	12,435		1.00	16	A	4		...					0....	15717
46-ECA	**LAI net**	1	1	10,732	12,435		1.00	16	A	4		...					0....	15718
46-ECAA	PALYU cluster	1	1	10,732	12,435		1.00	16	A	4		...					0....	15719
46-ECAA-a	palyu	1	1	10,732	12,435	0	1.00	16	A	4		...					0....	15720
46-F	**EAST MON-KHMER set**	11	100	14,317,862	20,596,942		3.68	49	A	72		PNB					2As.	15721
46-FA	KATUIC-BAHNARIC chain	5	81	2,358,606	3,455,950		19.16	50	B	42		PN.					0.s..	15722
46-FAA	**KATUIC-WEST net**	5	20	696,685	1,017,157		6.31	39	A	41		PN.					0.s..	15723
46-FAAA	SO-BRU cluster	4	16	400,699	624,587		9.88	44	A	41	So	PN.	1980				0.s..	15724
46-FAAA-a	kah-sô					1				41		pn.					0.s..	15725
46-FAAA-b	so-tri					1				41		pn.					0.s..	15729
46-FAAA-c	mangkong	4	8	98,214	130,798	1	7.50	37	A	41		pn.					0.s..	15732
46-FAAA-d	khua	2	2	7,828	12,894	1	1.00	24	A	41		pn.					0.s..	15733
46-FAAA-e	West bru	2	2	100,661	164,978	4	1.23	35	A	41		PN.					0.s..	15736
46-FAAA-f	West bru	1	1	67,897	91,886	4	45.00	90	B	41	Bru*	PN.	1968	1980-1981			0.s..	15739
46-FAAA-g	leung	1	1	5,433	9,653	1	0.99	24	A	41		pn.					0.s..	15742
46-FAAA-h	sapoin	1	1	2,717	4,826	1	1.99	26	A	41		pn.					0.s..	15743
46-FAAB	KUY-NYEU cluster	3	4	295,986	392,570		1.48	33	A	41		PN.					0....	15744
46-FAAB-a	kuy	3	3	294,144	390,388	0	1.48	33	A	41	Kuy	PN.	1965	1978-1992			0....	15745
46-FAAB-b	nyeu					0				41		pn.					0....	15752
46-FAB	**KATUIC-EAST net**	2	14	315,154	528,342		6.55	31	A	41		PN.					0....	15753
46-FABA	KATAANG cluster	1	1	20,000	34,000		1.00	16	A	0		...					0....	15754
46-FABA-a	kataang	1	1	20,000	34,000	0	1.00	16	A	0		...					0....	15755
46-FABB	TAOY cluster	2	3	78,636	131,260		1.94	26	A	12		...					0....	15756
46-FABB-a	ta'-oih	2	3	78,636	131,260	0	1.94	26	A	12	Taoih, Upper	...					0....	15757
46-FABB-b	tong					0				12		...					0....	15763
46-FABC	IN-ONG cluster	1	1	16,952	30,117		0.10	17	A	4		...					0....	15766
46-FABC-a	kha-in	1	1	16,952	30,117	0	0.10	17	A	4		...					0....	15767
46-FABC-b	ong					0				4		...					0....	15768
46-FABD	NGEQ-KHLOR cluster	1	1	16,613	29,515		28.91	53	B	12		...					0....	15769
46-FABD-a	North alak					0				12		...					0....	15770
46-FABD-b	ngeq	1	1	6,620	11,761	0	65.00	96	C	12	Ngeq	...					0....	15771
46-FABD-c	khlor	1	1	9,993	17,754	0	5.00	25	A	12		...					0....	15772
46-FABE	PACOH-PHUONG cluster	2	3	42,977	68,281		9.14	33	A	23		P..					0....	15773
46-FABE-a	pa-côh	2	2	34,283	56,516	0	8.92	34	A	23	Pacoh	P..	1965-1969				0....	15774
46-FABE-b	phuông	1	1	8,694	11,765	0	10.00	31	A	23		p..					0....	15777
46-FABF	KATU cluster	2	3	121,772	202,827		8.10	36	A	41		PN.					0....	15778
46-FABF-a	kantu	1	1	62,674	111,349	1	0.10	21	A	41		pn.					0....	15779
46-FABF-b	katu	2	2	59,098	91,478	4	16.59	52	B	41	Katu	PN.	1969	1978			0....	15783
46-FABF-c	thap					1				41		pn.					0....	15788
46-FABG	TARIANG cluster	1	1	8,275	14,701		1.99	20	A	4		...					0....	15789
46-FABG-a	tariang	1	1	8,275	14,701	0	1.99	20	A	4		...					0....	15790
46-FABH	KASENG cluster	1	1	9,929	17,641		1.50	20	A	3		...					0....	15791
46-FABH-a	kaseng	1	1	9,929	17,641	0	1.50	20	A	3		...					0....	15792
46-FAC	**NORTH BAHNARIC net**	3	23	549,687	763,896		23.12	57	B	41		PN.					0.s..	15793
46-FACA	EAST BAHNARIC cluster	2	17	372,531	519,063		25.67	56	B	23		P..					0....	15794
46-FACA-a	takua	1	1	13,044	17,653	1	25.00	52	B	23		p..					0....	15795
46-FACA-b	jeh	2	2	22,820	33,183	4	65.00	83	C	23	Jeh	P..	1967-1978				0....	15799
46-FACA-c	halang	2	2	22,777	33,106	4	20.20	56	B	23	Halang	P..	1970-1972				0....	15802
46-FACA-d	kayong	2	2	19,455	33,335	1	3.82	25	A	23		p..					0....	15805
46-FACA-e	cua	1	1	21,738	29,419	4	20.00	58	B	23	Cua	P..	1973				0....	15806

Continued opposite

Table 9-13 continued

Code 1	REFERENCE NAME / Autoglossonym 2	Coun 3	Peo 4	in 2000 5	in 2025 6	Media radio 7	AC% 8	E% 9	Wld 10	Tr 11	Biblioglossonym 12	Print 13-15	P-activity 16	N-activity 17	B-activity 18	J-year 19	Jayuh 20-24	Ref 25
46-FACA-f	katua	1	1	4,359	5,899	1	20.00	48	A	23		p..					0....	15814
46-FACA-g	doan	2	2	4,011	6,451	4	8.55	35	A	23		p..					0....	15815
46-FACA-h	rengao	1	1	26,081	35,296	4	25.00	55	B	23	Rengao	P..	1977				0....	15816
46-FACA-i	sedang	1	1	69,557	94,133	4	26.00	57	B	23		p..					0....	15820
46-FACA-j	todrah	1	2	18,034	24,405	1	23.11	51	B	23		p..					0....	15827
46-FACA-k	hre	1	1	145,222	196,530	4	26.00	58	B	23	Hre	P..	1967-1975				0....	15831
46-FACB	BAHNARIC-CENTRAL cluster	3	6	177,156	244,833		17.76	59	B	41		PN.					0.s..	15835
46-FACB-a	South alak	1	1	4,965	8,820	1	3.00	26	A	41		pn.					0.s..	15836
46-FACB-b	lamam	1	1	1,746	2,583	1	0.97	25	A	41		pn.					0.s..	15837
46-FACB-c	tampuan	1	2	21,839	32,319	1	1.00	28	A	41		pn.					0.s..	15838
46-FACB-d	bahnar	1	1	147,808	200,031	4	21.00	65	B	41	Bahnar	PN.	1952-1964	1971-1977			0.s..	15839
46-FAD	**WEST BAHNARIC net**	3	15	223,093	365,836		4.98	27	A	12		...					0....	15846
46-FADA	LAVEN cluster	2	4	122,420	203,978		8.12	30	A	2		...					0....	15847
46-FADA-a	laven	1	3	90,487	160,763	0	1.46	23	A	2		...					0....	15848
46-FADB	NYAHEUN-PROUAC cluster	1	1	6,628	11,776		2.01	26	A	2		...					0....	15849
46-FADB-a	nya-heun	1	1	6,628	11,776	0	2.01	26	A	2		...					0....	15850
46-FADB-b	prouac					0				2		...					0....	15851
46-FADC	BRAO-KRAVET cluster	3	5	57,325	84,844		1.00	22	A	12	Brao	...					0....	15852
46-FADC-a	brao	2	2	12,684	18,064	0	1.00	23	A	12	Brao	...					0....	15853
46-FADC-b	su	1	1	2,414	4,290	0	0.99	19	A	12		...					0....	15854
46-FADC-c	kravet	1	1	4,257	6,300	0	1.01	19	A	12		...					0....	15855
46-FADC-d	krung-2	1	1	37,970	56,190	0	1.00	23	A	12		...					0....	15856
46-FADD	OI-THE cluster	1	2	21,164	37,601		1.50	21	A	4		...					0....	15857
46-FADD-a	oi	1	1	17,542	31,166	0	1.50	22	A	4		...					0....	15858
46-FADD-b	the	1	1	3,622	6,435	0	1.49	21	A	4		...					0....	15863
46-FADE	SOK-SAPUAN cluster	1	3	15,556	27,637		0.87	21	A	4		...					0....	15864
46-FADE-a	sok	1	1	2,648	4,705	0	0.98	20	A	4		...					0....	15865
46-FADE-b	sapuan	1	1	3,972	7,056	0	0.50	23	A	4		...					0....	15866
46-FADE-c	cheng	1	1	8,936	15,876	0	1.00	20	A	4		...					0....	15867
46-FAE	**BAHNARIC SOUTHWEST net**	2	9	573,987	780,719		43.40	78	B	42		PN.					0.s..	15868
46-FAEA	MNONG cluster	2	4	253,942	347,074		23.97	61	B	22		P..					0.s..	15869
46-FAEA-a	pnong	2	2	114,779	158,744	4	22.71	61	B	22		p..					0.s..	15870
46-FAEA-b	biat					1				22		p..					0.s..	15877
46-FAEA-c	East mnong	1	1	69,709	94,338	4	25.00	63	B	22	Mnong, Eastern	P..	1977				0.s..	15878
46-FAEA-d	South mnong	1	1	69,454	93,992	4	25.00	58	B	22		p..					0.s..	15883
46-FAEB	KOHO cluster	1	2	214,867	290,781		67.80	97	C	42		PN.					0....	15889
46-FAEB-a	koho	1	2	214,867	290,781	4	67.80	97	C	42	Koho	PN.	1950-1966	1967			0....	15890
46-FAEC	STIENG-CHRAU cluster	2	3	105,178	142,864		40.45	80	B	41		PN.					0.s..	15904
46-FAEC-a	stieng	2	2	87,615	119,096	4	43.34	82	B	41	Stieng	Pn.	1971				0.s..	15905
46-FAEC-b	chrau	1	1	17,563	23,768	4	26.00	68	B	41	Chrau	PN.	1966-1985	1982			0.s..	15908
46-FB	KHMERIC chain	10	11	11,941,264	17,114,550		0.63	49	A	72		PNB					2A...	15918
46-FBA	**KHMERIC net**	10	11	11,941,264	17,114,550		0.63	49	A	72		PNB					2A...	15919
46-FBAA	KHMER cluster	10	11	11,941,264	17,114,550		0.63	49	A	72		PNB					2A...	15920
46-FBAA-a	Historical khmer	1	1	15,104	18,473	1	5.00	33	A	72	Khmer: Northern	PNb	1992	1994			1c...	15921
46-FBAA-b	khmae	8	8	10,838,278	15,807,818	5	0.67	49	A	72	Khmer*	PNB	1899-1933	1929-1993	1954	1980	2A...	15924
46-FBAA-c	North khmeer	1	1	1,087,061	1,287,440	5	0.10	45	A	72	Khmer, Northern	PNb		1996			1c...	15930
46-FBAA-d	West khmeer					1				72		pnb					1c...	15934
46-FBAA-e	kmer-krom					1				72		pnb					1c...	15938
46-FC	PEARIC chain	2	8	17,992	26,442		1.32	20	A	4		...					0....	15939
46-FCA	**WEST PEARIC net**	2	6	14,401	21,129		1.03	20	A	4		...					0....	15940
46-FCAA	SOMRAY cluster	1	2	3,840	5,682		0.99	20	A	4		...					0....	15941
46-FCAA-a	samrê	1	1	350	517	0	0.86	20	A	4		...					0....	15942
46-FCAA-b	somray	1	1	3,490	5,165	0	1.00	20	A	4		...					0....	15943
46-FCAB	CHONG cluster	2	3	10,211	14,930		1.03	20	A	4		...					0....	15946
46-FCAB-a	chong	2	2	9,339	13,639	0	1.03	20	A	4		...					0....	15947
46-FCAB-b	saoch	1	1	872	1,291	0	1.03	20	A	4		...					0....	15948
46-FCAC	SUOY cluster	1	1	350	517		1.43	21	A	4		...					0....	15949
46-FCAC-a	suoy					0				4		...					0....	15950
46-FCAC-b	angrak					0				4		...					0....	15951
46-FCB	**EAST PEARIC net**	1	2	3,591	5,313		2.48	21	A	3		...					0....	15952
46-FCBA	PEAR cluster	1	2	3,591	5,313		2.48	21	A	3		...					0....	15953
46-FCBA-a	pear	1	1	1,845	2,730	0	2.01	21	A	3		...					0....	15954
46-G	**SOUTH MON-KHMER set**	5	27	1,253,305	1,595,374		1.09	44	A	63		PNB					2.s..	15955
46-GA	MONIC chain	3	5	1,169,167	1,479,584		0.88	45	A	63		PNB					2....	15956
46-GAA	**MON-NYAHKUR net**	3	5	1,169,167	1,479,584		0.88	45	A	63		PNB					2....	15957
46-GAAA	MON cluster	3	4	1,165,729	1,475,512		0.88	45	A	63		PNB					2....	15958
46-GAAA-a	Historical mon					0				63		pnb					1....	15959
46-GAAA-b	Literary mon					0				63		pnb					1....	15960
46-GAAA-c	mon-te	1	1	1,056,469	1,346,216	0	0.90	46	A	63	Mon	PNB	1843-1904	1847	1928	1996	2....	15961
46-GAAA-d	mon-nya					0				63		pnb					1....	15965
46-GAAA-e	talaing	1	1	105,220	124,615	0	0.70	36	A	63		pnb					1....	15970
46-GAAA-f	mon-tang					0				63		pnb					1....	15971
46-GAAB	NYAH-KUR cluster	1	1	3,438	4,072		0.70	23	A	12	Nyahkur	...					0....	15972
46-GAAB-a	nyah-kur	1	1	3,438	4,072	0	0.70	23	A	12	Nyahkur	...					0....	15973
46-GB	NORTH ASLIAN chain	3	17	70,081	96,221		4.30	32	A	23		P..					0.s..	15977
46-GBA	**SEMANG net**	3	11	20,361	27,000		1.94	24	A	12		...					0....	15978
46-GBAA	NORTH SEMANG cluster	3	7	17,014	22,339		1.92	23	A	12		...					0....	15979
46-GBAA-a	tonga	1	1	111	155	0	0.90	22	A	12		...					0....	15980
46-GBAA-b	kensiu	3	5	16,719	21,966	0	1.90	23	A	12	Kensiu	...					0....	15985
46-GBAB	SOUTH SEMANG cluster	1	4	3,347	4,661		2.03	30	A	4		...					0....	16009
46-GBAB-a	jehai	1	1	1,973	2,747	0	1.01	29	A	4		...					0....	16010
46-GBAB-b	mendriq	1	1	198	276	0	1.52	27	A	4		...					0....	16014
46-GBAB-c	batek	1	1	1,103	1,536	0	3.99	31	A	4		...					0....	16015
46-GBAB-d	deq					0				4		...					0....	16021
46-GBAB-e	nong					0				4		...					0....	16023
46-GBAB-f	mintil	1	1	73	102	0	1.37	30	A	4		...					0....	16024
46-GBB	**CHEWONG net**	1	1	489	681		0.41	24	A	4		...					0....	16025
46-GBBA	CHEWONG cluster	1	1	489	681		0.41	24	A	4		...					0....	16026
46-GBBA-a	che'wong	1	1	489	681	0	0.41	24	A	4		...					0....	16027
46-GBC	**SENOIC net**	1	5	49,231	68,540		5.31	36	A	23		P..					0.s..	16031

Continued overleaf

Table 9-13 continued

Code 1	REFERENCE NAME Autoglossonym 2	Coun 3	Peo 4	Mother-tongue speakers in 2000 5	in 2025 6	Media radio 7	AC% 8	E% 9	Wld 10	Tr 11	Biblioglossonym 12	Print 13-15	P-activity 16	N-activity 17	B-activity 18	J-year 19	Jayuh 20-24	Ref 25
46-GBCA	LANOH-TEMIAR cluster	1	4	20,318	28,287		5.03	31	A	4		. . .					0....	16032
46-GBCA-a	lanoh	1	3	2,029	2,825	0	0.84	25	A	4		. . .					0....	16033
46-GBCA-b	temiar	1	1	18,289	25,462	0	5.50	31	A	4		. . .					0....	16038
46-GBCB	SEMAI cluster	1	1	28,913	40,253		5.50	40	A	23		P..					0.s..	16051
46-GBCB-a	semai	1	1	28,913	40,253	0	5.50	40	A	23	Senoi*	P..	1951-1962				0.s..	16052
46-GC	SOUTH ASLIAN chain	1	4	10,204	14,205		2.87	30	A	43		PN.					0....	16065
46-GCA	SEMELAIC net	1	4	10,204	14,205		2.87	30	A	43		PN.					0....	16066
46-GCAA	SEMELAI-TEMOQ cluster	1	3	8,064	11,226		3.40	30	A	4		. . .					0....	16067
46-GCAA-a	semaq-beri	1	1	3,281	4,568	0	2.99	31	A	4		. . .					0....	16068
46-GCAA-b	semelai	1	1	4,231	5,890	0	3.99	29	A	4		. . .					0....	16072
46-GCAA-c	semaq-palong					0				4		. . .					0....	16073
46-GCAA-d	chiong-biduanda					0				4		. . .					0....	16074
46-GCAA-e	temoq	1	1	552	768	0	1.27	29	A	4		. . .					0....	16075
46-GCAB	BESISI cluster	1	1	2,140	2,979		0.89	30	A	43		PN.					0....	16076
46-GCAB-a	besisi	1	1	2,140	2,979	0	0.89	30	A	43	Besisi	PN.		1933			0....	16077
46-GD	JAH-HUT chain	1	1	3,853	5,364		2.00	27	A	4		. . .					0....	16086
46-GDA	JAH-HUT net	1	1	3,853	5,364		2.00	27	A	4		. . .					0....	16087
46-GDAA	JAH-HUT cluster	1	1	3,853	5,364		2.00	27	A	4		. . .					0....	16088
46-GDAA-a	jah-hut	1	1	3,853	5,364	0	2.00	27	A	4		. . .					0....	16089
46-H	NICOBARESE set	1	7	47,742	62,664		81.10	100	C	62		PNB					0....	16097
46-HA	NICOBARESE chain	1	7	47,742	62,664		81.10	100	C	62		PNB					0....	16098
46-HAA	NICOBARESE net	1	5	47,438	62,265		81.42	100	C	62		PNB					0....	16099
46-HAAA	NICOBAR cluster	1	5	47,438	62,265		81.42	100	C	62		PNB					0....	16100
46-HAAA-a	car	1	1	31,119	40,845	0	81.00	100	C	62	Nicobarese: Car*	PNB	1913-1954	1940	1969		0....	16101
46-HAAA-b	tutet	1	1	2,027	2,661	0	80.02	100	C	62		pnb					0....	16102
46-HAAA-c	taih-long	1	1	2,027	2,661	0	80.02	100	C	62		pnb					0....	16103
46-HAAA-d	Central nicobar	1	1	7,197	9,446	0	84.99	100	C	62	Nicobarese, Central	Pnb	1884-1890				0....	16106
46-HAAA-e	nicobara	1	1	5,068	6,652	0	80.01	100	C	62		pnb					0....	16111
46-HAB	SHOM-PENGIC net	1	2	304	399		31.58	59	B	4		. . .					0....	16114
46-HABA	SHOM-PENG cluster	1	2	304	399		31.58	59	B	4		. . .					0....	16115
46-HABA-a	shom-peng	1	2	304	399	0	31.58	59	B	4		. . .					0....	16116
46-I	NORTH ANDAMANESE set									0		. . .					0....	16119
46-IA	NORTH ANDAMANESE chain									0		. . .					0....	16120
46-IAA	NORTH ANDAMANESE net									0		. . .					0....	16121
46-IAAA	AKA-CARI cluster			0	0		0.00	0		0		. . .					0....	16122
46-IAAA-a	aka-cari			0	0	0	0.00	0		0		. . .					0....	16123
46-IAAB	AKA-KORA cluster			0	0		0.00	0		0		. . .					0....	16124
46-IAAB-a	aka-kora			0	0	0	0.00	0		0		. . .					0....	16125
46-IAAC	AKA-BO cluster			0	0		0.00	0		0		. . .					0....	16126
46-IAAC-a	aka-bo			0	0	0	0.00	0		0		. . .					0....	16127
46-IAAD	AKA-JERU cluster			0	0		0.00	0		0		. . .					0....	16128
46-IAAD-a	aka-jeru			0	0	0	0.00	0		0		. . .					0....	16129
46-J	ANDAMANIC-CENTRAL set	1	1	101	133		29.70	65	B	9		. . .					0....	16130
46-JA	ANDAMANIC-CENTRAL chain	1	1	101	133		29.70	65	B	9		. . .					0....	16131
46-JAA	ANDAMANIC-CENTRAL net	1	1	101	133		29.70	65	B	9		. . .					0....	16132
46-JAAA	KEDE cluster			0	0		0.00	0		0		. . .					0....	16133
46-JAAA-a	aka-kede			0	0	0	0.00	0		0		. . .					0....	16134
46-JAAB	KOL cluster			0	0		0.00	0		9		. . .					0....	16135
46-JAAB-a	aka-kol			0	0	0	0.00	0		9		. . .					0....	16136
46-JAAC	JUWOI cluster			0	0		0.00	0		0		. . .					0....	16137
46-JAAC-a	oko-juwoi			0	0	0	0.00	0		0		. . .					0....	16138
46-JAAD	PUCIKWAR cluster	1	1	101	133		29.70	65	B	9		. . .					0....	16139
46-JAAD-a	a-pucikwar	1	1	101	133	0	29.70	65	B	9		. . .					0....	16140
46-JAAE	BALE cluster			0	0		0.00	0		0		. . .					0....	16141
46-JAAE-a	North akar-bale			0	0	0	0.00	0		0		. . .					0....	16142
46-JAAE-b	South akar-bale			0	0	0	0.00	0		0		. . .					0....	16143
46-JAAF	BEA cluster									0		. . .					0....	16144
46-JAAF-a	aka-bea					0				0		. . .					0....	16145
46-K	SOUTH ANDAMANIC set	1	3	608	798		9.05	37	A	4		. . .					0....	16146
46-KA	SOUTH ANDAMANIC chain	1	3	608	798		9.05	37	A	4		. . .					0....	16147
46-KAA	ANDAMANIC-SOUTH net	1	3	608	798		9.05	37	A	4		. . .					0....	16148
46-KAAA	SENTINEL cluster	1	1	101	133		4.95	30	A	4		. . .					0....	16149
46-KAAA-a	sentinel	1	1	101	133	0	4.95	30	A	4		. . .					0....	16150
46-KAAB	JARAWA cluster	1	1	304	399		9.87	39	A	4		. . .					0....	16151
46-KAAB-a	jarawa	1	1	304	399	0	9.87	39	A	4		. . .					0....	16152
46-KAAC	ONGE cluster	1	1	203	266		9.85	37	A	4		. . .					0....	16153
46-KAAC-a	onge	1	1	203	266	0	9.85	37	A	4		. . .					0....	16154
47	DAIC zone	18	125	96,885,339	116,954,462		1.43	49	A	82		PNB					3Asuh	16156
47-A	BE-KAM-TAI set	18	111	94,168,686	113,790,020		1.45	49	A	82		PNB					3Asuh	16157
47-AA	KAM-TAI chain	18	104	90,869,247	109,966,941		1.49	50	B	82		PNB					3Asuh	16158
47-AAA	TAI net	18	102	90,611,686	109,668,503		1.49	50	B	82		PNB					3Asuh	16159
47-AAAA	NORTHWEST TAI cluster	7	27	6,011,706	7,502,593		0.84	42	A	72		PNB					3.s..	16160
47-AAAA-a	ahom					1				72		pnb					1.s..	16161
47-AAAA-b	aiton	1	1	10,137	13,304	1	0.50	34	A	72		pnb					1.s..	16164
47-AAAA-c	phake	1	1	10,137	13,304	1	0.50	33	A	72		pnb					1.s..	16165
47-AAAA-d	khamti	2	2	4,756	6,086	1	0.69	32	A	72		pnb					1.s..	16166

Continued opposite

Table 9-13 continued

Code 1	REFERENCE NAME Autoglossonym 2	Coun 3	Peo 4	Mother-tongue speakers in 2000 5	in 2025 6	Media radio 7	AC% 8	E% 9	Wld 10	Tr 11	Biblioglossonym 12	Print 13-15	P-activity 16	N-activity 17	B-activity 18	J-year 19	Jayuh 20-24	Ref 25
47-AAAA-e	shan	3	5	4,291,485	5,330,628	4	0.75	47	A	72	Shan*	PNB	1871-1994	1994	1892	1993	3.s..	16170
47-AAAA-f	tai-neua	3	5	765,934	986,418	1	0.15	28	A	72	Chinese: Shanghai*	PNB	1847-1948	1870	1908		1.s..	16175
47-AAAA-g	tai-lü	5	7	673,519	839,093	1	1.83	33	A	72	Lu	PNb	1921-1932	1933			1.s..	16179
47-AAAA-h	tai-ya	1	4	218,044	252,648	1	1.00	25	A	72	Tai: Ya	Pnb	1922				1.s..	16185
47-AAAB	THAI cluster	14	25	39,481,120	47,015,671		1.77	59	B	71		PNB					3asuh	16189
47-AAAB-a	yuan	2	2	6,514,805	7,721,400	6	0.90	53	B	71	Tai, Northern	PNB	1867-1968	1914	1927		1csuh	16190
47-AAAB-b	lanna					1				71		pnb					1csuh	16191
47-AAAB-c	phuan	2	2	205,742	308,349	1	1.75	35	A	71		pnb					1csuh	16202
47-AAAB-d	Central thai	14	20	27,933,462	33,269,030	6	2.11	62	B	71	Thai*	PNB	1834-1967	1843-1977	1990	1980	3asuh	16209
47-AAAB-e	Literary thai					1				71		pnb					1csuh	16211
47-AAAB-f	pak-thai	1	1	4,827,111	5,716,892	1	1.00	47	A	71		pnb					1csuh	16214
47-AAAB-g	thai-islam					1				71		pnb					1csuh	16224
47-AAAC	LAOTIAN cluster	9	12	19,409,682	24,596,694	5	1.35	54	B	82		PNB					2As..	16236
47-AAAC-a	isan	2	4	16,325,136	19,335,316	5	1.40	53	B	82	Tai, Northeastern	PNB			1932		2cs..	16237
47-AAAC-b	lao	8	8	3,084,546	5,261,378	5	1.06	57	B	82	Lao	PNB	1906-1967	1926-1973	1932-1996	1992	2As..	16245
47-AAAD	PHU-TAI cluster	6	13	1,390,075	1,886,475		4.31	38	A	23		P..					0....	16256
47-AAAD-a	tai-dam	6	6	747,231	1,018,601	4	4.28	40	A	23	Tai: Dam*	P..	1982-1993				0....	16257
47-AAAD-b	tai-kao	4	4	476,746	629,600	4	4.28	36	A	23	Tai: White*	P..	1969				0....	16261
47-AAAD-c	tai-deng	2	2	160,877	231,208	1	4.00	29	A	23		p..					0....	16265
47-AAAD-d	tai-hang-tong					1				23		p..					0....	16268
47-AAAD-e	tai-man-tanh					1				23		p..					0....	16269
47-AAAD-f	tai-jo					1				23		p..					0....	16270
47-AAAD-g	tai-khang	1	1	5,221	7,066	1	20.00	49	A	23		p..					0....	16271
47-AAAE	HUANG-NUNG cluster	6	15	7,991,775	9,720,907		1.04	31	A	23		P..					0....	16272
47-AAAE-a	South Huang	4	10	6,964,853	8,339,383	4	0.95	33	A	23		P..					0....	16273
47-AAAE-b	tai-nung	4	5	1,026,922	1,381,524	1	1.67	22	A	23	Nung	P..	1971-1975				0....	16280
47-AAAE-c	lei-ping					1				23		p..					0....	16284
47-AAAE-d	kjang e					1				23		p..					0....	16285
47-AAAF	HUANG-CHIA cluster	4	5	566,455	683,611		1.78	22	A	20		...					0....	16286
47-AAAF-a	saek	2	2	44,335	71,493	0	0.20	25	A	20		...					0....	16287
47-AAAF-b	giay					0				20		...					0....	16290
47-AAAF-c	nhang	2	2	269,609	319,532	0	2.77	22	A	20		...					0....	16291
47-AAAF-d	gui-zhou					0				20		...					0....	16294
47-AAAF-e	biay					0				20		...					0....	16297
47-AAAF-f	ce-heng					0				20		...					0....	16298
47-AAAF-g	zhong-jia	1	1	252,511	292,586	0	1.00	22	A	20		...					0....	16299
47-AAAF-h	du-shan					0				20		...					0....	16305
47-AAAF-i	gui-yang					0				20		...					0....	16306
47-AAAF-j	ling-yün					0				20		...					0....	16307
47-AAAF-k	lung-an					0				20		...					0....	16308
47-AAAF-l	pa-di					0				20		...					0....	16309
47-AAAF-m	phu-la					0				20		...					0....	16310
47-AAAF-n	po-se					0				20		...					0....	16311
47-AAAF-o	tian-zhu					0				20		...					0....	16312
47-AAAF-p	tien-pa					0				20		...					0....	16313
47-AAAF-q	tu-di					0				20		...					0....	16314
47-AAAF-r	tu-lao					0				20		...					0....	16315
47-AAAF-s	xi-lin					0				20		...					0....	16316
47-AAAG	HUANG-CHUANG cluster	1	2	12,922,017	14,972,811		1.00	42	A	32		P..					1r...	16317
47-AAAG-a	qian-jang	1	1	126,256	146,293	1	0.50	25	A	32		p..					1c...	16318
47-AAAG-b	ching-hsi					1				32		p..					1c...	16319
47-AAAG-c	hung-ho					1				32		p..					1c...	16320
47-AAAG-d	kuei-pien					1				32		p..					1c...	16321
47-AAAG-e	kuang					1				32		p..					1c...	16322
47-AAAG-f	lin-chiang					1				32		p..					1c...	16323
47-AAAG-g	ma					1				32		p..					1c...	16324
47-AAAG-h	qiu-bei					1				32		p..					1c...	16325
47-AAAG-i	te					1				32		p..					1c...	16326
47-AAAG-j	tso-chiang					1				32		p..					1c...	16327
47-AAAG-k	t'u					1				32		p..					1c...	16328
47-AAAG-l	wen					1				32		p..					1c...	16329
47-AAAG-m	yen					1				32		p..					1c...	16330
47-AAAG-n	wu-ming	1	1	12,795,761	14,826,518	4	1.00	42	A	32	Zhuang, Northern	P..	1904			1992	1r...	16331
47-AAAG-o	yu-chiang					1				32		p..					1c...	16332
47-AAAG-p	yung-nan					1				32		p..					1c...	16333
47-AAAG-q	yung-pei					1				32		p..					1c...	16334
47-AAAH	BUYI cluster	2	3	2,838,856	3,289,741		2.00	32	A	20		...					0....	16335
47-AAAH-a	bu-yi	2	2	2,836,078	3,286,523	0	2.00	32	A	20	Bouyei	...					0....	16336
47-AAAH-b	ju-yi					0				20		...					0....	16339
47-AAB	**MAONAN net**	1	1	80,172	92,896		6.00	30	A	20		...					0....	16340
47-AABA	MAONAN cluster	1	1	80,172	92,896		6.00	30	A	20		...					0....	16341
47-AABA-a	mao-nan	1	1	80,172	92,896	0	6.00	30	A	20		...					0....	16342
47-AAC	**MULAO net**	1	1	177,389	205,542		1.50	26	A	20		...					0....	16343
47-AACA	MULAO cluster	1	1	177,389	205,542		1.50	26	A	20		...					0....	16344
47-AACA-a	mu-lao	1	1	177,389	205,542	0	1.50	26	A	20		...					0....	16345
47-AB	KAM-LAKA chain	1	7	3,299,439	3,823,079		0.28	23	A	43		PN.					0....	16346
47-ABA	**KAM-SUI net**	1	6	3,289,465	3,811,522		0.26	23	A	43		PN.					0....	16347
47-ABAA	KAM cluster	1	2	2,863,605	3,318,075		0.23	23	A	20		...					0....	16348
47-ABAA-a	kam	1	2	2,863,605	3,318,075	0	0.23	23	A	20		...					0....	16349
47-ABAB	CHING cluster	1	1	12,626	14,629		0.52	21	A	43		PN.					0....	16353
47-ABAB-a	ching-cham	1	1	12,626	14,629	0	0.52	21	A	43		pn.					0....	16354
47-ABAB-b	mak					0				43		pn.					0....	16355
47-ABAB-c	chi					0				43		pn.					0....	16356
47-ABAB-d	hwa					0				43	Miao: Hwa	PN.	1907	1917			0....	16357
47-ABAB-e	lyo					0				43		pn.					0....	16358
47-ABAB-f	mo-chia					0				43	Chung-chia	Pn.	1904				0....	16359
47-ABAC	SUI cluster	1	2	387,983	449,559		0.50	22	A	20		...					0....	16360
47-ABAC-a	sui-chia	1	1	385,332	446,487	0	0.50	23	A	20		...					0....	16361
47-ABAC-b	san-tung									20		...					0....	16362
47-ABAC-c	sui-ai	1	1	2,651	3,072	0	1.02	17	A	20		...					0....	16363
47-ABAC-d	sui-li					0				20		...					0....	16364
47-ABAC-e	sui-po					0				20		...					0....	16365
47-ABAD	TEN cluster	1	1	25,251	29,259		0.52	18	A	4		...					0....	16366
47-ABAD-a	ten	1	1	25,251	29,259	0	0.52	18	A	4		...					0....	16367
47-ABAD-b	yang-huang					0				4		...					0....	16368
47-ABAD-c	rau					0				4		...					0....	16369
47-ABB	**TAI-LAKA net**	1	1	9,974	11,557		4.00	26	A	24		P..					0....	16370
47-ABBA	LAKA cluster	1	1	9,974	11,557		4.00	26	A	24		P..					0....	16371
47-ABBA-a	laka	1	1	9,974	11,557	0	4.00	26	A	24	Laka	P..	1912-1936				0....	16372
47-B	**KADAI set**	2	14	2,716,653	3,164,442		0.80	22	A	24		P..					0....	16373
47-BA	BE chain	1	1	655,519	759,554		0.50	22	A	20		....					0....	16374

Continued overleaf

Table 9-13 continued

Code 1	REFERENCE NAME Autoglossonym 2	Coun 3	Peo 4	Mother-tongue speakers in 2000 5	in 2025 6	Media radio 7	CHURCH AC% 8	E% 9	Wld 10	Tr 11	Biblioglossonym 12	SCRIPTURES Print 13-15	P-activity 16	N-activity 17	B-activity 18	J-year 19	Jayuh 20-24	Ref 25
47-BAA	**BE net**	1	1	655,519	759,554		0.50	22	A	20		. . .					0	16375
47-BAAA	ONG-BE cluster	1	1	655,519	759,554		0.50	22	A	20		. . .					0	16376
47-BAAA-a	ong-be	1	1	655,519	759,554	0	0.50	22	A	20		. . .					0	16377
47-BB	LI-LAQUA chain	2	8	1,531,211	1,776,063		0.92	24	A	20		. . .					0	16381
47-BBA	**LI-NGAO net**	1	5	1,521,380	1,762,833		0.90	24	A	20		. . .					0	16382
47-BBAA	LI cluster	1	2	1,298,918	1,505,064		0.33	24	A	20		. . .					0	16383
47-BBAA-a	li	1	2	1,298,918	1,505,064	0	0.33	24	A	20		. . .					0	16384
47-BBAB	NGAO-FON cluster	1	3	222,462	257,769		4.23	23	A	20		. . .					0	16390
47-BBAB-a	ngao-fon	1	3	222,462	257,769	0	4.23	23	A	20		. . .					0	16391
47-BBB	**LAQUA-LAHA net**	2	3	9,831	13,230		3.84	22	A	4		. . .					0	16392
47-BBBA	LAQUA-LAHA cluster	2	3	9,831	13,230		3.84	22	A	4		. . .					0	16393
47-BBBA-a	laqua	2	2	7,644	10,270	0	4.80	24	A	4		. . .					0	16394
47-BBBA-b	laha	1	1	2,187	2,960	0	0.50	16	A	4		. . .					0	16395
47-BC	LATI chain	2	3	13,096	17,379		10.19	30	A	2		. . .					0	16396
47-BCA	**LATI net**	2	3	13,096	17,379		10.19	30	A	2		. . .					0	16397
47-BCAA	LATI cluster	2	3	13,096	17,379		10.19	30	A	2		. . .					0	16398
47-BCAA-a	lati	2	2	11,180	14,786	0	10.21	30	A	2		. . .					0	16399
47-BCAA-b	lipupo	1	1	1,916	2,593	0	10.02	32	A	2		. . .					0	16400
47-BD	GELO chain	2	2	496,827	577,446		0.38	18	A	24		P . .					0	16401
47-BDA	**KELAO net**	2	2	496,827	577,446		0.38	18	A	24		P . .					0	16402
47-BDAA	KELAO cluster	2	2	496,827	577,446		0.38	18	A	24		P . .					0	16403
47-BDAA-a	gelo	2	2	496,827	577,446	0	0.38	18	A	24	Gelao	P . .	1937				0	16404
47-BDB	**ANSHUN-GELO net**									0		. . .					0	16405
47-BDBA	ANSHUN cluster									0		. . .					0	16406
47-BDBA-a	anshun					0				0		. . .					0	16407
47-BDC	**SANSHONG-GELO net**									0		. . .					0	16408
47-BDCA	SANSHONG cluster									0		. . .					0	16409
47-BDCA-a	sanshong					0				0		. . .					0	16410
47-BE	MANAON-KADAI chain	1	1	20,000	34,000		5.00	24	A	0		. . .					0	16411
47-BEA	**MANAON-KADAI net**	1	1	20,000	34,000		5.00	24	A	0		. . .					0	16412
47-BEAA	MANAON cluster	1	1	20,000	34,000		5.00	24	A	0		. . .					0	16413
47-BEAA-a	manaon	1	1	20,000	34,000	0	5.00	24	A	0		. . .					0	16414
48	**MIENIC zone**	9	40	12,037,150	14,302,365		4.74	46	A	51		PN .					2As . .	16416
48-A	**HMONG-MIEN set**	9	40	12,037,150	14,302,365		4.74	46	A	51		PN .					2As . .	16417
48-AA	HMONG chain	9	26	8,102,481	9,627,690		6.67	51	B	47		PN .					2A . . .	16418
48-AAA	**HMONG net**	9	26	8,102,481	9,627,690		6.67	51	B	47		PN .					2A . . .	16419
48-AAAA	CHUANQIANDIAN cluster	9	16	4,685,219	5,636,395		8.27	58	B	47		PN .					2A . . .	16420
48-AAAA-a	hmong-daw	7	7	4,142,904	4,885,955	4	6.99	58	B	47	Hmong Daw*	PN .	1922-1984	1984		1988	2A . . .	16421
48-AAAA-b	hmong-njua	7	9	542,315	750,440	4	18.09	64	B	47	Hmong Njua	PN .	1932-1959	1975-1983		1988	1A . . .	16425
48-AAAA-c	lung-li					1				47		pn .					1c . . .	16430
48-AAAA-d	kwei-chu					1				47		pn .					1c . . .	16431
48-AAAA-e	kwang-shun					1				47		pn .					1c . . .	16432
48-AAAA-f	su-yung					1				47		pn .					1c . . .	16433
48-AAAA-g	hua-chieh					1				47		pn .					1c . . .	16434
48-AAAB	MEO-DO cluster	3	3	230,825	298,687		11.38	46	A	2		. . .					0r . . .	16435
48-AAAB-a	meo-do	3	3	230,825	298,687	4	11.38	46	A	2		. . .					0r . . .	16436
48-AAAC	QIANDONG-HE cluster	1	2	1,689,174	1,957,256		5.31	49	A	44		PN .					0r . . .	16440
48-AAAC-a	qiandong-miao	1	1	1,559,131	1,806,574	4	5.50	50	B	44	Hmong, Northern Qiandong	PN .	1937	1934			0r . . .	16441
48-AAAC-b	he-miao					1				44	Miao: He	PN .	1928	1934			0c . . .	16442
48-AAAC-c	tai-kung					1				44		pn .					0c . . .	16443
48-AAAC-d	kai-li					1				44		pn .					0c . . .	16444
48-AAAC-e	lu-shan					1				44		pn .					0c . . .	16445
48-AAAC-f	tai-chiang					1				44		pn .					0c . . .	16446
48-AAAC-g	cheng-feng					1				44		pn .					0c . . .	16447
48-AAAC-h	jung-chiang					1				44		pn .					0c . . .	16448
48-AAAC-i	keh-deo	1	1	130,043	150,682	1	3.00	29	A	44	Keh-deo	Pn .	1937				0c . . .	16449
48-AAAD	HSIANGSI cluster	1	1	857,529	993,623		3.50	43	A	2		. . .					0r . . .	16450
48-AAAD-a	xiangxi-miao	1	1	857,529	993,623	4	3.50	43	A	2		. . .					0r . . .	16451
48-AAAD-b	chi-wei					1				2		. . .					0c . . .	16452
48-AAAD-c	layi-ping					1				2		. . .					0c . . .	16453
48-AAAE	DANANSHAN-HMONG cluster	1	1	50,502	58,517		4.00	29	A	20		. . .					0	16454
48-AAAE-a	danan-shan	1	1	50,502	58,517	0	4.00	29	A	20		. . .					0	16455
48-AAAF	PUNU cluster	2	3	589,232	683,212		0.84	21	A	20		. . .					0	16456
48-AAAF-a	punu					0				20		. . .					0	16457
48-AAAF-b	pa-heng	2	2	35,853	42,009	0	3.00	21	A	20		. . .					0	16462
48-AB	YAO-PROPER chain	6	14	3,934,669	4,674,675		0.76	34	A	51		PN .					0as . .	16463
48-ABA	**MIEN-MUN net**	6	14	3,934,669	4,674,675		0.76	34	A	51		PN .					0as . .	16464
48-ABAA	MIEN-MUN cluster	6	13	3,232,687	3,861,285		0.86	35	A	51		PN .					0.s . .	16465
48-ABAA-a	mien	2	2	2,413,593	2,797,590	0	0.70	38	A	51	Mien	PN .	1932	1975			0.s . .	16466
48-ABAA-b	iu-mien	4	4	629,599	833,066	0	0.96	30	A	51	Iu Mien	PN .	1932-1968	1975-1991			0.s . .	16486
48-ABAA-c	biao-min	1	1	22,979	26,625	0	0.70	17	A	51		pn .					0.s . .	16487
48-ABAA-d	ba-pai	1	1	31,943	37,012	0	0.70	15	A	51		pn .					0.s . .	16488
48-ABAA-e	mun	4	4	134,194	166,553	0	3.24	28	A	51		pn .					0.s . .	16489
48-ABAA-f	yerong	1	1	379	439	0	1.06	23	A	51		pn .					0.s . .	16494
48-ABAB	SHE cluster	1	1	701,982	813,390		0.30	30	A	2		. . .					0a . . .	16495
48-ABAB-a	she					0				2		. . .					0c . . .	16496
49	**DRAVIDIC zone**	37	147	238,574,557	314,105,521		17.59	79	B	72		PNB					3Asu .	16499
49-A	**DRAVIDIC-NW set**	3	3	2,938,891	5,019,015		0.19	24	A	35		P . .					3	16500
49-AA	DRAVIDIC-NW chain	3	3	2,938,891	5,019,015		0.19	24	A	35		P . .					3	16501
49-AAA	**BRAHUI net**	3	3	2,938,891	5,019,015		0.19	24	A	35		P . .					3	16502

Continued opposite

Table 9-13 continued

Code 1	REFERENCE NAME / Autoglossonym 2	Coun 3	Peo 4	Mother-tongue speakers in 2000 5	in 2025 6	Media radio 7	AC% 8	E% 9	Wld 10	Tr 11	Biblioglossonym 12	Print 13-15	P–activity 16	N–activity 17	B–activity 18	J-year 19	Jayuh 20-24	Ref 25
49-AAAA	BRAHUI cluster	3	3	2,938,891	5,019,015		0.19	24	A	35		P..					3....	16503
49-AAAA-a	bra'uidi	3	3	2,938,891	5,019,015	0	0.19	24	A	35	Brahui	P..	1905-1978			1993	3....	16504
49-B	**NORTHEAST DRAVIDIC set**	4	7	2,086,471	2,745,279		41.19	84	B	43		PN.					2.s..	16509
49-BA	KURUKH-MALTO chain	4	7	2,086,471	2,745,279		41.19	84	B	43		PN.					2.s..	16510
49-BAA	**KURUKH-MALTO net**	4	7	2,086,471	2,745,279		41.19	84	B	43		PN.					2.s..	16511
49-BAAA	KURUKH cluster	4	5	1,978,009	2,602,921		42.96	87	B	43		PN.					2....	16512
49-BAAA-a	Nepal Kurukh	2	2	13,820	23,012	0	35.93	72	B	43	Kurux*	PN.	1895-1977	1989		1991	2....	16513
49-BAAA-b	Chota-Nagpur Kurukh	2	3	1,964,189	2,579,909	0	43.01	87	B	43	Kunrukh*	PN.	1895-1989	1950		1991	1....	16515
49-BAAB	MALTO cluster	1	2	108,462	142,358		9.00	42	A	35		P..					0.s..	16518
49-BAAB-a	malto	1	2	108,462	142,358	0	9.00	42	A	35	Malto	P..	1881				0.s..	16519
49-C	**DRAVIDIC-CENTRAL set**	1	6	247,466	332,553		0.45	19	A	20		...					0....	16523
49-CA	KOLAMI-PARJI chain	1	6	247,466	332,553		0.45	19	A	20		...					0....	16524
49-CAA	**KOLAMI-NAIKI net**	1	3	103,931	144,161		0.59	23	A	12		...					0....	16525
49-CAAA	KOLAMI cluster	1	3	83,931	110,161		0.50	25	A	12	Kolami, Northwestern	...					0....	16526
49-CAAA-a	mannyod	1	1	11,150	14,635	0	1.00	22	A	12		...					0....	16527
49-CAAA-b	wardha					0				12		...					0....	16528
49-CAAA-c	naikri					0				12		...					0....	16529
49-CAAB	NAIKI cluster	1	1	20,000	34,000		1.00	16	A	0		...					0....	16530
49-CAAB-a	naiki	1	1	20,000	34,000	0	1.00	16	A	0		...					0....	16531
49-CAB	**PARJI-GADABA net**	1	3	143,535	188,392		0.34	17	A	20		...					0....	16532
49-CABA	PARJI cluster	1	1	129,039	169,366		0.04	16	A	20		...					0....	16533
49-CABA-a	parji	1	1	129,039	169,366	0	0.04	16	A	20	Duruwa	...					0....	16534
49-CABB	GADABA cluster	1	2	14,496	19,026		3.00	25	A	4		...					0....	16539
49-CABB-a	gadaba	1	2	14,496	19,026	0	3.00	25	A	4		...					0....	16540
49-D	**SOUTH DRAVIDIC set**	13	40	80,601,392	105,788,052		12.36	70	B	72		PNB					3Asu.	16544
49-DA	GOND-KHOND chain	1	22	4,377,603	5,745,676		0.49	30	A	42		PN.					3as..	16545
49-DAA	**GOND net**	1	14	3,170,127	4,160,845		0.30	28	A	41		PN.					3.s..	16546
49-DAAA	GOND cluster	1	14	3,170,127	4,160,845		0.30	28	A	41		PN.					3.s..	16547
49-DAAA-a	gondi	1	2	1,576,143	2,068,715	0	0.07	29	A	41		PN.					3.s..	16548
49-DAAA-b	koya	1	2	1,058,871	1,389,787	0	0.70	29	A	41	Gondi: Koi*	Pn.	1882-1889				1.s..	16556
49-DAAA-c	maria	1	5	368,669	483,883	0	0.05	22	A	41	Maria*	pn.					1.s..	16561
49-DAB	**KONDA net**	1	4	67,511	88,608		0.67	22	A	12		...					0....	16568
49-DABA	KONDA cluster	1	4	67,511	88,608		0.67	22	A	12		...					0....	16569
49-DABA-a	konda-dora	1	2	46,426	60,935	0	0.64	23	A	12	Konda-dora	...					0....	16570
49-DABA-b	manna-dora	1	2	21,085	27,673	0	0.74	22	A	12		...					0....	16575
49-DAC	**MANDA-KHOND net**	1	4	1,139,965	1,496,223		0.99	35	A	42		PN.					2a...	16580
49-DACA	KHOND cluster	1	2	1,133,072	1,487,176		0.99	35	A	42		PN.					2....	16581
49-DACA-a	kui	1	1	753,962	989,588	0	1.10	38	A	42	Kui	PN.	1893-1965	1954-1975		1994	2....	16582
49-DACA-b	kuvi	1	1	379,110	497,588	0	0.78	29	A	42	Kuvi	PN.	1916-1962	1987			1....	16585
49-DACB	MANDA-PENGO cluster	1	2	6,893	9,047		0.04	17	A	12		...					0a...	16586
49-DACB-a	manda	1	1	4,055	5,322	4	0.00	19	A	12		...					0a...	16587
49-DACB-b	pengo	1	1	2,838	3,725	1	0.11	15	A	12	Pengo	...					0c...	16588
49-DB	TELEGU-SAVARA chain	13	18	76,223,789	100,042,376		13.04	73	B	72		PNB					2Asu.	16589
49-DBA	**TELUGU-SAVARA net**	13	18	76,223,789	100,042,376		13.04	73	B	72		PNB					2Asu.	16590
49-DBAA	SAVARA cluster	1	1	20,000	34,000		5.00	24	A	4		...					0....	16591
49-DBAA-a	savara	1	1	20,000	34,000	0	5.00	24	A	4		...					0....	16592
49-DBAB	TELUGU cluster	13	18	76,203,789	100,008,376		13.04	73	B	72		PNB					2Asu.	16593
49-DBAB-a	telugu	13	16	76,174,190	99,969,527	5	13.05	73	B	72	Telugu	PNB	1812-1966	1818-1995	1854-1990	1980	2Asu.	16594
49-DBAB-b	chenchu	1	1	22,706	29,802	1	0.35	28	A	72		pnb					1csu.	16616
49-DBAB-c	kannada south	1	1	6,893	9,047	1	1.00	33	A	72		pnb					1csu.	16617
49-E	**SOUTH DRAVIDIC set**	32	91	152,700,337	200,220,622		20.39	84	B	72		PNB					3Asu.	16618
49-EA	TULU-KORAGA chain	1	3	2,054,057	2,696,761		1.00	37	A	43		PN.					1.s..	16619
49-EAA	**TULU-BELLARI net**	1	2	2,050,131	2,690,833		1.00	37	A	43		PN.					1.s..	16620
49-EAAA	TULU-BELLARI cluster	1	2	2,050,131	2,690,833		1.00	37	A	43		PN.					1.s..	16621
49-EAAA-a	tulu	1	1	2,048,104	2,688,172	0	1.00	37	A	43	Tulu	PN.	1842-1912	1847-1892		1993	1.s..	16622
49-EAAA-b	bellari	1	1	2,027	2,661	0	0.99	27	A	43		pn.					1.s..	16623
49-EAB	**KORAGA net**	1	1	3,926	5,928		1.17	18	A	4		...					0....	16624
49-EABA	KORRA cluster	1	1	1,926	2,528		1.35	19	A	4		...					0....	16625
49-EABA-a	korra	1	1	1,926	2,528	0	1.35	19	A	4		...					0....	16626
49-EABB	MUDU cluster	1	1	2,000	3,400		1.00	16	A	4		...					0....	16627
49-EABB-a	mudu					0				4		...					0....	16628
49-EB	TAMIL-KANNADA chain	32	88	150,646,280	197,523,861		20.65	85	B	72		PNB					3Asu.	16629
49-EBA	**KANNADA net**	3	13	38,354,490	50,342,429		5.70	70	B	61		PNB					3Asu.	16630
49-EBAA	KANNADA cluster	3	9	37,440,674	49,143,029		5.81	71	B	61		PNB					3Asu.	16631
49-EBAA-a	kannada	3	4	37,219,190	48,852,326	5	5.80	71	B	61	Kannada	PNB	1812-1988	1823-1995	1831-1995	1980	2Asu.	16632
49-EBAA-b	badaga	1	1	188,642	247,597	1	9.80	48	A	61	Badaga	Pnb	1852-1992			1997	3csu.	16645
49-EBAB	KURUMBA cluster	1	4	913,816	1,199,400		1.23	30	A	20		...					0....	16646
49-EBAB-a	kurumba	1	2	889,083	1,166,937	0	1.01	30	A	20	Kurumba	...					0....	16647
49-EBAB-b	alu-kurumba	1	1	20,273	26,609	0	10.00	38	A	20	Alu	...					0....	16651
49-EBAB-c	jennu-kurumba					0				20		...					0....	16652
49-EBAB-d	betta-kurumba	1	1	4,460	5,854		5.00	34	A	20		...					0....	16653
49-EBB	**TODA-KOTA net**	1	2	3,953	5,189		5.92	30	A	24		P..					0....	16656
49-EBBA	TODA cluster	1	1	1,723	2,262		12.30	41	A	24		P..					0....	16657
49-EBBA-a	toda	1	1	1,723	2,262	0	12.30	41	A	24	Toda	P..	1897-1910				0....	16658
49-EBBB	KOTA cluster	1	1	2,230	2,927		0.99	21	A	12		...					0....	16659
49-EBBB-a	kota	1	1	2,230	2,927	0	0.99	21	A	12	Kota	...					0....	16660
49-EBC	**COORGI net**	1	1	133,905	175,752		0.20	20	A	20		...					0....	16663
49-EBCA	KODAGU cluster	1	1	133,905	175,752		0.20	20	A	20		...					0....	16664

Continued overleaf

Table 9-13 continued

Code 1	REFERENCE NAME / Autoglossonym 2	Coun 3	Peo 4	Mother-tongue speakers in 2000 5	in 2025 6	Media radio 7	CHURCH AC% 8	E% 9	Wld 10	Tr 11	Biblioglossonym 12	Print 13-15	P–activity 16	N–activity 17	B–activity 18	J-year 19	Jayuh 20-24	Ref 25
49-EBCA-a	kodagu	1	1	133,905	175,752	0	0.20	20	A	20	Kodagu	. . .					0	16665
49-EBD	**IRULA-YERUKULA net**	1	2	241,961	317,578		2.19	29	A	20		. . .					0	16666
49-EBDA	IRULA-YERUKULA cluster	1	2	241,961	317,578		2.19	29	A	20		. . .					0	16667
49-EBDA-a	irula	1	1	121,437	159,388	0	3.00	27	A	20	Irula	. . .					0	16668
49-EBDA-b	yerukala	1	1	120,524	158,190	0	1.37	31	A	20		. . .					0	16673
49-EBE	**TAMIL-MALAYALAM net**	32	68	111,898,590	146,665,351		25.84	90	B	72		PNB					2Asu.	16676
49-EBEA	WIDER-TAMIL cluster	28	35	72,690,134	95,141,635		19.36	86	B	71		PNB					2Asu.	16677
49-EBEA-a	Historical tamil					1				71		pnb					1csu.	16678
49-EBEA-b	tamil	28	32	72,292,272	94,619,434	6	19.47	86	B	71	Tamil	PNB	1714-1956	1715-1988	1727-1995	1980	2Asu.	16681
49-EBEB	MALAYALAM cluster	18	33	39,208,456	51,523,716		37.86	99	B	72		PNB					2Asu.	16699
49-EBEB-a	malayalam	18	21	39,147,333	51,443,490	4	37.91	99	B	72	Malayalam	PNB	1811-1968	1829-1980	1841-1996	1980	2Asu.	16700
49-EBEB-b	malapandaram	1	1	608	798	1	0.00	20	A	72		pnb					1csu.	16719
49-EBEB-c	malankuravan	1	1	6,487	8,515	1	3.25	35	A	72		pnb					1csu.	16720
49-EBEB-d	malaryan	1	2	18,956	24,880	1	2.09	34	A	72		pnb					1csu.	16724
49-EBEB-e	malavedan	1	1	2,534	3,326	1	0.67	28	A	72		pnb					1csu.	16725
49-EBF	**PANIYA net**	1	2	13,381	17,562		4.21	30	A	4		. . .					0	16728
49-EBFA	PANIYA cluster	1	2	13,381	17,562		4.21	30	A	4		. . .					0	16729
49-EBFA-a	paniyan	1	2	13,381	17,562	0	4.21	30	A	4		. . .					0	16730
5	**INDOEUROPEAN macrozone**	236	3148	2,683,096,073	3,348,034,971		45.60	78	B	82		PNB					4Bsuh	16731
50	**CELTIC zone**	11	23	6,037,407	6,704,642		80.59	100	C	66		PNB					2A.uh	16732
50-A	**CELTIC set**	11	23	6,037,407	6,704,642		80.59	100	C	66		PNB					2A.uh	16733
50-AA	GOIDELIC chain	4	5	1,129,728	1,313,043		93.68	100	C	66		PNB					2a.uh	16734
50-AAA	**GOIDELIC net**	4	5	1,129,728	1,313,043		93.68	100	C	66		PNB					2a.uh	16735
50-AAAA	GAEILGE cluster	4	5	1,129,728	1,313,043		93.68	100	C	66		PNB					2a.uh	16736
50-AAAA-a	Historical gaeilge					1				66		pnb					1c.uh	16737
50-AAAA-b	Standard gaidhlig	1	1	93,834	95,638	1	83.00	100	C	66	Gaelic*	PNB	1991	1767-1875	1801-1991		1c.uh	16738
50-AAAA-c	Religious gaidhlig					1				66		pnb					1c.uh	16739
50-AAAA-d	Northeast gaidhlig					1				66		pnb					1c.uh	16740
50-AAAA-e	West Central gaidhlig.					1				66		pnb					1c.uh	16741
50-AAAA-f	North gaidhlig-S.-gaeilge					1				66		pnb					1c.uh	16758
50-AAAA-g	gaeilge	3	3	1,035,736	1,217,203	4	94.65	100	C	66	Irish*	PNB	1976	1602-1951	1685-1989	1995	2a.uh	16761
50-AAAA-h	North gaeilge					1				66		pnb					1c.uh	16764
50-AAAA-i	Central gaeilge					1				66		pnb					1c.uh	16767
50-AAAA-j	South gaeilge					1				66		pnb					1c.uh	16772
50-AAAA-k	manaweg	1	1	158	202	1	89.87	100	C	66		PNB					1c.uh	16776
50-AB	BRITANNIC chain	8	10	4,851,454	5,333,885		77.68	100	C	63		PNB					2A.uh	16783
50-ABA	**NORTH BRITANNIC net**	7	8	3,521,808	3,946,134		80.58	100	C	61		PNB					2A.uh	16784
50-ABAA	CYMRAEG cluster	7	8	3,521,808	3,946,134		80.58	100	C	61		PNB					2A.uh	16785
50-ABAA-a	Historical cymraeg			0	0	1	0.00	0		61		pnb					1c.uh	16786
50-ABAA-b	Standard cymraeg	7	8	3,521,808	3,946,134	5	80.58	100	C	61		PNB					2A.uh	16787
50-ABAA-c	North cymraeg					1				61		pnb					1c.uh	16792
50-ABAA-d	South cymraeg					1				61		pnb					1c.uh	16798
50-ABB	**SOUTH BRITANNIC net**	2	2	1,329,646	1,387,751		70.01	100	C	63		PNB					0	16802
50-ABBA	KERNEWEK cluster	1	1	353	360		94.90	100	C	24		P . .					0	16803
50-ABBA-a	kernewek-H			0	0	0	0.00	0		24		p . .					0	16804
50-ABBA-b	kernewek-F	1	1	353	360	0	94.90	100	C	24	Cornish	P . .	1936				0	16805
50-ABBB	BREZONEG cluster	1	2	1,329,293	1,387,391		70.00	100	C	63		PNB					0	16806
50-ABBB-a	Historical brezoneg					1				63		pnb					0	16807
50-ABBB-b	General brezoneg					1				63		pnb					0	16811
50-ABBB-c	leoneg	1	1	1,329,293	1,387,391	1	70.00	100	C	63	Breton: Leon	PNB	1985	1827-1971	1866-1985		0	16816
50-ABBB-d	tregereg-kerneweg					1				63	Breton: Treguier	PNB		1853	1889		0	16823
50-ABBB-e	East gwenedeg					1				63	Breton: Vannes	Pnb	1857				0	16836
50-AC	SHELTA chain	6	8	56,225	57,714		67.97	100	C	20		. . .					0	16841
50-ACA	**SHELTA net**	6	8	56,225	57,714		67.97	100	C	20		. . .					0	16842
50-ACAA	SHELDRUU cluster	6	8	56,225	57,714		67.97	100	C	20		. . .					0	16843
50-ACAA-a	West sheldruu	6	7	55,947	57,388	8	67.91	100	C	20		. . .					0	16844
50-ACAA-b	North sheldruu	1	1	278	326	1	80.22	100	C	20		. . .					0	16845
51	**ROMANIC zone**	190	820	709,190,223	868,229,796		89.65	100	C	82		PNB					4Bsuh	16846
51-A	**ROMANCE set**	190	820	709,190,223	868,229,796		89.65	100	C	82		PNB					4Bsuh	16847
51-AA	ROMANCE chain	190	820	709,190,223	868,229,796		89.65	100	C	82		PNB					4Bsuh	16848
51-AAA	**PAN-ROMANCE net**	53	62	199,354	261,254		0.20	39	A	66		PNB					0A.u.	16849
51-AAAA	LATIN cluster	2	2	30	30		96.67	100	C	66		PNB					0A.u.	16850
51-AAAA-a	lingua-latina	2	2	30	30	4	96.67	100	C	66	Latin	PNB	1945	1943	1385-1906		0A.u.	16851
51-AAAA-b	latino-sine-flexione					1				66	Interlingua	Pnb	1978				0c.u.	16855
51-AAAB	JUDEO-ROMANCE cluster	8	8	199,090	260,988		0.11	39	A	63		PNB					0	16856
51-AAAB-a	ladino	3	3	33,417	41,174	1	0.42	37	A	63		pnb					0	16857
51-AAAB-b	hakitia	1	1	144,944	196,027	8	0.05	40	A	63	Ladino	PNB	1547-1873	1829	1829		0	16858
51-AAAB-c	tetauni					1				63		pnb					0	16859
51-AAAB-d	djudezmo	3	3	16,718	20,198	8	0.02	32	A	63	Spanish: Judaeo*	PNB	1547-1873	1743-1829	1829		0	16860
51-AAAB-e	judeo-veneziano			0	0	1	0.00	0		63		pnb					0	16871
51-AAAB-f	italkian	1	1	4,011	3,589	1	0.00	25	A	63		pnb					0	16872
51-AAAC	ESPERANTO cluster	51	52	234	236		69.66	100	C	63		PNB					0A . . .	16873
51-AAAC-a	Proper esperanto	51	52	234	236	5	69.66	100	C	63	Esperanto	PNB	1893	1912	1926		0A . . .	16874
51-AAAC-b	ido					1				63		pnb					0c . . .	16875
51-AAAC-c	novial					1				63		pnb					0c . . .	16876
51-AAB	**WEST ROMANCE net**	167	613	669,580,321	824,474,657		89.79	100	C	82		PNB					4Bsuh	16877
51-AABA	PORTUGUêS cluster	53	105	184,263,651	231,365,274		92.07	100	C	82		PNB					3Bsuh	16878
51-AABA-a	Historical português					1				82		pnb					1csuh	16879
51-AABA-b	galego	6	6	4,054,161	4,011,392	1	95.00	100	C	82	Galician	PNB	1861-1967	1974-1980	1989-1992	1993	1csuh	16880
51-AABA-c	North português					1				82		pnb					1csuh	16885
51-AABA-d	Literary português					1				82		PNB					1csuh	16888
51-AABA-e	General português	51	96	180,057,842	227,208,334	8	92.01	100	C	82	Portuguese	PNB	1505-1981	1681-1995	1751-1993	1998	2Bsuh	16891
51-AABA-f	madeirense					1				82		pnb					1csuh	16898
51-AABA-g	açoriano					1				82		pnb					1csuh	16901
51-AABA-h	General brasileiro	2	2	135,354	130,123	8	89.60	100	C	82	Portuguese: Brazilian	PNB	1877	1879	1917	1980	3csuh	16905
51-AABA-i	falares baianos					1				82		pnb					1csuh	16913

Continued opposite

Table 9-13 continued

Code 1	REFERENCE NAME / Autoglossonym 2	Coun 3	Peo 4	in 2000 5	in 2025 6	Media radio 7	AC% 8	E% 9	Wld 10	Tr 11	Biblioglossonym 12	Print 13-15	P–activity 16	N–activity 17	B–activity 18	J-year 19	Jayuh 20-24	Ref 25
51-AABA-j	mineiro					1				82		pnb					1csuh	16914
51-AABA-k	carioca					1				82		pnb					1csuh	16915
51-AABA-l	paulista					1				82		pnb					1csuh	16916
51-AABA-m	fronteiriço					1				82		pnb					1csuh	16917
51-AABB	ESPANOL cluster	71	211	336,908,562	443,334,913		92.75	100	C	72		PNB					4B.uh	16918
51-AABB-a	Historical castellano					1				72		pnb					1c.uh	16919
51-AABB-b	Standard castellano	1	1	28,221	38,530	8	96.00	100	C	72		pnb				1980	1A.uh	16920
51-AABB-c	General español	39	47	23,143,626	21,838,235	8	94.54	100	C	72	Spanish	PNB	1514-1985	1543-1994	1553-1979	1982	2B.uh	16923
51-AABB-d	andaluz					1				72		pnb					1c.uh	16939
51-AABB-e	español-canario					1				72		pnb					1c.uh	16940
51-AABB-f	español-sahariano	1	1	293	470	8	96.25	100	C	72		pnb					1B.uh	16941
51-AABB-g	español-guineo	1	2	23,539	41,325	8	96.61	100	C	72		pnb					1A.uh	16942
51-AABB-h	Latin American	39	155	300,758,068	406,262,801	8	93.02	100	C	72		pnb				1981	4B.uh	16943
51-AABB-i	rioplatense	1	1	6,674	7,813	8	83.01	100	C	72		pnb					1c.uh	16967
51-AABB-j	ucayaliano	1	1	2,566	3,552	1	90.02	100	C	72		pnb					1c.uh	16970
51-AABB-k	chicano	1	2	12,943,607	15,139,126	8	83.14	100	C	72		pnb					1B.uh	16971
51-AABC	ASTUR-LEONES cluster	2	2	505,247	467,577		90.12	100	C	22	Spanish: Asturian*	P..					0B.uh	16983
51-AABC-a	astur	1	1	495,372	458,229	8	90.00	100	C	22		P..	1861-1991				0B.uh	16984
51-AABC-b	mirandés	1	1	9,875	9,348	1	96.00	100	C	22		p..					0c.uh	16990
51-AABC-c	leonés					1				22		p..					0c.uh	16991
51-AABD	ARAGONéS cluster	1	1	1,981,489	1,832,915		95.00	100	C	12		...					0....	16996
51-AABD-a	Historical navarro-aragonés					0				12		...					0....	16997
51-AABD-b	aragonés	1	1	1,981,489	1,832,915	0	95.00	100	C	12	Aragonese	...					0....	16998
51-AABD-c	ansotano					0				12		...					0....	17007
51-AABD-d	cheso					0				12		...					0....	17008
51-AABD-e	tensino-pandicuto					0				12		...					0....	17009
51-AABD-f	belsetán					0				12		...					0....	17012
51-AABD-g	chistabín					0				12		...					0....	17013
51-AABD-h	benasqués					0				12		...					0....	17014
51-AABE	CATALAN cluster	8	9	11,731,170	10,997,560	1	94.07	100	C	63	Catalan	PNB			1478		2a..h	17015
51-AABE-a	Historical catalan									63	Catalan-valencian-balear	PNB					1c..h	17016
51-AABE-b	català	8	8	11,719,281	10,986,563	4	94.07	100	C	63	Catalan-valencian-balear	PNB	1928-1985	1832-1988	1478-1993	1985	2a..h	17017
51-AABE-c	alguerès					1				63		pnb					1c..h	17030
51-AABE-d	valencia	1	1	11,889	10,997	1	96.00	100	C	63		pnb					1c..h	17031
51-AABE-e	eivissenc					1				63		pnb					1c..h	17032
51-AABE-f	mallorquí					1				63	Mallorquin	PNb	1984	1987			1c..h	17033
51-AABE-g	menorquí					1				63		pnb					1c..h	17034
51-AABF	GASCON cluster	2	2	419,502	437,132		75.21	100	C	22	Gascon	P..					0....	17035
51-AABF-a	gascou	1	1	413,558	431,633	8	75.00	100	C	22		P..	1583-1983				0....	17036
51-AABF-b	biarnés					1				22		p..					0....	17045
51-AABF-c	bigordan					1				22		p..					0....	17049
51-AABF-d	comengés					1				22		p..					0....	17054
51-AABF-e	couseranés					1				22		p..					0....	17055
51-AABF-f	aranés	1	1	5,944	5,499	1	90.01	100	C	22	Gascon, Aranese	P..	1583-1983				0....	17056
51-AABG	OC cluster	2	5	11,754,244	12,241,962		75.75	100	C	43		PN.					0A...	17059
51-AABG-a	Historical proensal					1				43	Provencal: Ancient	PN.	1848	1887			0c...	17060
51-AABG-b	lengadocian	2	2	2,818,082	2,926,293	8	75.53	100	C	43	Provencal: Languedoc*	Pn.	1888				0c...	17061
51-AABG-c	prouvençau					1				43		Pn.					0c...	17077
51-AABG-d	nissart					1				43		pn.					0c...	17094
51-AABG-e	oc-cisalpin	1	1	74,206	66,399	8	86.00	100	C	43		pn.					0c...	17099
51-AABG-f	gavouot					1				43		pn.					0c...	17107
51-AABG-g	vivaro-dauphinois					1				43		pn.					0c...	17120
51-AABG-h	South auvergnat					1				43	Provencal: Auvergne*	Pn.	1824-1831				0c...	17131
51-AABG-i	North auvergnat					1				43		pn.					0c...	17136
51-AABG-j	lemozin					1				43		pn.					0c...	17144
51-AABG-k	marchois					1				43		pn.					0c...	17154
51-AABH	OIL-P. cluster	9	10	4,529,269	4,727,738		84.13	100	C	24		P..					0A.uh	17159
51-AABH-a	parlange					1				24		P..					0c.uh	17160
51-AABH-b	gallo					1				24		p..					0c.uh	17170
51-AABH-c	anglo-normand					1				24		P..					0c.uh	17176
51-AABH-d	normand					1				24		P..					0c.uh	17184
51-AABH-e	picard					1				24	French: Amiens-picard	P..	1863				0c.uh	17193
51-AABH-f	wallon	8	8	3,382,588	3,385,968	8	84.82	100	C	24	French: Walloon	P..	1934				0A.uh	17207
51-AABH-g	champaignat					1				24		p..					0c.uh	17213
51-AABH-h	lorrain					1				24		P..					0c.uh	17226
51-AABH-i	welche					1				24		P..					0c.uh	17233
51-AABH-j	jurassien					1				24		p..					0c.uh	17239
51-AABH-k	bourguignon					1				24		p..					0c.uh	17246
51-AABH-l	morvandiau					1				24		p..					0c.uh	17250
51-AABH-m	bourbonnais-berrichon					1				24		p..					0c.uh	17255
51-AABH-n	angevin-orléanais					1				24		p..					0c.uh	17261
51-AABH-o	acadjin	2	2	1,146,681	1,341,770	2	82.09	100	C	24		P..					0c.uh	17277
51-AABH-p	canadien					1				24		P..					0c.uh	17281
51-AABI	FRANCAIS cluster	135	171	48,628,802	53,770,223		73.50	99	C	71		PNB					4B.uh	17284
51-AABI-a	Historical français	4	4	10,075	11,267	8	22.55	65	B	71		pnb					1B.uh	17285
51-AABI-b	francien					1				71		pnb					1c.uh	17286
51-AABI-c	Standard français	3	6	817,853	858,420	8	71.64	98	C	71	French	PNB		1474	1530	1981	4B.uh	17287
51-AABI-d	General français	132	149	35,830,447	38,661,994	8	74.88	99	C	71	French	PNB	1483-1989	1474-1990	1530-1995		1B.uh	17292
51-AABI-e	français-belge					1				71		pnb					1c.uh	17312
51-AABI-f	français-suisse	2	2	1,272,555	1,307,722	8	84.81	100	C	71		pnb					1B.uh	17313
51-AABI-g	français-d'aoste					1				71		pnb					1c.uh	17314
51-AABI-h	français-germanique					1				71		pnb					1c.uh	17315
51-AABI-i	français-nord-américain	2	2	9,737,615	11,733,659	8	68.38	100	C	71		pnb					1B.uh	17320
51-AABI-j	français-antillais					1				71		pnb					1c.uh	17326
51-AABI-k	français-du-levant					1				71		pnb					1c.uh	17331
51-AABI-l	français-maghrebin					1				71		pnb					1c.uh	17335
51-AABI-m	français-d'afrique	6	6	909,596	1,127,730	8	59.57	100	B	71		pnb					1B.uh	17341
51-AABI-n	français d'inde					1				71		pnb					1c.uh	17365
51-AABI-o	français-du-sudest-asiatique					1				71		pnb					1c.uh	17371
51-AABI-p	français d'océanie	2	2	50,661	69,431	8	92.93	100	C	71		pnb					1A.uh	17375
51-AABJ	ROMAND cluster	2	2	745,897	775,945		88.79	100	C	43		PN.					0....	17381
51-AABJ-a	franc-comtois					1				43	French: Franche-comte	Pn.	1864				0....	17382
51-AABJ-b	lyonnais					1				43		pn.					0....	17388
51-AABJ-c	North dauphinois					1				43		pn.					0....	17394
51-AABJ-d	savoyard					1				43		pn.					0....	17400
51-AABJ-e	vaudois	2	2	745,897	775,945	8	88.79	100	C	43	French: Vaudois, Ancient*	PN.	1830-1848	1890			0....	17410
51-AABJ-f	valdôtain					1				43		pn.					0....	17415
51-AABK	RUMANTSCH cluster	2	5	130,174	126,458		89.71	100	C	63		PNB					0....	17429
51-AABK-a	sursilvan	1	3	75,334	77,387	3	90.92	100	C	63	Romansch: Sursilvan	PNB		1648	1718		0....	17430
51-AABK-b	sutsilvan-surmiran					1				63	Romansch: Ladin Sut	PNB	1562		1679		0....	17438
51-AABK-c	grischun	1	2	54,840	49,071	1	88.05	100	C	63	Romansch: Ladin Sura*	PNB	1964	1560-1954	1953		0....	17444
51-AABL	LADIN-DOLOMITIC cluster									0		...					0....	17451
51-AABL-a	nones					0				0		...					0....	17452
51-AABL-b	badio					0				0		...					0....	17453
51-AABL-c	gründno					0				0		...					0....	17456
51-AABL-d	fassa-fiamazzo					0				0		...					0....	17457
51-AABL-e	cadorino					0				0		...					0....	17460
51-AABM	FURLAN cluster	3	3	630,139	564,323		83.03	100	C	42	Friulian	PN.	1860	1972			0....	17464
51-AABM-a	carnico					0				42		pn.					0....	17465
51-AABM-b	West furlan					0				42		pn.					0....	17469
51-AABM-c	East Central furlan.					0				42		pn.					0....	17472

Continued overleaf

Table 9-13 continued

Code 1	REFERENCE NAME Autoglossonym 2	Coun 3	Peo 4	Mother-tongue speakers in 2000 5	in 2025 6	Media radio 7	CHURCH AC% 8	E% 9	Wld 10	Tr 11	SCRIPTURES Biblioglossonym 12	Print 13-15	P–activity 16	N–activity 17	B–activity 18	J-year 19	Jayuh 20-24	Ref 25
51-AABN	VENETAN cluster	1	1	2,172,318	1,943,766		90.00	100	C	24		P..					0....	17476
51-AABN-a	istrioto					0				24		p..					0....	17477
51-AABN-b	veneto	1	1	2,172,318	1,943,766	0	90.00	100	C	24		P..					0....	17481
51-AABO	GALLO-ITALIANO cluster	4	9	14,805,534	13,364,548		84.48	100	C	43		PN.					0B...	17491
51-AABO-a	trentino					1				43		pn.					0c...	17492
51-AABO-b	ticinese	1	1	813,905	836,087	7	94.00	100	C	43		pn.					0B...	17493
51-AABO-c	lombardo-alpino					1				43		pn.					0c...	17497
51-AABO-d	lombardo	1	1	131,350	117,530	1	89.00	100	C	43	Lombard	Pn.	1859-1860				0c...	17498
51-AABO-e	lombardo-siculo	1	1	8,798,073	7,872,421	1	85.00	100	C	43		pn.					0c...	17509
51-AABO-f	piemontese	1	1	3,089,336	2,764,304	1	80.00	100	C	43	Italian: Piedmontese*	PN.	1834-1861	1835			0c...	17510
51-AABO-g	brigasc					1				43		pn.					0c...	17520
51-AABO-h	ligure	3	4	1,955,681	1,758,825	8	84.98	100	C	43	Ligurian	Pn.	1860				0c...	17524
51-AABO-i	genovesi-di-corsica					1				43		pn.					0c...	17531
51-AABO-j	genovesi di sardegna					1				43		pn.					0c...	17534
51-AABO-k	emiliano-romagnolo	1	1	17,189	15,381	1	85.00	100	C	43	Italian: Romagnuolo	Pn.	1865				0c...	17537
51-AABP	CORSU cluster	3	5	1,042,748	1,007,630		79.96	100	C	24		P..					0....	17550
51-AABP-a	North corsu					1				24		p..					0....	17551
51-AABP-b	Central corsu	3	3	412,472	443,665	4	79.91	100	C	24	Italian: Corsican*	P..	1861-1994				0....	17559
51-AABP-c	South corsu					1				24		p..					0....	17567
51-AABP-d	gallurese	1	1	286,489	256,348	1	80.00	100	C	24	Sardinian: Tempiese*	P..	1861-1862				0....	17571
51-AABP-e	sassarese	1	1	343,787	307,617	1	80.00	100	C	24	Sardinian: Sassarese*	P..	1863-1866				0....	17572
51-AABQ	ITALIANO cluster	59	68	36,509,345	36,043,501		82.02	100	C	71		PNB					2B.uh	17573
51-AABQ-a	toscano-T.					1				71		Pnb					1c.uh	17574
51-AABQ-b	Historical italiano					1				71		pnb					1c.uh	17585
51-AABQ-c	Standard italiano	59	66	36,318,937	35,866,117	7	82.01	100	C	71	Italian	PNB	1984	1981	1471-1985	1982	2B.uh	17586
51-AABQ-d	General italiano	1	1	171,894	153,809	1	84.00	100	C	71		pnb					1A.uh	17587
51-AABR	NAPOLETANO cluster	1	2	12,077,358	10,806,688		81.20	100	C	24		P..					0....	17596
51-AABR-a	umbro-romanesco					0				24		p..					0....	17597
51-AABR-b	campano-molisano	1	1	7,257,259	6,493,716	0	80.00	100	C	24	Neapolitan-calabrese	P..	1861-1862				0....	17600
51-AABR-c	salentino					0				24		p..					0....	17609
51-AABR-d	calabrese					0				24	Italian: Calabrian	P..	1862				0....	17610
51-AABR-e	East Central siciliano.	1	1	4,820,099	4,312,972	0	83.00	100	C	24	Italian: Sicilian*	P..	1860				0....	17611
51-AABR-f	West siciliano					0				24		p..					0....	17619
51-AABS	SARDU cluster	1	2	744,872	666,504		80.00	100	C	24		P..					0....	17623
51-AABS-a	logudorese	1	1	401,085	358,887	0	80.00	100	C	24	Sardinian: Logudorese*	P..	1858-1861				0....	17624
51-AABS-b	nuorese					0				24		p..					0....	17628
51-AABS-c	gennargentese					0				24		p..					0....	17629
51-AABS-d	campidanese	1	1	343,787	307,617	0	80.00	100	C	24	Sardinian: Cagliaritan*	P..	1860-1900				0....	17630
51-AAC	**ROMANCE-CREOLE net**	51	89	16,003,975	21,867,624		89.95	99	C	82		PNB					4Asu.	17631
51-AACA	LUSO-CREOLE cluster	15	22	823,998	1,252,023		81.40	96	C	61	Crioulo	PNB	1979	1989			4a...	17632
51-AACA-a	caboverdense	6	7	433,114	661,769	8	97.67	100	C	61	Crioulo, Upper Guinea	PNB	1979	1989	1996		1c...	17633
51-AACA-b	guineense	3	3	169,147	279,174	8	60.82	100	C	61		PNB				1996	4c...	17636
51-AACA-c	sao-tomense-principense	1	2	116,499	172,355	8	90.71	100	C	61		pnb					1c...	17641
51-AACA-d	angolar	2	2	17,634	29,115	8	81.74	100	C	61		pnb					1a...	17644
51-AACA-e	fa-d'ambu	1	1	3,259	5,722	2	95.00	100	C	61		pnb					1c...	17645
51-AACA-f	cafundo	1	1	51	65	1	70.59	100	C	61		pnb					1c...	17646
51-AACA-g	indo-português	2	2	3,896	4,903	1	88.68	100	C	61	Indo-portuguese	PNb	1819-1851	1826-1852			1c...	17647
51-AACA-h	malaio-português	3	3	74,969	92,629	8	17.29	55	B	61		Pnb					1c...	17653
51-AACA-i	makista	1	1	5,429	6,291	1	95.01	100	C	61		pnb					1c...	17664
51-AACB	HISPANO-CREOLE cluster	7	8	857,030	1,243,418		89.19	100	C	72		PNB					1a.u.	17667
51-AACB-a	chavacano	2	2	428,845	611,075	1	90.00	100	C	72	Chavacano	PNb	1977	1981			1c.u.	17668
51-AACB-b	chocoano	1	1	12,696	17,927	1	80.00	100	C	72		pnb					1c.u.	17676
51-AACB-c	palanquero	1	1	3,271	4,619	8	97.00	100	C	72		pnb					1c.u.	17677
51-AACB-d	criollo-de-bobures	1	1	120,849	173,876	8	86.00	100	C	72		pnb					1c.u.	17678
51-AACB-e	papiamento	3	3	291,369	435,921	5	89.62	100	C	72	Papiamentu	PNB	1844-1987	1916	1996	1997	1a.u.	17679
51-AACC	GALLO-CREOLE cluster	34	59	14,322,947	19,372,183		90.49	99	C	82		PNB					3As..	17685
51-AACC-a	louisianais	1	1	1,897,895	2,219,819	8	85.00	100	C	82		pnb					1cs..	17686
51-AACC-b	haitien	7	8	9,338,730	13,331,200	4	92.66	100	C	82	Haitian*	PNB	1927-1993	1951-1996	1985	1982	3As..	17691
51-AACC-c	guadeloupéan	6	8	466,492	585,733	8	94.96	100	C	82	Creole French: Lesser Antill	Pnb	1894				1cs..	17695
51-AACC-d	dominiquais	3	6	767,719	914,021	2	95.83	100	C	82		pnb					1cs..	17700
51-AACC-e	martiniquais	6	9	641,394	718,614	8	93.12	100	C	82		pnb					1As..	17701
51-AACC-f	sainte-lucien					1				82	Lesser Antill Creole French	Pnb	1894-1992				1cs..	17702
51-AACC-g	trinidadien	1	1	8,366	7,520	8	93.00	100	C	82		pnb					1cs..	17703
51-AACC-h	guyanais	1	2	81,473	187,015	8	96.73	100	C	82		pnb					1cs..	17704
51-AACC-i	gallo-panamanéen					1				82		pnb					1cs..	17708
51-AACC-j	gallo-brasilien					1				82		pnb					1cs..	17709
51-AACC-k	seselwa	5	5	79,536	99,558	8	91.76	100	C	82	Creole: Seychelles*	PNb	1974-1984	1996			1cs..	17710
51-AACC-l	morisyen	4	6	520,107	618,691	8	52.11	82	B	82	Mauritius Creole*	Pnb	1885-1900			1998	1cs..	17716
51-AACC-m	réunioné	6	9	511,250	676,562	8	94.53	100	C	82		pnb					1cs..	17720
51-AACC-n	caldoche	1	1	1,070	1,428	1	70.00	100	C	82		pnb					1cs..	17721
51-AACC-o	Chinese Tahitian Creole	1	1	235	324	1	50.21	100	B	82		pnb					1cs..	17722
51-AACC-p	tay boi	1	1	7,983	10,804	8	38.01	88	B	82		pnb					1cs..	17723
51-AAD	**EAST ROMANCE net**	40	56	23,406,573	21,626,261		86.03	99	C	68		PNB					3A.u.	17724
51-AADA	ISTRO-ROMAN cluster	2	2	153,170	143,771		96.91	100	C	4		...					0....	17725
51-AADA-a	jeiani					0				4		...					0....	17726
51-AADA-b	susnjevica					0				4		...					0....	17727
51-AADB	AROMAN cluster	5	7	258,886	276,569		86.99	100	C	24		P..					0a...	17728
51-AADB-a	limba armâneasc-a	5	5	240,574	258,453	6	86.58	100	C	24	Romanian: Macedonian*	P..	1881-1889				0a...	17729
51-AADB-b	meglenitsa	2	2	18,312	18,116	6	92.36	100	C	24		p..					0c...	17736
51-AADC	DACO-ROMANCE cluster	38	47	22,994,517	21,205,921		85.95	99	C	68		PNB					3A.u.	17737
51-AADC-a	limba româneasca	38	47	22,994,517	21,205,921	6	85.95	99	C	68	Romanian	PNB	1553-1993	1648-1993	1688-1989		3A.u.	17738
51-AADC-b	General limba româneasca					1				68		pnb					1c.u.	17741
51-AADC-c	limba româneasca-T.					1				68		pnb					1c.u.	17742
51-AADC-d	moldavia					1				68		pnb					1c.u.	17751
52	**GERMANIC zone**	218	874	452,849,741	505,518,990		70.27	99	C	82		PNB					4Bsuh	17752
52-A	**GERMANIC set**	218	874	452,849,741	505,518,990		70.27	99	C	82		PNB					4Bsuh	17753
52-AA	NORDIC chain	19	49	29,369,127	31,827,301		79.44	100	C	72		PNB					2B.uh	17754
52-AAA	**NORDIC net**	19	49	29,369,127	31,827,301		79.44	100	C	72		PNB					2B.uh	17755
52-AAAA	HISTORICAL NORSE cluster									0		...					0....	17756
52-AAAA-a	Norse					0				0		...					0....	17757
52-AAAB	NORDIC-INSULAR cluster	5	6	374,598	422,739		94.66	100	C	72		PNB					0..uh	17758
52-AAAB-a	íslensk	4	4	327,838	381,995	2	94.87	100	C	72	Icelandic	PNB	1995	1540-1979	1584-1981		0..uh	17759
52-AAAB-b	foroysk	2	2	46,760	40,744	4	93.21	100	C	72	Faroese	PNB	1823-1931	1930-1937	1948-1961		0..uh	17770
52-AAAC	WEST NORDIC cluster	13	15	8,637,651	9,716,899		91.79	100	C	63		PNB					0B.uh	17782
52-AAAC-a	West norsk					1				63		pnb					0c.uh	17783
52-AAAC-b	midlands-norsk					1				63		pnb					0c.uh	17786
52-AAAC-c	trondelags-norsk	1	1	1,190	1,208	1	98.07	100	C	63		pnb					0c.uh	17787
52-AAAC-d	nordlands-norsk					1				63		pnb					0c.uh	17788
52-AAAC-e	ny-norsk	12	14	8,636,461	9,715,691	6	91.79	100	C	63	Norwegian*	PNB	1882-1930	1819-1961	1834-1938		0B.uh	17789
52-AAAC-f	West jysk					1				63		pnb					0c.uh	17792
52-AAAD	EAST NORDIC cluster	15	28	20,356,878	21,687,663		73.91	100	C	63		PNB					2B.uh	17799

Continued opposite

Table 9-13 continued

Code 1	REFERENCE NAME Autoglossonym 2	Coun 3	Peo 4	Mother-tongue speakers in 2000 5	in 2025 6	Media radio 7	CHURCH AC% 8	E% 9	Wld 10	Tr 11	Biblioglossonym 12	SCRIPTURES Print 13-15	P–activity 16	N–activity 17	B–activity 18	J-year 19	Jayuh 20-24	Ref 25
52-AAAD-a	Historical dansk					1				63		pnb					1c.uh	17800
52-AAAD-b	riks-dansk					1				63		pnb					1c.uh	17801
52-AAAD-c	General dansk	12	13	6,975,707	7,244,512	6	88.32	100	C	63	Danish	PNB	1987	1524-1989	1550-1993	1984	2A.uh	17802
52-AAAD-d	Standard norsk	1	1	1,026	1,107	6	0.19	52	B	63		PNB					1B.uh	17803
52-AAAD-e	by-mål					1				63		pnb					1c.uh	17806
52-AAAD-f	amerikansk-norsk					1				63		pnb					1c.uh	17807
52-AAAD-g	East norsk					1				63		pnb					1c.uh	17808
52-AAAD-h	East jysk					1				63		pnb					1c.uh	17809
52-AAAD-i	oen-dansk					1				63		pnb					1c.uh	17815
52-AAAD-j	bornholmsk					1				63		pnb					1c.uh	17823
52-AAAD-k	South svensk					1				63		pnb					1c.uh	17824
52-AAAD-l	Historical svensk					1				63		pnb					1c.uh	17829
52-AAAD-m	hög-svensk					1				63		pnb					1c.uh	17830
52-AAAD-n	tal-språk					1				63	Swedish	PNB		1526	1541		1c.uh	17831
52-AAAD-o	bohuslänsk					1				63		pnb					1c.uh	17832
52-AAAD-p	göta-svensk					1				63		pnb					1c.uh	17833
52-AAAD-q	värmlands-svensk					1				63		pnb					1c.uh	17841
52-AAAD-r	svea-svensk	12	14	13,380,145	14,442,044	6	66.41	100	C	63	Swedish	PNB	1536-1991	1526-1981	1541-1977	1984	1A.uh	17842
52-AAAD-s	dalarna-svensk					1				63		pnb					1c.uh	17846
52-AAAD-t	East svensk					1				63		pnb					1c.uh	17847
52-AAAD-u	jämtlands-svensk					1				63		pnb					1c.uh	17853
52-AAAD-v	norrlands-svensk					1				63		pnb					1c.uh	17856
52-AAAD-w	gotländsk					1				63		pnb					1c.uh	17859
52-AB	WEST GERMANIC chain	216	825	423,480,614	473,691,689		69.63	99	C	82		PNB					4Bsuh	17860
52-ABA	**ANGLO-SAXON net**	199	577	288,118,052	336,121,153		67.15	99	C	82		PNB					4Bsuh	17861
52-ABAA	HISTORICAL ENGLISH cluster									0		...					0....	17862
52-ABAA-a	Historical kentish					0				0		...					0....	17863
52-ABAA-b	Historical west-saxon					0				0		...					0....	17864
52-ABAA-c	Historical mercian					0				0		...					0....	17865
52-ABAA-d	Historical northumbrian					0				0		...					0....	17866
52-ABAB	NORTHUMB-SCOTS cluster	4	1	4,000,000	6,800,000		85.00	100	C	41		PN.					0....	17867
52-ABAB-a	shetlandic					0				41		pn.					0....	17868
52-ABAB-b	orcadian					0				41		pn.					0....	17873
52-ABAB-c	Northeast scots					0				41		pn.					0....	17878
52-ABAB-d	Central scots					0				41	Scots	PN.		1901-1983			0....	17887
52-ABAB-e	border-scots					0				41		pn.					0....	17902
52-ABAB-f	ulster-scots					0				41		pn.					0....	17906
52-ABAB-g	madeleine-scots					0				41		pn.					0....	17910
52-ABAB-h	otago-scots			0	0	0	0.00	0		41		pn.					0....	17911
52-ABAB-i	northumbrian					0				41		pn.					0....	17912
52-ABAB-j	cumbrian					0				41		pn.					0....	17921
52-ABAC	GLOBAL ENGLISH cluster	195	387	231,597,546	265,340,088		65.40	99	C	72		PNB					3Bsuh	17927
52-ABAC-a	English-M.					1				72	English: Old*	Pnb	1571-1936				1csuh	17928
52-ABAC-b	standard English	173	196	53,367,782	56,245,192	8	66.64	99	C	72	English	PNB	1526	1526	1535	1978	3Bsuh	17931
52-ABAC-c	Mercian-T.					1				72		pnb					1csuh	17954
52-ABAC-d	Southern-British-T.					1				72		pnb					1csuh	17969
52-ABAC-e	Cockney					1				72		pnb					1csuh	17985
52-ABAC-f	General Southern-British					1				72		pnb					1csuh	17989
52-ABAC-g	General Central-British					1				72		pnb					1csuh	17997
52-ABAC-h	General Scottish English	1	1	5,588,865	5,696,281	8	76.00	100	C	72	English: Scottish, Lowland	PNb	1856	1901			1Asuh	18013
52-ABAC-i	Irish-English	5	8	2,653,351	2,739,359	8	85.86	100	C	72		pnb					1Asuh	18014
52-ABAC-j	Newfie-T.					1				72		pnb					1csuh	18022
52-ABAC-k	Maritimes-T.					1				72		pnb					1csuh	18027
52-ABAC-l	Ottowan-T.					1				72		pnb					1csuh	18031
52-ABAC-m	New England-T.					1				72		pnb					1csuh	18032
52-ABAC-n	Newyorkese					1				72		pnb					1csuh	18036
52-ABAC-o	Mid-coast-T.					1				72		pnb					1csuh	18043
52-ABAC-p	Appalachian-T.					1				72		pnb					1csuh	18047
52-ABAC-q	Dixie-T.					1				72		pnb					1csuh	18050
52-ABAC-r	General Canadian	6	10	16,450,775	19,951,339	8	64.83	99	C	72		pnb					1Bsuh	18058
52-ABAC-s	General American	117	129	134,532,090	157,574,179	8	64.05	98	C	72	English*	PNB	1526	1526	1535	1978	1Bsuh	18067
52-ABAC-t	South-Atlantic-English	1	1	4,971	6,127	8	87.51	100	C	72		pnb					1Bsuh	18074
52-ABAC-u	South-British-African-English	2	3	1,102,621	1,256,688	8	80.25	93	C	72		pnb					1Bsuh	18079
52-ABAC-v	Afrikaans-English					1				72		pnb					1csuh	18084
52-ABAC-w	Strine					8				72		pnb					1Asuh	18085
52-ABAC-x	General Australian	16	18	14,493,293	17,729,961	8	65.66	99	C	72		pnb					1Bsuh	18091
52-ABAC-y	General New-Zealand	9	10	3,004,050	3,648,274	8	66.91	100	C	72		pnb					1Bsuh	18092
52-ABAD	ASIAN-ENGLISH cluster	16	24	1,445,567	1,725,273		43.59	87	B	0		...					0B.uh	18093
52-ABAD-a	south-asian-english	13	17	1,300,599	1,546,687	8	43.02	87	B	0		...					0B.uh	18094
52-ABAD-b	southeast-asian-english	2	4	112,967	141,959	8	43.59	85	B	0		...					0B.uh	18113
52-ABAD-c	east-asian-english	2	3	32,001	36,627	8	66.44	98	C	0		...					0B.uh	18117
52-ABAD-d	philippine-english					1				0		...					0c.uh	18123
52-ABAE	BLACK-ENGLISH cluster	31	45	38,975,582	45,665,971		75.58	100	C	61		PNB					0B.uh	18124
52-ABAE-a	talkin-black	14	16	32,741,317	38,296,620	8	75.21	100	C	61		pnb					0B.uh	18125
52-ABAE-b	samaná-english	2	2	9,706	12,752	8	89.80	100	C	61		pnb					0A.uh	18134
52-ABAE-c	caribbean-english	10	13	645,554	803,627	8	62.36	99	C	61		pnb					0B.uh	18135
52-ABAE-d	americo-liberian					1				61		pnb					0c.uh	18153
52-ABAE-e	west-african-english	3	3	154,740	165,803	8	88.60	100	C	61		pnb					0B.uh	18154
52-ABAE-f	black-south-african-english	4	5	74,107	96,847	8	76.00	90	C	61		PNB					0B.uh	18161
52-ABAE-g	east-african-english	1	2	13,611	18,895	8	60.35	92	C	61		pnb					0A.uh	18171
52-ABAE-h	seychellois-english					1				61		pnb					0c.uh	18175
52-ABAE-i	oceanian-english	3	4	5,336,547	6,271,427	8	79.11	100	C	61		pnb					0B.uh	18176
52-ABAF	CARIB-ANGLO-CREOL cluster	31	60	7,306,713	9,369,651		73.51	100	C	45	West Carib Creole English	PN.				1995	1a..h	18191
52-ABAF-a	sea-island-creole	1	1	158,163	184,990	8	85.00	100	C	45	Gullah*	Pn.	1994				1c..h	18192
52-ABAF-b	ghenna-creole					1				45		pn.					1c..h	18196
52-ABAF-c	afro-seminole-creole	2	2	149,067	175,806	1	89.34	100	C	45		pn.					1c..h	18199
52-ABAF-d	belizean-creole	1	2	104,371	160,447	8	82.37	100	C	45	Belize Creole English	pn.					1a..h	18203
52-ABAF-e	honduran-creole	1	2	38,912	63,936	8	97.00	100	C	45		pn.					1c..h	18206
52-ABAF-f	mískito-coastal-creole	1	3	457,794	784,558	8	86.77	100	C	45		pn.					1c..h	18212
52-ABAF-g	limón-coastal-creole	1	1	40,234	59,285	8	97.40	100	C	45		pn.					1c..h	18215
52-ABAF-h	san-andrés-providencia-creole					1				45		pn.					1c..h	18216
52-ABAF-i	colón-creole	1	2	274,145	362,800	8	96.02	100	C	45		pn.					1c..h	18219
52-ABAF-j	rio-abajo-creole					1				45		pn.					1c..h	18220
52-ABAF-k	bocas-del-toro-creole					1				45		pn.					1c..h	18221
52-ABAF-l	cayman-creole	2	3	29,695	60,288	8	69.89	100	C	45	Dutch Creole	PN.		1781-1833			1c..h	18222
52-ABAF-m	jamaican-creole	7	9	3,073,348	3,821,933	8	54.46	99	B	45	West Carib Creole English	pn.					1c..h	18225
52-ABAF-n	bahamian-creole	2	3	274,039	366,363	8	88.26	100	C	45		pn.					1a..h	18231
52-ABAF-o	turks-caicos-creole	1	1	12,905	26,002	8	80.00	100	C	45		pn.					1c..h	18239
52-ABAF-p	virgin-islands-creole	2	3	76,431	84,697	8	91.27	100	C	45		pn.					1c..h	18242
52-ABAF-q	anguillan-creole	1	2	8,126	10,743	8	86.89	100	C	45		pn.					1a..h	18248
52-ABAF-r	saint-martin-creole					1				45		pn.					1c..h	18251
52-ABAF-s	kittitian-creole	1	2	36,704	33,440	8	95.71	100	C	45		pn.					1c..h	18255
52-ABAF-t	antiguan-creole	1	2	58,034	64,494	8	79.90	100	C	45		pn.					1a..h	18258
52-ABAF-u	montserrat-creole	1	1	10,129	10,157	8	96.51	100	C	45		pn.					1c..h	18261
52-ABAF-v	vincentian-creole	1	2	96,861	111,163	8	71.43	100	C	45		pn.					1c..h	18262
52-ABAF-w	grenadan-creole	1	1	48,452	54,102	8	98.10	100	C	45		pn.					1c..h	18265
52-ABAF-x	tobagonian-creole					1				45		pn.					1c..h	18267
52-ABAF-y	trinidadian-ex-creole	2	3	804,074	928,700	8	87.98	100	C	45	Lesser Antill Creole French	Pn.	1894-1992				1c..h	18268
52-ABAF-z	bajan	1	2	251,734	276,218	8	73.31	100	C	45		pn.					1a..h	18269
52-ABAG	GUIANESE-CREOLE- cluster	6	19	1,292,243	1,548,640		58.26	89	B	43		PN.					4.s..	18270
52-ABAG-a	guyanese	3	6	879,710	1,065,488	8	48.65	84	B	43		pn.					1.s..	18271
52-ABAG-b	rupununi					1				43		pn.					1.s..	18275
52-ABAG-c	sranan-tongo	4	4	358,860	402,286	5	80.64	100	C	43	Sranan	PN.	1987	1829-1846		1986	4.s..	18276
52-ABAG-d	saramacca-tongo	2	2	27,932	38,895	1	63.25	100	C	43	Saramaccan	PN.	1974-1985	1991		1993	1.s..	18277
52-ABAG-e	matawari	1	1	1,155	1,453	1	7.97	47	A	43		pn.					1.s..	18280

Continued overleaf

Table 9-13 continued

Code 1	REFERENCE NAME Autoglossonym 2	Coun 3	Peo 4	Mother-tongue speakers in 2000 5	in 2025 6	Media radio 7	CHURCH AC% 8	E% 9	Wld 10	Tr 11	Biblioglossonym 12	SCRIPTURES Print 13-15	P–activity 16	N–activity 17	B–activity 18	J-year 19	Jayuh 20-24	Ref 25
52-ABAG-f	kwinti	1	1	384	483	1	70.05	100	C	43		pn.					1.s..	18281
52-ABAG-g	ndjuka	3	3	21,128	34,062	1	71.11	100	C	43	Aukan*	Pn.	1975-1987				1.s..	18282
52-ABAG-h	aluku	2	2	3,074	5,973	1	79.99	100	C	43		pn.					1.s..	18285
52-ABAG-i	paramaccan					1				43		pn.					1.s..	18286
52-ABAH	WEST-COAST-CREOLE- cluster	12	21	2,606,334	4,435,976		62.55	100	C	41		PN.					4.s.h	18287
52-ABAH-a	aku	1	2	11,226	18,497	8	59.99	100	B	41		pn.					1.s.h	18288
52-ABAH-b	krio	4	5	553,750	921,120	8	37.82	99	B	41	Krio	PN.	1992	1986-1992		1996	4.s.h	18289
52-ABAH-c	kroo-english	1	4	78,393	164,482	8	73.27	100	C	41		pn.					1.s.h	18294
52-ABAH-d	liberian-inland-creole					1				41		pn.					1.s.h	18295
52-ABAH-e	nigerian-creole	1	2	1,020,382	1,674,991	8	59.89	100	B	41	Pidgin, Nigerian	Pn.	1957				1.s.h	18296
52-ABAH-f	cameroonian-creole	3	3	891,629	1,564,958	8	78.99	100	C	41	Pidgin: Cameroon*	Pn.	1966			1989	4.s.h	18302
52-ABAI	OCEANIAN-CREOLE cluster	12	21	894,067	1,235,554		84.58	100	C	82		PNB					4asuh	18305
52-ABAI-a	australian-creole	1	2	12,936	15,822	1	75.73	100	C	82	Kriol	PNb	1981-1991	1991			1csuh	18306
52-ABAI-b	torres-strait-creole	1	1	26,528	32,445	1	70.00	100	C	82	Torres Strait Creole	pnb					1csuh	18313
52-ABAI-c	tok-pisin-creole	4	6	501,664	735,937	5	81.13	100	C	82	Tok Pisin	PNB	1956-1992	1969-1978	1989	1986	3asuh	18318
52-ABAI-d	solomonic-creole	2	2	24,517	41,931	4	95.47	100	C	82	Pijin: Solomon Islands	PNb	1976-1988	1993			1csuh	18319
52-ABAI-e	bislama	3	4	48,020	81,337	4	94.25	100	C	82	Bislama	PNB	1968-1988	1980	1996	1981	4ssuh	18320
52-ABAI-f	nauruan-creole					1				82		pnb				1980	4csuh	18321
52-ABAI-g	hawaiian-creole	1	1	278,357	325,573	8	90.00	100	C	82	Hawaii Creole English	pnb					1csuh	18322
52-ABAI-h	pitcairnese	4	4	1,186	1,476	8	98.40	100	C	82		pnb					1csuh	18327
52-ABAI-i	norfolk-island-creole	1	1	859	1,033	1	64.03	100	C	82		pnb					1csuh	18329
52-ABB	**FRISIAN net**	4	5	926,156	935,242		72.04	100	C	63		PNB					0....	18330
52-ABBA	WEST FRYSK cluster	3	3	846,713	854,094		72.00	100	C	63	Frisian	PNB	1755	1933	1943		0....	18331
52-ABBA-a	west-frysk	3	3	846,713	854,094	0	72.00	100	C	63		pnb					0....	18332
52-ABBB	EAST FRYSK cluster	1	1	11,429	11,153		72.00	100	C	4		...					0....	18337
52-ABBB-a	seeltersk					0				4		...					0....	18338
52-ABBB-b	wangeroogsk			0	0	0	0.00	0		4		...					0....	18339
52-ABBC	NORTHWEST FRYSK cluster	1	1	63,014	61,495		72.00	100	C	61	Frisian: Northern*	PNB	1755-1954	1933	1978		0....	18340
52-ABBC-a	sölring					0				61		pnb					0....	18341
52-ABBC-b	öömrang-fering					0				61		pnb					0....	18342
52-ABBD	FRASCH cluster	1	1	5,000	8,500		80.00	100	C	20		...					0....	18348
52-ABBD-a	wieding-mooring					0				20		...					0....	18349
52-ABBD-b	pellworm-nordstrand					0				20		...					0....	18361
52-ABC	**TEUTONIC net**	102	243	134,436,406	136,635,294		74.95	99	C	72		PNB					2Bsuh	18364
52-ABCA	NEDERLANDS cluster	28	41	21,735,728	22,093,257		73.78	100	C	72		PNB					2Bsuh	18365
52-ABCA-a	algemeen-nederlands	25	30	15,254,520	15,592,851	6	67.22	100	C	72	Dutch	PNB	1477-1986	1480-1992	1522-1988	1982	2Bsuh	18366
52-ABCA-b	hollands					1				72		pnb					1csuh	18369
52-ABCA-c	vries-hollands					1				72		pnb					1csuh	18380
52-ABCA-d	utrechts-alblasserwaards					1				72		pnb					1csuh	18385
52-ABCA-e	zeeuws-westhoeks					1				72		pnb					1csuh	18389
52-ABCA-f	westvlaemsch					1				72		pnb					1csuh	18395
52-ABCA-g	oostvlaandersch	11	11	6,481,208	6,500,406	6	89.22	100	C	72		pnb					1Bsuh	18404
52-ABCA-h	brussels					1				72		pnb					1csuh	18410
52-ABCA-i	antwerps					1				72		pnb					1csuh	18411
52-ABCA-j	brabants					1				72		pnb					1csuh	18412
52-ABCA-k	westplatt					1				72		pnb					1csuh	18425
52-ABCA-l	South geldersch					1				72		pnb					1csuh	18431
52-ABCB	AFRO-NEDERLANDS cluster	10	18	6,550,229	7,623,157		89.75	100	C	61		PNB					2B.uh	18437
52-ABCB-a	afrikaans	10	16	6,461,400	7,521,923	5	89.98	100	C	61	Afrikaans	PNB	1893-1929	1980	1933-1983	1987	2B.uh	18438
52-ABCB-b	kaaps					1				61		pnb					1c.uh	18439
52-ABCB-c	oorlans	1	1	28,264	32,211	1	80.00	100	C	61		pnb					1c.uh	18440
52-ABCB-d	negerhollands					1				61		pnb					1c.uh	18441
52-ABCB-e	berbice					1				61		pnb					1c.uh	18442
52-ABCB-f	skepi					1				61		pnb					1c.uh	18443
52-ABCB-g	fly taal	1	1	60,565	69,023	1	70.00	100	C	61		pnb					1c.uh	18444
52-ABCC	NORTH DEUTSCH cluster	12	13	10,408,212	10,302,801		89.59	100	C	63	German: Low*	PNB	1984-1986	1915-1987	1534	1994	2A.uh	18445
52-ABCC-a	North sächsisch	1	1	591,964	591,824	6	75.00	100	C	63	Saxon, Low	PNb		1915			1A.uh	18446
52-ABCC-b	mecklenburgisch-pommersch-T.					1				63		pnb					1c.uh	18464
52-ABCC-c	westfälisch-T.					1				63		pnb					1c.uh	18468
52-ABCC-d	engrisch-T.					1				63		pnb					1c.uh	18480
52-ABCC-e	ostfälisch-T.					1				63		pnb					1c.uh	18492
52-ABCC-f	brandenburgisch-T.					1				63		pnb					1c.uh	18497
52-ABCC-g	westpreussisch-T.					1				63		pnb					1c.uh	18507
52-ABCC-h	ostpreussisch-T.					1				63		pnb					1c.uh	18514
52-ABCC-i	mennoniten-plaut-T.					1				63		pnb					1c.uh	18518
52-ABCC-j	nataler-deutsch					1				63		pnb					1c.uh	18525
52-ABCD	CENTRAL DEUTSCH cluster	6	9	7,294,188	7,268,122		74.49	100	C	20		...					0A.uh	18526
52-ABCD-a	ripwarisch-T.					1				20		...					0c.uh	18527
52-ABCD-b	letzebürgesch-T.	5	5	413,388	445,786	8	93.53	100	C	20	Luxembourgeois	...					0a.uh	18533
52-ABCD-c	moselfränkisch-T.					1				20		...					0c.uh	18539
52-ABCD-d	lothringisch-T.					1				20		...					0c.uh	18545
52-ABCD-e	westpfälzisch-T.					1				20		...					0c.uh	18550
52-ABCD-f	vorderpfälzisch-T.					1				20		...					0c.uh	18560
52-ABCD-g	nordbadisch-T.					1				20		...					0c.uh	18566
52-ABCD-h	hessisch-nassauisch-T.					1				20		...					0c.uh	18572
52-ABCD-i	niederhessisch-T.					1				20		...					0c.uh	18582
52-ABCD-j	ostfränkisch-T.	3	4	6,880,800	6,822,336	8	73.34	100	C	20		...					0A.uh	18585
52-ABCD-k	thüringisch-obersächsisch-T.					1				20		...					0c.uh	18597
52-ABCD-l	schlesisch-T.					1				20		...					0c.uh	18609
52-ABCD-m	galizisch-pfälzisch					1				20		...					0c.uh	18624
52-ABCD-n	siebenbürgerisch					1				20		...					0c.uh	18625
52-ABCD-o	banater-schwäbisch					1				20		...					0c.uh	18629
52-ABCD-p	schwarzmeer-deutsch					1				20		...					0c.uh	18632
52-ABCD-q	texan-deutsch					1				20		...					0c.uh	18637
52-ABCD-r	lagunen-deutsch					1				20		...					0c.uh	18638
52-ABCE	HOCH-DEUTSCH cluster	86	98	71,117,305	71,383,421		71.61	100	C	61	German: Transylvania	PNB	1859				2B.uh	18639
52-ABCE-a	Standard hoch-deutsch	85	96	71,117,055	71,383,072	8	71.61	100	C	61	German*	PNB	1987	1983	1466-1982	1982	2B.uh	18640
52-ABCE-b	deutsche-umgangssprache					1				61		pnb					1c.uh	18645
52-ABCE-c	unser-deutsch	2	2	250	349	1	92.80	100	C	61		pnb					1c.uh	18656
52-ABCE-d	gastarbeiter-deutsch					1				61		pnb					1c.uh	18659
52-ABCF	SOUTH DEUTSCH cluster	16	25	10,496,461	10,797,862		85.70	100	C	41		PN.					0B.uh	18660
52-ABCF-a	nord-bayrisch-T.	3	4	292,259	417,892	8	85.68	100	C	41		pn.					0B.uh	18661
52-ABCF-b	donau-bayrisch-T.	12	14	8,754,958	8,881,675	8	86.07	100	C	41		pn.					0B.uh	18668
52-ABCF-c	donau-österreichisch-T.					1				41		pn.					0c.uh	18677
52-ABCF-d	steirisch-T.					1				41		pn.					0c.uh	18692
52-ABCF-e	kärntnerisch-T.					1				41		pn.					0c.uh	18700
52-ABCF-f	karnisch-T.					1				41		pn.					0c.uh	18710
52-ABCF-g	zimbrisch-T.	1	1	171,894	153,809	1	88.00	100	C	41		pn.					0c.uh	18714
52-ABCF-h	südtirolisch-T.					1				41		pn.					0c.uh	18718
52-ABCF-i	tirolisch-T.	1	1	5,762	6,739	1	90.00	100	C	41		pn.					0c.uh	18725
52-ABCF-j	schwäbisch-T.	1	1	822,205	802,382	8	80.00	100	C	41	Swabian	pn.					0c.uh	18734
52-ABCF-k	badisch-T.					1				41		pn.					0c.uh	18742
52-ABCF-l	elsässer-ditsch					1				41		pn.					0c.uh	18746
52-ABCF-m	oberwischauisch-T.					1				41		pn.					0c.uh	18750
52-ABCF-n	wolga-deutsch					1				41		pn.					0c.uh	18751
52-ABCF-o	kaukasus-deutsch					1				41		pn.					0c.uh	18754
52-ABCF-p	mittelasiatisches-deutsch					1				41		pn.					0c.uh	18755
52-ABCF-q	brazilinien-deutsch	1	1	73,252	93,841	8	87.00	100	C	41		pn.					0A.uh	18759
52-ABCF-r	hutterer-deutsch	1	1	19,227	23,394	1	90.00	100	C	41		pn.					0c.uh	18763
52-ABCF-s	sathmarisch					1				41		pn.					0c.uh	18764

Continued opposite

Table 9-13 continued

Code 1	REFERENCE NAME / Autoglossonym 2	Coun 3	Peo 4	Mother-tongue speakers in 2000 5	in 2025 6	Media radio 7	CHURCH AC% 8	E% 9	Wld 10	Tr 11	Biblioglossonym 12	SCRIPTURES Print 13-15	P-activity 16	N-activity 17	B-activity 18	J-year 19	Jayuh 20-24	Ref 25
52-ABCF-t	pennsylvanisch-dietsch	2	2	356,904	418,130	1	88.08	100	C	41	German: Pennsylvania*	PN.	1955-1975	1993-1994			0c.uh	18765
52-ABCF-u	templer-schwäbisch					1				41		pn.					0c.uh	18766
52-ABCG	SWISS-DEUTSCH-T. cluster	8	8	4,498,443	4,611,763		92.07	100	C	41	German: Erzgebirgisch*	PN.	1930-1986	1984			0B.uh	18767
52-ABCG-a	General schwytzer-tütsch	8	8	4,498,443	4,611,763	8	92.07	100	C	41	Schwyzerdutsch*	PN.	1936-1986	1984			0B.uh	18768
52-ABCG-b	basel-dytsch-T.					1				41		pn.					0c.uh	18771
52-ABCG-c	bärn-dütsch-T.					1				41	German: Bern	PN.	1936	1984			0c.uh	18779
52-ABCG-d	walserisch-T.					1				41		pn.					0c.uh	18787
52-ABCG-e	luzern-tütsch-T.					1				41		pn.					0c.uh	18793
52-ABCG-f	Proper schwyzer-tütsch					1				41		pn.					0c.uh	18800
52-ABCG-g	züri-tüütsch-T.					1				41		pn.					0c.uh	18806
52-ABCG-h	glarnertütsch-T.					1				41		pn.					0c.uh	18807
52-ABCG-i	bündner-deutsch-T.					1				41		pn.					0c.uh	18808
52-ABCG-j	Northeast schweizerisch					1				41		pn.					0c.uh	18809
52-ABCG-k	vorarlbergisch-liechtensteinisch-T.					1				41		pn.					0c.uh	18818
52-ABCG-l	argentinien-schwyzertütsch					1				41		pn.					0c.uh	18821
52-ABCH	YIDDISH cluster	30	30	2,319,396	2,538,863		0.32	52	B	63		PNB					0B..h	18822
52-ABCH-a	West yiddish	8	8	894,351	1,017,875	4	0.73	58	B	63	Yiddish	PNB	1544-1939	1678-1950	1821-1936		0B..h	18823
52-ABCH-b	East yiddish	2	2	719,618	664,704	5	0.02	47	A	63	Yiddish	PNB	1544-1939	1821-1950	1821-1936		0A..h	18829
52-ABCI	YENISH cluster	1	1	16,444	16,048		50.00	94	B	4		...					0....	18832
52-ABCI-a	jenisch					0				4		...					0....	18833
53	**SLAVONIC zone**	81	379	292,628,531	282,527,361		71.93	99	C	72		PNB					4Bsuh	18834
53-A	**SLAVONIC set**	81	379	292,628,531	282,527,361		71.93	99	C	72		PNB					4Bsuh	18835
53-AA	SLAVONIC chain	81	379	292,628,531	282,527,361		71.93	99	C	72		PNB					4Bsuh	18836
53-AAA	**SLAVONIC net**	81	379	292,628,531	282,527,361		71.93	99	C	72		PNB					4Bsuh	18837
53-AAAA	LITERARY SLAVONSKI cluster									72		PNB					0....	18838
53-AAAA-a	Historical slavonski					0				72	Slavonic, Old Church	PNB	1491-1580	1580	1581-1751		0....	18839
53-AAAA-b	russki-slavonski					0				72	Slavonic	PNB	1491	1580	1581		0....	18840
53-AAAA-c	srpski-slavonski					0				72		pnb					0....	18841
53-AAAA-d	bulgarski-slavonski					0				72		pnb					0....	18842
53-AAAB	SORB cluster	2	3	269,184	262,786		70.98	100	C	63		PNB					0....	18843
53-AAAB-a	dolno-serbska-roc			212,129	207,014	1	70.00	100	C	63	Sorbian: Lower*	PNB	1753	1709-1860	1796-1824		0....	18844
53-AAAB-b	hornjo-serbscina	1	1	212,129	207,014	2	70.00	100	C	63	Sorbian: Upper*	PNB	1670-1960	1706-1966	1728-1797		0....	18853
53-AAAC	LEKHITIC cluster	40	44	42,280,249	43,206,943		94.65	100	C	72		PNB					2A.uh	18860
53-AAAC-a	slovincki	1	1	233	234	1	88.84	100	C	72		pnb					1c.uh	18861
53-AAAC-b	kaszubi	1	1	153,897	155,105	1	90.00	100	C	72		pnb					1c.uh	18862
53-AAAC-c	polski	40	42	42,126,119	43,051,604	6	94.67	100	C	72	Polish	PNB	1522-1984	1553-1991	1561-1965	1980	2A.uh	18863
53-AAAD	CZECH-SLOVAK- cluster	24	40	18,554,921	18,468,153		60.91	100	C	72		PNB					2Asuh	18873
53-AAAD-a	czesky	20	21	11,220,468	10,795,368	6	48.76	99	B	72	Czech	PNB	1992	1475-1992	1488-1980	1990	2Asuh	18874
53-AAAD-b	slovensky	17	19	7,334,453	7,672,785	6	79.51	100	C	72	Slovak	PNB	1991	1993	1832-1926		1Asuh	18885
53-AAAE	EAST SLAVONIC cluster	78	154	200,869,728	190,440,249		67.53	99	C	72		PNB					4B..uh	18902
53-AAAE-a	rusyn	4	4	1,152,514	1,192,795	6	85.26	100	C	72		pnb					1c.uh	18903
53-AAAE-b	ukrainskiy	37	37	43,955,076	40,761,817	6	86.91	100	C	72	Ukrainian	PNB	1869-1942	1880-1942	1903-1962	1989	3A.uh	18906
53-AAAE-c	bielorusskiy	26	26	10,174,808	9,518,468	5	65.69	100	C	72	Byelorussian*	PNB	1517-1995	1931	1973	1991	3A.uh	18916
53-AAAE-d	russkiy	74	87	145,587,330	138,967,169	7	61.67	99	C	72	Russian	PNB	1815-1993	1821-1991	1680-1993	1982	4B.uh	18924
53-AAAF	SLOVENSKI cluster	14	15	2,265,163	2,130,896		88.93	100	C	72		PNB					1a..h	18933
53-AAAF-a	slovensko	14	15	2,265,163	2,130,896	6	88.93	100	C	72	Slovenian*	PNB	1993	1577-1985	1985	1990	1c..h	18934
53-AAAF-b	korosko-T.					1				72		pnb					1c..h	18939
53-AAAF-c	rezijansko					1				72		pnb					1c..h	18947
53-AAAF-d	benesko					1				72		pnb					1c..h	18948
53-AAAF-e	obosko					1				72		pnb					1c..h	18952
53-AAAF-f	krasko					1				72		pnb					1c..h	18956
53-AAAF-g	istrsko					1				72		pnb					1c..h	18959
53-AAAF-h	notranjsko					1				72		pnb					1c..h	18962
53-AAAF-i	gorenjsko-rovtarsko					1				72		pnb					1c..h	18963
53-AAAF-j	dolenjsko					1				72		pnb					1c..h	18973
53-AAAF-k	belo-krajinsko					1				72		pnb					1c..h	18977
53-AAAF-l	West stajersko					1				72		pnb					1c..h	18983
53-AAAF-m	East stajersko					1				72		pnb					1c..h	18989
53-AAAG	SRPSKO-HRVATSKI cluster	35	76	18,332,838	18,736,583		69.78	92	C	62		PNB					2Asuh	18996
53-AAAG-a	Standard srpski	33	52	12,512,967	12,978,347	6	58.21	88	B	62	Serbian*	PNB	1992	1563-1983	1804-1968	1988	1Asuh	18997
53-AAAG-b	Standard hrvatski	24	24	5,819,871	5,758,236	6	94.64	100	C	62	Croatian	PNB	1562-1987	1563-1981	1831-1968	1991	2Asuh	18998
53-AAAG-c	Standard ikavian					1				62		pnb					1csuh	18999
53-AAAG-d	General srpski					1				62		pnb				1988	1csuh	19000
53-AAAG-e	General hrvatski					1				62		pnb					1csuh	19001
53-AAAG-f	kajkavski-T.					1				62		pnb					1csuh	19002
53-AAAG-g	cakavski-T.					1				62		pnb					1csuh	19003
53-AAAG-h	stokavski-T.					1				62		pnb					1csuh	19004
53-AAAG-i	torlakski					1				62		pnb					1csuh	19014
53-AAAH	BULGARSKI cluster	31	47	10,056,448	9,281,751		84.67	98	C	71		PNB					2A.uh	19015
53-AAAH-a	makedonski	10	10	1,684,016	1,794,819	5	89.46	100	C	71	Macedonian*	PNB	1952-1959	1967-1976	1988-1990	1991	2a.uh	19016
53-AAAH-b	bulgarski	27	35	8,301,869	7,394,739	6	83.86	97	C	71	Bulgarian	PNB	1823-1994	1840-1927	1864-1923	1990	2A.uh	19027
54	**BALTIC zone**	20	35	5,586,833	5,316,882		87.84	100	C	72		PNB					3A.u.	19037
54-A	**BALTIC set**	20	35	5,586,833	5,316,882		87.84	100	C	72		PNB					3A.u.	19038
54-AA	LITHUANIAN-LATVIAN chain	20	35	5,586,833	5,316,882		87.84	100	C	72		PNB					3A.u.	19039
54-AAA	**LITHUANIAN net**	17	18	4,042,537	3,973,551		90.78	100	C	63		PNB					3A.u.	19041
54-AAAA	LIETUVISHKAI cluster	17	18	4,042,537	3,973,551		90.78	100	C	63		PNB					3A.u.	19042
54-AAAA-a	Standard lietuvishkai	17	18	4,042,537	3,973,551	5	90.78	100	C	63	Lithuanian	PNB	1625-1994	1701-1989	1735-1930	1990	3A.u.	19042
54-AAAA-b	aukshtaichiai					1				63		pnb					1c.u.	19043
54-AAAA-c	dzukai					1				63		pnb					1c.u.	19047
54-AAAA-d	zhemaichiai					1				63		pnb					1c.u.	19048
54-AAB	**LATVIAN net**	16	17	1,544,296	1,343,331		80.14	100	C	72		PNB					3A.u.	19049
54-AABA	LATVIASHU cluster	16	17	1,544,296	1,343,331		80.14	100	C	72		PNB					3A.u.	19050
54-AABA-a	Standard Latviashu	16	17	1,544,296	1,343,331	5	80.14	100	C	72	Latvian	PNB	1637-1994	1685-1937	1689-1995	1989	3A.u.	19051
55	**ALBANIC zone**	17	20	5,767,009	6,510,598		30.73	81	B	61		PNB					2A.u.	19055
55-A	**ALBANIAN set**	17	20	5,767,009	6,510,598		30.73	81	B	61		PNB					2A.u.	19056
55-AA	ALBANIAN chain	17	20	5,767,009	6,510,598		30.73	81	B	61		PNB					2A.u.	19057
55-AAA	**ALBANIAN net**	17	20	5,767,009	6,510,598		30.73	81	B	61		PNB					2A.u.	19058
55-AAAA	GHEG cluster	8	8	2,596,213	2,756,735		24.11	73	B	43		PN.					2a.u.	19059
55-AAAA-a	Standard gheg					1				43		pn.					1c.u.	19060
55-AAAA-b	Northwest gheg	6	6	416,154	499,648	6	34.25	79	B	43	Albanian: Gheg*	PN.	1866-1978	1872			2c.u.	19061
55-AAAA-c	kosove	2	2	2,180,059	2,257,087	6	22.17	72	B	43		pn.				1989	2c.u.	19062

Continued overleaf

Table 9-13 continued

Code 1	REFERENCE NAME / Autoglossonym 2	Coun 3	Peo 4	Mother-tongue speakers in 2000 5	in 2025 6	Media radio 7	AC% 8	E% 9	Wld 10	Tr 11	Biblioglossonym 12	Print 13-15	P-activity 16	N-activity 17	B-activity 18	J-year 19	Jayuh 20-24	Ref 25
55-AAAA-d	shkod`r					1				43		pn.					1c.u.	19063
55-AAAA-e	Central gheg					1				43		pn.				1993	2c.u.	19064
55-AAAA-f	South gheg					1				43		pn.					1c.u.	19065
55-AAAA-g	mandrica					1				43		pn.					1c.u.	19066
55-AAAB	TOSK cluster	11	12	3,170,796	3,753,863		36.16	87	B	61		PNB					0A...	19067
55-AAAB-a	Standard tosk	7	7	2,653,968	3,247,313	6	30.81	86	B	61	Albanian: Tosk*	PNB	1824-1914	1827-1913	1993		0A...	19068
55-AAAB-b	West tosk					1				61		pnb					0c...	19069
55-AAAB-c	South tosk					1				61		pnb					0c...	19070
55-AAAB-d	East tosk					1				61		pnb					0c...	19071
55-AAAB-e	srem					1				61		pnb					0c...	19072
55-AAAB-f	North arbanasi					1				61		pnb					0c...	19073
55-AAAB-g	East arbanasi					1				61		pnb					0c...	19074
55-AAAB-h	South arbanasi	1	1	160,629	148,826	6	64.80	100	C	61	Albanian, Arvanitika	PNb		1827			0c...	19075
55-AAAB-i	tosk-ukraine	1	1	4,879	4,418	6	4.00	56	B	61		pnb					0A...	19080
55-AAAB-j	tosk-anatolia	1	1	91,409	120,618	6	10.00	55	B	61		pnb					0c...	19081
55-AAAB-k	arbresh	1	1	259,537	232,230	6	83.00	100	C	61	Albanian, Arbereshe	Pnb	1868-1869				0c...	19082
56	**HELLENIC zone**	83	91	14,099,678	13,976,909		96.24	100	C	71		PNB					2B.uh	19088
56-A	**HELLENIC set**	83	91	14,099,678	13,976,909		96.24	100	C	71		PNB					2B.uh	19089
56-AA	HELLENIC chain	83	91	14,099,678	13,976,909		96.24	100	C	71		PNB					2B.uh	19090
56-AAA	**HELLENIC net**	83	90	14,088,182	13,966,257		96.24	100	C	71		PNB					2B.uh	19091
56-AAAA	HELLENIKI cluster	83	90	14,088,182	13,966,257		96.24	100	C	71		PNB					2B.uh	19092
56-AAAA-a	Historical helleniki					1				71		PNB					1c.uh	19093
56-AAAA-b	katharevusa					1				71		pnb					1c.uh	19098
56-AAAA-c	dhimotiki	80	85	13,559,937	13,462,127	7	96.41	100	C	71	Greek: Modern	PNB	1547-1949	1638-1989	1840-1994	1981	2B.uh	19099
56-AAAA-d	North helleniki					1				71		pnb					1c.uh	19114
56-AAAA-e	attica-euboea					1				71		pnb					1c.uh	19125
56-AAAA-f	Southwest helleniki					1				71		pnb					1c.uh	19128
56-AAAA-g	kritiki					1				71		pnb					1c.uh	19131
56-AAAA-h	Southeast helleniki					1				71		pnb					1c.uh	19132
56-AAAA-i	italiot	2	2	213,784	200,090	6	95.00	100	C	71		pnb					1A.uh	19140
56-AAAA-j	pontiki	2	2	314,410	303,971	1	90.00	100	C	71		pnb					1c.uh	19144
56-AAAA-k	yevanitika	1	1	51	69	1	0.00	24	A	71		pnb					1c.uh	19148
56-AAB	**TSAKONIA net**	1	1	11,496	10,652		95.01	100	C	4		...					0....	19149
56-AABA	TSAKONIA cluster	1	1	11,496	10,652		95.01	100	C	4		...					0....	19150
56-AABA-a	kastanitas-sitena-					0				4		...					0....	19151
56-AABA-b	leonidhion-prastos	1	1	11,496	10,652		95.01	100	C	4		...					0....	19152
57	**ARMENIC zone**	48	49	6,965,966	8,148,159		82.74	100	C	72		PNB					4A.u.	19153
57-A	**ARMENIC set**	48	49	6,965,966	8,148,159		82.74	100	C	72		PNB					4A.u.	19154
57-AA	ARMENIC chain	48	49	6,965,966	8,148,159		82.74	100	C	72		PNB					4A.u.	19155
57-AAA	**ARMENIC net**	48	49	6,965,966	8,148,159		82.74	100	C	72		PNB					4A.u.	19156
57-AAAA	HAY cluster	48	49	6,965,966	8,148,159		82.74	100	C	72		PNB					4A.u.	19157
57-AAAA-a	grabar					1				72	Armenian: Ancient	PNB	1565		1666		1c.u.	19158
57-AAAA-b	ashkharik	48	49	6,965,966	8,148,159	6	82.74	100	C	72	Armenian: Modern, Eastern	PNB	1831-1991	1825-1991	1853-1994	1991	4A.u.	19159
57-AAAA-c	arewmta-hayeren					1				72	Armenian: Modern, Western	PNB		1825	1853	1985	4c.u.	19171
58	**IRANIC zone**	57	252	123,198,333	192,248,670		0.41	38	A	63		PNB					3Asu.	19193
58-A	**IRANIAN-NURISTANI set**	57	252	123,198,333	192,248,670		0.41	38	A	63		PNB					3Asu.	19194
58-AA	WEST IRANIAN chain	55	187	89,821,226	133,599,336		0.16	36	A	63		PNB					3Asu.	19195
58-AAA	**KURDIC net**	32	50	19,197,333	27,509,770		0.07	29	A	48		PN.					3A...	19196
58-AAAA	KURDISH cluster	32	46	17,968,650	25,858,144		0.08	30	A	48		PN.					3A...	19197
58-AAAA-a	kurmanji	29	36	10,702,289	14,775,884	0	0.09	31	A	48	Kurdish: Kurmanji*	PN.	1856-1993	1872		1997	3c...	19198
58-AAAA-b	kurmanjiki	1	1	166,477	219,673	0	0.03	19	A	48	Kirmanjki	pn.					1A...	19206
58-AAAA-c	kurdi	5	8	7,093,696	10,855,064	0	0.06	29	A	48	Kurdi	PN.	1894-1972	1994			2c...	19207
58-AAAA-d	jafi					0				48		pn.					1c...	19216
58-AAAA-e	judeo-kurdish	1	1	6,188	7,523		0.00	20	A	48		pn.					1c...	19217
58-AAAB	DIMLI-GURANI cluster	3	4	1,228,683	1,651,626		0.00	12	A	20		...					0....	19218
58-AAAB-a	dimli	1	1	1,145,058	1,510,946	0	0.00	12	A	20	Dimli	...					0....	19219
58-AAAB-b	bajalani	1	1	40,199	71,327	0	0.07	19	A	20		...					0....	19223
58-AAAB-c	hawrami	2	2	43,426	69,353	0	0.05	12	A	20		...					0....	19226
58-AAB	**BALOCHI net**	13	17	8,752,237	14,553,861		0.00	20	A	35		P..					3.s..	19227
58-AABA	BALOCHI cluster	13	17	8,752,237	14,553,861		0.00	20	A	35		P..					3.s..	19228
58-AABA-a	East balochi	3	3	3,059,538	5,137,438	1	0.00	21	A	35	Baluchi: Eastern*	P..	1815-1906				1.s..	19229
58-AABA-b	West balochi	5	5	2,021,031	3,295,250	1	0.00	18	A	35	Baluchi: Western*	P..	198$-1984		1992		3.s..	19233
58-AABA-c	South balochi	7	7	3,652,917	6,096,156	1	0.00	20	A	35	Baluchi, Southern	P..	1992-1994				1.s..	19237
58-AABA-d	bashkardi	1	1	6,770	9,446	1	0.00	12	A	35		P..					1.s..	19243
58-AAC	**PERSIAN net**	46	120	61,871,656	91,535,705		0.21	40	A	63		PNB					2Asu.	19246
58-AACA	LURI-KUMZARI cluster	3	5	6,205,353	8,687,105		0.00	15	A	20		...					0....	19247
58-AACA-a	luri-bakhtiari	2	4	6,201,540	8,679,077	4	0.00	15	A	20		...					0....	19248
58-AACA-b	kumzari	1	1	3,813	8,028	1	0.00	11	A	20		...					0....	19255
58-AACB	LARI-FARS cluster	1	2	40,621	56,677		0.00	9	A	4		...					0....	19256
58-AACB-a	lari	1	1	33,851	47,231	0	0.00	9	A	4		...					0....	19257
58-AACB-b	fars	1	1	6,770	9,446	0	0.00	8	A	4		...					0....	19258
58-AACC	CENTRAL PERSIAN cluster	46	86	47,594,292	71,634,252		0.22	46	A	63		PNB					2Asu.	19259
58-AACC-a	parsi-I	4	4	216,052	283,508	4	0.05	38	A	63	Gujarati: Parsi	PNb	1861	1864			1Asu.	19260
58-AACC-b	parsi-II					1				63		pnb					1csu.	19261
58-AACC-c	Standard farsi	32	35	30,745,063	43,368,921	5	0.33	52	B	63		PNB					1Asu.	19264
58-AACC-d	General farsi	2	2	7,388	7,415	1	3.51	27	A	63		pnb					1csu.	19267
58-AACC-e	farsi-T.	3	3	2,229,183	4,210,279	4	0.03	29	A	63		pnb				1983	2asu.	19270
58-AACC-f	dari-T.	3	6	7,594,270	13,511,441	4	0.02	32	A	63	Dari*	PNb	1974	1982-1985		1995	2asu.	19287
58-AACC-g	pahlavani	1	1	2,272	4,493	1	0.00	11	A	63		pnb					1csu.	19293
58-AACC-h	darwazi	1	1	15,048	29,760	1	0.00	11	A	63		pnb					1csu.	19294
58-AACC-i	tangshewi	1	1	1,204	2,382	1	0.00	15	A	63		pnb					1csu.	19295
58-AACC-j	tajiki	13	15	5,433,949	7,669,998	4	0.02	40	A	63	Tajik*	PNB	1981	1983	1992	1991	2asu.	19296
58-AACC-k	judeo-persian	8	9	153,942	204,938	5	0.31	33	A	63	Panjabi: Persian*	PNB	1546-1885	1815-1912	1838		2asu.	19302
58-AACC-l	aimaq	2	7	1,176,777	2,307,592	1	0.00	15	A	63		pnb					1asu.	19305
58-AACC-m	warduji	1	1	4,544	8,987	1	0.00	13	A	63		pnb					1csu.	19316
58-AACC-n	dehwari	1	1	14,600	24,538	1	0.00	13	A	63		pnb					1csu.	19317
58-AACD	NORTH PERSIAN. cluster	1	9	107,558	150,072		0.01	11	A	4		...					0....	19318
58-AACD-a	ashtiani	1	1	20,311	28,339	0	0.03	13	A	4		...					0....	19319
58-AACD-b	vafsi	1	1	20,311	28,339	0	0.02	15	A	4		...					0....	19320
58-AACD-c	nayini	1	1	6,770	9,446	0	0.00	7	A	4		...					0....	19321
58-AACD-d	natanzi	1	1	6,770	9,446	0	0.00	7	A	4		...					0....	19322
58-AACD-e	soi	1	1	6,770	9,446	0	0.00	7	A	4		...					0....	19323

Continued opposite

Table 9-13 continued

Code 1	REFERENCE NAME / Autoglossonym 2	Coun 3	Peo 4	Mother-tongue speakers in 2000 5	in 2025 6	Media radio 7	CHURCH AC% 8	E% 9	Wld 10	Tr 11	Biblioglossonym 12	SCRIPTURES Print 13-15	P-activity 16	N-activity 17	B-activity 18	J-year 19	Jayuh 20-24	Ref 25
58-AACD-f	khunsari	1	1	20,311	28,339	0	0.00	5	A	4		. . .					0. . . .	19324
58-AACD-g	gazi	1	1	6,770	9,446	0	0.00	8	A	4		. . .					0. . . .	19325
58-AACD-h	sivandi	1	1	6,770	9,446	0	0.00	7	A	4		. . .					0. . . .	19326
58-AACD-i	gabri	1	1	12,775	17,825	0	0.05	25	A	4		. . .					0. . . .	19327
58-AACE	CASPIAN-PERSIAN cluster	2	9	7,773,443	10,819,076		0.24	25	A	20		. . .					1. . . .	19330
58-AACE-a	mazandarani	1	1	3,444,769	4,806,365	4	0.00	23	A	20	Mazanderani	. . .					1. . . .	19331
58-AACE-b	ghilaki	1	3	3,715,578	5,184,216	1	0.50	28	A	20	Gilaki	. . .					1. . . .	19337
58-AACE-c	takestani	1	1	301,092	420,103	1	0.00	12	A	20		. . .					1. . . .	19341
58-AACE-d	talishi	2	2	268,201	347,275	1	0.00	18	A	20		. . .					1. . . .	19347
58-AACE-e	karingani	1	1	16,722	23,332	1	0.00	7	A	20		. . .					1. . . .	19354
58-AACE-f	harzani	1	1	27,081	37,785	1	0.06	11	A	20		. . .					1. . . .	19355
58-AACF	WEST PERSIAN cluster	1	1	20,311	28,339		0.03	19	A	4		. . .					0. . . .	19356
58-AACF-a	semnani	1	1	20,311	28,339	5	0.03	19	A	4		. . .					0. . . .	19357
58-AACF-b	sangisari					1				4		. . .					0. . . .	19358
58-AACG	TAT-PERSIAN cluster	4	8	130,078	160,184		3.20	24	A	22		P. .					0. . . .	19359
58-AACG-a	muslim-tat	3	3	52,767	60,598	0	7.80	37	A	22	Tat*	P. .	1989				0. . . .	19360
58-AACG-b	judeo-tat	4	5	77,311	99,586	0	0.06	14	A	22	Judeo-tat	P. .	1980				0. . . .	19361
58-AACG-c	christian-tat					0				22		p. .					0. . . .	19366
58-AB	EAST IRANIAN chain	26	55	33,301,956	58,504,509		1.10	44	A	63		PNB					2As. .	19367
58-ABA	AVESTAN net									0		. . .					0. . . .	19368
58-ABAA	HISTORICAL AVESTAN cluster									0		. . .						19369
58-ABAA-a	Historical zoroastrian					0				0		. . .					0. . . .	19370
58-ABAA-b	Proper avestan					0				0		. . .					0. . . .	19371
58-ABB	OSSETIC net	15	15	730,815	758,498		43.98	86	B	41		PN.					2. . . .	19372
58-ABBA	OSETI cluster	15	15	730,815	758,498		43.98	86	B	41	Ossete*	PN.	1848-1984	1993		1992	2. . . .	19373
58-ABBA-a	digor					0				41		pn.					1. . . .	19374
58-ABBA-b	iron					0				41		pn.					1. . . .	19377
58-ABC	SOGDIAN net	1	1	2,552	3,653		0.00	18	A	2		. . .					0. . . .	19383
58-ABCA	HISTORICAL SUGHDIK cluster			0	0		0.00	0		0		. . .					0. . . .	19384
58-ABCA-a	great-wall-sogdian					0				0		. . .					0. . . .	19385
58-ABCA-b	buddhist-sogdian					0				0		. . .					0. . . .	19386
58-ABCA-c	christian-sogdian					0				0		. . .					0. . . .	19387
58-ABCA-d	manichean-sogdian					0				0		. . .					0. . . .	19388
58-ABCB	YAGHNOBI cluster	1	1	2,552	3,653		0.00	18	A	2		. . .					0. . . .	19389
58-ABCB-a	yaghnobi	1	1	2,552	3,653	0	0.00	18	A	2		. . .					0. . . .	19390
58-ABD	PUSHTU-PAMIR net	16	35	32,546,518	57,700,343		0.13	43	A	63		PNB					1As. .	19393
58-ABDA	PUSHTU cluster	15	22	32,312,991	57,334,495		0.12	43	A	63		PNB					1As. .	19394
58-ABDA-a	pashto	15	18	17,853,404	33,074,425	5	0.06	38	A	63		pnb				1985	1As. .	19395
58-ABDA-b	paktyan-pashto					1				63	Pashto, Southern	pnb					1cs. .	19404
58-ABDA-c	pakhto	2	3	14,351,363	24,078,179	5	0.20	50	B	63	Pashto*	PNB	1989	1818-1991	1895		1as. .	19408
58-ABDA-d	dera-ismail-khan					1				63		pnb					1cs. .	19418
58-ABDA-e	wanechi	1	1	108,224	181,891	1	0.00	14	A	63		pnb					1cs. .	19419
58-ABDB	MUNJI-YIDGHA cluster	2	2	10,740	19,218		0.06	10	A	4		. . .					0. . . .	19420
58-ABDB-a	munji	1	1	3,933	7,778	0	0.00	2	A	4		. . .					0. . . .	19421
58-ABDB-b	yidgha	1	1	6,807	11,440	0	0.09	15	A	4		. . .					0. . . .	19426
58-ABDC	WAKHI cluster	4	5	104,834	173,134		3.20	25	A	12	Wakhi	. . .					0. . . .	19427
58-ABDC-a	North wakhi					0				12		. . .					0. . . .	19428
58-ABDC-b	Central wakhi					0				12		. . .					0. . . .	19429
58-ABDC-c	South wakhi					0				12		. . .					0. . . .	19430
58-ABDC-d	East wakhi					0				12		. . .					0. . . .	19434
58-ABDD	SANGLECHI cluster	2	2	3,737	7,057		0.00	7	A	2		. . .					0. . . .	19435
58-ABDD-a	sanglechi	2	2	3,737	7,057	0	0.00	7	A	2		. . .					0. . . .	19436
58-ABDD-b	ishkashmi					0				2		. . .					0. . . .	19437
58-ABDD-c	zebaki					0				2		. . .					0. . . .	19440
58-ABDE	SHUGNI-ROSHANI cluster	3	3	110,045	160,469		0.00	11	A	12		. . .					0. . . .	19441
58-ABDE-a	shughni-bajuvi	2	2	72,673	117,166	0	0.00	10	A	12	Shughni	. . .					0. . . .	19442
58-ABDE-b	bartangi-oroshori					0				12		. . .					0. . . .	19445
58-ABDE-c	roshani-khufi					0				12		. . .					0. . . .	19448
58-ABDE-d	sarikoli	1	1	37,372	43,303	0	0.01	15	A	12		. . .					0. . . .	19451
58-ABDF	YAZGHULAMI cluster	1	1	4,171	5,970		0.00	19	A	12		. . .					0. . . .	19461
58-ABDF-a	yazghulami	1	1	4,171	5,970	0	0.00	19	A	12	Yazgulyam	. . .					0. . . .	19462
58-ABE	PARACHI-ORMURI net	2	4	22,071	42,015		0.13	7	A	4		. . .					0. . . .	19463
58-ABEA	PARACHI-ORMURI cluster	2	4	22,071	42,015		0.13	7	A	4		. . .					0. . . .	19464
58-ABEA-a	parachi	1	1	8,602	17,012	0	0.00	3	A	4		. . .					0. . . .	19465
58-ABEA-b	ormuri	2	3	13,469	25,003	0	0.21	9	A	4		. . .					0. . . .	19469
58-AC	NURISTANI chain	2	10	75,151	144,825		0.03	6	A	4		. . .					0. . . .	19473
58-ACA	ASHKUND net	1	2	16,854	33,332		0.00	4	A	4		. . .					0. . . .	19474
58-ACAA	ASHKUND cluster	1	2	16,854	33,332		0.00	4	A	4		. . .					0. . . .	19475
58-ACAA-a	ashkuni	1	1	10,947	21,649	0	0.00	3	A	4		. . .					0. . . .	19476
58-ACB	BASHGALI -PRASUNI net	2	6	40,121	75,546		0.06	8	A	4		. . .					0. . . .	19480
58-ACBA	BASH-GALI cluster	2	4	32,298	61,469		0.07	8	A	4		. . .					0. . . .	19481
58-ACBA-a	West kata-viri					0				4		. . .					0. . . .	19482
58-ACBA-b	lamert-viri					0				4		. . .					0. . . .	19487
58-ACBA-c	mum-viri					0				4		. . .					0. . . .	19490
58-ACBA-d	kam-viri	2	2	8,238	15,670	0	0.00	3	A	4		. . .					0. . . .	19494
58-ACBA-e	East kata-viri					0				4		. . .					0. . . .	19495
58-ACBB	PRASUNI cluster	2	2	7,823	14,077		0.00	7	A	4		. . .					0. . . .	19500
58-ACBB-a	prasuni	2	2	7,823	14,077	0	0.00	7	A	4		. . .					0. . . .	19501
58-ACC	WAI-GELI net	1	2	18,176	35,947		0.00	3	A	4		. . .					0. . . .	19505
58-ACCA	WAI-GELI cluster	1	2	18,176	35,947		0.00	3	A	4		. . .					0. . . .	19506
58-ACCA-a	wai-ala	1	1	13,632	26,960	0	0.00	3	A	4		. . .					0. . . .	19507
58-ACCA-b	tregami	1	1	4,544	8,987	0	0.00	4	A	4		. . .					0. . . .	19512
59	INDIC zone	137	605	1,066,772,352	1,458,852,964		2.59	53	B	80		PNB					4Bsuh	19513
59-A	INDIC set	137	605	1,066,772,352	1,458,852,964		2.59	53	B	80		PNB					4Bsuh	19514
59-AA	TRANS-INDIC chain	100	457	1,045,329,285	1,432,761,948		2.18	53	B	80		PNB					4Asuh	19515
59-AAA	PASHAYI-DARDIC net	3	9	226,422	434,556		0.29	5	A	20		. . .					0. . . .	19516
59-AAAA	NORTH PASHAYI cluster	1	1	159,338	315,123		0.00	2	A	20		. . .					0. . . .	19517
59-AAAA-a	gulbahar					0				20		. . .					0. . . .	19518
59-AAAA-b	kohnadeh					0				20		. . .					0. . . .	19519

Continued overleaf

Table 9-13 continued

Code 1	REFERENCE NAME / Autoglossonym 2	Coun 3	Peo 4	Mother-tongue speakers in 2000 5	in 2025 6	Media radio 7	AC% 8	E% 9	Wld 10	Tr 11	Biblioglossonym 12	Print 13-15	P-activity 16	N-activity 17	B-activity 18	J-year 19	Jayuh 20-24	Ref 25
59-AAAA-c	laurowan					0				20		. . .					0	19520
59-AAAA-d	sanjan					0				20		. . .					0	19521
59-AAAA-e	shutul					0				20		. . .					0	19522
59-AAAA-f	bolaghain					0				20		. . .					0	19523
59-AAAA-g	pachagan					0				20		. . .					0	19524
59-AAAA-h	alasai					0				20		. . .					0	19525
59-AAAA-i	shamakot					0				20		. . .					0	19526
59-AAAA-j	uzbin					0				20		. . .					0	19527
59-AAAA-k	pandau					0				20		. . .					0	19528
59-AAAA-l	najil					0				20		. . .					0	19529
59-AAAA-m	parazhghan					0				20		. . .					0	19530
59-AAAA-n	pashagar					0				20		. . .					0	19531
59-AAAA-o	wadau					0				20		. . .					0	19532
59-AAAA-p	nangarach					0				20		. . .					0	19533
59-AAAB	EAST PASHAYI cluster	1	1	6,016	11,899		0.00	2	A	4		. . .					0	19534
59-AAAB-a	chugari					0				4		. . .					0	19535
59-AAAB-b	chalas					0				4		. . .					0	19540
59-AAAB-c	kurangal					0				4		. . .					0	19541
59-AAAB-d	nangalami	1	1	6,016	11,899	0	0.00	2	A	4		. . .					0	19542
59-AAAC	WEST PASHAYI cluster	1	1	20,000	34,000		3.21	20	A	4		. . .					0	19543
59-AAAC-a	tagau					0				4		. . .					0	19544
59-AAAC-b	ishpi					0				4		. . .					0	19545
59-AAAC-c	isken					0				4		. . .					0	19546
59-AAAD	SOUTH PASHAYI cluster	2	2	2,578	4,435		0.00	11	A	4		. . .					0	19547
59-AAAD-a	darrai-nur					0				4		. . .					0	19548
59-AAAD-b	wegal					0				4		. . .					0	19552
59-AAAD-c	laghmani	2	2	2,578	4,435		0.00	11	A	4		. . .					0	19553
59-AAAD-d	alingar					0				4		. . .					0	19554
59-AAAE	KUNAR cluster	2	5	38,490	69,099		0.01	10	A	4		. . .					0	19555
59-AAAE-a	dameli	1	1	6,040	10,152	0	0.03	14	A	4		. . .					0	19556
59-AAAE-b	gawar-bati	2	2	15,600	30,270	0	0.00	4	A	4		. . .					0	19559
59-AAAE-c	shumasti	2	2	16,850	28,677	0	0.02	13	A	4		. . .					0	19562
59-AAB	**CHITRAL-DARDIC net**	3	5	304,678	506,807		0.01	10	A	20		. . .					0	19563
59-AABA	CHITRAL cluster	3	5	304,678	506,807		0.01	10	A	20		. . .					0	19564
59-AABA-a	kho-war	3	4	299,107	497,444	0	0.01	10	A	20		. . .					0	19565
59-AABA-b	kalasha	1	1	5,571	9,363	0	0.11	17	A	20	Kalasha	. . .					0	19571
59-AAC	**DARDIC-CENTRAL net**	3	11	473,040	798,727		0.01	12	A	20		. . .					0	19574
59-AACA	WOTAPURI cluster	1	1	5,907	11,683		0.00	2	A	4		. . .					0	19575
59-AACA-a	wotapuri	1	1	5,907	11,683	0	0.00	2	A	4		. . .					0	19576
59-AACA-b	katarqalai					0				4		. . .					0	19577
59-AACB	TIRAHI cluster	1	1	7,818	15,462		0.00	2	A	8		. . .					0	19578
59-AACB-a	tirahi	1	1	7,818	15,462	0	0.00	2	A	8		. . .					0	19579
59-AACC	KALAMI cluster	2	4	75,533	127,307		0.03	18	A	5		. . .					0	19580
59-AACC-a	kalami	2	4	75,533	127,307	0	0.03	18	A	5		. . .					0	19581
59-AACD	KALKOTI cluster	1	1	5,101	8,574		0.02	13	A	4		. . .					0	19586
59-AACD-a	kalkoti	1	1	5,101	8,574	0	0.02	13	A	4		. . .					0	19587
59-AACE	KHILI cluster	1	1	258,948	435,212		0.00	9	A	0		. . .					0	19588
59-AACE-a	maiya	1	1	258,948	435,212	0	0.00	9	A	0		. . .					0	19589
59-AACE-b	mani					0				0		. . .					0	19590
59-AACE-c	manzeri					0				0		. . .					0	19595
59-AACF	TORWALI cluster	2	3	119,733	200,489		0.03	18	A	20		. . .					0	19598
59-AACF-a	behrain					0				20		. . .					0	19599
59-AACF-b	chail					0				20		. . .					0	19600
59-AACF-c	bateri	2	2	32,087	53,183	0	0.10	14	A	20		. . .					0	19601
59-AAD	**SHINA-DARDIC net**	3	10	937,403	1,564,805		0.02	16	A	24		P . .					0	19602
59-AADA	DANGARIK cluster	2	2	15,547	27,469		0.08	12	A	4		. . .					0	19603
59-AADA-a	sau	1	1	4,515	8,928	0	0.00	3	A	4		. . .					0	19604
59-AADA-b	phalura	1	1	11,032	18,541	0	0.12	16	A	4		. . .					0	19605
59-AADB	SHINA cluster	2	8	921,856	1,537,336		0.02	16	A	24		P . .					0	19609
59-AADB-a	gilgit					0				24		p . .					0	19610
59-AADB-b	brokpa	1	1	22,503	29,536	0	0.02	17	A	24		p . .					0	19613
59-AADB-c	chilas-darel	1	2	530,916	892,305	0	0.02	17	A	24		p . .					0	19616
59-AADB-d	shinaki					0				24	Shina	P . .	1929				0	19619
59-AADB-e	kolai	2	2	362,240	605,080	0	0.02	14	A	24	Kohistani, Indus	p . .					0	19620
59-AADB-f	gurezi					0				24	Shina: Gurezi	P . .	1929				0	19621
59-AADB-g	ushojo	1	2	5,540	9,310	0	0.04	14	A	24		p . .					0	19622
59-AADB-h	dras					0				24		p . .					0	19623
59-AADB-i	dah					0				24		p . .					0	19624
59-AADB-j	hanu					0				24		p . .					0	19625
59-AADB-k	dumaki	1	1	657	1,105	0	0.00	16	A	24		p . .					0	19628
59-AADB-l	palasi					0				24		p . .					0	19629
59-AAE	**DANUWAR-DARAI net**	1	1	25,791	43,198		1.00	16	A	12		. . .					0	19632
59-AAEA	NORTH DANUWAR cluster	1	1	20,000	34,000		1.00	16	A	0		. . .					0	19633
59-AAEA-a	rai					0				0		. . .					0	19634
59-AAEA-b	done					0				0		. . .					0	19635
59-AAEA-c	kachariya					0				0		. . .					0	19638
59-AAEB	DARAI cluster	1	1	5,791	9,198		1.00	16	A	12		. . .					0	19639
59-AAEB-a	darai	1	1	5,791	9,198	0	1.00	16	A	12	Darai	. . .					0	19640
59-AAF	**INDIC-CENTRAL net**	99	421	1,043,361,951	1,429,413,855		2.18	53	B	80		PNB					4Asuh	19641
59-AAFA	KESHUR cluster	3	5	4,874,900	6,409,387		0.03	35	A	80		PNB					2	19642
59-AAFA-a	kashtawari					0				80		pnb					1	19643
59-AAFA-b	riasi					0				80		pnb					1	19646
59-AAFA-c	rambani					0				80		pnb					1	19647
59-AAFA-d	siraji-doda					0				80		pnb					1	19648
59-AAFA-e	siraji-kashmiri	3	3	4,832,935	6,354,306	0	0.03	35	A	80	Kashmiri	PNB	1954	1813-1884	1899	1994	2	19649
59-AAFA-f	kishtwari	1	1	21,692	28,472	0	0.02	18	A	80		pnb					1	19650
59-AAFA-g	bakawali					0				80		pnb					1	19651
59-AAFA-h	bunjwali					0				80		pnb					1	19652
59-AAFA-i	miraski					0				80		pnb					1	19653
59-AAFA-j	poguli					0				80		pnb					1	19654
59-AAFA-k	shah-mansuri					0				80		pnb					1	19655
59-AAFA-l	zayoli					0				80		pnb					1	19656
59-AAFA-m	zirak-boli	1	1	20,273	26,609	0	1.00	29	A	80	Vaagri Boli*	Pnb	1975				1	19657
59-AAFB	WEST PAHARI cluster	2	8	68,669,429	114,727,592	1	4.28	48	A	22		P . .					0 . s . .	19658
59-AAFB-a	potwari					1				22		p . .					0 . s . .	19659
59-AAFB-b	dhundi					1				22		p . .					0 . s . .	19660
59-AAFB-c	chibhali					1				22		p . .					0 . s . .	19661
59-AAFB-d	murree					1				22		p . .					0 . s . .	19662
59-AAFB-e	punchi					1				22		p . .					0 . s . .	19663
59-AAFB-f	bhadrawahi	1	1	71,767	94,196	1	0.10	17	A	22		p . .					0 . s . .	19664
59-AAFB-g	panjabi-pahari	2	2	67,717,499	113,478,167	4	4.34	48	A	22		P . .					0 . s . .	19667
59-AAFB-h	kului	1	2	702,164	921,602	1	0.09	20	A	22	Kului*	P . .	1932-1980				0 . s . .	19670

Continued opposite

Table 9-13 continued

Code 1	REFERENCE NAME Autoglossonym 2	Coun 3	Peo 4	Mother-tongue speakers in 2000 5	in 2025 6	Media radio 7	CHURCH AC% 8	E% 9	Wld 10	Tr 11	Biblioglossonym 12	SCRIPTURES Print 13-15	P–activity 16	N–activity 17	B–activity 18	J-year 19	Jayuh 20-24	Ref 25
59-AAFB-i	satlaji					1				22		p..					0.s..	19674
59-AAFB-j	baghati	1	1	8,920	11,708	1	0.06	15	A	22		p..					0.s..	19678
59-AAFB-k	sirmauri					1				22		p..					0.s..	19687
59-AAFB-l	chameali	1	1	151,441	198,769	1	0.05	20	A	22	Chambiali*	P..	1883-1979				0.s..	19692
59-AAFC	CENTRAL PAHARI cluster	3	7	5,865,015	7,730,101		0.19	26	A	44		PN.					1....	19695
59-AAFC-a	jaunsari	1	1	100,961	132,513	0	0.01	16	A	44	Jaunsari	Pn.	1895-1904				1....	19696
59-AAFC-b	garhwali	2	4	3,464,733	4,553,285	0	0.07	26	A	44	Garhwali*	PN.	1966	1827-1994		1992	1....	19697
59-AAFC-c	tehri					0				44		pn.					1....	19707
59-AAFC-d	kumauni	2	2	2,299,321	3,044,303	0	0.38	27	A	44	Kumaoni*	Pn.	1825-1876			1993	1....	19708
59-AAFD	EAST PAHARI cluster	7	11	22,100,449	32,848,732		2.28	58	B	70		PNB					2Asu.	19722
59-AAFD-a	palpa	1	1	7,562	12,011	1	0.04	21	A	70	Palpa	PNb		1827			1csu.	19723
59-AAFD-b	nepali	7	9	22,088,101	32,829,119	4	2.29	58	B	70	Nepali	PNB	1961	1821-1984	1914-1978	1987	2Asu.	19724
59-AAFE	PANJABI cluster	28	52	69,227,500	98,638,688		2.99	58	B	61		PNB					2Asu.	19736
59-AAFE-a	Religious panjabi	1	1	15,648	26,300	1	0.50	27	A	61		pnb					1csu.	19737
59-AAFE-b	Standard panjabi					1				61		pnb					1csu.	19738
59-AAFE-c	General panjabi	27	27	2,999,157	4,053,002	5	3.54	59	B	61		PNB					1Asu.	19742
59-AAFE-d	majhi	3	5	40,994,715	53,810,430	5	2.99	63	B	61	Panjabi*	PNB	1954	1815-1996	1959-1984		1asu.	19747
59-AAFE-e	lahnda	2	3	113,258	163,373	1	0.90	27	A	61	Panjabi, Western	PNb	1885-1922	1819-1952		1994	1csu.	19751
59-AAFE-f	doabi					1				61		pnb					1csu.	19765
59-AAFE-g	malwai					1				61		pnb					1csu.	19768
59-AAFE-h	patialwi	1	1	114,544	150,341	1	0.04	24	A	61		pnb					1csu.	19769
59-AAFE-i	awankari-ghebi					1				61		pnb					1csu.	19772
59-AAFE-j	gaddi	1	1	125,289	164,443	1	0.03	21	A	61		pnb					1csu.	19776
59-AAFE-k	bhateali	1	1	119,409	156,727	1	0.50	24	A	61		pnb					1csu.	19780
59-AAFE-l	dogri	2	4	3,506,212	4,964,926	5	0.63	42	A	61	Panjabi: Dogri*	PNb	1971	1826		1993	1asu.	19781
59-AAFE-m	kangri	1	1	98,832	129,719	1	0.10	24	A	61		pnb					1csu.	19786
59-AAFE-n	mirpuri	1	1	1,013,662	1,330,449	1	1.00	32	A	61		pnb					1csu.	19787
59-AAFE-o	hindki					1				61		pnb					1csu.	19788
59-AAFE-p	hindko	1	2	4,401,229	7,397,104	1	1.00	38	A	61	Hindko*	PNb	1929	1991			1csu.	19792
59-AAFE-q	kahluri	1	1	345,152	453,018	1	1.00	34	A	61		pnb					1csu.	19793
59-AAFE-r	siraiki	2	4	15,380,393	25,838,856	4	4.29	57	B	61	Siraiki*	PNb	1898	1819		1994	2asu.	19794
59-AAFF	SINDHI cluster	8	19	23,029,587	37,218,430		0.21	48	A	62		PNB					1as..	19803
59-AAFF-a	Standard sindhi	7	7	20,402,305	33,510,956	4	0.14	50	A	62	Sindhi	PNB	1825-1971	1890-1992	1954	1991	1as..	19804
59-AAFF-b	General sindhi					1				62		pnb					1cs..	19807
59-AAFF-c	vicholi					1				62		pnb					1cs..	19810
59-AAFF-d	thareli					1				62		pnb					1cs..	19813
59-AAFF-e	lasi	1	1	10,954	18,410	1	0.00	17	A	62		pnb					1cs..	19814
59-AAFF-f	lari					1				62		pnb					1cs..	19815
59-AAFF-g	macharia					1				62		pnb					1cs..	19816
59-AAFF-h	sindhi-bhil					1				62		pnb					1cs..	19817
59-AAFF-i	jad-gali	1	1	15,648	26,300	1	2.10	31	A	62		pnb					1cs..	19818
59-AAFF-j	kachchi	4	4	922,642	1,229,664	1	0.96	36	A	62	Kachchi	Pnb	1834				1cs..	19821
59-AAFF-k	wadiyara-koli	1	2	237,823	399,707	1	0.83	32	A	62	Koli, Kachi	Pnb	1834-1995				1cs..	19834
59-AAFF-l	tharadari-koli	1	1	55,035	92,497	1	1.00	31	A	62		pnb					1cs..	19837
59-AAFF-m	parkari-koli	1	1	275,176	462,485	1	1.00	33	A	62	Koli: Parkari*	PNb	1834	1996			1cs..	19840
59-AAFF-n	od	1	1	58,431	98,204	1	2.00	39	A	62		pnb					1cs..	19844
59-AAFF-o	mina	1	1	1,051,573	1,380,207	1	0.30	32	A	62		pnb					1cs..	19845
59-AAFG	RAJASTHANI cluster	3	22	19,522,754	26,031,699		1.18	36	A	57		PN.					4.s..	19846
59-AAFG-a	sindhi-marwari	2	2	162,296	266,797	0	0.18	25	A	57	Marwari	PN.	1867	1820-1821		1997	1.s..	19847
59-AAFG-b	rajasthani-marwari					0				57		pn.					1.s..	19856
59-AAFG-c	Standard rajasthani					0				57		pn.					1.s..	19857
59-AAFG-d	rajasthani-T.	1	1	65,723	110,460	0	0.20	32	A	57		pn.					1.s..	19858
59-AAFG-e	marwari-bhil	1	2	234,756	394,552	0	1.00	33	A	57		pn.					1.s..	19864
59-AAFG-f	bikaneri	1	1	1,013,662	1,330,449	0	0.12	34	A	57	Marwari: Bikaneri	PN.		1820			1.s..	19868
59-AAFG-g	mewati					0				57		pn.					1.s..	19871
59-AAFG-h	jaipuri	2	3	10,687,429	14,049,676	0	1.05	41	A	57	Jaipuri	Pn.	1815			1996	4.s..	19874
59-AAFG-i	ajmeri	1	1	1,318	1,730	0	0.23	24	A	57		pn.					1.s..	19881
59-AAFG-j	harauti	1	1	596,641	783,102	0	0.10	25	A	57	Harauti	PN.		1822		1995	1.s..	19882
59-AAFG-k	mewari	1	1	1,013,662	1,330,449	0	0.10	32	A	57	Marwari: Mewari	Pn.	1815			1994	1.s..	19885
59-AAFG-l	malvi	1	1	1,149,188	1,508,330	0	9.00	44	A	57	Malvi	PN.		1826		1997	1.s..	19890
59-AAFG-m	sondwari	1	1	56,157	73,707	0	0.10	23	A	57		pn.					1.s..	19901
59-AAFG-n	nimadi	1	1	1,417,302	1,860,233	0	0.10	24	A	57		pn.					1.s..	19902
59-AAFG-o	gujuri	3	3	996,802	1,442,742	0	0.30	25	A	57	Gujari	pn.					1.s..	19905
59-AAFG-p	bagri	2	2	2,118,999	2,867,897	0	0.20	25	A	57		pn.					1.s..	19910
59-AAFG-q	lambadi					0				57	Lambadi*	PN.	1963-1977	1995		1993	3.s..	19911
59-AAFG-r	lohari	1	1	5,068	6,652	0	0.10	21	A	57		pn.					1.s..	19915
59-AAFG-s	keer	1	1	3,751	4,923	0	0.00	15	A	57		pn.					1.s..	19920
59-AAFH	GUJARAATI cluster	29	29	50,142,354	66,412,421		2.28	63	B	61		PNB					2A.u.	19921
59-AAFH-a	Historical gujaraati					1				61		pnb					1c.u.	19922
59-AAFH-b	Standard gujaraati	29	29	50,142,354	66,412,421	6	2.28	63	B	61	Gujarati	PNB	1809-1965	1820-1985	1823-1994	1980	2A.u.	19925
59-AAFH-c	pattani					1				61		pnb					1c.u.	19929
59-AAFH-d	kaathiaawaadi					1				61		pnb					1c.u.	19930
59-AAFH-e	jhaalaawaadi					1				61		pnb					1c.u.	19931
59-AAFH-f	sorathi					1				61		pnb					1c.u.	19932
59-AAFH-g	haalaadi					1				61		pnb					1c.u.	19933
59-AAFH-h	gohilwaadi					1				61		pnb					1c.u.	19934
59-AAFH-i	bhavnagari					1				61		pnb					1c.u.	19935
59-AAFH-j	khaarawaa					1				61		pnb					1c.u.	19936
59-AAFH-k	Central gujaraati					1				61		pnb					1c.u.	19937
59-AAFH-l	bharuchi					1				61		pnb					1c.u.	19944
59-AAFH-m	surati					1				61		pnb					1c.u.	19945
59-AAFH-n	anawla					1				61		pnb					1c.u.	19946
59-AAFH-o	Urban mumbai					1				61		pnb					1c.u.	19947
59-AAFH-p	vhoraasaai					1				61		pnb					1c.u.	19948
59-AAFH-q	kaakari					1				61		pnb					1c.u.	19949
59-AAFH-r	ghisaadi					1				61		pnb					1c.u.	19950
59-AAFI	EAST SAURASHTRI cluster	1	1	325,994	427,872		1.00	29	A	22		P..					0....	19951
59-AAFI-a	East saurashtri	1	1	325,994	427,872	0	1.00	29	A	22	Sourashtra*	P..	1988				0....	19952
59-AAFJ	NORTH BHILI cluster	1	6	10,603,711	13,917,558		0.23	33	A	44		PN.					1.s..	19953
59-AAFJ-a	baaori					0				44		pn.					1.s..	19954
59-AAFJ-b	magra-ki-boli					0				44		pn.					1.s..	19955
59-AAFJ-c	giraasiaa-bhili	1	3	8,826,256	11,584,616	0	0.25	34	A	44	Bhili: Central*	PN.	1916-1927	1930		1993	1.s..	19956
59-AAFJ-d	wagadi-bhili	1	2	1,711,263	2,246,064	0	0.10	29	A	44	Wagdi*	pn.					1.s..	19957
59-AAFJ-e	dungari-bhili	1	1	66,192	86,878	0	1.00	27	A	44	Girasia, Rajput	pn.					1.s..	19958
59-AAFK	CENTRAL BHILI cluster	1	9	2,084,393	2,735,802		0.90	29	A	41		PN.					0as..	19959
59-AAFK-a	chodhari-bhili	1	1	249,969	328,089	1	0.50	31	A	41	Chodri	Pn.	1991				0cs..	19960
59-AAFK-b	gamati-bhili	1	1	243,076	319,042	1	1.50	39	A	41	Gamit	PN.	1975	1982			0cs..	19961
59-AAFK-c	naikadi					1				41		pn.					0cs..	19962
59-AAFK-d	raathvi					1				41		pn.					0cs..	19963
59-AAFK-e	pahaadi					1				41		pn.					0cs..	19964
59-AAFK-f	charani					1				41		pn.					0cs..	19965
59-AAFK-g	vasavi	1	1	395,328	518,875	1	0.90	33	A	41	Vasavi	pn.					0cs..	19966
59-AAFK-h	mawchi-bhili	1	1	78,964	103,642	1	0.10	31	A	41	Mawchi	PN.	1976-1978	1989			0cs..	19974
59-AAFK-i	dhanka-bhili	1	1	18,246	23,948	1	1.80	31	A	41		pn.					0cs..	19975
59-AAFK-j	patelia-bhili	1	1	84,033	110,294	5	0.10	33	A	41	Patelia	pn.					0as..	19978
59-AAFK-k	bhilala	1	1	643,777	844,968	1	0.01	18	A	41		pn.					0cs..	19979
59-AAFK-l	dubli bhili	1	1	235,980	309,728	1	4.00	39	A	41		pn.					0cs..	19980
59-AAFK-m	dhodiaa bhili	1	1	135,020	177,216	1	0.30	28	A	41		pn.					0cs..	19981
59-AAFK-n	konkani-bhili					1				41		pn.					0cs..	19982
59-AAFK-o	dehaawaali					1				41		pn.					0cs..	19983
59-AAFK-p	naahari-baaglani					1				41		pn.					0cs..	19984
59-AAFK-q	ahiri					1				41		pn.					0cs..	19985
59-AAFK-r	rajput-giraasia					1				41		pn.					0cs..	19986
59-AAFK-s	kotali					1				41		pn.					0cs..	19987
59-AAFK-t	bhimchaura					1				41		pn.					0cs..	19988

Continued overleaf

Table 9-13 continued

Code 1	REFERENCE NAME Autoglossonym 2	Coun 3	Peo 4	Mother-tongue speakers in 2000 5	in 2025 6	Media radio 7	CHURCH AC% 8	E% 9	Wld 10	Tr 11	Biblioglossonym 12	SCRIPTURES Print 13-15	P–activity 16	N–activity 17	B–activity 18	J-year 19	Jayuh 20-24	Ref 25
59-AAFK-u	haburi					1				41		pn.					0cs..	19989
59-AAFK-v	rana-bhili					1				41		pn.					0cs..	19990
59-AAFK-w	valvi					1				41		pn.					0cs..	19991
59-AAFL	EAST BHILI cluster	1	3	746,563	979,876		0.18	20	A	22		P..					0.s..	19992
59-AAFL-a	pawari-bhili	1	1	316,567	415,499	0	0.30	25	A	22	Pawri*	P..	1986				0.s..	19993
59-AAFL-b	bareli-bhili	1	1	410,432	538,699	0	0.10	16	A	22		p..					0.s..	19994
59-AAFL-c	paradhi-bhili	1	1	19,564	25,678	0	0.10	23	A	22		p..					0.s..	19995
59-AAFM	KHANDESI cluster	1	3	2,623,356	3,443,201		0.24	18	A	20		...					0....	20002
59-AAFM-a	khandesi	1	2	2,478,504	3,253,080	0	0.20	17	A	20	Khandesi*	...					0....	20003
59-AAFN	ARCHAIC-INDIC cluster	1	1	8,717	11,442		0.00	39	A	63		PNB					0a.u.	20007
59-AAFN-a	sanskrit	1	1	8,717	11,442	4	0.00	39	A	63	Sanskrit	PNB	1893	1808-1851	1822		0a.u.	20008
59-AAFN-b	paali					1				63	Pali	PNb	1827-1911	1835			0c.u.	20013
59-AAFN-c	praakrit					1				63		pnb					0c.u.	20018
59-AAFO	HINDI-URDU cluster	79	112	263,964,349	351,517,809		1.63	55	B	71		PNB					4Asuh	20027
59-AAFO-a	Historical urdu					1				71	Assamese	PNB		1819	1833		1csuh	20028
59-AAFO-b	Historical hindi	2	2	2,405,448	2,958,312	6	8.70	68	B	71	Hindi: Sarnami*	PNB	1806-1993	1960-1992	1987		1Asuh	20033
59-AAFO-c	Standard hindi	1	1	63,060,913	82,768,545	6	2.10	63	B	71	Hindi	PNB	1806	1811	1835		1Asuh	20034
59-AAFO-d	Standard urdu	29	31	66,314,208	91,727,637	5	0.12	54	B	71	Urdu	PNB	1747-1894	1758-1993	1843-1958	1980	2Asuh	20037
59-AAFO-e	General hindi	63	64	64,508,417	85,289,359	7	1.61	59	B	71		pnb				1980	3Asuh	20038
59-AAFO-f	General urdu	1	1	2,583	3,575	5	0.12	39	A	71		pnb					1asuh	20060
59-AAFO-g	khati-boli-T.					1				71		PNb					1csuh	20061
59-AAFO-h	baangaru	1	2	27,063,553	35,521,383	5	3.15	47	A	71	Haryanvi	pnb				1996	1asuh	20065
59-AAFO-i	braj-kannauji	1	3	27,379,613	35,936,218	1	2.19	42	A	71	Braj Bhasha	PNb	1822	1824		1996	4csuh	20069
59-AAFO-j	bundeli	1	2	12,593,734	16,529,495	6	1.49	51	B	71	Bundeli	pnb				1994	1asuh	20082
59-AAFO-k	bhojpuri-mauritius	2	2	396,925	470,687	6	3.02	61	B	71	Bhojpuri	PNB	1806-1962	1811-1992	1818-1987		1csuh	20095
59-AAFP	EAST HINDI cluster	8	14	39,143,616	51,613,510		2.46	33	A	44		PN.					2A.u.	20096
59-AAFP-a	awadhi	2	2	37,995,036	50,046,601	1	2.47	33	A	44	Awadhi	Pn.	1820-1911			1996	1c.u.	20097
59-AAFP-b	dang-tharu	1	1	357,105	567,211	1	0.02	18	A	44		pn.					1c.u.	20103
59-AAFP-c	bagheli	2	3	422,172	556,089	1	0.40	31	A	44	Bagheli	PN.		1821			1c.u.	20106
59-AAFP-d	South dhanuwar	1	1	37,708	49,493	1	1.00	25	A	44		pn.					1c.u.	20117
59-AAFP-e	caribbean-hindi	6	6	317,447	371,644	6	6.46	54	B	44	Hindi, Caribbean	Pn.	1980-1993			1986	2A.u.	20118
59-AAFQ	BIHARI cluster	6	20	89,664,851	118,934,978		1.01	37	A	43		PN.					1.s..	20123
59-AAFQ-a	bhojpuri	5	5	38,005,088	50,399,959	6	0.98	40	A	43	Bihari: Bhojpuri*	Pn.	1911-1982			1991	1.s..	20124
59-AAFQ-b	maithili	2	2	34,218,905	45,625,495	1	0.96	37	A	43	Maithili	Pn.	1983-1992			1996	1.s..	20136
59-AAFQ-c	bote-majhi	1	1	8,488	13,482	1	1.00	23	A	43		pn.					1.s..	20144
59-AAFQ-d	manjhi					1				43	Majhi	pn.					1.s..	20145
59-AAFQ-e	musasa	1	1	9,572	15,204	1	1.00	23	A	43		pn.					1.s..	20146
59-AAFQ-f	dehati	2	2	40,224	54,776	1	0.02	21	A	43	Maithili, Dehati	pn.					1.s..	20147
59-AAFQ-g	magahi	1	4	12,351,873	16,212,050	1	1.04	32	A	43	Bihari: Magahi*	PN.	1903	1826		1996	1.s..	20148
59-AAFQ-h	kortha	1	1	2,027,324	2,660,897	1	0.01	28	A	43	Bihari: Kortha	Pn.	1895				1.s..	20153
59-AAFQ-i	angikaa	1	1	755,685	991,850	1	0.02	25	A	43		pn.					1.s..	20154
59-AAFQ-j	gawari	1	1	37,607	49,360	1	0.02	20	A	43		pn.					1.s..	20155
59-AAFQ-k	sadani	1	1	2,054,388	2,696,420	1	0.02	30	A	43	Bihari: Nagpuria*	PN.	1919	1986		1997	1.s..	20156
59-AAFQ-l	oraon-sadri	1	1	155,697	215,485	1	48.00	84	B	43	Sadri	pn.					1.s..	20157
59-AAFR	CHHATTISGARHI cluster	1	7	12,855,461	16,873,017		1.22	44	A	35		P..					2as..	20158
59-AAFR-a	chhattisgarhi	1	3	12,026,590	15,785,109	6	1.30	45	A	35	Chhattisgarhi	P..	1904-1952			1991	2as..	20159
59-AAFR-b	halbi	1	1	758,219	995,176	1	0.01	25	A	35	Halbi	P..	1989				1cs..	20167
59-AAFR-c	bhunjia	1	1	6,792	8,914	1	0.00	13	A	35		p..					1cs..	20176
59-AAFR-d	East nahari	1	1	20,273	26,609	1	0.01	19	A	35		p..					1cs..	20177
59-AAFR-e	kawari	1	1	43,587	57,209	1	0.03	17	A	35		p..					1cs..	20178
59-AAFS	ORIYA cluster	3	17	34,209,857	44,899,341		1.38	57	B	61	Mirgan	PNB					3Asu.	20179
59-AAFS-a	odiaa	3	3	33,417,375	43,859,198	4	1.40	57	B	61	Oriya	PNB	1956	1809-1978	1815-1995	1980	3Asu.	20180
59-AAFS-b	bhuiya-oriya	1	1	9,934	13,038	1	29.00	59	B	61		pnb					1csu.	20190
59-AAFS-c	jharia-oriya	1	1	4,561	5,987	1	0.50	25	A	61		pnb					1csu.	20191
59-AAFS-d	jagannathi-oriya					1				61		pnb					1csu.	20192
59-AAFS-e	bhatri-oriya	1	1	185,196	243,073	1	0.02	24	A	61	Bhatri	pnb					1csu.	20193
59-AAFS-f	desia-oriya	1	1	252,807	331,814	4	0.10	35	A	61	Oriya: Adiwasi*	Pnb	1977-1982				1asu.	20194
59-AAFS-g	adiwasi-oriya	1	4	208,105	273,141	1	0.95	28	A	61	Girasia, Adiwasi*	pnb					1csu.	20195
59-AAFS-h	valmiki-oriya					1				61		pnb					1csu.	20198
59-AAFS-i	kupia-oriya	1	1	5,474	7,184	1	1.00	33	A	61	Kupia	PNb		1983			1csu.	20199
59-AAFS-j	bagata-oriya	1	1	100,454	131,847	1	0.09	27	A	61		pnb					1csu.	20200
59-AAFS-k	mali-oriya	1	1	2,129	2,794	1	0.05	21	A	61		pnb					1csu.	20201
59-AAFS-l	degaru	1	1	10,137	13,304	1	0.11	27	A	61		pnb					1csu.	20202
59-AAFT	BENGALI cluster	20	44	217,239,746	294,286,893		1.19	60	B	72		PNB					4Asuh	20203
59-AAFT-a	Historical baanglaa					1				72		pnb					1csuh	20204
59-AAFT-b	baanglaa-M.					1				72		pnb					1csuh	20205
59-AAFT-c	Standard baanglaa	1	1	102,111,536	141,322,748	6	0.14	59	B	72	Bengali	PNB	1800-1980	1801-1982	1809-1994		4Asuh	20206
59-AAFT-d	Central baanglaa					1				72		pnb					1csuh	20210
59-AAFT-e	West bengali	19	20	90,729,572	120,209,186	6	2.40	64	B	72	Bengali: Musalmani*	PNB	1800-1993	1801-1984	1996	1980	1Asuh	20211
59-AAFT-f	Southwest bengali					1				72		pnb					1csuh	20218
59-AAFT-g	North bengali	1	1	101,569	133,311	1	0.60	29	A	72		pnb					1csuh	20219
59-AAFT-h	West kamarupa	3	3	154,940	242,621	1	0.45	26	A	72		pnb					1csuh	20226
59-AAFT-i	East bengali	2	2	783,262	1,056,936	1	10.12	50	A	72		PNb					1csuh	20229
59-AAFT-j	kachari-bengali					1				72		pnb					1csuh	20235
59-AAFT-k	sylhetti-bengali	2	2	6,158,040	8,484,123	1	0.10	33	A	72		pnb				1996	3csuh	20236
59-AAFT-l	haijong-bangali	2	2	50,865	68,977	6	0.72	35	A	72		pnb					1csuh	20239
59-AAFT-m	tangchangya-bengali	1	1	25,172	34,839	1	1.00	28	A	72		pnb					1csuh	20240
59-AAFT-n	mahottari-tharu	2	4	210,480	326,378	1	0.01	17	A	72	Tharu, Mahotari*	Pnb	1977				1csuh	20241
59-AAFT-o	saptari-tharu	1	1	93,975	149,266	1	0.02	23	A	72		pnb					1csuh	20242
59-AAFT-p	rana-thakur-tharu	1	1	303,853	482,627	1	0.00	19	A	72		pnb					1csuh	20245
59-AAFT-q	deokri-tharu	1	2	149,230	237,031	1	0.07	24	A	72		pnb					1csuh	20246
59-AAFT-r	chitwan-tharu					1				72		pnb					1csuh	20249
59-AAFT-s	axamiyaa	3	3	16,232,334	21,361,767	4	1.09	57	B	72	Assamese	PNB	1822-1974	1819-1993	1833-1995	1991	3asuh	20250
59-AAFT-t	jiharwa					1				72		pnb					1csuh	20258
59-AAFU	MARATHI cluster	10	31	106,459,349	139,755,506		5.98	61	B	61		PNB					3Asu.	20259
59-AAFU-a	nagpuri-hindi					1				61		pnb					1csu.	20260
59-AAFU-b	varhaadi	1	2	7,558,774	9,921,023	1	2.00	34	A	61		pnb					1csu.	20261
59-AAFU-c	gowlan	1	2	30,410	39,913	1	5.67	42	A	61	Gowli	pnb					1csu.	20277
59-AAFU-d	ikrani					1				61		pnb					1csu.	20282
59-AAFU-e	kaatkari-kaathodi	1	1	11,049	14,502	1	0.08	23	A	61		pnb					1csu.	20283
59-AAFU-f	varli	1	1	676,822	888,341	1	1.00	36	A	61	Varli	pnb					1csu.	20286
59-AAFU-g	samvedi					1				61		pnb					1csu.	20287
59-AAFU-h	mangelas	1	1	10,137	13,304	1	0.50	36	A	61		pnb					1csu.	20288
59-AAFU-i	vadval-phudagi	1	1	1,014	1,330	1	0.99	33	A	61		pnb					1csu.	20289
59-AAFU-j	are	1	1	5,778	7,584	1	1.00	27	A	61		pnb					1csu.	20292
59-AAFU-k	bhalay	1	1	10,137	13,304	1	1.00	29	A	61		pnb					1csu.	20293
59-AAFU-l	thakuri	1	1	127,721	167,637	1	0.01	27	A	61		pnb					1csu.	20294
59-AAFU-m	deshi-marathi	5	7	88,392,817	116,015,923	4	4.45	63	B	61	Marathi*	PNB	1807-1957	1811-1982	1821-1989		2Asu.	20295
59-AAFU-n	konkan-marathi	1	2	5,754,355	7,552,691	4	1.95	40	A	61	Konkani: Kanara, Southern*	PNb	1970	1970-1995			1csu.	20302
59-AAFU-o	konkani-gomantaki	8	8	3,771,670	4,977,331	4	57.37	100	B	61	Konkani: Goan*	PNb	1966	1818-1976		1989	3asu.	20318
59-AB	INDIC-INSULAR chain	14	17	14,252,622	18,011,517		4.50	59	B	61		PNB					2asuh	20331
59-ABA	**MALDIVIAN net**	2	2	290,837	505,575		0.01	19	A	20		...					0....	20332
59-ABAA	MALDIVIAN cluster	2	2	290,837	505,575		0.01	19	A	20		...					0....	20333
59-ABAA-a	dhivehi	2	2	290,837	505,575	0	0.01	19	A	20		...					0....	20334
59-ABB	**SINHALESE net**	14	15	13,931,485	17,454,432		4.60	60	B	61		PNB					2asuh	20337
59-ABBA	SINHALA cluster	14	15	13,931,485	17,454,432		4.60	60	B	61		PNB					2asuh	20338
59-ABBA-a	Historical sinhala	12	13	13,908,295	17,421,567	6	4.60	60	B	61		PNB					2asuh	20339
59-ABC	**RODIYA net**	1	1	30,000	51,000		1.00	16	A	0		...					0....	20346

Continued opposite

Table 9-13 continued

Code 1	REFERENCE NAME / Autoglossonym 2	Coun 3	Peo 4	in 2000 5	in 2025 6	Media radio 7	AC% 8	E% 9	Wld 10	Tr 11	Biblioglossonym 12	Print 13-15	P–activity 16	N–activity 17	B–activity 18	J-year 19	Jayuh 20-24	Ref 25
59-ABCA	RODIYA cluster	1	1	30,000	51,000		1.00	16	A	0		...					0....	20347
59-ABCA-a	rodiya	1	1	30,000	51,000	0	1.00	16	A	0		...					0....	20348
59-ABD	**VEDDAH net**	1	1	300	510		50.00	86	B	4		...					0....	20349
59-ABDA	VEDDAH cluster	1	1	300	510		50.00	86	B	4		...					0....	20350
59-ABDA-a	veddah	1	1	300	510	0	50.00	86	B	4		...					0....	20351
59-AC	ROMINDIC chain	51	109	5,901,745	6,751,864		52.19	79	B	57		PN.					1A...	20352
59-ACA	**EAST ROMINDIC net**	15	15	916,240	1,328,763		1.92	29	A	4		...					0....	20353
59-ACAA	DOM cluster	15	15	916,240	1,328,763		1.92	29	A	4		...					0....	20354
59-ACAA-a	domari	15	15	916,240	1,328,763	7	1.92	29	A	4		...					0....	20355
59-ACB	**WEST ROMINDIC net**	42	94	4,985,505	5,423,101		61.43	89	C	57		PN.					1A...	20375
59-ACBA	SOUTHEAST ROM cluster	37	76	4,672,539	5,110,621		61.32	89	C	57		PN.					1A...	20376
59-ACBA-a	vlach-romani	32	50	3,186,558	3,667,237	6	78.68	99	C	57	Romani: Finnish*	PN.	1837-1991	1990-1995			1A...	20377
59-ACBA-b	balkan-romani	15	26	1,485,981	1,443,384	6	24.08	66	B	57		Pn.				1996	1A...	20400
59-ACBB	NORTHWEST ROM cluster	15	18	312,966	312,480		63.08	90	C	24		P..					0....	20413
59-ACBB-a	carpathian-romani	2	3	95,114	92,613	0	60.54	90	C	24		p..					0....	20414
59-ACBB-b	sinti	12	14	192,510	186,606	0	70.93	97	C	24	Romani: Sinti, Italian	P..	1875				0....	20420
59-ACBB-c	folditka-romá					0				24		p..					0....	20428
59-ACBB-d	fintika-romani	1	1	25,342	33,261	0	13.00	39	A	24	Romani: Lithuanian	P..	1996				0....	20433
59-ACBB-e	romnimos					0				24		p..					0....	20434
59-AD	ARMENIAN-ROMINDIC chain									0		...					0...	20435
59-ADA	**ARMENIANIZED-ROMINDIC net**									0		...					0....	20436
59-ADAA	LOM cluster									0		...					0....	20437
59-ADAA-a	lomavren					0				0		...					0....	20438
59-AEA	**ROMANICIZED-ROMINDIC net**	2	2	139,232	162,845		89.98	100	C	4		...					0....	20439
59-AEAA	CAL cluster	2	2	139,232	162,845		89.98	100	C	4		...					0....	20440
59-AEAA-a	caló	2	2	139,232	162,845	8	89.98	100	C	4		...					0....	20441
59-AF	ROMANIC-ROMINDIC chain	11	13	1,051,006	1,063,816		86.80	100	C	24		P..					0B.uh	20446
59-AFA	**NORDICIZED-ROMINDIC net**	11	13	1,051,006	1,063,816		86.80	100	C	24		P..					0B.uh	20447
59-AFAA	NORDIC-ROMANI cluster	11	13	1,051,006	1,063,816		86.80	100	C	24		P..					0B.uh	20448
59-AFAA-a	rodi	11	13	1,051,006	1,063,816	8	86.80	100	C	24	Calo	P..	1837-1872				0B.uh	20449
59-AG	ANGLICIZED-ROMINDIC chain	8	9	237,694	263,819		74.81	100	C	4		...					0....	20454
59-AGA	**ANGLICIZED-ROMINDIC net**	8	9	237,694	263,819		74.81	100	C	4		...					0....	20455
59-AGAA	ANGLO-ROMANI cluster	8	9	237,694	263,819		74.81	100	C	4		...					0....	20456
59-AGAA-a	pogadi-chib	8	9	237,694	263,819	0	74.81	100	C	4		...					0....	20457
6	**NORTHAMERICAN macrozone**	11	546	12,753,665	18,248,096		89.35	100	C	82		PNB					4Asuh	20462
60	**ARCTIC zone**	5	17	171,331	213,970		81.82	99	C	82		PNB					4A..h	20463
60-A	**ALEUT-INUITIC set**	5	17	171,331	213,970		81.82	99	C	82		PNB					4A..h	20464
60-AA	ALEUT chain	2	3	3,286	3,922		77.60	100	C	24		P..					0....	20465
60-AAA	**WEST ALEUT net**	1	1	340	578		75.29	97	C	0		...					0....	20466
60-AAAA	ATTUAN cluster	2	1	40	68		40.00	78	B	0		...					0....	20467
60-AAAA-a	attu			0	0	0	0.00	0		0		...					0....	20468
60-AAAA-b	mednov					0				0		...					0....	20469
60-AAAB	ATKAN cluster	1	1	300	510		80.00	100	C	0		...					0....	20470
60-AAAB-a	atka					0				0		...					0....	20471
60-AAB	**EAST ALEUT net**	2	3	2,946	3,344		77.87	100	C	24		P..					0....	20472
60-AABA	UNALASKA-KODIAK cluster	2	3	2,946	3,344		77.87	100	C	24		P..					0....	20473
60-AABA-a	pribilof					0				24		p..					0....	20474
60-AABA-b	umnak					0				24		p..					0....	20475
60-AABA-c	unalaska	2	3	2,946	3,344	0	77.87	100	C	24	Aleut: Eastern	P..	1840-1903				0....	20476
60-AABA-d	alaska					0				24		p..					0....	20477
60-AABA-e	kodiak-aleut					0				24		p..					0....	20478
60-AB	INUIT-YUPIK chain	5	14	168,045	210,048		81.90	99	C	82		PNB					4A..h	20479
60-ABA	**YUPIK net**	2	6	32,130	37,087		81.21	97	C	51		PN.					0A..h	20480
60-ABAA	SIRENIK cluster	1	1	30	51		40.00	77	B	8		...					0....	20481
60-ABAA-a	sirenik	1	1	30	51	0	40.00	77	B	8		...					0....	20482
60-ABAB	WEST YUPIK cluster	2	3	3,457	3,534		42.87	73	B	23		P..					0A...	20483
60-ABAB-a	Southwest yup'ik	2	2	3,016	3,120	4	46.22	75	B	23		P..					0A...	20484
60-ABAB-b	naukan	1	1	441	414	1	19.95	56	B	23		p..					0c...	20487
60-ABAC	CENTRAL YUPIK cluster	1	1	21,517	25,167		86.00	100	C	51		PN.					0...h	20488
60-ABAC-a	yukon-kuskokwim	1	1	21,517	25,167	4	86.00	100	C	51	Eskimo: Yupik, Central*	PN.	1915-1987	1956			0...h	20489
60-ABAC-b	kashunuk					1				51		pn.					0...h	20494
60-ABAC-c	nunivak					1				51		pn.					0...h	20495
60-ABAD	SUXTSTUN cluster	1	2	7,126	8,335		85.53	100	C	24		P..					0....	20496
60-ABAD-a	koniag					1				24		p..					0....	20497
60-ABAD-b	kodiak	1	2	7,126	8,335	5	85.53	100	C	24	Eskimo: Yupik, Pacific Gulf*	P..	1848				0....	20498
60-ABAD-c	chugach					1				24		p..					0....	20499
60-ABAD-d	tatitlek					1				24		p..					0....	20500
60-ABB	**INUKTITUT net**	4	8	135,915	172,961		82.07	100	C	82		PNB					4....	20501
60-ABBA	WEST INUPIAT cluster	1	1	9,047	10,581		86.00	100	C	22		P..					0....	20502
60-ABBA-a	qawiaraq	1	1	9,047	10,581	4	86.00	100	C	22	Inuktitut, Nw Inupiat	P..	1980-1984				0....	20503
60-ABBA-b	wales					1				22		p..					0....	20504
60-ABBB	NORTH INUPIAT cluster	2	2	14,772	17,718		91.69	100	C	41		PN.					0....	20511
60-ABBB-a	malimiut					1				41	Eskimo: Malimiut	PN.	1971				0....	20512
60-ABBB-b	kobuk	2	2	14,772	17,718	4	91.69	100	C	41		pn.					0....	20513
60-ABBB-c	noatak					1				41		pn.					0....	20514
60-ABBB-d	kivalina-kaktovik					1				41		PN.					0....	20515
60-ABBC	CENTRAL INUKTITUT cluster	4	4	64,014	69,245		72.11	100	C	68		PNB					1....	20520
60-ABBC-a	East mackenzie					1				68		pnb					1....	20521
60-ABBC-b	copper	2	2	12,396	14,951	8	93.43	100	C	68	Eskimo: Copper*	PNb	1920-1972	1983			1....	20522
60-ABBC-c	netsilik					1				68		pnb					1....	20528
60-ABBC-d	keewatin					1				68		pnb					1....	20529

Continued overleaf

Table 9-13 continued

Code 1	REFERENCE NAME / Autoglossonym 2	Coun 3	Peo 4	Mother-tongue speakers in 2000 5	in 2025 6	Media radio 7	CHURCH AC% 8	E% 9	Wld 10	Tr 11	Biblioglossonym 12	SCRIPTURES Print 13-15	P–activity 16	N–activity 17	B–activity 18	J-year 19	Jayuh 20-24	Ref 25
60-ABBC-e	iglulik			51,618	54,294	1	66.99	100	C	68		pnb					1....	20530
60-ABBC-f	North greenlandic	2	2	51,618	54,294	4	66.99	100	C	68	Greenlandic*	PNB	1744-1985	1766-1893	1900	1998	1....	20534
60-ABBD	SOUTH INUKTITUT cluster	1	1	13,082	15,917		95.99	100	C	82		PNB					1995 4....	20535
60-ABBD-a	ungava	1	1	13,082	15,917	3	95.99	100	C	82	Inuktitut: Eastern Arctic*	PNB	1810-1990	1871-1993	1871		1995 1....	20536
60-ABBE	TUNUNGAYUALOK cluster	1	1	3,000	5,100		90.00	99	C	0		. . .					0....	20545
60-ABBE-a	tunungayualok	1	1	3,000	5,100	0	90.00	99	C	0		. . .					0....	20546
60-ABBF	SOUTH BAFFIN cluster	1	1	2,000	3,400		90.00	99	C	0		. . .					0....	20547
60-ABBF-a	South Baffin	1	1	2,000	3,400	0	90.00	99	C	0		. . .					0....	20548
60-ABBG	KALAALLISUT cluster	2	1	30,000	51,000		90.00	99	C	0		. . .					0....	20549
60-ABBG-a	West kalaallisut					0				0		. . .					0....	20550
60-ABBG-b	East kalaallisut					0				0		. . .					0....	20551
61	**ATHABASKIC zone**	2	33	306,908	360,749		75.18	100	C	68		PNB					4As..	20552
61-A	**EYAK set**	1	1	28	33		10.71	39	A	8		. . .					0....	20553
61-AA	EYAK chain	1	1	28	33		10.71	39	A	8		. . .					0....	20554
61-AAA	**EYAK net**	1	1	28	33		10.71	39	A	8		. . .					0....	20555
61-AAAA	EYAK cluster	1	1	28	33		10.71	39	A	8		. . .					0....	20556
61-AAAA-a	eyak	1	1	28	33	0	10.71	39	A	8		. . .					0....	20557
61-B	**ATHABASKAN set**	2	32	306,880	360,716		75.18	100	C	68		PNB					4As..	20558
61-BA	NORTH ATHABASKAN chain	2	24	39,681	48,162		92.78	100	C	63		PNB					1a...	20559
61-BAA	**TANAINA-AHTNA net**	1	1	1,441	1,845		80.01	100	C	8		. . .					0....	20560
61-BAAA	TANAINA cluster	1	1	1,141	1,335		80.02	100	C	8		. . .					0....	20561
61-BAAA-a	kachemak					0				8		. . .					0....	20562
61-BAAA-b	kenai					0				8		. . .					0....	20563
61-BAAA-c	tyonee					0				8		. . .					0....	20564
61-BAAA-d	upper-inlet					0				8		. . .					0....	20565
61-BAAA-e	susitna					0				8		. . .					0....	20566
61-BAAA-f	iliamma					0				8		. . .					0....	20567
61-BAAB	AHTENA cluster	1	1	300	510		80.00	100	C	0		. . .					0....	20568
61-BAAB-a	ahtena	1	1	300	510	0	80.00	100	C	0		. . .					0....	20569
61-BAB	**INGALIK-KOYUKON net**	1	3	3,369	3,940		79.91	100	C	27		P..					0a...	20570
61-BABA	DEGEXITAN cluster	1	3	3,369	3,940		79.91	100	C	27		P..					0a...	20571
61-BABA-a	degexit'an	1	1	390	456	0	80.26	100	C	27		p..					0c...	20572
61-BABA-b	holikachuk	1	1	195	228	0	77.95	100	C	27		p..					0c...	20573
61-BABA-c	koyukon	1	1	2,784	3,256	0	79.99	100	C	27	Koyukon	P..	1974-1980				0a...	20574
61-BAC	**TUTCHONE net**	1	1	2,122	2,678		90.01	100	C	6		. . .					0....	20575
61-BACA	NORTH TUTCHONE cluster	1	1	1,922	2,338		91.05	100	C	6		. . .					0....	20576
61-BACA-a	mayo					0				6		. . .					0....	20577
61-BACA-b	selkirk	1	1	1,922	2,338	0	91.05	100	C	6		. . .					0....	20578
61-BACB	SOUTH TUTCHONE cluster	1	1	200	340		80.00	100	C	0		. . .					0....	20579
61-BACB-a	South tutchone	1	1	200	340	0	80.00	100	C	0		. . .					0....	20580
61-BAD	**TAHLTAN-KASKA net**	1	3	2,140	2,603		91.54	100	C	8		. . .					0....	20581
61-BADA	TAHLTAN-KASKA cluster	1	3	2,140	2,603		91.54	100	C	8		. . .					0....	20582
61-BADA-a	tagish	1	1	128	155	0	100.00	100	C	8		. . .					0....	20583
61-BADA-b	kaska	1	1	1,006	1,224	0	89.96	100	C	8		. . .					0....	20584
61-BADA-c	tsetsaut			0	0	0	0.00	0		8		. . .					0....	20585
61-BADA-d	tahltan	1	1	1,006	1,224	0	92.05	100	C	8		. . .					0....	20586
61-BAE	**NORTHEAST ATHABASKAN net**	2	16	30,609	37,096		95.08	100	C	63		PNB					1....	20587
61-BAEA	TANANA cluster	1	3	1,225	1,433		80.41	100	C	22		P..					0....	20588
61-BAEA-a	kolchan	1	1	195	228	0	80.00	100	C	22		p..					0....	20589
61-BAEA-b	North tanana					0				22		p..					0....	20590
61-BAEA-c	tanacross					0				22		p..					0....	20595
61-BAEA-d	minto-nenana					0				22		p..					0....	20596
61-BAEA-e	nabesna	1	2	1,030	1,205	0	80.49	100	C	22	Tanana: Upper*	P..	1970-1982				0....	20599
61-BAEB	HAN-KUTCHIN cluster	2	4	3,816	4,553		95.26	100	C	63		PNB					0....	20600
61-BAEB-a	han	2	2	589	705	0	91.17	100	C	63		pnb					0....	20601
61-BAEB-b	gwich'in	2	2	3,227	3,848	0	96.00	100	C	63	Gwichin: Western	PNB	1873-1986	1886	1898		0....	20604
61-BAEC	DENE cluster	1	3	15,676	19,074		95.82	100	C	43		PN.				1993	1....	20609
61-BAEC-a	mountain					0				43		pn.					1....	20610
61-BAEC-b	hare					0				43		pn.					1....	20611
61-BAEC-c	bearlake					0				43		pn.					1....	20612
61-BAEC-d	dogrib	1	1	2,909	3,540	0	95.02	100	C	43	Dogrib	pn.				1997	1....	20613
61-BAEC-e	yellowknife			0	0	0	0.00	0		43		pn.					1....	20614
61-BAEC-f	slavey	1	1	6,410	7,799	0	96.01	100	C	43	Slavey	PN.	1868-1973	1891		1998	1....	20615
61-BAEC-g	chipewyan	1	1	6,357	7,735	0	96.00	100	C	43	Chipewyan	PN.	1878	1881		1993	1....	20616
61-BAED	BEAVER-SEKANI cluster	1	3	2,271	2,763		93.22	100	C	23		P..					0....	20617
61-BAED-a	beaver	1	1	695	845	0	95.97	100	C	23	Beaver	P..	1886-1976				0....	20618
61-BAED-b	sekani					0				23		p..					0....	20619
61-BAED-c	sarsi	1	2	1,576	1,918	0	92.01	100	C	23	Sekani	P..	1969				0....	20620
61-BAEE	CARRIER-CHILCOTIN cluster	1	3	7,621	9,273		96.38	100	C	41		PN.					0....	20621
61-BAEE-a	babine-hagwilgate	1	1	2,803	3,411	0	97.00	100	C	41	Carrier: Northern*	Pn.	1978				0....	20622
61-BAEE-b	Central carrier					0				41	Carrier	PN.	1975-1980	1995			0....	20625
61-BAEE-c	South carrier	1	1	2,529	3,077	0	96.01	100	C	41		pn.					0....	20626
61-BAEE-d	chilcotin	1	1	2,289	2,785	0	96.02	100	C	41	Chilcotin	Pn.	1993				0....	20627
61-BAEE-e	nicola			0	0	0	0.00	0		41		pn.					0....	20628
61-BB	KWALHIOQUA chain									0		. . .					0....	20629
61-BBA	**KWALHIOQUA-TLATSKANAI net**									0		. . .					0....	20630
61-BBAA	KWALHIOQUA-TLATSKANAI cluster			0	0	0	0.00	0		0		. . .					0....	20631
61-BBAA-a	kwalhioqua			0	0	0	0.00	0		0		. . .					0....	20632
61-BBAA-b	tlatskanai			0	0	0	0.00	0		0		. . .					0....	20633
61-BC	ATHABASCAN-CENTRAL chain	1	2	1,543	1,826		90.21	100	C	8		. . .					0....	20634
61-BCA	**OREGON-ATHABASKAN net**	1	1	40	68		80.00	100	C	0		. . .					0....	20635
61-BCAA	TOLOWA-GALICE cluster	1	1	40	68		80.00	100	C	0		. . .					0....	20636
61-BCAA-a	mishikhwutmetunee			0	0	0	0.00	0		0		. . .					0....	20637
61-BCAA-b	South umpqua			0	0	0	0.00	0		0		. . .					20638
61-BCAA-c	galice			0	0	0	0.00	0		0		. . .					0....	20639
61-BCAA-d	tututni					0				0		. . .					0....	20640
61-BCAA-e	tolowa-chetco					0				0		. . .					0....	20644
61-BCAA-f	applegate			0	0	0	0.00	0		0		. . .					0....	20647

Continued opposite

Table 9-13 continued

Code 1	REFERENCE NAME / Autoglossonym 2	Coun 3	Peo 4	Mother-tongue speakers in 2000 5	in 2025 6	Media radio 7	AC% 8	E% 9	Wld 10	Tr 11	Biblioglossonym 12	Print 13-15	P-activity 16	N-activity 17	B-activity 18	J-year 19	Jayuh 20-24	Ref 25
61-BCB	**CALIFORNIA-ATHABASKAN net**	1	2	1,503	1,758		90.49	100	C	8		. . .					0....	20648
61-BCBA	HUPA-CHILULA cluster	1	1	1,392	1,628		91.45	100	C	8		. . .					0....	20649
61-BCBA-a	hupa	1	1	1,392	1,628	0	91.45	100	C	8		. . .					0....	20650
61-BCBA-b	chilula			0	0	0	0.00	0		8		. . .					0....	20651
61-BCBA-c	whilkut			0	0	0	0.00	0		8		. . .					0....	20652
61-BCBB	NONGATL-LASSIK cluster			0	0		0.00	0		0		. . .					0....	20653
61-BCBB-a	nongatl			0	0	0	0.00	0		0		. . .					0....	20654
61-BCBB-b	lassik			0	0	0	0.00	0		0		. . .					0....	20655
61-BCBC	MATTOLE-WAILAKI cluster	1	1	111	130		78.38	100	C	8		. . .					0....	20656
61-BCBC-a	mattole			0	0	0	0.00	0		8		. . .					0....	20657
61-BCBC-b	sinkyone			0	0	0	0.00	0		8		. . .					0....	20658
61-BCBC-c	wailaki			0	0	0	0.00	0		8		. . .					0....	20659
61-BCBC-d	kato	1	1	111	130		78.38	100	C	8		. . .					0....	20660
61-BD	APACHEAN chain	1	6	265,656	310,728		72.47	100	C	68		PNB					4As..	20661
61-BDA	**APACHE-NAVAJO net**	1	6	265,636	310,694		72.47	100	C	68		PNB					4As..	20662
61-BDAA	APACHE-NAVAJO cluster	1	5	263,131	307,764		72.47	100	C	68		PNB					4As..	20663
61-BDAA-a	navaho	1	1	244,119	285,527	1	72.00	100	C	68	Navajo*	PNB	1910-1994	1956-1959	1985	1989	4As..	20664
61-BDAA-b	West apache	1	4	19,012	22,237	1	78.53	100	C	68	Apache: Western*	PNb	1958	1966			1as..	20665
61-BDAB	EAST APACHE cluster	1	1	2,505	2,930		72.02	100	C	8		. . .					0....	20671
61-BDAB-a	jicarilla					0				8		. . .					0....	20672
61-BDAB-b	mescalero-chiricahua	1	1	2,505	2,930	0	72.02	100	C	8		. . .					0....	20673
61-BDAB-c	lipan					0				8		. . .					0....	20676
61-BDAC	TOBOSO cluster			0	0		0.00	0		0		. . .					0....	20677
61-BDAC-a	toboso			0	0	0	0.00	0		0		. . .					0....	20678
61-BDB	**KIOWA-APACHE net**	1	1	20	34		70.00	100	C	8		. . .					0....	20679
61-BDBA	KIOWA-APACHE cluster	1	1	20	34		70.00	100	C	8		. . .					0....	20680
61-BDBA-a	kiowa-apache	1	1	20	34	0	70.00	100	C	8		. . .					0....	20681
62	**ALGONKIC zone**	3	43	436,247	519,552		86.93	98	C	66		PNB					1as..	20682
62-A	**ALGONKIAN**	3	43	436,247	519,552		86.93	98	C	66		PNB					1as..	20683
62-AA	BLACKFOOT chain	2	2	19,775	23,746		91.27	100	C	22		P..					0a...	20684
62-AAA	**BLACKFOOT net**	2	2	19,775	23,746		91.27	100	C	22		P..					0a...	20685
62-AAAA	SOYI-TAPIX cluster	2	2	19,775	23,746		91.27	100	C	22		P..					0a...	20686
62-AAAA-a	sikasi-ka	2	2	19,775	23,746	0	91.27	100	C	22	Blackfoot	P..	1890-1980				0a...	20687
62-AAAA-b	kaina					0				22		p..					0c...	20688
62-AAAA-c	peigan					0				22		p..					0c...	20689
62-AB	ARAPAHO-ATSINA chain	1	2	7,822	9,149		87.69	100	C	24		P..					0....	20690
62-ABA	**ARAPAHO-ATSINA net**	1	2	7,822	9,149		87.69	100	C	24		P..					0....	20691
62-ABAA	ATSINA cluster	1	1	1,531	1,791		78.18	100	C	8		. . .					0....	20692
62-ABAA-a	hitowunena	1	1	1,531	1,791	0	78.18	100	C	8		. . .					0....	20693
62-ABAA-b	besawunena			0	0		0.00	0		8		. . .					0.?..	20694
62-ABAB	HINANA'EINA cluster	1	1	6,291	7,358		90.00	100	C	24	Arapahoe	P..	1903				0....	20695
62-ABAB-a	North hinana'eina					0				24		p..					0....	20696
62-ABAB-b	South hinana'eina					0				24		p..					0....	20697
62-AC	CHEYENNE chain	1	1	5,567	6,511		80.01	100	C	43		PN.					0....	20698
62-ACA	**CHEYENNE net**	1	1	5,567	6,511		80.01	100	C	43		PN.					0....	20699
62-ACAA	CHEYENNE cluster	1	1	5,567	6,511		80.01	100	C	43	Cheyenne	PN.	1902-1986	1934			0....	20700
62-ACAA-a	North cheyenne					0				43		pn.					0....	20701
62-ACAA-b	South cheyenne					0				43		pn.					0....	20702
62-AD	ALGONKIC-CENTRAL chain	3	25	330,837	394,741		90.99	100	C	63		PNB					1.s..	20703
62-ADA	**CREE-OJIBWA net**	2	17	297,917	355,599		91.20	100	C	63		PNB					1.s..	20704
62-ADAA	CREE cluster	2	6	94,932	114,194		95.77	100	C	63		PNB					1.s..	20705
62-ADAA-a	plains-cree	2	2	78,761	94,518	4	95.59	100	C	63	Cree: Saskatchewan, North*	PNB	1847-1992	1859-1986	1861-1862	1991	1.s..	20706
62-ADAA-b	woods-cree					1				63		pnb					1.s..	20707
62-ADAA-c	West swampy-cree					1				63		pnb					1.s..	20708
62-ADAA-d	East swampy-cree	1	1	3,426	4,169	3	96.99	100	C	63		pnb					1.s..	20709
62-ADAA-e	moose-cree	1	1	3,115	3,790	3	96.98	100	C	63	Cree: Moose*	PNb	1853-1894	1876-1976			1.s..	20710
62-ADAA-f	East cree	1	1	6,983	8,496	3	97.01	100	C	63	Cree: East Coast*	Pnb	1921-1996				1.s..	20711
62-ADAA-g	Southeast cree	1	1	2,647	3,221		95.01	100	C	63	Cree, Inland Eastern	Pnb	1853-1995				1.s..	20712
62-ADAB	MONTAGNAIS cluster	1	2	11,758	14,306		93.95	100	C	41		PN.					0....	20713
62-ADAB-a	mushau-innuts	1	1	922	1,122	0	69.96	100	C	41	Naskapi	pn.					0....	20714
62-ADAB-b	North montagnais	1	1	10,836	13,184		95.99	100	C	41	Montagnais	PN.	1986	1990-1991			0....	20715
62-ADAB-c	South montagnais					0				41		pn.					0....	20716
62-ADAC	ATIKAMEK cluster	1	1	3,918	4,767		96.02	100	C	22	Atikamekw	P..	1980-1983				0....	20717
62-ADAC-a	manawan					0				22		p..					0....	20718
62-ADAC-b	wemotaci					0				22		p..					0....	20719
62-ADAC-c	opitciwan					0				22		p..					0....	20720
62-ADAD	ALGONQUIN cluster	1	1	6,021	7,325		96.00	100	C	22		P..					0....	20721
62-ADAD-a	anissinapek	1	1	6,021	7,325	0	96.00	100	C	22	Algonquin	P..	1980-1993				0....	20722
62-ADAE	OTTAWA cluster	2	2	9,158	10,947		91.06	100	C	24		P..					0....	20723
62-ADAE-a	potawatomi	2	2	9,158	10,947	0	91.06	100	C	24	Pottawotomi*	P..	1844				0....	20724
62-ADAE-b	odawa					0				24	Ottawa	P..	1841				0....	20725
62-ADAF	OJIBWA cluster	2	5	172,130	204,060		88.22	100	C	43		PN.					0....	20726
62-ADAF-a	East ojibwa	2	2	80,258	94,898	0	80.70	100	C	43	Ojibwa, Eastern	Pn.	1841-1844				0....	20727
62-ADAF-b	South ojibwa					0				43	Ojibway: Southern	PN.	1831	1833			0....	20728
62-ADAF-c	Southwest ojibwa	2	2	81,133	96,095	0	94.63	100	C	43	Ojibway*	PN.	1831-1986	1988			0....	20729
62-ADAF-d	North ojibwa	1	1	10,739	13,067	0	96.01	100	C	43	Ojibway: Northern	PN.	1974-1986	1988			0....	20730
62-ADB	**MITCHIF net**	2	2	18,026	21,670		96.69	100	C	6		. . .					0....	20733
62-ADBA	MITCHIF cluster	2	2	18,026	21,670		96.69	100	C	6		. . .					0....	20734
62-ADBA-a	mitchif	2	2	18,026	21,670	3	96.69	100	C	6		. . .					0....	20735
62-ADC	**MENOMINI-FOX net**	2	5	12,361	14,509		77.71	92	C	22		P..					0....	20736
62-ADCA	MENOMINI cluster	1	1	4,426	5,177		95.71	100	C	8		. . .					0....	20737
62-ADCA-a	menomini	1	1	4,426	5,177	0	95.71	100	C	8		. . .					0....	20738
62-ADCB	FOX-KIKAPOO cluster	2	3	5,402	6,369		90.02	100	C	22		P..					0....	20739
62-ADCB-a	mesquaki	1	1	3,173	3,712	0	90.01	100	C	22	Mesquakie	P..	1986-1996				0....	20740
62-ADCB-b	kikapoo	2	2	2,229	2,657	0	90.04	100	C	22	Kikapoo	p..					0....	20743
62-ADCC	MIAMI-PEORIA cluster	1	1	2,533	2,963		20.02	59	B	9		. . .					0....	20746

Continued overleaf

Table 9-13 continued

Code 1	REFERENCE NAME / Autoglossonym 2	Coun 3	Peo 4	Mother-tongue speakers in 2000 5	in 2025 6	Media radio 7	CHURCH AC% 8	E% 9	Wld 10	Tr 11	Biblioglossonym 12	SCRIPTURES Print 13-15	P-activity 16	N-activity 17	B-activity 18	J-year 19	Jayuh 20-24	Ref 25
62-ADCC-a	North miami			0	0	1	0.00	0		9		. . .					0	20747
62-ADCC-b	South miami			0	0	1	0.00	0		9		. . .					0	20748
62-ADD	**SHAWNEE net**	1	1	2,533	2,963		90.01	100	C	24		P . .					0	20749
62-ADDA	SHAWNEE cluster	1	1	2,533	2,963		90.01	100	C	24		P . .					0	20750
62-ADDA-a	East shawnee	1	1	2,533	2,963	0	90.01	100	C	24	Shawnee	P . .	1842-1929				0	20751
62-ADDA-b	absent-shawnee					0				24		p . .					0	20752
62-AE	EAST ALGONKIAN chain	2	13	72,246	85,405		67.61	92	C	66		PNB					0	20753
62-AEA	**MICMAC-MALISEET net**	2	6	24,261	29,257		94.74	100	C	48		PN .					0	20754
62-AEAA	MICMAC cluster	2	2	17,551	21,223		95.09	100	C	48		PN .					0	20755
62-AEAA-a	restigouche					0				48		pn .					0	20756
62-AEAA-b	Southeast micmac	2	2	17,551	21,223	0	95.09	100	C	48	Micmac	PN .	1853-1980	1874			0	20757
62-AEAB	MALISEET cluster	2	2	3,417	4,079		95.99	100	C	24	Maliseet*	P . .	1870				0	20758
62-AEAB-a	maliseet					0				24		p . .					0	20759
62-AEAB-b	passamaquoddy					0				24		p . .					0	20760
62-AEAC	ABENAKI cluster	2	2	3,293	3,955		91.59	100	C	27	Abenaqui*	P . .	1844				0	20761
62-AEAC-a	West abenaki					0				27		p . .					0	20762
62-AEAC-b	penobscot					0				27		p . .					0	20763
62-AEB	**MASSACHUSET-DELAWARE net**	2	5	6,231	7,312		43.28	74	B	66		PNB					0	20764
62-AEBA	MASSACHUSET cluster	1	2	3,312	3,875		14.61	60	B	66		PNB					0	20765
62-AEBA-a	massachu-set	1	1	1,531	1,791	1	19.99	62	B	66	Massachusetts*	PNB	1655-1664	1661	1663-1685		0	20766
62-AEBA-b	nau-set					1				66		pnb					0	20767
62-AEBA-c	wampanoag					1				66		pnb					0	20768
62-AEBA-d	housetonic					1				66		pnb					0	20769
62-AEBA-e	nipmuc					1				66		pnb					0	20770
62-AEBA-f	pocomtuc					1				66		pnb					0	20771
62-AEBA-g	mahican					1				66		pnb					0	20772
62-AEBA-h	narragan-set					1				66		pnb					0	20773
62-AEBA-i	natick					1				66		pnb					0	20774
62-AEBA-j	pequot-mohegan					1				66		pnb					0	20775
62-AEBA-k	montauk	1	1	1,781	2,084	8	9.99	58	B	66		pnb					0	20776
62-AEBB	DELAWARE cluster	2	3	2,919	3,437		75.81	90	C	27		P . .					0	20777
62-AEBB-a	munsee	2	2	2,418	2,851	0	89.45	100	C	27	Delaware*	P . .	1818-1821				0	20778
62-AEBB-b	unami					0				27		p . .					0	20781
62-AEBB-c	nanticoke	1	1	501	586	0	9.98	41	A	27		p . .					0	20782
62-AEBB-d	conoy			0	0	0	0.00	0		27		p . .					0	20783
62-AEC	**SOUTHEAST ALGONKIAN net**	1	2	41,754	48,836		55.47	91	B	9		. . .					0	20784
62-AECA	POWHATAN cluster	1	1	3,786	4,428		10.01	40	A	9		. . .					0	20785
62-AECA-a	powhatan	1	1	3,786	4,428	0	10.01	40	A	9		. . .					0	20786
62-AECB	PAMLICO cluster	1	1	37,968	44,408		60.00	96	C	9		. . .					0	20787
62-AECB-a	pamlico			0	0	0	0.00	0		9		. . .					0	20788
62-AECB-b	lumbee	1	1	37,968	44,408	0	60.00	96	C	9		. . .					0	20789
63	**NORTH PACIFIC zone**	3	81	160,600	191,628		88.57	99	C	41		PN .					0	20790
63-A	**TLINGIT set**	2	2	11,194	13,246		93.00	100	C	23		P . .					0	20791
63-AA	TLINGIT chain	2	2	11,194	13,246		93.00	100	C	23		P . .					0	20792
63-AAA	**TLINGIT net**	2	2	11,194	13,246		93.00	100	C	23		P . .					0	20793
63-AAAA	NORTH TLINGIT cluster	2	2	11,154	13,178		93.01	100	C	23		P . .					0	20794
63-AAAA-a	North tlingit	2	2	11,154	13,178	0	93.01	100	C	23	Tlingit	P . .	1969				0	20795
63-AAAB	SOUTH TLINGIT cluster	1	1	40	68		90.00	100	C	0		. . .					0	20796
63-AAAB-a	tongass	1	1	40	68	0	90.00	100	C	0		. . .					0	20797
63-B	**HAIDA set**	2	2	3,499	4,681		92.17	100	C	24		P . .					0	20798
63-BA	HAIDA chain	2	2	3,499	4,681		92.17	100	C	24		P . .					0	20799
63-BAA	**HAIDA net**	2	2	3,499	4,681		92.17	100	C	24		P . .					0	20800
63-BAAA	NORTH HAIDA cluster	1	1	1,000	1,700		90.00	99	C	0		. . .					0	20801
63-BAAA-a	North masset					0				0		. . .					0	20802
63-BAAA-b	South masset					0				0		. . .					0	20803
63-BAAB	SOUTH HAIDA cluster	2	2	2,499	2,981		93.04	100	C	24		P . .					0	20804
63-BAAB-a	skidegate	2	2	2,499	2,981	0	93.04	100	C	24	Haida	P . .	1891-1899				0	20805
63-C	**TSIMSHIAN-NISKA set**	2	3	11,431	13,804		95.17	100	C	24		P . .					0	20806
63-CA	TSIMSHIAN-NISKA chain	2	3	11,431	13,804		95.17	100	C	24		P . .					0	20807
63-CAA	**TSIMSHIAN-NISHKA net**	2	3	11,431	13,804		95.17	100	C	24		P . .					0	20808
63-CAAA	TSIMSHIAN cluster	2	2	4,719	5,637		93.98	100	C	24		P . .					0	20809
63-CAAA-a	Northwest tsimshian					0				24		p . .					0	20810
63-CAAA-b	Southeast tsimshian	2	2	4,719	5,637	0	93.98	100	C	24	Tsimshian: Coastal	P . .	1885-1898				0	20811
63-CAAB	NASS-GITKSIAN cluster	1	1	6,712	8,167		96.01	100	C	24		P . .					0	20812
63-CAAB-a	niska					0				24		p . .					0	20813
63-CAAB-b	gitksian	1	1	6,712	8,167	0	96.01	100	C	24	Gitksian*	P . .	1906				0	20814
63-D	**BELLA-COOLA set**	1	1	200	340		90.00	99	C	6		. . .					0	20815
63-DA	BELLA-COOLA chain	1	1	200	340		90.00	99	C	6		. . .					0	20816
63-DAA	**BELLA-COOLA net**	1	1	200	340		90.00	99	C	6		. . .					0	20817
63-DAAA	NUXALK cluster	2	1	200	340		90.00	99	C	6		. . .					0	20818
63-DAAA-a	nuxalk	1	1	200	340	0	90.00	99	C	6		. . .					0	20819
63-E	**WAKASHAN set**	2	6	13,559	16,462		93.44	100	C	24		P . .					0	20820
63-EA	WAKASHAN chain	2	6	13,559	16,462		93.44	100	C	24		P . .					0	20821
63-EAA	**NORTH WAKASHAN net**	1	4	8,107	9,864		94.60	100	C	24		P . .					0	20822
63-EAAA	HAISLA-KITIMAT cluster	1	1	1,246	1,516		91.97	100	C	6		. . .					0	20823
63-EAAA-a	hais-la	1	1	1,246	1,516	0	91.97	100	C	6		. . .					0	20824
63-EAAA-b	kitimat					0				6		. . .					0	20825
63-EAAA-c	oowekya-la					0				6		. . .					0	20826
63-EAAB	HEILTSUK cluster	1	2	2,432	2,959		93.38	100	C	6		. . .					0	20827
63-EAAB-a	Proper heiltsuk	1	1	1,610	1,959	0	90.99	100	C	6		. . .					0	20828

Continued opposite

Table 9-13 continued

Code 1	REFERENCE NAME / Autoglossonym 2	Coun 3	Peo 4	Mother-tongue speakers in 2000 5	in 2025 6	Media radio 7	CHURCH AC% 8	E% 9	Wld 10	Tr 11	Biblioglossonym 12	SCRIPTURES Print 13-15	P-activity 16	N-activity 17	B-activity 18	J-year 19	Jayuh 20-24	Ref 25
63-EAAB-b	bella-bella			0	0	0	0.00	0		6		. . .					0. . . .	20829
63-EAAB-c	xaihai					0				6		. . .					0. . . .	20830
63-EAAC	KWAKWA-LA cluster	1	1	4,429	5,389		96.00	100	C	24		P. .					0. . . .	20831
63-EAAC-a	kwakwa-la	1	1	4,429	5,389	0	96.00	100	C	24	Kwakiutl	P. .	1882-1900				0. . . .	20832
63-EAB	**SOUTH WAKASHAN net**	2	2	5,452	6,598		91.71	100	C	6		. . .					0. . . .	20833
63-EABA	NOOTKA-NITINAT cluster	1	1	4,700	5,719		92.00	100	C	6		. . .					0. . . .	20834
63-EABA-a	nootka	1	1	4,700	5,719	0	92.00	100	C	6		. . .					0. . . .	20835
63-EABA-b	nitinat					0				6		. . .					0. . . .	20836
63-EABB	MAKAH cluster	1	1	752	879		89.89	100	C	6		. . .					0. . . .	20837
63-EABB-a	makah	1	1	752	879	0	89.89	100	C	6		. . .					0. . . .	20838
63-F	**CHIMAKUM-QUILEUTE set**	1	1	390	456		91.03	100	C	8		. . .					0. . . .	20839
63-FA	CHIMAKUM-QUILEUTE chain	1	1	390	456		91.03	100	C	8		. . .					0. . . .	20840
63-FAA	**QUILEUTE net**	1	1	390	456		91.03	100	C	8		. . .					0. . . .	20841
63-FAAA	QUILEUTE cluster	1	1	390	456		91.03	100	C	8		. . .					0. . . .	20842
63-FAAA-a	quileute	1	1	390	456	0	91.03	100	C	8		. . .					0. . . .	20843
63-FAAA-b	hoh					0				8		. . .					0. . . .	20844
63-FAAB	CHIMAKUM cluster			0	0		0.00	0		0		. . .					0. . . .	20845
63-FAAB-a	chimakum			0	0	0	0.00	0		0		. . .					0. . . .	20846
63-G	**SALISH set**	2	26	54,645	65,521		87.61	100	C	9		. . .					0. . . .	20847
63-GA	SALISH-CENTRAL chain	2	13	24,172	28,999		85.91	100	C	9		. . .					0. . . .	20848
63-GAA	**COMOX-CLALLAM net**	2	8	17,520	21,217		90.72	100	C	9		. . .					0. . . .	20849
63-GAAA	COMOX-SLIAMMON cluster	1	1	1,075	1,307		92.00	100	C	6		. . .					0. . . .	20850
63-GAAA-a	comox	1	1	1,075	1,307	0	92.00	100	C	6		. . .					0. . . .	20851
63-GAAA-b	sliammon					0				6		. . .					0. . . .	20852
63-GAAB	SECHELT cluster	1	1	738	898		89.02	100	C	8		. . .					0. . . .	20853
63-GAAB-a	sechelt	1	1	738	898	0	89.02	100	C	8		. . .					0. . . .	20854
63-GAAC	PENTLATCH cluster			0	0		0.00	0		9		. . .					0. . . .	20855
63-GAAC-a	pentlatch			0	0	0	0.00	0		9		. . .					0. . . .	20856
63-GAAD	SQUAMISH cluster	1	1	2,700	3,286		92.00	100	C	8		. . .					0. . . .	20857
63-GAAD-a	squamish	1	1	2,700	3,286	0	92.00	100	C	8		. . .					0. . . .	20858
63-GAAE	HALKOMELEM cluster	1	1	8,995	10,945		90.01	100	C	6		. . .					0. . . .	20859
63-GAAE-a	chiliwack					0				6		. . .					0. . . .	20860
63-GAAE-b	musqueam					0				6		. . .					0. . . .	20861
63-GAAE-c	cowichan					0				6		. . .					0. . . .	20862
63-GAAE-d	nanaimo					0				6		. . .					0. . . .	20863
63-GAAF	SAANICH-CLALLAM cluster	2	3	3,567	4,260		91.42	100	C	6		. . .					0. . . .	20864
63-GAAF-a	saanich					0				6		. . .					0. . . .	20865
63-GAAF-b	sooke					0				6		. . .					0. . . .	20866
63-GAAF-c	semiahmoo					0				6		. . .					0. . . .	20867
63-GAAF-d	songish					0				6		. . .					0. . . .	20868
63-GAAF-e	lummi					0				6		. . .					0. . . .	20869
63-GAAF-f	samish			0	0	0	0.00	0		6		. . .					0. . . .	20870
63-GAAF-g	clallam					0				6		. . .					0. . . .	20871
63-GAAG	NOOKSACK cluster	1	1	445	521		91.46	100	C	9		. . .					0. . . .	20872
63-GAAG-a	nooksack	1	1	445	521	0	91.46	100	C	9		. . .					0. . . .	20873
63-GAB	**PUGET-TWANA net**	1	5	6,652	7,782		73.23	99	C	9		. . .					0. . . .	20874
63-GABA	LUSHOOTSEED cluster	1	3	3,674	4,298		67.23	99	C	8		. . .					0. . . .	20875
63-GABA-a	skagit	1	1	445	521	0	79.10	100	C	8		. . .					0. . . .	20876
63-GABA-b	snohomish	1	1	1,002	1,172	0	78.04	100	C	8		. . .					0. . . .	20877
63-GABB	LUSHOOTSEEDSTH cluster	1	1	2,533	2,963		81.01	100	C	0		. . .					0. . . .	20878
63-GABB-a	duwamish					0				0		. . .					0. . . .	20879
63-GABB-b	muckleshoot					0				0		. . .					0. . . .	20880
63-GABB-c	nisqually					0				0		. . .					0. . . .	20881
63-GABB-d	puyallup					0				0		. . .					0. . . .	20882
63-GABB-e	snoqualmie					0				0		. . .					0. . . .	20883
63-GABB-f	suquamish					0				0		. . .					0. . . .	20884
63-GABC	TWANA cluster	1	1	445	521		78.43	100	C	9		. . .					0. . . .	20885
63-GABC-a	quilcene			0	0	0	0.00	0		9		. . .					0. . . .	20886
63-GABC-b	skokomish	1	1	445	521	0	78.43	100	C	9		. . .					0. . . .	20887
63-GB	TSAMOSAN chain	1	3	2,367	2,767		86.90	100	C	8		. . .					0. . . .	20888
63-GBA	**QUINAULT-CHEHALIS net**	1	2	2,144	2,507		89.69	100	C	8		. . .					0. . . .	20889
63-GBAA	QUINAULT cluster	1	1	1,893	2,214		91.28	100	C	8		. . .					0. . . .	20890
63-GBAA-a	quinault	1	1	1,893	2,214	0	91.28	100	C	8		. . .					0. . . .	20891
63-GBAB	WEST CHEHALIS cluster	1	1	251	293		77.69	100	C	8		. . .					0. . . .	20892
63-GBAB-a	West chehalis	1	1	251	293	0	77.69	100	C	8		. . .					0. . . .	20893
63-GBB	**COWLITZ-CHEHALIS net**	1	1	223	260		60.09	97	C	8		. . .					0. . . .	20894
63-GBBA	EAST CHEHALIS cluster									6		. . .					0. . . .	20895
63-GBBA-a	satsop					0				6		. . .					0. . . .	20896
63-GBBA-b	East chehalis					0				6		. . .					0. . . .	20897
63-GBBB	COWLITZ cluster	1	1	223	260		60.09	97	C	8		. . .					0. . . .	20898
63-GBBB-a	cowlitz	1	1	223	260	0	60.09	97	C	8		. . .					0. . . .	20899
63-GC	SALISH-INTERIOR chain	2	10	28,106	33,755		89.13	100	C	8		. . .					0. . . .	20900
63-GCA	**LILLOET-SHUSWAP net**	2	4	15,883	19,289		90.95	100	C	8		. . .					0. . . .	20901
63-GCAA	LILLOET cluster	1	1	3,759	4,574		93.00	100	C	6		. . .					0. . . .	20902
63-GCAA-a	leel-wat-ool	1	1	3,759	4,574	0	93.00	100	C	6		. . .					0. . . .	20903
63-GCAA-b	stla-tlei-mu-wh					0				6		. . .					0. . . .	20904
63-GCAB	SHUSWAP cluster	2	2	8,386	10,167		90.01	100	C	8		. . .					0. . . .	20905
63-GCAB-a	West shuswap					0				8		. . .					0. . . .	20906
63-GCAB-b	East shuswap					0				8		. . .					0. . . .	20907
63-GCAC	NTLAKYAPAMUK cluster	1	1	3,738	4,548		90.98	100	C	6		. . .					0. . . .	20908
63-GCAC-a	in-thla-cap-mu-wh	1	1	3,738	4,548	0	90.98	100	C	6		. . .					0. . . .	20909
63-GCB	**OKANAGAN-KALISPEL net**	2	5	11,583	13,717		87.14	100	C	8		. . .					0. . . .	20910
63-GCBA	OKANAGAN cluster	2	2	5,542	6,652		92.02	100	C	6		. . .					0. . . .	20911
63-GCBA-a	North okanagan	1	1	3,594	4,373	0	92.01	100	C	6		. . .					0. . . .	20912
63-GCBA-b	shwoy-el-pi	1	1	1,948	2,279	0	92.04	100	C	6		. . .					0. . . .	20913

Continued overleaf

Table 9-13 continued

Code 1	REFERENCE NAME / Autoglossonym 2	Coun 3	Peo 4	Mother-tongue speakers in 2000 5	in 2025 6	Media radio 7	CHURCH AC% 8	E% 9	Wld 10	Tr 11	Biblioglossonym 12	Print 13-15	P-activity 16	N-activity 17	B-activity 18	J-year 19	Jayuh 20-24	Ref 25
63-GCBA-c	methow					0				6		. . .					0. . . .	20914
63-GCBA-d	moses-lake					0				6		. . .					0. . . .	20915
63-GCBA-e	nespelim					0				6		. . .					0. . . .	20916
63-GCBB	KALISPEL cluster	1	2	5,039	5,893		80.00	100	C	8		. . .					0. . . .	20917
63-GCBB-a	flathead	1	1	3,786	4,428		80.01	100	C	8		. . .					0. . . .	20918
63-GCBB-b	pend-d'oreille					0				8		. . .					0. . . .	20919
63-GCBB-c	chewelah					0				8		. . .					0. . . .	20920
63-GCBB-d	spokane	1	1	1,253	1,465		79.97	100	C	8		. . .					0. . . .	20921
63-GCBC	SKITSAMISH cluster	1	1	1,002	1,172		96.01	100	C	8		. . .					0. . . .	20922
63-GCBC-a	skitsamish	1	1	1,002	1,172	0	96.01	100	C	8		. . .					0. . . .	20923
63-GCC	**WENATCHI-COLUMBIA net**	1	1	640	749		80.00	100	C	6		. . .					0. . . .	20924
63-GCCA	WENATCHI-COLUMBIA cluster	1	1	640	749		80.00	100	C	6		. . .					0. . . .	20925
63-GCCA-a	wenatchi					0				6		. . .					0. . . .	20926
63-GCCA-b	peskwaus					0				6		. . .					0. . . .	20927
63-GD	TILLAMOOK chain									0		. . .					0. . . .	20928
63-GDA	**TILLAMOOK net**									0		. . .					0. . . .	20929
63-GDAA	TILLAMOOK cluster			0	0		0.00	0		0		. . .					0. . . .	20930
63-GDAA-a	tillamook			0	0	0	0.00	0		0		. . .					0. . . .	20931
63-H	**KUTENAI set**	2	2	729	867		92.04	100	C	6		. . .					0. . . .	20932
63-HA	KUTENAI chain	2	2	729	867		92.04	100	C	6		. . .					0. . . .	20933
63-HAA	**KUTENAI net**	2	2	729	867		92.04	100	C	6		. . .					0. . . .	20934
63-HAAA	KUTENAI cluster	2	2	729	867		92.04	100	C	6		. . .					0. . . .	20935
63-HAAA-a	West kutenai					0				6		. . .					0. . . .	20936
63-HAAA-b	East kutenai					0				6		. . .					0. . . .	20937
63-I	**SAHAPTIN-MOLALA set**	1	5	14,308	16,735		88.52	100	C	24		P . .					0. . . .	20938
63-IA	SAHAPTIN chain	1	5	14,308	16,735		88.52	100	C	24		P . .					0. . . .	20939
63-IAA	**SAHAPTIN net**	1	5	14,308	16,735		88.52	100	C	24		P . .					0. . . .	20940
63-IAAA	SAHAPTIN cluster	1	5	14,308	16,735		88.52	100	C	24		P . .					0. . . .	20941
63-IAAA-a	nez-percé	1	1	1,893	2,214	0	90.02	100	C	24	Nez Perce	P . .	1845-1876				0. . . .	20942
63-IAAA-b	palus			0	0	0	0.00	0		24		p . .					0. . . .	20943
63-IAAA-c	walla-walla	1	1	891	1,042	0	80.36	100	C	24		p . .					0. . . .	20944
63-IAAA-d	umatilla	1	1	139	163	0	89.21	100	C	24		p . .					0. . . .	20945
63-IAAA-e	yakima	1	1	10,132	11,851	0	90.00	100	C	24		p . .					0. . . .	20946
63-IAAA-f	klikitat					0				24		p . .					0. . . .	20947
63-IAAA-g	tenino	1	1	1,253	1,465	0	79.97	100	C	24		p . .					0. . . .	20948
63-IB	MOLALA chain									0		. . .					0. . . .	20949
63-IBA	**MOLALA net**									0		. . .					0. . . .	20950
63-IBAA	MOLALA cluster			0	0		0.00	0		0		. . .					0. . . .	20951
63-IBAA-a	molala			0	0	0	0.00	0		0		. . .					0. . . .	20952
63-IC	CAYUSE chain									0		. . .					0. . . .	20953
63-ICA	**CAYUSE net**									0		. . .					0. . . .	20954
63-ICAA	CAYUSE cluster			0	0		0.00	0		0		. . .					0. . . .	20955
63-ICAA-a	cayuse			0	0	0	0.00	0		0		. . .					0. . . .	20956
63-J	**CHINOOKAN set**	2	4	1,568	1,840		65.56	88	C	27		P . .					0. . . .	20957
63-JA	CHINOOK chain	2	4	1,568	1,840		65.56	88	C	27		P . .					0. . . .	20958
63-JAA	**CHINOOK net**	2	4	1,568	1,840		65.56	88	C	27		P . .					0. . . .	20959
63-JAAA	EAST CHINOOK cluster	1	1	946	1,107		78.33	100	C	8		. . .					0. . . .	20960
63-JAAA-a	wasco					0				8		. . .					0. . . .	20961
63-JAAA-b	wishram					0				8		. . .					0. . . .	20962
63-JAAB	WEST CHINOOK cluster	1	1	390	456		20.00	51	B	9		. . .					0. . . .	20963
63-JAAB-a	clackama					0				9		. . .					0. . . .	20964
63-JAAB-b	clatsop	1	1	390	456	0	20.00	51	B	9		. . .					0. . . .	20965
63-JAAC	CHINOOK-WAWA cluster	2	2	232	277		90.09	100	C	27		P . .					0. . . .	20966
63-JAAC-a	chinook-wawa	2	2	232	277	0	90.09	100	C	27	Chinook*	P . .	1912				0. . . .	20967
63-K	**KALAPUYA-TAKELMA set**									0		. . .					0. . . .	20968
63-KA	KALAPUYAN-YONKALLA chain									0		. . .					0. . . .	20969
63-KAA	**KALAPUYAN-YONKALLA net**									0		. . .					20970
63-KAAA	KALAPUYA cluster			0	0		0.00	0		0		. . .					0. . . .	20971
63-KAAA-a	Northwest kalapuya			0	0	0	0.00	0		0		. . .					0. . . .	20972
63-KAAA-b	Central kalapuya			0	0	0	0.00	0		0		. . .					0. . . .	20973
63-KAAB	YONKALLA cluster			0	0		0.00	0		0		. . .					0. . . .	20974
63-KAAB-a	yonkalla			0	0	0	0.00	0		0		. . .					0. . . .	20975
63-KB	TAKELMA chain									0		. . .					0. . . .	20976
63-KBA	**TAKELMA net**									0		. . .					0. . . .	20977
63-KBAA	TAKELMA cluster			0	0		0.00	0		0		. . .					0. . . .	20978
63-KBAA-a	takelma			0	0	0	0.00	0		0		. . .					0. . . .	20979
63-L	**SIUSLAW-YAQUINA set**									0		. . .					0. . . .	20980
63-LA	YAQUINA-ALSEA chain									0		. . .					0. . . .	20981
63-LAA	**YAQUINA net**									0		. . .					0. . . .	20982
63-LAAA	YAQUINA cluster			0	0		0.00	0		0		. . .					0. . . .	20983
63-LAAA-a	yaquina			0	0	0	0.00	0		0		. . .					0. . . .	20984
63-LAB	**ALSEA net**									0		. . .					0. . . .	20985
63-LABA	ALSEA cluster			0	0		0.00	0		0		. . .					0. . . .	20986
63-LABA-a	alsea			0	0	0	0.00	0		0		. . .					0. . . .	20987
63-LB	SIUSLAW chain									0		. . .					0. . . .	20988
63-LBA	**SIUSLAW net**									0		. . .					0. . . .	20989

Continued opposite

Table 9-13 continued

Code 1	REFERENCE NAME / Autoglossonym 2	Coun 3	Peo 4	Mother-tongue speakers in 2000 5	in 2025 6	Media radio 7	CHURCH AC% 8	E% 9	Wld 10	Tr 11	Biblioglossonym 12	Print 13-15	P-activity 16	N-activity 17	B-activity 18	J-year 19	Jayuh 20-24	Ref 25
63-LBAA	SIUSLAW cluster			0	0		0.00	0		0		. . .					0	20990
63-LBAA-a	siuslaw			0	0	0	0.00	0		0		. . .					0	20991
63-M	**COOS set**	1	1	306	358		10.13	40	A	8		. . .					0	20992
63-MA	COOS chain	1	1	306	358		10.13	40	A	8		. . .					0	20993
63-MAA	**COOS net**	1	1	306	358		10.13	40	A	8		. . .					0	20994
63-MAAA	COOS cluster	1	1	306	358		10.13	40	A	8		. . .					0	20995
63-MAAA-a	coos	1	1	306	358	0	10.13	40	A	8		. . .					0	20996
63-N	**KLAMATH-MODOC set**	1	1	2,533	2,963		90.01	100	C	6		. . .					0	20997
63-NA	KLAMATH-MODOC chain	1	1	2,533	2,963		90.01	100	C	6		. . .					0	20998
63-NAA	**KLAMATH-MODOC net**	1	1	2,533	2,963		90.01	100	C	6		. . .					0	20999
63-NAAA	KLAMATH-MODOC cluster	1	1	2,533	2,963		90.01	100	C	6		. . .					0	21000
63-NAAA-a	klamath	1	1	2,533	2,963	0	90.01	100	C	6		. . .					0	21001
63-NAAA-b	modoc			0	0	0	0.00	0		6		. . .					0	21002
63-O	**YUROK set**	1	1	5,177	6,056		91.31	100	C	8		. . .					0	21003
63-OA	YUROK chain	1	1	5,177	6,056		91.31	100	C	8		. . .					0	21004
63-OAA	**YUROK net**	1	1	5,177	6,056		91.31	100	C	8		. . .					0	21005
63-OAAA	YUROK cluster	1	1	5,177	6,056		91.31	100	C	8		. . .					0	21006
63-OAAA-a	yurok	1	1	5,177	6,056	0	91.31	100	C	8		. . .					0	21007
63-P	**WIYOT set**	1	1	139	163		20.14	51	B	9		. . .					0	21008
63-PA	WIYOT chain	1	1	139	163		20.14	51	B	9		. . .					0	21009
63-PAA	**WIYOT net**	1	1	139	163		20.14	51	B	9		. . .					0	21010
63-PAAA	WIYOT cluster	1	1	139	163		20.14	51	B	9		. . .					0	21011
63-PAAA-a	wiyot	1	1	139	163	0	20.14	51	B	9		. . .					0	21012
63-Q	**YUKI set**									0		. . .					0	21013
63-QA	YUKI chain									0		. . .					0	21014
63-QAA	**YUKI net**									0		. . .					0	21015
63-QAAA	YUKI cluster			0	0		0.00	0		0		. . .					0	21016
63-QAAA-a	yuki			0	0	0	0.00	0		0		. . .					0	21017
63-R	**WAPPO set**	1	1	56	65		10.71	39	A	8		. . .					0	21018
63-RA	WAPPO chain	1	1	56	65		10.71	39	A	8		. . .					0	21019
63-RAA	**WAPPO net**	1	1	56	65		10.71	39	A	8		. . .					0	21020
63-RAAA	WAPPO cluster	1	1	56	65		10.71	39	A	8		. . .					0	21021
63-RAAA-a	North wappo			0	0	0	0.00	0		8		. . .					0	21022
63-RAAA-b	South wappo			0	0	0	0.00	0		8		. . .					0	21023
63-S	**WINTU-YOKUTS set**	1	4	2,478	2,898		78.17	100	C	9		. . .					0	21024
63-SA	WINTU chain	1	1	1,197	1,400		78.28	100	C	8		. . .					0	21025
63-SAA	**WINTU net**	1	1	1,197	1,400		78.28	100	C	8		. . .					0	21026
63-SAAA	WINTU cluster	1	1	1,197	1,400		78.28	100	C	8		. . .					0	21027
63-SAAA-a	Proper wintu	1	1	1,197	1,400	0	78.28	100	C	8		. . .					0	21028
63-SAAA-b	patwin					0				8		. . .					0	21029
63-SAAA-c	nomlaki					0				8		. . .					0	21030
63-SB	MAIDU chain	1	1	251	293		77.69	100	C	9		. . .					0	21031
63-SBA	**MAIDU net**	1	1	251	293		77.69	100	C	9		. . .					0	21032
63-SBAA	MAIDU-NISHINAM cluster	1	1	251	293		77.69	100	C	9		. . .					0	21033
63-SBAA-a	Northeast maidu					0				9		. . .					0	21034
63-SBAA-b	Northwest maidu					0				9		. . .					0	21035
63-SBAA-c	nisenan					0				9		. . .					0	21036
63-SC	YOKUTS chain	1	1	640	749		78.28	100	C	9		. . .					0	21037
63-SCA	**YOKUTS net**	1	1	640	749		78.28	100	C	9		. . .					0	21038
63-SCAA	YOKUTS cluster	1	1	640	749		78.28	100	C	9		. . .					0	21039
63-SCAA-a	yokuts	1	1	640	749	0	78.28	100	C	9		. . .					0	21040
63-SD	MIWOK-COSTANOAN chain	1	1	390	456		77.95	100	C	8		. . .					0	21041
63-SDA	**MIWOK-COSTANOAN net**	1	1	390	456		77.95	100	C	8		. . .					0	21042
63-SDAA	MIWOK cluster	1	1	390	456		77.95	100	C	8		. . .					0	21043
63-SDAA-a	coast-miwok					0				8		. . .					0	21044
63-SDAA-b	lake-miwok	1	1	390	456	0	77.95	100	C	8		. . .					0	21045
63-SDAA-c	plains-miwok					0				8		. . .					0	21046
63-SDAA-d	sierra-miwok					0				8		. . .					0	21047
63-SDAB	COSTANO cluster									0		. . .					0	21048
63-SDAB-a	rumsen					0				0		. . .					0	21049
63-SDAB-b	mutsun					0				0		. . .					0	21050
63-T	**KAROK-SHASTA set**	1	4	5,734	6,707		77.28	98	C	8		. . .					0	21051
63-TA	KAROK chain	1	1	4,509	5,274		80.31	100	C	6		. . .					0	21052
63-TAA	**KAROK net**	1	1	4,509	5,274		80.31	100	C	6		. . .					0	21053
63-TAAA	KAROK cluster	1	1	4,509	5,274		80.31	100	C	6		. . .					0	21054
63-TAAA-a	karok	1	1	4,509	5,274	0	80.31	100	C	6		. . .					0	21055
63-TB	CHIMARIKO chain									0		. . .					0	21056
63-TBA	**CHIMARIKO net**									0		. . .					0	21057
63-TBAA	CHIMARIKO cluster			0	0		0.00	0		0		. . .					0	21058
63-TBAA-a	chimariko			0	0	0	0.00	0		0		. . .					0	21059

Continued overleaf

Table 9-13 continued

Code 1	REFERENCE NAME / Autoglossonym 2	Coun 3	Peo 4	Mother-tongue speakers in 2000 5	in 2025 6	Media radio 7	AC% 8	E% 9	Wld 10	Tr 11	Biblioglossonym 12	Print 13-15	P-activity 16	N-activity 17	B-activity 18	J-year 19	Jayuh 20-24	Ref 25
63-TC	SHASTA-PALAIHNINAN chain	1	3	1,225	1,433		66.12	89	C	8		. . .					0	21060
63-TCA	**SHASTA net**	1	1	28	33		78.57	100	C	8		. . .					0	21061
63-TCAA	SHASTA cluster	1	1	28	33		78.57	100	C	8		. . .					0	21062
63-TCAA-a	shasta	1	1	28	33	0	78.57	100	C	8		. . .					0	21063
63-TCB	**PALAIHNINAN net**	1	2	1,197	1,400		65.83	89	C	8		. . .					0	21064
63-TCBA	ACHUMAWI cluster	1	1	946	1,107		78.01	100	C	8		. . .					0	21065
63-TCBA-a	achumawi	1	1	946	1,107	0	78.01	100	C	8		. . .					0	21066
63-TCBB	ATSUGEWI cluster	1	1	251	293		19.92	48	A	8		. . .					0	21067
63-TCBB-a	atsugewi	1	1	251	293	0	19.92	48	A	8		. . .					0	21068
63-TD	YANAN chain									0		. . .					0	21069
63-TDA	**YANA net**									0		. . .					0	21070
63-TDAA	YANA cluster			0	0		0.00	0		0		. . .					0	21071
63-TDAA-a	yana			0	0	0	0.00	0		0		. . .					0	21072
63-TDAB	YAHI cluster			0	0		0.00	0		0		. . .					0	21073
63-TDAB-a	yahi			0	0	0	0.00	0		0		. . .					0	21074
63-U	**WASHO set**	1	1	1,253	1,465		80.29	100	C	6		. . .					0	21075
63-UA	WASHO chain	1	1	1,253	1,465		80.29	100	C	6		. . .					0	21076
63-UAA	**WASHO net**	1	1	1,253	1,465		80.29	100	C	6		. . .					0	21077
63-UAAA	WASHO cluster	1	1	1,253	1,465		80.29	100	C	6		. . .					0	21078
63-UAAA-a	washo	1	1	1,253	1,465	0	80.29	100	C	6		. . .					0	21079
63-V	**POMO-YUMA set**	2	13	10,023	11,997		84.40	100	C	41		PN .					0	21080
63-VA	POMO-KASHAYA chain	1	1	1,263	1,482		80.36	100	C	8		. . .					0	21081
63-VAA	**POMO-KASHAYA net**	1	1	1,263	1,482		80.36	100	C	8		. . .					0	21082
63-VAAA	POMO-KASHAYA cluster	1	1	1,253	1,465		80.29	100	C	8		. . .					0	21083
63-VAAA-a	North pomo					0				8		. . .					0	21084
63-VAAA-b	Northeast pomo					0				8		. . .					0	21085
63-VAAA-c	Central pomo					0				8		. . .					0	21086
63-VAAA-d	kashaya	1	1	1,253	1,465	0	80.29	100	C	8		. . .					0	21087
63-VAAA-e	South pomo					0				8		. . .					0	21088
63-VAAB	SOUTHEAST POMO cluster	1	1	10	17		90.00	100	C	8		. . .					0	21089
63-VAAB-a	Southeast pomo	1	1	10	17	0	90.00	100	C	8		. . .					0	21090
63-VB	ESSELEN chain									0		. . .					0	21091
63-VBA	**ESSELEN net**									0		. . .					0	21092
63-VBAA	ESSELEN cluster									0		. . .					0	21093
63-VBAA-a	esselen					0				0		. . .					0	21094
63-VC	SALINA-CHUMASH chain									0		. . .					0	21095
63-VCA	**SALINA net**									0		. . .					0	21096
63-VCAA	SALINA cluster			0	0		0.00	0		0		. . .					0	21097
63-VCAA-a	North salina			0	0	0	0.00	0		0		. . .					0	21098
63-VCAA-b	South salina			0	0	0	0.00	0		0		. . .					0	21099
63-VCB	**CHUMASH net**									0		. . .					0	21100
63-VCBA	CHUMASH cluster									0		. . .					0	21101
63-VCBA-a	obispeño					0				0		. . .					0	21102
63-VCBA-b	ineseño					0				0		. . .					0	21103
63-VCBA-c	purisimeño					0				0		. . .					0	21104
63-VCBA-d	barbareño					0				0		. . .					0	21105
63-VCBA-e	ventureño					0				0		. . .					0	21106
63-VCBA-f	isleño					0				0		. . .					0	21107
63-VD	YUMA chain	2	11	7,979	9,486		86.44	100	C	23		P . .					0	21108
63-VDA	**NORTHEAST YUMA net**	1	1	1,893	2,214		79.98	100	C	22		. . .					0	21109
63-VDAA	WALAPAI-YAVAPAI cluster	1	1	1,893	2,214		79.98	100	C	22	Havasupai-walapai-yavapai	P . .	1980				0	21110
63-VDAA-a	walapai					0				22		p . .					0	21111
63-VDAA-b	havasupai					0				22		p . .					0	21112
63-VDAA-c	yavapai					0				22		p . .					0	21113
63-VDB	**CENTRAL YUMA net**	1	3	4,287	5,014		89.41	100	C	6		. . .					0	21114
63-VDBA	MOHAVE-QUECHAN cluster	1	3	4,287	5,014		89.41	100	C	6		. . .					0	21115
63-VDBA-a	mohave	1	1	1,893	2,214	0	90.02	100	C	6		. . .					0	21116
63-VDBA-b	quechan	1	1	1,893	2,214	0	90.02	100	C	6		. . .					0	21117
63-VDBA-c	maricopa	1	1	501	586	0	84.83	100	C	6		. . .					0	21118
63-VDBA-d	halchildoma					0				6		. . .					0	21119
63-VDBA-e	kavelchadom					0				6		. . .					0	21120
63-VDC	**WEST YUMA net**	2	7	1,799	2,258		86.16	100	C	23		P . .					0	21121
63-VDCA	COCOPA-DIEGUEñO cluster	2	5	1,423	1,763		85.59	100	C	23		P . .					0	21122
63-VDCA-a	cocopa	2	2	838	1,009	0	89.98	100	C	23	Cocopa	P . .	1972				0	21123
63-VDCA-b	diegueño	2	2	358	455	0	88.27	100	C	23		p . .					0	21124
63-VDCA-c	kamia					0				23		p . .					0	21125
63-VDCA-d	tipai	1	1	227	299	0	65.20	100	C	23		p . .					0	21126
63-VDCA-e	akwa'ala					0				23		p . .					0	21127
63-VDCA-f	halyikwamai					0				23		p . .					0	21128
63-VDCA-g	kahuana					0				23		p . .					0	21129
63-VDCB	PAIPAI cluster	1	1	346	456		89.88	100	C	5		. . .					0	21130
63-VDCB-a	paipai	1	1	346	456	0	89.88	100	C	5		. . .					0	21131
63-VDCC	KILIWI cluster	1	1	30	39		70.00	100	C	8		. . .					0	21132
63-VDCC-a	kiliwi	1	1	30	39	0	70.00	100	C	8		. . .					0	21133
63-VDCD	COCHIMI cluster									9		. . .					0	21134
63-VDCD-a	North cochimi					0				9		. . .					0	21135
63-VDCD-b	South cochimi					0				9		. . .					0	21136
63-VDCE	WAITURI-PERICú cluster									0		. . .					0	21137
63-VDCE-a	waituri					0				0		. . .					0	21138
63-VDCE-b	pericú					0				0		. . .					0	21139
63-VE	SERI chain	1	1	781	1,029		70.04	100	C	41		PN .					0	21140
63-VEA	**SERI net**	1	1	781	1,029		70.04	100	C	41		PN .					0	21141

Continued opposite

Table 9-13 continued

Code 1	REFERENCE NAME / Autoglossonym 2	Coun 3	Peo 4	Mother-tongue speakers in 2000 5	in 2025 6	Media radio 7	CHURCH AC% 8	E% 9	Wld 10	Tr 11	Biblioglossonym 12	SCRIPTURES Print 13-15	P–activity 16	N–activity 17	B–activity 18	J-year 19	Jayuh 20-24	Ref 25
63-VEAA	SERI cluster	1	1	781	1,029		70.04	100	C	41		PN.					0....	21142
63-VEAA-a	seri-tiburón	1	1	781	1,029	0	70.04	100	C	41	Seri	PN.	1966-1968	1982			0....	21143
63-VEAA-b	tepoca					0				41		pn.					0....	21144
63-VEAA-c	seri-salinero					0				41		pn.					0....	21145
63-VEAA-d	tastioteño					0				41		pn.					0....	21146
63-VEAA-e	guayma-upanguayma					0				41		pn.					0....	21147
63-W	**ZUÑI set**	1	1	7,237	8,465		92.00	100	C	23		P..					0....	21148
63-WA	ZUÑI chain	1	1	7,237	8,465		92.00	100	C	23		P..					0....	21149
63-WAA	**ZUÑI net**	1	1	7,237	8,465		92.00	100	C	23		P..					0....	21150
63-WAAA	ZUñI cluster	1	1	7,237	8,465		92.00	100	C	23		P..					0....	21151
63-WAAA-a	zuñi	1	1	7,237	8,465	0	92.00	100	C	23	Zuni	P..	1941-1970				0....	21152
63-X	**KERES set**	1	2	14,141	16,539		89.99	100	C	24		P..					0....	21153
63-XA	KERES chain	1	2	14,141	16,539		89.99	100	C	24		P..					0....	21154
63-XAA	**KERES net**	1	2	14,141	16,539		89.99	100	C	24		P..					0....	21155
63-XAAA	WEST KERES cluster	1	1	7,182	8,400		89.99	100	C	23		P..					0....	21156
63-XAAA-a	acoma	1	1	7,182	8,400	0	89.99	100	C	23	Keres, Western	P..	1966				0....	21157
63-XAAA-b	laguna					0				23		p..					0....	21158
63-XAAB	EAST KERES cluster	1	1	6,959	8,139		90.00	100	C	24	Keres: Eastern*	P..	1933-1936				0....	21159
63-XAAB-a	zia					0				24		p..					0....	21160
63-XAAB-b	santa ana					0				24		p..					0....	21161
63-XAAB-c	san felipe					0				24		p..					0....	21162
63-XAAB-d	santo domingo					0				24		p..					0....	21163
63-XAAB-e	cochiti					0				24		p..					0....	21164
64	**IROQUO-DAKOTIC zone**	2	37	206,688	243,551		79.59	99	C	63		PNB					0a...	21165
64-A	**DAKOTA-CATAWBA set**	2	19	89,301	105,541		82.72	98	C	63		PNB					0a...	21166
64-AA	DAKOTA-CROW chain	2	18	88,661	104,792		82.63	98	C	63		PNB					0a...	21167
64-AAA	**HIDATSA-CROW net**	1	2	9,409	11,004		88.51	100	C	22		P..					0a...	21168
64-AAAA	HIDATSA cluster	1	1	1,392	1,628		79.96	100	C	6		...					0....	21169
64-AAAA-a	hidatsa	1	1	1,392	1,628	0	79.96	100	C	6		...					0....	21170
64-AAAB	CROW cluster	1	1	8,017	9,376		90.00	100	C	22		P..					0a...	21171
64-AAAB-a	absaroka	1	1	8,017	9,376	0	90.00	100	C	22	Crow	P..	1980-1986				0a...	21172
64-AAB	**MANDAN net**	1	1	473	553		91.33	100	C	8		...					0....	21173
64-AABA	MANDAN cluster	1	1	473	553		91.33	100	C	8		...					0....	21174
64-AABA-a	mandan	1	1	473	553	0	91.33	100	C	8		...					0....	21175
64-AAC	**DAKOTA-WINNEBAGO net**	2	15	78,779	93,235		81.87	98	C	63		PNB					0....	21176
64-AACA	DAKOTA cluster	2	7	58,516	69,533		82.67	100	C	63		PNB					0....	21177
64-AACA-a	assiniboine	2	2	5,063	6,069	0	96.05	100	C	63		pnb					0....	21178
64-AACA-b	iyarhe-nakodabi	1	1	3,853	4,688	0	96.00	100	C	63	Stoney	Pnb	1970				0....	21179
64-AACA-c	nakota					0				63		pnb					0....	21180
64-AACA-d	lakota	2	2	23,593	28,182	0	85.28	100	C	63		pnb					0....	21181
64-AACA-e	East dakota	2	2	26,007	30,594	0	75.73	100	C	63	Dakota	PNB	1839-1976	1865	1879		0....	21182
64-AACB	DHEGIHA NET cluster	1	5	11,189	13,089		72.12	86	C	8		...					0....	21183
64-AACB-a	omaha	1	1	3,173	3,712	0	90.01	100	C	8		...					0....	21184
64-AACB-b	ponca	1	1	2,310	2,702	0	89.70	100	C	8		...					0....	21185
64-AACB-c	osage	1	1	2,895	3,386	0	92.30	100	C	8	Osage	...					0....	21186
64-AACB-d	quapaw	1	1	2,533	2,963	0	9.99	40	A	8		...					0....	21187
64-AACB-e	kansa	1	1	278	326	0	78.06	100	C	8		...					0....	21188
64-AACC	OTO-IOWA cluster	1	2	2,755	3,223		85.81	100	C	8		...					0....	21189
64-AACC-a	oto	1	1	1,614	1,888	0	89.71	100	C	8		...					0....	21190
64-AACC-b	missouri									8		...					0....	21191
64-AACC-c	iowa	1	1	1,141	1,335	0	80.28	100	C	8		...					0....	21192
64-AACD	WINNEBAGO cluster	1	1	6,319	7,390		90.00	100	C	24	Winnebago*	P..	1907				0....	21193
64-AACD-a	East winnebago					0				24		p..					0....	21194
64-AACD-b	West winnebago					0				24		p..					0....	21195
64-AB	CATAWBA chain	1	1	640	749		95.78	100	C	8		...					0....	21196
64-ABA	**CATAWBA net**	1	1	640	749		95.78	100	C	8		...					0....	21197
64-ABAA	CATAWBA cluster	1	1	640	749		95.78	100	C	8		...					0....	21198
64-ABAA-a	catawba	1	1	640	749	0	95.78	100	C	8		...					0....	21199
64-B	**CADDO-PAWNEE set**	1	4	6,987	8,172		90.87	100	C	6		...					0....	21200
64-BA	PAWNEE-WICHITA chain	1	3	4,732	5,535		91.29	100	C	6		...					0....	21201
64-BAA	**PAWNEE-ARIKARA net**	1	2	3,786	4,428		91.76	100	C	6		...					0....	21202
64-BAAA	ARIKARA cluster	1	1	1,253	1,465		94.89	100	C	6		...					0....	21203
64-BAAA-a	arikara	1	1	1,253	1,465	0	94.89	100	C	6		...					0....	21204
64-BAAB	PAWNEE cluster	1	1	2,533	2,963		90.21	100	C	6		...					0....	21205
64-BAAB-a	Proper pawnee	1	1	2,533	2,963	0	90.21	100	C	6		...					0....	21206
64-BAAB-b	skidi					0				6		...					0....	21207
64-BAB	**KITSAI net**									0		...					0....	21208
64-BABA	KITSAI cluster			0	0		0.00	0		0		...					0....	21209
64-BABA-a	kitsai			0	0	0	0.00	0		0		...					0....	21210
64-BAC	**WICHITA-WACO net**	1	1	946	1,107		89.43	100	C	6		...					0....	21211
64-BACA	WICHITA-TAWAKONI cluster	1	1	946	1,107		89.43	100	C	6		...					0....	21212
64-BACA-a	wichita	1	1	946	1,107	0	89.43	100	C	6		...					0....	21213
64-BACA-b	tawakoni			0	0		0.00	0		6		...					0....	21214
64-BACB	WACO cluster			0	0		0.00	0		0		...					0....	21215
64-BACB-a	waco			0	0	0	0.00	0		0		...					0....	21216
64-BB	CADDO chain	1	1	2,255	2,637		89.98	100	C	6		...					0....	21217
64-BBA	**CADDO net**	1	1	2,255	2,637		89.98	100	C	6		...					0....	21218
64-BBAA	CADDO cluster	1	1	2,255	2,637		89.98	100	C	6		...					0....	21219
64-BBAA-a	caddo	1	1	2,255	2,637	0	89.98	100	C	6		...					0....	21220
64-BC	ADAI chain									0		...					0....	21221

Continued overleaf

Table 9-13 continued

Code 1	REFERENCE NAME / Autoglossonym 2	Coun 3	Peo 4	Mother-tongue speakers in 2000 5	in 2025 6	Media radio 7	CHURCH AC% 8	E% 9	Wld 10	Tr 11	Biblioglossonym 12	SCRIPTURES Print 13-15	P-activity 16	N-activity 17	B-activity 18	J-year 19	Jayuh 20-24	Ref 25
64-BCA	**ADAI net**									0		. . .					0	21222
64-BCAA	ADAI cluster									0		. . .					0	21223
64-BCAA-a	adai					0				0		. . .					0	21224
64-C	**IROQUOIAN set**	2	14	110,400	129,838		76.34	99	C	42		PN.					0	21225
64-CA	IROQUOIAN chain	2	14	110,400	129,838		76.34	99	C	42		PN.					0	21226
64-CAA	**NORTH IROQUOIAN net**	2	13	29,676	35,422		88.14	97	C	25		P . .					0	21227
64-CAAA	LAURENTIAN cluster									25		P . .					0	21228
64-CAAA-a	laurentian					0				25	Iroquois	P . .	1880				0	21229
64-CAAB	HURON-PETUN cluster	1	1	1,392	1,628		9.99	40	A	9		. . .					0	21230
64-CAAB-a	wyandot	1	1	1,392	1,628	0	9.99	40	A	9		. . .					0	21231
64-CAAB-b	petun					0				9		. . .					0	21232
64-CAAB-c	neutral					0				9		. . .					0	21233
64-CAAB-d	wenrohronon					0				9		. . .					0	21234
64-CAAC	MOHAWK-ONEIDA cluster	2	4	13,541	16,248		93.74	100	C	24		P . .					0	21235
64-CAAC-a	mohawk	2	2	6,396	7,686	0	94.72	100	C	24	Mohawk	P . .	1787-1991				0	21236
64-CAAC-b	oneida	2	2	7,145	8,562	0	92.88	100	C	24	Oneida	P . .	1880-1942				0	21237
64-CAAD	SENECA-ONONDAGA cluster	2	6	12,940	15,379		90.44	100	C	24		P . .					0	21238
64-CAAD-a	seneca	2	2	5,785	6,776	0	89.71	100	C	24	Seneca	P . .	1829-1874				0	21239
64-CAAD-b	cayuga	2	2	4,228	5,092	0	91.89	100	C	24		p . .					0	21240
64-CAAD-c	onondaga	2	2	2,927	3,511	0	89.78	100	C	24		p . .					0	21241
64-CAAE	TUSCARORA cluster	2	2	1,803	2,167		89.79	100	C	8		. . .					0	21242
64-CAAE-a	susquehannock					0				8		. . .					0	21243
64-CAAE-b	tuscarora	2	2	1,803	2,167	0	89.79	100	C	8		. . .					0	21244
64-CAAE-c	nottoway					0				8		. . .					0	21245
64-CAB	**CHEROKEE net**	1	1	80,724	94,416		72.00	100	C	42		PN.					0	21246
64-CABA	TSALAGI cluster	1	1	80,724	94,416		72.00	100	C	42	Cherokee	PN.	1829-1953	1850-1951			0	21247
64-CABA-a	East cherokee					0				42		pn.					0	21248
64-CABA-b	West cherokee					0				42		pn.					0	21249
65	**CIRCUMGOLFIC zone**	1	8	58,789	68,761		86.79	100	C	44		PN.					0s . . .	21250
65-A	**COAHUILTEC-NAOLAN set**	1	1	111	130		9.91	40	A	9		. . .					0	21251
65-AA	NAOLAN chain									0		. . .					0	21252
65-AAA	**NAOLAN net**									0		. . .					0	21253
65-AAAA	NAOLAN cluster			0	0		0.00	0		0		. . .					0	21254
65-AAAA-a	naolan			0	0	0	0.00	0		0		. . .					0	21255
65-AB	TAMAULIPEC chain									0		. . .					0	21256
65-ABA	**TAMAULIPEC net**									0		. . .					0	21257
65-ABAA	TAMAULIPEC cluster			0	0		0.00	0		0		. . .					0	21258
65-ABAA-a	tamaulipec			0	0	0	0.00	0		0		. . .					0	21259
65-AC	COMECRUDO-GARZA chain									0		. . .					0	21260
65-ACA	**COMECRUDO-GARZA net**									0		. . .					0	21261
65-ACAA	COMECRUDO cluster									0		. . .					0	21262
65-ACAA-a	comecrudo					0				0		. . .					0	21263
65-ACAB	GARZA cluster									0		. . .					0	21264
65-ACAB-a	garza					0				0		. . .					0	21265
65-ACAC	MAMULIQUE cluster									0		. . .					0	21266
65-ACAC-a	mamulique					0				0		. . .					0	21267
65-AD	COTONAME chain									0		. . .					0	21268
65-ADA	**COTONAME net**									0		. . .					0	21269
65-ADAA	COTONAME cluster									0		. . .					0	21270
65-ADAA-a	cotoname					0				0		. . .					0	21271
65-AE	SOLANO chain									0		. . .					0	21272
65-AEA	**SOLANO net**									0		. . .					0	21273
65-AEAA	SOLANO cluster									0		. . .					0	21274
65-AEAA-a	solano					0				0		. . .					0	21275
65-AF	COAHUILTEC chain									0		. . .					0	21276
65-AFA	**COAHUILTEC net**									0		. . .					0	21277
65-AFAA	COAHUILTEC cluster									0		. . .					0	21278
65-AFAA-a	rio-grande					0				0		. . .					0	21279
65-AFAA-b	pajalate					0				0		. . .					0	21280
65-AFAA-c	san-antonio					0				0		. . .					0	21281
65-AG	ARANAMA-TAMIQUE chain									0		. . .					0	21282
65-AGA	**ARANAMA-TAMIQUE net**									0		. . .					0	21283
65-AGAA	ARANAMA-TAMIQUE cluster									0		. . .					0	21284
65-AGAA-a	aranama					0				0		. . .					0	21285
65-AGAA-b	tamique					0				0		. . .					0	21286
65-AH	TONKAWA chain	1	1	111	130		9.91	40	A	9		. . .					0	21287
65-AHA	**TONKAWA net**	1	1	111	130		9.91	40	A	9		. . .					0	21288
65-AHAA	TONKAWA cluster	1	1	111	130		9.91	40	A	9		. . .					0	21289
65-AHAA-a	tonkawa	1	1	111	130	0	9.91	40	A	9		. . .					0	21290
65-AI	KARANKAWA chain									0		. . .					0	21291
65-AIA	**KARANKAWA net**									0		. . .					0	21292
65-AIAA	KARANKAWA cluster									0		. . .					0	21293
65-AIAA-a	karankawa					0				0		. . .					0	21294
65-B	**ATAKAPA set**									0		. . .					0	21295
65-BA	ATAKAPA chain									0		. . .					0	21296

Continued opposite

Table 9-13 continued

Code 1	REFERENCE NAME / Autoglossonym 2	Coun 3	Peo 4	Mother-tongue speakers in 2000 5	in 2025 6	Media radio 7	CHURCH AC% 8	E% 9	Wld 10	Tr 11	Biblioglossonym 12	SCRIPTURES Print 13-15	P-activity 16	N-activity 17	B-activity 18	J-year 19	Jayuh 20-24	Ref 25
65-BAA	**ATAKAPA net**									0		. . .					0	21297
65-BAAA	ATAKAPA cluster			0	0		0.00	0		0		. . .					0	21298
65-BAAA-a	West atakapa			0	0	0	0.00	0		0		. . .					0	21299
65-BAAA-b	akokisa					0				0		. . .					0	21302
65-BAAA-c	East atakapa					0				0		. . .					0	21303
65-C	**CHITIMACHA set**									0		. . .					0	21306
65-CA	CHITIMACHA chain									0		. . .					0	21307
65-CAA	**CHITIMACHA net**									0		. . .					0	21308
65-CAAA	CHITIMACHA cluster			0	0		0.00	0		0		. . .					0	21309
65-CAAA-a	chitimacha			0	0	0	0.00	0		0		. . .					0	21310
65-D	**NATCHEZ set**									0		. . .					0	21311
65-DA	NATCHEZ chain									0		. . .					0	21312
65-DAA	**NATCHEZ net**									0		. . .					0	21313
65-DAAA	NATCHEZ cluster			0	0		0.00	0		0		. . .					0	21314
65-DAAA-a	natchez			0	0	0	0.00	0		0		. . .					0	21315
65-E	**TUNICA set**	1	1	195	228		9.74	40	A	9		. . .					0	21316
65-EA	TUNICA chain	1	1	195	228		9.74	40	A	9		. . .					0	21317
65-EAA	**TUNICA net**	1	1	195	228		9.74	40	A	9		. . .					0	21318
65-EAAA	TUNICA cluster	1	1	195	228		9.74	40	A	9		. . .					0	21319
65-EAAA-a	tunica	1	1	195	228	0	9.74	40	A	9		. . .					0	21320
65-F	**MUSKOGEE-CHOCTAW set**	1	5	56,590	66,189		87.40	100	C	44		PN.					0s . . .	21321
65-FA	CHOCTAW-MOBILIAN chain	1	1	28,587	33,436		95.00	100	C	43		PN.					0	21322
65-FAA	**CHOCTAW-MOBILIAN net**	1	1	28,587	33,436		95.00	100	C	43		PN.					0	21323
65-FAAA	CHOCTAW cluster	1	1	28,587	33,436		95.00	100	C	43		PN.					0	21324
65-FAAA-a	choctaw	1	1	28,587	33,436	0	95.00	100	C	43	Choctaw	PN.	1836-1993	1848			0	21325
65-FAAA-b	chickasaw					0				43		pn.					0	21330
65-FAAB	MOBILIAN cluster									5		. . .					0	21331
65-FAAB-a	mobilian					0				5		. . .					0	21332
65-FB	MUSKOGEE-ALABAMA chain	1	4	28,003	32,753		79.64	100	C	44		PN.					0s . . .	21333
65-FBA	**ALABAMA-KOASATI net**	1	2	1,169	1,367		71.43	99	C	6		. . .					0	21334
65-FBAA	ALABAMA-KOASATI cluster	1	2	1,169	1,367		71.43	99	C	6		. . .					0	21335
65-FBAA-a	koasati	1	1	501	586	0	60.08	97	C	6		. . .					0	21336
65-FBAA-b	alabama	1	1	668	781	0	79.94	100	C	6		. . .					0	21337
65-FBB	**MUSKOGEE-MIKASUKI net**	1	2	26,834	31,386		80.00	100	C	44		PN.					0s . . .	21338
65-FBBA	MIKASUKI-HITCHITI cluster	1	1	1,531	1,791		80.01	100	C	22		P . .					0s . . .	21339
65-FBBA-a	mikasuki	1	1	1,531	1,791	0	80.01	100	C	22	Mikasuki	P . .	1980-1985				0s . . .	21340
65-FBBA-b	hitchiti					0				22		p . .					0c . . .	21341
65-FBBB	MUSKOGEE cluster	1	1	25,303	29,595		80.00	100	C	44	Muskogee	PN.	1835-1896	1886-1891			0	21342
65-FBBB-a	creek					0				44		pn.					0	21343
65-FBBB-b	seminole					0				44		pn.					0	21344
65-FBC	**APALACHEE net**									0		. . .					0	21345
65-FBCA	APALACHEE cluster									0		. . .					0	21346
65-FBCA-a	apalachee					0				0		. . .					0	21347
65-G	**YUCHI set**	1	1	1,893	2,214		80.88	100	C	6		. . .					0	21348
65-GA	YUCHI chain	1	1	1,893	2,214		80.88	100	C	6		. . .					0	21349
65-GAA	**YUCHI net**	1	1	1,893	2,214		80.88	100	C	6		. . .					0	21350
65-GAAA	YUCHI cluster	1	1	1,893	2,214		80.88	100	C	6		. . .					0	21351
65-GAAA-a	yuchi	1	1	1,893	2,214	0	80.88	100	C	6		. . .					0	21352
65-H	**TIMUCUA set**									0		. . .					0	21353
65-HA	TIMUCUA chain									0		. . .					0	21354
65-HAA	**TIMUCUA net**									0		. . .					0	21355
65-HAAA	TIMUCUA cluster									0		. . .					0	21356
65-HAAA-a	Proper timucua					0				0		. . .					0	21357
65-HAAA-b	tawasa					0				0		. . .					0	21358
66	**AZTECOTANIC zone**	6	53	2,462,071	3,261,135		91.73	99	C	46		PN.					4A . uh	21359
66-A	**KIOWA-TANOAN set**	1	5	16,757	19,599		83.89	100	C	22		P . .					1A . . .	21360
66-AA	TEWA-TIWA chain	1	3	7,349	8,595		80.00	100	C	22		P . .					1A . . .	21361
66-AAA	**TIWA-PIRO net**	1	2	4,426	5,176		80.00	100	C	22		P . .					1A . . .	21362
66-AAAA	NORTH TIWA cluster	1	1	1,420	1,660		80.00	100	C	22	Tiwa: Northern*	P . .	1976-1992			1997	1A . . .	21363
66-AAAA-a	taos					0				22		p . .					1c . . .	21364
66-AAAA-b	picuris					0				22		p . .					1c . . .	21365
66-AAAB	SOUTH TIWA cluster	1	1	3,006	3,516		80.01	100	C	22	Tiwa: Southern*	P . .	1981-1987				0A . . .	21366
66-AAAB-a	isleta					0				22		p . .					0c . . .	21367
66-AAAB-b	sandia					0				22		p . .					0c . . .	21368
66-AAAB-c	South ysleta					0				22		p . .					0c . . .	21369
66-AAAC	PIRO cluster									0		. . .					0	21370
66-AAAC-a	piro					0				0		. . .					0	21371
66-AAB	**TEWA net**	1	1	2,923	3,419		79.99	100	C	20		. . .					0	21372
66-AABA	TEWA cluster	1	1	2,923	3,419		79.99	100	C	20		. . .					0	21373
66-AABA-a	hano					0				20		. . .					0	21374
66-AABA-b	san juan					0				20		. . .					0	21375
66-AABA-c	nambe					0				20		. . .					0	21376
66-AABA-d	pojoaque					0				20		. . .					0	21377

Continued overleaf

Table 9-13 continued

Code 1	REFERENCE NAME / Autoglossonym 2	Coun 3	Peo 4	Mother-tongue speakers in 2000 5	in 2025 6	Media radio 7	AC% 8	E% 9	Wld 10	Tr 11	Biblioglossonym 12	Print 13-15	P-activity 16	N-activity 17	B-activity 18	J-year 19	Jayuh 20-24	Ref 25
66-AABA-e	santa-clara					0				20		. . .					0	21378
66-AABA-f	san-ildefonso					0				20		. . .					0	21379
66-AABA-g	tesuque					0				20		. . .					0	21380
66-AB	KIOWA-TOWA chain	1	2	9,408	11,004		86.93	100	C	6		. . .					0	21381
66-ABA	**TOWA net**	1	1	1,809	2,116		95.02	100	C	4		. . .					0	21382
66-ABAA	JEMEZ cluster	1	1	1,809	2,116		95.02	100	C	4		. . .					0	21383
66-ABAA-a	jemez	1	1	1,809	2,116	0	95.02	100	C	4		. . .					0	21384
66-ABB	**KIOWA net**	1	1	7,599	8,888		85.00	100	C	6		. . .					0	21385
66-ABBA	KIOWA cluster	1	1	7,599	8,888		85.00	100	C	6		. . .					0	21386
66-ABBA-a	kiowa	1	1	7,599	8,888	0	85.00	100	C	6		. . .					0	21387
66-B	**UTO-AZTECAN set**	6	48	2,445,314	3,241,536		91.78	99	C	46		PN.					4A.uh	21388
66-BA	NUMIC chain	1	6	29,781	35,891		88.69	100	C	41		PN.					0A . . .	21389
66-BAA	**WEST NUMIC net**	1	2	4,816	5,632		89.37	100	C	41		PN.					0A . . .	21390
66-BAAA	MONO cluster	1	1	251	293		77.69	100	C	8		. . .					0	21391
66-BAAA-a	mono	1	1	251	293	0	77.69	100	C	8		. . .					0	21392
66-BAAB	NORTH PAIUTE cluster	1	1	4,565	5,339		90.01	100	C	41	Paiute: Northern*	PN.	1977	1985			0A . . .	21393
66-BAAB-a	North paviotso					0				41		pn.					0c . . .	21394
66-BAAB-b	South paviotso					0				41		pn.					0c . . .	21395
66-BAAB-c	bannock					0				41		pn.					0c . . .	21396
66-BAB	**NUMIC-CENTRAL net**	1	2	18,451	22,641		88.16	100	C	23		P..					0a . . .	21397
66-BABA	PANAMINT cluster									0		. . .					0	21398
66-BABA-a	panamint					0				0		. . .					0	21399
66-BABB	SHOSHONI cluster	1	1	8,852	10,353		85.00	100	C	22	Shoshone*	P..	1985-1986				0a . . .	21400
66-BABB-a	West shoshoni					0				22		p..					0c . . .	21401
66-BABB-b	East shoshoni					0				22		p..					0c . . .	21402
66-BABC	GOSIUTE cluster	1	1	2,000	3,400		80.00	100	C	0		. . .					0	21403
66-BABC-a	gosi-ute	1	1	2,000	3,400	0	80.00	100	C	0		. . .					0	21404
66-BABD	COMANCHE cluster	1	1	7,599	8,888		94.00	100	C	23		P..					0	21405
66-BABD-a	comanche	1	1	7,599	8,888	0	94.00	100	C	23	Comanche	P..	1958				0	21406
66-BAC	**SOUTH NUMIC net**	1	2	6,514	7,618		89.67	100	C	12		. . .					0	21407
66-BACA	KAWAIISU-UTE cluster	1	1	195	228		78.97	100	C	8		. . .					0	21408
66-BACA-a	kawaiisu	1	1	195	228	0	78.97	100	C	8		. . .					0	21409
66-BACB	UTE-CHEMEHUEVI cluster	1	1	6,319	7,390		90.00	100	C	12		. . .					0	21410
66-BACB-a	chemehuevi					0				12		. . .					0	21411
66-BACB-b	South pai-ute					0				12	Ute-southern Paiute	. . .					0	21412
66-BACB-c	ute	1	1	6,319	7,390	0	90.00	100	C	12		. . .					0	21413
66-BB	TUBATULABAL chain	1	1	56	65		78.57	100	C	8		. . .					0	21414
66-BBA	**TUBATULABAL net**	1	1	56	65		78.57	100	C	8		. . .					0	21415
66-BBAA	TUBATULABAL cluster	1	1	56	65		78.57	100	C	8		. . .					0	21416
66-BBAA-a	tubatulabal	1	1	56	65	0	78.57	100	C	8		. . .					0	21417
66-BC	TAKIC chain	1	3	3,118	3,646		80.31	100	C	8		. . .					0	21418
66-BCA	**SERRAÑO-KITANEMUK net**									0		. . .					0	21419
66-BCAA	SERRAñO cluster			0	0		0.00	0		0		. . .					0	21420
66-BCAA-a	serra-o			0	0	0	0.00	0		0		. . .					0	21421
66-BCAB	KITANEMUK cluster			0	0		0.00	0		0		. . .					0	21422
66-BCAB-a	kitanemuk			0	0	0	0.00	0		0		. . .					0	21423
66-BCB	**GABRIELEÑO net**									0		. . .					0	21424
66-BCBA	GABRIELEñO cluster									0		. . .					0	21425
66-BCBA-a	Proper gabrieleño					0				0		. . .					0	21426
66-BCBA-b	fernandeño					0				0		. . .					0	21427
66-BCBA-c	nicoleño					0				0		. . .					0	21428
66-BCC	**KAVIA-KUPA net**	1	2	1,225	1,432		80.33	100	C	8		. . .					0	21429
66-BCCA	KUPA cluster	1	1	223	260		78.03	100	C	8		. . .					0	21430
66-BCCA-a	kupa	1	1	223	260	0	78.03	100	C	8		. . .					0	21431
66-BCCB	KAVIA cluster	1	1	1,002	1,172		80.84	100	C	8		. . .					0	21432
66-BCCB-a	kavia	1	1	1,002	1,172	0	80.84	100	C	8		. . .					0	21433
66-BCD	**LUISEÑO-JUANEÑO net**	1	1	1,893	2,214		80.30	100	C	6		. . .					0	21434
66-BCDA	LUISEñO-JUANEñO cluster	1	1	1,893	2,214		80.30	100	C	6		. . .					21435
66-BCDA-a	luiseño	1	1	1,893	2,214	0	80.30	100	C	6		. . .					0	21436
66-BCDA-b	juaneño					0				6		. . .					0	21437
66-BD	HOPI chain	1	1	8,212	9,604		85.00	100	C	42		PN.					0	21438
66-BDA	**HOPI net**	1	1	8,212	9,604		85.00	100	C	42		PN.					0	21439
66-BDAA	HOPI cluster	1	1	8,212	9,604		85.00	100	C	42		PN.					0	21440
66-BDAA-a	hopi	1	1	8,212	9,604	0	85.00	100	C	42	Hopi	PN.	1929-1962	1972			0	21441
66-BE	SONORAN chain	3	18	264,040	344,424		72.17	92	C	42		PN.					4A . . .	21442
66-BEA	**TEPIMAN net**	3	8	59,162	74,882		69.79	90	C	42		PN.					0A . . .	21443
66-BEAA	PIMA-PAPAGO cluster	3	3	27,409	32,306		90.04	100	C	42	Papago-piman	PN.	1967	1975			0A . . .	21444
66-BEAA-a	pima					0				42		pn.					0c . . .	21445
66-BEAA-b	papago					0				42		pn.					0c . . .	21446
66-BEAB	NEVOME cluster	1	1	2,000	3,400		80.00	100	C	0		. . .					0	21447
66-BEAB-a	nevome	1	1	2,000	3,400	0	80.00	100	C	0		. . .					0	21448
66-BEAC	SOUTHEAST PIMA cluster	1	2	2,274	2,994		81.53	100	C	22		P..					0	21449
66-BEAC-a	Southeast pima	1	2	2,274	2,994	0	81.53	100	C	22	Pima Bajo, Sonora	P..	1994				0	21450
66-BEAD	NORTH TEPEHU cluster	1	1	9,354	12,317		5.00	36	A	41		PN.					0	21451
66-BEAD-a	North tepehuán	1	1	9,354	12,317	0	5.00	36	A	41	Tepehuan: Northern*	PN.	1962	1981-1982			0	21452
66-BEAE	SOUTH TEPEHUá cluster	1	2	18,125	23,865		70.00	100	C	22		P..					0	21453
66-BEAE-a	Southwest tepehuán	1	1	8,187	10,780	0	70.00	100	C	22	Tepehuan, Southwestern	P..					0	21454
66-BEAE-b	Southeast tepehuán	1	1	9,938	13,085	0	69.99	100	C	22	Tepehuan, Southeastern	P..	1991				0	21455
66-BEAE-c	tepecano			0	0	0	0.00	0		22		p..					0	21456
66-BEB	**TARAHUMARA-VAROHIO net**	1	5	79,609	104,821		71.39	100	C	42		PN.					4	21457

Continued opposite

Table 9-13 continued

Code 1	REFERENCE NAME / Autoglossonym 2	Coun 3	Peo 4	Mother-tongue speakers in 2000 5	in 2025 6	Media radio 7	CHURCH AC% 8	E% 9	Wld 10	Tr 11	Biblioglossonym 12	Print 13-15	P–activity 16	N–activity 17	B–activity 18	J-year 19	Jayuh 20-24	Ref 25
66-BEBA	TARAHUMARA cluster	1	4	74,230	97,738		70.04	100	C	42		PN.					4....	21458
66-BEBA-a	ariseachi	1	1	1,641	2,161	0	70.02	100	C	42		pn.					1....	21459
66-BEBA-b	rocoroibo	1	1	17,542	23,097	0	70.00	100	C	42	Tarahumara: Western*	Pn.	1975-1985			1997	1....	21460
66-BEBA-c	panalachi					0				42		pn.					1....	21461
66-BEBA-d	samachique	1	1	54,909	72,298	0	70.00	100	C	42	Tarahumara: Samachique*	PN.	1947-1963	1972		1985	4....	21462
66-BEBA-e	chinatu					0				42		pn.					1....	21463
66-BEBA-f	tubare	1	1	138	182	0	90.58	100	C	42		pn.					1....	21464
66-BEBB	VAROHIO cluster	1	1	5,379	7,083		90.00	100	C	22	Huarijio	P..	1995				0....	21465
66-BEBB-a	Upper varohio					0				22		p..					0....	21466
66-BEBB-b	Lower varohio					0				22		p..					0....	21467
66-BEBB-c	maculai					0				22		p..					0....	21468
66-BEC	**OPATA-EUDEVE net**									0		. . .					0....	21469
66-BECA	óPATA cluster									0		. . .					0....	21470
66-BECA-a	Proper ópata					0				0		. . .					0....	21471
66-BECA-b	batuc					0				0		. . .					0....	21472
66-BECA-c	nacosura					0				0		. . .					0....	21473
66-BECB	EUDEVE cluster									0		. . .					0....	21474
66-BECB-a	heve					0				0		. . .					0....	21475
66-BECB-b	dohema					0				0		. . .					0....	21476
66-BECC	JOVA cluster									0		. . .					0....	21477
66-BECC-a	jova					0				0		. . .					0....	21478
66-BECD	CONCHO cluster									0		. . .					0....	21479
66-BECD-a	chinarra					0				0		. . .					0....	21480
66-BECD-b	chizo					0				0		. . .					0....	21481
66-BED	**CAHITA-MAYO net**	2	3	93,093	122,356		90.36	100	C	41		PN.					1....	21482
66-BEDA	MAYO-YAQUI cluster	2	3	91,093	118,956		90.37	100	C	41		PN.					1....	21483
66-BEDA-a	yaqui	2	2	24,279	30,982	0	91.38	100	C	41	Yaqui	PN.	1959-1966	1977		1991	1....	21484
66-BEDA-b	mayo	1	1	66,814	87,974	0	90.00	100	C	41	Mayo: Sonora	Pn.	1962-1967				1....	21485
66-BEDB	CáHITA cluster	1	1	2,000	3,400		90.00	99	C	0		. . .					0....	21486
66-BEDB-a	bamoa					0				0		. . .					0....	21487
66-BEDB-b	sinaloa					0				0		. . .					0....	21488
66-BEDB-c	guasave					0				0		. . .					0....	21489
66-BEDB-d	ocoroni					0				0		. . .					0....	21490
66-BEDB-e	huite					0				0		. . .					0....	21491
66-BEDB-f	nio					0				0		. . .					0....	21492
66-BEDB-g	chínipa					0				0		. . .					0....	21493
66-BEDB-h	tahue					0				0		. . .					0....	21494
66-BEDB-i	tapahue					0				0		. . .					0....	21495
66-BEDB-j	macoyahui					0				0		. . .					0....	21496
66-BEDB-k	conicari					0				0		. . .					0....	21497
66-BEDB-l	baciroa					0				0		. . .					0....	21498
66-BEDB-m	temori					0				0		. . .					0....	21499
66-BEDB-n	topiame					0				0		. . .					0....	21500
66-BEDB-o	acaxee					0				0		. . .					0....	21501
66-BEDB-p	xixime					0				0		. . .					0....	21502
66-BEE	**TUBAR net**									9		. . .					0....	21503
66-BEEA	TUBAR cluster			0	0		0.00	0		9		. . .					0....	21504
66-BEEA-a	tubar			0	0	0	0.00	0		9		. . .					0....	21505
66-BEF	**CORA-HUICHOL net**	1	2	32,176	42,365		25.83	51	B	42		PN.					4....	21506
66-BEFA	HUICHOL cluster	1	1	23,395	30,804		1.00	33	A	42		PN.				1994	4....	21507
66-BEFA-a	West huichol					0				42		pn.					1....	21508
66-BEFA-b	East huichol	1	1	23,395	30,804	0	1.00	33	A	42	Huichol	PN.	1958-1967	1967			1....	21509
66-BEFA-c	coyultita					0				42		pn.					1....	21510
66-BEFA-d	tecual					0				42		pn.					1....	21511
66-BEFB	CORA cluster	1	1	8,781	11,561		91.99	100	C	32	Cora	P..	1961-1995			1992	1....	21512
66-BEFB-a	teresa					0				32	Cora, Santa Teresa	p..					1....	21513
66-BEFB-b	jesús-maría					0				32		p..					1....	21514
66-BEFB-c	corapan					0				32		p..					1....	21515
66-BEFB-d	mesa-del-nayar					0				32		p..					1....	21516
66-BEFC	COANO-TOTORAME cluster			0	0		0.00	0		0		. . .					0....	21517
66-BEFC-a	coano			0	0	0	0.00	0		0		. . .					0....	21518
66-BEFC-b	huaynamota			0	0	0	0.00	0		0		. . .					0....	21519
66-BEFC-c	zayahueco			0	0	0	0.00	0		0		. . .					0....	21520
66-BEFC-d	totorame			0	0	0	0.00	0		0		. . .					0....	21521
66-BF	AZTECAN chain	4	19	2,140,107	2,847,906		94.29	100	C	46		PN.					3A.uh	21522
66-BFA	**POCHUTEC net**									0		. . .					0....	21523
66-BFAA	POCHUTEC cluster			0	0		0.00	0		0		. . .					0....	21524
66-BFAA-a	pochutec			0	0	0	0.00	0		0		. . .					0....	21525
66-BFB	**NAWA net**	4	19	2,140,107	2,847,906		94.29	100	C	46		PN.					3A.uh	21526
66-BFBA	NAWA cluster	1	16	1,883,917	2,480,534		94.15	100	C	46	Nahuatl	PN.	1833				3A...	21527
66-BFBA-a	Historical nahuatl			0	0	0	0.00	0		46	Nahuatl, Classical	PN.		1833			1c...	21528
66-BFBA-b	nahuatlan	1	9	1,383,914	1,822,185	0	94.87	100	C	46		PN.					3A...	21529
66-BFBA-c	nahual	1	2	4,667	6,145	0	94.99	100	C	46		PN.					1c...	21543
66-BFBA-d	nahuat	1	5	495,336	652,204	0	92.13	100	C	46		PN.					1c...	21546
66-BFBB	PIPIL cluster	3	3	256,190	367,372		95.30	100	C	8		. . .					0A.uh	21553
66-BFBB-a	alagüilac					1				8		. . .					0c.uh	21554
66-BFBB-b	bagaces					1				8		. . .					0c.uh	21555
66-BFBB-c	chuchures					1				8		. . .					0c.uh	21556
66-BFBB-d	nicarao					1				8		. . .					0c.uh	21557
66-BFBB-e	toltec					1				8		. . .					0c.uh	21558
67	**OTO-MANGIC zone**	2	149	2,281,679	3,007,761		90.56	100	C	42		PN.					4a...	21559
67-A	**OTO-MANGUEAN set**	2	149	2,281,679	3,007,761		90.56	100	C	42		PN.					4a...	21560
67-AA	CHICHIMECA-JONAZ chain	1	1	1,810	2,383		90.94	100	C	4		. . .					0....	21561
67-AAA	**CHICHIMECA-JONAZ net**	1	1	1,810	2,383		90.94	100	C	4		. . .					0....	21562
67-AAAA	CHICHIMEC cluster	1	1	1,810	2,383		90.94	100	C	4		. . .					0....	21563
67-AAAA-a	chichimec	1	1	1,810	2,383	0	90.94	100	C	4		. . .					0....	21564
67-AB	OTOMI-PAME chain	1	15	670,618	884,915		91.98	100	C	42		PN.					3s...	21565
67-ABA	**PAME net**	1	2	8,901	12,488		90.21	100	C	32		P..					1....	21566
67-ABAA	NORTH PAME cluster	1	1	1,819	2,396		91.04	100	C	20		. . .					0....	21567
67-ABAA-a	North pame	1	1	1,819	2,396	0	91.04	100	C	20		. . .					0....	21568
67-ABAB	CENTRAL PAME cluster	1	1	5,082	6,692		90.00	100	C	32		P..					1....	21571
67-ABAB-a	chichimeca pame	1	1	5,082	6,692	0	90.00	100	C	32	Chichimeca: S Maria Acap*	P..	1953-1981			1994	1....	21572

Continued overleaf

Table 9-13 continued

Code 1	REFERENCE NAME / Autoglossonym 2	Coun 3	Peo 4	Mother-tongue speakers in 2000 5	in 2025 6	Media radio 7	CHURCH AC% 8	E% 9	Wld 10	Tr 11	Biblioglossonym 12	Print 13-15	P-activity 16	N-activity 17	B-activity 18	J-year 19	Jayuh 20-24	Ref 25
67-ABAC	SOUTH PAME cluster	1	1	2,000	3,400		90.00	99	C	0		...					0....	21573
67-ABAC-a	pame-S	1	1	2,000	3,400	0	90.00	99	C	0		...					0....	21574
67-ABB	**MATLATZINCA-OCUILTEC net**	1	2	6,738	10,021		90.00	99	C	8		...					0....	21575
67-ABBA	MATLATZINCA cluster	1	2	3,738	4,921		89.99	100	C	8		...					0....	21576
67-ABBA-a	matlatzinca	1	2	3,738	4,921	0	89.99	100	C	8		...					0....	21577
67-ABBB	OCUILTEC cluster	1	1	3,000	5,100		90.00	99	C	0		...					0....	21578
67-ABBB-a	ocuiltec					0				0		...					0....	21579
67-ABC	**OTOMI-MAZAHUA net**	1	11	654,979	862,406		92.02	100	C	42		PN.					3s...	21584
67-ABCA	OTOMí cluster	1	10	270,558	356,242		90.64	100	C	42		PN.					1s...	21585
67-ABCA-a	queretaro	1	1	38,603	50,829	0	95.00	100	C	42	Otomi, Western	pn.			1997	1c...	21586
67-ABCA-b	mezquital	1	1	116,996	154,048	0	95.00	100	C	42	Otomi: Mezquital*	PN.	1951-1991	1970	1993	1s...	21587
67-ABCA-c	texcatepec	1	1	14,031	18,475	0	95.00	100	C	42		pn.				1c...	21588
67-ABCA-d	huehuetla	1	2	27,518	36,233	0	91.41	100	C	42	Tepehua, Huehuetla*	PN.	1951-1968	1974-1976	1993	1c...	21589
67-ABCA-e	tenango	1	1	11,698	15,402	0	95.00	100	C	42	Otomi: Tenango*	PN.	1959-1967	1975		1c...	21590
67-ABCA-f	ixtenco	1	1	6,259	8,241	0	95.00	100	C	42		pn.				1c...	21591
67-ABCA-g	san-felipe	1	1	11,698	15,402	0	95.00	100	C	42	Otomi: San Felipe Santiago*	PN.	1957-1961	1975		1c...	21592
67-ABCA-h	tilapa	1	1	465	612	0	95.05	100	C	42		pn.				1c...	21593
67-ABCA-i	temoaya	1	1	43,290	57,000	0	70.00	100	C	42	Otomi, Temoaya	pn.				1s...	21594
67-ABCB	MAZAHUA cluster	1	1	384,421	506,164		93.00	100	C	42		PN.					3....	21595
67-ABCB-a	Central mazahua	1	1	384,421	506,164	0	93.00	100	C	42	Mazahua	PN.	1949-1987	1970	1996	3....	21596
67-ABCB-b	michoacán					0				42	Mazahua: Michoacan*	Pn.	1987			1....	21597
67-ABCB-c	jalapa-de-los-baños					0				42		pn.				1....	21598
67-ABCB-d	atlacomulco					0				42		pn.				1....	21599
67-AC	SUBTIABA-TLAPANEC chain	1	1	35,518	46,766		93.00	100	C	42		PN.					4....	21600
67-ACA	**TLAPENEC net**	1	1	35,518	46,766		93.00	100	C	42		PN.					4....	21601
67-ACAA	TLAPANEC cluster	1	1	35,518	46,766		93.00	100	C	42		PN.			1998	4....	21602
67-ACAA-a	tlacoapa					0				42	Tlapaneco: Tlacoapa	PN.	1953	1975		1....	21603
67-ACAA-b	malinaltepec					0				42	Tlapaneco: Huizapula*	PN.	1953-1994	1975	1998	4....	21604
67-ACB	**SUBTIABA net**									9		...					0....	21605
67-ACBA	SUBTIABA cluster			0	0		0.00	0		9		...					0....	21606
67-ACBA-a	subtiaba			0	0	0	0.00	0		9		...					0....	21607
67-AD	CHOCHO-MAZATEC chain	1	12	195,744	257,736		92.08	100	C	42		PN.					1a...	21608
67-ADA	**CHOCHO-IXCATEC net**	1	7	38,780	51,062		89.91	100	C	41		PN.					1....	21609
67-ADAA	POPOLOC-CHOCHO cluster	1	7	38,780	51,062		89.91	100	C	41	Popoloca, S Marcos Tlacoy	PN.	1976	1983		1....	21610
67-ADAA-a	West popoloc	1	1	6,595	8,684	0	90.01	100	C	41	Popoloca: Western*	Pn.	1955-1980		1993	1....	21611
67-ADAA-b	North popoloc	1	1	6,694	8,814	0	90.01	100	C	41	Popoloca: Northern	PN.	1976	1983		1....	21614
67-ADAA-c	ahuatempan	1	1	8,237	10,845	0	90.00	100	C	41	Popoloca: Ahuatempan*	Pn.	1994			1....	21615
67-ADAA-d	coyotepec	1	1	8,187	10,780	0	89.01	100	C	41		pn.				1....	21616
67-ADAA-e	East popoloc	1	1	5,468	7,200	0	90.00	100	C	41	Popoloca: Eastern*	PN.	1976-1995	1982	1993	1....	21617
67-ADAA-f	South popoloc	1	1	2,195	2,890	0	92.03	100	C	41		pn.				1....	21618
67-ADAA-g	chocho	1	1	1,404	1,849	0	90.03	100	C	41		pn.				1....	21619
67-ADAB	IXCATEC cluster									5		...					0....	21620
67-ADAB-a	ixcatec			0	0	0	0.00	0		5		...					0....	21621
67-ADB	**MAZATEC net**	1	5	156,964	206,674		92.62	100	C	42		PN.					1a...	21622
67-ADBA	MAZATEC cluster	1	5	156,964	206,674		92.62	100	C	42		PN.					1a...	21623
67-ADBA-a	ixcatlan	1	1	12,864	16,939	0	93.00	100	C	42	Mazateco, S Pedro Ixcatlan	pn.				1c...	21624
67-ADBA-b	Upper mazatec	1	1	84,237	110,914	0	93.00	100	C	42	Mazateco, Huautla Jimenez	PN.	1946-1958	1961		1c...	21625
67-ADBA-c	Lower mazatec	1	1	17,166	22,602	0	90.00	100	C	42	Mazateco: Jalapa De Diaz*	PN.	1968-1995	1996		1a...	21629
67-ADBA-d	tecoatl-soyaltepec	1	1	39,780	52,378	0	93.00	100	C	42		Pn.				1c...	21630
67-ADBA-e	chiquihuitlan	1	1	2,917	3,841	0	89.99	100	C	42	Mazateco: Chiquihuitlan*	PN.	1975-1987	1991		1c...	21633
67-AE	CHINANTEC chain	1	14	102,937	135,536		91.47	100	C	42		PN.					1a...	21634
67-AEA	**CHINANTEC net**	1	14	102,937	135,536		91.47	100	C	42		PN.					1a...	21635
67-AEAA	NORTH CHINANTEC cluster	1	3	37,427	49,279		92.12	100	C	42		PN.					0a...	21636
67-AEAA-a	ojitlán	1	1	25,739	33,890	0	93.00	100	C	42	Chinanteco: Ojitlan*	PN.	1955-1965	1968		0c...	21637
67-AEAA-b	chiltepec	1	1	1,167	1,536	0	91.95	100	C	42		pn.				0c...	21638
67-AEAA-c	usila	1	1	10,521	13,853	0	90.00	100	Wld	42	Chinanteco: Usila*	PN.	1964-1968	1983		0a...	21639
67-AEAB	CHINANTEC cluster	1	10	63,176	83,184		91.02	100	C	42		PN.					1....	21640
67-AEAB-a	palantla	1	1	14,031	18,475	0	93.00	100	C	42	Chinanteco: Palantla*	PN.	1965-1966	1973		1....	21641
67-AEAB-b	sochiapan	1	1	4,104	5,403	0	89.99	100	C	42	Chinanteco: Sochiapan*	PN.	1969	1986		1....	21642
67-AEAB-c	tlacoatzintepec	1	1	2,334	3,073	0	89.97	100	C	42	Chinanteco, Tlacoatzintepec	pn.				1....	21643
67-AEAB-d	valle-nacional	1	1	1,750	2,304	0	90.00	100	C	42		pn.				1....	21644
67-AEAB-e	tepetotutla	1	1	4,321	5,690	0	90.00	100	C	42	Chinanteco: Tepetotutla*	PN.	1974	1994	1992	1....	21645
67-AEAB-f	quiotepec	1	1	7,129	9,387	0	90.00	100	C	42	Chinanteco: Quiotepec*	PN.	1968	1983	1995	1....	21646
67-AEAB-g	yolox					0				42		pn.				1....	21647
67-AEAB-h	comaltepec-1	1	1	2,334	3,073	0	89.97	100	C	42	Chinanteco: Comaltepec*	Pn.	1976-1990			1....	21648
67-AEAB-i	ozumacín	1	1	4,371	5,755	0	89.98	100	C	42	Chinanteco: Ozumacin*	Pn.	1990-1995			1....	21649
67-AEAB-j	tepinapa	1	1	9,354	12,317	0	91.00	100	C	42		pn.				1....	21650
67-AEAB-k	lalana	1	1	13,448	17,707	0	91.00	100	C	42	Chinanteco: Lalana*	PN.	1962-1968	1974-1994		1....	21651
67-AEAC	SOUTH CHINANTEC cluster	1	1	2,334	3,073		92.97	100	C	41		PN.					0....	21652
67-AEAC-a	lealao	1	1	2,334	3,073	0	92.97	100	C	41	Chinanteco: Lealao*	PN.	1972	1980		0....	21653
67-AF	MIXTEC-TRIQUE chain	1	39	471,300	620,939		89.79	100	C	42		PN.					1a...	21654
67-AFA	**MIXTEC-CUICATEC net**	1	36	442,851	583,482		89.83	100	C	42		PN.					1a...	21655
67-AFAA	WEST MIXTEC cluster	1	4	124,908	164,464		90.24	100	C	23		P..					1....	21656
67-AFAA-a	ayutla	1	1	9,938	13,085	0	93.00	100	C	23	Mixteco: Ayutla	P..	1970			1....	21657
67-AFAA-b	metlatonoc	1	2	92,741	122,111	0	90.00	100	C	23	Mixteco: Metlatonoc*	P..	1959			1....	21658
67-AFAA-c	alacatlatzala	1	1	22,229	29,268	0	90.00	100	C	23	Mixteco, Alacatlatzala	P..	1990-1995		1997	1....	21662
67-AFAB	NORTH MIXTEC cluster	1	1	1,000	1,700		90.00	99	C	0		...					0....	21666
67-AFAB-a	chigmecatitlan					0				0		...					0....	21667
67-AFAB-b	tlatemplan					0				0		...					0....	21668
67-AFAC	NORTH MIXTEC cluster	1	8	80,756	106,331		86.77	100	C	41	Mixteco: Tonahuíxtla	PN.	1980			1....	21669
67-AFAC-a	acatlán					0				41	Mixteco: Puebla, Southern	PN.	1966	1978	1990	1....	21670
67-AFAC-b	chazumba					0				41		pn.				1....	21671
67-AFAC-c	coatzospan					0				41	Mixteco: Coatzospan*	Pn.	1971-1978			1....	21672
67-AFAC-d	teotitlán-de-camino	1	1	5,379	7,083	0	91.00	100	C	41		pn.				1....	21673
67-AFAC-e	cuyamecalco					0				41		pn.				1....	21674
67-AFAC-f	Northwest oaxaca	1	1	2,917	3,841	0	89.99	100	C	41	Mixteco, Northwest Oaxaca	pn.				1....	21675
67-AFAC-g	huajuapan	1	1	989	1,302	0	89.99	100	C	41		pn.				1....	21676
67-AFAC-h	cacaloxtepec					0				41		pn.				1....	21677
67-AFAC-i	cuatzoquitengo					0				41		pn.				1....	21678
67-AFAC-j	guadalupe-portezuelo					0				41		pn.				1....	21679
67-AFAC-k	santa-maria-peras					0				41		pn.				1....	21680
67-AFAC-l	silacayoapan	1	2	32,749	43,121	0	91.29	100	C	41	Mixteco: Silacayoapan*	PN.	1979-1986	1996	1993	1....	21681
67-AFAC-m	atenango					0				41		pn.				1....	21684
67-AFAC-n	tezoatlan-yucunuti	1	1	7,248	9,543	0	70.01	100	C	41	Mixteco: Tezoatlan*	PN.	1992			1....	21685
67-AFAC-o	zahuatlan					0				41		pn.				1....	21694
67-AFAC-p	West juxtlahuaca					0				41		pn.				1....	21695
67-AFAC-q	mixtepec					0				41	Mixteco: Mixtepec	Pn.	1974			1....	21696

Continued opposite

Table 9-13 continued

Code 1	REFERENCE NAME Autoglossonym 2	Coun 3	Peo 4	Mother-tongue speakers in 2000 5	in 2025 6	Media radio 7	CHURCH AC% 8	E% 9	Wld 10	Tr 11	Biblioglossonym 12	SCRIPTURES Print 13-15	P–activity 16	N–activity 17	B–activity 18	J-year 19	Jayuh 20-24	Ref 25
67-AFAC-r	ñumi-teposcolula	1	2	31,474	41,441	0	84.80	100	C	41	Mixteco: Tlaxiaco, Northern*	Pn.	1995				1....	21697
67-AFAD	CENTRAL MIXTEC cluster	1	8	67,990	89,523		89.94	100	C	42		PN.					1....	21700
67-AFAD-a	nuyoo-yucuhiti	1	1	7,011	9,231	0	90.00	100	C	42	Mixteco, S W Tlaxiaco	pn.					1....	21701
67-AFAD-b	atatlahuca	1	1	14,031	18,475	0	93.00	100	C	42	Mixteco: Atatlahuca*	PN.	1952-1964	1973			1....	21705
67-AFAD-c	yucuañe-teita	1	1	593	781	0	84.99	100	C	42		pn.					1....	21706
67-AFAD-d	molinos	1	1	11,698	15,402	0	90.00	100	C	42		PN.					1....	21710
67-AFAD-e	ocotepec	1	1	8,929	11,757	0	90.00	100	C	42	Mixteco: Ocotepec*	PN.	1958-1965	1977			1....	21713
67-AFAD-f	chocho-mixtec					0				42		pn.					1....	21714
67-AFAD-g	peñoles-tepantepec	1	1	12,864	16,939	0	93.00	100	C	42	Mixteco: Penoles*	PN.	1966	1979			1....	21715
67-AFAD-h	estetla					0				42		pn.					1....	21719
67-AFAD-i	nuxaá	1	1	8,187	10,780	0	80.00	100	C	42	Mixteco, S E Nochixtlan	pn.					1....	21720
67-AFAD-j	chalcatongo					0				42		pn.					1....	21724
67-AFAD-k	huitepec	1	1	4,677	6,158	0	89.99	100	C	42		pn.					1....	21725
67-AFAE	MIXTEC-NOCHIXTLáN cluster	1	4	22,278	29,333		91.01	100	C	23		P..					1a...	21726
67-AFAE-a	North nochixtlán	1	1	9,196	12,108	0	92.00	100	C	23		P..					1c...	21727
67-AFAE-b	tidaa	1	1	1,048	1,380	0	91.98	100	C	23		p..					1c...	21733
67-AFAE-c	diuxi-tilantongo	1	1	9,938	13,085	0	90.00	100	C	23	Mixteco: Diuxi-tilantongo*	P..	1973-1993			1997	1a...	21734
67-AFAE-d	East nochixtlán					0				23		p..					1c...	21737
67-AFAE-e	South nochixtlán					0				23		p..					1c...	21738
67-AFAF	SOUTH MIXTEC cluster	1	9	120,813	159,074		91.14	100	C	41		PN.					0a...	21739
67-AFAF-a	yosondua	1	1	5,844	7,695	0	89.99	100	C	41	Mixteco: Santiago Yosondua	PN.	1973	1988			0a...	21740
67-AFAF-b	sindihui					0				41		pn.					0c...	21741
67-AFAF-c	colorado	1	1	15,791	20,792	0	90.00	100	C	41	Mixteco: S Juan Colorado*	PN.	1986-1990	1994			0c...	21742
67-AFAF-d	South putla	1	1	6,724	8,853	0	90.01	100	C	41	Mixteco: Southern Putla*	Pn.	1996				0c...	21743
67-AFAF-e	itundujia	1	1	1,266	1,667	0	91.94	100	C	41		pn.					0c...	21748
67-AFAF-f	amoltepec	1	1	6,091	8,020	0	90.00	100	C	41		pn.					0c...	21749
67-AFAF-g	yoloxochitl					0				41		pn.					0c...	21750
67-AFAF-h	West jamiltepec	1	1	23,395	30,804	0	90.00	100	C	41		pn.					0c...	21751
67-AFAF-i	East jamiltepec	1	2	58,647	77,220	0	92.32	100	C	41	Mixteco: Jamiltepec, E.*	PN.	1962-1974	1979-1983			0c...	21755
67-AFAF-j	tututepec-acatepec	1	1	3,055	4,023	0	90.02	100	C	41		pn.					0c...	21758
67-AFAG	CUICATEC cluster	1	3	25,106	33,057		90.00	100	C	42		PN.					1....	21761
67-AFAG-a	tepeuxila	1	1	11,698	15,402	0	90.00	100	C	42	Cuicateco: Tepeuxila*	PN.	1951-1966	1974		1994	1....	21762
67-AFAG-b	papalo					0				42	Cuicateco: Papalo	Pn.	1951				1....	21763
67-AFAG-c	teutila	1	1	11,480	15,116	0	90.00	100	C	42	Cuicateco: Teutila*	PN.	1962-1965	1972			1....	21764
67-AFAG-d	teponaxtla					0				42		pn.					1....	21765
67-AFB	**TRIQUE net**	1	3	28,449	37,457		89.21	100	C	42		PN.					1....	21766
67-AFBA	NORTH TRIQUE cluster	1	1	17,542	23,097		91.00	100	C	41		PN.					1....	21767
67-AFBA-a	copala	1	1	17,542	23,097	0	91.00	100	C	41	Trique: San Juan Copala*	PN.	1969-1970	1987-1988		1993	1....	21768
67-AFBB	SOUTH TRIQUE cluster	1	2	10,907	14,360		86.32	100	C	42		PN.					0....	21769
67-AFBB-a	chicahuaxtla	1	1	8,237	10,845	0	90.00	100	C	42	Trique: Chicahuaxtla*	PN.	1951-1960	1968			0....	21770
67-AFBB-b	itunyoso	1	1	2,670	3,515	0	74.98	100	C	42	Trique: S Martin Itunyoso*	PN.		1996			0....	21771
67-AFBB-c	sabana					0				42		pn.					0....	21772
67-AFBB-d	san-miguel					0				42		pn.					0....	21773
67-AG	AMUZGO chain	1	3	43,403	58,298		92.21	100	C	42		PN.					1a...	21774
67-AGA	**AMUZGO net**	1	3	43,403	58,298		92.21	100	C	42		PN.					1a...	21775
67-AGAA	NORTH AMUZGO cluster	1	1	3,000	5,100		90.00	99	C	2		...					0....	21776
67-AGAA-a	ipalala, ipalapa	1	1	3,000	5,100	0	90.00	99	C	2		...					0....	21777
67-AGAB	CENTRAL AMUZGO cluster	1	3	40,403	53,198		92.37	100	C	42		PN.					1a...	21778
67-AGAB-a	san-pedro-amuzgos	1	1	4,677	6,158	.0	89.99	100	C	42	Amuzgo: Oaxaca*	PN.	1978-1980	1992-1993		1995	1a...	21779
67-AGAB-b	amuzgo-guerrero	1	2	35,726	47,040	0	92.69	100	C	42	Amuzgo: Guerrero*	PN.	1953-1990	1973		1997	1c...	21780
67-AH	ZAPOTEC-CHATINO chain	1	63	760,219	1,000,975		89.07	100	C	42		PN.					4a...	21785
67-AHA	**CHATINO net**	1	7	41,480	54,617		91.20	100	C	41		PN.					0....	21786
67-AHAA	ZENZONTEPEC cluster	1	1	9,354	12,317		90.00	100	C	12		...					0....	21787
67-AHAA-a	Proper zenzontepec	1	1	9,354	12,317	0	90.00	100	C	12	Chatino, Zenzontepec	...					0....	21788
67-AHAA-b	tlapanalquiahuitl					0				12		...					0....	21789
67-AHAB	TATALTEPEC cluster	1	1	4,677	6,158		89.99	100	C	41		PN.					0....	21790
67-AHAB-a	tataltepec	1	1	4,677	6,158	0	89.99	100	C	41	Chatino: Tataltepec*	PN.	1974	1981			0....	21791
67-AHAC	YOLOTEPEC cluster	1	2	3,362	4,426		90.01	100	C	20		...					0....	21792
67-AHAC-a	lachao					0				20		...					0....	21793
67-AHAC-b	yolotepec					0				20		...					0....	21794
67-AHAC-c	san-marcos-zacatepec	1	1	1,167	1,536	0	89.97	100	C	20	Chatino, Zacatepec	...					0....	21795
67-AHAD	CENTRAL CHATINO cluster	1	3	24,087	31,716		92.07	100	C	41		PN.					0....	21796
67-AHAD-a	panixtlahuaca	1	1	8,533	11,236	0	91.00	100	C	41	Chatino: West Highland*	PN.	1985	1992			0....	21797
67-AHAD-b	yaitepec	1	1	2,690	3,541	0	91.00	100	C	41	Chatino: Yaitepec*	Pn.	1966-1991				0....	21805
67-AHAD-c	nopala	1	1	12,864	16,939	0	93.00	100	C	41	Chatino, Nopala	pn.					0....	21806
67-AHB	**ZAPOTEC net**	1	56	718,739	946,358		88.95	100	C	42		PN.					4a...	21807
67-AHBA	WEST ZAPOTEC cluster	1	2	7,327	9,647		92.00	100	C	41		PN.					0....	21808
67-AHBA-a	texmelucan	1	1	4,588	6,041	0	92.00	100	C	41	Zapoteco: Texmelucan*	PN.	1983-1984	1989			0....	21809
67-AHBA-b	elotepec					0				41		pn.					0....	21810
67-AHBA-c	zaniza	1	1	2,739	3,606	0	92.00	100	C	41		pn.					0....	21811
67-AHBB	NORTH ZAPOTEC cluster	1	14	123,474	162,577		89.55	100	C	42		PN.					1a...	21812
67-AHBB-a	zoogocho	1	1	979	1,289	0	92.03	100	C	42	Zapoteco: S Bart Zoogocho*	PN.	1979	1987-1988			1a...	21813
67-AHBB-b	yatzachi	1	1	5,933	7,812	0	90.01	100	C	42	Zapoteco: Yatzachi*	PN.	1936-1966	1971			1c...	21818
67-AHBB-c	solaga	1	1	26,233	34,541	0	90.00	100	C	42		PN.					1c...	21821
67-AHBB-d	ixtlán	1	4	26,026	34,267	0	91.13	100	C	42	Zapoteco, Western Ixtlan	PN.	1966-1990				1c...	21825
67-AHBB-e	mazaltepec					0				42		pn.					1c...	21840
67-AHBB-f	villa-alta	1	5	52,971	69,747	0	89.39	100	C	42		PN.					1a...	21841
67-AHBB-g	yalalag	1	1	5,844	7,695	0	89.99	100	C	42	Zapoteco: Yalalag*	Pn.	1988-1992			1995	1c...	21850
67-AHBB-h	lachiruaj	1	1	5,488	7,226	0	79.99	100	C	42	Zapoteco, S Cristobal Lachir	pn.					1c...	21851
67-AHBC	WEST ZAPOTEC. cluster	1	13	64,430	84,835		85.33	100	C	41		PN.					0a...	21852
67-AHBC-a	zaachila	1	2	5,280	6,952	0	74.94	100	C	41		Pn.					0c...	21853
67-AHBC-b	zimatlán	1	4	11,974	15,767	0	90.48	100	C	41		Pn.					0c...	21857
67-AHBC-c	ocotlán	1	5	41,075	54,083	0	87.92	100	C	41	Zapoteco: Ocotlan*	PN.	1966	1983			0a...	21862
67-AHBC-d	ayoquesco	1	1	4,123	5,429	0	70.00	100	C	41		pn.					0c...	21867
67-AHBC-e	jalieza	1	1	1,978	2,604	0	60.01	99	C	41		pn.					0c...	21868
67-AHBD	EAST ZAPOTEC cluster	1	11	100,721	132,617		84.21	100	C	41		PN.					1a...	21869
67-AHBD-a	albarradas	1	2	8,168	10,754	0	82.60	100	C	41	Zapoteco, Albarradas	pn.					1c...	21870
67-AHBD-b	teotitlán-de-valle	1	1	1,978	2,604	0	69.97	100	C	41		pn.					1c...	21875
67-AHBD-c	tlacolula	1	2	34,470	45,386	0	74.25	99	C	41		PN.				1994	1c...	21876
67-AHBD-d	matatlán-ocotepec	1	2	46,820	61,648	0	92.64	100	C	41		PN.					1a...	21880
67-AHBD-e	yautepec	1	4	9,285	12,225	0	83.14	100	C	41	Zapoteco, S Catarina Quieri*	Pn.	1995				1c...	21885
67-AHBE	SOUTH ZAPOTEC cluster	1	7	139,225	183,317		88.81	100	C	42		PN.					0a...	21891
67-AHBE-a	West miahuatlán					0				42		pn.					0c...	21892
67-AHBE-b	Northeast miahuatlán	1	1	6,556	8,632	0	91.00	100	C	42	Zapoteco, N E Miahuatlan	Pn.	1992-1995				0c...	21895
67-AHBE-c	Central miahuatlán	1	1	109,867	144,661	0	90.00	100	C	42	Zapoteco: Miahuatlan*	PN.	1956-1968	1971			0a...	21898
67-AHBE-d	East miahuatlán	1	1	7,653	10,077	0	90.00	100	C	42	Zapoteco: Mixtepec*	Pn.	1980-1982				0c...	21899
67-AHBE-e	quioquitani	1	1	4,371	5,755	0	79.98	100	C	42	Zapoteco: Quioquitani	Pn.	1990				0c...	21900
67-AHBE-f	xanica	1	1	2,917	3,841	0	84.98	100	C	42	Zapoteco, Santiago Xanica	pn.					0c...	21901
67-AHBE-g	xanaguia	1	1	2,917	3,841	0	84.98	100	C	42	Zapoteco: Xanaguia*	Pn.	1996				0c...	21905
67-AHBE-h	lapaguía	1	1	4,944	6,510	0	70.00	100	C	42		pn.					0c...	21909

Continued overleaf

Table 9-13 continued

Code 1	REFERENCE NAME / Autoglossonym 2	Coun 3	Peo 4	in 2000 5	in 2025 6	Media radio 7	AC% 8	E% 9	Wld 10	Tr 11	Biblioglossonym 12	Print 13-15	P-activity 16	N-activity 17	B-activity 18	J-year 19	Jayuh 20-24	Ref 25
67-AHBF	SOUTHERN ZAPOTEC cluster	1	5	156,648	206,258		90.22	100	C	32		...					2....	21914
67-AHBF-a	South coatlán					0				32							1....	21915
67-AHBF-b	West loxicha	1	1	2,640	3,476	0	65.00	100	C	32		...				1992	2....	21916
67-AHBF-c	East loxicha	1	1	133,490	175,765	0	91.00	100	C	32	Zapoteco, Western Pochutla	...				1992	1....	21919
67-AHBF-d	ozolotepec	1	1	7,347	9,674	0	90.00	100	C	32	Zapoteco, Ozolotepec	...					1....	21922
67-AHBF-e	coatecas-altas	1	1	3,283	4,323	0	79.99	100	C	32	Zapoteco, Coatecas Altas	...					1....	21926
67-AHBF-f	xadani	1	1	9,888	13,020	0	90.00	100	C	32		...					1....	21927
67-AHBG	EAST ZAPOTEC cluster	1	4	126,914	167,107		92.35	100	C	42		PN.					4a...	21928
67-AHBG-a	petapa	1	1	9,354	12,317	0	90.00	100	C	42							1c...	21929
67-AHBG-b	lachiguiri	1	1	7,545	9,934	0	89.99	100	C	42	Zapoteco, N W Tehuantepec	pn.					1c...	21930
67-AHBG-c	zapotec-istmo	1	2	110,015	144,856	0	92.71	100	C	42	Zapoteco: Isthmus*	PN.	1912-1982	1972		1996	4a...	21934
67-AI	CHIAPANEC-MANGE chain	1	1	130	213		30.00	65	B	9		...					0....	21937
67-AIA	CHIAPANEC net	1	1	130	213		30.00	65	B	9		...					0....	21938
67-AIAA	CHIAPANEC cluster			0	0		0.00	0		0		...					0....	21939
67-AIAA-a	chiapanec			0	0	0	0.00	0		0		...					0....	21940
67-AIAB	CHOROTEGA-DIRIA cluster	1	1	130	213		30.00	65	B	9		...					0....	21941
67-AIAB-a	chorotega	1	1	130	213	0	30.00	65	B	9		...					0....	21942
67-AIAB-b	diria			0	0	0	0.00	0		9		...					0....	21943
67-AIAB-c	nagrandan			0	0	0	0.00	0		9		...					0....	21944
67-AIAB-d	nicoya			0	0	0	0.00	0		9		...					0....	21945
67-AIAB-e	orotinya			0	0	0	0.00	0		9		...					0....	21946
67-AIAB-f	orisi			0	0	0	0.00	0		9		...					0....	21947
68	**MAYANIC zone**	6	86	5,824,206	9,261,090		89.52	100	C	61		PNB					4As.	21948
68-A	**MAYAN set**	6	86	5,824,206	9,261,090		89.52	100	C	61		PNB					4As..	21949
68-AA	HUASTEC-CHICOMUCELTEC chain	2	5	147,409	194,157		83.08	100	C	42		PN.					4....	21950
68-AAA	**HUASTEC net**	1	3	145,197	191,180		82.97	100	C	42		PN.					4....	21951
68-AAAA	HUASTEC cluster	1	3	145,197	191,180		82.97	100	C	42		PN.					4....	21952
68-AAAA-a	West huastec	1	1	81,893	107,828	0	93.00	100	C	42	Huasteco: San Luis Potosi*	PN.	1952-1956	1971			1....	21953
68-AAAA-b	East huastec	1	2	63,304	83,352	0	70.00	100	C	42	Huasteco: Veracruz*	Pn.	1994			1997	4....	21954
68-AAB	**CHICOMUCELTEC net**	2	2	2,212	2,977		89.96	100	C	9		...					0....	21955
68-AABA	CHICOMUCELTEC cluster	2	2	2,212	2,977		89.96	100	C	9		...					0....	21956
68-AABA-a	West chicomuceltec			0	0	0	0.00	0		9		...					0....	21957
68-AABA-b	East chicomuceltec	1	1	155	269	0	89.68	100	C	9		...					0....	21958
68-AB	YUCATEC-ITZA chain	3	8	895,352	1,187,697		94.82	100	C	61		PNB					2a...	21959
68-ABA	**YUCATEC-ITZA net**	3	8	895,352	1,187,697		94.82	100	C	61		PNB					2a...	21960
68-ABAA	YUCATEC-LACANDóN cluster	2	4	873,738	1,152,036		94.99	100	C	61		PNB					2a...	21961
68-ABAA-a	yucatec-maya	1	2	865,825	1,140,024	0	95.00	100	C	61	Maya	PNB	1865-1985	1961-1977	1992	1994	2c...	21962
68-ABAA-b	South yucatec	1	1	7,221	11,101	0	94.00	100	C	61		pnb					1c...	21963
68-ABAA-c	icaiche					0				61		pnb					1c...	21964
68-ABAA-d	lacandón	1	1	692	911	0	90.03	100	C	61	Lacandon: Lacanja	PNb	1968	1978			1a...	21965
68-ABAB	MOPAN-ITZA cluster	2	4	21,614	35,661		87.95	100	C	41		PN.					0....	21966
68-ABAB-a	East itza			0	0	0	0.00	0		41		pn.					0....	21967
68-ABAB-b	petén-itza	2	2	9,489	16,368	0	85.91	100	C	41		pn.					0....	21968
68-ABAB-c	mopan	2	2	12,125	19,293	0	89.55	100	C	41	Maya: Mopan*	PN.	1965	1979			0....	21969
68-AC	CHOL-TZELTAL chain	3	13	928,728	1,239,522		90.68	100	C	61		PNB					1A...	21970
68-ACA	**CHOL-CHORTI net**	3	5	252,934	349,709		90.96	100	C	61		PNB					1A...	21971
68-ACAA	CHOL cluster	1	2	144,782	190,633		93.00	100	C	61		PNB					1A...	21972
68-ACAA-a	tila	1	1	43,874	57,768	0	93.00	100	C	61	Chol: Tila*	PNb	1966-1968	1976			1c...	21973
68-ACAA-b	sabanilla					0				61		pnb					1c...	21974
68-ACAA-c	tumbalá	1	1	100,908	132,865	0	93.00	100	C	61	Chol: Tumbala*	PNB	1947-1963	1960	1977-1992	1991	1A...	21975
68-ACAB	CHONTAL-TABASCO cluster	1	1	68,703	90,460		90.00	100	C	41		PN.					0....	21976
68-ACAB-a	chontal-tabasco	1	1	68,703	90,460	0	90.00	100	C	41	Chontal: Tabasco*	PN.	1952-1966	1977			0....	21977
68-ACAC	CHORTI cluster	2	2	39,449	68,616		85.14	100	C	41		PN.					0....	21978
68-ACAC-a	chortí	2	2	39,449	68,616	0	85.14	100	C	41	Chorti	PN.	1969-1981	1996			0....	21979
68-ACAC-b	choltí					0				41		pn.					0....	21980
68-ACB	**TZELTAL-TZOTZIL net**	1	8	675,794	889,813		90.58	100	C	61		PNB					1A...	21981
68-ACBA	TZELTAL cluster	1	2	329,492	433,840		90.00	100	C	61		PNB					1A...	21982
68-ACBA-a	bachajon	1	1	109,827	144,609	0	90.00	100	C	61	Tzeltal: Bachajon*	PNb	1959-1963	1964		1990	1c...	21983
68-ACBA-b	oxchuc	1	1	219,665	289,231	0	90.00	100	C	61	Tzeltal: Oxchuc*	PNB	1947-1967	1956-1981	1993	1990	1c...	21987
68-ACBB	TZOTZIL cluster	1	5	304,188	400,522		90.87	100	C	52	Tzotzil: Huixtan*	PN.	1951-1995	1975-1995			1A...	21988
68-ACBB-a	chamula	1	1	152,099	200,268	0	90.00	100	C	52	Tzotzil: Chamula*	PN.	1965	1979-1988		1996	1a...	21989
68-ACBB-b	chenalhó	1	1	40,947	53,914	0	90.00	100	C	52	Tzotzil: Chenalho*	PN.	1963-1966	1981			1a...	22003
68-ACBB-c	huixtán					0				52		pn.					1c...	22008
68-ACBB-d	larrainzar	1	1	58,498	77,024	0	93.00	100	C	52	Tzotzil: San Andres*	PN.	1963-1965	1983			1a...	22014
68-ACBB-e	zinacantec					0				52		pn.					1c...	22015
68-ACBC	TOJOLABAL cluster	1	1	42,114	55,451		93.00	100	C	42		PN.					1....	22016
68-ACBC-a	tojolabal	1	1	42,114	55,451	0	93.00	100	C	42	Tojolabal	PN.	1952-1967	1972		1994	1....	22017
68-AD	KANJOBAL-IXIL chain	3	26	909,506	1,527,279		85.65	100	C	61		PNB					4.s..	22018
68-ADA	**KANJOBAL-CHUJ net**	3	10	240,982	369,918		82.42	100	C	61		PNB					1....	22019
68-ADAA	CHUJ cluster	2	3	60,892	101,374		85.89	100	C	42		PN.					0....	22020
68-ADAA-a	chuj-ixtatán	2	2	37,491	60,644	0	86.45	100	C	42	Chuj: San Mateo Ixtatan*	PN.	1956-1994	1970-1994			0....	22021
68-ADAA-b	chuj-coatán	1	1	23,401	40,730	0	85.00	100	C	42	Chuj: S Sebastian Coatan*	PN.	1963-1966	1969			0....	22024
68-ADAB	JACALTEC cluster	2	3	57,197	94,456		77.79	100	C	41	Jacalteco	PN.	1977	1979			1....	22025
68-ADAB-a	West jacaltec	1	1	32,546	56,646	0	80.00	100	C	41	Jacalteco, Western	PN.	1969	1979		1992	1....	22026
68-ADAB-b	East jacaltec	1	1	12,627	21,978	0	70.00	100	C	41	Jacalteco: Eastern*	Pn.	1969-1991				1....	22029
68-ADAC	KANJOBAL cluster	2	3	122,705	173,841		82.84	100	C	61		PNB					0....	22030
68-ADAC-a	West kanjobal	1	1	28,907	50,313	0	80.00	100	C	61	K'anjobal: Western*	PNb	1975	1981			0....	22031
68-ADAC-b	East kanjobal	2	2	93,798	123,528	0	83.71	100	C	61	K'anjobal*	PNB	1942-1953	1955-1973	1994		0....	22032
68-ADAD	MOCHó cluster	1	1	188	247		89.89	100	C	6		...					0....	22033
68-ADAD-a	Proper motozintlec	1	1	188	247	0	89.89	100	C	6		...					0....	22034
68-ADAD-b	tuzantec					0				6		...					0....	22035
68-ADB	**MAM-AGUACATEC net**	2	13	602,998	1,043,313		87.41	100	C	61		PNB					4.s..	22036
68-ADBA	MAM cluster	2	12	582,325	1,007,331		87.50	100	C	61		PNB					4.s..	22037
68-ADBA-a	mam-huehuetenango	2	2	194,086	337,292	0	88.01	100	C	61	Mam: Huehuetenango*	PNB	1960-1961	1968	1993	1991	4.s..	22038
68-ADBA-b	mam-cuchumatan	2	2	37,985	61,484	0	90.00	100	C	61	Mam: Todos Santos*	Pnb	1981-1986				1.s..	22039
68-ADBA-c	mam-comitancillo									61	Mam: Comitancillo*	Pnb	1977-1989				1.s..	22040
68-ADBA-d	mam-tajumulco	1	1	40,891	71,172	0	80.00	100	C	61		pnb					1.s..	22041
68-ADBA-e	mam-quetzaltenango	1	2	162,748	283,263	0	85.92	100	C	61	Mam, Southern	PNb	1930	1939-1980			1.s..	22042
68-ADBA-f	tectitec	2	2	4,336	7,073	0	90.01	100	C	61	Tectiteco	pnb					1.s..	22046

Continued opposite

Table 9-13 continued

Code 1	REFERENCE NAME / Autoglossonym 2	Coun 3	Peo 4	Mother-tongue speakers in 2000 5	in 2025 6	Media radio 7	AC% 8	E% 9	Wld 10	Tr 11	Biblioglossonym 12	Print 13-15	P-activity 16	N-activity 17	B-activity 18	J-year 19	Jayuh 20-24	Ref 25
68-ADBA-g	tacanec	2	3	142,279	247,047	0	90.01	100	C	61		pnb					1.s..	22047
68-ADBB	AGUACATEC cluster	1	1	20,673	35,982		85.00	100	C	41		PN.					0....	22048
68-ADBB-a	aguacatec	1	1	20,673	35,982	0	85.00	100	C	41	Aguacateco	PN.	1958-1993	1971-1993			0....	22049
68-ADC	**IXIL net**	1	3	65,526	114,048		81.26	100	C	32		P..					1....	22050
68-ADCA	IXIL cluster	1	3	65,526	114,048		81.26	100	C	32		P..					1....	22051
68-ADCA-a	ixil-chajul	1	1	16,545	28,797	0	85.00	100	C	32	Ixil: Chajul*	P..	1981-1984				1....	22052
68-ADCA-b	ixil-ilom					0				32		p..					1....	22053
68-ADCA-c	ixil-nebaj	1	1	35,744	62,213	0	80.00	100	C	32	Ixil: Nebaj*	P..	1960-1993				1....	22054
68-ADCA-d	ixil-cotzal	1	1	13,237	23,038	0	80.00	100	C	32	Ixil: Cotzal*	P..	1978-1993				1....	22055
68-AE	QUICHE-KEKCHI chain	3	34	2,943,211	5,112,435		89.06	100	C	61		PNB					4As..	22056
68-AEA	**KEKCHI net**	3	3	441,990	762,455		92.35	100	C	61		PNB					4....	22057
68-AEAA	KEKCHI cluster	3	3	441,990	762,455		92.35	100	C	61	Kekchi	PNB	1937-1986	1961-1984	1988-1990	1983	4....	22058
68-AEAA-a	kekchí-cobán					0				61		pnb					1....	22059
68-AEAA-b	kekchí-petén					0				61		pnb					1....	22060
68-AEAA-c	West kekchí					0				61		pnb					1....	22061
68-AEAA-d	South kekchí					0				61		pnb					1....	22062
68-AEB	**POCOM net**	2	6	131,876	227,669		77.74	100	C	41		PN.					0.s..	22063
68-AEBA	POCOMAM cluster	2	4	65,963	112,948		80.95	100	C	22		P..					0....	22064
68-AEBA-a	Central pokomam	1	1	10,646	18,530	0	80.00	100	C	22	Pocomam: Central*	P..	1981-1982				0....	22065
68-AEBA-b	South pokomam	1	1	33,567	58,424	0	80.00	100	C	22		p..					0....	22066
68-AEBA-c	East pokomam	2	2	21,750	35,994	0	82.88	100	C	22	Pocomam: Eastern*	P..	1966-1982				0....	22067
68-AEBB	POCOMCHI cluster	1	2	65,913	114,721		74.53	100	C	41		PN.					0.s..	22068
68-AEBB-a	West pokomchi'	1	1	36,079	62,795	0	70.00	100	C	41	Pocomchi: Western*	Pn.	1957-1979				0.s..	22069
68-AEBB-b	East pokomchi'	1	1	29,834	51,926	0	80.00	100	C	41	Pocomchi: Eastern*	PN.		1983			0.s..	22072
68-AEC	**USPANTEC net**	1	1	2,476	4,310		85.02	100	C	22		P..					0....	22073
68-AECA	USPANTEC cluster	1	1	2,476	4,310		85.02	100	C	22		P..					0....	22074
68-AECA-a	uspantec	1	1	2,476	4,310	0	85.02	100	C	22	Uspanteco	P..	1978-1993				0....	22075
68-AED	**QUICHE net**	1	24	2,366,869	4,118,001		89.09	100	C	61		PNB					4As..	22076
68-AEDA	QUICHE cluster	1	12	1,660,159	2,889,510		90.09	100	C	61	Quiche: Sacapulas*	PNB	1961-1992	1983	1995	1995	4.s..	22077
68-AEDA-a	achi-cubulco	1	1	21,911	38,136	0	80.00	100	C	61	Achi: Cubulco*	PNB	1962-1968	1984			1.s..	22078
68-AEDA-b	achi-rabinal	1	1	46,175	80,368	0	80.00	100	C	61	Achi: Rabinal*	Pnb	1966-1993				1.s..	22079
68-AEDA-c	quiché-cunén	1	1	7,594	13,217	0	90.01	100	C	61		pnb					1.s..	22080
68-AEDA-d	Central quiché					0				61	Quiche: Central	PNB	1898	1946	1995		1.s..	22081
68-AEDA-e	quiché-chiché	1	2	381,125	663,349	0	88.68	100	C	61		pnb					1.s..	22082
68-AEDA-f	East quiché					0				61		pnb					1.s..	22085
68-AEDA-g	quiché-joyabaj	1	1	65,300	113,655	0	85.00	100	C	61	Quiche: Joyabaj*	PNb	1973	1984-1985			1.s..	22086
68-AEDA-h	quiché-cantel	1	2	511,726	890,660	0	85.93	100	C	61		pnb				1983	4.s..	22087
68-AEDB	TZUTUJIL cluster	1	2	101,387	176,464		80.00	100	C	41		PN.					0....	22090
68-AEDB-a	West tzutujil	1	1	41,842	72,826	0	80.00	100	C	41	Tzutujil*	PN.	1955-1983	1981-1989			0....	22091
68-AEDB-b	East tzutujil	1	1	59,545	103,638	0	80.00	100	C	41	Tzutujil: Eastern*	PN.	1985	1992			0....	22092
68-AEDC	CAKCHIQUEL cluster	1	10	567,323	987,427		88.39	100	C	41		PN.					4A...	22093
68-AEDC-a	North cakchiquel	1	1	24,838	43,231	1	80.00	100	C	41	Cakchiquel: Northern*	Pn.	1982-1984				1A...	22094
68-AEDC-b	West cakchiquel	1	1	12,255	21,330	1	80.00	100	C	41	Cakchiquel: Western	PN.	1982-1984	1996			1A...	22095
68-AEDC-c	Central cakchiquel	1	1	163,656	284,843	4	93.00	100	C	41	Cakchiquel*	PN.	1902-1993	1931-1980		1991	4A...	22100
68-AEDC-d	East cakchiquel	1	1	106,339	185,083	1	88.00	100	C	41	Cakchiquel: Eastern*	PN.	1982-1993	1986			1A...	22101
68-AEDC-e	cakchiquel-xenacoj	1	1	6,254	10,885	1	80.00	100	C	41	Cakchiquel: S. Domingo Xe*	Pn.	1982-1984				1A...	22102
68-AEDC-f	cakchiquel-acatenango	1	1	13,406	23,333	1	80.00	100	C	41							1A...	22103
68-AEDC-g	cakchiquel-yepocapa	1	2	101,022	175,829	1	86.57	100	C	41	Cakchiquel: S W Yepocapa*	PN.	1982	1990-1996			1A...	22104
68-AEDC-h	South Central cakchiquel.	1	1	90,741	157,935	1	88.00	100	C	41	Cakchiquel: South, Central*	Pn.	1982-1986				1A...	22105
68-AEDC-i	South cakchiquel	1	1	48,812	84,958	1	88.00	100	C	41	Cakchiquel: Southern*	PN.	1982	1993-1994			1A...	22106
68-AEDD	SIPACAPENSE cluster	1	1	3,000	5,100		80.00	100	C	0		...					0....	22107
68-AEDD-a	sipacapense	1	1	3,000	5,100	0	80.00	100	C	0		...					0....	22108
68-AEDE	SACAPULTEC cluster	1	1	35,000	59,500		80.00	100	C	22		P..					0....	22109
68-AEDE-a	sacapultec	1	1	35,000	59,500	0	80.00	100	C	22	Sacapulteco	P..	1980				0....	22110
69	**MESOMERIC zone**	5	39	845,146	1,119,899		88.64	100	C	51		PN.					1a...	22111
69-A	**TARASCO set**	1	1	140,402	184,866		93.00	100	C	42		PN.					1....	22112
69-AA	TARASCO chain	1	1	140,402	184,866		93.00	100	C	42		PN.					1....	22113
69-AAA	**TARASCO net**	1	1	140,402	184,866		93.00	100	C	42		PN.					1....	22114
69-AAAA	TARASCO cluster	1	1	140,402	184,866		93.00	100	C	42	Tarascan*	PN.	1946-1964	1964-1969		1988	1....	22115
69-AAAA-a	Historical tarasco					0				42		pn.					1....	22116
69-AAAA-b	tarasco-ichupio					0				42		pn.					1....	22117
69-AAAA-c	tarasco-purenchécuaro					0				42		pn.					1....	22118
69-B	**TOTONAC-TEPEHUA set**	2	12	375,805	494,711		91.02	100	C	42		PN.					0....	22119
69-BA	TOTONAC chain	1	8	363,804	479,017		91.51	100	C	42		PN.					0....	22120
69-BAA	**TOTONAC net**	1	8	363,804	479,017		91.51	100	C	42		PN.					0....	22121
69-BAAA	TOTONAC cluster	1	8	363,804	479,017		91.51	100	C	42		PN.					0....	22122
69-BAAA-a	totonac-juárez	1	1	13,735	18,084	0	90.00	100	C	42	Totonaco: Northern*	PN.	1957-1965	1978			0....	22123
69-BAAA-b	totonac-zihuateutla					0				42		pn.					0....	22124
69-BAAA-c	totonac-ozumatlán	1	1	4,677	6,158	0	89.99	100	C	42		pn.					0....	22125
69-BAAA-d	totonac-coahuitlán	1	1	15,109	19,894	0	91.00	100	C	42		pn.					0....	22126
69-BAAA-e	totonac-sierra	1	1	164,805	216,998	0	93.00	100	C	42	Totonaco: Highland*	PN.	1946-1956	1959			0....	22127
69-BAAA-f	totonac-coyutla	1	1	48,066	63,288	0	90.00	100	C	42	Totonaco: Coyutla*	PN.	1979	1986-1987			0....	22128
69-BAAA-g	totonac-papantla	1	1	109,867	144,661	0	91.00	100	C	42	Totonaco: Papantla*	PN.	1973-1990	1979			0....	22129
69-BAAA-h	totonac-patla	1	1	7,011	9,231	0	80.00	100	C	42	Totonaco: Patla*	PN.	1988-1995	1996			0....	22130
69-BAAA-i	totonac-yecuatla	1	1	534	703	0	90.07	100	C	42		pn.					0....	22131
69-BB	TEPEHUA chain	2	4	12,001	15,694		76.09	100	C	41		PN.					0....	22132
69-BBA	**TEPEHUA net**	2	4	12,001	15,694		76.09	100	C	41		PN.					0....	22133
69-BBAA	TEPEHUA cluster	2	4	12,001	15,694		76.09	100	C	41		PN.					0....	22134
69-BBAA-a	tepehua-hidalgo					0				41							0....	22135
69-BBAA-b	tepehua-puebla	2	4	12,001	15,694	0	76.09	100	C	41	Nahuatl: Puebla, Southeast*	PN.	1966-1992	1978			0....	22136
69-BBAA-c	tepehua-veracruz					0				41	Tepehua: Tlachichilco*	Pn.	1985-1993				0....	22137
69-C	**CUITLATEC set**									0		...					0....	22138
69-CA	CUITLATEC chain									0		...					0....	22139
69-CAA	**CUITLATEC net**									0		...					0....	22140
69-CAAA	CUITLATEC cluster			0	0		0.00	0		0		...					0....	22141
69-CAAA-a	cuitlatec			0	0	0	0.00	0%		0		...					0....	22142

Continued overleaf

Table 9-13 continued

Code 1	REFERENCE NAME / Autoglossonym 2	Coun 3	Peo 4	Mother-tongue speakers in 2000 5	in 2025 6	Media radio 7	AC% 8	E% 9	Wld 10	Tr 11	Biblioglossonym 12	Print 13-15	P-activity 16	N-activity 17	B-activity 18	J-year 19	Jayuh 20-24	Ref 25
69-D	**CHONTAL-OAXACA set**	1	2	5,309	6,991		90.81	100	C	41		PN.					0....	22143
69-DA	CHONTAL-OAXACA chain	1	2	5,309	6,991		90.81	100	C	41		PN.					0....	22144
69-DAA	**CHONTAL-OAXACA net**	1	2	5,309	6,991		90.81	100	C	41		PN.					0....	22145
69-DAAA	CHONTAL-OAXACA cluster	1	2	5,309	6,991		90.81	100	C	41		PN.					0....	22146
69-DAAA-a	huamelula	1	1	1,107	1,458	0	90.06	100	C	41	Chontal: Oaxaca, Lowland*	Pn.	1955				0....	22147
69-DAAA-b	tequistlatec	1	1	4,202	5,533	0	91.00	100	C	41	Chontal: Oaxaca, Highland*	PN.	1963-1980	1991			0....	22148
69-E	**HUAVE set**	1	2	18,421	24,256		90.00	100	C	41		PN.					1....	22149
69-EA	HUAVE chain	1	2	18,421	24,256		90.00	100	C	41		PN.					1....	22150
69-EAA	**HUAVE net**	1	2	18,421	24,256		90.00	100	C	41		PN.					1....	22151
69-EAAA	HUAVE cluster	1	2	18,421	24,256		90.00	100	C	41		PN.					1....	22152
69-EAAA-a	West huave	1	1	14,031	18,475	0	90.00	100	C	41	Huave*	PN.	1953-1995	1972-1995		1995	1....	22153
69-EAAA-b	East huave	1	1	4,390	5,781	0	90.00	100	C	41		pn.					1....	22154
69-F	**MIXE-ZOQUE set**	1	18	257,221	339,449		84.29	100	C	51		PN.					1a...	22157
69-FA	MIXE-ZOQUE chain	1	18	257,221	339,449		84.29	100	C	51		PN.					1a...	22158
69-FAA	**MIXE net**	1	11	152,040	200,190		81.35	100	C	51		PN.					1....	22159
69-FAAA	WEST MIXE cluster	1	3	35,528	46,780		77.48	100	C	51		PN.					0....	22160
69-FAAA-a	mixe-totontepec	1	2	30,060	39,580	0	74.65	100	C	51	Mixe, Totontepec*	PN.	1960-1994	1989			0....	22161
69-FAAA-b	mixe-tlahuitoltepec	1	1	5,468	7,200	0	93.00	100	C	51	Mixe: Tlahuitoltepec*	PN.	1965	1987-1988			0....	22162
69-FAAB	EAST MIXE cluster	1	6	100,137	131,850		81.26	100	C	41		PN.					1....	22163
69-FAAB-a	mixe-coatlán	1	2	13,724	18,072	0	90.00	100	C	41	Mixe: Camotlan*	PN.	1961-1967	1976		1990	1....	22164
69-FAAB-b	mixe-istmo	1	1	23,405	30,817	0	90.00	100	C	41		PN.					1....	22167
69-FAAB-c	mixe-juquila	1	1	16,474	21,691	0	90.00	100	C	41	Mixe: Juquila*	PN.	1975	1980			1....	22170
69-FAAB-d	mixe-mazatlán	1	1	19,213	25,297	0	80.00	100	C	41		pn.					1....	22171
69-FAAB-e	mixe-tutla					0				41		pn.					1....	22172
69-FAAB-f	Northeast mixe	1	1	27,321	35,973	0	65.00	100	C	41		pn.				1994	1....	22173
69-FAAC	MIXE-POPOLUCA cluster	1	2	16,375	21,560		90.28	100	C	42		PN.					0....	22182
69-FAAC-a	popoluca-oluta	1	1	11,698	15,402	0	90.00	100	C	42		pn.					0....	22183
69-FAAC-b	popoluca-sayula	1	1	4,677	6,158	0	91.00	100	C	42	Popoluca: Sayula*	PN.	1957-1964	1969			0....	22184
69-FAB	**ZOQUE net**	1	7	105,181	139,259		88.55	100	C	42		PN.					1a...	22185
69-FABA	ZOQUE-POPOLUCA cluster	1	2	49,707	65,450		90.00	100	C	41		PN.					1....	22186
69-FABA-a	popoluca-sierra	1	1	31,246	41,142	0	90.00	100	C	41	Popoluca: Highland*	PN.	1949-1965	1977		1994	1....	22187
69-FABA-b	popoluca-texistepec	1	1	18,461	24,308	0	90.00	100	C	41		pn.					1....	22188
69-FABB	ZOQUE-TABASCO cluster	1	3	17,917	23,591		92.25	100	C	27		P..					0a...	22189
69-FABB-a	zoque-tabasco	1	3	17,917	23,591	0	92.25	100	C	27	Zoque: Ostuacan	P..	1952				0a...	22190
69-FABC	ZOQUE-OAXACA cluster	1	1	2,000	3,400		80.00	100	C	2		...					0....	22191
69-FABC-a	North chimalapa					0				2		...					0....	22192
69-FABC-b	South chimalapa					0				2		...					0....	22193
69-FABD	ZOQUE-CHIAPAS cluster	1	2	35,557	46,818		85.14	100	C	42		PN.					1a...	22194
69-FABD-a	zoque-ostuacán					0				42		pn.					1c...	22195
69-FABD-b	zoque-ocotepec					0				42		pn.					1c...	22196
69-FABD-c	zoque-copainalá					0				42	Zoque: Copainala*	PN.	1948-1965	1967			1c...	22197
69-FABD-d	zoque-rayón	1	1	12,162	16,014	0	70.00	100	C	42		PN.					1c...	22198
69-FABD-e	zoque-francisco-león	1	1	23,395	30,804	0	93.00	100	C	42	Zoque: Francisco Leon*	PN.	1964-1995	1978		1993	1a...	22199
69-FABE	TAPACHULTEC cluster			0	0		0.00	0		0		...					0....	22200
69-FABE-a	tapachultec			0	0	0	0.00	0		0		...					0....	22201
69-G	**XINCA set**	1	1	293	509		89.76	100	C	9		...					0....	22202
69-GA	XINCA chain	1	1	293	509		89.76	100	C	9		...					0....	22203
69-GAA	**XINCA net**	1	1	293	509		89.76	100	C	9		...					0....	22204
69-GAAA	XINCA cluster	1	1	293	509		89.76	100	C	9		...					0....	22205
69-GAAA-a	chiquimulilla					0				9		...					0....	22206
69-GAAA-b	sinacatan					0				9		...					0....	22207
69-GAAA-c	yupiltepec					0				9		...					0....	22208
69-GAAA-d	jutiapa					0				9		...					0....	22209
69-H	**LENCA set**	2	2	46,949	67,892		79.68	100	C	8		...					0....	22210
69-HA	LENCA chain	2	2	46,949	67,892		79.68	100	C	8		...					0....	22211
69-HAA	**LENCA net**	2	2	46,949	67,892		79.68	100	C	8		...					0....	22212
69-HAAA	LENCA cluster	2	2	46,949	67,892		79.68	100	C	8		...					0....	22213
69-HAAA-a	Proper lenca	2	2	46,949	67,892	0	79.68	100	C	8		...					0....	22214
69-HAAA-b	chilanga			0	0	0	0.00	0		8		...					0....	22215
69-I	**TOL set**	1	1	746	1,225		80.03	100	C	41		PN.					0....	22216
69-IA	TOL chain	1	1	746	1,225		80.03	100	C	41		PN.					0....	22217
69-IAA	**TOL net**	1	1	746	1,225		80.03	100	C	41		PN.					0....	22218
69-IAAA	TOL cluster	1	1	746	1,225		80.03	100	C	41		PN.					0....	22219
69-IAAA-a	Proper tol	1	1	746	1,225	0	80.03	100	C	41	Tol	PN.	1977-1981	1993			0....	22220
69-IAAA-b	palmar			0	0	0	0.00	0		41		pn.					0....	22221
7	**SINOTIBETAN macrozone**	116	719	1,331,775,148	1,571,921,902		7.53	65	B	82		PNB					4Bsuh	22222
70	**BODIC zone**	9	123	13,431,685	17,744,335		1.51	32	A	63		PNB					1as..	22223
70-A	**BODIC-CENTRAL set**	9	123	13,431,685	17,744,335		1.51	32	A	63		PNB					1as..	22224
70-AA	BHOTIA-GURUNG chain	9	97	13,233,153	17,466,254		1.53	32	A	63		PNB					1as..	22225
70-AAA	**BHOTIA net**	8	76	10,901,368	13,480,180		0.72	33	A	63		PNB					1as..	22226
70-AAAA	PHöKE cluster	7	40	9,108,832	10,680,151		0.82	35	A	63		PNB					0a...	22227
70-AAAA-a	Literary phöke					1				63		pnb					0c...	22228
70-AAAA-b	choni-golog	1	5	1,070,649	1,240,566	1	0.00	17	A	63		pnb					0c...	22231
70-AAAA-c	utsang	7	22	5,596,449	6,577,057	4	1.32	46	A	63	Tibetan	PNB	1862-1991	1885-1973	1948		0a...	22243
70-AAAA-d	kham-atuence	1	2	2,286,238	2,649,077	1	0.04	18	A	63		PNb					0c...	22269
70-AAAA-e	sherpa	3	4	70,964	106,742	1	0.11	25	A	63	Sherpa*	Pnb	1977				0c...	22275

Continued opposite

Table 9-13 continued

Code 1	REFERENCE NAME / Autoglossonym 2	Coun 3	Peo 4	Mother-tongue speakers in 2000 5	in 2025 6	Media radio 7	CHURCH AC% 8	E% 9	Wld 10	Tr 11	Biblioglossonym 12	Print 13-15	P-activity 16	N-activity 17	B-activity 18	J-year 19	Jayuh 20-24	Ref 25
70-AAAA-f	dolpo-tichurong	1	4	15,608	24,790	1	0.00	14	A	63		pnb					0c...	22278
70-AAAB	TIBETAN-SOUTH cluster	4	15	531,023	871,975		0.22	23	A	41		PN.					1.s..	22284
70-AAAB-a	jirel	1	1	7,074	11,236	0	0.00	12	A	41	Jirel	PN.	1977	1992			1.s..	22285
70-AAAB-b	sikkim-bhotia	2	2	51,673	73,402	0	0.90	30	A	41		pn.					1.s..	22286
70-AAAB-c	groma	2	3	41,593	50,532	0	0.34	18	A	41		pn.					1.s..	22287
70-AAAB-d	spiti					0				41		pn.					1.s..	22290
70-AAAB-e	tomo					0				41		pn.					1.s..	22291
70-AAAB-f	dzongkha	3	3	304,002	526,153		0.08	25	A	41	Zongkhar*	Pn.	1970				1.s..	22292
70-AAAB-g	tshalingpa	1	1	8,071	14,835		0.10	12	A	41		pn.					1.s..	22293
70-AAAB-h	dagpakha					0				41		pn.					1.s..	22294
70-AAAB-i	tapadamteng					0				41		pn.					1.s..	22297
70-AAAB-j	laya-lingzhi					0				41		pn.					1.s..	22298
70-AAAB-k	adap					0				41		pn.					1.s..	22301
70-AAAB-l	sagtengpa	2	2	89,318	161,877		0.02	17	A	41		pn.					1.s..	22302
70-AAAC	TIBETAN-WEST cluster	3	12	1,207,955	1,844,800		0.19	21	A	44		PN.					1....	22303
70-AAAC-a	ladakhi	3	3	117,290	156,438	0	0.10	21	A	44	Ladakhi	Pn.	1904-1919				1....	22304
70-AAAC-b	changthang	1	1	10,137	13,304	0	0.01	20	A	44		PN.					1....	22311
70-AAAC-c	balti	2	2	398,387	643,180	0	0.24	23	A	44	Balti	Pn.	1903-1940				1....	22316
70-AAAC-d	purik	3	3	662,556	1,004,063	0	0.19	21	A	44	Purigskad*	PN.	1938-1940	1950			1....	22317
70-AAAC-e	zangskari	3	3	19,585	27,815	0	0.02	17	A	44	Zangskari	Pn.	1945-1951				1....	22318
70-AAAD	LARKYE cluster	2	2	10,568	14,912		0.00	7	A	4		...					0....	22319
70-AAAD-a	larkye	2	2	10,568	14,912	0	0.00	7	A	4		...					0....	22320
70-AAAE	LOYU cluster	3	4	35,320	55,547		0.01	7	A	4		...					0....	22321
70-AAAE-a	loyu	3	4	35,320	55,547	0	0.01	7	A	4		...					0....	22322
70-AAAF	THUDAM cluster	1	1	1,800	2,858		0.00	6	A	4		...					0....	22325
70-AAAF-a	thudam-bhotia	1	1	1,800	2,858	0	0.00	6	A	4		...					0....	22326
70-AAAG	SHERDUKPEN cluster	2	2	5,870	9,937		0.07	12	A	4		...					0....	22327
70-AAAG-a	sherdukpen	2	2	5,870	9,937	0	0.07	12	A	4		...					0....	22328
70-AAB	GURUNG net	3	12	1,136,665	1,800,487		10.93	44	A	41		PN.					0....	22331
70-AABA	TAMANG cluster	2	4	876,813	1,388,695		14.15	54	B	41		PN.					0....	22332
70-AABA-a	murmi	1	1	306,310	486,530	0	17.00	59	B	41	Tamang, Northwestern	PN.	1977-1986	1990			0....	22333
70-AABA-b	Southwest Tamang	1	1	128,267	203,735	0	15.00	51	B	41	Tamang	PN.	1977	1990			0....	22336
70-AABA-c	East Tamang	2	2	442,236	698,430	0	11.93	51	B	41	Tamang, Eastern	pn.					0....	22337
70-AABB	NORTH GURUNG cluster	2	2	9,498	14,387		0.41	16	A	41		PN.					0....	22341
70-AABB-a	manangba	1	1	6,964	11,061	0	0.09	15	A	41		pn.					0....	22342
70-AABB-b	North gurung	1	1	2,534	3,326	0	1.30	19	A	41	Gurung	PN.		1982			0....	22343
70-AABC	SOUTHWEST GURUNG cluster	1	1	127,327	202,241		0.02	13	A	0		...					0....	22344
70-AABC-a	kaski-gurung					0				0		...					0....	22345
70-AABC-b	syangja-gurung					0				0		...					0....	22346
70-AABD	EAST GURUNG cluster	2	2	86,196	136,662		0.02	12	A	22		P..	1994				0....	22347
70-AABD-a	lanjung	1	1	84,884	134,826	0	0.02	12	A	22		p..					0....	22348
70-AABE	MUSTANG cluster	1	1	8,615	13,684		0.01	11	A	4		...					0....	22351
70-AABE-a	thakali	1	1	8,615	13,684	0	0.01	11	A	4		...					0....	22352
70-AABE-b	baragaunle-1					0				4		...					0....	22353
70-AABE-c	baragaunle-2					0				4		...					0....	22354
70-AABF	GHALE cluster	1	2	28,216	44,818		0.02	10	A	12		...					0....	22355
70-AABF-a	ghale	1	2	28,216	44,818	0	0.02	10	A	12	Ghale, Southern	...					0....	22356
70-AAC	KEBUMTAMP net	1	3	719,516	1,322,484		0.07	11	A	20		...					0....	22357
70-AACA	KEBUMTAMP cluster	1	3	719,516	1,322,484		0.07	11	A	20		...					0....	22358
70-AACA-a	mangdi-kha					0				20		...					0....	22359
70-AACA-b	gungde-kha					0				20		...					0....	22360
70-AACA-c	khen-kha	1	1	135,722	249,459	0	0.10	7	A	20		...					0....	22361
70-AACA-d	bumthang-kha					0				20		...					0....	22362
70-AACA-e	tsamang-kha					0				20		...					0....	22363
70-AACA-f	kurtopa-kha	1	1	135,934	249,849	0	0.10	7	A	20		...					0....	22364
70-AACA-g	salabe-yangtsepa-kha					0				20		...					0....	22365
70-AAD	TSANGLA-SHARCHAGPA net	3	5	473,211	859,302		0.02	11	A	20		...					0....	22368
70-AADA	SHARCHAGPA cluster	1	2	305,640	561,770		0.03	11	A	20		...					0....	22369
70-AADA-a	sharchagpa-kha	1	1	237,885	437,236	0	0.01	12	A	20		...					0....	22370
70-AADA-b	monpa-kha					0				20		...					0....	22371
70-AADB	TSANGLA cluster	3	3	167,571	297,532		0.01	12	A	20		...					0....	22372
70-AADB-a	tsangla	3	3	167,571	297,532	0	0.01	12	A	20	Tsangla	...					0....	22373
70-AAE	KAIKE net	1	1	2,393	3,801		0.08	14	A	3		...					0....	22376
70-AAEA	KAIKE cluster	1	1	2,393	3,801		0.08	14	A	3		...					0....	22377
70-AAEA-a	tarali-kham	1	1	2,393	3,801	0	0.08	14	A	3		...					0....	22378
70-AB	KANAURI-THAMI chain	4	25	192,872	269,092		0.03	14	A	24		P..					0....	22381
70-ABA	KANAURI-LAHULI net	4	15	147,340	200,827		0.04	16	A	24		P..					0....	22382
70-ABAA	BUNAN-THEBOR cluster	3	7	41,670	60,811		0.04	13	A	24		P..					0....	22383
70-ABAA-a	bunan	2	2	6,178	7,876	0	0.11	16	A	24	Lahuli: Bunan*	P..	1911-1923				0....	22384
70-ABAA-b	lippa					0				24		p..					0....	22387
70-ABAA-c	zangram					0				24		p..					0....	22388
70-ABAA-d	thebor					0				24		p..					0....	22389
70-ABAA-e	sumchu	1	1	4,359	5,721	0	0.00	11	A	24		p..					0....	22390
70-ABAA-f	sungam	1	1	1,723	2,262	0	0.00	11	A	24		p..					0....	22391
70-ABAA-g	kanam					0				24		p..					0....	22392
70-ABAA-h	jangali	2	2	25,964	40,428	0	0.03	12	A	24		p..					0....	22393
70-ABAB	KANAURI-KANASHI cluster	2	4	71,696	95,833		0.01	17	A	24		P..					0....	22394
70-ABAB-a	kanashi	1	1	1,520	1,996	0	0.13	15	A	24		p..					0....	22395
70-ABAB-b	chikhuli	1	1	1,723	2,262	0	0.12	15	A	24		p..					0....	22396
70-ABAB-c	tukpa					0				24		p..					0....	22397
70-ABAB-d	kanauri	2	2	68,453	91,575	0	0.01	17	A	24	Kanauri	P..	1909				0....	22398
70-ABAC	CHAMBA-LAHULI cluster	2	2	5,520	7,051		0.09	17	A	24		P..					0....	22403
70-ABAC-a	chamba					0				24		p..					0....	22404
70-ABAC-b	manchati	2	2	5,520	7,051	0	0.09	17	A	24	Lahuli: Manchad	P..	1907				0....	22405
70-ABAC-c	patni					0				24		p..					0....	22406
70-ABAD	TINAN-LAHULI cluster	2	2	28,454	37,132		0.10	18	A	24		P..					0....	22407
70-ABAD-a	tinan	2	2	28,454	37,132	0	0.10	18	A	24	Lahuli: Tinan*	P..	1908-1915				0....	22408
70-ABAD-b	rangloi					0				24		p..					0....	22409
70-ABAD-c	gondla					0				24		p..					0....	22410
70-ABB	ALMORA net	2	7	10,496	15,327		0.00	8	A	4		...					0....	22411
70-ABBA	ALMORA cluster	2	7	10,496	15,327		0.00	8	A	4		...					0....	22412
70-ABBA-a	rangkas	2	2	1,421	1,976	0	0.00	10	A	4		...					0....	22413
70-ABBA-b	darmiya	2	2	3,224	4,562	0	0.00	9	A	4		...					0....	22414
70-ABBA-c	chaudangsi	2	2	3,022	4,296	0	0.00	7	A	4		...					0....	22415
70-ABBA-d	byangsi	1	1	2,829	4,493	0	0.00	6	A	4		...					0....	22416

Continued overleaf

Table 9-13 continued

Code 1	REFERENCE NAME / Autoglossonym 2	Coun 3	Peo 4	Mother-tongue speakers in 2000 5	in 2025 6	Media radio 7	CHURCH AC% 8	E% 9	Wld 10	Tr 11	Biblioglossonym 12	SCRIPTURES Print 13-15	P-activity 16	N-activity 17	B-activity 18	J-year 19	Jayuh 20-24	Ref 25
70-ABC	**THAMI-BARAAMU net**	2	3	35,036	52,938		0.00	5	A	4		. . .					0	22417
70-ABCA	THAMI-BARAAMU cluster	2	3	35,036	52,938		0.00	5	A	4		. . .					0	22418
70-ABCA-a	thami	2	2	34,608	52,258	0	0.00	5	A	4		. . .					0	22419
70-ABCA-b	baraamu	1	1	428	680	0	0.00	8	A	4		. . .					0	22420
70-AC	TANAHUN-HILLS chain									9		. . .					0	22421
70-ACA	**TANAHUN-HILLS net**									9		. . .					0	22422
70-ACAA	KUSANDA cluster			0	0		0.00	0		9		. . .					0	22423
70-ACAA-a	kusanda			0	0	0	0.00	0		9		. . .					0	22424
70-AD	CHANTEL chain	1	1	5,660	8,989		0.02	10	A	4		. . .					0	22425
70-ADA	**CHANTEL net**	1	1	5,660	8,989		0.02	10	A	4		. . .					0	22426
70-ADAA	CHENTEL-MAGAR cluster	1	1	5,660	8,989		0.02	10	A	4		. . .					0	22427
70-ADAA-a	chentel-magar	1	1	5,660	8,989	0	0.02	10	A	4		. . .					0	22428
71	**HIMALAYIC zone**	4	53	2,429,577	3,823,195		0.18	21	A	41		PN .					0a . . .	22429
71-A	**NEWARIC set**	2	2	728,967	1,151,905		0.13	27	A	41		PN .					0	22430
71-AA	NEWARIC chain	2	2	728,967	1,151,905		0.13	27	A	41		PN .					0	22431
71-AAA	**NEWARI-PAHRI net**	2	2	728,967	1,151,905		0.13	27	A	41		PN .					0	22432
71-AAAA	NEWARI-PAHRI cluster	2	2	728,967	1,151,905		0.13	27	A	41		PN .					0	22433
71-AAAA-a	newari	2	2	728,967	1,151,905	0	0.13	27	A	41	Newari	PN .	1964-1977	1986			0	22434
71-AAAA-b	dolkhali					0				41		pn .					0	22440
71-AAAA-c	pahri					0				41		pn .					0	22441
71-B	**WEST KIRANTI set**	3	15	693,542	1,103,458		0.27	18	A	41		PN .					0	22442
71-BA	WEST KIRANTI chain	3	15	693,542	1,103,458		0.27	18	A	41		PN .					0	22443
71-BAA	**VAYU-CHEPANG net**	1	3	33,349	52,971		4.95	21	A	41		PN .					0	22444
71-BAAA	VAYU cluster	1	1	2,826	4,489		0.00	5	A	4		. . .					0	22445
71-BAAA-a	vayu	1	1	2,826	4,489	0	0.00	5	A	4		. . .					0	22446
71-BAAB	CHEPANG-GHARTI cluster	1	2	30,523	48,482		5.41	22	A	41		PN .					0	22449
71-BAAB-a	chepang	1	1	27,472	43,636	0	6.00	23	A	41	Chepang	PN .	1977		1993		0	22450
71-BAAB-b	bujhel					0				41		pn .					0	22453
71-BAAB-c	gharti-2	1	1	3,051	4,846		0.13	16	A	41		pn .					0	22454
71-BAB	**MAGAR-RAJI net**	3	6	600,301	955,355		0.03	19	A	41		PN .					0	22455
71-BABA	MAGAR cluster	3	5	596,075	948,642		0.03	19	A	41		PN .					0	22456
71-BABA-a	West magar	1	1	239,305	380,102	0	0.03	16	A	41		pn .					0	22457
71-BABA-b	East magar	3	4	356,770	568,540	0	0.03	21	A	41	Magar*	PN .	1977-1984	1991			0	22458
71-BABB	RAJI cluster	1	1	4,226	6,713		0.00	6	A	4		. . .					0	22459
71-BABB-a	raji	1	1	4,226	6,713	0	0.00	6	A	4		. . .					0	22460
71-BAC	**SHESHI-KHAM net**	1	1	11,965	19,005		0.02	12	A	2		. . .					0	22463
71-BACA	SHESHI-KHAM cluster	1	1	11,965	19,005		0.02	12	A	2		. . .					0	22464
71-BACA-a	sheshi	1	1	11,965	19,005	0	0.02	12	A	2		. . .					0	22465
71-BAD	**GAMALE-KHAM net**	1	1	13,123	20,845		0.02	12	A	2		. . .					0	22466
71-BADA	GAMALE-KHAM cluster	1	1	13,123	20,845		0.02	12	A	2		. . .					0	22467
71-BADA-a	gamale	1	1	13,123	20,845	0	0.02	12	A	2		. . .					0	22468
71-BAE	**NISI-KHAM net**	1	1	11,965	19,005		0.02	12	A	2		. . .					0	22469
71-BAEA	NISI-KHAM cluster	1	1	11,965	19,005		0.02	12	A	2		. . .					0	22470
71-BAEA-a	nisi	1	1	11,965	19,005	0	0.02	12	A	2		. . .					0	22471
71-BAF	**TAKALE-KHAM net**	1	1	19,685	31,267		0.06	18	A	41		PN .					0	22472
71-BAFA	TAKALE-KHAM cluster	1	1	19,685	31,267		0.06	18	A	41		PN .					0	22473
71-BAFA-a	takale	1	1	19,685	31,267	0	0.06	18	A	41	Kham, Takale	PN .		1985			0	22474
71-BAG	**RAUTE net**	1	1	282	449		0.00	7	A	4		. . .					0	22475
71-BAGA	RAUTE cluster	1	1	282	449		0.00	7	A	4		. . .					0	22476
71-BAGA-a	raute	1	1	282	449	0	0.00	7	A	4		. . .					0	22477
71-BAH	**MAIKOTI net**	1	1	2,872	4,561		0.00	8	A	2		. . .					0	22478
71-BAHA	MAIKOTI cluster	1	1	2,872	4,561		0.00	8	A	2		. . .					0	22479
71-BAHA-a	maikoti	1	1	2,872	4,561	0	0.00	8	A	2		. . .					0	22480
71-C	**EAST KIRANTI set**	4	35	986,442	1,535,071		0.15	18	A	41		PN .					0a . . .	22481
71-CA	BAHING-DUMI chain	2	5	92,684	148,806		0.07	16	A	41		PN .					0	22482
71-CAA	**BAHING-TSAURASYA net**	2	3	51,963	81,893		0.06	17	A	41		PN .					0	22483
71-CAAA	BAHING-SUNWAR cluster	2	2	44,784	70,490		0.05	17	A	41		PN .					0	22484
71-CAAA-a	bahing					0				41		pn .					0	22485
71-CAAA-b	sunwar	2	2	44,784	70,490		0.05	17	A	41	Sunwar	PN .	1977	1992			0	22488
71-CAAB	TSAURASYA cluster	1	1	7,179	11,403		0.10	13	A	4		. . .					0	22489
71-CAAB-a	tsaurasya	1	1	7,179	11,403	0	0.10	13	A	4		. . .					0	22490
71-CAAB-b	umbule					0				4		. . .					0	22491
71-CAAB-c	jerung					0				4		. . .					0	22492
71-CAB	**DUMI-KHALING net**	1	2	40,721	66,913		0.09	16	A	41		PN .					0	22493
71-CABA	DUMI-KHALING cluster	1	2	20,721	32,913		0.07	18	A	41		PN .					22494
71-CABA-a	khaling	1	1	19,307	30,667	0	0.07	18	A	41	Khaling	PN .	1973-1977	1994			0	22495
71-CABA-b	dumi					0				41		pn .					0	22496
71-CABA-c	koi	1	1	1,414	2,246	0	0.07	20	A	41		pn .					0	22497
71-CABB	THULUNG cluster	1	1	20,000	34,000		0.10	14	A	2		. . .					0	22498
71-CABB-a	thulung					0				2		. . .					0	22499
71-CB	BANTAWA-LIMBU chain	4	13	585,247	901,938		0.17	20	A	20		. . .					0a . . .	22503
71-CBA	**CHAMLING-BANTAWA net**	1	2	70,743	112,365		0.07	13	A	4		. . .					0	22504
71-CBAA	CHAMLING-ARTHARE cluster	1	2	70,743	112,365		0.07	13	A	4		. . .					0	22505
71-CBAA-a	chamling	1	1	10,917	17,340	0	0.10	15	A	4		. . .					0	22506
71-CBAA-b	lambichong					0				4		. . .					0	22507
71-CBAA-c	arthare	1	1	59,826	95,025	0	0.07	12	A	4		. . .					0	22508

Continued opposite

Table 9-13 continued

Code 1	REFERENCE NAME / Autoglossonym 2	Coun 3	Peo 4	Mother-tongue speakers in 2000 5	in 2025 6	Media radio 7	CHURCH AC% 8	E% 9	Wld 10	Tr 11	Biblioglossonym 12	SCRIPTURES Print 13-15	P-activity 16	N-activity 17	B-activity 18	J-year 19	Jayuh 20-24	Ref 25
71-CBB	**BANTAWA-DEOSALI net**	1	1	45,292	72,275		0.10	13	A	8		. . .					0	22509
71-CBBA	BANTAWA-WALING cluster	1	1	42,292	67,175		0.10	13	A	8		. . .					0	22510
71-CBBA-a	bantawa	1	1	42,292	67,175	0	0.10	13	A	8		. . .					0	22511
71-CBBA-b	chhintang					0				8		. . .					0	22515
71-CBBA-c	dungmali					0				8		. . .					0	22516
71-CBBA-d	waling					0				8		. . .					0	22517
71-CBBA-e	rungchenbung					0				8		. . .					0	22518
71-CBBB	DEOSALI cluster	1	1	3,000	5,100		0.10	14	A	0		. . .					0	22519
71-CBBB-a	deosali	1	1	3,000	5,100	0	0.10	14	A	0		. . .					0	22520
71-CBC	**LOHORONG-LIMBU net**	4	10	469,212	717,298		0.19	22	A	20		. . .					0a . . .	22521
71-CBCA	LOHORONG cluster	1	2	21,214	33,696		0.02	7	A	4		. . .					0	22522
71-CBCA-a	lohorong	1	2	21,214	33,696	0	0.02	7	A	4		. . .					0	22523
71-CBCB	YAKHA cluster	2	2	11,711	18,378		0.00	6	A	4		. . .					0	22527
71-CBCB-a	yakha	2	2	11,711	18,378	0	0.00	6	A	4		. . .					0	22528
71-CBCC	LIMBU cluster	4	6	436,287	665,224		0.21	23	A	20		. . .					0a . . .	22532
71-CBCC-a	limbu	3	3	336,254	533,992	4	0.10	26	A	20	Limbu	. . .					0a . . .	22533
71-CBCC-b	panchthar					1				20		. . .					0c . . .	22536
71-CBCC-c	chhathar	1	1	18,426	29,268	1	0.09	14	A	20		. . .					0c . . .	22537
71-CBCC-d	moinba	2	2	81,607	101,964	1	0.70	15	A	20		. . .					0c . . .	22538
71-CC	KHAMBU-KULUNG chain	3	17	308,511	484,327		0.15	14	A	8		. . .					0	22541
71-CCA	**KHAMBU-KULUNG net**	3	17	308,511	484,327		0.15	14	A	8		. . .					0	22542
71-CCAA	NACHERENG cluster	1	1	3,000	5,100		0.10	14	A	4		. . .					0	22543
71-CCAA-a	nachereng	1	1	3,000	5,100	0	0.10	14	A	4		. . .					0	22544
71-CCAB	KULUNG-PELMUNG cluster	3	17	285,511	445,227		0.15	14	A	8		. . .					0	22545
71-CCAB-a	kulung	3	10	269,194	419,310	0	0.16	15	A	8		. . .					0	22546
71-CCAB-b	pelmung					0				8		. . .					0	22547
71-CCAB-c	sotang					0				8		. . .					0	22548
71-CCAB-d	namlung					0				8		. . .					0	22549
71-CCAC	KHAMBU cluster	1	1	20,000	34,000		0.10	14	A	4		. . .					0	22550
71-CCAC-a	khambu					0				4		. . .					0	22551
71-D	**DHIMALIC set**	1	1	20,626	32,761		0.00	5	A	2		. . .					0	22557
71-DA	DHIMALIC chain	1	1	20,626	32,761		0.00	5	A	2		. . .					0	22558
71-DAA	**DHIMAL-TOTO net**	1	1	20,626	32,761		0.00	5	A	2		. . .					0	22559
71-DAAA	DHIMAL-TOTO cluster	1	1	20,626	32,761		0.00	5	A	2		. . .					0	22560
71-DAAA-a	dhimal	1	1	20,626	32,761	0	0.00	5	A	2		. . .					0	22561
71-DAAA-b	toto					0				2		. . .					0	22564
72	**GARIC zone**	4	46	4,062,345	5,357,285		27.40	67	B	71		PNB					2as . .	22565
72-A	**BODO-GARO set**	3	23	3,306,007	4,366,829		16.07	60	B	70		PNB					2as . .	22566
72-AA	BODO-TRIPURA chain	3	12	2,046,417	2,696,001		6.46	51	B	70		PNB					2as . .	22567
72-AAA	**BODO-DIMASA net**	2	4	912,123	1,197,830		12.19	62	B	61		PNB					2as . .	22568
72-AAAA	BODO cluster	2	2	793,018	1,041,502		6.49	60	B	61		PNB					2a . . .	22569
72-AAAA-a	bodo	2	2	793,018	1,041,502	4	6.49	60	B	61	Boro*	PNB	1906-1961	1938-1991	1981	1997	2a . . .	22570
72-AAAA-b	mech					1				61		pnb					1c . . .	22571
72-AAAB	DIMASA cluster	1	2	119,105	156,328		50.09	72	B	24		P . .					0.s . .	22572
72-AAAB-a	dimasa	1	1	62,239	81,690	0	89.00	100	C	24	Dimasa	P . .	1905-1908				0.s . .	22573
72-AAAB-b	hariamba					0				24		p . .					0.s . .	22574
72-AAAB-c	kachari	1	1	56,866	74,638	0	7.50	42	A	24	Kachari	p . .					0.s . .	22575
72-AAB	**TRIPURI net**	2	7	1,110,574	1,467,038		1.88	43	A	70		PNB					1.s . .	22576
72-AABA	TRIPURI cluster	2	7	1,110,574	1,467,038		1.88	43	A	70		PNB					1.s . .	22577
72-AABA-a	kok-borok	2	4	937,329	1,239,563	0	1.26	43	A	70	Kok Borok	PNB	1959-1983	1976	1995		1.s . .	22578
72-AABA-b	riang	2	2	147,498	193,682	0	6.00	47	A	70	Riang	PNb	1950-1982	1990			1.s . .	22585
72-AABA-c	bhim	1	1	25,747	33,793	0	1.00	28	A	70		pnb					1.s . .	22586
72-AAC	**LALUNGIC net**	1	1	23,720	31,133		0.38	17	A	4		. . .					0	22587
72-AACA	LALUNG cluster	1	1	23,720	31,133		0.38	17	A	4		. . .					0	22588
72-AACA-a	lalung	1	1	23,720	31,133	0	0.38	17	A	4		. . .					0	22589
72-AB	DEORIC chain	1	1	20,476	26,875		0.56	19	A	4		. . .					0	22590
72-ABA	**DEORIC net**	1	1	20,476	26,875		0.56	19	A	4		. . .					0	22591
72-ABAA	DEORI cluster	1	1	20,476	26,875		0.56	19	A	4		. . .					0	22592
72-ABAA-a	deori	1	1	20,476	26,875	0	0.56	19	A	4		. . .					0	22593
72-AC	GARIC chain	2	10	1,239,114	1,643,953		32.19	76	B	61		PNB					0as . .	22596
72-ACA	**GARO net**	2	10	1,239,114	1,643,953		32.19	76	B	61		PNB					0as . .	22597
72-ACAA	PROPER GARO cluster	2	5	893,418	1,186,067		42.44	91	B	61		PNB					0as . .	22598
72-ACAA-a	Literary garo					1				61		pnb					0cs . .	22599
72-ACAA-b	achik	1	1	604,041	792,814	4	38.00	94	B	61	Garo: Achik	PNB	1875-1904	1894-1987	1924-1994		0as . .	22600
72-ACAA-c	abeng	2	2	229,707	310,670	4	62.98	96	C	61	Garo: Abeng	PNB	1887-1904	1987	1994		0as . .	22601
72-ACAA-d	awe					1				61		pnb					0cs . .	22604
72-ACAB	RABHA-MEGAM cluster	2	2	259,164	340,619		4.63	39	A	57		PN .					0	22605
72-ACAB-a	rabha	1	1	252,706	331,681	0	3.21	37	A	57	Rabha	PN .	1909-1986	1995			0	22606
72-ACAB-b	kamrup					0				57		pn .					0	22609
72-ACAB-c	chisak					0				57		pn .					0	22610
72-ACAB-d	ganching					0				57		pn .					0	22611
72-ACAB-e	mande					0				57		pn .					0	22612
72-ACAB-f	matchi					0				57		pn .					0	22613
72-ACAB-g	atong					0				57		pn .					0	22614
72-ACAB-h	ruga					0				57		pn .					0	22615
72-ACAB-i	dacca					0				57		pn .					0	22616
72-ACAB-j	megam	1	1	6,458	8,938	0	60.00	95	C	57		pn .					0	22617
72-ACAC	GARIC-KOCH cluster	2	3	86,532	117,267		8.89	30	A	4		. . .					0	22618
72-ACAC-a	koch	2	3	86,532	117,267	0	8.89	30	A	4		. . .					0	22619
72-ACAC-b	banai					0				4		. . .					0	22620
72-ACAC-c	harigaya					0				4		. . .					0	22621
72-ACAC-d	satpariya					0				4		. . .					0	22622
72-ACAC-e	tintekiya					0				4		. . .					0	22623
72-ACAC-f	wanang					0				4		. . .					0	22624
72-B	**KONYAKIC set**	2	23	756,338	990,456		76.95	98	C	71		PNB					0as . .	22625

Continued overleaf

Table 9-13 continued

Code 1	REFERENCE NAME 2 / Autoglossonym	Coun 3	Peo 4	Mother-tongue speakers in 2000 5	in 2025 6	Media radio 7	CHURCH AC% 8	E% 9	Wld 10	Tr 11	Biblioglossonym 12	Print 13-15	P-activity 16	N-activity 17	B-activity 18	J-year 19	Jayuh 20-24	Ref 25
72-BA	KONYAKIC chain	2	23	756,338	990,456		76.95	98	C	71		PNB					0as..	22626
72-BAA	KONYAK-WANCHO net	2	4	193,558	253,998		72.90	100	C	61		PNB					0....	22627
72-BAAA	PROPER KONYAK cluster	2	2	111,350	146,098	1	76.00	100	C	61		PNB					0....	22628
72-BAAA-a	tableng					1				61		pnb					0....	22629
72-BAAA-b	konyak-naga	2	2	111,350	146,098	4	76.00	100	C	61	Naga: Konyak*	PNB	1944-1980	1973	1992		0....	22630
72-BAAB	WANCHO cluster	1	1	46,831	61,467		70.00	100	C	12		...					0....	22656
72-BAAB-a	wancho-naga	1	1	46,831	61,467	0	70.00	100	C	12	Naga, Wancho	...					0....	22657
72-BAAC	PHOM cluster	1	1	35,377	46,433		67.00	100	C	51		PN.					0....	22665
72-BAAC-a	phom-naga	1	1	35,377	46,433	0	67.00	100	C	51	Naga: Phom*	PN.	1961	1978-1996			0....	22666
72-BAB	CHANG net	1	1	32,437	42,574		61.00	100	C	51		PN.					0....	22671
72-BABA	CHANG cluster	1	1	32,437	42,574		61.00	100	C	51		PN.					0....	22672
72-BABA-a	chang-naga	1	1	32,437	42,574	0	61.00	100	C	51	Naga: Chang*	PN.	1947-1964	1982			0....	22673
72-BAC	TASE net	2	2	70,243	90,171		70.00	100	C	57		PN.					0....	22674
72-BACA	TASE cluster	2	2	70,243	90,171		70.00	100	C	57		PN.					0....	22675
72-BACA-a	tase-nagaland	2	2	70,243	90,171	0	70.00	100	C	57	Naga, Tase	PN.	1979-1982	1992			0....	22676
72-BACA-b	tase-myanmar					0				57		pn.					0....	22692
72-BACA-c	hawa					0				57		pn.					0....	22702
72-BAD	MONSHANG-MOYON net	1	4	26,659	34,990		54.60	87	B	57		PN.					0....	22703
72-BADA	MONSHANG-MOYON cluster	1	4	26,659	34,990		54.60	87	B	57		PN.					0....	22704
72-BADA-a	monshang-naga	1	1	3,142	4,124	0	40.01	75	B	57		pn.					0....	22705
72-BADA-b	moyon-naga	1	3	23,517	30,866	0	56.55	89	B	57	Naga, Moyon*	PN.	1944-1959	1979			0....	22706
72-BAE	NOCTE net	1	1	34,363	45,102		70.00	100	C	12		...					0....	22707
72-BAEA	NOCTE cluster	1	1	34,363	45,102		70.00	100	C	12		...					0....	22708
72-BAEA-a	nocte-naga	1	1	34,363	45,102	0	70.00	100	C	12	Naga, Nocte	...					0....	22709
72-BAF	YIMCHUNGRU-AO net	2	5	232,229	304,630		89.14	100	C	71		PNB					0a...	22715
72-BAFA	YIMCHUNGRU cluster	2	2	42,979	56,236		75.90	100	C	51		PN.					0....	22716
72-BAFA-a	North yimchungru					1				51		pn.					0....	22717
72-BAFA-b	South yimchungru	2	2	42,979	56,236	4	75.90	100	C	51		PN.					0....	22722
72-BAFB	SANGTAM-POCHURI cluster	1	2	41,357	54,282		71.25	98	C	61		PNB					0....	22726
72-BAFB-a	pochuri-naga	1	1	9,731	12,772	0	50.01	92	B	61	Naga: Pochuri*	PNb		1994			0....	22727
72-BAFB-b	sangtam-naga	1	1	31,626	41,510	0	77.78	100	C	61	Naga: Sangtam*	PNB	1944-1950	1963	1995		0....	22728
72-BAFB-c	kizare-naga					0				61		pnb					0....	22735
72-BAFC	AO cluster	1	1	147,893	194,112		98.00	100	C	71		PNB					0a...	22736
72-BAFC-a	ao	1	1	147,893	194,112	4	98.00	100	C	71	Naga: Ao*	PNB	1883	1929-1995	1964		0a...	22737
72-BAG	MARING-TANGKHUL net	1	3	157,523	206,751		77.43	96	C	71		PNB					0.s..	22749
72-BAGA	MARING cluster	1	2	42,067	55,213		56.40	86	B	57		PN.					0.s..	22750
72-BAGA-a	maring-naga	1	2	42,067	55,213	0	56.40	86	B	57	Naga: Maring*	PN.		1988-1995			0.s..	22751
72-BAGB	TANGKHUL cluster	1	1	115,456	151,538		85.09	100	C	71		PNB					0....	22754
72-BAGB-a	tangkhul-naga	1	1	115,456	151,538	0	85.09	100	C	71	Naga: Tangkhul*	PNB	1904-1967	1927-1995	1976		0....	22755
72-BAH	CHOTHE net	1	1	3,548	4,657		29.99	61	B	2		...					0....	22763
72-BAHA	CHOTHE cluster	1	1	3,548	4,657		29.99	61	B	2		...					0....	22764
72-BAHA-a	chothe-naga	1	1	3,548	4,657	0	29.99	61	B	2		...					0....	22765
72-BAI	TARAO net	1	1	710	931		30.00	61	B	2		...					0....	22766
72-BAIA	TARAO cluster	1	1	710	931		30.00	61	B	2		...					0....	22767
72-BAIA-a	tarao-naga	1	1	710	931	0	30.00	61	B	2		...					0....	22768
72-BAJ	MELURI net	1	1	5,068	6,652		60.00	94	C	4		...					0....	22769
72-BAJA	MELURI cluster	1	1	5,068	6,652		60.00	94	C	4		...					0....	22770
72-BAJA-a	meluri-naga	1	1	5,068	6,652	0	60.00	94	C	4		...					0....	22771
73	KUKIC zone	6	100	5,641,980	7,417,427		41.88	76	B	82		PNB					1asu.	22774
73-A	NAGIC set	2	20	853,553	1,120,216		73.66	99	C	82		PNB					1.s..	22775
73-AA	LOTHA chain	1	1	83,931	110,161		99.00	100	C	72		PNB					0....	22776
73-AAA	LOTHA net	1	1	83,931	110,161		99.00	100	C	72		PNB					0....	22777
73-AAAA	LOTHA-NAGA cluster	1	1	83,931	110,161		99.00	100	C	72		PNB					0....	22778
73-AAAA-a	lotha-naga	1	1	83,931	110,161	0	99.00	100	C	72	Naga: Kyong*	PNB	1931-1966	1944-1992	1967		0....	22779
73-AB	RENGMA-ANGAMI chain	1	9	524,773	688,774		74.19	100	C	82		PNB					1.s..	22789
73-ABA	RENGMA net	1	1	35,681	46,832		58.45	100	B	82		PNB					0....	22790
73-ABAA	RENGMA-NAGA cluster	1	1	35,681	46,832		58.45	100	B	82		PNB					0....	22791
73-ABAA-a	rengma-naga	1	1	35,681	46,832	0	58.45	100	B	82	Naga: Rengma*	PNB	1928	1976	1996		0....	22792
73-ABB	SEMA-MAO net	1	8	489,092	641,942		75.34	100	C	71		PNB					1.s..	22799
73-ABBA	SEMA-NAGA cluster	1	1	138,162	181,340		91.67	100	C	71		PNB					0.s..	22800
73-ABBA-a	sema-naga	1	1	138,162	181,340	0	91.67	100	C	71	Naga: Sema*	PNB	1928-1961	1944-1960	1985		0.s..	22801
73-ABBB	MAO-NAGA cluster	1	2	125,390	164,577		76.94	100	C	61		PNB					0....	22807
73-ABBB-a	mao-naga	1	1	84,945	111,492	0	85.00	100	C	61	Mao Naga*	PNB	1945-1947	1960-1992	1995		0....	22808
73-ABBB-b	poumei	1	1	40,445	53,085	0	60.00	100	C	61	Naga: Poumei*	PNb		1992			0....	22814
73-ABBC	ANGAMI-NAGA cluster	1	5	225,540	296,025		64.45	100	C	70		PNB					1....	22815
73-ABBC-a	angami-naga	1	2	168,065	220,589	0	64.57	100	C	70	Angami Naga*	PNB	1890-1959	1927-1995	1970		1....	22816
73-ABBC-b	chokri-naga	1	1	23,314	30,600	0	65.00	100	C	70	Naga, Chokri	pnb					1....	22830
73-ABBC-c	khezha-naga	1	1	24,024	31,532	0	65.00	100	C	70		pnb					1....	22831
73-ABBC-d	naganese	1	1	10,137	13,304	0	60.00	100	B	70		pnb				1999	1....	22832
73-AC	LIANGMAI-RONGMAI chain	1	8	217,328	285,247		65.81	96	C	68		PNB					0....	22833
73-ACA	LIANGMAI-RONGMAI net	1	8	217,328	285,247		65.81	96	C	68		PNB					0....	22834
73-ACAA	MARAM-NAGA cluster	1	1	16,827	22,085		23.78	57	B	12		...					0....	22835
73-ACAA-a	maram-naga	1	1	16,827	22,085	0	23.78	57	B	12	Naga, Maram	...					0....	22836
73-ACAB	LIANGMAI-NAGA cluster	1	2	24,327	31,931		65.48	100	C	61		PNB					0....	22837
73-ACAB-a	liang-mai	1	2	24,327	31,931	0	65.48	100	C	61	Naga: Liangmei*	PNB	1978-1988	1983	1995		0....	22838
73-ACAC	ZEMI-NAGA cluster	1	1	29,700	38,982		70.00	100	C	61		PNB					0....	22841
73-ACAC-a	ze-mi	1	1	29,700	38,982	0	70.00	100	C	61	Naga: Zeme*	PNB	1928-1992	1978-1992	1992		0....	22842
73-ACAC-b	paren					0				61		pnb					0....	22848
73-ACAC-c	njauna					0				61		pnb					0....	22849

Continued opposite

Table 9-13 continued

Code 1	REFERENCE NAME / Autoglossonym 2	Coun 3	Peo 4	Mother-tongue speakers in 2000 5	in 2025 6	Media radio 7	CHURCH AC% 8	E% 9	Wld 10	Tr 11	Biblioglossonym 12	SCRIPTURES Print 13-15	P-activity 16	N-activity 17	B-activity 18	J-year 19	Jayuh 20-24	Ref 25
73-ACAD	MZIEME-NAGA cluster	1	1	30,410	39,913		70.00	100	C	61		PNB					0....	22850
73-ACAD-a	mzie-me	1	1	30,410	39,913	0	70.00	100	C	61	Naga: Mzieme*	PNB	1953	1981	1992		0....	22851
73-ACAE	RONGMAI-NAGA cluster	1	2	115,152	151,139		70.00	100	C	68		PNB	1959-1961	1979	1989		0....	22852
73-ACAE-a	songbu					0				68		pnb					0....	22853
73-ACAE-b	puiron	1	1	53,217	69,849	0	70.00	100	C	68		pnb					0....	22854
73-ACAF	KHOIRAO-NAGA cluster	1	1	912	1,197		45.07	79	B	12		...					0....	22857
73-ACAF-a	khoirao	1	1	912	1,197	0	45.07	79	B	12	Naga, Khoirao	...					0....	22858
73-ACAF-b	kolya					0				12		...					0....	22859
73-ACAF-c	mayang-khang					0				12		...					0....	22860
73-ACAF-d	ngari					0				12		...					0....	22861
73-ACAF-e	thanggal					0				12		...					0....	22862
73-ACAF-f	tukai-mi					0				12		...					0....	22863
73-AD	KHIAMNGAN chain	2	2	27,521	36,034		48.34	90	B	51		PN.					0....	22864
73-ADA	KHIAMNGAN net	2	2	27,521	36,034		48.34	90	B	51		PN.					0....	22865
73-ADAA	KHIAMNGAN-NAGA cluster	2	2	27,521	36,034		48.34	90	B	51	Naga, Khiamngan	PN.		1981			0....	22866
73-ADAA-a	West khiamngan					0				51	Naga: Khiamngan	PN.		1980			0....	22867
73-ADAA-b	East khiamngan					0				51		pn.					0....	22871
73-B	MRUIC set	3	3	121,278	159,339		0.20	24	A	24		P..					0....	22877
73-BA	MRUIC chain	3	3	121,278	159,339		0.20	24	A	24		P..					0....	22878
73-BAA	MRU net	3	3	121,278	159,339		0.20	24	A	24		P..					0....	22879
73-BAAA	MRU cluster	3	3	121,278	159,339		0.20	24	A	24		P..					0....	22880
73-BAAA-a	murung	3	3	121,278	159,339	0	0.20	24	A	24	Mro*	P..	1934				0....	22881
73-C	MIKIR-MEITHEI set	3	4	2,009,898	2,646,329		3.38	54	B	72		PNB					1as..	22884
73-CA	MIKIR-MEITHEI chain	3	4	2,009,898	2,646,329		3.38	54	B	72		PNB					1as..	22885
73-CAA	MEITHEI-BISHNUPURIYA net	3	3	1,508,541	1,988,289		1.08	54	B	69		PNB					1as..	22886
73-CAAA	MEITHEI cluster	3	3	1,508,541	1,988,289		1.08	54	B	69		PNB					1as..	22887
73-CAAA-a	meithei	3	3	1,508,541	1,988,289	4	1.08	54	B	69		PNB				1994	1as..	22888
73-CAAA-b	bishnupuriya					1				69		pnb					1cs..	22893
73-CAB	MIKIR net	1	1	501,357	658,040		10.28	55	B	72		PNB					0....	22894
73-CABA	MIKIR cluster	1	1	501,357	658,040		10.28	55	B	72		PNB					0....	22895
73-CABA-a	mikiri	1	1	501,357	658,040	0	10.28	55	B	72		PNB					0....	22896
73-CABA-b	amri					0				72		pnb					0....	22900
73-CABA-c	arleng					0				72		pnb					0....	22901
73-CABA-d	bhui					0				72		pnb					0....	22902
73-CABA-e	rhengkitang					0				72		pnb					0....	22903
73-D	KUKI-CHIN set	6	73	2,657,251	3,491,543		62.70	88	C	71		PNB					1asu.	22904
73-DA	NORTH KUKI-CHIN chain	3	19	957,435	1,242,345		62.20	93	C	71		PNB					0as..	22905
73-DAA	NORTH KUKI-CHIN net	3	19	957,435	1,242,345		62.20	93	C	71		PNB					0as..	22906
73-DAAA	RAL-TE cluster	2	2	13,987	17,835		60.00	95	B	4		...					0....	22907
73-DAAA-a	ral-te	2	2	13,987	17,835	0	60.00	95	B	4		...					0....	22908
73-DAAB	ZO-MI cluster	2	2	53,004	68,231		80.00	100	C	61		PNB					0....	22909
73-DAAB-a	zo-mi	2	2	53,004	68,231	4	80.00	100	C	61	Zomi*	PNB	1981	1967-1981	1992		0....	22910
73-DAAC	YO-TE cluster	1	1	4,301	5,481		15.00	36	A	4		...					0....	22911
73-DAAC-a	yo-te	1	1	4,301	5,481	0	15.00	36	A	4		...					0....	22912
73-DAAD	TIDDIM-CHIN cluster	2	2	391,143	505,465		60.00	100	B	71		PNB					0as..	22913
73-DAAD-a	tiddim	2	2	391,143	505,465	5	60.00	100	B	71	Chin: Tiddim*	PNB	1915-1964	1932	1983-1995		0as..	22914
73-DAAE	THADO-CHIN cluster	3	9	425,885	555,459		58.87	86	B	61	Chin, Cho	PNB		1995			0as..	22918
73-DAAE-a	thado	3	4	263,985	345,661	4	54.71	86	B	61	Chin, Thado	PNB	1924-1978	1942-1983	1971-1994		0as..	22919
73-DAAE-b	bai-te					1				61		pnb					0cs..	22920
73-DAAE-c	changsen					1				61		pnb					0cs..	22921
73-DAAE-d	kaokeep					1				61		pnb					0cs..	22922
73-DAAE-e	khongzai					1				61		pnb					0cs..	22923
73-DAAE-f	kipgen					1				61		pnb					0cs..	22924
73-DAAE-g	langiung					1				61		pnb					0cs..	22925
73-DAAE-h	sairang					1				61		pnb					0cs..	22926
73-DAAE-i	thangngen					1				61		pnb					0cs..	22927
73-DAAE-j	hawkip					1				61		pnb					0cs..	22928
73-DAAE-k	shithlou					1				61		pnb					0cs..	22929
73-DAAE-l	singson					1				61		pnb					0cs..	22930
73-DAAE-m	gang-te	2	2	74,630	97,736	1	85.86	100	C	61	Gangte	PNB	1952-1955	1959	1991		0cs..	22931
73-DAAE-n	sim-te	1	1	22,402	29,403	1	95.00	100	C	61	Simte	PNB	1957		1992		0cs..	22935
73-DAAE-o	minat	1	1	32,717	41,690	1	5.00	37	A	61		pnb					0cs..	22936
73-DAAF	PAITE-CHIN cluster	2	3	69,115	89,874		84.87	100	C	68		PNB					0....	22937
73-DAAF-a	pai-te	2	2	58,396	76,216	0	85.76	100	C	68	Paite*	PNB	1940-1960	1951-1995	1971		0....	22938
73-DAAF-b	hai-te					0				68		pnb					0....	22939
73-DAAF-c	vui-te					0				68		pnb					0....	22940
73-DAAF-d	siyin	1	1	10,719	13,658	0	80.00	100	C	68	Chin, Siyin	PNb		1995			0....	22941
73-DB	WEST KUKI-CHIN chain	1	2	43,486	57,076		7.87	22	A	4		...					0....	22942
73-DBA	WEST KUKI-CHIN net	1	2	43,486	57,076		7.87	22	A	4		...					0....	22943
73-DBAA	CHIRU cluster	1	2	43,486	57,076		7.87	22	A	4		...					0....	22944
73-DBAA-a	Proper chiru	1	2	43,486	57,076	0	7.87	22	A	4		...					0....	22945
73-DC	KUKI-CHIN-CENTRAL chain	4	19	849,460	1,110,287		88.40	98	C	62		PNB					0asu.	22947
73-DCA	LUSHAI-PANKHU net	4	6	630,102	826,558		99.27	100	C	62		PNB					0asu.	22948
73-DCAA	LUSHAI-MIZO cluster	4	4	574,352	753,154		99.35	100	C	62		PNB					0asu.	22949
73-DCAA-a	lushai	4	4	574,352	753,154	4	99.35	100	C	62	Lushai	PNB	1898-1956	1916-1986	1959-1995		0asu.	22950
73-DCAB	HMAR cluster	1	1	52,508	68,917		98.70	100	C	61		PNB					0....	22961
73-DCAB-a	hmar	1	1	52,508	68,917	0	98.70	100	C	61	Hmar	PNB	1920-1953	1946-1977	1968-1987		0....	22962
73-DCAC	PANKHU cluster	1	1	3,242	4,487		95.00	100	C	2		...					0....	22963
73-DCAC-a	pankhu	1	1	3,242	4,487	0	95.00	100	C	2		...					0....	22964
73-DCB	HAKA-SHONSHE net	3	6	164,763	210,610		59.02	99	B	61		PNB					0as..	22965
73-DCBA	HAKA-CHIN cluster	3	6	164,763	210,610		59.02	99	B	61		PNB					0as..	22966
73-DCBA-a	haka	3	3	118,493	151,509	4	59.75	99	B	61	Chin: Haka*	PNB	1920-1959	1940-1995	1978-1987		0cs..	22967
73-DCBA-b	lai					1				61		pnb					0cs..	22968
73-DCBA-c	klangklang					1				61		pnb					0cs..	22969
73-DCBA-d	banjogi	1	1	43,778	55,784	1	60.00	100	C	61	Chin: Zotung*	Pnb	1951				0cs..	22970
73-DCBA-e	zokhua					1				61		pnb					0cs..	22971
73-DCBA-f	shonshe					1				61		pnb					0cs..	22972

Continued overleaf

Table 9-13 continued

Code 1	REFERENCE NAME / Autoglossonym 2	Coun 3	Peo 4	Mother-tongue speakers in 2000 5	in 2025 6	Media radio 7	CHURCH AC% 8	E% 9	Wld 10	Tr 11	Biblioglossonym 12	Print 13-15	P-activity 16	N-activity 17	B-activity 18	J-year 19	Jayuh 20-24	Ref 25
73-DCC	**BAWM-CHIN net**	3	3	16,095	21,582		96.53	100	C	61		PNB					0as..	22973
73-DCCA	BAWM-CHIN cluster	3	3	16,095	21,582		96.53	100	C	61		PNB					0as..	22974
73-DCCA-a	bawm	3	3	16,095	21,582	0	96.53	100	C	61	Bawm*	PNB	1961	1977	1989		0as..	22975
73-DCD	**SENTHANG-CHIN net**	1	1	23,025	29,339		11.00	31	A	4		...					0....	22976
73-DCDA	SENTHANG-CHIN cluster	1	1	23,025	29,339		11.00	31	A	4		...					0....	22977
73-DCDA-a	senthang	1	1	23,025	29,339	0	11.00	31	A	4		...					0....	22978
73-DCE	**TAWR-CHIN net**	1	1	835	1,064		13.05	36	A	4		...					0....	22979
73-DCEA	TAWR-CHIN cluster	1	1	835	1,064		13.05	36	A	4		...					0....	22980
73-DCEA-a	tawr	1	1	835	1,064	0	13.05	36	A	4		...					0....	22981
73-DCF	**DARLONG-CHIN net**	2	2	10,640	14,334		67.38	93	C	41		PN.					0....	22982
73-DCFA	DARLONG cluster	2	2	10,640	14,334		67.38	93	C	41		PN.					0....	22983
73-DCFA-a	darlong	2	2	10,640	14,334	0	67.38	93	C	41	Darlong	PN.		1996			0....	22984
73-DCG	**LANGET-CHIN net**	1	1	4,000	6,800		70.00	98	C	0		...					0....	22985
73-DCGA	LANGET cluster	1	1	4,000	6,800		70.00	98	C	0		...					0....	22986
73-DCGA-a	langet	1	1	4,000	6,800	0	70.00	98	C	0		...					0....	22987
73-DD	OLD-KUKI chain	3	16	398,803	528,559		36.39	74	B	71		PNB					1.s..	22988
73-DDA	**LAMKANG-ANAL net**	2	3	31,930	41,664		63.24	92	C	51		PN.					0....	22989
73-DDAA	LAMKANG-NAGA cluster	1	1	9,630	12,639		40.00	75	B	41		PN.					0....	22990
73-DDAA-a	lamkang	1	1	9,630	12,639	0	40.00	75	B	41	Lamkang	PN.	1993	1995			0....	22991
73-DDAB	ANAL-NAGA cluster	2	2	22,300	29,025		73.28	100	C	51		PN.					0....	22992
73-DDAB-a	anal	2	2	22,300	29,025	0	73.28	100	C	51	Anal	PN.	1949-1983	1983			0....	22993
73-DDAB-b	namfau					0				51		pn.					0....	22994
73-DDAB-c	laizo					0				51		pn.					0....	22995
73-DDAB-d	mulsom					0				51		pn.					0....	22996
73-DDAB-e	moyon-monshang					0				51		pn.					0....	22997
73-DDB	**KOM-KOLHRENG net**	1	1	14,495	19,025		64.00	100	C	61		PNB					0....	22998
73-DDBA	KOM-KOLHRENG cluster	1	1	14,495	19,025		64.00	100	C	61		PNB					0....	22999
73-DDBA-a	kom	1	1	14,495	19,025	0	64.00	100	C	61	Kom Rem	PNB	1954-1960	1976-1977	1996		0....	23000
73-DDBA-b	kolh-reng					0				61		pnb					0....	23001
73-DDC	**OLD-KUKI-CENTRAL net**	2	2	632	812		33.70	55	B	4		...					0....	23002
73-DDCA	PURUM cluster	1	1	429	546		11.89	33	A	4		...					0....	23003
73-DDCA-a	purum	1	1	429	546	0	11.89	33	A	4		...					0....	23004
73-DDCB	AIMOL-LANGRONG cluster	1	1	203	266		79.80	100	C	4		...					0....	23005
73-DDCB-a	aimol	1	1	203	266	0	79.80	100	C	4		...					0....	23006
73-DDCB-b	langrong					0				4		...					0....	23007
73-DDD	**WEST OLD-KUKI net**	3	8	318,401	422,004		27.72	68	B	71		PNB					1.s..	23008
73-DDDA	NORTHWEST KUKI cluster	2	3	46,273	60,437		22.86	58	B	57		PN.					0....	23009
73-DDDA-a	hrangkhol	2	2	26,507	34,493	0	25.00	60	B	57	Hrangkhol	PN.		1996			0....	23010
73-DDDA-b	hadem					0				57		pn.					0....	23011
73-DDDA-c	biete	1	1	19,766	25,944	0	20.00	56	B	57	Biate*	PN.	1949-1991	1985-1991			0....	23012
73-DDDB	SOUTHWEST KUKI cluster	3	5	272,128	361,567		28.54	70	B	71	Kuki	PNB	1924	1942	1971		1.s..	23013
73-DDDB-a	falam	3	5	272,128	361,567	0	28.54	70	B	71	Chin: Falam*	PNB	1933-1964	1951-1973	1991	1998	1.s..	23014
73-DDDB-b	zahao-lyen-lyem					0				71		pnb					1.s..	23015
73-DDDB-c	zanniat					0				71	Chin: Zanniat	Pnb	1972				1.s..	23018
73-DDDB-d	tashon-shunkla					0				71		pnb					1.s..	23019
73-DDDB-e	laizo					0				71		pnb					1.s..	23022
73-DDDB-f	khualshim					0				71		pnb					1.s..	23023
73-DDDB-g	lente					0				71		pnb					1.s..	23024
73-DDDB-h	chorei					0				71		pnb					1.s..	23025
73-DDDB-i	chari-chong					0				71		pnb					1.s..	23026
73-DDDB-j	kaipang					0				71		pnb					1.s..	23027
73-DDDB-k	kalai					0				71		pnb					1.s..	23028
73-DDDB-l	khelma					0				71		pnb					1.s..	23029
73-DDDB-m	mursum					0				71		pnb					1.s..	23030
73-DDDB-n	rupini					0				71		pnb					1.s..	23031
73-DDDB-o	shekasip					0				71		pnb					1.s..	23032
73-DDDB-p	South luhuppa					0				71		pnb					1.s..	23033
73-DDE	**VAIPHEI-KUKI net**	2	2	29,345	38,254		83.03	100	C	41		PN.					0....	23034
73-DDEA	VAIPHEI cluster	2	2	29,345	38,254		83.03	100	C	41		PN.					0....	23035
73-DDEA-a	vaiphei	2	2	29,345	38,254	0	83.03	100	C	41	Vaiphei	PN.	1917-1989	1957-1989			0....	23036
73-DDF	**KYAO-KUKI net**	1	1	4,000	6,800		70.00	98	C	0		...					0....	23037
73-DDFA	KYAO cluster	1	1	4,000	6,800		70.00	98	C	0		...					0....	23038
73-DDFA-a	kyao	1	1	4,000	6,800	0	70.00	98	C	0		...					0....	23039
73-DE	SOUTH KUKI-CHIN chain	4	14	328,508	428,939		51.55	85	B	62		PNB					0.s..	23040
73-DEA	**KHUMI-KHAMI net**	3	4	172,213	221,045		60.00	100	B	41		PN.					0.s..	23041
73-DEAA	KHUMI-AWA-CHIN cluster	1	1	36,489	46,496		60.00	100	B	24		P..					0....	23042
73-DEAA-a	khumi-awa	1	1	36,489	46,496	0	60.00	100	B	24	Chin: Khumi, Awa*	P..	1939				0....	23043
73-DEAB	KHUMI-CHIN cluster	3	3	135,724	174,549		60.00	100	B	41		PN.					0.s..	23046
73-DEAB-a	khumi	3	3	135,724	174,549	0	60.00	100	B	41	Chin: Khumi*	PN.	1935-1950	1959-1991			0.s..	23047
73-DEAB-b	khimi					0				41		pn.					0.s..	23048
73-DEAB-c	yindi					0				41		pn.					0.s..	23049
73-DEAB-d	khami					0				41		pn.					0.s..	23050
73-DEAB-e	ngala					0				41		pn.					0.s..	23051
73-DEAB-f	matu					0				41		pn.					0.s..	23052
73-DEB	**LAKHER net**	2	2	35,528	46,160		95.00	100	C	62		PNB					0....	23053
73-DEBA	MARA-CHIN cluster	2	2	35,528	46,160		95.00	100	C	62		PNB					0....	23054
73-DEBA-a	mara	2	2	35,528	46,160	0	95.00	100	C	62	Mara*	PNB	1912-1954	1928-1939	1956		0....	23055
73-DEBA-b	zao					0				62		pnb					0....	23056
73-DEBA-c	tlongsai					0				62		pnb					0....	23057
73-DEBA-d	hlawthai					0				62		pnb					0....	23058
73-DEBA-e	sabeu					0				62		pnb					0....	23059
73-DEC	**MUN-CHIN net**	1	1	20,000	34,000		15.00	42	A	2		...					0....	23060
73-DECA	MUN-CHIN cluster	1	1	20,000	34,000		15.00	42	A	2		...					0....	23061
73-DECA-a	mün					0				2		...					0....	23062
73-DECA-b	ng'men					0				2		...					0....	23063
73-DED	**DAAI-CHIN net**	1	1	30,035	38,272		12.00	43	A	57		PN.					0....	23064
73-DEDA	DAAI-CHIN cluster	1	1	30,035	38,272		12.00	43	A	57		PN.					0....	23065
73-DEDA-a	daai	1	1	30,035	38,272	0	12.00	43	A	57	Dai Chin*	PN.		1996			0....	23066

Continued opposite

Table 9-13 continued

Code 1	REFERENCE NAME / Autoglossonym 2	Coun 3	Peo 4	Mother-tongue speakers in 2000 5	in 2025 6	Media radio 7	CHURCH AC% 8	E% 9	Wld 10	Tr 11	Biblioglossonym 12	SCRIPTURES Print 13-15	P-activity 16	N-activity 17	B-activity 18	J-year 19	Jayuh 20-24	Ref 25
73-DEE	**ASHO-CHIN net**	4	5	27,347	34,178		44.00	81	B	42		PN.					0.s..	23070
73-DEEA	ASHO-CHIN cluster	4	5	27,347	34,178		44.00	81	B	42		PN.					0.s..	23071
73-DEEA-a	chittagong-asho					1				42		pn.					0.s..	23072
73-DEEA-b	shendu	2	2	4,500	6,011	1	7.67	32	A	42		pn.					0.s..	23073
73-DEEA-c	asho	3	3	22,847	28,167	4	51.16	90	B	42	Chin: Asho*	PN.	1921-1986	1954			0.s..	23074
73-DEEA-d	thayetmyo					1				42		pn.					0.s..	23075
73-DEEA-e	minbu					1				42		pn.					0.s..	23076
73-DEEA-f	lemyo					1				42		pn.					0.s..	23077
73-DEEA-g	khyang					1				42		pn.					0.s..	23078
73-DEEA-h	saingbaun					1				42		pn.					0.s..	23079
73-DEEA-i	sandoway					1				42		pn.					0.s..	23080
73-DEF	**CHITBON-CHIN net**	1	1	24,794	31,594		10.00	36	A	3		...					0....	23081
73-DEFA	CHITBON-CHIN cluster	1	1	24,794	31,594		10.00	36	A	3		...					0....	23082
73-DEFA-a	chitbon	1	1	24,794	31,594	0	10.00	36	A	3		...					0....	23083
73-DEFA-b	ng'men					0				3		...						23087
73-DEG	**NGAWN-CHIN net**	1	1	18,591	23,690		60.00	100	C	23		P..					0....	23088
73-DEGA	NGAWN-CHIN cluster	1	1	18,591	23,690		60.00	100	C	23		P..					0....	23089
73-DEGA-a	ngawn	1	1	18,591	23,690	0	60.00	100	C	23	Chin: Ngawn*	P..	1951				0....	23090
73-DF	LEPCHAIC chain	3	3	79,559	124,337		2.25	30	A	41		PN.					1....	23091
73-DFA	**LEPCHAIC net**	3	3	79,559	124,337		2.25	30	A	41		PN.					1....	23092
73-DFAA	LEPCHA-ILAMMU cluster	3	3	79,559	124,337		2.25	30	A	41		PN.					1....	23093
73-DFAA-a	lepcha	3	3	79,559	124,337	0	2.25	30	A	41	Lepcha	PN.	1845-1989	1989			1....	23094
73-DFAA-b	ilam-mu					0				41		pn.					1....	23100
73-DFAA-c	tamsang-mu					0				41		pn.					1....	23101
73-DFAA-d	rengjong-mu					0				41		pn.					1....	23102
74	**MIRIC zone**	2	10	1,207,739	1,575,404		1.63	28	A	57		PN.					0....	23103
74-A	**MIRISH set**	2	10	1,207,739	1,575,404		1.63	28	A	57		PN.					0....	23104
74-AA	MIRISH chain	2	10	1,207,739	1,575,404		1.63	28	A	57		PN.					0....	23105
74-AAA	**ABOR net**	2	3	604,221	783,340		2.15	34	A	51		PN.					0....	23106
74-AAAA	ABOR cluster	2	3	604,221	783,340		2.15	34	A	51		PN.					0....	23107
74-AAAA-a	adi	2	2	551,713	714,423	0	1.92	34	A	51	Adi	PN.	1932-1986	1988			0....	23108
74-AAAA-b	miri					0				51		pn.					0....	23109
74-AAAA-c	galong	1	1	52,508	68,917	0	4.55	34	A	51	Galong	pn.		*			0....	23110
74-AAB	**NISI-APATANI net**	1	2	297,307	390,220		2.04	33	A	57		PN.					0....	23111
74-AABA	NISI-APATANI cluster	1	2	297,307	390,220		2.04	33	A	57		PN.					0....	23112
74-AABA-a	nisi	1	1	273,993	359,620	0	1.78	34	A	57	Nishi*	PN.	1957-1982	1995			0....	23113
74-AABA-b	aka-lel					0				57		pn.					0....	23117
74-AABA-c	apatani	1	1	23,314	30,600	0	5.10	30	A	57		pn.					0....	23118
74-AABA-d	tagen					0				57		pn.					0....	23119
74-AABA-e	tanang					0				57		pn.					0....	23120
74-AAC	**YANOIC net**	1	1	4,000	6,800		2.00	18	A	0		...					0....	23121
74-AACA	YANO cluster	1	1	4,000	6,800		2.00	18	A	0		...					0....	23122
74-AACA-a	yano					0				0		...					0....	23123
74-AAD	**LHO-PA net**	2	2	248,081	323,999		0.00	7	A	20		...					0....	23124
74-AADA	LHO-PA cluster	2	2	248,081	323,999		0.00	7	A	20		...					0....	23125
74-AADA-a	luo-ba	2	2	248,081	323,999	0	0.00	7	A	20		...					0....	23126
74-AAE	**MISHMI net**	1	3	54,130	71,045		1.00	20	A	4		...					0....	23130
74-AAEA	DIGARO-MIJU cluster	1	3	54,130	71,045		1.00	20	A	4		...					0....	23131
74-AAEA-a	digaro	1	1	34,870	45,767	0	1.00	18	A	4		...					0....	23132
74-AAEA-b	miju	1	1	10,137	13,304	0	1.00	24	A	4		...					0....	23137
74-AAEA-c	chulikata	1	1	9,123	11,974	0	1.00	21	A	4		...					0....	23140
75	**KACHINIC zone**	4	7	1,139,191	1,438,567		44.92	81	B	71		PNB					2as..	23143
75-A	**JINGPHO-KADO set**	4	7	1,139,191	1,438,567		44.92	81	B	71		PNB					2as..	23144
75-AA	JINGHPO-TAMAN chain	3	4	854,657	1,083,377		58.64	99	B	71		PNB					2as..	23145
75-AAA	**JINGPHO net**	3	4	834,657	1,049,377		59.09	99	B	71		PNB					2as..	23146
75-AAAA	JINGPHO cluster	3	4	834,657	1,049,377		59.09	99	B	71		PNB					2as..	23147
75-AAAA-a	jing-pho	3	4	834,657	1,049,377	5	59.09	99	B	71	Kachin: Jinghpaw*	PNB	1895-1912	1912	1927	1995	2as..	23148
75-AAAA-b	hka-ku					1				71		pnb					1cs..	23153
75-AAAA-c	kauri					1				71		pnb					1cs..	23154
75-AAAA-d	dzili					1				71		pnb					1cs..	23155
75-AAB	**TAMANIC net**	1	1	20,000	34,000		40.00	77	B	0		...					0....	23156
75-AABA	TAMAN cluster	1	1	20,000	34,000		40.00	77	B	0		...					0....	23157
75-AABA-a	taman	1	1	20,000	34,000	0	40.00	77	B	0		...					0....	23158
75-AB	LUIC chain	3	3	284,534	355,190		3.71	28	A	24		P..					0....	23159
75-ABA	**LUIC net**	3	3	284,534	355,190		3.71	28	A	24		P..					0....	23160
75-ABAA	KADO cluster	3	3	284,534	355,190		3.71	28	A	24		P..					0....	23161
75-ABAA-a	kado	3	3	284,534	355,190	0	3.71	28	A	24	Kadu*	P..	1939				0....	23162
75-ABAA-b	ganaan					0				24		p..					0....	23169
75-ABAA-c	andro					0				24		p..					0....	23170
75-ABAA-d	sengmai					0				24		p..					0....	23171
75-ABAA-e	chakpa					0				24		p..					0....	23172
75-ABAA-f	phayeng					0				24		p..					0....	23173
76	**NUNGIC zone**	3	15	674,278	805,366		12.32	33	A	61		PNB					0.s..	23174
76-A	**NUNGIC set**	3	11	276,826	344,835		29.86	64	B	61		PNB					0.s..	23175
76-AA	NUNG-NORRA chain	3	11	276,826	344,835		29.86	64	B	61		PNB					0.s..	23176
76-AAA	**NUNG-RAWANG net**	3	7	257,000	320,679		31.74	67	B	61		PNB					0.s..	23177
76-AAAA	NUNG cluster	2	4	73,757	92,148		47.04	74	B	4		...					0.s..	23178
76-AAAA-a	nung	2	2	10,304	12,036	0	5.08	25	A	4		...					0.s..	23179
76-AAAA-b	tulung	2	2	63,453	80,112	0	53.86	82	B	4		...					0.s..	23189
76-AAAB	RAWANG cluster	3	3	183,243	228,531		25.58	64	B	61		PNB					0....	23190
76-AAAB-a	rawang	3	3	183,243	228,531	4	25.58	64	B	61	Rawang	PNB	1952-1963	1974-1981	1986		0....	23191

Continued overleaf

Table 9-13 continued

Code 1	REFERENCE NAME / Autoglossonym 2	Coun 3	Peo 4	Mother-tongue speakers in 2000 5	in 2025 6	Media radio 7	AC% 8	E% 9	Wld 10	Tr 11	Biblioglossonym 12	Print 13-15	P-activity 16	N-activity 17	B-activity 18	J-year 19	Jayuh 20-24	Ref 25
76-AAB	**NORRA-LAMA net**	2	4	19,826	24,156		5.49	25	A	4		...					0....	23213
76-AABA	NORRA-LAMA cluster	2	4	19,826	24,156	0	5.49	25	A	4		...					0....	23214
76-AABA-a	norra	2	2	12,242	14,871	0	1.75	21	A	4		...					0....	23215
76-AABA-b	byabe					0				4		...					0....	23216
76-AABA-c	kizolo					0				4		...					0....	23217
76-AABA-d	lama	2	2	7,584	9,285	0	11.54	32	A	4		...					0....	23218
76-B	**GYARONGIC set**	1	1	111,231	128,884		0.03	8	A	20		...					0....	23219
76-BA	GYARONGIC chain	1	1	111,231	128,884		0.03	8	A	20		...					0....	23220
76-BAA	**GYARONG net**	1	1	111,231	128,884		0.03	8	A	20		...					0....	23221
76-BAAA	GYARONG cluster	1	1	111,231	128,884		0.03	8	A	20		...					0....	23222
76-BAAA-a	jiarong	1	1	111,231	128,884	0	0.03	8	A	20		...					0....	23223
76-C	**QIANGIC set**	1	2	228,901	265,230		0.11	11	A	20		...					0....	23227
76-CA	QIANGIC chain	1	2	228,901	265,230		0.11	11	A	20		...					0....	23228
76-CAA	**QIANG-DZORGAI net**	1	2	228,901	265,230		0.11	11	A	20		...					0....	23229
76-CAAA	QIANG cluster	1	2	228,901	265,230		0.11	11	A	20		...					0....	23230
76-CAAA-a	mawo					0				20		...					0....	23231
76-CAAA-b	taoping					0				20		...					0....	23232
76-CAAA-c	lofuchai					0				20		...					0....	23233
76-CAAA-d	wagsod					0				20		...					0....	23234
76-CAAA-e	dzorgai					0				20		...					0....	23235
76-CAAA-f	kortse					0				20		...					0....	23236
76-CAAA-g	pingfang					0				20		...					0....	23237
76-CAAA-h	thochu					0				20		...					0....	23238
76-D	**PRIMMIC set**	1	1	57,320	66,417		0.20	15	A	2		...					0....	23239
76-DA	PRIMMIC chain	1	1	57,320	66,417		0.20	15	A	2		...					0....	23240
76-DAA	**PRIMMI net**	1	1	57,320	66,417		0.20	15	A	2		...					0....	23241
76-DAAA	PRIMMI cluster	1	1	57,320	66,417		0.20	15	A	2		...					0....	23242
76-DAAA-a	p'umi	1	1	57,320	66,417	0	0.20	15	A	2		...					0....	23243
76-DAAA-b	jing-hua					0				2		...					0....	23245
77	**LOLO-BURMIC zone**	11	94	48,155,382	59,575,889		3.39	51	B	72		PNB					4Asu.	23246
77-A	**LOLO-BURMIC set**	11	31	30,920,865	39,425,044		0.92	57	B	72		PNB					4Asu.	23247
77-AA	BURMIC chain	11	31	30,920,865	39,425,044		0.92	57	B	72		PNB					4Asu.	23248
77-AAA	**NORTH BURMIC net**	4	11	378,982	464,923		4.13	27	A	41		PN.					0....	23249
77-AAAA	HPON cluster	3	3	4,581	6,381		1.55	21	A	4		...					0....	23250
77-AAAA-a	hpon	3	3	4,581	6,381	0	1.55	21	A	4		...					0....	23251
77-AAAB	ACHANG cluster	2	2	32,959	38,439		8.79	36	A	41		PN.					0....	23256
77-AAAB-a	achang	2	2	32,959	38,439	0	8.79	36	A	41	Achang	PN.		1992			0....	23257
77-AAAB-b	maingtha					0				41		pn.					0....	23260
77-AAAC	MARU cluster	2	6	341,442	420,103		3.71	26	A	37	Maru	P..	1940				0....	23261
77-AAAC-a	lawng					0				37	Maru	P..	1940				0....	23262
77-AAAC-b	lashi	2	2	108,091	133,359	0	0.04	17	A	37		p..					0....	23272
77-AAAC-c	atsi	2	2	94,598	111,541	0	5.35	26	A	37	Atsi	P..	1939				0....	23275
77-AAB	**SOUTH BURMIC net**	9	20	30,541,883	38,960,121		0.88	58	B	72		PNB					4Asu.	23279
77-AABA	BURMESE cluster	9	20	30,541,883	38,960,121		0.88	58	B	72		PNB					4Asu.	23280
77-AABA-a	bama	9	11	26,229,788	33,445,273	6	0.90	62	B	72	Burmese	PNB	1815-1985	1832-1987	1835-1995	1989	4Asu.	23281
77-AABA-b	arakan	3	4	2,389,041	3,064,378	1	1.02	36	A	72	Maghi*	Pnb	1914			1997	1csu.	23287
77-AABA-c	intha	1	1	178,504	227,460	1	0.10	25	A	72		pnb					1csu.	23292
77-AABA-d	toru	1	1	560,935	714,777	1	0.50	33	A	72		pnb					1csu.	23293
77-AABA-e	tawe-tavo					1				72		pnb					1csu.	23297
77-AABA-f	mergui					1				72		pnb					1csu.	23300
77-AABA-g	yangbye	1	1	1,025,093	1,306,235	1	0.50	28	A	72		pnb					1csu.	23303
77-AABA-h	chaungtha	1	1	153,961	196,186	1	0.10	25	A	72		pnb					1csu.	23304
77-AABA-i	palu	1	1	4,561	5,812	1	0.39	33	A	72		pnb					1csu.	23305
77-B	**LOLO set**	5	63	17,234,517	20,150,845		7.83	39	A	61		PNB					4as..	23306
77-BA	NORTH LOLO chain	5	19	6,003,994	6,990,552		13.28	43	A	61		PNB					4rs..	23307
77-BAA	**NORTH YI-LOLO net**	2	3	45,961	56,613		1.07	19	A	4		...					0....	23308
77-BAAA	LOLO-OUTER-NORTH cluster	2	3	45,961	56,613		1.07	19	A	4		...					0....	23309
77-BAAA-a	thongho					0				4		...					0....	23310
77-BAAA-b	pakishan					0				4		...					0....	23311
77-BAAA-c	kang-siang-ying	2	2	43,310	53,541	0	1.10	19	A	4		...					0....	23312
77-BAAA-d	kiaokio					0				4		...					0....	23313
77-BAAA-e	nee					0				4		...					0....	23314
77-BAAA-f	laichau					0				4		...					0....	23315
77-BAAA-g	tudza					0				4		...					0....	23316
77-BAAA-h	nuoku					0				4		...					0....	23317
77-BAAA-i	liangshan					0				4		...					0....	23318
77-BAAA-j	p'ou-la					0				4		...					0....	23319
77-BAAA-k	sani					0				4		...					0....	23320
77-BAB	**NAXI-LOLO net**	1	1	309,579	358,711		1.00	23	A	24		P..					0....	23321
77-BABA	NAXI cluster	1	1	309,579	358,711		1.00	23	A	24		P..					0....	23322
77-BABA-a	naxi	1	1	309,579	358,711	0	1.00	23	A	24	Naxi	P..	1932				0....	23323
77-BAC	**LISU-LOLO net**	3	6	892,316	1,051,837		74.53	97	C	61		PNB					4rs..	23326
77-BACA	LISU cluster	3	6	892,316	1,051,837		74.53	97	C	61		PNB					4rs..	23327
77-BACA-a	lisu	3	4	867,680	1,022,764	4	76.42	99	C	61	Lisu: Central*	PNB	1912-1950	1938-1978	1986	1996	4rs..	23328
77-BACA-b	taku	1	1	4,561	5,812	1	39.99	92	B	61		pnb					1cs..	23337
77-BACA-c	jino	1	1	20,075	23,261	1	1.00	24	A	61		pnb					1cs..	23338
77-BAD	**NASU-LOLO net**	3	4	1,270,485	1,476,968		2.38	38	A	44		PN.					1....	23339
77-BADA	NASU cluster	3	4	1,270,485	1,476,968		2.38	38	A	44		PN.					1....	23340
77-BADA-a	nasŏ	3	4	1,270,485	1,476,968	0	2.38	38	A	44	Nosu*	PN.	1913-1926	1948		1998	1....	23341
77-BAE	**SAMEI-LOLO net**	1	1	1,263	1,463		0.48	19	A	4		...					0....	23345
77-BAEA	SAMEI cluster	1	1	1,263	1,463		0.48	19	A	4		...					0....	23346
77-BAEA-a	samei					0				4		...					0....	23347
77-BAF	**KADUO-LOLO net**	1	1	14,000	23,800		1.00	16	A	0		...					0....	23348

Continued opposite

Table 9-13 continued

Code 1	REFERENCE NAME / Autoglossonym 2	Coun 3	Peo 4	Mother-tongue speakers in 2000 5	in 2025 6	Media radio 7	CHURCH AC% 8	E% 9	Wld 10	Tr 11	Biblioglossonym 12	SCRIPTURES Print 13-15	P-activity 16	N-activity 17	B-activity 18	J-year 19	Jayuh 20-24	Ref 25
77-BAFA	KADUO cluster	1	1	14,000	23,800		1.00	16	A	0		. . .					0. . . .	23349
77-BAFA-a	kaduo	1	1	14,000	23,800	0	1.00	16	A	0		. . .					0. . . .	23350
77-BAG	**YI-CENTRAL net**	1	4	3,470,390	4,021,160		2.84	34	A	20		. . .					0. . . .	23351
77-BAGA	YI-CENTRAL cluster	1	4	3,470,390	4,021,160		2.84	34	A	20		. . .					0. . . .	23352
77-BAGA-a	yi	1	1	329,401	381,679	0	2.80	35	A	20		. . .					0. . . .	23353
77-BAGA-b	chökö					0				20		. . .					0. . . .	23354
77-BAGA-c	axi					0				20		. . .					0. . . .	23355
77-BAGA-d	lolopho					0				20		. . .					0. . . .	23356
77-BAGA-e	phupha					0				20		. . .					0. . . .	23357
77-BB	SOUTH LOLO chain	5	39	3,092,364	3,728,410		14.45	47	A	61		PNB					4a. . .	23358
77-BBA	**HANI-LAHU net**	5	30	3,016,024	3,609,818		14.77	48	A	61		PNB					4a. . .	23359
77-BBAA	HANI cluster	5	20	2,350,528	2,817,548		6.00	35	A	41		PN.					1. . . .	23360
77-BBAA-a	menghua	1	1	3,788	4,389	0	0.37	21	A	41		pn.					1. . . .	23361
77-BBAA-b	ako					0				41		pn.					1. . . .	23362
77-BBAA-c	asong					0				41		pn.					1. . . .	23363
77-BBAA-d	akha	5	5	398,962	492,973	0	10.67	48	A	41	Akha	PN.	1939-1991	1968-1987			1. . . .	23364
77-BBAA-e	phana	1	1	8,275	14,701	0	5.00	33	A	41		pn.					1. . . .	23369
77-BBAA-f	kaduo	2	2	13,578	20,845	0	15.26	38	A	41		pn.					1. . . .	23370
77-BBAA-g	pudu									41		pn.					1. . . .	23371
77-BBAA-h	sansu	2	2	17,187	20,441	0	3.53	25	A	41		pn.					1. . . .	23372
77-BBAA-i	mahei	2	2	24,389	29,618	0	3.45	25	A	41		pn.					1. . . .	23373
77-BBAA-j	biyo	1	1	111,358	129,031	0	2.00	25	A	41		pn.					1. . . .	23374
77-BBAA-k	honi	1	1	111,358	129,031	0	3.00	25	A	41		pn.					1. . . .	23375
77-BBAB	LAHU cluster	5	10	665,496	792,270		45.74	96	B	61		PNB					4a. . .	23376
77-BBAB-a	lahu	5	5	621,858	739,171	4	48.29	99	B	61	Lahu*	PNB	1924-1962	1932-1962	1989	1992	4a. . .	23377
77-BBAB-b	kutsung	3	3	21,890	26,846	1	9.42	48	A	61	Lahu Shi	pnb					1a. . .	23378
77-BBAB-c	na					1				61	Na-hsi	Pnb	1932				1c. . .	23379
77-BBAB-d	nyi					1				61		pnb					1c. . .	23380
77-BBAB-e	shehleh					1				61		pnb					1c. . .	23381
77-BBAB-f	laopang	2	2	21,748	26,253	1	9.36	41	A	61		pnb					1c. . .	23382
77-BBAB-g	laba					1				61		pnb					1c. . .	23383
77-BBB	**PHUNOI-BISU net**	4	6	45,358	66,517		1.00	19	A	5		. . .					0. . . .	23384
77-BBBA	PHUNOI cluster	2	2	34,012	53,153		1.00	18	A	2		. . .					0. . . .	23385
77-BBBA-a	phunoi	2	2	34,012	53,153	0	1.00	18	A	2		. . .					0. . . .	23386
77-BBBA-b	khoany-black					0				2		. . .					0. . . .	23389
77-BBBA-c	khoany-white					0				2		. . .					0. . . .	23390
77-BBBA-d	mung					0				2		. . .					0. . . .	23391
77-BBBA-e	hwethom					0				2		. . .					0. . . .	23392
77-BBBA-f	khaskhong					0				2		. . .					0. . . .	23393
77-BBBB	BISU-MPI cluster	3	4	11,346	13,364		1.01	20	A	5		. . .					0. . . .	23394
77-BBBB-a	bisu	2	2	7,719	8,974	1	1.01	16	A	5		. . .					0. . . .	23395
77-BBBB-b	mpi	1	1	2,573	3,047	5	1.01	30	A	5		. . .					0. . . .	23396
77-BBBB-c	pyen	1	1	1,054	1,343	1	1.04	23	A	5		. . .					0. . . .	23397
77-BBC	**SILA-LOLO net**	2	2	26,421	46,263		1.54	20	A	2		. . .					0. . . .	23398
77-BBCA	SILA cluster	2	2	26,421	46,263		1.54	20	A	2		. . .					0. . . .	23399
77-BBCA-a	sila	2	2	26,421	46,263	0	1.54	20	A	2		. . .					0. . . .	23400
77-BBD	**LOPI-LOLO net**	1	1	4,561	5,812		16.01	34	A	4		. . .					0. . . .	23401
77-BBDA	LOPI cluster	1	1	4,561	5,812		16.01	34	A	4		. . .					0. . . .	23402
77-BBDA-a	lopi	1	1	4,561	5,812	0	16.01	34	A	4		. . .					0. . . .	23403
77-BC	HSIFAN-LOLO chain	1	1	4,561	5,812		0.11	22	A	4		. . .					0a. . .	23404
77-BCA	**HSIFAN-LOLO net**	1	1	4,561	5,812		0.11	22	A	4		. . .					0a. . .	23405
77-BCAA	HSIFAN cluster	1	1	4,561	5,812		0.11	22	A	4		. . .					0a. . .	23406
77-BCAA-a	Proper hsifan	1	1	4,561	5,812	4	0.11	22	A	4		. . .					0a. . .	23407
77-BCAA-b	manyak					1				4		. . .					0c. . .	23408
77-BCAA-c	horpa					1				4		. . .					0c. . .	23409
77-BCAA-d	menia					1				4		. . .					0c. . .	23410
77-BCAA-e	muli					1				4		. . .					0c. . .	23411
77-BD	UGONG-LOLO chain	1	1	111	131		0.90	24	A	4		. . .					0. . . .	23412
77-BDA	**UGONG-LOLO net**	1	1	111	131		0.90	24	A	4		. . .					0. . . .	23413
77-BDAA	UGONG cluster	1	1	111	131		0.90	24	A	4		. . .					0. . . .	23414
77-BDAA-a	ugong	1	1	111	131	0	0.90	24	A	4		. . .					0. . . .	23415
77-BE	PSEUDO-NUNG chain	1	1	4,641	7,002		12.07	35	A	4		. . .					0. . . .	23419
77-BEA	**PSEUDO-NUNG net**	1	1	4,641	7,002		12.07	35	A	4		. . .					0. . . .	23420
77-BEAA	NUSU cluster	1	1	3,000	5,100		5.00	24	A	0		. . .					0. . . .	23421
77-BEAA-a	nusu	1	1	3,000	5,100	0	5.00	24	A	0		. . .					0. . . .	23422
77-BEAB	ZAUZOU cluster	1	1	1,641	1,902		24.98	55	B	4		. . .					0. . . .	23423
77-BEAB-a	zauzou	1	1	1,641	1,902	0	24.98	55	B	4		. . .					0. . . .	23424
77-BF	TUJIA-LOLO chain	1	1	6,352,681	7,360,886		0.40	32	A	20		. . .					0a. . .	23425
77-BFA	**TUJIA-LOLO net**	1	1	6,352,681	7,360,886		0.40	32	A	20		. . .					0a. . .	23426
77-BFAA	TUJIA cluster	1	1	6,352,681	7,360,886		0.40	32	A	20		. . .					0a. . .	23427
77-BFAA-a	tujia	1	1	6,352,681	7,360,886	0	0.40	32	A	20		. . .					0a. . .	23428
77-BG	BAI-HYBRID chain	1	1	1,776,165	2,058,052		4.50	32	A	20		. . .					0. . . .	23431
77-BGA	**BAI net**	1	1	1,776,165	2,058,052		4.50	32	A	20		. . .					0. . . .	23432
77-BGAA	BAI cluster	1	1	1,776,165	2,058,052		4.50	32	A	20		. . .					0. . . .	23433
77-BGAA-a	minchia	1	1	1,776,165	2,058,052	0	4.50	32	A	20	Bai	. . .					0. . . .	23434
77-BGAA-b	eryuan					0				20		. . .					0. . . .	23438
77-BGAA-c	hoking					0				20		. . .					0. . . .	23439
77-BGAA-d	tali					0				20		. . .					0. . . .	23440
78	**KARENIC zone**	2	24	4,941,211	6,242,664		38.93	90	B	72		PNB					3.su.	23441
78-A	**KARENIC set**	2	24	4,941,211	6,242,664		38.93	90	B	72		PNB					3.su.	23442
78-AA	KAREN chain	2	24	4,941,211	6,242,664		38.93	90	B	72		PNB					3.su.	23443
78-AAA	**PHO net**	2	6	2,390,091	3,032,004		35.02	88	B	72		PNB					3.su.	23444
78-AAAA	PA'O-KAREN cluster	2	2	709,189	903,625		34.99	81	B	57		PN.					0. . . .	23445
78-AAAA-a	pa'o	2	2	709,189	903,625	0	34.99	81	B	57	Pa'o*	PN.	1912-1964	1961			0. . . .	23446
78-AAAB	PWO-KAREN cluster	2	4	1,680,902	2,128,379	4	35.03	91	B	72		PNB					3.su.	23450
78-AAAB-a	pwo	2	2	1,604,767	2,038,210	4	35.98	93	B	72	Pwo Kayin*	PNB	1845-1867	1860-1996	1883-1885	1995	3.su.	23451
78-AAAB-b	leke					1				72		pnb					1.su.	23462

Continued overleaf

Table 9-13 continued

Code 1	REFERENCE NAME Autoglossonym 2	Coun 3	Peo 4	Mother-tongue speakers in 2000 5	in 2025 6	Media radio 7	AC% 8	E% 9	Wld 10	Tr 11	Biblioglossonym 12	Print 13-15	P-activity 16	N-activity 17	B-activity 18	J-year 19	Jayuh 20-24	Ref 25
78-AAAB-c	phlong					1				72		pnb					1.su.	23463
78-AAAB-d	pwo-hua-hin					1				72		pnb					1.su.	23464
78-AAAB-e	pwo-kanchana-buri	1	1	73,679	87,260	1	15.00	60	B	72	Karen, Pwo Kanchana Buri	pnb					1.su.	23465
78-AAAB-f	pwo-phrae	1	1	2,456	2,909	1	12.01	55	B	72	Karen, Northern Pwo	pnb					1.su.	23466
78-AAB	**SGAW-BWE net**	2	18	2,551,120	3,210,660		42.61	92	B	72		PNB					3.s..	23467
78-AABA	BREK-KAREN cluster	1	1	20,999	26,759		80.00	100	C	3		...					0....	23468
78-AABA-a	brek	1	1	20,999	26,759	0	80.00	100	C	3		...					0....	23469
78-AABB	WEST BWE-KAREN cluster	1	1	50,729	64,642		80.00	100	C	4		...					0....	23470
78-AABB-a	geba	1	1	50,729	64,642	0	80.00	100	C	4		...					0....	23471
78-AABB-b	blimaw					0				4		...					0....	23472
78-AABC	CENTRAL KAREN cluster	2	3	33,737	42,822		40.81	78	B	24		P..					0....	23473
78-AABC-a	bghai	2	2	21,718	27,507	4	24.66	65	B	24	Karen: Bghai*	P..	1857-1862				0....	23474
78-AABC-b	gekho	1	1	12,019	15,315	1	70.00	100	C	24		p..					0....	23477
78-AABD	EAST KAREN cluster	2	3	63,319	80,465		17.84	50	A	2		...					0....	23478
78-AABD-a	pa-daung	2	2	54,197	68,841	0	20.00	53	B	2		...					0....	23479
78-AABD-b	lahta	1	1	9,122	11,624	0	5.00	30	A	2		...					0....	23483
78-AABE	KAYAH-KAREN cluster	2	3	355,537	444,374		25.13	64	B	20		...					0....	23484
78-AABE-a	kayah	2	2	346,301	432,605	4	25.00	64	B	20	Kayah, Western*	...					0....	23485
78-AABE-b	yinbaw	1	1	9,236	11,769	1	30.00	56	B	20		...					0....	23486
78-AABF	SGAW-KAREN cluster	2	3	1,977,448	2,488,712		45.62	99	B	72		PNB					3.s..	23489
78-AABF-a	sgaw	2	2	1,970,743	2,480,168	4	45.69	99	B	72	Sgaw Kayin*	PNB	1839-1995	1843-1995	1853-1996	1994	3.s..	23490
78-AABF-b	pa-ku	1	1	6,705	8,544	1	25.00	71	B	72		pnb					1.s..	23494
78-AABG	MANUMANAW-KAREN cluster	1	1	5,660	7,213		80.00	100	C	4		...					0....	23500
78-AABG-a	manumanaw	1	1	5,660	7,213	0	80.00	100	C	4		...					0....	23501
78-AABH	YINTALE-KAREN cluster	1	1	9,122	11,624		5.00	27	A	4		...					0....	23502
78-AABH-a	yintale	1	1	9,122	11,624	0	5.00	27	A	4		...					0....	23503
78-AABI	ZAYEIN-KAREN cluster	1	1	11,763	14,989		20.00	46	A	4		...					0....	23504
78-AABI-a	zayein	1	1	11,763	14,989	0	20.00	46	A	4		...					0....	23505
78-AABJ	WEWAW-KAREN cluster	1	1	22,806	29,060		25.00	57	B	4		...					0....	23508
78-AABJ-a	wewaw	1	1	22,806	29,060	0	25.00	57	B	4		...					0....	23509
79	**SINITIC zone**	114	247	1,250,091,760	1,467,941,770		7.39	66	B	72		PNB					3Bsuh	23510
79-A	**SINITIC set**	114	247	1,250,091,760	1,467,941,770		7.39	66	B	72		PNB					3Bsuh	23511
79-AA	**HAN-YU chain**	114	247	1,250,091,760	1,467,941,770		7.39	66	B	72		PNB					3Bsuh	23512
79-AAA	**HAN-YU net**	114	247	1,250,091,760	1,467,941,770		7.39	66	B	72		PNB					3Bsuh	23513
79-AAAA	WEN-LI cluster	3	1	5,000,000	8,500,000		1.00	16	A	63		PNB					0....	23514
79-AAAA-a	Literary wen-li					0				63	Chinese: Wenli, Easy*	PNB	1810-1880	1814-1885	1822-1902		0....	23515
79-AAAA-b	Historical wen-li					0				63		pnb					0....	23516
79-AAAA-c	wen-li-M.					0				63		pnb					0....	23517
79-AAAB	NORTH HAN-YU cluster	94	114	882,103,493	1,022,896,564		7.49	67	B	72		PNB					2Bsuh	23518
79-AAAB-a	guan-hua					1				72		pnb					1csuh	23519
79-AAAB-b	bei-jing-hua	93	109	834,677,668	967,939,308	7	7.51	68	B	72		PNB					2Bsuh	23520
79-AAAB-c	dong-bei-hua					1				72		pnb					1csuh	23530
79-AAAB-d	jiao-liao-hua					1				72		pnb					1csuh	23539
79-AAAB-e	ji-lu-hua					1				72		pnb					1csuh	23543
79-AAAB-f	zhong-yuan-hua					1				72	Chinese: Shantung	Pnb	1892				1csuh	23557
79-AAAB-g	lan-yin-hua					1				72		pnb					1csuh	23577
79-AAAB-h	xinan-guan-hua					1				72		pnb					1csuh	23582
79-AAAB-i	jiang-huai					1				72		pnb					1csuh	23605
79-AAAB-j	nanping-hua					1				72		pnb					1csuh	23612
79-AAAB-k	jun-hua					1				72		pnb					1csuh	23613
79-AAAB-l	hui-zu	5	5	47,425,825	54,957,256	7	6.99	47	A	72		pnb					1Asuh	23616
79-AAAB-m	judeo-mandarin					1				72		pnb					1csuh	23623
79-AAAB-n	jinyu					1				72		pnb					1csuh	23624
79-AAAC	JIN cluster	1	1	20,000,000	34,000,000		5.00	24	A	0		...					0....	23625
79-AAAC-a	jin-hua					0				0		...					0....	23626
79-AAAD	WU cluster	6	9	94,898,420	109,957,552		12.90	78	B	63	Chinese, Wu	PNB	1847-1908	1868-1908	1908-1914	1991	1A...	23642
79-AAAD-a	hui-hua					1				63		pnb					1c...	23643
79-AAAD-b	tai-hu	5	5	20,069	23,777	6	14.37	73	B	63		pnb					1A...	23649
79-AAAD-c	tai-gao					1				63		pnb					1c...	23657
79-AAAD-d	tong-jing					1				63		pnb					1c...	23661
79-AAAD-e	shi-ling					1				63		pnb					1c...	23672
79-AAAD-f	wu-zhou					1				63		pnb					1c...	23678
79-AAAD-g	tai-zhou					1				63		pnb					1c...	23687
79-AAAD-h	qing-jiang-ou-jiang	2	2	19,303	20,077	6	4.33	57	B	63		PNb					1c...	23697
79-AAAD-i	chu-qu					1				63		pnb					1c...	23706
79-AAAE	XIANG cluster	2	2	44,287,725	51,330,879		2.01	41	A	32		...					1....	23710
79-AAAE-a	xiang	2	2	44,287,725	51,330,879	0	2.01	41	A	32		...				1998	1....	23711
79-AAAF	GAN cluster	1	1	25,271,968	29,282,768		6.00	46	A	20		...					0....	23715
79-AAAF-a	gan	1	1	25,271,968	29,282,768	0	6.00	46	A	20		...					0....	23716
79-AAAG	HAKKA cluster	24	25	37,068,376	43,473,118		2.34	60	B	71		PNB					1A...	23726
79-AAAG-a	Literary hakka	24	25	37,068,376	43,473,118	7	2.34	60	B	71	Chinese: Hakka, Wukingfu*	PNB	1995	1883-1993	1916	1991	1A...	23727
79-AAAG-b	ting-zhou					1				71		pnb					1c...	23745
79-AAAH	MIN-INLAND cluster	2	2	367,415	503,815		9.95	68	B	43		PN.					0A...	23753
79-AAAH-a	min-bei	2	2	367,415	503,815	6	9.95	68	B	43	Chinese, Min Bei	PN.	1934	1934			0A...	23754
79-AAAH-b	min-zhong					1				43		pn.					0c...	23763
79-AAAI	MIN-COASTAL cluster	4	4	12,682,603	14,701,017		10.06	76	B	63		PNB					1A...	23767
79-AAAI-a	man-hua					1				63		pnb					1c...	23768
79-AAAI-b	North min-dong					1				63	Chinese, Min Dong	PNB	1852	1856	1884-1905		1c...	23773
79-AAAI-c	South min-dong	4	4	12,682,603	14,701,017	6	10.06	76	B	63		PNB					1A...	23780
79-AAAI-d	pu-xian					1				63	Chinese: Hinghua*	PNB	1892	1900	1912		1c...	23796
79-AAAJ	MIN-NAN cluster	19	23	48,924,773	57,491,181		10.16	76	B	72	Chinese, Min Nan	PNB	1875-1916	1896-1974	1933		2A..h	23800
79-AAAJ-a	datian					1				72		pnb					1c..h	23801
79-AAAJ-b	North quan-zhang					1				72		pnb					1c..h	23802
79-AAAJ-c	North Central quan-zhang.					1				72		pnb					1c..h	23805
79-AAAJ-d	East Central quan-zhang.					1				72		pnb					1c..h	23807
79-AAAJ-e	Central quan-zhang.					1				72		pnb				1980	1c..h	23814
79-AAAJ-f	South Central quan-zhang.					1				72		pnb					1c..h	23826
79-AAAJ-g	quan-zhang-penghu					1				72		pnb					1c..h	23831
79-AAAJ-h	quan-zhang-taiwan	6	6	22,250	27,952	5	18.11	78	B	72	Taiwanese	PNB	1852	1873	1884	1980	1A..h	23832
79-AAAJ-i	chao-shan	12	15	47,142,100	55,082,966	6	8.18	75	B	72		PNB				1989	1A..h	23847
79-AAAJ-j	lei-zhou					1				72		pnb					1c..h	23859
79-AAAK	MIN-HAINAN cluster	5	5	6,142,877	7,201,894		0.51	43	A	32	Chinese: Hainan	P..	1891				1a...	23871
79-AAAK-a	changgan					0				32		p..					1c...	23872
79-AAAK-b	yaxian					0				32		p..					1c...	23875
79-AAAK-c	wanning	5	5	6,142,877	7,201,894	0	0.51	43	A	32		p..				1989	1a...	23879
79-AAAK-d	wenchang					0				32		p..					1c...	23882

Continued opposite

Table 9-13 continued

Code 1	REFERENCE NAME / Autoglossonym 2	Coun 3	Peo 4	Mother-tongue speakers in 2000 5	in 2025 6	Media radio 7	CHURCH AC% 8	E% 9	Wld 10	Tr 11	Biblioglossonym 12	SCRIPTURES Print 13-15	P–activity 16	N–activity 17	B–activity 18	J-year 19	Jayuh 20-24	Ref 25
79-AAAK-e	fu-cheng					0				32		p..					1c...	23886
79-AAAL	MIN-TRANSITIONAL cluster	5	6	171,653	237,783		10.24	75	B	63		PNB					0a...	23891
79-AAAL-a	shao-jiang	5	6	171,653	237,783	7	10.24	75	B	63	Chinese: Cantonese	PNB	1862	1877	1894		0a...	23892
79-AAAM	YUE-HAI cluster	48	52	66,361,674	77,495,128		4.65	75	B	61		PNB					3A.uh	23897
79-AAAM-a	Central yue	48	52	66,361,674	77,495,128	8	4.65	75	B	61	Chinese, Yue	PNB	1862-1903	1877-1996	1894-1981	1980	3A.uh	23898
79-AAAM-b	si-yi					1				61		pnb					1c.uh	23914
79-AAAM-c	gao-yang					1				61		pnb					1c.uh	23923
79-AAAM-d	wu-hua					1				61		pnb					1c.uh	23942
79-AAAM-e	gou-lou					1				61		pnb					1c.uh	23943
79-AAAM-f	qin-lian					1				61		pnb					1c.uh	23957
79-AAAM-g	yong-xun					1				61		pnb					1c.uh	23961
79-AAAN	ZHANGZHOU-MAI cluster	1	1	70,000	119,000		4.00	22	A	0		...					0....	23965
79-AAAN-a	zhangzhou-hua					0				0		...					0....	23966
79-AAAN-b	mai-hua					0				0		...					0....	23969
79-AAAO	PING-HUA cluster	1	1	5,000,000	8,500,000		4.00	22	A	0		...					0....	23973
79-AAAO-a	gui-bei					0				0		...					0....	23974
79-AAAO-b	gui-nan					0				0		...					0....	23985
79-AAAP	TU-HUA cluster	4	4	1,740,783	2,251,071		12.72	68	B	63		PNB					0A...	24002
79-AAAP-a	West miao-chinese					1				63		pnb					0c...	24003
79-AAAP-b	North miao-chinese					1				63		pnb					0c...	24006
79-AAAP-c	East miao-chinese	3	3	1,425,144	1,885,338	4	14.43	76	B	63	Chinese: Swatow*	PNB	1852-1925	1896	1922		0A...	24007
79-AAAP-d	xiang-hua	1	1	315,639	365,733	1	5.00	31	A	63		pnb					0c...	24012
79-AAAP-e	daoxian-hua					1				63		pnb					0c...	24018
79-AAAP-f	jiangyong-hua					1				63		pnb					0c...	24019
79-AAAP-g	jiang-hua					1				63		pnb					0c...	24020
79-AAAP-h	shaozhou-hua					1				63		pnb					0c...	24021
8	**SOUTHAMERICAN macrozone**	21	522	23,006,180	34,211,667		91.02	99	C	61		PNB					4As.h	24030
80	**CARIBIC zone**	15	59	207,999	319,082		75.68	97	C	51		PN.					4.s..	24031
80-A	**CARIBAN set**	15	59	207,999	319,082		75.68	97	C	51		PN.					4.s..	24032
80-AA	YUKPA chain	2	3	6,309	8,957		74.16	99	C	12		...					0....	24033
80-AAA	**YUKPA net**	2	3	6,309	8,957		74.16	99	C	12		...					0....	24034
80-AAAA	YUCPA cluster	2	2	6,157	8,738		75.00	100	C	12	Yukpa	...					0....	24035
80-AAAA-a	césar					0				12		...					0....	24036
80-AAAA-b	codazzi					0				12		...					0....	24037
80-AAAA-c	maracas					0				12		...					0....	24038
80-AAAA-d	iroka					0				12		...					0....	24039
80-AAAB	YAPRERÍA cluster	1	1	152	219		40.13	70	B	4		...					0....	24040
80-AAAB-a	yaprería	1	1	152	219	0	40.13	70	B	4		...					0....	24041
80-AAAC	COYAIMA cluster			0	0		0.00	0		9		...					0....	24042
80-AAAC-a	coyaima			0	0	0	0.00	0		9		...					0....	24043
80-AB	OPON-KARARE chain									0		...					0....	24044
80-ABA	**OPON-KARARE net**									0		...					0....	24045
80-ABAA	OPóN-CARARE cluster			0	0		0.00	0		0		...					0....	24046
80-ABAA-a	opón			0	0	0				0		...					0....	24047
80-ABAA-b	carare			0	0	0	0.00	0		0		...					0....	24048
80-AC	CARIB chain	12	13	146,117	236,505		82.99	100	C	51		PN.					4.s..	24049
80-ACA	**CARIB net**	12	13	146,117	236,505		82.99	100	C	51		PN.					4.s..	24050
80-ACAA	CARINYA cluster	12	13	146,117	236,505		82.99	100	C	51		PN.					4.s..	24051
80-ACAA-a	West carinya	1	1	2,417	3,478	1	59.99	99	B	51		pn.					1.s..	24052
80-ACAA-b	Central carib	5	5	15,484	22,993	1	64.76	99	C	51	Carib*	Pn.	1994				1.s..	24056
80-ACAA-c	East carib					1				51		pn.					1.s..	24057
80-ACAA-d	garifuna	7	7	128,216	210,034	4	85.63	100	C	51	Garifuna	PN.	1847-1968	1983-1994		1985	4.s..	24063
80-AD	PANARE chain	1	1	1,631	2,347		50.03	84	B	22		P..					0....	24064
80-ADA	**PANARE net**	1	1	1,631	2,347		50.03	84	B	22		P..					0....	24065
80-ADAA	ENYAPA cluster	1	1	1,631	2,347		50.03	84	B	22		P..					0....	24066
80-ADAA-a	e'nyapa	1	1	1,631	2,347	0	50.03	84	B	22	Panare	P..	1984				0....	24067
80-AE	MAPOYO-MAQUIRITARI chain	4	7	10,661	15,440		71.59	93	C	42		PN.					0....	24068
80-AEA	**MAPOYO-YABARANA net**	1	2	322	462		34.78	66	B	8		...					0....	24069
80-AEAA	MAPOYO-WANAI cluster	1	1	213	306		39.91	70	B	8		...					0....	24070
80-AEAA-a	mapoyo	1	1	213	306	0	39.91	70	B	8		...					0....	24071
80-AEAA-b	wanai					0				8		...					0....	24072
80-AEAB	YABARANA cluster	1	1	109	156		24.77	57	B	8		...					0....	24073
80-AEAB-a	Proper yabarana	1	1	109	156	0	24.77	57	B	8		...					0....	24074
80-AEAB-b	curasicana					0				8		...					0....	24075
80-AEAB-c	wokiare					0				8		...					0....	24076
80-AEB	**MAKIRITARI-GUAYANA net**	2	2	9,092	13,030		80.00	100	C	42		PN.					0....	24077
80-AEBA	MAQUIRITARI cluster	2	2	9,092	13,030		80.00	100	C	42		PN.					0....	24078
80-AEBA-a	Proper maquiritari	2	2	9,092	13,030	0	80.00	100	C	42	Maquiritare*	PN.	1957-1968	1970			0....	24079
80-AEBA-b	ye'cuana					0				42		pn.					0....	24080
80-AEBA-c	de'cuana					0				42		pn.					0....	24081
80-AEBA-d	cunuana					0				42		pn.					0....	24082
80-AEBA-e	pawana					0				42		pn.					0....	24083
80-AEBA-f	soto					0				42		pn.					0....	24084
80-AEBA-g	ihuruana					0				42		pn.					0....	24085
80-AEBA-h	maitsi					0				42		pn.					0....	24086
80-AEBB	WAYUMARá cluster			0	0		0.00	0		0		...					0....	24087
80-AEBB-a	wayumará			0	0	0	0.00	0		0		...					0....	24088
80-AEC	**TIVERICOTO-YAO net**									0		...					0....	24089
80-AECA	TIVERICOTO cluster			0	0		0.00	0		0		...					0....	24090
80-AECA-a	tivericoto			0	0	0	0.00	0		0		...					0....	24091
80-AECB	YAO cluster			0	0		0.00	0		0		...					0....	24092
80-AECB-a	yao			0	0	0	0.00	0		0		...					0....	24093
80-AED	**GUAYANA net**	3	3	1,247	1,948		19.73	52	B	41		PN.					0....	24094
80-AEDA	GUAYANA cluster	3	3	1,247	1,948		19.73	52	B	41		PN.					0....	24095
80-AEDA-a	wayâna	3	3	1,247	1,948	0	19.73	52	B	41	Wajana*	PN.	1968-1970	1979			0....	24096

Continued overleaf

Table 9-13 continued

Code 1	REFERENCE NAME Autoglossonym 2	Coun 3	Peo 4	Mother-tongue speakers in 2000 5	in 2025 6	Media radio 7	CHURCH AC% 8	E% 9	Wld 10	Tr 11	Biblioglossonym 12	Print 13-15	P-activity 16	N-activity 17	B-activity 18	J-year 19	Jayuh 20-24	Ref 25
80-AEDA-b	rucuyen					0				41		pn.					0....	24097
80-AEDA-c	urucena					0				41		pn.					0....	24098
80-AEDA-d	upuruí					0				41		pn.					0....	24099
80-AF	YAWAPERI-PEMONG chain	4	15	34,501	44,346		53.59	89	B	42		PN.					0....	24100
80-AFA	**MAKUSHI-PEMONG net**	4	14	34,144	43,888		54.04	89	B	42		PN.					0....	24101
80-AFAA	MACUSHI cluster	3	3	14,397	18,094		39.99	81	B	41		PN.					0....	24102
80-AFAA-a	macushi	3	3	14,397	18,094	0	39.99	81	B	41	Makuchi*	PN.	1923-1975	1981			0....	24103
80-AFAB	PEMONG cluster	3	4	8,382	11,742		53.59	90	B	22		P..					0....	24104
80-AFAB-a	are-cuna	3	3	8,127	11,415	0	53.39	90	B	22	Pemon	P..	1990				0....	24105
80-AFAB-b	taulipang	1	1	255	327	0	60.00	90	C	22		p..					0....	24106
80-AFAB-c	camara-coto					0				22		p..					0....	24107
80-AFAB-d	dai-gok					0				22		p..					0....	24108
80-AFAB-e	potsawu-gok					0				22		p..					0....	24109
80-AFAC	KAPONG cluster	3	6	11,191	13,778		72.21	100	C	42		PN.					0....	24110
80-AFAC-a	acawayo	3	3	4,965	6,111	0	75.01	100	C	42	Acawaio*	Pn.	1873				0....	24111
80-AFAC-b	ingarí-kó									42							0....	24112
80-AFAC-c	patamona	3	3	6,226	7,667	0	69.98	100	C	42	Patamuna*	PN.	1963-1967	1974			0....	24113
80-AFAC-d	erema-gok					0				42		pn.					0....	24114
80-AFAD	PURUCOTO cluster	1	1	174	274		70.11	99	C	8		...					0....	24115
80-AFAD-a	puru-coto	1	1	174	274	0	70.11	99	C	8		...					0....	24116
80-AFB	**SAPARA-PAUXIANA net**									0		...					0....	24117
80-AFBA	SAPARá cluster			0	0		0.00	0		0		...					0....	24118
80-AFBA-a	sapará			0	0	0	0.00	0		0		...					0....	24119
80-AFBB	PAUXI-PARAVILHANA cluster			0	0		0.00	0		0		...					0....	24120
80-AFBB-a	pauxiana			0	0	0	0.00	0		0		...					0....	24121
80-AFBB-b	paravilhana			0	0	0	0.00	0		0		...					0....	24122
80-AFC	**YAWAPERI-BOANARI net**	1	1	357	458		10.08	41	A	2		...					0....	24123
80-AFCA	BOANARí cluster			0	0		0.00	0		0		...					0....	24124
80-AFCA-a	boanarí			0	0	0	0.00	0		0		...					0....	24125
80-AFCB	YAWAPERí cluster	1	1	357	458		10.08	41	A	2		...					0....	24126
80-AFCB-a	atruahí	1	1	357	458	0	10.08	41	A	2		...					0....	24127
80-AFCB-b	ki'nya					0				2		...					0....	24128
80-AFCB-c	waimirí					0				2		...					0....	24129
80-AFCB-d	jawaperí					0				2		...					0....	24130
80-AFCB-e	crishana					0				2		...					0....	24131
80-AFCB-f	piriutite									2		...					0....	24132
80-AFCB-g	tiquiría					0				2		...					0....	24133
80-AG	APALAI chain	2	2	851	1,082		75.68	100	C	41		PN.					0....	24134
80-AGA	**APALAI net**	2	2	851	1,082		75.68	100	C	41		PN.					0....	24135
80-AGAA	APALAí cluster	2	2	851	1,082		75.68	100	C	41		PN.					0....	24136
80-AGAA-a	apalaí	2	2	851	1,082	0	75.68	100	C	41	Apalai	PN.	1971-1975	1986			0....	24137
80-AH	TIRIYO-WAIWAI chain	6	13	6,165	8,059		48.18	79	B	41		PN.					1....	24138
80-AHA	**KARIHONA-TIRIYO net**	4	8	2,801	3,697		24.85	56	B	41		PN.					0....	24139
80-AHAA	CARIJONA cluster	3	4	1,315	1,815		11.10	36	A	8		...					0....	24140
80-AHAA-a	carijona-vaupés	1	1	174	245	0	9.77	38	A	8		...					0....	24141
80-AHAA-b	jianá-coto	2	2	379	494	0	31.93	63	B	8		...					0....	24142
80-AHAA-c	yari	1	1	762	1,076	0	1.05	22	A	8		...					0....	24143
80-AHAA-d	carijona-caqueta									8		...					0....	24144
80-AHAB	TIRIYó cluster	2	3	1,316	1,664		39.21	76	B	41		PN.					0....	24145
80-AHAB-a	Proper tiriyó	2	2	1,266	1,601	0	40.05	77	B	41	Trio	PN.	1974	1979			0....	24146
80-AHAB-b	piano-cotó					0				41		pn.					0....	24147
80-AHAB-c	akuriyo	1	1	50	63	0	18.00	56	B	41		pn.					0....	24148
80-AHAB-d	cumayena					0				41		pn.					0....	24149
80-AHAC	SALUMA cluster	1	1	170	218		20.00	47	A	4		...					0....	24150
80-AHAC-a	saluma	1	1	170	218	0	20.00	47	A	4		...					0....	24151
80-AHB	**SHIKUYANA-WAIWAI net**	3	5	3,364	4,362		67.60	98	C	41		PN.					1....	24152
80-AHBA	SHIKUYANA cluster	1	1	725	1,043		60.00	95	C	4		...					0....	24153
80-AHBA-a	sikiâna	1	1	725	1,043	0	60.00	95	C	4		...					0....	24154
80-AHBA-b	chiquiana			0	0	0	0.00	0		4		...					0....	24155
80-AHBB	KASHUYANA-WARIKYANA cluster	1	1	527	676		69.07	100	C	4		...					0....	24156
80-AHBB-a	kashuyana	1	1	527	676	0	69.07	100	C	4		...					0....	24157
80-AHBB-b	warikyana					0				4		...					0....	24158
80-AHBB-c	pawiyana					0				4		...					0....	24159
80-AHBC	WAIWAI cluster	2	3	2,112	2,643		69.84	99	C	41		PN.					1....	24160
80-AHBC-a	waiwai	2	2	1,534	1,902	0	59.97	99	B	41	Waiwai	PN.	1966-1976	1984		1997	1....	24161
80-AHBC-b	katawian					0				41		pn.					1....	24162
80-AHBC-c	charuma					0				41		pn.					1....	24163
80-AHBC-d	sherewyana					0				41		pn.					1....	24164
80-AHBC-e	hishkaryana	1	1	578	741	0	96.02	100	C	41	Hixkaryana	PN.	1966	1976			1....	24165
80-AHBC-f	chawiyana					0				41		pn.					1....	24166
80-AHBC-g	kumiyana					0				41		pn.					1....	24167
80-AHBC-h	sokaka					0				41		pn.					1....	24168
80-AHBC-i	wabui					0				41		pn.					1....	24169
80-AHBC-j	faruaru					0				41		pn.					1....	24170
80-AI	BAKAIRI-ARARA chain	1	5	1,764	2,346		52.32	80	B	22		P..					0....	24171
80-AIA	**CHICAO-YARUMA net**	1	1	625	885		40.48	73	B	4		...					0....	24172
80-AIAA	ARARA-AJUJURE cluster	1	1	200	340		20.00	51	B	0		...					0....	24173
80-AIAA-a	arara-parirí					0				0		...					0....	24174
80-AIAA-b	ajujure					0				0		...					0....	24175
80-AIAB	APIACá-APINGI cluster			0	0		0.00	0		0		...					0....	24176
80-AIAB-a	North apiacá			0	0	0	0.00	0		0		...					0....	24177
80-AIAB-b	apingi			0	0	0	0.00	0		0		...					0....	24178
80-AIAC	CHICAO cluster	1	1	425	545		50.12	83	B	4		...					0....	24179
80-AIAC-a	txikao	1	1	425	545	0	50.12	83	B	4		...					0....	24180
80-AIAC-b	tunuli					0				4		...					0....	24181
80-AIAD	YARUMá cluster			0	0		0.00	0		4		...					0....	24182
80-AIAD-a	yarumá			0	0	0	0.00	0		4		...					0....	24183
80-AIAE	YUMA cluster			0	0		0.00	0		0		...					0....	24184
80-AIAE-a	yuma			0	0	0	0.00	0		0		...					0....	24185
80-AIB	**BAKAIRI-AMONAP net**	1	4	1,139	1,461		58.82	84	B	22		P..					0....	24186
80-AIBA	BAKAIRí cluster	1	1	595	763		80.00	100	C	22		P..					0....	24187

Continued opposite

Table 9-13 continued

Code 1	REFERENCE NAME / Autoglossonym 2	Coun 3	Peo 4	Mother-tongue speakers in 2000 5	in 2025 6	Media radio 7	AC% 8	E% 9	Wld 10	Tr 11	Biblioglossonym 12	Print 13-15	P–activity 16	N–activity 17	B–activity 18	J-year 19	Jayuh 20-24	Ref 25
80-AIBA-a	bakairí	1	1	595	763	0	80.00	100	C	22	Bacairi*	P..	1969-1976				0....	24188
80-AIBB	AMONAP cluster	1	3	544	698		35.66	67	B	4		...					0....	24189
80-AIBB-a	kuikuro	1	1	272	349	0	40.07	70	B	4		...					0....	24190
80-AIBB-b	matipuhy	1	1	34	44	0	41.18	71	B	4		...					0....	24191
80-AIBB-c	mariape					0				4		...					0....	24192
80-AIBB-d	nahukuá					0				4		...					0....	24193
80-AIBB-e	kalapaló	1	1	238	305	0	29.83	62	B	4		...					0....	24194
80-AJ	PALMELA chain									0		...					0....	24195
80-AJA	PALMELA net									0		...					0....	24196
80-AJAA	PALMELA cluster			0	0		0.00	0		0		...					0....	24197
80-AJAA-a	palmela			0	0	0	0.00	0		0		...					0....	24198
80-AK	PIMENTEIRA chain									0		...					0....	24199
80-AKA	PIMENTEIRA net									0		...					0....	24200
80-AKAA	PIMENTEIRA cluster			0	0		0.00	0		0		...					0....	24201
80-AKAA-a	pimenteira			0	0	0	0.00	0		0		...					0....	24202
81	ARAWAKIC zone	8	59	530,212	745,045		37.27	75	B	46		PN.					0....	24203
81-A	NORTH MAIPURAN set	7	36	422,111	595,649		33.20	71	B	46		PN.					0....	24204
81-AA	TAINO chain									0		...					0....	24205
81-AAA	TAINO net									0		...					0....	24206
81-AAAA	TAINO cluster									0		...					0....	24207
81-AAAA-a	taino					0				0		...					0....	24208
81-AB	INYERI-KARIPONA chain									0		...					0....	24209
81-ABA	INYERI-KARIPONA net									0		...					0....	24210
81-ABAA	NORTH KALíPHONA cluster			0	0		0.00	0		0		...					0....	24211
81-ABAA-a	dominican			0	0	0	0.00	0		0		...					0....	24212
81-ABAB	SOUTH KALíPHONA cluster			0	0		0.00	0		0		...					0....	24213
81-ABAB-a	vincentian			0	0	0	0.00	0		0		...					0....	24214
81-AC	ARAWAK-WAHIRO chain	5	7	378,772	536,998		30.02	68	B	22		P..					0....	24215
81-ACA	WAHIRO net	2	3	359,080	512,280		26.62	66	B	22		P..					0....	24216
81-ACAA	GUAJIRO cluster	2	2	350,862	500,456		25.36	65	B	22		P..					0....	24217
81-ACAA-a	wayúu	2	2	350,862	500,456	0	25.36	65	B	22	Guajiro*	P..	1944-1989				0....	24218
81-ACAB	ANYU cluster	1	1	8,218	11,824		80.59	100	C	8		...					0....	24219
81-ACAB-a	alile					0				8		...					0....	24220
81-ACAB-b	toa					0				8		...					0....	24221
81-ACB	ARAWAK net	4	4	19,692	24,718		91.89	100	C	22		P..					0....	24222
81-ACBA	ARAWáK cluster	4	4	19,692	24,718		91.89	100	C	22	Arawak	P..	1850-1978				0....	24223
81-ACBA-a	West arawák					0				22		p..					0....	24224
81-ACBA-b	Central arawák					0				22		p..					0....	24225
81-ACBA-c	East arawák					0				22		p..					0....	24226
81-AD	WAPISHANA chain	2	2	11,338	13,877		59.99	99	B	22		P..					0....	24227
81-ADA	WAPISHANA net	2	2	11,338	13,877		59.99	99	B	22		P..					0....	24228
81-ADAA	WAPISHANA cluster	2	2	11,338	13,877		59.99	99	B	22		P..					0....	24229
81-ADAA-a	Proper wapishana	2	2	11,338	13,877	0	59.99	99	B	22	Wapishana	P..	1975-1994				0....	24230
81-ADAA-b	atoraí					0				22		p..					0....	24231
81-ADAA-c	mawakua					0				22		p..					0....	24232
81-ADAA-d	maopidyán					0				22		p..					0....	24233
81-ADAA-e	mawayana					0				22		p..					0....	24234
81-ADAA-f	amariba					0				22		p..					0....	24235
81-AE	PALIKUR chain	2	2	2,169	4,029		60.07	99	C	41		PN.					0....	24236
81-AEA	PALIKUR net	2	2	2,169	4,029		60.07	99	C	41		PN.					0....	24237
81-AEAA	PALIKúR cluster	2	2	2,169	4,029		60.07	99	C	41		PN.					0....	24238
81-AEAA-a	Proper palikúr	2	2	2,169	4,029	0	60.07	99	C	41	Palikur	PN.	1971	1982			0....	24239
81-AEAA-b	marawán-karipurá			0	0	0	0.00	0		41		pn.					0....	24240
81-AF	PIAPOKO-JUKUNA chain	3	10	13,035	18,446		61.24	91	C	41		PN.					0....	24241
81-AFA	PIAPOKO-ACHAWA net	2	4	5,475	7,736		52.13	91	B	41		PN.					0....	24242
81-AFAA	ACHAGUA cluster	2	2	584	826		70.03	100	C	12		....					0....	24243
81-AFAA-a	achagua	2	2	584	826	0	70.03	100	C	12	Achagua	...					0....	24244
81-AFAB	AMARIZANA cluster			0	0		0.00	0		0		...					0....	24245
81-AFAB-a	amarizana			0	0	0	0.00	0		0		...					0....	24246
81-AFAC	PIAPOCO cluster	2	2	4,891	6,910		49.99	90	B	41		PN.					0....	24247
81-AFAC-a	tsase	2	2	4,891	6,910	0	49.99	90	B	41	Piapoco	PN.	1960-1986	1966-1987			0....	24248
81-AFB	KAVIYARI net	1	1	42	60		80.95	100	C	8		...					0....	24249
81-AFBA	CAVIYARí cluster	1	1	42	60		80.95	100	C	8		...					0....	24250
81-AFBA-a	caviyarí	1	1	42	60	0	80.95	100	C	8		...					0....	24251
81-AFC	WAINUMA net									0		...					0....	24252
81-AFCA	WAINUMá cluster			0	0		0.00	0		0		...					0....	24253
81-AFCA-a	inahishana			0	0	0	0.00	0		0		...					0....	24254
81-AFD	ANAUYA net									0		...					0....	24255
81-AFDA	ANAUYá cluster			0	0		0.00	0		0		...					0....	24256
81-AFDA-a	anauyá			0	0	0	0.00	0		0		...					0....	24257
81-AFE	WAREKENA-MANDAWAKA net	2	4	5,965	8,371		67.61	91	C	4		...					0....	24258
81-AFEA	GUAREQUENA cluster	2	2	988	1,353		60.02	96	C	4		...					0....	24259
81-AFEA-a	walékhena	2	2	988	1,353	0	60.02	96	C	4		...					0....	24260
81-AFEB	MANDAHUACA cluster	1	1	4,075	5,863		80.00	100	C	4		...					0....	24261
81-AFEB-a	mandahuaca	1	1	4,075	5,863	0	80.00	100	C	4		...					0....	24262
81-AFEC	XIRIâNA-I cluster	1	1	902	1,155		19.96	49	A	0		...					0....	24263
81-AFEC-a	xiriâna-I	1	1	902	1,155	0	19.96	49	A	0		...					0....	24264
81-AFF	JUMANA-PASE net									0		...					0....	24265

Continued overleaf

Table 9-13 continued

Code 1	REFERENCE NAME / Autoglossonym 2	Coun 3	Peo 4	Mother-tongue speakers in 2000 5	in 2025 6	Media radio 7	CHURCH AC% 8	E% 9	Wld 10	Tr 11	Biblioglossonym 12	SCRIPTURES Print 13-15	P-activity 16	N-activity 17	B-activity 18	J-year 19	Jayuh 20-24	Ref 25
81-AFFA	JUMANA cluster			0	0		0.00	0		0		. . .					0. . . .	24266
81-AFFA-a	jumana			0	0	0	0.00	0		0		. . .					0. . . .	24267
81-AFFB	PASE cluster			0	0		0.00	0		0		. . .					0. . . .	24268
81-AFFB-a	pase			0	0	0	0.00	0		0		. . .					0. . . .	24269
81-AFFC	KAIWISHANA cluster			0	0		0.00	0		0		. . .					0. . . .	24270
81-AFFC-a	kaiwishana			0	0	0	0.00	0		0		. . .					0. . . .	24271
81-AFG	**JUKUNA-GARU net**	1	1	1,553	2,279		68.38	90	C	41		PN.					0. . . .	24272
81-AFGA	PROPER YUCUNA cluster	1	1	1,253	1,769		79.97	100	C	41		PN.					0. . . .	24273
81-AFGA-a	Proper yucuna	1	1	1,253	1,769	0	79.97	100	C	41	Yucuna	PN.	1970	1982			0. . . .	24274
81-AFGB	GARU cluster	1	1	300	510		20.00	50	B	0		. . .					0. . . .	24275
81-AFGB-a	garu	1	1	300	510	0	20.00	50	B	0		. . .					0. . . .	24276
81-AG	TARIANA-KARU chain	3	11	16,084	21,268		63.11	95	C	46		PN.					0. . . .	24277
81-AGA	**TARIANA net**	1	1	1,565	2,005		50.03	81	B	8		. . .					0. . . .	24278
81-AGAA	TARIANA cluster	1	1	1,565	2,005		50.03	81	B	8		. . .					0. . . .	24279
81-AGAA-a	tariana	1	1	1,565	2,005	0	50.03	81	B	8		. . .					0. . . .	24280
81-AGB	**KARU net**	3	10	14,519	19,263		64.52	97	C	46		PN.					0. . . .	24281
81-AGBA	IPECA-CURRIPACO cluster	3	4	4,247	5,871		59.97	98	B	42		PN.					0. . . .	24282
81-AGBA-a	kúrrim	3	3	4,043	5,609	0	59.98	98	B	42	Curripaco	PN.	1948	1959			0. . . .	24283
81-AGBA-b	unhun					0				42		pn.					0. . . .	24284
81-AGBA-c	ipeca	1	1	204	262	0	59.80	95	B	42		pn.					0. . . .	24285
81-AGBA-d	waliperi					0				42		pn.					0. . . .	24286
81-AGBB	HUHúTENI cluster	3	6	10,072	13,052		67.13	97	C	46		PN.					0. . . .	24287
81-AGBB-a	North baniva			0	0	0	0.00	0		46		pn.					0. . . .	24288
81-AGBB-b	quirruba			0	0	0	0.00	0		46		pn.					0. . . .	24289
81-AGBB-c	South baniwa	3	3	8,133	10,568	0	70.01	100	C	46	Baniua*	PN.	1959	1985			0. . . .	24290
81-AGBB-d	kohoroxitari	1	1	970	1,242	0	40.00	73	B	46		pn.					0. . . .	24291
81-AGBB-e	hohodene					0				46		pn.					0. . . .	24292
81-AGBB-f	siusí					0				46		pn.					0. . . .	24293
81-AGBB-g	adaru	1	1	374	479	0	70.05	100	C	46		pn.					0. . . .	24294
81-AGBB-h	arara					0				46		pn.					0. . . .	24295
81-AGBB-i	dzaui					0				46		pn.					0. . . .	24296
81-AGBB-j	adzáneni					0				46		pn.					0. . . .	24297
81-AGBB-k	jauarete					0				46		pn.					0. . . .	24298
81-AGBB-l	jurupari					0				46		pn.					0. . . .	24299
81-AGBB-m	máulieni					0				46		pn.					0. . . .	24300
81-AGBB-n	mapache					0				46		pn.					0. . . .	24301
81-AGBB-o	uadzoli					0				46		pn.					0. . . .	24302
81-AGBB-p	urubu	1	1	595	763	0	70.08	100	C	46	Urubu*	PN.	1970-1976	1986-1987			0. . . .	24303
81-AGBC	KATAPOLíTANI-MAPANAI cluster	1	1	200	340		30.00	65	B	0		. . .					0. . . .	24304
81-AGBC-a	katapolítani					0				0		. . .					0. . . .	24305
81-AGBC-b	moriwene					0				0		. . .					0. . . .	24306
81-AGBC-c	mapanai					0				0		. . .					0. . . .	24307
81-AGBD	YABAâNA cluster									0		. . .					0. . . .	24308
81-AGBD-a	yabaâna					0				0		. . .					0. . . .	24309
81-AH	BARE-YAVITERO chain	2	2	488	698		23.36	53	B	9		. . .					0. . . .	24310
81-AHA	**BARE net**	2	2	488	698		23.36	53	B	8		. . .					0. . . .	24311
81-AHAA	GINAO cluster			0	0		0.00	0		0		. . .					0. . . .	24312
81-AHAA-a	guinao					0				0		. . .					0. . . .	24313
81-AHAA-b	temomoyamo					0				0		. . .					0. . . .	24314
81-AHAB	BARé cluster	2	2	488	698		23.36	53	B	8		. . .					0. . . .	24315
81-AHAB-a	North baré					0				8		. . .					0. . . .	24316
81-AHAB-b	South barawâna					0				8		. . .					0. . . .	24317
81-AHAC	MARAWá cluster			0	0		0.00	0		0		. . .					0. . . .	24318
81-AHAC-a	marawá			0	0	0	0.00	0		0		. . .					0. . . .	24319
81-AHB	**YAVITERO net**									9		. . .					0. . . .	24320
81-AHBA	YAVITERO cluster			0	0		0.00	0		9		. . .					0. . . .	24321
81-AHBA-a	yavitero			0	0	0	0.00	0		9		. . .					0. . . .	24322
81-AI	RESIGARO chain	1	1	23	32		60.87	96	C	8		. . .					0. . . .	24323
81-AIA	**RESIGARO net**	1	1	23	32		60.87	96	C	8		. . .					0. . . .	24324
81-AIAA	RESíGARO cluster	1	1	23	32		60.87	96	C	8		. . .					0. . . .	24325
81-AIAA-a	resígaro	1	1	23	32	0	60.87	96	C	8		. . .					0. . . .	24326
81-AJ	MANAO-KARIAI chain									0		. . .					0. . . .	24327
81-AJA	**MANAO net**									0		. . .					0. . . .	24328
81-AJAA	MANAO cluster			0	0		0.00	0		0		. . .					0. . . .	24329
81-AJAA-a	manao			0	0	0	0.00	0		0		. . .					0. . . .	24330
81-AJB	**KARIAI net**									0		. . .					0. . . .	24331
81-AJBA	KARIAí cluster			0	0		0.00	0		0		. . .					0. . . .	24332
81-AJBA-a	kariaí			0	0	0	0.00	0		0		. . .					0. . . .	24333
81-AK	TUBARAO chain	1	1	202	301		35.15	66	B	12		. . .					0. . . .	24334
81-AKA	**TUBARAO net**	1	1	202	301		35.15	66	B	12		. . .					0. . . .	24335
81-AKAA	TUBARAO cluster	1	1	102	131		50.00	82	B	12		. . .					0. . . .	24336
81-AKAA-a	tubarao	1	1	102	131	0	50.00	82	B	12	Tubarao	. . .					0. . . .	24337
81-AKAB	MASAKá cluster	1	1	100	170		20.00	50	B	0		. . .					0. . . .	24338
81-AKAB-a	masaka	1	1	100	170	0	20.00	50	B	0		. . .					0. . . .	24339
81-B	**SOUTH MAIPURAN set**	3	23	108,101	149,396		53.16	90	B	42		PN.					0. . . .	24340
81-BA	AMOESHA-CHAMIKURO chain	1	2	7,827	10,833		45.68	90	B	41		PN.					0. . . .	24341
81-BAA	**CHAMICURO net**	1	1	208	288		70.19	100	C	8		. . .					0. . . .	24342
81-BAAA	CHAMICURO cluster	1	1	208	288		70.19	100	C	8		. . .					0. . . .	24343
81-BAAA-a	chamicuro	1	1	208	288	0	70.19	100	C	8		. . .					0. . . .	24344
81-BAB	**AMUESHA net**	1	1	7,619	10,545		45.01	90	B	41		PN.					0. . . .	24345
81-BABA	AMUESHA cluster	1	1	7,619	10,545		45.01	90	B	41		PN.					0. . . .	24346
81-BABA-a	yanesha	1	1	7,619	10,545	0	45.01	90	B	41	Amuesha	PN.	1956-1975	1978			0. . . .	24347
81-BB	CAMPA chain	2	8	61,333	84,857		61.14	99	C	42		PN.					0. . . .	24348

Continued opposite

Table 9-13 continued

Code 1	REFERENCE NAME / Autoglossonym 2	Coun 3	Peo 4	Mother-tongue speakers in 2000 5	in 2025 6	Media radio 7	AC% 8	E% 9	Wld 10	Tr 11	Biblioglossonym 12	Print 13-15	P–activity 16	N–activity 17	B–activity 18	J-year 19	Jayuh 20-24	Ref 25
81-BBA	**CAMPA net**	2	8	61,333	84,857		61.14	99	C	42		PN.					0....	24349
81-BBAA	NORTHWEST CAMPA cluster	2	4	45,184	62,506	0	61.84	99	C	42		PN.					0....	24350
81-BBAA-a	ashéni-nga	2	2	17,451	24,122	0	60.09	100	C	42		pn.					0....	24351
81-BBAA-b	asháni-nga	1	1	23,922	33,110	0	65.00	100	C	42	Campa: Ashaninca*	PN.	1960-1969	1972			0....	24352
81-BBAA-c	pajonal	1	1	3,811	5,274	0	49.99	90	B	42	Campa: Pajonal*	Pn.	1976-1986				0....	24353
81-BBAA-d	ats-iri					0				42		pn.					0....	24354
81-BBAA-e	ucay-ali					0				42		pn.					0....	24355
81-BBAA-f	unini					0				42		pn.					0....	24356
81-BBAA-g	pichis					0				42	Campa: Pichis Asheninca*	PN.	1982-1987	1996			0....	24357
81-BBAA-h	perene					0				42		pn.					0....	24358
81-BBAA-i	apurucay-ali					0				42		pn.					0....	24359
81-BBAA-j	cashar-ari					0				42		pn.					0....	24360
81-BBAB	SOUTHEAST CAMPA cluster	1	4	16,149	22,351		59.17	99	B	41		PN.					0....	24361
81-BBAB-a	no-matsigue-nga	1	1	5,381	7,448	0	60.01	100	B	41	Campa: Nomatsiguenga*	PN.	1969-1977	1980			0....	24362
81-BBAB-b	caquinte	1	1	362	501	0	30.11	62	B	41	Caquinte	Pn.	1984-1991				0....	24363
81-BBAB-c	machigue-nga	1	1	10,149	14,047	0	60.01	100	C	41	Machiguenga	PN.	1974	1956-1976			0....	24364
81-BBAB-d	mañaries					0				41		pn.					0....	24365
81-BBAB-e	cogapac-ori	1	1	257	355	0	49.81	87	B	41		pn.					0....	24366
81-BC	PIRO-APURINA chain	2	5	6,359	8,476		59.52	89	B	42		PN.					0....	24367
81-BCA	**PIRO net**	2	4	4,233	5,752		69.31	98	C	42		PN.					0....	24368
81-BCAA	PIRO cluster	2	4	4,233	5,752		69.31	98	C	42		PN.					0....	24369
81-BCAA-a	piro	2	2	3,725	5,090	0	69.96	100	C	42	Piro	PN.	1949-1956	1960			0....	24370
81-BCAA-b	contaquiro					0				42		pn.					0....	24371
81-BCAA-c	simirinch					0				42		pn.					0....	24372
81-BCAA-d	manitenerí	1	1	408	523	0	79.90	100	C	42	Piro: Manchineri*	Pn.	1960				0....	24373
81-BCAA-e	mashco-piro	1	1	100	139	0	2.00	35	A	42		pn.					0....	24374
81-BCAA-f	canamaré		0	0	0	0	0.00	0		42		pn.					0....	24375
81-BCB	**APURINYA net**	1	1	2,126	2,724		40.03	72	B	22		P..					0....	24376
81-BCBA	APURINYA cluster	1	1	2,126	2,724		40.03	72	B	22		P..					0....	24377
81-BCBA-a	Proper apurinya	1	1	2,126	2,724	0	40.03	72	B	22	Apurina	P..	1993				0....	24378
81-BCBA-b	kangite					0				22		p..					0....	24379
81-BCBA-c	popeng-are					0				22		p..					0....	24380
81-BCBA-d	zuruahá					0				22		p..					0....	24381
81-BD	BAURE-MOJO chain	1	3	11,726	18,512		25.29	60	B	41		PN.					0....	24382
81-BDA	**BAURE net**	1	1	333	525		60.06	99	C	27		P..					0....	24383
81-BDAA	BAURE cluster	1	1	333	525		60.06	99	C	27		P..					0....	24384
81-BDAA-a	baure	1	1	333	525	0	60.06	99	C	27	Baure	P..	1960-1966				0....	24385
81-BDB	MOJO net	1	2	11,393	17,987		24.27	59	B	41		PN.					0....	24386
81-BDBA	MOJO cluster	1	2	11,193	17,647		24.17	59	B	41	Trinitario	PN.	1962	1979			0....	24387
81-BDBA-a	ignaciano	1	1	5,656	8,917	0	39.99	77	B	41	Ignaciano	PN.	1967	1980			0....	24388
81-BDBA-b	loretano					0				41		pn.					0....	24389
81-BDBA-c	javierano					0				41		pn.					0....	24390
81-BDBB	BANURE cluster	1	1	200	340		30.00	65	B	0		...					0....	24391
81-BDBB-a	banure	1	1	200	340	0	30.00	65	B	0		...					0....	24392
81-BDBC	PAUNA-PAIKONE cluster		0	0	0		0.00	0		0		...					0....	24393
81-BDBC-a	pauna		0	0	0	0	0.00	0		0		...					0....	24394
81-BE	TERENA chain	1	1	19,189	24,582		45.00	83	B	41		PN.					0....	24395
81-BEA	**TERENA net**	1	1	19,189	24,582		45.00	83	B	41		PN.					0....	24396
81-BEAA	TERENA cluster	1	1	19,189	24,582		45.00	83	B	41		PN.					0....	24397
81-BEAA-a	Proper terena	1	1	19,189	24,582	0	45.00	83	B	41	Terena	PN.	1948-1974	1994			0....	24398
81-BEAB	GUANA cluster									0		...					0....	24399
81-BEAB-a	guana					0				0		...					0....	24400
81-BF	PARESI-SARAVE chain	1	1	1,276	1,634		69.98	100	C	41		PN.					0....	24401
81-BFA	**PARESSI net**	1	1	1,276	1,634		69.98	100	C	41		PN.					0....	24402
81-BFAA	PARESSI cluster	1	1	1,276	1,634		69.98	100	C	41		PN.					0....	24403
81-BFAA-a	paresí	1	1	1,276	1,634	0	69.98	100	C	41	Parecis	PN.	1971-1985	1995-1996			0....	24404
81-BFAA-b	haliti					0				41		pn.					0....	24405
81-BFAA-c	saraveca					0				41		pn.					0....	24406
81-BG	WAURA-YAWALAPITI chain	1	3	391	502		30.43	61	B	3		...					0....	24407
81-BGA	**WAURA-YAWALAPITI net**	1	3	391	502		30.43	61	B	3		...					0....	24408
81-BGAA	WAURA-KUSTENAU cluster	1	2	221	284		30.77	60	B	3		...					0....	24409
81-BGAA-a	custenau		0	0	0	0	0.00	0		3		...					0....	24410
81-BGAA-b	mehináku	1	1	119	153	0	40.34	72	B	3		...					0....	24411
81-BGAA-c	waurá					0				3		...					0....	24412
81-BGAA-d	agavotaguerra	1	1	102	131	0	19.61	45	A	3		...					0....	24413
81-BGAB	YAWALAPITí cluster	1	1	170	218		30.00	62	B	3		...					0....	24414
81-BGAB-a	yawalapiti	1	1	170	218	0	30.00	62	B	3		...					0....	24415
82	**TUPIC zone**	8	68	5,872,205	9,504,133		94.29	100	C	61		PNB					3a..h	24416
82-A	**INNER-TUPIAN set**	8	55	5,857,039	9,484,343		94.36	100	C	61		PNB					3a..h	24417
82-AA	INNER-TUPIAN chain	8	55	5,857,039	9,484,343		94.36	100	C	61		PNB					3a..h	24418
82-AAA	**WAYAMPI-EMERILLON net**	2	6	2,142	3,985		23.25	55	B	32		...					1...h	24419
82-AAAA	EMéRILLON cluster	2	2	510	1,067		10.20	40	A	4		...					0....	24420
82-AAAA-a	emerillon	2	2	510	1,067	0	10.20	40	A	4		...					0....	24421
82-AAAA-b	West emerillon					0				4		...					0....	24422
82-AAAA-c	East emerillon					0				4		...					0....	24423
82-AAAB	WAYAMPí cluster	2	2	1,190	2,352		20.25	53	B	32		...					1....	24424
82-AAAB-a	oyapock	1	1	816	1,873	0	20.34	53	B	32	Wayampi, Oiapoque	...					1....	24425
82-AAAB-b	oyampi-puku	1	1	374	479	0	20.05	51	B	32	Wayampi, Amapari	...				1995	1....	24429
82-AAAC	AMANAYé cluster	1	1	68	87		80.88	100	C	6		...					0....	24432
82-AAAC-a	amanayé	1	1	68	87		80.88	100	C	6		...					0....	24433
82-AAAD	URUBú-KAAPOR cluster									20		...					0...h	24434
82-AAAD-a	urubú					0				20		...					0...h	24435
82-AAAD-b	kaapor					0				20		...					0...h	24436
82-AAAE	TAKUNYAPé cluster		0	0	0		0.00	0		0		...					0....	24437
82-AAAE-a	takunyapé		0	0	0	0	0.00	0		0		...					0....	24438
82-AAAF	GUAJá cluster	1	1	374	479		40.11	72	B	2		...					0....	24439
82-AAAF-a	guajá	1	1	374	479	0	40.11	72	B	2		...					0....	24440

Continued overleaf

Table 9-13 continued

Code 1	REFERENCE NAME / Autoglossonym 2	Coun 3	Peo 4	Mother-tongue speakers in 2000 5	in 2025 6	Media radio 7	CHURCH AC% 8	E% 9	Wld 10	Tr 11	Biblioglossonym 12	SCRIPTURES Print 13-15	P-activity 16	N-activity 17	B-activity 18	J-year 19	Jayuh 20-24	Ref 25
82-AAB	**TENETEHARA-AKUAWA net**	1	5	14,368	18,533		59.52	98	B	41		PN.					0....	24441
82-AABA	TEMBé-GUAJAJáRA cluster	1	2	13,167	16,868		60.00	99	B	41		PN.					0....	24442
82-AABA-a	acará-tembé					0				41		pn.					0....	24443
82-AABA-b	capim-tembé					0				41		pn.					0....	24444
82-AABA-c	gurupi-tembé	1	1	885	1,133	0	60.00	98	C	41	Tembe	pn.					0....	24445
82-AABA-d	turiwára			0	0	0	0.00	0		41		pn.					0....	24446
82-AABA-e	guajajára	1	1	12,282	15,735	0	60.00	100	B	41	Guajajara	PN.	1930-1934	1985			0....	24447
82-AABA-f	tenetehar					0				41		pn.					0....	24448
82-AABA-g	pindare					0				41		pn.					0....	24449
82-AABA-h	zutiua					0				41		pn.					0....	24450
82-AABA-i	mearim					0				41		pn.					0....	24451
82-AABB	AKUAWA cluster	1	2	646	828		65.94	94	C	23		P..					0....	24452
82-AABB-a	parakana	1	1	459	588	0	60.13	92	C	23	Parakana	p..					0....	24453
82-AABB-b	Proper akuawa	1	1	187	240	0	80.21	100	C	23	Asurini, Xingu	P..	1973				0....	24454
82-AABB-c	suruí-tocantins					0				23		p..					0....	24455
82-AABC	TAPIRAPé cluster	1	1	255	327		65.10	98	C	4		...					0....	24456
82-AABC-a	tapirapé	1	1	255	327	0	65.10	98	C	4		...					0....	24457
82-AABD	AVá cluster	1	1	300	510		20.00	50	B	0		...					0....	24458
82-AABD-a	Northwest avá					0				0		...					0....	24459
82-AABD-b	Southeast avá					0				0		...					0....	24460
82-AAC	**KAMAYURA net**	1	1	289	370		60.21	94	C	2		...					0....	24461
82-AACA	KAMAYURA cluster	1	1	289	370		60.21	94	C	2		...					0....	24462
82-AACA-a	kamayurá	1	1	289	370	0	60.21	94	C	2		...					0....	24463
82-AAD	**JO'E net**	1	1	200	340		20.00	51	B	0		...					0....	24464
82-AADA	JO'E cluster	1	1	200	340		20.00	51	B	0		...					0....	24465
82-AADA-a	jo'e	1	1	200	340	0	20.00	51	B	0		...					0....	24466
82-AAE	**KAYABI-ASURINI net**	1	2	919	1,177		65.51	95	C	32		P..					1....	24467
82-AAEA	KAYABí cluster	1	1	851	1,090		69.92	100	C	32		P..					1....	24468
82-AAEA-a	Proper kayabí	1	1	851	1,090	0	69.92	100	C	32	Kayabi	P..	1986			1994	1....	24469
82-AAEA-b	parua					0				32		p..					1....	24470
82-AAEA-c	maquiri					0				32		p..					1....	24471
82-AAEB	SOUTH ASURINí cluster	1	1	68	87		10.29	35	A	8		...					0....	24472
82-AAEB-a	parakanan					0				8		...					0....	24473
82-AAEB-b	awaté					0				8		...					0....	24474
82-AAEB-c	anambé	1	1	68	87	0	10.29	35	A	8		...					0....	24475
82-AAF	**ARAWETE net**	1	1	187	240		80.21	100	C	2		...					0....	24476
82-AAFA	ARAWETé cluster	1	1	187	240		80.21	100	C	2		...					0....	24477
82-AAFA-a	araweté	1	1	187	240	0	80.21	100	C	2		...					0....	24478
82-AAG	**KAWAHIB-APIAKA net**	1	6	1,424	1,910		52.25	82	B	41		PN.					0....	24479
82-AAGA	KAGWAHIV cluster	1	5	1,139	1,461		57.51	89	B	41		PN.	1971-1976	1996			0....	24480
82-AAGA-a	tenharim	1	1	306	392	0	80.07	100	C	41	Tenharim	PN.	1971-1976	1996			0....	24481
82-AAGA-b	parintintín					0				41	Parintintin	Pn.	1971				0....	24482
82-AAGA-c	karipuna-paraná					0				41		pn.					0....	24483
82-AAGA-d	mialát					0				41		pn.					0....	24484
82-AAGA-e	diahói					0				41		pn.					0....	24485
82-AAGA-f	morerebi	1	1	119	153	0	5.04	29	A	41		pn.					0....	24486
82-AAGA-g	juma	1	3	714	916	0	56.58	94	B	41	Arara, Para	pn.					0....	24487
82-AAGA-h	nakazeti					0				41		pn.					0....	24488
82-AAGA-i	itoehebe					0				41		pn.					0....	24489
82-AAGA-j	amondawa					0				41		pn.					0....	24490
82-AAGB	URUEWAUWAU cluster	1	1	200	340		10.00	34	A	0		...					0....	24491
82-AAGB-a	uru-e-wauwau	1	1	200	340	0	10.00	34	A	0		...					0....	24492
82-AAGC	TUKUMANFéD cluster									0		...					0....	24493
82-AAGC-a	wiraféd					0				0		...					0....	24494
82-AAGC-b	Proper tukumanféd					0				0		...					0....	24495
82-AAGC-c	paranawát			0	0	0	0.00	0		0		...					0....	24496
82-AAGD	MAKIRí cluster			0	0		0.00	0		0		...					0....	24497
82-AAGD-a	makirí			0	0	0	0.00	0		0		...					0....	24498
82-AAGE	APIACA cluster	1	1	85	109		81.18	100	C	6		...					0....	24499
82-AAGE-a	apiaca	1	1	85	109	0	81.18	100	C	6		...					0....	24500
82-AAH	**KOKAMA-OMAWA net**	3	4	24,373	33,775		10.61	47	A	23		P..					0....	24501
82-AAHA	COCAMA-COCAMILLA cluster	3	4	24,173	33,435		10.62	47	A	23		P..					0....	24502
82-AAHA-a	cocama	3	3	21,607	29,883	0	10.10	47	A	23	Cocama*	P..	1961-1967				0....	24503
82-AAHA-b	cocamilla	1	1	2,566	3,552	0	15.00	51	B	23	Cocamilla	P..	1967				0....	24504
82-AAHA-c	ucayali					0				23		p..					0....	24505
82-AAHA-d	huallaga					0				23		p..					0....	24506
82-AAHA-e	xibitaona					0				23		p..					0....	24507
82-AAHB	OMAWA-CAMPEVA cluster	2	1	200	340		10.00	34	A	0		...					0....	24508
82-AAHB-a	omagua					0				0		...					0....	24509
82-AAHB-b	compeva					0				0		...					0....	24510
82-AAHB-c	aizuare					0				0		...					0....	24511
82-AAHB-d	curacirari					0				0		...					0....	24512
82-AAHB-e	paguana					0				0		...					0....	24513
82-AAHB-f	yhuata					0				0		...					0....	24514
82-AAHB-g	anapia					0				0		...					0....	24515
82-AAI	**TUPI-GUARANI net**	6	30	5,813,137	9,424,013		94.85	100	C	61		PNB					3a...	24516
82-AAIA	SIRIONó cluster	1	2	650	1,026		70.31	100	C	41		PN.					0....	24517
82-AAIA-a	Proper sirionó	1	1	635	1,002	0	70.08	100	C	41	Siriono	PN.	1964	1977			0....	24518
82-AAIA-b	jande					0				41		pn.					0....	24519
82-AAIA-c	nyeoze-nee					0				41		pn.					0....	24520
82-AAIA-d	tirinie					0				41		pn.					0....	24521
82-AAIA-e	jora	1	1	15	24	0	80.00	100	C	41		pn.					0....	24522
82-AAIB	YUQUI cluster	1	1	167	263		19.76	54	B	12		...					0....	24523
82-AAIB-a	yuqui	1	1	167	263	0	19.76	54	B	12	Yuqui	...					0....	24524
82-AAIC	PAUSERNA cluster	1	1	93,440	159,039		92.00	100	C	8		...					0....	24525
82-AAIC-a	pauserna					1				8		...					0....	24526
82-AAIC-b	guarani-ete	1	1	93,440	159,039	4	92.00	100	C	8		...					0....	24527
82-AAID	ACHé cluster	1	1	997	1,697		2.01	35	A	22		P..					0....	24528
82-AAID-a	aché	1	1	997	1,697	0	2.01	35	A	22	Ache	P..	1978				0....	24529
82-AAIE	XETá cluster	1	1	221	283		60.18	96	C	8		...					0....	24530
82-AAIE-a	xetá	1	1	221	283	0	60.18	96	C	8		...					0....	24531
82-AAIF	GUARANí cluster	4	21	5,705,200	9,244,634		94.95	100	C	61		PNB					3a...	24532
82-AAIF-a	Standard aba-ñeeme					1				61	Guarani: Paraguay*	PNB	1905-1994	1913-1977	1996	1990	3c...	24533
82-AAIF-b	Vehicular aba-ñeeme	3	3	5,586,681	9,069,018	5	95.63	100	C	61		pnb					1a...	24534
82-AAIF-c	guasurango-chiriguano	3	9	55,660	82,401	4	64.29	99	C	61		PNb					3a...	24535

Continued opposite

Table 9-13 continued

Code 1	REFERENCE NAME / Autoglossonym 2	Coun 3	Peo 4	Mother-tongue speakers in 2000 5	in 2025 6	Media radio 7	AC% 8	E% 9	Wld 10	Tr 11	Biblioglossonym 12	Print 13-15	P-activity 16	N-activity 17	B-activity 18	J-year 19	Jayuh 20-24	Ref 25
82-AAIF-d	chiripa-nhandeva	2	2	13,887	21,474	4	61.50	90	C	61		Pnb					1c...	24541
82-AAIF-e	pai-tavytera					1				61	Pai Tavytera	pnb					1c...	24547
82-AAIF-f	kaingwá	3	4	30,156	44,416	1	60.11	100	C	61	Kaiwa	PNb	1966-1972	1986			1c...	24548
82-AAIF-g	mbyá	3	3	18,816	27,325	4	65.00	100	C	61	Guarani: Brazil, Southern*	PNb	1971-1976	1987-1988			1c...	24553
82-AAIG	TUPI cluster	3	3	12,462	17,071		78.17	100	C	42		PN.					0....	24557
82-AAIG-a	nhengatu	3	3	12,462	17,071	0	78.17	100	C	42	Nyengato*	PN.	1960-1967	1973			0....	24558
82-AAIG-b	potiguara			0	0	0	0.00	0		42		pn.					0....	24559
82-AAIG-c	tupinamba					0				42		pn.					0....	24560
82-AAIG-d	tupinikin			0	0	0	0.00	0		42		pn.					0....	24561
82-AAIG-e	South tupi					0				42		pn.					0....	24562
82-B	**MAWE-SATERE set**	1	1	9,612	12,313		70.00	100	C	41		PN.					0....	24563
82-BA	MAWE-SATERE chain	1	1	9,612	12,313		70.00	100	C	41		PN.					0....	24564
82-BAA	**MAWE-SATERE net**	1	1	9,612	12,313		70.00	100	C	41		PN.					0....	24565
82-BAAA	MAWE-SATERE cluster	1	1	9,612	12,313		70.00	100	C	41	Satere-mawe	PN.	1968	1986			0....	24566
82-BAAA-a	mawé					0				41		pn.					0....	24567
82-BAAA-b	maragua					0				41		pn.					0....	24568
82-BAAA-c	arapium					0				41		pn.					0....	24569
82-BAAA-d	sataré					0				41		pn.					0....	24570
82-C	**MUNDURUKU-KURUAYA set**	1	1	2,112	2,715		59.61	99	B	41		PN.					0....	24571
82-CA	MUNDURUKU chain	1	1	2,092	2,681		59.99	100	B	41		PN.					0....	24572
82-CAA	**MUNDURUKU net**	1	1	2,092	2,681		59.99	100	B	41		PN.					0....	24573
82-CAAA	MUNDURUCú cluster	1	1	2,092	2,681		59.99	100	B	41		PN.					0....	24574
82-CAAA-a	Proper mundurucu	1	1	2,092	2,681	0	59.99	100	B	41	Munduruku	PN.	1967	1980			0....	24575
82-CAAA-b	weidyenye					0				41		pn.					0....	24576
82-CAAA-c	paiquize					0				41		pn.					0....	24577
82-CAAA-d	pari					0				41		pn.					0....	24578
82-CAAA-e	caras-pretas					0				41		pn.					0....	24579
82-CB	KURUAYA chain	1	1	20	34		20.00	50	B	6		...					0....	24580
82-CBA	**KURUAYA net**	1	1	20	34		20.00	50	B	6		...					0....	24581
82-CBAA	KURUáYA cluster	1	1	20	34		20.00	50	B	6		...					0....	24582
82-CBAA-a	curuáia					0				6		...					0....	24583
82-CBAA-b	xipaia					0				6		...					0....	24584
82-D	**RAMARAMA-ARARA set**	1	1	500	850		10.00	33	A	4		...					0....	24585
82-DA	RAMARAMA-ITOGAPUK chain	1	1	200	340		10.00	34	A	4		...					0....	24586
82-DAA	**RAMARAMA-ITOGAPUK net**	1	1	200	340		10.00	34	A	4		...					0....	24587
82-DAAA	RAMARAMA-URUMí cluster			0	0		0.00	0		0		...					0....	24588
82-DAAA-a	rama-rama			0	0	0	0.00	0		0		...					0....	24589
82-DAAA-b	urumí			0	0	0	0.00	0		0		...					0....	24590
82-DAAB	ITOGAPúC cluster	1	1	200	340		10.00	34	A	4		...					0....	24591
82-DAAB-a	itogapúc	1	1	200	340	0	10.00	34	A	4		...					0....	24592
82-DB	ARARA-URUKU chain	1	1	300	510		10.00	33	A	0		...					0....	24593
82-DBA	**ARARA-URUKU net**	1	1	300	510		10.00	33	A	0		...					0....	24594
82-DBAA	ARARA-URUKU cluster	1	1	300	510		10.00	33	A	0		...					0....	24595
82-DBAA-a	arara-jiparaná					0				0		...					0....	24596
82-DBAA-b	urukú					0				0		...					0....	24597
82-E	**MONDE-ARUA set**	1	5	1,904	2,460		65.28	87	C	22		P..					0....	24598
82-EA	MONDE-ARUA chain	1	5	1,854	2,375		66.50	87	C	22		P..					0....	24599
82-EAA	**MONDE net**	1	1	17	22		41.18	71	B	8		...					0....	24600
82-EAAA	MONDé cluster	1	1	17	22		41.18	71	B	8		...					0....	24601
82-EAAA-a	sanamay	1	1	17	22	0	41.18	71	B	8		...					0....	24602
82-EAB	**ARUA-GAVIAO net**	1	4	1,837	2,353		66.74	88	C	22		P..					0....	24603
82-EABA	ARUá-GAVIAO cluster	1	4	1,837	2,353		66.74	88	C	22		P..					0....	24604
82-EABA-a	aruá-shi					0				22		p..					0....	24605
82-EABA-b	ikoro	1	1	493	632	0	30.02	65	B	22	Gaviao*	P..	1988				0....	24606
82-EABA-c	digut					0				22		p..					0....	24607
82-EABA-d	suruí-jiparaná	1	2	306	392	0	47.06	83	B	22	Surui*	P..	1991				0....	24608
82-EABA-e	cinta-larga	1	1	1,038	1,329	0	89.98	100	C	22		p..					0....	24609
82-EABA-f	cabeça-seca					0				22		p..					0....	24610
82-EABA-g	zoró					0				22		p..					0....	24611
82-EB	MEKEM chain	1	1	50	85		20.00	50	B	4		...					0....	24612
82-EBA	**MEKEM net**	1	1	50	85		20.00	50	B	4		...					0....	24613
82-EBAA	MEQUEM cluster	1	1	50	85		20.00	50	B	4		...					0....	24614
82-EBAA-a	mequem	1	1	50	85	0	20.00	50	B	4		...					0....	24615
82-F	**KARITIANA-ARIKEM set**	1	1	353	536		28.61	61	B	22		P..					0....	24616
82-FA	KARITIANA-KABISHIANA chain	1	1	353	536		28.61	61	B	22		P..					0....	24617
82-FAA	**KARITIANA-KABISHIANA net**	1	1	353	536		28.61	61	B	22		P..					0....	24618
82-FAAA	CARITIANA cluster	1	1	153	196		39.87	76	B	22		P..					0....	24619
82-FAAA-a	caritiana	1	1	153	196	0	39.87	76	B	22	Karitiana	P..	1981				0....	24620
82-FAAB	CABIXIANA cluster	1	1	200	340		20.00	51	B	0		...					0....	24621
82-FAAB-a	cabixiana	1	1	200	340	0	20.00	51	B	0		...					0....	24622
82-FB	ARIKEM chain									0		...					0....	24623
82-FBA	**ARIKEM net**									0		...					0....	24624
82-FBAA	ARIQUEM cluster			0	0		0.00	0		0		...					0....	24625
82-FBAA-a	ariquem			0	0	0	0.00	0		0		...					0....	24626
82-G	**TUPARI-MAKURAP set**	1	2	226	328		52.65	77	B	8		...					0....	24627
82-GA	TUPARI-KURATEG chain	1	2	226	328		52.65	77	B	8		...					0....	24628
82-GAA	**TUPARI net**	1	1	50	85		20.00	50	B	8		...					0....	24629

Continued overleaf

Table 9-13 continued

Code 1	REFERENCE NAME 2 / Autoglossonym	Coun 3	Peo 4	Mother-tongue speakers in 2000 5	in 2025 6	Media radio 7	CHURCH AC% 8	E% 9	Wld 10	Tr 11	Biblioglossonym 12	SCRIPTURES Print 13-15	P–activity 16	N–activity 17	B–activity 18	J-year 19	Jayuh 20-24	Ref 25
82-GAAA	TUPARí cluster	1	1	50	85		20.00	50	B	8		. . .					0	24630
82-GAAA-a	tupari	1	1	50	85	0	20.00	50	B	8							0	24631
82-GAB	**KANOE-AMNIAPE net**	1	1	17	22		58.82	94	B	0		. . .					0	24632
82-GABA	CANOé-AMNIAPé cluster	1	1	17	22		58.82	94	B	0		. . .					0	24633
82-GABA-a	canoé					0				0		. . .					0	24634
82-GABA-b	guara-tégaya	1	1	17	22	0	58.82	94	B	0		. . .					0	24635
82-GABA-c	amniapé					0				0		. . .					0	24636
82-GABA-d	mequens					0				0		. . .					0	24637
82-GAC	**KEPKIRIWAT net**									0		. . .					0	24638
82-GACA	KEPKIRIWAT cluster			0	0		0.00	0		0		. . .					0	24639
82-GACA-a	kepkiriwat			0	0	0	0.00	0		0		. . .					0	24640
82-GAD	**MAKURAP net**	1	1	119	153		79.83	100	C	6		. . .					0	24641
82-GADA	MAKURAP cluster	1	1	119	153		79.83	100	C	6		. . .					0	24642
82-GADA-a	kurateg	1	1	119	153	0	79.83	100	C	6		. . .					0	24643
82-GADA-b	massaka									6		. . .					0	24644
82-GAE	**WAYORO net**	1	1	40	68		10.00	33	A	4		. . .					0	24645
82-GAEA	WAYORó cluster	1	1	40	68		10.00	33	A	4		. . .					0	24646
82-GAEA-a	ajurú					0				4		. . .					0	24647
82-GAEA-b	apichum					0				4		. . .					0	24648
82-H	**PURUBORA set**	1	1	255	327		20.00	50	B	12		. . .					0	24649
82-HA	PURUBORA chain	1	1	255	327		20.00	50	B	12		. . .					0	24650
82-HAA	**PURUBORA net**	1	1	255	327		20.00	50	B	12		. . .					0	24651
82-HAAA	PURUBORA cluster	1	1	255	327		20.00	50	B	12		. . .					0	24652
82-HAAA-a	Proper puroborá					0				12		. . .					0	24653
82-HAAA-b	kuyubi					0				12		. . .					0	24654
82-HAAA-c	aura	1	1	255	327	0	20.00	50	B	12	Waura	. . .					0	24655
82-I	**AWETI set**	1	1	51	65		39.22	71	B	4		. . .					0	24656
82-IA	AWETI chain	1	1	51	65		39.22	71	B	4		. . .					0	24657
82-IAA	**AWETI net**	1	1	51	65		39.22	71	B	4		. . .					0	24658
82-IAAA	AWETí cluster	1	1	51	65		39.22	71	B	4		. . .					0	24659
82-IAAA-a	awetí	1	1	51	65	0	39.22	71	B	4		. . .					0	24660
82-J	**JURUNA-MANITSAWA set**	1	1	153	196		69.93	100	C	3		. . .					0	24661
82-JA	JURUNA-MANITSAWA chain	1	1	153	196		69.93	100	C	3		. . .					0	24662
82-JAA	**JURUNA-SHIPAYA net**	1	1	153	196		69.93	100	C	3		. . .					0	24663
82-JAAA	YURUNA-XIPAYA cluster	1	1	153	196		69.93	100	C	3		. . .					0	24664
82-JAAA-a	yurúna	1	1	153	196	0	69.93	100	C	3		. . .					0	24665
82-JAAA-b	xipaya			0	0	0	0.00	0		3		. . .					0	24666
82-JAB	**MANITSAWA net**									0		. . .					0	24667
82-JABA	MANITSAWá cluster			0	0		0.00	0		0		. . .					0	24668
82-JABA-a	arupai					0				0		. . .					0	24669
83	**INTEROCEANIC zone**	8	50	715,694	1,058,894		74.97	96	C	42		PN.					4 . s . .	24670
83-A	**MISUMALPAN set**	2	4	216,880	370,616		89.53	100	C	42		PN.					4	24671
83-AA	MISUMALPAN chain	2	4	216,880	370,616		89.53	100	C	42		PN.					4	24672
83-AAA	**MISKITU net**	2	2	204,595	349,620		89.79	100	C	42		PN.					4	24673
83-AAAA	MíSKITU cluster	2	2	204,595	349,620		89.79	100	C	42	Miskito	PN. 1889-1958	1905-1975			1995	4	24674
83-AAAA-a	mam	1	1	14,313	23,518	0	87.00	100	C	42	Miskito	PN. 1889-1958	1905-1975				1	24675
83-AAAA-b	tawira					0				42		pn.					1	24676
83-AAAA-c	baymuna					0				42		pn.					1	24677
83-AAAA-d	wanki					0				42		pn.					1	24678
83-AAAA-e	cabo					0				42		pn.					1	24679
83-AAB	**SUMO net**	2	2	12,285	20,996		85.14	100	C	14		. . .					0	24680
83-AABA	SUMO cluster	2	2	12,285	20,996		85.14	100	C	14		. . .					0	24681
83-AABA-a	North sumo	1	1	817	1,343	0	87.03	100	C	14		. . .					0	24682
83-AABA-b	South sumo	1	1	11,468	19,653	0	85.00	100	C	14	Sumo	. . .					0	24686
83-AAC	**MATAGALPA-KAKAOPERA net**									9		. . .					0	24689
83-AACA	CACAOPERA cluster			0	0		0.00	0		9		. . .					0	24690
83-AACA-a	cacaopera			0	0	0	0.00	0		9		. . .					0	24691
83-AACB	MATAGALPA cluster			0	0		0.00	0		9		. . .					0	24692
83-AACB-a	matagalpa			0	0	0	0.00	0		9		. . .					0	24693
83-B	**PAYA set**	1	1	908	1,492		70.04	100	C	6		. . .					0	24694
83-BA	PAYA chain	1	1	908	1,492		70.04	100	C	6		. . .					0	24695
83-BAA	**PAYA net**	1	1	908	1,492		70.04	100	C	6		. . .					0	24696
83-BAAA	PECH cluster	1	1	908	1,492		70.04	100	C	6		. . .					0	24697
83-BAAA-a	pech	1	1	908	1,492	0	70.04	100	C	6		. . .					0	24698
83-C	**RAMA set**	1	1	50	85		40.00	76	B	0		. . .					0	24699
83-CA	RAMA chain	1	1	50	85		40.00	76	B	0		. . .					0	24700
83-CAA	**RAMA net**	1	1	50	85		40.00	76	B	0		. . .					0	24701
83-CAAA	RAMA cluster	1	1	50	85		40.00	76	B	0		. . .					0	24702
83-CAAA-a	rama	1	1	50	85	0	40.00	76	B	0		. . .					0	24703
83-D	**GUATUSO set**	1	1	556	819		80.04	100	C	6		. . .					0	24704
83-DA	GUATUSO chain	1	1	556	819		80.04	100	C	6		. . .					0	24705
83-DAA	**GUATUSO net**	1	1	556	819		80.04	100	C	6		. . .					24706

Continued opposite

Table 9-13 continued

Code 1	REFERENCE NAME / Autoglossonym 2	Coun 3	Peo 4	Mother-tongue speakers in 2000 5	in 2025 6	Media radio 7	CHURCH AC% 8	E% 9	Wld 10	Tr 11	Biblioglossonym 12	SCRIPTURES Print 13-15	P-activity 16	N-activity 17	B-activity 18	J-year 19	Jayuh 20-24	Ref 25
83-DAAA	MALéKU-KWERESA cluster	1	1	556	819		80.04	100	C	6		. . .					0	24707
83-DAAA-a	maléku-jaíka	1	1	556	819	0	80.04	100	C	6		. . .					0	24708
83-DAAA-b	kweresa			0	0	0	0.00	0		6		. . .					0	24709
83-E	**CHIBCHA-TERIBE set**	4	31	297,114	403,484		77.00	98	C	41		PN .					4 . s . .	24710
83-EA	TERIBE chain	2	2	2,607	3,497		67.32	100	C	22		P . .					0	24711
83-EAA	**TERIBE net**	2	2	2,607	3,497		67.32	100	C	22		P . .					0	24712
83-EAAA	NASO cluster	2	2	2,607	3,497		67.32	100	C	22		P . .					0	24713
83-EAAA-a	West naso	1	1	322	474	0	83.85	100	C	22	Teribe	P . .	1979-1984				0	24714
83-EAAA-b	East naso	1	1	2,285	3,023	0	64.99	100	C	22	Teribe	P . .	1979-1984				0	24715
83-EB	TALAMANKA chain	2	4	14,797	21,504		78.22	100	C	41		PN .					0 . s . .	24716
83-EBA	**BORUKA net**	1	1	1,303	1,920		85.03	100	C	8		. . .					0	24717
83-EBAA	BORUCA cluster	1	1	1,303	1,920		85.03	100	C	8		. . .					0	24718
83-EBAA-a	brunka	1	1	1,303	1,920	0	85.03	100	C	8		. . .					0	24719
83-EBB	**KABEKAR-BRIBRI net**	2	3	13,494	19,584		77.56	100	C	41		PN .					0 . s . .	24720
83-EBBA	CABéCAR cluster	1	1	4,444	6,549		78.02	100	C	41		PN .					0	24721
83-EBBA-a	cabécar	1	1	4,444	6,549	0	78.02	100	C	41		PN .					0	24722
83-EBBB	BRIBRI cluster	2	2	9,050	13,035		77.34	100	C	22		P . .					0 . s . .	24728
83-EBBB-a	bribri	2	2	9,050	13,035	0	77.34	100	C	22	Bribri	P . .	1905-1994				0 . s . .	24729
83-EC	GUAYMI-BUGLERE chain	1	3	114,570	151,621		84.40	100	C	41		PN .					0	24733
83-ECA	**GUAYMI-BUGLERE net**	1	3	114,570	151,621		84.40	100	C	41		PN .					0	24734
83-ECAA	NGOBERE cluster	1	2	111,372	147,388		84.67	100	C	23		P . .					0	24735
83-ECAA-a	West ngobere	1	1	74,248	98,259	0	92.00	100	C	23	Guaymi	P . .	1924-1995				0	24736
83-ECAA-b	East ngobere	1	1	37,124	49,129	0	70.00	100	C	23	Guaymi: Eastern	P . .	1968				0	24737
83-ECAB	BUGLERE cluster	1	1	3,198	4,233		75.02	100	C	41	Buglere	PN .	1980	1988			0	24738
83-ECAB-a	sabanero					0				41		pn .					0	24739
83-ECAB-b	bokotá					0				41		pn .					0	24740
83-ED	NORTH ARWAKO chain	1	3	17,410	24,584		44.55	78	B	12		. . .					0	24741
83-EDA	**COGUI net**	1	1	5,933	8,378		65.01	99	C	12		. . .					0	24742
83-EDAA	COGUI cluster	1	1	5,933	8,378		65.01	99	C	12		. . .					0	24743
83-EDAA-a	cówgi	1	1	5,933	8,378	0	65.01	99	C	12	Kogui	. . .					0	24744
83-EDB	**ICA net**	1	1	7,465	10,541		20.00	53	B	2		. . .					0	24745
83-EDBA	ICA cluster	1	1	7,465	10,541		20.00	53	B	2		. . .					0	24746
83-EDBA-a	ihka	1	1	7,465	10,541	0	20.00	53	B	2		. . .					0	24747
83-EDC	**MALAYO net**	1	1	4,012	5,665		60.00	95	B	12		. . .					0	24748
83-EDCA	MALAYO cluster	1	1	4,012	5,665		60.00	95	B	12		. . .					0	24749
83-EDCA-a	wiwa	1	1	4,012	5,665	0	60.00	95	B	12	Malayo	. . .					0	24750
83-EE	SOUTH ARWAKO chain	1	1	2,488	3,514		45.02	76	B	12		. . .					0	24751
83-EEA	**CHIMILA net**	1	1	2,488	3,514		45.02	76	B	12		. . .					0	24752
83-EEAA	CHIMILA cluster	1	1	2,488	3,514		45.02	76	B	12	Chimila	. . .					0	24753
83-EEAA-a	caca-weranos					0				12		. . .					0	24754
83-EEAA-b	san-jorge					0				12		. . .					0	24755
83-EF	CHIBCHA-TUNEBO chain	2	5	5,425	7,676		51.08	81	B	41		PN .					0	24756
83-EFA	**TUNEBO net**	2	5	5,425	7,676		51.08	81	B	41		PN .					0	24757
83-EFAA	WEST TUNEBO cluster	1	1	846	1,195		40.07	69	B	3		. . .					0	24758
83-EFAA-a	West tunebo	1	1	846	1,195	0	40.07	69	B	3		. . .					0	24759
83-EFAB	UPPER TUNEBO cluster	2	3	3,318	4,700		42.89	78	B	41		PN .					0	24760
83-EFAB-a	Central tunebo	2	2	2,836	4,019	0	39.99	75	B	41	Tunebo*	PN .	1972-1982	1987			0	24761
83-EFAB-b	tunebo-angosturas					0				41		pn .					0	24762
83-EFAB-c	East tunebo	1	1	482	681	0	59.96	94	B	41		pn .					0	24763
83-EFAC	CHIBCHA cluster	1	1	1,261	1,781		80.02	100	C	9		. . .					0	24764
83-EFAC-a	chibcha	1	1	1,261	1,781	0	80.02	100	C	9		. . .					0	24765
83-EG	CUNA chain	2	3	58,794	77,884		84.57	100	C	41		PN .					4	24766
83-EGA	**CUNA net**	2	3	58,794	77,884		84.57	100	C	41		PN .					4	24767
83-EGAA	CUNA cluster	2	3	58,794	77,884		84.57	100	C	41		PN .					4	24768
83-EGAA-a	cuna-sanblas	1	1	57,114	75,583	0	85.00	100	C	41	Kuna: San Blas*	PN .	1951-1965	1970-1995		1996	4	24769
83-EGAA-b	Southeast cuna	2	2	1,680	2,301	0	70.00	100	C	41		PN .					1	24774
83-EH	BARI chain	2	2	3,895	5,536		70.01	100	C	12		. . .					0	24777
83-EHA	**BARI net**	2	2	3,895	5,536		70.01	100	C	12		. . .					0	24778
83-EHAA	BARí cluster	2	2	3,895	5,536		70.01	100	C	12		. . .					0	24779
83-EHAA-a	barí	2	2	3,895	5,536	0	70.01	100	C	12	Motilon	. . .					0	24780
83-EI	EMBERA-NOANAMA chain	2	8	77,128	107,668		70.86	99	C	41		PN .					0	24781
83-EIA	**EMBERA-NOANAMA net**	2	8	77,128	107,668		70.86	99	C	41		PN .					0	24782
83-EIAA	EMBERá cluster	2	6	70,633	98,801		71.40	99	C	41		PN .					0	24783
83-EIAA-a	sambú	2	2	29,478	40,695	0	85.00	100	C	41	Embera, Northern	PN .	1972-1980	1993			0	24784
83-EIAA-b	atrato					0				41		pn .					0	24785
83-EIAA-c	tukurá					0				41		pn .					0	24786
83-EIAA-d	catío	2	2	23,571	33,277	0	60.08	97	C	41	Catio*	Pn .	1972-1987				0	24787
83-EIAA-e	caramanta-sitará					0				41		pn .					0	24793
83-EIAA-f	chamí	1	1	13,259	18,722	0	65.00	100	C	41	Embera-chami	pn .					0	24794
83-EIAA-g	tadó					0				41	Embera-tado	pn .					0	24795
83-EIAA-h	baudó					0				41		pn .					0	24796
83-EIAA-i	saija	1	1	4,325	6,107	0	60.00	97	C	41	Embera-saija	Pn .	1991				0	24797
83-EIAA-j	runa			0	0	0	0.00	0		41		pn .					0	24798
83-EIAB	NOANAMA cluster	2	2	6,495	8,867		64.99	100	C	41	Waunana*	PN .	1979-1982	1988			0	24799
83-EIAB-a	North noanama					0				41		pn .					0	24800
83-EIAB-b	South noanama					0				41		pn .					0	24801
83-F	**KOFAN set**	2	2	1,486	2,094		20.73	53	B	41		PN .					0	24802
83-FA	KOFAN chain	2	2	1,486	2,094		20.73	53	B	41		PN .					0	24803
83-FAA	**KOFAN net**	2	2	1,486	2,094		20.73	53	B	41		PN .					0	24804

Continued overleaf

Table 9-13 continued

Code 1	REFERENCE NAME / Autoglossonym 2	Coun 3	Peo 4	in 2000 5	in 2025 6	Media radio 7	AC% 8	E% 9	Wld 10	Tr 11	Biblioglossonym 12	Print 13-15	P-activity 16	N-activity 17	B-activity 18	J-year 19	Jayuh 20-24	Ref 25
83-FAAA	COFáN cluster	2	2	1,486	2,094		20.73	53	B	41		PN.					0....	24805
83-FAAA-a	North cofán	2	2	1,486	2,094		20.73	53	B	41	Cofan	PN.	1964	1980-1991			0....	24806
83-FAAA-b	santa-rosa					0				41		pn.					0....	24807
83-FAAA-c	aguarico					0				41		pn.					0....	24808
83-G	**PAEZ-KOKONUKO set**	1	2	125,216	176,891		65.52	100	C	41		PN.					0....	24809
83-GA	KOKONUKO-WAMBIANO chain	1	1	15,976	22,644		69.06	99	C	22		P..					0....	24810
83-GAA	**KOKONUKO-WAMBIANO net**	1	1	15,976	22,644		69.06	99	C	22		P..					0....	24811
83-GAAA	COCONUCO cluster	1	1	300	510		20.00	50	B	0		...					0....	24812
83-GAAA-a	coconuco	1	1	300	510	0	20.00	50	B	0		...					0....	24813
83-GAAB	TOTORó cluster			0	0		0.00	0		0		...					0....	24814
83-GAAB-a	totoró					0				0		...					0....	24815
83-GAAC	GUAMBIANO cluster	1	1	15,676	22,134		70.00	100	C	22		P..					0....	24816
83-GAAC-a	wambiano	1	1	15,676	22,134	0	70.00	100	C	22	Guambiano	P..	1982				0....	24817
83-GAAC-b	mogés					0				22		p..					0....	24818
83-GB	PAES-ANDAKI chain	1	1	109,240	154,247		65.00	100	C	41		PN.					0....	24819
83-GBA	**PAES-PANSALEO net**	1	1	109,240	154,247		65.00	100	C	41		PN.					0....	24820
83-GBAA	PAEZ cluster	1	1	109,240	154,247		65.00	100	C	41		PN.					0....	24821
83-GBAA-a	paez	1	1	109,240	154,247	0	65.00	100	C	41	Paez	PN.	1969-1985	1980			0....	24822
83-GBAA-b	pitayo					0				41		pn.					0....	24823
83-GBAA-c	paniquita					0				41		pn.					0....	24824
83-GBAB	PANZALEO cluster			0	0		0.00	0		0		...					0....	24825
83-GBAB-a	panzaleo			0	0	0	0.00	0		0		...					0....	24826
83-GBB	**ANDAKI net**									0		...					0....	24827
83-GBBA	ANDAQUí cluster			0	0		0.00	0		0		...					0....	24828
83-GBBA-a	andaquí					0				0		...					0....	24829
83-H	**KWAIKER-KAYAPA set**	2	4	38,733	54,644		54.15	88	B	41		PN.					0....	24830
83-HA	KWAIKER chain	2	2	30,067	42,449		65.00	99	C	22		P..					0....	24831
83-HAA	**KWAIKER net**	2	2	30,067	42,449		65.00	99	C	22		P..					0....	24832
83-HAAA	COAIQUER cluster	2	2	30,067	42,449		65.00	99	C	22		P..					0....	24833
83-HAAA-a	coaiquer	2	2	30,067	42,449	0	65.00	99	C	22	Cuaiquer	P..	1979-1982				0....	24834
83-HAAA-b	awa					0				22		p..					0....	24835
83-HAAB	BARBACOAS-PASTO cluster			0	0		0.00	0		9		...					0....	24836
83-HAAB-a	barbacoas			0	0	0	0.00	0		9		...					0....	24837
83-HAAB-b	muelyama			0	0	0	0.00	0		9		...					0....	24838
83-HAAB-c	pasto			0	0	0	0.00	0		9		...					0....	24839
83-HB	KAYAPA-KOLORADO chain	1	2	8,666	12,195		16.48	51	B	41		PN.					0....	24840
83-HBA	**KAYAPA net**	1	1	6,372	8,967		8.00	41	A	22		P..					0....	24841
83-HBAA	CAYAPA cluster	1	1	6,372	8,967		8.00	41	A	22		P..					0....	24842
83-HBAA-a	cayapa	1	1	6,372	8,967	0	8.00	41	A	22	Cayapa*	P..	1964-1980				0....	24843
83-HBB	**KOLORADO net**	1	1	2,294	3,228		40.02	78	B	41		PN.					0....	24844
83-HBBA	TSAFIKI cluster	1	1	2,294	3,228		40.02	78	B	41		PN.					0....	24845
83-HBBA-a	tsá-fiki	1	1	2,294	3,228	0	40.02	78	B	41	Colorado	PN.	1964-1990	1980-1990			0....	24846
83-I	**HIRAHARA-GAYON set**									0		...					0....	24847
83-IA	HIRAHARA-GAYON chain									0		...					0....	24848
83-IAA	**HIRAHARA-GAYON net**									0		...					0....	24849
83-IAAA	JIRAJARA cluster			0	0		0.00	0		0		...					0....	24850
83-IAAA-a	jirajara			0	0	0	0.00	0		0		...					0....	24851
83-IAAB	AYOMáN cluster			0	0		0.00	0		0		...					0....	24852
83-IAAB-a	ayomán			0	0	0	0.00	0		0		...					0....	24853
83-IAAC	GAYóN cluster			0	0		0.00	0		0		...					0....	24854
83-IAAC-a	gayón			0	0	0	0.00	0		0		...					0....	24855
83-J	**ESMERALDA set**									0		...					0....	24856
83-JA	ESMERALDA chain									0		...					0....	24857
83-JAA	**ESMERALDA net**									0		...					0....	24858
83-JAAA	TACAME cluster			0	0		0.00	0		0		...					0....	24859
83-JAAA-a	tacame			0	0	0	0.00	0		0		...					0....	24860
83-K	**YARURO set**	1	1	3,396	4,886		10.01	40	A	12		...					0....	24861
83-KA	YARURO chain	1	1	3,396	4,886		10.01	40	A	12		...					0....	24862
83-KAA	**YARURO net**	1	1	3,396	4,886		10.01	40	A	12		...					0....	24863
83-KAAA	PUME cluster	1	1	3,396	4,886		10.01	40	A	12		...					0....	24864
83-KAAA-a	pume	1	1	3,396	4,886	0	10.01	40	A	12	Yaruro	...					0....	24865
83-L	**TIMOTE-MUKUCHI set**	1	1	434	677		25.35	56	B	2		...					0....	24866
83-LA	TIMOTE-MUKUCHI chain	1	1	434	677		25.35	56	B	2		...					0....	24867
83-LAA	**TIMOTE-MUKUCHI net**	1	1	434	677		25.35	56	B	2		...					0....	24868
83-LAAA	TIMOTE cluster			0	0		0.00	0		0		...					0....	24869
83-LAAA-a	Proper timote			0	0	0	0.00	0		0		...					0....	24870
83-LAAA-b	cuica			0	0	0	0.00	0		0		...					0....	24871
83-LAAB	MUTúS cluster	1	1	234	337		29.91	61	B	2		...					0....	24872
83-LAAB-a	mutús	1	1	234	337	0	29.91	61	B	2		...					0....	24873
83-LAAB-b	loco					0				2		...					0....	24874
83-LAAC	MUCUCHí cluster	1	1	200	340		20.00	51	B	0		...					0....	24875
83-LAAC-a	Proper mucuchí					0				0		...					0....	24876
83-LAAC-b	maripú					0				0		...					0....	24877
83-M	**BETOY set**									0		...					0....	24878

Continued opposite

Table 9-13 continued

Code 1	REFERENCE NAME / Autoglossonym 2	Coun 3	Peo 4	Mother-tongue speakers in 2000 5	in 2025 6	Media radio 7	AC% 8	E% 9	Wld 10	Tr 11	Biblioglossonym 12	Print 13-15	P-activity 16	N-activity 17	B-activity 18	J-year 19	Jayuh 20-24	Ref 25
83-MA	BETOY chain									0		...					0....	24879
83-MAA	**BETOY net**									0		...					0....	24880
83-MAAA	BETOY cluster			0	0		0.00	0		0		...					0....	24881
83-MAAA-a	betoy			0	0	0	0.00	0		0		...					0....	24882
83-N	**YURIMANGI set**									0		...					0....	24883
83-NA	YURIMANGI chain									0		...					0....	24884
83-NAA	**YURIMANGI net**									0		...					0....	24885
83-NAAA	YURIMANGI cluster			0	0		0.00	0		0		...					0....	24886
83-NAAA-a	yurimangi			0	0	0	0.00	0		0		...					0....	24887
83-O	**KAMSA set**	1	1	5,036	7,111		39.99	76	B	41		PN.					0....	24888
83-OA	KAMSA chain	1	1	5,036	7,111		39.99	76	B	41		PN.					0....	24889
83-OAA	**KAMSA net**	1	1	5,036	7,111		39.99	76	B	41		PN.					0....	24890
83-OAAA	CAMSá cluster	1	1	5,036	7,111		39.99	76	B	41		PN.					0....	24891
83-OAAA-a	camsá	1	1	5,036	7,111	0	39.99	76	B	41	Camsa	PN.	1973	1990			0....	24892
83-P	**WARAO set**	2	2	25,885	36,095		25.89	63	B	42		PN.					0....	24893
83-PA	WARAO chain	2	2	25,885	36,095		25.89	63	B	42		PN.					0....	24894
83-PAA	**WARAO net**	2	2	25,885	36,095		25.89	63	B	42		PN.					0....	24895
83-PAAA	GUARAO cluster	2	2	25,885	36,095		25.89	63	B	42		PN.					0....	24896
83-PAAA-a	Proper guarao	2	2	25,885	36,095		25.89	63	B	42	Warao	PN.	1960-1967	1974			0....	24897
83-PAAA-b	guasay					0				42		pn.					0....	24898
83-PAAA-c	mariusa					0				42		pn.					0....	24899
83-PAAA-d	hoanarau					0				42		pn.					0....	24900
83-PAAA-e	cocuina					0				42		pn.					0....	24901
83-PAAA-f	changuane					0				42		pn.					0....	24902
84	**PRE-ANDINIC zone**	5	74	199,050	280,430		23.80	61	B	42		PN.					1....	24903
84-A	**KOFAN set**									0		...					0....	24904
84-AA	KOFAN chain									0		...					0....	24905
84-AAA	**KOFAN net**									0		...					0....	24906
84-AAAA	COFáN cluster									0		...					0....	24907
84-AAAA-a	Northwest cofán					0				0		...					0....	24908
84-AAAA-b	Southeast cofán					0				0		...					0....	24909
84-B	**MURUI-OKAINA set**	3	12	7,048	9,855		73.92	98	C	41		PN.					0....	24910
84-BA	MURUI-OKAINA chain	3	12	7,048	9,855		73.92	98	C	41		PN.					0....	24911
84-BAA	**MURUI net**	3	3	3,691	5,139		81.03	97	C	41		PN.					0....	24912
84-BAAA	MURUI cluster	3	3	3,691	5,139		81.03	97	C	41		PN.					0....	24913
84-BAAA-a	North murui					0				41		pn.					0....	24914
84-BAAA-b	Central murui	3	3	3,691	5,139	0	81.03	97	C	41	Huitoto: Murui*	PN.	1963-1980	1978			0....	24915
84-BAAA-c	South murui					0				41		pn.					0....	24916
84-BAB	**MENEKA net**	2	6	2,562	3,613		66.24	99	C	41		PN.					0....	24917
84-BABA	MENECA cluster	2	6	2,562	3,613		66.24	99	C	41	Huitoto: Minica*	PN.	1972-1973	1985			0....	24918
84-BABA-a	nüpode	2	2	174	244	0	60.34	91	C	41	Huitoto, Nipode	Pn.	1961				0....	24919
84-BABA-b	muinane-meneca	2	2	335	470	0	77.01	100	C	41	Huitoto: Muinani*	PN.	1961-1969	1981			0....	24920
84-BAC	**NONUYA net**									0		...					0....	24921
84-BACA	NONUñA cluster			0	0		0.00	0		0		...					0....	24922
84-BACA-a	nonuña			0	0	0	0.00	0		0		...					0....	24923
84-BAD	**KOERUNA net**									0		...					0....	24924
84-BADA	COERUNA cluster			0	0		0.00	0		0		...					0....	24925
84-BADA-a	coeruna			0	0	0	0.00	0		0		...					0....	24926
84-BAE	**ANDOKERO net**									0		...					0....	24927
84-BAEA	ANDOQUERO cluster			0	0		0.00	0		0		...					0....	24928
84-BAEA-a	andoquero			0	0	0	0.00	0		0		...					0....	24929
84-BAF	**OKAINA net**	2	2	390	542		71.54	100	C	23		P..					0....	24930
84-BAFA	OCAINA cluster	2	2	390	542		71.54	100	C	23		P..					0....	24931
84-BAFA-a	Proper ocaina	2	2	390	542	0	71.54	100	C	23	Ocaina	P..	1964-1971				0....	24932
84-BAFA-b	dukaiya					0				23		p..					0....	24933
84-BAFA-c	ibo'tsa					0				23		p..					0....	24934
84-BAG	**OREJON net**	1	1	405	561		60.00	98	C	22		P..					0....	24935
84-BAGA	OREJóN cluster	1	1	405	561		60.00	98	C	22		P..					0....	24936
84-BAGA-a	orejón	1	1	405	561	0	60.00	98	C	22	Orejon	P..	1967-1976				0....	24937
84-C	**ANDOKE set**	1	1	432	610		59.95	90	B	3		...					0....	24938
84-CA	ANDOKE chain	1	1	432	610		59.95	90	B	3		...					0....	24939
84-CAA	**ANDOKE net**	1	1	432	610		59.95	90	B	3		...					0....	24940
84-CAAA	ANDOQUE cluster	1	1	432	610		59.95	90	B	3		...					0....	24941
84-CAAA-a	andoque	1	1	432	610	0	59.95	90	B	3		...					0....	24942
84-D	**BORAN set**	3	3	5,114	7,671		31.44	65	B	41		PN.					0....	24943
84-DA	BORA-MUINANE chain	3	3	3,114	4,271		38.79	75	B	41		PN.					0....	24944
84-DAA	**BORA-MUINANE net**	3	3	3,114	4,271		38.79	75	B	41		PN.					0....	24945
84-DAAA	BORA-MUINANE cluster	3	3	3,114	4,271		38.79	75	B	41		PN.					0....	24946
84-DAAA-a	muinane-bora	3	3	3,114	4,271	0	38.79	75	B	41	Bora	PN.	1962-1976	1982			0....	24947
84-DAAA-b	faai					0				41		pn.					0....	24948
84-DAAA-c	imihita					0				41		pn.					0....	24949

Continued overleaf

Table 9-13 continued

Code 1	REFERENCE NAME 2 / Autoglossonym	Coun 3	Peo 4	Mother-tongue speakers in 2000 5	in 2025 6	Media radio 7	AC% 8	CHURCH E% 9	Wld 10	Tr 11	Biblioglossonym 12	SCRIPTURES Print 13-15	P-activity 16	N-activity 17	B-activity 18	J-year 19	Jayuh 20-24	Ref 25
84-DB	BORA-MIRANYA chain	1	1	2,000	3,400		20.00	50	B	0		...					0....	24950
84-DBA	**BORA-MIRANYA net**	1	1	2,000	3,400		20.00	50	B	0		...					0....	24951
84-DBAA	BORA-MIRAñA cluster	3	1	2,000	3,400		20.00	50	B	0		...					0....	24952
84-DBAA-a	bora-miraña	1	1	2,000	3,400	0	20.00	50	B	0		...					0....	24953
84-E	**HIVARO set**	2	5	99,988	139,544		7.75	49	A	42		PN.					1....	24954
84-EA	HIVARO chain	2	5	99,988	139,544		7.75	49	A	42		PN.					1....	24955
84-EAA	**HIVARO net**	2	5	99,988	139,544		7.75	49	A	42		PN.					1....	24956
84-EAAA	PROPER JíVARO cluster	2	4	63,743	89,378		8.18	48	A	42		PN.					1....	24957
84-EAAA-a	shuar	1	1	46,670	65,677	0	8.00	49	A	42	Shuar: Ecuador	PN.	1939-1966	1976-1983		1993	1....	24958
84-EAAA-b	achuara	2	2	7,740	10,783	0	13.05	52	B	42	Achual*	PN.	1972-1979	1981			1....	24959
84-EAAA-c	huambisa	1	1	9,333	12,918	0	5.00	43	A	42	Huambisa	PN.	1965-1971	1975			1....	24962
84-EAAB	AWAHUN cluster	1	1	36,245	50,166		7.00	49	A	42		PN.					0....	24963
84-EAAB-a	awahun	1	1	36,245	50,166	0	7.00	49	A	42	Aguaruna	PN.	1942-1971	1973			0....	24964
84-F	**CHAYAWITA-HEVERO set**	1	2	13,087	18,115		46.71	86	B	41		PN.					0....	24965
84-FA	CHAYAWITA-HEVERO chain	1	2	13,087	18,115		46.71	86	B	41		PN.					0....	24966
84-FAA	**CHAYAWITA net**	1	1	8,699	12,041		40.00	80	B	41		PN.					0....	24967
84-FAAA	CHAYAHUITA cluster	1	1	8,699	12,041		40.00	80	B	41		PN.					0....	24968
84-FAAA-a	Proper chayahuita	1	1	8,699	12,041	0	40.00	80	B	41	Chayahuita	PN.	1964-1975	1978			0....	24969
84-FAAA-b	cahuapana					0				41		pn.					0....	24970
84-FAAA-c	yamoraí					0				41		pn.					0....	24971
84-FAB	**HEVERO net**	1	1	4,388	6,074		60.00	98	C	23		P..					0....	24972
84-FABA	JEVERO cluster	1	1	4,388	6,074		60.00	98	C	23		P..					0....	24973
84-FABA-a	shewélo	1	1	4,388	6,074	0	60.00	98	C	23	Jebero	P..	1959				0....	24974
84-G	**URARINA set**	2	2	4,909	6,816		14.81	48	A	41		PN.					0....	24975
84-GA	URARINA chain	2	2	4,909	6,816		14.81	48	A	41		PN.					0....	24976
84-GAA	**URARINA net**	2	2	4,909	6,816		14.81	48	A	41		PN.					0....	24977
84-GAAA	URARINA cluster	2	2	4,909	6,816		14.81	48	A	41		PN.					0....	24978
84-GAAA-a	Proper urarina	1	1	3,988	5,520	0	9.00	41	A	41	Urarina	Pn.	1973-1990				0....	24979
84-GAAA-b	shimacu					0				41		pn.					0....	24980
84-GAAA-c	itucali					0				41		pn.					0....	24981
84-GAAA-d	singacuchusca					0				41		pn.					0....	24982
84-GAAA-e	arucuye					0				41		pn.					0....	24983
84-GAAA-f	chambira					0				41		pn.					0....	24984
84-GAAA-g	waorani	1	1	921	1,296	0	39.96	77	B	41	Waorani	PN.	1964-1981	1992			0....	24985
84-H	**ZAPARO-IKITO set**	2	5	956	1,391		56.49	89	B	41		PN.					0....	24986
84-HA	ZAPARO-ANDOA chain	2	3	758	1,117		53.30	87	B	41		PN.					0....	24987
84-HAA	**ZAPARO-KONAMBO net**	1	1	200	340		20.00	51	B	3		...					0....	24988
84-HAAA	ZAPARO-CONAMBO cluster	2	1	200	340		20.00	51	B	3		...					0....	24989
84-HAAA-a	cáyapwi					0				3		...					0....	24990
84-HAAA-b	conambo					0				3		...					0....	24991
84-HAB	**ARABELA-ANDOA net**	2	3	558	777		65.23	100	C	41		PN.					0....	24992
84-HABA	ARABELA-ANDOA cluster	2	3	558	777		65.23	100	C	41		PN.					0....	24993
84-HABA-a	chiripuno	1	1	362	501	0	59.94	100	B	41	Arabela	PN.	1965-1977	1986			0....	24994
84-HABA-b	aushiri	1		0	0	0	0.00	0		41		pn.					0....	24995
84-HABA-c	simicai	2	2	196	276	0	75.00	100	C	41		pn.					0....	24996
84-HB	IKITO-KAWARAN chain	1	2	198	274		68.69	98	C	23		P..					0....	24997
84-HBA	**IKITO-KAWARAN net**	1	2	198	274		68.69	98	C	23		P..					0....	24998
84-HBAA	IQUITO-CAHUARAN cluster	1	2	198	274		68.69	98	C	23		P..					0....	24999
84-HBAA-a	iquito	1	1	190	263	0	70.00	99	C	23	Iquito	P..	1963				0....	25000
84-HBAA-b	amacacore					0				23		p..					0....	25001
84-HBAA-c	puca-uma					0				23		p..					0....	25002
84-HBAA-d	cawarán	1		8	11	0	37.50	75	B	23		p..					0....	25003
84-I	**PEBA-YAGUA set**	1	1	5,123	7,107		15.05	51	B	41		PN.					0....	25004
84-IA	PEBA-YAGUA chain	1	1	5,123	7,107		15.05	51	B	41		PN.					0....	25005
84-IAA	**YAMEO net**	1	1	50	85		20.00	50	B	0		...					0....	25006
84-IAAA	YAMéO cluster	1	1	50	85		20.00	50	B	0		...					0....	25007
84-IAAA-a	yaméo	1	1	50	85	0	20.00	50	B	0		...					0....	25008
84-IAB	**PEBA net**									0		...					0....	25009
84-IABA	PEBA cluster			0	0		0.00	0		0		...					0....	25010
84-IABA-a	peba			0	0	0	0.00	0		0		...					0....	25011
84-IAC	**YAGUA net**	1	1	5,073	7,022		15.00	51	B	41		PN.					0....	25012
84-IACA	NIXAMWI cluster	1	1	5,073	7,022		15.00	51	B	41		PN.					0....	25013
84-IACA-a	nixamwi	1	1	5,073	7,022	0	15.00	51	B	41	Yagua	PN.	1964-1976	1994			0....	25014
84-J	**TAUSHIRO set**	1	1	31	43		58.06	94	B	8		...					0....	25015
84-JA	TAUSHIRO chain	1	1	31	43		58.06	94	B	8		...					0....	25016
84-JAA	**TAUSHIRO net**	1	1	31	43		58.06	94	B	8		...					0....	25017
84-JAAA	ITE'TSHI cluster	1	1	31	43		58.06	94	B	8		...					0....	25018
84-JAAA-a	ite'tshi	1	1	31	43	0	58.06	94	B	8		...					0....	25019
84-K	**OMURANO set**									9		...					0....	25020
84-KA	OMURANO chain									9		...					0....	25021
84-KAA	**OMURANO net**									9		...					0....	25022
84-KAAA	OMURANO cluster			0	0		0.00	0		9		...					0....	25023
84-KAAA-a	omurano					0				9		...					0....	25024

Continued opposite

Table 9-13 continued

Code 1	REFERENCE NAME / Autoglossonym 2	Coun 3	Peo 4	Mother-tongue speakers in 2000 5	in 2025 6	Media radio 7	CHURCH AC% 8	E% 9	Wld 10	Tr 11	Biblioglossonym 12	SCRIPTURES Print 13-15	P–activity 16	N–activity 17	B–activity 18	J-year 19	Jayuh 20-24	Ref 25
84-L	**KANDOSHI set**	1	1	4,350	6,020		6.00	41	A	41		PN.					0....	25025
84-LA	KANDOSHI chain	1	1	4,350	6,020		6.00	41	A	41		PN.					0....	25026
84-LAA	**KANDOSHI net**	1	1	4,350	6,020		6.00	41	A	41		PN.					0....	25027
84-LAAA	CANDOSHI cluster	1	1	4,350	6,020		6.00	41	A	41		PN.					0....	25028
84-LAAA-a	candoshi	1	1	4,350	6,020	0	6.00	41	A	41	Candoshi*	PN.	1958-1977	1979-1991			0....	25029
84-LAAA-b	chapara					0				41		pn.					0....	25030
84-LAAA-c	murato					0				41		pn.					0....	25031
84-M	**YURAKARE set**	1	1	2,768	4,365		25.00	54	B	23		P..					0....	25032
84-MA	YURAKARE chain	1	1	2,768	4,365		25.00	54	B	23		P..					0....	25033
84-MAA	**YURAKARE net**	1	1	2,768	4,365		25.00	54	B	23		P..					0....	25034
84-MAAA	YURACARE cluster	1	1	2,768	4,365		25.00	54	B	23	Yuracare	P..	1956-1965				0....	25035
84-MAAA-a	mansinyo					0				23		p..					0....	25036
84-MAAA-b	soloto					0				23		p..					0....	25037
84-N	**PANOAN set**	3	27	36,932	50,783		50.67	84	B	41		PN.					1....	25038
84-NA	PANO-AMAWAKA chain	3	22	34,394	47,210		51.58	85	B	41		PN.					1....	25039
84-NAA	**KASHIBO-NOKAMAN net**	1	1	1,812	2,508		15.01	55	B	41		PN.					0....	25040
84-NAAA	CASHIBO cluster	1	1	1,812	2,508		15.01	55	B	41		PN.					0....	25041
84-NAAA-a	cashi-bo	1	1	1,812	2,508	0	15.01	55	B	41	Cashibo*	PN.	1964-1975	1978			0....	25042
84-NAAA-b	cacatai-bo					0				41		pn.					0....	25043
84-NAAB	NOCAMAN cluster			0	0		0.00	0		9		...					0....	25044
84-NAAB-a	nocaman			0	0	0	0.00	0		9		...					0....	25045
84-NAB	**TAPICHE net**	2	2	883	1,268		4.53	19	A	4		...					0....	25046
84-NABA	TAPICHE cluster	2	2	683	928		0.00	10	A	4		...					0....	25047
84-NABA-a	mayu-bo	1	1	170	218	0	0.00	8	A	4		...					0....	25048
84-NABA-b	pisa-bo	1	1	513	710	0	0.00	11	A	4		...					0....	25049
84-NABB	CAPA-NAHUA cluster	1	1	200	340		20.00	51	B	0		...					0....	25050
84-NABB-a	capa-nahua					0				0		...					0....	25051
84-NABB-b	pahenbaque-bo					0				0		...					0....	25052
84-NAC	**SHIPIBO-MARUBO net**	2	5	24,306	33,454		59.90	94	B	41		PN.					1....	25053
84-NACA	SHIPIBO cluster	1	2	21,853	30,248		64.94	100	C	41		PN.					1....	25054
84-NACA-a	Proper shipi-bo					0				41		pn.					1....	25055
84-NACA-b	coni-bo	1	1	21,771	30,134	0	65.00	100	C	41	Shipibo-conibo	PN.	1954-1976	1983		1992	1....	25056
84-NACA-c	pisqui-bo					0				41		pn.					1....	25057
84-NACA-d	shete-bo					0				41		pn.					1....	25058
84-NACA-e	manoita					0				41		pn.					1....	25059
84-NACA-f	isco-nahua	1	1	82	114	0	50.00	90	B	41		pn.					1....	25060
84-NACA-g	picho-bo			0	0	0	0.00	0		41		pn.					1....	25061
84-NACA-h	saboi-bo					0				41		pn.					1....	25062
84-NACB	CAPANAHUA cluster	1	1	616	852		10.06	48	A	41		PN.					0....	25063
84-NACB-a	capanahua	1	1	616	852	0	10.06	48	A	41	Capanahua	PN.	1968-1973	1978			0....	25064
84-NACC	MARú-CORUBO cluster	1	1	612	785		30.07	60	B	12		...					0....	25065
84-NACC-a	marú-bo	1	1	612	785	0	30.07	60	B	12	Marubo	...					0....	25066
84-NACC-b	coru-bo					0				12		...					0....	25067
84-NACD	KATUKINA cluster	1	1	1,225	1,569		9.96	38	A	12	Katukina, Panoan	...					0....	25068
84-NACD-a	wanin-nawa					0				12		...					0....	25069
84-NACD-b	kama-nawa					0				12		...					0....	25070
84-NACD-c	arara-shawa-nawa					0				12		...					0....	25071
84-NACD-d	arara-wa					0				12		...					0....	25072
84-NACD-e	arara-pina					0				12		...					0....	25073
84-NACD-f	sanai-nawa					0				12		...					0....	25074
84-NACE	REMO cluster			0	0		0.00	0		9		...					0....	25075
84-NACE-a	remo					0				9		...					0....	25076
84-NAD	**PANA net**									9		...					0....	25077
84-NADA	PANOBO cluster			0	0		0.00	0		9		...					0....	25078
84-NADA-a	manoa					0				9		...					0....	25079
84-NADA-b	huaria-pano					0				9		...					0....	25080
84-NADA-c	pelado					0				9		...					0....	25081
84-NAE	**PUI-MORU net**	2	4	1,013	1,344		34.06	61	B	12		...					0....	25082
84-NAEA	PUI cluster	1	2	561	719		60.96	93	C	4		...					0....	25083
84-NAEA-a	shipi-nahua			0	0	0	0.00	0		4		...					0....	25084
84-NAEA-b	pui-nahua	1	1	323	414	0	69.04	100	C	4		...					0....	25085
84-NAEA-c	yahua-nahua	1	1	238	305	0	50.00	84	B	4		...					0....	25086
84-NAEB	PARQUE cluster	1	1	262	362		1.15	30	A	12		...					0....	25087
84-NAEB-a	parque-nahua	1	1	262	362	0	1.15	30	A	12	Yora	...					0....	25088
84-NAEB-b	tushi-nahua					0				12		...					0....	25089
84-NAEB-c	kama-nahua					0				12		...					0....	25090
84-NAEC	MORU cluster	1	1	190	263		0.00	9	A	4		...					0....	25091
84-NAEC-a	moru-nahua	1	1	190	263	0	0.00	9	A	4		...					0....	25092
84-NAEC-b	horu-nahua					0				4		...					0....	25093
84-NAEC-c	paco-nahua					0				4		...					0....	25094
84-NAF	**ANAWAKA-YAMINA net**	3	10	6,380	8,636		39.53	74	B	41		PN.					0....	25095
84-NAFA	AMAHUAKA cluster	2	2	760	1,029		23.95	56	B	22		P..					0....	25096
84-NAFA-a	ama-huaca	2	2	760	1,029	0	23.95	56	B	22	Amahuaca	P..	1963-1992				0....	25097
84-NAFA-b	sa-yaco					0				22		p..					0....	25098
84-NAFA-c	inu-vacen					0				22		p..					0....	25099
84-NAFA-d	viwi-vaceu					0				22		p..					0....	25100
84-NAFB	CASHI cluster	2	3	2,529	3,370		33.81	68	B	41		PN.					0....	25101
84-NAFB-a	cashi-nahua	2	2	2,223	2,978	0	35.72	70	B	41	Cashinahua	PN.	1971-1977	1980-1983			0....	25102
84-NAFB-b	nukuini	1	1	306	392	0	19.93	51	B	41		pn.					0....	25103
84-NAFB-c	nehanawa					0				41		pn.					0....	25104
84-NAFB-d	shemi-nahua					0				41		pn.					0....	25105
84-NAFC	SHARA cluster	2	2	1,095	1,472		70.05	100	C	41		PN.					0....	25106
84-NAFC-a	shara-nahua	2	2	1,095	1,472	0	70.05	100	C	41	Sharanahua	PN.	1973-1981	1996			0....	25107
84-NAFC-b	mari-nahua					0				41		pn.					0....	25108
84-NAFC-c	chandi-nahua					0				41		pn.					0....	25109
84-NAFD	YAMINA cluster	3	3	1,996	2,765		35.97	73	B	22		P..					0....	25110
84-NAFD-a	yami-nahua	3	3	1,996	2,765	0	35.97	73	B	22	Yaminahua	P..	1987-1992				0....	25111
84-NAFD-b	masta-nahua					0				22		p..					0....	25112
84-NAFD-c	masro-nahua					0				22		p..					0....	25113

Continued overleaf

Table 9-13 continued

Code 1	REFERENCE NAME / Autoglossonym 2	Coun 3	Peo 4	Mother-tongue speakers in 2000 5	in 2025 6	Media radio 7	AC% 8	E% 9	Wld 10	Tr 11	Biblioglossonym 12	Print 13-15	P-activity 16	N-activity 17	B-activity 18	J-year 19	Jayuh 20-24	Ref 25
84-NAFD-d	cujareño					0				22		p..					0....	25114
84-NAFD-e	nishi-nahua					0				22		p..					0....	25115
84-NAFD-f	chito-nahua					0				22		p..					0....	25116
84-NAFD-g	shao-nahua					0				22		p..					0....	25117
84-NAG	**ATSAWAKA net**									9		...					0....	25118
84-NAGA	ATSAHUACA-YAMIACA cluster			0	0		0.00	0		9		...					0....	25119
84-NAGA-a	Proper atsa-huaca					0				9		...					0....	25120
84-NAGA-b	yam-iaca					0				9		...					0....	25121
84-NB	MATSES chain	2	2	1,653	2,237		24.38	55	B	41		PN.					0....	25122
84-NBA	**MATSES net**	2	2	1,653	2,237		24.38	55	B	41		PN.					0....	25123
84-NBAA	MATSES cluster	2	2	1,653	2,237		24.38	55	B	41		PN.					0....	25124
84-NBAA-a	Proper matsés	2	2	1,653	2,237	0	24.38	55	B	41	Matses	PN.	1976-1988	1993			0....	25125
84-NBAA-b	mayoruna					0				41		pn.					0....	25126
84-NC	KASHARARI chain	1	1	221	283		60.63	95	C	2		...					0....	25127
84-NCA	**KASHARARI net**	1	1	221	283		60.63	95	C	2		...					0....	25128
84-NCAA	CASHARARí cluster	1	1	221	283		60.63	95	C	2		...					0....	25129
84-NCAA-a	cashar-arí	1	1	221	283	0	60.63	95	C	2		...					0....	25130
84-ND	KULINO chain									0		...					0....	25131
84-NDA	**KULINO net**									0		...					0....	25132
84-NDAA	CULINO cluster			0	0		0.00	0		0		...					0....	25133
84-NDAA-a	culino			0	0	0	0.00	0		0		...					0....	25134
84-NE	SHANINAWA chain									0		...					0....	25135
84-NEA	**SHANINAWA net**									0		...					0....	25136
84-NEAA	XANINAWA cluster			0	0		0.00	0		0		...					0....	25137
84-NEAA-a	xaninawa			0	0	0	0.00	0		0		...					0....	25138
84-NF	SENSI chain									9		...					0....	25139
84-NFA	**SENSI net**									9		...					0....	25140
84-NFAA	SENSI cluster			0	0		0.00	0		9		...					0....	25141
84-NFAA-a	Proper sensi					0				9		...					0....	25142
84-NFAA-b	inu-bu					0				9		...					0....	25143
84-NFAA-c	runu-bu					0				9		...					0....	25144
84-NFAA-d	casca					0				9		...					0....	25145
84-NFAA-e	mana-nahua					0				9		...					0....	25146
84-NG	KARIPUNA-CHAKOBO chain	1	2	664	1,053		65.66	95	C	41		PN.					0....	25147
84-NGA	**PACAWARA net**	1	1	16	25		75.00	100	C	8		...					0....	25148
84-NGAA	PACAHUARA cluster	1	1	16	25		75.00	100	C	8		...					0....	25149
84-NGAA-a	paca-huara	1	1	16	25	0	75.00	100	C	8		...					0....	25150
84-NGB	**CHAKOBO net**	1	1	598	943		70.07	100	C	41		PN.					0....	25151
84-NGBA	CHáCOBO cluster	1	1	598	943		70.07	100	C	41		PN.					0....	25152
84-NGBA-a	cháco-bo	1	1	598	943	0	70.07	100	C	41	Chacobo	PN.	1965	1979			0....	25153
84-NGC	**KARIPUNA net**	1	1	50	85		10.00	34	A	0		...					0....	25154
84-NGCA	CARIPUNA cluster	1	1	50	85		10.00	34	A	0		...					0....	25155
84-NGCA-a	Proper caripuna					0				0		...					0....	25156
84-NGCA-b	jau-navo					0				0		...					0....	25157
84-NGCA-c	jacaria					0				0		...					0....	25158
84-NGCA-d	pama-na					0				0		...					0....	25159
84-O	**CHAPAKURA-WANYAM set**	2	4	2,510	3,283		57.69	90	B	22		P..					0....	25160
84-OA	TORA chain	1	1	40	68		10.00	33	A	0		...					0....	25161
84-OAA	**TORA net**	1	1	40	68		10.00	33	A	0		...					0....	25162
84-OAAA	TORá cluster	1	1	40	68		10.00	33	A	0		...					0....	25163
84-OAAA-a	tora	1	1	40	68	0	10.00	33	A	0		...					0....	25164
84-OB	ITENE-WANYAM chain	2	4	2,470	3,215		58.46	91	B	22		P..					0....	25165
84-OBA	**ITENE net**	1	1	127	200		79.53	100	C	8		...					0....	25166
84-OBAA	ITENE cluster	1	1	127	200		79.53	100	C	8		...					0....	25167
84-OBAA-a	Proper itene	1	1	127	200		79.53	100	C	8		...					0....	25168
84-OBAA-b	itoreauhip					0				8		...					0....	25169
84-OBB	**WANYAM net**	1	1	149	204		49.66	83	B	4		...					0....	25170
84-OBBA	WANHAM cluster									0		...					0....	25171
84-OBBA-a	Proper wanham					0				0		...					0....	25172
84-OBBA-b	pawumwa					0				0		...					0....	25173
84-OBBA-c	cujuna					0				0		...					0....	25174
84-OBBA-d	mataua					0				0		...					0....	25175
84-OBBA-e	urunumacan					0				0		...					0....	25176
84-OBBB	ABITANA-KUMANá cluster	1	1	30	51		10.00	33	A	0		...					0....	25177
84-OBBB-a	abitana					0				0		...					0....	25178
84-OBBB-b	cumana					0				0		...					0....	25179
84-OBBB-c	cutinaa					0				0		...					0....	25180
84-OBBC	KABIXI cluster	1	1	119	153		59.66	95	B	4		...					0....	25181
84-OBBC-a	cabishí	1	1	119	153	0	59.66	95	B	4		...					0....	25182
84-OBC	**CHAPAKURA-JARU net**	1	2	2,194	2,811		57.84	92	B	22		P..					0....	25183
84-OBCA	URUPA-JARU cluster	1	1	238	305		39.92	71	B	4		...					0....	25184
84-OBCA-a	urupá	1	1	238	305	0	39.92	71	B	4		...					0....	25185
84-OBCA-b	jarú					0				4		...					0....	25186
84-OBCB	OROWARI cluster	1	1	1,956	2,506		60.02	94	C	22		P..					0....	25187
84-OBCB-a	oro-wari	1	1	1,956	2,506	0	60.02	94	C	22	Pacaas Novos*	P..	1975-1984				0....	25188
84-OBCB-b	uomo					0				22		p..					0....	25189
84-OBCC	KITEMO-NAPE cluster			0	0		0.00	0		0		...					0....	25190
84-OBCC-a	quitemo-ca			0	0	0	0.00	0		0		...					0....	25191
84-OBCC-b	nape-ca			0	0	0	0.00	0		0		...					0....	25192
84-OBCD	CHAPAKURA cluster			0	0		0.00	0		0		...					0....	25193
84-OBCD-a	Proper chapacura			0	0	0	0.00	0		0		...					0....	25194
84-OBCD-b	huachin			0	0	0	0.00	0		0		...					0....	25195

Continued opposite

Table 9-13 continued

Code 1	REFERENCE NAME / Autoglossonym 2	Coun 3	Peo 4	Mother-tongue speakers in 2000 5	in 2025 6	Media radio 7	CHURCH AC% 8	E% 9	Wld 10	Tr 11	Biblioglossonym 12	SCRIPTURES Print 13-15	P-activity 16	N-activity 17	B-activity 18	J-year 19	Jayuh 20-24	Ref 25
84-P	**ITONAMA set**	1	1	218	344		80.28	100	C	27		P..					0....	25196
84-PA	ITONAMA chain	1	1	218	344		80.28	100	C	27		P..					0....	25197
84-PAA	**ITONAMA net**	1	1	218	344		80.28	100	C	27		P..					0....	25198
84-PAAA	ITONAMA cluster	1	1	218	344		80.28	100	C	27		P..					0....	25199
84-PAAA-a	itonama	1	1	218	344	0	80.28	100	C	27	Itonama	P..	1967				0....	25200
84-PAAA-b	machoto									27		p..					0....	25201
84-PAAA-c	saramo					0				27		p..					0....	25202
84-Q	**CAYUBABA set**	1	1	1,114	1,756		80.97	100	C	8		...					0....	25203
84-QA	CAYUBABA chain	1	1	1,114	1,756		80.97	100	C	8		...					0....	25204
84-QAA	**CAYUBABA net**	1	1	1,114	1,756		80.97	100	C	8		...					0....	25205
84-QAAA	CAYUBABA cluster	1	1	1,114	1,756		80.97	100	C	8		...					0....	25206
84-QAAA-a	cayubaba	1	1	1,114	1,756	0	80.97	100	C	8		...					0....	25207
84-R	**TAKANA-KAVINENYA set**	2	6	8,339	13,056		17.30	53	B	41		PN.					0....	25208
84-RA	TOROMO-ESE'EHA chain	2	2	1,513	2,295		39.99	78	B	41		PN.					0....	25209
84-RAA	**ESE'EHA net**	2	2	1,513	2,295		39.99	78	B	41		PN.					0....	25210
84-RAAA	ESE-EJJA cluster	2	2	1,513	2,295		39.99	78	B	41	Ese Ejja	PN.	1967-1981	1984			0....	25211
84-RAAA-a	bagua-ja					0				41		pn.					0....	25212
84-RAAA-b	mohino					0				41		pn.					0....	25213
84-RAAA-c	chun-cho					0				41		pn.					0....	25214
84-RAAA-d	echo-ja					0				41		pn.					0....	25215
84-RAAA-e	guara-yo					0				41		. pn.					0....	25216
84-RAAA-f	huana-yo					0				41		pn.					0....	25217
84-RAAA-g	quinaqui					0				41		pn.					0....	25218
84-RAB	**TOROMONA net**									4		...					0....	25219
84-RABA	TOROMO-NA cluster			0	0		0.00	0		4		...					0....	25220
84-RABA-a	toromo-na			0	0	0	0.00	0		4		...					0....	25221
84-RB	KAVINENYA chain	1	1	2,249	3,545		16.01	50	B	41		PN.					0....	25222
84-RBA	**KAVINENYA net**	1	1	2,249	3,545		16.01	50	B	41		PN.					0....	25223
84-RBAA	CAVINENYA cluster	1	1	2,249	3,545		16.01	50	B	41		PN.					0....	25224
84-RBAA-a	cavineña	1	1	2,249	3,545	0	16.01	50	B	41	Cavinena	PN.	1979	1985			0....	25225
84-RC	TAKANA-ARAONA chain	1	3	4,577	7,216		10.44	45	A	41		PN.					0....	25226
84-RCA	**ARAONA net**	1	1	100	158		60.00	98	C	22		P..					0....	25227
84-RCAA	ARAONA cluster	1	1	100	158		60.00	98	C	22		P..					0....	25228
84-RCAA-a	Proper arao-na	1	1	100	158	0	60.00	98	C	22	Araona	P..	1974-1981				0....	25229
84-RCAA-b	cavi-na					0				22		p..					0....	25230
84-RCAA-c	capeche-ne					0				22		p..					0....	25231
84-RCAA-d	mabenaro					0				22		p..					0....	25232
84-RCB	**TAKANA net**	1	1	4,452	7,019		9.01	44	A	41		PN.					0....	25233
84-RCBA	TACANA cluster	1	1	4,452	7,019		9.01	44	A	41	Tacana	PN.	1969-1973	1981			0....	25234
84-RCBA-a	ayaychu-na					1				41		pn.					0....	25235
84-RCBA-b	babaya-na					1				41		pn.					0....	25236
84-RCBA-c	chiliuvo					1				41		pn.					0....	25237
84-RCBA-d	chiva-mo-na					1				41		pn.					0....	25238
84-RCBA-e	idia-ma					1				41		pn.					0....	25239
84-RCBA-f	isia-ma					1				41		pn.					0....	25240
84-RCBA-g	pamaino					1				41		pn.					0....	25241
84-RCBA-h	pasara-mo-na					1				41		pn.					0....	25242
84-RCBA-i	sapuru-na					1				41		pn.					0....	25243
84-RCBA-j	silia-ma					1				41		pn.					0....	25244
84-RCBA-k	tumapasa					1				41		pn.					0....	25245
84-RCBA-l	uchupia-mo-na					1				41		pn.					0....	25246
84-RCBA-m	yabaypura					1				41		pn.					0....	25247
84-RCBA-n	yubamo-na					1				41		pn.					0....	25248
84-RCC	**REYESAN net**	1	1	25	39		68.00	100	C	9		...					0....	25249
84-RCCA	REYESANO cluster	1	1	25	39		68.00	100	C	9		...					0....	25250
84-RCCA-a	Proper reyesano	1	1	25	39	0	68.00	100	C	9		...					0....	25251
84-RCCA-b	san-borjano					0				9		...					0....	25252
84-S	**MOSETEN-CHIMANE set**	1	1	6,091	9,603		12.00	42	A	22		P..					0....	25253
84-SA	MOSETEN-CHIMANE chain	1	1	6,091	9,603		12.00	42	A	22		P..					0....	25254
84-SAA	**MOSETEN-CHIMANE net**	1	1	6,091	9,603		12.00	42	A	22		P..					0....	25255
84-SAAA	MOSETEN-TSIMANé cluster	1	1	6,091	9,603		12.00	42	A	22		P..					0....	25256
84-SAAA-a	tsimané	1	1	6,091	9,603	0	12.00	42	A	22	Chimane*	P..	1963-1986				0....	25257
84-SAAA-b	moseten					0				22		p..					0....	25258
84-T	**CHON set**	1	1	40	68		50.00	88	B	8		...					0....	25259
84-TA	TEWELCHE chain	1	1	40	68		50.00	88	B	0		...					0....	25260
84-TAA	**TEWELCHE net**	1	1	40	68		50.00	88	B	0		...					0....	25261
84-TAAA	TEHUELCHE cluster	1	1	40	68		50.00	88	B	0		...					0....	25262
84-TAAA-a	tewesh					0				0		...					0....	25263
84-TAAA-b	South tehuelche					0				0		...					0....	25264
84-TAAA-c	tsóneka					0				0		...					0....	25265
84-TB	ONA-HAUSH chain									8		...					0....	25266
84-TBA	**ONA net**									8		...					0....	25267
84-TBAA	ONA cluster			0	0		0.00	0		8		...					0....	25268
84-TBAA-a	ona			0	0	0	0.00	0		8		...					0....	25269
84-TBB	**HAUSH net**									0		...					0....	25270
84-TBBA	HAUSH cluster			0	0		0.00	0		0		...					0....	25271
84-TBBA-a	haush			0	0	0	0.00	0		0		...					0....	25272
85	**ANDINIC zone**	6	63	14,300,993	20,732,687		95.90	100	C	61		PNB					3As..	25273
85-A	**CHIMUAN set**									0		...					0....	25274

Continued overleaf

Table 9-13 continued

Code 1	REFERENCE NAME / Autoglossonym 2	Coun 3	Peo 4	Mother-tongue speakers in 2000 5	in 2025 6	Media radio 7	CHURCH AC% 8	E% 9	Wld 10	Tr 11	Biblioglossonym 12	SCRIPTURES Print 13-15	P-activity 16	N-activity 17	B-activity 18	J-year 19	Jayuh 20-24	Ref 25
85-AA	KANYARI-PURUWA chain									0		...					0....	25275
85-AAA	**KANYARI net**									0		...					0....	25276
85-AAAA	PURUWá cluster			0	0		0.00	0		0		...					0....	25277
85-AAAA-a	puruwá					0				0		...					0....	25278
85-AAAB	CANYARI cluster			0	0		0.00	0		0		...					0....	25279
85-AAAB-a	canyari			0	0	0	0.00	0		0		...					0....	25280
85-AAB	**MOCHIKA net**									0		...					0....	25281
85-AABA	MOCHIKA cluster			0	0		0.00	0		0		...					0....	25282
85-AABA-a	mochika			0	0	0	0.00	0		0		...					0....	25283
85-B	**SECHURA set**									0		...					0....	25284
85-BA	SECHURA chain									0		...					0....	25285
85-BAA	**SECHURA net**									0		...					0....	25286
85-BAAA	SECHURA cluster			0	0		0.00	0		0		...					0....	25287
85-BAAA-a	sec					0				0		...					0....	25288
85-BAAA-b	tallán					0				0		...					0....	25289
85-C	**KATAKAO-KOLAN set**									0		...					0....	25290
85-CA	KATAKAO-KOLAN chain									0		...					0....	25291
85-CAA	**KATAKAO net**									0		...					0....	25292
85-CAAA	CATACAO cluster			0	0		0.00	0		0		...					0....	25293
85-CAAA-a	katakao					0				0		...					0....	25294
85-CAB	**KOLAN net**									0		...					0....	25295
85-CABA	COLáN cluster			0	0		0.00	0		0		...					0....	25296
85-CABA-a	kolan					0				0		...					0....	25297
85-D	**CHOLON-HIBITO set**	1	1	30	51		30.00	63	B	9		...					0....	25298
85-DA	HIBITO chain									9		...					0....	25299
85-DAA	**HIBITO net**									9		...					0....	25300
85-DAAA	HIBITO cluster			0	0		0.00	0		9		...					0....	25301
85-DAAA-a	hibito			0	0	0	0.00	0		9		...					0....	25302
85-DB	CHOLON chain	1	1	30	51		30.00	63	B	0		...					0....	25303
85-DBA	**CHOLON net**	1	1	30	51		30.00	63	B	0		...					0....	25304
85-DBAA	CHOLóN cluster	1	1	30	51		30.00	63	B	0		...					0....	25305
85-DBAA-a	cholón	1	1	30	51	0	30.00	63	B	0		...					0....	25306
85-E	**KULYI set**									0		...					0....	25307
85-EA	KULYI chain									0		...					0....	25308
85-EAA	**KULYI net**									0		...					0....	25309
85-EAAA	CULYI cluster			0	0		0.00	0		0		...					0....	25310
85-EAAA-a	culyi			0	0	0	0.00	0		0		...					0....	25311
85-F	**KECHUA-KICHWA set**	6	50	11,284,190	16,183,342		97.16	100	C	61		PNB					3As..	25312
85-FA	KECHUA-KICHWA chain	6	50	11,284,190	16,183,342		97.16	100	C	61		PNB					3As..	25313
85-FAA	**KECHUA-KICHWA net**	6	50	11,284,190	16,183,342		97.16	100	C	61		PNB					3As..	25314
85-FAAA	INGA cluster	1	2	21,241	29,992		48.37	79	B	41		PN.					0....	25315
85-FAAA-a	sibundoy	1	1	12,053	17,019	0	70.00	100	C	41	Inga: Highland	PN.	1971-1987	1996			0....	25316
85-FAAA-b	caquetá	1	1	9,188	12,973	0	20.00	52	B	41		pn.					0....	25320
85-FAAB	INGANO cluster	3	7	50,120	70,145		92.33	100	C	42		PN.					0....	25324
85-FAAB-a	quixo	3	3	27,590	38,598	5	93.78	100	C	42		PN.					0....	25325
85-FAAB-b	North pastaza	2	3	18,907	26,532	4	94.48	100	C	42	Quichua: Pastaza, North*	PN.		1992			0....	25330
85-FAAB-c	South pastaza	1	1	3,623	5,015	4	70.00	100	C	42	Quechua: Pastaza*	Pn.	1981-1990				0....	25335
85-FAAC	QUICHUA-ALTIPLANO cluster	1	6	1,896,783	2,669,236		99.10	100	C	61		PNB					3.s..	25340
85-FAAC-a	imbabura	1	1	505,843	711,844	4	99.00	100	C	61	Quichua: Imbabura*	PNB		1976	1994		1.s..	25341
85-FAAC-b	pichincha	1	1	35,050	49,324	4	99.00	100	C	61		pnb					1.s..	25342
85-FAAC-c	chimborazo	1	2	1,208,823	1,701,108	4	99.39	100	C	61	Quichua: Chimborazo*	PNB	1917-1968	1954-1973	1989	1995	3.s..	25345
85-FAAC-d	salasaca					1				61		pnb					1.s..	25350
85-FAAC-e	cuenca	1	2	147,067	206,960	4	97.13	100	C	61		Pnb					1.s..	25351
85-FAAD	WEST QUECHUA cluster	1	4	106,659	147,628		92.90	100	C	41		PN.					0....	25356
85-FAAD-a	lambayeque	1	1	26,870	37,191	4	99.00	100	C	41		Pn.					0....	25357
85-FAAD-b	cajamarca	1	1	50,743	70,234	4	99.00	100	C	41	Quechua: Cajamarca*	Pn.	1985-1993				0....	25364
85-FAAD-c	chachapoyas	1	1	6,623	9,167	4	99.00	100	C	41		pn.					0....	25368
85-FAAD-d	lamista	1	1	22,423	31,036	5	70.00	100	C	41	Quechua: San Martin*	PN.	1970-1986	1992			0....	25372
85-FAAE	CHINCHAYSUYO cluster	1	3	365,546	505,950		89.76	100	C	24		P..					3....	25377
85-FAAE-a	North ancash	1	2	29,165	40,367	4	87.00	100	C	24		p..					1....	25378
85-FAAE-b	Central ancash	1	1	336,381	465,583	1	90.00	100	C	24		P..					3....	25381
85-FAAF	CENTRAL QUECHUA cluster	1	14	882,614	1,221,623		93.14	100	C	22		P..					3....	25385
85-FAAF-a	East ancash	1	2	287,333	397,698	4	90.00	100	C	22		P..					3....	25386
85-FAAF-b	North lima	1	1	28,846	39,926	4	99.00	100	C	22		p..					1....	25389
85-FAAF-c	huánuco	1	5	209,625	290,141	5	89.59	100	C	22	Quechua: Huanuco*	P..	1917-1995				1....	25393
85-FAAF-d	ambo-pasco	1	2	84,096	116,396	5	91.67	100	C	22	Quechua: S Rafael, Huaria*	P..	1993				1....	25401
85-FAAF-e	Upper pasco	1	1	37,576	52,009	4	99.00	100	C	22		p..					1....	25404
85-FAAF-f	junín-tarma	1	1	73,318	101,479	5	99.00	100	C	22	Quechua: Junin*	P..	1954-1989				1....	25407
85-FAAF-g	huanca	1	2	161,820	223,974	4	99.00	100	C	22	Quechua, Huanca, Huaylla	P..	1991-1992				1....	25410
85-FAAG	YAUYOS cluster	1	1	33,080	45,787		99.00	100	C	4		...					0....	25415
85-FAAG-a	huacarpana					1				4		...					0....	25416
85-FAAG-b	apurí					1				4		...					0....	25417
85-FAAG-c	madeán-viñac					1				4		...					0....	25418
85-FAAG-d	huangáscar					1				4		...					0....	25421
85-FAAG-e	cacra-hongos					1				4		...					0....	25425
85-FAAG-f	tana-lincha					1				4		...					0....	25428
85-FAAG-g	tomás-alis					1				4		...					0....	25431
85-FAAG-h	huancaya-vitis					1				4		...					0....	25434
85-FAAH	SOUTH QUECHUA cluster	4	13	7,928,147	11,492,981		97.69	100	C	61	Quechua: Classical*	PNB	1880				3As..	25437
85-FAAH-a	ayucucho	1	2	1,655,591	2,291,496	5	99.00	100	C	61		PNB				1990	3As..	25438
85-FAAH-b	arequipa	1	1	29,329	40,594	4	99.00	100	C	61		Pnb					1cs..	25443

Continued opposite

Table 9-13 continued

Code 1	REFERENCE NAME / Autoglossonym 2	Coun 3	Peo 4	Mother-tongue speakers in 2000 5	in 2025 6	Media radio 7	CHURCH AC% 8	E% 9	Wld 10	Tr 11	Biblioglossonym 12	SCRIPTURES Print 13-15	P-activity 16	N-activity 17	B-activity 18	J-year 19	Jayuh 20-24	Ref 25
85-FAAH-c	cuzco	1	2	1,848,829	2,558,955	5	96.92	100	C	61	Quechua: Cuzco*	PNB	1901-1965	1947-1971	1988	1995	3cs..	25447
85-FAAH-d	apolo-sandia	1	2	218,106	343,870	4	93.47	100	C	61	Quechua: Bolivia, North*	PNb		1985			1as..	25450
85-FAAH-e	potosí	2	2	4,074,444	6,128,319	4	97.84	100	C	61	Quechua, South Bolivian	PNB	1907-1949	1922-1977	1986-1993	1984	2as..	25455
85-FAAH-f	jujuy	1	1	5,728	7,294	4	93.99	100	C	61		pnb					1as..	25460
85-FAAH-g	santiagueno	1	1	91,557	116,589	4	94.00	100	C	61		pnb					1as..	25463
85-G	**TUYONERI set**	1	2	587	822		10.05	47	A	41		PN.					0....	25464
85-GA	TUYONERI chain	1	2	587	822		10.05	47	A	41		PN.					0....	25465
85-GAA	**TUYONERI net**	1	2	587	822		10.05	47	A	41		PN.					0....	25466
85-GAAA	HARAKMBET cluster	1	1	311	430		9.97	45	A	4		. . .					0....	25467
85-GAAA-a	huachipa-eri	1	1	311	430	0	9.97	45	A	4		. . .					0....	25468
85-GAAA-b	kochimb-eri					0				4		. . .					0....	25469
85-GAAA-c	manuqui-ari					0				4		. . .					0....	25470
85-GAAA-d	pukiri-eri					0				4		. . .					0....	25471
85-GAAB	AMARAKAERI cluster	1	1	246	341		10.16	50	B	41		PN.					0....	25472
85-GAAB-a	amaraca-eri	1	1	246	341	0	10.16	50	B	41	Amarakaeri	PN.	1972-1976	1986			0....	25473
85-GAAB-b	toy-eri					0				41		pn.					0....	25474
85-GAAB-c	kisamba-eri					0				41		pn.					0....	25475
85-GAAB-d	sapit-eri					0				41		pn.					0....	25476
85-GAAB-e	ipitin-eri					0				41		pn.					0....	25477
85-GAAB-f	küpondirid-eri					0				41		pn.					0....	25478
85-GAAB-g	wintap-eri					0				41		pn.					0....	25479
85-GAAB-h	wakitan-eri					0				41		pn.					0....	25480
85-GAAB-i	karen-eri					0				41		pn.					0....	25481
85-GAAC	ARASA-IRI cluster	1	1	30	51		10.00	33	A	0		. . .					0....	25482
85-GAAC-a	arasa-iri	1	1	30	51	0	10.00	33	A	0		. . .					0....	25483
85-H	**LAPACHU set**									0		. . .					0....	25484
85-HA	LAPACHU chain									0		. . .					0....	25485
85-HAA	**LAPACHU net**									0		. . .					0....	25486
85-HAAA	LAPACHU cluster			0	0		0.00	0		0		. . .					0....	25487
85-HAAA-a	lapachu					0				0		. . .					0....	25488
85-I	**LEKO set**									9		. . .					0....	25489
85-IA	LEKO chain									9		. . .					0....	25490
85-IAA	**LEKO net**									9		. . .					0....	25491
85-IAAA	LECO cluster									9		. . .					0....	25492
85-IAAA-a	leco					0				9		. . .					0....	25493
85-J	**AYMARA-HAKARU set**	4	9	3,013,829	4,544,744		91.23	100	C	61		PNB					2.s..	25494
85-JA	HAKI chain	4	9	3,013,829	4,544,744		91.23	100	C	61		PNB					2.s..	25495
85-JAA	**HAKARU-KAUKI net**	1	1	2,476	3,428		80.01	100	C	4		. . .					0....	25496
85-JAAA	JAQARU-CAUQUI cluster	1	1	2,476	3,428		80.01	100	C	4		. . .					0....	25497
85-JAAA-a	jaqaru	1	1	2,476	3,428	0	80.01	100	C	4		. . .					0....	25498
85-JAAA-b	cauqui					0				4		. . .					0....	25499
85-JAB	**AYMARA net**	4	8	3,011,353	4,541,316		91.23	100	C	61		PNB					2.s..	25500
85-JABA	AYMARA cluster	4	8	3,011,353	4,541,316		91.23	100	C	61		PNB					2.s..	25501
85-JABA-a	Central aymara	4	7	2,469,990	3,687,789	4	91.07	100	C	61	Aymara*	PNB	1829-1966	1954-1977	1986-1993	1984	2.s..	25502
85-JABA-b	South aymara	1	1	541,363	853,527	1	92.00	100	C	61		pnb					1.s..	25509
85-K	**PUKINA set**									0		. . .					0....	25512
85-KA	PUKINA chain									0		. . .					0....	25513
85-KAA	**PUKINA net**									0		. . .					0....	25514
85-KAAA	PUQUINA cluster			0	0		0.00	0		0		. . .					0....	25515
85-KAAA-a	puquina			0	0	0	0.00	0		0		. . .					0....	25516
85-L	**KALLAWAYA set**	1	1	17	26		76.47	100	C	0		. . .					0....	25517
85-LA	KALLAWAYA chain	1	1	17	26		76.47	100	C	0		. . .					0....	25518
85-LAA	**KALLAWAYA net**	1	1	17	26		76.47	100	C	0		. . .					0....	25519
85-LAAA	CALLAHUAYA cluster	1	1	17	26		76.47	100	C	0		. . .					0....	25520
85-LAAA-a	callahuaya	1	1	17	26	0	76.47	100	C	0		. . .					0....	25521
85-M	**URU-CHIPAYA set**	1	1	2,340	3,702		73.93	99	C	41		PN.					0....	25522
85-MA	URU-CHIPAYA chain	1	1	2,340	3,702		73.93	99	C	41		PN.					0....	25523
85-MAA	**URU-CHIPAYA net**	1	1	2,340	3,702		73.93	99	C	41		PN.					0....	25524
85-MAAA	URU cluster	1	1	100	170		50.00	86	B	4		. . .					0....	25525
85-MAAA-a	uru	1	1	100	170	0	50.00	86	B	4		. . .					0....	25526
85-MAAB	CHIPAYA cluster	1	1	2,240	3,532		75.00	100	C	41		PN.					0....	25527
85-MAAB-a	chipaya	1	1	2,240	3,532	0	75.00	100	C	41	Chipaya	PN.	1967	1978			0....	25528
86	**CHACONIC zone**	5	42	917,742	1,208,259		68.45	99	C	61		PNB					4.s..	25529
86-A	**MATACO-CHOROTI set**	3	13	65,332	95,273		65.77	94	C	61		PNB					0.s..	25530
86-AA	MATAKO chain	3	5	28,413	37,808		82.62	99	C	41		PN.					0.s..	25531
86-AAA	**MATAKO net**	3	5	28,413	37,808		82.62	99	C	41		PN.					0.s..	25532
86-AAAA	WICHÍ cluster	3	5	28,413	37,808		82.62	99	C	41		PN.					0.s..	25533
86-AAAA-a	noctén	2	2	2,394	3,734	0	84.71	100	C	41	Wichi Lhamtes Nocten	pn.					0.s..	25534
86-AAAA-b	vejoz	2	2	23,797	31,245	0	85.46	100	C	41	Mataco*	PN.	1919-1989	1962-1993			0.s..	25535
86-AAAA-c	güisnay	1	1	2,222	2,829	0	50.00	92	B	41	Wichi Lhamtes Guisnay	pn.					0.s..	25538
86-AAAA-d	matahuayo					0				41		pn.					0.s..	25539
86-AB	CHOROTI-MAKA chain	3	8	36,919	57,465		52.80	91	B	61		PNB					0....	25540
86-ABA	**CHOROTI net**	3	5	12,913	16,716		77.56	100	C	35		P..					0....	25541
86-ABAA	CHOROTÍ cluster	3	5	12,913	16,716		77.56	100	C	35		P..					0....	25542

Continued overleaf

Table 9-13 continued

Code 1	REFERENCE NAME / Autoglossonym 2	Coun 3	Peo 4	Mother-tongue speakers in 2000 5	in 2025 6	Media radio 7	CHURCH AC% 8	E% 9	Wld 10	Tr 11	Biblioglossonym 12	SCRIPTURES Print 13-15	P-activity 16	N-activity 17	B-activity 18	J-year 19	Jayuh 20-24	Ref 25
86-ABAA-a	yofúaha	3	5	12,913	16,716	0	77.56	100	C	35	Chorote*	P..	1961-1993				0....	25543
86-ABB	**CHULUPI net**	2	2	22,756	38,622		40.00	87	B	61		PNB					0....	25544
86-ABBA	NIWACLé cluster	2	2	22,756	38,622		40.00	87	B	61	Nivacle*	PNB	1969	1973	1994-1995		0....	25545
86-ABBA-a	West niwaclé					0				61		pnb					0....	25546
86-ABBA-b	East niwaclé					0				61		pnb					0....	25547
86-ABC	**MAKA net**	1	1	1,250	2,127		30.00	68	B	41		PN.					0....	25551
86-ABCA	MAC'á cluster	1	1	1,250	2,127		30.00	68	B	41		PN.					0....	25552
86-ABCA-a	mac'á					0				41		pn.					0....	25553
86-ABCA-b	eni-maca	1	1	1,250	2,127	0	30.00	68	B	41	Maca	PN.		1985			0....	25554
86-B	**AYOREO-CHAMAKOKO set**	2	4	9,033	15,177		46.37	85	B	41		PN.					0....	25555
86-BA	AYOREO chain	2	2	5,340	8,890		55.00	97	B	41		PN.					0....	25556
86-BAA	**AYOREO net**	2	2	5,340	8,890		55.00	97	B	41		PN.					0....	25557
86-BAAA	AYOREO cluster	2	2	5,340	8,890		55.00	97	B	41		PN.					0....	25558
86-BAAA-a	North ayoré	1	1	1,590	2,507	0	54.97	98	B	41	Ayore*	PN.	1957-1985	1982			0....	25559
86-BAAA-b	morotoco	1	1	3,750	6,383	0	55.01	97	B	41	Ayoreo	PN.	1957-1985	1982			0....	25560
86-BAAA-c	tsiricua					0				41		pn.					0....	25561
86-BAAA-d	pyeta					0				41		pn.					0....	25562
86-BAAA-e	yovai					0				41		pn.					0....	25563
86-BB	CHAMAKOKO chain	1	2	3,693	6,287		33.90	68	B	22		P..					0....	25564
86-BBA	**CHAMAKOKO net**	1	2	3,693	6,287		33.90	68	B	22		P..					0....	25565
86-BBAA	CHAMACOCO cluster	1	2	3,693	6,287		33.90	68	B	22		P..					0....	25566
86-BBAA-a	ebitoso	1	1	1,443	2,457	0	39.99	73	B	22		p..					0....	25567
86-BBAA-b	chamacoco-bravo	1	1	2,250	3,830	0	30.00	65	B	22	Chamacoco	P..	1992-1995				0....	25568
86-C	**MASKOI set**	2	10	36,193	60,967		85.78	100	C	61		PNB					0....	25569
86-CA	MASKOI chain	2	10	36,193	60,967		85.78	100	C	61		PNB					0....	25570
86-CAA	**MASKOI net**	2	10	36,193	60,967		85.78	100	C	61		PNB					0....	25571
86-CAAA	ENLHIT cluster	2	9	30,697	51,612		86.82	100	C	61		PNB					0....	25572
86-CAAA-a	cashquiha	1	1	688	1,170	0	60.03	100	C	61		pnb					0....	25573
86-CAAA-b	sanapaná	1	2	5,935	10,101	0	95.00	100	C	61	Sanapana	pnb					0....	25574
86-CAAA-c	maskoy	1	2	4,190	7,132	0	83.72	100	C	61		pnb					0....	25575
86-CAAA-d	angaite					0				61	Angaite	Pnb	1994-1995				0....	25576
86-CAAA-e	North lengua	2	3	14,111	23,382	0	85.52	100	C	61	Lengua: Northern	PNB	1900-1987	1970-1992	1995-1996		0....	25577
86-CAAA-f	South lengua	1	1	5,773	9,827	0	87.01	100	C	61	Lengua: Southern	Pnb	1969				0....	25578
86-CAAB	MASCOY-PIDGIN cluster	1	1	5,496	9,355		80.00	100	C	0		...					0....	25579
86-CAAB-a	mascoy-pidgin	1	1	5,496	9,355	0	80.00	100	C	0		...					0....	25580
86-D	**LULE-VILELA set**	1	1	37	47		81.08	100	C	0		...					0....	25581
86-DA	LULE chain									0		...					0....	25582
86-DAA	**LULE net**									0		...					0....	25583
86-DAAA	LULE cluster	0	0	0	0		0.00	0		0		...					0....	25584
86-DAAA-a	gran-lule	0	0	0	0	0	0.00	0		0		...					0....	25585
86-DAAA-b	lule-pequeño	0	0	0	0	0	0.00	0		0		...					0....	25586
86-DB	VILELA chain	1	1	37	47		81.08	100	C	0		...					0....	25590
86-DBA	**VILELA net**	1	1	37	47		81.08	100	C	0		...					0....	25591
86-DBAA	VILELA cluster	1	1	37	47		81.08	100	C	0		...					0....	25592
86-DBAA-a	chulupí-chaco					0				0		...					0....	25593
86-DBAA-b	ipa	0	0	0	0	0	0.00	0		0		...					0....	25597
86-DBAA-c	omoampa	0	0	0	0	0	0.00	0		0		...					0....	25598
86-DBAA-d	pasain	0	0	0	0	0	0.00	0		0		...					0....	25599
86-DBAA-e	takete	0	0	0	0	0	0.00	0		0		...					0....	25600
86-DBAA-f	vacaa	0	0	0	0	0	0.00	0		0		...					0....	25601
86-DBAA-g	yocnoampa	0	0	0	0	0	0.00	0		0		...					0....	25602
86-DC	CHARRUA-CHANA chain									0		...					0....	25603
86-DCA	**CHARRUA-CHANA net**									0		...					0....	25604
86-DCAA	MIÑUANE cluster	0	0	0	0		0.00	0		0		...					0....	25605
86-DCAA-a	minuane	0	0	0	0	0	0.00	0		0		...					0....	25606
86-DCAB	CHARRUA cluster	0	0	0	0		0.00	0		0		...					0....	25607
86-DCAB-a	charrua	0	0	0	0	0	0.00	0		0		...					0....	25608
86-DCAC	GüENOA cluster	0	0	0	0		0.00	0		0		...					0....	25609
86-DCAC-a	güenoa	0	0	0	0	0	0.00	0		0		...					0....	25610
86-DCAD	CHANá cluster	0	0	0	0		0.00	0		0		...					0....	25611
86-DCAD-a	chaná	0	0	0	0	0	0.00	0		0		...					0....	25612
86-E	**WAIKURU-QOM set**	4	7	28,123	36,344		82.13	95	C	57		PN.					1.s..	25613
86-EA	WAIKURU chain	1	1	1,565	2,005		30.03	65	B	32		P..					1....	25614
86-EAA	**WAIKURU net**	1	1	1,565	2,005		30.03	65	B	32		P..					1....	25615
86-EAAA	KADIWéU cluster	1	1	1,565	2,005		30.03	65	B	32		P..					1....	25616
86-EAAA-a	Proper kadiwéu	1	1	1,565	2,005	0	30.03	65	B	32	Kadiweu	P..	1981			1997	1....	25617
86-EAAA-b	mbayá-guaikurú					0				32		p..					1....	25618
86-EB	QOM-MOKAVI chain	3	6	26,558	34,339		85.20	97	C	57		PN.					0.s..	25619
86-EBA	**QOM-PILAGA net**	3	5	22,033	28,577		94.49	100	C	57		PN.					0.s..	25620
86-EBAA	QOM cluster	3	3	19,535	25,294		94.99	100	C	41	Toba	PN.	1964-1994	1980			0.s..	25621
86-EBAA-a	Southeast nam-qom					0				41		pn.					0.s..	25622
86-EBAA-b	Northeast nam-qom					0				41		pn.					0.s..	25623
86-EBAA-c	North nam-qom					0				41		pn.					0.s..	25624
86-EBAA-d	Northwest nam-qom					0				41		pn.					0.s..	25625
86-EBAB	PILAGá cluster	2	2	2,498	3,283		90.51	100	C	57		PN.					0.s..	25626
86-EBAB-a	toba-pilagá	2	2	2,498	3,283	0	90.51	100	C	57	Pilaga*	PN.	1938-1978	1981-1993			0.s..	25627
86-EBAB-b	chaco-pilagá					0				57		pn.					0.s..	25628
86-EBB	**MOKOVI net**	1	1	4,525	5,762		40.00	82	B	41		PN.					0.s..	25629
86-EBBA	MOQOYT cluster	1	1	4,525	5,762		40.00	82	B	41		PN.					0.s..	25630
86-EBBA-a	moqoyt	1	1	4,525	5,762	0	40.00	82	B	41	Mocovi	PN.	1976	1988			0.s..	25631

Continued opposite

Table 9-13 continued

Code 1	REFERENCE NAME / Autoglossonym 2	Coun 3	Peo 4	Mother-tongue speakers in 2000 5	in 2025 6	Media radio 7	AC% 8	E% 9	Wld 10	Tr 11	Biblioglossonym 12	Print 13-15	P-activity 16	N-activity 17	B-activity 18	J-year 19	Jayuh 20-24	Ref 25
86-EBC	**ABIPON net**									0		. . .					0. . . .	25632
86-EBCA	ABIPON cluster			0	0		0.00	0		0		. . .					0. . . .	25633
86-EBCA-a	abipon			0	0	0	0.00	0		0		. . .					0. . . .	25634
86-EC	WACHI-PAYAWA chain									0		. . .					0. . . .	25635
86-ECA	**WACHI net**									0		. . .					0. . . .	25636
86-ECAA	GUACHí cluster			0	0		0.00	0		0		. . .					0. . . .	25637
86-ECAA-a	guachí			0	0	0	0.00	0		0		. . .					0. . . .	25638
86-ECB	**PAYAWA net**									0		. . .					0. . . .	25639
86-ECBA	PAYAGUá cluster			0	0		0.00	0		0		. . .					0. . . .	25640
86-ECBA-a	payaguá			0	0	0	0.00	0		0		. . .					0. . . .	25641
86-F	**KUNSA set**									0		. . .					0. . . .	25642
86-FA	KUNSA chain									0		. . .					0. . . .	25643
86-FAA	**KUNSA net**									0		. . .					0. . . .	25644
86-FAAA	CUNZA cluster			0	0		0.00	0		0		. . .					0. . . .	25645
86-FAAA-a	cunza			0	0	0	0.00	0		0		. . .					0. . . .	25646
86-G	**MAPUCHE set**	3	4	778,946	1,000,351		67.63	100	C	35		P . .					4. . . .	25647
86-GA	MAPUCHE chain	3	4	778,946	1,000,351		67.63	100	C	35		P . .					4. . . .	25648
86-GAA	**MAPUCHE net**	3	4	778,946	1,000,351		67.63	100	C	35		P . .					4. . . .	25649
86-GAAA	MAPU-DUNGUN cluster	3	4	778,946	1,000,351		67.63	100	C	35		P . .					4. . . .	25650
86-GAAA-a	pehuenche					0				35		p . .					1. . . .	25651
86-GAAA-b	picunche					0				35		p . .					1. . . .	25652
86-GAAA-c	Proper mapuche	2	2	595,304	764,356	0	70.00	100	C	35	Mapudungun	P . .	1901-1930			1995	4. . . .	25655
86-GAAA-d	East mapuche					0				35		p . .					1. . . .	25661
86-GAAA-e	huilliche	1	1	183,098	235,298	0	60.00	100	C	35		p . .					1. . . .	25665
86-H	**PUELCHE set**	1	2	14	18		85.71	100	C	8		. . .					0. . . .	25669
86-HA	PUELCHE chain	1	2	14	18		85.71	100	C	8		. . .					0. . . .	25670
86-HAA	**PUELCHE net**	1	2	14	18		85.71	100	C	8		. . .					0. . . .	25671
86-HAAA	GüNüA-KüNE cluster	1	2	14	18		85.71	100	C	8		. . .					0. . . .	25672
86-HAAA-a	West günüa-küne	1	1	7	9	0	85.71	100	C	8		. . .					0. . . .	25673
86-HAAA-b	East günüa-küne	1	1	7	9	0	85.71	100	C	8		. . .					0. . . .	25674
86-I	**QAWASQAR set**	1	1	64	82		59.38	91	B	4		. . .					0. . . .	25675
86-IA	QAWASQAR chain	1	1	64	82		59.38	91	B	4		. . .					0. . . .	25676
86-IAA	**QAWASQAR net**	1	1	64	82		59.38	91	B	4		. . .					0. . . .	25677
86-IAAA	QAWASQAR cluster	1	1	64	82		59.38	91	B	4		. . .					0. . . .	25678
86-IAAA-a	kawaskar	1	1	64	82	0	59.38	91	B	4		. . .					0. . . .	25679
86-IAAA-b	cacahue			0	0	0	0.00	0		4		. . .					0. . . .	25680
86-J	**YAMANA set**									27		P . .					0. . . .	25681
86-JA	YAMANA chain									27		P . .					0. . . .	25682
86-JAA	**YAMANA net**									27		P . .					0. . . .	25683
86-JAAA	YAMANA cluster			0	0		0.00	0		27	Yahgan*	P . .	1881-1886				0. . . .	25684
86-JAAA-a	West yamana					0				27		p . .					0. . . .	25685
86-JAAA-b	Central yamana					0				27		p . .					0. . . .	25686
86-JAAA-c	East yamana					0				27		p . .					0. . . .	25687
86-JAAA-d	Southwest yamana					0				27		p . .					0. . . .	25688
86-JAAA-e	Southeast yamana					0				27		p . .					0. . . .	25689
87	**MATOGROSSIC zone**	3	26	80,865	113,036		50.38	91	B	41		PN .					1. . . .	25690
87-A	**KANICHANA-MOVIMA set**	1	2	1,488	2,346		70.03	100	C	27		P . .					0. . . .	25691
87-AA	KANICHANA-MOVIMA chain	1	2	1,488	2,346		70.03	100	C	27		P . .					0. . . .	25692
87-AAA	**MOVIMA net**	1	1	870	1,372		70.00	100	C	27		P . .					0. . . .	25693
87-AAAA	MOVIMA cluster	1	1	870	1,372		70.00	100	C	27		P . .					0. . . .	25694
87-AAAA-a	movima	1	1	870	1,372	0	70.00	100	C	27	Movima	P . .	1967				0. . . .	25695
87-AAB	**CANICHANA net**	1	1	618	974		70.06	100	C	8		. . .					0. . . .	25696
87-AABA	CANICHANA cluster	1	1	618	974		70.06	100	C	8		. . .					0. . . .	25697
87-AABA-a	canichana	1	1	618	974	0	70.06	100	C	8		. . .					0. . . .	25698
87-B	**CHIQUITO set**	1	1	29,070	45,833		40.00	88	B	41		PN .					0. . . .	25699
87-BA	CHIQUITO chain	1	1	29,070	45,833		40.00	88	B	41		PN .					0. . . .	25700
87-BAA	**CHIQUITO net**	1	1	29,070	45,833		40.00	88	B	41		PN .					0. . . .	25701
87-BAAA	CHIQUITO cluster	1	1	29,070	45,833		40.00	88	B	41	Chiquitano	PN .	1974	1980			0. . . .	25702
87-BAAA-a	concepción					1				41		pn .					0. . . .	25703
87-BAAA-b	velazco					1				41		pn .					0. . . .	25704
87-BAAA-c	javierano					1				41		pn .					0. . . .	25705
87-BAAA-d	santiago					1				41		pn .					0. . . .	25706
87-BAAA-e	san-miguel					1				41		pn .					0. . . .	25707
87-C	**BORORO-UMUTINA set**	1	2	1,072	1,373		28.45	60	B	41		PN .					0. . . .	25708
87-CA	BORORO-UMUTINA chain	1	2	1,072	1,373		28.45	60	B	41		PN .					0. . . .	25709
87-CAA	**BORORO net**	1	1	902	1,155		18.96	52	B	41		PN .					0. . . .	25710
87-CAAA	BORöRO cluster	1	1	902	1,155		18.96	52	B	41		PN .					0. . . .	25711
87-CAAA-a	borôro	1	1	902	1,155	0	18.96	52	B	41	Bororo	PN .	1977-1995	1993			0. . . .	25712
87-CAB	**UMOTINA net**	1	1	170	218		78.82	100	C	9		. . .					0. . . .	25713
87-CABA	UMOTINA cluster	1	1	170	218		78.82	100	C	9		. . .					0. . . .	25714
87-CABA-a	umotina	1	1	170	218	0	78.82	100	C	9		. . .					0. . . .	25715

Continued overleaf

Table 9-13 continued

Code 1	REFERENCE NAME / *Autoglossonym* 2	Coun 3	Peo 4	Mother-tongue speakers in 2000 5	in 2025 6	Media radio 7	CHURCH AC% 8	E% 9	Wld 10	Tr 11	Biblioglossonym 12	SCRIPTURES Print 13-15	P–activity 16	N–activity 17	B–activity 18	J-year 19	Jayuh 20-24	Ref 25
87-CAC	**OTUKE net**									0		. . .					0. . . .	25716
87-CACA	OTUKé cluster									0		. . .					0. . . .	25717
87-CACA-a	Proper otuké					0				0		. . .					0. . . .	25718
87-CACA-b	louxiru					0				0		. . .					0. . . .	25719
87-CACA-c	covareca			0	0	0	0.00	0		0		. . .					0. . . .	25720
87-CACA-d	curuminaca			0	0	0	0.00	0		0		. . .					0. . . .	25721
87-CACA-e	coraveca			0	0	0	0.00	0		0		. . .					0. . . .	25722
87-CACA-f	curucaneca			0	0	0	0.00	0		0		. . .					0. . . .	25723
87-CACA-g	tapii			0	0	0	0.00	0		0		. . .					0. . . .	25724
87-D	**GUATO set**	1	1	408	523		20.10	51	B	5		. . .					0. . . .	25725
87-DA	GUATO chain	1	1	408	523		20.10	51	B	5		. . .					0. . . .	25726
87-DAA	**GUATO net**	1	1	408	523		20.10	51	B	5		. . .					0. . . .	25727
87-DAAA	GUATó cluster	1	1	408	523		20.10	51	B	5		. . .					0. . . .	25728
87-DAAA-a	guató	1	1	408	523	0	20.10	51	B	5		. . .					0. . . .	25729
87-E	**YABUTI-ARIKAPU set**	1	1	50	85		20.00	50	B	0		. . .					0. . . .	25730
87-EA	YABUTI-ARIKAPU chain	1	1	50	85		20.00	50	B	0		. . .					0. . . .	25731
87-EAA	**YABUTI net**	1	1	30	51		20.00	50	B	0		. . .					0. . . .	25732
87-EAAA	JABUTí cluster	1	1	30	51		20.00	50	B	0		. . .					0. . . .	25733
87-EAAA-a	jabutí	1	1	30	51	0	20.00	50	B	0		. . .					0. . . .	25734
87-EAB	**ARIKAPU-MASHUBI net**	1	1	20	34		20.00	50	B	0		. . .					0. . . .	25735
87-EABA	ARICAPú cluster	1	1	20	34		20.00	50	B	0		. . .					0. . . .	25736
87-EABA-a	aricapú	1	1	20	34	0	20.00	50	B	0		. . .					0. . . .	25737
87-EABB	MAXUBí cluster			0	0		0.00	0		0		. . .					0. . . .	25738
87-EABB-a	maxubí			0	0	0	0.00	0		0		. . .					0. . . .	25739
87-F	**KAPISHANA set**	1	1	200	340		20.00	51	B	0		. . .					0. . . .	25740
87-FA	KAPISHANA chain	1	1	200	340		20.00	51	B	0		. . .					0. . . .	25741
87-FAA	**KAPISHANA net**	1	1	200	340		20.00	51	B	0		. . .					0. . . .	25742
87-FAAA	CAPIXANá cluster	1	1	200	340		20.00	51	B	0		. . .					0. . . .	25743
87-FAAA-a	capixaná	1	1	200	340	0	20.00	51	B	0		. . .					0. . . .	25744
87-G	**CABIXI-SABANE set**	1	5	1,684	2,158		44.83	81	B	41		PN.				1. . . .		25745
87-GA	CABIXI-SABANE chain	1	5	1,684	2,158		44.83	81	B	41		PN.				1. . . .		25746
87-GAA	**CABIXI-SARARE net**	1	4	1,633	2,093		43.72	81	B	41		PN.				1. . . .		25747
87-GAAA	CABIXI-OURO cluster	1	2	374	480		40.11	72	B	32		P. .				1. . . .		25748
87-GAAA-a	tawadnde					0				32		p. .				1. . . .		25749
87-GAAA-b	lacondê					0				32		p. .				1. . . .		25750
87-GAAA-c	taiatê					0				32		p. .				1. . . .		25751
87-GAAA-d	yalunte					0				32		p. .				1. . . .		25752
87-GAAA-e	tawente					0				32		p. .				1. . . .		25753
87-GAAA-f	mameleto					0				32		p. .				1. . . .		25754
87-GAAA-g	cabixi	1	1	119	153	0	40.34	77	B	32		P. .				1. . . .		25755
87-GAAA-h	negarotê	1	1	255	327	0	40.00	69	B	32		p. .				1. . . .		25758
87-GAAB	SARARé-MANDUCA cluster	1	2	1,259	1,613		44.80	83	B	41	Nambikwara*	PN.	1972-1980	1992			0. . . .	25759
87-GAAB-a	manduca					0				41		pn.					0. . . .	25760
87-GAAB-b	campo					0				41		pn.					0. . . .	25764
87-GAAB-c	guaporé					0				41		pn.					0. . . .	25771
87-GAAB-d	sararé	1	1	204	262	0	69.61	100	C	41		pn.					0. . . .	25781
87-GAB	**SABANE net**	1	1	51	65		80.39	100	C	6		. . .					0. . . .	25782
87-GABA	SABANê cluster	1	1	51	65		80.39	100	C	6		. . .					0. . . .	25783
87-GABA-a	sabanê	1	1	51	65	0	80.39	100	C	6		. . .					0. . . .	25784
87-H	**RIKBAKTSA set**	1	1	851	1,090		79.91	100	C	32		P. .				1. . . .		25785
87-HA	RIKBAKTSA chain	1	1	851	1,090		79.91	100	C	32		P. .				1. . . .		25786
87-HAA	**RIKBAKTSA net**	1	1	851	1,090		79.91	100	C	32		P. .				1. . . .		25787
87-HAAA	RIKBAKTSA cluster	1	1	851	1,090		79.91	100	C	32		P. .				1. . . .		25788
87-HAAA-a	rikbaktsa	1	1	851	1,090	0	79.91	100	C	32	Rikbaktsa	P. .	1977-1993			1997	1. . . .	25789
87-I	**OPAYE set**	1	1	10	17		20.00	50	B	0		. . .					0. . . .	25790
87-IA	OPAYE chain	1	1	10	17		20.00	50	B	0		. . .					0. . . .	25791
87-IAA	**OPAYE net**	1	1	10	17		20.00	50	B	0		. . .					0. . . .	25792
87-IAAA	OPAYé cluster	1	1	10	17		20.00	50	B	0		. . .					0. . . .	25793
87-IAAA-a	Proper opayé					0				0		. . .					0. . . .	25794
87-IAAA-b	guachi					0				0		. . .					0. . . .	25795
87-J	**TRUMAI set**	1	1	70	119		30.00	64	B	4		. . .					0. . . .	25796
87-JA	TRUMAI chain	1	1	70	119		30.00	64	B	4		. . .					0. . . .	25797
87-JAA	**TRUMAI net**	1	1	70	119		30.00	64	B	4		. . .					0. . . .	25798
87-JAAA	TRUMAí cluster	1	1	70	119		30.00	64	B	4		. . .					0. . . .	25799
87-JAAA-a	trumaí	1	1	70	119	0	30.00	64	B	4		. . .					0. . . .	25800
87-K	**HALO-TE-SU set**	1	1	50	85		30.00	64	B	0		. . .					0. . . .	25801
87-KA	HALO-TE-SU chain	1	1	50	85		30.00	64	B	0		. . .					0. . . .	25802
87-KAA	**HALO-TE-SU net**	1	1	50	85		30.00	64	B	0		. . .					0. . . .	25803
87-KAAA	HALó-Té-Sú cluster	1	1	50	85		30.00	64	B	0		. . .					0. . . .	25804
87-KAAA-a	haló-té-sú	1	1	50	85	0	30.00	64	B	0		. . .					0. . . .	25805
87-L	**NUMBIAI set**	1	1	30	51		30.00	63	B	0		. . .					0. . . .	25806
87-LA	NUMBIAI chain	1	1	30	51		30.00	63	B	0		. . .					0. . . .	25807
87-LAA	**NUMBIAI net**	1	1	30	51		30.00	63	B	0		. . .					0. . . .	25808

Continued opposite

Table 9-13 continued

Code 1	REFERENCE NAME / Autoglossonym 2	Coun 3	Peo 4	in 2000 5	in 2025 6	Media radio 7	AC% 8	E% 9	Wld 10	Tr 11	Biblioglossonym 12	Print 13-15	P-activity 16	N-activity 17	B-activity 18	J-year 19	Jayuh 20-24	Ref 25
87-LAAA	NUMBIAI cluster	1	1	30	51		30.00	63	B	0		...					0....	25809
87-LAAA-a	numbiai	1	1	30	51	0	30.00	63	B	0		...					0....	25810
87-M	**ENAWENE set**	1	1	200	340		30.00	65	B	0		...					0....	25811
87-MA	ENAWENE chain	1	1	200	340		30.00	65	B	0		...					0....	25812
87-MAA	**ENAWENE net**	1	1	200	340		30.00	65	B	0		...					0....	25813
87-MAAA	ENAWENE cluster	1	1	200	340		30.00	65	B	0		...					0....	25814
87-MAAA-a	enawené-nawé					0				0		...					0....	25815
87-MAAA-b	enawené-maré					0				0		...					0....	25816
87-N	**IRANCHE set**	1	1	187	240		19.79	52	B	4		...					0....	25817
87-NA	IRANCHE chain	1	1	187	240		19.79	52	B	4		...					0....	25818
87-NAA	**IRANCHE net**	1	1	187	240		19.79	52	B	4		...					0....	25819
87-NAAA	MUNDU cluster	1	1	187	240		19.79	52	B	4		...					0....	25820
87-NAAA-a	menku					0				4		...					0....	25821
87-NAAA-b	irántxe	1	1	187	240	0	19.79	52	B	4		...					0....	25822
87-O	**KARAYA set**	1	1	1,786	2,288		60.02	100	C	41		PN.					0....	25823
87-OA	KARAYA chain	1	1	1,786	2,288		60.02	100	C	41		PN.					0....	25824
87-OAA	**KARAYA net**	1	1	1,786	2,288		60.02	100	C	41		PN.					0....	25825
87-OAAA	CARAJá cluster	1	1	1,786	2,288		60.02	100	C	41	Karaja	PN.	1965	1983			0....	25826
87-OAAA-a	carajá-X.					0				41		pn.					0....	25827
87-OAAA-b	carajá-Y.					0				41		pn.					0....	25828
87-OAAA-c	javaé					0				41		pn.					0....	25829
87-P	**GE set**	2	12	43,709	56,148		57.16	94	B	41		PN.					1....	25830
87-PA	NORTHEAST GE chain	1	7	10,254	13,221		52.03	88	B	41		PN.					0....	25831
87-PAA	**KREEN-AKARORE net**	1	1	119	153		40.34	70	B	3		...					0....	25832
87-PAAA	KREEN-AKARORE cluster	1	1	119	153		40.34	70	B	3		...					0....	25833
87-PAAA-a	kreen-akarore	1	1	119	153	0	40.34	70	B	3		...					0....	25834
87-PAB	**KAYAPO net**	1	1	4,270	5,470		60.00	99	C	41		PN.					0....	25835
87-PABA	CAYAPO cluster	1	1	4,270	5,470		60.00	99	C	41		PN.					0....	25836
87-PABA-a	cayapó	1	1	4,270	5,470	0	60.00	99	C	41	Kayapo	PN.	1975-1978	1996			0....	25837
87-PABA-b	kokraimoró					0				41		pn.					0....	25838
87-PABA-c	diore					0				41		pn.					0....	25839
87-PABA-d	kararaó					0				41		pn.					0....	25840
87-PABA-e	kuben-krag-no-ti-re					0				41		pn.					0....	25841
87-PABA-f	men-tuk-ti-re					0				41		pn.					0....	25842
87-PABA-g	pacajá					0				41		pn.					0....	25843
87-PABA-h	txukuhamai					0				41		pn.					0....	25844
87-PABA-i	goro-ti-re					0				41		pn.					0....	25845
87-PABA-j	South cayapó					0				41		pn.					0....	25846
87-PABB	CRADAHú cluster			0	0		0.00	0		0		...					0....	25847
87-PABB-a	cradahú			0	0	0	0.00	0		0		...					0....	25848
87-PAC	**APINAYE net**	1	1	851	1,090		79.91	100	C	22		P..					0....	25849
87-PACA	APINAYé cluster	1	1	851	1,090		79.91	100	C	22		P..					0....	25850
87-PACA-a	apinayé	1	1	851	1,090	0	79.91	100	C	22	Apinaye	P..	1967-1989				0....	25851
87-PAD	**TIMBIRA net**	1	3	4,610	5,906		39.54	75	B	41		PN.					0....	25852
87-PADA	TIMBIRA cluster	1	3	4,610	5,906		39.54	75	B	41		PN.					0....	25853
87-PADA-a	canela	1	2	4,185	5,361	0	40.00	76	B	41	Canela	PN.	1981	1990			0....	25854
87-PADA-b	apanjekra					0				41		pn.					0....	25855
87-PADA-c	ramkókamekra					0				41		pn.					0....	25856
87-PADA-d	krinkatí	1	1	425	545	0	35.06	70	B	41	Krikati-timbira	pn.					0....	25857
87-PADA-e	crenye					0				41		pn.					0....	25858
87-PADA-f	pukobyé					0				41		pn.					0....	25859
87-PADA-g	parakáteye					0				41		pn.					0....	25860
87-PADA-h	taze					0				41		pn.					0....	25861
87-PAE	**SUYA net**	1	1	204	262		59.80	93	B	3		...					0....	25862
87-PAEA	SUYA cluster	1	1	204	262		59.80	93	B	3		...					0....	25863
87-PAEA-a	suyá	1	1	204	262	0	59.80	93	B	3		...					0....	25864
87-PAEA-b	tapayuna									3		...					0....	25865
87-PAF	**IPEWI net**	1	1	200	340		50.00	87	B	0		...					0....	25866
87-PAFA	IPEWí cluster	1	1	200	340		50.00	87	B	0		...					0....	25867
87-PAFA-a	ipewí	1	1	200	340	0	50.00	87	B	0		...					0....	25868
87-PB	GE-CENTRAL chain	1	2	9,833	12,596		62.63	95	C	22		P..					1....	25869
87-PBA	**SHAVANTE net**	1	1	8,540	10,940		60.00	94	C	22		P..					1....	25870
87-PBAA	XAVáNTE cluster	1	1	8,540	10,940		60.00	94	C	22		P..					1....	25871
87-PBAA-a	Proper xavánte	1	1	8,540	10,940	0	60.00	94	C	22	Xavante	P..	1970-1993				1....	25872
87-PBAA-b	akuen					0				22		p..					1....	25873
87-PBAA-c	crisca					0				22		p..					1....	25874
87-PBAA-d	pusciti					0				22		p..					1....	25875
87-PBAA-e	tapacua					0				22		p..					1....	25876
87-PBB	**AKROA net**									0		...					0....	25877
87-PBBA	ACROá cluster			0	0		0.00	0		0		...					0....	25878
87-PBBA-a	acroá			0	0	0	0.00	0		0		...					0....	25879
87-PBC	**SHERENTE net**	1	1	1,293	1,656		79.97	100	C	22		P..					0....	25880
87-PBCA	XERéNTE cluster	1	1	1,293	1,656		79.97	100	C	22		P..					0....	25881
87-PBCA-a	xerénte	1	1	1,293	1,656	0	79.97	100	C	22	Xerente	P..	1970-1990				0....	25882
87-PBD	**SHAKRIABA net**									0		...					0....	25883
87-PBDA	XAKRIABá cluster			0	0		0.00	0		0		...					0....	25884
87-PBDA-a	xakriabá			0	0	0	0.00	0		0		...					0....	25885
87-PC	KAINGANG chain	2	3	23,622	30,331		57.11	97	B	41		PN.					0....	25886
87-PCA	**KAINGANG net**	2	3	23,422	29,991		57.25	97	B	41		PN.					0....	25887
87-PCAA	KAINGáNG cluster	2	3	23,422	29,991		57.25	97	B	41		PN.					0....	25888
87-PCAA-a	kaingáng-sao-paulo					0				41		pn.					0....	25889

Continued overleaf

Table 9-13 continued

Code 1	REFERENCE NAME / Autoglossonym 2	Coun 3	Peo 4	Mother-tongue speakers in 2000 5	in 2025 6	Media radio 7	CHURCH AC% 8	E% 9	Wld 10	Tr 11	Biblioglossonym 12	SCRIPTURES Print 13-15	P-activity 16	N-activity 17	B-activity 18	J-year 19	Jayuh 20-24	Ref 25
87-PCAA-b	kaingáng-paraná					0				41		pn.					0....	25890
87-PCAA-c	Central kaingáng	2	2	22,639	28,989		58.37	98	B	41	Kaingang	PN.	1967-1968	1977			0....	25891
87-PCAA-d	Southwest kaingáng					0				41		pn.					0....	25892
87-PCAA-e	Southeast kaingáng					0				41		pn.					0....	25893
87-PCB	**SHOKLENG net**	1	1	200	340		40.00	77	B	0		...					0....	25894
87-PCBA	XOKLENG cluster	1	1	200	340		40.00	77	B	0		...					0....	25895
87-PCBA-a	xokleng	1	1	200	340	0	40.00	77	B	0		...					0....	25896
87-PCC	**WAYANA net**									0		...					0....	25897
87-PCCA	GUAYANá cluster			0	0		0.00	0		0		...					0....	25898
87-PCCA-a	guayaná			0	0		0.00	0		0		...					0....	25899
88	**AMAZONIC zone**	5	79	177,528	245,032		44.57	74	B	42		PN.					1.s..	25900
88-A	**AMIKOANA set**									4		...					0....	25901
88-AA	AMIKOANA chain									4		...					0....	25902
88-AAA	**AMIKOANA net**									4		...					0....	25903
88-AAAA	AMIKOANA cluster									4		...					0....	25904
88-AAAA-a	amikoana					0				4		...					0....	25905
88-B	**IAPAMA set**	1	1	10	17		50.00	90	B	4		...					0....	25906
88-BA	IAPAMA chain	1	1	10	17		50.00	90	B	4		...					0....	25907
88-BAA	**IAPAMA net**	1	1	10	17		50.00	90	B	4		...					0....	25908
88-BAAA	IAPAMA cluster	1	1	10	17		50.00	90	B	4		...					0....	25909
88-BAAA-a	iapama	1	1	10	17	0	50.00	90	B	4		...					0....	25910
88-C	**ARUTANI-SAPE set**	1	2	193	279		59.07	89	B	8		...					0....	25911
88-CA	SAPE chain	1	1	140	202		70.00	100	C	8		...					0....	25912
88-CAA	**SAPE net**	1	1	140	202		70.00	100	C	8		...					0....	25913
88-CAAA	SAPé cluster	1	1	140	202		70.00	100	C	8		...					0....	25914
88-CAAA-a	sapé	1	1	140	202	0	70.00	100	C	8	Sape	...					0....	25915
88-CB	ARUTANI chain	1	1	53	77		30.19	60	B	8		...					0....	25916
88-CBA	**ARUTANI net**	1	1	53	77		30.19	60	B	8		...					0....	25917
88-CBAA	ARUTANI cluster	1	1	53	77		30.19	60	B	8		...					0....	25918
88-CBAA-a	arutani	1	1	53	77	0	30.19	60	B	8		...					0....	25919
88-D	**YANOMAM-NINAM set**	2	7	44,289	59,965		18.05	52	B	41		PN.					1.s..	25920
88-DA	YANOMAM-NINAM chain	2	7	44,289	59,965		18.05	52	B	41		PN.					1.s..	25921
88-DAA	**NINAM net**	2	2	849	1,110		70.08	100	C	23		P..					0....	25922
88-DAAA	NINAM cluster	2	2	849	1,110		70.08	100	C	23	Ninam	P..	1970				0....	25923
88-DAAA-a	jawarib					0				23		p..					0....	25924
88-DAAA-b	yanam					0				23		p..					0....	25925
88-DAAA-c	South ninam					0				23		p..					0....	25926
88-DAB	**SANUMA net**	2	2	5,326	7,550		29.70	64	B	12		...					0....	25927
88-DABA	SANUMá cluster	2	2	5,326	7,550		29.70	64	B	12	Sanuma	...					0....	25928
88-DABA-a	guaika					0				12		...					0....	25929
88-DABA-b	samatari					0				12		...					0....	25930
88-DABA-c	chirichano					0				12		...					0....	25931
88-DAC	**YANOMAM net**	2	3	38,114	51,305		15.26	49	A	41		PN.					1.s..	25932
88-DACA	YANOMAMö cluster	2	2	17,649	25,088		15.55	51	B	41	Yanomamo	PN.	1961-1968	1984		1991	1....	25933
88-DACA-a	West yanomamö	1	1	15,710	22,604	0	15.00	50	B	41	Guaica	Pn.	1961				1....	25934
88-DACA-b	East yanomamö	1	1	1,939	2,484	0	20.01	59	B	41		pn.					1....	25935
88-DACB	YANOMáMI cluster	1	1	20,465	26,217		15.00	48	A	12		...					0.s..	25936
88-DACB-a	patimitheri					0				12		...					0.s..	25937
88-DACB-b	guaicá	1	1	20,465	26,217	0	15.00	48	A	12	Yanomami	...					0.s..	25938
88-DACB-c	naomam					0				12		...					0.s..	25939
88-DACB-d	guadema					0				12		...					0.s..	25940
88-DACB-e	toototobi					0				12		...					0.s..	25941
88-DACB-f	nanomam					0				12		...					0.s..	25942
88-DACB-g	jauari					0				12		...					0.s..	25943
88-E	**YUWANA set**	1	1	684	984		3.07	28	A	12		...					0....	25944
88-EA	YUWANA chain	1	1	684	984		3.07	28	A	12		...					0....	25945
88-EAA	**YUWANA net**	1	1	684	984		3.07	28	A	12		...					0....	25946
88-EAAA	HOTí cluster	1	1	684	984		3.07	28	A	12	Yuwana	...					0....	25947
88-EAAA-a	North hotí					0				12		...					0....	25948
88-EAAA-b	South hotí					0				12		...					0....	25949
88-F	**PIAROA-SALIVA set**	2	4	19,491	27,954		26.02	65	B	41		PN.					0....	25950
88-FA	PIAROA-SALIVA chain	2	4	19,491	27,954		26.02	65	B	41		PN.					0....	25951
88-FAA	**PIAROA-SALIVA net**	2	4	19,491	27,954		26.02	65	B	41		PN.					0....	25952
88-FAAA	PIAROA cluster	1	1	15,875	22,840		20.00	60	B	41		PN.					0....	25953
88-FAAA-a	Proper piaroa	1	1	15,875	22,840	0	20.00	60	B	41	Piaroa	PN.	1961-1964	1986			0....	25954
88-FAAA-b	itoto					0				41		pn.					0....	25955
88-FAAB	SALIBA cluster	2	3	3,616	5,114		52.43	86	B	12		...					0....	25956
88-FAAB-a	sáliba	2	2	3,438	4,863	0	55.09	89	B	12	Saliba	...					0....	25957
88-FAAB-b	chipiajes					0				12		...					0....	25958
88-G	**WAHIVO-KUIVA set**	2	7	41,177	58,366		69.66	88	C	41		PN.					0....	25959
88-GA	WAHIVO-KUIVA chain	2	7	41,177	58,366		69.66	88	C	41		PN.					0....	25960
88-GAA	**WAHIVO-KUIVA net**	2	7	41,177	58,366		69.66	88	C	41		PN.					0....	25961
88-GAAA	HIWI cluster	2	5	33,112	46,959		84.29	100	C	41		PN.					0....	25962
88-GAAA-a	Proper guahibo	2	2	31,115	44,138	0	85.00	100	C	41	Guajibo*	PN.	1960-1968	1982			0....	25963

Continued opposite

Table 9-13 continued

Code 1	REFERENCE NAME / Autoglossonym 2	Coun 3	Peo 4	Mother-tongue speakers in 2000 5	in 2025 6	Media radio 7	CHURCH AC% 8	E% 9	Wld 10	Tr 11	Biblioglossonym 12	SCRIPTURES Print 13-15	P–activity 16	N–activity 17	B–activity 18	J-year 19	Jayuh 20-24	Ref 25
88-GAAA-b	playero	1	1	245	347	0	50.20	88	B	41		pn.					0....	25964
88-GAAA-c	guahibo-tomo					0				41		pn.					0....	25965
88-GAAA-d	macaguán	1	1	207	293	0	50.24	83	B	41		pn.					0....	25966
88-GAAA-e	guayabero	1	1	1,545	2,181	0	80.00	100	C	41	Guayabero	Pn.	1961-1995				0....	25967
88-GAAA-f	churuya					0				41		pn.					0....	25968
88-GAAB	CUIBA cluster	2	2	8,065	11,407		9.56	41	A	41		PN.					0....	25969
88-GAAB-a	Proper cuiba	2	2	8,065	11,407	0	9.56	41	A	41	Cuiba	PN.	1974-1993	1987-1988			0....	25970
88-GAAB-b	chiricoa					0				41		pn.					0....	25971
88-GAAB-c	masiware					0				41		pn.					0....	25972
88-GAAB-d	chiripo					0				41		pn.					0....	25973
88-GAAB-e	yarahuuraxi					0				41		pn.					0....	25974
88-GAAB-f	mayayero					0				41		pn.					0....	25975
88-GAAB-g	mochuelo					0				41		pn.					0....	25976
88-GAAB-h	tampiwi					0				41		pn.					0....	25977
88-GAAB-i	mella					0				41		pn.					0....	25978
88-GAAB-j	ptamo					0				41		pn.					0....	25979
88-GAAB-k	casibara					0				41		pn.					0....	25980
88-GAAB-l	hermosa					0				41		pn.					0....	25981
88-H	PUINAVE set	2	2	3,940	5,575		60.00	98	C	42		PN.					0....	25982
88-HA	PUINAVE chain	2	2	3,940	5,575		60.00	98	C	42		PN.					0....	25983
88-HAA	PUINAVE net	2	2	3,940	5,575		60.00	98	C	42		PN.					0....	25984
88-HAAA	PUINAVE cluster	2	2	3,940	5,575		60.00	98	C	42		PN.					0....	25985
88-HAAA-a	West puinave	1	1	3,483	4,918	0	60.01	98	C	42	Puinave	PN.	1955	1964			0....	25986
88-HAAA-b	East puinave	1	1	457	657	0	59.96	96	B	42	Puinave	PN.	1955	1964			0....	25987
88-I	KAKWA-HUPDE set	2	9	3,435	4,522		33.77	66	B	23		P..					0....	25988
88-IA	KAKWA chain	2	2	373	509		66.49	99	C	23		P..					0....	25989
88-IAA	KAKWA net	2	2	373	509		66.49	99	C	23		P..					0....	25990
88-IAAA	CACUA cluster	2	2	373	509		66.49	99	C	23	Cacua	P..	1975				0....	25991
88-IAAA-a	kakwa-querari					0				23		p..					0....	25992
88-IAAA-b	kakwa-vaupés					0				23		p..					0....	25993
88-IAAA-c	kakwa-papuri					0				23		p..					0....	25994
88-IAAA-d	kakwa-paraná					0				23		p..					0....	25995
88-IAAA-e	bará	1	1	136	174	0	60.29	99	C	23		p..					0....	25996
88-IB	HUPDE chain	2	3	1,959	2,536		35.48	69	B	12		...					0....	25997
88-IBA	HUPDE net	2	3	1,959	2,536		35.48	69	B	12		...					0....	25998
88-IBAA	HUPDE cluster	2	3	1,959	2,536		35.48	69	B	12		...					0....	25999
88-IBAA-a	Proper hupde	2	2	1,449	1,882	0	37.41	71	B	12	Hupde	...					0....	26000
88-IBAA-b	tuhup					0				12		...					0....	26001
88-IBAA-c	nehup					0				12		...					0....	26002
88-IBAA-d	yahup	1	1	510	654	0	30.00	62	B	12	Yuhup	...					0....	26003
88-IBAA-e	tikié					0				12		...					0....	26004
88-IBAA-f	papurí					0				12		...					0....	26005
88-IC	WARIVA-KABURI chain	2	4	1,103	1,477		19.67	49	A	12		...					0....	26006
88-ICA	WARIVA net	1	1	238	305		39.92	71	B	0		...					0....	26007
88-ICAA	GUARIBA cluster	1	1	238	305		39.92	71	B	0		...					0....	26008
88-ICAA-a	guariba	1	1	238	305	0	39.92	71	B	0		...					0....	26009
88-ICB	KABURI net	1	1	374	479		29.95	65	B	12		...					0....	26010
88-ICBA	NADEB cluster	1	1	374	479		29.95	65	B	12		...					0....	26011
88-ICBA-a	nadeb-P.	1	1	374	479	0	29.95	65	B	12	Nadeb	...					0....	26012
88-ICBA-b	kabori.					0				12		...					0....	26013
88-ICBA-c	xiriwai					0				12		...					0....	26014
88-ICBA-d	kamán					0				12		...					0....	26015
88-ICC	WAVIARE net	1	2	491	693		2.04	25	A	12		...					0....	26016
88-ICCA	GUAVIARE cluster	1	2	491	693		2.04	25	A	12		...					0....	26017
88-ICCA-a	guaviare	1	1	360	508	0	1.94	25	A	12		...					0....	26018
88-ICCA-b	nukak maku	1	1	131	185	0	2.29	26	A	12	Nukak Maku	...					0....	26019
88-J	TINGUA-PAMIGUA set									0		...					0....	26020
88-JA	TINGUA-PAMIGUA chain									0		...					0....	26021
88-JAA	TINGUA net									0		...					0....	26022
88-JAAA	TINGUA cluster			0	0		0.00	0		0		...					0....	26023
88-JAAA-a	tingua			0	0	0	0.00	0		0		...					0....	26024
88-JAB	PAMIGUA net									0		...					0....	26025
88-JABA	PAMIGUA cluster			0	0		0.00	0		0		...					0....	26026
88-JABA-a	pamigua			0	0	0	0.00	0		0		...					0....	26027
88-K	TUCANOAN set	4	28	20,244	28,188		59.05	89	B	41		PN.					0....	26028
88-KA	TUCANOAN chain	4	28	20,244	28,188		59.05	89	B	41		PN.					0....	26029
88-KAA	TUCANOAN net	4	28	20,244	28,188		59.05	89	B	41		PN.					0....	26030
88-KAAA	WEST TUCANOAN cluster	3	7	4,042	5,699		28.75	66	B	41		PN.					0....	26031
88-KAAA-a	correguaje-tama	1	1	2,163	3,054	0	20.02	59	B	41	Coreguaje*	PN.	1981-1986	1991			0....	26032
88-KAAA-b	piohé-siona	3	4	1,339	1,882	0	42.27	78	B	41	Siona	PN.	1965	1982			0....	26035
88-KAAA-c	teteté	1	1	3	4	0	66.67	100	C	41		pn.					0....	26042
88-KAAA-d	yaúna-opaina	1	1	537	759	0	29.98	62	B	41	Tanimuca-retuara	pn.					0....	26043
88-KAAB	SOUTHWEST TUCANOAN cluster	1	1	200	340		30.00	65	B	0		...					0....	26048
88-KAAB-a	coto					0				0		...					0....	26049
88-KAAC	CENTRAL TUCANOAN cluster	2	2	6,366	8,965		80.00	100	C	41		PN.					0....	26055
88-KAAC-a	cubeo	2	2	6,366	8,965	0	80.00	100	C	41	Cubeo	PN.	1958-1986	1970-1989			0....	26056
88-KAAC-b	Vehicular cubeo					0				41		pn.					0....	26057
88-KAAC-c	dyuremawa					0				41		pn.					0....	26058
88-KAAC-d	hehénawa					0				41		pn.					0....	26059
88-KAAC-e	bahúkiwa									41		pn.					0....	26060
88-KAAD	NORTH TUCANOAN cluster	2	6	3,005	4,023		62.26	97	C	41		PN.					0....	26061
88-KAAD-a	dahseyé	1	2	340	435	0	43.24	81	B	41	Tucano	PN.	1967-1981	1988-1989			0....	26062
88-KAAD-b	cótiria	2	2	1,251	1,693	0	70.02	100	C	41	Guanano	PN.	1968	1982			0....	26072
88-KAAD-c	pirá-tapuyo	2	2	1,414	1,895	0	59.97	100	B	41	Piratapuyo	PN.		1990-1991			0....	26073
88-KAAE	EAST TUCANOAN. cluster	2	9	4,858	6,657		59.41	92	B	41		PN.					0....	26077
88-KAAE-a	waimaha	2	2	895	1,202	0	60.00	97	C	41	Waimaha	Pn.	1975-1994				0....	26078
88-KAAE-b	winá	2	3	2,304	3,121	0	61.41	97	C	41		PN.					0....	26083

Continued overleaf

Table 9-13 continued

Code 1	REFERENCE NAME / Autoglossonym 2	Coun 3	Peo 4	Mother-tongue speakers in 2000 5	in 2025 6	Media radio 7	CHURCH AC% 8	E% 9	Wld 10	Tr 11	Biblioglossonym 12	SCRIPTURES Print 13-15	P–activity 16	N–activity 17	B–activity 18	J-year 19	Jayuh 20-24	Ref 25
88-KAAE-c	tatuyo-carpano	2	4	1,659	2,334	0	56.30	84	B	41		PN.					0....	26086
88-KAAF	SOUTH TUCANOAN cluster	1	4	1,773	2,504		49.80	85	B	41		PN.					0....	26092
88-KAAF-a	macuna-barasano	1	4	1,773	2,504	0	49.80	85	B	41	Barasano: Northern*	PN.	1973-1975				0....	26093
88-KAAF-b	yupuá-durina			0	0	0	0.00	0		41		pn.					0....	26101
88-KAAF-c	cueretú			0	0	0	0.00	0		41		pn.					0....	26104
88-L	**ABISHIRA set**	1	1	10	17		50.00	90	B	9		...					0....	26105
88-LA	ABISHIRA chain	1	1	10	17		50.00	90	B	9		...					0....	26106
88-LAA	**ABISHIRA net**	1	1	10	17		50.00	90	B	9		...					0....	26107
88-LAAA	ABISHIRA cluster	1	1	10	17		50.00	90	B	9		...					0....	26108
88-LAAA-a	abishira	1	1	10	17	0	50.00	90	B	9		...					0....	26109
88-M	**TIKUNA set**	3	3	30,123	40,176		52.03	83	B	41		PN.					0....	26110
88-MA	TIKUNA chain	3	3	30,123	40,176		52.03	83	B	41		PN.					0....	26111
88-MAA	**TIKUNA net**	3	3	30,123	40,176		52.03	83	B	41		PN.					0....	26112
88-MAAA	TICUNA cluster	3	3	30,123	40,176		52.03	83	B	41		PN.					0....	26113
88-MAAA-a	ticuna	3	3	30,123	40,176	0	52.03	83	B	41	Ticuna	PN.	1964-1975	1986			0....	26114
88-N	**XIRIANA set**	1	1	20	34		50.00	85	B	4		...					0....	26115
88-NA	XIRIANA chain	1	1	20	34		50.00	85	B	4		...					0....	26116
88-NAA	**XIRIANA net**	1	1	20	34		50.00	85	B	4		...					0....	26117
88-NAAA	XIRIáNA-2 cluster	2	1	20	34		50.00	85	B	4		...					0....	26118
88-NAAA-a	xiriâna-2	1	1	20	34	0	50.00	85	B	4		...					0....	26119
88-O	**MUNICHE set**	1	1	3	4		66.67	100	C	8		...					0....	26120
88-OA	MUNICHE chain	1	1	3	4		66.67	100	C	8		...					0....	26121
88-OAA	**MUNICHE net**	1	1	3	4		66.67	100	C	8		...					0....	26122
88-OAAA	MUNICHE cluster	1	1	3	4		66.67	100	C	8		...					0....	26123
88-OAAA-a	muniche	1	1	3	4	0	66.67	100	C	8		...					0....	26124
88-P	**ARAUAN set**	2	8	4,937	7,000		41.16	74	B	41		PN.					0....	26125
88-PA	JAMAMADI-KULINA chain	2	7	4,206	6,063		36.14	69	B	22		P..					0....	26126
88-PAA	**JAMAMADI net**	2	7	4,206	6,063		36.14	69	B	22		P..					0....	26127
88-PAAA	PROPER YAMAMADí cluster	1	1	204	262		29.90	65	B	22	Jamamadi	P..	1991				0....	26128
88-PAAA-a	bom-futuro					0				22		p..					0....	26129
88-PAAA-b	juruá					0				22		p..					0....	26130
88-PAAA-c	pauiní					0				22		p..					0....	26131
88-PAAA-d	mamoría					0				22		p..					0....	26132
88-PAAA-e	cuchudua					0				22		p..					0....	26133
88-PAAB	TUKURINA cluster	1	1	200	340		40.00	77	B	0		...					0....	26134
88-PAAB-a	tucurina	1	1	200	340	0	40.00	77	B	0		...					0....	26135
88-PAAC	ARAWA cluster									0		...					0....	26136
88-PAAC-a	araua					0				0		...					0....	26137
88-PAAD	PAMA cluster	1	1	300	510		40.00	77	B	0		...					0....	26138
88-PAAD-a	pama	1	1	300	510	0	40.00	77	B	0		...					0....	26139
88-PAAE	SEWACU cluster	1	1	100	170		40.00	77	B	0		...					0....	26140
88-PAAE-a	sewacu	1	1	100	170	0	40.00	77	B	0		...					0....	26141
88-PAAF	SIPO cluster	1	1	200	340		40.00	77	B	0		...					0....	26142
88-PAAF-a	sipo	1	1	200	340	0	40.00	77	B	0		...					0....	26143
88-PAAG	YUBERI cluster	1	1	200	340		40.00	77	B	0		...					0....	26144
88-PAAG-a	yuberi	1	1	200	340	0	40.00	77	B	0		...					0....	26145
88-PAAH	JARAWARA cluster	1	1	153	196		30.07	66	B	12		...					0....	26146
88-PAAH-a	jarawara	1	1	153	196	0	30.07	66	B	12	Jaruara	...					0....	26147
88-PAAI	BANAWá cluster	1	1	119	153		20.17	50	B	12		...					0....	26148
88-PAAI-a	banawá	1	1	119	153	0	20.17	50	B	12	Banawa	...					0....	26149
88-PAAJ	KANAMANTI cluster	1	1	200	340		30.00	65	B	0		...					0....	26150
88-PAAJ-a	kanamanti	1	1	200	340	0	30.00	65	B	0		...					0....	26151
88-PAAK	DENí cluster	1	1	731	937		9.99	38	A	12		...					0....	26152
88-PAAK-a	dení	1	1	731	937	0	9.99	38	A	12	Deni	...					0....	26153
88-PAAL	INAUINí cluster	1	1	300	510		30.00	65	B	0		...					0....	26154
88-PAAL-a	inauiní	1	1	300	510	0	30.00	65	B	0		...					0....	26155
88-PAAM	MADIJá cluster	2	2	1,346	1,769		53.49	85	B	22		P..					0....	26156
88-PAAM-a	madijá	2	2	1,346	1,769	0	53.49	85	B	22	Culina	P..	1965-1985				0....	26157
88-PAAN	ZURUAHA cluster	1	1	153	196		30.07	62	B	12		...					0....	26158
88-PAAN-a	zuruaha	1	1	153	196	0	30.07	62	B	12	Suruaha	...					0....	26159
88-PB	PAUMARI chain	1	1	731	937		70.04	100	C	41		PN.					0....	26160
88-PBA	**PAUMARI net**	1	1	731	937		70.04	100	C	41		PN.					0....	26161
88-PBAA	PAUMARI cluster	1	1	731	937		70.04	100	C	41		PN.					0....	26162
88-PBAA-a	Proper paumarí	1	1	731	937	0	70.04	100	C	41	Paumari	PN.	1972-1976	1995			0....	26163
88-PBAA-b	curucurú					0				41		pn.					0....	26164
88-PBAA-c	uaiai					0				41		pn.					0....	26165
88-Q	**NEREYAMA set**	1	1	20	34		20.00	50	B	0		...					0....	26166
88-QA	NEREYAMA chain	1	1	20	34		20.00	50	B	0		...					0....	26167
88-QAA	**NEREYAMA net**	1	1	20	34		20.00	50	B	0		...					0....	26168
88-QAAA	NEREYAMA cluster	1	1	20	34		20.00	50	B	0		...					0....	26169
88-QAAA-a	nereyama	1	1	20	34	0	20.00	50	B	0		...					0....	26170
88-R	**MURA set**	1	1	1,565	2,005		19.81	53	B	22		P..					0....	26171
88-RA	MURA chain	1	1	1,565	2,005		19.81	53	B	22		P..					0....	26172

Continued opposite

Table 9-13 continued

Code 1	REFERENCE NAME / Autoglossonym 2	Coun 3	Peo 4	Mother-tongue speakers in 2000 5	in 2025 6	Media radio 7	CHURCH AC% 8	E% 9	Wld 10	Tr 11	Biblioglossonym 12	SCRIPTURES Print 13-15	P-activity 16	N-activity 17	B-activity 18	J-year 19	Jayuh 20-24	Ref 25
88-RAA	**MURA net**	1	1	1,565	2,005		19.81	53	B	22		P..					0....	26173
88-RAAA	MúRA-PIRAHA cluster	1	1	1,565	2,005		19.81	53	B	22		P..					0....	26174
88-RAAA-a	múra-piraha	1	1	1,565	2,005	0	19.81	53	B	22	Mura-piraha	P..	1987				0....	26175
88-RAB	**MATANAWI net**									0		...					0....	26176
88-RABA	MATANAUI cluster			0	0		0.00	0		0		...					0....	26177
88-RABA-a	matanaui			0	0	0	0.00	0		0		...					0....	26178
88-S	**BARA-MAKU set**	1	1	20	34		20.00	50	B	0		...					0....	26179
88-SA	BARA-MAKU chain	1	1	20	34		20.00	50	B	0		...					0....	26180
88-SAA	**BARA-MAKU net**	1	1	20	34		20.00	50	B	0		...					0....	26181
88-SAAA	BARA-MAKU cluster	1	1	20	34		20.00	50	B	0		...					0....	26182
88-SAAA-a	bara-maku	1	1	20	34	0	20.00	50	B	0		...					0....	26183
88-T	**HIMARIMA set**	1	1	30	51		20.00	50	B	4		...					0....	26184
88-TA	HIMARIMA chain	1	1	30	51		20.00	50	B	4		...					0....	26185
88-TAA	**HIMARIMA net**	1	1	30	51		20.00	50	B	4		...					0....	26186
88-TAAA	HIMARIMA cluster	1	1	30	51		20.00	50	B	4		...					0....	26187
88-TAAA-a	himarima	1	1	30	51	0	20.00	50	B	4		...					0....	26188
88-U	**KARAHAWYANA set**	1	1	10	17		50.00	90	B	8		...					0....	26189
88-UA	KARAHAWYANA chain	1	1	10	17		50.00	90	B	8		...					0....	26190
88-UAA	**KARAHAWYANA net**	1	1	10	17		50.00	90	B	8		...					0....	26191
88-UAAA	KARAHAWYANA cluster	1	1	10	17		50.00	90	B	8		...					0....	26192
88-UAAA-a	karahawyana	1	1	10	17	0	50.00	90	B	8		...					0....	26193
88-V	**DJAPA-HEWADIE set**	2	5	7,157	9,592		51.80	84	B	12		...					0....	26194
88-VA	HEWADIE chain	1	1	20	34		50.00	85	B	0		...					0....	26195
88-VAA	**HEWADIE net**	1	1	20	34		50.00	85	B	0		...					0....	26196
88-VAAA	HEWADIE cluster	1	1	20	34		50.00	85	B	0		...					0....	26197
88-VAAA-a	hewadie	1	1	20	34	0	50.00	85	B	0		...					0....	26198
88-VB	DJAPA chain	2	5	7,137	9,558		51.80	84	B	12		...					0....	26199
88-VBA	**KATUKINA net**									0		...					0....	26200
88-VBAA	CATUQUINA cluster									0		...					0....	26201
88-VBAA-a	weri-djapá					0				0		...					0....	26202
88-VBAA-b	pidá-djapá					0				0		...					0....	26203
88-VBAA-c	cutia-djapá					0				0		...					0....	26204
88-VBAA-d	tarauacá					0				0		...					0....	26205
88-VBB	**KANAMARI net**	2	5	7,137	9,558		51.80	84	B	12		...					0....	26206
88-VBBA	CANAMARí cluster	2	5	7,137	9,558		51.80	84	B	12		...					0....	26207
88-VBBA-a	Proper canamarí	1	1	663	850	0	30.02	61	B	12	Kanamari	...					0....	26208
88-VBBA-b	ben-dyapá					0				12		...					0....	26209
88-VBBA-c	chunyuán-dyapá	1	1	85	109	0	30.59	58	B	12		...					0....	26210
88-VBBA-d	tucano-dyapá	2	3	6,389	8,599	0	54.34	87	B	12		...					0....	26211
88-W	**PAPAVO set**	1	1	170	218		1.18	20	A	5		...					0....	26212
88-WA	PAPAVO chain	1	1	170	218		1.18	20	A	5		...					0....	26213
88-WAA	**PAPAVO net**	1	1	170	218		1.18	20	A	5		...					0....	26214
88-WAAA	PAPAVó cluster	1	1	170	218		1.18	20	A	5		...					0....	26215
88-WAAA-a	papavó	1	1	170	218	0	1.18	20	A	5		...					0....	26216
89	**BAHIANIC zone**	1	2	3,892	5,069		60.95	97	C	41		PN.					0....	26217
89-A	**WAMOE set**									0		...					0....	26218
89-AA	WAMOE chain									0		...					0....	26219
89-AAA	**WAMOE net**									0		...					0....	26220
89-AAAA	UAMOé cluster			0	0		0.00	0		0		...					0....	26221
89-AAAA-a	uamoé			0	0	0	0.00	0		0		...					0....	26222
89-B	**TUSHA set**									0		...					0....	26223
89-BA	TUSHA chain									0		...					0....	26224
89-BAA	**TUSHA net**									0		...					0....	26225
89-BAAA	TUXá cluster			0	0		0.00	0		0		...					0....	26226
89-BAAA-a	tuxá			0	0	0	0.00	0		0		...					0....	26227
89-C	**PANKARARU-KIRIRI set**									9		...					0....	26228
89-CA	PANKARARU chain									9		...					0....	26229
89-CAA	**PANKARARU net**									9		...					0....	26230
89-CAAA	PANKARARU cluster			0	0		0.00	0		9		...					0....	26231
89-CAAA-a	pancararú			0	0	0	0.00	0		9		...					0....	26232
89-CAAA-b	pancараré			0	0	0	0.00	0		9		...					0....	26233
89-CB	KARIRI-SHOKO chain									0		...					0....	26234
89-CBA	**KARIRI net**									0		...					0....	26235
89-CBAA	CARIRí cluster			0	0		0.00	0		0		...					0....	26236
89-CBAA-a	quipeá					0				0		...					0....	26237
89-CBAA-b	camurú					0				0		...					0....	26238
89-CBAA-c	dzubucuá					0				0		...					0....	26239
89-CBAA-d	sabujá					0				0		...					0....	26240
89-CBB	**SHUKURU net**									0		...					0....	26241

Continued overleaf

Table 9-13 continued

Code 1	REFERENCE NAME / Autoglossonym 2	Coun 3	Peo 4	Mother-tongue speakers in 2000 5	in 2025 6	Media radio 7	CHURCH AC% 8	E% 9	Wld 10	Tr 11	Biblioglossonym 12	SCRIPTURES Print 13-15	P-activity 16	N-activity 17	B-activity 18	J-year 19	Jayuh 20-24	Ref 25
89-CBBA	XUCURú cluster			0	0		0.00	0		0		...					0....	26242
89-CBBA-a	xucurú			0	0	0	0.00	0		0		...					0....	26243
89-CBC	**SHOKO net**									0		...					0....	26244
89-CBCA	XOCó cluster			0	0		0.00	0		0		...					0....	26245
89-CBCA-a	xocó			0	0	0	0.00	0		0		...					0....	26246
89-D	**FULNIO set**	1	1	2,926	3,748		60.01	98	C	4		...					0....	26247
89-DA	FULNIO chain	1	1	2,926	3,748		60.01	98	C	4		...					0....	26248
89-DAA	**FULNIO net**	1	1	2,926	3,748		60.01	98	C	4		...					0....	26249
89-DAAA	FULNIô cluster	1	1	2,926	3,748		60.01	98	C	4		...					0....	26250
89-DAAA-a	fulniô	1	1	2,926	3,748	0	60.01	98	C	4		...					0....	26251
89-E	**NATU set**									0		...					0....	26252
89-EA	NATU chain									0		...					0....	26253
89-EAA	**NATU net**									0		...					0....	26254
89-EAAA	NATú cluster			0	0		0.00	0		0		...					0....	26255
89-EAAA-a	natú			0	0	0	0.00	0		0		...					0....	26256
89-F	**KATEMBRI set**									0		...					0....	26257
89-FA	KATEMBRI chain									0		...					0....	26258
89-FAA	**KATEMBRI net**									0		...					0....	26259
89-FAAA	CATEMBRí cluster			0	0		0.00	0		0		...					0....	26260
89-FAAA-a	catembrí			0	0	0	0.00	0		0		...					0....	26261
89-G	**KAMAKAN set**									9		...					0....	26262
89-GA	KAMAKAN chain									9		...					0....	26263
89-GAA	**KAMAKAN net**									9		...					0....	26264
89-GAAA	KAMAKAN cluster			0	0		0.00	0		9		...					0....	26265
89-GAAA-a	kamakan			0	0	0	0.00	0		9		...					0....	26266
89-H	**MASHAKALI set**	1	1	766	981		69.97	100	C	41		PN.					0....	26267
89-HA	MASHAKALI chain	1	1	766	981		69.97	100	C	41		PN.					0....	26268
89-HAA	**MASHAKALI net**	1	1	766	981		69.97	100	C	41		PN.					0....	26269
89-HAAA	MAXAKALí cluster	1	1	766	981		69.97	100	C	41		PN.					0....	26270
89-HAAA-a	Proper maxakalí	1	1	766	981	0	69.97	100	C	41	Maxakali	PN.	1968	1981			0....	26271
89-HAAA-b	cumanasho					0				41		pn.					0....	26272
89-HAAA-c	monoxo					0				41		pn.					0....	26273
89-HAAA-d	capoxo					0				41		pn.					0....	26274
89-HAAA-e	macuni					0				41		pn.					0....	26275
89-I	**PURI set**									9		...					0....	26276
89-IA	PURI chain									9		...					0....	26277
89-IAA	**PURI net**									9		...					0....	26278
89-IAAA	PURI cluster			0	0		0.00	0		9		...					0....	26279
89-IAAA-a	puri			0	0	0	0.00	0		9		...					0....	26280
89-J	**KRENAK set**	1	1	200	340		40.00	77	B	4		...					0....	26281
89-JA	KRENAK chain	1	1	200	340		40.00	77	B	4		...					0....	26282
89-JAA	**KRENAK net**	1	1	200	340		40.00	77	B	4		...					0....	26283
89-JAAA	KRENAK cluster	1	1	200	340		40.00	77	B	4		...					0....	26284
89-JAAA-a	krenak	1	1	200	340	0	40.00	77	B	4		...					0....	26285
89-K	**OTI set**									9		...					0....	26286
89-KA	OTI chain									9		...					0....	26287
89-KAA	**OTI net**									9		...					0....	26288
89-KAAA	OTI cluster			0	0		0.00	0		9		...					0....	26289
89-KAAA-a	oti			0	0	0	0.00	0		9		...					0....	26290
9	**TRANSAFRICAN macrozone**	58	2033	391,501,719	663,425,063		61.68	88	C	82		PNB					4Bsuh	26291
90	**ATLANTIC zone**	21	127	27,196,658	47,027,949		2.27	44	A	61		PNB					4As..	26292
90-A	**WOLOF set**	8	8	3,754,870	6,587,173		0.27	47	A	41		PN.					4.s..	26293
90-AA	WOLOF chain	8	8	3,754,870	6,587,173		0.27	47	A	41		PN.					4.s..	26294
90-AAA	**WOLOF net**	8	8	3,754,870	6,587,173		0.27	47	A	41		PN.					4.s..	26295
90-AAAA	WOLOF cluster	8	8	3,754,870	6,587,173		0.27	47	A	41		PN.					4.s..	26296
90-AAAA-a	Vehicular wolof	7	7	3,566,898	6,277,453	4	0.08	47	A	41	Wolof: Senegal	PN.	1873-1982	1988		1989	4.s..	26297
90-AAAA-b	jolof					1				41		pn.					1.s..	26298
90-AAAA-c	baol					1				41		pn.					1.s..	26299
90-AAAA-d	cayor					1				41		pn.					1.s..	26300
90-AAAA-e	ndyanger					1				41		pn.					1.s..	26301
90-AAAA-f	lebu					1				41		pn.					1.s..	26302
90-AAAA-g	wolof-gambia	1	1	187,972	309,720	1	4.00	47	A	41	Wolof: Gambia*	Pn.	1882-1967				1.s..	26303
90-B	**FULA-SERER set**	21	50	20,872,384	36,133,087		1.34	43	A	61		PNB					4As..	26304
90-BA	FULA chain	21	46	19,765,625	34,183,246		0.59	42	A	61		PNB					4As..	26305
90-BAA	**FULA net**	21	46	19,765,625	34,183,246		0.59	42	A	61		PNB					4As..	26306
90-BAAA	PULAAR-FULFULDE cluster	21	46	19,765,625	34,183,246		0.59	42	A	61		PNB					4As..	26307

Continued opposite

Table 9-13 continued

Code 1	REFERENCE NAME / Autoglossonym 2	Coun 3	Peo 4	Mother-tongue speakers in 2000 5	in 2025 6	Media radio 7	CHURCH AC% 8	E% 9	Wld 10	Tr 11	Biblioglossonym 12	Print 13-15	P–activity 16	N–activity 17	B–activity 18	J-year 19	Jayuh 20-24	Ref 25
90-BAAA-a	haal-pulaar	6	7	1,526,848	2,676,983	4	2.75	37	A	61	Fula: Pulaar*	Pnb	1982-1993			1994	2As..	26308
90-BAAA-b	futa-tooro	2	3	521,459	931,337	4	0.07	32	A	61		pnb					1cs..	26309
90-BAAA-c	fula-kunda	4	4	1,417,461	2,469,762	4	0.07	38	A	61	Pulaar: Fulakunda	Pnb	1991				1as..	26310
90-BAAA-d	futa-jalon	4	5	3,168,729	5,348,844	4	0.01	38	A	61	Fula: Futa-jalon*	Pnb	1929-1975			1996	2as..	26311
90-BAAA-e	fula-masina	2	2	1,090,857	2,066,881	4	0.99	45	A	61	Fula: Macina*	Pnb	1934			1991	4cs..	26314
90-BAAA-f	East fula-masina					1				61		pnb					1cs..	26315
90-BAAA-g	fula-barani					1				61		pnb					1cs..	26316
90-BAAA-h	fula-jelgooji	1	1	119,368	233,213	4	0.10	35	A	61	Fulfulde, Jelgoore	pnb					1cs..	26317
90-BAAA-i	fula-bogandé					1				61		pnb					1cs..	26320
90-BAAA-j	fula-liptaako	1	1	406,014	793,243	4	0.70	43	A	61		pnb					1cs..	26321
90-BAAA-k	fula-gurma	1	1	179,052	349,820	4	0.20	36	A	61	Fulfulde, Gourmantche	pnb					1cs..	26322
90-BAAA-l	fula-atakora	1	1	285,935	521,041	4	1.00	46	A	61	Fulfulde, Benin-togo	pnb					1as..	26323
90-BAAA-m	fula-borgu					1				61		pnb					1cs..	26324
90-BAAA-n	fula-sokoto	6	9	6,434,476	10,968,281	4	0.23	47	A	61	Fulfulde	PNB	1919	1963	1983		1cs..	26325
90-BAAA-o	fula-bororo	5	5	2,163,414	3,641,067	4	0.05	36	A	61	Fulfide, Kano-katsina	pnb					1cs..	26328
90-BAAA-p	fula-gombe					1				61		pnb					1cs..	26329
90-BAAA-q	fula-adamawa	2	3	2,132,703	3,646,291	4	1.81	51	B	61	Fulfulde, Adamawa	PNB	1919-1966	1963-1964	1983	1987	1cs..	26330
90-BAAA-r	fula-bagirmi	2	2	102,011	174,625	4	0.02	30	A	61		pnb					1cs..	26331
90-BAAA-s	fula-fellata	2	2	217,298	361,858	4	0.39	37	A	61	Fulfulde, Adamawa	PNB	1919-1966	1963-1964	1983		1cs..	26332
90-BB	SERER chain	4	4	1,106,759	1,949,841		14.82	59	B	41		PN.					2....	26335
90-BBA	SERER net	4	4	1,106,759	1,949,841		14.82	59	B	41		PN.					2....	26336
90-BBAA	SERER cluster	4	4	1,106,759	1,949,841		14.82	59	B	41		PN.					2....	26337
90-BBAA-a	sine	4	4	1,106,759	1,949,841	0	14.82	59	B	41	Seereer*	PN.	1978-1979	1987		1989	2....	26338
90-BBAA-b	segum					0				41		pn.					1....	26339
90-BBAA-c	fadyut					0				41		pn.					1....	26340
90-BBAA-d	dyegem					0				41		pn.					1....	26341
90-C	CANGIN set	1	5	110,381	194,919		20.00	54	B	12		...					0....	26342
90-CA	CANGIN chain	1	5	110,381	194,919		20.00	54	B	12		...					0....	26343
90-CAA	SAFEN-NON net	1	3	74,762	132,020		17.15	53	B	12		...					0....	26344
90-CAAA	LEHAR cluster	1	1	3,524	6,223		9.99	40	A	2		...					0....	26345
90-CAAA-a	lehar	1	1	3,524	6,223	0	9.99	40	A	2		...					0....	26346
90-CAAB	SERER-NON cluster	1	1	26,683	47,119		15.00	52	B	12		...					0....	26347
90-CAAB-a	non	1	1	26,683	47,119	0	15.00	52	B	12	Noon	...					0....	26348
90-CAAB-b	niominka					0				12		...					0....	26349
90-CAAC	SAFEN cluster	1	1	44,555	78,678		19.00	54	B	12		...					0....	26350
90-CAAC-a	safen	1	1	44,555	78,678	0	19.00	54	B	12	Safen	...					0....	26351
90-CAB	PALOR-NDUT net	1	2	35,619	62,899		25.97	56	B	12		...					0....	26352
90-CABA	PALOR-NDUT cluster	1	2	35,619	62,899		25.97	56	B	12		...					0....	26353
90-CABA-a	palor	1	1	8,936	15,780	0	5.00	31	A	12		...					0....	26354
90-CABA-b	ndut	1	1	26,683	47,119	0	33.00	64	B	12	Ndut	...					0....	26355
90-D	JOLA-CENTRAL set	4	15	593,930	1,026,288		9.55	43	A	37		P..					4....	26356
90-DA	NORTH JOLA chain	4	12	575,639	994,427		9.69	43	A	37		P..					4....	26357
90-DAA	JOLA-FOGNY net	3	3	323,580	564,764		13.68	56	B	37		P..					4....	26358
90-DAAA	FOONYI cluster	3	3	323,580	564,764		13.68	56	B	37		P..					4....	26359
90-DAAA-a	Proper foonyi	3	3	323,580	564,764	0	13.68	56	B	37	Diola*	P..	1961			1996	4....	26360
90-DAAA-b	Vehicular foonyi					0				37		p..					1....	26361
90-DAB	JOLA-BULUF net	1	1	32,000	54,400		3.00	20	A	0		...					0....	26362
90-DABA	BULUF cluster	1	1	30,000	51,000		3.00	20	A	0		...					0....	26363
90-DABA-a	ku-ricaak-aay					0				0		...					0....	26364
90-DABA-b	jaang					0				0		...					0....	26365
90-DABA-c	tenduuk					0				0		...					0....	26366
90-DABA-d	elana					0				0		...					0....	26367
90-DABA-e	kanyobong					0				0		...					0....	26368
90-DABA-f	kabunaye					0				0		...					0....	26369
90-DABA-g	narang					0				0		...					0....	26370
90-DABB	KOMBO cluster	1	1	2,000	3,400		3.00	20	A	0		...					0....	26371
90-DABB-a	kombo	1	1	2,000	3,400	0	3.00	20	A	0		...					0....	26372
90-DAC	JOLA-MLOMP net	1	1	4,529	7,998		3.00	26	A	4		...					0....	26373
90-DACA	MLOMP cluster	1	1	4,529	7,998		3.00	26	A	4		...					0....	26374
90-DACA-a	mlomp	1	1	4,529	7,998	0	3.00	26	A	4		...					0....	26375
90-DAD	JOLA-ENDUNGO net	1	2	21,807	38,508		5.00	29	A	4		...					0....	26376
90-DADA	GUSILAY cluster	1	1	16,118	28,462		5.00	32	A	3		...					0....	26377
90-DADA-a	gu-siil-aay	1	1	16,118	28,462	0	5.00	32	A	3		...					0....	26378
90-DADA-b	afinyaam					0				3		...					0....	26379
90-DADB	BANJAAL cluster	1	1	5,689	10,046		4.99	21	A	4		...					0....	26380
90-DADB-a	banjaal	1	1	5,689	10,046	0	4.99	21	A	4		...					0....	26381
90-DAE	JOLA-HULON net	1	1	1,258	2,222		3.97	27	A	0		...					0....	26382
90-DAEA	KULUNAY cluster	1	1	1,258	2,222		3.97	27	A	0		...					0....	26383
90-DAEA-a	ku-luun-aay	1	1	1,258	2,222	0	3.97	27	A	0		...					0....	26384
90-DAF	JOLA-KASA net	1	1	137,759	236,677		5.49	27	A	23		P..					0....	26385
90-DAFA	BILIS cluster	1	1	30,000	51,000		6.00	26	A	0		...					0....	26386
90-DAFA-a	bilis	1	1	30,000	51,000	0	6.00	26	A	0		...					0....	26387
90-DAFB	KASA cluster	1	1	37,759	66,677		6.00	35	A	23		P..					0....	26388
90-DAFB-a	kasa	1	1	37,759	66,677	0	6.00	35	A	23	Jola-kasa	P..	1961				0....	26389
90-DAFC	ESULALU cluster	1	1	40,000	68,000		5.00	24	A	0		...					0....	26390
90-DAFC-a	e-suu-laalu					0				0		...					0....	26391
90-DAFC-b	kata-hu-toongaat					0				0		...					0....	26392
90-DAFD	HULUF cluster	1	1	30,000	51,000		5.00	24	A	0		...					0....	26393
90-DAFD-a	hu-luf	1	1	30,000	51,000	0	5.00	24	A	0		...					0....	26394
90-DAG	JOLA-HER net	1	1	11,112	19,622		3.00	26	A	12		...					0....	26395
90-DAGA	HER cluster	1	1	11,112	19,622		3.00	26	A	12		...					0....	26396
90-DAGA-a	ke-era-ku	1	1	11,112	19,622	0	3.00	26	A	12	Kerak	...					0....	26397
90-DAH	JOLA-FLUP net	2	3	43,594	70,236		3.25	28	A	4		...					0....	26398
90-DAHA	FLUP cluster	2	3	43,594	70,236		3.25	28	A	4		...					0....	26399
90-DAHA-a	ku-jamut-aay	2	3	43,594	70,236	0	3.25	28	A	4		...					0....	26400
90-DAHA-b	e-fok					0				4		...					0....	26401
90-DAHA-c	youtou					0				4		...					0....	26402
90-DAHA-d	calequisse					0				4		...					0....	26403

Continued overleaf

Table 9-13 continued

Code 1	REFERENCE NAME / Autoglossonym 2	Coun 3	Peo 4	in 2000 5	in 2025 6	Media radio 7	AC% 8	E% 9	Wld 10	Tr 11	Biblioglossonym 12	Print 13-15	P-activity 16	N-activity 17	B-activity 18	J-year Jayuh 19 20-24	Ref 25
90-DAHA-e	mazonimi					0				4		...				0....	26404
90-DB	**WEST JOLA chain**	2	3	18,291	31,861		5.00	29	A	12		...				0....	26405
90-DBA	**KARON net**	2	2	9,886	17,282		5.01	31	A	2		...				0....	26406
90-DBAA	KAROON cluster	2	2	9,886	17,282		5.01	31	A	2		...				0....	26407
90-DBAA-a	karoon	2	2	9,886	17,282	0	5.01	31	A	2		...				0....	26408
90-DBB	**LOMPAY net**	1	1	4,000	6,800		5.00	24	A	0		...				0....	26409
90-DBBA	GULOMPAAY cluster	1	1	4,000	6,800		5.00	24	A	0		...				0....	26410
90-DBBA-a	gu-lomp-aay	1	1	4,000	6,800	0	5.00	24	A	0		...				0....	26411
90-DBC	**WATAY net**	1	1	4,405	7,779		4.99	29	A	12		...				0....	26412
90-DBCA	KUWAATAAY cluster	1	1	4,405	7,779		4.99	29	A	12		...				0....	26413
90-DBCA-a	ku-waat-aay	1	1	4,405	7,779	0	4.99	29	A	12	Kwatay	...				0....	26414
90-E	**SOUTH JOLA set**	3	3	17,047	29,198		4.75	26	A	3		...				0....	26415
90-EA	SOUTH JOLA chain	3	3	17,047	29,198		4.75	26	A	3		...				0....	26416
90-EAA	**ESING net**	3	3	14,047	24,098		4.48	26	A	3		...				0....	26417
90-EAAA	BAYOT cluster	3	3	9,047	15,598		4.19	27	A	3		...				0....	26418
90-EAAA-a	bayot	3	3	9,047	15,598	0	4.19	27	A	3		...				0....	26419
90-EAAB	KUXINGE cluster	2	1	5,000	8,500		5.00	24	A	0		...				0....	26420
90-EAAB-a	ku-xinge	1	1	5,000	8,500	0	5.00	24	A	0		...				0....	26421
90-EAB	**GUBAARE net**	1	1	3,000	5,100		6.00	26	A	0		...				0....	26422
90-EABA	GUBAARE cluster	2	1	3,000	5,100		6.00	26	A	0		...				0....	26423
90-EABA-a	gu-baare	1	1	3,000	5,100	0	6.00	26	A	0		...				0....	26424
90-F	**MANDYAK-PEPEL set**	6	11	467,547	759,009		17.17	51	B	41		PN.				0....	26425
90-FA	MANDYAK-PEPEL chain	6	11	467,547	759,009		17.17	51	B	41		PN.				0....	26426
90-FAA	**MANDYAK-BABOK net**	5	5	317,186	512,494		13.11	45	A	23		P..				0....	26427
90-FAAA	MANDYAK cluster	5	5	297,186	478,494		13.65	47	A	23		P..				0....	26428
90-FAAA-a	Proper mandyak	5	5	297,186	478,494	0	13.65	47	A	23	Manjako*	P..	1967-1968			0....	26429
90-FAAA-b	kanyop					0				23		p..				0....	26430
90-FAAB	BABOK cluster	2	1	4,000	6,800		5.00	24	A	0		...				0....	26431
90-FAAB-a	Proper ba-bok					0				0		...				0....	26432
90-FAAB-b	tsaam					0				0		...				0....	26433
90-FAAB-c	sarar					0				0		...				0....	26434
90-FAAC	LIKES-UTSIA cluster	2	1	3,000	5,100		5.00	24	A	0		...				0....	26435
90-FAAC-a	baraa					0				0		...				0....	26436
90-FAAC-b	kalkus					0				0		...				0....	26437
90-FAAD	CUUR cluster	2	1	5,000	8,500		5.00	24	A	0		...				0....	26438
90-FAAD-a	cuur	1	1	5,000	8,500	0	5.00	24	A	0		...				0....	26439
90-FAAE	LUND cluster	2	1	2,000	3,400		5.00	24	A	0		...				0....	26440
90-FAAE-a	lund	1	1	2,000	3,400	0	5.00	24	A	0		...				0....	26441
90-FAAF	YU cluster	2	1	6,000	10,200		5.00	24	A	0		...				0....	26442
90-FAAF-a	Proper yu					0				0		...				0....	26443
90-FAAF-b	siis					0				0		...				0....	26444
90-FAAF-c	pulhilh					0				0		...				0....	26445
90-FAB	**PAPEL net**	3	3	84,184	136,044		25.17	65	B	41		PN.				0....	26446
90-FABA	PAPEL cluster	3	3	84,184	136,044		25.17	65	B	41		PN.				0....	26447
90-FABA-a	Proper papel	3	3	84,184	136,044	0	25.17	65	B	41	Papel	PN.	1981		1996	0....	26448
90-FABA-b	moium					0				41		pn.				0....	26449
90-FABA-c	oium					0				41	Oium	Pn.	1981			0....	26450
90-FAC	**MANKANYA net**	3	3	63,177	105,371		27.42	62	B	2		...				0....	26451
90-FACA	MANKANYA cluster	3	3	63,177	105,371		27.42	62	B	2		...				0....	26452
90-FACA-a	mankany	3	3	63,177	105,371	0	27.42	62	B	2		...				0....	26453
90-FACA-b	shadal					0				2		...				0....	26454
90-FAD	**BURAMA net**	1	1	3,000	5,100		6.00	26	A	0		...				0....	26455
90-FADA	BURAMA cluster	2	1	3,000	5,100		6.00	26	A	0		...				0....	26456
90-FADA-a	buraam	1	1	3,000	5,100	0	6.00	26	A	0		...				0....	26457
90-G	**BALANTA-GANJA set**	4	6	576,498	950,657		13.35	44	A	35		P..				0....	26458
90-GA	BALANTA-GANJA chain	4	6	576,498	950,657		13.35	44	A	35		P..				0....	26459
90-GAA	**GANJA net**	2	2	5,954	10,317		6.00	39	A	2		...				0....	26460
90-GAAA	GANJA cluster	2	2	5,954	10,317		6.00	39	A	2		...				0....	26461
90-GAAA-a	ganja-blip	2	2	5,954	10,317	4	6.00	39	A	2		...				0....	26462
90-GAAA-b	bandal					1				2		...				0....	26463
90-GAB	**BALANTA net**	4	4	570,544	940,340		13.42	44	A	35		P..				0....	26464
90-GABA	NORTH BALANTA cluster	4	4	470,544	770,340		15.42	48	A	35	Frase*	P..	1980			0....	26465
90-GABA-a	balanta-naaga					0				35		p..				0....	26466
90-GABA-b	balanta-maane					0				35		p..				0....	26467
90-GABB	SOUTH BALANTA cluster	2	1	100,000	170,000		4.00	22	A	0		...				0....	26468
90-GABB-a	balanta-kuntoi					0				0		...				0....	26469
90-GABB-b	balanta-foora					0				0		...				0....	26470
90-H	**BAINUK-KOBIANA set**	2	6	35,142	60,693		15.55	47	A	12		...				0....	26471
90-HA	BAINUK chain	2	2	33,450	57,872		15.91	48	A	12		...				0....	26472
90-HAA	**BAINUK net**	2	2	33,450	57,872		15.91	48	A	12		...				0....	26473
90-HAAA	BAINUK cluster	2	2	33,450	57,872		15.91	48	A	12		...				0....	26474
90-HAAA-a	gu-nyamolo					0				12	Bainouk	...				0....	26475
90-HAAA-b	gu-jaaxut					0				12		...				0....	26476
90-HB	KOBIANA-KASANGA chain	2	4	1,692	2,821		8.39	33	A	5		...				0....	26477
90-HBA	**KOBIANA net**	2	2	777	1,292		9.91	34	A	5		...				0....	26478
90-HBAA	BUY cluster	2	2	777	1,292		9.91	34	A	5		...				0....	26479
90-HBAA-a	buy	2	2	777	1,292	0	9.91	34	A	5		...				0....	26480

Continued opposite

Table 9-13 continued

Code 1	REFERENCE NAME / Autoglossonym 2	Coun 3	Peo 4	Mother-tongue speakers in 2000 5	in 2025 6	Media radio 7	CHURCH AC% 8	E% 9	Wld 10	Tr 11	Biblioglossonym 12	Print 13-15	P-activity 16	N-activity 17	B-activity 18	J-year 19	Jayuh 20-24	Ref 25
90-HBB	**KASANGA net**	2	2	915	1,529		7.10	31	A	5		. . .					0	26481
90-HBBA	HAAL cluster	2	2	915	1,529		7.10	31	A	5		. . .					0	26482
90-HBBA-a	haal	2	2	915	1,529	0	7.10	31	A	5		. . .					0	26483
90-I	**BIAFADA-PAJADE set**	3	5	63,610	104,401		4.40	29	A	12		. . .					0	26484
90-IA	BIAFADA chain	2	2	43,721	70,598		5.95	33	A	2		. . .					0	26485
90-IAA	**BIAFADA net**	2	2	43,721	70,598		5.95	33	A	2		. . .					0	26486
90-IAAA	BIAFADA cluster	2	2	43,721	70,598		5.95	33	A	2		. . .					0	26487
90-IAAA-a	Proper bia-fada	2	2	43,721	70,598	0	5.95	33	A	2		. . .					0	26488
90-IAAA-b	b-ool					0				2		. . .					0	26489
90-IAAA-c	bii-nala					0				2		. . .					0	26490
90-IAAA-d	bu-baasu					0				2		. . .					0	26491
90-IAAA-e	kakande					0				2		. . .					0	26492
90-IB	PAJADE chain	3	3	19,889	33,803		1.00	22	A	12		. . .					0	26493
90-IBA	**PAJADE net**	3	3	19,889	33,803		1.00	22	A	12		. . .					0	26494
90-IBAA	BAJAR cluster	3	3	19,889	33,803		1.00	22	A	12		. . .					0	26495
90-IBAA-a	ba-jar	3	3	19,889	33,803	0	1.00	22	A	12	Badyara	. . .					0	26496
90-IBAA-b	bi-gola					0				12		. . .					0	26497
90-J	**TENDA set**	4	8	60,956	105,053		16.78	43	A	44		PN .					0	26498
90-JA	TENDA chain	4	8	60,956	105,053		16.78	43	A	44		PN .					0	26499
90-JAA	**TENDA net**	4	8	60,956	105,053		16.78	43	A	44		PN .					0	26500
90-JAAA	TENDA cluster	4	8	60,956	105,053		16.78	43	A	44		PN .					0	26501
90-JAAA-a	o-ni-yan	4	5	34,306	58,353	0	5.69	29	A	44	Basari	PN .		1988			0	26502
90-JAAA-b	wa-meyny	2	2	19,854	34,699	0	41.33	72	B	44	Wamei	pn .					0	26503
90-JAAA-c	mo-peny					0				44		pn .					0	26504
90-JAAA-d	o-nik	1	1	6,796	12,001	0	1.00	30	A	44	Budik	pn .					0	26505
90-K	**SUA set**	2	2	14,250	22,916		5.46	31	A	4		. . .					0	26506
90-KA	SUA chain	2	2	14,250	22,916		5.46	31	A	4		. . .					0	26507
90-KAA	**SUA net**	2	2	14,250	22,916		5.46	31	A	4		. . .					0	26508
90-KAAA	SUA cluster	2	2	14,250	22,916		5.46	31	A	4		. . .					0	26509
90-KAAA-a	sua	2	2	14,250	22,916	0	5.46	31	A	4		. . .					0	26510
90-L	**NALU set**	2	2	22,815	37,789		0.16	12	A	4		. . .					0	26511
90-LA	NALU chain	2	2	22,815	37,789		0.16	12	A	4		. . .					0	26512
90-LAA	**NALU net**	2	2	22,815	37,789		0.16	12	A	4		. . .					0	26513
90-LAAA	NALUU cluster	2	2	22,815	37,789		0.16	12	A	4		. . .					0	26514
90-LAAA-a	naluu	2	2	22,815	37,789	0	0.16	12	A	4		. . .					0	26515
90-M	**MBULUNGISH set**	1	2	45,416	76,384		17.72	45	A	4		. . .					0	26516
90-MA	MBULUNGISH chain	1	2	45,416	76,384		17.72	45	A	4		. . .					0	26517
90-MAA	**MBULUNGISH net**	1	2	45,416	76,384		17.72	45	A	4		. . .					0	26518
90-MAAA	MBULUNGISH cluster	1	2	45,416	76,384		17.72	45	A	4		. . .					0	26519
90-MAAA-a	mbulungish					0				4		. . .					0	26520
90-N	**BAGA-MBOTENI set**	1	1	4,000	6,800		2.00	18	A	4		. . .					0	26521
90-NA	BAGA-MBOTENI chain	1	1	4,000	6,800		2.00	18	A	4		. . .					0 . . . :	26522
90-NAA	**BAGA-MBOTENI net**	1	1	4,000	6,800		2.00	18	A	4		. . .					0	26523
90-NAAA	BAGA-MBOTENI cluster	1	1	4,000	6,800		2.00	18	A	4		. . .					0	26524
90-NAAA-a	baga-mboteni	1	1	4,000	6,800	0	2.00	18	A	4		. . .					0	26525
90-O	**BIJOGO set**	1	1	28,923	46,397		20.20	58	B	42		PN .					0	26526
90-OA	BIJOGO chain	1	1	28,923	46,397		20.20	58	B	42		PN .					0	26527
90-OAA	**BIJOGO net**	1	1	28,923	46,397		20.20	58	B	42		PN .					0	26528
90-OAAA	BIJOGO cluster	1	1	28,923	46,397		20.20	58	B	42	Bijago*	PN .	1973	1975			0	26529
90-OAAA-a	orango					0				42		pn .					0	26530
90-OAAA-b	anhaqui					0				42		pn .					0	26531
90-P	**LIMBA set**	2	3	528,889	887,185		10.79	47	A	42		PN .					0	26532
90-PA	LIMBA chain	2	3	528,889	887,185		10.79	47	A	42		PN .					0	26533
90-PAA	**LIMBA net**	2	3	528,889	887,185		10.79	47	A	42		PN .					0	26534
90-PAAA	NORTH LIMBA cluster	2	1	30,000	51,000		4.00	22	A	0		. . .					0	26535
90-PAAA-a	kamuke					0				0		. . .					0	26536
90-PAAA-b	warawara					0				0		. . .					0	26537
90-PAAB	CENTRAL LIMBA cluster	1	1	150,000	255,000		5.00	24	A	22	Limba: Western	P . .	1979				0	26538
90-PAAB-a	sela					0				22		p . .					0	26539
90-PAAB-b	tonka					0				22		p . .					0	26540
90-PAAB-c	keleng					0				22		p . .					0	26541
90-PAAB-d	tamiso					0				22		p . .					0	26542
90-PAAB-e	gbongogbo					0				22		p . .					0	26543
90-PAAC	SOUTH LIMBA cluster	2	3	348,889	581,185		13.87	60	B	42	Limba	PN .	1911	1966			0	26544
90-PAAC-a	biriwa					1				42		pn .					0	26545
90-PAAC-b	safroko					1				42		pn .					0	26546
90-PAAC-c	kalantuba					1				42		pn .					0	26547
90-PAAC-d	sunko					1				42		pn .					0	26548
91	**VOLTAIC zone**	11	165	23,960,073	44,064,019		16.68	63	B	71		PNB					4Asu .	26549
91-A	**DOGON set**	3	3	868,535	1,609,376		11.27	49	A	41		PN .					4	26550
91-AA	BANGERI chain	1	1	3,000	5,100		1.00	16	A	0		. . .					0	26551
91-AAA	**BANGERI net**	1	1	3,000	5,100		1.00	16	A	0		. . .					0	26552

Continued overleaf

Table 9-13 continued

Code 1	REFERENCE NAME / Autoglossonym 2	Coun 3	Peo 4	Mother-tongue speakers in 2000 5	in 2025 6	Media radio 7	CHURCH AC% 8	E% 9	Wld 10	Tr 11	Biblioglossonym 12	SCRIPTURES Print 13-15	P–activity 16	N–activity 17	B–activity 18	J-year 19	Jayuh 20-24	Ref 25
91-AAAA	BANGERI cluster	1	1	3,000	5,100		1.00	16	A	0		...					0....	26553
91-AAAA-a	bangeri-me	1	1	3,000	5,100	0	1.00	16	A	0		...					0....	26554
91-AB	WEST DOGON chain	1	1	20,000	34,000		1.00	16	A	0		...					0....	26555
91-ABA	**WEST DOGON net**	1	1	20,000	34,000		1.00	16	A	0		...					0....	26556
91-ABAA	DULERI-EJENGE cluster	1	1	20,000	34,000		1.00	16	A	0		...					0....	26557
91-ABAA-a	duleri-dom					0				0		...					0....	26558
91-ABAA-b	ejenge-don					0				0		...					0....	26559
91-AC	DOGON-CENTRAL chain	3	3	845,535	1,570,276		11.55	50	A	41		PN.					4....	26560
91-ACA	**NORTH DOGON net**	1	1	30,000	51,000		1.00	16	A	0		...					0....	26561
91-ACAA	BONDUM-DOGUL cluster	1	1	30,000	51,000		1.00	16	A	0		...					0....	26562
91-ACAA-a	bondum-dom					0				0		...					0....	26563
91-ACAA-b	dogul-dom					0				0		...					0....	26564
91-ACB	**NANGA net**	1	1	2,000	3,400		1.00	16	A	0		...					0....	26565
91-ACBA	NANGA cluster	1	1	2,000	3,400		1.00	16	A	0		...					0....	26566
91-ACBA-a	nanga-tegu	1	1	2,000	3,400	0	1.00	16	A	0		...					0....	26567
91-ACC	**ORU net**	1	1	3,000	5,100		1.00	16	A	0		...					0....	26568
91-ACCA	ORU cluster	1	1	3,000	5,100		1.00	16	A	0		...					0....	26569
91-ACCA-a	oru-yille	1	1	3,000	5,100	0	1.00	16	A	0		...					0....	26570
91-ACD	**YANDA net**	1	1	5,000	8,500		1.00	16	A	0		...					0....	26571
91-ACDA	YANDA cluster	1	1	5,000	8,500		1.00	16	A	0		...					0....	26572
91-ACDA-a	yanda-dom	1	1	5,000	8,500	0	1.00	16	A	0		...					0....	26573
91-ACE	**DOGON-CENTRAL net**	3	3	655,535	1,247,276		14.38	59	B	41		PN.					4....	26574
91-ACEA	CENTRAL DOGON cluster	3	3	655,535	1,247,276		14.38	59	B	41		PN.					4....	26575
91-ACEA-a	tombo-so					0				41		pn.					1....	26576
91-ACEA-b	toro-so	3	3	655,535	1,247,276	0	14.38	59	B	41	Dogon	PN.	1933-1984	1957-1994		1991	4....	26577
91-ACEA-c	kamba-so					0				41		pn.					1....	26578
91-ACF	**DOGON-PLAINS net**	1	1	150,000	255,000		2.00	18	A	0		...					0....	26579
91-ACFA	DOGON-PLAINS cluster	1	1	150,000	255,000		2.00	18	A	0		...					0....	26580
91-ACFA-a	tomo-kan					0				0		...					0....	26581
91-ACFA-b	tene-kan					0				0		...					0....	26582
91-ACFA-c	togo-kan					0				0		...					0....	26583
91-ACFA-d	toro-tegu					0				0		...					0....	26584
91-ACFA-e	jamsay-tegu					0				0		...					0....	26585
91-B	**SENUFO set**	5	22	2,962,280	5,140,425		5.35	43	A	41		PN.					3.s..	26586
91-BA	SENUFO-CENTRAL chain	4	18	2,830,613	4,918,588		4.91	43	A	41		PN.					3.s..	26587
91-BAA	**SENARI-SUPYIRE net**	4	11	2,434,552	4,258,796		3.62	42	A	41		PN.					3.s..	26588
91-BAAA	MAMARA cluster	1	1	590,818	1,119,988		1.50	37	A	32	Senoufo, Mamara	P..	1967-1975			1999	1....	26589
91-BAAA-a	soghoo					1				32		p..					1....	26590
91-BAAA-b	bajii					1				32		p..					1....	26591
91-BAAA-c	nafaa					1				32		p..					1....	26592
91-BAAA-d	mijuu					1				32		p..					1....	26593
91-BAAA-e	kle					1				32		p..					1....	26594
91-BAAA-f	noehmo					1				32		p..					1....	26595
91-BAAA-g	nejuu					1				32		p..					1....	26596
91-BAAA-h	koloo					1				32		p..					1....	26597
91-BAAA-i	kujaa					1				32		p..					1....	26598
91-BAAA-j	sunoo					1				32		p..					1....	26599
91-BAAB	SUPYIRE cluster	2	2	530,472	973,802		2.00	31	A	22		P..					0....	26600
91-BAAB-a	supyi-re	2	2	530,472	973,802	5	2.00	31	A	22	Suppire*	P..	1979-1982				0....	26601
91-BAAC	SENARI-CEBAARA cluster	4	8	1,313,262	2,165,006		5.22	49	A	41		PN.					3.s..	26602
91-BAAC-a	sena-ri	2	2	1,117,936	1,816,185	5	5.26	50	B	41	Senoufo, Shempire	pn.					1.s..	26603
91-BAAC-b	papa-ra					1				41		pn.					1.s..	26604
91-BAAC-c	takpa-syee-ri					1				41		pn.					1.s..	26605
91-BAAC-d	niango-lo	1	1	7,906	15,446	1	5.00	33	A	41		pn.					1.s..	26606
91-BAAC-e	sicite	1	1	32,601	63,693	5	5.00	43	A	41	Senoufo: Sicite*	Pn.	1995				1.s..	26607
91-BAAC-f	nane-ri-ge	1	1	75,770	148,035	1	6.00	36	A	41	Senoufo, Nanerige	pn.					1.s..	26608
91-BAAC-g	cebaa-ra	1	1	29,572	46,690	1	3.00	36	A	41	Cebaara*	PN.	1960	1982-1996		1997	3.s..	26609
91-BAAC-h	kande-re					1				41		pn.					1.s..	26611
91-BAAC-i	tagba-ri					1				41		pn.					1.s..	26612
91-BAAC-j	poga-ra					1				41		pn.					1.s..	26613
91-BAAC-k	tene-re					1				41		pn.					1.s..	26614
91-BAAC-l	kasan-ra					1				41		pn.					1.s..	26616
91-BAAC-m	nowo-lo					1				41		pn.					1.s..	26617
91-BAAC-n	tanga-ra					1				41		pn.					1.s..	26618
91-BAAC-o	gbato					1				41		pn.					1.s..	26619
91-BAAC-p	kafi-re					1				41		pn.					1.s..	26620
91-BAAC-q	kufu-ru					1				41		pn.					1.s..	26621
91-BAAC-r	fodon-ro					1				41		pn.					1.s..	26622
91-BAAC-s	nafa-nan					1				41		pn.					1.s..	26623
91-BAAC-t	nyarafolo	1	1	43,569	68,791	1	4.00	40	A	41	Senoufo, Niarafolo	pn.					1.s..	26624
91-BAAC-u	tafi-re					1				41		pn.					1.s..	26625
91-BAAC-v	Southwest senari					1				41		pn.					1.s..	26626
91-BAB	**KARABORO net**	2	3	114,715	213,036		5.71	33	A	41		PN.					0....	26627
91-BABA	WEST KARABORO cluster	1	1	40,067	78,280		4.00	28	A	41	Karaboro	PN.		1993			0....	26628
91-BABA-a	tenyer					0				41		pn.					0....	26629
91-BABA-b	syer	1	1	40,067	78,280	0	4.00	28	A	41		pn.					0....	26630
91-BABB	EAST KARABORO cluster	2	2	74,648	134,756		6.62	35	A	41	Karaboro, Eastern	PN.	1985	1994			0....	26631
91-BABB-a	kar	2	2	74,648	134,756	0	6.62	35	A	41		pn.					0....	26632
91-BAC	**TAGWANA-JIMINI net**	1	3	246,401	390,856		17.48	57	B	41		PN.					0....	26633
91-BACA	NORTH TAGWANA cluster	1	1	153,344	242,112		26.00	68	B	41	Tagbana*	PN.		1987			0....	26634
91-BACA-a	gbozo-ro					0				41		pn.					0....	26635
91-BACA-b	tafi-re					0				41		pn.					0....	26636
91-BACA-c	niediekaha					0				41		pn.					0....	26637
91-BACA-d	niangbo					0				41		pn.					0....	26638
91-BACB	SOUTH TAGBWANA cluster	1	1	15,000	25,500		10.00	33	A	0		...					0....	26639
91-BACB-a	takper					0				0		...					0....	26640
91-BACB-b	fondebugu					0				0		...					0....	26641
91-BACB-c	jidanan					0				0		...					0....	26642
91-BACB-d	furgu-la					0				0		...					0....	26643
91-BACB-e	kacaa-la					0				0		...					0....	26644
91-BACB-f	kacoolo					0				0		...					0....	26645
91-BACB-g	cedaan-le					0				0		...					0....	26646
91-BACC	JIMINI cluster	1	2	78,057	123,244		2.17	39	A	41	Djimini*	PN.	1985-1989	1993			0....	26647
91-BACC-a	dofa-na					1				41		pn.					0....	26648

Continued opposite

Table 9-13 continued

Code 1	REFERENCE NAME / Autoglossonym 2	Coun 3	Peo 4	Mother-tongue speakers in 2000 5	in 2025 6	Media radio 7	AC% 8	E% 9	Wld 10	Tr 11	Biblioglossonym 12	Print 13-15	P-activity 16	N-activity 17	B-activity 18	J-year 19	Jayuh 20-24	Ref 25
91-BACC-b	dyafo-lo					1				41		pn.					0....	26649
91-BACC-c	dofa-na					1				41		pn.					0....	26650
91-BACC-d	fo-lo					1				41		pn.					0....	26651
91-BACC-e	bandogo					1				41		pn.					0....	26652
91-BACC-f	singa-la					1				41		pn.					0....	26653
91-BACC-g	jama-la	1	1	13,643	21,541	1	3.00	35	A	41		pn.					0....	26654
91-BAD	**TYELERI net**	1	1	6,000	10,200		10.00	33	A	0		...					0....	26655
91-BADA	TYELI-RI cluster	1	1	6,000	10,200		10.00	33	A	0		...					0....	26656
91-BADA-a	tyeli-ri	1	1	6,000	10,200	0	10.00	33	A	0		...					0....	26657
91-BAE	**KULERE net**	1	1	28,945	45,700		3.00	28	A	0		...					0....	26658
91-BAEA	KULE-RE cluster	1	1	28,945	45,700		3.00	28	A	0		...					0....	26659
91-BAEA-a	kule-re	1	1	28,945	45,700	0	3.00	28	A	0		...					0....	26660
91-BB	EAST SENUFO chain	2	4	131,667	221,837		14.71	50	A	41		PN.					0....	26661
91-BBA	**KPALAGHA net**	1	1	8,298	13,101		3.00	30	A	12		...					0....	26662
91-BBAA	KPALAGHA cluster	1	1	8,298	13,101		3.00	30	A	12		...					0....	26663
91-BBAA-a	kpalagha	1	1	8,298	13,101	0	3.00	30	A	12	Senoufo, Palaka	...					0....	26664
91-BBB	**NAFAANRA net**	2	3	123,369	208,736		15.50	51	B	41		PN.					0....	26665
91-BBBA	NAFAANRA cluster	2	3	123,369	208,736		15.50	51	B	41	Nafaanra	PN.	1982	1984			0....	26666
91-BBBA-a	pante-ra					0				41		pn.					0....	26667
91-BBBA-b	fante-ra					0				41		pn.					0....	26670
91-C	**TUSYAN set**	1	2	41,026	80,156		5.00	33	A	12		...					0....	26671
91-CA	TUSYAN chain	1	2	41,026	80,156		5.00	33	A	12		...					0....	26672
91-CAA	**TUSYAN net**	1	2	41,026	80,156		5.00	33	A	12		...					0....	26673
91-CAAA	TUSYAN cluster	1	2	41,026	80,156		5.00	33	A	12		...					0....	26674
91-CAAA-a	Proper tusyan	1	1	20,513	40,078	0	5.00	33	A	12	Toussian, Southern	...					0....	26675
91-CAAA-b	win	1	1	20,513	40,078	0	5.00	34	A	12		...					0....	26676
91-D	**TIEFO set**	1	1	16,044	30,838		4.75	27	A	5		...					0....	26677
91-DA	TIEFO chain	1	1	16,044	30,838		4.75	27	A	5		...					0....	26678
91-DAA	**TIEFO net**	1	1	16,044	30,838		4.75	27	A	5		...					0....	26679
91-DAAA	TIEFO cluster	1	1	14,044	27,438		5.00	28	A	5		...					0....	26680
91-DAAA-a	kumandara	1	1	14,044	27,438	0	5.00	28	A	5		...					0....	26681
91-DAAB	NYARAFO cluster	1	1	2,000	3,400		3.00	20	A	0		...					0....	26682
91-DAAB-a	nyarafo	1	1	2,000	3,400	0	3.00	20	A	0		...					0....	26683
91-E	**WARA-NATIORO set**	1	2	8,853	17,298		6.28	29	A	4		...					0....	26684
91-EA	WARA-NATIORO chain	1	2	8,853	17,298		6.28	29	A	4		...					0....	26685
91-EAA	**WARA-NATIORO net**	1	2	8,853	17,298		6.28	29	A	4		...					0....	26686
91-EAAA	WARA cluster	1	1	5,691	11,120		6.99	30	A	4		...					0....	26687
91-EAAA-a	negeni					0				4		...					0....	26688
91-EAAA-b	waturu					0				4		...					0....	26689
91-EAAA-c	sulani					0				4		...					0....	26690
91-EAAB	NATIORO cluster	1	1	3,162	6,178		5.00	27	A	4		...					0....	26691
91-EAAB-a	kawara					0				4		...					0....	26692
91-EAAB-b	ginawuru					0				4		...					0....	26693
91-F	**DOGOSO-KHE set**	1	2	8,380	16,372		4.51	25	A	4		...					0....	26694
91-FA	DOGOSO-KHE chain	1	2	8,380	16,372		4.51	25	A	4		...					0....	26695
91-FAA	**DOGOSO net**	1	1	6,324	12,356		5.00	26	A	4		...					0....	26696
91-FAAA	DOGOSO cluster	1	1	6,324	12,356		5.00	26	A	4		...					0....	26697
91-FAAA-a	dogoso	1	1	6,324	12,356	0	5.00	26	A	4		...					0....	26698
91-FAB	**KHE net**	1	1	2,056	4,016		3.02	22	A	4		...					0....	26699
91-FABA	KHE cluster	1	1	2,056	4,016		3.02	22	A	4		...					0....	26700
91-FABA-a	khe	1	1	2,056	4,016	0	3.02	22	A	4		...					0....	26701
91-G	**GUR set**	11	133	20,050,955	37,162,754		18.63	66	B	71		PNB					4Asu.	26702
91-GA	VIEMO chain	1	1	8,854	17,297		3.00	25	A	2		...					0....	26703
91-GAA	**VIEMO net**	1	1	8,854	17,297		3.00	25	A	2		...					0....	26704
91-GAAA	VIEMO cluster	1	1	8,854	17,297		3.00	25	A	2		...					0....	26705
91-GAAA-a	vige					0				2		...					0....	26706
91-GB	LOBI-MORU chain	3	5	531,615	963,380		1.52	37	A	41		PN.					0....	26707
91-GBA	**LOBI net**	3	4	505,945	922,851		1.45	38	A	41		PN.					0....	26708
91-GBAA	LOBI cluster	3	3	487,289	886,402		1.20	38	A	41		PN.					0....	26709
91-GBAA-a	lobi-ri	3	3	487,289	886,402	4	1.20	38	A	41	Lobiri	PN.	1940-1961	1965-1985			0....	26710
91-GBAA-b	gongon-lobi					1				41		pn.					0....	26711
91-GBAA-c	miwa					1				41		pn.					0....	26712
91-GBAB	DYAN cluster	1	1	18,656	36,449		8.00	33	A	2		...					0....	26713
91-GBAB-a	jaane	1	1	18,656	36,449	0	8.00	33	A	2		...					0....	26714
91-GBAB-b	zanga					0				2		...					0....	26715
91-GBB	**MORU net**	1	1	25,670	40,529		3.00	28	A	4		...					0....	26716
91-GBBA	MORU cluster	1	1	25,670	40,529		3.00	28	A	4		...					0....	26717
91-GBBA-a	moru	1	1	25,670	40,529	0	3.00	28	A	4		...					0....	26718
91-GC	KULANGO-TEGE chain	3	7	391,005	626,107		5.61	41	A	44		PN.					0....	26719
91-GCA	**TEGE net**	2	2	8,818	14,515		2.99	31	A	22		P..					0....	26720
91-GCAA	TEGE cluster	2	2	8,818	14,515		2.99	31	A	22		P..					0....	26721
91-GCAA-a	teen	2	2	8,818	14,515	0	2.99	31	A	22	Teen	P..	1985-1995				0....	26722
91-GCAA-b	loghon					0				22		p..					0....	26723
91-GCB	**LOMA net**	1	1	7,393	11,673		3.00	28	A	5		...					0....	26724
91-GCBA	LOMA cluster	1	1	7,393	11,673		3.00	28	A	5		...					0.....	26725

Continued overleaf

Table 9-13 continued

Code 1	REFERENCE NAME / Autoglossonym 2	Coun 3	Peo 4	Mother-tongue speakers in 2000 5	in 2025 6	Media radio 7	CHURCH AC% 8	E% 9	Wld 10	Tr 11	Biblioglossonym 12	SCRIPTURES Print 13-15	P-activity 16	N-activity 17	B-activity 18	J-year 19	Jayuh 20-24	Ref 25
91-GCBA-a	loma	1	1	7,393	11,673	0	3.00	28	A	5		. . .					0	26726
91-GCC	**KULANGO net**	2	4	374,794	599,919		5.72	42	A	44		PN.					0	26727
91-GCCA	KULANGO cluster	2	4	374,794	599,919		5.72	42	A	44	Koulango	PN.	1967				0	26728
91-GCCA-a	kong					1				44		pn.					0	26729
91-GCCA-b	bonduku	1	1	157,675	248,950	4	4.00	42	A	44	Kulango, Bondoukou	PN.	1967-1989	1975			0	26730
91-GCCA-c	nasion					1				44		pn.					0	26731
91-GCCA-d	buna	2	3	217,119	350,969	1	6.98	41	A	44		pn.					0	26732
91-GD	CURAMA-CERMA chain	2	3	140,900	274,523		8.46	37	A	22		P . .					0	26735
91-GDA	**CURAMA-CERMA net**	2	3	140,900	274,523		8.46	37	A	22		P . .					0	26736
91-GDAA	CURA-MA cluster	1	1	59,665	116,569		5.00	29	A	12	Turka	. . .					0	26737
91-GDAA-a	duna					0				12		. . .					0	26738
91-GDAA-b	beregadugu					0				12		. . .					0	26739
91-GDAB	CER-MA cluster	2	2	81,235	157,954		11.00	43	A	22	Cerma	P . .	1995				0	26740
91-GDAB-a	banfora					0				22		p . .					0	26741
91-GDAB-b	niangoloko					0				22		p . .					0	26742
91-GDAB-c	subaka					0				22		p . .					0	26743
91-GDAB-d	gwinduguba					0				22		p . .					0	26744
91-GDAB-e	wangolodugu					0				22		p . .					0	26745
91-GE	GAN-DOGHO chain	2	5	44,554	84,822		3.93	28	A	12		. . .					0	26746
91-GEA	**DOGHO-KHI net**	2	3	35,688	67,502		4.11	29	A	12		. . .					0	26747
91-GEAA	DOGHOSE cluster	1	1	25,804	50,414		5.00	30	A	12	Doghosie	. . .					0	26748
91-GEAA-a	klamaasi-se					0				12		. . .					0	26749
91-GEAA-b	mAisi-se					0				12		. . .					0	26750
91-GEAA-c	luti-se					0				12		. . .					0	26751
91-GEAA-d	gbAnya-se					0				12		. . .					0	26752
91-GEAA-e	sukura-se					0				12		. . .					0	26753
91-GEAA-f	gbogoro-se					0				12		. . .					0	26754
91-GEAB	KHI cluster	2	2	9,884	17,088		1.80	27	A	12		. . .					0	26755
91-GEAB-a	khi-sa	2	2	9,884	17,088	0	1.80	27	A	12	Khisa	. . .					0	26756
91-GEB	**GAN-DOGHO net**	1	2	8,866	17,320		3.20	23	A	12		. . .					0	26757
91-GEBA	GAN cluster	1	1	7,962	15,555		3.00	22	A	12		. . .					0	26758
91-GEBA-a	kaan-se	1	1	7,962	15,555	0	3.00	22	A	12	Kaanse	. . .					0	26759
91-GEBB	KPATOGO cluster	1	1	904	1,765		4.98	29	A	4		. . .					0	26760
91-GEBB-a	kpatogo-so	1	1	904	1,765	0	4.98	29	A	4		. . .					0	26761
91-GF	GRUSI chain	7	41	3,510,898	6,616,367		15.29	56	B	51		PN.					4asu.	26762
91-GFA	**NORTH GRUSI net**	4	8	894,087	1,731,475		11.59	48	A	41		PN.					1	26763
91-GFAA	PANA cluster	2	2	13,807	26,723		2.69	24	A	3		. . .					0	26764
91-GFAA-a	North lu-pana					0				3		. . .					0	26765
91-GFAA-b	South lu-pana					0				3		. . .					0	26766
91-GFAB	LYELE cluster	1	1	303,081	592,138		10.00	45	A	22	Lyele	P . .	1968-1995				0	26767
91-GFAB-a	North lyele					1				22		p . .					0	26768
91-GFAB-b	Central lyele					1				22		p . .					0	26769
91-GFAC	NUNI cluster	2	2	314,194	613,751		12.99	48	A	22	Nuni*	P . .	1987				0	26770
91-GFAC-a	mica-ri					1				22		p . .					0	26771
91-GFAC-b	basinya-ri					1				22		p . .					0	26772
91-GFAC-c	sundo-ni					1				22		p . .					0	26773
91-GFAC-d	yati-ni					1				22		p . .					0	26774
91-GFAC-e	go-ri	1	1	727	1,321	1	10.04	31	A	22		p . .					0	26775
91-GFAC-f	bwana					1				22		p . .					0	26776
91-GFAC-g	sankura					1				22		p . .					0	26777
91-GFAC-h	nebo-li					1				22		p . .					0	26778
91-GFAD	KASEM cluster	2	2	248,505	470,535		12.33	54	B	41		PN.					1	26779
91-GFAD-a	fu-ri					1				41		pn.					1	26780
91-GFAD-b	East kasem	2	2	248,505	470,535	4	12.33	54	B	41	Kasem	PN.	1948-1990	1988			1	26781
91-GFAE	SAMO-KALAMSE cluster	1	1	14,500	28,328		10.00	35	A	4		. . .					0	26782
91-GFAE-a	kaso-ma					0				4		. . .					0	26783
91-GFAE-b	logrem-ma					0				4		. . .					0	26784
91-GFB	**WEST GRUSI net**	3	12	362,550	667,726		15.07	51	B	41		PN.					0	26785
91-GFBA	KO cluster	1	1	20,554	40,157		5.00	28	A	12		. . .					0	26786
91-GFBA-a	ko-lsi	1	1	20,554	40,157	0	5.00	28	A	12	Ko	. . .					0	26787
91-GFBB	PWO cluster	1	1	13,880	27,118		3.00	25	A	0		. . .					0	26788
91-GFBB-a	phwi	1	1	13,880	27,118	0	3.00	25	A	0		. . .					0	26789
91-GFBC	SISALA cluster	2	4	234,827	430,593		11.35	48	A	41		PN.					0	26790
91-GFBC-a	sisaa-li	1	1	16,772	32,769	0	10.00	40	A	41	Sisaala*	PN.	1972-1995	1984			0	26791
91-GFBC-b	busil-lu	1	1	28,609	52,195	0	10.00	44	A	41	Sisaala, Western	pn.					0	26792
91-GFBC-c	n-si-haa					0				41		pn.					0	26793
91-GFBC-d	potu-le					0				41		pn.					0	26794
91-GFBC-e	gil-baga-le	1	1	157,957	288,180	0	12.00	51	B	41	Sisaala, Tumulung	PN.	1972	1984			0	26795
91-GFBC-f	paasa-li	1	1	31,489	57,449	0	10.00	44	A	41	Pasaale	Pn.	1994-1996				0	26796
91-GFBD	TAMPUL cluster	1	1	48,977	89,355		23.00	61	B	41		PN.					0	26797
91-GFBD-a	tampul-ma	1	1	48,977	89,355	0	23.00	61	B	41	Tampulma	PN.	1972	1978-1994			0	26798
91-GFBE	CHAKALI cluster	1	1	5,722	10,440		1.50	25	A	6		. . .					0	26799
91-GFBE-a	chaka-li	1	1	5,722	10,440	0	1.50	25	A	6		. . .					0	26800
91-GFBF	VAGHLA cluster	2	2	12,706	23,161		39.76	78	B	41		PN.					0	26801
91-GFBF-a	Proper vaghla	2	2	12,706	23,161	0	39.76	78	B	41	Vagla	PN.	1969	1977			0	26802
91-GFBF-b	bole					0				41		pn.					0	26803
91-GFBF-c	buge					0				41		pn.					0	26804
91-GFBF-d	siti					0				41		pn.					0	26805
91-GFBG	DEG cluster	2	2	25,884	46,902		39.14	81	B	41		PN.					0	26806
91-GFBG-a	Proper deg	2	2	25,884	46,902	0	39.14	81	B	41	Deg	PN.		1990			0	26807
91-GFBG-b	boe					0				41		pn.					0	26808
91-GFBG-c	longoro					0				41		pn.					0	26809
91-GFBG-d	mangum					0				41		pn.					0	26810
91-GFC	**EAST GRUSI net**	3	15	1,338,231	2,449,448		17.66	61	B	41		PN.					3a.u.	26811
91-GFCA	CHALA cluster	1	1	2,860	5,218		2.97	29	A	4		. . .					0	26812
91-GFCA-a	chala	1	1	2,860	5,218	0	2.97	29	A	4		. . .					0	26813
91-GFCB	KABIYE-LAMA cluster	3	11	1,010,278	1,849,175		21.13	69	B	41		PN.					3a . . .	26814
91-GFCB-a	kabiye	3	3	690,248	1,264,163	4	22.20	75	B	41	Kabiye	PN.	1955-1987	1996		1988	3a . . .	26815
91-GFCB-b	lama	2	2	219,389	401,292	1	13.80	54	B	41	Lama: Togo	PN.		1993			1c . . .	26818
91-GFCB-c	delo	2	2	19,512	35,651	1	89.67	100	C	41	Delo	pn.					1c . . .	26823
91-GFCB-d	bago	1	1	7,751	14,203	1	1.01	27	A	41		pn.					1c . . .	26824
91-GFCB-e	lukpa	3	3	73,378	133,866	2	16.83	53	B	41	Lokpa*	PN.	1955-1991	1977			1c . . .	26825

Continued opposite

Table 9-13 continued

Code 1	REFERENCE NAME / Autoglossonym 2	Coun 3	Peo 4	Mother-tongue speakers in 2000 5	in 2025 6	Media radio 7	CHURCH AC% 8	E% 9	Wld 10	Tr 11	Biblioglossonym 12	SCRIPTURES Print 13-15	P-activity 16	N-activity 17	B-activity 18	J-year 19	Jayuh 20-24	Ref 25
91-GFCC	TEM cluster	3	3	325,093	595,055		7.00	38	A	20		. . .					2..u.	26826
91-GFCC-a	tem	3	3	325,093	595,055	0	7.00	38	A	20	Tem	. . .					2..u.	26827
91-GFD	**BWAMU net**	2	5	740,632	1,425,037		16.59	60	B	51		PN.					4.s..	26828
91-GFDA	BO-MU cluster	2	4	735,015	1,414,389		16.68	60	B	51	Boomu*	PN.	1937-1994	1954-1980		1991	4.s..	26829
91-GFDA-a	ouarkoye	1	1	11,234	21,295	0	6.00	42	A	51	Bwamu*	Pn.	1957-1995				1.s..	26830
91-GFDA-b	dwe-mu					0				51		pn.					1.s..	26831
91-GFDA-c	dahan-mu					0				51		pn.					1.s..	26832
91-GFDA-d	pwe					0				51	Pwe	pn.					1.s..	26833
91-GFDA-e	sankura					0				51		pn.					1.s..	26834
91-GFDA-f	tara					0				51		pn.					1.s..	26835
91-GFDA-g	nyenyege					0				51		pn.					1.s..	26836
91-GFDA-h	mandia-kuy					0				51		pn.					1.s..	26837
91-GFDA-i	bomboro-kuy					0				51		pn.					1.s..	26838
91-GFDA-j	sanaba					0				51		pn.					1.s..	26839
91-GFDA-k	solenso					0				51		pn.					1.s..	26840
91-GFDA-l	mao					0				51		pn.					1.s..	26841
91-GFDA-m	masala					0				51		pn.					1.s..	26842
91-GFDA-n	dedugu					0				51		pn.					1.s..	26843
91-GFDA-o	bondu-koy					0				51		pn.					1.s..	26844
91-GFDA-p	wakara					0				51		pn.					1.s..	26845
91-GFDA-q	sara					0				51		pn.					1.s..	26846
91-GFDA-r	hunde					0				51		pn.					1.s..	26847
91-GFDA-s	yaho					0				51		pn.					1.s..	26848
91-GFDA-t	mamu					0				51		pn.					1.s..	26849
91-GFDA-u	bagasi					0				51		pn.					1.s..	26850
91-GFDB	CHAN cluster	1	1	5,617	10,648		5.00	37	A	0		. . .					0....	26851
91-GFDB-a	kyan					0				0		. . .					0....	26852
91-GFE	**KURUMFE net**	1	1	175,398	342,681		11.00	45	A	20		. . .					0....	26853
91-GFEA	KURUMFE cluster	1	1	175,398	342,681		11.00	45	A	20	Koromfe	. . .					0....	26854
91-GFEA-a	a-kurum-fe	1	1	175,398	342,681	2	11.00	45	A	20		. . .					0....	26855
91-GFEA-b	nyonyo-si					1				20		. . .					0....	26856
91-GG	OTI-VOLTA chain	10	65	14,882,518	27,604,417		20.91	71	B	71		PNB					4Asu.	26857
91-GGA	**MOORE-DAGBANE net**	9	37	12,082,576	22,420,701		22.22	75	B	71		PNB					4A...	26858
91-GGAA	MOORE-DAGAARI cluster	9	25	10,336,631	19,233,148		24.75	79	B	71		PNB					2A...	26859
91-GGAA-a	moo-re	9	10	8,053,292	14,996,100	4	26.67	84	B	71	Moore	PNB	1930-1960	1939-1960	1983	1993	2A...	26860
91-GGAA-b	yan-ga	1	1	20,840	40,717	1	2.00	29	A	71		pnb					1c...	26866
91-GGAA-c	zao-re	1	1	33,776	65,990	1	2.00	29	A	71		pnb					1c...	26867
91-GGAA-d	waa-li	1	1	129,154	235,632	1	3.00	43	A	71	Wali	PNb	1968	1984			1c...	26868
91-GGAA-e	guren-ge	2	3	884,767	1,618,485	1	9.37	54	B	71	Frafra*	PNb	1962-1992	1986			1c...	26872
91-GGAA-f	kanto-si	1	1	2,607	4,757	1	1.00	34	A	71		pnb					1c...	26873
91-GGAA-g	safala	1	1	3,473	6,335	1	30.00	74	B	71		pnb					1c...	26874
91-GGAA-h	dagaa-ri	2	2	932,605	1,742,443	4	30.56	77	B	71	Dagaare*	Pnb	1970-1980				1c...	26875
91-GGAA-i	dagaari-jula	1	1	11,937	23,321	1	0.10	24	A	71		pnb					1c...	26878
91-GGAA-j	North birifor	3	3	262,890	496,847	4	13.88	60	B	71	Birifor*	PNb		1993			1c...	26879
91-GGAA-k	nura					1				71		pnb					1c...	26882
91-GGAA-l	lob-r					1				71	Birifor: Southern*	Pnb	1993				1c...	26883
91-GGAA-m	bam-ge					1				71		pnb					1c...	26884
91-GGAA-n	sininkere	1	1	1,290	2,521	1	3.02	36	A	71		pnb					1c...	26885
91-GGAB	BULBA cluster	1	1	1,021	1,861		5.00	30	A	4		. . .					0....	26886
91-GGAB-a	not-re	1	1	1,021	1,861	0	5.00	30	A	4		. . .					0....	26887
91-GGAC	DAGBANI-KUSAAL cluster	3	11	1,744,924	3,185,692		7.26	47	A	41		PN.					4....	26888
91-GGAC-a	kusaal	3	3	603,808	1,103,680	1	14.69	54	B	41	Kusaal*	PN.	1965	1976-1995			1....	26889
91-GGAC-b	nab-t	1	1	52,427	95,650	1	9.00	47	A	41		pn.					1....	26893
91-GGAC-c	tal-ne	1	1	104,034	189,802	1	9.00	46	A	41		pn.					1....	26894
91-GGAC-d	mampru-li	2	2	304,841	556,235	1	0.59	37	A	41	Mampruli	Pn.	1943-1994				1....	26895
91-GGAC-e	dagba-ne	2	2	632,337	1,153,707	4	3.01	47	A	41	Dagbani	PN.	1935-1955	1974-1995		1994	4....	26896
91-GGAC-f	nanu-ne	1	1	41,165	75,102	1	4.00	37	A	41		pn.					1....	26897
91-GGAC-g	hanga	1	1	6,312	11,516	1	23.00	60	B	41	Hanga	PN.	1982	1983			1....	26898
91-GGB	**BULI-KONNI net**	2	3	210,633	394,296		6.36	46	A	41		PN.					4....	26904
91-GGBA	BULI-KONNI cluster	2	3	210,633	394,296		6.36	46	A	41		PN.					4....	26905
91-GGBA-a	kon-ni	1	1	2,894	5,281	0	13.99	43	A	41	Konni	pn.					1....	26906
91-GGBA-b	bu-li	2	2	207,739	389,015	0	6.25	46	A	41	Buli	PN.	1962-1991	1995-1996			4....	26907
91-GGC	**YOM-NAWDM net**	2	2	254,584	465,790		23.72	62	B	41		PN.					0....	26908
91-GGCA	NAWDM cluster	1	1	185,016	339,020		30.00	68	B	22		P..					0....	26909
91-GGCA-a	nawd-m	1	1	185,016	339,020	0	30.00	68	B	22	Nawdm	P..	1992				0....	26910
91-GGCB	PILA cluster	1	1	69,568	126,770		7.00	45	A	41		PN.					0....	26911
91-GGCB-a	yo-m	1	1	69,568	126,770	2	7.00	45	A	41	Yom*	PN.	1954-1966	1985			0....	26912
91-GGCB-b	tangel-em					1				41		pn.					0....	26913
91-GGD	**GURMA-MOBA net**	6	16	1,974,643	3,666,838		15.55	59	B	61		PNB					3Asu.	26914
91-GGDA	GURMA cluster	5	5	703,409	1,343,348		12.74	58	B	51		PN.					3.s..	26915
91-GGDA-a	North gulma-ncema					1				51		pn.					1.s..	26916
91-GGDA-b	Central gulma-ncema	1	1	157,141	287,942	4	25.00	73	B	51	Gourma*	PN.	1947-1988	1958-1990		1994	3.s..	26917
91-GGDA-c	South gulma-ncema					1				51		pn.					1.s..	26918
91-GGDB	NGANGAM cluster	2	3	569,486	1,039,829		14.33	64	B	61		PNB					2A.u.	26919
91-GGDB-a	mi-gangam	1	1	42,569	78,002	0	6.00	45	A	61	Ngangam	pnb					1c.u.	26920
91-GGDB-b	ku-mongu					0				61		pnb					1c.u.	26921
91-GGDB-c	li-jem					0				61		pnb					1c.u.	26922
91-GGDB-d	mi-gbeen					0				61		pnb					1c.u.	26925
91-GGDB-e	mi-dokm					0				61		pnb					1c.u.	26926
91-GGDB-f	mi-felm					0				61		pnb					1c.u.	26927
91-GGDB-g	le-kpekpam	2	2	526,917	961,827	0	15.00	65	B	61	Konkomba	PNB	1969	1977-1984	1996		2A.u.	26928
91-GGDC	MOBA cluster	3	3	339,049	620,781		23.86	64	B	41		PN.					0..u.	26929
91-GGDC-a	Central moba					0				41	Moba	Pn.	1941-1984				0..u.	26930
91-GGDC-b	bi-moba	3	3	339,049	620,781	0	23.86	64	B	41	Bimoba	PN.	1971-1973	1986			0..u.	26931
91-GGDC-c	bem					0				41		pn.					0..u.	26932
91-GGDC-d	nachaba					0				41		pn.					0..u.	26933
91-GGDD	BASAAL cluster	2	3	301,713	551,749		15.72	52	B	51		PN.					0..u.	26934
91-GGDD-a	n-can-m	2	2	258,128	471,884	0	15.00	51	B	51	Ntcham	PN.	1969	1986-1990			0..u.	26935
91-GGDD-b	n-taapu-m					0				51		pn.					0..u.	26936
91-GGDD-c	li-nangman-li					0				51		pn.					0..u.	26937
91-GGDD-d	a-kasele-m	1	1	43,585	79,865	0	20.00	54	B	51		pn.					0..u.	26938
91-GGDD-e	tobote					0				51		pn.					0..u.	26939
91-GGDE	KPAKPA cluster	1	1	6,096	11,108		70.00	100	C	4		. . .					0....	26940
91-GGDE-a	li-koon-li					0				4		. . .					0....	26941
91-GGDE-b	li-chaboo-l					0				4		. . .					0....	26942
91-GGDE-c	li-monkpe-l					0				4		. . .					0....	26943
91-GGDE-d	li-nafie-l					0				4		. . .					0....	26944
91-GGDE-e	li-gbe-ln	1	1	6,096	11,108	0	70.00	100	C	4		. . .					0....	26945
91-GGDF	NATENI-TAYARI cluster	1	1	54,890	100,023		6.00	34	A	12		. . .					0....	26946
91-GGDF-a	nate-ni	1	1	54,890	100,023	0	6.00	34	A	12	Nateni	. . .					0....	26947
91-GGDF-b	taya-ri					0				12		. . .					0....	26948
91-GGDF-c	kunte-ni					0				12		. . .					0....	26949

Continued overleaf

Table 9-13 continued

Code 1	REFERENCE NAME 2 / Autoglossonym	Coun 3	Peo 4	Mother-tongue speakers in 2000 5	in 2025 6	Media radio 7	CHURCH AC% 8	E% 9	Wld 10	Tr 11	Biblioglossonym 12	SCRIPTURES Print 13-15	P–activity 16	N–activity 17	B–activity 18	J-year 19	Jayuh 20-24	Ref 25
91-GGDF-d	oko-ni					0				12		. . .					0	26950
91-GGE	**BIALI-TAMARI net**	3	7	360,082	656,792		13.01	48	A	41		PN.					0	26951
91-GGEA	BIALI cluster	2	2	84,347	153,964		6.00	37	A	12		. . .					0	26952
91-GGEA-a	bia-li	2	2	84,347	153,964	2	6.00	37	A	12	Biali	. . .					0	26953
91-GGEB	WAAMA-TANGAM cluster	2	2	66,121	120,608		9.29	45	A	41		PN.					0	26954
91-GGEB-a	waa-ma	2	2	66,121	120,608	2	9.29	45	A	41	Waama	PN.	1986	1994			0	26955
91-GGEB-b	tangam-ma					1				41		pn.						26956
91-GGEC	TAMARI cluster	2	3	209,614	382,220		17.00	53	B	41		PN.					0	26957
91-GGEC-a	li-tanmari-1					0				41		pn.					0	26958
91-GGEC-b	di-tammari	2	2	178,340	325,232	0	17.00	54	B	41	Ditamari*	PN.	1991	1989			0	26959
91-GGEC-c	nyende					0				41		pn.					0	26960
91-GGEC-d	mbelime	1	1	31,274	56,988	0	17.00	52	B	41	Mbelime	pn.					0	26961
91-GH	YOBE chain	2	2	11,096	20,242		6.00	33	A	12		. . .					0	26962
91-GHA	**YOBE net**	2	2	11,096	20,242		6.00	33	A	12		. . .					0	26963
91-GHAA	YOBE cluster	2	2	11,096	20,242		6.00	33	A	12		. . .					0	26964
91-GHAA-a	mi-yobe	2	2	11,096	20,242	0	6.00	33	A	12	Sola	. . .					0	26965
91-GI	BARIBA chain	4	4	529,515	955,599		8.00	58	B	61		PNB					3	26966
91-GIA	**BARIBA net**	4	4	529,515	955,599		8.00	58	B	61		PNB					3	26967
91-GIAA	BARIBA cluster	4	4	529,515	955,599		8.00	58	B	61		PNB					3	26968
91-GIAA-a	baatonum	4	4	529,515	955,599	4	8.00	58	B	61	Bariba	PNB	1953-1986	1977	1996	1992	3	26969
91-H	**CENKA set**	1	1	4,000	6,800		7.00	28	A	4		. . .					0	26970
91-HA	CENKA chain	1	1	4,000	6,800		7.00	28	A	4		. . .					0	26971
91-HAA	**CENKA net**	1	1	4,000	6,800		7.00	28	A	4		. . .					0	26972
91-HAAA	CENKA cluster	1	1	4,000	6,800		7.00	28	A	4		. . .					0	26973
91-HAAA-a	cenka	1	1	4,000	6,800	0	7.00	28	A	4		. . .					0	26974
92	**ADAMAWIC zone**	4	104	2,809,978	4,782,010		27.31	62	B	61		PNB					0 . su .	26975
92-A	**WAJA-JEN set**	1	24	441,576	724,987		21.33	50	B	41		PN.					0	26976
92-AA	WAJA-LOTSU chain	1	9	130,115	213,591		14.97	45	A	24		P . .					0	26977
92-AAA	**WAJA-TULA net**	1	4	94,757	155,549		9.09	40	A	24		P . .					0	26978
92-AAAA	WAJA cluster	1	2	54,849	90,038		9.61	41	A	24		P . .					0	26979
92-AAAA-a	waja	1	1	52,675	86,469	0	10.00	42	A	24	Wuya*	P . .	1926-1935				0	26980
92-AAAB	TULA cluster	1	1	33,363	54,766		10.00	42	A	24		P . .					0	26981
92-AAAB-a	tula	1	1	33,363	54,766	0	10.00	42	A	24	Kutele*	P . .	1929				0	26982
92-AAAC	BANGWINJI cluster	1	1	6,545	10,745		0.05	17	A	4		. . .					0	26983
92-AAAC-a	bangwinji	1	1	6,545	10,745	0	0.05	17	A	4		. . .					0	26984
92-AAB	**YEBU-KAMO net**	1	2	8,463	13,893		5.00	29	A	4		. . .					0	26985
92-AABA	YEBU cluster	1	1	5,062	8,310		5.00	28	A	4		. . .					0	26986
92-AABA-a	yiin-yebu	1	1	5,062	8,310	0	5.00	28	A	4		. . .					0	26987
92-AABB	KAMO cluster	1	1	3,401	5,583		5.00	31	A	4		. . .					0	26988
92-AABB-a	kamo	1	1	3,401	5,583	0	5.00	31	A	4		. . .					0	26989
92-AAC	**DIYA net**	1	1	4,037	6,626		0.10	20	A	4		. . .					0	26990
92-AACA	DIYA cluster	1	1	4,037	6,626		0.10	20	A	4		. . .					0	26991
92-AACA-a	loo-diya	1	1	4,037	6,626	0	0.10	20	A	4		. . .					0	26992
92-AACA-b	tunga					0				4		. . .					0	26993
92-AAD	**LOTSU-DIJIM net**	1	2	22,858	37,523		45.66	76	B	4		. . .					0	26994
92-AADA	DIJIM cluster	1	1	16,391	26,907		40.00	71	B	4		. . .					0	26995
92-AADA-a	cham					0				4		. . .					0	26996
92-AADA-b	mwana					0				4		. . .					0	26997
92-AADB	LOTSU-PIRI cluster	1	1	6,467	10,616		60.00	89	B	4		. . .					0	26998
92-AADB-a	lotsu	1	1	6,467	10,616	0	60.00	89	B	4		. . .					0	26999
92-AADB-b	piri					0				4		. . .					0	27000
92-AB	BURAK-JANJO chain	1	8	58,038	95,274		34.07	61	B	4		. . .					0	27001
92-ABA	**BURAK-PANYAM net**	1	6	35,336	58,006		18.26	43	A	4		. . .					0	27002
92-ABAA	BURAK cluster	1	2	13,091	21,489		13.37	37	A	4		. . .					0	27003
92-ABAA-a	burak	1	1	4,360	7,157	0	0.09	19	A	4		. . .					0	27004
92-ABAA-b	lo	1	1	8,731	14,332	0	20.00	46	A	4		. . .					0	27005
92-ABAB	PANYAM cluster	1	1	5,575	9,152		40.00	67	B	4		. . .					0	27006
92-ABAB-a	lee-mak	1	1	5,575	9,152	0	40.00	67	B	4		. . .					0	27007
92-ABAC	BAMBUKA cluster	1	1	11,318	18,579		10.00	35	A	4		. . .					0	27008
92-ABAC-a	kyak	1	1	11,318	18,579	0	10.00	35	A	4		. . .					0	27009
92-ABAC-b	kanawa					0				4		. . .					0	27010
92-ABAD	LAU cluster	1	1	3,345	5,491		40.00	66	B	4		. . .					0	27011
92-ABAD-a	lee-lau	1	1	3,345	5,491	0	40.00	66	B	4		. . .					0	27012
92-ABAE	GWOMU cluster	1	1	2,007	3,295		0.05	19	A	4		. . .					0	27013
92-ABAE-a	gwomu	1	1	2,007	3,295	0	0.05	19	A	4		. . .					0	27014
92-ABB	**JANJO-MUNGA net**	1	2	22,702	37,268		58.69	90	B	4		. . .					0	27015
92-ABBA	DZA cluster	1	1	19,714	32,362		60.00	92	C	4		. . .					0	27016
92-ABBA-a	West dza					0				4		. . .					0	27017
92-ABBA-b	East dza					0				4		. . .					0	27018
92-ABBB	MUNGA cluster	1	1	2,988	4,906		50.00	78	B	4		. . .					0	27019
92-ABBB-a	munga	1	1	2,988	4,906	0	50.00	78	B	4		. . .					0	27020
92-AC	LONGUDA chain	1	2	63,826	104,772		42.01	78	B	41		PN.					0	27021
92-ACA	**LONGUDA net**	1	2	63,826	104,772		42.01	78	B	41		PN.					0	27022
92-ACAA	LONGURA-MA cluster	1	2	63,826	104,772		42.01	78	B	41		PN.					0	27023
92-ACAA-a	nya-ceri-ya					0				41		pn.					0	27024
92-ACAA-b	nya-gwanda					0				41		pn.					0	27025
92-ACAA-c	nya-guyuwa	1	1	56,188	92,234	0	45.00	82	B	41	Longuda: Guyuk	PN.	1975	1978			0	27026
92-ACAA-d	nya-dele					0				41		pn.					0	27027
92-ACAA-e	nya-tariya					0				41		pn.					0	27028

Continued opposite

Table 9-13 continued

Code 1	REFERENCE NAME / Autoglossonym 2	Coun 3	Peo 4	in 2000 5	in 2025 6	Media radio 7	AC% 8	E% 9	Wld 10	Tr 11	Biblioglossonym 12	Print 13-15	P-activity 16	N-activity 17	B-activity 18	J-year 19	Jayuh 20-24	Ref 25
92-AD	YUNGUR-MBOI chain	1	5	187,597	307,950		14.90	41	A	4		. . .					0....	27029
92-ADA	**YUNGUR-LALA net**	1	3	155,941	255,984		13.12	40	A	4		. . .					0....	27030
92-ADAA	LALA-ROBA cluster	1	1	48,717	79,971		20.00	47	A	2		. . .					0....	27031
92-ADAA-a	roba					0				2		. . .					0....	27032
92-ADAA-b	lala	1	1	48,717	79,971	0	20.00	47	A	2		. . .					0....	27033
92-ADAB	YUNGUR cluster	1	2	107,224	176,013		10.00	37	A	4		. . .					0....	27034
92-ADAB-a	e-buna	1	1	3,512	5,766	0	9.99	33	A	4		. . .					0....	27035
92-ADB	**MBOI-HANDA net**	1	1	20,740	34,046		15.00	39	A	4		. . .					0....	27036
92-ADBA	MBOI-HANDA cluster	1	1	20,740	34,046		15.00	39	A	4		. . .					0....	27037
92-ADBA-a	mboi	1	1	20,740	34,046	0	15.00	39	A	4		. . .					0....	27038
92-ADBA-b	handa					0				4		. . .					0....	27039
92-ADBA-c	banga					0				4		. . .					0....	27040
92-ADC	**LIBO net**	1	1	10,916	17,920		40.01	67	B	4		. . .					0....	27041
92-ADCA	LIBO cluster	1	1	10,916	17,920		40.01	67	B	4		. . .					0....	27042
92-ADCA-a	libo	1	1	10,916	17,920	0	40.01	67	B	4		. . .					0....	27043
92-AE	KWA chain	1	1	2,000	3,400		10.00	33	A	0		. . .					0....	27044
92-AEA	**KWA net**	1	1	2,000	3,400		10.00	33	A	0		. . .					0....	27045
92-AEAA	KWA cluster	1	1	2,000	3,400		10.00	33	A	0		. . .					0....	27046
92-AEAA-a	ba					0				0		. . .					0....	27047
92-B	**LEKO-NIMBARI set**	2	36	1,192,850	2,001,039		17.26	51	B	41		PN.					0.s..	27048
92-BA	MUMUYE-YANDANG chain	2	11	779,959	1,292,883		10.32	45	A	41		PN.					0....	27049
92-BAA	**MUMUYE-GENGLE net**	2	6	662,354	1,099,830		10.01	46	A	41		PN.					0....	27050
92-BAAA	WAKA cluster	1	1	5,453	8,951		20.01	45	A	4		. . .					0....	27051
92-BAAA-a	waka	1	1	5,453	8,951	0	20.01	45	A	4		. . .					0....	27052
92-BAAB	TEME cluster	1	1	3,345	5,491		40.00	66	B	4		. . .					0....	27053
92-BAAB-a	teme	1	1	3,345	5,491	0	40.00	66	B	4		. . .					0....	27054
92-BAAC	GENGLE cluster	1	1	11,151	18,304		0.04	21	A	4		. . .					0....	27055
92-BAAC-a	gengle	1	1	11,151	18,304	0	0.04	21	A	4		. . .					0....	27056
92-BAAD	GONGLA cluster	1	1	11,151	18,304		10.00	35	A	0		. . .					0....	27057
92-BAAD-a	gongla	1	1	11,151	18,304	0	10.00	35	A	0		. . .					0....	27058
92-BAAE	WEST MUMUYE cluster	2	2	431,254	708,780		9.91	53	B	41	Mumuye	PN.	1938	1994-1995			0....	27059
92-BAAE-a	lankaviri					0				41		pn.					0....	27060
92-BAAE-b	gola					0				41		pn.					0....	27061
92-BAAE-c	kasaa					0				41		pn.					0....	27062
92-BAAE-d	saawa					0				41		pn.					0....	27063
92-BAAE-e	pangseng					0				41		pn.					0....	27064
92-BAAE-f	jalingo					0				41		pn.					0....	27065
92-BAAE-g	nyaaja					0				41		pn.					0....	27066
92-BAAF	EAST MUMUYE cluster	1	1	200,000	340,000		10.00	33	A	0		. . .					0....	27067
92-BAAF-a	zing					0				0		. . .					0....	27068
92-BAAF-b	dong					0				0		. . .					0....	27069
92-BAAF-c	yoro					0				0		. . .					0....	27070
92-BAAF-d	jeng					0				0		. . .					0....	27071
92-BAAF-e	gnoore					0				0		. . .					0....	27072
92-BAAF-f	yaa					0				0		. . .					0....	27073
92-BAAF-g	rang					0				0		. . .					0....	27074
92-BAAF-h	sagbee					0				0		. . .					0....	27075
92-BAAF-i	shaari					0				0		. . .					0....	27076
92-BAAF-j	kugong					0				0		. . .					0....	27077
92-BAAF-k	mang					0				0		. . .					0....	27078
92-BAAF-l	kwaji					0				0		. . .					0....	27079
92-BAAF-m	meeka					0				0		. . .					0....	27080
92-BAAF-n	yakoko					0				0		. . .					0....	27081
92-BAB	**YANDANG-KPASAM net**	1	5	117,605	193,053		12.07	38	A	4		. . .					0....	27082
92-BABA	KPASAM cluster	1	1	16,369	26,870		30.00	59	B	4		. . .					0....	27083
92-BABA-a	kpasam	1	1	16,369	26,870	0	30.00	59	B	4		. . .					0....	27084
92-BABB	YENDANG cluster	1	2	82,693	135,743		10.81	37	A	4		. . .					0....	27085
92-BABB-a	Proper yendang	1	1	79,348	130,252	0	10.00	36	A	4		. . .					0....	27086
92-BABB-b	kuseki					0				4		. . .					0....	27087
92-BABB-c	yofo					0				4		. . .					0....	27088
92-BABB-d	kumba	1	1	3,345	5,491	0	30.01	57	B	4		. . .					0....	27089
92-BABC	KUGAMA cluster	1	1	3,345	5,491		10.01	33	A	4		. . .					0....	27090
92-BABC-a	kugama	1	1	3,345	5,491	0	10.01	33	A	4		. . .					0....	27091
92-BABD	BALI cluster	1	1	15,198	24,949		0.07	26	A	4		. . .					0....	27092
92-BABD-a	bali	1	1	15,198	24,949	0	0.07	26	A	4		. . .					0....	27093
92-BB	DII-DULI chain	1	5	106,456	186,903		8.67	39	A	23		P..					0.s..	27094
92-BBA	**DII-PANON net**	1	4	105,702	185,579		8.70	39	A	23		P..					0.s..	27095
92-BBAA	DII-PANON cluster	1	4	105,702	185,579		8.70	39	A	23		P..					0.s..	27096
92-BBAA-a	n-duupa	1	1	6,162	10,819	0	10.00	40	A	23	Duupa	P..	1982				0.s..	27097
92-BBAA-b	panon	1	1	6,162	10,819	0	40.00	71	B	23	Dugun*	P..	1982				0.s..	27098
92-BBAA-c	saa					0				23		p..					0.s..	27099
92-BBAA-d	goom					0				23		p..					0.s..	27100
92-BBAA-e	dii	1	2	93,378	163,941	0	6.55	37	A	23	Duru*	P..	1966				0.s..	27101
92-BBB	**DULI net**	1	1	754	1,324		5.04	30	A	9		. . .					0....	27111
92-BBBA	DULI cluster	1	1	754	1,324		5.04	30	A	9		. . .					0....	27112
92-BBBA-a	duli	1	1	754	1,324	0	5.04	30	A	9		. . .					0....	27113
92-BC	VOKO-DOWAYO chain	2	10	132,222	225,559		30.94	65	B	41		PN.					0....	27114
92-BCA	**KUTIN net**	2	2	26,404	45,754		38.00	73	B	41		PN.					0....	27115
92-BCAA	PEERE cluster	2	2	26,404	45,754		38.00	73	B	41	Peere	PN.		1985-1986			0....	27116
92-BCAA-a	peer-muure					0				41		pn.					0....	27117
92-BCAA-b	dan-muure					0				41		pn.					0....	27118
92-BCAA-c	zongbi					0				41		pn.					0....	27119
92-BCB	**KOMA-DOYAYO net**	2	7	101,849	172,837		28.76	63	B	41		PN.					0....	27120
92-BCBA	DOYAYO cluster	1	1	28,423	49,902		26.00	63	B	41		PN.					0....	27121
92-BCBA-a	doyayo	1	1	28,423	49,902	0	26.00	63	B	41	Dooyaayo*	PN.	1979	1991			0....	27122
92-BCBA-b	marke					0				41		pn.					0....	27123
92-BCBA-c	teere					0				41		pn.					0....	27124
92-BCBA-d	sewe					0				41		pn.					0....	27125

Continued overleaf

Table 9-13 continued

Code 1	REFERENCE NAME / Autoglossonym 2	Coun 3	Peo 4	Mother-tongue speakers in 2000 5	in 2025 6	Media radio 7	AC% 8	E% 9	Wld 10	Tr 11	Biblioglossonym 12	Print 13-15	P-activity 16	N-activity 17	B-activity 18	J-year 19	Jayuh 20-24	Ref 25
92-BCBB	KOMA-VERE cluster	2	6	73,426	122,935		29.83	63	B	12		...					0....	27126
92-BCBB-a	gimme	1	1	4,960	8,708	0	5.00	32	A	12	Gimme	...					0....	27127
92-BCBB-b	gimnime	1	1	4,963	8,713	0	6.00	33	A	12		...					0....	27128
92-BCBB-c	ritime					0				12		...					0....	27129
92-BCBB-d	leelu					0				12		...					0....	27130
92-BCBB-e	bangru					0				12		...					0....	27131
92-BCBB-f	zanu					0				12		...					0....	27132
92-BCBB-g	liu	2	2	38,501	63,718	0	40.00	73	B	12		...					0....	27133
92-BCBB-h	yeru					0				12		...					0....	27134
92-BCBB-i	ndera					0				12		...					0....	27135
92-BCBB-j	damti					0				12		...					0....	27136
92-BCBB-k	mom-jango	2	2	25,002	41,796	0	23.82	59	B	12		...					0....	27137
92-BCBB-l	momi					0				12		...					0....	27138
92-BCC	**VOKO net**	1	1	3,969	6,968		40.01	70	B	4		...					0....	27139
92-BCCA	VOKO cluster	1	1	3,969	6,968		40.01	70	B	4		...					0....	27140
92-BCCA-a	longto	1	1	3,969	6,968	0	40.01	70	B	4		...					0....	27141
92-BD	SAMBA-KOLBILA chain	2	8	164,403	279,073		44.01	77	B	22		P..					0....	27142
92-BDA	**SAMBA-KOLBILA net**	2	8	164,403	279,073		44.01	77	B	22		P..					0....	27143
92-BDAA	KOLBILA cluster	1	1	3,820	6,706		40.00	72	B	22		P..					0....	27144
92-BDAA-a	kolbila	1	1	3,820	6,706	0	40.00	72	B	22	Kolbila	P..	1982-1986				0....	27145
92-BDAB	SAMBA-LEKO cluster	2	7	160,583	272,367		44.10	77	B	12		...					0....	27146
92-BDAB-a	Proper samba-leko	2	2	91,744	154,142	0	50.00	85	B	12	Samba Leko	...					0....	27147
92-BDAB-b	samba-bali					0				12		...					0....	27148
92-BDAB-c	deenu					0				12		...					0....	27149
92-BDAB-d	bangla					0				12		...					0....	27150
92-BDAB-e	samba-wangai					0				12		...					0....	27151
92-BDAB-f	sampara					0				12		...					0....	27152
92-BDAB-g	daga-nyonga					0				12		...					0....	27153
92-BDAB-h	nyong	2	2	34,408	59,252	0	41.15	74	B	12		...					0....	27154
92-BDAB-i	dong	1	1	7,482	12,282	0	0.09	19	A	12		...					0....	27155
92-BDAB-j	wom	2	2	26,949	46,691	0	40.00	70	B	12		...					0....	27156
92-BE	NIMBARI chain	1	1	4,525	7,945		30.01	60	B	4		...					0....	27157
92-BEA	**NIMBARI net**	1	1	4,525	7,945		30.01	60	B	4		...					0....	27158
92-BEAA	NIMBARI cluster	1	1	4,525	7,945		30.01	60	B	4		...					0....	27159
92-BEAA-a	nimbari	1	1	4,525	7,945	0	30.01	60	B	4		...					0....	27160
92-BF	KAM chain	1	1	5,285	8,676		30.01	57	B	0		...					0....	27161
92-BFA	**KAM net**	1	1	5,285	8,676		30.01	57	B	0		...					0....	27162
92-BFAA	KAM cluster	1	1	5,285	8,676		30.01	57	B	0		...					0....	27163
92-BFAA-a	kam	1	1	5,285	8,676	0	30.01	57	B	0		...					0....	27164
92-C	**MBUM-BUA set**	4	44	1,175,552	2,055,984		39.75	78	B	61		PNB					0.su.	27165
92-CA	BUA-LUA chain	1	8	31,831	57,628		6.93	29	A	8		...					0....	27166
92-CAA	**BUA-LUA net**	1	8	31,831	57,628		6.93	29	A	8		...					0....	27167
92-CAAA	NOY cluster	1	1	2,000	3,400		5.00	24	A	8		...					0....	27168
92-CAAA-a	noy	1	1	2,000	3,400	0	5.00	24	A	8		...					0....	27169
92-CAAB	LUA cluster	1	1	6,565	11,935		1.01	22	A	2		...					0....	27170
92-CAAB-a	niellim	1	1	6,565	11,935	0	1.01	22	A	2		...					0....	27171
92-CAAB-b	chini			0	0	0	0.00	0		2		...					0....	27172
92-CAAB-c	niou					0				2		...					0....	27173
92-CAAC	TUNYA cluster	1	1	2,869	5,216		20.01	42	A	0		...					0....	27174
92-CAAC-a	tunya	1	1	2,869	5,216	0	20.01	42	A	0		...					0....	27175
92-CAAC-b	perim			0	0	0	0.00	0		0		...					0....	27176
92-CAAD	BUA-KOKE cluster	1	2	10,575	19,222		2.26	24	A	5		...					0....	27177
92-CAAD-a	bua	1	1	9,811	17,834	0	0.10	21	A	5		...					0....	27178
92-CAAD-b	koke	1	1	764	1,388	0	29.97	57	B	5		...					0....	27181
92-CAAE	BOLGO cluster	1	1	2,296	4,174		30.01	53	B	2		...					0....	27182
92-CAAE-a	petit-bolgo	1	1	2,296	4,174	0	30.01	53	B	2		...					0....	27183
92-CAAE-b	grand-bolgo					0				2		...					0....	27184
92-CAAF	GULA-GUéRA cluster	1	1	1,528	2,777		4.97	25	A	3		...					0....	27185
92-CAAF-a	zan-gula					0				3		...					0....	27186
92-CAAF-b	taat-aal	1	1	1,528	2,777	0	4.97	25	A	3		...					0....	27187
92-CAAG	KULAAL cluster	1	1	4,599	8,360		10.00	37	A	3		...					0....	27188
92-CAAG-a	pon-aal					0				3		...					0....	27189
92-CAAG-b	ti-aala					0				3		...					0....	27190
92-CAAG-c	tiit-aal					0				3		...					0....	27191
92-CAAG-d	pat-ool					0				3		...					0....	27192
92-CAAG-e	korint-al					0				3		...					0....	27193
92-CAAH	FANIA cluster	1	1	1,399	2,544		0.07	16	A	2		...					0....	27194
92-CAAH-a	Proper fania	1	1	1,399	2,544	0	0.07	16	A	2		...					0....	27195
92-CAAH-b	mana					0				2		...					0....	27196
92-CB	DAY chain	1	1	63,544	115,511		50.00	88	B	41		PN.					0....	27197
92-CBA	**DAY net**	1	1	63,544	115,511		50.00	88	B	41		PN.					0....	27198
92-CBAA	DAY cluster	1	1	63,544	115,511		50.00	88	B	41		PN.					0....	27199
92-CBAA-a	day	1	1	63,544	115,511	0	50.00	88	B	41	Day	PN.		1989			0....	27200
92-CC	KIM-BESME chain	2	4	27,484	49,441		47.51	83	B	42		PN.					0....	27201
92-CCA	**KIM-BESME net**	2	4	27,484	49,441		47.51	83	B	42		PN.					0....	27202
92-CCAA	BESME cluster	2	2	3,732	6,263		30.01	56	B	4		...					0....	27203
92-CCAA-a	besme	2	2	3,732	6,263	0	30.01	56	B	4		...					0....	27204
92-CCAB	KIM cluster	1	2	23,752	43,178		50.26	87	B	42		PN.					0....	27205
92-CCAB-a	kim	1	1	19,545	35,530	0	60.00	99	C	42	Kim	PN.	1948	1955			0....	27206
92-CCAB-b	ere					0				42		pn.					0....	27207
92-CCAB-c	jumam	1	1	4,207	7,648	0	4.99	33	A	42		pn.					0....	27208
92-CCAB-d	kolobo					0				42		pn.					0....	27209
92-CCAB-e	kosop					0				42		pn.					0....	27210
92-CCAB-f	kilop					0				42		pn.					0....	27211
92-CD	MBUM-MAMBAI chain	4	29	993,166	1,728,894		41.96	82	B	61		PNB					0.su.	27212
92-CDA	**MBUM-MAMBAI net**	4	29	993,166	1,728,894		41.96	82	B	61		PNB					0.su.	27213
92-CDAA	TUPURI cluster	2	2	285,891	509,115		48.09	87	B	41	Tupuri	PN.		1988			0.s..	27214
92-CDAA-a	bang-ling					0				41		pn.					0.s..	27215
92-CDAA-b	bang-go					0				41		pn.					0.s..	27216
92-CDAA-c	bang-were					0				41		pn.					0.s..	27217

Continued opposite

Table 9-13 continued

Code 1	Reference Name / Autoglossonym 2	Coun 3	Peo 4	Mother-tongue speakers in 2000 5	in 2025 6	Media radio 7	AC% 8	E% 9	Wld 10	Tr 11	Biblioglossonym 12	Print 13-15	P-activity 16	N-activity 17	B-activity 18	J-year 19	Jayuh 20-24	Ref 25
92-CDAA-d	faale-piyew					0				41		pn.					0.s..	27218
92-CDAA-e	podokge					0				41		pn.					0.s..	27219
92-CDAA-f	kaele					0				41		pn.					0.s..	27220
92-CDAA-g	mata					0				41		pn.					0.s..	27221
92-CDAA-h	ndore					0				41		pn.					0.s..	27222
92-CDAB	MUNDANG cluster	2	2	304,247	546,818		38.66	81	B	61	Mundang	PNB	1933-1941	1948-1956	1983		0..u.	27223
92-CDAB-a	kiziere					0				61		pnb					0..u.	27224
92-CDAB-b	imbana					0				61		pnb					0..u.	27225
92-CDAB-c	yasing					0				61		pnb					0..u.	27226
92-CDAB-d	gelama					0				61		pnb					0..u.	27227
92-CDAC	MAMBAI cluster	2	2	4,165	7,383		49.99	81	B	4		...					0....	27228
92-CDAC-a	mambai	2	2	4,165	7,383	0	49.99	81	B	4		...					0....	27229
92-CDAD	DAMA-GALKE cluster	1	2	1,849	3,247		74.26	99	C	8		...					0....	27230
92-CDAD-a	mono	1	1	1,819	3,194	0	74.99	100	C	8		...					0....	27231
92-CDAD-b	ndai	1	1	30	53	0	30.00	57	B	8		...					0....	27232
92-CDAD-c	dama					0				8		...					0....	27233
92-CDAE	KARANG-MBUM cluster	4	21	397,014	662,331		39.84	78	B	44		PN.					0.s..	27234
92-CDAE-a	nzak-mbay	1	1	1,508	2,648	1	14.99	50	B	44	Nzakmbay	PN.		1968-1994			0.s..	27235
92-CDAE-b	gonge					1				44		pn.					0.s..	27236
92-CDAE-c	karang	3	4	125,668	203,090	1	36.67	79	B	44	Karre*	PN.	1931-1945	1947			0.s..	27237
92-CDAE-d	sakpu	1	1	11,575	20,321	1	60.00	98	C	44		pn.					0.s..	27238
92-CDAE-e	mbere	2	2	9,649	16,298	4	72.50	100	C	44	Gbaya: Mbere*	PN.	1933	1951			0.s..	27239
92-CDAE-f	kuo	2	2	14,493	26,159	1	20.00	52	B	44	Kuo	Pn.	1987-1993				0.s..	27240
92-CDAE-g	tale					1				44		pn.					0.s..	27244
92-CDAE-h	pana	4	4	117,709	192,042	1	48.68	86	B	44	Pana	Pn.	1953				0.s..	27245
92-CDAE-i	man					1				44		pn.					0.s..	27246
92-CDAE-j	pondo	1	1	15,085	26,484	1	40.00	78	B	44		pn.					0.s..	27247
92-CDAE-k	mbum	4	4	94,835	164,459	1	32.68	71	B	44	Mboum*	PN.	1936-1965	1965			0.s..	27248
92-CDAE-l	gbete					1				44		pn.					0.s..	27249
92-CDAE-m	oblo	1	1	1,508	2,648	1	30.04	64	B	44		pn.					0.s..	27250
92-CDAE-n	to					1				44		pn.					0.s..	27251
92-CE	FALI chain	1	2	59,527	104,510		6.00	34	A	42		PN.					0....	27252
92-CEA	**FALI net**	1	2	59,527	104,510		6.00	34	A	42		PN.					0....	27253
92-CEAA	NORTH FALI cluster	1	1	26,456	46,448		1.00	23	A	5		...					0....	27254
92-CEAA-a	durbayi					0				5		...					0....	27255
92-CEAA-b	North gobri					0				5		...					0....	27256
92-CEAA-c	bveri					0				5		...					0....	27257
92-CEAB	SOUTH FALI cluster	1	1	33,071	58,062		10.00	43	B	42	Fali*	PN.		1975			0....	27258
92-CEAB-a	South gobri					0				42		pn.					0....	27259
92-CEAB-b	kangu					0				42		pn.					0....	27260
92-CEAB-c	bele					0				42		pn.					0....	27261
92-CEAB-d	bonum					0				42		pn.					0....	27262
92-CEAB-e	yingilum					0				42		pn.					0....	27263
92-CF	GEY chain									9		...					0....	27264
92-CFA	**GEY net**									9		...					0....	27265
92-CFAA	GEY cluster			0	0		0.00	0		9		...					0....	27266
92-CFAA-a	gey			0	0	0	0.00	0		9		...					0....	27267
93	**UBANGIC zone**	8	130	6,794,446	12,185,523		68.85	95	C	72		PNB					4As..	27268
93-A	**BANDA-GBAYA set**	8	120	4,892,940	8,635,677		61.97	93	C	72		PNB					4.s..	27269
93-AA	GBAYA-NGBAKA chain	6	18	1,749,372	2,922,742		62.07	98	C	71		PNB					0.s..	27270
93-AAA	**GBAYA net**	6	18	1,749,372	2,922,742		62.07	98	C	71		PNB					0.s..	27271
93-AAAA	GBAYA cluster	6	16	1,742,492	2,910,246		62.10	98	C	71		PNB					0.s..	27272
93-AAAA-a	Vehicular gbaya	5	6	1,064,939	1,720,294	4	57.51	99	B	71	Gbaya: Gbea*	PNB	1933-1980	1982	1994		0.s..	27273
93-AAAA-b	gbeya					1				71		pnb					0.s..	27274
93-AAAA-c	suma					1				71		pnb					0.s..	27275
93-AAAA-d	manja	2	2	241,706	382,682	1	55.78	100	B	71	Manza	pnb					0.s..	27276
93-AAAA-e	budigri					1				71		pnb					0.s..	27277
93-AAAA-f	gbanu	1	1	101,116	159,531	1	40.00	85	B	71	Banu*	Pnb	1932-1939				0.s..	27278
93-AAAA-g	ali					1				71		pnb					0.s..	27279
93-AAAA-h	gbofi	1	1	25,013	39,463	1	60.00	90	C	71		pnb					0.s..	27280
93-AAAA-i	bokari					1				71		pnb					0.s..	27281
93-AAAA-j	somo					1				71		pnb					0.s..	27282
93-AAAA-k	Central gbaya	3	3	17,057	28,776	1	41.64	74	B	71		PNB					0.s..	27283
93-AAAA-l	ngbaka-gbaya	2	2	289,718	573,811	1	93.23	100	C	71		pnb					0.s..	27308
93-AAAA-m	bonjo	1	1	2,943	5,689	1	70.00	100	C	71		pnb					0.s..	27309
93-AAAB	BANGANDU cluster	2	2	6,880	12,496		55.15	91	B	2		...					0....	27310
93-AAAB-a	North bangandu					0				2		...					0....	27311
93-AAAB-b	South bangandu					0				2		...					0....	27312
93-AB	UBANGI-CENTRAL chain	6	52	2,372,359	4,299,626		64.25	93	C	72		PNB					4.s..	27313
93-ABA	**BANDA net**	5	41	1,444,583	2,649,100		64.04	91	C	22		P..					0....	27314
93-ABAA	YANGERE cluster	1	1	8,526	13,452		40.00	71	B	5		...					0....	27315
93-ABAA-a	yangere					0				5		...					0....	27316
93-ABAB	CENTRAL BANDA cluster	4	6	528,717	887,333		50.60	91	B	20		...					0....	27319
93-ABAB-a	banda-ndele	4	4	526,186	883,340	0	50.62	91	B	20	Banda, South Central	...					0....	27320
93-ABAB-b	tangbago	1	1	1,446	2,282	0	45.02	81	B	20		...					0....	27321
93-ABAB-c	ngao					0				20		...					0....	27322
93-ABAB-d	junguru	1	1	1,085	1,711	0	44.98	81	B	20		...					0....	27323
93-ABAB-e	banda-kpaya					0				20		...					0....	27324
93-ABAC	NDI cluster	2	4	11,453	18,044		38.49	71	B	4		...					0....	27329
93-ABAC-a	mbiyi					0				4		...					0....	27330
93-ABAC-b	Proper ndi	1	1	3,443	5,432	0	49.99	85	B	4		...					0....	27331
93-ABAC-c	ngalabo					0				4		...					0....	27332
93-ABAC-d	ngola	1	1	3,615	5,704	0	40.00	72	B	4		...					0....	27333
93-ABAC-e	vidiri	2	2	4,395	6,908	0	28.24	59	B	4		...					0....	27334
93-ABAC-f	North gbaga					0				4		...					0....	27335
93-ABAC-g	gbambiya					0				4		...					0....	27336
93-ABAC-h	hai					0				4		...					0....	27337
93-ABAC-i	ka					0				4		...					0....	27338
93-ABAC-j	banda-banda					0				4		...					0....	27339
93-ABAC-k	bereya					0				4		...					0....	27340
93-ABAD	TOGBO-NDOKPA cluster	2	2	31,404	58,912		56.45	87	B	4		...					0....	27341
93-ABAD-a	togbo	2	2	31,404	58,912	0	56.45	87	B	4		...					0....	27342
93-ABAD-b	baba					0				4		...					0....	27343
93-ABAD-c	bada					0				4		...					0....	27344
93-ABAD-d	baragra					0				4		...					0....	27345
93-ABAD-e	gbakpatili					0				4		...					0....	27346
93-ABAD-f	kana					0				4		...					0....	27347
93-ABAD-g	ndara					0				4		...					0....	27348
93-ABAD-h	pata					0				4		...					0....	27349

Continued overleaf

Table 9-13 continued

Code 1	REFERENCE NAME / Autoglossonym 2	Coun 3	Peo 4	Mother-tongue speakers in 2000 5	in 2025 6	Media radio 7	AC% 8	E% 9	Wld 10	Tr 11	Biblioglossonym 12	Print 13-15	P-activity 16	N-activity 17	B-activity 18	J-year 19	Jayuh 20-24	Ref 25
93-ABAD-i	vara					0				4		. . .					0. . . .	27350
93-ABAE	LINDA-JETO cluster	1	1	72,408	114,237		40.00	74	B	0		. . .					0. . . .	27351
93-ABAE-a	joto					0				0		. . .					0. . . .	27352
93-ABAE-b	ndokpa					0				0		. . .					0. . . .	27353
93-ABAE-c	ngapo					0				0		. . .					0. . . .	27354
93-ABAE-d	linda					0				0		. . .					0. . . .	27355
93-ABAE-e	ngasa					0				0		. . .					0. . . .	27356
93-ABAE-f	mbala					0				0		. . .					0. . . .	27357
93-ABAF	GUBU-YAKPA cluster	4	10	222,019	434,732		57.83	89	B	20		. . .					0. . . .	27358
93-ABAF-a	mono	1	1	112,498	228,217	0	70.00	100	C	20	Mono	. . .					0. . . .	27359
93-ABAF-b	wasa	1	1	1,446	2,282		30.01	60	B	20		. . .					0. . . .	27364
93-ABAF-c	bongo					0				20		. . .					0. . . .	27365
93-ABAF-d	dukpu	1	1	5,898	9,253	0	20.01	49	A	20		. . .					0. . . .	27366
93-ABAF-e	wojo	1	1	1,446	2,282		50.00	87	B	20		. . .					0. . . .	27367
93-ABAF-f	yakpa	3	3	48,659	88,692	0	30.97	60	B	20		. . .					0. . . .	27368
93-ABAF-g	gubu	2	2	24,380	47,829		64.07	94	C	20		. . .					0. . . .	27369
93-ABAF-h	belingo					0				20		. . .					0. . . .	27370
93-ABAF-i	buru					0				20		. . .					0. . . .	27371
93-ABAF-j	mbulu					0				20		. . .					0. . . .	27372
93-ABAF-k	nori					0				20		. . .					0. . . .	27373
93-ABAF-l	gbende					0				20		. . .					0. . . .	27374
93-ABAF-m	ngbundu	1	1	27,692	56,177	0	60.00	98	B	20		. . .					0. . . .	27375
93-ABAG	WADA-BUKA cluster	2	4	10,961	17,240		32.91	62	B	0		. . .					0. . . .	27376
93-ABAG-a	sabanga	1	1	2,170	3,423	0	40.00	66	B	0		. . .					0. . . .	27377
93-ABAG-b	maraba	1	1	1,085	1,711	0	49.95	81	B	0		. . .					0. . . .	27378
93-ABAG-c	mbre					0				0		. . .					0. . . .	27379
93-ABAG-d	buka					0				0		. . .					0. . . .	27380
93-ABAG-e	wada	2	2	7,706	12,106		28.51	58	B	0		. . .					0. . . .	27381
93-ABAH	LAGBA-NGBUGU cluster	2	3	58,098	98,660		38.91	70	B	4		. . .					0. . . .	27382
93-ABAH-a	langba					0				4		. . .					0. . . .	27383
93-ABAH-b	langbashe	2	2	47,767	77,702	0	34.35	65	B	4		. . .					0. . . .	27384
93-ABAH-c	ngbugu	1	1	10,331	20,958	0	60.00	92	C	4		. . .					0. . . .	27385
93-ABAI	GBI-GOLO cluster	3	3	24,878	43,869		42.78	78	B	0		. . .					0. . . .	27386
93-ABAI-a	gbi	1	1	10,331	20,958	0	50.00	86	B	0		. . .					0. . . .	27387
93-ABAI-b	dakpwa	1	1	10,056	15,865	0	50.00	89	B	0		. . .					0. . . .	27388
93-ABAI-c	vita					0				0		. . .					0. . . .	27389
93-ABAI-d	golo	1	1	4,491	7,046	0	10.00	35	A	0		. . .					0. . . .	27390
93-ABAI-e	South gbaga					0				0		. . .					0. . . .	27391
93-ABAJ	NGUNDU-KPAGUA cluster	2	3	14,055	26,835		64.10	83	C	4		. . .					0. . . .	27392
93-ABAJ-a	ngundu	1	1	5,165	10,479	0	80.00	100	C	4		. . .					0. . . .	27393
93-ABAJ-b	kpagua	2	2	8,890	16,356	0	54.86	74	B	4		. . .					0. . . .	27396
93-ABAK	MBANJA-MBANZA cluster	3	4	462,064	935,786		92.81	100	C	22		P. .					0. . . .	27397
93-ABAK-a	mbanja	1	1	193,358	392,251	0	92.00	100	C	22		p. .					0. . . .	27398
93-ABAK-b	mbanza	3	3	268,706	543,535	0	93.40	100	C	22	Mbanza	P. .	1986				0. . . .	27399
93-ABB	**NGBANDI-SANGO net**	5	11	927,776	1,650,526		64.58	96	C	72		PNB					4.s. .	27402
93-ABBA	NGBANDI-SANGO cluster	5	11	927,776	1,650,526		64.58	96	C	72		PNB					4.s. .	27403
93-ABBA-a	sango	5	5	468,719	770,975	4	53.19	100	B	72	Sango	PNB	1927-1993	1935-1993	1966	1988	4.s. .	27404
93-ABBA-b	ngbandi	2	3	335,179	678,405	1	92.51	100	C	72	Ngbandi	PNb	1935-1959	1988			1.s. .	27405
93-ABBA-c	yakoma	2	2	119,088	193,590	1	31.59	72	B	72		pnb					1.s. .	27414
93-ABBA-d	kpatili	1	1	4,790	7,556	1	44.99	87	B	72		pnb					1.s. .	27415
93-ABBA-e	mongoba					1				72		pnb					1.s. .	27416
93-ABBA-f	kazibati					1				72		pnb					1.s. .	27417
93-AC	SERE-FEROGE chain	3	13	113,136	192,380		31.01	64	B	22		P. .					0. . . .	27418
93-ACA	**NDOGO-SERE net**	3	8	61,694	111,677		46.37	81	B	22		P. .					0. . . .	27419
93-ACAA	SERE cluster	2	2	6,471	13,113		44.86	78	B	4		. . .					0. . . .	27420
93-ACAA-a	North sere					0				4		. . .					0. . . .	27421
93-ACAA-b	South sere					0				4		. . .					0. . . .	27422
93-ACAB	NDOGO-TAGBU cluster	3	6	55,223	98,564		46.55	82	B	22		P. .					0. . . .	27423
93-ACAB-a	ndogo	3	3	29,472	48,632	0	48.75	84	B	22	Ndogo	P. .	1985-1990				0. . . .	27424
93-ACAB-b	tagbu	3	3	25,751	49,932	0	44.03	78	B	22		p. .					0. . . .	27425
93-ACB	**BAI-VIRI net**	1	2	38,178	59,894		10.00	41	A	12		. . .					0. . . .	27426
93-ACBA	BAI-VIRI cluster	1	2	38,178	59,894		10.00	41	A	12		. . .					0. . . .	27427
93-ACBA-a	b-viri	1	1	33,020	51,802	0	10.00	42	A	12	Belanda Viri	. . .					0. . . .	27428
93-ACBA-b	bai	1	1	5,158	8,092	0	10.00	37	A	12		. . .					0. . . .	27429
93-ACC	**INDRI-KALI net**	1	3	13,264	20,809		20.00	49	A	9		. . .					0. . . .	27430
93-ACCA	INDRI-TOGOYO cluster	1	1	920	1,443		20.00	47	A	9		. . .					0. . . .	27431
93-ACCA-a	togoyo					0				9		. . .					0. . . .	27432
93-ACCA-b	indri	1	1	920	1,443		20.00	47	A	9		. . .					0. . . .	27433
93-ACCB	KALI-BUGA cluster	1	2	12,344	19,366		20.00	49	A	5		. . .					0. . . .	27434
93-ACCB-a	buga	1	1	510	800	0	20.00	47	A	5		. . .					0. . . .	27435
93-ACCB-b	kali-gi	1	1	11,834	18,566	0	20.00	49	A	5		. . .					0. . . .	27436
93-AD	NGBAKA-YANGO chain	5	28	378,669	679,365		57.07	82	B	61		PNB					0.s. .	27437
93-ADA	**GBANZIRI-BURAKA net**	3	5	25,418	43,475		34.68	63	B	4		. . .					0. . . .	27438
93-ADAA	GBANZIRI cluster	2	2	20,325	34,272		37.59	66	B	4		. . .					0. . . .	27439
93-ADAA-a	North gbanziri					0				4		. . .					0. . . .	27440
93-ADAA-b	South gbanziri					0				4		. . .					0. . . .	27441
93-ADAB	BURAKA cluster	3	3	5,093	9,203		23.05	49	A	4		. . .					0. . . .	27442
93-ADAB-a	buraka	3	3	5,093	9,203	0	23.05	49	A	4		. . .					0. . . .	27443
93-ADB	**NGBAKA-GILIMA net**	3	6	227,924	411,332		78.09	99	C	61		PNB					0.s. .	27444
93-ADBA	NGBAKA cluster	3	5	207,154	369,197		78.90	99	C	61	Ngbaka	PNB	1936-1989	1983	1995		0.s. .	27445
93-ADBA-a	ngbaka-ma'bo	3	4	203,592	362,313	0	78.88	99	C	61	Ngbaka: Ma'bo*	Pnb	1936-1937				0.s. .	27446
93-ADBA-b	ngbaka-limba					0				61		pnb					0.s. .	27447
93-ADBB	GILIMA cluster	1	1	20,770	42,135		70.00	100	C	2		. . .					0. . . .	27448
93-ADBB-a	bogon					0				2		. . .					0. . . .	27449
93-ADBB-b	mbanza-balakpa	1	1	20,770	42,135	0	70.00	100	C	2		. . .					0. . . .	27450
93-ADBB-c	bandi-gilima					0				2		. . .					0. . . .	27451
93-ADC	**NZOMBO-KPALA net**	4	6	32,524	62,421		41.97	75	B	6		. . .					0. . . .	27452
93-ADCA	NZOMBO cluster	3	3	17,504	34,115		37.48	71	B	4		. . .					0. . . .	27453
93-ADCA-a	mo-nzombo	3	3	17,504	34,115	0	37.48	71	B	4		. . .					0. . . .	27454
93-ADCB	KPALA cluster	1	1	4,892	9,923		40.00	77	B	4		. . .					0. . . .	27455
93-ADCB-a	kpala	1	1	4,892	9,923	0	40.00	77	B	4		. . .					0. . . .	27456
93-ADCC	YANGO cluster	2	2	10,128	18,383		50.68	83	B	6		. . .					0. . . .	27457
93-ADCC-a	yango	2	2	10,128	18,383	0	50.68	83	B	6		. . .					0. . . .	27458
93-ADD	**BAKA-GUNDI net**	5	11	92,803	162,137		16.89	45	A	12		. . .					0. . . .	27459

Continued opposite

Table 9-13 continued

Code 1	REFERENCE NAME / Autoglossonym 2	Coun 3	Peo 4	Mother-tongue speakers in 2000 5	in 2025 6	Media radio 7	AC% 8	E% 9	Wld 10	Tr 11	Biblioglossonym 12	Print 13-15	P-activity 16	N-activity 17	B-activity 18	J-year 19	Jayuh 20-24	Ref 25
93-ADDA	BAKA-NGOMBE cluster	5	11	92,803	162,137		16.89	45	A	12		...					0....	27460
93-ADDA-a	baka	3	3	57,927	99,304	0	10.00	38	A	12		...					0....	27461
93-ADDA-b	yaka					0				12		...					0....	27465
93-ADDA-c	ganzi	2	2	4,139	7,471	0	50.81	80	B	12		...					0....	27466
93-ADDA-d	gundi	3	4	18,863	31,970	0	27.03	55	B	12		...					0....	27467
93-ADDA-e	bayanga					0				12		...					0....	27468
93-ADDA-f	ngombe-kaka	1	1	1,543	2,434	0	39.99	67	B	12		...					0....	27469
93-ADDA-g	mbunjo					0				12		...					0....	27470
93-ADDA-h	bomassa	1	1	10,331	20,958	0	20.00	49	A	12		...					0....	27471
93-AE	MAYOGO-MUNDU chain	2	5	214,454	409,804		62.85	84	C	22		P..					0....	27472
93-AEA	**MAYOGO-BANGBA net**	1	2	154,411	313,242		80.99	97	C	20		...					0....	27473
93-AEAA	MAYOGO cluster	1	1	140,635	285,295		85.00	100	C	20		...					0....	27474
93-AEAA-a	mangbele-mayogo	1	1	140,635	285,295	0	85.00	100	C	20	Mayogo	...					0....	27475
93-AEAA-b	mabozo					0				20		...					0....	27476
93-AEAA-c	dimadoko					0				20		...					0....	27477
93-AEAA-d	magbai					0				20		...					0....	27478
93-AEAA-e	ba-lika					0				20		...					0....	27479
93-AEAB	BANGBA cluster	1	1	13,776	27,947		40.00	70	B	3		...					0....	27480
93-AEAB-a	alo					0				3		...					0....	27481
93-AEAB-b	koko					0				3		...					0....	27482
93-AEAB-c	merei					0				3		...					0....	27483
93-AEAB-d	makudukudu					0				3		...					0....	27484
93-AEAB-e	moco					0				3		...					0....	27485
93-AEAB-f	tibu					0				3		...					0....	27486
93-AEB	**MUNDU net**	2	3	60,043	96,562		16.23	49	A	22		P..					0....	27487
93-AEBA	MUNDU cluster	2	3	60,043	96,562		16.23	49	A	22		P..					0....	27488
93-AEBA-a	o-mundu					0				22							0....	27489
93-AEBA-b	mundu-shatt	2	3	60,043	96,562	0	16.23	49	A	22	Mundu	P..	1983-1995				0....	27490
93-AEBA-c	yogo					0				22		p..					0....	27491
93-AF	MBA-NDUNGA chain	1	2	41,969	85,140		64.41	96	C	4		...					0....	27492
93-AFA	**MBA net**	1	1	36,587	74,221		68.00	100	C	2		...					0....	27493
93-AFAA	MBA cluster	1	1	36,587	74,221		68.00	100	C	2		...					0....	27494
93-AFAA-a	mba-ni	1	1	36,587	74,221	0	68.00	100	C	2		...					0....	27495
93-AFB	**NDUNGA net**	1	1	5,382	10,919		40.00	68	B	4		...					0....	27496
93-AFBA	NDUNGA cluster	1	1	5,382	10,919		40.00	68	B	4		...					0....	27497
93-AFBA-a	ndunga-le	1	1	5,382	10,919	0	40.00	68	B	4		...					0....	27498
93-AG	MA-DONGO chain	1	2	22,981	46,620		40.00	73	B	4		...					0....	27499
93-AGA	**MA net**	1	1	10,114	20,517		40.00	73	B	4		...					0....	27500
93-AGAA	MA cluster	1	1	10,114	20,517		40.00	73	B	4		...					0....	27501
93-AGAA-a	a-ma-ro	1	1	10,114	20,517	0	40.00	73	B	4		...					0....	27502
93-AGB	**DONGO net**	1	1	12,867	26,103		40.00	73	B	4		...					0....	27503
93-AGBA	DONGO cluster	1	1	12,867	26,103		40.00	73	B	4		...					0....	27504
93-AGBA-a	dongo-ko	1	1	12,867	26,103	0	40.00	73	B	4		...					0....	27505
93-B	**ZANDE-PAMBIA set**	3	10	1,901,506	3,549,846		86.55	100	C	61		PNB					4As..	27506
93-BA	ZANDE chain	3	10	1,901,506	3,549,846		86.55	100	C	61		PNB					4As..	27507
93-BAA	**ZANDE net**	3	7	1,795,260	3,348,472		87.46	100	C	61		PNB					4As..	27508
93-BAAA	ZANDE cluster	3	7	1,795,260	3,348,472		87.46	100	C	61		PNB					4As..	27509
93-BAAA-a	pa-zande	3	4	1,739,906	3,260,441	0	87.54	100	C	61	Pazande*	PNB	1918-1952	1938-1952	1978	1990	4As..	27510
93-BAAA-b	patri					0				61		pnb					1cs..	27511
93-BAAA-c	kporo-nzakara	2	2	54,769	87,108	0	85.00	100	C	61		pnb					1cs..	27512
93-BAAA-d	ma-karaka					0				61		pnb					1cs..	27513
93-BAAA-e	dio					0				61		pnb					1cs..	27514
93-BAAA-f	geme	1	1	585	923	0	64.96	94	C	61		pnb					1cs..	27515
93-BAB	**BARAMBU-PAMBIA net**	2	3	106,246	201,374		71.13	95	C	4		...					0....	27516
93-BABA	PAMBIA cluster	2	2	69,112	126,042		66.37	93	C	4		...					0....	27517
93-BABA-a	pa-pambia	2	2	69,112	126,042	0	66.37	93	C	4		...					0....	27518
93-BABB	BARAMBU cluster	1	1	37,134	75,332		80.00	100	C	4		...					0....	27519
93-BABB-a	barambu-ro	1	1	37,134	75,332	0	80.00	100	C	4		...					0....	27520
93-BABB-b	pa-miangba					0				4		...					0....	27521
94	**MELIC zone**	3	13	2,154,278	3,697,735		6.32	50	B	57		PN.					3....	27522
94-A	**NORTH MEL set**	2	3	1,240,021	2,066,291		5.48	52	B	42		PN.					3....	27523
94-AA	NORTH MEL chain	2	3	1,240,021	2,066,291		5.48	52	B	42		PN.					3....	27524
94-AAA	**NORTH MEL net**	2	3	1,240,021	2,066,291		5.48	52	B	42		PN.					3....	27525
94-AAAA	LANDUMA-TYAPI cluster	1	1	18,040	30,341		5.00	29	A	2		...					0....	27526
94-AAAA-a	tyapi			0	0	0	0.00	0	A	2		...					0....	27527
94-AAAA-b	landuma	1	1	18,040	30,341	0	5.00	29	A	2		...					0....	27528
94-AAAB	BAGA cluster	1	1	11,000	18,700		5.00	24	A	0		...					0....	27529
94-AAAB-a	baga-maduri					0				0		...					0....	27530
94-AAAB-b	baga-sitemu					0				0		...					0....	27531
94-AAAB-c	baga-binari					0				0		...					0....	27532
94-AAAB-d	baga-sobane					0				0		...					0....	27533
94-AAAB-e	baga-koba					0				0		...					0....	27534
94-AAAC	TEMNE cluster	2	2	1,210,981	2,017,250		5.49	52	B	42		PN.					3....	27535
94-AAAC-a	ka-themne	2	2	1,210,981	2,017,250	4	5.49	52	B	42	Themne	PN.	1865-1993	1868-1955			3....	27536
94-B	**SOUTH MEL set**	3	10	914,257	1,631,444		7.47	48	A	57		PN.					3....	27543
94-BA	KISI-BOLOM chain	3	8	787,199	1,368,870		8.32	50	B	57		PN.					3....	27544
94-BAA	**BOLOM-KRIM net**	1	4	171,506	285,659		7.89	43	A	27		P..					0....	27545
94-BAAA	BULLOM cluster	1	3	159,807	266,173		7.74	43	A	27		P..					0....	27546
94-BAAA-a	bolom	1	1	8,350	13,907	0	4.99	35	A	27	Bullom*	P..	1816				0....	27547
94-BAAA-b	shebra	1	1	145,777	242,806	0	8.00	44	A	27		p..					0....	27550
94-BAAA-c	bom	1	1	5,680	9,460	0	5.00	29	A	27		p..					0....	27553
94-BAAB	KRIM cluster	1	1	11,699	19,486		10.00	41	A	6		...					0....	27554
94-BAAB-a	krim	1	1	11,699	19,486	0	10.00	41	A	6		...					0....	27555
94-BAB	**KISI net**	3	4	615,693	1,083,211		8.44	53	B	57		PN.					3....	27556

Continued overleaf

Table 9-13 continued

Code 1	REFERENCE NAME / Autoglossonym 2	Coun 3	Peo 4	Mother-tongue speakers in 2000 5	in 2025 6	Media radio 7	AC% 8	E% 9	Wld 10	Tr 11	Biblioglossonym 12	Print 13-15	P-activity 16	N-activity 17	B-activity 18	J-year 19	Jayuh 20-24	Ref 25
94-BABA	KISI cluster	3	4	615,693	1,083,211		8.44	53	B	57		PN.					3....	27557
94-BABA-a	North kisi	2	2	404,510	679,594	5	7.66	53	B	57	Kisi: Northern*	PN.	1935-1968	1966-1986		1997	3....	27558
94-BABA-b	South kisi	2	2	211,183	403,617	1	9.93	52	B	57	Kisi: Southern*	PN.	1982-1987	1991			1....	27563
94-BB	GOLA chain	2	2	127,058	262,574		2.17	33	A	20		...					0....	27564
94-BBA	**GOLA net**	2	2	127,058	262,574		2.17	33	A	20		...					0....	27565
94-BBAA	GOLA cluster	2	2	127,058	262,574		2.17	33	A	20	Gola	...					0....	27566
94-BBAA-a	mana-gobla					1				20		...					0....	27567
94-BBAA-b	kongbaa					1				20		...					0....	27568
94-BBAA-c	kpo					1				20		...					0....	27569
94-BBAA-d	senje					1				20		...					0....	27570
94-BBAA-e	tege					1				20		...					0....	27571
94-BBAA-f	toldil					1				20		...					0....	27572
95	**KRU-GREBIC zone**	8	52	2,879,971	5,166,301		40.79	82	B	57		PN.					0....	27573
95-A	**KRU set**	7	51	2,860,403	5,128,070		41.03	82	B	57		PN.					0....	27574
95-AA	KUWAA chain	1	1	15,183	31,855		45.00	86	B	41		PN.					0....	27575
95-AAA	**KUWAA net**	1	1	15,183	31,855		45.00	86	B	41		PN.					0....	27576
95-AAAA	KUWAA cluster	1	1	15,183	31,855		45.00	86	B	41		PN.					0....	27577
95-AAAA-a	kuwaa	1	1	15,183	31,855	1	45.00	86	B	41	Kuwaa	PN.	1982	1989			0....	27578
95-AB	KRU-CENTRAL chain	7	49	2,829,442	5,071,303		40.73	82	B	57		PN.					0....	27581
95-ABA	**KRU-CENTRAL net**	7	49	2,829,442	5,071,303		40.73	82	B	57		PN.					0....	27582
95-ABAA	DE cluster	1	1	9,608	20,159		42.00	81	B	4		...					0....	27583
95-ABAA-a	dewen-wulu	1	1	9,608	20,159	0	42.00	81	B	4		...					0....	27584
95-ABAB	BASOO cluster	2	2	418,037	874,622		45.95	99	B	51		PN.					0....	27590
95-ABAB-a	Central basoo	2	2	418,037	874,622	4	45.95	99	B	51	Bassa: Liberia	PN.	1844-1988	1970			0....	27591
95-ABAB-b	gbezon					1				51		pn.					0....	27592
95-ABAB-c	nasan					1				51		pn.					0....	27593
95-ABAB-d	hwen-gbakon					1				51		pn.					0....	27594
95-ABAB-e	gibii					1				51		pn.					0....	27595
95-ABAB-f	kokoja					1				51		pn.					0....	27596
95-ABAB-g	gboo					1				51		pn.					0....	27597
95-ABAB-h	koo					1				51		pn.					0....	27598
95-ABAB-i	nibune-xwinin					1				51		pn.					0....	27599
95-ABAB-j	gme-wiin					1				51		pn.					0....	27600
95-ABAB-k	ni-xwinin					1				51		pn.					0....	27601
95-ABAB-l	mabahn					1				51		pn.					0....	27602
95-ABAC	LOWOLU-BELETO cluster	1	1	2,000	3,400		40.00	77	B	0		...					0....	27603
95-ABAC-a	lowolu					0				0		...					0....	27604
95-ABAC-b	beleto					0				0		...					0....	27605
95-ABAD	GBII-LOBOO cluster	1	1	6,643	13,937		40.00	77	B	2		...					0....	27606
95-ABAD-a	kpoloo					1				2		...					0....	27607
95-ABAD-b	loboo					1				2		...					0....	27608
95-ABAD-c	gbii	1	1	6,643	13,937	1	40.00	77	B	2		...					0....	27609
95-ABAE	KLAO cluster	4	5	262,498	539,708		53.16	99	B	41		PN.					0....	27610
95-ABAE-a	kabo					1				41		pn.					0....	27611
95-ABAE-b	Southeast klao					1				41		pn.					0....	27612
95-ABAE-c	troo					1				41		pn.					0....	27628
95-ABAE-d	tajuoson	1	1	11,387	23,892	1	40.00	79	B	41	Tajuasohn	pn.					0....	27629
95-ABAE-e	tatue-kweatuo					1				41		pn.					0....	27635
95-ABAE-f	Northwest klao					1				41		pn.					0....	27638
95-ABAE-g	Central klao	4	4	251,111	515,816	4	53.75	100	B	41	Kru*	PN.	1921-1989	1996			0....	27644
95-ABAF	WEDEBO-KPLEBO cluster	1	1	28,112	58,983		60.00	100	B	2		...					0....	27659
95-ABAF-a	kple-bo					0				2		...					0....	27660
95-ABAF-b	gbweta					0				2		...					0....	27661
95-ABAF-c	wede-bo	1	1	28,112	58,983	0	60.00	100	B	2		...					0....	27662
95-ABAF-d	sikli					0				2		...					0....	27663
95-ABAG	FOPO-BUA cluster	1	1	19,928	41,811		55.00	95	B	2		...					0....	27664
95-ABAG-a	fo-po					0				2		...					0....	27665
95-ABAG-b	bua					0				2		...					0....	27666
95-ABAG-c	gboa-o					0				2		...					0....	27667
95-ABAH	CHEDEPO-JEDEPO cluster	2	3	100,257	169,432		27.98	60	B	41		PN.					0....	27668
95-ABAH-a	jede-po	2	3	100,257	169,432	1	27.98	60	B	41	E Je*	PN.	1838-1987	1989			0....	27669
95-ABAH-b	kle-po					1				41		pn.					0....	27670
95-ABAH-c	chede-po					1				41		pn.					0....	27671
95-ABAH-d	tiem-po					1				41		pn.					0....	27672
95-ABAH-e	gbe-po					1				41		pn.					0....	27673
95-ABAH-f	pali-po					1				41		pn.					0....	27674
95-ABAI	NITIABO-KITIABO cluster	1	1	23,605	49,526		40.00	80	B	2		...					0....	27675
95-ABAI-a	kitia-po					0				2		...					0....	27676
95-ABAI-b	sa-bo					0				2		...					0....	27677
95-ABAI-c	nitia-bo	1	1	23,605	49,526	0	40.00	80	B	2		...					0....	27678
95-ABAI-d	we-bo					0				2		...					0....	27679
95-ABAJ	GBOLOO cluster	1	1	66,781	140,116		38.90	80	B	12	Grebo, Gboloo	...					0....	27680
95-ABAJ-a	gedere-bo					1				12		...					0....	27681
95-ABAJ-b	nyanoun					1				12		...					0....	27682
95-ABAJ-c	North tuo-bo					1				12		...					0....	27683
95-ABAJ-d	bia-bo					1				12		...					0....	27684
95-ABAJ-e	dedie-po					1				12		...					0....	27685
95-ABAK	GLOBO-GEDEBO cluster	1	1	31,540	66,175		49.00	88	B	2		...					0....	27686
95-ABAK-a	boro-bo					0				2		...					0....	27687
95-ABAK-b	nyene-bo					0				2		...					0....	27688
95-ABAK-c	doro-bo					0				2		...					0....	27689
95-ABAK-d	gede-bo					0				2		...					0....	27690
95-ABAK-e	glo-bo	1	1	31,540	66,175	0	49.00	88	B	2		...					0....	27691
95-ABAK-f	West trem-bo					0				2		...					0....	27692
95-ABAK-g	South tuo-bo					0				2		...					0....	27693
95-ABAL	GLEBO-JABO cluster	2	4	145,643	282,546		53.66	95	B	2		...					0....	27694
95-ABAL-a	ja-bo	1	2	67,243	141,085	1	49.31	92	B	2		...					0....	27695
95-ABAL-b	nya-bo					1				2		...					0....	27696
95-ABAL-c	wrel-po					1				2		...					0....	27697
95-ABAL-d	gle-bo	2	2	78,400	141,461	1	57.39	98	B	2		...					0....	27698
95-ABAM	TEPO-GLAWLO cluster	2	3	56,784	91,293		62.69	91	C	41		PN.					0....	27699
95-ABAM-a	glawlo					0				41		pn.					0....	27700
95-ABAM-b	ba-po-wi					0				41		pn.					0....	27701
95-ABAM-c	pla-wi					0				41		pn.					0....	27702
95-ABAM-d	hom-po					0				41		pn.					0....	27703
95-ABAM-e	wlo-po					0				41		pn.					0....	27704
95-ABAM-f	da-po					0				41		pn.					0....	27705
95-ABAM-g	te-po	2	3	56,784	91,293	0	62.69	91	C	41	Krumen: Southern*	PN.	1981	1995-1996			0....	27706
95-ABAM-h	yre-po					0				41		pn.					0....	27707

Continued opposite

Table 9-13 continued

Code 1	REFERENCE NAME / Autoglossonym 2	Coun 3	Peo 4	Mother-tongue speakers in 2000 5	in 2025 6	Media radio 7	CHURCH AC% 8	E% 9	Wld 10	Tr 11	Biblioglossonym 12	Print 13-15	P–activity 16	N–activity 17	B–activity 18	J-year 19	Jayuh 20-24	Ref 25
95-ABAN	DUGBO-PIE cluster	1	1	20,000	34,000		60.00	93	C	0		...					0....	27708
95-ABAN-a	abri-wi					0				0		...					0....	27709
95-ABAN-b	ule					0				0		...					0....	27710
95-ABAN-c	tre-wi					0				0		...					0....	27711
95-ABAN-d	dugbo					0				0		...					0....	27712
95-ABAN-e	pie					0				0		...					0....	27713
95-ABAN-f	hwane					0				0		...					0....	27720
95-ABAO	GLARO-TWABO cluster	1	1	4,626	9,706		42.00	80	B	12	Glaro-twabo	...					0....	27721
95-ABAO-a	glaro					1				12	Glaro-twabo	...					0....	27722
95-ABAO-b	twa-bo					1				12		...					0....	27723
95-ABAP	GLIO-UBI cluster	2	2	7,118	13,394		44.17	79	B	4		...					0....	27724
95-ABAP-a	glio					0				4		...					0....	27725
95-ABAP-b	ubi					0				4		...					0....	27726
95-ABAQ	DAHO-DOO cluster	1	1	7,025	11,091		20.00	53	B	4		...					0....	27727
95-ABAQ-a	daho					0				4		...					0....	27728
95-ABAQ-b	East doo					0				4		...					0....	27729
95-ABAR	WEE cluster	2	7	696,325	1,177,268		19.66	66	B	57	Guere*	PN.		1982-1987			0....	27730
95-ABAR-a	go-bo					1				57		pn.					0....	27731
95-ABAR-b	kana					1				57		pn.					0....	27732
95-ABAR-c	kono-bo					1				57		pn.					0....	27733
95-ABAR-d	cien	2	2	63,142	128,643	1	23.24	67	B	57	Krahn: Tchien*	PN.	1953-1994	1996		1997	0....	27734
95-ABAR-e	sa-po	1	1	37,483	78,644	1	30.00	71	B	57	Sapo	Pn.	1956				0....	27735
95-ABAR-f	gbazon					1				57		pn.					0....	27742
95-ABAR-g	plo					1				57		pn.					0....	27743
95-ABAR-h	gbo-bo	2	2	70,244	140,347	1	16.11	54	B	57	Krahn: Western*	PN.	1987	1995			0....	27744
95-ABAR-i	gba-bo					1				57		pn.					0....	27745
95-ABAR-j	kpeaply					1				57		pn.					0....	27746
95-ABAR-k	biai					1				57		pn.					0....	27747
95-ABAR-l	pewa					1				57		pn.					0....	27748
95-ABAR-m	nidru					1				57		pn.					0....	27749
95-ABAR-n	nia-bo					1				57		pn.					0....	27750
95-ABAR-o	welea					1				57		pn.					0....	27751
95-ABAR-p	beu-zarabaon					1				57		pn.					0....	27752
95-ABAR-q	fleo					1				57		pn.					0....	27755
95-ABAR-r	zaa					1				57		pn.					0....	27756
95-ABAR-s	nyeo					1				57		pn.					0....	27757
95-ABAR-t	zagna					1				57		pn.					0....	27758
95-ABAR-u	zibiao					1				57		pn.					0....	27759
95-ABAR-v	wobe	1	1	173,553	274,020	4	27.00	74	B	57	Wobe	PN.	1979	1984			0....	27760
95-ABAS	NYA-NYEDEBWA cluster	1	1	47,315	74,704		40.00	83	B	41		PN.					0....	27764
95-ABAS-a	nya-bwa	1	1	47,315	74,704	0	40.00	83	B	41	Nyabwa	PN.	1977	1991			0....	27765
95-ABAS-b	nyede-bwa					0				41		pn.					0....	27766
95-ABAT	KUYA cluster	1	1	11,233	17,735		40.00	79	B	22		P..					0....	27767
95-ABAT-a	kuya	1	1	11,233	17,735	0	40.00	79	B	22	Kouya	P..	1992				0....	27768
95-ABAU	WEST BETE cluster	2	3	364,233	588,415		44.72	83	B	57	Bete*	PN.	1978-1993	1982-1996			0....	27769
95-ABAU-a	dakwia					1				57		pn.					0....	27770
95-ABAU-b	deba-yo					1				57		pn.					0....	27771
95-ABAU-c	yoko-lo					1				57		pn.					0....	27772
95-ABAU-d	joko-lo					1				57		pn.					0....	27773
95-ABAU-e	gaponoroguhe					1				57		pn.					0....	27774
95-ABAU-f	tagura					1				57		pn.					0....	27775
95-ABAU-g	bog-wi					1				57		pn.					0....	27776
95-ABAU-h	gbalwa-no					1				57		pn.					0....	27777
95-ABAU-i	lob-we					1				57		pn.					0....	27778
95-ABAU-j	broku-ya					1				57		pn.					0....	27779
95-ABAU-k	gib-wa					1				57		pn.					0....	27780
95-ABAU-l	loz-wa					1				57		pn.					0....	27781
95-ABAU-m	zelmogbo					1				57		pn.					0....	27782
95-ABAU-n	jivo					1				57		pn.					0....	27783
95-ABAV	EAST BETE cluster	1	2	199,400	314,830		34.81	66	B	20		...					0....	27784
95-ABAV-a	Proper shyen	1	1	192,007	303,157	0	35.00	66	B	20	Bete, Gagnoa	...					0....	27785
95-ABAV-b	gbadi	1	1	7,393	11,673	0	30.00	60	B	20		...					0....	27786
95-ABAV-c	zehireku					0				20		...					0....	27787
95-ABAV-d	nekeide					0				20		...					0....	27788
95-ABAV-e	mahi-huo					0				20		...					0....	27789
95-ABAV-f	baru-hio					0				20		...					0....	27790
95-ABAW	SOUTHEAST BETE cluster	1	1	30,000	51,000		30.00	65	B	0		...					0....	27791
95-ABAW-a	ziko-bwe					0				0		...					0....	27792
95-ABAW-b	gida-bwe					0				0		...					0....	27793
95-ABAW-c	ge-bye					0				0		...					0....	27794
95-ABAX	DIDA cluster	1	2	216,317	341,539		70.00	100	C	24		P..					0....	27795
95-ABAX-a	vata					1				24		p..					0....	27796
95-ABAX-b	Central dida	1	1	103,501	163,416	2	70.00	100	C	24	Dida	P..	1930				0....	27801
95-ABAX-c	South dida	1	1	112,816	178,123	1	70.00	100	C	24	Dida, Yocoboue	P..	1930-1972				0....	27809
95-ABAY	GODYE cluster	1	3	40,645	64,174		37.62	74	B	22		P..					0....	27814
95-ABAY-a	koyi					0				22		p..					0....	27815
95-ABAY-b	kagbu					0				22		p..					0....	27816
95-ABAY-c	dagli					0				22		p..					0....	27817
95-ABAY-d	tiglu					0				22		p..					0....	27818
95-ABAY-e	nugbo					0				22		p..					0....	27819
95-ABAY-f	jluko					0				22		p..					0....	27820
95-ABAY-g	dlogo					0				22		p..					0....	27821
95-ABAY-h	nyago					0				22		p..					0....	27822
95-ABAY-i	glibe					0				22		p..					0....	27823
95-ABAY-j	kwadia-kotrohu	1	2	30,295	47,832	0	50.31	90	B	22	Godie	P..	1977				0....	27824
95-ABAY-k	ne-wole	1	1	10,350	16,342	0	0.50	27	A	22		p..					0....	27827
95-ABAZ	BAKWE cluster	1	2	13,769	21,739		44.16	80	B	12	Bakwe	...					0....	27828
95-ABAZ-a	da-prele					0				12		...					0....	27829
95-ABAZ-b	da-fale					0				12		...					0....	27830
95-ABAZ-c	da-ghaye					0				12		...					0....	27831
95-ABAZ-d	da-katele					0				12		...					0....	27832
95-ABAZ-e	magba					0				12		...					0....	27833
95-ABAZ-f	ngwane	1	1	2,332	3,682	0	40.01	73	B	12		...					0....	27834
95-AC	AIZI chain	1	1	15,778	24,912		91.00	100	C	4		...					0....	27835
95-ACA	**AIZI net**	1	1	15,778	24,912		91.00	100	C	4		...					0....	27836
95-ACAA	EDEYI cluster	1	1	15,778	24,912		91.00	100	C	4		...					0....	27837
95-ACAA-a	a-ïzi					0				4		...					0....	27838
95-ACAA-b	a-prwe					0				4		...					0....	27839
95-ACAA-c	a-brako					0				4		...					0....	27840
95-B	**SEME set**	1	1	19,568	38,231		5.00	28	A	12		...					0....	27841
95-BA	SEME chain	1	1	19,568	38,231		5.00	28	A	12		...					0....	27842
95-BAA	**SEME net**	1	1	19,568	38,231		5.00	28	A	12		...					0....	27843
95-BAAA	SEME cluster	1	1	19,568	38,231		5.00	28	A	12		...					0....	27844
95-BAAA-a	siamou	1	1	19,568	38,231	0	5.00	28	A	12	Siamou	...					0....	27845

Continued overleaf

Table 9-13 continued

Code 1	REFERENCE NAME / Autoglossonym 2	Coun 3	Peo 4	Mother-tongue speakers in 2000 5	in 2025 6	Media radio 7	CHURCH AC% 8	E% 9	Wld 10	Tr 11	Biblioglossonym 12	SCRIPTURES Print 13-15	P-activity 16	N-activity 17	B-activity 18	J-year 19	Jayuh 20-24	Ref 25
95-BAAA-b	bandugu					0				12		. . .					0. . . .	27846
96	**WEST AKANIC zone**	10	120	23,770,724	42,301,980		54.08	94	B	80		PNB					4Asu.	27847
96-A	**AVIKAM-ALADIAN set**	1	2	48,855	77,137		90.00	100	C	35		P . .					0. . . .	27848
96-AA	AVIKAM chain	1	1	23,317	36,815		90.00	100	C	23		P . .					0. . . .	27849
96-AAA	**AVIKAM net**	1	1	23,317	36,815		90.00	100	C	23		P . .					0. . . .	27850
96-AAAA	AVIKAM cluster	1	1	23,317	36,815		90.00	100	C	23		P . .					0. . . .	27851
96-AAAA-a	a-vikam	1	1	23,317	36,815	0	90.00	100	C	23	Avikam	P . .	1957				0. . . .	27852
96-AB	ALADIAN chain	1	1	25,538	40,322		90.00	100	C	35		P . .					0. . . .	27853
96-ABA	**ALADIAN net**	1	1	25,538	40,322		90.00	100	C	35		P . .					0. . . .	27854
96-ABAA	ALADIAN cluster	1	1	25,538	40,322		90.00	100	C	35		P . .					0. . . .	27855
96-ABAA-a	a-ladian	1	1	25,538	40,322	0	90.00	100	C	35	Alladian*	P . .	1937-1968				0. . . .	27856
96-B	**ABE-JUKRU set**	1	3	339,361	535,811		90.00	100	C	22		P . .					0.s . .	27857
96-BA	JUKRU chain	1	1	106,930	168,830		90.00	100	C	22		P . .					0.s . .	27858
96-BAA	**JUKRU net**	1	1	106,930	168,830		90.00	100	C	22		P . .					0.s . .	27859
96-BAAA	JUKRU cluster	1	1	106,930	168,830		90.00	100	C	22		P . .					0.s . .	27860
96-BAAA-a	mo-jukru	1	1	106,930	168,830	2	90.00	100	C	22	Adioukrou	P . .	1927-1994				0.s . .	27861
96-BB	ABIJI chain	1	1	56,074	88,534		90.00	100	C	22		P . .					0. . . .	27862
96-BBA	**ABIJI net**	1	1	56,074	88,534		90.00	100	C	22		P . .					0. . . .	27863
96-BBAA	ABIJI cluster	1	1	56,074	88,534		90.00	100	C	22	Abidji	P . .	1978-1988				0. . . .	27864
96-BBAA-a	a-ri					0				22		p . .					0. . . .	27865
96-BBAA-b	ogbru					0				22		p . .					0. . . .	27866
96-BBAA-c	enyembe					0				22		p . .					0. . . .	27867
96-BC	ABE chain	1	1	176,357	278,447		90.00	100	C	22		P . .					0. . . .	27868
96-BCA	**ABE net**	1	1	176,357	278,447		90.00	100	C	22		P . .					0. . . .	27869
96-BCAA	A-BE cluster	1	1	176,357	278,447		90.00	100	C	22	Abe	P . .	1967-1980				0. . . .	27870
96-BCAA-a	morie					0				22		p . .					0. . . .	27871
96-BCAA-b	ve					0				22		p . .					0. . . .	27872
96-BCAA-c	khos					0				22		p . .					0. . . .	27873
96-BCAA-d	tiofo					0				22		p . .					0. . . .	27874
96-C	**ATYE set**	1	1	422,875	667,670		88.00	100	C	41		PN .					0.s . .	27875
96-CA	ATYE chain	1	1	422,875	667,670		88.00	100	C	41		PN .					0.s . .	27876
96-CAA	**ATYE net**	1	1	422,875	667,670		88.00	100	C	41		PN .					0.s . .	27877
96-CAAA	ATYE cluster	1	1	422,875	667,670		88.00	100	C	41	Attie	PN .	1931-1991	1995			0.s . .	27878
96-CAAA-a	ketin					1				41		pn .					0.s . .	27879
96-CAAA-b	boden					1				41		pn .					0.s . .	27880
96-CAAA-c	nedin					1				41		pn .					0.s . .	27881
96-D	**EBRIE-MBATO set**	1	3	129,068	203,784		90.03	100	C	57		PN .					0.s . .	27882
96-DA	EBRIE chain	1	1	100,156	158,135		90.00	100	C	57		PN .					0.s . .	27883
96-DAA	**EBRIE net**	1	1	100,156	158,135		90.00	100	C	57		PN .					0.s . .	27884
96-DAAA	CAMA cluster	1	1	100,156	158,135		90.00	100	C	57		PN .					0.s . .	27885
96-DAAA-a	cama-ncan	1	1	100,156	158,135	2	90.00	100	C	57	Ebrie	PN .	1930-1991	1996			0.s . .	27886
96-DB	MBATO chain	1	1	27,759	43,828		90.00	100	C	2		. . .					0. . . .	27887
96-DBA	**MBATO net**	1	1	27,759	43,828		90.00	100	Wld	2		. . .					0. . . .	27888
96-DBAA	GWIA cluster	1	1	27,759	43,828		90.00	100	C	2		. . .					0. . . .	27889
96-DBAA-a	domolon					0				2		. . .					0. . . .	27890
96-DBAA-b	dabre					0				2		. . .					0. . . .	27891
96-DC	ESUMA chain	1	1	1,153	1,821		93.06	100	C	9		. . .					0. . . .	27892
96-DCA	**ESUMA net**	1	1	1,153	1,821		93.06	100	C	9		. . .					0. . . .	27893
96-DCAA	E-SUMA cluster	1	1	1,153	1,821		93.06	100	C	9		. . .					0. . . .	27894
96-DCAA-a	esuma					0				9		. . .					0. . . .	27895
96-E	**EGA set**	1	1	322	509		50.00	82	B	6		. . .					0. . . .	27896
96-EA	EGA chain	1	1	322	509		50.00	82	B	6		. . .					0. . . .	27897
96-EAA	**EGA net**	1	1	322	509		50.00	82	B	6		. . .					0. . . .	27898
96-EAAA	EGA cluster	1	1	322	509		50.00	82	B	6		. . .					0. . . .	27899
96-EAAA-a	e-ga	1	1	322	509	0	50.00	82	B	6		. . .					0. . . .	27900
96-F	**VOLTA-COMOÉ set**	6	49	13,100,867	23,148,528		50.93	96	B	80		PNB					4Asu.	27901
96-FA	ABULE-BETIBE chain	1	2	65,431	103,309		89.07	100	C	2		. . .					0. . . .	27902
96-FAA	**ABULE net**	1	1	61,204	96,635		89.00	100	C	2		. . .					27903
96-FAAA	A-BULE cluster	1	1	61,204	96,635		89.00	100	C	2		. . .					27904
96-FAAA-a	e-yive					0				2		. . .					0. . . .	27905
96-FAAA-b	e-hie					0				2		. . .					0. . . .	27906
96-FAAA-c	o-suan					0				2		. . .					0. . . .	27907
96-FAB	**BETIBE net**	1	1	4,227	6,674		90.02	100	C	0		. . .					0. . . .	27908
96-FABA	BE-TIBE cluster	1	1	4,227	6,674		90.02	100	C	0		. . .					0. . . .	27909
96-FABA-a	betibe-bassam					0				0		. . .					0. . . .	27910
96-FABA-b	betibe-adiake					0				0		. . .					0. . . .	27911
96-FB	KROBU chain	1	1	11,014	17,390		90.00	100	C	4		. . .					0. . . .	27912
96-FBA	**KROBU net**	1	1	11,014	17,390		90.00	100	C	4		. . .					0. . . .	27913
96-FBAA	KROBU cluster	1	1	11,014	17,390		90.00	100	C	4		. . .					0. . . .	27914
96-FBAA-a	krobu	1	1	11,014	17,390	0	90.00	100	C	4		. . .					0. . . .	27915
96-FC	BAULE-NZEMA chain	6	31	12,063,694	21,282,122		51.52	97%	B	80		PNB					4Asu.	27916

Continued opposite

Table 9-13 continued

Code 1	REFERENCE NAME / Autoglossonym 2	Coun 3	Peo 4	Mother-tongue speakers in 2000 5	in 2025 6	Media radio 7	CHURCH AC% 8	E% 9	Wld 10	Tr 11	Biblioglossonym 12	Print 13-15	P-activity 16	N-activity 17	B-activity 18	J-year 19	Jayuh 20-24	Ref 25
96-FCA	**BAULE-ANYI net**	4	8	3,081,114	5,010,118		49.54	97	B	80		PNB					4As..	27917
96-FCAA	BAULE cluster	1	1	1,803,052	2,846,811		49.00	99	B	80		PNB					4As..	27918
96-FCAA-a	Central baule	1	1	1,803,052	2,846,811	4	49.00	99	B	80	Baoule*	PNB	1946-1994	1953-1975	1996	1989	4As..	27919
96-FCAA-b	kode					1				80		pnb					1cs..	27920
96-FCAB	ANYI cluster	2	2	908,826	1,491,807		52.54	98	B	41		PN.					0....	27921
96-FCAB-a	Central a-nyi	2	2	908,826	1,491,807	2	52.54	98	B	41	Agni*	PN.	1927-1993	1995			0....	27922
96-FCAB-b	moronu-fwe					1				41		pn.					0....	27923
96-FCAB-c	bini					1				41		pn.					0....	27924
96-FCAB-d	bona					1				41		pn.					0....	27925
96-FCAB-e	joablin					1				41		pn.					0....	27926
96-FCAB-f	a-be					1				41	Abbey	Pn.	1967				0....	27927
96-FCAB-g	indenie					1				41		pn.					0....	27928
96-FCAB-h	sanvi					1				41		pn.					0....	27929
96-FCAB-i	e-bolosa					1				41		pn.					0....	27930
96-FCAB-j	a-no					1				41		pn.					0....	27931
96-FCAB-k	tiasale					1				41		pn.					0....	27932
96-FCAB-l	abiji-anyin					1				41		pn.					0....	27933
96-FCAB-m	a-fema					1				41		pn.					0....	27934
96-FCAB-n	aowin					1				41		pn.					0....	27935
96-FCAC	SEHWI cluster	2	2	241,977	438,929		64.36	99	C	20		. . .					0....	27936
96-FCAC-a	sehwi	2	2	241,977	438,929	0	64.36	99	C	20	Sehwi	. . .					0....	27937
96-FCAD	ANUFO cluster	3	3	127,259	232,571		7.59	44	A	22		P..					0....	27938
96-FCAD-a	anu-fo	3	3	127,259	232,571	0	7.59	44	A	22	Anufo	P..	1993				0....	27939
96-FCB	**NZEMA-AHANTA net**	2	4	586,098	1,051,140		66.55	99	C	41		PN.					1.s..	27940
96-FCBA	NZEMA cluster	2	2	446,405	796,281		67.22	100	C	41		PN.					1.s..	27941
96-FCBA-a	nzema	2	2	446,405	796,281	4	67.22	100	C	41	Nzema	PN.	1984	1985			1.s..	27942
96-FCBB	JWIRA-PEPESA cluster	1	1	16,793	30,637		60.00	92	C	2		. . .					0....	27943
96-FCBB-a	jwira					0				2		. . .					0....	27944
96-FCBB-b	pepesa					0				2		. . .					0....	27945
96-FCBC	AHANTA cluster	1	1	122,900	224,222		65.00	100	C	20		. . .					0....	27946
96-FCBC-a	a-hanta	1	1	122,900	224,222	0	65.00	100	C	20	Ahanta	. . .					0....	27947
96-FCC	**AKAN-BRONG net**	6	19	8,396,482	15,220,864		51.19	97	B	63		PNB					4ssu.	27948
96-FCCA	BRONG cluster	2	2	936,805	1,673,225		35.61	80	B	20		. . .					0....	27949
96-FCCA-a	gyaman					1				20		. . .					0....	27950
96-FCCA-b	brong-ahafo	2	2	936,805	1,673,225	4	35.61	80	B	20		. . .					0....	27951
96-FCCB	AKAN cluster	5	15	7,230,326	13,129,209		52.94	100	B	63		PNB					4ssu.	27957
96-FCCB-a	Standard akan					1				63	Akan	PNB	1859-1957	1863-1981	1871-1964	1994	1csu.	27958
96-FCCB-b	fante	3	3	2,330,566	4,256,949	4	48.57	99	B	63	Fante	PNB	1877	1896	1948	1994	2csu.	27959
96-FCCB-c	twi	5	12	4,899,760	8,872,260	4	55.02	100	B	63		PNB				1983	4ssu.	27966
96-FCCC	WASA cluster	1	1	228,074	416,104		60.00	100	B	20		. . .					0....	27979
96-FCCC-a	a-menfi					1				20		. . .					0....	27980
96-FCCC-b	fianse					1				20		. . .					0....	27981
96-FCCD	BASA cluster	1	1	1,277	2,326		10.02	39	A	6		. . .					0....	27982
96-FCCD-a	basa	1	1	1,277	2,326	0	10.02	39	A	6		. . .					0....	27983
96-FD	GUANG chain	3	15	960,728	1,745,707		40.53	76	B	41		PN.					1....	27984
96-FDA	**WUTU-GUA net**	1	4	366,720	669,053		60.00	99	C	20		. . .					0....	27985
96-FDAA	WUTU cluster	1	1	143,046	260,977		60.00	100	C	20		. . .					0....	27986
96-FDAA-a	Proper a-wutu	1	1	143,046	260,977	0	60.00	100	C	20		. . .					0....	27987
96-FDAA-b	e-futu					0				20		. . .					0....	27988
96-FDAB	GUA cluster	1	3	223,674	408,076		60.00	98	B	3		. . .					0....	27989
96-FDAB-a	okere-mmiri	1	1	101,315	184,842	0	60.00	97	C	3		. . .					0....	27990
96-FDAB-b	late	1	1	67,219	122,636	0	60.00	100	B	3		. . .					0....	27991
96-FDAB-c	a-num	1	1	55,140	100,598	0	60.00	100	C	3		. . .					0....	27992
96-FDAB-d	boso					0				3		. . .					0....	27993
96-FDB	**GONJA-DUMPO net**	2	2	361,945	654,071		13.13	51	B	41		PN.					1....	27994
96-FDBA	GONJA cluster	1	1	289,534	528,233		14.00	55	B	41	Gonja	PN.	1967-1974	1984			1....	27995
96-FDBA-a	n-gbandzi-to					0				41		pn.					1....	27996
96-FDBA-b	n-gbanye					0				41		pn.					1....	27999
96-FDBA-c	n-gbanyi-to					0				41		pn.					1....	28006
96-FDBB	CHORUBA cluster	1	1	30,000	51,000		14.00	41	A	0		. . .					0....	28011
96-FDBB-a	choruba					0				0		. . .					0....	28012
96-FDBC	DOMPO cluster	1	1	20,000	34,000		14.00	41	A	0		. . .					0....	28013
96-FDBC-a	n-dmpo	1	1	20,000	34,000	0	14.00	41	A	0		. . .					0....	28014
96-FDBD	PODO cluster	1	1	22,411	40,838		0.02	18	A	12		. . .					0....	28015
96-FDBD-a	foodo	1	1	22,411	40,838	0	0.02	18	A	12	Foodo	. . .					0....	28016
96-FDC	**YEJI-KRACHI net**	1	5	169,365	308,122		58.04	81	B	41		PN.					0....	28017
96-FDCA	KPLANG cluster	1	1	10,036	18,309		59.99	98	B	4		. . .					0....	28018
96-FDCA-a	kplang	1	1	10,036	18,309	0	59.99	98	B	4		. . .					0....	28019
96-FDCB	YEJI cluster	1	1	4,000	6,800		20.00	50	B	0		. . .					0....	28020
96-FDCB-a	yeji	1	1	4,000	6,800	0	20.00	50	B	0		. . .					0....	28021
96-FDCC	CHUMBURUNG cluster	1	1	50,503	92,139		8.00	44	A	41	Chumburung	PN.		1988			0....	28022
96-FDCC-a	North chumburung					0				41		pn.					0....	28023
96-FDCC-b	South chumburung					0				41		pn.					0....	28024
96-FDCD	CHUMBULU cluster	1	1	1,694	3,090		59.98	95	B	4		. . .					0....	28030
96-FDCD-a	n-chumbulu	1	1	1,694	3,090	0	59.98	95	B	4		. . .					0....	28031
96-FDCE	TSUMUNU cluster	1	1	14,304	26,097		60.00	95	C	3		. . .					0....	28032
96-FDCE-a	dwang	1	1	14,304	26,097	0	60.00	95	C	3		. . .					0....	28033
96-FDCE-b	kwame-danso					0				3		. . .					0....	28034
96-FDCE-c	bassa					0				3		. . .					0....	28035
96-FDCE-d	ewoase					0				3		. . .					0....	28036
96-FDCF	KRACHI cluster	1	1	85,828	156,587		90.00	100	C	20		. . .					0....	28037
96-FDCF-a	nkatekwan					0				20		. . .					0....	28038
96-FDCF-b	chantai					0				20		. . .					0....	28039
96-FDCG	TSUMBULI cluster	3	1	3,000	5,100		20.00	50	B	0		. . .					0....	28040
96-FDCG-a	tsumbuli	1	1	3,000	5,100	0	20.00	50	B	0		. . .					0....	28041
96-FDD	**NAWURI net**	1	1	11,580	21,126		25.00	64	B	12		. . .					0....	28042
96-FDDA	NAWURI cluster	1	1	11,580	21,126		25.00	64	B	12	Nawuri	. . .					0....	28043
96-FDDA-a	na-wura					0				12		. . .					0....	28044
96-FDDA-b	ka-wuri					0				12		. . .					0....	28045
96-FDE	**NKONYA net**	1	1	28,936	52,792		60.00	96	C	12		. . .					0....	28046

Continued overleaf

Table 9-13 continued

Code 1	REFERENCE NAME / Autoglossonym 2	Coun 3	Peo 4	Mother-tongue speakers in 2000 5	in 2025 6	Media radio 7	CHURCH AC% 8	E% 9	Wid 10	Tr 11	Biblioglossonym 12	SCRIPTURES Print 13-15	P–activity 16	N–activity 17	B–activity 18	J-year 19	Jayuh 20-24	Ref 25
96-FDEA	NKONYA cluster	1	1	28,936	52,792		60.00	96	C	12		. . .					0	28047
96-FDEA-a	n-konya	1	1	28,936	52,792	0	60.00	96	C	12	Nkonya	. . .					0	28048
96-FDF	**CHODE-NYANGA net**	2	2	22,182	40,543		14.72	48	A	22		P . .					0	28049
96-FDFA	GIKYODE cluster	1	1	13,033	23,778		4.00	38	A	22		P . .					0	28050
96-FDFA-a	gi-kyode	1	1	13,033	23,778	0	4.00	38	A	22	Gikyode	P . .	1986-1988				0	28051
96-FDFB	ANYANGA cluster	1	1	9,149	16,765		30.00	62	B	4		. . .					0	28052
96-FDFB-a	a-nyanga	1	1	9,149	16,765	0	30.00	62	B	4		. . .					0	28053
96-G	**ANI-LOGBA set**	3	5	41,990	76,239		32.77	68	B	41		PN .					0	28054
96-GA	ANI-ADELE chain	3	5	37,990	69,439		34.11	69	B	41		PN .					0	28055
96-GAA	**ADELE net**	2	2	23,845	43,609		20.56	56	B	41		PN .					0	28056
96-GAAA	ADELE cluster	2	2	23,845	43,609		20.56	56	B	41	Adele	PN .	1992-1993	1996			0	28057
96-GAAA-a	West gi-dire					0				41		pn .					0	28058
96-GAAA-b	East gi-dire					0				41		pn .					0	28059
96-GAB	**ANI-AKPE net**	2	3	14,145	25,830		56.95	91	B	4		. . .					0	28060
96-GABA	AKPE cluster	1	1	4,320	7,917		50.00	87	B	4		. . .					0	28061
96-GABA-a	gi-seme	1	1	4,320	7,917	0	50.00	87	B	4		. . .					0	28062
96-GABA-b	a-nanjubi					0				4		. . .					0	28063
96-GABB	ANII cluster	2	2	9,825	17,913		60.01	93	C	2		. . .					0	28064
96-GABB-a	gi-lempla					0				2		. . .					0	28065
96-GABB-b	gi-kolodjya					0				2		. . .					0	28066
96-GABB-c	gi-sida					0				2		. . .					0	28067
96-GB	LOGBA chain	1	1	4,000	6,800		20.00	50	B	0		. . .					0	28068
96-GBA	**LOGBA net**	1	1	4,000	6,800		20.00	50	B	0		. . .					0	28069
96-GBAA	EKPANA cluster	1	1	4,000	6,800		20.00	50	B	0		. . .					0	28070
96-GBAA-a	e-kpana	1	1	4,000	6,800	0	20.00	50	B	0		. . .					0	28071
96-H	**LELEMI-SANTROKOFI set**	3	7	166,732	294,032		62.40	80	C	41		PN .					0	28072
96-HA	LELEMI-AKPAFU chain	3	5	138,600	242,707		56.80	75	B	41		PN .					0	28073
96-HAA	**LELEMI net**	2	2	53,270	97,225		90.00	100	C	41		PN .					0	28074
96-HAAA	LELEMI cluster	2	2	53,270	97,225		90.00	100	C	41		PN .					0	28075
96-HAAA-a	le-lemi	2	2	53,270	97,225	0	90.00	100	C	41	Lelemi	PN .	1984	1995			0	28076
96-HAB	**AKPAFU-LOLOBI net**	2	3	85,330	145,482		36.07	60	B	4		. . .					0	28077
96-HABA	AKPAFU-LOLOBI cluster	2	3	85,330	145,482		36.07	60	B	4		. . .					0	28078
96-HABA-a	si-wu	1	1	20,983	38,281	0	90.00	100	C	4		. . .					0	28079
96-HABA-b	lo-lobi	1	1	8,594	15,680	0	80.00	100	C	4		. . .					0	28080
96-HB	LIKPE-SANTROKOFI chain	1	2	28,132	51,325		90.00	100	C	4		. . .					0	28081
96-HBA	**SANTROKOFI net**	1	1	8,582	15,658		90.00	100	C	2		. . .					0	28082
96-HBAA	SELE cluster	1	1	8,582	15,658		90.00	100	C	2		. . .					0	28083
96-HBAA-a	se-le	1	1	8,582	15,658	0	90.00	100	C	2		. . .					0	28084
96-HBB	**LIKPE net**	1	1	19,550	35,667		90.00	100	C	4		. . .					0	28085
96-HBBA	LIKPE cluster	1	1	19,550	35,667		90.00	100	C	4		. . .					0	28086
96-HBBA-a	se-kpele	1	1	19,550	35,667	0	90.00	100	C	4		. . .					0	28087
96-HBBA-b	se-kwa					0				4		. . .					0	28088
96-I	**KEBU-ANIMERE set**	2	2	54,578	99,985		27.10	64	B	4		. . .					0	28089
96-IA	KEBU-ANIMERE chain	2	2	54,578	99,985		27.10	64	B	4		. . .					0	28090
96-IAA	**ANIMERE net**	1	1	2,860	5,218		65.00	100	C	4		. . .					0	28091
96-IAAA	ANIMERE cluster	1	1	2,860	5,218		65.00	100	C	4		. . .					0	28092
96-IAAA-a	kecheibi					0				4		. . .					0	28093
96-IAAA-b	kunda	1	1	2,860	5,218	0	65.00	100	C	4		. . .					0	28094
96-IAB	**KEBU net**	1	1	51,718	94,767		25.00	62	B	4		. . .					0	28095
96-IABA	KEBU cluster	1	1	51,718	94,767		25.00	62	B	4		. . .					0	28096
96-IABA-a	ke-gberi-ke	1	1	51,718	94,767	0	25.00	62	B	4		. . .					0	28097
96-J	**KPOSO-AHLO set**	2	4	150,556	275,703		75.83	100	C	20		. . .					0	28098
96-JA	KPOSO-BOWILI chain	2	3	142,277	260,532		75.59	100	C	20		. . .					0	28099
96-JAA	**BOWILI net**	1	1	14,310	26,108		90.00	100	C	2		. . .					0	28100
96-JAAA	LIWULI cluster	1	1	14,310	26,108		90.00	100	C	2		. . .					0	28101
96-JAAA-a	li-wuli	1	1	14,310	26,108	0	90.00	100	C	2		. . .					0	28102
96-JAB	**KPOSO net**	2	2	127,967	234,424		73.98	100	C	20		. . .					0	28103
96-JABA	I-KPOSO cluster	2	2	127,967	234,424		73.98	100	C	20	Akposo	. . .					0	28104
96-JABA-a	uma					0				20		. . .					0	28105
96-JABA-b	logbo					0				20		. . .					0	28106
96-JABA-c	i-kponu					0				20		. . .					0	28107
96-JABA-d	i-wi					0				20		. . .					0	28108
96-JABA-e	litime					0				20		. . .					0	28109
96-JABA-f	amu-oblo					0				20		. . .					0	28110
96-JABA-g	apesokubi					0				20		. . .					0	28111
96-JB	IGO-AHLO chain	1	1	8,279	15,171		80.00	100	C	12		. . .					0	28112
96-JBA	**IGO-AHLO net**	1	1	8,279	15,171		80.00	100	C	12		. . .					0	28113
96-JBAA	IGO-AHLO cluster	1	1	8,279	15,171		80.00	100	C	12		. . .					0	28114
96-JBAA-a	i-go					0				12	Igo	. . .					0	28115
96-JBAA-b	anlo					0				12		. . .					0	28116
96-K	**AVATIME-NYANGBO set**	1	3	23,982	43,753		90.00	100	C	4		. . .					0	28117
96-KA	AVATIME-NYANGBO chain	1	3	23,982	43,753		90.00	100	C	4		. . .					0	28118
96-KAA	**AVATIME-NYANGBO net**	1	3	23,982	43,753		90.00	100	C	4		. . .					0	28119
96-KAAA	TAFI-NYANGBO cluster	1	2	8,863	16,170		90.00	100	C	4		. . .					0	28120
96-KAAA-a	te-gbo	1	1	3,780	6,896	0	90.00	100	C	4		. . .					0	28121
96-KAAA-b	tu-trugbu	1	1	5,083	9,274	0	90.01	100	C	4		. . .					0	28122

Continued opposite

Table 9-13 continued

Code 1	REFERENCE NAME / Autoglossonym 2	Coun 3	Peo 4	Mother-tongue speakers in 2000 5	in 2025 6	Media radio 7	AC% 8	E% 9	Wld 10	Tr 11	Biblioglossonym 12	Print 13-15	P-activity 16	N-activity 17	B-activity 18	J-year 19	Jayuh 20-24	Ref 25
96-KAAB	AVATIME cluster	1	1	15,119	27,583		90.00	100	C	2		. . .					0. . . .	28123
96-KAAB-a	si-ya-se	1	1	15,119	27,583	0	90.00	100	C	2		. . .					0. . . .	28124
96-L	**GA-DANGME set**	3	5	1,485,351	2,710,121		57.19	98	B	70		PNB					4.s..	28125
96-LA	GA-DANGME chain	3	5	1,485,351	2,710,121		57.19	98	B	70		PNB					4.s..	28126
96-LAA	**GA-DANGME net**	3	5	1,485,351	2,710,121		57.19	98	B	70		PNB					4.s..	28127
96-LAAA	GA cluster	3	3	511,331	933,093		60.87	100	C	70	Ga-adangme-krobo	PNB	1843-1966	1859-1994	1866-1909	1994	1.s..	28128
96-LAAA-a	accra	3	3	511,331	933,093	4	60.87	100	C	70	Ga*	PNB	1843-1966	1859-1978	1866-1909		1.s..	28129
96-LAAA-b	teshi					1				70		pnb					1.s..	28130
96-LAAA-c	osu					1				70		pnb					1.s..	28131
96-LAAB	KROBO cluster	1	1	489,593	893,227		55.00	96	B	0		. . .					0. . . .	28132
96-LAAB-a	krobo	1	1	489,593	893,227	2	55.00	96	B	0		. . .					0. . . .	28133
96-LAAC	ADANGME cluster	1	1	484,427	883,801		55.50	100	B	41	Dangme	PN.	1935	1977		1994	4.s..	28134
96-LAAC-a	kpone					0				41		pn.					1.s..	28135
96-LAAC-b	ningo					0				41		pn.					1.s..	28136
96-LAAC-c	prampram					0				41		pn.					1.s..	28137
96-LAAC-d	osuduku					0				41		pn.					1.s..	28138
96-LAAC-e	shai					0				41		pn.					1.s..	28139
96-LAAC-f	ada					0				41		pn.					1.s..	28140
96-M	**GBE set**	9	35	7,806,187	14,168,708		54.14	90	B	72		PNB					4Asu.	28141
96-MA	GBE chain	9	35	7,806,187	14,168,708		54.14	90	B	72		PNB					4Asu.	28142
96-MAA	**GBE net**	9	35	7,806,187	14,168,708		54.14	90	B	72		PNB					4Asu.	28143
96-MAAA	EWE cluster	7	7	3,483,504	6,307,170		77.49	100	C	72		PNB					4Asu.	28144
96-MAAA-a	Standard ewe	7	7	3,483,504	6,307,170	4	77.49	100	C	72	Ewe	PNB	1858-1988	1877-1991	1913-1931	1987	1csu.	28145
96-MAAA-b	agblodome					1				72		pnb					1csu.	28146
96-MAAA-c	agoe-nyive					1				72		pnb					1csu.	28147
96-MAAA-d	agome					1				72		pnb					1csu.	28148
96-MAAA-e	agotime					1				72		pnb					1csu.	28149
96-MAAA-f	agu					1				72		pnb					1csu.	28154
96-MAAA-g	anhlo					1				72		pnb					1csu.	28155
96-MAAA-h	awuna					1				72		pnb					1csu.	28156
96-MAAA-i	axefe					1				72		pnb					1csu.	28157
96-MAAA-j	dayin					1				72		pnb					1csu.	28158
96-MAAA-k	gbin					1				72		pnb					1csu.	28159
96-MAAA-l	ho					1				72		pnb					1csu.	28160
96-MAAA-m	kotafo					1				72		pnb					1csu.	28161
96-MAAA-n	kpandu					1				72		pnb					1csu.	28162
96-MAAA-o	kpele					1				72		pnb					1csu.	28163
96-MAAA-p	lavye					1				72		pnb					1csu.	28167
96-MAAA-q	lome					1				72		pnb					1csu.	28168
96-MAAA-r	ngotse					1				72		pnb					1csu.	28171
96-MAAA-s	tomety-kodzi					1				72		pnb					1csu.	28172
96-MAAA-t	tsekpo-dedekpoe					1				72		pnb					1csu.	28173
96-MAAA-u	tsevie					1				72		pnb					1csu.	28174
96-MAAA-v	tove					1				72		pnb					1csu.	28175
96-MAAA-w	towun					1				72		pnb					1csu.	28176
96-MAAA-x	vli					1				72		pnb					1csu.	28177
96-MAAA-y	vo					1				72		pnb					1csu.	28178
96-MAAA-z	wance					1				72		pnb					1csu.	28183
96-MAAB	KPESI cluster	1	1	4,014	7,354		15.99	50	B	4		. . .					0. . . .	28184
96-MAAB-a	kpesi	1	1	4,014	7,354	0	15.99	50	B	4		. . .					0. . . .	28185
96-MAAC	WACI-WUDU cluster	2	2	595,927	1,090,629		26.03	66	B	20		. . .					0. . . .	28186
96-MAAC-a	waci	2	2	595,927	1,090,629	4	26.03	66	B	20		. . .					0. . . .	28187
96-MAAC-b	wudu					1				20		. . .					0. . . .	28188
96-MAAD	GEN cluster	2	2	408,883	747,739		70.13	100	C	51	Mina*	PN.	1920-1994	1962			0. . . .	28189
96-MAAD-a	gliji					1				51		pn.					0. . . .	28190
96-MAAD-b	anexo					1				51		pn.					0. . . .	28191
96-MAAD-c	agoe					1				51		pn.					0. . . .	28192
96-MAAE	AJA cluster	2	3	532,019	970,942		26.57	71	B	20		. . .					0. . . .	28193
96-MAAE-a	dogbo					1				20		. . .					0. . . .	28194
96-MAAE-b	tado					1				20		. . .					0. . . .	28195
96-MAAE-c	hwe	1	1	5,337	9,779	1	50.01	87	B	20		. . .					0. . . .	28196
96-MAAE-d	sikpi					1				20		. . .					0. . . .	28197
96-MAAF	AYIZO-XWLA cluster	1	7	487,404	888,162		23.11	55	B	4		. . .					0. . . .	28198
96-MAAF-a	movolo					1				4		. . .					0. . . .	28199
96-MAAF-b	se					1				4		. . .					0. . . .	28200
96-MAAF-c	saxwe					1				4		. . .					0. . . .	28201
96-MAAF-d	ko	1	1	25,531	46,523	1	5.00	35	A	4		. . .					0. . . .	28202
96-MAAF-e	ci					1				4		. . .					0. . . .	28203
96-MAAF-f	xwla	1	1	38,295	69,782	1	5.00	33	A	4		. . .					0. . . .	28204
96-MAAF-g	xwela	1	1	12,193	22,219	1	5.00	32	A	4		. . .					0. . . .	28205
96-MAAF-h	xweda	1	1	68,931	125,608	1	4.00	31	A	4		. . .					0. . . .	28206
96-MAAF-i	kada					1				4		. . .					0. . . .	28207
96-MAAF-j	ayizo	1	1	257,853	469,868	2	35.00	69	B	4		. . .					0. . . .	28208
96-MAAF-k	toli	1	1	6,096	11,108	1	2.00	28	A	4		. . .					0. . . .	28209
96-MAAF-l	tofin	1	1	78,505	143,054	1	20.00	54	B	4		. . .					0. . . .	28210
96-MAAG	FON-GUN cluster	6	13	2,294,436	4,156,712		36.20	91	B	72		PNB					2As..	28211
96-MAAG-a	Standard fon	5	5	1,674,510	3,035,512	4	32.93	91	B	72	Fon*	PNb	1967	1993		1992	2as..	28212
96-MAAG-b	maxi	2	2	115,121	210,104	2	32.79	79	B	72		pnb					1cs..	28213
96-MAAG-c	arohun					1				72		pnb					1cs..	28214
96-MAAG-d	kpase					1				72		pnb					1cs..	28215
96-MAAG-e	agbome					1				72		pnb					1cs..	28216
96-MAAG-f	glexwe					1				72		pnb					1cs..	28217
96-MAAG-g	weme-nu	1	1	76,590	139,565	1	15.00	56	B	72		pnb					1cs..	28218
96-MAAG-h	seto	2	2	7,211	12,938	1	4.78	40	A	72		pnb					1cs..	28219
96-MAAG-i	alada					1				72		pnb					1cs..	28220
96-MAAG-j	gun	3	3	421,004	758,593	4	54.51	99	B	72	Gun-alada*	PNB	1886-1910	1892-1919	1923-1972		1As..	28221
97	**DELTIC zone**	2	12	1,282,243	2,110,392		87.45	100	C	62		PNB					0. . . .	28222
97-A	IJO-KALABARI set	2	11	1,281,161	2,108,617		87.49	100	C	62		PNB					0. . . .	28223
97-AA	IJO-KALABARI chain	2	11	1,281,161	2,108,617		87.49	100	C	62		PNB					0. . . .	28224
97-AAA	**IJO-CENTRAL net**	1	1	518,782	851,599		94.00	100	C	24		P..					0. . . .	28225
97-AAAA	IZON cluster	1	1	518,782	851,599		94.00	100	C	24		P..					0. . . .	28226
97-AAAA-a	mein					1				24		p..					0. . . .	28227
97-AAAA-b	kabo					1				24		p..					0. . . .	28228
97-AAAA-c	tarakiri					1				24		p..					0. . . .	28229
97-AAAA-d	tuomo					1				24		p..					0. . . .	28232
97-AAAA-e	o-peremo					1				24		p..					0. . . .	28233
97-AAAA-f	seimbri					1				24		p..					0. . . .	28234
97-AAAA-g	kumbo					1				24		p..					0. . . .	28235
97-AAAA-h	i-duwini					1				24		p..					0. . . .	28236

Continued overleaf

Table 9-13 continued

Code 1	REFERENCE NAME / Autoglossonym 2	Coun 3	Peo 4	Mother-tongue speakers in 2000 5	in 2025 6	Media radio 7	CHURCH AC% 8	E% 9	Wld 10	Tr 11	Biblioglossonym 12	SCRIPTURES Print 13-15	P-activity 16	N-activity 17	B-activity 18	J-year 19	Jayuh 20-24	Ref 25
97-AAAA-i	o-gulagha					1				24		p..					0....	28237
97-AAAA-j	o-poroza					1				24		p..					0....	28238
97-AAAA-k	o-gbe					1				24		p..					0....	28239
97-AAAA-l	a-rogbo					1				24		p..					0....	28240
97-AAAA-m	e-gbema					1				24		p..					0....	28241
97-AAAA-n	o-lodiama					1				24		p..					0....	28242
97-AAAA-o	furupagha					1				24		p..					0....	28245
97-AAAA-p	kolokuma	1	1	518,782	851,599	2	94.00	100	C	24	Ijo: Central*	P..	1912-1924				0....	28246
97-AAAA-q	gbanrain					1				24		p..					0....	28247
97-AAAA-r	e-kpetiama					1				24		p..					0....	28248
97-AAAA-s	i-kbiri					1				24		p..					0....	28249
97-AAAA-t	boma					1				24		p..					0....	28250
97-AAAA-u	bumo					1				24		p..					0....	28251
97-AAAA-v	a-poi					1				24		p..					0....	28252
97-AAAA-w	bassan					1				24		p..					0....	28253
97-AAAA-x	o-poroma					1				24		p..					0....	28254
97-AAAA-y	o-iakiri					1				24		p..					0....	28255
97-AAAA-z	o-gboin					1				24		p..					0....	28256
97-AAB	**BISENI-OKORDIA net**	1	3	25,870	42,466		65.40	99	C	4		...					0....	28257
97-AABA	BISENI cluster	1	2	20,406	33,497		66.84	100	C	4		...					0....	28258
97-AABA-a	Proper biseni	1	1	12,868	21,123	0	65.00	100	C	4		...					0....	28259
97-AABA-b	amegi	1	1	7,538	12,374	0	69.99	100	C	4		...					0....	28260
97-AABB	OKODIA cluster	1	1	5,464	8,969		59.99	97	B	4		...					0....	28261
97-AABB-a	o-kodia	1	1	5,464	8,969	0	59.99	97	B	4		...					0....	28262
97-AAC	**ORUMA net**	1	1	4,984	8,182		60.01	82	C	4		...					0....	28263
97-AACA	ORUMA cluster	1	1	4,984	8,182		60.01	82	C	4		...					0....	28264
97-AACA-a	o-ruma	1	1	4,984	8,182	0	60.01	82	C	4		...					0....	28265
97-AAD	**KALABARI-NKOROO net**	2	5	622,015	1,026,605		82.22	100	C	41		PN.					0....	28266
97-AADA	KALABARI-IBANI cluster	2	4	617,187	1,018,679		82.35	100	C	41		PN.					0....	28267
97-AADA-a	kalabari	2	2	304,011	504,589	0	89.10	100	C	41	Kalabari	PN.	1980-1991	1996			0....	28268
97-AADA-b	i-bani	1	1	65,655	107,775	0	60.00	100	C	41	Ibani	Pn.	1892-1986				0....	28269
97-AADA-c	o-krika	1	1	247,521	406,315	0	80.00	100	C	41	Okrika	Pn.	1979-1991				0....	28270
97-AADB	NKOROO cluster	1	1	4,828	7,926		65.00	99	C	4		...					0....	28271
97-AADB-a	nkoroo	1	1	4,828	7,926	0	65.00	99	C	4		...					0....	28272
97-AAE	**NEMBE-AKASSA net**	1	1	109,510	179,765		93.00	100	C	62		PNB					0....	28273
97-AAEA	NEMBE-AKASSA cluster	1	1	109,510	179,765		93.00	100	C	62		PNB					0....	28274
97-AAEA-a	nembe	1	1	109,510	179,765	0	93.00	100	C	62	Ijo: Brass*	PNB	1886-1943	1927	1956		0....	28275
97-AAEA-b	akassa					0				62		pnb					0....	28276
97-B	**DEFAKA set**	1	1	1,082	1,775		40.02	69	B	4		...					0....	28277
97-BA	DEFAKA chain	1	1	1,082	1,775		40.02	69	B	4		...					0....	28278
97-BAA	**DEFAKA net**	1	1	1,082	1,775		40.02	69	B	4		...					0....	28279
97-BAAA	DEFAKA cluster	1	1	1,082	1,775		40.02	69	B	4		...					0....	28280
97-BAAA-a	defaka	1	1	1,082	1,775	0	40.02	69	B	4		...					0....	28281
98	**BENUIC zone**	14	298	63,005,681	103,784,533		70.37	95	C	82		PNB					4asu.	28282
98-A	**YORUBA-IGALA set**	13	28	26,053,438	43,064,803		60.74	99	C	62		PNB					4asu.	28283
98-AA	YORUBA-IGALA chain	13	28	26,053,438	43,064,803		60.74	99	C	62		PNB					4asu.	28284
98-AAA	**YORUBA-IGALA net**	13	28	26,053,438	43,064,803		60.74	99	C	62		PNB					4asu.	28285
98-AAAA	YORUBA cluster	13	25	25,111,413	41,518,434		60.92	99	C	62		PNB					3asu.	28286
98-AAAA-a	Standard yoruba	12	12	20,575,737	33,937,896	5	57.27	100	B	62	Yoruba	PNB	1850-1960	1862-1993	1884-1966	1985	3asu.	28287
98-AAAA-b	General yoruba					1				62		pnb					1csu.	28288
98-AAAA-c	West yoruba	4	10	4,001,480	6,704,696	5	75.83	95	C	62		Pnb					1csu.	28289
98-AAAA-d	Central yoruba	1	1	8,030	8,662	5	54.99	100	B	62		pnb					1csu.	28303
98-AAAA-e	East Central yoruba.					1				62		pnb					1csu.	28309
98-AAAA-f	Northeast yoruba					1				62		pnb					1csu.	28312
98-AAAA-g	Southeast yoruba					1				62		pnb					1csu.	28329
98-AAAA-h	i-shekiri	1	1	507,018	832,288	1	93.00	100	C	62	Isekiri	PNb	1974-1985	1985			1csu.	28333
98-AAAA-i	aguna	1	1	19,148	34,892	1	30.00	73	B	62		pnb					1csu.	28334
98-AAAB	NORTH AKOKO cluster	1	1	55,753	91,521		30.00	66	B	4		...					0....	28335
98-AAAB-a	oyin					0				4		...					0....	28336
98-AAAB-b	arigidi					0				4		...					0....	28337
98-AAAB-c	uro					0				4		...					0....	28338
98-AAAB-d	ahan					0				4		...					0....	28339
98-AAAB-e	ayere					0				4		...					0....	28340
98-AAAB-f	erushu					0				4		...					0....	28341
98-AAAB-g	amgbe					0				4		...					0....	28342
98-AAAB-h	okeagbe					0				4		...					0....	28343
98-AAAC	IGALA cluster	1	2	886,272	1,454,848		57.41	99	B	62		PNB					4.s..	28348
98-AAAC-a	i-gala	1	2	886,272	1,454,848	5	57.41	99	B	62	Igala	PNB	1924-1958	1935-1948	1970	1995	4.s..	28349
98-B	**NIGER-CENTRAL set**	1	19	4,788,415	7,860,355		38.53	79	B	82		PNB					4....	28355
98-BA	NUPE-GADE chain	1	5	2,204,474	3,618,724		30.43	73	B	61		PNB					4....	28356
98-BAA	**NUPE-GWARI net**	1	4	2,110,642	3,464,695		31.11	74	B	61		PNB					4....	28357
98-BAAA	NUPE cluster	1	1	1,094,198	1,796,165		2.80	58	B	61		PNB					4....	28358
98-BAAA-a	ezi-nupe	1	1	1,094,198	1,796,165	5	2.80	58	B	61	Nupe	PNB	1877-1950	1915-1982	1953-1989	1995	4....	28359
98-BAAA-b	ganagana					1				61		pnb					1....	28363
98-BAAA-c	ka-kakanda					1				61		pnb					1....	28367
98-BAAA-d	eggan					1				61		pnb					1....	28371
98-BAAA-e	ibara					1				61		pnb					1....	28372
98-BAAA-f	nupe-tako					1				61		pnb					1....	28373
98-BAAA-g	edzu					1				61		pnb					1....	28374
98-BAAA-h	agbi					1				61		pnb					1....	28375
98-BAAA-i	gupa					1				61		pnb					1....	28376
98-BAAA-j	kami					1				61		pnb					1....	28377
98-BAAA-k	gbanmi-sokun					1				61		pnb					1....	28378
98-BAAA-l	asu					1				61		pnb					1....	28379
98-BAAB	GWARI cluster	1	3	1,016,444	1,668,530		61.59	92	C	41		PN.					2....	28380
98-BAAB-a	gbari	1	1	298,245	489,580	0	35.00	77	B	41	Gbari	Pn.	1925-1926				1....	28381
98-BAAB-b	gbagyi	1	2	718,199	1,178,950	0	72.63	99	C	41	Gbagyi: Gayegi*	PN.	1913-1938	1995			2....	28391
98-BAB	**GADE net**	1	1	93,832	154,029		15.00	51	B	20		...					0....	28400
98-BABA	GADE cluster	1	1	93,832	154,029		15.00	51	B	20		...					0....	28401
98-BABA-a	gade	1	1	93,832	154,029	0	15.00	51	B	20		...					0....	28402
98-BB	EBIRA chain	1	1	1,194,665	1,961,085		24.00	69	B	41		PN.					0....	28403

Continued opposite

Table 9-13 continued

Code 1	REFERENCE NAME / Autoglossonym 2	Coun 3	Peo 4	Mother-tongue speakers in 2000 5	in 2025 6	Media radio 7	CHURCH AC% 8	E% 9	Wld 10	Tr 11	Biblioglossonym 12	SCRIPTURES Print 13-15	P-activity 16	N-activity 17	B-activity 18	J-year 19	Jayuh 20-24	Ref 25
98-BBA	**EBIRA net**	1	1	1,194,665	1,961,085		24.00	69	B	41		PN.					0....	28404
98-BBAA	EBIRA cluster	1	1	1,194,665	1,961,085		24.00	69	B	41		PN.					0....	28405
98-BBAA-a	Central e-bira	1	1	1,194,665	1,961,085	0	24.00	69	B	41	Ebira	PN.	1891-1960	1981			0....	28406
98-BBAA-b	i-hima					0				41		pn.					0....	28410
98-BC	IDOMA-ETULO chain	1	13	1,389,276	2,280,546		63.87	95	C	82		PNB					0....	28413
98-BCA	**ELOYI net**	1	1	28,311	46,474		1.00	30	A	20		...					0....	28414
98-BCAA	AFO cluster	1	1	28,311	46,474		1.00	30	A	20	Eloyi	...					0....	28415
98-BCAA-a	mbeci					0				20		...					0....	28416
98-BCAA-b	mbamu					0				20		...					0....	28417
98-BCB	**IDOMA-YALA net**	1	8	1,298,209	2,131,057		65.43	97	C	82		PNB					0....	28418
98-BCBA	IDOMA cluster	1	4	893,944	1,467,442		71.92	100	C	82		PNB					0....	28419
98-BCBA-a	North i-doma	1	1	280,661	460,715	1	69.00	100	C	82		PNb					0....	28420
98-BCBA-b	Central i-doma	1	1	256,464	420,995	2	68.00	100	C	82	Idoma	PNB	1927-1957	1970	1995		0....	28423
98-BCBA-c	West i-doma	1	1	278,765	457,603	2	79.00	100	C	82		pnb					0....	28427
98-BCBA-d	Southwest i-doma					1				82		pnb					0....	28430
98-BCBA-e	South i-doma	1	1	78,054	128,129	2	70.00	100	C	82		pnb					0....	28431
98-BCBB	ALAGO cluster	1	1	61,462	100,892		16.70	55	B	24	Alago	P..	1929				0....	28435
98-BCBB-a	agwatashi					0				24		p..					0....	28436
98-BCBB-b	assaikio					0				24		p..					0....	28437
98-BCBB-c	doma					0				24		p..					0....	28438
98-BCBB-d	keana					0				24		p..					0....	28439
98-BCBC	IGEDE cluster	1	2	255,003	418,596		60.76	100	C	41		PN.					0....	28440
98-BCBC-a	o-ju	1	1	248,536	407,980	0	60.00	100	C	41	Igede	PN.	1937	1980-1981			0....	28441
98-BCBC-b	i-to	1	1	6,467	10,616	0	90.01	100	C	41		pn.					0....	28442
98-BCBC-c	worku					0				41		pn.					0....	28443
98-BCBC-d	gabu					0				41		pn.					0....	28444
98-BCBD	YALA cluster	1	1	87,800	144,127		47.00	89	B	41		PN.					0....	28445
98-BCBD-a	i-yala	1	1	87,800	144,127	0	47.00	89	B	41	Iyala*	PN.	1974	1979			0....	28446
98-BCC	**ETULO net**	1	1	12,299	20,189		60.00	92	B	2		...					0....	28450
98-BCCA	ETULU cluster	1	1	12,299	20,189		60.00	92	B	2		...					0....	28451
98-BCCA-a	e-tulu	1	1	12,299	20,189	0	60.00	92	B	2		...					0....	28452
98-BCD	**AKPA-YACHE net**	1	3	50,457	82,826		60.08	92	C	22		P..					0....	28453
98-BCDA	AKPA-YACHE cluster	1	3	50,457	82,826		60.08	92	C	22		P..					0....	28454
98-BCDA-a	akpa					0				22		p..					0....	28455
98-BCDA-b	i-yace	1	3	50,457	82,826	0	60.08	92	C	22	Ekpari	P..	1980				0....	28458
98-BCDA-c	ekpari					0				22		p..					0....	28459
98-C	**UKAAN-AKPES set**	1	2	42,528	69,812		30.00	61	B	4		...					0....	28460
98-CA	AKPES chain	1	1	10,916	17,920		30.00	62	B	4		...					0....	28461
98-CAA	**AKPES net**	1	1	10,916	17,920		30.00	62	B	4		...					0....	28462
98-CAAA	AKPES cluster	1	1	10,916	17,920		30.00	62	B	4		...					0....	28463
98-CAAA-a	akunnu					0				4		...					0....	28464
98-CAAA-b	daja					0				4		...					0....	28465
98-CAAA-c	efifa					0				4		...					0....	28466
98-CAAA-d	gedegede					0				4		...					0....	28467
98-CAAA-e	i-baram					0				4		...					0....	28468
98-CAAA-f	i-keram					0				4		...					0....	28469
98-CAAA-g	i-yani					0				4		...					0....	28470
98-CB	UKAAN chain	1	1	31,612	51,892		30.00	61	B	4		...					0....	28471
98-CBA	**UKAAN net**	1	1	31,612	51,892		30.00	61	B	4		...					0....	28472
98-CBAA	UKAAN cluster	1	1	31,612	51,892		30.00	61	B	4		...					0....	28473
98-CBAA-a	i-she					0				4		...					0....	28474
98-CBAA-b	auga					0				4		...					0....	28475
98-CBAA-c	kakumo					0				4		...					0....	28476
98-CBAA-d	anyaran					0				4		...					0....	28479
98-D	**OKO set**	1	1	10,615	17,426		2.00	24	A	4		...					0....	28480
98-DA	OKO chain	1	1	10,615	17,426		2.00	24	A	4		...					0....	28481
98-DAA	**OKO net**	1	1	10,615	17,426		2.00	24	A	4		...					0....	28482
98-DAAA	OGORI-OSAYEN cluster	1	1	10,615	17,426		2.00	24	A	4		...					0....	28483
98-DAAA-a	ogori					0				4		...					0....	28484
98-DAAA-b	osayen					0				4		...					0....	28485
98-DAAA-c	eni					0				4		...					0....	28486
98-E	**EDO-OKPAMHERI set**	1	23	3,006,904	4,938,568		73.77	92	C	61		PNB					0....	28487
98-EA	EDO-OKPAMHERI chain	1	23	3,006,904	4,938,568		73.77	92	C	61		PNB					0....	28488
98-EAA	**OKPAMHERI net**	1	3	83,149	136,494		27.30	56	B	4		...					0....	28489
98-EAAA	OKPAMHERI cluster	1	1	52,675	86,469		27.00	57	B	4		...					0....	28490
98-EAAA-a	okulosho					0				4		...					0....	28491
98-EAAA-b	West okpamheri					0				4		...					0....	28497
98-EAAA-c	emhalhe					0				4		...					0....	28516
98-EAAB	OKPE-AKUKU cluster	1	2	30,474	50,025		27.82	55	B	4		...					0....	28517
98-EAAB-a	North okpe					0				4		...					0....	28518
98-EAAB-b	idesa					0				4		...					0....	28519
98-EAAB-c	oloma					0				4		...					0....	28520
98-EAAB-d	akuku					0				4		...					0....	28521
98-EAB	**UKUE-IYAYU net**	1	3	65,187	107,006		30.00	55	B	4		...					0....	28522
98-EABA	UKUE-EHUEN cluster	1	1	27,743	45,541		30.00	57	B	4		...					0....	28523
98-EABA-a	ukue					0				4		...					0....	28524
98-EABA-b	ehueun					0				4		...					0....	28525
98-EABB	IYAYU cluster	1	2	37,444	61,465		30.00	53	B	4		...					0....	28526
98-EABB-a	uhami	1	1	13,303	21,837	0	30.00	57	B	4		...					0....	28527
98-EABB-b	iyayu	1	1	24,141	39,628	0	30.00	51	B	4		...					0....	28528
98-EAC	**EDO-CENTRAL net**	1	10	1,947,190	3,197,255		72.67	95	C	61		PNB					0....	28529
98-EACA	OSOSO cluster	1	1	18,644	30,604		30.00	57	B	4		...					0....	28530
98-EACA-a	ososo	1	1	18,644	30,604	0	30.00	57	B	4		...					0....	28531
98-EACB	GHOTUO-UNEME cluster	1	1	19,436	31,904		30.00	57	B	4		...					0....	28532
98-EACB-a	uneme	1	1	19,436	31,904	0	30.00	57	B	4		...					0....	28533

Continued overleaf

Table 9-13 continued

Code 1	REFERENCE NAME / Autoglossonym 2	Coun 3	Peo 4	Mother-tongue speakers in 2000 5	in 2025 6	Media radio 7	AC% 8	E% 9	Wld 10	Tr 11	Biblioglossonym 12	Print 13-15	P-activity 16	N-activity 17	B-activity 18	J-year 19	Jayuh 20-24	Ref 25
98-EACC	YEKHEE cluster	1	1	273,469	448,908		79.00	100	C	22	Etsako*	P..	1980				0....	28536
98-EACC-a	auchi					0				22		p..					0....	28537
98-EACC-b	uzairue					0				22		p..					0....	28538
98-EACC-c	South ibie					0				22		p..					0....	28539
98-EACC-d	uwepa-uwano					0				22		p..					0....	28540
98-EACC-e	avianwu					0				22		p..					0....	28541
98-EACC-f	aviele					0				22		p..					0....	28542
98-EACC-g	ivhiadaobi					0				22		p..					0....	28543
98-EACD	GHOTUO cluster	1	1	29,092	47,755		30.00	58	B	4		...					0....	28544
98-EACD-a	ghotuo	1	1	29,092	47,755	0	30.00	58	B	4		...					0....	28545
98-EACE	SASARU-ENWAN cluster	1	1	12,199	20,025		30.00	56	B	4		...					0....	28546
98-EACE-a	enwan					0				4		...					0....	28547
98-EACE-b	sasaru					0				4		...					0....	28548
98-EACE-c	igwe					0				4		...					0....	28549
98-EACF	ATTE cluster	1	1	15,000	25,500		30.00	65	B	0		...					0....	28550
98-EACF-a	North ivbie					0				0		...					0....	28551
98-EACF-b	okpela					0				0		...					0....	28552
98-EACF-c	arhe					0				0		...					0....	28553
98-EACG	IKPESHI cluster	1	1	5,207	8,548		27.00	54	B	4		...					0....	28554
98-EACG-a	ikpeshi	1	1	5,207	8,548	0	27.00	54	B	4		...					0....	28555
98-EACH	KUNIBUM cluster	1	1	126,671	207,935		27.00	57	B	24		P..					0....	28556
98-EACH-a	ivhimion					0				24		p..					0....	28557
98-EACH-b	emai	1	1	126,671	207,935	0	27.00	57	B	24	Emai-iuleha-ora	P..	1908-1910				0....	28558
98-EACH-c	iuleha					0				24		p..					0....	28559
98-EACH-d	ora					0				24	Ora	P..	1908				0....	28560
98-EACI	ESAN cluster	1	1	351,200	576,506		80.00	100	C	23		P..					0....	28561
98-EACI-a	Proper esan	1	1	351,200	576,506	2	80.00	100	C	23	Esan	P..	1974				0....	28562
98-EACI-b	ekpon					1				23		p..					0....	28563
98-EACI-c	igueben					1				23		p..					0....	28564
98-EACJ	PROPER EDO cluster	1	2	1,096,272	1,799,570		77.90	100	C	61		PNB					0....	28565
98-EACJ-a	Proper edo	1	1	1,094,198	1,796,165	2	78.00	100	C	61	Edo	PNB	1914-1935	1981	1996		0....	28566
98-EAD	**SOUTHWEST EDO net**	1	4	851,298	1,399,190		87.48	96	C	61		PNB					0....	28567
98-EADA	SOUTH OKPE cluster	1	1	30,000	51,000		30.00	65	B	0		...					0....	28568
98-EADA-a	South okpe	1	1	30,000	51,000	0	30.00	65	B	0		...					0....	28569
98-EADB	URHOBO-ISOKO cluster	1	2	746,154	1,224,838		94.80	100	C	61		PNB					0....	28570
98-EADB-a	urhobo	1	1	597,037	980,057	2	95.00	100	C	61	Urhobo	PNB	1927-1963	1951	1977		0....	28571
98-EADB-b	isoko	1	1	149,117	244,781	1	94.00	100	C	61	Isoko	PNB	1920-1932	1970	1977		0....	28574
98-EADC	UVBIE cluster	1	1	19,391	31,831		60.00	89	C	4		...					0....	28575
98-EADC-a	uvbie	1	1	19,391	31,831	0	60.00	89	C	4		...					0....	28576
98-EADD	ERUWA cluster	1	1	55,753	91,521		30.00	61	B	4		...					0....	28577
98-EADD-a	eruwa	1	1	55,753	91,521	0	30.00	61	B	4		...					0....	28578
98-EAE	**EDO-DELTA net**	1	3	60,080	98,623		26.89	60	B	41		PN.					0....	28579
98-EAEA	NGENE cluster	1	1	27,687	45,449		26.00	63	B	41		PN.					0....	28580
98-EAEA-a	Proper ngene	1	1	27,687	45,449	0	26.00	63	B	41	Engenni	PN.	1968	1977			0....	28581
98-EAEA-b	ediro					0				41		pn.					0....	28582
98-EAEA-c	inedua					0				41		pn.					0....	28583
98-EAEA-d	ogua					0				41		pn.					0....	28584
98-EAEB	EPIE-ATISSA cluster	1	1	21,075	34,595		28.00	58	B	4		...					0....	28585
98-EAEB-a	epie	1	1	21,075	34,595	0	28.00	58	B	4		...					0....	28586
98-EAEB-b	atissa					0				4		...					0....	28587
98-EAEC	DEGEMA cluster	1	1	11,318	18,579		27.00	55	B	4		...					0....	28588
98-EAEC-a	u-dekama	1	1	11,318	18,579	0	27.00	55	B	4		...					0....	28589
98-EAEC-b	atala					0				4		...					0....	28590
98-EAEC-c	u-sokun					0				4		...					0....	28591
98-F	**IGBO-EKPEYE set**	5	16	16,870,295	27,709,883		95.32	99	C	61		PNB					2..u.	28592
98-FA	IGBO-EKPEYE chain	5	16	16,870,295	27,709,883		95.32	99	C	61		PNB					2..u.	28593
98-FAA	**IGBO net**	5	15	16,817,620	27,623,414		95.41	99	C	61		PNB					2..u.	28594
98-FAAA	CENTRAL IGBO cluster	5	6	15,008,300	24,653,353		97.87	100	C	61		PNB					2..u.	28595
98-FAAA-a	Standard igbo	4	4	124,578	221,199	4	87.68	100	C	61	Igbo	PNB	1860-1950	1900-1981	1906-1988	1992	2..u.	28596
98-FAAA-b	union-igbo					1				61		pnb					1..u.	28597
98-FAAA-c	General igbo					1				61		pnb					1..u.	28598
98-FAAA-d	North Central igbo.	1	1	55,753	91,521	5	86.00	100	C	61		pnb					1..u.	28599
98-FAAA-e	South Central igbo.	1	1	14,827,969	24,340,633	5	98.00	100	C	61		pnb					1..u.	28606
98-FAAB	IKA cluster	1	1	22,301	36,608		57.00	91	B	4		...					0....	28614
98-FAAB-a	ika	1	1	22,301	36,608	0	57.00	91	B	4		...					0....	28615
98-FAAB-b	enuani									4		...					0....	28616
98-FAAC	WEST IGBO cluster	1	1	169,835	278,790		90.00	100	C	20		...					0....	28617
98-FAAC-a	aboh					0				20		...					0....	28618
98-FAAC-b	ukwuani					0				20		...					0....	28619
98-FAAD	SOUTHWEST IGBO cluster	1	1	180,071	295,593		50.00	87	B	12		...					0....	28620
98-FAAD-a	egi					0				12		...					0....	28621
98-FAAD-b	ogba	1	1	180,071	295,593	0	50.00	87	B	12	Ogbah	...					0....	28622
98-FAAE	IKWERE cluster	1	1	351,200	576,506		40.00	76	B	20		...					0....	28625
98-FAAE-a	obio					0				20		...					0....	28626
98-FAAE-b	akpo					0				20		...					0....	28627
98-FAAE-c	ogbakiri					0				20		...					0....	28631
98-FAAE-d	emowhua					0				20		...					0....	28632
98-FAAE-e	ndele					0				20		...					0....	28633
98-FAAE-f	elele					0				20		...					0....	28634
98-FAAE-g	omerelu					0				20		...					0....	28635
98-FAAE-h	egbeda					0				20		...					0....	28636
98-FAAE-i	aluu					0				20		...					0....	28637
98-FAAE-j	igwuruta					0				20		...					0....	28638
98-FAAE-k	ibaa					0				20		...					0....	28639
98-FAAE-l	isiokpo					0				20		...					0....	28640
98-FAAE-m	omagwa					0				20		...					0....	28641
98-FAAF	EAST IGBO cluster	1	1	44,602	73,216		85.00	100	C	0		...					0....	28642
98-FAAF-a	ada					1				0		...					0....	28643
98-FAAF-b	abam					1				0		...					0....	28644
98-FAAF-c	aro					1				0		...					0....	28645
98-FAAG	NORTHEAST IGBO cluster	1	4	1,041,311	1,709,348		88.63	100	C	41	Izi-ezaa-ikwo-mgbo	PN.		1980			0..u.	28646
98-FAAG-a	ishielu					0				41		pn.					0..u.	28647
98-FAAG-b	ezaa					0				41	Ezaa	PN.	1980				0..u.	28648
98-FAAG-c	ikwo					0				41	Ikwo	PN.		1980			0..u.	28649
98-FAAG-d	mgbo					0				41		pn.					0..u.	28650
98-FAAG-e	izi					0				41	Izi	PN.		1980			0..u.	28651

Continued opposite

Table 9-13 continued

Code 1	REFERENCE NAME Autoglossonym 2	Coun 3	Peo 4	Mother-tongue speakers in 2000 5	in 2025 6	Media radio 7	AC% 8	E% 9	Wld 10	Tr 11	Biblioglossonym 12	Print 13-15	P-activity 16	N-activity 17	B-activity 18	J-year 19	Jayuh 20-24	Ref 25
98-FAB	**EKPEYE net**	1	1	52,675	86,469		67.00	100	C	4		. . .					0	28652
98-FABA	EKPEYE cluster	1	1	52,675	86,469		67.00	100	C	4		. . .					0	28653
98-FABA-a	ako					0				4		. . .					0	28654
98-FABA-b	upata					0				4		. . .					0	28655
98-FABA-c	ubye					0				4		. . .					0	28656
98-FABA-d	igbuduyaa					0				4		. . .					0	28657
98-G	**KAINJI set**	1	46	1,295,761	2,127,346		22.39	55	B	42		PN.					0	28658
98-GA	WEST KANJI chain	1	22	844,546	1,386,352		24.33	59	B	42		PN.					0	28659
98-GAA	**LOPA-LARU net**	1	2	6,991	11,476		32.86	60	B	4		. . .					0	28660
98-GAAA	LOPA-LARU cluster	1	2	6,991	11,476		32.86	60	B	4		. . .					0	28661
98-GAAA-a	kirikjir	1	1	1,996	3,276	0	39.98	69	B	4		. . .					0	28662
98-GAAA-b	laru	1	1	4,995	8,200	0	30.01	56	B	4		. . .					0	28663
98-GAB	**RESHE net**	1	1	52,675	86,469		10.00	42	A	23		P. .					0	28664
98-GABA	RESHE cluster	1	1	52,675	86,469		10.00	42	A	23	Reshe	P. .	1970				0	28665
98-GABA-a	yauri					0				23		P. .					0	28666
98-GABA-b	gunga					0				23		P. .					0	28667
98-GAC	**KAMBARI net**	1	5	234,597	385,101		15.00	45	A	22		P. .					0	28668
98-GACA	WEST KAMBARI cluster	1	1	49,899	81,911		15.00	50	B	12		. . .					0	28669
98-GACA-a	agwara					0				12		. . .					0	28670
98-GACA-b	auna					0				12		. . .					0	28673
98-GACB	EAST KAMBARI cluster	1	4	184,698	303,190		15.00	43	A	22		P. .					0	28676
98-GACB-a	ci-shingini	1	1	78,054	128,129	0	15.00	37	A	22	Kambari*	P. .	1933-1994				0	28677
98-GACB-b	tsi-vadi					0				22		P. .					0	28678
98-GACB-c	tsi-gadi	1	2	92,104	151,192	0	15.00	50	B	22		P. .					0	28679
98-GACB-d	ci-baangi	1	1	14,540	23,869	0	15.00	36	A	22		P. .					0	28680
98-GAD	**DUKA-LELA net**	1	4	233,695	383,617		21.65	55	B	24		P. .					0	28681
98-GADA	PUKU-WIPSI cluster	1	1	26,338	43,234		1.00	30	A	2		. . .					0	28682
98-GADA-a	puku					0				2		. . .					0	28683
98-GADA-b	geeri					0				2		. . .					0	28687
98-GADA-c	wipsi					0				2		. . .					0	28690
98-GADA-d	et-us					0				2		. . .					0	28693
98-GADB	LYASE cluster	1	1	14,050	23,063		5.00	27	A	4		. . .					0	28694
98-GADB-a	gwamhi					0				4		. . .					0	28695
98-GADB-b	wuri					0				4		. . .					0	28696
98-GADC	LELA-DOMA cluster	1	1	95,327	156,482		50.00	85	B	24		P. .					0	28697
98-GADC-a	chi-lela	1	1	95,327	156,482	0	50.00	85	B	24	Lela	P. .	1931				0	28698
98-GADC-b	dabai					0				24		P. .					0	28699
98-GADC-c	a-doma					0				24		P. .					0	28700
98-GADD	DUKA cluster	1	1	97,980	160,838		2.00	36	A	22	Dukanci	P. .	1979				0	28703
98-GADD-a	et-hun					0				22		P. .					0	28704
98-GADD-b	es-saare					0				22		P. .					0	28705
98-GAE	**KAMUKU-PONGU net**	1	6	95,505	156,774		16.53	51	B	4		. . .					0	28706
98-GAEA	CEP-BOROMA cluster	1	1	7,237	11,879		19.99	56	B	4		. . .					0	28707
98-GAEA-a	ta-cep	1	1	7,237	11,879	0	19.99	56	B	4		. . .					0	28708
98-GAEA-b	ta-boroma					0				4		. . .					0	28709
98-GAEB	KAMUKU cluster	1	2	60,715	99,666		10.00	47	A	4		. . .					0	28710
98-GAEB-a	te-gina	1	1	30,776	50,519	0	10.00	48	A	4		. . .					0	28711
98-GAEB-b	regi					0				4		. . .					0	28712
98-GAEC	NGWOI cluster	1	1	1,996	3,276		30.01	56	B	4		. . .					0	28713
98-GAEC-a	hungworo	1	1	1,996	3,276	0	30.01	56	B	4		. . .					0	28714
98-GAED	URA cluster	1	1	959	1,574		30.03	55	B	4		. . .					0	28715
98-GAED-a	fungwa	1	1	959	1,574	0	30.03	55	B	4		. . .					0	28716
98-GAEE	PONGU cluster	1	1	24,598	40,379		30.00	57	B	3		. . .					0	28717
98-GAEE-a	pongu	1	1	24,598	40,379	0	30.00	57	B	3		. . .					0	28718
98-GAF	**BAUSHI-GURMANA net**	1	2	25,412	41,715		10.00	36	A	4		. . .					0	28719
98-GAFA	BAUSHI cluster	1	1	21,833	35,839		10.00	36	A	4		. . .					0	28720
98-GAFA-a	baushi	1	1	21,833	35,839	0	10.00	36	A	4		. . .					0	28721
98-GAFB	GURMANA cluster	1	1	3,579	5,876		10.00	34	A	4		. . .					0	28722
98-GAFB-a	gurmana	1	1	3,579	5,876	0	10.00	34	A	4		. . .					0	28723
98-GAG	**BASA net**	1	2	195,671	321,200		47.95	94	B	42		PN.					0	28724
98-GAGA	BASA-KADUNA cluster	1	1	20,071	32,947		30.00	63	B	9		. . .					0	28725
98-GAGA-a	West basa-kaduna					0				9		. . .					0	28726
98-GAGA-b	East basa-kaduna					0				9		. . .					0	28727
98-GAGB	BASA-KONTAGORA cluster			0	0		0.00	0		8		. . .					0	28728
98-GAGB-a	basa-kontagora			0	0	0	0.00	0		8		. . .					0	28729
98-GAGC	BASA-BENUE cluster	1	1	175,600	288,253		50.00	98	B	42		PN.					0	28730
98-GAGC-a	ru-bassa	1	1	175,600	288,253	0	50.00	98	B	42	Rubassa*	PN.	1946-1965	1972			0	28731
98-GB	EAST KAINJI chain	1	24	451,215	740,994		18.75	47	A	24		P. .					0	28735
98-GBA	**JERA-SANGA net**	1	10	95,326	156,499		25.73	53	B	9		. . .					0	28736
98-GBAA	KUDU-CAMO cluster	1	1	4,594	7,541		5.01	29	A	5		. . .					0	28737
98-GBAA-a	kudu					0				5		. . .					0	28738
98-GBAA-b	camo					0				5		. . .					0	28739
98-GBAB	GAMO-NINGI cluster	1	1	16,369	26,870		0.02	17	A	9		. . .					0	28740
98-GBAB-a	gamo					0				9		. . .					0	28741
98-GBAB-b	ningi					0				9		. . .					0	28742
98-GBAC	GYEM cluster	1	1	300	510		30.00	65	B	0		. . .					0	28743
98-GBAC-a	gyem	1	1	300	510	0	30.00	65	B	0		. . .					0	28744
98-GBAD	TAURA-TAKAYA cluster			0	0		0.00	0		8		. . .					0	28745
98-GBAD-a	ta-ura			0	0	0	0.00	0		8		. . .					0	28746
98-GBAD-b	ta-kaya			0	0	0	0.00	0		8		. . .					0	28747
98-GBAE	SHENI cluster	1	1	401	659		4.99	28	A	8		. . .					0	28748
98-GBAE-a	sheni	1	1	401	659	0	4.99	28	A	8		. . .					0	28749
98-GBAF	ZORA cluster	1	1	1,818	2,984		5.01	31	A	4		. . .					0	28750
98-GBAF-a	i-zora	1	1	1,818	2,984	0	5.01	31	A	4		. . .					0	28751
98-GBAG	JERA-MORO cluster	1	3	60,917	99,996		34.38	64	B	4		. . .					0	28752
98-GBAG-a	e-moro	1	1	11,753	19,293	0	40.00	71	B	4		. . .					0	28753

Continued overleaf

Table 9-13 continued

Code 1	REFERENCE NAME / Autoglossonym 2	Coun 3	Peo 4	Mother-tongue speakers in 2000 5	in 2025 6	Media radio 7	AC% 8	E% 9	Wld 10	Tr 11	Biblioglossonym 12	Print 13-15	P-activity 16	N-activity 17	B-activity 18	J-year 19	Jayuh 20-24	Ref 25
98-GBAG-b	i-sanga	1	1	8,776	14,405	0	1.00	21	A	4		...					0....	28754
98-GBAG-c	e-zelle					0				4		...					0....	28755
98-GBAG-d	e-boze					0				4		...					0....	28756
98-GBAG-e	i-bunu					0				4		...					0....	28757
98-GBAG-f	gurum					0				4		...					0....	28758
98-GBAH	DUGUZA cluster	1	1	3,512	5,766		1.99	24	A	4		...					0....	28759
98-GBAH-a	duguza	1	1	3,512	5,766	0	1.99	24	A	4		...					0....	28760
98-GBAI	GUTA cluster	1	1	6,289	10,324		40.01	67	B	4		...					0....	28761
98-GBAI-a	i-guta	1	1	6,289	10,324	0	40.01	67	B	4		...					0....	28762
98-GBAJ	JANJI cluster	1	1	1,126	1,849		50.00	78	B	4		...					0....	28763
98-GBAJ-a	ti-janji	1	1	1,126	1,849	0	50.00	78	B	4		...					0....	28764
98-GBB	**KAURU net**	1	11	91,140	149,900		8.72	35	A	4		...					0....	28765
98-GBBA	KURAMI cluster	1	1	39,451	64,760		15.00	46	A	4		...					0....	28766
98-GBBA-a	ti-kurami	1	1	39,451	64,760	0	15.00	46	A	4		...					0....	28767
98-GBBB	RUMA cluster	1	1	7,928	13,014		4.99	27	A	4		...					0....	28768
98-GBBB-a	tu-ruma	1	1	7,928	13,014	0	4.99	27	A	4		...					0....	28769
98-GBBC	MALA cluster	1	1	6,490	10,653		4.99	27	A	4		...					0....	28770
98-GBBC-a	mala	1	1	6,490	10,653	0	4.99	27	A	4		...					0....	28771
98-GBBD	TUMI cluster	1	1	2,219	3,643		5.00	26	A	4		...					0....	28772
98-GBBD-a	ki-timi	1	1	2,219	3,643	0	5.00	26	A	4		...					0....	28773
98-GBBE	GBIRI-NIRAGU cluster	1	1	16,157	26,523		2.00	27	A	4		...					0....	28774
98-GBBE-a	i-gbiri					0				4		...					0....	28775
98-GBBE-b	niragu	1	1	16,157	26,523	0	2.00	27	A	4		...					0....	28776
98-GBBF	KAIVI cluster	1	1	2,275	3,734		1.98	23	A	4		...					0....	28777
98-GBBF-a	kaivi	1	1	2,275	3,734	0	1.98	23	A	4		...					0....	28778
98-GBBG	DUNGI cluster	1	1	1,082	1,775		4.99	28	A	4		...					0....	28779
98-GBBG-a	dungi	1	1	1,082	1,775	0	4.99	28	A	4		...					0....	28780
98-GBBH	KIBALLO cluster	1	1	881	1,446		4.99	28	A	4		...					0....	28781
98-GBBH-a	kiballo	1	1	881	1,446	0	4.99	28	A	4		...					0....	28782
98-GBBI	KONO cluster	1	1	3,000	5,100		5.00	24	A	0		...					0....	28783
98-GBBI-a	kono	1	1	3,000	5,100	0	5.00	24	A	0		...					0....	28784
98-GBBJ	KINUKU cluster	1	1	881	1,446		4.99	28	A	4		...					0....	28785
98-GBBJ-a	kinuku	1	1	881	1,446	0	4.99	28	A	4		...					0....	28786
98-GBBK	BINA cluster	1	1	2,000	3,400		5.00	24	A	0		...					0....	28787
98-GBBK-a	bina	1	1	2,000	3,400	0	5.00	24	A	0		...					0....	28788
98-GBBL	SURUBU cluster	1	1	7,025	11,532		5.00	27	A	4		...					0....	28789
98-GBBL-a	surubu	1	1	7,025	11,532	0	5.00	27	A	4		...					0....	28790
98-GBBM	SHUWA-ZAMANI cluster	1	1	1,751	2,874		5.03	26	A	4		...					0....	28791
98-GBBM-a	ku-zamani	1	1	1,751	2,874	0	5.03	26	A	4		...					0....	28792
98-GBBM-b	ri-shuwa					0				4		...					0....	28793
98-GBC	**MAP net**	1	1	204,848	336,265		20.00	48	A	20		...					0....	28794
98-GBCA	MAP cluster	1	1	204,848	336,265		20.00	48	A	20		...					0....	28795
98-GBCA-a	ti-map	1	1	204,848	336,265	0	20.00	48	A	20		...					0....	28796
98-GBD	**PITI-ATSAM net**	1	2	59,901	98,330		18.64	56	B	24		P..					0....	28797
98-GBDA	PITI-RIBAN cluster	1	1	5,419	8,896		5.00	31	A	4		...					0....	28798
98-GBDA-a	piti	1	1	5,419	8,896	0	5.00	31	A	4		...					0....	28799
98-GBDA-b	ri-ban					0				4		...					0....	28800
98-GBDB	ATSAM cluster	1	1	54,482	89,434		20.00	58	B	24		P..					0....	28801
98-GBDB-a	atsam	1	1	54,482	89,434	0	20.00	58	B	24	Chawai*	P..	1923-1932				0....	28802
98-H	**PLATEAU-BENUE set**	2	74	3,119,360	5,128,435		39.38	71	B	42		PN.					4....	28803
98-HA	PLATEAU chain	1	45	2,452,073	4,025,166		38.74	70	B	42		PN.					4....	28804
98-HAA	**ADARA-ANKWA net**	1	6	137,354	225,469		12.83	44	A	4		...					0....	28805
98-HAAA	ADARA cluster	1	1	72,646	119,251		18.00	55	B	4		...					0....	28806
98-HAAA-a	k-ajuru					0				4		...					0....	28807
98-HAAA-b	iri					0				4		...					0....	28808
98-HAAA-c	kachia					0				4		...					0....	28809
98-HAAA-d	minna					0				4		...					0....	28810
98-HAAB	DOKA cluster	1	1	11,151	18,304		1.00	21	A	0		...					0....	28811
98-HAAB-a	doka	1	1	11,151	18,304	0	1.00	21	A	0		...					0....	28812
98-HAAC	IDON cluster	1	1	11,151	18,304		5.00	28	A	4		...					0....	28813
98-HAAC-a	i-don	1	1	11,151	18,304	0	5.00	28	A	4		...					0....	28814
98-HAAD	KUTURMI cluster	1	1	10,303	16,913		20.00	51	B	4		...					0....	28815
98-HAAD-a	kuturmi	1	1	10,303	16,913	0	20.00	51	B	4		...					0....	28816
98-HAAE	GORA-ANKWA cluster	1	1	11,151	18,304		5.00	27	A	4		...					0....	28817
98-HAAE-a	i-ku					0				4		...					0....	28818
98-HAAE-b	gora					0				4		...					0....	28819
98-HAAE-c	ankwa					0				4		...					0....	28820
98-HAAF	KULU cluster	1	1	20,952	34,393		6.00	30	A	4		...					0....	28821
98-HAAF-a	i-kulu	1	1	20,952	34,393	0	6.00	30	A	4		...					0....	28822
98-HAB	**HYAM-KORO net**	1	7	499,423	819,823		8.46	43	A	24		P..					0....	28823
98-HABA	KORO cluster	1	1	307,623	504,974		10.00	46	A	4		...					0....	28824
98-HABA-a	ashe					0				4		...					0....	28825
98-HABA-b	ala					0				4		...					0....	28826
98-HABA-c	begbere					0				4		...					0....	28827
98-HABA-d	ejar					0				4		...					0....	28828
98-HABA-e	mia-mia					0				4		...					0....	28829
98-HABB	UNGU cluster	1	1	18,164	29,817		10.00	39	A	4		...					0....	28830
98-HABB-a	i-dun	1	1	18,164	29,817	0	10.00	39	A	4		...					0....	28831
98-HABC	YESKWA cluster	1	1	22,825	37,469		5.00	33	A	2		...					0....	28832
98-HABC-a	yeskwa	1	1	22,825	37,469	0	5.00	33	A	2		...					0....	28833
98-HABD	HYAM-SHAMANG cluster	1	2	107,781	176,928		5.23	39	A	24		P..					0....	28834
98-HABD-a	hyam	1	1	102,797	168,746	0	5.00	40	A	24	Hyam*	P..	1921-1923				0....	28835
98-HABD-b	chori					0				24		p..					0....	28836
98-HABD-c	shamang	1	1	4,984	8,182	0	9.99	28	A	24		p..					0....	28837
98-HABD-d	zhire					0				24		p..					0....	28838
98-HABE	KAMANTON cluster	1	1	18,164	29,817		9.00	37	A	4		....					0....	28839

Continued opposite

Table 9-13 continued

Code 1	REFERENCE NAME / Autoglossonym 2	Coun 3	Peo 4	in 2000 5	in 2025 6	Media radio 7	AC% 8	E% 9	Wld 10	Tr 11	Biblioglossonym 12	Print 13-15	P-activity 16	N-activity 17	B-activity 18	J-year 19	Jayuh 20-24	Ref 25
98-HABE-a	ka-manton	1	1	18,164	29,817	0	9.00	37	A	4		. . .					0. . . .	28840
98-HABF	KAGOMA cluster	1	1	24,866	40,818		5.00	29	A	4		. . .					0. . . .	28841
98-HABF-a	ka-goma	1	1	24,866	40,818	0	5.00	29	A	4		. . .					0. . . .	28842
98-HAC	**NINZAM-RUKUBA net**	1	8	523,051	858,610		19.55	48	A	24		P. .					0. . . .	28843
98-HACA	MADA cluster	1	1	105,373	172,974		50.00	89	B	22		P. .					0. . . .	28844
98-HACA-a	mada	1	1	105,373	172,974	0	50.00	89	B	22	Mada: Nigeria	P. .	1990				0. . . .	28845
98-HACB	NINZAM cluster	1	1	61,462	100,892		5.00	33	A	2		. . .					0. . . .	28846
98-HACB-a	ninzam	1	1	61,462	100,892	0	5.00	33	A	2		. . .					0. . . .	28847
98-HACC	NUMANA-GWANTU cluster	1	1	16,982	27,877		5.00	32	A	4		. . .					0. . . .	28848
98-HACC-a	nunku					0				4		. . .					0. . . .	28849
98-HACC-b	numana					0				4		. . .					0. . . .	28850
98-HACC-c	gwantu					0				4		. . .					0. . . .	28851
98-HACC-d	numbu					0				4		. . .					0. . . .	28852
98-HACD	KANUFI-NIDEM cluster	1	1	10,147	16,657		10.00	35	A	4		. . .					0. . . .	28853
98-HACD-a	kanufi					0				4		. . .					0. . . .	28854
98-HACD-b	i-nidem					0				4		. . .					0. . . .	28855
98-HACD-c	kaningkon					0				4		. . .					0. . . .	28856
98-HACE	CHE cluster	1	1	87,800	144,127		40.00	74	B	24	Rukuba	P. .	1924				0. . . .	28857
98-HACE-a	ku-che	1	1	87,800	144,127	0	40.00	74	B	24	Che	P. .	1924-1931				0. . . .	28858
98-HACF	KWANKA-LEGERI cluster	1	1	229,970	377,504		3.00	25	A	4		. . .					0. . . .	28859
98-HACF-a	kwanka					0				4		. . .					0. . . .	28860
98-HACF-b	boi					0				4		. . .					0. . . .	28861
98-HACF-c	bijim					0				4		. . .					0. . . .	28862
98-HACF-d	legeri					0				4		. . .					0. . . .	28863
98-HACG	SHALL-ZWALL cluster	1	1	7,805	12,813		20.00	48	A	4		. . .					0. . . .	28864
98-HACG-a	shall					0				4		. . .					0. . . .	28865
98-HACG-b	zwall					0				4		. . .					0. . . .	28866
98-HACH	PAI cluster	1	1	3,512	5,766		30.01	56	B	4		. . .					0. . . .	28867
98-HACH-a	pai	1	1	3,512	5,766	0	30.01	56	B	4		. . .					0. . . .	28868
98-HAD	**NUNGU-EGGON net**	1	5	184,878	303,482		46.26	83	B	42		PN.					0. . . .	28869
98-HADA	YASHI cluster	1	1	457	750		40.04	66	B	4		. . .					0. . . .	28870
98-HADA-a	yashi	1	1	457	750	0	40.04	66	B	4		. . .					0. . . .	28871
98-HADB	IBUT cluster	1	1	11,151	18,304		40.00	67	B	4		. . .					0. . . .	28872
98-HADB-a	i-but	1	1	11,151	18,304	0	40.00	67	B	4		. . .					0. . . .	28873
98-HADC	NUNGU cluster	1	1	28,735	47,170		30.00	57	B	4		. . .					0. . . .	28874
98-HADC-a	nungu					0				4		. . .					0. . . .	28875
98-HADC-b	rindre					0				4		. . .					0. . . .	28876
98-HADC-c	gudi					0				4		. . .					0. . . .	28877
98-HADD	EGGON cluster	1	1	144,200	236,709		50.00	90	B	42		PN.					0. . . .	28878
98-HADD-a	mada-eggon	1	1	144,200	236,709	0	50.00	90	B	42	Eggon	PN.	1935	1974			0. . . .	28879
98-HADD-b	mata-tarwa					0				42		pn.					0. . . .	28880
98-HADD-c	mate-ngala					0				42		pn.					0. . . .	28881
98-HADE	HAKE cluster	1	1	335	549		49.85	79	B	4		. . .					0. . . .	28882
98-HADE-a	ake	1	1	335	549	0	49.85	79	B	4		. . .					0. . . .	28883
98-HAE	**AYU net**	1	1	4,527	7,431		4.99	27	A	4		. . .					0. . . .	28884
98-HAEA	AYU cluster	1	1	4,527	7,431		4.99	27	A	4		. . .					0. . . .	28885
98-HAEA-a	ayu	1	1	4,527	7,431	0	4.99	27	A	4		. . .					0. . . .	28886
98-HAF	**BEROM-TEN net**	1	3	368,104	604,255		82.74	97	C	41		PN.					4. . . .	28887
98-HAFA	TEN cluster	1	1	49,208	80,776		50.00	80	B	24		P. .					0. . . .	28888
98-HAFA-a	ten	1	1	49,208	80,776	0	50.00	80	B	24	Aten	P. .	1940				0. . . .	28889
98-HAFB	BEROM cluster	1	1	317,781	521,649		88.00	100	C	41	Berom	PN.	1916-1936	1984		1995	4. . . .	28890
98-HAFB-a	gyell-vwang					0				41		pn.					1. . . .	28891
98-HAFB-b	fan-heikpang					0				41		pn.					1. . . .	28895
98-HAFB-c	bachit-gashish					0				41		pn.					1. . . .	28899
98-HAFB-d	du-rim					0				41		pn.					1. . . .	28902
98-HAFB-e	hoss					0				41		pn.					1. . . .	28906
98-HAFC	CHARA cluster	1	1	1,115	1,830		30.04	55	B	4		. . .					0. . . .	28907
98-HAFC-a	n-fa-chara	1	1	1,115	1,830	0	30.04	55	B	4		. . .					0. . . .	28908
98-HAG	**ZERE-KATAB net**	1	9	625,069	1,026,075		54.94	94	B	41		PN.					4. . . .	28909
98-HAGA	KAJE cluster	1	1	329,277	540,521		54.70	97	B	41		PN.					0. . . .	28910
98-HAGA-a	j-ju	1	1	329,277	540,521	0	54.70	97	B	41	Jju	PN.		1982			0. . . .	28911
98-HAGB	KATAB cluster	1	5	194,299	318,950		63.96	99	C	32		P. .					4. . . .	28912
98-HAGB-a	ka-chichere					0				32		p. .					1. . . .	28913
98-HAGB-b	ka-fanchan	1	1	4,014	6,589	0	60.01	97	C	32		p. .					1. . . .	28914
98-HAGB-c	ka-goro	1	1	17,841	29,287	0	60.00	99	C	32		p. .					1. . . .	28915
98-HAGB-d	a-takat	1	1	16,235	26,651	0	65.00	100	C	32		p. .					1. . . .	28916
98-HAGB-e	ka-tab	1	1	137,699	226,038	0	65.00	100	C	32	Katab	P. .	1940			1995	4. . . .	28917
98-HAGB-f	a-sholio	1	1	18,510	30,385	0	60.00	99	C	32		p. .					1. . . .	28918
98-HAGC	ZERE cluster	1	2	54,638	89,690		50.00	88	B	24		P. .					0. . . .	28919
98-HAGC-a	Northwest i-zere					0				24	Izere	P. .	1940				0. . . .	28920
98-HAGC-b	Northeast i-zere					0			·	24		p. .					0. . . .	28923
98-HAGC-c	jos-zarazon					0				24		p. .					0. . . .	28927
98-HAGC-d	South i-zere					0				24		p. .					0. . . .	28928
98-HAGC-e	ganang-faishang					0				24		p. .					0. . . .	28931
98-HAGC-f	fi-ran	1	1	1,684	2,764		50.00	72	B	24		p. .					0. . . .	28934
98-HAGD	RIGWE cluster	1	1	46,855	76,914		25.00	60	B	24		P. .					0. . . .	28935
98-HAGD-a	nka-rigwe	1	1	46,855	76,914	0	25.00	60	B	24	Rigwe*	P. .	1923-1935				0. . . .	28936
98-HAH	**NANDU-TARI net**	1	1	7,025	11,532		49.99	78	B	4		. . .					0. . . .	28937
98-HAHA	NANDU-TARI cluster	1	1	7,025	11,532		49.99	78	B	4		. . .					0. . . .	28938
98-HAHA-a	nandu					0				4		. . .					0. . . .	28939
98-HAHA-b	tari					0				4		. . .					0. . . .	28940
98-HAI	**JILI net**	1	1	58,563	96,133		50.00	86	B	41		PN.					0. . . .	28941
98-HAIA	JILI cluster	1	1	58,563	96,133		50.00	86	B	41		PN.					0. . . .	28942
98-HAIA-a	li-jili	1	1	58,563	96,133	0	50.00	86	B	41	Migili*	PN.	1980	1986			0. . . .	28943
98-HAJ	**FYAM-HOROM net**	1	4	44,079	72,356		48.34	78	B	4		. . .					0. . . .	28944
98-HAJA	FYAM cluster	1	2	37,623	61,758		49.77	80	B	4		. . .					0. . . .	28945
98-HAJA-a	fyam	1	2	37,623	61,758	0	49.77	80	B	4		. . .					0. . . .	28946
98-HAJB	MABO-BARKUL cluster	1	1	5,575	9,152		40.00	67	B	4		. . .					0. . . .	28947
98-HAJB-a	mabo					0				4		. . .					0. . . .	28948
98-HAJB-b	barkul					0				4		. . . .					0. . . .	28949

Continued overleaf

Table 9-13 continued

Code 1	REFERENCE NAME / Autoglossonym 2	Coun 3	Peo 4	Mother-tongue speakers in 2000 5	in 2025 6	Media radio 7	CHURCH AC% 8	E% 9	Wld 10	Tr 11	Biblioglossonym 12	SCRIPTURES Print 13-15	P-activity 16	N-activity 17	B-activity 18	J-year 19	Jayuh 20-24	Ref 25
98-HAJC	HOROM cluster	1	1	881	1,446		39.95	66	B	4		. . .					0....	28950
98-HAJC-a	horom	1	1	881	1,446	0	39.95	66	B	4		. . .					0....	28951
98-HB	BENUE chain	2	29	667,287	1,103,269		41.75	74	B	41		PN.					4....	28952
98-HBA	**TAROK-TURKWAM net**	1	4	211,204	346,697		57.52	89	B	41		PN.					4....	28953
98-HBAA	TURKWAM-CESU cluster	1	2	21,688	35,601		40.28	68	B	4		. . .					0....	28954
98-HBAA-a	turkwam	1	1	10,537	17,297	0	30.00	57	B	4		. . .					0....	28955
98-HBAA-b	arum-cesu	1	1	11,151	18,304	0	50.00	78	B	4		. . .					0....	28956
98-HBAB	TAROK cluster	1	1	158,885	260,815		67.10	100	C	41	Tarok	PN.	1917-1966	1988		1983	4....	28959
98-HBAB-a	Upper tarok					0				41		pn.					1....	28960
98-HBAB-b	Lower tarok					0				41		pn.					1....	28961
98-HBAC	BASHAR cluster	1	1	30,631	50,281		20.00	48	A	4		. . .					0....	28962
98-HBAC-a	bashar	1	1	30,631	50,281	0	20.00	48	A	4		. . .					0....	28963
98-HBB	**KPAN-CEN net**	1	2	60,281	98,952		20.00	47	A	4		. . .					0....	28964
98-HBBA	KPAN cluster	1	1	11,151	18,304		20.00	47	A	4		. . .					0....	28965
98-HBBA-a	bissaula			0	0	0	0.00	0		4		. . .					0....	28966
98-HBBA-b	kumbo					0				4		. . .					0....	28967
98-HBBA-c	tissa					0				4		. . .					0....	28968
98-HBBA-d	takum					0				4		. . .					0....	28969
98-HBBA-e	donga					0				4		. . .					0....	28970
98-HBBA-f	gayi					0				4		. . .					0....	28971
98-HBBA-g	hwaye					0				4		. . .					0....	28972
98-HBBA-h	hwaso					0				4		. . .					0....	28973
98-HBBA-i	nyatso					0				4		. . .					0....	28974
98-HBBA-j	nyonyo					0				4		. . .					0....	28975
98-HBBA-k	abakan					0				4		. . .					0....	28976
98-HBBA-l	yorda					0				4		. . .					0....	28977
98-HBBA-m	i-bukwa					0				4		. . .					0....	28978
98-HBBA-n	kente					0				4		. . .					0....	28979
98-HBBA-o	apa					0				4		. . .					0....	28980
98-HBBB	CEN cluster	1	1	49,130	80,648		20.00	47	A	2		. . .					0....	28981
98-HBBB-a	i-cen	1	1	49,130	80,648	0	20.00	47	A	2		. . .					0....	28982
98-HBC	**WURBO net**	1	3	32,382	53,155		27.60	55	B	4		. . .					0....	28983
98-HBCA	SHOO-MINDA cluster	1	1	17,886	29,360		40.00	69	B	4		. . .					0....	28984
98-HBCA-a	shoo					0				4		. . .					0....	28985
98-HBCA-b	minda					0				4		. . .					0....	28986
98-HBCA-c	nyem					0				4		. . .					0....	28987
98-HBCB	COMO-KARIM cluster	1	1	11,151	18,304		10.00	35	A	4		. . .					0....	28988
98-HBCB-a	como					0				4		. . .					0....	28989
98-HBCB-b	karim					0				4		. . .					0....	28990
98-HBCC	JIRU-KIR cluster	1	1	3,345	5,491		20.00	45	A	4		. . .					0....	28991
98-HBCC-a	jiru	1	1	3,345	5,491	0	20.00	45	A	4		. . .					0....	28992
98-HBCC-b	wiyap									4		. . .					0....	28993
98-HBCC-c	kir					0				4		. . .					0....	28994
98-HBCC-d	atak					0				4		. . .					0....	28995
98-HBD	**JUKUN net**	2	11	211,826	348,073		42.15	78	B	41		PN.					0....	28996
98-HBDA	NJIKUM-JIBU cluster	2	11	211,826	348,073		42.15	78	B	41	Jibu	PN.	1973				0....	28997
98-HBDA-a	Vehicular jukun					0				41		pn.					0....	28998
98-HBDA-b	wase	1	1	22,301	36,608	0	20.00	55	B	41		pn.					0....	28999
98-HBDA-c	diyi	2	3	2,495	4,380	0	59.92	99	B	41	Jukun Takum	PN.	1918	1980			0....	29002
98-HBDA-d	donga					0				41		pn.					0....	29003
98-HBDA-e	gayam					0				41		pn.					0....	29004
98-HBDA-f	garbabi					0				41		pn.					0....	29005
98-HBDA-g	kona	1	1	3,066	5,034		50.00	85	B	41	Jukun: Kona*	Pn.	1927				0....	29006
98-HBDA-h	wukan					0				41	Jukun: Wukari	PN.	1914	1994			0....	29007
98-HBDA-i	wapan	1	1	105,362	172,956	0	60.00	98	B	41	Wapan	PN.	1914	1994			0....	29008
98-HBDA-j	abinsi	1	1	22,301	36,608	0	10.00	39	A	41		pn.					0....	29009
98-HBDA-k	wurkum	1	1	25,646	42,099	0	50.00	88	B	41	Wurkum*	Pn.	1927-1950				0....	29012
98-HBDA-l	beezen	1	1	582	1,022	0	45.02	78	B	41		pn.					0....	29013
98-HBE	**TIGON net**	2	3	85,766	147,686		10.21	38	A	4		. . .					0....	29014
98-HBEA	TIGON cluster	2	3	85,766	147,686		10.21	38	A	4		. . .					0....	29015
98-HBEA-a	nzare	1	1	25,334	41,587	0	10.00	34	A	4		. . .					0....	29016
98-HBEA-b	kporo					0				4		. . .					0....	29017
98-HBEA-c	eneeme					0				4		. . .					0....	29018
98-HBEA-d	nama	1	1	905	1,589	0	30.06	57	B	4		. . .					0....	29019
98-HBEA-e	ashuku					0				4		. . .					0....	29020
98-HBF	**YUKUBEN-KUTEP net**	2	4	63,453	104,550		58.17	91	B	41		PN.					0....	29021
98-HBFA	KUTEP cluster	2	2	45,702	75,254		65.22	100	C	41	Kuteb*	PN.		1986-1995			0....	29022
98-HBFA-a	jenuwa					0				41		pn.					0....	29023
98-HBFA-b	lissam					0				41		pn.					0....	29024
98-HBFA-c	fikyu					0				41		pn.					0....	29025
98-HBFA-d	kunabe					0				41		pn.					0....	29026
98-HBFA-e	kentin	1	1	2,036	3,575	0	70.04	100	C	41		pn.					0....	29027
98-HBFB	YUKUBEN cluster	2	2	17,751	29,296		40.00	67	B	4		. . .					0....	29028
98-HBFB-a	yukuben	2	2	17,751	29,296	0	40.00	67	B	4		. . .					0....	29029
98-HBFB-b	uuhum-gigi					0				4		. . .					0....	29030
98-HBG	**FURU net**	1	1	2,263	3,973		49.98	84	B	8		. . .					0....	29031
98-HBGA	BISHUO cluster	1	1	2,263	3,973		49.98	84	B	8		. . .					0....	29032
98-HBGA-a	bishuo	1	1	2,263	3,973	0	49.98	84	B	8		. . .					0....	29033
98-HBH	**TAPSHIN net**	1	1	112	183		9.82	34	A	4		. . .					0....	29034
98-HBHA	TAPSHIN cluster	1	1	112	183		9.82	34	A	4		. . .					0....	29035
98-HBHA-a	tapshin	1	1	112	183	0	9.82	34	A	4		. . .					0....	29036
98-I	**CROSS-RIVER set**	4	69	7,404,858	12,172,164		90.47	99	C	62		PNB					4as..	29037
98-IA	CENTRAL-DELTA chain	1	8	280,838	461,007		87.53	99	C	41		PN.					0....	29038
98-IAA	**KUGBO-OGBIA net**	1	6	234,552	385,027		90.98	99	C	20		. . .					0....	29039
98-IAAA	OGBOGOLO cluster	1	1	9,980	16,382		60.00	89	C	4		. . .					0....	29040
98-IAAA-a	o-gbogolo	1	1	9,980	16,382	0	60.00	89	C	4		. . .					0....	29041
98-IAAB	OGBIA cluster	1	1	212,363	348,602		94.00	100	C	20		. . .					0....	29042
98-IAAB-a	Proper o-gbia	1	1	212,363	348,602	0	94.00	100	C	20	Ogbia	. . .					0....	29043
98-IAAB-b	kolo					0				20		. . .					0....	29044
98-IAAB-c	anyama					0				20		. . .					0....	29045
98-IAAB-d	o-loibiri					0				20		. . .					0....	29046
98-IAAC	MINI cluster	1	1	3,345	5,491		70.01	100	C	4		. . .					0....	29047
98-IAAC-a	mini	1	1	3,345	5,491	0	70.01	100	C	4		. . .					0....	29048

Continued opposite

Table 9-13 continued

Code 1	REFERENCE NAME / Autoglossonym 2	Coun 3	Peo 4	Mother-tongue speakers in 2000 5	in 2025 6	Media radio 7	AC% 8	E% 9	Wld 10	Tr 11	Biblioglossonym 12	Print 13-15	P-activity 16	N-activity 17	B-activity 18	J-year 19	Jayuh 20-24	Ref 25
98-IAAD	KUGBO cluster	1	1	3,512	5,766		59.99	90	B	2		. . .					0	29049
98-IAAD-a	kugbo	1	1	3,512	5,766	0	59.99	90	B	2		. . .					0	29050
98-IAAE	OBULOM cluster	1	2	5,352	8,786		62.52	91	C	4		. . .					0	29051
98-IAAE-a	o-gbronuagum	1	1	2,007	3,295	0	50.02	79	B	4		. . .					0	29052
98-IAAE-b	Proper o-bulom	1	1	3,345	5,491	0	70.01	98	C	4		. . .					0	29053
98-IAB	**ABUA-ODUAL net**	1	2	46,286	75,980		70.00	100	C	41		PN.					0	29054
98-IABA	ODUAL cluster	1	1	19,112	31,373		70.00	100	C	41		PN.					0	29055
98-IABA-a	o-dual	1	1	19,112	31,373	0	70.00	100	C	41	Odual	PN.		1981			0	29056
98-IABB	ABUA cluster	1	1	27,174	44,607		70.00	100	C	41		PN.					0	29057
98-IABB-a	Central abua	1	1	27,174	44,607	0	70.00	100	C	41	Abuan	PN.	1973	1978			0	29058
98-IABB-b	emughan					0				41		pn.					0	29059
98-IABB-c	o-tabha					0				41		pn.					0	29060
98-IABB-d	o-kpeden					0				41		pn.					0	29061
98-IB	OGONI chain	1	3	367,368	603,047		78.77	100	C	62		PNB					0	29062
98-IBA	**WEST OGONI net**	1	1	60,180	98,787		60.00	99	C	22		P . .					0	29063
98-IBAA	ELEME cluster	1	1	60,180	98,787		60.00	99	C	22		P . .					0	29064
98-IBAA-a	eleme	1	1	60,180	98,787	0	60.00	99	C	22	Eleme	P . .	1988				0	29065
98-IBB	**EAST OGONI net**	1	2	307,188	504,260		82.44	100	C	62		PNB					0	29066
98-IBBA	GOKANA cluster	1	1	94,825	155,658		70.00	100	C	41		PN.					0	29067
98-IBBA-a	gokana	1	1	94,825	155,658	0	70.00	100	C	41	Gokana	PN.	1993	1996			0	29068
98-IBBB	KHANA cluster	1	1	212,363	348,602		88.00	100	C	62	Khana*	PNB	1930-1935	1961	1968		0	29069
98-IBBB-a	North kana					0				62		pnb					0	29070
98-IBBB-b	South kana					0				62		pnb					0	29071
98-IBBB-c	tai					0				62		pnb					0	29072
98-IC	LOWER-CROSS chain	4	21	5,587,547	9,185,138		95.35	100	C	61		PNB					4as . .	29073
98-ICA	**ANDONI-ORON net**	1	8	272,711	447,665		80.80	100	C	41		PN.					4	29074
98-ICAA	OBOLO cluster	1	1	102,731	168,636		94.00	100	C	41		PN.					4	29075
98-ICAA-a	ngo					0				41		pn.					1	29076
98-ICAA-b	ataba					0				41		pn.					1	29077
98-ICAA-c	unyeada					0				41		pn.					1	29078
98-ICAA-d	o-koroete					0				41		pn.					1	29079
98-ICAA-e	ibot-obolo	1	1	102,731	168,636	0	94.00	100	C	41	Obolo	PN.	1988	1991			4	29080
98-ICAA-f	iko					0				41		pn.					1	29081
98-ICAB	IBINO cluster	1	4	28,401	46,621		82.52	100	C	4		. . .					0	29082
98-ICAB-a	ibino	1	2	16,971	27,859	0	77.49	100	C	4		. . .					0	29083
98-ICAC	ORON cluster	1	2	85,313	140,045		71.44	100	C	4		. . .					0	29084
98-ICAC-a	o-ron	1	2	85,313	140,045	0	71.44	100	C	4		. . .					0	29085
98-ICAD	OKOBO cluster	1	1	56,266	92,363		70.00	100	C	4		. . .					0	29086
98-ICAD-a	o-kobo	1	1	56,266	92,363	0	70.00	100	C	4		. . .					0	29087
98-ICB	**IBIBIO-EKIT net**	4	13	5,314,836	8,737,473		96.09	100	C	61		PNB					3as . .	29088
98-ICBA	IBIBIO-EFIK cluster	4	12	5,075,912	8,345,271		97.32	100	C	61		PNB					3as . .	29089
98-ICBA-a	anaang	1	1	1,159,663	1,903,628	2	96.00	100	C	61		pnb					1cs . .	29090
98-ICBA-b	ibibio	4	4	3,463,212	5,696,080	4	98.77	100	C	61	Ibibio	pnb				1996	3cs . .	29091
98-ICBA-c	efik	2	5	434,483	715,105	4	89.62	100	C	61	Efik	PNB	1850-1866	1862-1947	1868-1995		1as . .	29095
98-ICBB	EKIT cluster	1	1	238,924	392,202		70.00	100	C	4		. . .					0	29096
98-ICBB-a	ekit	1	1	238,924	392,202	0	70.00	100	C	4		. . .					0	29097
98-ID	UPPER-CROSS chain	2	26	678,377	1,115,091		76.43	99	C	41		PN.					0	29098
98-IDA	**KIONG-KOROP net**	2	4	25,684	43,575		78.73	100	C	8		. . .					0	29099
98-IDAA	KOROP cluster	2	2	22,439	38,249		79.99	100	C	4		. . .					0	29100
98-IDAA-a	ko-rop	2	2	22,439	38,249	0	79.99	100	C	4		. . .					0	29101
98-IDAB	KIONG cluster	1	1	558	915		69.89	100	C	8		. . .					0	29102
98-IDAB-a	ki-yong	1	1	558	915	0	69.89	100	C	8		. . .					0	29103
98-IDAC	ODUT cluster	1	1	2,687	4,411		70.00	100	C	5		. . .					0	29106
98-IDAC-a	o-dut	1	1	2,687	4,411	0	70.00	100	C	5		. . .					0	29107
98-IDB	**AGOI-IYONIYONG net**	1	4	22,613	37,121		74.09	99	C	4		. . .					0	29108
98-IDBA	IYONIYONG cluster	1	1	3,345	5,491		60.00	92	C	4		. . .					0	29109
98-IDBA-a	i-yoniyong	1	1	3,345	5,491	0	60.00	92	C	4		. . .					0	29110
98-IDBA-b	u-wet					0				4		. . .					0	29111
98-IDBB	IKO-AGOI cluster	1	3	19,268	31,630		76.54	100	C	4		. . .					0	29112
98-IDBB-a	u-yanga	1	1	223	366	0	69.96	100	C	4		. . .					0	29113
98-IDBB-b	do-sanga					0				4		. . .					0	29114
98-IDBB-c	i-ko	1	1	6,300	10,342	0	90.00	100	C	4		. . .					0	29115
98-IDBB-d	a-goi	1	1	12,745	20,922	0	70.00	100	C	4		. . .					0	29116
98-IDBB-e	bami					0				4		. . .					0	29117
98-IDC	**UBAGHARA-UMON net**	1	4	109,600	179,911		66.79	99	C	24		P . .					0	29118
98-IDCA	UBAGHARA cluster	1	1	35,136	57,676		60.00	96	B	22		P . .					0	29119
98-IDCA-a	u-tuma					0				22		p . .					0	29120
98-IDCA-b	u-gbem					0				22		p . .					0	29121
98-IDCA-c	biakpan	1	1	35,136	57,676	0	60.00	96	B	22	Ubaghara	P . .	1984				0	29122
98-IDCA-d	i-kun					0				22		p . .					0	29123
98-IDCA-e	South e-tono					0				22		p . .					0	29124
98-IDCB	UMON cluster	1	1	19,960	32,764		70.00	100	C	24		P . .					0	29125
98-IDCB-a	u-mon	1	1	19,960	32,764	0	70.00	100	C	24	Umon	P . .	1895				0	29126
98-IDCC	HUMONO cluster	1	1	31,857	52,295		70.00	100	C	2		. . .					0	29127
98-IDCC-a	ho-humono					0				2		. . .					0	29128
98-IDCC-b	e-diba	1	1	31,857	52,295	0	70.00	100	C	2		. . .					0	29129
98-IDCD	AGWAGWUNE cluster	1	1	22,647	37,176		70.00	100	C	24		P . .					0	29130
98-IDCD-a	a-gwa-gwune	1	1	22,647	37,176	0	70.00	100	C	24	Agwagwune	P . .	1894				0	29131
98-IDCD-b	a-bini					0				24		p . .					0	29132
98-IDCD-c	North e-tono					0				24		p . .					0	29133
98-IDCD-d	e-rei					0				24		p . .					0	29134
98-IDCD-e	a-dim					0				24		p . .					0	29135
98-IDCD-f	a-ba-yongo					0				24		p . .					0	29136
98-IDD	**ORING-UKELE net**	1	3	189,282	310,712		77.43	100	C	41		PN.					0	29137
98-IDDA	UKELE cluster	1	1	100,868	165,579		80.00	100	C	41	Kukele	PN.	1974	1979			0	29138
98-IDDA-a	South u-kele					0				41		pn.					0	29139
98-IDDA-b	North u-kele					0				41		pn.					0	29143
98-IDDB	UZEKWE cluster	1	1	8,776	14,405		70.00	99	C	4		. . .					0	29144
98-IDDB-a	u-zekwe	1	1	8,776	14,405	0	70.00	99	C	4		. . .					0	29145

Continued overleaf

Table 9-13 continued

Code 1	REFERENCE NAME / Autoglossonym 2	Coun 3	Peo 4	Mother-tongue speakers in 2000 5	in 2025 6	Media radio 7	CHURCH AC% 8	E% 9	Wld 10	Tr 11	Biblioglossonym 12	Print 13-15	P-activity 16	N-activity 17	B-activity 18	J-year 19	Jayuh 20-24	Ref 25
98-IDDC	ORING cluster	1	1	79,638	130,728		75.00	100	C	2		...					0....	29146
98-IDDC-a	Proper o-ring	1	1	79,638	130,728	0	75.00	100	C	2		...					0....	29147
98-IDDC-b	o-kpoto					0				2		...					0....	29148
98-IDDC-c	u-fiom					0				2		...					0....	29149
98-IDDC-d	u-fia					0				2		...					0....	29150
98-IDE	**UKPET-EHOM net**	1	1	11,151	18,304		69.99	99	C	4		...					0....	29151
98-IDEA	UKPET-EHOM cluster	1	1	11,151	18,304		69.99	99	C	4		...					0....	29152
98-IDEA-a	u-kpet					0				4		...					0....	29153
98-IDEA-b	e-hom					0				4		...					0....	29154
98-IDEA-c	u-beteng					0				4		...					0....	29155
98-IDF	**LOKÖ-LUBILA net**	1	2	12,902	21,178		69.99	99	C	22		P..					0....	29156
98-IDFA	LOKUKOLI cluster	1	1	1,751	2,874		69.96	100	C	4		...					0....	29157
98-IDFA-a	lo-ku-koli	1	1	1,751	2,874	0	69.96	100	C	4		...					0....	29158
98-IDFB	LOKÖ cluster									22		P..					0....	29159
98-IDFB-a	lo-kö					0				22	Loke*	P..	1972-1984				0....	29160
98-IDFB-b	u-gep					0				22		p..					0....	29161
98-IDFB-c	n-kpani					0				22		p..					0....	29162
98-IDFC	LUBILA cluster	1	1	11,151	18,304		69.99	99	C	4		...					0....	29163
98-IDFC-a	lu-bila	1	1	11,151	18,304	0	69.99	99	C	4		...					0....	29164
98-IDFC-b	West o-jo					0				4		...					0....	29165
98-IDFC-c	East o-jo					0				4		...					0....	29166
98-IDG	**LEGBO-LEYIGHA net**	1	3	74,441	122,199		67.08	97	C	4		...					0....	29167
98-IDGA	LEGBO cluster	1	2	63,826	104,773		68.25	98	C	4		...					0....	29168
98-IDGA-a	le-gbo	1	1	52,675	86,469	7	70.00	100	C	4		...					0....	29169
98-IDGA-b	le-tatama					1				4		...					0....	29170
98-IDGA-c	le-nyima	1	1	11,151	18,304	1	59.99	90	B	4		...					0....	29171
98-IDGB	LEYIGHA cluster	1	1	10,615	17,426		60.00	93	C	4		...					0....	29172
98-IDGB-a	le-yigha	1	1	10,615	17,426	0	60.00	93	C	4		...					0....	29173
98-IDH	**WEST MBEMBE net**	1	1	129,659	212,840		88.00	100	C	41		PN.					0....	29174
98-IDHA	WEST MBEMBE cluster	1	1	129,659	212,840		88.00	100	C	41		PN.					0....	29175
98-IDHA-a	a-dun	1	1	129,659	212,840	0	88.00	100	C	41	Mbembe: Adun*	PN.	1975	1985			0....	29176
98-IDHA-b	o-sopong					0				41		pn.					0....	29177
98-IDHA-c	o-fom-bonga					0				41		pn.					0....	29178
98-IDHA-d	o-kom					0				41		pn.					0....	29179
98-IDHA-e	o-fon-okpan					0				41		pn.					0....	29184
98-IDHA-f	o-kam					0				41		pn.					0....	29185
98-IDHA-g	o-ferikpe					0				41		pn.					0....	29186
98-IDHA-h	o-deriga					0				41		pn.					0....	29187
98-IDI	**OLULUMO-IKOM net**	1	1	95,561	156,866		80.00	100	C	4		...					0....	29188
98-IDIA	OLULUMO-IKOM cluster	1	1	95,561	156,866		80.00	100	C	4		...					0....	29189
98-IDIA-a	o-lu-lumo	1	1	95,561	156,866	0	80.00	100	C	4		...					0....	29190
98-IDIA-b	i-kom					0				4		...					0....	29191
98-IDIA-c	o-kuni					0				4		...					0....	29192
98-IDJ	**AKUM net**	1	1	872	1,531		50.00	86	B	4		...					0....	29193
98-IDJA	AKUM cluster	1	1	872	1,531		50.00	86	B	4		...					0....	29194
98-IDJA-a	a-kum	1	1	872	1,531	0	50.00	86	B	4		...					0....	29195
98-IDK	**TITA net**	1	1	3,345	5,491		40.00	66	B	4		...					0....	29196
98-IDKA	TITA cluster	1	1	3,345	5,491		40.00	66	B	4		...					0....	29197
98-IDKA-a	tita	1	1	3,345	5,491	0	40.00	66	B	4		...					0....	29198
98-IDL	**NORTH BETE net**	1	1	3,267	5,363		80.99	100	C	8		...					0....	29199
98-IDLA	NORTH BETE cluster	1	1	3,267	5,363		80.99	100	C	8		...					0....	29200
98-IDLA-a	North bete	1	1	3,267	5,363	0	80.99	100	C	8		...					0....	29201
98-IE	BENDI chain	2	11	490,728	807,881		64.82	91	C	61		PNB					0.s..	29202
98-IEA	**BENDI net**	2	11	490,728	807,881		64.82	91	C	61		PNB					0.s..	29203
98-IEAA	BEKWARRA cluster	1	1	106,176	174,292		20.00	60	B	41		PN.					0....	29204
98-IEAA-a	Proper be-kwarra	1	1	106,176	174,292	0	20.00	60	B	41	Bekwarra	PN.	1970	1983			0....	29205
98-IEAA-b	be-ten					0				41		pn.					0....	29206
98-IEAB	MBE-AFAL cluster	1	1	21,075	34,595		70.00	100	C	4		...					0....	29207
98-IEAB-a	o-be					0				4		...					0....	29208
98-IEAB-b	o-tugwang	1	1	21,075	34,595	0	70.00	100	C	4		...					0....	29209
98-IEAB-c	o-korogung					0				4		...					0....	29210
98-IEAB-d	o-korotung					0				4		...					0....	29211
98-IEAB-e	a-frike					0				4		...					29212
98-IEAB-f	o-boso					0				4		...					0....	29213
98-IEAC	OBANLIKU-ALEGE cluster	2	4	106,531	176,596		81.84	100	C	4		...					0....	29214
98-IEAC-a	a-lege	1	1	1,360	2,233	0	70.00	98	C	4		...					0....	29215
98-IEAC-b	u-kpe	1	1	21,075	34,595	0	70.00	100	C	4		...					0....	29216
98-IEAC-c	ba-yobiri					0				4		...					0....	29217
98-IEAC-d	o-banliku	2	2	84,096	139,768	0	85.00	100	C	4		...					0....	29218
98-IEAD	BETE-BENDE cluster	1	1	88,435	145,170		70.00	100	C	41		PN.					0....	29224
98-IEAD-a	South bete	1	1	88,435	145,170	0	70.00	100	C	41	Bette*	PN.	1977	1982			0....	29225
98-IEAE	BUMAJI cluster	1	1	11,151	18,304		69.99	100	C	4		...					0....	29226
98-IEAE-a	bu-maji	1	1	11,151	18,304	0	69.99	100	C	4		...					0....	29227
98-IEAF	UBANG cluster	1	1	3,345	5,491		60.00	89	C	4		...					0....	29228
98-IEAF-a	u-bang	1	1	3,345	5,491	0	60.00	89	C	4		...					0....	29229
98-IEAG	BOKYI cluster	2	2	154,015	253,433		80.00	100	C	61		PNB					0.s..	29230
98-IEAG-a	u-ki	2	2	154,015	253,433	0	80.00	100	C	61	Bokyi	PNB		1978	1985-1987		0.s..	29231
98-IEAG-b	East u-ki					0				61		pnb					0.s..	29232
98-IEAG-c	ba-sua					0				61		pnb					0.s..	29233
98-IEAG-d	i-ruan					0				61		pnb					0.s..	29234
98-IEAG-e	a-bu					0				61		pnb					0.s..	29235
98-IEAG-f	bo-je					0				61		pnb					0.s..	29236
98-IEAG-g	kwakwagom					0				61		pnb					0.s..	29237
98-IEAG-h	nsadop					0				61		pnb					0.s..	29238
98-IEAG-i	o-sokom					0				61		pnb					0.s..	29239
98-IEAG-j	o-yokom					0				61		pnb					0.s..	29240
98-IEAG-k	wula					0				61		pnb					0.s..	29241
98-IEAG-l	o-ku					0				61	Oku	pnb					0.s..	29242
98-IEAG-m	bo-orim					0				61		pnb					0.s..	29243
98-IEAG-n	ndir					0				61		pnb					0.s..	29244
98-IEAG-o	u-kwese					0				61		pnb					0.s..	29245
98-IEAG-p	u-tang					0				61		pnb					0.s..	29246
98-IEAG-q	yon					0				61		pnb					0.s..	29247
98-J	**MAMBILA-SAMBA set**	2	20	413,507	695,741		33.43	69	B	41		PN.					0.s..	29248

Continued opposite

Table 9-13 continued

Code 1	REFERENCE NAME / Autoglossonym 2	Coun 3	Peo 4	in 2000 5	in 2025 6	Media radio 7	AC% 8	E% 9	Wld 10	Tr 11	Biblioglossonym 12	Print 13-15	P-activity 16	N-activity 17	B-activity 18	J-year 19	Jayuh 20-24	Ref 25
98-JA	NDOOLA chain	2	2	13,301	22,078		55.65	86	B	4		...					0....	29249
98-JAA	**NDOOLA net**	2	2	13,301	22,078		55.65	86	B	4		...					0....	29250
98-JAAA	NDOOLA cluster	2	2	13,301	22,078		55.65	86	B	4		...					0....	29251
98-JAAA-a	ndola	2	2	13,301	22,078	0	55.65	86	B	4		...					0....	29252
98-JB	MAMBILA-KONJA chain	2	8	189,988	318,808		32.82	69	B	41		PN.					0....	29253
98-JBA	**KONJA net**	1	2	25,882	45,442		33.58	65	B	20		...					0....	29254
98-JBAA	KONJA cluster	1	2	25,882	45,442		33.58	65	B	20	Kwanja	...					0....	29255
98-JBAA-a	nya-sunda					0				20		...					0....	29256
98-JBAA-b	nya-ndung					0				20		...					0....	29257
98-JBAA-c	nya-njang					0				20		...					0....	29258
98-JBB	**MVANON-KAMKAM net**	2	4	25,673	42,348		33.71	59	B	4		...					0....	29259
98-JBBA	MVANON-KAMKAM cluster	2	4	25,673	42,348		33.71	59	B	4		...					0....	29260
98-JBBA-a	mvanon	1	1	11,597	19,036	0	44.99	72	B	4		...					0....	29261
98-JBBA-b	kamkam	2	2	2,925	5,008	0	79.38	100	C	4		...					0....	29262
98-JBBA-c	somyewe	1	1	11,151	18,304	0	10.00	34	A	4		...					0....	29263
98-JBC	**MAMBILA net**	2	2	138,433	231,018		32.51	72	B	41		PN.					0....	29264
98-JBCA	MAMBILA cluster	2	2	138,433	231,018		32.51	72	B	41	Mambila*	PN.	1973-1992	1977			0....	29265
98-JBCA-a	ju-ba					0				41		pn.					0....	29266
98-JBCA-b	ju-naare					0				41		pn.					0....	29267
98-JBCA-c	ju-li					0				41		pn.					0....	29268
98-JBCA-d	sunu-torbi					0				41		pn.					0....	29269
98-JBCA-e	ble					0				41		pn.					0....	29270
98-JBCA-f	koti					0				41		pn.					0....	29271
98-JBCA-g	kuma					0				41		pn.					0....	29272
98-JBCA-h	kumchun					0				41		pn.					0....	29273
98-JBCA-i	kurun					0				41		pn.					0....	29274
98-JBCA-j	lagubi					0				41		pn.					0....	29275
98-JBCA-k	lingan					0				41		pn.					0....	29276
98-JBCA-l	nasarao					0				41		pn.					0....	29277
98-JBCA-m	sarka-mbaka					0				41		pn.					0....	29278
98-JBCA-n	somie					0				41		pn.					0....	29279
98-JBCA-o	son-kalong					0				41		pn.					0....	29280
98-JBCA-p	tagbo					0				41		pn.					0....	29281
98-JBCA-q	tep					0				41		pn.					0....	29282
98-JBCA-r	vam-ngo					0				41		pn.					0....	29283
98-JBCA-s	yokasala					0				41		pn.					0....	29284
98-JBD	**NJERUP net**									8		...					0....	29285
98-JBDA	NJERUP cluster			0	0		0.00	0		8		...					0....	29286
98-JBDA-a	njerup			0	0	0	0.00	0		8		...					0....	29287
98-JC	SUGA-VUTE chain	2	4	65,375	114,577		54.47	87	B	22		P..					0....	29288
98-JCA	**SUGA net**	1	1	15,280	26,826		80.00	100	C	2		...					0....	29289
98-JCAA	SUGA cluster	1	1	15,280	26,826		80.00	100	C	2		...					0....	29290
98-JCAA-a	North suga					0				2		...					0....	29291
98-JCAA-b	South suga					0				2		...					0....	29292
98-JCB	**VUTE net**	2	3	50,095	87,751		46.68	84	B	22		P..					0....	29293
98-JCBA	BUTE cluster	2	3	50,095	87,751		46.68	84	B	22	Vute	P..	1988				0....	29294
98-JCBA-a	North bute					0				22		p..					0....	29295
98-JCBA-b	wawa	1	1	3,697	6,491	0	5.00	31	A	22		p..					0....	29306
98-JD	DAKA-TARAM chain	2	5	141,471	234,627		22.71	58	B	24		P..					0.s..	29318
98-JDA	**DAKA-TARAM net**	2	5	141,471	234,627		22.71	58	B	24		P..					0.s..	29319
98-JDAA	SAMBA-DAKA cluster	2	3	133,661	221,297		22.53	58	B	24		P..					0.s..	29320
98-JDAA-a	samba-daka	2	2	123,837	205,171	0	24.00	60	B	24	Chamba*	P..	1907-1933				0.s..	29321
98-JDAA-b	samba-gurum					0				24		p..					0.s..	29322
98-JDAA-c	dirim	1	1	9,824	16,126	0	4.00	33	A	24		p..					0.s..	29323
98-JDAB	LAMJA cluster	1	1	3,345	5,491		20.00	44	A	4		...					0....	29324
98-JDAB-a	lamja	1	1	3,345	5,491	0	20.00	44	A	4		...					0....	29325
98-JDAC	TARAM cluster	1	1	4,465	7,839		30.01	59	B	4		...					0....	29326
98-JDAC-a	taram	1	1	4,465	7,839	0	30.01	59	B	4		...					0....	29327
98-JE	FAM chain	1	1	1,372	2,251		40.01	60	B	4		...					0....	29328
98-JEA	**FAM net**	1	1	1,372	2,251		40.01	60	B	4		...					0....	29329
98-JEAA	FAM cluster	1	1	1,372	2,251		40.01	60	B	4		...					0....	29330
98-JEAA-a	fam	1	1	1,372	2,251	0	40.01	60	B	4		...					0....	29331
98-JF	TIBA chain	1	1	2,000	3,400		10.00	33	A	4		...					0....	29332
98-JFA	**TIBA net**	1	1	2,000	3,400		10.00	33	A	4		...					0....	29333
98-JFAA	TIBA cluster	1	1	2,000	3,400		10.00	33	A	4		...					0....	29334
98-JFAA-a	tiba	1	1	2,000	3,400	0	10.00	33	A	4		...					0....	29335
99	**BANTUIC zone**	38	1012	237,647,667	398,304,621		72.29	94	C	82		PNB					4Bsuh	29336
99-A	**BANTU set**	38	1012	237,647,667	398,304,621		72.29	94	C	82		PNB					4Bsuh	29337
99-AA	GONGOLA-PAI chain	2	15	359,551	590,392		27.26	60	B	24		P..					0....	29338
99-AAA	**MAMA net**	1	1	35,124	57,658		20.00	51	B	2		...					0....	29339
99-AAAA	MAMA cluster	1	1	35,124	57,658		20.00	51	B	2		...					0....	29340
99-AAAA-a	kwarra					0				2		...					0....	29341
99-AAAA-b	kantana					0				2		...					0....	29342
99-AAB	**WEST LAME net**	1	2	5,396	8,859		14.75	38	A	4		...					0....	29343
99-AABA	LAME cluster	1	1	3,512	5,766		19.99	44	A	4		...					0....	29344
99-AABA-a	bambaro					0				4		...					0....	29345
99-AABA-b	gura					0				4		...					0....	29346
99-AABB	GWA cluster	1	1	1,884	3,093		4.99	26	A	4		...					0....	29347
99-AABB-a	gwa	1	1	1,884	3,093	0	4.99	26	A	4		...					0....	29348
99-AAC	**SHIKI net**	1	1	1,048	1,721		10.02	34	A	4		...					0....	29349
99-AACA	SHIKI cluster	1	1	1,048	1,721		10.02	34	A	4		...					0....	29350
99-AACA-a	gubi	1	1	1,048	1,721	0	10.02	34	A	4		...					0....	29351
99-AACA-b	guru					0				4		...					0....	29352

Continued overleaf

Table 9-13 continued

Code 1	REFERENCE NAME / Autoglossonym 2	Coun 3	Peo 4	Mother-tongue speakers in 2000 5	in 2025 6	Media radio 7	CHURCH AC% 8	E% 9	Wld 10	Tr 11	Biblioglossonym 12	SCRIPTURES Print 13-15	P–activity 16	N–activity 17	B–activity 18	J-year 19	Jayuh 20-24	Ref 25
99-AAD	**JARAWA net**	1	5	208,060	341,537		21.34	55	B	24		P..					0....	29353
99-AADA	JAR cluster	1	3	196,764	322,995		22.00	56	B	24	Jarawa	P..	1940				0....	29354
99-AADA-a	bankal					0				24		p..					0....	29355
99-AADA-b	bobar					0				24		p..					29358
99-AADA-c	gingwak					0				24		p..					0....	29359
99-AADA-d	duguri	1	1	21,075	34,595	0	5.00	29	A	24		p..					0....	29360
99-AADA-e	m-bada	1	1	11,318	18,579	0	10.00	39	A	24		p..					0....	29365
99-AADA-f	kanam					0				24		p..					0....	29366
99-AADA-g	ligri					0				24		p..					0....	29367
99-AADB	DULBU cluster	1	1	145	238		9.66	35	A	4		...					0....	29368
99-AADB-a	dulbu	1	1	145	238	0	9.66	35	A	4		...					0....	29369
99-AADC	JAKU cluster	1	1	11,151	18,304		10.00	35	A	4		...					0....	29370
99-AADC-a	labir	1	1	11,151	18,304	0	10.00	35	A	4		...					0....	29371
99-AAE	**KULUNG net**	1	1	16,982	27,877		60.00	91	B	24		P..					0....	29372
99-AAEA	KULUNG cluster	1	1	16,982	27,877		60.00	91	B	24		P..					0....	29373
99-AAEA-a	ku-kulung	1	1	16,982	27,877	0	60.00	91	B	24	Kulung	P..	1950				0....	29374
99-AAF	**NUMAN-BILE net**	1	3	90,308	148,245		38.49	69	B	4		...					0....	29377
99-AAFA	MBULA-BWAZZA cluster	1	2	57,559	94,486		31.94	63	B	4		...					0....	29378
99-AAFA-a	mbula	1	1	39,718	65,199	0	40.00	71	B	4		...					0....	29379
99-AAFA-b	bwazza	1	1	17,841	29,287	0	14.00	45	B	4		...					0....	29380
99-AAFB	BILE cluster	1	1	32,749	53,759		50.00	79	B	4		...					0....	29381
99-AAFB-a	bile	1	1	32,749	53,759	0	50.00	79	B	4		...					0....	29382
99-AAG	**NGONG-NAGUMI net**	1	1	10	17		10.00	20	A	9		...					0....	29383
99-AAGA	NGONG-NAGUMI cluster	1	1	10	17		10.00	20	A	9		...					0....	29384
99-AAGA-a	ngong					0				9		...					0....	29385
99-AAGA-b	nagumi			0	0	0	0.00	0		9		...					0....	29386
99-AAH	**MBONGA net**	2	2	2,623	4,478		27.14	54	B	4		...					0....	29387
99-AAHA	MBONGA cluster	2	2	2,623	4,478		27.14	54	B	4		...					0....	29388
99-AAHA-a	m-bonga	2	2	2,623	4,478	0	27.14	54	B	4		...					0....	29389
99-AB	BENUE-KATSINA chain	2	18	3,106,013	5,112,872		92.45	99	C	62		PNB					4s...	29390
99-ABA	**TIV net**	1	1	2,871,082	4,713,157		94.56	100	C	62		PNB					4s...	29391
99-ABAA	TIV cluster	1	1	2,868,082	4,708,057		94.60	100	C	62		PNB					4s...	29392
99-ABAA-a	dzwa-tiv	1	1	2,868,082	4,708,057	2	94.60	100	C	62	Tiv	PNB	1916-1959	1936-1942	1964	1991	4s...	29393
99-ABAA-b	i-harev					1				62		pnb					1c...	29396
99-ABAA-c	shitire					1				62		pnb					1c...	29397
99-ABAA-d	u-tisha					1				62		pnb					1c...	29398
99-ABAB	IYIVE cluster	1	1	3,000	5,100		60.00	93	C	5		...					0....	29399
99-ABAB-a	i-yive					0				5		...					0....	29400
99-ABAB-b	i-njobo					0				5		...					0....	29401
99-ABB	**BITARE-ABONG net**	2	3	90,060	148,711		61.95	84	C	4		...					0....	29402
99-ABBA	BITARE cluster	2	3	87,060	143,611		63.74	86	C	4		...					0....	29403
99-ABBA-a	njwande	2	2	58,749	97,137	0	80.00	100	C	4		...					0....	29404
99-ABBA-b	batu	1	1	28,311	46,474	0	30.00	58	B	4		...					0....	29407
99-ABBB	ABONG cluster	1	1	3,000	5,100		10.00	33	A	0		...					0....	29408
99-ABBB-a	abong	1	1	3,000	5,100	0	10.00	33	A	0		...					0....	29409
99-ABC	**WEST ASUMBO net**	2	2	25,241	43,209		57.68	89	B	3		...					0....	29410
99-ABCA	WEST ASUMBO cluster	2	2	25,241	43,209		57.68	89	B	3		...					0....	29411
99-ABCA-a	e-vand	2	2	25,241	43,209	0	57.68	89	B	3		...					0....	29412
99-ABCA-b	ba-legete					0				3		...					0....	29413
99-ABD	**NORTH ASUMBO net**	2	2	6,755	11,606		85.02	100	C	12		...					0....	29414
99-ABDA	NORTH ASUMBO cluster	2	2	6,755	11,606		85.02	100	C	12		...					0....	29415
99-ABDA-a	o-lithi					0				12		...					0....	29416
99-ABDA-b	i-ceve	2	2	6,755	11,606	0	85.02	100	C	12	Iceve-maci	...					0....	29417
99-ABDA-c	u-tse					0				12		...					0....	29418
99-ABE	**ASUMBO-CENTRAL net**	1	1	3,187	5,596		85.00	100	C	12		...					0....	29419
99-ABEA	CENTRAL ASUMBO cluster	1	1	3,187	5,596		85.00	100	C	12		...					0....	29420
99-ABEA-a	i-pulo	1	1	3,187	5,596	0	85.00	100	C	12	Ipulo	...					0....	29421
99-ABF	**EAST ASUMBO net**	2	2	12,171	20,094		40.00	68	B	5		...					0....	29422
99-ABFA	EAST ASUMBO cluster	2	2	12,171	20,094		40.00	68	B	5		...					0....	29423
99-ABFA-a	e-man	2	2	12,171	20,094	0	40.00	68	B	5		...					0....	29424
99-ABG	**ESIMBI net**	1	1	33,071	58,062		85.00	100	C	12		...					0....	29427
99-ABGA	ESIMBI cluster	1	1	33,071	58,062		85.00	100	C	12		...					0....	29428
99-ABGA-a	e-simbi	1	1	33,071	58,062	0	85.00	100	C	12	Esimbi	...					0....	29429
99-ABH	**UGARE net**	1	1	23,149	40,643		80.00	100	C	12		...					0....	29430
99-ABHA	UGARE cluster	1	1	23,149	40,643		80.00	100	C	12		...					0....	29431
99-ABHA-a	u-gare	1	1	23,149	40,643	0	80.00	100	C	12	Mesaka	...					0....	29432
99-ABI	**BATOMO net**	1	1	2,000	3,400		40.00	77	B	0		...					0....	29433
99-ABIA	BATOMO cluster	1	1	2,000	3,400		40.00	77	B	0		...					0....	29434
99-ABIA-a	ba-tomo	2	1	2,000	3,400	0	40.00	77	B	0		...					0....	29435
99-ABJ	**MANTA net**	1	4	34,034	59,754		66.99	91	C	4		...					0....	29436
99-ABJA	MANTA cluster	1	4	34,034	59,754		66.99	91	C	4		...					0....	29437
99-ABJA-a	m-anta	1	1	22,487	39,480	0	80.00	100	C	4		...					0....	29438
99-ABJA-b	amasi					0				4		...					0....	29439
99-ABJA-c	i-hatum	1	1	1,508	2,648	0	45.03	80	B	4		...					0....	29440
99-ABJA-d	caka	1	1	7,776	13,653	0	40.01	72	B	4		...					0....	29441
99-ABK	**OTANK net**	1	1	5,263	8,640		50.01	78	B	4		...					0....	29442
99-ABKA	OTANK cluster	1	1	5,263	8,640		50.01	78	B	4		...					0....	29443
99-ABKA-a	o-tank	1	1	5,263	8,640	0	50.01	78	B	4		...					0....	29444
99-AC	CROSS-MIDDLE chain	2	10	275,941	459,809		75.11	100	C	42		PN.					0....	29447
99-ACA	**EKAJUK net**	1	6	145,158	238,283		70.00	100	C	42		PN.					0....	29448
99-ACAA	NKEM-NKUM cluster	1	1	43,699	71,734		70.00	100	C	12		...					0....	29449
99-ACAA-a	n-kem	1	1	43,699	71,734	0	70.00	100	C	12	Nkem-nkum	...					0....	29450
99-ACAA-b	n-kum					0				12		...					0....	29454

Continued opposite

Table 9-13 continued

Code 1	REFERENCE NAME / Autoglossonym 2	Coun 3	Peo 4	Mother-tongue speakers in 2000 5	in 2025 6	Media radio 7	AC% 8	E% 9	Wld 10	Tr 11	Biblioglossonym 12	Print 13-15	P-activity 16	N-activity 17	B-activity 18	J-year 19	Jayuh 20-24	Ref 25
99-ACAB	NNAM cluster	1	3	59,198	97,176		70.00	100	C	42		PN.					0....	29455
99-ACAB-a	n-nam	1	1	3,791	6,223	0	70.01	100	C	42		pn.					0....	29456
99-ACAB-b	e-kajuk	1	1	39,116	64,211	0	70.00	100	C	42	Ekajuk	PN.		1971			0....	29457
99-ACAB-c	a-banyom	1	1	16,291	26,742	0	70.00	100	C	42		pn.					0....	29458
99-ACAC	NDE-NTA cluster	1	1	24,699	40,544		70.00	100	C	4		. . .					0....	29459
99-ACAC-a	n-de	1	1	24,699	40,544	0	70.00	100	C	4		. . .					0....	29460
99-ACAC-b	n-sele					0				4		. . .					0....	29466
99-ACAC-c	n-ta					0				4		. . .					0....	29467
99-ACAD	EFUTOB cluster	1	1	17,562	28,829		70.00	100	C	4		. . .					0....	29468
99-ACAD-a	e-futob	1	1	17,562	28,829	0	70.00	100	C	4		. . .					0....	29469
99-ACB	NDOE net	1	1	11,422	18,867		70.01	99	C	4		. . .					0....	29470
99-ACBA	BALEP cluster	1	1	2,000	3,400		70.00	98	C	0		. . .					0....	29471
99-ACBA-a	ba-lep	1	1	2,000	3,400	0	70.00	98	C	0		. . .					0....	29472
99-ACBB	KPARAGBONG cluster	1	1	9,422	15,467		70.01	100	C	4		. . .					0....	29473
99-ACBB-a	e-kparagbong	1	1	9,422	15,467	0	70.01	100	C	4		. . .					0....	29474
99-ACBB-b	be-ndeghe-affi					0				4		. . .					0....	29475
99-ACC	EJAGHAM net	2	3	119,361	202,659		81.82	100	C	41		PN.					0....	29476
99-ACCA	WEST EJAGHAM cluster	1	1	1,137	1,867		50.04	80	B	4		. . .					0....	29477
99-ACCA-a	be-ndeghe-e-tung					0				4		. . .					0....	29478
99-ACCA-b	North e-tung	1	1	1,137	1,867		50.04	80	B	4		. . .					0....	29482
99-ACCA-c	South e-tung					0				4		. . .					0....	29483
99-ACCA-d	ekwe					0				4		. . .					0....	29484
99-ACCA-e	akamkpa					0				4		. . .					0....	29485
99-ACCB	EAST EJAGHAM cluster	2	2	116,224	197,392		82.51	100	C	41		PN.					0....	29486
99-ACCB-a	ke-aka					0				41		pn.					0....	29487
99-ACCB-b	Proper e-jagham	2	2	116,224	197,392		82.51	100	C	41	Ejagham	PN.	1985	1996			0....	29488
99-ACCB-c	babong-mbakem					0				41		pn.					0....	29489
99-ACCB-d	o-bang					0				41		pn.					0....	29490
99-ACCC	SOUTH EJAGHAM cluster	1	1	2,000	3,400		60.00	93	C	0		. . .					0....	29491
99-ACCC-a	e-kin	1	1	2,000	3,400	0	60.00	93	C	0		. . .					0....	29492
99-AD	OGOJA-HILLS chain	1	1	25,111	41,221		60.00	96	C	22		P . .					0....	29493
99-ADA	OGOJA-HILLS net	1	1	25,111	41,221		60.00	96	C	22		P . .					0....	29494
99-ADAA	WEST MBUBE cluster	1	1	25,111	41,221		60.00	96	C	22		P . .					0....	29495
99-ADAA-a	m-be	1	1	25,111	41,221	0	60.00	96	C	22	Mbe	P . .	1992				0....	29496
99-AE	MAMFE-HILLS chain	1	3	86,278	151,475		52.15	89	B	12		. . .					0....	29497
99-AEA	DENYA net	1	1	18,520	32,515		60.00	98	C	12		. . .					0....	29498
99-AEAA	DENYA cluster	1	1	18,520	32,515		60.00	98	C	12	Denya	. . .					0....	29499
99-AEAA-a	ba-sho					1				12		. . .					0....	29500
99-AEAA-b	ba-jwa					1				12		. . .					0....	29501
99-AEAA-c	takamanda					1				12		. . .					0....	29502
99-AEAA-d	bi-tieku					1				12		. . .					0....	29503
99-AEB	KENDEM net	1	1	1,610	2,826		50.00	84	B	4		. . .					0....	29504
99-AEBA	KENDEM-BOKWA cluster	1	1	1,610	2,826		50.00	84	B	4		. . .					0....	29505
99-AEBA-a	kendem-bokwa	1	1	1,610	2,826	0	50.00	84	B	4		. . .					0....	29506
99-AEC	KENYANG net	1	1	66,148	116,134		50.00	86	B	12		. . .					0....	29509
99-AECA	KENYANG cluster	1	1	66,148	116,134		50.00	86	B	12		. . .					0....	29510
99-AECA-a	ke-nyang	1	1	66,148	116,134	0	50.00	86	B	12	Kenyang	. . .					0....	29511
99-AECA-b	ki-ngwa					0				12		. . .					0....	29512
99-AECA-c	ki-twii					0				12		. . .					0....	29513
99-AF	KATSINA-UPPER-HILLS chain	1	11	68,618	120,473		54.26	88	B	12		. . .					0....	29514
99-AFA	WEST BEBOID net	1	4	11,905	20,901		61.27	91	C	4		. . .					0....	29515
99-AFAA	WEST BEBOID cluster	1	4	11,905	20,901		61.27	91	C	4		. . .					0....	29516
99-AFAA-a	bu-naki	1	1	4,363	7,659	0	60.00	93	C	4		. . .					0....	29517
99-AFAA-b	bu	1	1	1,508	2,648	0	50.00	82	B	4		. . .					0....	29521
99-AFAA-c	misong	1	1	3,017	5,297	0	49.98	82	B	4		. . .					0....	29525
99-AFAA-d	kosin	1	1	3,017	5,297	0	80.01	100	C	4		. . .					0....	29531
99-AFB	EAST BEBOID net	1	7	56,713	99,572		52.79	88	B	12		. . .					0....	29534
99-AFBA	EAST BEBOID cluster	1	7	56,713	99,572		52.79	88	B	12		. . .					0....	29535
99-AFBA-a	bebe	1	1	1,508	2,648	0	50.00	83	B	12		. . .					0....	29536
99-AFBA-b	ke-mezung	1	1	3,017	5,297	0	80.01	100	C	12		. . .					0....	29540
99-AFBA-c	n-cane	1	1	1,508	2,648	0	50.00	81	B	12		. . .					0....	29541
99-AFBA-d	n-sari	1	1	3,017	5,297	0	49.98	84	B	12		. . .					0....	29542
99-AFBA-e	noni	1	1	43,138	75,737	0	50.00	87	B	12	Noone	. . .					0....	29543
99-AFBA-f	cung	1	1	1,508	2,648	0	55.04	87	B	12		. . .					0....	29544
99-AG	GRASSFIELD-WIDER chain	2	63	4,110,074	7,197,456		71.47	94	C	62		PNB					0.s..	29545
99-AGA	MENCHUM net	1	2	68,602	120,276		87.37	99	C	4		. . .					0....	29546
99-AGAA	NORTH MENCHUM cluster	1	1	3,000	5,100		40.00	77	B	0		. . .					0....	29547
99-AGAA-a	ushe-ida					0				0		. . .					0....	29548
99-AGAA-b	ushe-ku					0				0		. . .					0....	29549
99-AGAB	SOUTH MENCHUM cluster	1	2	65,602	115,176		89.54	100	C	4		. . .					0....	29550
99-AGAB-a	ge	1	1	6,034	10,594	0	85.00	100	C	4		. . .					0....	29551
99-AGAB-b	ba-ngwe	1	1	59,568	104,582	0	90.00	100	C	4		. . .					0....	29552
99-AGAB-c	o-komanjang					0				4		. . .					0....	29553
99-AGAB-d	o-bang-2					0				4		. . .					0....	29554
99-AGB	WEST MOMO net	1	4	25,193	44,233		74.62	96	C	4		. . .					0....	29555
99-AGBA	WEST MOMO cluster	1	4	25,193	44,233		74.62	96	C	4		. . .					0....	29556
99-AGBA-a	a-tong	1	1	1,508	2,648	0	50.00	82	B	4		. . .					0....	29557
99-AGBA-b	n-gamambo	1	2	22,177	38,937	0	77.96	98	C	4		. . .					0....	29562
99-AGBA-c	bu-sam	1	1	1,508	2,648	0	50.00	82	B	4		. . .					0....	29568
99-AGC	SOUTH MOMO net	1	6	314,424	552,028		80.48	99	C	22		P . .					0....	29572
99-AGCA	SOUTH MOMO cluster	1	6	314,424	552,028	1	80.48	99	C	22		P . .					0....	29573
99-AGCA-a	n-gwo	1	3	110,431	193,882	1	79.30	100	C	22		p . .					0....	29574
99-AGCA-b	mo-ghamo	1	2	154,686	271,579	1	81.48	99	C	22		p . .					0....	29586
99-AGCA-c	mun-dani	1	1	49,307	86,567	1	80.00	100	C	22	Mundani	P . .	1989-1990				0....	29592
99-AGD	RING net	2	17	666,789	1,170,287		72.73	99	C	41		PN.					0....	29598
99-AGDA	WEST RING cluster	1	6	105,665	185,514		75.57	96	C	24		P . .					0....	29599
99-AGDA-a	e-su	1	2	63,446	111,391	0	72.32	94	C	24	Isu	P . .	1852				0....	29600
99-AGDA-b	wi	1	1	8,086	14,196	0	70.00	100	C	24		p . .					0....	29601
99-AGDA-c	a-ghem	1	1	27,103	47,585	0	85.00	97	C	24		p . .					0....	29602
99-AGDA-d	zoa					0				24		p . .					0....	29603

Continued overleaf

Table 9-13 continued

Code 1	REFERENCE NAME / Autoglossonym 2	Coun 3	Peo 4	Mother-tongue speakers in 2000 5	in 2025 6	Media radio 7	AC% 8	E% 9	Wld 10	Tr 11	Biblioglossonym 12	Print 13-15	P-activity 16	N-activity 17	B-activity 18	J-year 19	Jayuh 20-24	Ref 25
99-AGDA-e	kumfutu					0				24		p..					0....	29604
99-AGDA-f	kung					0				24		p..					0....	29605
99-AGDA-g	kuk					0				24		p..					0....	29606
99-AGDA-h	fungom	1	1	1,171	2,055	0	49.96	83	B	24		p..					0....	29607
99-AGDA-i	cha'					0				24		p..					0....	29608
99-AGDA-j	nyos	1	1	5,859	10,287	0	80.00	100	C	24		p..					0....	29609
99-AGDB	CENTRAL RING cluster	2	7	472,578	829,314		72.50	99	C	41		PN.					0....	29610
99-AGDB-a	bum	1	1	15,085	26,484	1	80.00	100	C	41		pn.					0....	29611
99-AGDB-b	m-mem	1	1	7,542	13,242	1	60.00	98	B	41		pn.					0....	29614
99-AGDB-c	n-kom	1	1	209,996	368,687	1	68.00	100	C	41	Kom	pn.					0....	29615
99-AGDB-d	ba-banki	1	1	6,034	10,594	1	80.00	100	C	41		pn.					0....	29616
99-AGDB-e	ba-banki-tungo					1				41		pn.					0....	29617
99-AGDB-f	kuo	1	1	49,301	86,556	1	70.00	100	C	41		pn.					0....	29618
99-AGDB-g	lam-nso	2	2	184,620	323,751	1	77.93	99	C	41	Nso*	PN.		1990			0....	29619
99-AGDC	SOUTH RING cluster	1	4	88,546	155,459		70.56	97	C	41		PN.					0....	29620
99-AGDC-a	vengo	1	1	22,323	39,192	0	70.00	100	C	41	Babungo*	PN.	1985	1993			0....	29621
99-AGDC-b	ke-nswei	1	1	20,669	36,289	0	80.00	100	C	41		pn.					0....	29622
99-AGDC-c	ba-munka	1	1	25,133	44,126	0	80.00	100	C	41		pn.					0....	29623
99-AGDC-d	wushi	1	1	20,421	35,852	0	50.00	87	B	41		pn.					0....	29624
99-AGE	**MBAM-NKAM net**	2	34	3,035,066	5,310,632		69.88	93	C	62		PNB					0.s..	29625
99-AGEA	NGEMBA cluster	1	7	289,748	508,707		78.02	99	C	20		...					0....	29626
99-AGEA-a	beba					1				20	Bafut	...					0....	29627
99-AGEA-b	bufe	1	1	72,510	127,305	1	80.00	100	C	20		...					0....	29632
99-AGEA-c	mbili-mbui	1	1	15,551	27,303	1	60.00	93	C	20		...					0....	29633
99-AGEA-d	mundum	1	1	33,071	58,062	1	94.00	100	C	20	Ngomba	...					0....	29636
99-AGEA-e	Proper n-gemba	1	1	115,745	203,212	1	74.00	100	C	20		...					0....	29639
99-AGEA-f	ba-freng					1				20		...					0....	29648
99-AGEA-g	menda-nkwe	1	1	15,551	27,303	1	85.00	100	C	20		...					0....	29649
99-AGEA-h	awing	1	1	10,864	19,074	1	70.00	100	C	20		...					0....	29650
99-AGEA-i	pinyin	1	1	26,456	46,448	1	80.00	100	C	20		...					0....	29653
99-AGEB	EAST GRASSFIELD cluster	2	9	233,788	409,184		75.86	97	C	41		PN.					0....	29656
99-AGEB-a	li-mbum	1	2	129,900	228,062	0	83.31	100	C	41	Limbum	pn.					0....	29657
99-AGEB-b	mfumte	1	4	49,892	87,595	0	80.00	100	C	41		pn.					0....	29662
99-AGEB-c	yamba	2	3	53,996	93,527	0	54.13	90	B	41	Yamba	PN.	1990	1992			0....	29670
99-AGEC	DSCHANG-NGWE cluster	1	1	300,000	510,000		75.00	99	C	0		...					0....	29676
99-AGEC-a	ngwe					0				0		...					0....	29677
99-AGEC-b	dschang					0				0		...					0....	29681
99-AGED	NGOMBA-BAGAM cluster	1	5	621,679	1,091,472		83.72	100	C	61		PNB					0.s..	29697
99-AGED-a	ngombale	1	1	49,605	87,091	1	90.00	100	C	61		pnb					0.s..	29698
99-AGED-b	ngyemboong	1	2	403,851	709,193	1	82.72	100	C	61	Ngiemboon	PNB	1984				0.s..	29702
99-AGED-c	me-gaka	1	1	4,525	7,945	1	94.01	100	C	61		pnb					0.s..	29708
99-AGED-d	ngomba	1	1	163,698	287,401	1	84.00	100	C	61		pnb					0.s..	29712
99-AGEE	GHOMALA cluster	1	2	810,671	1,423,279		81.12	100	C	35		P..					0....	29718
99-AGEE-a	Northwest ghomala					1				35		p..					0....	29719
99-AGEE-b	Southwest ghomala					1				35		p..					0....	29725
99-AGEE-c	Northeast ghomala					1				35		p..					0....	29729
99-AGEE-d	Southeast ghomala	1	2	810,671	1,423,279	1	81.12	100	C	35		P..					0....	29732
99-AGEF	FE'FE' cluster	1	1	204,539	359,105		82.00	100	C	2		...					0....	29737
99-AGEF-a	North fe'fe'					0				2		...					0....	29738
99-AGEF-b	Central fe'fe'	1	1	204,539	359,105	0	82.00	100	C	2		...					0....	29745
99-AGEG	NDANDA cluster	1	1	15,538	27,279		94.00	100	C	4		...					0....	29753
99-AGEG-a	Northwest ndanda					0				4		...					0....	29754
99-AGEG-b	Northeast ndanda	1	1	15,538	27,279	0	94.00	100	C	4		...					0....	29757
99-AGEG-c	South ndanda					0				4		...					0....	29762
99-AGEH	KWA cluster	1	1	14,221	24,967		74.99	100	C	4		...					0....	29767
99-AGEH-a	Northeast kwa					0				4		...					0....	29768
99-AGEH-b	Central kwa	1	1	14,221	24,967	0	74.99	100	C	4		...					0....	29774
99-AGEI	MUNGAKA-BAMUM cluster	1	8	544,882	956,639		22.27	62	B	62		PNB					0....	29784
99-AGEI-a	mu-nga'ka	1	2	103,924	182,457	1	41.01	84	B	62	Mungaka	PNB	1929-1952	1933	1961		0....	29785
99-AGEI-b	shu-pamem	1	5	435,333	764,306	1	17.05	56	B	62	Bamun	PNB	1925-1980	1967	1988		0....	29791
99-AGEI-c	ma-menyan	1	1	5,625	9,876	1	80.00	100	C	62		pnb					0....	29799
99-AH	VOURI-UPPER chain	1	1	6,034	10,594		9.99	33	A	4		...					0....	29800
99-AHA	**NDEMLI net**	1	1	6,034	10,594		9.99	33	A	4		...					0....	29801
99-AHAA	NDEMLI cluster	1	1	6,034	10,594		9.99	33	A	4		...					0....	29802
99-AHAA-a	ndem-li	1	1	6,034	10,594	0	9.99	33	A	4		...					0....	29803
99-AI	MBAM-UPPER chain	1	1	35,955	62,958		10.00	42	A	41		PN.					0....	29804
99-AIA	**TIKAR net**	1	1	35,955	62,958		10.00	42	A	41		PN.					0....	29805
99-AIAA	TIKARI cluster	1	1	32,955	57,858		10.00	43	A	41	Tikar	PN.	1987	1989			0....	29806
99-AIAA-a	le-twumwu					0				41		pn.					0....	29807
99-AIAA-b	kong					0				41		pn.					0....	29808
99-AIAA-c	ti-ge					0				41		pn.					0....	29809
99-AIAA-d	nditam					0				41		pn.					0....	29810
99-AIAB	BANDOBO cluster	1	1	3,000	5,100		10.00	33	A	0		...					0....	29811
99-AIAB-a	ba-ndobo					0				0		...					0....	29812
99-AJ	N'KONGSAMBA-HILLS chain	1	9	622,767	1,091,989		69.66	97	C	20		...					0....	29813
99-AJA	**OROKO net**	1	4	244,757	429,717		58.16	94	B	20		...					0....	29814
99-AJAA	WEST OROKO cluster	1	2	124,877	219,246		63.02	98	C	4		...					0....	29815
99-AJAA-a	ba-rondo					0				4		...					0....	29816
99-AJAA-b	ngoro					0				4		...					0....	29817
99-AJAA-c	do-tanga	1	1	87,165	153,035	0	60.00	97	C	4		...					0....	29818
99-AJAA-d	b-ima					0				4		...					0....	29821
99-AJAB	EAST OROKO cluster	1	2	119,880	210,471		53.10	89	B	20		...					0....	29822
99-AJAB-a	e-kombe					0				20		...					0....	29823
99-AJAB-b	lo-lue	1	1	12,403	21,775	0	80.00	100	C	20		...					0....	29824
99-AJAB-c	mbonge					0				20		...					0....	29825
99-AJAB-d	lo-kundu					0				20		...					0....	29826
99-AJB	**MBO-BALONG net**	1	5	378,010	662,272		77.10	99	C	20		...					0....	29827
99-AJBA	WEST NGOE cluster	1	1	13,889	24,384		85.00	100	C	4		...					0....	29828
99-AJBA-a	le-fo'	1	1	13,889	24,384	0	85.00	100	C	4		...					0....	29829
99-AJBA-b	ba-long					0				4		...					0....	29830
99-AJBB	NORTHWEST MBO cluster	1	1	105,595	185,391		70.00	100	C	20	Mbo	...					0....	29833
99-AJBB-a	mi-enge					0				20		...					0....	29834
99-AJBB-b	n-swase	1	1	105,595	185,391	0	70.00	100	C	20		...					0....	29835
99-AJBC	NORTHEAST MBO cluster	1	1	20,000	34,000		70.00	98	C	0		...					0....	29836
99-AJBC-a	nlaa-mboo					0				0		...					0....	29837
99-AJBC-b	nlee-mbuu					0				0		...					0....	29840
99-AJBC-c	eho-mbo'					0				0		...					0....	29843

Continued opposite

Table 9-13 continued

Code 1	REFERENCE NAME / Autoglossonym 2	Coun 3	Peo 4	Mother-tongue speakers in 2000 5	in 2025 6	Media radio 7	CHURCH AC% 8	E% 9	Wld 10	Tr 11	Biblioglossonym 12	SCRIPTURES Print 13-15	P-activity 16	N-activity 17	B-activity 18	J-year 19	Jayuh 20-24	Ref 25
99-AJBD	CENTRAL MBO cluster	1	2	150,850	264,844		78.20	100	C	0		. . .					0	29846
99-AJBD-a	ehow-mba'					0				0		. . .					0	29847
99-AJBD-b	mwa-neka					0				0		. . .					0	29848
99-AJBD-c	ma-nenguba					0				0		. . .					0	29849
99-AJBD-d	ehobe-be-lon	1	1	15,085	26,484	0	80.00	100	C	0		. . .					0	29850
99-AJBD-e	eho-mkaa'					0				0		. . .					0	29851
99-AJBD-f	mwa-hed					0				0		. . .					0	29852
99-AJBD-g	ma-nehas					0				0		. . .					0	29853
99-AJBD-h	ihobe-mbog					0				0		. . .					0	29854
99-AJBD-i	mbwase-nghuy					0				0		. . .					0	29855
99-AJBE	AKOOSE cluster	1	1	82,676	145,153		86.20	100	C	12	Akoose	. . .					0	29856
99-AJBE-a	ba-nyue					0				12		. . .					0	29857
99-AJBE-b	e-lung					0				12		. . .					0	29858
99-AJBE-c	ba-bubog					0				12		. . .					0	29861
99-AJBE-d	e-bamut					0				12		. . .					0	29862
99-AJBE-e	ngemenge					0				12		. . .					0	29863
99-AJBE-f	mbw-ogmut					0				12		. . .					0	29864
99-AJBE-g	n-nenong					0				12		. . .					0	29865
99-AJBE-h	ma-nyue.					0				12		. . .					0	29866
99-AJBE-i	mwa-mbong					0				12		. . .					0	29867
99-AJBE-j	mwa-menam					0				12		. . .					0	29868
99-AJBE-k	mw-etan					0				12		. . .					0	29869
99-AJBE-l	mw-etug					0				12		. . .					0	29872
99-AJBF	LEKONGO cluster	1	1	2,000	3,400		50.00	86	B	0		. . .					0	29875
99-AJBF-a	le-kongo	1	1	2,000	3,400	0	50.00	86	B	0		. . .					0	29876
99-AJBG	BONGKENG cluster	1	1	3,000	5,100		50.00	86	B	0		. . .					0	29877
99-AJBG-a	bongkeng	1	1	3,000	5,100	0	50.00	86	B	0		. . .					0	29878
99-AK	BUBI chain	1	1	45,311	79,552		97.00	100	C	24		P . .					0	29879
99-AKA	**BUBI net**	1	1	45,311	79,552		97.00	100	C	24		P . .					0	29880
99-AKAA	BUBI cluster	1	1	45,311	79,552		97.00	100	C	24	Bube	P . .	1849				0	29881
99-AKAA-a	North bubi					1				24		p . .					0	29882
99-AKAA-b	Southwest bubi					1				24		p . .					0	29883
99-AKAA-c	Southeast bubi					1				24		p . .					0	29884
99-AL	WOURI-UPPER chain	1	3	84,844	148,126		51.77	88	B	22		P . .					0	29885
99-ALA	**NYOKON-NEN net**	1	1	73,368	127,976		52.04	89	B	10		. . .					0	29886
99-ALAA	NYOKON cluster	1	1	15,000	25,500		60.00	93	C	0		. . .					0	29887
99-ALAA-a	ni-nyo'o					0				0		. . .					0	29888
99-ALAA-b	fung					0				0		. . .					0	29889
99-ALAB	TUNEN cluster	1	1	58,368	102,476		50.00	88	B	10		. . .					0	29890
99-ALAB-a	to-boan					0				10		. . .					0	29891
99-ALAB-b	tu-ling					0				10		. . .					0	29892
99-ALAB-c	mese					0				10		. . .					0	29893
99-ALAB-d	i-tundu					0				10		. . .					0	29894
99-ALAB-e	lo-gananga					0				10		. . .					0	29895
99-ALAB-f	ndog-bang					0				10		. . .					0	29896
99-ALAB-g	ndok-biakat					0				10		. . .					0	29897
99-ALAB-h	ndok-tuna					0				10		. . .					0	29898
99-ALB	**MANDI net**	1	2	11,476	20,150		50.01	85	B	22		P . .					0	29899
99-ALBA	MANDI cluster	1	2	11,476	20,150		50.01	85	B	22		P . .					0	29900
99-ALBA-a	no-maande	1	1	9,921	17,419	0	50.01	85	B	22	Nomaande	P . .	1994				0	29901
99-ALBA-b	tuo-tomp	1	1	1,555	2,731	0	50.03	83	B	22		p . .					0	29902
99-AM	MBAM-LOWER chain	1	5	91,438	160,535		66.95	99	C	41		PN .					0 . s . .	29903
99-AMA	**HIJUK net**	1	1	495	869		49.90	82	B	5		. . .					0	29904
99-AMAA	HIJUK cluster	1	1	495	869		49.90	82	B	5		. . .					0	29905
99-AMAA-a	hijuk	1	1	495	869	0	49.90	82	B	5		. . .					0	29906
99-AMB	**BAFIA net**	1	4	90,943	159,666		67.05	99	C	41		PN .					0 . s . .	29907
99-AMBA	BAFIA cluster	1	4	90,943	159,666		67.05	99	C	41	Bafia	PN .	1964-1990	1996			0 . s . .	29908
99-AMBA-a	le-fa'					1				41		pn .					0 . s . .	29909
99-AMBA-b	ti-ngong					1				41		pn .					0 . s . .	29910
99-AMBA-c	zakan					1				41		pn .					0 . s . .	29911
99-AMBA-d	di-mbong	1	2	15,257	26,786	1	69.77	100	C	41		pn .					0 . s . .	29912
99-AMBA-e	ri-kpa'	1	1	73,953	129,837	1	67.00	100	C	41		pn .					0 . s . .	29913
99-AMBA-f	maja					1				41		pn .					0 . s . .	29914
99-AMBA-g	ri-pey					1				41		pn .					0 . s . .	29915
99-AMBA-h	ti-bea	1	1	1,733	3,043	1	45.01	80	B	41		pn .					0 . s . .	29916
99-AN	SANAGA chain	1	11	181,084	317,705		70.07	93	C	12		. . .					0	29917
99-ANA	**NIGI net**	1	2	9,135	16,039		43.39	75	B	4		. . .					0	29918
99-ANAA	NIGI cluster	1	2	9,135	16,039		43.39	75	B	4		. . .					0	29919
99-ANAA-a	ni-gii					0				4		. . .					0	29920
99-ANAA-b	ne-dek	1	1	3,017	5,297	0	30.00	59	B	4		. . .					0	29921
99-ANB	**YAMBASA net**	1	6	74,084	130,070		70.55	95	C	12		. . .					0	29922
99-ANBA	DUMBULE cluster	1	1	1,508	2,648		50.00	83	B	4		. . .					0	29923
99-ANBA-a	du-mbule	1	1	1,508	2,648	0	50.00	83	B	4		. . .					0	29924
99-ANBB	GUNU cluster	1	1	50,756	89,112		80.00	100	C	12		. . .					0	29925
99-ANBB-a	nu-tongi					0				12		. . .					0	29926
99-ANBB-b	nu-gunu	1	1	50,756	89,112	0	80.00	100	C	12	Nugunu	. . .					0	29929
99-ANBC	CENTRAL YAMBASA cluster	1	3	20,883	36,665		50.00	83	B	3		. . .					0	29930
99-ANBC-a	nu-libie	1	1	9,921	17,419	0	50.01	83	B	3		. . .					0	29931
99-ANBC-b	nu-yangben	1	2	10,962	19,246	0	50.00	84	B	3		. . .					0	29932
99-ANBD	SOUTH YAMBASA cluster	1	1	937	1,645		49.95	82	B	5		. . .					0	29937
99-ANBD-a	nu-baca	1	1	937	1,645	0	49.95	82	B	5		. . .					0	29938
99-ANC	**TI net**	1	2	54,874	96,118		66.09	89	C	5		. . .					0	29939
99-ANCA	BATI cluster	1	1	4,000	6,800		40.00	77	B	0		. . .					0	29940
99-ANCA-a	ba-ti-ba-ngong					0				0		. . .					0	29941
99-ANCB	LETI cluster	1	2	50,874	89,318		68.14	90	C	5		. . .					0	29942
99-ANCB-a	le-ti	1	2	50,874	89,318	0	68.14	90	C	5		. . .					0	29943
99-AND	**KI net**	1	1	42,991	75,478		80.00	100	C	3		. . .					0	29944
99-ANDA	TUKI cluster	1	1	42,991	75,478		80.00	100	C	3		. . .					0	29945
99-ANDA-a	tu-ngoro					0				3		. . .					0	29946
99-ANDA-b	tu-kombe					0				3		. . .					0	29947
99-ANDA-c	to-njo					0				3		. . .					0	29948
99-ANDA-d	tu-tsingo					0				3		. . .					0	29949
99-ANDA-e	to-cenga					0				3		. . .					0	29950
99-ANDA-f	tu-mbele					0				3		. . .					0	29951

Continued overleaf

Table 9-13 continued

Code 1	REFERENCE NAME / Autoglossonym 2	Coun 3	Peo 4	Mother-tongue speakers in 2000 5	in 2025 6	Media radio 7	CHURCH AC% 8	E% 9	Wld 10	Tr 11	Biblioglossonym 12	Print 13-15	P-activity 16	N-activity 17	B-activity 18	J-year 19	Jayuh 20-24	Ref 25
99-AO	CORISCO-BAY chain	2	2	16,805	28,991		93.91	100	C	4		...					0....	29952
99-AOA	**SEKI net**	2	2	16,805	28,991		93.91	100	C	4		...					0....	29953
99-AOAA	SEKI cluster	2	2	16,805	28,991		93.91	100	C	4		...					0....	29954
99-AOAA-a	sekya-ni	2	2	16,805	28,991	0	93.91	100	C	4		...					0....	29955
99-AP	OGOOUÉ-INNER chain	1	6	99,632	161,241		95.06	100	C	63		PNB					0..u.	29958
99-APA	**MYENE net**	1	2	52,687	85,133		96.94	100	C	63		PNB					0....	29959
99-APAA	MPONGWE cluster	1	1	49,695	80,299		97.00	100	C	43		PN.					0....	29960
99-APAA-a	m-pongwe	1	1	49,695	80,299	2	97.00	100	C	43	Omyene: Mpongwe	PN.	1850	1869			0....	29961
99-APAB	GALWA-NKOMI cluster	1	1	2,992	4,834		95.99	100	C	63		PNB					0....	29964
99-APAB-a	o-myene	1	1	2,992	4,834	0	95.99	100	C	63	Omyene*	PNB	1850-1925	1869-1919	1927		0....	29965
99-APAB-b	o-rungu					0				63		pnb					0....	29968
99-APAB-c	n-komi					0				63		pnb					0....	29969
99-APAB-d	e-nenga					0				63		pnb					0....	29970
99-APB	**JUMBA-TSOGO net**	1	4	46,945	76,108		92.95	100	C	41		PN.					0..u.	29971
99-APBA	JUMBA cluster	1	1	3,000	5,100		80.00	100	C	4		...					0....	29972
99-APBA-a	a-jumba	1	1	3,000	5,100	0	80.00	100	C	4		...					0....	29973
99-APBB	PINJI cluster	1	1	5,236	8,460		95.00	100	C	5		...					0....	29974
99-APBB-a	a-pinji	1	1	5,236	8,460	0	95.00	100	C	5		...					0....	29975
99-APBC	WEST KANDE cluster	1	1	1,042	1,684		90.02	100	C	4		...					0....	29976
99-APBC-a	o-kande	1	1	1,042	1,684	0	90.02	100	C	4		...					0....	29977
99-APBD	TSOGO cluster	1	1	32,431	52,404		96.00	100	C	41		PN.					0..u.	29978
99-APBD-a	ge-tsogo	1	1	32,431	52,404	2	96.00	100	C	41	Ghetsogo*	PN.	1955-1957	1983			0..u.	29979
99-APBE	POVE cluster	1	1	5,236	8,460		79.98	100	C	4		...					0....	29980
99-APBE-a	i-bubi	1	1	5,236	8,460	0	79.98	100	C	4		...					0....	29981
99-AQ	KADEI chain	1	1	2,943	5,689		71.02	100	C	4		...					0....	29982
99-AQA	**NGONDI net**	1	1	2,943	5,689		71.02	100	C	4		...					0....	29983
99-AQAA	NGONDI cluster	1	1	2,943	5,689		71.02	100	C	4		...					0....	29984
99-AQAA-a	i-ngondi	1	1	2,943	5,689	0	71.02	100	C	4		...					0....	29985
99-AR	MAMBÉRÉ chain	1	1	12,324	19,689		36.49	66	B	4		...					0....	29988
99-ARA	**PANDE-GONGO net**	1	1	12,324	19,689		36.49	66	B	4		...					0....	29989
99-ARAA	PANDE cluster	1	1	10,324	16,289		30.00	60	B	4		...					0....	29990
99-ARAA-a	mambere-pande	1	1	10,324	16,289	0	30.00	60	B	4		...					0....	29991
99-ARAA-b	mbaere-pande					0				4		...					0....	29992
99-ARAA-c	bodengue-pande					0				4		...					0....	29993
99-ARAA-d	kongwala					0				4		...					0....	29994
99-ARAA-e	i-kenga					0				4		...					0....	29995
99-ARAB	GONGO cluster	1	1	2,000	3,400		70.00	98	C	0		...					0....	29996
99-ARAB-a	bu-gongo	1	1	2,000	3,400	0	70.00	98	C	0		...					0....	29997
99-AS	CONGO-MIDDLE chain	4	31	1,880,923	3,815,022		79.33	96	C	24		P..					0.s..	29998
99-ASA	**BWA-KANGO net**	2	3	286,427	580,614		86.79	99	C	24		P..					0....	29999
99-ASAA	NAPAGISENE cluster	1	1	1,604	2,815		84.98	100	C	5		...					0....	30000
99-ASAA-a	li-benge					0				5		...					0....	30001
99-ASAA-b	li-baati	1	1	1,604	2,815	0	84.98	100	C	5		...					0....	30002
99-ASAA-c	li-gbaase					0				5		...					0....	30005
99-ASAA-d	bo-ganga					0				5		...					0....	30006
99-ASAA-e	li-gbe					0				5		...					0....	30009
99-ASAB	APAGIBETI cluster	1	1	42,047	85,297		51.00	91	B	12		...					0....	30015
99-ASAB-a	e-gulu					0				12		...					0....	30016
99-ASAB-b	e-bugbuma					0				12		...					0....	30017
99-ASAB-c	e-gezon					0				12		...					0....	30018
99-ASAB-d	e-gbuta					0				12		...					0....	30021
99-ASAB-e	a-pakebeti-yambuku					0				12		...					0....	30022
99-ASAB-f	i-lombo					0				12		...					0....	30023
99-ASAB-g	e-gezon-2					0				12		...					0....	30024
99-ASAB-h	ndaayi					0				12		...					0....	30025
99-ASAB-i	mo-ngbapele					0				12		...					0....	30026
99-ASAB-j	mo-mveda	1	1	42,047	85,297	0	51.00	91	B	12	Pagabete	...					0....	30027
99-ASAC	NAPAGITENE cluster	1	1	242,776	492,502		93.00	100	C	24		P..					0....	30028
99-ASAC-a	li-bwa-li	1	1	242,776	492,502	0	93.00	100	C	24	Libwa*	P..	1938				0....	30029
99-ASAC-b	yewu					0				24		p..					0....	30040
99-ASAC-c	li-ngingita					0				24		p..					0....	30044
99-ASAC-d	le-lisi					0				24		p..					0....	30045
99-ASAC-e	li-wiinza					0				24		p..					0....	30050
99-ASAC-f	li-ganzulu					0				24		p..					0....	30053
99-ASB	**KANGO-CREOLE net**	1	1	7,232	14,670		89.99	100	C	4		...					0....	30054
99-ASBA	KANGO-CREOLE cluster	1	1	7,232	14,670		89.99	100	C	4		...					0....	30055
99-ASBA-a	li-kango	1	1	7,232	14,670	0	89.99	100	C	4		...					0....	30056
99-ASC	**ANGBA-BEO net**	1	1	51,654	104,788		95.00	100	C	4		...					0....	30057
99-ASCA	BORO-ANGBA cluster	1	1	51,654	104,788		95.00	100	C	4		...					0....	30058
99-ASCA-a	le-boro					0				4		...					0....	30059
99-ASCA-b	le-angba	1	1	51,654	104,788	0	95.00	100	C	4		...					0....	30060
99-ASCA-c	babendja-kalumete					0				4		...					0....	30061
99-ASCA-d	bagenza-ibembo					0				4		...					0....	30062
99-ASCA-e	le-salia					0				4		...					0....	30063
99-ASCA-f	le-lima					0				4		...					0....	30064
99-ASCA-g	le-bendia					0				4		...					0....	30065
99-ASCA-h	le-tungu					0				4		...					0....	30066
99-ASCA-i	le-beo					0				4		...					0....	30069
99-ASD	**LIKA net**	1	1	89,967	182,509		80.00	100	C	20		...					0....	30074
99-ASDA	LIKA cluster	1	1	89,967	182,509		80.00	100	C	20		...					0....	30075
99-ASDA-a	li-lika	1	1	89,967	182,509	0	80.00	100	C	20	Lika	...					0....	30076
99-ASE	**BALI net**	1	1	66,350	134,600		90.00	100	C	12		...					0.s..	30080
99-ASEA	BALI cluster	1	1	66,350	134,600		90.00	100	C	12		...					0.s..	30081
99-ASEA-a	li-baali	1	1	66,350	134,600	0	90.00	100	C	12	Bali	...					0.s..	30082
99-ASF	**BUDU-NYALI net**	1	6	360,321	730,958		85.29	100	C	20		...					0....	30087
99-ASFA	BUDU cluster	1	6	360,321	730,958		85.29	100	C	20		...					0....	30088
99-ASFA-a	e-budu	1	1	253,148	513,543	0	87.00	100	C	20	Budu	...					0....	30089
99-ASFA-b	i-ndaaka	1	1	30,347	61,563	0	80.00	100	C	20		...					0....	30099
99-ASFA-c	i-beeke	1	1	1,214	2,463	0	79.98	100	C	20		...					0....	30102

Continued opposite

Table 9-13 continued

Code / Autoglossonym	Coun	Peo	in 2000	in 2025	Media radio	AC%	E%	Wld	Tr	Biblioglossonym	Print	P-activity	N-activity	B-activity	J-year	Jayuh	Ref
99-ASFA-d i-mbo	1	1	13,353	27,088	0	89.99	100	C	20		...					0....	30105
99-ASFA-e li-nyaali	1	1	53,870	109,283	0	80.00	100	C	20		...					0....	30106
99-ASFA-f li-vanuma	1	1	8,389	17,018	0	80.00	100	C	20		...					0....	30111
99-ASG **KUMU-BILA net**	1	4	372,495	755,655		75.88	94	C	22		P..					0.s..	30112
99-ASGA KUMU cluster	1	2	306,889	622,565		84.63	100	C	22		P..					0.s..	30113
99-ASGA-a ki-kuumu	1	1	284,399	576,940	0	85.00	100	C	22	Komo	P..	1991				0.s..	30114
99-ASGA-b e-bhele	1	1	22,490	45,625	0	80.00	100	C	22	Ipere*	P..	1939-1986				0.s..	30123
99-ASGB BILA cluster	1	2	65,606	133,090		34.94	66	B	4		...					0....	30131
99-ASGB-a e-bila					0				4		...					0....	30132
99-ASGB-b ki-bila	1	1	50,110	101,654	0	21.00	56	B	4		...					0....	30136
99-ASGB-c mbuti					0				4		...					0....	30141
99-ASGB-d i-kaiku	1	1	15,496	31,436	0	80.00	100	C	4		...					0....	30142
99-ASH **BIRA net**	2	6	443,397	900,360		67.17	90	C	24		P..					0....	30143
99-ASHA BIRA cluster	2	6	443,397	900,360		67.17	90	C	24		P..					0....	30144
99-ASHA-a ki-bira	2	3	239,618	486,105	1	68.12	89	C	24	Kibira*	P..	1930				0....	30145
99-ASHA-b ku-amba	2	3	203,779	414,255	4	66.04	92	C	24		p..					0....	30146
99-ASI **KARI net**	1	1	1,632	3,311		80.02	100	C	4		...					0....	30152
99-ASIA KARI cluster	1	1	1,632	3,311		80.02	100	C	4		...					0....	30153
99-ASIA-a li-kari-li	1	1	1,632	3,311	0	80.02	100	C	4		...					0....	30154
99-ASJ **LINGBE net**	1	1	77,213	156,637		80.00	100	C	4		...					0....	30157
99-ASJA LINGBE cluster	1	1	77,213	156,637		80.00	100	C	4		...					0....	30158
99-ASJA-a li-ngbee	1	1	77,213	156,637	0	80.00	100	C	4		...					0....	30159
99-ASK **SUDANIC-FRINGE net**	1	1	5,565	11,159		30.01	60	B	9		...					0....	30162
99-ASKA BODO cluster	3	1	400	680		30.00	65	B	8		...					0....	30163
99-ASKA-a South bodo					0				8		...					0....	30164
99-ASKA-b North bodo			0	0	0	0.00	0		8		...					0....	30165
99-ASKB HOMA-GURU cluster	1	1	5,165	10,479		30.01	60	B	9		...					0....	30166
99-ASKB-a ba-banga					0				9		...					0....	30167
99-ASKB-b North homa			0	0	0	0.00	0		9		...					0....	30168
99-ASKB-c bo-guru	1	1	5,165	10,479	0	30.01	60	B	9		...					0....	30169
99-ASL **NGBINDA net**	1	1	5,165	10,479		80.00	100	C	4		...					0....	30173
99-ASLA NGBINDA cluster	1	1	5,165	10,479		80.00	100	C	4		...					0....	30174
99-ASLA-a South bu-ngbinda					0				4		...					0....	30175
99-ASLA-b North bu-ngbinda			0	0	0	0.00	0		4		...					0....	30176
99-ASM **NYANGA-GBATI net**	2	4	113,505	229,282		87.70	100	C	4		...					0....	30177
99-ASMA NYANGA-GBATI cluster	2	4	113,505	229,282		87.70	100	C	4		...					0....	30178
99-ASMA-a li-nyanga-le	1	1	59,682	121,072	0	95.00	100	C	4		...					0....	30179
99-ASMA-b gbati-ri	1	1	25,827	52,394	0	90.00	100	C	4		...					0....	30180
99-ASMA-c ma-yeka	2	2	27,996	55,816	0	70.00	100	C	4		...					0....	30181
99-AT LUALABA-LOWER chain	1	14	893,449	1,804,097		87.35	100	C	44		PN.					0....	30182
99-ATA **MBESA-POKE net**	1	3	149,168	300,962		93.83	100	C	44		PN.					0....	30183
99-ATAA MBESA cluster	1	1	10,331	20,958		80.00	100	C	4		...					0....	30184
99-ATAA-a um-mbesa	1	1	10,331	20,958	0	80.00	100	C	4		...					0....	30185
99-ATAB SO cluster	1	1	15,445	31,331		80.00	100	C	44		PN.					0....	30186
99-ATAB-a li-ge-sogo	1	1	15,445	31,331	0	80.00	100	C	44	Heso*	PN.	1909-1915	1920			0....	30187
99-ATAC POKE cluster	1	1	118,392	240,173		97.00	100	C	24		P..					0....	30188
99-ATAC-a lo-mbooki					0				24		p..					0....	30189
99-ATAC-b li-ombo					0				24		p..					0....	30190
99-ATAC-c wenge					0				24		p..					0....	30191
99-ATAC-d ba-uma					0				24		p..					0....	30192
99-ATAC-e ya-ba-undu					0				24		p..					0....	30193
99-ATAC-f lu-olambila					0				24		p..					0....	30194
99-ATAC-g li-kolo					0				24		p..					0....	30195
99-ATAC-h li-u-twa	1	1	118,392	240,173	0	97.00	100	C	24	Poke	P..	1923				0....	30196
99-ATAD NGA cluster	1	1	5,000	8,500		90.00	99	C	0		...					0....	30197
99-ATAD-a li-nga	1	1	5,000	8,500	0	90.00	99	C	0		...					0....	30198
99-ATB **MBOLE net**	1	6	493,371	994,295		86.53	100	C	42		PN.					0....	30199
99-ATBA LOMBO cluster	1	1	20,000	34,000		80.00	100	C	0		...					0....	30200
99-ATBA-a East o-lombo					0				0		...					0....	30201
99-ATBA-b West o-lombo					0				0		...					0....	30202
99-ATBB EAST KELE cluster	1	1	313,331	635,631		85.00	100	C	42		PN.					0....	30203
99-ATBB-a lo-kele	1	1	313,331	635,631	0	85.00	100	C	42	Lokele*	PN.	1903-1936	1918-1958			0....	30204
99-ATBB-b ya-wembe					0				42		pn.					0....	30205
99-ATBB-c li-leko					0				42		pn.					0....	30206
99-ATBB-d mo-ngabe					0				42		pn.					0....	30207
99-ATBB-e mo-lwa					0				42		pn.					0....	30208
99-ATBB-f m-booso					0				42		pn.					0....	30209
99-ATBB-g ya-li-koka					0				42		pn.					0....	30210
99-ATBB-h yuani					0				42		pn.					0....	30211
99-ATBC FOMA cluster	1	1	15,496	31,436		80.00	100	C	4		...					0....	30212
99-ATBC-a ya-li-hila					0				4		...					0....	30213
99-ATBC-b ya-li-kanza					0				4		...					0....	30214
99-ATBD EAST MBOLE cluster	1	4	144,544	293,228		91.44	100	C	4		...					0....	30215
99-ATBD-a lo-mbole					0				4		...					0....	30216
99-ATBD-b ya-ikole					0				4		...					0....	30217
99-ATBD-c ya-amba					0				4		...					0....	30218
99-ATBD-d ya-ngonda					0				4		...					0....	30219
99-ATBD-e bo-tunga					0				4		...					0....	30220
99-ATBD-f bo-kuma					0				4		...					0....	30221
99-ATBD-g ya-tanda					0				4		...					0....	30222
99-ATBD-h ya-tulia					0				4		...					0....	30223
99-ATBD-i ya-isa					0				4		...					0....	30224
99-ATBD-j inja					0				4		...					0....	30225
99-ATBD-k nkembe					0				4		...					0....	30226
99-ATBD-l l-ombo	1	1	25,739	52,216	0	80.00	100	C	4		...					0....	30227
99-ATBD-m langa					0				4		...					0....	30228
99-ATBD-n jonga					0				4		...					0....	30229
99-ATBD-o mpundu					0				4		...					0....	30230
99-ATBD-p hambo					0				4		...					0....	30231
99-ATBD-q mbuli					0				4		...					0....	30232
99-ATBD-r kuti					0				4		...					0....	30233
99-ATBD-s lu-amba					0				4		...					0....	30234
99-ATBD-t North kamba					0				4		...					0....	30235
99-ATBD-u lo-ombo	1	1	10,331	20,958	0	90.00	100	C	4		...					0....	30236
99-ATBD-v kori					0				4		...					0....	30237
99-ATC **ENYA-MITUKU net**	1	2	66,722	135,355		80.00	100	C	4		...					0....	30238

Continued overleaf

Table 9-13 continued

Code 1	REFERENCE NAME / Autoglossonym 2	Coun 3	Peo 4	Mother-tongue speakers in 2000 5	in 2025 6	Media radio 7	CHURCH AC% 8	E% 9	Wld 10	Tr 11	Biblioglossonym 12	SCRIPTURES Print 13-15	P-activity 16	N-activity 17	B-activity 18	J-year 19	Jayuh 20-24	Ref 25
99-ATCA	ENYA-MITUKU cluster	1	2	66,722	135,355		80.00	100	C	4		. . .					0. . . .	30239
99-ATCA-a	c-eenya	1	1	15,068	30,567	0	80.00	100	C	4		. . .					0. . . .	30240
99-ATCA-b	ki-nya-mituku	1	1	51,654	104,788	0	80.00	100	C	4		. . .					0. . . .	30241
99-ATD	**LENGOLA net**	1	1	51,654	104,788		70.00	100	C	4		. . .					0. . . .	30242
99-ATDA	LENGOLA cluster	1	1	51,654	104,788		70.00	100	C	4		. . .					0. . . .	30243
99-ATDA-a	ki-lengola	1	1	51,654	104,788	0	70.00	100	C	4		. . .					0. . . .	30244
99-ATE	**BINJA net**	1	2	132,534	268,697		93.59	100	C	4		. . .					0. . . .	30245
99-ATEA	SONGOLA cluster	1	1	3,347	6,790		80.01	100	C	4		. . .					0. . . .	30246
99-ATEA-a	ke-songola	1	1	3,347	6,790	0	80.01	100	C	4		. . .					0. . . .	30247
99-ATEB	ZIMBA cluster	1	1	128,687	261,057		94.00	100	C	2		. . .					0. . . .	30248
99-ATEB-a	zimba	1	1	128,687	261,057	0	94.00	100	C	2		. . .					0. . . .	30249
99-ATEB-b	South c-eenya					0				2		. . .					0. . . .	30250
99-ATEC	GENGELE cluster	1	1	500	850		80.00	100	C	0		. . .					0. . . .	30251
99-ATEC-a	ke-gengele	1	1	500	850	0	80.00	100	C	0		. . .					0. . . .	30252
99-AU	BANTU-INNER chain	37	805	225,642,572	376,924,735		72.01	94	C	82		PNB					4Bsuh	30253
99-AUA	**CAMEROON-COAST net**	3	14	295,361	518,187		78.66	100	C	63		PNB					0. . . .	30254
99-AUAA	KPWE-MBOKO cluster	1	4	60,410	106,062		84.87	100	C	24		P. .					0. . . .	30255
99-AUAA-a	mo-kpwe	1	1	53,242	93,477	1	85.00	100	C	24		p. .					0. . . .	30256
99-AUAA-b	bo-bea	1	1	1,131	1,986	1	85.06	100	C	24		p. .					0. . . .	30257
99-AUAA-c	bo-mboko	1	1	4,714	8,276	1	85.00	100	C	24		p. .					0. . . .	30258
99-AUAA-d	i-su	1	1	1,323	2,323	1	78.99	100	C	24	Subu	P. .	1843				0. . . .	30259
99-AUAA-e	ba-kole					1				24		p. .					0. . . .	30260
99-AUAB	DUALA cluster	1	2	202,085	354,799		75.18	100	C	62		PNB					0. . . .	30261
99-AUAB-a	Proper duala	1	1	194,644	341,734	1	75.00	100	C	62	Duala	PNB	1848-1933	1861-1909	1872-1970		0. . . .	30262
99-AUAB-b	bodiman					1				62		pnb					0. . . .	30263
99-AUAB-c	oli					1				62		pnb					0. . . .	30264
99-AUAB-d	pongo					1				62		pnb					0. . . .	30265
99-AUAB-e	mungo					1				62		pnb					0. . . .	30266
99-AUAB-f	mu-límba	1	1	7,441	13,065	1	80.00	100	C	62		pnb					0. . . .	30267
99-AUAC	SOUTH BATANGA cluster	2	2	17,797	31,247		86.64	100	C	23		P. .					0. . . .	30268
99-AUAC-a	South ba-tanga	1	1	9,921	17,419	0	80.00	100	C	23	Batanga	P. .	1953				0. . . .	30269
99-AUAC-b	ba-no'o					0				23	Bano'o	P. .	1953				0. . . .	30270
99-AUAC-c	ba-puku	1	1	7,876	13,828	0	95.00	100	C	23		p. .					0. . . .	30271
99-AUAD	YASA cluster	2	4	9,203	16,157		89.59	100	C	44		PN.					0. . . .	30272
99-AUAD-a	yasa	2	2	2,413	4,237	1	83.80	100	C	44		pn.					0. . . .	30273
99-AUAD-b	kombe	2	2	6,790	11,920	2	91.65	100	C	44	Combe*	PN.	1958	1940			0. . . .	30274
99-AUAE	BENGA cluster	2	2	5,866	9,922		93.23	100	C	63		PNB					0. . . .	30275
99-AUAE-a	benga	2	2	5,866	9,922	0	93.23	100	C	63	Benga	PNB	1858-1929	1871-1893	1898		0. . . .	30276
99-AUB	**SANAGA-LOWER net**	1	3	413,965	725,120		70.24	100	C	72		PNB					2. . . .	30277
99-AUBA	ROMBI-NKON cluster	1	2	3,658	6,422		67.63	93	C	4		. . .					0. . . .	30278
99-AUBA-a	ba-rombi	1	1	2,150	3,774	0	80.00	100	C	4		. . .					0. . . .	30279
99-AUBA-b	ba-nkon	1	1	1,508	2,648	0	50.00	83	B	4		. . .					0. . . .	30280
99-AUBB	BASAA cluster	1	1	380,307	667,698		69.50	100	C	72	Bassa: Cameroon*	PNB	1922-1967	1939-1967	1969		2. . . .	30281
99-AUBB-a	mbene					1				72		pnb					1. . . .	30282
99-AUBB-b	basaa-ba-duala					1				72		pnb					1. . . .	30286
99-AUBB-c	Northwest basaa					1				72		pnb					1. . . .	30287
99-AUBB-d	ba-kem					1				72		pnb					1. . . .	30290
99-AUBB-e	bo					1				72		pnb					1. . . .	30291
99-AUBB-f	bi-beng					1				72		pnb					1. . . .	30292
99-AUBB-g	log					1				72		pnb					1. . . .	30293
99-AUBB-h	lombi					1				72		pnb					1. . . .	30294
99-AUBB-i	West mpo					1				72		pnb					1. . . .	30295
99-AUBB-j	mbang					1				72		pnb					1. . . .	30296
99-AUBB-k	ndokama					1				72		pnb					1. . . .	30297
99-AUBB-l	ndokbele					1				72		pnb					1. . . .	30298
99-AUBB-m	ndokpenda					1				72		pnb					1. . . .	30299
99-AUBB-n	nyamtam					1				72		pnb					1. . . .	30300
99-AUBC	KOKO cluster	1	1	30,000	51,000		80.00	100	C	0		. . .					0. . . .	30301
99-AUBC-a	Central ba-koko					0				0		. . .					0. . . .	30302
99-AUBC-b	bi-soo					0				0		. . .					0. . . .	30303
99-AUBC-c	ya-kalag					0				0		. . .					0. . . .	30304
99-AUBC-d	ya-sug					0				0		. . .					0. . . .	30305
99-AUBC-e	West ba-koko					0				0		. . .					0. . . .	30306
99-AUBC-f	di-mbambang					0				0		. . .					0. . . .	30309
99-AUC	**SANAGA-OGOOUÉ net**	5	14	2,833,116	4,922,486		79.84	100	C	72		PNB					1. . . .	30310
99-AUCA	EKI-MVELE cluster	1	2	82,820	145,405		59.11	95	B	3		. . .					0. . . .	30311
99-AUCA-a	gbilgbil	1	1	7,395	12,983	0	49.99	85	B	3		. . .					0. . . .	30312
99-AUCA-b	be-bele	1	1	75,425	132,422	0	60.00	96	C	3		. . .					0. . . .	30313
99-AUCA-c	a-vek					0				3		. . .					0. . . .	30314
99-AUCA-d	le-pek					0				3		. . .					0. . . .	30315
99-AUCA-e	mengang					0				3		. . .					0. . . .	30316
99-AUCA-f	ya-nga-fuk					0				3		. . .					0. . . .	30317
99-AUCA-g	eki					0				3		. . .					0. . . .	30318
99-AUCA-h	a-song					0				3		. . .					0. . . .	30319
99-AUCA-i	ya-sem					0				3		. . .					0. . . .	30320
99-AUCA-j	ye-kaba					0				3		. . .					0. . . .	30321
99-AUCA-k	ye-samba					0				3		. . .					0. . . .	30322
99-AUCA-l	mvele					0				3		. . .					0. . . .	30323
99-AUCA-m	Vehicular ye-zum									3		. . .					0. . . .	30324
99-AUCB	ETON cluster	1	1	120,680	211,875		70.00	100	C	5		. . .					0. . . .	30325
99-AUCB-a	Proper eton	1	1	120,680	211,875	1	70.00	100	C	5		. . .					0. . . .	30326
99-AUCB-b	esele					1				5		. . .					0. . . .	30327
99-AUCB-c	mvog-namve					1				5		. . .					0. . . .	30328
99-AUCB-d	mvo-nangkok					1				5		. . .					0. . . .	30329
99-AUCB-e	be-yidzolo					1				5		. . .					0. . . .	30330
99-AUCB-f	njowi					1				5		. . .					0. . . .	30331
99-AUCC	EWONDO-FANG cluster	5	11	2,629,616	4,565,206		80.94	100	C	72	Beti	PNB	1955	1959	1970		1. . . .	30332
99-AUCC-a	ewondo	1	1	1,221,882	2,145,237	1	80.50	100	C	72	Ewondo	PNb	1955-1957	1959-1962			1. . . .	30333
99-AUCC-b	Vehicular ewondo					1				72		pnb					1. . . .	30334
99-AUCC-c	bene					1				72		pnb					1. . . .	30335
99-AUCC-d	enoa					1				72		pnb					1. . . .	30336
99-AUCC-e	evuzog					1				72		pnb					1. . . .	30337
99-AUCC-f	fong					1				72		pnb					1. . . .	30338
99-AUCC-g	mbida-mbani					1				72		pnb					1. . . .	30339
99-AUCC-h	mvete					1				72		pnb					1. . . .	30340
99-AUCC-i	mvog-nyenge					1				72		pnb					1. . . .	30341
99-AUCC-j	ngoe					1				72		pnb					1. . . .	30342
99-AUCC-k	ya-be-ka					1				72		pnb					1. . . .	30343
99-AUCC-l	ya-be-kanga					1				72		pnb					1. . . .	30344
99-AUCC-m	ya-be-kolo					1				72		pnb					1. . . .	30345
99-AUCC-n	bulu	3	4	636,635	1,118,232	4	74.60	100	C	72	Bulu	PNB	1896-1991	1926	1940		1. . . .	30346
99-AUCC-o	ye-bekolo					1				72		pnb					1. . . .	30347
99-AUCC-p	o-mvang					1				72		pnb					1. . . .	30348

Continued opposite

Table 9-13 continued

Code 1	REFERENCE NAME / Autoglossonym 2	Coun 3	Peo 4	Mother-tongue speakers in 2000 5	in 2025 6	Media radio 7	AC% 8	E% 9	Wld 10	Tr 11	Biblioglossonym 12	Print 13-15	P–activity 16	N–activity 17	B–activity 18	J-year 19	Jayuh 20-24	Ref 25
99-AUCC-q	ye-linda					1				72		pnb					1.....	30349
99-AUCC-r	ye-mbana					1				72		pnb					1.....	30350
99-AUCC-s	ye-ngono					1				72		pnb					1.....	30351
99-AUCC-t	zaman					1				72		pnb					1.....	30352
99-AUCC-u	fang	2	2	20,565	33,093	8	85.71	100	C	72	Fang: Gabon*	PNB	1894-1938	1927	1951		1.....	30353
99-AUCC-v	ntumu	3	3	461,045	800,875	2	81.26	100	C	72		pnb					1.....	30354
99-AUCC-w	make	1	1	289,489	467,769	2	95.90	100	C	72		pnb					1.....	30355
99-AUCC-x	mvany					1				72		pnb					1.....	30356
99-AUD	**SANGHA-UPPER net**	5	31	647,952	1,144,796		62.46	94	C	24		P..					0.....	30357
99-AUDA	KAKO cluster	3	3	97,479	170,737		32.72	66	B	22	Yaka	P..					0.....	30358
99-AUDA-a	East kako	3	3	97,479	170,737	1	32.72	66	B	22	Kako*	P..	1993				0.....	30359
99-AUDA-b	West bera					1				22		p..					0.....	30360
99-AUDA-c	mbe-sembo					1				22		p..					0.....	30361
99-AUDA-d	mbo-butu					1				22		p..					0.....	30362
99-AUDA-e	mbo-do					1				22		p..					0.....	30363
99-AUDA-f	mbo-ngendi					1				22		p..					0.....	30364
99-AUDA-g	mbo-njo					1				22		p..					0.....	30365
99-AUDA-h	mbo-rong					1				22		p..					0.....	30366
99-AUDA-i	ngbako					1				22		p..					0.....	30367
99-AUDA-j	ngonje					1				22		p..					0.....	30368
99-AUDA-k	ngweje					1				22		p..					0.....	30369
99-AUDB	POL-KWAKUM cluster	3	4	58,230	102,787		66.01	96	C	4		...					0.....	30370
99-AUDB-a	baki					0				4		...					0.....	30371
99-AUDB-b	kinda					0				4		...					0.....	30372
99-AUDB-c	asom					0				4		...					0.....	30373
99-AUDB-d	beten					0				4		...					0.....	30376
99-AUDB-e	til					0				4		...					0.....	30377
99-AUDB-f	pori	2	2	49,943	88,623	0	67.88	98	C	4		...					0.....	30378
99-AUDB-g	pomo					0				4		...					0.....	30379
99-AUDB-h	kwakum	1	1	6,118	10,742	0	60.00	93	C	4		...					0.....	30380
99-AUDC	MAKAA cluster	2	4	147,121	258,297		60.25	97	C	20		...					0.....	30381
99-AUDC-a	b-yep	1	1	12,944	22,726	1	60.00	96	C	20		...					0.....	30382
99-AUDC-b	be-kol	2	3	134,177	235,571	1	60.27	98	C	20	Makaa	...					0.....	30383
99-AUDC-c	be-sep					1				20		...					0.....	30384
99-AUDC-d	m-bwas					1				20		...					0.....	30385
99-AUDC-e	be-bende					1				20		...					0.....	30386
99-AUDD	SSO cluster	1	1	2,000	3,400		70.00	98	C	5		...					0.....	30387
99-AUDD-a	emvane-so					0				5		...					0.....	30388
99-AUDD-b	melan-so					0				5		...					0.....	30389
99-AUDE	KWASIO-MVUMBO cluster	2	2	26,158	45,926		97.39	100	C	23		P..					0.....	30390
99-AUDE-a	mvumbo	2	2	26,158	45,926	0	97.39	100	C	23	Ngumba	P..	1957				0.....	30391
99-AUDE-b	mabi					0				23		p..					0.....	30392
99-AUDE-c	kwa-sio					0				23		p..					0.....	30393
99-AUDE-d	ba-gyeli					0				23	Gyele	P..	1969				0.....	30394
99-AUDE-e	ba-kola					0				23		p..					0.....	30395
99-AUDF	KOOZIME cluster	2	2	106,952	192,986		66.38	100	C	22	Koozime	P..	1986				0.....	30396
99-AUDF-a	ba-jue					0				22		p..					0.....	30397
99-AUDF-b	n-gyeme					0				22		p..					0.....	30398
99-AUDG	MPO cluster	2	6	114,206	195,681		67.57	100	C	3		...					0.....	30399
99-AUDG-a	me-dzime					1				3		...					0.....	30400
99-AUDG-b	m-pobyeng					1				3		...					0.....	30401
99-AUDG-c	popyeet					1				3		...					0.....	30402
99-AUDG-d	ba-gheto					1				3		...					0.....	30403
99-AUDG-e	m-pompo	1	1	18,188	31,932	1	70.00	100	C	3		...					0.....	30404
99-AUDG-f	m-pyemo	2	3	33,303	53,640	1	70.00	100	C	3		...					0.....	30405
99-AUDG-g	bi-jugi					1				3		...					0.....	30406
99-AUDG-h	bi-akumbo					1				3		...					0.....	30407
99-AUDG-i	bi-kum					1				3		...					0.....	30408
99-AUDG-j	kpabili					1				3		...					0.....	30409
99-AUDG-k	kunabeeb	1	1	7,251	12,731	1	70.00	100	C	3		...					0.....	30410
99-AUDG-l	m-pomam					1				3		...					0.....	30411
99-AUDH	BEKWEL cluster	3	3	37,034	67,023		75.03	100	C	12		...					0.....	30412
99-AUDH-a	be-kwil	3	3	37,034	67,023	0	75.03	100	C	12	Bekwel	...					0.....	30413
99-AUDH-b	e-sel					0				12		...					0.....	30414
99-AUDI	BOMWALI cluster	2	2	38,540	73,400		69.20	99	C	3		...					0.....	30415
99-AUDI-a	bo-mwali	2	2	38,540	73,400	0	69.20	99	C	3		...					0.....	30416
99-AUDJ	UNGOM cluster	2	2	12,630	21,808		79.76	100	C	24	Ngom	P..	1910				0.....	30417
99-AUDJ-a	ngom-mekambo					0				24		p..					0.....	30418
99-AUDJ-b	ngom-ogooué					0				24		p..					0.....	30419
99-AUDJ-c	ngom-koulamoutou					0				24		p..					0.....	30420
99-AUDJ-d	ngom-sindara					0				24		p..					0.....	30421
99-AUDK	SAKE cluster	1	1	2,452	3,962		80.02	100	C	4		...					0.....	30422
99-AUDK-a	a-sake	1	1	2,452	3,962	0	80.02	100	C	4		...					0.....	30423
99-AUDL	MBANGWE cluster	2	2	5,150	8,789		82.29	99	C	4		...					0.....	30424
99-AUDL-a	m-bangwe	2	2	5,150	8,789	0	82.29	99	C	4		...					0.....	30425
99-AUE	**OGOOUÉ-UPPER net**	2	10	111,913	194,914		84.88	100	C	24		P..					0.....	30426
99-AUEA	KELE-KOTA cluster	2	6	80,890	141,520		86.25	100	C	24		P..					0.....	30427
99-AUEA-a	a-kele	2	2	34,480	63,729	2	93.00	100	C	24	Dikele*	P..	1855-1910				0.....	30428
99-AUEA-b	le-sighu	1	1	1,042	1,684	1	80.04	100	C	24		p..					0.....	30429
99-AUEA-c	i-kota	2	2	42,916	72,145	2	81.91	100	C	24	Ikota*	P..	1938-1948				0.....	30430
99-AUEA-d	ma-hongwe	1	1	2,452	3,962	1	70.02	100	C	24		p..					0.....	30435
99-AUEB	WUMVU cluster	2	2	24,156	40,898		82.56	100	C	4		...					0.....	30438
99-AUEB-a	wumvu	2	2	24,156	40,898	0	82.56	100	C	4		...					0.....	30439
99-AUEC	NDASA cluster	2	2	6,867	12,496		76.79	100	C	4		...					0.....	30440
99-AUEC-a	ndasa	2	2	6,867	12,496	0	76.79	100	C	4		...					0.....	30441
99-AUF	**OUBANGI-CONGO net**	3	20	1,590,049	3,052,258		80.55	97	C	44		PN.					4.....	30442
99-AUFA	MBATI cluster	1	1	63,863	100,756		10.00	42	A	5		...					0.....	30443
99-AUFA-a	mbati	1	1	63,863	100,756	0	10.00	42	A	5		...					0.....	30444
99-AUFB	NGANDO-KOTA cluster	1	1	5,322	8,396		90.00	100	C	4		...					0.....	30449
99-AUFB-a	di-kota					0				4		...					0.....	30450
99-AUFB-b	di-kuta					0				4		...					0.....	30451
99-AUFB-c	di-ngando	1	1	5,322	8,396	0	90.00	100	C	4		...					0.....	30452
99-AUFC-a	North m-bomitaba	1	1	291	459	0	39.86	71	B	0		...					0.....	30453
99-AUFC-b	Central m-bomitaba	1	1	9,360	18,091	0	75.00	100	C	0		...					0.....	30454
99-AUFC-c	Southern Mbomitaba	1	1	5,357	10,354	0	80.01	100	C	12	Babole	...					0.....	30455
99-AUFD	BUNGILI cluster	1	1	6,417	12,402		75.00	100	C	43		PN.					0.....	30456
99-AUFD-a	Proper bu-ngili	1	1	6,417	12,402	0	75.00	100	C	43	Bungili*	PN.	1930-1931	1947			0.....	30457
99-AUFD-b	ndaanda					0				43		pn.					0.....	30458
99-AUFD-c	West bo-mboli					0				43		pn.					0.....	30459
99-AUFE	MBOKO-NGARE cluster	1	1	26,491	51,202		65.00	100	C	4		...					0.....	30460
99-AUFE-a	mboko	1	1	26,491	51,202	0	65.00	100	C	4		...					0.....	30461
99-AUFE-b	ngare					0				4		...					0.....	30462

Continued overleaf

Table 9-13 continued

Code 1	REFERENCE NAME / Autoglossonym 2	Coun 3	Peo 4	Mother-tongue speakers in 2000 5	in 2025 6	Media radio 7	AC% 8	CHURCH E% 9	Wld 10	Tr 11	Biblioglossonym 12	SCRIPTURES Print 13-15	P-activity 16	N-activity 17	B-activity 18	J-year 19	Jayuh 20-24	Ref 25
99-AUFF	AKWA cluster	1	1	23,548	45,513		75.00	100	C	4		. . .					0. . . .	30463
99-AUFF-a	akwa	1	1	23,548	45,513	0	75.00	100	C	4		. . .					0. . . .	30464
99-AUFG	KOYO cluster	1	1	26,491	51,202		65.00	100	C	3		. . .					0. . . .	30465
99-AUFG-a	koyo	1	1	26,491	51,202	0	65.00	100	C	3		. . .					0. . . .	30466
99-AUFH	MBOSHI cluster	1	1	158,947	307,214		84.50	100	C	32		. . .					4. . . .	30467
99-AUFH-a	Proper mboshi					0				32		. . .					1. . . .	30468
99-AUFH-b	bosi					0				32		. . .					1. . . .	30469
99-AUFH-c	mbosi	1	1	158,947	307,214	0	84.50	100	C	32	Mbosi	. . .				1997	4. . . .	30470
99-AUFH-d	boshi					0				32		. . .					1. . . .	30471
99-AUFI	LIKUBA cluster	1	1	29,435	56,891		65.00	100	C	4		. . .					0. . . .	30472
99-AUFI-a	South li-kuba	1	1	29,435	56,891	0	65.00	100	C	4		. . .					0. . . .	30473
99-AUFJ	LIKWALA cluster	1	1	23,548	45,513		60.00	96	C	4		. . .					0. . . .	30474
99-AUFJ-a	li-kwala	1	1	23,548	45,513	0	60.00	96	C	4		. . .					0. . . .	30475
99-AUFK	LOBALA-TANDA cluster	2	2	100,739	201,540		52.92	91	B	12		. . .					0. . . .	30476
99-AUFK-a	lo-bala	2	2	100,739	201,540	0	52.92	91	B	12	Lobala	. . .					0. . . .	30477
99-AUFK-b	m-poko					0				12		. . .					0. . . .	30478
99-AUFK-c	South lo-bala					0				12		. . .					0. . . .	30479
99-AUFK-d	tanda					0				12		. . .					0. . . .	30480
99-AUFK-e	n-kolo					0				12		. . .					0. . . .	30481
99-AUFK-f	li-koka					0				12		. . .					0. . . .	30482
99-AUFK-g	manganzi					0				12		. . .					0. . . .	30483
99-AUFL	LIKAW-BOBA cluster	1	1	40,998	83,170		80.00	100	C	2		. . .					0. . . .	30484
99-AUFL-a	bomboma	1	1	40,998	83,170	0	80.00	100	C	2		. . .					0. . . .	30485
99-AUFL-b	li-kaw					0				2		. . .					0. . . .	30486
99-AUFL-c	li-ngonda					0				2		. . .					0. . . .	30487
99-AUFL-d	ebuku					0				2		. . .					0. . . .	30488
99-AUFL-e	bokonzi					0				2		. . .					0. . . .	30489
99-AUFM	LEMOI cluster	1	1	2,943	5,689		80.02	100	C	4		. . .					0. . . .	30490
99-AUFM-a	nkoboko					0				4		. . .					0. . . .	30491
99-AUFM-b	nsangasi					0				4		. . .					0. . . .	30492
99-AUFM-c	bolobo					0				4		. . .					0. . . .	30493
99-AUFM-d	North li-kuba					0				4		. . .					0. . . .	30494
99-AUFN	BOBANGI cluster	2	2	110,523	218,571		79.67	100	C	44		PN.					0. . . .	30495
99-AUFN-a	lo-bo-bangi	2	2	110,523	218,571	0	79.67	100	C	44	Bobangi*	PN.	1892-1928	1909-1922			0. . . .	30496
99-AUFN-b	Vehicular bobangi			0	0	0	0.00	0		44		pn.					0. . . .	30497
99-AUFN-c	bobangi-mpombo					0				44		pn.					0. . . .	30498
99-AUFN-d	bobangi-ubangi					0				44		pn.					0. . . .	30499
99-AUFO	DOKO cluster	1	1	10,331	20,958		95.00	100	C	4		. . .					0. . . .	30500
99-AUFO-a	ingbeele					0				4		. . .					0. . . .	30501
99-AUFO-b	ndeke					0				4		. . .					0. . . .	30507
99-AUFO-c	bwela	1	1	10,331	20,958	0	95.00	100	C	4		. . .					0. . . .	30508
99-AUFO-d	mongombo					0				4		. . .					0. . . .	30509
99-AUFO-e	bo-kutu					0				4		. . .					0. . . .	30510
99-AUFO-f	ingundji					0				4		. . .					0. . . .	30511
99-AUFO-g	bu-mbiya					0				4		. . .					0. . . .	30512
99-AUFO-h	mongala-boko					0				4		. . .					0. . . .	30513
99-AUFP	TEMBO cluster	1	2	190,238	385,922		89.57	100	C	22	Chitembo	P. .	1977				0. . . .	30514
99-AUFP-a	tembo-bosanga					0				22		p. .					0. . . .	30515
99-AUFP-b	tembo-mbinga					0				22		p. .					0. . . .	30516
99-AUFP-c	bo-mbenga					0				22		p. .					0. . . .	30517
99-AUFP-d	tembo-banga-melo					0				22		p. .					0. . . .	30518
99-AUFP-e	tembo-mongala					0				22		p. .					0. . . .	30519
99-AUFP-f	tembo-banga-bolu					0				22		p. .					0. . . .	30522
99-AUFP-g	tembo-sumba					0				22		p. .					0. . . .	30523
99-AUFP-h	tembo-ukaturaka					0				22		p. .					0. . . .	30524
99-AUFP-i	tembo-malundja					0				22		p. .					0. . . .	30525
99-AUFQ	NDOKO cluster	1	1	20,000	34,000		80.00	100	C	0		. . .					0. . . .	30526
99-AUFQ-a	n-doko					0				0		. . .					0. . . .	30527
99-AUFQ-b	mimbo					0				0		. . .					0. . . .	30528
99-AUFQ-c	gomba					0				0		. . .					0. . . .	30532
99-AUFR	BINZA cluster	1	1	70,105	142,218		80.00	100	C	6		. . .					0. . . .	30533
99-AUFR-a	i-bindja					0				6		. . .					0. . . .	30534
99-AUFR-b	li-binza					0				6		. . .					0. . . .	30535
99-AUFR-c	li-gendza-bumba					0				6		. . .					0. . . .	30536
99-AUFR-d	li-gendza-yambuku					0				6		. . .					0. . . .	30537
99-AUFR-e	di-gendja					0				6		. . .					0. . . .	30538
99-AUFR-f	binza-wiinza									6		. . .					0. . . .	30539
99-AUFR-g	di-baali-ligendza	1	1	70,105	142,218	0	80.00	100	C	6		. . .					0. . . .	30542
99-AUFR-h	di-baali-wiinza					0				6		. . .					0. . . .	30543
99-AUFS	SOUTH BUJA cluster	1	1	380,110	771,101		99.00	100	C	20		. . .					0. . . .	30544
99-AUFS-a	manga					0				20		. . .					0. . . .	30545
99-AUFS-b	buja-itimbiri	1	1	380,110	771,101	0	99.00	100	C	20		. . .					0. . . .	30550
99-AUFT	NORTH BUJA cluster	1	1	300,000	510,000		80.00	100	C	0		. . .					0. . . .	30554
99-AUFT-a	bo-sambi-yamwando					0				0		. . .					0. . . .	30555
99-AUFT-b	bo-sambi-yamuwa					0				0		. . .					0. . . .	30556
99-AUFT-c	bo-sambi-botsholi					0				0		. . .					0. . . .	30557
99-AUFT-d	bo-sambi-yamoloto					0				0		. . .					0. . . .	30558
99-AUFT-e	yamiekoli					0				0		. . .					0. . . .	30562
99-AUFT-f	libute-yanzila					0				0		. . .					0. . . .	30565
99-AUFT-g	yamandika					0				0		. . .					0. . . .	30566
99-AUFT-h	e-bango					0				0		. . .					0. . . .	30567
99-AUFT-i	bo-mbanga					0				0		. . .					0. . . .	30568
99-AUG	KASAI-MIDDLE net	1	1	15,331	29,458		86.74	100	C	4		. . .					0. . . .	30569
99-AUGA	NJAAL cluster	1	1	5,000	8,500		80.00	100	C	0		. . .					0. . . .	30570
99-AUGA-a	njaal	1	1	5,000	8,500	0	80.00	100	C	0		. . .					0. . . .	30571
99-AUGB	NGUL-NGWI cluster	1	1	10,331	20,958		90.00	100	C	4		. . .					0. . . .	30572
99-AUGB-a	i-ngul	1	1	10,331	20,958	0	90.00	100	C	4		. . .					0. . . .	30573
99-AUGB-b	e-ngwi					0				4		. . .					0. . . .	30574
99-AUH	KWENGE-UPPER net	2	7	1,398,881	2,835,695		95.95	100	C	61		PNB					0. . . .	30575
99-AUHA	MBALA cluster	1	1	499,804	1,013,914		97.00	100	C	24	Mbala	P. .	1931-1968				0. . . .	30576
99-AUHA-a	North ki-mbala					0				24		p. .					0. . . .	30577
99-AUHA-b	South ki-mbala									24	Gimbala	P. .	1931				0. . . .	30578
99-AUHB	PHENDE-SOONDE cluster	1	2	782,297	1,586,987		97.63	100	C	61		PNB					0. . . .	30579
99-AUHB-a	gi-phende	1	1	663,492	1,345,976	0	99.00	100	C	61	Giphende*	PNB	1926-1962	1935-1977	1996		0. . . .	30580
99-AUHB-b	ki-soonde	1	1	118,805	241,011	0	90.00	100	C	61		pnb					0. . . .	30581
99-AUHB-c	ki-lua					0				61		pnb					0. . . .	30582
99-AUHC	KWEZO cluster	1	1	70,591	143,203		95.00	100	C	24		P. .					0. . . .	30583
99-AUHC-a	ki-kwezo	1	1	70,591	143,203	0	95.00	100	C	24	Kikwese*	P. .	1929				0. . . .	30584
99-AUHD	HOLU-SAMBA cluster	2	3	46,189	91,591		57.57	88	B	23		P. .					0. . . .	30585
99-AUHD-a	ki-holu	2	2	41,024	81,112	0	53.49	87	B	23	Kiholu*	P. .	1943-1956				0. . . .	30586
99-AUHD-b	u-samba	1	1	5,165	10,479	0	90.01	100	C	23		p. .					0. . . .	30587

Continued opposite

Table 9-13 continued

Code 1	REFERENCE NAME Autoglossonym 2	Coun 3	Peo 4	Mother-tongue speakers in 2000 5	in 2025 6	Media radio 7	CHURCH AC% 8	E% 9	Wld 10	Tr 11	Biblioglossonym 12	SCRIPTURES Print 13-15	P-activity 16	N-activity 17	B-activity 18	J-year 19	Jayuh 20-24	Ref 25
99-AUI	**CONGO-BASIN net**	11	61	11,115,203	22,402,103		93.61	100	C	72		PNB					4asu.	30588
99-AUIA	SOUTHWEST NGIRI cluster	2	4	29,882	60,479		87.28	100	C	4		...					0....	30589
99-AUIA-a	ba-loi	2	3	19,551	39,521	0	85.85	100	C	4		...					0....	30590
99-AUIA-b	ma-mpoko			0	0	0	0.00	0		4		...					0....	30591
99-AUIA-c	li-kila	1	1	10,331	20,958	0	90.00	100	C	4		...					0....	30592
99-AUIA-d	mbondo			0	0	0	0.00	0		4		...					0....	30593
99-AUIA-e	bo-mbemda					0				4		...					0....	30594
99-AUIA-f	ba-ngele			0	0	0	0.00	0		4		...					0....	30595
99-AUIA-g	dzamba					0				4		...					0....	30596
99-AUIA-h	batu-baloi					0				4		...					0....	30597
99-AUIA-i	mpundza			0	0	0	0.00	0		4		...					0....	30598
99-AUIA-j	mbonzi			0	0	0	0.00	0		4		...					0....	30599
99-AUIA-k	bo-laba					0				4		...					0....	30600
99-AUIA-l	mbonzo-buburu					0				4		...					0....	30601
99-AUIA-m	mbonzo-imese					0				4		...					0....	30602
99-AUIA-n	mbonzo-boyele					0				4		...					0....	30603
99-AUIA-o	mbonzo-mikinda					0				4		...					0....	30604
99-AUIA-p	nunu					0				4		...					0....	30605
99-AUIB	NORTHEAST NGIRI cluster	1	5	76,532	155,254		73.16	97	C	6		...					0....	30606
99-AUIB-a	East bo-mboli	1	1	4,076	8,268	0	50.00	88	B	6		...					0....	30607
99-AUIB-b	li-binza-2	1	1	16,302	33,071	0	80.00	100	C	6		...					0....	30608
99-AUIB-c	ba-lobo					0				6		...					0....	30609
99-AUIB-d	bu-jaba	1	1	9,804	19,889	0	50.00	85	B	6		...					0....	30610
99-AUIB-e	li-ngundu-ebuku					0				6		...					0....	30611
99-AUIB-f	Upper koto					0				6		...					0....	30612
99-AUIB-g	Lower koto					0				6		...					0....	30613
99-AUIB-h	ba-mwe	1	1	35,652	72,324	0	80.00	100	C	6		...					0....	30614
99-AUIB-i	dzandu	1	1	10,698	21,702	0	69.99	100	C	6		...					0....	30615
99-AUIB-j	lo-liba					0				6		...					0....	30616
99-AUIB-k	bo-niange			0	0	0	0.00	0		6		...					0....	30617
99-AUIB-l	e-waku			0	0	0	0.00	0		6		...					0....	30618
99-AUIB-m	monia					0				6		...					0....	30619
99-AUIC	BOLOKI cluster	2	3	21,383	42,815		79.66	100	C	24	Boleki*	P..	1895-1904				0....	30620
99-AUIC-a	Lower bo-loki					0				24		p..					0....	30621
99-AUIC-b	Upper bo-loki					0				24		p..					0....	30622
99-AUIC-c	ndoobo	1	1	10,331	20,958	0	85.00	100	C	24		p..					0....	30623
99-AUID	MABALE cluster	5	6	65,082	128,573		73.84	91	C	20		...					0....	30624
99-AUID-a	lo-mabaale	1	1	51,654	104,788	0	85.00	100	C	20		...					0....	30625
99-AUID-b	li-panja					0				20		...					0....	30626
99-AUID-c	ma-banza					0				20		...					0....	30627
99-AUID-d	ma-bembe	1	1	2,943	5,689	0	70.00	100	C	20		...					0....	30628
99-AUID-e	m-binga	4	4	10,485	18,096	0	19.94	47	A	20		...					0....	30629
99-AUID-f	bo-nkembe					0				20		...					0....	30630
99-AUID-g	bo-kula					0				20		...					0....	30631
99-AUID-h	bo-djinga					0				20		...					0....	30632
99-AUID-i	dibali					0				20		...					0....	30633
99-AUID-j	i-boko					0				20		...					0....	30636
99-AUID-k	doko-ngiri					0				20		...					0....	30637
99-AUIE	LUSENGO cluster	1	5	91,923	186,481		83.34	100	C	24		P..					0....	30638
99-AUIE-a	li-kangana					0				24		p..					0....	30639
99-AUIE-b	bo-londo	1	1	5,346	10,846	0	95.01	100	C	24		p..					0....	30640
99-AUIE-c	n-dolo	1	2	19,427	39,411	0	83.67	100	C	24		P..					0....	30641
99-AUIE-d	li-poto	1	2	67,150	136,224	0	82.31	100	C	24	Lipoto	P..	1898				0....	30645
99-AUIF	NGALA cluster	9	14	3,322,092	6,599,718		91.83	100	C	72		PNB					4asu.	30660
99-AUIF-a	Literary lingala					1				72		pnb					1csu.	30661
99-AUIF-b	Vehicular lingala	9	9	2,475,469	4,902,837	5	91.21	100	C	72	Lingala	PNB	1908-1968	1942-1992	1970	1984	4asu.	30662
99-AUIF-c	bangala-3	4	4	842,208	1,688,347	4	93.74	100	C	72	Bangala	PNB	1916-1932	1928-1977	1953-1995		1csu.	30663
99-AUIF-d	mangala-4	1	1	4,415	8,534	1	80.00	100	C	72		pnb					1csu.	30664
99-AUIG	NGOMBE cluster	1	1	386,055	783,162		95.00	100	C	42		PN.					0....	30665
99-AUIG-a	dianga					0				42		pn.					0....	30666
99-AUIG-b	li-ngombe	1	1	386,055	783,162	0	95.00	100	C	42	Lingombe*	PN.	1903-1940	1915-1956			0....	30667
99-AUIG-c	kipoto					0				42		pn.					0....	30676
99-AUIG-d	li-sena					0				42		pn.					0....	30677
99-AUIG-e	ngombe-wiinza					0				42		pn.					0....	30678
99-AUIG-f	ngbolo					0				42		pn.					0....	30679
99-AUIG-g	Northeast ngombe					0				42		pn.					0....	30680
99-AUIH	SENGELE cluster	1	1	20,662	41,915		90.00	100	C	24		P..					0....	30681
99-AUIH-a	ke-sengele	1	1	20,662	41,915	0	90.00	100	C	24	Kesengele*	P..	1915-1917				0....	30682
99-AUII	SOUTH NTOMBA cluster	1	2	1,698,141	3,444,893		98.77	100	C	24		P..					0....	30683
99-AUII-a	lo-sakani					0				24		p..					0....	30684
99-AUII-b	nkole					0				24		p..					0....	30685
99-AUII-c	yeli					0				24		p..					0....	30686
99-AUII-d	lo-lia	1	1	96,852	196,477	0	95.00	100	C	24	Bolia	P..	1936				0....	30687
99-AUII-e	jombo					0				24		p..					0....	30688
99-AUII-f	jale					0				24		p..					0....	30689
99-AUII-g	e-konda	1	1	1,601,289	3,248,416	0	99.00	100	C	24		p..					0....	30690
99-AUII-h	i-yembe					0				24		p..					0....	30691
99-AUII-i	ya-jima					0				24		p..					0....	30698
99-AUII-j	e-twa-oli					0				24		p..					0....	30699
99-AUII-k	e-diki					0				24		p..					0....	30700
99-AUII-l	lo-kala					0				24		p..					0....	30701
99-AUII-m	lo-longo					0				24		p..					0....	30702
99-AUII-n	lo-lendo					0				24		p..					0....	30703
99-AUII-o	nkole-2					0				24		p..					0....	30704
99-AUII-p	i-moma					0				24		p..					0....	30705
99-AUII-q	mpongo					0				24		p..					0....	30706
99-AUII-r	lo-oli					0				24		p..					0....	30707
99-AUIJ	NORTH MONGO cluster	1	3	1,864,273	3,781,911		97.41	100	C	63		PNB					4....	30708
99-AUIJ-a	ba-enga					0				63		pnb					1....	30709
99-AUIJ-b	North lo-ntomba	1	1	195,833	397,271	0	96.00	100	C	63	Lontomba*	Pnb	1916-1947				1....	30710
99-AUIJ-c	basi-mongo	1	2	1,668,440	3,384,640	0	97.57	100	C	63		PNB					4....	30713
99-AUIK	WEST MBOLE cluster	1	2	732,595	1,486,161		96.30	100	C	20		...					0....	30720
99-AUIK-a	Northwest lo-mbole					0				20		...					0....	30721
99-AUIK-b	West Central lo-mbole.	1	1	257,374	522,115	0	95.00	100	C	20		...					0....	30722
99-AUIK-c	Southwest lo-mbole					0				20		...					0....	30723
99-AUIK-d	bo-ngongombe					0				20		...					0....	30724
99-AUIK-e	li-kalo					0				20		...					0....	30725
99-AUIK-f	i-kongo					0				20		...					0....	30726
99-AUIK-g	North ba-kutu					0				20		...					0....	30727
99-AUIK-h	nkole-3					0				20		...					0....	30732
99-AUIK-i	lionje					0				20		...					0....	30733
99-AUIK-j	bo-saka	1	1	475,221	964,046	0	97.00	100	C	20		...					0....	30734
99-AUIL	NGANDO cluster	2	3	380,818	772,401		96.54	100	C	44		PN.					0....	30735
99-AUIL-a	ya-sayama					0				44		pn.					0....	30736
99-AUIL-b	lalia	1	1	68,902	139,776	0	90.00	100	C	44		pn.					0....	30737
99-AUIL-c	lalia-ngulu					0				44		pn.					0....	30738
99-AUIL-d	lo-ngando	1	1	311,420	631,754	0	98.00	100	C	44	Longandu*	PN.	1920-1929	1941			0....	30739
99-AUIL-e	North bo-kala					0				44		pn.					0....	30740
99-AUIL-f	lo-kole	1	1	496	871	0	85.08	100	C	44		pn.					0....	30741
99-AUIL-g	bo-onde					0				44		pn.					0....	30742
99-AUIM	MPAMA-WANGATA cluster	1	1	4,000	6,800		85.00	100	C	0		...					0....	30743

Continued overleaf

Table 9-13 continued

Code 1	REFERENCE NAME / Autoglossonym 2	Coun 3	Peo 4	Mother-tongue speakers in 2000 5	in 2025 6	Media radio 7	CHURCH AC% 8	E% 9	Wld 10	Tr 11	Biblioglossonym 12	SCRIPTURES Print 13-15	P–activity 16	N–activity 17	B–activity 18	J-year 19	Jayuh 20-24	Ref 25
99-AUIM-a	wangata					0				0		...					0....	30744
99-AUIM-b	mpama					0				0		...					0....	30745
99-AUIN	KUTU cluster	1	5	842,691	1,709,505		91.94	100	C	24		P..					0....	30746
99-AUIN-a	o-kela	1	1	449,823	912,522	0	93.00	100	C	24	Okela*	P..	1940				0....	30747
99-AUIN-b	lo-yela	1	1	71,025	144,083	0	90.00	100	C	24		p..					0....	30748
99-AUIN-c	lo-nkutu	1	1	99,962	202,785	0	90.00	100	C	24	Lonkutu*	P..	1937-1940				0....	30749
99-AUIN-d	lo-nkucu	1	1	154,963	314,363	0	94.00	100	C	24		p..					0....	30750
99-AUIN-e	lo-kutsu	1	1	66,918	135,752	0	85.00	100	C	24		p..					0....	30751
99-AUIO	SANKURU cluster	1	3	149,059	302,385		38.87	73	B	24		P..					0....	30752
99-AUIO-a	ba-shobwa					0				24		p..					0....	30753
99-AUIO-b	lo-lengese	1	1	8,611	17,468	0	90.00	100	C	24		p..					0....	30754
99-AUIO-c	lodi									24		p..					0....	30755
99-AUIO-d	songo-mene	1	2	140,448	284,917	0	35.73	72	B	24	Songo	P..	1936				0....	30756
99-AUIO-e	ma-luk									24							0....	30759
99-AUIO-f	ba-ngoombe					0				24		p..					0....	30760
99-AUIO-g	ba-mbeengi					0				24		p..					0....	30761
99-AUIP	LUKUBA cluster	1	3	241,205	489,316		94.02	100	C	63		PNB					0....	30762
99-AUIP-a	ba-wongo	1	1	12,867	26,103	0	90.00	100	C	63	Wongo	Pnb	1938-1940				0....	30763
99-AUIP-b	u-si-lele	1	1	66,918	135,752	0	90.00	100	C	63		pnb					0....	30764
99-AUIP-c	ba-shi-domai					0				63		pnb					0....	30765
99-AUIP-d	ba-ileo					0				63		pnb					0....	30766
99-AUIP-e	ba-kel					0				63		pnb					0....	30767
99-AUIP-f	bu-shoong	1	1	161,420	327,461	0	96.00	100	C	63	Bushoong	PNB		1927			0....	30768
99-AUIP-g	kayuweeng					0				63		pnb					0....	30769
99-AUIP-h	kaam			0	0	0	0.00	0		63		pnb					0....	30772
99-AUIP-i	bi-eng					0				63		pnb					0....	30773
99-AUIP-j	bu-laang					0				63		pnb					0....	30774
99-AUIP-k	bu-piaang					0				63		pnb					0....	30775
99-AUIP-l	bu-ngeende					0				63		pnb					0....	30776
99-AUIP-m	i-sambo					0				63		pnb					0....	30777
99-AUIQ	NGONGO cluster	1	1	4,000	6,800		40.00	77	B	0		...					0....	30778
99-AUIQ-a	bu-ngongo					0				0		...					0....	30779
99-AUIQ-b	ba-twa					0				0		...					0....	30780
99-AUIR	TETELA cluster	1	1	1,184,810	2,403,534		94.00	100	C	62		PNB					4....	30781
99-AUIR-a	sungu	1	1	1,184,810	2,403,534	0	94.00	100	C	62	Otetela*	PNB	1919-1986	1938-1993	1966	1996	4....	30782
99-AUIR-b	West hamba					0				62		pnb					4....	30783
99-AUIR-c	West pina					0				62		pnb					1....	30784
99-AUIR-d	East pina					0				62		pnb					1....	30785
99-AUJ	NYANGA-LEGA net	2	9	1,300,751	2,637,426		80.94	98	C	61		PNB					0.s..	30786
99-AUJA	NYANGA cluster	1	1	64,341	130,523		45.00	77	B	2		...					0....	30787
99-AUJA-a	ki-nyanga	1	1	64,341	130,523	0	45.00	77	B	2		...					0....	30788
99-AUJB	KWAME cluster	1	1	10,331	20,958		80.00	100	C	4		...					0....	30789
99-AUJB-a	ki-kwame	1	1	10,331	20,958	0	80.00	100	C	4		...					0....	30790
99-AUJC	EAST LEGA cluster	1	1	45,518	92,339		40.00	77	B	12		...					0....	30791
99-AUJC-a	ki-lega-mwenga	1	1	45,518	92,339	0	40.00	77	B	12	Lega-mwenga	...					0....	30792
99-AUJC-b	imuzimu					0				12		...					0....	30793
99-AUJD	WEST LEGA cluster	1	2	744,016	1,509,329		86.92	100	C	42		PN.					0....	30794
99-AUJD-a	ki-lega-shabunda	1	1	735,007	1,491,054	0	87.00	100	C	42	Kilega*	PN.	1934-1942	1957			0....	30795
99-AUJD-b	West ki-gala					0				42		pn.					0....	30796
99-AUJD-c	ki-gyoma					0				42		pn.					0....	30797
99-AUJD-d	li-liga					0				42		pn.					0....	30798
99-AUJD-e	ki-sede					0				42		pn.					0....	30799
99-AUJD-f	ki-nyabanga					0				42		pn.					0....	30800
99-AUJD-g	ki-nyamunsange					0				42		pn.					0....	30801
99-AUJD-h	ki-kaanu	1	1	9,009	18,275	0	80.00	100	C	42		pn.					0....	30802
99-AUJE	BUYU-KALANGA cluster	2	4	436,545	884,277		80.36	100	C	61		PNB					0.s..	30803
99-AUJE-a	kya-wakabango					0				61		pnb					0.s..	30804
99-AUJE-b	i-beembe	1	1	398,096	807,588	0	80.00	100	C	61	Ebembe*	PNB	1936-1966	1979	1991		0.s..	30805
99-AUJE-c	ki-buyu	1	1	15,496	31,436	0	90.00	100	C	61		pnb					0.s..	30806
99-AUJE-d	ki-holoholo	2	2	22,953	45,253	0	80.00	100	C	61	Holoholo	Pnb	1948				0.s..	30809
99-AUJE-e	ki-kalanga					0				61	Kikalanga	Pnb	1948				0.s..	30812
99-AUJE-f	ki-lumbu					0				61		pnb					0.s..	30813
99-AUJE-g	e-tumbwe					0				61		pnb					0.s..	30814
99-AUK	SOUTHEAST KAVIRONDO net	2	2	1,924,301	2,685,254		86.32	100	C	61		PNB					3....	30815
99-AUKA	GUSII cluster	2	2	1,924,301	2,685,254		86.32	100	C	61		PNB					3....	30816
99-AUKA-a	i-ki-gusii	2	2	1,924,301	2,685,254	4	86.32	100	C	61	Ekegusii*	PNB	1929-1967	1948-1975	1988	1990	3....	30817
99-AUL	NATRON-LAKE net	1	1	22,580	39,020		7.00	36	A	2		...					0....	30818
99-AULA	SONJO cluster	1	1	22,580	39,020		7.00	36	A	2		...					0....	30819
99-AULA-a	ba-temi	1	1	22,580	39,020	0	7.00	36	A	2		...					0....	30820
99-AUM	KENYA-HIGHLANDS net	3	15	11,844,675	16,532,935		84.57	99	C	72		PNB					3as..	30821
99-AUMA	THAGICU cluster	3	13	11,744,820	16,380,830		85.29	100	C	72		PNB					3as..	30822
99-AUMA-a	gi-gikuyu	3	4	5,805,829	8,109,917	4	91.61	100	C	72	Gigikuyu*	PNB	1903-1964	1926-1995	1951-1965	1985	3as..	30823
99-AUMA-b	ki-embu	1	1	471,955	655,143	1	72.00	100	C	72	Embu	pnb					1cs..	30830
99-AUMA-c	mbeere	1	1	111,634	154,965	1	34.00	92	B	72		pnb					1cs..	30833
99-AUMA-d	cuka	1	1	126,578	175,709	1	40.00	95	B	72		pnb					1cs..	30836
99-AUMA-e	nithi	1	1	126,602	175,743	1	40.00	91	B	72		pnb					1cs..	30837
99-AUMA-f	igoji					1				72		pnb					1cs..	30841
99-AUMA-g	ki-meru	1	1	1,673,774	2,323,445	1	81.00	100	C	72	Kimeru*	PNB	1921-1955	1952-1988	1964	1996	2cs..	30844
99-AUMA-h	ki-tharaka	1	1	123,212	171,037	1	37.20	95	B	72	Kitharaka*	Pnb	1934-1993				1cs..	30850
99-AUMA-i	ki-kamba	3	3	3,305,236	4,614,871	4	85.25	100	C	72	Kikamba*	PNB	1850-1936	1920	1956	1983	1cs..	30855
99-AUMB	DAISO cluster	2	2	99,855	152,105		0.01	23	A	2		...					0....	30861
99-AUMB-a	ki-daiso	2	2	99,855	152,105	0	0.01	23	A	2		...					0....	30862
99-AUN	KILIMANJARO net	2	8	1,862,734	3,214,766		90.91	100	C	43		PN.					0....	30863
99-AUNA	CHAGA cluster	2	7	1,829,217	3,156,848		91.11	100	C	43		PN.					0....	30864
99-AUNA-a	ki-arusha	1	1	130,029	224,694	0	80.00	100	C	43		pn.					0....	30865
99-AUNA-b	ki-rwo	1	1	123,185	212,867	0	64.90	100	C	43	Kichaga: Kirwa*	PN.		1964			0....	30866
99-AUNA-c	ki-hai					0				43		pn.					0....	30867
99-AUNA-d	siha					0				43		pn.					0....	30868
99-AUNA-e	ng'uni					0				43		pn.					0....	30869
99-AUNA-f	ki-mashamï	2	2	414,236	711,722	0	94.27	100	C	43	Chagga: Machame	PN.	1932	1964			0....	30870
99-AUNA-g	masama					0				43		pn.					0....	30871
99-AUNA-h	ki-bosho					0				43		pn.					0....	30872
99-AUNA-i	ki-bombo					0				43		pn.					0....	30873
99-AUNA-j	ki-wunjo	1	1	603,306	1,042,530	0	95.00	100	C	43	Chagga: Vunjo	Pn.	1995				0....	30874
99-AUNA-k	uru					0				43		pn.					0....	30880
99-AUNA-l	mbokom					0				43		pn.					0....	30881
99-AUNA-m	ki-mochi	1	1	554,764	958,647	0	93.00	100	C	43	Kichaga: Mochi*	PN.	1892	1939			0....	30882
99-AUNA-n	ki-kahe	1	1	3,697	6,388	0	80.01	100	C	43		pn.					0....	30883
99-AUNA-o	ki-rombo					0				43		pn.					0....	30884
99-AUNB	GWENO cluster	1	1	33,517	57,918		80.00	100	C	4		...					0....	30889
99-AUNB-a	ki-gweno	1	1	33,517	57,918	0	80.00	100	C	4		...					0....	30890
99-AUO	TAITA-HILLS net	2	3	292,789	412,316		67.85	100	C	82		PNB					1....	30891

Continued opposite

Table 9-13 continued

Code 1	REFERENCE NAME / Autoglossonym 2	Coun 3	Peo 4	Mother-tongue speakers in 2000 5	in 2025 6	Media radio 7	AC% 8	E% 9	Wld 10	Tr 11	Biblioglossonym 12	Print 13-15	P–activity 16	N–activity 17	B–activity 18	J-year 19	Jayuh 20-24	Ref 25
99-AUOA	DAWIDA cluster	2	2	282,111	396,246		68.00	100	C	82	Taita	PNB	1904-1985	1922-1990	1996		1.....	30892
99-AUOA-a	bura					0				82		pnb					1.....	30893
99-AUOA-b	ch-awia					0				82		pnb					1.....	30894
99-AUOA-c	ch-azi					0				82		pnb					1.....	30899
99-AUOA-d	ki-daya					0				82		pnb					1.....	30900
99-AUOA-e	East ki-gala					0				82		pnb					1.....	30901
99-AUOA-f	ki-gombo					0				82		pnb					1.....	30902
99-AUOA-g	North ki-shamba					0				82		pnb					1.....	30903
99-AUOA-h	m-bale					0				82		pnb					1.....	30904
99-AUOA-i	m-baramgondi					0				82		pnb					1.....	30909
99-AUOA-j	m-gange					0				82		pnb					1.....	30910
99-AUOA-k	m-korore					0				82		pnb					1.....	30911
99-AUOA-l	m-ragua					0				82		pnb					1.....	30912
99-AUOA-m	m-wanda					0				82		pnb					1.....	30913
99-AUOA-n	n-dile					0				82		pnb					1.....	30914
99-AUOA-o	n-dom					0				82		pnb					1.....	30915
99-AUOA-p	n-geranyi					0				82		pnb					1.....	30916
99-AUOA-q	ronge					0				82		pnb					1.....	30917
99-AUOA-r	selemba					0				82		pnb					1.....	30918
99-AUOA-s	u-mingu					0				82		pnb					1.....	30919
99-AUOA-t	w-eruga					0				82		pnb					1.....	30920
99-AUOA-u	w-esu					0				82		pnb					1.....	30923
99-AUOA-v	wu-mari					0				82		pnb					1.....	30924
99-AUOA-w	wu-ndanyi					0				82		pnb					1.....	30925
99-AUOA-x	wu-ngonyi					0				82		pnb					1.....	30926
99-AUOB	DAMBI-DALIO cluster	1	1	4,000	6,800		70.00	98	C	0		...					0.....	30927
99-AUOB-a	dambi					0				0		...					0.....	30928
99-AUOB-b	dalio					0				0		...					0.....	30929
99-AUOC	KASIGAU cluster	1	1	6,678	9,270		60.00	100	C	0		...					0.....	30930
99-AUOC-a	ki-kasigau	1	1	6,678	9,270	0	60.00	100	C	0		...					0.....	30931
99-AUP	SAGALA-HILL net	1	1	12,032	16,702		37.00	87	B	41		PN.					0.....	30932
99-AUPA	SAGHALA cluster	1	1	12,032	16,702		37.00	87	B	41		PN.					0.....	30933
99-AUPA-a	ki-saghala	1	1	12,032	16,702	0	37.00	87	B	41	Kisagalla*	PN.	1892-1994	1994			0.....	30934
99-AUQ	TANA-MIDDLE net	1	1	45,214	62,763		15.00	47	A	12		...					0.....	30935
99-AUQA	ILWANA cluster	1	1	45,214	62,763		15.00	47	A	12	Malakote	...					0.....	30936
99-AUQA-a	utuli					0				12		...					0.....	30937
99-AUQA-b	masa					0				12		...					0.....	30938
99-AUQA-c	chewele					0				12		...					0.....	30939
99-AUR	WEST BANTU-INNER net	11	201	42,560,660	82,170,367		88.27	99	C	72		PNB					4Asu.	30940
99-AURA	SHIRA-PUNU cluster	3	10	261,979	440,913		93.29	100	C	61		PNB					0.s..	30941
99-AURA-a	yi-barama	1	1	6,278	10,144	1	79.99	100	C	61		pnb					0.s..	30942
99-AURA-b	ghi-sira	1	1	39,359	63,598	2	97.00	100	C	61	Yichira*	Pnb	1954				0.s..	30945
99-AURA-c	yi-sangu	1	1	23,909	38,634	2	97.00	100	C	61	Yisangou*	Pnb	1943-1959				0.s..	30946
99-AURA-d	yi-punu	2	2	134,140	219,549	2	96.10	100	C	61	Yipunu*	PNB	1939-1955	1977	1994		0.s..	30947
99-AURA-e	i-bwisi	3	3	35,487	71,203	1	78.82	100	C	61		pnb					0.s..	30948
99-AURA-f	i-lumbu	2	2	22,806	37,785	1	92.65	100	C	61	Ilumbu*	Pnb	1933-1966				0.s..	30949
99-AURB	NZEBI-CAANGI cluster	3	9	219,185	383,813		90.37	100	C	41		PN.					0As..	30950
99-AURB-a	li-duma	1	1	9,809	15,850	1	97.00	100	C	41		pn.					0cs..	30951
99-AURB-b	wandji	1	1	10,447	16,880	1	85.00	100	C	41		pn.					0cs..	30952
99-AURB-c	yi-nzebi	2	2	114,890	187,510	2	95.10	100	C	41	Yinzebi*	PN.	1958-1959	1968-1979			0cs..	30953
99-AURB-d	i-vili	3	3	62,455	124,500	5	88.29	100	C	41		pn.					0As..	30954
99-AURB-e	i-caangi	2	2	21,584	39,073	1	70.79	100	C	41	Tsaangi	pn.					0cs..	30955
99-AURC	MBEDE-NDUUMU cluster	2	7	148,971	267,399		75.60	99	C	4		...					0.....	30956
99-AURC-a	li-mbede	2	2	104,236	187,089	0	76.53	100	C	4		...					0.....	30957
99-AURC-b	ngwii					0				4		...					0.....	30958
99-AURC-c	le-mbaama	2	2	23,570	42,751	0	73.77	98	C	4		...					0.....	30959
99-AURC-d	le-nduumu	2	2	14,887	27,415	0	70.09	96	C	4		...					0.....	30960
99-AURC-e	le-kaningi	1	1	6,278	10,144	0	79.99	100	C	4		...					0.....	30965
99-AURD	TEKE cluster	3	15	647,453	1,258,424		81.33	100	C	24	Kiteke	P..	1889				0.....	30966
99-AURD-a	ka-tege	2	2	63,761	118,264	0	79.25	100	C	24		p..					0.....	30967
99-AURD-b	m-pumpu					0				24		p..					0.....	30970
99-AURD-c	n-gungwel	1	1	70,143	135,572	0	75.50	100	C	24		p..					0.....	30971
99-AURD-d	ngu-ngwoni	1	1	5,887	11,378	0	70.00	100	C	24		p..					0.....	30972
99-AURD-e	nci-ncege	1	1	2,943	5,689	0	70.00	100	C	24		p..					0.....	30973
99-AURD-f	ge-tsaayi	2	2	127,016	234,889	0	78.69	100	C	24	Teke, Western	P..	1933				0.....	30974
99-AURD-g	laali-yaa					0				24		p..					0.....	30975
99-AURD-h	kwe					0				24		p..					0.....	30978
99-AURD-i	e-tyee					0				24		P..					0.....	30979
99-AURD-j	ku-kuya	1	1	37,824	73,105	0	65.00	100	C	24		p..					0.....	30980
99-AURD-k	n-jinju					0				24		p..					0.....	30981
99-AURD-l	a-boong	2	2	101,294	199,673	0	76.59	100	C	24	Teke, Central	p..					0.....	30982
99-AURD-m	i-wuumu	1	1	15,496	31,436	0	73.00	100	C	24		p..					0.....	30983
99-AURD-n	i-fuumu					0				24		p..					0.....	30984
99-AURD-o	i-fuumu-2	1	1	7,947	15,361	0	50.01	90	B	24		p..					0.....	30985
99-AURD-p	i-tyoo					0				24		p..					0.....	30986
99-AURD-q	m-finu	1	1	10,331	20,958	0	90.00	100	C	24		p..					0.....	30987
99-AURD-r	n-tsiam					0				24		p..					0.....	30988
99-AURD-s	n-tswar					0				24		p..					0.....	30989
99-AURD-t	m-puono					0				24		p..					0.....	30990
99-AURD-u	esi-ngee					0				24		p..					0.....	30991
99-AURD-v	mosiee					0				24		p..					0.....	30992
99-AURD-w	li-bali	2	2	204,811	412,099	0	92.86	100	C	24	Teke, Eastern	P..	1889-1905				0.....	30993
99-AURE	YANS-DZING cluster	1	5	879,536	1,784,250		95.60	100	C	23		P..					0.s..	30994
99-AURE-a	ki-tiene	1	1	52,729	106,967	0	90.00	100	C	23		p..					0.s..	30995
99-AURE-b	ki-boma	1	1	20,589	41,768	0	90.00	100	C	23		p..					0.s..	30996
99-AURE-c	i-yans	1	1	238,918	484,674	0	97.00	100	C	23		p..					0.s..	30999
99-AURE-d	i-yeei					0				23		p..					0.s..	31002
99-AURE-e	i-tsong					0				23		p..					0.s..	31003
99-AURE-f	m-piin					0				23		p..					0.s..	31006
99-AURE-g	i-mbuun	1	1	412,337	836,478	0	96.00	100	C	23	Gimbunda*	P..	1935-1951				0.s..	31009
99-AURE-h	i-dzing	1	1	154,963	314,363	0	95.00	100	C	23		p..					0.s..	31012
99-AURE-i	i-ding					0				23		p..					0.s..	31016
99-AURF	SAKATA cluster	1	1	137,814	279,573		95.00	100	C	23		P..					0.....	31020
99-AURF-a	ki-djia					0				23		p..					0.....	31021
99-AURF-b	ki-bai					0				23		p..					0.....	31022
99-AURF-c	ki-sakata	1	1	137,814	279,573	0	95.00	100	C	23	Kisakata*	P..	1932-1951				0.....	31023
99-AURF-d	ki-lesa					0				23		p..					0.....	31024
99-AURG	KONGO cluster	4	19	9,780,115	19,581,159		93.41	100	C	72		PNB					4as..	31025
99-AURG-a	ki-tuba	3	3	3,481,150	7,048,529	5	92.41	100	C	72	Kituba	PNB	1934-1968	1950-1973	1990	1982	4as..	31026
99-AURG-b	ki-fiote	2	2	2,325,121	4,614,651	5	93.17	100	C	72		PNB					1as..	31032
99-AURG-c	ki-yombe	3	4	1,565,775	3,140,825	5	95.33	100	C	72	Yombe	Pnb					1cs..	31037
99-AURG-d	ki-kunyi	1	2	353,216	682,697	5	89.33	100	C	72		Pnb					1cs..	31042
99-AURG-e	ki-doondo	1	1	2,943	5,689	5	60.01	100	C	72		pnb					1cs..	31046
99-AURG-f	Central ki-koongo	4	4	1,180,352	2,346,156	5	92.26	100	C	72	Kongo	PNB	1885-1931	1891-1993	1905-1933	1982	4as..	31049
99-AURG-g	ki-ntaandu					1				72		pnb					1cs..	31062
99-AURG-h	ki-dikidiki					1				72		pnb					1cs..	31066
99-AURG-i	ki-mbeeko					1				72		pnb					1cs..	31067
99-AURG-j	ki-nzamba					1				72		pnb					1cs..	31068
99-AURG-k	ki-mbata					1				72		pnb					1cs..	31069
99-AURG-l	ki-nkanu					1				72		pnb					1cs..	31070

Continued overleaf

Table 9-13 continued

Code 1	REFERENCE NAME Autoglossonym 2	Coun 3	Peo 4	Mother-tongue speakers in 2000 5	in 2025 6	Media radio 7	CHURCH AC% 8	E% 9	Wld 10	SCRIPTURES Tr 11	Biblioglossonym 12	Print 13-15	P–activity 16	N–activity 17	B–activity 18	J-year 19	Jayuh 20-24	Ref 25
99-AURG-m	ki-patu					1				72		pnb					1cs..	31071
99-AURG-n	ki-zoombo					1				72		pnb					1cs..	31072
99-AURG-o	ki-ndibu					1				72		pnb					1cs..	31073
99-AURG-p	ki-shi-koongo	2	2	866,393	1,732,133	5	98.00	100	C	72		PNB					1as..	31074
99-AURG-q	ki-mbamba					1				72		pnb					1cs..	31080
99-AURG-r	ki-pombo					1				72		pnb					1cs..	31081
99-AURG-s	ki-hungu					1				72		pnb					1cs..	31082
99-AURG-t	hungaan	1	1	5,165	10,479	1	90.01	100	C	72	Kihungana*	Pnb	1920-1935				1cs..	31087
99-AURH	YAKA-BEMBE cluster	2	6	266,813	539,128		94.52	100	C	23		P..					0....	31091
99-AURH-a	ki-beembe					0				23		p..					0....	31092
99-AURH-b	South ki-yaka	2	6	266,813	539,128	0	94.52	100	C	23	Iyaka: Congo*	P..	1933-1957				0....	31096
99-AURI	MBUNDU-SONGO cluster	2	6	3,121,829	6,087,432		83.44	100	C	61		PNB					0....	31111
99-AURI-a	ki-mbundu	2	2	2,991,987	5,834,297	4	83.90	100	C	61	Kimbundu: Luanda*	PNB	1888-1936	1922	1980		0....	31112
99-AURI-b	ki-sama	1	1	16,557	32,280	1	65.00	100	C	61		pnb					0....	31127
99-AURI-c	lu-bolo	1	1	2,576	5,021	1	64.98	100	C	61		pnb					0....	31128
99-AURI-d	njinga					1				61		pnb					0....	31129
99-AURI-e	ki-songo	1	1	88,816	173,152	2	80.00	100	C	61	Nsongo	Pnb	1936-1978				0....	31133
99-AURI-f	ci-mbangala	1	1	21,893	42,682	1	50.00	89	B	61		pnb					0....	31134
99-AURI-g	lu-shinji					1				61		pnb					0....	31135
99-AURJ	UMBUNDU cluster	1	2	3,267,305	6,369,822		83.71	100	C	62		PNB					0a...	31136
99-AURJ-a	u-mbundu	1	1	3,245,412	6,327,140	4	84.00	100	C	62	Umbundu	PNB	1889-1952	1897-1939	1963		0a...	31137
99-AURJ-b	n-dombe	1	1	21,893	42,682	1	40.00	78	B	62		pnb					0c...	31147
99-AURK	NYANEKA-HANDA cluster	1	2	523,209	1,020,029		89.16	100	C	22		P..					0.s..	31148
99-AURK-a	o-lu-nyaneka	1	1	501,316	977,347	2	90.00	100	C	22	Nyaneka	p..					0.s..	31149
99-AURK-b	o-lu-ci-lenge-muso					1				22		p..					0.s..	31153
99-AURK-c	o-lu-nkumbi	1	1	21,893	42,682	1	70.00	100	C	22	Nkhumbi	P..	1985-1987				0.s..	31154
99-AURK-d	o-lu-handa					1				22		p..					0.s..	31161
99-AURL	KWANYAMA-HERERO cluster	3	11	1,685,702	2,824,455		85.31	100	C	62		PNB					4asu.	31166
99-AURL-a	o-shi-kwanyama	2	3	735,311	1,317,607	5	90.59	100	C	62	Oshikwanyama*	PNB	1894-1960	1927	1974	1989	3asu.	31167
99-AURL-b	kwambi	1	1	64,409	87,239	1	80.00	100	C	62	Otjikwambi*	PNb		1951			1csu.	31178
99-AURL-c	o-ci-ndonga	2	2	656,240	1,042,121	5	78.29	100	C	62	Oshindonga*	PNB	1891-1944	1903-1925	1954-1986		1asu.	31179
99-AURL-d	o-ci-herero	3	4	134,819	248,920	4	88.70	100	C	62	Otjiherero*	PNB	1875-1912	1878-1912	1987	1989	4asu.	31180
99-AURL-e	mbandieru	1	1	94,923	128,568	3	91.80	100	C	62		pnb					1csu.	31188
99-AURM	YEI cluster	2	2	22,581	31,155		19.12	47	A	2		...					0....	31189
99-AURM-a	ci-yei	2	2	22,581	31,155	0	19.12	47	A	2		...					0....	31190
99-AURN	LUYANA-KAVANGO cluster	4	20	666,357	1,092,276		63.67	96	C	61		PNB					4as..	31191
99-AURN-a	e-si-luyana	2	2	126,041	222,526	4	71.95	100	C	61		pnb					1as..	31192
99-AURN-b	kwandi	1	1	27,090	46,140	4	46.00	90	B	61		pnb					1cs..	31193
99-AURN-c	kwangwa					1				61		pnb					1cs..	31194
99-AURN-d	e-si-mbowe	1	1	6,050	10,304	4	42.99	86	B	61		pnb					1cs..	31195
99-AURN-e	mbumi					1				61		pnb					1cs..	31196
99-AURN-f	liyuwa					1				61		pnb					1cs..	31197
99-AURN-g	mwenyi	1	1	13,069	22,259	1	45.00	88	B	61		pnb					1cs..	31198
99-AURN-h	makoma	1	1	28,445	48,448	1	40.00	87	B	61		pnb					1cs..	31199
99-AURN-i	nyengo	2	2	32,007	56,781	1	52.14	95	B	61		pnb					1cs..	31200
99-AURN-j	i-milangu	1	1	13,308	22,667	4	70.00	100	C	61		pnb					1cs..	31201
99-AURN-k	simaa	1	1	94,167	160,387	5	47.00	99	B	61		pnb					1cs..	31202
99-AURN-l	mulonga					1				61		pnb					1cs..	31203
99-AURN-m	kwandu					1				61		pnb					1cs..	31204
99-AURN-n	ca-mashi	1	1	46,731	79,593	4	37.00	79	B	61		pnb					1cs..	31207
99-AURN-o	North mbukushu	2	2	18,599	32,871	3	59.49	92	B	61	Mbukushu	PNb	1976-1986	1986			1cs..	31208
99-AURN-p	South thi-mbukushu	2	2	40,484	64,784	4	68.73	93	C	61	Thimbukushu*	PNb	1976-1986	1986		1997	1cs..	31209
99-AURN-q	shi-sambyu					1				61		pnb					1cs..	31210
99-AURN-r	shi-mo					1				61		pnb					1cs..	31211
99-AURN-s	si-kwangali	3	3	197,133	286,383	4	81.23	99	C	61	Rukwangali*	PNB	1960	1974	1987	1990	4as..	31212
99-AURN-t	mbundza					1				61		pnb					1cs..	31213
99-AURN-u	ru-gciriku	2	2	23,233	39,133	3	63.37	97	C	61	Gciriku*	PNb	1979-1985	1988			1cs..	31214
99-AURO	NKOYA-LUSHANGE cluster	1	3	136,044	231,713		57.36	97	B	41		PN.					0....	31215
99-AURO-a	shi-nkoya	1	1	67,874	115,604	0	55.00	96	B	41	Shinkoya*	PN.	1929-1995	1936-1991			0....	31216
99-AURO-b	shi-mbwera	1	2	68,170	116,109	0	59.71	98	B	41		pn.					0....	31221
99-AURP	COKWE-LUNDA cluster	3	23	4,887,082	9,468,096		82.60	100	C	71		PNB					0....	31225
99-AURP-a	nyemba	1	1	215,067	419,287	1	85.00	100	C	71	Nyemba	Pnb	1955				0....	31226
99-AURP-b	nkangala	1	1	25,756	50,214	1	40.00	79	B	71		pnb					0....	31227
99-AURP-c	shi-mbwela	1	1	215,067	419,287	1	80.00	100	C	71		pnb					0....	31228
99-AURP-d	ci-luimbi	1	1	43,013	83,857	1	60.00	97	C	71	Chiluimbi*	Pnb	1935				0....	31229
99-AURP-e	mbande					1				71		pnb					0....	31230
99-AURP-f	ki-cokwe	3	3	1,495,745	2,965,291	2	78.33	100	C	71	Chokwe	PNB	1916-1964	1927-1958	1970-1990		0....	31231
99-AURP-g	mi-nungu					1				71		pnb					0....	31232
99-AURP-h	lwena-luvale	3	3	1,410,972	2,712,419	4	84.90	100	C	71	Chiluvale*	PNB	1902-1951	1928-1945	1955-1961		0....	31233
99-AURP-i	ci-lucazi	2	2	369,274	703,052	2	88.85	100	C	71	Chiluchazi*	PNB	1957	1935	1963		0....	31236
99-AURP-j	ci-mbunda	2	4	280,513	514,116	1	64.09	97	C	71	Chimbunda*	PNb	1919-1995	1983			0....	31239
99-AURP-k	ci-lunda	3	4	342,703	622,275	4	85.89	100	C	71	Lunda	PNB	1914-1946	1918-1929	1962		0....	31242
99-AURP-l	i-shindi					1				71		pnb					0....	31247
99-AURP-m	West ci-na-luunda					1				71		pnb					0....	31248
99-AURP-n	u-ruund	2	2	359,836	716,329	1	96.52	100	C	71	Uruund*	PNb	1914-1956	1933-1963			0....	31249
99-AURP-o	kanincin					1				71		pnb					0....	31250
99-AURP-p	ci-salampahu	1	1	129,136	261,969	1	98.00	100	C	71	Tshisalampasu*	Pnb	1938				0....	31251
99-AURQ	LUBA-SONGYE cluster	2	16	8,920,099	17,993,404		92.80	99	C	63		PNB					4Asu.	31254
99-AURQ-a	lwalwa	1	1	54,046	109,639	1	95.00	100	C	63		pnb					1csu.	31255
99-AURQ-b	mbal					1				63		pnb					1csu.	31256
99-AURQ-c	mbagani					1				63		pnb					1csu.	31257
99-AURQ-d	South lu-kete	1	1	10,331	20,958	1	95.00	100	C	63		pnb					1csu.	31258
99-AURQ-e	North lu-kete					1				63		pnb					1csu.	31259
99-AURQ-f	ci-binji	1	1	164,716	334,147	1	97.00	100	C	63	Binji	PNb		1962			1csu.	31262
99-AURQ-g	bu-ilande					1				63		pnb					1csu.	31265
99-AURQ-h	ki-budya					1				63		pnb					1csu.	31274
99-AURQ-i	ki-songe	1	2	1,585,400	3,216,183	1	97.11	100	C	63	Kisongye*	PNb	1920-1981	1952-1978			1csu.	31275
99-AURQ-j	mi-lembwe					1				63		pnb					1csu.	31278
99-AURQ-k	ki-n-ekiiye					1				63		pnb					1csu.	31281
99-AURQ-l	Vehicular ci-luba	1	2	3,202,579	6,496,831	3	93.48	100	C	63	Tshiluba*	PNB	1913-1962	1920-1982	1927-1995	1983	4csu.	31285
99-AURQ-m	East ci-luba					1				63		pnb					1csu.	31286
99-AURQ-n	Central ci-luba	1	1	65,597	111,725	4	52.00	95	B	63		pnb					1csu.	31294
99-AURQ-o	West ci-luba					1				63		pnb					1csu.	31297
99-AURQ-p	South ci-luba					1				63		pnb					1csu.	31302
99-AURQ-q	ki-na-luluwa					1				63		pnb					1csu.	31305
99-AURQ-r	bu-kwa-mputu					1				63		pnb					1csu.	31308
99-AURQ-s	luna	1	1	81,516	165,365	1	43.00	94	B	63	Kuba: Inkongo*	PNB	1905-1927	1911-1930	1927-1932		1csu.	31309
99-AURQ-t	bu-kwa-luntu					1				63		pnb					1csu.	31310
99-AURQ-u	ci-kanyoka	1	1	281,274	570,600	1	98.00	100	C	63	Kanyok	PNb	1979-1991	1995			1csu.	31311
99-AURQ-v	ki-luba	1	1	2,118,496	4,297,633	1	97.10	100	C	63	Kiluba*	PNB	1921-1948	1923-1980	1951	1998	2csu.	31312
99-AURQ-w	ki-hemba	1	1	183,466	372,185	3	97.00	100	C	63		pnb					1csu.	31318
99-AURQ-x	ki-sanga	1	1	680,868	1,381,226	1	98.00	100	C	63	Kisanga*	PNB	1903-1985	1904-1988	1928-1994		1csu.	31321
99-AURQ-y	ki-bangubangu	1	1	201,194	408,148	1	10.00	48	A	63		pnb					1csu.	31322
99-AURQ-z	ci-kaonde	2	2	290,616	508,764	4	88.29	100	C	63	Kikaonde*	PNB	1923-1962	1938-1962	1975		2Asu.	31325
99-AURR	BEMBA-LAMBA cluster	5	30	5,368,342	9,831,557		91.49	100	C	71		PNB					4.su.	31330
99-AURR-a	ki-lomotwa					1				71		pnb					1.su.	31331
99-AURR-b	ki-nwenshi					1				71		pnb					1.su.	31332
99-AURR-c	ki-na-kunda					1				71		pnb					1.su.	31333
99-AURR-d	ki-lembwe					1				71		pnb					1.su.	31336
99-AURR-e	i-ci-taabwa	2	2	684,289	1,368,791	3	92.95	100	C	71		pnb					1.su.	31337
99-AURR-f	ki-bwile	2	2	60,251	113,164	3	79.24	100	C	71		pnb					1.su.	31338
99-AURR-g	ki-shila	2	2	99,505	198,053	3	80.70	100	C	71		pnb					1.su.	31339
99-AURR-h	i-ci-bemba	5	6	2,286,834	4,002,185	8	90.72	100	C	71	Chibemba*	PNB	1904-1948	1916-1934	1956-1983	1981	4.su.	31340

Continued opposite

Table 9-13 continued

Code 1	REFERENCE NAME Autoglossonym 2	Coun 3	Peo 4	Mother-tongue speakers in 2000 5	in 2025 6	Media radio 7	CHURCH AC% 8	E% 9	Wld 10	Tr 11	Biblioglossonym 12	SCRIPTURES Print 13-15	P–activity 16	N–activity 17	B–activity 18	J-year 19	Jayuh 20-24	Ref 25
99-AURR-i	East ci-na-luunda					1				71		pnb					1.su.	31345
99-AURR-j	ngoma	1	1	72,137	122,866	3	89.00	100	C	71		pnb					1.su.	31346
99-AURR-k	ci-shinga	1	1	37,921	64,587	1	70.00	100	C	71		pnb					1.su.	31347
99-AURR-l	mukululu	1	1	15,107	25,731	3	87.00	100	C	71		pnb					1.su.	31348
99-AURR-m	ngumbo	1	1	95,287	162,293	3	95.00	100	C	71		pnb					1.su.	31349
99-AURR-n	i-ci-biisa	1	1	147,722	251,601	1	93.00	100	C	71	Chibiza-chilala*	PNb	1909-1995	1947-1977			1.su.	31350
99-AURR-o	i-ci-lamba	2	2	234,678	406,429	1	90.00	100	C	71	Ichilamba*	PNB	1914-1950	1921-1938	1959		1.su.	31354
99-AURR-p	ki-seba	1	1	206,618	419,150	1	97.00	100	C	71		pnb					1.su.	31357
99-AURR-q	i-c-aushi	2	2	439,147	824,900	4	92.23	100	C	71		pnb					1.su.	31358
99-AURR-r	kabende	1	1	63,465	108,094	3	90.00	100	C	71		pnb					1.su.	31359
99-AURR-s	unga-twa	1	1	31,628	53,870	3	93.00	100	C	71		pnb					1.su.	31360
99-AURR-t	i-ci-lala	2	2	798,772	1,548,070	1	94.97	100	C	71	Lala-bisa	PNb	1909-1995	1947-1977			1.su.	31363
99-AURR-u	ambo	1	1	2,272	3,870	1	87.98	100	C	71		pnb					1.su.	31364
99-AURR-v	vu-lima	1	1	26,348	44,876	1	90.00	100	C	71		pnb					1.su.	31365
99-AURR-w	i-ci-swaka	1	1	59,725	101,724	1	82.00	100	C	71		pnb					1.su.	31366
99-AURR-x	luano	1	1	6,636	11,303	1	70.00	100	C	71		pnb					1.su.	31367
99-AURS	TONGA-LENJE cluster	4	14	1,620,244	2,685,769		70.97	99	C	61		PNB					4..u.	31368
99-AURS-a	lenje	1	1	171,213	291,612	1	68.00	100	C	61	Chilenje*	PNb	1927-1994	1996			1..u.	31369
99-AURS-b	soli	1	1	68,485	116,644	1	58.00	100	B	61	Soli	pnb					1..u.	31374
99-AURS-c	ci-ila	1	2	102,728	174,966	2	56.25	97	B	61	Chiila*	PNb	1907-1937	1915-1945			1..u.	31378
99-AURS-d	West ci-tonga	2	4	1,174,514	1,944,050	4	74.51	100	C	61	Chitonga*	PNB	1911-1957	1949-1989	1963-1996	1983	4..u.	31388
99-AURS-e	leya	1	1	10,616	18,082	2	40.01	80	B	61		pnb					1..u.	31394
99-AURS-f	ci-ikuhane	3	3	35,291	52,288	4	61.69	92	C	61		pnb					1..u.	31395
99-AURS-g	fwe	1	1	27,614	37,401	1	80.00	100	C	61		pnb					1..u.	31396
99-AURS-h	e-ci-totela	1	1	29,783	50,726	2	43.00	81	B	61		pnb					1..u.	31397
99-AURS-i	shanjo					1				61		pnb					1..u.	31398
99-AUS	**EAST BANTU-INNER net**	26	292	97,879,626	170,450,242		60.52	89	C	82		PNB					4Bsuh	31399
99-AUSA	NYIHA-FIPA cluster	3	20	5,133,158	8,868,175		41.77	85	B	72		PNB					4....	31400
99-AUSA-a	i-cii-na-mwanga	2	2	290,292	497,384	0	72.98	100	C	72	Ichinamwanga*	PNB	1903-1953	1930-1941	1982		1....	31401
99-AUSA-b	ci-kuulwe					0				72		pnb					1....	31402
99-AUSA-c	i-wa	1	1	32,869	55,983	0	75.00	100	C	72		pnb					1....	31403
99-AUSA-d	tambo	1	1	16,036	27,313	0	58.00	100	B	72		pnb					1....	31404
99-AUSA-e	i-ci-lambya	2	2	104,744	185,939	0	67.09	93	C	72		pnb				1996	4....	31405
99-AUSA-f	i-shi-malila	1	1	71,173	122,990	0	10.00	53	B	72		pnb					1....	31406
99-AUSA-g	i-shi-safwa	1	1	216,255	373,695	0	11.80	56	B	72		pnb					1....	31407
99-AUSA-h	i-shi-nyiha	2	2	427,994	739,358	0	25.26	73	B	72	Shinyiha*	PNb	1904-1963	1913-1966			1....	31408
99-AUSA-i	i-ci-wanda	1	1	32,850	56,766	0	20.00	64	B	72		pnb					1....	31409
99-AUSA-j	mambwe-lungu	2	4	403,309	690,216	0	56.40	90	B	72	Ichimambwe-ichilungu*	PNb	1893-1924	1901-1991			1....	31410
99-AUSA-k	i-ci-fipa	2	3	3,473,304	6,007,362	0	40.68	87	B	72	Ichifipa*	PNB		1988			1....	31414
99-AUSA-l	i-ci-rungwa	1	1	24,638	42,576	0	50.00	93	B	72		pnb					1....	31422
99-AUSA-m	i-ci-pimbwe	1	1	39,694	68,593	0	70.00	100	C	72		pnb					1....	31423
99-AUSB	KIMBU-BUNGU cluster	1	2	156,031	269,627		68.63	100	C	20		...					0....	31424
99-AUSB-a	i-ki-bungu	1	1	49,273	85,146	0	70.00	100	C	20		...					0....	31425
99-AUSB-b	ki-kimbu	1	1	106,758	184,481	0	68.00	100	C	20		...					0....	31426
99-AUSC	BENDE-TONGWE cluster	1	2	57,485	99,336		84.76	100	C	4		...					0....	31427
99-AUSC-a	bende	1	1	27,373	47,302	0	90.00	100	C	4		...					0....	31428
99-AUSC-b	ki-tongwe	1	1	30,112	52,034	0	80.00	100	C	4		...					0....	31429
99-AUSD	WEST NYANZA cluster	7	42	23,838,842	42,444,073		83.07	99	C	72		PNB					4Asu.	31430
99-AUSD-a	vinza	1	1	13,688	23,654	1	39.00	87	B	72		pnb					1csu.	31431
99-AUSD-b	i-ki-ha	1	2	975,221	1,685,209	1	65.02	99	C	72	Giha*	Pnb	1960-1962				1csu.	31432
99-AUSD-c	i-ki-ruundi	5	7	7,544,716	13,105,622	4	78.43	99	C	72	Kirundi*	PNB	1920-1986	1951	1967	1982	4csu.	31433
99-AUSD-d	u-ru-shubi	1	1	209,414	361,874	1	80.00	100	C	72		pnb					1csu.	31437
99-AUSD-e	ki-hangaza	1	1	205,305	354,773	1	70.00	100	C	72	Kihangaza*	Pnb	1938				1csu.	31438
99-AUSD-f	i-ki-nya-rwanda	6	12	9,710,502	16,468,293	4	84.59	99	C	72	Kinyarwanda*	PNB	1914-1986	1931-1989	1954-1993	1981	2Asu.	31439
99-AUSD-g	i-gi-kiga					1				72		pnb					1csu.	31450
99-AUSD-h	ki-joba	2	2	18,347	36,212	1	87.26	100	C	72		pnb					1csu.	31451
99-AUSD-i	i-ki-fuliru	1	1	386,753	784,576	1	98.00	100	C	72	Kifuliiru*	Pnb	1929-1991				1csu.	31454
99-AUSD-j	kabwari	1	1	10,331	20,958	1	90.00	100	C	72		pnb					1csu.	31455
99-AUSD-k	a-ma-shi	2	2	1,033,610	2,096,659	1	92.96	100	C	72	Mashi*	PNB	1953-1977	1961-1977	1996	1982	4csu.	31456
99-AUSD-l	e-ki-haavu	1	1	625,438	1,268,779	1	98.00	100	C	72		pnb					1csu.	31463
99-AUSD-m	e-ki-hunde	1	2	401,996	815,500	1	84.87	100	C	72	Kihunde*	PNb	1930-1935	1987			1csu.	31466
99-AUSD-n	o-ru-kobi					1				72		pnb					1csu.	31471
99-AUSD-o	e-ki-songoora					1				72		pnb					1csu.	31472
99-AUSD-p	e-ki-shu					1				72		pnb					1csu.	31473
99-AUSD-q	e-ki-nande	2	4	1,760,576	3,571,679	1	97.00	100	C	72	Kinandi*	PNB	1932-1962	1962	1980-1996	1982	4csu.	31476
99-AUSD-r	o-ru-konzo	2	3	653,147	1,329,950	1	85.70	100	C	72	Lhukonzo*	Pnb	1914				1csu.	31484
99-AUSD-s	ki-yaaka					1				72		pnb					1csu.	31487
99-AUSD-t	talinga-bwisi	1	1	62,620	127,765	1	70.00	100	C	72	Talinga-bwisi	pnb					1csu.	31488
99-AUSE	CENTRAL NYANZA cluster	6	27	12,576,975	24,896,665		83.87	99	C	63		PNB					4Bs.h	31491
99-AUSE-a	ru-gungu	1	1	29,279	59,739	1	80.00	100	C	63		pnb					1cs.h	31492
99-AUSE-b	o-ru-ruli	1	1	79,655	162,522	1	80.00	100	C	63		pnb					1cs.h	31493
99-AUSE-c	nyoro-toro	2	3	1,277,151	2,604,335	4	91.53	100	C	63	Runyoro-rutooro*	PNB	1900-1902	1905-1978	1912	1982	4cs.h	31494
99-AUSE-d	o-ru-tagwenda					1				63		pnb					1cs.h	31498
99-AUSE-e	ru-nya-ruguru					1				63		pnb					1cs.h	31499
99-AUSE-f	o-ru-nya-nkore	5	8	3,746,195	7,632,246	4	96.67	100	C	63	Runyankore*	PNB	1907-1957	1962	1964-1989	1983	3As.h	31500
99-AUSE-g	ru-nyambo	1	1	9,583	16,559	1	49.99	97	B	63		pnb					1cs.h	31505
99-AUSE-h	ru-haya	2	2	1,548,930	2,717,403	1	85.22	100	C	63	Ruhaya*	PNb	1920-1986	1930-1968			1as.h	31509
99-AUSE-i	e-ci-jinja	1	1	188,882	326,393	1	93.80	100	C	63	Kizinza*	PNb	1930-1958				1cs.h	31520
99-AUSE-j	e-ci-kerebe	1	1	136,870	236,515	1	87.00	100	C	63	Kikerewe*	PNb		1936-1946			1cs.h	31521
99-AUSE-k	kwaya	1	1	139,608	241,247	1	35.00	84	B	63		pnb					1cs.h	31522
99-AUSE-l	e-ci-jita	1	1	297,011	513,243	1	45.20	97	B	63	Ecijita*	PNb	1934-1941	1943-1960			1cs.h	31525
99-AUSE-m	ki-kara	1	1	117,708	203,403	1	14.50	59	B	63		pnb					1cs.h	31526
99-AUSE-n	o-lu-sese					1				63		pnb					1cs.h	31527
99-AUSE-o	o-lu-kome					1				63		pnb					1cs.h	31528
99-AUSE-p	o-lu-vuma					1				63		pnb					1cs.h	31529
99-AUSE-q	o-lu-gaya					1				63		pnb					1cs.h	31530
99-AUSE-r	o-lu-ganda	3	3	3,075,679	6,245,149	4	71.57	100	C	63	Luganda*	PNB	1887-1953	1893-1993	1896-1968	1983	3Bs.h	31531
99-AUSE-s	o-lu-soga	2	2	1,607,626	3,279,295	4	83.88	100	C	63	Lusoga*	Pnb	1896-1899			1991	2cs.h	31534
99-AUSE-t	o-lu-diope					1				63		pnb					1cs.h	31538
99-AUSE-u	o-lu-lamogi					1				63		pnb					1cs.h	31539
99-AUSE-v	o-lu-siki					1				63		pnb					1cs.h	31540
99-AUSE-w	o-lu-gwere	1	1	322,798	658,616	1	93.00	100	C	63	Gwere	pnb					1cs.h	31541
99-AUSE-x	o-ru-nyara					1				63		pnb					1cs.h	31542
99-AUSF	NORTH NYANZA cluster	4	14	6,354,986	9,883,723		88.73	100	C	72		PNB					4.s..	31543
99-AUSF-a	u-lu-masaba	2	2	917,750	1,847,800	1	81.30	100	C	72	Lumasaaba*	PNb	1904-1910	1977-1992		1995	3.s..	31544
99-AUSF-b	u-lu-bukusu	1	1	767,600	1,065,542	1	80.00	100	C	72	Lubukusu*	PNb	1984-1995	1993			1.s..	31548
99-AUSF-c	o-ru-syan					1				72		pnb					1.s..	31549
99-AUSF-d	o-lu-nyore	2	2	485,123	848,268	1	94.21	100	C	72	Lunyore*	PNb	1915-1995	1936-1996			1.s..	31550
99-AUSF-e	o-lu-saamia	2	2	718,644	1,169,448	1	93.10	100	C	72	Saamia	Pnb	1904				1.s..	31551
99-AUSF-f	Standard o-lu-luyia	2	2	2,326,842	3,233,769	4	90.99	100	C	72	Oluluyia	PNB	1954	1968	1975	1994	1.s..	31558
99-AUSF-g	o-lu-wanga	2	2	440,165	738,847	1	91.69	100	C	72	Oluhanga	PNb	1914	1939		1994	2.s..	31559
99-AUSF-h	Northeast lu-nyala					1				72		pnb					1.s..	31563
99-AUSF-i	taconi					1				72		pnb					1.s..	31564
99-AUSF-j	kabras					1				72		pnb					1.s..	31565
99-AUSF-k	lu-tsotso					1				72		pnb					1.s..	31568
99-AUSF-l	lu-marama					1				72	Luyia	PNB	1914-1968	1939-1968	1975		1.s..	31569
99-AUSF-m	lu-shisa					1				72		pnb					1.s..	31570
99-AUSF-n	o-lu-nyuli					1				72	Nyole	pnb					1.s..	31571
99-AUSF-o	lw-isuxa					1				72		pnb					1.s..	31572
99-AUSF-p	lw-idaxo					1				72		pnb					1.s..	31573
99-AUSF-q	lu-tiriki	1	1	415,726	577,089	1	91.00	100	C	72		pnb					1.s..	31574
99-AUSF-r	u-lu-logooli	1	1	267,640	371,524	1	90.00	100	C	72	Lulogooli*	PNB	1911-1939	1925	1951	1994	4.s..	31575
99-AUSG	EAST NYANZA cluster	2	9	837,713	1,377,791		58.54	99	B	57		PN.					0a...	31576
99-AUSG-a	e-ke-koria	2	4	537,964	859,816	4	59.32	100	B	57	Igikuria*	PN.	1969-1975	1996			0a...	31577
99-AUSG-b	zanaki-koma	1	5	299,749	517,975	1	57.15	97	B	57	Ikizanaki*	Pn.	1948				0c...	31601

Continued overleaf

Table 9-13 continued

Code 1	REFERENCE NAME Autoglossonym 2	Coun 3	Peo 4	Mother-tongue speakers in 2000 5	in 2025 6	Media radio 7	CHURCH AC% 8	E% 9	Wld 10	Tr 11	Biblioglossonym 12	SCRIPTURES Print 13-15	P–activity 16	N–activity 17	B–activity 18	J-year 19	Jayuh 20-24	Ref 25
99-AUSH	SOUTH NYANZA cluster	2	7	2,820,824	4,875,082		40.39	79	B	42		PN.					0....	31612
99-AUSH-a	ki-sumbwa	1	1	261,423	451,746	0	26.00	61	B	42		pn.					0....	31613
99-AUSH-b	ki-gwe					0				42		pn.					0....	31614
99-AUSH-c	ki-nyamwezi	1	2	1,273,603	2,200,820	0	30.68	77	B	42	Kinyamwezi*	PN.	1897-1940	1909-1951			0....	31619
99-AUSH-d	i-ki-ni-lyamba	2	3	648,646	1,121,500	0	33.24	71	B	42		PN.					0....	31628
99-AUSH-e	ki-nya-turu	1	1	637,152	1,101,016	0	73.00	100	C	42	Nyaturu	Pn.	1956-1964				0....	31633
99-AUSI	LANGI-MBUGWE cluster	1	2	398,296	688,267		30.37	65	B	20		...					0....	31638
99-AUSI-a	ki-langi	1	1	376,396	650,423	0	26.90	63	B	20		...					0....	31639
99-AUSI-b	mbugwe	1	1	21,900	37,844	0	90.00	100	C	20		...					0....	31640
99-AUSJ	TUVETA-PARE cluster	2	4	456,454	781,301		46.62	91	B	44		PN.					0....	31641
99-AUSJ-a	ki-tuveta	2	2	22,303	32,098	0	67.55	100	C	44	Kitaveta*	PN.	1892-1905	1906			0....	31642
99-AUSJ-b	ci-athu	2	2	434,151	749,203	0	45.55	91	B	44	Chasu*	PN.	1910-1960	1922-1967			0....	31643
99-AUSJ-c	ci-mbughu					0				44		pn.					0....	31646
99-AUSK	POKOMO cluster	1	2	69,305	96,205		22.48	69	B	43		PN.					1....	31647
99-AUSK-a	ki-pokomo	1	1	37,402	51,919	0	24.00	70	B	43	Kipokomo	PN.	1894	1902			1....	31648
99-AUSK-b	ndura-gwano					0				43		pn.					1....	31651
99-AUSK-c	malachini	1	1	31,903	44,286	0	20.70	69	B	43	Pokomo, Lower	PN.	1894-1993	1902		1999	1....	31656
99-AUSL	MIJI-KENDA cluster	2	10	1,378,066	1,953,895		23.71	73	B	63		PNB					4....	31665
99-AUSL-a	ki-giryama	1	1	475,505	660,070	0	35.30	89	B	63	Kigiryama*	PNB	1878-1951	1901-1951	1901-1908		2....	31666
99-AUSL-b	ki-kauma	1	1	18,340	25,459	0	20.00	61	B	63		pnb					1....	31667
99-AUSL-c	ki-conyi	1	1	133,115	184,783	0	22.00	64	B	63		pnb					1....	31668
99-AUSL-d	ki-jibana	1	1	21,056	29,229	0	20.00	60	B	63		pnb					1....	31669
99-AUSL-e	ki-kambe	1	1	13,536	18,790	0	20.00	61	B	63		pnb					1....	31670
99-AUSL-f	ki-ribe	1	1	6,016	8,351	0	22.01	68	B	63	Kinyika: Ribe	Pnb	1878				1....	31671
99-AUSL-g	ki-rabai	1	1	79,208	109,952	0	30.00	78	B	63		pnb					1....	31672
99-AUSL-h	ki-duruma	1	1	271,731	377,203	0	34.40	84	B	63	Duruma	Pnb	1848-1992				1....	31673
99-AUSL-i	ki-digo	2	2	359,559	540,058	0	0.11	45	A	63	Kidigo*	Pnb	1982-1993			1996	4....	31674
99-AUSL-j	chwaka					0				63		pnb					1....	31675
99-AUSM	SWAHILI cluster	25	43	3,750,992	6,772,467		21.93	58	B	82	Swahili	PNB	1868-1968	1879-1989	1891-1996		4Asu.	31676
99-AUSM-a	Literary ki-swahili					1				82	Kiswahili: Central	PNB	1878	1909	1914		1csu.	31677
99-AUSM-b	Standard ki-swahili	18	19	682,088	1,155,117	5	1.37	50	A	82	Kiswahili*	PNB	1868-1968	1879-1989	1890-1996	1981	4Asu.	31678
99-AUSM-c	ci-miini	1	1	36,913	82,456	5	0.00	32	A	82	Swahili	PNB	1868-1968	1879-1989	1891-1996		1Asu.	31679
99-AUSM-d	ki-tikuu	3	3	91,423	137,015	5	0.01	35	A	82		pnb					1csu.	31680
99-AUSM-e	ki-siyu					1				82		pnb					1csu.	31683
99-AUSM-f	ki-pate					1				82		pnb					1csu.	31684
99-AUSM-g	matondoni					1				82		pnb					1csu.	31685
99-AUSM-h	ki-amu					1				82		pnb					1csu.	31686
99-AUSM-i	ki-mvita	1	1	98,363	136,542	5	0.03	46	A	82		pnb					1Asu.	31689
99-AUSM-j	ci-jomvu					1				82		pnb					1csu.	31693
99-AUSM-k	ki-ngare					1				82		pnb					1csu.	31694
99-AUSM-l	shirazi					1				82		pnb					1csu.	31695
99-AUSM-m	ki-vumba					1				82		pnb					1csu.	31700
99-AUSM-n	ki-mtangata					1				82		pnb					1csu.	31706
99-AUSM-o	pemba	1	1	1,431	2,473	5	0.28	45	A	82		pnb					1csu.	31707
99-AUSM-p	zanzibari	1	2	159,544	275,697	5	0.00	33	A	82		pnb					1csu.	31718
99-AUSM-q	ki-unguja	6	6	882,537	1,583,916	5	5.52	42	A	82		pnb					1Asu.	31723
99-AUSM-r	ki-mrima					1				82		pnb					1csu.	31724
99-AUSM-s	shi-ngazidya	5	5	384,652	652,322	5	0.03	38	A	82	Comorian*	PNb	1976	1994			1csu.	31727
99-AUSM-t	ki-mwali	1	1	26,674	44,528	5	0.02	29	A	82		pnb					1csu.	31728
99-AUSM-u	shi-nzuani	1	1	259,268	432,814	5	0.02	35	A	82	Comorian	PNb	1983	1995			1csu.	31729
99-AUSM-v	shi-maore	1	1	93,806	172,165	5	0.02	39	A	82		pnb				1997	1csu.	31733
99-AUSM-w	ki-shamba					1				82	Kiswahili: Kishamba	Pnb	1931				1csu.	31736
99-AUSM-x	ki-hindi	1	1	1,203	1,670	1	0.17	35	A	82		pnb					1csu.	31737
99-AUSM-y	ki-settla					1				82		pnb					1csu.	31738
99-AUSM-z	ki-ngwana	1	1	1,033,090	2,095,752	5	74.00	100	C	82	Kiswahili: Zaire*	PNB	1921-1955	1929-1992	1960	1982	2Asu.	31739
99-AUSN	MWANI cluster	1	2	158,178	246,037		10.00	43	A	20	Mwani	...					0....	31744
99-AUSN-a	North mwani					0				20		...					0....	31745
99-AUSN-b	mwani-ki-sanga					0				20		...					0....	31746
99-AUSN-c	mwani-ibo					0				20		...					0....	31747
99-AUSN-d	South mwani					0				20		...					0....	31748
99-AUSN-e	West mwani	1	1	32,473	50,510	0	10.00	29	A	20		...					0....	31749
99-AUSN-n	rungi					0				20		...					0....	31750
99-AUSO	SHAMBALA-SAGARA cluster	2	16	5,387,684	9,333,945		38.60	78	B	72		PNB					0a...	31751
99-AUSO-a	ki-shambala	1	1	663,825	1,147,107	0	44.00	90	B	72	Kishambala*	PNb	1896-1960	1908			0c...	31752
99-AUSO-b	ki-bondei	1	1	109,497	189,213	0	22.00	67	B	72	Kibondei*	Pnb	1887-1895				0c...	31753
99-AUSO-c	ki-ngulu	1	1	180,670	312,203	0	10.00	53	B	72		pnb					0c...	31754
99-AUSO-d	ki-zigula	1	1	459,887	794,697	0	10.00	57	B	72	Kizigula*	Pnb	1906				0c...	31755
99-AUSO-e	ki-mushu-ngulu	1	1	47,219	105,477	0	1.00	26	A	72		pnb					0c...	31756
99-AUSO-f	doe	1	1	32,850	56,766	0	20.00	64	B	72		pnb					0c...	31757
99-AUSO-g	ki-zalamo	1	1	626,869	1,083,246	0	2.00	46	A	72	Kizaramo*	PNb	1967	1975			0c...	31758
99-AUSO-h	ki-nghwele	1	2	167,652	289,707	0	19.92	64	B	72		pnb					0c...	31759
99-AUSO-i	ki-kutu	1	1	61,591	106,431	0	20.00	60	B	72		pnb					0c...	31760
99-AUSO-j	ci-lugulu	1	1	659,052	1,138,860	0	53.40	99	B	72		pnb					0c...	31761
99-AUSO-k	ki-kami	1	1	431,143	745,027	0	2.00	42	A	72		pnb					0c...	31766
99-AUSO-l	ci-vidunda	1	1	43,800	75,688	0	60.00	100	C	72		pnb					0c...	31767
99-AUSO-m	ki-sagara	1	1	108,129	186,850	0	60.00	100	C	72		pnb					0c...	31768
99-AUSO-n	ci-kagulu	1	1	315,110	544,519	0	32.30	77	B	72	Chikaguru*	Pnb	1885-1894				0c...	31774
99-AUSO-o	ci-megi					0				72		pnb					0c...	31775
99-AUSO-p	ci-gogo	1	1	1,480,390	2,558,154	0	73.00	100	C	72	Chigogo*	PNB	1886-1990	1899-1993	1962		0a...	31776
99-AUSP	NGINDO-RUIHI cluster	1	4	896,011	1,548,330		15.90	50	B	20		...					0....	31780
99-AUSP-a	ki-ndengereko	1	1	150,558	260,169	0	2.00	34	A	20		...					0....	31781
99-AUSP-b	ki-ruihi	1	1	273,744	473,036	0	5.00	40	A	20		...					0....	31782
99-AUSP-c	ki-matumbi	1	1	170,592	294,787	0	15.50	49	A	20		...					0....	31783
99-AUSP-d	ki-chi					0				20		...					0....	31784
99-AUSP-e	ki-ngindo	1	1	301,117	520,338	0	33.00	68	B	20		...					0....	31785
99-AUSQ	MAKONDE-YAO cluster	6	13	3,929,248	6,735,531		17.30	68	B	63		PNB					4.s..	31786
99-AUSQ-a	ci-mwera	1	1	472,204	815,982	1	28.30	74	B	63		pnb					1.s..	31787
99-AUSQ-b	macinga	1	1	49,273	85,146	1	25.00	69	B	63		pnb					1.s..	31788
99-AUSQ-c	ci-ndonde	1	1	45,168	78,051	1	10.00	53	B	63		pnb					1.s..	31789
99-AUSQ-d	ci-makonde	4	4	1,477,644	2,489,667	1	16.00	63	B	63	Makonde	pnb					1.s..	31790
99-AUSQ-e	ci-mabiha	2	2	170,237	293,495	1	7.30	47	A	63		pnb					1.s..	31796
99-AUSQ-f	ci-yao	4	4	1,714,722	2,973,190	4	16.36	72	B	63	Chiyao*	PNB	1880-1935	1898-1994	1920	1993	4.s..	31797
99-AUSR	MANDA-MATENGO cluster	3	7	442,922	769,145		40.73	75	B	43		PN.					0....	31801
99-AUSR-a	ci-manda	1	1	24,638	42,576	0	70.00	100	C	43	Chimanda*	PN.	1913-1928	1937			0....	31802
99-AUSR-b	ci-mpoto	2	2	85,088	151,136	0	56.34	91	B	43	Chimpoto*	Pn.	1913-1924				0....	31803
99-AUSR-c	ci-matengo	2	2	207,273	357,834	0	44.75	80	B	43		pn.					0....	31804
99-AUSR-d	North ci-ngoni					0				43	Kingoni	Pn.	1891				0....	31805
99-AUSR-e	kisi	1	1	17,794	30,749	0	35.00	73	B	43		pn.					0....	31809
99-AUSR-f	ndendeule	1	1	108,129	186,850	0	15.00	47	A	43		pn.					0....	31810
99-AUSS	POGOLU cluster	1	1	253,211	437,556		72.70	100	C	20		...					0....	31811
99-AUSS-a	ci-pogolu	1	1	253,211	437,556	0	72.70	100	C	20		...					0....	31812
99-AUST	NDAMBA-MBUNGA cluster	1	2	114,975	198,678		51.01	82	B	4		...					0....	31813
99-AUST-a	ndamba	1	1	75,279	130,085	0	70.00	100	C	4		...					0....	31814
99-AUST-b	mbunga	1	1	39,694	68,593	0	15.00	47	A	4		...					0....	31815
99-AUSU	HEHE-BENA cluster	1	6	2,200,144	3,801,909		78.77	96	C	43		PN.					0....	31818
99-AUSU-a	e-ki-hehe	1	1	871,442	1,505,876	0	90.00	100	C	43	Hehe	pn.					0....	31819
99-AUSU-b	e-ki-bena	1	1	637,152	1,101,016	0	88.00	100	C	43	Ekibena*	PN.		1914-1920			0....	31820
99-AUSU-c	e-ki-pangwa	1	1	242,261	418,634	0	80.00	100	C	43		pn.					0....	31828
99-AUSU-d	e-shi-sangu	1	1	102,653	177,386	0	36.30	74	B	43		pn.					0....	31829
99-AUSU-e	ki-wanji	1	1	82,123	141,911	0	30.00	70	B	43	Kivwanji*	Pn.	1979-1985				0....	31830
99-AUSU-f	e-ki-kinga	1	1	264,513	457,086	0	50.00	89	B	43	Kikinga*	PN.		1961			0....	31831

Continued opposite

Table 9-13 concluded

Code 1	REFERENCE NAME / Autoglossonym 2	Coun 3	Peo 4	Mother-tongue speakers in 2000 5	in 2025 6	Media radio 7	CHURCH AC% 8	E% 9	Wld 10	Tr 11	Biblioglossonym 12	Print 13-15	P-activity 16	N-activity 17	B-activity 18	J-year 19	Jayuh 20-24	Ref 25
99-AUSV	NYAKYUSA-NGONDE cluster	2	3	1,516,105	2,658,078		85.95	100	C	61	Nyakyusa-ngonde	PNB	1895-1961	1908-1966	1993-1996	1997	1....	31832
99-AUSV-a	i-ki-nyakyusa					0				61	Ikinyakyusa	PNB	1895	1908	1996		1....	31833
99-AUSV-b	i-ci-ndali	1	1	205,305	354,773	0	65.00	100	C	61		pnb					1....	31842
99-AUSV-c	i-ki-ngonde					0				61	Ikingonde	PNB	1895	1908	1993		1....	31843
99-AUSV-d	sukwa					0				61		pnb					1....	31844
99-AUSW	TUMBUKA-SENGA cluster	4	7	1,731,663	3,089,556		85.33	100	C	71		PNB					3....	31845
99-AUSW-a	senga	1	1	45,393	77,314	0	71.00	100	C	71		pnb					1....	31846
99-AUSW-b	yombe	1	1	2,319	3,949	0	86.98	100	C	71		pnb					1....	31847
99-AUSW-c	ci-tumbuka	4	4	1,397,426	2,484,865	0	86.13	100	C	71	Chitumbuka*	PNB	1904-1994	1911	1957-1980	1995	3....	31848
99-AUSW-d	East ci-tonga	1	1	286,525	523,428	0	83.70	100	C	71	Chitonga: Malawi*	PNB	1890-1948	1921-1939	1987	1997	1....	31861
99-AUSX	NYANJA-SENA cluster	7	29	12,033,890	20,456,796		59.42	95	B	72		PNB					3.su.	31862
99-AUSX-a	nyanja-cewa	7	10	5,813,332	9,977,349	5	63.82	100	C	72	Chinyanja: Eastern*	PNB	1884-1892	1886-1898	1905	1981	3.su.	31863
99-AUSX-b	ci-peta					1				72		pnb					1.su.	31871
99-AUSX-c	South ci-ngoni	4	4	1,607,118	2,857,891	5	67.97	99	C	72	Ngoni	Pnb	1891-1898				1.su.	31872
99-AUSX-d	ci-manganja	1	1	1,329,601	2,428,931	1	81.00	100	C	72		pnb					1.su.	31873
99-AUSX-e	South ci-kunda	4	4	199,643	283,074	1	36.20	80	B	72	Kunda	Pnb	1988				1.su.	31874
99-AUSX-f	ci-nsenga	3	3	546,979	910,019		56.21	97	B	72	Chinsenga*	PNb	1919-1943	1923			1.su.	31877
99-AUSX-g	pimbi					1				72		pnb					1.su.	31881
99-AUSX-h	ci-nyungwe	3	3	461,319	714,405	1	25.51	71	B	72	Chinyungwi*	Pnb	1897			1997	1.su.	31882
99-AUSX-i	ci-sena	3	3	1,983,837	3,141,931	1	36.62	84	B	72	Chisena*	PNb	1897	1983		1995	1.su.	31883
99-AUSX-j	ci-rue					1				72		pnb					1.su.	31887
99-AUSX-k	gombe					1				72		pnb					1.su.	31888
99-AUSX-l	sangwe					1				72		pnb					1.su.	31889
99-AUSX-m	ci-podzo	1	1	92,061	143,196	1	51.00	91	B	72	Shiputhsu*	Pnb	1911				1.su.	31890
99-AUSX-n	mazaro					1				72		pnb					1.su.	31891
99-AUSX-o	hwesa					1				72		pnb					1.su.	31892
99-AUSY	MAKHUA cluster	8	18	11,386,470	18,168,074		24.67	70	B	61	Kimakhua	PNB	1927		1982		2.s..	31893
99-AUSY-a	e-meeto	6	6	2,424,224	3,890,754	0	23.09	71	B	61		pnb				1994	2.s..	31894
99-AUSY-b	i-ngulu	1	1	1,070,617	1,665,284	0	20.00	65	B	61		pnb					1.s..	31895
99-AUSY-c	e-mwuikari	1	1	451,979	703,029	0	20.00	66	B	61		pnb					1.s..	31896
99-AUSY-d	i-makhuani	1	1	3,009,142	4,680,551	0	15.00	60	B	61	Makhuwa-makhuwana	PNB	1927-1946		1982		1.s..	31903
99-AUSY-e	e-sakaji	1	1	19,371	30,131	0	20.00	61	B	61		pnb					1.s..	31904
99-AUSY-f	e-koti	1	1	67,181	104,497	0	30.00	74	B	61		pnb					1.s..	31905
99-AUSY-g	i-lomwe	2	2	2,236,327	3,707,093	0	46.49	90	B	61	Ilomwe*	PNb	1917-1993	1930-1983			1.s..	31906
99-AUSY-h	ci-cuabo	2	3	1,877,011	2,973,763	0	20.34	64	B	61	Chwabo	PNb		1978		1997	1.s..	31907
99-AUSY-i	e-shirima					0				61		pnb					1.s..	31912
99-AUSY-j	i-mithupi					0				61		pnb					1.s..	31913
99-AUSY-k	i-korovere					0				61		pnb					1.s..	31914
99-AUT	**SOUTH BANTU-INNER net**	11	111	49,475,439	62,877,927		70.18	98	C	72		PNB					4Asuh	31915
99-AUTA	SHONA cluster	7	28	9,811,536	13,148,822		58.01	99	B	72		PNB					3asuh	31916
99-AUTA-a	Standard chi-shona	5	5	3,015,705	3,915,301	4	60.83	100	C	72	Shona: Standard	PNB	1897-1994	1907-1993	1949-1980		3csuh	31917
99-AUTA-b	chi-korekore	3	5	590,397	822,572	4	55.91	99	B	72		pnb					1csuh	31918
99-AUTA-c	chi-zezuru	3	4	1,983,935	2,698,411	4	61.46	99	C	72	Chishona: Chizezuru	PNb	1898	1907			1csuh	31930
99-AUTA-d	North chi-manyika					1				72		pnb					1csuh	31942
99-AUTA-e	Central chi-manyika	2	2	995,486	1,339,952	4	56.38	100	B	72	Chishona: Chimanyika*	PNb	1903-1922	1908			1csuh	31954
99-AUTA-f	chi-karanga	3	3	1,830,060	2,393,950	4	64.36	100	C	72	Chishona: Chikaranga	PNb	1897	1919			1asuh	31962
99-AUTA-g	chi-ndau	2	3	562,416	765,979	4	31.66	93	B	72	Chindau*	PNB	1906-1989	1956	1957		1csuh	31969
99-AUTA-h	chi-shanga	2	2	306,057	505,701	1	36.78	88	B	72	Chixanga	PNb	1935	1949			1csuh	31975
99-AUTA-i	chi-kalanga	3	3	444,786	600,002	1	56.03	100	B	72	Kalanga	Pnb	1904-1993				1csuh	31976
99-AUTA-j	chi-nambya	1	1	82,694	106,954	1	35.00	84	B	72	Chinambya*	Pnb	1961				1csuh	31977
99-AUTA-k	chi-lilima					1				72		pnb					1csuh	31981
99-AUTB	VENDA cluster	2	2	894,064	1,036,511		22.63	83	B	61		PNB					4.su.	31988
99-AUTB-a	chi-venda	2	2	894,064	1,036,511	4	22.63	83	B	61	Tshivenda*	PNB	1920-1989	1923-1989	1936-1996	1992	4.su.	31989
99-AUTC	CHOPI-TONGA cluster	1	2	906,157	1,409,476		40.43	85	B	48		PN.					0.s..	31994
99-AUTC-a	gi-tonga	1	1	364,437	566,861	0	50.00	96	B	48	Gitonga*	PN.	1888-1989	1890-1996			0.s..	31995
99-AUTC-b	ki-lenge					0				48		pn.					0.s..	31999
99-AUTC-c	shi-copi	1	1	541,720	842,615	0	34.00	78	B	48	Txopi*	Pn.	1910-1986				0.s..	32000
99-AUTD	TSWA-RONGA cluster	4	9	5,155,121	7,370,856		56.19	93	B	72		PNB					3.s..	32005
99-AUTD-a	shi-tswa	3	3	1,290,966	1,962,936	4	16.37	72	B	72	Xitshwa*	PNB	1891-1908	1903-1928	1910-1955		1.s..	32006
99-AUTD-b	shi-hlengwe					1				72		pnb					1.s..	32012
99-AUTD-c	shi-shangana	4	4	3,093,819	4,243,281	5	69.50	100	C	72	Tsonga	PNB	1892-1968	1894-1986	1907-1989	1991	3.s..	32015
99-AUTD-d	shi-ronga	2	2	770,336	1,164,639	5	69.48	100	C	72	Shironga*	PNB	1896-1905	1903-1914	1923		1.s..	32023
99-AUTE	SOTHO-TSWANA cluster	8	44	12,061,122	15,226,613		69.64	98	C	63		PNB					4Asu.	32029
99-AUTE-a	khe-lobedu	3	4	233,210	270,378	1	24.72	71	B	63		pnb					1csu.	32030
99-AUTE-b	thi-pulana					1				63		pnb					1csu.	32038
99-AUTE-c	khutswe	1	1	403,766	460,153	2	65.00	100	C	63		pnb					1csu.	32039
99-AUTE-d	se-pedi	3	3	3,046,035	3,494,693	4	88.93	100	C	63	Sesotho: Northern	PNB		1890	1904	1990	2asu.	32040
99-AUTE-e	se-sotho	4	5	4,019,364	5,448,048	5	80.50	100	C	63	Sesotho: Southern*	PNB	1839-1993	1855-1982	1878-1989	1989	3asu.	32050
99-AUTE-f	si-lozi	4	4	631,796	1,017,740	5	77.78	100	C	63	Silozi*	PNB	1922-1957	1925-1939	1951-1987	1996	3asu.	32056
99-AUTE-g	se-tswana	4	26	3,688,764	4,482,828	5	44.29	97	B	63	Tswana: Central*	PNB	1830-1966	1840-1994	1857-1993	1990	4Asu.	32057
99-AUTE-h	kxalaxari	1	1	38,187	52,773	5	27.00	77	B	63		pnb					1csu.	32072
99-AUTF	NGONI cluster	8	26	20,647,439	24,685,649		83.13	100	C	62		PNB					4Asu.	32076
99-AUTF-a	i-si-xhosa	4	6	7,451,797	8,508,939	5	83.79	100	C	62	Xhosa	PNB	1833-1987	1846-1987	1859-1996	1989	2Asu.	32077
99-AUTF-b	i-si-hlubi					1				62		pnb					1csu.	32088
99-AUTF-c	phuthi	1	1	43,051	70,128	5	80.00	100	C	62		pnb					1csu.	32089
99-AUTF-d	i-si-bhaca					1				62		pnb					1csu.	32090
99-AUTF-e	i-si-swati	4	4	1,873,299	2,683,853	4	68.73	100	C	62	Siswati*	PNB	1976-1986	1981-1986	1996	1998	2csu.	32091
99-AUTF-f	pai					1				62		pnb					1csu.	32095
99-AUTF-g	i-si-zulu	7	7	8,876,600	10,433,700	5	91.46	100	C	62	Isizulu*	PNB	1848-1986	1865-1986	1883-1959	1989	3asu.	32096
99-AUTF-h	fanakolo	4	4	34,254	46,689	1	69.82	100	C	62		pnb				1989	1csu.	32102
99-AUTF-i	South i-si-ndebele	1	1	816,390	930,401	5	69.00	100	C	62	Isindebele: Southern	PNb	1977	1986			1csu.	32103
99-AUTF-j	i-si-nrebele	1	1	27,578	38,112	4	43.00	99	B	62	Ndebele	PNB	1884-1986	1884-1986	1978	1994	4asu.	32106
99-AUTF-k	North i-si-ndebele	2	2	1,524,470	1,973,827	5	57.78	100	B	62	Isindebele	PNB		1884	1978		1Asu.	32107

Part 10

METROSCAN

Metropolises of the world:
7,000 city profiles

*The angel who spoke to me had a gold measuring stick to measure
the city and its gates and its walls.*

—Revelation 21:15, Contemporary English Version

Part 10 contains data on 7,000 cities each over 50,000 in population. Each is described by means of 7 or more measurements.

Metropolises of the world: 7,000 city profiles

The rise of the world's cities
Historian of the cities Lewis Mumford states that since their origin, humans have 'swung between two poles: movement and settlement.' This tendency provides the initial clues needed to trace the rough outlines of the world's first cities. Evidences of early settlement, such as burial grounds, shrines, and caves, all point toward small villages with relatively short histories. Hunting and gathering could sustain less than ten people per square mile. Only with the rise of agriculture would people be able to congregate in larger groups—the forerunners of today's cities.

The Greek city state or polis was one of the most important developments in urban settlement. As agricultural techniques improved, people moved less. Soon the territorial association of various kindred groups became the basis for the city state. Kindred relations were still strong but the polis vied for the citizens' loyalty as they became more dependent on each other economically. William McNeill identified the polis as 'the cell of civilization'. It was from this context that peoples came into greater proximity and societies beyond the tribal barriers emerged.

Religion and the cities
Religion was not dependent on cities for its development. However, religion did play an important role in the development of the world's cities.

In the Greek context, as wealth increased in the polis, the state cults flourished. At the same time, skepticism increased, particularly among the most educated—influenced no doubt by anti-religious philosophy and intellectualism. For the vast majority, however, religion played an important part in daily life.

Alexander's conquests transformed both the city states of Greece and their religions. The power of the states, already diminished, gave way to Alexander's ambitions abroad. The people in Greece began to practice more personalized religion, looking to Isis, Fortune, and a host of other gods for assistance.

Cities of the Old Testament
The cities of the Old Testament suffered diverse fates. Many seemed destined for destruction, and, in some cases, rebuilding. The Tower of Babel is recorded as an example of people coming together to form a community around a highrise building. This experiment failed with the result being the confusion of human languages. Later one finds the Canaanite city of Jericho falling to the Israelites. Many cities were taken at the time of the Israelite invasion of Canaan. Cities often had specialized purposes, such as the cities of refuge in the time of the Judges.

However, Jerusalem stands out as the premier city of the Old Testament. Over time, this city became the focus of royal, governmental, and religious life. The Temple became the focal point of the emerging Jewish faith.

After the exile, Baghdad, Alexandria, Antioch and many other places became centers of Jewish thought until the rise of Islam. After this Cordoba, Spain, was a major center of Jewish scholarship (Maimonides).

Cities and early Christianity
The life of Jesus moved from a largely rural and small town setting to that of urban Jerusalem. His disciples then took their ministries for the most part to urban centers. The Apostle Paul based his mission strategy on targeting urban centers from which the Christian message could spread to surrounding areas. This was especially true for cities such as Antioch, Corinth, Ephesus, and Phillipi.

The expansion of Christianity and cities
Throughout the history of the Christian church, cities have played key roles—ranging from training centers for missionaries to targets for evangelistic rallies.

Christian merchants and traders built on centuries of Jewish proselytism by first evangelizing both Jews and Gentile God-fearers in the synagogues of the great cities of the Mediterranean. Church leaders later met in leading cities beginning in Nicea in the great ecumenical councils. One of the greatest Christian theological treatises was penned by the bishop of a leading Roman port, Hippo. Augustine wrote *The city of God* and his *Confessions* there.

Christian rulers have often been involved in more than secular administration of urban centers. Constantine established Constantinople as an administrative center for churches. Justinian and Theodora built up Constantinople as a great center of religious devotion, art, and architecture. The Hagia Sophia, one of the most beautiful churches in the world, was a magnet for Christian pilgrims. Later Charlemagne would utilize great urban centers as the focus of Carolingian renewal.

The Church of the East also used cities as strategic centers for administration and evangelistic activity. In most cases, these cities were predominately non-Christian and stretched out across Asia on the Silk Route.

With the advent of the friars, cities throughout Europe once again became important centers of evangelism and renewal. Franciscans and Dominicans worked closely with local parishes in major urban centers. The scholastic age was based in universities in cities in Europe. Magnus taught in Paris and Cologne. His student, Aquinas, spent most of his career in Paris. Aquinas' detractors Duns Scotus and William of Occam studied in Oxford and Paris.

The Protestant Reformation took place in the context of cities: Luther in Wittenberg, Zwingli in Zurich, Calvin in Geneva, and so on. Similarly, the Catholic Reformation found its genesis in cities. Ignatius Loyola launched the Society of Jesus (Jesuits) in Paris and this movement spread to cities throughout Europe but also to major non-Christian cities such as Goa, Macao, and, later, Peking.

The rise of the world-class city
By the mid-1800s the dominant means of livelihood in Europe began to shift from agriculture to production of goods and materials. This phenomenon made it more efficient for people to live close to their work. More people lived closer together as a result and urban density increased. By the year 1900 half of Great Britain's population were living in cities.

The first world-class city on the face of the globe in recent times has been London, England—since the year 1806, in fact. London has pioneered in every type of evangelism. In London's streets every day for the last 15 centuries, preachers have stood on soapboxes to evangelize the lunchtime crowds. One day in the 1950s the Methodist evangelist Donald Soper was preaching Christ to a crowd of a thousand on Tower Hill when a scruffy, unwashed heckler on the fringes bellowed out: 'Christianity has been in existence 2,000 years and look at the state of the world!' In a flash Soper shot back: 'Water has been in existence 2,000 million years and look at the state of this man's neck!' The crowd saw the point and roared with laughter.

Communicating the good news of Jesus Christ effectively has always been closely associated with the world's cities. Two things, in parallel, illustrate this. First, the evidence concerning the past, present, and future of world urbanization and of urban missions in the world's cities as engaged in by Christians. And second, quantification and measurement of this past history of urban evangelization, its present status, and its future prospects.

URBAN TRENDS AND CHRISTIANITY

A twentieth-century decline
A glance at the graphs in this section illustrates that something remarkable has been happening in the urban world of the twentieth century. The graphs all cover the period AD 1775-2050, or 1900-2050, shown along the same horizontal scale. Graphs 1, 2, and 3 give the picture of urban growth. Graphs 3-8 show non-Christian urban growth. Graphs 3, 4, 9 and 10 show Christian urban growth. The vertical scales of Graphs 3-10 are all based on the presence or absence of Christians (disciples) and Graphs 3 and 10 specifically enumerate disciples.

From AD 1400 until 1700, all the world's five

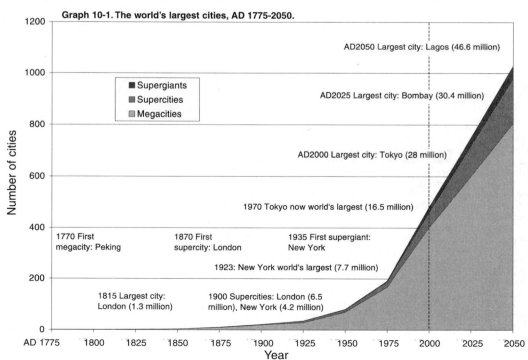

Graph 10-1. The world's largest cities, AD 1775-2050.

AD2050 Largest city: Lagos (46.6 million)

AD2025 Largest city: Bombay (30.4 million)

AD2000 Largest city: Tokyo (28 million)

1970 Tokyo now world's largest (16.5 million)

1770 First megacity: Peking

1870 First supercity: London

1935 First supergiant: New York

1923: New York world's largest (7.7 million)

1815 Largest city: London (1.3 million)

1900 Supercities: London (6.5 million), New York (4.2 million)

■ Supergiants
■ Supercities
□ Megacities

Number of cities

Year

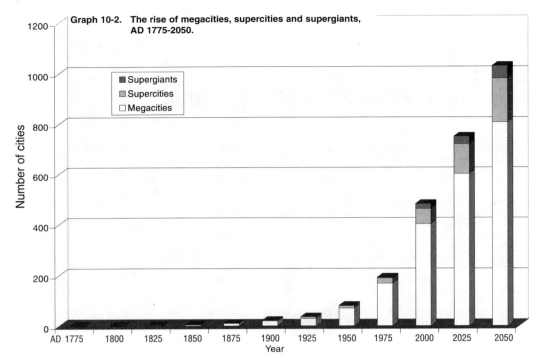

Graph 10-2. The rise of megacities, supercities and supergiants, AD 1775-2050.

largest cities were non-Christian and even anti-Christian capitals. Certainly, they were hostile to Christian missions. By 1800, the story shown on the graphs begins. Graph 10-9 shows that by 1800, two of the world's five largest cities had become bulwarks of Christian life and missions: London and Paris. Then began what church historians call the Great Century, when Christian missions expanded rapidly across the world and achieved phenomenal success. By the year 1900, all of the world's five largest cities had become strongholds of Christian life, discipleship, urban evangelism, urban missions, foreign missions and global missions: in order of size, London, New York, Paris, Berlin, Chicago. This represented a major achievement in urban missions since AD 1700.

But by AD 2000, in Graph 10-8, two of the five were non-Christian, in fact 97% so; by AD 2025, four of the top five will be cities hostile to Christianity; and by AD 2050, four of the top five will be non-Christian and even anti-Christian giants of around 40 million inhabitants each: in order of size, Karachi, Bombay, Dhaka, Calcutta (see Table 10-1). The fortunes of Christians in the cities have thus reversed since 1900 and have declined startlingly. In contrast to the favorable urban situation in 1900, across the world huge non-Christian supercities are materializing as it were out of nowhere and impeding Christian advance.

The plain facts are that Christians are decreasing as a proportion of all urban dwellers. In this vital area of urbanized life, as expressed in the world's cities, discipling the world's cities as measured by the presence of Christians (the number of baptized or affiliated church members of all confessions) has not been advancing proportionately but, instead, has been declining markedly throughout the twentieth century. Graph 10-10 tells the story. It is entitled 'Discipling the Urban Masses: Proportion of Urban Christians, AD 1800-2050.' In the year 1800, 31% of all urban dwellers in the world were Christians. Near the close of the Great Century in 1900, this had risen spectacularly to 69%. Then the tide suddenly turned. Today that proportion has dropped once more, to under 40%; by the year AD 2025, given current trends, it is likely still to be less than 40%, but by AD 2050 perhaps back over 40%.

The predominant cause of this decline is massive population increase in Third World countries where non-Christian world religions have long been strongly entrenched, combined with massive migration to their cities. Graph 10-6 shows how pronounced the result has become. Non-Christian megacities have mushroomed phenomenally from five in the year 1900 to 229 today, and to 536 by AD 2050. Non-Christian supercities also are exploding from nil in 1900 to 36 today, and to 116 by AD 2050.

Moreover, huge non-Christian supergiants, cities with over 10 million inhabitants each, are suddenly

erupting across the globe. In 1958 came Tokyo as the first to reach 10 million, then in 1967 Shanghai, 1976 Beijing, 1982 Osaka, 1986 Calcutta and Bombay. Next to follow will be five Islamic supergiants: 1998 Karachi and Cairo, 1999 Dhaka, 2001 Jakarta, and 2003 Istanbul (as well as one Hindu/Muslim city— 1996 Delhi); and so on into the twenty-first century.

Since the proportion of Christians in a city reflects, to some extent, the amount and relative effectiveness of Christian presence, Christian influence, Christian witness, Christian evangelism, Christian evangelization, and Christian urban missions in those cities, by this first criterion or measure (discipling) the churches have suffered a marked and progressive decline throughout this century. They are fast losing the battle to disciple the cities. The exact rate in AD 2000 shows the churches losing the cities at the rate of 47.1 million new urban non-Christians every year—which is 129,000 a day, or one every second. By AD 2025— in 25 years' time—this is likely on present trends to nearly double to 200,000 a day.

The history of urban Christians
To understand how the current situation can have come about, consider the history of urbanization as

it relates to Christians. The history of the Christian mission in urbanized society goes back to the days of Jesus himself. Some of the major events of this history have been compiled here under the title 'Christianity and the world's cities; past, present, future' (Table 10-4). Even a brief skimming of the table will show that Christians have been concerned, from the very beginning, with reaching the world's great cities for Christ and that their urban mission has been remarkably effective in cities across the world from apostolic times.

The table is divided into 13 major sections or periods. Eleven are history, referring to the past. Two are forecasts, referring to the future.

In the historical part, each section or period focuses on a new development, each of which is characterized with one particular city.

1. Background: the origins of urbanization. (8900 BC: city of Jericho)
2. Migration of proto-Hebrew nation to Palestine. (1950 BC: Ur of the Chaldees; call of Abram)
3. Birth of Christianity as an urban phenomenon. (AD 33: Jerusalem; Pentecost regarded as urban missions outreach)
4. Christianity becomes organized with metropolitan structures. (AD 249: Paris)
5. The Dark Ages: decline of cities and of urban Christendom. (AD 500: sack of Rome)
6. Protestant Reformation spreads via German and Swiss cities. (AD 1517: city of Wittenberg)
7. Modern missionary movement emphasizes urban ministry. (AD 1705: city of Halle)
8. Large-scale urban team evangelism begins. (AD 1857: Chicago)
9. New types of urban missions emerge: radio, television, et al. (AD 1921: Pittsburgh)
10. Global international mass evangelism develops. (AD 1970: Amsterdam)
11. Christians focus on supercities. (AD 1985: Tokyo, Mexico City)

Such an overall historical outlook is necessary to comprehend today's situation.

The future of urban Christians
By studying the past and by consulting church historians, urbanologists, and experts on aspects of the future, it is possible to get an idea of what is likely to develop in the cities of the future. A handful of such future scenarios is given in Table 10-4.

They are divided into two major sections or periods, as follows:

12. Massive urban growth and problems continue. (Horrific events are going to be hard to avoid; e.g., see item for 1999)
13. A new age of urban supergiants arrives. (This is the period from AD 2025 on)

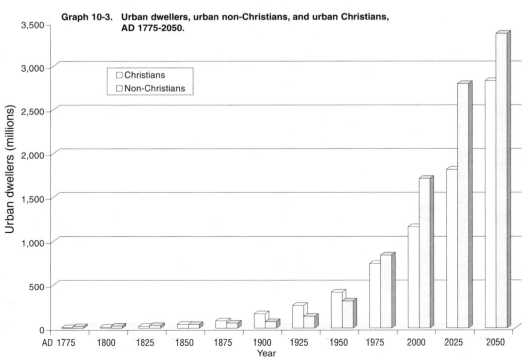

Graph 10-3. Urban dwellers, urban non-Christians, and urban Christians, AD 1775-2050.

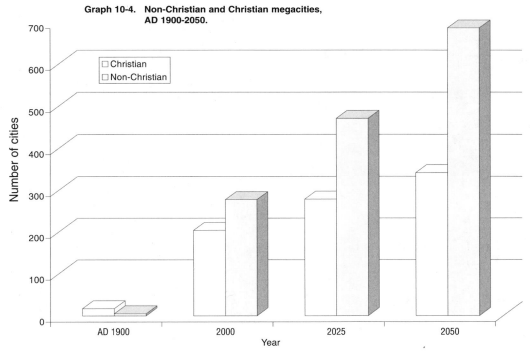

Graph 10-4. Non-Christian and Christian megacities, AD 1900-2050.

THE PHENOMENON OF CITIES

Major secular features of cities have developed in recent decades and they are likely to develop in future decades.

The past, present, and future of cities
In their 1982 collection of essays entitled *Cities in the 21st Century*, urbanologists G. Gappert and R. V. Knight have depicted some of the major features of cities throughout the Christian era and up to today and beyond.

Past. The principal role of the city in history may be seen as the passing on of a culture from one generation to the next. In the traditional definition, cities are centers of civilization, the centers of power that provide order to the civilizations over which they dominate. A city has thus been the anvil of civilization, the place where new values are forged and administered for the civilization that uses them.

Up until the Industrial Revolution in 1775, there had been one predominant type of city, the imperial cities which presided over empires. Then after the abolition of the Holy Roman Empire in 1806, commercial or mercantile cities were established. In commercial cities, power was based on liquid capital or exchange values.

In the early nineteenth century, North American cities served primarily as commercial centers funneling primary products to external markets and and receiving finished goods, capital, and immigrant labor in return. Up until about 1840, urbanization and industrialization were not necessarily related; it was possible to have the one without the other. Industrial know-how became a new form of capital. Investment in the production of know-how or knowledge can be referred to as human capital rather than physical capital.

Present. Urbanologists describe today's cities in self-explanatory terms such as Senior Citizen City, Human Services City, Abandoned City (where the inner city has become too expensive for city officials to spend money on), Learning City, and many others.

Urban writer A. Shostak has recently put forward a seven-part set of alternative urban scenarios describing cities in the present and in the future. These are:

1. Conflict City (example: Detroit; current US cities in the Northeast and Midwest)
2. Wired City (examples: Manhattan; London; the world's 70 operational data teleports including Hong Kong and San Antonio, Texas; hi-tech, information technology, total communications)
3. Neighborhood City (examples: Seattle; Boulder, Colorado: local communities, urban homesteading, with individual owners restoring dilapidated areas or shops)

4. Conservation City (examples: Tokyo; Hong Kong; energy conservation)
5. International City (examples: Paris; Toronto; multilingual, relation to emerging global economy, headquarters of multinationals)
6. Regional City (example: Miami; regional response, political power sharing, multicentric, multinodal rather than with one power center)
7. Leisure City (examples: Reno; Palm Beach; for all ages, including over 65s).

Of particular interest is International City, a city where foreign, international, and global ideas, people, and products circulate with relative freedom, an example often cited is Philadelphia (USA), which plays host to 1 million foreign visitors every year.

A new kind of international city is developing, dating from the London of 1806, which urbanologists have for some years termed a *world-class city*. Depending on its size, it can also be termed a *megacity*, *a supercity*, or even a *supergiant*.

Other major urban trends are observable. In Europe, it is clear that migrations from rural to urban areas have ceased; the 200-year shift of labor from field to factory is now over so far as the original citizens are concerned. Factories these days are being moved not only out of Europe's cities but out of Europe altogether and into newly industrializing nations in Asia and Africa. Some factories may be moved out into space, where certain types of manufacturing facilities benefit from zero-gravity conditions.

Future. In thinking about the future of cities, a voluminous literature by urbanologists exists. They visualize the cities of an advanced industrial society—the future megalopolis—which will be primarily engaged in indirect, and partially abstract, transactional activities.

A major new development is that the world's dominant activity is rapidly becoming the deepening and spreading of information and knowledge. The real success of any city in the future, as in the past, will depend on its ability to pass on its knowledge base from one generation to another. This means that urban development is likely to be led by those cities that can be characterized as knowledge-adequate, let alone knowledge-deficient. The successful cities of the future will be those that learn to (1) manage knowledge (by which is meant information-intensive technologies, global business services, etc.) and its development, transmittal, and utilization; (2) promote innovation; and (3) guide scarce resources towards strategic priorities. Another characteristic of successful cities is that, instead of being based on a single nerve and power center, they will be decentralized, poly-nucleated, multiple-activity centers. They will have multiple-use megastructures, new leisure industries, new mass housing developments, and the like.

A leading criterion by which to judge the success of any future city will be the extent to which it is people-oriented. Industrial cities in the past and present have too often been product-oriented rather than people-oriented. Nowadays, it is recognized that the existence of a large and dominant middle-class, together with local autonomy, is the critical attribute of progressive cities. In the future, therefore, high priority will likely be given to creating the amenity-rich environments that attract the middle class. Such environments are needed in order to develop, retain, and recruit talent required by knowledge-intensive activities. Thus, it is likely that the great industrial cities of the past and present, such as Manchester, Birmingham (UK), Detroit, Pittsburgh, or Cleveland, will shift to become more people-oriented, and their success will then depend on how attractive their environments are in relation to other cities also competing for knowledge workers. And the critical attribute of success will be leadership, especially the ability to envision the future of world cities, and to formulate strategies for their design and development.

Graph 10-5. The proportion of non-Christians to all urban dwellers, AD 1800-2050.

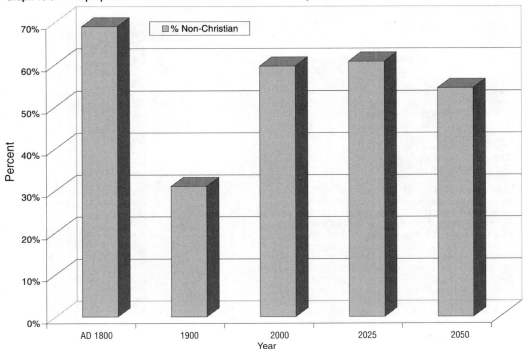

Graph 10-6. Non-Christian megacities, supercities, and supergiants, AD 1800-AD 2050.

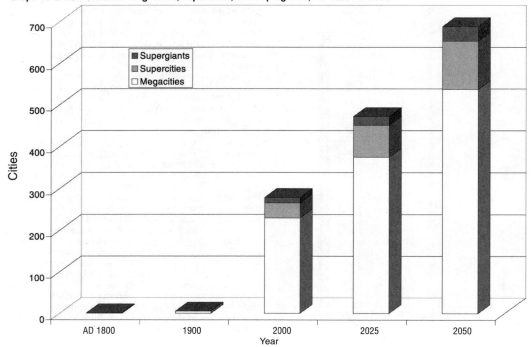

chronology for the year 1870. London was the first supercity, in 1870; today there are 60 supercities, with 118 anticipated by AD 2025, and 174 by AD 2050 (see Tables 10-3, 10-4, and Graphs 10-1, 10-2). This is dramatic growth indeed.

The volcanic eruption of urban supergiants
A third major category is necessary: supergiants, which are defined as cities with populations of 10 million or over. The term comes from astronomy, where it refers to 'a star of great intrinsic luminosity and enormous size' (Webster's). In urban usage, supergiants are, by definition, also supercities, also world-class cities and also megacities at one and the same time. They are also, of course, metropolises. Table 10-3 will help to get these relationships and statistics clear, and to show geographic distribution.

The first supergiant was New York in 1935, the second, Tokyo, in 1958. Suddenly supergiants were erupting everywhere; by AD 2000 some 20 will have arisen and by AD 2050 as many as 50. Graphs 10-1 and 10-2 illustrate this phenomenon.

The Top 25: the world's most awesome cities
One final category has been coined—The Top 25. A very revealing listing of the largest of the world-class cities is given in Table 10-1, which is taken from the UN report *World urbanization prospects; the 1996 revision*. A list of the 25 ranked by size is given for every five years during the 75-year period, 1950-2025, and then a single projection for AD 2050. Its makeup changes constantly. It is very instructive to see how the first supercity, London, declines in population (after 1965) and finally is thrown off the list after AD 2000. Chicago is pushed off the list by 1990, Paris by 2010. Even New York, the original supergiant, drops rapidly down the list to No. 18 by 2050. Others enter the list at the bottom and rise in meteoric fashion; still others rise only to fall again.

In 1950 the world's largest supercity was New York, replaced in 1975 by Tokyo-Yokohama, to be replaced in 2025 by Bombay, probably to be replaced in turn in 2050 by Lagos. As described earlier, in 1950 only 7 of the 25 were non-Christian cities, but in only 50 years, by AD 2000, 14 of the 25 will be non-Christian cities. Graphs 10-6 through 10-9 illustrate this evolution.

MEASURING CHRISTIAN PROGRESS

The comprehensive work of Christians, which includes witness, compassion, confrontation, seed-sowing, pre-evangelism, proclamation, hearing with understanding, evangelism which may or may not result in churches in particular cases, discipling, the formation of cores or nucleuses of disciples, church

As for Christian patterns of urban ministry, they will have to be based on and related directly to all of these secular realities. Such approaches should not be too difficult, especially if Christians and their theologians let their imaginations play over the fact that the major new concept describing future cities—knowledge—is also a major concept in the New Testament (*gnosis*, knowledge). And at the global level, expert strategists and planners are needed who are thoroughly familiar with both the realities of today's Christian world mission and also the whole literature of future-oriented urbanology.

The mushrooming of megacities, 1900-2000
A megacity is defined simply as a city which has reached or passed the size of 1 million inhabitants (the prefix *mega-* means large or 1 million). The most startling aspect of megacities, from the standpoint of Christianity, is the meteoric rise of over 400 of them across the world in the twentieth century. (This is illustrated in Graphs 10-1 and 10-2.) There was, of course, only one megacity in the ancient world, namely the Rome of the time of Christ. It achieved this status because huge numbers of the empire's 16 million slaves were concentrated in the capital. Throughout Europe's Dark Ages and its Middle Ages, city populations fell drastically, with Rome itself falling from 1.1 million in AD 100, to only 19,000 by AD 1360 under the Black Death. (It did not reach 1 million again until 1930.)

From AD 200 to 1770, there were no megacities. A brief summary of their subsequent statistics is given for the year 1770 (Table 10-4), and a breakdown by continent is given in Table 10-3. By 1900 there were 22 such cities, all being Christian strongholds in Europe or North America except for Tokyo, Calcutta, and a couple of others; then 183 by 1975, 276 by 1985, 482 by AD 2000, and with future numbers estimated by the UN as high as 750 by AD 2025, 550 of which will be in developing countries. And by AD 2050, one might see a phenomenal 1,030 such megacities.

What are world-class cities?
Definitions can be sharpened further. What is meant by a 'world-class city'? Urbanologist L. Wirth formulated the concept of urbanism around the notions of size, density, and heterogeneity. Today one should add institutional vitality (such as would come from embracing the information explosion or knowledge revolution). Size, however, is the major criterion. Some speak of world-class cities as all with 5 million or more inhabitants; others say 4 million; most usually define a world-class city as one with 1 million or over. A world-class city is a megacity. But there must also be, as with the category called International City, something additional—a genuine international ele-

ment in its makeup.

In short, a world-class city is one that is international, multinational, transnational, and has a million or more inhabitants. This definition excludes a large number of megacities which have little or no international makeup and are virtually unknown outside their own country—such as 25 of China's megacities today. This internationalism or its absence is very difficult to measure, however, so in practice one (as with the UN) has to settle for enumerating megacities rather than world-class cities.

The rise and explosion of supercities
So many megacities and world-class cities are arising that it is now necessary to coin the term *supercities* to define an even larger entity—all those cities with populations of 4 million or over. Supercities, it must be clearly noted, are also megacities—a group of larger megacities. All supercities are sufficiently international to be called world-class. Their impact on the modern world is as sensational as the sudden explosion of supernovas in the astronomical world. Their explosive rise is recorded in the entry in the

Graph 10-7. Non-Christians megacities, supercities, and supergiants, AD 1800-AD 2050.

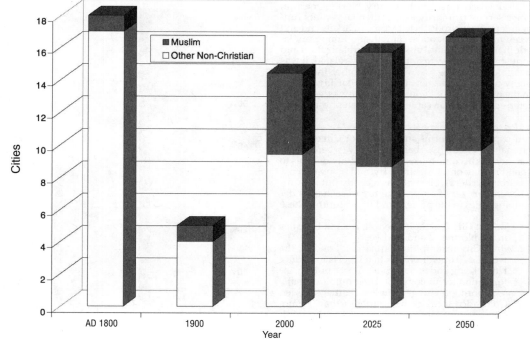

Table 10-1.   The Top 25: the world's 25 largest urban agglomerations, ranked by size, with populations, AD 1950-2050.

RANK	1950	Population	RANK	1955	Population	RANK	1960	Population	RANK	1965	Population	RANK	1970	Population
1.	New York	12,339,000	1.	New York	13,220,000	1.	New York	14,164,000	1.	New York	15,177,000	1.	Tokyo	16,468,000
2.	London	8,733,000	2.	London	8,930,000	2.	Tokyo	10,976,000	2.	Tokyo	12,943,000	2.	New York	16,191,000
3.	Tokyo	6,920,000	3.	Tokyo	8,823,000	3.	London	9,131,000	3.	Shanghai	10,872,000	3.	Shanghai	11,154,000
4.	Paris	5,441,000	4.	Shanghai	6,866,000	4.	Shanghai	8,839,000	4.	London	8,900,000	4.	Osaka	9,387,000
5.	Moscow	5,356,000	5.	Paris	6,272,000	5.	Paris	7,230,000	5.	Paris	7,979,000	5.	Mexico City	9,067,000
6.	Shanghai	5,333,000	6.	Buenos Aires	5,843,000	6.	Buenos Aires	6,772,000	6.	Beijing	7,653,000	6.	London	8,594,000
7.	Essen	5,296,000	7.	Essen	5,823,000	7.	Los Angeles	6,530,000	7.	Buenos Aires	7,557,000	7.	Paris	8,498,000
8.	Buenos Aires	5,042,000	8.	Moscow	5,749,000	8.	Essen	6,404,000	8.	Los Angeles	7,408,000	8.	Buenos Aires	8,417,000
9.	Chicago	4,945,000	9.	Chicago	5,441,000	9.	Beijing	6,269,000	9.	Osaka	7,291,000	9.	Los Angeles	8,378,000
10.	Calcutta	4,446,000	10.	Los Angeles	5,155,000	10.	Osaka	6,228,000	10.	Mexico City	7,028,000	10.	Beijing	8,087,000
11.	Osaka	4,147,000	11.	Osaka	5,121,000	11.	Moscow	6,170,000	11.	Moscow	6,622,000	11.	Sao Paulo	8,064,000
12.	Los Angeles	4,046,000	12.	Beijing	4,953,000	12.	Chicago	5,977,000	12.	Essen	6,541,000	12.	Moscow	7,107,000
13.	Beijing	3,913,000	13.	Calcutta	4,945,000	13.	Calcutta	5,500,000	13.	Chicago	6,345,000	13.	Rio de Janeiro	7,040,000
14.	Milan	3,633,000	14.	Milan	4,045,000	14.	Mexico City	5,427,000	14.	Sao Paulo	6,163,000	14.	Calcutta	6,912,000
15.	Berlin	3,337,000	15.	Mexico City	3,959,000	15.	Rio de Janeiro	4,915,000	15.	Calcutta	6,162,000	15.	Chicago	6,716,000
16.	Philadelphia	2,939,000	16.	Rio de Janeiro	3,752,000	16.	Sao Paulo	4,700,000	16.	Rio de Janeiro	5,891,000	16.	Essen	6,568,000
17.	St. Petersburg	2,903,000	17.	Bombay	3,432,000	17.	Milan	4,504,000	17.	Milan	4,994,000	17.	Bombay	5,812,000
18.	Bombay	2,901,000	18.	Sao Paulo	3,375,000	18.	Bombay	4,060,000	18.	Bombay	4,854,000	18.	Milan	5,528,000
19.	Mexico City	2,885,000	19.	Berlin	3,318,000	19.	Cairo	3,712,000	19.	Cairo	4,606,000	19.	Cairo	5,333,000
20.	Rio de Janeiro	2,864,000	20.	Philadelphia	3,277,000	20.	Philadelphia	3,644,000	20.	Tianjin	4,426,000	20.	Seoul	5,312,000
21.	Detroit	2,769,000	21.	St. Petersburg	3,141,000	21.	Tianjin	3,618,000	21.	Philadelphia	3,833,000	21.	Tianjin	5,222,000
22.	Naples	2,750,000	22.	Detroit	3,140,000	22.	Detroit	3,548,000	22.	Detroit	3,759,000	22.	Philadelphia	4,023,000
23.	Manchester	2,537,000	23.	Cairo	2,991,000	23.	St. Petersburg	3,398,000	23.	St. Petersburg	3,677,000	23.	St. Petersburg	3,980,000
24.	Sao Paulo	2,423,000	24.	Naples	2,963,000	24.	Berlin	3,299,000	24.	Seoul	3,453,000	24.	Detroit	3,966,000
25.	Cairo	2,410,000	25.	Tianjin	2,931,000	25.	Naples	3,192,000	25.	Naples	3,394,000	25.	Jakarta	3,916,000

RANK	1975	Population	RANK	1980	Population	RANK	1985	Population	RANK	1990	Population	RANK	1995	Population
1.	Tokyo	19,771,000	1.	Tokyo	21,854,000	1.	Tokyo	23,322,000	1.	Tokyo	25,069,000	1.	Tokyo	26,959,000
2.	New York	15,880,000	2.	New York	15,601,000	2.	New York	15,827,000	2.	New York	16,056,000	2.	Mexico City	16,562,000
3.	Shanghai	11,443,000	3.	Mexico City	13,888,000	3.	Mexico City	14,474,000	3.	Mexico City	15,130,000	3.	Sao Paulo	16,533,000
4.	Mexico City	11,236,000	4.	Sao Paulo	12,497,000	4.	Sao Paulo	13,758,000	4.	Sao Paulo	15,082,000	4.	New York	16,332,000
5.	Sao Paulo	10,047,000	5.	Shanghai	11,739,000	5.	Shanghai	12,396,000	5.	Shanghai	13,342,000	5.	Bombay	15,138,000
6.	Osaka	9,844,000	6.	Osaka	9,990,000	6.	Buenos Aires	10,522,000	6.	Bombay	12,246,000	6.	Shanghai	13,584,000
7.	Buenos Aires	9,144,000	7.	Buenos Aires	9,920,000	7.	Los Angeles	10,445,000	7.	Los Angeles	11,456,000	7.	Los Angeles	12,410,000
8.	Los Angeles	8,926,000	8.	Los Angeles	9,523,000	8.	Osaka	10,351,000	8.	Buenos Aires	11,144,000	8.	Calcutta	11,923,000
9.	Paris	8,885,000	9.	Calcutta	9,030,000	9.	Calcutta	9,946,000	9.	Calcutta	10,890,000	9.	Buenos Aires	11,802,000
10.	Beijing	8,545,000	10.	Beijing	9,029,000	10.	Bombay	9,907,000	10.	Beijing	10,820,000	10.	Seoul	11,609,000
11.	London	8,169,000	11.	Paris	8,938,000	11.	Beijing	9,797,000	11.	Seoul	10,544,000	11.	Beijing	11,299,000
12.	Calcutta	7,888,000	12.	Rio de Janeiro	8,741,000	12.	Seoul	9,549,000	12.	Osaka	10,486,000	12.	Osaka	10,609,000
13.	Rio de Janeiro	7,854,000	13.	Seoul	8,284,000	13.	Rio de Janeiro	9,208,000	13.	Rio de Janeiro	9,682,000	13.	Lagos	10,287,000
14.	Moscow	7,623,000	14.	Moscow	8,136,000	14.	Paris	9,105,000	14.	Paris	9,334,000	14.	Rio de Janeiro	10,181,000
15.	Bombay	6,856,000	15.	Bombay	8,067,000	15.	Moscow	8,580,000	15.	Moscow	9,048,000	15.	Delhi	9,948,000
16.	Seoul	6,808,000	16.	London	7,741,000	16.	Tianjin	8,133,000	16.	Tianjin	8,786,000	16.	Karachi	9,733,000
17.	Chicago	6,749,000	17.	Tianjin	7,268,000	17.	Cairo	7,691,000	17.	Cairo	8,633,000	17.	Cairo	9,690,000
18.	Essen	6,448,000	18.	Cairo	6,852,000	18.	London	7,666,000	18.	Delhi	8,207,000	18.	Paris	9,523,000
19.	Tianjin	6,160,000	19.	Chicago	6,780,000	19.	Metro Manila	6,888,000	19.	Metro Manila	7,968,000	19.	Tianjin	9,415,000
20.	Cairo	6,079,000	20.	Essen	6,331,000	20.	Jakarta	6,788,000	20.	Karachi	7,945,000	20.	Metro Manila	9,286,000
21.	Milan	5,529,000	21.	Jakarta	5,985,000	21.	Chicago	6,786,000	21.	Lagos	7,742,000	21.	Moscow	9,269,000
22.	Metro Manila	5,000,000	22.	Metro Manila	5,955,000	22.	Delhi	6,770,000	22.	London	7,653,000	22.	Jakarta	8,621,000
23.	Jakarta	4,814,000	23.	Delhi	5,559,000	23.	Karachi	6,336,000	23.	Jakarta	7,650,000	23.	Dhaka	8,545,000
24.	Delhi	4,426,000	24.	Milan	5,334,000	24.	Essen	6,217,000	24.	Chicago	6,792,000	24.	Istanbul	7,911,000
25.	St. Petersburg	4,326,000	25.	Teheran	5,073,000	25.	Lagos	5,827,000	25.	Istanbul	6,544,000	25.	London	7,640,000

RANK	2000	Population	RANK	2005	Population	RANK	2010	Population	RANK	2015	Population	RANK	2020	Population
1.	Tokyo	28,025,000	1.	Tokyo	28,605,000	1.	Tokyo	28,840,000	1.	Tokyo	28,887,000	1.	Tokyo	28,887,000
2.	Mexico City	18,131,000	2.	Bombay	20,926,000	2.	Bombay	23,653,000	2.	Bombay	26,218,000	2.	Bombay	28,499,000
3.	Bombay	18,042,000	3.	Sao Paulo	18,748,000	3.	Lagos	20,956,000	3.	Lagos	24,640,000	3.	Lagos	27,884,000
4.	Sao Paulo	17,711,000	4.	Mexico City	18,452,000	4.	Sao Paulo	19,659,000	4.	Sao Paulo	20,320,000	4.	Karachi	22,135,000
5.	New York	16,626,000	5.	Lagos	17,154,000	5.	Mexico City	18,682,000	5.	Dhaka	19,486,000	5.	Dhaka	21,951,000
6.	Shanghai	14,173,000	6.	New York	16,910,000	6.	New York	17,232,000	6.	Karachi	19,377,000	6.	Sao Paulo	20,703,000
7.	Lagos	13,488,000	7.	Shanghai	15,216,000	7.	Karachi	16,669,000	7.	Mexico City	19,180,000	7.	Mexico City	19,967,000
8.	Los Angeles	13,129,000	8.	Calcutta	14,132,000	8.	Dhaka	16,663,000	8.	Shanghai	17,969,000	8.	Shanghai	19,377,000
9.	Calcutta	12,900,000	9.	Karachi	14,091,000	9.	Shanghai	16,578,000	9.	New York	17,602,000	9.	Calcutta	19,143,000
10.	Buenos Aires	12,431,000	10.	Dhaka	13,726,000	10.	Calcutta	15,640,000	10.	Calcutta	17,305,000	10.	Delhi	18,435,000
11.	Seoul	12,215,000	11.	Los Angeles	13,575,000	11.	Delhi	15,175,000	11.	Delhi	16,860,000	11.	New York	18,023,000
12.	Beijing	12,033,000	12.	Delhi	13,442,000	12.	Beijing	14,339,000	12.	Beijing	15,572,000	12.	Beijing	16,759,000
13.	Karachi	11,774,000	13.	Beijing	13,085,000	13.	Los Angeles	13,896,000	13.	Metro Manila	14,657,000	13.	Cairo	15,640,000
14.	Delhi	11,680,000	14.	Buenos Aires	13,025,000	14.	Metro Manila	13,700,000	14.	Cairo	14,418,000	14.	Metro Manila	15,149,000
15.	Dhaka	10,979,000	15.	Seoul	12,612,000	15.	Buenos Aires	13,515,000	15.	Los Angeles	14,217,000	15.	Jakarta	14,943,000
16.	Metro Manila	10,818,000	16.	Metro Manila	12,371,000	16.	Cairo	13,174,000	16.	Jakarta	13,923,000	16.	Los Angeles	14,538,000
17.	Cairo	10,772,000	17.	Cairo	11,931,000	17.	Seoul	12,913,000	17.	Buenos Aires	13,856,000	17.	Tianjin	14,537,000
18.	Osaka	10,609,000	18.	Tianjin	11,280,000	18.	Jakarta	12,658,000	18.	Tianjin	13,530,000	18.	Buenos Aires	14,036,000
19.	Rio de Janeiro	10,556,000	19.	Jakarta	11,229,000	19.	Tianjin	12,433,000	19.	Seoul	12,980,000	19.	Seoul	12,980,000
20.	Tianjin	10,239,000	20.	Rio de Janeiro	10,974,000	20.	Istanbul	11,715,000	20.	Istanbul	12,328,000	20.	Istanbul	12,512,000
21.	Jakarta	9,815,000	21.	Istanbul	10,737,000	21.	Rio de Janeiro	11,450,000	21.	Rio de Janeiro	11,860,000	21.	Rio de Janeiro	12,196,000
22.	Paris	9,638,000	22.	Osaka	10,609,000	22.	Osaka	10,609,000	22.	Hangzhou	11,407,000	22.	Hangzhou	11,693,000
23.	Istanbul	9,413,000	23.	Paris	9,685,000	23.	Hangzhou	10,301,000	23.	Osaka	10,609,000	23.	Lahore	11,529,000
24.	Moscow	9,299,000	24.	Moscow	9,299,000	24.	Paris	9,694,000	24.	Hyderabad	10,489,000	24.	Teheran	11,482,000
25.	London	7,640,000	25.	Hangzhou	8,611,000	25.	Hyderabad	9,382,000	25.	Teheran	10,309,000	25.	Kinshasa	11,468,000

RANK	2025	Population	RANK	2050	Population
1.	Bombay	30,378,000	1.	Lagos	46,566,000
2.	Lagos	30,372,000	2.	Karachi	44,284,000
3.	Tokyo	28,887,000	3.	Bombay	41,803,000
4.	Karachi	24,847,000	4.	Dhaka	35,841,000
5.	Dhaka	23,820,000	5.	Calcutta	35,027,000
6.	Calcutta	21,171,000	6.	Kinshasa	34,624,000
7.	Mexico City	21,078,000	7.	Addis Ababa	31,876,000
8.	Sao Paulo	20,793,000	8.	Shanghai	29,534,000
9.	Shanghai	20,787,000	9.	Tokyo	28,887,000
10.	Delhi	19,838,000	10.	Delhi	28,627,000
11.	New York	18,498,000	11.	Mexico City	27,632,000
12.	Beijing	17,875,000	12.	Beijing	24,674,000
13.	Cairo	16,816,000	13.	Cairo	24,163,000
14.	Jakarta	15,649,000	14.	Lahore	23,687,000
15.	Tianjin	15,421,000	15.	Bangkok	22,325,000
16.	Metro Manila	15,149,000	16.	Sao Paulo	21,249,000
17.	Los Angeles	14,858,000	17.	Teheran	21,234,000
18.	Buenos Aires	14,049,000	18.	New York	21,068,000
19.	Kinshasa	13,787,000	19.	Tianjin	20,716,000
20.	Lahore	12,999,000	20.	Jakarta	19,712,000
21.	Seoul	12,980,000	21.	Madras	18,423,000
22.	Teheran	12,721,000	22.	Ho Chi Minh	18,201,000
23.	Istanbul	12,512,000	23.	Los Angeles	16,567,000
24.	Rio de Janeiro	12,450,000	24.	Luanda	16,508,000
25.	Bangkok	12,397,000	25.	Hyderabad	16,112,000

Notes. Source: *World urbanization prospects, the 1996 revision.* New York: United Nations, 1997. Urban agglomerations included in the chart are those of one million population or more in 1996. The concept of agglomeration defines the population contained within the contours of contiguous territory inhabited at urban levels of residential density without regard to administrative boundaries. Population figures for each urban agglomeration for 2050 were calculated by using the following formula: pop 2050 = pop 2025 * UN urbanites 2050/UN urbanites 2025. These were then ranked by size to produce a 'Top 25'. The extent of Christianity and evangelization for each of the urban agglomerations above is enumerated in Table 10-5. In addition, suburbs over 50,000 in population are indented below each of these urban agglomerations in Table 10-5.

Graph 10-8. Non-Christian cities in the Top 5, AD 1800-AD 2050.

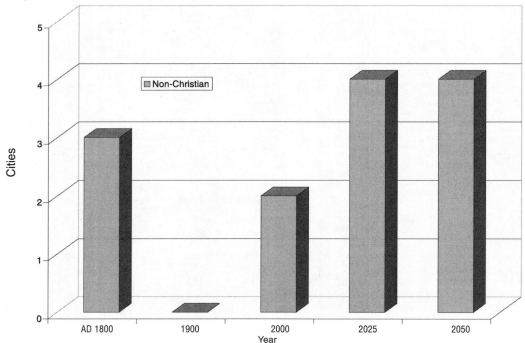

Next, there are the world's 2.9 billion urban dwellers today. They are more evangelized than rural dwellers, and the level approximates to 78%. This leaves 22%, which is 629 million unevangelized urban dwellers. Their annual natural increase rate is 2.5%, i.e., 15.7 million, or 393 million more over the next 25 years. So the grand total to be evangelized by AD 2025 is 1,022 million, which is 41 million unevangelized urban dwellers a year or 112,000 a day (one a second). The present level of achievement is about 50,000 newly evangelized urban dwellers a day.

Whichever interpretation of the Great Commission is considered, achieving closure by AD 2025 involves statistics of millions of people. The only kinds of ministry likely to have any influence on meeting this goal can likewise be termed 'megaministries,' which are defined as outreach ministries of any type which reach somewhere around 1 million people a day, or somewhat over 100 million unevangelized people every year. These figures approximate two totals of great significance for world evangelization: (a) the world's annual population increase of 72 million, and (b) the world's annual birth rate (new human beings) of 124 million. These are, respectively, 196,000 and 341,000 a day.

It is probably better to define a megaministry as one that reaches a minimum of 100,000 unevangelized people every day, with a preferable optimum of more than 1 million a day.

It is interesting to note that these figures are roughly 1% of the world's population (i.e., roughly equal to annual population increase). Thus, an alternative definition could be used: a megaministry is one which reaches over 1% of world population every year. On this definition, the world's first megaministry was the Bible societies' distributing of the Scriptures, which reached 1% about 1870 (the year in which London became the world's first supercity).

In a nutshell, then, megacities demand megaministries. Only this variety of ministries can face up to the prospect of 471 massive non-Christian megacities, supercities, and supergiants which today are growing at the rate of 129,000 urban non-Christians every day.

METHODOLOGY

Historical background is valuable, but more detailed contemporary information on individual cities is needed if to fully analyze and comprehend the present urban situation.

Surveying the world's 7,000 metropolises
Since 1980 a number of Christian research centers sponsored by many denominations worldwide have been working on how to get such new data. Secular

planting and church growth—this comprehensive work of Christians is what is measured in this study.

The twentieth century as progress or decline
A further graph measures not disciples nor Christians nor church members, but evangelized persons— all those urban dwellers who have been witnessed to, have had the gospel preached to them, have heard the gospel, have had the gospel presented to them, have had the gospel shared with them, or have otherwise been given the opportunity to respond to the gospel.

Graph 10-11, 'The Urban Masses: the Extent of Global Urban Evangelization, AD 1800-2050,' presents a quite different picture of the fortunes of world evangelization. Instead of going up over the years, these fortunes are going down. The graph indicates that evangelization of the urban world has decreased proportionally since 1900. This is due to the massive increase of non-Christian megacities, rising from only 5 in 1900 to 229 by AD 2000. In 1900, 72% of all urban dwellers had become adequately evangelized (i.e., adequately meaning having had opportunity to hear the gospel, although this does not signal the end of further evangelizing efforts on their behalf). Today the percentage is 55%, and present trends indicate that, without any further new endeavors, by AD 2025 it will probably be around 65% and by AD 2050 around 75%.

The increasing role of megaministries
Since large numbers of Christians, churches, and agencies have committed themselves publicly to the global task of evangelization (some with the fixed deadline of AD 2025), the magnitude of what remains to be accomplished needs to be understood. Clearly, it depends on the measurement of 'evangelization.' There are two component parts of the definition.

First, there is the *discipling* component. Progress in discipling is measured by the numbers of baptized church members (see Graph 10-10). Many church workers today expect the whole world to be won for Christ. Since church members number only 31% of the world, a staggering 69% remain to be discipled. This is 4.2 billion people. To disciple this population in 25 short years (by AD 2025) Christians must persuade 168 million every year to accept Christ. Each year, also, the world's total population increases, due to births minus deaths, by 72 million. Hence, protagonists of discipling the world face an awesome unfinished task of discipling 6.4 billion people, which means 256 million people a year (700,000 a day) for the next 25 years. The likely outcome of urban Christianity is illustrated in Graph 10-12 where past and present trends are projected to the year AD 2050.

Second, there is the *evangelizing* component. Progress in evangelizing is measured by the the impact of all Christian ministries on a population segment. Many parachurch workers today think only in terms of their own seed-sowing ministries. In this interpretation, the task of world evangelization is virtually completed today. The seed of the gospel has been sown in every country of the world, Christian broadcasting is universal, the message has been proclaimed to the ends of the earth. The whole world of 6 billion people, they feel, is now evangelized.

Combining the two components, discipling and evangelizing, produces the situation depicted in Graph 10-11. By this criterion, the world is computed to be 73% adequately evangelized (including the 31% who have been discipled), which leaves 27% or 1,629 million unevangelized. To this figure must be added the natural increase each year: at 1.7% per annum this is 27 million a year, or 675 million by AD 2025. This means a total of 2,304 million to be evangelized by AD 2025, or 92 million a year (252,000 a day). The present level of achievement is running at about 87,000 a day.

Graph 10-9. Christian cities in the Top 5, AD 1800-AD 2050.

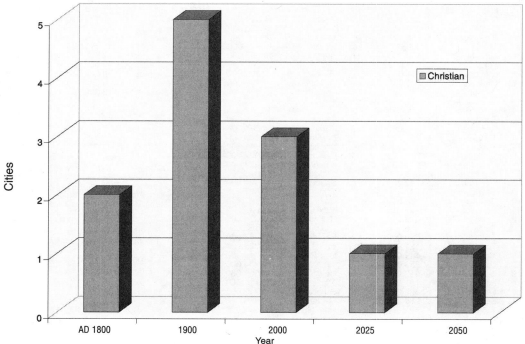

Graph 10-10. The urban masses: proportion of urban Christians, AD 1800-2050.

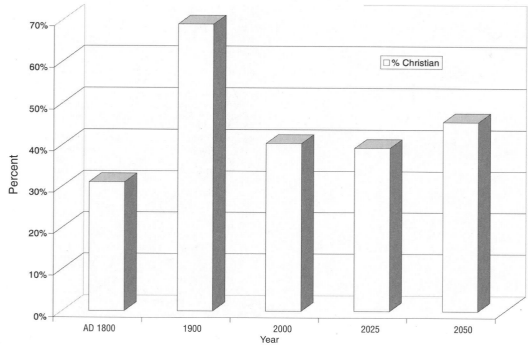

First of all, cities known to be over 50,000 in population from other sources (see bibliography) have been added. This includes many suburbs that are not listed on the Rand McNally list. Second, the Rand McNally cities have populations relating to a wide variety of dates (e.g. 1970-1994). Thus a city of 42,000 in 1970 in a rapidly-growing country will likely have 50,000 by AD 2000 (see column 3 explanation below).

Meaning of columns
1. Rec. No. Record number. These are sequential beginning with Afghanistan and include the categories 'rural areas', 'urban areas', non-metropolitan areas', and 'metropolitan areas' for every country. Thus the total number of cities in the listing is the final record number 7,904 minus (4 additional categories times 238 countries) which equals 6,952.
2. Country. Standard name of 238 countries. For more details on individual countries see Part 4 "Countries". The entire country line is in bold. All data on this line relates to the entire country, not to any individual city below.
City. In most cases the city name is an autometronym or the name of a city as it is known to its inhabitants. One example is Krung Thep for Bangkok, Thailand. Capitals are given in capital letters.
3. Pop 2000. Population figures are for mid-2000 and are derived in the following fashion: A population figure is supplied by Rand McNally or another source for a particular date. To calculate the year 2000 population of a city, the following formula is used (note that an asterisk * in a formula is standard notation for 'multiplied by'):

= UN urban population (AD 2000) * city population (McNally)/UN urban population (McNally date)

Cities included in the United Nations list of 431 urban agglomerations include projections for AD 2000 and these are used instead of the formula above.
4. AC%. Percent affiliated church members. Totals for country are derived from Tables 1 in Part 4 "Countries". Certain guidelines were followed to determine the percentage of Christians within a particularly city. The 100% rule always applied. Metro Christians + Non-metro Christians + Rural Christians always equals the total number of Christians in a country according to Table 1 for that country. Urban Christians is always the total of Metro and Non-metro Christians.

Apart from these overall guidelines, the following techniques were used:
a. Urban surveys. For a number of cities an urban survey, usually filled out by missionaries or church workers in that city, was available. This often gave a detailed breakdown of Christians by denomination. Numbers were often provided for other religions.

data on cities, such as demographic populations, are collected by the United Nations Population Division in New York City. The UN has pushed forward its projections of population for all countries and cities from its previous limit, the year AD 2025, to the year AD 2050. But comparable religious data for the past and present is more difficult to obtain. In fact, no Christian denomination in the world collects or publishes its statistical data of membership divided up by or based on the urban criterion, i.e., for particular cities within their secular boundaries.

Here is the problem. The world today has 1,160 million urban Christians. Some 20,000 different Christian denominations enumerate them within ecclesiastical jurisdictions (dioceses, synods, districts, deaneries, presbyteries, conventions, etc.) whose boundaries virtually never coincide with the political city boundaries within which secular statistics are collected. So one cannot benefit by comparing Christian figures with secular analysis.

Since 1980 Christian researchers have cooperated to compile a short four-page questionnaire entitled 'Urban Mission and Evangelization' and to attempt to get one completed for every metropolis (which means 'mother city') in the world, defined as every large city with over 100,000 population. These cities number 3,180. Full replies were received from 700 cities, partial data on another 400, scattered Christian data on another 1,000, and basic comparative Christian data (six variables) on the whole 3,180. A vast amount of totally new data has thus been generated. A number of analyses have been done, and results are incorporated in this present report.

A large part of these data is quite new and unexpected. Questions asking for the ethnic, linguistic, and religious composition of each city have revealed that the world's cities have entered a whole new era of multiracial, multiethnic, multilingual, and multireligious pluralism unprecedented in the entire history of urbanization. Thus one learns of Paris now being 14% Arab and Berber; the English cathedral city of Leicester being 20% Gujarati, 10% Pakistani, and 5% West Indian; Japanese sects including Soka Gakkai and Tenrikyo in African cities; Chinese Buddhists in the staunchly Catholic city of Dublin, Ireland; Los Angeles expected to become 60% Hispanic with 500 ethnic groups; and so on.

On the whole, placing the churches' data within the secular context is succeeding beyond original expectation. Problems remain, one of which relates to exactly how many metropolises (cities of over 50,000) there are, how many megacities, how many world-class cities and how many supercities. For the past twenty years, data sets published by the UN and other sources have varied widely in their answers to these questions.

There are three reasons for these fluctuations: (a) New census data is continually coming in from member countries of the UN, revealing more cities which have passed 50,000 or 100,000 inhabitants. (b) The overall total is gradually decreasing because large numbers of pairs of cities are physically meeting and joining up, each to form one single megacity. Thus today the UN lists the world's largest city as, not Tokyo, but the single continuous urban agglomeration named Tokyo-Yokohama. Two huge cities have now, de facto, become one. Also, (c) large numbers of entities formerly regarded as separate cities are now being reclassified as suburbs of larger megacities. These continual mergers and reclassifications have understandably complicated analysis of the status of Christianity in the urban world.

Codebook
The listing of 7,000 cities in Table 10-5 is derived from Rand McNally's *The new international atlas* (1993), pages 301-316. These cities are over 50,000 in population or are capital cities under 50,000 in population. However, a number of adjustments have been made.

Graph 10-11. The urban masses: the extent of global urban evangelization, AD 1800-2050.

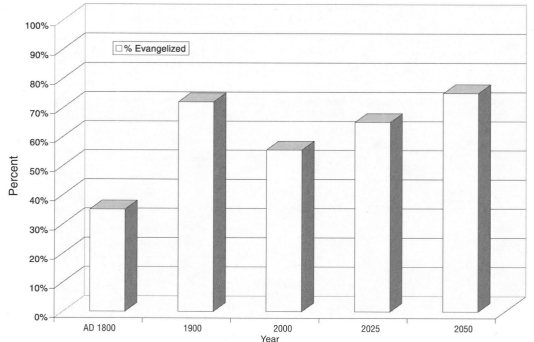

Graph 10-12. The rise and fall of urban Christianity, AD 1775-2050.

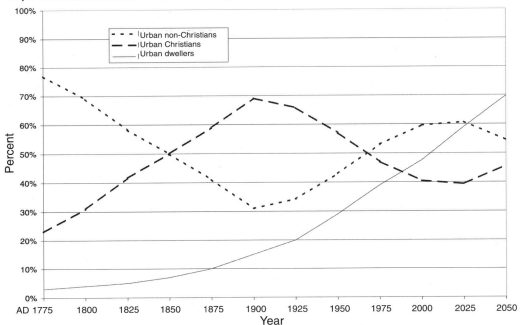

---

b. Country reports. The number of Christians could be determined for many cities by country reports done by missionaries and church workers. Often, detailed information on cities within these countries was included.

c. Censuses. For many countries, such as India, detailed census reports give some figures for religions, including Christianity.

d. Denominational reports. For many denominations, precise church membership figures are reported for cities. From this information a fuller picture of Christianity can often be constructed.

e. Ethnic affiliation. In many cities, the Christian situation can be derived from ethnic data. For example, it may be known that a city is composed predominately of one or two ethnic groups. Since the percentage Christian is known for all ethnic groups, the percentage of Christians in a city can be calculated using ethnic data.

f. Literature. A vast number of books, articles, and other published works exist on the subject of Christians and the urban world. A selection is present in the 4-page Bibliography following Table 10-4.

g. Contextual information. In the absence of any of the resources named above there is almost always a series of contextual clues related to the status of Christianity in a city. For example, in some areas of China, little is known at the city level. However, much work has been done on Christianity in China's provinces. One can apply the 100% rule to the province and calculate where the Christians reside.

5. Church members. Number of affiliated church members. Calculated by multiplying column 3 (Pop 2000) by column 4 (%AC) divided by 100. These fig-

ures are not meant to convey exactitude, i.e. 'There are exactly 33 Christians in Herat, Afghanistan', but rather 'There are very few Christians in Herat, perhaps only 0.01% of the population'.

6. E%. Percent evangelized. The percentage of this city (or category) who have received an adequate opportunity to become Christians. Evangelization of a city is measured by setting up a proportion related to the church members in the city and the evangelization of the country. The formula is as follows:

% evangelized of a city= church members (city)/church members (country)*% evangelized (country)

This result is then adjusted (figure available on the related CD *World Christian database*) to reconcile it with the total urban evangelized derived from Tables 1 in Part 4 "Countries".

7. W. Worlds. Using the church membership and evangelization data, one can determine where a city fits into the World A, B, C trichotomy. Worlds A, B, and C are defined in Part 2 "Glossary".

8. Pop 2025. Population in mid-2025. To calculate the year 2025 population of a city, the following formula is used:

=urban population (UN AD 2025) * city population (AD 2000)/urban population (UN AD 2000)

However, cities included in the United Nations list of 431 urban agglomerations include projections for AD 2025 and these are used instead of the formula. AD 2050 projections for all cities (available on the re-

lated CD *World Christian database*) use a formula similar to those above for population 2000 and population 2025.

9. Notes. Several different types of additional information are provided here.

On the country line. The first data on this line are the two largest ecclesiastical megablocs in this country expressed as a percentage of the country's population. In some countries the title 'Marginal Christians' has been shortened to 'Marginals' in the interest of space. Following this are the three trans-megabloc groupings. Pentecostals/ Charismatics is shortened to Pent-Char, followed by Evangelicals, and finally GCC (all defined in Part 2 "Glossary"), the short form for Great Commission Christians. Each of these it followed by the percentage they represent of the country's population. Fuller descriptions of these data can be found in Country Tables 1 in Part 4 "Countries."

On the rural areas line. The percentage of the country's population that is rural is given for six dates in parentheses: 1950, 1970, 1990, 2000, 2010, and 2025. The main source of this data is from the United Nations *World urbanization prospects.*

On the urban areas line. The percentage of the country's population that is urban is given for six dates in parentheses: 1950, 1970, 1990, 2000, 2010, and 2025. The main source of this data is from the United Nations *World urbanization prospects.*

On the non-metropolitan areas line. Sources of data for urbanization, urban demographics and metropolitan demographics are given. Most are taken from the United Nations *World urbanization prospects.*

On the metropolitan areas line. The standard definition for urban areas and, in some cases, cities, is given here. Most are taken from the United Nations *World urbanization prospects.*

On the cities line. Here the reader is presented with a sequence of facts about a particular city. Normally the first word on this line refers to the major civil division of this city. This is usually followed by facts related to the geography or location. Often there are data on the main economic activity of each city. The code 'F=' refers to the date in which the city was founded. This normally differs from the date a city was incorporated. The founding date refers to the earliest date of known settlement. This is usually followed with data on ethnic groups and religions, accompanied by percentages where these are known. Finally the code 'D=' refers to denominations active in the city and the code 'M=' to mission agencies working there. The meaning of abbreviations can be found in Part 15 "Indexes".

Table 10-2. Megacities, supercities, supergiants by continent, AD 1800-2050.

This table and Table 10-3, overleaf, describe the rise of megacities from AD 1775 to AD 2050. The table below presents the summary data by Worlds A, B, and C (see Part 2 "Glossary" for definitions) and by the six UN regions. *Definitions.* Megacities = all cities over 1 million each (includ-

ing supergiants and supercities when reported in the final 5 columns). Supercities = all cities over 4 million each (including supergiants when reported under 'total supercities'). Table 10-3 presents the data in more detail globally, by UN region, and by Worlds A, B, and C within each of these

regions. The final six columns under each region enumerates total population, urban population and Christian population. *Source of urban data. World urbanization prospects, 1996* (UN 1998).

Year	Megacities Under 4m					Supercities Under 10m					Supergiants Over 10m					Total Supercities					Total Megacities				
	1800	1900	2000	2025	2050	1800	1900	2000	2025	2050	1800	1900	2000	2025	2050	1800	1900	2000	2025	2050	1800	1900	2000	2025	2050
World	1	20	402	601	806	0	2	60	118	174	0	0	20	31	49	0	2	80	149	223	1	22	482	750	1029
World A	1	5	41	80	141	0	0	2	12	26	0	0	0	3	6	0	0	2	15	32	1	5	43	95	173
World B	0	0	188	294	395	0	0	34	64	90	0	0	13	18	29	0	0	47	82	119	0	0	235	376	514
World C	0	15	173	227	270	0	2	24	42	58	0	0	7	10	14	0	2	31	52	72	0	17	204	279	342
Africa	0	2	40	79	129	0	2	40	79	129	0	0	4	21	39	0	2	44	100	168	0	4	84	179	297
Asia	1	3	195	321	450	0	0	0	3	6	0	0	0	3	6	0	0	0	6	12	1	3	195	327	462
Europe	0	11	66	71	73	0	1	7	7	7	0	0	0	0	0	0	1	7	7	7	0	12	73	78	80
Latin America	0	0	52	65	78	0	0	8	17	19	0	0	4	5	6	0	0	12	22	25	0	0	64	87	103
North America	0	4	43	59	69	0	1	7	9	13	0	0	2	2	3	0	1	9	11	16	0	5	52	70	85
Oceania	0	0	6	6	7	0	0	0	1	2	0	0	0	0	0	0	0	0	1	2	0	0	6	7	9

Table 10-3. Megacities, supercities, and supergiants by Worlds A, B, and C, AD 1775 – AD 2050.

	GLOBAL Mega	Super	Giant	Worlds A	B	C	Global Pop	Urban Pop	%	Christians Pop	%	Non-Christians Pop	%	World A Mega	Super	Giant	World B Mega	Super	Giant	World C Mega	Super	Giant
AD1775	1	-	-	1	-	-	768.7	23.1	3%	5.2	23%	17.8	77%	1	—	—	—	—	—	—	—	—
AD1800	1	-	-	1	—	-	900.0	36.0	4%	11.2	31%	24.8	69%	1	—	—	—	—	—	—	—	—
AD1825	2	—	-	1	—	1	1,053.8	52.7	5%	22.2	42%	30.4	58%	1	—	—	—	—	—	1	—	—
AD1850	3	—	-	1	—	2	1,233.9	86.4	7%	44.4	51%	42.0	49%	1	—	—	—	—	—	2	—	—
AD1875	6	1	—	1	—	5	1,444.7	144.5	10%	88.4	61%	56.0	39%	1	—	—	—	—	—	5	1	—
AD1900	20	2	—	5	—	17	1,619.5	266.4	16%	176.3	66%	90.1	34%	5	—	—	—	—	—	15	2	—
AD1925	29	7	—	8	—	28	2,010.0	434.3	22%	267.0	61%	167.2	39%	5	3	—	—	—	—	24	4	—
AD1950	70	10	1	25	8	48	2,521.4	749.8	30%	433.3	58%	316.5	42%	22	3	—	7	1	—	41	6	1
AD1975	168	21	3	64	31	97	4,074.5	1,541.7	38%	767.4	50%	774.3	50%	56	7	1	25	5	1	87	9	1
AD2000	402	60	20	43	235	204	6,054.9	2,877.2	48%	1,254.3	44%	1,622.9	56%	41	2	—	188	34	13	173	24	7
AD2025	601	118	31	95	376	279	7,823.5	4,620.0	59%	1,814.9	39%	2,805.1	61%	80	12	3	294	64	18	227	42	10
AD2050	806	174	49	173	514	342	8,909.0	6,188.6	69%	2,536.1	41%	3,652.5	59%	141	26	6	395	90	29	270	58	14

AFRICA

	Mega	Super	Giant	World A Mega	Super	Giant	World B Mega	Super	Giant	World C Mega	Super	Giant	Pop	% of Globe	Urban Pop	%	Christians AC	%AC
AD1775	—	—	—	—	—	—	—	—	—	—	—	—						
AD1800	—	—	—	—	—	—	—	—	—	—	—	—						
AD1825	—	—	—	—	—	—	—	—	—	—	—	—						
AD1850	—	—	—	—	—	—	—	—	—	—	—	—						
AD1875	—	—	—	—	—	—	—	—	—	—	—	—						
AD1900	2	—	—	2	—	—	—	—	—	—	—	—	107.8	6.7%	4.3	4.0%	0.3	0.3%
AD1925	2	—	—	2	—	—	—	—	—	—	—	—	154.0	7.7%	11.7	7.6%	1.7	1.1%
AD1950	2	—	—	2	—	—	—	—	—	—	—	—	220.9	8.8%	32.3	14.6%	8.8	4.0%
AD1975	8	1	—	4	—	—	2	1	—	2	—	—	405.9	10.0%	102.2	25.2%	42.4	10.4%
AD2000	40	4	2	5	—	—	20	3	2	15	1	—	784.4	13.0%	295.2	37.8%	135.6	17.3%
AD2025	79	21	4	9	1	—	37	12	2	33	8	2	1,298.3	16.6%	666.8	51.7%	325.5	25.1%
AD2050	129	39	11	18	2	1	64	19	6	47	18	4	1,766.0	19.8%	1,143.8	64.8%	781.3	44.2%

ASIA

	Mega	Super	Giant	World A Mega	Super	Giant	World B Mega	Super	Giant	World C Mega	Super	Giant	Pop	% of Globe	Urban Pop	%	Christians AC	%AC
AD1775	1	—	—	1	—	—	—	—	—	—	—	—						
AD1800	1	—	—	1	—	—	—	—	—	—	—	—						
AD1825	1	—	—	1	—	—	—	—	—	—	—	—						
AD1850	1	—	—	1	—	—	—	—	—	—	—	—						
AD1875	1	—	—	1	—	—	—	—	—	—	—	—						
AD1900	3	—	—	3	—	—	—	—	—	—	—	—	956.2	59.0%	62.2	6.5%	0.1	0.0%
AD1925	3	3	—	3	3	—	—	—	—	—	—	—	1,157.0	57.6%	122.6	10.6%	0.8	0.1%
AD1950	26	3	—	20	3	—	4	—	—	2	—	—	1,402.0	55.6%	244.1	17.4%	5.1	0.4%
AD1975	70	10	2	52	7	1	15	2	1	3	1	—	2,405.6	59.0%	592.7	24.6%	32.7	1.4%
AD2000	195	34	12	36	2	—	155	31	11	4	1	1	3,682.5	60.8%	1,384.6	37.6%	117.9	3.2%
AD2025	321	63	20	71	11	3	246	50	16	4	2	1	4,723.1	60.4%	2,475.4	52.4%	243.4	5.2%
AD2050	450	94	29	123	24	5	319	68	23	8	2	1	5,268.4	59.1%	3,398.1	64.5%	350.0	6.6%

EUROPE

	Mega	Super	Giant	World A Mega	Super	Giant	World B Mega	Super	Giant	World C Mega	Super	Giant	Pop	% of Globe	Urban Pop	%	Christians AC	%AC
AD1775	—	—	—	—	—	—	—	—	—	—	—	—						
AD1800	—	—	—	—	—	—	—	—	—	—	—	—						
AD1825	1	—	—	—	—	—	—	—	—	1	—	—						
AD1850	2	—	—	—	—	—	—	—	—	2	—	—						
AD1875	4	1	—	—	—	—	—	—	—	4	1	—						
AD1900	11	1	—	—	—	—	—	—	—	11	1	—	402.6	24.9%	153.0	38.0%	134.7	33.5%
AD1925	15	3	—	—	—	—	—	—	—	15	3	—	469.0	23.3%	209.2	44.6%	183.1	39.0%
AD1950	25	4	—	—	—	—	2	1	—	23	3	—	547.3	21.7%	286.8	52.4%	248.7	45.4%
AD1975	41	6	—	—	—	—	5	2	—	36	4	—	676.3	16.6%	454.5	67.2%	336.0	49.7%
AD2000	66	7	—	—	—	—	9	—	—	57	7	—	728.9	12.0%	545.9	74.9%	419.3	57.5%
AD2025	71	7	—	—	—	—	4	1	—	67	6	—	702.3	9.0%	573.7	81.7%	453.4	64.6%
AD2050	73	7	—	—	—	—	5	1	—	68	6	—	627.7	7.0%	553.0	88.1%	445.0	70.9%

LATIN AMERICA

	Mega	Super	Giant	World A Mega	Super	Giant	World B Mega	Super	Giant	World C Mega	Super	Giant	Pop	% of Globe	Urban Pop	%	Christians AC	%AC
AD1775	—	—	—	—	—	—	—	—	—	—	—	—						
AD1800	—	—	—	—	—	—	—	—	—	—	—	—						
AD1825	—	—	—	—	—	—	—	—	—	—	—	—						
AD1850	—	—	—	—	—	—	—	—	—	—	—	—						
AD1875	—	—	—	—	—	—	—	—	—	—	—	—						
AD1900	—	—	—	—	—	—	—	—	—	—	—	—	65.1	4.0%	8.5	13.0%	7.1	10.9%
AD1925	1	—	—	—	—	—	—	—	—	1	—	—	104.0	5.2%	24.1	23.2%	21.3	20.5%
AD1950	6	1	—	—	—	—	1	—	—	5	1	—	167.0	6.6%	69.2	41.4%	64.0	38.3%
AD1975	20	1	—	—	—	—	2	—	—	18	1	—	321.9	7.9%	197.1	61.2%	181.0	56.2%
AD2000	52	8	4	—	—	—	1	—	—	51	8	4	519.1	8.6%	391.2	75.4%	362.7	69.9%
AD2025	65	17	5	—	—	—	2	—	—	63	17	5	696.6	8.9%	572.2	82.1%	527.3	75.7%
AD2050	78	19	6	—	—	—	2	—	—	76	19	6	808.9	9.1%	719.9	89.0%	650.0	80.4%

NORTHERN AMERICA

	Mega	Super	Giant	World A Mega	Super	Giant	World B Mega	Super	Giant	World C Mega	Super	Giant	Pop	% of Globe	Urban Pop	%	Christians AC	%AC
AD1775	—	—	—	—	—	—	—	—	—	—	—	—						
AD1800	—	—	—	—	—	—	—	—	—	—	—	—						
AD1825	—	—	—	—	—	—	—	—	—	—	—	—						
AD1850	—	—	—	—	—	—	—	—	—	—	—	—						
AD1875	1	—	—	—	—	—	—	—	—	1	—	—						
AD1900	4	1	—	—	—	—	—	—	—	4	1	—	81.6	5.0%	35.9	44.0%	32.5	39.8%
AD1925	8	1	—	—	—	—	—	—	—	8	1	—	118.0	5.9%	56.9	53.0%	56.9	48.2%
AD1950	11	2	1	—	—	—	—	—	—	11	2	1	171.6	6.8%	109.7	63.9%	99.7	58.1%
AD1975	27	3	1	—	—	—	—	—	—	27	3	1	243.4	6.0%	179.8	73.9%	162.0	66.6%
AD2000	43	7	2	—	—	—	—	—	—	43	7	2	309.6	5.1%	239.0	77.2%	201.2	65.0%
AD2025	59	9	2	—	—	—	—	—	—	59	9	2	363.6	4.6%	302.8	83.3%	241.8	66.5%
AD2050	69	13	3	—	—	—	—	—	—	69	13	3	391.8	4.4%	338.5	86.4%	280.0	71.5%

OCEANIA

	Mega	Super	Giant	World A Mega	Super	Giant	World B Mega	Super	Giant	World C Mega	Super	Giant	Pop	% of Globe	Urban Pop	%	Christians AC	%AC
AD1775	—	—	—	—	—	—	—	—	—	—	—	—						
AD1800	—	—	—	—	—	—	—	—	—	—	—	—						
AD1825	—	—	—	—	—	—	—	—	—	—	—	—						
AD1850	—	—	—	—	—	—	—	—	—	—	—	—						
AD1875	—	—	—	—	—	—	—	—	—	—	—	—						
AD1900	—	—	—	—	—	—	—	—	—	—	—	—	6.2	0.4%	2.6	42.0%	1.6	25.4%
AD1925	—	—	—	—	—	—	—	—	—	—	—	—	8.0	0.4%	4.1	50.9%	3.3	41.3%
AD1950	—	—	—	—	—	—	—	—	—	—	—	—	12.6	0.5%	7.8	61.6%	7.0	55.6%
AD1975	2	—	—	—	—	—	1	—	—	1	—	—	21.4	0.5%	15.4	71.8%	13.3	62.1%
AD2000	6	—	—	—	—	—	3	—	—	3	—	—	30.4	0.5%	21.3	70.0%	17.6	57.9%
AD2025	6	1	—	—	—	—	5	1	—	1	—	—	39.6	0.5%	29.1	73.5%	23.5	59.2%
AD2050	7	2	—	—	—	—	5	2	—	2	—	—	46.2	0.5%	35.2	76.2%	29.8	64.5%

Table 10-4. Christianity and the world's cities: past, present, future.

1. Background: The origins of urbanization

BC

8900 World's first permanent city: sudden growth and explosive expansion of Jericho, to a population of 3,000, after introduction of cultivation 'techniques of wheat and barley: as commercial enterprise and trade (salt, sulphur) lead to wealth, city is fortified and surrounded by a massive wall for flood protection; occupied for next 7,000 years.

5000 Development of temple towns, concurrent with human sacrifice, inflicted death, and religiously-related warfare; rise of city-states, specialized trades and industries.

4400 Ubaid culture in southern Mesopotamia leads by 3100 BC into Sumerian civilization (world's oldest urban literate culture); numerous cities arise, with monumental mud-brick temples.

2500 Mohenjo Daro and Harappa built as largest cities of Indus Valley civilization, whose script is similar to that of Easter Island, in Pacific; other far-flung global urban links.

2000 First stirrings of urban-industrial mass society: vast bureaucracies rule Egypt and Babylonia, embryonic mass-production factories in ancient Greece and Rome, oil drilled in Greece in 400 BC and in Burma in AD 100.

2. Migration of proto-Hebrew nation to Palestine

BC

1950 Abraham moves from Ur of the Chaldees to Palestine. Hebrew nation begins its record around cities (1,230 references in Bible, with hundreds more on specific cities) with negative image of cities as evil from Enoch, Babel, Sodom (Genesis 4-19) on through to Christian Great Babylon (Revelation 17), but later includes positive image from refugee cities (Joshua 20) to Christian New Jerusalem (Revelation 22).

1900 Destruction of cities of Sodom and Gomorrah by earthquake, then covered by Dead Sea in Palestine.

1500 Heyday of kingdom of Tartessus, 'Venice of the West,' Atlantic Spanish port (biblical Tarshish—21 references); with records and a literature since 6500 BC; 533 BC destroyed by Carthaginians, vanishes without trace.

1360 World's 5 largest cities:
Thebes 100,000
Memphis 74,000
Babylon 54,000
Chengchow 40,000
Khattushas (Hattusa) 40,000

950 Large-scale spread of urbanization in northern Chinese independent city-states.

650 World's 5 largest cities:
Nineveh 120,000
Loyang (Honan) 117,000
Yenhsiatu 108,000
Memphis 99,000
Chicheng 91,000

586 Final fall of Jerusalem, obliterated by Nebuchadnezzar II.

430 World's 5 largest cities:
Babylon 250,000
Ecbatana 200,000
Athens 155,000
Sravasti (Savatthi, Set Mahet) 150,000
Champa (Lin-Yi) 150,000

300 Cursus Publicus, highly-developed postal system and extensive messenger service of ancient Roman world linking its cities, with relay stages covering 170 miles in 24 hours; persists until AD 820.

200 World's 5 largest cities:
Patna (Pataliputra) 350,000
Alexandria 300,000
Seleucia 300,000
Changan 239,000
Loyang 189,000

3. Birth of Christianity as an urban phenomenon

AD

33 Day of Pentecost in Jerusalem: 3,000 converted among Diaspora Jews and Gentiles from 'every nation under heaven,' from North Africa to Persia; converts return home taking gospel to cities across world.

39 City of Antioch (population 200,000): wider mission to Gentiles inaugurated; AD 46, first of Paul's three missionary journeys visiting urban centers utilizing a strategy of urban evangelization.

55 Paul's 'Letter to the Romans' sent to 3,000 Christians in 5 congregations in Rome (population 800,000).

64 First imperial Roman persecution of Christians, under emperor Nero; many martyrs including Apostles Peter and Paul.

70 Obliteration of Jerusalem by Titus with 4 Roman legions; 10,000 Jews crucified, 90,000 Jews to Rome as slaves; destruction of Jewish Christianity and end of Judaizers.

79 Cities of Pompeii, Stabiae, and Herculaneum in Italy destroyed by eruption of Mount Vesuvius.

100 Christianity predominantly urban, based on Roman cities, spreading from city to city along trade routes; later missions to Armenia, Ethiopia, China (under Nestorians) all center on capital cities.
World's 5 largest cities:
Rome 1,100,000
Loyang 510,000
Alexandria 400,000
Seleucia 300,000
Changan 245,000
Rome the first and only metropolis in ancient world to reach or pass 1 million population (60% being slaves); by AD 450 falls to under 250,000, by AD 650 to under 50,000, and to under 19,000 by 1360 due to Black Death; then rises to over 100,000 by 1600 and to 1 million by 1930.
Teotihuacan (Mexico) established as America's first urban civilization; at its height in AD 590, contains 160,000 people and controls empire covering all Meso-America.

130 Christianity spreads principally and normally, though not exclusively, through (as prevailing strategy) the planting of urban churches which then serve as missionary communities to evangelize their areas by continuing to attract and enlist converts; most converts are reached through casual contacts, witnessing a martyrdom, hospitality and care of strangers, et al.

132 Second Jewish rebellion under alleged messiah Bar Kokeba; 134, second destruction of Jerusalem by Romans, 580,000 Jews killed in battle; final dispersal of the Jews.

200 First permanent church buildings constructed (all worship being previously in homes); only in cities at first.
Edessa (now Urfa) first city-state to make Christianity its state religion; conversion of its king Abgar IX, first Christian political ruler; missionary center for eastern Syria.

4. Christianity becomes organized with metropolitan structures

249 Seven missionary bishops sent to cities in Gaul by Cornelius of Rome (to Tours, Arles, Narbonne, Toulouse, Paris, Limoges, Clermont).

250 Bishoprics in southern Italy total over 100, all centered on cities.

251 City of Rome: 45,000 Christians (5% of population of 900,000), 46 presbyters, 14 deacons, 42 acolytes, 52 exorcists, supporting 1,500 widows and persons in distress; by AD 300, church buildings in Rome increase to over 40.

290 Roman Empire reorganized by emperor Diocletian into 4 prefectures, 15 dioceses (secular areas governed by imperial vicars), 120 provinces; Christians begin to relate their ecclesiastical jurisdictions to these political boundaries.

303 Tenth and last imperial Roman persecution, under Diocletian; aimed at clergy and bishops, with destruction of church buildings and Scriptures ordered; around 500,000 Christians systematically executed or killed, mostly in urban centers.

330 Constantine moves capital of Roman Empire to Byzantium, renames it Constantinople; Christianity now overwhelmingly an urban phenomenon.

361 World's 5 largest cities:
Constantinople 350,000
Loyang 296,000
Rome 250,000
Patna 224,000
Ctesiphon 200,000

380 City of Antioch: of 200,000 population, 50% are Christians, increasing rapidly.

410 Episcopate in Proconsular Africa, Numidia and Mauretania expands to 768 bishops; total episcopate across North Africa numbers 1,200 bishops all based on metropolises or other urban centers.

426 Augustine bishop of Hippo completes in 13 years his treatise *The City of God* (De Civitate Dei) against background of fall and sack of Rome by Barbarian Alaric and his Visigoths, followed by collapse of western Roman Empire.

5. The Dark Ages: decline of cities and of urban Christendom

500 Cities empty as Europe returns to village and town life, until 11th-century revival of urban development.

526 150,000, including many Christians, killed by earthquake in city of Antioch.

622 World's 5 largest cities:
Constantinople 500,000
Changan 447,000
Loyang 400,000
Ctesiphon 283,000
Alexandria 200,000

640 Eighty percent of 6.5 million Berbers across North Africa (2.6 million urbanized) now Christians; but by 950 all become converted to Islam.

697 City of Carthage captured by Muslims; North Africa in Muslim hands.

800 World's 5 largest cities:
Changan 800,000
Baghdad 700,000
Constantinople 300,000
Loyang 245,000
Kyoto 200,000

999 Multitudes journey to city of Jerusalem to await Second Coming of Christ in AD 1000 as believed prophesied in Apocrypha.

1000 World's 5 largest cities:
Cordova 450,000
Constantinople 450,000
Kaifeng 400,000
Sian (Changan) 300,000
Kyoto 200,000
Nestorian (East Syrian) church most extensive in world, with 250 dioceses across Asia and 12 million adherents, dioceses being based on cities organized under 15 metropolitan provinces within Arab caliphate and 5 abroad including India and China.
Patriarchate of Constantinople oversees 624 dioceses in cities around eastern Mediterranean.

1150 Widest expansion of West Syrian (Jacobite) church; 20 metropolitan sees and 103 bishoprics based on urban centers.

1200 World's 5 largest cities:
Hangchow (Quinsay) 255,000
Fez 250,000
Cairo 200,000
Constantinople 200,000
Canton 200,000

1305 House of Taxis (Vienna) operates express message postal system through Europe's cities with (by 1628) 20,000 liveried couriers; a mass communications total monopoly for the rich, privileged, and powerful.

1306 John of Montecorvino builds two churches in city of Cambaluc (Peking) with 6,000 converts, translates New Testament into Ongut (Tatar) and Uighur.

1325 Aztecs found capital city Tenochtitlan in Valley of Mexico; by 1500, population 500,000; 1523, destroyed and razed by Cortes and conquistadors.

1347 Black Death (bubonic plague pandemic) from Crimea sweeps across Europe killing 40% of entire urban population.

1400 World's 5 largest cities:
Nanking 473,000
Cairo 450,000
Vijayanagar (Hampi) 350,000
Hangchow 325,000
Peking 320,000

6. Protestant Reformation spreads via German and Swiss cities

1517 Luther at Wittenberg begins Reformation, which achieves its greatest response in German and Swiss cities.

1530 Anabaptist leader Melchior Hofmann predicts imminent end of world in 1533 with Strasbourg to be the New Jerusalem.

1536 City of Geneva becomes first Reformed city in Europe, a theocracy under John Calvin.

1540 Population census of Venice (Italy), conducted by church authorities: 129,971 persons.

1600 World's 5 largest cities:
Peking 706,000
Istanbul (Constantinople) 700,000
Agra 500,000
Cairo 400,000
Osaka 400,000

1610 Spanish Jesuit missionary Peter Claver, 'Apostle to the Blacks,' arrives at slave-trade capital Cartagena (Colombia), ministers to 1,000 African arrivals a month for 44 years, baptizing 300,000 negro slaves.

1623 Twenty-three Jesuit reductions (urban settlements) with 100,000 population established in Paraguay.
German Lutherans arrive in New York, organizing a congregation by 1649; 1628, Dutch organize first Christian Reformed church on Manhattan Island.

1631 Entire Christian population of city of Mombasa, Kenya, massacred by apostate Swahili sultan Chingulia.

1670 City of Paris begins publishing records of baptisms, births and burials (up to present day).

1680 Penny Post set up as first urban postal service in London by William Dockwra, prepaid and with hourly deliveries.

7. Modern missionary movement emphasizes urban ministry

1705 City of Halle (Germany) becomes center of foreign missionary activity and training; Canstein House as first Bible society, and revivals and evangelistic campaigns of Lutheran professor of Hebrew A. H. Francke.

1738 Conversion of John Wesley (1703-1791), beginning of 18th-century Evangelical Revival with its urban outreach to the poor, orphans, the uneducated and unemployed.

1770 Chinese capital Peking becomes first city in modern times to reach 1 million in population; meteoric rise begins of megacities (over 1 million persons each) across world, escalating to (year, world total, total in developing countries):
1900, *20*
1950, *81* (35)
1955, *95* (42)
1960, *115* (53)
1965, *136* (63)
1970, *161* (79)
1975, *183* (95)
1980, *227* (125)
1985, *276* (163)
1990, *330* (205)
AD 2000, *482* (330)

Continued opposite

Table 10-4 continued

AD 2025, *750* (580)
AD 2050, *1,029* (850)

1775 Industrial revolution begins in Holland first, then in Britain; urban working classes become permanently alienated from churches.

1800 World's 10 largest cities:
Peking 1,100,000
London 861,000
Canton 800,000
Istanbul 570,000
Paris 547,000
Hangchow 500,000
Yedo (Tokyo) 492,000
Naples 430,000
Soochow 392,000
Osaka 380,000

1812 New York City Mission movement founded by Evangelicals, lasts till 1870.

1824 USA: beginnings of interdenominational city-wide cooperative evangelism.

1832 London City Mission founded, first of 50 city missions begun in Britain's largest cities (Bristol, Chester, Edinburgh, Glasgow, Leeds, Liverpool, York, et alia), still thriving into 1980s.

1850 World's 10 largest cities:
London 2,320,000
Peking 1,648,000
Paris 1,314,000
Canton 800,000
Istanbul 785,000
Hangchow 700,000
New York 682,000
Bombay 575,000
Yedo 567,000
Soochow 550,000

8. Large-scale urban team evangelism begins

1857 USA: evangelist D. L. Moody preaches in Chicago, over next 40 years has personal evangelistic dealings with 750,000 persons; beginnings of large-scale, lay-centered urban evangelism.

1865 Christian Revival Association (from 1878 named Salvation Army) founded in London for urban social outreach and street evangelism.

1870 Heyday of British city evangelists: William Booth, C. H. Spurgeon, Henry Drummond, Wilson Carlile, Gipsy Smith.
Rise of supercities across world (cities with over 4 million population each), beginning with London (4.2 million by 1875); escalating over next century to 60 by AD 2000 (40 in developing countries); by AD 2025, 118 (85); by AD 2050, 174 (150).
Rise of first Christian megaministry (a ministry reaching over 1% of the world, i.e., 14 million people a year in 1870); British and Foreign Bible Society's, American Bible Society's, and other Bible societies' distribution rises to 38,000 Scriptures a day.

1871 Great fire of Chicago: 50 churches and missions destroyed.
Sermon preached before Baptist Missionary Society in London emphasizes gospel could easily be preached to every creature in world by 1886, or by 1891 at latest.

1875 World's 10 largest cities:
London 4,241,000
Paris 2,250,000
New York 1,900,000
Peking 1,310,000
Berlin 1,045,000
Vienna 1,001,000
Canton 944,000
Philadelphia 791,000
Tokyo 780,000
St. Petersburg 764,000

1884 Citywide evangelists in USA proliferate: Samuel Porter Jones (1847-1906 and E. O. Excell (from 1885-1906, 25 million attenders and 500,000 converts, most in South), B. Fay Mills (1857-1916), J. Wilbur Chapman (1859-1918).

1885 Wesleyan Forward Movement in British Methodism under Hugh Price Hughes (1847-1902) of West London Mission, founding Methodist central halls in cities and stressing social evangelism.

1887 Canada: evangelistic campaigns under evangelists Crossley and Hunter.

1895 City of Trebizond: 80,000 Armenian Christians massacred by Turks.

1898 Nyasaland: Providence Industrial Mission founded by US blacks, later becomes a leading African indigenous church.

1900 World's 10 largest cities:
London 6,480,000
New York 4,242,000
Paris 3,330,000
Berlin 2,424,000
Chicago 1,717,000
Vienna 1,662,000
Tokyo 1,497,000
St. Petersburg 1,439,000
Philadelphia 1,418,000
Manchester 1,255,000

1901 After first Industrial Revolution (fueled by steam power and coal in Britain, 1775), second revolution arises due to electrical and chemical industries in Germany.

1905 Evangelistic Council of London sponsors Greater London crusade with Torrey and Alexander team; 202 meetings, 1.1 million attenders, 14,000 conversions.

1908 J. Wilbur Chapman's six-week evangelistic campaign in Philadelphia: 400 churches, 1.5 million attenders, 7,000 inquirers.

1910 USA team evangelism: 1910-30, Billy Sunday (1862-1935) and H. Rodeheaver; the former preaches to 100 million, with 1 million converts.
Edinburgh Conference states: 'The Church is confronted today with a literally worldwide opportunity to make Christ known.'

1912 USA team evangelism: 1912-45, Mordecai Ham and W. J. Ramsay.

9. New types of urban missions emerge: radio, television, et alia

1921 Pittsburgh (USA): first broadcast of a church worship service; Sunday, January 2, from Calvary Episcopal Church.

1925 World's 10 largest cities:
New York 7,774,000
London 7,742,000
Tokyo 5,300,000
Paris 4,800,000
Berlin 4,013,000
Chicago 3,564,000
Ruhr 3,400,000
Buenos Aires 2,410,000
Osaka 2,219,000
Philadelphia 2,085,000

1927 In USA, 50 radio stations now licensed to religious bodies in cities.

1930 Telephone system now serves 10% of humanity, and 20% in cities.

1933 Shanghai Christian Broadcasting Association organized (XMHD), covering entire Far East; also 1935 XLKA (Peking).

1935 Rise of urban supergiants (cities with over 10 million population each) across the world, the first being New York in 1935, escalating to 8 by 1985, 20 by AD 2000, 31 by AD 2025, and 49 by AD 2050.

1936 BBC (Britain) begins first television broadcasting, including regular worship services.

1943 Britain: Christian Commando Campaigns 1943-47, led by Methodists, in London, Edinburgh, Glasgow, et al.

1950 After first Industrial Revolution (steam and coal, 1775) and second (electrical and chemical, 1901), third revolution from 1950 on is fueled by nuclear power, microchips and genes.
Mass immigration from Third World into industrialized Western world begins, totaling by 1960 3.2 million; by 1974, 9.5 million.
World's 10 largest cities:
New York/Northeast New Jersey 12,339,000
London 8,733,000
Tokyo/Yokohama 6,920,000
Paris 5,441,000
Moscow 5,356,000
Shanghai 5,533,000
Essen 5,300,000
Buenos Aires 5,042,000
Chicago 4,945,000
Calcutta 4,446,000

1954 International radio stations begun: ELWA (Liberia), TWR (Tangiers, later closed), also several national stations.

1960 World's 10 largest cities:
New York/NENJ 14,164,000
Tokyo-Yokohama 10,976,000
London 9,130,000
Shanghai 8,840,000
Paris 7,230,000
Buenos Aires 6,772,000
Los Angeles/Long Beach 6,530,000
Essen 6,400,000
Beijing 6,270,000
Osaka 6,230,000

10. Global international mass evangelism develops

1970 Euro-70 Crusade, largest evangelistic campaign in Europe, using radio/TV; 839,000 attenders.
World's 10 largest cities:
Tokyo/Yokohama 16,468,000
New York/NENJ 16,191,000
Shanghai 11,154,000
Osaka 9,387,000
Mexico City 9,067,000
London 8,594,000
Paris 8,500,000
Buenos Aires 8,417,000
Los Angeles/Long Beach 8,378,000
Beijing 8,087,000

1973 Largest preaching service in history: 1.1 million at one rally in Seoul (Korea) to hear evangelist Billy Graham during five-day Crusade.

1975 Here's Life, America (two-year media campaign in over 200 major cities): 179 million in USA exposed to gospel; 543,000 recorded decisions.
Continente-75, Latin American mass media campaign under Argentinian evangelist Luis Palau, utilizing 56 radio and 100 TV stations in 23 countries; 1978, Palau preaches to over 2 million persons face-to-face; holds that every city should have a citywide crusade three times in a generation (once every 10 years).

1980 Urban dwellers rise from 14.4% of world in 1900 to 37.4% (1970), 41.1% (1980), 43.3% (1985), increasing at a mil-

lion a week.
Christian broadcasting based on cities expands from origin in 1921 to global force heard or seen regularly by 23% of world's population.
World's 10 largest cities:
Tokyo/Yokohama 21,854,000
New York/NENJ 15,601,000
Mexico City 13,888,000
São Paulo 12,497,000
Shanghai 11,739,000
Osaka 9,990,000
Buenos Aires 9,920,000
Los Angeles/Long Beach 9,523,000
Calcutta 9,030,000
Beijing 9,029,000

1984 Series of conferences for 5,000 Spanish-speaking evangelists in 15 cities in Central and South America (July-September).

11. Christians focus on supercities

Supercities (over 4 million population) in Africa escalate from 1 in 1985 (Cairo) to 6 by AD 2000, to 25 by AD 2025 and to 50 by AD 2050.

1985 World's 10 largest cities:
Tokyo/Yokohama 23,322,000
New York/NENJ 15,827,000
Mexico City 14,474,000
Sao Paulo 13,758,000
Shanghai 12,396,000
Buenos Aires 10,522,000
Los Angeles/Long Beach 10,445,000
Osaka 10,351,000
Calcutta 9,946,000
Bombay 9,907,000
Explosive rise of 121 anti-Christian megacities and 20 supercities hostile to Christian mission, especially 3 Muslim supercities over 6 million each in 1985 (Jakarta, Cairo, Karachi), increasing to 4 Islamic supergiants over 10 million each by AD 2000.

1987 After first Industrial Revolution (1775), second in 1901, and third in 1950 (nuclear power, microchips, genes), fourth revolution from 1987 on is noological, knowledge-based, information-based; with people-supervised cybernated machines based on inexhaustible resources in space.
Urbanization is boosted by greatest migration in history, with 400 million Third-World country-dwellers streaming into urban centers.
Mega-industries: 300 multinational corporations using goods and services totaling US $300 billion a year produce destabilizing effect on smaller and poorer nations.

1988 Explosive growth in cities and supercities of charismatic, evangelical and fundamentalist 'video churches.'

1989 Satellites enable living maps (animated color displays, movie x-rays in motion) of any city or area on Earth, at any scale desired, to be inspected for activities as they take place.

1990 Massive urban growth (7,000-year-old trend of urban flow or clustering) slows and reverses in most high-technology developed countries as offices and factories relocate in countryside, taking large populations with them.

1990 World's 10 largest cities:
Tokyo/Yokohama 25,069,000
New York/NENJ 16,056,000
Mexico City 15,130,000
Sao Paulo 15,082,000
Shanghai 13,342,000
Bombay 12,246,000
Los Angeles 11,456,000
Buenos Aires 11,144,000
Calcutta 10,890,000
Beijing 10,820,000

1992 Blackmail and terrorism become rampant in all cities on all continents.

1996 Billy Graham satellite broadcasts reach 70 million.

1999 Pollution: urban pollution becomes deadly, with Mexico City as world's most polluted city, with 6 million cars and 1,100,000 more people each year; also, uncontrolled sewage, industrial wastes, slums, crime, mass cholera, typhoid, hepatitis et al.
Urban supergiants (each with over 10 million population) now number 20, including 3 Islamic supergiants hostile to Christian mission (Cairo, Karachi, Dhaka); resurgence in them of Islamic neo-fundamentalism and sectarian violence.

12. Massive urban growth and problems continue

2000 World's 10 largest cities:
Tokyo/Yokohama 28,025,000
Mexico City 18,131,000
Bombay 18,042,000
Sao Paulo 17,711,000
New York/NENJ 16,626,000
Shanghai 14,173,000
Lagos 13,488,000
Los Angeles 13,129,000
Calcutta 12,900,000
Buenos Aires 12,431,000
Postindustrialism: half of all urban mankind live in cities with postindustrial (transindustrial) knowledge-intensive economies, where producing necessities of life becomes trivially easy technologically, and in which therefore knowledge and information replace capital

Continued overleaf

Table 10-4 concluded

as society's most important resource.
Urbanization: supercities (urban agglomerations with over 4 million inhabitants) total 80 (60 in developing countries): megacities (with over 1 million) 482; urban dwellers number 47.6% of world, increasing by 1.3 million a week; urban slums (totaling 700 million people) expand far faster than cities, producing 'a planet of slums.'

2010 World's 10 largest cities:
Tokyo/Yokohama 28,840,000
Bombay 23,653,000
Lagos 20,956,000
Sao Paulo 19,659,000
Mexico City 18,682,000
New York/NENJ 17,232,000
Karachi 16,669,000
Dhaka 16,663,000
Shanghai 16,578,000
Calcutta 15,640,000

2020 World's 10 largest cities:
Tokyo/Yokohama 28,887,000
Bombay 28,499,000
Lagos 27,884,000
Karachi 22,135,000
Dhaka 21,951,000
Sao Paulo 20,703,000
Mexico City 19,967,000
Shanghai 19,377,000
Calcutta 19,143,000
Delhi 18,435,000

13. A new age of urban supergiants arrives

2025 World's 10 largest cities:
Bombay 30,378,000
Lagos 30,372,000
Tokyo/Yokohama 28,887,000
Karachi 24,847,000
Dhaka 23,820,000
Calcutta 21,171,000
Mexico City 21,078,000
Sao Paulo 20,793,000
Shanghai 20,787,000
Delhi 19,838,000
Total urban supergiants now 31.

2050 World's 5 largest cities:
Lagos 46,5665,000
Karachi 44,284,000
Bombay 41,803,000
Dhaka 35,841,000
Calcutta 35,027,000
All but the first non-Christian. Total urban supergiants now 49.

BIBLIOGRAPHY

'A basic bibliography for metropolitan ministry,' C. E. Stockwell, *Church and society*, 78, 1 (September–October 1987), 59–62.
'A biblical and systematic analysis of church growth with emphasis on urban ministry.' W. W. Elliott. D.Miss. thesis, Fuller Theological Seminary, School of World Mission, Pasadena, CA, 1986.
A biblical approach to urban culture: a general bibliography of materials on Paul's letters to the Corinthians. C. E. Stockwell. Chicago: Urban Church Resource Center, SCUPE, 1982.
'A biblical theology of the city,' W. C. Kaiser, *Urban mission*, 7, 1 (September 1989), 6–18.
'A changing city—an adapting church,' D. Araujo, W. Boggs & C. S. Lee, *New world outlook*, 45, n.s., 5 (February 1985), 12–15. (Concerns Wilshire United Methodist Church in Los Angeles, an urban congregation seeking to address multi-ethnic ministries).
'A church planning strategy for world class cities,' B. A. Sawatsky, *Urban mission*, 3, 2 (November 1985), 7–19.
'A church planting strategy for the urban poor.' T. J. Courtney. D.Min. thesis, Westminster Theological Seminary, Chestnut Hill, PA, 1987.
A clarified vision for urban mission: dispelling the urban stereotypes. H. M. Conn. Grand Rapids, MI: Zondervan Publishing House, 1987.
'A computerized church and community research model.' D. L. Finnell. Ed.D. thesis, Southwestern Baptist Theological Seminary, Fort Worth, TX, 1984.
'A critical analysis of selected urban church and community classifications.' J. H. Furr. Ph.D. dissertation, Southern Baptist Theological Seminary, Louisville, KY, 1987.
'A 'David' church in a Goliath' city,' E. Smith & C. Smith, *The Alliance Witness*, 122, 4 (February 1988), 16–17.
'A family life education for the Church's ministry to urban migrants in Nigeria.' Y. Y. Akpem. D.Miss. thesis, Fuller Theological Seminary, Pasadena, CA, 1982.
'A few tested ways to keep an urban church from growing,' H. M. Conn, *Urban mission*, 7, 1 (September 1989), 3–6.
A general bibliography for urban ministers. C. E. Stockwell. Chicago: Urban Church Resource Center, SCUPE, 1980.
A handbook for urban congregations. J. Eller et al (eds). Boston: Unitarian Universalist Association, Urban Church Coalition, 1984.
'A mission in the city,' H. Krover, *Church herald*, 45, 20 (November 18, 1988), 12–14.
A mission in the city: The Sheffield inner city ecumenical mission. M. Lowndes. New City Special No. 5. Sheffield, England: Urban Theology Unit, 1988. (A pamphlet).
'A multipoint approach to urban community ministry,' E. R. Dill, *Christian ministry*, 22, 4 (September–October 1991), 12–13.
'A postscript to the practice of urban ministry,' P. D. Simmons, *Review and expositor*, 80 (Fall 1983), 537–41.
'A project of the inner–city church growth.' Y. K. Chung. D.Min. thesis, Fuller Theological Seminary, Pasadena, CA, 1983. (text in Korean).
A selected annotated bibliography for urban ministries. C. E. Stockwell. Chicago: Urban Church Resource Center, SCUPE, 1983.
A selected bibliography: the city, Church and ministry. G. W. Bennett & D. T. Britt. *Occasional paper*, no. 5. Atlanta, GA: Metropolitan Missions Department, Home Mission Board of the Southern Baptist Convention, 1982.
A statement on urban theology. S. K. Reus. Victoria, Australia: Department of Education, University of Melbourne, 1980. (A pamphlet).
'A theology as big as the city,' R. J. Bakke, *Urban mission*, 6, 5 (May 1989), 8–19.
'A theology for ministry to the urban poor,' D. Clarebaut, *Covenant quarterly*, 38, 2 (1980), 29–37.
'Address to participants in a meeting of the World Federation of Towns and Cities saying their peace is an objective to pursue and realize concretely'. John Paul II. October 28, 1988.
'Affirming faith in the city,' D. Worlock (archbp), *Christian action journal*, (Summer 1986), 3–10.
African cities and Christian communities. M. Peil et al. Eldoret, Kenya: Gaba Publications, 1982.
'African cities and the Church,' M. Peil, *Pro Mundi Vita, Africa Dossier*, No. 17 (October 1981), 1–19.
'African urban people groups,' H. C. Schreck Jr., *Urban mission*, 4, 4 (March 1987), 42–51.
'Africa's cities beckon new missionaries,' T. Burns & G. Burns, *Impact*, 39 (January 1982), 12–13.
'Ahmadiyya and urbanization: easing the integration of rural women in Abidjan,' M. M. Yacoob, *Asian and African studies*, 20, 1 (1986), 125–140.
Al–Kūfa: naissance de la ville islamique: Islam d'hier et d'aujourd'hui. H. Djait. Paris: G.-P. Maissoneuve et Larose, 1986. No. 29.
'An annotated bibliography on Christian leadership development for urban ministries using andragogical methods.' D. J. Teague. M.A. thesis, Fuller Theological Seminary, School of World Mission, Pasadena, CA, 1984.
'An annotated bibliography on evangelism and church growth in urban areas,' J. F. Eaves, *Southwestern journal of theology*, 24 (Spring 1982), 76–83.
'An ecumenical approach to urban ministry,' D. C. Bloom, *Church and society*, 78, 1 (September 1987), 13–15.
'An evaluation of approaches for urban mission: discovering indicators of effectiveness.' D. W. Cross. D.Min. thesis, Westminster Theological Seminary, Chestnut Hill, PA, 1989.
An introduction to the study of the problem of urban evangelism. B. de Amorim Pimentel. Rio de Janeiro, Brazil: The Author, 1980. (a pamphlet).
'An urban missionary encounters Jane Jacobs,' F. L. Tink, *Urban mission*, 3, 3 (January 1986), 21–29.
An urban world: churches face the future. L. L. Rose & C. K. Hadaway (eds). Nashville, TN: Broadman Press, 1984.
'Annotated bibliography on the urban church,' R. D. Boan et al, *Review and expositor*, 80 (Fall 1983), 583–94.
Announcing the reign of God: evangelization and the subversive memory of Jesus. M. Arias. Philadelphia: Fortress Press, 1984.
'Anti–urbanism in the Bible: a critique,' H. Brodsky, *Urbanism past and present*, 9 (Winter 1984), 36–39.
'Any faith dies in the city,' H. M. Conn, *Missiology: an international review*, 13, 4 (October 1985), 6–19.
''Any faith dies in the city:' the secularization myth,' H. M. Conn, *Urban mission*, 3, 5 (May 1986), 6–19.
'Audio–visual resources for urban ministry,' C. O'Neill, *Cities*, 5, 1 (Spring 1985), 6–8.
Backs against the wall: urban–oriented colleges and universities and the urban poor and disadvantaged. P. S. J. Cafferty. New York: Ford Foundation, 1983.
'Barriers and bridges to evangelization in urban neighborhoods,' C. E. Stockwell, in *Signs of the kingdom in the secular city*, p.95–104. D. Frenchak et al (eds). Chicago: Covenant Press, 1984.
Bauen mit Geschichte. R. Bürgel. Gütersloh, West Germany: Gütersloher Verlagshaus, G. Mohn, 1980.
'Bible and mission in an inner–city congregation,' B. Jurgensen, in *Bible and mission: biblical foundations and working models for congregational ministry*, p.111–119. W. C. Stumme (ed). Minneapolis: Augsburg, 1986.
Biblical and theological resources for urban ministry. C. E. Stockwell. Chicago: Urban Church Resource Center, SCUPE, 1982.
'Biblical theology of the city.' W. C. Kaiser. Paper no. 1, Moody Bible Institute, Trinity Evangelical Divinity School, Wheaton College and Graduate School. The Trinary Study Conference on the Evangelization of the World, Wheaton, IL, March 14–17, 1986.
'Big work in the city,' C. Van Eyl, *Church herald*, 45, 20 (November 18, 1988), 8–11.
'Billy Sunday: evangelist to urban America,' L. W. Dorsett, *Urban mission*, 8, 1 (September 1990), 6–13.
Black Pentecostalism: Southern religion in an urban world. A. E. Paris. Amherst, MA: University of Massachusetts Press, 1982.
Blue collar ministry: problems and opportunities for mainline 'middle' congregations. S. W. Martin. Washington, D.C.: Alban Institute, 1989. (A pamphlet).
'Case study: African cities—choosing new urban fields,' T. Monsma, *Urban mission*, 3, 5 (May 1986), 49–50.
'Case study: disciples downtown,' D. Taliaferro, *Urban mission*, 3, 4 (March 1986), 34–35.
'Case study: effective evangelization in modern cities,' D. A. McGavran & K. McKean, *Urban mission*, 2, 4 (March 1985), 40–43.
'Case study: Kinshasa, Zaire—an African strategy for urban church growth,' M. F. Polding, *Urban mission*, 3, 4 (March 1986), 36–38.
'Case study: Taiwan's urban population—time for a spiritual harvest,' S. E. Mumper, *Urban mission*, 4, 1 (September 1986), 35–38.
'Case study: urban missions in Tanzania, East Africa,' S. Mwantila, *Urban mission*, 2, 4 (March 1985), 44–47.
Centesimus annus (On the hundredth anniversary of Rerum novarum). Pope John Paul II. Città del Vaticano: The Vatican, 1991.
'Christ and the city,' H. M. Conn, *Urban mission*, 1 (November 1983), 25–30.
'Christian broadcasting and the urban crisis,' A. T. Evans, *Religious broadcasting*, 19, 2 (February 1987), 80+.
'Christian perspectives on the city,' R. Trabold, *The city of God*, 2 (Winter 1980), 3–18.
'Christian witness in the city: an annotated bibliography,' C. E. Stockwell, *TSF bulletin*, (7 (November 1983), 17–19; 7 (January 1984), 20–22).
'Christianity and metrocenter do not mix ...?,' J. Hammersley, *Crucible*, 27, 2 (April–June 1988), 57–61.
Christianity in the inner city: some sociological issues. G. Smith. London: MARC Europe, 1988.
'Church and city: Black Christianity's ministry,' R. M. Franklin, *The Christian ministry*, 20, 2 (March–April 1989), 17–19.
'Church growth in Nairobi, Kenya,' L. L. Niemeyer, *Urban mission*, 8, 1 (September 1990), 45–54.
'Church life in the inner city,' P. Dearnley, *Shaft*, 41 (1984), 13–16.
'Church planting among the urban poor,' G. Houghton & E. Sargunam, *Africa pulse*, 15 (May 1982), 1–6.
'Church seeks to heal pain of inner city,' J. Sly, *National Catholic register*, 59 (October 2, 1983), 1+.
'Churches for the cities,' *Impact*, 43, 1 (February 1986), 6–11. (A publication of the Conservative Baptist Foreign Missions Society).
Cities and caliphs: on the genesis of Arab Muslim urbanism. N. Al Sayyad. New York: Greenwood Press, 1991. 207p.
Cities and churches: an international bibliography. L. H. Hartley. *ATLA bibliography series*, no. 31. Metuchen, NJ: Scarecrow Press, 1992. 3 vols.
Cities and development in the Third World. R. B. Potter & A. T. Salau (eds). London: Mansell, 1991. 200p.
Cities and New Testament times. C. Ludwig. Denver: Accent Books, 1976.
Cities: mission's new frontier. R. S. Greenway & T. M. Monsma. Grand Rapids, MI: Baker, 1989.
Cities of change: urban growth and God's people in ten Latin American cities. J. Maust. Coral Gables, FL: Latin American Mission, 1984.
Cities of the world. M. M. Hubbard & B. Baer (eds). 4th ed. Detroit, Mich.: Gale Research, 1993. 4 vols;. ('A compilation of current information on cultural, geographical, and political conditions in the countries and cities of six continents, based on the Department of State's 'Post Reports'.').
City of God, city of Satan: a biblical theology of the urban church. R. C. Linthicum. Grand Rapids, MI: Zondervan, 1991.
City of God? pastoral care in the inner city. N. Bradbury. London: SPCK, 1989.
'City, seminaries and Christian colleges,' R. S. Greenway, *Urban Mission*, 3, 1 (September 1985), 3–6.
Civitas: religious interpretations of the city. P. S. Hawkins (ed). Atlanta: Scholar's Press, 1986.
Class and culture in urban India: fundamentalism in a Christian community. L. Caplan. Oxford, UK: Clarendon Press, 1987.
'Community context and metropolitan church growth,' A. M. Guest, *Urban affairs quarterly*, 24 (March 1989), 435–459.
'Community forms and urban church profiles,' L. McSwain, *Review and expositor*, 80 (Fall 1983), 501–514.
Companion to the poor. V. Grigg. Sutherland, Australia: Albatross Books, 1984.
'Comparative study of religiosity among the rural and the urban poor,' S. P. Gupta, *The journal of sociological studies*, 6 (January 1987), 173–178.
'Comportamenti religiosi nell'area urbana,' C. Martino, in *Religione e morale popolare cristiana ricera interdisciplinare*, p.277–290. T. Tentori et al. Bologna, Italy: Edisioni Dehoniane, 1980.
'Crisis ministry in inner–city churches,' D. Watkins, *Southwestern journal of theology*, 24 (Spring 1982), 40–54. (theme of entire issue is urban ministry).
Crisis of the church in the inner city: pastoral options for inner city parishes. P. J. Murnion & A. Wenzel. New York: Pastoral Life Center, 1989.
'Crusade preparation for large cities in Africa,' D. Richardson, in *The work of an evangelist: International Conference for Itinerant Evangelists, Amsterdam, The Netherlands*, p.335–41. J. D. Douglas (ed). Minneapolis, MN: World-Wide Publications, 1984.
'Crusade preparation for large cities in Asia,' A. Yeo, *The work of an evangelist*, p.343–350. J. D. Douglas (ed). Minneapolis: World-Wide Publications, 1984.
'Crusade preparation for large cities in Europe,' A. Schulte, in *The work of an evangelist.* J. D. Douglaas (ed). Minneapolis: World-Wide Publications, 1984.
'Crusade preparation for large cities in North America,' S. W. Huston, in *The work of an evangelist: International Conference for Itinerant Evangelists, Amsterdam, The Netherlands*, p.319–26. J. D. Douglas (ed). Minneapolis, MN: World-Wide Publications, 1984.

Death and new life in urban churches: case study of selected CIT churches, 1977-1985. P.A. Terpenning. Manuscript of a pamphlet at Chicago Theological Seminary, 1985.
'De–evangelism: exploring the mystery of the deserted urban churches,' D. Hall, *Urban mission*, 6, 1 (September 1988), 6–12.
'Developing laity as ministers in an urban church.' A. P. Rowe. D.Min. thesis, Eastern Baptist Theological Seminary, Wynnewood, PA, 1982.
'Developing mission strategies for larger metropolitan areas,' G. W. Bullard, *Church administration*, 25 (February 1983), 33–35.
'Die große Stadt, der kleine Glaube: zehn Anmerkungen nach dem Buch Jona,' C. Jahn, *Zeitschrift für mission*, 11, 4 (1985), 194–197.
'Discipling in three Sri Lankan cities,' R. De Silva, *Urban mission*, 2, 4 (March 1985), 33–40.
'Discipling inner city peoples: models for church growth among ethnic groups in Los Angeles.' R. M. Elmore. Th.M. thesis, Fuller Theological Seminary, Pasadena, CA, 1981.
Discovering faith in the city. London: Church House Publishing, 1988.
'Distinctives of African urban ministry,' J. J. Shane, *Urban ministry*, 6, 5 (May 1989), 31–40.
'Doing effective ministry in the city,' R. C. Linthicum, *Together*, (April–June 1988).
'Doing your own urban church research,' L. L. Falk, in *Urban church education*, p.114–126. D. B. Rogers (ed). Birmingham, AL: Religious Education Press, 1989.
'Don't be an urban missionary unless . . .,' R. S. Greenway, *Evangelical missions quarterly*, 19 (April 1983), 86–94.
'Ecumenism in metropolis,' C. Green, *JSAC Grapevine*, 18, 1 (June 1986), 1–18.
'Editorial: mission to an urban world,' R. S. Greenway, *Urban mission*, 1 (September 1983), 1–2.
'Effective church evangelism in the city,' J. F. Eaves, *Southwestern journal of theology*, 24 (Spring 1982), 66–76.
Effective urban church ministry. G. W. Bennett. Nashville, TN: Broadman Press, 1983.
'Effective urban preaching,' J. Gregory, *Urban review*, 1, 2 (July 1985), 16–24.
'Elites, evangelicals, and the London poor,' D. M. Fahey, *Journal of urban history*, 17, 3 (May 1991), 293–295.
'Emerging church planting strategies for world class cities,' J. E. Westgate, *Urban mission*, 4, 2 (November 1986), 6–13.
Empowering the poor: community organizing among the city's ragtag and bobtail. R. C. Linthicum. Monrovia, California: MARC, 1991.
'Equipping congregations for urban ministry.' C. Michael. D.Min. thesis, Bethany Theological Seminary, Oak Brook, Illinois, 1984.
'Essentials for urban ministry,' A. P. Johnston, *Alliance witness*, 120, 5 (February 27, 1985), 8–10.
EthniCity:geographic perspectives on ethnic change in modern cities. C. C. Roseman & H. D. Laux (eds). Lanham, Maryland: Rowman & Littlefield, 1996. 344p.
'Evangelical spirituality in the inner city,' N. Black, in *Can spirituality be taught?* J. Robson & D. Lonsdale (eds). England: Association of Centers of Adult Theological Association, 1987.
Evangelio y comunidad cristiana. C. M. Martini. Bogotá: Ediciones Paulinas, 1985.
''Evangelism Explosion': a tool God is using in many cities,' E. P. Gant, *Urban mission*, 3, 2 (November 1985), 32–36.
'Evangelism in the city,' R. Mitchell, *Urban mission*, 1 (January 1984), 30–35.
'Evangelistic crusades in inner cities, I,' C. W. Loritts Jr., in *The work of an evangelist: International Conference for Itinerant Evangelists, Amsterdam, The Netherlands*, p.449–50. J. D. Douglas (ed). Minneapolis, MN: World-Wide Publications, 1984.
'Evangelistic crusades in inner cities, II,' G. Carney, in *The work of an evangelist: International Conference for Itinerant Evangelists, Amsterdam, The Netherlands*, p.451–54. J. D. Douglas (ed). Minneapolis, MN: World-Wide Publications, 1984.
'Evangelizing high–rise dwellers,' W. Leslie, *Urban review*, 2, 1 (April 1986), 3–12.
Evangelizing neo–pagan North America. A. C. Krass. Scottdale, PA: Herald Press, 1982. ('Has appendix with 11 church statements or declarations on evangelism.').
'Evangelizing the central city: problems and possibilities,' V. Miller, in *Missions, evangelism, and church growth*, p.123–39. C. N. Kraus (ed). Scottdale, PA: Herald Press, 1980.
'Evangelizing the homeless,' M. Hollowell, *Urban mission*, 7, 3 (January 1990), 36–42.
'Faith in the city: a Jewish response,' D. Cohn-Sherbok, in *Theology in the city: a theological response to faith in the city.* A. Harvey (ed). London: SPCK, 1989.
'Faithful to the cities of the world,' R. J. Bakke, in *Faithful witness: the Urbana 84 compendium*, p.88–98. J. McLeish (ed). Downers Grove, Illinois: InterVarsity Press, 1985.
'Feeding the urban poor,' W. D. Lockard, *Urban review*, 2, 1 (April 1986), 40+.
'Films about the city: a selected bibliography of films for sensitizing Christians to urban life and its problems,' R. W. Carlson, *Urban mission*, 4, 1 (September 1986), 24–34.
'Formación del pueblo de Dios in las grandes urbes,' S. Escobar, *Boletín teológico*, (July/September 1982), 37–83.
'Formulating a mission statement in an inner city congregation.' L. J. Grubbs. D.Min. thesis, Drew University, Madison, NJ, 1986.
'Free cities, free churches, and urbanized societies,' P. Peachey, *Brethren life and thought*, 27 (Autumn 1982), 199–205.
'From city to community: Christian community in the modern metropolis,' C. Lewis, *Epiphany*, 1 (Summer 1981), 38–47.
'From jungle to city: enduring yet endangered, tribal people look for hope in the urban world,' L. Willems, *World Christian magazine*, 3, 1 (January–February 1984), 16–19.
'From Lausanne 1974 to Manila 1989: the pilgrimage of urban mission,' S. Escobar, *Urban mission*, 7, 4 (March 1990), 21–29.
'Gentrification: challenge for urban churches,' D. Mader, *Church herald*, 39 (May 1982), 9–11.
'Glimpses of the kingdom in the urban church,' C. Michael, in *Urban church education*, p.41–49. D. B. Rogers (ed). Birmingham, AL: Religious Education Press, 1989.
'God in Metropolis: ministering to the urban soul,' M. Olson (ed), *The other side*, 24, 4 (May 1988), 20–47.
'God's agenda for the city: some biblical perspectives,' J. W. Olley, *Urban mission*, 8, 1 (September 1990), 14–23.
'God's city,' B. Dew, *Crucible*, 22 (January–March 1983), 27–32.
God's inner city address: crossing the boundaries. M. Van Houten. Grand Rapids, MI: Ministry Resources Library, Zondervan, 1988.
'God's sacred place: the city,' H. J. Recinos, *Circuit rider*, 14, 10 (December 1990), 28–30.
Good news to the poor: the church and city problems. Albingdon, Oxon, England: [Roman Catholic] Commission for Social Welfare, 1980.
Gospel in industrial society. M. Kane. London: SCM Press, 1980.
Growing churches Singapore style: ministry in an urban context. K. Hinton. Singapore: Overseas Missionary Fellowship, 1985. 234p.
Gutter feelings: Christian youth work in the inner city. P. Wilson. Basingstoke, U.K.: Marshalls, 1985.
'Habitat and values in Islam: a conceptual formulation of an Islamic city,' G. Haider, in *The touch of Midas: science, values, and environment in Islam and West*, p.170–208. Z. Sardar (ed). Manchester, England: Manchester University Press, 1984.
'Habitat for Humanity: a new frontier in Christian mission,' M. Fuller, *Cities*, 1 (July 1981), 15–17.
Habits of the heart: individualism and commitment in American life. R. N. Bellah et al. Berkeley, CA: University of California Press, 1985. (An influential study of the loss of the 'second language' of piety in American culture).
Hacia la ciudad unida: problema de las ciudades modernas desde la perspectiva cristiana (Towards a united city: problems of the modern city from a Christian perspective). C. M. Martini. Madrid: n.p., 1985.
Healing for the city: counseling for the urban setting. C. W. Ellison & E. S. Maynard. Grand Rapids, MI: Zondervan, 1991.
'Hispanic urban ministry comes of age,' E. E. Vásquez, *The Christian ministry*, 20, 2 (March–April 1989), 20–21.
'History of evangelizing world class cities.' R. S. Greenway. Paper no. 4, Moody Bible Institute, Trinity Evangelical Divinity School, Wheaton College and Graduate School; The Trinary Study Conference on the Evangelization of the World, Wheaton, IL, March 14, 1986.
'Homogeneous networks—a Babel that promotes good urban strategy,' T. Monsma, *Urban mission*, 5, 3 (January 1988), 11–17.
Hope in the city: a response to the Archbishop's Commission Report on Urban Priority Areas. G. Forster (ed.). Bramcote, England: Grove Books, Grove Booklet on Ethics No. 61, 1986.
'Hope of Bangkok: a visionary model of church growth and church planting,' K. Chareonwongsak, *Urban mission*, 7, 3 (January 1990), 25–35.
How Christianity grows in the city. A. R. Jennings. Fort Worth: Star Bible Publications, 1985.
'How do you pray for a city?,' D. Brynt, *Latin American evangelist*, 69, 1 (January–March 1989).
'How effective are city–wide crusades?,' G. Firebaugh, *Christianity today*, 25 (March 27, 1981), 24–29.
'How shall we work the cities—from within?,' G. Oosterwal, *Ministry*, 53 (June 1980), 18–22+. (Seventh-day Adventist).
'How to grow churches in Manila,' R. Lenz, *Urban mission*, 7, 1 (September 1989), 42–47.
'How to reach urban ethnics,' T. Yamamori, *Urban mission*, 1, 4 (March 1984), 29–35.
'How to study an urban church,' G. W. Bennett, *Urban review*, 1, 1 (April 1985).
'Human services in the church's urban evangelization.' P. J. Cascia. D.Min. thesis, Hartford Seminary, Hartford, CT, 1989.
'Inner city evangelism,' E. V. Hill, *Religious broadcasting*, 13 (October 1981), 52–53.
'Inner–city street ministry: a christology,' M. Van Houten, *Urban mission*, 7, 1 (September 1989), 35–43.
'Interview: urban Black churches and foreign missions,' D. Canty, *Urban mission*, 1 (January 1984), 36–39.
Into all the city: the urban mission strategy of World Vision International. R. C. Linthicum. Pasadena: Technical Services, World Vision International, 1987.
Iranian cities: formation and development. M. Kheirabadi. Austin: University of Texas Press, 1991. 146p.
'Is there faith in the city?,' R. McCloughry, *Grass roots*, 12, 2 (1986), 16–17.
'Islam and Adat among South Tapanuli migrants in three Indonesian cities,' B. H. Harahap, in *Indonesian religion in transition.* R. S. Kipp & S. Rodgers (eds). Tucson, AZ: University of Arizona Press, 1987.
'Jerusalem—city of religions: the universality of Jerusalem,' I. Lippel, *Christian Jewish relations*, 21, 2 (Summer 1988), 6–16.
Jesus and his towns. S. E. Johnson. Wilmington, Delaware: Michael Glazier, 1989.
Jesus and the forgotten city: new light on Sepphoris and the urban world of Jesus. R. A. Batey. Grand Rapids, MI: Baker, 1991.
'Jesus Christ, the life of the city?,' P. Dearnley & P. Broadbent, *Churchman: journal of Anglican theology*, 97, 1 (1983), 41–54.
Justice and urban ministry: a bibliography of philosophical and theological resources. H. M. Conn & C. Stockwell. Chicago: Urban Church Resource Center, Seminary Consortium for Urban Pastoral Education, 1984.
'Kamuning, Philippines—an urban church–planting model,' F. W. Allen, *Urban mission*, 6, 2 (November 1988), 56–60.
'Kirche in dieser Stadt, zu einer Gesamtkonzeption kirchlicher Arbeit in der Großstadt,' H. W. Dannowski, *Theologica practica*, 19 (1984), 186–92.
'La misión del pueblo de Dios en la ciudad,' O. E. Costas, *Boletín Teológico*, 7 (1982), 85–96.
'La patoral de las grandes cuidades: Bogotá,' A. C. Hualde, *Pro Mundi Vita, Dossier Africain*, 38 (1985), 2–34.
Lagos: the city is the people. M. Peil. Boston, MA: G. K. Hall, 1991. 224p.
Latin American urbanization. D. Butterworth & J. K. Chance. Cambridge: University of Cambridge Press, 1981.
'Learning from urban church research,' C. K. Hadaway, *Review and expositor*, 80 (Fall 1983), 543–52.
'Lucan perspectives and the city,' H. M. Conn, *Missiology: an international review*, 13, 4 (October 1985), 409–428.
'Making the dream come true: discipleship for all God's people in the urban church,' C. D. Newbern, in *Urban church education*, p.102–113. D. B. Rogers (ed). Birmingham, AL: Religious Education Press, 1989.
'Mass evangelism—reaching your city in the Eighties,' J. McWilliam, *Urban mission*, 3, 1 (September 1985), 7–14.
'Meeting God in the city,' T. Boogart, *Church herald*, 45, 20 (November 18, 1988), 6–7.
Mega focus cities: a plan of megalopolitan strategy development. G. W. Bullard. Atlanta, GA: Metropolitan Missions Department, Home Mission Board of the Southern Baptist Convention, 1983?
Mega–city growth and the future. New York: United Nations University Press, 1992, 428p.
Met het oog op de stad: enkele overwengingen met betrekking tot 'urban mission' in Nederland. K. A. Schippers. Kampen, Nedterlands: J.H. Kok, 1984. (Covers urban missions in the Netherlands).
'Ministering in the urban world,' H. Brown, *Mission focus*, 10, 2 (1982), 17–18.
'Ministries in an urban settlement,' H. Janssen, *Point series*, , 7 (1985), 184–190.
Ministry and mission in the city. J. Stein. Edinburgh: Handsel, 1987.
Ministry in an urban world: responding to the city. T. Costello (ed). Canberra: Acorn Press, 1991.
'Ministry in Bombay,' D. Franklin, *New World outlook*, 46 n.s., 9 (July–August 1986), 31–34.
'Ministry in the inner city,' A. Smith, *New Blackfriars*, 68, 810 (November 1987), 516–528.
'Ministry in the urban context,' B. Schwarz, *Point: Forum for Melanesian Affairs*, , Series No. 7 (1985), 166–183.
'Ministry on the urban frontier,' P. A. Amerson, in *Signs of the kingdom in the secular city*, p.83–94. D. Frenchak et al (eds). Chicago: Covenant Press, 1984.
'Mission among metropolitan Muslims,' G. Jennings, *Urban Mission*, 5, 2 (November 1987), 12–18.
'Mission and evangelism in urban rural mission,' E. Castro, *International review of mission*, 74, 303 (July 1987), 324–330.
'Mission in an urban world,' E. Rubingh, *Reformed Ecumenical Synod Mission bulletin*, 7, 1 (1987), 1–10.
'Mission in the cities of Latin America,' J. W. Hall Jr., *Urban mission*, 7, 1 (September 1989), 25–34.
Mission in urban Hong Kong. D. Ngai & K. Lo (eds). Kowloon, Hong Kong: Chinese Coordinating Center of World Evangelism, 1988. (Text in Chinese).
'Mission to the urban poor,' T. Courtney, *Urban mission*, 1 (November 1983), 17–24.
Mobilizing social movement organizations: the formation, institutionalization, and effectiveness of ecumenical urban ministries. J. D. Davidson. Storrs, Connecticut: Society for the Scientific Study of Religion, 1985.
'Models for urban witness,' P. Shen, *The Mennonite*, 97 (April 13, 1982), 170–72. (theme of entire issue is 'Church in the city').
'Models for urban youth ministry: goals, styles, and contexts,' W. R. Myers, in *Urban church education*, p.127–134. D. B. Rogers (ed). Birmingham, AL: Religious Education Press, 1989.
'Muslim cities: recent history and possible future,' A. Malik, in *An early crescent.* Z. Sarder (ed). London: Mansell, 1989.
'Mysterious fall kills a minister,' M. Howe, *New York Times*, 140 (December 20, 1990), A20. (Concerns the death of Noah Lewis).
'Networking: hope for the church in the city,' R. C. Linthicum, *Urban mission*, 4, 3 (January 1987), 32–50.
New church in the city: the work of the Chicago Fellowship of Friends. M. M. Pedigo. Richmond, IN: Friends United Press, 1988.
'New evidence on religious pluralism, urbanism and religious participation,' K. D. Breault, *American sociological review*, 54, 6 (December 1989), 1048–1053.
'New patterns of urban ministry,' K. Byrne, *Clergy review*, 69 (January 1984), 31–33.
'New urban faces of the church,' D. McGavran, *Urban mission*, 1 (September 1983), 2–11.
New York, New York: how the apartment house transformed the life of the city. E. Hawes. Holt.
No stranger in the city: God's concern for urban people. I. Coffey et al. Leicester, U.K.: InterVarsity, 1989.
'Non–Christian religion and culture in the cities of the world,' M. T. Starkes, *An urban world*, p.95–116. L. L. Rose & C. K. Hadaway (eds). Nashville: Broadman Press, 1984.
'O problema da pastoral urbana,' A. Cheuiche, *Teocomunicação* (Porto Alegre), 13, 1 (1983), 5–10.
'On asking a fish to jump into a barrel: reflections on urban evangelization,' P. A. Amerson, *Covenant quarterly*, 40 (May 1982), 19–30.
'One in body: how an urban church learned to thrive on diversity,' D. L. Buttry, *Christian ministry*, 17, 2 (March 1986), 12–15.
'One ministry: a case study in urban evangelism,' B. Spring, *Christianity today*, 25 (February 6, 1981), 75.

'One strategy for inner city mission and ministry.' P. A. Meyers. D.Min. thesis, United Theological Seminary, Dayton, OH, 1984.

'Out of the city/into the city: two competing models for the urban church,' R. L. Stackpole & R. Robotham, in *Urban church education*, p.162–181. D. B. Rogers (ed). Birmingham, AL: Religious Education Press, 1989.

Passion for the inner city: a personal view. A. Smith. London: Sheed and Ward, 1983.

'Pastoral care for supercities,' P. Delooz, *Pro Mundi Vita bulletin*, Bulletin 99 (1984), 29–52.

'Personal evangelism in the inner city,' R. M. Sowel, *Urban mission*, 5, 2 (November 1987), 19–24.

'Plan for developing the ministry of city missionary by formulating a program of urban evangelism.' J. W. Bruce. D.Min. thesis, Southwestern Baptist Theological Seminary, Fort Worth, TX, 1981.

'Planning a holistic strategy for urban witness,' A. C. Scanlon, *An urban world*, p.51–74. L. L. Rose & C. K. Hadaway (eds). Nashville: Broadman Press, 1984.

'Planning for the urban poor: basic needs and priorities,' E. F. N. Ribeiro, *Social action* (India), 32 (April 1982), 127–50.

Planting the house church. C. A. Chilton. Baltimore, MD: Prince George's Baptist Association, 1980.

'Preparing for holistic church planting among Mexico's urban poor.' L. D. Long. M.A. thesis, Fuller Theological Seminary, Pasadena, CA, 1982.

'Professing Christ in the city,' G. D. McKinney, in *Confessing Christ as Lord*, Urbana '81, p.217–27. J. Alexander (ed). Downers Grove, Illinois: InterVarsity Press, 1982.

'Public transportation and urban witness,' J. Lingenfelter, *Urban mission*, 5, 4 (March 1988), 5–10.

'Quito, Ecuador, transferable principles of urban outreach,' J. P. Klassen, *Urban mission*, 3, 1 (September 1985), 32–40.

'Reaching apartment dwellers,' R. S. Greenway, *Urban mission*, 1 (March 1984), 2–3.

'Reaching Canada's cities for Christ,' G. Smith, *Urban mission*, 8, 1 (September 1990), 27–36.

'Reaching cities with home cells,' P. Y. Cho, *Urban mission*, 1 (January 1984), 4–14.

'Reaching Muslims in French cities,' J. F. Haines, *Urban mission*, 2 (September 1984), 20–32.

'Reaching our cities for Christ,' C. W. Moorhous, *Christian standard*, 123, 31 (July 31, 1988), 700–701.

'Reaching the unreached in the cities,' R. S. Greenway, *Urban mission*, 2, 5 (May 1985), 3–5.

Reconciling heaven and earth: the transcendental enthusiasm and growth of an urban Protestant community, Bogotá, Colombia. K. W. Westmeier. New York: Verlag Peter Lang, 1986.

Redeeming the city: theology, politics, and urban policy. R. D. Pasquariello, D. W. Shriver Jr. & A. Geyer. New York: Pilgrim Press, 1982.

'Redeveloping the urban congregation,' R. P. Poethig (ed), *Justice ministries: resources for urban mission*, nos. 15-16 (Winter/Spring 1982), 1–67.

'Religion in the secular city: a symposium,' H. G. Cox, *Christianity and crisis*, 44 (February 20, 1984), 35–45.

'Religion in the city of man,' C. J. Bourg, *Sociological analysis*, 45 (Summer 1984), 99–106.

Religion in the megacity: Catholic and Protestant portraits from Latin America. P. Berryman. Maryknoll, New York: Orbis Books, 1996. 216p.

Religion in the secular city: towards a post–modern theology. H. G. Cox. New York: Simon and Schuster, 1984.

Religious groups in urban America: a bibliography. D. E. Casper. Monticello, Illinois: Vance bibliographies, 1983.

'Religious, social, and physical qualities of Islamic urbanization,' F. de Montêquin, *Hamdard Islamicus*, 6 (Spring 1983), 63–86.

'Research as a tool for urban evangelism in developing countries.' H. G. Shipp. D.Miss thesis, Fuller Theological Seminary, School of World Mission, Pasadena, CA, 1986.

'Resources for urban ministry,' C. E. Stockwell, *The other side*, 24, 4 (May 1988), 36–47.

Resources for urban ministry: a bibliographic essay. C. E. Stockwell. Atlanta: Metropolitan Missions Department, Home Missions Board, Southern Baptist Convention, 1984. Occasional Paper No. 9.

'Resources for urban ministry—a bibliographic essay,' C. E. Stockwell, *Covenant quarterly*, 40 (May 1982), 3–18.

'Revisioning seminary as ministry–centered,' G. Hope, *The Christian century*, 106, 4 (February 1–8, 1989), 107–111.

'Revitalizing an urban church: the role of pastor and deacons,' J. D. Aderhold, *Urban review* ([Southern Baptist]), 1, 2 (July 1985), 5–15.

San'a': an Arabian Islamic city. R. B. Serjeant & R. Lewcock. London: World of Islam Festival Trust, 1983.

'Savior in the city,' G. Gaither, *Christian herald*, 109, 10 (November 1986), 20–25.

'Scaffolding: urban mission in Australia,' V. Bowie, *Urban mission*, 2, 5 (May 1985), 46–51.

'Secularization and sociology: the history of an idea,' D. Lyon, *Fides et historia*, 13 (Spring 1981), 38–52.

Seeing cities with the eyes of God. F. McClung. Tarrytown, NY: Chosen Books, 1991.

'Seeking justice and shalom in the city,' C. M. Barbour, *International review of mission*, 73 (July 1984), 303–309.

'Serving Christ in the city,' W. O'Brien, *The other side*, 21, 5 (July 1985), 8–9.

'Shifting urban mission into the future tense,' T. W. Sine Jr., in *Urban ministry*. R. C. Linthicum (ed). Pasadena: Technical Services, World Vision International, 1986. Vol. 2.

Signs of the kingdom in the secular city. D. Frenchak, C. Stockwell & H. Ujvarosy (eds). Chicago: Covenant Press, 1984.

'Singapore: urbanism, culture, and the church,' J. Clammer, *Urban mission*, 7, 4 (March 1990), 6–20.

'Stages in the life of our urban congregations,' R. T. Roberts, *Alban Institute Action Information*, 14, 5 (September 1988), 12–14.

Starting all over again: hints of Jesus in the city. J. J. Vincent. *Risk book series*, no. 13. Geneva: World Council of Churches, 1981.

'Strategic thinking for urban ministry,' J. P. Wogaman, *Cities*, 2 (March–April 1982), 8–11.

'Strategies for cities,' J. R. W. Stott, *Beacon*, 60, 13 (June 22, 1987), 8–10.

Strategies for evangelization in cities. E. Rubingh. Grand Rapids, MI: Centennial Missions Scholarship Committee, Christian Reformed Church, 1986.

'Strategy and urban ministry,' P. A. Amerson, *Cities*, 3 (Summer 1983), 25–31.

'Strategy for urban ministry,' R. J. Bakke, *TSF bulletin*, 8, 4 (March–April 1985), 20–21.

'Stress and urban ministry,' C. W. Ellison, *Urban mission*, 1 (November 1983), 5–16.

'Students in urban ministry,' S. Pohorski, *World Christian*, 9, 5 (May 1990), 32+.

'Studies in the Church and the city,' J. A. Brooks (ed), *Southwestern journal of theology*, 24 (Spring 1982), 5–83.

'Summer urban church–planting internships for seminary students: Nigeria,' P. J. Fritz, *Urban mission*, 5, 5 (May 1988), 38–42.

Taking on faith in the city. D. Newman et al. *Grove Pastoral Series No. 26.* Bramcote, England: Grove Books, 1986.

Taking our cities for God: how to break spiritual strongholds. J. Dawson. Lake Mary, FL: Creation House, 1989.

'Taking the Gospel to urban Africa,' A. Dobra, *Impact*, 43, 1 (February 1986), 12–14.

'Teams multiply churches in Malaysia/Singapore,' L. Childs, *Urban mission*, 2, 5 (May 1985), 33–39.

Ten inner city churches. M. Eastman (ed). Eastbourne, England: MARC, 1988.

'Tent evangelism in Argentine cities,' G. Krätzig, *Urban mission*, 3, 5 (May 1986), 51–56.

'The Bible in the city,' J. Goldingay, *Theology*, 92, 745 (January 1989), 5–15.

'The Bible, the city, and urban reform,' R. D. Pasquariello, *Cities*, 5, 1 (Spring 1985), 10–14.

'The birth of a downtown Tokyo church,' J. Davidson, *Urban mission*, 8, 1 (September 1990), 37–44.

'The Bresee Institute for Urban Training: a study in the analysis of urban training.' D. McConnell. M.A. thesis, Fuller Theological Seminary, School of World Mission, Pasadena, CA, 1985.

'The call to freedom: salvation in the city,' M. G. Etling, *Priest*, 40 (December 1984), 36–41.

'The challenge of the ethnic mosaic,' H. R. Baird, *Christian standard*, 122, 4 (January 25, 1987), 71–72.

'The challenge of world urbanization to mission thinking and strategy: perspective on demographic realities,' R. J. Bakke, *Urban mission*, 4, 1 (September 1986), 6–17. (Reprinted as Occasional Paper No. 12. Atlanta: Metropolitan Missions Department, Home Mission Board, Southern Baptist Convention, 1987.)

The church in the city. G. E. Nelson. Springfield, MO: Division of Foreign Missions, Assemblies of God, 1987.

'The church and its community,' D. Hall, *Urban mission*, 4, 2 (November 1986), 36–44.

'The church and questions of ministry in the urban environment,' J. M. Shopshire, *AME Zion quarterly review*, 96, 1 (April, 1984), 2–12.

'The church and the city in transition,' F. Milligan (guest ed), *The Christian ministry*, 20, 2 (March–April 1989), 3–34. (Special thematic issue, 'Urban ministry today').

'The church and the city: signs of despair, signs of hope,' *JSAC grapevine*, 13 (July 1981), 1–4.

'The church and urban priorities,' K. Slack, *Christian Century*, 103, 9 (March 12, 1986), 261–262.

The church and urban problems. E. Gondolf. Elsah, Illinois: Principia College, 1981.

The church in the African city. A. Shorter. London: Geoffrey Chapman, 1991.

The church in the city: Samuel C. Kinchloe and the sociology of the city church. S. C. Kinchloe. Chicago: Explorations Press, 1989. (Edited and introduced by Yoshio Fukuyama).

'The Church in the urban setting,' C. K. Hadaway, in *The urban challenge*, p.80–99. L. Rose & C. K. Hadaway (eds). Nashville, TN: Broadman, 1982.

'The church in the immigrant city,' J. J. Bukowczyk, *Journal of urban history*, 13, 2 (February 1987), 207–217.

'The church in urban America: excerpts from a paper delivered at the Urban Forum, 1985,' S. J. Winger, *Christian standard*, 121, 2 (January 12, 1986), 33–34.

The church in urban society: a bibliography for the Congress on Urban Ministry. C. E. Stockwell. Chicago: Urban Church Resource Center, SCUPE, 1984.

'The church situation in European cities,' C. H. Koetsier, *Urban mission*, 3, 3 (January 1986), 45–47.

'The church, the city, and the compassionate Christ,' C. Rosado, *Apuntes: reflexiones teologicas desde el margen Hispano*, 9 (Summer 1989), 27–35.

'The church, the city, and the poor: a challenge,' *(Conference, St. John's Church, Bronx, NY, Lutheran Church Leadership)*, *Lutheran Forum*, 19, 3 (1985), 9–10+.

'The city and the Scriptures,' R. J. Bakke, *Christianity today*, 28 (June 15, 1984), 14–18.

'The city as church, the church as city,' J. F. Baldovin, *Liturgy*, 3 (Fall 1983), 69–73.

'The city as context for biblical faith,' R. H. Luecke, *The Christian ministry*, 20, 2 (March–April 1989), 10–12.

'The city as mission field,' R. J. Bakke, *Christianity today*, 34, 8 (May 1990), 53–54. (Interview).

The city as sacred center: essays on six Asian contexts. B. L. Smith & H. B. Reynolds (eds.). Leiden: E.J. Brill, 1987.

'The city in the Bible,' D. S. Lim, *Evangelical review of theology*, 12, 2 (April 1988), 138–156.

'The city in the missions of God,' G. Rubingh, *Urban mission*, 5, 2 (November 1987), 5–11.

'The city: the new frontier,' H. M. Conn, *Evangelical missions*

quarterly, 29 (October 1984), 395–98.

'The city—the eschatological garden,' G. Waldecker, *Urban mission*, 5, 4 (March 1988), 18–26.

'The development of an urban ministry program and model.' R. M. Gilmore Sr. M.Div. thesis, Houston Graduate School of Theology, Houston, TX, 1989.

'The downtown priest,' C. D. Gorman, *Homiletic and pastoral review*, 81 (August–September 1981), 19–23.

'The effects of modernization on religious change,' M. Douglas, *Daedalus*, 11 (Winter 1982), 1–19.

The experience of hope: mission and ministry in changing urban communities. W. Stumme (ed). Minneapolis: Augsburg, 1991.

'The explosion, the slumber, and the city of light: three South American cities encounter the Gospel,' L. Willems, *World Christian*, 3, 3 (May 1984), 30–33.

'The field is the world and the world is increasingly urban,' S. Wilson, *Signs of the kingdom in the secular city*, p.9–18. D. Frenchak et al (eds). Chicago: Covenant Press, 1984.

The fivesquare city: the city in the religious imagination. J. Dougherty. Notre Dame, IN: Notre Dame Press, 1980.

'The forgotten Christians of the Middle East,' B. M. Madany, *Urban mission*, 1 (March 1984), 4–9.

The future of cities: essays based on a series of lectures sponsored by the Worcester Municipal Research Bureau. D. L. Schaefer & R. R. Schaefer (eds). Lanham, Maryland: University Press of America, 1996. 100p.

The future of religion: secularization, revival, and cult formation. R. Stark & W. Bainbridge. Berkeley: University of California Press, 1985. 579p.

'The future of the church in the inner city,' P. J. Murnion, *America*, 163, 19 (December 15, 1990), 478–485.

The good society. R. N. Bellah et al. New York: Knopf, 1991.

The gospel and urbanization: a workbook/reader for participants in a seminar held April 22–26, 1985. R. T. Coote (ed). Ventnor, NJ: Overseas Ministries Study Center, 1984.

'The Gospel to the urban Zulu: three cultures in conflict,' K. C. Fleming, *Evangelical missions quarterly*, 22, 1 (January 1986), 24–31.

'The homeless on our streets: how can the Church minister to them?,' R. S. Greenway, *Urban mission*, 2 (September 1984), 44–46.

'The homeless poor: what is the church doing for America's destitute?,' M. Hope & J. Young, *Christianity today*, 29, 14 (October 14, 1985), 30–35.

The house of the Lord: God's plan to liberate your city from darkness. F. Frangipane. Lake Mary, FL: Creation House, 1991.

'The inner city church: its problems and its potential.' P. L. Livingston. D.Min. thesis, San Francisco Theological Seminary, San Anselmo, CA, 1984.

'The Islamic city—historic myth, Islamic essence, and contemporary relevance,' J. L. Abu-Lughod, *International journal of Middle East studies*, 19, 2 (1987), 155–176.

'The kingdom of God, its advance, and the city,' H. M. Conn, *Urban mission*, 1 (May 1984), 16–25.

'The mission of Christ in urban America,' A. T. Eastman, in *Crossroads are for meeting: essays on the mission and common life of the church in a global society.* P. W. Turner & F. Sugeno (eds). Sewanee, TN: SPCK, 1986.

'The paradox of urban ministry today,' P. J. Murnion, *Origins*, 12 (April 21, 1983), 741–44.

'The pastor's opportunities VI: evangelism in the city,' L. Newbigin, *The expository times*, 98, 12 (September 1987), 355–358.

The pivot of the four quarters: a preliminary inquiry into the origins and character of the ancient Chinese city. P. Wheatley. New York: Aldine-Atherson, 1971. 602p.

The poor in the city. Y. Kim. Seoul: Achim, 1985. (Text in Korean).

'The practice of urban ministry: a postscript,' D. E. Hammer, *Review and expositor*, 80 (Fall 1983), 537–41.

'The practice of urban ministry: Christian social ministries,' C. A. Davis, *Review and expositor*, 80 (Fall 1983), 523–28.

'The practice of urban ministry: relating to issues through social action,' P. D. Simmons, *Review and expositor*, 80 (Fall 1983), 529–36.

'The practice of urban ministry: urban evangelism,' F. M. DuBose, *Review and expositor*, 80 (Fall 1983), 515–21.

'The pre–conditions necessary for evangelism in the urban context: a study of Toronto Baptist Churches (Canada).' G. V. Nelson. D.Min. thesis, Fuller Theological Seminary, Pasadena, CA, 1987.

'The renewal of the city church.' D. E. Bonner. D.Min. thesis, Boston University, Boston, 1982.

'The role of theological education in church planting among the urban poor: a case study from Madras,' G. Houghton & E. Sargunam, *Evangelical review of theology*, 6 (April 1982), 141–44.

'The rule of God: agenda for the city,' M. C. Lind, *Covenant quarterly*, 40 (May 1982), 3–18.

'The rural–urban myth and world mission,' H. M. Conn, *Reformed review*, 37 (Spring 1984), 125–36.

'The sacred sojourner: a prescriptive model for an urban church.' J. E. Smith. D.Min. Thesis, Pacific Lutheran Theological Seminary, Berkeley, CA, 1985.

The Thailand report on the urban poor: Report of the Lausanne Committee for World Evangelization, Consultation on World Evangelization, Mini–Consultation on Reaching the Urban Poor, Pattaya, Thailand. Thailand report, no. 22. Wheaton, Illinois: The Committee, 1980.

'The thriving urban parish,' R. G. Ensman Jr., *Today's Parish*, 19, 4 (April–May 1987), 9–11.

The urban challenge: reaching America's cities with the gospel. L. L. Rose & C. K. Hadaway (eds). Nashville, TN: Broadman Press, 1982.

The urban Christian: effective ministry in today's urban world. R. J. Bakke & J. Hart. Downer's Grove, Illinois: InterVarsity Press, 1987.

'The urban church,' R. L. Honeycutt (ed), *Review and exposi-*

tor, 80 (Fall 1983), 487–607. (Thematic issue).

'The urban church,' E. M. Miller, in *Parish: a place for worship*, p.121–36. M. Searle (ed). Collegeville, MN: Liturgical Press, 1981.

The urban church as community builder: proceedings of the 1989 ICUIS Urban/Metropolitan Leadership Workshop. J. C. Montgomery (ed). Chicago: Institute on the Church in Urban-Industrial Society, 1989.

'The urban church: choosing between two gods,' C. Belknap, *The witness* (Ambler, PA), 64 (February 1981), 16–17.

'The urban church: flight time or staying power?,' P. A. Amerson, *Circuit rider*, 14, 10 (December 1990), 4–5.

'The urban church in the 1990s,' B. Whiten Jr., in *The urban church as community builder: proceedings of the 1989 ICUIS Urban/Metropolitan Leadership Workshop*, p.1–11. J. C. Montgomery (ed). Chicago: Institute on the Church in Urban-Industrial Society, 1989.

'The urban church: symbol and reality,' J. S. Spong, *Christian Century*, 101, 27 (September 12, 1984), 828–831.

'The urban church: the role of active churches in urban design.' R. B. Kemendo. Master of Architecture in urban design thesis, Harvard University, Cambridge, MA, 1981.

'The urban mission of the Church from an urban anthropological perspective.' V. Roberts. D.Miss. thesis, Fuller Theological Seminary, Pasadena, CA, 1981.

'The urban Muslims of Ivory Coast,' D. Schreiber, *Urban mission*, 3, 3 (January 1986), 39–43.

The urban pastor as leader. R. D. Dale. *Occasional paper of the Metropolitan Missions Board*. Atlanta, GA: Home Mission Board, Southern Baptist Convention, 1980.

'The urban poor: prime missionary research,' V. Grigg, *Evangelical review of missions*, 11, 3 (July 1987), 3–5.

Theirs is the kingdom: celebrating the gospel in urban America. R. D. Lupton. San Francisco: Harper and Row, 1989.

'Theological education for urban mission,' J. J. Vincent, *Ministerial formation*, 27 (July 1984), 20–22.

'Theological education in the urban context,' D. Hall, in *One faith, many cultures: the Boston Theological Institute annual*. R. O. Costa (ed). 2 ed. Maryknoll, New York: Orbis Books, 1988.

Theology in the City: a theological response to Faith in the City. A. Harvey (ed). London: SPCK, 1989.

Third World cities: problems, policies, and prospects. J. D. Kasarda & A. M. Parnell (eds). Newbury Park: Sage Publications, 1993. 327p.

'Tips for urban church planters,' E. Eckbald, *Urban mission*, 1 (January 1984), 24–29.

To build the city—too long to dream: studies of urban churches. W. A. Yon (ed). Washington, DC: Alban Institute, 1982.

To synchronon astikon perivallon hos poimantikon provlema: melete 'poimantikes koinoniologias. E. Stylios. Athens: Heptalophos, 1980.

'Toward a biblical theology for the urban context.' V. L. Blackwood. Graduate student paper, Northern Baptist Theological Seminary, New Orleans, LA, 1988.

'Toward a biblical urban mission,' F. W. Allen, *Urban mission*, 3, 3 (May 1986), 6–15.

'Toward a theology of the city,' R. J. Bakke, *Cities*, 1 (September 1981), 7–12.

'Toward an urban strategy for Mindanao, Philippines,' M. Shelley, *Urban mission*, 4, 5 (May 1987), 21–31.

'Towards a biblical urban theology,' R. C. Linthicum, *Together*, (April–June 1988).

'Towards an urban theology,' J. J. Vincent, *New Blackfriars*, 64 (January 1983), 4–17.

'Training for urban evangelism,' S. M. Jones, in *An urban world*, p.51–74. L. L. Rose & C. K. Hadaway (eds). Nashville, TN: Broadman Press, 1984.

Two cities: Hanoi and Saigon today. N. Sheehan. London: Cape, 1992. 131p.

Types of churches: the urban fringe. D. McCarty. *Occasional paper*, no. 3. Atlanta, GA: Home Mission Board, Southern Baptist Convention, 1981.

'Unbabbling Pentecost: a case for multi–ethnic church planting,' P. Steinhouer, *Urban mission*, 4, 5 (May 1987), 32–35.

'Understanding life in the city: context for Christian ministry,' L. L. McSwain, *Southwestern journal of theology*, 24 (Spring 1982), 6–19.

Urban America examined: a bibliography. D. E. Casper. New York: Garland, 1985.

'Urban apostolate in Kisumu,' H. Burgman, *AFER*, 24 (December 1982), 337-42; 25 (February 1983), 7-15 (1982–83).

'Urban Black churches: conservators of value and sustainers of community,' L. N. Jones, *Journal of religious thought*, 39 (Fall–Winter 1982–83), 41–50.

'Urban church growth through adult religious education,' B. Gambrell, in *Urban religious education*, p.135–141. D. B. Rogers (ed). Birmingham, AL: Religious Education Press, 1989.

Urban church research: methods and models, collected readings. H. M. Conn (comp.). Chestnut Hill, PA: Urban Missions Program, Westminster Theological Seminary, 1985.

'Urban churches in cross–cultural ministries.' T. Patnaik. D.Min. thesis, San Francisco Theological Seminary, San Anselmo, CA, 1984.

'Urban cities and the gospel in Asia,' B. R. Ro, *Urban mission*, 6, 5 (May 1989), 20–20.

'Urban evangelism and evangelization: an annotated bibliography,' P. A. Amerson et al, *Urban mission*, 1 (May 1984), 26–37.

'Urban evangelism: kosher style,' M. Glaser, *Urban mission*, 2, 4 (March 1985), 6–11.

'Urban evangelization: a Lausanne strategy since 1980,' R. J. Bakke, *International bulletin of missionary research*, 8 (October 1984), 149–54.

'Urban explosion and missions strategy,' T. Monsma, *Evangelical missions quarterly*, 17 (January 1981), 5–12.

Urban heartbeat: the human touch in metropolitan missions. D. R. Wilkinson & P. Obregón. Atlanta, GA: Home Mission Board, Southern Baptist Convention, 1981.

Urban history, policy and the history of urban Christianity. C. E. Stockwell. Chicago: Urban Church Resource Center, SCUPE, 1982. (A bibliography).

Urban ministries training: evaluating for effectiveness. C. D. McConnel. Altadena, California: Barnabas Resources, 1985.

'Urban ministry,' in *The Brethren encyclopedia*, p.1295–97. Philadelphia: The Brethren Encyclopedia, 1983.

'Urban ministry,' E. C. Byford (ed), *St. Mark's review*, no. 119 (June 1983), 1–27.

Urban ministry. D. Claerbaut. Grand Rapids, MI: Zondervan, 1983.

'Urban ministry,' R. Wright, *Christian herald*, 108, 9 (October 1985), 39–43.

'Urban ministry: a partnership model for the white suburban church in the South.' L. B. Lloyd. D.Min. thesis, Fuller Theological Seminary, Pasadena, CA, 1988.

Urban ministry activity report. E. G. David. Madras: World Vision India, March, 1987.

'Urban ministry as Exodus,' T. Arthur, *The Christian ministry*, 20, 2 (March–April 1989), 8–9.

'Urban ministry enters a new phase,' R. D. Pasquariello, *Modern ministries*, 2 (November 1981), 17–19.

Urban ministry in Asia: cities, the exploding mission field. B. R. Ro. Taichung, Taiwan: Asia Theological Association, 1989.

Urban ministry in Indonesia. Jakarta: World Vision International, Indonesia Office, 1990. (Pamphlet).

'Urban ministry in third world cities: three examples,' J. K. Maroney, R. Hill & D. Finnell, in *An urban world*, p.117–46. L. L. Rose & C. K. Hadaway (eds). Nashville, TN: Broadman Press, 1984.

'Urban ministry in today's new social context,' J. R. Jennings, *New Catholic world*, 225 (May 1982), 131–34.

'Urban ministry: sacrament in the city,' P. J. Murnion, *Christianity and crisis*, 43 (May 16, 1983), 187–91.

'Urban ministry: strategy and faith for the city,' D. Heim & E. C. Roehlkepartain, *Christian Century*, 103, 17 (May 14, 1986), 491–495.

'Urban ministry: the bricks without straw syndrome,' D. Schaper, *The other side*, 26, 4 (July 1990), 49–52.

'Urban minorities and Christian higher education,' A. L. Nieves, *Urban mission*, 3, 2 (November 1985), 20–28.

'Urban mission: an annotated bibliography.' H. M. Conn. Instructional resource, Westminster Theological Seminary, Chestnut Hill, PA, 1986.

Urban mission, God's concern for the city: papers presented at the 15th InterVarsity Students Missions Convocation, December 27, 1987 at the University of Illinois, Urbana–Champaign. J. E. Kyle (ed). Downers Grove, Illinois: InterVarsity Press, 1988.

'Urban mission in Japan,' M. Sumiya, *Christian quarterly*, 54, 4 (Fall 1988), 197–203.

'Urban missions: a historical perspective,' B. R. Ro, *Evangelical review of theology*, 12, 2 (April 1988), 157–173.

'Urban people in poverty: towards an alternative model of ministry,' S. Hopkins, B. Bosworth & B. Lennon, in *Justice as mission: an agenda for the church: essays in appreciation of Marjorie and Cyril Powles*, p.153–161. C. Lind & T. Brown (eds). Burlington, Ontario: The Trinity Press, 1985.

'Urban perspectives: on stewardship—reflections on the gospel and the poor,' R. D. Lupton, *Urban mission*, 3, 3 (March 1986), 39.

'Urban poor–ology: a theology of ministry to the world's urban poor,' B. K. Yuen, *Urban mission*, 5, 1 (September 1987), 13–19.

'Urban poverty as a world challenge,' F. M. DuBose, in *An urban world*, p.51–74. L. L. Rose & C. K. Hadaway (eds). Nashville, TN: Broadman Press, 1984.

'Urban theology, 1960-1990,' M.S. Nortcott, *Crucible* vol. 29, no. 4 (October-December 1989) 161-170; *Crucible* vol. 30, no. 1 (January-March 1990) 17-24.

'Urban training needs for the foreign missionary,' J. K. Maroney, *Urban review*, 2, 2 (July 1986), 24–33.

'Urbanism and religion: community, hierarchy and sanctity in urban Thai Buddhist temples.' R. A. O'Connor. Ph.D. dissertation, Cornell University, Ithaca, NY, 1978.

'Urbanization and Christian ministry in world history,' W. Crawley, in *An urban world*, p.37–50. L. L. Rose & C. K. Hadaway (eds). Nashville, TN: Broadman Press, 1984.

'Urbanization and evangelization in South Asia,' R. E. Hedlund, *Urban mission*, 4, 3 (January 1987), 16–30.

'Urbanization and the environment: an Islamic perspective,' H. M. Ateshin, in *An early crescent*. Z. Sarder (ed). London: Mansell, 1989.

'Urbanization as a world trend: a challenge to the churches,' R. J. Siebert, *Missiology: an international review*, 13, 4 (October 1985), 429–443.

'Urbanization: today's missionary reality in Africa,' A. Shorter, *AFER: African ecclesial review*, 32, 5 (October 1990), 290–300.

'Using the media to reach the city for Christ,' A. Fasol, *Southwestern journal of theology*, 24 (Spring 1982), 55–65.

Voices from the corner: poverty and racism in the inner city. R. S. Ezekiel. Philadelphia: Temple University Press, 1984.

'We can solve urban problems,' A. Garvin, *World order*, 17 (Winter 1982–83), 31–42. (Baha'i Faith perspective).

'Why the church fails the city,' R. Darwin (S.J.), *Month*, 19 n.s., 7-8 (July–August 1986), 267–270.

'Will the 'Back to the City' movement revive the urban church,' D. Spain, *Urban review*, 1, 1 (April 1985), 12–24.

Winning the cities: the preoccupation of evangelism. D. Gomes. Rio de Janeiro, Brazil: The Author, 1980 (pamphlet).

'Women and the evangelization of Indian cities,' A. J. John, *Urban mission*, 3, 1 (September 1985), 15–25.

World encyclopedia of cities. G. T. Kurian. Santa Barbara, California: ABC-CLIO, 1994 (multivolume).

World–class cities and world evangelization. D. B. Barrett. Birmingham, AL: New Hope, 1986. (Commissioned by the Southern Baptist Foreign Mission Board as the first of the 'AD 2000' series).

World urbanization prospects: the 1996 revision. New York: United Nations, 1997. 180p. (Updated every 2 years).

You shall be my witnesses: how to reach your city for Christ. L. Rosenbaum. San Francisco: SOS Ministries Press, 1986.

Youth ministry in city churches. E. C. Roehlkepartain. Loveland, Colorado: Groups Publishers, 1989.

'Youth ministry is the urban context,' M. R. Gornick, *Urban mission*, 4, 2 (November 1986), 28–37.

Table 10-5. Profiles of 7,000 cities in 238 nations of the world.

Rec No 1	Country City 2	Pop 2000 3	AC% 4	Church Members 5	E% 6	W 7	Pop 2025 8	Notes 9
	AFGHANISTAN	**22,720,000**	**0.03**	**6,900**	**29.58**	**A**	**44,934,000**	**INDEPENDENTS 0.01%, PROTESTANTS 0.01%. PENT-CHAR 0.01%, EVANGELICAL 0.00%, GCC 0.02%**
1	rural areas	17,681,000	0.01	1,400	28.56	A	28,488,000	94.2% (1950), 88.9% (1970), 81.7% (1990), 77.8% (2000), 73.0% (2010), 63.4% (2025)
2	urban areas	5,039,000	0.11	5,500	33.16	A	16,446,000	5.8% (1950), 11.0% (1970), 18.2% (1990), 22.1% (2000), 26.9% (2010), 36.6% (2025)
3	non-metropolitan areas	185,000	0.10	180	33.07	A	2,284,598	*Sources of data:* Census of 1979; estimates for 1950, 1966, 1971, and 1988.
4	metropolitan areas	4,854,000	0.11	5,400	33.16	A	14,161,000	*Definition:* Sixty-three localities.
5	Baghlan	264,000	0.01	26	27.56	A	863,000	Sugar, cotton. Site of Zoroastrian temple. 37% Uzbek, 35% Tajik, 13% Pathan, 5% Turkmen. 97% Muslim.
6	Balkh (Vazirabad)	223,000	0.01	22	27.56	A	727,000	Formerly Bactra. F=500 BC. Ancient ruins. 39% Tajik, 20% Pathan, 20% Uzbek, 5% Arab. 95% Muslim.
7	Charikar (Charekar)	206,000	0.01	21	27.56	A	673,000	Capital of Parvan. Pottery, grapes, cutlery. 42% Tajik, 15% Pathan, 13% Uzbek, 8% Hazara, 5% Turkmen.
8	Herat (Heroiva)	330,000	0.01	33	27.56	A	1,077,000	Capital of Herat. Agriculture, carpets. 30% Tajik, 28% Pathan, 10% Persian, 10% Uzbek. 1 house church.
9	Jalalabad (Jalalkot)	99,600	0.15	150	34.70	A	325,000	Capital of Nangarhar. Strategic position. Fruit, almonds, rice, grain. Mainly Pathans. University (1963).
10	KABOL (Kabul)	2,716,000	0.17	4,600	36.52	A	7,184,000	Mud-walled compounds. 5,800 ft. F=1500 BC. 50% Pathan. RC church; Irish Sisters of Jesus. M=IAM.
11	Kandahar (Qandahar)	420,000	0.05	210	29.60	A	1,370,000	Chief commercial center. Food processing, textiles. 66% Pathan, 10% Tajik. 96% Muslim. 1 house church.
12	Mazar-e Sharif (Mazan-Sharifi)	243,000	0.01	24	27.56	A	793,000	Shiite shrine. Cotton, grain, fruit. 42% Tajik, 20% Uzbek, 20% Pathan, Turkmen. 95% Muslim. 1 house church.
13	Qonduz (Kunduz, Konduz)	97,900	0.01	10	27.56	A	319,000	Capital of Konduz. 40% Uzbek, 35% Tajik, 13% Pathan. 97% Muslim.
14	Tagab (Tageb)	255,000	0.10	260	32.65	A	831,000	58% Pathan, 20% Hazara, 10% Tajik. 98% Muslim.
	ALBANIA	**3,113,000**	**34.38**	**1,070,000**	**85.41**	**B**	**3,820,000**	**ROMAN CATHOLICS 16.7%, ORTHODOX 16.0%. PENT-CHAR 3.2%, EVANGELICAL 0.1%, GCC 19.7%**
15	rural areas	1,895,000	32.89	623,000	82.77	B	1,765,000	79.6% (1950), 68.2% (1970), 64.2% (1990), 60.8% (2000), 55.6% (2010), 46.2% (2025)
16	urban areas	1,219,000	36.70	447,000	89.53	B	2,055,000	20.3% (1950), 31.7% (1970), 35.7% (1990), 39.1% (2000), 44.3% (2010), 53.8% (2025)
17	non-metropolitan areas	528,000	36.63	193,000	89.46	B	890,116	*Sources of data:* Censuses of 1950, 1960, 1969, 1979 and 1989.
18	metropolitan areas	691,000	36.75	254,000	89.58	B	1,165,000	*Definition:* Towns and other industrial centers with more than 400 inhabitants.
19	Durres	92,600	35.00	32,400	86.03	B	156,000	Capital of Durres on Adriatic Sea. Seaport. Shipbuilding,tobacco. F=600 BC. D=Albanian Orthodox.
20	Elbasan	90,400	35.00	31,600	86.03	B	152,000	On Shkumbin River. Timber, olive oil, cement, soap. F=1466. 60% Muslim. D=Albanian Orthodox.
21	Korce (Korcha, Kortcha)	71,200	35.00	24,900	86.03	B	120,000	Wheat, sugar, apples, grapes. F=c1200. First Albanian school. D=Albanian Orthodox.
22	Shkoder (Shkodra)	89,500	36.00	32,200	89.03	B	151,000	Grains, tobacco, fruits, cotton, silk. F=c500 BC. Muslims. D=RCC,Albanian Orthodox.
23	TIRANE (Tirana)	267,000	39.50	105,000	94.53	B	450,000	Capital. Food processing, tourism. 90% Albanian, 3% Greek. F=c1650. D=Albanian Orthodox.
24	Vlore (Vlora)	80,300	34.00	27,300	85.03	B	135,000	Seaport. Fishing, canning, olive oil. Muslims. D=Albanian Orthodox,RCC.
	ALGERIA	**31,471,000**	**0.29**	**90,900**	**49.55**	**A**	**46,611,000**	**INDEPENDENTS 0.2%, ROMAN CATHOLICS 0.06%. PENT-CHAR 0.1%, EVANGELICAL 0.02%, GCC 0.2%**
25	rural areas	12,818,000	0.13	16,300	45.76	A	13,200,000	77.7% (1950), 60.5% (1970), 48.2% (1990), 40.7% (2000), 34.8% (2010), 28.3% (2025)
26	urban areas	18,653,000	0.40	74,600	52.16	B	33,410,000	22.2% (1950), 39.5% (1970), 51.7% (1990), 59.2% (2000), 65.2% (2010), 71.6% (2025)
27	non-metropolitan areas	7,303,000	0.23	17,000	52.28	B	14,323,308	*Sources of data:* Censuses of 1954, 1960, 1966, 1977 and 1987.
28	metropolitan areas	11,350,000	0.51	57,600	52.08	B	19,087,000	*Definition:* All communes having as *chef-lieu* either a city, a rural town or an urban agglomeration.
29	Ain el Beida (Daoud)	83,500	0.01	8	44.27	A	150,000	Grain-producing area, trading center. F=1848. Harakta Berbers.
30	Ain Oussera	59,700	0.01	6	44.27	A	107,000	Es Salam Research Reactor, 200 km. south of Algiers, 32 miles SSE of Baghari. Sheep, wool.
31	Ain Temouchent	64,000	0.01	6	44.27	A	115,000	Vineyards, orchards. F=1851. Built on site of ruined Roman Albula.
32	Annaba (Bone, Bona)	412,000	0.80	3,300	55.06	B	737,000	Mediterranean port. Formerly Hippo Regius (St. Augustine's bishopric). Minerals, iron, steel. F=c1200 BC.
33	Barika	76,100	0.01	8	44.27	A	136,000	Batna. Hodna Plain on Barika Wadi.
34	Batna	245,000	0.90	2,200	54.16	B	438,000	Agriculture, forest products. Tourist base for Roman ruins. F=1844.
35	Bechar (Colomb-Bechar)	145,000	0.01	14	44.27	A	259,000	Leatherwork, jewelry, dates, cereals, figs, trade center.
36	Bejaia (Bougie)	154,000	0.80	1,200	55.06	B	276,000	Iron ore, phosphates, olive oil, wine, cork, Saharan oil. Market town. Kabyles.
37	Beskra (Biskra)	173,000	0.01	17	44.27	A	310,000	Winter resort. Dates, figs, pomegranates, apricots. Nucleus is Fort Saint-Germain (1849).
38	Blida (El-Boulaida)	303,000	0.90	2,700	55.16	B	543,000	Oranges, flour. F=1553 by Moorish refugees. French in character.
39	Bordj Bou Arreridj	114,000	0.01	11	44.27	A	203,000	Bordj Bou Arreridj. West of Stif.
40	Bou Saada	89,900	0.01	9	44.27	A	161,000	Oasis. Daily market of jewelry, metal works, carpets, knives. Winter resort.
41	Boufarik	55,700	0.20	110	49.46	A	99,700	Grapes, citrus fruits, cereals, tobacco, flowers. F=1836 on malarial swampland.
42	EL DJAZAIR (Alger, Algiers)	4,447,000	0.70	31,100	55.46	B	6,723,000	Wine, oranges, iron ore, phosphates. Chief seaport. Fortress of the Kasbah. 70% Berber. D=RCC.
43	Bab Ezzouar	74,400	0.80	600	55.06	B	133,000	Residential. Oranges. Berber.
44	Bordj el Kiffan	82,200	0.70	580	54.96	B	147,000	Residential. Wine. 70% Berber.
45	Ech Cheliff (Al Asnam, Orleansville)	175,000	0.20	350	49.46	A	314,000	Wheat, barley, leatherworks. F=1843. Name changed in 1981 because of earthquake disasters.
46	El Djelfa	113,000	0.01	11	44.27	A	203,000	Djelfa near Mont des Oulad Nail. Meeting place for nomadic Ouled Nail. F=1852.
47	El Eulma	91,500	0.01	9	44.27	A	164,000	Bordj Bou Arreridj. East of Stif.
48	El Wad	94,400	0.01	9	44.27	A	169,000	Biskra. East of Touggourt near Tunisian border.
49	Ghardaia	120,000	0.01	12	44.27	A	216,000	Oasis. Chief town of the M'zab. F=c1050. Cave of female Saint Daia. Jews.
50	Ghilizane	108,000	0.01	11	44.27	A	193,000	Mostaganem. Inland.
51	Guelma	105,000	0.01	10	44.27	A	188,000	Originally pre-Roman Calama. Capital of Guelma. Agricultural center, large cattle market. F=1836.
52	Jijel (Djidjelli)	84,600	0.10	85	49.36	A	152,000	Seaside resort. Cork, leather, steel. Arabs, Kabyles.
53	Khemis	74,600	0.01	7	44.27	A	134,000	Ech Chleff on Wadi Cheliff near Melyana.
54	Khenchla	94,000	0.01	9	44.27	A	168,000	Khenchela near Garaet et Tarf.
55	Laghouat	90,600	0.05	45	49.31	A	162,000	Dates, fruits, woven wall hangings, carpets. Cathedral of the bishop of the Sahara.
56	Lemdiyya (Medea)	115,000	0.01	11	44.27	A	206,000	Pumps, irrigation equipment, wines, handicrafts. F=c950. Lambdia, Roman military post.
57	M'Sila	88,700	0.01	9	44.27	A	159,000	M'Sila north of Chott el Hodna. Near Atlas Mountains.
58	Maghniya	70,400	0.01	7	44.27	A	126,000	Far west across the border from Oujda, Morocco.
59	Messaad	63,900	0.01	6	44.27	A	115,000	Market town. Dates, fruits.
60	Mestghanem (Mostaganem)	154,000	0.01	15	44.27	A	275,000	Sugar refining, paper pulp, wine, fruit, diatomite.
61	Mouaskar (Mascara)	87,200	0.05	44	49.31	A	156,000	Wine, leather goods, grains, olive oil. F=1701. Jews.
62	Oran (Wahran, Ouahran)	1,043,000	0.60	6,300	54.86	B	1,868,000	Port. Wine, cereals, vegetables, fruits. F=900. Jews.
63	Qacentina (Constantine)	594,000	0.80	4,800	55.06	B	1,064,000	Ancient Cirta. Walled fortress. Women wear black veil. F=313.
64	Saida	109,000	0.01	11	44.27	A	195,000	Strategic militarily. Sheep, wool, cereals, leatherworks, mineral water.
65	Setif (Stif)	229,000	0.20	460	49.46	A	411,000	Center for cereal cultivation. Roman necropolis. Byzantine ruins. Carpets, flour. Elevation 3,600 ft.
66	Sidi-bel-Abbes	206,000	1.00	2,100	55.26	B	369,000	Wheat, barley, grapes, farm machinery. F=1843.
67	Skikda (Philippeville)	173,000	0.10	170	49.36	A	311,000	Port. Oil, minerals, agriculture, sardines. F=1838. Roman ruins.
68	Souq Ahras	112,000	0.01	11	44.27	A	200,000	Souk Ahras near Tunisian border. Ancient Thagaste. Birthplace of Augustine (354).
69	Tbessa (Tebessa)	145,000	0.02	29	45.28	A	260,000	Walled Byzantine citadel. Sheep, esparto grass, grain, carpets. Roman ruins. Christian basilica.
70	Tihert (Tiaret, Tagdempt)	129,000	0.01	13	44.27	A	231,000	Agricultural center. Noted for Arabian horses. Djedar-Berber monuments.
71	Tilimsen (Tlemcen, Tiemcem)	171,000	0.90	1,500	54.16	B	306,000	Agricultural trade. Many 12-15th century buildings. Hadars, Koulouglis, Jews.
72	Tizi-Ouzou	82,400	1.00	820	55.26	B	148,000	Basketry trade center. Olives, figs, grapes. Built by Turks. 'Capital of the Kabyle'. D=Independents.
73	Touggourt	95,200	0.01	10	44.27	A	170,000	Oasis on trade routes. Date palms, livestock, carpets, clothes. Medjara, Rouarha.
74	Wargla (Ouargla)	110,000	0.01	11	44.27	A	197,000	Settled by Berbers. Agriculture, livestock, carpets, basketry. Saharan museum.
	AMERICAN SAMOA	**68,100**	**81.13**	**55,200**	**99.63**	**C**	**143,000**	**PROTESTANTS 52.5%, ROMAN CATHOLICS 13.9%. PENT-CHAR 14.5%, EVANGELICAL 8.0%, GCC 44.4%**
75	rural areas	32,200	79.04	25,500	99.33	C	49,000	62.6% (1950), 58.1% (1970), 51.9% (1990), 47.3% (2000), 42.0% (2010), 34.3% (2025)
76	urban areas	35,900	83.00	29,800	99.90	C	93,700	37.3% (1950), 41.8% (1970), 48.1% (1990), 52.7% (2000), 57.9% (2010), 65.6% (2025)
77	non-metropolitan areas	29,900	83.00	24,800	99.90	C	78,065	*Sources of data:* Censuses of 1970, 1980 and 1990.
78	metropolitan areas	6,000	83.01	5,000	99.90	C	15,600	*Definition:* Places with 2,500 or more inhabitants and urbanized areas.
79	PAGO PAGO (Pango-Pango)	6,000	83.00	5,000	99.90	C	15,600	Port, capital. Canned tuna, tourist industry. F=1872. D=Congregational,RCC.
	ANDORRA	**78,000**	**90.02**	**70,200**	**99.06**	**C**	**154,000**	**ROMAN CATHOLICS 89.1%, MARGINALS 0.5%. PENT-CHAR 1.0%, EVANGELICAL 0.03%, GCC 34.0%**
80	rural areas	3,600	90.51	3,300	96.34	C	5,600	2.8% (1950), 3.6% (1970), 4.6% (1990), 4.6% (2000), 4.3% (2010), 3.6% (2025)
81	urban areas	74,400	90.00	67,000	99.19	C	149,000	97.1% (1950), 96.3% (1970), 95.3% (1990), 95.3% (2000), 95.6% (2010), 96.3% (2025)
82	non-metropolitan areas	44,000	90.00	39,600	99.15	C	87,858	*Sources of data:* Estimates for 1978 and 1986.
83	metropolitan areas	30,400	90.00	27,400	99.24	C	60,800	*Definition:* Urban centers.
84	ANDORRA LA VELLA	30,400	90.00	27,400	99.24	C	60,800	Center for imported goods. Tourist industry, skiing, cattle and sheep raising, tobacco. D=RCC.
	ANGOLA	**12,878,000**	**84.91**	**10,934,000**	**99.29**	**C**	**25,107,000**	**ROMAN CATHOLICS 62.1%, PROTESTANTS 14.9%. PENT-CHAR 15.8%, EVANGELICAL 9.5%, GCC 12.0%**
85	rural areas	8,474,000	83.30	7,058,000	99.12	C	12,423,000	92.4% (1950), 85.0% (1970), 72.4% (1990), 65.8% (2000), 59.1% (2010), 49.4% (2025)
86	urban areas	4,404,000	88.00	3,876,000	99.63	C	12,684,000	7.5% (1950), 14.9% (1970), 27.5% (1990), 34.2% (2000), 40.8% (2010), 50.5% (2025)
87	non-metropolitan areas	518,000	88.54	459,000	99.53	C	2,105,045	*Sources of data:* Censuses of 1950, 1960 and 1970.
88	metropolitan areas	3,886,000	87.93	3,417,000	99.64	C	10,579,000	*Definition:* Localities with a population of 2,000 or more.
89	Benguela (Benguella)	268,000	88.00	236,000	99.98	C	771,000	Benguela. Political/economic center. Sugar, fish, soap, pottery. F=1617 by Portuguese. D=RCC.
90	Huambo (Nova Lisboa)	351,000	89.00	312,000	99.93	C	1,010,000	Huambo. Transportation center. Large rail repair shop. F=1912. Heavily-damaged in civil war. D=RCC.
91	LUANDA (Loanda)	2,665,000	87.50	2,332,000	99.50	C	7,063,000	Capital, seaport. Coffee, cotton, diamonds, iron, salt. F=1576. Cubans. D=RCC(Archdiocese).
92	Lobito	259,000	90.00	233,000	99.98	C	746,000	Benguela on Atlantic Ocean. Largest and busiest port. Food processing, shipbuilding. F=1843. D=RCC.
93	Lubango (Sa de Bandeira)	161,000	88.00	142,000	99.98	C	465,000	Huila. Elevation 5,774 ft. F=1885. D=RCC.
94	Namibe (Mocamedes, Mossamedes)	182,000	89.00	162,000	99.93	C	524,000	Namibe. Atlantic Ocean port. Iron ore, fishing. F=mid 19th century by Brazilians. D=RCC.
	ANGUILLA	**8,300**	**86.48**	**7,200**	**99.80**	**C**	**11,000**	**PROTESTANTS 49.6%, ANGLICANS 31.8%. PENT-CHAR 12.5%, EVANGELICAL 9.6%, GCC 13.2%**
95	rural areas	7,000	86.96	6,100	99.96	C	8,400	90.0% (1950), 90.0% (1970), 89.6% (1990), 84.0% (2000), 84.2% (2010), 76.6% (2025)
96	urban areas	1,300	84.00	1,100	98.92	C	2,600	10.0% (1950), 10.0% (1970), 10.3% (1990), 16.0% (2000), 15.7% (2010), 23.4% (2025)
97	non-metropolitan areas	48	84.08	40	99.26	C	93	*Sources of data:* Censuses.
98	metropolitan areas	1,300	84.00	1,100	98.91	C	2,500	*Definition:* The Valley.
99	THE VALLEY	1,300	84.00	1,100	98.92	C	2,500	Marigot Island. Southern coast. Salt, fishing, tourism. D=Anglican,Methodist.
	ANTIGUA	**67,600**	**79.50**	**53,700**	**99.77**	**C**	**75,100**	**ANGLICANS 33.4%, PROTESTANTS 31.0%. PENT-CHAR 12.4%, EVANGELICAL 10.3%, GCC 15.2%**
100	rural areas	42,700	79.22	33,800	99.71	C	37,800	54.0% (1950), 66.1% (1970), 64.5% (1990), 63.1% (2000), 59.4% (2010), 50.3% (2025)
101	urban areas	24,900	80.00	19,900	99.87	C	37,300	45.9% (1950), 33.8% (1970), 35.4% (1990), 36.8% (2000), 40.5% (2010), 49.7% (2025)
102	non-metropolitan areas	–	–	–	–	–	–	*Sources of data:* Censuses of 1960, 1970 and 1991.
103	metropolitan areas	27,800	80.00	22,200	99.87	C	41,700	*Definition:* St. John's.
104	ST JOHN'S CITY	27,800	80.00	22,200	99.87	C	41,700	On Deep Water Harbor. Cruise ship docks. Sugar. F=1703 as Fort James. D=Anglican. Cathedral (1722).

Table 10-5–continued opposite

Table 10-5–continued

Rec No 1	Country City 2	Pop 2000 3	AC% 4	Church Members 5	E% 6	W 7	Pop 2025 8	Notes 9
	ARGENTINA	**37,027,000**	**91.79**	**33,986,000**	**99.34**	**C**	**47,150,000**	**ROMAN CATHOLICS 91.1%, PROTESTANTS 6.2%. PENT-CHAR 22.6%, EVANGELICAL 5.2%, GCC 7.4%**
105	rural areas	3,943,000	95.86	3,780,000	99.96	C	3,385,000	34.6% (1950), 21.6% (1970), 13.4% (1990), 10.6% (2000), 8.7% (2010), 7.1% (2025)
106	urban areas	33,084,000	91.30	30,206,000	99.27	C	43,765,000	65.3% (1950), 78.3% (1970), 86.5% (1990), 89.3% (2000), 91.2% (2010), 92.8% (2025)
107	non-metropolitan areas	10,351,000	92.26	9,550,000	99.28	C	16,405,598	*Sources of data:* Censuses of 1947, 1960, 1970, 1980, and 1991.
108	metropolitan areas	22,733,000	90.86	20,656,000	99.27	C	27,359,000	*Definition:* Population centers with 2,000 or more inhabitants.
109	BUENOS AIRES	12,431,000	90.80	11,287,000	99.65	C	14,049,000	Capital, major port. Banking, flour mills, meat-packing, auto manufacturing. F=1536. D=RCC.
110	Almirante Brown (Adroque)	499,000	91.00	454,000	99.55	C	660,000	Livestock, textile mills, dairies. F= 1873. D=RCC.
111	Avellaneda (Barracas Al Sur)	385,000	91.00	351,000	99.55	C	510,000	Rio de la Plata Port. Hides, wool, meat, oil refineries. F=1852. D=RCC.
112	Bahia Blanca (Gran Bahia Blanca)	292,000	94.00	274,000	97.65	C	386,000	Port. 'White Bay'. Grains, meat, fruit, petrochemicals. F=1828. National University of the South (1956). D=RCC.
113	Berazategui	271,000	91.00	247,000	99.55	C	358,000	Created out of existing Quilmes. Beef, textiles. F=1960. D=RCC.
114	Berisso	82,300	94.00	77,300	97.65	C	109,000	Heavy industrial zone. Meat packing, steel mill. F=1957. D=RCC.
115	Campana	71,500	90.00	64,300	98.55	C	94,600	Northwest on Parana de las Palmas. D=RCC.
116	Caseros (Tres de Febrero)	388,000	91.00	353,000	99.55	C	514,000	Industrial center. Metal goods, paper, glass, textiles, bricks. F=1959. D=RCC.
117	Esteban Echeverria	307,000	91.00	279,000	99.55	C	406,000	Dairy farms, fruit orchards. F=1913. D=RCC.
118	Florencio Varela	282,000	91.00	256,000	99.55	C	373,000	Formerly San Juan. RR junction, agriculture center, corn, alfalfa, grapes, silk textiles. F=1873. D=RCC.
119	General San Martin (San Martin)	453,000	90.00	408,000	98.55	C	599,000	Industrial center. Linseed oil, cigarettes, liquor, textiles, dairy products. F=1856. D=RCC.
120	General Sarmiento (San Miguel)	719,000	90.00	647,000	98.55	C	951,000	Northwest. Cattle raising, dairy products. F=1862. D=RCC.
121	La Plata (Gran La Plata, Eva Peron)	603,000	85.00	513,000	97.55	C	798,000	Capital of Buenos Aires. Universities. Modeled after Washington D.C. Horse racing. F=1882. D=RCC.
122	Lanus (Cuatro de Junio)	519,000	90.00	467,000	98.55	C	686,000	Paper, wire, ammunition, textiles. F=1944. High population density. D=RCC.
123	Lomas de Zamora	637,000	90.00	573,000	98.55	C	842,000	Industrial center. Chemicals, electrical-manufacturing. F=1861. Formerly owned by Jesuits (1767). D=RCC.
124	Merlo	434,000	90.00	390,000	98.55	C	574,000	Trade center. Agricultural, pastoral lands. F=1865. D=RCC.
125	Moreno	319,000	91.00	291,000	99.55	C	422,000	West. Buenos Aires. Industry. F=1865. D=RCC.
126	Moron (Seis de Septiembre)	713,000	91.00	649,000	99.55	C	943,000	Industrial center. Meat-packing, dairy, canning, tanning. F=1870. D=RCC.
127	Pilar	145,000	90.00	130,000	98.55	C	191,000	Northwest on General San Martin railroad. D=RCC.
128	Quilmes	566,000	90.00	510,000	98.55	C	749,000	Breweries, textiles, ironware, glass. F=1730. D=RCC.
129	San Fernando	161,000	92.00	148,000	99.55	C	213,000	River port. Dairy, fruit, cattle, fish, furniture. F=1909. D=RCC.
130	San Isidro	332,000	91.00	302,000	99.55	C	440,000	Resort. Meat, dairy, tires, paper, ceramics, horse racing. F=1784. D=RCC.
131	San Justo	1,246,000	88.00	1,097,000	98.55	C	1,649,000	Industrial center. Auto parts, paper, rubber. F=1856. Y=1860. D=RCC.
132	San Vincente	96,100	92.00	88,500	99.55	C	127,000	South. Near Lake Tucuru. D=RCC.
133	Tigre	285,000	91.00	259,000	99.55	C	376,000	River trade center, resort. Fruit market. F=1678. Y=1678. D=RCC.
134	Vicente Lopez	321,000	91.00	292,000	99.55	C	425,000	Beach resort, residential. Presidential residence. F=1905. D=RCC.
135	Caseros (Tres de Febrero)	447,000	92.00	411,000	99.55	C	591,000	Industrial center. Metal goods, paper, glass, textiles, perfume, bricks. F=1959. D=RCC.
136	Catamarca (San Fernando del Valle)	116,000	90.00	105,000	99.05	C	154,000	Capital of Catamarca. Grapes, alfalfa. F=1694. Pilgrimage center. Church of the Virgin of the Valley. D=RCC.
137	Comodoro Rivada	126,000	90.00	114,000	98.55	C	167,000	San Jorge Gulf port city. Oil wells. Air Force base. F=1901. D=RCC.
138	Concordia	123,000	90.00	111,000	99.05	C	162,000	On Uruguay River. Commercial center. Tanneries, sawmills, flour & rice mills, lime kilns. F=1832. D=RCC.
139	Cordoba (Gran Cordoba)	1,407,000	89.00	1,252,000	99.15	C	1,729,000	Capital of Cordoba. Tourist trade, manufacturing. University (1613). F=1573. Y=1599 (Jesuits). D=RCC.
140	Corrientes	235,000	92.00	217,000	99.55	C	311,000	Capital and Parana River port. Agriculture, trade. F=1588. Pilgrimage center-cross of Torres de Vera. D=RCC.
141	Formosa	122,000	93.00	113,000	99.05	C	161,000	Agriculture & cattle raising. F=1879. Large numbers of indigenous Indians. M=SJ. D=RCC.
142	Gualeguaychu	67,000	94.00	63,000	99.55	C	88,600	Entre Rios near Uruguay River and Uruguay border. D=RCC.
143	Guaymallen (Villa Nueva)	200,000	92.00	184,000	99.55	C	265,000	Suburb of Mendoza. Wine, grapes, peaches, apples, plums, olives. D=RCC.
144	Junin	81,400	94.00	76,500	99.55	C	108,000	Agriculture, commercial, manufacturing center. F=1906. D=RCC.
145	La Rioja	87,400	93.00	81,300	99.05	C	116,000	Capital of La Rioja. Minerals, agriculture. F=1591. 16th century Jesuit church. D=RCC.
146	Mar del Plata	541,000	91.00	492,000	98.55	C	715,000	Ocean resort. Large casino. F=1907. Originally Jesuit reduction (1746). D=RCC.
147	Melincue	154,000	91.00	140,000	98.55	C	204,000	Sante Fe near Venado Tuerto. D=RCC.
148	Mendoza (Gran Mendoza)	943,000	90.00	849,000	97.55	C	1,182,000	Capital of Mendoza. Wine, fruit preservation, petrochemicals. Known for museums & parks. F=1516. D=RCC.
149	Godoy Cruz	200,000	90.00	180,000	97.55	C	264,000	Industrial center. Wineries, canneries, meat-packing, breweries, flour mills. D=RCC.
150	Las Heras	132,000	90.00	119,000	97.55	C	175,000	North. Near Andes Mountains. D=RCC.
151	Villa Nueva (Guaymallen)	247,000	90.00	222,000	97.55	C	327,000	Wine, grapes, peaches, apples, plums, olives. D=RCC.
152	Mercedes (Villa Mercedes)	66,500	95.00	63,100	99.55	C	87,900	San Luis on Quinto River. West of Buenos Aires. Named after 'Virgin of Mercy'. D=RCC.
153	Necochea	66,600	95.00	63,200	99.55	C	88,100	Buenos Aires. Atlantic port south of Mar del Plata. D=RCC.
154	Neuquen	117,000	93.00	109,000	99.05	C	155,000	Capital of Neuquen. Market center for fruit. Ski resort. F=1896. D=RCC.
155	Olavarria	83,600	95.00	79,400	99.15	C	111,000	Buenos Aires on Canal No. 11 near Azul. D=RCC.
156	Parana	211,000	90.00	190,000	97.55	C	279,000	Capital of Entre Rios. F=1730 as Bajada de Sante Fe. Y=1730. Cathedral of Parana. D=RCC.
157	Pergamino	89,400	94.00	84,100	99.05	C	118,000	Agriculture, furniture, metals, textiles. F=1784. D=RCC.
158	Posadas	188,000	96.00	180,000	99.55	C	248,000	Capital of Misiones. Public service, wood, iron. Originally Paraguayan trading post. D=RCC.
159	Presidencia Roque Saenz Pena	64,300	94.00	60,500	99.05	C	85,100	Chaco on railroad northwest of Resistencia. D=RCC.
160	Punta Alta	73,800	93.00	68,600	98.95	C	97,600	Buenos Aires on Blanca Bay near Bahia Blanca. D=RCC.
161	Rafaela	69,400	93.00	64,600	98.95	C	91,900	Sante Fe Province. Northwest of Sante Fe. Rail junction. D=RCC.
162	Resistencia (Gran Resistencia)	287,000	91.00	261,000	98.55	C	380,000	Capital of Chaco on Parana River. Cotton, quebracho, lumber, cattle, sugarcane. F=1878. M=SJ. D=RCC.
163	Rio Cuarto	144,000	93.00	134,000	98.95	C	190,000	Rail junction. Fruit, meat packing, flour milling. F=1794. Y=1797. D=RCC.
164	Rosario (Gran Rosario)	1,228,000	89.00	1,093,000	99.05	C	1,505,000	Parana River port. Grain export, steel, automobiles. F=1689. Church erected in 1731. D=RCC.
165	San Lorenzo	126,000	89.00	112,000	96.55	C	167,000	Port. Manufacturing, petrochemicals, agriculture. F=1944. Originally Catholic monastery. D=RCC.
166	Salta	340,000	78.00	265,000	95.55	C	450,000	Capital of Salta in Lerma Valley. Tourists, farming, lumber, mining. F=1582. Annual Fiesta del Milagro. D=RCC.
167	San Carlos de Bariloche (Bariloche)	63,800	94.00	60,000	99.05	C	84,500	Tourism, skiing, fishing. D=RCC.
168	San Francisco	76,300	94.00	71,700	99.05	C	101,000	Rail center. Linseed oil, batteries, leather goods. F=1886. D=RCC.
169	San Juan (Gran San Juan)	333,000	95.00	317,000	99.15	C	441,000	Capital of San Juan. Meats, wines, fruits, grains. F=1562, M=SJ. Destroyed by earthquake (1944). D=RCC.
170	Villa Krause	86,900	95.00	82,600	99.15	C	115,000	Southwest. Andes Mountains. D=RCC.
171	San Luis	92,500	97.00	89,800	99.25	C	122,000	Capital of San Luis province. Irrigated agriculture, meat-packing, food processing. F=1594. D=RCC.
172	San Miguel de Tucuman	684,000	92.00	630,000	99.05	C	905,000	Capital of Tucuman. Center of sugar industry, maize, tourism. Our Lady of Mercy shrine. F=1565. D=RCC.
173	San Nicolas de los Arroyos	128,000	91.00	117,000	98.55	C	170,000	Port. River trade in grains, iron ore, manufactured goods. F=1748. D=RCC.
174	San Rafael	92,500	92.00	85,100	99.05	C	122,000	Agriculture, wineries, canneries, dairies, petroleum. F=1805. D=RCC.
175	San Salvador de Jujuy	163,000	94.00	153,000	99.05	C	215,000	Capital of Jujuy. Agriculture, tourism. F=1593. First cathedral (1606). D=RCC.
176	Santa Fe	381,000	92.00	350,000	99.05	C	504,000	Capital of Sante Fe. Most inland seaport in world (250 miles). F=1573. Jesuit center (1660). D=RCC.
177	Santiago del Estero	261,000	95.00	248,000	99.55	C	345,000	Capital of Santiago del Estero. Food processing, Agriculture. F=1553. Cathedral (1590). D=RCC.
178	Tandil	104,000	93.00	96,300	99.05	C	137,000	Agriculture, health resort, tourism. F=1895. Holy week festivities. D=RCC.
179	Trelew	68,300	93.00	63,500	99.05	C	90,300	Chubut on Chubut River. Inland from Rawson. D=RCC.
180	Villa Maria	88,100	93.00	81,900	99.05	C	116,000	Rail junction, commercial center. Livestock, grain, military explosives. F=1867. D=RCC.
181	Zarate (General Uriburu)	87,500	94.00	82,300	99.15	C	116,000	Manufacturing & transportation center. F=1825. D=RCC.
	ARMENIA	**3,520,000**	**83.92**	**2,954,000**	**97.79**	**C**	**3,946,000**	**ORTHODOX 78.2%, ROMAN CATHOLICS 4.5%. PENT-CHAR 2.1%, EVANGELICAL 0.05%, GCC 11.2%**
182	rural areas	1,058,000	81.65	864,000	95.49	C	862,000	57.1% (1950), 40.5% (1970), 32.5% (1990), 30.0% (2000), 26.8% (2010), 21.8% (2025)
183	urban areas	2,462,000	84.90	2,090,000	98.77	C	3,084,000	42.9% (1950), 59.4% (1970), 67.4% (1990), 69.9% (2000), 73.1% (2010), 78.1% (2025)
184	non-metropolitan areas	678,000	85.05	577,000	98.43	C	910,072	*Sources of data:* Censuses of 1959, 1970, 1979 and 1989.
185	metropolitan areas	1,784,000	84.84	1,513,000	98.90	C	2,174,000	*Definition:* Cities and urban-type localities, officially designated as such by each of the constituent republics.
186	Abovjan	61,700	85.00	52,500	98.87	C	77,300	Northeast of Jerevan. D=AAC.
187	JEREVAN (Erevan, Yerevan)	1,322,000	85.00	1,124,000	98.87	C	1,596,000	On Razdan River. Focus of trade. Long history of siege & storm. Ancient Armenian manuscripts. D=AAC.
188	Ecmiadzin (Echmiadzin)	61,700	90.00	55,600	99.57	C	77,300	On plain of Araks River. Armenian Apostolic Seminary. Clear view of Mt. Ararat. D=AAC.
189	Kirovakan (Karaklis)	197,000	83.00	163,000	98.87	C	247,000	On Pambak, Tandzut & Vanadzoriget Rivers. Carbide, ammonia, textiles. F=1826. Earthquake (1988). D=AAC.
190	Kumajri (Gumry, Gyumri)	138,000	83.00	114,000	98.87	C	173,000	Formerly Leninabad, Alexandropol. Textile center. Bicycles. F=401 BC. Earthquake (1988). D=AAC.
191	Razdan	65,200	91.00	59,400	99.67	C	81,700	On Razdan River northeast of Jerevan. D=AAC.
	ARUBA	**103,000**	**92.69**	**95,200**	**99.54**	**C**	**250,000**	**ROMAN CATHOLICS 82.0%, PROTESTANTS 7.3%. PENT-CHAR 8.2%, EVANGELICAL 3.9%, GCC 5.2%**
192	rural areas	30,400	94.35	28,700	99.98	C	53,300	32.1% (1950), 32.1% (1970), 31.6% (1990), 29.5% (2000), 26.1% (2010), 21.2% (2025)
193	urban areas	72,400	92.00	66,600	99.35	C	197,000	67.9% (1950), 67.9% (1970), 68.3% (1990), 70.4% (2000), 73.8% (2010), 78.7% (2025)
194	non-metropolitan areas	49,600	92.00	45,700	99.35	C	135,197	*Sources of data:* Censuses.
195	metropolitan areas	22,700	92.00	20,900	99.35	C	61,900	*Definition:* Oranjestad.
196	ORANJESTAD	22,700	92.00	20,900	99.35	C	61,900	Seaport. Petroleum processing, shipping. Seven-mile long Palm Beach. Hotels, tourism.
	AUSTRALIA	**18,880,000**	**66.68**	**12,588,000**	**98.37**	**C**	**23,091,000**	**ROMAN CATHOLICS 28.6%, ANGLICANS 21.5%. PENT-CHAR 13.0%, EVANGELICAL 13.7%, GCC 34.3%**
197	rural areas	2,890,000	73.18	2,115,000	96.59	C	2,842,000	24.9% (1950), 14.8% (1970), 14.9% (1990), 15.3% (2000), 14.7% (2010), 12.3% (2025)
198	urban areas	15,989,000	65.50	10,473,000	98.69	C	20,248,000	75.1% (1950), 85.1% (1970), 85.0% (1990), 84.6% (2000), 85.2% (2010), 87.6% (2025)
199	non-metropolitan areas	2,164,000	68.65	1,486,000	98.63	C	3,502,265	*Sources of data:* Estimate for 1950; censuses of 1961, 1966, 1971, 1976, 1981, 1986, and 1991.
200	metropolitan areas	13,825,000	65.01	8,987,000	98.70	C	16,746,000	*Definition:* Population clusters of 1,000 or more inhabitants; and some areas of lower population.
201	Adelaide	1,063,000	65.30	694,000	98.99	C	1,300,000	Capital of South Australia on River Torrens. Petroleum. F=1836. 'City of churches'. D=Anglican,RCC.
202	Enfield	74,000	65.00	48,100	96.69	C	93,700	North. Agriculture, industry, textile, dairy products, wine and fruit. D=Anglican,RCC.
203	Marion	86,200	65.50	56,500	97.19	C	109,000	South near Brighton. Grains, fruit, agriculture, industry. D=Anglican,RCC.
204	Mitcham	73,100	65.00	47,500	96.69	C	92,600	South near Unley. Textiles, service industries, livestock. D=Anglican,RCC.
205	Noarlunga	89,400	65.50	58,500	97.19	C	113,000	South on Gulf Saint Vincent, Port Noarlunga nearby on Gulf St. Vincent. Fruit growing, dairying center. D=RCC.
206	Salisbury	123,000	65.00	79,700	96.69	C	155,000	Northeast near Elizabeth. RR junction, wheat supply, supply center for former rocket base at Woomera. D=RCC.
207	Tea Tree Gully	95,100	65.00	61,800	96.69	C	120,000	East, beyond Hope Valley. Textiles, industry, fruit, livestock. D=Anglican,RCC.
208	West Torrens	51,700	65.00	33,600	96.69	C	65,400	West. Adelaide Airport. Gulf Saint Vincent. Industry, wine, textiles. D=Anglican,RCC.
209	Woodville	95,400	65.00	62,000	96.69	C	121,000	West near Port Adelaide. Automobile plants, metropolitan area. D=Anglican,RCC.
210	Albury - Wodonga	76,900	67.00	51,500	98.69	C	97,300	Twin cities. Agriculture, livestock, heavy industry. Wine, produce, distribution, electronics, printing. D=Anglican.
211	Ballarat (Ballaarat)	92,500	67.00	62,000	98.69	C	117,000	Aboriginal name Victoria, SE, Eureka Stockade Uprising 1854. Gold rush 1860s. Paper, brick. D=Anglican.
212	Bendigo	78,500	67.00	52,600	98.69	C	99,400	Sandhurst until 1891. Livestock, fruit, poultry, wheat. F=1840. D=Anglican,RCC.
213	Brisbane	1,591,000	65.50	1,042,000	99.69	C	1,967,000	Port and capital of Queensland. Tropical vegetation. Agricultural export, shipyards, oil. F=1834. D=Anglican, RCC.
214	Ipswich	87,000	66.00	57,400	97.69	C	110,000	West. Inland. Amberley R.A.A.F. Base. D=Anglican,RCC.
215	Logan	164,000	65.00	107,000	96.69	C	208,000	South. Logan River. Railroad, tourism. D=Anglican,RCC.
216	Redcliffe	55,600	67.00	37,300	98.69	C	70,400	North on Moreton Bay. Commercial, industrial, and cultural center, shipyards, food processing. D=Anglican.
217	CANBERRA	328,000	65.00	213,000	96.69	C	416,000	Federal capital. Light industry, tourism. Australia National University. F=1836. Ch. of St. John the Baptist (1845).
218	Coffs Harbour	55,300	67.00	37,100	98.69	C	70,100	New South Wales. Pacific Ocean near New England National Park. D=Anglican,RCC.
219	Darwin	84,700	67.00	56,700	98.69	C	107,000	Port & capital of Northern Territory. Formerly Palmerston. Service center for hinterland, export. F=1869. D=RCC.
220	Geelong	172,000	63.00	108,000	94.69	C	218,000	Corio Bay port. 40% parks. Wool, petroleum, grains, meat, resort. Education center. F=1837. D=RCC.
221	Gold Coast (Southport)	244,000	65.00	159,000	96.69	C	309,000	Beach resorts. Population swells at Christmas. Fauna reserve, bird sanctuary. D=Anglican,RCC.

Table 10-5–continued overleaf

Table 10-5–continued

Rec No 1	Country City 2	Pop 2000 3	AC% 4	Church Members 5	E% 6	W 7	Pop 2025 8	Notes 9
222	Gosford	146,000	64.50	94,300	96.19	C	185,000	New South Wales. On Brisbane Water near Brisbane Water National Park. D=Anglican,RCC.
223	Hobart	209,000	67.00	140,000	98.69	C	265,000	Port & capital of Tasmania. Communication & trade, fishing. F=1804. First Jews (1843). D=Anglican,RCC.
224	Launceston	107,000	64.00	68,300	95.69	C	135,000	Tasmanian port. Commercial center, export. F=1826. St. John's Church 1824. D=Anglican,RCC.
225	MacKay	58,800	65.00	38,200	96.69	C	74,400	Queensland. On Coral Sea near Great Barrier Reef Marine Park. D=Anglican,RCC.
226	Melbourne	3,188,000	65.20	2,079,000	99.39	C	3,764,000	Capital of Victoria. Finance. F=1835. Italians, Greeks, Yugoslavs, Vietnamese, Khmer. D=RCC.
227	Berwick	74,100	65.00	48,100	96.69	C	93,800	Southeast beyond Dandenong. D=RCC,Anglican.
228	Box Hill	55,100	65.50	36,100	97.19	C	69,800	East. South Victoria, 9 miles east of Melbourne. Textiles, electrical goods. D=RCC,Anglican.
229	Broadmeadows	122,000	66.00	80,400	97.69	C	154,000	North near Essendon Airport. D=Anglican,RCC.
230	Brunswick	47,500	65.00	30,900	96.69	C	60,100	North. Royal Park. Zoo. Ethnically diverse. Manufacturing, textiles, recording label. D=RCC,Anglican.
231	Camberwell	101,000	65.00	65,900	96.69	C	128,000	East. Victorian Lawn Tennis Association Courts. 5 miles east of Melbourne. D=Anglican,RCC.
232	Caulfield	81,000	66.00	53,500	97.69	C	103,000	Southeast. Caulfield Race Course. D=Anglican,RCC.
233	Coburg	63,000	65.00	40,900	96.69	C	79,700	North. Merri Creek. 5 miles north of Melbourne. D=Anglican,RCC.
234	Dandenong	68,600	65.00	44,600	96.69	C	86,900	Southeast on Eastern Railway. Dandenong Creek. Dairy, vegetable dehydration plant. D=Anglican,RCC.
235	Doncaster	124,000	65.00	80,600	96.69	C	157,000	East, south of Templestowe. D=Anglican,RCC.
236	Essendon	63,900	65.00	41,500	96.69	C	80,900	North. Essendon Airport. Industrial manufacturing. D=Anglican,RCC.
237	Footscray	56,300	65.00	36,600	96.69	C	71,300	West on Yarra River. Rope manufacturing. Flemington Race Course. D=Anglican,RCC.
238	Frankston	105,000	63.00	65,900	94.69	C	132,000	South on Port Phillip Bay. Summer resort, orchards, ham, bacon. D=Anglican,RCC.
239	Heidelberg	73,400	64.00	47,000	95.69	C	92,900	Northeast on Yarra River. La Trobe University. D=Anglican,RCC.
240	Keilor	120,000	63.50	76,100	95.19	C	152,000	Northwest. Maribyrnong Creek. Tullamarine International Airport. Organ Pipes Natl. Park. D=Anglican,RCC.
241	Knox	140,000	65.00	91,100	96.69	C	177,000	Residential. Manufacturing. D=Anglican,RCC.
242	Malvern	50,100	64.00	32,100	95.69	C	63,500	Southeast beyond Prahran. Residential metro area. D=Anglican,RCC.
243	Moorabbin	114,000	63.50	72,600	95.19	C	145,000	Southeast. Moorabbin Airport. Truck gardening. D=Anglican,RCC.
244	Northcote	56,700	65.00	36,900	96.69	C	71,800	North. Merri Creek. Apparel manufacturing, printing, paper. D=Anglican,RCC.
245	Nunawading	111,000	64.00	71,300	95.69	C	141,000	East beyond Box Hill. D=Anglican,RCC.
246	Oakleigh	66,500	65.00	43,300	96.69	C	84,300	Southeast beyond Caulfield. Monash University. D=Anglican,RCC.
247	Prahran	50,700	65.00	33,000	96.69	C	64,200	Southeast. Light industrial and residential. Fawkner Gardens. D=Anglican,RCC.
248	Preston	94,700	65.00	61,600	96.69	C	120,000	North beyond Northcote. Manufacturing, automotive products, coffee, sheep. D=Anglican,RCC.
249	Saint Kilda	53,600	66.00	35,400	97.69	C	67,900	Southeast on Hobsons Bay. D=Anglican,RCC.
250	Springvale	102,000	65.00	66,600	96.69	C	130,000	Southeast. Sandown Park Racecourse. Great ethnic diversity, immigrant hostels. D=RCC,Anglican.
251	Sunshine	113,000	63.50	71,700	95.19	C	143,000	West on Northern Railway. Kororoit Creek. 6 miles west of Melbourne. D=Anglican,RCC.
252	Waverley	146,000	65.00	94,800	96.69	C	185,000	Southeast beyond Caulfield. Bathing beach on Bondi Bay, tourism. D=Anglican,RCC.
253	Newcastle (King's Town)	492,000	66.00	325,000	97.69	C	623,000	Port of NSW. Coal, farm produce. War Memorial Cultural Centre. F=1801 as penal colony. D=RCC.
254	Lake Macquarie	187,000	65.00	121,000	96.69	C	237,000	South. Lake Macquarie. D=RCC,Anglican.
255	Perth	1,313,000	64.00	840,000	97.69	C	1,622,000	Capital of Western Australia. Heavy industry, metals. F=1829. Italians. D=Anglican,RCC. M=YWAM.
256	Canning	79,800	66.00	52,700	97.69	C	101,000	Southeast on Canning River. D=Anglican,RCC.
257	Cockburn	57,500	65.50	37,700	97.19	C	72,900	South. Cockburn Sound. D=Anglican,RCC.
258	Wanneroo	189,000	65.00	123,000	96.69	C	239,000	North. Lake Joondalup. D=Anglican,RCC.
259	Gosnells	83,000	64.00	53,100	95.69	C	105,000	Southeast on Canning River. D=Anglican,RCC.
260	Melville	98,900	66.00	65,300	97.69	C	125,000	South on Swan River. D=Anglican,RCC.
261	Stirling	210,000	66.00	138,000	97.69	C	266,000	North near North Beach. D=Anglican,RCC.
262	Randwick	138,000	65.00	89,500	96.69	C	174,000	Southeast. University of New South Wales. Randwick Racecourse. D=Anglican,RCC.
263	Rockhampton	71,300	67.00	47,800	98.69	C	90,300	Queensland. Commercial center. Grain, cattle, sheep. F=1858. D=Anglican,RCC.
264	Shoalhaven	74,000	68.00	50,300	99.69	C	93,700	New South Wales. Shoalhaven Bight. Dairying. D=Anglican,RCC.
265	Sydney	3,665,000	64.50	2,364,000	99.19	C	4,288,000	Capital of NSW. Manufacturing, government, water sports. F=1788. Muslims, Jews, Buddhists. D=Anglican,RCC.
266	Auburn	57,700	65.00	37,500	96.69	C	73,100	West. Site of Olympic Stadium. Industrial center, chemicals, office supplies. D=Anglican,RCC.
267	South Sydney	85,600	64.00	54,800	95.69	C	108,000	South. University of Sydney. D=Anglican,RCC.
268	Bankstown	183,000	65.00	119,000	96.69	C	232,000	Southwest. Bankstown Aerodrome. Manufacturing, stationary, oil cans, tire pumps, aircraft. D=Anglican,RCC.
269	Blacktown	244,000	64.00	156,000	95.69	C	309,000	Northwest. North of Prospect Reservoir. D=Anglican,RCC.
270	Blue Mountains	81,800	65.00	53,200	96.69	C	104,000	West in Great Dividing Range. Blue Mountains National Park. Tourism. D=Anglican,RCC.
271	Campbelltown	161,000	65.00	105,000	96.69	C	204,000	Southwest on Southern Railway. Former coal mining center. Historic-tourist destination. F=1810. D=Anglican.
272	Canterbury	156,000	64.00	100,000	95.69	C	198,000	Southwest. Canterbury Park Racecourse. Commercial, retail, light industry, ethnically diverse. D=RCC,Anglican.
273	Fairfield	204,000	64.00	130,000	95.69	C	258,000	West. Prospect Creek. Southwest RR node. Light manufacturing, hardware. D=Anglican,RCC.
274	Holroyd	95,300	63.00	60,000	94.69	C	121,000	West. Prospect Reservoir. Manufacturing, electrical equipment, generators. D=Anglican,RCC.
275	Hurstville	76,700	64.00	49,100	95.69	C	97,100	South near Georges River. Residential with retail , light industry. D=Anglican,RCC.
276	Kogarah	55,300	65.00	35,900	96.69	C	70,000	South near Botany Bay. Commercial, retail and light industries. Sydney Intl. Airport nearby. D=Anglican,RCC.
277	Leichhardt	68,100	64.00	43,600	95.69	C	86,200	West near Iron Cove Bay. Highly diversified light industries, commercial and retail. D=Anglican,RCC.
278	Liverpool	115,000	64.00	73,800	95.69	C	146,000	Southwest. Warwick Farm Racecourse and Motor Race Track. D=Anglican,RCC.
279	Marrickville	97,800	65.00	63,600	96.69	C	124,000	South near Kingsford Smith Airport. Manufacturers, pet food and footwear. D=Anglican,RCC.
280	North Sydney	61,700	66.00	40,700	97.69	C	78,100	North across Sydney Harbour Bridge. Large manufacturing district, shipyard. 'Second Downtown'. D=Anglican.
281	Parramatta	156,000	64.00	99,500	95.69	C	197,000	West. Parramatta Park. Rosehill Racecourse. 2nd oldest settlement in Australia. F=1788. D=Anglican.
282	Penrith	176,000	64.00	113,000	95.69	C	223,000	Far west on Main Western Railway. Nepean River. Hawkesburg River. Dairying, fruit. D=Anglican,RCC.
283	Rockdale	102,000	65.00	66,200	96.69	C	129,000	Southwest near Botany Bay. Metro area, light industries. Intl. airport nearby. D=Anglican,RCC.
284	Ryde	109,000	65.00	70,900	96.69	C	138,000	Northwest. Meadowbank Park. Parramatta River. Electronics, consumer goods, shipyards. D=Anglican,RCC.
285	Waverley	71,500	66.00	47,200	97.69	C	90,500	East. Queens Park. Pacific Ocean. Bathing beach on Bondi Bay, tourism. D=Anglican,RCC.
286	Willoughby	62,300	66.00	41,100	97.69	C	78,900	North beyond North Sydney. Manufacturers, greeting cards. D=Anglican,RCC.
287	Woollahra	62,200	66.00	41,100	97.69	C	78,800	East. Cricket Ground. Southeast suburb. D=Anglican,RCC.
288	Toowoomba (The Swamps)	93,700	67.00	62,800	98.69	C	119,000	Rail & road junction in Queensland. Tourism, livestock, dairies, grain. F=1849. D=Anglican,RCC.
289	Townsville	129,000	65.00	84,100	96.69	C	164,000	Queensland port. Beef cattle, sheep, sugar, fishing, tourism. F=1864. D=Anglican,RCC.
290	Wagga Wagga	60,300	66.00	39,800	97.69	C	76,300	New South Wales. Service center for wheat, sheep, rubber goods, iron. F=1849. D=Anglican,RCC.
291	Wollongong (Greater Wollongong)	293,000	64.00	187,000	95.69	C	371,000	New South Wales coastal port. Dairy farming, coal, fishing. F=1816. University. D=Anglican,RCC.
292	Bayswater	53,600	65.00	34,900	96.69	C	67,900	Northeast. Swan River. Residential. D=Anglican,RCC.
	AUSTRIA	**8,211,000**	**84.16**	**6,910,000**	**98.59**	**C**	**8,186,000**	**ROMAN CATHOLICS 75.5%, PROTESTANTS 5.0%. PENT-CHAR 3.6%, EVANGELICAL 0.5%, GCC 20.9%**
293	rural areas	2,902,000	86.27	2,504,000	97.79	C	2,246,000	36.2% (1950), 34.6% (1970), 35.4% (1990), 35.3% (2000), 33.2% (2010), 27.4% (2025)
294	urban areas	5,308,000	83.00	4,406,000	99.03	C	5,940,000	63.8% (1950), 65.3% (1970), 64.5% (1990), 64.6% (2000), 66.7% (2010), 72.5% (2025)
295	non-metropolitan areas	1,556,000	83.57	1,300,000	98.88	C	1,940,159	*Sources of data:* Censuses of 1951, 1961, 1971, 1981, and 1991.
296	metropolitan areas	3,752,000	82.76	3,106,000	99.09	C	3,999,000	*Definition:* Communes (*Gemeinden*) with 5,000 or more inhabitants.
297	Bruck an der Mur (Bruck)	51,500	86.00	44,300	99.73	C	57,700	Styria on Mur River. Rail junction. Iron, steel, copper, cable, paper, wood. F=1263. Gothic parish church. D=RCC.
298	Graz	342,000	83.00	283,000	98.43	C	382,000	Capital of Styria on Mur River. Iron, steel, breweries, textiles, tourism. F=c1240. Protestants (c1530). D=RCC.
299	Innsbruck	194,000	84.00	163,000	98.43	C	218,000	Capital of Tirol on Inn River. Tourist & health resort. Market center. F=1239. Franciscan church (1533). D=RCC.
300	Klagenfurt	121,000	83.00	100,000	98.43	C	135,000	Capital of Karnten. Communication & tourist center. Popular winter resort. Theological seminary. F=1279. D=RCC.
301	Leoben	54,600	84.00	45,900	98.43	C	61,100	Styria on Mur River. Lignite mining, iron, beer, tourism. F=1263. Maria am Waasen Church c1150. D=RCC.
302	Linz	352,000	83.00	292,000	98.43	C	394,000	Capital of Oberosterreich. Danube River. Formerly Roman fort Lentia. Church of St. Martin (799). D=RCC.
303	Neunkirchen	47,300	83.00	39,300	98.43	C	52,900	Pinzgau. Salzach River. D=RCC.
304	Salzburg	231,000	83.00	192,000	98.43	C	259,000	Capital of Salzburg on Salzach River. Celtic settlement. Benedictine Abbey 696. RCC Archbishopric (c800).
305	Sankt Polten	70,400	86.00	60,600	99.73	C	78,800	Rail junction, manufacturing. Roman settlement Aelium Cetium. 8th century abbey. D=RCC.
306	Steyr	68,300	86.00	58,700	99.73	C	76,400	On Steyr River. Iron, steel. F=c950. Hospital dating from 1305. Gothic church (15th century). D=RCC.
307	Villach	68,300	86.00	58,700	99.73	C	76,400	Karnten on Drau River. Tourism. Roman Bilachinium. Parish church St. Jakob. (15th century). D=RCC.
308	Wels	79,900	85.00	67,900	99.43	C	89,400	Oberosterreich. Railway junction, cattle. Originally Roman Ovilava. F=15 BC. Gothic parish church c1350. D=RCC.
309	WIEN (Vienna)	2,072,000	82.00	1,699,000	99.43	C	2,119,000	Danube River. 30 museums. St. Stephen's Cathedral c1150. Roman Vindobonda. D=RCC.
	AZERBAIJAN	**7,734,000**	**4.63**	**358,000**	**36.99**	**A**	**9,403,000**	**ORTHODOX 4.4%, ROMAN CATHOLICS 0.1%. PENT-CHAR 0.1%, EVANGELICAL 0.01%, GCC 1.6%**
310	rural areas	3,306,000	0.64	21,200	29.00	A	2,949,000	53.7% (1950), 50.0% (1970), 45.5% (1990), 42.7% (2000), 38.4% (2010), 31.3% (2025)
311	urban areas	4,428,000	7.60	337,000	42.96	A	6,454,000	46.2% (1950), 49.9% (1970), 54.4% (1990), 57.2% (2000), 61.5% (2010), 68.6% (2025)
312	non-metropolitan areas	1,813,000	7.60	138,000	42.95	A	2,687,709	*Sources of data:* Censuses of 1959, 1970, 1979, and 1989.
313	metropolitan areas	2,616,000	7.60	199,000	42.97	A	3,766,000	*Definition:* Cities and urban-type localities, officially designated as such by each of the constituent republics.
314	Ali-Bajramly	68,000	2.00	1,400	34.36	A	99,100	East. Kura River. Textiles. 98% Muslim.
315	BAKU	1,946,000	8.60	167,000	44.46	A	2,790,000	On Caspian Sea. Oil industry, most wells now dried up. Cultural center for Azerbaijanis. F=BC. D=AAC.
316	Sumgait	261,000	8.00	20,900	43.86	A	381,000	Mouth of Sumgait River. Major chemical & metallurgy center, aluminum, steel. F=1944.
317	Kirovabad (Gandzha, Gyandzha)	302,000	8.00	24,200	43.86	A	440,000	On Gyandzha River. Alumina, machinery, instruments, agriculture, carpets. F=5th century. Mosque (1920).
318	Mingecaur	101,000	2.00	2,000	34.36	A	146,000	On Kura River. Cotton textile mill. Large reservoir provides hydroelectric power.
319	Nachicevan	68,200	1.00	680	33.36	A	99,400	Nakhichevan Republic near Iranian border. Wine, dairy products, furniture. F=1500 BC(myth-by Noah).
320	Seki (Nucha)	69,900	2.00	1,400	34.36	A	102,000	In Great Caucasus Range. Historic palaces, mosques, baths. Silk weaving. Ancient origins.
321	Stepanakert	61,000	3.00	1,800	35.36	A	89,000	Nagorno-Karabakh. Mountainous. Majority Azerbaijani but many Armenians. Early 1990s conflict. D=AAC.
	BAHAMAS	**307,000**	**87.06**	**267,000**	**99.72**	**C**	**415,000**	**PROTESTANTS 54.5%, ROMAN CATHOLICS 15.6%. PENT-CHAR 15.9%, EVANGELICAL 29.5%, GCC 13.2%**
322	rural areas	35,200	95.20	33,500	99.87	C	31,200	23.2% (1950), 28.2% (1970), 16.3% (1990), 11.4% (2000), 9.1% (2010), 7.5% (2025)
323	urban areas	271,000	86.00	233,000	99.70	C	383,000	76.7% (1950), 71.7% (1970), 83.6% (1990), 88.5% (2000), 90.9% (2010), 92.4% (2025)
324	non-metropolitan areas	109,000	86.00	93,400	99.76	C	153,509	*Sources of data:* Censuses of 1963, 1970, 1980, and 1990.
325	metropolitan areas	163,000	86.00	140,000	99.66	C	230,000	*Definition:* Urban centers.
326	NASSAU	163,000	86.00	140,000	99.66	C	230,000	Capital & resort on New Providence Island. Tourism. F=1729. Anglican Christ Church Cathedral. D=Baptist.
	BAHRAIN	**617,000**	**10.16**	**62,700**	**57.21**	**B**	**858,000**	**INDEPENDENTS 4.3%, ROMAN CATHOLICS 4.0%. PENT-CHAR 4.6%, EVANGELICAL 0.6%, GCC 3.4%**
327	rural areas	47,900	2.53	1,200	34.09	A	38,400	36.1% (1950), 21.3% (1970), 12.4% (1990), 7.7% (2000), 5.5% (2010), 4.4% (2025)
328	urban areas	569,000	10.80	61,500	59.15	B	820,000	63.8% (1950), 78.6% (1970), 87.5% (1990), 92.2% (2000), 94.4% (2010), 95.5% (2025)
329	non-metropolitan areas	193,000	10.80	20,800	59.15	B	277,784	*Sources of data:* Censuses of 1950, 1959, 1965, 1971, 1981, and 1991.
330	metropolitan areas	376,000	10.80	40,700	59.15	B	542,000	*Definition:* Communes or villages with 2,500 or more inhabitants.
331	AL-MANAMAH (Manama)	376,000	10.80	40,700	59.15	B	542,000	On Persian Gulf. Finance, fishing, oil. F=1345. American Mission Hospital. 'Place of Sleeping'.
332	Al-Muharraq	108,000	11.00	11,800	59.35	B	155,000	On Al Muharraq island. Traditional Arab town. Many Manama commuters. Bahrain International Airport. Arab Fort.
333	Jidd Hafs	66,200	11.00	7,300	59.35	B	95,300	Many Manama commuters. One of world's hottest places.
	BANGLADESH	**129,155,000**	**0.72**	**932,000**	**57.21**	**B**	**178,751,000**	**INDEPENDENTS 0.4%, ROMAN CATHOLICS 0.1%. PENT-CHAR 0.3%, EVANGELICAL 0.06%, GCC 0.4%**
334	rural areas	101,800,000	0.59	603,000	56.27	B	112,041,000	95.7% (1950), 92.3% (1970), 84.3% (1990), 78.8% (2000), 72.5% (2010), 62.6% (2025)
335	urban areas	27,355,000	1.20	328,000	60.69	B	66,710,000	4.2% (1950), 7.6% (1970), 15.6% (1990), 21.1% (2000), 27.5% (2010), 37.3% (2025)

Table 10-5–continued opposite

Table 10-5–continued

Rec No 1	Country City 2	Pop 2000 3	AC% 4	Church Members 5	E% 6	W 7	Pop 2025 8	Notes 9
336	non-metropolitan areas	7,570,000	1.24	94,200	60.55	B	22,399,916	*Sources of data:* Censuses of 1951, 1961, 1974, and 1981; estimate for 1991.
337	metropolitan areas	19,785,000	1.18	234,000	60.74	B	44,310,000	*Definition:* Places having a municipality (*Pourashava*), a town committee (*shahar*) or a cantonment board.
338	Barisal (Bakerganj)	257,000	1.80	4,600	61.29	B	627,000	On Ganges River delta. Jute, rice. F=1876. 2% Bihari, 2% Urdu. D=Baptists,Anglicans,RCC.
339	Begamganj	103,000	0.30	310	55.79	B	252,000	Chittagong. Near Bay of Bengal. Rice, tea, jute.
340	Bhairab Bazar	94,500	0.30	280	55.79	B	230,000	Dhaka. Meghna River. RR junction, river port. Trade center, rice, jute, oilseeds, salt, fish, cattle.
341	Bogra (Bagura)	102,000	0.30	310	55.79	B	249,000	Rajshahi. Commercial center. Rice, soap, matches, 6 colleges. F=1876.
342	Brahmanbaria	130,000	0.30	390	55.79	B	317,000	Chittagong. Near Bhairab Bazar, Meghna River. Rice, jute, oilseeds, bricks, brassware.
343	Chandpur	127,000	0.30	380	55.79	B	311,000	River port. Meghna River. Major jute pressing center, matches, plywood, oilseeds, RR terminus. F=1897.
344	Chittagong (Chittagram)	2,906,000	0.80	23,200	61.29	B	6,361,000	Port near Bay of Bengal. Rice, tea, jute. F=1864, but ancient origins. 10% tribals. D=RCC,BUB. M= ABWE.
345	Sitakunda	353,000	0.10	350	53.59	B	861,000	Chittagong. Bay of Bengal. Heavy annual rainfall. Rice, oilseeds, tobacco, noted Hindu temples, pilgrimage center.
346	Chuadanga	113,000	0.30	340	55.79	B	276,000	Khulna near India border. Trades in rice, jute, linseeds, sugarcane, large sugar processing plant.
347	Comilla (Kumilla)	274,000	0.63	1,700	57.12	B	667,000	Hides & skins, jute. F=1864. Strongly Hindu (22%) area; as many temples as mosques. 73% Muslim. 10% tribals.
348	DHAKA (Dacca)	10,979,000	1.40	154,000	61.89	B	23,820,000	On Dhaleswari River. 700 Mosques. 85% Muslim, 9% Hindu. 470 Christian workers (300 aliens). D=RCC.
349	Gulshan	320,000	0.50	1,600	56.99	B	781,000	North on Railway. Cottage industries, handicrafts. New housing developments. Golf course.
350	Mirpur	519,000	0.50	2,600	56.99	B	1,265,000	Northwest. Turag River. Zia International Airport.
351	Narayanganj	603,000	1.50	9,000	60.99	B	1,470,000	Southeast on Lakhya River. Large industrial concentration. Textiles, paper. Kadam Rasal shrine.
352	Tongi	141,000	0.30	420	55.79	B	343,000	North of Gulshan. New houses. Many bicycles.
353	Dinajpur	144,000	0.30	430	55.79	B	351,000	Rice, jute, sugarcane. Pala ruins (900 AD). University of Rajshahi.
354	Faridpur	99,000	0.30	300	55.79	B	241,000	Rail junction. Jute. F=1869. Muslim saint Farid-ud Din Masud shrine.
355	Gopalpur	47,200	0.30	140	55.79	B	115,000	Dhaka north of Tangail. Small branch of Jamuna River. Trading center for jute. College.
356	Jamalpur	136,000	0.30	410	55.79	B	333,000	Trade center for rice, jute, oilseeds, sugarcane, tobacco.
357	Jessore	221,000	0.70	1,600	57.19	B	540,000	On Bhairab River. Rice, sugarcane. F=1864. Muslim saint shrines. 67% Bengali, 15% Bihari, 7% Hindi, 5% Urdu.
358	Jhenida	71,300	0.30	210	55.79	B	174,000	Khulna near Tropic of Cancer. On distributary of Madhamati River. Rice, jute, linseed, sugarcane, pepper.
359	Khulna	1,229,000	0.64	7,900	60.13	B	2,739,000	Ganges River port. F=1884. 66% Bengali, 16% Bihari. 25% Hindu. D=BUB,AoG,RCC,CoG,Church of Bangladesh.
360	Kishorganj	77,700	0.30	230	55.79	B	190,000	Kundali Khal River port. Sugar & paper mills. F=1869. Rice, jute, oilseeds, large annual fair, sugar milling.
361	Kurigram	70,800	0.30	210	55.79	B	173,000	Northern Rajshahi on Jamuna River. Terminus of RR from Tista Village. Rice, jute, tobacco, oilseeds.
362	Kushtia	111,000	0.30	330	55.79	B	271,000	Trade center. Cotton, sugar, pottery. Originally part of Srn Kingdom. Overcome in 13th century by Afghans.
363	Madaripur	95,000	0.30	290	55.79	B	232,000	Dhaka on Arial Khan River. Faridpur district. Jute trade center, rice, oilseeds, sugar cane.
364	Mymensingh (Nasirabad)	284,000	8.00	22,700	74.49	B	692,000	On Brahmaputra River. Cotton, sugar. F=1869. 75% Bengali, 10% Garo. D=BBU(ABMS), Garo Baptist Union.
365	Naogaon	78,700	0.30	240	55.79	B	192,000	Rajshahi north of Rajshahi. Ganja growing center, silk weaving factory, rice, jute, oilseeds.
366	Narsingdi	114,000	0.30	340	55.79	B	279,000	Dhaka near Meghna River. Jute collecting and trading center.
367	Nawabganj	130,000	0.30	390	55.79	B	318,000	Rajshahi near Indian border. RR terminus, rice, wheat, oilseed, jute, silk.
368	Noakhali (Sudharam)	87,800	0.30	260	55.79	B	214,000	Port. Cotton weaving, rice, jute. F=1876.
369	Pabna (Pubna)	162,000	1.20	1,900	59.69	B	395,000	On Ichamati River. Jute mills. F=1876. Hindu temple. 66% Bengali, 15% Bihari. 25% Hindu. D=BBU(ABMS),RCC.
370	Patuakhali	71,500	0.30	220	55.79	B	174,000	Trade center for rice, jute, oilseeds, sugarcane, betel nuts.
371	Rajshahi (Rampur Boalia)	377,000	1.80	6,800	61.29	B	920,000	On Ganges River. Silk. Industrial center. F=1876. 25% Hindu. D=Church of Sylhet,BUB,CoG,RCC.
372	Rangpur	228,000	0.20	460	54.69	B	555,000	On Little Ghaghet River. Cotton carpets. F=1869. 57% Bengali, 18% Bihari, 10% Hindi. 15% Hindu. D=BBU.
373	Saidpur	188,000	0.23	430	54.72	B	459,000	Railway terminus. Jute, exports. 56% Bengali, 18% Bihari, 10% Hindi, 6% tribal. 16% Hindu. D=BBU.
374	Satkhira	77,500	0.30	230	55.79	B	189,000	Khulna in Ganges Delta. Near Basirhat, India.
375	Sherpur	71,700	0.30	220	55.79	B	175,000	Dhaka near Jamalpur. Trade center, jute, rice, mustard, sugarcane, ancient fort ruins.
376	Sirajganj	159,000	0.10	160	53.59	B	387,000	Trade center for jute. F=1869. Three colleges. 66% Bengali. 72% Muslim, 25% Hindu. No organized churches.
377	Sylhet (Srihatta)	250,000	0.80	2,000	57.29	B	610,000	Center of Islamic culture. F=1878. Shah Jalal Mosque. 66% Bengali, 12% Bihari. D=Church of Sylhet,RCC.
378	Tangail	115,000	0.30	350	55.79	B	281,000	Handloom & cotton weaving, rice, jute.
	BARBADOS	**270,000**	**72.79**	**197,000**	**99.20**	**C**	**297,000**	**PROTESTANTS 31.4%, ANGLICANS 28.5%. PENT-CHAR 18.0%, EVANGELICAL 29.7%, GCC 18.4%**
379	rural areas	135,000	73.58	99,500	99.99	C	108,000	66.1% (1950), 62.9% (1970), 55.2% (1990), 50.0% (2000), 44.3% (2010), 36.3% (2025)
380	urban areas	135,000	72.00	97,300	98.41	C	189,000	33.8% (1950), 37.0% (1970), 44.7% (1990), 49.9% (2000), 55.6% (2010), 63.6% (2025)
381	non-metropolitan areas	11,500	72.00	8,300	98.41	C	16,061	*Sources of data:* Censuses of 1960, 1970, 1980 and 1990.
382	metropolitan areas	124,000	72.00	89,100	98.41	C	173,000	*Definition:* Bridgetown.
383	BRIDGETOWN	124,000	72.00	89,100	98.41	C	173,000	Formerly St. Michael's. Sugar, rum, gardens. F=1628. St. Michael's Anglican Church. D=Anglican,RCC,SDA.
	BELGIUM	**10,161,000**	**83.84**	**8,519,000**	**97.84**	**C**	**9,918,000**	**ROMAN CATHOLICS 80.9%, PROTESTANTS 1.2%. PENT-CHAR 2.9%, EVANGELICAL 0.2%, GCC 46.0%**
384	rural areas	269,000	88.83	239,000	99.32	C	177,000	8.5% (1950), 5.6% (1970), 3.4% (1990), 2.6% (2000), 2.1% (2010), 1.7% (2025)
385	urban areas	9,892,000	83.70	8,280,000	97.80	C	9,741,000	91.4% (1950), 94.3% (1970), 96.5% (1990), 97.3% (2000), 97.8% (2010), 98.2% (2025)
386	non-metropolitan areas	5,160,000	84.08	4,339,000	97.81	C	5,063,690	*Sources of data:* Censuses of 1947, 1961, 1970, and 1981; estimate for 1991.
387	metropolitan areas	4,732,000	83.29	3,941,000	97.79	C	4,678,000	*Definition:* Cities, urban agglomerations and urban communes.
388	BRUXELLES (Brussels)	1,122,000	82.50	926,000	96.50	C	1,123,000	World port. Headquarters of European Community & NATO. F=c AD 200. Church of la Chappelle. D=RCC.
389	Antwerpen (Antwerp)	1,141,000	81.00	924,000	96.00	C	1,123,000	Capital of Antwerp on Schelde River. Flemish. World trade center. Cathedral of the Holy Virgin c1350. F=c 800.
390	Brugge (Bruges)	231,000	83.00	192,000	98.50	C	228,000	Capital of West Flanders. Tourism. Evangelized by St. Eloi (c850). Many Cathedrals. 'City of bridges'. D=RCC.
391	Aalst (Alost)	80,000	82.00	65,600	97.00	C	78,800	On Dender River. F=c850. First Belgian printing press (1473). Gothic St. Martin's Church c1480. D=RCC.
392	Anderlecht	92,100	84.00	77,400	99.00	C	90,700	Original site of Brussels. Church of Saints Peter & Guidon (c1000). Home of Erasmus. D=RCC.
393	Bruxelles	143,000	83.00	119,000	98.50	C	141,000	World port. Headquarters of European Community & NATO. Banking, finance. Free University. D=RCC.
394	Etterbeek	45,900	83.00	38,100	98.50	C	45,200	Primarily industrial. F=c1120. D=RCC.
395	Forest (Vorst)	50,100	82.00	41,000	98.00	C	49,300	Vehicles, chemicals, paper, beer. Abbey of Saint Benoit 1106. D=RCC.
396	Ixelles (Elsene)	79,100	81.50	64,400	96.50	C	77,900	Metals, chemicals, textiles. Cistercian Abbey of La Cambre 1201. D=RCC.
397	Molenbeek-St-Jean	72,300	84.00	60,800	99.00	C	71,200	Leather, clothing, chemicals. Many foreigners. D=RCC.
398	Schaerbeek (Schaarbeek)	109,000	83.00	90,300	98.00	C	107,000	Rail junction, industry. Domed church Sainte-Marie (1845). Brussels American School (BAS). D=RCC.
399	Uccle (Ukkel)	78,700	82.00	64,500	97.00	C	77,500	Residential. F=c1150. Russian Orthodox church. Royal observatory. D=RCC.
400	Woluwe-Saint-Lambert	49,700	82.50	41,000	98.50	C	48,900	East near Schaerbeek. D=RCC.
401	Charleroi	498,000	80.00	398,000	96.00	C	490,000	On Sambre River. Coal mining, iron, steel, machinery, glass blowing. F=1666.
402	Gent (Gand, Ghent)	482,000	85.00	410,000	99.00	C	475,000	Capital of East Flanders. Chief textile center. F=650. 7th century monasteries. 'City of flowers'. D=RCC.
403	Hasselt	301,000	83.00	250,000	98.00	C	296,000	Capital of Limburg province. Market town, distilleries. Church of St. Quentin c1350. D=RCC.
404	Genk (Genck)	63,700	83.00	52,800	98.50	C	62,700	Resorts, coal, automobiles, natural gas. D=RCC.
405	Kortrijk (Courtrai)	209,000	83.00	174,000	98.50	C	206,000	On Leie River. Rail junction, flax, linen center. F=1190. 7th century chapel. Church of Notre Dame. D=RCC.
406	La Louviere	152,000	80.00	122,000	97.00	C	150,000	Coal, steel, ceramics. F=c1350. D=RCC.
407	Leuven (Louvain)	179,000	88.00	158,000	99.50	C	177,000	On Dijle River. Major cultural center. F=c850. Catholic University of Louvain (1425). D=RCC.
408	Liege (Luik)	778,000	85.00	661,000	99.00	C	766,000	Meuse & Ourthe river port. Glassworks. F=721. St. Lambert martyred 705. RCC, Bishopric since c750.
409	Seraing	64,000	85.00	54,400	99.00	C	63,000	Southwest. Meuse River. D=RCC.
410	Mechelen (Malines)	125,000	90.00	113,000	99.80	C	124,000	On Dijle River. Lace. F=756. Church of St. Rumoldus (c1250). Van Dyke's 'Crucifixion'. R=CCC.
411	Mons (Bergen)	251,000	82.00	206,000	98.00	C	247,000	Capital of Hainaut. City of schools. F=c650. Church of St. Waudru (1450). Annual St. George festival. D=RCC.
412	Mouscron (Moeskroen)	55,700	88.00	49,000	99.50	C	54,900	Textiles, wheat, flax. Saint Bartholomew's Church (c1450). D=RCC.
413	Namur (Namen)	152,000	80.00	122,000	97.00	C	150,000	Capital of Namur. Rail junction, art, tourism. F=908. Many cathedrals & convents. D=RCC.
414	Oostende (Ostende)	127,000	80.00	101,000	97.00	C	125,000	On North Sea. Fishing port, seaside resort, rail junction. F=c850. D=RCC.
415	Roeselare (Roulers)	53,900	85.00	45,800	99.00	C	53,100	Textiles, linen. Church of St. Michael (1497). D=RCC.
416	Sint-Niklaas (Saint-Nicolas)	70,600	85.00	60,000	99.00	C	69,500	Rail junction, huge marketplace, textiles. F=1241. Church of Saint-Niklaas (c1450).
417	Tournai (Doornik)	69,500	85.00	59,100	99.00	C	68,400	Ardennes mountains. Tapestry, copperware. F=c450. Cathedral of Notre Dame (c1050). D=RCC.
418	Verviers	105,000	83.00	86,900	98.00	C	103,000	On Schelde River near French border. Wool. D=RCC.
	BELIZE	**241,000**	**81.90**	**197,000**	**97.86**	**C**	**370,000**	**ROMAN CATHOLICS 56.8%, PROTESTANTS 16.4%. PENT-CHAR 13.0%, EVANGELICAL 7.1%, GCC 11.9%**
419	rural areas	129,000	80.94	104,000	96.90	C	159,000	42.9% (1950), 49.0% (1970), 52.5% (1990), 53.4% (2000), 51.2% (2010), 43.0% (2025)
420	urban areas	112,000	83.00	92,900	98.96	C	211,000	57.1% (1950), 50.9% (1970), 47.4% (1990), 46.5% (2000), 48.7% (2010), 56.9% (2025)
421	non-metropolitan areas	48,600	82.86	40,200	98.96	C	91,430	*Sources of data:* Censuses of 1960, 1970, 1980, and 1991.
422	metropolitan areas	63,400	83.11	52,700	98.96	C	119,000	*Definition:* Urban centers.
423	Belize City (Belice)	56,600	83.00	47,000	98.96	C	107,000	Former capital. Chief seaport. Sugar, timber, fishing. St. John's Anglican Cathedral (1812). D=RCC,Anglican.
424	BELMOPAN	6,800	84.00	5,700	98.96	C	12,800	Capital since 1970. F=1966 after hurricane devastated Belize City in 1961. D=RCC,Anglican.
	BELORUSSIA	**10,236,000**	**64.32**	**6,584,000**	**99.15**	**C**	**9,496,000**	**ORTHODOX 48.7%, ROMAN CATHOLICS 13.1%. PENT-CHAR 0.9%, EVANGELICAL 0.3%, GCC 21.1%**
425	rural areas	2,618,000	65.26	1,709,000	99.50	C	1,628,000	77.3% (1950), 56.1% (1970), 33.1% (1990), 25.5% (2000), 21.0% (2010), 17.1% (2025)
426	urban areas	7,618,000	64.00	4,875,000	99.03	C	7,868,000	22.6% (1950), 43.8% (1970), 66.8% (1990), 74.4% (2000), 79.0% (2010), 82.8% (2025)
427	non-metropolitan areas	2,347,000	64.32	1,510,000	99.01	C	2,444,703	*Sources of data:* Censuses of 1959, 1970, 1979, and 1989.
428	metropolitan areas	5,270,000	63.86	3,365,000	99.04	C	5,423,000	*Definition:* Cities and urban-type localities, officially designated as such by each of the constituent republics.
429	Baranovici (Baranovichi)	164,000	63.00	103,000	98.63	C	170,000	Brest in Novogrudok Hills. Cotton, food-processing, machines. F=19th century. D=ROC.
430	Bobrujsk (Bobruisk)	220,000	64.00	141,000	99.03	C	227,000	Mogilyov on Berezina River. Engineering, machine building. F=16th century. Major WWII battle. D=ROC.
431	Borisov	148,000	63.00	93,200	98.63	C	153,000	Minsk on Berezina river. Timber working, plastics. F=12th century. D=ROC.
432	Brest (Brest Litovsk, Brzesc)	273,000	62.00	169,000	98.43	C	282,000	Brest on Bug River. River port. F=1019 as Berestye. 1918 treaty between Russians & Germans. D=ROC.
433	Gomel' (Homei)	496,000	63.00	312,000	98.63	C	512,000	Gomel on Sozh River. Important port, fertilizer, machinery, forestry research. F=1142. D=ROC.
434	Grodno (Gardinas)	281,000	64.00	180,000	98.83	C	290,000	Grodno on Neman River. Fertilizers, synthetic fibers. F=1128. Capital of Lithuania in 14th century. D=ROC.
435	Lida	93,600	66.00	61,800	99.83	C	96,700	Grodno. Food processing, agricultural machinery. F=13th century. 14th century Gediminas Castle. D=ROC.
436	MINSK	1,862,000	64.00	1,192,000	99.03	C	1,903,000	On Svisloch River. Educational, cultural, printing center. F=1067. 40% Jewish before WWII. D=ROC.
437	Mogil'ov (Mogilev, Mogilyov)	358,000	65.00	232,000	99.83	C	369,000	Mogilyov on Dnepr River. Synthetic fibers, industrial equipment. F=1267. Four 16-17th century churches. D=ROC.
438	Molodecno	92,100	66.00	60,800	99.83	C	95,200	Minsk. Diverse food & other light industries. Railway junction since late 19th century. Destroyed in WWII. D=ROC.
439	Mozyr'	101,000	66.00	67,000	99.83	C	105,000	Gomel on Pripyat River. Oil refining, machine building, salt deposits, handicraft. F=12th century. D=ROC.
440	Novopolock	95,200	65.00	61,900	99.83	C	98,300	Vitebsk near Polock on western Dvina River. D=ROC.
441	Orsa (Orsha)	123,000	64.00	79,000	99.03	C	128,000	Vitebsk on Dnepr River. Major focus of trade routes throughout history. F=1067. D=ROC.
442	Pinsk	122,000	65.00	79,300	99.83	C	126,000	Brest at confluence of Pina & Pripyat rivers. River port, woodworking, metalworking. F=1097. D=ROC.
443	Polock (Polotsk)	77,500	62.00	48,100	98.43	C	80,100	Vitebsk on western Dvina River. Oil refining, petrochemicals, glass fibers. Major trade centers. F=862. D=ROC.
444	Recica (Rechitsa)	68,400	65.00	44,400	99.83	C	70,600	Gomel on Dnepr River. Furniture, engineering, nails, pipes, petroleum. F=12th century. D=ROC.
445	Sluck (Slutsk)	59,200	66.00	39,100	99.83	C	61,200	Minsk. Weaving, working of gold & silver, furniture, linens. F=12th century. Incorporated 1795. D=ROC.
446	Soligorsk	94,600	66.00	62,400	99.83	C	97,700	Minsk. Potash, precast concrete. Chemical engineering college. F=1949. D=ROC.
447	Svetlogorsk	70,500	64.00	45,100	99.03	C	72,900	Near Gomel. North Gomel Oblast, Berczina River. Power plant, concrete, baker, pulp. D=ROC.
448	Vitebsk	356,000	62.00	221,000	98.43	C	368,000	Vitebsk on Western Dvina River. Textiles, meat & dairy products. F=1021 as major fortress. D=ROC.
449	Zlobin	59,900	63.00	37,700	98.63	C	61,900	Gomel on Dneper River. D=ROC.
450	Zodino	55,200	64.00	35,300	99.03	C	57,000	Minsk northeast of Minsk. D=ROC.

Table 10-5–continued overleaf

Table 10-5–continued

Rec No 1	Country City 2	Pop 2000 3	AC% 4	Church Members 5	E% 6	W 7	Pop 2025 8	Notes 9
	BENIN	**6,097,000**	**27.63**	**1,684,000**	**74.18**	**B**	**11,109,000**	**ROMAN CATHOLICS 20.7%, PROTESTANTS 3.7%. PENT-CHAR 5.6%, EVANGELICAL 1.8%, GCC 16.4%**
451	rural areas	3,520,000	21.49	756,000	67.32	B	4,585,000	95.0% (1950), 83.3% (1970), 65.5% (1990), 57.7% (2000), 50.3% (2010), 41.2% (2025)
452	urban areas	2,577,000	36.00	928,000	83.55	B	6,525,000	4.9% (1950), 16.6% (1970), 34.4% (1990), 42.2% (2000), 49.6% (2010), 58.7% (2025)
453	non-metropolitan areas	1,304,000	36.08	470,000	83.51	B	3,301,522	*Sources of data:* Survey of 1961; census of 1992; estimate for 1979.
454	metropolitan areas	1,273,000	35.92	457,000	83.59	B	3,223,000	*Definition:* Localities with 10,000 or more inhabitants.
455	Abomey	85,700	30.00	25,700	76.55	B	217,000	Southern Zou near Bohicon. Former capital of Dahomean Empire. Palm nuts, peanuts, weaving.
456	Cotonou	773,000	37.00	286,000	85.05	B	1,958,000	De facto capital & port city. Breweries, palm oil. Supreme Court & National Assembly. F=1851. D=RCC.
457	Parakou	149,000	30.00	44,600	76.55	B	377,000	Southern Borgou. Rail junction. Transport route with links to Niger. D=RCC.
458	PORTO-NOVO	265,000	38.00	101,000	85.55	B	672,000	National archives, library. F=c1580. Old Portuguese cathedral. Historical center of slave trade. D=RCC.
	BERMUDA	**64,600**	**86.20**	**55,700**	**99.81**	**C**	**75,600**	**ANGLICANS 37.4%, PROTESTANTS 30.1%. PENT-CHAR 20.7%, EVANGELICAL 11.9%, GCC 17.5%**
459	rural areas	–	–	–	–	–	–	0.0% (1950), 0.0% (1970), 0.0% (1990), 0.0% (2000), 0.0% (2010), 0.0% (2025)
460	urban areas	64,600	86.20	55,700	99.81	C	75,600	100.0% (1950), 100.0% (1970), 100.0% (1990), 100.0% (2000), 100.0% (2010), 100.0% (2025)
461	non-metropolitan areas	47,100	86.20	40,600	99.81	C	55,195	*Sources of data:* Censuses of 1950, 1960, 1970, 1980, and 1991.
462	metropolitan areas	17,400	86.20	15,000	99.81	C	20,400	*Definition:* Entire population.
463	HAMILTON	17,400	86.20	15,000	99.81	C	20,400	Tourism. F=1790. Gothic cathedral on Church St. D=Anglican,RCC,Methodist,SDA.
	BHUTAN	**2,124,000**	**0.45**	**9,600**	**20.76**	**A**	**3,904,000**	**INDEPENDENTS 0.2%, PROTESTANTS 0.1%. PENT-CHAR 0.2%, EVANGELICAL 0.05%, GCC 0.4%**
464	rural areas	1,972,000	0.37	7,400	20.44	A	3,296,000	97.9% (1950), 96.9% (1970), 94.8% (1990), 92.8% (2000), 90.1% (2010), 84.4% (2025)
465	urban areas	152,000	1.50	2,300	24.81	A	608,000	2.1% (1950), 3.1% (1970), 5.1% (1990), 7.1% (2000), 9.8% (2010), 15.5% (2025)
466	non-metropolitan areas	130,000	1.43	1,900	24.77	A	521,630	*Sources of data:* Estimates for 1950, 1960, and 1970.
467	metropolitan areas	21,500	1.94	420	25.05	A	86,200	*Definition:* Urban centers.
468	Paro	4,400	1.70	74	24.01	A	17,400	Administrative capital. Agriculture. Cultural center. Fort Paro with seven story tower. Temples, lamas.
469	THIMPHU (Thimbu)	17,200	2.00	340	25.31	A	68,800	Rice, corn, wheat. Monasteries. 50% Bhotia, 25% Nepali, 20% Assamese. 47% Buddhist. D=Assemblies,RCC.
	BOLIVIA	**8,329,000**	**93.49**	**7,786,000**	**99.71**	**C**	**13,131,000**	**ROMAN CATHOLICS 88.2%, PROTESTANTS 6.3%. PENT-CHAR 14.5%, EVANGELICAL 4.5%, GCC 20.7%**
470	rural areas	2,928,000	94.39	2,764,000	99.68	C	3,006,000	62.2% (1950), 59.2% (1970), 44.4% (1990), 35.1% (2000), 28.5% (2010), 22.8% (2025)
471	urban areas	5,400,000	93.00	5,022,000	99.72	C	10,125,000	37.7% (1950), 40.7% (1970), 55.5% (1990), 64.8% (2000), 71.4% (2010), 77.1% (2025)
472	non-metropolitan areas	1,604,000	93.40	1,499,000	99.70	C	3,295,231	*Sources of data:* Censuses of 1950, 1976 and 1992.
473	metropolitan areas	3,796,000	92.83	3,524,000	99.73	C	6,830,000	*Definition:* Localities with 2,000 or more inhabitants.
474	Cochabamba	524,000	93.00	487,000	99.92	C	982,000	Capital of Cochabamba. El. 8,392 ft. Architecture, gardens, agriculture. F=1574 as Villa de Oropeza. D=RCC.
475	LA PAZ	1,458,000	92.00	1,341,000	99.42	C	2,510,000	Seat of government. World's highest capital 10,650-13,250 ft. F=1548 by Spanish conquistadors. D=RCC.
476	Oruro	263,000	93.00	245,000	99.92	C	493,000	Capital of Oruro. El. 12,160 ft. Tin refinery. F=1606 as Real Villa de San Felipe de Austria. D=RCC.
477	Potosi	152,000	95.00	145,000	99.92	C	285,000	Highest city in the world (14,000 ft). Leading industrial city, mining. F=1545. Pop. 160,000 in 1650. D=RCC.
478	Santa Cruz	1,110,000	93.00	1,032,000	99.92	C	2,018,000	Trade center for tropical & subtropical crops. F=1561. Early Jesuit missionary center. D=RCC.
479	Sucre (La Plata, Charcas)	128,000	94.50	121,000	99.92	C	241,000	Constitutional Capital city. Commercial & agricultural center. F=1539. RCC archbishopric.
480	Tarija	94,500	95.00	89,800	99.92	C	177,000	Agriculture for local consumption. Vineyards & orchards. F=1574. Outdoor religious processions. D=RCC.
481	Trinidad	65,800	95.00	62,500	99.92	C	123,000	Capital of Beni on Mamore River. Sugar refinery. Sugarcane, rice, beef, cotton. University. D=RCC.
	BOSNIA-HERZEGOVINA	**3,972,000**	**34.89**	**1,386,000**	**73.67**	**B**	**4,324,000**	**ORTHODOX 17.6%, ROMAN CATHOLICS 17.1%. PENT-CHAR 0.8%, EVANGELICAL 0.01%, GCC 9.2%**
482	rural areas	2,258,000	35.57	803,000	73.59	B	1,861,000	86.3% (1950), 72.8% (1970), 60.6% (1990), 56.8% (2000), 51.8% (2010), 43.0% (2025)
483	urban areas	1,713,000	34.00	583,000	73.78	B	2,463,000	13.6% (1950), 27.2% (1970), 39.3% (1990), 43.1% (2000), 48.1% (2010), 56.9% (2025)
484	non-metropolitan areas	519,000	34.00	176,000	74.02	B	745,582	*Sources of data:* Censuses of 1953, 1961, and 1971 and 1981.
485	metropolitan areas	1,195,000	34.00	406,000	73.68	B	1,718,000	*Definition:* Urban centers.
486	Banja Luka	196,000	36.00	70,700	75.78	B	282,000	On Vrbas River. Turkish character. Leather goods, iron. Thermal springs. F=c200 as Roman fort. Mosque. D=RCC.
487	Mostar	118,000	20.00	23,600	53.78	B	170,000	On Neretva River. Surrounded by vineyards. Wine, textiles, tobacco. F=1566 by Turks. D=RCC.
488	Prijedor	116,000	36.00	41,900	75.78	B	167,000	North, Kozara mountains. On Sana River. Wood pulp mfg., iron ore, coal deposits. D=RCC.
489	SARAJEVO	486,000	35.00	170,000	76.28	B	698,000	On Miljacka River. Strong Muslim character. Carpets. F=14th century. Mosque (1530). D=RCC.
490	Tuzla	132,000	37.00	48,700	76.78	B	189,000	In Tuzla Basin. Salt deposits, lignite mining, agriculture. F=10th century as Soli (salts). D=SOC,RCC.
491	Zenica	147,000	35.00	51,400	73.78	B	211,000	Central, Bosna River. Near Sarajevo. Railroad, lignite mine, iron and steel works, paper mills. D=SOC,RCC.
	BOTSWANA	**1,622,000**	**46.30**	**751,000**	**94.86**	**B**	**2,242,000**	**INDEPENDENTS 30.7%, PROTESTANTS 10.9%. PENT-CHAR 32.9%, EVANGELICAL 3.1%, GCC 23.6%**
492	rural areas	429,000	47.13	202,000	95.71	B	222,000	99.6% (1950), 91.5% (1970), 58.4% (1990), 26.4% (2000), 13.5% (2010), 9.9% (2025)
493	urban areas	1,193,000	46.00	549,000	94.56	B	2,020,000	0.3% (1950), 8.4% (1970), 41.5% (1990), 73.5% (2000), 86.4% (2010), 90.1% (2025)
494	non-metropolitan areas	934,000	45.96	429,000	94.54	B	1,580,830	*Sources of data:* Censuses of 1964, 1971, and 1981; estimate for 1993.
495	metropolitan areas	259,000	46.15	120,000	94.62	B	439,000	*Definition:* Agglomeration of 5,000 or more inhabitants where 75% of economic activity is non-agricultural.
496	Francistown	84,800	30.00	25,400	88.56	B	144,000	Administrative & commercial center. Tati River. Farming. First mine discovered in South Africa (1880s). D=RCC.
497	GABORONE (Gaberone)	175,000	54.00	94,200	97.56	B	295,000	Capital since 1965. University of Botswana. Gaborone Dam. D=UCCSA,RCC.
	BOUGAINVILLE	**198,000**	**93.37**	**185,000**	**99.87**	**C**	**286,000**	**ROMAN CATHOLICS 74.7%, PROTESTANTS 11.4%. PENT-CHAR 4.6%, EVANGELICAL 2.6%, GCC 8.1%**
498	rural areas	159,000	93.46	148,000	99.99	C	186,000	91.7% (1950), 91.0% (1970), 85.4% (1990), 80.0% (2000), 74.4% (2010), 64.9% (2025)
499	urban areas	39,700	93.00	36,900	99.40	C	100,000	8.2% (1950), 8.9% (1970), 14.5% (1990), 20.0% (2000), 25.5% (2010), 35.0% (2025)
500	non-metropolitan areas	19,700	93.00	18,300	99.40	C	49,701	*Sources of data:* Censuses.
501	metropolitan areas	20,000	93.00	18,600	99.40	C	50,500	*Definition:* Arawa.
502	Arawa	20,000	93.00	18,600	99.40	C	50,500	Southwest Pacific, Solomon Islands chain. Copra, ivory nuts, green snails. F=1768. D=RCC.
	BRAZIL	**170,115,000**	**91.39**	**155,476,000**	**99.75**	**C**	**217,930,000**	**ROMAN CATHOLICS 90.1%, PROTESTANTS 17.7%. PENT-CHAR 47.0%, EVANGELICAL 16.3%, GCC 14.2%**
503	rural areas	31,846,000	95.28	30,341,000	99.97	C	25,846,000	64.0% (1950), 44.1% (1970), 25.2% (1990), 18.7% (2000), 14.7% (2010), 11.8% (2025)
504	urban areas	138,270,000	90.50	125,134,000	99.70	C	192,083,000	35.9% (1950), 55.8% (1970), 74.7% (1990), 81.2% (2000), 85.2% (2010), 88.1% (2025)
505	non-metropolitan areas	46,000,000	91.45	42,068,000	99.68	C	73,477,681	*Sources of data:* Censuses of 1950, 1960, 1970, 1980, and 1991.
506	metropolitan areas	92,270,000	90.03	83,066,000	99.71	C	118,606,000	*Definition:* Urban and suburban zones of administrative centers of municipalities and districts.
507	Alagoinhas	151,000	89.00	135,000	99.36	C	210,000	Bahia. Oranges, bananas, lemons, dairies. F=1880. D=RCC.
508	Alegrete	93,100	90.00	83,800	99.61	C	129,000	Rio Grande do Sul. Meat-processing center. Cattle, sheep. F=1817. D=RCC.
509	Americana	202,000	90.00	182,000	99.61	C	281,000	Sao Paulo. Agriculture, corn, sugarcane, grapes, silk milling, hydroelectric plant. F=1868. D=RCC.
510	Anapolis	292,000	90.50	265,000	99.66	C	406,000	Goias. Commercial center. Lumber, rice, coffee. Praca Bom Jesus square. F=1907. D=RCC.
511	Apucarana	120,000	91.00	109,000	99.76	C	167,000	Northern Parana near Londrina. Railroad junction. Coffee region, rice, cotton, potatoes, kidney beans. D=RCC.
512	Aracaju	466,000	92.00	429,000	99.76	C	647,000	Port city and capital of Sergipe near mouth of Sergipe River. Leather, bananas, cassava. F=1855. D=RCC.
513	Aracatuba	167,000	90.00	151,000	99.61	C	233,000	Sao Paulo. Tiete River. Agriculture, cotton, coffee roasting, alcohol distilling, dairying. F=1908. D=RCC.
514	Araguari (Freguesia do Brejo Alegre)	124,000	92.00	114,000	99.76	C	173,000	Minas Gerais. Cattle, rice, corn, soybeans, shipping center, hulling, tanneries, diamonds. F=1882. D=RCC.
515	Arapiraca	191,000	92.00	176,000	99.76	C	266,000	Alagoas north of Sao Francisco River. Cotton, fruit, mineral springs, phosphate deposits. D=RCC.
516	Araraquara	188,000	92.00	173,000	99.76	C	261,000	Sao Paulo. Sugarcane, coffee, textiles, very rich agriculture, milk products, cottonseed, distilling. F=1817. D=RCC.
517	Araras	92,800	90.00	83,500	99.61	C	129,000	Sao Paulo north of Campinas. Dairying center, food processing, brandy distilling, textile milling. D=RCC.
518	Araxa	79,500	90.00	71,600	99.61	C	110,000	Minas Gerais west of Belo Horizonte. Railroad, resort, sulphur springs, dairying, titanium mine, airport. D=RCC.
519	Assis	96,100	91.00	87,500	99.76	C	134,000	Sao Paulo. Coffee, cotton, corn, rice, cattle raising, railroad. F=1915. D=RCC.
520	Atibaia	97,400	90.00	87,700	99.61	C	135,000	Sao Paulo on Atibaia River. Sugarcane, corn, potatoes, meat packing, distilling. D=RCC.
521	Bacabal	117,000	89.00	104,000	99.36	C	163,000	Northeast Maranhao on Mearim River. Babasser nuts, rice, cotton. D=RCC.
522	Bage	137,000	90.00	124,000	99.61	C	191,000	Rio Grande do Sul. Cattle, sheep, wheat, beef jerking, wool shearing, horse trading, alfalfa. F=1811. D=RCC.
523	Barbacena	129,000	89.50	115,000	99.46	C	179,000	Minas Gerais. Trade, manufacturing, textiles, silk, ceramic, tobacco, footwear, glass, silk institute. F=1791. D=RCC.
524	Barra do Pirai	101,000	90.00	91,100	99.61	C	141,000	Rio de Janeiro. Textiles, metals, chemicals. Railroad, dairying, paper mill. D=RCC.
525	Barretos (Amaral dos Barretos)	104,000	90.00	93,400	99.61	C	144,000	Sao Paulo. Cattle, rice, bottled water, coffee, cotton, corn, sugar mills, dairies. F=1895. D=RCC.
526	Bauru (Divino Espirito da Fortaleza)	285,000	89.00	254,000	99.36	C	396,000	Sao Paulo. Agricultural & manufacturing center, cotton, citrus fruit, vinegar. F=1887. D=RCC.
527	Belem (Para)	1,634,000	88.00	1,438,000	99.36	C	2,099,000	Amazon port. Nuts, pepper. F=1655. Santo Alexandre church 1616. 10,000 Japanese. D=RCC.
528	Belo Horizonte	4,160,000	88.00	3,661,000	99.76	C	5,180,000	Minas Gerais. Agriculture, commerce, heavy industry. F=1897. 'Beautiful Horizon'. D=RCC. M=YWAM.
529	Betim	125,000	90.00	113,000	99.61	C	174,000	Minas Gerais. Railroad, agriculture, trade, intermittent streams. D=RCC.
530	Contagem	198,000	90.00	178,000	99.61	C	275,000	Espirito Santo on Doce River, states second largest city, industrial suburb. D=RCC.
531	Parque Industrial	296,000	90.00	266,000	99.61	C	411,000	Minas Gerais. Industry, agriculture. D=RCC.
532	Birigui	85,800	92.00	78,900	99.76	C	119,000	Parana on Tiete River near Aracatuba. Coffee growing center, cotton and rice, sawmilling. D=RCC.
533	Blumenau	249,000	90.00	224,000	99.61	C	345,000	Santa Catarina. Textiles. F=1852 by Germans. Heavily German. D=RCC.
534	Boa Vista	89,300	91.00	81,300	99.76	C	124,000	Roraima on Branco River near Guyana. Gold, bauxite, diamonds, alcohol, petroleum. D=RCC.
535	Botucatu	92,100	90.00	82,900	99.61	C	128,000	Sao Paulo. Crops, textiles, foundries, mills, machinery, footwear, clothing. F=1855. D=RCC.
536	Braganca Paulista	136,000	90.00	122,000	99.61	C	189,000	Para. Cotton, tobacco, cassava, lime kilns, coffee, rice, citrus fruit, grain, sugar. D=RCC.
537	BRASILIA	1,985,000	89.00	1,767,000	99.36	C	2,541,000	Governmental center, construction, printing, publishing. F=1956. 'City of the Sky'. D=RCC.
538	Cabo	162,000	90.00	145,000	99.61	C	224,000	Pernambuco. South of Recife on Atlantic Ocean. Sugar milling, alcohol distilling, coffee, coconuts. D=RCC.
539	Cacapava	83,100	93.00	77,300	99.76	C	115,000	Sao Paulo on President Dutra Road midway between Sao Jose dos Campos and Taubate. D=RCC.
540	Caceres	111,000	90.00	99,700	99.61	C	154,000	Southern Mato Grosso on Paraguai River near Bolivian border. D=RCC.
541	Cachoeira do Sul	118,000	89.00	105,000	99.36	C	165,000	Rio Grande do Sul. Rice, wool, wheat, fruit, livestock, grain, molybendom deposits. F=1819. D=RCC.
542	Cachoeiro de Itapemirim	179,000	90.50	162,000	99.66	C	248,000	Espirito Santo. Manufacturing, livestock, cement, cotton goods, rum, refined sugar. F=1889. D=RCC.
543	Campina Grande	362,000	94.00	341,000	99.76	C	503,000	Paraiba. Commercial center. Cotton, beans, textiles. F=1864. Art museum, regional university. D=RCC.
544	Campinas (Sao Carlos)	1,857,000	88.50	1,643,000	99.46	C	2,420,000	Sao Paulo. Coffee, industry. F=1797. Pontificia Universidade Catolica de Campinas, 1941. D=RCC.
545	Campo Grande	498,000	91.00	453,000	99.76	C	691,000	Capital of Mato Grosso do Sul. Agriculture, cattle, tea, coffee, corn. D=RCC.
546	Campos	475,000	88.00	418,000	98.76	C	660,000	Rio de Janeiro. Cacao, sugarcane, oil, rice, beans, coffee, distilleries. F=early 17th century. D=RCC.
547	Carazinho	80,400	91.00	73,200	99.76	C	112,000	Rio Grande do Sul on Rio de Vaizea. Near Passo Fundo. D=RCC.
548	Carpina	86,000	92.00	79,200	97.36	C	120,000	Pernambuco near Recife. Near Atlantic coast. Railroad, sugar, farming. D=RCC.
549	Caruaru	247,000	90.00	222,000	99.61	C	343,000	Pernambuco. Market center, agriculture, livestock. F=1857. Religious festivals. D=RCC.
550	Cascavel	260,000	89.00	231,000	99.36	C	361,000	Western Parana near Paraguay. Livestock, airport. D=RCC.
551	Castanhal	116,000	90.00	105,000	99.61	C	161,000	Para east of Belem, near Guama River. Nuts, jute, pepper, major highway. D=RCC.
552	Cataguases	74,400	92.00	68,500	99.76	C	103,000	Minas Gerais on Pomba River, Novo River. Railroad, primary roads, livestock, rural farming. D=RCC.
553	Catanduva	104,000	91.00	94,600	99.76	C	144,000	Sao Paulo. Coffee, hides & skins. F=1909. Originally Vila Adolfo. D=RCC.
554	Caxias	192,000	92.00	177,000	99.76	C	267,000	Maranhao. Formerly Sao Jose das Aldeias Altas. F=1837. RCC bishopric.
555	Caxias do Sul	345,000	90.00	311,000	99.61	C	480,000	Rio Grande do Sul. Metals, vineyards. F=1875 by Italian immigrants. Annual wine festival. D=RCC.
556	Chapeco	131,000	90.00	118,000	99.61	C	182,000	Western Santa Catarina near Uruguay River. Lumber, livestock, mate. D=RCC.
557	Colatina	138,000	90.50	124,000	99.11	C	191,000	Espirito Santo. Transportation, trade, manufacturing center. Coffee, lumber. F=1921. D=RCC.
558	Conselheiro Lafaiete (Lueluz)	101,000	91.00	91,800	99.76	C	140,000	Minas Gerais. Agriculture, livestock, manganese mining, steel industry. F=1886. D=RCC.
559	Corumba	104,000	92.00	96,100	99.76	C	145,000	Mato Grosso do Sul. River port. Manganese, iron ore. Wildlife preserve. F=1778 by Jesuits. D=RCC.

Table 10-5–continued opposite

Table 10-5–continued

Rec No 1	Country City 2	Pop 2000 3	AC% 4	Church Members 5	E% 6	W 7	Pop 2025 8	Notes 9
560	Crato	112,000	92.00	103,000	99.76	C	155,000	Southern Ceara near Juazeiro do Norte. Railroad, cattle, hides, skins, cotton, rubber, gypsum quarry. D=RCC.
561	Criciuma	166,000	90.00	150,000	99.61	C	231,000	Santa Catarina. Coal mining center, hog, cattle, lard and bacon processing, export. F=1925. D=RCC.
562	Cruz Alta	93,000	94.00	87,400	99.76	C	129,000	Rio Grande do Sul. Cattle raising, agricultural area. F=1834. D=RCC.
563	Cruzeiro (Embau, Boa Vista)	82,700	93.00	77,000	99.76	C	115,000	Sao Paulo. Food processing, sugarcane, manufacturing. F=1801. D=RCC.
564	Cuiaba	362,000	90.00	326,000	99.61	C	503,000	Capital of Mato Grosso. Agriculture, stock raising. F=1719 by gold hunters. D=RCC.
565	Curitiba	2,519,000	89.00	2,242,000	99.56	C	3,207,000	Capital of Parana. Textiles, autos. Tourism. F=1654. Catholic University (1959). D=RCC.
566	Colombo	85,300	92.00	78,500	99.76	C	119,000	Parana. North of Curitiba. Trade, livestock, farming, ceramics, paints, soft drinks. D=RCC.
567	Pinheirinho	66,800	93.00	62,100	99.76	C	92,800	Eastern Parana. D=RCC.
568	Sao Jose dos Pinhais	83,000	90.00	74,700	99.61	C	115,000	South. Textiles industry, market, railroad. D=RCC.
569	Divinopolis	181,000	89.00	161,000	99.36	C	252,000	Minas Gerais. Cassava, corn, coffee, textiles, dairies. F=1911. D=RCC.
570	Dourados	160,000	90.00	144,000	99.61	C	223,000	Southern Mato Grosso do Sul near Paraguay. D=RCC.
571	Erechim	91,500	91.00	83,300	99.76	C	127,000	North Rio Grande do Sul, 45 miles north of Passo Fundo. Grain, flax, hogs, distilling, meat processing. D=RCC.
572	Feira de Santana (Feira de Sant' Anna)	460,000	92.00	423,000	99.76	C	639,000	Bahia state. Livestock, meat export, tobacco. F=1873. D=RCC.
573	Florianopolis	473,000	93.00	439,000	99.76	C	656,000	Port and capital of Santa Catarina. Wharves, beaches. F=1700. University (6,000 students). D=RCC.
574	Fortaleza	3,007,000	90.00	2,706,000	99.61	C	3,845,000	Port and capital of Ceara. Exports sugar, coffee, cashews. Lace-making. F=1654. 'Fortress'. RC Bishopric (1854).
575	Caucaia	102,000	91.00	92,500	99.76	C	141,000	North on Atlantic Ocean. Port, fishing, railroad, coffee, oats, sugar. D=RCC.
576	Foz do Iguacu	236,000	90.50	213,000	99.66	C	327,000	Western Parana on Iguacu River on Paraguayan border. D=RCC.
577	Franca (Vila Franca del Rei)	237,000	91.00	215,000	99.76	C	329,000	Sao Paulo. Sugar refinery, coffee, rice, leather goods, furniture, cigarettes, diamond area nearby. F=1824. D=RCC.
578	Garanhuns	94,600	93.00	88,000	99.76	C	131,000	Pernambuco. Resort, trade, manufacturing, coffee, cotton. F=1874. D=RCC.
579	Goiania	1,103,000	91.00	1,004,000	99.76	C	1,428,000	Capital of Goias. Agriculture, livestock, nickel. F=1933. Sunday hippie fair. Catholic university. D=RCC.
580	Governador Valadares (Figuira)	281,000	91.00	256,000	99.76	C	390,000	Minas Gerais. Agricultural trade, gem trading, lumbering, mining, beans, rice, sugarcane. F=1937. D=RCC.
581	Guaratingueta	121,000	91.00	110,000	99.76	C	168,000	Sao Paulo. Crop processing, textiles, explosives, soft drinks. F=1651. D=RCC.
582	Ijui	106,000	90.00	95,600	99.61	C	148,000	Rio Grande do Sul on Ijui River. Cattle and hog raising, meat, grain, mate, airfield. D=RCC.
583	Ilheus	189,000	90.50	171,000	99.66	C	262,000	Bahia. Major cacao port, rubber, timber, chemicals. F=c1532 as Sao Jorge dos Ilheos. D=RCC.
584	Imperatriz	305,000	92.00	280,000	99.76	C	423,000	Southwestern Maranhao on Tocantins River. Manioc meal, babassu, copaiba oil, cotton. D=RCC.
585	Ipatinga	350,000	91.00	318,000	99.76	C	486,000	Minas Gerais on Doce River. East of Belo Horizonte. Rio Doce Valley, Vitoria-Minas railroad. D=RCC.
586	Itapetininga	137,000	90.00	123,000	99.61	C	190,000	Sao Paulo. Corn, rice, cotton, furniture, cheese factories, livestock, cottonseed oil. F=1770. D=RCC.
587	Itabira	106,000	90.00	95,300	99.61	C	147,000	Minas Gerais east of Belo Horizonte. Leading iron mining center, semi-precious stones, graphite. D=RCC.
588	Itabuna	217,000	91.00	197,000	99.76	C	301,000	Bahia. Trade center for cacao, livestock, agriculture, chemical factory. F=1910. D=RCC.
589	Itajai	135,000	92.00	124,000	99.76	C	187,000	Santa Catarina. Commercial port. Wrapping paper, textiles. F=c1850 by Germans/Italians. D=RCC.
590	Itajuba	90,200	93.00	83,900	99.76	C	125,000	Minas Gerais. Textile center, agriculture. F=1848. D=RCC.
591	Itapeva	110,000	90.50	100,000	99.66	C	153,000	Sao Paulo near Itapetininga. Railroad, farming, agriculture. D=RCC.
592	Itatiba	70,200	93.00	65,200	99.76	C	97,500	Sao Paulo north of Jundiai, southeast of Campirias. Secondary roads, trade. D=RCC.
593	Itu	120,000	90.00	108,000	99.61	C	167,000	Sao Paulo on Tiete River. West of Sao Paulo. D=RCC.
594	Ituiutaba	111,000	89.00	98,400	99.36	C	154,000	Minas Gerais. Commercial center for agriculture. F=1901. D=RCC.
595	Itumbiara	102,000	91.00	92,900	99.76	C	142,000	Southern Goias on Paranaiba River. Fruit. D=RCC.
596	Jacarei	193,000	90.00	174,000	99.61	C	268,000	Sao Paulo. Dairying, food processing. F=1653. D=RCC.
597	Jaquie (Jeguie, Jequie)	191,000	89.50	171,000	99.56	C	265,000	Bahia. Trade center for cacao & livestock. F=1910. D=RCC.
598	Jatai	78,400	93.00	72,900	99.76	C	109,000	Goias on Claro River. Primary road, corn, cattle, livestock. D=RCC.
599	Jau	120,000	91.00	109,000	99.76	C	166,000	Sao Paulo near Tiete River. Railroad, large lakes, fishing, farming. D=RCC.
600	Jequie	165,000	90.00	148,000	99.61	C	229,000	Bahia on Contas River. Primary road, contas tributaries, tobacco, petroleum. D=RCC.
601	Joao Monlevade	72,800	92.00	67,000	99.76	C	101,000	Elevation 680m, Piracicaba River. Steel milling, manganese. D=RCC.
602	Joao Pessoa (Frederikstad, Paraiba)	712,000	89.00	634,000	99.36	C	989,000	Port & capital of Paraiba. Chemicals, plastics. F=1585. Paraiba University. Many old churches. D=RCC.
603	Bayeux	87,000	93.00	80,900	99.76	C	121,000	West. Railroad, industry, chemicals, sugar, cotton. D=RCC.
604	Santa Rita	77,800	92.00	71,600	99.76	C	108,000	Paraiba. East of Joao Pessoa. Industry, trade. D=RCC.
605	Joinville	392,000	90.00	353,000	99.61	C	545,000	Santa Catarina. Iron, steel, flour, cotton. F=1887. Heavily German. D=RCC.
606	Juazeiro do Norte	207,000	89.50	185,000	99.56	C	287,000	Ceara. Sugar, cotton, livestock, rural farming. F=1914. D=RCC.
607	Juiz de Fora (Paraibuna)	453,000	88.50	401,000	98.86	C	629,000	Minas Gerais. Agriculture, textiles, plastics, knitwear, bananas. Mariano Procopio museum. D=RCC.
608	Jundiai (Porta do Sertao)	406,000	90.00	365,000	99.61	C	564,000	Sao Paulo. Ferrova Paulista railroad, Jundiai River. Agriculture, industry. F=1865. D=RCC.
609	Lajes (Lages)	185,000	90.00	167,000	99.61	C	258,000	Santa Catarina. Livestock, industry. F=1800 by Germans. D=RCC.
610	Lavras	67,400	91.00	61,400	99.76	C	93,700	Minas Gerais near Grande River. Railroad, primary highway. D=RCC.
611	Leme	77,900	92.00	71,700	99.76	C	108,000	Sao Paulo north of Araras. Primary roads, agriculture. D=RCC.
612	Limeira (Tatuibi)	242,000	91.00	220,000	99.76	C	336,000	Sao Paulo. Crop processing. F=1863. D=RCC.
613	Linhares	159,000	90.50	143,000	99.66	C	220,000	Espirito Santo on Doce River, Doce inlet. Fishing, coastal plain. D=RCC.
614	Lins	71,300	91.00	64,900	99.76	C	99,100	Sao Paulo near Tiete River. Coffee growing and processing, furniture, pottery, dairy produce. RC Bishopric.
615	Londrina	449,000	90.50	406,000	99.66	C	623,000	Parana. Coffee, cotton, livestock. German, Slavic. F=1930 by Germans & Japanese. D=RCC.
616	Lorena (Porto de Guaipacare)	81,900	92.00	75,300	99.76	C	114,000	Sao Paulo. Agricultural trade center, sugar, alcohol distilling, meat drying, talc quarries. F=1782. D=RCC.
617	Luziania	127,000	93.00	118,000	99.76	C	177,000	E. Goias south of Brasilia. Cheese, fruit processing, tobacco, coffee, nitrate deposits. D=RCC.
618	Macapa	219,000	91.00	199,000	99.76	C	304,000	Capital of Amapa territory on Amazon river. Gold, lumber, fish. F=1688. D=RCC.
619	Maceio (Macayo)	624,000	90.00	562,000	99.61	C	867,000	Capital of Alagoas. Textiles, sugar, steel. F=1815. Church of Bom Jesus des Martires. D=RCC.
620	Mage (Maje)	270,000	89.50	242,000	99.56	C	375,000	Rio de Janeiro. North of Guanabara Bay. Railroad, junction, cotton mill, match factory, pottery works. D=RCC.
621	Manaus (Manaos)	1,432,000	89.00	1,274,000	99.36	C	1,924,000	River port & capital of Amazonas. Duty-free zone. Trade. F=1669. Episcopal see (1892). D=RCC. M=YWAM.
622	Maraba	173,000	91.00	157,000	99.76	C	240,000	Para south of Belem on Tocantins River. Rubber, Brazil nuts, fishing, diamonds nearby. D=RCC.
623	Marilia	176,000	90.00	159,000	99.61	C	245,000	Sao Paulo. Agriculture, livestock, lumbering, leading cotton growing center, cotton ginning. F=1611. D=RCC.
624	Maringa	255,000	89.00	227,000	99.36	C	354,000	Parana. Coffee. F=1947. Many Japanese. D=RCC.
625	Mogi-Guacu (Mojiguacu)	119,000	91.00	108,000	99.76	C	165,000	Sao Paulo north of Campinas on Mojiguacu River. D=RCC.
626	Mojimirim	82,000	92.00	75,400	99.76	C	114,000	Sao Paulo north of Campinas. Cotton ginning, meat packing, rice, breweries. F=18th century. D=RCC.
627	Montes Claros	278,000	91.00	253,000	99.76	C	386,000	Minas Gerais. Livestock, cassava, furniture, textiles. F=1831. D=RCC.
628	Mossoro (Santa Luiza de Mossoro)	205,000	90.00	185,000	99.61	C	285,000	Rio Grande do Norte. Salt, clay, textiles. F=1870. D=RCC.
629	Muriae	104,000	91.50	95,300	99.26	C	145,000	Southern Minas Gerais on Muriae River. Sugar, coffee, cereals, dairy, distilleries, white marble quarries. D=RCC.
630	Natal	660,000	89.50	591,000	99.56	C	917,000	Capital of Rio Grande do Norte. Major port. Silk & cotton textiles. F=1597. 'Christmas'. D=RCC.
631	Nova Friburgo	186,000	91.00	169,000	99.76	C	258,000	Rio de Janeiro. Summer mountain resort. Alpine style resort built by Swiss who first settled here in 1818. D=RCC.
632	Ourinhos (Jacarezinho)	85,200	93.00	79,300	99.76	C	118,000	Sao Paulo. Agricultural products, food processing, coffee, cotton, alfalfa, fruits, livestock, timber. F=1948. D=RCC.
633	Paranagua	123,000	90.00	110,000	99.61	C	171,000	Port, Parana. Brazil's largest coffee export port. F=1585. Sao Benedictus church (c1600). D=RCC.
634	Paranavai	97,800	92.00	89,900	99.76	C	136,000	Parana northwest of Maringa. Coffee. D=RCC.
635	Parnaiba	150,000	89.00	134,000	99.36	C	209,000	Port, Piaui. Carnauba wax, cotton, babussa palm oil, sugar livestock. F=1761. D=RCC.
636	Passo Fundo	178,000	91.00	162,000	98.72	C	248,000	Rio Grande do Sul. Agriculture, livestock, meat processing, lumber, manganese. F=1857. D=RCC.
637	Passos	103,000	90.00	92,500	99.61	C	143,000	Minas Gerais. Rice, corn, sugarcane, cattle, cement plant. F=1848. D=RCC.
638	Patos	96,200	92.50	89,000	99.26	C	134,000	Paraiba. Commercial center for agriculture. Railroad, cotton, sugar, corn, beans. F=1903. D=RCC.
639	Patos de Minas	128,000	90.50	116,000	99.66	C	178,000	Minas Gerais. Agriculture, livestock, dairies, experimental wheat, diamond washing. F=1866. D=RCC.
640	Paulo Afonso	112,000	91.50	102,000	99.26	C	155,000	Bahia. Sao Francisco River. Commercial center for agriculture. F=1958. D=RCC.
641	Pelotas	360,000	92.00	331,000	99.76	C	499,000	Coastal city, Rio Grande do Sul. Jerked beef, meat-packing. F=1780. D=RCC.
642	Petrolina	291,000	90.00	262,000	99.61	C	405,000	Pernambuco. Sao Francisco River. Cotton, textiles, chemicals, ships, tobacco, airfield. D=RCC.
643	Juazeiro	102,000	93.00	94,600	99.76	C	141,000	Bahia. Transportation center for agriculture & livestock. F=1878. D=RCC.
644	Petropolis	341,000	91.00	310,000	99.76	C	474,000	Rio de Janeiro. Fashionable resort, flower gardens, cathedral, university. F=1845 by Bavarians. D=RCC.
645	Pindamonhangaba	113,000	92.00	104,000	99.76	C	156,000	Sao Paulo northeast of Taubate. Near Paraiba do Sul River. Sugarcane. D=RCC.
646	Piracicaba (Santo Antonio)	326,000	89.00	290,000	99.36	C	453,000	Sao Paulo. Sugarcane, distilleries, cotton, rice, maize, coffee, agricultural institute. F=1821. D=RCC.
647	Pocos de Caldas	129,000	92.00	119,000	99.76	C	180,000	Minas Gerais. Resort, thermal baths, aluminum. Leading bauxite mining district, hotels, casinos. D=RCC.
648	Ponta Grossa	289,000	90.00	260,000	99.61	C	401,000	Parana. Tea, timber, meat-packing, hog raising, lumbering, sawmilling, talc quarries. D=RCC.
649	Porto Alegre	3,699,000	89.20	3,300,000	99.76	C	4,629,000	Capital of Rio Grande do Sul on Guaiba River. Center of inland navigation. Rice, corn, wheat. F=1742. D=RCC.
650	Alvorada	138,000	89.50	124,000	99.56	C	192,000	Rio Grande do Sul. Varied processing industries. D=RCC.
651	Cachoeirinha	94,700	93.00	88,000	99.76	C	131,000	Rio Grande do Sul, 8 miles northeast of Porto Alegre. D=RCC.
652	Canoas	338,000	91.00	308,000	99.76	C	470,000	Rio Grande do Sul. Glass, chemicals, meat-packing. F=1839. D=RCC.
653	Esteio	76,300	92.00	70,200	99.76	C	106,000	North beyond Canoas. Rio Grande do Sul, 14 miles north of Porto Alegre. D=RCC.
654	Novo Hamburgo	217,000	89.50	194,000	99.56	C	302,000	Rio Grande do Sul. Shoes, hides, leather. F=1927 by Germans. D=RCC.
655	Sao Leopoldo	148,000	90.00	133,000	99.61	C	205,000	Rio Grande do Sul. Serves agricultural region. F=1824 by Germans. D=RCC.
656	Sapucaia do Sul	119,000	91.00	108,000	99.76	C	165,000	Rio Grande do Sul. Varied processing industries. D=RCC.
657	Porto Velho	262,000	89.00	233,000	99.36	C	363,000	Capital of Rondonia. Head of navigation on Madeira river. F=1915. D=RCC.
658	Pouso Alegre	85,400	92.00	78,600	99.76	C	119,000	Southern Minas Gerais on Sapucai River. Textiles, hats, matches, coffee, sugar, fruit, wine. D=RCC.
659	Presidente Prudente (Corrego)	202,000	91.00	184,000	99.76	C	280,000	Sao Paulo. Agriculture, lumbering, dairy, flour products, machinery, tile, pottery, beverages. F=1921. D=RCC.
660	Recife	3,307,000	91.00	3,009,000	99.76	C	4,105,000	Capital of Pernambuco. Built on two islands on Capibaribe & Beberibe Rivers. Sugar 'Venice of Brazil'. D=RCC.
661	Cavaleiro	138,000	91.00	126,000	99.76	C	192,000	Pernambuco. Sugar, cotton, coffee, railroad, industry. D=RCC.
662	Jaboatao	113,000	92.00	104,000	99.76	C	157,000	Pernambuco. Commercial center for agriculture. F=c1650. D=RCC.
663	Muribeca dos Guararapes	235,000	90.00	212,000	99.61	C	326,000	Pernambuco. South of Recife. D=RCC.
664	Olinda	410,000	89.00	365,000	99.36	C	569,000	Pernambuco. 16-17th century ornate churches. Beachfront seafood houses. Night clubs. F=1537. D=RCC.
665	Sao Lourenco da Mata	85,400	92.00	78,500	99.76	C	119,000	Pernambuco. Capiberibe River. Sugar, corn, cotton, fruit, sugar milling. D=RCC.
666	Ribeirao Preto (Entre Rios)	496,000	91.00	451,000	99.76	C	689,000	Sao Paulo. Coffee, cotton, sugar, textiles, cloth, oil, food products, alcoholic beverages. F=1856. D=RCC.
667	Rio Branco	188,000	91.50	172,000	99.26	C	262,000	Capital of Acre. Exports rubber, metals, petroleum, Brazil nuts, Trans-Amazon Highway. D=RCC.
668	Rio Claro	168,000	90.50	152,000	99.66	C	234,000	Sao Paulo. Trade & processing center for agriculture. F=1845. D=RCC.
669	Rio de Janeiro (Rio)	10,556,000	88.90	9,384,000	99.96	C	12,450,000	Capital of Rio de Janeiro. Tourism, finance. F=1565. Carnaval festival. Statue of Christ the Redeemer.
670	Belford Roxo	441,000	90.00	397,000	99.61	C	613,000	Northwest beyond Sao Joao de Meriti. D=RCC.
671	Campos Elyseos	244,000	91.00	222,000	99.76	C	338,000	North. Near Guanabara Bay. D=RCC.
672	Coelho da Rocha	213,000	90.50	193,000	99.66	C	296,000	Northwest beyond San Joao de Meriti, on federal district border. D=RCC.
673	Duque de Caxias (Meriti Station)	457,000	88.50	405,000	99.46	C	635,000	Rio de Janeiro. Commercial & manufacturing center. D=RCC.
674	Ipiiba	150,000	90.00	135,000	99.61	C	209,000	Far east beyond Sao Goncalo, near Guanabara Bay. D=RCC.
675	Mesquita	209,000	89.00	186,000	99.36	C	290,000	Northwest near Belford Roxo. D=RCC.
676	Monjolo	147,000	90.00	133,000	99.61	C	205,000	East of Sao Goncalo. D=RCC.
677	Neves	212,000	89.00	188,000	99.36	C	294,000	Rio de Janeiro. Minerals. Originally a Guarulhos Indian village. Nossa Senhora de Neves chapel (1566). D=RCC.
678	Nilopolis	146,000	91.00	133,000	99.76	C	203,000	Rio de Janeiro. Metals, meats, oranges. D=RCC.
679	Niteroi	572,000	88.00	503,000	99.46	C	794,000	Rio de Janeiro. Residential, ship building. F=1671. D=RCC.
680	Nova Iguacu (Maxambamba)	767,000	88.30	678,000	99.76	C	1,066,000	Rio de Janeiro. Marmalade & orange juice. D=RCC.
681	Queimados	147,000	90.00	132,000	99.61	C	204,000	Northwest beyond Nova Iguacu. D=RCC.
682	Sao Goncalo	340,000	89.00	302,000	99.36	C	472,000	Rio de Janeiro, Guanabara Bay. Chemicals, cement, citrus fruits, distribution center. D=RCC.
683	Sao Joao de Meriti (Meriti)	313,000	90.00	282,000	99.61	C	435,000	Rio de Janeiro. Sugarcane, livestock, residential. F=1647. D=RCC.

Table 10-5–continued overleaf

Table 10-5–continued

Rec No 1	Country City 2	Pop 2000 3	AC% 4	Church Members 5	E% 6	W 7	Pop 2025 8	Notes 9
684	Sete Pontes	93,600	92.00	86,100	99.76	C	130,000	East. Near Neves on Guanabara Bay. D=RCC.
685	Rio do Sul	58,600	93.00	54,500	99.76	C	81,400	Santa Catarina on Itajai do Sul. Inland from Blumenau. D=RCC.
686	Rio Grande	213,000	91.00	193,000	99.76	C	295,000	Port, Rio Grande do Sul. Jerked beef, hides. F=1745. D=RCC.
687	Rio Verde	120,000	91.00	110,000	99.76	C	167,000	Goias on Rio Verde. Trade center for livestock, rice, corn, caster beans, tobacco, sugar. D=RCC.
688	Rondonopolis	132,000	90.00	118,000	99.61	C	183,000	Southern Mato Grosso. River port. Important center for soybean cultivation, airfield. D=RCC.
689	Salto	71,400	93.00	66,400	99.76	C	99,200	Sao Paulo, Tirte River. Siemens mfg., electronic relays, sensors. cotton milling, paper, sugar, grain. D=RCC.
690	Salvador (Sao Salvador, Bahia)	3,180,000	92.00	2,926,000	99.96	C	4,029,000	Port & capital of Bahia. Cocoa, sugar. F=1549. Church of convent of Third Order of St. Francis (1701). D=RCC.
691	Santa Barbara d'Oeste	124,000	92.00	114,000	99.76	C	172,000	East central Sao Paulo, WNW of Campinas. Distilling, silk, cotton weaving, sugar milling. D=RCC.
692	Santa Cruz do Sul	149,000	90.00	134,000	99.61	C	207,000	Rio Grande do Sul west of Porto Alegre. Tobacco growing center, iron founding, chemicals, airfield. D=RCC.
693	Santa Maria	255,000	89.50	228,000	99.56	C	354,000	Rio Grande do Sul. Railroad, meats, food stuffs, railroad machinery. Important military base. F=1797. D=RCC.
694	Santa Rosa	80,200	93.00	74,600	99.76	C	111,000	Northern Rio Grande do Sul near Argentinian border. Corn, mate tobacco, airfield. D=RCC.
695	Santana do Livramento	91,300	91.00	83,000	99.76	C	127,000	Rio Grande do Sul. Cattle, sheep, meat packing, leather working, amethysts. F=1833. D=RCC.
696	Santarem (Tapajos)	293,000	90.00	264,000	99.61	C	408,000	Para. River port. Rosewood oil, lumber, rubber. F=1661 as Jesuit Mission. D=RCC.
697	Santo Angelo	139,000	90.50	126,000	99.66	C	193,000	Rio Grande do Sul. Trade & transportation for agriculture. F=1707. D=RCC.
698	Santos	1,257,000	85.00	1,068,000	99.36	C	1,604,000	Port. Sao Paulo on island of Sao Vicente. World's largest coffee port. Soft drinks. Beaches. F=1543. D=RCC.
699	Cubatao	1,257,000	91.00	1,144,000	99.76	C	1,746,000	Sao Paulo. Bananas, petroleum, steel, leading hydroelectric plant, paper mills, chemicals. F=1948. D=RCC.
700	Guaruja	108,000	90.50	97,800	99.66	C	150,000	Sao Paulo. Santo Amaro Island. Beach resort, casino, ship yards. D=RCC.
701	Praia Grande	87,800	93.00	81,600	99.76	C	122,000	South on Santos Bay. D=RCC.
702	Sao Vicente	310,000	91.00	282,000	99.76	C	431,000	Sao Paulo. Resort with large beach. First permanent Portuguese settlement, island, resort. F=1532. D=RCC.
703	Sao Borja	85,500	93.00	79,500	99.76	C	119,000	Rio Grande do Sul on Uruguay River at Argentinian border. D=RCC.
704	Sao Carlos	182,000	90.00	164,000	99.61	C	252,000	Sao Paulo. Agriculture, cattle, industry, cotton milling, meat packing, brewing. Cathedral. F=1865. D=RCC.
705	Sao Joao da Boa Vista	79,800	92.00	73,400	99.76	C	111,000	Sao Paulo near Pocos de Caldas. Brazil's principle zirconium mine, coffee, potatoes, corn, hats. D=RCC.
706	Sao Joao del Rei	96,300	91.00	87,600	99.76	C	134,000	Minas Gerais. Minerals, manufacturing, livestock. F=1838. 18th century churches. D=RCC.
707	Sao Jose do Rio Preto (Rio Preto)	297,000	90.50	269,000	99.66	C	412,000	Sao Paulo. Service center for agriculture, livestock trade, pharmacy and dentistry schools. F=1894. D=RCC.
708	Sao Jose dos Campos	949,000	92.00	873,000	99.76	C	1,287,000	Sao Paulo. Service center for agriculture. F=1767 as Jesuit mission. D=RCC.
709	Sao Luiz (San Luis, Maranhao)	948,000	90.00	853,000	99.61	C	1,269,000	Capital of Maranhao. Chief seaport. Sugar, rum, cotton. F=1612. D=RCC.
710	Sao Paulo	17,711,000	90.50	16,028,000	99.86	C	20,793,000	Capital of Sao Paulo. Foremost industrial center. International banking. F=1554 as Jesuit mission. D=RCC.
711	Carapicuiba	344,000	90.00	310,000	99.61	C	478,000	West on Tiete River. Manufacturing. D=RCC.
712	Suzano	167,000	92.00	154,000	99.76	C	232,000	Far east beyond Poa, 20 miles east of Sao Paulo city. Railroad, vegetables. D=RCC.
713	Diadema	415,000	89.50	371,000	99.56	C	576,000	South on Billings Reservoir. Residential, manufacturing. D=RCC.
714	Embu	155,000	91.00	141,000	99.76	C	215,000	Southwest beyond Taboao da Serra, 14 miles west of Sao Paulo. Weekly artist fairs. D=RCC.
715	Ferraz de Vasconcelos	89,100	92.00	82,000	99.76	C	124,000	Far east near Poa. Manufacturing. D=RCC.
716	Guarulhos	740,000	89.50	662,000	99.56	C	1,028,000	Sao Paulo. Industry, steel, motorcycles, cotton and silk textiles. Old cathedral, major airport. F=1560. D=RCC.
717	Itapecerica da Serra	84,800	91.00	77,200	99.76	C	118,000	Southwest near Embu-mirim River. Timber, kaolin quarries, mica, gold deposits. D=RCC.
718	Itapevi	86,500	91.00	78,700	99.76	C	120,000	West beyond Carapicuiba. Livestock center, cotton processing, cheese factories. D=RCC.
719	Itaquaquecetuba	118,000	90.00	106,000	99.61	C	164,000	East on Tiete River. Manufacturing. D=RCC.
720	Maua	349,000	89.50	312,000	99.56	C	484,000	Southeast on Tamanduatei River, on Sao Paulo-Santos railroad. D=RCC.
721	Mogi das Cruzes (M'bbaygi)	331,000	90.00	298,000	99.61	C	460,000	Sao Paulo. Beans, fruits, sawmills, ceramics. F=1611. D=RCC.
722	Osasco	766,000	89.50	685,000	99.56	C	1,064,000	Sao Paulo. Meat-packing, metals, autos. D=RCC.
723	Poa	85,500	91.00	77,800	99.76	C	119,000	East on Tiete River. Manufacturing. D=RCC.
724	Santo Andre	822,000	90.00	740,000	99.61	C	1,142,000	Sao Paulo. Textiles, metals, chinaware. F=1553. D=RCC.
725	Sao Bernardo do Campo	728,000	89.50	652,000	99.56	C	1,012,000	Sao Paulo. Furniture, autos, tanning, vegetables, chemicals, fabrics, ceramics. F=1553. D=RCC.
726	Sao Caetano do Sul	221,000	91.00	201,000	99.76	C	308,000	Sao Paulo. Minerals, autos, textiles. F=1631 by Benedictine monks. D=RCC.
727	Tabao da Serra	158,000	90.00	142,000	99.61	C	220,000	West on Poa River. Residential. D=RCC.
728	Sertaozinho	86,900	92.00	79,900	99.76	C	121,000	Minas Gerais near Pouso Alegre. Sugar milling, distilling, coffee, cotton, fruit, sugar. D=RCC.
729	Sete Lagoas	157,000	91.00	143,000	99.76	C	218,000	Minas Gerais. Service center for agricultural region. Marble quarrying, quartz crystal mining. D=RCC.
730	Sobral	145,000	91.00	132,000	99.76	C	202,000	Ceara. Cotton, agriculture, chemicals, cloth, carnauba wax, sugar, alcohol, cattle. F=1773. D=RCC.
731	Sorocaba	424,000	90.00	382,000	99.61	C	589,000	Sao Paulo. Cotton & silk textiles, cement. F=1661. D=RCC.
732	Tatui	89,800	93.00	83,500	99.76	C	125,000	Sao Paulo, elev. 645 m. Dr. Carlos de Campos Conservatory of Drama & Music. 'Music Capital'. D=RCC.
733	Taubate	266,000	94.00	250,000	99.76	C	369,000	Sao Paulo. Coffee, dolomite, cotton, jute. 17th century convent, old cathedral. F=c1600. D=RCC.
734	Teofilo Otoni	163,000	90.00	147,000	99.61	C	227,000	Minas Gerais. Trade center for agriculture, livestock. Noted for semiprecious stones. F=1878. D=RCC.
735	Teresina	680,000	89.00	605,000	99.36	C	944,000	Capital of Piaui. Textiles, sugar, cattle. Named for Brazilian empress Teresa Cristina Marra.F=1852. D=RCC.
736	Timon	88,400	91.00	80,500	99.76	C	123,000	West of Teresina in Maranhao state on Parnaiba River. Babassu oil, carnauba wax, sugar milling.
737	Teresopolis (Therezopolis)	150,000	92.00	138,000	99.76	C	208,000	Rio de Janeiro. Summer resort. Numerous villas and estates, flowers, furniture, vegetables. F=1890. D=RCC.
738	Tres Rios	113,000	91.00	102,000	99.76	C	156,000	Rio de Janeiro on Paraiba do Sul. Soap, chemicals, distilling, cotton milling, rice, dairying. D=RCC.
739	Tubarao	106,000	90.00	95,600	99.61	C	148,000	Santa Catarina. Grains, beans, coffee, iron ore. F=1870. D=RCC.
740	Tupa	79,000	92.00	72,700	99.76	C	110,000	Sao Paulo northwest of Bauru. Sawmilling, cotton ginning, coffee, rice processing. D=RCC.
741	Uba	80,500	91.00	73,300	99.76	C	112,000	Minas Gerais northeast of Juiz de Fora. Coffee, tobacco, sugar, school of pharmacy and dentistry. D=RCC.
742	Uberaba	317,000	90.00	285,000	99.61	C	440,000	Minas Gerais. Trade center. Cattle, oranges, cement. F=1856. D=RCC.
743	Uberlandia	404,000	91.00	368,000	99.76	C	561,000	Minas Gerais. Cotton, corn, rice, cattle, soybean center, airfield. F=1892. D=RCC.
744	Uruguaiana (Uruguayana)	137,000	90.50	124,000	99.66	C	190,000	Rio Grande do Sul. River port. Livestock, perfumes. Founded by Jesuit ministers. F=1839. D=RCC.
745	Varginha	96,600	92.00	88,900	99.76	C	134,000	Minas Gerais near Furnas Reservoir. D=RCC.
746	Varzea Grande	149,000	91.00	136,000	99.76	C	207,000	Mato Grosso on Cuiaba River near Cuiaba. D=RCC.
747	Vitoria	952,000	92.00	875,000	99.76	C	1,322,000	Capital of Espirito Santo on Atlantic Ocean. Textiles, sugar, export. F=1535. D=RCC.
748	Cariacica	96,200	94.00	90,400	99.76	C	134,000	Espirito Santo. West of Vitoria. D=RCC.
749	Itaquari	212,000	92.50	196,000	99.46	C	295,000	Espirito Santo. Southwest. D=RCC.
750	Vila Velha (Espirito Santo)	119,000	93.00	111,000	99.76	C	165,000	Espirito Santo. Chocolate & candy making. F=1535. 16th century convent Our Lady of Penha. D=RCC.
751	Vitoria da Conquista (Conquista)	257,000	93.00	239,000	99.76	C	356,000	Bahia. Trade & transport for livestock. F=1891. D=RCC.
752	Vitoria de Santo Antao	87,800	92.00	80,800	99.76	C	122,000	Pernambuco west of Recife. Fruit and vegetables, tobacco, sugar milling, alcohol distilling. D=RCC.
753	Volta Redonda	284,000	91.00	258,000	99.76	C	394,000	Rio de Janeiro. Steel manufacturing. F=1941. D=RCC.
754	Barra Mansa	193,000	92.00	178,000	99.76	C	268,000	Rio de Janeiro. Nestle's food & chocolate. D=RCC.
	BRITAIN	**58,830,000**	**66.38**	**39,053,000**	**98.10**	**C**	**59,961,000**	**ANGLICANS 44.6%, ROMAN CATHOLICS 9.5%. PENT-CHAR 9.8%, EVANGELICAL 19.6%, GCC 35.9%**
755	rural areas	6,189,000	73.89	4,573,000	99.22	C	4,869,000	15.8% (1950), 11.5% (1970), 10.9% (1990), 10.5% (2000), 9.7% (2010), 8.1% (2025)
756	urban areas	52,641,000	65.50	34,480,000	97.97	C	55,092,000	84.1% (1950), 88.4% (1970), 89.0% (1990), 89.4% (2000), 90.2% (2010), 91.8% (2025)
757	non-metropolitan areas	15,809,000	68.95	10,900,000	98.87	C	17,194,203	*Sources of data:* Censuses of 1951, 1961, 1971, and 1981.
758	metropolitan areas	36,832,000	64.02	23,580,000	97.59	C	37,898,000	*Definition:* Continuous area of land extending for 20 hectares or more.
759	Aberdeen	217,000	64.00	139,000	97.72	C	227,000	Seaport of Scotland. Fishing. University town. F=580 by St. Machar, disciple of St. Columba. D=RCC.
760	Aldershot-Farnborough-Camberley	232,000	64.00	149,000	97.72	C	243,000	Surrey. Largest permanent military base in U.K. Birthplace of Irish patriot Maud Gonne. D=COE.
761	Aldershot	56,200	64.50	36,300	96.22	C	58,800	Surrey. Largest permanent military base in U.K. Birthplace of Irish patriot Maud Gonne. D=COE.
762	Aylesbury	54,500	65.00	35,400	96.72	C	57,000	Buckinghamshire county. Food processing, printing. D=COE,Methodist.
763	Ayr	105,000	65.50	68,600	99.22	C	110,000	Seaport of Scotland. Tourism, resort, fishing, coal. F=1202. D=COS,RCC,SEC.
764	Bangor	74,600	65.50	48,900	97.22	C	78,100	Wales. Cathedral city. Cultural center. F=c550. Center of Celtic Christianity (600). D=CIW Diocese.
765	Barnsley	80,400	64.50	51,900	96.22	C	84,200	South Yorkshire. River Dearne. Coal mining. Mining and technical college. D=COE.
766	Barrow-in-Furness	52,500	65.00	34,200	96.72	C	55,000	Cumbrin country. Extensive shipyards, submarines. D=COE.
767	Basildon	99,300	64.00	63,500	95.72	C	104,000	Essex county. 230 factories, 400 shops. F=1494. D=COE.
768	Basingstoke	76,500	65.00	49,700	96.72	C	80,000	Market town in Hampshire county. Cloth industry, cereal. D=COE.
769	Bath	88,300	65.00	57,400	96.72	C	92,400	Avon county. Hot mineral springs, classical buildings, literary associations. Founded by Romans. D=COE Diocese.
770	Bedford	79,200	65.00	51,500	96.72	C	82,900	Bedfordshire county. Center for large agricultural area. F=Roman fording station. John Bunyan museum. D=COE.
771	Belfast	704,000	63.00	444,000	96.72	C	737,000	Capital of Northern Ireland. Ships, linen. F=1611. Violence between Catholics and Protestants. 70% Protestant.
772	Castlereagh	59,700	65.00	38,800	96.72	C	62,500	Northern Ireland. Residential, agriculture. F=1973. D=COL,RCC.
773	Newtownabbey	74,900	65.00	48,700	96.72	C	78,400	Northern Ireland. Tires, telephones, textiles. F=1958. D=COL,RCC.
774	Birmingham-West Midlands	2,271,000	64.50	1,465,000	99.52	C	2,271,000	West Midlands county. Metal, autos. Extensive WWII damage. 7% Muslims. D=COE.
775	Birmingham	1,062,000	64.00	680,000	98.72	C	1,111,000	West Midlands county. Metal, autos. St. Philip's Cathedral (1715). 3% Hindus. D=COE Diocese,RCC.
776	Solihull	98,400	61.00	60,000	92.72	C	103,000	West Midlands county. Residential area. Automobiles. D=COE,RCC,Baptist.
777	Cannock (Chase)	57,100	65.00	37,100	96.72	C	59,700	Staffordshire county. Coal mining, metals, open forests. D=COE,AoG.
778	Dudley	195,000	64.00	125,000	97.72	C	204,000	West Midlands county. Metal working, crystal glassware. D=COE,Methodist.
779	Halesowen	60,300	65.00	39,200	96.72	C	63,100	West Midlands. River Stour. Birthplace of English novelist Francis Brett Young. D=COE,Methodist.
780	Oldbury-Smethwick	161,000	64.00	103,000	97.72	C	168,000	West Midlands county. Famous ironworks Soho Manufactory (1761). D=COE,RCC.
781	Redditch	64,600	65.00	42,000	96.72	C	67,600	Hereford & Worcester county. Needle, fish hook, bicycles. D=COE,RCC.
782	Stourbridge	57,700	65.00	37,500	96.72	C	60,400	West Midlands county. River Stour. Famous glassmaking industry (16th century). Tools, heating units. D=COE.
783	Sutton Coldfield	107,000	64.50	69,300	98.22	C	112,000	Borough in West Midlands (1886), then Warrickshire. Residential, light industries. D=COE,RCC.
784	Walsall	186,000	64.00	119,000	97.72	C	195,000	West Midlands. Industrial center, lock & key making, nuts & bolts. 2% Muslims. D=COE,Methodist,RCC.
785	West Bromwich	161,000	64.00	103,000	97.72	C	168,000	West Midlands. Metallurgical industries, electrical engineering. D=COE.
786	Wolverhampton	276,000	60.50	167,000	94.22	C	289,000	West Midlands county. Metal manufacturing, paints, rubber tires. Many South Asian immigrants. D=COE,RCC.
787	Blackburn-Darwen	232,000	64.50	150,000	98.22	C	243,000	Lancashire county. Wool, textiles, paper, electronics. F=c1250. D=COE Diocese.
788	Blackpool-Lytham St Ames-Fleetwood	293,000	63.50	186,000	97.22	C	307,000	Lancashire county. Irish sea coast. Resort, bathing, conferences. F=c1780. D=COE.
789	Bognor Regis	52,700	65.00	34,300	96.72	C	55,200	West Sussex. English channel. Resort. William Blake lived in nearby Felpham. D=COE.
790	Bootle	74,200	65.00	48,200	96.72	C	77,700	Merseyside on Irish Sea. Main dock facilities. Grain milling. Office development, banking. D=COE.
791	Bournemouth-Poole-Christchurch	330,000	63.00	208,000	96.72	C	345,000	Dorset. Poole Bay, popular resort and fine arts center, small fishing village. D=COE.
792	Bournemouth	150,000	64.50	96,500	96.22	C	157,000	Dorset. Seaside resort. Retirees. Conferences. F=1810. 2.4% Jews. D=COE and 70 others.
793	Poole	129,000	64.50	83,000	96.22	C	135,000	Dorset. Pottery, boatbuilding, pottery making, residential. Brownsea Island bird sanctuary. D=COE,RCC.
794	Brighton-Hove-Worthing	440,000	63.00	277,000	96.72	C	460,000	East and West Sussex. Seaside resort, fishing, conferences. D=COE,RCC.
795	Brighton	141,000	64.50	90,900	98.22	C	148,000	East Sussex. Seaside resort, fishing, conferences. Royal Pavilion. D=COE,RCC.
796	Hove	68,700	65.00	44,600	96.72	C	71,900	East Sussex county on English Channel. Seaside resort, residential. D=COE,RCC.
797	Worthing	95,000	65.00	61,700	96.72	C	99,400	West Sussex county. Seaside resort, retirees. Fruits, flowers, prehistoric and Roman ruins. D=COE,RCC.
798	Bristol	660,000	62.50	412,000	96.22	C	691,000	Avon county. Sugar, chocolate. F=1155. Abbey of St. Augustine (1142). D=COE Diocese,RCC,Methodist.
799	Kingswood	57,300	65.00	37,300	96.72	C	60,000	Avon county. Printing, brushes. Closely associated with Wesley & Whitefield. D=COE,Methodist.
800	Burnley-Nelson-Colne	168,000	64.50	108,000	98.22	C	175,000	Lancashire county. Textiles. Historically a coal mining and cotton weaving town. 5% Muslims. D=COE,RCC.
801	Burnley	80,000	65.00	52,000	96.72	C	83,700	Lancashire county. Textiles. Kitchen equipment, electrical heating appliances. D=COE,RCC.
802	Burton upon Trent	61,800	65.00	40,200	96.72	C	64,700	Staffordshire county. Breweries, foundries. Benedictine abbey (1002). D=COE.
803	Cambridge	91,200	64.50	58,800	96.22	C	95,500	Cambridgeshire county. University of Cambridge & related industry. Many old churches. D=COE.
804	Cardiff-Rhondda	655,000	63.00	412,000	96.72	C	685,000	Wales. Great coal-shipping port. Iron, steel, autos, fishing. 13th century church. D=CIW,RCC.
805	Cardiff (Caerdydd)	275,000	63.50	174,000	97.22	C	288,000	Capital of Wales. Shopping & service center. F=c75. D=CIW,RCC.

Table 10-5–continued opposite

Table 10-5–continued

Rec No 1	Country City 2	Pop 2000 3	AC% 4	Church Members 5	E% 6	W 7	Pop 2025 8	Notes 9
806	Rhondda	74,300	65.00	48,300	96.72	C	77,800	Wales. Coal mining. 170,000 in 1924. Many pit closures since 1948. D=CIW.
807	Carlisle	75,600	65.00	49,200	96.72	C	79,100	Cumbria county. Textiles, food, confectionery. Cathedral (1093). D=COE Diocese.
808	Cheltenham	91,300	65.00	59,400	96.72	C	95,600	Gloucestershire county. Educational center. Y=803. D=COE.
809	Chester	83,900	65.00	54,600	96.72	C	87,900	Cheshire county. Commercial & ecclesiastical center. Roman outpost for 20th legion. D=COE Diocese.
810	Chesterfield	133,000	65.00	86,500	96.72	C	139,000	Derbyshire county. Market town. 14th century crooked church spire. D=COE.
811	Coatbridge	53,200	65.00	34,600	96.72	C	55,700	Scotland. Iron, steel, tinplate. F=1885 as a burgh. D=COE.
812	Colchester	91,600	65.00	59,500	96.72	C	95,900	Essex county. Clothing, oysters, printing. Pre-Roman origins. Holy Trinity Church (1050). D=COE.
813	Corby	51,000	65.00	33,200	96.72	C	53,400	Northhamptonshire county. Iron ore. F=1931 as steel-making city. D=COE.
814	Coventry-Bedworth	676,000	63.00	426,000	96.72	C	707,000	West Midlands county. Autos, engineering, machine tools. Monastery found by Lady Godiva (d. 1067). D=COE.
815	Coventry	334,000	63.00	210,000	96.72	C	349,000	West Midlands and Warwickshire counties. Autos, machine tools. 5% Sikhs. D=RCC,COE Diocese.
816	Nuneaton	63,200	65.00	41,100	96.72	C	66,100	Warwickshire county. Coal mining. F=c1150 as Benedictine nunnery. D=COE.
817	Royal Leamington Spa	59,200	65.00	38,500	96.72	C	62,000	Warwickshire county. Residential & resort town. F=c1780. D=COE.
818	Crewe	61,900	65.00	40,200	96.72	C	64,800	Cheshire county. Railroads, autos, clothing. F=1837 by Railway Company. D=COE.
819	Darlington-Auckland-Aycliffe	89,600	64.00	57,300	95.72	C	93,700	Durham county. Heavy construction engineering. Church of St. Cuthbert (c1150). D=COE.
820	Derby	288,000	63.50	183,000	97.22	C	301,000	Derbyshire county. Cattle markets, china. F=c850 by Danes as Deoraby. 6% Sikhs. D=COE Diocese,RCC.
821	Doncaster-Bentley	139,000	64.50	89,700	96.22	C	146,000	South Yorkshire county. Service center for mining. F=1194, first charter. D=COE.
822	Doncaster	78,300	65.00	50,900	96.72	C	81,900	South Yorkshire county. Service center for mining. F=1194, first charter. D=COE.
823	Dundee	178,000	64.00	114,000	97.72	C	186,000	Seaport in Scotland. Fishing, textiles, confectionery. F=1892. D=COS,RCC,SEC.
824	Dunfermline	132,000	65.00	85,600	96.72	C	138,000	Scotland. Linen, damask, Carnegie Trusts. Early Celtic monks. D=COS,RCC,SEC.
825	Eastbourne	90,800	65.00	59,000	96.72	C	95,000	East Sussex county. Residential, resorts, conferences. F=c1800. D=COE.
826	Edinburgh (Duneideann)	648,000	63.00	408,000	96.72	C	678,000	Capital of Scotland. Food processing, tobacco, finance. F=617. Educational center. D=COS,RCC,SEC.
827	Exeter	92,400	65.00	60,100	96.72	C	96,700	Devon county. Metal, leather, paper. Ancient origins. St. Peter's (1133). D=COE Diocese,RCC,Methodist.
828	Falkirk	155,000	65.50	102,000	97.22	C	162,000	Scotland. Iron, aluminum, brewing. Roman Antonine Wall. D=COS,RCC,SEC.
829	Glasgow	1,851,000	64.50	1,194,000	99.72	C	1,937,000	Scotland on River Clyde. Textiles. F=550 by St. Kentigern. St. Mungo's Cathedral (13th cent). D=RCC,SEC,COS.
830	Clydebank	54,300	65.00	35,300	96.72	C	56,800	Southwestern Scotland. Declining heavy industry. Offshore oil rigs. D=RCC,SEC,COS.
831	Cumbernauld	53,100	65.00	34,500	96.72	C	55,600	Scotland. Residential (80% from Glasgow), manufacturing. F=1956. D=RCC,SEC,COS.
832	East Kilbride	72,500	65.00	47,100	96.72	C	75,900	Scotland. Milk, agriculture. Celtic origins (St. Bride). D=RCC,SEC,COS.
833	Hamilton	54,100	65.00	35,200	96.72	C	56,600	Scotland. Center for orchards, market gardens. Prehistoric origins. D=RCC,SEC,COS.
834	Paisley	88,300	65.00	57,400	96.72	C	92,400	Scotland. Cotton, dyes, shipbuilding, textiles. F=1163 as Cluniac abbey. D=RCC,SEC,COS.
835	Gloucester	120,000	64.50	77,700	96.22	C	126,000	Gloucestershire county. Fishing, railway, aircraft, agriculture. F=AD 96. D=COE Diocese,COS.
836	Great Yarmouth	57,400	65.00	37,300	96.72	C	60,000	Norfolk county. Gas & oil, herring, holiday resort. F=1208. D=COE.
837	Greenock	106,000	65.00	68,800	96.72	C	111,000	Shipbuilding port of Scotland. Birthplace of James Watt, the discoverer of steam power. D=COS,Presbyterian.
838	Grimsby-Cleethorpes	152,000	64.50	97,900	96.22	C	159,000	Humberside county. Fishing port. F=c1800. D=COE.
839	Halifax	80,300	65.00	52,200	96.72	C	84,000	West Yorkshire county. Wool, cotton, carpet, machine tools. D=COE.
840	Harrogate	66,600	65.00	43,300	96.72	C	69,700	North Yorkshire county. 88 springs. Resort, spa, research, residential. F=c1650. D=COE.
841	Hastings-Bexhill	117,000	64.50	75,500	96.22	C	123,000	East Sussex county. Seaside resort, antiques. Medieval ruins. D=COE,RCC,Methodist,SA.
842	Hastings	78,500	65.00	51,000	96.72	C	82,200	East Sussex county. Seaside resort, antiques. Medieval ruins. D=COE,RCC,Baptist,SA.
843	Hereford	50,600	65.00	32,900	96.72	C	52,900	Hereford & Worcester county on River Wye. Agriculture. F=c650. First bishop Putta. D=COE Diocese.
844	High Wycombe	164,000	64.50	106,000	98.22	C	172,000	Buckinghamshire county. Furniture. Roman ruins. F=1237. Wycliffe/SIL headquarters. D=COE.
845	Huddersfield	395,000	64.00	253,000	97.72	C	414,000	West Yorkshire metropolitan area. Textiles, dyestuff, chemicals. F=c1750. D=COE.
846	Ipswich	136,000	64.50	87,600	96.22	C	142,000	North Sea port in Suffolk county. Engineering, agriculture. F=1200. D=COE.
847	Irvine	96,600	65.50	63,300	97.22	C	101,000	Scotland. Rehouse overflow from Glasgow. Chemicals, engineering. F=1967. D=COS,RCC.
848	Kidderminster	52,800	65.00	34,300	96.72	C	55,200	Hereford & Worcester county. Carpet, spinning, dyeing, metal forging. F=736. D=COE.
849	Kilmarnock	88,000	65.00	57,200	96.72	C	92,100	Scotland. Whisky, textiles. Robert Burns' first poems published here. F=1975. D=COS,RCC.
850	Kingston upon Hull (Hull)	367,000	63.00	231,000	96.72	C	384,000	Humberside county. National seaport. Medieval origins. Parish church of Holy Trinity. D=COE,RCC,Methodist.
851	Kirkcaldy	155,000	65.00	101,000	96.72	C	162,000	Seaport. Linen, linoleum. F=Dunfermline Abbey c700. D=COE.
852	Leeds-Bradford (West Yorkshire)	1,433,000	60.00	860,000	94.72	C	1,433,000	West Yorkshire county. Clothing, engineering, electronics. F=1376. Kirkstall Abbey (1152). D=COE,RCC.
853	Bradford	307,000	59.00	181,000	90.72	B	322,000	West Yorkshire. Wool, dyestuffs. St. Peter's Church (1458). Large Pakistani population. D=COE Diocese.
854	Dewsbury	52,200	61.00	31,800	92.72	C	54,600	West Yorkshire. Weaving, coal mining, engineering. Tradition that Paulinus preached here in AD 627. D=COE.
855	Keighley	51,500	61.00	31,400	92.72	C	53,900	West Yorkshire county, River Worth. Wool, textiles, silk, rayon, machinery, consumer goods. D=COE.
856	Leeds	466,000	60.00	280,000	91.72	C	488,000	West Yorkshire county. Clothing, engineering, electronics. F=1376. D=COE,RCC.
857	Wakefield	78,300	61.00	47,800	92.72	C	81,900	West Yorkshire. Textiles, wool, dyestuffs. F=1086. D=COE Diocese.
858	Leicester-Wigston	518,000	63.00	327,000	96.72	C	543,000	Leicestershire county. Footwear, light engineering. F=Roman settlement. Abbey (1143). 14% Hindus. D=COE.
859	Leicester	340,000	63.00	214,000	96.72	C	356,000	Leicestershire county. Footwear. F=Roman settlement. Abbey (1143). 14% Hindus. D=COE Diocese.
860	Lincoln	83,800	65.00	54,400	96.72	C	87,700	Lincolnshire county. Major agricultural center. F=AD 71 as Roman settlement. D=COE Diocese.
861	Liverpool-Merseyside	912,000	62.50	570,000	97.22	C	944,000	Seaport. Import/export. F=1207. Heavy WWII damage. Cathedral Church of Christ (1903).
862	Bebington	65,600	65.00	42,600	96.72	C	68,600	Merseyside. Model village (Lady Lever Art Gallery, 1922). D=COE,RCC.
863	Birkenhead	104,000	64.50	66,900	96.22	C	109,000	Seaport in Merseyside county. Flour milling, ships, import/export. F=c1810. D=COE,RCC.
864	Crosby	56,700	65.00	36,800	96.72	C	59,300	Merseyside. Irish Sea. Boys' school (1620). Girls' school (1888). D=COE,RCC.
865	Ellesmere Port	68,900	65.00	44,800	96.72	C	72,200	Cheshire county. Petroleum, chemicals, autos, oil refinery. D=COE,RCC.
866	Greasby / Moreton	59,100	65.00	38,400	96.72	C	61,800	Merseyside county. West of Birkenhead. Light engineering, residential. D=COE,RCC.
867	Huyton-with-Roby	64,900	65.00	42,200	96.72	C	68,000	Merseyside metropolitan area. Residential. F=1086. D=COE,RCC.
868	Kirkby	55,300	65.00	36,000	96.72	C	57,900	Merseyside. North of Liverpool-East Lancashire Road. D=COE,RCC.
869	Liverpool	564,000	62.50	353,000	97.22	C	591,000	Seaport. Previously known for import/export. F=1207. Major missions conference (1860). D=COE Diocese,RCC.
870	Runcorn	67,000	65.00	43,600	96.72	C	70,100	Cheshire county. Chemicals. Manchester ship canal, shipbuilding, iron works. D=COE,RCC.
871	Southport	92,800	64.50	59,800	96.22	C	97,100	Merseyside metropolitan area. Residential, Irish Sea coastal resort. D=COE,RCC.
872	Wallasey	65,400	65.00	42,500	96.72	C	68,500	Merseyside. Shipyards, docks. Wirral peninsula, flour milling, ship repairing, seaside resort. D=COE,RCC.
873	LONDON (Greater London)	7,640,000	65.00	4,966,000	97.72	C	7,640,000	On Thames River. International trade & finance. F=AD 43 by Romans as Londinium. St. Paul's Cathedral. D=ZOO.
874	Barking-Dagenham	157,000	65.00	102,000	96.72	C	164,000	Ford Motor Company, power station, chemical products. Remains of a Benedictine abbey c670. D=COE.
875	Barnet	306,000	65.00	199,000	96.72	C	320,000	Residential. Motor vehicle parts. F=1965. Chipping Barnet Church (1250). Battle of Barnet 1471. D=COE.
876	Benfleet	53,200	65.00	34,600	96.72	C	55,700	Essex county. Rapid residential growth in 1960s and 1970s. District seat. D=COE.
877	Bexley	224,000	65.00	145,000	96.72	C	234,000	Southern bank of River Thames. Oil-seed processing, paper, plastics. St. Paulinus Church (c1050). D=COE.
878	Bracknell	54,700	65.00	35,600	96.72	C	57,300	Berkshire county. Engineering, furniture, clothing. F=1949. D=COE.
879	Brent	265,000	65.00	172,000	96.72	C	277,000	Major industrial area. Wembley Stadium. Clocks. Hindu temple, Kensal Green Cemetery. D=COE.
880	Brentwood	53,600	65.00	34,900	96.72	C	56,100	Essex. Residential. Farm lands, agricultural equipment, film. White-Hart Coaching Inn. D=COE,RCC.
881	Bromley	295,000	65.00	192,000	96.72	C	309,000	Residential, shopping, entertainment. 19th century chalk mines. D=COE.
882	Camden	180,000	65.00	117,000	96.72	C	188,000	Diamond, gold & silver trades. Medieval manors. D=COE.
883	Chatham	68,900	65.00	44,800	96.72	C	72,200	Kent county. Shopping center. F=1086 as Cetaham. 5% Jews. D=COE,Methodist,Baptist.
884	Chelmsford	95,400	65.00	62,000	96.72	C	99,900	Essex county. Agricultural market, light engineering. F=1227. D=COE Diocese.
885	Cheshunt	52,000	65.00	33,800	96.72	C	54,400	Hertfordshire county. River Lea. Parks and woodlands. District headquarters. D=COE.
886	Crawley	83,900	64.50	54,100	96.22	C	87,800	West Sussex county. Engineering, printing, plastics, London commuters. F=1202. D=COE.
887	Croydon	314,000	65.00	204,000	96.72	C	329,000	Office space, shopping and cultural center. F=1965. D=COE.
888	Dartford	65,000	65.00	42,200	96.72	C	68,000	Kent county. Paper, chalk, cement, flour milling, pharmaceuticals, chemicals. D=COE.
889	Ealing	292,000	65.00	190,000	96.72	C	306,000	Popular health resort in Acton. Motor vehicles, scientific instruments. Thames Valley University, mosque. D=COE.
890	Enfield	270,000	65.00	176,000	96.72	C	283,000	Farmland, parkland, consumer-goods industries, timber. D=COE.
891	Epsom and Ewell	68,900	65.00	44,800	96.72	C	72,200	Surrey county. Mineral springs, horse racing. D=COE.
892	Gillingham	96,900	65.00	63,000	96.72	C	101,000	Kent county. River Medway. Dockyard, light industries. F=1903. D=COE.
893	Gravesend	56,100	65.00	36,400	96.72	C	58,700	Kent county. River Thames. Paper, cement, ships, customs. D=COE.
894	Greenwich	223,000	65.00	145,000	96.72	C	233,000	South bank of River Thames. Henry VIII's birthplace. D=COE.
895	Guildford	64,400	65.00	41,900	96.72	C	67,400	Surrey county. Residential, motor vehicles. F=1257. Pre-Norman churches. D=COE Diocese.
896	Hackney	188,000	65.00	123,000	96.72	C	197,000	Furniture, cabinet making. London's first theatre 1575. Elizabethan church, several colleges. D=COE.
897	Hammersmith-Fulham	156,000	65.00	101,000	96.72	C	163,000	BBC Studios. Wharves, pottery kilns, Fulham palace. Residence of London Bishop. D=COE.
898	Haringey (Harringay)	213,000	65.00	138,000	96.72	C	223,000	Residential, light engineering, furniture, clothing, footwear. D=COE.
899	Harlow	82,900	65.00	53,900	96.72	C	86,800	Essex county. Offices, printing, metallurgy. F=1947. D=COE.
900	Harrow	204,000	65.00	133,000	96.72	C	214,000	Residential, shopping centers. Harrow school. Medieval Church of St. Mary. D=COE.
901	Havering	250,000	65.00	163,000	96.72	C	262,000	Commuters. Engineering, manufacturing. Plastics, chemicals, clothing, beer, mostly residential. D=COE.
902	Hemel Hempstead	83,900	65.00	54,500	96.72	C	87,800	Hertfordshire county on River Gade. Papermaking, electrical. F=1539. D=COE.
903	Hillingdon	240,000	65.00	156,000	96.72	C	252,000	Residential, open spaces. Heathrow airport. Printing, motion picture production, musical instruments. D=COE.
904	Hounslow	210,000	65.00	136,000	96.72	C	220,000	Thames valley. Picturesque riverside communities. Factories. Monastery at Isleworth (1415). D=COE.
905	Islington	168,000	65.00	109,000	96.72	C	176,000	Light industries. Burial place of John Bunyan, Isaac Watts, William Blake, John Wesley's chapel. D=COE.
906	Kensington-Chelsea	145,000	65.00	94,300	96.72	C	152,000	Residential. Shops, restaurants, Hyde Park, Albert Hall, literary and artistic center. D=COE.
907	Kingston upon Thames	138,000	65.00	90,000	96.72	C	145,000	Residential. Major shopping center. Marymount International School (1955). D=CODE.
908	Lambeth	257,000	65.00	167,000	96.72	C	269,000	Residential. Commercial & government offices. Lambeth Palace. D=COE.
909	Lewisham	242,000	65.00	157,000	96.72	C	253,000	Light engineering, electrical engineering. Christopher Marlowe killed here. Goldsmith's College. D=COE.
910	Maidenhead	62,600	65.00	40,700	96.72	C	65,600	Berkshire county on River Thames. Residential, summer resort. D=COE.
911	Merton	174,000	65.00	113,000	96.72	C	182,000	Residential. Extensive open spaces. Wimbledon. D=COE.
912	Newham	219,000	65.00	142,000	96.72	C	229,000	Residential. Engineering, milling, manufacturing. D=COE.
913	Redbridge	239,000	65.00	155,000	96.72	C	250,000	Residential. Major suburban shopping center. D=COE.
914	Reigate/Redhill	50,500	65.00	32,800	96.72	C	52,900	Surrey county. Residential, parks, recreation, light industry. D=COE.
915	Richmond upon Thames	167,000	65.00	108,000	96.72	C	175,000	Residential. Boat building and repair. Home of Henry VIII, Oxford Cambridge boat race. D=COE.
916	Slough	111,000	64.50	71,800	96.22	C	117,000	Berkshire county. Light industry, home to astronomer William Herschel. D=COE.
917	Southend-on-Sea	163,000	64.00	104,000	95.72	C	171,000	Essex county. Thames estuary and North Sea. Nearest seaside resort to London. Millions of visitors. D=COE.
918	Southwark	221,000	65.00	144,000	96.72	C	232,000	Food processing, newspaper publishing & printing, spas, resorts, inns. D=COE Diocese.
919	Staines	54,400	65.00	35,400	96.72	C	56,900	Surrey county. Residential, Thames River water works for London. D=COE. D=COE.
920	Sutton	175,000	65.00	113,000	96.72	C	183,000	Greater London. Private housing. Parkland. Medieval buildings. D=COE.
921	Tower Hamlets	149,000	65.00	97,000	96.72	C	156,000	Wharves, marina. F=1965. Large scale urban renewal. Many Indians, Pakistanis. D=COE.
922	Waltham Forest	226,000	65.00	147,000	96.72	C	236,000	Residential. Roman and Saxon antiquities. Hunting lodge of Queen Elizabeth I. D=COE.
923	Walton and Weybridge	52,400	65.00	34,100	96.72	C	54,800	Surrey county. Largely residential. Sandown racecourse (1875). D=COE.
924	Wandsworth	266,000	65.00	173,000	96.72	C	279,000	Beer, gas, paint, candles, printing inks. Battersea Park. D=COE.
925	Watford	115,000	65.00	74,500	96.72	C	120,000	Commuters, printing, breweries, chemicals. Engineering. D=COE.
926	Watford	115,000	64.50	74,000	96.22	C	120,000	Hertfordshire county. Residential community for London. Printing. D=COE.
927	Westminster	200,000	65.00	130,000	96.72	C	209,000	North bank of River Thames. Big Ben, 10 Downing St. F=AD 785 by Monks. D=COE,RCC.
928	Woking	97,100	64.50	62,600	96.22	C	102,000	Surrey county. Residential town in heathlands. Mosque (1889). D=COE.
929	Londonderry (Derry, Doire)	103,000	65.00	67,200	96.72	C	108,000	Northern Ireland. On River Foyle. Clothing, foods. St. Columba monastery c550. D=COE Diocese,RCC.

Table 10-5–continued overleaf

Table 10-5–continued

Rec No 1	Country City 2	Pop 2000 3	AC% 4	Church Members 5	E% 6	W 7	Pop 2025 8	Notes 9
930	Lowestoft	62,200	65.00	40,500	96.72	C	65,100	Suffolk county. Fishing, resort. North Sea, easternmost town in England, birthplace of Thomas Nashe. D=COE.
931	Lurgan	64,800	65.50	42,400	97.22	C	67,800	Northern Ireland. Craigavon district. Market town. Lurgan Castle (1836). D=RCC.
932	Luton-Dunstable	230,000	63.50	146,000	95.22	C	241,000	Bedfordshire county. Hats, motor vehicles, aircraft parts, ball bearings, printing. 7% Muslims. D=COE,RCC.
933	Dunstable	50,700	65.00	33,000	96.72	C	53,100	Bedfordshire county. Light engineering, autos, cement plants. Whipsnade Zoo. D=COE,RCC,Methodist.
934	Luton	171,000	64.00	109,000	95.72	C	179,000	Bedfordshire county. Hats, motor vehicles, largest town in Bedfordshire, ball bearings, aircraft parts. D=COE.
935	Maidstone	90,100	65.00	58,600	96.72	C	94,300	Kent county. Major agricultural market center. Paper, breweries. F=c1250. D=COE.
936	Manchester (Greater Manchester)	2,252,000	64.50	1,453,000	99.22	C	2,252,000	On Irwell River. Printing, finance. F=AD 78 as Roman Mancunium. 15th century cathedral. D=COE.
937	Bolton	151,000	64.50	97,200	96.22	C	158,000	Greater Manchester. Cotton, engineering, printing. D=COE,RCC.
938	Bury	64,700	65.00	42,100	96.72	C	67,700	Greater Manchester. Textiles, paper, metals, hats, paper, machines, boilers. D=COE,RCC.
939	Cheadle and Gatley	62,300	65.00	40,500	96.72	C	65,200	Greater Manchester. South, 8 miles east of Stoke-on-Trent. Light industrial, marketplace. D=COE,RCC.
940	Middleton	53,800	65.00	35,000	96.72	C	56,300	Greater Manchester. North. Major golf driving range, engineering. D=COE,RCC.
941	Oldham	112,000	64.50	72,300	96.22	C	117,000	Greater Manchester metropolitan county. Agriculture, cotton, weaving, electronics. D=COE,RCC.
942	Rochdale	102,000	64.50	65,700	96.22	C	107,000	Greater Manchester metropolitan area. Heavy textiles. Medieval origins. D=COE,RCC.
943	Sale	60,600	65.00	39,400	96.72	C	63,400	Greater Manchester. Southwest. Bridgewater Canal (1761). D=COE,RCC.
944	Salford	101,000	64.50	65,200	96.22	C	106,000	Greater Manchester metropolitan area. Textiles, chemicals, plastics. F=1228. D=COE,RCC.
945	Stockport	142,000	64.50	91,500	96.22	C	149,000	Greater Manchester metropolitan area. Clothing, electronics, residential. F=1220. D=COE,RCC.
946	Wigan-Skelmersdale	92,900	64.00	59,500	95.72	C	97,200	Greater Manchester metropolitan area. Coal, cotton, food processing. D=COE,RCC.
947	Manchester	458,000	66.00	302,000	97.72	C	480,000	Printing, finance, schools, 15th century cathedral. D=COE Diocese,RCC,Reformed,Methodist.
948	Mansfield-Sutton	207,000	64.00	133,000	97.72	C	217,000	Nottinghamshire county. Coal mining, hosiery, shoes, medieval church. D=COE.
949	Mansfield	74,700	65.00	48,600	96.72	C	78,200	Nottinghamshire county. Coal mining, hosiery, shoes, prehistoric cave dwelling remains. D=COE.
950	Margate	55,700	65.00	36,200	96.72	C	58,200	Kent county. Bathing resort. Founded as Roman villa. D=COE.
951	Rochester upon Medway	153,000	63.50	97,100	97.22	C	160,000	Kent county. River Medway. Major naval dockyards. Cathedral city. D=COE.
952	Newcastle-upon-Tyne (Tyneside)	979,000	61.50	602,000	98.22	C	1,019,000	Tyne & Wear Metropolitan area. Marine, heavy engineering. Education. F=1080. D=COE Diocese,RCC.
953	South Shields	90,600	65.00	58,900	96.72	C	94,800	Tyne & Wear metropolitan area. North Sea port. Shipbuilding. F=c1250 by Convent of Durham. D=COE,RCC.
954	Sunderland	204,000	63.50	130,000	95.22	C	214,000	Tyne & Wear county. Coal, ships, glass. F=674 as monastery. Venerable Bede studied here. D=COE,RCC.
955	Washington	51,200	65.00	33,300	96.72	C	53,500	Sunderland district. River Wear. Coal mining. American president George Washington's forebears. D=COE,RCC.
956	Gateshead	95,800	64.00	61,300	95.72	C	100,000	Tyne and Wear. Medieval origins. Iron, steel, engineering, and food industries. D=COE,Methodist.
957	Newport	122,000	64.50	78,600	96.22	C	128,000	Isle of Wight county. Agricultural center, plastics, beverages, woodworking. F=1177. Parkhurst. D=COE.
958	Newport (Casnewydd)	325,000	64.50	209,000	98.22	C	340,000	Wales. Steel, paper, chemicals, timber, tea, motor vehicles, semiconductors, cathedral. F=c1126. D=CIW.
959	Northampton	161,000	64.00	103,000	95.72	C	169,000	Northamptonshire county. Shoes, leather, electronics, brewing. F=1100. D=COE,RCC.
960	Norwich	241,000	64.00	154,000	95.72	C	252,000	Norfolk county. Footwear, printing, mustard, agriculture, livestock. F=1158. D=COE Diocese.
961	Nottingham	686,000	64.50	442,000	98.22	C	718,000	Nottinghamshire county. Hosiery, lace, pharmaceuticals, tobacco. Robin Hood statue. F=c550. D=COE,RCC.
962	Beeston and Stapleford	67,800	65.00	44,100	96.72	C	71,000	Nottinghamshire county. Pharmaceuticals. F=c1850 around coal mining. D=COE,RCC.
963	Oxford	241,000	64.50	155,000	98.22	C	252,000	Oxfordshire county. Oxford University. Tourism, Sheldonian theatre, St. Michael church. D=COE Diocese.
964	Peterborough	119,000	64.50	76,600	96.22	C	124,000	Cambridge county. Warehousing, trade. F=c1100. D=COE Diocese.
965	Plymouth	304,000	63.50	193,000	97.22	C	318,000	Devon county. Machine tools, precision instruments. Navy dockyard (1640). D=COE,RCC,Methodist.
966	Port Talbot	136,000	65.50	89,200	97.22	C	142,000	Wales. Seaside resort, mouth of Avon River. Steel works, oil refinery. D=CIW.
967	Portsmouth-Havant-Gosport	508,000	65.00	330,000	98.72	C	532,000	Hampshire county. Naval base, seaside resort. F=1194. D=COE,RCC.
968	Fareham / Portchester	58,200	65.00	37,800	96.72	C	60,900	Hampshire county. Grain, timber, coal, boat-building. Roman fortress. D=COE,RCC.
969	Gosport	73,000	65.00	47,400	96.72	C	76,400	Hampshire county. Naval port, shares harbour with Portsmouth. Ship and yacht building. D=COE,RCC.
970	Havant	52,500	65.00	34,100	96.72	C	54,900	Hampshire county. Light engineering, plastics, yachting. 12th century church. D=COE,RCC.
971	Portsmouth	182,000	64.00	117,000	95.72	C	191,000	Hampshire county. Naval base, seaside resort. F=1194. Birthplace of C. Dickens. D=COE Diocese,RCC.
972	Waterlooville	60,000	65.00	39,000	96.72	C	62,800	Hampshire county. London Road. Homes and factories, yachting. D=COE,RCC.
973	Preston-Chorley-Leyland	262,000	63.50	166,000	97.22	C	274,000	Lancashire county. Agricultural center, cattle, engineering. F=1179. D=COE.
974	Preston	175,000	64.00	112,000	95.72	C	183,000	Lancashire county. Agricultural center, cattle, engineering. F=1179. D=COE.
975	Reading	209,000	63.50	133,000	97.22	C	219,000	Berkshire county. Biscuit making, printing, engineering. F=871. Benedictine abbey 1121. D=COE,Methodist.
976	Royal Tunbridge Wells (Tunbridge Wells)	60,400	65.00	39,300	96.72	C	63,200	Kent county. Spa, shopping, administration. F=c1650. Church of St. Charles the Martyr (1684). D=COE.
977	Rugby	61,800	65.00	40,200	96.72	C	64,700	Warwickshire county. Railway junction. Rugby School (1567). D=COE.
978	Saint Helens	120,000	64.50	77,300	96.22	C	125,000	Merseyside county. Glassmaking, iron and brass foundries, Pilkington glass museum. D=COE.
979	Scunthorpe	82,800	65.00	53,800	96.72	C	86,600	Humberside county. Sits on an ironstone field. Steelmaking, iron, apparel manufacturing. F=1870. D=COE.
980	Sheffield-South Yorkshire	744,000	64.50	480,000	99.22	C	778,000	South Yorkshire county. Metallurgy, cutlery, steelworks. Medieval origins. University (1905). D=COE.
981	Rotherham	128,000	64.50	82,700	96.22	C	134,000	South Yorkshire county. Rivers Don and Rother. Clothing manufacturing. Ironworks (1746). D=COE.
982	Sheffield	493,000	63.00	311,000	94.72	C	516,000	South Yorkshire county. Metallurgy, cutlery, steelworks. Medieval origins. D=COE Diocese.
983	Shrewsbury	60,500	65.00	39,300	96.72	C	63,300	Shropshire county. Market center for dairy farming. D=COE,RCC.
984	Southampton-Eastleigh	435,000	63.50	276,000	98.22	C	455,000	Hampshire county. Shipbuilding, oil. F=AD 43 as Roman settlement. 3% Sikhs. D=COE,RCC.
985	Eastleigh	61,400	65.00	39,900	96.72	C	64,200	Hampshire county. Railroad, residential. D=COE,RCC,Baptist,Methodist.
986	Southampton	221,000	63.50	141,000	97.22	C	232,000	Hampshire county. Britain's second largest port. Shipbuilding, oil. F=AD 43 as Roman settlement. D=COE,RCC.
987	St. Albans-Hatfield	115,000	64.50	74,400	98.22	C	121,000	Hertfordshire county. Printing. F=c50 BC. St Alban martyred here in 304. D=COE.
988	Saint Albans	80,300	65.00	52,200	96.72	C	84,100	Hertfordshire county. Printing. F=c50 BC. St Alban martyred here in 304. D=COE Diocese.
989	Stafford	63,800	65.00	41,500	96.72	C	66,800	Staffordshire county on River Sow. Salt, shoes. Founded by Aethelflaed c900. D=COE.
990	Stevenage	78,300	65.00	50,900	96.72	C	81,900	Hertfordshire county. Electronics. Cameras, photographic goods, pharmaceutical research. F=c1150. D=COE.
991	Stirling	63,900	65.50	41,800	97.22	C	66,900	Scotland. Agricultural center, coal mining, tourism. F=1130. D=COE,RCC.
992	Stoke-on-Trent-Newcastle (Potterie)	461,000	63.00	290,000	96.72	C	482,000	Staffordshire county. Coal mining, ceramics, iron and steel. D=COE.
993	Newcastle-under-Lyme	76,700	65.00	49,800	96.72	C	80,200	Staffordshire county. Coal mining, brick & tile making. F=1173. D=COE.
994	Stoke-on-Trent	285,000	63.50	181,000	97.22	C	299,000	Staffordshire county. Coal mining, rubber, iron and steel. 'The Potteries' (ceramics). D=COE.
995	Swansea (Abertane)	288,000	63.00	181,000	96.72	C	301,000	Wales on Bristol Channel. Coal, copper, lead, zinc, nickel. Birthplace of D. Thomas (1914). D=CIW Diocese.
996	Neath (Castell-Nedd)	51,000	65.00	33,100	96.72	C	53,400	Wales. Petrochemicals, steel manufacturing. F=AD 75 as Roman fort. D=CIW.
997	Swindon	133,000	64.50	86,000	96.22	C	140,000	Wiltshire county. Railway, engineering, clothes, tobacco. D=COE,RCC,Methodist,Reformed.
998	Tanworth	66,300	65.00	43,100	96.72	C	69,300	Midlands. Near Birmingham. Metal, engineering, autos. D=Anglican.
999	Teesside (Stockton-Middlesbrough)	607,000	63.00	383,000	97.72	C	636,000	Cleveland county. River Tees. Large-scale industrial development. D=COE.
1000	Hartlepool	96,100	65.00	62,500	96.72	C	101,000	Cleveland county. Port servicing North Sea petroleum. F=1201. D=COE.
1001	Middlesbrough	166,000	64.00	106,000	95.72	C	174,000	Cleveland county. Heavy engineering. F=1830. D=COE.
1002	Stockton-on-Tees	90,800	65.00	59,000	96.72	C	95,000	Cleveland county. Market town, port, petrochemicals. F=1310. D=COE.
1003	Telford	108,000	64.50	69,900	96.22	C	113,000	Shropshire county. Housing, factories. F=1968. 2% Muslims, 2% Sikhs. D=COE,RCC,Methodist.
1004	Thanet (Broadstairs-Margate)	120,000	64.50	77,200	96.22	C	125,000	Kent county. Seaside resorts, green vegetables, potatoes. D=COE.
1005	Thurrock	133,000	64.50	85,500	96.22	C	139,000	Essex county. River port. Soap, margarine, cement. D=COE.
1006	Torquay	118,000	65.00	76,500	96.72	C	123,000	Devon county. All-year resort, conferences. Premonstratensian abbey (1196). D=COE,RCC,Baptist.
1007	Warrington	85,200	64.50	55,000	96.22	C	89,200	Cheshire county. Sawmills, breweries, printing, warehouses. Founded in pre-Roman times. D=COE.
1008	Weston-super-Mare	63,700	65.00	41,400	96.72	C	66,700	Avon county. Beach, extensive marine promenade. D=COE.
1009	Widnes	58,600	65.00	38,100	96.72	C	61,300	Cheshire county on River Mersey. Britain's principal chemical center. D=COE.
1010	Worcester	79,000	65.00	51,400	96.72	C	82,700	Hereford & Worcester county. Porcelain industry. First bishop, Bosel (679). D=COE Diocese.
1011	York	152,000	64.50	97,900	98.22	C	159,000	North Yorkshire county. Tourism. F=AD 71 as Roman Eboracum. Cathedral city. D=COE Diocese.
	BRITISH INDIAN OCEAN	**2,000**	**45.00**	**900**	**96.25**	**B**	**2,000**	**ROMAN CATHOLICS 35.0%, ANGLICANS 10.0%. PENT-CHAR 5.6%, EVANGELICAL 0.5%, GCC 24.0%**
1012	rural areas	–	–	–	–	–	–	0.0% (1950), 0.0% (1970), 0.0% (1990), 0.0% (2000), 0.0% (2010), 0.0% (2025)
1013	urban areas	2,000	45.00	900	96.25	B	2,000	100.0% (1950), 100.0% (1970), 100.0% (1990), 100.0% (2000), 100.0% (2010), 100.0% (2025)
1014	non-metropolitan areas	1,000	45.00	450	96.20	B	1,000	*Sources of data:* Censuses.
1015	metropolitan areas	1,000	45.00	450	96.30	B	1,000	*Definition:* Total population.
1016	DIEGO GARCIA	1,000	45.00	450	96.25	B	1,000	Southern Indian ocean. Copra from coconut palms. U.S. military communications center. D=RCC.
	BRITISH VIRGIN IS	**21,400**	**69.70**	**14,900**	**99.58**	**C**	**36,700**	**PROTESTANTS 45.8%, ANGLICANS 13.1%. PENT-CHAR 12.5%, EVANGELICAL 17.0%, GCC 29.1%**
1017	rural areas	17,100	69.62	11,900	99.50	C	0	0.0% (1950), 0.0% (1970), 0.0% (1990), 80.0% (2000), 0.0% (2010), 0.0% (2025)
1018	urban areas	4,300	70.00	3,000	99.88	C	36,700	100.0% (1950), 100.0% (1970), 100.0% (1990), 20.0% (2000), 100.0% (2010), 100.0% (2025)
1019	non-metropolitan areas	480	70.02	340	99.97	C	4,120	*Sources of data:* Censuses.
1020	metropolitan areas	3,800	70.00	2,700	99.87	C	32,500	*Definition:* Road Town.
1021	ROAD TOWN	3,800	70.00	2,700	99.88	C	32,500	Port of Tortola Island, capital and largest town. F=1840. D=Methodist,Anglican.
	BRUNEI	**328,000**	**7.50**	**24,600**	**45.13**	**A**	**459,000**	**INDEPENDENTS 2.5%, PROTESTANTS 1.8%. PENT-CHAR 2.7%, EVANGELICAL 1.9%, GCC 5.5%**
1022	rural areas	91,100	3.59	3,300	33.43	A	85,500	73.2% (1950), 38.3% (1970), 34.1% (1990), 27.7% (2000), 23.0% (2010), 18.6% (2025)
1023	urban areas	237,000	9.00	21,300	49.63	A	373,000	26.7% (1950), 61.6% (1970), 65.8% (1990), 72.2% (2000), 76.9% (2010), 81.3% (2025)
1024	non-metropolitan areas	137,000	9.00	12,300	49.63	A	216,074	*Sources of data:* Censuses of 1960, 1971, and 1981.
1025	metropolitan areas	99,900	9.00	9,000	49.63	A	157,000	*Definition:* Municipalities and areas having urban socio-economic characteristics.
1026	BANDAR SERI BEGAWAN (Brunei town)	99,900	9.00	9,000	49.63	A	157,000	Brunei River port. Rebuilt following WWII. Saifuddin Mosque. Malay Muslim, 20% Chinese. D=RCC,Anglican.
	BULGARIA	**8,225,000**	**80.95**	**6,658,000**	**94.48**	**C**	**7,023,000**	**ORTHODOX 71.5%, INDEPENDENTS 7.0%. PENT-CHAR 1.7%, EVANGELICAL 1.4%, GCC 6.0%**
1027	rural areas	2,461,000	87.85	2,162,000	99.05	C	1,509,000	74.4% (1950), 48.2% (1970), 33.5% (1990), 29.9% (2000), 26.3% (2010), 21.4% (2025)
1028	urban areas	5,764,000	78.00	4,496,000	92.53	C	5,514,000	25.6% (1950), 51.8% (1970), 66.4% (1990), 70.0% (2000), 73.6% (2010), 78.5% (2025)
1029	non-metropolitan areas	1,832,000	78.47	1,437,000	92.70	C	1,700,604	*Sources of data:* Censuses of 1956, 1965, 1975 and 1985
1030	metropolitan areas	3,932,000	77.78	3,059,000	92.45	C	3,813,000	*Definition:* Towns, that is, localities legally established as urban.
1031	Blagoevgrad (Dzhumaya)	70,700	81.00	57,300	94.53	C	67,600	Chief center of Macedonia. Oriental tobacco, wood, canning, textiles. Mineral Springs. D=BOC.
1032	Burgas (Bourgas)	191,000	76.00	145,000	92.53	C	183,000	Port on Gulf of Burgas, Black Sea. Fish, food processing, engineering. F=c1650. D=BOC.
1033	Dimitrovgrad	54,400	82.00	44,600	95.53	C	52,000	Rail junction in Maritsa River Valley. Chemicals, cement, hothouse vegetables. F=1947. D=BOC.
1034	Gabrovo	77,100	80.00	61,700	93.53	C	73,700	Yantra River in Balkan Mountains. Large textile industry, footwear. F=c1450. D=BOC.
1035	Haskovo (Khaskovo)	89,200	79.00	70,400	92.53	C	85,300	Near Rhodope Mountains. Silk & cotton textiles. Refugees from Macedonia & Aegean Thrace. D=BOC.
1036	Jambol (Yambol)	92,800	78.00	72,400	91.53	C	88,800	On Tundzha River. Textiles, machinery, ceramics, furniture. D=BOC.
1037	Kardzali (Kurdzhali, Kurdzali)	56,200	80.00	45,000	93.53	C	53,800	Tobacco growing center, lead & zinc refining. Famous rock formations. F=1913. D=BOC.
1038	Kazanlak (Kazanluk)	60,700	81.00	49,200	94.53	C	58,100	Famous for roses. Lavender, peppermint, ancient craft center. D=BOC.
1039	Kjustendil (Kyustendi, Kustendil)	53,000	80.00	42,400	93.53	C	50,700	Carpets, woolens, fruit canning. Mineral springs, & extensive orchards. D=BOC.
1040	Lovec (Lovech)	48,500	82.00	39,700	95.53	C	46,400	On Osum River. Bicycles, motorcycles, autos, leather goods. Prehistoric settlement. D=BOC.
1041	Mihajlovgrad (Mihailovgrad)	52,600	79.00	41,500	92.53	C	50,300	On Ogosta River. Center of fertile agricultural region. D=BOC.
1042	Pazardzik (Pazardjik, Pazarzhik)	79,500	78.00	62,000	91.53	C	76,000	Upper Maritsa River. Textile, rubber, furniture. Founded by Russian Tatars. Church of the Virgin Mary. D=BOC.
1043	Pernik (Dimitrovo)	93,300	76.00	70,900	89.53	C	89,200	Struma River. Coal mining, leading industrial city. Originally a Bulgarian fortress. D=BOC.
1044	Pleven (Plevene)	130,000	75.00	97,400	88.53	C	124,000	Near Vir River. Service center for agricultural hinterland. Grains, grapes, fruits, cattle. Thracian settlement. D=BOC.
1045	Plovdiv	347,000	77.00	267,000	94.53	C	332,000	Maritsa River. Food processing center, metals, agriculture. Thracian origins. (c700 BC). D=BOC.

Table 10-5–continued opposite

Table 10-5–continued

Rec No 1	Country City 2	Pop 2000 3	AC% 4	Church Members 5	E% 6	W 7	Pop 2025 8	Notes 9
1046	Razgrad (Rasgrad)	53,800	80.00	43,000	93.53	C	51,500	On Beli Lom River. Largest producer of antibiotics, concrete, porcelain, glass. D=BOC.
1047	Ruse (Rousse, Russe)	182,000	77.00	140,000	90.53	C	174,000	On Danube River. Oil, railway, textiles. F=c50 BC as Sexantaprista. Old churches & mosques. D=BOC.
1048	SOFIJA (Sofia, Sophia, Sofiya)	1,188,000	78.00	927,000	92.53	C	1,188,000	Sofia Basin. Engineering, metals. F=c750 BC by Thracians. Ancient Orthodox monasteries. D=BOC.
1049	Silistra	54,200	82.00	44,400	95.53	C	51,900	On Danube River. Textiles, furniture, brick & tile, livestock, grains. F=c150.D=BOC.
1050	Sliven (Slivno)	104,000	79.00	82,300	92.53	C	99,700	Balkan Mountains.Handicrafts, carpets. F=1153. Roman ruins. Mosques. D=BOC.
1051	Stara Zagora	151,000	78.00	118,000	94.53	C	144,000	Cotton, textiles, chemicals, fertilizers, cigarettes. Thracian origins. D=BOC.
1052	Sumen (Shumen)	103,000	77.00	79,200	90.53	C	98,400	Road & rail center. Tobacco, canning & brewing, furniture. Thracian origins. Tumbul Mosque. D=BOC.
1053	Tolbuhin (Tolbukhin, Dobrich)	101,000	80.00	80,400	93.53	C	96,200	Market town. Agricultural industries: milling, baking, oil-extraction. D=BOC.
1054	Varna	292,000	72.00	210,000	88.53	C	279,000	Black Sea port. Economic, cultural, resort center. F=c500 BC by Greeks. Ancient monasteries. D=BOC.
1055	Veliko Tarnovo	68,300	81.00	55,300	94.53	C	65,300	Jantra River. Beverages. Prehistoric settlement. Church of the Forty Martyrs (1230). D=BOC.
1056	Vidin (Widyn)	62,800	82.00	51,500	95.53	C	60,000	Danube River port. Agricultural & trade center. F=c250 BC as Celtic settlement. D=BOC.
1057	Vraca (Vratsa, Vratca)	78,100	79.00	61,700	92.53	C	74,700	Chemicals, textiles, furniture, ceramics. F=c1420. D=BOC.
	BURKINA FASO	**11,937,000**	**16.62**	**1,984,000**	**63.09**	**B**	**23,321,000**	**ROMAN CATHOLICS 9.4%, PROTESTANTS 6.6%. PENT-CHAR 7.0%, EVANGELICAL 6.4%, GCC 12.7%**
1058	rural areas	9,733,000	13.59	1,323,000	59.60	B	15,453,000	96.1% (1950), 94.2% (1970), 86.4% (1990), 81.5% (2000), 75.7% (2010), 66.2% (2025)
1059	urban areas	2,204,000	30.00	661,000	78.47	B	7,869,000	3.8% (1950), 5.7% (1970), 13.5% (1990), 18.4% (2000), 24.2% (2010), 33.7% (2025)
1060	non-metropolitan areas	598,000	28.99	173,000	78.58	B	2,338,235	*Sources of data:* Censuses of 1960, 1975 and 1985; estimate for 1991.
1061	metropolitan areas	1,606,000	30.38	488,000	78.43	B	5,530,000	*Definition:* The sum of 14 towns.
1062	Bobo-Dioulasso	340,000	5.00	17,000	46.47	A	1,213,000	Trade center. F=c1450. 60% Bobo Fing, Red Bobo, Mossi. 47% Muslim, 40% animist. D=C&MA,AoG.
1063	Koudougou	77,200	10.00	7,700	53.47	B	276,000	Capital of BoulkimdA. Peanut, tobacco, cotton, textiles, Shea nuts, chromium, manganese. D=RCC.
1064	OUAGADOUGOU (Wagadugu)	1,131,000	39.00	441,000	89.27	B	3,835,000	Textiles, carbonated beverages. 79% Mossi, 3% Bobo. 48% Muslim, 10% animist. D=AoG,RCC,SDA.
1065	Ouahigouya	57,800	38.00	22,000	87.47	B	206,000	Northwest of Ouagadougou. Kingdom of former Mossi empire. Mosques. D=RCC.
	BURUNDI	**6,695,000**	**76.97**	**5,153,000**	**99.18**	**C**	**11,569,000**	**ROMAN CATHOLICS 57.1%, PROTESTANTS 11.9%. PENT-CHAR 11.5%, EVANGELICAL 12.7%, GCC 17.1%**
1066	rural areas	6,095,000	76.37	4,655,000	99.13	C	9,349,000	98.2% (1950), 97.6% (1970), 93.7% (1990), 91.0% (2000), 87.5% (2010), 80.8% (2025)
1067	urban areas	600,000	83.00	498,000	99.71	C	2,220,000	1.7% (1950), 2.3% (1970), 6.2% (1990), 8.9% (2000), 12.4% (2010), 19.1% (2025)
1068	non-metropolitan areas	151,000	82.94	125,000	99.70	C	559,647	*Sources of data:* Censuses of 1965, 1970, 1979 and 1990; estimate for 1987.
1069	metropolitan areas	449,000	83.02	372,000	99.71	C	1,660,000	*Definition:* Commune of Bujumbura.
1070	BUJUMBURA	302,000	84.00	254,000	99.81	C	1,118,000	Lake Tanganyika port. Textiles, leather, paper, bananas. Scenic beaches. Zairians, Belgians, Indians. D=RCC.
1071	Gitega	146,000	81.00	119,000	99.51	C	542,000	Center for religion & education. Livestock, agriculture, tanning. National Museum. D=RCC.
	CAMBODIA	**11,168,000**	**1.06**	**118,000**	**49.09**	**A**	**16,526,000**	**INDEPENDENTS 0.6%, ROMAN CATHOLICS 0.2%. PENT-CHAR 0.5%, EVANGELICAL 0.1%, GCC 0.9%**
1072	rural areas	8,546,000	0.93	79,100	48.89	A	9,994,000	89.8% (1950), 88.3% (1970), 82.5% (1990), 76.5% (2000), 70.2% (2010), 60.4% (2025)
1073	urban areas	2,622,000	1.50	39,300	49.73	A	6,533,000	10.2% (1950), 11.7% (1970), 17.4% (1990), 23.4% (2000), 29.7% (2010), 39.5% (2025)
1074	non-metropolitan areas	1,537,000	1.51	23,200	49.94	A	3,828,538	*Sources of data:* Censuses of 1962 and 1980; estimates for 1950, 1966, 1970 and 1975.
1075	metropolitan areas	1,085,000	1.49	16,200	49.44	A	2,704,000	*Definition:* Municipalities of Phnom Penh, Bokor and Kep, and 13 urban centers.
1076	Batdambang	124,000	0.80	990	48.83	A	310,000	Capital of Batdambang on Sangke River. Rice-growing region. Ancient Khmer temples.
1077	Kampong Saom	88,800	0.10	89	43.13	A	221,000	Kampot on Kampong Saom Bay. Major port. F=1960 by French.
1078	PHNUM-PENH (Phnom Penh)	629,000	2.30	14,500	52.13	B	1,567,000	Three rivers. Cultural center. 77% Khmer, Vietnamese, Chinese. 80% Buddhist. F=1434. M=WVI,YWAM.
1079	Prey Veng	54,600	0.10	55	43.13	A	136,000	Capital of Prey Veng. East of Phnom Penh.
1080	Siemreab	101,000	0.20	200	43.23	A	251,000	Capital of Siemreab. North of Tonle Sab. Pharmaceuticals. Angkor Wat nearby.
1081	Sisophon	88,200	0.40	350	48.43	A	220,000	Northwest near Thai border. Railroad, customs station, market center, rice growing.
	CAMEROON	**15,085,000**	**51.45**	**7,762,000**	**79.93**	**B**	**26,484,000**	**ROMAN CATHOLICS 26.4%, PROTESTANTS 20.6%. PENT-CHAR 6.5%, EVANGELICAL 4.1%, GCC 22.4%**
1082	rural areas	7,705,000	54.28	4,182,000	79.89	B	9,521,000	90.2% (1950), 79.7% (1970), 59.7% (1990), 51.0% (2000), 43.9% (2010), 35.9% (2025)
1083	urban areas	7,380,000	48.50	3,579,000	79.98	B	16,963,000	9.7% (1950), 20.3% (1970), 40.2% (1990), 48.9% (2000), 56.0% (2010), 64.0% (2025)
1084	non-metropolitan areas	3,260,000	47.98	1,564,000	80.03	B	7,773,268	*Sources of data:* Censuses of 1976 and 1987; estimates for 1959, 1965 and 1970.
1085	metropolitan areas	4,120,000	48.91	2,015,000	79.94	B	9,190,000	*Definition:* Urban centers.
1086	Bafoussam	136,000	45.00	61,200	73.48	B	313,000	Capital of Ouest.Trading center of the Bamileke peoples. Coffee, kola nuts, tobacco, tea. D=RCC.
1087	Bamenda	110,000	40.00	44,000	66.48	B	253,000	Capital of Nord-Ouest. Trade & export center for hides, coffee, tobacco. Elaborate wood & ivory carvings. D=RCC.
1088	Douala	1,672,000	48.00	803,000	78.48	B	3,676,000	Capital of Littoral. Chief port. Overseas trade, breweries, textiles, palm oil, soap. Nigerians, French. D=RCC.
1089	Foumban	76,400	45.00	34,400	73.48	B	176,000	Ouest northeast of Bafoussam. Former capital of Bamum Kingdom. Center for art. D=RCC.
1090	Garoua (Garua)	147,000	50.00	73,400	82.48	B	337,000	Capital of Nord on Benue River. Weaving, textiles, leatherwork, fishing. F=c1825. Tourism. D=RCC.
1091	Kumba	102,000	50.00	51,200	82.48	B	235,000	Soud-Ouest north of Buea. Near Mont Koupe. Known for scenic waterfalls. Cocoa, bananas. D=RCC.
1092	Maroua	154,000	50.00	77,000	82.48	B	354,000	Capital of Extreme-Nord. Near Mandara Mountains and Parc National de Waza. Pottery, jewelry. D=RCC.
1093	Ngaoundere	93,300	30.00	28,000	50.48	B	214,000	Capital of Adamoua. Tourism related to game reserves. Traditional Fulani capital. D=RCC.
1094	Nkongsamba	183,000	50.00	91,400	82.48	B	420,000	Littoral north of Douala. Tobacco, coffee. Banana & coffee plantations. D=RCC.
1095	YAOUNDE	1,446,000	52.00	752,000	84.48	B	3,211,000	Capital of Centre. International Airport. El. 2,500 ft. More than 5,000 Europeans. D=RCC.
	CANADA	**31,147,000**	**64.98**	**20,238,000**	**97.79**	**C**	**37,896,000**	**ROMAN CATHOLICS 41.8%, PROTESTANTS 17.1%. PENT-CHAR 14.2%, EVANGELICAL 8.1%, GCC 40.4%**
1096	rural areas	7,142,000	71.62	5,115,000	99.40	C	6,681,000	39.1% (1950), 24.3% (1970), 23.4% (1990), 22.9% (2000), 21.3% (2010), 17.6% (2025)
1097	urban areas	24,005,000	63.00	15,123,000	97.31	C	31,215,000	60.8% (1950), 75.6% (1970), 76.5% (1990), 77.0% (2000), 78.6% (2010), 82.3% (2025)
1098	non-metropolitan areas	2,913,000	62.95	1,834,000	97.98	C	5,540,196	*Sources of data:* Censuses of 1951, 1961, 1966, 1971, 1976, 1981, 1986, and 1991.
1099	metropolitan areas	21,092,000	63.01	13,289,000	97.22	C	25,675,000	*Definition:* Incorporated cities, towns and villages with a population of 1,000 or more and their urbanized fringes.
1100	Barrie	57,000	68.00	38,800	99.81	C	74,100	Ontario. Summer & winter resort. F=1828. D=RCC,UCC.
1101	Brantford	107,000	67.00	71,600	99.81	C	139,000	Ontario. Agriculture. F=1784. Her Majesty's Chapel of the Mohawks (1785). Six Nations Indians. D=RCC,UCC.
1102	Calgary	888,000	63.00	559,000	96.81	C	1,068,000	Alberta. Petroleum refining, flour milling, meat packing, brewing. F=1875 as Mountie's post. D=RCC,UCC.
1103	Charlottetown	63,600	68.00	43,200	99.86	C	82,700	Capital of Prince Edward Island. Tourism, government, fishing. F=1720 as French settlement. D=RCC.
1104	Chicoutimi-Jonquiere	187,000	67.00	125,000	99.81	C	243,000	Quebec. Lumber, pulp, paper, furniture. Tourist base for Saguenay area. F=1676 as Jesuit mission. D=RCC.
1105	Jonquiere	69,000	67.00	46,300	99.81	C	89,800	Quebec. Lumber & wood pulp center, railway. F=c1850. D=RCC.
1106	Cornwall	61,100	68.00	41,500	99.86	C	79,400	Ontario on St. Lawrence River. Paper, textiles, dairy & farming. F=1784. D=RCC,UCC.
1107	Drummondville	66,500	67.00	44,500	99.81	C	86,400	Quebec on Saint-Francois River. Textiles, lumber, heavy machinery. F=1815. D=RCC.
1108	Edmonton	913,000	65.00	593,000	98.81	C	1,091,000	Capital of Alberta. Agriculture & oil-based economy. F=1795 as trading post. 'Gateway to the North'. D=RCC,UCC.
1109	Fredericton	77,700	69.00	53,600	99.91	C	101,000	Capital of New Brunswick. Administrative & educational center. F=1692. River Jubilee Festival. D=RCC,UCC.
1110	Guelph	101,000	67.00	68,000	99.81	C	132,000	Ontario on Speed River. Clothing, glass, yarn. F=1827. University of Guelph (1964). Spring Festival. D=RCC,UCC.
1111	Halifax	349,000	66.00	231,000	98.81	C	454,000	Capital of Nova Scotia. Ice-free harbor. Exports fish, lumber, agriculture. F=c1700. D=RCC,UCC.
1112	Dartmouth	77,000	66.00	50,800	98.81	C	100,000	Nova Scotia. Petroleum refining, shipbuilding, molasses. F=1784 as Quaker whaling company. D=RCC,UCC.
1113	Hamilton	658,000	66.00	434,000	98.81	C	855,000	Ontario on Lake Ontario. Royal Botanical gardens. Iron, steel, automobiles, financial hub, fruit. F=1778. D=RCC.
1114	Burlington	140,000	67.00	93,700	99.81	C	182,000	Ontario. Beach resort, fruit growing, lakeside residential area. F=1810. D=RCC,UCC.
1115	Kamloops	72,900	68.00	49,600	99.86	C	94,800	British Columbia. Service center for ranching and lumbering. F=c1850. D=RCC,UCC.
1116	Kelowna	106,000	67.00	71,000	99.81	C	138,000	British Columbia. Focal point of fruit-growing industry. F=1859 by Oblates of Mary Immaculate. D=RCC.
1117	Kingston	144,000	67.00	96,800	99.81	C	188,000	Busy port of Ontario on Rideau Canal. Aluminum, ceramics. F=1673. 19th century buildings. D=RCC.
1118	Kitchener	367,000	66.00	242,000	98.81	C	478,000	Ontario. Industrial, financial center. F=1807 by German immigrants. St. Jerome's College (1864). D=RCC.
1119	Cambridge (Galt)	94,400	67.00	63,200	99.81	C	123,000	Ontario. Milling town: flour, lumber, textiles. F=1973. Scottish immigrants. D=RCC,Mennonites.
1120	Waterloo	69,300	67.00	46,400	99.81	C	90,200	Northwest. Furniture, textiles, large insurance company center, settled by Mennonites from Pennsylvania. D=RCC.
1121	Lethbridge	65,800	69.00	45,400	99.91	C	85,500	Alberta on Oldman River. Coal, oil, natural gas. F=1880. D=RCC,UCC.
1122	London	404,000	66.00	267,000	98.81	C	526,000	Ontario on Thames River. Many museums. Service center for large agricultural region. F=1826. D=RCC,UCC.
1123	Matsqui	97,500	67.00	65,300	99.81	C	127,000	British Columbia on Fraser River near USA border. Lumbering fruit, hops, tobacco. D=RCC,UCC.
1124	Medicine Hat	60,400	67.00	40,500	99.81	C	78,600	Alberta on South Saskatchewan River. Natural gas, glassblowing, pottery. F=1882 as Mounties post. D=RCC.
1125	Moncton	121,000	68.00	82,000	99.86	C	157,000	New Brunswick. Food processing, woodworking, lobster. F=1698. D=RCC.
1126	Montreal	3,401,000	61.00	2,075,000	93.81	C	3,879,000	Major seaport of Quebec. Finance, education. F=1535. World's 2nd French-speaking city. D=RCC.
1127	Brossard	67,800	62.00	42,000	94.81	C	88,200	Southeast across the St. Lawrence Seaway. Furniture, electronic products, explosives. D=RCC.
1128	Gatineau	95,900	62.00	59,500	94.81	C	125,000	North on Gatineau River, 5th largest city in Quebec. Plastics, metal doors, structured lumber, pulp mill. D=RCC.
1129	Gloucester	106,000	63.00	66,800	95.81	C	138,000	Southeast near Ottawa International Airport. Dairying, electronics, mixed farming. D=RCC.
1130	Hull	69,300	62.00	43,000	94.81	C	90,200	North bank of Ottawa River, Quebec. Timber, hydroelectric, meat-packing. F=c1800. D=RCC.
1131	La Salle	89,300	62.00	55,400	94.81	C	116,000	Quebec. Primarily residential. Food products, plastics. F=1668. D=RCC.
1132	Laval	336,000	61.00	205,000	93.81	C	436,000	On Jesus Island, Quebec. Television, printed materials, dairy foods. F=1681 (Society of Jesus). D=RCC.
1133	Longueuil	148,000	61.00	90,300	93.81	C	193,000	On St. Lawrence River, Quebec. Residential & industrial. F=1657. D=RCC.
1134	Montreal-Nord	107,000	60.00	64,000	92.81	C	139,000	North on Prairies River, 6 miles northwest of downtown Montreal, St. Leonard to the east. D=RCC.
1135	Nepean	113,000	62.00	69,900	94.81	C	147,000	South on Rideau River near Ottawa International Airport. D=RCC.
1136	Saint-Hubert	78,200	63.00	49,300	95.81	C	102,000	Quebec. Residential. D=RCC.
1137	Saint-Laurent	79,100	63.00	49,800	95.81	C	103,000	Quebec. Aircraft, railway, foundry. F=1845 on mission site (1720). D=RCC.
1138	Saint-Leonard	89,700	63.00	56,500	95.81	C	117,000	North near Montreal-Nord, 5 miles north of Montreal on Montreal Island. D=RCC.
1139	Verdun	71,100	62.00	44,100	94.81	C	92,500	Quebec. Primarily residential, numerous parks. F=1672. D=RCC.
1140	Nanaimo	71,300	68.00	48,500	98.81	C	92,800	British Columbia. Lumbering, fishing, agriculture, tourism. F=1849. D=RCC,UCC.
1141	North Bay	69,600	67.00	46,600	99.81	C	90,500	Ontario on Lake Nipissing. Railway junction, lumbering, dairying, furs, summer resort. F=1882. D=RCC,UCC.
1142	Oshawa	240,000	66.00	159,000	98.81	C	313,000	Ontario on Lake Ontario. Auto Industry center, port of entry, woolen mills, foundries. F=1795. D=RCC.
1143	OTTAWA	1,085,000	63.00	684,000	95.81	C	1,311,000	Ontario. Government, commerce, finance. F=1613. 35% Francophone. D=RCC,UCC.
1144	Peterborough	103,000	66.00	67,900	98.81	C	134,000	Ontario. Large outdoor skating rink. Boats, watches, tourism. F=1821. 'Near the Water'. D=RCC.
1145	Prince George	79,800	67.00	53,500	98.81	C	104,000	British Columbia. Forest industries, minerals, oil, natural gas. F=1807 by Simon Fraser. D=UCC,RCC.
1146	Quebec	712,000	62.00	442,000	96.81	C	926,000	Port and capital of Quebec. Newsprint, milled grain, cigarettes, tourism. F=1535. 96% French-speaking.D=RCC.
1147	Beauport	74,200	63.00	46,800	95.81	C	96,500	Quebec. On St. Lawrence River. Residential. F=1634. D=RCC.
1148	Charlesbourg	81,500	63.00	51,300	95.81	C	106,000	St. Lawrence Seaway. One of the oldest parishes in the province. D=RCC.
1149	Sainte-Foy	82,200	63.00	51,800	95.81	C	107,000	Quebec. Residential. F=1698. Y=1698. D=RCC.
1150	Red Deer	56,400	64.00	36,100	96.81	C	73,400	Alberta. Dairy produce, oil and gas wells. F=1891 as railway junction. D=UCC,RCC.
1151	Regina	220,000	65.00	143,000	97.81	C	286,000	Capital of Saskatchewan. Service center for vast agricultural area. F=1857. Canadian Bible College. D=RCC
1152	Saint Catharines	405,000	63.00	255,000	95.81	C	527,000	On south shore of Lake Ontario, Ontario. Fruit, industry. F=1790. 'The Garden City'. (1941). D=UCC.
1153	Niagara Falls	85,100	64.00	54,500	96.81	C	111,000	Across from Niagara Falls, USA. Tourism, silverware. Casino Niagara, Queen Victoria Park. D=UCC.
1154	Saint John	143,000	67.00	95,900	99.81	C	186,000	New Brunswick. Shipping, lumbering, oil, textiles, fisheries. Known for museums. F=1783. D=RCC,UCC.
1155	Saint John's	191,000	66.00	126,000	98.81	C	249,000	Capital of Newfoundland. Major ocean port. Fishing, shipbuilding. F=1593. D=RCC,Anglican.
1156	Saint-Jean-sur-Richelieu (Saint Jean)	70,800	68.00	48,100	99.81	C	92,100	Quebec. Trade center. Sewing machines, ribbons, textiles. F=1666. D=RCC.
1157	Sarnia	101,000	67.00	67,800	99.81	C	132,000	Ontario on Saint Clair River. White, sandy beaches. Petroleum, chemicals, salt, grain elevators. F=1807. D=RCC.
1158	Saskatoon	237,000	66.00	156,000	98.81	C	308,000	Saskatchewan. Distribution centers for potash mining and wheat growing. F=1883. Ukrainians. D=RCC.
1159	Sault Saint Marie	112,000	67.00	75,200	99.81	C	146,000	Ontario on St. Mary's River. Locks & canal industry. Heavy industry. F=1669 as Jesuit mission. D=RCC,UCC.

Table 10-5–continued overleaf

Table 10-5–continued

Rec No 1	Country City 2	Pop 2000 3	AC% 4	Church Members 5	E% 6	W 7	Pop 2025 8	Notes 9
1160	Shawinigan (Shawinigan Falls)	73,200	67.00	49,000	98.81	C	95,100	Quebec. Chemicals, aluminum, pulp & paper, textiles, clothing. F=1900. D=RCC.
1161	Sherbrooke	153,000	66.00	101,000	98.81	C	200,000	Quebec. Textiles, heavy machinery, pulp & paper, dairy products. F=1818. D=RCC.
1162	Sudbury	176,000	67.00	118,000	99.81	C	229,000	Ontario. One of world's richest mining centers. F=1893. 'Nickel capital of the World'. D=RCC,UCC.
1163	Sydney	141,000	66.00	93,100	98.81	C	183,000	Ocean port of Nova Scotia. Aluminum, auto-assembly, concrete. F=1783 by United Empire Loyalists. D=RCC.
1164	Thunder Bay (Lakehead)	144,000	65.00	93,800	97.81	C	188,000	Ontario on St. Lawrence Seaway. One of world's largest grain storage & transshipment depots. F=c1850. D=RCC.
1165	Toronto	4,657,000	60.50	2,817,000	97.81	C	5,350,000	Capital of Ontario. Financial center. Many European immigrants. F=1750 as French trading post. D=RCC.
1166	Brampton	223,000	62.00	138,000	94.81	C	289,000	Ontario. Flower growing, tanning, lumbering. F=1830. 'Flower City'. D=RCC,UCC.
1167	East York	119,000	61.00	72,800	93.81	C	155,000	Ontario. Planned industrial & residential complex. F=1967. D=RCC,UCC.
1168	Etobicoke	358,000	62.00	222,000	94.81	C	465,000	Ontario. Large tire & rubber plant. 1,600 acres of parks. F=1967. D=RCC,UCC.
1169	Markham	135,000	63.00	85,200	95.81	C	176,000	Northeast on Lake Ontario. Rouge River. High technology industry, medical supplies, book publishing. D=RCC.
1170	Mississauga	442,000	60.00	265,000	92.81	C	574,000	On Lake Ontario in Ontario. Aircraft, engines, motor vehicles. F=1974. D=RCC.
1171	North York	657,000	62.00	407,000	94.81	C	854,000	Ontario. 4,000 acres of parks, Humber River, Ontario Science Center. Air force base. F=1922. D=RCC.
1172	Oakville	103,000	61.00	62,700	93.81	C	134,000	Southwest on Lake Ontario. Wealthy community. Autos, plastics. Summer resort, golfing. D=RCC,UCC.
1173	Scarborough	572,000	60.00	343,000	92.81	C	744,000	Ontario. Well planned industrial & residential complex. Originally Glasgow. F=1850. D=RCC,UCC.
1174	Vaughn	71,700	62.00	44,500	94.81	C	93,300	Northwest on Humber River. D=RCC,UCC.
1175	York	160,000	61.00	97,500	93.81	C	208,000	Ontario. Originally Dublin. Primarily residential Weston Recreation Centre. F=1793.
1176	Trois-Rivieres (Three Rivers)	152,000	66.00	100,000	98.81	C	198,000	Quebec. Deepwater port & industrial center. Newsprint. F=1634. Ursuline convent (1697). D=RCC,Anglican.
1177	Vancouver	1,987,000	60.30	1,198,000	96.11	C	2,364,000	British Columbia. Financial center. Wood processing, fishing. Many Chinese. F=1870. Stanley Park. D=RCC.
1178	Burnaby	171,000	60.00	103,000	92.81	C	223,000	British Columbia. Trucking, warehousing, petroleum. F=c1875. Simon Fraser University (1963). D=RCC,UCC.
1179	Richmond	128,000	60.00	76,900	92.81	C	167,000	On Lulu Island near Vancouver International Airport. Shipbuilding, book publishing, fruit growing. D=RCC,UCC.
1180	Coquitlam	92,600	61.00	56,500	93.81	C	120,000	East on Pitt River. Residential, wineries, electrical machinery, petroleum refinery. D=RCC,UCC.
1181	Surrey	270,000	61.00	165,000	93.81	C	351,000	British Columbia. Southeast of Vancouver. Residential, surgical supplies, gypsum products. D=RCC.UCC.
1182	Delta	98,100	62.00	60,800	94.81	C	128,000	British Columbia, Fraser River. Logging, fruit, dairying, shipbuilding, furniture. D=RCC,UCC.
1183	Victoria	302,000	64.00	193,000	96.81	C	392,000	Capital of British Columbia on Vancouver Island. English character. Butchard Gardens (1904). F=1843. D=RCC.
1184	Saanich	105,000	63.00	66,400	95.81	C	137,000	North. Saanich Inlet. University of Victoria, Butchard Gardens, parks. Dairying, fruit, metal doors. D=RCC,UCC.
1185	Windsor	300,000	65.00	195,000	97.81	C	390,000	Ontario, Detroit River. Farming. F=1701. Assumption University (1857). 'City of Roses'. D=RCC.
1186	Winnipeg	738,000	66.00	487,000	98.81	C	960,000	Capital of Manitoba on Red and Assiniboine Rivers. Major grain market. F=1738 as trading post. D=RCC.
	CAPE VERDE	**428,000**	**95.13**	**407,000**	**99.95**	**C**	**671,000**	**ROMAN CATHOLICS 97.4%, PROTESTANTS 3.6%. PENT-CHAR 7.4%, EVANGELICAL 2.5%, GCC 13.0%**
1187	rural areas	162,000	97.31	157,000	99.99	C	155,000	92.1% (1950), 80.4% (1970), 55.8% (1990), 37.7% (2000), 28.3% (2010), 23.1% (2025)
1188	urban areas	266,000	93.80	250,000	99.93	C	516,000	7.9% (1950), 19.5% (1970), 44.1% (1990), 62.2% (2000), 71.6% (2010), 76.9% (2025)
1189	non-metropolitan areas	123,000	93.72	116,000	99.94	C	239,073	*Sources of data:* Censuses of 1950, 1960, 1970, 1980, and 1990.
1190	metropolitan areas	143,000	93.87	134,000	99.92	C	277,000	*Definition:* Urban centers.
1191	Mindelo (Porto Grande)	61,900	95.00	58,800	99.92	C	120,000	Sao Vicente main port. Refueling point for freighters, shipyard. Pre-Lenten Carnaval. D=RCC,SDA,Nazarene.
1192	PRAIA	80,900	93.00	75,300	99.92	C	157,000	Sao Tiago Port. Bananas, coffee. Submarine cable station. D=RCC,SDA,Nazarene.
	CAYMAN ISLANDS	**38,400**	**67.29**	**25,800**	**98.05**	**C**	**77,900**	**PROTESTANTS 53.9%, INDEPENDENTS 10.5%. PENT-CHAR 16.9%, EVANGELICAL 14.5%, GCC 19.3%**
1193	rural areas	–	–	–	–	–	–	0.0% (1950), 0.0% (1970), 0.0% (1990), 0.0% (2000), 0.0% (2010), 0.0% (2025)
1194	urban areas	38,400	67.29	25,800	98.05	C	77,900	100.0% (1950), 100.0% (1970), 100.0% (1990), 100.0% (2000), 100.0% (2010), 100.0% (2025)
1195	non-metropolitan areas	17,800	67.28	12,000	98.04	C	36,187	*Sources of data:* Censuses of 1960, 1970, 1979, and 1989.
1196	metropolitan areas	20,600	67.30	13,800	98.06	C	41,800	*Definition:* Entire population.
1197	GEORGETOWN	20,600	67.30	13,800	98.06	C	41,800	On Grand Cayman Island. Finance & tourism. 25% European, 25% African. D=Presbyterians, Baptists.
	CENTRAL AFRICAN REPUBLIC	**3,615,000**	**44.51**	**1,609,000**	**83.99**	**B**	**5,704,000**	**ROMAN CATHOLICS 18.3%, PROTESTANTS 14.4%. PENT-CHAR 13.4%, EVANGELICAL 17.4%, GCC 22.4%**
1198	rural areas	2,126,000	40.66	864,000	78.05	B	2,524,000	84.0% (1950), 69.8% (1970), 62.5% (1990), 58.8% (2000), 53.4% (2010), 44.2% (2025)
1199	urban areas	1,489,000	50.00	745,000	92.48	B	3,180,000	15.9% (1950), 30.1% (1970), 37.4% (1990), 41.1% (2000), 46.5% (2010), 55.7% (2025)
1200	non-metropolitan areas	514,000	49.85	256,000	92.59	B	1,096,701	*Sources of data:* Survey of 1960; censuses of 1966, 1975 and 1988.
1201	metropolitan areas	976,000	50.08	489,000	92.42	B	2,083,000	*Definition:* Twenty principal centers with a population of over 3,000.
1202	Bambari	63,500	44.00	27,900	83.48	B	136,000	Capital of Ouaka on Ouaka River. Fishing, coffee. Picturesque scenery. D=RCC.
1203	BANGUI	697,000	52.00	362,000	95.48	B	1,489,000	On Ubangi River. Commercial center, soap making, breweries. F=1889. French. 'The Rapids'. D=RCC.
1204	Berberati	141,000	46.00	64,900	85.48	B	301,000	Capital of Mambere-Kadei. Transport center for overland exports. Sawmills. D=RCC.
1205	Bouar	73,900	45.00	33,300	84.48	B	158,000	Capital of Nana-Mambere on Mambere River. Ancient stone monuments. Ivory & wood handicrafts. D=RCC.
	CHAD	**7,651,000**	**18.80**	**1,438,000**	**50.09**	**B**	**13,908,000**	**PROTESTANTS 10.2%, ROMAN CATHOLICS 6.5%. PENT-CHAR 3.2%, EVANGELICAL 8.5%, GCC 9.3%**
1206	rural areas	5,831,000	16.23	947,000	46.72	A	8,697,000	96.1% (1950), 88.2% (1970), 78.9% (1990), 76.2% (2000), 71.8% (2010), 62.5% (2025)
1207	urban areas	1,820,000	27.00	491,000	60.89	B	5,211,000	3.8% (1950), 11.7% (1970), 21.0% (1990), 23.7% (2000), 28.1% (2010), 37.4% (2025)
1208	non-metropolitan areas	478,000	26.65	127,000	60.84	B	1,623,682	*Sources of data:* Survey of 1964; estimates for 1972 and 1978; census of 1993.
1209	metropolitan areas	1,342,000	27.13	364,000	60.91	B	3,588,000	*Definition:* Ten urban centers.
1210	Abeche	54,900	7.00	3,800	33.29	A	157,000	Seat of Ouanddao. Capital of pre-French Muslim sultanate. Camel-hair industry. Many mosques.
1211	Moundou	137,000	5.00	6,900	30.29	A	393,000	On Lagone River. Center of cotton-growing, cattle-raising, fishing. F=1900.
1212	N'DJAMENA (Fort-Lamy)	1,044,000	30.30	316,000	65.34	B	2,735,000	Commercial center. Textiles, fishing. Sara people. Largely destroyed in civil war (1979-82). D=RCC.
1213	Sarh (Fort-Archambault)	106,000	35.00	36,900	71.29	B	302,000	Capital of Moyen-Chari on Chari River. Cotton, fish, textiles. Sara people. D=RCC.
	CHANNEL ISLANDS	**153,000**	**65.91**	**101,000**	**99.53**	**C**	**173,000**	**ANGLICANS 44.1%, ROMAN CATHOLICS 14.5%. PENT-CHAR 5.4%, EVANGELICAL 13.0%, GCC 26.5%**
1214	rural areas	61,200	71.03	43,400	99.84	C	97,900	57.3% (1950), 65.0% (1970), 70.5% (1990), 40.0% (2000), 66.3% (2010), 56.4% (2025)
1215	urban areas	91,700	62.50	57,300	99.32	C	75,500	42.6% (1950), 34.9% (1970), 29.4% (1990), 60.0% (2000), 33.6% (2010), 43.5% (2025)
1216	non-metropolitan areas	2,800	64.29	1,800	99.32	C	2,275	*Sources of data:* Censuses of 1951, 1961, 1971, and 1981; estimate for 1986.
1217	metropolitan areas	89,000	62.44	55,600	99.32	C	73,200	*Definition:* Guernsey, Civil Parish of St. Peter Port; Jersey, Civil Parish of St. Helier.
1218	Saint Peter Port	39,500	63.00	24,900	99.32	C	32,500	Capital of Guernsey. Resort, port of call. F=c1250. St. Peter's Church (c1250). D=Anglican.
1219	ST HELIER	49,400	62.00	30,600	99.32	C	40,700	Capital of Jersey. Resort. St. Helier (Frankish missionary) martyred in 555. D=Anglican.
	CHILE	**15,211,000**	**87.82**	**13,358,000**	**99.60**	**C**	**19,548,000**	**ROMAN CATHOLICS 77.5%, INDEPENDENTS 25.1%. PENT-CHAR 36.4%, EVANGELICAL 1.6%, GCC 14.6%**
1220	rural areas	2,344,000	95.06	2,228,000	99.92	C	2,240,000	41.5% (1950), 24.7% (1970), 16.7% (1990), 15.4% (2000), 13.8% (2010), 11.4% (2025)
1221	urban areas	12,867,000	86.50	11,130,000	99.54	C	17,308,000	58.4% (1950), 75.2% (1970), 83.2% (1990), 84.5% (2000), 86.1% (2010), 88.5% (2025)
1222	non-metropolitan areas	2,596,000	88.17	2,289,000	99.51	C	4,212,964	*Sources of data:* Censuses of 1952, 1960, 1970, 1982, and 1992.
1223	metropolitan areas	10,272,000	86.08	8,842,000	99.55	C	13,095,000	*Definition:* Populated centers with definite urban characteristics, such as certain public and municipal services.
1224	Antofagasta	255,000	86.00	219,000	99.58	C	343,000	Capital of Antofagasta. Pacific port. Mining, foundries, refineries. F=1870. D=RCC.
1225	Arica	206,000	86.00	177,000	99.58	C	278,000	Capital of Arica near border with Peru. Fish-meal, auto assembly, beach resort. Mild climate. F=1883. D=RCC.
1226	Calama	109,000	85.00	92,500	99.48	C	146,000	Capital of El Loa. Mining & agricultural market center, cattle. D=RCC.
1227	Chillan	170,000	85.00	144,000	99.48	C	229,000	Capital of Nuble. Service center for agricultural region. Skiing. Birthplace of B. O'Higgins. F=1580. D=RCC.
1228	Concepcion	826,000	86.00	711,000	99.58	C	1,112,000	Capital of Concepcion. Near mouth of Bio-Bio River. Mining, railway, textiles, resort. F=1550. D=RCC.
1229	Talcahuano	287,000	87.00	250,000	99.78	C	387,000	Northwest on Punta Tumbes on Pacific Ocean. Textiles, resort. D=RCC.
1230	Copiapo	92,000	85.00	78,200	99.48	C	124,000	Capital of Copiapo. Mining. F=1540. D=RCC.
1231	Coquimbo	82,800	85.00	70,400	99.48	C	111,000	Port of Elqui. Chilean Navy, cement, fertilizer, agriculture. F=1850. D=RCC.
1232	Coronel	87,800	85.00	74,600	99.48	C	118,000	Port of Concepcion. Major source of Chile's coal, lumber. F=1851. D=RCC.
1233	Curico	80,600	90.00	72,600	99.58	C	108,000	Capital of Curico. Wine, flour mills, distilleries. Center for cowboys. F=1743. D=RCC.
1234	Iquique	173,000	99.00	171,000	99.78	C	233,000	Capital of Iquique. Pacific port. Fish-meal, canneries, tourism. Deep sea fishing. F=c1550. D=RCC.
1235	La Serena	123,000	85.00	104,000	99.48	C	165,000	Capital of Coquimbo. Popular beach resort. Center for agriculture, dairy, tourism. F=1543. D=RCC.
1236	Linares	61,800	85.00	52,600	99.48	C	83,200	Capital of Linares. Commercial & agricultural center, wine, grapes, grains. F=1755. D=RCC.
1237	Los Angeles (Los Anjeles)	93,900	85.00	79,800	99.48	C	126,000	Capital of Bio-Bio. Commercial & agricultural center, lumbering. F=1739. D=RCC.
1238	Lota	62,800	85.00	53,400	99.48	C	84,400	Concepcion. Major coal mining center, brick, copper. F=1662. D=RCC.
1239	Osorno	137,000	83.00	113,000	99.38	C	184,000	Capital of Osorno. Grain, lumber, milk, meat, tourism. F=1553. D=RCC.
1240	Ovalle	57,300	85.00	48,700	99.48	C	77,100	Coquimbo on Limar River. South of Coquimbo. D=RCC.
1241	Puerto Montt	124,000	85.00	105,000	99.48	C	167,000	Port & capital of Llanquihue on Gulf of Ancud. Agriculture, fishing. F=1853. American School. D=RCC.
1242	Punta Arenas	140,000	83.00	116,000	99.38	C	188,000	Capital of Magallanes on Strait of Magellan. Exports wool. F=1849. Southernmost city in the world. D=RCC.
1243	Rancagua	222,000	83.00	184,000	99.38	C	298,000	Capital of Cachapoal. Beef, grain, fruit, vegetables, auto assembly. F=1743. D=RCC.
1244	San Antonio	81,900	85.00	69,600	99.48	C	110,000	Valparaiso on Pacific Ocean. South of Valparaiso. Textiles, sugar. D=RCC.
1245	SANTIAGO (Gran Santiago)	5,261,000	86.50	4,551,000	99.58	C	6,355,000	On canalized Mapocho River. European character. Foodstuffs, textiles, shoes, clothes. F=1541. D=RCC.
1246	Apoquindo	234,000	86.00	201,000	99.58	C	315,000	East near Cerro Alto de las Vizcachas. Thermal alkaline waters which are bottled commercially. D=RCC.
1247	Cerrillos	89,200	87.00	77,600	99.78	C	120,000	Southwest. Aeropuerto los Cerrillos. Textiles. D=RCC.
1248	Cerro Navia	183,000	86.00	158,000	99.58	C	247,000	West beyond Renca on Mapocho River. Textiles. D=RCC.
1249	Conchali	210,000	85.00	179,000	99.48	C	283,000	North near Recoleta. Village and canton, 5 miles north of Santiago. Foodstuffs. D=RCC.
1250	El Bosque	191,000	85.00	163,000	99.48	C	257,000	South beyond La Cisterna. Textiles. D=RCC.
1251	Huechuraba	75,000	86.00	64,500	99.58	C	101,000	North beyond Conchali. Food processing. D=RCC.
1252	Independencia	115,000	86.00	99,300	99.58	C	155,000	North. Hipodromo Chile. Residential. D=RCC.
1253	La Cisterna	128,000	85.00	109,000	99.48	C	172,000	South near El Bosque, 6 miles south of Santiago. Railroad. D=RCC.
1254	La Florida	256,000	85.00	217,000	99.48	C	344,000	Southeast near La Granja. Residential. D=RCC.
1255	La Granja	145,000	86.00	125,000	99.58	C	196,000	South beyond San Miguel. Textiles. D=RCC.
1256	La Pintana	98,500	87.00	85,700	99.78	C	132,000	South on Canal Eyzaguirre. Food processing. D=RCC.
1257	La Reina	107,000	86.00	92,100	99.58	C	144,000	East. Aerodromo Tobalaba Eulogio Sanchez. Residential. D=RCC.
1258	La Rejas	197,000	86.00	169,000	99.58	C	265,000	West on Alameda Bernardo O'Higgins. Residential. D=RCC.
1259	Lo Espejo	166,000	85.00	141,000	99.48	C	223,000	South on Carretera Panamericana. 6 miles south of Santiago on railroad. D=RCC.
1260	Lo Prado Arriba	138,000	86.00	119,000	99.58	C	186,000	West near Pudahuel. Textiles. D=RCC.
1261	Macul	151,000	86.00	130,000	99.58	C	203,000	Southeast on Canal San Carlo Viejo. Residential. D=RCC.
1262	Maipu	152,000	85.00	129,000	99.48	C	204,000	Southwest beyond Cerrillos. Site of the battle of Maipu fought in 1818. D=RCC.
1263	Nunoa	225,000	86.00	193,000	99.58	C	303,000	East. Estadio Nacional. Residential. D=RCC.
1264	Pedro Aguirre Cerda	193,000	86.00	166,000	99.58	C	260,000	Southwest. Textiles, food processing. D=RCC.
1265	Penalolen	183,000	85.00	155,000	99.48	C	246,000	East on Canal Los Perdices. Residential. D=RCC.
1266	Providencia	154,000	87.00	134,000	99.78	C	207,000	East. North of Nunoa. Food processing. D=RCC.
1267	Pudahuel	130,000	86.00	112,000	99.58	C	175,000	West north of La Prado. Textiles. D=RCC.
1268	Puente Alto	218,000	85.00	185,000	99.48	C	293,000	South near Maipo River. Cereals, fruit, grapes, livestock, forest products, textiles, chemicals.
1269	Quinta Normal	172,000	86.00	148,000	99.58	C	231,000	Northwest near downtown. Manufacturing. D=RCC.
1270	Recoleta	219,000	86.00	188,000	99.58	C	294,000	North near Conchali. Residential. D=RCC.
1271	Renca	125,000	87.00	109,000	99.78	C	168,000	Northwest on Mapocho River. Residential. D=RCC.

Table 10-5–continued opposite

Table 10-5–continued

Rec No 1	Country City 2	Pop 2000 3	AC% 4	Church Members 5	E% 6	W 7	Pop 2025 8	Notes 9
1272	San Bernardo	219,000	86.00	188,000	99.58	C	295,000	South on Ochagavia. Corrals, fruits, grapes, livestock, chemical industry, metal working. D=RCC.
1273	San Miguel	118,000	86.00	102,000	99.58	C	159,000	South. Parque O'Higgins. Residential. D=RCC.
1274	San Joaquin	165,000	87.00	144,000	99.78	C	222,000	South beyond Nunoa. Textiles. D=RCC.
1275	San Ramon	132,000	86.00	114,000	99.58	C	178,000	Residential. Textiles, food processing. D=RCC.
1276	Santiago	577,000	85.00	490,000	99.48	C	776,000	On canalized Mapocho River. Foodstuffs, textiles, shoes, clothes. F=1541. D=RCC.
1277	Vitacura	95,900	86.00	82,500	99.58	C	129,000	Northeast east of Recoleta. Residential. D=RCC.
1278	Talca	191,000	84.00	161,000	99.38	C	258,000	Capital of Talca. Wine, matches, shoes, biscuits. F=1692 but destroyed by earthquakes 1742, 1928. D=RCC.
1279	Temuco	246,000	85.00	209,000	99.48	C	331,000	Capital of Cautin on Cautin River. Wheat, apples, cattle. F=1881. Several missionary schools. D=RCC.
1280	Valdivia	132,000	85.00	112,000	99.48	C	178,000	Capital of Valdivia. Railroad shops, factories, boatyards. F=1552. Germans. D=RCC.
1281	Vallenar	51,100	87.00	44,500	99.78	C	68,700	Southern Atacama on Huasco River. Railroad, copper mining, grapes, wines, fruit, gold & silver mining. D=RCC.
1282	Valparaiso	803,000	85.00	683,000	99.48	C	1,080,000	Capital of Valparaiso. Chief port. Severe earthquakes (1907, 1971). Chemicals, sugar. F=1536. D=RCC.
1283	Quilpue	125,000	86.00	108,000	99.58	C	168,000	Inland to the east. Resort and agricultural center, fruit, grapes, cereals, vegetables, cattle. D=RCC.
1284	Villa Alemana	74,300	87.00	64,600	99.78	C	99,900	Pacific Ocean resort. Casinos, beaches, hotels, residential. D=RCC.
1285	Vina del Mar	327,000	85.00	278,000	99.48	C	440,000	North on Pacific Ocean. Popular tourist resort, beaches. Textiles. D=RCC.
	CHINA	**1,262,557,000**	**7.05**	**88,955,000**	**64.82**	**B**	**1,462,931,000**	**INDEPENDENTS 6.3%, ROMAN CATHOLICS 0.5%. PENT-CHAR 4.3%, EVANGELICAL 0.2%, GCC 6.4%**
1286	rural areas	828,995,000	7.23	59,907,000	65.26	B	698,842,000	87.4% (1950), 82.6% (1970), 73.8% (1990), 65.6% (2000), 57.6% (2010), 47.7% (2025)
1287	urban areas	433,562,000	6.70	29,049,000	63.97	B	764,089,000	12.5% (1950), 17.4% (1970), 26.2% (1990), 34.3% (2000), 42.3% (2010), 52.2% (2025)
1288	non-metropolitan areas	103,916,000	6.72	6,980,000	63.80	B	213,296,823	*Sources of data:* Censuses of 1953, 1982, and 1990; estimates for 1964, 1970, 1975 and 1987.
1289	metropolitan areas	329,646,000	6.69	22,068,000	64.02	B	550,792,000	*Definition:* Population living in areas under the administration of cities and towns.
1290	Abagnar Qi	119,000	12.00	14,300	69.77	B	210,000	Eastern Inner Mongolian Autonomous Region. Agriculture, pastoralism. D=house churches.
1291	Acheng (A-ch'eng)	120,000	1.30	1,600	59.07	B	212,000	Heilungkiang. Collecting & commercial center for agricultural district, brickworks.
1292	Aihui (Heihe)	160,000	1.20	1,900	58.97	B	281,000	Heilungkiang on Amur River across from Blagovescensk, Russia. Agriculture.
1293	Aksu	409,000	0.10	410	37.87	A	721,000	Sinkiang Uighur on Toxkan River. Agriculture and light industry. Grain, cotton, fruits, ancient Buddhist statues.
1294	Anci (Langfang)	618,000	2.70	16,700	60.47	B	1,089,000	Hopeh. Grains, vegetables, fruits, oil crops, cotton, textiles, chemicals. D=TSPM,house churches.
1295	Anda (Anta)	1,388,000	0.90	12,500	38.67	A	2,302,000	Heilungkiang northwest of Zhaodong. Important oil field. D=TSPM, house churches.
1296	Ankang (Hsing-an)	107,000	4.50	4,800	62.27	B	189,000	Southern Shensi on Han River. Important agricultural trade center. F=AD 250. D=house churches.
1297	Anqing (Anching, An King, Huaining)	513,000	8.00	41,000	65.77	B	904,000	Anhwei on Yangtze River. Tea market. D=RC Diocese(1949: 134 churches),house churches.
1298	Anshan	1,567,000	1.00	15,700	58.77	B	2,507,000	Liaoning. Industrial, with extreme air pollution. Iron, steel. F=c100 BC. D=TSPM,house churches.
1299	Anshun	254,000	3.00	7,600	60.77	B	447,000	Kweichow. Chief market & commercial center for district. F=1958. D=house churches.
1300	Anyang (Zhangde)	641,000	5.00	32,000	62.77	B	1,129,000	Honan. Agriculture, textiles. 1981, RC church opened. D=RC Diocese(1949: 70 churches),house churches.
1301	Baicheng (Paicheng, Pai-ch'eng)	333,000	7.00	23,300	64.77	B	588,000	Inner Mongolian Autonomous Region. Agriculture, pastoralism. D=Baicheng Church(TSPM).
1302	Baiquan	61,200	1.30	800	59.07	B	108,000	Heilungkiang north of Harbin. Road junction, grain, flax, sugar beets, food processing, textiles, coal mining.
1303	Baiyin	357,000	5.30	18,900	63.07	B	629,000	Kansu north of Lanzhou. Heavy industry, vegetables, fruits, hogs, coal mining. D=house churches.
1304	Baoding (Pao-ting, Qingyuan)	633,000	3.00	19,000	60.77	B	1,115,000	Hopeh.Education. 1984, RC bishop jailed 10 years for ordaining underground priests. D=TSPM,house churches.
1305	Baoji (Paochi, Paohi, Paoki)	425,000	4.00	17,000	61.77	B	749,000	Shensi. Transportation center, textiles, chemicals. Coal-mining regional city. D=house churches.
1306	Baoshan	814,000	1.50	12,200	59.27	B	1,434,000	Yunnan between Mekong River and Myanmar border. Animal husbandry, light industry. D=house churches.
1307	Baotou (Paotaw, Baotau, Paotow)	1,481,000	12.00	178,000	69.77	B	2,387,000	Inner Mongolian Autonomous Region. Trade with NW China & Mongolia. D=TSPM,house churches.
1308	Baoying	60,600	10.00	6,100	67.77	B	107,000	Kiangsu north of Gaoyou Lake on Grand Canal. Rice, cotton, oil seeds, chemicals. D=house churches.
1309	Bei'an	521,000	1.30	6,800	59.07	B	918,000	Heilungkiang south of Keshan. Railroad junction. Grains, oil crops, milk, machinery, tractors.
1310	Beihai (Pei-hai, Pak-hoi)	208,000	2.00	4,200	59.77	B	367,000	Kwangsi Chuang Autonomous Region. Fishing. D=TSPM church,RC Diocese(1949: 38 churches).
1311	BEIJING (Pei-Ching, Peking)	12,033,000	1.40	168,000	60.17	B	17,875,000	On Yangon River. Capital since 1272. Steel, handicrafts. YWCA active, YMCA 16-story building. D=RCC,TSPM.
1312	Beipiao (Pei-piao)	714,000	2.50	17,800	60.27	B	1,258,000	Liaoning. Mining town. Textiles, coal mining, archaeological excavations. D=house churches,TSPM church.
1313	Bengbu (Pengpu, Pangfu)	918,000	8.00	73,400	65.77	B	1,530,000	Anhwei. Light industrial center, animal husbandry, pharmaceuticals. D=RC Diocese(1949: 86 churches).
1314	Benxi (Penki, Pen-hsi, Pen-chi)	1,170,000	2.30	26,900	60.07	B	1,911,000	Liaoning. Iron, coal, cement. Railroad, smelting, non-ferrous metals, crude oil refining. D=TSPM.
1315	Bijie	65,900	9.00	5,900	66.77	B	116,000	Kweichow north of Dafang. Rice, tobacco, oilseeds, jute, tobacco processing. D=house churches.
1316	Binxian (Pin-hsien)	210,000	1.30	2,700	59.07	B	371,000	Heilungkiang. Communications center for agricultural region, food processing.
1317	Boli	74,400	1.30	970	59.07	B	131,000	Heilungkiang northwest of Jixi. Grain, tobacco, flax, sugar beets, textiles, food processing, mining.
1318	Bose (Po-se, Pai-se, Baise)	321,000	1.00	3,200	58.77	B	566,000	Kwangsi Chuang Autonomous Region. Sugar refining, trade. Center for non-Chinese tribes.
1319	Boshan (Po-shan)	138,000	6.00	8,300	63.77	B	244,000	Shantung. Center for ceramic & glass industry, mining, heavy industry. D= TSPM,house church.
1320	Boxian	75,900	7.50	5,700	65.27	B	134,000	Northern Anhwei on Guo River. Tea. D=house churches.
1321	Boxing	72,100	5.50	4,000	63.27	B	127,000	Shantung on Xiaoqing River. North of Boshan. Grain, cotton, textiles, crafts. D=house churches.
1322	Boyang	72,900	6.00	4,400	63.77	B	128,000	Kiangsi on Boyang Lake. Commercial center, rice, cotton, jute, oilseeds. D=house churches.
1323	Butha Qi (Zalantun)	461,000	12.00	55,300	69.77	B	812,000	Inner Mongolian Autonomous Region on Yalu River. D=house churches.
1324	Cangshan (Bianzhuang)	99,400	1.00	990	58.77	B	175,000	Northern Heilungkiang on Huma River. Grain, tobacco, flax.
1325	Cangzhou (Tsiang-chou, Sienhsien)	347,000	3.00	10,400	60.77	B	612,000	Hopeh. Agriculture, salt. D=RC Diocese(1949: 88 churches),house churches.
1326	Chang-chun (Kuachengzi)	5,566,000	8.00	445,000	65.77	B	9,340,000	Capital of Kirin. Automotive. 1981, Korean Christian Churches Conference. D=RCC & 10 others.
1327	Changde (Ch'ang-te)	1,371,000	2.80	38,400	60.57	B	2,190,000	Hunan. Agricultural central market. D=RC Diocese(1949: 33 churches),house churches.
1328	Changge	83,900	16.00	13,400	73.77	B	148,000	Honan on Shuangji River. Grain, oilseeds, tobacco, cotton, clothing, papermaking. D=house churches.
1329	Changji	276,000	0.20	550	37.97	A	486,000	Sinkiang Uighur northwest of Urumchi. Crop growing, animal husbandry, grain and oil crops, leather.
1330	Changqing	81,500	5.50	4,500	63.27	B	144,000	Shantung southwest of Jinan. Grain, cotton, oilseeds, machinery, metalwork. D=house churches.
1331	Changsha (Tan, Tanzhou, Ch'ang-sha)	1,738,000	3.00	52,100	60.77	B	2,833,000	Capital of Hunan. Major port, rice, cotton. Changsha Church (TSPM). 1981: first service since 1965. RC Diocese.
1332	Changshou	62,300	5.00	3,100	62.77	B	110,000	Szechwan on Yangtze River. East of Chongqing. Rice, tobacco, oilseeds, jute, dyes, paper. D=house churches.
1333	Changshu (Ch'ang-shu)	1,180,000	10.70	126,000	68.47	B	2,080,000	Kiangsu. Dense network of canals. Textiles, leather, furniture, chemicals. D=house churches.
1334	Changtu	60,000	2.50	1,500	60.27	B	106,000	Northern Liaoning north of Tieling. Oilseeds, sugar beets, machinery, chemicals. D=house churches.
1335	Changyi	80,800	5.80	4,700	63.57	B	142,000	Shantung on Wen River northeast of Weifang. Wheat, rice, cotton, oilseeds, textiles, crafts.
1336	Changzhi (Ch'ang-chih, Lu-an)	548,000	8.00	43,800	65.77	B	966,000	Shansi. Local ginseng, pig iron. D=RC Diocese(1949: 196 churches),house churches.
1337	Changzhou (Chang, Changshu)	618,000	11.00	68,000	68.77	B	1,089,000	Kiangsu. Agricultural center, engineering. D=Changzhou City Church (TSPM), opened 1985,house churches.
1338	Chaoxian	874,000	7.50	65,600	65.27	B	1,541,000	Anhwei on Chao Lake southeast of Hefei. Tea, textiles. D=house churches.
1339	Chaoyang	103,000	2.50	2,600	60.27	B	182,000	Liaoning. Rice, cotton, textiles. D=TSPM church.
1340	Chaoyang	377,000	4.50	17,000	62.27	B	665,000	Kwangtung on South China Sea near Shantou. Rice, oilseeds, textiles, machinery. D=house churches.
1341	Chaozhou (Chao, Chaochow)	1,436,000	6.00	86,200	63.77	B	2,531,000	Eastern Kwangtung. Agricultural district center. D=Chaozhou County Church(TSPM)house churches.
1342	Chengde (Ch'eng-te, Jehol)	391,000	3.00	11,700	60.77	B	688,000	Hopeh. Commercial and collecting center. D=RC Diocese,1 bishop,house churches.
1343	Chengdu (Chleng-tu, Yizhou)	5,293,000	6.00	318,000	63.77	B	8,521,000	Szechwan. Textiles. F=c200 BC. D=Christian Worship Church(TSPM),RC Diocese,20 others.
1344	Chenghai	60,800	4.50	2,700	62.27	B	107,000	Kwangtung north of Shantou, Han River Delta. Rice, oilseeds, aquatic products. D=house churches.
1345	Chenxian	227,000	2.60	5,900	60.37	B	400,000	Hunan southwest of Liyujiang. Crop growing, animal husbandry, tobacco, textiles. D=house churches.
1346	Chifeng (Ulanhad, Chih-feng)	1,044,000	4.00	41,800	61.77	B	1,840,000	Collecting point for Mongolian products. D=RC Diocese(1949: 52 churches),house churches.
1347	Chongqing (Chungking)	3,896,000	6.00	234,000	63.77	B	6,127,000	Szechwan on Yangtse & Chia-ling rivers. 'Fog city'. D=Christian Worship Church (TSPM),RCC, & 20 others.
1348	Chuxian	432,000	8.00	34,500	65.77	B	761,000	Anhwei northwest of Nanjing. Tea, textiles. D=house churches.
1349	Chuxiong	449,000	2.80	12,600	60.57	B	791,000	Yunnan west of Kunming. Center for light industry, crop growing, animal husbandry. D=house churches.
1350	Da'an	84,700	6.80	5,800	64.57	B	149,000	Kirin east of Baicheng, Singhua River. Grains, oil crops, hogs, eggs, machinery. D=house churches.
1351	Dachangzhen	69,200	11.00	7,600	68.77	B	122,000	Kiangsu on Yangtze River near Nanjing. Agricultural center, engineering. D=house churches.
1352	Dalian (Luda, Lute, Dalny, Dairen)	3,153,000	2.50	78,800	60.27	B	5,157,000	Liaoning. Port, railways, chemicals, cement, fishing. Summer resort. D=Dalian Church,TSPM.
1353	Dandong (Andong, Tantung, An-tung)	860,000	5.00	43,000	62.77	B	1,439,000	Liaoning. Textiles, agriculture. 80% Korean. D=TSPM church(numerous Koreans),house churches..
1354	Dashiqiao	82,700	2.50	2,100	60.27	B	146,000	Liaoning. Northwest of Shenyang. Textiles, agriculture. D=house churches.
1355	Datong (Ta-t'ung)	1,191,000	8.00	95,300	65.77	B	2,099,000	Shansi. Food processing. D=Datong Church (TSPM),RC Diocese(1949: 71 churches),and 20 others.
1356	Datong	1,801,000	1.20	21,600	58.97	B	2,968,000	Western Heilungkiang southwest of Anda. Agricultural center, food processing. D=house churches.
1357	Dawa	171,000	2.70	4,600	60.47	B	302,000	Liaoning northeast of Shenyang. Textiles, agriculture. D=house churches.
1358	Daxian (Ta-hsien)	248,000	6.00	14,900	63.77	B	436,000	Szechwan. Qu River. Food processing, textiles, iron and steel, coal mining, grain, hogs. D=TSPM.
1359	Dehui	72,300	6.80	4,900	64.57	B	127,000	Northeast. Kirin north of Changchun. Railroad, grain, sugar beets, flax, beverages. D=house churches.
1360	Dengfeng	62,300	17.00	10,600	74.77	B	110,000	Honan northwest of Yuxian. Song Mountains. Grain, tobacco, oilseeds, coal mining. D=house churches.
1361	Deqing	61,000	16.00	9,800	73.77	B	108,000	Chekiang on Dongtiao River north of Hangzhou. Rice, oilseeds, animal husbandry. D=house churches.
1362	Deyang	891,000	5.00	44,500	62.77	B	1,570,000	Szechwan north of Chengdu. Agriculture and heavy industry, crop growing, animal husbandry. D=house churches.
1363	Dezhou (Te-chou)	327,000	5.50	18,000	63.27	B	576,000	Shangtung. Grain milling, cotton, agricultural center, textiles, chemicals, machinery. D=TSPM.
1364	Didao	69,200	1.20	830	58.97	B	122,000	Heilungkiang near Jixi. Agricultural center, textiles.
1365	Dinghai	60,200	15.50	9,300	73.27	B	106,000	Chekiang on Zhoushan Island. Silk, wool, agricultural products. D=house churches.
1366	Dongying	608,000	5.00	30,400	62.77	B	1,072,000	Shantung in Yellow River Delta. Second largest oilfield in China. Grains, cotton, lamb. D=house churches.
1367	Dongchuan (Xincun)	325,000	1.80	5,900	59.57	B	573,000	Yunnan north of Kunming. Crop growing, animal husbandry, beef, hogs. D=house churches.
1368	Dongguan	1,429,000	4.50	64,300	62.27	B	2,518,000	Kwangtung on Dong River. North of Hong Kong. Pharmaceuticals, plastics, fruits, leather. D=house churches.
1369	Dongsheng	143,000	12.00	17,200	69.77	B	253,000	Inner Mongolian Autonomous Region south of Baotou. Light industry, textiles, machinery. D=house churches.
1370	Dongtai	79,000	11.00	8,700	68.77	B	139,000	Kiangsu northeast of Taizhou. Grain, oil crops, cotton, vegetables, fruit, eggs, fishing. D=house churches.
1371	Dukou (Tukou)	652,000	6.00	39,100	63.77	B	1,149,000	Szechwan.Textiles. D=TSPM,house churches.
1372	Dunhua	530,000	7.00	37,100	64.77	B	934,000	Kirin southeast of Jiaohe. Mudan River. Heavy industry, grains, vegetables, hogs, logging. D=house churches.
1373	Duyun	457,000	9.00	41,100	66.77	B	806,000	Kweichow. Transport center. Coal, paper, chemicals. Textiles, electronics, grain. D=house churches.
1374	Echeng	1,109,000	5.00	55,500	62.77	B	1,955,000	Hupeh. Textiles. D=TSPM,house church.
1375	Enshi	803,000	5.40	43,400	63.17	B	1,415,000	Southwest Hupeh on Qing River. Grain, hogs, chemicals, machinery, food processing. D=house churches.
1376	Ergun Zuoqi	67,200	10.00	6,700	67.77	B	118,000	Northern Inner Mongolian Autonomous Region on Gen River. D=house churches.
1377	Feixian	91,700	5.50	5,000	63.27	B	162,000	Shantung on Beng River northwest of Linyi. Agricultural products. D=house churches.
1378	Fengcheng	80,100	5.50	4,400	63.27	B	141,000	Kiangsi. Coal-mining center. Railroad, agricultural products, boron ore mining. D=TSPM.
1379	Foshan (Fatshan, Fo-shan)	370,000	4.50	16,600	62.27	B	652,000	Kwangtung. Prosperous trade center. Popular religion center. D=TSPM,1982,Foshan Church.
1380	Fujin	73,200	1.30	950	59.07	B	129,000	Heilungkiang on Songhua River east of Jiamusi. Grains, hogs, eggs, poultry, food processing.
1381	Fuling	1,151,000	6.00	69,100	63.77	B	2,029,000	Szechwan on Yangtze River east of Chongqing. Crop growing, animal husbandry, chemicals. D=house churches.
1382	Fushun (Fu-shun)	1,698,000	2.30	39,100	60.07	B	2,737,000	Liaoning. Coal, aluminum. D=TSPM,RC Diocese(1949: 17 churches), & 10 others.
1383	Fuxian (Wafangdian, Fu-hsien)	1,136,000	2.70	30,700	60.47	B	2,002,000	Liaoning. Market center for agriculture & fruit, chemicals, salt extraction, machinery. D=house churches.
1384	Fuxin (Foushin, Fusin)	901,000	2.00	18,000	59.77	B	1,485,000	Liaoning. Market center for Mongolian trade, iron ore. D=TSPM,house church.
1385	Fuyang	231,000	8.00	18,500	65.77	B	407,000	Anhwei. 1984 crackdown prohibited evangelizing and hearing gospel radio. D=house churches.
1386	Fuyu	58,400	1.30	760	59.07	B	103,000	Heilungkiang near Wuyur River northeast of Qiqihar. Grain, sugar beets, pulp, paper.
1387	Fuyu	118,000	7.00	8,300	64.77	B	208,000	Kirin on Songhua River near Qian Gorlos. Heavy industry, grains, hogs, marine products. D=house churches.
1388	Fuzhou	1,420,000	5.00	71,000	62.77	B	2,502,000	Kiangsi. Railroad, vegetables, poultry, food, textiles, chemicals, transportation equipment. D=TSPM.
1389	Fuzhou (Foochow, Fu-chou)	1,827,000	20.00	365,000	77.77	B	2,966,000	Fukien capital on Minjiang River. Seaport, handicrafts, tea. F=202 BC. D=34 TSPM churches,TSPM seminary.
1390	Gaixian	81,200	2.70	2,200	60.47	B	143,000	Liaoning on Liaodong Peninsula near Gulf of Liaotung. Tea, agricultural products. D=house churches.
1391	Ganhe	57,800	8.00	4,600	65.77	B	102,000	Northern Inner Mongolian Autonomous Region near Orogen Zizhiqi. Agriculture. D=house churches.
1392	Ganzhou (Kan-chou, Ganxian)	409,000	5.00	20,500	62.77	B	721,000	Kiangsi. Engineering, papermaking, tin. D=RC Diocese(1949: 52 churches),house churches.
1393	Gaoqing (Tianzhen)	88,200	5.50	4,900	63.27	B	155,000	Shantung near Yellow River west of Boxing. Peanuts, grain, cotton, textiles. D=house churches.

Table 10-5–continued overleaf

Table 10-5–continued

Rec No 1	Country City 2	Pop 2000 3	AC% 4	Church Members 5	E% 6	W 7	Pop 2025 8	Notes 9
1394	Gaoyou	69,500	10.00	6,900	67.77	B	122,000	Kiangsu on Gaoyou Lake. Food processing, textiles, important ancient postal station. D=house churches.
1395	Gejiu (Ko-chiu, Kokin)	404,000	3.00	12,100	60.77	B	712,000	Yunnan. Largest tin reserve in country, crops, animal husbandry. D=house churches.
1396	Golmud (Ge'ermu, Ko-erh-mu)	71,300	1.00	710	58.77	B	126,000	Tsinghai. Ancient highway junction. Chemicals, fertilizer.
1397	Gongchangling	61,700	2.30	1,400	60.07	B	109,000	Liaoning southeast of Liaoyang. Tea, agricultural products.
1398	Guanghua (Kuang-hua, Laohekou)	497,000	5.40	26,800	63.17	B	875,000	Hupeh. Communications and commercial center. Trade declining. Bank branches. D=TSPM,house churches.
1399	Guangyuan	952,000	5.10	48,600	62.87	B	1,678,000	Northern Szechwan on Jialing River. Railroad, forestry, coal mining, nonferrous metals. D=house churches.
1400	Guangzhou (Canton, Kwangchow)	5,162,000	5.00	258,000	62.77	B	8,109,000	Kwangtung capital on Pearl River. Textiles. YMCA, YWCA. D=RCC,TSPM, & 20 others.
1401	Guanxian	62,300	5.50	3,400	63.27	B	110,000	Shantung west of Liacheng. Handicrafts, food processing. D=house churches.
1402	Guanxian	78,100	5.10	4,000	62.87	B	138,000	Szechwan on Min River northwest of Chengdu. Grain, eggs. D=house churches.
1403	Guilin (Kweilin, Guizhou, Kuei-lin)	541,000	2.00	10,800	59.77	B	953,000	Kwangsi Chuang Autonomous Region on Lijiang River. Food processing. F=c300 BC. D=Guilin Church(TSPM).
1404	Guixian	74,400	1.00	740	58.77	B	131,000	Kwangsi Chuang Autonomous Region. East of Nanning. Agriculture, timber.
1405	Guiyang (Kweiyang, Kuei-yang)	2,230,000	9.00	201,000	66.77	B	3,612,000	Kweichow capital on Nan-ming Ho River. Coal. D=Guiyang Church(TSPM),RC Diocese(1949: 82 churches).
1406	Hai-kou (Zhuyai)	342,000	2.50	8,600	60.27	B	603,000	Hainan Island port. Exporting agricultural produce & livestock. Ethnoreligionists strong.D=TSPM.
1407	Haicheng	1,164,000	2.70	31,400	60.47	B	2,052,000	Liaoning on Haicheng River southwest of Anshan. Heavy industry, textiles, iron and steel. D=house churches.
1408	Haifeng	60,500	4.50	2,700	62.27	B	107,000	Kwangtung near South China Sea. West of Lufeng. Sugarcane, oilseeds, fisheries, saltworks. D=house churches.
1409	Hailar (Hailaerh, Hulun)	193,000	12.00	23,200	69.77	B	341,000	Inner Mongolian Autonomous Region. Trades in meat, hides, dairy products. D=house churches.
1410	Hailin	70,700	1.30	920	59.07	B	125,000	Heilungkiang west of Mudanjiang. Railroad, tobacco, sugarbeets, sugar refining, lumbering.
1411	Hailong (Meihekou)	632,000	6.50	41,100	64.27	B	1,113,000	Kirin on Liu River near Huinan. Trading point, food processing, paper, beverages. D=house churches.
1412	Hailun	100,000	1.30	1,300	59.07	B	177,000	Heilungkiang north of Suileng. Agriculture and light industry, grain, tobacco, jute, milk, hogs, plastics.
1413	Haiyang (Dongcun)	96,600	5.50	5,300	63.27	B	170,000	Shantung on Yellow Sea on Shantung Peninsula, 65 miles NE of Qingdao. Grain, oilseeds. D=house churches.
1414	Hami (Ha-mi)	320,000	0.30	960	38.07	A	563,000	Sinkiang Uighur. Coal, iron & steel. On silk road, home to 24 ethnic groups, 270 mosques. Uighurs. D=RCC.
1415	Hancheng	360,000	4.50	16,200	62.27	B	634,000	Shensi on Yellow River. Crop growing, forestry, coal, iron and steel, animal husbandry. D=house churches.
1416	Handan (Han-tan)	3,763,000	3.00	113,000	60.77	B	6,646,000	Hopeh. Communications center. Coal, iron & steel, cotton. D=TSPM,house churches, & 10 others.
1417	Hangzhou (Hangchow, Hang-chou)	6,389,000	16.00	1,022,000	73.77	B	11,693,000	Chekiang capital on Qiantang River. Tourism, silk. D=6 TSPM churches,RC Diocese, & 30 others.
1418	Hanzhong (Han-chung)	491,000	4.80	23,600	62.57	B	865,000	Shensi. Agricultural market, cotton. D=RC Diocese(1949: 94 churches).
1419	Harbin (Haerbin, Huining)	5,475,000	2.00	110,000	59.77	B	8,802,000	Heilungkiang capital on Sung-hua River. D=RCC,Orthodox, & 20 others. Many Korean Christians.
1420	Hebi (Ho-pi)	380,000	15.00	57,000	72.77	B	670,000	Honan. Center of coal-mining district. Heavy industry, cotton, fruit, eggs, hogs, chemicals, coal. D=TSPM.
1421	Hechi	315,000	1.00	3,200	58.77	B	556,000	Northern Kwangsi Chuang Autonomous Region on Long River. Agriculture, textiles, D=house churches.
1422	Hechuan (Ho-ch'uan)	78,300	5.10	4,000	62.87	B	138,000	Szechwan Province. Important market, grain milling, eggs, weaving. D=house churches.
1423	Hefei (Ho-fei, Lu, Luzhou)	1,574,000	9.00	142,000	66.77	B	2,615,000	Anhwei capital. Chemicals, fertilizers, cotton. D=Hefei Church(TSPM),RC,house churches.
1424	Hegang (Ho-kang, Hao-li)	696,000	0.90	6,300	38.67	A	1,226,000	Heilungkiang. Coal production. Railroad, heavy mining. D=Hegang Church(TSPM),house churches.
1425	Helong	75,200	6.00	4,500	63.77	B	133,000	Eastern Kirin near North Korean border. Tumen River. Tobacco, jute, lumbering, coal mining. D=house churches.
1426	Hengshui	339,000	2.00	6,800	59.77	B	597,000	Hopeh. D=Hengshui Church (TSPM),RC Diocese(1949: 319 churches),house churches.
1427	Hengyang (Hengzhou, Heng-yang)	866,000	2.50	21,700	60.27	B	1,444,000	Hunan. Center of learning. D=TSPM church,RC Diocese(1949: 59 churches),house churches.
1428	Heshan	130,000	1.00	1,300	58.77	B	228,000	Kwangsi Chuang Autonomous Region on Hongshui River north of Nanning. Textiles.
1429	Heze (Caozhou)	1,184,000	5.50	65,100	63.27	B	2,087,000	Southwestern Shantung west of Jining. Birthplace of numerous historic figures. Coal. D=house churches.
1430	Hohhat (Huhhot, Guisui, Kewisue)	1,261,000	13.00	164,000	70.77	B	2,087,000	Inner Mongolian Autonomous Region capital. D=TSPM, RC Diocese(1949: 81 churches), & 20 others.
1431	Hongjiang	79,200	2.60	2,100	60.37	B	140,000	Hunan on Wu River near Qingyang. Port, light industry, crop growing, animal husbandry. D=house churches.
1432	Horqin Youyi Qianqi (Ulanhot)	227,000	10.00	22,700	67.77	B	400,000	Inner Mongolian Autonomous Region. Dairying, tobacco, steel, hogs. D=Ulanhot Church(TSPM).
1433	Hotan (Ho-t'ien, Khotan)	145,000	0.30	440	38.07	A	256,000	Oasis town in Sinkiang Uighur Autonomous Region. Jade, cotton, fruit, grains, jewelry.
1434	Houma	187,000	7.50	14,100	65.27	B	330,000	Shansi. Vegetables, grain, swine, eggs, machinery, electrical equipment. D=TSPM,house churches.
1435	Huadian	90,300	7.00	6,300	64.77	B	159,000	Kirin on Songhua Lake south of Jilin. Songhua River. Nonferrous mineral mining, rubber. D=house churches.
1436	Huai'an (Huai-an)	78,900	10.70	8,400	68.47	B	139,000	Kiangsu. River port. Shipping, agriculture and light industries, textiles, chemicals. D=house churches.
1437	Huaibei (Huaipei)	529,000	8.00	42,300	65.77	B	932,000	Anhwei. Industrial center, crop growing, animal husbandry, cotton, mining. D=TSPM.
1438	Huaide	1,063,000	7.50	79,800	65.27	B	1,874,000	Kirin southwest of Changchun. Crop growing, animal husbandry, light industry. D=house churches.
1439	Huaihua	505,000	3.00	15,200	60.77	B	890,000	Hunan. Grain, oilseeds, hogs, food processing, textiles, chemicals, electronics. D=TSPM.
1440	Huainan (Hwainan, Huai-nan)	1,271,000	7.00	89,000	64.77	B	2,240,000	Anhwei. Coal, chemical, engineering. Nitrogenous fertilizer, thermal power generation. D=TSPM,house churches.
1441	Huaiyin (Wangying)	452,000	11.00	49,700	68.77	B	797,000	Kiangsu across the Yanyun River from Qingliang. Crop growing, synthetic fibers, rubber. D=house churches.
1442	Huanan	80,000	1.30	1,000	59.07	B	141,000	Heilungkiang east of Yilan. Food processing, tobacco.
1443	Huanggang	82,600	5.40	4,500	63.17	B	146,000	Eastern Hupeh on Yangtze River. Light and heavy industries, fishing, grain, oil crops, hogs. D=house churches.
1444	Huangshi (Hwangshih, Huang-shih)	510,000	5.80	29,600	63.57	B	900,000	Hupeh. Coal, iron, steel. Oldest cement factory in China. D=TSPM,house churches.
1445	Huayun	371,000	5.00	18,500	62.77	B	653,000	Szechwan. Railroad, commercial center, rice, cotton, oilseeds. D=TSPM church,house churches.
1446	Huinan (Chaoyang)	63,000	6.80	4,300	64.57	B	111,000	Kirin on Liu River east of Dongfeng. Industry and construction, grains, oil crops, lamb. D=house churches.
1447	Huizhou (Hui-chow, Hui-chou)	215,000	7.00	15,100	64.77	B	379,000	Kwangtung. Agricultural market. D=TSPM,1985, Huizhou Church opened,house churches.
1448	Hulan (Hu-lan)	90,000	1.30	1,200	59.07	B	159,000	Northeast. Heilungkiang. Grain, flax, sugar beets, jute, tobacco, precious metal ore mining, linen textiles.
1449	Hunjiang (Badaojiang, Hun-chiang)	813,000	10.00	81,300	67.77	B	1,433,000	Kirin. Logging, textiles, plastics, nonferrous metals, coal. 70% Koreans. Many Korean Christians. D=TSPM.
1450	Huzhou (Hu, Huchou, Wu-hsing)	1,140,000	12.00	137,000	69.77	B	2,010,000	Chekiang. Rice, sheep, silk, oilseeds, leather, chemicals, iron and steel. D=TSPM.
1451	Ji'an (Chi-an, Kian)	218,000	6.00	13,100	63.77	B	384,000	Kiangsi. F=180 AD. Academic center. D=Diocese(1949: 25 churches),house churches.
1452	Jiading	72,900	17.00	12,400	74.77	B	128,000	Shanghai. Northwest beyond Nanxiang. Stone Buddha, sacred peak Emei. D=house churches & 10 others.
1453	Jiamusi (Kiamusze, Chia-mu-ssu)	1,127,000	0.80	9,000	38.57	A	1,913,000	Heilungkiang. Wood pulp, newsprint, sugar refining. D=TSPM, 1982 Jiamusi City Church opened.
1454	Jian'ou	66,300	13.40	8,900	71.17	B	117,000	Fukien on Song River north of Nanping. Commercial center in major rice growing region. D=house churches.
1455	Jiangling	93,500	5.40	5,100	63.17	B	165,000	Hupeh on Yangtze River near Shashi. Rice, sugarcane, oilseeds, cotton, ancient walled city dating from 1000 BC.
1456	Jiangmen (Chiang-men, Kongmoon)	274,000	6.00	16,400	63.77	B	483,000	Kwangtung on Hsi River. Agriculture center. D= RC Diocese,TSPM.
1457	Jiangyin	79,800	10.70	8,500	68.47	B	141,000	Kiangsu on Yangtze River north of Wuxi. Rice growing region, textiles, chemicals, rubber. D=house churches.
1458	Jiangyou	87,200	5.80	5,100	63.57	B	154,000	Szechwan on Fu River north of Mianyang. Heavy industry, oil, iron and steel, non-metallic materials, tobacco.
1459	Jiaohe	61,800	7.00	4,300	64.77	B	109,000	Kirin on Songhua Lake southeast of Jilin. Agriculture, heavy industry, grain, tobacco, logging, coal mining.
1460	Jiaojiang (Haimen)	455,000	15.00	68,300	72.77	B	803,000	Chekiang. Outer port on East China Sea, at mouth of Ling River. Fishing, agriculture. D=TSPM.
1461	Jiaoxian	62,300	5.90	3,700	63.67	B	110,000	Shantung west of Qingdao. Handicrafts, bamboo.
1462	Jiaozuo (Chiao-tso, Ts'iao-tso)	603,000	15.00	90,400	72.77	B	1,062,000	Honan. Ceramics, coal-mining, forestry, chemicals. D=TSPM,house churches.
1463	Jiawang	69,200	10.70	7,400	68.47	B	122,000	Northern Kiangsu near Xuzhou, Tianjin-Pukou River. Iron mining settlement. D=house churches.
1464	Jiaxing (Chia-hsing)	812,000	15.00	122,000	72.77	B	1,430,000	Chekiang. Silk, wool, cigarette paper, agricultural products. D=TSPM,house churches, &10 others.
1465	Jiayuguan	121,000	5.30	6,400	63.07	B	213,000	Kansu on Silk Road, at west end of Great Wall. 'Steel city of the Northwest'. D=house churches.
1466	Jiexiu	61,600	8.00	4,900	65.77	B	109,000	Shansi on Fen River. Railroad, coal mining center, grain, cotton, oilseeds. D=house churches.
1467	Jieyang	118,000	4.50	5,300	62.27	B	208,000	Kwangtung near Shantou. River port on coastal stream. Rice, chemicals, plastics, textiles. D=house churches.
1468	Jilin (Kirin, Chi-lin)	1,586,000	7.00	111,000	64.77	B	2,573,000	Kirin. Lumber, matches, sugar. D=TSPM,many Korean Christians,RC Diocese.
1469	Jinan (Ji, Qi, Licheng, Tsi-nan)	4,789,000	6.50	311,000	64.27	B	8,235,000	Capital of Shantung. Textiles, flour, chemicals. D=Jinan Church(TSPM),RC Diocese(1949: 317 churches).
1470	Jinchang (Baijiazui)	161,000	5.00	8,000	62.77	B	283,000	Kansu. Nuclear industry, major military research laboratory, animal husbandry. D=house churches.
1471	Jincheng	724,000	7.60	55,100	65.37	B	1,277,000	Shansi near Jiaozuo. Heavy industrial center, grains, fruits, hogs, eggs, cattle, sheep. D=house churches.
1472	Jingdezhen (Ching-te-chen, Fou-liang)	674,000	5.00	33,700	62.77	B	1,187,000	Kiangsi. Produces world-renowned porcelain. D=Jingdezhen Church(TSPM),house churches.
1473	Jingmen	1,119,000	5.00	56,000	62.77	B	1,972,000	Hupeh. Food processing, textiles, oil refining, chemicals, cotton, oil crops. D=TSPM.
1474	Jinhua (Chin-hua)	946,000	16.00	151,000	73.77	B	1,667,000	Chekiang. Rice, bamboo, hogs. D=TSPM, 1985, Lanxi Church, Jinhua opened house churches.
1475	Jining (Chi-ning)	193,000	12.00	23,200	69.77	B	340,000	Inner Mongolian Autonomous Region. Trade junction. Crops & meat. D=RC Diocese.
1476	Jining (Chi-ning, Jizhou, Tsin-ing)	905,000	6.00	54,300	63.77	B	1,596,000	Shantung. Trade junction. Handicrafts, food processing, wood, bamboo. D=TSPM,house churches.
1477	Jinshi (Chin-shih)	260,000	2.60	6,800	60.37	B	458,000	Hunan. Port on Li River. Collecting center for grain, cotton, timber, tea, salt mining. D=house churches.
1478	Jinxi	750,000	2.70	20,200	60.47	B	1,322,000	Liaoning on Gulf of Liadong. Annexed by Huludao. Rice, jute. D=house churches.
1479	Jinxian (Dalinghe)	115,000	2.70	3,100	60.47	B	203,000	Liaoning on Daling River east of Jinzhou. Rice, cotton, jute, papermaking, crafts, engineering.
1480	Jinzhou (Chin-chou, Jingzhou)	825,000	2.50	20,600	60.27	B	1,349,000	Liaoning. Engineering industry, papermaking. D=Jinzhou Christian Church(TSPM),1980,house churches.
1481	Jishou	230,000	2.60	6,000	60.37	B	405,000	Western Hunan west of Yuanling. Railroad, agriculture, light industry, textiles, chemicals. D=house churches.
1482	Jishu	90,800	5.80	5,300	63.57	B	160,000	Kirin on Qiacha River south of Shulan. Lumber, sugar. D=house churches.
1483	Jiujiang (Chiu-chiang)	452,000	6.00	27,100	63.77	B	797,000	Kiangsi. River port. Textiles. D=TSPM (CIM background), supported from rental income,house churches.
1484	Jiutai	75,700	6.80	5,100	64.57	B	133,000	Kirin northeast of Changchun. Agriculture, soybeans, grain, food processing, machinery. D=house churches.
1485	Jixi (Chi-hsi)	950,000	1.20	11,400	58.97	B	1,539,000	Heilungkiang. Coal mining, lumber, engineering. D=Jixi Church(TSPM),house churches.
1486	Jixian	71,700	17.20	12,300	74.97	B	126,000	Honan on Wei River near Xinxiang. Ceramics, coal mining. D=house churches.
1487	Juancheng	67,800	5.50	3,700	63.27	B	119,000	Western Shantung north of Heze. Grain, oilseeds, cotton, medicinal herbs, textiles.
1488	Junan (Shizilu)	113,000	5.80	6,600	63.57	B	199,000	Shantung east of Linyi. Handicrafts, textiles. D=house churches.
1489	Junxian	501,000	5.40	27,000	63.17	B	882,000	Hupeh on Danjiangkou Reservoir near Guanghua. Rice, sugarcane, oilseeds. D=house churches.
1490	Juxian	64,700	5.50	3,600	63.27	B	114,000	Shantung on Shu River. Handicrafts, bamboo. D=house churches.
1491	Kaifeng (Dongjing, K'ai-feng)	835,000	17.00	142,000	74.77	B	1,370,000	Honan. Textiles. 30% Muslims, 60 mosques, 20 schools, one Muslim hospital. D=TSPM,RC churches,Yellers.
1492	Kaili	404,000	9.00	36,400	66.77	B	713,000	Kweichow east of Guiyang. Agriculture and heavy industry, crop growing, animal husbandry.
1493	Kaiping	65,000	4.00	2,600	61.77	B	115,000	Kwangtung southwest of Guangzhou, river port. Rice, wheat, cotton, sugarcane, fruits, polyester fiber, knitwear.
1494	Kaiyuan	103,000	2.00	2,100	59.77	B	181,000	Liaoning northeast of Shenyang. Old walled city dating from 13th century. Soybeans, grain, food, machinery.
1495	Kaiyuan (K'ai-yuan)	404,000	2.50	10,100	60.27	B	713,000	Yunnan. Coal mining, lumber, crop growing, animal husbandry, grain, hogs, chemicals. D=house churches.
1496	Karamay (Karamai, K'o-la-ma-i)	200,000	0.50	1,000	38.27	A	352,000	Sinkiang Uighur Autonomous Region. Oil. D=house churches.
1497	Kashi (Kashgar, Shufu)	230,000	0.80	1,800	38.57	A	405,000	Sinkiang Uighur. Oasis city and trade center. 78% Muslims. Id Kah, China's biggest mosque, seats 10,000.
1498	Keshan	78,200	1.10	860	58.87	B	138,000	Heilungkiang near Wuyur River east of Yi'an. Grain, sugarbeets, oilseed, jute, machinery. D=house churches.
1499	Korla	259,000	0.10	260	37.87	A	456,000	Sinkiang Uighur Autonomous Region south of Bosten Lake and Yanqi. Textiles.
1500	Kunming (Yunnanfu, K'un-ming)	1,909,000	3.00	57,300	60.77	B	3,053,000	Yunnan capital. Copper. D=Holy Zion Church(TSPM),RC Diocese(1949: 44 churches),house churches.
1501	Kunshan	53,600	11.00	5,900	68.77	B	94,500	Kiangsu west of Shanghai. Textiles, leather, pharmaceuticals, synthetic fibers. D=house churches.
1502	Kuga	76,700	0.10	77	37.87	A	135,000	Sinkiang Uighur near Muzat River. Muslims.
1503	Kuytun	71,200	0.10	71	37.87	A	125,000	Sinkiang Uighur Autonomous Region northwest of Urumchi. Light industry (food processing and textiles).
1504	Laiwu	1,232,000	2.80	34,500	60.57	B	2,171,000	Shantung south of Boshan. Heavy industry and agriculture, non metallic mineral mining. D=house churches.
1505	Langxiang	77,600	1.00	780	58.77	B	137,000	Heilungkiang east of Tieli. Coal mining, lumber.
1506	Lanxi	717,000	16.00	115,000	73.77	B	1,264,000	Chekiang on Qu River northwest of Jinhua. Zhuge ancestry temples. D=house churches.
1507	Lanxi	63,900	1.20	770	58.97	B	113,000	Heilungkiang, north of Harbin. Grain, tobacco, jute, sugar beets, linen textiles.
1508	Lanzhou (Lanchow, Lanchou)	2,021,000	10.00	202,000	67.77	B	3,247,000	Kansu. Petrochemicals. D=Lanzhou Church (TSPM),90,000 active.
1509	Lechang	67,300	4.00	2,700	61.77	B	119,000	Northern Kwangtung on Wu River. Rice, oil seeds, cotton, jute, textiles. D=house churches.
1510	Lengshuijiang (Leng-shui-chiang)	328,000	6.00	19,700	63.77	B	578,000	Szechwan south of Chongqing. Heavy industry, crop growing, livestock raising. D=TSPM,house churches.
1511	Lengshuitan	428,000	3.00	12,800	60.77	B	754,000	Hunan on Xiang River north of Lingling. Agriculture and heavy industry, hogs. D=house churches.
1512	Leshan (Jiading, Le-shan)	1,150,000	6.00	69,000	63.77	B	2,026,000	Szechwan on Min River. Silk textiles. D=Leshan Church(TSPM),RC Diocese(1949: 23 churches).
1513	Lhasa (La-sa)	127,000	0.60	760	38.37	A	224,000	Tibet capital. Trade. Tantrayana (Lamaist Buddhism). 1,600 Muslims, 2 mosques, 1 school.
1514	Liaocheng	856,000	5.50	47,100	63.27	B	1,509,000	Shantung on Grand Canal west of Jinan. Coal, crude oil. Ancient city built 5,800 years ago. D=house churches.
1515	Liaoyang (Dingliao, Liao-yang)	984,000	2.00	19,700	59.77	B	1,676,000	Liaoning. Hun River. Chemicals, Buddhist temples built in 18th century. D=Liaoyang City Church(TSPM).
1516	Liaoyuan (Tung-liao, Liao-yuan)	912,000	6.00	54,700	63.77	B	1,608,000	Kirin. Coal-mining, agricultural products. Originally a Manchu hunting preserve. D=TSPM,house churches.
1517	Lien-yun-kang (Lianyungang, Xinpu)	492,000	10.00	49,200	67.77	B	868,000	Kiangsu. Fishing port, salt. D=ISPM,1985,Lianyungang City Church opened.

Table 10-5–continued opposite

Table 10-5–continued

Rec No	Country City	Pop 2000	AC%	Church Members	E%	W	Pop 2025	Notes
1	2	3	4	5	6	7	8	9
1518	Liling	1,012,000	2.80	28,300	60.57	B	1,784,000	Hunan southeast of Zhuzhou. Agriculture, crafts, porcelain, construction materials. D=house churches.
1519	Linfen (Pingyang, Jin)	627,000	7.00	43,900	64.77	B	1,105,000	Shansi. Coal, food processing, agricultural implements. D=TSPM,house churches.
1520	Lingling	609,000	3.00	18,300	60.77	B	1,074,000	Hunan on Xiang River. Agriculture and light industry, animal husbandry, hogs, tobacco. D=house churches.
1521	Lingyuan	80,200	2.20	1,800	59.97	B	141,000	Western Liaoning west of Chaoyang. Agriculture, chemicals, iron and steel. D=house churches.
1522	Linhai	63,200	16.00	10,100	73.77	B	111,000	Chekiang on Yong'an River northwest of Haimen. Taizhou Bay. Grains, fruits, textiles, crafts. D=house churches.
1523	Linhe	433,000	12.70	54,900	70.47	B	762,000	Inner Mongolian Autonomous Region on Yellow River. Hetao Oasis. Grains, fruits. D=house churches.
1524	Linkou	63,600	1.00	640	58.77	B	112,000	Heilungkiang east of Jixi. Railroad junction. Agriculture, tobacco, medicinal herbs.
1525	Linqing	713,000	5.80	41,400	63.57	B	1,256,000	Shantung on Grand Canal west of Jinan. Wei River. Grains. 'Land of the Beijing Opera'. D=house churches.
1526	Linqu	105,000	5.30	5,600	63.07	B	186,000	Shantung on Mi River south of Yidu. Scenic setting, Yi Mountains. Tobacco, oilseeds. D=house churches.
1527	Linxia	178,000	5.00	8,900	62.77	B	313,000	Kansu southeast of Lanzhou. Gateway to Tibetan areas: Qinghai and Sichuan. Leather. D=house churches.
1528	Linyi	1,614,000	6.50	105,000	64.27	B	2,844,000	Southern Shantung on Yi River. Agriculture and light industry, fruits, poultry, coal mining. D=house churches.
1529	Liuzhou (Liuc-hou, Liuchow, Maping)	1,027,000	2.00	20,500	59.77	B	1,723,000	Kwangsi Chuang Autonomous Region. Agricultural products, timber, textiles. D=TSPM,house churches.
1530	Longjiang	61,400	1.00	610	58.77	B	108,000	Western Heilungkiang on Yalu River east of Qiqihar. Grain, tobacco
1531	Longyan (Lung-yen)	448,000	13.00	58,200	70.77	B	789,000	Fukien. Coal mining, iron ore, agriculture, other minerals. D= TSPM house churches.
1532	Loudi	301,000	3.00	9,000	60.77	B	530,000	Hopeh northwest of Xingtai. Heavy industry, animal husbandry, iron, steel, coal. D=TSPM,house churches.
1533	Luan	193,000	6.00	11,600	63.77	B	340,000	Anhwei on Pi River east of Hefei. Food processing, textiles, paper, chemicals, crop growing. D=TSPM.
1534	Lufeng	63,700	4.50	2,900	62.27	B	112,000	Kwangtung on Jieshi Bay on South China Sea. Rice, wheat, sugarcane, oilseeds, crafts, plastics, machinery.
1535	Luohe (Lo-ho, T'a-ho, Tahe)	188,000	15.00	28,200	72.77	B	332,000	Honan on Sha River. Agricultural produce, light bulbs. High tech industrial park. D=TSPM.
1536	Luoyang (Xijing, Honan, Lo-yang)	1,569,000	12.00	188,000	69.77	B	2,557,000	Honan. Buddhist center. D=Chengguan Church (TSPM),RC Diocese(1949: 24 churches).
1537	Luzhou (Lu, Lu-chou, Luchow)	426,000	6.00	25,600	63.77	B	751,000	Szechwan. River port. Market & commercial center for T'o River. D=RCC,house churches.
1538	Ma'anshan (Ma-an-shan)	434,000	8.00	34,700	65.77	B	765,000	Anhwei on Yangtze River. Iron, steel, sulfur. Industrial center. Chemicals. D=house churches.
1539	MACAU (Macao, Aomen)	450,000	9.60	43,200	67.37	B	793,000	On Pearl River estuary. Free port, trade. Exports textiles, garments, tourism. D=RCC.
1540	Manzhouli (Man-chou-li, Lupin)	138,000	10.00	13,800	67.77	B	243,000	Inner Mongolian Autonomous Region on Soviet border. Customs station, coal. D=house churches.
1541	Maoming (Mao-ming)	514,000	4.00	20,600	61.77	B	906,000	Kwangtung. Oil, gasoline, chemicals, heavy industry, textiles, crafts, poultry, eggs, fruit. D=TSPM.
1542	Meixian (Mei-hsien)	876,000	4.50	39,400	62.27	B	1,543,000	Kwangtung on Mei River. Collecting center for produce. Predominantly Hakka. D=house churches.
1543	Mengyin	88,400	5.50	4,900	63.27	B	156,000	Shantung on Wen River southeast of Xinwen. Grain, oilseeds, tobacco, textiles, engineering. D=house churches.
1544	Mianyang (Mien-yang)	1,003,000	6.00	60,200	63.77	B	1,768,000	Szechwan. Natural communication center. Silk, cotton. D=RCC,house churches.
1545	Minhang	83,100	17.30	14,400	75.07	B	146,000	Shanghai on Huangpu River south of Shanghai. Engineering, coking coal industry, rice. D=house churches.
1546	Mishan	65,900	1.10	730	58.87	B	116,000	Heilungkiang on Muling River north of Chanka Lake. Grain, tobacco, sugarbeets, aquatic products, milk, hogs.
1547	Mixian	81,100	17.20	14,000	74.97	B	143,000	Honan on Shuangji River north of Yuxian. Ceramics, coal mining. D=house churches.
1548	Mudanjiang (Mu-tan-chiang)	665,000	2.00	13,300	59.77	B	1,173,000	Heilungkiang. Rubber, aluminum, asbestos. D=TSPM church. Many Korean Christians.
1549	N'aizishen	62,400	6.80	4,200	64.57	B	110,000	Kirin east of Jiaohe. Agriculture, coal mining. D=house churches.
1550	Nahe	59,700	1.00	600	58.77	B	105,000	Western Heilungkiang on Nemor River. Grain, tobacco.
1551	Nancha	69,200	1.30	900	59.07	B	122,000	Heilungkiang on Tangwang River west of Jiamusi. Agricultural center.
1552	Nanchang (Hongzhou)	1,582,000	6.20	98,100	63.97	B	2,571,000	Capitol of Kiangsi. F=201 BC. D=TSPM,(Methodist),RC Diocese (1949: 21 churches).
1553	Nanchong (Nan-ch'ung, Shunking)	282,000	6.00	16,900	63.77	B	496,000	Szechwan. Major grain market, silk. D=RC Diocese(1949: 15 churches),house churches.
1554	Nanjing (Nanking, Jinling)	3,375,000	11.00	371,000	68.77	B	5,369,000	Capital of Kiangsu on Yangtze River. F=c500 BC. D=TSPM,RC,house churches. Jin Ling Seminary.
1555	Nanning (Nan-ning, Yung-ning)	1,610,000	1.50	24,200	59.27	B	2,653,000	Kwangsi Chuang Autonomous Region capital. Chuang peoples. D=Nanning Christian Church(TSPM),RC Diocese.
1556	Nanpiao	84,300	2.70	2,300	60.47	B	148,000	Liaoning west of Jinzhou. Agriculture, chemicals. D=house churches.
1557	Nanping (Yanping, Nan-p'ing)	498,000	12.00	59,700	69.77	B	877,000	Fukien. Timber, paper, cement, chemicals. D=Gospel Church(TSPM),house churches. Christian nursery school.
1558	Nantong (Nan-tung)	486,000	10.00	48,600	67.77	B	856,000	Kiangsu. Major port on Yangzi River. Salt, rice, cotton, textiles, fibers, plastics, fishing. D=house churches.
1559	Nanyang (Nan-yang)	349,000	15.00	52,300	72.77	B	614,000	Honan on Pai River. Grains, tobacco, silk. D=RC Diocese,Nanyang Church(TSPM), & 10 others.
1560	Neihuang	70,200	17.20	12,100	74.97	B	124,000	Honan near Wei River east of Anyang. Grain, cotton, textiles, food and beverage production. D=house churches.
1561	Neijiang (Neikiang, Nei-chiang)	1,424,000	6.00	85,400	63.77	B	2,262,000	Szechwan. Sugarcane, molasses, textiles, grain, cotton, vegetables, fruit. D=TSPM.
1562	Ning'an	59,200	1.30	770	59.07	B	104,000	Southern Heilungkiang on Mudan River south of Mudanjiang. Grain, tobacco, sugar refining.
1563	Ningbo (Ning-po, Yin-hsien)	1,202,000	14.00	168,000	71.77	B	2,119,000	Chekiang. Cotton, textiles. 1842 Treaty Port. D=Ningbo Century Church(TSPM),RC Diocese,house churches.
1564	Ningyang	69,400	5.80	4,000	63.57	B	122,000	Shantung north of Yanzhou. Grain, oilseeds, cotton, jute, coal mining, chemicals, textiles. D=house churches.
1565	Nong'an	67,200	7.00	4,700	64.77	B	118,000	Kirin north of Changchun. Livestock, soybeans, sugarbeets, tobacco, chemicals. D=house churches.
1566	Nunjiang	71,200	1.50	1,100	59.27	B	125,000	Northwestern Heilungkiang on Gan River on Inner Mongolian border. Soybeans, sugar beets.
1567	Orogen Zizhiqi	57,700	12.00	6,900	69.77	B	102,000	Northern Inner Mongolian Autonomous Region on Gan River. Grains. D=house churches.
1568	Panshan	406,000	2.70	11,000	60.47	B	715,000	Liaoning on Shuangtaizi River north of Gulf of Liaotung. Grain, crude oil extraction. D=house churches.
1569	Panshi	71,200	7.00	5,000	64.77	B	125,000	Northwest. Kirin north of Huinan. Railroad, limestone quarrying, copper mining, copper and iron smelting.
1570	Pingdingshan (Ping-ting-shan)	969,000	14.00	136,000	71.77	B	1,708,000	Honan. Coal mining. Fengxue temple, burial site of Northern Song dynasty and poet Su Dongbo. D=TSPM.
1571	Pingliang (P'ing-liang)	429,000	5.30	22,700	63.07	B	755,000	Kansu. Wheat, wool, tobacco, crop growing, animal husbandry, grain food, textiles, machinery. D=house churches.
1572	Pingxiang (P'ing-hsiang)	1,521,000	6.00	91,300	63.77	B	2,681,000	Kiangsi. Coal, iron, steel, ceramics. Catholic Patriotic Association at work. D=TSPM,house churches.
1573	Pingxiang (P'ing-hsiang)	101,000	0.50	510	38.27	A	178,000	Kwangsi Chuang Autonomous Region. Many non-Han Chinese. Trade with Vietnam.
1574	Pingyi	112,000	5.70	6,400	63.47	B	197,000	Shantung south of Xinwen. Grains, oilseeds, cotton. D=house churches.
1575	Pingyin	78,700	5.50	4,300	63.27	B	139,000	Shantung on Huang River southeast of Jinan. Grain, oilseeds, cotton. D=house churches.
1576	Potou	550,000	11.00	60,500	68.77	B	969,000	Honan on Huang River across from Mengjin. Coal mining. D=house churches.
1577	Puqi	78,300	5.40	4,200	63.17	B	138,000	Southern Hupeh east of Honghu, on Guangzhou-Wuhan railroad. Grain, hogs, textiles. D=house churches.
1578	Putian	314,000	12.50	39,200	70.27	B	553,000	Fukien near Hanjiang. Xinghua Bay. Fishing, forestry, grains, oil crops, leather, milk. D=house churches.
1579	Putuo	61,200	16.60	10,200	74.37	B	108,000	Chekiang on Zhoushan Island. Buddhist holy mountain, numerous temples and monasteries. D=house churches.
1580	Puyang	1,284,000	17.00	218,000	74.77	B	2,263,000	Northern Honan near Anyang. Heavy industry, crop growing, animal husbandry, oil. D=house churches.
1581	Qian Gorlos	95,400	7.00	6,700	64.77	B	168,000	Kirin on Songhua River across from Fuyu. Livestock, soybeans. D=house churches.
1582	Qingdao (Tsingtao, Chl'ing-tao)	4,376,000	6.00	263,000	63.77	B	7,596,000	Shantung. Brewery, fishing. Major holiday resort and port. Two gothic churches restored. D=TSPM,RC Diocese.
1583	Qinggang	51,700	1.30	670	59.07	B	91,100	Heilungkiang north of Harbin. Soybeans, grain, jute, sugar beets, engineering, chemicals.
1584	Qingjiang	51,300	6.00	3,100	63.77	B	90,400	Kiangsi on Gan River south of Nanchang. Coal mining, ceramics. D=house churches.
1585	Qingjiang (Ch'ing-chiang, Hwai-yin)	309,000	11.00	34,000	68.77	B	544,000	Kiangsu on Grand Canal. Water transport. Communication and marketing center. D=TSPM,house churches.
1586	Qingyuan	62,100	4.50	2,800	62.27	B	110,000	Kwangtung on Bei River north of Guangzhou. Transportation center, grain, fruits. D=house churches.
1587	Qinhuangdao (Ch'in-huang-tao)	516,000	2.50	12,900	60.27	B	909,000	Hopeh seaport. Coal export, peanuts, soybeans, summer resorts. D=RCC,house churches.
1588	Qinzhou	1,092,000	1.00	10,900	58.77	B	1,924,000	Kwangsi Chuang Autonomous Region on Gulf of Tonkin. Grains, fruits, hogs, fish, crafts. D=house churches.
1589	Qiqihaer (Tsitsihar, Ch'i-ch'i-ha-erh)	1,681,000	1.00	16,800	58.77	B	2,702,000	Heilungkiang. F=1333 by Mongols. Engineering industry, timber. D=RCC,Qiqihar Church(TSPM).
1590	Qitaihe (Chitaiho)	366,000	0.50	1,800	38.27	A	646,000	Heilungkiang east of Boli. Heavy industry, grain, swine, eggs, coal mining. D=Qitaihe Church (TSPM).
1591	Qixia	67,800	5.60	3,800	63.37	B	120,000	Shantung on Shantung Peninsula north of Laiyang. Grain, peanuts, textiles, tobacco. D=house churches.
1592	Qixian	62,700	17.20	10,800	74.97	B	111,000	Honan on Huiji River. Grains, tobacco, silk. D=house churches.
1593	Quanzhou (Zaytou, Chuanchow)	516,000	14.00	72,200	71.77	B	909,000	Fukien. Agriculture. F=AD 700. Medieval ruins. D=Nanjie Church(TSPM),2 Christian factories,house churches.
1594	Qujing	896,000	6.00	53,800	63.77	B	1,579,000	Kiangsi on Gan River across from Fengcheng. Coal mining, ceramics. D=house churches.
1595	Quxian (Quzhou, Qu Xian, Ch'u-hsien)	833,000	13.00	108,000	70.77	B	1,469,000	Chekiang. Collecting center. Food processing, woodworking, chemicals, electricity. D=TSPM church.
1596	Raoping	65,800	4.50	3,000	62.27	B	116,000	Kwangtung on South China Sea northeast of Shantou. Rice, wheat, sugarcane, paper making, plastics.
1597	Rizhao	1,147,000	5.90	67,700	63.67	B	2,022,000	Shantung near Yellow Sea, 38 mile coastline. Silt and mud free water, 2 major piers. D=house churches.
1598	Rongcheng	66,200	5.50	3,600	63.27	B	117,000	Shantung on Shantung Peninsula on Yellow Sea. Grain, oilseeds, textiles, rubber, plastics, machinery, crafts.
1599	Rugao	60,800	11.00	6,700	68.77	B	107,000	Kiangsu north of Nantong. Agriculture, rice, cotton, oilseeds, textiles, crafts. D=house churches.
1600	Rui'an	69,600	16.60	11,600	74.37	B	123,000	Chekiang on Feiyun River south of Wenzhou. Fishing port, rice, oilseeds, textiles. D=house churches.
1601	Sanmenxia (San-men-hsia)	177,000	17.00	30,200	74.77	B	313,000	Honan. Large dam & hydroelectric plant, flooding displaced 600,000. F=1957. D=TSPM house churches.
1602	Sanming (San-ming)	253,000	13.00	32,900	70.77	B	447,000	Fukien. Market center, iron & steel, animal husbandry, chemicals, plastics. D=22 TSPM churches.
1603	Shanghai (Shang-hai)	14,173,000	17.50	2,480,000	77.77	B	20,787,000	Major seaport. F=11th century. Strong YMCA, YWCA. D=RC Diocese(1949: 425 churches),TSPM
1604	Shangqiu (Suiyang, Zhuji)	236,000	14.00	33,000	71.77	B	415,000	Honan. Collecting center. Agriculture, flour milling, tobacco, oil-processing. D=TSPM, house churches.
1605	Shangrao (Shang-jao)	168,000	6.00	10,100	63.77	B	297,000	Kiangsi. Commercial center, paper, tea. D=TSPM,house churches.
1606	Shangshui	62,900	17.20	10,800	74.97	B	111,000	Honan on Ying River west of Huaiyang. Grain, tobacco, cotton, textiles, engineering. D=house churches.
1607	Shantou (Swatow)	1,146,000	11.00	126,000	68.77	B	1,891,000	Kwangtung. Sugar. Up to 80% are young people. Rapid growth. D=RCC,house churches.
1608	Shanwei	73,500	4.50	3,300	62.27	B	130,000	Kwangtung on South China Sea. Honghai Bay. Grain, oil crops, poultry, eggs. D=house churches.
1609	Shao-yang (Shaozhou, Baoching)	551,000	3.00	16,500	60.77	B	971,000	Hunan. Collecting center for agriculture. Handicrafts, paper, coal. D=TSPM,house churches.
1610	Shaoguan (Shao-kuan, Shiuchou)	408,000	7.00	28,500	64.77	B	719,000	Kwangtung. Heavy industry. 130,000 in 32 Minority tribes (93,000 Yao). D=TSPM,RCC.
1611	Shaowu	315,000	13.40	42,300	71.17	B	556,000	Fukien on Futun River. Grain, hogs, heavy industry, rubber, forestry. D=house churches.
1612	Shaoxing (Shaozing, Shao-hsing)	297,000	13.00	38,600	70.77	B	523,000	Chekiang. Wine, tea, rice, oil, flour. Ancient relics. D=TSPM,house churches.
1613	Shashi (Sha-shih)	300,000	5.00	15,000	62.77	B	529,000	Hupeh. Handicraft textiles, satins, cotton weaving. D=TSPM,1984 Shashi City Church opened,house churches.
1614	Shenxian	62,900	2.70	1,700	60.47	B	111,000	Hopeh east of Shijiazhuang. Grain, cotton, oilseeds, textiles, machinery and equipment manufacturing.
1615	Shenyang (Mukden, Fengtian)	5,681,000	2.00	114,000	59.77	B	8,793,000	Liaoning on Hun River. F=2nd cent BC. D=6 TSPM,60 house churches,RCC.
1616	Shenzhen (Shen-chen)	1,042,000	7.00	72,900	64.77	B	1,702,000	Kwangtung. Special economic zone. 30,000 in 1980. Tourists. D=TSPM(1984),house churches.
1617	Sheung Shui	94,300	14.00	13,200	71.77	B	166,000	North New Territories, Hong Kong. Vegetables, rice, hog raising, light industry. D=RCC.
1618	Shiguaigou	69,200	12.70	8,800	70.47	B	122,000	Inner Mongolian Autonomous Region east of Baotou. Agriculture. D=house churches.
1619	Shihezi (Shih-ho-tzu)	639,000	2.00	12,800	59.77	B	1,126,000	Sinkiang Uighur Autonomous Region. State farms, corn, wheat. Mainly ethnic Chinese. D=house churches.
1620	Shijiazhuang (Shihkiachwong)	1,875,000	3.00	56,300	60.77	B	3,072,000	Hopeh capital. Textiles, chemicals. D=Shijiazhuang Church(TSPM),RC metropolitan Diocese.
1621	Shiyan	393,000	5.00	19,700	62.77	B	693,000	Northern Hupeh near Yunxian. Wudang mountains. Heavy industry, crop growing, rubber. D=TSPM.
1622	Shizuishan (Dawukou)	375,000	1.00	3,800	58.77	B	661,000	Ningsia Hui Autonomous Region north of Yinchuan. Crop growing, hogs, coal mining. D=house churches.
1623	Shouguang	104,000	5.50	5,700	63.27	B	184,000	Shantung near Mi River. Grain, cotton, oilseeds, tobacco, textiles. D=house churches.
1624	Shuangcheng	109,000	1.50	1,600	59.27	B	193,000	Heilungkiang south of Harbin. Lalin River. Grain, sugarbeets, dairying, hogs, aquatic products. D=house churches.
1625	Shuangliao	80,800	6.80	5,500	64.57	B	142,000	Kirin on Liao River. Agriculture, light industry, grains.
1626	Shuangyashan (Chien-shan)	505,000	0.90	4,500	38.67	A	890,000	Heilungkiang. Coal production as single industry. D=Shuangyashan Church(TSPM),house churches.
1627	Shuicheng	2,621,000	9.00	236,000	66.77	B	4,619,000	Kweichow near Sancha River west of Anshun. Grain, food processing, tobacco. D=house churches.
1628	Shulan	59,800	6.80	4,100	64.57	B	105,000	Kirin northeast of Jilin. Food and beverages, building materials, textiles, coal mining. D=house churches.
1629	Shunde	60,300	5.00	3,000	62.77	B	106,000	Kwangtung south of Guangzhou. Pearl River delta, Qinghui gardens. Textiles, apparel. D=house churches.
1630	Siping (Szepingkai, Ssu-p'ing)	423,000	5.00	21,200	62.77	B	746,000	Kirin. Petrochemicals, agriculture. D=RC Diocese(1949: 16 churches),TSPM,house churches.
1631	Sishui	104,000	6.00	6,200	63.77	B	183,000	Shantung on Si River east of Yanzhou. Wheat, oilseeds, tobacco, engineering, textiles. D=house churches.
1632	Songjiang (Sung-chiang)	86,300	17.30	14,900	75.07	B	152,000	Shanghai municipality. Cotton textiles, waterway communications, perch fisheries. D=house churches.
1633	Songjianghe	63,700	6.50	4,100	64.27	B	112,000	Kirin southeast of Fusong. Textiles, coal mining. D=house churches.
1634	Suihua	866,000	1.30	11,300	59.07	B	1,526,000	Heilungkiang north of Harbin. Agriculture, light industry, hogs, milk, eggs, tobacco. D=house churches.
1635	Suileng	82,100	1.20	990	58.97	B	145,000	Heilungkiang south of Hailun. Soybeans, grain, sugarbeets, jute, tobacco, logging, food processing, textiles.
1636	Suining	1,389,000	6.00	83,400	63.77	B	2,448,000	Szechwan on Fu River northwest of Chongqing. Crop growing, animal husbandry, cotton, fruit.
1637	Suixian	1,515,000	5.40	81,800	63.17	B	2,671,000	Northern Hupeh on Jue River. Textiles, river trade. D=house churches & 10 others.
1638	Suqian	60,900	10.70	6,500	68.47	B	107,000	Kiangsu on Grand Canal. Agriculture and light industry, cotton, non-metallic materials. D=house churches.
1639	Suxian	258,000	7.00	18,100	64.77	B	456,000	Northern Anhwei north of Bengbu. Tea, agriculture. D=house churches.
1640	Suzhou (Hsuchow, Suchow, Jiuquan)	1,272,000	12.00	153,000	69.77	B	2,121,000	Kiangsu on Chang Jiang River. Historic garden city. F=514 BC. Great Pagoda (1131). D=TSPM,RCC.
1641	Tai'an	1,567,000	6.00	94,000	63.77	B	2,762,000	Shantung south of Jinan. Foot of Taishan Mountain, China's most sacred mountain. D=RCC.

Table 10-5–continued overleaf

Table 10-5–continued

Rec No 1	Country City 2	Pop 2000 3	AC% 4	Church Members 5	E% 6	W 7	Pop 2025 8	Notes 9
1642	Tai Po	129,000	13.00	16,800	70.77	B	228,000	North of Kowloon. Tai Po Lake, Tolo Harbor. Largely residential, Guamgzhou-Kowloon railroad. D=RCC.
1643	Taiyuan (T'ai-yuan)	2,280,000	8.50	194,000	66.27	B	3,613,000	Shansi capital. Heavy industry. D=Taiyuan Church(TSPM),RCC.
1644	Taizhou (Taichow, Tai-chou)	245,000	10.00	24,500	67.77	B	432,000	Kiangsu. Transshipment point. Salt, flour, textiles, fishing nets. D=large TSPM church.
1645	Tancheng	77,500	5.80	4,500	63.57	B	137,000	Southern Shantung south of Linyi. Grain, oilseeds, chemicals, crafts, engineering. D=house churches.
1646	Tangshan (T'ang-shan)	1,626,000	2.50	40,700	60.27	B	2,570,000	Hopeh. Steel, ceramics. 1976 earthquake leveled city, killing over 700,000. D=RC Diocese of Tangshan.
1647	Tao'an	91,600	7.20	6,600	64.97	B	161,000	Kirin on Tao'er River south of Baicheng. Agriculture, light industry, grains. Lamasery. Taonan Double Pagodas.
1648	Tengxian	63,900	6.00	3,800	63.77	B	113,000	Southern Shantung near Dushan Lake. Food processing, rice.
1649	Tianjin (Tientsin, T'ien-ching)	10,239,000	1.30	133,000	59.07	B	15,421,000	Gulf of Chihli port. YMCA, YWCA. D=RCC,TSPM,house churches.
1650	Tianshui (T'ien-shui, Tsinchow)	1,127,000	5.50	62,000	63.27	B	1,986,000	Kansu. Cotton, matches. Large Muslim minority. D=RC Diocese(1949: 77 churches),house churches.
1651	Tiefa	183,000	2.00	3,700	59.77	B	323,000	Liaoning northwest of Tieling. Construction, industry, coal mining. D=TSPM,house churches.
1652	Tieli	123,000	1.30	1,600	59.07	B	217,000	Heilungkiang on Hulan River. Grains, milk, hogs, eggs, logging, heavy industry. D=house churches.
1653	Tieling (Tiehling)	537,000	2.50	13,400	60.27	B	946,000	Liaoning near Liao River. D=Tieling Christian Church(TSPM),opened 1981,house churches.
1654	Tongchuan (Tung-chuan)	465,000	2.00	9,300	59.77	B	819,000	Yunnan. Copper industry. D=TSPM,house churches.
1655	Tonghua (Tung-hua, Dunhua)	434,000	7.00	30,400	64.77	B	766,000	Kirin. Paper, engineering, iron & steel. 70% Koreans. D=TSPM,many Korean Christians.
1656	Tongliao (T'ung-liao)	299,000	12.00	35,900	69.77	B	527,000	Inner Mongolian Autonomous Region. Collecting point for pastoral products. D=house churches.
1657	Tongling (Tung-ling)	256,000	8.00	20,500	65.77	B	451,000	Anhwei. Iron, copper, chemicals. Mining center. D=TSPM,house churches.
1658	Tongren	60,400	9.00	5,400	66.77	B	106,000	Eastern Kweichow. Da and Xiao rivers. Grain, oil crops, tobacco. Dates to ancient times. D=house churches.
1659	Tongxian	117,000	1.40	1,600	59.17	B	206,000	Beijing municipality. East on Chaobai River. D=house churches.
1660	Tumen	118,000	7.00	8,300	64.77	B	208,000	Kirin on Tumen River on North Korean border. Animal husbandry, paper, oil refining. D=house churches.
1661	Tunxi (T'un-hsi)	124,000	8.00	9,900	65.77	B	218,000	Anhwei. Famous tea production center. D=Tunxi Church(TSPM),house churches.
1662	Turpan	233,000	0.30	700	38.07	A	410,000	Sinkiang Uighur near Urumchi. Turfan Depression. Cotton, silk, wheat, grapes, melons, oil.
1663	Urumqi (Wulumuchi, Luntai, Urumchi)	1,481,000	0.40	5,900	38.17	A	2,412,000	Sinkiang Uighur capital. Uighurs, Kazaks, Manchus, Dungans. D=TSPM, Orthodox & 10 others.
1664	VICTORIA (Xianggang)	6,097,000	13.40	817,000	71.17	B	6,334,000	On Hong Kong Island. International banks, tourism, foreign trade. F=1841. D=RCC,Baptist.
1665	Kowloon (Jiulong)	838,000	14.00	117,000	71.77	B	1,477,000	Kowloon Peninsula. Port, textile manufacturing, tourism. International airport. Shopping, dining. D=RCC.
1666	Kwai Chung	142,000	15.00	21,300	72.77	B	250,000	South New Territories, Ma Wa Channel. Industrial town, Chek Lap Kok airport motorway. D=RCC.
1667	New Kowloon (Xinjiulong)	1,652,000	13.20	218,000	70.97	B	2,911,000	North of Kowloon. New Territories, recent town developments. D=RCC,Baptist.
1668	Sha Tin	385,000	14.00	53,900	71.77	B	678,000	New Territories. North of Kowloon near Tai Po Lake. Site of Chinese University. D=RCC,Baptist.
1669	Tsuen Wan (Quanwan, Kwai Chung)	556,000	13.60	75,700	71.37	B	980,000	New Territories port. Recent town developments with industries. Incorporated in 1960's. D=RCC.
1670	Tuen Mun	284,000	14.00	39,700	71.77	B	500,000	Western New Territories. Hong Kong, recent town developments. F=1960's, formerly Castle Peak.
1671	Wangkui	62,500	1.00	630	58.77	B	110,000	Heilungkiang north of Harbin. Sugar refining, textiles, soybeans, grain, tobacco, sugar beets.
1672	Wangqing	73,500	7.00	5,100	64.77	B	130,000	Eastern Kirin west of Vladivostok, Russia. Logging, food industry, oil. D=house churches.
1673	Wanxian (Wan-hsien)	332,000	6.00	19,900	63.77	B	585,000	Szechwan. River port. D=RC Diocese(1949: 4 churches),TSPM,house churches.
1674	Weifang (Wei, Weixian)	1,232,000	6.20	76,400	63.97	B	2,172,000	Shantung. Agricultural produce, oil-pressing, cloth export. D=TSPM,Weifang City Church,house churches.
1675	Weihai (Weihaiwei)	261,000	5.80	15,100	63.57	B	460,000	Shantung. Small commercial and fishing port, textiles, silk. Navy Base. D=TSPM,house churches.
1676	Weinan	827,000	4.50	37,200	62.27	B	1,457,000	Shensi on Wei River east of Xi'an. Heavy industry, grain, oil crops, cotton, eggs. D=house churches.
1677	Weishan (Xiazhen)	72,600	5.70	4,100	63.47	B	128,000	Southern Shantung on Weishan Lake. Rice, wheat, millet, beans, tobacco, logging. D=house churches.
1678	Weixian (Hanting)	62,800	5.50	3,500	63.27	B	111,000	Shantung north of Weifang. Agricultural, textiles. D=house churches.
1679	Wenzhou (Yung-chia, Wen-chow)	1,540,000	21.00	323,000	78.77	B	2,661,000	Chekiang. River port, trade. D=550 TSPM meeting places,RCC,Yellers sect & 20 others.
1680	Wuchang (Wu-ch'ang)	77,300	1.30	1,000	59.07	B	136,000	Southern Heilungkiang on Lalin River. Oldest of 3 Wuhan cities. Huanghi pavilion, Wuhan University.
1681	Wuhai (Uhai)	315,000	12.00	37,700	69.77	B	554,000	Inner Mongolian Autonomous Region on Yellow River north of Yinchuan. D=Wuhai Church(TSPM),RCC.
1682	Wuhan (Hankou-Hanyang-Wuchang)	4,750,000	6.00	285,000	63.77	B	7,416,000	Hupeh capital on Yangtze River. Tea, silk, temples. YMCA, YWCA. D=RCC,TSPM & 20 others.
1683	Wuhu (Wu-hu)	594,000	8.00	47,500	65.77	B	1,046,000	Anhwei. Communication center. D=Wuhu Church(TSPM),RC Diocese(1949: 199 churches).
1684	Wulian (Hongning)	64,800	5.00	3,200	62.77	B	114,000	Eastern Shantung south of Zhucheng. Agriculture, textiles. D=house churches.
1685	Wusong	80,200	17.30	13,900	75.07	B	141,000	Shanghai municipality north of Shanghai on Huangpu River. Rice growing region. D=house churches.
1686	Wuwei (Liangzhou, Wu-wei)	951,000	5.30	50,400	63.07	B	1,675,000	Kansu. Chief market & collecting center, esp. for pastoral nomads. Silk Road junction. D=house churches.
1687	Wuxi (Wu-hsi, Nandongwan, Wu)	1,053,000	11.00	116,000	68.77	B	1,715,000	Kiangsu. Silk reeling center. Buddhists, Taoists strong. D=TSPM,RCC,SDA, & 10 others.
1688	Wuzhong	476,000	1.50	7,100	59.27	B	838,000	Ningsia Hui on Yellow River south of Yinchuan. Agriculture, paper, chemicals, electronics. D=house churches.
1689	Wuzhou (Wu-chow, Ts'ang-wu)	309,000	1.50	4,600	59.27	B	545,000	Kwangsi Chuang Autonomous Region. River port. D=Wuzhou Church(TSPM),RC Diocese(1949: 41 churches).
1690	Xiaguan (Hsia-Kuan)	468,000	2.00	9,400	59.77	B	825,000	Yunnan. Collecting center for cotton, grain, tea, fish. Light engineering. D=house churches.
1691	Xiamen (Amoy, Hsia-men)	646,000	13.00	84,000	70.77	B	1,139,000	Fukien. Port. D=8 large TSPM churches,RC Diocese,house churches. YMCA hostel.
1692	Xian (Hsi-an, Jingchao, Sian)	3,352,000	5.00	168,000	62.77	B	5,312,000	Capital of Shensi. Buddhist Center. Start of 'Silk Road'. D=TSPM,house churches,RCC & 10 others.
1693	Xiangfan (Hsiang-fan)	498,000	5.50	27,400	63.27	B	878,000	Hupeh. Collecting & commercial center, textiles. D=TSPM,house churches.
1694	Xiangtan (Hsiang-tlan, Siangtan)	604,000	3.00	18,100	60.77	B	1,065,000	Hunan. Important river port & collecting center, textiles. F=AD 749. D=Xiangtan Church(TSPM),house churches.
1695	Xianning	476,000	5.50	26,200	63.27	B	838,000	Hupeh south of Wuhan. Grain, oil crops, hogs, tobacco, textiles, machinery. D=house churches.
1696	Xianyang (Hsienyang)	759,000	4.00	30,400	61.77	B	1,337,000	Shensi on Wei River. Market center. Grains, tobacco, cotton, textiles. D=TSPM,house churches.
1697	Xiaogan	1,424,000	5.80	82,600	63.57	B	2,510,000	Hupeh on Huan River northwest of Wuhan. Grain, oil crops, hogs, eggs. D=house churches.
1698	Xiaoshan	75,700	16.50	12,500	74.27	B	133,000	Chekiang south of Hanzhou. Food, beverages, textiles, chemicals, rice, wheat, beans. D=house churches.
1699	Xichang	190,000	5.10	9,700	62.87	B	335,000	Southern Szechwan south of Zhaojue. Trading center, highway hub, tobacco, iron, steel. D=house churches.
1700	Xinghua	90,700	10.90	9,900	68.67	B	160,000	Kiangsu east of Gaoyou. Agriculture, rice, cotton, food, textiles, chemicals, machinery. D=house churches.
1701	Xinglongzhen	66,300	1.30	860	59.07	B	117,000	Heilungkiang south of Suihua. Soybeans, jute.
1702	Xingtai (Hsing, Xing, Geng, Hsing-t'ai)	415,000	3.00	12,400	60.77	B	731,000	Hopeh. Local market & commercial center. D= Xingtai Church(TSPM),RC Diocese (1949: 39 churches).
1703	Xinhui	92,900	4.50	4,200	62.27	B	164,000	Kwangtung south of Guangzhou. Xi river delta. Fruit orchards, tungsten, machine shops. D=house churches.
1704	Xining (Sinju, Hsi-ning, Sining)	902,000	0.80	7,200	38.57	A	1,505,000	Tsinghai capital. Wool, leather. Large lamasery. D=Xining Christian Church,30 Protestant(TSPM),house groups.
1705	Xinmin	57,500	2.70	1,600	60.47	B	101,000	Liaoning west of Shenyang. Northeast. Apparel, paper, food, soybean oil. Kaoliang.
1706	Xintai	1,368,000	6.00	82,100	63.77	B	2,412,000	Shantung near Xinwen. Heavy industry, grain, oilseeds, chemicals, fabricated metals, coal. D=house churches.
1707	Xinwen (Suncun)	69,200	6.20	4,300	63.97	B	122,000	Shantung south of Boshan. Grains, textiles. D=house churches.
1708	Xinxian	471,000	8.00	37,700	65.77	B	831,000	Shansi north of Taiyuan. Cotton, agriculture. D=house churches.
1709	Xinxiang (Hsin-hsiang, Sinsiang)	639,000	17.00	109,000	74.77	B	1,126,000	Honan. Cotton, textiles, spinning, dyeing, flour milling. Transport route, canal. D=TSPM,house churches.
1710	Xinyang (Hsin-yang, Sinyang)	277,000	15.00	41,500	72.77	B	488,000	Honan. Collecting point for grain, cotton. D=RC Diocese(1949: 63 churches),house churches.
1711	Xinyu	722,000	5.80	41,900	63.57	B	1,272,000	Kiangsi on Yuan River east of Yichun. Iron ore, coal, steel, fruit, hogs, chemicals. D=house churches.
1712	Xuancheng	62,900	8.00	5,000	65.77	B	111,000	Northern Anhwei on Shuiyang River. Grains, oil crops, hogs, eggs, textiles. D=house churches.
1713	Xuanhua (Suanhwa, Hsuan-hua)	194,000	2.80	5,400	60.57	B	342,000	Hopeh. Industrial center. Iron, steel, mines. D=RC Diocese,3 bishops(1949: 258 churches).
1714	Xuanwei	87,800	2.50	2,200	60.27	B	155,000	Northern Yunnan north of Qujing. Chemicals, electric power generation, rice, wheat, millet, tobacco, coal.
1715	Xuchang (Hsu-chang)	292,000	16.00	46,800	73.77	B	515,000	Honan. Handicrafts, ceramics, tobacco. D=TSPM,1984, Xuchang City Church opened.
1716	Xuguit Qi (Yakeshi)	461,000	12.70	58,600	70.47	B	813,000	Northern Inner Mongolian Autonomous Region on Hailar River. Agriculture, pastoralism. D=house churches.
1717	Xuzhou (Soochow, Hsuchow)	1,833,000	11.50	211,000	69.27	B	3,086,000	Kiangsu. D=13 TSPM churches,135 meeting points(1 per village). Tents used. RC Diocese,house churches.
1718	Yaan (Ya-an)	328,000	5.10	16,700	62.87	B	578,000	Szechwan. Tea market. Iron ore, tanneries. Communications center. D=house churches.
1719	Yanan (Yen-an)	307,000	4.00	12,300	61.77	B	541,000	Shensi. Coal, iron. Communist capital during World War II. D=RC Diocese(1949: 95,000 Catholics).
1720	Yancheng (Yen-ch'eng)	1,480,000	10.70	158,000	68.47	B	2,608,000	Kiangsu. Market for agricultural produce. Cotton. Famous dikes. D=house churches,20 others.
1721	Yangcheng	71,700	8.00	5,700	65.77	B	126,000	Southern Shansi on Qin River. Iron smelting, grain, cotton, beans, jute, sugarcane. D=house churches.
1722	Yangjiang	108,000	4.50	4,900	62.27	B	191,000	Kwangtung on South China Sea west of Guangzhou. Trade center, textiles. D=house churches.
1723	Yangquan (Yang-ch'uan)	566,000	6.00	34,000	63.77	B	998,000	Shansi. Mining center. Iron ore smelting. D=TSPM,house churches.
1724	Yangzhou (Yangchow, Yang-chou)	493,000	10.00	49,300	67.77	B	870,000	Kiangsu. Transportation & market center. Handicrafts. D=large Yangzhou Church(TSPM),house churches.
1725	Yanji (Longjing)	256,000	6.80	17,400	64.57	B	452,000	Kirin south of larger Yanji metropolitan area. Tobacco, textiles. D=house churches.
1726	Yanji (Yen-chi, Yenki)	66,100	18.00	11,900	75.77	B	116,000	Kirin. Collecting center for agriculture. 80% Korean. Christian stronghold. D=TSPM,RC Diocese,house churches.
1727	Yanling	66,000	15.00	9,900	72.77	B	116,000	Honan on Shuangji River south of Kaifeng. Grain, cotton, tobacco, oilseeds. D=house churches.
1728	Yantai (Chefoo, Zhefu, Yen-tÍai)	848,000	5.00	42,400	62.77	B	1,495,000	Shantung. Agriculture, fishing. D=Yantai Church(TSPM),RC Diocese(1949: 62 churches),house churches.
1729	Yanzhou	58,800	6.00	3,500	63.77	B	104,000	Shantung on Si River north of Jining. Wheat, peanuts, millet, beans, cotton. D=house churches.
1730	Yexian	380,000	16.50	62,800	74.27	B	670,000	Honan on Sha River south of Pingdingshan. Grain, cotton, textiles. D=house churches.
1731	Yi'an	64,100	1.00	640	58.77	B	113,000	Heilungkiang on Wuyur River near Keshan. Food processing, grain, sugar beets, jute, oilseeds.
1732	Yibin (I-pin, Rong, Xu, Shuifu)	753,000	6.00	45,200	63.77	B	1,326,000	Szechwan. Communications center, salt, paper. D=RC Diocese(1949: 102 churches),house churches.
1733	Yichang (I-chang)	485,000	5.00	24,300	62.77	B	855,000	Hupeh. River port, trade.D=RC Diocese(1949: 31 churches),St James Church(TSPM),house churches.
1734	Yichuan	73,800	4.00	3,000	61.77	B	130,000	Shensi near Yellow River. Grain, tobacco. D=house churches.
1735	Yinchuan (Yichuan)	463,000	0.10	460	37.87	A	816,000	Ningsia Hui Autonomous Region capital. 50% Muslims. China's first Islamic Cultural Center. D=RCC.
1736	Yichun (I-ch'un, Ichun)	962,000	1.20	11,500	58.97	B	1,695,000	Heilungkiang in mountains among forests. Timber is dominant industry. D=house churches.
1737	Yichun	902,000	5.00	45,100	62.77	B	1,454,000	Kiangsi east of Gaokeng. Grains, hogs, eggs, chemicals, machinery. D=TSPM,house churches.
1738	Yidu	65,800	5.30	3,500	63.07	B	116,000	Shantung west of Weifang. Railroad, grain, tobacco. D=house churches.
1739	Yilan	60,600	1.30	790	59.07	B	107,000	Heilungkiang on Songhua River. Sugar refining, sugar beets, tobacco, jute, vehicle engine parts.
1740	Yima	100,000	6.60	6,600	64.37	B	177,000	Kirin northwest of Huadian. Coal mining. D=house churches.
1741	Yinan (Jiehu)	84,900	5.50	4,700	63.27	B	150,000	Shantung north of Linyi. Grain, tobacco. D=house churches.
1742	Yingchengzi	70,900	7.00	5,000	64.77	B	125,000	Kirin near Jiutai. Coal mining, agriculture. D=house churches.
1743	Yingkou (Yingkow, Newchwang)	568,000	2.50	14,200	60.27	B	1,000,000	Liaoning. River port, cotton mills, fishing industry. D=TSPM,RC Diocese,house churches.
1744	Yingtan	137,000	6.00	8,200	63.77	B	242,000	Kiangsi on Xin River. Grain, oil crops, vegetables, hogs, food, timber, chemicals. D=house churches.
1745	Yining (I-ning, Gulja, Kuldja)	274,000	0.60	1,600	38.37	A	483,000	Sinkiang Uihgur. Agricultural market. Kazakhs, Mongols, Sibos. D=house churches.
1746	Yiyang (I-yang)	432,000	2.60	11,200	60.37	B	761,000	Hunan. Agriculture, wood & bamboo handicrafts. D=TSPM,house churches.
1747	Yiyuan (Nanma)	67,400	6.00	4,000	63.77	B	119,000	Shantung on Yi River south of Boshan. Grain, tobacco. D=house churches.
1748	Yong'an (Yung-an)	318,000	13.40	42,600	71.17	B	561,000	Fukien on Sha Hsi River. Collection & distribution center for agriculture & timber. D=house churches & 10 others.
1749	Yongchuan	84,600	5.80	4,900	63.57	B	149,000	Szechwan west of Chongqing. Rice, wheat, kaoliang, rapeseed, sugarcane, coal mines. D=house churches.
1750	Yuci (Yu-tzu, Yu-tze)	497,000	7.50	37,300	65.27	B	877,000	Shansi. Road & railway center. Cotton manufacturing. D=RC Diocese(1949: 77 churches),house churches.
1751	Yuen Long	81,900	15.00	12,300	72.77	B	144,000	Northwestern New Territories, Hong Kong. Former market town, incorporated in 1970's. D=RCC.
1752	Yueyang (Yueh-yang, Yech-chou)	1,237,000	2.60	32,200	60.37	B	1,995,000	Hunan. Domestic trade, water traffic & transshipment of timber. D=TSPM, house churches.
1753	Yulin	1,453,000	1.00	14,500	58.77	B	2,561,000	Kwangsi Chuang Autonomous Region. Grains, vegetables, fruit, hogs, food processing. D=house churches.
1754	Yulin	62,000	4.50	2,800	62.27	B	109,000	Northern Shensi near Great Wall. Agriculture, grains, hogs, textiles, utilities. D=house churches.
1755	Yumen (Laojunmiao, Yu-men)	189,000	4.00	7,600	61.77	B	334,000	Kansu on ancient Silk Road. Oil drilling and refineries. D=house churches.
1756	Yuncheng	68,000	5.00	3,400	62.77	B	120,000	Western Shantung west of Jining. Grains, cottons, fruits, hogs, eggs, chemicals, machinery. D=house churches.
1757	Yuncheng	514,000	7.00	36,000	64.77	B	906,000	Southern Shansi. Peanuts, wheat. D=house churches & 10 others.
1758	Yunyang	68,800	5.50	3,800	63.27	B	121,000	Szechwan on Yangtze River east of Wanxian. Chemicals, rice, jute, oilseeds, coal mining. D=house churches.
1759	Yushu	68,700	6.50	4,500	64.27	B	121,000	Northern Kirin north of Jilin. Grain, soybeans, sugar beets, tobacco, indigo. D=house churches.
1760	Yuyao	914,000	16.50	151,000	74.27	B	1,610,000	Chekiang northwest of Ningbo. Heavy industry, textiles, chemicals, plastics. D=house churches & 10 others.
1761	Zaozhuang (Tsao-chuang)	1,882,000	6.00	113,000	63.77	B	3,317,000	Shantung. Includes dispersed coal mines. D=RC Diocese(1949: 44,000 Catholics),house churches.
1762	Zhangjiakou (Kalgan, Changchiaku)	902,000	3.00	27,100	60.77	B	1,488,000	Hopeh. On trade routes. Light industry, furs, tanning. D=Zhangjiakou City Church(TSPM),house churches.
1763	Zhangye	466,000	5.00	23,300	62.77	B	821,000	Kansu on Hei River. On Silk Road. Grain, oil crops, fruits, nonferrous mineral mining. D=house churches.
1764	Zhangzhou (Changchow, Longxi)	367,000	13.00	47,700	70.77	B	647,000	Fukien. Collecting center for fruit, jute. D=large Zhangzhou Tan Phoa-Au Church (TSPM),RCC.
1765	Zhanjiang (Leizhou, Chan-chiang)	1,089,000	5.00	54,400	62.77	B	1,919,000	Kwangtung. Major seaport. Trade, shipyards, textiles. D=Zhanjiang Church(TSPM),house churches.

Table 10-5–continued opposite

Table 10-5–continued

Rec No 1	Country City 2	Pop 2000 3	AC% 4	Church Members 5	E% 6	W 7	Pop 2025 8	Notes 9
1766	Zhaodong	120,000	1.20	1,400	58.97	B	211,000	Heilungkiang northwest of Harbin. Grains, vegetables, milk, hogs, eggs, poultry, chemicals. D=house churches.
1767	Zhaoqing (Chao-chĭng)	222,000	7.00	15,500	64.77	B	391,000	Kwangtung on Hsi River. Agriculture. Great scenic beauty. D=Zhaoqing Church(TSPM),house churches.
1768	Zhaotong (Chao-t'ung)	646,000	2.50	16,200	60.27	B	1,139,000	Yunnan. Chin dynasty frescoes uncovered. D=Zhaotong City Church(RC),house churches.
1769	Zhaoyuan	50,900	2.00	1,000	59.77	B	89,800	Southern Heilungkiang on Lalin River. Sugar, tobacco, jute. D=house churches.
1770	Zhaoyuan	70,600	5.00	3,500	62.77	B	124,000	Shantung on Shantung Peninsula. Nonferrous mineral mining, chemicals, machinery. D=house churches.
1771	Zhengzhou (Cheng-chow, Kiangan)	2,275,000	17.00	387,000	74.77	B	3,671,000	Honan capital. Textile. F=c1500 BC. 15% Muslims, 100 mosques. D=RC Diocese,house churches & 20 others.
1772	Zhenjiang (Chenkiang, Chen-chiang)	488,000	11.00	53,600	68.77	B	859,000	Kiangsu. Yangtze River port. D=large Zhenjiang Church (TSPM), opened 1982,house churches.
1773	Zhongshan (Shiqizhen, Chung-shan)	1,253,000	4.50	56,400	62.27	B	2,208,000	Kwangtung. Network of waterways. Collecting center for agriculture. D=house churches & 10 others.
1774	Zhoucun	69,200	6.00	4,200	63.77	B	122,000	Shantung north of Boshan. Food processing, chemical. D=house churches.
1775	Zhoukouzhen (Chou-kĭou-chen)	261,000	12.00	31,300	69.77	B	459,000	Honan on Ying Ho River. Collecting center for agriculture, ceramics. D=TSPM,house churches.
1776	Zhuhai	183,000	6.00	11,000	63.77	B	323,000	Kwangtung north of Macao. Industrial center, crops, fishing, textiles, electronics. D=house churches.
1777	Zhumadian (Chumatien)	177,000	15.00	26,500	72.77	B	312,000	Honan east of Runan. D=RC Diocese(1949: 14 churches),house churches.
1778	Zhuoxian	65,500	2.70	1,800	60.47	B	115,000	Hopeh south of Beijing. Coal, cotton. D=house churches.
1779	Zhuzhou (Chuchow, Chu-chou)	591,000	2.50	14,800	60.27	B	1,041,000	Hunan. Transport center, chemicals, minerals, railroad cars. D=TSPM,house churches.
1780	Zibo (Tzu-po, Tzepo, Zhangdian)	2,714,000	5.60	152,000	63.37	B	4,783,000	Shantung. Mining, silk, porcelain. F=c200 BC. D=TSPM opened 1982,house churches.
1781	Zigong (Tzu-kung, Tzekung, Tzekun)	1,075,000	5.50	59,100	63.27	B	1,895,000	Szechwan. Salt, oil, natural gas, chemicals. D=TSPM, with ordinations in 1984,house churches.
1782	Zixing	395,000	3.00	11,900	60.77	B	697,000	Hunan east of Liyujiang. Grain, hogs, manufacturing, coal mining. D=house churches.
1783	Ziyang	68,900	6.00	4,100	63.77	B	121,000	Szechwan on Tuo River south of Chengdu. Machinery, rice, sweet potatoes, tobacco. D=house churches.
1784	Zouping	61,700	5.80	3,600	63.57	B	109,000	Shantung north of Zhoucun. Textiles, melons, peanuts, wheat, cotton. D=house churches.
1785	Zouxian	73,900	5.50	4,100	63.27	B	130,000	Shantung east of Jining. Wheat, peanuts, cotton, coal mining. D=house churches.
1786	Zunyi (Tsun-i)	411,000	9.00	37,000	66.77	B	724,000	Kweichow. Silk textiles, rice & flour mills, chemicals. D=Zunyi City Church(TSPM),house churches.
	CHRISTMAS ISLAND	**3,400**	**12.91**	**440**	**64.87**	**B**	**4,100**	**ROMAN CATHOLICS 7.3%, PROTESTANTS 3.5%. PENT-CHAR 2.9%, EVANGELICAL 1.9%, GCC 7.2%**
1787	rural areas	860	12.64	110	61.58	B	910	35.0% (1950), 32.0% (1970), 27.0% (1990), 25.0% (2000), 25.0% (2010), 22.0% (2025)
1788	urban areas	2,600	13.00	330	65.96	B	3,200	65.0% (1950), 68.0% (1970), 73.0% (1990), 75.0% (2000), 75.0% (2010), 78.0% (2025)
1789	non-metropolitan areas	1,000	13.02	130	65.94	B	1,285	*Sources of data:* Censuses.
1790	metropolitan areas	1,500	12.99	200	65.97	B	1,900	*Definition:* Flying Fish Cove.
1791	FLYING FISH COVE	1,500	13.00	200	65.96	B	1,900	Eastern part of the Island on Indian Ocean. D=RCC,Anglican.
	COCOS (KEELING) IS	**730**	**16.94**	**120**	**49.59**	**A**	**870**	**ANGLICANS 11.4%, ROMAN CATHOLICS 5.5%. PENT-CHAR 2.0%, EVANGELICAL 1.3%, GCC 8.6%**
1792	rural areas	150	8.71	12	33.33	A	140	40.0% (1950), 30.0% (1970), 25.0% (1990), 20.0% (2000), 18.0% (2010), 16.0% (2025)
1793	urban areas	580	19.00	110	53.65	B	730	60.0% (1950), 70.0% (1970), 75.0% (1990), 80.0% (2000), 82.0% (2010), 84.0% (2025)
1794	non-metropolitan areas	29	17.96	5	52.35	B	37	*Sources of data:* Censuses.
1795	metropolitan areas	550	19.06	110	53.72	B	700	*Definition:* West Island.
1796	WEST ISLAND	550	19.00	110	53.65	B	700	Main export is copra. Mostly Malay origin, many Muslims. D=Anglicans,RCC.
	COLOMBIA	**42,321,000**	**96.73**	**40,936,000**	**99.72**	**C**	**59,758,000**	**ROMAN CATHOLICS 96.1%, PROTESTANTS 2.6%. PENT-CHAR 29.7%, EVANGELICAL 1.3%, GCC 6.3%**
1797	rural areas	10,606,000	98.90	10,489,000	99.65	C	10,428,000	62.9% (1950), 42.8% (1970), 30.0% (1990), 25.0% (2000), 21.3% (2010), 17.4% (2025)
1798	urban areas	31,716,000	96.00	30,447,000	99.74	C	49,330,000	37.0% (1950), 57.2% (1970), 69.9% (1990), 74.9% (2000), 78.6% (2010), 82.5% (2025)
1799	non-metropolitan areas	10,569,000	95.50	10,094,000	99.77	C	19,963,021	*Sources of data:* Censuses of 1951, 1964, 1973 and 1985.
1800	metropolitan areas	21,146,000	96.25	20,353,000	99.73	C	29,367,000	*Definition:* Population living in a nucleus of 1,500 or more inhabitants.
1801	Armenia	240,000	97.00	233,000	99.99	C	373,000	Capital of Quindio. Elevation 4,865 ft. Coffee, corn, beans, coal. F=1889 by Jesus Maria Ocampo. D=RCC.
1802	Barrancabermeja	176,000	97.00	171,000	99.99	C	274,000	Santander on Magdalena River. Ranching, beef, oil. F=1536. Cathedral of Sacred Heart of Jesus. D=RCC.
1803	Barranquilla	1,246,000	98.00	1,221,000	99.99	C	1,693,000	Atlantico capital. Coffee, petroleum, natural gas. Carnival festival. F=1629. 'Gateway to Colombia'. D=RCC.
1804	Malambo	67,500	98.00	66,100	99.99	C	105,000	Atlantico. South. Magdalena River, Caribbean lowlands. Cotton, sugarcane, corn, bananas, planting. D=RCC.
1805	Soledad	213,000	98.00	208,000	99.99	C	331,000	Atlantico. Commercial and manufacturing center. International airport. F=1640. D=RCC.
1806	BOGOTA	6,834,000	95.50	6,526,000	99.69	C	8,829,000	Elevation 8,660 ft. Banks, commerce, tires, chemicals, pharmaceuticals. F=1538. 6,000 Americans. D=RCC.
1807	Soacha	140,000	96.00	134,000	98.99	C	218,000	Cundinamarca. Southwest. Railroad, main highway, coffee, corn, potatoes. D=RCC.
1808	Bucaramanga	706,000	96.00	677,000	98.99	C	1,097,000	Capital of Santander. Coffee, tobacco, cigars, cigarettes, textiles. F=1622. 'Garden City'. D=RCC.
1809	Floridablanca	185,000	97.00	179,000	99.99	C	287,000	Southeast. Santander. Sugarcane, coffee, corn, horticultural gardens. D=RCC.
1810	Buenaventura	206,000	97.00	200,000	99.99	C	320,000	Valle del Cauca port. Main Pacific port. Fishing port. Sugar, coffee, cotton. F=1540. D=RCC.
1811	Buga	106,000	97.00	103,000	99.99	C	166,000	Valle del Cauca. Agricultural center for coffee and cotton. Milagroso Cristo de Buga shrine. F=1650. D=RCC.
1812	Cali	2,082,000	96.00	1,999,000	99.69	C	2,793,000	Capital of Valle del Cauca. Collection and distribution center. Sugar cane, paper. F=1536. D=RCC.
1813	Cartagena	918,000	97.00	890,000	99.99	C	1,272,000	Capital of Bolivar. Petroleum, oil, exports. F=1533. Church of San Pedro Claver (1603). D=RCC.
1814	Cartago	125,000	97.00	122,000	99.99	C	195,000	Valle de Cauca on Cauca River. Railroad, sugarcane, sorghum, soybeans. D=RCC.
1815	Cienaga	72,900	98.00	71,500	99.99	C	113,000	Caribbean port, Magdalena. Shipping, fishing, marble, coffee. F=1518. D=RCC.
1816	Cucuta	571,000	96.50	551,000	99.49	C	888,000	Capital of Norte de Santander. Livestock, agriculture, center of contraband. F=1733. D=RCC.
1817	Villa Rosario	81,600	97.00	79,200	99.99	C	127,000	Near Venezuela border. Coffee, oil, mineral deposits. D=RCC.
1818	Duitama	72,300	98.00	70,900	99.99	C	113,000	Boyaca. Elevation 8,300 ft. Resort, flour milling, cigars, silver, copper. D=RCC.
1819	Florencia	85,200	98.00	83,500	99.99	C	133,000	Capital of Caqueta. Cattle, rice, trade center. F=1908 by Capuchin missionaries. D=RCC.
1820	Girardot	89,900	98.00	88,100	99.99	C	140,000	River port, Cundinamarca. Numerous acacia trees. Coffee, hides. F=1844 as San Miguel parish. D=RCC.
1821	Ibague	376,000	96.50	363,000	99.49	C	585,000	Capital of Tolima. Coffee, cacao, tobacco, rice, sugar cane. F=1550 on site of Indian village. D=RCC.
1822	Magangue	63,100	98.00	61,800	99.99	C	98,100	Bolivar. Grain, fishing, fruits. F=1610. Once part of Christianized-Indian estate. D=RCC.
1823	Maicao	59,100	98.00	57,900	99.99	C	91,900	La Guajra on Venezuela border. Northeast, reportedly a center of contraband trade with Venezuela. D=RCC.
1824	Manizales	423,000	97.00	411,000	99.99	C	658,000	Capital of Caldas. Center of most important coffee growing area. Elevation 6,975 ft. F=1848. D=RCC.
1825	Medellin	3,831,000	96.00	3,678,000	99.69	C	5,082,000	Capital of Antioquia. On Porce River. Steel, coffee, heavy industry. Illegal drugs. F=1675. D=RCC.
1826	Bello	273,000	96.50	264,000	99.49	C	425,000	On Porce River. Industrial complex. Textiles, brushes. Elevation 4,905 ft. D=RCC.
1827	Envigado	117,000	97.00	114,000	99.99	C	182,000	Industrial complex. Textile manufacturing. Elevation 5,085 ft. D=RCC.
1828	Itagui	177,000	96.50	170,000	99.49	C	275,000	Industrial complex. Textile milling. Formerly a resort. Elevation 5,148 ft. D=RCC.
1829	Monteria	202,000	97.00	196,000	99.99	C	314,000	Capital of Cordoba. Sinu River port. Stock raising, lumbering, mining, nuts. F=1744. 'Hunting'. D=RCC.
1830	Neiva	250,000	97.00	242,000	99.99	C	388,000	Capital of Huila. Agricultural center for cotton, rice, corn. F=1612. D=RCC.
1831	Ocana	66,000	98.00	64,700	99.99	C	103,000	Norte de Santander. Barium mining, onions. F=1570. D=RCC.
1832	Palmira	225,000	97.00	218,000	99.99	C	350,000	Valle del Cauca. Major agricultural center, tobacco, coffee, sugar cane, rice. F=1688. D=RCC.
1833	Pasto	253,000	97.00	246,000	99.99	C	394,000	Capital of Narino. Elevation 8,291 ft. Agriculture, gold mining. F=1539. Large Indian population. D=RCC.
1834	Pereira	500,000	96.00	480,000	98.99	C	778,000	Capital of Risaralda. Coffee, cattle, textiles. Cathedral of Our Lady of the Poor (1890). D=RCC.
1835	Dos Quebradas	130,000	97.00	126,000	99.99	C	202,000	Risaralda near Pereira. West central. Coffee, plantains, sugarcane. D=RCC.
1836	Popayan	182,000	97.00	177,000	99.99	C	283,000	Capital of Cauca. Coffee. F=1535. University of Cauca (1827). Religious processions. D=RCC.
1837	Santa Marta	228,000	97.00	221,000	99.99	C	355,000	Capital of Magdalena. Bananas. Oldest city in Colombia (1525). Tourism, beaches. D=RCC.
1838	Sincelejo	155,000	97.00	150,000	99.99	C	241,000	Capital of Sucre. Cattle raising, sugar refining, clothing. F=1776. D=RCC.
1839	Sogamoso	82,700	98.00	81,000	99.99	C	129,000	Boyaca. Elevation 8,428 ft. Agriculture, flour, textiles, coal mining. D=RCC.
1840	Tulua	128,000	97.00	124,000	99.99	C	199,000	Valle del Cauca. Beef, milk, yeast, foodstuffs. Settled by Putimaes Indians. F=1636 as cattle ranch. D=RCC.
1841	Tunja	120,000	97.50	117,000	99.49	C	187,000	Capital of Boyaca. Cattle, gold, emeralds. F=1539. Pedagogical & Technological University. D=RCC.
1842	Valledupar	183,000	97.00	178,000	99.99	C	285,000	Capital of Cesar. Agriculture, ice, bricks, sawmill. F=1550. D=RCC.
1843	Villavicencio	229,000	97.00	222,000	99.99	C	357,000	Capital of Meta on Meta River. Distillery, brewery, soap, coffee. F=1840. D=RCC.
1844	Zipaquira	58,600	98.00	57,400	99.99	C	91,100	Cundinamarca north of Bogota. Cattle, corn, coffee. Cathedral in underground salt mine. D=RCC.
	COMOROS	**593,000**	**1.19**	**7,100**	**37.35**	**A**	**990,000**	**ROMAN CATHOLICS 0.9%, PROTESTANTS 0.1%. PENT-CHAR 0.09%, EVANGELICAL 0.04%, GCC 0.6%**
1845	rural areas	396,000	1.14	4,500	36.31	A	504,000	96.7% (1950), 80.6% (1970), 72.1% (1990), 66.7% (2000), 60.6% (2010), 50.9% (2025)
1846	urban areas	197,000	1.30	2,600	39.46	A	486,000	3.3% (1950), 19.3% (1970), 27.9% (1990), 33.2% (2000), 39.3% (2010), 49.0% (2025)
1847	non-metropolitan areas	166,000	1.30	2,200	39.46	A	408,841	*Sources of data:* Censuses of 1966 and 1980; estimate for 1950.
1848	metropolitan areas	31,200	1.30	410	39.46	A	76,900	*Definition:* Administrative centers of prefectures and localities with 5,000 or more inhabitants.
1849	MORONI	31,200	1.30	410	39.46	A	76,900	On Grand Comore (Njazidja) Island. Vanilla, cacao, coffee exported. Muslim pilgrimage. D=RCC.
	CONGO-BRAZZAVILLE	**2,943,000**	**79.26**	**2,333,000**	**99.03**	**C**	**5,689,000**	**ROMAN CATHOLICS 49.3%, PROTESTANTS 16.9%. PENT-CHAR 20.0%, EVANGELICAL 6.6%, GCC 19.2%**
1850	rural areas	1,103,000	86.36	952,000	99.66	C	1,482,000	69.1% (1950), 67.1% (1970), 46.6% (1990), 37.4% (2000), 32.0% (2010), 26.0% (2025)
1851	urban areas	1,841,000	75.00	1,380,000	98.65	C	4,207,000	30.8% (1950), 32.8% (1970), 53.3% (1990), 62.5% (2000), 67.9% (2010), 73.9% (2025)
1852	non-metropolitan areas	–	–	–	–	–	–	*Sources of data:* Censuses of 1960, 1974, and 1984.
1853	metropolitan areas	1,845,000	74.84	1,380,000	98.53	C	4,218,000	*Definition:* Sum of the Brazzaville and Pointe-Noire communes.
1854	BRAZZAVILLE	1,234,000	74.61	921,000	98.38	C	2,822,000	Congo River port. Transit trade for Central Africa. Seriously overcrowded. F=1883. D=RCC,EEC.
1855	Loubomo (Dolisie)	79,500	76.00	60,500	99.27	C	182,000	Gold and lead mining center. Leather, sisal and cattle center. Important transit center for Zaire. D=RCC,EEC.
1856	Nkayi (formerly Jacob)	50,700	77.00	39,100	99.77	C	116,000	Major sugar-producing center in the Niari Valley. Peanut oil, cattle feed, flour. D=RCC,EEC.
1857	Pointe-Noire	480,000	75.00	360,000	98.67	C	1,098,000	Principal Atlantic port for transit trade. Light industries, mineral processing, petroleum. F=1883. D=RCC,EEC.
	CONGO-ZAIRE	**51,654,000**	**91.28**	**47,152,000**	**99.11**	**C**	**104,788,000**	**ROMAN CATHOLICS 50.9%, INDEPENDENTS 23.3%. PENT-CHAR 34.3%, EVANGELICAL 8.6%, GCC 7.5%**
1858	rural areas	36,014,000	91.80	33,059,000	99.75	C	56,732,000	80.9% (1950), 69.7% (1970), 72.0% (1990), 69.7% (2000), 64.0% (2010), 54.1% (2025)
1859	urban areas	15,641,000	90.10	14,093,000	97.63	C	48,056,000	19.1% (1950), 30.3% (1970), 27.9% (1990), 30.2% (2000), 35.9% (2010), 45.8% (2025)
1860	non-metropolitan areas	3,358,000	90.38	3,035,000	98.02	C	12,289,590	*Sources of data:* Censuses.
1861	metropolitan areas	12,283,000	90.02	11,057,000	97.52	C	35,766,000	*Definition:* Agglomerations of 2,000 or more inhabitants where main economic activity is non-agricultural.
1862	Bandundu (Banningville)	106,000	90.00	95,500	97.83	C	326,000	At junction of Kwango & Kwilu Rivers. Palm oil, kernels, peanuts, manioc, rope making. D=RCC,ECZ.
1863	Beni	73,600	90.00	66,200	97.83	C	226,000	Northern Kivu north of Lake Edward. Trading and tourist center, Virunga Natl. Park. Leprosarium. D=RCC,ECZ.
1864	Boma (Lombi, Embomma)	329,000	90.00	296,000	97.83	C	1,012,000	On Congo River. Palm oil, bananas, timber. Slave market center in 19th century. Tribal chief graves. D=RCC.
1865	Bukavu (Costermansville)	280,000	88.00	246,000	95.83	C	860,000	On Lake Kivu. Tourist city. Coffee, tea, tobacco. 1970's refugees. 'Mountains of the Moon'. D=RCC.
1866	Bumba	85,300	91.00	77,700	98.83	C	262,000	Northern Equateur on Congo River. Congo-Nile highway. Rice milling. Roman Catholic mission. D=RCC,EJCSK.
1867	Bunia	99,300	91.00	90,400	98.83	C	305,000	Eastern Haut-Zaire on Ituri River near Lake Albert. Gold mining, cattle raising, rice. D=RCC,ECZ,EJCSK.
1868	Butembo	122,000	90.00	110,000	97.83	C	375,000	Northern Kivu north of Lake Edward. Coffee, tea, bananas. Gold mining. RC church, hospital. D=RCC.
1869	Gandajika	108,000	90.00	97,300	97.83	C	332,000	Southern Kasai-Oriental near Mbuji-Mayi. Agricultural research station, cotton, cotton ginning. D=RCC,EJCSK.
1870	Gemena	105,000	90.00	94,600	97.83	C	323,000	Northern Equateur near Central African Republic. Cotton ginning, airport. D=RCC,ECZ,EJCSK.
1871	Goma	130,000	89.00	116,000	96.83	C	399,000	Kivu on Lake Kivu on Rwandan border. Rwandan refugees (1990s). Lava fields. D=RCC,EJCSK.
1872	Ilebo (Port Francqui)	89,800	90.00	80,800	97.83	C	276,000	On Kasai River. Transshipment point for copper & other minerals. Hotel des Palmes (1920). D=RCC,EJCSK.
1873	Isiro (Paulis)	130,000	89.00	116,000	96.83	C	401,000	Central Haut-Zaire. Cotton production, palm products, auto repair shops, coffee. Protestant mission. D=ECZ.
1874	KINSHASA (Leopoldville)	5,068,000	92.40	4,683,000	99.43	C	13,787,000	On Congo River. Manufacturing, transportation center. High unemployment. F=1881 by H. M. Stanley. D=RCC.
1875	Kalemie (Albertville, Kalemi, Lukuga)	123,000	90.00	110,000	97.83	C	377,000	Lake Tanganyika. Port handles most imports. Fishing, textiles, cement. F=1915. D=RCC,ECZ.
1876	Kamina	105,000	91.00	95,200	98.83	C	322,000	Shaba on Lovoi River. Military air base, cotton, tobacco, vegetables. D=RCC,EJCSK.
1877	Kananga (Luluabourg)	498,000	90.00	448,000	97.83	C	1,530,000	On Lulua River. Diamonds, livestock, coffee, cotton, brewing, printing. D=RCC,ECZ.

Table 10-5–continued overleaf

Table 10-5–continued

Rec No 1	Country City 2	Pop 2000 3	AC% 4	Church Members 5	E% 6	W 7	Pop 2025 8	Notes 9
1878	Kikwit	249,000	90.00	224,000	97.83	C	765,000	Kwilu River port. Palm oil & kernels, casava, peanuts, corn. F=1901. D=RCC,ECZ,EJCSK.
1879	Kindu (Kindu-Port-Empain)	111,000	90.00	100,000	97.83	C	342,000	On Lualaba River. Important for commercial transport-between railway & boats. Sawmills. D=RCC,ECZ.
1880	Kipushi	88,700	90.00	79,800	97.83	C	272,000	Southern Shaba on Zambian border southwest of Lubumbashi. D=RCC,ECZ.
1881	Kisangani (Stanleyville)	529,000	88.00	466,000	95.83	C	1,626,000	On Congo River. Major center for Northern Congo. Brewing, furniture, clothing, palm, rice. F=1883. D=RCC.
1882	Kolwezi	694,000	90.00	624,000	97.83	C	2,131,000	Near Zilo Gorges of Lualaba River. Copper-mining center. Attacked by Shaba rebels (1978). D=RCC,ECZ.
1883	Likasi (Jadotville)	356,000	89.00	317,000	96.83	C	1,095,000	On Likasi River. Mineral processing center (copper, cobalt). Chemicals, brewery. D=RCC,EJCSK.
1884	Lubumbashi (Elisabethville)	967,000	85.00	822,000	92.83	C	2,784,000	Southern Shaba. Copper, cobalt, zinc mining. Printing, brewing. F=1910 by Belgians. RC Cathedral. D=RCC.
1885	Matadi	231,000	80.00	185,000	87.83	C	711,000	On Congo River. Nation's principal port. Railroad, palm products, coffee, cotton, rubber, bananas. D=RCC.
1886	Mbandaka (Coquilhatville)	229,000	88.00	201,000	95.83	C	703,000	On the Equator. Busy river port on Congo & Ruki rivers. Shipping, agriculture. F=1886. D=RCC,ECZ.
1887	Mbuji-Mayi (Bakwanga)	810,000	88.00	713,000	95.83	C	2,490,000	On Mbuji-Mayi River. Produces 1/3 of world's industrial diamonds. F=1909. Pop. 30,000 in 1960. D=RCC.
1888	Mwene-Ditu	158,000	90.00	142,000	97.83	C	484,000	Southern Kasai-Oriental south of Mbuji-Mayi. Railroad, sawmilling, cotton ginning. D=RCC,EJCSK.
1889	Tshikapa	193,000	88.00	170,000	95.83	C	594,000	Kasai-Oriental on Kasai River. Diamond mining (1907-1970). Gravel quarrying. D=RCC,ECZ.
1890	Uvira	124,000	89.00	110,000	96.83	C	381,000	Kivu on Lake Tanganyika near Bujumbura, Burundi. Cotton. RC and Protestant missions. D=RCC,ECZ.
1891	Yangambi	89,000	88.00	78,300	95.83	C	273,000	On Congo River. Average temp. 76 degrees F. (24 degrees C.). D=RCC,ECZ,EJCSK.
	COOK ISLANDS	**19,500**	**94.72**	**18,500**	**99.95**	**C**	**23,700**	**PROTESTANTS 72.7%, ROMAN CATHOLICS 18.7%. PENT-CHAR 15.8%, EVANGELICAL 7.8%, GCC 12.9%**
1892	rural areas	7,200	95.79	6,900	99.96	C	6,200	54.9% (1950), 46.6% (1970), 42.2% (1990), 36.9% (2000), 32.1% (2010), 26.1% (2025)
1893	urban areas	12,300	94.10	11,600	99.94	C	17,500	45.0% (1950), 53.3% (1970), 57.7% (1990), 63.0% (2000), 67.8% (2010), 73.8% (2025)
1894	non-metropolitan areas	630	94.13	590	99.78	C	892	*Sources of data:* Censuses of 1966, 1971, 1976, 1986, and 1991.
1895	metropolitan areas	11,700	94.10	11,000	99.95	C	16,600	*Definition:* Avarua (on Rarotonga).
1896	AVARUA	11,700	94.10	11,000	99.95	C	16,600	On Rarotonga. Tourism. Extinct volcanoes. International finance-tax haven. D=CICC,RCC.
	COSTA RICA	**4,023,000**	**96.19**	**3,870,000**	**99.89**	**C**	**5,929,000**	**ROMAN CATHOLICS 90.9%, PROTESTANTS 8.2%. PENT-CHAR 12.2%, EVANGELICAL 6.9%, GCC 12.7%**
1897	rural areas	1,936,000	96.72	1,873,000	99.98	C	2,057,000	66.4% (1950), 60.3% (1970), 53.0% (1990), 48.1% (2000), 42.4% (2010), 34.7% (2025)
1898	urban areas	2,087,000	95.70	1,998,000	99.80	C	3,871,000	33.5% (1950), 39.6% (1970), 46.9% (1990), 51.8% (2000), 57.5% (2010), 65.3% (2025)
1899	non-metropolitan areas	942,000	95.90	903,000	99.81	C	1,891,002	*Sources of data:* Censuses of 1950, 1973, and 1984.
1900	metropolitan areas	1,146,000	95.54	1,095,000	99.79	C	1,980,000	*Definition:* Administrative centers of cantons, except Coto Brus, Guatusa, Los Chiles, Sarapiqu' and Upala.
1901	Limon	82,700	96.00	79,400	99.70	C	153,000	Capital of Limon on Caribbean Sea. Bananas, freight export, coffee. Tourism. F=1874. D=RCC.
1902	SAN JOSE	1,063,000	95.50	1,015,000	99.80	C	1,827,000	Settled in 1736 as Villa Nueva. El. 3,814 ft. Tobacco, coffee. Educational center. 20,000 USA citizens. D=RCC.
1903	Desamparados	64,100	96.00	61,600	99.70	C	119,000	South. San Jose province, central valley, residential suburb. Light manufacturing. D=RCC.
	CROATIA	**4,473,000**	**95.17**	**4,256,000**	**99.24**	**C**	**4,193,000**	**ROMAN CATHOLICS 88.5%, ORTHODOX 5.5%. PENT-CHAR 2.8%, EVANGELICAL 0.1%, GCC 5.2%**
1904	rural areas	1,891,000	98.81	1,868,000	99.88	C	1,302,000	77.7% (1950), 59.8% (1970), 45.9% (1990), 42.2% (2000), 37.9% (2010), 31.0% (2025)
1905	urban areas	2,582,000	92.50	2,388,000	98.77	C	2,892,000	22.3% (1950), 40.2% (1970), 54.0% (1990), 57.7% (2000), 62.0% (2010), 68.9% (2025)
1906	non-metropolitan areas	623,000	93.13	580,000	98.96	C	733,775	*Sources of data:* Censuses of 1953, 1961, 1971, 1981, and 1991.
1907	metropolitan areas	1,959,000	92.30	1,808,000	98.71	C	2,158,000	*Definition:* Urban centers.
1908	Cakovec	122,000	92.00	112,000	98.57	C	137,000	Near Hungary. North Croatia. Wine growing area, textiles, furniture, machinery. D=RCC.
1909	Osijek	160,000	93.00	149,000	98.67	C	179,000	On Drava River. Textiles, tanneries, footwear, rubber, cereals. Old fortress. D=RCC.
1910	Rijeka	196,000	93.00	183,000	98.67	C	220,000	Major port on Adriatic Sea. Naval base, shipping. F=Roman Tarsatica 3rd century. 14th century church. D=RCC.
1911	Slavanski Brod (Slavonski Brod)	111,000	93.00	103,000	98.67	C	124,000	On Sava River. E. Croatia, Dilj mountain. Locomotives, autos, steam rollers, fishing, woodworking. D=RCC.
1912	Split	188,000	92.00	173,000	98.57	C	211,000	Dalmatia seaport. Shipyard. Palace of Diocletian (305). Mausoleum converted to cathedral (635). D=RCC.
1913	Zadar	121,000	93.00	113,000	98.67	C	136,000	Dalmatia. Deepwater harbor. Fish canning. Resort. F=9th century. St. Donati church (9th century). D=RCC.
1914	ZAGREB	1,060,000	92.00	975,000	98.77	C	1,151,000	On Sava River. Heavy machinery. International trade fair. F=1093. Y=1093. University (1874). D=RCC.
1915	Novi Zagreb	118,000	92.00	109,000	98.57	C	132,000	Across the Sava River to the south. High-rise apartment buildings. F=c1950. D=RCC.
1916	Tresnjevka	120,000	92.00	110,000	98.57	C	134,000	Southwest Zagreb, Dom Sportova Arena, Kazaliste Mladih Youth Theater, Erikson-Tesla Industrial Firm. D=RCC.
	CUBA	**11,201,000**	**43.06**	**4,823,000**	**99.10**	**B**	**11,798,000**	**ROMAN CATHOLICS 39.0%, PROTESTANTS 1.7%. PENT-CHAR 5.1%, EVANGELICAL 1.2%, GCC 23.0%**
1917	rural areas	2,473,000	50.33	1,245,000	99.50	B	1,791,000	50.6% (1950), 39.8% (1970), 26.5% (1990), 22.0% (2000), 18.6% (2010), 15.1% (2025)
1918	urban areas	8,728,000	41.00	3,578,000	98.99	B	10,007,000	49.3% (1950), 60.2% (1970), 73.4% (1990), 77.9% (2000), 81.3% (2010), 84.8% (2025)
1919	non-metropolitan areas	3,500,000	41.46	1,451,000	99.02	B	4,229,179	*Sources of data:* Censuses of 1953, 1970, and 1981; estimate for 1988.
1920	metropolitan areas	5,227,000	40.69	2,127,000	98.97	B	5,778,000	*Definition:* Population living in a nucleus of 2,000 or more inhabitants.
1921	Bayamo	148,000	41.00	60,700	99.04	B	170,000	Capital of Granma on Bayamo River. Cattle, dairy, tanning. F=1513 as San Salvador de Bayamo. D=RCC.
1922	Camaguey	305,000	38.00	116,000	98.04	B	350,000	Capital of Camaguey. Livestock, sugar cane, chromite. F=1514. D=RCC.
1923	Cardenas	90,100	44.00	39,600	99.54	B	103,000	Matanzas. Fishing port. Chief sugar port. Rope, rum, beach resort. F=1828. D=RCC.
1924	Ciego de Avila	108,000	42.00	45,400	99.04	B	124,000	Capital of Ciego de Avila. Sugarcane, honey, sawmills, distilleries. D=RCC.
1925	Cienfuegos	145,000	41.00	59,500	99.04	B	166,000	Capital of Cienfuegos. Chief sugar port. Numerous parks. Coffee, tobacco, shrimp. F=1819. D=RCC.
1926	Florida	54,800	44.00	24,100	99.54	B	62,800	Camaguey on Jiqui River. Trading and agricultural center. Sugarcane, oranges, cattle. D=RCC.
1927	Guantanamo	230,000	40.00	91,900	99.04	B	264,000	Capital of Guantanamo. Sugarcane, coffee, chocolate. F=1819. Heavy air traffic. US Navy Base (1903). D=RCC.
1928	Holguin	252,000	39.00	98,400	98.04	B	289,000	Capital of Holguin. Communications and trading center. Sugar cane, tobacco. F=c1500. D=RCC.
1929	Kanzanillo	100,000	42.00	42,100	99.04	B	115,000	Unhealthful swamplands. Port. Sugar, fruit, rice, cattle, fishing. F=1784. D=RCC.
1930	LA HABANA (Havana)	2,302,000	41.00	944,000	99.04	B	2,424,000	Administrative center. Food processing (sugar), ship building, fishing. University (1721). F=1519. D=RCC.
1931	Las Tunas	135,000	41.00	55,300	99.04	B	155,000	Capital of Las Tunas. Sugarcane, bananas, oranges, cattle, iron ore, marble. D=RCC.
1932	Manzanillo	116,000	42.00	48,600	99.04	B	133,000	Granma on Gulf of Guacanayabo. Sugarcane, rice, tobacco. F=1784. D=RCC.
1933	Matanzas	127,000	40.00	50,900	99.04	B	146,000	Capital of Matanzas. Chief port for sugar. F=1693. The 'Athens of Cuba'. D=RCC.
1934	Moron	53,000	44.00	23,300	99.54	B	60,800	Ciego de Avila near Laguna de la Leche. Railroad, sugarcane, tobacco, cacao, coffee, fruit, cattle. D=RCC.
1935	Palma Soriano	133,000	41.00	54,400	99.04	B	152,000	Santiago de Cuba. On Rio Cauto. Sugarcane, cacao, coffee, soft drinks, furniture. D=RCC.
1936	Pinar del Rio	145,000	42.00	60,900	99.04	B	166,000	Capital of Pinar del Rio. Hilly pinelands. Tobacco, sugar. F=1775. D=RCC.
1937	Sancti-Spiritus	104,000	41.00	42,600	99.04	B	119,000	Capital of Sancti-Spiritus. Narrow, crooked streets and old churches. Sugar, tobacco. F=1516. D=RCC.
1938	Santa Clara	217,000	39.00	84,600	99.54	B	249,000	Capital of Villa Clara. Sugar, tobacco. F=1689. On ancient site of Cubanacan. University (1948). D=RCC.
1939	Santiago de Cuba	463,000	40.00	185,000	99.04	B	530,000	Capital of Santiago de Cuba. Coffee, cacao, cattle, dairy products. F=1514. D=RCC.
	CYPRUS	**601,000**	**91.85**	**552,000**	**99.82**	**C**	**688,000**	**ORTHODOX 87.4%, ROMAN CATHOLICS 1.6%. PENT-CHAR 0.5%, EVANGELICAL 0.5%, GCC 11.0%**
1940	rural areas	260,000	92.98	241,000	99.88	C	213,000	70.2% (1950), 59.2% (1970), 48.6% (1990), 43.2% (2000), 37.9% (2010), 30.9% (2025)
1941	urban areas	341,000	91.00	310,000	99.77	C	475,000	29.7% (1950), 40.7% (1970), 51.4% (1990), 56.7% (2000), 62.0% (2010), 69.0% (2025)
1942	non-metropolitan areas	54,200	89.61	48,600	99.77	C	75,618	*Sources of data:* Censuses of 1960 and 1973; estimates for 1956 and 1991.
1943	metropolitan areas	287,000	91.26	262,000	99.77	C	400,000	*Definition:* Six district towns and Nicosia suburbs.
1944	Ammokhostos (Famagusta)	62,100	92.00	57,200	99.77	C	86,600	On Famagusta Bay. Richest medieval city in Christendom. Major port. Agriculture, dairy, fishing. D=Orthodox.
1945	Larnax (Larnaca)	58,900	92.00	54,200	99.77	C	82,100	Modern port exports potatoes, cement. Schools. Tradition says Lazarus of Bethany first bishop. D=Orthodox.
1946	Lemesos (Limassol)	120,000	91.00	109,000	99.77	C	167,000	On Akrotiri Bay. Chief port and tourist center. Exports wine, beverages, fruits. Many Arab refugees. D=Orthodox.
1947	LEVKOSIA (Nicosia-I)	45,900	90.00	41,300	99.77	C	63,900	On the Pedieos River. Textiles. Ancient origins. Seat of autocephalous Church of Cyprus. D=Orthodox.
	CZECH REPUBLIC	**10,244,000**	**47.04**	**4,819,000**	**99.42**	**B**	**9,512,000**	**ROMAN CATHOLICS 40.3%, PROTESTANTS 3.1%. PENT-CHAR 2.5%, EVANGELICAL 1.2%, GCC 25.3%**
1948	rural areas	3,456,000	49.09	1,697,000	99.89	B	2,430,000	59.1% (1950), 47.9% (1970), 35.0% (1990), 33.7% (2000), 31.0% (2010), 25.5% (2025)
1949	urban areas	6,788,000	46.00	3,122,000	99.18	B	7,082,000	40.8% (1950), 52.0% (1970), 64.9% (1990), 66.2% (2000), 68.9% (2010), 74.4% (2025)
1950	non-metropolitan areas	2,359,000	44.92	1,060,000	99.30	B	2,507,777	*Sources of data:* Censuses of 1950, 1961, 1970, 1980, and 1991.
1951	metropolitan areas	4,429,000	46.57	2,063,000	99.12	B	4,574,000	*Definition:* Localities with 5,000 or more inhabitants.
1952	Brno	452,000	46.00	208,000	99.38	B	471,000	Capital of Jihomoravsky. Cultural capital of Moravia. Wool industry. Augustinian monastery. F=Celts. D=RCC.
1953	Ceske Budejovice	114,000	50.00	57,200	99.38	B	119,000	Capital of Jihocesky on Vltava River. Original home of Budweiser beer. F=1265 by Dominicans. D=RCC.
1954	Chomutov	80,300	49.00	39,400	99.48	B	83,800	Severocesky. At foot of Ore Mountains. Metals, mining. Near German border. Czech in origin. D=RCC.
1955	Decin	72,300	50.00	36,200	99.38	B	75,400	Severocesky. In gorge of Elbe River. Scenic tourist region, boats, metals, textiles. F=c1150. D=RCC.
1956	Hradec Kralove	113,000	48.00	54,500	99.53	B	118,000	Capital of Vychodocesky on Elbe River. F=1225. Gothic Cathedral of the Holy Ghost (1307). D=RCC.
1957	Jihlava	52,500	49.00	25,700	99.48	B	54,800	Jihomoravsky. Destroyed in 1523. Cloth, tobacco, vehicles, precision instruments. D=RCC.
1958	Karlovy Vary (Carlsbad)	56,500	48.00	27,100	99.53	B	59,000	Zapadocesky. Spa city on Tepla River. Porcelain, glassware. Coal mining caused air pollution. D=RCC.
1959	Kladno	88,900	50.00	44,400	99.38	B	92,700	Stredocasky. Mining city. Blast furnaces, rolling mill, steelworks. D=RCC.
1960	Liberec	176,000	50.00	87,900	99.38	B	183,000	Severocesky on Neisse River. Textiles, glass. F=c1250. 'Bohemian Manchester'. D=RCC.
1961	Most	136,000	48.00	65,100	99.53	B	141,000	Severocesky. Coalfield, ignite-mining, steel, chemicals, ceramics. D=RCC.
1962	Olomouc	127,000	55.00	69,600	99.93	B	132,000	Severomoravsky on Morava River. Steel, chocolate. RC Bishopric established in 1063. University (1566).
1963	Opava	78,300	45.00	35,200	97.38	B	81,700	Severomoravsky on Opava River. Market center, clothing, machinery. Near Polish border. D=RCC.
1964	Ostrava	763,000	44.00	336,000	98.98	B	796,000	Capital of Severomoravsky. Heavy industry, mining, metal working. F=1267. Formerly Moravska. D=RCC.
1965	Frydek-Mistek	65,300	46.00	30,100	99.38	B	68,200	On the Ostravice River. Coal, iron, heavy industry, rolled steel, cotton textiles. Institute of ethnography. D=RCC.
1966	Havirov	86,600	46.00	39,800	99.38	B	90,400	On the Lucina River. Machinery, rubber, tanning, food processing, mining. F=1947. D=RCC.
1967	Karvina	68,700	46.00	31,600	99.38	B	71,600	Mining city on the Olse River. High-grade coal, chemicals, iron, glassworks. D=RCC.
1968	Pardubice	95,300	51.00	48,600	98.83	B	99,400	Vychodocesky in Elbe Valley. Horse racing, sugar. F=c1250. 13th century church. D=RCC.
1969	Plzen	211,000	45.00	94,900	97.38	B	220,000	Capital of Zapadocesky. Medieval town square. Pilsner beer. F=1290. Church of St. Bartholomew. D=RCC.
1970	PRAHA (Prague)	1,233,000	44.00	543,000	98.98	B	1,240,000	On Vltava River. Precision equipment. F=c850. Charles University (1848). 'City of a hundred spires'. D=RCC.
1971	Prerov	51,600	49.00	25,300	99.48	B	53,800	Severni Morava. Precision instruments, optical equipment, textiles. F=11th century. D=RCC.
1972	Prostejov	50,300	57.00	28,700	99.98	B	52,500	Jihomoravsky. Publishing center of Czech & Hebrew books after 1500. Hana Harvest Festival. D=RCC.
1973	Tabor	55,700	53.00	29,500	99.88	B	58,100	Jihocesky. S. Bohemia. Cheese, fish, textiles, furniture, brewing. Hussite relics. F=1420. D=RCC.
1974	Teplice	94,400	48.00	45,300	99.53	B	98,500	Severocesky. Radioactive springs. Wood processing, health resort. Convent founded by Judith (1156). D=RCC.
1975	Trinec	87,900	53.00	46,600	99.88	B	91,700	Severni Morava near Poland border. Iron works, mining, coal, lime, museum of metallurgy. F=15th cent. D=RCC.
1976	Usti nad Labem	115,000	47.00	54,300	99.38	B	120,000	Capital of Severocesky. Port on Elbe River. Major tourist spot. Mining, glass. F=c950. Church (1186). D=RCC.
1977	Zlin (Gottwaldov)	125,000	49.00	61,000	99.48	B	130,000	Jihomoravsky. Cultural center. Shoemaking, knitting, orchestra, film studies. F=1948. D=RCC.
	DENMARK	**5,293,000**	**89.76**	**4,751,000**	**99.22**	**C**	**5,238,000**	**PROTESTANTS 87.6%, MARGINAL CHRISTIANS 0.6%. PENT-CHAR 3.8%, EVANGELICAL 4.9%, GCC 12.8%**
1978	rural areas	755,000	91.31	689,000	99.60	C	563,000	32.0% (1950), 20.2% (1970), 15.2% (1990), 14.2% (2000), 12.9% (2010), 10.7% (2025)
1979	urban areas	4,538,000	89.50	4,062,000	99.16	C	4,676,000	67.9% (1950), 79.7% (1970), 84.7% (1990), 85.7% (2000), 87.0% (2010), 89.2% (2025)
1980	non-metropolitan areas	2,244,000	89.80	2,015,000	99.19	C	2,352,267	*Sources of data:* Censuses of 1950, 1955, 1960, 1965, 1970, and 1981; estimate for 1992.
1981	metropolitan areas	2,294,000	89.21	2,047,000	99.13	C	2,324,000	*Definition:* Provincial capitals plus capital city.
1982	Alborg (Aalborg)	158,000	90.00	142,000	99.96	C	163,000	Nordjyllands port on Arhus Bay. Conferences, cement. F=c1000. Cathedral of St. Botolph. D=Lutheran.
1983	Arhus (Aarhus)	271,000	89.00	241,000	99.46	C	279,000	Arhus on Arhus Bay. Busy port, chemicals. F=c948. Episcopal See (11th century). D=Lutheran.
1984	Esbjerg	82,700	91.00	75,200	99.96	C	85,200	Ribe on North Sea. Largest fishing port, meat, dairy, tourism. F=1868. D=Lutheran.
1985	Fredericia	47,100	92.00	43,300	99.86	C	48,500	Vejle port. Silverware, frozen fish, textiles. Oil, Danish industries fair. F=1650. D=Lutheran.
1986	Horsens	55,700	92.00	51,200	99.86	C	57,400	Vejle on Horsens Fjord. Dairy, tobacco, textiles. 13th century monastery. D=Lutheran.
1987	KOBENHAVN (Copenhagen)	1,326,000	88.50	1,174,000	98.66	C	1,326,000	Zealand and Amager islands. Shipbuilding. F=c950. Bishop Absalon (1167). 'Paris of the North'. D=Lutheran.

Table 10-5–continued opposite

Table 10-5–continued

Rec No 1	Country City 2	Pop 2000 3	AC% 4	Church Members 5	E% 6	W 7	Pop 2025 8	Notes 9
1988	Ballerup	45,900	89.00	40,900	99.46	C	47,300	West. Northeast Sjaelland. Barley, wheat, kitchen utensils, pharmaceuticals. D=Lutheran.
1989	Frederiksberg	87,200	87.00	75,900	99.16	C	89,900	Royal Porcelain Factory, Carlsberg breweries, cable, wireworks. F=1651. D=Lutherans.
1990	Gentofte	66,700	88.00	58,700	99.26	C	68,800	Foreign embassies, horse-trotting course, Tuborg breweries, residential. Kronborg Castle (1554). D=Lutheran.
1991	Gladsakse	61,200	89.00	54,500	99.46	C	63,100	Northwest. Manufacturing. D=Lutheran.
1992	Helsingor (Elsinore)	57,400	88.00	50,500	99.26	C	59,100	Frederiksberg. Ship building, rubber, tourism. Connected to Sweden by 2 ferries. D=Lutheran.
1993	Hvidovre	49,200	88.00	43,300	99.26	C	50,700	West. Residential. D=Lutheran.
1994	Kongens Lyngby	50,100	89.00	44,600	99.46	C	51,600	North. Manufacturing. D=Lutheran.
1995	Radovre	36,900	88.00	32,500	99.46	C	38,000	West beyond Frederiksberg. Distilleries. D=Lutheran.
1996	Roskilde	50,700	89.00	45,100	99.46	C	52,200	Roskilde. Tanneries, distilleries, bacon. F=c950. Y=c960 by King Harald Bluetooth. D=Lutheran.
1997	Tarnby	41,000	90.00	36,900	99.96	C	42,200	South on Island. International airport. Amager Island, Copenhagen country. D=Lutheran.
1998	Kolding	58,600	92.00	53,900	99.96	C	60,300	Vejle commune. Rail junction, cement, machinery. F=c950. Church of St. Nicholas (c1250). D=Lutheran.
1999	Odense	181,000	88.00	160,000	99.76	C	187,000	Fyns. Tobacco, iron. F=c950. as bishop's seat. Center for religious pilgrimage in Middle Ages. D=Lutheran.
2000	Randers	62,000	93.00	57,700	99.96	C	63,900	Arhus on Gudena River. Beer, bacon. Medieval market. F=1086. Church of St. Morton (15th century). D=Lutheran.
2001	Vejle	52,400	94.00	49,200	99.96	C	53,900	Vejle seaport. Agricultural distribution center, textiles. F=1327. Church of St. Nikolaj (c1250). D=Lutheran.
	DJIBOUTI	**638,000**	**4.42**	**28,200**	**45.84**	**A**	**1,026,000**	**ORTHODOX 2.9%, ROMAN CATHOLICS 1.3%. PENT-CHAR 0.1%, EVANGELICAL 0.01%, GCC 1.8%**
2002	rural areas	106,000	1.54	1,600	27.99	A	123,000	59.0% (1950), 38.0% (1970), 19.7% (1990), 16.7% (2000), 14.6% (2010), 12.0% (2025)
2003	urban areas	531,000	5.00	26,600	49.42	A	903,000	40.9% (1950), 62.0% (1970), 80.2% (1990), 83.3% (2000), 85.3% (2010), 88.0% (2025)
2004	non-metropolitan areas	177,000	5.00	8,800	49.42	A	300,265	*Sources of data:* Estimates for 1956, 1963, and 1970.
2005	metropolitan areas	355,000	5.00	17,700	49.42	A	603,000	*Definition:* Capital city.
2006	DJIBOUTI (Jibuti)	355,000	5.00	17,700	49.42	A	603,000	Gulf of Aden. Port. F=1888. 72% Somali, 11% Arab, 8% Afar. 86% Muslim. Christians are 88% French.
	DOMINICA	**70,700**	**94.40**	**66,800**	**99.91**	**C**	**73,400**	**ROMAN CATHOLICS 79.6%, PROTESTANTS 15.8%. PENT-CHAR 7.0%, EVANGELICAL 6.6%, GCC 7.1%**
2007	rural areas	20,500	95.39	19,600	99.92	C	15,400	51.7% (1950), 53.1% (1970), 32.2% (1990), 28.9% (2000), 25.6% (2010), 20.9% (2025)
2008	urban areas	50,200	94.00	47,200	99.91	C	58,100	48.2% (1950), 46.8% (1970), 67.7% (1990), 71.0% (2000), 74.3% (2010), 79.0% (2025)
2009	non-metropolitan areas	41,100	94.00	38,600	99.91	C	47,520	*Sources of data:* Censuses.
2010	metropolitan areas	9,100	94.00	8,600	99.91	C	10,600	*Definition:* Roseau.
2011	ROSEAU	9,100	94.00	8,600	99.91	C	10,600	Port. Exports limes, lime juice, oils, spices. Near total destruction by hurricane (1979). D=RCC,Anglican.
	DOMINICAN REPUBLIC	**8,495,000**	**94.48**	**8,027,000**	**99.93**	**C**	**11,164,000**	**ROMAN CATHOLICS 88.5%, PROTESTANTS 4.2%. PENT-CHAR 12.1%, EVANGELICAL 3.1%, GCC 5.8%**
2012	rural areas	2,958,000	96.89	2,866,000	99.97	C	2,647,000	76.2% (1950), 59.7% (1970), 41.6% (1990), 34.8% (2000), 29.3% (2010), 23.7% (2025)
2013	urban areas	5,537,000	93.20	5,161,000	99.90	C	8,517,000	23.7% (1950), 40.2% (1970), 58.3% (1990), 65.1% (2000), 70.6% (2010), 76.2% (2025)
2014	non-metropolitan areas	–	–	–	–	–	–	*Sources of data:* Censuses of 1950, 1960, 1970, and 1981.
2015	metropolitan areas	6,516,000	93.12	6,068,000	99.86	C	9,321,000	*Definition:* Administrative centers of municipalities and municipal districts.
2016	Barahona	96,100	95.00	91,300	99.95	C	148,000	Caribbean Port, fishing center, sugarcane, molasses, coffee, hardwoods, fruits. D=RCC.
2017	La Romana	177,000	94.50	167,000	99.95	C	272,000	Capital of La Romana. Sugar, coffee, tobacco, fishing. Luxury resorts. 'The Scales'. D=RCC.
2018	La Vega	230,000	94.00	216,000	99.45	C	353,000	Capital of La Vega. Cacao, coffee, tobacco, rice, fruits. F=1495 by Bartolomeo Colombo. D=RCC.
2019	Mao	69,800	95.00	66,300	99.95	C	107,000	Northwest of Santiago on Yague del Norte River. Rice growing and milling, lumber, gold washing. D=RCC.
2020	Puerto Plata	113,000	94.50	107,000	99.95	C	174,000	Capital of Puerto Plata. Tobacco, coffee. F=c1550 as pirate port. North of Santiago on Macoris Bay. D=RCC.
2021	San Cristobal	164,000	95.00	156,000	99.95	C	253,000	Capital of San Cristobal. Rice, coffee, sugarcane. F=1575 by Spaniards. Signing of Constitution (1844). D=RCC.
2022	San Francisco de Macoris	197,000	94.00	186,000	99.45	C	304,000	Capital of Duarte. Cacao, coffee, fruits, rice, beeswax, hides. F=1777. D=RCC.
2023	San Juan de la Maguana	155,000	95.00	147,000	99.95	C	238,000	Central south of Santiago. Rice, fruit, corn. Battle of Santome (1844). F=1508. D=RCC.
2024	San Pedro de Macoris	172,000	94.50	163,000	99.95	C	265,000	Capital of San Pedro de Macoris. Modern port handles most of country's exports, sugar. Baseball.
2025	Santiago de los Caballeros	1,540,000	94.50	1,455,000	99.95	C	2,230,000	Capital of Santiago on Yaque River. F=1494 by Christopher Columbus. Catholic University (c1970). D=RCC.
2026	SANTO DOMINGO	3,601,000	92.00	3,313,000	99.85	C	4,976,000	Commercial, and finance center. F=1496. Oldest RCC archbishopric in Western Hemisphere.
	ECUADOR	**12,646,000**	**97.33**	**12,308,000**	**99.44**	**C**	**17,796,000**	**ROMAN CATHOLICS 94.1%, PROTESTANTS 1.9%. PENT-CHAR 11.1%, EVANGELICAL 2.3%, GCC 5.1%**
2027	rural areas	4,754,000	98.69	4,692,000	99.64	C	4,554,000	71.7% (1950), 60.4% (1970), 44.9% (1990), 37.5% (2000), 31.7% (2010), 25.5% (2025)
2028	urban areas	7,892,000	96.50	7,616,000	99.31	C	13,242,000	28.2% (1950), 39.5% (1970), 55.0% (1990), 62.4% (2000), 68.2% (2010), 74.4% (2025)
2029	non-metropolitan areas	2,426,000	96.13	2,332,000	99.36	C	4,588,060	*Sources of data:* Censuses of 1950, 1962, 1974, 1982, and 1990.
2030	metropolitan areas	5,466,000	96.67	5,284,000	99.29	C	8,654,000	*Definition:* Capitals of provinces and cantons.
2031	Ambato	153,000	96.00	147,000	99.11	C	257,000	Capital of Tungurahua. On Ambato River at 8,500 ft. Agriculture-trade center. Fruits, sugar, resort. D=RCC.
2032	Babahoyo	62,000	97.00	60,100	99.11	C	104,000	Capital of Los Rios on Babahoyo River. Rice, fruits, balsa wood, tagua nuts. University (1971). D=RCC.
2033	Cuenca	240,000	96.50	232,000	98.61	C	403,000	Capital of Azuay. 8,517 ft. on Rio Matadero. Agriculture, cattle, marble. Weekly Indian market. F=1557. D=RCC.
2034	Esmeraldas	121,000	97.00	118,000	99.11	C	204,000	Capital of Esmeraldas and Pacific seaport. Trading center for agriculture & lumber. Oil, bananas. D=RCC.
2035	Guayaquil	2,127,000	96.50	2,053,000	99.21	C	3,254,000	Capital of Guayas on Guayas River. Growing slums. Sugar, iron, machines, shrimp, oil. F=1530s. D=RCC.
2036	Alfaro	101,000	97.00	98,400	99.11	C	170,000	Across the Guayas River. Sugar, agricultural. D=RCC.
2037	Ibarra	99,800	97.00	96,800	99.11	C	167,000	7,300 ft. Trade center for cotton, sugarcane, cereals, coffee, livestock. Wood carvings. F=1606. D=RCC.
2038	La Libertad	65,400	98.00	64,100	99.81	C	110,000	Processing and trading center, sugarcane, rice, cacao, tropical fruit, sugar refining. D=RCC.
2039	Loja	116,000	97.00	113,000	99.11	C	195,000	Capital of Loja. Regional agricultural trade. Sugarcane, tanning, textiles. F=1553. Local quarries. D=RCC.
2040	Machala	178,000	97.00	172,000	99.11	C	298,000	Capital of El Oro. Trade in bananas, cocoa, coffee, hides. Handles 1/4 Ecuador's banana export. D=RCC.
2041	Manta	155,000	98.00	152,000	99.81	C	259,000	Port city of Manabi. Exports Panama hats, coffee, cocoa. Tuna, tourism. F=3000 BC. D=RCC.
2042	Milagro	115,000	97.00	112,000	99.11	C	194,000	East of Guayaquil. Processing and trading center, sugarcane, rice, cacao, tropical fruit, sugar refining. D=RCC.
2043	Portoviejo	164,000	97.00	159,000	99.81	C	275,000	Capital of Manabi. Coffee, cocoa, sugar cane, cotton, balsa wood. Bishopric (1871). F=1535. D=RCC.
2044	Quevedo	107,000	97.50	104,000	99.61	C	180,000	Los Rios. Upper Vinces River. Cacao, papaya, bananas, oil palm, sugarcane, rice, tropical fruit. D=RCC.
2045	QUITO	1,505,000	96.40	1,451,000	99.41	C	2,323,000	9,350 ft. Colonial atmosphere. City-center slums. Indian markets. Religious art center. F=c1535. D=RCC.
2046	Riobamba	116,000	97.00	113,000	99.11	C	195,000	Capital of Chimborazo. 9,000 ft. Pre-Inca origins. Fertile agriculture, native artifacts. RCC diocese(1863).
2047	Santa Domingo de los Colorados	141,000	98.00	138,000	99.81	C	237,000	Pichincha on Toachi River. Tropical fruits. Colorado Indians. D=RCC.
	EGYPT	**68,470,000**	**15.07**	**10,320,000**	**77.65**	**B**	**95,615,000**	**ORTHODOX 13.6%, PROTESTANTS 0.8%. PENT-CHAR 1.1%, EVANGELICAL 0.6%, GCC 11.9%**
2048	rural areas	37,015,000	12.33	4,564,000	73.12	B	39,021,000	68.0% (1950), 57.7% (1970), 56.0% (1990), 54.0% (2000), 49.5% (2010), 40.8% (2025)
2049	urban areas	31,455,000	18.30	5,756,000	82.98	B	56,595,000	31.9% (1950), 42.2% (1970), 43.9% (1990), 45.9% (2000), 50.4% (2010), 59.1% (2025)
2050	non-metropolitan areas	7,281,000	18.38	1,338,000	82.94	B	16,398,012	*Sources of data:* Censuses of 1947, 1960, 1966, 1976, and 1986.
2051	metropolitan areas	24,174,000	18.28	4,418,000	82.99	B	40,197,000	*Definition:* Governorates of Cairo, Alexandria, Port Said, Ismailia and Suez and frontier governorates.
2052	Abnub	65,700	30.00	19,700	92.58	B	118,000	Asyut on Nile River north of Asyut. D=COC.
2053	Abu Kabir	94,200	10.00	9,400	72.58	B	169,000	Ash-Sharqiyah northeast of az-Zaqaziq. 90% Muslim.
2054	Abu Tij	66,000	25.00	16,500	87.58	B	119,000	Asyut on Nile River south of Asyut. D=COC.
2055	Akhmim	95,700	24.00	23,000	86.58	B	172,000	On Nile River north of Sawhaj. Ancient Theban city. Silk, sugar, cotton. D=COC.
2056	Al-Arish	91,600	2.00	1,800	64.58	B	165,000	Sinai Peninsula on Mediterranean Sea. 98% Muslim.
2057	Al-Fayyum	288,000	19.50	56,200	82.08	B	518,000	Al-Fayyum capital west of Nile River. D=COC.
2058	Al-Iskandariyah (Alexandria)	3,995,000	27.30	1,091,000	93.38	B	6,456,000	Chief seaport. Cotton, trade. F=332 BC. Large-scale Christian activities: youth work, radio, Bible sales. D=COC.
2059	Kafr ad-Dawwar (Kafr-El-Dwar)	219,000	16.40	35,900	78.98	B	394,000	Southeast on Tur'at al-Mahmudiyah canal. Cotton ginning, cigarettes, rice, cereals. D=COC.
2060	Al-Ismailiyah	318,000	10.30	32,800	72.88	B	573,000	Al-Ismailiyah capital on Suez Canal and Lake Timsah. Canal administration. F=1863 as base of operations.
2061	Al-Mahallah al-Kubra	486,000	9.90	48,100	72.48	B	875,000	Al-Gharbiyah northeast of Tanta. 90% Muslim.
2062	Al-Mansurah	508,000	10.40	52,800	72.98	B	914,000	Ad-Daqahiyah on Damietta Branch. Cotton, cereals.
2063	Talkha	75,500	10.50	7,900	73.08	B	136,000	North across Damietta Branch of Nile River. Railroad, cotton, cereals, rice, fruit.
2064	Al-Manzilah	74,600	9.00	6,700	71.58	B	134,000	Ad-Daqahiyah on Lake Manzilah. 90% Muslim.
2065	Al-Matariyah	101,000	8.00	8,100	70.58	B	182,000	Ad-Daqahiyah on Lake Manzilah. 90% Muslim.
2066	Al-Minya (Menia)	243,000	32.10	77,900	94.68	B	437,000	Al-Minya capital on Nile River. D=COC.
2067	AL-QAHIRAH-AL-JIZAH (Cairo)	10,772,000	18.30	1,971,000	84.38	B	16,816,000	On Nile River. 1,500 Ahmadis, 1,500 Baha'is, 300 Jews. Large-scale activities; charismatic renewal. D=COC.
2068	Al-Hawamidiyah	99,000	18.00	17,800	80.58	B	178,000	Al-Jizah. South on Nile River. D=COC.
2069	Al-Jizah (Giza)	2,534,000	20.00	507,000	82.58	B	4,560,000	Al-Jizah capital on Nile River. Resort. Center of motion-picture industry. Cotton textiles. Pyramids. D=COC.
2070	Bahtim	374,000	19.00	71,000	81.58	B	672,000	North near Heliopolis. 5 miles North northeast of Cairo city center. D=COC.
2071	Bulaq ad-Dakrur	202,000	18.00	36,300	80.58	B	363,000	Central. University of Cairo. Formerly known for great museum. F=15th century. D=COC.
2072	Shubra al-Khaymah	963,000	19.00	183,000	81.58	B	1,733,000	North of al-Qahirah on Nile River. Large concentration of factories, cotton textiles, lead smelters. D=COC.
2073	Warraq al-Arab	172,000	18.50	31,900	81.08	B	310,000	North beyond Cairo Airport. 4 miles Northwest of Cairo city center. D=COC.
2074	Al-Qanatir al-Khayriyah	66,300	6.00	4,000	68.58	B	119,000	Al-Qalyubiyah west of Qalyub on Nile River. 94% Muslim.
2075	Al-Uqsur (Luxor)	170,000	8.00	13,600	70.58	B	306,000	On Nile River near Armant. Thebes nearby. Valley of the Kings. King Tut's tomb. Tourism.
2076	Armant	74,000	8.00	5,900	70.58	B	133,000	On Nile River near al-Uqsur. Valley of the Kings to the north. 90% Muslim.
2077	As-Sinbillawayan	81,700	9.00	7,400	71.58	B	147,000	Ad-Daqahiyah south of al-Mansurah. 90% Muslim.
2078	As-Suways (Suez)	443,000	11.30	50,000	73.88	B	797,000	As-Suways capital on Suez Canal and Gulf of Suez. Oil refining, petroleum products. Pilgrims to Mecca.
2079	Ashmun	73,800	5.00	3,700	67.58	B	133,000	Al-Minufiyah on Rosetta Branch of Nile River. Railroad, rich agricultural area, cereals, cotton, flax, cigarettes.
2080	Aswan (Assuan, Assouan)	259,000	24.90	64,600	87.48	B	467,000	Capital of Aswan. Copper, steel, granite quarries, resort. Aswan Dam. One of world's driest cities. D=COC.
2081	Asyut (Assiut)	370,000	32.70	121,000	95.28	B	666,000	Capital of Asyut. Silver shawls. Largely Christian population. CEOSS (social services). D=COC.
2082	Az-Zaqaziq (Zagazig)	333,000	12.30	40,900	74.88	B	598,000	Ash-Shariqiyah, on Nile Delta and Ismailia Canal. Cotton, grain. Near ancient Bubastis.
2083	Banha (Benha)	157,000	6.00	9,400	68.58	B	282,000	Capital of al-Qalyubiyah. Honey, cotton, oranges, grapes, rug weaving, food processing. 94% Muslim.
2084	Bani Suwayf (Beni-Suef)	206,000	23.70	48,800	86.28	B	370,000	Capital of Bani Suwayf. Agricultural trade center. Flour, cotton, textiles, alabaster. D=COC.
2085	Bani-Mazar	65,000	25.00	16,200	87.58	B	117,000	Al-Minya on Nile River south of Maghaghah. D=COC.
2086	Bilbays (Bilbeis, Bilbis)	131,000	6.00	7,800	68.58	B	235,000	Southeastern ash-Sharqiyah in Eastern Nile Delta. Textile manufacturing, railway junction.
2087	Bilqas Qism Awwal	99,100	9.00	8,900	71.58	B	178,000	Ad-Daqahiyah north of al-Mansurah. Cotton, cotton ginning.
2088	Biyala	64,700	8.00	5,200	70.58	B	116,000	Southern Kafr ash-Shaykh on Bahr Tiral. Cotton. 90% Muslim.
2089	Bur Said (Port Said)	542,000	11.40	61,800	73.98	B	975,000	Suez Canal at Mediterranean Sea. Textiles, glass, fishing, salt. F=1859 by canal builders.
2090	Bush	73,800	20.00	14,800	82.58	B	133,000	Bani-Suwayf on Nile River north of Bani-Suwayf. Cotton, cereal, sugarcane. D=COC.
2091	Damanhur	259,000	10.00	25,900	72.58	B	465,000	Capital of Al-Buhayrah. Railway transports cotton, dates, vegetables, cereals. 90% Muslim.
2092	Disuq	106,000	6.00	6,400	68.58	B	190,000	Kafr ash-Shaykh on Rosetta Branch of Nile River. Cotton ginning, cigarette mfg.
2093	Dumyat (Damietta, Dimyat)	121,000	10.00	12,100	72.58	B	218,000	Capital of Dumyat in the Nile Delta. Trade center, leather, flour, fishing.
2094	Faqus	65,900	10.00	6,600	72.58	B	119,000	Central ash-Sharqiyah east of Abu Kabir. Railroad, cotton.
2095	Hawsh Isa	84,700	3.00	2,500	65.58	B	152,000	Al-Buhayrah south of Damanhur. 30 miles SE of Alexandria. 95% Muslim.
2096	Hulwan (Helwan, Hilwan)	483,000	12.00	58,000	74.58	B	869,000	Southern suburb of Cairo. Prehistoric settlement. Spa, heavy industry, flour, textiles, natural gas.
2097	Idku	95,800	5.00	4,800	67.58	B	172,000	Northern al-Buhayrah on Lake Idku. Rice milling, silk weaving, fisheries.
2098	Jirja	96,100	30.00	28,800	92.58	B	173,000	On Nile River south of al-Manshah. Noted for its pottery, RC monastery, sugar refining. D=COC,RCC.
2099	Kafr ash-Shaykh (Kafr El-Sheikh)	139,000	8.00	11,200	70.58	B	251,000	Capital of Kafr ash-Shaykh. Cotton, cigarettes, rice, chemicals. Fertile plain.
2100	Kafr az-Zayyat	78,700	8.00	6,300	70.58	B	142,000	Al-Gharbiyah on Rosetta Branch on Nile River. Railroad, cotton ginning, wool spinning, cigarettes, chemicals.
2101	Kawm Umbu	70,600	23.00	16,200	85.58	B	127,000	On Nile River north of Aswan. D=COC.

Table 10-5–continued overleaf

Table 10-5–continued

Rec No 1	Country City 2	Pop 2000 3	AC% 4	Church Members 5	E% 6	W 7	Pop 2025 8	Notes 9
2102	Maghaghah	68,800	24.00	16,500	86.58	B	124,000	Al-Minya on Nile River north of Bani Mazar. Railroad, cotton ginning, wood, sugar milling, livestock. D=COC.
2103	Mallawi	134,000	25.00	33,600	87.58	B	241,000	Al-Minya on Nile River south of al-Minya. Farming region, railroad, textiles, handicrafts. D=COC.
2104	Manfalut	71,300	30.00	21,400	92.58	B	128,000	Asyut on Nile River north of Asyut. Pottery, cereals, wood carving, weaving, wool, dates. D=COC.
2105	Marsa Matruh	58,500	2.00	1,200	64.58	B	105,000	Matruh on Mediterranean Sea. Gas, oil fields, railroad, major tourist resorts. 98% Muslim.
2106	Minuf	94,700	8.00	7,600	70.58	B	170,000	Al-Minufiyah. Cotton ginning, agricultural trade center, corn, grain, cotton, dairy products.
2107	Mit Ghamir	135,000	10.00	13,500	72.58	B	244,000	Ad-Daqahliyah across Damietta Branch of Nile River from Zifta. Cotton ginning, cotton-seed oil.
2108	Zifta	93,600	10.00	9,400	72.58	B	168,000	Al-Gharbiyah on Damietta Branch of Nile River. Cotton center, cereals, rice, fruits.
2109	Qalyub (Kalyub)	117,000	8.00	9,400	70.58	B	211,000	Al-Qalyubiyah. Cotton, Silk weaving. F=AD 641 from ruins of Heliopolis. Great Mosque (1182).
2110	Qina (Qena)	162,000	11.00	17,900	73.58	B	292,000	Capital of Qina. Market town. Porous clay water vessels. Many ancient ruins, pottery, sugarcane, grains.
2111	Rashid (Rosetta)	70,500	8.00	5,600	70.58	B	127,000	Al-Buhayrah on Rosetta Branch of Nile River. Rice milling, fish processing. Rosetta stone found here.
2112	Rummanah	67,800	2.00	1,400	64.58	B	122,000	Sinai Peninsula near Pelusium Bay on Mediterranean Sea. 98% Muslim.
2113	Samalut	84,600	26.00	22,000	88.58	B	152,000	Al-Minya on Nile River north of al-Minya. Woolen milling, sugar milling, cotton, cereals, railroad. D=COC.
2114	Saqiyat Makki	69,200	20.00	13,800	82.58	B	124,000	Al-Jizah on Nile River just south of al-Jizah. Opposite Cairo. D=COC.
2115	Sawhaj (Sohag, Suhag)	180,000	32.10	57,800	94.68	B	324,000	Capital of Sawhaj. Market town. Porous clay water vessels. Cotton ginning, 2 Coptic monasteries, silk. D=COC.
2116	Shibin al-Kawm (Shebin-El-Kom)	180,000	11.70	21,000	74.28	B	324,000	Capital of Al-Minutiyah. Textiles, cigarettes, irrigates rich alluvial region. Agricultural market, cotton processing.
2117	Sinnuris	75,000	18.00	13,500	80.58	B	135,000	Al-Fayyum north of al-Fayyum. Railroad, cotton ginning, dyeing, cereals, sugarcane, fruits. D=COC.
2118	Tahta	79,300	24.00	19,000	86.58	B	143,000	On Nile River south of Asyut. Railroad, wood weaving, dairying, cotton, cereals, dates, sugar. D=COC.
2119	Tanta	453,000	10.80	48,900	73.38	B	815,000	Capital of al-Gharbiyah. Oil, cotton. Tanta Institute (1276). Arab pilgrimage center. Coptic bishopric (1895).
2120	Tima	64,000	25.00	16,000	87.58	B	115,000	Sohag. On Nile River south of Asyut. Railroad, cotton ginning, pottery, dairying, cereals, dates. D=COC.
	EL SALVADOR	**6,276,000**	**97.16**	**6,098,000**	**99.90**	**C**	**9,062,000**	**ROMAN CATHOLICS 91.1%, INDEPENDENTS 11.3%. PENT-CHAR 23.5%, EVANGELICAL 6.7%, GCC 8.1%**
2121	rural areas	3,350,000	98.18	3,289,000	99.86	C	3,685,000	63.4% (1950), 60.6% (1970), 56.1% (1990), 53.3% (2000), 49.0% (2010), 40.6% (2025)
2122	urban areas	2,927,000	96.00	2,809,000	99.94	C	5,378,000	36.5% (1950), 39.4% (1970), 43.8% (1990), 46.6% (2000), 50.9% (2010), 59.3% (2025)
2123	non-metropolitan areas	1,132,000	96.51	1,092,000	99.94	C	2,231,734	*Sources of data:* Censuses of 1950, 1961, 1971, and 1992; estimate for 1982.
2124	metropolitan areas	1,795,000	95.68	1,717,000	99.94	C	3,146,000	*Definition:* Administrative centers of municipalities.
2125	Nueva San Salvador (Santa Tecla)	72,800	96.50	70,200	99.94	C	134,000	Densely settled agricultural region. Salvadorean Institute for Coffee Research. F=1854. D=RCC.
2126	San Miguel	120,000	96.00	115,000	99.94	C	221,000	Capital of San Miguel at foot of San Miguel volcano (6,057 ft.). Textiles, rope, leather. F=1530. D=RCC.
2127	SAN SALVADOR	1,415,000	95.50	1,351,000	99.94	C	2,448,000	At foot of San Salvador volcano (6,398). Financial center. Textiles, clothing, leather. F=1525. D=RCC.
2128	Delgado	91,800	96.00	88,100	99.94	C	169,000	East of downtown. Pottery making. Formed in 1935 by union of 3 adjoining towns. D=RCC.
2129	Mejicanos	124,000	95.50	118,000	99.84	C	228,000	North of downtown. Residential, 2 miles north of San Salvador. D=RCC.
2130	Soyapango	81,400	95.50	77,700	99.84	C	149,000	East near the airport. Inter-American Hwy. Grain, sugarcane, poultry farming. D=RCC.
2131	Santa Ana	187,000	96.50	180,000	99.94	C	344,000	Capital of Santa Ana near Santa Ana volcano (7,828 ft.). Coffee, alcohol, cotton. Historic churches. D=RCC.
	EQUATORIAL GUINEA	**453,000**	**87.20**	**395,000**	**98.57**	**C**	**795,000**	**ROMAN CATHOLICS 86.3%, INDEPENDENTS 3.9%. PENT-CHAR 5.5%, EVANGELICAL 2.4%, GCC 14.0%**
2132	rural areas	234,000	89.24	209,000	99.69	C	268,000	84.0% (1950), 73.2% (1970), 64.2% (1990), 51.7% (2000), 42.0% (2010), 33.6% (2025)
2133	urban areas	218,000	85.00	185,000	97.37	C	527,000	16.0% (1950), 26.7% (1970), 35.7% (1990), 48.2% (2000), 57.9% (2010), 66.3% (2025)
2134	non-metropolitan areas	86,200	85.00	73,300	97.37	C	208,166	*Sources of data:* Censuses of 1950, 1960, and 1983; estimate for 1991.
2135	metropolitan areas	132,000	85.00	112,000	97.37	C	319,000	*Definition:* Urban centers.
2136	MALABO (Santa Isabel)	132,000	85.00	112,000	97.37	C	319,000	Bioko Island. Cocoa, timber, coffee. Volcano. Beaches. 60% Bubi, Fang. D=RCC,SDA.
	ERITREA	**3,850,000**	**50.24**	**1,934,000**	**73.57**	**B**	**6,681,000**	**ORTHODOX 46.0%, ROMAN CATHOLICS 3.3%. PENT-CHAR 0.9%, EVANGELICAL 0.3%, GCC 7.4%**
2137	rural areas	3,129,000	51.22	1,602,000	73.63	B	4,512,000	94.1% (1950), 88.9% (1970), 84.2% (1990), 81.2% (2000), 76.7% (2010), 67.5% (2025)
2138	urban areas	722,000	46.00	332,000	73.33	B	2,169,000	5.9% (1950), 11.0% (1970), 15.8% (1990), 18.7% (2000), 23.2% (2010), 32.4% (2025)
2139	non-metropolitan areas	228,000	45.99	105,000	73.32	B	685,784	*Sources of data:* Census of 1984; estimates for 1950, 1967, and 1989.
2140	metropolitan areas	493,000	46.00	227,000	73.33	B	1,483,000	*Definition:* Localities with 2,000 or more inhabitants.
2141	ASMERA (Asmara)	440,000	45.40	200,000	72.73	B	1,323,000	Former hamlet of Tigrai people. Textiles, footwear. 50% Christian, 50% Muslim. D=Orthodox,RCC.
2142	Assab (Aseb)	53,100	51.00	27,100	78.33	B	160,000	Red Sea port on Assab Bay. Petroleum refinery, saltworks, water distillation. D=Orthodox,RCC.
	ESTONIA	**1,396,000**	**37.95**	**530,000**	**98.07**	**B**	**1,131,000**	**PROTESTANTS 17.1%, ORTHODOX 16.4%. PENT-CHAR 4.3%, EVANGELICAL 5.1%, GCC 20.9%**
2143	rural areas	359,000	29.14	105,000	97.93	B	211,000	50.3% (1950), 35.0% (1970), 28.2% (1990), 25.7% (2000), 22.8% (2010), 18.6% (2025)
2144	urban areas	1,037,000	41.00	425,000	98.12	B	921,000	49.6% (1950), 64.9% (1970), 71.8% (1990), 74.3% (2000), 77.1% (2010), 81.3% (2025)
2145	non-metropolitan areas	268,000	40.17	108,000	98.56	B	238,042	*Sources of data:* Census of 1959, 1970, 1979, and 1989.
2146	metropolitan areas	769,000	41.29	318,000	97.97	B	683,000	*Definition:* Cities and urban-type localities according to the criteria of number of inhabitants.
2147	Kohtla-Jarve	71,000	43.00	30,600	99.12	B	63,100	Near Gulf of Finland. Oil shale processing, petroleum products, fertilizer. F=1900. D=EAOC,Lutheran.
2148	Narva	78,900	43.00	33,900	99.12	B	70,100	On Narva River 9 miles from Gulf of Finland. Cotton textile center. F=1223 by Danes. D=EAOC,Lutheran.
2149	Parnu	51,500	42.00	21,700	98.62	B	45,800	At mouth of Darnu River on Gulf of Riga. Holiday resort, leather. F=1251(Hanseatic League). D=EAOC,Lutheran.
2150	TALLINN (Revel)	458,000	40.00	183,000	97.12	B	406,000	On Gulf of Finland. Major commercial & fishing port, shipbuilding. F=c1000 BC. D=EAOC,Lutheran.
2151	Tartu (Dorpat)	110,000	44.00	48,300	99.62	B	97,300	Old university city on Emajogi River. F=5th century. 13th century cathedral. D=EAOC,Lutheran.
	ETHIOPIA	**62,565,000**	**49.81**	**31,161,000**	**84.48**	**B**	**115,382,000**	**ORTHODOX 36.5%, PROTESTANTS 13.6%. PENT-CHAR 6.5%, EVANGELICAL 10.5%, GCC 15.5%**
2152	rural areas	51,522,000	47.30	24,370,000	83.22	B	78,425,000	95.4% (1950), 91.4% (1970), 86.5% (1990), 82.3% (2000), 77.1% (2010), 67.9% (2025)
2153	urban areas	11,043,000	61.50	6,791,000	90.37	C	36,957,000	4.6% (1950), 8.6% (1970), 13.4% (1990), 17.6% (2000), 22.8% (2010), 32.0% (2025)
2154	non-metropolitan areas	6,917,000	61.40	4,247,000	90.38	C	23,167,799	*Sources of data:* Census of 1984; estimates for 1950, 1967, and 1989.
2155	metropolitan areas	4,126,000	61.66	2,544,000	90.36	C	13,789,000	*Definition:* Localities with 2,000 or more inhabitants.
2156	ADIS ABEBA (Addis Ababa)	3,112,000	70.00	2,178,000	98.17	C	10,395,000	Educational center. F=1887. 45% Amharic, 25% Oromo, 15% Tigre. 430 house churches. 'New Flower'. D=EOC.
2157	Akaki Beseka	89,000	70.00	62,300	98.17	C	298,000	South near the airport. Textiles. D=EOC.
2158	Bahir Dar	90,500	30.00	27,200	57.67	B	303,000	Gojam at southern end of Lake Tana. Tis-Abay Falls. Coffee, cereals, fishing, industry. D=EOC.
2159	Debre Zeyit	84,500	45.00	38,000	79.67	B	283,000	Shewa southeast of Adis Abeba. Formerly Emperor's summer residence. Cereals, vegetables. D=EOC.
2160	Dese (Dessye, Dessie)	116,000	40.00	46,500	74.67	B	389,000	7,500 ft. Amharic: Market for grains, oilseeds, hides, honey. Artisan industries. 'My Joy'. D=EOC.
2161	Dire Dawa	161,000	30.00	48,400	57.67	B	540,000	Historically a caravan center. Textiles, cement, coffee, meats. Oromo, Somali, Afars, Arabs. 'Empty Plain'. D=EOC.
2162	Gonder (Gondar)	133,000	60.00	79,700	94.67	C	444,000	Capital of Gonder. 7,500 ft. Subsistence farming. Center of Ethiopian Church. Muslims, Falashas. D=EOC.
2163	Harer (Harar)	103,000	30.00	30,800	57.67	B	343,000	6,000 ft. Coffee, grain, basket weaving. Ancient walled city. Hareri (adeve), Oromo, Amharas, Somalis. D=EOC.
2164	Jima (Jimma)	101,000	40.00	40,400	74.67	B	338,000	Capital of Kefa. Coffee, potassium & sodium nitrate mines. 5,740 ft. in forested region. D=EOC.
2165	Mekele (Makalle)	99,600	30.00	29,900	57.67	B	333,000	Capital of Tigre. Principal center of salt trade, incense, resin. 6,778 ft. D=EOC.
2166	Nazret (Nazareth)	125,000	20.00	25,100	44.67	A	419,000	Shewa. Sugar, civet cats, oil cakes, oilseeds, pulses. Hot springs. D=EOC.
	FAEROE ISLANDS	**42,700**	**92.61**	**39,600**	**99.93**	**C**	**36,600**	**PROTESTANTS 90.9%, INDEPENDENTS 0.9%. PENT-CHAR 6.9%, EVANGELICAL 17.5%, GCC 27.5%**
2167	rural areas	27,900	92.40	25,800	99.94	C	17,900	82.5% (1950), 72.1% (1970), 69.8% (1990), 65.2% (2000), 58.6% (2010), 48.9% (2025)
2168	urban areas	14,800	93.00	13,800	99.92	C	18,700	17.4% (1950), 27.8% (1970), 30.1% (1990), 34.7% (2000), 41.3% (2010), 51.0% (2025)
2169	non-metropolitan areas	–	–	–	–	–	–	*Sources of data:* Censuses of 1950, 1955, 1960, 1966, 1970, and 1977
2170	metropolitan areas	15,100	93.00	14,100	99.92	C	19,000	*Definition:* Torshavn.
2171	THORSHAVN (Torshavn)	15,100	93.00	14,100	99.92	C	19,000	Southern tip of Streymoy Island. Fish and whale processing, dairying, tourism. D=Lutheran.
	FALKLAND ISLANDS	**2,300**	**79.07**	**1,800**	**99.78**	**C**	**2,500**	**ANGLICANS 36.5%, PROTESTANTS 29.2%. PENT-CHAR 13.3%, EVANGELICAL 15.0%, GCC 33.5%**
2172	rural areas	230	79.66	190	99.94	C	110	55.7% (1950), 46.0% (1970), 25.5% (1990), 10.3% (2000), 5.6% (2010), 4.2% (2025)
2173	urban areas	2,000	79.00	1,600	99.76	C	2,400	44.2% (1950), 53.9% (1970), 74.4% (1990), 89.6% (2000), 94.3% (2010), 95.7% (2025)
2174	non-metropolitan areas	720	78.94	570	99.74	C	850	*Sources of data:* Censuses of 1972, 1980, 1986, and 1991.
2175	metropolitan areas	1,300	79.03	1,000	99.77	C	1,500	*Definition:* Stanley.
2176	STANLEY (Port Stanley)	1,300	79.00	1,000	99.76	C	1,500	Base for Antarctic whaling operations. Exports wool, sheepskins, seal oil. Penguin rookeries. D=Anglican.
	FIJI	**817,000**	**56.28**	**460,000**	**88.78**	**B**	**1,104,000**	**PROTESTANTS 45.9%, INDEPENDENTS 10.5%. PENT-CHAR 22.6%, EVANGELICAL 13.0%, GCC 12.8%**
2177	rural areas	471,000	57.22	270,000	89.14	B	480,000	75.6% (1950), 65.2% (1970), 60.7% (1990), 57.6% (2000), 52.6% (2010), 43.5% (2025)
2178	urban areas	346,000	55.00	190,000	88.30	B	624,000	24.3% (1950), 34.7% (1970), 39.2% (1990), 42.3% (2000), 47.3% (2010), 56.4% (2025)
2179	non-metropolitan areas	130,000	54.98	71,500	88.30	B	234,699	*Sources of data:* Censuses of 1956, 1966, 1976, and 1986.
2180	metropolitan areas	216,000	55.01	119,000	88.30	B	389,000	*Definition:* Places with a population of 1,000 or more.
2181	Lautoka	46,700	50.00	23,400	82.50	B	84,300	Viti Levu island. Sugarcane. Originally called Namoli. Inter-island cruises. Indian shopkeepers. D=Methodist,RCC.
2182	SUVA	169,000	56.40	95,300	89.90	B	305,000	Viti Levu island shipping port. Tourism. F=1849. University of the South Pacific. D=Methodist,RCC.
	FINLAND	**5,176,000**	**88.48**	**4,579,000**	**99.71**	**C**	**5,254,000**	**PROTESTANTS 89.5%, INDEPENDENTS 1.5%. PENT-CHAR 12.8%, EVANGELICAL 14.3%, GCC 19.9%**
2183	rural areas	1,812,000	93.08	1,686,000	99.86	C	1,334,000	67.9% (1950), 49.7% (1970), 38.5% (1990), 35.0% (2000), 31.1% (2010), 25.4% (2025)
2184	urban areas	3,364,000	86.00	2,893,000	99.63	C	3,919,000	32.0% (1950), 50.2% (1970), 61.4% (1990), 65.0% (2000), 68.8% (2010), 74.6% (2025)
2185	non-metropolitan areas	992,000	85.89	852,000	99.44	C	1,215,157	*Sources of data:* Censuses of 1950, 1960, 1970, 1975, 1980, and 1990.
2186	metropolitan areas	2,373,000	86.05	2,042,000	99.71	C	2,704,000	*Definition:* Urban communes.
2187	HELSINKI (Helsingfors)	1,163,000	85.00	989,000	99.63	C	1,295,000	Seaport on excellent harbor. Shipyards, printing. F=1550 by Swedes. Great Church (1832). D=Lutheran.
2188	Espoo (Esbo)	182,000	85.00	154,000	99.63	C	212,000	West on Gulf of Finland. Institute of Technology. Prehistoric origins. Granite Church (15th century). D=Lutheran.
2189	Vaanta (Vanda)	163,000	85.00	138,000	99.63	C	189,000	Northeast near airport. Commercial & tourist hub. F=1974. St. Lauri Church (13th century). D=Lutheran.
2190	Jyvaskyla	97,000	90.00	87,300	99.93	C	113,000	Capital of Keksi-Suomi. Educational center. Paper & plywood mills. F=1837. D=Lutheran.
2191	Kotka	58,400	92.00	53,700	99.93	C	68,000	Kymi. Lumber, pulp, cellulose, phosphate, petroleum. F=1878. Greek Orthodox Church (1795). D=Lutheran.
2192	Kouvola	55,600	91.00	50,600	99.93	C	64,800	Capital of Kymi. Kymijoki River. Pulp and paper milling center, natural gas pipeline. D=Lutheran.
2193	Kuopio	84,300	90.00	75,900	99.93	C	98,200	Capital of Kuopio. Wood production, flour, tourism. F=1653. Center for Finnish Orthodox Church. D=Lutheran.
2194	Lahti	112,000	88.00	98,200	99.73	C	130,000	Hame on shores of Lake Vesijarvi. Furniture, radio & TV production, winter sports. F=1878. D=Lutheran.
2195	Lappeenranta	57,200	89.00	50,900	99.83	C	66,700	Kymi. Major harbor. Sulphuric acid, lumber, lime, cement, mineral baths. F=1649. D=Lutheran.
2196	Oulu	126,000	87.00	110,000	99.73	C	147,000	Capital of Oulu. Wood tar, lumber, flour, shipyards. F=1590. Educational center. Bishopric (1906). D=Lutheran.
2197	Pori	79,000	87.00	68,700	99.73	C	92,000	Turkuja Pori. Seaport exports wood & lumber. Nickel, copper. F=c1150. D=Lutheran.
2198	Tampere (Tammerfors)	249,000	84.00	209,000	99.83	C	290,000	Hameen. Textiles, leather, lumber. F=1779. Cathedral (1907). Messukyla Stone Church. D=Lutheran.
2199	Turku (Abo)	236,000	85.00	200,000	99.63	C	275,000	Capital of Turku ja Pori. Cradle of Finnish culture. Naval shipyards. F=c1200. Cathedral (1290). D=Lutheran.
2200	Vaasa (Vasa)	55,600	87.00	48,300	99.73	C	64,700	Capital of Vaasa. Exports timber, raw materials; flour, textiles. F=1606. 66% Finns, 34% Swedes. D=Lutheran.
	FRANCE	**59,080,000**	**69.60**	**41,117,000**	**96.30**	**C**	**61,662,000**	**ROMAN CATHOLICS 82.2%, INDEPENDENTS 2.2%. PENT-CHAR 2.4%, EVANGELICAL 0.4%, GCC 41.5%**
2201	rural areas	14,433,000	77.63	11,204,000	99.07	C	11,074,000	43.8% (1950), 28.9% (1970), 25.9% (1990), 24.4% (2000), 22.0% (2010), 17.9% (2025)
2202	urban areas	44,647,000	67.00	29,913,000	95.40	C	50,587,000	56.1% (1950), 71.0% (1970), 74.0% (1990), 75.5% (2000), 77.9% (2010), 82.0% (2025)
2203	non-metropolitan areas	14,398,000	67.44	9,710,000	95.40	C	17,890,897	*Sources of data:* Censuses of 1954, 1962, 1968, 1975, 1982, and 1990.
2204	metropolitan areas	30,249,000	66.79	20,203,000	95.40	C	32,696,000	*Definition:* Communes containing an agglomeration of more than 2,000 inhabitants living in contiguous houses.
2205	Aix-en-Provence	129,000	68.00	87,600	94.70	C	146,000	Bouches-du-Rhone. Residential suburb of Marseille. Olives. F=123 BC. Birthplace of Cezanne (1839). D=RCC.

Table 10-5–continued opposite

Table 10-5–continued

Rec No 1	Country City 2	Pop 2000 3	AC% 4	Church Members 5	E% 6	W 7	Pop 2025 8	Notes 9
2206	Ajaccio	60,700	73.00	44,300	99.70	C	68,800	Capital of Corse-du-Sud on West coast of Corsica. Tourism, shipping. D=RCC.
2207	Albi	56,600	73.00	41,300	99.70	C	64,100	Capital of Tarn. Medieval center. Tourism, cement, dyes. Sainte-Cecile cathedral (1277). D=RCC.
2208	Ales	80,000	73.00	58,400	99.70	C	90,600	Gard. Chemicals, coal, metalwork, textiles, cattle feed, wine. F=1200. D=RCC.
2209	Amiens	162,000	68.00	110,000	94.70	C	184,000	Capital of Somme. Notre-Dame Cathedral, largest Gothic cathedral in France. Y=c350; St. Firmin. D=RCC.
2210	Angers	217,000	68.00	147,000	94.70	C	246,000	Capital of Maine-et-Loire on Maine River. Slate, ropes. 12th century Cathedral of Mt. Maurice. D=RCC.
2211	Angouleme	107,000	68.00	72,800	94.70	C	121,000	Capital of Charente on Charente River. Papermaking, felt. F=507. Cathedral of Saint-Pierre (1105). D=RCC.
2212	Annecy	132,000	62.00	81,800	88.70	C	149,000	Haute-Savoie on Lake Annecy. 20 miles south of Geneva. Tourist resort. 12th century castle. D=RCC.
2213	Arles	56,500	73.00	41,300	99.70	C	64,000	Bouches-du-Rhone on Grand Rhone River. Home of painters Van Gogh & Gaugin. 11th cent church. D=RCC.
2214	Armentieres	60,100	73.00	43,900	99.70	C	68,100	Nord on Lys River. Flax, printing, dyes, clothing. F=BC 57. Rebuilt after WWI. D=RCC.
2215	Arras	82,800	73.00	60,500	99.70	C	93,900	Capital of Pas-de-Calais on Scarpe River. Metals, textiles. Roman origins. Episcopal see (500). D=RCC.
2216	Avignon	189,000	68.00	128,000	94.70	C	214,000	Capital of Vaucluse on Rhone River. Wine, flour, dye. Medieval papal center. Annual theatre festivals. D=RCC.
2217	Bastia	54,600	73.00	39,800	99.70	C	61,800	Capital of Haute-Corse. Cigarettes, preserves. F=1383. D=RCC.
2218	Bayonne	171,000	68.00	116,000	94.70	C	194,000	Pyrenees-Atlantiques. Oil, natural gas, tuna. Cathedral de Sainte-Marie (13th cent). D=RCC.
2219	Beauvais	60,100	73.00	43,800	99.70	C	68,000	Capital of Oise. Carpets, blankets. Roman origins. Cathedral of Saint-Pierre (10th century). D=RCC.
2220	Belfort	81,000	73.00	59,100	99.70	C	91,800	Capital of Territoire de Belfort. Electrical, metals, textiles. Important fortress town. F=1307. D=RCC.
2221	Besancon	128,000	68.00	86,800	94.70	C	145,000	Capital of Doubs. Archbishopric from 2nd century. University (1422). Birthplace of V. Hugo (1802). D=RCC.
2222	Bethune	272,000	72.00	196,000	98.70	C	308,000	Pas-de-Calais. Automobiles. F=c1150. 14th century belfry. D=RCC.
2223	Beziers	79,400	73.00	58,000	99.70	C	90,000	Herault. Alcohol, fertilizers. Town massacred by Simon de Montfort (1209). D=RCC.
2224	Blois	67,800	73.00	49,500	99.70	C	76,800	Capital of Loir-et-Cher on Loire River. 17th century cathedral. Tourism, corn, chocolate. D=RCC.
2225	Bordeaux	791,000	70.00	554,000	96.70	C	896,000	Capital of Gironde on Garonne River. Wine, shipping, trade. Celtic origins. University of Bordeaux. D=RCC.
2226	Merignac	59,600	70.00	41,700	96.70	C	67,500	Gironde east near airport. Produces diverse consumer goods, pharmaceuticals, Bordeaux airport. D=RCC.
2227	Pessac	53,100	70.00	37,200	96.70	C	60,200	Site of Gallo-Roman villa of patrician Pesus. Noted for red wines. D=RCC.
2228	Boulogne-sur-Mer	95,000	68.00	64,600	94.70	C	108,000	Pas-de-Calais. English channel port. Fishing, canneries. Known for herring catches. Ancient Roman port. D=RCC.
2229	Bourg-en-Bresse	58,100	73.00	42,400	99.70	C	65,800	Capital of Ain. Manufacturing, trade, tourism. F=c1100. 16th century Gothic cathedral. D=RCC.
2230	Bourges	98,600	73.00	72,000	99.70	C	112,000	Capital of Cher. Market center. St. Ursin brought Christianity in 3rd century. Roman Avaricum. D=RCC.
2231	Brest	210,000	68.00	143,000	94.70	C	238,000	Port city of Finistere. Navy, metals, precision mechanics. F=1240. D=RCC.
2232	Brive-la-Gaillarde	67,000	73.00	48,900	99.70	C	75,900	Correze. Agricultural market. St. Anthony of Padua monastery (1226). D=RCC.
2233	Bruay-en-Artois (Bruay-la-BuisseÇre)	25,900	68.00	17,600	94.70	C	29,400	Pas-de-Calais west of Lille. Once a coal mining center, now textile and construction industry. D=RCC.
2234	Caen	199,000	68.00	136,000	94.70	C	226,000	Capital of Calvados on Orne River. Import/export, steel. Saint-Etienne (1060). Church of St. Nicholas. D=RCC.
2235	Calais	106,000	68.00	72,000	94.70	C	120,000	Industrial seaport, Pas-de-Calais. Lace, channel crossing, mail. D=RCC.
2236	Cambrai	50,100	73.00	36,600	99.70	C	56,800	Nord on Escaut River. Center of farming district, textiles. Rights from bishop (1227). D=RCC.
2237	Cannes	349,000	70.00	245,000	96.70	C	396,000	Resort city of French Riviera. Tourism, International Film Festival. Monks of Lerins (10th century). D=RCC.
2238	Antibes	65,800	71.00	46,700	97.70	C	74,600	Originally Greek trading post Antipolis. Tourism, flowers. D=RCC.
2239	Carcassonne	45,200	73.00	33,000	99.70	C	51,300	Capital of Aude on Aude River. Farm trade center. Tourism. Church of Saint-Vincent (13th century). D=RCC.
2240	Castres	48,400	73.00	35,300	99.70	C	54,800	Tarn on Agout River. Textiles, machine tools. Founded around Benedictine monastery (647). D=RCC.
2241	Chalon-sur-Saone	80,900	73.00	59,100	99.70	C	91,700	Saone-et-Loire. River port, manufacturing town, iron, steel. D=RCC.
2242	Chalons-sur-Marne	64,000	73.00	46,700	99.70	C	72,500	Capital of Marne. Hat-making, paper-making, confectionaries. D=RCC.
2243	Chambery	107,000	68.00	73,100	94.70	C	122,000	Capital of Savoie. Metals, glass, confectionaries. D=RCC.
2244	Charleville-Mezieres	69,900	73.00	51,100	99.70	C	79,300	Joint capital of Ardennes on Meuse River. Cranes, agriculture. D=RCC.
2245	Chartres	89,400	71.00	63,500	97.70	C	101,000	Capital of Eure-et-Loir on Eure River. Market town. Famous Notre Dame cathedral (c1150). D=RCC.
2246	Chateauroux	69,800	73.00	51,000	99.70	C	79,100	Capital of Indre. Agriculture, metal equipment, chemicals, paper. D=RCC.
2247	Chatellerault	37,800	74.00	28,000	99.90	C	42,800	Vienne on Vienne River. Armaments, cutlery. Descartes' childhood home. D=RCC.
2248	Cherbourg	95,800	73.00	69,900	99.70	C	109,000	Naval station & seaport, Manche. Channel traffic, yachting, fishing. D=RCC.
2249	Cholet	57,400	73.00	41,900	99.70	C	65,000	Maine-et-Loire on Moine River. Cattle market, agriculture. F=c1050. D=RCC.
2250	Clermont-Ferrand	265,000	72.00	191,000	98.70	C	300,000	Capital of Puy-de-Dome on Tiretaine River. St. Austremanius (c250). Crusades launched 1095. D=RCC.
2251	Colmar	87,200	73.00	63,700	99.70	C	98,800	Capital of Haut-Rhin. Tourism, wines, metals. F=800. Collegiate Church of St. Martin (1235). D=RCC.
2252	Compiegne	69,800	73.00	50,900	99.70	C	79,100	Oise. Tourism, petroleum, metals. F=557. 13th century churches. D=RCC.
2253	Creil	85,400	73.00	62,400	99.70	C	96,800	Oise on Oise River. Metal works, railroad workshops. Gothic church Saint-Medard. D=RCC.
2254	Dijon	240,000	70.00	168,000	96.70	C	272,000	Capital of Cote d'Or. Market & tourist town. Mustard. Ancient origins. University of Dijon (1722). D=RCC.
2255	Douai (Douay)	208,000	72.00	150,000	98.70	C	235,000	Nord on Scarpe River. Coal-mining center, chemicals, university town. D=RCC.
2256	Dunkerque (Dunkirk)	199,000	71.00	141,000	97.70	C	225,000	Seaport in Nord. Import/export, ferry service, oil, metals. F=1067. D=RCC.
2257	Elbeuf	56,100	73.00	40,900	99.70	C	63,500	Seine-Maritime on Seine river. Traditional center for wool & cloth manufacture. D=RCC.
2258	Epinal	64,700	72.00	46,600	98.70	C	73,300	Capital of Vosges on Moselle River. Cotton, rubber, textiles, printing. F=10th century monastery. D=RCC.
2259	Evreux	60,300	73.00	44,000	99.70	C	68,400	Eure on Iton River. Normandy, Notre Dame Cathedral. Industrial center, pharmaceuticals, printing. D=RCC.
2260	Evry	47,400	74.00	35,100	99.90	C	53,700	Essonne south of Paris on Seine River. Aeronautical equipment. Resurrection cathedral(20th century). D=RCC.
2261	Forbach	103,000	73.00	75,000	99.70	C	116,000	Moselle. Mining equipment, cokery, saar coal basin, specialty coke ovens, petrochemicals, metals. D=RCC.
2262	Frejus	77,000	73.00	56,200	99.70	C	87,200	Var. Tourism, wine, peaches. F=50 BC as naval base. 5th century baptistery. D=RCC.
2263	Grenoble	421,000	70.00	295,000	96.70	C	477,000	Capital of Isere on Isere River. Surrounded by the Alps. University (1339). 10th century cathedral. D=RCC.
2264	Hagondange	117,000	71.00	82,800	97.70	C	132,000	Moselle on Moselle River north of Metz. Steel mill, located in the iron mining district. D=RCC.
2265	La Rochelle	104,000	68.00	71,000	94.70	C	118,000	Atlantic seaport & capital of Charente-Maritime. Fishing, import/export. D=RCC.
2266	Laval	59,200	73.00	43,200	99.70	C	67,000	Capital of Mayenne. Textiles (linen & cotton), shoes. 10th century cathedral. D=RCC.
2267	Le Havre	264,000	72.00	190,000	98.70	C	299,000	Seaport, Seine-Maritime. Machinery, automobiles, rope, timber, transatlantic passenger liners. F=1517. D=RCC.
2268	Le Mans	197,000	68.00	134,000	94.70	C	223,000	Capital of Sarthe. Plastics, automobile race. Pre-Roman origins. Evangelized by St. Julian (c250). D=RCC.
2269	Lens	336,000	70.00	235,000	96.70	C	381,000	Pas-de-Calais. Center of coal mining & industry. D=RCC.
2270	Lille	991,000	66.00	654,000	92.70	C	1,031,000	Capital of Nord. Traditional textile center. RCC university. F=1030. Two 15th century churches. D=RCC.
2271	Roubaix	102,000	67.00	68,200	93.70	C	115,000	Industrial town. Over 200 textile factories, mail-order sales, chemicals. F=1469. D=RCC.
2272	Tourcoing	97,600	68.00	66,400	94.70	C	111,000	Center for wool and cotton textiles. Soap, sugar. F=1491. Seriously damaged in WWI. D=RCC.
2273	Villeneuve-d'Ascq	68,000	67.00	45,500	93.70	C	77,000	Nord. East near Belgian border. Created in 1970 by combining suburbs. Art museums. D=RCC.
2274	Wattrelos	45,500	68.00	30,900	94.70	C	51,500	Known as Waterloz in 1030. Textiles, chemicals, metals, wool and cotton. D=RCC.
2275	Limoges	177,000	68.00	120,000	94.70	C	201,000	Capital of Haute-Vienne on Vienne River. Porcelain. Destroyed by Edward (1370). Y=c250 by St. Martial. D=RCC.
2276	Longwy	43,000	73.00	31,400	99.70	C	48,700	Meurthe-et-Moselle. Heavy industry center in iron-mining area. Lorraine iron and steel industry. D=RCC.
2277	Lorient	120,000	68.00	81,700	94.70	C	136,000	Maritime town in Morbihan. Fish cannery, shipbuilding. F=17th century. D=RCC.
2278	Lyon (Lyons)	1,359,000	66.00	897,000	92.70	C	1,407,000	Capital of Rhone on Rhone & Saone rivers. Renaissance architecture. Medical center. F=43 BC. Y=c150. D=RCC.
2279	Villeurbanne	122,000	67.00	81,500	93.70	C	138,000	Metallurgy, chemicals, rayon. First skyscrapers in France. University, theatre. D=RCC.
2280	Macon	48,600	73.00	35,500	99.70	C	55,100	Capital of Saone-et-Loire. Communications center. Episcopal see from 536-1790. D=RCC.
2281	Mantes-la-Jolie	46,900	68.00	31,900	94.70	C	53,200	Yvelines west of Paris on Seine River. Industrial and trade center, beer, metalworking, musical institute. D=RCC.
2282	Marseille (Marseilles)	1,243,000	61.00	758,000	87.70	C	1,282,000	Capital of Bouches-du-Rhone. Major Mediterranean seaport. Tourism. F=c650 BC. D=RCC.
2283	Maubeuge	107,000	68.00	72,700	94.70	C	121,000	Nord. Blast furnaces, breweries, chemicals. F=c650 around Sainte-Aldegonde monastery. D=RCC.
2284	Meaux	65,600	73.00	47,900	99.70	C	74,300	Seine-et-Marne. Agricultural market center. Metals, chemicals. Episcopal see since c350. D=RCC.
2285	Melun	112,000	73.00	81,800	99.70	C	127,000	Capital of Seine-et-Marne. Mechanical, aeronautical, food-processing plants. 11th century church. D=RCC.
2286	Metz	201,000	68.00	137,000	94.70	C	228,000	Capital of Moselle. Autos, electrical equipment. Pre-Roman origins. Cathedral (1221).Y=c250. D=RCC.
2287	Montargis	55,000	73.00	40,100	99.70	C	62,300	Loiret on Canal du Loing. Poultry, dairy products, machinery, furniture, shoes, rubber goods, tanneries. D=RCC.
2288	Montbeliard	122,000	68.00	83,200	94.70	C	139,000	Doubs. Peugeot autos, museums. F=c750. Huguenot refuge during Reformation. D=RCC.
2289	Montceau-les-Mines	49,200	73.00	35,900	99.70	C	55,800	Saone-de-Loire on Canal du Centre. Coal mining, rubber tires, faucets, pipes, plastics. D=RCC.
2290	Montlucon	65,600	73.00	47,900	99.70	C	74,300	Allier on Cher River. Metals, plastics, tires, coal. Former Ursuline convent. Church of Saint Pierre. D=RCC.
2291	Montpellier	258,000	72.00	186,000	98.70	C	293,000	Capital of Herault. Tourist center, wines. French paintings. University (1220). Algerians refugees. F=900. D=RCC.
2292	Moyeuvre-Grande	9,600	73.00	7,000	99.70	C	10,900	Moselle on Orne River southwest of Thionville. Former active iron-mining center, metal works. D=RCC.
2293	Mulhouse (Mulhausen)	233,000	72.00	168,000	98.70	C	264,000	Haut-Rhin. Metal industries, chemicals, 200 botanical gardens. F=c850. 13-14th century churches. D=RCC.
2294	Nancy	343,000	72.00	247,000	98.70	C	388,000	Capital of Meucthe-et-Moselle. Chemicals, clothing, iron industry. 15th century church. F=c1050. D=RCC.
2295	Nantes	516,000	70.00	361,000	96.70	C	585,000	Capital of Loire-Atlantique on Loire River. Ancient origins. Shipbuilding, chemicals, metals, museums. D=RCC.
2296	Nevers	61,300	73.00	44,800	99.70	C	69,500	Capital of Nievre on Loire River. Machinery, rubber, ceramics. 11th century cathedral. D=RCC.
2297	Nice	538,000	68.00	366,000	94.70	C	609,000	Seaport, capital of Alpes-Maritimes. Tourist center of French Riviera. Cut flower trade. F=350 BC. D=RCC.
2298	Nimes	144,000	68.00	98,000	94.70	C	163,000	Capital of Gard. F=121 BC as Menausus. 11th cent cathedral built on ruins of temple of Apollo. D=RCC.
2299	Niort	68,500	73.00	50,000	99.70	C	77,600	Capital of Deux-Sevres. Agricultural market town, chamois leather, plywood. D=RCC.
2300	Orleans	253,000	72.00	182,000	98.70	C	287,000	Capital of Loriet. Market gardening & horticulture center. F=52 BC. Annual feast of Joan of Arc. D=RCC.
2301	PARIS	9,638,000	61.00	5,879,000	93.70	C	9,694,000	Auto & aeronautical industry, printing. Louvre museum. 12th century Notre Dame. D=RCC.
2302	Antony	60,100	64.00	38,500	90.70	C	68,100	Hauts-de-Seine south of Chateaux de Sceaux. 12th century church, University of Paris, residential. D=RCC.
2303	Argenteuil	96,900	62.00	60,100	88.70	C	110,000	Heavy industry & suburban housing. F=c650 around a convent. Basilica of Saint-Denis; robe of Christ. D=RCC.
2304	Asnieres-sur-Seine	74,800	61.00	45,600	87.70	C	84,700	Hauts-de-Seine north of Paris on Seine River. Motor vehicle assembly plant, steel rolling mill. D=RCC.
2305	Aubervilliers	70,300	63.00	44,300	89.70	C	79,700	St.-Denis north of Paris. Metals, chemicals, pharmaceuticals, leather goods, pilgrimage site. D=RCC.
2306	Aulnay-sous-Bois	85,700	61.00	52,300	87.70	C	97,100	Seine-St.-Denis near Sevran. Northeast of Paris proper. Motor vehicles, chemical industry, near airport. D=RCC.
2307	Bondy	48,600	64.00	31,100	90.70	C	55,000	Seine-St.-Denis east of Paris on Canal de l'Ourcq. Transportation equipment, forest of Bondy. D=RCC.
2308	Boulogne-Billancourt	106,000	61.00	64,600	87.70	C	120,000	Hauts-de-Seine west of Paris on Seine River. Auto factories, chemicals, electrical goods. Residential. D=RCC.
2309	Champigny-sur-Marne	82,700	62.00	51,300	88.70	C	93,700	Val-de-Marne southeast of Paris on Marne River. Museum of French resistance of WWII. D=RCC.
2310	Clamart	49,100	63.00	31,000	89.70	C	55,700	Hauts-de-Seine south of Boulogne-Billancourt. Pharmaceutical laboratories, tobacco factories, nurseries. D=RCC.
2311	Clichy	50,000	62.00	31,000	88.70	C	56,600	Northern suburb. Beaujon Hospital. Mechanical, chemical products. Saint-Vincent-de-Paul church. D=RCC.
2312	Colombes	81,700	61.00	49,800	87.70	C	92,600	Northwestern suburb. Auto tires. Yves-du-Manoir sports stadium seats 65,000. D=RCC.
2313	Courbevoie	68,000	62.00	42,200	88.70	C	77,100	Northwestern industrial suburb. High-rise buildings with flats & offices. D=RCC.
2314	Creteil	101,000	61.00	61,700	87.70	C	115,000	Val-de-Marne beyond Maisons-Alfort. Appliances. University of Paris branch, amusement park. D=RCC.
2315	Drancy	63,200	62.00	39,200	88.70	C	71,600	Northeastern industrial suburb. World War II concentration camp. Motor vehicle parts, aircraft parts. D=RCC.
2316	Epinay-sur-Seine	50,700	62.00	31,500	88.70	C	57,500	Northern suburb. Chemical industry, film studios. Originally called Spinogelum. D=RCC.
2317	Fontenay-sous-Bois	54,000	63.00	34,000	89.70	C	61,200	Val-de-Marne near Chateaux de Vincennes. Furniture, pharmaceuticals, Gothic church. D=RCC.
2318	Gennevilliers	46,600	63.00	29,400	89.70	C	52,800	Hauts-de-Seine west of Saint-Denis. Steel products, aircraft equipment, chemicals, ball bearings. D=RCC.
2319	Issy-les-Moulineaux	48,000	62.00	29,800	88.70	C	54,400	Southwestern suburb. Aeronautics, metals, chemicals, cigarettes. Quietism gathering (1694-95). D=RCC.
2320	Ivry-sur-Seine	55,800	61.00	34,000	87.70	C	63,200	Southeastern industrial suburb. Machinery, food-processing, chemicals, wood, paper. D=RCC.
2321	Le Blanc-Mesnil	48,900	62.00	30,300	88.70	C	55,400	Seine-St.-Denis east of Saint-Denis. Metal works, chemical laboratories, railroad yards. D=RCC.
2322	Levallois-Perret	49,500	62.00	30,700	88.70	C	56,100	Northwestern industrial & residential suburb. Autos, taxi garages, perfume, metro subway. D=RCC.
2323	Maisons-Alfort	55,500	63.00	35,000	89.70	C	62,900	Val-de-Marne southeast of Paris. Chemical, cement, metalworking, veterinary school. D=RCC.
2324	Meudon	47,200	62.00	29,300	88.70	C	53,500	Southwestern suburb. Machinery, aeronautical museum. Home of Richard Wagner and Auguste Rodin. D=RCC.
2325	Montreuil-sous-Bois	98,600	61.00	60,200	87.70	C	112,000	Eastern industrial suburb. Processing hides & skins, cookies, textiles. 12th century church. D=RCC.
2326	Nanterre	88,000	61.00	53,700	87.70	C	99,700	Capital of Hauts-de-Seine on Seine River. Basilica of St. Genevieve. Western industrial suburb. Autos. D=RCC.
2327	Neuilly-sur-Seine	64,300	61.00	39,200	87.70	C	72,800	Northwestern well-to-do residential suburb. American Hospital of Paris. D=RCC.
2328	Noisy-le-Grand	56,200	72.00	40,500	98.70	C	63,700	Seine-St.-Denis east of Paris. Left bank of the Marne. Rubber, paints, surgical instruments. D=RCC.
2329	Noisy-le-Sec	37,800	62.00	23,400	88.70	C	42,800	Seine-St.-Denis east of Paris. Ourcq Canal. Railroad yards, metal works, cement products. D=RCC.

Table 10-5–continued overleaf

Table 10-5–continued

Rec No 1	Country City 2	Pop 2000 3	AC% 4	Church Members 5	E% 6	W 7	Pop 2025 8	Notes 9
2330	Pantin	49,200	63.00	31,000	89.70	C	55,800	Seine-St.-Denis northeast of Paris on Canal de l'Ourcq. Consumer goods, cigarettes, chemicals. D=RCC.
2331	Paris	2,315,000	60.00	1,389,000	91.70	C	2,623,000	Central district. Eiffel Tower, hotels, banking, tourism. D=RCC.
2332	Poissy	38,200	63.00	24,100	89.70	C	43,300	Yvelines. Autos, kitchen equipment, cables. 12th century collegiate church of Notre-Dame. D=RCC.
2333	Rueil-Malmaison	69,100	62.00	42,800	88.70	C	78,300	Western residential & industrial suburb. Auto parts, film, engraving, distilling, museums. D=RCC.
2334	Saint-Denis	93,600	61.00	57,100	87.70	C	106,000	Northern suburb. Machinery assembly, electronics. 7th century abbey, important church architecture. D=RCC.
2335	Saint-Maur-des-Fosses	80,300	61.00	49,000	87.70	C	91,000	Southeastern residential suburb. Gardens. Founded around 7th century abbey. D=RCC.
2336	Saint-Ouen	44,100	62.00	27,300	88.70	C	49,900	Northern industrial suburb. Liqueur distilling, tourists, flea markets. D=RCC.
2337	Sarcelles	59,100	61.00	36,100	87.70	C	67,000	Val-d'Oise north of Saint-Denis. Light industry, pharmaceuticals, plastics. D=RCC.
2338	Versailles	91,400	61.00	55,700	87.70	C	104,000	Capital of Yvelines. Palace of Versailles, tourist center. WWI treaty signed here. D=RCC.
2339	Villejuif	50,400	62.00	31,200	88.70	C	57,100	Southern suburb. Glass, sheet metal, cancer research institute. D=RCC.
2340	Vitry-sur-Seine	85,800	61.00	52,300	87.70	C	97,200	Val-de-Marne. Southeastern residential & industrial suburb. Market gardening. D=RCC.
2341	Pau	151,000	68.00	102,000	94.70	C	171,000	Capital of Pyrenees-Atlantiques. Spa & winter sports center. Wool. F=11th century. University (1724). D=RCC.
2342	Perigueux	65,900	73.00	48,100	99.70	C	74,700	Dordogne. Hogs, truffles, wine. Saint-Front (c1150) with 50 lofty domes. D=RCC.
2343	Perpignan	164,000	68.00	112,000	94.70	C	186,000	Capital of Pyrenees-Orientales on Tet River. Wines, tourism. F=10th century. Cathedral(14th century). D=RCC.
2344	Poitiers	112,000	68.00	76,200	94.70	C	127,000	Capital of Vienne. Printing. University (1431). 4th century Baptistere Saint-Jean, oldest in France. D=RCC.
2345	Quimper	68,600	73.00	50,100	99.70	C	77,800	Capital of Finistere. Pottery, tourism. St. Corentin (5th century bishop). D=RCC.
2346	Reims (Rheims)	215,000	72.00	155,000	98.70	C	243,000	Marne. Champagne wine, aircraft, autos. 13th century Notre-Dame cathedral. Joan of Arc (1429). D=RCC.
2347	Rennes	255,000	72.00	184,000	98.70	C	289,000	Capital of Ille-et-Vilaine. Railway, autos, petroleum. Celtic origins. Archiepiscopal see. D=RCC.
2348	Roanne	80,300	73.00	58,600	99.70	C	91,000	Loire. Hatmaking, textiles, machine tooling, cotton, synthetic products, paper. F=c1050. D=RCC.
2349	Romans-sur-Isere	51,200	73.00	37,400	99.70	C	58,000	Drome on Isere River northeast of Valence. Shoes. Abbey founded by St. Bernard in 837. D=RCC.
2350	Rouen	396,000	72.00	285,000	98.70	C	448,000	Capital of Seine-Maritime. Cotton, museums. Y=c250 by Saint Mellon. Joan of Arc martyred (1431). D=RCC.
2351	Saint-Brieuc	87,300	73.00	63,700	99.70	C	98,900	Capital of Cotes-du-Nord on Gouet River. Tourism. Founded by Welsh monk, St. Briocus (c550). D=RCC.
2352	Saint-Chamond	85,100	73.00	62,100	99.70	C	96,400	Lorie on Gier River northeast of Saint-Etienne. Cereals, cattle. D=RCC.
2353	Saint-Etienne	326,000	72.00	235,000	98.70	C	369,000	Capital of Loire. Steel for arms and armor plating. In coal basin. Bicycles. 15th century church. D=RCC.
2354	Saint-Malo	50,000	73.00	36,500	99.70	C	56,700	Seaport, Ille-et-Vilaine on English Channel. Fishing. Named after Welsh monk (6th century). D=RCC.
2355	Saint-Nazaire	137,000	68.00	93,100	94.70	C	155,000	Seaport, Loire-Atlantique on Bay of Biscay. Fishing, shipbuilding. Ancient origins as Roman Carbilo. D=RCC.
2356	Saint-Quentin	74,000	73.00	54,000	99.70	C	83,900	Aisne. Wool center since Middle Ages. Named after Gaius Quentinius (3rd century martyr). D=RCC.
2357	Sartrouville	52,400	72.00	37,700	98.70	C	59,300	Yvelines on Seine River northwest of Paris. Electronics industry, industrial district, railroad. D=RCC.
2358	Sevran	50,400	71.00	35,800	97.70	C	57,200	Seine-St.-Denis. Northeast of Paris on Canal de l'Ourcq. Light mfg., wooded park east along canal. D=RCC.
2359	Soissons	48,000	73.00	35,100	99.70	C	54,400	Aisne. In rich agricultural valley. Market town for produce. Evangelized in 3rd century. D=RCC.
2360	Strasbourg	432,000	70.00	302,000	96.70	C	489,000	Capital of Bas-Rhin. Seat of the Council of Europe. Coal. Originally a Celtic village. Cathedral. D=RCC.
2361	Tarbes	80,900	73.00	59,100	99.70	C	91,700	Capital of the Hautes-Pyrenees on Adour River. Arabian horses, arsenal. D=RCC.
2362	Thionville	138,000	68.00	93,700	94.70	C	156,000	Moselle. Center of iron-mining district, heavy metallurgical industries. D=RCC.
2363	Hayange	16,300	73.00	11,900	99.70	C	18,400	Moselle. West southwest of Thionville. Metallurgical industry. D=RCC.
2364	Toulon	455,000	72.00	328,000	98.70	C	516,000	Mediterranean port, capital of Var. Naval base, shipbuilding. F=c250. 13th century cathedral. D=RCC.
2365	La Seyne-sur-Mer	62,400	72.00	44,900	98.70	C	70,700	Southwestern suburb, shipbuilding, summer & art festivals. D=RCC.
2366	Toulouse	676,000	70.00	474,000	96.70	C	766,000	Capital of Haute-Garonne on Garonne River. University (1229). Aerospace. Bishopric since 4th century. D=RCC.
2367	Tours	294,000	72.00	211,000	98.70	C	333,000	Capital of Indre-et-Loire. Tourism. Evangelized in 250 by Gatien, later by St. Martin. Archdiocese (853). D=RCC.
2368	Troyes	128,000	68.00	86,900	94.70	C	145,000	Capital of Aube on Seine River. Tire manufacturing. Y=c250. Once housed 25 churches. D=RCC.
2369	Valence	112,000	68.00	76,400	94.70	C	127,000	Capital of Drome on Rhone River. Fruits, vegetables. Bishopric from 4th century. 11th century cathedral. D=RCC.
2370	Valenciennes	352,000	72.00	254,000	98.70	C	399,000	Nord on Escaut River. Traditional fine lace industry, petroleum, autos. D=RCC.
2371	Vichy	64,100	73.00	46,800	99.70	C	72,600	Allier. Spa, alkaline springs, bottled water, sports complex, hotels, villas, entertainment, beauty products. D=RCC.
2372	Villefranche	57,500	72.00	41,400	98.70	C	65,100	Rhone on Saone River north of Lyon. Cereals, sugar beets, wines. D=RCC.
	FRENCH GUIANA	**181,000**	**84.24**	**153,000**	**98.76**	**C**	**416,000**	**ROMAN CATHOLICS 79.9%, PROTESTANTS 3.8%. PENT-CHAR 5.7%, EVANGELICAL 1.9%, GCC 13.1%**
2373	rural areas	39,700	81.52	32,300	95.71	C	64,500	46.3% (1950), 32.5% (1970), 25.3% (1990), 21.8% (2000), 18.9% (2010), 15.4% (2025)
2374	urban areas	142,000	85.00	120,000	99.62	C	352,000	53.6% (1950), 67.4% (1970), 74.6% (1990), 78.1% (2000), 81.0% (2010), 84.5% (2025)
2375	non-metropolitan areas	52,100	85.00	44,200	99.62	C	129,238	*Sources of data:* Censuses of 1954, 1961, 1967, 1982, and 1990.
2376	metropolitan areas	89,600	85.00	76,200	99.62	C	222,000	*Definition:* Urban centers.
2377	CAYENNE	89,600	85.00	76,200	99.62	C	222,000	At mouth of Cayenne River. Timber, gold, pineapples. F=1643. Pasteur Institute. D=RCC.
	FRENCH POLYNESIA	**235,000**	**84.54**	**199,000**	**98.64**	**C**	**324,000**	**PROTESTANTS 46.8%, ROMAN CATHOLICS 42.5%. PENT-CHAR 10.5%, EVANGELICAL 2.6%, GCC 13.7%**
2378	rural areas	101,000	87.90	89,000	99.36	C	105,000	69.7% (1950), 46.0% (1970), 43.6% (1990), 43.0% (2000), 39.7% (2010), 32.4% (2025)
2379	urban areas	134,000	82.00	110,000	98.10	C	219,000	30.2% (1950), 53.9% (1970), 56.3% (1990), 56.9% (2000), 60.2% (2010), 67.5% (2025)
2380	non-metropolitan areas	30,900	82.00	25,300	98.10	C	50,532	*Sources of data:* Censuses of 1962, 1971, 1977, 1983, and 1988.
2381	metropolitan areas	103,000	82.00	84,500	98.10	C	169,000	*Definition:* Places with a population of 1,000 or more.
2382	PAPEETE	103,000	82.00	84,500	98.10	C	169,000	Major stop for transpacific ships & airlines. Tourism, sugarcane, vanilla. Chinese. D=EEPF,RCC.
	GABON	**1,226,000**	**88.55**	**1,086,000**	**98.09**	**C**	**1,981,000**	**ROMAN CATHOLICS 60.7%, PROTESTANTS 19.0%. PENT-CHAR 7.3%, EVANGELICAL 4.6%, GCC 8.3%**
2383	rural areas	549,000	86.23	474,000	97.23	C	583,000	88.6% (1950), 75.2% (1970), 55.4% (1990), 44.8% (2000), 36.7% (2010), 29.4% (2025)
2384	urban areas	677,000	90.44	612,000	98.78	C	1,398,000	11.4% (1950), 24.8% (1970), 44.5% (1990), 55.1% (2000), 63.2% (2010), 70.5% (2025)
2385	non-metropolitan areas	–	–	–	–	–	–	*Sources of data:* Census of 1961; estimate for 1950.
2386	metropolitan areas	721,000	90.43	652,000	98.64	C	1,490,000	*Definition:* Towns with a population of 2,000 or more.
2387	Franceville	90,500	90.00	81,500	97.54	C	187,000	Capital of La Passa on Ogooue River. Trading center in mining region. Coffee. F=1880. D=RCC.
2388	LIBREVILLE	363,000	90.00	327,000	98.74	C	750,000	On Gabon Estuary. Lumber as major export. Settled by Pongove (c1550) then Fang. Y=1844. D=RCC.
2389	Lambarene	76,200	89.00	67,800	97.24	C	157,000	Capital of Des Lacs on Ogooue River. Paris Mission Society (1876). Schweitzer's hospital. D=RCC.
2390	Port Gentil	192,000	92.00	176,000	99.54	C	396,000	Capital of Bendje. Chief port & industrial center. Oil & lumber. D=RCC.
	GAMBIA	**1,305,000**	**3.62**	**47,200**	**44.07**	**A**	**2,151,000**	**ROMAN CATHOLICS 2.3%, INDEPENDENTS 0.6%. PENT-CHAR 0.8%, EVANGELICAL 0.09%, GCC 2.3%**
2391	rural areas	882,000	2.66	23,500	40.71	A	1,098,000	89.4% (1950), 84.9% (1970), 74.3% (1990), 67.5% (2000), 60.8% (2010), 51.0% (2025)
2392	urban areas	424,000	5.60	23,700	51.05	B	1,053,000	10.5% (1950), 15.0% (1970), 25.7% (1990), 32.4% (2000), 39.1% (2010), 48.9% (2025)
2393	non-metropolitan areas	127,000	5.60	7,100	51.05	B	316,491	*Sources of data:* Censuses of 1951, 1963, and 1973; estimate for 1980.
2394	metropolitan areas	296,000	5.60	16,600	51.05	B	737,000	*Definition:* Banjul.
2395	BANJUL (Bathurst)	296,000	5.60	16,600	51.05	B	737,000	St. Mary's Island. Peanuts. F=1816. 30% Mandinka, 30% Wolof, Jola, Fula. 90% Muslim. M=WEC,MMS. D=RCC.
	GEORGIA	**4,968,000**	**60.57**	**3,009,000**	**88.61**	**C**	**5,178,000**	**ORTHODOX 58.1%, ROMAN CATHOLICS 1.1%. PENT-CHAR 0.6%, EVANGELICAL 0.1%, GCC 14.9%**
2396	rural areas	1,952,000	67.63	1,320,000	91.03	C	1,457,000	61.3% (1950), 52.5% (1970), 43.9% (1990), 39.3% (2000), 34.5% (2010), 28.1% (2025)
2397	urban areas	3,015,000	56.00	1,689,000	87.04	B	3,722,000	38.6% (1950), 47.4% (1970), 56.0% (1990), 60.7% (2000), 65.4% (2010), 71.8% (2025)
2398	non-metropolitan areas	943,000	55.95	528,000	86.81	B	1,198,107	*Sources of data:* Censuses of 1959, 1970, 1979, and 1989.
2399	metropolitan areas	2,072,000	56.02	1,161,000	87.14	B	2,523,000	*Definition:* Cities and urban-type localities, officially designated as such by each of the constituent republics.
2400	Batumi	140,000	53.00	74,100	81.04	B	173,000	Capital of Adzhar on Black Sea. Important port, oil, shipyard. Popular resort. F=Middle Ages. D=Orthodox.
2401	Gori	71,300	46.00	32,800	74.04	B	88,000	Gori on Kura River. Fruits, vegetables, textiles. F=7th century AD as Tontio. Stalin b.1879. D=Orthodox.
2402	Kutaisi	242,000	59.00	143,000	90.04	B	299,000	On Rioni River. One of oldest cities in Transcaucasia. Trucks, pumps. 11th & 12th century cathedrals. D=Orthodox.
2403	Poti	56,300	53.00	29,800	81.04	B	69,500	On mouth of Rioni River at Black Sea. Fishing, dredger building works. F=ancient Greek Phasis. D=Orthodox.
2404	Suchumi (Sukhumi)	122,000	53.00	64,700	81.04	B	151,000	Capital of Abkhazia on Black Sea coast. Popular resort. Wine, fruits. Ancient Greek Dioscurias. D=Orthodox.
2405	TBILISI (Tiflis)	1,389,000	56.60	786,000	88.64	B	1,680,000	On Kura River. Strategic position between east & west. Cultural center. F=458. 5th century cathedral. D=Orthodox.
2406	Rustavi	165,000	57.00	93,900	89.04	B	203,000	On Kura River. Large iron & steel works. F=post WWII. D=Orthodox.
2407	Zugdidi	51,500	59.00	30,400	89.04	B	63,500	West near Abkhazia. Paper, cannery, silkworm farm, tea, botanical garden. C=1500. D=Orthodox.
	GERMANY	**82,220,000**	**71.49**	**58,783,000**	**97.64**	**C**	**80,238,000**	**PROTESTANTS 37.0%, ROMAN CATHOLICS 34.9%. PENT-CHAR 3.1%, EVANGELICAL 1.6%, GCC 31.8%**
2408	rural areas	10,245,000	82.00	8,400,000	98.95	C	7,125,000	28.0% (1950), 20.3% (1970), 14.7% (1990), 12.4% (2000), 10.7% (2010), 8.8% (2025)
2409	urban areas	71,976,000	70.00	50,383,000	97.45	C	73,113,000	71.9% (1950), 79.6% (1970), 85.3% (1990), 87.5% (2000), 89.2% (2010), 91.1% (2025)
2410	non-metropolitan areas	19,635,000	70.46	13,835,000	97.95	C	20,055,577	*Sources of data:* Censuses of 1950, 1961, 1970 in former FRG, and 1950, 1964, 1971, 1981 in former GDR.
2411	metropolitan areas	52,341,000	69.83	36,548,000	97.26	C	53,057,000	*Definition:* Communes with 2,000 or more inhabitants.
2412	Aachen (Aix-la-Chapelle)	1,069,000	71.00	759,000	97.15	C	1,083,000	North Rhine-Westphalia. Iron & steel industry. Palace chapel of Charlemagne (790). D=EKO,RCC.
2413	Alsdorf	48,000	72.00	34,600	98.15	C	48,800	Koln north of Aachen near Netherlands border. Pharmaceuticals. Moated castle (15th century). D=EKD,RCC.
2414	Eschweiler	55,900	73.00	40,800	99.15	C	56,800	Koln on Inde River east of Aachen. Lignite, iron, steel, rubber goods, limestone. F=9th century. D=EKD.
2415	Stolberg	58,600	72.00	42,200	98.15	C	59,500	Koln east on Inde River. Center for German brass industry. Chemicals, glass, textiles, furniture, needles. D=EKD.
2416	Aalen	79,800	74.00	59,100	99.65	C	81,100	Baden-Wurttemberg on Kocher River. Communications center, metal, textiles, chemicals. F=Roman fort. D=EKD.
2417	Ahlen	55,400	75.00	41,600	99.65	C	56,300	Munster north of Hamm. Enamel, iron ware, coal mining. Gothic church, Strontium mine in 1880's. D=EKD.
2418	Albstadt	50,200	75.00	37,600	99.65	C	50,900	Baden-Wurttemberg, southwest. Textiles, machinery, vehicles. Created in 1975 by merging villages. D=EKD.
2419	Altenburg	50,100	60.00	30,000	86.15	C	50,800	Saxony on Pleisse River. Known for playing cards. Sewing machines, hats, cigars. F=976. D=EKD.
2420	Amberg	44,100	75.00	33,100	99.65	C	44,800	Bayern on Vils River. Iron-ore mining & working, glass grinding. F=1034. St George's (14th century). D=EKD.
2421	Arnsberg	77,600	73.00	56,700	99.15	C	78,800	North Rhine-Westphalia on Ruhr River. Spa & summer resort. F=11th century. Wedinghausen Abbey. D=EKD.
2422	Aschaffenburg	153,000	71.00	109,000	97.15	C	156,000	Bavaria on Main River. Clothing, colored paper. Many parks. Roman settlement. 12th century church. D=EKD.
2423	Augsburg	430,000	69.00	297,000	95.15	C	436,000	Bavaria on Wertach & Lech rivers. Heavy engineering. Early Bronze Age origins. Bishopric state 739. D=RCC.
2424	Bad Oeynhausen	47,500	74.00	35,200	99.65	C	48,300	Detmold northeast of Herford near Weser River. Paper, electronics, mineral springs. F=1232. D=RCC.
2425	Baden-Baden	53,000	74.00	39,300	99.65	C	53,900	Baden-Wurttemberg on Oos River in Black Forest. Spas. Roman origins. Lichtemal convent (1254). D=RCC.
2426	Bamberg	72,200	71.00	51,200	97.15	C	73,300	Bavaria on Regnitz River. Internationally known symphony orchestra. F=902. Bishopric since 1007. D=RCC.
2427	Bautzen	49,700	65.00	32,300	91.15	C	50,500	Saxony. Railway junction. Wagon & vehicle building, iron foundries. Cultural center of Lusatian Sorbs. D=EKD.
2428	Bayreuth	74,000	74.00	54,800	99.65	C	75,200	Bavaria on Red Main River. Known for composer Richard Wagner. Annual music festivals. F=1194. D=EKD.
2429	Berlin	3,337,000	70.50	2,353,000	97.65	C	3,347,000	Capital of Germany 1871-1945. Manufacturing, trading. F=1237. Under tripartite jurisdiction. D=EKD,RCC.
2430	Bielefeld	1,304,000	71.00	926,000	97.65	C	1,325,000	North Rhine-Westphalia. Center of Ravensberg linen industry, bicycles. F=1214 by Count Hermann. D=EKD.
2431	Gutersloh	88,800	73.00	64,800	99.15	C	90,200	Garden atmosphere. Textiles, meat processing, machinery, metal products. F=1825. D=EKD.
2432	Bitterfeld	107,000	60.00	64,500	86.15	C	109,000	Arnhalt northeast of Halle near Mulde River. Industrial center, polluted. F=mid-12th century. D=RCC.
2433	Bocholt	70,500	74.00	52,200	99.65	C	71,600	North Rhine-Westphalia on the Aa River. Railroad, textiles, machinery, electronics, foundries. F=1222. D=EKD.
2434	BONN	588,000	71.00	418,000	97.15	C	598,000	North Rhine-Westphalia on Rhine River. Only light industry. Musical arts. F=1st century BC. D=EKD.
2435	Sankt Augustin	53,100	72.00	38,200	98.15	C	53,900	Koln across Rhine River to the east. Computers, machinery. Created in 1968 by merging 6 villages. D=EKD.
2436	Brandenburg	92,000	65.00	59,800	91.15	C	93,400	Brandenburg on Havel River. Steel, textiles, leather. F=928. Y=948 as bishopric. D=EKD,RCC.
2437	Braunschweig (Brunswick)	327,000	70.00	229,000	96.15	C	333,000	Lower Saxony on Oker River. Scientific research, sausages. F=12th cent. St. Blasius Cathedral (1173). D=EKD.
2438	Wolfenbuttel	53,200	73.00	38,900	99.15	C	54,100	Canning, agricultural machinery, chemicals. Herzog-August Library. F=1118. D=EKD.
2439	Bremen	887,000	70.00	621,000	97.15	C	897,000	Capital of Bremen on Weser River. Large port. Base of missions under Charlemagne (787). D=EKD.
2440	Delmenhorst	76,900	72.00	55,400	98.15	C	78,100	Weser-Ems west of Bremen. Largely industrial, chemicals, textiles, plastics, furniture, food, machinery. D=EKD.
2441	Bremerhaven	184,000	72.00	133,000	98.15	C	187,000	Bremen on Weser River. Largest fishing port. Shipbuilding. F=1827. Heavy damage in WWII. D=EKD.

Table 10-5–continued opposite

Table 10-5–continued

Rec No 1	Country City 2	Pop 2000 3	AC% 4	Church Members 5	E% 6	W 7	Pop 2025 8	Notes 9
2442	Celle	73,900	73.00	54,000	99.15	C	75,100	Lower Saxony on Aller River. Forestry, agricultural, virus research. Horse breeding. F=1248. D=EKD.
2443	Chemnitz (Karl-Marx-Stadt)	512,000	65.00	333,000	96.15	C	520,000	Saxony on Chemnitz River. Engineering, textiles, autos. F=1143 as trading center. D=EKD.
2444	Cottbus (Kottbus)	129,000	60.00	77,300	86.15	C	131,000	Extensive lignite fields, coal products, chemicals. Last of the Sorbian language neighborhoods. D=EKDG.
2445	Cuxhaven	57,400	74.00	42,500	99.65	C	58,300	Lower Saxony port at mouth of Elbe. Fishing, fish processing, beach resort, spa. F=1394. D=EKD.
2446	Darmstadt	322,000	71.00	229,000	97.15	C	327,000	Hesse. Chemicals, machinery, radios, kitchen ranges. F=11th century. Russian church (1898). D=EKD.
2447	Dessau	141,000	60.00	84,700	86.15	C	143,000	Saxony-Anhalt State on Mulde River. Shipyard, vehicles, machinery, chemicals. F=1213. D=EKD.
2448	Detmold	71,700	73.00	52,300	99.15	C	72,800	North Rhine-Westphalia on Werre River. Picturesque residential city. Furniture making. F=12th century. D=EKD.
2449	Dresden	890,000	55.00	490,000	96.15	B	904,000	Capital of Saxony. Music, opera, education, precision instruments. Major art collections. F=1216. D=RCC.
2450	Duren	110,000	74.00	81,800	99.65	C	112,000	North Rhine-Westphalia on Ruhr River. Paper, metal goods, textiles, glass. F=748. D=EKD.
2451	Eberswalde-Finow	53,800	63.00	33,900	89.15	C	54,700	Brandenburg. Europe's largest marine & industrial crane factory, rolling mills, gravel, brick. F=c1300. D=EKD.
2452	Eisenach	46,300	60.00	27,800	86.15	C	47,000	Thuringia. Tourism, auto factories, machinery, metal, woods. Wartburg castle. F=c1150. D=EKD,RCC.
2453	Eisenhuttenstadt	51,400	60.00	30,800	86.15	C	52,200	Brandenburg on Oder River. Pig iron, steel, shipyards, glass, trade center. F=1961. D=EKD,RCC.
2454	Emden	51,900	75.00	38,900	99.65	C	52,700	Lower Saxony near North Sea. Busy port, shipping, shipbuilding, herring fishing. F=800. D=EKD.
2455	Erfurt	214,000	60.00	128,000	86.15	C	217,000	Thuringia. Wheat, barley, sugar beets, metalworking. Germany's oldest university (14th century). D=RCC.
2456	Euskirchen	50,800	75.00	38,100	99.65	C	51,600	Koln on Erft River west of Bonn. Paper, machinery, sugar, glass, animal feeds. 14th century town hall. D=EKD.
2457	Flensburg	100,000	72.00	72,200	98.15	C	102,000	Schleswig-Holstein on Flensburger Forde. Shipbuilding, rum, eels. F=1240. Churches (1284). D=EKD.
2458	Frankfurt am Main	3,700,000	73.50	2,720,000	99.65	C	3,747,000	Hesse on Main River. Trade fairs since 1240. Heavy industry. F=1st century BC. 25% Expatriates. D=EKD,RCC.
2459	Bad Homburg	53,000	74.00	39,200	99.65	C	53,900	North. Near wooded Tavnus Mountains. Internationally fashionable spa. Residential. F=1200. D=EKD,RCC.
2460	Offenbach am Main	118,000	73.00	85,900	99.15	C	120,000	Main River port. Tanning, leather goods. Meteorological services. F=977. D=EKD,RCC.
2461	Frankfurt an der Oder	88,100	65.00	57,300	91.15	C	89,500	Brandenburg. Transit trade center, machinery, furniture, foodstuffs, shoes. F=1253. D=EKD,RCC.
2462	Freiberg	49,700	64.00	31,800	90.15	C	50,500	Saxony. Historically a mining (silver) center. Oldest mining school in the world (1765). F=c1190. D=EKD.
2463	Freiburg im Breisgau	240,000	72.00	173,000	98.15	C	244,000	Baden-Wurttemberg in Black Forest. Tourist & conference center, trade in timber & wine. F=1120. D=RCC.
2464	Friedrichshafen	55,400	75.00	41,500	99.65	C	56,300	Baden-Wurttemberg on Lake Constance. Lake resort, annual fair. F=1811. Benedictine convent (1050). D=EKD.
2465	Fulda	75,700	73.00	55,300	99.15	C	76,900	Hesse on Fulda River. Banking. Medieval missionary center. F=744 by Sturmi, Bonaface disciple. D=RCC.
2466	Garbsen	62,200	72.00	44,800	98.15	C	63,200	Hannover on Leine River west of Hannover. Lower Saxony, chartered in 1468. D=EKD.
2467	Gera	132,000	60.00	79,200	86.15	C	134,000	Thuringia. Textiles, metal products, machinery, fats, oils, uranium mines. F=c1230. D=EKD,RCC.
2468	Giessen	159,000	72.00	114,000	98.15	C	161,000	Hesse on Lahn River. Machinery, textiles. F=1197. Schiffenberg Monastery. D=EKD,RCC.
2469	Goppingen	159,000	72.00	114,000	98.15	C	161,000	Baden-Wurttemberg on Fils River. Textiles, plastics, toys. F=c1150. Gothic church 1436. D=EKD,RCC.
2470	Gorlitz	73,900	63.00	46,600	89.15	C	75,100	Saxony on Neisse River. Lignite-mining, textiles, railway cars, machinery. F=1071. D=RCC.
2471	Goslar	73,700	74.00	54,500	99.65	C	74,800	Lower Saxony near Harz Mountains. Tourism, men's clothing, chemicals. F=922. D=EKD,RCC.
2472	Gotha	55,800	64.00	35,700	90.15	C	56,700	Thuringia. Machinery, textiles, chemicals, china. Historical seat of Justus Perthes publisher. F=775. D=EKD.
2473	Gottingen	125,000	71.00	88,500	97.15	C	127,000	Lower Saxony on Leine River. University city. Printing, optical & precision instruments. F=953. D=EKD.
2474	Greifswald	67,800	64.00	43,400	90.15	C	68,900	Macklenburg-West Pomerania. Trades in grains, wood, coal. F=1209 as market for Eldena Monastery. D=EKD.
2475	Gummersbach	52,100	75.00	39,100	99.65	C	53,000	Koln east of Koln. Metalworking, electronics, boilers, wallpaper, tourism, 12th century church. F=1857. D=EKD.
2476	Halberstadt	46,400	65.00	30,200	91.15	C	47,100	Saxony-Anhalt. Sugar, metal, engineering, sausage. F=c814 as bishopric. D=RCC,EKO.
2477	Halle	466,000	60.00	279,000	94.15	C	473,000	Saxony-Anhalt on Saale River. Industrial center. F=806 as fortress. Center for Protestant learning. D=EKD.
2478	Halle-Neustadt	96,000	63.00	60,500	89.15	C	97,500	Residential and service center. Chemicals, refined sugar, rubber, cement, lignite, potash. F=1964. D=EKD.
2479	Merseburg	43,900	63.00	27,700	89.15	C	44,600	Anhalt south on Saale River. One of most polluted regions in Europe. Bricks, aluminum foil, beer. D=EKD.
2480	Hamburg	2,680,000	71.00	1,903,000	98.15	C	2,707,000	On Alster and Elbe Rivers. Largest port. F=825 as missions base. Five historic churches. D=RCC,EKD.
2481	Norderstedt	70,000	74.00	51,800	99.65	C	71,100	Vast new business district.
2482	Hameln	66,500	73.00	48,500	99.15	C	67,600	Lower Saxony on Weser River. Scenic center & nature park. Carpets, chemicals, electric goods. D=EKD.
2483	Hannau	88,900	72.00	64,000	98.15	C	90,300	Kinzig River, east of Frankfurt. Jewel industry, lumber. F=1303, birthplace of Brothers Grimm. D=EKD.
2484	Hannover (Hanover)	1,293,000	71.00	918,000	97.15	C	1,307,000	Capital of Lower Saxony on Leine River. 60% destroyed in WWII. World's largest industrial fair. Gardens. D=EKD.
2485	Heidenheim	81,800	74.00	60,600	99.65	C	83,100	Baden-Wurttemberg on Brenz River. International shepherd's competitions. Roman settlement. D=EKD.
2486	Heilbronn	251,000	72.00	180,000	98.15	C	255,000	Baden-Wurttemberg on Neckar River. Port, commercial & industrial center, machinery, automotive parts. D=EKD.
2487	Herford	123,000	71.00	87,200	97.15	C	125,000	North Rhine-Westphalia on Aa & Weere rivers. Furniture. F=789 around Benedictine nunnery. D=RCC,EKD.
2488	Bad Salzuflen	55,000	74.00	40,700	99.65	C	55,900	Detmold southeast of Herford. Spa with warm salt springs. Furniture, fibers, shoes, food processing. D=EKD.
2489	Hildesheim	129,000	72.00	92,800	98.15	C	131,000	Lower Saxony on Innerste River. Industrial & transportation center, televisions, radio, dairy. D=RCC.
2490	Hof	54,100	75.00	40,600	99.65	C	55,000	Bavaria on Saale River. Textiles, machinery. Cultural center. F=c1200 by dukes of Andechs-Meran. D=EKD.
2491	Hoyerswerda	66,400	64.00	42,500	90.15	C	67,400	Saxony. Lignite mines, coal processing, glass, bricks. F=1268. D=EKD,RCC.
2492	Ingolstadt	148,000	72.00	107,000	98.15	C	151,000	Bavaria on Danube & Schutter Rivers. Center for heavy industry. F=806. D=EKD.
2493	Iserlohn	98,500	73.00	71,900	99.15	C	100,000	North Rhine-Westphalia. Machinery, chemicals. F=11th century. St. Pan Kratius Church (11th century). D=RCC.
2494	Jena	105,000	60.00	62,900	86.15	C	107,000	Thuringia on Saale River. Optical precision instruments, pharmaceuticals. F=1230. University (1554). D=EKD.
2495	Kaiserslauten	133,000	70.00	93,100	96.15	C	135,000	Rhineland-Palatinate. Important banking & rail transshipment center. F=c 8th century. D=RCC,EKD.
2496	Karlsruhe	985,000	69.00	680,000	95.15	C	999,000	Baden-Wurttemberg in Black Forest. Nuclear reactor & research center. Technical University (1825). D=EKD.
2497	Kassel	384,000	71.00	272,000	97.15	C	390,000	Hesse on Fulda River. Internationally known art collection. Home of Grimm brothers. Castles, museums. D=EKD.
2498	Kempten (Allgau)	63,300	75.00	47,500	99.65	C	64,300	Bavaria on Iller River. Dairy market (esp. cheeses). Celtic origins. Benedictine abbey (752). D=RCC,EKD.
2499	Kiel	333,000	71.00	236,000	97.15	C	338,000	Capital of Schleswig-Holstein on Baltic Sea. Institute of world economics. F=1242. St Nicholas Church (c1240).
2500	Kleve (Cleve)	47,000	74.00	34,800	99.65	C	47,800	North Rhine-Westphalia. Tourism, food processing. F=11th century. Minorite Church (1427). D=EKD.
2501	Koblenz (Loblenz)	174,000	73.00	127,000	99.15	C	177,000	Rhineland-Palatinate on Rhine & Mosel rivers. Wine. F=9BC as Roman town. St. Castor's (836). D=RCC.
2502	Koln (Cologne)	3,067,000	70.00	2,147,000	97.15	C	3,108,000	North Rhineland-Westphalia on Rhine River. Banking, wine. F=50 BC Cathedral (11th century). D=RCC,EKD.
2503	Bergheim	59,500	72.00	42,800	98.15	C	60,400	Koln east on Erft River. Coal mining, metal working, horse breeding. F=1317. D=EKD,RCC.
2504	Bergisch Gladbach	106,000	71.00	75,600	97.15	C	108,000	Tourist base for Bergisches Land. Paper, machinery. F=1856. 12th century Romanesque church. D=RCC.
2505	Dormagen	59,600	73.00	43,500	99.15	C	60,500	Dusseldorf north on Rhine River. Center of chemical industry, sugar refining, brewing, agriculture. D=EKD.
2506	Hurth	52,000	73.00	37,900	99.15	C	52,800	Center of truck farming & lignite mining. Coal, stoneware. Kottenforst-Ville nature park. Roman origins. D=RCC.
2507	Kerpen	58,700	74.00	43,400	99.65	C	59,600	Koln near Erft River southwest of Koln. Former lignite mining. Motor vehicles, ancient castles. D=EKD.
2508	Leverkusen	165,000	71.00	117,000	97.15	C	167,000	Bayer works (chemicals, pharmaceuticals). Iron, textiles. Numerous parks. F=1930. D=EKD.
2509	Konstanz	76,800	74.00	56,900	99.65	C	78,000	Baden-Wurttemberg on Lake Constance. Important Christian center (medieval). F=Roman fort. D=EKD.
2510	Landshut	60,400	75.00	45,300	99.65	C	61,400	Bavaria on Isar River. Electrotechnics. Medieval character. F=1204. St. Martin's (1389)D=EKD.
2511	Leipzig	737,000	55.00	405,000	96.15	B	748,000	Saxony. Parks & gardens. Traditional furs, book publishing. Intellectual & cultural center. F=1015. D=RCC.
2512	Lingen	50,300	72.00	36,200	98.15	C	51,100	17 miles NNW of Rheine, Dortmund-Ens Canal. Oil wells, textile. Nuclear power plant built in 1988. D=EKD.
2513	Lippstadt	63,800	74.00	47,200	99.65	C	64,800	North Rhine-Westphalia on Lippe River. Iron, metalworking. F=1168. 13th century churches. D=EKD.
2514	Lubeck	256,000	70.00	179,000	96.15	C	260,000	Schleswig-Holstein on Trave & Wakenitz Rivers. Seaport, shipbuilding. F=1143. 12th century church. D=EKD.
2515	Ludenscheid	81,200	73.00	59,300	99.15	C	82,500	North Rhine Westphalia. Aluminum, plastics. F=9th century by Franks. Church (1072). D=EKD.
2516	Luneburg	63,300	74.00	46,800	99.65	C	64,300	Lower Saxony on Ilmenau River. Chemicals, wood products. F=956. St. John's church (13th century). D=EKD.
2517	Magdeburg	410,000	60.00	246,000	96.15	C	416,000	Saxony-Anhalt on Elbe River. F=805. Sugar & flour milling, coal. 20,000 martyrs (1631). D=RCC.
2518	Mannheim	1,617,000	71.00	1,148,000	97.15	C	1,640,000	Baden-Wurttemberg on Rhine River. One of Europe's largest inland ports. Trade in coal & iron. F=764. D=EKD.
2519	Heidelberg	140,000	72.00	101,000	98.15	C	142,000	On Neckar River. University city (founded by Pope Urban VI in 1386). Castle (13th century). F=1196. D=RCC.
2520	Ludwigshafen am Rhein	166,000	73.00	121,000	99.15	C	169,000	Rhineland-Palatinate on Rhine River. Gateway to wine-growing region. Chemical industry. F=1606. D=EKD.
2521	Worms	78,300	74.00	57,900	99.65	C	79,500	Rhineland-Palatinate on Rhine River. Wine. 100 diets held here. Celtic origins. Bishopric (c600). D=EKD.
2522	Marburg	75,900	74.00	56,100	99.65	C	77,100	Hesse on Lahn River. Tourism, applied arts. F=1130. St. Elizabeth of Hungary (1228). D=EKD.
2523	Menden	57,800	75.00	43,400	99.65	C	58,700	Arnsberg on Ruhr River tributary west of Arnsberg. Electronic equipment, forestry. F=1276. D=EKD.
2524	Minden	124,000	72.00	89,100	98.15	C	126,000	North Rhine-Westphalia on Weser River. Textiles, farming. Charlemagne organized bishopric (800). D=EKD.
2525	Monchengladbach (Munchengladbach)	419,000	71.00	298,000	97.15	C	426,000	North Rhine-Westphalia. Cotton,textiles. Developed around a Benedictine Abbey. F=972. D=EKD.
2526	Viersen	79,200	73.00	57,800	99.15	C	80,500	Dusseldorf north on Niers River. Textile mfg., machinery, leather goods, plastics, chemicals. D=EKD.
2527	Munchen (Munich)	2,306,000	69.00	1,591,000	96.15	C	2,339,000	Capital of Bavaria on Isar River. Center for the arts. Numerous conventions. D=EKD,ECC.
2528	Munster	260,000	72.00	187,000	98.15	C	264,000	North Rhine-Westphalia on Munster-Aa River. Cattle. F=804 by missionary. 13th cent churches. D=RCC.
2529	Neubrandenburg	91,300	63.00	57,500	89.15	C	92,800	Mecklenburg-West Pomerania State. Engineering, food processing, wood, leather, paper. F=1248. D=EKD.
2530	Neumunster	82,600	72.00	59,500	98.15	C	83,900	Schleswig-Holstein north of Hamburg. Transportation and industrial center, machinery, leather, textiles. D=EKD.
2531	Neunkirchen/Saar	128,000	73.00	93,400	99.15	C	130,000	Saarland. Predominately Roman Catholic. Metalworking, coal mining until 1968. D=RCC.
2532	Neustadt an der Weinstrasse	53,200	75.00	39,900	99.65	C	54,000	Rhineland-Palatinate at mouth of Speyer-Bach. Wine trade, tourism. F=1220. Stifts church (14th century). D=EKD.
2533	Neuwied	161,000	71.00	114,000	97.15	C	163,000	Rhineland-Palatinate on Rhine River. F=1653 for religious refugees. Moravian school (1756-1910). D=EKD.
2534	Nordhausen	47,500	65.00	30,900	91.15	C	48,200	Thuringia. Brewing, distilling, chewing tobacco, machinery, clothing. F=927 as Royal Castle. D=EKD.
2535	Nordhorn	50,500	73.00	36,900	99.15	C	51,300	Weser-Ems on Vechte River near Netherlands border. Textile center, cotton. 15th century church. D=RCC.
2536	Nurnberg (Nuremberg)	1,199,000	70.00	839,000	96.15	C	1,218,000	Bavaria on Pegnitz River. Optical goods. Higher education center. F=c1050. Melanchthon's home (c1520). D=EKD.
2537	Erlangen	105,000	71.00	74,400	97.15	C	106,000	On Schwabach & Regnitz rivers. Gloves, hats, drapery. F=8th century. Huguenots settled here (1686). D=EKD.
2538	Furth	106,000	72.00	76,100	98.15	C	107,000	At junction of Pegnitz & Regnitz rivers. Gold leaf, metals. F=8th century. D=RCC,EKD.
2539	Offenburg	54,200	75.00	40,600	99.65	C	55,000	Baden-Wurttemberg on edge of Black Forest. Wine & fruit growing, tourism, F=1101. D=EKD.
2540	Oldenburg	146,000	69.00	101,000	95.15	C	149,000	Lower Saxony on Hunte River. Cattle & horse auctions. F=1108. Lamberti Church (1270). D=EKD.
2541	Osnabruck	276,000	73.00	202,000	99.15	C	281,000	Lower Saxony on Hase River. Steel, machinery. F=785 as bishopric by Charlemagne. D=EKD,RCC.
2542	Paderborn	123,000	71.00	87,700	97.15	C	125,000	North Rhine-Westphalia on Pader River. Bread, cattle, beer. F=799. Birthplace of Holy Roman Empire. D=RCC.
2543	Passau	51,500	75.00	38,600	99.65	C	52,300	Bavaria at Danube, Inn & Ilz Rivers. Salt, knives, swords. F=Celtic Bojodurum. Episcopal see (739). D=RCC.
2544	Peine	47,700	74.00	35,300	99.65	C	48,500	Braunschweig on Fuhse River west of Braunschweig. Oil district, iron ore, rolling mill, silk spinning. D=EKD.
2545	Pforzheim	235,000	70.00	165,000	96.15	C	239,000	Baden-Wurttemberg near Black Forest. Center of watch & jewelry industry. F=Roman fort. D=EKD.
2546	Pirmasens	48,800	75.00	36,600	99.65	C	49,600	Rhineland-Palatinate near French border. Shoes. F=8th century by St. Pirmin. D=RCC.
2547	Plauen	73,400	63.00	46,300	89.15	C	74,600	Saxony. Lace making, textile craft school, textiles. F=1220. 12th century St. John's Church. D=EKD.
2548	Potsdam	143,000	60.00	85,800	86.15	C	145,000	Brandenburg on Havel River. Textiles, pharmaceuticals. WWII Potsdam Conference (1945). D=EKD.
2549	Ravensburg	76,700	73.00	56,000	99.15	C	77,900	Baden-Wurttemberg on Schussen River. Textiles, paper. F=12th century. St. Jodok's church. D=RCC.
2550	Regensburg (Ratisbon)	184,000	71.00	131,000	97.15	C	187,000	Bavaria on Danube River. Tourism, electronics. F=Celts. Bishopric (739). Cathedral of St. Peter (1275). D=RCC.
2551	Reutlingen	174,000	72.00	125,000	98.15	C	177,000	Baden-Wurttemberg on Echaz River. Textiles, leather tanning. Church of St. Mary (13th century). D=RCC.
2552	Rhein-Ruhr (Ruhrgebiet)	6,559,000	70.00	4,591,000	99.15	C	6,663,000	North Rhine-Westphalia. Coal, steel, chemicals. Densely populated. D=EKD,RCC.
2553	Bergkamen	50,900	73.00	37,200	99.15	C	51,700	Arnsberg northeast of Dortmund. Chemicals, pharmaceuticals, coal mining. D=EKD.
2554	Bochum	406,000	70.00	284,000	96.15	C	412,000	Metallurgy. F=1298. Seat of Ruhr University (1965). Diocese Church (1599), Old Parish Church (1008). D=EKD.
2555	Bottrop	122,000	72.00	87,600	98.15	C	124,000	On Rhine-Herne-Kanal. Coal mining & coking. F=Middle Ages. Churches date from 1860. D=EKD.
2556	Castrop-Rauxel	80,900	72.00	58,200	98.15	C	82,100	Near Rhine-Herne Canal. Coal mining, chemicals. F=834. Church of St. Lambert (13th century). D=EKD.
2557	Dinslaken	66,800	72.00	48,100	98.15	C	67,900	Coal mining, sawmilling, residential. Open air theater. F=1163. Castle of Count of Cleve (1273). D=EKD.
2558	Dorsten	79,800	71.00	56,700	97.15	C	81,100	On Lippe River and Wesel-Datteln Canal. Coal-gas works. F=Roman village. Medieval monastery center. D=RCC.
2559	Dortmund	613,000	70.00	429,000	96.15	C	623,000	Extensive port at head of Dortmund-Ems Canal. Steel, coal, beer. F=885. Large Westphalia Hall (1952). D=EKD.
2560	Duisburg	548,000	70.00	383,000	96.15	C	556,000	At junction of Rhine & Ruhr. Coal, iron, steel, heavy machinery. F=Roman Castrum Deutonis. D=EKD.
2561	Dusseldorf	3,251,000	67.00	2,178,000	93.15	C	3,363,000	Capital of North Rhine-Westphalia on Rhine River. Major financial center. F=1159. 13th century church. D=EKD.
2562	Essen	6,559,000	66.00	4,329,000	92.15	C	6,596,000	On Baldeney Lake. Coal, steel, construction. F=852 as aristocratic convent. Abbey church (796). D=RCC,EKD.
2563	Gelsenkirchen	301,000	70.00	210,000	96.15	C	305,000	On Rhine-Horne-Kanal. Inland port. Coal mining, iron, steel. F=1850 (1,00 inhabitants). D=EKD,RCC.
2564	Gladbeck	82,100	71.00	58,300	97.15	C	83,400	Coal mining, iron working, chemicals, textiles. F=1019. Heavily damaged in WWII. D=EKD,RCC.
2565	Grevenbroich	62,200	72.00	44,800	98.15	C	63,200	Dusseldorf on Erft River. Machinery, aluminum, power stations. Developed around abbey. D=RCC.

Table 10-5–continued overleaf

Table 10-5–continued

Rec No 1	Country City 2	Pop 2000 3	AC% 4	Church Members 5	E% 6	W 7	Pop 2025 8	Notes 9
2566	Hagen	219,000	71.00	156,000	97.15	C	223,000	At confluence of Ennepe & Volme rivers. Ironworking, steelworking, die-casting. F=8th century. D=EKD.
2567	Hamm	184,000	72.00	132,000	98.15	C	187,000	On Lippe and Ahse rivers. Wire & cables. F=1226. St. Paul's church (medieval). D=EKD.
2568	Hattingen	59,600	72.00	42,900	98.15	C	60,500	On Ruhr River. Steelworks, rolling mills, coal. F=1396. St. Georges church (1450). D=EKD.
2569	Herne	183,000	72.00	132,000	98.15	C	186,000	On Rhine-Herne-Kanal. Coal mines, foundries textiles. F=10th century as Haranni. D=EKD.
2570	Herten	70,800	72.00	51,000	98.15	C	72,000	Coal mining, food processing. 16th century castle. F=9th century. Gothic church (1433). D=EKD.
2571	Hilden	56,000	71.00	39,800	97.15	C	56,900	On the Itter River. Metals, textiles. Nature preserve. F=1169. Parish church (1136). D=EKD.
2572	Krefeld (Crefeld)	250,000	69.00	172,000	95.15	C	254,000	Rhine River port. Silks, velvets (begun by 17th century Protestant refugees). F=1373. D=EKD.
2573	Langenfeld	54,700	72.00	39,400	98.15	C	55,600	Dusseldorf south near Monheim on Rhine River. Steelware, motor vehicles, medical equipment. D=EKD.
2574	Lunen	89,900	71.00	63,800	97.15	C	91,300	On Lippe River. Coal mining, iron foundries, aluminum. F=1336. Former monastery. D=RCC.
2575	Marl	93,600	71.00	66,400	97.15	C	95,100	Coal & iron-ore mining, chemicals. F=800. North Rhine-Westphalia, Ruhr industrial district. D=EKD.
2576	Meerbusch	53,300	72.00	38,400	98.15	C	54,200	Dusseldorf west across Rhine River. North Rhine-Westhalia. Steel, metalworking, 2 castles. D=EKD.
2577	Moers (Mors)	107,000	71.00	76,000	97.15	C	109,000	Fortification wall & moat. Coal & salt mining. F=Roman Asciburgium. Protestant school (1582). D=EKD.
2578	Mulheim and der Ruhr	182,000	70.00	127,000	96.15	C	185,000	River port. Heavy industry. Formerly coal-mining center. F=1093. St. Peter's church (11th century). D=EKD.
2579	Neuss	150,000	71.00	107,000	97.15	C	153,000	On Erft Canal. Grain market, chemicals. F=12BC as Roman fortress. Church of St. Quirinius (1209). D=RCC.
2580	Oberhausen	229,000	70.00	160,000	96.15	C	233,000	On Rhine-Herne-Kanal. Steel, coal, zinc, dye works. Sterkrade Abbey (1150). D=RCC.
2581	Ratingen	93,100	71.00	66,100	97.15	C	94,600	Dusseldorf north towards Essen. North Rhine-Westphalia. Machinery, paper, iron, glass, textile. F=1276. D=EKD.
2582	Recklinghausen	128,000	72.00	92,100	98.15	C	130,000	Rhine-Herne-Kanal port. Annual art & music drama. Chemicals. Saxon settlement. St. Peter's (1276). D=RCC.
2583	Remscheid	126,000	71.00	89,500	97.15	C	128,000	On Wupper River. Slate houses. Iron, tools. F=11th century by Knights of St. John. D=RCC.
2584	Solingen	169,000	71.00	120,000	97.15	C	172,000	On Wupper River. Internationally known cutlery. Museum of Blades. F=965. D=EKD,RCC.
2585	Unna	63,000	72.00	45,300	98.15	C	64,000	Arnsberg far east of Dortmund. Westphalia-Lippe. Coal mining. Founded by Charlemagne. F=1290. D=RCC.
2586	Velbert	91,300	75.00	68,500	99.65	C	92,800	Dusseldorf south of Essen. Rhineland. Fittings for vehicles, ships, furniture, windows, textiles. D=EKD.
2587	Witten	108,000	72.00	77,600	98.15	C	110,000	North Rhine-Westphalia. On Ruhr River. Heavily-wooded surroundings. Steel. F=1825. D=RCC.
2588	Wuppertal	865,000	68.00	588,000	94.15	C	878,000	On Wupper River. Textiles, velvets, silk, rubber, pharmaceuticals. F=11th century. D=EKD.
2589	Rheine	72,200	75.00	54,100	99.65	C	73,300	On Ems River. Important textile industry. Popular saline spa. F=838. St. Dionysius Church (1484). D=EKD.
2590	Riesa	46,500	65.00	30,200	91.15	C	47,200	Saxony on Elbe River. Steelworks, rolling mills. F=1111 as Benedictine monastery. D=RCC.
2591	Rosenheim	57,600	75.00	43,200	99.65	C	58,600	Bavaria at confluence of Inn & Mangfall rivers. Important timber industry. F=1864. D=EKD.
2592	Rostock	254,000	55.00	140,000	81.15	B	258,000	Mecklenburg-West Pomerania. Fishing, shipbuilding. F=1218. University (1419). Many gothic churches. D=RCC.
2593	Saarbrucken	898,000	71.00	638,000	97.15	C	902,000	Capital of Saarland on Saar River. International fair. Coal, iron, and steel industries. D=EKD.
2594	Saarlouis	118,000	72.00	84,700	98.15	C	120,000	Saarland on Saar River. Coal, iron, steel. F=1680 by Louis XIV of France. D=EKD.
2595	Salzgitter	117,000	73.00	85,400	99.15	C	119,000	Lower Saxony near Harz Mountains. Iron-ore, metallurgical works. Well-known spa. F=1937. D=EKD.
2596	Schwabisch Gmund	61,500	75.00	46,100	99.65	C	62,400	Baden-Wurttemberg on Rems River. Jewelry, glassware. F=1162. 14th century cathedral. D=EKD.
2597	Schwedt	51,800	65.00	33,700	91.15	C	52,600	Brandenburg on Westoder River. Oil refining, fertilizer, paper plants. F=1265. D=EKD.
2598	Schweinfurt	107,000	74.00	79,500	99.65	C	109,000	Bavaria on Main River. Center of wine-growing area, breweries, F=791. St. Johannes' Church (1554). D=RCC.
2599	Schwerin	130,000	60.00	78,200	86.15	C	132,000	Capital of Mecklenburg on Lake Schwerin. Dairy, agriculture. F=1018 by Wends. D=EKD,RCC.
2600	Schwerte	51,900	70.00	36,300	96.15	C	52,700	North Rhine-Westphalia. Iron foundries, nickel, copper refining. Town first mentioned in 926. D=EKD.
2601	Siegburg	179,000	72.00	129,000	98.15	C	182,000	Koln on Sieg River north of Sankt Augustin. Machinery, tools, chemicals. Benedictine Abbey. F=1064. D=RCC.
2602	Troisdorf	65,900	73.00	48,100	99.15	C	67,000	Koln northwest of Siegburg. North Rhine-Westphalia. Railroad, plastics, machinery, celluloid. D=EKD.
2603	Siegen	196,000	72.00	141,000	98.15	C	200,000	North Rhine-Westphalia on Sieg River. Center of iron-ore mining. 13th century St. Nicholas Church. D=EKD.
2604	Stralsund	74,500	63.00	46,900	89.15	C	75,600	Baltic port in Meckleaburg-West Pomerania. Ship building, fishing. F=1234. D=EKD.
2605	Stuttgart	2,688,000	72.00	1,935,000	99.15	C	2,728,000	Capital of Baden-Wurttemberg on Neckar River. Major concentration of small industries. D=RCC.
2606	Esslingen (Esslingen Am Neckar)	93,800	73.00	68,500	99.15	C	95,300	On Neckar River. Wine, fruit. F=777. St. Paul's Church (1233)-oldest Dominican church in Germany. D=RCC.
2607	Ludwigsburg	84,200	73.00	61,500	99.15	C	85,600	On Neckar River. Machinery, iron & wire goods, organs, china. F=1704. Scenic park. D=RCC.
2608	Sindelfingen	60,200	72.00	43,300	98.15	C	61,100	Stuttgart southwest near Boblingen. Textiles, shoes, motor vehicles. F=1263. D=RCC.
2609	Suhl	56,000	64.00	35,800	90.15	C	56,900	Thuringia on Lauter River. Motorcycles, machinery, guns, toys. F=1239. D=EKD.
2610	Trier	125,000	73.00	91,100	99.15	C	127,000	Rhineland-Palatinate on Mosel River. Wines. F=15 BC. Y=4th century. Birthplace of St. Ambrose (c339). D=RCC.
2611	Tubingen	82,200	79.00	65,000	99.95	C	83,500	Baden-Wurttemberg. University of Tubingen (1477). Publishing. F=1078. Seminary (1534). D=EKD.
2612	Ulm/Neu-Ulm	220,000	73.00	161,000	99.15	C	223,000	Baden-Wurttemberg on Danube River. Motor vehicles. Bread museum. F=854. Cathedral (1377). D=EKD.
2613	Neu-Ulm	47,200	74.00	35,000	99.65	C	48,000	Bavaria on Danube River. Railroad, textiles, leather, metal, woodworking, brewing. F=1810. D=EKD.
2614	Villingen-Schwenningen	80,000	75.00	60,000	99.65	C	81,300	Baden-Wurttemberg north of Singen. Black Forest. Airport, watchmaking, climatic health resort. D=EKD.
2615	Weimar	61,700	63.00	38,900	89.15	C	62,700	Thuringia on Ilm River. Combine harvester plant. Buchenwald concentration camp. F=975. D=EKD.
2616	Wesel	61,000	76.00	46,400	99.85	C	62,000	North Rhine-Westphalia on Rhine & Lippe rivers. Large harbor installations, metals. F=1241. D=EKD.
2617	Wetzlar	98,200	73.00	71,700	99.15	C	99,800	Giessen on Lahn River west of Giessen. Iron ore, metallurgical industry, cameras, microscopes. D=EKD.
2618	Wiesbaden	808,000	72.00	582,000	98.15	C	821,000	Capital of Hesse on Rhine River. Mineral springs, mild climate. Pottery, boats. F=by Celts 3rd century BC. D=RCC.
2619	Mainz	184,000	71.00	130,000	97.15	C	187,000	Capital of Rhineland-Palatinate on Rhine River. F=Celtic Moguntiacum. Gutenberg (1440). Bishopric (747).
2620	Russelsheim	60,800	75.00	45,600	99.65	C	61,800	Hesse on Main River. Opel automobile plant. F=Frankish Prince Ruzilo. D=EKD.
2621	Wilhelmshaven	125,000	72.00	89,900	98.15	C	127,000	Lower Saxony. North Sea port. Oil, metalworking, machinery. Tourist resort. F=1853. D=EKD.
2622	Wismar	56,800	64.00	36,300	90.15	C	57,700	Mecklenburg-West Pomerania. Shipbuilding, fishing, sugar refining, metalworking. F=1229. D=EKD.
2623	Wittenberg	50,800	65.00	33,000	91.15	C	51,600	Saxony-Anhalt on Elbe River. Chemicals, fertilizers. Wittenberg University (1502). F=1180. D=EKD.
2624	Wolfsburg	131,000	71.00	93,400	97.15	C	134,000	Lower Saxony on Mittelland Canal. Volkswagen plant. F=1938. D=EKD.
2625	Wurzburg	200,000	71.00	142,000	97.15	C	203,000	Bavaria on Main River. Grape growing. F=Celtic settlement. Bishopric by Boniface (741). D=RCC.
2626	Zweibrucken	102,000	73.00	74,700	99.15	C	104,000	Rhineland-Palatinate on Schwarz River. Leather goods, machinery, horse breeding center. F=1352. D=EKD.
2627	Zwickau	184,000	60.00	110,000	86.15	C	187,000	Saxony. Coal mining, automobiles, machinery, cloth. F=1118. St. Catherine's Church (1212). D=EKD.
	GHANA	**20,212,000**	**42.88**	**8,667,000**	**84.63**	**B**	**36,876,000**	**PROTESTANTS 16.6%, INDEPENDENTS 14.4%. PENT-CHAR 22.1%, EVANGELICAL 7.3%, GCC 19.4%**
2628	rural areas	12,459,000	35.96	4,480,000	80.83	B	16,978,000	85.5% (1950), 71.0% (1970), 66.1% (1990), 61.6% (2000), 55.4% (2010), 46.0% (2025)
2629	urban areas	7,754,000	54.00	4,187,000	90.75	B	19,898,000	14.4% (1950), 28.9% (1970), 33.8% (1990), 38.3% (2000), 44.5% (2010), 53.9% (2025)
2630	non-metropolitan areas	3,747,000	53.87	2,018,000	90.56	B	10,122,666	*Sources of data:* Censuses of 1948, 1960, 1970, and 1984.
2631	metropolitan areas	4,007,000	54.13	2,169,000	90.93	B	9,776,000	*Definition:* Localities with a population of 5,000 or more.
2632	ACCRA (Accra-Tema)	2,010,000	65.00	1,307,000	97.75	C	4,651,000	On Gulf of Guinea. Administrative, economic & educational center. Portuguese settled in 1482. D=RCC.
2633	Ashiaman	81,700	65.00	53,100	97.75	C	210,000	Large slum area consisting of shacks with open sewage in muddy streets. D=RCC.
2634	Tema	165,000	65.00	107,000	97.75	C	422,000	Africa's largest man-made harbour. Industrial-residential complex. F=1962. Golf course. D=RCC.
2635	Teshie	104,000	65.00	67,600	97.75	C	267,000	Brewery. Annual Teshie Festival, Aokwei Art Gallery, Odahe Center for Drumming and Dancing. D=RCC.
2636	Cape Coast	143,000	60.00	85,900	95.75	C	367,000	Educational center. Fishing, trade, government administration. F=1655 by Swedes. Castle museum. D=RCC.
2637	Koforidua	89,900	40.00	36,000	78.75	B	231,000	Capital of Eastern Region. Cocoa producing center. Granite quarrying. D=RCC.
2638	Kumasi	992,000	50.00	496,000	94.75	B	2,547,000	Humid, wet climate. Seat of Ashanti Kings. Handicrafts, cocoa. 'Garden city of West Africa'. F=c1650.
2639	Tafo	83,300	50.00	41,700	91.75	B	214,000	Eastern region. West African Cocoa Research Institute. Railroad. D=RCC.
2640	Obuasi	99,300	20.00	19,900	53.75	B	255,000	Ashanti Region. World's richest gold mine, cocoa. Mosque. D=RCC,Presbyterian.
2641	Sekondi-Takoradi	393,000	50.00	196,000	91.75	B	1,008,000	Port city on Gulf of Guinea. Terminus of several Ghana railways. Women street vendors. D=RCC.
2642	Sekondi	291,000	50.00	145,000	91.75	B	747,000	Old & new buildings on a hilly site. Fishing & pleasure craft. D=RCC.
2643	Takoradi	102,000	50.00	50,800	91.75	B	261,000	Well-planned, modern buildings, tree-shaded residential area. Horse racing. D=RCC.
2644	Tamale	279,000	10.00	27,900	41.75	A	717,000	North central region. Educational center, agricultural trade, cotton milling, shea nut. D=RCC,Presbyterian.
	GIBRALTAR	**25,100**	**85.19**	**21,400**	**94.58**	**C**	**21,400**	**ROMAN CATHOLICS 84.5%, ANGLICANS 7.5%. PENT-CHAR 15.5%, EVANGELICAL 1.3%, GCC 9.1%**
2645	rural areas	–	–	–	–	–	–	0.0% (1950), 0.0% (1970), 0.0% (1990), 0.0% (2000), 0.0% (2010), 0.0% (2025)
2646	urban areas	25,100	85.19	21,400	94.58	C	21,400	100.0% (1950), 100.0% (1970), 100.0% (1990), 100.0% (2000), 100.0% (2010), 100.0% (2025)
2647	non-metropolitan areas	–	–	–	–	–	–	*Sources of data:* Censuses of 1951, 1961, 1970, and 1981; estimate for 1989.
2648	metropolitan areas	25,100	85.19	21,400	94.58	C	21,400	*Definition:* Entire population.
2649	GIBRALTAR	25,100	85.19	21,400	94.58	C	21,400	Provisioning of ships & military, tourism, re-export trade. Jews. Ancient origins. D=RCC,Anglicans.
	GREECE	**10,645,000**	**94.52**	**10,061,000**	**98.44**	**C**	**9,863,000**	**ORTHODOX 93.0%, INDEPENDENTS 2.1%. PENT-CHAR 1.1%, EVANGELICAL 0.1%, GCC 2.4%**
2650	rural areas	4,247,000	96.80	4,111,000	99.23	C	3,001,000	62.7% (1950), 47.4% (1970), 41.1% (1990), 39.9% (2000), 36.9% (2010), 30.4% (2025)
2651	urban areas	6,397,000	93.00	5,950,000	97.92	C	6,861,000	37.2% (1950), 52.5% (1970), 58.8% (1990), 60.1% (2000), 63.0% (2010), 69.5% (2025)
2652	non-metropolitan areas	1,053,000	92.81	977,000	97.80	C	1,309,943	*Sources of data:* Censuses of 1951, 1961, 1971, and 1981.
2653	metropolitan areas	5,344,000	93.04	4,972,000	97.94	C	5,551,000	*Definition:* Municipalities and communes in which the largest center has 10,000 or more inhabitants.
2654	Akharnai	61,700	96.00	59,200	99.92	C	66,200	North of Athens. Textiles, soap, alcoholic beverages, using charcoal to supply armor to Athens. G=GOC.
2655	Amarousion	65,400	95.00	62,100	98.92	C	70,100	Northeast of Athens near Kifisia. Pottery making center, summer resort. D=GOC.
2656	ATHINAI (Greater Athens)	3,103,000	92.00	2,855,000	96.92	C	3,118,000	On Aegean Sea. Birthplace of Western civilization. Tourism, publishing. F=c700BC. Ancient temples. D=Orthodox.
2657	Aiyaleo	81,800	95.00	77,700	98.92	C	87,700	West of downtown on Kifisos River. Tourism. D=GOC.
2658	Ayios Dhimitrios	59,000	96.00	56,600	99.92	C	63,200	South near Ilioupolis. D=GOC.
2659	Galatsion	58,500	95.00	55,600	98.92	C	62,800	Northeast. D=GOC.
2660	Ilioupolis	74,600	94.00	70,100	97.92	C	80,000	South near Ayios Dhimitrios.
2661	Kallithea	114,000	93.00	106,000	96.92	C	122,000	Southwest near Ilisos River. Attica prefecture, 9km from city center. Cotton textile manufacturing. D=GOC.
2662	Keratsinion	73,800	95.00	70,100	98.92	C	79,200	Far west beyond Nikaia. D=GOC.
2663	Khalandrion	74,300	95.00	70,600	98.92	C	79,700	East near Ayia Paraskevi. Attica prefecture, 8km from city center. Summer resort. D=GOC.
2664	Koridhallos	64,800	94.00	60,900	97.92	C	69,500	West near Nikaia. Tourism. D=GOC.
2665	Nea Ionia	62,000	95.00	58,900	98.92	C	66,500	North beyond Galatsion. Attica prefecture, 6.4 km from city center. Cotton textile manufacturing. D=GOC.
2666	Nea Liosia	80,200	94.00	75,400	97.92	C	86,000	North beyond Ayioi Anaryiroi. D=GOC.
2667	Nea Smirni	71,200	95.00	67,700	98.92	C	76,400	South near Kallithea. Developed after 1922 settlement of refugees from Smyrna. D=GOC.
2668	Nikaia	90,300	93.00	84,000	96.92	C	96,900	West near Kordhallos. Attica prefecture, Attica dept., 8km from city center. D=GOC.
2669	Palaion Faliron	62,700	95.00	59,500	98.92	C	67,200	South on Saronikos Bay. Attica prefecture, east shore of Phaleron Bay. Seaside resort. D=GOC.
2670	Peristerion	150,000	93.00	139,000	96.92	C	161,000	Northwest across Kifisos River. D=GOC.
2671	Piraieus (Piraeus)	174,000	93.00	162,000	96.92	C	187,000	Largest port. Engineering, chemicals, shipyards. Naval academy. F=c600 BC. Damaged in WWII. D=GOC.
2672	Viron	58,700	95.00	55,800	98.92	C	63,000	Southeast near Kaisariani. Attica prefecture, 4km from city center. Also Vyron, Byron, Virona. D=GOC.
2673	Zografos	80,700	96.00	77,500	99.92	C	86,600	East near Kaisariani Monastery. D=GOC.
2674	Glifadha	64,000	95.00	60,800	98.92	C	68,700	South of Athens beyond Ellininko International Airport. D=GOC.
2675	Ioannina (Yannina, Janina)	58,100	96.00	55,700	99.92	C	62,300	Capital of Ioannina. Agricultural & commercial center, metals, embroidery. Y=c850. D=GOC.
2676	Iraklion (Heraklion)	121,000	95.00	115,000	98.92	C	129,000	Principal port of Crete. Exports, grapes, olives, wines. Tourism. F=832. Many churches and mosques. D=GOC.
2677	Kalamai (Kalamata)	47,000	96.00	45,100	99.92	C	50,400	Capital of Messenia. Silk cloth, flour, tobacco. Principal outlet for exports. Bishopric. D=GOC.
2678	Kavala (Kavalla)	60,200	96.00	57,800	99.92	C	64,600	Seaport of Macedonia. Tobacco, vineyards. Y=c50 by St. Paul. Near ruins of Philippi. D=GOC.
2679	Khalkis (Chalcis)	52,900	96.00	50,800	99.92	C	56,700	Capital of Euboea. Agricultural trade, resort. Aristotle died here in 322 BC. D=GOC.
2680	Khania (Canea)	67,400	96.00	64,700	99.92	C	72,300	Capital of Crete. Exports citrus fruits, olive oil, wine. Heavily damaged in WWII. D=GOC,RCC.
2681	Larisa (Larissa)	129,000	95.00	123,000	98.92	C	138,000	Capital of Larisa. Agriculture, silk cloth. Y=Seat of Bishop since 9th century. Ancient capital of Delagian. D=GOC.
2682	Patrai (Patras)	168,000	95.00	160,000	98.92	C	180,000	Capital of Achaea on Gulf of Patraikos. Currents. Pre-Lenten Carnival. St. Andrew crucified here. D=GOC.
2683	Rodhos (Rhodes)	44,800	96.00	43,000	99.92	C	48,100	Island of Rhodes. Ancient origins. Resort. Colossus of Rhodes. F=408 BC. Church of the Evangelismos. D=GOC.

Table 10-5–continued opposite

Table 10-5–continued

Rec No 1	Country City 2	Pop 2000 3	AC% 4	Church Members 5	E% 6	W 7	Pop 2025 8	Notes 9
2684	Serrai	52,300	95.00	49,700	98.92	C	56,100	North near Strimon River northeast of Thessaloniki. D=GOC.
2685	Thessaloniki (Salonica)	1,083,000	93.50	1,013,000	99.42	C	1,191,000	Capital of Thessaloniki. Oil. F=315 BC. Jewish synagogue. First Bishop-Gaius. D=GOC.
2686	Ampelokipoi	43,500	94.00	40,900	97.92	C	46,700	Theatre Keron. D=GOC.
2687	Kalamaria	56,200	95.00	53,400	98.92	C	60,300	Philharmonic Orchestra. D=GOC.
2688	Trikala (Trikkala)	50,200	96.00	48,200	99.92	C	53,800	Capital of Trikala. Agricultural & grazing center. Winter migration of Vlach herdsmen. D=GOC.
2689	Volos	117,000	95.00	111,000	98.92	C	125,000	Capital of Magnisia on Gulf of Volos. Cereals, wines, cotton. Orthodox bishop of Demetrias. D=GOC.
	GREENLAND	**56,200**	**70.07**	**39,400**	**99.70**	**C**	**59,600**	**PROTESTANTS 69.2%, MARGINAL CHRISTIANS 0.4%. PENT-CHAR 9.9%, EVANGELICAL 3.7%, GCC 22.1%**
2690	rural areas	9,900	70.41	7,000	99.96	C	7,400	23.6% (1950), 26.6% (1970), 20.5% (1990), 17.6% (2000), 15.2% (2010), 12.4% (2025)
2691	urban areas	46,300	70.00	32,400	99.65	C	52,200	76.3% (1950), 73.3% (1970), 79.4% (1990), 82.3% (2000), 84.8% (2010), 87.5% (2025)
2692	non-metropolitan areas	33,200	70.00	23,200	99.65	C	37,491	*Sources of data:* Censuses of 1960, 1970, and 1976.
2693	metropolitan areas	13,000	70.00	9,100	99.65	C	14,700	*Definition:* Localities designated.
2694	GODTHAB (Nuuk)	13,000	70.00	9,100	99.65	C	14,700	Hunting, fishing, reindeer. Founded by Hans Egede, Norwegian missionary (1721). D=Lutheran.
	GRENADA	**93,700**	**96.83**	**90,700**	**99.97**	**C**	**105,000**	**ROMAN CATHOLICS 56.2%, PROTESTANTS 20.3%. PENT-CHAR 15.1%, EVANGELICAL 10.7%, GCC 6.8%**
2695	rural areas	58,200	97.03	56,500	99.99	C	48,800	71.5% (1950), 67.7% (1970), 65.7% (1990), 62.0% (2000), 56.0% (2010), 46.6% (2025)
2696	urban areas	35,500	96.50	34,300	99.94	C	55,900	28.5% (1950), 32.2% (1970), 34.2% (1990), 37.9% (2000), 43.9% (2010), 53.4% (2025)
2697	non-metropolitan areas	9,700	96.50	9,300	99.95	C	15,220	*Sources of data:* Censuses.
2698	metropolitan areas	25,900	96.50	24,900	99.94	C	40,700	*Definition:* St. George's.
2699	ST GEORGE'S	25,900	96.50	24,900	99.94	C	40,700	Tourist resort, exports, cocoa, nutmeg, mace, bananas. F=1650 by French. D=RCC, Anglican, Presbyterian.
	GUADELOUPE	**456,000**	**95.01**	**433,000**	**99.90**	**C**	**569,000**	**ROMAN CATHOLICS 95.0%, PROTESTANTS 4.9%. PENT-CHAR 5.0%, EVANGELICAL 3.0%, GCC 14.4%**
2700	rural areas	1,200	91.30	1,100	97.97	C	570	64.2% (1950), 24.5% (1970), 1.4% (1990), 0.2% (2000), 0.1% (2010), 0.1% (2025)
2701	urban areas	454,000	95.02	432,000	99.91	C	569,000	35.7% (1950), 75.4% (1970), 98.5% (1990), 99.7% (2000), 99.8% (2010), 99.9% (2025)
2702	non-metropolitan areas	226,000	94.98	214,000	99.93	C	282,393	*Sources of data:* Censuses of 1954, 1982, and 1990; estimates for 1961 and 1967.
2703	metropolitan areas	229,000	95.06	217,000	99.89	C	286,000	*Definition:* Localities with 2,000 or more inhabitants.
2704	BASSE-TERRE	36,700	96.00	35,200	99.91	C	45,900	Capital on southern Basse Terre Island. Bananas. Black beaches. F=1643 by French. D=RCC.
2705	Les Abymes	77,500	95.00	73,600	99.89	C	97,000	Grande Island near International Airport. D=RCC.
2706	Pointe-a-Pitre	115,000	94.80	109,000	99.89	C	143,000	Grande Island on Petit Cul-de-Sac Marin. Over 900 ships call p.a. Rum, coffee, sugar. Yachting. D=RCC.
	GUAM	**168,000**	**93.49**	**157,000**	**98.98**	**C**	**228,000**	**ROMAN CATHOLICS 83.2%, PROTESTANTS 10.4%. PENT-CHAR 5.9%, EVANGELICAL 5.0%, GCC 10.1%**
2707	rural areas	102,000	93.81	95,500	99.30	C	107,000	82.8% (1950), 74.1% (1970), 61.8% (1990), 60.7% (2000), 56.5% (2010), 47.0% (2025)
2708	urban areas	65,700	93.00	61,100	98.49	C	121,000	17.2% (1950), 25.8% (1970), 38.1% (1990), 39.2% (2000), 43.4% (2010), 52.9% (2025)
2709	non-metropolitan areas	4,500	93.00	4,200	98.49	C	8,202	*Sources of data:* Censuses of 1960, 1970, 1980, and 1990.
2710	metropolitan areas	61,300	93.00	57,000	98.49	C	112,000	*Definition:* Places with 2,500 or more inhabitants and urbanized areas.
2711	AGANA	61,300	93.00	57,000	98.49	C	112,000	Government administration. Completely destroyed in WWII. Cathedral, Dulce Nombre de Maria. D=RCC.
	GUATEMALA	**11,385,000**	**93.84**	**10,684,000**	**99.93**	**C**	**19,816,000**	**ROMAN CATHOLICS 84.3%, PROTESTANTS 12.7%. PENT-CHAR 21.8%, EVANGELICAL 10.3%, GCC 8.5%**
2712	rural areas	6,791,000	97.12	6,596,000	99.99	C	9,022,000	70.5% (1950), 64.4% (1970), 62.0% (1990), 59.6% (2000), 54.8% (2010), 45.5% (2025)
2713	urban areas	4,594,000	89.00	4,089,000	99.84	C	10,794,000	29.5% (1950), 35.5% (1970), 38.0% (1990), 40.3% (2000), 45.1% (2010), 54.4% (2025)
2714	non-metropolitan areas	1,693,000	89.02	1,507,000	99.89	C	4,272,574	*Sources of data:* Censuses of 1964, 1973, and 1981.
2715	metropolitan areas	2,901,000	88.99	2,582,000	99.81	C	6,521,000	*Definition:* Municipality of Guatemala Department, including suburbs that border the municipality.
2716	Escuintla	83,000	90.00	74,700	99.29	C	195,000	Capital of Escuintla. Winter resort, cotton, meat-packing, agricultural trade. D=RCC.
2717	GUATEMALA (Guatemala City)	2,697,000	89.00	2,400,000	99.84	C	6,041,000	Temperate mountain climate at 4,897 ft. Center of trade, commerce, government, education. F=1776. D=RCC.
2718	Quezaltenango (Quetzaltenango)	121,000	88.00	107,000	99.49	C	285,000	Capital of Quetzaltenango at 7,656 ft. Trade center, textiles, mills, breweries. Hot sulfur baths. D=RCC.
	GUINEA	**7,430,000**	**3.11**	**231,000**	**41.63**	**A**	**12,497,000**	**ROMAN CATHOLICS 1.5%, PROTESTANTS 0.9%. PENT-CHAR 0.8%, EVANGELICAL 0.7%, GCC 2.2%**
2719	rural areas	4,995,000	3.01	150,000	39.82	A	6,328,000	94.5% (1950), 86.1% (1970), 74.3% (1990), 67.2% (2000), 60.4% (2010), 50.6% (2025)
2720	urban areas	2,436,000	3.32	80,900	45.34	A	6,168,000	5.5% (1950), 13.8% (1970), 25.6% (1990), 32.7% (2000), 39.5% (2010), 49.3% (2025)
2721	non-metropolitan areas	9,900	3.34	330	44.86	A	–	*Sources of data:* Census of 1955; estimates for 1950, 1960, 1972, and 1983.
2722	metropolitan areas	2,426,000	3.32	80,500	45.34	A	6,344,000	*Definition:* Urban centers.
2723	CONAKRY (Konakry)	1,896,000	4.00	75,800	47.32	A	5,002,000	Chief Atlantic port on Tombo Island. Textiles, fish. Exports alumina & bananas. F=1884 by French. D=RCC.
2724	Kankan	151,000	1.00	1,500	39.52	A	384,000	On Milo River. Traditional crafts. Diamonds. F=c1750 by Soninke merchants. Malinke, Diula. D=RCC.
2725	Kindia	121,000	0.50	610	34.02	A	307,000	Chief trading center for rice, cattle, bananas. F=1904. Muslim Susu & Fulani. M=RCC(1908). D=RCC.
2726	Labe	167,000	1.00	1,700	39.52	A	422,000	Chief trading center for cattle, rice, millet, oranges. Muslim center. Fulani. F=1720 by Dialonke. M=RCC (1954).
2727	Nzerekore	90,500	1.00	910	39.52	A	229,000	South near Liberian border. Gold and iron deposits, timber, rice, palm kernals, coffee, tobacco. D=RCC.
	GUINEA-BISSAU	**1,213,000**	**12.83**	**156,000**	**48.17**	**A**	**1,946,000**	**ROMAN CATHOLICS 11.6%, INDEPENDENTS 2.5%. PENT-CHAR 2.8%, EVANGELICAL 0.7%, GCC 8.0%**
2728	rural areas	925,000	12.16	112,000	45.94	A	1,201,000	89.9% (1950), 84.8% (1970), 79.9% (1990), 76.2% (2000), 71.2% (2010), 61.7% (2025)
2729	urban areas	288,000	15.00	43,200	55.34	B	745,000	10.0% (1950), 15.1% (1970), 20.0% (1990), 23.7% (2000), 28.7% (2010), 38.2% (2025)
2730	non-metropolitan areas	127,000	15.00	19,000	55.34	B	327,618	*Sources of data:* Censuses of 1950, 1960, and 1979.
2731	metropolitan areas	161,000	15.00	24,200	55.34	B	417,000	*Definition:* Urban centers.
2732	BISSAU	161,000	15.00	24,200	55.34	B	417,000	Port city. F=1687. 95% speak Crioulo (24% Papel, 22% Balanta, 10% Manjaco). 60% Muslim. D=RCC.
	GUYANA	**861,000**	**43.43**	**374,000**	**81.25**	**B**	**1,045,000**	**PROTESTANTS 19.5%, ROMAN CATHOLICS 10.0%. PENT-CHAR 14.6%, EVANGELICAL 12.1%, GCC 12.1%**
2733	rural areas	532,000	45.54	242,000	82.13	B	479,000	71.9% (1950), 70.5% (1970), 66.7% (1990), 61.8% (2000), 55.2% (2010), 45.8% (2025)
2734	urban areas	329,000	40.00	132,000	79.82	B	566,000	28.0% (1950), 29.4% (1970), 33.2% (1990), 38.1% (2000), 44.7% (2010), 54.1% (2025)
2735	non-metropolitan areas	116,000	40.00	46,400	79.82	B	199,606	*Sources of data:* Censuses of 1950, 1960, 1970, and 1980.
2736	metropolitan areas	213,000	40.00	85,200	79.82	B	366,000	*Definition:* Cities of Georgetown, New Amsterdam, and Upper Demerara River.
2737	GEORGETOWN	213,000	40.00	85,200	79.82	B	366,000	Port at mouth of Demerara River. Sugar, rice. F=1781 by British. Predominately African. D=Anglican,RCC.
	HAITI	**8,222,000**	**92.91**	**7,639,000**	**99.93**	**C**	**11,988,000**	**ROMAN CATHOLICS 79.3%, PROTESTANTS 17.5%. PENT-CHAR 18.2%, EVANGELICAL 14.2%, GCC 6.5%**
2738	rural areas	5,353,000	93.40	5,000,000	99.99	C	5,857,000	87.8% (1950), 80.2% (1970), 71.1% (1990), 65.1% (2000), 58.5% (2010), 48.8% (2025)
2739	urban areas	2,869,000	92.00	2,639,000	99.82	C	6,131,000	12.1% (1950), 19.7% (1970), 28.8% (1990), 34.8% (2000), 41.4% (2010), 51.1% (2025)
2740	non-metropolitan areas	935,000	91.59	857,000	99.81	C	1,928,386	*Sources of data:* Censuses of 1950, 1971, and 1982; estimate for 1990.
2741	metropolitan areas	1,933,000	92.20	1,783,000	99.82	C	4,202,000	*Definition:* Administrative centers of communes.
2742	Cap-Haitien (Le Cap)	94,100	95.00	89,400	99.92	C	201,000	Capital of Nord. Bananas, pineapples, rope fibers. F=1670 by the French. D=RCC.
2743	Gonaives	48,300	94.00	45,400	99.82	C	103,000	Capital of L'Artibonite on Gulf of Gonave. Commercial port. Coffee, sugar. Musee du Centenaire (1904). D=RCC.
2744	PORT-AU-PRINCE	1,791,000	92.00	1,648,000	99.82	C	3,898,000	On Gulf of Gonave. Textiles, cottonseed oil, tourism. F=1749 by French. Voodoo. D=RCC.
	HOLY SEE	**1,000**	**98.00**	**980**	**100.00**	**C**	**1,000**	**ROMAN CATHOLICS 98.0%. PENT-CHAR 12.0%, EVANGELICAL 2.0%, GCC 46.1%**
2745	rural areas	–	–	–	–	–	–	0.0% (1950), 0.0% (1970), 0.0% (1990), 0.0% (2000), 0.0% (2010), 0.0% (2025)
2746	urban areas	1,000	98.00	980	100.00	C	1,000	100.0% (1950), 100.0% (1970), 100.0% (1990), 100.0% (2000), 100.0% (2010), 100.0% (2025)
2747	non-metropolitan areas	–	–	–	–	–	–	*Sources of data:* Censuses.
2748	metropolitan areas	1,000	98.00	980	100.00	C	1,000	*Definition:* Entire population.
2749	CITTA DEL VATICANO (Vatican City)	1,000	98.00	980	100.00	C	1,000	Enclave of Rome on Tibre River. All supplies imported. Vatican library, Sistine Chapel, St. Peter's (c350). All RCC.
	HONDURAS	**6,485,000**	**93.40**	**6,058,000**	**99.90**	**C**	**10,656,000**	**ROMAN CATHOLICS 86.1%, PROTESTANTS 6.5%. PENT-CHAR 13.2%, EVANGELICAL 4.7%, GCC 6.3%**
2750	rural areas	3,443,000	94.38	3,250,000	99.99	C	4,096,000	82.4% (1950), 71.1% (1970), 59.3% (1990), 53.0% (2000), 46.8% (2010), 38.4% (2025)
2751	urban areas	3,042,000	92.30	2,808,000	99.80	C	6,560,000	17.5% (1950), 28.9% (1970), 40.6% (1990), 46.9% (2000), 53.1% (2010), 61.5% (2025)
2752	non-metropolitan areas	1,156,000	92.27	1,067,000	99.86	C	2,742,234	*Sources of data:* Censuses of 1961, 1974, and 1988.
2753	metropolitan areas	1,886,000	92.32	1,742,000	99.77	C	3,818,000	*Definition:* Localities with 2,000 or more inhabitants.
2754	Choluteca	76,000	94.00	71,400	99.83	C	164,000	On Choluteca River. Coffee, cattle, bees. F=1522 as mining center by Spanish. D=RCC.
2755	El Progreso	78,400	94.00	73,700	99.83	C	169,000	On Ulua River. Cement, metals, shoes, coffee. F=1927 as banana trade center. D=RCC.
2756	La Ceiba	96,400	93.00	89,700	99.70	C	208,000	Atlantida on Gulf of Honduras. International school. Coconuts, citrus fruits, beaches. D=RCC.
2757	San Pedro Sula	395,000	92.50	365,000	99.65	C	851,000	Capital of Cortes. Agricultural center, manufacturing. F=1536 by Spanish. International school. D=RCC.
2758	TEGUCIGALPA	1,241,000	92.00	1,142,000	99.80	C	2,426,000	El. 3,200 ft. Universities, textiles. F=1578 as mining center. 'Mountain of silver'. D=RCC.
	HUNGARY	**10,036,000**	**87.19**	**8,750,000**	**99.35**	**C**	**8,900,000**	**ROMAN CATHOLICS 63.0%, PROTESTANTS 25.5%. PENT-CHAR 6.8%, EVANGELICAL 4.5%, GCC 10.6%**
2759	rural areas	3,317,000	91.62	3,039,000	99.32	C	2,079,000	60.7% (1950), 51.4% (1970), 37.9% (1990), 33.0% (2000), 28.7% (2010), 23.3% (2025)
2760	urban areas	6,719,000	85.00	5,711,000	99.36	C	6,821,000	39.2% (1950), 48.5% (1970), 62.0% (1990), 66.9% (2000), 71.2% (2010), 76.6% (2025)
2761	non-metropolitan areas	2,691,000	85.25	2,294,000	99.31	C	2,762,634	*Sources of data:* Censuses of 1949, 1960, 1970, 1980, and 1990.
2762	metropolitan areas	4,028,000	84.83	3,417,000	99.39	C	4,059,000	*Definition:* Budapest and all legally designated towns.
2763	BUDAPEST	2,017,000	85.00	1,714,000	99.16	C	2,017,000	On Danube River. Heavy industry, foreign trade. F=3rd century BC. Matthias Church (13th century). D=RCC.
2764	Bekescsaba	65,200	85.00	55,400	99.66	C	66,200	Seat of Bekes. Flour milling, tobacco, sausage. Largely Slovak. D=Lutheran,RCC(since 13th century).
2765	Debrecen	206,000	83.00	171,000	99.46	C	209,000	Seat of Hadju-Bihar. Market center, horses, livestock, pottery. F=13th century. Center of Hungarian Protestantism.
2766	Dunaujvaros	56,700	85.00	48,200	99.66	C	57,600	Fejer county on Danube River. Iron works, textiles. Roman ruins. Greek Orthodox Church. D=RCC.
2767	Eger	60,200	86.00	51,800	99.76	C	61,100	Seat of Heves. Tourism, spa, wine. F=old Magyar tribal city. Y=11th century. RCC center.
2768	Gyor	125,000	85.00	106,000	99.66	C	127,000	Capital of Gyor-Sopron on Raba River. Horse breeding, grain. F=Roman Arabona. 12th century cathedral.
2769	Hodmezovasarhely	49,300	86.00	42,400	99.76	C	50,100	Csongrad. Grain & fiber processing, dairying. Calvinist, Greek Orthodox churches. D=RCC.
2770	Kaposvar	68,800	85.00	58,500	99.66	C	69,800	Seat of Somogy. Rye, potatoes, textiles. Center of Hungarian art & poetry. 11th century Benedictine monastery.
2771	Kecskemet	99,800	84.00	83,800	99.56	C	101,000	Seat of Bacs-Kiskun. Handicrafts, cattle rearing, fruit growing region. D=RCC.
2772	Miskolc	187,000	85.00	159,000	99.66	C	190,000	Borsod-Abauj-Zemplen. Cement, glass, textiles, wine. Many old churches. Ancient origin. Protestant bishopric.
2773	Nagykanizsa	51,700	84.00	43,500	99.56	C	52,500	Zala near Croatian border. D=RCC.
2774	Nyiregyhaza	110,000	83.00	91,700	99.46	C	112,000	Seat of Szabolcs-Szatmer. Natural gas, health resort. Destroyed under Turks (16th century). D=RCC.
2775	Ozd	41,500	86.00	35,700	99.76	C	42,100	Borsod-Abauj-Zemplen near Slovakian border. Wine, iron ore.
2776	Pecs	164,000	85.00	139,000	99.66	C	166,000	Capital of Baranya on Danube & Drava Rivers. Handicrafts. F=Celtic origins. RC Bishopric since 1009.
2777	Salgotarjan	45,800	86.00	39,400	99.76	C	46,500	Seat of Nograd. Coal mines, cast iron foundry, glassworks. D=RCC.
2778	Sopron	53,100	85.00	45,200	99.66	C	53,900	Gyor-Sopron. Fruit, sugar, tourism, mercantile center. Ancient origins. Medieval city center. D=RCC.
2779	Szeged	170,000	85.00	144,000	99.66	C	172,000	Seat of Csongrad on Tisza River. Paprika, salami. Protected by dikes. Annual summer festival. D=RCC.
2780	Szekesfehervar	105,000	85.00	89,400	99.66	C	107,000	Seat of Fejer. Market for truck farmers, wine growers. Destroyed in 1688 & 1945. Burial site for Kings. D=RCC.
2781	Szolnok	75,800	84.00	63,700	99.56	C	77,000	Seat of Szolnok. Transportation center & river port, baths. F=10th century. D=RCC.
2782	Szombathely	82,600	85.00	70,200	99.66	C	83,800	Seat of Vos on Gyongyos River. Wines, fruits, honey. F=AD 43 as Sabaria, Roman town. Cathedral. D=RCC.
2783	Tatabanya	71,200	84.00	59,800	99.56	C	72,300	Seat of Komarom. Main mining center, lignite, aluminum, cement. D=RCC.

Table 10-5–continued overleaf

Table 10-5–continued

Rec No 1	Country City 2	Pop 2000 3	AC% 4	Church Members 5	E% 6	W 7	Pop 2025 8	Notes 9
2784	Veszprem	61,900	86.00	53,300	99.76	C	62,900	Seat of Veszprem on Sed River. Textiles, wine. Bishop's palace (1765). Cathedral of St. Michael. D=RCC.
2785	Zalaegerszeg	60,100	85.00	51,100	99.66	C	61,000	Seat of Zala on Zala River. Clothing. Medieval origins. Barogue parish church (1760). D=RCC.
	ICELAND	**281,000**	**94.41**	**265,000**	**99.95**	**C**	**328,000**	**PROTESTANTS 89.1%, INDEPENDENTS 3.9%. PENT-CHAR 8.1%, EVANGELICAL 2.3%, GCC 10.8%**
2786	rural areas	21,600	94.15	20,300	99.65	C	17,900	26.2% (1950), 15.1% (1970), 9.4% (1990), 7.6% (2000), 6.5% (2010), 5.4% (2025)
2787	urban areas	259,000	94.43	245,000	99.97	C	310,000	73.8% (1950), 84.9% (1970), 90.6% (1990), 92.3% (2000), 93.4% (2010), 94.5% (2025)
2788	non-metropolitan areas	95,600	94.48	90,300	99.99	C	114,390	*Sources of data:* Estimates for 1950, 1960, 1970, 1980, and 1990.
2789	metropolitan areas	164,000	94.40	155,000	99.96	C	196,000	*Definition:* Localities with 200 or more inhabitants.
2790	REYKJAVIK	164,000	94.40	155,000	99.96	C	196,000	On Faxa Bay. Major fishing port. Hot water springs. F=874 by Norsemen. Y=1000. 'Smokey bay'. D=Lutheran.
	INDIA	**1,013,662,000**	**6.14**	**62,244,000**	**59.34**	**B**	**1,330,449,000**	**INDEPENDENTS 3.3%, PROTESTANTS 1.6%. PENT-CHAR 3.3%, EVANGELICAL 0.9%, GCC 4.9%**
2791	rural areas	725,376,000	6.68	48,435,000	61.87	B	764,609,000	82.7% (1950), 80.2% (1970), 74.4% (1990), 71.5% (2000), 67.0% (2010), 57.4% (2025)
2792	urban areas	288,285,000	4.79	13,809,000	52.99	B	565,840,000	17.2% (1950), 19.7% (1970), 25.5% (1990), 28.4% (2000), 33.0% (2010), 42.5% (2025)
2793	non-metropolitan areas	82,180,000	4.77	3,916,000	53.17	B	186,095,811	*Sources of data:* Censuses of 1951, 1961, 1971, 1981, and 1991.
2794	metropolitan areas	206,106,000	4.80	9,893,000	52.92	B	379,744,000	*Definition:* Towns and all places having 5,000 or more inhabitants.
2795	Abohar	126,000	0.09	110	28.29	A	247,000	Punjab near Rajasthan and Pakistan. Wheat, cotton, rice, hand loom weaving, cotton ginning, metalworks. D=CNI.
2796	Achalpur	113,000	0.40	450	38.60	A	222,000	Maharashtra near Amravati, foot of Gawilgarh hills, off branch of Purha River.
2797	Adilabad (Edlabad)	99,200	2.20	2,200	50.40	B	195,000	Andhra Pradesh. Agricultural trade center. Teak, ebony, mining, rice. D=CSI,COG.
2798	Adoni	160,000	2.20	3,500	50.40	B	314,000	Andhra Pradesh. Cotton cloth, carpets. Stronghold of Medieval Hindu Kingdom. Jami Masjid (1680). D=CSI,JS.
2799	Agartala	186,000	0.31	580	38.51	A	365,000	Capital of Tripura State. Commercial center on Haroa River. D=RCC.
2800	Agra	1,167,000	1.00	11,700	44.20	A	2,094,000	Uttar Pradesh on Yamuna River. Tourism. Taj Mahal, Red fort. F=c1520. Agra University. D=RCC,Methodist.
2801	Agra Cantonment	58,900	1.00	590	44.20	A	116,000	Uttar Pradesh. Millet, barley, tourism. F=c1520. Taj Mahal, Red Fort. D=CNI,CBAF,RCC.
2802	Ahmadabad (Ahmedabad)	4,154,000	1.60	66,500	44.80	A	7,164,000	Gujarat. Largest inland industrial center in India. F=1411 by Muslims. Jains (100 temples). D=CNI,RCC.
2803	Vejalpur	105,000	1.50	1,600	44.70	A	206,000	Gujarat. Sabarmati River. North of Ahmedabad. Cotton, sugarcane. D=CNI,Independent,RCC.
2804	Ahmadnagar (Ahmednagar)	261,000	10.00	26,100	63.20	B	513,000	Maharashtra on Sina River. Cotton, leather, millet, sugarcane, herbal medicines. D=CNI,IPLOG,RCC,SA.
2805	Aizawl	182,000	90.00	164,000	99.20	C	357,000	Mizoram. Aluminum utensils, textiles, furniture. Mizo Hills tribes. D=CBCNEI.
2806	Ajmer (Ajmere, Ajmir)	474,000	1.75	8,300	44.95	A	929,000	Rajasthan. Trade center for salt, mica, cloth, handicrafts. Ancient Jaina temple. F=1100. D=CNI,Brethren.
2807	Akola	386,000	1.10	4,300	44.30	A	758,000	Maharashtra on Murna River. Cotton, textiles, vegetable oils. D=CNI,COG,CMA,COC.
2808	Akot	77,400	0.30	230	38.50	A	152,000	Maharashtra in Gawilgarh Hills. North of Purha River, NW of Amravati. M=GFA,IOM.
2809	Aligarh (Koil, Kol)	565,000	0.44	2,500	38.64	A	1,110,000	Uttar Pradesh. Agricultural trade center. Fort. Tombs of Muslim saints. D=CNI.
2810	Alipur Duar	122,000	0.02	24	28.22	A	239,000	West Bengal. Market center for rice, tobacco, jute. Rice milling. D=CNI.
2811	Allahabad	1,061,000	1.10	11,700	44.30	A	1,916,000	Uttar Pradesh. Ganges & Jumna Rivers. Every 12th year Kumbha Mela. D=CNI. M=FMPB.
2812	Alleppey	312,000	27.00	84,300	90.20	B	613,000	Kerala on Arabian Sea. Coconuts, pepper, rice, tapioca. D=OSC,RCC.
2813	Alwar (Alwur)	249,000	0.18	450	38.38	A	488,000	Rajasthan. Cloth, oilseed, flour. Surrounded by wall and moat. Ancient mosques. D=CNI,IPCOG.
2814	Amalner	90,000	0.30	270	38.50	A	177,000	Maharashtra near Tapi River. North. Cloth fabric trades, millet, wheat, cotton, ginning.
2815	Ambajogai	67,200	0.30	200	38.50	A	132,000	Maharashtra. Balaghat Range. Near Latur. D=Methodist,Brethren.
2816	Ambala (Umbala)	141,000	0.57	800	38.77	A	276,000	Haryana. Grain, cotton, sugarcane trade center, bamboo furniture making. Air force academy. D=CNI,IPC,IPA.
2817	Ambala Sadar	57,600	0.60	350	38.80	A	113,000	Haryana. Main highway, railroad, grain, cotton. Processed foods, flour. D=CNI,Independent.
2818	Ambasamudram	70,100	9.00	6,300	62.20	B	138,000	Tamil Nadu. Agricultural center, cotton goods, oil cake, metal industry supplies bells to temples in state. d=csi.
2819	Ambikapur	62,700	0.80	500	39.00	A	123,000	Madhya Pradesh. Ramgarh Hills. Rice, oilseeds, bamboo, coal deposits. D=Mennonite,IPC,MTSC.
2820	Ambur	89,200	5.00	4,500	58.20	B	175,000	Tamil Nadu near Vaniyambadi. Tanbark, tamarind, hemp, narcotics, tannery, sugar mills. D=CSI,FFNI,AoG.
2821	Amravati (Amraoti)	511,000	0.35	1,800	38.55	A	1,003,000	Maharashtra on Purna River. Cotton ginning, agricultural market. Great Stupa temple (2nd century). D=CNI,CMA
2822	Amreli (Amaravalli)	81,600	0.02	16	28.22	A	160,000	Gujarat. Cotton, tanning, chemicals, pharmaceuticals. Ancient religious center at Venivala River. D=Methodist.
2823	Amritsar	829,000	0.70	5,800	38.90	A	1,490,000	Punjab. Textiles, silk. Center of Sikh faith. F=1577 by Ram Pas, fourth Guru of the Sikhs. D=BCOG,SA,IPC.
2824	Amroha	161,000	0.08	130	28.28	A	317,000	Uttar Pradesh on Sot River. Handloom weaving, pottery, sugar. Shrine of Sheikh Saddu.
2825	Anakapalle	99,400	4.60	4,600	57.80	B	195,000	Andhra Pradesh on Bay of Bengal. Sugar, rice, oilseed, agricultural research. Buddhist stupa nearby. D=CSI,AELC.
2826	Anand	130,000	1.40	1,800	44.60	A	255,000	Gujarat near Nadiad, Mahi River. Railroad, commerce, trade, livestock. D=Methodist,GFA.
2827	Anantapur	206,000	2.10	4,300	50.30	B	404,000	Andhra Pradesh. Colleges of science, arts, engineering. Medieval origins. D=CSI,ECI.
2828	Anjar	60,300	0.20	120	38.40	A	118,000	Gujarat near Gulf of Kachchh. Railroad junction, wheat, cotton, barley, embroidery. D=CNI.
2829	Ankleshwar	92,000	0.70	640	38.90	A	181,000	Gujarat on Gulf of Khambhat. Near Bharuch. Major industrial center, soap, stone cutting, crude oil. D=CNI.
2830	Arcot	135,000	5.70	7,700	58.90	B	266,000	Tamil Nadu on Palar River. Fortified Muslim capital in 17th & 18th centuries. Weaving. D=CSI,ECI,RCC.
2831	Arakkonam	84,200	3.00	2,500	51.20	B	165,000	Tamil Nadu west of Madras. Ambedkar district. Railroad junction, workshops. D=CSI,AoG,ECI.
2832	Arni	64,700	0.10	65	38.30	A	127,000	Tamil Nadu. Chingleput. Rice, cotton, peanuts, silk-weaving, madras, tamarind, sesame. D=TFGC.
2833	Arrah (Ara)	185,000	0.14	260	38.34	A	363,000	Bihar. Agricultural trade, oilseed milling, rice, sugarcane, limestone deposits, 3 colleges. M=GEMS,OM.
2834	Asansol	1,423,000	0.93	13,200	39.13	A	2,734,000	West Bengal. Coal trading & railway center, textiles, iron, steel, pharmaceuticals. D=CNI,AoG,Methodist.
2835	Kulti	128,000	0.90	1,200	39.10	A	252,000	West Bengal west of Asansol near Panchet Reservoir. Major iron, steelworks. D=CNI,Lutheran.
2836	Attur	65,400	3.50	2,300	51.70	B	128,000	Tamil Nadu east of Salem, Kalrayan Hills. Rice, cotton, sugar, castor oil, bamboo, sandalwood. D=CSI.
2837	Auraiya	59,800	0.40	240	38.60	A	117,000	Uttar Pradesh near Yamuna River. Near Kanpur. Pearl millet, wheat, barley, cotton, corn. F=16th century.
2838	Aurangabad	1,010,000	1.63	16,500	44.83	A	1,930,000	Maharashtra on Kaum River. Artistic silk fabrics. F=1610 as Khadki. Temple caves. D=CNI,RCC. M=GEMS.
2839	Azamgarh	92,300	0.06	55	28.26	A	181,000	Uttar Pradesh on Tons Rivers. Sugar milling, cotton weaving. F=1665 by A'zam Khan. D=EHC.
2840	Badagara	121,000	5.00	6,000	58.20	B	237,000	Kerala. Port, fishing & trade center for pepper, copra, timber. D=OSC,RCC.
2841	Bagaha	76,100	0.20	150	38.40	A	149,000	Bihar on Gandak River. Near Nepal border. M=Independent.
2842	Bagalkot	90,500	0.40	360	38.60	A	178,000	Karnataka on Ghatprabha River. Market center, cotton, peanuts, millet, wheat, slate, flagstone. D=CSI. M=NMS.
2843	Bahadurgarh	67,400	0.10	67	38.30	A	132,000	Haryana near Delhi. Railroad, traditional handcrafts, market, trade. Millet, grain, salt, wheat. D=NICOG,GFA.
2844	Baharampur (Berhampur, Berhampore)	149,000	0.20	300	38.40	A	292,000	West Bengal. Agricultural trade, silk weaving, rice milling, ivory carving. F=1757. D=CNI,AoG.
2845	Bahraich	159,000	0.04	64	28.24	A	313,000	Uttar Pradesh. Trade center with Nepal. Afghan warrior-saint tomb. Buddhist monastery ruins.
2846	Bal'y (Bally, Bali)	86,300	0.50	430	38.70	A	169,000	West Bengal. Jute, paper, bone-milling, chemical fertilizer, textiles, construction materials, iron, steel.
2847	Balaghat	79,100	0.80	630	39.00	A	155,000	Madhya Pradesh. Agricultural trade, manganese mining, sugar milling. D=Methodist,CFIM,IPC.
2848	Balangir	82,500	3.60	3,000	51.80	B	162,000	Orissa near Tel River. Paved highway, rice, minerals, oilseeds, cloth, metalware, graphite, gold, silver. D=RCC.
2849	Balasore (Baleshwar)	121,000	1.10	1,300	44.30	A	237,000	Orissa. Rice, fish, cotton goods, kerosene, salt, hand loom weaving. F=1633 as British settlement. D=JKPS,EHC.
2850	Ballarpur	109,000	1.40	1,500	44.60	A	214,000	Maharashtra on Wardha River south of Chandrapur. Coal mining, sawmilling, teak, ceramics. D=CNI,COG.
2851	Ballia	99,900	0.30	300	38.50	A	196,000	Uttar Pradesh on Ganges River. Annual cattle fair, trade center. Grains, sugarcane.
2852	Balrampur	70,800	0.20	140	38.40	A	139,000	Uttar Pradesh north of Faizabad. Road junction. Sugar, rice, wheat, corn, grain, oilseeds. F=17th century.
2853	Balurghat	149,000	0.11	160	38.31	A	292,000	West Bengal. Chief distributing center trading in rice, jute, sugarcane, oilseeds. D=BBU,CNI,EHC,NELC.
2854	Banda	115,000	0.70	800	38.90	A	225,000	Uttar Pradesh. Agricultural marketplace, agates. Mosques & Hindu temples.
2855	Bangalore	5,554,000	7.51	417,000	65.71	B	9,614,000	Capital of Karnataka. Pharmaceuticals. Limited water supply. Tourist resorts. F=1537. University. D=CSI,RCC.
2856	Bangaon	93,600	0.10	94	38.30	A	184,000	West Bengal near Bangladesh border. Rice, jute, linseed, sugarcane. D=CNI.
2857	Bankura	135,000	0.60	810	38.80	A	266,000	West Bengal. Agricultural distributing center. Rice, oilseeds. Focus of Hindu culture. D=CNI,AoG.
2858	Banswara	80,100	1.80	1,400	45.00	A	157,000	Rajasthan. Agricultural market center. Cotton, flour, handweaving, woodworking. D=CNI,FFCI,CBA.
2859	Banur	65,600	0.10	66	38.30	A	129,000	Punjab. Near Rajpura. Paved highway, rice, minerals, near Ghegghar River, cotton. D=IPC.
2860	Bapatla	73,900	4.70	3,500	57.90	B	145,000	Andhra Pradesh south of Guntur. Rice milling, tobacco, palmyra and betel palms, agricultural college. D=AELC.
2861	Baran	68,000	0.10	68	38.30	A	133,000	Rajasthan near Parbati River. Trade center, wheat, millet, grain, cotton, handicraft cloth weaving. D=IPCOG.
2862	Barauni (Baruni, Beruni)	84,400	0.40	340	38.60	A	166,000	Bihar. Industrial complex. Part of Begusarai. Petroleum refinery, thermal power plant. D=CNI,NSS.
2863	Baraut	79,700	1.00	800	44.20	A	156,000	Uttar Pradesh on Hindan River north of Delhi. Manufacturing of iron implements, wheat, millet, sugarcane.
2864	Barddhaman (Burdewan, Burdwan)	288,000	0.04	120	28.24	A	566,000	West Bengal. Rice, oilseed, hosiery. Ancient Muslim tombs. Maharaja's palace. D=CNI.
2865	Bareilly	716,000	0.75	5,400	38.95	A	1,405,000	Uttar Pradesh on Ramganga River. Trade, sugar, cotton. F=1537. Many mosques. D=EHC,RSP.
2866	Bargarh	60,200	0.50	300	38.70	A	118,000	Orissa. Bargarh College. Iron ore, Bargarth cement factory. D=RCC.
2867	Baripada	81,200	1.00	810	44.20	A	159,000	Orissa. Trade center for rice & other crops, timber. F=1800. D=RCC.
2868	Barmer	81,700	0.20	160	38.40	A	160,000	Rajasthan. Trade center for camels, sheep, wool & salt. F=13th century. D=CBA,FFCI. M=NMM.
2869	Barnala	88,800	0.60	530	38.80	A	174,000	Punjab near Sangrur. Railroad, wheat, cotton, commerce. D=IDC.
2870	Barsi	105,000	1.00	1,000	44.20	A	205,000	Maharashtra north of Solapur. Cotton milling center, oilseed milling, hand loom weaving. D=Independent.
2871	Basirhat	120,000	0.20	240	38.40	A	235,000	West Bengal. Major trade depot for rice, jute, mustard, legumes. Sugar milling. F=1869. D=CNI.
2872	Basti	103,000	0.07	72	28.27	A	202,000	Uttar Pradesh. Agricultural trade center with light industry. Rice, mustard, wheat, sugarcane. M=FMPB.
2873	Batala	125,000	1.99	2,500	45.19	A	245,000	Punjab. Cotton ginning, weaving, sugar refining. 2 colleges. D=CNI,Methodist,SA,IDC.
2874	Bathinda	187,000	1.00	1,900	44.20	A	368,000	Punjab. Railroad junction. Branch of Sirhind Canal. Trading and commerce. D=GFA,IPC,AoG.
2875	Beawar	126,000	1.40	1,800	44.60	A	247,000	Rajasthan. Woolen market center. Cotton, handloom weaving, hosiery. F=1835. D=CNI.
2876	Begusarai	98,900	0.40	400	38.60	A	194,000	Bihar. Commercial center. Subsistence agriculture, rice, legumes, textiles. D=CNI,NSS.
2877	Bela	78,800	0.08	63	28.28	A	155,000	Uttar Pradesh on Sai River. Agricultural trade, rice, barley, grain, mustard. F=1802 as a cantonment.
2878	Belampalli	78,500	1.60	1,300	44.80	A	154,000	Andhra Pradesh. North of Godavari. Railroad, paved highway. Chemical fertilizer, coal mining. D=Baptist.
2879	Belgaum	473,000	2.50	11,800	50.70	B	929,000	Karnataka. Leather, cotton. F=c1150. Kannada, Konkani, Marathi, Goan cultures. D=Methodist,RCC.
2880	Bellary	290,000	1.86	5,400	45.06	A	568,000	Karnataka. Cotton, distillery, sugar, railroad, domestic airport, iron, manganese deposits. D=CSI,AoG.
2881	Bettiah	109,000	0.40	440	38.60	A	214,000	Bihar. Agricultural trade center. Brass, metalwork, leather. RCC mission established 1740. D=RCC,AoG.
2882	Betul	74,800	1.70	1,300	44.90	A	147,000	Madhya Pradesh. Agricultural trade center. Sawmilling, silk growing, weekly cattle mart. D=AoG,FPCGI.
2883	Bhadohi	74,900	0.40	300	38.60	A	147,000	Uttar Pradesh on Varuna River. Near Varanasi. Carpet manufacturing, rice, barley, grain, wheat.
2884	Bhadrak	90,000	1.00	900	44.20	A	177,000	Orissa northeast of Cuttack. Rice, canals, railroad, salt, hides, hand loom weaving, palm-mat making. D=RCC.
2885	Bhadravati	176,000	5.88	10,300	59.08	B	345,000	Karnataka. Iron, steel, manganese, charcoal, tar, cement. Major industrial center. D=Lutheran,EHC,CSI.
2886	Bhadravati New Town	88,200	1.00	880	44.20	A	173,000	Karnataka. Business district. Cement, wood products, bricks, coal, paper plants. D=CSI.
2887	Bhagalpur	309,000	0.50	1,500	38.70	A	606,000	Bihar. Silk, rice, sugar, trade center for agriculture & cloth, railroad, fabric weaving. D=CNI,RCC. M=FMPB.
2888	Bhandara	84,500	0.47	400	38.67	A	166,000	Maharashtra on Wainganga River. Brassware, cigarettes, mineral resources. D=CNI,EHC.
2889	Bharatpur (Bhurtpore)	185,000	0.16	300	38.36	A	363,000	Rajasthan. Oil mills, metal, small-cars, handicrafted chowries. F=1733. D=CNI. M=TPM.
2890	Bharuch (Broach)	163,000	0.86	1,400	39.06	A	320,000	Gujarat on Narmada River. Ancient Indian harbour. Cotton, handloom weaving. D=CNI,Methodist.
2891	Bhatinda (Bathinda)	195,000	0.46	900	38.66	A	382,000	Punjab. Agricultural trade, flour, handloom weaving. Muslim Saint Shrine, Baba Ratan. D=Independent.
2892	Bhaunagar (Bhavnagar)	475,000	0.31	1,500	38.51	A	933,000	Gujarat on Gulf of Cambay. Spinning & weaving mills, metalworks, tile & bricks. F=1723. D=CNI.
2893	Bhavani	114,000	5.00	5,700	58.20	B	224,000	Tamil Nadu west of Erode. Rice, peanut oil extraction. Steatile, Shivaife, Vishnuite temples. D=CSI,COG.
2894	Kumarapalaiyam	67,800	5.00	3,400	58.20	B	133,000	Tamil Nadu on Kaveri River north of Erode. Rice, peanuts, caster beans, corundum deposits nearby. D=COG.
2895	Bhawanipatna	60,100	2.00	1,200	50.20	B	118,000	Orissa near Tel River. Trade center for timber, hides, handicrafts, clothweaving. D=RCC.
2896	Bhilwara	217,000	0.22	480	38.42	A	425,000	Rajasthan. Aravalli Range. Market town, cotton, headloom weaving. D=Methodist,FFCI,PCA.
2897	Bhimavaram (Bheemavaram)	148,000	7.27	10,700	60.47	B	290,000	Andhra Pradesh on Godavari Delta. Rice, oilseed milling, rope, mats, tobacco, sugarcane, college. D=AELC.
2898	Bhind (Bhind-Bhanwara)	129,000	0.03	39	28.23	A	254,000	Madhya Pradesh. Market center, grain, hand loom weaving, cotton, brassware. Old fort, Gauri Tal. M=FMPB.
2899	Bhiwani (Bhawani)	143,000	0.29	420	38.49	A	281,000	Haryana. Cotton milling, ginning, and pressing. Trade center with Rajasthan. F=1817. D=NICOG,Baptist.
2900	Bhopal	1,574,000	1.80	28,300	45.00	A	2,886,000	Capital of Madhya Pradesh. 2,500 killed in industrial accident (1984). F=1728. Taj-ul-Masjid. D=RCC,OSC.
2901	Bhubaneswar (Bhuvanesvara)	485,000	0.59	2,900	38.79	A	952,000	Capital of Orissa. 30 ancient temples. F=3rd century BC. Center of Saivite faith. Utkal University (1943). D=Union.
2902	Bhuj	130,000	0.20	260	38.40	A	256,000	Gujarat. Commercial center for wheat, barley, cattle, cotton, and salt. D=CNI.
2903	Bhusawal	188,000	1.89	3,600	45.09	A	369,000	Maharashtra on Tapti River. Cotton, bananas, millet, peanuts. D=AoG,CMA,COG,IFGM,RCC.

Table 10-5–continued opposite

Table 10-5–continued

Rec No 1	Country City 2	Pop 2000 3	AC% 4	Church Members 5	E% 6	W 7	Pop 2025 8	Notes 9
2904	Bid (Beed)	132,000	0.50	660	38.70	A	260,000	Maharashtra in Balaghat Range. Sorghum, secondary road. D=AoG,CON.
2905	Bidar	154,000	5.00	7,700	58.20	B	302,000	Karnataka. Ornamented metal articles. Medieval Hindu dynasties. D=Methodist,Baptist,NAC.
2906	Bihar (Biharsharif)	237,000	0.10	240	38.30	A	465,000	Bihar. Agricultural trade center. Buddhist college ruins, 5th century Gupta pillar. M=GEMS,GFA.
2907	Bijapur	227,000	0.25	570	38.45	A	446,000	Karnataka. Deccan Islamic architecture. Tourism, cotton, oilseed. D=CSI,BYM,EHC.
2908	Bijnor	86,700	0.15	130	38.35	A	170,000	Uttar Pradesh. Thread manufacturing, agricultural trade, sugar.
2909	Bikaner	489,000	0.15	730	38.35	A	960,000	Rajasthan. Trade center for wool, hides, building stone, salt. F=1488. D=CNI,FFCI.
2910	Bilaspur	275,000	2.90	8,000	51.10	B	540,000	Madhya Pradesh. Agricultural trade, rice, flour, sawmilling, shellac. D=RCC,CNI,MTSC,AoG,OSC.
2911	Bilimora	60,000	0.20	120	38.40	A	118,000	Gujarat on Gulf of Khambhat. Near Navsari. Trade center, cotton, millet, molasses, timber, fish. D=FPCGI.
2912	Bir (Bhir)	120,000	0.50	600	38.70	A	236,000	Maharashtra. Leatherwork. Kankalesvar Temple (Hindu). Millet, wheat, oilseeds.
2913	Birlapur	77,000	0.25	190	38.45	A	151,000	West Bengal, near Calcutta. Rice, markets, livestock.
2914	Birnagar	109,000	0.30	330	38.50	A	213,000	West Bengal near Churni River north of Ranaghat. Rice, jute, linseed, sugarcane. D=CNI.
2915	Bishnupur (Vishnupur)	66,100	0.50	330	38.70	A	130,000	West Bengal. Agricultural trade, silk weaving. Dozen temples. F=8th century AD. D=BBU,ECI,JKPS.
2916	Bodhan	75,900	2.00	1,500	50.20	B	149,000	Northwestern Andhra Pradesh near Manjira River. Sugar factory, distillery, experimental farm (sugarcane). D=CSI.
2917	Bodinayakkanur	77,800	10.00	7,800	63.20	B	153,000	Tamil Nadu in mountains near Vaigai River. Coffee, tea, silk, cotton. F=1336. D=CSI,IPA.
2918	Bokaro Steel City	490,000	2.00	9,800	50.20	B	961,000	Bihar on Damodar River near Bermo. One of Asia's largest steel plants, coalfields nearby. D=CNI,RCC,GELC.
2919	Bolpur	62,300	0.60	370	38.80	A	122,000	West Bengal near Ajay River. Trade center, rice, grain, wheat, sugarcane, oilseed milling, cotton weaving. D=CNI.
2920	Botad	76,000	0.20	150	38.40	A	149,000	Gujarat on Kathiawar Peninsula northwest of Bhavnagar. Grain, cotton, salts, hand loom weaving. D=CNI.
2921	Brahmapur	248,000	1.10	2,700	44.30	A	487,000	Orissa. Trade center for rice, sugarcane. Rice milling, distilling, silk. Road and railroad junction. D=RCC.
2922	Brajrajnagar	81,900	0.40	330	38.60	A	161,000	Orient Bpor Industries, near river Mahanadi. Rice, timber, hides, paper manufacturing.
2923	Budaun	137,000	0.35	480	38.55	A	270,000	Uttar Pradesh. Agricultural trade center. F=AD 905 by Hindu raja. Jami Masjid (1223).
2924	Bulandshahr	149,000	0.14	210	38.34	A	293,000	Uttar Pradesh on Kali River. Trade in grains, cotton, sugarcane. M=IET.
2925	Buldana	62,100	0.40	250	38.60	A	122,000	Maharashtra in Ajanta Range. Near Khamgaon. Industrial school, large college, teak forest, oilseed. D=CNI.
2926	Bundi	76,600	0.16	120	38.36	A	150,000	Rajasthan. Agricultural market center. Palace frescoes. D=CBA.
2927	Burhanpur	204,000	0.25	510	38.45	A	400,000	Madhya Pradesh. Walled with massive gates. Textiles, muslin, gold & silver. F=1399. Mosques. D=Methodist.
2928	Calcutta	12,900,000	2.00	258,000	55.20	B	21,171,000	Capital of West Bengal on Hooghly River. Swampy. Jute. F=1690 by East India company. D=CNI,RCC.
2929	Baidyabati	107,000	0.40	430	38.60	A	210,000	West Bengal. North of Calcutta along Hugli River, eastern railroad. 50% Bengali Hindu. D=CNI,RCC.
2930	Bally (Bali or Baly)	214,000	0.33	710	38.53	A	421,000	Jute, paper, bone-milling. Steamer station for traffic on the Hooghly River. D=CNI,RCC.
2931	Bansbaria	110,000	0.50	550	38.70	A	216,000	West Bengal. North on Hugli River. Shivaite and Hanseswari temples. Rice and jute milling. D=CNI,RCC.
2932	Baranagar (Barahanagar)	264,000	0.22	580	38.42	A	517,000	Jute, cotton milling & ginning, chemicals, castor oil. Founded as Portuguese settlement. D=CNI,RCC.
2933	Barasat	121,000	0.20	240	38.40	A	237,000	Trade center for rice, legumes, sugarcane, potatoes, cotton weaving. Annual Muslim saint fair. D=ECI,RCC.
2934	Barrackpur (Barrakpore, Chanak)	174,000	0.24	420	38.44	A	342,000	Jute, rice, sawmilling, hosiery. F=1869. Colleges. D=CNI,NF,RCC.
2935	Bhadreswar	85,300	0.20	170	38.40	A	167,000	West Bengal north on Hugli River beyond Champdani. Rice, jute milling, old residential settlement. D=CNI.
2936	Bhatpara	359,000	0.08	290	28.28	A	704,000	Jute, cotton, paper milling. Ancient of Sanskrit learning. Hugliside industrial complex. D=CNI,RCC.
2937	Budge Budge (Baj Baj)	86,400	0.50	430	38.70	A	170,000	Jute, cotton milling, oil deport, boot & shoe factory. Thermal power plant. D=CNI,ECI,RCC.
2938	Champdani	116,000	0.40	470	38.60	A	229,000	West Bengal. North of Calcutta, eastern railroad, Hugli River. Jute milling center. D=CNI,RCC.
2939	Chandannagar (Chandernagore)	144,000	0.38	550	38.58	A	283,000	Colleges. F=1673 by the French. Hugli district, ceded by France to India in 1951. D=CNI,RCC.
2940	Garulia	95,300	0.20	190	38.40	A	187,000	West Bengal north of Calcutta on Hugli River. Across from Bhadreswar. D=CNI,RCC.
2941	Halisahar (Kumarhata)	134,000	0.30	400	38.50	A	263,000	Paper milling center. Noted home of Sanskrit scholars. D=CNI,RCC.
2942	Haora	1,115,000	0.07	780	28.27	A	2,189,000	West Bengal. River port. Jute, flour, rice, chemicals, glass. Botanical gardens. D=CNI,RCC.
2943	Hugli (Hooghly) Chinsurah	168,000	0.45	760	38.65	A	329,000	Rice milling, rubber goods. F=1537 by Portuguese. Road and railroad junction. D=CNI,BBU,EHC,RCC.
2944	Kamarhati	314,000	0.03	94	28.23	A	617,000	Jute, cotton milling, leather tanning, rubber goods. Rani Rasmani's Nabaratna (temples).
2945	Kanchrapara	118,000	0.30	350	38.50	A	231,000	Railway workshop, jute. Bangladesh refugee colony. Krishna temple. D=CNI,RCC.
2946	Konnagar	73,300	0.20	150	38.40	A	144,000	North on Hugli River near Rishra. Chemicals, glass, cotton milling, jute pressing, liquor distilling. D=CNI,RCC.
2947	Naihati	156,000	0.03	47	28.23	A	305,000	North on Hugli River north of Bhatpara. Railroad, jute, rice, oilseed, paper milling, paint processing. D=CNI,RCC.
2948	Nangi	62,300	0.50	310	38.70	A	122,000	South on Hugli River near Budge Budge. Agriculture, jute, livestock. D=CNI,RCC.
2949	North Barrackpore (North Barakpur)	118,000	0.40	470	38.60	A	232,000	North on Hugli River. North of Barakpur, West Bengal State. D=CNI,NF,RCC.
2950	North Dum-Dum	178,000	0.60	1,100	38.80	A	350,000	Large rural enclaves. Jute, tanneries. Suburban Calcutta, West Bengal State. D=CNI,ECI,AoG,RCC.
2951	Panihati	324,000	0.05	160	28.25	A	637,000	Rice trading center. Cotton, tanneries, chemicals, glass, cement, apparel. F=1900. Suburban Calcutta. D=CNI.
2952	Rishra	121,000	0.50	610	38.70	A	237,000	North on Hugli River beyond Konnagar. Cotton, jute, rice milling, chemical manufacturing. D=CNI,RCC.
2953	Serampore (Shrirampur, Serampur)	93,100	2.00	1,900	50.20	B	183,000	Jute, paper mills. F=18th century by Danes. Y=1793 Baptist mission (William Carey). D=Baptist,CNI.
2954	South Dum-Dum	272,000	0.41	1,100	38.61	A	533,000	Jute, tanneries, glass, soap. West Bengal State, residential area. D=CNI,ECI,OSC,RCC.
2955	Titagarh (Tittagarh)	134,000	0.05	67	28.25	A	263,000	Jute, paper milling, glass, textiles, tea. F=1895. Once residence for Europeans. D=CNI,RCC.
2956	Uttapara-Kotrung	119,000	0.50	590	38.70	A	233,000	North on Hugli River north of Bally. Chemical and bone meal manufacturing, college, large public library. D=CNI.
2957	Cambay (Khambhat)	103,000	0.80	820	39.00	A	202,000	Gujarat. Trade in cotton, grains, tobacco, textiles. Once a major port, now silted up. D=CNI.
2958	Cannanore	76,900	4.00	3,100	57.20	B	151,000	Arabian sea port in Kerala. Spinning, weaving, hosiery mills. Portuguese church. Many mosques. D=RCC,OSC.
2959	Chaibasa	66,800	1.00	670	44.20	A	131,000	Bihar near Jamshedpur. Railroad, minerals, secondary roads, rice. M=CNI,FMPB,EHC.
2960	Chakdaha	88,100	0.50	440	38.70	A	173,000	West Bengal north of Calcutta on Hugli River. Rice, jute, linseeds, sugarcane, wheat. D=CNI.
2961	Chakradharpur	56,900	3.00	1,700	51.20	B	112,000	Southern Bihar west of Jamshedpur. Trade center, salt, timber, rice, oilseeds, corn. D=CNI.
2962	Chalisgaon	91,100	2.00	1,800	50.20	B	179,000	Maharashtra south of Girna River, east of Malegaon. Millet, wheat, cotton milling, matches, ironworks. D=CNI.
2963	Chandausi	97,500	0.50	490	38.70	A	191,000	Uttar Pradesh in Rohilkhand Plains south of Moradabad. Wheat, rice, pearl millet, mustard, cotton.
2964	Chandigarh	593,000	1.04	6,200	44.24	A	1,163,000	Joint capital of Haryana & Punjab. Communications junction. Education center. D=CNI,RCC.
2965	Chandpur	65,800	0.05	33	28.25	A	129,000	Uttar Pradesh. Near Amroha. Rice, wheat, grain, barley, sugarcane.
2966	Chandrapur (Chanda)	266,000	0.98	2,600	39.18	A	522,000	Maharashtra on Wardha River. Cotton, collieries, glassworks, silk, copper, iron ore. D=CNI,Methodist,IPC.
2967	Changanacheri	61,800	30.00	18,500	93.20	B	121,000	Kerala east of Alleppey. Malabor Coast, railroad. Rice milling, pottery, nut processing, jute. D=OSC,RCC.
2968	Channapatna	65,000	3.70	2,400	51.90	B	128,000	Southern Karnataka southwest of Bangalore. Silk milling center, textiles, lacquerware, silk growing. D=RCC,CSI.
2969	Chapra	161,000	0.07	110	28.27	A	316,000	Bihar. River mart. Agricultural trade center. Saltpeter, linseed-oil. D=Methodist,NSS.
2970	Chas	76,800	0.20	150	38.40	A	151,000	Bihar near West Bengal, west of Asanol, near Parchet Reservoir. Minerals, surface mines. D=CNI.
2971	Chennai (Madras)	6,639,000	10.00	664,000	73.20	B	11,225,000	Capital of Tamil Nadu on Bay of Bengal. Educational center. F=1639. 800 churches. D=CSI,RCC.
2972	Alandur	147,000	9.00	13,300	62.20	B	289,000	Tamil Nadu. South of Madras, near airport. Navigable canal. Residential, textiles. D=CSI,AoG,RCC.
2973	Ambattur	263,000	8.50	22,400	61.70	B	516,000	Tamil Nadu. Residential. Chemical plants, textiles, agriculture, market, cattle trade. D=CSI,Baptist,Methodist.
2974	Avadi	212,000	9.00	19,100	62.20	B	417,000	Tamil Nadu. Residential. Trade, industry, handicrafts, cotton, handloom weaving. D=CSI,JS,PCOG,RCC.
2975	Madhavaram	57,700	8.00	4,600	61.20	B	113,000	Tamil Nadu. Trade, textile mills, chemical plants, industry, motor vehicle parts, market. D=CSI,COG,ECI,RCC.
2976	Pallavaram	131,000	10.00	13,100	63.20	B	257,000	Tamil Nadu. Schools, market, trade, industrial, warehouses, residential, agriculture. D=CSI,CFBI,JS,RCC.
2977	Tambaram	126,000	10.00	12,600	63.20	B	246,000	International Missionary Conference (1938). Railroad workshops. Madras Christian College. D=CSI,ECI,RCC.
2978	Tiruvottiyur	198,000	7.66	15,100	60.86	B	388,000	Tamil Nadu. North on Bay of Bengal. Navigable canals, railroads. Matches, tanning, rice milling. D=CSI,SA.
2979	Chhatarpur	89,000	0.50	450	38.70	A	175,000	Madhya Pradesh. Trade center for agriculture & cloth products. F=1707 by Bundela king. D=COG,IPC.
2980	Chhindwara	114,000	1.60	1,800	44.80	A	224,000	Madhya Pradesh. Cotton trade, coal shipping, sawmilling. F=1867. D=CNI,EVGLC,FPCGI,BYM.
2981	Chidambaram	81,100	5.50	4,500	58.70	B	159,000	Tamil Nadu. Food processing, silk, cotton, handloom weaving. Hindu temple & religious center. D=CSI.
2982	Chikmagalur	71,600	5.00	3,600	58.20	B	141,000	Karnataka. Major center for coffee. Lacquer ware & rattan products. D=Independent.
2983	Chilakalurupet	93,200	9.00	8,400	62.20	B	183,000	Andhra Pradesh southwest of Guntur. Tobacco curing, cotton ginning, steatite mines. D=Lutheran,AMG.
2984	Chingleput	63,400	1.40	890	44.60	A	124,000	Tamil Nadu on Palar River. Near Kanchipuram. Agriculture, livestock, handcrafts. D=CSI,AoG,COI.
2985	Chintamani	59,400	8.00	4,700	61.20	B	116,000	Karnataka near Kolar. Andhra Pradesh border. Secondary roads, mines. D=PNLC.
2986	Chirala	168,000	9.00	15,100	62.20	B	330,000	Andhra Pradesh on Bay of Bengal north of Ongole. Tobacco curing, rice, betel palms. D=ECI,IPCOG.
2987	Chitradurga (Chitaldrug)	122,000	1.40	1,700	44.60	A	239,000	Karnataka. Cotton trading center. Arid region subject to famine. Sugarcane, groundnuts. D=CSI,Brethren.
2988	Chittaranjan	68,700	1.00	690	44.20	A	135,000	West Bengal north of Asansol. Locomotive factory. Formerly called Mihijans.
2989	Chittaurgarh	84,300	0.20	170	38.40	A	165,000	Rajasthan near Aravalli Range. Near Bhilwara. Cotton, millet, corn, limestone, ancient ruins. D=CBA,FFCI.
2990	Chittoor	157,000	2.90	4,600	51.10	B	308,000	Andhra Pradesh. Rice, oilseed, Indian steatite, sugarcane, cotton, mango and tamarind groves. D=CSI,JS.
2991	Chopda	57,900	0.25	150	38.45	A	114,000	Maharashtra near Tapi River. Near Amalner. Market center for cotton, handicraft, cloth weaving.
2992	Churu	97,600	0.05	49	28.25	A	192,000	Rajasthan. Local market for wool, millet cattle, salt, handloom weaving. D=Independent.
2993	Cochin	1,759,000	36.25	638,000	94.45	B	3,249,000	Major port of Kerala. Navy training center. Y=1510 by Portuguese. Jews date to 4th century. D=CSI,OSC,RCC.
2994	Thirippunithura	60,100	35.00	21,000	93.20	B	118,000	Kerala. D=CSI,OSC,Mar Thoma Syrian Church,IPC.
2995	Coimbatore	1,290,000	15.00	194,000	73.20	B	2,284,000	Tamil Nadu on Noyil River. Agricultural trade center, tea, coffee. F=1866. Temple of Perur. D=CLJC,TELC,RCC.
2996	Kurichi	75,000	15.00	11,300	73.20	B	147,000	Tamil Nadu. Cotton milling, Nogil River. Agriculture livestock. D=ECI,CSI,RCC,TELC.
2997	Contai	62,900	0.50	320	38.70	A	124,000	West Bengal on Kanthi Coastal Plain. Hugli River and Bay of Bengal. D=AoG,JKPS. M=YWAM.
2998	Cooch Behar (Kuch Bihar, Koch Bihar)	123,000	0.30	370	38.50	A	241,000	West Bengal. Agricultural market center, leather goods. D=NELC,JKPS,EHC.
2999	Coonoor	117,000	8.00	9,400	61.20	B	230,000	Western Tamil Nadu in Kunda Hills. Famous sanatorium, medical research, botanical garden. D=CSI,ECI.
3000	Cuddalore	169,000	5.50	9,300	58.70	B	332,000	Tamil Nadu on Bay of Bengal. Ancient seaport. Fishing, shipbuilding. D=CSI,AoG,TELC,Pentecostal,RCC.
3001	Cuddapah	254,000	4.10	10,400	57.30	B	498,000	Andhra Pradesh. Peanuts, cotton, melons, fine-grained limestones. D=RCC,CSI,SALC.
3002	Cuttack	518,000	2.50	12,900	50.70	B	1,016,000	Orissa. River port & trade center. Handicrafts. Numerous temples, monuments. D=AJI,EHC,Baptist.
3003	Dabgram	173,000	0.50	870	38.70	A	340,000	East of Jalpaiguri. West Bengal. Rice, jute, tannery, bicycle rim and spoke production. D=CNI.
3004	Dabhoi	59,600	0.80	480	39.00	A	117,000	Gujarat north of Narmada River, southeast of Vadodara. D=CNI,AMM,Methodist.
3005	Dahod	114,000	1.00	1,100	44.20	A	223,000	Gujarat near Madhya Pradesh. Near Godhra. Timber, oilseeds, agriculture, livestock, handcrafts. D=FPCGI,SA.
3006	Daltonganj	66,500	9.00	6,000	62.20	B	130,000	Bihar. Agricultural trade center, shellac manufacture. F=1862 by British. D=CNI,CGM,DOC.
3007	Damoh	124,000	0.80	990	39.00	A	243,000	Madhya Pradesh. Agricultural trade, oilseeds, handloom weaving & dyeing. D=CNI. M=CICM,MICM.
3008	Dandeli	62,100	5.00	3,100	58.20	B	122,000	Karnataka on Kalinadi River. Near Goa. Railroad spur terminus, timber depot, teak, sandalwood. D=CSI,NLF.
3009	Darbhanga	257,000	0.12	310	38.32	A	505,000	Bihar. Trades in produce, mangoes & fish. Rice, jute, sugar. M=GEMS,AGA.
3010	Darjeeling (Darjiling)	86,100	3.00	2,600	51.20	B	169,000	West Bengal. Hill resort in Sikkim Himalayas at 7,000 ft. Mahakal Temple, sacred to Hindus & Buddhists. D=CNI.
3011	Datia	77,200	0.15	120	38.35	A	152,000	Madhya Pradesh. Trade in grain & cotton goods. Surrounded by stone wall. D=Independent. M=NMS.
3012	Davangere	338,000	1.05	3,600	44.25	A	664,000	Karnataka. Textiles, trade center for cotton & grain. Machine tool factory. D=CSI.
3013	Dehra Dun	433,000	1.47	6,400	44.67	A	850,000	Utter Pradesh in Himalayan foothills. Hill resort, tea. F=1699 by heretical Sikh. D=Agape,IET,KEF.
3014	Dehri	111,000	0.33	370	38.53	A	219,000	Bihar. Railway workshops. Son canal system headworks. Sugar, ghee, sawmilling. D=CNI.
3015	Delhi	11,680,000	3.00	350,000	54.20	B	19,838,000	On Yamuna River. Economic center. Electronics, engineering, traditional handicrafts. Jama Masjid. D=CNI,RCC.
3016	Delhi Cantonment	111,000	2.00	2,200	50.20	B	218,000	Southwest of central district. Indira Gandhi International Airport. Hindus, Muslims. D=RCC,CNI,Methodist.
3017	Faridabad New Township	723,000	0.75	5,400	38.95	A	1,419,000	Haryana south of Delhi. Railroad, commerce, trade, industry. D=CNI,FGCOG,AoG,Independent.
3018	NEW DELHI	347,000	3.82	13,200	52.02	B	680,000	Administrative center on Yamuna River. Well planned streets, low population density. D=CNI,RCC.
3019	Deoband	73,600	0.45	330	38.65	A	144,000	Uttar Pradesh. Leading Muslim theological center.
3020	Deoghar (Deogarh)	101,000	1.80	1,800	45.00	A	199,000	Bihar. Ancient town, Buddhist ruins, Hindu temples (22 Shivan), leper asylum. M=CNI,EHC.
3021	Deoria	96,500	0.10	97	38.30	A	189,000	Uttar Pradesh. Agricultural trade center, sugar milling. Near Buddhist pilgrimage center.
3022	Dewas	193,000	0.47	910	38.67	A	379,000	Madhya Pradesh. Agricultural trade center. Cotton & flour milling, soap. Devivasini shrine. D=CNI,MTSC.
3023	Dhamtari	81,600	2.30	1,900	50.50	B	160,000	Madhya Pradesh. Trade center for agriculture & forest products. Rice, flour, shellac. D=CNI.
3024	Dhanbad	960,000	0.43	4,100	38.63	A	1,717,000	Bihar. Coal, agriculture. India School of Mines. Rice, corn, oilseeds. D=CNI,AoG,Methodist,RCC.
3025	Jharia	81,900	0.40	330	38.60	A	161,000	Bihar. Near Panchet Reservoir, Damodar River. Coalfield. Mining center. D=CNI,RCC.
3026	Sindri	85,200	0.40	340	38.60	A	167,000	East near Panchet Reservoir, west northwest of Asansol. Railroad, trails, mines. D=Methodist,RCC.
3027	Dhar	69,600	0.50	350	38.70	A	137,000	Madhya Pradesh. Cotton ginning, handicraft weaving. On northern slopes of Vindhya Range. Mosques. D=CNI.

Table 10-5–continued overleaf

Table 10-5–continued

Rec No 1	Country City 2	Pop 2000 3	AC% 4	Church Members 5	E% 6	W 7	Pop 2025 8	Notes 9
3028	Dharapuram	57,000	14.00	8,000	72.20	B	112,000	Tamil Nadu on Amaravati River. Near Palani. Trade center in tobacco region, cotton rice, millet, silk. D=IPA,IPC.
3029	Dharmapuri	69,600	3.40	2,400	51.60	B	137,000	Tamil Nadu. Agricultural trade center, light industry. Nearby pilgrimage & healing center. D=AoG,FGPC.
3030	Dharmavaram	92,800	3.00	2,800	51.20	B	182,000	Southern Andhra Pradesh on Chitravati River south of Anantapur. D=CSI,Lutheran.
3031	Dhaulpur	80,700	0.10	81	38.30	A	158,000	Rajasthan. Between Agra and Gwalior. On Madhya Pradesh border.
3032	Dholka	64,000	0.40	260	38.60	A	126,000	Gujarat. Near Ahmadabad. Marsh, crafts, secondary roads. D=CMA.
3033	Dhoraji	93,600	0.18	170	38.38	A	184,000	Gujarat on Kathiawar Peninsula south of Rajkot. Oilseeds, millet, cotton, cloth fabrics, copper, brassware. D=CNI.
3034	Dhrangadhra	64,000	0.30	190	38.50	A	126,000	Gujarat north of Surendranagar. Marsh. Cotton, salt, millet, clothweaving. Built c1730. D=CNI,Brethren.
3035	Dhubri	71,800	4.00	2,900	57.20	B	141,000	Assam on Brahmaputra River. Trade center for rice, jute, fish, match factory. D=Baptist.
3036	Dhuburi	77,600	4.00	3,100	57.20	B	152,000	Assam. Brahmaputra River. Near Bangladesh border. Cotton, jute, rice, agriculture. D=Baptist.
3037	Dhulia (Dhule)	327,000	0.40	1,300	38.60	A	643,000	Maharashtra. Cotton textiles, cotton ginning, cigarettes, oil. 13 colleges. D=Methodist,EHC.
3038	Dibrugarh	146,000	4.00	5,800	57.20	B	286,000	Assam on Brahmaputra River. Tea, rice, oilseed, port. Heavy earthquake damage (1950). D=Baptist.
3039	Dimapur	67,100	6.00	4,000	59.20	B	132,000	Assam. Near Nagaland. Near Lumding. Rice, cotton, oranges, potatoes, temple ruins. D=Baptist.
3040	Dindigul	215,000	15.08	32,400	73.28	B	422,000	Tamil Nadu. Cotton spinning & weaving mills, silk, jewelry. D=CSI,AoG,IELC,TELL,RCC.
3041	Disa	72,900	0.30	220	38.50	A	143,000	Gujarat. Near Palanpur. Secondary roads, canal, handicrafts. D=CNI,GFA,NICOG.
3042	Dod Ballapur	64,200	6.50	4,200	59.70	B	126,000	Karnataka. Near Bangalore. Railroad, valley, Nandi Drug mountain. D=CSI.
3043	Durg-Bhilai Nagar (Bhilai)	924,000	3.25	30,000	51.45	B	1,692,000	Madhya Pradesh. Milling, rice, industry, cotton. Agriculture, trade center, markets. D=CNI,Methodist,MTSC.
3044	Bhilai	811,000	3.00	24,300	51.20	B	1,593,000	Large steel project. Sawmills. Maitri Bagh (Garden of Friendship)-Indian/Russian cooperation. D=CNI,OSC.
3045	Durg (Drug)	177,000	3.00	5,300	51.20	B	348,000	Agricultural market. Milling rice & pigeon peas. Remains of an ancient fortress. D=Methodist,COG.
3046	Durgapur	490,000	1.20	5,900	44.40	A	962,000	West Bengal. Steel producing center, coal, brick & tile. Coke gas, hydroelectric power. D=CNI,AoG,RCC.
3047	Eluru (Ellore)	251,000	4.90	12,300	58.10	B	492,000	Andhra Pradesh. Textiles, leather, pile carpets. Rice, oilseeds, tobacco. Buddhist ruins. D=RCC,AELC,CSI.
3048	English Bazar (Angrezabad)	118,000	0.10	120	38.30	A	232,000	West Bengal. Silk, agriculture. F=1676 by British East India Company for silk factories. D=CNI.
3049	Erode	421,000	5.00	21,100	58.20	B	827,000	Tamil Nadu on Cauvery River. Cotton, transport equipment. Cola temple. D=AoG,FOC,TELC,CSI,RCC.
3050	Veerappanchattiram	72,600	5.00	3,600	58.20	B	142,000	Tamil Nadu. Cotton growing region, milling, agriculture, livestock. D=COG,Independent,CSI,RCC.
3051	Etah	92,400	0.50	460	38.70	A	181,000	Uttar Pradesh. Agricultural marketplace. 3 colleges.
3052	Etawah	146,000	0.01	15	28.21	A	287,000	Uttar Pradesh on Yamuna River. Cotton, silk, oilseeds, ghee. 16th century Mosque. D=CBAF. M=FMPB.
3053	Faizabad-Ayodhya	215,000	0.27	580	38.47	A	423,000	Uttar Pradesh on Ghaghara River. Sugar, oilseed, agriculture. F=1730 by Sadat Ali Khan.
3054	Faridkot	66,000	0.50	330	38.70	A	130,000	Punjab on Indira Gandhi Canal. Near Kot Kapura. Grain, wheat, cotton, drugs, chemicals. D=IPC.
3055	Farrukhabad-Fategarh	233,000	0.50	1,200	38.70	A	458,000	Uttar Pradesh. Potatoes, tobacco, watermelons. Ancient temples. Buddhist pilgrimage center. D=CNI.
3056	Fatehpur	138,000	0.70	970	38.90	A	271,000	Uttar Pradesh. Agricultural trade center. F=15th century by Pathans. M=IET.
3057	Fathpur (Fatehpur)	78,200	0.05	39	28.25	A	154,000	Rajasthan, NNW of Sikar. Secondary roads, wool, millet. Railroad, hides, hand looming, pottery making. D=CBA.
3058	Fazilka	67,600	0.20	140	38.40	A	133,000	Punjab near Pakistan border, near Thar Desert. Secondary roads. D=IPC.
3059	Firozabad	319,000	0.10	320	38.30	A	626,000	Uttar Pradesh east of Agra, 20 miles of Taj Mahal. Railroad, primary roads.
3060	Firozpur (Ferozepore)	91,300	2.70	2,500	50.90	B	179,000	Punjab. Agricultural trade, weaving, confections. F=14th century. 5 miles from Pakistan. D=CNI,IDC.
3061	Gadag	158,000	5.50	8,700	58.70	B	310,000	Karnataka near Hubli-Dharwar. Rice, livestock. Cotton, millet, wheat, chemical disinfectants. D=CSI,ECI.
3062	Gandhidham	123,000	0.50	620	38.70	A	241,000	Gujarat, Gulf of Kachchh, Kandla Port. Bluedart Air Express. Railway station, Jain pilgrimage center.
3063	Gandhinagar	143,000	2.00	2,900	50.20	B	282,000	Capital of Gujarat on Sabarmati River. F=1966. D=CNI,GFA,COG,Independent.
3064	Ganga Ghat	59,500	0.50	300	38.70	A	117,000	Northern Uttar Pradesh near Nepal. Tourism.
3065	Gangapur	81,300	0.20	160	38.40	A	160,000	Rajasthan. Aravalli Range. Near Bhilwara. Millet, cotton, wheat, cotton ginning. D=CNI,IPCOG.
3066	Gangawati	95,600	3.20	3,100	51.40	B	188,000	Karnataka. Near Hospet. Tuggabhadra River. Secondary road, rice, millet. D=Baptist,Methodist. M=OM.
3067	Gauhati	347,000	4.00	13,900	57.20	B	681,000	Assam on Brahmaputra River. River port, oil refinery, tea, soap. Hindu pilgrimage centers nearby.
3068	Gaya	346,000	0.30	1,000	38.50	A	680,000	Bihar on Phalgu River. Hindu pilgrimage center (30,000 annually). M=CNI,GEMS,RCC.
3069	Ghaziabad (Ghaziuddinnagar)	612,000	0.30	1,800	38.50	A	1,201,000	Uttar Pradesh. Vegetable oil, electroplating. Commuters to Delhi. F=1740. D=CNI.
3070	Ghazipur	90,800	0.43	390	38.63	A	178,000	Uttar Pradesh on Ganges River. Agricultural market. British cantonment with church. D=CNI.
3071	Giridih	91,800	1.80	1,700	45.00	A	180,000	Bihar on Usri River. Mica, coal, trade, rice, mustard, corn, sugarcane, barley. College. D=CNI,EHC.
3072	Godhra (Godrh)	118,000	1.40	1,700	44.60	A	232,000	Gujarat. Timber, agricultural produce, oilseeds, flour, glass, cotton, peanuts, tanning, railroad. D=Methodist.
3073	Gokak	61,300	2.20	1,300	50.40	B	120,000	Karnataka on Ghatprabha River. Near Belgaum. Cotton, jaggery, chili, millet, wooden toys. D=Methodist.
3074	Gonda	125,000	0.18	230	38.38	A	245,000	Uttar Pradesh, Sarayu River. Trade center, rice & sugar milling, maize, sugarcane, wheat, oilseeds. M=FMPB.
3075	Gondal	96,100	0.29	280	38.49	A	189,000	Gujarat on Kathiawar Peninsula south of Rajkot. Oilseeds, cotton, several temples, cloth weaving. D=IPC.
3076	Gondia	129,000	1.80	2,300	45.00	A	253,000	Maharashtra near Nagpur. Rice, tile, glassworks, paper-free cigarettes. D=CNI,Baptist.
3077	Gopichettipalaiyam	57,000	3.50	2,000	51.70	B	112,000	Tamil Nadu near Erode. Canal. Bhavani River. Tobacco, rice, millet, corundum mines. D=AoG,CSI,IPC.
3078	Gorakhpur	577,000	2.00	11,500	50.20	B	1,133,000	Uttar Pradesh on Rapti River. Agriculture, textiles, printing, sugar. F=1400. Named for Hindu saint. D=CNI,RCC.
3079	Gudivada	120,000	4.50	5,400	57.70	B	235,000	Andhra Pradesh in Krishna Delta east of Guntur. Rice milling, sugarcane, oilseeds, tobacco. D=CSI,JS.
3080	Gudiyattam	106,000	7.40	7,800	60.60	B	208,000	Northern Tamil Nadu on Palar River west of Vellore. Cotton milling, trade center, hides, skins. D=CSI,AoG,PCA.
3081	Gudur	65,900	6.00	4,000	59.20	B	129,000	Andhra Pradesh near Bay of Bengal. Near Nellore. Ceramics, rice, oilseed, mica quarries nearby. D=CSI,MFGC.
3082	Gulbarga	365,000	0.95	3,500	39.15	A	717,000	Karnataka. Cotton trade, flour oil. Ancient monuments, notable mosque. D=Methodist,Mennonite Brethren.
3083	Guna (Goona)	118,000	0.23	270	38.43	A	232,000	Madhya Pradesh. Major agricultural center, cotton, oilseeds, handloom weaving. D=FFCI,KEF,GFA.
3084	Guntakal	127,000	2.00	2,500	50.20	B	249,000	Western Andhra Pradesh north of Anantapur. Major railroad junction, cotton ginning, grain trade. D=CSI,AoG.
3085	Guntur	555,000	8.17	45,300	61.37	B	1,089,000	Andhra Pradesh in Krishna River Delta. Jute, rice. Andhra Christian College. F=c1750. D=AELC,RCC.
3086	Gurdaspur	64,300	1.50	960	44.70	A	126,000	Punjab near Jammu and Kashmir border. South of Pathanket. Canal. D=CNI,SA,Baptist.
3087	Gurgaon (Hidayatpur)	159,000	0.40	630	38.60	A	311,000	Haryana. Agricultural trade center. South of Delhi, primary road, railroad. D=CNI,Lutheran,COG.
3088	Guruvayur	140,000	0.20	280	38.40	A	274,000	Kerala. Rail station, Hindu temple premises. Trichur District.
3089	Guwahati	680,000	5.00	34,000	58.20	B	1,336,000	Assam on Brahmaputra River. Marsh, rice, center of tea industry. University and law school. D=Baptist.
3090	Gwalior	897,000	0.25	2,200	38.45	A	1,631,000	Madhya Pradesh. Walled fortress, music center, agricultural produce, cloth, iron ore. D=CNI,Independent.
3091	Habra	231,000	0.12	280	38.32	A	454,000	West Bengal northeast of Calcutta on Eastern Railway. D=CNI,AoG.
3092	Ashoknagar-Kalyangarh	113,000	0.10	110	38.30	A	223,000	West Bengal. Eastern railway, primary roads. D=CNI.
3093	Hajipur	103,000	0.40	410	38.60	A	203,000	Bihar. Ganga River. Rice, wheat, engineering, glass, metal & steel containers. 4 colleges. M=GEMS.
3094	Haldwani	121,000	0.76	920	38.96	A	238,000	Uttar Pradesh, foot of Siwalik Range. Rail station, sugar, rice, wheat. Founded 1834.
3095	Hansi	70,300	0.22	160	38.42	A	138,000	Haryana. Ancient town. Cotton ginning, handloom weaving, metal work. 12th century mosques. D=Independent.
3096	Hanumangarh (Sadulgarh)	97,500	0.18	180	38.38	A	191,000	Rajasthan on Ghaggar River. Agricultural market center, cotton, wool. M=FMPB.
3097	Hapur	173,000	0.45	780	38.65	A	339,000	Uttar Pradesh near Delhi. Railroad, primary roads, east of Delhi, handicrafts.
3098	Hardoi	104,000	0.65	680	38.85	A	205,000	Uttar Pradesh. Grain market, sugar milling, potassium nitrate.
3099	Haridwar	223,000	0.19	420	38.39	A	437,000	Uttar Pradesh near Himalayan Mountains. Ganga River. Hindu temple, pilgrimages to sacred bathing area.
3100	Harihar	78,500	1.50	1,200	44.70	A	154,000	Karnataka. Northwest of Davangere, Varada River branch. Railroad, primary roads. D=CSI,AoG,Baptist.
3101	Hassan	128,000	2.75	3,500	50.95	B	251,000	Karnataka. Cool, humid climate. Rice, engineering, cement. F=12th century. D=CSI,ECI,IPC,Brethren.
3102	Hathras	134,000	0.60	800	38.80	A	263,000	Uttar Pradesh. Agricultural trade center, oilseeds, cotton, pearl millet, glass and cutlery.
3103	Hazaribagh	115,000	3.00	3,500	51.20	B	226,000	Bihar. Agricultural trade center. F=1869 as municipality. Near a national park. D=Independent,CNI,RCC.
3104	Himatnagar	60,000	0.10	60	38.30	A	118,000	Gujarat near Visnagar. Near Sabarmati River. Grain, cloth fabrics, cotton ginning, sandstone. D=CNI,IPC.
3105	Hindaun	71,600	0.10	72	38.30	A	141,000	Rajasthan in East Rajasthan uplands. Cotton, wheat, barley, millet, sandstone, cotton milling.
3106	Hindupur	123,000	3.00	3,700	51.20	B	242,000	Southern Andhra Pradesh south of Anantapur. Penner River. Jaggery, peanut milling. D=CSI,CBA.
3107	Hinganghat	92,700	0.40	370	38.60	A	182,000	Eastern Maharashtra on Wardha River south of Nagpur. Major cotton textile center. Millet, wheat, turmeric.
3108	Hingoli	64,100	0.30	190	38.50	A	126,000	Maharashtra near Penganga River tributary. Railroad. Hindu temple is example of medieval Hindu architecture.
3109	Hisar	213,000	0.22	470	38.42	A	418,000	Haryana northwest of Delhi near Hansi. Livestock, cotton and silk fabrics. University. F=1356. D=AoG.
3110	Hoshangabad	83,400	1.50	1,300	44.70	A	164,000	Madhya Pradesh on Narmada River. Hoshangabad Plain. Brass wire, bamboo canes. D=ECI.
3111	Hoshiarpur	144,000	0.50	720	38.70	A	283,000	Punjab. Manufacturing and trade center. Silk, oilseeds. Wheat, grain, maize, mangoes, sugar. D=BCOG,CNI.
3112	Hospet	159,000	3.30	5,200	51.50	B	312,000	Karnataka on Tungabhadra Reservoir. Famous ruins of ancient Vijayanagar. Irrigation, hydroelectric. D=CJI,MFGC.
3113	Hubli-Dharwar (Dharwar-Hubli)	763,000	5.60	42,700	58.80	B	1,498,000	Karnataka. Education and trading center. Cotton, newspaper. Mosques & temples. D=CSI,Lutheran,RCC.
3114	Hyderabad	6,833,000	4.30	294,000	61.50	B	12,089,000	Capital of Andhra Pradesh on Musi River. Former Deccan capital. F=1591. Char Minar (1591). D=RCC,CSI,AELC.
3115	Alwal	77,800	4.00	3,100	57.20	B	153,000	Loyola Academy, syndicate bank, theatre. Millet, rice, oilseeds, commerce. D=RCC,CSI.
3116	Kapra	103,000	4.20	4,300	57.40	B	203,000	Andhra Pradesh. Rice, sugarcane, tobacco, peanuts, coal, chrome, manganese. D=RCC,CSI.
3117	Kukatpelle	218,000	4.50	9,800	57.70	B	429,000	Andhra Pradesh. Textiles, cigarettes, industry, tobacco, peanuts, cotton handcrafts. D=RCC,CSI,FGCI.
3118	Malkajgiri	149,000	4.00	5,900	57.20	B	292,000	Andhra Pradesh. Markets, industry textiles, cotton milling, rice, commerce. D=CSI,Methodist,RCC,Baptist.
3119	Qutubullapur	124,000	4.40	5,500	57.60	B	244,000	Andhra Pradesh. Millet, rice, oilseeds, agriculture trading, peanuts, residential, textiles. D=RCC,CSI.
3120	Rajendranagar	98,800	4.10	4,100	57.30	B	194,000	Andhra Pradesh. Agriculture University, Natl. Institute of Rural Development. Genetics cooperative. D=RCC,CSI.
3121	Secunderabad Cantonment	197,000	7.18	14,200	60.38	B	387,000	Wholesale commerce. St. John's Church, St. Mary's Church (1847), center of Christian missions. D=RCC,CSI.
3122	Serilungampalle	85,600	4.00	3,400	57.20	B	168,000	Andhra Pradesh. Commerce, millet, rice, tobacco products, handcrafts. D=CSI,RCC,Baptist.
3123	Uppal Kalan	88,400	4.10	3,600	57.30	B	174,000	Andhra Pradesh. Industry, business, agriculture, cotton milling, textiles. D=Methodist,CSI,RCC.
3124	Ichalkaranji	278,000	0.46	1,300	38.66	A	545,000	Maharashtra near Karnataka border. Near Kolhapur. Trade center for sugarcane, tobacco, cotton, wheat. D=CNI.
3125	Imphal	236,000	5.60	13,200	58.80	B	464,000	Capital of Manipur. Weaving, brassware, bronzeware. Mainly Manipuris. D=Baptist.
3126	Indore (Indur)	1,427,000	1.05	15,000	44.25	A	2,566,000	Madhya Pradesh. Distribution center of Malwa Region. Grain milling. F=1715 as trade mart. D=RCC,CNI.
3127	Ingraj Bazar	209,000	0.20	420	38.40	A	409,000	West Bengal near Ganges River, near Gouri ruins. Canal, railroad, primary roads. D=CNI.
3128	Itarsi	101,000	1.60	1,600	44.80	A	198,000	Madhya Pradesh. Railway workshops, trade center for forest products, weekly cattle mart. D=CNI.
3129	Jabalpur (Jubbulpore)	1,026,000	2.57	26,400	50.77	B	1,830,000	Madhya Pradesh. Military headquarters, food processing, sawmilling. Lakes, temples. D=CNI,Methodist,RCC.
3130	Jagdalpur (Jagadelpur, Bastar)	99,600	2.30	2,300	50.50	B	196,000	Madhya Pradesh. Dense forest. Agricultural trade, 2 colleges. D=Methodist,CFIMCOG.
3131	Jagtial	80,100	2.00	1,600	50.20	B	157,000	Andhra Pradesh northwest of Karimnagar. Forest supply, bamboo pulp to Sirpur paper mills. D=CSI,JS.
3132	Jahanabad	61,100	0.50	310	38.70	A	120,000	Bihar near Patna. South Bihar plains, railroad, canals. Ganga River. Barley, jowar, sugarcane. D=GEMS.
3133	Jaipur (Jeypore)	2,143,000	0.37	7,900	38.57	A	3,861,000	Capital of Rajasthan. Walled town. Ivory and enamel, glassware, marble. Pink houses. F=1727. D=CMI,RCC.
3134	Jalandhar (Jullundur)	612,000	0.76	4,700	38.96	A	1,201,000	Punjab. Ancient city. Agricultural trade, tanning, weaving, sporting goods. 13 colleges. D=COG,IPC,Baptist.
3135	Jalgaon	285,000	0.28	800	38.48	A	559,000	Maharashtra. Cotton, millet, oilseeds, thread, fireworks. Educational center. D=CMA,EHC,GFA.
3136	Jalna	206,000	3.83	7,900	52.03	B	405,000	Maharashtra east of Aurangabad near Dudna River. Chiefly cotton, millet, wheat, peanuts. D=CNI,CGC.
3137	Jalpaiguri	79,500	1.50	1,200	44.70	A	156,000	West Bengal. Agricultural distributing center, jute, sawmills, matches. 5 colleges. D=JKPS.
3138	Jamalpur	101,000	0.37	380	38.57	A	199,000	Bihar. Locomotive engineering workshops, iron, steel, slate. F=1862. D=CNI.
3139	Jamkhandi	56,700	0.50	280	38.70	A	111,000	Karnataka near Krishna River. Near Ichalkaronji. Cotton, silk fabrics, wheat, millet, hand loom weaving. D=BYM.
3140	Jammu	324,000	1.54	5,000	44.74	A	637,000	Winter capital of Indian held Jammu & Kashmir. Railroad & manufacturing center. D=CNI,IPC,ECI,RCC.
3141	Jamnagar	431,000	0.57	2,500	38.77	A	845,000	Gujarat. Cement, pottery, textiles, salt, tye-dyeing. Historic temples & palaces. D=CNI,Methodist.
3142	Jamshedpur (Tatanagar)	1,001,000	2.20	22,000	50.40	B	1,798,000	Bihar. Iron, steel, vehicle assembly. National Metallurgical Laboratory. F=1907. D=CNI,Baptist,Brethren,RCC.
3143	Adityapur	92,100	2.00	1,800	50.20	B	181,000	Bihar. Rivers, canal, craft, industry, machinery, coal and iron deposits. D=CNI,Baptist,RCC.
3144	Mango	130,000	2.00	2,600	50.20	B	254,000	Bihar. Railroad, canals, livestock, crafts, industry, coal and iron deposits. D=CNI,Baptist,RCC.
3145	Jaora	66,000	1.60	1,100	44.80	A	129,000	Western Madhya Pradesh north of Ratlam. Corn, millet, cotton, sugarcane, opium, loom weaving. D=CNI.
3146	Jaunpur	161,000	0.08	130	28.28	A	315,000	Uttar Pradesh on Gomati River. Agricultural market, gardening, perfume. F=11th century.
3147	Jaypur	77,300	2.00	1,500	50.20	B	152,000	Orissa near Sabari River, Eastern Ghats. Railway, primary roads. D=RCC.
3148	Jetpur	112,000	0.30	340	38.50	A	220,000	Gujarat on Kathiawar Peninsula east of Dhoraji. Millet, oilseeds, wheat, cotton, handicraft, cloth weaving. D=CNI.
3149	Jhansi	434,000	1.98	8,600	45.18	A	852,000	Uttar Pradesh. Agricultural market, steel-rolling mill. Walled city. F=1613. D=RCC,CNI. M=FMPB.
3150	Jharsuguda	76,600	3.00	2,300	51.20	B	150,000	Orissa near Hirakud Reservoir north of Sambalpur. Railroad workshops, timber, hides, rice.
3151	Jhunjhunun	84,800	0.05	42	28.25	A	166,000	Rajasthan near Churu. Great Indian Desert. Wool, livestock, hides, grain. D=NICOG.

Table 10-5–continued opposite

Table 10-5–continued

Rec No 1	Country City 2	Pop 2000 3	AC% 4	Church Members 5	E% 6	W 7	Pop 2025 8	Notes 9
3152	Jind (Jhind)	101,000	0.22	220	38.42	A	197,000	Haryana. Grain-trade center, cotton ginning. Ancient origins & temple. D=Independent. M=PTL.
3153	Jodhpur	846,000	0.58	4,900	38.78	A	1,551,000	Rajasthan. Trade center for agricultural crops, wool, cattle, ivory goods, glass bangles. D=CNI,FFCI,RCC.
3154	Jorhat	131,000	4.70	6,200	57.90	B	258,000	Assam. Commercial center of productive agricultural area, jewelry. Assam Agricultural College. D=Baptist.
3155	Junagadh	196,000	0.30	590	38.50	A	386,000	Gujarat. Manufacturing center. Buddhist, Taina, Hindu temples, mosques. Ancient origins. D=CNI,BYM.
3156	Kadaiyanallur	81,100	11.50	9,300	64.70	B	159,000	Southern Tamil Nadu north of Tirunelveli. Major cotton weaving center. D=CSI.
3157	Kadiri	74,700	6.50	4,900	59.70	B	147,000	Southern Andhra Pradesh west of Rayachoti. HQ of regional malaria supply, sheep grazing. D=CSI.
3158	Kagaznagar	67,900	1.50	1,000	44.70	A	133,000	Andhra Pradesh near Maharashtra in the north. Cotton, millet, livestock, rice. D=Lutheran.
3159	Kairana	66,100	1.00	660	44.20	A	130,000	Uttar Pradesh near Shamli. Secondary roads, handicrafts, rice. D=CNI.
3160	Kaithal	84,000	0.15	130	38.35	A	165,000	Haryana. Agricultural market center, cotton, saltpeter. Historically, Muslim cultural center, many tombs.
3161	Kakinada (Cocanada)	386,000	5.00	19,300	58.20	B	757,000	Andhra Pradesh seaport. Exports cotton, peanuts, sugar. Salt-evaporating plant. D=RCC,AELC,Independent.
3162	Kalol	109,000	1.50	1,600	44.70	A	213,000	Gujarat north of Ahmadabad. Local market for timber, millet, wheat. D=FPCGI,GFA.
3163	Kambam	61,200	2.90	1,800	51.10	B	120,000	Tamil Nadu on Kerala border north of Gudalur, Suruli River. Teak, turmeric. D=CSI.
3164	Kanchipuram (Conjeeveram)	200,000	1.04	2,100	44.24	A	393,000	Tamil Nadu on Palar River. Important pilgrimage center (130 Saiva & Vaishnava temples). D=CSI,ECI,MFGC.
3165	Kannangad	139,000	0.50	700	38.70	A	273,000	Road junction, agricultural trade.
3166	Kannauj	70,300	0.40	280	38.60	A	138,000	Uttar Pradesh on Ganges River. Railroad, commerce, trade, cereals. M=IET,FMPB.
3167	Kanpur (Cawnpore)	2,447,000	0.76	18,600	48.96	A	4,269,000	Uttar Pradesh on Ganges River. Major industrial center. Hindu glass temple. 1857 mutiny. D=RCC. M=FMPB.
3168	Kanpur Cantonment	110,000	0.75	820	38.95	A	215,000	Uttar Pradesh on Ganges River. Railroad, Ganga-yamuna Doab. Industrial center. D=RCC,Methodist.
3169	Kapurthala	91,600	0.50	460	38.70	A	180,000	Punjab. Agricultural market, chemicals, paints, pharmaceuticals. F=11th century. D=CNI,IPC.
3170	Karad	66,800	1.90	1,300	45.10	A	131,000	Maharashtra on Krishna River south of Pune. Road junction, millet, peanuts, cotton and silk milling. D=CNI.
3171	Karaikal	72,900	16.00	11,700	74.20	B	143,000	Tamil Nadu on Bay of Bengal. Kaveri River branch. Secondary roads. Pondicherry Union territory. D=CSI.
3172	Karaikkudi	130,000	4.20	5,500	57.40	B	255,000	Tamil Nadu south of Pudukkottai. Residential and financial center of Chettia merchant. D=RCC,CSI,AoG.
3173	Karanja	57,600	1.00	580	44.20	A	113,000	Maharashtra near Akola. Plains, canal, livestock, cotton ginning, oilseed milling.
3174	Karauli	57,700	0.20	120	38.40	A	113,000	Rajastan near Madhya Pradesh. East Rajasthan Uplands. Grain, wheat, cotton, carpets.
3175	Karimnagar	175,000	1.75	3,100	44.95	A	343,000	Andhra Pradesh. Millet, oilseeds, rice, cotton center., teak, ebony forest. D=CSI,BGC,Independent.
3176	Karnal	207,000	0.15	310	38.35	A	407,000	Haryana on Yamuna River. Trade center for grain, salt, metal, cotton. Annual horse fair. D=CNI,CON.
3177	Karur	130,000	4.20	5,500	57.40	B	256,000	Tamil Nadu on Amaravati River south of Erode. Brassware, 'place of the sacred cow', cotton fabrics. D=CSI,IPA.
3178	Karwar	60,100	6.00	3,600	59.20	B	118,000	Karnataka on Kalinadi River and Arabian Sea. Near Goa. Rice, fish, coconuts, timber, fruit canning. D=RCC.
3179	Kasaragod	59,100	5.00	3,000	58.20	B	116,000	Kerala on Arabian Sea. Near Mangalore. Fish curing, coconuts, mangoes, rice, pottery-clay pits. D=RCC,OSC.
3180	Kasganj	89,100	0.50	450	38.70	A	175,000	Uttar Pradesh. Agricultural market, cotton, sugar. Near Hindu pilgrimage center.
3181	Kashipur	82,300	0.75	620	38.95	A	162,000	Uttar Pradesh north of Moradabad. Ramganga River. Rice, wheat, corn, cloth, Hindu temple, fort ruins.
3182	Katihar (Saifganj)	182,000	0.13	240	38.33	A	356,000	Bihar on Saura River. Railway workshops, agricultural trade, rice, jute, oilseeds. D=FPCOB. M=GFA.
3183	Katwa	65,400	0.01	7	28.21	A	128,000	West Bengal near Bhagitathi River north of Navadwip.
3184	Kavali	77,500	5.10	4,000	58.30	B	152,000	Eastern Andhra Pradesh on Bay of Bengal. Cashew and casuarina plantations, laterite quarries. D=CSI,COG.
3185	Kayankulam	79,100	25.00	19,800	88.20	B	155,000	Western Kerala on Lakshadweep Sea south of Alleppey. Mats, rice, cassava, cashews. D=RCC.,OSC.
3186	Keshod	59,100	0.30	180	38.50	A	116,000	Gujarat near Veraval and Arabian Sea. Local market for cotton, millet, oilseeds, handloom weaving.D=FPCGI.
3187	Khambhat	106,000	0.20	210	38.40	A	208,000	Gujarat on Gulf of Khambhat. Marsh, fishing, textile weaving, carpets, petroleum refining, salt ornaments. D=CNI.
3188	Khamgaon	86,800	0.43	370	38.63	A	170,000	Maharashtra west of Akola. Base of Ajanta Range. Primary roads. Cotton ginning, industrial schools. D=CMA.
3189	Khammam	175,000	5.50	9,600	58.70	B	344,000	Andhra Pradesh. Trade center. Rice, sorghum, corn, oilseed milling, pulses, garnet. D=RCC,CSI,AoG.
3190	Khandwa	171,000	3.60	6,200	51.80	B	336,000	Madhya Pradesh. Cotton, timber. 12th century center of Jaina worship. D=FPCGI,RCC,Methodist.
3191	Khanna	85,000	0.60	510	38.80	A	167,000	Punjab southeast of Ludhiana. Railroad. Hosiery, several schools and colleges. D=IPC.
3192	Kharagpur (Kharakpur)	330,000	3.70	12,200	51.90	B	647,000	West Bengal. Rail junction, rice milling, chemicals, shoes, silk. Muslim saint shrine. D=CNI,Baptist,IPC,RCC.
3193	Khardaha	104,000	0.10	100	38.30	A	204,000	West Bengal on Hugli River north of Calcutta. Jute milling center, woodworking. Vishnuite temple.
3194	Khargone (Khargon)	78,700	1.40	1,100	44.60	A	154,000	Madhya Pradesh. Agricultural produce & timber market. Cotton, rice, oilseeds. D=CNI.
3195	Khurja	94,700	0.43	410	38.63	A	186,000	Uttar Pradesh southeast of Delhi. Secondary roads, canal, railroad, handicrafts.
3196	Kishanganj	75,900	0.38	290	38.58	A	149,000	Eastern Bihar on Mahananda River. West Bengal border, north Bihar plains. D=FBC,Independent.
3197	Kishangarh (Kishengarh)	96,500	1.73	1,700	44.93	A	189,000	Rajasthan on banks of Lake Gundalao. Cotton, agricultural trade. F=1611 by Rajput warrior. D=Methodist.
3198	Koch Bihar	109,000	0.02	22	28.22	A	214,000	West Bengal on Amo River. North of Bangladesh. Torsa River. Rice, jute, tobacco, sugarcane, leather goods.
3199	Kodarma (Koderma)	63,100	0.10	63	38.30	A	124,000	Bihar. Near Hazaribag Plateau, Koderma district. Mica mining center. D=CNI.
3200	Kohima	62,600	85.00	53,200	99.70	C	123,000	Nagaland, capital. State museum. Japanese advance halted (April 1944). D=CBNEI.
3201	Kolar	98,000	10.25	10,100	63.45	B	192,000	Karnataka. Woolen blankets, leather, pencils, silk & cotton fabrics. D=Methodist,CSI.
3202	Kolar Gold Fields	184,000	22.20	40,900	85.40	B	362,000	Karnataka. Gold mines nationalized in 1950. First mined in 1881. D=CSI.,Lutheran,RCC.
3203	Robertsonpet	80,000	20.00	16,000	83.20	B	157,000	Karnataka. Residential area. Commercial college, cotton products. D=RCC,CSI,AoG. M=OM.
3204	Kolhapur	492,000	1.12	5,500	44.32	A	965,000	Maharashtra on Pancaganga River. Sugar, textiles. Early center of Buddhism. D=CNI,Brethren,EHC.
3205	Korba	147,000	1.00	1,500	44.20	A	288,000	Madhya Pradesh on Hasdo River. Major coalfields nearby, thermal power station. D=COG,Mennonite.
3206	Kot Kapura	73,500	0.50	370	38.70	A	144,000	Punjab. Rail junction near Firozpur. Trade center, grain, wheat, cotton, oilseeds, millet, hand loom weaving.
3207	Kotah (Kota)	632,000	0.64	4,000	38.84	A	1,240,000	Rajasthan. Oil, textiles, paper, cotton, bone mills. F=14th century as walled city. D=CNI,SFC,CBA,IPCOG.
3208	Kottagudem	120,000	5.50	6,600	58.70	B	236,000	Northern Andhra Pradesh northeast of Khammam. Mining center in Singareni, coalfields, railroad. D=CSI.
3209	Kottayam	196,000	45.00	88,100	98.20	B	384,000	Kerala. Market center for tea, rubber. Center of Syrian Orthodox. F=AD 53 by St. Thomas. D=OSC,RCC.
3210	Kovilpatti (Koilpatti)	91,900	25.00	23,000	88.20	B	180,000	Southern Tamil Nadu north of Tirunelveli. Major cotton-milling center. D=CSI,CBA,AoG.
3211	Kozhikode (Calicut)	1,114,000	3.96	44,100	52.16	B	2,048,000	Kerala on Malabar Coast. Coconut, ginger, coffee. Calicut University. F=1664 by British.D=OSC,RCC.
3212	Krishnagiri	71,000	7.30	5,200	60.50	B	139,000	Northern Tamil Nadu west of Vaniyambadi. Trade center, tanning, grapes, mangoes, castor oil. D=AoG,FFNI.
3213	Krishnanagar (Krishnagar)	142,000	0.01	14	28.21	A	280,000	West Bengal. Agricultural distribution. Sugar milling, colored clay. Christian evangelism center. D=CNI,JKDS.
3214	Kumbakonam	177,000	4.16	7,400	57.36	B	348,000	Tamil Nadu on Cauvery River Delta. Trade in rice & betel leaves. F=7th century as Cola capital. D=CSI,IPA,IDC.
3215	Kundla	77,400	0.03	23	28.23	A	152,000	Gujarat on Kathiawar Peninsula. Gir range. Rice, cotton, millet, wheat, handcraft cloth, weaving. D=CNI.
3216	Kurasia	84,400	0.40	340	38.60	A	166,000	Madhya Pradesh. Grain, cotton cloth, livestock, transmitter.
3217	Kurnool	324,000	4.10	13,300	57.30	B	635,000	Andhra Pradesh. Trade center. Colleges of arts, sciences, medicine. Hindu shrines. D=RCC,CSI,MBCI,AoG.
3218	Ladnun	56,800	0.01	6	28.21	A	111,000	Rajasthan near Sikar. Great Indian desert. Hides, livestock, wool, grain, salt, gold ornaments, sandstone.
3219	Lakhimpur	93,700	0.42	390	38.62	A	184,000	Uttar Pradesh on North-Eastern railway. Tea, rice, jute, silkworms, wheat, grain, corn, barley.
3220	Lalitpur	81,000	0.51	410	38.71	A	159,000	Uttar Pradesh on Shahjad River. Tanning, sawmilling, shoemaking, soap.
3221	Latur	232,000	0.26	600	38.46	A	456,000	Maharashtra. Balaghat Range. Manjra River. Cotton ginning, wheat. Devastating 1993 earthquake. D=CNI,AoG.
3222	Luckeesarai	62,700	0.20	130	38.40	A	123,000	Bihar near Mokama. South Bihar range. Railroad, canal. Rice, corn, wheat, grain, barley. D=CNI.
3223	Lucknow	2,565,000	0.76	19,500	38.96	A	4,658,000	Capital of Uttar Pradesh on Gomati River. Agricultural. Notable architecture. D=RCC. M=FMPB.
3224	Lucknow Cantonment	59,100	0.60	350	38.80	A	116,000	Gomati River. Great Imambara (c1780). Botanical gardens. Lucknow University. D=BYM,EHC. M=FMPB.
3225	Ludhiana	1,652,000	0.47	7,800	38.67	A	3,065,000	Punjab. Agricultural market, hosiery, cotton textiles. U.S. Presbyterian mission college & hospital. D=CNI,IPC.
3226	Machilipatnam (Masulipatam, Bandar)	187,000	3.36	6,300	51.56	B	368,000	Andhra Pradesh. Seaport, carpet weaving, rice. F=1611 as first British industrial settlement. D=CSI,Apostolic.
3227	Madanapalle	86,900	2.90	2,500	51.10	B	170,000	Southern Andhra Pradesh near Karnataka. Rice milling, sugarcane, millet. Tuberculosis sanatorium. D=CSI.
3228	Madgaon (Margao)	84,900	31.20	26,500	94.40	B	167,000	Goa. Cold storage for fish, agricultural produce, beaches, rice, copra, cashews, mangoes, sheep. D=RCC.
3229	Madhubani	63,100	0.10	63	38.30	A	124,000	Bihar in North Bihar Plains near Nepal border. Rice, corn, wheat, barley, sugarcane, jute. M=GEMS.
3230	Madurai	1,273,000	6.60	84,000	61.80	B	2,249,000	Tami Nadu on Vaigai River. Cotton. Many temples, thousands of pilgrims. Ancient origins. D=CSI,TELC,RCC.
3231	Mahbubnagar	138,000	2.00	2,800	50.20	B	270,000	Andhra Pradesh. Cotton ginning & pressing, oilseeds, rice milling, teak, ebony, livestock. D=MBCI,MCI.
3232	Mahesana	129,000	1.50	1,900	44.70	A	253,000	Gujarat near Ahmadabad. Railroads. Millet, wheat, oilseeds, cotton, chemical manufacturing. D=CNI.
3233	Mahoba	66,200	0.60	400	38.80	A	130,000	Uttar Pradesh near Madhya Pradesh. Grain. 24 rock hewn images dating around 1149. F=c800. D=CNI.
3234	Mahuva	75,200	0.27	200	38.47	A	148,000	Gujarat on Kathiawar Peninsula and Gulf of Khambhat. Grain, cotton, oilseeds, woodcarving, sawmills. D=CNI.
3235	Mainpuri	90,400	0.12	110	38.32	A	177,000	Uttar Pradesh. Agricultural trade, cotton, oilseeds, lamps, glass, wooden sculpture, tobacco.
3236	Makrana	78,500	0.01	8	28.21	A	154,000	Rajasthan near Sambhar Lake. Railroad, desert, handicrafts, agriculture, marble, salt, hides, quarries.
3237	Malappuram	168,000	0.50	840	38.70	A	329,000	Karnataka, WNW of Bellary, Tungabhadra River. Rail station, rice, milling. Coconuts, mangoes, cashews. D=CSI.
3238	Malaut	67,000	0.10	67	38.30	A	131,000	Punjab near Abohar. Indira Gandhi Canal. Primary roads.
3239	Malegaon	403,000	0.12	480	38.32	A	792,000	Maharashtra on Girna River. Agricultural produce, handloom weaving, cotton, silk. D=CNI,Independent.
3240	Malerkotla	104,000	0.20	210	38.40	A	205,000	Muslim community attacked by Sikhs (c1870). Punjab, wheat, millet, cotton, sugar.
3241	Malkapur	60,400	1.50	910	44.70	A	119,000	Maharashtra near Bhusawal, north of Ajanta range. Railroad, handicrafts, cotton ginning, oilseed milling.
3242	Mancheriyal (Mancheral)	62,000	1.60	990	44.80	A	122,000	Andhra Pradesh on Godavari River. Rice, sorghum, fruits, marsh, fishing. D=COG,CSI.
3243	Mandasor (Mandsaur)	113,000	0.55	620	38.75	A	221,000	Madhya Pradesh on Sau River. Trade center for grain, cotton, cloth. Sugar milling. Ancient origins. D=CNI.
3244	Mandya	141,000	2.58	3,600	50.78	B	277,000	Karnataka. Center of sugarcane region. Alcohol, tobacco, vegetable oil. D=CSI,EHC,IDC.
3245	Mangalagiri	69,800	7.00	4,900	60.20	B	137,000	Andhra Pradesh near Vijayawada. Railroad, nearby Hindu ruins, cotton. D=Baptist,COG.
3246	Mangalore	502,000	16.93	84,900	75.13	B	985,000	Karnataka. Arabian seaport. Coconuts, cotton weaving, roofing tiles, boatbuilding. D=RCC,Lutheran,CSI.
3247	Manjeri	81,700	2.10	1,700	50.30	B	160,000	Kerala east of Calicut. Western Ghots, inland waterway. Fishing, tea. D=OSC,RCC.
3248	Manmad	72,200	0.10	72	38.30	A	142,000	Maharashtra south of Malegaon. Market center for cotton, peanuts, millet, handcraft cloth weaving. D=CNI,COG.
3249	Mannargudi	66,600	6.90	4,600	60.10	B	131,000	Tamil Nadu on Kaveri tributary west of Nagappattinam. Brass and copper vessels, Hindu temples. D=CSI,AoG.
3250	Mansa	64,900	0.10	65	38.30	A	127,000	Punjab near Haryana. Canal, railroad, irrigation projects, millet. Market, wheat, cotton.
3251	Mathura (Muttra)	275,000	0.43	1,200	38.63	A	539,000	Uttar Pradesh on Yamuna River. Agricultural trade center. Traditional birthplace of Krishna. Hindu center. M=CCC.
3252	Maunath Bhanjan	161,000	0.33	530	38.53	A	316,000	Eastern Uttar Pradesh east of Azamgarh. Millet, cotton, jute, corn, wheat, agriculture.
3253	Mawana	60,800	1.40	850	44.60	A	119,000	Uttar Pradesh near Ganges River. Near Meerut. Wheat, millet, sugarcane, oilseeds.
3254	Mayuram	90,800	8.00	7,300	61.20	B	178,000	Tamil Nadu on Kaveri tributary. Hindu pilgrimage center, cotton and silk weaving. D=CSI.
3255	Meerut	1,259,000	1.49	18,800	44.69	A	2,328,000	Uttar Pradesh. Agricultural trade, manufacturing, smelting, handicrafts. Old temples & mosques. D=RCC,CNI.
3256	Meerut Cantonment	112,000	1.50	1,700	44.70	A	219,000	Uttar Pradesh. Flour, sugar, cotton, textiles, leather, smelting, vegetable oils. D=RCC,CNI,Methodist.
3257	Mehsana	109,000	0.17	190	38.37	A	214,000	Gujarat. Market & manufacturing center. F=12th century. D=CNI,Independent.
3258	Mettuppalaiyam	74,500	4.20	3,100	57.40	B	146,000	Southern Tamil Nadu near Tirunelveli. Livestock grazing, tannery, shellac manufacturing. D=CSI.
3259	Mhow	98,600	0.90	890	39.10	A	193,000	Madhya Pradesh on southern Malwa Plateau. Dairy farming. F=1818 as British cantonment. D=CNI,IFGM.
3260	Midnapore (Midnapur, Medinipur)	129,000	1.50	1,900	44.70	A	253,000	West Bengal. Agricultural trade center, rice, chemicals, silk, educational center. F=1865. D=CNI,Baptist.
3261	Miryalaguda	77,600	0.50	390	38.70	A	152,000	Andhra Pradesh. Legume tumma, Nizam sugar factory, rice milling, cotton ginning, castor oil. D=CSI,JS.
3262	Mirzapur-cum-Vindhyachal	186,000	0.31	580	38.51	A	365,000	Uttar Pradesh on Ganges River. Cotton milling, sandstone. Many temples. F=1700. D=CNI. M=GEMS.
3263	Modinagar	146,000	1.40	2,000	44.60	A	287,000	Uttar Pradesh south of Meerut. Railroad, agriculture, handicrafts, cotton, millet, trade center. D=CNI.
3264	Moga	131,000	0.40	520	38.60	A	256,000	Punjab near Firozpur, west of Ludhiana. Railroad, wheat, millet, annual fair, cotton, oilseeds. D=CNI,IPC.
3265	Mokama	70,100	0.20	140	38.40	A	138,000	Bihar on Ganges River near Barauni. Railroad ferry, site of projected steel plant, sugarcane, barley, corn. D=CNI.
3266	Monghyr (Munger)	177,000	0.40	710	38.60	A	347,000	Bihar on Ganges River. Grain market, firearms, cigarettes. F=4th century by Guptas. D=CNI,Baptist.
3267	Moradabad	509,000	0.97	4,900	39.17	A	1,000,000	Uttar Pradesh. Agricultural trade center, cotton milling, weaving. F=1625. Large mosque. D=CNI.
3268	Morena	173,000	0.06	100	28.26	A	340,000	Madhya Pradesh. Agricultural trade center, oilseed milling, cotton weaving. D=PTL,Independent.
3269	Mormugao	108,000	31.20	33,600	94.40	B	211,000	Goa on Arabian Sea. Port, fruit, fishing, iron ore, cotton, rice, cashews, industrial and commercial. D=RCC.
3270	Morvi (Morbi)	110,000	0.30	330	38.50	A	215,000	Gujarat. Trade center for agricultural produce, cotton processing. Kathiawar peninsula. D=IPCOG,CLC.
3271	Motihari	97,700	0.40	390	38.60	A	192,000	Bihar on bank of lake. Oilseeds, sugar, cotton, road center, weaving, milling. F=1869. M=GFA,Independent.
3272	Mubarakpur	73,900	0.05	37	28.25	A	145,000	Uttar Pradesh near Azamgarh. Hand loom cotton weaving center, silk weaving, sugar milling.
3273	Muktsar	78,200	0.48	380	38.68	A	153,000	Punjab near Indira Gandhi Canal south of Firozpur. Grain, cotton, oilseeds. Annual Sikh festival. D=CNI.
3274	Mumbai (Bombay)	18,042,000	15.00	2,706,000	75.20	B	30,378,000	Capital of Maharashtra on Arabian Sea. Finance, port. Severe overcrowding. Indian films. D=RCC,CNI.
3275	Ambarnath (Amarnath)	144,000	8.00	11,500	61.20	B	283,000	Maharashtra, NE of Bombay. Railroad. Chemical products, pharmaceuticals. Shivaite temple. D=CNI.

Table 10-5–continued overleaf

Table 10-5–continued

Rec No 1	Country City 2	Pop 2000 3	AC% 4	Church Members 5	E% 6	W 7	Pop 2025 8	Notes 9
3276	Bhiwandi	461,000	0.29	1,300	38.49	A	906,000	Maharashtra northeast of Bombay. Glass, timber, cloth weaving, bricks, textiles. D=CNI,AoG.
3277	Bulsar (Valsad)	132,000	10.00	13,200	63.20	B	258,000	Gujarat, gulf of Khambat. Railroad, engineering workshops, wheat, molasses, tiles. Lighthouse. D=CMI.
3278	Dombivli	149,000	10.00	14,900	63.20	B	292,000	Maharashtra. Textiles, industry, machinery, clothing, chemicals, electronic goods. D=CNI.
3279	Kalyan	1,195,000	2.93	35,000	51.13	B	2,345,000	On Ulhas River. Chemicals, synthetics, electrical equipment, handloom cotton. D=Brethren.
3280	Mira Bhayandar	207,000	10.00	20,700	63.20	B	406,000	Maharashtra. Thane District, W. Central India. Chemicals, machinery, clothing, textiles. D=Methodist,CNI.
3281	Nalasopara	79,600	8.00	6,400	61.20	B	156,000	Maharashtra. Industrial center, cotton textiles, clothing, fish processing, chemicals. D=CNI,RCC.
3282	New Bombay	362,000	15.00	54,300	68.20	B	711,000	Maharashtra. Engineering, commerce, trade, business, exports, glass, motor vehicles. D=CNI,RCC.
3283	Thana (Thane)	939,000	2.59	24,300	50.79	B	1,842,000	Residential suburb. Chemical, textiles, engineering, medicines. Two Christian churches. D=CNI.
3284	Ulhasnagar (Kalyan Camp)	435,000	2.48	10,800	50.68	B	853,000	Chemicals, silk, nylon. Industrial training institute. Sindhi community. Textile factory. D=Methodist,IPC.
3285	Virar	67,800	10.00	6,800	63.20	B	133,000	Maharashtra. Cotton textiles, heavy industry, chemicals, electronic goods, cloth production. D=CNI.
3286	Murwara (Katni)	192,000	1.33	2,600	44.53	A	378,000	Madhya Pradesh trade center, rice, flour, limestone, cement, pots, varnishes, mining. F=1874. D=CNI,PCA.
3287	Muzaffarnagar	292,000	0.17	500	38.37	A	573,000	Uttar Pradesh. Agricultural marketplace, wheat, sugarcane. F=1633 by Khan-e Jahan. M=PTL.
3288	Muzaffarpur	283,000	0.04	110	28.24	A	556,000	Bihar. Trade center on Patna-Nepal route, rice, sugar, cutlery. F=18th century. Buddhist pilgrimage center. D=CNI.
3289	Mysore	768,000	3.24	24,900	51.44	B	1,508,000	Karnataka. Rice, oil mills, ivory, wood art work. Pilgrimage center. Ancient origins. D=RCC,CSI,Methodist.
3290	Nabadwip (Nadia, Navadwip)	195,000	0.01	19	28.21	A	382,000	West Bengal. Traditional Sanskrit schools, important pilgrimage center. F=1063.
3291	Nabha	63,700	0.20	130	38.40	A	125,000	Punjab near Patiala. Canal, railroad, millet, cotton, handicrafts, loomweaving, college. D=AT,Independent.
3292	Nadiad	200,000	3.40	6,800	51.60	B	393,000	Gujarat. Industrial & commercial center. Railroad, textiles, sugarcane. D=Methodist,SA.
3293	Nagaon	110,000	5.00	5,500	58.20	B	216,000	Assam near Brahmaputra River. Railroad, jute timber, rice, mustard, tea, sugarcane, silk and lace. D=Baptist.
3294	Nagappattinam (Negapattam)	117,000	17.00	19,800	75.20	B	229,000	Tamil Nadu on Bay of Bengal. Ship repair, fishing. Ancient port. D=AoG,TELC,Zion Church of Christ.
3295	Nagaur (Nagor)	80,200	0.06	48	28.26	A	157,000	Rajasthan. Walled town. Trade center for bullock, wool, hides, cotton. D=CBA,GFA,FFCI.
3296	Nagda	93,600	0.70	660	38.90	A	184,000	Western Madhya Pradesh on Chambal River northwest of Ujjain. Cotton, oilseeds. D=CNI,RCC.
3297	Nagercoil	223,000	24.28	54,200	87.48	B	438,000	Tamil Nadu. Cotton, rice, rubber. Tourist center. Important Christian center. D=RCC,CSI,AoG,BYM,MFGC.
3298	Nagina	68,900	0.45	310	38.65	A	135,000	Uttar Pradesh near Najibabad, on tributary of Ramganga River. Sugar trade, noted carved ebony works, glass.
3299	Nagpur	2,060,000	1.91	39,300	50.11	B	3,630,000	Maharashtra on Nag River. Cotton, educational & cultural center. F=18th century. D=CNI,Baptist,RCC.
3300	Kamthi (Kamptee)	155,000	1.80	2,800	45.00	A	305,000	Maharashtra. Feromanganese products, transport equipment, metals, quarries. D=Methodist,RCC.
3301	Najibabad	78,700	0.45	350	38.65	A	155,000	Uttar Pradesh east of Muzaffarnagar. Afghan fort built 1775. Rice, wheat, barley, cotton, timber.
3302	Nalgonda	99,800	3.50	3,500	51.70	B	196,000	Andhra Pradesh east of Hyderabad. Krishna River. Millet, oilseeds, rice, cotton ginning. D=RCC,CSI,MBCI.
3303	Nanded (Nander)	364,000	0.53	1,900	38.73	A	714,000	Maharashtra on Godavari River. Commercial center, cotton, weaving. Sanskrit learning center. D=AoG.
3304	Nandurbar	92,300	0.64	590	38.84	A	181,000	Northern Maharashtra near Tapi River. Cotton, wheat, linseed, timber, tanning, hand loom weaving, melons.
3305	Nandyal	142,000	6.00	8,500	59.20	B	278,000	Andhra Pradesh on Kunderu. Agriculture center, cotton ginning, oilseed milling, handmade paper. D=CSI.
3306	Narasapur	66,400	10.00	6,600	63.20	B	130,000	Andhra Pradesh in Godavari Delta. Rice milling, tobacco, coconuts, ceded to English in 1759. D=ECI,ALEC.
3307	Narasaraopet	105,000	11.50	12,000	64.70	B	205,000	Andhra Pradesh west of Guntur. Trade center, rice and oilseed milling, cotton ginning. D=Lutheran.
3308	Narnaul	61,100	0.08	49	28.28	A	120,000	Haryana near Rajasthan border. Cotton, grain, ghee, salt, hand loom weaving, cart manufacturing.
3309	Nasik	1,135,000	1.82	20,700	45.02	A	2,130,000	Maharashtra on Godavari River. Silk & cotton weaving. Important religious center for pilgrimage. D=CNI,CMA.
3310	Deolali Cantonment	60,200	1.50	900	44.70	A	118,000	Maharashtra. Buddhist, Jaina, & Hindu temples. Agriculture, cotton, rice. D=CNI,NLF,CMA.
3311	Navsari (Naosari)	224,000	0.23	520	38.43	A	439,000	Gujarat on Purna River. Cotton, wood carvings, perfume. Home of Parsees. Important fire temples. D=FPCGI.
3312	Nawabganj	91,400	0.26	240	38.46	A	179,000	Utter Pradesh. Agricultural market, cotton weaving. Rice, wheat, grain, oilseeds, barley, sugarcane.
3313	Nawada	62,500	0.30	190	38.50	A	123,000	Bihar near Gaya. Railroad, rice, corn, handicrafts, wheat, grain, barley, oilseeds, mica mining. D=CNI.
3314	Nawalgarh	60,300	0.01	6	28.21	A	118,000	Rajasthan near Sikar, desert. Salt, wool, grain, livestock, cotton, hand loom weaving, enamel work.
3315	Nedumangad	58,700	0.50	290	38.70	A	115,000	Neyyar Sanctuary. D= Salvation Army.
3316	Neemuch (Nimach)	107,000	0.50	530	38.70	A	209,000	Madhya Pradesh on a barren ridge. Handloom weaving, building stone. Wheat, cotton, opium, airport. D=FFCI.
3317	Nellore	373,000	6.30	23,500	59.50	B	732,000	Andhra Pradesh on Penneru River near Bay of Bengal. Cotton and oilseed market, milling. D=RCC,COG.
3318	New Barakpur	75,200	0.25	190	38.45	A	148,000	West Bengal on Hugli River. 6 miles SE of Barakpur. Fish, ice, old fashioned bungalows.
3319	Neyveli	149,000	12.54	18,700	65.74	B	293,000	Tamil Nadu, South Arrot Vallalur district, South India. Cotton, oilseeds, rice, milling. D=CSI,AoG,RCC.
3320	Nipani	60,800	0.50	300	38.70	A	119,000	Karnataka near Maharashtra, Western Ghats range. Highway, rice, cotton, timber. D=CSI.
3321	Nirmal	68,100	2.00	1,400	50.20	B	134,000	Andhra Pradesh near Godavari River. Primary highway, rice, wheat, cotton. D=Lutheran.
3322	Nizamabad (Indur)	284,000	2.00	5,700	50.20	B	557,000	Andhra Pradesh. Sugarcane, vegetable oil. College of arts & sciences. Administrative center. D=CSI,CFIM.
3323	Nowgong (Naogaon)	84,600	0.50	420	38.70	A	166,000	Madhya Pradesh. Agricultural distribution center, chemicals, military. Ganja growing center. M=FMPB.
3324	Ongole	151,000	5.00	7,500	58.20	B	296,000	Andhra Pradesh on Bay of Bengal, Coromandel Coast. Railroad, navigable canal, agriculture. D=IPCOG.
3325	Ootacamund (Uthagamandalam)	117,000	22.50	26,300	85.70	B	230,000	Tamil Nadu in Nilgir Hills at 7,500 ft. Tourist resort, tea, textiles. F=1821. D=CSI,Brethren,Baptist.
3326	Orai	116,000	0.06	70	28.26	A	228,000	Uttar Pradesh. Trade center for agriculture. Trades in grain, wheat, oilseeds, jowar.
3327	Palakodu	67,100	7.00	4,700	60.20	B	132,000	Andhra Pradesh on Godavari Delta. Rice, trade, markets, handicrafts. D=CSI,Lutheran.
3328	Palani	89,500	15.00	13,400	68.20	B	176,000	Tamil Nadu on Amaravati River. Near Dindigul. Tobacco, coffee, cardamom, turmeric, silk, livestock. D=CSI.
3329	Palanpur	106,000	0.32	340	38.52	A	209,000	Gujarat. Trade center for agricultural produce, handicrafts. Grain, cloth fabrics, ghee. D=CNI,CMA.
3330	Palghat	212,000	4.71	10,000	57.91	B	416,000	Kerala on Ponnani River. Grain, tobacco, textiles, timber, rice milling. D=OSC,RCC.
3331	Pali	161,000	0.21	340	38.41	A	316,000	Rajasthan. Divided into ancient & modern. Historic temples. Agricultural market center. D=CBA,Independent.
3332	Palwal	69,700	0.57	400	38.77	A	137,000	Haryana south of Delhi, west of Yamuna River. Railroad, trade center, sugar agriculture. D=Baptist.
3333	Palwancha	62,300	0.50	310	38.70	A	122,000	Andhra Pradesh. Sugarcane, cotton, palm oil, paddy, maize.
3334	Panaji (Panjim)	100,000	31.20	31,300	94.40	B	197,000	Capital of Goa on Mandari River. Colonial houses & plazas. Administrative center. D=RCC & 20 others.
3335	Pandharpur	94,000	1.10	1,000	44.30	A	185,000	Maharashtra on Bhima River. Hindu pilgrimage center, 4 annual festivals. D=CNI.
3336	Panipat (Ponipat)	225,000	0.03	68	28.23	A	442,000	Haryana north of Delhi. Site of 3 famous battles: 1526, 1556, 1761. Cotton, textiles. D=GFA,PTL.
3337	Panruti	60,600	5.50	3,300	58.70	B	119,000	Tamil Nadu west of Cuddalore. Sugarcane, cotton, trade, near ruins of Ft. St. David (fort). D=CSI.
3338	Panvel	69,300	8.00	5,500	61.20	B	136,000	Maharashtra near Bombay. Port, rice, millet, ghee, oilseed, bridge connection to Mumbai. D=CNI,AoG.
3339	Paramakkudi	85,000	6.00	5,100	59.20	B	167,000	Tamil Nadu near Madurai. Vagai River. Railroad, agriculture, silk weaving. D=CSI,AoG,TELC.
3340	Parbhani	224,000	0.34	760	38.54	A	440,000	Maharashtra. Commercial center. Prabhavati Temple converted to mosque. Cotton, millet, peanuts. D=CNI,BCOG.
3341	Parli	85,500	0.30	260	38.50	A	168,000	Maharashtra in Balaghat Range south of Parbhani. Cotton, millet, wheat. Hindu place of pilgrimage. D=BCOG.
3342	Patan	114,000	0.32	370	38.52	A	224,000	Gujarat on Saraswati River. Cotton, weaving, embroidery, pottery, swords. D=CNI.
3343	Pathankot	173,000	1.56	2,700	44.76	A	340,000	Punjab near Jammu and Kashmir and Himachal Pradesh. Grain, wool, timber, hides, hand loom weaving. D=CNI.
3344	Patiala	316,000	0.21	660	38.41	A	621,000	Punjab on Sirhind Canal. Weaving, cotton ginning, distilling. Punjabi University. F=1763. D=IPC,CPH,GFA.
3345	Patna	1,289,000	0.54	7,000	38.74	A	2,283,000	Capital of Bihar. Extensive archaeological excavations. Mosques, Sikh temple. F=450 BC. D=CNI,RCC.
3346	Danapur (Dinapore, Dinapur)	99,100	0.50	500	38.70	A	194,000	Agricultural trade center, printing, oilseeds, metalworks. F=1887. Bihar State. D=CNI,AoG,RCC.
3347	Pattukkottai	68,200	7.00	4,800	60.20	B	134,000	Tamil Nadu inland from Palk Strait near Atirampattinam. Grand Anicut Canal. Sugarcane, soybeans. D=AoG.
3348	Payyannur	75,400	0.50	380	38.70	A	148,000	Tamil Nadu. Service Cooperative Bank, Mandalam Congress. D=CSI.
3349	Periyakulam	55,100	10.00	5,500	63.20	B	108,000	Tamil Nadu west of Madurai. Lake, secondary road. Sugarcane, timber, tea, coffee, fruit. D=CSI,MFGC,AoG.
3350	Petlad	57,200	1.40	800	44.60	A	112,000	Gujarat north of Khambhat, near Gulf of Khambar. Rice, cotton, fruits, matches, bobbins, pencils. D=CNI.
3351	Phagwara	105,000	1.00	1,000	44.20	A	205,000	Punjab southeast of Jalandhar. Grain, sugar, salts, industrial mills, chemical and metalworks, college. D=IPC.
3352	Pilibhit	125,000	0.22	280	38.42	A	246,000	Uttar Pradesh. Sugar processing, agricultural products. 18th century mosque.
3353	Pilkhua	59,200	0.50	300	38.70	A	116,000	Uttar Pradesh near Hapur, west of Delhi. Sugarcane, textiles, cotton weaving, wheat, millet, sugarcane.
3354	Pollachi	150,000	3.28	4,900	51.48	B	294,000	Tamil Nadu south of Coimbatore. Railroad sleeper cars, tea, coffee, rubber. 1st century Roman coins. D=CSI.
3355	Pondicherry	473,000	13.88	65,600	67.08	B	928,000	Pondicherry Union Territory on Coromandel Coast. Seaside tourist resort. F=1674 as French trade center. D=OSC.
3356	Ponnani	61,000	2.00	1,200	50.20	B	120,000	Kerala on Arabian Sea. Malabar Coast. Fishing, port, tea. Ponnami River. Muslim cultural center. D=OSC,RCC.
3357	Ponnuru Nidubrolu	64,000	9.00	5,800	62.20	B	126,000	Andhra Pradesh on Bay of Bengal near Chirala. Rice, milling, tanning. D=CSI,Lutheran.
3358	Porbandar	189,000	0.22	420	38.42	A	370,000	Gujarat on Arabian Sea. Building stone. Birthplace of Mahatma Gandhi. Fishing, textiles, cement. D=CNI.
3359	Port Blair	88,100	16.00	14,100	74.20	B	173,000	Capital of Andaman Islands. Timber, Andaman redwood, coconuts. British penal colony 1789-1945. D=RCC.
3360	Proddatur	158,000	6.50	10,300	59.70	B	310,000	Andhra Pradesh on Penneru River northwest of Cuddapah. Cotton ginning, rice, dairy farm, limestone. D=CSI.
3361	Pudukkottai	116,000	7.00	8,100	60.20	B	228,000	Tamil Nadu. Peanut & sesame oil, perfume, tannery, red ocher, granite. Founded by Raghunath. D=AoG,TELC.
3362	Puliyangudi	62,700	3.50	2,200	51.70	B	123,000	Tamil Nadu in Southern Ghats. Cotton, timber, agriculture, sesame growing area, cotton weaving. D=CSI.
3363	Pune (Poona)	3,485,000	4.00	139,000	61.20	B	6,160,000	Maharashtra on Bima River. Tourist resort. Educational center. Maratha. M=YWAM. D=RCC,CNI.
3364	Pimpri-Chinchwad	608,000	3.00	18,200	56.20	B	1,193,000	Maharashtra. Textiles, handicrafts, market place. Fast growing industrial suburb. D=RCC,CNI,Methodist.
3365	Pune Cantonment	96,600	3.50	3,400	51.70	B	190,000	Maharashtra on Bima River. Public gardens, palaces, temples. Meteorological center in area. D=CNI,EHC,RCC.
3366	Puri	147,000	0.71	1,000	38.91	A	289,000	Orissa on Bay of Bengal. Market center, seaside resort. Hindu pilgrimage center. Temples and caves. D=BYM,CNI.
3367	Purnea (Purnia)	160,000	0.60	960	38.80	A	314,000	Bihar. Agricultural trade, rice, jute milling, corn, tobacco, wheat, sugarcane. F=1864. D=EMS.
3368	Purulia	109,000	2.10	2,300	50.30	B	214,000	West Bengal. Agricultural distribution center, oilseed milling, silk weaving. Jaina temple ruins. D=CNT,AoG.
3369	Pusad	65,900	0.40	260	38.60	A	129,000	Maharashtra near Digras, Panganga tributary. Wheat, manganese, cotton ginning, oilseed milling, teak, college.
3370	Quilon	427,000	22.20	94,800	85.40	B	838,000	Kerala on Arabian Sea. Active export trade, cashew nuts. 5 colleges. D=OSC,RCC.
3371	Rabkavi Banhatti	71,400	0.20	140	38.40	A	140,000	Northern Karnataka north of Belgaum. Cotton, wheat, peanuts, silkweaving, handicraft cloth weaving. D=RCC.
3372	Rae Bareli	153,000	0.43	660	38.63	A	301,000	Uttar Pradesh on Sai River. Agricultural trade, handloom weaving. 15th century fort.
3373	Raichur	201,000	1.28	2,600	44.48	A	394,000	Karnataka. Commercial center, oilseed, cotton, soap. Palace-citadel (1294). D=Methodist,Baptist,SA.
3374	Raiganj (Rayganj)	188,000	0.90	1,700	39.10	A	369,000	West Bengal on Kulik River. Agricultural trade, jute exporting, rice milling. D=BBU,EHC,NF.
3375	Raigarh (Kolaba)	109,000	5.60	6,100	58.80	B	214,000	Madhya Pradesh. Jute milling, handloom weaving, bamboo, silk, soap, glass, lace. D=CNI,FPCGI.
3376	Raipur	544,000	2.30	12,500	50.50	B	1,068,000	Madhya Pradesh. Sawmills, musical. F=14th century. D=Lutheran,CNI,RCC.
3377	Raj-Nandgaon	148,000	1.60	2,400	44.80	A	290,000	Madhya Pradesh. Agricultural trade, cotton-textiles, rice, oilseeds, jute, chemical manufacturing. D=Methodist.
3378	Rajahmundry	476,000	7.25	34,500	60.45	B	934,000	Andhra Pradesh on Godavari River Delta. Lumber. Pushkaram festival every 12 years. D=LAELC,CSI,PCA.
3379	Rajapalaiyam (Rajapalayam)	134,000	3.70	5,000	51.90	B	264,000	Tamil Nadu in Western Ghats. Cotton handlooming and weaving, cement, sugar, timber, livestock. D=CSI,RCC.
3380	Rajhara-Jharandalli	65,900	0.50	330	38.70	A	129,000	Madhya Pradesh. Iron ore. Road junction, agricultural trade.
3381	Rajkot	912,000	0.35	3,200	38.55	A	1,691,000	Gujarat. Cotton and woolen textiles, grains, sugarcane. On Kathiawar Peninsula. D=CNI,SFC.
3382	Rajpur	102,000	0.72	730	38.92	A	200,000	West Bengal south of Jadabpur. Rice, rice milling, jute, pulses.
3383	Rajpura	83,500	0.20	170	38.40	A	164,000	Punjab near Patiala. Railroad junction, cotton, wheat, distilling, primary roads. D=CNI,SF.
3384	Ramanagaram	59,400	3.50	2,100	51.70	B	117,000	Karnataka near Bangalore. Road junction, agricultural trade. D=CSI.
3385	Ramanathapuram	62,000	6.00	3,700	59.20	B	122,000	Tamil Nadu near Gulf of Mannar. Railroad, primary road, sugarcane, handicrafts. D=CSI,TELC.
3386	Ramgarh	96,800	9.00	8,700	62.20	B	190,000	Bihar north of Ranchi, Chotonagpur plateau. Secondary road junction, railroad, coal, iron ore, wheat. M=GEMS.
3387	Rampur	286,000	0.35	1,000	38.55	A	561,000	Uttar Pradesh on Kosi River. Sugar processing, cotton milling. Library with 12,000 rare manuscripts. D=CNI.
3388	Ranaghat	149,000	0.50	750	38.70	A	293,000	West Bengal north of Calcutta on Eastern Railway. Rice, jute, linseeds, sugarcane, wheat. D=CNI,JKPS.
3389	Ranchi	724,000	10.00	72,400	63.20	B	1,421,000	Bihar on Subarnarekha River (summer capital). Cotton & tea trade. F=1869. D=CNI,Independent.
3390	Ranibennur	79,400	1.00	790	44.20	A	156,000	Karnataka northwest of Davangere. Railroad, primary highway, timber, cotton, rice. D=CSI.
3391	Raniganj	183,000	0.30	550	38.50	A	360,000	West Bengal, near Damoder River. Railroad, rice, jute, coalfields. D=CNI.
3392	Ratangarh	64,900	0.05	32	28.25	A	127,000	Rajasthan. Railroad, secondary road, wool, desert, salt, grain, leather, ivory products.
3393	Ratlam (Rutlam)	231,000	1.68	3,900	44.88	A	453,000	Madhya Pradesh. Agricultural trade, cotton, silk, sugar. Jaina temples. D=CNI,Independent,RCC.
3394	Ratnagiri	66,600	3.46	2,300	51.66	B	131,000	Maharashtra on Arabian Sea. Marine biology research, popular resort. Fish, bamboo, rice. D=Independent.
3395	Raurkela (Rourkela)	470,000	8.00	37,600	61.20	B	922,000	Northern Orissa near Mandira Lake, Mandira River. Railroad junction, iron ore, chromite, timber. D=RCC,CNI.
3396	Raurkela Civil Township	165,000	8.00	13,200	61.20	B	324,000	Northern Orissa. Industrial agricultural, minerals, fertilizers, chemicals. D=RCC,CNI,Lutheran.
3397	Rayagada	57,000	0.50	290	38.70	A	112,000	Bauxite, manganese ore, rail station. Society for Natives Education, Health, and Agriculture.
3398	Rewa (Rewah, Riwa)	152,000	0.44	670	38.64	A	298,000	Madhya Pradesh. Trade center for grain, building stone, timber. Cloth weaving, wood carving. D=FPCGI.
3399	Rewari (Riwari)	88,700	0.09	80	28.29	A	174,000	Haryana. Commercial & transport center, agricultural market, millet, cotton, grain, copper, brass. F=1867. D=CNI.

Table 10-5–continued opposite

Table 10-5–continued

Rec No 1	Country City 2	Pop 2000 3	AC% 4	Church Members 5	E% 6	W 7	Pop 2025 8	Notes 9
3400	Rishikesh	84,200	0.15	130	38.35	A	165,000	Uttar Pradesh near Himalayan Mountains. On Ganges River. Wheat, rice, oilseeds, barley, corn, pilgrimage center.
3401	Rohtak	254,000	0.05	130	28.25	A	499,000	Haryana. Grain & cotton trade center. Dini mosque (1140). Buddhist sculpture from 600 BC, university. D=NKOG.
3402	Roorkee	106,000	0.20	210	38.40	A	208,000	Northern Uttar Pradesh east of Saharanpur. HQ of Ganga Canal. Workshops, civil engineering, university.
3403	Rudarpur	71,900	0.50	360	38.70	A	141,000	Uttar Pradesh, Rapti River. Saltpeter processing, rice, wheat, barley, oilseeds, noted Hindu temple.
3404	Sagar (Saugor)	303,000	1.50	4,500	44.70	A	594,000	Madhya Pradesh on a lake. Agricultural trade, oil & flour milling. F=1660 by Udan Singh. D=CNI,IPC,RCC.
3405	Saharanpur	441,000	0.44	1,900	38.64	A	865,000	Uttar Pradesh. Railway workshops, cotton, sugar, paper. F=1340 named for Muslim saint. D=IET,KEF.
3406	Saharsa	94,300	0.20	190	38.40	A	185,000	Bihar. Major rail & road hub. Wheat, barley, sugarcane, vegetables, livestock. F=1961. M=NSS.
3407	Sahaswan	60,200	0.30	180	38.50	A	118,000	Uttar Pradesh on Ganges River. Rice, sugarcane, perfume manufacture, mustard.
3408	Sahibganj (Sahebganj)	57,900	1.00	580	44.20	A	114,000	Bihar on Ganges River. Near West Bengal. Railroad junction, trade center, rice, corn, barley. M=CNI,Baptist.
3409	Salem	676,000	5.00	33,800	58.20	B	1,327,000	Tamil Nadu. Cotton & silk handloom weaving, electrical and chemical factories. D=RCC,CSI,IPC,ECI.
3410	Samalkot	57,400	5.00	2,900	58.20	B	113,000	Andhra Pradesh on Bay of Bengal. Railroad, navigable canal, handicrafts, market. D=CSI,AELC,COG.
3411	Sambalpur	227,000	2.95	6,700	51.15	B	446,000	Orissa on Mahanadi River. Milling of rice, weaving, metalworking. Vaishnavite temple. D=RCC,CNI. M=FMPB.
3412	Sambhal	177,000	0.01	18	28.21	A	347,000	Uttar Pradesh. Ancient settlement. Agricultural trade, sugar, calico printing. Annual Hindu & Muslim fair.
3413	Sangamner	57,600	1.00	580	44.20	A	113,000	Maharashtra. Godavari tributaries, Harischandra range. Wheat, cotton, silk yarn, millet, salt. D=Methodist,COG.
3414	Sangareddi	59,000	0.50	300	38.70	A	116,000	Andhra Pradesh, NW of Hyderabed. Ramalingeswara Temple. Rail station, rice, sugarcane, oilseeds. D=CSI,JS.
3415	Sangli	429,000	1.89	8,100	45.09	A	841,000	Maharashtra on Krishna River. Oilseeds, turmeric. Ganapati temple, many pilgrims. D=CNI,AoG,Brethren.
3416	Miraj	143,000	3.96	5,700	52.16	B	281,000	Medical colleges, musical instruments. Railroad, engineering, textiles. D=CNI,AoG,Brethren,Baptist.
3417	Sangrur	66,400	0.80	530	39.00	A	130,000	Punjab near Sunam. Railroad, secondary road junction, canals, irrigation. D=Methodist,CNI.
3418	Sankarankovil	57,400	3.00	1,700	51.20	B	113,000	Tamil Nadu. Eastern foothills of Southern Ghats. Timber, bell-metal industry, seasonal cattle trade. D=CSI,AoG.
3419	Santipur (Shantipur)	129,000	0.50	650	38.70	A	254,000	West Bengal. Cotton weaving, agricultural trade, pottery. Pilgrimage center, sacred bath.
3420	Sardarshahr	80,100	0.15	120	38.35	A	157,000	Northern Rajasthan west of Churu. Thar desert. Exports, wool, livestock, leather goods, pottery making.
3421	Sarni	99,200	0.50	500	38.70	A	195,000	Central School. Road junction, agricultural trade.
3422	Sasaram (Sahsaram)	116,000	0.33	380	38.53	A	227,000	Bihar. Agricultural trade, carpet, pottery, rice, wheat, grain, oilseeds. Mausoleums. M=GEMS.
3423	Satara	112,000	0.83	930	39.03	A	220,000	Maharashtra. Engineering works, sugar processing, animal husbandry. Museum containing many relics. D=CNI.
3424	Satna	189,000	0.36	680	38.56	A	370,000	Madhya Pradesh on Tons River. Agricultural trade, cloth, flour & oilseed milling. D=CNI,MTSC,AoG.
3425	Sawai Madhopur	91,400	0.60	550	38.80	A	179,000	Rajasthan. Walled town. Metalware, agricultural produce, handmade copper & brass. D=CNI,CBA,IPCOG.
3426	Sehore (Sihor)	84,200	0.50	420	38.70	A	165,000	Madhya Pradesh. Agricultural trade center, sugar, cotton, handloom weaving. D=CNI,FPCGI.
3427	Seoni	75,800	1.20	910	44.40	A	149,000	Madhya Pradesh. Chief commercial center, cloth weaving, sawmilling. F=1774. D=CNI,Free Mission Church.
3428	Shahdol (Sahdol)	71,400	0.93	660	39.13	A	140,000	Madhya Pradesh on Murna River. Agricultural market, Hindu ruins. D=EVGLC,FPCGI,MTSC.
3429	Shahjahanpur	307,000	0.45	1,400	38.65	A	602,000	Uttar Pradesh on Deotta River. Carpet weaving, distilling. F=1647. D=CNI.
3430	Shamli	82,900	1.00	830	44.20	A	163,000	Uttar Pradesh near Haryana border. Railroad, textiles, cotton, sugarcane.
3431	Shikohabad	74,500	0.10	75	38.30	A	146,000	Uttar Pradesh east of Firozabad. Ganges tributaries. Railroad, primary roads.
3432	Shillong	262,000	41.02	107,000	99.22	B	514,000	Capital of Meghalaya (4,990 ft.). Agricultural trade, research stations, summer resort, university. D=Presbyterian.
3433	Shimoga	227,000	3.30	7,500	51.50	B	445,000	Karnataka on Tunga River. Rice, oilseed, cloth handlooming, coffee, sugarcane. D=CSI. M=CCC.
3434	Shivpuri (Sipri)	128,000	0.12	150	38.32	A	250,000	Madhya Pradesh on elevated watershed. Agriculture, forest products, wildlife sanctuary. M=Alliance Mission.
3435	Sholapur (Solapur)	769,000	1.20	9,200	44.40	A	1,509,000	Maharashtra on Sina River. Cotton textiles, agricultural produce. Muslim fort ruins. D=CNI,Brethren.
3436	Shrirampur	93,100	0.20	190	38.40	A	183,000	Sugar, tobacco products, cotton textiles, wool, silk. D=Salvation Army.
3437	Siddipet	63,600	1.60	1,000	44.80	A	125,000	Andhra Pradesh near Karimnagar. Secondary roads, rice, wheat, cotton, handicrafts. D=CSI,JS.
3438	Sikandarabad	71,900	0.15	110	38.35	A	141,000	Uttar Pradesh near Upper Ganges Canal. Near Delhi. Hand loom cotton weaving center, wheat barley.
3439	Sikar	175,000	0.01	17	28.21	A	343,000	Rajasthan. Agricultural trade, textiles, pottery, enamel work. 2 colleges. D=CBA,CLC. M=FMPB.
3440	Silchar	136,000	4.70	6,400	57.90	B	266,000	Assam on Surma River near Bangladesh. Trade for tea, rice, agriculture. D=Baptist.
3441	Siliguri (Shiliguri)	267,000	0.48	1,300	38.68	A	524,000	West Bengal. Hub of trade between Darjeeling, Sikkim & Tibet. Refugee center. D=CNI,UCNI,Brethren.
3442	Simla	129,000	1.10	1,400	44.30	A	254,000	Capital of Himachal Pradesh at 7,100 ft. Summer resort, agricultural trade. F=1816 by British. D=Independent.
3443	Sircilla	58,900	0.50	300	38.70	A	116,000	Road junction, agricultural trade. BCC, FUBA, India Ltd.
3444	Sirsa	133,000	0.30	400	38.50	A	260,000	Haryana on edge of Great Indian (Thar) Desert. Handloom weaving, cattle fair. F=c250. D=Methodist.
3445	Sitamarhi	79,300	0.10	79	38.30	A	156,000	Bihar in North Bihar Plains near Nepal border. Ganga River tributary. Rice, wheat, barley, oilseeds. D=NSS.
3446	Sitapur	142,000	0.69	980	38.89	A	279,000	Uttar Pradesh on Sarayan River. Grain & crop marketplace, sugar, plywood. Eye disease hospital. D=CNI.
3447	Siuri	63,900	0.50	320	38.70	A	126,000	West Bengal near Bihar. Railroad, secondary road junction, coal, jute. Annual livestock, agricultural fair.
3448	Sivakasi	120,000	3.50	4,200	51.70	B	236,000	Tamil Nadu east of Rajapalaiyam. East of Southern Ghats, livestock, agriculture, railroad. D=CSI.
3449	Siwan	95,500	0.08	76	28.28	A	188,000	Bihar on Daha River. Pottery, brassware, phul, rice, wheat, barley, corn, oilseeds, sugar milling. M=FMPB.
3450	Sonipat	168,000	0.17	290	38.37	A	331,000	Haryana north of Delhi. Railroad, livestock, agriculture, sugarcane, millet, gur, mangoes. D=IPC,CNC.
3451	Sri Ganganagar (Ganganagar)	185,000	0.14	260	38.34	A	362,000	Rajasthan. Agricultural distribution center, sugar, rice, camel and sheep breeding, grain, vegetables. D=CNI,CBA.
3452	Srikakulam (Chicacole)	104,000	0.92	960	39.12	A	205,000	Andhra Pradesh on Nagavali River. Government colleges. Mosque (1641). Once a Muslim capital. D=RCC,JS.
3453	Sri Kalahasti	72,500	6.00	4,400	59.20	B	142,000	Southern Andhra Pradesh west of Pulicat Lake. Rice and oilseed milling, ceramics, metalworks. D=CSI,ECI,SALC.
3454	Srinagar	880,000	0.04	350	28.24	A	1,727,000	Summer capital of Jammu & Kashmir on Thelum River. Tourist economy, mosques & temples. D=CNI,AoG.
3455	Srivilliputtur	80,800	3.50	2,800	51.70	B	159,000	Tamil Nadu near Rajapalaiyam, foothills of southern Ghats. Railroad, primary road, agriculture. D=CSI.
3456	Sujangarh	82,900	0.01	8	28.21	A	163,000	Rajasthan west of Sikar. Desert, wool, gypsum, salt, hides, leather goods, pottery, ivory crafts.
3457	Sultanpur	90,200	0.08	72	28.28	A	177,000	Uttar Pradesh on Gomati River. Agricultural trade center. Ancient origins. Extensive mango groves, grains.
3458	Surat	2,341,000	0.31	7,300	43.51	A	4,270,000	Gujarat near Gulf of Cambay. Fine muslin, cotton, silk, brocades. F=1514 by Brahmins. D=FDCGI,GFA.
3459	Surendranagar	196,000	0.26	510	38.46	A	385,000	Gujarat. Agricultural trade, textiles, soap, glass, cotton, grain, ghee, cloth fabrics, hides. D=CNI,Brethren.
3460	Wadhwan	58,600	0.18	110	38.38	A	115,000	Gujarat. Textiles, market, livestock, soap, glass, grain. Capital of former princely state of Wadhwan. D=CNI.
3461	Suriapet	71,400	5.00	3,600	58.20	B	140,000	Andhra Pradesh on Musi River. Near Khammam. Road center, rice milling, peanut oil extraction, farming. D=CSI.
3462	Tadepallegudem	105,000	5.00	5,200	58.20	B	206,000	Andhra Pradesh in Godavari Delta near Eluru. Cotton textile, rice milling, oilseeds, tobacco, sugarcane. D=AELC.
3463	Tadpatri	83,700	2.00	1,700	50.20	B	164,000	Andhra Pradesh on Penneru River west of Proddatur. Silk and cotton cloth, peanut milling, fruit canning. D=CSI.
3464	Talipparamba	71,000	4.00	2,800	57.20	B	139,000	Kerala on Malabar Coast near Cannanore. Fertile rice growing region, coconuts, tapioca, spices. D=OSC,RCC.
3465	Tanda	82,500	0.25	210	38.45	A	162,000	Uttar Pradesh on Ghangara River east of Faizabad. Hand loom cotton weaving center, rice, wheat, grain.
3466	Tanuku	74,100	5.00	3,700	58.20	B	145,000	Andhra Pradesh in Godavari Delta near Eluru. Rice and oilseed milling, hand loom weaving, tobacco. D=AELC.
3467	Tellicherry	547,000	4.00	21,900	57.20	B	1,073,000	Kerala on low hills. Major port for pepper, coffee, sandalwood, coconuts. Rope & mat making. D=OSC,RCC.
3468	Tenali	169,000	6.45	10,900	59.65	B	333,000	Andhra Pradesh near Guntur. Railroad, navigable canals, agriculture, trade. Market center for rice. D=CSI.
3469	Tenkasi	64,900	11.00	7,100	64.20	B	127,000	Southern Tamil Nadu near Kerala. Railroad junction, health resort, sesame oil, cotton weaving. D=CSI,IPM.
3470	Tezpur	64,800	5.00	3,200	58.20	B	127,000	Assam on Brahmaputra River. Near Nagaon.Tea, rice, mustard, sugarcane, jute, temple ruins. D=Baptist.
3471	Thanesar	95,800	0.20	190	38.40	A	188,000	Northern Haryana south of Ambala. Wheat, maize, grain, pilgrimage site. M=FMPB.
3472	Thanjavur (Thanjore, Tanjore)	236,000	16.90	39,900	75.10	B	463,000	Tami Nadu on Cauvery Delta. Tourist center. Cola temples. Leading music and dance center. D=RCC,CSI.
3473	Theni-Allinagaram	77,700	6.00	4,700	59.20	B	153,000	Tamil Nadu on Vaigai River. Madurai district, Road center, trades in products of Cardamom Hills. D=CSI.
3474	Thiruvarur	58,000	16.00	9,300	74.20	B	114,000	Tamil Nadu near Bay of Bengal and Nagappattinam. Peanuts, cotton, silk, livestock, vegetables tobacco. D=IPA.
3475	Tikamgarh	63,800	0.50	320	38.70	A	125,000	Madhya Pradesh near Lalitpur. Millet, wheat, timber, ghee, flour milling, sawmill, stud farm. D=Independent.
3476	Tindivanam	72,700	5.50	4,000	58.70	B	143,000	Tamil Nadu north of Pondicherry. Rice, textiles, cashews, peanut oil, granite quarries nearby. D=CSI,AoG.
3477	Tinsukia	86,900	4.70	4,100	57.90	B	171,000	Assam in Brahmaputra River Valley. Tea processing, rice, jute, sugarcane, rope, mustard. D=Baptist.
3478	Tiruchchirappalli (Trichinopoly)	818,000	15.53	127,000	78.73	B	1,462,000	Tamil Nadu at Cauvery Delta. Industrial & education center. Rock fortress. Shrine of Srirangam. D=CSI,RCC.
3479	Ponmalai	82,700	9.00	7,400	62.20	B	162,000	Tamil Nadu. Kaveri River. Agriculture, market. Commercial, very industrial, several schools. D=CSI,AoG,RCC.
3480	Srirangam	82,400	10.00	8,200	63.20	B	162,000	Most frequently visited pilgrimage center in South India. Ranganatha temple (Hall of a Thousand Pillars). D=CSI.
3481	Tirunelveli (Tinnevelly)	431,000	12.00	51,700	75.20	B	846,000	Tamil Nadu. Industrial town, jewelry, motor workshops. Christian mission activity. D=CSI,RCC. M=CCC.
3482	Melappalaiyam	80,500	12.00	9,700	75.20	B	158,000	Tamil Nadu. Railroad, primary roads, handicrafts, market, towel and carpet weaving center. D=CSI,RCC,Brethren.
3483	Palayankottai (Palamcottah)	115,000	12.00	13,800	75.20	B	226,000	On Tambraparni River. Residential & educational center. Major center of Christian missions. D=CSI,RCC,AoG.
3484	Tirupati	223,000	0.90	2,000	39.10	A	437,000	Andhra Pradesh. Known as abode of Hindu god Venkatesvara. Tirumala hill temple. Pilgrimage center. D=ECIL.
3485	Tiruppattur	64,700	5.00	3,200	58.20	B	127,000	Tamil Nadu in Javadi Hills south of Vaniyambadi. Road center, trades in cotton fabrics, peanuts. D=AoG,TELC.
3486	Tiruppur	360,000	4.22	15,200	57.42	B	707,000	Tamil Nadu. Cotton ginning & distribution center. Saiva temple attracts large crowds of pilgrims. D=RCC,CSI.
3487	Tirur	58,300	4.00	2,300	57.20	B	114,000	Kerala on Arabian Sea. Near Calicut. Malappuram district. Transport canal linking. D=OSC,RCC.
3488	Tiruvalla	64,500	26.00	16,800	89.20	B	127,000	Kerala on Malabar Coast. Near Alleppey. Coir rope, mats, tiles. D=OSC,RCC.
3489	Tonk	118,000	0.13	150	38.33	A	231,000	Rajasthan. Agricultural mart, manufacturing center, cotton, wool, leather. F=1643. D=CBA.
3490	Trichur	324,000	40.94	133,000	99.14	B	636,000	Kerala. Cotton weaving, rice & oilseed milling. Vatakkunatha temple, annual festival. D=OSC,RCC.
3491	Trivandrum	973,000	16.61	162,000	79.81	B	1,909,000	Capital of Kerala. Minerals, sugar, textiles. Large fort with Vaisnava temple, pilgrimage center. D=RCC,CSI,OSC.
3492	Ttruchchendur	88,800	30.00	26,700	93.20	B	174,000	Tamil Nadu on Gulf of Mannar. Near Tuticorin. Fishing. D=CSI,AoG.
3493	Tumkur	211,000	6.50	13,700	59.70	B	415,000	Karnataka at foot of Devarayadurga Hill. Health resort (3,900 ft.). Vegetable oil, tobacco. D=CSI,RCC,EHC.
3494	Tuticorin	335,000	30.00	100,000	93.20	B	657,000	Tamil Nadu on Gulf of Mannar. Fishing. 7 colleges. Seaport, pearl oysters. F=c1540. D=CSI,RCC.
3495	Udagamandalam (Ootacamund)	96,300	12.00	11,600	65.20	B	189,000	Tamil Nadu in Kunda Hills. Famous hot weather resort, tourism. Tea, coffee, sandalwood, textiles. D=CSI.
3496	Udaipur (Udaypur)	362,000	0.40	1,500	38.60	A	711,000	Rajasthan. Walled town. Agricultural distribution center, chemicals, asbestos. D=CBA,FFCI,CNI.
3497	Udamalpet	69,100	3.00	2,100	51.20	B	136,000	Tamil Nadu east of Pollachi. Cotton, tea, coffee, rubber, peanut oil extraction. D=CSI.
3498	Udgir	83,000	0.25	210	38.45	A	163,000	Maharashtra east of Latur. South of Ballaghat range. Railroad, textiles, wheat. D=Methodist,NAC.
3499	Ujjain	432,000	0.70	3,000	38.90	A	848,000	Madhya Pradesh. Sacred Hindu city. Ancient origins. Many temples (Hindu & Buddhist). D=CNI,MTSC,RCC.
3500	Ulubaria (Uluberia)	183,000	0.50	910	38.70	A	359,000	West Bengal on Hugli River. Southwest of Calcutta. Developing industrial center. D=COG. M=NMS.
3501	Unjha	60,000	0.15	90	38.35	A	118,000	Gujarat near Visnagar. Railroad, cotton, sugarcane, millet, wheat, oilseeds, hand loom weaving. D=AMM.
3502	Unnao	126,000	0.75	950	38.95	A	248,000	Uttar Pradesh east of Kanpur. Trades in grain, oilseeds, sugarcane, cotton, bone meal. F=8th century. M=FMPB.
3503	Upleta	60,700	0.15	91	38.35	A	119,000	Gujarat on Kathiawar Peninsula west of Dhoraji. Peanuts, millet, oilseeds, cotton ginning. D=CNI.
3504	Vadodara (Baroda)	1,606,000	1.25	20,100	49.45	A	2,922,000	Gujarat on Visvamitra River. Many palaces, gates, parks. Cotton, cloth. F=812. D=CNI,Methodist,AMM.
3505	Valparai	125,000	18.56	23,200	81.76	B	246,000	Tamil Nadu near Kerala and Anai Mudi mountain. Coimbatore district. D=TELC,CLJC.
3506	Vaniyambadi	109,000	5.00	5,400	58.20	B	213,000	Northern Tamil Nadu south of Ambur. Tan bark, nux vomica, hemp narcotics, hides and skins. D=CSI.
3507	Varanasi (Benares, Banaras, Kasi)	1,290,000	0.60	7,700	38.80	A	2,314,000	Uttar Pradesh on Ganges River. Sacred Hindu city. 1,000,000 pilgrims p.a. World's oldest city. D=RCC,CNI.
3508	Vasai (Bassein)	98,500	3.50	3,400	51.70	B	193,000	Maharashtra on Arabian Sea. Fishing, agricultural export, silk & cotton handloom. D=CNI.
3509	Vellore	359,000	10.00	35,900	63.20	B	705,000	Tamil Nadu on Palar River. Major Christian medical center, fort (British). D=CSI,CON,ECI,RCC.
3510	Veraval	141,000	0.33	470	38.53	A	277,000	Gujarat on Arabian Sea. Timber, agriculture, matches, fishing. Ancient city ruins. D=FPCGI.
3511	Vidisha (Vidisa)	109,000	0.29	320	38.49	A	215,000	Madhya Pradesh. Great antiquity. Agriculture, flour, handloom weaving. Religious ruins. M=CICM.
3512	Vijayawada (Vijayavada, Bezwada)	1,236,000	6.10	75,400	59.30	B	2,276,000	Andhra Pradesh on Krishna River. Hindu pilgrimage center. Toys. D=RCC,CSI,AELC.
3513	Vikramasingapuram	57,800	9.00	5,200	62.20	B	113,000	Southern Tamil Nadu west of Tirunelveli. Cotton market, textile mills. D=CSI.
3514	Villupuram	105,000	5.00	5,200	58.20	B	206,000	Tamil Nadu west of Pondicherry. Railroad junction, agriculture, livestock, sugar milling. D=AoG,MFGC,TELC.
3515	Viramgam	60,200	0.25	150	38.45	A	118,000	Gujarat west of Ahmadabad. Railroad junction, salt, minerals, agriculture. D=CMA.
3516	Virudunagar	83,600	7.50	6,300	60.70	B	164,000	Tamil Nadu south of Madurai. Railroad junction, agriculture, market, trade. D=CSI.
3517	Vishakhapatnam	1,702,000	3.19	54,300	51.39	B	3,169,000	Andhra Pradesh on Bay of Bengal. Shipbuilding, manganese. Medical college. D=RCC,Lutheran,Baptist,CSI.
3518	Visnagar	70,300	0.17	120	38.37	A	138,000	Gujarat near Ahmadabad. Salt, minerals, agriculture. D=CNI.
3519	Vizianagaram (Vizianagram)	208,000	1.02	2,100	44.22	A	407,000	Andhra Pradesh. Shipping center for sunn hemp, jute. D=CSI,Lutheran,Baptist.
3520	Vriddhachalam	62,200	4.00	2,500	57.20	B	122,000	Tamil Nadu near Vellar River. Sugarcane, cotton. D=AoG,MFGC,Lutheran.
3521	Warangal	550,000	6.90	38,000	60.10	B	1,080,000	Andhra Pradesh. Carpets, silks. Thousand pillar temple (1162). 12th century Telugu capital. D=RCC,Baptist,CSI.
3522	Wardha	121,000	0.40	490	38.60	A	238,000	Maharashtra. Important in national freedom movement, Sevagram ashram. D=CNI,EHC.
3523	Washim	57,900	0.40	230	38.60	A	114,000	Maharastra near Akola, Ajanta range. Secondary roads, agriculture, livestock.

Table 10-5–continued overleaf

Table 10-5–continued

Rec No 1	Country City 2	Pop 2000 3	AC% 4	Church Members 5	E% 6	W 7	Pop 2025 8	Notes 9
3524	Yamunanagar	259,000	0.51	1,300	38.71	A	508,000	Northern Haryana on Yamuna River near Jagadhri. Agriculture, cotton, sugar, oilseeds. D=CNI,FGCOG,COC.
3525	Jagadhri	79,400	0.50	400	38.70	A	156,000	Northern Haryana north of Yamunanagar. Agriculture, livestock, farming. D=CNI,MFGA,MI.
3526	Yavatmal	144,000	0.65	930	38.85	A	282,000	Maharashtra south of Amravati. Market center for peanuts, cotton, timber, sawmills, ice factory. M=FMPB.
3527	Yemmiganur	76,700	3.50	2,700	51.70	B	151,000	Andhra Pradesh. Cotton ginning, peanut milling, weaving. D=CSI,Lutheran,Baptist.
	INDONESIA	**212,107,000**	**12.43**	**26,365,000**	**62.85**	**B**	**273,442,000**	**PROTESTANTS 5.7%, INDEPENDENTS 3.9%. PENT-CHAR 4.4%, EVANGELICAL 1.9%, GCC 6.8%**
3528	rural areas	126,840,000	12.05	15,280,000	63.81	B	114,135,000	87.6% (1950), 82.9% (1970), 69.4% (1990), 59.8% (2000), 51.1% (2010), 41.7% (2025)
3529	urban areas	85,267,000	13.00	11,085,000	61.42	B	159,307,000	12.4% (1950), 17.0% (1970), 30.5% (1990), 40.2% (2000), 48.8% (2010), 58.2% (2025)
3530	non-metropolitan areas	46,010,000	12.98	5,972,000	61.56	B	90,771,362	*Sources of data:* Censuses of 1961, 1971, 1980, and 1990; estimate for 1950.
3531	metropolitan areas	39,257,000	13.02	5,113,000	61.25	B	68,536,000	*Definition:* Municipalities, regency capitals and other places with urban characteristics.
3532	Ambon (Amboina)	321,000	59.00	189,000	94.42	B	600,000	Capital of Maluku. Banda Sea port city. Stone houses. F=1574 by Portuguese. D=RCC,HKBP,GPI.
3533	Balikpapan	400,000	3.00	12,000	38.42	A	748,000	Kalimantan Timur. Makasar Strait Inlet. Major oil refinery. Pipeline to Samarinda oil fields, airport.
3534	Banda Aceh (Kuturaja)	215,000	0.10	220	30.52	A	401,000	Capital of Aceh, Sumatra. Trade center, copra, pepper. Trans-Sumatra Highway, large Mosque, 1879.
3535	Bandung (Bandoeng)	3,420,000	11.50	393,000	65.92	B	5,719,000	Capital of Jawa Barat. Center of Sundanese cultural life. Textiles, quinine industry. F=1810. D=RCC.
3536	Cimahi	125,000	8.00	10,000	58.42	B	233,000	Jawa Barar, Java west of Bandung. Rubber, rice, tea, textile mills. Dutch military center until 1949.
3537	Banjarmasin (Bandjarmasin)	559,000	2.00	11,200	32.42	A	1,045,000	Capital of Kalimantan Selatan on Tapas Island. Rubber, pepper, timber. Houses raised on piles. D=RCC.
3538	Banyuwang (Banjuwangi)	127,000	1.00	1,300	31.42	A	238,000	Jawa Timur. Exports copra, lumber, rubber. Predominately Javanese.
3539	Batang	69,500	4.00	2,800	54.42	B	130,000	Jawa Tengah on Java Sea. Near Pekalongan. Trade center for agriculture, rice, sugar, rubber, tobacco, textile mill.
3540	Bengkulu (Bencoolen, Benkoelen)	198,000	1.00	2,000	31.42	A	370,000	Capital of Bengkulu, Sumatra. Indian ocean port. Trade center for mining & agriculture.
3541	Binjai	212,000	6.00	12,700	51.42	B	395,000	Sumatera Utara, Sumatra west of Medan. Trade center, tea, rubber, palm oil, fibers, tobacco.
3542	Blitar	175,000	2.00	3,500	32.42	A	326,000	Jawa Timur, Java. Coffee, rice, sugar, peanuts. Ancient temples, rural character. Javanese.
3543	Bogor	652,000	3.00	19,500	38.42	A	1,217,000	Jawa Barat, Java. Botanical gardens (1817), residential city. F=1745 by Dutch. D=RCC.
3544	Bojonegoro	81,000	4.00	3,200	39.42	A	151,000	Jawa Timur, Java on Solo River east of Cepu. Trade center for forest and agriculture, teak, tobacco, rice, corn.
3545	Bukittinggi (Fort de Kock)	97,500	3.00	2,900	38.42	A	182,000	Sumatera Barat, Sumatra. 3000 ft. Houses with saddle-shaped roofs. Minangkabau.
3546	Cianjur	149,000	6.00	8,900	51.42	B	278,000	Jawa Barat, Java south of Jakarta. Mt. Pangrango. Rice, corn, tea, fruits, trade center.
3547	Cibinong	123,000	20.00	24,700	70.42	B	231,000	Jawa Barat, Java south of Jakarta, near Depok. Textiles, market. D=RCC,GPI,Independents.
3548	Cilacap (Chilachap, Tjilatjap)	179,000	5.00	9,000	45.42	A	334,000	Port of Jawa Tengah. Wharves. Exports copra, rubber, tea, cassava.
3549	Ciparay	94,200	10.00	9,400	60.42	B	176,000	Jawa Barat, Java near Bandung. Textiles, industry, market. D=Independents.
3550	Cirebon (Tjirebon, Cherebon)	320,000	5.00	16,000	45.42	A	598,000	Jawa Barat on Java Sea. Tea, rice, tobacco, horses. Volcano Gunung Ciremay. Center for Islam.
3551	Denpasar	224,000	3.00	6,700	38.42	A	419,000	Capital of Bali. Food processing, handicrafts. Balinese. Arab & Indian merchants. D=RCC.
3552	Garut	205,000	6.00	12,300	51.42	B	383,000	Jawa Barat, Java southeast of Bandung. Vacation resort and trade center, tea, rice, tobacco, cotton milling.
3553	Genteng	83,800	0.90	750	31.32	A	157,000	Jawa Timur, Java near Banyuwangi.
3554	Gorontalo	139,000	1.00	1,400	31.42	A	260,000	Sulawesi Utara, Sulawesi on Molucca Sea. Trade center, timber, resin, rattan, kapok, copra, hides, airport.
3555	Gresik	122,000	3.00	3,700	38.42	A	228,000	Jawa Timur, Java on Lintasan Barat near Surabaya. Cement plant, shipbuilding, fishing, oil, silver, gold.
3556	JAKARTA (Batavia)	9,815,000	21.00	2,061,000	84.42	B	15,649,000	Major center for finance, industry, education. Mixture of Western & Oriental styles. Overcrowding. D=RCC.
3557	Bekasi	203,000	20.00	40,700	70.42	B	380,000	Jawa Barat. South of Jakarta. Javanese, Chinese. Industry, manufacturing. D=GBIP,Independent.
3558	Depok	179,000	20.00	35,700	70.42	B	334,000	Jawa Barat, Java south of Jakarta. Trade, market, textiles. D=GPM,Independent. D=RCC,GPI,Independents.
3559	Jayapura (Hollandia, Sukarnapura)	85,500	92.00	78,600	98.42	C	160,000	Capital of Irian Jaya province. Port. Furniture, textiles, beverages.
3560	Jember (Djember)	241,000	2.00	4,800	32.42	A	451,000	Jawa Timur, Java. Agricultural trade, sugar, tobacco, corn. Javanese, Tenggarese. Islam.
3561	Jombang	82,900	4.00	3,300	39.42	A	155,000	Jawa Timur, Java north of Kediri. Brantas River. Rice, corn, cassava, peanuts, highway and railroad hub.
3562	Karawang	102,000	15.00	15,300	65.42	B	190,000	Jawa Barat, Java on Tarum River east of Jakarta. D=RCC,GPI,Independents.
3563	Kediri	352,000	4.50	15,800	42.92	A	657,000	Jawa Timur, Java on Brantas River. Center of the sugar industry. Hindu ruins.
3564	Kisaran	81,900	1.00	820	51.42	B	153,000	Sumatera Utara on Silau River near Tanjungbalai. Designated in 1980's as capital and administrative center.
3565	Klangenang	90,200	4.50	4,100	54.92	B	169,000	Jawa Barat near Cirebon. Sugar, rice, tobacco, livestock.
3566	Klaten	166,000	12.00	19,900	62.42	B	310,000	Jawa Tengah, Java east of Yogyakarta. Tobacco, rice, peanuts, textile mills, meteorological station.
3567	Kudus	218,000	6.00	13,100	51.42	B	407,000	Jawa Tengah, Java near Serang River east of Semarang. Sugar, rice, cassava, textile mills.
3568	Kupang (Koepang)	119,000	88.00	105,000	97.92	C	223,000	Capital of Nusa Tenggara Timur. Trade center: copra, hides, sandalwood. Papuan peoples. F=c1620. D=RCC.
3569	Lumajang	82,400	3.00	2,500	38.42	A	154,000	Jawa Timur, Java south of Probolinggo. Sugar, tobacco, coffee, rubber, tea, sugar mills, cinchonda bark.
3570	Madiun (Madioen)	233,000	4.00	9,300	39.42	A	435,000	Jawa Timur, Java. Rice & sugarcane, cassava, corn, lumber. Indonesian & Chinese.
3571	Magelang	186,000	3.60	6,700	39.02	A	348,000	Jawa Tengah, Java. Rice, tobacco, sugar. Tourist center for temples. RCC seminary.
3572	Majalaya	123,000	10.00	12,300	60.42	B	230,000	Jawa Barat on Tarum River. Near Bandung. Textiles, agriculture, vegetables.
3573	Malang	809,000	3.50	28,300	38.92	A	1,511,000	Jawa Timur, Java. Agricultural, vegetables, fruits, flowers. Palace ruins-tourism. D=RCC.
3574	Manado (Menado)	373,000	91.00	339,000	98.22	C	697,000	Capital of Sulawesi Utara, Celebes. Agricultural & lumber trade. Chinese. D=RCC.
3575	Mataram	297,000	1.00	3,000	31.42	A	554,000	Capital of Nusa Tenggara Barat, Lombok. Agricultural trade. Mostly Sassaks (Muslims).
3576	Medan	1,910,000	10.00	191,000	65.42	B	3,197,000	Capital of Sumatera Utara on Deli River. Tobacco. Chinese, Malay, Javanese, Batak. F=c1900. D=RCC,HKBP.
3577	Mojokerto	116,000	4.00	4,600	39.42	A	217,000	Jawa Timur, Java on Brantas and Porong rivers southwest of Surabaya.
3578	Muncar	66,200	0.80	530	51.22	B	124,000	Jawa Timur, Java on Bali Strait.
3579	Padang	735,000	4.00	29,400	39.42	A	1,372,000	Capital of Sumatera Barat. Chief port. Coffee, copra. Minangkabau. D=RCC.
3580	Padangsidempuan	80,300	1.00	800	31.42	A	150,000	Sumatera Utara, Sumatra south of Sibolga. Trade for rubber-growing region. Destroyed by fire in 1885.
3581	Palangkaraya	131,000	2.00	2,600	37.42	A	245,000	Capital of Kalimantan Tengah, Borneo. Wood carving, plaiting, weaving. Dayaks, Chinese, Japanese.
3582	Palembang	1,429,000	2.00	28,600	37.42	A	2,460,000	Capital of Sumatera Selatan on Musi River. Port exports rubber, coffee, timber. Great Mosque (1740). D=RCC.
3583	Palu	420,000	55.00	231,000	95.42	B	785,000	Capital of Sulawesi Tengah. Seafarers, wood carving, fishing. Buginese, Makassarese. D=Independents.
3584	Pangkalpinang	132,000	2.00	2,600	32.42	A	246,000	Sumatera Selatan, Bangka island. Port. Fishing, wood carving. Mainly Hakka Creoles.
3585	Pare	66,600	4.00	2,700	54.42	B	124,000	Jawa Timur, Java near Kediri. Trade center for rice, corn, cassava, peanuts, railroad workshops.
3586	Parepare	118,000	2.00	2,400	32.42	A	220,000	Sulawesi Selatan, Sulawesi on Makassar Strait. Trade center and port, shipping, copra.
3587	Pasuruan	221,000	4.00	8,800	39.42	A	413,000	Jawa Timur, Java on Madura Strait. Forestry, copper mining, rice milling. F=1707 by Dutch.
3588	Pati	70,700	5.00	3,500	45.42	A	132,000	Jawa Tengah, Java east of Kudus. Trade center for agriculture, sugar, rice, peanuts, cassava.
3589	Payakumbuh	106,000	3.00	3,200	38.42	A	197,000	Sumatera Barat, Sumatra north of Padang. Agricultural center, coffee, tea, tobacco, rubber, airfield.
3590	Pekalongan (Pakalongan, Pecalongan)	442,000	4.50	19,900	42.92	A	826,000	Jawa Tengah, Java. Harbor exports tea, rubber, sugar, batik, textiles.
3591	Pemalang	102,000	5.00	5,100	45.42	A	191,000	Northern Jawa Tengah, Java west of Pekalongan. Sugar, rice, tobacco, peanuts.
3592	Pematang Siantar	291,000	5.00	14,500	45.42	A	544,000	Sumatera Utara, Sumatra. Rubber, palm plantations. Tobacco, tea, soap, oil. Mainly Batak.
3593	Ponorogo	78,200	4.00	3,100	39.42	A	146,000	Western Jawa Timur, Java south of Madiun. Sugar, rice, corn, peanuts, paper mills.
3594	Pontianak	462,000	6.20	28,600	56.62	B	862,000	Capital of Kalimantan Barat, Borneo. Shipbuilding, palm oil, rubber. F=1772. D=RCC.
3595	Pringsewu	79,100	1.00	790	51.42	B	148,000	Lampung. Near Tanjungkarang-Telukbetung
3596	Probolinggo (Prabalingga)	206,000	3.50	7,200	38.92	A	385,000	Jawa Timur, Java. Good harbour, fishing, pottery, sarongs. Mainly Madurese, some Chinese.
3597	Purwokerto	203,000	5.00	10,100	50.42	B	379,000	Jawa Tenga, Java north of Cilacap. Trade center, rice, rubber, sugar, peanuts, cassava, coffee, tea. D=RCC.
3598	Puwakarta	87,400	6.00	5,200	51.42	B	163,000	Jawa Barat, Java near Waduk Jatiluhur. Preanger highlands. Trade center for rice growing, railroad.
3599	Salatiga	114,000	4.00	4,600	39.42	A	213,000	Jawa Tengah, Java. Trade center for rice, corn, rubber. Wood carving. Satya Wacana Christian University.
3600	Samarinda	474,000	1.00	4,700	31.42	A	885,000	Capital of Kalimantan Timur, Borneo. Extensive timber & logging industries. D=RCC.
3601	Semarang	826,000	15.00	124,000	65.42	B	1,379,000	Capital of Jawa Tengah, Java. Fishing, glass, electrical equipment. Deponegoro University (1957). D=RCC.
3602	Serang	110,000	3.00	3,300	38.42	A	206,000	Western Jawa Barat, Java south of Banten Bay. Trade center for rice growing, machine shops, shoes.
3603	Sibolga	83,300	1.00	830	31.42	A	156,000	Sumatera Utara, Sumatra. Port. Rubber, coffee, fishing. Achinese, Minangkabau, Coastal Malays. D=RCC.
3604	Sidoarjo	79,000	3.50	2,800	38.92	A	148,000	Jawa Timur near Salat Madura. Trade center for Brantas Delta. Rice, corn growing, textiles.
3605	Sing Kawang	82,700	6.00	5,000	56.42	B	155,000	Kalimantan Barat on Serasan Strait. Trade center, shipping rubber, copra, rubber, pepper, airport.
3606	Singaraja	75,200	2.00	1,500	37.42	A	141,000	Bali on Bali Sea. Hindu temples, once capital of Balinese kingdom. Metal working, weaving, carving.
3607	Situbondo	82,200	2.00	1,600	32.42	A	153,000	Eastern Jawa Timur, Java on Madura Strait. Trade center for agriculture. Rice, sugar, corn, peanuts.
3608	Sorong	73,300	80.00	58,700	95.42	C	137,000	Irian Jaya on Dampier Strait. Oil shipping port, copra, resin. Japanese base in WWII. D=RCC.
3609	Subang	73,300	7.00	5,100	57.42	B	137,000	Jawa Barat near Asem River. Near Purwakarta. Trade center for rice, lumber mills.
3610	Sukabumi (Soekaboemi)	262,000	2.60	6,800	38.02	A	489,000	Jawa Barat, Java. Agricultural trade, rubber plantations, health resort. Javanese, Balinese.
3611	Surabaja (Surabaya)	2,507,000	15.70	394,000	71.12	B	4,143,000	Capital of Jawa Timur on Surabaya Strait. Chief trade port for Java. Fishing. Javanese, Madurese. D=RCC.
3612	Surakarta (Solo)	687,000	22.00	151,000	82.42	B	1,283,000	Jawa Tengah on Solo River. Educational & cultural center, batik. Hindu & Buddhist temples. D=Independents.
3613	Taman	90,700	4.00	3,600	54.42	B	169,000	Jawa Timur near Salat Madura.
3614	Tandjung-Karang-Telukbetung	741,000	3.00	22,200	38.42	A	1,384,000	Lampung, Sumatra. Port, rubber, coffee. Javanese, Sudanese = 1/3 pop. Destroyed by Krakatoa in 1883. D=RCC.
3615	Tangerang	137,000	10.00	13,700	60.42	B	256,000	Jawa Barat, Java on Sadane River west of Jakarta. Apparel manufacturing.
3616	Tanjungbalai	125,000	1.00	1,300	31.42	A	234,000	Sumatera Utara on Strait of Malacca. Ships, rubber, copra, palm oil, tea, gambir, fruit.
3617	Tanjungpinang	123,000	5.00	6,200	55.42	B	230,000	Riau Islands near Singapore. Ships, bauxite, copra, gambier, pepper. Dutch fort built in 1824.
3618	Tarakan	65,700	20.00	13,200	80.42	B	123,000	Kalimantan Timur on Celebes Sea. Swampy coastal areas. Oil, refinery, shipping. D=RCC,Independents.
3619	Tasikmalaya (Tasikmalaja)	271,000	9.00	24,400	59.42	B	506,000	Jaina Barat, Java. Agricultural trade, rattan, batik. Devout Javanese Muslims.
3620	Tebingtinggi	136,000	1.00	1,400	31.42	A	254,000	Sumatera Utara. Rubber, tobacco, tea, fibers, palm oil, rice.
3621	Tegal	524,000	5.00	26,200	45.42	A	978,000	Java seaport in Jawa Tengah, Java. Agricultural shipment, sugar, fish, cotton.
3622	Telanaipura (Jambi, Djambi)	336,000	1.00	3,400	31.42	A	628,000	Jambi, Sumatra. Rubber-processing center. Minangkabau, Batak, Chinese, Arabs, Indians.
3623	Tembilahan	73,500	4.00	2,900	54.42	B	137,000	Riau on Sumatra near Indragiri River. Oil production, mining, fishing, tourism.
3624	Tuban	68,400	6.00	4,100	56.42	B	128,000	Jawa Timur on Java Sea. Fishing port, trade, center for rice, corn, former opium smuggling.
3625	Tulungagung	129,000	3.00	3,900	38.42	A	241,000	Southern Jawa Timur near Brantas River south of Kedin. Sugar, opra, rice, corn, tobacco, textiles, marble.
3626	Ujung Pandang (Makassar)	1,063,000	3.00	31,900	43.42	A	1,823,000	Capital of Sulawesi Selatan, Celebes. Copra, rubber. Makassarese. Pilgrimage center. D=RCC.
3627	Watampone (Bone)	77,900	2.00	1,600	32.42	A	146,000	Sulawesi Tengah, Celebes. 17th century Muslim state capital. Corn and rice growing region.
3628	Yogyakarta (Jogjakarta)	593,000	19.00	113,000	79.42	B	1,109,000	Capital of Yogyakarta, Java. Handtooled silver. Ancient Hindu & Buddhist temples. F=1755. D=Independents.
	IRAN	**67,702,000**	**0.46**	**314,000**	**37.21**	**A**	**94,463,000**	**ORTHODOX 0.3%, INDEPENDENTS 0.1%. PENT-CHAR 0.1%, EVANGELICAL 0.03%, GCC 0.1%**
3629	rural areas	25,991,000	0.12	30,400	33.66	A	25,684,000	73.0% (1950), 58.1% (1970), 43.6% (1990), 38.3% (2000), 33.4% (2010), 27.1% (2025)
3630	urban areas	41,711,000	0.68	284,000	39.43	A	68,778,000	26.9% (1950), 41.9% (1970), 56.3% (1990), 61.6% (2000), 66.5% (2010), 72.8% (2025)
3631	non-metropolitan areas	10,601,000	0.63	66,900	39.51	A	14,561,628	*Sources of data:* Censuses of 1956, 1966, 1976, 1986, and 1991.
3632	metropolitan areas	31,111,000	0.70	217,000	39.40	A	54,217,000	*Definition:* All *shahrestan* (county) centers, regardless of size; and all places having municipal centers.
3633	Abadan	643,000	0.60	3,900	41.35	A	1,060,000	Khuzestan. Oil. 77% Arab, 15% Persian. F=c750. D=RCC,SDA,GOC,Khuzestan Church Council.
3634	Agha Jari	112,000	0.01	11	26.76	A	184,000	Southern Khuzestan east of Bandar-e Mah Shahr. Linked to Abadan by pipeline, oil field opened 1944.
3635	Ahar	90,700	0.01	9	26.76	A	150,000	Azarbayjan-e Sharqi on Ahar River northeast of Tabriz. Mountainous Arasbaran district, grain, fruit, iron.
3636	Ahvaz (Ahwaz)	1,018,000	0.35	3,600	40.10	A	1,958,000	Khuzestan on Karun River. Oil. 79% Arab, 15% Persian. D=Khuzestan Church Council,RCC,SDA.
3637	Aligudarz	78,800	0.01	8	36.76	A	130,000	Lorestan in Zagros Mountains. Tribal Bakhtiari population, grain, fruit.
3638	Amol (Amul)	173,000	0.01	17	26.76	A	285,000	Mazandaran on Harhaz River. Ceramics, oranges, rice. Nestorian episcopate in Sasanian period.
3639	Andimeshk	92,500	0.01	9	26.76	A	152,000	Khuzestan near Dezful. Luristan nomads. Railroad maintenance point, citrus fruit, rice, Trans-Iranian railroad.
3640	Arak	389,000	0.12	470	36.87	A	641,000	Markazi. 35% Persian, 30% Azerbaijani. 95% Muslim. D=Armenian Apostolic Ch,AoG.
3641	Ardabil	413,000	0.01	41	26.76	A	681,000	Azarbayjan-e Sharqi. Carpets, mineral springs. 55% Azerbaijani, 20% Persian, 12% Kurd. 96% Muslim.
3642	Babol (Babul, Barfurush)	169,000	0.01	17	26.76	A	278,000	Mazandaran on Babol River. Resort, bazaars. Caspian Sea. Processed foods, fruits, tea, tobacco, cotton.
3643	Bakhtaran (Kermanshah)	949,000	0.43	4,100	40.18	A	1,853,000	Bakhtaran. Textiles. F=c350. 55% Kurd, 30% Persian, 96% Muslim. Christian hospital, school; TEE.

Table 10-5–continued opposite

Table 10-5–continued

Rec No 1	Country City 2	Pop 2000 3	AC% 4	Church Members 5	E% 6	W 7	Pop 2025 8	Notes 9
3644	Bandar-e Abbas	295,000	0.02	59	26.77	A	487,000	Strait of Hormuz. Import/export. Pleasant winters. Arabs, African Blacks.
3645	Bandar-e Anzali (Bandar-e Pahlavi)	145,000	0.01	14	26.76	A	239,000	Gilan on Caspian Sea near Rasht.
3646	Bandar-e Mah Shahr	154,000	0.01	15	26.76	A	253,000	Southern Khuzestan on Persian Gulf east of Abadan.
3647	Behbehan (Behbahan)	147,000	0.01	15	26.76	A	242,000	Khuzestan near Zagros mountains. Tribal populations. Gas producing region, grain, rice, dates, oranges, oil.
3648	Birjand	119,000	0.01	12	26.76	A	196,000	Khorasan on Khusf River (usually dry). In an oasis. Carpets, felt, woolen fabrics, copper, lead.
3649	Bojnurd	143,000	0.01	14	26.76	A	236,000	Northern Khorasan near Atrak River. Near Turkmenistan border. Wool rugs, wheat, walnuts, airfield.
3650	Borazjan	92,500	0.01	9	26.76	A	152,000	Bushehr inland from Bandar-e Bushehr. Road junction, grain dates. Formerly known as Dashtistan.
3651	Borujerd (Boroojerd)	269,000	0.01	27	26.76	A	444,000	Lorestan. Regional center. Ancient ruins. 25% Luri, 25% Azerbaijani, 23% Persian. 95% Muslim.
3652	Bushehr (Bushire)	213,000	0.00	0	26.75	A	351,000	Capital of Bushehr. Persian Gulf port. Oil distribution, fisheries. Suffered extensive damage in Iran-Iraq war.
3653	Dezful (Dezfool, Dizful)	222,000	0.01	22	26.76	A	366,000	Khuzestan on Dez River. Winter market for Luristan nomads. 30% Persian, 25% Arab, 20% Bakhtiari, 20% Luri.
3654	Do Rud	90,700	0.01	9	26.76	A	150,000	Eastern Lorestan near Oshtoran Mountain. Serves as station for Borujerd on Trans-Iranian railroad. Grain, fruit.
3655	Emamshahr (Shahrud)	119,000	0.01	12	26.76	A	196,000	Semnan southeast of Gorgan. Cotton, wheat, fruit, lumbering, matches, rugs, airfield.
3656	Esfahan (Isfahan, New Julfa)	2,644,000	3.00	79,300	54.75	B	5,162,000	Esfahan. Major textile center. Christian hospitals and schools. 4% Baha'i, 1% Jewish. D=AAC,RCC.
3657	Eslamabad-e Gharb	124,000	0.01	12	26.76	A	204,000	Bakhtaran west of Bakhtaran. Sugar beets, grain, tobacco, wool, dairy products, sugar processing.
3658	Fasa	117,000	0.01	12	26.76	A	193,000	Fars south of Kharman Mountain. Grain, sugarbeets, cotton, rice, tobacco.
3659	Gonbad-e Qabus	131,000	0.01	13	26.76	A	216,000	Gorgan region. Turkish mausoleum. 200 ft. tower (1006-7). Cotton, tobacco, flax, sesame, rice, citrus fruit.
3660	Gorgan (Gurgan)	204,000	0.01	20	26.76	A	337,000	Mazandaran. Caspian seaport. Cereal, soap, carpets, rug weaving, flax, sesame, rice, citrus fruit.
3661	Hamadan (Ecbatana)	399,000	0.80	3,200	37.55	A	658,000	Hamadan. Resort. 6,158 ft. Mentioned in Ezra 6:2. 28% Azerbaijani, 24% Kurd, 23% Persian. D=Assyrians,AAC.
3662	Ilam	131,000	0.00	0	26.75	A	216,000	Ilam. Rural appearance. Bricks, woven cloth, coarse carpets. Mainly Kurds, Lurs.
3663	Jahrom	119,000	0.01	12	26.76	A	196,000	Fars south of Fasa. Dates, tobacco, cotton, grain.
3664	Kashan	203,000	0.02	41	26.77	A	335,000	Markazi. Ancient city. Ceramics, woolen & silk carpets, rose water, Ardebil carpet. 13th century minaret.
3665	Kazerun	110,000	0.01	11	26.76	A	181,000	Fars. Date palms, citrus orchards, wheat, tobacco. High limestone ridges.
3666	Kerman (Kirman)	377,000	0.03	110	26.78	A	621,000	Capital of Kerman. Largest carpet-exporting. 81% Persian, 10% Arab. 96% Muslim. D=Episcopal Church of Iran.
3667	Khomeynishahr	153,000	0.01	15	26.76	A	253,000	Esfahan northwest of Esfahan. Central Iran, barley cultivation.
3668	Khorramabad (Khurramabad)	305,000	0.01	31	26.76	A	504,000	Lorestan. Summer market for nomadic Lurs. 30% Persian, 20% Arab, 15% Luri, 15% Kurd. 97% Muslim.
3669	Khorramshahr (Mohammerah)	319,000	0.27	860	37.02	A	525,000	Khuzestan port on Kuran River. Date palms. 63% Arab, 20% Persian, 8% Luri. D=RCC(1 school),SDA.
3670	Khvorasgan (Khorasgan)	74,900	0.01	7	36.76	A	123,000	Esfahan east of Esfahan city. Major textile center. D=AAC,RCC.
3671	Khvoy (Khoi)	169,000	0.01	17	26.76	A	278,000	Azarbayjan-e Gharbi. Cool streams, willows. Agricultural trade center. Grain, fruit, timber, fertile irrigated region.
3672	Mahabad (Mehabad)	110,000	0.01	11	26.76	A	181,000	Southern Azarbayjan-e Gharbi. Little economic development. Center of Kurdish nationalism. Many Kurds.
3673	Malayer	152,000	0.01	15	26.76	A	250,000	Southern Hamadan north of Borujerd. Grain, fruit, grapes, rug and textile weaving, railroad.
3674	Maragheh (Maraghah)	147,000	0.01	15	26.76	A	243,000	Southern Azarbayjan-e Sharqi. Fruit-growing area, dried fruits, marble. Ancient ruins.
3675	Marand	103,000	0.01	10	26.76	A	170,000	Northern Azarbayjan-e Sharqi northwest of Tabriz. Grains, cotton, dry fruit, many gardens and fruit orchards.
3676	Marv Dasht	126,000	0.01	13	26.76	A	207,000	Fars on Kor River north of Shiraz. Sugar beets, sugar refinery, ruins of Persopolis.
3677	Mashhad (Meshed)	2,378,000	0.16	3,800	41.91	A	4,405,000	Capital of Khorasan. Wool. 4 million Muslim pilgrims p.a. 75% Persian, 25% Afghans. Christian Service Board.
3678	Masjed Soleyman (Masjid-i Sulaiman)	153,000	0.01	15	26.76	A	253,000	Khuzestan. Leading oil center. Karun River. Petroleum(1908).
3679	Mehr Shani	84,200	0.01	8	36.76	A	139,000	Dates, tobacco, cotton, grain. 99% Muslim.
3680	Miandoab	90,700	0.01	9	26.76	A	150,000	Southern Azarbayjan-e Gharbi east of Mahabad. Zarineh River. Grain, fruit, sugar beets, sheep.
3681	Mianeh	99,400	0.01	10	26.76	A	164,000	Southern Azarbayjan-e Sharqi on Sefid River. Railroad, grain, cotton, grapes.
3682	Naqadeh	76,500	0.01	8	36.76	A	126,000	Southern Azarbayjan-e Gharbi on Lake Urmia.
3683	Najafabad	189,000	0.01	19	26.76	A	312,000	Esfahan west of Esfahan. West central. Trade center for an agricultural region. Noted for pomegranates.
3684	Neyshabur (Nishapur)	160,000	0.01	16	26.76	A	264,000	Khorasan. Cereals, cottons, carpets, pottery. Nearby tomb of Omar Khayyam.
3685	Orumiyeh (Rezaiyeh, Urmia)	440,000	6.00	26,400	52.75	B	726,000	Mainly Azeri Turks. In 1900 1/2 Christian. 40% Persian, 20% Kurd. Assyrian and Chaldean (RC) churches.
3686	Qa'emshahr	160,000	0.01	16	26.76	A	264,000	Mazandaran near Babol. Textiles, food processing, thermal power plant, road and railroad transport center.
3687	Qarchaqah	114,000	0.01	11	36.76	A	188,000	Carpets, processed hides & skins. 99% Muslim.
3688	Qazvin (Kazvin)	364,000	0.31	1,100	40.06	A	600,000	Markazi. Cloth-weaving. F=250. 35% Persian, 30% Azerbaijani, 10% Luri. 93% Muslim. D=ROC,AAC.
3689	Qom (Qum, Ghom)	795,000	0.01	80	26.76	A	1,311,000	Markazi. Center of fundamentalist Islam (pilgrimages). 100 Muslim saints' tombs. No Christian visitors.
3690	Qomsheh	117,000	0.01	12	26.76	A	193,000	Esfahan south of Esfahan. Fruit gardens, cotton, cotton spinning factory. Esfahan-Shirae road.
3691	Quchan (Kuchan)	106,000	0.01	11	26.76	A	175,000	Northern Khorasan. Atrek River. Mainly Kurds. Many still nomads. Grain, vineyards, distillery, earthquake zone.
3692	Rafsanjan	106,000	0.01	11	26.76	A	175,000	Central Kerman west of Kerman. Rich agricultural area. Grain, cotton, opium, noted pistachio production.
3693	Ramhormoz	92,500	0.01	9	26.76	A	152,000	Southern Khuzestan north of Bandar-e Mah Shahr. Oil, petroleum, dates, rice, citrus fruits, vegetables.
3694	Rasht (Resht)	426,000	0.38	1,600	37.13	A	702,000	Capital of Gilan. Rice. 32% Persian, 25% Azerbaijani, 15% Kurd. 91% Muslim. D=GOC,Armenian,Evangelical Ch.
3695	Sabzevar	189,000	0.01	19	26.76	A	312,000	Northern Khorasan on Shur River west of Mashhad. Trade center of cotton growing region, textiles, rugs.
3696	Sanandaj (Sisar)	299,000	0.02	60	26.77	A	494,000	Kordestan. Carpets, processed hides & skins. Mainly Kurds, Armenians. Handicrafts, area of Kurdish unrest.
3697	Saqqez (Saqqiz)	133,000	0.01	13	26.76	A	219,000	Northern Kordestan. One-time capital of Scythians (c600 B.C.). Tobacco, wheat, gums, sheep raising.
3698	Sari	206,000	0.01	21	26.76	A	340,000	Capital of Mazandaran. Bricks, mosaics. Persians, Turks, Kurds, Bangladeshis, Afghans, Turkomans.
3699	Semnan (Samnan)	94,200	0.01	9	26.76	A	155,000	Semnan. Local grains, cotton, tobacco. Known for sweet almond paste.
3700	Shiraz	1,113,000	0.25	2,800	39.00	A	2,045,000	Capital of Fars. Wine. 83% Persian, 5% Turk. 95% Muslim. D=Armenian Apostolic, SDA, Episcopal (1 hospital).
3701	Shirvan	71,300	0.01	7	26.76	A	118,000	Northern Khorasan on Atrak River east of Bojnurd. NW of Quchan. Grain, raisins, melons, woolen textiles.
3702	Shushtar	96,400	0.01	10	26.76	A	159,000	Khuzestan on Karun River north of Ahvaz. Known for brocaded textiles, metalworks, engineering.
3703	Sirjan	117,000	0.01	12	26.76	A	193,000	Western Kerman. Cotton ginning, metalworks, pistashios, fruit, gum, road junction.
3704	Tabriz	1,624,000	1.10	17,900	48.85	A	2,980,000	Azarbayjan-e Sharqi. Carpets. The Blue Mosque. 70% Azerbaijani, 13% Persian. D=AAC(32 churches).
3705	TEHRAN (Teheran)	7,380,000	0.90	66,400	48.65	A	12,721,000	Textiles, cement, sugar, chinaware. 60% Persian. 80,000 Baha'is, 30,000 Jews. F=c400.
3706	Eslamshahr	315,000	1.00	3,200	45.75	A	519,000	Southwest beyond international airport. D=AAC.
3707	Karaj	403,000	1.00	4,000	45.75	A	664,000	48% Persian, 25% Azerbaijani, 10% Mazanderani, 7% Kurd. 96% Muslim. D=AAC.
3708	Shahr Kord	110,000	1.00	1,100	45.75	A	181,000	Bricks, mosaics, milled rice, carpets, rugs. D=AAC.
3709	Torbat-e Heydariyeh	108,000	0.01	11	26.76	A	178,000	Khorasan south of Mashhad. Road junction and trade center, saffron, wool, silk, grain, sugar beets.
3710	Varamin	89,000	0.01	9	26.76	A	147,000	Tehran south of Tehran. Fertile plain irrigated by the Jaj River. Grain, sugar beets, cotton, fruit, paper.
3711	Yazd	337,000	0.03	100	26.78	A	556,000	Yazd. Last center of Zoroastrianism in Iran. F=c500. 81% Persian, 10% Arab. D=Episcopal Church.
3712	Zabol	101,000	0.01	10	26.76	A	167,000	Northern Sistan va Baluchestan near Lake Daryacheh. Nomadic herding and some cereal crops.
3713	Zahedan	413,000	0.02	83	26.77	A	681,000	Sistan va Baluchestan. Economically backward. Bricks, ceramics. Persians, Baloch.
3714	Zanjan (Zenjan)	315,000	0.01	32	26.76	A	520,000	Zanjan on Zanjan River. Grains. 64% Azerbaijani, 15% Persian, 15% Kurd. 94% Muslim, 2% Baha'i.
3715	Zarrin Shahr	120,000	0.01	12	26.76	A	198,000	Esfahan on Zayandeh River south of Esfahan. Central Iran. Railroad terminus from Yazd.
	IRAQ	**23,115,000**	**3.14**	**725,000**	**48.44**	**A**	**41,014,000**	**INDEPENDENTS 1.3%, ROMAN CATHOLICS 1.1%. PENT-CHAR 1.1%, EVANGELICAL 0.3%, GCC 0.8%**
3716	rural areas	5,358,000	0.93	49,900	36.33	A	6,591,000	64.8% (1950), 43.8% (1970), 28.1% (1990), 23.1% (2000), 19.6% (2010), 16.0% (2025)
3717	urban areas	17,757,000	3.80	675,000	52.10	B	34,423,000	35.1% (1950), 56.1% (1970), 71.8% (1990), 76.8% (2000), 80.3% (2010), 83.9% (2025)
3718	non-metropolitan areas	5,447,000	3.82	208,000	52.01	B	12,270,667	*Sources of data:* Censuses of 1947, 1957, 1965, 1977, and 1987; estimate for 1970.
3719	metropolitan areas	12,310,000	3.79	467,000	52.14	B	22,152,000	*Definition:* Area within the boundaries of municipality councils (Al-Majlis Al-Baldei).
3720	Ad-Diwaniyah	158,000	0.10	160	30.40	A	307,000	Al-Qadisiyah on Nahr al-Furat. Hilla Canal (branch off the Euphrates). Rice, dates.
3721	Al Basrah (Basra)	956,000	6.00	57,400	57.30	B	1,854,000	Principal port. Petroleum refining & export, dates, corn. F=638. Much destroyed in Iran-Iraq war. D=RCC.
3722	Al-'Amarah	204,000	0.10	200	30.40	A	396,000	Capital of Maysan. Agricultural trade, livestock, wool, weaving, silverware.
3723	Al-Hillah (Hilla)	334,000	1.00	3,300	46.30	A	647,000	River port, grain market. F=10th century. On former pilgrimage route.
3724	Al-Kut	113,000	0.20	230	30.50	A	220,000	Wasit on Tigris River. Port and market center. Grains, dates, vegetables, fruits, vast destruction in WWI.
3725	Al-Mawsil (Mosul)	1,034,000	6.00	62,000	57.30	B	1,862,000	Capital of Ninawa on Tigris River. Near ancient Nineveh. Ancient mosques and churches. D=RCC,SOC.
3726	An-Najaf (Najaf)	376,000	0.50	1,900	35.80	A	729,000	Capital of an-Najaf. Holy city. Mosque with tomb of Ali, fourth caliph. F=791.
3727	An-Nasiryah	215,000	0.10	220	30.40	A	417,000	On Euphrates River. Boatbuilding, carpentry, silverware. Near ancient Ur. F=1870.
3728	Ar-Ramadi	213,000	0.10	210	30.40	A	413,000	Capital of al-Anbar on Euphrates River. F=1869 to settle nomadic Dulaym tribes.
3729	As-Samawah	117,000	0.10	120	30.40	A	226,000	Al-Muthanna on Euphrates River. Baghdad-Basra Railroad. Rice, dates, trade center, building materials.
3730	As-Sulaymaniyah (Sulaimaniya)	433,000	4.20	18,200	55.50	B	840,000	Center of Kurdish nationalism. Northeast Iraq. Tobacco, fruit, cereals. F=1781. D=RCC.
3731	Ba'qubah	178,000	0.10	180	30.40	A	344,000	Capital of Diyala. Regional agricultural trade, livestock. Many Assyrian Christians (WWI).
3732	BAGHDAD	4,796,000	4.20	201,000	55.50	B	8,051,000	On Tigris River. Center of finance, industry, oil trade. Many mosques & Islamic schools. F=c750. D=RCC,SOC.
3733	Irbil (Arbil)	2,368,000	4.00	94,700	55.30	B	4,267,000	One of the world's oldest continuously inhabited cities. Early Christian presence. Kurds. D=RCC.
3734	Karbala (Kerbala)	286,000	1.00	2,900	41.30	A	555,000	Holy city. Battle of Karbala (680) between Sunni & Shia Muslims. Burial here assures paradise for Muslims.
3735	Kirkuk	528,000	4.50	23,800	55.80	B	1,023,000	Kurdistan. Agricultural trade & export. Oil center. F=3000 BC. Kurds, Turkomen. D=RCC.
	IRELAND	**3,730,000**	**89.95**	**3,355,000**	**99.72**	**C**	**4,404,000**	**ROMAN CATHOLICS 84.7%, ANGLICANS 3.5%. PENT-CHAR 13.1%, EVANGELICAL 3.3%, GCC 48.4%**
3736	rural areas	1,547,000	92.71	1,434,000	99.94	C	1,386,000	58.9% (1950), 48.2% (1970), 43.0% (1990), 41.4% (2000), 38.2% (2010), 31.4% (2025)
3737	urban areas	2,183,000	88.00	1,921,000	99.57	C	3,018,000	41.0% (1950), 51.7% (1970), 56.9% (1990), 58.5% (2000), 61.7% (2010), 68.5% (2025)
3738	non-metropolitan areas	926,000	87.96	814,000	99.65	C	1,483,497	*Sources of data:* Censuses of 1951, 1956, 1961, 1966, 1971, 1981, 1986, and 1991.
3739	metropolitan areas	1,257,000	88.03	1,107,000	99.51	C	1,534,000	*Definition:* Cities and towns, including suburbs with 1,500 or more inhabitants.
3740	Cork (Corcaigh)	177,000	90.00	159,000	99.57	C	244,000	Seaport on River Lee. World's first yachting club (1720). F=7th century monastery. 'Marsh'. D=RCC.
3741	DUBLIN (Baile Atha Cliath)	913,000	87.00	794,000	99.47	C	1,058,000	Chief port on Irish Sea. Guinness brewery. F=c850 as Norse stronghold. D=RCC.
3742	Dun Laoghaire	55,700	92.00	51,200	99.67	C	77,000	Seaport. Residential, hotels. F=5th century. Formerly fishing village. James Joyce museum. D=RCC.
3743	Galway (Gaillimh)	47,900	92.00	44,100	99.67	C	66,300	Seaport. Strong Gaelic character. Wool, marble. F=c1270. Franciscan friary(1296). D=RCC.
3744	Limerick	77,900	91.00	70,900	99.62	C	108,000	Seaport. Salmon fishing, agricultural produce. F=812. Protestant Cathedral of St. Mary (1142). D=RCC.
3745	Waterford (Port Lairge)	41,800	92.00	38,400	99.67	C	57,700	Port. Salmon fisheries, lead crystal. 13th century monasteries. D=Anglican,RCC.
	ISLE OF MAN	**79,200**	**66.24**	**52,400**	**99.63**	**C**	**101,000**	**ANGLICANS 42.4%, PROTESTANTS 14.1%. PENT-CHAR 7.5%, EVANGELICAL 22.3%, GCC 32.3%**
3746	rural areas	18,500	71.92	13,300	99.93	C	17,000	47.0% (1950), 44.1% (1970), 26.1% (1990), 23.4% (2000), 20.6% (2010), 16.8% (2025)
3747	urban areas	60,600	64.50	39,100	99.54	C	83,900	52.9% (1950), 55.8% (1970), 73.8% (1990), 76.5% (2000), 79.3% (2010), 83.1% (2025)
3748	non-metropolitan areas	26,700	63.86	17,000	99.54	C	36,887	*Sources of data:* Censuses of 1951, 1961, 1966, 1971, 1976, 1981, and 1986.
3749	metropolitan areas	34,900	65.00	22,100	99.54	C	47,000	*Definition:* Borough of Douglas; town and village districts.
3750	DOUGLAS	34,000	65.00	22,100	99.54	C	47,000	Dhoo & Glass Rivers. Tourism, breweries, mineral water. F=1869. D=COE,Methodist.
	ISRAEL	**5,122,000**	**5.74**	**294,000**	**56.02**	**B**	**6,927,000**	**ROMAN CATHOLICS 2.7%, INDEPENDENTS 1.6%. PENT-CHAR 2.0%, EVANGELICAL 0.6%, GCC 3.7%**
3751	rural areas	452,000	3.08	13,900	32.64	A	455,000	35.3% (1950), 15.8% (1970), 9.7% (1990), 8.8% (2000), 7.9% (2010), 6.5% (2025)
3752	urban areas	4,669,000	6.00	280,000	58.28	B	6,472,000	64.6% (1950), 84.2% (1970), 90.2% (1990), 91.1% (2000), 92.0% (2010), 93.4% (2025)
3753	non-metropolitan areas	658,000	5.99	39,400	58.16	B	1,305,997	*Sources of data:* Censuses of 1961, 1972, and 1983; estimate for 1955, 1991, and 1993.
3754	metropolitan areas	4,012,000	6.00	241,000	58.30	B	5,166,000	*Definition:* All settlements with more than 2,000 inhabitants.
3755	Ashdod	107,000	1.00	1,100	48.28	A	148,000	Southern Palestine. Ancient Philistine city (1 Sam 5). Exports citrus crop, textiles.
3756	Ashqelon (Ashkelon)	75,900	1.00	760	48.28	A	105,000	Palestine. Textiles, plastics, wristwatches. Resort center. F=2000 BC.
3757	Beer Sheva (Beersheba)	155,000	0.50	780	45.78	A	215,000	Center of the Negev. Chemicals, porcelain. Very few Muslims or Christians. 'City of Abraham'.
3758	Hefa (Haifa)	572,000	4.00	22,900	56.28	B	792,000	Principal port. Jews, Arabs (Muslims). HQ of Baha'i. Crusades (1960). D=RCC,ROC,Seamen's Mission.
3759	Lod (Lydda)	55,000	1.00	550	48.28	A	76,300	Southern Hamerkaz on Kinneret-Negev Conduit. Paper, oil. Settled by Jewish immigrants (1948).

Table 10-5–continued overleaf

Table 10-5–continued

Rec No 1	Country City 2	Pop 2000 3	AC% 4	Church Members 5	E% 6	W 7	Pop 2025 8	Notes 9
3760	Nazerat (Nazareth)	97,800	5.00	4,900	55.28	B	136,000	Lower Galilee. Mainly Arab. Christian pilgrimage center. Church of the Annunciation. D=RCC,GOC.
3761	Ra'ananna	68,100	1.00	680	48.28	A	94,400	Hamerkaz north of Tel Aviv. Plain of Sharon. Large residential satellite of Tel-Aviv. Large medical center.
3762	Tel Aviv-Yafo (Jaffa)	2,170,000	8.00	174,000	61.28	B	2,613,000	On Mediterranean Sea. Commercial center. F=1909. Jewish, Arab, 1.5% Muslim. D=GOC,RCC.
3763	Bat Yam	180,000	7.00	12,600	57.28	B	249,000	Plain of Sharon & Mediterranean coast. Seaside resort. Printing and publishing. F=1926.
3764	Bene Beraq	148,000	7.50	11,100	57.78	B	206,000	Citrus groves, industry. Citadel of Orthodox Judaism. Mentioned in Joshua 19. Modern settlement.
3765	Giv'atayim	59,200	8.00	4,700	58.28	B	82,100	Food processing, printing. First suburban workers development. Diamond polishing. F=1922.
3766	Herzliyya	98,100	7.50	7,400	57.78	B	136,000	Suburban residences, luxury hotels. Center of Israeli electronics industry. F=1924 by American Zionists.
3767	Holon	199,000	8.00	15,900	58.28	B	276,000	Textiles, rubbers, metal, plastics. Samaritan community. Leather goods, furniture, glassware. F=1925.
3768	Kefar Sava	77,600	7.00	5,400	57.28	B	108,000	Citrus, mixed farming, dairying. F=1903 as first Jewish settlement in South Sharon. Destroyed in WWI.
3769	Netanya (Natanya)	168,000	7.50	12,600	57.78	B	233,000	Coastal city. Diamond cutting & polishing, textiles, breweries, resort. F=1928. Jews, Arabs. D=RCC et alia.
3770	Petah Tiqwa (Petach Tikva)	183,000	7.70	14,100	57.98	B	254,000	Hamerkaz. New urban center east of Tel Aviv. Canned fruits, oil & soaps, textiles. F=1878. Mainly Jewish.
3771	Ramat Gan	152,000	8.00	12,100	58.28	B	210,000	Residential, parks & gardens. Chocolate, citrus products, textiles. F=1921. Bar Ilan University (1953).
3772	Rehovot	102,000	7.00	7,100	57.28	B	141,000	Citrus groves, imitation leather, cereals, pharmaceuticals. F=1890 by Warsaw Jews. Institute of Science.
3773	Rishon leZiyyon (Rishon Letsion)	177,000	6.50	11,500	56.78	B	246,000	Extensive vineyards. F=1882. Jews (65% secular, 25% traditional, 10% Orthodox). No Arabs. D=RCC. TEE.
3774	Yerushalayim (Jerusalem, Al-Quds)	712,000	5.00	35,600	58.28	B	986,000	Holy city to Jews, Christians, Muslims. Tourism. F=1800 BC. 27% Arab (13% Christian). D=RCC,GOC.
ITALY		**57,298,000**	**81.89**	**46,922,000**	**99.24**	**C**	**51,270,000**	**ROMAN CATHOLICS 97.1%, PROTESTANTS 0.7%. PENT-CHAR 7.3%, EVANGELICAL 0.5%, GCC 42.2%**
3775	rural areas	18,908,000	85.73	16,210,000	99.62	C	13,084,000	45.6% (1950), 35.7% (1970), 33.2% (1990), 33.0% (2000), 30.9% (2010), 25.5% (2025)
3776	urban areas	38,390,000	80.00	30,712,000	99.05	C	38,186,000	54.3% (1950), 64.2% (1970), 66.7% (1990), 67.0% (2000), 69.0% (2010), 74.4% (2025)
3777	non-metropolitan areas	12,096,000	79.53	9,620,000	99.22	C	11,963,110	*Sources of data:* Censuses of 1951, 1961, 1971, 1981, and 1991.
3778	metropolitan areas	26,294,000	80.22	21,092,000	98.97	C	26,222,000	*Definition:* Communes with 10,000 or more inhabitants.
3779	Agrigento	53,100	82.80	44,000	99.15	C	52,900	Capital of Agrigento, Sicily. Sulfur & potash mining, tourism. Many Greek ruins. F=581 BC. D=RCC.
3780	Alessandria	93,700	84.60	79,300	99.95	C	93,200	Capital of Alessandria, Piedmont. Hat making, agriculture, wine. F=1168. Bishopric (1175). D=RCC.
3781	Altamura	57,700	84.70	48,800	99.55	C	57,300	Bari, Puglia. Cattle, almonds, wine, wool. F=c1200. Romanesque Cathedral of the Assumption (1232). D=RCC.
3782	Ancona	104,000	82.50	85,500	99.85	C	103,000	Capital of Ancona, Marche on Adriatic Sea. Port. Shipbuilding. Many cathedrals. F=390 BC. D=RCC.
3783	Andria	82,800	80.80	66,900	99.15	C	82,400	Bari, Puglia. Vines, olives, almonds. F=c100 BC. 10th century cathedral. D=RCC.
3784	Arezzo	92,000	83.80	77,100	99.15	C	91,500	Capital of Arezzo, Toscana. Agricultural economy. Roman origins. Cathedral (1286). D=RCC.
3785	Ascoli Piceno	55,500	84.50	46,900	99.85	C	55,200	Capital of Ascoli Piceno, Marche. Agriculture. F=c300 BC. Roman ruins. 7th century cathedral. D=RCC.
3786	Asti	74,800	83.00	62,100	99.85	C	74,400	Capital of Asti, Piedmont. Wines & fruits. Roman origins. Bishopric since 932. D=RCC.
3787	Avellino	54,500	85.00	46,300	99.85	C	54,200	Capital of Avellino, Campania on Sabato River. Benedictine monastery of Montevergine (1119). D=RCC.
3788	Bari	477,000	79.50	379,000	96.85	C	474,000	Capital of Bari & Puglia. Adriatic port. Boat-building, exports wine, olive oil, almonds. F=1500 BC. D=RCC.
3789	Barletta	86,500	80.10	69,300	97.45	C	86,000	Bari, Puglia. Adriatic port & resort. Fishing, wines, almonds, olives. Ancient origins. Cathedral (1150). D=RCC.
3790	Benevento	62,900	83.50	52,500	98.85	C	62,600	Capital of Benevento, Campania. Agriculture center for wheat, grapes, olives. Cathedral (c800). D=RCC.
3791	Bergamo	346,000	82.00	284,000	99.35	C	344,000	Capital of Bergamo, Lombardy. Textiles, engineering, cement. F=196 BC. Basilica (1137). D=RCC.
3792	Biella	51,200	84.50	43,300	99.85	C	50,900	Vercelli, Piedmont. Woollen industry. Pilgrimage resort Santuario Oi Dropa (369). St. Eusebius. D=RCC.
3793	Bitonto	50,000	80.60	40,300	97.95	C	49,700	Bari, Puglia. Wines, olives, almonds. Romanesque Cathedral (1175). Church of St. Francis (1286). D=RCC.
3794	Bologna	527,000	81.00	427,000	98.35	C	524,000	Capital of Bologna, Emilia-Romagna. Agriculture, machinery. Oldest university in Europe (c1050). D=RCC.
3795	Bolzano	101,000	84.10	84,800	99.45	C	100,000	Capital of Bolzano, Trentino-Alto Adige. Agricultural & tourist center. Austrian character. D=RCC.
3796	Brescia	198,000	81.00	160,000	98.35	C	197,000	Capital of Brescia, Lombardy. Art treasures in numerous churches. F=c200 BC. 8th century church. D=RCC.
3797	Brindisi	92,100	84.30	77,600	99.65	C	91,600	Capital of Brindisi, Puglia on Adriatic Sea. Wine, tourist center. End of Appian Way. F=226 BC. D=RCC.
3798	Cagliari	306,000	83.90	257,000	99.25	C	305,000	Capital of Cagliari, Sardinia. Port exports lead, zinc. F=by Phoenicians. Basilica of St. Saturnino (c450). D=RCC.
3799	Caltanissetta	63,100	83.90	52,900	99.25	C	62,800	Capital of Caltanissetta, Sicily. Agricultural market center, sulfur industry. Episcopal see. D=RCC.
3800	Campobasso	51,500	84.10	43,300	99.45	C	51,200	Capital of Campobasso & Molise. Pears, cheese. Romanesque churches. D=RCC.
3801	Carpi	61,000	84.70	51,700	99.55	C	60,700	Modena, Emilia-Romagna. Great piazza. Food processing, straw plaiting. Many old churches. D=RCC.
3802	Caserta	69,000	68.50	47,300	95.85	C	68,700	Capital of Caserta, Campania. Agricultural trade. Bourbon Royal Palace. F=8th century. D=RCC.
3803	Catania	552,000	81.80	451,000	99.15	C	549,000	Capital of Catania, Sicily. Busy port. Chemicals, fishing, sulfur. Built on lava. F=729 BC by Greeks. D=RCC.
3804	Catanzaro	104,000	83.30	86,800	99.85	C	104,000	Capital of Catanzaro, Calabria. Silk weaving, olive oil. F=10th century. Baroque church of San Domenico. D=RCC.
3805	Cerignola	55,200	83.10	45,800	99.85	C	54,900	Foggia, Puglia. Communications & market center. Wine, olive oil, almonds, wool. D=RCC.
3806	Cesena	89,900	84.00	75,500	99.35	C	89,400	Forli, Emilia-Romagna on Savio River. Agriculture. Ancient origins. Rocca Malatestiana (1381). D=RCC.
3807	Chieti	57,800	83.30	48,100	99.85	C	57,500	Capital of Chieti, Abruzzi. Textile, cellulose, sugar, wire, tobacco. Ancient origins. 11th century cathedral. D=RCC.
3808	Civitavecchia	51,000	75.00	38,300	92.35	C	50,800	Roma, Lazio. Tyrrhenian Sea. F=2nd century BC. Episcopal see. Three fourths destroyed in WWII. D=RCC.
3809	Como	166,000	84.20	139,000	99.55	C	165,000	Capital of Como, Lombardia. Printing, silk. Bishopric (379). Church of San Carpoforo (4th century). D=RCC.
3810	Cosenza	151,000	83.70	126,000	99.05	C	150,000	Capital of Cosenza, Calabria. Agriculture, furniture, woolens. Many medieval churches. Ancient origins. D=RCC.
3811	Cremona	75,500	82.60	62,300	99.95	C	75,100	Capital of Cremona, Lombardia on Po River. Famous for violins & violas. F=218 BC. Cathedral (1190). D=RCC.
3812	Crotone	62,100	83.90	52,100	99.25	C	61,700	Catanzaro, Calabria. Port. Chemicals, zinc. F=710 BC by Greeks. Pythagoras & 300 disciples. D=RCC.
3813	Cuneo	56,100	84.50	47,400	99.85	C	55,800	Capital of Cuneo, Piemonte. Raw silk, chestnuts. F=1198. Gothic cathedral (10th century). D=RCC.
3814	Empoli	42,900	84.50	36,300	99.85	C	42,700	Firenze, Toscana on Lower Arno River. Glass, matches. Heavily damaged in WWII. Church (1093). D=RCC.
3815	Ferrara	141,000	83.60	118,000	98.95	C	140,000	Capital of Ferrara, Emilia-Romagna. Agriculture, chemicals, sugar, alcohol. 15th-16th century palaces. D=RCC.
3816	Firenze (Florence)	778,000	79.00	615,000	97.35	C	778,000	Capital of Firenze, Toscana on Arno River. Tourism, center of the arts. Baptistery of St. John (c1000). D=RCC.
3817	Scandicci	53,400	80.00	42,800	97.35	C	53,200	Firenze southwest on Greve River. Tourism, glassware, metalware, leatherworks, ceramics, shoes. D=RCC.
3818	Sesto Fiorentino	47,100	81.00	38,100	98.35	C	46,800	Firenze north on railway. Porcelain, soaps, cement, clothing, straw hats, candy, paper, metal products. D=RCC.
3819	Foggia	156,000	84.00	131,000	99.35	C	155,000	Capital of Foggia, Puglia. Major wool market, wheat, cheese. Severely damaged in WWII. D=RCC.
3820	Foligno	53,700	84.60	45,500	99.95	C	53,400	Perugia, Umbria. Sugar, metals, textiles. Cathedral (1133). Romanesque cathedrals. D=RCC.
3821	Forli	110,000	83.90	92,500	99.25	C	110,000	Capital of Forli, Emilia-Romagna. Agriculture. F=2nd century BC. Earliest bishops 4th century. D=RCC.
3822	Gela	80,000	84.50	67,600	99.85	C	79,600	Caltanissetta on Gulf of Gela. Archaeological center, cotton, fishing. Temple of Athena (5th century BC). D=RCC.
3823	Genova (Genoa)	890,000	79.70	709,000	97.05	C	890,000	Capital of Genoa, Liguria. Center of Italian Riviera on Mediterranean Sea. Shipping F=3rd century BC. D=RCC.
3824	Grosseto	71,700	80.70	57,800	98.05	C	71,300	Capital of Grosseto, Toscana. Agriculture, mineral springs. Romanesque Cathedral (1294). D=RCC.
3825	Imola	62,600	82.10	51,400	99.45	C	62,300	Bologna, Emilia-Romagna. Pottery, glassware, strawberries. Church of S. Domenico (1430). D=RCC.
3826	Imperia	41,400	84.40	35,000	99.75	C	41,200	Capital of Imperia, Liguria. Production & export of olive oil & flowers. Tourism. F=1923. D=RCC.
3827	L'Aquila	68,100	79.80	54,300	97.15	C	67,700	Capital of L'Aquila & Abruzzi. Skiing center, summer resort. Medieval walls extant. F=1270. D=RCC.
3828	La Spezia	186,000	83.90	156,000	99.25	C	185,000	Capital of La Spezia, Liguria. Major naval base. Shipbuilding, iron. Roman origins. D=RCC.
3829	Latina	106,000	80.10	84,800	97.45	C	105,000	Capital of Latina, Lazio. Beet-sugar, fruit, vegetables, glass. F=1932. D=RCC.
3830	Lecce	103,000	83.40	85,700	98.75	C	102,000	Capital of Lecce, Puglia. Flour milling, olive oil, religious paper-mache. Diocese (6th century). D=RCC.
3831	Lecco	46,000	84.50	38,900	99.85	C	45,800	Como, Lombardia. Tourist center, metals, mechanical, textiles, food-canning, local cheese. D=RCC.
3832	Livorno	172,000	83.70	144,000	99.05	C	171,000	Capital of Livorno, Toscana. Large port. Import/export. Shipbuilding. Cathedral (1595). D=RCC.
3833	Lucca	86,800	84.20	73,100	99.55	C	86,300	Capital of Lucca, Toscana. Market town, olive oil, silk. Early episcopal see. Numerous churches. D=RCC.
3834	Manfredonia	58,400	82.00	47,800	99.35	C	58,000	Foggia, Puglia. Archepiscopal see. Agriculture, fishing. F=1260. 1st century Christianity nearby. D=RCC.
3835	Mantova (Mantua)	54,400	84.10	45,800	99.45	C	54,200	Capital of Mantova, Lombardia. Processing & shipping agricultural produce. Cathedral (16th century). D=RCC.
3836	Marsala	77,500	84.50	65,500	99.85	C	77,100	Trapani, Sicily. Marsala wine, fishing. F=397 BC. Named by Saracens. D=RCC.
3837	Massa	146,000	84.40	123,000	99.75	C	145,000	Capital of Massa-Carrara, Toscana. Marble, office furniture. 15th century cathedral. D=RCC.
3838	Carrara	68,800	85.00	58,400	99.65	C	68,400	Processing & export of marble. Ligurian Sea. Medieval cathedral, damaged in WWII. D=RCC.
3839	Matera	55,100	84.20	46,400	99.55	C	54,800	Capital of Matera, Basilicata. Tufa quarrying, ceramics. Cavelike houses. Cathedral (1268). D=RCC.
3840	Messina	276,000	82.20	227,000	99.55	C	274,000	Capital of Messina, Sicily. Port, trade, citrus fruit. F=c730 BC. Byzantine church. D=RCC.
3841	Milano (Milan)	4,251,000	77.00	3,273,000	99.35	C	4,251,000	Capital of Milan, Lombardia in Po River Valley. Leading financial center. Medieval Duomo church. D=RCC.
3842	Busto Arsizio	77,300	80.00	61,800	97.35	C	76,800	Textiles, cotton. Renaissance church of Santa Maria di Piazza (1515). Center of cotton industry. D=RCC.
3843	Cinisello Balsamo	75,900	79.00	59,900	96.35	C	75,500	Milano. North of downtown. Highly diversified industries, fabricated metals, machinery, chemicals, paper. D=RCC.
3844	Cologno Monzese	51,000	80.00	40,800	97.35	C	50,800	Milano. Northeast. East of Sesto San Giovanni. Industry, tourism, chemicals. D=RCC.
3845	Legnano	50,200	80.00	40,200	97.35	C	50,000	On Olona River. Metals, cotton, machinery. Church of San Magno (1529). D=RCC.
3846	Monza	122,000	79.00	96,000	96.35	C	121,000	On Lambro River. Felt hats, carpets, textiles. Cathedral (595) by Theodelinda. Autodromo. D=RCC.
3847	Rho	51,800	80.00	41,500	97.35	C	51,500	Milano. Northwest of the city. Railroad junction, metallurgy, chemicals, textiles, paper, food processing. D=RCC.
3848	Sesto San Giovanni	85,500	79.00	67,500	96.35	C	85,000	Blast furnaces, foundries, glassworks, chemicals, aircraft, textiles. Bastion of Italian communism. D=RCC.
3849	Modena	178,000	83.90	150,000	99.25	C	177,000	Capital of Modena, Emilia-Romagna. Auto industry. Urban renewal. F=218 BC. Cathedral (1099). D=RCC.
3850	Molfetta	66,900	84.30	56,400	99.65	C	66,500	Bari, Puglia. Port on Adriatic Sea. Fishing, boatbuilding. Episcopal see. Old Cathedral (12th century). D=RCC.
3851	Napoli (Naples)	3,012,000	79.00	2,379,000	99.35	C	3,012,000	Capital of Naples, Campania. Tyrrhenian Seaport. Intellectual and financial center. Duomo (1279). D=RCC.
3852	Afragola	60,100	80.00	48,100	97.35	C	59,800	North beyond Capodichino Airport. Cereals, fruit, hemp, canning, poultry farming. Angevin castle. D=RCC.
3853	Aversa	50,500	83.00	41,900	99.75	C	50,300	Caserta, Campania. Shoemaking, wine. F=1030 by Normans. 11th century cathedral. Episcopal see. D=RCC.
3854	Casoria	79,600	82.00	65,300	99.35	C	79,200	Napoli. North of downtown near Capodichino Airport. Heavy damage by earthquake in 1980. D=RCC.
3855	Castellammare di Stabia	69,000	80.00	55,200	97.35	C	68,600	Hot mineral springs, beaches, summer resort, shipyard, arsenal. Episcopal see. D=RCC.
3856	Ercolano (Resina)	61,100	81.00	49,500	98.35	C	60,700	Built on lava. Bathing resort, excursions to Mt. Vesuvius. Tears of Christ wine. D=RCC.
3857	Giugliano in Campania	59,300	83.00	49,200	99.75	C	59,000	Napoli. North beyond Marano di Napoli. Secondary manufacturing center. D=RCC.
3858	Portici	68,100	84.00	57,200	99.85	C	67,700	Fishing, agriculture. Destroyed by Mt. Vesuvius in 1631. Royal palace of Two Sicilies. D=RCC.
3859	Pozzuoli	76,000	80.00	60,800	97.35	C	75,600	Bathing resort, food-processing, fishing. F=c529 BC by Greeks. Roman ruins. Episcopal see. D=RCC.
3860	San Giorgio a Cremano	62,400	84.00	52,400	99.85	C	62,000	Napoli. West of downtown. North of Mt Vesuvius. Tomato canning, clothing. D=RCC.
3861	Torre Annunziata	50,500	83.00	41,900	99.75	C	50,200	Napoli. Southeast on Gulf of Naples near Pompei. Foot of Mt. Vesuvius. Port, resort area. D=RCC.
3862	Torre del Greco	102,000	79.00	80,400	96.35	C	101,000	Built on lava. Bathing resort, fishing, coral craftsmanship, chemicals. 2/3 destroyed in 1631. D=RCC.
3863	Nicastro	69,900	84.50	59,100	99.85	C	69,600	Northern Catanzaro west of Catanzaro. Wine, olive oil, wheat, fruit. Ancient castle ruins. D=RCC.
3864	Nocera Inferiore	49,200	81.30	40,000	98.65	C	48,900	Salerno, Campania. Episcopal see. Agricultural exports, lumbering, textiles. Old churches & convents. D=RCC.
3865	Novara	104,000	80.40	83,400	97.75	C	103,000	Capital of Novara, Piedmont. Rice, cotton, silk. Ancient baptistery. Roman origins. D=RCC.
3866	Padova (Padua)	271,000	84.70	230,000	99.55	C	270,000	Capital of Padova, Veneto. Botanical garden (1545). Medieval churches. F=302 BC. University (1222). D=RCC.
3867	Palermo	700,000	80.50	563,000	98.85	C	696,000	Capital of Sicily. Manufacturing, citrus fruits. Endemic poverty. F=8th century BC. D=RCC.
3868	Parma	175,000	83.20	145,000	99.75	C	174,000	Capital of Parma, Emilia-Romagna on Parma River. Cheese. F=183 BC. Episcopal see (4th cent). D=RCC.
3869	Paterno	46,200	84.50	39,000	99.85	C	45,900	Catania, Sicily. Holiday resort, hot springs, fruits, grapes. Ancient origins. Medieval churches. D=RCC.
3870	Pavia	80,400	84.50	67,900	99.85	C	80,000	Capital of Pavia, Lombardia. Communications, agriculture. Ancient Ticinum. Carthusian monastery. D=RCC.
3871	Perugia	151,000	84.10	127,000	99.45	C	150,000	Capital of Perugia & Umbria. Chocolate. Ancient origins. Church of S. Angelo (5th century). D=RCC.
3872	Pesaro	90,700	83.90	76,100	99.25	C	90,200	Capital of Pesaro e Urbino, Marche. Adriatic Seaport. Resort, agriculture. Museum of majolica. D=RCC.
3873	Pescara	129,000	83.20	107,000	99.75	C	128,000	Capital of Pescara, Abruzzi. Adriatic Seaport. Resort, fishing. Founded as Roman Arternum. D=RCC.
3874	Piacenza	103,000	83.30	85,500	99.75	C	102,000	Capital of Piacenza, Emilia-Romagna on Po River. Cereal, viticulture. F=218 BC as Placentia. D=RCC.
3875	Pisa	102,000	84.10	85,700	99.45	C	101,000	Capital of Pisa, Tuscanyen Arno River. Tourism, leaning tower. Christian bishopric since 313. D=RCC.
3876	Pistoia	87,600	82.10	71,900	99.45	C	87,100	Capital of Pistoia, Tuscany. Lace, flowers. Medieval city center. Bishopric since 5th century. D=RCC.
3877	Pordenone	50,400	84.20	42,500	99.55	C	50,200	Capital of Pordenone, Friuli-Venezia. Giulia. Motor vehicles. Founded as Roman Portus Naonis. D=RCC.
3878	Potenza	68,800	84.40	58,000	99.75	C	68,400	Capital of Potenza, Basilicata. Orchards. F=2nd century BC. Episcopal see. Medieval churches. D=RCC.
3879	Prato (Prato in Toscana)	216,000	83.90	181,000	99.25	C	215,000	Firenze, Toscana on Bisenzio River. Wool, cement, textiles. Medieval churches. D=RCC.
3880	Quartu Sant'Elena	61,100	80.00	48,900	97.35	C	60,800	Southern Cagliari, Sicily on Gulf of Cagliari. Distilleries, paper mills, brickworks, nuts. D=RCC.
3881	Ragusa	69,700	74.80	52,100	92.15	C	69,300	Capital of Ragusa, Sicily. Asphalt mining, oil, cement. Ancient Hybla Heraea. Episcopal see. D=RCC.

Table 10-5–continued opposite

Table 10-5–continued

Rec No 1	*Country City* 2	*Pop 2000* 3	*AC%* 4	*Church Members* 5	*E%* 6	*W* 7	*Pop 2025* 8	*Notes* 9
3882	Ravenna	137,000	80.20	110,000	97.55	C	137,000	Capital of Ravenna, Emilia-Romagna. Petroleum. F=1400 BC. Oldest Christian mosaics extant. D=RCC.
3883	Reggio di Calabria	179,000	82.90	149,000	99.75	C	178,000	Capital of Reggio di Calabria, Calabria. Port on Strait of Messina. Tourism, perfume. F=720 BC. D=RCC.
3884	Reggio nell'Emilia	132,000	83.70	111,000	99.05	C	132,000	Capital of Reggio nell'Emilia, Emilia-Romagna. Agriculture, wine, cheese. F=2nd century BC. D=RCC.
3885	Rimini	131,000	80.00	105,000	97.35	C	131,000	Forli, Emilia-Romagna. Beach resort, tourism. Site of Council of Rimini (359) over Arian controversy. D=RCC.
3886	ROMA (Rome)	2,688,000	77.00	2,070,000	99.35	C	2,688,000	Capital of Rome, Lazio. Tourism, commerce, government. F=1500 BC. Spiritual capital of RCC. 'Eternal City'.
3887	Tivoli	52,200	83.00	43,300	99.75	C	51,900	Landmark in history of architecture. Tourism, paper-making. Inhabited since prehistoric times. D=RCC.
3888	Rovigo	52,900	84.60	44,800	99.95	C	52,600	Capital of Rovigo, Veneto. Agricultural market. First mentioned in 838. D=RCC.
3889	Salerno	251,000	79.10	198,000	96.45	C	250,000	Capital of Salerno, Campania. Tyrrhenian sea port. Foodstuffs. San Matteo Church (845). D=RCC.
3890	Cava de'Tirreni	52,800	79.00	41,700	96.35	C	52,500	Resort, international sports events. Benedictine abbey (1011). 7th century Visogothic Bible. D=RCC.
3891	San Benedetto del Tronto	45,400	84.10	38,200	99.45	C	45,200	Ascoli Piceno on Adriatic Sea north of Pescara. Important seaport, metals, machinery, apparel. D=RCC.
3892	San Remo	59,500	81.50	48,500	98.85	C	59,200	Imperia. Liguria. Rivera resort. Important flower market. 12th century cathedral of S. Siro. D=RCC.
3893	San Severo	55,600	82.70	46,000	99.55	C	55,300	Foggia, Puglia. Agricultural products. Baroque churches. Earthquake (1627). D=RCC.
3894	Sassari	120,000	83.50	101,000	98.85	C	120,000	Capital of Sassari, Sardinia. Agriculture. G.A. Sanna National Museum. Romanesque churches. D=RCC.
3895	Savona	112,000	76.00	85,500	93.35	C	112,000	Capital of Savona, Liguria. Seaport. Imports coal, oil. Iron industry. Roman origins. D=RCC.
3896	Siena	58,000	82.40	47,800	99.75	C	57,700	Capital of Siena, Tuscany. Tourism, wine, agriculture. Medieval city center. Beautiful architecture & art. D=RCC.
3897	Siracusa (Syracuse)	126,000	82.00	103,000	99.35	C	125,000	Capital of Siracusa, Sicily. Tourism, fishing, agriculture. F=734 BC. Archeological remains. D=RCC.
3898	Taranto	233,000	84.30	196,000	99.65	C	232,000	Capital of Taranto, Puglia. Naval base, iron, steel. F=706 BC. Greek & Roman ruins. D=RCC.
3899	Teramo	52,700	84.20	44,400	99.55	C	52,400	Capital of Teramo, Abruzzi. Agricultural center, wool, textiles. Ancient origins. 12th century cathedral. D=RCC.
3900	Terni	110,000	83.80	92,400	99.15	C	110,000	Capital of Terni, Umbria. Metallurgy, machinery. Neolithic ruins. 5th century round church. D=RCC.
3901	Torino (Turin)	1,294,000	79.50	1,029,000	99.35	C	1,294,000	Capital of Torino, Piemonte on Po River. Wine. Ecclesiastical architecture. Ancient Roman origins. D=RCC.
3902	Collegno	47,400	82.00	38,800	99.35	C	47,100	Torino. West of downtown. North of Grugliasco. Dora Riparia River. Industrial center, foundries. D=RCC.
3903	Moncalieri	58,600	81.00	47,500	98.35	C	58,300	Foundries, canneries. Saint Maria della Scala church (14th century). Textiles, paper products, plastics. D=RCC.
3904	Rivoli	52,100	80.00	41,600	97.35	C	51,800	Textiles. Patrician residences. Castle (1712). Fabricated metals, plastics, 18th century villas. D=RCC.
3905	Trani	49,500	80.00	39,600	97.35	C	49,200	Northern Bari on Adriatic Sea west of Bari. Seaport, resort, famous for wine. 13th century castle. D=RCC.
3906	Trapani	69,500	67.10	46,600	89.45	C	69,100	Capital of Trapani, Sicily. Port. Exports salt, wine. Tunny fishing. 14th century church of San Agortino. D=RCC.
3907	Trento	103,000	82.20	84,300	99.55	C	102,000	Capital of Trento, Trentino-Alto Adige. First Bishop, St. Vigilius, converts whole city (4th century). D=RCC.
3908	Treviso	84,200	84.50	71,200	99.85	C	83,800	Capital of Treviso, Veneto. Agricultural market center, rice, paper. Celtic origins. Christian frescoes. D=RCC.
3909	Trieste	232,000	81.90	190,000	99.25	C	231,000	Capital of Friuli-Venezia Giulia, Trieste. Adriatic seaport. Roman ruins. Cathedrals. 10% Slovene. D=RCC.
3910	Udine	127,000	83.10	105,000	99.75	C	126,000	Capital of Udine, Friuli-Venezia Giulia. Ironworks, cotton mills, tanneries. RCC patriarchate (1238-1751). D=RCC.
3911	Varese	85,700	84.50	72,500	99.85	C	85,300	Capital of Varese, Lombardia. Leather goods, shoes. Pilgrimage church Sante Maria del Monte (1684). D=RCC.
3912	Venezia (Venice)	422,000	81.00	342,000	98.85	C	419,000	Capital of Venezia, Veneto. Major seaport. 400 bridges. Tourism, music. Church of San Zanipolo (1430). D=RCC.
3913	Mestre	183,000	83.00	152,000	99.75	C	182,000	Marghera & Porto Marghera industrial districts. Chemical, glass. Roman origins. D=RCC.
3914	Vercelli	50,400	84.60	42,600	99.95	C	50,100	Capital of Vercelli, Piemonte on Sesia River. Rice market. Ancient origins. Bishopric since 4th century. D=RCC.
3915	Verona	260,000	81.60	212,000	98.95	C	259,000	Capital of Verona, Veneto. Many roman remains. Cereal market, horse Fair. Medieval painting center. D=RCC.
3916	Viareggio	60,800	84.50	51,400	99.85	C	60,500	Lucca, Toscana on Ligurian Sea. Seaside resort, famous beach, yachts, fishing port. D=RCC.
3917	Vicenza	110,000	84.20	92,400	99.55	C	109,000	Capital of Vicenza, Veneto. Engineering, food-processing. Episcopal see. 4th century church. D=RCC.
3918	Vigevano	61,600	84.60	52,100	99.95	C	61,300	Pavia, Lombardia on Ticino River. International Shoe Fair & Market, textiles. Bishopric. D=RCC.
3919	Viterbo	60,500	84.40	51,000	99.75	C	60,100	Capital of Viterbo, Lazio. Etruscan origin. Agriculture. Episcopal see (1193). Tombs of 2 popes. D=RCC.
3920	Vittoria	57,200	83.50	47,800	98.85	C	56,900	Ragusa, Sicily. Wine, olive oil, fruit, vegetables. F=1607. Madre church (18th century). D=RCC.
	IVORY COAST	**14,786,000**	**29.45**	**4,354,000**	**72.75**	**B**	**23,345,000**	**ROMAN CATHOLICS 14.7%, INDEPENDENTS 9.2%. PENT-CHAR 8.2%, EVANGELICAL 4.5%, GCC 13.7%**
3921	rural areas	7,906,000	31.58	2,496,000	71.40	B	9,058,000	86.8% (1950), 72.5% (1970), 59.5% (1990), 53.4% (2000), 47.2% (2010), 38.8% (2025)
3922	urban areas	6,880,000	27.00	1,858,000	74.30	B	14,287,000	13.1% (1950), 27.4% (1970), 40.4% (1990), 46.5% (2000), 52.7% (2010), 61.2% (2025)
3923	non-metropolitan areas	2,178,000	27.17	592,000	74.34	B	5,102,604	*Sources of data:* Censuses of 1960, 1975, and 1988.
3924	metropolitan areas	4,702,000	26.92	1,266,000	74.28	B	9,185,000	*Definition:* Urban agglomeration containing more than 10,000 inhabitants.
3925	ABIDJAN	3,359,000	30.00	1,008,000	79.10	B	6,395,000	Port, center of French-speaking West Africa. Coffee, cocoa. Petroleum docks. F=1903. D=RCC,TBH.
3926	Bouake	501,000	35.00	175,000	86.30	B	1,040,000	Commercial hub of the interior. Cotton, tobacco. Trade center for Baule people. RCC bishopric.
3927	Daloa	195,000	3.00	5,800	38.30	A	405,000	Chief collecting point for forest region. Beta, Guro, Baule, Diula, Mossi. D=RCC bishopric,Protestant church.
3928	Gagnoa	178,000	4.00	7,100	39.30	A	370,000	Collecting point for exports. Market center for Bete & Gagu peoples. D=RCC diocese,Independents.
3929	Korhogo	228,000	3.00	6,800	38.30	A	473,000	Chief trade center for Senufo farmers, Muslim Fulani. French Catholics (19th century). D=RCC,TBH.
3930	Man	95,800	5.00	4,800	40.30	A	199,000	Ko River. Chief trade center for Dau & Guereor Wobe peoples. Diula craftsmen. D=RCC,Independents.
3931	YAMOUSSOUKRO	146,000	40.00	58,300	91.30	B	303,000	President Felix Houphouet-Boigny's home. Fishing, forestry. Basilica-largest church in the world. D=RCC.
	JAMAICA	**2,583,000**	**43.43**	**1,122,000**	**98.93**	**B**	**3,245,000**	**PROTESTANTS 24.9%, INDEPENDENTS 8.9%. PENT-CHAR 14.9%, EVANGELICAL 11.7%, GCC 24.6%**
3932	rural areas	1,134,000	42.07	477,000	98.21	B	1,033,000	73.2% (1950), 58.4% (1970), 48.5% (1990), 43.9% (2000), 38.9% (2010), 31.8% (2025)
3933	urban areas	1,449,000	44.50	645,000	99.50	B	2,212,000	26.7% (1950), 41.5% (1970), 51.4% (1990), 56.0% (2000), 61.0% (2010), 68.1% (2025)
3934	non-metropolitan areas	400,000	44.56	178,000	99.42	B	610,226	*Sources of data:* Censuses of 1960, 1970, 1982, and 1991.
3935	metropolitan areas	1,049,000	44.48	467,000	99.53	B	1,602,000	*Definition:* Kingston metropolitan area and selected main towns.
3936	KINGSTON-St Andrew	882,000	44.00	388,000	99.50	B	1,346,000	Recreational & tourist resort. F=1692. University of the West Indies (1962). Church of St. Thomas (1699). D=SDA.
3937	Portmore	84,600	45.00	38,100	99.80	B	129,000	West on Caribbean Sea. D=Baptists,Church of God,Anglican,SDA,RCC.
3938	Spanish Town	386,000	44.00	170,000	99.50	B	589,000	Bananas, sugarcane, annatto. F=c1523 by Diego Columbus. St. Catherine's Cathedral (1655). D=SDA,JBU,RCC.
3939	Montego Bay	167,000	47.00	78,700	99.70	B	256,000	Tourism resort, commercial center & port. Exports fruit. Arawak village (1494). St. James Church (1775). D=SDA.
	JAPAN	**126,714,000**	**2.71**	**3,437,000**	**66.94**	**B**	**121,150,000**	**INDEPENDENTS 1.2%, MARGINAL CHRISTIANS 0.5%. PENT-CHAR 1.3%, EVANGELICAL 0.3%, GCC 2.4%**
3940	rural areas	26,762,000	2.95	788,000	52.23	B	19,081,000	49.7% (1950), 28.7% (1970), 22.6% (1990), 21.1% (2000), 19.1% (2010), 15.7% (2025)
3941	urban areas	99,952,000	2.65	2,649,000	70.88	B	102,069,000	50.3% (1950), 71.2% (1970), 77.3% (1990), 78.8% (2000), 80.8% (2010), 84.2% (2025)
3942	non-metropolitan areas	16,476,000	2.65	436,000	70.40	B	16,556,105	*Sources of data:* Censuses of 1970, 1975, 1980, 1985, and 1990; estimates for 1950, 1955, 1960 and 1965.
3943	metropolitan areas	83,476,000	2.65	2,212,000	70.97	B	85,513,000	*Definition:* City (*shi*) having 50,000 or more inhabitants with 60% or more of the houses in main areas.
3944	Aizu-wakamatsu	122,000	1.00	1,200	65.23	B	124,000	Fukushima, Honshu. Lacquer ware, ceramics, tourism. Hot springs. F=1590.
3945	Akita	310,000	1.00	3,100	65.23	B	316,000	Akita, Honshu. Petroleum, chemicals. HQ of Lutheran Brethren Mission of Japan (begun 1949).
3946	Ako	52,300	0.30	160	64.53	B	53,500	Hyogo, Honshu. Polluted industrial city, chemicals, steel mills. F=794. Kabuki theatre.
3947	Anan	60,400	0.40	240	64.63	B	61,700	Tokushima, Shikoku on Naka-gawa. Lime, timber, ships, wooden goods. F=1958.
3948	Anjo	146,000	1.00	1,500	65.23	B	149,000	Aichi, Honshu. Textiles, model farm community (rice, wheat). Automotive parts, annual festival.
3949	Aomori	295,000	0.96	2,800	65.19	B	301,000	Aomori, Honshu. Transportation center. 468 Koreans. 85% Buddhist. D=RCC,UCCJ,&c. Aomori Christian Centre.
3950	Asahikawa (Asahigawa)	368,000	1.00	3,700	65.23	B	375,000	Hokkaido on Ishikari River. Brewing, pulp, paper. F=1889. Ainu reservation nearby.
3951	Ashikaga	172,000	1.00	1,700	65.23	B	175,000	Tochigi, Honshu on Watarase River. Textiles, agriculture. F=9th century. Confucian shrine, 2 Buddhist temples.
3952	Atami	48,400	0.30	150	64.53	B	49,400	Shizouka, Honshu. Built on extinct volcano crater. Resort since AD 500. Atami tropical garden, art museum.
3953	Beppu	133,000	1.00	1,300	65.23	B	136,000	Oita, Kyushu. Hot Springs resort, tourism, bamboo industry, volcanic research institute.
3954	Chichibu	62,400	0.40	250	64.63	B	63,700	Saitama, Honshu on Ara River. 450 silk textile mills. Tourism. Shinto shrine. Night Festival.
3955	Chitose	80,800	0.50	400	64.73	B	82,500	Hokkaido. Tourist center for Shikotsu-Toya National Park. Chitose River. Adzuki beans, lumber, dairying, airport.
3956	Chosi	87,200	0.50	440	64.73	B	89,000	Chiba, Honshu on Tone River. Deep sea fishing, soy sauce, tourism. F=17th century.
3957	Eniwa	56,900	1.00	570	65.23	B	58,100	Hokkaido near Sapporo. Pumpkins, goldfish, crayfish, turtles. Training grounds for Japan self-defense.
3958	Fuchu	51,300	1.80	920	66.03	B	52,300	Hiroshima, Honshu. Aluminum products, furniture, precision equipment. Known for splash patterned cloth.
3959	Fuji	379,000	1.00	3,800	65.23	B	387,000	Shizuoka, Honshu at Mt. Fuji. Chemicals, automobiles. Base for ascent of Mt. Fugi.
3960	Fujinomiya	120,000	1.00	1,200	65.23	B	122,000	Sengen Shrine (9th century). Pilgrims, tourists, dairies, paper pulp. Tea, tobacco.
3961	Fuji-yoshida	56,100	0.40	220	64.63	B	57,300	Yamanashi north of Mt. Fuji. Katsura River. Communications center for Mt. Fuji region. Fire festival, watercress.
3962	Fujioka	62,400	1.00	620	65.23	B	63,800	Gumma, Honshu near Takasaki. Tone River. Clay tiles, Edo-era mathematician Seki Takakazu born here.
3963	Fukaya	96,300	0.50	480	64.73	B	98,300	Saitama, Honshu. Early market & post town. Ceramic tile production. Televisions, earthenware pipe, spring onions.
3964	Fukuchiyama	68,100	0.40	270	64.63	B	69,500	Kyoto, Honshu on Yura River west of Ayabe. Important railroad junction, major castle town during the Edo era.
3965	Fukui	259,000	1.25	3,200	65.48	B	264,000	Honshu. Silk, textiles. 65% Buddhist, 14% New-Religionist, 10% nonreligious. 10 clergy, 4 kindergartens.
3966	Fukuoka	1,792,000	3.00	53,700	72.23	B	1,830,000	Capital of Fukuoka, Kyushu. Ancient port, fishing. 5,200 Koreans. D=Spirit of Jesus Church,RCC.
3967	Chikushino	72,000	2.60	1,900	66.83	B	73,500	Fukuoka, Kyushu south of Fukuoka. Near Dazaifu. Computer components, textiles, fishing, railroad.
3968	Dazaifu	63,900	2.70	1,700	66.93	B	65,200	Fukuoka, Kyushu south of Fukuoka beyond Onojo. Fishing, railroad, heavy electronics, industry, colleges.
3969	Kasuga	90,800	2.70	2,500	66.93	B	92,700	Fukuoka south of Fukuoka city near Onojo. Fishing industry, electronics industry, chemicals, university.
3970	Onojo	77,000	0.40	310	64.63	B	78,600	Fukuoka, Kyushu south of Fukuoka near Kasuga. Fishing, textiles, computers, electronics, many schools.
3971	Fukushima	284,000	1.00	2,800	65.23	B	290,000	Honshu. Agriculture. HQ of Central Japan Pioneer Mission (1925), Baptist Mid-Missions in Japan (1949).
3972	Fukuyama	374,000	2.00	7,500	66.23	B	382,000	Hiroshima, Honshu. Spinning industry, kotos (harps), machinery. Originally small fishing village.
3973	Furukawa	65,800	0.40	260	64.63	B	67,100	Miyagi, Honshu. Northeast Japan on the Eai River. Electrical appliances, rice, other agriculture.
3974	Gamagori	86,800	0.50	430	64.73	B	88,700	Aichi, Honshu on Mikawa Bay. Cotton textiles, mandarin oranges, seaside resort, hot springs. Take-shima.
3975	Gifu	420,000	2.00	8,400	66.23	B	429,000	Gifu, Honshu. Paper lanterns, trout fishing, forestry, agriculture. Frequent earthquakes.
3976	Ginowan	70,900	0.40	280	64.63	B	72,400	Okinawa south of Okinawa city. Southwest Japan. Large United States Kadena Air Force base nearby.
3977	Gotemba	81,500	0.50	410	64.73	B	83,200	Shizuoka, Honshu. Recreational & tourist center. Mulberry trees for silkworms. Base for ascent of Mt. Fuji.
3978	Gushikawa	55,300	1.20	660	65.43	B	56,500	East Okinawa on Philippine Sea. Sugarcane, sweet potatoes, rice, sugar refineries, livestock, fishing.
3979	Gyoda	85,200	0.50	430	64.73	B	87,000	Saitama, Honshu. Clothing, electric appliances, rubber goods. Ancient origins.
3980	Hachinohe	247,000	1.00	2,500	65.23	B	252,000	Aomori, Honshu on Pacific Ocean. Deep sea fishing port, scenic beauty, marine products.
3981	Hagi	51,800	0.30	160	64.53	B	52,900	Yamaguchi, Honshu on Abu River delta. Pottery, bamboo work. Sho Temple, Hagi Castle. F=1600.
3982	Hakodate	315,000	1.00	3,100	65.23	B	321,000	Hokkaido. Fishing. Ainu, Gilyak peoples. Trappist convent for women (1898). Russian church (1859).
3983	Hamada	50,300	0.30	150	64.53	B	51,400	Shimane, Honshu on Sea of Japan. Fishing and commercial port, dried globefish. Iwami Kagura temple.
3984	Hamakita	83,100	0.50	420	64.73	B	84,800	Shizouka, Honshu on Tenryu River. 500 cotton factories, agriculture. Engine manufacturing. Bonsai technology.
3985	Hamamatsu	547,000	2.00	10,900	66.23	B	559,000	Shizouka, Honshu on Pacific coast. Pianos, motorcycles, eel cultivation, tea, textiles.
3986	Hashima	62,900	0.40	250	64.63	B	64,300	Gifu on Kiso River east of Ogaki. 5 miles south of Gifu. Textiles, agriculture, markets, fishing.
3987	Hekinan	67,500	0.30	200	64.53	B	68,900	Aichi, Honshu. Transport equipment, rice, salt, sake, pottery, roof tile. F=1948 by merger.
3988	Hikone	102,000	0.60	610	64.83	B	104,000	Shiga, Honshu on Lake Biwa. Tourist center, textiles, cement, pulp. F=1603 around castle.
3989	Himeji	676,000	2.00	13,500	66.23	B	690,000	Hyogo, Honshu. Iron, steel, textiles, leather goods. F=14th century around castle. 'Egret castle'.
3990	Himi	62,200	0.40	250	64.63	B	63,500	Toyama, Honshu on Toyama Bay north of Takaoka. 16 miles north of Toyama. Fisheries.
3991	Hirosaki	179,000	1.00	1,800	65.23	B	183,000	Aomori, Honshu. Green laquerware, apple products. F=1611 around castle.
3992	Hiroshima	912,000	1.90	17,300	74.13	B	931,000	Capital of Hiroshima, Honshu. Spiritual center of peace movement. 8,400 Koreans. D=RCC,YMCA,YWCA.
3993	Hatsukaichi	64,900	0.40	260	64.63	B	66,300	Hiroshima southwest on Hiroshima Bay. Oysters, wood working, tallest Buddha statue in Japan.
3994	Higashihiroshima	96,400	0.50	480	64.73	B	98,500	Hiroshima east of Fuchu. Rebuilt in post-WWII years. 16 miles east of Hiroshima. Stereos, electronics, sake.
3995	Kure	222,000	1.65	3,700	65.88	B	227,000	Natural harbour. Merchant ships, oil tankers. Large shipbuilding, semiconductors, whetstone, dried cuttlefish.
3996	Hita	66,200	0.40	270	64.63	B	67,600	Oita, Kyushu. Market for rice, wheat, vegetables. Lumber, wooden clogs. Summer resort, Mikuma Rapids.
3997	Hitachi	207,000	1.00	2,100	65.23	B	211,000	Ibaraki, Honshu. Commercial harbour, copper mining (1591), electric appliances, machinery.
3998	Hofu	120,000	0.67	810	64.90	B	123,000	Yamaguchi, Honshu on Inland Sea. Textiles, chemicals. Prehistoric remains. Temman Shrine (9th century)
3999	Honjo	60,500	0.40	240	64.63	B	61,800	Northern Saitama, Honshu near Tone River. Communications equipment, spring onions, cucumbers.

Table 10-5–continued overleaf

Table 10-5–continued

Rec No 1	Country City 2	Pop 2000 3	AC% 4	Church Members 5	E% 6	W 7	Pop 2025 8	Notes 9
4000	Hyuga	59,800	0.40	240	64.63	B	61,100	Miyazaki, Kyushu on Hyuga Strait. Citrons, clams, traditional game pieces, tables, research center.
4001	Ichinoseki	63,400	0.40	250	64.63	B	64,800	Iwate, Honshu. Near Mt. Kurikona. Computers, Sukawa hot spring, Gembi Gorge nearby.
4002	Iida	94,000	0.50	470	64.73	B	96,000	Nagano, Honshu near Tenryu River. Hot springs, mountainous, raw silk industry, rice growing, lumbering.
4003	Iizuka	113,000	0.60	680	64.83	B	115,000	Fukuoka, Kyushu. On Onga River. Former mining center. Commercial center & railway hub.
4004	Imabari	126,000	1.00	1,300	65.23	B	129,000	Ehime, Shikoku on Inland Sea. 150 cotton cloth factories. Brisk trade. First port opened to foreign trade.
4005	Imari	62,300	0.40	250	64.63	B	63,700	Saga, Kyushu. Porcelain, lumber, marine products. Protected harbour. Former base for Japanese pirates.
4006	Ina	61,500	0.40	250	64.63	B	62,800	Nagano, Honshu on Tenryu River south of Okaya. Agricultural. Microscopes, resistors, condensers.
4007	Isahaya	92,800	0.50	460	64.73	B	94,800	Nagasaki, Kyushu. National park. Agriculture, tourism. Rice cakes, baked eel, electronics. F=13th century.
4008	Ise (Uji-yamada)	107,000	1.50	1,600	65.73	B	109,000	Mie, Honshu. Many Shinto shrines. 65% Shinto, 14% Buddhist, 10% New-Religionist. 5 clergy, 3 kindergartens.
4009	Isesaki	119,000	1.00	1,200	65.23	B	121,000	Gumma, Honshu. Silk weaving, textiles. F=17th century around castle.Castle town of Sakai family.
4010	Ishinomaki	125,000	0.50	620	64.73	B	128,000	Miyagi, Honshu. 2 clinics. F=4th century. 99% Buddhist. D=RCC,UCCJ,Orthodox.
4011	Ito	72,900	0.40	290	64.63	B	74,500	Shizouka, Honshu on Izu Peninsula. 400 hot springs, resort, fishing. Otonashi shrine.
4012	Iwaki (Taira)	364,000	1.00	3,600	65.23	B	372,000	Fukushima, Honshu on Pacific Ocean. Chemicals, tobacco, lumber, mining. F=17th century.
4013	Iwakuni	112,000	4.00	4,500	68.23	B	115,000	Yamaguchi, Honshu. Petrochemicals. F=1603. 4% USA at USAF military base. D=RCC,C&MA,Nazarene.
4014	Iwamizawa	82,300	0.50	410	64.73	B	84,100	Hokkaido east of Sapporo. Vegetables, onions, cabbage lily roots, trench diggers.
4015	Iwata	85,500	0.50	430	64.73	B	87,300	Southern Shizouka on Enshu Strait near mouth of Tenryu River. Motorcycles, sushi-making machines, melons.
4016	Izumo	84,600	0.50	420	64.73	B	86,400	Shimane, Honshu. Agriculture, stock raising, silk. Shinto religious center. In October festival of the gods.
4017	Joetsu	133,000	1.00	1,300	65.23	B	136,000	Niigata, Honshu inland from Sea of Japan. Textiles, agricultural machinery, wooden furniture, lace. Castle ruins.
4018	Kaga	70,800	0.40	280	64.63	B	72,300	Ishikawa, Honshu on Daishoji River. Electrical machinery. Tourist center for temples, hot springs. F=1958.
4019	Kagoshima	549,000	2.60	14,300	66.83	B	561,000	Kagoshima, Kyushu. Well-protected harbor. Naval yard, rockets, silk. Y=1549 (F. Xavier). D=RCC.
4020	Kakamigahara	133,000	1.00	1,300	65.23	B	136,000	Southern Gifu east of Gifu. Central Honshu. Agricultural and commercial center, aircraft manufacturing.
4021	Kakegawa	74,500	0.40	300	64.63	B	76,100	Southern Shizuoka east of Hamamatsu. Agricultural center for tea, Kappu textiles.
4022	Kamaishi	53,700	0.30	160	64.53	B	54,900	Iwate, Honshu on Pacific Ocean. Fishing port, mining, iron & steel imports.
4023	Kameoka	87,300	0.50	440	64.73	B	89,200	Kyoto on Katsura River west of Kyoto. Beef cattle, matsutake mushrooms, chestnuts, adzuki beans, bamboo.
4024	Kanazawa	453,000	1.50	6,800	65.73	B	463,000	Capital of Ishikawa on Sai River. Porcelain, silk. 1 college, 15 kindergartens. D=7 UCCJ churches.
4025	Kanoya	79,500	0.50	400	64.73	B	81,200	Kagoshima, Kyushu. Sweet potatoes, cereals, alcohol, starch. Former Navy base.
4026	Kanuma	92,200	0.50	460	64.73	B	94,100	Tochigi, Honshu. Lumber, furniture, rope, brooms. Source of gardening soil.
4027	Karatsu	81,100	0.50	410	64.73	B	82,800	Saga, Kyushu on Karatsu Bay. Chemicals, ceramics, fishing, tourism. Ancient trade port with China.
4028	Kasai	53,000	0.30	160	64.53	B	54,100	Hyogo, Honshu north of Himeji. 24 miles north of Kobe. Appliance manufacturing.
4029	Kasaoka	61,000	0.40	240	64.63	B	62,300	Okayama, Honshu on Inland Sea. Old temple town. Textiles, fruit, flowers.
4030	Kashiwazaki	90,400	0.50	450	64.73	B	92,300	Niigata, Honshu on Sea of Japan. Oil refineries. Hot springs resort.
4031	Katsuta	112,000	1.00	1,100	65.23	B	115,000	Ibaraki, Honshu on Naka River. Electric locomotives, electric machinery.
4032	Kesennuma	67,100	0.40	270	64.63	B	68,600	Miyagi, Honshu on Pacific Ocean. Deep sea fishing, oysters, textiles.
4033	Kimitsu	91,400	0.50	460	64.73	B	93,300	Chiba, Honshu on Boso Peninsula and Koito River. Tokyo Bay. Iron and steel products, toothpicks, chickens.
4034	Kiryu	129,000	1.00	1,300	65.23	B	132,000	Gumma, Honshu. Brocades, satins, fine silks, rayon. Major silk production since 8th century.
4035	Kisarazu	126,000	1.00	1,300	65.23	B	129,000	Chiba, Honshu. Chemicals, iron, steel, electrical machinery. Tokyo suburb noted for Shojoji (Buddhist) temples.
4036	Kitaibaraki	52,300	0.90	470	65.13	B	53,400	Ibaraki, Honshu on Pacific Ocean. 31 miles north of Mito. Fish processing, pumpkins.
4037	Kitakyushu	2,898,000	1.90	55,100	71.13	B	3,052,000	9,900 aliens (9,138 Koreans). F=1963. D=Baptist(17 churches),UCCJ(12),RCC,Lutheran, etc.
4038	Nakama	50,400	0.30	150	64.53	B	51,500	Yamaguchi, Honshu. Heavy industry, Shimonoseki Aquarium, Akama Shrine.
4039	Shimonoseki (Aka-maga-seki)	269,000	1.46	3,900	65.69	B	275,000	2.0% aliens (5,285 Koreans). Little activity. D=UCCJ(6 churches),RCC,Lutheran,Anglican.
4040	Kitami	110,000	1.00	1,100	65.23	B	112,000	Hokkaido on Sea of Okhotsk. Peppermint refinery. Originally an Ainu settlement.
4041	Kochi	325,000	1.00	3,200	65.23	B	331,000	Kochi, Shikoku. Agricultural machinery, coral, seafood. Kochi Castle (1603).
4042	Kofu	205,000	1.00	2,100	65.23	B	210,000	Capital of Yamanashi, Honshu. Textiles, silk, hot springs. Takeda Shrine.
4043	Komatsu	109,000	1.00	1,100	65.23	B	111,000	Ishikawa, Honshu on Kakehashi River. Synthetic fibers, copper-mining machinery. F=1639.
4044	Koriyama	322,000	0.30	970	64.53	B	329,000	Fukushima, Honshu. Annual Light of the World campaign (Akira Hatori, also on radio). 99.5% Buddhist-Shintoist.
4045	Kumagaya	156,000	1.00	1,600	65.23	B	159,000	Saitama, Honshu on Ara River. Silk reeling, heavy industry. Tokyo commuters.
4046	Kumamoto	593,000	1.00	5,900	65.23	B	606,000	Capital of Kumamoto, Kyushu. F=16th century. HQ of Christian Church of the Glorious Gospel (1936).
4047	Kurashiki	425,000	0.75	3,200	64.98	B	434,000	Okayama, Honshu on Takahashi River. Cultural center, rayon textiles, heavy industry. Ohara Museum.
4048	Kuroiso	53,600	0.30	160	64.53	B	54,700	Northern Tochigi on Tohoku-Honsen Railway. 28 miles north of Utsunomiya. Tire manufacturing, dairying.
4049	Kurume	234,000	2.80	6,500	67.03	B	239,000	Fukuoka, Kyushu on Chikugo River. Patterned cotton textiles, rubber industry. Suiten Shrine (12th century).
4050	Kushiro	211,000	1.00	2,100	65.23	B	215,000	Hokkaido on Kushiro River at Pacific Ocean. Commercial & fishing port. F=1870 by 537 Japanese.
4051	Maebashi	293,000	1.00	2,900	65.23	B	299,000	Capital of Gumma, Honshu. Silk yarn. F=1338. HQ of Evangelical Missionary Church (an indigenous body).
4052	Maizuru	98,600	0.50	490	64.73	B	101,000	Kyoto, Honshu on Wakasa Bay. Natural port. Ships, textiles, pottery. F=14th century.
4053	Marugame	77,400	0.40	310	64.63	B	79,000	Kagawa, Shikoku on Inland Sea. Rice, barley. Former pilgrimage port. F=1597.
4054	Matsue	146,000	0.75	1,100	64.98	B	149,000	Capital of Shimane, Honshu. 98% Buddhist. D=RCC(1 secondary school),UCCJ(3 churches),&c.
4055	Matsumoto	205,000	1.00	2,100	65.23	B	210,000	Nagano, Honshu. Silk, tourism. HQ of Universal Evangelical Church (a Japanese indigenous denomination).
4056	Matsusaka (Matsuzaka)	122,000	1.05	1,300	65.28	B	124,000	Mie, Honshu. Beef cattle. 442 Koreans, 55 Chinese. 60% Buddhist. No public evangelism, training or media work.
4057	Matsuyama	454,000	1.22	5,500	65.45	B	463,000	Ehime, Shikoku. 793 aliens. Evangelistic radio from Tokyo. D=RCC,UCCJ(9 churches),Lutheran, et alia.
4058	Mihara	87,500	0.50	440	64.73	B	89,400	Hiroshima, Honshu. Inland Sea port. Fibers, cement, chemicals. F=1582 around castle.
4059	Mito	241,000	0.91	2,200	65.14	B	246,000	Capital of Ibaraki, Honshu. Evangelistic radio weekly from Tokyo. D=UCCJ(3 churches),RCC, etc.
4060	Miyako	59,900	0.40	240	64.63	B	61,200	Iwate, Honshu. Fishing port, fertilizer, metals, imports timber, seaweed, kombu, wakame.
4061	Miyakonojo	133,000	1.00	1,300	65.23	B	136,000	Miyazaki, Kyushu on Oyodo River. Textiles, dairy, lumber, railroad junction, pigs, beef cattle. F=11th century.
4062	Miyazaki	294,000	1.00	2,900	65.23	B	300,000	Capital of Miyazaki, Kyushu on Oyodo River. Shinto shrine. HQ of Kyushu Mennonite Christian Church.
4063	Mobara	85,400	0.50	430	64.73	B	87,200	Chiba, Honshu on Boso Peninsula. 12 miles south of Chiba. Appliance manufacturing, peanut farms.
4064	Morioka	241,000	1.00	2,400	65.23	B	246,000	Capital of Iwate, Honshu on Kitakami River. Traditional ironware, annual horse fairs. Feudal atmosphere.
4065	Moriyama	60,000	0.90	540	65.13	B	61,200	Shiga, Honshu near Biwa-Ko. Melons, flowers. Known for a 262 foot high fountain.
4066	Munakata	69,900	0.40	280	64.63	B	71,400	Fukuoka, Kyushu west of Kitakyushu. 19 miles north of Fukuoka. Agriculture, livestock.
4067	Muroran	200,000	1.00	2,000	65.23	B	204,000	Hokkaido on Cape Chikyu. Steel, iron, coal, machinery. Industrial growth after 1906.
4068	Mutsu	49,600	0.30	150	64.53	B	50,700	Northern Aomori on Mutsu Bay. Scallops, fishing. Osore-zan Reitai festival held here.
4069	Nabari	70,600	0.40	280	64.63	B	72,100	Western Mie on Nabari River near Kochi-Dani. Matsutake mushrooms, paint. Kochi Gorge and Akame waterfalls.
4070	Nagahama	56,800	0.30	170	64.53	B	58,000	Shiga, Honshu on Biwa Lake north of Hikone. 37 miles north of Otsu.
4071	Nagano (Zenkoji)	355,000	1.00	3,600	65.23	B	363,000	Nagano, Honshu. 7th century Buddhist temple. HQ of Church of the Resurrected Christ (indigenous body).
4072	Nagaoka	190,000	1.00	1,900	65.23	B	194,000	Niigata, Honshu. Chemicals, machinery, oil. F=1600 as castle town. Near Mt. Yukyu.
4073	Nagasaki	455,000	5.60	25,500	69.83	B	465,000	Nagasaki, Kyushu. Tourism. Y=1549 (F. Xavier). Original Catholic center. D=RCC,with numerous schools.
4074	Nagoya	3,377,000	3.50	118,000	74.73	B	3,516,000	Capital of Aichi, Honshu. F=1610. 1960 Nagoya Christian Council (100 churches). 4 major crusades.
4075	Bisai	57,200	1.50	860	65.73	B	58,400	Aichi west of Ichinomiya. 12 miles north of Nagoya. Woolen textile industry.
4076	Chiryu	55,300	1.60	890	65.83	B	56,500	Aichi southeast of Nagoya near Kariya. 12 miles south of Nagoya. Formed in 1970 by merger of smaller towns.
4077	Chita	77,200	1.50	1,200	65.73	B	78,900	Aichi south on Ise Bay near Tokai. 12 miles south of Nagoya. Oil manufacturing, heavy industry.
4078	Handa	102,000	1.80	1,800	66.03	B	104,000	Brewing, food processing, cotton, vegetable & flower market. Commercial port since 1603.
4079	Ichinomiya	269,000	2.00	5,400	66.23	B	274,000	Woolen & cotton textiles, kimonos. F=7th century around Shinto temple. Industry, woolen textiles, televisions.
4080	Inazawa	98,600	1.40	1,400	65.63	B	101,000	Aichi north beyond airport. Textiles, machinery, residential, elevators, bonsai plants, garden plants.
4081	Inuyama	71,500	1.50	1,100	65.73	B	73,000	Aichi far north beyond Konan. 12 miles north of Nagoya. Inuyama castle has oldest castle tower in Japan.
4082	Kani	81,900	1.20	980	65.43	B	83,600	Southern Gifu near Hida and Kiso rivers. 19 miles east of Gifu. Industry includes manufacturing automotive parts.
4083	Kariya	123,000	1.80	2,200	66.03	B	126,000	Automobile parts, textiles, farm machinery, industrial center, transportation equipment. F=1533 by Mizuno clan.
4084	Kasugai	273,000	2.00	5,500	66.23	B	279,000	6 miles north of Nagoya. Paper manufacturing, peaches, residential, manufacturing of motors. Cacti.
4085	Komaki	127,000	1.70	2,200	65.93	B	130,000	6 miles north of Nogoya. Pottery, rubber, machines, residential, helicopters, airplane parts, peaches.
4086	Konan	96,100	1.00	960	65.23	B	98,100	Synthetic fibers, textiles. Center of sericulture since 1603. 12 miles north of Nagoya.
4087	Kuwana	100,000	1.50	1,500	65.73	B	102,000	Mie, Honshu. Center of Northern Ise Industrial Zone. Metal, textiles. F=10th century.
4088	Obu	71,400	1.20	860	65.43	B	72,900	Aichi south near Kariya. 12 miles south of Nagoya. Industry, electronics.
4089	Owariashi	67,200	1.60	1,100	65.83	B	68,700	Aichi, Honshu east of Nagoya. 9 miles north of Nogoya. Computers, traditional ceramic zodiac ornaments.
4090	Tajimi	96,300	1.70	1,600	65.93	B	98,300	Gifu, Honshu on Toki River. Mino Kiln sites. Ceramic tile, dinnerware. Site of Roman Catholic Shingon Abbey.
4091	Tokai	99,700	1.50	1,500	65.73	B	102,000	Aichi, Honshu south on Ise Bay. 9 miles south of Nagoya. Iron, steel, butterburs, orchids, onions.
4092	Tokoname	53,000	1.40	740	65.63	B	54,100	Aichi, Honshu on Ise Bay. Pottery produced here since 8th century. Ceramic pipes, teapots.
4093	Toyoake	63,600	1.30	830	65.53	B	65,000	Aichi, Honshu south of Nagoya near Obu. 9 miles south of Nagoya.
4094	Tsushima	60,800	1.20	730	65.43	B	62,000	Western Aichi, Honshu west of Nagoya. Strawberries, traditional footwear, taiko drums, woolen textiles.
4095	Naha	312,000	1.00	3,100	65.23	B	319,000	Capital of Okinawa. Deepwater port. Sogen Temple. Chinese exodus to Guam. D=RC Diocese.
4096	Nakatsu	68,000	0.40	270	64.63	B	69,400	Oita, Kyushu. Porcelain, steel, rice, commercial center, traditional umbrellas, port. F=1587 around a castle.
4097	Nakatsugawa	55,000	0.40	220	64.63	B	56,200	Gifu, Honshu near Kiso River. Electronic equipment manufacturing, chestnut processing. Ena Gorge nearby.
4098	Nanao	51,300	0.40	210	64.63	B	52,400	Ishikawa, Honshu. Imports wood & ore from Russia. Once visited by 7,000 ships annually.
4099	Narita	88,800	0.50	440	64.73	B	90,600	Chiba, Honshu. Agricultural. Shinsho Temple (millions of Buddhist pilgrims annually). International airport.
4100	Naruto	66,100	0.40	260	64.63	B	67,500	Tokushima, Shikoku on Naruto Strait. Salt, chemicals, medicines, socks, fishing. Tourism for whirlpools.
4101	Naze	47,400	0.80	380	65.03	B	48,400	Okinawa. Amami Islands.
4102	Niigata	498,000	1.00	5,000	65.23	B	508,000	Capital of Niigata, Honshu. Rice. F=1616. D=RC Diocese; HQ of Japan Evangelical Mission (Canada; 1949).
4103	Niihama	132,000	1.00	1,300	65.23	B	135,000	Ehime, Shikoku on Inland Sea. Copper, aluminum, chemicals. Originally small fishing village.
4104	Niitsu	65,500	0.40	260	64.63	B	66,900	Niigata, Honshu. Residential suburb of Niigata. Tulip & hyacinth bulbs.
4105	Nishio	97,500	0.50	490	64.73	B	99,500	Aichi, Honshu on Yahagi River. Tea, textiles, metal castings. Castle town (1603-1867).
4106	Nobeoka	134,000	1.00	1,300	65.23	B	137,000	Miyazaki, Kyushu on Gokase River delta. Fertilizers, medicine, pearls, fishing. F=12th century.
4107	Noboribetsu	56,900	0.40	230	64.63	B	58,100	Most visited hot spring resort in Japan. Cement, pottery, chemicals.
4108	Nogata	64,000	0.40	260	64.63	B	65,400	Fukuoka, Kyushu. Machinery, Industrial goods. Suburb of Kita-Kyushu. F=1626.
4109	Noshiro	57,200	0.30	170	64.53	B	58,500	Akita, Honshu on Yoneshiro River. Cedar lumber. Large vegetation planting to prevent beach sand erosion.
4110	Numazu	507,000	1.00	5,100	65.23	B	517,000	Shizouka, Honshu on Kano River. Machinery, port. HQ of Swedish Evangelical Orient Mission (begun 1950).
4111	Mishima	108,000	0.60	650	64.83	B	110,000	On Izu Peninsula at foot of Mount Hakone. Dairy cattle, spas, paper, machinery. Mishima shrine.
4112	Obihiro	171,000	1.00	1,700	65.23	B	175,000	Hokkaido on Tokachi River. Agricultural trade, food-processing, beet-sugar. F=1883.
4113	Odate	69,800	0.40	280	64.63	B	71,300	Akita, Honshu on Yoneshiro River. Lumbering center, wood products, copper, lead zinc.
4114	Odawara	198,000	1.00	2,000	65.23	B	202,000	Kanagawa, Honshu. F=1192. HQ of Living Water Christian Church (indigenous pentecostal denomination).
4115	Ogaki	152,000	1.00	1,500	65.23	B	155,000	Gifu, Honshu on Ibi River. Textiles, chemicals. F=1533 around castle. Tokiwa Shrine.
4116	Oita	418,000	0.54	2,300	64.77	B	427,000	Capital of Oita, Kyushu. 1,318 aliens (1,022 Koreans, 202 Chinese). D=UCCJ(12 churches),RCC.
4117	Okawa	46,800	0.30	140	64.53	B	47,800	Fukuoka, Kyushu on mouth of Chikugo River. Wood working. Former fishing port.
4118	Okaya	61,300	0.40	250	64.63	B	62,600	Nagano, Honshu on Suwa lake. Watches, clocks, cameras, music boxes.
4119	Okayama	608,000	0.70	4,300	64.93	B	621,000	Okayama, Honshu on Inland Plain. Agricultural market, machinery. Koraku-en garden (1786). F=1573.
4120	Okazaki	314,000	1.00	3,100	65.23	B	321,000	Aichi, Honshu on Yahagi River. Textiles, foods, machinery. F=1455 around castle.
4121	Okinawa	104,000	1.40	1,500	65.63	B	106,000	Okinawa. U.S. Kadena military base. Botanical garden. New city (1975).
4122	Omura	75,200	0.50	380	64.73	B	76,800	Nagasaki, Kyushu on Omura Bay. Processed foods, pearls. Center of Christianity in late 16th century.
4123	Omuta	230,000	1.00	2,300	65.23	B	235,000	Fukuoka, Kyushu on Ariake Sea. Chemicals. Decline of coal mining has hurt economy.

Table 10-5–continued opposite

Table 10-5–continued

Rec No 1	Country City 2	Pop 2000 3	AC% 4	Church Members 5	E% 6	W 7	Pop 2025 8	Notes 9
4124	Arao	60,900	0.40	240	64.63	B	62,200	Kumamoto. Residential suburb. Former coal mine and factory.
4125	Onomichi	99,400	1.07	1,100	65.30	B	102,000	Hiroshima, Honshu on Inland Sea. Busy port. F=1168. Trade with China. Buddhist Senko Temple (9th century).
4126	Osaka-Kobe	10,609,000	3.60	382,000	71.83	B	10,609,000	Massive industrialization. 23,000 Koreans. D=RCC,UCCJ(60 churches), et alia. YMCA, YWCA.
4127	Akashi	277,000	1.00	2,800	65.23	B	283,000	Steel industry. HQ of Japan Jesus Christ Church, a very large indigenous pentecostal denomination.
4128	Amagasaki	511,000	1.00	5,100	65.23	B	522,000	Iron & steel, electrical machinery, transport vehicles. Serious land subsidence.
4129	Ashiya	89,600	0.90	810	65.13	B	91,500	Renowned residential area. Known for beauty since 794. Osaka Bay. Industrial suburb, Ashiya University.
4130	Daito	129,000	1.00	1,300	65.23	B	132,000	Residential. South Honshu, 6 miles east of Osaka. Metal products, electrical appliances, electronics production.
4131	Fujiidera	67,500	1.00	680	65.23	B	68,900	Osaka on Yamato River south of Yao Airport. 9 miles south of Osaka.
4132	Habikino	118,000	1.00	1,200	65.23	B	120,000	Osaka south of Fujidera. South Honshu, 9 miles south of Osaka.
4133	Higashiosaka	531,000	1.00	5,300	65.23	B	542,000	East Osaka. Residential. 7th century shrine. HQ of Next Towns Crusade in Japan (1957; M=Revival Temple).
4134	Hirakata	400,000	1.00	4,000	65.23	B	409,000	On Yodo River. Residential, educational center, tractors, noodles, local sake.
4135	Ibaraki	260,000	1.00	2,600	65.23	B	266,000	Osaka, Honshu northeast beyond Settsu. 9 miles north of Osaka, appliance manufacturing.
4136	Ikeda	107,000	1.00	1,100	65.23	B	109,000	Residential. Brewing, woodworking, garden trees. Ancient origins. 99% Japanese.
4137	Ikoma	102,000	0.90	920	65.13	B	104,000	Nara, Honshu east of Daito. Railroad junction, mountain resort, Buddhist temple on nearby Mt. Ikoma.
4138	Itami	191,000	1.00	1,900	65.23	B	195,000	Hyogo. Residential. Osaka International Airport. Muko River, Osaka Bay. Bread, automotive parts manufacturing.
4139	Izumi (Osaka)	150,000	1.00	1,500	65.23	B	153,000	Osaka south on Osaka Bay. Residential and commercial suburb. Numerous textile mills, artificial pearls, glass.
4140	Izumi-otsu	68,600	0.80	550	65.03	B	70,100	Port since 8th century. Woolen & cotton blankets. 16 miles south of Osaka.
4141	Izumi-sano	91,000	0.90	820	65.13	B	92,900	On Osaka Bay. Market for cotton, fish, onions. Textiles, towels, machinery. F=8th century.
4142	Joyo	86,800	0.80	690	65.03	B	88,600	Kyoto, Honshu south of Uji. 12 miles south of Kyoto. Rice fields, textiles, woodworking, handicrafts.
4143	Kadoma	146,000	1.00	1,500	65.23	B	149,000	On Yodo River. Lotus flowers, appliances, plastics. Furu River. Matsushita Electric Industrial Co.
4144	Kaizuka	81,100	1.00	810	65.23	B	82,800	Osaka far south on Osaka Bay. Commercial port, fibers, textiles, ropes, vegetables, taro, mandarin oranges.
4145	Kakogawa	246,000	1.00	2,500	65.23	B	251,000	Hygo on Kako River. Residential. Woolen textiles, fertilizer, iron, steel, machinery.
4146	Kashihara	118,000	0.81	960	65.04	B	121,000	Nara. Archeology. 2% Korean. Japanese are Shinto at New Year, Christian on wedding day, Buddhist at funeral.
4147	Kashiwara	78,600	0.90	710	65.13	B	80,300	Osaka on Yamato River south of Yao. South Honshu, 9 miles south of Osaka. Agriculture.
4148	Katano	66,900	1.00	670	65.23	B	68,300	Osaka east of Neyagawa. South Honshu, 12 miles north of Osaka.
4149	Kawachi-nagano	111,000	1.10	1,200	65.33	B	114,000	Osaka on Ishi River east of Izumi. South Honshu, 16 miles south of Osaka.
4150	Kawanishi	145,000	1.00	1,400	65.23	B	148,000	Hyogo on Ina River. Dyed cloth, bleached and tanned leather. Fruit, flowers.
4151	Kishiwada	193,000	1.60	3,100	65.83	B	197,000	On Osaka Bay. F=14th century. 15% New-Religionist, 14% nonreligious. D=RCC,UCCJ,Anglican.
4152	Kobe	1,513,000	1.00	15,100	65.23	B	1,545,000	Capital of Hyogo. Important port on Inland Sea. Shipbuilding, steel. Koreans, Chinese. D=RCC,UCCJ,AoG.
4153	Kusatsu	97,000	1.00	970	65.23	B	99,100	Shiga, Honshu near Biwa Lake east of Otsu. Railroad junction, appliance, gourds, bamboo works.
4154	Kyoto	1,703,000	1.92	32,700	66.15	B	1,703,000	Cultural center of Buddhism. F=794. 1960, Kyoto Christian Council (RCC, UCCJ, Anglican). 160 clergy.
4155	Matsubara	139,000	1.00	1,400	65.23	B	142,000	Yamato River. Residential. Pearls, ivory, industrial. Ancient tomb of Otsukayama, one of Japan's largest.
4156	Miki	78,300	1.00	780	65.23	B	80,000	Hyogo. Satellite city of Kobe. F=1468 around castle.
4157	Mino (Minoo)	125,000	1.00	1,300	65.23	B	128,000	Osaka north of Toyonaka. South Honshu, 9 miles north of Osaka.
4158	Moriguchi	161,000	1.00	1,600	65.23	B	165,000	On Yodo River. Electrical machinery, appliances, textiles. Residential suburb.
4159	Muko	54,200	0.80	430	65.03	B	55,300	Southern Kyoto south of Kyoto. Bamboo shoots, handicrafts, agriculture, markets.
4160	Nagaokakyo	79,000	0.90	710	65.13	B	80,700	Kyoto, Honshu south of Muko. 9 miles south of Kyoto. Television, bamboo shoots.
4161	Nara	358,000	1.23	4,400	65.46	B	365,000	Ancient Buddhist buildings and temples. F=710. 11% New-Religionist. D=UCCJ(4 churches),RCC(3).
4162	Neyagawa	263,000	1.00	2,600	65.23	B	268,000	Residential suburb. Metal products, transportation equipment, textiles.
4163	Nishinomiya	437,000	1.00	4,400	65.23	B	446,000	Hyogo on Osaka Bay. Known for sake. 4,500 Koreans, 400 Chinese. D=UCCJ(13 churches),RCC, et alia.
4164	Omi-hachiman	67,600	0.90	610	65.13	B	69,100	Shiga, Honshu on Biwa Lake north of Kusatsu. Rice, pearl farming and processing, tile, pottery. Konnyaku
4165	Osaka	17,302,000	1.00	173,000	65.23	B	17,668,000	Machinery, electric machinery, iron & steel, chemicals. Large financial center. News media.
4166	Otsu	266,000	1.85	4,900	66.08	B	272,000	Capital of Shiga on Lake Biwa. 16% nonreligious, 13% New-Religionist. D=UCCJ(6 churches),RCC (2 churches)
4167	Sakai	827,000	1.00	8,300	65.23	B	845,000	On Osaka Bay. Large mausoleum. HQ of Christian Canaan Church (1948; indigenous pentecostal church).
4168	Sanda	66,100	0.90	600	65.13	B	67,500	Hyogo, Honshu on Muko River north of Kobe. Railroad junction, livestock, beef cattle.
4169	Sayama	55,600	0.90	500	65.13	B	56,800	Osaka, Honshu south of Mihara. Iruma River, Lake Sayama. Motor vehicles, tea, resort, Tanabata Festival.
4170	Sennan	61,500	0.90	550	65.13	B	62,800	Osaka, Honshu far south on Osaka Bay. 25 miles south of Osaka.
4171	Settsu	89,500	0.80	720	65.03	B	91,400	Osaka, Honshu northeast on Tokaido Honsen Railway. 6 miles north of Osaka.
4172	Shijonawate	51,200	0.80	410	65.03	B	52,300	Eastern Osaka, Honshu near Neyagawa. 9 miles north of Osaka.
4173	Suita	353,000	1.00	3,500	65.23	B	361,000	On Yodo River. Beer brewery, large railway freight year, metals, chemicals. F=1603 as river port.
4174	Takaishi	66,600	1.00	670	65.23	B	68,000	Osaka, Honshu south of Sakai on Osaka Bay.
4175	Takarazuka	207,000	1.00	2,100	65.23	B	211,000	Near Mount Rokko. Hot springs resort, female opera company, 4,000 seat opera house.
4176	Takasago	95,500	0.90	860	65.13	B	97,500	On Inland Sea. Ceramics, heavy chemicals. Noise & air pollution.
4177	Takatsuki	368,000	1.00	3,700	65.23	B	376,000	On Yodo River. Electrical appliances, pharmaceuticals. F=1338 as castle town.
4178	Tondabayashi	113,000	1.00	1,100	65.23	B	115,000	Osaka, Honshu on Ishi River south of Habikino. 12 miles south of Osaka, synthetic resins.
4179	Toyonaka	420,000	1.00	4,200	65.23	B	428,000	Residential suburb. Machinery, metal, knitting plants, petroleum. Former rural town.
4180	Uji	181,000	1.00	1,800	65.23	B	185,000	On Uji River. Known for tea since 1338. Many historic temples. Residential.
4181	Yamato-koriyama (Koriyama-Kingyo)	95,200	1.00	950	65.23	B	97,200	Nara prefecture, South Honshu, south of Nara. Appliance manufacturing, goldfish breeding, Jiko Temple, tourism.
4182	Yamato-takada	69,900	0.90	630	65.13	B	71,300	Nara, Honshu west of Kashihara. 13 miles south of Nara.
4183	Yao	284,000	1.00	2,800	65.23	B	290,000	Osaka, Honshu on Nagase River. Residential, large-scale machinery, chemicals, textiles.
4184	Yawata	77,600	0.90	700	65.13	B	79,200	Kyoto, Honshu on Kizu River northeast of Takatsuki. 9 miles south of Kyoto.
4185	Ota	143,000	1.00	1,400	65.23	B	146,000	Gumma, Honshu on Tone River. Automobiles, aircraft, fruits, vegetables.
4186	Oyama	146,000	1.00	1,500	65.23	B	149,000	Tochigi, Honshu on Omoi River. Oyama Radio transmitting station, mining & transport equipment.
4187	Sabae	63,800	0.40	260	64.63	B	65,100	Fukui, Honshu. Optical frames, roof tiles, silk, synthetic fibers. Formed around Buddhist Josho temple.
4188	Saga	174,000	1.00	1,700	65.23	B	178,000	Saga, Kyushu. Cotton textiles, ceramics. Feudal character (thatched roofs, castle moats).
4189	Saijo	58,200	0.40	230	64.63	B	59,400	Ehime, Shikoku in Kamo River delta. Pulp, paper mills. Pilgrimages to Ishizuchi Shrine.
4190	Saiki (Saeki)	53,600	0.40	210	64.63	B	54,700	Oita, Kyushu on Saiki Bay. Ships, pulp, cement. Castle town since 1338.
4191	Sakaide	65,400	0.50	330	64.73	B	66,800	Kagawa, Shikoku on Seto Inland Sea near Marugame. Mandarin oranges, carrots, oil, ships, noodles.
4192	Sakata	103,000	0.30	310	64.53	B	105,000	Yamagata, Honshu. Seaport. 99.8% are both Shintoists and Buddhists. D=UCCJ(2 churches),RCC,&c.
4193	Saku	63,500	0.40	250	64.63	B	64,800	Nagano, Honshu on Chikuma River southeast of Ueda. Magnetic tape, carp fishing.
4194	Sakurai	61,700	0.40	250	64.63	B	63,000	Nara, Honshu east of Kashihara, 12 miles south of Nara. Noodles. Buddhist temple from the 7th century.
4195	Sanjo	87,900	0.50	440	64.73	B	89,700	Niigata, Honshu on Shinano River delta. 2,000 small workshops, carpenter tools, hardware. F=16th century.
4196	Sano	85,500	0.50	430	64.73	B	87,300	Southern Tochigi east of Ashikaga. 25 miles south of Utsunomiya. Strawberry cultivation.
4197	Sapporo	1,827,000	1.23	22,500	70.46	B	1,930,000	Capital of Hokkaido. Skiing, winter sports. 2,000 Koreans. D=UCCJ(16 churches),RCC,Baptist (6),&c.
4198	Ebetsu	99,500	0.60	600	64.83	B	102,000	On Ishikari River. Residential area, food processing, metal, pottery, paper. F=1868 by 10 families.
4199	Otaru	167,000	1.00	1,700	65.23	B	171,000	On Ishikari Bay. Large commercial & industrial center, important seaport. D=RCC.
4200	Sasebo	251,000	1.00	2,500	65.23	B	256,000	Nagasaki, Kyushu on Omaru Bay. Commercial & fishing port. Base for Maritime Self-Defense Force (1973).
4201	Satte	55,600	1.90	1,100	66.13	B	56,800	Saitama, Honshu. North of Tokyo. 16 miles north of Urawa.
4202	Seki	70,000	0.50	350	64.73	B	71,500	Southern Gifu near Nagara River northeast of Gifu. Cutlery, master swordsmiths in feudal times.
4203	Sendai (Kagoshima)	73,400	0.40	290	64.63	B	75,000	Kagoshima, Kyushu on Sendai River. Large paper-pulp plants. F=17th century as castle town.
4204	Sendai (Miyagi)	821,000	2.50	20,500	71.73	B	839,000	Educational center. 2,000 Koreans. 98% Buddhist. D=UCCJ(14 churches, 2 universities),RCC(many schools).
4205	Izumi (Miyagi)	127,000	0.37	470	64.60	B	130,000	98% Shinto-Buddhist. 99.9% Japanese, 130 aliens (100Koreans, 10 USA).
4206	Shiogama	63,500	0.40	250	64.63	B	64,800	On Matsushima Bay. Long known for production of salt, major fishing center, shipbuilding.
4207	Tagajo	59,800	0.40	240	64.63	B	61,100	Miyagi, Honshu east of Sendai on Ishinomaki Bay. Electrical appliance manufacturing, rice, Taga castle, ruins.
4208	Seto	129,000	1.00	1,300	65.23	B	132,000	Aichi, Honshu. Known for porcelain (900 factories, 1000 kilns). F=1230.
4209	Shibata	80,000	0.50	400	64.73	B	81,700	Niigata, Honshu northeast of Niigata near Sea of Japan. Rice, sake, traditional confections, pickles.
4210	Shimada	75,600	0.40	300	64.63	B	77,200	Shizouka, Honshu on Oi River. Trade center for timber, paper mills, tea, oranges.
4211	Shimodate	67,600	0.40	270	64.63	B	69,000	Ibaraki, Honshu on Kokai River. Commercial & transport center, cotton textiles.
4212	Shizuoka	998,000	2.50	25,000	71.73	B	1,019,000	Shizouka, Honshu on Suruga Bay. Fishing port, motor vehicles, ships, famous for green tea.
4213	Fujieda	123,000	1.00	1,200	65.23	B	125,000	On Oi River delta. Tea, mandarin oranges, mushrooms. Central Honshu, Paulownia furniture.
4214	Shimizu	247,000	1.00	2,500	65.23	B	252,000	On Suruga Bay. Commercial port, deep-sea fishing,motorcycles. Ryuge Temple (1,000 year old fern palm).
4215	Yaizu	115,000	1.00	1,100	65.23	B	117,000	Important coastal fishing port, canning, freezing plants, 9 miles south of Shizuoka.
4216	Suwa	53,700	0.30	160	64.53	B	54,800	Nagano, Honshu on Lake Suwa. Watches, cameras, music boxes. Tourist center for shrines.
4217	Suzuka	178,000	1.00	1,800	65.23	B	182,000	Mie, Honshu on Ise Bay. Stencil paper, dyeing kimonos. Automobile speedway.
4218	Tagawa (Takawa)	59,100	0.30	180	64.53	B	60,300	Fukuoka, Kyushu on Onga River. Former coal mining town. Cement.
4219	Takamatsu	338,000	1.00	3,400	65.23	B	345,000	Capital of Kagawa, Shikoku. Tourist center. D=RC Diocese(begun 1904), 48 priests.
4220	Takaoka	225,000	1.00	2,300	65.23	B	230,000	Toyama, Honshu on Shu River. F=1609. HQ of Fellowship of Evangelical Baptist Churches (begun 1964).
4221	Takasaki	242,000	1.00	2,400	65.23	B	247,000	Gumma, Honshu on Karasu River. Silk-reeling, woodworking. Statue of Kannon (Buddhist).
4222	Takayama	66,800	0.40	270	64.63	B	68,200	Gifu, Honshu on Miya River. Laquerware, tourist center. Kokubun Temple (1588).
4223	Takefu	71,900	0.40	290	64.63	B	73,400	Fukui, Honshu on Hino River. Cutlery, silk, papers, fertilizer. F=1603.
4224	Takikawa	50,800	0.90	460	65.13	B	51,800	Hokkaido on Ishikari River, 47 miles north of Sapporo, agricultural machinery industry.
4225	Tamano	75,000	0.40	300	64.63	B	76,600	Okayama, Honshu on Inland Sea. Shipbuilding. Kibitsu Temple (4th century).
4226	Tanabe	71,500	0.40	290	64.63	B	73,000	Wakayama, Honshu on Pacific Ocean south of Gobo, Tanabe Bay. Commercial and fishing port, Japanese plums.
4227	Tatebayashi	78,000	0.40	310	64.63	B	79,700	Gumma, Honshu. Woven cotton, textiles, beverages, processed foods. F=16th century as castle town.
4228	Tenri	70,500	0.40	280	64.63	B	71,900	Nara, Honshu. Headquarters of Tenrikyo. Many religious & cultural facilities. Many burial mounds.
4229	Tochigi	88,300	0.50	440	64.73	B	90,100	Tochigi, Honshu. Ceramics, rice wheat, tobacco, cattle, silk, electrical appliances, copper, manganese.
4230	Toki	66,500	0.40	270	64.63	B	67,900	Gifu, Honshu on Toki River. Kilns for Oribe ware. Tableware, tiles, pottery, uranium deposits.
4231	Tokushima	270,000	1.00	2,700	65.23	B	275,000	Tokushima, Shikoku on Pacific Ocean. Cotton textiles, chemicals. Annual folk festival.
4232	Hikari	48,700	0.90	440	65.13	B	49,800	Yamaguchi on Suo Strait southeast of Tokuyama, formed in 1940's. Medicines, vitamins, steel manufacturing.
4233	Kudamatsu	54,300	0.90	490	65.13	B	55,400	Port on Suo Sea. Heavy machinery, petrochemicals, tinware, heavy industry.
4234	Tokuyama	256,000	1.00	2,600	65.23	B	261,000	Yamaguchi, Honshu on Inland Sea. Petroleum, chemicals, petrochemicals.
4235	TOKYO-Yokohama	28,025,000	4.20	1,177,000	76.43	B	28,887,000	Ancient origin. Financial center, 8,000 factories. Crusades. D=UCCJ(152 churches),RCC (60),Japan Baptist(40).
4236	Abiko	123,000	3.00	3,700	67.23	B	126,000	Chiba east of Kashiwa, important railroad junction, resort town, residential suburb. Tega Marsh nearby.
4237	Ageo	200,000	2.00	4,000	66.23	B	204,000	Saitama, Honshu, 9 miles north of Urawa. Machinery, rubber, metallurgy, vegetable farming, kiwi.
4238	Akigawa	51,600	2.00	1,000	66.23	B	52,700	Tokyo prefecture, east central Honshu, 16 miles south of Shinjuku.
4239	Akishima	108,000	2.50	2,700	66.73	B	110,000	Western Tokyo west of Tachikawa, 25 miles west of Shinjuku.
4240	Asaka	106,000	2.80	3,000	67.03	B	108,000	Saitama, Honshu on Kurume River. Copper-rolling military base, residential.
4241	Atsugi	202,000	2.00	4,000	66.23	B	206,000	Kanagawa, Honshu. Sweetfish fishing, center for agriculture, auto parts, electric equipment.
4242	Ayase	79,800	2.00	1,600	66.23	B	81,500	Kanagawa west of Yokohama. Near Atsugi-Hikojo. Livestock, agriculture, gardens, pigs.
4243	Chiba	849,000	2.50	21,200	66.73	B	867,000	Capital of Chiba. Large steel mill. Chiba University (1949). F=1126.
4244	Chigasaki	206,000	2.00	4,100	66.23	B	211,000	Kanagawa, Honshu. Garden agriculture, electric equipment, chinaware. F=1880.
4245	Chofu	202,000	2.00	4,000	66.23	B	207,000	Machinery, electrical equipment, chemicals. Race track, Jindai Temple (733).
4246	Ebina	108,000	3.00	3,300	67.23	B	111,000	Kanagawa on Sagami River near Atsugi, 16 miles west of Yokohama. Automotive parts industry.
4247	Fuchu	214,000	2.00	4,300	66.23	B	219,000	On Tama River. Heavy industry, residential suburb. F=7th century AD.

Table 10-5–continued overleaf

Table 10-5–continued

Rec No 1	Country City 2	Pop 2000 3	AC% 4	Church Members 5	E% 6	W 7	Pop 2025 8	Notes 9
4248	Fujimi	97,100	2.50	2,400	66.73	B	99,200	Tokyo northwest beyond Shiki, 5 miles west of Urawa. Market, shops, handcrafts.
4249	Fujisawa	359,000	2.00	7,200	66.23	B	366,000	Kanagawa on Sagami Bay. Residential, resorts. Yugyo Temple (1325), main temple of Buddhist & Ji sect.
4250	Funabashi	546,000	2.00	10,900	66.23	B	558,000	Chiba on Tokyo Bay. Iron, steel, petrochemicals, residential. Agricultural zone.
4251	Fussa	59,400	2.50	1,500	66.73	B	60,700	Western Tokyo near Akishima. East central Henshu, 16 miles south of Shinjuku. Rice, fruits, vegetables.
4252	Hachioji	477,000	2.00	9,500	66.23	B	488,000	Residential, silk-weaving, textiles, electrical machinery. Castle town in Middle Ages.
4253	Hadano (Hatano)	159,000	2.00	3,200	66.23	B	163,000	Kanagawa. Tobacco-trading center. Tsurumaki spa, known for its scenic beauty. Computers, peanuts.
4254	Hanno	75,000	2.80	2,100	67.03	B	76,500	Saitama on Iruma River west of Iruma, Naguri River. Lumber, fishing, vegetables, fruit.
4255	Hasuda	61,100	2.50	1,500	66.73	B	62,400	Tokyo north on Moto-ara River beyond Iwatsuki, 9 miles north of Urawa. Fruit, vegetables, pears.
4256	Hatogaya	57,800	2.20	1,300	66.43	B	59,000	Tokyo north beyond Kawaguchi, Saitama prefecture, residential suburb. Industry, markets.
4257	Higashikurume	117,000	2.00	2,300	66.23	B	119,000	Western Tokyo beyond Hoya. Christian Academy (1950), 19 miles west of Shinjuku.
4258	Higashimurayama	137,000	2.00	2,700	66.23	B	140,000	Western Tokyo south of Tokorozawa.Commercial hub of tea-producing region. Residential.
4259	Higashiyamato	76,900	2.30	1,800	66.53	B	78,500	Western Tokyo near Murayama Reservoir, 6 miles north of Shinjuku. Vegetables, fruits.
4260	Hino	170,000	2.00	3,400	66.23	B	173,000	On Tama River. Automobiles, electric machinery, precision instruments. Takahata Temple.
4261	Hiratsuka	252,000	2.00	5,000	66.23	B	257,000	Kanagawa on Sagami Bay. Rubber, chemicals, vegetables, dairy cattle. Annual Star Festival.
4262	Hoya	97,400	2.50	2,400	66.73	B	99,500	Western Tokyo near Tanashi. Residential suburb, commercial, industry, fruits, vegetables.
4263	Ichihara	264,000	2.50	6,600	66.73	B	269,000	Chiba, Tokyo Bay. Agriculture, fishing, petrochemicals, steel. Serious air pollution.
4264	Ichikawa	447,000	2.60	11,600	66.83	B	456,000	Chiba on Edo River. Educational center. 99.66% Japanese, 0.34% alien (895 Koreans). D=RCC,UCCJ,Anglican.
4265	Inagi	60,000	2.80	1,700	67.03	B	61,300	Western Tokyo south of Fuchu, 31 miles southwest of Shinjuku. Computers, electronic technology.
4266	Iruma	141,000	2.70	3,800	66.93	B	144,000	Saitama on Iruma River. Renowned for Sayama green tea. Rich archaeological sites damaged by urbanization.
4267	Isehara	91,700	2.50	2,300	66.73	B	93,600	Kanagawa far west of Yokohama. Vegetables, fruit, market, handcrafts, residential commercial.
4268	Iwatsuki	109,000	2.60	2,800	66.83	B	111,000	Saitama, Honshu north on Moto-ara River, 6 miles north of Urawa. Fishing, vegetables, traditional dolls.
4269	Kamagaya	97,300	2.00	1,900	66.23	B	99,400	Chiba east of Ichikawa, 9 miles north of Chiba. Pottery, vegetables, traditional doll making.
4270	Kamakura	178,000	2.00	3,600	66.23	B	182,000	Kanagawa on Pacific Ocean. Historic site. 49 foot high statue of Great Buddha, a noted pilgrimage center.
4271	Kamifukuoka	60,100	2.50	1,500	66.73	B	61,400	Southern Saitama south of Kawagoe, 6 miles west of Urana. Computer park, electronics.
4272	Kashiwa	312,000	2.40	7,500	66.63	B	319,000	Chiba. Residential. F=1954. HQ of Japan Baptist Association (begun 1952; M=American Baptist Association).
4273	Kasukabe	193,000	2.00	3,900	66.23	B	197,000	Southern Saitama on Furu-tone River, 9 miles north of Urawa. Paulownia furniture, battledores, hats.
4274	Kawagoe	312,000	2.80	8,700	67.03	B	319,000	Saitama. Residential, textiles, food processing. F=15th century as castle town.
4275	Kawaguchi	449,000	2.90	13,000	67.13	B	459,000	Saitama. Ajikawa and Kizagawa Rivers, residential, commercial. Textiles, precision instruments, brewing.
4276	Kawasaki	1,201,000	3.00	36,000	67.23	B	1,227,000	Port in Kanagawa on Tokyo Bay. Automobiles, machines, tools, chemicals. Buddhist Heigen Temple.
4277	Kitamoto	65,500	2.50	1,600	66.73	B	66,800	Saitama, Honshu north of Okegawa, 9 miles north of Urawa. Vegetables, crafts.
4278	Kiyose	69,100	2.30	1,600	66.53	B	70,600	Western Tokyo, Honshu near Niiza, 12 miles south of Shinjuku. Fruits, vegetables.
4279	Kodaira	168,000	2.90	4,900	67.13	B	171,000	Residential, 93 miles west of Shinjuku. Automobile tires. Mulberry trees for silk.
4280	Koga	59,600	2.40	1,400	66.63	B	60,900	Important river port in Ibaraki. Major trade center, 43 miles southwest of Mito. Umbrellas.
4281	Koganei	108,000	2.00	2,200	66.23	B	111,000	Residential, educational center. HQ of Brethren in Christ Church (begun 1953).
4282	Kokubunji	103,000	2.60	2,700	66.83	B	106,000	Residential, agriculture. Kokubun Temple (built in 8th century for Buddhist nuns).
4283	Komae	76,000	2.50	1,900	66.73	B	77,600	Tokyo near Tama River and Chofu, immediately southwest of Tokyo. Residential, commercial, industry.
4284	Konosu	74,200	2.40	1,800	66.63	B	75,700	Saitama, Honshu north of Okegawa, 16 miles north of Urawa. Residential, markets.
4285	Koshigaya	292,000	2.90	8,500	67.13	B	298,000	Saitama. Motoara River. Chemicals, leather, machinery, Paulownia item manufacturing, paper tumblers, dolls.
4286	Kuki	68,400	2.50	1,700	66.73	B	69,900	Saitama, Honshu near Furu-tone River north of Hasuda, 12 miles north of Urawa.
4287	Kunitachi	67,400	2.60	1,800	66.83	B	68,800	Western Tokyo, Honshu west of Fuchu. Hitotsubashi University. 124 miles west of Shinjuku.
4288	Machida	357,000	2.80	10,000	67.03	B	365,000	Residential. On southern slopes of Tama Hills. Industrial, residential, important transportation hub.
4289	Matsudo	467,000	3.00	14,000	67.23	B	477,000	Chiba, 12 miles north of Chiba. Residential, ironworks, engineering, spring onions, motors, rice flour.
4290	Misato	131,000	2.80	3,700	67.03	B	134,000	Saitama, Honshu north on Furu-tone River near Soka, 12 miles east of Urawa.
4291	Mitaka	169,000	2.70	4,600	66.93	B	173,000	Residential. Electrical machinery, transport equipment. International Christian University (1958).
4292	Miura	53,700	2.50	1,300	66.73	B	54,800	Kanagawa on Miura Peninsula on Sagami Bay, Miura coast nearby. Watermelon, cabbage, daikon, pickled fish.
4293	Musashimurayama	67,100	2.00	1,300	66.23	B	68,500	Western Tokyo near Yokota Air Base, 9 miles south of Shinjuku, residential. Motor vehicle production.
4294	Musashino	142,000	2.50	3,600	66.73	B	145,000	Residential. F=1659 as Kichijoji. Sumida River. Commercial, medical products, electrical machinery.
4295	Nagareyama	143,000	2.70	3,900	66.93	B	146,000	Chiba, Honshu west of Kashiwa, 16 miles north of Chiba, Tone canal nearby. Sweet-sake brewing.
4296	Narashino	155,000	2.60	4,000	66.83	B	158,000	Chiba on Tokyo Bay. Residential, truck farming, weekend vacation area. Educational center.
4297	Niza	142,000	2.80	4,000	67.03	B	145,000	Southern Saitama, Honshu near Asaka, Yonase River, 6 miles south of Urawa. Residential, commercial. Printing.
4298	Noda	117,000	3.00	3,500	67.23	B	120,000	Chiba on Edo River. Residential. Numerous soy sauce factories, rice cracker, food processing.
4299	Okegawa	70,700	2.90	2,000	67.13	B	72,200	Saitama, Honshu north of Ageo, 9 miles north of Urawa.
4300	Ome	129,000	2.00	2,600	66.23	B	132,000	On Tama River. Cotton textiles, lumber, woodworking. Early trade center.
4301	Omiya	413,000	2.80	11,600	67.03	B	422,000	Saitama. Railway workshops. Known for cherry blossoms. Shinto Hikawa Shrine (5th century BC).
4302	Sagamihara	544,000	3.10	16,900	67.33	B	556,000	Kanagawa. Metal products, machinery, rice, wheat. Residential.
4303	Sakado	98,000	2.80	2,700	67.03	B	100,000	Saitama, Honshu on Koma River north of Kawagoe, 16 miles north of Urawa. Residential, commercial.
4304	Sakura	148,000	2.00	3,000	66.23	B	151,000	Chiba, Honshu east of Yachiyo, seat of Sakura castle. Railroad junction, cable, peanuts.
4305	Sayama	161,000	2.50	4,000	66.73	B	164,000	Southern Saitama, Honshu on Iruma River, Lake Sayama. Motor vehicle production, tea, resort, festival.
4306	Shiki	65,000	2.50	1,600	66.73	B	66,400	Southern Saitama, Honshu north of Niiza, 3.7 miles west of Urawa. Residential, industrial, markets.
4307	Soka	211,000	2.80	5,900	67.03	B	215,000	Saitama on Ayase River. 9 miles east of Urawa. Pulp, leather, metal, machinery, residential, fruits, vegetables.
4308	Tachikawa	156,000	2.60	4,100	66.83	B	160,000	Commercial center & railway hub. Residential. Takao quasi-national park. Mt. Takao.
4309	Tama	148,000	2.70	4,000	66.93	B	151,000	Tokyo, Honshu south of Fuchu, 12 miles west of Shinjuku, Tama new town project.
4310	Tanashi	76,900	2.60	2,000	66.83	B	78,600	Tokyo, Honshu near Hoya, 186 miles west of Shinjuku. Timepiece manufacturing.
4311	Toda	89,700	2.50	2,200	66.73	B	91,600	Saitama, 3.1 miles south of Urgwa. Industrial suburb. Boat racing. Some residential, commercial, markets.
4312	Tokorozawa	310,000	2.80	8,700	67.03	B	317,000	Saitama. Residential. Distribution center for Sayama green tea, Video production, baseball stadium.
4313	Tokyo	8,722,000	3.20	279,000	67.43	B	8,907,000	Tokyo, Honshu. Ancient origin. Crusades. D=UCCJ(152 churches),RCC(60),Japan Baptist(40).
4314	Toride	83,600	2.80	2,300	67.03	B	85,400	Southern Ibaraki, Honshu near Abiko, port on Tone River. Commercial, office equipment, railroad junction.
4315	Urawa	428,000	2.90	12,400	67.13	B	437,000	Capital of Saitama. Residential. D=RC Diocese; HQ of Evangelical Free Church in Japan (1949).
4316	Urayasu	118,000	2.50	3,000	66.73	B	121,000	Chiba, Honshu east of Tokyo on Tokyo Bay, 9 miles west of Chiba, Tokyo Disneyland here.
4317	Wako	58,200	2.00	1,200	66.23	B	59,500	Southern Saitama near Camp Asaka and Niiza, 5 miles west of Urawa. Automotive parts manufacturing.
4318	Warabi	75,400	2.60	2,000	66.83	B	77,000	Saitama. Cotton fabric, woolen textiles, electric industries. Residential, commuters.
4319	Yachiyo	152,000	2.00	3,000	66.23	B	155,000	Chiba, Honshu west of Sakura, 2.5 miles south of Urawa between Urawa and Kawaguchi.
4320	Yamato	199,000	2.80	5,600	67.03	B	204,000	Kanagawa. Vehicles. 708 Koreans. D=RCC,UCCJ(3 churches),Cumberland Presbyterian. 12 clergy. YMCA.
4321	Yashio	74,200	2.50	1,900	66.73	B	75,800	Southern Saitama near Furu-tone River east of Soka. Yukata (cotton kimonos), dumplings.
4322	Yokohama	3,297,000	3.00	98,900	67.23	B	3,367,000	Capital of Kanagawa. Major port on Tokyo Bay. Educational center. D=UCCJ,Presbyterian,RCC.
4323	Yokosuka	444,000	2.80	12,400	67.03	B	453,000	Kanagawa seaport. Fishing. 50% Buddhist, 27% Shintoist. D=UCCJ(8 churches),Presbyterian(3),RCC, et alia.
4324	Yono	80,900	2.70	2,200	66.93	B	82,700	Saitama. Residential. 1.9 miles north of Urawa. Machinery, metals, heavy industry, commercial.
4325	Yotsukaido	73,900	2.90	2,100	67.13	B	75,400	Chiba, Honshu northeast of Chiba. Commercial, industrial, residential, markets.
4326	Zama	115,000	2.50	2,900	66.73	B	117,000	Kanagawa, Honshu west of Yokohama. U.S. Army base. Motor vehicle manufacturing.
4327	Zushi	58,100	2.70	1,600	66.93	B	59,300	Southern Kanagawa, Honshu on Mura Peninsula near Kamakura, 19 miles north of Yokohama.
4328	Tomakomai	164,000	0.71	1,200	64.94	B	167,000	Hokkaido. Paper. 284 Koreans. D=RCC(2 churches),&c. 1977 Takiyawa crusade. 5 child centers.
4329	Tosu	57,200	0.40	230	64.63	B	58,400	Saga, Kyushu on Chikugo River. Food processing, grain, tobacco.
4330	Tottori	146,000	1.00	1,500	65.23	B	149,000	Tottori, Honshu on Sea of Japan. Tourism, machinery, paper. Noted for its university.
4331	Toyama	329,000	1.60	5,300	65.83	B	336,000	Medicines, drugs. 14% New-Religionist, 10% Shintoist, 9% nonreligious. 3 kindergartens, YMCA.
4332	Toyohashi	346,000	1.00	3,500	65.23	B	353,000	Aichi, Honshu on Atsumi Bay. Known in the past for silk. Cotton & synthetic textiles.
4333	Toyokawa	114,000	1.00	1,100	65.23	B	117,000	Aichi, Honshu on Toyo River. Auto parts, toys. Inari Shrine attracts many pilgrims.
4334	Toyota	340,000	1.00	3,400	65.23	B	347,000	Aichi, Honshu on Yahagi River. Automobiles. Formerly Koromo.
4335	Tsu	161,000	2.07	3,300	66.30	B	164,000	Capital of Mie, Honshu. 20% nonreligious, 14% New-Religionist, 10% Shintoist. D=UCCJ(3 churches).
4336	Tsuchiura	130,000	1.00	1,300	65.23	B	133,000	Ibaraki, Honshu on Lake Kasumi. Fishing, commercial and cultural center, carp fishing, lotus roots.
4337	Tsuruga	69,700	0.40	280	64.63	B	71,100	Fukui, Honshu on Sea of Japan. Center of communication with Asia. Synthetic fibers.
4338	Tsuruoka	102,000	1.00	1,000	65.23	B	104,000	Yamagata, Honshu, 43 miles north of Yamagata City. Candles, silk, sake, persimmons, rice.
4339	Tsuyama	91,500	0.50	460	64.73	B	93,500	Okayama, Honshu on Yoshii River. Socks, sickles, silk textiles. F=1442 as castle town.
4340	Ube	235,000	0.48	1,100	64.71	B	240,000	Yamaguchi. 0.4% Korean. 99.5% Buddhist. D=RCC(1 church),Methodist (3),Lutheran(1). 7 clergy. 3 child centers.
4341	Ueda	122,000	1.00	1,200	65.23	B	125,000	Nagano, Honshu on Chikuma River. Tourist gateway, synthetic fibers, processed foods.
4342	Ueno	61,700	0.40	250	64.63	B	63,000	Mie, Honshu. Sake, textiles, stoneware, umbrellas. F=1611 around a castle.
4343	Uozu	50,700	0.30	150	64.53	B	51,800	Toyama, Honshu on Toyama Bay east of Toyama. Computer components, fishery, squid processing.
4344	Urasoe	92,100	0.50	460	64.73	B	94,100	Southern Okinawa north of Naha on East China Sea. Residential, markets, fruits, vegetables.
4345	Usa	52,000	0.30	160	64.53	B	53,100	Oita, Kyushu. Textiles, rice products. Usa Hachiman Shrine (717). Annual festival, March 18.
4346	Ushiku	62,100	1.00	620	65.23	B	63,500	Ibaraki, Honshu, 34 miles south of Mito. Watermelons, wine, Ushiku Chateau: Japan's first winery.
4347	Utsunomiya	437,000	1.00	4,400	65.23	B	446,000	Capital of Tochigi, Honshu. Tourism around old temples. Railway cars, aircraft, tobacco. F=11th century.
4348	Uwajima	69,700	0.40	280	64.63	B	71,100	Ehime, Shikoku on Bungo Channel. Active fishing center. Many shrines & festivals. F=16th century.
4349	Wakayama	507,000	1.60	8,100	70.83	B	517,000	Wakayama on Kino River. 15% Shintoist, 15% New-Religionist, 14% nonreligious. 5 kindergartens.
4350	Kainan	49,800	1.50	750	65.73	B	50,800	Kuroe-nuri lacquerware, umbrellas, petrochemicals, port railroad, industrial center, rope nets. F=1934.
4351	Wakkanai	49,400	0.30	150	64.53	B	50,400	Hokkaido on Soya Bay, Cape Noshappu, Cape Soya Park. Deep sea fishing, marine products, dairying.
4352	Yamagata	255,000	1.00	2,600	65.23	B	261,000	Consumer goods, cast metal. HQ of Conservative Baptist Association of Churches (begun 1947).
4353	Yamaguchi	133,000	2.18	2,900	66.41	B	135,000	F=14th century. 90% Buddhist, 5% nonreligious. D=RCC (1 church), UCCJ (2), Plymouth Brethren (2).
4354	Yatsushiro	111,000	1.00	1,100	65.23	B	113,000	Kumamoto, Kyushu on Kuma River delta. Fishing, pottery, cement, paper, rayon. F=9th century.
4355	Yokkaichi	281,000	1.09	3,100	65.32	B	287,000	Mie, Honshu on Ise Bay. 24% New-Religionist, 10% Shintoist, 10% nonreligious. 16 clergy, 12 nuns.
4356	Yonago	135,000	1.30	1,700	65.53	B	137,000	Tottori, Honshu on Hino River. Pulp, iron & steel, textiles. Railroad junction, vegetables, agriculture.
4357	Yonezawa	97,000	0.50	490	64.73	B	99,100	Yamagata, Honshu. Electrical appliances, lumber. F=1338 as castle town. Matsugasaki Park.
4358	Yukuhashi	67,300	0.40	270	64.63	B	68,700	Fukuoka, Kyushu on Ima River south of Kitakyushu.
	JORDAN	**6,669,000**	**4.10**	**274,000**	**54.25**	**B**	**12,063,000**	**ORTHODOX 1.9%, INDEPENDENTS 1.1%. PENT-CHAR 1.3%, EVANGELICAL 0.4%, GCC 3.4%**
4359	rural areas	1,721,000	1.52	26,100	40.16	A	2,130,000	65.3% (1950), 49.4% (1970), 32.0% (1990), 25.8% (2000), 21.6% (2010), 17.6% (2025)
4360	urban areas	4,948,000	5.00	247,000	59.15	B	9,933,000	34.6% (1950), 50.5% (1970), 67.9% (1990), 74.1% (2000), 78.3% (2010), 82.3% (2025)
4361	non-metropolitan areas	2,672,000	4.94	132,000	59.09	B	5,582,841	*Sources of data:* Censuses of 1952, 1961, and 1979; estimates for 1967 and 1989.
4362	metropolitan areas	2,276,000	5.07	115,000	59.22	B	4,350,000	*Definition:* Localities with 10,000 or more inhabitants and each subdistrict center irrespective of size of population.
4363	AMMAN	1,449,000	5.00	72,500	59.15	B	2,690,000	Amman, central Jordan at 2,950 ft. Biblical Ramoth Amman. Many Palestinian Arabs. D=GOC,RCC.
4364	Al-Baq'ah	99,200	6.00	6,000	60.15	B	199,000	Eastern Al-Balqa north of Amman. Palestinian Arabs. Textiles, quarrying, leather goods. D=GOC.
4365	Ar-Rusayfah	112,000	5.00	5,600	59.15	B	226,000	Western Az-Zarqa north of Amman. Palestinian Arabs. Textiles, livestock, leather goods. D=COG.
4366	As-Salt	73,800	5.00	3,700	59.15	B	148,000	Capital of Al-Balqa. Agricultural market, grapes, grain. Byzantine bishopric. D=GOC,RCC.
4367	Az-Zarqa (Zarka)	493,000	4.80	23,700	58.95	B	990,000	Capital on Az-Zarqa north of Amman. Former Circassian center. Many Palestinian Arabs. D=GOC,RCC.
4368	Irbid	260,000	6.00	15,600	60.15	B	522,000	Capital of Irbid. Agricultural center. D=GOC(Arabs),RCC(1 hospital, schools),SDA,Anglican.

Table 10-5–continued opposite

Table 10-5–continued

Rec No 1	Country City 2	Pop 2000 3	AC% 4	Church Members 5	E% 6	W 7	Pop 2025 8	Notes 9
	KAZAKHSTAN	**16,223,000**	**15.98**	**2,592,000**	**64.25**	**B**	**17,698,000**	**ORTHODOX 8.6%, INDEPENDENTS 4.0%. PENT-CHAR 0.5%, EVANGELICAL 0.06%, GCC 8.9%**
4369	rural areas	6,215,000	14.33	890,000	62.61	B	4,879,000	60.9% (1950), 49.7% (1970), 42.3% (1990), 38.3% (2000), 33.8% (2010), 27.5% (2025)
4370	urban areas	10,008,000	17.00	1,701,000	65.27	B	12,819,000	39.0% (1950), 50.2% (1970), 57.6% (1990), 61.6% (2000), 66.1% (2010), 72.4% (2025)
4371	non-metropolitan areas	2,557,000	17.23	441,000	65.19	B	3,172,476	*Sources of data:* Censuses of 1959, 1970, 1979, and 1989.
4372	metropolitan areas	7,450,000	16.92	1,261,000	65.30	B	9,646,000	*Definition:* Cities and urban-type localities, officially designated as such by each of the constituent republics.
4373	Aktau	178,000	12.00	21,400	60.27	B	228,000	Karaganda. North of Karaganda. Caspian Sea. Oil and gas industry, nuclear plant, desalinization. D=ROC.
4374	Akt'ubinsk (Aktyubinsk)	281,000	10.00	28,100	58.27	B	360,000	Aktyubinsk on Ilek River. Chromium compounds, x-ray apparatus. F=1869 as Aktyube(White Hill). D=ROC.
4375	Almaty (Alma-ata, Vyermyi)	1,309,000	28.00	367,000	80.27	B	1,780,000	Educational center. Earthquakes & mudslides. Destroyed by Mongols (13th century). D=Baptist,Presbyterian,ROC.
4376	Arkalyk	68,400	1.00	680	44.27	A	87,600	Turgay. Bauxite deposits. Tobyl-Akmsla railroad, population doubled from 1970-1979. F=1956.
4377	ASTANA (Tselinograd, Akmola)	301,000	20.00	60,300	68.27	B	386,000	Tselinograd on Ishim River. Railways. Research & educational center. D=ROC,Ukrainian Orthodox.
4378	Aterau (Gurjev)	165,000	1.00	1,700	44.27	A	212,000	Guryev on Ural River near Caspian Sea. Oil, fishing, trade. F=17th century.
4379	Balchas (Balkhash)	92,300	1.00	920	44.27	A	118,000	Dzhezkazgan on Lake Balkhash. Major center of nonferrous metallurgy. Fish canning. F=1937.
4380	Cimkent (Chimkent)	463,000	22.00	102,000	70.27	B	592,000	Chimkent on Sayram River. Lead, automatic press, cement works, petroleum. F=12th century. D=ROC.
4381	Dzambul (Dzhambul, Aulie Ata)	329,000	17.00	56,000	65.27	B	422,000	Dzhambul on Talas River. Phosphate-processing, sugar, leather, footwear. Ancient origins. D=ROC.
4382	Dzetygara	51,500	12.00	6,200	60.27	B	66,000	Kustaney near Tobol River. Near Russian border. Agriculture, chemical fibers, building materials, iron. D=ROC.
4383	Dzezkazgan (Dzhezkazgan)	117,000	12.00	14,100	60.27	B	150,000	Capital of Dzhezkazgen on Kara-Kengir River reservoir. Copper mining, smelting. F=1938.
4384	Ekibastuz	146,000	10.00	14,600	58.27	B	188,000	Pavlodar on Irtysh-Karaganda Canal. Coal mining center. F=1876.
4385	Karaganda	642,000	25.00	160,000	73.27	B	822,000	Karaganda at center of coal basin. Iron & steel works, cement. F=1856. D=ROC,Ukrainian Orthodox.
4386	Kentau	68,600	1.00	690	44.27	A	87,900	Chimkent in Karatau Mountains. Mining, polymetallic ores.
4387	Kokcetav (Kokchetav)	151,000	19.00	28,700	67.27	B	193,000	Kokchetav along Ishim steppe. Substantial industrial center, agriculture. F=1824. D=ROC.
4388	Kustanaj (Kustanai)	247,000	18.00	44,400	66.27	B	316,000	Kustaney on Tobol River. Food processing, mineral wealth. F=1879 by Russian settlers. D=ROC.
4389	Kzyl-Orda (Perovsk)	167,000	12.00	20,000	60.27	B	214,000	Kyzl-Orda on Syr River. Former capital of Kazakhstan (1925-29). Kazakh theater. F=c1800.
4390	Leninogorsk (Ridder)	73,300	1.00	730	44.27	A	93,800	Vostochno-Kazakhstan on Ulba River in Altai mountains at 3,300 ft. Lead & zinc industry. F=1786.
4391	Leninsk	76,900	2.00	1,500	45.27	A	98,600	On Syr Darya. Irrigation, cotton cultivation, hydroelectric power, railroad.
4392	Pavlodar	361,000	16.00	57,800	64.27	B	462,000	Pavlodar on Irtysh River. Tractor, aluminum, chemical plants, oil refinery. F=1720. D=ROC.
4393	Petropavlovsk	262,000	15.00	39,300	63.27	B	335,000	Capital of Severo Kazakhstan on Ishim River. Trade & industry. F=1752 as Russian fort. D=ROC.
4394	Rudnyj (Rudny)	136,000	15.00	20,400	63.27	B	174,000	Kustanay on Tobol River. Heavy machinery, construction, thermoelectric power plant, iron, steel. D=ROC.
4395	Sachtinsk	68,800	1.00	690	44.27	A	88,200	Near Karaganda. Metalworks, machinery, consumer goods, food processing, mining, railroad, livestock.
4396	Saptajev	64,700	1.00	650	44.27	A	82,900	Dzezkazgan northwest of Dzezkazgan. Mining, irrigation, vegetables, livestock.
4397	Saran'	66,000	1.00	660	44.27	A	84,500	Karaganda. Major coal-mining center, chemicals, rubber products. F=1946.
4398	Scucinsk (Shchuchinsk)	59,000	1.00	590	44.27	A	75,600	Kokchetav on Lake Shchuchye. Health resort. Agricultural center. F=1828 by Cossacks.
4399	Semipalatinsk	363,000	18.00	65,400	66.27	B	465,000	Semipalatinsk on Irtysh River. Food processing, meat-packing. Nuclear-related sickness. F=1718. D=ROC.
4400	Taldy-Kurgan	143,000	10.00	14,300	58.27	B	184,000	Taldy-Kurgan on Karatal River. Construction materials, large parks. F=19th century. D=ROC.
4401	Temirtau	225,000	13.00	29,200	61.27	B	288,000	Karaganda on Samarkand Reservoir of Nura River. Iron & steel, chemicals, calcium carbide. F=1934. D=ROC.
4402	Turkestan	85,600	1.00	860	44.27	A	110,000	Chimkent in syrdarya plain. Ancient center of caravan trade. 12th century Muslim Saint Yasawi pilgrimage center.
4403	Ural'sk	226,000	19.00	42,900	67.27	B	289,000	Uralsk on Ural river. Leather, footwear, meat-packing. Oldest Theater in Kazakhstan. F=1612. D=ROC.
4404	Ust'Kamenogorsk (Ust-Kamenogorsk)	351,000	16.00	56,100	64.27	B	449,000	Vostochno-Kazakhstan at junction of Ulba & Irtysh rivers. Major center of nonferrous metallurgy. F=1720. D=ROC.
4405	Zanatas	55,900	5.00	2,800	53.27	B	71,600	Dzhambul in Karatau Mountains. Sugar beets, cotton, sheep, cattle, horses, phosphorite mining, chemicals.
4406	Zyr'anovsk	56,700	1.00	570	49.27	A	72,600	Vostochno-Kazakhstan on Beryozovka River near Lake Zajsan. Center of lead and zinc mining. F=1794.
	KENYA	**30,080,000**	**74.72**	**22,477,000**	**94.21**	**C**	**41,756,000**	**ROMAN CATHOLICS 23.2%, INDEPENDENTS 21.9%. PENT-CHAR 27.7%, EVANGELICAL 22.4%, GCC 12.2%**
4407	rural areas	20,124,000	76.72	15,438,000	95.21	C	20,494,000	94.4% (1950), 89.7% (1970), 75.9% (1990), 66.9% (2000), 58.7% (2010), 49.0% (2025)
4408	urban areas	9,957,000	70.70	7,039,000	92.19	C	21,262,000	5.5% (1950), 10.3% (1970), 24.0% (1990), 33.1% (2000), 41.2% (2010), 50.9% (2025)
4409	non-metropolitan areas	6,028,000	70.75	4,265,000	92.24	C	12,778,510	*Sources of data:* Censuses of 1948, 1962, 1969, and 1979.
4410	metropolitan areas	3,928,000	70.62	2,774,000	92.12	C	8,484,000	*Definition:* Towns with 2,000 or more inhabitants.
4411	Eldoret	103,000	60.00	61,600	84.49	C	219,000	Uasin Gishu Plateau. 6,857 ft. Corn, wheat, pyrethum, cattle. D=RCC bishopric.
4412	Kisumu	284,000	79.00	224,000	98.49	C	605,000	Capital of Nyanza. Port on Lake Victoria. 2% Muslim (2 mosques). D=RCC,Anglican,SDA,30 AICs.
4413	Machakos	162,000	60.00	97,300	84.49	C	346,000	Eastern southeast of Nairobi. Agricultural trade center, fruit, corn, dairy farming. D=Independents.
4414	Meru	147,000	60.00	87,900	84.49	C	313,000	Eastern near Mount Kenya National Park. Coffee, wheat, tea, corn, fruits. D=Independents.
4415	Mombasa	741,000	50.00	370,000	72.49	B	1,582,000	Capital of Coast. Chief port on Indian Ocean. Agricultural market. F=11th century. Hindus. D=Anglican,RCC.
4416	NAIROBI	2,320,000	77.00	1,786,000	98.49	C	5,049,000	Industrial center. Universities and research institutes. Tourism. F=1895. RCC cathedral. D=Independents.
4417	Nakuru	173,000	85.00	147,000	98.49	C	368,000	Capital of Rift Valley. Agricultural center. Kikuyu heartland. Egerton College. D=RCC,Independents.
	KIRGHIZIA	**4,699,000**	**9.91**	**466,000**	**47.37**	**A**	**6,096,000**	**ORTHODOX 7.7%, INDEPENDENTS 1.5%. PENT-CHAR 0.3%, EVANGELICAL 0.06%, GCC 4.7%**
4418	rural areas	2,816,000	8.91	251,000	45.78	A	2,801,000	68.9% (1950), 62.6% (1970), 61.8% (1990), 59.9% (2000), 55.3% (2010), 45.9% (2025)
4419	urban areas	1,883,000	11.40	215,000	49.76	A	3,295,000	31.0% (1950), 37.3% (1970), 38.1% (1990), 40.0% (2000), 44.6% (2010), 54.0% (2025)
4420	non-metropolitan areas	477,000	11.51	54,900	49.76	A	833,934	*Sources of data:* Censuses of 1959, 1970, 1979, and 1989.
4421	metropolitan areas	1,407,000	11.36	160,000	49.76	A	2,461,000	*Definition:* Cities and urban-type localities, officially designated as such by each of the constituent republics.
4422	BISHKEK (Pishpek, Frunze)	744,000	16.00	119,000	56.46	B	1,301,000	Chu River Valley. Cultural center. Museums, opera. Machine building, metalworking, orchards. F=1878. D=ROC.
4423	Dzalal-Abad	92,600	0.50	460	32.96	A	162,000	Osh. Food, light industry, food processing. Nearby Mount Ayubtav spa. F=1877.
4424	Kara-Balta	63,700	1.00	640	35.46	A	112,000	Cu near Bishkek. Orchards. 99% Muslim.
4425	Karakol (Przevalsk)	74,500	2.00	1,500	37.46	A	130,000	Issyk-Kul on eastern Issyk-Kul Lake. Wheat, wines, fruit juices, food processing, furniture, machine shops.
4426	Os (Osh)	276,000	13.00	35,900	51.46	B	483,000	Osh at 3,300 ft on Akbura River. Silk. Muslim pilgrimage (Takht-i-Suleyman) F=9th century. Uzbeks. D=ROC.
4427	Przeval'sk (Przhevalsk)	73,700	1.00	740	35.46	A	129,000	Issyk-Kul on Karakol River. Health resorts, sanatoriums. F=1869. Formerly Karakol.
4428	Tokmak (Bolshoy Tokmak)	82,500	2.00	1,700	37.46	A	144,000	On Chu River. Industrial development followed railway (1938). Originally 19th century fort. D=ROC.
	KIRIBATI	**83,400**	**92.74**	**77,300**	**99.93**	**C**	**119,000**	**ROMAN CATHOLICS 52.8%, PROTESTANTS 44.3%. PENT-CHAR 15.2%, EVANGELICAL 7.1%, GCC 12.2%**
4429	rural areas	52,300	93.18	48,700	99.93	C	58,500	90.4% (1950), 74.3% (1970), 65.3% (1990), 62.7% (2000), 58.2% (2010), 49.0% (2025)
4430	urban areas	31,100	92.00	28,600	99.92	C	60,800	9.5% (1950), 25.6% (1970), 34.6% (1990), 37.2% (2000), 41.7% (2010), 50.9% (2025)
4431	non-metropolitan areas	28,400	92.00	26,100	99.92	C	55,576	*Sources of data:* Censuses of 1968, 1973, 1978, 1985, and 1990.
4432	metropolitan areas	2,700	92.00	2,500	99.93	C	5,300	*Definition:* Tarawa.
4433	BAIRIKI (Tarawa)	2,700	92.00	2,500	99.94	C	5,300	Copra, mother-of-pearl. Government hospital, leper station, teacher's training college. D=RCC,GIPC.
	KUWAIT	**1,972,000**	**12.55**	**248,000**	**64.46**	**B**	**2,974,000**	**ROMAN CATHOLICS 8.8%, INDEPENDENTS 3.2%. PENT-CHAR 3.4%, EVANGELICAL 0.9%, GCC 8.3%**
4434	rural areas	47,500	6.68	3,200	38.31	A	48,800	40.9% (1950), 22.2% (1970), 4.1% (1990), 2.4% (2000), 1.9% (2010), 1.6% (2025)
4435	urban areas	1,924,000	12.70	244,000	65.11	B	2,926,000	59.0% (1950), 77.7% (1970), 95.8% (1990), 97.5% (2000), 98.0% (2010), 98.3% (2025)
4436	non-metropolitan areas	436,000	12.75	55,600	64.82	B	851,548	*Sources of data:* Censuses of 1957, 1965, 1970, 1975, 1980, and 1985.
4437	metropolitan areas	1,488,000	12.68	189,000	65.20	B	2,074,000	*Definition:* Agglomerations of 10,000 or more inhabitants.
4438	Al-Ahmadi	301,000	7.50	22,600	60.41	B	458,000	Capital of Al-Ahmadi. Oasis town. Kuwait Oil Company. F=1946. Natural History Society. D=Anglican.
4439	Ac-Fuhayhil	52,900	8.00	4,200	59.91	B	80,500	Pleasant gardens. D=RCC,Anglican.
4440	Subahiya	64,300	7.00	4,500	58.91	B	97,700	Industrial area. Oil refinery, chemical fertilizer. D=RCC.
4441	AL-KUWAYT	1,187,000	14.00	166,000	66.41	B	1,616,000	On Kuwait Bay and Persian Gulf. Commercial center. Banking. Modern hotels. Damaged in 1990-91. D=RCC.
4442	Abraq Khitan	47,700	13.00	6,200	64.91	B	72,500	Experimental farm. Fertilizers, various consumer goods, vegetables, livestock.
4443	Al-Farwaniyah	72,600	13.00	9,400	64.91	B	110,000	1 of 5 governorates. Located at head of Persian Gulf, desalinization.
4444	Al-Jahrah	118,000	14.00	16,500	65.91	B	179,000	West of Kuwait City. Center of agriculture region, fruits, vegetables. Oasis town. Ancient origins. Camel market.
4445	Al-Salimiyah (Salmuja)	162,000	14.00	22,700	65.91	B	247,000	Agricultural market. D=RCC.
4446	Al-Sulaybiyah	54,200	13.00	7,100	64.91	B	82,500	Oasis town. D=RCC.
4447	Hawalli	153,000	14.00	21,500	65.91	B	233,000	Five miles southeast of Kuwait City. American School. Site of first water well in Kuwait. D=RCC.
4448	Qalib ash-Shuyukh	121,000	14.00	17,000	65.91	B	184,000	Oil refinery. D=RCC.
4449	South Khitan	73,200	13.00	9,500	64.91	B	111,000	Vegetables, livestock. D=RCC.
	LAOS	**5,433,000**	**2.07**	**113,000**	**47.55**	**A**	**9,653,000**	**INDEPENDENTS 0.8%, PROTESTANTS 0.6%. PENT-CHAR 0.9%, EVANGELICAL 0.7%, GCC 1.8%**
4450	rural areas	4,158,000	1.79	74,300	46.75	A	5,859,000	92.7% (1950), 90.3% (1970), 81.9% (1990), 76.5% (2000), 70.5% (2010), 60.7% (2025)
4451	urban areas	1,275,000	3.00	38,200	50.18	B	3,793,000	7.2% (1950), 9.6% (1970), 18.0% (1990), 23.4% (2000), 29.5% (2010), 39.3% (2025)
4452	non-metropolitan areas	444,000	3.04	13,500	50.20	B	1,322,456	*Sources of data:* Census of 1973; estimates for 1958 and 1966.
4453	metropolitan areas	830,000	2.98	24,700	50.17	B	2,471,000	*Definition:* Sum of five largest towns: Vientiane, Luang Prabang, Savannakhet, Kammouan and Pakse.
4454	Louangphrabang (Luang Prabang)	70,600	0.50	350	46.98	A	210,000	Mekong River port. Indian & Chinese merchants. F=1353. Religious center. More than 20 Buddhist pagodas.
4455	Pakxe (Pakse)	73,300	0.50	370	46.98	A	218,000	Confluence of Xedon & Mekong Rivers. Distributing center for teak, tea. Sawmills. Chief port before 1966.
4456	Savannakhet	98,200	0.50	490	46.98	A	292,000	Mekong River port. Soft drinks, ice-making, sawmill. Education center. Alak, So, Souei peoples.
4457	VIANGCHAN (Vientiane)	588,000	4.00	23,500	51.48	B	1,751,000	Mekong River port. Brewing, lumber. F=13th century. That Luang temple (1566). 'City of Sandalwood'. D=RCC.
	LATVIA	**2,357,000**	**66.90**	**1,576,000**	**99.04**	**C**	**1,936,000**	**PROTESTANTS 23.7%, ORTHODOX 23.5%. PENT-CHAR 3.8%, EVANGELICAL 7.1%, GCC 20.0%**
4458	rural areas	606,000	72.09	437,000	99.33	C	357,000	48.4% (1950), 37.9% (1970), 28.7% (1990), 25.7% (2000), 22.6% (2010), 18.4% (2025)
4459	urban areas	1,751,000	65.10	1,140,000	98.94	C	1,579,000	51.5% (1950), 62.0% (1970), 71.2% (1990), 74.3% (2000), 77.3% (2010), 81.5% (2025)
4460	non-metropolitan areas	487,000	65.05	317,000	98.94	C	348,910	*Sources of data:* Censuses of 1959, 1970, 1979, and 1989.
4461	metropolitan areas	1,264,000	65.12	823,000	98.94	C	1,230,000	*Definition:* Cities and urban-type localities according to the criteria of number of inhabitants.
4462	Daugavpils (Dvinsk)	120,000	65.00	77,900	98.64	C	108,000	On western Dvina River. Locomotive repair shops. F=1270 by Brothers of the Sword. D=ROC,LOC.
4463	Jelgava (Mitava)	69,200	66.00	45,700	98.14	C	62,400	On Lielupe River. Agricultural machinery, locks. linen. F=1226 by Brothers of the Sword. D=Lutheran.
4464	Liepaja (Liepaya, Libau)	107,000	70.00	74,700	99.64	C	96,300	On Baltic Sea. Naval port, grain export, steel, deep-sea fishing. F=1253 as Kurdish settlement. D=ROC,LOC.
4465	RIGA	921,000	64.00	589,000	98.91	C	921,000	On western Dvina River. Ships. F=1201 by Bishop Albert I. Done. Cathedral (1215). D=LOC,ROC.
4466	Jurmala	61,800	65.00	40,200	97.14	C	55,700	On Gulf of Riga west of Riga. Textiles, museums. D=Lutheran,LOC,ROC.
4467	Ventspils	46,800	75.00	35,100	99.84	C	42,200	At mouth of Venta River on Baltic Sea. Ice-free port for oil export, fishing. F=2000 BC. D=Lutheran.
	LEBANON	**3,282,000**	**52.86**	**1,735,000**	**91.87**	**B**	**4,400,000**	**ROMAN CATHOLICS 42.5%, ORTHODOX 16.3%. PENT-CHAR 5.0%, EVANGELICAL 1.7%, GCC 21.9%**
4468	rural areas	337,000	42.91	144,000	72.32	B	287,000	77.3% (1950), 40.6% (1970), 15.8% (1990), 10.2% (2000), 7.8% (2010), 6.5% (2025)
4469	urban areas	2,945,000	54.00	1,590,000	94.11	B	4,113,000	22.6% (1950), 59.3% (1970), 84.1% (1990), 89.7% (2000), 92.1% (2010), 93.4% (2025)
4470	non-metropolitan areas	205,000	53.80	110,000	93.18	B	575,998	*Sources of data:* Census of 1970; estimate for 1958 and 1988.
4471	metropolitan areas	2,740,000	54.02	1,480,000	94.18	B	3,537,000	*Definition:* Localities with 5,000 or more inhabitants.
4472	BAYRUT (Beirut)	2,058,000	53.70	1,105,000	93.71	B	2,584,000	On Mediterranean Sea. Former banking center. Civil war seriously damaged city. D=RCC,GOC.
4473	Sayda (Sidon)	129,000	57.00	73,800	96.01	B	181,000	Fishing & market center. F=3rd century BC. Ancient ruins. Christian Maronites. Palestinian refugees. D=RCC.
4474	Tarabulus (Tripoli)	270,000	55.00	149,000	96.01	B	377,000	Mediterranean port. Oil, soap. Beach resort. F=700 BC. Many historical ruins & sites. Sunni Muslim. D=RCC.
4475	Zahlah (Zahle)	283,000	54.00	153,000	95.01	B	395,000	In Lebanon Mountains at 3,150 ft. Agricultural market, summer resort. Fruit, vineyards, arrack. D=RCC.

Table 10-5–continued overleaf

Table 10-5–continued

Rec No 1	Country City 2	Pop 2000 3	AC% 4	Church Members 5	E% 6	W 7	Pop 2025 8	Notes 9
	LESOTHO	**2,153,000**	**67.14**	**1,445,000**	**99.62**	**C**	**3,506,000**	**ROMAN CATHOLICS 37.4%, PROTESTANTS 12.9%. PENT-CHAR 15.8%, EVANGELICAL 3.5%, GCC 23.7%**
4476	rural areas	1,551,000	66.04	1,024,000	99.60	C	1,911,000	99.0% (1950), 91.4% (1970), 79.9% (1990), 72.0% (2000), 64.4% (2010), 54.5% (2025)
4477	urban areas	602,000	70.00	421,000	99.68	C	1,595,000	0.9% (1950), 8.5% (1970), 20.0% (1990), 27.9% (2000), 35.6% (2010), 45.5% (2025)
4478	non-metropolitan areas	443,000	70.00	310,000	99.68	C	1,173,905	*Sources of data:* Censuses of 1956, 1966, 1976, and 1986.
4479	metropolitan areas	159,000	70.00	111,000	99.68	C	422,000	*Definition:* The district headquarters and other settlements of rapid population growth.
4480	MASERU-Roma-Morija	159,000	70.00	111,000	99.68	C	422,000	On Caledon River at 5,000 ft. Farm produce. National Assembly. Radio Lesotho. F=1869. D=RCC,Ev Church.
	LIBERIA	**3,154,000**	**29.55**	**932,000**	**72.51**	**B**	**6,618,000**	**INDEPENDENTS 17.0%, PROTESTANTS 13.6%. PENT-CHAR 16.4%, EVANGELICAL 10.6%, GCC 17.2%**
4481	rural areas	1,643,000	23.62	388,000	66.57	B	2,501,000	87.0% (1950), 73.9% (1970), 57.9% (1990), 52.0% (2000), 46.1% (2010), 37.7% (2025)
4482	urban areas	1,511,000	36.00	544,000	78.96	B	4,117,000	12.9% (1950), 26.0% (1970), 42.0% (1990), 47.9% (2000), 53.9% (2010), 62.2% (2025)
4483	non-metropolitan areas	98,100	36.00	35,300	78.96	B	706,762	*Sources of data:* Censuses of 1962, 1974, and 1984; estimate for 1993.
4484	metropolitan areas	1,413,000	36.00	509,000	78.96	B	3,410,000	*Definition:* Localities with 2,000 or more inhabitants.
4485	MONROVIA	1,413,000	36.00	509,000	78.96	B	3,410,000	On Bushrod Island. Growing rapidly. Latex, iron ore. Educational center. F=1822. D=Baptist.
	LIBYA	**5,605,000**	**3.04**	**170,000**	**46.12**	**A**	**8,647,000**	**ORTHODOX 1.9%, ROMAN CATHOLICS 0.8%. PENT-CHAR 0.3%, EVANGELICAL 0.1%, GCC 1.6%**
4486	rural areas	693,000	0.49	3,400	37.94	A	736,000	81.4% (1950), 54.6% (1970), 18.1% (1990), 12.3% (2000), 10.3% (2010), 8.5% (2025)
4487	urban areas	4,911,000	3.40	167,000	47.28	A	7,911,000	18.5% (1950), 45.3% (1970), 81.8% (1990), 87.6% (2000), 89.7% (2010), 91.4% (2025)
4488	non-metropolitan areas	1,352,000	3.38	45,700	47.40	A	1,211,137	*Sources of data:* Censuses of 1954, 1964, 1973, and 1984.
4489	metropolitan areas	3,559,000	3.41	121,000	47.23	A	6,700,000	*Definition:* Total population of Tripoli and Banghazi, plus the urban parts of Beida and Derna.
4490	Al-Bayda (Beida)	118,000	0.50	590	35.58	A	190,000	Seaport on Gulf of Sidra. National government buildings. Salt, oil, cement. Founded by Greeks.
4491	Banghazi (Benghazi)	975,000	4.00	39,000	49.08	A	1,916,000	Coastal oasis. Market economy, textiles & hardware. Arab, Turkish & European architecture. F=500 BC. D=COC.
4492	Darnah	109,000	0.50	550	33.58	A	176,000	Northern Barqah on Mediterranean Sea near Tobruk. Great Mosque. Fruits, winter resort. F=15th century.
4493	Misratah (Misurata)	184,000	0.50	920	35.58	A	296,000	Chief seaport. Olives, vegetables, fishing, tanning. Ancient origins. Old mosques. New steel plant (1990).
4494	TARABULUS (Tripoli)	2,041,000	3.80	77,600	48.88	A	3,909,000	Port. Ancient Greek origins. Olives, citrus fruits, tobacco. Gurgi mosque. D=COC,RCC.
4495	Tubruq (Tobruk)	132,000	2.00	2,600	46.08	A	213,000	Northern Barqah on Mediterranean Sea. World War II battlefield. Major oil terminal.
	LIECHTENSTEIN	**32,800**	**82.36**	**27,100**	**98.36**	**C**	**41,300**	**ROMAN CATHOLICS 74.2%, PROTESTANTS 7.6%. PENT-CHAR 2.4%, EVANGELICAL 0.3%, GCC 43.1%**
4496	rural areas	25,400	82.76	21,000	98.76	C	25,700	80.1% (1950), 79.8% (1970), 79.9% (1990), 77.3% (2000), 72.0% (2010), 62.3% (2025)
4497	urban areas	7,400	81.00	6,000	97.00	C	15,500	19.8% (1950), 20.1% (1970), 20.1% (1990), 22.6% (2000), 27.9% (2010), 37.6% (2025)
4498	non-metropolitan areas	2,000	81.01	1,600	96.99	C	4,110	*Sources of data:* Censuses of 1950, 1960, and 1981.
4499	metropolitan areas	5,500	81.00	4,400	97.00	C	11,400	*Definition:* Urban centers.
4500	VADUZ	5,500	81.00	4,400	97.00	C	11,400	Tourism. Art collections. Rhine River, medieval castle (art museum), grapes, wine, construction materials. D=RCC.
	LITHUANIA	**3,670,000**	**87.55**	**3,213,000**	**99.60**	**C**	**3,399,000**	**ROMAN CATHOLICS 84.6%, ORTHODOX 3.1%. PENT-CHAR 1.4%, EVANGELICAL 0.2%, GCC 11.7%**
4501	rural areas	930,000	92.13	856,000	99.75	C	591,000	68.9% (1950), 50.4% (1970), 31.2% (1990), 25.3% (2000), 21.3% (2010), 17.3% (2025)
4502	urban areas	2,741,000	86.00	2,357,000	99.55	C	2,808,000	31.0% (1950), 49.5% (1970), 68.7% (1990), 74.6% (2000), 78.6% (2010), 82.6% (2025)
4503	non-metropolitan areas	1,190,000	86.44	1,029,000	99.53	C	1,219,572	*Sources of data:* Censuses of 1959, 1970, 1979, and 1989.
4504	metropolitan areas	1,550,000	85.66	1,328,000	99.57	C	1,588,000	*Definition:* Cities and urban-type localities according to the inhabitants.
4505	Alytus (Alitus)	71,900	80.00	57,500	99.05	C	73,600	On Neman River. Iron foundry, turpentine, linen, clothing. Agricultural college. F=14th century. D=RCC.
4506	Kaunas (Kovno)	423,000	86.00	363,000	99.55	C	433,000	On Neman River. Metal castings, radios. F=1030 as fortress. 84% Lithuanian. Vytautas church (1400). D=RCC.
4507	Klaipeda (Memel)	204,000	84.00	171,000	99.25	C	209,000	On Baltic Sea. Ice-free port. Shipbuilding & repair, fishing, cotton textiles. F=13th century. D=RCC.
4508	Panavezys (Panevezhis)	126,000	85.00	107,000	99.35	C	129,000	On Nevezis River. Agricultural trade, sugar refining, metal works. Drama theater. F=1503. D=RCC.
4509	Siauliai (Shaulyay)	145,000	85.00	123,000	99.35	C	148,000	Leather, footwear, metalworking, precision instruments. F=13th century. May be Saule of 1236 battle. D=RCC.
4510	VILNIUS (Wilno)	581,000	87.00	506,000	99.85	C	596,000	Confluence of Nevis & Vilnia Rivers. F=10th century. Y=1387. Cathedral (1387). Jesuit academy (1579). D=RCC.
	LUXEMBOURG	**431,000**	**93.51**	**403,000**	**99.09**	**C**	**463,000**	**ROMAN CATHOLICS 94.5%, PROTESTANTS 1.7%. PENT-CHAR 4.6%, EVANGELICAL 0.2%, GCC 17.5%**
4511	rural areas	38,500	97.70	37,600	99.16	C	24,600	40.9% (1950), 32.2% (1970), 13.7% (1990), 8.9% (2000), 6.6% (2010), 5.3% (2025)
4512	urban areas	392,000	93.10	365,000	99.08	C	439,000	59.0% (1950), 67.7% (1970), 86.3% (1990), 91.0% (2000), 93.3% (2010), 94.7% (2025)
4513	non-metropolitan areas	151,000	93.15	140,000	99.07	C	168,427	*Sources of data:* Censuses of 1947, 1960, 1966, 1970; estimates for 1981 and 1991.
4514	metropolitan areas	242,000	93.07	225,000	99.08	C	270,000	*Definition:* Communes having more than 2,000 inhabitants in the administrative center.
4515	Esch-sur-Alzette	91,600	94.00	86,100	99.58	C	102,000	On Alzette River near French border. Phosphoric iron ore, iron & steel, fertilizer, foodstuffs. D=RCC.
4516	LUXEMBOURG-Ville	150,000	92.50	139,000	98.78	C	168,000	On Alzette and Petrusse rivers. International financial center. F=963. 'Gibraltar of the North'. D=RCC.
	MACEDONIA	**2,024,000**	**63.61**	**1,287,000**	**88.05**	**C**	**2,258,000**	**ORTHODOX 59.3%, ROMAN CATHOLICS 3.4%. PENT-CHAR 0.3%, EVANGELICAL 0.1%, GCC 10.5%**
4517	rural areas	769,000	66.24	509,000	89.05	C	619,000	76.5% (1950), 52.9% (1970), 42.2% (1990), 38.0% (2000), 33.6% (2010), 27.4% (2025)
4518	urban areas	1,255,000	62.00	778,000	87.44	C	1,639,000	23.4% (1950), 47.0% (1970), 57.7% (1990), 62.0% (2000), 66.3% (2010), 72.5% (2025)
4519	non-metropolitan areas	321,000	62.97	202,000	87.44	C	419,244	*Sources of data:* Censuses of 1953, 1961, 1971, 1981, and 1991.
4520	metropolitan areas	934,000	61.67	576,000	87.44	C	1,220,000	*Definition:* Urban centers.
4521	Bitola (Bitol)	163,000	63.00	103,000	87.44	C	213,000	On Dragor River. Cereals, tobacco. F=Greek settlement,1014 by Slavs. Monastery of Obitelj. D=MOC.
4522	Kumanovo	147,000	63.00	92,900	87.44	C	193,000	Tobacco processing . Staro Nagoricane Monastery (1318). Matejic Monastery (16th century). D=MOC.
4523	SKOPJE	623,000	61.00	380,000	87.44	C	814,000	On Vardar River. 80% destroyed by 1963 earthquake. F=Illyrian Scupi. Church of Sveti Pantelejmon. D=MOC.
	MADAGASCAR	**15,942,000**	**47.86**	**7,629,000**	**82.99**	**B**	**28,964,000**	**PROTESTANTS 25.6%, ROMAN CATHOLICS 22.9%. PENT-CHAR 4.6%, EVANGELICAL 5.9%, GCC 15.6%**
4524	rural areas	11,237,000	46.75	5,254,000	82.21	B	15,672,000	92.2% (1950), 85.9% (1970), 76.5% (1990), 70.4% (2000), 64.0% (2010), 54.1% (2025)
4525	urban areas	4,704,000	50.50	2,376,000	84.83	B	13,291,000	7.8% (1950), 14.1% (1970), 23.4% (1990), 29.5% (2000), 36.0% (2010), 45.8% (2025)
4526	non-metropolitan areas	1,815,000	50.50	917,000	84.82	B	5,108,343	*Sources of data:* Surveys of 1966 and 1975; estimates for 1950 and 1970.
4527	metropolitan areas	2,889,000	50.50	1,459,000	84.84	B	8,183,000	*Definition:* Centers with 5,000 or more inhabitants.
4528	ANTANANARIVO (Tananarive)	1,128,000	65.00	733,000	94.13	C	3,207,000	Capital of Antananarivo. Tobacco. F=c1625 by Hova. 'City of a thousands warriors'. D=RCC,FJKM.
4529	Antsirabe	147,000	50.00	73,400	89.13	B	415,000	Southern Antananarivo in Ankaratra Mountains. Thermal springs. American Lutheran Missionary School (1916).
4530	Antsiranana (Diego-Suarez)	323,000	30.00	96,900	66.13	B	912,000	Capital of Antsiranana. Northern tip of Madagascar. Ship construction & repair. Coffee, peanuts. D=RCC,FJKM.
4531	Fianarantsoa	440,000	50.00	220,000	89.13	B	1,244,000	Capital of Fianarantsoa. Rice, beans, cattle herding, sports facilities, university. D=RCC,FJKM.
4532	Mahajanga (Majunga)	294,000	40.00	117,000	77.13	B	829,000	On mouth of Betsiboka River. Fishing, lumbering, transshipment. F=18th century. D=RCC,FJKM,FLM.
4533	Toamasina (Tamatave)	338,000	45.00	152,000	83.13	B	954,000	On Indian Ocean. Exports coffee, vanilla, pepper. Holiday resorts nearby. Destroyed by hurricane (1927). D=RCC.
4534	Toliara (Toliary)	220,000	30.00	66,000	66.13	B	622,000	Port on Mozambique Channel. Beaches. Agricultural products, marine products, sisal. D=RCC,FJKM.
	MALAWI	**10,925,000**	**64.37**	**7,032,000**	**96.05**	**C**	**19,958,000**	**ROMAN CATHOLICS 24.6%, PROTESTANTS 19.5%. PENT-CHAR 17.7%, EVANGELICAL 8.6%, GCC 22.4%**
4535	rural areas	9,248,000	63.26	5,850,000	95.68	C	14,242,000	96.4% (1950), 93.9% (1970), 88.1% (1990), 84.6% (2000), 80.0% (2010), 71.3% (2025)
4536	urban areas	1,677,000	70.50	1,182,000	98.08	C	5,716,000	3.5% (1950), 6.0% (1970), 11.8% (1990), 15.3% (2000), 19.9% (2010), 28.6% (2025)
4537	non-metropolitan areas	821,000	70.41	578,000	98.15	C	2,798,640	*Sources of data:* Censuses of 1966, 1977, and 1987; estimate for 1956.
4538	metropolitan areas	856,000	70.59	604,000	98.01	C	2,917,000	*Definition:* All townships, town planning areas and district centers.
4539	Blantyre-Limbe	502,000	71.00	356,000	97.68	C	1,710,000	Shoes, corn milling, brewing, tobacco auctions. F=1876 as Church of Scotland mission. D=RCC,CCAP.
4540	LILONGWE	354,000	70.00	248,000	98.48	C	1,207,000	Agriculture market center, tobacco. Government buildings & embassies. Capital since 1975.D=RCC,CCAP.
	MALAYSIA	**22,244,000**	**7.96**	**1,771,000**	**63.67**	**B**	**30,968,000**	**ROMAN CATHOLICS 3.2%, PROTESTANTS 2.9%. PENT-CHAR 2.4%, EVANGELICAL 2.2%, GCC 6.0%**
4541	rural areas	9,509,000	7.24	689,000	61.94	B	9,114,000	79.6% (1950), 66.5% (1970), 50.2% (1990), 42.7% (2000), 36.4% (2010), 29.4% (2025)
4542	urban areas	12,735,000	8.50	1,082,000	64.96	B	21,854,000	20.3% (1950), 33.4% (1970), 49.7% (1990), 57.2% (2000), 63.6% (2010), 70.5% (2025)
4543	non-metropolitan areas	6,969,000	8.50	593,000	64.95	B	12,178,704	*Sources of data:* Censuses of 1947, 1957, and 1991; estimates for 1970 and 1980.
4544	metropolitan areas	5,766,000	8.50	490,000	64.97	B	9,676,000	*Definition:* Gazetted areas with their adjoining built-up areas that have a combined population of 10,000 or more.
4545	Alor Setar (Alor Star)	112,000	5.00	5,600	60.71	B	193,000	Capital of Kedah on Kedah River. Major distribution center, paddy rice. Residence of Sultan of Kedah.
4546	Batu Pahat (Bandar Penggaram)	105,000	6.00	6,300	61.71	B	180,000	On Strait of Malacca. Fishing town & distribution center. Sago palms, rubber, coconuts.
4547	Ipoh	476,000	10.00	47,600	66.71	B	817,000	Capital of Perak on Kinta River. Tin mining by Chinese. Caves used as Chinese temples. D=RCC,Methodist.
4548	Johor Bharu (Johore, Johor Baharu)	399,000	5.20	20,800	60.91	B	685,000	Capital of Johor. 45% Malay, 40% Chinese, 10% Indian. D=RCC. Evangelistic crusades 1983, 1984.
4549	Kelang (Port Kelang, Klang)	311,000	4.00	12,400	52.71	B	534,000	Selangor. On Kelang River. Administrative center for fruit & rubber, pineapple canning, seafood.
4550	Keluang	81,500	6.00	4,900	61.71	B	140,000	Central Johor north of Johor Baharu. Rubber, oil palm, rice, copra, pineapples, mining.
4551	Kota Baharu (Kota Bahru)	272,000	5.00	13,600	60.71	B	467,000	Capital of Kelantan on Kelantan River. Industrial nucleus. Handicrafts, hotels, beach resorts. D=RCC.
4552	Kota Kinabalu (Jesselton)	90,700	25.00	22,700	85.71	B	156,000	Capital of Sabah. Rubber, flour milling, woodworking. F=1899. Mainly Chinese. D=RCC,Ev. Church.
4553	KUALA LUMPUR	1,378,000	4.50	62,000	63.21	B	2,145,000	Banking. F=1857. 46% Chinese, 35% Malay, 13% Tamil. D=RCC,Anglican,Methodist.
4554	Petaling Jaya	337,000	4.00	13,500	62.71	B	578,000	Industrial estate. Food processing, iron works, engineering, rubber. D=RCC,Anglican,Methodist.
4555	Kuala Terengganu (Kuala Trengganu)	292,000	4.00	11,700	52.71	B	501,000	At mouth of Terengganu River. Sprawling town with houses on stilts. Agricultural trade, weaving.
4556	Kuantan	213,000	5.00	10,700	60.71	B	366,000	Capital of Pahang. At mouth of Kuantan River. Exports tin, rubber, copra. Fishing, textiles, dolls.
4557	Kuching	118,000	30.00	35,300	90.71	B	202,000	Capital & port of Sarawak. Rubber, pepper. Many cathedrals, mosques & temples. F=1839. D=RCC.
4558	Melaka (Malacca)	142,000	30.00	42,500	90.71	B	243,000	Port on Strait of Malacca. Rubber. F=1400. Mostly Chinese, Baba Chinese. Francis Xavier. D=RCC.
4559	Miri	84,400	29.00	24,500	89.71	B	145,000	Sarawak port on South China Sea. Rubber, rice. F=1911. D=RCC,Methodist.
4560	Muar (Bandar Maharani)	106,000	25.00	26,400	85.71	B	181,000	Port on Strait of Malacca. Food, beverages, oils, fats, chemicals. F=14th century.
4561	Pinang (George Town, Penang)	802,000	6.00	48,100	61.71	B	1,376,000	Island. Tourist center. Chinese by race. European in character. F=1786 by British. D=RCC. Dalat School (CMA).
4562	Butterworth	126,000	6.00	7,600	61.71	B	217,000	Transshipment port. Hub of rubber plantations. Oil import, tin smelting. D=RCC,Methodist,Anglican.
4563	Sandakan	114,000	20.00	22,800	80.71	B	196,000	Principal port of Sabah. Timber, copra, manila hemp. Mainly Cantonese Chinese. F=1847. D=RCC,Methodist.
4564	Seremban	215,000	5.00	10,800	60.71	B	370,000	On Linggi River. Rubber, tin, rice. Hot springs resort nearby. F=1840 around tin mining.
4565	Sibu	138,000	30.00	41,400	90.71	B	237,000	Sarawak at confluence of Rajang & Igan rivers. Exports timber, rubber, & pepper. D=RCC,Methodist.
4566	Taiping	237,000	5.00	11,800	60.71	B	406,000	Tin, paddy rice, rubber. Bukit Maxwell tourism. F=1840 by Chinese for tin mining.
4567	Telok Anson	79,600	10.00	8,000	66.71	B	137,000	Southern Perak near Perak River mouth and Andaman Sea. D=RCC,Anglican,Methodist.
	MALDIVES	**286,000**	**0.13**	**360**	**19.60**	**A**	**501,000**	**PROTESTANTS 0.09%, ROMAN CATHOLICS 0.03%. PENT-CHAR 0.02%, EVANGELICAL 0.02%, GCC 0.1%**
4568	rural areas	205,000	0.06	120	17.16	A	286,000	89.3% (1950), 86.4% (1970), 74.0% (1990), 71.6% (2000), 66.9% (2010), 57.0% (2025)
4569	urban areas	81,100	0.29	240	25.76	A	215,000	10.6% (1950), 13.5% (1970), 25.9% (1990), 28.3% (2000), 33.0% (2010), 42.9% (2025)
4570	non-metropolitan areas	5,100	0.14	7	25.61	A	13,456	*Sources of data:* Censuses of 1946, 1965, 1967, 1977, 1985, and 1990.
4571	metropolitan areas	76,000	0.30	230	25.77	A	202,000	*Definition:* Male, the capital.
4572	MALE	76,000	0.30	230	25.77	A	202,000	Trade & tourist center. Coconuts, breadfruits, fish, woven palm mats. Muslim (99%). D=CSI,RCC.
	MALI	**11,234,000**	**2.00**	**224,000**	**43.56**	**A**	**21,295,000**	**ROMAN CATHOLICS 1.1%, PROTESTANTS 0.7%. PENT-CHAR 0.2%, EVANGELICAL 0.7%, GCC 1.7%**
4573	rural areas	7,859,000	1.35	106,000	41.29	A	11,368,000	91.5% (1950), 85.6% (1970), 76.2% (1990), 69.9% (2000), 63.2% (2010), 53.3% (2025)
4574	urban areas	3,375,000	3.50	118,000	48.86	A	9,928,000	8.4% (1950), 14.3% (1970), 23.8% (1990), 30.0% (2000), 36.7% (2010), 46.6% (2025)
4575	non-metropolitan areas	1,636,000	3.53	57,800	48.86	A	5,027,220	*Sources of data:* Censuses of 1976 and 1987; estimate for 1960.
4576	metropolitan areas	1,738,000	3.47	60,300	48.86	A	4,901,000	*Definition:* Localities with 5,000 or more inhabitants and district centers.

Table 10-5–continued opposite

Table 10-5–continued

Rec No 1	Country City 2	Pop 2000 3	AC% 4	Church Members 5	E% 6	W 7	Pop 2025 8	Notes 9
4577	BAMAKO	1,160,000	4.40	51,000	51.56	B	3,199,000	Koulikoro on Niger River. Mud brick buildings. 50% Bambara, 17% Fulani, 10% Arab. D=RCC,ECEM,EEPM.
4578	Gao	82,000	1.00	820	40.56	A	241,000	Southern Gao on Niger River. Sahara desert. Capital of Songhai empire. Rice, wheat.
4579	Kayes	72,100	1.00	720	40.56	A	212,000	Capital of Kayes on Senegal River. Peanuts, livestock. Subsistence agriculture. D=RCC.
4580	Koutiala	71,800	1.00	720	40.56	A	211,000	Northern Sikasso east of Bamako. Cotton gin, research institute, peanuts, kapok, iron deposits. D=ECEM.
4581	Mopti	111,000	1.00	1,100	40.56	A	325,000	Capital of Mopti on Niger and Bani rivers. Fishing. Dogon, Bambara. D=RCC,ECEM,EEPM.
4582	Segou	133,000	2.00	2,700	46.56	A	391,000	Capital of Segou on Niger River. Trade center. Textiles, rice, livestock. Headquarters of irrigation system. D=RCC.
4583	Sikasso	109,000	3.00	3,300	48.56	A	321,000	Capital of Sikasso. Cotton ginning. Bambara. Former capital of Kingdom of Kenedougou. D=RCC,EEPM.
	MALTA	**389,000**	**95.58**	**371,000**	**99.94**	**C**	**430,000**	**ROMAN CATHOLICS 94.5%, ANGLICANS 0.2%. PENT-CHAR 24.9%, EVANGELICAL 0.1%, GCC 43.7%**
4584	rural areas	36,800	95.42	35,100	99.78	C	27,900	38.8% (1950), 22.6% (1970), 12.3% (1990), 9.4% (2000), 7.8% (2010), 6.5% (2025)
4585	urban areas	352,000	95.60	336,000	99.96	C	402,000	61.1% (1950), 77.4% (1970), 87.6% (1990), 90.5% (2000), 92.1% (2010), 93.5% (2025)
4586	non-metropolitan areas	124,000	95.60	119,000	99.96	C	141,840	*Sources of data:* Censuses of 1948, 1957, 1967, and 1985.
4587	metropolitan areas	228,000	95.60	218,000	99.96	C	260,000	*Definition:* Towns with 1,500 or more inhabitants.
4588	VALLETTA (Valetta)	228,000	95.60	218,000	99.96	C	260,000	Seaport. Tourism. Most heavily-bombed site of WWII. F=1565. St. John's Co-Cathedral (1573). D=RCC.
	MARSHALL ISLANDS	**64,200**	**93.59**	**60,100**	**99.93**	**C**	**127,000**	**PROTESTANTS 105.0%, INDEPENDENTS 12.6%. PENT-CHAR 47.0%, EVANGELICAL 30.9%, GCC 11.3%**
4589	rural areas	18,100	95.09	17,200	100.00	C	24,700	28.3% (1950), 37.0% (1970), 34.3% (1990), 28.1% (2000), 23.7% (2010), 19.3% (2025)
4590	urban areas	46,100	93.00	42,900	99.91	C	102,000	71.6% (1950), 62.9% (1970), 65.7% (1990), 71.8% (2000), 76.2% (2010), 80.6% (2025)
4591	non-metropolitan areas	30,600	93.00	28,500	99.91	C	67,995	*Sources of data:* Censuses of 1973, 1980, and 1988.
4592	metropolitan areas	15,500	93.00	14,400	99.91	C	34,500	*Definition:* The entire population of Majuro atoll and Ebeye on Kwajalein atoll.
4593	MAJURO (D.U.D. or Darrit-Uliga-Dalap)	15,500	93.00	14,400	99.91	C	34,500	Port facilities, international airport. D=UCCMI,AoG,RCC.
	MARTINIQUE	**395,000**	**94.44**	**373,000**	**99.87**	**C**	**450,000**	**ROMAN CATHOLICS 92.5%, PROTESTANTS 5.9%. PENT-CHAR 3.9%, EVANGELICAL 4.0%, GCC 10.8%**
4594	rural areas	20,200	95.14	19,200	99.90	C	13,600	72.2% (1950), 38.9% (1970), 9.4% (1990), 5.1% (2000), 3.6% (2010), 3.0% (2025)
4595	urban areas	375,000	94.40	354,000	99.87	C	436,000	27.7% (1950), 61.0% (1970), 90.5% (1990), 94.8% (2000), 96.3% (2010), 96.9% (2025)
4596	non-metropolitan areas	236,000	94.40	222,000	99.87	C	274,177	*Sources of data:* Censuses of 1954, 1982, and 1990; estimates for 1961 and 1967.
4597	metropolitan areas	139,000	94.40	132,000	99.87	C	162,000	*Definition:* Total population of the commune of Fort-de-France, plus the agglomerations of the other communes.
4598	FORT-DE-FRANCE	139,000	94.40	132,000	99.87	C	162,000	At mouth of Madame River. Exports sugarcane, cacao, rum. Hot springs. Capital since 1680. French. D=RCC.
	MAURITANIA	**2,670,000**	**0.24**	**6,500**	**31.89**	**A**	**4,766,000**	**ROMAN CATHOLICS 0.1%, INDEPENDENTS 0.06%. PENT-CHAR 0.08%, EVANGELICAL 0.02%, GCC 0.1%**
4599	rural areas	1,128,000	0.06	670	26.23	A	1,305,000	97.6% (1950), 86.3% (1970), 56.5% (1990), 42.2% (2000), 33.6% (2010), 27.3% (2025)
4600	urban areas	1,541,000	0.38	5,900	36.03	A	3,461,000	2.3% (1950), 13.7% (1970), 43.4% (1990), 57.7% (2000), 66.3% (2010), 72.6% (2025)
4601	non-metropolitan areas	1,146,000	0.38	4,400	36.03	A	2,572,583	*Sources of data:* Censuses of 1964 and 1977.
4602	metropolitan areas	396,000	0.38	1,500	36.03	A	889,000	*Definition:* Urban centers.
4603	NOUAKCHOTT	396,000	0.38	1,500	36.03	A	889,000	Between agricultural south & mineral rich north. Major refugee center. 'Place of the winds'.
	MAURITIUS	**1,156,000**	**31.94**	**369,000**	**74.86**	**B**	**1,377,000**	**ROMAN CATHOLICS 26.8%, PROTESTANTS 9.5%. PENT-CHAR 25.5%, EVANGELICAL 8.8%, GCC 7.6%**
4604	rural areas	679,000	26.21	178,000	67.72	B	624,000	71.2% (1950), 57.9% (1970), 59.5% (1990), 58.7% (2000), 54.6% (2010), 45.3% (2025)
4605	urban areas	478,000	40.10	191,000	85.02	B	753,000	28.7% (1950), 42.0% (1970), 40.5% (1990), 41.2% (2000), 45.3% (2010), 54.6% (2025)
4606	non-metropolitan areas	4,800	40.09	1,900	85.01	B	7,518	*Sources of data:* Censuses of 1952, 1962, 1972, 1983, and 1990.
4607	metropolitan areas	473,000	40.10	190,000	85.02	B	746,000	*Definition:* Towns with proclaimed legal limits.
4608	Beau Bassin-Rose Hill	106,000	40.00	42,400	82.92	B	167,000	Busy market & shopping center. Residential suburb. British Council Library. D=RCC,AoG.
4609	Curepipe	75,100	40.50	30,400	83.42	B	118,000	Import companies. Mauritius Broadcasting Company. F=1867 after malaria epidemic in Port Louis. D=RCC,AoG.
4610	PORT LOUIS	473,000	40.10	190,000	85.02	B	746,000	Central collecting point for imports & exports. Sugar (90% of exports). F=1736. D=RCC,Anglican,AoG.
4611	Quatre Bornes	74,000	40.00	29,600	82.92	B	117,000	Middle class urban center. Sugarcane. Named after four boundary stones of four sugar estates. D=RCC,AoG.
4612	Vacoas-Phoenix	63,400	40.50	25,700	83.42	B	100,000	Beer brewing, cosmetics, garments, sugarcane, vegetables. Separate until 1963. D=RCC,AoG.
	MAYOTTE	**102,000**	**1.84**	**1,900**	**40.71**	**A**	**187,000**	**ROMAN CATHOLICS 1.2%, PROTESTANTS 0.3%. PENT-CHAR 0.2%, EVANGELICAL 0.1%, GCC 0.9%**
4613	rural areas	67,900	0.51	350	36.90	A	95,000	96.7% (1950), 80.6% (1970), 72.1% (1990), 66.7% (2000), 60.6% (2010), 50.9% (2025)
4614	urban areas	33,800	4.50	1,500	48.37	A	91,600	3.3% (1950), 19.3% (1970), 27.9% (1990), 33.2% (2000), 39.3% (2010), 49.0% (2025)
4615	non-metropolitan areas	21,300	4.50	960	48.37	A	57,665	*Sources of data:* Censuses.
4616	metropolitan areas	12,500	4.50	560	48.37	A	33,900	*Definition:* Mamoundzou.
4617	MAMOUNDZOU	12,500	4.50	560	48.37	A	33,900	On main island. Former capital Dzaoudzi. Ylang-ylang and vanilla exported. Radio broadcasting. D=RCC,EJCC.
	MEXICO	**98,881,000**	**94.87**	**93,807,000**	**99.85**	**C**	**130,196,000**	**ROMAN CATHOLICS 93.8%, PROTESTANTS 3.3%. PENT-CHAR 13.2%, EVANGELICAL 1.7%, GCC 5.1%**
4618	rural areas	25,323,000	98.84	25,030,000	100.00	C	25,219,000	57.3% (1950), 40.9% (1970), 27.5% (1990), 25.6% (2000), 23.3% (2010), 19.3% (2025)
4619	urban areas	73,558,000	93.50	68,777,000	99.80	C	104,977,000	42.6% (1950), 59.0% (1970), 72.4% (1990), 74.3% (2000), 76.6% (2010), 80.6% (2025)
4620	non-metropolitan areas	17,050,000	94.87	16,175,000	99.91	C	30,444,791	*Sources of data:* Censuses of 1950, 1960, 1970, 1980, and 1990.
4621	metropolitan areas	56,508,000	93.09	52,602,000	99.77	C	74,532,000	*Definition:* Localities with 2,500 or more inhabitants.
4622	Acambaro	63,300	92.00	58,200	99.68	C	90,400	Guanajato on Lake Solis. Lerma River. Corn, wheat, sugar, vegetables, tanneries. F=1526. D=RCC.
4623	Acapulco de Juarez	625,000	87.00	543,000	99.48	C	891,000	Guerrero. Resort & port. Excellent natural harbor. Coffee, sugar. 300,000 visitors annually. F=1550. D=RCC.
4624	Aguascalientes	534,000	92.00	491,000	99.68	C	762,000	Capital of Aguascalientes. Extensive networks of tunnels. Orchards, vineyards. F=1522. 'Hot water'. D=RCC.
4625	Ahome	324,000	94.00	304,000	99.78	C	462,000	Sonora on Fuerte River near Los Mochis. Irrigation, grains, sugarcane, tomatoes. D=RCC.
4626	Apatzingan de la Constitucion	92,900	92.00	85,400	99.68	C	133,000	Michoacan on Apatzingan River. Corn, beans, sesame, silver, gypsum. Constitution signed here (1814). D=RCC.
4627	Apodaca	125,000	92.00	115,000	99.68	C	179,000	Calcium carbonate, industrial, Milwhite Inc., Rhone Poulenc Ag Co. D=RCC.
4628	Atlixco	90,000	94.00	84,600	99.78	C	128,000	Puebla. Wheat, corn, beans, fruits, cotton & woolen mills. F=1579 as Villa de Carrion. D=RCC.
4629	Buenavista	139,000	92.00	128,000	99.68	C	198,000	Baja California Norte near Tijuana and USA border. Trade. D=RCC.
4630	Campeche	182,000	93.00	170,000	99.48	C	260,000	Capital of Campeche, on Gulf of Mexico. Oil. F=1540. Colonial churches. Cortes' first landing (1517). D=RCC.
4631	Cancun	203,000	90.00	183,000	99.58	C	290,000	Quintana Roo on Yucatan Peninsula. Gulf of Mexico resort, built in early 1970's, luxurious hotels. D=RCC.
4632	Cardenas	73,900	93.00	68,800	99.48	C	106,000	Tabasco near Mezcalapa River. Grijalva River. Agriculture center, bananas, tobacco, coffee, rice. D=RCC.
4633	Celaya	260,000	91.00	237,000	99.58	C	372,000	Guanajuato. Agricultural & livestock center. F=1571. Church of Nuestra Senora del Carmen (1807). D=RCC.
4634	Chicoloapan de Juarz	69,400	94.00	65,300	99.78	C	99,100	East shore of Lake Texcoco, 14 miles east of Mexico City. Maguey, cereals, stock. D=RCC.
4635	Chihuahua	625,000	92.00	575,000	99.58	C	893,000	Capital of Chihuahua. Center of cattle raising area. F=1709. Church of San Francisco (18th century). D=RCC.
4636	Chilpancingo	108,000	91.00	97,800	99.58	C	153,000	Capital of Guerrero. Corn, sugarcane, bananas. F=1591. Site of first Mexican congress. D=RCC.
4637	Chetumal	114,000	95.00	108,000	99.88	C	163,000	Capital of Quintana Roo. Forestry, forest products. Local market fishing. F=1899 as Payo Obispo. D=RCC.
4638	Chilpancingo de los Bravo	118,000	95.00	112,000	99.88	C	168,000	Guerrero in Sierra Madre del Sur Mountains. Names for its heroes in war against Spain. Corn, bananas. D=RCC.
4639	Chimalhuacan	285,000	92.00	263,000	99.68	C	407,000	Anixter Fiber Optics, Chimal Falls. Cereals, maguey. D=RCC,Victory Outreach Church.
4640	Ciudad Acuna	64,200	95.00	61,000	99.88	C	91,600	Coahuila on Rio Grande and US border. Neighboring Del Rio, Texas. Cattle, sheep, wheat, cereals. D=RCC.
4641	Ciudad de Mexico (Mexico City)	18,131,000	94.50	17,134,000	99.88	C	21,078,000	Distrito Federal. Mountains. Serious air pollution. One third of Mexico's industrial production. D=RCC.
4642	Azcapotzalco	1,066,000	94.00	1,002,000	99.98	C	1,521,000	Livestock & dairying. Textiles, auto & bus assembly. 7,350 ft. elevation. F=12th century. D=RCC.
4643	Chalco	272,000	93.50	254,000	99.98	C	388,000	Distrito Federal southeast of downtown. Chemicals, textiles, machinery, consumer goods, crafts. D=RCC.
4644	Ciudad de Mexico	14,068,000	94.00	13,224,000	99.98	C	20,077,000	Distrito Federal. Serious air pollution. University of Mexico (325,000 students). Cathedral (1525). D=RCC,JWS.
4645	Coyoacan	662,000	94.00	622,000	99.98	C	945,000	Distrito Federal. South of city center. Cortes' palace. Dominican monastery (1530). RC church (1583). D=RCC.
4646	Cuautitlan Izcalli	380,000	93.50	355,000	99.88	C	542,000	Mexico on Cuautitlan River at Guadalupe Reservoir north of Mexico City. Pharmaceuticals. D=RCC.
4647	Ecatepec de Morelos	1,476,000	94.00	1,388,000	99.98	C	2,107,000	Mexico northeast of Mexico City. 12th century Indian kingdom, monument to Morelos y Pav—n. D=RCC.
4648	Naucalpan de Juarez	1,153,000	94.00	1,084,000	99.98	C	1,646,000	Mexico on Hondo River west of Mexico City. An industrial extension of Mexico City. D=RCC.
4649	Netzahualcoyotl (Nezahualcoyotl)	1,521,000	94.00	1,430,000	99.98	C	2,171,000	Residential. Dependent on Mexico City's economy. F=1900 but many problems with marshy land. D=RCC.
4650	Texcoco de Mora	89,900	95.00	85,400	99.98	C	128,000	Mexico northeast of Mexico City. Lake Texcoco, ancient Aztec capital, pyramid, temple ruins, schools. D=RCC.
4651	Tlalnepantla	851,000	94.00	800,000	99.98	C	1,215,000	7,474 ft. on Rio Tlalnepantla. Industrial suburb, iron & bronze, chemicals. Founded by Otomi. Y=1583. D=RCC.
4652	Ciudad Valles	111,000	92.00	102,000	99.68	C	158,000	San Luis Potosi on Tampaon River. Sugarcane, citrus fruits, avocados, coffee. Lumbering. D=RCC.
4653	Ciudad del Carmen	102,000	95.00	96,500	99.88	C	145,000	Campeche on Isla del Carmen. On Gulf of Mexico. Most important shrimp port, lizard and shark skins. D=RCC.
4654	Ciudad Guzman	88,000	91.00	80,100	99.63	C	126,000	Jalisco. Near Lake Zapotlan. Beans, corn, wheat, mercury ore. Nevado de Colima (14,206 ft.). D=RCC.
4655	Ciudad Hidalgo	58,700	94.00	55,200	99.78	C	83,800	Michoacan on Tuzuntla River. Resins, turpentine, sugarcane, beans, fruit, livestock, tanning. D=RCC.
4656	Ciudad Juarez (in El Paso, Texas)	1,168,000	94.00	1,098,000	99.78	C	1,618,000	Chihuahua on Rio Grande. Border trade, marketing center for cotton. Guadalupe mission (1659). D=RCC.
4657	Ciudad Lopez Mateos	382,000	91.00	347,000	99.63	C	545,000	Mexico northeast of Mexico City. Railroad, cereals, livestock, an important manufacturing center. D=RCC.
4658	Ciudad Madero	194,000	92.00	179,000	99.68	C	277,000	Tamaulipas. Port on Gulf of Mexico. Near Tampico. Petroleum producing, oil refining center. D=RCC.
4659	Ciudad Mante	93,100	93.00	86,600	99.48	C	133,000	Tamaulipas. Heart of sugar producing region, tomatoes, lemons, livestock, fishing, hunting. D=RCC.
4660	Ciudad Obregon	267,000	92.00	245,000	99.68	C	380,000	Sonora near Yaqui River. Cotton, wheat, rice, sesame. Duck hunting. D=RCC.
4661	Ciudad Victoria	236,000	90.00	213,000	99.58	C	337,000	Capital of Tamaulipas on San Marcos River. Tourist center. Henequen, livestock. F=1750. D=RCC.
4662	Coacalco	183,000	90.00	165,000	99.58	C	262,000	Mexico north of Mexico City. Commercial, industrial, textiles, machinery, consumer goods. D=RCC.
4663	Coatzacoalcos	241,000	93.00	224,000	99.48	C	344,000	Veracruz on Gulf of Campeche. Port & transport center. Exports hardwood, cereals. D=RCC.
4664	Colima	130,000	94.00	122,000	99.78	C	185,000	Capital of Colima on Colima River. Cotton, rice, corn. Difficult access. F=1522. D=RCC.
4665	Comitan de Dominguez	58,500	94.00	55,000	99.78	C	83,500	Chiapas near Guatemala border. Tojolabal Maya population. Trading, distilling, textiles, colonial churches. D=RCC.
4666	Comondu	90,100	91.00	82,000	99.63	C	129,000	Baja California Sur. Wheat, corn, beans, cotton, papaya, copper mining, livestock, Mexico highway. D=RCC.
4667	Cordoba	158,000	93.00	147,000	99.48	C	226,000	Veracruz on San Antonio River. Tropical landscape. Coffee, sugarcane, tobacco. F=1618. D=RCC.
4668	Cortazar	55,200	91.00	50,300	99.63	C	78,800	Guanajuato on Laja River. Near Celaya. Vegetable, fruits, sugarcane center, other agriculture. D=RCC.
4669	Cuauhtemoc	84,700	92.00	77,900	99.68	C	121,000	CuauntÁmoc, Zacatecas, north central on plateau. Agriculture is main industry. D=RCC.
4670	Cuernavaca	338,000	92.00	311,000	99.68	C	483,000	Capital of Morelos. Retreat center, corn, beans, fruit. Cortes' Palace (1531). Franciscan cathedral (1529). D=RCC.
4671	Culiacan	503,000	92.00	463,000	99.68	C	718,000	Capital of Sinaloa. Corn, sugarcane, tobacco, fruits, vegetables. F=1531. D=RCC.
4672	Delicias	106,000	92.00	97,500	99.68	C	151,000	Chihuahua near Conchos River. Vast irrigation area, cotton growing center, wheat, grapevines, dams. D=RCC.
4673	Durango (Vitoria de Durango)	422,000	90.00	380,000	99.58	C	602,000	Capital of Durango. 6,197 ft. Health resort. Commercial & mining center. Movie studios. F=1556. D=RCC.
4674	Ensenada	205,000	93.00	191,000	99.48	C	293,000	Baha California Norte. Tourism. Important Pacific port, agriculture, fishing. D=RCC.
4675	Fresnillo	91,000	94.00	85,600	99.78	C	130,000	Zacatecas. Silver-mining center, mining school. Livestock, cereals, beans. 7,000 ft. F=1554. D=RCC.
4676	Guadalajara	3,908,000	94.00	3,674,000	99.88	C	4,933,000	Capital of Jalisco. Shoes, chemicals. F=1531. Seat of bishopric since 1549. More than 50 churches. D=RCC.
4677	Tlaquepaque	398,000	94.00	374,000	99.88	C	567,000	Jalisco. Handicrafts center, pottery, textiles, hand-blown glass. Agricultural processing. D=RCC.
4678	Zapopan	810,000	94.00	761,000	99.88	C	1,156,000	Manufacturing center for surrounding agriculture. Livestock. Pilgrimage center, 17th century basilica. D=RCC.
4679	Guamuchil	60,100	94.00	56,500	99.78	C	85,800	Sinaloa near Gulf of California. Mocorito River. Fuerte irrigation district, chickpeas, sugarcane, tomatoes. D=RCC.
4680	Guanajuato	88,600	92.00	81,500	99.68	C	126,000	Capital of Guanajuato. Tourism, mining. 16th century silver mining. Richly endowed churches. F=1554. D=RCC.
4681	Guasave	59,800	93.00	55,600	99.48	C	85,300	Sinaloa on Sinaloa River. Fuerte irrigation district. Cotton, livestock. F=1595 as a Spanish mission. D=RCC.
4682	Guaymas	106,000	93.00	98,600	99.48	C	151,000	Sonora on Bay of California. Resort, sport fishing, port, manufacturing. F=1760 by Indians. D=RCC.
4683	Hermosillo	492,000	92.00	453,000	99.58	C	703,000	Capital of Sonora. Commercial center for surrounding farmlands. Winter resort, copper. 'Pretty little place'.D=RCC.
4684	Heroica Nogales (Nogales)	128,000	93.00	119,000	99.48	C	183,000	Port of entry, Sonora, US border. Mexican-U.S. trading center in cattle & minerals, graphite, silver, gold. D=RCC.
4685	Heroica Zitacuaro	81,200	93.00	75,500	99.48	C	116,000	Michoacan on Tuzuntla River. Sawmilling, tanning, soapmaking, vegetables, mineral water spa. D=RCC.
4686	Hidalgo del Parral (Parral)	107,000	92.00	98,300	99.58	C	153,000	Chihuahua on Rio Parral. Processes & exports lead, zinc, copper, & gold. Colonial atmosphere. D=RCC.

Table 10-5–continued overleaf

Table 10-5–continued

Rec No 1	Country City 2	Pop 2000 3	AC% 4	Church Members 5	E% 6	W 7	Pop 2025 8	Notes 9
4687	Iguala	101,000	93.00	94,000	99.48	C	144,000	Guerrero on Cocula River. Corn, beans, sugarcane, peanuts, lemons. F=1750. D=RCC.
4688	Irapuato	321,000	91.00	292,000	99.63	C	458,000	Guanajuato on Irapuato River. Agricultural & livestock-raising center. Known for strawberries. F=1547. D=RCC.
4689	Ixtapaluca	140,000	94.00	132,000	99.78	C	200,000	Mexico state, 19 miles southeast of Mexico City. Cereals, maguey, vegetables, livestock. D=RCC.
4690	Jalapa Enriquez (Jalapa)	326,000	94.00	307,000	99.78	C	466,000	Capital of Veracruz. Flowers, coffee, tobacco. Spanish-Moorish architecture. Indian village in 1519. D=RCC.
4691	Jiutepec	100,000	91.00	91,400	99.63	C	143,000	Morelos, central 5 miles southeast of Cuernavaca. Sugarcane, rice, fruit, livestock. D=RCC.
4692	Juchitan de Zaragoza	65,000	92.00	59,800	99.68	C	92,800	Oaxaca on Laguna Superior near Gulf of Tehuantepec. Rio de los Perros. Straw hat production. D=RCC.
4693	La Paz	167,000	94.00	157,000	99.78	C	238,000	Capital of Baja California Sur on La Paz Bay. Fishing, tourism. F=1811 by Spanish. D=RCC.
4694	La Piedad (Cavadas)	75,600	93.00	70,300	99.48	C	108,000	Michoacan on Rio Lerma. Livestock, dairying, cheese, butter, corn, beans. F=1871. D=RCC.
4695	La Piedad de Cabadas	75,900	93.00	70,600	99.48	C	108,000	Michoacan on Lerma River. Cereals, sugarcane, livestock, tanneries, rayon mills, native shawls. D=RCC.
4696	Lagos de Moreno	77,100	92.00	71,000	99.68	C	110,000	Jalisco. Sierra Madre Occidental. Resort, silver mining, beans, chili, corn, Colonial churches. D=RCC.
4697	Las Choapas	53,200	95.00	50,500	99.88	C	75,900	Veracruz on Tonala River. Railroad, roads, petroleum center, very hot climate. D=RCC.
4698	Las Truchas	64,900	93.00	60,400	99.48	C	92,700	Michoacan on Grande River at Pacific Ocean. Near Lazaro Cardenas. D=RCC.
4699	Leon	1,050,000	91.00	956,000	99.88	C	1,370,000	Guanajuato on Turbio River. Protected by large dam. Leather goods, gold & silver embroidery. F=1552. D=RCC.
4700	Los Mochis	197,000	93.00	183,000	99.48	C	281,000	Sinaloa. Corn, cotton, sugarcane, sugar refineries, tourism. Winter resort. D=RCC.
4701	Los Reyes la Paz	163,000	91.00	148,000	99.63	C	233,000	Mexico, east of Mexico City. Near Nezahualcoyotl. Railroad junction, rapidly urbanizing, some agriculture. D=RCC.
4702	Matamoros (in Brownsville, Texas)	322,000	92.00	297,000	99.68	C	460,000	Tamaulipas on Rio Grande. Chief port of entry for tourists. Import/export. Cotton, sugar. F=1824. D=RCC.
4703	Matehuala	66,300	93.00	61,700	99.48	C	94,600	San Luis Potosi near Sierra de Catorce. Gold, silver mining, tanning, textiles, liquor, maguey. D=RCC.
4704	Mazatlan	318,000	92.00	293,000	99.68	C	454,000	Pacific port & resort in Sinaloa. Known for sandy beaches. Popular tourist resort. Shrimp. F=1837. D=RCC.
4705	Merida	634,000	89.00	565,000	99.48	C	905,000	Capital of Yucatan. Sisal hemp. Tourist base. Strong Indian influence. F=1542 on Ancient Mayan site. D=RCC.
4706	Metepec	141,000	92.00	130,000	99.68	C	201,000	Mexico near Toluca. Pottery, colorful market, agricultural center, grain, fruit, livestock, dairying. D=RCC.
4707	Mexicali	557,000	93.00	518,000	99.48	C	796,000	Capital of Baja California Norte. Cotton, fruits, vegetables, cereals. Tourism. University. D=RCC.
4708	Minatitlan	172,000	94.00	162,000	99.78	C	246,000	Veracruz river port on Rio Coatzacoalcos. Petrochemical center, lumbering, agriculture. F=1822. D=RCC.
4709	Monclova	215,000	93.00	200,000	99.48	C	307,000	Coahuila on Salado de los Nadadores River. Iron, steel, agriculture, livestock. D=RCC.
4710	Monterrey	3,416,000	94.00	3,211,000	99.88	C	4,335,000	Capital of Nuevo Leon. Heavy industries, ore-processing, beer, cigarettes, pottery, glass. F=1579. D=RCC.
4711	Garza Garcia	137,000	94.00	129,000	99.88	C	195,000	Nuevo Leon. Sierra Madre Oriental. Upper class residential suburb with very little industry. D=RCC.
4712	Guadalupe	649,000	94.00	610,000	99.88	C	926,000	Nuevo Leon. Corn, chick-peas, cattle, sheep. Santa Catalina River. Working class suburb. D=RCC.
4713	San Nicolas de los Garzas	529,000	94.00	497,000	99.88	C	755,000	Nuevo Leon. North of Monterrey. Working class suburb. Industry, consumer goods. D=RCC.
4714	Santa Catarina	197,000	95.00	187,000	99.98	C	281,000	Nuevo Leon. West of Monterrey. Sierra Madre Oriental. Crafts, consumer goods, vegetables. D=RCC.
4715	Morelia	519,000	91.00	473,000	99.63	C	741,000	Capital of Michoacan. Processing center for agricultural region. Baroque cathedral (1744). F=1541. D=RCC.
4716	Navojoa	100,000	93.00	93,100	99.48	C	143,000	Sonora. Lower Mayo River, Gulf of California. Cotton, corn, dates, cattle, native handicrafts. D=RCC.
4717	Nuevo Laredo (Laredo, Texas)	265,000	92.00	243,000	99.58	C	378,000	Port of entry, Tamaulipas on Rio Grande. Cattle, natural gas. Bullring attracts tourists. D=RCC.
4718	Oaxaca de Juarez	258,000	89.00	230,000	99.48	C	368,000	Capital of Oaxaca. Handicrafts. Noted for 16th century art & architecture. F=1486 as Aztec garrison. D=RCC.
4719	Ocotlan	75,900	92.00	69,800	99.68	C	108,000	Jalisco. Important transportation hub. Tourist gateway to Chapala resorts. Agriculture, fishing. D=RCC.
4720	Orizaba	261,000	94.00	245,000	99.78	C	372,000	Veracruz. Tobacco, textiles, tourist resort. F=16th century by Spaniards. Colonial atmosphere. D=RCC.
4721	Pachuca (Pachuca de Soto)	211,000	93.00	196,000	99.48	C	301,000	Capital of Hidalgo in Sierra Madre Oriental (7,959 ft). Extensive mining. Church of San Francisco (1596). D=RCC.
4722	Papantla de Olarte	55,800	94.00	52,500	99.78	C	79,700	Veracruz near the Gulf of Mexico. Largest supplier of vanilla in Mexico, oil production, orchids, El Taj. D=RCC.
4723	Piedras Negras	117,000	93.00	108,000	99.48	C	166,000	Coahuila on Rio Grande. Customs station (USA border), international transport hub. F=1849. D=RCC.
4724	Poza Rica de Hidalgo	184,000	94.00	173,000	99.78	C	262,000	Veracruz on Rio Cazones. Hot, humid. Petrochemical center. Major air pollution disaster (1950). D=RCC.
4725	Puebla	1,968,000	94.00	1,850,000	99.88	C	2,535,000	Capital of Puebla at 7,183 ft. Onyx, glazed tiles. Spanish architecture. Bishopric since 1550. F=1532. D=RCC.
4726	Cholula	65,000	94.00	61,100	99.78	C	92,800	West of Puebla. Teocali de Cholula, most massive pyramid in Americas. Tourism. D=RCC.
4727	Puerto Vallarta	113,000	92.00	104,000	99.68	C	162,000	Jalisco on Banderas Bay. Exports bananas, coconut oil, hides, tourism, aquatic sports. D=RCC.
4728	Queretaro	467,000	90.00	420,000	99.58	C	667,000	Capital of Queretaro at 5,900 ft. Spanish colonial city. Cotton textiles. F=Otomi Indians,Franciscans. D=RCC.
4729	Reynosa	322,000	91.00	293,000	99.63	C	459,000	Tamaulipas on Rio Grande. Cattle raising, cotton, sugarcane, oil. F=1749. D=RCC.
4730	Rio Bravo	81,300	93.00	75,600	99.48	C	116,000	Tamaulipas on Rio Grande, gulf coastal flatlands. Highway, railroad, subtropical climate, corn, cotton. D=RCC.
4731	Sahuayo de Jose Maria Morelos	61,200	93.00	56,900	99.48	C	87,300	Michoacan near Laguna de Chapala. Cereals, sugarcane, tobacco, beans, fruit, livestock. D=RCC.
4732	Salamanca	149,000	92.00	137,000	99.68	C	213,000	Guanajuato on Lerma River. Agricultural & commercial center, oil refining center. D=RCC.
4733	Salina Cruz	74,700	90.00	67,200	99.58	C	107,000	Oaxaca on Gulf of Tehuantepec. Pacific coast oil port, fishing, lumber, milling, fruit. D=RCC.
4734	Saltillo	510,000	91.00	464,000	99.63	C	728,000	Capital of Coahuila at 5,244 ft. Summer resort. Woolen fabrics, knitted goods. F=1575 by Spanish. D=RCC.
4735	San Andres Tuxtla	60,200	94.00	56,600	99.78	C	85,900	Veracruz near Laguna Catemaco. Agriculture center, fruit, high grade tobacco, cigars. D=RCC.
4736	San Cristobal de las Casas	88,900	94.00	83,600	99.78	C	127,000	Chiapas in mountains near Guatemala. Inter-American Highway. Art and Science Institute. F=c1530. D=RCC.
4737	San Francisco del Rincon	63,400	93.00	58,900	99.48	C	90,400	Guanajuato on Turbio River near Leon. Grain, sugarcane, fruit, vegetables, livestock, flour mills. D=RCC.
4738	San Juan del Rio	74,700	94.00	70,200	99.78	C	107,000	QuerÁtaro, central plateau. Opals mined at La Trinidad, corn, wheat, sugarcane, beans. D=RCC.
4739	San Luis Potosi	931,000	90.00	838,000	99.78	C	1,314,000	Capital of San Luis Potosi. Silver mining. Spanish Baroque Cathedral. F=1583 as Franciscan mission. D=RCC.
4740	Soledad Diez Gutierrez	78,400	92.00	72,100	99.68	C	112,000	San Luis Potosi northeast of San Luis Potosi. Agricultural community, interior plateau. D=RCC.
4741	San Luis Rio Colorado	116,000	92.00	106,000	99.68	C	165,000	Sonora on Colorado River. On US border. Near Yuma, Arizona. Citrus fruit, wheat, corn, rice, beans. D=RCC.
4742	San Martin Texmelucan	69,700	92.00	64,100	99.68	C	99,500	Puebla. Franciscan, Carmelite convents. Jewelry, pottery, Emper industrial, aluminum sulfate producers. D=RCC.
4743	San Miguel de Allende	59,300	93.00	55,100	99.48	C	84,600	Guanajuato near Presa Begonias. Known for atmosphere, art, & climate. Tourist center. F=1542. D=RCC.
4744	San Pablo de las Salinas	102,000	91.00	92,900	99.63	C	146,000	Corn, beans, livestock, maize. D=RCC.
4745	Silao	61,600	93.00	57,300	99.48	C	87,900	Guanajuato near Leon. Motor vehicle assembly plant, corn, wheat, beans, mineral springs. F=1537. D=RCC.
4746	Soledad de Graciano Sanchez	150,000	91.00	137,000	99.63	C	214,000	San Luis Potosi. Elevation 6,100 m. Interior plateau, agricultural community. Returmos Church of Christ. D=RCC.
4747	Tampico	533,000	92.00	491,000	99.68	C	761,000	Tamaulipas port on Panuco River. Oil, tourist resort. F=1532 by Franciscan friar. D=RCC.
4748	Tapachula	168,000	93.00	156,000	99.48	C	240,000	Chiapas on Coatan River. Coffee, bananas, cacao, sugarcane. Distilleries, saddleries. D=RCC.
4749	Tecoman	73,800	95.00	70,200	99.88	C	105,000	Colima near Armeria River. Coconuts, cotton, tropical fruits, lemon oil, cottonseed oil. D=RCC.
4750	Tehuacan	169,000	93.00	157,000	99.48	C	241,000	Puebla (5,500 ft.). One of oldest Spanish settlements in Mexico. Corn, beans, silver. Mixtec Indians. D=RCC.
4751	Temixco	78,800	93.00	73,300	99.48	C	113,000	Morelos near Cuernavaca. Elevation 4,081 ft. Sugarcane, rice, wheat, coffee, fruit, livestock. D=RCC.
4752	Tepatitlan de Morelos	65,500	92.00	60,200	99.68	C	93,400	Jalisco near Guadalajara. Corn, beans, dairy products. Commercial and industrial region of Los Altos. D=RCC.
4753	Tepic	251,000	95.00	238,000	99.88	C	358,000	Capital of Nayarit on Rio Tepic. Corn, sugarcane. F=1542. Huichol & Cora Indians. Cathedral(1750). D=RCC.
4754	Tijuana (in San Diego, USA)	1,167,000	90.00	1,050,000	99.78	C	1,709,000	Baja California Norte on Rio Tecate. Wheat, barley, wine grapes. American tourists. F=1862. D=RCC.
4755	Tlaxcala de Xicotencatl	61,200	95.00	58,100	99.88	C	87,300	Tlaxcala east of Mexico City. Oldest Christian church in Mexico. F=1521 by CortÁs, shrine. D=RCC.
4756	Toluca de Lerdo	1,184,000	93.00	1,101,000	99.78	C	2,056,000	Capital of Mexico at 8,793 ft. Textile, brewing, food processing. F=1530. Oldest church 1585. D=RCC.
4757	Tonala	183,000	91.00	167,000	99.63	C	261,000	Jalisco near Guadalajara. Agriculture center, grain, sugarcane, tobacco, vegetables, fruit, pottery. D=RCC.
4758	Torreon	953,000	92.00	877,000	99.68	C	1,285,000	Coahuila on Rio Nazas. Cotton, wheat, dairy, livestock. Mining center. F=1893. D=RCC.
4759	Ciudad Lergo	56,500	93.00	52,500	99.48	C	80,600	Durango. Cotton, grain, wine, fruit, vegetables, foundries, tobacco, fruit canning. D=RCC.
4760	Gomez Palacio	199,000	92.00	183,000	99.68	C	284,000	Durango west of Torreon. Nazas River. Distilling, tanning, foundries, chemicals, soaps, wine, cotton. D=RCC.
4761	Tulancingo	91,500	94.00	86,000	99.78	C	131,000	Hidalgo on Rio Grande de Tulancingo. Agricultural center, wool. F=1520s. Bishopric(1862). D=RCC.
4762	Tuxpan	83,900	93.00	78,000	99.48	C	120,000	Veracruz on Tuxpan River and Gulf of Mexico. Corn, sugarcane, fruit, timber, bananas, plant fibers. D=RCC.
4763	Tuxpan de Rodriguez Cano	89,300	95.00	84,800	99.88	C	127,000	Veracruz on Tuxpan River. Hot, humid. Petroleum, corn, bananas, shipyards, timber, rubber, vanilla. D=RCC.
4764	Tuxtepec	76,100	90.00	68,500	99.58	C	109,000	Oaxaca on Santo Domingo River. Very hot climate, coffee, tobacco, sugarcane, cedar, mahogany. D=RCC.
4765	Tuxtla Gutierrez	351,000	91.00	319,000	99.63	C	501,000	Capital of Chiapas. Corn, cotton, cacao, coffee. Tourists in December (Fair of Guadalupe). D=RCC.
4766	Uruapan del Progreso	227,000	91.00	207,000	99.63	C	324,000	Michoacan. Spanish colonial atmosphere. Lacquerware, Indian handicrafts, tourism. D=RCC.
4767	Valle de Santiago	67,900	93.00	63,100	99.48	C	96,900	Guanajuato south of Salamanca. Lerma River basin. Wheat, fruit, sweet potatoes, shoes, lumber. D=RCC.
4768	Veracruz (Veracruz Llave)	654,000	92.00	602,000	99.68	C	934,000	Veracruz port on Gulf of Mexico. Rainy, humid. Caribbean creole influences. Cigars. F=1519. D=RCC.
4769	Villa Frontera (Frontera)	70,500	92.00	64,900	99.68	C	101,000	NW of Monterey, altitude 1,926 ft. Cereal, fruit, cattle, flower milling. Built around a railroad station. D=RCC.
4770	Villa Nicolas Romera	180,000	90.00	162,000	99.58	C	257,000	Mexico state, 18 miles northwest of Mexico City. Railroad, industrial center, grain, fruit, livestock. D=RCC.
4771	Villahermosa	317,000	94.00	298,000	99.78	C	452,000	Capital of Tabasco on Rio Grijalva. Tropical products, sugar. F=1596. Cathedral(1614). D=RCC.
4772	Xalapa	339,000	92.00	312,000	99.68	C	483,000	Veracruz near Coatepec. Parks, artificial lakes, popular resort, rich agriculture. University of Veracruz. D=RCC.
4773	Zacatecas	121,000	94.00	114,000	99.78	C	173,000	Capital of Zacatecas at 8,189 ft. Silver. Mining center, agriculture. F=1548. Cathedral(1612). D=RCC.
4774	Zamora de Hidalgo	133,000	92.00	122,000	99.68	C	190,000	Michoacan in Zamora Valley. Livestock, corn, dairy, handicrafts. F=1540. D=RCC.
	MICRONESIA	**119,000**	**91.55**	**109,000**	**99.63**	**C**	**190,000**	**ROMAN CATHOLICS 62.8%, PROTESTANTS 39.6%. PENT-CHAR 7.9%, EVANGELICAL 11.7%, GCC 18.9%**
4775	rural areas	83,400	92.21	76,900	99.86	C	103,000	77.1% (1950), 75.7% (1970), 73.7% (1990), 70.3% (2000), 64.3% (2010), 54.4% (2025)
4776	urban areas	35,300	90.00	31,700	99.08	C	86,300	22.8% (1950), 24.2% (1970), 26.2% (1990), 29.7% (2000), 35.6% (2010), 45.5% (2025)
4777	non-metropolitan areas	25,700	90.00	23,100	99.08	C	62,850	*Sources of data:* Censuses of 1973 and 1980.
4778	metropolitan areas	9,600	90.00	8,600	99.08	C	23,400	*Definition:* Localities with 1,000 or more inhabitants.
4779	KOLONIA	9,600	90.00	8,600	99.08	C	23,400	On Pohnpei, formerly called Ascension. Volcanic, basaltic rock, Mt. Totolom. Copra, dried bonito. D=RCC,UCC.
	MOLDAVIA	**4,380,000**	**63.89**	**2,799,000**	**94.23**	**C**	**4,547,000**	**ORTHODOX 44.5%, INDEPENDENTS 15.3%. PENT-CHAR 1.1%, EVANGELICAL 0.4%, GCC 19.1%**
4780	rural areas	1,963,000	64.98	1,276,000	95.32	C	1,431,000	83.4% (1950), 68.1% (1970), 52.2% (1990), 44.8% (2000), 38.6% (2010), 31.4% (2025)
4781	urban areas	2,417,000	63.00	1,523,000	93.34	C	3,116,000	16.6% (1950), 31.8% (1970), 47.7% (1990), 55.1% (2000), 61.3% (2010), 68.5% (2025)
4782	non-metropolitan areas	1,015,000	63.38	644,000	93.31	C	1,313,959	*Sources of data:* Censuses of 1959, 1970, 1979, and 1989
4783	metropolitan areas	1,402,000	62.73	879,000	93.36	C	1,802,000	*Definition:* Cities and urban-type localities, officially designated as such by each of the constituent republics.
4784	Bel'cy (Beltsy)	170,000	64.00	109,000	94.34	C	219,000	On Reut River. Processing farm products, furniture, fur clothing. F=15th century. D=MOC,ROC.
4785	Bendery (Bender)	146,000	64.00	93,200	94.34	C	188,000	On Dnester River. 16th century Turkish fortress. Destroyed in WWII. F=2nd century BC. D=MOC,ROC.
4786	KISIN'OV (Kishinev)	830,000	62.00	515,000	92.84	C	1,065,000	On Byk River. Wine, tobacco. Nearly destroyed in WWII. F=1466. Cathedral of the Nativity. D=MOC.
4787	Rybnica	64,800	65.00	42,100	95.34	C	83,500	On Dnestr River. Transnistria Republic. Cement, sugar milling, limestone, dairying. D=MOC,ROC.
4788	Tiraspol'	191,000	63.00	121,000	93.34	C	247,000	On Dnestr River. Wine, textiles, carpets, glass. Heavily damaged in WWII. F=1795. D=MOC.
	MONACO	**33,600**	**92.57**	**31,100**	**98.83**	**C**	**40,700**	**ROMAN CATHOLICS 89.2%, PROTESTANTS 2.0%. PENT-CHAR 3.1%, EVANGELICAL 0.1%, GCC 26.1%**
4789	rural areas	–	–	–	–	–	–	0.0% (1950), 0.0% (1970), 0.0% (1990), 0.0% (2000), 0.0% (2010), 0.0% (2025)
4790	urban areas	33,600	92.57	31,100	98.83	C	40,700	100.0% (1950), 100.0% (1970), 100.0% (1990), 100.0% (2000), 100.0% (2010), 100.0% (2025)
4791	non-metropolitan areas	–	–	–	–	–	–	*Sources of data:* Censuses of 1956, 1962, 1968, and 1982.
4792	metropolitan areas	33,600	92.57	31,100	98.83	C	40,700	*Definition:* City of Monaco.
4793	MONACO-Ville	33,600	92.57	31,100	98.83	C	40,700	Resort on French Riviera. Beaches, boating, sports car race, gambling. French is official language. D=RCC.
	MONGOLIA	**2,662,000**	**1.25**	**33,400**	**42.82**	**A**	**3,709,000**	**PROTESTANTS 0.8%, INDEPENDENTS 0.3%. PENT-CHAR 0.3%, EVANGELICAL 0.04%, GCC 1.1%**
4794	rural areas	971,000	0.83	8,000	34.56	A	955,000	81.0% (1950), 54.9% (1970), 42.0% (1990), 36.4% (2000), 31.6% (2010), 25.7% (2025)
4795	urban areas	1,691,000	1.50	25,400	47.57	A	2,754,000	18.9% (1950), 45.0% (1970), 57.9% (1990), 63.5% (2000), 68.3% (2010), 74.2% (2025)
4796	non-metropolitan areas	907,000	1.50	13,600	47.56	A	1,477,596	*Sources of data:* Censuses of 1956, 1963, 1969, and 1979; estimate for 1989.
4797	metropolitan areas	784,000	1.50	11,800	47.58	A	1,277,000	*Definition:* Capital and district centers.
4798	Darchan (Darhan)	97,300	0.10	97	35.67	A	159,000	Large industrial complex. Concrete, woolen textiles, carpets. F=1961 by Soviet Union. D=MP.
4799	ULAANBAATAR (Ulan Bator)	686,000	1.70	11,700	49.27	A	1,118,000	On Tuul River. Air pollution. Leather. High priest of Tibetan Buddhism. F=1639. 'Red Hero'. D=MP.
	MONTSERRAT	**10,600**	**95.68**	**10,200**	**99.93**	**C**	**10,700**	**PROTESTANTS 51.7%, ANGLICANS 29.1%. PENT-CHAR 33.3%, EVANGELICAL 24.9%, GCC 18.3%**
4800	rural areas	8,700	96.96	8,400	99.98	C	7,100	78.1% (1950), 88.8% (1970), 85.3% (1990), 81.6% (2000), 76.2% (2010), 66.9% (2025)

Table 10-5–continued opposite

Table 10-5–continued

Rec No 1	Country City 2	Pop 2000 3	AC% 4	Church Members 5	E% 6	W 7	Pop 2025 8	Notes 9
4801	urban areas	2,000	90.00	1,800	99.75	C	3,500	21.8% (1950), 11.1% (1970), 14.6% (1990), 18.3% (2000), 23.7% (2010), 33.0% (2025)
4802	non-metropolitan areas	500	90.02	450	99.82	C	908	*Sources of data:* Censuses of 1960, 1970, and 1980.
4803	metropolitan areas	1,400	89.99	1,300	99.72	C	2,600	*Definition:* Town of Plymouth.
4804	PLYMOUTH	1,400	90.00	1,300	99.75	C	2,600	Southwestern part of island on Guadeloupe Passage. Medical school, cotton, citrus fruit. D=Anglican.
	MOROCCO	**28,221,000**	**0.62**	**174,000**	**42.19**	**A**	**38,530,000**	**INDEPENDENTS 0.5%, ROMAN CATHOLICS 0.08%. PENT-CHAR 0.5%, EVANGELICAL 0.1%, GCC 0.3%**
4805	rural areas	12,609,000	0.52	65,200	38.87	A	12,002,000	73.8% (1950), 65.4% (1970), 51.7% (1990), 44.6% (2000), 38.4% (2010), 31.1% (2025)
4806	urban areas	15,612,000	0.70	109,000	44.87	A	26,528,000	26.1% (1950), 34.5% (1970), 48.2% (1990), 55.3% (2000), 61.5% (2010), 68.8% (2025)
4807	non-metropolitan areas	4,973,000	0.69	34,200	44.95	A	9,251,566	*Sources of data:* Censuses of 1952, 1960, 1971, and 1982; estimate for 1992.
4808	metropolitan areas	10,638,000	0.71	75,100	44.83	A	17,276,000	*Definition:* Urban centers.
4809	Agadir	161,000	0.10	160	41.67	A	274,000	Atlantic port. Fishing, olives. Destroyed by two earthquakes (1960). Ancient Roman origins. F=c1550.
4810	Beni Mellal	139,000	0.05	69	41.62	A	235,000	In Middle Atlas mountains. Oranges, olives, figs, livestock. Kasba bel-Kush (17th century).
4811	Berkane	88,200	0.01	9	37.58	A	150,000	Northern Oriental north of Oujda. Agricultural trade center, citrus fruit, wine, almonds, potatoes, wheat, barley.
4812	Casablanca (Dar el Beida)	3,535,000	0.90	31,800	47.47	A	5,396,000	Principal Atlantic port. Berber origins. D=RCC(12 schools), White Russian Orthodox, GOC(Arabs), &c.
4813	El Jadida (Mazagan)	119,000	0.50	590	42.07	A	202,000	Atlantic port, provincial capital. Seaside resort. Portuguese origins (1502). Some churches remain.
4814	Fes (Fez)	780,000	0.30	2,300	44.87	A	1,326,000	Crafts, olives. Oldest university in the world. F=789. 60% Arab, 35% Berber, 4% French. 1,300 Jews. D=RCC.
4815	Kenitra	274,000	0.20	550	41.77	A	466,000	Sebou River. Port. Shipping center for agriculture, citrus. D=Churches of Christ (among US military).
4816	Khemisset	85,900	0.01	9	37.58	A	146,000	West of Meknes, Rabat region. Agricultural trade center, cereals, livestock, wool, weekly carpet market.
4817	Khouribga	185,000	0.01	19	37.58	A	315,000	Provincial capital. Phosphates. Subsistence agriculture, mineral drying, superphosphate manufacturing.
4818	Ksar-el-Kebir	107,000	0.01	11	37.58	A	182,000	On Lucas River. Agricultural market. Old mosque built with inscribed stones of Christian church-Greek origins.
4819	Larache	93,200	0.01	9	37.58	A	158,000	Atlantic port. Agricultural & fishing center. Spanish influence. Phonecian origins.
4820	Marrakech	780,000	0.30	2,300	41.87	A	1,326,000	Provincial capital. Famous parks, tourism, winter sports. F=1062. Koutoubia mosque (12th century). D=RCC.
4821	Meknes	547,000	0.08	440	41.65	A	929,000	Berber embroidery & carpets. Tourist center. F=10th century. D=RCC,French Reformed.
4822	Mohammedia (Fedala)	153,000	0.20	310	41.77	A	260,000	Atlantic port. Seaside resort, crude oil, fish cannery, chemicals. Christian merchant port in 18th-19th centuries.
4823	Nador	90,500	3.00	2,700	49.57	A	154,000	Mediterranean port. Trading center for fish, fruits, livestock, cement, sugar refinery, barley, olives, airfield, fruits.
4824	Oued-Zem	85,700	0.01	9	37.58	A	146,000	East of Khouribga. Livestock, fruit, agriculture, sugar, cereals, potatoes, handicrafts, market.
4825	Oujda (Udja)	379,000	0.40	1,500	41.97	A	644,000	Frontier post with Algeria. Tourist center. Coal, lead, zinc, olives, grapes. F=944 by Zanatah Berbers.
4826	RABAT-Sale	1,493,000	1.00	14,900	47.57	A	2,347,000	Atlantic port. Textiles. 50% Arab, 35% Berber. D=RCC,Baptist,Russian Orthodox,Pentecostal.
4827	Sale	422,000	0.80	3,400	42.37	A	717,000	Walled city on mouth on Wadi Bou Regreg. Many mosques & museums. F=10th century by Orthodox Muslims.
4828	Temera	70,900	0.80	570	42.37	A	121,000	On Atlantic Ocean. Public beaches. Carpets, tourism, textiles, airport, handicrafts.
4829	Safi (Saffi)	288,000	0.10	290	41.67	A	489,000	Atlantic port city, provincial capital. Fishing, textiles, phosphates. Founded by Canaanites.
4830	Settat	95,100	0.20	190	41.77	A	162,000	Market center of fertile Chaouia plain. Truck gardening. 17th century casbah.
4831	Sidi Kacem	81,400	0.01	8	37.58	A	138,000	North of Meknes. Industrial and agricultural processing center, Gharib plain, oil refinery.
4832	Sidi Slimane	73,600	0.01	7	37.58	A	125,000	North of Meknes. El Kansera Dam. Center of citrus and cotton growing area, essential oil processing.
4833	Tan-Tan	60,400	0.01	6	37.58	A	103,000	Far south on Atlantic Ocean. Tan Tan province, left bank of Oued Dra, port for offshore fishing, airport.
4834	Tanger (Tangiers)	540,000	2.00	10,800	48.57	A	917,000	Strait of Gibraltar. Tourism. 50% Arab, 40% Berber. D=RCC,Baptist,Reformed,Anglican,SFM.
4835	Taza	113,000	0.10	110	41.67	A	191,000	Provincial capital. Cereals, cattle, olives, citrus fruits. F=c7th century by MeKnassa Berbers.
4836	Tetouan (Tetuan)	291,000	2.00	5,800	43.57	A	495,000	On Wadi Martin. Crafts, light manufacturing, cereals. School of music. F=9th century. D=RCC.
	MOZAMBIQUE	**19,680,000**	**32.83**	**6,461,000**	**77.03**	**B**	**30,612,000**	**ROMAN CATHOLICS 15.8%, PROTESTANTS 8.8%. PENT-CHAR 11.8%, EVANGELICAL 6.8%, GCC 18.0%**
4837	rural areas	11,763,000	26.65	3,135,000	69.84	B	13,035,000	97.6% (1950), 94.3% (1970), 73.3% (1990), 59.7% (2000), 51.6% (2010), 42.5% (2025)
4838	urban areas	7,917,000	42.00	3,325,000	87.70	B	17,577,000	2.3% (1950), 5.6% (1970), 26.6% (1990), 40.2% (2000), 48.3% (2010), 57.4% (2025)
4839	non-metropolitan areas	3,565,000	41.78	1,489,000	87.62	B	7,503,964	*Sources of data:* Censuses of 1950, 1960, 1970, and 1980.
4840	metropolitan areas	4,353,000	42.18	1,836,000	87.77	B	10,073,000	*Definition: Conselho* of Maputo and Beira.
4841	Beira	395,000	49.00	194,000	93.20	B	878,000	Capital of Sofala. On Indian Ocean. Exports ores, tobacco, cotton, hides, fishing, resorts. F=1891. D=RCC.
4842	Chimoio (Vila Pery)	121,000	30.00	36,200	74.20	B	268,000	Manica province, Beira railroad. Cotton, steel, saw mills, textiles, bananas, sisal, tobacco, corn, cattle. D=RCC.
4843	Inhambane	89,100	30.00	26,700	74.20	B	198,000	Seaport on Inhambane Bay. Market center. Cashew nuts, rice, cattle. Tsonga, Chopi peoples. D=RCC.
4844	MAPUTO (Lourenco Marques)	3,017,000	46.00	1,388,000	92.20	B	7,108,000	Port on Delagoa Bay. Formerly tourist resort. Brewing, shipbuilding. F=1787(Portuguese). D=RCC,Independents.
4845	Nacala	138,000	20.00	27,500	64.20	B	306,000	Northeast, Mozambique channel. Sheltered, modern harbor. Railroad spur terminus, sisal, copra. D=RCC.
4846	Nampula	268,000	22.00	58,900	66.20	B	594,000	Nampula province. International airport. Rail & road junction, agriculture trade center. D=RCC.
4847	Pemba	69,600	30.00	20,900	74.20	B	155,000	Southern Cabo Delgado on Indian Ocean. Pemba Bay. Cotton, sisal, coffee, airfield. D=RCC.
4848	Quelimane	106,000	30.00	31,900	74.20	B	236,000	Seaport, capital of Zambezia. Fishing. One of world's largest coconut plantations. F=1544. D=RCC.
4849	Tete	77,900	35.00	27,300	79.20	B	173,000	Capital of Tete on Zambezi River. Cattle, cassava, coal mines. F=1531. Cathedral (1563). D=RCC.
4850	Xai-Xai	71,600	35.00	25,100	79.20	B	159,000	Sul do Save. Capital of Gaza on Limpopo River. Sugar, rice corn, agriculture station, railroad, airfield. D=RCC.
	MYANMAR	**45,611,000**	**8.20**	**3,741,000**	**60.86**	**B**	**58,120,000**	**PROTESTANTS 5.5%, ROMAN CATHOLICS 1.2%. PENT-CHAR 2.1%, EVANGELICAL 2.4%, GCC 4.9%**
4851	rural areas	32,981,000	9.43	3,110,000	61.55	B	32,931,000	83.8% (1950), 77.1% (1970), 75.3% (1990), 72.3% (2000), 66.5% (2010), 56.6% (2025)
4852	urban areas	12,630,000	5.00	631,000	59.06	B	25,189,000	16.1% (1950), 22.8% (1970), 24.6% (1990), 27.6% (2000), 33.4% (2010), 43.3% (2025)
4853	non-metropolitan areas	4,229,000	5.15	218,000	59.08	B	9,038,486	*Sources of data:* Censuses of 1953, 1973, and 1983; survey of 1957.
4854	metropolitan areas	8,400,000	4.92	414,000	59.05	B	16,151,000	*Definition:* Urban centers.
4855	Bago (Pegu)	216,000	4.40	9,500	57.06	B	430,000	Bago on Pegu River. Rice, timber. F=573 by Mon. 61% Burmese, 18% Karen, 5% Shan. D=Baptists,RCC.
4856	Chauk	73,600	2.00	1,500	54.66	B	147,000	Magway on Irrawaddy River north of Yenangyaung. Oil production in Sengu oil fields, refinery.
4857	Dawei (Tavoy)	100,000	2.00	2,000	54.66	B	200,000	Tanintharyi at head of Tavoy River estuary on Andaman Sea. Weaving center, coastal trade, popular beach area.
4858	Henzada	117,000	3.00	3,500	55.66	B	234,000	Ayeyarwady on Irrawaddy River. Port for rice & tobacco. Major irrigation site. Mainly Burmese, and Buddhist.
4859	Kale	75,400	1.00	750	53.66	B	150,000	SE of Kayes. Dakar-Niger railroad. Caltex lubricants, peanuts, livestock.
4860	Lashio	127,000	1.00	1,300	53.66	B	253,000	Central Shan northeast of Mandalay. Famous in WWII as starting point of Burma Road. Railroad. D=RCC.
4861	Magway (Magwe)	78,600	2.00	1,600	54.66	B	157,000	Capital of Magway on Irrawaddy River south of Yenangyaung. Rice, cotton, sesame, peanuts, teak forest.
4862	Mandalay	763,000	5.60	42,700	60.26	B	1,522,000	On Irrawaddy River. Tea, silk. F=1860. Center of Burmese Buddhism. 62% Burmese. D=Baptists,RCC.
4863	Mawlamyine (Moulmein)	315,000	15.00	47,200	73.66	B	628,000	Mon port on Gulf of Martaban. 57% Burmese, 20% Karen, 10% Mon. D=HQ Burma Baptist Union,RCC.
4864	Maymyo	91,300	3.00	2,700	55.66	B	182,000	Mandalay east of Mandalay. British hill station and summer capital. Golf, tennis.
4865	Meiktila	138,000	2.00	2,800	54.66	B	276,000	Mandalay east of Chauk. Ancient Burmese irrigation reservoir. Major road, railroad hub, cotton, airfield.
4866	Mergui (Myeik)	127,000	1.00	1,300	53.66	B	253,000	Tanintharyi on Andaman Sea. Tenasserim River. Rice, salt, fish, tin, tungsten.
4867	Mogok	70,700	1.00	710	53.66	B	141,000	North of Mandalay. Centuries-old ruby trade. Rice, sesame, sugarcane, cotton, teak.
4868	Monywa	153,000	2.00	3,100	54.66	B	305,000	Southern Sagaing on Chindwin River. Paddy rice, sesame, millet, peas, wheat, textiles, wood products.
4869	Myingyan	110,000	2.00	2,200	54.66	B	220,000	Northern Mandalay. Port on Irrawaddy River. Cotton-trading center. Strongly Buddhist.
4870	Myitkyina	80,800	5.00	4,000	57.66	B	161,000	Kachin on Irrawaddy River. Trade center for teak and jade, railroad. Liberated in 1944 by U.S. in WWII.
4871	Nyaunglebin	79,000	2.00	1,600	54.66	B	158,000	Bago near Sittoung River north of Bago. Railroad, 90 miles north northeast of Yangon. Rice growing region.
4872	Pakokku	103,000	1.50	1,500	54.16	B	205,000	Northern Magway on Irrawaddy River. Port, peanuts, sesame, rice, oil fields, trading-shipping center.
4873	Pathein (Bassein)	206,000	3.30	6,800	55.96	B	412,000	Ayeyarwady port on Bassein River. Rice. 14% Karen. D=Burma Baptist Union,RCC.
4874	Prome (Pye)	119,000	3.00	3,600	55.66	B	238,000	Northern Bago on Irrawaddy River. Trading center. Ancient origins. Old capital of Pyu people (Sri Ksetra). D=RCC.
4875	Pyinmana	75,800	1.50	1,100	54.16	B	151,000	Southern Mandalay on Sittoung River. Extensive teak forest nearby, forestry college, railroad.
4876	Sagaing	66,200	4.00	2,600	56.66	B	132,000	Capital of Sagaing west of Mandalay. Ancient & modern pagodas. Cotton, sesame, salt, fruit.
4877	Shawebo (Shwebo)	74,700	2.00	1,500	54.66	B	149,000	Sagaing north of Mandalay. Shwebo irrigation canal, army cantonment, ruins, rice, cotton, corn, sesame.
4878	Sittwe (Akyab)	154,000	3.00	4,600	55.66	B	307,000	Rakhine on Bay of Bengal. Important port. Exports rice. Muslims outnumber Buddhist Arakanese.
4879	Taunggyi	155,000	3.00	4,600	55.66	B	309,000	On Thazi-Keng Tung road at 4,712 ft. Kan-Kambawza College. Hunting reserve nearby. D=RCC.
4880	Thaton	88,500	6.00	5,300	58.66	B	176,000	Mon near Gulf of Martaban. Shwezayan Pagoda (believed to contain 4 of Buddha's teeth). F=534 BC.
4881	Toungoo	94,300	2.00	1,900	54.66	B	188,000	Northern Pago on Sittoung River south of Pyinmara. Teak forest, coffee, sugarcane, rice, railroad. D=RCC.
4882	YANGON (Rangoon)	4,458,000	5.60	250,000	60.26	B	8,288,000	On Yangon River. Shwe Dagon Pagod. Rice. F=6th century. 64% Burmese. D=Rangoon Council of Churches.
4883	Karnbe (Kanbe)	371,000	5.20	19,300	57.86	B	739,000	Mandalay. 83% Burmese, 8% Karen. 90% Buddhist. Rice, cotton, mills. D=Baptists.
4884	Yenangyaung	89,600	2.00	1,800	54.66	B	179,000	Magway on Irrawaddy River north of Magway. Leading oil production center in Myanmar, pipeline.
	NAMIBIA	**1,726,000**	**78.18**	**1,349,000**	**97.73**	**C**	**2,338,000**	**PROTESTANTS 47.5%, ROMAN CATHOLICS 17.7%. PENT-CHAR 13.3%, EVANGELICAL 9.2%, GCC 17.1%**
4885	rural areas	1,021,000	80.37	820,000	99.24	C	960,000	90.5% (1950), 81.4% (1970), 68.9% (1990), 59.1% (2000), 50.4% (2010), 41.0% (2025)
4886	urban areas	705,000	75.00	529,000	95.55	C	1,378,000	9.4% (1950), 18.6% (1970), 31.0% (1990), 40.8% (2000), 49.6% (2010), 58.9% (2025)
4887	non-metropolitan areas	548,000	75.00	411,000	95.55	C	1,070,827	*Sources of data:* Censuses of 1951, 1960, 1981, and 1991.
4888	metropolitan areas	157,000	75.00	118,000	95.55	C	307,000	*Definition:* Urban centers.
4889	WINDHOEK	157,000	75.00	118,000	95.55	C	307,000	At 5,428 ft. Hot springs. Furriers, cattle, sheep. F=by Khoikhoin & Herero peoples. D=UELC,RCC.
	NAURU	**11,500**	**72.41**	**8,300**	**96.44**	**C**	**17,800**	**PROTESTANTS 50.7%, ROMAN CATHOLICS 25.3%. PENT-CHAR 9.5%, EVANGELICAL 2.6%, GCC 18.9%**
4890	rural areas	–	–	–	–	–	–	0.0% (1950), 0.0% (1970), 0.0% (1990), 0.0% (2000), 0.0% (2010), 0.0% (2025)
4891	urban areas	11,500	72.41	8,300	96.44	C	17,800	100.0% (1950), 100.0% (1970), 100.0% (1990), 100.0% (2000), 100.0% (2010), 100.0% (2025)
4892	non-metropolitan areas	11,000	72.39	7,900	96.41	C	16,987	*Sources of data:* Censuses of 1977, 1983, and 1992.
4893	metropolitan areas	540	72.91	390	97.03	C	830	*Definition:* Nauru.
4894	YARAN (Yaren)	540	73.00	390	97.03	C	830	Phosphate. Y=1899 by Protestants, 1902 by Catholics. D=Congregational,RCC.
	NEPAL	**23,930,000**	**2.41**	**576,000**	**46.23**	**A**	**38,010,000**	**INDEPENDENTS 2.3%, PROTESTANTS 0.06%. PENT-CHAR 2.1%, EVANGELICAL 0.7%, GCC 2.2%**
4895	rural areas	21,088,000	2.33	491,000	45.88	A	29,108,000	97.7% (1950), 96.0% (1970), 91.0% (1990), 88.1% (2000), 84.2% (2010), 76.5% (2025)
4896	urban areas	2,843,000	3.00	85,300	48.82	A	8,902,000	2.2% (1950), 3.9% (1970), 8.9% (1990), 11.8% (2000), 15.7% (2010), 23.4% (2025)
4897	non-metropolitan areas	2,090,000	3.00	62,700	49.04	A	6,544,487	*Sources of data:* Censuses of 1953, 1961, 1971, and 1981.
4898	metropolitan areas	753,000	3.00	22,600	48.20	A	2,357,000	*Definition:* Localities with 9,000 or more inhabitants.
4899	Bhaktapur (Bhatgaon, Bhadgaon)	78,800	0.70	550	44.52	A	247,000	In Nepal Valley. Center of medieval art. Pottery. Old Palace (1700). 18th century Najatapola Dewai. F=865.
4900	Biratnagar (Wiratnagar)	154,000	0.80	1,200	44.62	A	482,000	In Terai plain. Nepal's principal industrial and foreign trade center, jute, sugar, cotton.
4901	KATHMANDU	520,000	4.00	20,800	49.82	A	1,629,000	At 4,500 ft. Agriculture. Palaces. F=723. 31% Nepali, 15% Maithili. M=UMN. D=NCFIN,Christ Groups.
4902	Lalitpur (Patan)	131,000	4.00	5,300	49.82	A	411,000	Headquarters for Banra sect of Newar people. 'City of Beauty'. Buddhist temples. F=AD 299. D=NCF/N.
	NETHERLANDS	**15,786,000**	**65.14**	**10,283,000**	**97.63**	**C**	**15,782,000**	**ROMAN CATHOLICS 34.5%, PROTESTANTS 26.8%. PENT-CHAR 6.5%, EVANGELICAL 3.8%, GCC 41.2%**
4903	rural areas	1,681,000	74.71	1,256,000	99.68	C	1,258,000	17.3% (1950), 13.9% (1970), 11.3% (1990), 10.6% (2000), 9.6% (2010), 7.9% (2025)
4904	urban areas	14,105,000	64.00	9,027,000	97.39	C	14,524,000	82.6% (1950), 86.1% (1970), 88.7% (1990), 89.3% (2000), 90.3% (2010), 92.0% (2025)
4905	non-metropolitan areas	5,494,000	64.32	3,534,000	97.95	C	5,692,041	*Sources of data:* Censuses of 1947 and 1960; estimates for 1947, 1970, 1975, 1981, and 1990.
4906	metropolitan areas	8,610,000	63.79	5,493,000	97.04	C	8,832,000	*Definition:* Municipalities with 2,000 or more inhabitants.
4907	'S-GRAVENHAGE (The Hague)	817,000	62.00	506,000	97.49	C	841,000	Center of international law. Trade, banking, insurance, conferences. Museums. F=1248. D=NHK.
4908	Delft	94,600	64.00	60,500	96.49	C	97,400	Tin-glazed earthenware, ceramics, spirits, oils, penicillin. The Gothic New Church (1384). F=1075. D=NHK.
4909	Rijswijk	50,500	65.00	32,800	97.49	C	52,000	On Vliet River. Primarily residential, oil wells, laboratories. Treaties of Rijswijk (1697). D=NHK.
4910	Zoetermeer	105,000	63.00	66,100	95.49	C	108,000	Machinery, tobacco, cereals, livestock, oil & gas fields. On polder created in 17th century. D=NHK.

Table 10-5–continued overleaf

Table 10-5–continued

Rec No 1	Country City 2	Pop 2000 3	AC% 4	Church Members 5	E% 6	W 7	Pop 2025 8	Notes 9
4911	's-Hertogenbosch (Den Bosch)	212,000	64.00	135,000	96.49	C	218,000	Capital of Noordbrabant. Important cattle market, shoes, cigars. F=1185. St. John's Cathedral.
4912	Alkmaar	131,000	65.00	85,300	97.49	C	135,000	Noordholland on North Holland Canal. Cattle, cheese, vegetables. F=10th century. Y=8th century. D=RCC.
4913	Almelo	66,300	66.00	43,800	98.49	C	68,300	Overijssel. Textiles, metallurgical center. F=1350. 17th century Dutch Reformed Church. D=NHK.
4914	Alphen aan den Rijn	66,000	66.00	43,600	98.49	C	68,000	Zuidholland on Oude Rijn north of Gouda. Dairying, cattle, hogs, poultry, flowers, vegetables, chocolate. D=NHK.
4915	Amersfoort	108,000	65.00	70,100	97.49	C	111,000	Utrecht on Eem River. Poultry raising, market gardening. F=12th century. 13th century church. D=NHK.
4916	Soest	43,800	66.00	28,900	98.49	C	45,100	Residential, light industry. F=1029. Gothic church (c1400). Royal residence, air base. D=RCC,NHK.
4917	AMSTERDAM	1,149,000	60.00	689,000	95.49	C	1,171,000	On North Sea. 90 islands connected by 1,000 bridges. Finance. F=1275. 13th century old church. D=RCC,NHK.
4918	Amstelveen	74,400	65.00	48,400	97.49	C	76,600	Near Amstel River. Residential. Water-sports center. Shoes, apparel, vegetables, dairying, flowers. D=RCC.
4919	Haarlem	158,000	64.00	101,000	96.49	C	163,000	Capital of Noordholland. Printing, shipbuilding, flowers. F=10th century. Jansenists. D=RCC diocese seat(1559).
4920	Hilversum	89,500	64.00	57,300	96.49	C	92,200	Center of Gooiland district of lakes & woods. Health & summer resort. Center of Dutch radio/TV. D=RCC,NHK.
4921	IJmuiden	63,600	63.00	40,100	95.49	C	65,500	Port. Fishing, fertilizer, cement. National park, institute for fisheries research. D=RCC,NHK.
4922	Purmerend	64,600	65.00	42,000	97.49	C	66,500	Noordholland north of Amsterdam. Dairying, cattle, apples, printing, publishing, flowers, vegetables. D=RCC,NHK.
4923	Zaanstad	138,000	64.00	88,500	96.49	C	142,000	Noordholland on Zaan River. Peter the Great learned shipbuilding here. (1697). D=RCC.
4924	Apeldoorn	157,000	66.00	103,000	98.49	C	161,000	Gelderland. Residential, many gardens, paper, pharmaceuticals. Near Soeren Forest and Het Loo. D=RCC,NHK.
4925	Arnhem	323,000	64.00	207,000	96.49	C	332,000	Capital of Gelderland on Lower Rhine River. Tourist center, metallurgy. Roman origins. D=RCC,NHK.
4926	Assen	53,300	68.00	36,200	98.49	C	54,900	Capital of Drenthe. Agricultural & dairy center. F=1257. 13th century Cistercian convent church. D=RCC,NHK.
4927	Bergen op Zoom	49,600	69.00	34,200	98.99	C	51,100	Noordbrabant on Zoom River. Fishing, oysters, asparagus, distillery. F=c850. Grote Kerk(c1400). D=RCC,NHC.
4928	Breda	172,000	66.00	114,000	98.49	C	178,000	Noordbrabant. Food processing, machinery, rayon, matches. F=c1100. Many historic churches. D=RCC,NHK.
4929	Den Helder	65,000	68.00	44,200	98.49	C	67,000	Noordholland at Marsdiep on North Sea. Shipbuilding, Royal Naval Institute. Sheep, cattle, flowers. D=RCC.
4930	Deventer	71,400	68.00	48,500	98.49	C	73,500	Overijssel on Ijssel River. Carpets, tapestries, honey cakes. F=8th century by St. Lebuinus. D=RCC,NHK.
4931	Dordrecht-Zwijndrecht (Dort, Dordt)	221,000	63.00	139,000	95.49	C	228,000	Zuidholland. Port, timber, shipbuilding, aquatic sports. F=1008. Medieval character. Groote Kerk (c1400). D=RCC.
4932	Ede	100,000	67.00	67,100	98.49	C	103,000	Gelderland. Metallurgy, rayon, pianos, dairy foods. F=8th century by Saxons. 15th century church. D=RCC,NHK.
4933	Eindhoven	406,000	63.00	256,000	95.49	C	418,000	Noordbrabant on Dommel River. Electrical manufacturing, tobacco, textiles. F=1232. D=RCC,NHK.
4934	Emmen	98,300	66.00	64,900	98.49	C	101,000	Drenthe on Hondsrug Ridge. Textiles, metallurgy, chemicals, timber. Prehistoric boulders. D=RCC,NHK.
4935	Enschede	267,000	64.00	171,000	96.49	C	275,000	Overijssel on Twente Canal. Cotton textiles, metallurgy, rubber goods. F=1325. Natural history museum. D=RCC.
4936	Hengelo	80,800	67.00	54,100	98.49	C	83,200	Textiles, metallurgy, electrical engineering, salt. Twickel Castle (1347). D=NHK,RCC.
4937	Geleen-Sittard	189,000	65.00	123,000	97.49	C	195,000	Limburg. Quarrying, fertilizer, chemicals. F=1243. Churches(14th, 15th, 17th centuries). D=RCC,NHK.
4938	Gouda	69,700	68.00	47,400	98.49	C	71,800	Zuidholland. Famous for Gouda cheese. Clay pipes, pottery. F=1272. St. John's church(1552). D=RCC,NHK.
4939	Groningen	220,000	65.00	143,000	97.49	C	227,000	Capital of Groningen. Cereals, lumber, cattle. University (1614). F=9th century. Gothic church (1253). D=RCC.
4940	Haarlemmermeer	104,000	67.00	69,500	98.49	C	107,000	Noordholland. Wheat, beets, potatoes, dairy. Dikes & polders. F=c1850s. D=RCC,NHK.
4941	Heerlen	283,000	66.00	187,000	98.49	C	291,000	Limburg. On Roman settlement Coriovallum. Petrochemicals, automobiles. St. Pancras Church (1180). D=RCC.
4942	Kerkrade	56,400	68.00	38,300	98.49	C	58,000	Coal-mining center from 1113 to 1970. Abbey of Rolduc (1104). International music contests. D=RCC,NHK.
4943	Helmond	74,000	68.00	50,300	98.49	C	76,200	Noordbrabant on Aa River. Textiles, iron, engineering. Castle (1402). D=RCC,NHK.
4944	Hoorn	61,600	68.00	41,900	98.49	C	63,400	Noordholland on Lake IJssel. Market center for vegetables & dairy, fishing. F=1300. Medieval churches. D=RCC.
4945	Leeuwarden	90,700	67.00	60,800	98.49	C	93,400	Capital of Friesland. Cattle market, tin, wood, paper. Frisian Museum. F=1300. D=RCC,NHK.
4946	Leiden (Leyden)	201,000	65.00	131,000	97.49	C	207,000	Zuidholland on Old Rhine River. Graphic arts. University of Leiden (1575). F=922. St. Peter's Church. D=RCC.
4947	Maastricht	172,000	64.00	110,000	96.49	C	178,000	Capital of Limburg on Maas River. Pottery. Roman origins. Bishopric (382-721). 6th century church. D=RCC.
4948	Nieuwegein	62,300	68.00	42,400	98.49	C	64,200	Utrecht south of Utrecht. Merewede Canal. Dairying, cattle, poultry, nursery stock, sugar beets. D=RCC.
4949	Nijmegen	256,000	67.00	172,000	98.49	C	264,000	Gelderland on Waal River. Roman Noviomagus. Industrial center. 16-sided baptistry (799). D=RCC.
4950	Oss	54,700	69.00	37,700	98.69	C	56,300	Noordbrabant. Food-processing town, margarine, meat, pharmaceuticals. F=1399. Mainly RCC.
4951	Roosendaal	64,300	64.00	41,100	96.49	C	66,200	Noordbrabant near Belgium. Railway repair, paper, graphics. F=1268 with founding of church. D=RCC.
4952	Rotterdam	1,078,000	61.00	658,000	96.49	C	1,088,000	Port in Zuid-Holland on New Waterway. Rebuilt after WWII. Economy based on shipping. F=1283. D=RCC,NHK.
4953	Ridderkerk	48,700	65.00	31,600	97.49	C	50,100	Zuidholland southeast of Rotterdam. Livestock, seeds, fruit, polymers, motors, kitchen equipment. D=RCC.
4954	Schiedam	74,300	65.00	48,300	97.49	C	76,500	Port. Gin & liquor distilleries, shipbuilding, iron founding, machinery. St. John's church(15th century). D=RCC.
4955	Spijkenisse	73,100	65.00	47,500	97.49	C	75,300	Zuidholland south of Rotterdam. Old Maas River. Large oil refineries, engines, dairying, poultry. D=RCC.
4956	Vlaardingen	78,000	65.00	50,700	97.49	C	80,300	Large seaport, shipyards, herring, dairies, phosphates. Grote Kerk (1643). D=RCC,NHK.
4957	Tilburg	247,000	68.00	168,000	98.49	C	254,000	Noordbrabant on Wilhelmina Canal. Woolen textiles. Small village until 1860. D=RCC,NHK.
4958	Utrecht	558,000	64.00	357,000	96.49	C	574,000	Capital of Utrecht on Winding Rhine. Market city, fairs. F=AD 48 by Romans. Bishopric since 696. D=RCC.
4959	Zeist	62,800	69.00	43,300	98.69	C	64,700	Residential & resort town. HQ of the Dutch Province of the Moravian Church (17th century-present).
4960	Veenendaal	52,600	63.00	33,100	95.49	C	54,100	Eastern Utrecht west of Arnhem. Furniture, tobacco products, vegetables, dairying, flowers. D=RCC.
4961	Venlo	92,100	69.00	63,500	98.69	C	94,800	Limburg on Maas River. Greenhouse market gardening, vegetables. F=1343. Medieval St. Martin's. D=RCC.
4962	Vlissingen (Flushing)	46,300	70.00	32,400	98.99	C	47,700	Zeeland on Walcheren Island. Commercial port, fishing, resort. Church of St. James (1308). D=RCC,NHK.
4963	Zwolle	101,000	65.00	65,700	97.49	C	104,000	Capital of Overijssel on Zwarte River. Shipbuilding. F=1230. Mount Saint Agnes (Thomas a' Kempis). D=RCC.
	NETHERLANDS ANTILLES	**217,000**	**85.30**	**185,000**	**99.29**	**C**	**258,000**	**ROMAN CATHOLICS 69.5%, PROTESTANTS 10.6%. PENT-CHAR 4.7%, EVANGELICAL 3.2%, GCC 17.5%**
4964	rural areas	64,100	86.02	55,200	99.52	C	55,000	32.1% (1950), 32.1% (1970), 31.6% (1990), 29.5% (2000), 26.1% (2010), 21.2% (2025)
4965	urban areas	153,000	85.00	130,000	99.19	C	203,000	67.9% (1950), 67.9% (1970), 68.3% (1990), 70.4% (2000), 73.8% (2010), 78.7% (2025)
4966	non-metropolitan areas	–	–	–	–	–	–	*Sources of data:* Censuses of 1960 and 1981.
4967	metropolitan areas	154,000	85.00	131,000	99.19	C	205,000	*Definition:* Population of urban agglomeration of Willemstad, Philipsburg, and Kralendijk.
4968	WILLEMSTAD	154,000	85.00	131,000	99.19	C	205,000	On Curacao. Oil refinery, tourism. Synagogue (1732). F=1499. D=RCC,NHK.
	NEW CALEDONIA	**214,000**	**75.54**	**162,000**	**98.61**	**C**	**286,000**	**ROMAN CATHOLICS 54.2%, PROTESTANTS 14.0%. PENT-CHAR 5.5%, EVANGELICAL 5.0%, GCC 18.8%**
4969	rural areas	76,700	74.72	57,300	97.80	C	73,200	51.1% (1950), 47.9% (1970), 40.1% (1990), 35.8% (2000), 31.5% (2010), 25.6% (2025)
4970	urban areas	137,000	76.00	104,000	99.07	C	212,000	48.8% (1950), 52.0% (1970), 59.8% (1990), 64.1% (2000), 68.4% (2010), 74.3% (2025)
4971	non-metropolitan areas	22,100	76.00	16,800	99.07	C	34,112	*Sources of data:* Censuses of 1963, 1976, 1983, and 1989.
4972	metropolitan areas	115,000	76.00	87,600	99.07	C	178,000	*Definition:* NoumÂa urban agglomeration.
4973	NOUMEA (Numea)	115,000	76.00	87,600	99.07	C	178,000	Excellent deepwater harbor. St. Joseph's Cathedral. F=1854 as Port-de-France. D=RCC,Evangelical Church.
	NEW ZEALAND	**3,862,000**	**66.35**	**2,562,000**	**99.07**	**C**	**4,695,000**	**PROTESTANTS 24.1%, ANGLICANS 21.3%. PENT-CHAR 15.2%, EVANGELICAL 17.0%, GCC 39.9%**
4974	rural areas	506,000	75.28	381,000	99.72	C	437,000	27.4% (1950), 18.8% (1970), 15.2% (1990), 13.0% (2000), 11.3% (2010), 9.3% (2025)
4975	urban areas	3,356,000	65.00	2,182,000	98.97	C	4,258,000	72.5% (1950), 81.1% (1970), 84.7% (1990), 86.9% (2000), 88.6% (2010), 90.6% (2025)
4976	non-metropolitan areas	872,000	64.88	566,000	99.25	C	1,104,142	*Sources of data:* Censuses of 1951, 1956, 1961, 1966, 1971, 1976, 1981, 1986, and 1991.
4977	metropolitan areas	2,484,000	65.04	1,616,000	98.87	C	3,154,000	*Definition:* Twenty-four urban areas plus all boroughs, town districts, townships and country towns 1,000 or more.
4978	Auckland	1,014,000	64.80	657,000	99.52	C	1,289,000	Largest port. Steel, dairy products, meats, tourism. F=1840 by British. Many Maoris. D=CPNZ,PCNZ,RCC.
4979	Takapuna	82,300	64.00	52,700	99.22	C	104,000	Residential. Suburb within North Shore City, Waitemata Harbour. Many Maoris. D=CPNZ,PCNZ.
4980	Waitemata	151,000	64.50	97,600	99.22	C	192,000	Waitemata Harbour. One-day festival. Hauraki Gulf, North-South Auckland Harbour Bridge. D=PCNZ,CPNZ.
4981	Manukau	250,000	63.00	158,000	97.72	C	317,000	Agriculture, butter, cheese, wool storage works. Residential. F=1965 by merger. D=CPNZ,PCNZ,RCC.
4982	Christchurch	340,000	65.50	223,000	99.42	C	431,000	South Island on Avon River. Meat-freezing, wool, agriculture. Educational center. Gardens. F=1850. D=PCNZ.
4983	Dunedin	129,000	65.00	83,800	97.72	C	164,000	South Island port. Wool, textiles, ship repair, iron & brass. F=1848 by Scottish Free Church. D=RCC,CPNZ.
4984	Hamilton	164,000	65.00	107,000	97.72	C	209,000	North Island on Waikato River. Lumber. Military settlement on deserted Maori village. University (1964). D=PCNZ.
4985	Invercargill	62,100	66.00	41,000	98.72	C	78,800	Southern part of South Island on Foveaux Strait. Scottish atmosphere. Scenic areas. F=1856. D=PCNZ,RCC.
4986	Napier-Hastings	122,000	64.00	78,100	96.72	C	155,000	North Island port on Hawke Bay. Wool, agriculture, livestock. Winter resort. F=1856. Anglican cathedral. D=CPNZ.
4987	Palmerston North	78,500	66.00	51,800	98.72	C	99,600	North Island on Manawatu River. Service center for pastoral & farming. University center. F=1866. D=PCNZ.
4988	Rotorua	59,400	65.00	38,600	97.72	C	75,400	North Island on Lake Rotorua. Hot springs, geysers, spa, resort. F=1870. Maori settlements. D=PCNZ.
4989	Tauranga	78,300	65.00	50,900	96.62	C	99,400	North Island port. Services agricultural region. Oil, fishing. Many Maoris. F=1834(Anglican mission). D=CPNZ.
4990	WELLINGTON	387,000	65.30	253,000	99.22	C	491,000	North Island port on Cook Strait. Trade. Victoria University (1962). F=1839. Anglican cathedral. D=CPNZ.
4991	Lower Hutt	105,000	64.00	67,000	98.72	C	133,000	Research organizations. Auto assembly, oil, plastics, paint, metalworking. D=CPNZ,RCC.
4992	Whangarei	49,900	65.00	31,800	96.62	C	62,000	Northern part of North Island on Bream Bay. Livestock raising. Deep sea fishing. Clock museum. D=CPNZ,PCNZ.
	NICARAGUA	**5,074,000**	**95.73**	**4,857,000**	**99.86**	**C**	**8,696,000**	**ROMAN CATHOLICS 85.1%, PROTESTANTS 11.6%. PENT-CHAR 14.1%, EVANGELICAL 8.7%, GCC 6.0%**
4993	rural areas	1,791,000	98.90	1,771,000	99.97	C	2,177,000	65.0% (1950), 52.9% (1970), 40.6% (1990), 35.2% (2000), 30.7% (2010), 25.0% (2025)
4994	urban areas	3,284,000	94.00	3,087,000	99.80	C	6,519,000	34.9% (1950), 47.0% (1970), 59.3% (1990), 64.7% (2000), 69.2% (2010), 74.9% (2025)
4995	non-metropolitan areas	1,338,000	94.01	1,258,000	99.78	C	3,028,286	*Sources of data:* Censuses of 1950, 1963, and 1971; estimate for 1980.
4996	metropolitan areas	1,946,000	93.99	1,829,000	99.81	C	3,491,000	*Definition:* Administrative centers of departments and municipalities.
4997	Chinandega	120,000	95.00	114,000	99.83	C	238,000	Capital of Chinandega. Pacific coastal lowlands. Cotton, sugarcane, bananas, sawmills, tanneries. D=RCC.
4998	Granada	116,000	95.00	110,000	99.83	C	230,000	Foot of Mombacho Volcano on Lake Nicaragua. Furniture, soap, clothing. Spanish style. F=1523. D=RCC.
4999	Leon	162,000	94.00	152,000	99.78	C	321,000	Liberal political & intellectual center. Cotton, sugarcane, rice. F=1524 but moved in 1610. D=RCC.
5000	MANAGUA	1,319,000	93.80	1,237,000	99.83	C	2,247,000	On Lake Managua. Meat, coffee, cotton. Center of commerce. Disastrous earthquake (1972). F=1855. D=RCC.
5001	Masaya	120,000	95.00	114,000	99.83	C	238,000	Foot of Masaya Volcano. Large Indian population, handicrafts, festivals. Sandanista fighting (1978-1979). D=RCC.
5002	Matagalpa	109,000	93.00	101,000	99.63	C	216,000	Capital of Matagalpa east of Esteli at 2,100 ft. Cattle, coffee, furniture, resorts. D=RCC.
	NIGER	**10,730,000**	**0.54**	**58,300**	**42.14**	**A**	**21,495,000**	**INDEPENDENTS 0.2%, ROMAN CATHOLICS 0.1%. PENT-CHAR 0.2%, EVANGELICAL 0.1%, GCC 0.4%**
5003	rural areas	8,523,000	0.40	34,000	41.40	A	13,839,000	95.1% (1950), 91.4% (1970), 83.9% (1990), 79.4% (2000), 73.9% (2010), 64.3% (2025)
5004	urban areas	2,207,000	1.10	24,300	45.00	A	7,657,000	4.8% (1950), 8.5% (1970), 16.1% (1990), 20.5% (2000), 26.0% (2010), 35.6% (2025)
5005	non-metropolitan areas	1,121,000	1.07	12,000	45.10	A	3,889,918	*Sources of data:* Censuses of 1977 and 1988; estimates for 1956, 1962, and 1966.
5006	metropolitan areas	1,086,000	1.13	12,300	44.90	A	3,767,000	*Definition:* Urban centers (27 towns).
5007	Agadez	71,300	0.10	71	39.70	A	247,000	Capital of Agadez. Desert oasis. Air Mountains. Sahara tours. F=15th century.
5008	Maradi	168,000	0.10	170	39.70	A	583,000	On Maradi River. Peanuts, cotton, leather. Mainly Hausa. Destroyed by flood in 1945.
5009	NIAMEY	593,000	2.00	11,900	49.60	A	2,057,000	On Niger River. Yoruba, Hausa. 30% Zerma, 20% Gourma. D=RCC (95% expatriate), ECWA.
5010	Tahoua	73,300	0.01	7	36.61	A	254,000	Capital of Tahoua. Farming. Tuareg & Fulani nomads. Gypsum & phosphate.
5011	Zinder	180,000	0.10	180	39.70	A	624,000	Capital of Zinder. Peanut processing and marketing. Tannery. Capital of 18th century Muslim dynasty.
	NIGERIA	**111,506,000**	**45.71**	**50,965,000**	**79.77**	**B**	**183,041,000**	**INDEPENDENTS 21.5%, ANGLICANS 18.0%. PENT-CHAR 32.1%, EVANGELICAL 20.0%, GCC 10.0%**
5012	rural areas	62,455,000	48.46	30,265,000	78.83	B	71,551,000	89.8% (1950), 80.0% (1970), 64.9% (1990), 56.0% (2000), 48.0% (2010), 39.0% (2025)
5013	urban areas	49,052,000	42.20	20,700,000	80.96	B	111,490,000	10.1% (1950), 20.0% (1970), 35.0% (1990), 43.9% (2000), 52.0% (2010), 60.9% (2025)
5014	non-metropolitan areas	13,369,000	42.05	5,621,000	80.78	B	30,617,786	*Sources of data:* Censuses of 1953, 1963, and 1991; estimates for 1970, 1975, and 1983.
5015	metropolitan areas	35,683,000	42.26	15,079,000	81.03	B	80,873,000	*Definition:* Towns with 20,000 or more inhabitants whose occupations are not mainly agrarian.
5016	Aba	351,000	75.00	263,000	99.06	C	797,000	Imo on Aba River. Handicrafts, natural gas, textiles. Traditional market for Igbo before 1900. D=RCC.
5017	Abakaliki	83,100	67.00	55,700	98.06	C	189,000	Anambra. Agricultural trade center (yams, cassava, rice) for Igbo. Lead, zinc, limestone. D=RCC.
5018	Abeokuta	499,000	30.70	153,000	64.76	B	1,135,000	Capital of Ogun on Ogun River. Rice, yams, cassava. F=1830 by Egba refugees. Olumo Rock. D=RCC.
5119	ABUJA	520,000	40.00	208,000	74.06	B	1,182,000	Federal Capital Territory. Capital since 1991. Scenic location. Airport, central location. D=RCC,Anglican.
5020	Ado-Ekiti	420,000	30.00	126,000	64.06	B	954,000	Ondo in Yoruba Hills. Cotton weaving, shoes, pottery. Founded by Ekiti (Yoruba subgroup). D=RCC.
5021	Afikpo	96,300	69.00	66,400	98.06	C	219,000	Abia. Imo near Cross River. Near Ugep. Palm oil, cacao, kola nuts, rice, port. D=Anglican,Independents.
5022	Agege	123,000	41.00	50,300	75.06	B	279,000	Ikeja. North of the international airport. Trade center in cacao, citrus fruit drinks. D=Anglican.

Table 10-5–continued opposite

Table 10-5–continued

Rec No 1	Country City 2	Pop 2000 3	AC% 4	Church Members 5	E% 6	W 7	Pop 2025 8	Notes 9
5023	Akure	190,000	45.00	85,300	79.06	B	431,000	Capital of Ondo. Agricultural trade center (yams, cassava, corn), cocoa, weaving, hunting. D=RCC,Anglican.
5024	Amaigbo	78,600	40.00	31,400	74.06	B	179,000	Imo, yams, cassava, handicrafts, corn.
5025	Apomu	72,500	38.00	27,600	72.06	B	165,000	Osun, yams, cassava, corn, brasswork, woven cloth.
5026	Aramoko	70,600	40.00	28,300	74.06	B	161,000	Ekih State, Ondo. Cotton, tobacco, rubber.
5027	Asaba	69,400	67.00	46,500	98.06	C	158,000	Bendel on Niger River. Palm oil and kernels, kola nuts, lignite deposits, agricultural trade center. D=Anglican.
5028	Awka	130,000	67.00	87,000	98.06	C	295,000	Anambra. Ibo blacksmiths, agricultural trade (yams, cassava, taro) for Ibo people. D=RCC,Anglican.
5029	Azare	73,200	50.00	36,600	84.06	B	166,000	Plateau on Ankwe River. Cotton, peanuts, millet, durra. Hospital, leper community. D=Anglican.
5030	Bauchi	101,000	42.00	42,300	76.06	B	229,000	Capital of Bauchi. Peanuts, cotton, asbestos, auto assembly. F=1800 by Yakubu, a Gerawa. D=Independents.
5031	Benin City (Edo)	268,000	45.00	121,000	79.06	B	609,000	Capital of Bendel on Benin River. Brass work, rubber. Former Edo kingdom. D=RCC,Anglican.
5032	Bida	147,000	32.00	46,900	66.06	B	333,000	Niger on Bako River. Brass & copper crafts. Mud houses. Rice collection. Mainly Nupe. D=Independents.
5033	Calabar	205,000	80.00	164,000	99.06	C	465,000	Capital of Cross River State. Palm produce, rubber. Slave trading center in 18th century. Y=1846. D=RCC.
5034	Deba	162,000	42.00	68,000	76.06	B	368,000	Bauchi near Gongola River. Near Gombe and Kumo. Collecting point for peanuts, cotton, corn. D=Anglican.
5035	Duku	77,400	35.00	27,100	69.06	B	176,000	Bauchi near Gongola River. Cassava, millet, durra, agriculture. D=RCC,Anglican.
5036	Ede	359,000	32.00	115,000	66.06	B	815,000	Oyo on Oshun River. Local trading center for cotton, palm produce, cocoa. F=1500 by Yoruba. D=RCC.
5037	Effon-Alaiye (Efon-Alaye)	179,000	44.00	78,700	78.06	B	407,000	Ondo in Yoruba Hills. Cocoa, cotton & palm oil. F=late 19th century. Ilesha & Effon Yoruba. D=Anglican.
5038	Ejigbo	124,000	43.00	53,200	77.06	B	281,000	Oyo, southwest, 15 miles southeast of Ogbomosho. Market, millet, yams, cassava.
5039	Emure-Ekiti	86,000	40.00	34,400	74.06	B	195,000	Ondo in Yoruba Hills. Agricultural trade, cocoa. D=RCC,Anglican.
5040	Enugu	369,000	73.00	270,000	99.06	C	840,000	Capital of Anambra State. Coal mining. Trade center for Ibo. Educational center. F=1906. D=RCC,Anglican.
5041	Epe	118,000	42.00	49,500	76.06	B	268,000	Lagos port. Exports fish, cassava, corn. Barge production. F=18th century by Ijebu Yoruba. D=Anglican.
5042	Erin-Oshogbo	87,700	35.00	30,700	69.06	B	199,000	Eastern Oyo near Ede. Oshun River. Cotton, steel, textiles, cigarettes, food processing, airport. F=17th century.
5043	Eruwa	71,900	35.00	25,200	69.06	B	163,000	Oyo, southwest, 30 miles west northwest of Ibandun. Market town, yams, maize. D=Anglican,Independents.
5044	Fiditi	72,300	32.00	23,100	66.06	B	164,000	Oyo near Iwo. On main road, 15 miles south of Oyo. Market town, millet, plantains, yams.
5045	Gboko	72,300	55.00	39,700	89.06	B	164,000	Benue. South of Makurdi. Capital of Gboko local government area. Shea nuts, sesame. D=Anglican,RCC.
5046	Gbongan	79,000	40.00	31,600	74.06	B	180,000	Osun State. Afribank. Market town, yams, millet, plantains. D=Anglican,Episcopal Bishop of Oke-Osun
5047	Gombe	126,000	43.00	54,200	77.06	B	286,000	Bauchi. Peanuts, cotton, textiles. F=1804 by Fulani Buba Yero. Arabic teacher-training college. D=Anglican.
5048	Gusau	185,000	10.00	18,500	39.06	A	420,000	Sokoto. Major collecting point for cotton & peanuts. F=1927. Hausa & Fulani peoples.
5049	Ibadan	1,739,000	35.00	609,000	69.06	B	4,006,000	Capital of Oyo. Many markets, local crafts. Cacao. Yoruba. Educational center. F=1829. D=RCC,Anglican.
5050	Idah	74,000	50.00	37,000	84.06	B	168,000	Kogi on Niger River. Agriculture trade center. Shea nut processing, cotton, palm oil, corn, plantains. D=RCC.
5051	Idanre	82,100	40.00	32,800	74.06	B	186,000	Ogan State. Afribank, annual Ogan Festival. Cacao, palm oil, timber, rubber, cotton. D=Anglican.
5052	Ife (Ife-lodun)	347,000	36.00	125,000	70.06	B	788,000	Oyo. Considered by Yoruba as holy city & birthplace of mankind. Town-dwelling farmers. F=1300. D=Anglican.
5053	Ifon-Oshogbo	96,500	30.00	29,000	64.06	B	219,000	Ondo near Owo, 45 miles south of Akure. Market town, kola nuts, maize, cocoyams. D=RCC,Anglican.
5054	Igbasa-Odo	70,300	40.00	28,100	74.06	B	160,000	Agricultural trade center (yams, cassava, corn). D=Anglican, Independents.
5055	Igbo-Ora	99,600	31.00	30,900	65.06	B	226,000	Oyo near Ogun River. North of Abeokuta. Cotton weaving, shea nut processing, cattle, yams. D=RCC.
5056	Igboho	125,000	30.00	37,400	64.06	B	283,000	Oyo in the north near Kishi. Cotton weaving, maize, oil palms, cassava, millet, pottery. D=Anglican.
5057	Igede-Ekiti	82,800	40.00	33,100	74.06	B	188,000	Niger State, 50 miles west northwest of Minna. Market town, yams, cassava, livestock. D=RCC.
5058	Ihiala	107,000	60.00	64,300	94.06	C	244,000	Anambra near Onitsha. Oil palms, rice, yams, cassava, maize, cocoyams, poultry, pigs, cotton. D=Anglican.
5059	Ijebu-Igbo	115,000	35.00	40,300	69.06	B	262,000	Ogun, north of Lagos. Road center, market town in cocoa belt. Hardwood, rubber, palm oil, kernals, kola nuts.
5060	Ijebu-Ode	183,000	43.00	78,600	77.06	B	415,000	Ogun. Major collecting station for Kola nuts. Iron handiwork. Muslim & Christian training colleges. D=RCC.
5061	Ijero-Ekiti	112,000	40.00	44,700	74.06	B	254,000	Ondo State, southwest on road, 45 miles north of Akure. Market town, yams, rice. D=Anglican.
5062	Ikare	165,000	35.00	57,600	69.06	B	374,000	Ondo in Yoruba Hills. Agricultural trade center (yams, cassava, corn). Christian schools & hospitals. D=Anglican.
5063	Ikerre (Ikere-Ekiti)	286,000	45.00	129,000	79.06	B	650,000	Ondo. Major collecting point for cocoa. Agricultural trade center for Ekiti Yoruba. Christian colleges. D=RCC.
5064	Ikire	138,000	29.00	40,100	63.06	B	314,000	Oyo. Collecting point for local cash crops (cocoa, corn, palm oils). Traditional cotton weaving. D=Anglican.
5065	Ikirun	212,000	30.00	63,600	64.06	B	482,000	Oyo. Local trading center (yams, corn, cassava). Cotton weaving. Mainly Yoruba. D=Anglican.
5066	Ikole	105,000	30.00	31,500	64.06	B	239,000	Ondo north of Ado-Ekiti. Cacao industry, palm oil, kernel seeds, kola nuts, agriculture. D=RCC,Anglican.
5067	Ikorodu	216,000	42.00	90,800	76.06	B	491,000	Lagos. Traditional settlement of Awori Yoruba. Fish, poultry, cassava. Truck farms. D=Independents,Anglican.
5068	Ikot Ekpene	102,000	65.00	66,000	99.06	C	231,000	Akwa Ibom. Chief trade center (yams, cassava, taro, corn). Cane furniture by Anang Ibibio. D=RCC.
5069	Ila (Illa, Ila Orangun)	308,000	30.00	92,500	64.06	B	701,000	Oyo in Yoruba Hills. Collecting center for tobacco. Traditional Yoruba settlement. D=Anglican,Independents.
5070	Ilawe-Ekiti (Ilawe)	216,000	35.00	75,400	69.06	B	490,000	Ondo in Yoruba Hills. Collecting point for cocoa. Yoruba (Ilesha, Ekiti, & Ondo). D=Anglican.
5071	Ilesha	442,000	30.00	133,000	64.06	B	1,005,000	Oyo in Yoruba Hills. Exports cocoa. Traditional cultural center for Ilesha Yoruba. King's palace.
5072	Ilobu	233,000	29.00	67,500	63.06	B	529,000	Oyo. Trade center (yams, cassava, corn, palm oil). Cotton weaving. Mainly Yoruba.
5073	Ilorin	556,000	28.00	156,000	62.06	B	1,264,000	Capital of Kwara on Awun River. Market for yams, cassava, corn. Industrial center. Yoruba. D=Anglican,RCC.
5074	Inisa	140,000	30.00	42,000	64.06	B	318,000	Oyo. Local market center (yams, cassava, corn). Cash crops (cotton, tobacco). Mainly Yoruba.
5075	Ipoti-Ekiti	77,900	40.00	31,100	74.06	B	177,000	Ondo in Yoruba Hills. Agricultural trade, cocoa. D=Anglican,RCC.
5076	Ise-Ekiti	121,000	40.00	48,300	74.06	B	275,000	Ondo State. Agriculture trade, kola nuts, yams, cassava, corn palm oil, kernels, maize. D=RCC.
5077	Iseyin	254,000	30.00	76,200	64.06	B	577,000	Oyo. Dyeing heavy cloth. Cotton, tobacco, teak. Y=1860s by Anglican Yoruba Mission. D=Anglican.
5078	Iwo	423,000	29.00	123,000	63.06	B	961,000	Oyo. Cultivation & export of cocoa. Cotton weaving & dyeing. Mainly Muslim. D=Baptist,RCC.
5079	Jega	72,900	17.00	12,400	51.06	B	166,000	Kebbi on Zamfara River. Agricultural trade center, cotton, millet, rice, cattle, skins. D=RCC.
5080	Jimeta	96,800	45.00	43,500	79.06	B	220,000	Gongola near Benue River. Peanuts, cotton, cattle, cassava, millet, sorghum, trading. D=Anglican.
5081	Jos	241,000	50.00	120,000	84.06	B	548,000	Capital of Plateau on Delimi River. Tin, columbite, sorghum, millet. Hill resort. D=Independents,RCC.
5082	Kaduna	400,000	35.00	140,000	69.06	B	909,000	Capital of Kaduna. Financial center. Cotton textiles. Educational center. F=1917. D=RCC.
5083	Kano	788,000	13.00	102,000	47.06	A	1,790,000	Capital of Kano State on Jakara River. Peanuts, hides & skins. Mostly Hausa. Ancient origins. D=RCC.
5084	Katsina	241,000	16.00	38,600	50.06	B	549,000	Katsina near Niger. Collecting point for peanuts, hides, skins. Hausa weaving. F=1100. Fulani emirs. D=RCC.
5085	Kaura Namoda	77,400	19.00	14,700	53.06	B	176,000	Sokoto on Gagere River. Cotton shipping point, gold, diamond mining, peanuts, cattle millet. D=RCC.
5086	Keffi	84,600	52.00	44,000	86.06	B	192,000	Plateau. Tin and columbite mining, millet, sorghum, yams, cotton. Gwandara people. F=1800. D=Independents.
5087	Kishi	113,000	30.00	33,900	64.06	B	257,000	Oyo near Moshi River, 60 miles northwest of Ilorin, cotton weaving, shea nut processing, cattle. D=Anglican.
5088	Kumo	173,000	41.00	70,900	75.06	B	393,000	Bauchi. Peanuts, cotton, corn. Trade center for Tangale, Fulani, Hausa. Gombe emirate. D=RCC.
5089	Lafia	143,000	50.00	71,600	84.06	B	325,000	Plateau. Collecting point for sesame seeds, soybeans. Cotton weaving, dyeing. Arago, Tiv, Kanuri. D=RCC.
5090	Lafiagi	84,200	35.00	29,500	69.06	B	191,000	Kwara on Niger River. Rice, yams, sorghum, cotton, tobacco. Majority are Muslim Nupe. F=1810. D=Anglican.
5091	Lagos	13,488,000	47.00	6,339,000	95.06	B	30,372,000	Chief port on Lagos island. Fishing. F=late 15th century. D=Anglican,RCC,Independents.
5092	Mushin	389,000	46.00	179,000	94.06	B	885,000	Overcrowding, poor sanitation. Spinning & weaving cotton, shoes. Predominantly Yoruba. D=Anglican.
5093	Shomolu (Somolu)	177,000	48.00	84,800	96.06	B	401,000	Residential suburb. Overcrowding, poor housing, inadequate sanitation. Leather. Mainly Yoruba. D=RCC.
5094	Lalupon	82,100	20.00	16,400	54.06	B	187,000	Agricultural trade center, palm oil and kernels, yams, cassava. D=RCC.
5095	Lere (Leri)	72,700	40.00	29,100	74.06	B	165,000	Bauchi near Sara Peak, 55 miles southwest of Bauchi. Tin mining center, cassava, millet, cotton. D=Anglican.
5096	Maiduguri (Yerwa, Yerwa-Maiduguri)	373,000	40.00	149,000	74.06	B	848,000	Capital of Borno. Livestock, leather, dried fish, food processing. F=1907. Muslim Kanuri & Shuwa. D=RCC.
5097	Makurdi	144,000	55.00	79,100	89.06	B	327,000	Capital of Benue. Transshipment point for cattle. Sesame seeds, cotton. Trade center for Tiv. F=1927. D=RCC.
5098	Minna	160,000	32.00	51,200	66.06	B	363,000	Capital of Niger. Collecting point for peanuts, cotton, yams. Woven & dyed cloth. Gbari people. D=RCC.
5099	Mubi	74,900	43.00	32,200	77.06	B	170,000	Gongola on Yedseram River near Cameroon border. Peanuts, pepper, hemp, rice, cotton, cattle. D=Anglican.
5100	Nguru	115,000	40.00	46,100	74.06	B	262,000	Borno. Major collecting point for gum arabic. Trade center for Muslim Kanuri, Bede, and Manga peoples. D=RCC.
5101	Nsukka	69,900	65.00	45,400	99.06	C	159,000	Enugu State north of Enugu. Agricultural trade center, palm oil and kernels, yams, cassava. D=RCC.
5102	Ode-Ekiti	71,600	40.00	28,600	74.06	B	163,000	Ogun State. Cacao industry, cotton weaving, indigo dyeing, palm oil and kernels, rice. D=Anglican.
5103	Offa	230,000	35.00	80,700	69.06	B	524,000	Kwara. Traditional settlement of Yoruba. Collecting point for yams, cassava. Cotton weaving & dyeing. D=RCC.
5104	Ogbomosho	853,000	29.00	247,000	63.06	B	1,938,000	Oyo. Mainly Yoruba farmers, traders, and artisans. Traditional Yoruba cloth. D=American Baptists headquarters.
5105	Oka (Oka-Akoko)	167,000	35.00	58,600	69.06	B	380,000	Ondo in Yoruba Hills. Yoruba agricultural market center. Cocoa, palm produce, tobacco, cotton. D=Anglican.
5106	Oke-Mesi	80,500	40.00	32,200	74.06	B	183,000	Peanuts, cotton, cattle, cassava, millet, sorghum, trading. D=Anglican.
5107	Ondo	198,000	45.00	89,100	79.06	B	450,000	Ondo in Yoruba Hills. Collecting point for cocoa & palm oil. Wooden doors, furniture. Educational center. D=RCC.
5108	Onitsha	436,000	72.00	314,000	99.06	C	992,000	Anambra port on Niger River. Exports palm oil & kernals. Christian schools. D=RCC,Anglican.
5109	Opobo	94,500	65.00	61,500	99.06	C	215,000	Rivers State on Gulf of Guinea, Niger River delta. Palm oil, fishing, boat building. F=1869. D=Anglican,RCC.
5110	Oron (Idua Oron)	91,100	65.00	59,200	99.06	C	207,000	Akwa Ibom. Coastal trade center for yams, cassava, fish. Ancestral carvings of the Ibibio. D=Anglican.
5111	Oshogbo	557,000	35.00	195,000	69.06	B	1,266,000	Oyo on Oshun River. Cocoa, weaving & dyeing of cotton cloth. Yoruba king (Oba). Yonba shrines. D=RCC.
5112	Owerri	57,400	70.00	40,200	99.06	C	130,000	Capital of Imo. Chief trade center (yams, cassava). Handicraft centers. Christian Ibo people. D=RCC,Anglican.
5113	Owo	214,000	45.00	96,500	79.06	B	488,000	Ondo. Major collecting point for cocoa. Cotton, teak. St. John's Teacher Training College. D=Anglican.
5114	Oyan	74,500	40.00	29,800	74.06	B	169,000	Collecting point for local cash crops (cocoa, corn, palm oils). Traditional cotton weaving. D=Anglican.
5115	Oyo	299,000	30.00	89,800	64.06	B	681,000	Oyo. Agriculture & handicrafts. Traditional center of cotton spinning, weaving & dyeing. D=RCC.
5116	Pindiga	93,800	40.00	37,500	74.06	B	213,000	Bauchi near Yankari Game Reserve. Cassava, millet, durra, corn, tomatoes, peanuts. D=Anglican.
5117	Port Harcourt	479,000	75.00	359,000	99.06	C	1,088,000	Capital of Rivers on Bonny River. Palm oil, timber, coal, tin. Radio & TV broadcasting. F=1912. D=RCC.
5118	Potiskum	82,700	40.00	33,100	74.06	B	188,000	Yobe. Cotton, peanuts, cassava, millet, cotton, cattle, diatomite deposits. D=Independents.
5119	Sapele	163,000	65.00	106,000	99.06	C	370,000	Port of Rivers. Sawmilling, plywood & veneer manufacturing, rubber. F=Colonial period. Urhobo people. D=RCC.
5120	Shagamu	137,000	30.00	41,100	64.06	B	311,000	Ogun on Ibu River. Largest collecting point for Kola nuts. Thorn carvings. F=19th century by Yoruba. D=Anglican.
5121	Shaki (Saki)	203,000	33.00	67,100	67.06	B	462,000	Oyo. Exports cotton, swamp rice, teak, tobacco. F=1835. Y=1860 by Anglicans. D=Anglican,Independents.
5122	Sokoto	240,000	20.00	47,900	54.06	B	544,000	Capital of Sokoto. Major trade center in leather crafts. Muslim pilgrimage center. F=1804. Hausa, Fulani. D=RCC.
5123	Ugep	120,000	70.00	83,900	99.06	C	272,000	Cross River State on Cross River. Oil palms, yams, cassava, maize, groundnuts, bananas, fishing. D=RCC.
5124	Umuahia	76,900	68.00	52,300	98.56	C	175,000	Abia. Palm oil and kernels, kola nuts. Hospital, University of Agriculture. D=Anglican,RCC.
5125	Uyo	88,500	65.00	57,500	99.06	C	201,000	Capital of Akwa Ibom. Collecting station for palm oil & kernels. Local trade center for Ibibio. D=RCC.
5126	Warri	147,000	40.00	58,900	74.06	B	335,000	Port in Bendel on Warri River. Natural gas, petroleum. F=15th century. D=RCC.
5127	Zaria	443,000	30.00	133,000	64.06	B	1,007,000	Kaduna on Kubanni River. Cotton. Educational center. Hausa, Fulani peoples. Gbari. F=c1000. D=Anglican.
	NIUE ISLAND	**1,900**	**92.54**	**1,700**	**99.95**	**C**	**1,400**	**PROTESTANTS 57.3%, MARGINAL CHRISTIANS 23.4%. PENT-CHAR 11.7%, EVANGELICAL 3.7%, GCC 17.5%**
5128	rural areas	1,300	93.59	1,200	99.96	C	870	76.5% (1950), 78.9% (1970), 69.1% (1990), 70.6% (2000), 68.9% (2010), 60.0% (2025)
5129	urban areas	550	90.00	500	99.86	C	580	23.4% (1950), 21.0% (1970), 30.8% (1990), 29.4% (2000), 31.0% (2010), 39.9% (2025)
5130	non-metropolitan areas	–	–	–	–	–	–	*Sources of data:* Censuses of 1966, 1971, 1986, and 1991.
5131	metropolitan areas	590	90.09	530	99.83	C	610	*Definition:* Alofi.
5132	ALOFI	590	90.00	530	99.86	C	610	Passion fruit, coconuts, tourism. F=AD 900(Samoans). Y=1830(LMS) . D=Ekalesia Niue,Mormon.
	NORFOLK ISLAND	**2,100**	**65.20**	**1,400**	**99.66**	**C**	**2,500**	**ANGLICANS 29.4%, PROTESTANTS 22.8%. PENT-CHAR 5.3%, EVANGELICAL 20.4%, GCC 28.6%**
5133	rural areas	620	65.68	410	99.90	C	500	40.0% (1950), 35.0% (1970), 30.0% (1990), 30.0% (2000), 25.0% (2010), 20.0% (2025)
5134	urban areas	1,500	65.00	940	99.56	C	2,000	60.0% (1950), 65.0% (1970), 70.0% (1990), 70.0% (2000), 75.0% (2010), 80.0% (2025)
5135	non-metropolitan areas	220	65.09	150	99.38	C	309	*Sources of data:* Censuses.
5136	metropolitan areas	1,200	64.98	800	99.59	C	1,700	*Definition:* Kingston-Norfolk.
5137	KINGSTON-NORFOLK	1,200	65.00	800	99.56	C	1,700	Tourism. One-third descended from Pitcairners (1856). Citrus, passion fruit. D=Anglican,Methodist.
	NORTH KOREA	**24,039,000**	**2.08**	**500,000**	**49.97**	**A**	**29,388,000**	**INDEPENDENTS 1.8%, ROMAN CATHOLICS 0.2%. PENT-CHAR 1.8%, EVANGELICAL 0.08%, GCC 1.9%**
5138	rural areas	8,940,000	2.22	198,000	47.41	A	7,955,000	69.0% (1950), 45.8% (1970), 40.1% (1990), 37.1% (2000), 33.2% (2010), 27.0% (2025)
5139	urban areas	15,099,000	2.00	302,000	51.49	B	21,432,000	31.0% (1950), 54.2% (1970), 59.9% (1990), 62.8% (2000), 66.7% (2010), 72.9% (2025)
5140	non-metropolitan areas	8,136,000	2.03	165,000	51.55	B	11,885,843	*Sources of data:* Estimates for 1950, 1960, 1967, 1970, 1975, 1980, 1982, and 1986.

Table 10-5–continued overleaf

Table 10-5–continued

Rec No 1	Country City 2	Pop 2000 3	AC% 4	Church Members 5	E% 6	W 7	Pop 2025 8	Notes 9
5141	metropolitan areas	6,963,000	1.97	137,000	51.42	B	9,547,000	*Definition:* Urban centers.
5142	Chongjin	685,000	0.80	5,500	48.69	A	972,000	On Kyongsong Bay. Iron, steel, shipbuilding, chemicals. F=1908 as open port.
5143	Haeju	288,000	1.20	3,500	49.09	A	409,000	On Haeju Bay. Fishing, cement, chemicals. Does not freeze over in winter.
5144	Hamhung-Huangan	267,000	1.60	4,300	49.49	A	378,000	Capital of South Hamgyong. Synthetic textiles, scenic beaches. Chemical research. F=15th century.
5145	Hungnam	399,000	0.80	3,200	48.69	A	567,000	Hamgyong Namdo on Sea of Japan near Hamhung, Tongsongchon River. Gold refinery, aluminum, fisheries, coal.
5146	Kaesong	362,000	1.20	4,300	49.09	A	514,000	Near border with South Korea. Textiles, medicinal herbs. Many temples, tombs, palaces.
5147	Kanggye	255,000	0.80	2,000	48.69	A	362,000	Chagang Do on Tongno-gang River near Chinese border. Mining, ceramics, timber.
5148	Kimchaek (Songjin)	519,000	0.80	4,200	48.69	A	737,000	North Hamgyong port. Iron, magnesium marble, fishing. F=1899 as open port.
5149	Namp'o (Chinnamp'o)	337,000	1.20	4,000	49.09	A	478,000	Chief seaport on Taedong River. Market center for marine products, copper & gold refining. Apples.
5150	PYONGYANG	2,726,000	3.50	95,400	55.39	B	3,533,000	On Taedong River. Textiles. F=1122 BC. In 1880s, 100 churches and many missionaries. D=house churches.
5151	Sinuiju	426,000	0.80	3,400	48.69	A	605,000	Near mouth of Yalu River. Lumber, chemicals, ironware. Trade with China.
5152	Songnim	142,000	0.80	1,100	48.69	A	201,000	North Hwanghae province. Largest iron & steel center. Taedong River port. Mining center, chemical plants.
5153	Wonsan	556,000	1.10	6,100	48.99	A	790,000	On Sea of Japan. Fishing & marine products, shipbuilding. Recreational beaches. F=Yi dynasty.
	NORTHERN CYPRUS	**185,000**	**8.70**	**16,100**	**56.02**	**B**	**212,000**	**ORTHODOX 7.5%, INDEPENDENTS 1.2%. PENT-CHAR 1.1%, EVANGELICAL 0.1%, GCC 2.4%**
5154	rural areas	80,000	5.69	4,600	53.01	B	65,700	70.2% (1950), 59.2% (1970), 48.6% (1990), 43.2% (2000), 37.9% (2010), 30.9% (2025)
5155	urban areas	105,000	11.00	11,600	58.32	B	147,000	29.7% (1950), 40.7% (1970), 51.4% (1990), 56.7% (2000), 62.0% (2010), 69.0% (2025)
5156	non-metropolitan areas	63,000	11.00	6,900	58.32	B	87,986	*Sources of data:* Censuses.
5157	metropolitan areas	42,100	11.00	4,600	58.32	B	58,800	*Definition:* Urban areas.
5158	LEFKOSE (Levkosia-2, Nicosia-2)	42,100	11.00	4,600	58.32	B	58,800	Northern section of Nicosia under UN forces.Textiles, cigarettes, flour. Ancient origins. Turkish. D=GOC.
	NORTHERN MARIANA IS	**78,400**	**88.39**	**69,300**	**98.93**	**C**	**245,000**	**ROMAN CATHOLICS 88.4%, INDEPENDENTS 8.5%. PENT-CHAR 10.5%, EVANGELICAL 4.2%, GCC 9.2%**
5159	rural areas	35,400	92.50	32,800	99.89	C	82,600	47.0% (1950), 47.0% (1970), 47.0% (1990), 45.2% (2000), 41.2% (2010), 33.6% (2025)
5160	urban areas	42,900	85.00	36,500	98.14	C	163,000	53.0% (1950), 53.0% (1970), 53.0% (1990), 54.7% (2000), 58.7% (2010), 66.3% (2025)
5161	non-metropolitan areas	30,500	85.00	25,900	98.14	C	115,462	*Sources of data:* Censuses of 1980 and 1990.
5162	metropolitan areas	12,400	85.00	10,600	98.14	C	47,100	*Definition:* Places with a population of 1,000 or more.
5163	SUSUPE (Saipan)	12,400	85.00	10,600	98.14	C	47,100	Tourism. Copra, fishing, pig & cattle raising. Chamorro. Mass suicide in 1944. D=RCC,UCC.
	NORWAY	**4,461,000**	**94.18**	**4,201,000**	**98.63**	**C**	**4,812,000**	**PROTESTANTS 94.1%, INDEPENDENTS 3.0%. PENT-CHAR 28.0%, EVANGELICAL 10.8%, GCC 24.0%**
5164	rural areas	1,152,000	96.41	1,110,000	99.44	C	923,000	49.8% (1950), 34.6% (1970), 27.6% (1990), 25.8% (2000), 23.3% (2010), 19.1% (2025)
5165	urban areas	3,309,000	93.40	3,091,000	98.35	C	3,889,000	50.1% (1950), 65.4% (1970), 72.3% (1990), 74.1% (2000), 76.6% (2010), 80.8% (2025)
5166	non-metropolitan areas	1,677,000	93.45	1,568,000	98.35	C	1,971,183	*Sources of data:* Censuses of 1950, 1960, 1970, 1980, and 1990.
5167	metropolitan areas	1,632,000	93.34	1,523,000	98.35	C	1,917,000	*Definition:* Localities with 200 or more inhabitants.
5168	Bergen	253,000	93.00	235,000	97.45	C	297,000	Hordaland port on North Sea. Fishing. 12th century Church of St. Mary. F=1070 by King Olaf III. D=NK.
5169	Drammen	77,800	96.00	74,700	99.45	C	91,400	Buskerud seaport. Wood products, plastics, abrasives, granite. Spiraltoppen tunnel. D=NK.
5170	Fredrikstad (Halden)	55,800	96.00	53,600	99.45	C	65,600	Ostfold. Year-round harbor. Sawmilling, shipping, and fishing. Glass, silver, textile workshops. F=1567. D=NK.
5171	Kristiansand	66,300	96.00	63,700	99.45	C	77,900	Vest-Agder seaport on Otra River. Holiday resort. Shipyards, textiles. F=1641. Y=11th century. D=NK.
5172	OSLO	761,000	91.50	697,000	97.95	C	895,000	On Oslo Fjord. Center of trade, banking, shipbuilding. Maritime museums. Skiing. F=11th century. D=NK.
5173	Baerum	88,500	94.00	83,200	98.45	C	104,000	West of Oslo. Fishing, industrial, residential, textiles, machinery, technological, electronics. D=NK.
5174	Skien	83,100	97.00	80,600	99.45	C	97,700	Telemark. Lumber & pulp, copper mining. Birthplace of H. Ibsen (1828). F=1110. Originally a monastery. D=NK.
5175	Stavanger	141,000	95.00	134,000	98.45	C	165,000	Rogaland seaport. Canning of sardines & fish. North Sea oil. F=8th century. Bishopric from 12th century. D=NK.
5176	Tromso	51,000	97.00	49,400	99.45	C	59,900	Troms on Tromsoy Island. Largest city above Arctic Circle. Continuous sun (May-July). F=1250. D=NK.
5177	Trondheim	143,000	95.00	136,000	99.45	C	168,000	Sor-Trondelag port. F=997. Pilgrimage center (St. Olaf). Nidaros Cathedral (12th-14th centuries). D=NK.
	OMAN	**2,542,000**	**4.80**	**122,000**	**46.97**	**A**	**5,352,000**	**ROMAN CATHOLICS 2.0%, INDEPENDENTS 1.7%. PENT-CHAR 1.8%, EVANGELICAL 0.2%, GCC 2.1%**
5178	rural areas	407,000	1.11	4,500	27.58	A	342,000	97.6% (1950), 88.5% (1970), 37.8% (1990), 16.0% (2000), 8.5% (2010), 6.3% (2025)
5179	urban areas	2,135,000	5.50	117,000	50.67	B	5,010,000	2.4% (1950), 11.4% (1970), 62.1% (1990), 83.9% (2000), 91.4% (2010), 93.6% (2025)
5180	non-metropolitan areas	2,073,000	5.50	114,000	50.67	B	4,864,635	*Sources of data:* Estimates for 1950, 1960, and 1990.
5181	metropolitan areas	61,900	5.50	3,400	50.67	B	145,000	*Definition:* Two main towns, Muscat and Matrah.
5182	MASQAT	61,900	5.50	3,400	50.67	B	145,000	On Gulf of Oman. Hottest climate in world. Oil. Architecture shows Asian, African, European influence. D=RCC.
	PAKISTAN	**156,483,000**	**2.44**	**3,812,000**	**46.76**	**A**	**263,000,000**	**PROTESTANTS 1.1%, ROMAN CATHOLICS 0.7%. PENT-CHAR 0.5%, EVANGELICAL 0.4%, GCC 2.2%**
5183	rural areas	98,522,000	2.10	2,073,000	45.96	A	123,847,000	82.4% (1950), 75.1% (1970), 68.1% (1990), 62.9% (2000), 56.6% (2010), 47.0% (2025)
5184	urban areas	57,961,000	3.00	1,739,000	48.12	A	139,153,000	17.5% (1950), 24.8% (1970), 31.8% (1990), 37.0% (2000), 43.4% (2010), 52.9% (2025)
5185	non-metropolitan areas	19,265,000	2.84	548,000	48.09	A	52,684,668	*Sources of data:* Censuses of 1951, 1961, 1972, and 1981.
5186	metropolitan areas	38,696,000	3.08	1,191,000	48.14	A	86,468,000	*Definition:* Places with municipal corporation, town committee or cantonment.
5187	Abbottabad	121,000	0.20	240	39.52	A	291,000	North-West Frontier. District market center. Iron-ore. 2 colleges. F=1853.
5188	Ahmadpur East	104,000	0.40	420	39.72	A	251,000	Punjab near Thar Desert. Near Bahawalpur. Cotton, grain, livestock.
5189	Bahawalnagar	137,000	0.60	820	39.92	A	328,000	Punjab. East of Sutlej River. Wheat, rice, sorghum, cotton. Several government colleges.
5190	Bahawalpur	331,000	0.50	1,700	39.82	A	794,000	Punjab near Sutlej River. Soapmaking. F=1748. Jat & Baluchi. D=Church of Pakistan(Methodist tradition).
5191	Bannu	79,200	0.20	160	39.52	A	190,000	North-West Frontier. Wheat, corn, large woolen mill. Weekly fair, college. F=1848. Mainly Pashtun.
5192	Charsadda	115,000	0.30	340	39.62	A	275,000	North-West Frontier on Kabul River. Near Peshawar, Swat River. Felt mats, saddlecloth, leather goods, poultry.
5193	Chichawatni	92,100	2.50	2,300	46.82	A	221,000	Punjab in Bari Doab. Near Sahiwal. Cotton, grain, handcrafts, markets.
5194	Chiniot	194,000	3.00	5,800	47.32	A	465,000	Punjab on Chenab River. Woodcarving & marquetry, formerly known for its masons. D=COP.
5195	Chishtian Mandi	114,000	0.30	340	39.62	A	273,000	Punjab, near India border. Near Bahawalnagar. Cotton, livestock, markets, trading.
5196	Daska	102,000	5.00	5,100	49.32	A	245,000	Punjab, near Gujranwala, 15 miles southwest of Sialkot, sometimes called Hardo Daska.
5197	Dera Ghazi Khan (D.G. Khan)	187,000	0.30	560	39.62	A	449,000	Punjab. Rug & carpet weaving. F=1867. Christians almost all Punjabis. M=International Missions.
5198	Dera Ismail Khan	125,000	0.50	630	39.82	A	300,000	North-West Frontier in Indus River Valley. Laquered woodwork, glasswork. Junction of Pashtun & Baluchi.
5199	Faisalabad (Lyallpur)	2,228,000	5.00	111,000	51.32	B	4,986,000	Punjab. Chemicals, cotton. F=1890. D=RCC. HQ Pakistan Bible Correspondence.
5200	Gojra	125,000	4.00	5,000	48.32	A	299,000	Punjab in Rechna Doab. Near Faisalabad. Cotton, wheat, grains, cloth, dairy products, agriculture.
5201	Gujranwala	2,048,000	6.00	123,000	52.32	B	4,616,000	Punjab. Grains, melons, sugarcane. F=1867. Major Christian center. D=UP Church,plus large schisms out of it.
5202	Gujranwala Cantonment	106,000	6.00	6,400	50.32	B	254,000	Punjab. Grains, melons, sugarcane. F=1867. D=UP Church, plus large schisms out of it.
5203	Gujrat (Gujarat)	284,000	4.00	11,400	48.32	A	683,000	Punjab. Furniture, pottery, electric fans. F=1580 by Mughal emperor Akbar.
5204	Hafizabad	153,000	3.00	4,600	47.32	A	367,000	Punjab near Rechna Doab. Trade center, grains, cotton, fruits, vegetables, hides, irrigation, rice.
5205	Hasan Abdal (Campbellpore)	81,400	2.50	2,000	46.82	A	195,000	Punjab near Wah Cantonment. Textile & communications center. Buddhist site since 2nd century BC.
5206	Hyderabad (Haiderabad)	1,302,000	0.80	10,400	42.12	A	2,965,000	Sind on Indus River. Silk embroidery. F=1768. Hindus. D=RCC,AoG,COP.
5207	Hyderabad Cantonment	89,800	0.80	720	40.12	A	216,000	Textiles, sugar, cement, hide tanneries, ornamented silks, silverware. Numerous mosques. D=RCC.
5208	Jacobabad	146,000	0.60	870	39.92	A	349,000	Sind near Baluchistan. Consistent high temperatures. Cotton carpets, wooden toys, grain markets. F=1847.
5209	Jaranwala	127,000	3.00	3,800	47.32	A	306,000	Punjab in Rechna Doab. Cotton, wheat, rice, railroad junction, jute, sugarcane, sulphuric acid mfg.
5210	Jhang Sadar (Jhang Maghiana)	359,000	1.00	3,600	45.32	A	861,000	Punjab. Twin towns. Wool collecting, handlooms, textiles, wheat, cotton. F=1462.
5211	Jhelum	195,000	4.00	7,800	48.32	A	469,000	Punjab. Timber market, textiles, sawmills. F=4th century BC as Bucephala. Ruined Buddhist temples.
5212	Kamalia	112,000	2.00	2,200	46.32	A	269,000	Punjab near Ravi River, 55 miles south southwest of Faisalabad. Cotton, wheat, livestock, various trading.
5213	Kamoke	130,000	3.00	3,900	47.32	A	313,000	Punjab in Rechna Doab. Near Gujranwala. Market center, hides, leather goods, vegetables, fruits, livestock.
5214	Karachi	11,774,000	3.26	384,000	50.58	B	24,847,000	Capital of Sind. Seaport. Textiles. F=c1870. Many Hindus. 20,000 Goans (all RCC). D=RCC,COP.
5215	Drigh Road Cantonment	104,000	2.00	2,100	46.32	A	250,000	Sind. Modern architecture. Congestion, pollution. Fishing. D=RCC.
5216	Karachi Cantonment	334,000	3.00	10,000	47.32	A	801,000	Sind. 50% of population are migrants or offspring since 1947. Center of banking & insurance. D=RCC.
5217	Malir Cantonment	87,300	2.50	2,200	46.82	A	210,000	Sind. Many mosques. Parsi burial towers of silence. Fishing. D=RCC.
5218	Kasur	285,000	3.50	10,000	47.82	A	685,000	Punjab. Tanning, cotton, oil pressing. F=1867. Well churched area (Presbyterian tradition of Praying Hyde).
5219	Khairpur (Khairpur Mirs)	113,000	1.50	1,700	45.82	A	271,000	Sind. Textiles, silk, leather, agriculture, fruits. Kot Diji (15 miles south) dates from 3000 BC.
5220	Khanewal	163,000	0.80	1,300	40.12	A	392,000	Punjab in Bari Doab. Near Multan. Cotton, fruits, livestock, grain, agriculture, trading, market, handcrafts.
5221	Khanpur	129,000	0.50	650	39.82	A	311,000	Sind near Thar Desert. Wheat, rice, millet, dates, cotton, rice husking, metalware.
5222	Kharian	94,500	3.00	2,800	47.32	A	227,000	Punjab near Jhelum, 20 miles northwest of Grujrat. Cotton, grains, millet, handcrafts, livestock.
5223	Khushab	103,000	1.00	1,000	45.32	A	248,000	Punjab on Jhelum River. Near Salt Range. Cotton milling, oilseed, textiles, dairy, agricultural goods.
5224	Kohat	142,000	0.20	290	39.52	A	342,000	North-West Frontier. Cotton loincloths, turbans, textiles, wheat, millet, camels. F=14th century by Buddhists.
5225	Lahore	6,030,000	5.10	308,000	52.42	B	12,999,000	Capital of Punjab. Main cultural center. F=c950. Publishing house. D=RCC & Church of Pakistan, Bhais.
5226	Lahore Cantonment	450,000	5.00	22,500	52.32	B	1,081,000	Punjab. Commercial & banking center. Engineering, textiles. University (1882). Badshahi Mosque. D=RCC,COP.
5227	Larkana	227,000	1.00	2,300	45.32	A	545,000	Sind. Grain marketing & trade center. Brass, metal. Camels. F=1855. Larka people.
5228	Leiah	94,400	0.20	190	39.52	A	227,000	Punjab on Indus River. Near Thal Desert. Market center for wheat, millet, rice, dates, hand loom weaving, textile.
5229	Mandi Burewala	158,000	0.70	1,100	40.02	A	380,000	Punjab in Bari Doab. Near Vihari. Road center, wheat, cotton, cotton ginning, rice, drug manufacturing.
5230	Mardan	271,000	0.50	1,400	39.82	A	652,000	North-West Frontier. Textiles, vegetable oils, sugar refinery. Punjabi churches, with 1 Pushtu congregation.
5231	Mianwali	108,000	0.60	650	39.92	A	260,000	Punjab near Indus River. Cotton, wheat, barley, sheep & camel breeding. F=1868.
5232	Mingaora	162,000	0.20	320	39.52	A	388,000	North-West Frontier on Swat River in Kohistan. Wheat, fruit, barley, sugarcane, timber harvesting.
5233	Mirpur Khas	228,000	0.70	1,600	40.02	A	548,000	Sind. Trade center for grain, fabrics, cotton. F=1806 by Mir Ali Murad Talpur.
5234	Multan	1,498,000	0.90	13,500	41.22	A	3,389,000	Punjab. Ceramics, camel skin. F=c400 BC. Christians all Punjabis. D=RCC,COP,Bhai Mission.
5235	Muzaffargarh	97,200	0.80	780	40.12	A	233,000	Punjab on Chenab River near Multan. Area subject to periodic flooding. Rice, wheat, livestock, vegetables, fruit.
5236	Nawabshah	187,000	6.50	12,200	53.82	B	450,000	Sind. Small boats, refined sugar. Originally Nasrat. Hinduism widespread. One Church of Pakistan church.
5237	Nowshera (Naushahra)	137,000	0.20	280	39.52	A	330,000	North-West Frontier on Kabul River. Cotton, wool, paperboard mills.
5238	Okara	281,000	2.00	5,600	46.32	A	676,000	Punjab. Textile, hosiery, carpet, grains, livestock. F=1869 as headquarters of Okara.
5239	Pakpattan	128,000	0.80	1,000	40.12	A	307,000	Punjab in Bari Doab. Near India border. Railroad workshop. Visited by Timur in 1398, Muslim pilgrimage.
5240	Peshawar	2,094,000	0.30	6,300	40.62	A	4,732,000	North-West Frontier. Many Hindus. Vast influx of refugees from Afghanistan. F=1519. Christians mostly Punjabis.
5241	Peshawar Cantonment	109,000	0.30	330	39.62	A	261,000	Buddhist origins. Textile & sugar mills. Great historic center of transit caravan trade.
5242	Quetta (Kwatah)	524,000	1.20	6,300	45.52	A	1,258,000	Baluchistan at 5,500 ft. Market center. Baluchis, Brahuis (Muslims). M=CMS(strong medical tradition).
5243	Rahimyar Khan	243,000	0.70	1,700	40.02	A	584,000	Punjab. Cotton. F=1751. Many Hindus. Sindhi, Saraiki, Punjabi. Scattered Christian community.
5244	Rawalpindi (Pindi)	1,529,000	1.80	27,500	48.12	A	3,463,000	Punjab. Strong Presbyterian area. D=UPC, RCC, Anglican (Ch of Pakistan), Bhais, SDA, TEAM (HQ).
5245	ISLAMABAD	1,066,000	1.30	13,900	47.62	A	2,473,000	Administrative center. Foreigners' union church. F=1961. Large and prominent RC hospital.House churches.
5246	Rawalpindi Cantonment	619,000	1.80	11,200	48.12	A	1,487,000	Capital of Pakistan from 1959-1969. Military base. Bazaars. Alexander the Great (326 BC). D=RCC.
5247	Sadiqabad	117,000	0.60	700	39.92	A	282,000	Punjab in Thar Desert near Rahimyar Khan. Sheep, camels, irrigation, sparse agriculture.
5248	Sahiwal (Montgomery)	277,000	3.00	8,300	47.32	A	665,000	Punjab. Cotton center. F=1865. D=Associate Reformed Presbyterian Church. M=ICF,IM.
5249	Sargodha	534,000	4.20	22,400	50.52	B	1,283,000	Punjab. Grain & cash crop market, textiles, hosiery. F=1903. Several institutions.
5250	Sargodha Cantonment	109,000	4.20	4,600	50.52	B	262,000	Punjab. Grain & cash crop market, textiles, hosiery. F=1903. Several institutions.
5251	Sheikhu Pura (Shekhupura)	259,000	3.50	9,100	47.82	A	622,000	Punjab. Fertilizer. Rice, wheat, cotton. Long established Christian work, mainly Punjabis. D=SDA, RCC.
5252	Shikarpur	162,000	1.00	1,600	45.32	A	388,000	Sind. Historical trade center. Brass, metal, carpets, cotton cloth. Great bazaar. F=1617.
5253	Sialkot	554,000	6.00	33,200	53.32	B	1,330,000	Punjab. Bicycles. Guru Nanak (d. 1538). Numerous schools, colleges. D=Presbyterian,Sialkot Convention.
5254	Sukkur	349,000	0.80	2,800	40.12	A	839,000	Sind on Indus River. Trade center. Since 1880, strong Anglican tradition (CMS hospital until 1975). D=RCC,SDA.

Table 10-5–continued opposite

Table 10-5–continued

Rec No 1	Country City 2	Pop 2000 3	AC% 4	Church Members 5	E% 6	W 7	Pop 2025 8	Notes 9
5255	Tando Adam	115,000	0.70	810	40.02	A	276,000	Sind north of Hyderabad. Irrigation, wheat, rice, millet, cotton, oilseeds, sugarcane, fruits, cattle, sheep, camel.
5256	Turbat	96,000	0.10	96	39.42	A	230,000	Baluchistan on Kech River. Marketplace for dates. Sorghum, barley, millet, cotton, wheat.
5257	Vihari (Vehari)	98,700	0.70	690	40.02	A	237,000	Punjab. Market & processing center for cotton & oilseeds. Wheat, millet, livestock.
5258	Wah (Wah Cantonment)	224,000	3.00	6,700	47.32	A	539,000	Punjab. Large cement factory. Garden built by Akbar (16th century). Agricultural development projects.
5259	Wazirabad	115,000	4.00	4,600	48.32	A	276,000	Punjab. Important rail junction. Boatbuilding, cutlery. F=18th century by Wazir Khan.
	PALAU	**19,400**	**94.57**	**18,400**	**99.94**	**C**	**33,200**	**ROMAN CATHOLICS 44.2%, PROTESTANTS 28.8%. PENT-CHAR 6.5%, EVANGELICAL 10.0%, GCC 14.4%**
5260	rural areas	5,300	96.10	5,100	99.98	C	6,500	53.8% (1950), 41.1% (1970), 30.5% (1990), 27.1% (2000), 23.8% (2010), 19.4% (2025)
5261	urban areas	14,100	94.00	13,300	99.93	C	26,800	46.1% (1950), 58.8% (1970), 69.4% (1990), 72.8% (2000), 76.1% (2010), 80.5% (2025)
5262	non-metropolitan areas	2,300	93.98	2,100	99.92	C	4,277	*Sources of data:* Censuses of 1973, 1986, and 1990.
5263	metropolitan areas	11,900	94.00	11,200	99.93	C	22,500	*Definition:* Koror.
5264	KOROR (Corrora)	11,900	94.00	11,200	99.93	C	22,500	Commercial & tourist center. Pop. 30,000 before WWII. Volcanic island. D=RCC,Modekne.
	PALESTINE	**2,215,000**	**8.50**	**188,000**	**70.64**	**B**	**4,133,000**	**INDEPENDENTS 4.6%, ORTHODOX 2.1%. PENT-CHAR 4.8%, EVANGELICAL 0.6%, GCC 7.6%**
5265	rural areas	121,000	5.01	6,000	58.48	B	165,000	49.5% (1950), 17.8% (1970), 6.5% (1990), 5.4% (2000), 4.8% (2010), 4.0% (2025)
5266	urban areas	2,095,000	8.70	182,000	71.34	B	3,967,000	50.5% (1950), 82.1% (1970), 93.4% (1990), 94.5% (2000), 95.1% (2010), 96.0% (2025)
5267	non-metropolitan areas	1,194,000	8.70	104,000	71.31	B	2,260,834	*Sources of data:* Estimates for 1950 and 1975.
5268	metropolitan areas	901,000	8.70	78,400	71.38	B	1,706,000	*Definition:* Urban centers.
5269	Al Quds (EAST JERUSALEM)	183,000	9.10	16,700	72.24	B	347,000	Government, public service employment. Pilgrims & tourists. Large number of churches. D=GOC,RCC.
5270	Ghazzah (Gaza)	303,000	9.00	27,300	72.14	B	574,000	Continuous habitation for 3,000 years. Headquarters of Israeli forces. Citrus truck farms. D=GOC,RCC.
5271	Khan Yunus	136,000	8.00	10,900	70.14	B	257,000	Southern Gaza near Egyptian border. 13th century mosque, Khan Yunis refugee camp (pop. 53,800). D=GOC.
5272	Nabulus (Nablus)	151,000	8.00	12,000	70.14	B	285,000	Biblical Sheckem. Springs. Market center of natural oasis. Samaritans, Muslims. D=GOC,RCC.
5273	Rafah	128,000	9.00	11,500	71.14	B	242,000	Southern Gaza. Mentioned in ancient Egyptian documents. Rafah refugee camp (pop. 90,000).
	PANAMA	**2,856,000**	**86.04**	**2,457,000**	**98.35**	**C**	**3,779,000**	**ROMAN CATHOLICS 77.3%, PROTESTANTS 11.9%. PENT-CHAR 17.1%, EVANGELICAL 9.2%, GCC 15.5%**
5274	rural areas	1,207,000	88.15	1,064,000	99.09	C	1,156,000	64.2% (1950), 52.3% (1970), 46.2% (1990), 42.2% (2000), 37.5% (2010), 30.6% (2025)
5275	urban areas	1,649,000	84.50	1,394,000	97.81	C	2,623,000	35.7% (1950), 47.6% (1970), 53.7% (1990), 57.7% (2000), 62.4% (2010), 69.4% (2025)
5276	non-metropolitan areas	369,000	84.77	312,000	97.93	C	708,568	*Sources of data:* Censuses of 1950, 1960, 1970, 1980, and 1990.
5277	metropolitan areas	1,281,000	84.42	1,081,000	97.78	C	1,914,000	*Definition:* Localities with 1,500 or more inhabitants having essentially urban characteristics.
5278	Colon	114,000	86.00	98,300	98.31	C	182,000	Capital of Colon. Important port of Caribbean Sea. Tourist center. Largely Black. F=1850 by Americans. D=RCC.
5279	David	78,200	88.00	68,800	99.31	C	124,000	Capital of Chiriqui on Rio David. Meat-packing, sugar, coffee, cocoa, saddles. F=1738. D=RCC.
5280	PANAMA (Panama City)	1,088,000	84.00	914,000	97.61	C	1,608,000	Economy is based on Canal traffic. F=1519. Cathedral (1673). University of Panama (1935). D=RCC.
5281	San Miguelito	289,000	86.00	248,000	98.31	C	459,000	On Gulf of Panama. D=RCC.
	PAPUA NEW GUINEA	**4,608,000**	**82.15**	**3,786,000**	**97.53**	**C**	**7,174,000**	**PROTESTANTS 56.6%, ROMAN CATHOLICS 29.9%. PENT-CHAR 16.3%, EVANGELICAL 17.5%, GCC 11.3%**
5282	rural areas	3,806,000	82.50	3,140,000	97.45	C	5,037,000	99.3% (1950), 90.2% (1970), 85.0% (1990), 82.5% (2000), 78.7% (2010), 70.2% (2025)
5283	urban areas	802,000	80.50	646,000	97.88	C	2,137,000	0.6% (1950), 9.8% (1970), 14.9% (1990), 17.4% (2000), 21.2% (2010), 29.7% (2025)
5284	non-metropolitan areas	461,000	80.44	371,000	97.88	C	1,229,308	*Sources of data:* Censuses of 1966, 1971, 1980, and 1990.
5285	metropolitan areas	341,000	80.58	275,000	97.88	C	908,000	*Definition:* Centers with a population of 500 or more.
5286	Lae	98,200	82.00	80,600	97.88	C	262,000	Near mouth of Markham River on Huan Gulf. Timber, coffee. Originated as Lehe mission. D=RCC,ELCONG.
5287	PORT MORESBY	243,000	80.00	194,000	97.88	C	646,000	On Gulf of Papua. Shipping, tourism. National Botanical Gardens. F=1873. Chinese. D=RCC,ELCONG.
	PARAGUAY	**5,496,000**	**94.13**	**5,174,000**	**99.82**	**C**	**9,355,000**	**ROMAN CATHOLICS 90.0%, PROTESTANTS 3.6%. PENT-CHAR 4.4%, EVANGELICAL 2.8%, GCC 7.8%**
5288	rural areas	2,420,000	96.19	2,327,000	99.98	C	2,857,000	65.4% (1950), 62.9% (1970), 51.3% (1990), 44.0% (2000), 37.7% (2010), 30.5% (2025)
5289	urban areas	3,077,000	92.50	2,846,000	99.69	C	6,498,000	34.5% (1950), 37.0% (1970), 48.7% (1990), 55.9% (2000), 62.2% (2010), 69.4% (2025)
5290	non-metropolitan areas	1,415,000	92.49	1,308,000	99.66	C	3,198,921	*Sources of data:* Censuses of 1950, 1962, 1972, 1982, and 1992.
5291	metropolitan areas	1,662,000	92.51	1,538,000	99.72	C	3,299,000	*Definition:* Cities, towns and administrative centers of departments and districts.
5292	ASUNCION	1,262,000	92.00	1,161,000	99.69	C	2,454,000	Principal distribution & export center for cotton, sugarcane, coffee. Large parks. F=1537 as stockade. D=RCC.
5293	Fernando de la Mora	117,000	95.00	111,000	99.79	C	247,000	Central on Paraguay River and border with Argentina. Large German population. D=RCC.
5294	San Lorenzo	164,000	93.00	152,000	99.69	C	346,000	On Paraguay River and border with Argentina. Soap, vegetable oil plants. F=1775. D=RCC.
5295	Lambare	122,000	93.00	114,000	98.69	C	258,000	On Paraguay River and border with Argentina. Liquor distilling, salt works, heavy industry. D=RCC.
5296	Capiata	102,000	94.00	96,000	99.69	C	216,000	Mythological museum with religious wooden statues. Honey, lumbering, cotton, sugarcane. F=1640. D=RCC.
5297	Ciudad del Este	164,000	93.50	154,000	99.89	C	347,000	Alto Parana on Parana River and border with Brazil. Iquacu Falls nearby. F=1957. D=RCC.
5298	Encarnacion	68,000	95.00	64,600	99.79	C	144,000	Itapua on Parana River on Argentinian border. Lumber, tobacco. Japanese farms. F=1614. D=RCC.
5299	Pedro Juan Caballero	65,800	95.00	62,500	99.79	C	139,000	Capital of Amambay on Brazilian border. Cattle ranching, coffee growing. D=RCC.
	PERU	**25,662,000**	**96.26**	**24,702,000**	**99.73**	**C**	**35,518,000**	**ROMAN CATHOLICS 95.6%, PROTESTANTS 5.7%. PENT-CHAR 13.4%, EVANGELICAL 4.4%, GCC 3.7%**
5300	rural areas	6,988,000	98.29	6,868,000	99.96	C	6,862,000	64.4% (1950), 42.5% (1970), 31.1% (1990), 27.2% (2000), 23.7% (2010), 19.3% (2025)
5301	urban areas	18,674,000	95.50	17,834,000	99.65	C	28,656,000	35.5% (1950), 57.4% (1970), 68.9% (1990), 72.7% (2000), 76.2% (2010), 80.6% (2025)
5302	non-metropolitan areas	6,623,000	95.92	6,353,000	99.71	C	11,546,574	*Sources of data:* Censuses of 1961, 1972, and 1981; estimate for 1989.
5303	metropolitan areas	12,051,000	95.27	11,481,000	99.62	C	17,110,000	*Definition:* Populated centers with 100 or more occupied dwellings.
5304	Arequipa	656,000	96.00	630,000	99.87	C	1,007,000	Capital of Arequipa. 7,550 ft. Wool processing, tourism. Incan origins. F=1540. Cathedral (1612). D=RCC.
5305	Ayacucho (Huamanga)	102,000	96.00	98,000	99.47	C	157,000	Capital of Huamanga. 9,007 ft. Agricultural. Many colonial buildings. F=1539. D=RCC. Archbishopric.
5306	Cajamarca	91,400	96.50	88,200	99.97	C	140,000	Capital of Cajamarca. 9,022 ft. Mining, agricultural, tourism. Ancient Inca city. F=1532. D=RCC.
5307	Cerro de Pasco	97,500	96.50	94,000	99.97	C	150,000	Capital of Pasco. One of the world's highest cities at 14,232 ft. Mining (silver, copper, gold, lead). F=1630. D=RCC.
5308	Chiclayo	410,000	95.50	392,000	98.97	C	630,000	Capital of Chiclayo. Sugarcane, cotton, rice. Many parks & gardens. F=1720. University (1962). D=RCC.
5309	Chimbote	328,000	95.50	313,000	98.97	C	503,000	Capital of Santa. Natural harbor. Exports fish meal, fish oil. F=1822. Destroyed by earthquake (1970). D=RCC.
5310	Chosica	95,600	96.00	91,800	99.47	C	147,000	Lima inland from Lima on Rio Rimac. D=RCC.
5311	Cuzco (Cusco)	271,000	96.00	260,000	99.47	C	416,000	Capital of Cuzco. Incan capital. F=1533. Destroyed by earthquake (1650). 'City of the Sun'. D=RCC.
5312	Huacho	63,700	97.00	61,800	99.77	C	97,800	Northern Lima on Huaura River at Pacific Ocean. Cotton ginning, soap, candles, salt. D=RCC.
5313	Huancayo	242,000	95.50	231,000	98.97	C	372,000	Capital of Huancayo on Montaro River. 10,659 ft. Quecha settlement. Tourism. F=1823. D=RCC.
5314	Huanuco	90,800	96.00	87,100	99.47	C	139,000	Capital of Huanuco on Huallaga River. Agricultural trade center, tourism. F=1539. D=RCC.
5315	Ica	169,000	96.00	162,000	99.47	C	259,000	Capital of Ica on Ica River. Cotton, grapes. F=1569. Collection of Nazca pottery (200 BC-AD 600). D=RCC.
5316	Iquitos	262,000	95.50	251,000	98.97	C	403,000	Capital of Loreto. Amazon river port. Religious & tourist center of eastern Peru. Rubber, coffee. F=1864. D=RCC.
5317	Juliaca	129,000	95.50	123,000	98.97	C	197,000	Puno near Lake Titicaca north of Puno. Railroad junction, native woolen textiles, hides, cereals. D=RCC.
5318	LIMA-Callao (Gran Lima)	7,443,000	95.00	7,071,000	99.87	C	10,039,000	Textiles, plastics, wood. Many banks. Squatter towns. Colonial style. F=1535 by Spanish. 'City of Kings'. D=RCC.
5319	Barranco	68,200	96.00	65,500	99.47	C	105,000	Seaside resort town. Residential. Zoo. Colonial museum. Artist community, national park. F=1874. D=RCC.
5320	Barrio Obrero Industrial	641,000	95.00	609,000	98.47	C	984,000	On Rio Rimac. Working class residential area. Educational and recreational facilities. D=RCC.
5321	Brena	165,000	95.50	158,000	98.97	C	253,000	Central near downtown. Parque de la Reserva. Commercial, residential, educational facilities. D=RCC.
5322	Callao	388,000	95.00	368,000	98.47	C	595,000	International airport. Principal seaport. Totally destroyed by earthquake (1746). F=1537. D=RCC.
5323	Chorrillos	208,000	95.50	199,000	98.97	C	320,000	Seaside resort town. Middle income residential. Swimming, boating resort, La Herradura beach. F=1824. D=RCC.
5324	Jesus Maria	122,000	95.50	117,000	98.97	C	187,000	Central Lima south of Brena. Parque de la Reserva. Plastics, clothing, financial, markets. D=RCC.
5325	La Victoria	398,000	95.00	378,000	98.47	C	610,000	Residential. Slums in the north. Large wholesale & retail market. Houses highland migrants. D=RCC.
5326	Lince	118,000	96.00	113,000	99.47	C	181,000	Lima south of La Victoria. Industrial, commercial, textiles, consumer goods, food processing. D=RCC.
5327	Magdalena Nueva (Magdalena del Mar)	88,000	96.50	84,900	99.97	C	135,000	Bordered by cliffs overlooking Pacific Ocean. Resort. Largely residential. D=RCC.
5328	Miraflores	152,000	95.00	144,000	98.47	C	233,000	Seaside resort town. Residential. Known for bougainvillea. Huaca Juliana shrine. F=1850. D=RCC.
5329	Pueblo Libre	123,000	96.00	118,000	99.47	C	189,000	Residential community. Museum of indigenous cultures. Pontifica Universidad Catolica (1917). F=1822. D=RCC.
5330	Rimac	271,000	95.00	257,000	98.47	C	416,000	Lower income residential district. F=1921. Monastery of the Barefoot Brethren. D=RCC.
5331	San Isidro	105,000	95.00	99,300	98.47	C	160,000	Large homes. Numerous gardens & parks. Pre-Inca ruins, just north of Miraflores. D=RCC.
5332	San Martin de Porras	594,000	94.00	559,000	97.47	C	912,000	Lima northwest of downtown. Commercial, industrial, financial, residential, textiles, shoes, clothing. D=RCC.
5333	Santiago de Surco	232,000	95.00	221,000	98.47	C	356,000	South on Surco River. Upper income housing. Private schools. F=1824. D=RCC.
5334	Surquillo	197,000	96.00	189,000	99.47	C	302,000	South near Miraflores. Crafts, market, industrial, textiles, factories. D=RCC.
5335	Vitarte	214,000	95.50	204,000	98.97	C	328,000	Rimac River, coastal plain. Heavy industry. Railroad, highway, sugarcane, fodder. D=RCC.
5336	Pisco	81,600	96.50	78,800	99.97	C	125,000	Ica. Pacific port at mouth of Rio Pisco. Brandy from muscat grapes. Resort. F=1640. D=RCC.
5337	Piura	305,000	95.00	290,000	98.47	C	469,000	Capital of Piura. Warm coastal desert. Cotton, rice, sugarcane. F=1532. Church of San Francisco. D=RCC.
5338	Pucallpa	165,000	95.50	157,000	98.97	C	253,000	Capital of Coronel Portillo. Amazon rain forest. Sawmills. F=1534. Numerous missionary HQs. D=RCC.
5339	Puno	99,000	96.00	95,000	99.47	C	152,000	Capital of Puno on Lake Titicaca. 12,549 ft. Tourism, wool trade. F=1668. Colonial churches & cathedral. D=RCC.
5340	Sullana	131,000	95.50	125,000	98.97	C	201,000	Capital of Sullana on Rio Chiva. Cotton industry, irrigated rice growing region, charcoal. F=1821. D=RCC.
5341	Tacna	143,000	96.00	137,000	99.47	C	219,000	Capital of Tacna on Rio Caplina. Agricultural processing center. Originally settled by Aymara. D=RCC.
5342	Talara	84,200	96.50	81,300	99.97	C	129,000	Piura on Pacific Ocean. Refining & shipping port for oil. Asphalt works, tar, turpentine, machine shops. D=RCC.
5343	Trujillo	520,000	95.00	494,000	98.47	C	798,000	Capital of Trujilla. Sugar refineries. Beach resorts. F=1534. University of La Libertad (1824). D=RCC.
5344	Tumbes (Tumbez)	70,400	97.00	68,300	99.77	C	108,000	Capital of Tumbes. Tobacco, cotton, rice, fishing, tourism. Pizarro began conquest here in 1532. F=1942. D=RCC.
	PHILIPPINES	**75,967,000**	**87.67**	**66,600,000**	**94.44**	**C**	**108,251,000**	**ROMAN CATHOLICS 82.3%, INDEPENDENTS 18.8%. PENT-CHAR 26.3%, EVANGELICAL 2.4%, GCC 5.1%**
5345	rural areas	31,435,000	95.70	30,084,000	99.93	C	30,419,000	72.8% (1950), 67.0% (1970), 51.2% (1990), 41.3% (2000), 34.5% (2010), 28.1% (2025)
5346	urban areas	44,532,000	82.00	36,516,000	90.57	C	77,833,000	27.1% (1950), 32.9% (1970), 48.8% (1990), 58.6% (2000), 65.4% (2010), 71.9% (2025)
5347	non-metropolitan areas	22,606,000	82.04	18,545,000	91.51	C	43,548,792	*Sources of data:* Censuses of 1948, 1960, 1970, 1975, 1980, and 1990.
5348	metropolitan areas	21,926,000	81.96	17,971,000	89.60	C	34,284,000	*Definition:* All cities and municipalities with a density of at least 1,000 persons per square kilometer.
5349	Angeles	290,000	90.00	261,000	96.77	C	506,000	Pampanga, Luzon. Clark Air Force Base (USA). F=1963. RCC seminary. D=RCC.
5350	Antipolo	106,000	40.00	42,500	47.77	A	186,000	Luzon. Image of Virgin of Peace and Good Voyage brought from Mexico in early 17th century. Rice, fruit. D=RCC.
5351	Bacolod	447,000	85.00	380,000	91.77	C	781,000	Negros island. Important seaport, shipping center for sugarcane industry. Airport, university. D=RCC.
5352	Baguio	225,000	80.00	180,000	86.77	C	392,000	Benguet, Luzon. Foremost resort. Earthquake (1991-1,600 killed). F=c1900. 'Summer capital'. D=RCC.
5353	Baliuag	109,000	60.00	65,300	66.77	C	190,000	Bulacan north of Manila. Known for handmade buri-palm hats, market, trade, rice milling. D=RCC.
5354	Basilan City (Isabela)	77,000	89.00	68,500	95.77	C	135,000	Capital of Basilan Island. Rubber latex, palm oil, coffee. Muslim Yakans, Filipino Christians. D=RCC.
5355	Batangas	226,000	45.00	102,000	51.77	B	395,000	Luzon. Trade & food processing center for rice, sugarcane, coconuts. Beef cattle. D=RCC.
5356	Binangonan	125,000	60.00	75,000	66.77	C	218,000	Rizal on northern shore of Laguna de Bay near Pasig. Agricultural center for rice and fruit. D=RCC.
5357	Bislig	126,000	80.00	101,000	86.77	C	220,000	Eastern Mindanao on Bislig Bay. Port, airport, major farm and lumber processing complex, paper. D=RCC.
5358	Bocaue	76,700	70.00	53,700	76.77	C	134,000	Bulacan north of Manila. Near railroad. agriculture center for rice, sugar, corn. D=RCC.
5359	Butuan	280,000	20.00	56,000	26.77	A	489,000	Capital of Agusan del Norte, Mindanao. Logging, petroleum trade center. Jesuit mission (16th century). D=RCC.
5360	Cabanatuan	212,000	75.00	159,000	81.77	C	371,000	Nueva Ecija, Luzon on Pampanga River. Commercial center, rice , corn. Railroad terminus. D=RCC.
5361	Cadiz	204,000	80.00	163,000	86.77	C	357,000	Negros Occidental, Negros Island. Port. Fishing, lumbering and agricultural center, rice, sugarcane. D=RCC.
5362	Cagayan de Oro	417,000	25.00	104,000	31.77	A	729,000	Capital of Misamis Oriental, Mindanao. Exports rice, corn, copra. F=Mission station(17th century). D=RCC.
5363	Calamba	187,000	85.00	159,000	91.77	C	327,000	Laguna on southern Laguna de Bay. Rice, coconuts, sugarcane. JosÂ Rizal born here. D=RCC.
5364	Calbayog	167,000	90.00	151,000	96.77	C	292,000	Samar Island. Religious & educational center. Fishing, mat making. Exports abaca & copra. D=RCC.

Table 10-5–continued overleaf

Table 10-5–continued

Rec No 1	Country City 2	Pop 2000 3	AC% 4	Church Members 5	E% 6	W 7	Pop 2025 8	Notes 9
5365	Cavite	239,000	85.00	203,000	91.77	C	418,000	Cavite on Manila Bay. Residential center for Manila commuters. F=1940. D=RCC.
5366	Cebu (Cebu City)	1,012,000	94.00	952,000	99.77	C	1,769,000	Cebu Island. Nation's oldest settlement. Main collection center. F=1521. Y=1521. D=RCC.
5367	Cotabato	156,000	25.00	39,000	31.77	A	272,000	Mindanao. Trade & commercial center. Rice, corn, coconuts, sugarcane, coffee, bananas. D=RCC.
5368	Dagupan	150,000	80.00	120,000	86.77	C	262,000	Luzon Island port. Fish, salt, rice, fruit. F=1590 by Augustinian missionaries. D=RCC.
5369	Davao	1,196,000	70.00	837,000	96.77	C	1,811,000	Mindanao. 50 small ports. Copra, corn, rice. F=1849. 150 missionaries. D=RCC.
5370	Dumaguete	98,200	90.00	88,300	96.77	C	172,000	Negros Island. Educational center. Silliman University (American Presbyterian)(1901). Pottery, matting. D=RCC.
5371	General Santos (Dadiangas, Buayan)	307,000	88.00	270,000	94.77	C	536,000	Mindanao. Bananas, pineapples, cassava. Pioneer settlement by Christian Filipinos. D=RCC.
5372	Guagua	112,000	80.00	89,700	86.77	C	196,000	Pampanga west of San Fernando. Railroad, local markets, industry, fish canning, meat packing. D=RCC.
5373	Iligan	263,000	30.00	79,000	36.77	A	460,000	Capital of Lanao del Norte, Mindanao. Major industries. Steel, calcium-carbide. F=1950. D=RCC.
5374	Iloilo	382,000	85.00	324,000	96.77	C	667,000	Capital of Iloilo, Panay. Regional center for sugar exports, major fishing port. Many old churches. D=RCC.
5375	Jolo	80,900	25.00	20,200	31.77	A	141,000	Jolo Island, Sulu. International & interisland trade port. Fishing. Settled before Islam (14th century). D=RCC.
5376	Lapu-Lapu (Opan)	179,000	75.00	134,000	81.77	C	313,000	Mactan Island. Coconut growing & fishing center. Named for Chief Capulapu who killed Magellan (1521). D=RCC.
5377	Legazpi	148,000	50.00	74,200	56.77	B	259,000	Capital of Albay, Luzon. Export port for copra & abaca. On southern base of active volcano. F=1639. D=RCC.
5378	Lipa	191,000	65.00	124,000	71.77	C	333,000	Batangas, Luzon. Market center for fruit. Clothing, military air base. Destroyed by volcano(1754). D=RCC.
5379	Lucena	185,000	60.00	111,000	66.77	C	324,000	Luzon. Major fishing port, regional wholesale distributing point, food processing. Predates Spaniards. D=RCC.
5380	Mabalacat	125,000	70.00	87,500	76.77	C	218,000	Northern Pampanga north of Clark Air Force Base. Sugar, north terminal of expressway from Manila. D=RCC.
5381	Malolos	117,000	75.00	88,100	81.77	C	205,000	Luzon. Trade center for rice & vegetables, major fish-pond-culture areas. College of Arts and Trades. D=RCC.
5382	Mandaue	221,000	88.00	194,000	94.77	C	386,000	Industrial suburb. Brewery, sugar refining, food processing, fishing. F=17th century(Jesuits). D=RCC.
5383	Mangaldan	77,800	85.00	66,200	96.77	C	136,000	Northern Pangasinan on Lingayen Gulf near Dagupan. Rice, copra, corn. D=RCC.
5384	MANILA-Quezon (Metro Manila)	10,818,000	94.00	10,169,000	99.27	C	15,149,000	Luzon on Manila Bay. Port of entry. Banks, insurance. Education center. Squatters. F=1571. D=RCC.
5385	Bacoor	139,000	94.00	131,000	99.27	C	244,000	Cavite south of Manila on Bacoor Bay. Fishing, rice, fruit, coconuts, aquaculture, salt production. D=RCC.
5386	Binan	129,000	95.00	123,000	99.37	C	226,000	Manila. Laguna province, Luzon, Laguna de Bay, agricultural center, rice, coconuts, sugarcane. D=RCC.
5387	Cainta	91,100	94.00	85,600	99.27	C	159,000	Rizal east of Pasig on Sapang Baho River. Las Pinas Church w/Bamboo Organ(1815). D=RCC.
5388	Caloocan	915,000	94.00	860,000	99.27	C	1,600,000	Manila Bay. Residential suburb. Processed foods, textiles, engineering products. F=1762(Augustinians). D=RCC.
5389	Carmona	100,000	95.00	95,300	99.37	C	175,000	Cavite west of Laguna de Bay. Residential suburb, vegetables, fruits, flowers for Manila market. D=RCC.
5390	Las Pinas	266,000	94.00	250,000	99.27	C	465,000	Rizal south of Paranaque on Manila Bay. National capital region, agricultural center for rice and fruit. D=RCC.
5391	Makati	571,000	94.00	537,000	99.27	C	998,000	Southern residential & industrial suburb. Modern manufacturing complex. Many foreign residents. D=RCC.
5392	Malabon	297,000	95.00	283,000	99.37	C	520,000	10km N of downtown Manila, Island of Luzon, Gregorian Araneta University Foundation. Zoo. D=RCC.
5393	Mandaluyong	317,000	94.00	298,000	99.27	C	553,000	Rizal east of Manila on Pasig River, national capital region. Sugar refining, pulp and paper milling. D=RCC.
5394	Manila	2,596,000	92.00	2,388,000	98.77	C	4,537,000	Rizal on Manila Bay and Pasig River. University of the Philippines(1908). Zoo, botanical gardens. D=RCC.
5395	Marikina	347,000	94.00	326,000	99.27	C	606,000	Rizal east of Quezon City on Marikina River, national capital region. Rice, sugarcane, shoe making. D=RCC.
5396	Meycauayan	129,000	95.00	123,000	99.37	C	225,000	Southern Bulacan north of Manila inland from Manila Bay. Rice growing center, knife and cutlery mfg. D=RCC.
5397	Muntinglupa	241,000	94.00	226,000	99.27	C	421,000	15km SSE of downtown Manila. Rail station, penitentiary, Johnson Matthey Electronics. D=RCC.
5398	Navotas	205,000	94.00	193,000	99.27	C	359,000	Northern suburb. Fishing center (1/2 of total Philippine commercial fishing). Prawn paste. D=RCC.
5399	Paranaque	353,000	94.00	332,000	99.27	C	617,000	Southern suburb. Intricate hand embroidery. Fishing from rafts. Manila Beach Resort Park. D=RCC.
5400	Pasay (Rizal City)	434,000	95.00	413,000	99.37	C	759,000	Major southern residential suburb. Nightclubs. Araneta University (1946). Rizal Museum. D=RCC.
5401	Pasig	445,000	94.00	419,000	99.27	C	778,000	Market town on Pasig River. International School (Brent). D=Anglican,RCC.
5402	Quezon City	2,002,000	94.00	1,882,000	99.27	C	3,500,000	Northeast. Capital from 1948-76. Light industry. Ateneo de Manila University (1859 by Jesuits). D=RCC.
5403	San Juan del Monte	194,000	95.00	185,000	99.37	C	340,000	Eastern residential & industrial suburb, national capital region. Agricultural center, rice, fruit, vegetables. D=RCC.
5404	Santa Rosa	99,300	95.00	94,300	99.37	C	174,000	SSE of Manila, on Laguna de Bay, 22 miles south southeast of Manila. Rice, coconuts, sugar. D=RCC.
5405	Tagig	183,000	94.00	172,000	99.27	C	319,000	Rizal south of Pasig near Laguna de Bay. Fishing, railroad, rice, fruit, vegetables, sugar. D=RCC.
5406	Taytay	116,000	95.00	110,000	99.37	C	203,000	Rizal east of Pasig. Railroad terminus, trade center, rice, sugarcane, fruit, vegetables, handcrafts. D=RCC.
5407	Valenzuela	385,000	94.00	362,000	99.27	C	673,000	Southern Bulacan north of Caloocan. Industrial suburb, machinery, motors, metalworks, factories. D=RCC.
5408	Marawi (Dansalan)	113,000	20.00	22,600	31.77	A	197,000	Capital of Lanao del Sur, Mindanao. Trade center, Muslim handicrafts, bladed weapons. Muslims. D=RCC.
5409	Naga (Nueva Caceres)	141,000	55.00	77,600	61.77	B	247,000	Luzon on Bicol River. Important center of Spanish culture. F=1573. Y=1573. D=RCC.
5410	Olongapo	236,000	75.00	177,000	86.77	C	412,000	Zambales, Luzon. Major tourist center. Beaches, resorts. Near Subic Bay Naval Station (U.S.). F=1959. D=RCC.
5411	Ormoc	165,000	80.00	132,000	86.77	C	288,000	Leyte on Ormoc Bay. Sugarcane, rice, copra, corn. Fell in WWII in 1944. Rebuilt city. D=RCC.
5412	Pagadian	131,000	60.00	78,800	66.77	C	229,000	Western Mindanao on Pagadian Bay. Commercial center, early native trade center, coconuts, corn. D=RCC.
5413	Puerto Princesa	113,000	70.00	79,000	76.77	C	197,000	Central Palawan on Sulu Sea, Honda Bay. Trade center, copra, rattan. Iwahig Penal Colony. D=RCC.
5414	San Carlos	159,000	88.00	140,000	94.77	C	279,000	Negros Island. Deepwater port. Sugar plantations. Many migrant workers. F=1912. D=RCC.
5415	San Fernando	171,000	70.00	120,000	76.77	C	299,000	Luzon on South China Sea. Tobacco & rice-growing. Church ruins (1674). D=RCC.
5416	San Pablo	198,000	75.00	148,000	81.77	C	345,000	Laguna, Luzon. Copra & dried coconut. Seven crater lakes & 43 villages. Originally missionary post. D=RCC.
5417	San Pedro	115,000	88.00	101,000	94.77	C	201,000	Laguna, Luzon. Industrial suburb of Manila. 19 m southeast of city center. D=RCC.
5418	Santa Cruz	93,600	90.00	84,200	96.77	C	164,000	Laguna on southern Laguna de Bay. Railroad, trade center for agriculture area, sugarcane, coconuts. D=RCC.
5419	Silay	175,000	85.00	149,000	91.77	C	306,000	Negros Occidental, Negros Island. Large sugar mill. Fishing port, sulphur mining. D=RCC.
5420	Tacloban	169,000	85.00	144,000	91.77	C	296,000	Capital of Leyte on San Pedro Bay. Deepwater port. Hemp, copra, lumber exports. F=1874. D=RCC.
5421	Tagbilaran	68,700	80.00	55,000	86.77	C	120,000	Southwestern Boho Island on Maribojoc Bay. Trade center for agricultural region, rice, coconuts. D=RCC.
5422	Zamboanga	545,000	50.00	272,000	71.77	B	952,000	Zamboanga del Sur, Mindanao. Busy port. Exports rubber, pearls. F=1635. 17th century Christian shrine. D=RCC.
	PITCAIRN ISLANDS	**47**	**89.36**	**42**	**100.00**	**C**	**47**	**PROTESTANTS 89.3%, ROMAN CATHOLICS 92.2%. PENT-CHAR 4.2%, EVANGELICAL 10.6%, GCC 40.4%**
5423	rural areas	–	–	–	–	–	–	0.0% (1950), 0.0% (1970), 0.0% (1990), 0.0% (2000), 0.0% (2010), 0.0% (2025)
5424	urban areas	47	89.36	42	100.00	C	47	100.0% (1950), 100.0% (1970), 100.0% (1990), 100.0% (2000), 100.0% (2010), 100.0% (2025)
5425	non-metropolitan areas	–	–	–	–	–	–	*Sources of data:* Censuses of 1986 and 1991.
5426	metropolitan areas	47	89.36	42	100.00	C	47	*Definition:* No urban population.
5427	ADAMSTOWN	47	89.36	42	100.00	C	47	On north coast near Bounty Bay. Fishing, garden produce, crops. Postage stamp sales. D=SDA (1887).
	POLAND	**38,765,000**	**96.73**	**37,498,000**	**99.96**	**C**	**39,069,000**	**ROMAN CATHOLICS 92.2%, ORTHODOX 2.6%. PENT-CHAR 5.2%, EVANGELICAL 0.3%, GCC 7.6%**
5428	rural areas	13,351,000	98.12	13,100,000	99.99	C	9,724,000	61.3% (1950), 47.6% (1970), 38.1% (1990), 34.4% (2000), 30.5% (2010), 24.8% (2025)
5429	urban areas	25,414,000	96.00	24,398,000	99.94	C	29,345,000	38.7% (1950), 52.3% (1970), 61.8% (1990), 65.5% (2000), 69.4% (2010), 75.1% (2025)
5430	non-metropolitan areas	7,860,000	97.83	7,689,000	99.97	C	9,638,566	*Sources of data:* Censuses of 1960, 1978, and 1988; estimates for 1950, 1969, and 1987.
5431	metropolitan areas	17,555,000	95.18	16,709,000	99.93	C	19,706,000	*Definition:* Towns and settlements of urban type, e.g., workers' and fishermen's settlements.
5432	Belchatow	58,300	96.00	55,900	99.93	C	67,300	Piotrkow west of Piotrkow Trybunalski. Textile manufacturing, cement ware, tanning, sawmilling. D=RCC.
5433	Biala Podlaska	53,900	96.00	51,800	99.93	C	62,200	Capital of Biala Podlaska on Krzna River. Pottery, carpet. F=15th century. Church of St. Anne (1524). D=RCC.
5434	Bialystok	275,000	94.00	258,000	99.93	C	317,000	Capital of Bialystok. Linens, meats. F=1320. WWII center of Polish Jewry (40,000)-1/2 killed by Nazis. D=RCC.
5435	Bielsko-Biala	184,000	95.00	175,000	99.93	C	213,000	Capital of Bielsko-Biala. Major textile center, wool since Middle Ages. Tourist resort. F=13th century. D=RCC.
5436	Bydgoszcz (Bromberg)	387,000	92.00	356,000	99.93	C	447,000	Capital of Bydgoszcz. Forest products, textiles, metals. Important water & rail junction. F=1346. D=RCC.
5437	Chelm	67,400	96.00	64,700	99.93	C	77,800	Capital of Chelm on Uherka River. Minerals, wood, flour, brewing. F=1233. D=RCC.
5438	Czestochowa	262,000	94.00	246,000	99.93	C	302,000	Capital of Czestochowa. Textiles. Major pilgrimage center. F=13th century. Jasna Gora monastery (1382). D=RCC.
5439	Dzierzoniow (Reichenbach)	90,400	96.00	86,700	99.93	C	104,000	On Pilawa River. Cotton & wood textiles, machinery, electrical equipment. F=12th century. D=RCC.
5440	Elblag (Elbing)	128,000	93.00	119,000	99.93	C	148,000	Capital of Elblag on Elblag River. Metals, heavy machinery, sawmills. F=1237 by Teutonic Knights. D=RCC.
5441	Elk	53,200	98.00	52,100	99.93	C	61,400	Southern Suwalki. Masurian Lakes region. Grain and cattle market, Teaton Knight castle in 14th century. D=RCC.
5442	Gdansk (Danzig)	893,000	96.00	857,000	99.93	C	1,000,000	Capital of Gdansk on Baltic Sea. Shipyards, metals, chemicals. Solidarity (1980). F=987. Y=1148. D=RCC.
5443	Gdynia	255,000	95.00	243,000	99.93	C	295,000	Passenger port. Shipyards. Homeport of Polish Navy. Exports lumber, coal, sugar. Live theater. D=RCC.
5444	Sopot	47,400	95.00	45,000	99.93	C	54,700	Large & popular seaside & health resort, Baltic Sea. School of Economics and Music. F=13th century. D=RCC.
5445	Glogow	74,400	94.00	69,900	99.88	C	85,900	Legnica or Oder River. Railway & road center. Food processing, copper electroplating. F=1253. D=RCC.
5446	Gniezno	71,500	96.00	68,600	99.93	C	82,500	Poznan. Trade center. F=8th century. RCC archdiocese capital (AD1000). 14th century church. D=RCC.
5447	Gorzow Wielkopolski	126,000	94.00	119,000	99.88	C	146,000	Capital of Gorzow on Warta River. Synthetic textiles, lumber, food processing. F=13th century.D=RCC.
5448	Grudziadz	104,000	94.00	97,600	99.88	C	120,000	Torun on Vistula River. Foundries, lumber mills, breweries textiles, chemicals. F=10th century. D=RCC.
5449	Inowroclaw	78,900	95.00	74,900	99.93	C	91,100	Bydgoszcz. Salt, chemicals, health spa. F=1185. 12th century church of the Blessed Virgin. D=RCC.
5450	Jastrzebie-Zdroj	105,000	94.00	99,000	99.93	C	122,000	Katowice. Thermal spa, coking-coal deposits. Educational and cultural center, mining. F=1963. D=RCC.
5451	Jelenia Gora (Hirschberg)	94,800	95.00	90,100	99.93	C	109,000	Capital of Jelenia Gora. In Sudeten mountains. Coal mining, metals. F=11th century. 14th century parish. D=RCC.
5452	Kalisz (Wlaclawek)	108,000	94.00	101,000	99.88	C	124,000	Capital of Kalisz on Prosna River. Textiles, scenic parks. Ancient origins. D=RCC.
5453	Katowice	3,488,000	96.50	3,366,000	99.93	C	3,732,000	Capital of Katowice. Coal mining, heavy industry. Cultural center. F=1598. D=RCC.
5454	Bedzin	77,400	96.00	74,300	99.93	C	89,300	Coal mining, heavy industry. WWII concentration camp. 13th century castle. D=RCC.
5455	Bytom (Beuthen)	235,000	95.00	223,000	99.93	C	271,000	Silver foundry, iron & steel works. Mining coal, zinc, lead, silver. F=11th century. D=RCC.
5456	Chorzow	134,000	95.00	127,000	99.93	C	155,000	Iron & steel works (1802). Historical & ethnographic museum. F=1136. D=RCC.
5457	Dabrowa Gornicza	139,000	95.00	132,000	99.93	C	160,000	Located over world's thickest coal deposit (80ft). Mining school (1889). Coal mining since 1796. D=RCC.
5458	Gliwice (Gleiwitz)	217,000	94.50	205,000	99.93	C	251,000	Iron foundry (1794), coke furnace (1798). Chemical production. Many parks. F=1276. D=RCC.
5459	Jaworzno	101,000	95.50	96,500	99.93	C	117,000	Zinc, lead ore, coal, chemicals, ceramics, cement. F=18th century. D=RCC.
5460	Myslowice	95,200	96.00	91,400	99.93	C	110,000	Katowice east of Katowice, Czarna Przemsza. Metal industry, brickworks, coal mine, chemicals. D=RCC.
5461	Piekary Slaskie	69,500	96.50	67,100	99.93	C	80,300	Katowice. Mining and industrial region, manufacturing includes mining equipment and various metals. D=RCC.
5462	Ruda Slaska	174,000	95.00	165,000	99.93	C	200,000	Coal mining since 1751. Iron mining in Middle Ages. Steel mill, incorporated after 1946. F=Middle Ages. D=RCC.
5463	Siemianowice Slaskie	82,300	96.00	79,000	99.93	C	95,100	Northern suburb. Coal mining, iron working, boilers, first coal mine opened in 1797, castle. D=RCC.
5464	Sosnowiec	263,000	95.00	250,000	99.93	C	304,000	On Czarna Przemsza River. Heavy industry, coal mining, glassworks. Mining museum. F=17th century. D=RCC.
5465	Swietochlowice	61,400	97.00	59,600	99.83	C	70,900	Northwestern suburb. Coal mining, iron & steel. Metals, machinery, incorporated after 1946. D=RCC.
5466	Tarnowskie Gory	75,200	96.50	72,600	99.73	C	86,900	Katowice northwest of Katowice. Mining and industrial region, coal, zinc, lead. F=1526. D=RCC.
5467	Tychy	195,000	96.00	187,000	99.93	C	225,000	Beer since 1629. Automobile assembly. Largely residential. Developed 1950 for industrial workers. D=RCC.
5468	Zabrze (Hindenburg)	208,000	95.50	199,000	99.93	C	240,000	Mining since 1790. Coal & coke industry, metalworks, chemicals. Railroad junction. F=13th century. D=RCC.
5469	Kedzierzyn Kozle	72,800	96.00	69,900	99.93	C	84,000	Opole near Odra River west of Katowice. Railroad junction, fertilizer mfg., thermal power plant. D=RCC.
5470	Kielce	217,000	94.00	204,000	99.93	C	251,000	Capital of Kielce in Holy Cross Mountains. F=11th century. Episcopal property (14th-16th century). D=RCC.
5471	Konin	81,500	96.00	78,300	99.93	C	94,100	Konin on Warta River. Chemicals, building materials. F=13th century. 14th century church. D=RCC.
5472	Koszalin (Koslin)	110,000	95.00	105,000	99.93	C	127,000	Capital of Koszalin on Dzierzecinka River. Resort, timber, woodworking. F=1214. D=RCC.
5473	Krakow (Cracow)	857,000	94.00	806,000	99.93	C	957,000	Krakow on Vistula River. Known for grand historical style. 60 old churches. F=965. University (1364). D=RCC.
5474	Krosno	50,500	96.00	48,400	99.93	C	58,300	Capital of Krosno near Carpathian Mountains. Wislok River. Petroleum, natural gas, glass, rubber. D=RCC.
5475	Kutno	51,200	97.00	49,600	99.83	C	59,100	Southern Plock west of Warsaw. Railroad junction, agricultural machinery, cement, bricks, brewing. D=RCC.
5476	Legionowo	51,600	96.00	49,500	99.93	C	59,500	North on Wisla River. Soap, beet sugar, flour milling, timber, sawmilling, distilling, vegetables. D=RCC.
5477	Legnica (Liegnitz)	107,000	95.00	101,000	99.93	C	123,000	Capital of Legnica on Kaczawa River. Metalworking, textiles. 12th century Silesian stronghold. D=RCC.
5478	Leszno	59,200	96.00	56,800	99.93	C	68,300	Leszno. Agricultural & manufacturing center. F=15th century. Center of the Reformation. D=RCC.
5479	Lodz	1,055,000	96.00	1,013,000	99.93	C	1,170,000	Capital of Lodz. Major textiles center. Over 40% Poland's cotton goods. Center of film industry. F=1423. D=RCC.
5480	Pabianice	76,300	95.00	72,500	99.93	C	88,100	On Dobrzynka River. Textiles. Settled in 11th century. Small castle, 16th century church. D=RCC.
5481	Zgierz	59,900	95.00	56,900	99.93	C	69,200	Lodz north of Lodz. Textile center, chemicals, textile machinery, metals, chartered around 1300. D=RCC.
5482	Lomza	60,200	96.00	57,800	99.93	C	69,500	Lomza. Food processing, paper milling, textiles. Destroyed in WWII. 16th century Gothic cathedral. D=RCC.
5483	Lubin	83,600	95.00	79,400	99.93	C	96,500	Legnica north of Legnica. Copper mining, food products, furniture, pianos, woodworking. D=RCC.
5484	Lublin	395,000	91.00	359,000	99.88	C	456,000	Capital of Lublin on Bystrzyca River. Agricultural machinery, chemicals. F=9th century. Catholic university. D=RCC.

Table 10-5–continued opposite

Table 10-5–continued

Rec No 1	Country City 2	Pop 2000 3	AC% 4	Church Members 5	E% 6	W 7	Pop 2025 8	Notes 9
5485	Mielec	62,700	96.00	60,200	99.93	C	72,400	Western Rzeszow on Wisloka River. Ceramics, perfume, lumbering, flour milling, oil deposits, tannery. D=RCC.
5486	Nowy Sacz	79,400	95.00	75,400	99.93	C	91,700	Nowy Sacz on Dunajec River. Apples, tourist center, lignite, petroleum. F=1298. Prehistoric origins. D=RCC.
5487	Olsztyn (Allenstein)	165,000	94.00	155,000	99.93	C	191,000	Capital of Olsztyn on Lyna River. Many lakes. Trade center, tires. Teutonic Knights (1334). D=RCC.
5488	Opole (Oppeln)	130,000	94.00	123,000	99.93	C	151,000	Capital of Opole on Oder River. River port, iron. Historic buildings. F=9th century by Slavic Opolanie. D=RCC.
5489	Ostroteka	51,500	96.00	49,400	99.93	C	59,400	Capital of Ostroteka on Narew River. Pulp, paper. F=1427. Churches (14th-17th centuries). D=RCC.
5490	Ostrow Wielkopolski	74,400	95.50	71,100	99.93	C	85,900	Kalisz. Rail junction. Machine tools, railroad cars, lumber, textiles, ceramics, F=13th century. D=RCC.
5491	Ostrowiec Swieokrzyski	79,800	96.00	76,600	99.93	C	92,100	Kielce on Kamienna River. Iron industry. Food processing, ceramics, building materials. F=15th century. D=RCC.
5492	Pila (Schneidemuhl)	73,400	95.50	70,100	99.93	C	84,700	Capital of Pila on Guda River. Lumber mills, railway shops, potatoes. F=15th century. D=RCC.
5493	Piotrkow Tybunalski	82,200	95.00	78,100	99.93	C	94,900	Capital of Piotrkow Tybunalski. Textile mills, woodworks, glassworks. F=13th century. D=RCC.
5494	Plock	125,000	94.00	118,000	99.93	C	145,000	Capital of Plock on Vistula River. Oil refining, petrochemicals, plastics. F=10th century. D=RCC.
5495	Poznan	682,000	95.00	648,000	99.93	C	788,000	Capital of Poznan on Warta River. Metals, textiles. Academic center. F=9th century. Y=968(cathedral). D=RCC.
5496	Przemysil	69,500	96.00	66,800	99.93	C	80,300	Capital of Przemysl. Marketing center. Metal, timber, textiles. F=1340. D=RCC.
5497	Pulawy	87,000	96.00	83,500	99.93	C	100,000	Western Lublin on Wisla River. Port, cement products, shipbuilding, sawmilling, agriculture institute. D=RCC.
5498	Raciborz (Ratibor)	65,400	96.00	62,800	99.93	C	75,500	Katowice on Oder River. Electrotechnical, chemical, woodworking industries. F=9th century by Slavs. D=RCC.
5499	Radom	232,000	93.00	216,000	99.93	C	268,000	Capital of Radom. Textile milling, glass & chemical works, processed foods, machinery. F=1154. D=RCC.
5500	Radomsko	51,200	96.00	49,100	99.93	C	59,100	Southern Piotrkow northeast of Czestochowa. Furniture, machinery, brewing, flour milling. D=RCC.
5501	Rybnik	146,000	95.00	139,000	99.93	C	169,000	Katowice on Nacyna River. Coal mining, vocational schools. F=10th century as fishing village. D=RCC.
5502	Rzeszow	155,000	95.00	148,000	99.93	C	179,000	Capital of Rzesnow on Wislok River. Metals, textiles. Ethnographical museum. F=14th century. D=RCC.
5503	Siedlce	73,100	95.50	69,800	99.93	C	84,400	Capital of Siedlce. Food processing, textiles, toys. Five Nazi concentration camps in WWI. F=1448. D=RCC.
5504	Skarzysko-Kamienna	51,700	96.00	49,600	99.93	C	59,700	Northern Kielce north of Kielce. Klasztor Wachock (church). Ironworks, cutting stones, tiles, resort. D=RCC.
5505	Slupsk (Stolp)	103,000	95.50	98,100	99.93	C	119,000	Capital of Slupsk on Slupin River. Exports furniture. F=8th century Slavic stronghold. D=RCC.
5506	Stalowa Wola	71,100	96.00	68,200	99.93	C	82,100	Tarnobrzeg on San River. Railroad, iron and steel industry. Establised in 1930's. D=RCC.
5507	Starachowice	57,500	96.00	55,200	99.93	C	66,300	Kielce on Kamienna River. Iron mining, trucks, buses, machinery. F=16th century as mining center. D=RCC.
5508	Stargard Szczecinski	72,100	95.50	68,800	99.93	C	83,200	Szczecin on Ina River. Flour mills, cosmetics. F=12th century. St. Mary's Church (13th century). D=RCC.
5509	Starogard Gdanski	50,300	97.00	48,700	99.93	C	58,000	Central Gdansk on Wierzyca River. Lumber industry, chemicals, beer, furniture, 14th century church. D=RCC.
5510	Suwalki	62,200	96.00	59,700	99.93	C	71,900	Capital of Suwalki bordering Lithuania and Russia. Furniture, flour milling, brewing, tanning. D=RCC.
5511	Swidnica (Schweidnitz)	64,300	96.00	61,700	99.93	C	74,200	Walbrzych on Bystrzyca River. Metals, chemicals, wood. F=12th century Slavic settlement. D=RCC.
5512	Swinoujscie (Swinemunde)	44,000	96.50	42,400	99.93	C	50,800	Szczecin on an island. Major fishing port, resorts, beaches. F=1181. D=RCC.
5513	Szczecin (Stettin)	456,000	94.00	428,000	99.93	C	526,000	Capital of Czczecin on Oder River. Inhabited 2,500 years ago. Birthplace of Catherine the Great. D=RCC.
5514	Tarnow	123,000	94.50	116,000	99.93	C	142,000	Capital of Tarnow. Chemicals, building materials, processed foods. F=1330. D=RCC.
5515	Tczew	60,400	95.00	57,400	99.93	C	69,700	Gdansk on Vistula River. Major river port. Shipyards, railway workshops. F=1252. D=RCC.
5516	Tomaszow Mazowiecki	71,000	96.00	68,100	99.93	C	81,900	Piotrkow on Pilica River. Major textile center, synthetic silk, carpets. F=late 18th century. D=RCC.
5517	Torun	205,000	94.00	193,000	99.93	C	237,000	Capital of Torun on Vistula River. River port. Wool, gingerbread, electronics. F=1230. D=RCC.
5518	Walbrzych (Waldenburg)	210,000	94.00	198,000	99.93	C	243,000	Capital of Walbrzych in Sudeten mountains. Center of heavy industry, coke & chemicals. F=1290. D=RCC.
5519	WARSZAWA (Warsaw)	2,269,000	96.00	2,178,000	99.93	C	2,464,000	On Vistula River. Metallurgy, printing. Education center. Gardening. 80% destroyed in WWII. F=1300. D=RCC.
5520	Pruszkow	54,500	94.00	51,200	99.93	C	62,900	Warszawa southwest of Warsaw. Near airport. Many parks & squares. D=RCC.
5521	Wloclawek	124,000	94.00	117,000	99.93	C	143,000	Capital of Wloclawek on Vistula River. Cellulose. F=11th century. Kujavian bishopric. Y=11th century. D=RCC.
5522	Wodzislaw Slaski	113,000	94.00	107,000	99.93	C	131,000	Katowice. Coal mining center, coke production. F=12th century. Franciscan monks (15th century). D=RCC.
5523	Wroclaw (Breslau)	653,000	93.00	607,000	99.93	C	754,000	Capital of Wroclaw on Oder River. Largest flour mills. Ancient origins. 13th century cathedral. D=RCC.
5524	Zamosc	62,700	96.00	60,200	99.93	C	72,400	Zamosc. City classified as a historical monument. F=16th century. Renaissance church (1593). D=RCC.
5525	Zawiercie	57,500	96.00	55,200	99.93	C	66,300	Northern Katowice north of Katowice. Metals, glass, machinery, chemicals, lignite, iron ore, mining. D=RCC.
5526	Zielona Gora (Grunberg)	116,000	94.00	109,000	99.93	C	134,000	Capital of Zielona Gora. Textiles, metals. Cultural center (theatre, folk culture). F=13th century. D=RCC.
5527	Zory (Zary, Sorau)	68,000	96.00	65,300	99.93	C	78,500	Zielona Gora near German border. Paper, machinery, sawmilling, flour milling, coal mine. D=RCC.
	PORTUGAL	**9,875,000**	**91.95**	**9,080,000**	**99.64**	**C**	**9,348,000**	**ROMAN CATHOLICS 90.8%, INDEPENDENTS 2.8%. PENT-CHAR 6.5%, EVANGELICAL 1.0%, GCC 36.1%**
5528	rural areas	6,122,000	94.07	5,759,000	99.91	C	4,405,000	80.8% (1950), 74.0% (1970), 66.5% (1990), 62.0% (2000), 56.4% (2010), 47.1% (2025)
5529	urban areas	3,752,000	88.50	3,321,000	99.19	C	4,943,000	19.1% (1950), 25.9% (1970), 33.4% (1990), 38.0% (2000), 43.5% (2010), 52.8% (2025)
5530	non-metropolitan areas	325,000	88.69	288,000	99.64	C	600,739	*Sources of data:* Censuses of 1950, 1960, 1970, 1981, and 1991.
5531	metropolitan areas	3,427,000	88.48	3,033,000	99.15	C	4,343,000	*Definition:* Agglomerations of 10,000 or more inhabitants.
5532	Braga	62,800	90.00	56,500	99.19	C	82,700	Capital of Braga. Jewelry. F=296 BC by Carthaginians. 12th century cathedral. Pilgrimage center. D=RCC.
5533	Coimbra	74,300	90.00	66,900	99.19	C	97,900	Capital of Coimbra on Rio Mondego. Pottery, fabrics. 1 million volume Baroque library. Ancient origins. D=RCC.
5534	LISBOA (Lisbon)	1,971,000	86.00	1,695,000	99.09	C	2,424,000	On Sea of Palha. Chief port. Cement, cork. Museums, churches. Education center. Ancient origins. D=RCC.
5535	Amadora	95,200	90.00	85,700	99.69	C	125,000	Lisboa northwest of Lisboa city. Residential suburb, railroad, industrial, commercial. D=RCC.
5536	Barreiro	50,700	92.00	46,600	99.69	C	66,800	Setubal across Tagus Bay from Lisboa. Fishing port, industrial suburb, cork, soap. D=RCC.
5537	Ponta Delgada	21,100	94.00	19,800	99.69	C	27,800	Capital of the Azores in North Atlantic Ocean. Tourist resort. Holy Christ of the Miracles Church. D=RCC.
5538	Porto (Oporto)	1,221,000	92.00	1,123,000	99.19	C	1,608,000	Capital of Porto on Douro River. World famous port wine. Roman origins. 12th century cathedral. Pilgrims. D=RCC.
5539	Vita Nova de Gaia	62,200	90.00	56,000	99.69	C	82,000	Porto south of Douro River on Atlantic Ocean. Wine production, pottery. D=RCC.
5540	Setubal (Saint Yves)	77,600	92.00	71,400	99.69	C	102,000	Capital of Setubal. Salt, oranges, wine, grapes. Destroyed by earthquake (1755). 14th century church. D=RCC.
	PUERTO RICO	**3,869,000**	**96.22**	**3,722,000**	**99.90**	**C**	**4,478,000**	**ROMAN CATHOLICS 74.9%, PROTESTANTS 13.0%. PENT-CHAR 26.5%, EVANGELICAL 9.0%, GCC 14.0%**
5541	rural areas	959,000	98.40	943,000	99.99	C	785,000	59.4% (1950), 41.6% (1970), 28.6% (1990), 24.7% (2000), 21.4% (2010), 17.5% (2025)
5542	urban areas	2,910,000	95.50	2,779,000	99.87	C	3,693,000	40.5% (1950), 58.3% (1970), 71.3% (1990), 75.2% (2000), 78.5% (2010), 82.4% (2025)
5543	non-metropolitan areas	886,000	95.54	846,000	99.85	C	1,215,964	*Sources of data:* Censuses of 1950, 1960, 1970, 1980, and 1990.
5544	metropolitan areas	2,024,000	95.48	1,933,000	99.88	C	2,477,000	*Definition:* Places with 2,500 or more inhabitants and densely settled urban fringes or urbanized areas.
5545	Arecibo	174,000	96.00	167,000	99.88	C	221,000	On Arecibo River. Largest rum distilleries, sugarcane, pineapples. Radar-radio telescope. F=1537. D=RCC.
5546	Mayaguez	217,000	95.50	208,000	99.88	C	276,000	Deepwater harbor, chief shipping port. Needlework. F=1760. D=RCC.
5547	Ponce	252,000	95.00	239,000	99.88	C	320,000	Port. Canning, sugar refining, cement. F=1670. Catholic University (1948). D=RCC.
5548	SAN JUAN	1,381,000	95.50	1,319,000	99.88	C	1,661,000	Major port & tourist resort. Petroleum & sugar refining. Executive mansion La Fortaleza (1533). F=1508. D=RCC.
5549	Bayamon	239,000	94.00	224,000	99.68	C	303,000	Residential. Clothing, furniture, auto parts, metals, medicines, plastics, pharmaceuticals. F=1772. D=RCC.
5550	Caguas	145,000	95.00	137,000	99.68	C	183,000	Diamond cutting, tobacco, leather. F=1775 named for early Indian chief convert to Christianity. D=RCC.
5551	Carolina	193,000	94.00	181,000	99.68	C	244,000	Sugarcane, tobacco, textiles, pharmaceuticals, electronics. Many colleges and universities. F=1816. D=RCC.
5552	Guaynabo	101,000	95.00	95,600	99.68	C	128,000	South-southwest. Commercial center. Oil, pharmaceuticals, cement, paper. Historic museum. F=1769. D=RCC.
	QATAR	**599,000**	**9.95**	**59,600**	**56.37**	**B**	**779,000**	**ROMAN CATHOLICS 6.0%, INDEPENDENTS 1.7%. PENT-CHAR 2.4%, EVANGELICAL 0.7%, GCC 5.0%**
5553	rural areas	45,100	3.26	1,500	37.30	A	39,900	37.1% (1950), 20.1% (1970), 10.1% (1990), 7.5% (2000), 6.1% (2010), 5.1% (2025)
5554	urban areas	554,000	10.50	58,200	57.92	B	739,000	62.8% (1950), 79.9% (1970), 89.8% (1990), 92.4% (2000), 93.8% (2010), 94.8% (2025)
5555	non-metropolitan areas	67,900	10.50	7,100	57.92	B	90,565	*Sources of data:* Census of 1986; estimates for 1956 and 1963.
5556	metropolitan areas	486,000	10.50	51,000	57.92	B	648,000	*Definition:* Urban centers.
5557	AD-DAWHAH (Doha)	486,000	10.50	51,000	57.92	B	648,000	On Persian Gulf. New construction, rapid growth. Formerly pearls, now oil. 33% South Asian. D=RCC.
	REUNION	**699,000**	**86.80**	**607,000**	**97.19**	**C**	**880,000**	**ROMAN CATHOLICS 87.3%, PROTESTANTS 4.5%. PENT-CHAR 7.8%, EVANGELICAL 3.8%, GCC 8.0%**
5558	rural areas	204,000	88.76	181,000	98.41	C	175,000	76.5% (1950), 56.3% (1970), 36.1% (1990), 29.1% (2000), 24.3% (2010), 19.8% (2025)
5559	urban areas	496,000	86.00	426,000	96.69	C	705,000	23.4% (1950), 43.6% (1970), 63.8% (1990), 70.8% (2000), 75.6% (2010), 80.1% (2025)
5560	non-metropolitan areas	383,000	86.00	329,000	96.69	C	544,616	*Sources of data:* Censuses of 1954, 1967, and 1982; estimate for 1990.
5561	metropolitan areas	113,000	86.00	97,000	96.69	C	160,000	*Definition:* Urban centers.
5562	SAINT-DENIS	113,000	86.00	97,000	96.69	C	160,000	Administrative town. Education center. Arab minority runs commerce. Sugar, molasses, bananas, rum. D=RCC.
	ROMANIA	**22,327,000**	**87.91**	**19,627,000**	**99.27**	**C**	**19,945,000**	**ORTHODOX 85.1%, ROMAN CATHOLICS 14.5%. PENT-CHAR 6.0%, EVANGELICAL 6.2%, GCC 8.3%**
5563	rural areas	9,330,000	89.18	8,321,000	99.70	C	6,020,000	74.5% (1950), 58.1% (1970), 46.3% (1990), 41.7% (2000), 36.9% (2010), 30.1% (2025)
5564	urban areas	12,996,000	87.00	11,307,000	98.96	C	13,926,000	25.5% (1950), 41.8% (1970), 53.6% (1990), 58.2% (2000), 63.0% (2010), 69.8% (2025)
5565	non-metropolitan areas	4,069,000	87.21	3,548,000	98.97	C	4,444,013	*Sources of data:* Censuses of 1956, 1966, 1977, and 1992.
5566	metropolitan areas	8,928,000	86.90	7,759,000	98.95	C	9,482,000	*Definition:* Cities, towns and 183 other localities having certain urban socio-economic characteristics.
5567	Alba-Iulia (Alba Julia)	69,700	88.00	61,300	99.36	C	74,700	On Mures River. One of oldest settlements in Romania. Leatherworking. Batthyaneum Library (1794). D=RCC.
5568	Alexandria	57,300	89.00	51,000	99.56	C	61,400	Capital of Teleorman on Vedea River. Railroad, manufacturing, foodstuffs, textiles, machines, metallurgy. D=ROC.
5569	Arab	186,000	85.00	158,000	98.36	C	199,000	Capital of Arab on Muresul River. Neolithic settlement. Magyars. Seminary. D=ROC.
5570	BUCURESTI (Bucharest)	2,130,000	88.00	1,874,000	99.36	C	2,198,000	Cultural & administrative center. Engineering. F=1459. Many churches. Earthquake (1977). D=ROC,RCC.
5571	Bacau	200,000	86.00	172,000	98.56	C	214,000	Capital of Bacau on Bistrita River. Fighter airplanes, paper mill, footwear. Cultural center. F=1408. D=ROC.
5572	Baia-Mare (Neustadt)	146,000	88.00	128,000	99.36	C	156,000	Capital of Mamamures. Chemicals, metals. F=12th century by Saxons. Until 1948 Eastern-rite see. D=ROC.
5573	Birlad	75,300	89.00	67,000	99.56	C	80,700	Vaslui. Machinery. Residence of princes of Moldavia in 14th century. 17th century churches. D=ROC.
5574	Bistrita	85,800	89.00	76,400	99.56	C	92,000	Capital of Bistrita-Nasavd. Foodstuffs, building materials, timber, wines. F=12th century by Germans. D=ROC.
5575	Botosani	123,000	88.00	109,000	99.36	C	132,000	Capital of Botosani. Rich farming area near Moldova. Textiles, wines. F=1439. Y=1496 (Popauti Church). D=ROC.
5576	Braila	230,000	86.00	197,000	98.56	C	246,000	Capital of Braila on Danube River. Metalworking. F=1350. Cathedral of St. Michael. D=ROC.
5577	Brasov	317,000	86.00	272,000	98.56	C	339,000	Capital of Brasov in Alps. First Romanian book(16th cent). F=1211. St. Bartholomew's (13th cent). D=ROC.
5578	Buzau	145,000	86.00	125,000	98.56	C	155,000	Capital of Buzau. Orchards, market gardens, vineyards. F=1431. Romanian Orthodox (1500). D=ROC.
5579	Calarasi	75,200	85.00	63,900	98.36	C	80,600	Capital of Calarasi. River port & trading center. Fish, flour. F=1593. D=ROC.
5580	Cluj-Napoca	321,000	84.00	269,000	98.16	C	344,000	Capital of Cluj. Historic capital of Transylvania. F=12th century. Church of St. Michael (1321). D=ROC,RCC.
5581	Constanta	343,000	84.00	288,000	98.16	C	367,000	Capital of Constanta on Black Sea. Principal seaport. F=7th century BC. Ovid's exile (AD 17). D=ROC.
5582	Craiova	297,000	84.00	249,000	98.16	C	318,000	Capital of Dolj on Jiul River. Locomotives. Roman origins. University (1966). St. Dimitru Church (1652). D=ROC.
5583	Deva	76,600	89.00	68,200	99.56	C	82,100	Capital of Hunedoara on Mures River. Little industry. 13th century Citadel. Magna Curia (1621). D=ROC.
5584	Drobeta-Turnu-Severin	113,000	88.00	99,400	99.36	C	121,000	Capital of Mehedinti on Danube River. Tourism. F=2nd century. Iron Gates Museum. 13th century church. D=ROC.
5585	Focsani	99,100	89.00	88,200	99.56	C	106,000	Capital of Vrancea on Milcov River. Center for wine-making region. Dairy products, furniture. D=ROC.
5586	Galati	319,000	87.00	277,000	99.86	C	341,000	Capital of Galati on Danube & Siret Rivers. Timber. F=15th century. Precista Church (15th Century). D=ROC.
5587	Gheorghe Gheorghiu-Dej	99,800	88.00	87,800	99.36	C	107,000	Bacau. Oil, chemical, industrial complex. F=15th century. New town since 1953. D=ROC.
5588	Giurgiu	72,600	89.00	64,600	99.56	C	77,800	Capital of Giurgiu on Danube River. Shipyard, sugar. F=10th century. 14th century fortress. D=ROC.
5589	Hunedoara	79,400	88.00	69,900	99.36	C	85,100	Hunedoara. Major metallurgical center. Hunedoara Castle (1453). Roman origins of ore mining. D=ROC.
5590	Iasi(Jassy)	335,000	86.00	288,000	98.56	C	359,000	Capital of Iasi on Bahlui River. Educational institutes. F=7th century. Byzantine church(1635). D=ROC,RCC.
5591	Lugoj	49,900	89.00	44,400	99.56	C	53,400	Timis on Timis River. Textiles, silk, wood-processing. F=1st century BC. Seat of Orthodox bishopric. D=ROC,RCC.
5592	Medias	63,100	89.00	56,100	99.56	C	67,600	Sibiu on Tirnava Mare River. Natural gas, kitchen utensils, vineyards. F=13th century by Germans. D=ROC.
5593	Onesti	57,700	86.00	49,600	98.56	C	61,800	Bacau. Power station, petrochemical plant, gymnastics training center. D=ROC.
5594	Oradea	216,000	86.00	186,000	98.56	C	231,000	Capital of Bihor on Crisul Repede River. Museums. Ancient settlement. RCC bishopric (1080). D=ROC.
5595	Petrosani	74,300	87.00	64,700	98.66	C	79,600	Hunedoara on Jiu River. Coal mining center & cultural center. F=17th century. D=ROC.
5596	Piatra Neamt	120,000	87.00	105,000	98.66	C	129,000	Capital of Neamt. Fertilizer. F=15th century. Church of St. John (1497). Bistrita monastery (15th cent). D=ROC.
5597	Pitesti	176,000	86.00	151,000	98.56	C	188,000	Capital of Arges. Famous for wines & resorts. F=Middle Ages. Roman relics in the area. D=ROC.
5598	Ploesti	303,000	86.00	261,000	98.56	C	325,000	Capital of Prahova. Petroleum industry. Six museums. F=16th century by Father Ploaie. D=ROC.

Table 10-5–continued overleaf

Table 10-5–continued

Rec No 1	Country City 2	Pop 2000 3	AC% 4	Church Members 5	E% 6	W 7	Pop 2025 8	Notes 9
5599	Resita (Recita)	94,700	87.00	82,300	98.66	C	101,000	Capital of Caras-Severin in Transylvania. Center of coal & metal-mining region. Roman settlement. D=ROC.
5600	Rimnicu-Vilcea	111,000	88.00	97,500	98.56	C	119,000	Capital of Vilcea on Olt River. Chemicals, timber, oil-drilling machines. F=14th century. Cetatvia church. D=ROC.
5601	Roman	78,400	89.00	69,800	99.56	C	84,000	Neamt on Moldova & Siret Rivers. Sugar refinery. F=1392. Church of Precista Marc (16th century). D=ROC.
5602	Satu-Mare	129,000	87.00	112,000	98.66	C	138,000	Capital of Satu Mare on Somes River. Textiles. F=1214. Treaty of Szatmar (1711)-religious freedom. D=ROC,RCC.
5603	Sfintu-Gheorghe	66,600	88.00	58,600	99.36	C	71,300	Capital of Covasna on Olt River. Regional Museum. Daco-Roman settlement. Fortified church. D=ROC.
5604	Sibiu	166,000	86.00	143,000	98.56	C	178,000	Capital of Sibiu on Cibin River. Large industrial base. Roman origins. Many Germans. D=Lutheran,ROC,RCC.
5605	Slatina	83,400	89.00	74,300	99.56	C	89,400	Capital of Olt on Olt River. Aluminum works. Once a fort. Roman relics. D=ROC.
5606	Slobozia	54,400	89.00	48,400	99.56	C	58,300	Capital of Ialomita on Ialomita River. Cattle market, textiles, bricks, dairy products, Amara Health Resort. D=ROC.
5607	Suceava	112,000	88.00	98,400	99.36	C	120,000	Capital of Suceava. Meat processing, timber. F=14th century. Mirauti church (14th century). D=ROC.
5608	Timisoara	327,000	86.00	281,000	98.56	C	350,000	Timis on Bega River. Cultural center. Roman origins. Demonstrations sparked 1989 revolution. D=RCC,,ROC.
5609	Tirgoviste	95,700	87.00	83,300	98.66	C	103,000	Capital of Dimbovita on Ialomita River. Center of oil industry. Roman origins. 17th century church. D=ROC.
5610	Tirgu Mures	160,000	86.00	138,000	98.56	C	171,000	Capital of Mures on Muresul River. Sugar. Important cultural center. F=14th century. 50% Hungarian. D=ROC.
5611	Tirgu-Jiu	96,100	88.00	84,600	99.36	C	103,000	Capital of Gorj on Jiu River. Timber, clothing. Roman settlement. D=ROC.
5612	Tulcea	95,300	88.00	83,900	99.36	C	102,000	Capital of Tulcea on Danube River. Important port, fishing, tourism. F=7th century BC. D=ROC.
5613	Turda	59,800	88.00	52,600	99.36	C	64,100	Cluj on Aries River. Cement, glass, ceramics, tourism. Dacian settlement (Dierna). D=ROC.
5614	Vaslui	78,400	89.00	69,800	99.56	C	84,000	Capital of Vaslui on Birlad River. Trading center, tile, bricks. St. John the Baptist Church (1490). D=ROC.
5615	Zalau	66,800	89.00	59,500	99.56	C	71,600	Capital of Salaj in Mezes Mountains. Local market center, furniture. Roman origins. D=ROC.
	RUSSIA	**146,934,000**	**56.91**	**83,618,000**	**93.25**	**B**	**137,933,000**	**ORTHODOX 51.6%, INDEPENDENTS 5.3%. PENT-CHAR 4.4%, EVANGELICAL 0.3%, GCC 19.9%**
5616	rural areas	32,796,000	63.55	20,842,000	97.44	C	21,766,000	55.3% (1950), 37.5% (1970), 26.0% (1990), 22.3% (2000), 19.3% (2010), 15.7% (2025)
5617	urban areas	114,138,000	55.00	62,776,000	92.04	B	116,167,000	44.7% (1950), 62.4% (1970), 74.0% (1990), 77.6% (2000), 80.7% (2010), 84.2% (2025)
5618	non-metropolitan areas	35,787,000	56.43	20,195,000	92.07	B	36,966,814	*Sources of data:* Censuses of 1959, 1970, 1979, and 1989.
5619	metropolitan areas	78,351,000	54.35	42,581,000	92.02	B	79,200,000	*Definition:* Cities and urban-type localities, officially designated as such by each of the constituent republics.
5620	Abakan	155,000	62.00	95,800	98.34	C	157,000	Khakassia on Abakan River. Metalworking, footwear, food processing, coal & iron ore. D=ROC.
5621	Achtubinsk	49,900	60.00	29,900	96.34	C	50,800	Astrakhan near Volga River. Near Kazakhstan border. Cattle, vegetables, metal goods, woodworking. D=ROC.
5622	Acinsk (Achinsk)	120,000	55.00	65,900	91.34	B	122,000	Kransnoyarsk on Chulym River. Alumina plant, petroleum refinery. F=1621. D=ROC.
5623	Al'metjevsk (Almetevsk)	130,000	25.00	32,600	61.34	B	133,000	Tatarstan on Stepnoy Zay River. Crude oil, petroleum, tires. F=1950. D=ROC.
5624	Alapajevsk (Alapayevsk)	49,400	56.00	27,700	92.34	B	50,300	Sverdlovsk on Neyva River. Oldest iron & steel works in Urals (1704). Machine-tool, timber. D=ROC.
5625	Alatyr'	46,900	44.00	20,600	80.34	B	47,700	Chuvashia on Alatyr River. Volga River basin. River port, railroad junction, clothing. F=1552. D=ROC.
5626	Aleksandrov	67,400	62.00	41,800	98.34	C	68,600	Vladimir on Seraja River. Radio/TV supplies, folk industries, embroidery, first printing in Russia. D=ROC.
5627	Aleksin	72,900	60.00	43,700	96.34	C	74,200	Tula on Oka River. Engineering, building materials, chemicals, cardboard. F=1236. D=ROC.
5628	Amursk	58,600	58.00	34,000	94.34	B	59,600	Khabarovsk on Amur River. Wood-processing complex, paper products.. F=1958. D=ROC.
5629	Anapa	54,900	60.00	33,000	96.34	C	55,900	Krasnodar Kraj on Black Sea. Wine growing region, port, children's climate and bathing resort. D=ROC.
5630	Angarsk	264,000	53.00	140,000	94.34	B	268,000	Irkutsk on Trans-Siberian Railroad. Oil refining, petrochemicals, synthetic fibers. F=1948. D=ROC.
5631	Anzero-Sudzensk	105,000	48.00	50,500	84.34	B	107,000	Kemerovo on Trans-Siberian Railroad. Coal mining, pharmaceuticals. F=1928. D=ROC.
5632	Apatity	87,000	45.00	39,200	81.34	B	88,600	South of Murmansk on Lake Imandra. Arose in 1935 for processing of phosphate ores. D=ROC.
5633	Archangel'sk (Arkhangelsk, Archangel)	413,000	40.00	165,000	81.34	B	420,000	Arkhangelsk on Northern Dvina River. Largest timber export. Fishing fleet. F=1584 as monastery. D=ROC.
5634	Armavir	159,000	60.00	95,600	96.34	C	162,000	Krasnodar on Kuban River. Food-processing industries, large meat-packing combines. F=1839. D=ROC.
5635	Arsenjev	70,000	51.00	35,700	87.34	B	71,200	Primorsky. North of Vladivostok. Machinery, aviation and construction, woodworking,. F=1902. D=ROC.
5636	Art'om (Artyom)	68,900	53.00	36,500	89.34	B	70,100	Primorsky. Lignite production. Building materials, porcelain, pianos. F=1924. D=ROC.
5637	Arzamas	110,000	58.00	63,700	94.34	B	112,000	Gorky on Tyosha River. Agricultural equipment, food processing. School of painting (1802-1862). F=1366. D=ROC.
5638	Asbest	83,400	60.00	50,000	96.34	C	84,900	Sverdlovsk in Ural Mountains. Largest producer of asbestos in former USSR. F=1720. D=ROC.
5639	Astrachan' (Astrakhan)	503,000	55.00	277,000	96.34	B	512,000	Astrakhan in Volga River Delta. City of bridges & water canals. Fishing. Medieval origins. Cathedral. D=ROC.
5640	Azov (Azak, Tana)	79,300	60.00	47,600	96.34	C	80,700	On Don River near Sea of Azov. Fish processing, lumber milling. F=6th century BC as Greek Tanais. D=ROC.
5641	Balakovo	198,000	59.00	117,000	95.34	B	201,000	Saratov on Volga River. Chemical industry. Nuclear power plant. Engine manufacture. F=1762. D=ROC.
5642	Balasov	95,600	60.00	57,400	96.34	C	97,300	Saratov on Chop'or River. Wheat and sunflower region, auto trailers, mica, furniture, dairy. F=1780. D=ROC.
5643	Barnaul	661,000	47.00	311,000	88.34	B	673,000	Altay on Ob River. Hub of mining. Engineering, cotton textiles. Agricultural research. F=1738. D=ROC.
5644	Novoaltajsk	54,200	48.00	26,000	84.34	B	55,200	Near Ob River. Center of agriculture area, paper mill, metal goods, flourmilling. F=1942. D=ROC.
5645	Belebej	53,500	30.00	16,100	66.34	B	54,500	Bashkortostan near Usen River. Rapid growth of oil production, auto parts, machinery. F=1757. D=ROC.
5646	Belgorod	306,000	59.00	181,000	95.34	B	311,000	Belgorod on Donets River. Light engineering. F=10th century. Stronghold against Tatars. D=ROC.
5647	Belogorsk	73,000	40.00	29,200	76.34	B	74,300	Amur on Tom River near Chinese border. Agriculture center, meat packing, flour milling. F=1860. D=ROC.
5648	Belorecensk	51,000	60.00	30,600	96.34	C	51,900	Krasnodar Kraj on Beleja River. Near Majkop. Sunflower oil press, wood working, furniture. D=ROC.
5649	Beloreck (Beloretsk)	71,800	25.00	18,000	61.34	B	73,100	Bashkortostan near headwaters of Belaya River. Metallurgical center. F=1762. D=ROC.
5650	Belovo	91,300	58.00	52,900	94.34	B	92,900	Kemerovo on Bachat River. Coal mining, zinc, sulphuric acid. F=1930. D=ROC.
5651	Berezniki	196,000	54.00	106,000	90.34	B	200,000	Perm on Kama River. Salt, potassium deposits. Huge chemical industry. F=1932. D=ROC.
5652	Berezovskiy	51,000	59.00	30,100	95.34	B	51,900	Kemerovo near Jaja River. Near Kemerovo, West Siberia. Coal mining. F=1965 from 3 settlements. D=ROC.
5653	Bijsk (Biisk, Bisk, Biysk)	230,000	53.00	122,000	89.34	B	235,000	Altay on Biya River. Engineering, consumer goods. Linked by highway with Mongolia. F=1709. D=ROC.
5654	Birobidzan	84,800	58.00	49,200	94.34	B	86,300	Yevreyskaya on Bira River. Sawmilling, woodworking. On Trans-Siberian Railroad. F=1928. D=ROC.
5655	Blagoveshchensk (Amurskaya)	201,000	30.00	60,400	66.34	B	205,000	Amur on Amur & Zeya Rivers. Major center of Soviet Far East. Timber, gold-mining machines. F=1856. D=ROC.
5656	Borisoglebsk	70,800	60.00	42,500	96.34	C	72,100	Voronezh on Vorona River. Grain collection center, flour milling. F=1646 as fortress against Tatars. D=ROC.
5657	Borovici	61,700	55.00	33,900	91.34	B	62,800	Borovichi on Msta River. Old handicrafts, hosiery, ceramics, paper, wood. F=1770. D=ROC.
5658	Br'ansk (Bryansk, Briansk)	451,000	58.00	262,000	96.34	B	459,000	Bryansk on Desna river. Engineering, building materials, cement. F=1146. Moscow-Ukraine trade. D=ROC.
5659	Bratsk	255,000	52.00	133,000	93.34	B	259,000	Irkutsk on Angara River. Aluminum, timber. One of world's largest hydroelectric plants. F=1631. D=ROC.
5660	Bud'onnovsk	56,500	55.00	31,100	91.34	B	57,500	Stavropol Kraj on Kuma River. Chemical polymers, food industries, flour milling, wine, railroad terminus. D=ROC.
5661	Bugul'ma	89,500	27.00	24,200	63.34	B	91,100	Tatarstan. Center of petroleum mining, machinery production. Grain, meat processing. F=1736. D=ROC.
5662	Buguruslan	53,200	58.00	30,800	94.34	B	54,100	Orenburg in Ural Mountains on Great Kinel River. Petroleum production, sawmilling. F=1748. D=ROC.
5663	Buj	61,800	55.00	34,000	91.34	B	62,900	Kostroma on Kostroma River. Chemicals, metalworking, sawmilling, electronics, flax. D=ROC.
5664	Bujnaksk	56,900	8.00	4,600	44.34	A	57,900	Dagestan near Caspian Sea. Fruit canning center, shoes, furniture, petroleum. F=end of 14th century. D=ROC.
5665	Buzuluk	83,600	55.00	46,000	91.34	B	85,100	Orenburg in Ural Mountains on Samara river. Heavy metallurgy, agricultural machines. F=1736. D=ROC.
5666	Cajkovskij	86,800	48.00	41,600	84.34	B	88,300	Perm on Kama River. Mining region, rye, oats, flax, potatoes, wheat, clover, livestock, leather, lumbering. D=ROC.
5667	Capajevsk (Chapayevsk)	94,300	56.00	52,800	92.34	B	96,000	Kuybyshev on Volga River. Nitrogen, ammonia. Formerly center of defense industry. D=ROC.
5668	Cebarkul	49,800	61.00	30,400	97.34	C	50,700	Celabinsk in Ural Mountains near Celabinsk. Heavy industry, mining, wheat, rye, oats, sheep, dairying. D=ROC.
5669	Ceboksary (Cheboksary)	428,000	45.00	193,000	86.34	B	436,000	Capital of Chuvashia on Volga River. Cotton textiles, heavy tractors. F=15th century. D=ROC.
5670	Cechov	59,100	60.00	35,500	96.34	C	60,200	South of Moscow on Lopasna River. Industrial region, electric power, chemicals, metallurgy, dairy. D=ROC.
5671	Cel'abinsk (Chelyabinsk)	1,183,000	57.00	674,000	96.34	B	1,183,000	Chelyabinsk in Ural Mountains on Miass River. Important industrial center. Iron, steel. Tractors. F=1736. D=ROC.
5672	Kopejsk (Kopeisk)	76,900	58.00	44,600	94.34	B	78,300	Center of lignite mining. Declining population since 1960s due to mechanization. F=1920. D=ROC.
5673	Ceremchovo (Cheremchovo)	72,300	50.00	36,200	86.34	B	73,600	Irkutsk on Trans-Siberian Railroad. Formerly mining center-declining since 1960s. F=1772. D=ROC.
5674	Cerepovec (Cherepovets)	310,000	57.00	177,000	95.34	B	316,000	Vologda on Sheksna River. Iron & steel, shipbuilding, fertilizer. Volga-Baltic waterway. D=ROC.
5675	Cerkessk (Cherkessk, Batalpashinsk)	115,000	26.00	29,900	62.34	B	117,000	Karachay-Cherkessia on Kuban River near Caucasus Mountains. Refrigerators, shoes. F=1825. D=ROC.
5676	Cernogorsk (Chernogorsk)	78,300	63.00	49,300	98.34	C	79,700	Khakassia on Yenisey River. Center of coal mining since 1917. F=1936. D=ROC.
5677	Chabarovsk (Khabarovsk, Habarovsk)	603,000	45.00	271,000	86.34	B	613,000	Khabarovsk on Amur River. Engineering, machine-building. Attractive waterfront park. F=1858. D=ROC.
5678	Chasavjurt	71,500	7.00	5,000	43.34	A	72,800	Dagestan on Yaryksu River. Cotton, fruits, vegetables, natural resources, winter wheat, corn, textiles. D=ROC.
5679	Cholmsk	50,900	40.00	20,400	76.34	B	51,800	Sakhalin Island on Sea of Japan. Lumbering, offshore gas production, herring fishing, paper milling. D=ROC.
5680	Cistopol' (Chistopol)	65,400	25.00	16,400	61.34	B	66,600	Tatarstan on Volga River. Ship repairing, flour milling, sawmilling. F=1781. D=ROC.
5681	Cita (Chita)	370,000	53.00	196,000	94.34	B	376,000	Chita at confluence of Chita & Ingoda rivers. Trade & transportation center. F=1653. D=ROC.
5682	Cusovoj	57,000	49.00	27,900	85.34	B	58,000	Perm on Cusovaja River near Ural Mountains. Extensive mining district, livestock, sawmilling. D=ROC.
5683	Derbent	80,100	7.00	5,600	43.34	A	81,500	Dagestan. Wool spinning, wine making, large cannery. F=AD 438 as fortress to guard caravan route. D=ROC.
5684	Dmitrov	64,500	62.00	40,000	98.34	C	65,600	North of Moscow on Moscow canal. Light manufacturing. Cathedrals (16th century). F=1154. D=ROC.
5685	Dimitrovgrad (Melekess)	125,000	59.00	73,600	95.34	B	127,000	Ulyanovsk at confluence of Melekes and Bolshoy Cheremshan Rivers. Agricultural center. F=1714. D=ROC.
5686	Doneck	48,000	58.00	27,900	94.34	B	48,900	Rostov on Severskij Donec River near Ukraine border. Steppe region. Tobacco, wheat, sunflower, melons. D=ROC.
5687	Dubna	66,000	56.00	37,000	92.34	B	67,200	Moscow on Volga River. Hydroelectric station. F=1956 as seat of Joint Institute for Nuclear Research. D=ROC.
5688	Elektrostal' (Zatishye)	150,000	60.00	90,200	96.34	C	153,000	Moscow. Steel metallurgical equipment, steel-milling center, stainless steel products, tractor parts. D=ROC.
5689	Elista	91,100	25.00	22,800	61.34	B	92,700	Capital of Kalymkia. Diverse government, educational, cultural, industrial establishments. F=1865. D=ROC.
5690	Gatcina	79,200	60.00	47,500	96.34	C	80,600	Machine building, metalworking. 600 room summer palace (1766) now a museum. F=1499. D=ROC.
5691	Georgijevsk	62,600	55.00	34,400	91.34	B	63,700	Stavropol Kraj near Kuma River. Treaty between Russia & Georgia (1783). D=ROC.
5692	Georgiu-Dez (Georgiu-Dezh)	53,600	58.00	31,100	94.34	B	54,600	Voronezh on Don River. Locomotives, meat packing, flour milling. F=1937. Known as Svoboda & Liski. D=ROC.
5693	Glazov	104,000	56.00	58,300	92.34	B	106,000	Udmurtia on Cheptsa River. Timber milling, woodworking, metal working. F=1780. D=ROC.
5694	Gor'kij (Gorky, Nizhni Novgorod)	1,461,000	60.00	877,000	96.34	C	1,461,000	Gorky on Volga & Oka Rivers. Heavy industry, motor vehicles, ships. Known for trade fairs. F=1221. D=ROC.
5695	Bor	63,400	57.00	36,100	93.34	B	64,500	Glass, ship repair, port equipment. Major center for ships, known since 14th century. F=1938. D=ROC.
5696	Dzerzinsk (Dzerzhinsk)	282,000	55.00	155,000	91.34	B	287,000	Chemicals, fertilizers, materials for synthetic textiles, plastics, port. Oka River, formed in 1930. D=ROC.
5697	Kstovo	64,200	59.00	37,900	95.34	B	65,300	Port on Cheboksary Reservoir, Volga River. Major oil refinery. Vitamins, thermoelectric power station. D=ROC.
5698	Gorno-Altajsk	46,700	55.00	25,700	91.34	B	47,500	Gorno-Altay on Mayma River. Agricultural center, sawmilling. F=1928. D=ROC.
5699	Gr'azi	46,900	57.00	26,700	93.34	B	47,700	Lipeck on Matyra River. Moderate climate. Ferrous metallurgy, machines, appliances, furniture. D=ROC.
5700	Groznyj (Grozny)	394,000	5.00	19,700	41.34	A	401,000	Checheno-Ingushetia on Sunzha River. Major oil center. Petroleum institute (1920). F=1818. D=ROC.
5701	Gubkin	75,100	58.00	43,500	94.34	B	76,400	Belgorod. Important iron-ore mining center. Kursk magnetic anomaly, mineral pigments. F=1930s. D=ROC.
5702	Gukovo	66,500	60.00	39,900	96.34	C	67,700	Rostov, Donets basin. Center of coal industry, construction, railroad. F=1955. D=ROC.
5703	Gus'-Chrustal'nyj (Gus-Khrustalny)	75,700	57.00	43,100	93.34	B	77,000	Vladimir on Gus River. Famous as center of glass industry, crystal works, peat works. F=1931. D=ROC.
5704	Inta	59,800	40.00	23,900	76.34	B	60,900	Komi. Far north. Near Ural Mountains, Inta River. Coal mining center in Pechora basin. F=1940. D=ROC.
5705	Irbit	50,400	56.00	28,200	92.34	B	51,300	Sverdlovsk on Nica River. Near Ural Mountains. Agricultural center. Motorcycles, bricks. D=ROC.
5706	Irkutsk	629,000	48.00	302,000	89.34	B	640,000	Irkutsk on Angara River. Engineering products, mica processing. Cultural center of Siberia. F=1652. D=ROC.
5707	Isim (Ishim)	64,700	50.00	32,400	86.34	B	65,900	Tyumen on Isim River. Agricultural center, machinery, food products, shoes, old trading village. D=ROC.
5708	Isimbaj (Ishimbay)	69,800	27.00	18,800	63.34	B	71,100	Bashkortostan on Belaya River. Earliest center of oil industry in Volga-Urals. Petrochemicals. F=1932. D=ROC.
5709	Iskitim	67,500	53.00	35,800	89.34	B	68,700	Novosibirsk near Novosibirsk reservoir, south of Novosibirsk, Turksib River. Plumbing, furniture. D=ROC.
5710	Ivanovo	474,000	58.00	275,000	95.34	B	482,000	Ivanovo on Uvod River. Blended yarns, worsteds, cotton cloth, mining cranes, chemicals, wood. D=ROC.
5711	Izevsk (Izhevsk, Ustinov)	626,000	56.00	351,000	94.34	B	637,000	Capital of Udmurtia on Izh River. Steel armaments, motorcycles. Udmudt cultural center. F=1760. D=ROC.
5712	Jakutsk (Yakutsk)	190,000	57.00	108,000	95.34	B	193,000	Capital of Yakut-Sakha on Lena River. Wooden houses. River port. F=1632. D=ROC.
5713	Jarcevo	53,100	62.00	32,900	98.34	C	54,000	Smolensk on Vop River near Smolensk. Flax, linseed oil, fodder grasses, grain, wheat, sawmilling. D=ROC.
5714	Jaroslavl' (Yaroslavl)	627,000	58.00	364,000	96.34	B	638,000	Yaroslavl on Volga River. Diesel engines, petroleum, textiles. F=1010. Transfiguration Cathedral (1505). D=ROC.
5715	Jefremov	55,600	60.00	33,400	96.34	C	56,600	Tula on Krasivaja Meca River. Mining, potatoes, wheat, flour milling, distilling, sugar refining. D=ROC.
5716	Jegorjevsk (Yegoryevsk)	72,900	62.00	45,200	98.34	C	74,200	Moscow on Glushitsy River. Textile machinery, clothing, footwear, phosphates. F=1778. D=ROC.
5717	Jejsk (Yeysk)	78,000	58.00	45,200	94.34	B	79,400	Krasnodar on Sea of Azov. Fishing, agriculture, health resort-mud baths. F=1848. D=ROC.
5718	Jelec (Elets, Yelets)	119,000	59.00	70,300	95.34	B	121,000	Lipetsk on Sosna River. Flour milling. Noted for hand-made lace. F=1146. D=ROC.
5719	Jelizovo	47,800	60.00	28,700	96.34	C	48,700	Southern Mogilov on Berezina River north of Bobrujsk. Wood products, furniture, chemicals, shoes. D=ROC.
5720	Jermolajevo	64,500	30.00	19,300	66.34	B	65,600	Bashkortostan south of Sterlitamak. Wheat, rye, oats, natural gas, petroleum, mining, sawmilling. D=ROC.

Table 10-5–continued opposite

Table 10-5–continued

Rec No 1	Country City 2	Pop 2000 3	AC% 4	Church Members 5	E% 6	W 7	Pop 2025 8	Notes 9
5721	Jessentuki (Yessentuki)	84,800	56.00	47,500	92.34	B	86,300	Stavropol in valley of Podkumok River. Major health resort, mud baths, springs. F=1798. D=ROC.
5722	Joskar-Ola (Yoshkar-Ola)	243,000	70.00	170,000	98.34	C	248,000	Capital of Mari El on Malaya Koshaga River. Light engineering. F=1578. D=ROC.
5723	Jurga	92,400	55.00	50,800	91.34	B	94,000	Kemerovo on Tom River. Coal and iron mining, ferrous metallurgy, fertilizers, plastics, fur, cattle. D=ROC.
5724	Juzno-Sachalinsk (Toyohara)	161,000	42.00	67,700	78.34	B	164,000	Sakhalin on Susuya River. Furniture, footwear. Japanese (Toyohara) until 1945. D=ROC.
5725	Kalinin (Tver)	451,000	58.00	261,000	95.34	B	459,000	Kalinin on Volga and Tvertsa Rivers. Flax, textiles, river port. F=1134. D=ROC.
5726	Kaliningrad (Konigsberg)	401,000	53.00	213,000	94.34	B	408,000	Kaliningrad seaport on Pregolya River. Major Baltic Sea naval port. German until 1945. F=1255. D=ROC.
5727	Kaluga	310,000	50.00	155,000	91.34	B	315,000	Kaluga on Oka River. Turbines, railway equipment. F=14th century stronghold against Tatars.D=ROC.
5728	Kamensk-Sachtinskij	71,800	57.00	40,900	93.34	B	73,100	Rostov on Seversky Donets River. Formerly coal-mining. Agricultural & mining machinery. F=1686. D=ROC.
5729	Kamensk-Ural'skij (Kamensk-Uralsky)	205,000	58.00	119,000	94.34	B	209,000	Sverdlovsk on Kamenka & Iset Rivers. Aluminum products. F=1700. First state iron foundry. D=ROC.
5730	Kamysin (Kamyshin)	122,000	55.00	67,200	91.34	B	124,000	Volgograd on Volga River. Center of agricultural region. F=1697 as fort. D=ROC.
5731	Kanas	55,100	42.00	23,100	78.34	B	56,100	Chuvashia near Kazan. Machinery, metal goods, auto parts, chemicals, food industry. F=1925. D=ROC.
5732	Kandalaksa	53,300	45.00	24,000	81.34	B	54,300	Murmansk on White Sea, Niva River. Seaport, aluminum. F=1938, settlement 11th century. D=ROC.
5733	Kansk	108,000	58.00	62,600	94.34	B	110,000	Krasnoyarsk on Kan River. Large coal mining area. Cotton, timber hydrolysis. F=1640 as fort. D=ROC.
5734	Kaspijsk	60,800	7.00	4,300	43.34	A	61,900	Dagestan on Caspian Sea. Industrial center, engines, precision machines. F=1932. D=ROC.
5735	Kazan'	1,135,000	25.00	284,000	66.34	B	1,135,000	Capital of Tatarstan on Volga River. Chief manufacturing city. Center of Tatar culture. F=13th century. D=ROC.
5736	Kemerovo	512,000	60.00	307,000	96.34	C	521,000	Kemerovo on Tom River. Coal mining center, chemicals, sawmilling. F=1830. D=ROC.
5737	Kimry	60,900	58.00	35,300	94.34	B	62,000	Kalinin on Volga River. Traditional handicrafts, leatherworking shoes. F=1917. D=ROC.
5738	Kinesma (Kineshma)	103,000	60.00	61,800	96.34	C	105,000	Ivanovo on Volga River. Cotton, petroleum, timber, grain. River port. F=16th century. D=ROC.
5739	Kingisepp	49,700	63.00	31,300	98.34	C	50,600	Leningrad near Estonian border. Luga River. Phosphorite, furniture, leather, shoes, wood. D=ROC.
5740	Kirisi	52,200	62.00	32,300	98.34	C	53,100	Leningrad on Volchov River. Petroleum products, oil pipeline, electric power station. D=ROC.
5741	Kirov (Vyatka)	483,000	58.00	280,000	95.34	B	491,000	Kirov on Vyatka River. Nonferrous metalworking, engineering, tires, timber. F=1181. D=ROC.
5742	Kirovo-Cepeck	93,900	57.00	53,500	93.34	B	95,600	Kirov. Near Kirov, Cheptsa River. Electrical machinery, metal working, food and textile industries. D=ROC.
5743	Kislovodsk	115,000	59.00	67,700	95.34	B	117,000	Stavropol on Podkumok River. Health resort, mineral springs. F=1803. D=ROC.
5744	Klin	93,400	62.00	57,900	98.34	C	95,100	Moscow. Center of chemical industry. Synthetic fibers, glass. Tchaikovsky Museum. F=1234. D=ROC.
5745	Klincy	70,000	53.00	37,100	89.34	B	71,200	Bryansk near Uneca River. Near Belorussian border. Turosna River. Fine woolen cloth, leather. D=ROC.
5746	Kolomna	161,000	62.00	99,600	98.34	C	163,000	Moscow near Moskva & Oka Rivers. Diesel engines, heavy machinery, synthetic rubber. F=1177. D=ROC.
5747	Kolpino	142,000	61.00	86,600	97.34	C	144,000	South. Road junction, agricultural trade. D=ROC.
5748	Komsomol'sk-Na-Amure	313,000	55.00	172,000	96.34	B	319,000	Khabarovsk on Amur River. Heavy industry, oil refining. F=1932 by Young Communist League. D=ROC.
5749	Korkino	44,000	57.00	25,100	93.34	B	44,800	Chelyabinsk in southern Ural Mountains. Center of lignite mining, truck production. F=1934. D=ROC.
5750	Korsakov	44,500	45.00	20,000	81.34	B	45,300	Sakhalin on Aniva Gulf. Ship repairing, fish processing. F=1853 as fortified post. Japanese (1905-45). D=ROC.
5751	Kostroma	277,000	59.00	163,000	95.34	B	282,000	Kostroma on Volga River. Major textile center flax-processing. F=1152. Cathedral (1239). D=ROC.
5752	Kotlas	67,700	48.00	32,500	84.34	B	68,900	Arkhangelsk at confluence of Northern Dvina & Vychegda Rivers. Coal, timber. F=1917. D=ROC.
5753	Kovrov	159,000	60.00	95,400	96.34	C	162,000	Vladimir on Klyazma River. Textiles, cotton cloth, heavy engineering, excavators. D=ROC.
5754	Krasnodar	620,000	57.00	353,000	95.34	B	631,000	Krasnodar on Kuban River. Processing agricultural products, refining petroleum. F=1793. D=ROC.
5755	Krasnojarsk (Krasnoyarsk)	975,000	59.00	575,000	96.34	B	976,000	Krasnoyarsk on Yenisey River. Aluminum, timber industry. Huge hydroelectric station. F=1628. D=ROC.
5756	Krasnokamensk	56,800	60.00	34,100	96.34	C	57,800	Near Lake Baikal, Chita. Rail station, largest uranium site in former Soviet Union. D=ROC.
5757	Krasnokamsk	65,800	57.00	37,500	93.34	B	67,000	Perm on Kama River. Oil refining & metalworking. F=1929 as paper mill site. D=ROC.
5758	Krasnoturjinsk	66,000	56.00	37,000	92.34	B	67,200	Sverdlovsk on Turya River in Ural mountains. Aluminum industry. F=1758. D=ROC.
5759	Kropotkin	75,300	58.00	43,700	94.34	B	76,600	Krasnodar on Kuban River. Transport (30% of labor force), agriculture. F=19th century. D=ROC.
5760	Krymsk	50,200	58.00	29,100	94.34	B	51,100	Krasnodar Kraj near Novorossijsk. Near Black Sea. Canned goods, dairy products, feed, wine, beer. D=ROC.
5761	Kujbysev (Kuybyshev, Samara)	1,260,000	55.00	693,000	96.34	B	1,260,000	Kuybyshev on Volga River. Network of pipelines. Oil refining, petrochemicals. F=1586 as Samara. D=ROC.
5762	Novokujbysevsk (Novokuibyshevsk)	111,000	55.00	61,200	91.34	B	113,000	Amid Volga-Urals oil field. Oil refining, petrochemicals, metal industries. F=1948. D=ROC.
5763	Kungur	80,400	52.00	41,800	88.34	B	81,800	Perm at confluence of Sylva, Iren & Shakva Rivers. Machine building. Alabaster caves. F=1648. D=ROC.
5764	Kurgan	357,000	59.00	211,000	95.34	B	364,000	Kurgan on Tobol River. Agricultural & other machinery. F=1553 as Tsaryovo Gorodishche. D=ROC.
5765	Kursk	426,000	60.00	255,000	96.34	C	433,000	Kursk on Seym River. One of oldest cities in Russia. Machine building. F=1032. D=ROC.
5766	Kuzneck	98,200	55.00	54,000	91.34	B	100,000	Penza near Sura River. Instruments, condensers, polymer machinery, textiles, shoes. F=1780. D=ROC.
5767	Kyzyl (Belotsarsk, Khem-Beldyr)	86,500	25.00	21,600	61.34	B	88,000	Capital of Tuva on Yenisey River. Tanning, timberworking, brickworking, furniture, sawmills. D=ROC.
5768	Labinsk	57,600	58.00	33,400	94.34	B	58,600	Krasnodar on Laba River. Agricultural center, canning, timer, sugar, dairy products. F=1840 as fortress. D=ROC.
5769	Leninogorsk (Tatarskaja)	62,200	22.00	13,700	58.34	B	63,300	Tatarstan near Zaj River. Petroleum, motor vehicle parts. Arose from oil field discovery in 1948. D=ROC.
5770	Leninsk-Kuzneckij (Leninsk-Kuznetsky)	131,000	56.00	73,400	92.34	B	133,000	Kemerovo on Inya River. Coal-mining center, chemicals. F=1912 by French mining company. D=ROC.
5771	Lesosibirsk	68,100	51.00	34,700	87.34	B	69,300	Krasnojarsk Kraj on Yenisey River. Lumbering, chemicals. F=settlements from 1640. D=ROC.
5772	Lipeck (Lipetsk)	452,000	57.00	258,000	95.34	B	460,000	Lipetsk on Voronezh River. Steelworks, nitrogenous fertilizers. F=1703 by Peter the Great. D=ROC.
5773	Livny	51,700	59.00	30,500	95.34	B	52,600	Orel on Sosna River near Jelec. Railroad, machinery, plastics, flour milling, distilling. Chartered in 1586. D=ROC.
5774	Lys'va	76,400	57.00	43,600	93.34	B	77,800	Perm on Lysva River in Ural mountains. Metallurgical center (tinplate, steel). F=c1650. D=ROC.
5775	Machackala (Makhachkala)	328,000	5.00	16,400	41.34	A	333,000	Dagestan on Caspian Sea. Chemicals, textiles. Oil pipeline terminus. F=1844 as fortress. D=ROC.
5776	Magadan	152,000	56.00	85,200	92.34	B	155,000	Magadan on Sea of Okhotsk. Ship repair. F=1933 as port & supply center for Kolyma goldfields. D=ROC.
5777	Magnitogorsk	436,000	58.00	253,000	95.34	B	444,000	Chelyabinsk on Ural River. Iron & steelworks. F=1929 for magnetite ore. D=ROC.
5778	Majkop (Maikop, Maykop)	150,000	40.00	59,900	76.34	B	152,000	Capital of Adygea on Belaya River. Machinery, lumber, wood pulp, electric power station. F=1858. D=ROC.
5779	Mcensk	48,300	60.00	29,000	96.34	C	49,200	Orel on Zusa River northeast of Orel. Hemp, potatoes, wheat, sugarbeets, hogs, distilling. D=ROC.
5780	Meleuz	54,200	32.00	17,400	68.34	B	55,200	Bashkortostan on Belaja River south of Sterlitamak. Chemical industry, milk, sugar, wood industries. D=ROC.
5781	Mezdurecensk (Mezhdurechensk)	106,000	57.00	60,200	93.34	B	107,000	Kemerovo on Usa & Tom Rivers. Coal mining, reinforced concrete forms. F=1955 as town. D=ROC.
5782	Miass	167,000	58.00	96,700	94.34	B	170,000	Chelyabinsk on Miass River. Commercial vehicles, gold mining. F=1773 as copper smelting center. D=ROC.
5783	Michajlovka (Mikhaylovka)	57,700	60.00	34,600	96.34	C	58,700	Volgograd on Medveditsa River. Flour milling, meat packing, canning, cement factories. D=ROC.
5784	Micurinsk (Michurinsk)	107,000	56.00	60,200	92.34	B	109,000	Tambov on Lesnoy Voronezh River. Locomotive repair, fruit, vegetables. F=1636 as Kozlov. D=ROC.
5785	Mineral'nyje Vody	71,200	57.00	40,600	93.34	B	72,500	Stavropol on Kuma River. Freight yards, railroad workshops, resorts, mineral springs, water bottling. D=ROC.
5786	Minusinsk	72,900	50.00	36,500	86.34	B	74,200	Krasnojarsk Kraj near Abakan, Khakassia. River port, agriculture, gold and coal mining basin. F=1739. D=ROC.
5787	Moncegorsk	66,900	59.00	39,500	95.34	B	68,100	Murmansk on Lake Imandra. Copper, nickel, fishing, forestry. F=1930s, made city in 1937. D=ROC.
5788	Morsansk	49,600	57.00	28,300	93.34	B	50,500	Tambov on Cna River. Center of agriculture area, machinery and metal industries, clothing. F=1779. D=ROC.
5789	MOSKVA (Moscow)	9,299,000	62.00	5,765,000	98.34	C	9,299,000	On Moscow River. Industry, science, research. Kremlin, Red Square. 15th century cathedrals. D=ROC.
5790	Balasicha (Balashikha)	135,000	62.00	83,800	98.34	C	138,000	East on Pekhorka River. Machine building. F=19th century for cloth, later papermaking. D=ROC.
5791	Chimki (Khimki)	133,000	62.00	82,500	98.34	C	135,000	Northwest. Engineering, tile, glass. F=1939 as small summer cottages. D=ROC.
5792	Dolgoprudnyj (Dolgoprudny)	69,900	63.00	44,000	98.34	C	71,100	North. Airship construction, machine building. Agrochemical laboratory. D=ROC.
5793	Domodedovo	55,300	65.00	36,000	98.34	C	56,300	Southeast. Machinery, woolen mills, building materials, one of area airports. F=1947. D=ROC.
5794	Fr'azino	53,100	63.00	33,400	98.34	C	54,000	Northeast. Railroad junction, electronic appliances, residential suburb, commuters. F=1951. D=ROC.
5795	Ivantejevka	52,300	60.00	31,400	96.34	C	53,200	Northeast. Woolen and cotton milling center, knitwear. Known since 1586. F=1938.
5796	Kaliningrad (Moskovskaya)	159,000	62.00	98,400	98.34	C	161,000	Northeastern outskirts. Silk textiles, food processing. Developed after 1928. D=ROC.
5797	Klimovsk	56,600	63.00	35,700	98.34	C	57,600	South. Textile machinery since 1883, agricultural machinery, toys. F=1940. D=ROC.
5798	Krasnogorsk	90,100	62.00	55,900	98.34	C	91,700	In greenbelt. Cameras, building machinery, plasterwork. Known as Banki before 1940. D=ROC.
5799	L'ubercy (Lyubertsy)	162,000	63.00	102,000	98.34	C	165,000	In greenbelt southeast. Machine building, oil refining, consumer goods. Formerly agriculture center. D=ROC.
5800	Lobn'a	59,900	63.00	37,800	98.34	C	61,000	North. Plywood for construction, electrical equipment, cotton spinning. F=1961. D=ROC.
5801	Lytkarino	50,800	62.00	31,500	98.34	C	51,700	Southeast, 20 miles from Moscow, Moskva River. Optical glass. Became city in 1957. D=ROC.
5802	Moskva (Moscow)	9,049,000	60.00	5,430,000	96.34	C	9,210,000	Vast number of large apartment buildings. Moscow State University (1755). Public transportation. D=ROC.
5803	Mytisci (Mytishchi)	151,000	62.00	93,700	98.34	C	154,000	Northeast. Machine building, transport machinery. Between Moscow & Trinity-St. Sergius monastery. D=ROC.
5804	Odincovo (Odintsovo)	126,000	63.00	79,500	98.34	C	128,000	Southwest. Railroad, building materials, bricks, furniture, chemicals, plastics, refractories. F=1957. D=ROC.
5805	Podol'sk (Podolsk)	205,000	63.00	129,000	98.34	C	208,000	South. Engineering, nonferrous-metallurgical, cement, food-processing industries. F=1781. D=ROC.
5806	Ramenskoje	87,200	62.00	54,100	98.34	C	88,800	Southwest. Textile & engineering center. Residential, medical school. F=1820s for cotton. D=ROC.
5807	Reutov	67,700	63.00	42,600	98.34	C	68,900	East. Railroad junction, cotton spinning, weaving, orthopaedic devices, toys, armaments. F=1940. D=ROC.
5808	Scelkovo	108,000	63.00	67,800	98.34	C	110,000	Northeast. Railroad junction, machinery, heavy industry, distilling, metalworks, residential, financial. D=ROC.
5809	Solnecnogorsk	55,700	63.00	35,100	98.34	C	56,700	Northwest. Senezh Lake. Railroad, highway, metal, nets, glassworks. F=1938. D=ROC.
5810	Zelenograd	160,000	63.00	101,000	98.34	C	163,000	Northwest. Skhodnya River, Moscow-St. Petersburg highway. Electronics, planned community. F=1960. D=ROC.
5811	Zeleznodoroznyj	97,600	62.00	60,500	98.34	C	99,300	East. Railroad shops, wood products, ceramic facing materials, cotton mill. F=1952. D=ROC.
5812	Murmansk	465,000	58.00	269,000	94.34	B	473,000	Murmansk on Kola Bay. Ice free port. Fishing. Largest city in world north of Arctic circle. D=ROC.
5813	Murom	124,000	57.00	70,600	93.34	B	126,000	Vladimir on Oka River. Textiles, sawmilling. F=862. Trinity & Annunciation monasteries. D=ROC.
5814	Naberezhnie Chelni Breznev	445,000	25.00	111,000	66.34	B	453,000	Tatarstan on Kama River. World's largest truck plant, hydroelectric station. D=ROC.
5815	Nachodka (Nakhodka)	162,000	40.00	64,600	76.34	B	164,000	Primorsky on Sea of Japan. Large shipping port, fish industry, ship repair yard, tin can factory. F=1950. D=ROC.
5816	Nadym	51,300	30.00	15,400	66.34	B	52,200	Yamalo-Nenets on Nadym River. Kara Sea. System of natural gas pipelines that feed central Russia. D=ROC.
5817	Nal'cik (Nalchik)	236,000	20.00	47,300	56.34	B	241,000	Capital of Kabardino-Balkaria on Nalchik River. Popular health resort. F=1818 as Russian fort. D=ROC.
5818	Naro-Fominsk	57,800	60.00	34,700	96.34	C	58,800	Moscow on Nara River. Silk weaving combine. Totally destroyed in WWII. F=1926. D=ROC.
5819	Nazarovo	64,100	52.00	33,300	88.34	B	65,200	Krasnojarsk Kraj on Culym River. South of Acinsk. Lignite mining area, agricultural machinery. F=1700. D=ROC.
5820	Neftejugansk	64,400	58.00	37,300	94.34	B	65,500	Siberia. On Channel of the Ob River. Oil production, arose from oil discovery, pipeline. F=1967. D=ROC.
5821	Ner'ungri	75,800	55.00	41,700	91.34	B	77,200	Siberia, Sakha Republic. Railroad, mining and processing of bituminous coal, machine repair shop. F=1975.
5822	Nevinnomyssk	121,000	56.00	67,800	92.34	B	123,000	Stavropol on Kuban River. Chemical complex, fertilizer, plastics. Until 1950s agricultural town. D=ROC.
5823	Nikolo-Berjozovka	109,000	27.00	29,300	63.34	B	110,000	Bashkortostan near Kama River. Flour milling, saw milling, timber, agriculture. D=ROC.
5824	Niznekamsk (Nizhnekamsk)	193,000	27.00	52,000	63.34	B	196,000	Tatarstan on Kama River. Petrochemical center, synthetic rubber plant (one of world's largest). D=ROC.
5825	Niznevartosk	243,000	58.00	141,000	94.34	B	247,000	Tyumen on Ob River. Major administrative center for Ob oil fields. Pop. 1970 (16,000). D=ROC.
5826	Niznij Tagil (Nizhny Tagil)	432,000	59.00	255,000	95.34	B	439,000	Sverdlovsk on Tagil River. One of oldest smelting centers in Urals. Metallurgy. F=1725. D=ROC.
5827	Njagan	58,800	55.00	32,300	91.34	B	59,800	Siberia. Airport, center of oil production in Krasnoleninsk oil field. F=1985. D=ROC.
5828	Noginsk (Bogorodsk)	121,000	61.00	73,500	97.34	C	123,000	Moscow on Klyazma River. Large textile center, cotton. Originally Yamskaya village. F=1781. D=ROC.
5829	Nojabr'sk	87,300	58.00	50,700	94.34	B	88,900	Airport, Yamalo Nenezskiy. Center for development and servicing of natural gas, petroleum, airport. D=ROC.
5830	Noril'sk	166,000	59.00	98,000	95.34	B	169,000	Krasnoyarsk in Rybraya Valley. World's leading producer for nickel & platinum. F=1935. D=ROC.
5831	Novgorod	230,000	60.00	138,000	96.34	C	234,000	Novgorod on Volkhov River. One of oldest Russian cities. Tourist center. F=859. St. Sophia Cathedral. D=ROC.
5832	Novoceboksarsk	117,000	45.00	52,700	81.34	B	119,000	Chuvashia on Volga River. Chemical center. Hydroelectric station. D=ROC.
5833	Novocerkassk (Novocherkassk)	185,000	58.00	107,000	94.34	B	188,000	Rostov at confluence of Tuzlov & Aksay Rivers. Electric locomotives, mining machinery. F=1805. D=ROC.
5834	Novodvinsk	49,400	45.00	22,200	81.34	B	50,300	Arkhangelsk near Archangelsk, North Dvina River. Wood pulp combine. F=1977. D=ROC.
5835	Novokuzneck (Novokuznetsk, Stalinsk)	591,000	59.00	349,000	95.34	B	602,000	Kemerovo on Tom River. Ironworks, ferroalloys, mining machinery. F=1617 as Kuznetz. D=ROC.
5836	Novomoskovsk (Bobriki, Stalinogorsk)	359,000	58.00	208,000	95.34	B	365,000	Tula on Don River. Major chemical center, fertilizers, plastics. F=1930 as Bobriki. D=ROC.
5837	Novorossijsk	185,000	59.00	109,000	95.34	B	189,000	Krasnodar at head of Tsemes Bay of Black Sea. Major port with naval base, cement. F=1838. D=ROC.
5838	Novosachtinsk (Novoshakhtinsk)	105,000	60.00	63,300	96.34	C	107,000	Rostov on Maly Nesvetay River. Major coal mining center, anthracite mining. F=1863. D=ROC.
5839	Novosibirsk	1,476,000	55.00	812,000	96.34	B	1,476,000	Novosibirsk on Ob River. Heart of Siberia. Metallurgy. Gold refinery. Academy of Science. F=1893. D=ROC.
5840	Berdsk	79,000	60.00	47,400	96.34	C	80,400	On Novosibirsk Reservoir. Flour milling, radio production, recreation center. F=18th century as fortress. D=ROC.
5841	Novotroick	106,000	57.00	60,300	93.34	B	108,000	Orenburg on Ural River. Ferrous metallurgy center, chemical production, high quality steel, chromium. D=ROC.
5842	Novyj Urengoj	92,000	55.00	50,600	91.34	B	93,600	Yamalo-Nenezskiy, Taz Bay, near Arctic circle. Airport, oil, Urengoy Gas Industry. F=1982. D=ROC.
5843	Obninsk	102,000	60.00	61,100	96.34	C	104,000	Kaluga near Pratva River. Southwest of Moscow. Scientific center, research institute, uranium. D=ROC.
5844	Okt'abr'skij (Oktyabriskii)	105,000	24.00	25,200	60.34	B	107,000	Bashkortostan on Ik River. Clothing, footwear, ceramic tiles. F=1937 on oil industry. D=ROC.

Table 10-5–continued overleaf

Table 10-5–continued

Rec No 1	Country City 2	Pop 2000 3	AC% 4	Church Members 5	E% 6	W 7	Pop 2025 8	Notes 9
5845	Omsk	1,214,000	56.00	680,000	96.34	B	1,215,000	Omsk on Irtysh River. Petrochemicals, refineries, synthetic rubber, timber. F=1716. D=ROC.
5846	Or'ol (Orel, Oryol)	337,000	58.00	196,000	94.34	B	343,000	Oryol on Oka River. Many homes of writers & poets. F=1564 as fortress against Tatars. D=ROC.
5847	Orechovo-Zujevo (Orekhovo-Zuevo)	201,000	60.00	121,000	96.34	C	205,000	Moscow on Klyazma River. One of largest textile cities in ex-USSR, cotton. F=1917. D=ROC.
5848	Orenburg (Chkalov)	547,000	58.00	317,000	95.34	B	556,000	Orenburg on Ural River. Heavy industrial & agricultural machinery. F=1735 as fortress. D=ROC.
5849	Orsk	267,000	59.00	158,000	95.34	B	272,000	Orenburg at confluence of Ural and Or Rivers. Large oil refinery, nickel, cobalt. F=1735 as fortress. D=ROC.
5850	Osinniki	62,100	58.00	36,000	94.34	B	63,200	Kemerovo at confluence of Kandalep and Kondoma rivers. Coal-mining center. F=1930s. D=ROC.
5851	Otradnyj	48,700	50.00	24,400	86.34	B	49,600	Samara on Bolsaja Kinel River. East of Samara. Developed with exploitation of Mukhanovsk oil fields. D=ROC.
5852	P'atigorsk (Pyatigorsk)	129,000	60.00	77,300	96.34	C	131,000	Stavropol on Podkumok River. Famous spa, mineral springs. Lermontov (port) House. F=1780. D=ROC.
5853	Partizansk (Suchan)	49,100	55.00	27,000	91.34	B	50,000	Primorsky on Partizanskaya River. Coal mining, clothing. F=1932. Mining college. D=ROC.
5854	Pavlovo	70,900	61.00	43,300	97.34	C	72,200	Gorky on Oka River. Metalworking industry, buses. Long handicraft tradition in metals. D=ROC.
5855	Pavlovskij Posad	69,600	62.00	43,100	98.34	C	70,800	Moscow on Klyazma River. Silk, paper, cotton, wool, ceramics. F=18th century as monastic village. D=ROC.
5856	Pecora (Pechora)	64,400	50.00	32,200	86.34	B	65,500	Komi on Pecora River near Ural mountains. Pechova coal basin, timber transfer point, sawmill, furniture. D=ROC.
5857	Penza	541,000	58.00	314,000	94.34	B	551,000	Penza at confluence of Penza & Sura Rivers. Machinery, diesel engines, agriculture. F=1666 as fortress. D=ROC.
5858	Perm' (Perm, Molotov)	1,117,000	55.00	614,000	95.34	B	1,117,000	Perm on Kama River. Large-scale engineering industries, oil refining. F=1723 as copper-smelting works. D=ROC.
5859	Pervoural'sk	141,000	58.00	81,900	94.34	B	144,000	Sverdlovsk on Chusovaya River. Steel pipe factories, mining machinery. F=1732 as ironworks. D=ROC.
5860	Petrodvorec	82,300	60.00	49,400	96.34	C	83,800	Port & resort center. Grand Palace museum. F=1709 as country estate. D=ROC.
5861	Petropavlovsk-Kamcatskij	268,000	40.00	107,000	81.34	B	273,000	Kamchatka on Pacific Coast. Fishing center, fish processing, net-making, ship repair. F=1740. D=ROC.
5862	Petrozavodsk	273,000	67.00	183,000	98.34	C	277,000	Capital of Karelia on Lake Omega. Engineering, timberworking. F=1703 by Peter the Great. D=ROC.
5863	Polevskoj	70,600	60.00	42,400	96.34	C	71,900	Sverdlovsk near Chusovaya River in Ural Mountains. Coal mining, chemicals. F=1724. D=ROC.
5864	Prochladnyj	57,500	22.00	12,600	58.34	B	58,500	Kabardino-Balkaria on Terek River. Near Nal'cik. Major railroad junction, workshops, freight yards. D=RCC.
5865	Prokopjevsk (Prokopyevsk)	419,000	58.00	243,000	94.34	B	427,000	Kemerovo on Aba Rivers. Coal-mining center, flour, machinery. F=18th century. D=ROC.
5866	Kisel'ovsk (Kiselevsk)	125,000	55.00	68,600	91.34	B	127,000	Coal used for coking, drilling equipment, trucks, mechanical horses for coal trains. F=1930s. D=ROC.
5867	Pskov (Pihkva)	204,000	55.00	112,000	91.34	B	207,000	Pskov on Velikaya River. Machine building, flax. 13th century population 60,000. F=903. D=ROC.
5868	Puskin (Pushkin)	93,600	61.00	57,100	97.34	C	95,300	Leningrad. Residential and resort suburb, canals, lakes, parks. F=1708. D=ROC.
5869	Puskino	74,500	60.00	44,700	96.34	C	75,800	Northeast of Moscow, Ucha River. Woolen industry, jute, furniture, chemicals. F=1499.
5870	R'azan' (Ryazan, Riazan)	518,000	55.00	285,000	96.34	B	527,000	Ryazan on Oka River. Engineering, petrochemicals, oil-refining. F=1095. 13th century bishopric. D=ROC.
5871	Rasskazovo	48,900	56.00	27,400	92.34	B	49,800	Tambov east of Tambov. Textiles, brewery, machinery repair, biochemicals. F=1698. D=ROC.
5872	Revda	64,800	60.00	38,900	96.34	C	66,000	Sverdlosvsk on Revda River. Copper smelting, ferrous, metallurgy, fertilizers. F=1734. D=ROC.
5873	Roslavl'	59,600	60.00	35,800	96.34	C	60,700	Smolensk on Ostyor River. Near Belorussia. Railroad junction, auto parts, diamond cutting, glass. D=ROC.
5874	Rossos'	57,900	58.00	33,600	94.34	B	58,900	Voronez near Ukraine. Poultry, meat packing, flour milling, sunflower, oil extraction, chemical fertilizers. D=ROC.
5875	Rostov-na-Donu	1,048,000	61.00	639,000	97.34	C	1,048,000	Rostov on Don River. Trade, commerce, agricultural machinery. Strategic location. F=1749 as Temernika. D=ROC.
5876	Batajsk (Bataysk)	91,700	58.00	53,200	94.34	B	93,300	Rostov. Transport center, railway shops, freight yards. Grain, livestock, metal working. F=1938. D=ROC.
5877	Rubcovsk (Rubtsovsk)	169,000	48.00	81,300	84.34	B	172,000	Altay on Aley River. Nonferrous mining center, diesel tractors, flour, dairying, industrialized during WWII. D=ROC.
5878	Ruzajevka	51,200	58.00	29,700	94.34	B	52,100	Mordvinia. Railroad enterprises, chemicals, machinery, plastics, textiles, brick industry. F=1893. D=ROC.
5879	Rybinsk (Andropov)	258,000	58.00	150,000	95.34	B	262,000	Jaroslavl on Volga River at Rybinsk Reservoir. Engineering. F=12th century. D=ROC.
5880	Rzev (Rzhev)	69,700	59.00	41,100	95.34	B	70,900	Kalinin on Volga River. Light engineering, agricultural products. F=1216. Held by various princes. D=ROC.
5881	Sachty (Shakhty)	224,000	60.00	134,000	96.34	C	228,000	Rostov on Upper Grushevka River. Major anthracite mining center, machinery, textiles, clothing. D=ROC.
5882	Sadrinsk (Shadrinsk)	86,000	57.00	49,000	93.34	B	87,500	Kurgan on Iset River & Trans-Siberian Railroad. Manufacturing & agricultural center. F=1662. D=ROC.
5883	Safonovo	55,300	60.00	33,200	96.34	C	56,300	Smolensk, Vopets River, west part of Moscow. Coal mining, plastics, electrical machinery. D=ROC.
5884	Sajanogorsk	52,100	63.00	32,800	98.34	C	53,000	Khakassia on Yenisey River. Sayan aluminum factory, electric power, stone working, marble deposits. D=ROC.
5885	Sal'sk	60,600	59.00	35,800	95.34	B	61,700	Rostov. Don River basin. Railroad junction, agricultural center, feed industries. F=1830. D=ROC.
5886	Salavat	149,000	25.00	37,200	61.34	B	151,000	Bashkortostan on Belaya River. Oil refinery, chemicals, technical glass. F=1948. D=ROC.
5887	Sankt-Peterburg	5,132,000	60.00	3,079,000	98.34	C	5,132,000	Leningrad. Gulf of Finland seaport. Engineering, printing. education. F=1703 by Peter the Great. D=ROC.
5888	Saransk	314,000	58.00	182,000	96.34	B	320,000	Capital of Mordvinia on Insar River. Machinery, penicillin, cables, chemicals, textiles. F=1641. D=ROC.
5889	Sarapul	109,000	54.00	58,700	90.34	B	111,000	Udmurtia on Kama River. Port. Machine tools, radios. F=16th century as Russian stronghold. D=ROC.
5890	Saratov	917,000	40.00	367,000	81.34	B	917,000	Saratov on Volga River. Engineering, electrical equipment, flour milling. F=1590. D=ROC.
5891	Engels' (Pokrovsk)	180,000	58.00	105,000	94.34	B	184,000	Main trolley bus manufacturer in ex-USSR. Artificial fibers. F=1747 as military base. D=ROC.
5892	Satka	50,200	50.00	25,100	86.34	B	51,100	Celabinsk near Bashkortostan. Magnesite, metallurgy, fireproof brick, low-phosphorous iron. F=1758. D=ROC.
5893	Scekino (Shchyokino)	71,800	52.00	37,300	88.34	B	73,100	Tula. Coal mining, chemicals, wheat, potatoes, sugarbeets, ironworks, distilling. F=1870 for lignite mining. D=ROC.
5894	Scokino	67,600	60.00	40,600	96.34	C	68,800	Tula south of Tula. Iron ores, marble, gypsum, gravel, vegetable produce, wheat, flour milling, sugar. D=ROC.
5895	Selechov	47,700	52.00	24,800	88.34	B	48,600	Irkutsk on Irkut River near Irkutsk. Industrial and cultural region, machine tools, textiles, chemicals. D=ROC.
5896	Serov (Nadezhdinsk)	102,000	58.00	59,100	94.34	B	104,000	Sverdlovsk on Kavka River. Center of Urals mining & metals. Iron & steel. F=1890s. D=ROC.
5897	Serpuchov (Serpukhov)	139,000	60.00	83,200	96.34	C	141,000	Moscow on Nara River at confluence with Oka. Cotton, artificial silk. F=1374. D=ROC.
5898	Severodvinsk (Molotovsk)	247,000	48.00	119,000	89.34	B	251,000	Archangelsk on White Sea's Gulf of Dvina. Shipbuilding, timber, fishing. F=1917. D=ROC.
5899	Severomorsk	65,000	45.00	29,300	81.34	B	66,200	Murmansk on Kola River. Near Murmansk and Barents Sea. Fishing port, naval flotilla station. F=1951. D=ROC.
5900	Shchelkovo (Shchyolkovo)	106,000	61.00	64,600	97.34	C	108,000	Moscow on Klyazma River. Renowned for handicraft silkweaving. Textiles. D=ROC.
5901	Slav'ansk-Na-Kubani	57,500	58.00	33,300	94.34	B	58,500	Krasnodar on Protoka River. Agricultural processing and studies. Cossack village until 1958. D=ROC.
5902	Smolensk	344,000	59.00	203,000	95.34	B	350,000	Smolensk on Dnepr River. Old Russian city. F=863. Cathedral of the Assumption (12th century). D=ROC.
5903	Soci (Sochi)	336,000	57.00	191,000	95.34	B	341,000	Krasnodar on Black Sea. Greater Sochi-87 miles of coast. Holiday & health resorts. F=1896. D=ROC.
5904	Sokol	45,900	60.00	27,500	96.34	C	46,700	Vologda on Sukhona River. Paper, woodworking, river port. F=1932. D=ROC.
5905	Solikamsk	108,000	54.00	58,500	90.34	B	110,000	Perm on Usolka River. Major salt and potassium mining center, magnesium. F=15th century. D=ROC.
5906	Sosnovyj Bor	55,700	60.00	33,400	96.34	C	56,700	Leningrad on Gulf of Finland near Leningrad. Leningrad nuclear power station. F=1973. D=ROC.
5907	Spassk-Dal'nij	60,000	50.00	30,000	86.34	B	61,100	Near China and Lake Chanka. Cement, concrete, cement-asbestos products, sanitary equipment. D=ROC.
5908	Staryj Oskol (Stary Oskol)	179,000	58.00	104,000	94.34	B	182,000	Belgorod on Oskol River. Machinery, large cement plant, iron & steel complex. F=1593 as Oskol. D=ROC.
5909	Stavropol' (Voroshilovsk)	323,000	60.00	194,000	96.34	C	328,000	Stavropol near source of Grachovka River. Processing farm produce. Grid pattern. F=1777 as fortress. D=ROC.
5910	Sterlitamak	248,000	25.00	61,900	63.34	B	252,000	Bashkortostan on Belaya River. Synthetic rubber, chemicals, cement. F=1781. D=ROC.
5911	Stupino	73,300	62.00	45,400	98.34	C	74,600	Moscow on Oka River. Metalworking, concrete, cotton, electric locomotives, fiberglass. F=1938. D=ROC.
5912	Suja (Shuya)	67,800	58.00	39,300	94.34	B	69,000	Ivanovo on Teza River. Trade center. Cotton & synthetic fabric processing. F=16th century. D=ROC.
5913	Surgut	257,000	51.00	131,000	89.34	B	261,000	Tyumen on Ob River. Main administrative center of western Siberian oilfields. F=1965. D=ROC.
5914	Sverdlovsk (Ekaterinburg)	1,429,000	59.00	843,000	96.34	B	1,429,000	Sverdlovsk on Iset River. Important for heavy engineering, 200 factories. F=1672 by Old Believers. D=ROC.
5915	Verchn'aga Pysma	52,600	60.00	31,500	96.34	C	53,500	Sverdlovsk north of Sverdlovsk. Anthracite mining region, machine building, sewing, livestock. D=ROC.
5916	Svobodnyj (Svobodny)	79,500	50.00	39,700	86.34	B	80,900	Amur on Zeya River. Transportation center on Trans-Siberian Railroad. Steamship repair. F=1912. D=ROC.
5917	Syktyvkar (Ust Sysolsk)	220,000	50.00	110,000	91.34	B	224,000	Capital of Komi at confluence on Vychegda & Sysola rivers. Shipbuilding, timber. F=1586. D=ROC.
5918	Syzran'	172,000	58.00	99,700	94.34	B	175,000	Kuybyshev on Volga River. Major oil field center & river port. Oil refining. F=1683 as stronghold. D=ROC.
5919	T'umen' (Tyumen)	486,000	56.00	272,000	92.34	B	494,000	Tyumen on Tura River. Transshipment point. Oldest Russian city in Siberia. F=14th century; 1586. D=ROC.
5920	Taganrog	288,000	59.00	170,000	95.34	B	294,000	Rostov on Sea of Azov. Port for coal basin. Birthplace of playwright Anton Chekhov. F=1698 by Peter I. D=ROC.
5921	Talnach	64,500	55.00	35,400	91.34	B	65,600	Krasnoyarsk territory, Kharayel mountains. Majakite, polarite. Copper and nickel ore mines, metallurgy. D=ROC.
5922	Tambov	304,000	60.00	183,000	96.34	C	310,000	Tambov on upper Tsna River. Engineering, chemicals. Gridiron pattern. F=1636 as fortress. D=ROC.
5923	Tichoreck	66,400	58.00	38,500	94.34	B	67,600	Krasnodar. Railway junction & grain center. Flour mills, locomotive repair, oil. D=ROC.
5924	Tichvin	70,500	60.00	42,300	96.34	C	71,800	Leningrad on Sas River. Logging, timber, machine building, metallurgy, chemicals, dairying. D=ROC.
5925	Tobol'sk	95,100	58.00	55,200	94.34	B	96,800	Tyumen on confluence of Irtysh and Tobol Rivers. Large petrochemical complex. F=1587. D=ROC.
5926	Toljatti (Tolyatti, Stavropol)	643,000	57.00	367,000	95.34	B	655,000	Kuybyshev on Volga River. Important chemical center, machinery, large auto works. F=1738. D=ROC.
5927	Tomsk	497,000	58.00	288,000	95.34	B	506,000	Tomsk on Tom River. Bearings, electric equipment. First Siberian university (1888). F=1604 as fort. D=ROC.
5928	Torzok (Torzhok)	49,600	55.00	27,300	91.34	B	50,500	Kalinin on Tvertsa River. Gold embroidery (since 13th century). Traditional wooden architecture. F=1139. D=ROC.
5929	Troick (Troitsk)	88,200	59.00	52,100	95.34	B	89,800	Chelyabinsk on Uy River. Agricultural center, hides, milk, beer, meat. F=1743 as fortress. D=ROC.
5930	Tuapse	62,700	57.00	35,700	93.34	B	63,800	Krasnodar on Black Sea. Ship repair, oil refining and exports. F=1838 around a fortress. D=ROC.
5931	Tujmazy	58,800	28.00	16,500	64.34	B	59,800	Bashkortostan on Usen River. Near Oktabrskij. Sawmilling, plywood, paper, wheat, rye, oats. D=ROC.
5932	Tula	629,000	56.00	352,000	94.34	B	640,000	Tula on Upa River. Lignite, iron, steel, chemicals, samovars. F=1146 as Taydula. D=ROC.
5933	Tulun	52,800	54.00	28,500	90.34	B	53,700	Irkutsk on Iya River and Trans-Siberian Railroad. Lignite, wood, forest industry. F=1922. D=ROC.
5934	Tyndinskij (Tynda)	63,600	48.00	30,500	84.34	B	64,700	Amur. Near Manchuria, China. Food industries, gold fields nearby. F=1975. D=ROC.
5935	Uchta (Ushta, Ukhta)	110,000	50.00	55,100	86.34	B	112,000	Komi on Ukhta River. Oil refining, center of petroleum and natural gas fields. F=1931 as Chibyu. D=ROC.
5936	Ufa	1,138,000	28.00	319,000	67.34	B	1,138,000	Capital of Bashkortostan on Belaya River. Oil refining, power & mining machinery. F=1574. D=ROC.
5937	Ulan-Ude	356,000	45.00	160,000	81.34	B	362,000	Capital of Buryatia at confluence of Selenga and Uda rivers. Major rail junction, glassmaking. F=1666. D=ROC.
5938	Uljanovsk (Ulyanovsk, Simbirsk)	637,000	59.00	376,000	95.34	B	648,000	Ulyanovsk on Volga River. Busses, trucks, machine tools. F=1648 as key fortress. D=ROC.
5939	Usinsk	51,400	45.00	23,100	81.34	B	52,300	Komi on Usa River. South of Arctic Circle. Railroad, oil district, natural gas processing, building materials. D=ROC.
5940	Usolje-Sibirskoje (Usolye-Sibirskoye)	105,000	55.00	57,700	91.34	B	107,000	Irkutsk on Angara river and Trans-Siberian Railroad. Salt, caustic soda, health resort. D=ROC.
5941	Ussurijsk (Voroshilov)	157,000	57.00	89,700	93.34	B	160,000	Primorsky on Trans-Siberian Railroad. Food-processing, footwear. F=1866 as Nikolskoye. D=ROC.
5942	Ust'Ilimsk	110,000	54.00	59,500	90.34	B	112,000	Irkutsk on Angara River. Dam & hydroelectric power station, timber. F=1973. D=ROC.
5943	Ust'Kut	60,700	56.00	34,000	92.34	B	61,800	Irkutsk on Kuta River. River-road transshipment center, ship repair, lumbering, salt deposits. F=1954. D=ROC.
5944	V'az'ma (Vyazma)	58,900	60.00	35,300	96.34	C	59,900	Smolensk on Vazma River. Machinery, furs, food products, lumbering, flax processing. F=1239. D=ROC.
5945	Velikije Luki (Velikige Luki)	113,000	58.00	65,800	94.34	B	115,000	Pskov on Lovat River. Locomotive repair, machinery, radios, clothing, woodworking. F=1166. D=ROC.
5946	Verchn'aja Salda	54,100	53.00	28,700	89.34	B	55,100	Sverdlovsk on Ural mountains. Anthracite mining region, livestock, agriculture, machinery, tools, textiles. D=ROC.
5947	Vicuga (Vichuga)	48,800	57.00	27,800	93.34	B	49,700	Ivanovo. Textiles, cotton, linen milling, wood processing, castings. F=1920 from a number of villages. D=ROC.
5948	Vidnoje	55,900	61.00	34,100	97.34	C	56,900	Moscow, south. Coke gas works, aluminum structural components, gypsum concrete forms. D=ROC.
5949	Vladikavkaz (Ordzhonikidze)	312,000	50.00	156,000	91.34	B	317,000	Capital of North Ossetia on Terek River. Nonferrous metals. F=1784 as Vladicaukaz. D=ROC.
5950	Vladimir	349,000	60.00	210,000	96.34	C	356,000	Vladimir on Klyazma River. F=1108 by Vladimir II Monomakh. Cathedral of the Assumption (1158). D=ROC.
5951	Vladivostok	637,000	50.00	318,000	91.34	B	648,000	Primorsky Kray on Sea of Japan. Major seaport, fish processing. F=1860 as Russian military outpost. D=ROC.
5952	Vol'sk	64,400	55.00	35,400	91.34	B	65,500	Saratov on Volga River. Largest center for cement in ex-USSR. F=18th century as Malykovka. D=ROC.
5953	Volchov	49,200	60.00	29,500	96.34	C	50,100	Rostov on Volkhov River. First hydroelectric station in Soviet Union (1926). D=ROC.
5954	Volgodonsk	178,000	57.00	101,000	93.34	B	181,000	Rostov on Chimlyanskoye reservoir. Hydroelectric station, Volga-Don canals, chemicals, food industries. D=ROC.
5955	Volgograd (Stalingrad)	1,021,000	60.00	613,000	97.34	C	1,021,000	Volgograd on Volga River. Steel, aluminum, chemicals. Major WWII battle (1942-1943). F=1589. D=ROC.
5956	Votzskij	251,000	60.00	151,000	96.34	C	256,000	Volgograd on Volga River. Major petrochemical industry. Electrical energetics, grains. F=1951. D=ROC.
5957	Vologda	284,000	57.00	162,000	95.34	B	289,000	Vologda on Vologda River. Timber, furniture, dairying region, optical goods. Monastery (1147). D=ROC.
5958	Volzsk	60,900	55.00	33,500	91.34	B	62,000	Saratov on Volga River. Natural gas, phosphorite, wheat, rye, oats, potatoes, chemicals, textiles. D=ROC.
5959	Vorkuta	115,000	50.00	57,700	86.34	B	117,000	Komi on Vorkuta River. Stalinist forced-labor camps. F=1932 for coal mining. D=ROC.
5960	Voronez (Voronezh)	938,000	59.00	553,000	95.34	B	939,000	Voronezh on Voronezh River. Center for grain trade & flour milling. F=1586 as fortress. D=ROC.
5961	Voskresensk	80,000	61.00	48,800	97.34	C	81,400	Moscow on Moskva River. Concentrated fertilizers, building materials. D=ROC.
5962	Votkinsk	103,000	56.00	57,500	92.34	B	104,000	Udmurtia on Votka River. Birthplace of Tchaikovsky, museum. F=1759. D=ROC.
5963	Vyborg (Viipuri)	79,700	61.00	48,600	97.34	C	81,100	Leningrad on Gulf of Finland. Fishing port, ship repair, beach resorts. F=12th century. D=ROC.
5964	Vyksa	61,100	57.00	34,800	93.34	B	62,200	Nizhny Novgorod near Oka River. Arose around ferrous metallurgy plant from late 18th century. D=ROC.
5965	Vysnij Volocok (Vyshny Volochyok)	63,500	56.00	35,500	92.34	B	64,600	Kalinin. Textiles, hosiery, wood working, pianos, sawmilling, glass works. F=1770. D=ROC.
5966	Zagorsk (Sergiyev)	116,000	61.00	70,900	97.34	C	118,000	Moscow. Principal seminary in ex-USSR (1742). F=1337 as Trinity-St. Sergius monastery. D=ROC.
5967	Zel'onodol'sk (Zelenodosk)	95,300	27.00	25,700	63.34	B	97,000	Tatarstan on Volga River. Port. Grain milling, wood working, food processing, agricultural machinery. D=ROC.
5968	Zeleznogorsk	87,600	57.00	50,000	93.34	B	89,200	Kursk. Flour milling, sugar refining, distilling, canning, tanning, machine building, chemical enterprises. D=ROC.

Table 10-5–continued opposite

Table 10-5–continued

Rec No 1	Country City 2	Pop 2000 3	AC% 4	Church Members 5	E% 6	W 7	Pop 2025 8	Notes 9
5969	Zigulevsk	44,200	58.00	25,600	94.34	B	45,000	Samara on Volga River near Toljatti. Tanning, flour and sugar milling, metalworks, woodworking. D=ROC.
5970	Zima	52,300	55.00	28,800	91.34	B	53,200	Irkutsk on Zima River. Lumber industry, prefabricated homes, concrete forms, clothing, poultry. D=ROC.
5971	Zlatoust	205,000	58.00	119,000	94.34	B	208,000	Chelyabinsk on Ay River. Important metallurgy center in Ural Mountains. F=1754. D=ROC.
5972	Zukovskij	99,500	60.00	59,700	96.34	C	101,000	Southeast of Moscow. Electric power, chemicals, machinery, metallurgy, urban markets, dairy. D=ROC.
	RWANDA	**7,733,000**	**81.94**	**6,337,000**	**98.86**	**C**	**12,427,000**	**ROMAN CATHOLICS 50.9%, PROTESTANTS 20.9%. PENT-CHAR 16.0%, EVANGELICAL 19.4%, GCC 12.4%**
5973	rural areas	7,258,000	82.07	5,956,000	98.92	C	10,911,000	98.2% (1950), 96.8% (1970), 94.6% (1990), 93.8% (2000), 92.2% (2010), 87.8% (2025)
5974	urban areas	476,000	80.00	380,000	97.92	C	1,516,000	1.8% (1950), 3.1% (1970), 5.3% (1990), 6.1% (2000), 7.7% (2010), 12.2% (2025)
5975	non-metropolitan areas	174,000	80.00	139,000	97.92	C	555,119	*Sources of data:* Censuses of 1970, 1978, and 1991; estimate for 1960.
5976	metropolitan areas	301,000	80.00	241,000	97.92	C	961,000	*Definition:* Kigali, administrative centers of prefectures and important agglomerations and their surroundings.
5977	KIGALI	301,000	80.00	241,000	97.92	C	961,000	On Ruganwa River. Four hills. Shoes, paints, tanning. Squatter's settlement. Muslim quarter. D=RCC,EAR.
	SAHARA	**293,000**	**0.17**	**490**	**24.62**	**A**	**470,000**	**INDEPENDENTS 0.1%, ROMAN CATHOLICS 0.05%. PENT-CHAR 0.1%, EVANGELICAL 0.01%, GCC 0.1%**
5978	rural areas	13,500	0.08	11	16.45	A	8,800	32.1% (1950), 56.6% (1970), 12.2% (1990), 4.6% (2000), 2.4% (2010), 1.8% (2025)
5979	urban areas	280,000	0.17	480	25.02	A	461,000	67.8% (1950), 43.3% (1970), 87.7% (1990), 95.3% (2000), 97.5% (2010), 98.1% (2025)
5980	non-metropolitan areas	64,200	0.14	87	24.99	A	105,810	*Sources of data:* Censuses of 1960 and 1970; estimate for 1974.
5981	metropolitan areas	216,000	0.18	390	25.03	A	355,000	*Definition:* El Aaiun.
5982	EL AAIUN (Laayoun)	216,000	0.18	390	25.03	A	355,000	Northern Sahara near Moroccan border. International Airport. D=RCC.
	SAINT HELENA	**6,300**	**84.73**	**5,300**	**99.86**	**C**	**7,800**	**ANGLICANS 70.1%, PROTESTANTS 8.2%. PENT-CHAR 14.7%, EVANGELICAL 2.4%, GCC 18.5%**
5983	rural areas	1,800	86.48	1,600	99.92	C	1,300	70.5% (1950), 74.8% (1970), 48.3% (1990), 29.3% (2000), 21.0% (2010), 17.1% (2025)
5984	urban areas	4,400	84.00	3,700	99.83	C	6,400	29.5% (1950), 25.1% (1970), 51.6% (1990), 70.6% (2000), 79.0% (2010), 82.8% (2025)
5985	non-metropolitan areas	2,900	84.00	2,400	99.84	C	4,149	*Sources of data:* Censuses of 1966, 1976, and 1987; estimate for 1950.
5986	metropolitan areas	1,600	84.00	1,300	99.81	C	2,300	*Definition:* Jamestown.
5987	JAMESTOWN	1,600	84.00	1,300	99.83	C	2,300	Wharfage, stamps. F=1659 by British East India Company. Cathedral of St. Paul's. D=Anglican.
	SAINT KITTS & NEVIS	**38,500**	**93.57**	**36,000**	**99.93**	**C**	**35,100**	**PROTESTANTS 57.8%, ANGLICANS 25.2%. PENT-CHAR 18.5%, EVANGELICAL 18.4%, GCC 5.4%**
5988	rural areas	25,300	94.90	24,100	99.96	C	19,000	77.6% (1950), 65.8% (1970), 65.3% (1990), 65.8% (2000), 63.2% (2010), 54.1% (2025)
5989	urban areas	13,100	91.00	11,900	99.86	C	16,100	22.3% (1950), 34.1% (1970), 34.6% (1990), 34.1% (2000), 36.7% (2010), 45.8% (2025)
5990	non-metropolitan areas	–	–	–	–	–	–	*Sources of data:* Censuses of 1960, 1970, and 1980.
5991	metropolitan areas	13,700	91.00	12,500	99.86	C	16,800	*Definition:* Basseterre.
5992	BASSETERRE	13,700	91.00	12,500	99.86	C	16,800	Chief port. Sugar refinery. F=1627, rebuilt in 1867 after fire. St. George's church. D=Methodist,Anglican.
	SAINT LUCIA	**154,000**	**93.50**	**144,000**	**98.98**	**C**	**208,000**	**ROMAN CATHOLICS 75.1%, PROTESTANTS 13.2%. PENT-CHAR 8.2%, EVANGELICAL 6.7%, GCC 6.1%**
5993	rural areas	96,000	93.81	90,100	99.16	C	104,000	62.0% (1950), 59.9% (1970), 62.7% (1990), 62.2% (2000), 58.9% (2010), 49.9% (2025)
5994	urban areas	58,300	93.00	54,200	98.68	C	104,000	37.9% (1950), 40.0% (1970), 37.2% (1990), 37.7% (2000), 41.0% (2010), 50.0% (2025)
5995	non-metropolitan areas	–	–	–	–	–	–	*Sources of data:* Censuses of 1960, 1970, 1980, and 1991.
5996	metropolitan areas	64,200	93.00	59,700	98.68	C	115,000	*Definition:* Castries.
5997	CASTRIES	64,200	93.00	59,700	98.68	C	115,000	Deepwater harbor. Exports bananas, sugarcane, rum, molasses, cacao, coconuts. D=RCC.
	SAINT PIERRE & MIQUELON	**6,600**	**97.27**	**6,400**	**99.94**	**C**	**7,200**	**ROMAN CATHOLICS 98.4%, PROTESTANTS 1.0%. PENT-CHAR 2.4%, EVANGELICAL 0.1%, GCC 34.2%**
5998	rural areas	520	98.13	510	99.81	C	420	20.0% (1950), 12.3% (1970), 9.1% (1990), 7.9% (2000), 6.9% (2010), 5.8% (2025)
5999	urban areas	6,000	97.20	5,900	99.95	C	6,800	80.0% (1950), 87.6% (1970), 90.8% (1990), 92.0% (2000), 93.0% (2010), 94.2% (2025)
6000	non-metropolitan areas	55	97.85	54	99.96	C	62	*Sources of data:* Censuses of 1962, 1982, and 1990; estimate for 1950.
6001	metropolitan areas	6,000	97.19	5,800	99.95	C	6,700	*Definition:* St. Pierre.
6002	SAINT-PIERRE	6,000	97.20	5,800	99.95	C	6,700	Subsidized by France. Cod fishing. French speaking, many Basques. F=1604. Mainly RCC.
	SAINT VINCENT	**114,000**	**68.83**	**78,400**	**98.78**	**C**	**131,000**	**PROTESTANTS 29.7%, ANGLICANS 17.3%. PENT-CHAR 21.0%, EVANGELICAL 13.2%, GCC 21.1%**
6003	rural areas	51,500	69.84	36,000	99.79	C	36,500	87.4% (1950), 84.7% (1970), 59.3% (1990), 45.2% (2000), 35.2% (2010), 27.9% (2025)
6004	urban areas	62,400	68.00	42,500	97.95	C	94,300	12.5% (1950), 15.2% (1970), 40.6% (1990), 54.7% (2000), 64.7% (2010), 72.0% (2025)
6005	non-metropolitan areas	30,000	68.00	20,400	97.95	C	45,284	*Sources of data:* Censuses of 1960, 1970, 1980, and 1991.
6006	metropolitan areas	32,400	68.00	22,100	97.95	C	49,000	*Definition:* Urban centers.
6007	KINGSTOWN	32,400	68.00	22,100	97.95	C	49,000	Exports bananas, arrowroot, coconuts, cotton. Few tourists. Botanical gardens (1763). D=Anglican,Methodist.
	SAMOA	**180,000**	**93.92**	**169,000**	**99.94**	**C**	**271,000**	**PROTESTANTS 71.0%, ROMAN CATHOLICS 21.9%. PENT-CHAR 15.7%, EVANGELICAL 14.9%, GCC 47.4%**
6008	rural areas	141,000	94.45	133,000	99.97	C	182,000	87.1% (1950), 79.7% (1970), 79.0% (1990), 78.4% (2000), 75.6% (2010), 66.9% (2025)
6009	urban areas	38,800	92.00	35,700	99.82	C	89,700	12.8% (1950), 20.2% (1970), 21.0% (1990), 21.5% (2000), 24.3% (2010), 33.0% (2025)
6010	non-metropolitan areas	–	–	–	–	–	–	*Sources of data:* Censuses of 1951, 1956, 1961, 1966, 1971, 1976, 1981, 1986, and 1991.
6011	metropolitan areas	39,000	92.00	35,900	99.82	C	90,200	*Definition:* Urban area of Apia, comprising the Faipule districts of Vaimuga West and Foleata East.
6012	APIA	39,000	92.00	35,900	99.82	C	90,200	Exports copra, bananas, cocoa, coffee. Home of Scottish writer Robert Louis Stevenson. D=CCCS,RCC.
	SAN MARINO	**26,500**	**89.68**	**23,800**	**99.88**	**C**	**32,400**	**ROMAN CATHOLICS 88.6%, MARGINALS 1.0%. PENT-CHAR 1.8%, EVANGELICAL 0.00%, GCC 48.6%**
6013	rural areas	1,100	93.83	1,100	99.73	C	800	81.7% (1950), 39.1% (1970), 8.4% (1990), 4.2% (2000), 2.9% (2010), 2.4% (2025)
6014	urban areas	25,400	89.50	22,700	99.89	C	31,600	18.2% (1950), 60.9% (1970), 91.5% (1990), 95.7% (2000), 97.0% (2010), 97.5% (2025)
6015	non-metropolitan areas	22,100	89.50	19,800	99.89	C	27,526	*Sources of data:* Census of 1976; estimate for 1989.
6016	metropolitan areas	3,300	89.49	2,900	99.88	C	4,100	*Definition:* Urban centers.
6017	SAN MARINO	3,300	89.50	2,900	99.89	C	4,100	On Mount Titano. Tourism, wine, building stone, silk. Many Italians. F=4th century AD by Christians. D=RCC.
	SAO TOME & PRINCIPE	**147,000**	**90.00**	**132,000**	**99.90**	**C**	**217,000**	**ROMAN CATHOLICS 75.3%, INDEPENDENTS 10.5%. PENT-CHAR 14.3%, EVANGELICAL 3.1%, GCC 14.7%**
6018	rural areas	78,200	91.76	71,800	99.91	C	83,300	87.0% (1950), 76.6% (1970), 61.1% (1990), 53.2% (2000), 46.7% (2010), 38.3% (2025)
6019	urban areas	68,600	88.00	60,300	99.90	C	134,000	13.0% (1950), 23.3% (1970), 38.9% (1990), 46.7% (2000), 53.2% (2010), 61.6% (2025)
6020	non-metropolitan areas	33,700	88.00	29,600	99.90	C	65,719	*Sources of data:* Censuses of 1950, 1960, and 1970.
6021	metropolitan areas	34,900	88.00	30,700	99.90	C	68,200	*Definition:* Sao TomÂ and Pantufo.
6022	SAO TOME	34,900	88.00	30,700	99.90	C	68,200	On Sao TomÂ Island. Agriculture & fishing. Cocoa. Portuguese, Creole languages, D=RCC,NAC.
	SAUDI ARABIA	**21,607,000**	**3.64**	**787,000**	**54.94**	**B**	**39,965,000**	**ROMAN CATHOLICS 2.9%, INDEPENDENTS 0.3%. PENT-CHAR 0.5%, EVANGELICAL 0.1%, GCC 1.9%**
6023	rural areas	3,081,000	1.49	46,000	46.78	A	3,625,000	84.1% (1950), 51.3% (1970), 21.4% (1990), 14.2% (2000), 11.0% (2010), 9.0% (2025)
6024	urban areas	18,526,000	4.00	741,000	56.30	B	36,340,000	15.9% (1950), 48.6% (1970), 78.5% (1990), 85.7% (2000), 89.0% (2010), 90.9% (2025)
6025	non-metropolitan areas	8,672,000	4.04	350,000	56.39	B	17,705,133	*Sources of data:* Censuses of 1962 and 1974; estimates for 1950 and 1986.
6026	metropolitan areas	9,853,000	3.96	391,000	56.22	B	18,635,000	*Definition:* Cities with 5,000 or more inhabitants.
6027	Abha	93,100	0.10	93	51.40	B	183,000	Capital of Asir. Gardens, fields, streams nearby. Fortress in Manadhir quarter.
6028	Ad-Dammam (Damman)	443,000	3.20	14,200	55.50	B	868,000	On Persian Gulf. Oil, dairying. 93% Arab, 1% European, 1% USA. D=RCC,20 house groups(USA nationals).
6029	Al Jubayl (Jubail)	243,000	0.80	1,900	53.10	B	477,000	On Persian Gulf. New industrial complex. Ancient fishing & pearling village. Huge civil engineering project.
6030	Al-Hufuf (Hofuf)	313,000	0.80	2,500	53.10	B	613,000	Ash Sharqiyah. Agricultural market center, rice & date processing. 94% Arab. 93% Muslim. House of Sa'ud (1700).
6031	Al-Khubar (Al-Khobar)	151,000	0.10	150	51.40	B	296,000	Oasis & port, ash Sharqiyah, on Persian Gulf. Good wells, fertile soil. Dates, watermelon. Aramco.
6032	Al-Madinah (Medina, Yathric)	642,000	0.15	960	51.45	B	1,259,000	Hejaz. Second holiest city in Islam. Pilgrims. Date palms. F=AD135 by Jews. Islamic University.
6033	Al-Mubarraz	168,000	0.40	670	51.70	B	329,000	Ash Sharqiyah north of Al-Hufuf. Arabian horse breeding, dates, wheat, fruit.
6034	Ar-RIYAD (Riyadh)	3,328,000	10.50	349,000	63.80	B	6,098,000	Oil commerce. No churches permitted. Numerous radio believers and house groups. 20,000 USA.
6035	At-Ta'if (Taif, Tayif)	664,000	0.20	1,300	51.50	B	1,302,000	Principal summer resort at 6,165 ft. University city. No Christian activities permitted. One house group (expats).
6036	Buraydah	216,000	0.10	220	51.40	B	424,000	Capital of al-Qasim. Oasis & agricultural center, dates, lemons, oranges.
6037	Ha'il	125,000	0.10	130	51.40	B	245,000	On pilgrimage route from Iraq to Mecca. Regional market & oasis.
6038	Jiddah (Jedda)	1,812,000	1.00	18,100	53.30	B	3,362,000	Hejaz. Red Sea. Oil. Port. Many nationalities and races. No Christian activities permitted; 10 house groups.
6039	Khamis Mushayt	153,000	0.10	150	51.40	B	300,000	Army & air force bases. Wheat, rice, coffee, henna. Thursday market of Mushayt clan.
6040	Makkah (Mecca)	920,000	0.01	92	51.31	B	1,734,000	In Sirat mountains. Chief city of Islam: 3 million pilgrims p.a. No Christians permitted. Great Mosque & Kabbah.
6041	Najran	147,000	0.10	150	51.40	B	288,000	Asir oasis along Yemen frontier. Dates, grains. Once important Christian colony (500-635).
6042	Tabuk	231,000	0.10	230	51.40	B	453,000	Oasis amid grove of date palms. Turkish fort (1694). Fast growing industrial center.
6043	Yanbu (Yenbo)	206,000	0.10	210	51.40	B	404,000	On Red Sea. Main port for Medina. Pilgrim trade. Petroleum industry.
	SENEGAL	**9,481,000**	**4.93**	**467,000**	**46.01**	**A**	**16,743,000**	**ROMAN CATHOLICS 4.6%, INDEPENDENTS 0.1%. PENT-CHAR 0.3%, EVANGELICAL 0.06%, GCC 3.1%**
6044	rural areas	5,024,000	2.03	102,000	39.57	A	6,371,000	69.5% (1950), 66.5% (1970), 59.6% (1990), 52.9% (2000), 46.5% (2010), 38.0% (2025)
6045	urban areas	4,457,000	8.20	365,000	53.28	B	10,372,000	30.4% (1950), 33.4% (1970), 40.3% (1990), 47.0% (2000), 53.5% (2010), 61.9% (2025)
6046	non-metropolitan areas	1,423,000	8.28	118,000	53.58	B	3,661,113	*Sources of data:* Censuses of 1976 and 1988; survey for 1961.
6047	metropolitan areas	3,034,000	8.16	248,000	53.14	B	6,711,000	*Definition:* Agglomerations of 10,000 or more inhabitants.
6048	DAKAR	2,077,000	9.00	187,000	55.08	B	4,484,000	Chief West African seaport. Peanut-oil refining. F=1857 by French. 'Paris of Africa'. D=RCC,NAC,AoG.
6049	Diourbel	106,000	2.00	2,100	43.58	A	247,000	Market for peanut growing area. Peanut oil, beverages, perfumes. Beautiful mosque. D=RCC.
6050	Kaolack	208,000	11.00	22,900	55.08	B	484,000	Ocean & river port on Saloum River. Exports peanuts, salt. Center of Tijaniyah order of Islam. D=RCC.
6051	Saint-Louis (Ndar)	220,000	1.20	2,600	42.28	A	512,000	Island city & seaport near mouth of Senegal River. Fishing center. F=1659 as earliest French West African colony.
6052	Thies	253,000	5.00	12,600	47.08	A	589,000	Important transportation center. Light industries, processing plants. Peanuts, aluminum phosphate. D=RCC.
6053	Ziguinchor	170,000	12.00	20,400	56.08	B	396,000	Casamance River port. Sawmills, peanut-oil processing. F=1457 by Portuguese. D=RCC.
	SEYCHELLES	**77,400**	**92.72**	**71,800**	**99.55**	**C**	**98,000**	**ROMAN CATHOLICS 90.4%, ANGLICANS 6.7%. PENT-CHAR 5.2%, EVANGELICAL 3.2%, GCC 11.9%**
6054	rural areas	32,100	95.14	30,600	99.72	C	28,000	73.0% (1950), 73.9% (1970), 50.2% (1990), 41.5% (2000), 35.0% (2010), 28.5% (2025)
6055	urban areas	45,300	91.00	41,200	99.43	C	70,000	26.9% (1950), 26.0% (1970), 49.8% (1990), 58.4% (2000), 64.9% (2010), 71.4% (2025)
6056	non-metropolitan areas	17,800	91.00	16,200	99.43	C	27,545	*Sources of data:* Censuses of 1947, 1960, 1971, and 1977; estimate for 1990.
6057	metropolitan areas	27,500	91.00	25,000	99.43	C	42,500	*Definition:* Victoria.
6058	PORT VICTORIA	27,500	91.00	25,000	99.43	C	42,500	On Mahe Island. Deepwater port. Tourism, fishing. 2,000 expats, mainly British. D=RCC,Anglican.
	SIERRA LEONE	**4,854,000**	**10.52**	**510,000**	**59.18**	**B**	**8,085,000**	**PROTESTANTS 3.5%, ROMAN CATHOLICS 3.4%. PENT-CHAR 4.1%, EVANGELICAL 1.7%, GCC 8.0%**
6059	rural areas	3,076,000	9.08	279,000	55.60	B	3,804,000	93.3% (1950), 82.4% (1970), 70.0% (1990), 63.3% (2000), 56.5% (2010), 47.0% (2025)
6060	urban areas	1,779,000	13.00	231,000	65.36	B	4,281,000	6.7% (1950), 17.5% (1970), 30.0% (1990), 36.6% (2000), 43.4% (2010), 52.9% (2025)
6061	non-metropolitan areas	691,000	12.87	88,900	65.34	B	1,662,258	*Sources of data:* Censuses of 1963 and 1974.
6062	metropolitan areas	1,088,000	13.08	142,000	65.37	B	2,619,000	*Definition:* Towns with 2,000 or more inhabitants.
6063	FREETOWN	743,000	16.00	119,000	69.66	B	1,789,000	Chief port, deepwater harbor. Palm oil. F=1787 as haven for slaves. Mosques. D=RCC,NAC,Methodist.
6064	Koindu (Koidu)	117,000	9.00	10,500	59.66	B	281,000	Trade center for rice, palm oil & kernels, cattle. Diamond-mining area. D=RCC,Methodist.

Table 10-5–continued overleaf

Table 10-5–continued

Rec No 1	Country City 2	Pop 2000 3	AC% 4	Church Members 5	E% 6	W 7	Pop 2025 8	Notes 9
6065	Bo	84,600	6.00	5,100	54.66	B	204,000	Capital of Southern province. Commercial center of interior. Ginger, palm oil, coffee. Large hospital. D=RCC.
6066	Kenema	74,300	5.00	3,700	53.66	B	179,000	Capital of Eastern province on Moa River. Timber industry, diamonds. Mende people. D=RCC,Methodist.
6067	Makeni	69,400	6.00	4,200	54.66	B	167,000	Capital of Northern province near Mabole River. Rice, palm oil. Trade center for Temne. D=RCC,Methodist.
	SINGAPORE	**3,567,000**	**11.30**	**403,000**	**72.69**	**B**	**4,168,000**	**ROMAN CATHOLICS 4.0%, PROTESTANTS 3.5%. PENT-CHAR 4.0%, EVANGELICAL 3.3%, GCC 8.2%**
6068	rural areas	–	–	–	–	–	–	0.0% (1950), 0.0% (1970), 0.0% (1990), 0.0% (2000), 0.0% (2010), 0.0% (2025)
6069	urban areas	3,567,000	11.30	403,000	72.69	B	4,168,000	100.0% (1950), 100.0% (1970), 100.0% (1990), 100.0% (2000), 100.0% (2010), 100.0% (2025)
6070	non-metropolitan areas	–	–	–	–	–	86,756	*Sources of data:* Censuses of 1957, 1970, 1980, and 1990.
6071	metropolitan areas	3,587,000	11.24	403,000	72.69	B	4,081,000	*Definition:* City of Singapore.
6072	SINGAPORE	3,587,000	11.30	403,000	72.69	B	4,081,000	Busiest port in Asia. F=1819. St Andrews Cathedral (1862). Chinese, Malay, Indian. D=RCC,Methodist.
	SLOVAKIA	**5,387,000**	**80.27**	**4,324,000**	**99.53**	**C**	**5,393,000**	**ROMAN CATHOLICS 67.9%, PROTESTANTS 11.1%. PENT-CHAR 4.5%, EVANGELICAL 2.1%, GCC 14.1%**
6073	rural areas	2,095,000	80.14	1,679,000	99.40	C	1,505,000	69.9% (1950), 58.9% (1970), 43.5% (1990), 38.8% (2000), 34.2% (2010), 27.9% (2025)
6074	urban areas	3,292,000	80.35	2,645,000	99.61	C	3,888,000	30.0% (1950), 41.0% (1970), 56.4% (1990), 61.1% (2000), 65.7% (2010), 72.1% (2025)
6075	non-metropolitan areas	1,928,000	80.35	1,549,000	99.58	C	2,277,539	*Sources of data:* Census of 1950, 1961, 1970, 1980, and 1991.
6076	metropolitan areas	1,364,000	80.36	1,096,000	99.65	C	1,611,000	*Definition:* Large towns, usually with 5,000 or more inhabitants.
6077	Banska Bystrica	88,100	81.00	71,400	99.86	C	104,000	Capital of Stredoslovensky. Ancient town, mining center since 1200s. 13th century church. D=RCC.
6078	BRATISLAVA	458,000	80.00	366,000	99.56	C	540,000	Capital of Zapadoslovensky. On Danube river. Cultural center, textiles, chemicals. F=Roman Posonium. D=RCC.
6079	Kosice	243,000	80.00	195,000	99.56	C	287,000	Capital of Vychodoslovensky region. Heavy industry, farm products. Many medieval churches. F=c850.
6080	Martin	60,500	82.00	49,600	99.96	C	71,400	Capital of Martin district on Vah River. Furniture, brewery. Slovak National Museum. D=RCC.
6081	Nitra	93,200	80.00	74,500	99.56	C	110,000	Zapadoslovensky region on Nitra River. Religious center, Cyril and Methodius consecrated first church (830).
6082	Poprad	54,800	80.00	43,800	99.56	C	64,700	Capital of Poprad district on Poprad River. F=12th century by Saxon immigrants. D=Lutheran.
6083	Presov	91,000	81.00	73,700	99.86	C	107,000	Vchodoslovensky region. Brewery. F=1247. D=Orthodox bishopric.
6084	Prievidza	55,300	82.00	45,400	99.96	C	65,400	Capital of Prievidza district on Nitra River. 17th century Piarist monastery. Lignite mines. F=12th century. D=RCC.
6085	Trencin	58,800	80.00	47,000	99.56	C	69,400	Capital of Trencin district on Vah River. Trade center, wheat, barley, potatoes, textiles, apparel, food. D=RCC.
6086	Trnava	74,200	81.00	60,100	99.86	C	87,700	Zapadoslovensky region. Railway car manufacturing. 'Slovak Rome' - Heart of Catholicism. F=c650. D=RCC.
6087	Zilina	86,900	80.00	69,500	99.56	C	103,000	Stredoslovensky region. On Vah River. Rail junction, wood processing, cellulose, plastics. F=c1200. D=RCC.
	SLOVENIA	**1,986,000**	**87.47**	**1,737,000**	**99.80**	**C**	**1,818,000**	**ROMAN CATHOLICS 83.5%, PROTESTANTS 1.6%. PENT-CHAR 3.5%, EVANGELICAL 0.7%, GCC 13.3%**
6088	rural areas	941,000	85.44	804,000	99.77	C	655,000	80.0% (1950), 63.0% (1970), 49.5% (1990), 47.3% (2000), 43.6% (2010), 36.0% (2025)
6089	urban areas	1,045,000	89.30	933,000	99.83	C	1,163,000	19.9% (1950), 37.0% (1970), 50.4% (1990), 52.6% (2000), 56.3% (2010), 63.9% (2025)
6090	non-metropolitan areas	527,000	89.23	471,000	99.82	C	587,274	*Sources of data:* Censuses of 1953, 1961, 1971, and 1981.
6091	metropolitan areas	517,000	89.37	462,000	99.84	C	576,000	*Definition:* Urban centers.
6092	LJUBLJANA	325,000	89.00	289,000	99.78	C	362,000	On Ljubljanica River. Turbines, textiles. F=Roman Emona (1st century BC). Bishopric (1461). D=RCC
6093	Maribor (Marburg)	192,000	90.00	173,000	99.93	C	214,000	On Drava River. Popular resort & winter sports center. Heavy industry. F=1147. 12th century cathedral. D=RCC.
	SOLOMON ISLANDS	**444,000**	**90.88**	**403,000**	**99.89**	**C**	**817,000**	**ANGLICANS 38.2%, PROTESTANTS 35.8%. PENT-CHAR 13.9%, EVANGELICAL 22.4%, GCC 13.5%**
6094	rural areas	356,000	92.57	330,000	99.99	C	531,000	91.7% (1950), 91.0% (1970), 85.4% (1990), 80.3% (2000), 74.4% (2010), 64.9% (2025)
6095	urban areas	87,300	84.00	73,300	99.51	C	286,000	8.2% (1950), 8.9% (1970), 14.5% (1990), 19.6% (2000), 25.5% (2010), 35.0% (2025)
6096	non-metropolitan areas	38,900	84.00	32,700	99.51	C	127,598	*Sources of data:* Censuses of 1970, 1976, and 1986.
6097	metropolitan areas	48,300	84.00	40,600	99.51	C	158,000	*Definition:* Places with a population of 1,000 or more.
6098	HONIARA	48,300	84.00	40,600	99.51	C	158,000	On Mataniko River. Port trades in coconuts, timber, fish. National museum. D=Ch of Melanesia.
	SOMALIA	**7,265,000**	**1.36**	**98,600**	**43.83**	**A**	**16,227,000**	**ORTHODOX 1.2%, INDEPENDENTS 0.08%. PENT-CHAR 0.1%, EVANGELICAL 0.01%, GCC 0.1%**
6099	rural areas	5,267,000	1.02	53,700	42.36	A	9,327,000	87.2% (1950), 79.6% (1970), 75.7% (1990), 72.5% (2000), 67.3% (2010), 57.4% (2025)
6100	urban areas	1,997,000	2.25	44,900	47.72	A	6,900,000	12.7% (1950), 20.3% (1970), 24.2% (1990), 27.4% (2000), 32.6% (2010), 42.5% (2025)
6101	non-metropolitan areas	540,000	2.20	11,900	47.65	A	2,389,961	*Sources of data:* Census of 1986; estimates for 1953 and 1963.
6102	metropolitan areas	1,457,000	2.27	33,000	47.75	A	4,510,000	*Definition:* Towns with 5,000 or more inhabitants.
6103	Kismaayo (Chismayu, Kismayu)	97,100	0.80	780	39.27	A	335,000	Indian Ocean seaport. Banana export industry, meat-processing. F=1872 by Sultan of Zanzibar.
6104	MUQDISHO (Mogadishu)	1,277,000	2.50	31,900	48.97	A	3,887,000	Indian Ocean seaport. Bananas. F=10th century by Arabs. D=RCC(1,000 Somalis),radio believers.
6105	Merca (Marca, Marka, Merka)	83,200	0.40	330	38.87	A	287,000	Indian Ocean seaport. Banana exports. F=10th century by Arab or Persian traders.
	SOMALILAND	**2,833,000**	**0.30**	**8,400**	**44.69**	**A**	**4,984,000**	**ORTHODOX 0.1%, INDEPENDENTS 0.1%. PENT-CHAR 0.1%, EVANGELICAL 0.02%, GCC 0.1%**
6106	rural areas	2,054,000	0.22	4,500	43.63	A	2,865,000	87.2% (1950), 79.6% (1970), 75.7% (1990), 72.5% (2000), 67.3% (2010), 57.4% (2025)
6107	urban areas	779,000	0.50	3,900	47.49	A	2,119,000	12.7% (1950), 20.3% (1970), 24.2% (1990), 27.4% (2000), 32.6% (2010), 42.5% (2025)
6108	non-metropolitan areas	581,000	0.50	2,900	47.49	A	1,580,612	*Sources of data:* Surveys.
6109	metropolitan areas	198,000	0.51	1,000	47.49	A	539,000	*Definition:* Urban areas.
6110	Berbera	95,300	0.20	190	44.59	A	259,000	On Gulf of Aden. Exports sheep, hides & skins. Soviet-built naval base. Medieval Muslim settlement.
6111	Hargeyisa (Hargeisa)	103,000	0.80	820	50.19	B	279,000	El. 4,377 ft. Former summer capital. Important nomadic center. Destroyed in 1980s civil war.
	SOUTH AFRICA	**40,377,000**	**78.76**	**31,801,000**	**98.06**	**C**	**46,015,000**	**INDEPENDENTS 45.8%, PROTESTANTS 30.7%. PENT-CHAR 52.5%, EVANGELICAL 11.2%, GCC 19.1%**
6112	rural areas	20,047,000	85.62	17,163,000	99.24	C	17,592,000	56.9% (1950), 52.1% (1970), 51.1% (1990), 49.6% (2000), 46.1% (2010), 38.2% (2025)
6113	urban areas	20,330,000	72.00	14,637,000	96.90	C	28,424,000	43.1% (1950), 47.8% (1970), 48.8% (1990), 50.3% (2000), 53.8% (2010), 61.7% (2025)
6114	non-metropolitan areas	6,989,000	71.99	5,032,000	97.11	C	5,717,904	*Sources of data:* Censuses of 1951, 1960, 1970, and 1985.
6115	metropolitan areas	13,340,000	72.00	9,606,000	96.79	C	22,706,000	*Definition:* All population agglomerations of an urban nature, without regard to local boundaries and status.
6116	Bloemfontein	329,000	71.00	233,000	95.80	C	460,000	Capital of Orange Free State. El. 4,568 ft. Gold mining. F=1846 as fort. D=RCC,NGK.
6117	Botshabelo	134,000	72.00	96,300	91.30	C	187,000	Birthplace of Jan Gerard Sekoto. Muslim Youth Movement, Mpuma Langa. 'Place of Refuge'. D=RCC.
6118	Mangaung	112,000	71.00	79,300	90.30	C	156,000	Orange Free State. Agriculture, maize, sorghum, potatoes, wheat, sheep, cattle, mining, chemicals.
6119	CAPE TOWN (KAAPSTAD)	3,092,000	72.00	2,226,000	97.30	C	5,356,000	Scenic city & seaport at 3,500 ft. Petroleum refining, chemicals. F=1652 by Dutch. D=RCC,NGK.
6120	Bellville	96,400	73.00	70,400	92.30	C	135,000	On Elsies River. Wheat growing region, metal working, machinery, fertilizer, large research hospital. D=RCC.
6121	Elsies River	98,000	71.00	69,600	90.30	C	137,000	Western Cape. Commercial, industrial, motor vehicles, leather, plastic goods, clothing, fruits, vegetables. D=NGK.
6122	Grassy Park	70,200	71.00	49,800	90.30	C	98,100	Western Cape. Was low-income. Black residential area before 1994, during apartheid era. D=Methodist.
6123	Guguleto	89,400	72.00	64,300	91.30	C	125,000	Western Cape. Food products, chemicals, fertilizer processing, leather, tourism, markets. D=RCC.
6124	Nyanga	208,000	70.00	146,000	89.30	C	291,000	Western Cape. Ship repair, tourism, wine, fruit, leather goods, financial and industrial, plastics, metals. D=RCC.
6125	Paarl	89,100	71.00	63,200	90.30	C	125,000	On Groot-Berg River. Vineyards, citrus fruits, tobacco, olives. Educational center. F=1688 by Huguenots. D=NGK.
6126	Parow	84,300	70.00	59,000	89.30	C	118,000	Western Cape. Inland to the east. Wingfield military airport. Now merged with Bellville fertilizers. D=RCC.
6127	Carletonville	169,000	71.00	120,000	94.80	C	236,000	Principal gold-mining center. Suffers from Sinkhole destruction. World's deepest gold mine 11,837 ft. D=RCC.
6128	Durban	1,379,000	72.00	993,000	96.30	C	2,418,000	Chief seaport & major container port. Headquarters of sugar industry. Many parks. Tourism. F=1824. D=ZCC.
6129	Empumalanga	67,000	72.00	48,300	91.30	C	93,700	Natal. Sugar refineries, textiles, clothing, rubber, fertilizer, detergent, paper, food processing, tanneries. D=ZCC.
6130	Kwa Makuta	99,800	71.00	70,900	90.30	C	140,000	Natal. Railroad, timber industries, textiles, tanning, sugar, chemicals, citrus fruits, sorghum, bananas. D=ZCC.
6131	Kwa Mashu	156,000	71.00	111,000	90.30	C	218,000	Natal. Began acting as Black residencies to provide segregated housing for Durban. D=ZCC.
6132	Ntuzuma	86,500	72.00	62,300	91.30	C	121,000	Natal. Railroad, textiles, detergents, fertilizers, paper products, food processing, rubber, clothing. D=ZCC.
6133	Pinetown	78,000	73.00	56,900	92.30	C	109,000	Natal. Inland to the west. Palmist River valley. Fruit growing, commercial poultry production, high income. D=ZCC.
6134	Umlazi	273,000	72.00	196,000	91.30	C	381,000	Natal. Commercial, industrial, financial, textiles, rubber, paper, markets, clothing, shoes, sugar refining. D=ZCC.
6135	East London (Oos Londen)	448,000	71.00	318,000	96.30	C	626,000	Indian Ocean port. Beach resort, fishing, natural history museum. F=1836 by British. D=RCC,ZCC.
6136	Mdantsane	332,000	70.00	232,000	89.30	C	464,000	Ciskei near East London. Maize, wool, fruit, motor vehicles, furniture, textiles, footwear, glass, fishing. D=RCC.
6137	Ga-Rankuwa	76,500	75.00	57,400	96.30	C	107,000	Bophuthatswana. D=RCC,Independents.
6138	Johannesburg	2,412,000	72.00	1,737,000	95.30	C	4,178,000	Transvaal. Center of gold-mining industry. El. 5,709 ft. Commercial center. F=1886. D=ZCC,RCC.
6139	Alberton	92,500	73.00	67,500	92.30	C	129,000	Gauteng. Southeast beyond Rand Airport. Heavy industry, steel, iron production, large population growth. D=RCC.
6140	Alexandra	94,100	72.00	67,700	91.30	C	132,000	Gaukng. North beyond Bramley. High population density, almost entire population in Black commuters. D=ZCC.
6141	Benoni	133,000	71.00	94,300	90.30	C	186,000	Iron & steel works, brass foundry. El. 5,419 ft. F=1887 as gold-mining camp. D=RCC,NOK.
6142	Boksburg	155,000	71.00	110,000	90.30	C	217,000	Gold mining in deep shafts. Electric motors, cranes, glazed ceramics. F=1887. D=RCC,NGK.
6143	Brakpan	64,900	73.00	47,400	92.30	C	90,800	Mining & industrial complex. Wide, tree-lined streets. Residential. F=1886. D=ZCC,NGK.
6144	Daveyton	139,000	72.00	99,800	91.30	C	194,000	Gauteng. East beyond Benoni. Gold mining district, iron, steel, electrical equipment, sports. D=ZCC.
6145	Diepmeadow	269,000	71.00	191,000	90.30	C	377,000	Gauteng. Gold mining, diamond cutting, industrial chemicals, cement, paper and paper products. D=RCC.
6146	Germiston	163,000	72.00	118,000	91.30	C	228,000	El. 5,550 ft. Rail repair shops. Largest gold bullion refinery in the world. Chemicals. F=1886. D=RCC.
6147	Kagiso	70,800	73.00	51,700	92.30	C	99,000	Gauteng. PG Glass Co., Kagiso Trust Investment. Gold mining, iron and steel processing. D=NGK.
6148	Katlehong	193,000	72.00	139,000	91.30	C	269,000	Gautoong. South beyond Alberton. Steel and iron production, plastics, cement, electrical equipment. D=RCC.
6149	Kempton Park	123,000	72.00	88,300	91.30	C	172,000	Northeast near Johannesburg Airport. Iron, brick, cement works, gold mining region. D=NGK.
6150	Krugersdorp	103,000	73.00	75,300	92.30	C	144,000	Mining center. Uranium as by-product since 1952. El. 5,709 ft. F=1887. Annual pilgrimage center. D=ZCC.
6151	Kwa-Thema	110,000	72.00	79,200	91.30	C	154,000	South of Brakpan. Gold and coal mining district, iron and steel industry, machinery. D=NGK,ZCC.
6152	Randburg	104,000	73.00	75,900	92.30	C	145,000	Residential town, numerous suburbs. Garden city, many parks. Vintage car museum. D=NGK,RCC.
6153	Randfontein	61,200	73.00	44,700	92.30	C	85,600	Gold mining, uranium, engineering, food processing, textiles. Mainly black. F=1887. D=ZCC.
6154	Roodepoort-Maraisburg	198,000	71.00	141,000	90.30	C	277,000	Gold mining. Diversified manufacturing, modern residential area. F=1886. D=NGK.
6155	Sandton	120,000	73.00	87,900	92.30	C	168,000	Brewery, Astra Pharmaceuticals, Delhi Palace, Rand Merchant Bank. D=NGK,Methodist.
6156	Soweto (Meadowlands-Jabavu)	730,000	71.00	518,000	90.30	C	1,021,000	Black townships. Shanty towns, slums. Soweto Rebellion (1976). Mainly commuters. D=ZCC.
6157	Springs	95,400	73.00	69,700	92.30	C	133,000	Manufacturing (paper, foodstuffs, cosmetics), gold mining. F=1885 as coal mine. El. 5,338 ft. D=RCC.
6158	Tembisa	209,000	72.00	150,000	91.30	C	292,000	North. Dormitory town for workers from Johannesburg and Pretoria. D=ZCC.
6159	Vosloosrus	72,800	73.00	53,200	92.30	C	102,000	Gauteng. Gold and coal mining, plastics, cement, heavy industry, mining equipment, machinery. D=RCC.
6160	Westonaria	65,100	73.00	47,500	92.30	C	91,000	Far west south of Donaldson Dam. Residential, industrial, chemicals, electrical equipment. D=NGK.
6161	Kimberley	203,000	71.00	144,000	94.80	C	284,000	Cape. Diamond-mining center. Gardens & squares. F=1869. D=Anglican,RCC,NGK.
6162	Galeshewe	88,400	71.00	62,800	90.30	C	124,000	Northern Cape. Diamond mining region, textiles, construction material, railroad. D=RCC,NGK,Methodist.
6163	Klerksdorp	287,000	71.00	204,000	94.80	C	401,000	Principal goldfields center. Grains. F=1837 as first Boer settlement in Transvaal. D=RCC,NGK.
6164	Newcastle	281,000	71.00	200,000	94.90	C	393,000	Natal. Ncandu River. Coal mining. Construction materials, wool market. F=1864 by British. D=ZCC.
6165	Madadeni	92,100	71.00	65,400	90.30	C	129,000	Natal. Coal mining, steel and iron works, building materials, livestock, textiles. D=ZCC,Methodist.
6166	Oziweni	72,600	72.00	52,300	91.30	C	102,000	Natal. Coal mining, steel and iron works, grain markets, dairying, textiles. D=ZCC.
6167	Pietermaritzburg	322,000	70.00	225,000	97.30	C	450,000	Capital of Natal. University of Natal. Rubber, aluminum. Queen Elizabeth Nature Reserve. D=ZCC.
6168	Edendale	65,700	70.00	46,000	89.30	C	91,900	Natal. West on the river. Residential and commercial, industrial, markets, plastics, chemicals, textiles. D=ZCC.
6169	Port Elizabeth-Uitenhage	1,226,000	73.00	895,000	99.30	C	2,233,000	Cape. Port on Algoa Bay, Indian Ocean. Automotive industry, tourism, exports ores. F=1820. D=RCC.
6170	Kayamnandi	308,000	73.00	225,000	92.30	C	431,000	Western Cape. Algoabaai. Automotive parts, leather goods, clothing, fruit, vegetables. D=RCC.
6171	Kwanobuhle	73,300	74.00	54,200	93.30	C	102,000	Western Cape. Residential, vegetables, fruit, leather goods, fertilizers, metal working, machinery. D=RCC.
6172	Uitenhage	76,900	74.00	56,900	93.30	C	108,000	Auto assembly, railway workshops, textiles. Sheep and goat farming district. F=1804 by Dutch. D=RCC.
6173	PRETORIA	1,558,000	72.00	1,122,000	96.30	C	2,813,000	Capital of Transvaal. On Apies River. Government-based economy. Well planned. Parks. F=1855. D=RCC,NGK.
6174	Atteridgeville-Saulsville	103,000	73.00	75,000	92.30	C	144,000	Transvaal. Iron and steel industries, residential, many museums, machine shops, flour mills. D=RCC,ZCC.

Table 10-5–continued opposite

Table 10-5–continued

Rec No 1	Country City 2	Pop 2000 3	AC% 4	Church Members 5	E% 6	W 7	Pop 2025 8	Notes 9
6175	Mamelodi	178,000	72.00	128,000	91.30	C	248,000	Transvaal. East. Residential, jacaranda trees, colleges, university, commercial, textiles, mills. D=RCC,NGK.
6176	Soshanguve	95,900	74.00	71,000	93.30	C	134,000	Transvaal. Glass, commercial, motor vehicle assembly nearby, machinery, textiles. D=Methodist.
6177	Verwoerdburg	68,400	73.00	49,900	92.30	C	95,600	Transvaal. Educational and cultural region, universities, administrative, railroad, machinery. D=RCC.
6178	Vereeniging	1,259,000	73.00	919,000	99.30	C	2,332,000	Transvaal on Vaal River. Coal, iron, steel, glass. F=1892 around coal mine. Demonstrations (1960). D=ZCC.
6179	Evaton	73,500	73.00	53,700	92.30	C	103,000	Transvaal. Iron and steel production, coal, brickworks, glass, textiles, diverse heavy industry. D=RCC.
6180	Sasolburg	87,900	74.00	65,000	93.30	C	123,000	Orange Free State. Coal, oil, petrochemicals, maize, sorghum, potatoes, wheat, livestock. F=1954. D=RCC.
6181	Vanderbijlpark	83,700	73.00	61,100	92.30	C	117,000	Transvaal on Vaal River. Major steel-producing center of south Africa. F=1942. D=RCC,NGK.
6182	Welkom	301,000	71.00	213,000	95.00	C	420,000	Orange Free State. Gold mining, uranium, slaughtering, steel making, sawmilling. F=1947. D=RCC,ZCC.
6183	Thabong	60,800	71.00	43,200	90.30	C	85,000	Orange Free State. Sheep cattle, potatoes, wheat, sorghum, agricultural center, mining, markets. D=RCC.
	SOUTH KOREA	**46,844,000**	**39.88**	**18,682,000**	**98.80**	**B**	**52,533,000**	**PROTESTANTS 18.9%, INDEPENDENTS 16.4%. PENT-CHAR 16.1%, EVANGELICAL 19.5%, GCC 28.4%**
6184	rural areas	6,483,000	31.05	2,013,000	99.32	B	3,598,000	78.6% (1950), 59.2% (1970), 26.1% (1990), 13.8% (2000), 8.8% (2010), 6.8% (2025)
6185	urban areas	40,361,000	41.30	16,669,000	98.72	B	48,934,000	21.3% (1950), 40.7% (1970), 73.8% (1990), 86.1% (2000), 91.1% (2010), 93.1% (2025)
6186	non-metropolitan areas	9,139,000	41.19	3,764,000	99.27	B	13,912,866	*Sources of data:* Censuses of 1955, 1960, 1966, 1970, 1975, 1980, 1985, and 1990.
6187	metropolitan areas	31,222,000	41.33	12,905,000	98.56	B	35,021,000	*Definition:* Population living in cities irrespective of size of population.
6188	Andong	129,000	30.00	38,600	88.92	B	156,000	Kyongsang-pukto on Naktong River. Alcohol, hemp cloth, silk. F=c57BC. Confucian Academy. D=RCC.
6189	Ch'onan (Cheonan, Chionan)	232,000	45.00	105,000	99.42	B	282,000	Ch'ungch'ong-namdo. Market center for rice barley. Hot springs. Songbul Temple. D=Presbyterian.
6190	Ch'unch'on (Chuncheon)	192,000	40.00	76,600	98.92	B	232,000	Capital of Kangwon-do. Market center for rice, millet, soybeans. Education center. D=RCC.
6191	Ch'ungmu	101,000	30.00	30,400	88.92	B	123,000	Kyongsang-namdo. Deep water port. Fishing, lacquerwork (pearl). Formerly Tongyong. D=Presbyterian.
6192	Chech'on	112,000	50.00	56,100	99.92	B	136,000	Northern Ch'ungch'ong-pukto south of Wonju. Limestone, silicon, cement, paper, ancient irrigation system.
6193	Cheju (Jeju)	256,000	30.00	76,800	88.92	B	310,000	Capital of Cheju-do on Cheju Island. Canning. Samsong-hyol (historic cradle of three families). D=RCC.
6194	Chinhae	132,000	43.00	56,800	98.92	B	160,000	Kyongsang-namdo on Korean Strait. Near Masan. Fishing port, naval base. D=Presbyterian.
6195	Chinju (Jinju)	284,000	33.00	93,800	91.92	B	345,000	Kyongsang-namdo on Mam'ch-on River. Transportation junction. Historic remains. F=578c. D=Presbyterian.
6196	Chongju	547,000	55.00	301,000	99.92	B	663,000	Ch'ungchong pukto. Old inland rural city. Tobacco products, silk weaving. Educational center. D=RCC.
6297	Chonju	569,000	35.00	199,000	99.42	B	690,000	Cholla-pukto near Iri. Rice, primary producer of traditional paper, hanji. D=RCC.
6198	Chungju	547,000	52.00	284,000	99.92	B	663,000	Ch'ungchong-pukto. Fruit, farming, tobacco, waterskiing, boating, fishing, textiles. D=Presbyterian.
6199	Iri	224,000	30.00	67,100	88.92	B	271,000	Cholla-pukto. Market center, largest granary in South Korea, mainly rice. Lack of water. D=Presbyterian.
6200	Kangnung (Gangneung, Gangreung)	168,000	30.00	50,400	88.92	B	203,000	Kangwon-do on Sea of Japan. Administrative center. Tourism, beaches. Ojukhyon shrine. D=RCC.
6201	Kimch'on	89,500	33.00	29,500	91.92	B	108,000	Kyongsang-pukto. Service center. Important market town in Yi dynasty (1392-1910). D=Presbyterian.
6202	Kimhae	117,000	40.00	46,700	98.92	B	142,000	Kyongsang-pukto near Pusan. Nakgong River. Rice, fruit, husbandry, prehistoric remains. D=RCC.
6203	Kimje	143,000	30.00	42,900	88.92	B	173,000	Cholla-pukto south of Iri. Rice, highly developed irrigation system, rye. Confucian shrine. D=Presbyterian.
6204	Kongju	71,700	38.00	27,200	96.92	B	86,900	Ch'ungch'ong-namdo. Rice, barley, sweet potatoes, tobacco. Kyeryong Mountain Natl. Park. D=Presbyterian.
6205	Kumi (Gumi)	227,000	35.00	79,300	93.92	B	275,000	Kyongsang-pukto. Near Kumi & Naktong river junction. Electronics. Point Hanksa Temple. D=RCC.
6206	Kumsong	68,100	35.00	23,800	93.92	B	82,500	Silla Royal Tombs, Badminton Association. 'City of Gold'. D=Presbyterian,RCC.
6207	Kunsan (Gunsan, Gusan)	240,000	34.00	81,600	92.92	B	291,000	Cholla-pukto. Processing, storing, transporting rice. Paper, lumber, rubber. D=Presbyterian,RCC.
6208	Kwangju (Kwangchu, Gwangju)	1,655,000	41.00	679,000	99.42	B	1,996,000	Capital of Cholla-namdo. Center of trade since 57 BC. Cotton textiles. Many old temples & tombs. D=RCC.
6209	Kyongju (Gyeongju)	156,000	30.00	46,800	88.92	B	189,000	Kyongsang-pukto. One million tourists p.a. Hundreds of temples. Sokkuram shrine. F=57 BC. D=RCC.
6210	Kyongsan	66,600	35.00	23,300	93.92	B	80,700	Kyongsang-pukto. Nam River. Vegetables, dairy, apples. Yongnam University. D=Presbyterian.
6211	Masan	687,000	35.00	241,000	98.92	B	833,000	Kyongsang-namdo on Masan Bay. Large commercial & industrial city. Free export zone. Market center. D=RCC.
6212	Changwon (Changweon)	355,000	35.00	124,000	98.92	B	431,000	Kyongsang-namdo on Chinghae Bay. Fishing, soy sauce production, salt. D=Presbyterian.
6213	Miryang	58,300	35.00	20,400	93.92	B	70,700	Kyongsang-namdo. Nakdong River. Rice, barley, persimmon, pears. Buddhist temples. D=Presbyterian.
6214	Mokp'o (Mogpo, Mokpo)	279,000	30.00	83,600	93.92	B	338,000	Cholla-namdo port. Door to largest granary. Marine products, salt chemicals. Opened to trade 1879. D=RCC.
6215	Naju	60,800	40.00	24,300	98.92	B	73,700	Cholla-namdo on Yongsan River. Fruit growing area, pears, peaches. D=Presbyterian.
6216	Namwon	69,400	40.00	27,800	98.92	B	84,200	Southern Cholla-pukto. Home of Chunyang, heroine of famous Korean story. Raw silk spinning. D=Presbyterian.
6217	Onyang	73,000	35.00	25,600	93.92	B	88,500	Kyongsang-namdo near Ulsan. Famed hot springs, Onyang folk museum, tourism. D=RCC.
6218	Osan	65,400	45.00	29,400	99.42	B	79,300	Kyonggi-do south of Suwon. Rapid industrialization, textiles, chemistry, paper, railroad. D=Presbyterian.
6219	P'ohang	350,000	69.00	242,000	99.92	C	425,000	Kyongsang-pukto on Yongil Gulf. Fishing port. Iron & steel, shipbuilding, wine, brandy. Beaches. D=Presbyterian.
6220	P'yongt'aek	87,100	35.00	30,500	93.92	B	106,000	Southern Kyonggi-do near Asan Bay. Gold mining nearby, famous rice, apples, pears, dairying. D=RCC.
6221	Pusan (Busan)	4,239,000	42.00	1,780,000	99.62	B	4,523,000	Capital of Kyongsang-namdo. Largest Korean port. Trade, fishing, plywood, aerospace. Old temples. D=RCC.
6222	Samch'onp'o	69,100	35.00	24,200	93.92	B	83,800	Kyongsang-namdo deep water port. Fishing, pottery, tiles, seafood plants. Samhak cranes. D=Presbyterian.
6223	Sangju	57,100	30.00	17,100	88.92	B	69,200	Western Kyongsang-pukto north of Kimch'on. Rice, mining, graphite, gold, silver. D=RCC.
6224	Sogwipo	97,100	36.00	35,000	94.92	B	118,000	Cheju Island, Sanbanggulsa Temple, Chonjiyon Waterfall, Cheju Art Park. Scuba diving. D=Presbyterian.
6225	Sokch'o	81,200	30.00	24,300	88.92	B	98,400	Kangwon-do on Sea of Japan. Cuttlefish, pollack, mackerel. Chongcho Lagoon. D=Presbyterian,RCC.
6226	Songtan	85,200	35.00	29,800	93.92	B	103,000	Kyonggi-do. Yong Motor Company. U.S. Army base nearby. Rice, barley, beans, poultry. D=Presbyterian.
6227	Sosan	61,500	35.00	21,500	93.92	B	74,600	Ch'ungch'ong-namdo near Yellow Sea. Rice, soybeans, cotton, ginger, garlic, national park on coast. D=RCC.
6228	SOUL (Seoul, Kyongsong)	12,215,000	45.00	5,497,000	99.52	B	12,980,000	On Han River. Capital since 1394. Textiles. Congestion. Educational center. D=Presbyterian,RCC.
6229	Ansan	277,000	45.00	125,000	99.92	B	336,000	Kyonggi-do. Yellow Sea. Metals, chemistry, textiles, paper, famous fishing center. D=Presbyterian.
6230	Anyang	529,000	46.00	243,000	99.92	B	641,000	Kyonggi-do. Largest industrial satellite. Brewing. Yombul-am & Jungcho-sa temples, 9th century. D=RCC.
6231	Bucheon (Puchon)	1,264,000	46.00	581,000	99.92	B	1,705,000	Kyonggi-do. Wigs, sewing machines, cement. Known for peaches. F=1973. D=Presbyterian,RCC.
6232	Hanam	111,000	47.00	52,400	99.92	B	135,000	Kyonggi-do. Han River, Paldong Dam, Seoul bedroom community. Rice farming. D=RCC.
6233	Inch'on (Incheon)	2,837,000	45.00	1,277,000	99.92	B	3,492,000	Kyonggi-do. Fishing port since Yi Dynasty. Seaside recreation. U.S. troops landed 1950. D=Presbyterian.
6234	Kunp'o	110,000	46.00	50,600	99.92	B	133,000	Kyonggi-do. Rail station, golf. Machinery, metals, electronics, traditional folk festival. D=RCC.
6235	Kwachon	79,500	47.00	37,400	99.92	B	96,400	Kyonggi-do. Large amusement park, horticulture, famous flower market. D=Presbyterian.
6236	Kwangmyong	362,000	46.00	166,000	99.92	B	438,000	Kurum Mountain Cultural Festival, Oh Ree Cultural Festival, Lee Won Yk Graveyard. D=Presbyterian.
6237	Mikum	82,100	47.00	38,600	99.92	B	99,600	Kyonggi-do. Electronic, glassware, machinery, textiles, rice, wheat, barley, fruits, vegetables.
6238	Shihung	118,000	46.00	54,200	99.92	B	143,000	Kyonggi-do southwest across Han River from Soul. D=Presbyterian,RCC,Jesus Assembly.
6239	Songnam (Seangnam)	595,000	47.00	280,000	99.92	B	721,000	Kyonggi-do. Rapidly absorbing Seoul industries & population. Highest growth rate. F=1973. D=RCC.
6240	Suwon (Suweon, Powan, Puwan)	1,268,000	46.00	583,000	99.92	B	1,737,000	Capital of Kyonggi-do. Agricultural research center. Many historic remains. F=14th century. D=Presbyterian.
6241	Uijongbu (Eujeongbu)	234,000	45.00	105,000	99.92	B	283,000	Kyonggi-do. Kwangju mountains. Fruits, vegetables, textiles, chemicals, metals, electronics. D=Presbyterian.
6242	Sunch'on (Suncheon)	184,000	31.00	57,000	89.92	B	223,000	Cholla-namdo on Yosu Peninsula. Service center. Songgwang Temple, center of Son Buddhism. D=RCC.
6243	T'aebaek	98,700	30.00	29,600	88.92	B	120,000	Northern Kyongsang-pukto near T'aebaek Mountain. Corn, potatoes, coal mining, lime grottos. D=RCC.
6244	Taech'on	62,600	38.00	23,800	96.92	B	75,900	Ch'ungch'ong-nam on Yellow Sea. Nation's two most important expressways converge here. D=Presbyterian.
6245	Taegu (Daegu, Taiku)	2,559,000	35.00	896,000	99.92	B	2,785,000	Capital of Kyongsang-puk on Kum River. Textiles. Apples. Kyongbuk National University. D=RCC.
6246	Taejon (Daejeon)	1,431,000	39.00	558,000	99.92	B	1,685,000	Capital of Chungchong-nam. Cotton textiles, machines, chemicals. 70% destroyed in WWII. D=RCC.
6247	Tongduchon	78,600	38.00	29,900	96.92	B	95,300	U.S. military camps, north of Seoul, Soyo Mountain. Barley, beans, potatoes, fruit. D=Presbyterian,RCC.
6248	Tongkwang	77,100	37.00	28,500	95.92	B	93,500	Pusan Bank. Plastics, chemicals, ceramics, electronics, clothing, fishing equipment. D=Presbyterian.
6249	Tongnae (Tonghae, Dongnae)	98,100	36.00	35,300	94.92	B	119,000	Kangwon. Pusan-si northeast of Pusan. Fishery (pike, squid), largest cement factory in Korea. D=Presbyterian.
6250	Uiwang	107,000	40.00	42,600	98.92	B	129,000	Railway Museum, Korean Railroad Research Institute. Rail station, paints and resins. D=Presbyterian.
6251	Ulsan	967,000	34.00	329,000	98.92	B	1,164,000	Kyongsang-namdo on Sea of Japan. Major industrial complex and open port. Shipbuilding. D=RCC.
6252	Wonju (Weonju)	190,000	40.00	76,100	98.92	B	231,000	Kangwon-do on South Han River. Military. Market for forest products. Traditional laquerware. D=RCC.
6253	Yoch'on	70,200	35.00	24,600	93.92	B	85,100	Mt. Youngchi Azalea Festival. Oil refinery, polyethylene, polypropylene, Buddhist hermitage. D=Presbyterian.
6254	Yongch'on	53,800	36.00	19,400	94.92	B	65,200	Southern Kyongsang-pukto northwest of Kyongju. Rice, fruit, red peppers, garlic, tobacco. D=Presbyterian.
6255	Yongju	92,800	30.00	27,800	88.92	B	112,000	Northern Kyongsang-pukto north of Andong. Rice, soybeans, cotton, hemp, ramie, raw silk. D=Presbyterian.
6256	Yosu (Yeosu)	190,000	31.00	59,000	97.92	B	231,000	Cholla-namdo on Yosu peninsula. Fishing, petrochemicals. Navy headquarters (1392-1910). D=RCC.
	SPAIN	**39,630,000**	**93.55**	**37,074,000**	**99.68**	**C**	**36,658,000**	**ROMAN CATHOLICS 96.0%, INDEPENDENTS 0.8%. PENT-CHAR 2.7%, EVANGELICAL 0.3%, GCC 43.2%**
6257	rural areas	8,869,000	94.07	8,343,000	99.98	C	5,994,000	48.1% (1950), 33.9% (1970), 24.6% (1990), 22.3% (2000), 19.9% (2010), 16.3% (2025)
6258	urban areas	30,761,000	93.40	28,730,000	99.60	C	30,665,000	51.8% (1950), 66.0% (1970), 75.3% (1990), 77.6% (2000), 80.0% (2010), 83.6% (2025)
6259	non-metropolitan areas	11,467,000	93.37	10,707,000	99.64	C	11,403,400	*Sources of data:* Censuses of 1950, 1960, 1970, 1981, and 1991.
6260	metropolitan areas	19,294,000	93.41	18,023,000	99.58	C	19,261,000	*Definition:* Municipalities with 10,000 or more inhabitants.
6261	Albacete	129,000	95.00	122,000	99.83	C	128,000	Capital of Albacete on Don Juan River. Market center for fruit & saffron. Christian/Moor battles (1146). D=RCC.
6262	Alcala de Guadaira	52,100	95.00	49,500	99.83	C	51,900	Andalucia east of Seville beyond the airport. Parks, artistic interest, olives, pimientos, ruined castle. D=RCC.
6263	Alcoy	67,500	96.00	64,800	99.93	C	67,300	Alicante, Valencia. Center for textile industry. Festival of St. George. Founded by Moors. D=RCC.
6264	Algeciras	102,000	96.00	97,700	99.93	C	101,000	Cadiz, Andalusia on mouth of Rio de la Miel. Shipment port, tourism. F=713 by Moors. D=RCC.
6265	Alicante	267,000	95.00	253,000	99.83	C	266,000	Capital of Alicante, Valencia on Mediterranean Sea. Commercial port of Madrid. F=325 BC by Greeks. D=RCC.
6266	Almeria	161,000	95.00	153,000	99.83	C	161,000	Capital of Almeria, Andalusia on Mediterranean Sea. Resort center. Moroccan appearance. D=RCC.
6267	Aviles	134,000	95.00	127,000	99.83	C	133,000	Oviedo, Asturias on inlet of Bay of Biscay. Resort, iron & steel, fishing. Medieval churches. D=RCC.
6268	Badajoz	125,000	95.00	119,000	99.83	C	125,000	Capital of Badajoz, Extremadura on Guadiana River. Roman origins. 13th century cathedral. D=RCC.
6269	Barcelona	2,819,000	92.50	2,608,000	99.63	C	2,819,000	Capital of Barcelona, Catalonia. Major Mediterranean port. Tourism. F=680 BC. 6th century basilica. D=RCC.
6270	Badalona	230,000	92.00	212,000	98.13	C	229,000	Northeast industrial suburb on Mediterranean coast. Chemicals, textiles. 15th century monastery. D=RCC.
6271	Granollers	50,100	93.00	46,600	99.13	C	50,000	Catalunya north inland from Mataro. Chemicals, cotton spinning, flour milling. 14th century church.D=RCC.
6272	Hospitalet de Llobregat	285,000	92.00	262,000	98.13	C	284,000	Southwestern industrial suburb. On coastal delta of Llobregat River. Hospital for pilgrims since c1300. D=RCC.
6273	Rubi	49,900	94.00	46,900	99.63	C	49,700	Northwest on Rubi River. Metal manufacturing, electrical equipment, chemicals, construction materials. D=RCC.
6274	San Baudilio de Llobregat	79,200	92.00	72,900	98.13	C	79,000	West across the Llobregat River. North of international airport. Textiles, chemicals, wine making. D=RCC.
6275	Santa Coloma de Gramanet	139,000	93.00	129,000	99.13	C	139,000	Northern industrial suburb. Metallurgical goods, textiles, chemicals. Pre-Roman settlement. D=RCC.
6276	Tarrasa	165,000	92.00	152,000	98.13	C	164,000	Northwest. Woollens. Many medieval churches. Episcopal see from 450. 6th century baptistry. D=RCC.
6277	Bilbao (Vizcaya)	1,011,000	93.00	941,000	99.83	C	1,008,000	Capital of Biscay, Basque country. Most important Spanish port. Metallurgical & chemical industries. D=RCC.
6278	Baracaldo	116,000	94.00	109,000	99.63	C	116,000	On Nervion River. Leading iron and steel center of Spain, machinery, shipbuilding. D=RCC.
6279	Portugalete	59,100	94.00	55,500	99.63	C	58,900	Northwestern suburb on Nervion. Metalworks. Bilbao Bay. Hog market, swimming resort. D=RCC.
6280	Santurce-Antiguo	53,500	93.00	49,700	99.13	C	53,300	Euskal Herriko near Bay of Biscay. Vegetables, fishing, canning, metallurgy, thermal heat station. D=RCC.
6281	Burgos	164,000	95.00	156,000	99.83	C	164,000	Capital of Burgos, Castile-Leon on Arlanzon River. Tourism. F=884. Convents & monasteries. D=RCC.
6282	Caceres	73,200	95.00	69,500	99.83	C	72,900	Capital of Caceres, Extremadura. Cork, leather goods. Medieval, Moorish character. D=RCC.
6283	Cadiz	245,000	94.00	231,000	99.63	C	245,000	Capital of Cadiz, Andalusia on Gulf of Cadiz. Wine, olives. F=1100 BC. 13th century cathedraL D=RCC.
6284	San Fernando	83,800	95.00	79,600	99.83	C	83,500	On rocky island. Spanish naval headquarters, salt, stone. Naval academy, marshes, workshops. F=1776. D=RCC.
6285	Cartagena	177,000	94.00	166,000	99.63	C	176,000	Murcia. Chief Mediterranean naval base. Olive oil, dried fruits. F=3rd century BC. Medieval cathedral. D=RCC.
6286	Castellon de la Plana	135,000	95.00	128,000	99.83	C	134,000	Capital of Castellon, Valencia. Orange, hemp, colored tiles. 14th century Gothic Santa Maria church. D=RCC.
6287	Ciudad Real	57,500	96.00	55,200	99.93	C	57,400	Capital Cuidad Real, Castile-La Mancha. Agricultural market center. F=1255 by Alfonso X the Wise. D=RCC.
6288	Cordoba	309,000	93.00	287,000	98.13	C	308,000	Capital of Cordoba, Andalusia on Guadalquivir River. Moorish character. Capital of Muslim Spain. D=RCC.
6289	Dos Hermanas	70,000	96.00	67,200	99.93	C	69,700	Sevilla, Andalusia. Processing and agricultural center, olive industry, industrial satellite of Seville. D=RCC.
6290	El Ferrol del Caudillo	88,400	95.00	84,000	99.83	C	88,100	La Coruna, Galicia on inlet of Atlantic Ocean. Naval station. Fishing, textiles, canning, food processing. D=RCC.
6291	El Puerto de Santa Maria	63,700	96.00	61,100	99.93	C	63,500	Cadiz, Andalusia on Bay of Cadiz. Sherry wines. F=Roman Portus Menesthei. D=RCC.
6292	Elche	184,000	94.00	173,000	99.63	C	184,000	Alicante, Valencia on Rio Vinalopo. Dates, fronds, olive oil. Annual August medieval drama. D=RCC.
6293	Elda	58,000	96.00	55,700	99.93	C	57,800	Alicante, Valencia. Fertile grain & fruit producing area. F=ancient Idella. D=RCC.
6294	Gerona	133,000	94.00	125,000	99.63	C	133,000	Capital of Gerona, Catalonia on Onar River. Dairying, flour mills, textiles. Gothic cathedral (1292). D=RCC.

Table 10-5–continued overleaf

Table 10-5–continued

Rec No 1	Country City 2	Pop 2000 3	AC% 4	Church Members 5	E% 6	W 7	Pop 2025 8	Notes 9
6295	Gijon	268,000	93.00	249,000	98.13	C	267,000	Oviedo, Asturias on Bay of Biscay. International port of call. Coal. Summer resort. Pre-Roman origins. D=RCC.
6296	Granada	269,000	93.00	250,000	98.13	C	268,000	Capital of Granada, Andalusia on Genil River. Tourism. F=5th century BC. Christian & Moorish bldgs. D=RCC.
6297	Guadalajara	62,700	96.00	60,200	99.93	C	62,500	Capital of Guadalajara, Castile-La Mancha on Rio Henares. Agriculture. Ancient Arriaca. D=RCC.
6298	Huelva	141,000	95.00	134,000	99.83	C	140,000	Capital of Huelva, Andalusia on Gulf of Cadiz. Ore-shipping port, fishing. Ancient origins. D=RCC.
6299	Irun	56,100	96.00	53,900	99.93	C	55,900	Guipuzcoa, Basque on Rio Bidasoa. Customs station for overland travel. Ironworks. D=RCC.
6300	Jaen	109,000	95.00	103,000	99.83	C	108,000	Capital of Jaen, Andalusia. Olive oil. F=Roman Aurinx. Cathedral (1540). D=RCC.
6301	Jerez de la Frontera	187,000	95.00	178,000	99.83	C	186,000	Cadiz, Andalusia on Guadalete River. Sherry wine, horses. Roman origins. Gothic churches. D=RCC.
6302	La Coruna	254,000	94.00	239,000	99.63	C	254,000	Northern Galicia on Rio de Betanzos. Summer resort fishing, shipyards. 13th century church. D=RCC.
6303	La Linea	62,300	96.00	59,800	99.93	C	62,100	Cadiz, Andalusia on Bay of Gibraltar. Fruit, vegetables, cork, fish paste. Military garrison. D=RCC.
6304	Las Palmas de Gran Canaria (Canarias)	374,000	93.00	348,000	98.13	C	373,000	Capital of Las Palmas, Spanish Canary Islands. Main port between Europe & South America. D=RCC.
6305	Leon	163,000	95.00	154,000	99.83	C	162,000	Capital of Leon, Castile-Leon. Tourism based on Christian art. Roman origins. 13th century cathedral. D=RCC.
6306	Lerida	112,000	95.00	107,000	99.83	C	112,000	Capital of Lerida, Catalonia on Segre River. Cattle, agriculture, fruit. Iberian origin. D=RCC.
6307	Linares	59,900	96.00	57,500	99.93	C	59,700	Jaen, Andalusia. Mining, gunpowder, dynamite, rope. Lead smelting. D=RCC.
6308	Logrono	122,000	94.00	114,000	99.63	C	121,000	Capital of La Rioja on Ebro River. Agriculture, wine. Ancient walled town. Santa Maria del Palacio. D=RCC.
6309	Lugo	80,500	96.00	77,300	99.93	C	80,300	Capital of Lugo, Galacia on Rio Mino, Agricultural markets. Romanesque Cathedral (1129). D=RCC.
6310	MADRID	4,072,000	91.50	3,726,000	99.63	C	4,072,000	Madrid at 2,100 ft. Major publishing center, manufacturing, government, tourism. F=10th century. D=RCC.
6311	Alcala de Henares	152,000	91.00	139,000	97.13	C	152,000	University of Alcala de Henaras (16th century). Chemicals, cotton goods. F=Complutum by Romans. D=RCC.
6312	Alcobendas	75,100	93.00	69,800	99.13	C	74,800	North near San Sebastian de los Reyes. International College Spain (1980). D=RCC.
6313	Alcorcon	143,000	92.00	131,000	98.13	C	142,000	Southwest near Mostoles. Railroad, 9 miles southwest from Madrid. Residential, commercial, industrial. D=RCC.
6314	Coslada	70,300	94.00	66,100	99.63	C	70,100	East of Madrid, south of Aeropuerto Barajas. Commercial, printing, clothing, food processing, metals. D=RCC.
6315	Fuenlabrada	132,000	93.00	122,000	99.13	C	131,000	Southwest beyond Leganes. Grain, woolen goods, artificial flowers, sweets, residential, commuters. D=RCC.
6316	Getafe	138,000	92.00	127,000	98.13	C	138,000	South. Military aviation center. Large Piarist seminary, 16th century church of Santa Maria Magadelena. D=RCC.
6317	Leganes	172,000	91.00	157,000	97.13	C	172,000	Southwest beyond Arroyo de Butarque. Mainly residential commuter suburb, some commercial. D=RCC.
6318	Madrid	4,199,000	91.00	3,821,000	97.13	C	4,186,000	Madrid at 2,100 ft. Major publishing center, manufacturing, government, tourism. F=10th century. D=RCC.
6319	Mostoles	186,000	93.00	173,000	99.13	C	185,000	Southwest beyond Alcorcon. Meat packing, celebrated for its declaration of war on Napoleon. D=RCC.
6320	Parla	67,700	93.00	63,000	99.13	C	67,500	Madrid south beyond Getafe, 12 miles south of Madrid. Residential, commercial, clothing, textiles, flowers. D=RCC.
6321	Torrejon de Ardoz	85,100	93.00	79,100	99.13	C	84,800	Northeast on Henares River near airport. Railroad, 11 miles east of Madrid. Fruits, vegetables. D=RCC.
6322	Malaga	587,000	93.00	546,000	99.13	C	585,000	Capital of Malaga, Andalusia on Mediterranean Sea. F=12th century BC. Birthplace of P. Picasso. D=RCC.
6323	Manresa	67,100	96.00	64,400	99.93	C	66,800	Barcelona, Catalonia on Cardoner River. Metallurgy, textiles. Roman origins (Minorisa). D=RCC.
6324	Mataro	103,000	92.00	94,800	98.13	C	103,000	Barcelona Catalonia on Mediterranean Sea. Wine, carnations, potatoes. Roman Iluro center. D=RCC.
6325	Merida	53,500	96.00	51,400	99.93	C	53,400	Extremadira on Guadiana River east of Badajoz. Agricultural hub, textiles, leather, cork, Roman buildings. D=RCC.
6326	Murcia	321,000	95.00	305,000	99.83	C	320,000	Capital of Murcia. Citrus fruits, almonds, cereals, silk. Ermita de Jesus (pilgrimage center). D=RCC.
6327	Orense	108,000	96.00	104,000	99.93	C	108,000	Capital of Orenge, Galacia on Rio Mino. Sawmills. Medieval family mansions. Roman Urentae. D=RCC.
6328	Oviedo	194,000	95.00	185,000	99.83	C	194,000	Capital of Oviedo, Asturias. Mining. F=757 as monastery by Fruela I. Cathedral (1388). D=RCC.
6329	Palencia	78,400	96.00	75,200	99.93	C	78,100	Capital of Palencia, Castile-Leon. Communications center. Iron, rugs. Gothic cathedral (1321). D=RCC.
6330	Palma de Mallorca	325,000	95.00	308,000	99.83	C	324,000	Capital of Balearic Islands. Tourism, furniture. embroidery. Ancient origins. Gothic cathedral (1230). D=RCC.
6331	Pamplona	185,000	95.00	175,000	99.83	C	184,000	Capital of Navarra on Rio Arga. Fiesta de San Fermin (July 6-14). F=75 BC. Gothic cathedral (c1400).
6332	Ponferrada	58,200	96.00	55,900	99.93	C	58,000	Leon, Castile-Leon at Sil & Boeza rivers. Coal & iron mining. 10th century Mozalapic church. D=RCC.
6333	Puertollano	53,400	96.00	51,300	99.93	C	53,300	Cuidad Real, Castile-La Mancha. Mining, metallurgy, chemicals. Mineral baths. D=RCC.
6334	Reus	85,600	96.00	82,200	99.93	C	85,400	Tarragona, Catalonia. Textiles, wine. Salou Beach nearby. F=13th century. Church of San Pedro. D=RCC.
6335	Sabadell	194,000	95.00	184,000	99.83	C	193,000	Barcelona, Catalonia. Textiles, metallurgy. Iberian origins. Churches destroyed in riots 1835, 1909. D=RCC.
6336	Salamanca	163,000	95.00	155,000	99.83	C	162,000	Capital of Salamanca. Ancient origins. University (1218). Bishopric since 7th century. D=RCC.
6337	San Cristobal de la Laguna	114,000	95.00	108,000	99.83	C	114,000	Canary Islands on Tenerife on Atlantic Ocean. Bananas, tomatoes, potatoes, tobacco, beaches, tourism. D=RCC.
6338	San Sebastian (Guipuzcoa, Donostia)	52,800	95.00	50,200	99.83	C	52,600	Capital of Guipuzcoa, Basque on Bay of Biscay. Seaside resort, fishing. F=1014. Gothic church (1507). D=RCC.
6339	Santa Cruz de Tenerife	220,000	95.00	209,000	99.83	C	219,000	Capital of Tenerife, Canary Islands. Oil bunkering port. Tourism, bananas, tomatoes. F=1494. D=RCC.
6340	Santander	195,000	95.00	185,000	99.83	C	194,000	Capital of Cantabria on Bay of Biscay. Fishing, iron refining, shipbuilding. Roman origins. Episcopal see. D=RCC.
6341	Santiago de Compostela	90,100	95.00	85,600	99.83	C	89,800	La Coruna, Galacia at confluence of Sar and Sarela rivers. Agriculture. Shrine of St. James (pilgrimage). D=RCC.
6342	Segovia	55,600	96.00	53,400	99.93	C	55,400	Capital of Segovia, Castile-Leon. Agriculture. F=700 BC. Many medieval churches. D=RCC.
6343	Sevilla (Seville)	678,000	94.00	637,000	99.63	C	676,000	Capital of Seville, Andalusia. Ancient origins. One of largest cathedrals in the world (1403). D=RCC.
6344	Talavera de la Reina	69,700	96.00	66,900	99.93	C	69,400	Toledo, Castile-La Mancha on Tagus River. Cereals. Birthplace of historian Juan de Mariana. D=RCC.
6345	Tarragona	112,000	95.00	106,000	99.83	C	112,000	Capital of Tarragona, Catalonia on Rio Francoli. Exports, tourism. Iberian origins. Y=AD 60 by St Paul. D=RCC.
6346	Toledo	60,900	96.00	58,400	99.93	C	60,700	Capital of Toledo, on Tagus River. Urban area is a national monument. Pre-Roman origins. D=RCC.
6347	Valencia	754,000	93.00	701,000	99.13	C	758,000	Capital of Valencia on Mediterranean Sea and Turia River. Textiles. F=2nd century BC by Romans. D=RCC.
6348	Torrente	57,000	96.00	54,700	99.93	C	56,800	Inland from Gulf of Valencia. Rich farming region, chocolate, wine making, cereals, olives. D=RCC.
6349	Valladolid	339,000	94.00	318,000	99.63	C	338,000	Capital of Valladolid, on Pisuerga River. C. Columbus (d. 1506). F=1074. University(1346). D=RCC.
6350	Vigo	277,000	95.00	263,000	99.83	C	276,000	Pontevedra, Galacia on Atlantic Ocean. Fishing, naval station. Medieval chapel. D=RCC.
6351	Vitoria	209,000	95.00	198,000	99.83	C	208,000	Capital of Alava, Basque on Rio Zadorra. Furniture. F=581 by Visigoths. Cathedral (1180). D=RCC.
6352	Zamora	63,400	96.00	60,900	99.93	C	63,200	Capital of Zamora, Castile-Leon on Duero River. Agricultural trade. Four 12th century churches. D=RCC.
6353	Zaragoza (Saragossa)	595,000	93.00	553,000	99.83	C	593,000	Capital of Zaragoza, Aragon on Rio Ebro. Roman origins. Bishop since 3rd century. D=RCC.
	SPANISH NORTH AFRICA	**130,000**	**80.25**	**104,000**	**93.42**	**C**	**140,000**	**ROMAN CATHOLICS 79.1%, INDEPENDENTS 0.6%. PENT-CHAR 2.3%, EVANGELICAL 0.2%, GCC 8.7%**
6354	rural areas	13,000	77.99	10,100	91.20	C	14,000	20.0% (1950), 20.0% (1970), 15.0% (1990), 10.0% (2000), 10.0% (2010), 10.0% (2025)
6355	urban areas	117,000	80.50	94,200	93.67	C	126,000	80.0% (1950), 80.0% (1970), 85.0% (1990), 90.0% (2000), 90.0% (2010), 90.0% (2025)
6356	non-metropolitan areas	–	–	–	–	–	–	*Sources of data:* Censuses.
6357	metropolitan areas	154,000	80.55	124,000	93.72	C	166,000	*Definition:* Urban areas.
6358	CEUTA	84,000	81.00	68,100	94.17	C	90,500	Free port on Mediterranean coast of Morocco. Fishing, tourism. European character. Jebel Musa. D=RCC.
6359	Melilla	69,700	80.00	55,800	93.17	C	75,100	Old walled town built on a huge rock on Mediterranean coast. Iron ore. Colonized by Phoenicians. D=RCC.
	SRI LANKA	**18,827,000**	**9.32**	**1,755,000**	**64.57**	**B**	**23,547,000**	**ROMAN CATHOLICS 6.6%, INDEPENDENTS 1.7%. PENT-CHAR 2.1%, EVANGELICAL 0.4%, GCC 7.4%**
6360	rural areas	14,391,000	7.94	1,143,000	62.14	B	14,453,000	85.5% (1950), 78.1% (1970), 78.7% (1990), 76.4% (2000), 71.1% (2010), 61.3% (2025)
6361	urban areas	4,436,000	13.80	612,000	72.45	B	9,094,000	14.4% (1950), 21.8% (1970), 21.2% (1990), 23.5% (2000), 28.8% (2010), 38.6% (2025)
6362	non-metropolitan areas	1,538,000	13.81	212,000	72.47	B	3,152,547	*Sources of data:* Censuses of 1953, 1963, 1971, and 1981.
6363	metropolitan areas	2,898,000	13.79	400,000	72.44	B	5,941,000	*Definition:* Municipalities, urban councils and towns.
6364	Batticaloa	57,300	6.00	3,400	61.25	B	118,000	East coast on Indian Ocean south of Trincomalee. Beaches. D=RCC.
6365	COLOMBO	2,351,000	15.00	353,000	74.25	B	4,820,000	Indian Ocean port. Processing raw materials for export. F=cAD 500. Dutch church (1749). D=RCC.
6366	Battaramulla	73,100	15.00	11,000	74.25	B	150,000	On Indian Ocean. Beaches. Flowering trees, gardens. Overseas Childrens School. D=RCC.
6367	Dehiwala-Mount Lavinia	221,000	17.00	37,600	76.25	B	454,000	Southern residential suburb. Zoo, seaside resort known for its beaches. D=RCC.
6368	Kotte	131,000	16.00	20,900	75.25	B	268,000	Southeast. Rice paddies & plantations. Natural defense of lagoons, rivers & swamps. D=RCC.
6369	Moratuwa	190,000	16.00	30,500	75.25	B	390,000	South on Indian Ocean. Beach resorts. gardens, gems, ivory. D=RCC.
6370	Galle (Point de Galle)	95,200	10.00	9,500	65.25	B	195,000	Indian Ocean port. Shipping, cement factory. F=13th century. Chief fort under Portuguese (1507-1640). D=RCC.
6371	Jaffna	147,000	12.30	18,100	70.55	B	301,000	Capital of Northern Province. Agricultural trade center, fishing. Tamil character. D=RCC.
6372	Kandy	118,000	5.00	5,900	60.25	B	242,000	Kandy Plateau on Mahaweli River. Most of Sri Lanka's tea, rice. Temple of the Tooth (Buddhist). D=RCC,SDA.
6373	Negombo	73,400	10.00	7,300	65.25	B	150,000	North of Colombo on Indian Ocean. Beach resorts. Fishing, coconuts, ceramics. International airport.
6374	Trincomalee	56,200	5.00	2,800	60.25	B	115,000	East coast on Indian Ocean. Natural harbor. Beach resorts. Tea, coconut plantations. F=1676. D=RCC.
	SUDAN	**29,490,000**	**16.53**	**4,874,000**	**53.81**	**B**	**46,264,000**	**ROMAN CATHOLICS 10.6%, ANGLICANS 7.8%. PENT-CHAR 2.2%, EVANGELICAL 2.6%, GCC 6.4%**
6375	rural areas	18,838,000	15.41	2,904,000	51.28	B	20,911,000	93.6% (1950), 83.6% (1970), 73.3% (1990), 63.8% (2000), 55.0% (2010), 45.2% (2025)
6376	urban areas	10,652,000	18.50	1,971,000	58.28	B	25,353,000	6.3% (1950), 16.3% (1970), 26.6% (1990), 36.1% (2000), 44.9% (2010), 54.8% (2025)
6377	non-metropolitan areas	5,883,000	18.53	1,090,000	58.40	B	14,682,348	*Sources of data:* Censuses of 1956, 1973, and 1983.
6378	metropolitan areas	4,769,000	18.47	881,000	58.13	B	10,670,000	*Definition:* Localities of administrative and/or commercial importance or with a population of 5,000 or more.
6379	Al-Fashir (El Fasher)	133,000	0.50	670	34.78	A	317,000	Capital of Darfur ash-Shamaliyah. Historic caravan center. Cereals, fruits, gum.
6380	AL-KHARTUM (3 Towns of Khartoum)	2,748,000	23.00	632,000	66.78	B	5,861,000	Conurbation. Tanning. Mainly Arab. 22% Black. F=1823. D=RCC.
6381	Umm Durman (Omdurman)	831,000	25.00	208,000	67.28	B	1,977,000	Left bank of main Nile River. Hides, gumarabic, textiles. Islamic University (1912). Traditional markets. D=RCC.
6382	Al-Khartum Bahri (Khartoum North)	538,000	18.00	96,800	59.28	B	1,280,000	East bank of The Nile. Main industrial center, dockyards, marine & rail workshops. Cotton, grains. D=RCC.
6383	Al-Qadarif (El Gedaref)	184,000	0.50	920	34.78	A	439,000	Commercial center for cotton, cereals, sesame seeds. Arabs, Nubians, Beja.
6384	Al-Ubayyid (El Obeid)	217,000	8.08	17,500	49.36	A	517,000	Surrounded by forest. Gumarabic. F=1821. D=RC Diocese,Coptic Orthodox church (1 priest).
6385	Atbarah (Atbara)	115,000	0.50	580	34.78	A	274,000	An Nil on Nile River. Commercial & agricultural center, government railways, cement.
6386	Bur Sudan (Port Sudan)	325,000	0.50	1,600	34.78	A	774,000	Capital of al-Bahr al-Ahmar on Red Sea. Principal seaport. Exports cotton, gum arabic. Arabs, Nubians, Beja.
6387	Juba	133,000	85.00	113,000	97.28	C	317,000	Capital of al-Istumyah ash-Sharqiyah. Tobacco, coffee. 50% Bari, 20% Zande. D=RCC,Anglican.
6388	Kassala	223,000	8.00	17,900	49.28	A	531,000	Capital of Kassala. Extensive market trade, fruit gardens. F=1834 by Egyptians.
6389	Kusti (Kosti)	141,000	0.50	700	34.78	A	335,000	Al-Bahr, al-Abyad on White Nile River. Agricultural economy.
6390	Nyala	176,000	0.50	880	34.78	A	420,000	Capital of Darfur al-Janubiyah. Textiles, processed food, leather. Trade center for gumarabic.
6391	Wad Madani (Medoni)	229,000	0.60	1,400	34.88	A	545,000	Capital of al-Jazirah on Blue Nile River. Peanuts, wheat, cotton. F=19th century by Egyptians. University (1975).
6392	Waw (Wau)	144,000	65.00	93,300	95.28	C	342,000	On River Jur. Cotton, tobacco. Destroyed 1965, rebuilt 1972. D=RCC,Anglican.
	SURINAME	**417,000**	**41.31**	**172,000**	**83.77**	**B**	**525,000**	**ROMAN CATHOLICS 22.3%, PROTESTANTS 17.1%. PENT-CHAR 2.6%, EVANGELICAL 2.8%, GCC 17.0%**
6393	rural areas	199,000	26.34	52,500	72.07	B	180,000	53.1% (1950), 54.0% (1970), 53.1% (1990), 47.7% (2000), 41.9% (2010), 34.2% (2025)
6394	urban areas	218,000	55.00	120,000	94.46	B	345,000	46.8% (1950), 45.9% (1970), 46.8% (1990), 52.2% (2000), 58.0% (2010), 65.7% (2025)
6395	non-metropolitan areas	–	–	–	–	–	–	*Sources of data:* Censuses of 1950, 1964, and 1971.
6396	metropolitan areas	275,000	55.00	151,000	94.46	B	436,000	*Definition:* Greater Paramaribo.
6397	PARAMARIBO	275,000	55.00	151,000	94.46	B	436,000	On Suriname River. Tourism. Dutch colonial architecture. F=French (c1640). D=RCC,EGBS.
6398	Wanica	62,800	55.00	34,500	94.46	B	99,400	Across bay from Paramaribo on Atlantic Ocean. D=RCC,EGBS.
	SVALBARD & JAN MAYEN	**3,700**	**47.58**	**1,700**	**99.37**	**B**	**4,700**	**PROTESTANTS 27.2%, ORTHODOX 20.3%. PENT-CHAR 2.5%, EVANGELICAL 4.0%, GCC 29.0%**
6399	rural areas	740	45.89	340	97.71	B	700	40.0% (1950), 30.0% (1970), 25.0% (1990), 20.0% (2000), 20.0% (2010), 15.0% (2025)
6400	urban areas	2,900	48.00	1,400	99.79	B	4,000	60.0% (1950), 70.0% (1970), 75.0% (1990), 80.0% (2000), 80.0% (2010), 85.0% (2025)
6401	non-metropolitan areas	2,300	48.02	1,100	99.78	B	3,173	*Sources of data:* Censuses.
6402	metropolitan areas	600	47.93	290	99.83	B	820	*Definition:* Longyearbyen.
6403	LONGYEARBYEN (Longyear City)	600	48.00	290	99.79	B	820	Administrative center. Tourism, mining, trapping. No indigenous inhabitants. D=Ch of Norway,ROC.
	SWAZILAND	**1,008,000**	**67.55**	**681,000**	**99.36**	**C**	**1,785,000**	**INDEPENDENTS 45.6%, PROTESTANTS 15.2%. PENT-CHAR 52.0%, EVANGELICAL 12.2%, GCC 26.9%**
6404	rural areas	648,000	67.63	438,000	99.44	C	832,000	98.6% (1950), 90.2% (1970), 73.6% (1990), 64.2% (2000), 56.0% (2010), 46.6% (2025)
6405	urban areas	360,000	67.40	243,000	99.21	C	953,000	1.3% (1950), 9.7% (1970), 26.3% (1990), 35.7% (2000), 43.9% (2010), 53.3% (2025)
6406	non-metropolitan areas	260,000	67.38	175,000	99.19	C	687,423	*Sources of data:* Censuses of 1956, 1966, 1976, and 1986.

Table 10-5–continued opposite

Table 10-5–continued

Rec No 1	Country City 2	Pop 2000 3	AC% 4	Church Members 5	E% 6	W 7	Pop 2025 8	Notes 9
6407	metropolitan areas	100,000	67.44	67,600	99.25	C	265,000	*Definition:* Localities proclaimed as urban.
6408	Manzini (Bremersdorp)	44,100	68.00	30,000	99.81	C	117,000	Near Great Usutu River. Corn, cotton, dairies, beef, meat-processing. F=1887 by trader (Bremer). D=Nazarene.
6409	MBABANE	56,200	67.00	37,700	98.81	C	149,000	Capital. Light industry. Small town atmosphere. D=Anglican,RCC,Methodist,Zionist.
	SWEDEN	**8,910,000**	**67.34**	**6,000,000**	**98.43**	**C**	**9,097,000**	**PROTESTANTS 94.5%, ROMAN CATHOLICS 1.9%. PENT-CHAR 6.9%, EVANGELICAL 9.9%, GCC 28.0%**
6410	rural areas	1,486,000	74.05	1,101,000	99.60	C	1,180,000	34.1% (1950), 18.8% (1970), 16.9% (1990), 16.6% (2000), 15.6% (2010), 12.9% (2025)
6411	urban areas	7,424,000	66.00	4,900,000	98.19	C	7,917,000	65.8% (1950), 81.1% (1970), 83.1% (1990), 83.3% (2000), 84.4% (2010), 87.0% (2025)
6412	non-metropolitan areas	2,769,000	67.15	1,860,000	98.33	C	2,999,953	*Sources of data:* Censuses of 1950, 1960, 1965, 1970, 1975, 1980, 1985, and 1990; estimate for 1992.
6413	metropolitan areas	4,655,000	65.31	3,040,000	98.11	C	4,917,000	*Definition:* Built-up areas with at least 200 inhabitants and usually not more than 200 meters between houses.
6414	Boras	106,000	65.00	69,000	96.09	C	113,000	Alvborg on Viskan River. Leading textile center, cotton & woolen mills. F=1622. Kinnarumma church. D=SK.
6415	Eskilstuna	93,600	67.00	62,700	98.09	C	99,800	Sodermanland on Eskilstuna River. Metal industry, cutlery, precision instruments. F=12th century. D=SK.
6416	Gavle	92,300	67.00	61,900	98.09	C	98,500	Capital of Gavleborg on Gulf of Bothnia. Export city, paper, leather. F=8th century. Popular resort. D=SK.
6417	Goteborg (Gothenburg)	763,000	65.00	496,000	99.09	C	806,000	Capital of Goteborg och Bohus on Gota River estuary. Chief port. Paper, timber. F=1603. Y=1633. D=SK.
6418	Molndal	54,200	68.00	36,900	99.09	C	57,900	Southern Goteborg south of Goteborg. Industrial suburb, paper products, metals, fisheries. D=SK.
6419	Halmstad	83,500	67.00	55,900	98.09	C	89,000	Capital of Halland on the Kattegat. Engineering, smoked salmon. F=14th century. 14th century church. D=SK.
6420	Helsingborg (Halsingborg)	114,000	65.00	74,100	99.09	C	121,000	Malmohus on the Sound. Leading shipping center, shipbuilding. F=1085. 13th century Gothic church. D=SK.
6421	Jonkoping	116,000	65.00	75,600	99.09	C	124,000	Capital of Jonkoping on Lake Vatter. Matches, paper, textiles. F=1283 by Franciscans. D=SK.
6422	Karlstad	79,700	67.00	53,400	98.09	C	85,000	Capital of Varmland on Lake Vanern. Forest products, heavy machinery. F=1584. Cathedral city (1645). D=SK.
6423	Linkoping	127,000	65.00	82,900	96.09	C	136,000	Capital of Ostergotland on Stang River. Aircraft, freight cars, autos. Ancient origins. 15th century cathedral. D=SK.
6424	Lulea	71,300	67.00	47,800	98.09	C	76,100	Norrbotten on Gulf of Bothnia. F=1621. Seat of Lutheran bishop. Gammelstad church (c.1400). D=SK.
6425	Lund	91,400	67.00	61,300	98.09	C	97,500	Malmohus. Educational center-university founded 1671. F=1020 by Danes. Bishopric (1060). D=SK.
6426	Malmo	464,000	66.00	306,000	99.09	C	495,000	Malmohus on The Sound. Shipbuilding. Busy port. F=13th century. 14th century St Peter's Church. D=SK.
6427	Norrkoping	126,000	65.00	81,700	99.09	C	134,000	Ostergotland on Motala Strom. Engineering, textiles, paper. F=1350. Medieval churches. D=SK.
6428	Orebro	126,000	65.00	82,000	99.09	C	134,000	Capital of Orebro on Svart River. Commercial center by 13th century. Gothic church 13th century. D=SK.
6429	STOCKHOLM	1,582,000	64.50	1,020,000	97.09	C	1,648,000	On Lake Malar and Baltic Sea. Metal industries, paper, printing. F=1252. Riddarholm church (c1250). D=SK.
6430	Huddinge	77,000	64.00	49,300	97.09	C	82,100	Southern suburb. Wooded & rolling. 50 sq. miles. Hosiery, metal, concrete. Commuter residences. D=SK.
6431	Jarfalla	58,800	65.00	38,200	98.09	C	62,700	Stockholm. Residential, commercial, industrial, vegetables, metals, clothing, textiles, flour milling. D=SK.
6432	Nacka	66,800	64.00	42,700	97.09	C	71,200	Southeastern suburb on Sodertorn peninsula. Chemical technology, flour milling, motors. D=SK.
6433	Sodertalje (Talje)	85,300	64.00	54,600	97.09	C	90,900	Southwestern suburb. 19th century spa. Manufacturing. F=10th century. St. Ragnhild's Church (1200). D=SK.
6434	Sollentuna	53,600	66.00	35,400	99.09	C	57,100	Stockholms northwest of Stockholm. Residential suburb, textiles, clothing, metals, printing, porcelain. D=SK.
6435	Solna	54,100	65.00	35,100	98.09	C	57,600	Northwestern suburb. Manufacturing, medical center. Ancient settlement. 12th century church. D=SK.
6436	Taby	59,100	64.00	37,800	97.09	C	63,100	Stockholms north of Stockholm. 15th century church, several stones with runic inscriptions. D=SK.
6437	Tumba	71,500	65.00	46,500	98.09	C	76,200	Stockholms southwest of Stockholm near Sodertalje. Bank notes paper mill (1755). D=SK.
6438	Sundsvall	97,800	67.00	65,500	98.09	C	104,000	Vasternorrland on Gulf of Bothnia. One of world's most important pulp-producing regions. F=1621. D=SK.
6439	Trollhattan	53,200	68.00	36,200	99.09	C	56,800	Alvsborg on Gota River. Hydroelectric power stations. Once known for waterfalls. F=1916. D=SK.
6440	Umea	95,200	67.00	63,800	98.09	C	101,000	Capital of Vasterboten on Umea River. Educational & cultural center for northern Sweden. F=1622. D=SK.
6441	Uppsala	175,000	65.00	114,000	99.09	C	186,000	Capital of Uppsala. Originally Ostra Aros. Center for religion & education. Gothic cathedral (1435). D=SK.
6442	Vasteras	125,000	65.00	81,200	99.09	C	133,000	Capital of Vastmanland on Lake Malar. Largest inland port. F=1100. 13th century cathedral. Bishopric. D=SK.
6443	Vaxjo	72,500	68.00	49,300	99.09	C	77,300	Capital of Kronoberg on Lake Vaxjo. Matches, furniture, paper. F=medieval trade center. Bishopric. D=SK.
	SWITZERLAND	**7,386,000**	**87.27**	**6,446,000**	**98.23**	**C**	**7,587,000**	**ROMAN CATHOLICS 44.1%, PROTESTANTS 41.1%. PENT-CHAR 6.4%, EVANGELICAL 4.0%, GCC 34.4%**
6444	rural areas	2,764,000	89.40	2,471,000	98.69	C	2,096,000	55.6% (1950), 45.5% (1970), 40.3% (1990), 37.4% (2000), 33.7% (2010), 27.6% (2025)
6445	urban areas	4,622,000	86.00	3,975,000	97.96	C	5,491,000	44.3% (1950), 54.4% (1970), 59.6% (1990), 62.5% (2000), 66.2% (2010), 72.3% (2025)
6446	non-metropolitan areas	624,000	85.92	536,000	97.80	C	800,886	*Sources of data:* Censuses of 1950, 1960, 1970, and 1980; estimate for 1991.
6447	metropolitan areas	3,998,000	86.01	3,438,000	97.98	C	4,691,000	*Definition:* Communes with 10,000 or more inhabitants, including suburbs.
6448	Aarau	64,600	88.00	56,800	98.96	C	76,700	Capital of Aarau on Aare River. Tourism. Electrical goods. F=1240. German-speaking. 75% Protestant. D=FEPS.
6449	Baden	78,700	88.00	69,300	98.96	C	93,500	Aargau on Limmat River. Hot sulphur springs. F=1291 by Habsburgs. German-speaking. Mainly Catholic. D=RCC.
6450	Basel (Basle, Bale)	631,000	86.00	542,000	98.96	C	749,000	Capital of Basel-Stadt on Rhine River. Pharmaceuticals. F=Celts. Bishopric since 5th century. D=RCC.
6451	BERN (Berne)	327,000	85.00	278,000	97.96	C	389,000	On Aare River. Government, precision instruments. Tourism. F=1191 as military post. Cathedrals. D=RCC.
6452	Biel (Bienne)	91,200	88.00	80,200	98.96	C	108,000	Bern on Lake Biel. Watchmaking. 2/3 German, 1/3 French. Celtic origins. F=11th century. D=RCC.
6453	Fribourg (Freiburg)	64,900	89.00	57,700	98.96	C	77,100	Capital of Fribourg on La Sarine River. Chocolate. French-speaking. F=1157. Center of Swiss Catholicism.
6454	Geneve (Genf, Geneva)	515,000	85.00	438,000	97.96	C	612,000	Capital of Geneve on Lake Geneva. HQ of many international agencies. F=c100 BC by Celts. WCC HQ.
6455	Lausanne	289,000	87.00	251,000	97.96	C	343,000	Capital of Vaud on Lake Geneva. Precision instruments. Cathedral de Notre-Dame. M=YWAM.
6456	Locarno (Luggarus)	46,400	88.00	40,900	98.96	C	55,200	Ticino on Lake Maggiore. Noted health & tourist resort. Prehistoric origins. Italian-speaking. D=RCC.
6457	Lugano (Lauis)	104,000	87.00	90,400	97.96	C	124,000	Ticino on Lake. Tourism, international finance. F=6th century. Italian-speaking. D=RCC.
6458	Luzern (Lucerne)	179,000	86.00	154,000	97.96	C	212,000	Capital of Luzern on Reuss River. Tourism. F=8th century as monastery. German-speaking. D=RCC.
6459	Neuchatel (Neuenburg)	72,900	88.00	64,100	98.96	C	86,600	Capital of Neuchatel on Lake Neuchatel. Watches. Collegiate Notre Dame (12th century). F=11th century. D=RCC.
6460	Sankt Gallen (Saint-Gall)	139,000	86.00	120,000	96.96	C	165,000	Capital of Sankt Gallen. Textiles. Library w/2000 rare manuscripts. F=612 by Celt St. Gall. Monastery (720).
6461	Schaffhausen (Schaff-House)	58,700	88.00	51,600	98.96	C	69,700	Capital of Schaffhausen on Rhine River. Tourism. F=1045. Monastery (1049). German-speaking Protestant.
6462	Thun (Thoune)	86,600	88.00	76,200	98.96	C	103,000	Bern on Aare River. Cheese, watches. F=12th century. Scherzligen Church (12th century). D=FEPS.
6463	Vevey	71,400	88.00	62,800	98.96	C	84,800	Vaud on Lake Geneva east of Lausanne. Popular tourist resort, NestlÃ corporation headquarters. D=RCC.
6464	Winterthur	119,000	86.00	103,000	96.96	C	142,000	Zurich. Heavy engineering, cotton textiles. F=1175. Town church of St. Laurenz (1264). D=FEPS.
6465	Zug (Zoug)	75,300	88.00	66,300	98.96	C	89,500	Capital of Zug on Lake Zug. F=1242. German-speaking. Capuchin monastery (1597). D=RCC.
6466	Zurich	984,000	85.00	836,000	96.96	C	1,110,000	Capital of Zurich. Tourism, conferences. Prehistoric origins. Zwingli residence. D=FEPS.
	SYRIA	**16,125,000**	**7.80**	**1,258,000**	**62.21**	**B**	**26,292,000**	**ORTHODOX 4.9%, ROMAN CATHOLICS 2.0%. PENT-CHAR 0.6%, EVANGELICAL 0.2%, GCC 4.9%**
6467	rural areas	7,342,000	3.37	248,000	54.20	B	8,695,000	69.3% (1950), 56.6% (1970), 49.8% (1990), 45.5% (2000), 40.5% (2010), 33.0% (2025)
6468	urban areas	8,783,000	11.50	1,010,000	68.91	B	17,597,000	30.6% (1950), 43.3% (1970), 50.2% (1990), 54.4% (2000), 59.4% (2010), 66.9% (2025)
6469	non-metropolitan areas	1,697,000	11.54	196,000	68.85	B	4,183,980	*Sources of data:* Censuses of 1960, 1970 and 1981; estimate for 1990.
6470	metropolitan areas	7,087,000	11.49	814,000	68.92	B	13,413,000	*Definition:* Cities, *mohafaza* centers and *mantika* centers.
6471	Al-Hasakah (Hassaka, Hasakeh)	141,000	1.00	1,400	52.41	B	283,000	On Khabur River. Center of irrigated farming region. Wheat, rice, cotton, oil. Assyrian refugees from Iraq (1932).
6472	Al-Ladhiqiyar (Latakia)	375,000	13.00	48,700	72.41	B	751,000	Capital of Al-Ladhiqiyar on Mediterranean Sea. Principal port. Bitumen. Phoenician Ramitha. D=RCC.
6473	Al-Qamishli (Qamishliye)	190,000	0.50	950	49.91	A	381,000	On Turkish border. Cotton. F=1926. Armenians, Kurds, Assyrians. Bishopric of Syrian Catholics, Armenians.
6474	Ar-Raqqah (Raqqa, Rakka)	170,000	2.00	3,400	54.41	B	341,000	Capital of Ar-Raqqah on Euphrates River. Market center, Tabaqah Dam. Ancient Greek origins.
6475	Dar'a (Der'a, Edrei)	95,400	10.00	9,500	67.41	B	191,000	Hawran. Market center, garrison town. Wheat, barley. Greco-Roman ruins. Mosque (1253).
6476	Dayr az-Zawr (Deir ez-zor)	169,000	1.00	1,700	52.41	B	338,000	Capital of Dayr az-Zawr on Euphrates River. Farming, cattle breeding. F=1867 by Ottomans.
6477	DIMASHQ (Damas, Damascus)	2,335,000	11.00	257,000	69.41	B	4,258,000	Capital of Dimashq on Barada River. Oldest continuously inhabited city in the world (4,000 years). D=GOC,RCC.
6478	Darayya	80,100	11.00	8,800	68.41	B	160,000	Dimashq southwest of Damascus near international airport. Apartment buildings.
6479	Duma	99,600	11.00	11,000	68.41	B	199,000	Dimashq northeast of Damascus. Inlaid wood, silk.
6480	Jaramanah	146,000	10.00	14,600	67.41	B	292,000	Dimashq southeast of Damascus. Jewelry, handicrafts.
6481	Halab (Alep, Aleppo)	2,173,000	15.00	326,000	73.41	B	3,989,000	Capital of Halab. Silk weaving. Muslim schools. F=2000 BC. Great Mosque (715). Byzantine citadel (12th century).
6482	Hamar (Hama, Hamah)	334,000	10.00	33,400	67.41	B	670,000	On Orontes River. Market, famous gardens. Biblical Hamath. Churches became mosques (7th century).
6483	Hims (Homs)	673,000	15.00	101,000	73.41	B	1,348,000	On Orontes River. Wheat, corn, jewelry, oil. Ancient Emesa. Christians martyred by Muslims (855). D=GOC,RCC.
6484	Idlib	99,500	15.00	14,900	73.41	B	199,000	Capital of Idlib. Textile & agricultural market. Spinning, olive oil pressing.
6485	Kabir as Saghir	71,900	0.50	360	49.91	A	144,000	Market center, garrison town. Wheat, barley. D=GOC,RCC.
6486	Madinat ath Thawrah	87,600	0.70	610	50.11	B	175,000	Ar-Raqqah on Euphrates River west of Ar-Raqqah.
6487	Salamiyah	70,500	0.50	350	49.91	A	141,000	Hamah southeast of Hamah.
6488	Tartus (Tartous)	101,000	15.00	15,200	74.41	B	203,000	Capital of Tartus on Mediterranean Sea. Ancient Antaradus. Cathedral of Our Lady of Tortosa (c1250). D=RCC.
	TAIWAN	**22,401,000**	**5.27**	**1,180,000**	**68.85**	**B**	**25,730,000**	**INDEPENDENTS 2.0%, PROTESTANTS 1.7%. PENT-CHAR 1.6%, EVANGELICAL 0.9%, GCC 3.6%**
6489	rural areas	5,376,000	5.48	294,000	62.74	B	5,146,000	36.0% (1950), 31.0% (1970), 27.0% (1990), 24.0% (2000), 22.0% (2010), 20.0% (2025)
6490	urban areas	17,025,000	5.20	885,000	70.78	B	20,584,000	64.0% (1950), 69.0% (1970), 73.0% (1990), 76.0% (2000), 78.0% (2010), 80.0% (2025)
6491	non-metropolitan areas	6,367,000	5.34	340,000	70.80	B	6,078,582	*Sources of data:* Censuses.
6492	metropolitan areas	10,658,000	5.12	545,000	70.77	B	14,505,000	*Definition:* Urban areas.
6493	Banqiao (Panchiao, Taipei-hsien)	588,000	6.00	35,300	69.58	B	711,000	Southwest of Taipei. Electronics, electrical equipment, metals, machinery, food products, motorcycles. D=RCC.
6494	Changhua (Zhanghua, Chenghua)	235,000	6.00	14,100	69.58	B	284,000	Chang-hua. Market for local products. Sugar refining, textiles. F=c1650. D=Presbyterian.
6495	Chi-lung (Jilong, Chilong, Keelung)	385,000	3.00	11,500	66.58	B	465,000	Principal port of Taipei. Importing, fishing. 85% Taiwanese, 14% Mainlander. Buddhist, folk-religionist. D=RCC.
6496	Chiai (Jiayi, Chiayi, Chia-i)	279,000	1.60	4,500	65.18	B	337,000	Chia-i. Rice market trade. 95% Taiwanese, 4% Mainlander. 90% folk-religionist. D=RCC,Presbyterian.
6497	Chungli (Chung-li)	295,000	6.00	17,700	69.58	B	356,000	Tao-yuan on Hsin-Chien River. Sugar, rice milling, textiles. Chung Yuan Christian University. M=YWAM.
6498	Chutung	119,000	6.00	7,100	69.58	B	144,000	Southeast of Hsinchu. Natural gas producing center, cement, rice milling, tea processing, ginger.
6499	Fangshan (Kaohsiung-hsien)	364,000	5.50	20,000	69.08	B	440,000	Capital of Kao-hsiung South China Sea. World's third largest container port. Dragon & Tiger pagodas. D=RCC.
6500	Fengyuan (Feng-yuan, Hulutun)	166,000	5.00	8,300	68.58	B	200,000	T'ai-chung. High grade rice, tobacco, marketing center, sawmills, hemp processing. D=Presbyterian.
6501	Hsinchu (Xinzhu, Chinchow)	356,000	4.00	14,300	67.58	B	431,000	Hsin-chu. Marketing center for rice and tea. Petroleum. Advanced technology park. D=RCC,Presbyterian.
6502	Hualien (Hua-lien)	117,000	4.00	4,700	67.58	B	142,000	Hua-lien on Pacific Ocean. Highly volcanic region. Japanese farmers, fishing. Earthquake (1951). D=RCC.
6503	Ilan	104,000	2.50	2,600	66.08	B	126,000	Capital of I-lan on east coast on Pacific Ocean. One of largest rice markets in Taiwan, wood, paper. D=RCC.
6504	Kangshan	99,100	3.00	3,000	66.58	B	120,000	Southeastern coast on South China Sea. Agricultural center for sugarcane, rice, bananas. D=RCC.
6505	Kaohsiung (Gaoxiong, Dagon)	1,534,000	5.00	76,700	73.58	B	2,446,000	Kao-hsiung. Major export port. 80% Taiwanese, 18% Mandarin, 1% Hakka. TEE. D=RCC,Presbyterian.
6506	Lotung	73,600	2.50	1,800	66.08	B	88,900	I'lan on Pacific Ocean south of I-lan. Lumber milling, carbide, manganese, camphor oil. D=RCC.
6507	Lukang	91,400	2.50	2,300	66.08	B	111,000	Changhua on South China Sea south of T'aichung. Minor port, saltworks, sugar refining, fishing.
6508	Miao-li	103,000	4.00	4,100	67.58	B	125,000	Miao-li. On Hou-lung Hsi (river). Market center for watermelons, sugar cane, citrus fruits. D=Presbyterian.
6509	Nant'ou	107,000	2.00	2,100	65.58	B	129,000	Capital of Nant'ou in central Taiwan. Agricultural center, oranges, bananas, pineapple. D=RCC.
6510	Pingtung (Ping-tung, Pingdong, Akow)	230,000	5.00	11,500	68.58	B	278,000	Ping-tung. Leading sugar-refining city, metal goods, machinery, chemicals, alcohol. D=Presbyterian.
6511	T'oufen	84,500	4.00	3,400	67.58	B	102,000	Miaoli county. Metallurgy, rice, banking, fruit, vegetables. Mostly Hakka-speaking. D=Presbyterian.
6512	Tach'i	85,300	4.00	3,400	67.58	B	103,000	Chunbg Cheng Institute of Technology. Tanshui River. Wood mfg., tea processing, rice milling, coal mining.
6513	Tainan (Tai-nan)	746,000	4.00	29,800	67.58	B	902,000	Tai-nan county. Tourism. 85% Taiwanese. 204 Taoist and Buddhist temples. D=RCC,Presbyterian.
6514	TAIPEI (Taibei, Tai-Pei, T'aipei)	2,880,000	7.20	207,000	75.78	B	4,510,000	National Palace Museum. F=17th century. 74% Taiwanese, 15% Mandarin. D=RCC,Presbyterian.
6515	Chungho (Chung-ho)	409,000	5.00	20,400	68.58	B	494,000	T'aipei south of Hsintien River. Canned goods, residential suburb, electronics, machinery, metals, textiles. D=RCC.
6516	Hsichih	88,900	5.00	4,400	68.58	B	108,000	T'aipei east on Tanshui River. Household appliances, railroad, coal mining, iron foundry, tea processing. D=RCC.
6517	Hsinchuang (Hsin-chuang)	327,000	5.00	16,300	68.58	B	395,000	T'aipei west across the Tanshui River. Buddhist temple, Hsintien River. Black tea center, tea industry. D=RCC.
6518	Hsintien (Hsin-tien)	246,000	4.00	9,800	67.58	B	298,000	T'aipei south on Hsintien River. Center for tea, rice, citrus fruits. Major campground. D=RCC.
6519	P'ingchen (Ping-chen)	160,000	5.00	8,000	68.58	B	194,000	T'aipei. Handicrafts, markets, tea, vegetables, fruits, sugar milling, rice. D=Presbyterian.
6520	Sanchung (Shanzhong, Shanchong)	410,000	4.00	16,400	67.58	B	496,000	West of Taipei. Commercial center for agriculture. Woodworking. Residential area. D=Presbyterian.
6521	Shulin	122,000	5.00	6,100	68.58	B	148,000	T'aipei. Machinery. Electrical equipment, textiles, metals, machinery, chemicals, food processing. D=RCC.
6522	T'uch'eng	149,000	5.00	7,500	68.58	B	181,000	T'aipei southwest on Tanshui River. Fast growth suburban area, residential, educational, technology. D=RCC.

Table 10-5–continued overleaf

Table 10-5–continued

Rec No 1	Country City 2	Pop 2000 3	AC% 4	Church Members 5	E% 6	W 7	Pop 2025 8	Notes 9
6523	Yungho	273,000	4.00	10,900	67.58	B	330,000	T'aipei south across Hsintien River. Market center for tea, rice. Several colleges. D=Presbyterian.
6524	Taitung (Tai-tung, P'i-nan)	118,000	4.00	4,700	67.58	B	143,000	T'ai-tung county. Coastal city. Agricultural market center. Sugar milling, cotton ginning. Hot springs. D=RCC.
6525	Taizhong (Taichung, Tai-chung)	846,000	3.40	28,800	66.98	B	1,023,000	Taiwan Province. F=1721. Happy Buddha Statue (88 ft.). 25% Hakka. D=RCC.
6526	Taoyuan (Tao-yuan)	263,000	4.00	10,500	67.58	B	318,000	Tao-yuan county. Agricultural market, cement, tourist and recreational center. D=Presbyterian.
6527	Yangmei	107,000	4.00	4,300	67.58	B	129,000	Leofoo Safari and Theme Park, Formosa Golf and Country Club, Chunghwa Picture Tubes. D=RCC.
6528	Yuanlin	132,000	4.00	5,300	67.58	B	160,000	Changhua south of Changhua. Oranges, pineapples, bananas, rice, sugarcane. D=RCC.
6529	Yungkang	149,000	4.00	6,000	67.58	B	180,000	Tainan. Furniture, martial arts equipment, wood working, furniture, tea. D=Presbyterian.
	TAJIKISTAN	**6,188,000**	**2.09**	**130,000**	**44.12**	**A**	**8,857,000**	**ORTHODOX 1.5%, PROTESTANTS 0.2%. PENT-CHAR 0.05%, EVANGELICAL 0.03%, GCC 0.8%**
6530	rural areas	4,155,000	2.01	83,700	43.65	A	4,723,000	70.6% (1950), 63.1% (1970), 67.8% (1990), 67.1% (2000), 63.2% (2010), 53.3% (2025)
6531	urban areas	2,033,000	2.26	46,000	45.09	A	4,134,000	29.3% (1950), 36.8% (1970), 32.2% (1990), 32.8% (2000), 36.8% (2010), 46.6% (2025)
6532	non-metropolitan areas	901,000	2.25	20,200	45.09	A	1,830,536	*Sources of data:* Censuses of 1959, 1970, 1979, and 1989.
6533	metropolitan areas	1,133,000	2.27	25,700	45.09	A	2,303,000	*Definition:* Cities and urban-type localities, officially designated as such by each of the constituent republics.
6534	DUSANBE (Dushanbe, Stalinabad)	746,000	3.00	22,400	47.13	A	1,516,000	On Varzob River. One story buildings. Textiles, embroidery workshops. Well planned streets & parks. 60% Tajik.
6535	Kul'ab	102,000	0.10	100	37.13	A	206,000	Near Afghan border. Many Uzbeks. Cotton ginning, cotton oilseed extraction, metal working, salt deposits.
6536	Kurgan-T'ube	74,800	0.10	75	37.13	A	152,000	Khatlon. Food processing, clothing, cotton ginning, sheep. F=17th century.
6537	Khudzhand (Leninabad, Khojend)	211,000	1.50	3,200	44.53	A	428,000	Leninabad on Syr River. Ancient city on Silk Road. Silk, cotton. D=ROC,German Ev Lutheran.
	TANZANIA	**33,517,000**	**46.91**	**15,723,000**	**81.42**	**B**	**57,918,000**	**ROMAN CATHOLICS 24.7%, PROTESTANTS 16.5%. PENT-CHAR 10.2%, EVANGELICAL 14.5%, GCC 16.7%**
6538	rural areas	24,189,000	49.30	11,926,000	84.01	B	31,919,000	96.2% (1950), 93.3% (1970), 79.2% (1990), 72.1% (2000), 65.0% (2010), 55.1% (2025)
6539	urban areas	9,328,000	40.70	3,796,000	74.71	B	26,000,000	3.7% (1950), 6.6% (1970), 20.8% (1990), 27.8% (2000), 34.9% (2010), 44.8% (2025)
6540	non-metropolitan areas	4,304,000	40.69	1,751,000	74.75	B	12,509,284	*Sources of data:* Censuses of 1957, 1967, and 1978; estimates for 1973, 1985, and 1990.
6541	metropolitan areas	5,024,000	40.71	2,045,000	74.68	B	13,490,000	*Definition:* Gazetted townships.
6542	Arusha	111,000	70.00	78,000	97.51	C	311,000	Capital of Arusha. Coffee, tourism (big-game hunting). Arusha, Meru, Iraqw, & Masai. F=1963. D=ROC,ELCT.
6543	DAR ES SALAAM (Dar as-salam)	2,051,000	40.00	820,000	74.51	B	5,255,000	Industrial center, major port. Serengeti Research Institute. Capital 1894-1974. D=RCC,ELCT.
6544	DODOMA	87,200	60.00	52,300	94.51	C	243,000	Capital since 1974. Market center for peanuts, castor beans. Gogo, Sanawe, Rangi, Burungi. D=RCC.
6545	Iringa	108,000	50.00	54,100	84.51	B	302,000	Iringa (est. 1963). Tobacco, pyrethrum, wattle extract, tea. Mainly Hehe. Also Bena, Kinga, Nyakyusa. D=RCC.
6546	Kigoma	97,700	60.00	58,600	94.51	C	272,000	Capital of Kigoma on Lake Tanganyika. Fish, corn, wheat, rice, ivory. Slave trading (1850's-1890). D=RCC.
6547	Mbeya	150,000	50.00	75,100	84.51	B	419,000	Capital of Mbeya in Poroto Mountains north of Lake Nyasa. Final rail stop before Zambia. D=RCC,ELCT.
6548	Morogoro	116,000	30.00	34,900	64.51	B	324,000	Capital of Morogoro west of Dar es Salaam. International school. Sisal, tobacco, sugar. D=RCC,ELCT.
6549	Moshi	100,000	80.00	80,100	99.51	C	279,000	Capital of Kilimanjaro south of Mount Kilimanjaro. International school. Wheat. International airport. D=RCC.
6550	Mtwara	94,700	10.00	9,500	44.51	A	264,000	Capital of Mtwara on Indian Ocean just north of Mozambique. D=RCC,ELCT.
6551	Mwanza	216,000	65.00	140,000	97.51	C	602,000	Capital of Mwanza on southern shore of Lake Victoria. Major port & terminus. D=RCC,ELCT.M=AIM.
6552	Tabora (Kazeh)	1,488,000	40.00	595,000	74.51	B	4,096,000	On Central Plateau at 4,000 ft. Capital of Nyamwezi people. Tobacco, cassava. F=1820 by Arabs. D=RCC.
6553	Tanga	195,000	20.00	39,100	54.51	B	545,000	On Pemba Channel of Indian Ocean. Sisal, cotton, salt. F=14th century by Persian traders. D=RCC.
6554	Zanzibar	208,000	3.60	7,500	38.11	A	580,000	Island of Zanzibar. Cloves, coconuts. Slave trade in 19th century. Home of David Livingstone. D=ELCT.
	THAILAND	**61,399,000**	**2.19**	**1,345,000**	**56.82**	**B**	**72,717,000**	**INDEPENDENTS 1.2%, PROTESTANTS 0.4%. PENT-CHAR 1.3%, EVANGELICAL 0.3%, GCC 1.9%**
6555	rural areas	48,149,000	2.06	994,000	55.60	B	46,684,000	89.5% (1950), 86.7% (1970), 81.2% (1990), 78.4% (2000), 73.7% (2010), 64.2% (2025)
6556	urban areas	13,250,000	2.65	351,000	61.28	B	26,033,000	10.4% (1950), 13.2% (1970), 18.7% (1990), 21.5% (2000), 26.2% (2010), 35.8% (2025)
6557	non-metropolitan areas	4,214,000	2.64	111,000	61.19	B	10,069,669	*Sources of data:* Censuses of 1947, 1960, 1970, 1980, and 1990.
6558	metropolitan areas	9,036,000	2.65	240,000	61.32	B	15,963,000	*Definition:* Municipalities.
6559	Chiang Mai (Chiengmai)	188,000	4.50	8,500	61.13	B	370,000	On Ping River. Appearance of large village. Cultural center for Northern Thailand. Hill tribes. D=RCC.
6560	Chon Buri (Chonburi)	54,300	0.50	270	55.13	B	107,000	On Gulf of Thailand. Food-processing. Rice, sugarcane, cassava, fishing, salt extraction.
6561	Hat Yai	159,000	0.10	160	54.73	B	312,000	Songkhla. Trade with Malaysia. Center of rubber industry. Thai silks. In Muslim south.
6562	Khon Kaen	151,000	0.50	750	55.13	B	296,000	Capital of Khon Kaen. Rice trading center. University (1966).
6563	KRUNG THEP (Bangkok-Thonburi)	7,221,000	3.00	217,000	62.63	B	12,397,000	On Chao Phraya River. Port economy. (687 Buddhist temples), 171 mosques. D=Hope of Bangkok,RCC.
6564	Nonthaburi	251,000	2.00	5,000	56.63	B	493,000	North of Bangkok on Chao Phraya River. Residential. International school. D=RCC,CCT.
6565	Samut Prakan (Paknam)	84,200	2.00	1,700	56.63	B	166,000	On Gulf of Thailand. South of Bangkok. Rice & fishing. Marshy coastline. D=RCC,CCT.
6566	Thon Buri (Thonburi)	979,000	2.00	19,600	56.63	B	1,924,000	On Chao Phraya River. National capital from 1767-1782. Merged in 1972. Wat Arun. D=Hope of Bangkok.
6567	Nakhon Ratchasima (Khorat)	235,000	2.00	4,700	56.63	B	463,000	Commercial center of Northeast on Mum River. Silk, rice, 11th century Khmer ruins. D=RCC.
6568	Nakhon Sawan	121,000	1.50	1,800	56.13	B	237,000	On Chao Phraya River. Buddhist temples. Rice, corn, cotton. Chinese New Year celebrations. D=RCC.
6569	Nakhonsi Thammarat	83,200	0.10	83	54.73	B	163,000	Walled city. Metalwork, rice, fruit, coconuts. F=c AD1000. Wat Mahathudu Temple. Strongly Muslim area.
6570	Pattaya	64,800	0.80	520	55.43	B	127,000	Resort city south of Chonburi on Gulf of Thailand. Prostitution and gambling. Many foreign tourists. D=Baptist.
6571	Phitsanulok	89,200	0.50	450	55.13	B	175,000	On Nan River. Rice, cotton, tobacco. Walled city dates to 13th century. Wat Phia Si Rattana Mahathat.
6572	Phra Nakhon Si Ayutthaya (Ayuthia)	69,900	0.50	350	55.13	B	137,000	On Lop Buri River. Krung Kao (ancient capital) for 400 years. F=1350. Tourism to numerous shrines & temples.
6573	Sakon Nakhon	28,800	0.50	140	55.13	B	56,700	On Han Lake. Agricultural market. Rice, fish. Nam Pung Dam. Phuthai people.
6574	Samut Saknon	62,000	1.00	620	55.63	B	122,000	South of Bangkok on Gulf of Thailand. Rice, fruit, rice milling, fisheries, various manufacturing.
6575	Saraburi	70,300	0.30	210	54.93	B	138,000	Central Thailand on Pa Sak River north of Ayutthaya. Rice growing, cattle trading. Friendship highway starts here.
6576	Songkhla (Singora)	97,000	0.50	490	55.13	B	191,000	Capital of Songkhla on Gulf of Thailand. Tourism. Rubber, oil exploration. Strongly Muslim area. D=SDA.
6577	Trang	55,200	0.50	280	55.13	B	108,000	Southern Thailand on Malay Peninsula north of Hat Yai. Trang River. Industrial center, rubber, tin processing.
6578	Ubon Ratchathani	115,000	1.80	2,100	56.43	B	227,000	Capital of Ubon Ratchatchani on Khorat Plateau. Lao, Khmer. D=RCC.
6579	Udon Thani (Udorn)	93,300	1.50	1,400	56.13	B	183,000	Northern Khorat Plateau near Laos. Rice, livestock, timber, fish. U.S. Air Force (1970s). Temples. D=RCC.
6580	Yala	77,400	0.50	390	55.13	B	152,000	Capital of Yala on Mae Nam Pattani. Thai Muslim, Malay Muslim, Chinese. Rubber, tin.
	TIMOR	**885,000**	**92.18**	**815,000**	**98.79**	**C**	**1,185,000**	**ROMAN CATHOLICS 89.9%, PROTESTANTS 5.3%. PENT-CHAR 5.2%, EVANGELICAL 0.5%, GCC 4.4%**
6581	rural areas	818,000	92.76	759,000	99.21	C	1,031,000	90.1% (1950), 90.6% (1970), 92.1% (1990), 92.5% (2000), 91.5% (2010), 87.0% (2025)
6582	urban areas	66,300	85.00	56,300	93.61	C	154,000	9.8% (1950), 9.3% (1970), 7.8% (1990), 7.4% (2000), 8.4% (2010), 12.9% (2025)
6583	non-metropolitan areas	–	–	–	–	–	–	*Sources of data:* Censuses for 1950, 1960, and 1990.
6584	metropolitan areas	147,000	85.00	125,000	93.61	C	343,000	*Definition:* Dili.
6585	OEKUSI (Dili, Dilly, Dilli)	147,000	85.00	125,000	93.61	C	343,000	On Selat Owbai. Soap, perfume. Exports cotton, coffee. Basketry. Mainly Timorese, Atonese. D=RCC,AoG.
	TOGO	**4,629,000**	**37.78**	**1,749,000**	**75.84**	**B**	**8,482,000**	**ROMAN CATHOLICS 24.2%, PROTESTANTS 10.3%. PENT-CHAR 8.1%, EVANGELICAL 3.0%, GCC 19.8%**
6586	rural areas	3,089,000	34.19	1,056,000	70.75	B	4,325,000	92.7% (1950), 86.8% (1970), 71.5% (1990), 66.7% (2000), 60.7% (2010), 50.9% (2025)
6587	urban areas	1,540,000	45.00	693,000	86.06	B	4,157,000	7.2% (1950), 13.1% (1970), 28.4% (1990), 33.2% (2000), 39.2% (2010), 49.0% (2025)
6588	non-metropolitan areas	709,000	45.69	324,000	86.04	B	1,913,625	*Sources of data:* Censuses of 1959 and 1970; estimates for 1974, 1981, and 1985.
6589	metropolitan areas	831,000	44.41	369,000	86.08	B	2,244,000	*Definition:* Seven urban communes.
6590	LOME	749,000	46.00	344,000	88.06	B	2,021,000	On Gulf of Guinea. Phosphates, cocoa, coffee. F=1897 as capital of German Togo Island. D=RCC,JWS.
6591	Sokode	82,400	30.00	24,700	68.06	B	222,000	Capital of Centrale near Mo River. Trade center for northern region. Hunting. Cotton, sugar. Muslims. D=RCC.
	TOKELAU ISLANDS	**1,500**	**91.20**	**1,400**	**99.93**	**C**	**1,500**	**PROTESTANTS 66.6%, ROMAN CATHOLICS 37.3%. PENT-CHAR 5.0%, EVANGELICAL 6.0%, GCC 18.8%**
6592	rural areas	1,100	91.23	960	99.99	C	980	80.0% (1950), 80.0% (1970), 75.0% (1990), 70.0% (2000), 70.0% (2010), 65.0% (2025)
6593	urban areas	450	91.12	410	99.79	C	530	20.0% (1950), 20.0% (1970), 25.0% (1990), 30.0% (2000), 30.0% (2010), 35.0% (2025)
6594	non-metropolitan areas	80	90.05	72	100.07	C	93	*Sources of data:* Censuses of 1982, 1986, and 1991.
6595	metropolitan areas	370	91.35	340	99.73	C	430	*Definition:* Nukunonu.
6596	Nukunonu	370	91.30	340	99.86	C	430	New Zealand dependency. Central atoll. Tuna fishing, tourism. D=Congregational,RCC.
	TONGA	**98,500**	**91.01**	**89,700**	**99.91**	**C**	**105,000**	**PROTESTANTS 42.9%, INDEPENDENTS 21.1%. PENT-CHAR 12.4%, EVANGELICAL 7.4%, GCC 28.3%**
6597	rural areas	52,900	91.89	48,600	99.99	C	38,900	87.1% (1950), 79.7% (1970), 64.9% (1990), 53.6% (2000), 45.1% (2010), 36.9% (2025)
6598	urban areas	45,700	90.00	41,100	99.81	C	66,300	12.8% (1950), 20.3% (1970), 35.0% (1990), 46.3% (2000), 54.8% (2010), 63.0% (2025)
6599	non-metropolitan areas	22,100	90.00	19,900	99.81	C	32,037	*Sources of data:* Censuses of 1956, 1966, 1976, and 1986; estimate for 1950.
6600	metropolitan areas	23,600	90.00	21,200	99.81	C	34,200	*Definition:* Greater Nuku'alofa (Kolomotu'a and Kolof'ou districts).
6601	NUKU'ALOFA	23,600	90.00	21,200	99.81	C	34,200	On Tongatapu. Copra, bananas, vanilla. Traditional handicrafts. Chapel (1862). D=FWCT,RCC,LDS.
	TRINIDAD & TOBAGO	**1,295,000**	**61.46**	**796,000**	**91.55**	**C**	**1,493,000**	**ROMAN CATHOLICS 30.7%, PROTESTANTS 13.8%. PENT-CHAR 10.5%, EVANGELICAL 12.6%, GCC 22.2%**
6602	rural areas	336,000	62.77	211,000	92.86	C	270,000	36.0% (1950), 37.0% (1970), 30.9% (1990), 25.9% (2000), 22.1% (2010), 18.0% (2025)
6603	urban areas	959,000	61.00	585,000	91.09	C	1,224,000	63.9% (1950), 63.0% (1970), 69.1% (1990), 74.0% (2000), 77.8% (2010), 81.9% (2025)
6604	non-metropolitan areas	442,000	61.22	270,000	91.31	C	563,243	*Sources of data:* Censuses of 1946, 1960, 1970, 1980, and 1990.
6605	metropolitan areas	518,000	60.81	315,000	90.90	C	660,000	*Definition:* Port-of-Spain, Arima borough and San Fernando town.
6606	PORT OF SPAIN	434,000	60.00	260,000	90.09	C	554,000	Chief port on Gulf of Paria. Not dependent on tourism. Rum, beer, sawmills. D=RC,Archbishop,RIC.
6607	San Fernando	83,700	65.00	54,400	95.09	C	107,000	Western Trinidad on Guapo Bay on Gulf of Paria. Seaport, business, industry. Horse-racing. D=RCC,Anglican.
	TUNISIA	**9,586,000**	**0.53**	**50,500**	**48.91**	**A**	**12,843,000**	**INDEPENDENTS 0.3%, ROMAN CATHOLICS 0.2%. PENT-CHAR 0.1%, EVANGELICAL 0.07%, GCC 0.3%**
6608	rural areas	3,305,000	0.25	8,400	43.51	A	2,969,000	68.7% (1950), 55.4% (1970), 42.0% (1990), 34.4% (2000), 28.7% (2010), 23.1% (2025)
6609	urban areas	6,280,000	0.67	42,100	51.75	B	9,874,000	31.2% (1950), 44.5% (1970), 57.9% (1990), 65.5% (2000), 71.2% (2010), 76.8% (2025)
6610	non-metropolitan areas	2,966,000	0.67	19,700	51.76	B	4,908,409	*Sources of data:* Censuses of 1946, 1956, 1966, 1975, and 1984.
6611	metropolitan areas	3,314,000	0.67	22,300	51.74	B	4,965,000	*Definition:* Population living in communes.
6612	Bizerte (Bizerta, Banzart)	129,000	0.50	650	48.88	A	203,000	Capital of Banzart on Mediterranean Sea. Beach resort. Exports fish, phosphates, oil refining. F=Phoenicians.
6613	Gabes (Qabis)	126,000	0.10	130	48.48	A	198,000	Capital of Qabis on Gulf of Gabes. Fishing port, date palms, textiles.
6614	Gafsa (Qafsah)	83,400	0.05	42	48.43	A	131,000	Capital of Qafsah on Oued el Leben. Irrigated fruit growing oasis. Phosphates. Mainly nomads.
6615	Houmt Essouk (Hawmat as-Suq)	126,000	0.10	130	48.48	A	198,000	On Jerba Island in Gulf of Gabes. Jewish colony. Olives, figs, dates, grapes, silk, tourism, airport.
6616	Kairouan (Al-Qayrawan, Qairovan)	98,800	0.10	99	48.48	A	155,000	Al-Kairouan on Low Steppes. Holy city of Islam. Carpets. F=670. Center of Islamic offensive in Maghrib (c700).
6617	Kasserine (Al-Qasrayn)	65,100	0.05	33	48.43	A	102,000	Capital of Al-Qasrayn. Olives, cellulose and paper industries, zinc and lead deposits, ancient Roman ruins.
6618	Menzel Bourguiba	70,300	0.05	35	48.43	A	111,000	Banzart across the bay from Bizerte. Named after president. Heavy industry. Naval base.
6619	Sfax (Safaqis)	424,000	0.70	3,000	52.08	B	667,000	Major port on Gulf of Gabes. Phosphates, fishing. Early Islamic trade center. F=Ancient.
6620	Susah (Sousse)	219,000	0.50	1,100	48.88	A	344,000	Capital of Susah on Mediterranean Sea. Fishing, tourism. F=Ancient Hadrumetum. Christian mosaics.
6621	TUNIS (Tunus)	1,905,000	0.90	17,100	53.28	B	2,750,000	On Lake of Tunis. Olives, cereals, carpets. Thermal baths. F=c1100 BC by Libyans. Arab League HQ. D=RCC.
6622	Aryanah (Ariana)	135,000	0.30	410	51.68	B	212,000	Tunis. Woolen mill, orange groves, olive groves, vineyards, cereals, markets, trading.
6623	Bardo	89,800	0.50	450	51.88	B	141,000	Tunis. Treaty establishing French authority (1881).
6624	Ben Arous	71,300	1.00	710	53.38	B	112,000	Tunis. Steelworks, chemicals, food products, cement factories, railroad workshops.
6625	Hammam Lif	64,300	0.90	580	53.28	B	101,000	Tunis east on Gulf of Tunis. Bathing and health resort, medicinal hot springs, cement, brick works.
6626	La Goulette	84,300	0.80	670	52.18	B	132,000	Tunis east on Gulf of Tunis. Yacht clubs. Principal import/export center. Bathing resort.
6627	Zarzis	67,100	0.05	34	48.43	A	105,000	Madanin on Gulf of Gades. Oasis, port, olive processing, tuna and sponge fishing, Roman ruins.

Table 10-5–continued opposite

Table 10-5–continued

Rec No 1	Country City 2	Pop 2000 3	AC% 4	Church Members 5	E% 6	W 7	Pop 2025 8	Notes 9
	TURKEY	**66,591,000**	**0.56**	**373,000**	**48.58**	**A**	**87,869,000**	**ORTHODOX 0.3%, INDEPENDENTS 0.1%. PENT-CHAR 0.1%, EVANGELICAL 0.02%, GCC 0.3%**
6628	rural areas	16,428,000	0.23	37,100	44.56	A	11,941,000	78.6% (1950), 61.5% (1970), 38.8% (1990), 24.6% (2000), 17.3% (2010), 13.5% (2025)
6629	urban areas	50,163,000	0.67	336,000	49.89	A	75,928,000	21.3% (1950), 38.4% (1970), 61.1% (1990), 75.3% (2000), 82.6% (2010), 86.4% (2025)
6630	non-metropolitan areas	17,741,000	0.67	119,000	49.99	A	29,932,873	*Sources of data:* Censuses of 1950, 1955, 1960, 1965, 1970, 1975, 1980, 1985, and 1990.
6631	metropolitan areas	32,422,000	0.67	218,000	49.83	A	45,995,000	*Definition:* Population of localities within municipality limits of administrative centers of provinces and districts.
6632	Adana (Ataniya, Seyhan)	1,289,000	0.30	3,900	48.32	A	1,789,000	On Sarus River. Cotton. F=1440 BC. 65% Turk, 25% Arab, Kurd. 93% Muslim. Arab Orthodox Church.
6633	Adapazari (Sakarya)	207,000	0.20	410	48.22	A	313,000	Sakarya. On fertile plain near Sakarya River. Sugar beets, agriculture. 90% Turk, 5% Kurd. 94% Muslim.
6634	Adiyaman (Hisn Mansur)	121,000	0.05	60	48.07	A	183,000	Adiyaman. Local agricultural market, cereals, cotton. F=8th century by Umayyad Arabs.
6635	Afyon	116,000	0.10	120	48.12	A	175,000	Afyon on Akar River at 3,392 ft. Grain growing region, opium poppies (banned in 1971), carpets.
6636	Agri (Karakose)	70,100	0.05	35	48.07	A	106,000	On Murat River at 5,380 ft. Livestock trade. Named for nearby Mount Ararat. Mainly Kurds in countryside.
6637	Akhisar (Thyatira)	89,300	0.20	180	48.22	A	135,000	Akhisar, Manisa on Great Zab River. Cotton. Founded by Lydinasas Pelopia. One of 7 churches of Revelation.
6638	Aksaray	110,000	0.10	110	48.12	A	166,000	Nigde. Near Lake Tuz. Lignite, wheat, rye, barley, vetch, beans, onions.
6639	Aksehir	62,500	0.10	62	48.12	A	94,600	Konya. Near Lake Aksehir. Railroad, carpet mfg., wheat, barley, thought to be part of ancient Pergamum.
6640	Alanya	63,400	0.20	130	48.22	A	95,900	Pamphylia on Mediterranean Sea. Copper, chromium, barley, wheat, onions, cotton, port.
6641	Amasya	69,200	0.10	69	48.12	A	105,000	Capital of Amasya on Yesil River. On narrow gorge with renowned orchards. Seljuk ruins. F=c200 BC.
6642	ANKARA (Ancyra, Angora)	3,190,000	0.20	6,400	48.22	A	4,199,000	Museums. F=Stone age. 77% Turk, 10% Kurd. D=RCC,AAC,Gospel Believers(OM). TEE.
6643	Antakya (Antioch, Hatay)	150,000	0.46	690	48.48	A	226,000	Hatay on Orontes River. Wheat, cotton. Famous city in biblical times. 60% Arab, 30% Turk. D=Arab Orthodox.
6644	Antalya (Adalia, Attalea, Attalia)	457,000	0.30	1,400	48.32	A	691,000	Mediterranean port. Chief tourist resort, fruit, timber. Paul & Barnabas (c50). F=200 BC. 90% Turk, 5% Kurd.
6645	Aydin	129,000	0.15	190	48.17	A	196,000	Capital of Aydin near Menderes River. Near ancient Tralles. Tobacco, wheat. Trade center.
6646	Bafra	79,200	0.10	79	48.12	A	120,000	Samsun on Kizil River near Black Sea, 29 miles northwest of Samsun. Tobacco center.
6647	Balikesir	206,000	0.20	410	48.22	A	312,000	Balikesir. Numerous Ottoman inns & mosques. Cotton textiles, flour, leather goods. 90% Turk, 5% Kurd.
6648	Bandirma (Panderma, Panormos)	93,500	0.30	280	48.32	A	142,000	Balikesir. On Sea of Marmara. Protected harbor exports cereals. Used by 13th century Latin crusaders.
6649	Batman	178,000	0.03	53	48.05	A	269,000	Siirt near Tigris River. Oil-producing region. Beverages, chemicals, furniture, footwear. Refinery & pipeline.
6650	Bolu	73,400	0.40	290	48.42	A	111,000	Bolu on Yenice River. At 2,434 ft. on bare hill. Leather products, school of forestry, lumber, industry. F=c500 BC.
6651	Burdur (Buldur)	68,200	0.05	34	48.07	A	103,000	Capital of Burdur near Burdur Lake. Textiles, copper. Called Polydorion in Middle Ages.
6652	Bursa (Brusa)	1,299,000	0.10	1,300	48.12	A	1,863,000	Bursa near Ulu Dag mountain. Orchards, silk, baths. Mosque (1421). F=AD300. 89% Turk, 5% Kurd.
6653	Canakkale	65,200	0.15	98	48.17	A	98,700	Canakkale on Canakkale Strait. At mouth of Koca River. Dardanelles, pottery, fish canning. 15th century fort.
6654	Ceyhan	103,000	0.25	260	48.27	A	156,000	Adana on Ceyhan River. Wheat, barley, oats, legumes, sesame, onions, tobacco, cotton.
6655	Cizre	60,400	0.02	12	48.04	A	91,400	Eastern Turkey on Tigris River on Syrian border. Lignite, wheat, barley millet, lentils, rice, chickpeas.
6656	Corlu	90,200	0.40	360	48.42	A	137,000	Tekirdag near Ergene River. European Turkey. Railroad, grain market, textile and clothing center, tile.
6657	Corum	141,000	0.08	110	48.10	A	214,000	Capital of Corum. Famous for hand-spinning & weaving industries. On old trade routes. Copper.
6658	Darica	64,700	0.40	260	48.42	A	97,900	Kocaeli on Sea of Marmara. Near Gebze. Railroad, vetch, cereals, ancient ruins, handicrafts.
6659	Denizli (Laodicea)	247,000	0.10	250	48.12	A	373,000	Denizli near Curuksu River. Woven & embroidered products. Gardens. 90% Turk, 5% Kurd, 3% Tatar. 92% Muslim.
6660	Diyarbakir (Amida, Amid, Diyarbekir)	460,000	1.72	7,900	52.74	B	697,000	Diyarbakir on Tigris River. Gold & silver filigree. 60% Kurd. Longstanding Christian center (Armenian, Syrian)
6661	Duzce	74,700	0.50	370	48.52	A	113,000	Bolu. Near Bolu. Agricultural center, markets, trade, tobacco, corn, fruit, flax, garlic.
6662	Edirne (Adrianople, Hadrianople)	124,000	1.00	1,200	51.02	B	187,000	At Tunca & Maritsa Rivers. Known for peynir (white cheese). Cotton, woolens. F=BC.
6663	Elazig	247,000	0.05	120	48.07	A	374,000	Elazig near Keban Reservoir. Vineyards & orchards, wine. F=Ottoman garrison. 65% Turk, 30% Kurd.
6664	Elbistan	66,100	0.03	20	48.05	A	100,000	Kahraman Maras on Ceyhan River tributary. Wheat, barley, rye, vetch, potatoes, sugarbeets. 'The Garden'.
6665	Eregli	89,700	0.04	36	48.06	A	136,000	Konya near Taurus Mountains. Center of cotton-textile manufacturing. Great Mosque (16th century).
6666	Eregli	77,300	0.08	62	48.10	A	117,000	Zonguldak on Black Sea. Heavy industry, coal export. F=c560 BC as Heraclea Pontica.
6667	Erzincan	111,000	0.01	11	48.03	A	168,000	Capital of Erzincan on Karasu River. Cotton & silk textiles, copper utensils. Severe earthquakes.
6668	Erzurum	293,000	0.03	88	48.05	A	443,000	Capital of Erzurum at 6,400 ft. Sugar beets. 12th century mosque. 55% Turk, 40% Kurd. 97% Muslim.
6669	Eskisehir (Dorylaeum)	499,000	0.10	500	48.12	A	755,000	Eskisehir on Porsuk River. Sugar, textiles, bricks. 89% Turk, 5% Kurd. 10th century monastery.
6670	Gaziantep (Aintab)	926,000	0.23	2,100	48.25	A	1,335,000	Gaziantep near the Sacirsuyu. Ancient origins. 86% Turk, 5% Kurd. Jesusists (Followers of Jesus), all Turks.
6671	Gemlik	60,700	0.10	61	48.12	A	91,800	Bursa on Sea of Marmara. Near Bursa. Port, artificial silk factory, olive growing center, small chromium deposits.
6672	Giresun (Keresun)	81,600	0.07	57	48.09	A	124,000	Capital of Giresun on Black Sea. Hazelnuts, walnuts, hides. English 'cherry' is derived from name.
6673	Golcuk	78,400	0.20	160	48.22	A	119,000	Kocaeli on Sea of Marmara. Near Adapazari. Shipyards, trade, repair, naval base, cereal trading.
6674	Inegol	85,900	0.08	69	48.10	A	130,000	Bursa near Ulu Dag mountain, 25 miles east southeast of Bursa. Wheat, barley, corn.
6675	Iskenderun (Alexandretta)	187,000	0.10	190	48.12	A	283,000	Hatay. Turkist naval port. 50% Turk, 50% Arab. 93% Muslim. Some Arab Orthodox.
6676	Isparta	135,000	0.08	110	48.10	A	205,000	Isparta. Roses, fragrant rose oil, carpets. Known as Baris under Byzantines. 90% Turk. 93% Muslim.
6677	Istanbul (Stambul, Constantinople)	9,413,000	1.40	132,000	52.42	B	12,512,000	Located in both Europe & Asia. Byzantium. F=c660 BC. D=HQ Ecumenical Patriarchate of Constantinople,RCC.
6678	Esenyurt	84,900	1.60	1,400	52.62	B	128,000	Istanbul. Commercial, industrial, textiles, glass, shoes, ships, chemicals, printing tourism. D=Orthodox.
6679	Gebze	192,000	1.50	2,900	52.52	B	291,000	On Sea of Marmara. Istanbul-Izmit railroad. Cereals, vetch, ruins of ancient Libyssa to the east. D=RCC.
6680	Kucukkoy	152,000	1.30	2,000	52.32	B	231,000	European side. West of Istanbul. Tourism, financial, commercial, colleges, university, textiles, chemicals. D=RCC.
6681	Sultanbeyli	99,400	1.40	1,400	52.42	B	150,000	Ataturk statue. Sabanci Creche Pre-school and Library. Textiles, glass, cement, chemicals. D=Orthodox.
6682	Yalova	79,500	1.40	1,100	52.42	B	120,000	N.E. of Armutla Peninsula Yalava Springs. Kemal Ataturk statue, ferry station, resort area. D=Orthodox.
6683	Izmir (Smyrna)	2,399,000	1.74	41,700	52.76	B	3,248,000	On Gulf of Izmir, Aegean Sea. 5,000 years of continuous historical importance. D=RCC.
6684	Izmit (Kocaeli, Nicomedia)	310,000	0.50	1,600	48.52	A	470,000	Kocaeli on Gulf of Izmit. 90% Turk, 5% Kurd. 94% Muslim. Tobacco, olives, petrochemicals. F= c 712 BC.
6685	Kadirli	66,500	0.20	130	48.22	A	101,000	Adana near Aslantas Reservoir, 50 miles northeast of Adana. Grains, trading.
6686	Kahramanmaras (Maras)	276,000	0.10	280	48.12	A	417,000	Kahraman Maras near Ahir Mountains. Capital of Hittite Kingdom (c12th century BC). Dolomite, limes.
6687	Karabuk	126,000	0.15	190	48.17	A	190,000	Zonguldak on Soganli River. 1st Turkish iron and steel plant, Zonguldak coal fields, iron ore.
6688	Karaman	92,400	0.02	18	48.04	A	140,000	Konya near Taurus Mountains. Karamanid castle ruins, 2 fine mosques, once an independent Muslim state.
6689	Kars	94,700	0.01	9	48.03	A	143,000	Capital of Kars at 5,740 ft. Livestock trade, cheese. Kumbet Camii (originally ancient Armenian church).
6690	Kastamonu (Castamon)	62,300	0.10	62	48.12	A	94,200	Kastamonu near Gok River. Copper utensils, sugar. Byzantine fortress. Mosque, theological school.
6691	Kayseri	509,000	0.01	51	48.03	A	770,000	Kayseri near extinct volcano Mount Erciyes. Agricultural market. F=c400. 65% Turk, 30% Kurd. D=AAC.
6692	Kilis	100,000	0.05	50	48.07	A	152,000	Gaziantep near Syrian border. Silk & cotton manufacturing. Olives, grapes, pistachios.
6693	Kirikhan	82,800	0.10	83	48.12	A	125,000	Hatay near Askenderun, 23 miles north northeast of Antakya. Grain, market, handicrafts.
6694	Kirikkale	224,000	0.15	340	48.17	A	339,000	Ankara near Kizil River. Steel mills, cereals, livestock. 40 miles east of Ankara. 90% Turk. 94% Muslim.
6695	Kirsehir	88,800	0.05	44	48.07	A	134,000	Kirsehir on tributary of Kizil River. Carpet making. Ahi brotherhood (14th-18th century).
6696	Kiziltepe	72,600	0.05	36	48.07	A	110,000	Mardin near Syrian border, 11 miles southwest of Mardin. Grain, legumes, mohair goats.
6697	Konya (Iconium)	620,000	0.10	620	48.12	A	938,000	Konya. One of oldest cities in world. Y=AD 47 by Apostle Paul. 90% Turk, 5% Kurd. Islamic fundamentalism.
6698	Korfez	79,400	0.10	79	48.12	A	120,000	Izmir refinery management.
6699	Kozan	65,800	0.07	46	48.09	A	99,500	Adana on Ceyhan River tributary, 40 miles northeast of Adana. Wheat, barley, oats, cotton, medieval church.
6700	Kutahya	158,000	0.10	160	48.12	A	239,000	Capital of Kutahya. Sugar refining, tanning. Center of Ottoman ceramic industry. 89% Turk. 95% Muslim.
6701	Luleburgaz	63,300	1.00	630	49.02	A	95,800	Kirklareli near Evros River. In European Turkey. Grain, sugarbeets, beans, potatoes, trade centers.
6702	Malatya (Melitene)	340,000	0.25	850	48.27	A	515,000	Capital of Malatya. Textiles. F=1838. 65% Turk, 30% Kurd. D=Armenian,Catholic, and Gregorian, churches.
6703	Manisa	192,000	0.10	190	48.12	A	291,000	Manisa on Gediz River near Mount Sipylus. F=12th century BC. Many Ottoman buildings. 90% Turk. 92% Muslim.
6704	Mardin	64,000	0.10	64	48.12	A	96,900	Mardin near Syrian border. Agriculture center, barley, wheat, tobacco, onions. D=Syrian Orthodox.
6705	Mersin (Icel, Mersina)	443,000	0.51	2,300	48.53	A	671,000	Mediterranean seaport. Oil refinery. F=c3600 BC. 45% Turk, 45% Arab, 5% Kurd. D=Arab Orthodox.
6706	Mus	53,200	0.03	16	48.05	A	80,500	Capital of Mus. Oak scrub & vineyards. Destroyed by earthquake (1966). Many Kurds.
6707	Nazilli	96,900	0.10	97	48.12	A	147,000	Aydin on Buyukmenderes River. Railroad, cotton goods, olives, valonia, barley, antimony, emery, lignite.
6708	Nevsehir	63,700	0.05	32	48.07	A	96,400	Nevsehir. Agricultural products. Mosque Kursunlu Cami with attached Madrasah (18th century).
6709	Nigde	66,500	0.04	27	48.06	A	101,000	Nigde at 4,100 ft. Possibly Hittite Nakida. Flour, wine, cement. Many medieval mosques.
6710	Nizip (Nezib)	70,800	0.07	50	48.09	A	107,000	Gaziantep. Site of battle in which Ali Pasha, viceroy of Egypt, defeated Ottomans (June 24, 1839).
6711	Nusaybin	60,000	0.05	30	48.07	A	90,800	Mardin on Syrian border. Commercial and transportation center. Residence of Armenian kings in past.
6712	Odemis	62,300	0.20	130	48.22	A	94,400	Izmir near Boz Dag. Emery, mercury, antimony, arsenic, iron, olives, figs, valonia, tobacco, barley.
6713	Ordu	123,000	0.10	120	48.12	A	187,000	Ordu. Black Sea port. Ancient Cotyora (5th century BC). Hazelnut processing & export.
6714	Osmaniye	149,000	0.15	220	48.17	A	225,000	Adana on Ceyhan River tributary, 50 miles east of Adana. Wheat, cotton, railroad.
6715	Polatli	72,700	0.10	73	48.12	A	110,000	Ankara near ancient Gordion. Railroad, agricultural center, grain, fruit, mohair goats.
6716	Rize	62,800	0.08	50	48.10	A	95,100	Rize on Black Sea in wooded hills. Tea processing & export. Tea research institute (1958).
6717	Salihli	85,600	0.10	86	48.12	A	130,000	Manisa on Gediz River. Raisins, valonia, wheat, barley, sugarbeets, cotton, tobacco.
6718	Samsun (Amisus)	367,000	0.09	330	48.11	A	556,000	Capital of Samsun on Black Sea. Tobacco. F=7th century BC. 73% Turk, 20% Kurd. 96% Muslim.
6719	Siirt	82,500	0.16	130	48.18	A	125,000	Siirt on Buhtan River. Goat-hair blankets. 70% Kurd, 20% Turk, 5% Arab. D=Syrian and Chaldean churches.
6720	Silvan (Miyafarkin)	72,300	0.30	220	48.32	A	109,000	45 miles east northeast of Diyarbakir. Wheat, barley.
6721	Sivas (Sebastea)	268,000	0.38	1,000	48.40	A	405,000	Capital of Sivas. Armenian monastery of the Holy Cross. 65% Turk, 30% Kurd. D=Gregorian,RCC,AAC.
6722	Siverek	76,100	0.03	23	48.05	A	115,000	Urfa near Ataturk Reservoir. Wheat, barley, rice, chickpeas, lentils, cotton, tobacco.
6723	Soke	61,400	0.50	310	48.52	A	93,000	Buyukmenderes River valley. Near ancient Ephesus. Tobacco, figs, olives.
6724	Soma	60,400	0.20	120	48.22	A	91,400	Manisa on Bakir River. Near Akhisar. Railroad, lignite, wheat, barley, sugarbeets, cotton, tobacco.
6725	Tarsus	226,000	0.10	230	48.12	A	343,000	Icel. Ancient city on Cydnus River. Birthplace of St. Paul. Cotton milling. 50% Turk, 40% Arab. D=Arab Orthodox.
6726	Tatvan	65,300	0.04	26	48.06	A	98,800	Bitlis on Lake Van. Railroad terminal from Elazig, ferry across Lake Van. Grain.
6727	Tekirdag (Rodosto)	97,100	0.30	290	48.32	A	147,000	Capital of Tekirdag on Sea of Marmara. F=7th century BC as Bisanthe. Agricultural market.
6728	Tokat	100,000	0.05	50	48.07	A	152,000	Capital of Tokat on Yesil River surrounded by orchards & gardens. Copper utensils. Gok Madrasch (13th cent).
6729	Trabzon (Trapezus, Trebizond)	174,000	0.20	350	48.22	A	263,000	Trabzon on Black Sea. F=756BC. 13th century Hagia Sophia. 1895: 80,000 Armenian Christians murdered.
6730	Turgutlu	88,900	0.30	270	48.32	A	135,000	Manisa near Izmir. Noted for melons known by town's former name: Kassaba (Cassaba).
6731	Turhal	82,600	0.04	33	48.06	A	125,000	Tokat on Yesil River.
6732	Urfa (Edessa, Sanliurfa)	418,000	0.10	420	48.12	A	632,000	Urfa. Butter, wool. Former Christian center. 60% Kurd, 35% Turk. Y=150. Important Syrian bishopric.
6733	Usak (Ushak)	127,000	0.08	100	48.10	A	192,000	Usak. Near ruins of ancient Flaviopolis. Noted for carpet industry. Sugar refining.
6734	Van	185,000	0.10	190	48.12	A	280,000	Van on Lake Van. Chief city of 7th century BC kingdom of Urartu. 80% Kurd. A few Assyrian Christians.
6735	Viransehir	69,400	0.05	35	48.07	A	105,000	Ursa on Habur River. Near Syrian border. Malatya-Adana railroad, 30 miles southwest of Malatya. Grains.
6736	Yalova	79,500	0.50	400	48.52	A	120,000	Istanbul on Sea of Marmara across from Gebze. South shore of Gulf of Izmit. Hot springs, tourism.
6737	Yozgat	60,800	0.10	61	48.12	A	92,000	Yozgat. East of Ankara. Mountain valley, wheat, barley, mohair goats, horses.
6738	Zonguldak	266,000	0.07	190	48.09	A	402,000	Capital of Zonguldak on Black Sea. Exports coal. 72% Turk, 20% Kurd, 2% Circassian. 20 Catholics only.
	TURKMENISTAN	**4,459,000**	**2.22**	**98,900**	**34.54**	**A**	**6,287,000**	**ORTHODOX 1.6%, INDEPENDENTS 0.4%. PENT-CHAR 0.2%, EVANGELICAL 0.02%, GCC 1.0%**
6739	rural areas	2,430,000	1.90	46,100	32.98	A	2,627,000	55.0% (1950), 52.2% (1970), 55.1% (1990), 54.4% (2000), 50.7% (2010), 41.7% (2025)
6740	urban areas	2,029,000	2.60	52,800	36.44	A	3,660,000	44.9% (1950), 47.7% (1970), 44.8% (1990), 45.5% (2000), 49.3% (2010), 58.2% (2025)
6741	non-metropolitan areas	821,000	2.63	21,600	36.44	A	1,480,310	*Sources of data:* Censuses of 1959, 1970, 1979, and 1989.
6742	metropolitan areas	1,209,000	2.58	31,200	36.41	A	2,180,000	*Definition:* Cities and urban-type localities, officially designated as such by each of the constituent republics.
6743	ASCHABAD (Ashkhabad)	501,000	4.00	20,000	40.32	A	903,000	In Akhal oasis on edge of Kara-Kum Desert. Glassworks, carpets. F=1881 by Russian military. D=RCC,AAC.
6744	Cardzou (Chardzhou, Charjui)	202,000	3.00	6,100	37.32	A	365,000	Chardzhou on Amu Darya. Cotton ginning, silk mills, Astra Khan furs. F=1886 by Russian military. D=ROC,AAC.
6745	Chodzejli	67,500	0.20	140	29.52	A	122,000	On Uzbekistan border. Mining, irrigation region, various agriculture, sheep, livestock, carpets, handicrafts.
6746	Krasnovodsk	72,300	0.20	150	29.52	A	130,000	Krasnovodsk on Caspian Sea. Important transshipment center, link to Baku. Oil. F=1869.
6747	Mary	115,000	0.60	690	30.92	A	208,000	Mary on Murgab River. Gas field center, transport junction, plastics. F=1884.
6748	Nebit-Dag	108,000	0.50	540	30.82	A	195,000	Krasnovodsk at Great Balkhan Ridge. Oil industry. 'Oil mountain'.

Table 10-5–continued overleaf

Table 10-5–continued

Rec No 1	Country City 2	Pop 2000 3	AC% 4	Church Members 5	E% 6	W 7	Pop 2025 8	Notes 9
6749	Tasauz (Tashauz)	142,000	2.50	3,600	36.82	A	256,000	Tashauz in western Khorezm oasis. Cotton gin, carpet making. Founded as fort & bazaar. D=ROC,AAC.
	TURKS & CAICOS IS	**16,800**	**79.13**	**13,300**	**99.79**	**C**	**33,800**	**PROTESTANTS 48.4%, ANGLICANS 11.9%. PENT-CHAR 25.6%, EVANGELICAL 17.9%, GCC 20.9%**
6750	rural areas	9,200	83.36	7,700	99.98	C	13,900	59.0% (1950), 59.2% (1970), 57.3% (1990), 54.8% (2000), 50.0% (2010), 41.2% (2025)
6751	urban areas	7,600	74.00	5,600	99.56	C	19,800	41.0% (1950), 40.8% (1970), 42.6% (1990), 45.1% (2000), 49.9% (2010), 58.7% (2025)
6752	non-metropolitan areas	2,300	73.98	1,700	99.55	C	5,974	*Sources of data:* Censuses of 1960, 1970, 1975, and 1980.
6753	metropolitan areas	5,300	74.01	3,900	99.57	C	13,900	*Definition:* Grand Turk.
6754	GRAND TURK (Cockburn Town)	5,300	74.00	3,900	99.56	C	13,900	Tourism, offshore banking, spiny lobster. Seat of the government. D=RCC,Jamaica Baptist Union.
	TUVALU	**11,700**	**83.16**	**9,700**	**99.83**	**C**	**20,700**	**PROTESTANTS 102.4%, MARGINAL CHRISTIANS 2.4%. PENT-CHAR 17.9%, EVANGELICAL 4.7%, GCC 19.1%**
6755	rural areas	5,600	89.88	5,000	99.89	C	6,500	90.7% (1950), 79.0% (1970), 59.1% (1990), 47.7% (2000), 39.0% (2010), 31.3% (2025)
6756	urban areas	6,100	77.00	4,700	99.77	C	14,200	9.2% (1950), 20.9% (1970), 40.9% (1990), 52.2% (2000), 60.9% (2010), 68.6% (2025)
6757	non-metropolitan areas	2,900	77.01	2,200	99.75	C	6,645	*Sources of data:* Censuses of 1979 and 1991.
6758	metropolitan areas	3,300	76.99	2,500	99.78	C	7,600	*Definition:* Funafuti.
6759	FONGAFELA-Funafuti	3,300	77.00	2,500	99.77	C	7,600	Center of government and commerce. Copra, stamp sales. Imports most fuel & food. Few automobiles. D=EKT.
	UGANDA	**21,778,000**	**86.99**	**18,944,000**	**99.10**	**C**	**44,435,000**	**ROMAN CATHOLICS 41.9%, ANGLICANS 39.4%. PENT-CHAR 23.0%, EVANGELICAL 17.8%, GCC 13.8%**
6760	rural areas	18,695,000	88.14	16,477,000	99.15	C	32,704,000	96.9% (1950), 92.0% (1970), 88.8% (1990), 85.8% (2000), 81.7% (2010), 73.6% (2025)
6761	urban areas	3,084,000	80.00	2,467,000	98.81	C	11,731,000	3.0% (1950), 7.9% (1970), 11.1% (1990), 14.1% (2000), 18.2% (2010), 26.4% (2025)
6762	non-metropolitan areas	1,660,000	79.74	1,324,000	98.80	C	6,701,566	*Sources of data:* Censuses of 1959, 1969, 1980, and 1991.
6763	metropolitan areas	1,424,000	80.31	1,143,000	98.83	C	5,029,000	*Definition:* Population of all settlements as small as trading centers with as few as 100 inhabitants.
6764	Jinja	80,700	78.00	63,000	97.11	C	307,000	Nile flows out of Lake Victoria here. Owen Falls Dam. Steel, copper, plywood. F=1901. D=RCC,CURBZ.
6765	KAMPALA	1,207,000	81.00	978,000	99.11	C	4,205,000	On Lake Victoria. Coffee, cotton, tea. F=1895. Mosques, Hindu temples. D=RCC,Anglican,CURBZ.
6766	Masaka	65,000	75.00	48,700	97.11	C	247,000	Capital of South Buganda on Lake Victoria. Historic Fort Masaka. Meat, fish. D=RCC,CURBZ.
6767	Mbale	71,000	76.00	54,000	97.51	C	270,000	Capital of East Buganda west of Mount Elgon. Agricultural trading center, dairies. D=RCC,CURBZ.
	UKRAINE	**50,456,000**	**82.59**	**41,669,000**	**98.51**	**C**	**45,688,000**	**ORTHODOX 54.3%, INDEPENDENTS 16.8%. PENT-CHAR 8.0%, EVANGELICAL 2.0%, GCC 12.1%**
6768	rural areas	13,870,000	89.40	12,401,000	99.27	C	8,781,000	60.8% (1950), 45.3% (1970), 32.4% (1990), 27.4% (2000), 23.5% (2010), 19.2% (2025)
6769	urban areas	36,586,000	80.00	29,269,000	98.22	C	36,907,000	39.1% (1950), 54.6% (1970), 67.5% (1990), 72.5% (2000), 76.4% (2010), 80.7% (2025)
6770	non-metropolitan areas	11,638,000	80.87	9,411,000	98.22	C	11,745,117	*Sources of data:* Censuses of 1959, 1970, 1979, and 1989.
6771	metropolitan areas	24,948,000	79.59	19,857,000	98.22	C	25,162,000	*Definition:* Cities and urban-type localities, officially designated as such by each of the constituent republics.
6772	Achtyrka	51,600	85.00	43,900	97.92	C	52,100	Sumy west of Char'kov. Wheat, sugarbeets, corn, potatoes, hemp, flax, furniture, clothing. D=UOC.
6773	Aleksandrija (Aleksandriya)	104,000	81.00	83,900	96.92	C	104,000	Kirovograd on Ingulets River. Lignite field, rayon fibers. F=1754 as Usovka. D=UOC.
6774	Art'omovsk (Artyomovsk, Artemovsk)	89,600	82.00	73,500	97.92	C	90,400	Donetsk on Bakhmut River. Largest salt operations in ex-USSR. Chemicals. F=17th century. D=UOC.
6775	Belaja Cerkov' (Belaya Tserkov)	202,000	79.00	159,000	98.92	C	203,000	Kiev on Ros River. Flax, potatoes, buckwheat, wheat, sugarbeets, flour milling, distilling. D=UOC.
6776	Belgorod-Dnestrovskij	56,100	82.00	46,000	97.92	C	56,500	Odessa on Dnestr Estuary. Fish canning. F=6th century by Greeks on Tyras. D=UOC.
6777	Berd'ansk	137,000	81.00	111,000	96.92	C	138,000	Zaporozhye on Berdyansk Gulf of Sea of Azov. Holiday & health resort. Engineering, oil. F=1827. D=UOC.
6778	Berdicev	92,200	80.00	73,700	95.92	C	93,000	Zhitomir. Sugar, tannery. F=1482 as Lithuanian fortress. 16th century Catholic church. D=UOC.
6779	Cerkassy (Cherkassy)	298,000	78.00	233,000	93.92	C	301,000	Cherkassy on Dnepr River. Growing chemical industry. F=15th century by Polish Ukraine. D=UOC.
6780	Cernigov (Chernigov)	302,000	79.00	238,000	94.92	C	304,000	Chernigov on Desna River. Pianos. F=7th century. Chief town of Kievan Rus. Spassky Cathedral 1024. D=UOC.
6781	Cernovcy (Chernovtsy, Cernauti)	255,000	80.00	204,000	95.92	C	258,000	Chernovtsy on Prut River. Trade center. Woolen, cotton textiles, meat, sugar, timber. F=1407. D=UOC.
6782	Cervonograd	73,000	82.00	59,900	97.92	C	73,700	Near Polish border on Bug River. Coal mining center, wood working, dairy products. D=UOC.
6783	Char'kov (Kharkov, Kharkiv)	1,701,000	80.00	1,361,000	99.92	C	1,711,000	Kharkov at confluence of Udy, Lopan & Kharkov Rivers. Engineering. Rebuilt after WWII. F=1656. D=UOC.
6784	Cherson (Kherson)	361,000	80.00	288,000	95.92	C	364,000	Kherson on Dnepr River. Major shipbuilding center, oil refinery. F=1778 as military fortress. D=UOC.
6785	Chmel'nickij (Khmelnitsky, Proskuton)	241,000	79.00	191,000	94.92	C	243,000	Khmelnitsky on Bug River. Light engineering, food processing. F=15th century as Polish military fort. D=UOC.
6786	Dnepropetrovsk (Ekaterinoslav)	1,244,000	79.00	983,000	99.42	C	1,250,000	Dnepropetrovsk on Dnepr River. Huge iron & steel industry, electric locomotives. F=1783. D=UOC.
6787	Dneprodzerzinsk (Kamenskoye)	281,000	79.00	222,000	94.92	C	283,000	High grade steels, rolling stock, cement, coke-chemical, fertilizer. F=1750 as Cossack settlement. D=UOC.
6788	Doneck (Donetsk, Stalino)	1,158,000	79.00	915,000	98.92	C	1,162,000	Donetsk on Kalmius River. 40 coalpits in city. One of largest metallurgy centers in former-USSR. F=1872. D=UOC.
6789	Charcyzsk	68,400	80.00	54,700	95.92	C	69,000	Wire & cable drawing, tubes & pipes, foundries. Metallurgy, coking plants, furniture. F=1869. D=UOC.
6790	Makejevka (Makeyevka)	418,000	80.00	335,000	98.92	C	422,000	On Gruzskaya River. Large integrated iron & steel works. Residential. F=1899. D=UOC.
6791	Drogobyc	78,200	82.00	64,100	97.92	C	78,800	Lvov. Mining center for petroleum, natural gas, potassium. Known for salt in 11th & 12th centuries. D=UOC.
6792	Dzankoj	53,800	85.00	45,700	97.92	C	54,300	Crimea north of Simferopol. Fishing, coastal tourism, wine, tobacco, fruit, vegetables. D=UOC.
6793	Enakievo (Yenakiyevo)	119,000	80.00	95,500	95.92	C	120,000	Donetsk on Bulavina river. Metallurgy, iron & steel, coke-based chemicals. F=1858. D=UOC.
6794	Fastov	53,400	70.00	37,400	85.92	C	53,900	Southwest of Kiev on Irpen River. Machinery, furniture, 18th century wooden church. F=1390. D=UOC.
6795	Feodosija (Feodosiya)	84,500	81.00	68,400	96.92	C	85,200	Crimean coastal & fishing port. Major resort. F=7th century BC by Miletan Greeks. D=UOC.
6796	Gorlovka	691,000	80.00	553,000	98.92	C	697,000	Konetsk on Korsun River. Large coal-mining center, waste heaps. F=1867. D=UOC.
6797	Dzerzinsk	49,800	83.00	41,400	98.92	C	50,300	Doneck northwest of Gorlovka. Heavy industry and coal mining region, sewing, wood working. D=UOC.
6798	Jenakijevo	119,000	81.00	96,000	96.92	C	120,000	Doneck southeast of Gorlovka. Coke-chemical complex, food processing, building materials. D=UOC.
6799	Ivano-Frankovsk (Stanislav)	238,000	80.00	190,000	95.92	C	240,000	Ivano-Frankovsk on Bystritsa River. Timber, furniture. Medical, teacher-training. F=1661 by Poles. D=UOC,RCC.
6800	Iz'um (Izyum, Izium)	63,900	82.00	52,400	97.92	C	64,500	Kharkov on Donets River. Railroad repair shop. Brickworks, brewery. F=1571. D=UOC.
6801	Izmail	93,800	81.00	76,000	96.92	C	94,700	Odessa on Danube River. Port & transshipment point. F=16th century as Turkish fortress. D=UOC.
6802	Jalta (Yalta)	88,100	81.00	71,400	96.92	C	88,900	Crimea on Crimean Peninsula. Popular holiday & health resort, wine, fruit. WWII conference. F=1838. D=UOC.
6803	Jevpatorija (Evpatoriya, Yevpatoriya)	109,000	80.00	87,200	95.92	C	110,000	Crimea on Kalamit Bay. Popular resort, coastal & fishing port. F=6th century BC as Greek colony. D=UOC.
6804	Kalus (Kalush)	68,500	82.00	56,200	97.92	C	69,100	Ivano-Frankovsk. Food processing, clothing, chemicals, concrete. F=1939. D=UOC.
6805	Kamenec-Podol'skij	104,000	81.00	83,900	96.92	C	104,000	Khmelnitsky on Smotrich River. Scientific industries, cement. F=11th century. D=UOC,RCC.
6806	Kerc' (Kerch)	176,000	80.00	141,000	95.92	C	177,000	Crimea on Strait of Kerch. Ore-sintering, cast-iron piping, fishing. F=6th century BC by Miletan Greeks. D=UOC.
6807	KIJEV (Kiyev, Kiev)	2,897,000	79.00	2,289,000	99.92	C	2,939,000	Kiev on Dnepr River. Chemicals. F=8th century. Cathedral of St. Sophia (11th century). D=UOC,RCC.
6808	Borispol	52,000	80.00	41,600	95.92	C	52,500	Kijev east of Kiev near international airport. Rayon center, instruments, flour, clothing, metal work. D=UOC.
6809	Brovay	83,700	80.00	66,900	95.92	C	84,400	Kijev east of Kiev. Rayon center, industrial agglomeration, knitting factory, tech school. D=UOC.
6810	Kirovograd (Zinovievsk)	274,000	79.00	217,000	94.92	C	277,000	Kirovograd on Ingul River. Agricultural trade & machinery. F=1754 as fortress. D=UOC.
6811	Kolomyja	65,300	83.00	54,200	98.92	C	65,900	Ivano-Frankovsk on Prut River. Trade center, agriculture, paper, brewing. F=1240. D=UOC,RCC.
6812	Komsomolsk	55,300	84.00	46,400	97.92	C	55,700	Oil refinery, polytechnical institute, rail station, NASA Crustal Dynamics site. D=UOC.
6813	Konotop	96,400	82.00	79,100	97.92	C	97,300	Sumy. Railway, electrical engineering. College of building technology. F=1652 as fort. D=UOC.
6814	Konstantinovka	106,000	80.00	85,100	95.92	C	107,000	Donetsk on Krivoy Torets River. Ironworks, steelworks, zinc smelter, chemicals, glass-making. D=UOC.
6815	Korosten'	66,600	81.00	54,000	96.92	C	67,200	Zhitomir on Uzh River. Railway junction, chemical industry, woodworking. Granite. F=1926. D=UOC.
6816	Kovel'	68,800	82.00	56,400	97.92	C	69,400	Near Polish border. Tura River. Rayon center, agriculture machines, flax, cheese, starch flour, meat. D=UOC.
6817	Kramatorsk	508,000	79.00	401,000	98.92	C	513,000	Donetsk on Kazyonny Torets. Metallurgy, iron & steel, heavy machinery, machine tools. D=UOC.
6818	Druzkovka	73,400	80.00	58,700	95.92	C	74,100	Important machine works & metal working. Working of fireclays, mining, gas equipment. F=1863. D=UOC.
6819	Slav'ansk (Slavyansk)	135,000	80.00	108,000	95.92	C	136,000	Unusual combination of health resort & industrial town. Chemical industry. F=1676 as Tor. D=UOC.
6820	Krasnoarmejsk	178,000	80.00	142,000	95.92	C	179,000	Donetsk. Old coal-mining center. Significant agricultural area. Before 1938 known as Srishino. D=UOC.
6821	Dimitrov	367,000	81.00	297,000	96.92	C	370,000	Doneck. Bituminous coal mines, mining technical school, other professional technical schools. D=UOC.
6822	Krasnodon	163,000	79.00	129,000	94.92	C	164,000	Voroshilovgrad on Bolshaya Kamenda River. Coal mining. Before 1938-Sorokino. D=UOC.
6823	Krasnyj Luc (Krasniy Luch)	316,000	80.00	253,000	95.92	C	319,000	Voroshilovgrad on Donetsk Ridge. Anthracite mining center, coal enriching plats. F=1900. D=UOC.
6824	Antracit	71,800	80.00	57,500	95.92	C	72,500	Anthracite-mining rise due to Soviet five-year plans. Mining technical school, metal working. F=1938. D=UOC.
6825	Kremencug (Kremenchug)	237,000	80.00	190,000	95.92	C	240,000	Doltava on Dnepr River. Metallurgical & engineering industries, steel castings. F=1571 as fortress. D=UOC.
6826	Krivoj Rog	714,000	79.00	564,000	98.92	C	721,000	Dnepropetrovsk at Ingulets & Saksagan Rivers. Iron-mining center. F=17th century. D=UOC.
6827	L'vov (Lvov, Lwow, Lwiw)	876,000	78.00	683,000	98.92	C	888,000	Lvov on Roztoche upland. Ukrainian culture & publishing center. F=c1250. RC Cathedral (1270). D=UOC,RCC.
6828	Lisicansk (Lisichansk)	410,000	79.00	324,000	98.92	C	413,000	Voroshilovgrad on Donets River. Coal-mining, chemicals, glassmaking. F=1710 as Cossacks village. D=UOC.
6829	Rubeznoje	74,100	80.00	59,300	95.92	C	74,800	Important chemical industry, aniline dyes, paints, hosiery, metal working, glass. F=18th century. D=UOC.
6830	Severodoneck (Severodonetsk)	132,000	80.00	105,000	95.92	C	133,000	Chemical industries based on coke, woodworking, airport. F=1934 as chemical combine. D=UOC.
6831	Lozovaja	73,100	79.00	57,800	94.92	C	73,800	Near Krepopetrovsk. Rayon center, machinery, building materials, flour, cheese, meat, history museum. D=UOC.
6832	Lubny	59,500	83.00	49,400	98.92	C	60,000	Poltava on Sula River. Port. Textiles, clothing, furniture, construction. F=12th century. Incorporated(1783).
6833	Luck (Lutsk)	207,000	80.00	165,000	98.92	C	209,000	Volyn on Styr River. Scientific instruments, trucks. F=1000 by Vladimir. 3 monasteries. D=UOC,RCC.
6834	Marganec	54,000	82.00	44,300	97.92	C	54,500	Near Nikopol. Kakhovka reservoir, major manganese mining center, mining machinery repair shops. D=UOC.
6835	Melitopol'	175,000	80.00	140,000	95.92	C	176,000	Zaporozhye on Molochnaya River. Center of fruit-growing area. F=late 18th century. D=UOC.
6836	Mukacevo (Mukachevo, Mukachovo)	86,800	81.00	70,300	96.92	C	87,600	Zakarpatskaya on Latoritsa River. Timber. F=10th century. ROC wood church. D=RCC,UOC.
6837	Nezin	80,900	82.00	66,400	97.92	C	81,600	Chernigov. Engineering & food industries. F=11th century. Cathedrals of St. Nicholas & Annunciation. D=UOC.
6838	Nikolajev (Nikolaev, Nikolayev)	505,000	79.00	399,000	94.92	C	509,000	Nikolayev on Yuzhay Bug River. Important Black Sea port. Shipbuilding. F=1788 as naval base. D=UOC.
6839	Nikopol'	157,000	80.00	126,000	95.92	C	158,000	Dnepropetrovsk on Kakhovka Reservoir. World's largest manganese deposit. F=1630 as Nikitin Rog. D=UOC.
6840	Novaja Kachovka	58,200	82.00	47,700	97.92	C	58,700	On Kakhovka Reservoir. Major manganese mining region, railroad, machinery, fabricated metal products. D=UOC.
6841	Novograd-Volynskij	55,400	82.00	45,400	97.92	C	55,800	Zhitomir at confluence of Sluch & Smolka Rivers. Machine building. F=1257. 14th century castle. D=UOC.
6842	Novomoskovsk	75,600	81.00	61,200	96.92	C	76,300	Dnepropetrovsk on Samara River. Metal pipes, railroad ties, furniture. F=1650. 18th century cathedral. D=UOC.
6843	Novovolynsk	55,400	70.00	38,800	85.92	C	55,900	Volyn near Bug River. Near Polish border. Coal mining center, machine construction, woodworking. D=UOC.
6844	Odessa	1,123,000	80.00	898,000	98.92	C	1,123,000	Odessa seaport on Black Sea. Popular resort. Fishing. F=14th century. Greek Orthodox monastery. D=UOC.
6845	Iljicovsk	55,300	80.00	44,200	95.92	C	55,700	Odessa south of Odessa on Black Sea. Resorts. Fishing, tourism, food processing, clothing. D=UOC.
6846	Pavlograd	133,000	81.00	107,000	96.92	C	134,000	Dnepropetrovsk. Major railway center in Donets Coal Basin. Chemical industry. F=1797. D=UOC.
6847	Pervomajsk	82,700	80.00	66,200	95.92	C	83,400	Nikolayev at confluence of Sinyukha and Yuzhny Bug Rivers. Machines, furniture. F=1773. D=UOC.
6848	Poltava	316,000	79.00	250,000	98.92	C	319,000	Poltava on Vorskla River. Textiles, processing farm produce. F=8th century. Destroyed in WWII. D=UOC.
6849	Priluki	71,900	80.00	57,600	95.92	C	72,600	Chernigov on Uday River. Center of oil industry, textiles. F=1092. D=UOC.
6850	Romny	56,900	82.00	46,700	97.92	C	57,400	Sumy on Sula River. Engineering, consumer-goods production. F=11th century as fortress. D=UOC.
6851	Roven'ki	57,700	81.00	46,800	96.92	C	58,200	Voroshilovgrad. Coal-mining region, woodworking, stone products. F=1934. D=UOC.
6852	Rovno (Rowne)	236,000	80.00	189,000	98.92	C	238,000	Rovno on Ustye River. Chemicals, machine building. Branch of Kiev University. F=1282. D=UOC.
6853	Sepetovka	51,200	85.00	43,500	97.92	C	51,700	Chmel'nickij north of Starokonstantinov. Rayon center, sugar refinery, brewery, dairying, clothing. D=UOC.
6854	Sevastopol' (Sebastopol)	361,000	79.00	285,000	98.92	C	365,000	Crimean on Black Sea. Major naval base. Ancient Greek Chetsonesus nearby (421 BC). F=1783. D=UOC.
6855	Simferopol'	348,000	78.00	271,000	98.92	C	351,000	Crimean on Salgir River. Wine, tobacco, cigarettes. Near Neapolis (3rd century BC). F=1784. D=UOC.
6856	Smela	80,100	80.00	64,100	95.92	C	80,800	Near Cherkasgy. Tyasmyn River. Rayon center, sugar refining, flour milling, brewing, woodworking. D=UOC.
6857	Sostka (Shostka)	93,900	81.00	76,100	96.92	C	94,800	Sumy on Shostka River. Photographic materials, veneers, chemicals. F=1730 as powder mill. D=UOC.
6858	Stachanov (Kadievka, Sergo)	691,000	85.00	587,000	99.42	C	697,000	Voroshilovgrad in Donets Coal Basin. Coal mining though pits are worked out. F=19th century. D=UOC.
6859	Br'anka	63,700	80.00	50,900	95.92	C	64,200	Lugansk. Barley, wheat, corn for grain and silage, coal mining, steel, metallurgy. D=UOC.
6860	Kommunarsk (Alchevsk, Voroshilovsk)	128,000	86.00	110,000	98.92	C	129,000	Major bituminous coal-mining center, ironworks, coke-chemicals. Modern apartment blocks. F=1895. D=UOC.
6861	Pervomajsk	51,300	83.00	42,600	98.92	C	51,800	Lugansk on Lugan River northwest of Stachanov. Manufacturing industries, vegetable produce, mining. D=UOC.
6862	Stryj (Stry)	67,300	82.00	55,200	97.92	C	67,900	Lvov on Stryy River. Machine building, center of gas industry. F=1396. D=UOC.
6863	Sumy	299,000	81.00	242,000	98.92	C	302,000	Sumy on Psyol River. Electron microscopes, sugar refining. F=1652. Cathedrals (18th century). D=UOC.
6864	Sverdlovsk	143,000	80.00	114,000	98.92	C	144,000	Voroshilorgrad in Donets Coal Basin. Coal mining, anthracite. Near Provalsky Steppe reserve. F=1938. D=UOC.

Table 10-5–continued opposite

Table 10-5–continued

Rec No 1	Country City 2	Pop 2000 3	AC% 4	Church Members 5	E% 6	W 7	Pop 2025 8	Notes 9
6865	Svetlovodsk	56,900	72.00	41,000	87.92	C	57,400	Kirovograd on Kremenchug Reservoir. Near Kremenchug. Ceramics, furniture. D=UOC.
6866	Ternopol' (Tarnopol)	216,000	80.00	173,000	98.92	C	218,000	Ternopol on upper Seret River. Heavy damage from WWII. F=1524. 16th century Nativity. D=UOC,RCC.
6867	Torez	316,000	79.00	249,000	98.92	C	319,000	Donetsk on Donets Coal Basin. Electrical engineering, building materials. D=UOC.
6868	Sacht'orsk (Shakhtyorsk)	72,100	80.00	57,700	95.92	C	72,800	Mining town. High-quality anthracite coal. Building materials. Incorporated in 1953. D=UOC.
6869	Sneznoje	68,000	80.00	54,400	95.92	C	68,600	Mining, chemicals. Center of rich agricultural area cereal grains. F=1938. D=UOC.
6870	Uman'	96,400	79.00	76,200	94.92	C	97,300	Cherkassy at confluence of Uman & Kamenka rivers. Scientific instrument. F=Middle Ages. Inc.=1795. D=UOC.
6871	Uzgorod (Uzhgorod, Ungvar)	121,000	80.00	96,800	95.92	C	122,000	Zakarpatskaya on Uzh River. Furniture, veneer, margarine. Military & trade center. F=903. D=UOC.
6872	Vinnica (Vinnitsa)	376,000	78.00	293,000	98.92	C	379,000	Vinnitsa on Yuzhny Bug River. Agricultural center, fertilizers. F=1363 as fortress. Destroyed in WWII. D=UOC.
6873	Vorosilovgrad (Lugansk)	651,000	78.00	508,000	98.92	C	657,000	Voroshilovgrad on Lugan River. Diesel locomotives, steel tubes. F=1795 as Lugansk. D=UOC.
6874	Zaporozje (Zaporozhye)	949,000	79.00	750,000	98.92	C	957,000	Zaporozhye on Dnepr River. Metallurgy industry. F=1770 as fortress. D=UOC.
6875	Zdanov (Zhdanov, Mariupol)	536,000	80.00	429,000	98.92	C	541,000	Donetsk on Kalmius-Kalchik estuary. Major port for coal basin, fishing. F=18th century Pavlovsk. D=UOC.
6876	Zitomir (Zhitomir, Jitomir)	294,000	79.00	232,000	98.92	C	296,000	Zhitomir on Teterev River. Major trade focus. Wood, flax, musical instruments. F=9th century. D=UOC,RCC
6877	Zoltyje Vody	63,800	70.00	44,600	85.92	C	64,300	Dnepropetrovsk north of Krivoj Rog. Heavy machinery, chemicals, footwear, mining, metallurgy. D=UOC.
	UNITED ARAB EMIRATES	**2,441,000**	**10.76**	**263,000**	**57.88**	**B**	**3,284,000**	**ROMAN CATHOLICS 5.0%, ORTHODOX 2.8%. PENT-CHAR 2.2%, EVANGELICAL 0.5%, GCC 5.6%**
6878	rural areas	344,000	3.23	11,100	34.48	A	323,000	75.0% (1950), 42.8% (1970), 19.0% (1990), 14.1% (2000), 11.9% (2010), 9.8% (2025)
6879	urban areas	2,097,000	12.00	252,000	61.72	B	2,961,000	25.0% (1950), 57.1% (1970), 80.9% (1990), 85.8% (2000), 88.0% (2010), 90.1% (2025)
6880	non-metropolitan areas	59,500	11.88	7,100	60.66	B	158,478	*Sources of data:* Census of 1980; estimates for 1950, 1960, and 1975.
6881	metropolitan areas	2,037,000	12.00	245,000	61.75	B	2,803,000	*Definition:* Urban centers.
6882	ABU ZABY (Abu Dhabi)	928,000	14.30	133,000	65.42	B	1,236,000	Island off Persian Gulf coast. F=1760. Revolutionized by discovery of oil (1958). D=RCC,Anglican.
6883	Al'Ayn (Ap-Ain, Al Ain)	211,000	6.00	12,700	51.12	B	298,000	East on Oman border. Airport, zoo, museum.
6884	Ash-Shariqah (Sharjah)	260,000	5.00	13,000	50.12	B	367,000	Capital of Ash-Shariqah. Commemorative stamps. Deepwater port, fishing tourism. British base til 1971.
6885	Dubayy (Dubai)	551,000	15.00	82,700	67.12	B	779,000	Capital of Dubayy. Banks, insurance companies, freegold trade, oil industry. International airport. D=RCC.
6886	Ra's al-Khaymah	87,200	4.00	3,500	49.12	A	123,000	Capital of Ra's al-Khaymah on Persian Gulf near Oman border. Ancient seaport. Vegetables, dates, oil (1982).
	USA	**278,357,000**	**68.91**	**191,828,000**	**98.53**	**C**	**325,573,000**	**INDEPENDENTS 28.2%, PROTESTANTS 23.2%. PENT-CHAR 27.0%, EVANGELICAL 14.6%, GCC 35.4%**
6887	rural areas	63,438,000	73.71	46,757,000	99.96	C	54,078,000	35.8% (1950), 26.4% (1970), 24.7% (1990), 22.7% (2000), 20.3% (2010), 16.6% (2025)
6888	urban areas	214,920,000	67.50	145,071,000	98.11	C	271,495,000	64.1% (1950), 73.6% (1970), 75.2% (1990), 77.2% (2000), 79.6% (2010), 83.3% (2025)
6889	non-metropolitan areas	26,688,000	69.48	18,544,000	99.03	C	42,721,937	*Sources of data:* Censuses of 1950, 1960, 1970, 1980, and 1990.
6890	metropolitan areas	188,231,000	67.22	126,526,000	97.98	C	228,773,000	*Definition:* Places with 2,500 or more inhabitants and urbanized areas.
6891	Abilene, TX	132,000	72.50	95,500	98.82	C	166,000	Taylor County seat. Petroleum, natural gas, livestock. F=1881. Abilene. Christian University (1906). D=SBC,RCC.
6892	Albany, GA	124,000	70.50	87,400	98.62	C	157,000	Dougherty County on Flint River. Pecans, peanuts, livestock. F=1836 as cotton market. D=SBC,NBC.
6893	Albany-Schenectady-Troy, NY	962,000	71.00	683,000	99.12	C	1,216,000	Capital on Hudson River Channel. Administration, historical landmarks. F=1600s by Dutch. D=RCC,NBC.
6894	Albany, NY	111,000	70.80	78,800	98.67	C	141,000	Capital on Hudson River Channel. Administration, historical landmarks. F=1600s by Dutch. D=RCC,NBC.
6895	Schenectady, NY	72,300	73.00	52,800	99.32	C	91,300	Schenectady County on Mohawk River. General Electric Co., sporting goods. F=1661 by Dutch. D=RCC,NBC.
6896	Troy, NY	59,700	70.50	42,100	99.07	C	75,500	Rensselaer County on Hudson River. Iron & steel, autos. Troy Female Seminary (1821). F=1629. DRCC,NBC.
6897	Albuquerque, NM	529,000	67.50	357,000	97.12	C	668,000	Bernalillo County on Rio Grande. Encircled by Indian pueblos. 5,314 ft. Health center. F=1706. D=RCC,SBC.
6898	Alexandria, LA	145,000	72.50	105,000	98.82	C	183,000	Rapides Paris on Red River. Distribution center for farm products, timber, livestock. F=1810. D=RCC,SBC.
6899	Allentown-Bethlehem, PA-NJ	756,000	68.50	518,000	98.12	C	955,000	Lehigh County on Lehigh River. Iron ore, zinc, limestone. F=1762. D=Quakers Amish,RCC,ELCA.
6900	Allentown, PA	116,000	68.50	79,200	98.12	C	146,000	Lehigh County on Lehigh River. Iron ore, zinc, limestone. F=1762. D=Quakers,Amish,ELCA.
6901	Bethlehem, PA	78,600	70.50	55,400	99.07	C	99,300	Northampton and Lehigh counties on Lehigh River. Steel. F=1741 by Moravians. D=RCC,ELCA.
6902	Altoona, PA	144,000	70.50	101,000	98.62	C	182,000	Blair County on Allegheny Front. Diversified industries & railroad shops. F=1760s. D=RCC,ELCA.
6903	Amarillo, TX	206,000	71.50	148,000	98.72	C	261,000	Potter County. Oil, farming, ranching, copper, helium. F=1887 as railroad construction camp. D=SBC,RCC.
6904	Ames, IA	71,600	71.00	50,800	99.12	C	90,400	Story County on Skunk River. Institute for Atomic Research. Oldest veterinary college (1879). F=1865. D=ELCA.
6905	Anchorage, AK	273,000	59.80	164,000	89.42	B	345,000	Port on Cook Inlet. Defense industry, oil, tourism. Severe earthquake (1964). F=1914 by Alaska railroad. D=RCC.
6906	Anderson, IN	144,000	65.50	94,200	95.12	C	182,000	Madison County on White River. Corn, wheat. F=1823 on Delaware Indian village. D=Church of God HQ.
6907	Anderson, SC	160,000	71.50	114,000	98.72	C	202,000	Anderson County in Blue Ridge Mountains. Glass fibers. Johnson Female Seminary (1848). F=1826. D=SBC.
6908	Anniston, AL	128,000	72.50	92,600	98.82	C	161,000	Calhoun County in Appalachian foothills. Cast-iron pipe, textiles, chemicals. F=1872. D=SBC,NBC,UMC.
6909	Appleton-Oshkosh-Neenah, WI	347,000	71.50	248,000	98.72	C	438,000	Outagamie County on Fox River. Paper industry. Lawrence College (1847). F=1847, as Grand Chute. D=RCC.
6910	Appleton, WI	72,300	72.00	52,100	99.22	C	91,400	Outagamie County on Fox River. Paper industry. Lawrence College (1847). F=1847, as Grand Chute. D=RCC.
6911	Oshkosh, WI	60,600	72.00	43,600	99.22	C	76,500	Winnebago County seat on Lake Winnebago. Lumber, trucks, apparel. F=1836 by Menominee Indians. D=RCC.
6912	Asheville, NC	192,000	73.50	141,000	98.77	C	243,000	Buncombe County. Blue Ridge Mountains. Textiles, furniture. F=1794. Biltmore estate. D=SBC,NBC.
6913	Athens, GA	172,000	69.50	120,000	98.57	C	217,000	Clarke County on Oconee River. Dairy, beef cattle, poultry. F=1801 as seat of University of Georgia. D=SBC,NBC.
6914	Atlanta, GA	2,689,000	67.00	1,802,000	98.72	C	3,228,000	Capital. Fulton County. Communications hub. Financial center of Southeast. HQ of Coca-Cola. F=1837. D=SBC.
6915	Auburn, AL	67,300	74.80	50,300	99.22	C	85,000	Lee County. Auburn University (originally Methodist-1856). F=1836. D=SBC,NBC,UMC.
6916	Auburn, NY	58,200	74.00	43,100	99.22	C	73,600	Cayuga County or Owasco Lake. Shoes, rope, rugs. Auburn Theological Seminary (1822-1939). F=1793. D=RCC.
6917	Augusta, ME	62,400	66.00	41,200	95.62	C	78,800	Capital. Kennebec County on Kennebec River. Paper, textiles, tourism. F=1628. Inc=1797. D=RCC,UCC.
6918	Augusta, GA	437,000	69.50	304,000	98.57	C	552,000	Richmond County on Savannah River. Cotton trading, textiles. F=1735. D=SBC,NBC.
6919	Austin, TX	860,000	69.50	598,000	98.57	C	1,087,000	Capital. Travis County on Colorado River. Research for defense & consumer industries. F=1839. D=SBC,RCC.
6920	Bakersfield, CA	598,000	66.50	398,000	96.12	C	756,000	Kern County. Grain, livestock, oil, vineyards, tourism. F=1869 by Thomas Baker. D=RCC,LDS.
6921	Bangor, ME	97,700	64.50	63,000	94.12	C	123,000	Penobscot County on Penobscot River. Lumber, paper. F=1769. Bangor Theological Seminary (1814). D=RCC.
6922	Baton Rouge, LA	582,000	71.50	416,000	98.72	C	735,000	Capital. On Mississippi River. Oil industry, transportation. F=1719 as French fort. D=RCC,SBC.
6923	Battle Creek, MI	150,000	67.50	101,000	97.12	C	189,000	Calhoun County on Battle Creek. Cereal. F=1831, later Seventh-day Adventist colony. 'Health City'. D=RCC.
6924	Beaumont-Port Arthur, TX	398,000	71.00	282,000	98.67	C	502,000	Jefferson County on Neches River. 'Golden Triangle' industrial complex. Petrochemicals. F=1825. D=SBC,RCC.
6925	Beaumont, TX	126,000	70.50	88,700	98.62	C	159,000	Jefferson County on Neches River. 'Golden Triangle' industrial complex. Petrochemicals. F=1825. D=SBC,RCC.
6926	Port Arthur, TX	64,600	73.00	47,200	99.32	C	81,700	Jefferson County on Sabine Lake. Petrochemicals, shipbuilding. Major deepwater port. F=1895. D=SBC,RCC.
6927	Beckley, WV	70,800	66.00	46,700	95.62	C	89,400	Raleigh County. Commercial center for coal mining & agriculture. F=1838. Beckley College (1933). D=UMC,ABC.
6928	Bellingham, WA	141,000	63.50	89,300	93.12	C	178,000	Whatcom County on Bellingham Ray. Timber pulp, fish canneries, pleasure boats. F=1852. D=RCC,ELCA.
6929	Benton Harbor, MI	178,000	66.50	118,000	96.12	C	224,000	Berrien County on Lake Michigan. Industry declined in 1980s-city facing insolvency. 90% Black. F=1869. D=RCC.
6930	Billings, MT	125,000	63.50	79,300	93.12	C	158,000	Yellowstone County on Yellowstone River. Rangeland, sugar beets. F=1882. 'Midland Empire'. D=RCC,ELCA.
6931	Biloxi-Gulfport, MS	217,000	72.00	156,000	98.82	C	274,000	Harrison County on Gulf Coast peninsula. Seafood, tourism. F=1719. D=SBC,NBC.
6932	Binghamton, NY	291,000	70.50	205,000	98.62	C	368,000	Broome County on Chenango & Susquehanna rivers. Shoes, photo supplies. SUNY (1946). F=1787. D=RCC.
6933	Birmingham, AL	999,000	70.50	705,000	98.62	C	1,262,000	Jefferson County. Coal, limestone in past. Now aircraft, acetylene. Higher education center. F=1813. D=SBC.
6934	Bismarck, ND	92,300	76.00	70,100	99.32	C	117,000	Capital. Burleigh County on Missouri River. Grain & livestock distribution center. F=1830s. D=ELCA,RCC.
6935	Bloomington, IN	120,000	66.50	79,800	96.12	C	152,000	Monroe County. Center of limestone belt. Refrigerators. Indiana University (1820). F=1818. D=RCC,UMC.
6936	Bloomington-Normal, IL	142,000	68.50	97,400	98.12	C	180,000	McLean County. Farming, livestock, agricultural equipment. Illinois Wesleyan University (1850). F=1822. D=RCC.
6937	Bloomington, IL	57,200	69.50	39,800	99.12	C	72,300	McLean County. Farming, livestock, agricultural equipment. Illinois Wesleyan University (1850). F=1822. D=RCC.
6938	Boise City, ID	227,000	65.50	148,000	95.12	C	286,000	Capital. Ada County on Boise River. On Oregon Trail & Mining center. Boise National Forest. F=1863. D=RCC.
6939	Boston-Lawrence-Salem, MA-NH	3,553,000	68.00	2,416,000	99.62	C	4,489,000	Capital. Suffolk County on Atlantic Ocean. Finance, insurance. F=1630. Harvard University (1636). D=RCC.
6940	Boston, MA (PMSA)	2,915,000	68.00	1,982,000	99.62	C	3,440,000	Capital. Suffolk County on Atlantic Ocean. Finance, insurance. F=1630. Harvard University (1636). D=RCC.
6941	Brookline, MA	60,200	72.00	43,400	99.22	C	76,100	Norfolk County. Suburban residential area w/light industries. Birthplace of J.F. Kennedy. F=1638. D=RCC.
6942	Cambridge, MA	105,000	70.50	74,300	98.62	C	133,000	Middlesex County on Charles River. Harvard University (1636). Scientific & industrial research. F=1630. D=RCC.
6943	Framingham, MA	71,500	70.00	50,100	99.07	C	90,400	Middlesex County on Sudbury River. Textiles, printing & publishing, computers. Shopper's world. F=1650. D=RCC.
6944	Malden, MA	59,300	73.00	43,300	99.32	C	74,900	Middlesex County north of Boston. Mystic River valley. Birthplace of Saul Cohen. F=1640. D=RCC.
6945	Medford, MA	63,200	73.00	46,100	99.32	C	79,800	Middlesex County on Mystic River. Residential. Tufts University (1852). F=1630. 'Middle ford'. D=RCC.
6946	Newton, MA	90,900	72.00	65,500	99.22	C	115,000	Middlesex County on Charles River. Andover Newton Theological School (1808). F=1639. D=RCC.
6947	Quincy, MA	93,600	71.50	66,900	99.17	C	118,000	Norfolk County on Boston Harbor. Adams family home. United First Parish Church (1828). F=1625. D=RCC.
6948	Somerville, MA	83,900	71.00	59,600	99.12	C	106,000	Middlesex County on Mystic River. Meat-packing. F=1630 as Cow Commons. D=RCC.
6949	Waltham, MA	63,700	70.00	44,600	99.07	C	80,500	Middlesex County on Charles River. First cotton-cloth textile mill (1813). F=1630s. D=RCC.
6950	Weymouth, MA	59,500	69.50	41,400	99.12	C	75,200	Norfolk County on Hingham Bay. Mainly residential. Fertilizers, shoes (1853). F=1622 as plantation. D=RCC.
6951	Brockton, MA (PMSA)	260,000	67.50	175,000	97.12	C	328,000	Plymouth County. Shoes, boots, clothing. Electricity since 1884. F=1649 as part of Plymouth Colony. D=RCC.
6952	Lawrence-Haverhill, MA-NH (PMSA)	433,000	68.50	297,000	98.12	C	547,000	Essex County on Merrimack River. Large woolen-textile center. Labor strike (1912). F=1845. D=RCC.
6953	Lawrence, MA	77,300	69.00	53,300	98.62	C	97,600	Essex County on Merrimack River. Large woolen-textile center. Labor strike (1912). F=1845. D=RCC.
6954	Haverhill, MA	56,600	72.00	40,800	99.22	C	71,500	Essex County on Merrimack River north of Lawrence. Leather, John Greenleaf Whittier birthplace. D=RCC.
6955	Lowell, MA-NH (PMSA)	301,000	69.50	209,000	98.57	C	380,000	Middlesex County on Concord & Merrimack rivers. Textile center until 1924. Electronics. F=1653. D=RCC.
6956	Lowell, MA	114,000	70.00	79,700	98.57	C	144,000	Middlesex County on Concord & Merrimack rivers. Textile center until 1924. Electronics. F=1653. D=RCC.
6957	Manchester, NH	163,000	63.50	103,000	93.12	C	206,000	Hillsborough County near Amoskeag Falls. Cotton milling. St. Anselm's College (1889). F=1722. D=RCC.
6958	Nashua, NH (PMSA)	199,000	63.50	126,000	93.12	C	251,000	Hillsborough County on Merrimack & Nashua rivers. Shoes. Rivier College (1933, RCC). F=1655. D=RCC.
6959	New Bedford, MA	193,000	70.50	136,000	98.62	C	244,000	Bristol County Acushnet River. 19th century whaling port. Fishing. Seaman's Bethel. F=1652. D=RCC.
6960	Portsmouth-Dover-Rochester, NH-ME	246,000	62.50	154,000	92.12	C	311,000	Rockingham County, Atlantic coast. Seaport, naval yard, resort. F=1623. St. John's Church (1807). D=RCC.
6961	Worcester, MA	481,000	68.50	329,000	98.12	C	608,000	Worcester County on Blackstone River. Metals. College of Holy Cross (1843, RCC). F=1713. D=RCC.
6962	Bowling Green, KY	65,100	72.00	46,800	99.22	C	82,200	Warren County on Barren River. River & rail transportation, tobacco, agriculture. F=1780. D=SBC,RCC,UMC.
6963	Bradenton, FL	194,000	65.00	126,000	94.62	C	245,000	Manatee County on Manatee River. Winter resort, farm market. F=1854. D=RCC,SBC.
6964	Bremerton, WA	209,000	62.50	131,000	92.12	C	264,000	Kitsup County on Puget Sound. Naval Shipyard. Dairy, lumber. F=1891. D=RCC,ELCA.
6965	Brownsville-Harlingen-San Ben, TX	506,000	72.50	367,000	98.82	C	640,000	Cameron County on Rio Grande. Deepwater port. Fuel oil, ores, grains. Tourism. F=1846. D=SBC,RCC.
6966	Brownsville, TX	109,000	71.50	77,900	98.72	C	138,000	Cameron County on Rio Grande. Deepwater port. Fuel oil, ores, grains. Tourism. F=1846. D=SBC,RCC.
6967	Harlingen, TX	53,600	72.00	38,600	99.22	C	67,800	Cameron County. Food processing. Transport for cotton, citrus, vegetables. F=1900s. D=SBC,RCC.
6968	Bryan-College Station, TX	134,000	70.50	94,600	98.62	C	169,000	Brazos County. Cotton, dairying, poultry. F=1820s. Texas A&M University. D=SBC,RCC.
6969	Bryan, TX	60,500	71.00	43,000	99.12	C	76,500	Brazos County. Cotton, dairying, poultry. F=1820s. Education, research, building materials. D=SBC,RCC.
6970	College Station, TX	57,700	70.00	40,400	99.07	C	72,900	Brazos County. Cotton, dairying, poultry. F=1820s. Education, research, laboratory equipment. D=SBC,RCC.
6971	Buffalo-Niagara Falls, NY	983,000	68.50	673,000	98.12	C	1,209,000	Erie County on Lake Erie. Grain, coal, iron ore. State University (1846). F=1780. 'Beautiful river'. D=RCC.
6972	Buffalo, NY (PMSA)	361,000	68.20	246,000	97.82	C	456,000	Erie County on Lake Erie. Grain, limestone, coal. State University (1846). F=1780. 'Beautiful river'. D=RCC.
6973	Cheektowaga, NY	92,900	70.00	65,000	99.07	C	117,000	Erie County east of Buffalo. Buffalo International Airport. Settled in 1809, incorporated in 1834. D=RCC.
6974	Lockport, NY	63,300	69.50	44,000	99.12	C	80,000	Niagara County. Fruit, paper, textiles. Built around five double locks (Lake Erie). F=1821. D=RCC,NBC.
6975	West Seneca, NY	52,700	72.80	38,400	99.22	C	66,600	Erie County in lee of Lake Erie. Nurseries. F=1842 by Ebenezer Society(German religious sect). D=RCC.
6976	Niagara Falls, NY (PMSA)	243,000	68.50	166,000	98.12	C	307,000	Niagra County on Niagra River. Hydroelectric power, tourism. F=1761 as Fort Schlosser by British. D=RCC.
6977	Burlington, NC	119,000	72.50	86,400	98.82	C	150,000	Alamance County. Textiles, electronic equipment, furniture, chemicals. Coffin factory (1884). F=1855. D=SBC.
6978	Burlington, VT	145,000	64.50	93,300	94.12	C	183,000	Chittenden County on Lake Champlain. Famous for sunset views. Aircraft, computers. F=1763. D=RCC.
6979	Butler, PA	95,200	72.00	68,600	99.22	C	120,000	Butler County north of Pittsburgh. Moraine State Park. Natural gas, oil, coal, limestone. D=RCC,ELCA.
6980	Canton, OH	434,000	69.50	302,000	98.57	C	548,000	Stark County. Farm equipment, safes & bank vaults. Football Hall of Fame (1963). F=1805. D=RCC,UMC,NBC.
6981	Cape Girardeau, MO	65,100	71.00	46,200	99.12	C	82,200	Cape Girardeau County on Mississippi River. Paper products, clothing, shoes. F=1793. D=SBC,RCC.
6982	Casper, WY	67,400	66.50	44,800	96.12	C	85,100	Natrona County on North Platte River. Oil fields, natural gas. Cattle, sheep. F=1888 as tent town. D=RCC,LDS.
6983	Cedar Rapids, IA	186,000	69.50	129,000	98.57	C	235,000	Linn County on Cedar River. Grain & livestock, farm-related industry. Quaker Oats. F=1830s. D=ELCA,RCC.
6984	Champaign-Urbana-Rantoul, IL	190,000	69.50	132,000	98.57	C	241,000	Champaign County. University of Illinois (1868), agriculture, light manufacturing. F=1853. D=RCC,ELCA.

Table 10-5–continued overleaf

Table 10-5–continued

Rec No 1	Country City 2	Pop 2000 3	AC% 4	Church Members 5	E% 6	W 7	Pop 2025 8	Notes 9
6985	Champaign, IL	69,900	70.00	48,900	99.07	C	88,300	Champaign County. University of Illinois (1868), agriculture, light manufacturing. F=1853. D=RCC,ELCA.
6986	Charleston, SC	558,000	70.50	393,000	98.62	C	705,000	Atlantic port. Hub of Southern culture. Paper, metalworking. Devastated by hurricane (1989). F=1670. D=SBC.
6987	North Charleston, SC	77,300	71.00	54,900	99.12	C	97,600	Atlantic port. Hub of Southern culture. Paper, pulp. Devastated by hurricane (1989). F=1670. D=SBC.
6988	Charleston, WV	276,000	64.50	178,000	94.12	C	348,000	Kanawha County on Elk & Kanawha Rivers. Coal, chemicals, glass, steel, nylon, lucite. F=1788. D=UMC,ABC.
6989	Charlotte-Gastonia-Rock Hill, NC-SC	1,279,000	66.00	844,000	98.62	C	1,616,000	Mecklenburg County in Piedmont region. Textiles, machinery, metal, food products. F=1750s. D=SBC,NBC,UMC.
6990	Charlotte, NC	436,000	65.00	283,000	94.62	C	551,000	Mecklenburg County in Piedmont region. Textiles, machinery, metal, food products. F=1750s. D=SBC,NBC,UMC.
6991	Gastonia, NC	60,200	67.00	40,400	96.62	C	76,100	Gaston County seat in Piedmont Plateau. Textile-manufacturing center. F=late 1700s. D=SBC,NBC,UMC.
6992	Charlottesville, VA	144,000	66.00	95,300	95.62	C	182,000	Albemarle County on Rivanna River. University of Virginia. T. Jefferson's home. F=1730s. D=SBC.
6993	Chattanooga, TN-GA	477,000	68.50	327,000	98.12	C	602,000	Hamilton County on Tennessee River. HQ of Tennessee Valley Authority (TVA). Tourism. F=1815. D=SBC,UMC.
6994	Chattanooga, TN	168,000	68.30	115,000	97.92	C	212,000	Seventh-day Adventist Southern Missionary College (1916). D=SBC,UMC.
6995	Cheyenne, WY	80,500	66.50	53,500	96.12	C	102,000	Capital. Laramie County on Crow Creek. Oil, timber, livestock. Frontier Days (July). F=1867. D=RCC,LDS.
6996	Chicago-Gary-Lake County, IL-IN-WI	8,158,000	65.50	5,344,000	99.12	C	10,306,000	Cook County on Lake Michigan. Steel, food products, printing & publishing. Ethnically diverse. F=1837. D=RCC.
6997	Aurora-Elgin, IL (PMSA)	393,000	65.50	257,000	99.12	C	496,000	Kane & Du Page counties on Fox River. Tractors, telephones. Aurora College (Advent) 1893. F=1834. D=RCC.
6998	Aurora, IL	110,000	70.50	77,300	98.62	C	138,000	Kane & Du Page counties on Fox River. Tractors, telephones. Aurora College (Advent) 1893. F=1834. D=RCC.
6999	Elgin, IL	84,800	65.50	55,500	95.12	C	107,000	Cook & Kane counties on Fox River. From Scottish hymn 'The Song of Elgin'. Dairying. F=1835. D=RCC.
7000	Chicago, IL (PMSA)	6,945,000	66.00	4,584,000	99.62	C	7,951,000	Cook County on Lake Michigan. Steel, food products, printing & publishing. Ethnically diverse. F=1837. D=RCC.
7001	Arlington Heights, IL	83,100	67.00	55,700	96.62	C	105,000	Cook County. Northwestern residential suburb of Chicago. F-1836. Known as Dunton until 1871. D=RCC.
7002	Cicero, IL	74,200	67.00	49,700	96.62	C	93,800	Cook County. Al Capone's headquarters (1920s). Manufacturing. F=1830s. Nouton College (1902). D=RCC.
7003	Des Plaines, IL	58,600	66.00	38,700	95.62	C	74,000	Cook County on Des Plaines River. Residential until 1950s (O'Hare Intl. Airport). F=1873. D=RCC.
7004	Evanston, IL	80,600	66.50	53,600	96.12	C	102,000	Cook County on Lake Michigan. Northwestern University (1853). 2nd assembly WCC (1954). F=1863. D=RCC.
7005	Mount Prospect, IL	58,500	69.00	40,400	98.62	C	73,900	Cook County north of Chicago near Des Plaines. Residential, commercial, some industry. D=RCC.
7006	Naperville, IL	94,000	71.00	66,700	99.12	C	119,000	Du Page County west of Chicago near Aurora. Major office and corporate center. D=RCC.
7007	Oak Lawn, IL	61,800	68.00	42,100	97.62	C	78,100	Cook County south of Chicago near Chicago-Midway Airport. Metal working, wood products. D=RCC.
7008	Oak Park, IL	59,100	66.00	39,000	95.62	C	74,600	Cook County. Primarily residential. Birthplace of Ernest Hemmingway. F=1833 as Oak Ridge. D=RCC.
7009	Schaumburg, IL	75,500	67.50	51,000	97.12	C	95,400	Cook County northwest of Chicago beyond O'Hare International Airport. D=RCC.
7010	Skokie, IL	65,400	66.50	43,500	96.12	C	82,600	Cook County. Publishing (Rand McNally). Hebrew Theological College (1922). F=1834. 'Swamp'. D=RCC.
7011	Waukegan, IL	76,400	70.00	53,500	99.07	C	96,500	Lake County seat on Lake Michigan. Port of call. F=1695 as fort by French. 'Little Fort'. D=RCC.
7012	Wheaton, IL	56,700	73.00	41,400	99.32	C	71,600	Du Page County seat. Headquarters for many Protestant Evangelical groups. Wheaton College (1860). F=1837.
7013	Gary-Hammond, IN (PMSA)	665,000	65.70	437,000	95.32	C	841,000	Lake County on Lake Michigan. Steel industry base. Many Blacks. F=1906 for steel. D=RCC.
7014	Hammond, IN	92,700	67.00	62,100	96.62	C	117,000	Lake County on Grand Calumet River. Diversified light manufacturing. F=1869 as Hohman. D=RCC,UMC.
7015	Joliet, IL (PMSA)	429,000	65.50	281,000	98.12	C	542,000	Will County seat on Des Plaines River. Known for limestone. Agriculture. State penitentiary. F=1833. D=RCC.
7016	Kenosha, WI (PMSA)	141,000	69.50	98,100	98.57	C	178,000	Kenosha County seat on Lake Michigan. Port. Autos, furniture. Carthage College (1847). F=1835. 'Pike'. D=RCC.
7017	Chico, CA	200,000	67.00	134,000	96.62	C	253,000	Central Valley north of Yuba City near Sacramento River. D=Independents,RCC,LDS.
7018	Cincinnati-Hamilton, OH-KY-IN	1,680,000	68.00	1,142,000	97.62	C	2,122,000	Hamilton County on Ohio River. Inland coal port. Noted cultural center. Xavier Univ. (1831). F=1788. D=RCC.
7019	Cincinnati, OH-KY-IN (PMSA)	1,315,000	69.00	907,000	98.62	C	1,603,000	Hamilton County on Ohio River. Inland coal port. Noted cultural center. Xavier Univ. (1831). F=1788. D=RCC.
7020	Hamilton-Middletown, OH (PMSA)	321,000	69.00	221,000	98.62	C	405,000	Butler County on Great Miami River. Agriculture trade, safes, auto parts, paper. F=1794 as Fairfield. D=RCC.
7021	Hamilton, OH	67,600	69.00	46,600	98.62	C	85,300	Butler County on Great Miami River. Agriculture trade, safes, auto parts, paper. F=1794 as Fairfield. D=RCC.
7022	Middletown, OH	118,000	66.50	78,500	96.12	C	149,000	Butler County midway between Cincinnati and Dayton.
7023	Clarksburg, WV	59,200	68.00	40,300	97.62	C	74,800	Harrison County on Monongahela River. Coal mining, oil & gas, glassware. F=1765. D=UMC,ABC.
7024	Clarksville-Hopkinsville, TN-KY	187,000	71.50	133,000	98.72	C	236,000	Montgomery County at confluence of Cumberland & Red rivers. Farm economy, tobacco, meat. F=1784. D=SBC.
7025	Clarksville, TN	83,100	71.00	59,000	99.12	C	105,000	Montgomery County at confluence of Cumberland & Red rivers. Farm economy, tobacco, meat. F=1784. D=SBC.
7026	Cleveland-Akron-Loraine, OH	2,424,000	66.50	1,612,000	98.12	C	3,062,000	Cuyahoga County on Lake Erie. Steel, aluminum. 400 medical & industrial research centers. D=RCC.
7027	Akron, OH (PMSA)	724,000	67.50	489,000	97.12	C	914,000	Summit County on Cuyahoga River. 'High place'. 'Rubber capital of the world'. F=1825. D=RCC.
7028	Akron, OH	246,000	67.50	166,000	97.12	C	310,000	Summit County on Cuyahoga River. 'High place'. 'Rubber capital of the world'. F=1825. D=RCC.
7029	Cleveland, OH (PMSA)	1,724,000	66.50	1,146,000	98.12	C	2,074,000	Cuyahoga County on Lake Erie. Steel, aluminum. 400 medical & industrial research centers. D=RCC.
7030	Cleveland Heights, OH	59,500	67.10	39,900	96.72	C	75,200	Cuyahoga County. Residential suburb of Cleveland. Cain Park (summer theater). F=1903. D=RCC.
7031	Euclid, OH	60,400	69.00	41,700	98.62	C	76,300	Cuyahoga County on Lake Erie. Noted for grapes before 1940. Airplane parts castings. F=1798. D=RCC.
7032	Lakewood, OH	65,700	67.00	44,000	96.62	C	83,000	Cuyahoga County on Lake Erie. Residential. Great Lakes Shakespeare Festival (summer). F=1806. D=RCC.
7033	Parma, OH	96,700	68.00	65,800	97.62	C	122,000	Cuyahoga County. Auto parts, tools, dies, metal stampings. F=1816 as Greenbriar. D=RCC.
7034	Lorain-Elyria, OH (PMSA)	298,000	67.50	201,000	97.12	C	377,000	Lorain County on Lake Erie. Major shipping center for coal, iron ore. F=1807 as trading post. D=RCC.
7035	Elyria, OH	62,500	70.00	43,700	99.07	C	78,900	Lorain County seat on Black River. Alloy castings, autoparts. Caves, waterfalls. F=1817 by Herman Ely. D=RCC.
7036	Lorain, OH	78,400	68.00	53,300	97.62	C	99,100	Lorain County on Lake Erie. Major shipping center for coal, iron ore. F=1807 as trading post. D=RCC.
7037	Colorado Springs, CO	437,000	71.50	312,000	98.72	C	552,000	El Paso County at 6,000 ft. Tourism, resorts. Air Force Academy (1954). Pike's Peak (14,000 ft.). F=1871. D=RCC.
7038	Columbia, MO	124,000	69.50	86,000	98.57	C	156,000	Boone County near Missouri River. Schools, professional associations, insurance. F=1819 as Smithton. D=SBC.
7039	Columbia, SC	499,000	69.50	347,000	98.57	C	630,000	Capital. Richland County on Congaree River. Cotton, peaches, tobacco. F=1786. D=SBC.
7040	Columbus, MS	57,400	74.00	42,400	99.32	C	72,400	Columbus Lake on Tombigbee River. Columbus Air Force Base. D=SBC,NBC.
7041	Columbus, IN	64,900	68.00	44,200	97.62	C	82,000	Bartholomew County on White River. Known for architecture, particularly churches. F=1821. D=RCC,UMC.
7042	Columbus, GA-AL	268,000	69.50	186,000	98.57	C	338,000	Muscogee County on Chattahoochee River. One of largest textile centers of the South. F=1827. D=SBC,NBC.
7043	Columbus, OH	1,060,000	67.00	710,000	98.62	C	1,298,000	Capital. Fairfield & Franklin counties. Industry, government agencies, education, research. F=1812. D=RCC.
7044	Concord, NH	80,700	65.00	52,400	94.62	C	102,000	Capital. Merrimack County on Merrimack River. Printing, manufacturing, insurance. F=1725. D=RCC,UCC.
7045	Corpus Christi, TX	385,000	71.50	275,000	98.72	C	487,000	Nueces County on Corpus Christi Bay. Deepwater port (bulk cargoes), gas, oil. Resort facilities. F=1838. D=SBC.
7046	Corvallis, OR	109,000	60.50	65,700	90.12	C	137,000	Benton County. Oregon State University (1868). F=1851 as Marysville. 'Heart of the Valley'. D=RCC,LDS,ELCA.
7047	Cumberland, MD-WV	112,000	66.50	74,400	96.12	C	141,000	Allegany County on Potomac River. Coal mining, rubber, textiles. F=1750 as trading post. D=RCC,NBC.
7048	Dallas-Fort Worth, TX	3,912,000	69.00	2,699,000	99.62	C	4,644,000	Dallas County on Trinity River. Cotton, oil, insurance, computer science, medical center. F=1856. D=SBC,RCC.
7049	Dallas, TX	2,946,000	68.50	2,018,000	99.62	C	3,721,000	Dallas County on Trinity River. Cotton, oil, insurance, computer science, medical center. F=1856. D=SBC,RCC.
7050	Carrollton, TX	90,500	69.50	62,900	99.12	C	114,000	Dallas County north of Dallas near Dallas-Fort Worth Regional Airport. D=SBC,RCC.
7051	Denton, TX	73,000	72.00	52,500	99.22	C	92,200	Denton County. Cultural, research, & education center. North Texas State University (1890). F=1857. D=SBC,RCC.
7052	Garland, TX	199,000	69.50	138,000	98.57	C	251,000	Dallas County. Farm crops, electronic equipment, chemicals. F=1887 by consolidation. D=SBC,RCC.
7053	Irving, TX	171,000	68.50	117,000	98.12	C	216,000	Dallas County northwest of Dallas. Dallas-Fort Worth Regional Airport. Texas Stadium. D=SBC,RCC.
7054	Mesquite, TX	112,000	69.50	77,600	98.57	C	141,000	Dallas County. Power, gas, telephone headquarters. F=1873 by Texas & Pacific Railway. D=SBC,RCC.
7055	Plano, TX	142,000	68.50	97,100	98.12	C	179,000	Collin County north of Dallas. Southfork ranch from TV series 'Dallas'. J.C. Penney museum. D=SEC,RCC.
7056	Richardson, TX	82,400	70.00	57,700	99.07	C	104,000	Dallas & Collin counties. Residential suburb of Dallas, research center. F=1872. D=SBC,RCC.
7057	Fort Worth-Arlington, TX (PMSA)	1,498,000	70.00	1,049,000	99.62	C	1,893,000	Tarrent County seat on Trinity River. Aircraft, cattle, oil. Southwest Baptist (1908). F=1849. D=SBC,RCC.
7058	Arlington, TX	288,000	70.50	203,000	98.62	C	364,000	Tarrant County. Automotive & aerospace industries. University of Texas (1895). F=1843. D=SBC,RCC.
7059	Fort Worth, TX	493,000	70.00	345,000	98.57	C	622,000	Tarrent County seat on Trinity River. Aerospace, cattle, oil. Southwest Baptist (1908). F=1849. D=SBC,RCC.
7060	Grand Prairie, TX	110,000	70.50	77,300	98.62	C	139,000	Dallas County west of Dallas near Mountain Creek Lake. D=SBC,RCC.
7061	Danville, IL	74,900	71.00	53,100	99.12	C	94,600	Vermilion County on Vermilion River. Automotive products. Former Piankashaw village. F=1827. D=RCC.
7062	Danville, VA	58,400	70.00	40,900	99.07	C	73,800	Within Pittsylvania County on Dan River. Textiles, tobacco. Lady Astor (b. 1870). F=1830. D=SBC,NBC.
7063	Davenport-Rock Island-Moline, IA-IL	386,000	69.00	266,000	98.62	C	488,000	'Quad Cities' urban complex. Scott County on Mississippi River. Trading center, farm machinery. D=ELCA,RCC.
7064	Davenport, IA	105,000	69.50	72,900	98.57	C	133,000	Scott County on Mississippi River. Trading center, farm machinery. D=ELCA,RCC.
7065	Dayton-Springfield, OH	1,047,000	66.50	696,000	99.12	C	1,323,000	Montgomery County. Agriculture. National aviation center. F=1805. United Theological Seminary 1871. D=RCC.
7066	Dayton, OH	200,000	65.50	131,000	95.12	C	253,000	Montgomery County. Agriculture. National aviation center. F=1805. United Theological Seminary 1871. D=RCC.
7067	Kettering, OH	66,700	67.50	45,000	97.12	C	84,200	Montgomery County in the Miami Valley. Mainly residential. Testing laboratories. F=1841. D=RCC.
7068	Springfield, OH	77,600	67.00	52,000	96.62	C	98,000	Clark County seat on Buck Creek & Mad River. Wittenberg University (1845-Lutheran). F=1801. D=RCC.
7069	Daytona Beach, FL	408,000	63.50	259,000	93.12	C	516,000	Volusia County on Atlantic Ocean. Year-round beach resort. Daytona Speedway. F=1870. D=RCC,SBC.
7070	De Kalb, IL	57,500	72.00	41,400	99.22	C	72,600	DeKalb County on Kishwaukee River. Hybrid seed corn. Northern Illinois U. (1895). F=1838. D=RCC.
7071	Decatur, IA	145,000	72.30	105,000	98.92	C	183,000	Morgan County on Tennessee River. Port traffic, recreational development. F=1820 as Rhodes Ferry. D=SBC.
7072	Decatur, IL	129,000	68.50	88,400	98.12	C	163,000	Macon County on Sangamon River. Corn, soybeans, tractors. Home of A. Lincoln (1839-31). F=1829. D=RCC.
7073	Denver-Boulder, CO	1,687,000	61.00	1,029,000	96.62	C	2,048,000	Capital of Colorado. Denver County. Denver Mint (1906). Ski resorts. F=1861. 'Mile High City'. D=RCC.
7074	Boulder-Longmont, CO (PMSA)	248,000	59.50	148,000	89.12	B	313,000	Boulder County on Boulder Creek at 5,354 ft. Environment research. New Age organizations. F=1858. D=RCC.
7075	Boulder, CO	91,700	59.00	54,100	88.62	B	116,000	Boulder County on Boulder Creek at 5,354 ft. Environment research. New Age organizations. F=1858. D=RCC.
7076	Longmont, CO	56,800	66.50	37,700	96.12	C	71,700	North of Denver near Boulder and Front Range Mountains. D=RCC,UMC.
7077	Denver, CO (PMSA)	515,000	61.00	314,000	90.62	C	650,000	Capital of Colorado. Denver County. Denver Mint (1906). Ski resorts. F=1861. 'Mile High City'. D=RCC.
7078	Arvada, CO	98,200	65.00	63,900	94.62	C	124,000	Northwest suburb of Denver. Youth With A Mission (YWAM) base. D=RCC,UMC.
7079	Aurora, CO	244,000	63.50	155,000	93.12	C	309,000	Adams & Arapahoe counties. Eastern suburb of Denver. Mainly residential. F=1891 during silver boom. D=RCC.
7080	Thornton, CO	60,600	66.00	40,000	95.62	C	76,500	North of Denver near Westminster. Computer graphics systems, coffee, tea, infant furniture. D=RCC,UMC.
7081	Westminster, CO	82,100	64.20	52,700	93.82	C	104,000	North of Denver near Arvada. Electronics, leather goods, aerial lifts. D=RCC,UMC.
7082	Des Moines, IA	433,000	66.50	288,000	96.12	C	546,000	Capital of Iowa. Polk County. Insurance, publishing farm journals, farm machinery. F=1851. D=ELCA,RCC.
7083	Detroit-Ann Arbor, MI	4,697,000	63.80	2,997,000	97.42	C	5,934,000	Wayne County on Detroit River. Automobile capital of the world. Racial tensions. F=1701. D=RCC.
7084	Ann Arbor, MI (PMSA)	311,000	66.70	208,000	96.32	C	393,000	Washtenaw County on Huron River. University of Michigan (1837). F=1824. D=RCC.
7085	Detroit, MI (PMSA)	3,785,000	63.50	2,403,000	98.12	C	4,431,000	Wayne County on Detroit River. Automobile capital of the world. Racial tensions. F=1701. D=RCC.
7086	Clinton Township, MI	85,800	65.00	55,700	94.62	C	108,000	Worcester County on Nashua River. Lace, carpet mills (Bigelow since 1850s). F=1654. D=RCC.
7087	Dearborn Heights, MI	67,000	64.50	43,200	94.12	C	84,600	Wayne County on River Rouge. Headquarters of Ford Motor Company. Automotive industry. F=1795. D=RCC.
7088	Dearborn, MI	98,300	66.00	64,900	95.62	C	124,000	Wayne County on River Rouge. Headquarters of Ford Motor Company. Automotive industry. F=1795. D=RCC.
7089	Farmington Hills, MI	82,200	65.00	53,400	94.62	C	104,000	Oakland County northwest of Detroit and south of Pontiac. D=RCC,NBC,LCMS.
7090	Flint, MI	474,000	67.00	317,000	96.62	C	599,000	Genesee County seat on Flint River. Automobile industry (General Motors Co.). F=1819 as trading post. D=RCC.
7091	Livonia, MI	111,000	64.50	71,600	94.12	C	140,000	Wayne County. Western suburb of Detroit. Madonna College (1937), Detroit Race Course. F=1834. D=RCC.
7092	Monroe, MI	68,900	66.00	45,500	95.62	C	87,100	Monroe County seat on Raisin River. Paper, auto parts. Raisin River Massacre (1813). F=1780s. D=RCC.
7093	Pontiac, MI	78,300	64.00	50,100	93.62	C	99,000	Oakland County on Clinton River. Automobiles, auto parts. Silverdome sports arena. F=1820. D=RCC,NBC.
7094	Redford Township, MI	59,900	66.00	39,500	95.62	C	75,600	Wayne County north of Livonia, Middle River. Metal stampings, steel forging, diesel engines, ink, tools. D=RCC.
7095	Roseville, MI	56,600	65.00	36,800	94.62	C	71,500	Macomb County near Lake St. Clair. Mainly residential, light industry. F=1836 as post office. D=RCC,NBC.
7096	Royal Oak, MI	72,000	65.00	46,800	94.62	C	91,000	Oakland County. F=1819. Radio priest C. Coughlin at Shrine of The Little Flower (1930s). D=RCC.
7097	Saint Clair Shores, MI	75,000	64.50	48,400	94.12	C	94,700	Macomb County on Lake Saint Clair north of Detroit. Retail and office industries, light manufacturing. D=RCC.
7098	Southfield, MI	83,400	65.00	54,200	94.62	C	105,000	Oakland County northwest of Detroit and south of Pontiac. Electronic research, rubber products.D=RCC.
7099	Sterling Heights, MI	130,000	63.50	82,400	93.12	C	164,000	Oakland County north of Detroit beyond Warren. Transportation equipment, aerospace center, parks. D=RCC.
7100	Taylor, MI	77,900	66.00	51,400	95.62	C	98,500	Wayne County south of Detroit near Wyandotte. Adhesive mfg., building materials, furniture. F=1847. D=RCC.
7101	Troy, MI	80,200	65.00	52,200	94.62	C	101,000	Oakland County north of Detroit and east of Pontiac. Automobiles, auto parts, chemicals. D=RCC.
7102	Warren, MI	159,000	64.50	103,000	94.12	C	201,000	Macomb County. General Motors Technical Center, Detroit Arsenal. Residential. F=1837. D=RCC.
7103	Westland, MI	93,300	66.00	61,600	95.62	C	118,000	Wayne County west of Dearborn. Transportation equipment, Nankin Mills Nature Center. D=RCC.
7104	Dothan, AL	144,000	72.50	105,000	98.82	C	182,000	Houston County. Farm trade center. National Peanut Festival (October). F=1858 as Poplar Head. D=SBC.
7105	Dover, DE	86,900	67.00	58,200	96.62	C	110,000	Capital of Delaware. Kent County on St. Jones River. Farm trade center. Wesley College (1873). F=1717. D=RCC.
7106	Dubuque, IA	95,100	72.00	68,500	99.22	C	120,000	Dubuque County on Mississippi River. Meat packing, wood products. Trappist abbey (1849). F=1837. D=ELCA.
7107	Duluth, MN-WI	264,000	72.50	192,000	98.82	C	334,000	St. Louis County on Lake Superior. Coal & iron-ore docks, grain elevators. F=1856. D=ELCA,RCC.
7108	Eau Claire, WI	151,000	72.50	110,000	98.82	C	191,000	Eau Claire County on Eau Claire & Chippewa Rivers. Dairying, rubber tires. F=1855. 'Clear Water'. D=RCC,ELCA.

Table 10-5–continued opposite

Table 10-5–continued

Rec No 1	Country City 2	Pop 2000 3	AC% 4	Church Members 5	E% 6	W 7	Pop 2025 8	Notes 9
7109	El Paso, TX	716,000	73.50	526,000	98.82	C	904,000	El Paso County on Rio Grande. On US-Mexican border. Cotton. Spanish culture. F=1859. D=SBC,RCC.
7110	Elkhart-Goshen, IN	172,000	67.50	116,000	97.12	C	217,000	Elkhart County at confluence of St. Joseph & Elkhart Rivers. Band instruments. F=1832. D=RCC,UMC.
7111	Elmira, NY	105,000	73.00	76,500	98.82	C	132,000	Chemung County seat on Chemung River. Woodlawn National Cemetery. Mark Twain's study. F=1815. D=RCC.
7112	Enid, OK	62,500	74.00	46,200	99.32	C	78,900	Garfield County seat. Wheat, cattle, oil. F=Sept 16, 1893 as tent city. Phillips University (1906). D=RCC,UMC.
7113	Erie, PA	303,000	70.50	214,000	98.62	C	383,000	Erie County seat on Lake Erie. PA's only port on St. Lawrence seaway. Shipping lumber, coal. F=1795. D=RCC.
7114	Eugene-Springfield, OR	311,000	61.50	192,000	91.12	C	393,000	Lane County seat on Willamette River. Lumber-plywood economy. University of Oregon (1872). F=1852. D=RCC.
7115	Eureka, CA	98,900	60.00	59,300	89.62	C	125,000	Humboldt County on Humboldt Bay. Lumber & fishing center. 'I have found it'. F=1850. D=RCC,LDS.
7116	Evansville, IN-KY	307,000	65.50	201,000	95.12	C	388,000	Vanderburgh County on Ohio River. River terminal. Coal, oil, farm lands. F=1812 by Hugh McGary, Jr. D=RCC.
7117	Evansville, IN	139,000	66.00	91,700	95.62	C	176,000	Vanderburgh County on Ohio River. River terminal. Coal, oil, farm lands. F=1812 by Hugh McGary, Jr. D=RCC.
7118	Fairbanks, AK	65,500	64.30	42,100	93.92	C	82,700	On Chena river. Supply center for oil. Mining, lumbering, fur trading. F=1902 during gold strike. D=RCC.
7119	Fairmont, WV	59,100	69.00	40,800	98.62	C	74,700	North on Monongahela River south of Morgantown. D=UMC,ABC.
7120	Fargo-Moorhead, ND-MN	169,000	73.50	124,000	98.72	C	213,000	Cass County seat on Red River. Wheat. North Dakota State University (1890). F=1871. D=ELCA,RCC.
7121	Fargo, ND	81,600	74.50	60,800	99.32	C	103,000	Cass County seat on Red River. Wheat. North Dakota State University (1890). F=1871. D=ELCA,RCC.
7122	Farmington, NM	55,400	72.00	39,900	99.22	C	69,900	San Juan County at confluence of San Juan, Animas & La Plata Rivers. Coal, oil, gas. F=1876. D=RCC,SBC.
7123	Fayetteville, NC	302,000	70.50	213,000	98.62	C	382,000	Cumberland County seat on Cape Fear River. Textiles, wood products. F=1739, renamed 1783. D=SBC,NBC.
7124	Fayetteville-Springdale, AR	125,000	72.50	90,500	98.82	C	158,000	Washington County seat in Ozarks on White River. Poultry. Female Seminary (1839). F=1836. D=SBC.
7125	Fitchburg-Leominster, MA	113,000	71.50	80,900	98.72	C	143,000	Worchester County on Mohawk Trail. Machinery, paper, steel. F=1740 as Turkey Hills. D=RCC,UCC.
7126	Florence, AL (Muscle Shoals)	145,000	72.30	105,000	98.72	C	183,000	Lauderdale County seat on Tennessee River. Wilson Dam. Indian Mound. F=1818. D=SBC,NBC,UMC.
7127	Florence, SC	126,000	72.50	91,300	98.82	C	159,000	Florence County seat. Tobacco, cotton, film, electronics. F=1850s as rail junction. D=SBC,NBC,UMC.
7128	Fond du Lac, WI	57,700	74.00	42,700	99.32	C	72,900	Fond du Lac County on Lake Winnebago. Dairy farming. F=1835. 'Farther end of lake'. D=RCC,ELCA,LCMS.
7129	Fort Collins-Loveland, CO	205,000	65.50	134,000	95.12	C	259,000	Larimer County seat on Cache la Poudre River. 5,004 ft. Sugar beets, lamb feeding. F=1864. D=RCC,UMC.
7130	Fort Meyers-Cape Coral, FL	369,000	68.50	253,000	98.12	C	466,000	Lee County seat on Caloosahatchee River. Citrus fruits, flowers, cattle. Retirees. F=1839 as fort. D=RCC,SBC.
7131	Fort Myers, FL	49,800	69.50	34,600	99.12	C	62,900	Lee County seat on Caloosahatchee River. Citrus fruits, flowers, cattle. Retirees. F=1839 as fort. D=RCC,SBC.
7132	Cape Coral, FL	82,600	69.00	57,000	98.62	C	104,000	Lee County on Caloosahatchee River. Retirement community. D=RCC,SBC.
7133	Fort Pierce, FL	276,000	66.50	184,000	96.12	C	349,000	St. Lucie County seat on Indian River. Commercial fishing, shrimp, cattle. F=1838 as fort. D=RCC,SBC.
7134	Fort Smith, AR-OK	194,000	71.50	138,000	98.72	C	245,000	Sebastian County on Arkansas River. Coal, natural gas, manufacturing. F=1817 as army fort. D=SBC,UMC.
7135	Fort Smith, AK	80,100	73.00	58,500	99.32	C	101,000	Sebastian County on Arkansas River. Coal, natural gas, manufacturing. F=1817 as army fort. D=SBC,UMC.
7136	Fort Walton Beach, FL	158,000	65.50	104,000	95.12	C	200,000	Okaloosa County on Gulf of Mexico. Residential resort. Pre-Columbian Indian Temple Mound. F=1820s. D=RCC.
7137	Fort Wayne, IN	400,000	65.50	262,000	95.12	C	506,000	Allen County seat on Maumee River. Machinery. Concordia Theological Seminary (1839). F=1794. D=RCC,UMC.
7138	Fresno, CA	735,000	65.50	481,000	95.12	C	928,000	Fresno County seat in San Joaquin Valley. Cotton, fruits. Sun Maid Raisin. 'Ash tree'. F=1872. D=RCC,LDS.
7139	Clovis, CA	55,400	68.00	37,700	97.62	C	70,000	Sacramento County in Central Valley. California State University (Fresno), airport, dairying, almonds. D=RCC.
7140	Gadsden, AL	110,000	73.00	80,200	98.72	C	139,000	Etowah County seat on Coosa River. Hydropower, iron, coal, timber. F=1846 as Double Springs. D=SBC,NBC.
7141	Gainesville, FL	225,000	66.50	149,000	96.12	C	284,000	Alachua County. Tung-oil. University of Florida (1903). East Florida State Seminary. (1853). F=1830. D=RCC.
7142	Glens Falls, NY	130,000	69.50	90,700	98.57	C	165,000	Warren County on Hudson River. Waterpower driven lumbering, paper, clothing. F=1760s by Quakers. D=RCC.
7143	Goldsboro, NC	104,000	73.50	76,200	98.82	C	131,000	Wayne County seat near Neuse River. Tobacco,furniture. Odd Fellows' Orphans Home. F=1838. D=SBC.
7144	Grand Forks, ND	77,800	77.00	59,900	99.32	C	98,300	Grand Forks County seat. Red & Red Lake Rivers. Grains, potatoes. University (1883). F=1801. D=ELCA,RCC.
7145	Grand Junction, CO	93,800	67.00	62,800	96.62	C	118,000	Mesa County seat in Grand Valley. Uranium, mining, irrigated farms. F=1881 by ranchers. D=RCC,UMC.
7146	Grand Rapids, MI	758,000	70.50	534,000	98.62	C	957,000	Kent County seat on Grand River. Furniture. Calvin College & Theo. Seminary (1876). F=1826. D=RCC.
7147	Wyoming, MI	70,300	67.00	47,100	96.62	C	88,800	Kent County southwest of Grand Rapids on Grand River. Native American mounds, settled in 1832. D=RCC.
7148	Great Falls, MT	85,500	65.00	55,600	94.62	C	108,000	Cascade County seat on Missouri River. Wheat, livestock. College of Great Falls (RCC, 1932). F=1883. D=RCC.
7149	Greeley, CO	145,000	66.50	96,500	96.12	C	183,000	Weld County seat at 4,665 ft. Food processing, canning, cattle. F=1870 as Union Colony. D=RCC,UMC.
7150	Green Bay, WI	214,000	69.50	149,000	98.57	C	271,000	Brown County seat on inlet of Lake Michigan. Wood pulp, paper, cheese. F=1634. Jesuit mission (1671). D=RCC.
7151	Greensboro-Winston Salem-High Pt	1,037,000	71.00	736,000	99.12	C	1,310,000	Guilford County. Textiles, insurance. Native Dolley Madison. F=1808 for General Greene. D=SBC,UMC.
7152	Greensboro, NC	202,000	70.50	142,000	98.62	C	255,000	Guilford County. Textiles, insurance. Native Dolley Madison. F=1808 for General Greene. D=SBC,UMC.
7153	High Point, NC	76,400	70.00	53,500	99.07	C	96,600	Guilford County. Furniture manufacturing. Hosiery. High Point College (Meth., 1924). F=1750. D=SBC,UMC.
7154	Winston-Salem, NC	158,000	70.50	111,000	98.62	C	200,000	Forsyth County. Piedmont Plateau. Tobacco (R.J. Reynolds, 1875). Wake Forest U. (1834). F=1766. D=SBC,UMC.
7155	Greenville, MS	53,400	75.00	40,000	99.32	C	67,400	Washington County on Mississippi River. Agriculture-based economy. Textiles, wood. F=1827. F=1760s. D=SBC.
7156	Greenville-Spartanburg, SC	705,000	72.50	511,000	98.82	C	891,000	Greenville County seat on Reedy River. Textile mills, eggs, dairy products. Bob Jones University (1927). D=SBC.
7157	Greenville, SC	64,200	72.00	46,200	99.22	C	81,000	Greenville County seat on Reedy River. Textile mills, eggs, dairy products. Bob Jones University (1927). D=SBC.
7158	Harrisburg-Lebanon-Carlisle, PA	647,000	70.00	453,000	98.57	C	818,000	Capital of PA. Dauphin County seat on Susquehanna River. Transportation hub. Steel. F=1718. D=RCC.
7159	Harrisburg, PA	57,700	70.00	40,400	99.07	C	72,800	Capital of PA. Dauphin County seat on Susquehanna River. Transportation hub. Steel. F=1718. D=RCC.
7160	Hartford-New Britain-Middletown, CT	1,195,000	69.00	825,000	98.62	C	1,510,000	Capital of CT. Port of entry on Connecticut River. Insurance since 1794. F=1635. Y=1636. D=RCC,UCC.
7161	Hartford, CT (PMSA)	154,000	69.00	106,000	98.62	C	194,000	Seat of Trinity College (1823). Hartford Seminary Foundation (1834). First Church of Christ (1636). D=RCC,UCC.
7162	Bristol, CT	87,500	71.00	62,100	99.12	C	111,000	Hartford. Southwest midway between Hartford and Waterbury. D=RCC,UCC.
7163	East Hartford, CT	55,500	70.50	39,200	99.07	C	70,200	Hartford County on Connecticut River. Papermaking, gunpowder. F=1639 by John Crow. D=RCC,UCC.
7164	Manchester, CT	56,100	71.00	39,900	99.12	C	70,900	Hartford County on Hockanum River. Sawmills, glass, cotton mills, silk mills (1838). F=1672. D=RCC,UCC.
7165	West Hartford, CT	65,100	69.00	44,900	98.62	C	82,200	Hartford County. Birthplace of Noah Webster. AM School for the Deaf (1817). F=1679. D=RCC,UCC.
7166	New Britain, CT (PMSA)	163,000	70.00	114,000	98.57	C	206,000	Hartford County. Metalworking, hardware, machinery. F=1686 as Great Swamp. D=RCC,UCC.
7167	Hattiesburg, MS	78,800	73.00	57,500	99.32	C	99,600	Forrest County on Leaf & Bowie rivers. Textiles, metals. William Carey College (1906). F=1881. D=SBC.
7168	Hickory, NC	244,000	73.50	179,000	98.82	C	308,000	Catawba County near Appalachian Mountains. Lenoir Rhyne College (Lutheran, 1891). F=1870. D=SBC.
7169	Hilo, HI	52,600	63.50	33,400	93.12	C	66,500	On Hawaii Island. Hawaii County on Hilo Bay. Sugarcane, orchids, tourism. Lyman Mission House (1839). D=RCC.
7170	Honolulu, HI	921,000	61.50	566,000	91.12	C	1,163,000	Capital of HI. On Oahu Island. Honolulu County. Trans-Pacific shipping. Pineapple. Tourism. F=1845. D=RCC.
7171	Hot Springs National Park, AR	62,200	73.50	45,700	99.12	C	78,600	Southwest of Little Rock. Lake Hamilton and Lake Ouachita. D=SBC,UMC.
7172	Houma-Thibodaux, LA	201,000	72.50	146,000	98.82	C	254,000	Terrebonne Parish seat on Intercoastal Waterway. Oil, gas, sugar. F=1810. Southdown Plantation (1850). D=RCC.
7173	Houma, LA	107,000	72.50	77,400	98.82	C	135,000	Terrebonne Parish seat on Intercoastal Waterway. Oil, gas, sugar. F=1810. Southdown Plantation (1850). D=RCC.
7174	Houston-Galveston-Brazoria, TX	3,657,000	70.00	2,560,000	99.62	C	4,620,000	Harris County on Houston Ship Canal. Leading oil & petrochemical center. Space center. F=1837. D=SBC,RCC.
7175	Galveston-Texas City, TX (PMSA)	239,000	71.50	171,000	98.72	C	302,000	Galveston County seat on Gulf Intercoastal Waterway. Shipping, oil refining. F=1834. D=SBC,RCC.
7176	Galveston, TX	65,000	72.00	46,800	99.22	C	82,100	Galveston County seat on Gulf Intercoastal Waterway. Shipping, oil refining. F=1834. D=SBC,RCC.
7177	Houston, TX (PMSA)	3,365,000	70.00	2,356,000	99.62	C	3,996,000	Harris County on Houston Ship Canal. Leading oil & petrochemical center. Space center. F=1837. D=SBC,RCC.
7178	Freeport, TX	97,500	71.00	69,200	99.12	C	123,000	Brazoria County on Brazos River at Gulf of Mexico. Ranching, oil, natural gas, shrimping, tourism. D=SBC.
7179	Baytown, TX	70,300	72.00	50,600	99.22	C	88,800	Harris County. Oil refineries, petrochemicals, steel-plate mills. F=1822. Lee College (1934). D=SBC,RCC.
7180	Pasadena, TX	131,000	69.50	91,300	98.57	C	166,000	Harris County southeast of Houston. Oil refineries, chemical plants, meat, Johnson Space Center. D=SBC.
7181	Huntington-Ashland, WV-KY-OH	344,000	64.50	222,000	94.12	C	435,000	Wayne & Cabell counties at confluence of Ohio & Guyandotte rivers. Coal, oil, natural gas. F=1870. D=UMC,ABC.
7182	Huntington, WV	60,400	65.00	39,200	94.62	C	76,300	Wayne & Cabell counties at confluence of Ohio & Guyandotte rivers. Coal, oil, natural gas. F=1870. D=UMC,ABC.
7183	Huntsville, AL	263,000	72.00	189,000	98.82	C	332,000	Madison County near Tennessee River. Hay, cotton, corn. Space Center (1959). F=1810. D=SBC.
7184	Hutchinson, KS	51,500	70.00	36,100	99.07	C	65,100	Reno County on Arkansas River. Salt beds (1887). Hard wheat, oil. F=1872 by Indian agent. D=RCC,UMC.
7185	Idaho Falls, ID	80,000	67.20	53,800	96.82	C	101,000	Bonneville County on Upper Snake river. Potatoes, livestock. F=1863. Mormon temple (1944). D=RCC.
7186	Indianapolis, IN	1,002,000	65.00	651,000	98.62	C	1,229,000	Capital of IN. Marion County on White River. Corn, coal. Motor speedway (1911). F=1821. D=RCC.
7187	Iowa City, IA	106,000	70.50	74,600	98.62	C	134,000	Johnson County seat on Iowa River. University of Iowa (1847). Medical center. F=1839. D=ELCA.
7188	Ithaca, NY	91,000	71.00	64,600	99.12	C	115,000	Tompkins County seat on Cayuga Lake. Agriculture, lumber. Cornell University (1865). F=1789. D=RCC,NBC.
7189	Jackson, TN	85,800	74.00	63,500	99.32	C	108,000	Madison County seat on Forked Deer River. Textiles, food processing. Union University (1825). F=c1820. D=SBC.
7190	Jackson, MI	165,000	68.50	113,000	98.12	C	208,000	Jackson County seat on Grand River. Auto parts & tires. Michigan Space Center. F=1829. D=RCC,NBC,LCMS.
7191	Jackson, MS	435,000	71.50	311,000	98.72	C	550,000	Capital of MS. Hinds County on Pearl River. Natural gas. Education. Millsaps College (1890). F=1792. D=SBC.
7192	Jacksonville, FL	877,000	65.50	574,000	95.12	C	1,090,000	Duval County on St. John's River. 841 sq. miles. Port of entry, major shipyards. Tourism. F=1822. D=RCC,SBC.
7193	Jacksonville, NC	165,000	74.50	123,000	98.82	C	208,000	Onslow County seat on New River. Marine base Camp Lejeune. Hunting & fishing resort. F=1757. D=SBC,NBC.
7194	Jamestown, NY	156,000	70.00	109,000	98.57	C	197,000	Chautauqua County on Lake Chautauqua. Tools, fruit & dairy farms, resort. F=1811. D=RCC,NBC.
7195	Janesville-Beloit, WI	154,000	69.00	106,000	98.62	C	194,000	Rock County seat on Rock River. Trade center for dairy, grains, logging. Autos. F=1835. D=RCC,ELCA,LCMS.
7196	Janesville, WI	57,400	69.00	39,600	98.62	C	72,500	Rock County seat on Rock River. Trade center for dairy, grains, logging. Autos. F=1835. D=RCC,ELCA,LCMS.
7197	Jefferson City, MO	66,200	72.00	47,600	99.22	C	83,600	Capital of MO. Cole County on Missouri River. Farming. Lincoln University (1866). F=1821. D=SBC.
7198	Johnson City-Kingsport-Bristol, TN	480,000	72.50	348,000	98.82	C	606,000	Washington County in Great Appalachian Valley. Cattle, alfalfa, tobacco, mining. F=1857 around railroad. D=SBC.
7199	Johnson City, TN	54,400	72.00	39,100	99.22	C	68,700	Washington County in Great Appalachian Valley. Cattle, alfalfa, tobacco, mining. F=1857 around railroad. D=SBC.
7200	Johnstown, PA	266,000	71.50	190,000	98.72	C	335,000	Cambria County on Conemaugh River. Leading steel center in 1873. 1889 flood killed 2,000. F=1800. D=RCC.
7201	Jonesboro, AK	54,300	74.00	40,200	99.32	C	68,600	Craighead County, Crowley's Ridge. Home of Hattie Caraway (first woman U.S. Senator-1932). F=1859. D=SBC.
7202	Joplin, MO	149,000	72.00	107,000	98.82	C	188,000	Jasper & Newton Counties in Ozark mountains. Farm products. Named for Methodist missionary. F=1871. D=SBC.
7203	Kalamazoo, MI	246,000	67.50	166,000	97.12	C	311,000	Kalamazoo County seat on Kalamazoo River. Paper industry (since 1874). Celery. F=1829. D=RCC.
7204	Kankakee, IL	106,000	69.50	73,600	98.57	C	134,000	Kankakee County seat on Kankakee River. Agricultural. Olivet Nazarene College (1907). F=1853. D=RCC.
7205	Kansas City, MO-KS	1,451,000	67.20	975,000	99.32	C	1,772,000	Clay, Jackson, & Platte counties on Missouri River. Agricultural & livestock. F=1833. D=SBC.
7206	Kansas City, MO	479,000	65.50	314,000	95.12	C	605,000	Clay, Jackson, & Platte counties on Missouri River. Agricultural & livestock. F=1833. D=SBC.
7207	Independence, MO	124,000	67.50	83,400	97.12	C	156,000	Jackson County seat on Missouri River. Agriculture. Reorganized LDS (Mormons) hdqtrs. F=1827. D=SBC.
7208	Kansas City, KS	165,000	67.50	111,000	97.12	C	208,000	Wyandotte County seat at Kansas & Missouri rivers. Shawnee Methodist Mission (1839). F=1857. D=RCC.
7209	Olathe, KS	69,700	70.00	48,800	99.07	C	88,100	Southwest of Kansas City beyond Overland Park. D=RCC,UMC,LCMS.
7210	Overland Park, KS	123,000	68.00	83,700	97.62	C	155,000	Johnson County on old Sante Fe Trail. Residential for Kansas City. F=1906. D=RCC,UMC,LCMS.
7211	Killeen-Temple, TX	281,000	70.50	198,000	98.62	C	355,000	Bell County. Service center for Ft. Hood (1942). F=1882 by Santa Fe Railway. D=SBC,RCC.
7212	Killeen, TX	69,900	71.00	49,700	99.12	C	88,400	Bell County. Service center for Ft. Hood (1942). F=1882 by Santa Fe Railway. D=SBC,RCC.
7213	Kingston, NY	97,100	72.00	69,900	99.22	C	123,000	Ulster County seat on Hudson River. Computers, fruit lands. First NY capital (1777). F=1652. D=RCC.
7214	Knoxville, TN	666,000	69.50	463,000	98.57	C	841,000	Knox County seat on Tennessee River. TVA headquarters, tobacco, textiles. F=1785 as White's Fort. D=SBC.
7215	Kokomo, IN	107,000	67.50	72,000	97.12	C	135,000	Howard County on Wildcat Creek. Machinery, auto parts. 'Horseless carriage' road test (1894). F=1844. D=RCC.
7216	La Crosse, WI	108,000	71.50	77,100	98.72	C	136,000	La Crosse County seat on Mississippi River. Rubber footwear, beer. Oktoberfest (200,000 annually). D=RCC.
7217	Lafayette, LA	230,000	73.50	169,000	98.82	C	290,000	Lafayette Parish seat on Vermilion River. Oil & gas industry. French & Cajun influence. F=1824. D=RCC,SBC.
7218	Lafayette-West Lafayette, IN	144,000	66.00	94,900	95.62	C	182,000	Tippercanoe County on Wabash River. Aluminum, grains. Purdue University (1869). F=1825. D=RCC.
7219	Lake Charles, LA	185,000	74.50	138,000	98.82	C	234,000	Calcasieu Parish seat on Calcasieu River. Petrochemicals, furs, rice. F=1781. D=RCC,SBC.
7220	Lakeland-Winter Haven, FL	446,000	66.00	295,000	95.62	C	564,000	Polk County. Pebble phosphate mining, citrus fruits. Winter resort. Christian Colleges. F=1883. D=RCC,SBC.
7221	Lakeland, FL	77,700	66.50	51,700	96.12	C	98,100	Polk County. Pebble phosphate mining, citrus fruits. Winter resort. Christian Colleges. F=1883. D=RCC,SBC.
7222	Lakewood, CO	139,000	63.50	88,400	93.12	C	176,000	West of Denver near Golden. Medical equipment, Red Rock natural amphitheater, Belmar museum. D=RCC,UMC.
7223	Lancaster, PA	465,000	73.50	342,000	98.82	C	588,000	Lancaster County seat. Cattle, dairy, grain, watches. Amish & Mennonites. F=1729. D=Quakers,Amish,RCC,ELCA.
7224	Lansing-East Lansing, MI	476,000	66.70	318,000	96.32	C	602,000	Capital of MI. Ingham County on Grand River. Auto production. School for the blind (1879). F=1847. D=RCC.
7225	East Lansing, MI	55,800	66.00	36,800	95.62	C	70,500	Ingham County on Red Cedar River. Michigan State University (1855). F=1855. D=RCC,NBC,LCMS.
7226	Lansing, MI	140,000	67.00	93,900	96.62	C	177,000	Capital of MI. Ingham County on Grand River. Auto production. School for the blind (1879). F=1847. D=RCC.
7227	Laredo, TX	390,000	71.50	279,000	98.72	C	492,000	Webb County seat on Rio Grande. Frontier character. Indian wars & bandits. Trade. F=1755. D=SBC,RCC.
7228	Las Cruces, NM	149,000	68.50	102,000	98.12	C	188,000	Dona Ana County seat on Rio Grande. Cotton. White Sands Missile Range. F=1848. 'The crosses'. D=SBC.
7229	Las Vegas, NV	989,000	55.50	549,000	95.12	B	1,239,000	Clark County seat. Desert resort, gambling, mining. F=1855 by Mormons, 1864 by Army. 'The Meadows'. D=RCC.
7230	Henderson, NV	71,500	58.00	41,500	87.62	B	90,300	Southeast of Las Vegas on way to Hoover Dam. Limestone, plastics, defense related industries. D=RCC.
7231	Paradise, NV	137,000	58.50	80,300	88.12	B	173,000	South of Las Vegas near airport, unincorporated area where most of casinos are located. D=RCC.
7232	Sunrise Manor, NV	105,000	58.50	61,400	88.12	B	133,000	East of Las Vegas. Nellis Air Force Base. Residential. Sunrise Mountain. Natural gas. D=RCC.

Table 10-5–continued overleaf

Table 10-5–continued

Rec No 1	Country City 2	Pop 2000 3	AC% 4	Church Members 5	E% 6	W 7	Pop 2025 8	Notes 9
7233	Laurel, MS	52,100	76.00	39,600	99.32	C	65,800	Jones County seat on Tallahala Creek. Masonite. Southeastern Baptist College (1948). F=1882. D=SBC,NBC.
7234	Lawrence, KS	90,000	69.00	62,100	98.62	C	114,000	Douglas County seat on Kansas River. University of Kansas (1866). F=1854. D=RCC.
7235	Lawton, OK	123,000	72.50	89,000	98.82	C	155,000	Comanche County seat on Cache Creek. Farms. Cameron University (1901). F=1901. D=SBC,UMC.
7236	Lewiston, ME	97,000	65.00	63,100	94.62	C	123,000	Androscoggin County on Androscoggin River. Textile center. Bates College (1864). F=1770. D=RCC,UCC.
7237	Lexington-Fayette, KY	384,000	68.50	263,000	98.12	C	485,000	Focus of the Bluegrass region. Major center for horse breeding & racing. 'Athens of the West'. F=1775. D=SBC.
7238	Lexington, KY	248,000	68.50	170,000	98.12	C	313,000	Focus of the Bluegrass region. Major center for horse breeding & racing. 'Athens of the West'. F=1775. D=SBC.
7239	Lima, OH	170,000	68.50	116,000	98.12	C	215,000	Allen County seat on Ottawa River. Pipeline & refining center, former oil fields. F=1831. D=RCC,UMC,NBC.
7240	Lincoln, NE	235,000	71.50	168,000	98.72	C	297,000	Capital of NE. Lancaster County seat. Major grain market, insurance. U of NE (1869). F=1859. D=RCC,UMC.
7241	Little Rock-North Little Rock, AR	565,000	68.50	387,000	98.12	C	714,000	Capital of AR. Pulaski County seat on Arkansas River. Agricultural market, transportation center. F=1821. D=SBC.
7242	Little Rock, AK	194,000	68.50	133,000	98.12	C	244,000	Capital of AR. Pulaski County seat on Arkansas River. Agricultural market, transportation center. F=1821. D=SBC.
7243	North Little Rock, AK	68,000	70.00	47,600	99.07	C	85,900	Pulaski County on Arkansas River. Freight yards. Shorter College (1886; AME). F=1812 as De Cantillon. D=SBC.
7244	Logan, UT	66,400	77.00	51,100	99.32	C	83,900	Cache County seat on Logan River. Grains, sugar beets, pianos. Mormon Temple (1884). F=1859. D=LDS.
7245	Longview, WA	73,900	64.00	47,300	93.62	C	93,300	Cowlitz County on Cowlitz River. One of world's great lumber centers. F=1922. D=RCC,ELCA.
7246	Longview-Marshall, TX	179,000	72.50	130,000	98.82	C	226,000	Gregg County near Sabine River. Oil derricks and refineries. F=1870 by Texas & Pacific Railroad. D=SBC,RCC.
7247	Longview, TX	77,400	73.00	56,500	99.32	C	97,800	Gregg County near Sabine River. Oil derricks and refineries. F=1870 by Texas & Pacific Railroad. D=SBC,RCC.
7248	Los Angeles-Anaheim-Riverside, CA	13,129,000	65.30	8,573,000	97.92	C	14,858,000	Los Angeles County seat. Severe air & water pollution. Banks, insurance, media center, tourism. F=1781. D=RCC.
7249	Anaheim-Santa Ana, CA (PMSA)	2,654,000	68.00	1,804,000	97.62	C	3,352,000	Orange County on Santa Ana River. Large influx of Asian immigrants in 1980s and 1990s. D=RCC,LDS.
7250	Anaheim, CA	293,000	67.50	198,000	97.12	C	370,000	Orange County on Santa Ana River. Disneyland (1955). F=1857 by Germans. D=RCC,LDS.
7251	Buena Park, CA	75,700	67.00	50,700	96.62	C	95,700	Orange County. Aircraft & food industries. Knott's Berry Farm. F=1887. D=RCC,LDS.
7252	Costa Mesa, CA	106,000	67.50	71,600	97.12	C	134,000	Orange County at mouth of Santa Ana River. F=1906 as Harper. Southern California College (A of G). D=RCC.
7253	El Toro, CA	69,000	66.00	45,500	95.62	C	87,200	Orange County on Aliso Creek near Mission Viejo. New residential development. D=RCC,LDS.
7254	Fountain Valley, CA	59,100	68.00	40,200	97.62	C	74,700	Orange County inland from Huntington Beach. Residential, consumer goods, apparel, computer. D=RCC.
7255	Fullerton, CA	126,000	67.00	84,200	96.62	C	159,000	Orange County. Citrus center after 1888. Residential. Pacific Christian College (1928). F=1887. D=RCC,LDS.
7256	Garden Grove, CA	157,000	67.50	106,000	97.12	C	199,000	Orange County. Robert Schuller's Crystal Cathedral. Aerospace and defense installations. D=RCC,LDS.
7257	Huntington Beach, CA	200,000	62.50	125,000	92.12	C	252,000	Orange County on Pacific Coast resort. Offshore oil. F=1901 as Shell Beach. D=RCC,LDS.
7258	Irvine, CA	121,000	66.00	80,200	95.62	C	153,000	Orange County. University of California. New residential development. D=Independents,RCC,LDS.
7259	La Habra, CA	56,400	67.00	37,800	96.62	C	71,300	Orange County near Brea. Settled in 1840's. Oil research center, printing, computers. D=RCC.
7260	Mission Viejo, CA	80,200	68.00	54,500	97.62	C	101,000	Orange County. New residential development. Pharmaceuticals. Mission San Juan Capistrano. D=RCC.
7261	Newport Beach, CA	73,400	67.00	49,200	96.62	C	92,700	Orange County on Pacific Ocean. Yachting, sport fishing, beach resort. F=1865 by Capt. Dunnels. D=RCC,LDS.
7262	Orange, CA	122,000	68.50	83,400	98.12	C	154,000	Orange County on Santa Ana River. Orange groves. Chapman College (1861 in L.A.) F=1868. D=RCC.
7263	Santa Ana, CA	323,000	66.50	215,000	96.12	C	408,000	Orange County seat on Santa Ana River. Produce, military installations, residential, tourism. F=1869. D=RCC.
7264	Tustin, CA	55,800	69.00	38,500	98.62	C	70,500	Orange County east of Santa Ana. Trinity Broadcasting Network (TBN) headquarters. D=RCC,LDS.
7265	Westminster, CA	86,000	68.00	58,500	97.62	C	109,000	Orange County near Garden Grove. Seal Beach U.S. Naval Weapons Station, 'Little Saigon'. F=1870. D=RCC.
7266	Yorba Linda, CA	57,700	68.00	39,300	97.62	C	72,900	Orange County northwest of Anaheim. Seventh-day Adventist hospital. D=RCC,LDS.
7267	Los Angeles-Long Beach, CA	9,756,000	65.00	6,342,000	97.62	C	12,325,000	Los Angeles County seat. Severe air & water pollution. Banks, insurance, media center, tourism. F=1781. D=RCC.
7268	Alhambra, CA	90,400	66.00	59,700	95.62	C	114,000	Los Angeles residential suburb.Iron, aluminum foundry, Mt. Wilson Observatory. 'The red' (Arabic). D=RCC,LDS.
7269	Baldwin Park, CA	76,300	64.00	48,800	93.62	C	96,400	Los Angeles County. San Gabriel River. Fabricated metals, printing, plastics. Settled in 1870. D=RCC.
7270	Bellflower, CA	68,000	64.00	43,500	93.62	C	86,000	Los Angeles County. Chiefly residential with some industry, fabricated metal products, rubber goods. D=RCC.
7271	Burbank, CA	103,000	63.50	65,500	93.12	C	130,000	Los Angeles County. Lockheed aircraft, Disney, Warner Bros., NBC. Universal Studios. F=1887. D=RCC.
7272	Carson, CA	92,500	63.00	58,300	92.62	C	117,000	Los Angeles County between Long Beach and Torrance. Oil refining, paper, California State University. D=RCC.
7273	Cerritos, CA	58,600	63.50	37,200	93.12	C	74,000	Los Angeles County north of Long Beach. Furniture, sheet metal, printing, publishing, consumer goods. D=RCC.
7274	Compton, CA	99,600	65.00	64,700	94.62	C	126,000	Los Angeles County. Residential suburb & market center. F=1867 as Methodist colony. D=RCC,LDS.
7275	Diamond Bar, CA	59,100	64.00	37,800	93.62	C	74,600	Eastern Los Angeles County near Pomona, Puente Hills. Paper products, construction materials. D=RCC.
7276	Downey, CA	101,000	64.50	64,900	94.12	C	127,000	Los Angeles. Heavy industry. Metals, rubber, communications equipment, dairy, aerospace mfg. D=RCC,LDS.
7277	East Los Angeles, CA	139,000	67.50	93,900	97.12	C	176,000	Los Angeles County. Heavily Hispanic. Residential suburb, industrial region. D=RCC,LDS.
7278	El Monte, CA	117,000	63.50	74,200	93.12	C	148,000	Los Angeles County on San Gabriel River. Residential suburb with light industry. F=1849. D=RCC,LDS.
7279	Gardena, CA	54,900	64.00	35,100	93.62	C	69,300	Los Angeles County north of Torrance. Aircraft components, tools, plant nurseries. 'Freeway City'. D=RCC.
7280	Glendale, CA	198,000	64.50	128,000	94.12	C	250,000	Los Angeles County in Verdugo Hills. Optical instruments. Forest Lawn Memorial Park. F=1886. D=RCC,LDS.
7281	Hacienda Heights, CA	64,100	63.00	40,400	92.62	C	80,900	Los Angeles County near Whittier. Electrical and electronic equipment. Puente Hills, residential. D=RCC,LDS.
7282	Hawthorne, CA	78,500	64.00	50,300	93.62	C	99,200	Los Angeles County north of Torrance. Manhattan State Beach. Oil, gas, solar panels. D=RCC,LDS.
7283	Huntington Park, CA	61,700	62.00	38,300	91.62	C	78,000	Los Angeles County south of Los Angeles. Metal fabrication, glass, rubber products, industrial. D=RCC.
7284	Inglewood, CA	121,000	63.50	76,600	93.12	C	152,000	Los Angeles County. Poultry-raising. Hollywood Park racetrack. L.A. International Airport. F=1873. D=RCC,LDS.
7285	Lakewood, CA	81,000	64.00	51,800	93.62	C	102,000	Los Angeles County south of Bellflower. Extensive aerospace, high technology. D=RCC.
7286	Lancaster, CA	208,000	67.50	141,000	97.12	C	263,000	Unincorporated in Antelope Valley. Agriculture. Edwards Air Force Base. F=1882. D=RCC,LDS.
7287	Long Beach, CA	473,000	65.50	310,000	95.12	C	597,000	Los Angeles County on San Pedro Bay. Oil since 1921. Severe earthquake damage (1933). F=1881. D=RCC,LDS.
7288	Los Angeles, CA	3,837,000	64.00	2,456,000	93.62	C	4,847,000	Los Angeles County seat. Severe pollution. Banks, insurance, media center, tourism. F=1781. D=RCC,LDS.
7289	Lynwood, CA	68,200	63.00	43,000	92.62	C	86,100	Los Angeles County near Compton. Chiefly residential, printing presses, furniture. F=1896. D=RCC.
7290	Montebello, CA	65,600	64.00	42,000	93.62	C	82,800	Los Angeles County near Pico Rivera. Diversified manufacturing, residential, oil wells. D=RCC,LDS.
7291	Monterey Park, CA	66,900	60.00	40,100	89.62	C	84,500	Los Angeles County. Predominantly Chinese. Retail center, 1st city in U.S. with Asian majority. D=RCC,LDS.
7292	Norwalk, CA	104,000	64.50	66,900	94.12	C	131,000	Los Angeles County. Formerly logging, dairying, ranching. Cerritos College (1955). F=1868 as Corvallis. D=RCC.
7293	Pasadena, CA	145,000	65.50	94,900	95.12	C	183,000	Los Angeles County in San Gabriel Valley. Cal Tech (1891), research. JPL. Fuller Seminary. F=1874. D=RCC.
7294	Pico Rivera, CA	65,100	67.00	43,600	96.62	C	82,300	Los Angeles County south of Montebello. Furniture, machinery, exercise equipment, B-2 aircraft. D=RCC.
7295	Pomona, CA	145,000	64.50	93,500	94.12	C	183,000	Los Angeles County in Pomona Valley. Fruit center. Residential. Cal State Polytechnic U. (1938). F=1875. D=RCC.
7296	Redondo Beach, CA	66,200	65.00	43,100	94.62	C	83,700	Los Angeles County on Santa Monica Bay. Beach resort, modern marina. F=1892. D=RCC,LDS.
7297	Rosemead, CA	56,800	64.00	36,400	93.62	C	71,800	Los Angeles County near Arcadia. Directory publishing, furniture, electronics, printing. F=1867. D=RCC,LDS.
7298	Santa Monica, CA	95,700	62.00	59,300	91.62	C	121,000	Los Angeles County on Santa Monica Bay. Oceanside resort, residential, aerospace. F=1875. D=RCC,LDS.
7299	South Gate, CA	95,000	64.00	60,800	93.62	C	120,000	Los Angeles County south of Los Angeles near Florence. Furniture, publishing, iron foundry, chemicals. D=RCC.
7300	South Whittier, CA	56,300	66.00	37,100	95.62	C	71,100	Los Angeles County near La Habra. Residential, 12 miles, southeast of downtown LA. D=RCC,LDS.
7301	Torrance, CA	147,000	64.50	94,500	94.12	C	185,000	Los Angeles County in South Bay area. Oil, iron, steel. El Camino College (1947). F=1911. D=RCC.
7302	West Covina, CA	106,000	63.50	67,200	93.12	C	134,000	Los Angeles County in San Gabriel Valley. Mainly single-family homes; residential. F=1905. D=RCC,LDS.
7303	Whittier, CA	85,500	66.00	56,400	95.62	C	108,000	Los Angeles County at Puente Hills. Citrus-growing, residential. Whittier College (1901). F=1887. D=RCC.
7304	Oxnard-Ventura, CA (PMSA)	736,000	66.50	490,000	96.12	C	930,000	Ventura County on Pacific Ocean. Sugar beets, military, agriculture. F=1898. D=RCC,LDS.
7305	Camarillo, CA	57,600	66.00	38,000	95.62	C	72,700	Ventura County. Strawberries, citrus fruits, avocados, nursery, Oxnard Air Force Base. D=RCC.
7306	Oxnard, CA	157,000	67.50	106,000	97.12	C	198,000	Ventura County on Pacific Ocean. Sugar beets, military, agriculture. F=1898. D=RCC,LDS.
7307	Simi Valley, CA	110,000	62.50	68,900	92.12	C	139,000	Ventura County on Arroyo Simi. High-tech companies. D=RCC,LDS.
7308	Thousand Oaks, CA	115,000	63.50	72,900	93.12	C	145,000	Southern Ventura County near Santa Monica Mountains National Recreation Area. D=RCC,LDS.
7309	Ventura (San Buenaventura), CA	102,000	65.50	66,700	95.12	C	129,000	Ventura County on Pacific Coast. Lemons, petroleum, tourism. F=1782 as last mission of J. Serra. D=RCC,LDS.
7310	Riverside-San Bernardino (PMSA)	1,688,000	66.00	1,114,000	96.62	C	2,087,000	Riverside County on Santa Ana River. Originally silk-growing, citrus fruits. F=1870 as Jorupa. D=RCC,LDS.
7311	Chino, CA	65,700	66.00	43,400	95.62	C	83,000	Southwestern San Bernardino County south of Ontario. 'Prison without Walls' institute for men. F=1887.
7312	Corona, CA	83,800	64.00	53,600	93.62	C	106,000	Riverside County near Prado Flood Control Basin. Fruit, pharmaceuticals, prisons, Chino Hills State Park. D=RCC.
7313	Cucamonga, CA	112,000	66.00	73,700	95.62	C	141,000	Southern San Bernardino County near San Gabriel Mountains. Ontario International Airport. D=RCC,LDS.
7314	Fontana, CA	96,400	66.50	64,100	96.12	C	122,000	San Bernardino County near San Gabriel Mountains west of San Bernardino. D=RCC,LDS.
7315	Ontario, CA	147,000	66.00	96,800	95.62	C	185,000	San Bernardino County. Fruit processing, electrical appliances. Motor speedway, airport. F=1882. D=RCC.
7316	Redlands, CA	66,500	66.00	43,900	95.62	C	84,000	San Bernardino County east of San Bernardino. Missionary Aviation Fellowship headquarters. D=RCC,LDS.
7317	Rialto, CA	79,700	65.00	51,800	94.62	C	101,000	San Bernardino County west of San Bernardino. Cucamonga Wilderness area. Beverage industries. D=RCC.
7318	Riverside, CA	249,000	66.00	165,000	95.62	C	315,000	Riverside County on Santa Ana River. Originally silk-growing, citrus fruits. F=1870 as Jorupa. D=RCC,LDS.
7319	San Bernardino, CA	181,000	63.50	115,000	93.12	C	228,000	San Bernardino County at San Bernardino Mountains. Citrus groves, vineyards, aerospace. F=1852. D=RCC.
7320	Upland, CA	69,800	65.00	45,300	94.62	C	88,100	San Bernardino County north of Ontario. Electronics, textiles, building materials, consumer goods, skiing. D=RCC.
7321	Louisville, KY-IN	780,000	70.50	550,000	98.62	C	965,000	Jefferson County seat on Ohio River. Cigarettes. American Printing House for the Blind (1858). F=1779. D=SBC.
7322	Louisville, KY	296,000	70.50	209,000	98.62	C	374,000	Jefferson County seat on Ohio River. Whiskey. American Printing House for the Blind (1858). F=1779. D=SBC.
7323	Lubbock, TX	245,000	72.00	176,000	98.82	C	310,000	Lubbock County seat. Cotton, cattle. Reese Air Force Base. Severe damage/tornado (1970). F=1890. D=SBC.
7324	Lufkin, TX	61,600	74.00	45,600	99.32	C	77,900	Angelina County in Piney Woods. Sawmilling center. Forestry-based economy. F=1882. D=SBC,RCC.
7325	Lynchburg, VA	157,000	73.50	115,000	98.82	C	198,000	Campbell and Bedford counties on James River. Tobacco, corn, grains. Liberty University (1971). F=1757. D=SBC.
7326	Macon-Warner Robins, GA	309,000	70.00	217,000	98.57	C	391,000	Bibb County on Ocmulgee River. Textiles, brick, tile. Mercer University (1833). D=SBC,NBC.
7327	Macon, GA	117,000	70.50	82,700	98.62	C	148,000	Bibb County on Ocmulgee River. Textiles, brick, tile. Mercer University (1833). Cherry Blossom Festival. D=SBC.
7328	Madison, WI	404,000	70.50	285,000	98.62	C	510,000	Capital of WI. Dane County on four lakes. University of Wisconsin (1848). International students. F=1836. D=RCC.
7329	Manhattan, KS	52,200	69.50	36,300	99.12	C	65,900	Pottawatomie & Riley counties, Big Blue & Kansas Rivers. 'Beecher Bible and Rifle' Church (1862). D=RCC.
7330	Manitowoc, WI	63,100	74.00	46,700	99.32	C	79,700	Manitowoc County on Lake Michigan. Shipbuilding, aluminum. Silver Lake College (RCC, 1869). F=1837. D=RCC.
7331	Mankato, MN	53,300	74.00	39,400	99.32	C	67,300	Blue Earth County on Minnesota River. Hog market. Mankato State U. (1867). F=1852. 'Blue Clay'. D=ELCA.
7332	Mansfield, OH	139,000	69.50	96,500	98.57	C	175,000	Richland County seat on Mohican River. Electric appliances, auto parts. Winter Sports Center. F=1808. D=RCC.
7333	Marion, IN	84,700	67.00	56,700	96.62	C	107,000	Grant County on Mississinewa River. Oil, gas, auto, radio. Marion College (1920). F=1826. D=RCC,UMC.
7334	Marion, OH	59,300	71.00	42,100	99.12	C	75,000	Marion County seat. Excavating machinery. F=c1820 as Jacob's Well. Renamed 1822. 'Shovel City'. D=RCC.
7335	Martinsville, VA	73,900	71.00	52,400	99.12	C	93,300	Smith River near Danville. Fairy Stone State Park. Patrick Henry Community College, museums. D=SBC,NBC.
7336	McAllen-Edinburg-Mission, TX	422,000	70.50	298,000	98.62	C	533,000	Hidalgo County in Lower Rio Grande Valley. Oil, gas, winter resort, citrus fruits. F=1905. D=SBC,RCC.
7337	McAllen, TX	92,500	71.00	65,700	99.12	C	117,000	Hidalgo County in Lower Rio Grande Valley. Oil, gas, winter resort, citrus fruits. F=1905. D=SBC,RCC.
7338	Medford, OR	161,000	63.50	102,000	93.12	C	204,000	Jackson County seat on Bear Creek. Timber, pears, tourism. F=1833. D=RCC,LDS,ELCA.
7339	Melbourne-Titusville-Palm Bay, FL	439,000	64.50	283,000	94.12	C	555,000	Brevard County on Indian River. Yachting, sport fishing, space complex, citrus. F=1878. D=RCC,SBC.
7340	Melbourne, FL	65,700	65.30	42,900	94.92	C	82,900	Brevard County on Indian River. Yachting, sport fishing, space complex, citrus. F=1878. D=RCC,SBC.
7341	Memphis, TN-AR-MS	889,000	69.00	613,000	98.62	C	1,093,000	Shelby County above Mississippi River. Cotton, hard wood lumber, medicine, education. F=1819. D=SBC,UMC.
7342	Memphis, TN	672,000	69.00	464,000	98.62	C	849,000	Shelby County above Mississippi River. Cotton, hard wood lumber, medicine, education. F=1819. D=SBC,UMC.
7343	Merced, CA	196,000	69.50	136,000	98.57	C	248,000	Merced County on Bear Creek. Agricultural produce, metals. F=1872 by Central Pacific Railroad. D=RCC,LDS.
7344	Meridian, MS	66,700	74.00	49,400	99.32	C	84,300	Lauderdale County. Farm produce, timber, textiles. Country western music festival. F=1854. D=SBC,NBC.
7345	Miami-Fort Lauderdale, FL	3,672,000	63.50	2,333,000	93.13	C	4,438,000	Dade County seat on Atlantic Ocean. Luxury winter resort. 300,000 Cubans. F=1567. 'Sweetwater'. D=RCC,SBC.
7346	Fort Lauderdale-Hollywood (PMSA)	1,462,000	65.50	958,000	95.12	C	1,784,000	Broward County seat on Atlantic Ocean. Port of entry. Recreational waterways. F=1838 as fort. D=RCC,SBC.
7347	City of Sunrise, FL	70,900	66.00	46,800	95.62	C	89,600	Broward County north of Plantation. Major office and commercial center, factory outlet mall, hockey team. D=RCC.
7348	Fort Lauderdale, FL	164,000	65.50	108,000	95.12	C	208,000	Broward County seat on Atlantic Ocean. Port of entry. Recreational waterways. F=1838 as fort. D=RCC,SBC.
7349	Hollywood, FL	134,000	62.50	83,700	92.12	C	169,000	Broward County on Atlantic Ocean. Residential, resort. F=1921 by Joseph W. Young. D=RCC,SBC.
7350	Pembroke Pines, FL	72,100	65.00	46,800	94.62	C	91,000	Broward County west of Hollywood near Hollywood Indian Reservation. D=RCC,SBC.
7351	Plantation, FL	73,400	65.00	47,700	94.62	C	92,700	Broward County west of Fort Lauderdale. Major housing developments, banking industry. D=RCC,SBC.
7352	Pompano Beach, FL	79,700	66.00	52,600	95.62	C	101,000	Broward County north of Fort Lauderdale. Resorts, beaches, fishing, harness-racing track, tourism. D=RCC.
7353	Miami-Hialeah, FL (PMSA)	2,210,000	62.20	1,375,000	91.82	C	2,654,000	Dade County seat on Atlantic Ocean. Luxury winter resort. 300,000 Cubans. F=1567. 'Sweetwater'. D=RCC,SBC.
7354	Carol City, FL	58,100	66.00	38,400	95.62	C	73,400	Northern Dade County. Pro Player Stadium. Miami Dolphins, FL Marlins, Orange Bowl. D=RCC,SBC.
7355	Hialeah, FL	207,000	63.50	131,000	93.12	C	261,000	Dade County on Miami River Canal. Residential suburb. Racetrack. F=1910. 'Pretty Prairie'. D=RCC,SBC.
7356	Kendall, FL	58,500	67.00	39,200	96.62	C	73,800	Dade County south of Miami near South Miami. Major retail and business complexes, chiefly residential.

Table 10-5–continued opposite

Table 10-5–continued

Rec No 1	Country City 2	Pop 2000 3	AC% 4	Church Members 5	E% 6	W 7	Pop 2025 8	Notes 9
7357	Miami Beach, FL	102,000	61.50	62,700	91.12	C	129,000	Dade County between Bay of Biscayne and Atlantic Ocean. Convention center. F=1912. D=RCC.
7358	Michigan City, IN	61,200	68.00	41,600	97.62	C	77,300	La Porte County on Lake Michigan. Lumber. Vacation spot. IN state prison (1860). F=1830. D=RCC,UMC.
7359	Midland, TX	117,000	71.50	83,900	98.72	C	148,000	Midland County on High Plains. National oil center. F=1884 as depot for Texas and Pacific Railway. D=SBC,RCC.
7360	Milwaukee-Racine, WI	1,576,000	70.00	1,103,000	99.62	C	1,991,000	Milwaukee County on Lake Michigan. Coal & grain port. Machinery, metals, beer. F=1831. D=RCC,ELCA,LCMS.
7361	Milwaukee, WI (PMSA)	1,277,000	70.00	894,000	99.62	C	1,554,000	Milwaukee County on Lake Michigan. Coal & grain port. Machinery, metals, beer. F=1831. D=RCC,ELCA,LCMS.
7362	Waukesha, WI	62,700	71.50	44,800	99.17	C	79,200	Waukesha County seat on Fox River. Limestone quarries. Carroll College (1846). F=1834. D=RCC.
7363	Wauwatosa, WI	54,300	71.00	38,600	99.12	C	68,600	Milwaukee on Menomonee River west of downtown. Transportation equipment. Settled in 1835. D=RCC.
7364	West Allis, WI	69,600	70.50	49,100	99.07	C	87,900	Milwaukee County. Allis-Chambers Manufacturing Co. (heavy machinery). Annual state fair. F=1880.
7365	Racine, WI (PMSA)	193,000	70.50	136,000	98.62	C	243,000	Racine County on Lake Michigan. Publishing, farm machinery. F=1834 as Port Gilbert. D=RCC,ELCA,LCMS.
7366	Minneapolis-St Paul, MN-WI	2,363,000	68.00	1,607,000	99.62	C	2,835,000	Hennepin County on Mississippi River. 22 lakes & 150 parks. Billy Graham HQ. F=1823. D=ELCA.
7367	Bloomington, MN	95,000	71.00	67,500	99.12	C	120,000	Hennepin County near Minnesota River. Mall of America. Medical products, art center. F=1843. D=ELCA.
7368	Brooklyn Park, MN	62,100	69.00	42,800	98.62	C	78,400	Hennepin County north of Minneapolis on Mississippi River. Medical supplies, pharmaceuticals. D=ELCA.
7369	Burnsville, MN	56,500	70.00	39,500	99.07	C	71,300	Hennepin County south of Minneapolis near Minnesota River. Pharmaceuticals, aerospace. D=ELCA.
7370	Coon Rapids, MN	58,300	71.00	41,400	99.12	C	73,700	Anoka County northeast of Minneapolis on Mississippi River. Medical equipment, printing. D=ELCA.
7371	Minneapolis, MN	406,000	67.00	272,000	98.62	C	512,000	Hennepin County on Mississippi River. 22 lakes & 150 parks. Grain market. Billy Graham HQ. F=1823. D=ELCA.
7372	Plymouth, MN	56,000	69.00	38,700	98.62	C	70,800	Hennepin County northwest of Minneapolis. Small lakes, highly diversified manufacturing. D=ELCA.
7373	Saint Paul, MN	300,000	66.50	199,000	98.12	C	379,000	Capital of MN. Ramsey County seat on Mississippi River. Livestock market. Many seminaries. F=1838. D=ELCA.
7374	Missoula, MT	72,300	65.50	47,400	95.12	C	91,400	Missoula County seat on Columbia River. Lumber & paper milling. University of MT (1893). F=1860's. D=RCC.
7375	Mobile, AL	525,000	70.50	370,000	98.62	C	663,000	Mobile County on Gulf of Mexico. Paper, chemicals. Spring Hill College (RCC, 1830). F=1711. D=RCC.
7376	Modesto, CA	408,000	68.50	279,000	98.12	C	515,000	Stanislaus County seat on Tuolumne River. Shipping center for agriculture (peaches). F=1870. 'Modest'. D=RCC.
7377	Monroe, LA	157,000	72.50	113,000	98.82	C	198,000	Northern Louisiana on Ouachita River. Monroe national gas fields, zoo, antebellum homes. D=RCC.
7378	Montgomery, AL	322,000	71.50	230,000	98.72	C	407,000	Capital of AL. Montgomery County seat on Alabama River. Cotton, livestock, fertilizer, furniture. F=1819. D=SBC.
7379	Montpelier, VT	58,100	67.00	38,900	96.62	C	73,400	Capital of VT. Washington County seat on Winooski River. Granite, insurance, ski areas. F=1781. D=RCC.
7380	Morgantown, WV	78,700	69.00	54,300	98.62	C	99,400	Monongalia County seat on Monongahela River. Coal. West Virginia University (1867). F=1766. D=UMC.
7381	Muncie, IN	132,000	66.00	86,900	95.62	C	166,000	Delaware County seat on White River. Subject of Middletown (1929). Ball State U. (1918). D=RCC.
7382	Muskegon, MI	175,000	67.00	117,000	96.62	C	221,000	Muskegon County on Lake Michigan. Large port, tools & dies. F=1849. 'Marshy river'. D=RCC,NBC.
7383	Muskogee, OK	54,500	75.00	40,900	99.32	C	68,800	Muskogee County seat. Port with access to Gulf of Mexico. Five Civilized Tribe HQ. F=1872. D=SBC.
7384	Nampa, ID	77,600	67.50	52,400	97.12	C	98,000	West of Boise near Lake Lowell. Food processing, large sugar factory, furniture, wildlife refuge. D=LDS.
7385	Naples, FL	167,000	67.50	113,000	97.12	C	212,000	Collier County at edge of Everglades on Gulf of Mexico. Tourism, truck gardening. F=late 19th century. D=RCC.
7386	Nashville-Davidson, TN	1,084,000	70.50	764,000	99.32	C	1,370,000	Davidson County on Cumberland River. Educational center. Many denominational HQ. F=1780. D=SBC.
7387	Nashville, TN	537,000	69.50	373,000	98.57	C	679,000	Davidson County on Cumberland River. Educational center. Many denominational HQ. F=1780. D=SBC.
7388	New Castle, PA	75,300	70.00	52,700	99.07	C	95,100	New Castle County on Delaware River. Rayon, steel. Immanuel Church (1703). F=1651 as Santhoeck. D=RCC.
7389	New Iberia, LA	53,900	74.00	39,900	99.32	C	68,100	Iberia parish seat on Bayou Teche. Salt, sugarcane, rice. Strong French influence. F=1835. D=RCC.
7390	New London-Norwich, CT-RI	294,000	67.50	198,000	97.12	C	371,000	New London County on Long Island Sound. Deep harbor. U.S. Coast Guard Academy (1876). F=1646. D=RCC.
7391	New Orleans, LA	1,072,000	67.00	718,000	98.62	C	1,314,000	At mouth of Mississippi River. Harbor. Strong French & Black influence. Mardi Gras. F=1717. D=RCC.
7392	Kenner, LA	79,300	68.00	53,900	97.62	C	100,000	West of New Orleans near the airport. Commercial, retail, electronics, foods, chemicals, machinery. D=RCC.
7393	Metairie, LA	164,000	68.50	113,000	98.12	C	208,000	Western suburb of New Orleans south of Lake Pontchartrain. Cultured marble, fabricated metals. D=RCC.
7394	New York-N New Jersey-Long Island	16,626,000	65.00	10,807,000	98.62	C	18,498,000	On Hudson River, Manhattan & Staten islands, Long Island. Center of world trade & finance. F=1625. D=RCC.
7395	Bridgeport-Milford, CT (PMSA)	488,000	68.50	335,000	98.12	C	617,000	Fairfield County on Long Island Sound. Electrical & transportation equipment. P.T. Barnum. F=1639. D=RCC.
7396	Bridgeport, CT	156,000	70.00	109,000	98.57	C	197,000	Fairfield County on Long Island Sound. Electrical & transportation equipment. P.T. Barnum. F=1639. D=RCC.
7397	Fairfield, CT	58,800	71.00	41,800	99.12	C	74,300	Fairfield County on Long Island Sound near Bridgeport. Firearms, hats, chemicals, rubber, paper. D=RCC.
7398	Milford, CT	53,400	72.00	38,400	99.22	C	67,400	New Haven County on Long Island Sound. Oysters, clams. F=1639 purchased from Paugusset Indians. D=RCC.
7399	Stratford, CT	54,400	71.00	38,600	99.12	C	68,700	Fairfield County on Long Island Sound. Shipbuilding, aircraft engines. Shakespeare Theatre. F=1639. D=RCC.
7400	Danbury, CT (PMSA)	207,000	69.50	144,000	98.57	C	261,000	Fairfield County on Still River. Known for hat industry. Electrical equipment. F=1685. D=RCC,UCC.
7401	Jersey City, NJ (PMSA)	609,000	70.00	426,000	98.57	C	769,000	Hudson County opposite Manhattan Island, NY. Major transportation & communications center. F=1618. D=RCC.
7402	Bayonne, NJ	67,600	72.00	48,700	99.22	C	85,400	Hudson County. Oil refining, machinery. Connected by bridge with Staten Island. F=1646 by Dutch. D=RCC.
7403	Jersey City, NJ	252,000	69.00	174,000	98.62	C	318,000	Hudson County opposite Manhattan Island, NY. Major transportation & communications center. F=1618. D=RCC.
7404	Union City, NJ	63,900	69.00	44,100	98.62	C	80,700	Union County southwest of Newark, Palisades, Hudson River. Embroidery industry, machinery, apparel. D=RCC.
7405	Newark, NJ (PMSA)	2,008,000	68.00	1,366,000	97.62	C	2,537,000	On Passaic River and Newark Bay. Leather, shoes, leading industrial center. Racial riots (1967). F=1666. D=RCC.
7406	East 0range, NJ	81,000	71.00	57,500	99.12	C	102,000	Essex County. Residential. Electric motors, clothing, paint. Upsala College (Lutheran) 1893. F=1666. D=RCC.
7407	Elizabeth, NJ	121,000	68.50	82,900	98.12	C	153,000	Union County seat on Newark Bay. Shipping operations, sewing machines. F=1664. D=RCC.
7408	Irvington, NJ	65,800	73.00	48,000	99.32	C	83,100	Essex County. Textiles, metals, rubber, paper. Named after Washington Irving. F=1666 as Camp town. D=RCC.
7409	Union, NJ	55,100	74.00	40,700	99.32	C	69,600	Union County on Elizabeth River. Newark State College (f1855, moved 1958). F=1740s. D=RCC.
7410	New Haven-Meriden, CT	584,000	66.50	388,000	96.12	C	737,000	New Haven County on Long Island Sound. Yale University/Divinity School (1701). Eli Whitney. F=1638. D=RCC.
7411	Hamden, CT	58,500	68.00	39,700	97.62	C	73,800	New Haven County. Diversified industry. Many old mills. Eli Whitney (muskets, 1798). F=1786. D=RCC.
7412	Meriden, CT	65,500	70.50	46,200	99.07	C	82,700	New Haven County on Quinnipiac River. Silverware, pewter. F=1661 by Jonathan Gilbert. D=RCC.
7413	New Haven, CT	144,000	67.00	96,200	96.62	C	181,000	New Haven County on Long Island Sound. Yale University/Divinity School (1701). Eli Whitney. F=1638. D=RCC.
7414	West Haven, CT	59,500	68.00	40,400	97.62	C	75,100	New Haven County on New Haven Bay. Fishing, buckles (1853). U. of New Haven (1920). F=1640s. D=RCC.
7415	New York, NY (PMSA)	9,409,000	66.00	6,210,000	95.62	C	11,885,000	On Hudson River, Manhattan & Staten islands, Long Island. Center of world trade & finance. F=1625. D=RCC.
7416	Brick Township, NJ	73,200	71.00	52,000	99.12	C	92,400	Northcentral NJ on Metedeconk River near Point Pleasant. Residential and resort area. Inc in 1850. D=RCC.
7417	Clifton, NJ	79,000	70.00	55,300	99.07	C	99,800	Passaic County near Passaic. D=RCC,SBC.
7418	Edison, NJ	97,800	70.00	68,500	99.07	C	124,000	Middlesex County. Site of Menlo Park, Thomas Edison's research laboratory. F=1954. D=RCC.
7419	Hempstead, NY	54,400	71.40	38,900	99.02	C	68,800	Nassau County on Long Island north of Valley Stream. Most populous town in the U.S. Settled in 1644. D=RCC.
7420	Levittown, NY	58,700	70.00	41,100	99.07	C	74,100	Nassau County, Long Island. Completely preplanned & mass produced housing complex. F=1946. D=RCC.
7421	Mount Vernon, NY	73,900	69.00	51,000	98.62	C	93,400	Westchester County on Bronx & Hutchinson rivers. Petroleum. St. Paul's church (1761). F=1664. D=RCC.
7422	New Rochelle, NY	74,000	69.50	51,500	99.12	C	93,500	Westchester County on Long Island Sound. Parks, golf courses, residential. F=1688. D=RCC.
7423	Newburgh, NY	113,000	71.50	80,500	98.72	C	142,000	Orange County on Hudson River. Shipbuilding, textiles, dairy, fruit. F=1709 by Germans. D=RCC.
7424	Passaic, NJ	63,900	71.00	45,400	99.12	C	80,700	Passaic County on Passaic River. Rubber goods, television parts. Formerly textiles. F=1678. D=RCC.
7425	Paterson, NJ	155,000	71.50	111,000	98.72	C	196,000	Passaic County seat on Passaic River. Textiles. Great Falls. First submarine (1881). F=c1765. D=RCC.
7426	Yonkers, NY	207,000	68.50	142,000	98.12	C	262,000	Westchester County on Hudson River. Printing & publishing. St Joseph's Seminary (1886). F=1639. D=RCC.
7427	Stamford, CT (PMSA)	223,000	68.00	152,000	97.62	C	282,000	Fairfield County on Rippowan River at Long Island Sound. Concentration of corporate hdqtrs. F=1641. D=RCC.
7428	Norwalk, CT (PMSA)	140,000	68.50	96,000	98.12	C	177,000	Fairfield County on Long Island Sound. Hats, textiles, summer resort. F=1651. D=RCC,UCC.
7429	Greenwich, CT	64,300	69.00	44,400	98.62	C	81,300	Fairfield County on Long Island Sound. F=1640, purchased from Indians for 25 coats. D=RCC.
7430	Newport, RI	71,000	75.00	53,300	99.32	C	89,700	Newport County on Narragansett Bay. Trinity Church (1726), Touro Synagogue (1763). F=1639. D=RCC.
7431	Norfolk-VA Beach-Newport News, VA	1,951,000	65.50	1,278,000	98.12	C	2,405,000	Tidewater region at mouth of Chesapeake Bay. Shipbuilding, naval activities. F=1682. D=SBC,NBC.
7432	Chesapeake, VA	167,000	64.50	108,000	94.12	C	211,000	On Elizabeth River. Dismal Swamp. Farmlands. Port facilities, oil storage. Settled 1630s. F=1963. D=SBC.
7433	Hampton, VA	147,000	65.50	96,500	95.12	C	186,000	On Chesapeake Bay. Military. Oldest continuously settled community of English origin (1610). F=1609. D=SBC.
7434	Newport News, VA	187,000	65.50	123,000	95.12	C	236,000	Port of Hampton Roads. One of world's largest shipyards. F=1621 by Irish. D=SBC,NBC.
7435	Norfolk, VA	288,000	64.50	185,000	94.12	C	363,000	Tidewater region at mouth of Chesapeake Bay. Shipping, shipbuilding, naval activities. F=1682. D=SBC,NBC.
7436	Portsmouth, VA	114,000	65.50	74,900	95.12	C	144,000	Southwest of Norfolk on Elizabeth River. Seaport, naval hospital, huge naval installation. F=1752. D=SBC.
7437	Suffolk, VA	57,400	66.00	37,900	95.62	C	72,500	On Nansemond River. Peanut center, tea, bricks, fishing. F=1720 as Constant's Warehouse. D=SBC,NBC.
7438	Virginia Beach, VA	433,000	65.00	281,000	94.62	C	547,000	On Atlantic Coast & Chesapeake Bay. Resort city, tourism, military. F=1887. Regent University. D=SBC.
7439	Ocala, FL	214,000	66.50	143,000	96.12	C	271,000	Marion County seat. Mixed farming center. Limestone, tourism. F=1827 as Fort King. D=RCC,SBC.
7440	Odessa, TX	131,000	71.00	93,000	98.67	C	165,000	Ector County seat on High Plains. Petrochemical industries, ranching. F=1886. D=SBC,RCC.
7441	Oklahoma City, OK	896,000	70.50	632,000	98.62	C	1,113,000	Capital of OK. Oklahoma County on North Canadian River. Cotton. Aviation center. F=1889. D=SBC.
7442	Edmond, OK	57,600	71.00	40,900	99.12	C	72,700	North of Oklahoma City. Oil field, University of Central OK, wood products. Settled in 1889. D=SBC.
7443	Midwest City, OK	57,500	70.00	40,300	99.07	C	72,700	Oklahoma County. Residential suburb of Oklahoma City. Tinker Air Force Base. F=1942. D=SBC,UMC.
7444	Norman, OK	88,100	72.00	63,500	99.22	C	111,000	Cleveland County seat on South Canadian River. University of Oklahoma (1892). F=1889. D=SBC.
7445	Olympia, WA	177,000	63.00	112,000	92.62	C	224,000	Capital of WA. Thurston County on Puget Sound. Port, lumber, oysters. F=1851 as Smithfield. D=RCC,ELCA.
7446	Omaha, NE-IA	681,000	69.50	473,000	98.57	C	860,000	Douglas County seat on Missouri River. Largest meat-packing/livestock center in world. F=1854. D=RCC.
7447	Council Bluffs, IA	59,800	72.00	43,000	99.22	C	75,500	Pottawattamie County on Missouri River. Railroad-agricultural economy. F=1846 by Mormons. D=ELCA,RCC.
7448	Omaha, NE	370,000	68.50	253,000	98.12	C	467,000	Douglas County seat on Missouri River. Largest meat-packing/livestock center in world. F=1854. D=RCC.
7449	Orlando, FL	1,218,000	69.00	840,000	98.62	C	1,514,000	Orange County. Citrus, tourism. Walt Disney World (1971). HQ Campus Crusade. F=1844. D=RCC.
7450	Owensboro, KY	96,000	72.00	69,100	99.22	C	121,000	Daviess County on Ohio River. Oil, tobacco, bourbon. Kentucky Wesleyan College (1858). F=1800. D=SBC.
7451	Paducah, KY	69,400	72.00	49,900	99.22	C	87,600	McCracken County seat at Ohio & Tennessee rivers. Tobacco, timber. TVA power. F=1827. D=SBC,RCC,UMC.
7452	Panama City, FL	140,000	65.50	91,600	95.12	C	177,000	Bay County on St. Andrew Bay. Shipbuilding, fish paper, sport fishing. F=c1765. D=RCC,SBC.
7453	Parkersburg-Marietta, WV-OH	164,000	66.50	109,000	96.12	C	207,000	Wood County at Ohio & Little Kanawha rivers. Oil-well equipment, glass, porcelain. F=C1785. D=UMC.
7454	Pascagoula, MS	127,000	72.50	92,000	98.82	C	160,000	Jackson County seat on Mississippi Sound. Seaport, fishing, shipbuilding. F=1718. D=SBC.
7455	Pensacola, FL	379,000	69.50	263,000	98.57	C	479,000	Escambia County on Pensacola Bay. Lumbering, fishing. F=1698 around Spanish Ft. San Carlos. D=RCC.
7456	Peoria, IL	373,000	67.50	252,000	97.12	C	472,000	Peoria County seat on Illinois River. Corn, livestock. Caterpillar Tractor Company. F=1813. D=RCC.
7457	Philadelphia-Wilmington-Trenton	5,418,000	67.00	3,630,000	98.62	C	6,844,000	Philadelphia County at Delaware & Schuylkill rivers. Major shipping port, research, banking. F=1681. D=RCC.
7458	Atlantic City, NJ	352,000	63.50	223,000	93.12	C	444,000	Atlantic County on Atlantic Ocean. Resort, casinos, boardwalk. Trade & shipping center. F=1820. D=RCC.
7459	Philadelphia, PA-NJ (PMSA)	4,398,000	67.20	2,955,000	98.52	C	5,127,000	Philadelphia County at Delaware & Schuylkill rivers. Major shipping port, research, banking. F=1681. D=RCC.
7460	Abington, PA	65,300	70.50	46,000	99.07	C	82,500	Montgomery County. Pressed steel, chemicals, metal & plastic products. F=1700s. D=Quakers,RCC.
7461	Bensalem, PA	62,500	70.00	43,800	99.07	C	79,000	Northeast of Philadelphia beyond Philadelphia Airport. Philadelphia Park Race Track. D=Quakers,RCC.
7462	Bristol, PA	62,900	69.50	43,700	99.12	C	79,400	Northeast on Delaware River. Third oldest borough in PA, Friends meetinghouse (1710). Settled in 1697. D=RCC.
7463	Camden, NJ	96,300	70.00	67,400	99.07	C	122,000	Camden County on Delaware River. 'Box like' row houses. Campbell Soup Co. F=1773. D=RCC.
7464	Cherry Hill, NJ	76,300	69.00	52,700	98.62	C	96,400	Camden County east of Philadelphia. New Jersey Turnpike. Residential, racetrack, electronics. D=RCC.
7465	Coatesville, PA	103,000	69.50	71,500	98.57	C	130,000	Chester County midway between Philadelphia and Lancaster. Steel plant, grain, apples, vegetables. D=RCC.
7466	Haverford, PA	54,900	71.00	39,000	99.12	C	69,300	Haverford College founded by Quakers in 1833 as men's college. Co-ed since 1980. D=Quakers,RCC.
7467	Lower Merion Township, PA	63,900	69.00	44,100	98.62	C	80,700	Montgomery County northwest. St. Joseph's University. Eastern Baptist Theological Seminary. D=RCC.
7468	Pottstown, PA	97,200	70.00	68,000	99.07	C	123,000	Montgomery County on Schuylkill River. Farm, steel. F=1752. Augustus Lutheran Church (1943). D=RCC.
7469	Upper Darby, PA	92,500	71.00	65,700	99.12	C	117,000	Southwest of Philadelphia. Arab World Ministries headquarters. Residential, light manufacturing. D=RCC.
7470	Trenton, NJ (PMSA)	359,000	69.50	249,000	98.57	C	453,000	Capital of NJ. Mercer County seat on Delaware River. Iron, rubber, Lennox china. F=1679. D=RCC.
7471	Vineland-Millville-Bridgeton, NJ	152,000	70.50	107,000	98.62	C	192,000	Cumberland County on Maurice River. Market center for truck farming & poultry, glass. F=1861. D=RCC.
7472	Vineland, NJ	60,300	71.00	42,800	99.12	C	76,200	Cumberland County on Maurice River. Market center for truck farming & poultry, glass. F=1861. D=RCC.
7473	Wilmington, DE-NJ-MD (PMSA)	565,000	65.50	370,000	95.12	C	713,000	New Castle County seat on Delaware River. Flour mills. F=1638. Old Swede Church (1698). D=RCC.
7474	Wilmington, DE	78,700	66.50	52,400	96.12	C	99,500	New Castle County seat on Delaware River. Chemicals. F=1638. Old Swede Church (1698). D=RCC.
7475	Phoenix, AZ	2,607,000	63.00	1,642,000	98.62	C	3,149,000	Capital of AZ. Maricopa County on Salt River. Diversified manufacturing, mining, tourism. F=1867. D=RCC,SBC.
7476	Chandler, AZ	99,700	66.50	66,300	96.12	C	126,000	Southeast of Phoenix near Williams Air Force Base. Salt River valley, resort, airport, tourism. D=RCC.
7477	Glendale, AZ	163,000	64.00	104,000	93.62	C	206,000	Maricopa County in Salt River Valley. Agricultural trade center (fruits, vegetables, cotton). F=1892. D=RCC,SBC.
7478	Mesa, AZ	315,000	63.70	201,000	96.32	C	398,000	Maricopa County. Agriculture, fruit, tourism. Mormon Temple (1927). F=1878. D=RCC,SBC.
7479	Scottsdale, AZ	143,000	64.70	92,600	94.32	C	181,000	Maricopa County. Arts & crafts center. Lettuce, grain, cotton. F=1895 by W. Scott. D=RCC,SBC.
7480	Pine Bluff, AR	94,100	72.00	67,800	99.22	C	119,000	Jefferson County seat overlooking Arkansas River. Cotton, archery supplies. F=1819 as trading post. D=SBC.

Table 10-5–continued overleaf

Table 10-5–continued

Rec No 1	Country City 2	Pop 2000 3	AC% 4	Church Members 5	E% 6	W 7	Pop 2025 8	Notes 9
7481	Pittsburgh-Beaver Valley, PA	1,724,000	68.00	1,172,000	97.62	C	2,067,000	Allegheny County seat at Allegheny & Monongahela rivers. Formerly steel industry. Research. F=1758. D=RCC.
7482	Pittsburgh, PA	407,000	67.00	273,000	96.62	C	514,000	Allegheny County seat at Allegheny & Monongahela rivers. Formerly steel industry. Research. F=1758. D=RCC.
7483	Penn Hills, PA	56,600	69.00	39,100	98.62	C	71,500	Allegheny County, includes communities of Rodi, Churchill Valley, Penn Ridge. D=Quakers,Amish,RCC.
7484	Uniontown, PA	58,600	70.00	41,000	99.07	C	74,000	Fayette County seat on Redstone Creek. Coal, steel, textiles. F=1767 by H. Beeson, Quaker. D=RCC.
7485	Washington, PA	72,700	71.00	51,600	99.12	C	91,800	Washington County on Chartiers Creek southwest of Pittsburgh. Coal, home of Dr Francis Le Mayne. D=RCC.
7486	Pittsfield, MA	87,200	72.00	62,800	99.22	C	110,000	Berkshire County seat on Housatonic River. Insurance, tourism. Herman Melville home. F=c1740. D=RCC.
7487	Pocatello, ID	62,400	67.00	41,800	96.62	C	78,800	Bannock County seat in Portneuf Valley. Phosphate reduction. Caribou National Forrest. F=1882. D=LDS.
7488	Portland, ME	237,000	61.50	146,000	91.12	C	299,000	Cumberland County seat on Casco Bay. Fishing, shipping, petroleum port, publishing. F=1632. D=RCC,UCC.
7489	Portland-Vancouver, OR-WA	1,320,000	61.50	812,000	91.12	C	1,620,000	Multnomah County on Willamette River. Port, hydroelectric power. Rose festival (June). F=1829. D=RCC.
7490	Portland, OR (PMSA)	481,000	60.50	291,000	90.12	C	608,000	Multnomah County on Willamette River. Port, hydroelectric power. Rose festival (June). F=1829. D=RCC.
7491	Beaverton, OR	58,700	61.00	35,800	90.62	C	74,100	Washington County west of Portland. Silicon forest high tech mfg. complex. Nike HQ, electronics. D=RCC.
7492	Gresham, OR	75,100	62.00	46,600	91.62	C	94,900	Multnomah County east of Portland. Construction materials, electronics equipment, nuts, poultry, college. D=RCC.
7493	Salem, OR	306,000	62.50	191,000	92.12	C	387,000	Capital of OR. Marion County on Willamette River. Food processing. F=1840. Willamette U. (1842). D=RCC.
7494	Portsmouth, OH	70,800	70.00	49,500	99.07	C	89,400	Scioto County seat on Ohio River. Sandstone quarries, steel. Floods (1937). F=1803 by H. Massie. D=RCC.
7495	Pottsville, PA	59,700	71.00	42,400	99.12	C	75,400	Schuylkill County seat on Schuylkill River. Textiles, aluminum, shoes. F=1816 by J. Potts. D=RCC.
7496	Poughkeepsie, NY	286,000	72.00	206,000	98.82	C	361,000	Dutchess County on Hudson River. Computers, printing. Vassar College (1861). F=1683. 'Waterfall'. D=RCC.
7497	Providence-Pawtucket-Fall River, RI	910,000	72.50	660,000	98.82	C	1,122,000	Capital of RI. Providence County seat on Narragansett Bay. F=1636. First Baptist Church (1775). D=RCC.
7498	Fall River, MA-RI (PMSA)	173,000	70.50	122,000	98.62	C	219,000	Bristol County on Mount Hope Bay. Textiles, clothing. Axe-murderer Lizzie Borden (1892). 'Falling water'. D=RCC.
7499	Providence, RI (PMSA)	177,000	71.50	127,000	98.72	C	224,000	Capital of RI. Providence County seat on Narragansett Bay. F=1636. First Baptist Church (1775). D=RCC.
7500	Cranston, RI	83,700	74.00	62,000	99.32	C	106,000	Providence County on Narragansett Bay. Residential, textiles. F=1636 by William Arnold. D=RCC,ECUS.
7501	East Providence, RI	55,500	73.00	40,500	99.32	C	70,100	Providence County on Seekonk & Providence rivers. Primarily residential, chemicals, jewelry. F=1644. D=RCC.
7502	Fall River, MA	102,000	70.50	71,900	98.62	C	129,000	Bristol County on Mount Hope Bay. Textiles, clothing. Axe-murderer Lizzie Borden (1892). 'Falling water'. D=RCC.
7503	Warwick, RI	94,000	74.00	69,600	99.32	C	119,000	Kent County on Narragansett Bay. Residential suburb of Providence. Jewelry. Music theater. F=1642. D=RCC.
7504	Pawtucket-Woonsocket, RI-MA	363,000	73.50	267,000	98.82	C	458,000	Providence County on Blackstone River. Highly industrialized. F=1671. 'At the falls'. D=RCC,ECUS.
7505	Pawtucket, RI	80,000	73.00	58,400	99.32	C	101,000	Providence County on Blackstone River. Highly industrialized. F=1671. 'At the falls'. D=RCC,ECUS.
7506	Provo-Orem, UT	290,000	74.50	216,000	98.82	C	367,000	Utah County on Provo River. Silver, lead, copper, gold. Brigham Young University (1875). F=1849. D=LDS.
7507	Orem, UT	74,400	74.00	55,000	99.32	C	93,900	Utah County on Provo River. Silver, lead, copper, gold. Brigham Young University (1875). F=1849. D=LDS.
7508	Provo, UT	95,600	74.00	70,700	99.32	C	121,000	Utah County on Provo River. Silver, lead, copper, gold. Brigham Young University (1875). F=1849. D=LDS.
7509	Pueblo, CO	135,000	64.50	87,400	94.12	C	171,000	Pueblo County on Arkansas River at 4,690 ft. Coal fields, trucking. F=1842 as trading post. D=RCC.
7510	Quincy, IL	55,700	69.00	38,400	98.62	C	70,400	Adams County on Mississippi River. Agriculture, manufacturing. F=1822 as Bluffs. Franciscan seminary. D=RCC.
7511	Raleigh-Durham, NC	810,000	69.50	563,000	98.57	C	1,023,000	Capital of NC. Wake County seat. Educational center, N.C. State U. (1887), research. F=1792. D=SBC,NBC.
7512	Durham, NC	150,000	69.50	105,000	98.57	C	190,000	Durham County seat. Tobacco, medical & research center. Duke University (1924). F=1867. D=SBC.
7513	Raleigh, NC	229,000	69.50	159,000	98.57	C	289,000	Capital of NC. Wake County seat. Educational center, N.C. State U. (1887), research. F=1792. D=SBC,NBC.
7514	Rapid City, SD	89,500	72.00	64,500	99.22	C	113,000	Pennington County seat on Rapid Creek near Black Hills. Tourism. Floods (1972-200 killed). F=1876. D=RCC.
7515	Reading, PA	370,000	70.00	259,000	98.57	C	468,000	Berks County seat on Schuylkill River. Iron & steel, clothing, bricks. Albright College (1856). F=1748. D=RCC.
7516	Redding, CA	162,000	60.50	97,900	90.12	C	204,000	Shasta County seat in Sacramento Valley. Lumbering, tourism. F=1872 on Poverty Flat. D=Independents,RCC.
7517	Reno, NV	280,000	60.50	170,000	90.12	C	354,000	Washoe County seat on Truckee River. Divorce & marriage center, gambling, vacation spot. F=1871. D=RCC.
7518	Sparks, NV	58,700	62.00	36,400	91.62	C	74,200	East of Reno on Truckee River. Airport. D=RCC,LDS.
7519	Richmond, IN	70,600	68.50	48,300	98.12	C	89,100	Wayne County seat on Whitewater River. Agricultural marketing. Quaker center. F=1806. D=RCC.
7520	Richmond-Petersburg, VA	953,000	67.50	643,000	97.12	C	1,204,000	Henrico County. Tobacco, banking. U. of Richmond (1830). Union Theo. Seminary (1812). F=1637. D=SBC.
7521	Richmond, VA	224,000	66.50	149,000	96.12	C	282,000	Capital. James River. Tobacco. Union Theological Seminary (1812). F=1637. Medical College of VA. D=SBC.
7522	Roanoke, VA	247,000	68.50	169,000	98.12	C	312,000	On Roanoke River in Shenandoah Valley. Steel, textiles, trucking, tourism. F=1740. D=SBC,NBC.
7523	Rochester, MN	117,000	72.50	85,000	98.82	C	148,000	Olmsted County seat on Zumbro River. Mayo Medical Center (1889). F=1854. Minn. Bible College. D=ELCA.
7524	Rochester, NY	1,103,000	70.00	772,000	99.07	C	1,394,000	St. Lawrence Seaway. F=1789. Spiritualist center (1840s). Theological seminary (1850). D=RCC.
7525	Irondequoit, NY	57,600	72.00	41,500	99.22	C	72,800	North of Rochester on Lake Ontario and Irondequoit Bay. Partly enclosed by city, settled in 1791. D=RCC.
7526	Rockford, IL	312,000	66.50	208,000	96.12	C	395,000	Winnebago County on rock River. Tools, furniture. F=1834. Rockford college (1847 as seminary). D=RCC.
7527	Rocky Mount, NC	91,800	71.00	65,200	99.12	C	116,000	Nash & Edgecombe counties. Bright-leaf tobacco mart, textiles. F=1816. N.C. Wesleyan College (1956). D=SBC.
7528	Rome, GA	82,500	66.00	54,400	95.62	C	104,000	Northwest of Atlanta on Coosa River near Alabama border. D=SBC,NBC.
7529	Roswell, NM	55,700	73.00	40,700	99.32	C	70,400	Chaves County on Hondo River. Ranching, cotton. Walker Air Force Base (1941). F=1871. D=RCC.
7530	Rutland, VT	58,300	67.50	39,400	97.12	C	73,700	Rutland County seat between Green & Taconic mountains. Quarrying, winter sports, tourism. F=1759. D=RCC.
7531	Sacramento, CA	1,399,000	67.00	937,000	97.62	C	1,726,000	Capital of CA. Sacramento County in Central Valley. Deepwater port. Agriculture, beef cattle. F=1839. D=RCC.
7532	Arden, CA	69,200	69.00	47,800	98.62	C	87,500	Sacramento County in Central Valley. McClellan Air Force Base, Sacramento Army Depot. D=RCC.
7533	Citrus Heights, CA	124,000	66.50	82,600	96.12	C	157,000	Sacramento County in Central Valley. Folson Lake Reservoir, state recreation area, citrus, poultry. D=RCC.
7534	Carmichael, CA	53,600	68.00	36,500	97.62	C	67,700	Sacramento County in Central Valley, American River. Metal work, printing, publishing, corn. D=RCC.
7535	Rancho Cordova, CA	53,600	67.00	35,900	96.62	C	67,800	Sacramento County in Central Valley near Mather Air Force Base. Nursery, citrus, grain, dairying. D=RCC.
7536	Saginaw-Bay City-Midland, MI	440,000	65.00	286,000	94.62	C	555,000	Saginaw County on Saginaw River. Agriculture, auto parts. F=1816. 'Land of the Sauks'. D=RCC.
7537	Saginaw, MI	76,500	66.00	50,500	95.62	C	96,700	Saginaw County on Saginaw River. Agriculture, auto parts. F=1816. 'Land of the Sauks'. D=RCC.
7538	Saint Joseph (Saint Joe), MO	91,500	71.50	65,400	99.17	C	116,000	Buchanan County seat on Missouri River. Livestock-grain market. F=1826. D=SBC,RCC.
7539	Lynn, MA	89,400	72.00	64,400	99.22	C	113,000	Essex County on Massachusetts Bay. General Electric Co. Mary Baker Eddy home (1860s). F=1629. D=RCC.
7540	Salinas-Seaside-Monterey, CA	392,000	67.50	264,000	97.12	C	495,000	Monterey County seat in Salinas Valley. Lettuce, artichokes. J. Steinbeck birthplace. F=1856. D=RCC.
7541	Salinas, CA	120,000	68.50	82,000	98.12	C	151,000	Monterey County seat in Salinas Valley. Lettuce, artichokes. J. Steinbeck birthplace. F=1856. D=RCC.
7542	Tempe, AZ	156,000	65.50	102,000	95.12	C	197,000	Maricopa County on Salt River. Agriculture, residential. Arizona State University. F=1872. D=RCC.
7543	Salisbury, MD	79,700	68.00	54,200	97.62	C	101,000	Wicomico County on Wicomico River. Agriculture, duck hunting, fishing. F=1732. All Hallows churches. D=RCC.
7544	Salt Lake City-Ogden, UT	905,000	72.50	656,000	98.82	C	1,120,000	Capital of UT. Salt Lake County on Jordan River. World capital of Mormon Church. F=1847 by B. Young. D=LDS.
7545	Ogden, UT	70,400	75.00	52,800	99.32	C	88,900	Weber County seat at Weber & Ogden rivers. Transportation, income tax processing. F=1850. D=LDS.
7546	Salt Lake City, UT	176,000	72.50	128,000	98.82	C	222,000	Capital of UT. Salt Lake County on Jordan River. World capital of Mormon Church. F=1847 by B. Young. D=LDS.
7547	Sandy, UT	82,600	75.00	62,000	99.32	C	104,000	South of Salt Lake City near Timpanogos Cave National Monument, Twin Peaks. Natural gas and oil. D=LDS.
7548	West Valley City, UT	95,700	74.00	70,900	99.32	C	121,000	Immediately south of Salt Lake City. Utah's second largest city, flour, beverages. Formed in 1980. D=LDS.
7549	San Angelo, TX	108,000	72.50	78,600	98.82	C	137,000	Tom Green County seat. Wool & mohair market. Livestock raising. F=1869 as Over-The-River. D=SBC,RCC.
7550	San Antonio, TX	1,310,000	72.00	943,000	99.22	C	1,604,000	Bexar County seat on San Antonio River. Cattle, military, tourism. F=1718 as mission 'Alamo'. D=SBC.
7551	San Diego, CA	2,983,000	66.00	1,969,000	97.62	C	3,586,000	San Diego County on San Diego Bay. Pacific port & military (naval) base. Farm products. F=1769. D=RCC.
7552	Carlsbad, CA	69,500	67.00	46,600	96.62	C	87,800	San Diego County south of Oceanside on Gulf of Santa Catalina. Spas, aircraft industries. D=RCC.
7553	Chula Vista, CA	149,000	68.50	102,000	98.12	C	188,000	San Diego County on San Diego Bay. Citrus center, truck gardening, aircraft. F=1888. 'Pretty view'. D=RCC.
7554	El Cajon, CA	97,600	69.00	67,400	98.62	C	123,000	San Diego County inland from San Diego near Santee. Aircraft parts, orthopaedic supplies. D=RCC.
7555	Escondido, CA	120,000	67.00	80,100	96.62	C	151,000	San Diego County. Secluded valley. Fruits, wine. cereals, grain, tourism. F=1885. 'Hidden'. D=RCC.
7556	La Mesa, CA	58,300	67.00	39,000	96.62	C	73,600	San Diego County inland from San Diego near Lemon Grove. Pacific Southwest Railway Museum. D=RCC.
7557	National City, CA	59,700	66.00	39,400	95.62	C	75,400	San Diego County south of San Diego on San Diego Bay. HQs of Pacific Reserve Fleet, residential. D=RCC.
7558	Oceanside, CA	141,000	65.50	92,600	95.12	C	179,000	San Diego County on Pacific Ocean. Agricultural trade, beach. Mission San Luis Rey de Francis. (1798). D=RCC.
7559	Santee, CA	58,200	67.00	39,000	96.62	C	73,600	San Diego County on San Diego River north of San Diego. Electrical equipment, printing, publishing. D=RCC.
7560	Spring Valley, CA	60,100	67.00	40,300	96.62	C	75,900	San Diego County east of San Diego. Bancroft Ranch House Museum, transportation equipment, paper. D=RCC.
7561	Vista, CA	79,100	66.00	52,200	95.62	C	99,900	San Diego County east of Carlsbad. Resort, Camp Pendleton Marine Corps Base, computer supplies. D=RCC.
7562	San Francisco-Oakland-San Jose	4,051,000	61.50	2,491,000	96.12	C	4,761,000	On San Francisco Bay. Cultural & financial center of western U.S. Chinese, Hispanic. F=1796. D=RCC.
7563	Oakland, CA (PMSA)	2,293,000	63.00	1,445,000	96.62	C	2,896,000	Alameda County seat on San Francisco Bay. Deepwater port. Severe earthquake (1989). F=1852. D=RCC.
7564	Alameda, CA	84,200	63.00	53,000	92.62	C	106,000	Alameda County. On island in San Francisco Bay. Port, shipbuilding. F=1850s. D=Independents,RCC.
7565	Antioch, CA	68,500	64.00	43,800	93.62	C	86,500	Contra Costa County on Sacramento River east of Concord. Calaveras Aqueduct, gypsum. D=RCC.
7566	Berkeley, CA	113,000	61.50	69,500	91.12	C	143,000	Alameda County on San Francisco Bay. Pacific School of Religion (1866). F=1853. D=RCC.
7567	Concord, CA	123,000	61.50	75,400	91.12	C	155,000	Contra Costa County. Residential. Naval weapons station. F=1868 as Todos Santos(All Saints). D=RCC.
7568	Fremont, CA	191,000	61.50	117,000	91.12	C	241,000	Alameda County on San Francisco Bay. Residential. On site of Mission San Jose de Guadalupe (1797). D=RCC.
7569	Hayward, CA	123,000	61.50	75,500	91.12	C	155,000	Alameda County on San Francisco Bay. Livestock, agricultural, manufacturing. F=1797. D=Independents,RCC.
7570	Livermore, CA	62,500	63.00	39,400	92.62	C	78,900	Alameda County. Cattle, roses, dry white wines. Lawrence Laboratory (1952). F=c1860. D=Independents,RCC.
7571	Pleasanton, CA	55,600	62.00	34,500	91.62	C	70,300	Alameda County west of Livermore. Electronic equipment, printing, publishing, vineyard and dairy. D=RCC.
7572	Richmond, CA	96,200	64.00	61,600	93.62	C	122,000	Contra Costa County on San Francisco Bay. Oil, petroleum, naval yards. Ancient Indian mounds. F=1823. D=RCC.
7573	San Leandro, CA	75,100	62.00	46,600	91.62	C	94,900	Alameda County on San Francisco Bay. Residential, waterfront industry, commercial trade. F=1839. D=RCC.
7574	Union City, CA	59,200	63.00	37,300	92.62	C	74,800	Alameda County east of San Francisco Bay north of Fremont. Metal, plastic products, iron foundry. D=RCC.
7575	Walnut Creek, CA	66,700	64.00	42,700	93.62	C	84,200	Contra Costa County in San Ramon Valley. Fruits, walnuts. F=1849 during Gold Rush as 'the corners'. D=RCC.
7576	San Francisco, CA (PHSA)	1,766,000	59.00	1,042,000	92.62	B	2,231,000	On San Francisco Bay. Cultural & financial center. F=1796. Earthquake (1906) destroyed city. D=RCC.
7577	Daly City, CA	102,000	62.50	63,500	92.12	C	128,000	San Mateo County immediately south of San Francisco. Livestock Exhibition bldg., printing, chemicals. D=RCC.
7578	Redwood City, CA	72,700	62.00	45,100	91.62	C	91,900	San Mateo County seat on San Francisco Bay. Deepwater port, cut-flowers, electronics. F=1854. D=RCC.
7579	San Mateo, CA	94,100	63.00	59,300	92.62	C	119,000	San Mateo County on San Francisco Bay. Race Track, College of San Mateo (1922). F=1793. D=RCC.
7580	South San Francisco, CA	59,800	61.00	36,500	90.62	C	75,500	San Mateo County on San Francisco Bay. Heavy industry, meat-packing, steel. S.F. Intl. Airport. D=RCC.
7581	San Jose, CA (PMSA)	1,649,000	60.00	989,000	89.62	C	2,083,000	Santa Clara County along Coyote River. Near Silicon Valley. Dried fruits, electronics, computers. F=1777. D=RCC.
7582	Milpitas, CA	55,800	61.00	34,000	90.62	C	70,500	Santa Clara County north of San Jose. Auto assembly plant, high-tech mfg., vegetables, strawberries. D=RCC.
7583	Mountain View, CA	74,300	62.00	46,000	91.62	C	93,800	Santa Clara County on San Francisco Bay. Fruit & grain shipping, religious book publishing. F=1852. D=RCC.
7584	Palo Alto, CA	61,500	63.00	38,800	92.62	C	77,700	Santa Clara County on San Francisco Bay. Research industries. Stanford University (1891). F=1891. D=RCC.
7585	Santa Clara, CA	103,000	63.50	65,400	93.12	C	130,000	Santa Clara County on Guadalupe River. Manufacturing, fruit. Santa Clara U. (1851, Jesuit). F=1777. D=RCC.
7586	Sunnyvale, CA	129,000	61.50	79,400	91.12	C	163,000	Santa Clara County on San Francisco Bay. Fruit-processing, U.S. Navy electronics. F=1850. D=RCC.
7587	Santa Cruz, CA (PMSA)	253,000	65.50	166,000	95.12	C	319,000	Santa Cruz County on Monterey Bay. Lumbering, fishing, agriculture, tourism. F=1791 as mission. D=RCC.
7588	Santa Rosa-Petaluma, CA (PMSA)	427,000	65.50	280,000	95.12	C	540,000	Sonoma County on Santa Rosa Creek. Formerly lumbering, retail service, residential. F=1833. D=RCC.
7589	Santa Rosa, CA	125,000	66.00	82,300	95.62	C	158,000	Sonoma County on Santa Rosa Creek. Formerly lumbering, retail service, residential. F=1833. D=RCC.
7590	Vallejo-Fairfield-Napa, CA (PMSA)	497,000	62.50	310,000	92.12	C	627,000	Lolano County on San Pablo Bay. Naval shipyard, flour-milling, meat-packing. F=1850. D=RCC.
7591	Fairfield, CA	85,000	64.00	54,400	93.62	C	107,000	Solano County seat. Fruits, cereal, livestock. Wineries. F=1859 by Robert Waterman. D=RCC.
7592	Napa, CA	68,100	64.00	43,600	93.62	C	86,000	Napa County on Napa River. Table wines, farm produce, steel pipes. F=1848. D=Independents,RCC.
7593	Vacaville, CA	78,700	62.00	48,800	91.62	C	99,400	Solano County on Ulatis Creek north of Fairfield. Travis Air Force Base, state prison medical facility. D=RCC.
7594	Vallejo, CA	120,000	61.50	73,900	91.12	C	152,000	Lolano County on San Pablo Bay. Naval shipyard, flour-milling, meat-packing. F=1850. D=RCC.
7595	Sandusky, OH	87,800	71.00	62,400	99.12	C	111,000	Erie County seat on Lake Erie. Summer recreation, fishing, wineries, steel. F=c1750. 'Cola'. D=RCC.
7596	Santa Barbara-Santa Maria-Lompoc	407,000	65.50	266,000	95.12	C	514,000	Santa Barbara County on Pacific Coast. Resort, tourism, citrus, oil. Westmont College (1940). F=1782. D=RCC.
7597	Santa Barbara, CA	94,200	67.00	63,100	96.62	C	119,000	Santa Barbara County on Pacific Coast. Resort, tourism, citrus, oil. Westmont College (1940). F=1782. D=RCC.
7598	Santa Maria, CA	67,500	67.00	45,200	96.62	C	85,200	Between Santa Barbara and San Luis Obispo. Agriculture, oil, Vandenburg Air Force Base nearby. D=RCC.
7599	Santa Fe, NM	129,000	65.50	84,400	95.12	C	163,000	Capital of NM. Santa Fe County on Santa Fe River. Resort. Cultural capital of Southwest. F=1610. D=RCC.
7600	Sarasota, FL	306,000	67.50	206,000	97.12	C	386,000	Sarasota County on Sarasota Bay. Tourism, cattle, vegetables. Museum of the Circus. F=1885. D=RCC.
7601	Savannah, GA	267,000	71.00	190,000	98.67	C	337,000	Chatham County on Savannah River. Industrial seaport, shipbuilding, paper. Tourist center. F=1733. D=SBC.
7602	Scranton-Wilkes Barre, PA	808,000	68.50	554,000	98.12	C	1,021,000	Lackawanna River Valley. Noted for Nottingham lace. Publishing. F=1788 as Deep Hollow. D=RCC.
7603	Scranton, PA	90,100	68.50	61,700	98.12	C	114,000	Lackawanna County in Lackawanna River Valley. Noted for Nottingham lace. Textiles. F=1788. D=RCC.
7604	Wilkes-Barre, PA	52,300	70.00	36,600	99.07	C	66,100	Luzerne County on Susquehanna River. Coal (til 1930s), pencils. Severe floods (1972). F=1769. D=RCC.

Table 10-5–continued opposite

Table 10-5–continued

Rec No 1	Country City 2	Pop 2000 3	AC% 4	Church Members 5	E% 6	W 7	Pop 2025 8	Notes 9
7605	Seattle-Tacoma, WA	2,238,000	60.00	1,343,000	96.62	C	2,827,000	King County on Puget Sound. 50 mi. of wharves. Aerospace, forest products. F=1853 for Indian Chief. D=RCC.
7606	Seattle, WA (PMSA)	2,084,000	60.00	1,250,000	96.62	C	2,511,000	King County on Puget Sound. 50 mi. of wharves. Aerospace, forest products. F=1853 for Indian Chief. D=RCC.
7607	Bellevue , WA	95,600	61.00	58,300	90.62	C	121,000	Seattle suburb. Connected to Seattle by 2 floating bridges, office complexes, medical equipment. D=RCC.
7608	Everett, WA	77,000	62.00	47,700	91.62	C	97,300	Western Snohomish County on Possession Sound north of Seattle. Lumber, Boeing tour center. D=RCC.
7609	Tacoma, WA (PMSA)	645,000	60.50	390,000	90.12	C	815,000	Pierce County seat on Puget Sound. Lumber, shipyards. Pacific Lutheran University (1890). F=1864. D=RCC.
7610	Lakes District, WA	64,300	62.50	40,200	92.12	C	81,200	Pierce County on Puget Sound southwest of Tacoma. Fish hatcheries, Fort Lewis Military Reservation. D=RCC.
7611	Sharon, PA	133,000	72.50	96,600	98.82	C	168,000	Mercer County on Shenango River. Electric transformers, steel. F=1802 around gristmill. D=Quakers,RCC.
7612	Sheboygan, WI	114,000	71.50	81,800	98.72	C	144,000	Sheboygan County seat on Lake Michigan. Port. Enamelware, bratwurst. Germans. F=1818. 'Wind'. D=RCC.
7613	Sherman, TX	105,000	73.50	76,900	98.82	C	132,000	Grayson County seat on Red & Trinity Rivers. Cotton-ginning, oil & gas, electronics. F=c1840. D=SBC,RCC.
7614	Shreveport, LA	368,000	71.50	263,000	98.72	C	465,000	Caddo Parish seat on Red River. Petroleum, natural gas, cotton. Spring festival. F=1837 for $80,000. D=RCC.
7615	Bossier City, LA	58,000	69.00	40,000	98.62	C	73,300	Across Red River from Shreveport. Barksdale Air Force Base. Marble, pecans, thoroughbred race track. D=RCC.
7616	Sioux City, IA-NE	127,000	71.00	89,900	98.67	C	160,000	Woodbury County on Missouri River. Transportation, stockyards, grain. Pop 70,000 (1920). F=1848. D=RCC,UMC.
7617	Sioux City, IA	88,600	72.00	63,800	99.22	C	112,000	Woodbury County on Missouri River. Transportation, stockyards, grain. Pop 70,000 (1920). F=1848. D=RCC,UMC.
7618	Sioux Falls, SD	136,000	71.00	96,800	98.67	C	172,000	Minnehaha County on Big Sioux River. Divorce mill (1890-1910). Augustana College (1860). F=1857. D=RCC.
7619	South Bend-Mishawaka, IN	272,000	65.00	177,000	94.62	C	344,000	St. Joseph County seat on St. Joseph River. Financial center. University of Notre Dame (1842). F=1820. D=RCC.
7620	South Bend, IN	116,000	65.30	75,800	94.92	C	147,000	St. Joseph County seat on St. Joseph River. Financial center. University of Notre Dame (1842). F=1820. D=RCC.
7621	Spokane, WA	398,000	62.50	249,000	92.12	C	503,000	Spokane County at falls of Spokane River. Lumber, aluminum. Gateway to resorts. F=1871. D=RCC,ELCA.
7622	Springfield, IL	209,000	70.50	147,000	98.62	C	264,000	Capital of IL. Sangamon County on Sangamon River. Tourism. A. Lincoln home & tomb. F=1818. D=RCC.
7623	Springfield, MA	583,000	68.50	399,000	98.12	C	736,000	Hampden County seat on Connecticut River. Machinery, publishing (Merriam Co.). F=1636. D=RCC,UCC.
7624	Chicopee, MA	62,300	73.00	45,500	99.32	C	78,800	Hampden County at Chicopee & Connecticut rivers. Radios, tires, textiles. F=1650s. 'Cedar tree'. D=RCC,UCC.
7625	Springfield, MO	265,000	68.50	181,000	98.12	C	335,000	Green County near James River. Dairy, poultry, steel, television. Central Bible College (1922). F=1829. D=SBC.
7626	St Cloud, MN	210,000	74.50	157,000	98.82	C	265,000	Stearns County on Mississippi & Sauk rivers. F=1854. St. John's Abbey & Univ. (1857). 'Granite City'. D=ELCA.
7627	St Louis, MO-IL	2,071,000	67.00	1,388,000	97.62	C	2,485,000	On Mississippi River. Major transportation hub. Education center, seminaries, Bible schools. F=1764. D=SBC.
7628	Florissant, MO	56,400	69.00	38,900	98.62	C	71,200	St. Louis County near Missouri River. Old St. Ferdinand's Shrine (1821). Jesuit Seminary (1831). F=1785. D=SBC.
7629	Saint Charles, MO	60,100	69.00	41,400	98.62	C	75,900	St. Charles County on Missouri River northwest of St. Louis. D=SBC,RCC.
7630	Saint Louis, MO	437,000	68.70	300,000	98.32	C	552,000	On Mississippi River. Major transportation hub. Education center, seminaries, Bible schools. F=1764. D=SBC.
7631	State College, PA	136,000	71.50	97,400	98.72	C	172,000	Centre County in Nittany River Valley. Oats, swine. Pennsylvania State U. (1855). F=1859. D=Quakers,Amish,RCC.
7632	Steubenville-Weirton, OH-WV	157,000	70.50	111,000	98.62	C	198,000	Jefferson County on Ohio River. Steel, tin, chemicals. College of Steubenville. F=1765. D=RCC.
7633	Stockton, CA	529,000	64.50	341,000	94.12	C	668,000	San Joaquin County seat on San Joaquin River. Inland port. Farm produce, wines. F=1847. D=RCC.
7634	Lodi, CA	57,100	68.00	38,800	97.62	C	72,100	San Joaquin County on Mokelumne River north of Stockton. Settled by wheat farmers, in 1869. D=RCC.
7635	Sumter, SC	99,400	73.00	72,600	99.32	C	126,000	Sumter County seat. Commercial & trucking center. Tobacco. Morris College (1908, Baptist). F=1785. D=SBC.
7636	Syracuse, NY	726,000	71.50	519,000	98.72	C	918,000	Onondaga County seat on Lake Onondaga. Pharmaceuticals. Syracuse University (1878). F=1786. D=RCC.
7637	Tallahassee, FL	257,000	65.50	168,000	95.12	C	325,000	Capital of FL. Leon County seat. Cotton, cattle. Florida State U. (1857). F=1824. 'Old town'. D=RCC,SBC.
7638	Tampa-St Petersburg-Clearwater, FL	2,051,000	67.00	1,374,000	97.62	C	2,480,000	Hillsborough County seat on Tampa Bay. Citrus, phosphates, cigars, tourism. F=1824 (Ft. Brooke). D=RCC,SBC.
7639	Clearwater, FL	109,000	66.50	72,300	96.12	C	137,000	Pinellas County on Clearwater Bay. Sport-fishing fleet, tourism. F=1830s. D=RCC,SBC.
7640	Saint Petersburg, FL	263,000	66.50	175,000	96.12	C	332,000	Pinellas County on Tampa Bay. Resort, retirees. F=1876. Eckard College (Presbyterian, 1958). D=RCC,SBC.
7641	Tampa, FL	308,000	66.50	205,000	96.12	C	389,000	Hillsborough County seat on Tampa Bay. Citrus, phosphates, cigars, tourism. F=1824 (Ft. Brooke). D=RCC,SBC.
7642	Brandon, FL	63,800	66.00	42,100	95.62	C	80,600	Hillsborough County east of Tampa. Citrus fruits, vegetables, cattle, dairy farms, retail and service. D=RCC,SBC.
7643	Taunton, MA	65,700	73.00	48,000	99.32	C	83,000	Bristol County seat on Taunton River. Silverware, kitchen ranges. F=1639 by Elizabeth Poole. D=RCC,UCC.
7644	Terre Haute, IN	144,000	66.00	95,000	95.62	C	182,000	Vigo County seat near Wabash River. Coal, oil, chemicals. Union formation. F=1816. 'Highground'. D=RCC,UMC.
7645	Texarkana, TX-AR	132,000	71.50	94,600	98.72	C	167,000	Bowie County. Marketing & distribution for agriculture. Wood products, tank cars. F=1874. D=SBC,RCC.
7646	Toledo, OH	676,000	65.50	443,000	95.12	C	854,000	Lucas County seat on Lake Erie. Principal Great Lakes port. Coal, shipping, glassmaking. F=1817. D=RCC,UMC.
7647	Topeka, KS	177,000	68.50	121,000	98.12	C	224,000	Capital. Shawnee County on Kansas River. Agriculture. Menninger Foundation (psychiatry). F=1854. D=RCC.
7648	Torrington, CT	64,700	71.50	46,300	99.17	C	81,800	Litchfield County on Naugatuck River. Woolen mills, brass. First condensed milk (1850). F=1735. D=RCC.
7649	Tucson, AZ	734,000	63.50	466,000	93.12	C	927,000	Pima County seat on Santa Cruz River. Silver, copper. Tourist & health resort. U. of AZ (1885). F=1697. D=RCC.
7650	Tulsa, OK	780,000	71.50	558,000	98.72	C	986,000	Tulsa County on Arkansas River. 800 major oil companies. Oral Roberts U. (1963). F=1836. D=SBC,UMC.
7651	Broken Arrow, OK	63,900	72.00	46,000	99.22	C	80,700	Southeast of Tulsa. Medical equipment, aircraft-engine parts, Rhema Bible College. D=SBC,UMC.
7652	Tuscaloosa, AL	166,000	72.00	119,000	98.82	C	209,000	Tuscaloosa County seat on Black Warrior River. Coal, minerals. U. of Alabama (1831). F=1816. D=SBC,NBC.
7653	Tyler, TX	167,000	72.50	121,000	98.82	C	210,000	Smith County seat. Oil companies, flower industry. Many small lakes. F=1846. M=YWAM HQ. D=SBC,RCC.
7654	Utica-Rome, NY	349,000	71.00	247,000	98.67	C	440,000	Oneida County seat on Mohawk River. Metals, dairying. F. W. Woolworth stores (1879). F=1758. D=RCC.
7655	Utica, NY	75,600	71.50	54,000	99.17	C	95,400	Oneida County seat on Mohawk River. Metals, dairying. F. W. Woolworth stores (1879). F=1758. D=RCC.
7656	Valdosta, GA	70,500	72.00	50,700	99.22	C	89,000	Lowndes County seat. Tobacco, timber, cattle, naval stores market, tourism. F=1825. D=SBC,NBC.
7657	Victoria, TX	81,900	74.00	60,600	99.32	C	103,000	Victoria County seat on Guadalupe River. Cattle center, petroleum industry. F=1824. D=SBC,RCC.
7658	Visalia-Tulane-Porterville, CA	343,000	66.50	228,000	96.12	C	434,000	Tulare County seat in San Joaquin Valley. Olives, grapes, cotton. College of the Sequoias (1926). D=RCC.
7659	Visalia, CA	83,300	68.00	56,600	97.62	C	105,000	Tulare County seat in San Joaquin Valley. Olives, grapes, cotton. College of the Sequoias (1926). D=RCC.
7660	Washington-Baltimore CMSA	7,355,000	68.20	5,016,000	98.82	C	9,291,000	On Potomoc River. Government, tourism. Historical markers. Smithsonian Institution. F=1790. D=NBC.
7661	Baltimore, MD	2,040,000	67.00	1,367,000	99.62	C	2,453,000	Patapsco River estuary. Seaport, shipbuilding. F=1729. RCC diocese (1789) & cathedral (1806). D=RCC,NBC.
7662	Columbia, MD	83,500	66.00	55,100	95.62	C	106,000	Howard County. Planned community with nine villages & town center. Merriweather-Post Pavillon. D=RCC,NBC.
7663	Dundalk, MD	72,400	66.00	47,800	95.62	C	91,500	Baltimore County southeast of Baltimore near Chesapeake Bay. One of world's largest steel plants. D=RCC,NBC.
7664	Hagerstown, MD	134,000	66.00	88,200	95.62	C	169,000	Washington County seat in Cumberland River valley. Agriculture, aircraft, textiles. F=1762. D=RCC,NBC.
7665	Towson, MD	54,400	65.00	35,400	94.62	C	68,800	Baltimore County. Residential-industrial suburb of Baltimore. Goucher College (1885). F=1750. D=RCC,NBC.
7666	Washington, DC-MD-VA	3,927,000	68.00	2,670,000	97.62	C	4,631,000	On Potomoc River. Government, tourism. Historical markers. Smithsonian Institution. F=1790. D=NBC.
7667	Alexandria, VA	122,000	63.50	77,700	93.12	C	155,000	On Potomac River. Mainly residential for Washington, D.C. Many colonial buildings. F=1695. D=SBC,NBC.
7668	Annandale, VA	56,100	65.00	36,500	94.62	C	70,900	Fairfax County inside the Capital Beltway. Light manufacturing, North VA Community College. D=SBC,NBC.
7669	Arlington, VA	188,000	63.50	119,000	93.12	C	238,000	Across the Potomac River from D.C. Arlington National Cemetary, Pentagon, CIA HQ. D=SBC.
7670	Bethesda-Chevy Chase, MD	69,300	65.00	45,000	94.62	C	87,500	Montgomery County. Suburbs of D.C. Research Institutes. Bethesda Presbyterian Church (1820). D=RCC.
7671	Silver Spring, MD	83,700	64.50	54,000	94.12	C	106,000	Montgomery County north of Washington D.C. Major train derailment (1995). D=RCC,NBC.
7672	WASHINGTON, DC	668,000	68.00	454,000	97.62	C	844,000	On Potomoc River. Government, tourism. Monuments. Smithsonian Institution. F=1790. D=NBC.
7673	Wheaton, MD	65,500	67.00	43,900	96.62	C	82,700	Montgomery County. Named for General Frank Wheaton. D=RCC, Korean-American churches.
7674	Waco, TX	208,000	73.50	153,000	98.82	C	263,000	McLennan County on Brazos River. Cotton, livestock. Baylor University (1845, S. Baptist). F=1849. D=SBC.
7675	Waterbury, CT	244,000	68.50	167,000	98.12	C	308,000	New Haven County on Naugatuck River. Brass products, clocks. F=1674 as Mattatuck Plantation. D=RCC.
7676	Waterloo-Cedar Falls, IA	161,000	72.00	116,000	98.82	C	204,000	Black Hawk County seat on Cedar River. Meat-packing. National Dairy Cattle Congress. F=1845. D=ELCA.
7677	Waterloo, IA	73,200	72.50	53,000	99.32	C	92,400	Black Hawk County seat on Cedar River. Meat-packing. National Dairy Cattle Congress. F=1845. D=ELCA.
7678	Wausau, WI	127,000	71.50	90,800	98.72	C	160,000	Marathon County seat on Wisconsin River. Dairying, tourism. F=1839 as Big Bull Falls. 'Faraway Place'. D=RCC.
7679	West Palm Beach-Boca Raton-Delray	1,136,000	64.00	727,000	98.62	C	1,419,000	Palm Beach County on Lake Worth. Winter resort, tourism, commercial fishing. F=1880 by I. Henry. D=RCC,SBC.
7680	Boca Raton, FL	67,700	66.00	44,700	95.62	C	85,500	Palm Beach County on Atlantic Coast. Resort-retirement community. Bibletown U.S.A. F=1925. D=RCC,SBC.
7681	West Palm Beach, FL	74,500	64.00	47,700	93.62	C	94,100	Palm Beach County on Lake Worth. Winter resort, tourism, commercial fishing. F=1880 by I. Henry. D=RCC,SBC.
7682	Wheeling, WV-OH	175,000	65.50	115,000	95.12	C	222,000	Ohio County seat on Ohio River. Iron, steel, coal, gas. Bethany College (1840). F=1769. 'Head'. D=UMC.
7683	Wichita Falls, TX	135,000	70.50	95,000	98.62	C	170,000	Wichita County seat on Wichita River. Petroleum, cotton, cattle. Severe tornado (1964). F=1876. D=SBC,RCC.
7684	Wichita, KS	534,000	67.50	361,000	97.12	C	675,000	Sedgwick County seat on Arkansas River. Livestock marketing. Friends U. (1898). F=1864. D=RCC,UMC.
7685	Wichita, KS	335,000	67.50	226,000	97.12	C	423,000	Wichita County seat on Wichita River. Petroleum, cotton, cattle. Severe tornado (1964). F=1876. D=RCC,UMC,LCMS.
7686	Williamsport, PA	131,000	70.50	92,100	98.62	C	165,000	Lycoming County on Susquehanna River. Little League Baseball HQ. Lycoming College (1812). F=1795. D=RCC.
7687	Wilmington, NC	132,000	73.50	97,300	98.82	C	167,000	New Hanover County seat on Cape Fear River. Chief seaport of NC. Textiles. F=1730s. D=SBC,UMC.
7688	Yakima, WA	208,000	63.00	131,000	92.62	C	263,000	Yakima County seat on Yakima River. Apples, pears, food processing. Yakima Indians. F=1884 by railroad. D=RCC.
7689	York, PA	460,000	68.50	315,000	98.12	C	581,000	York County on Cororus Creek. Agriculture, refrigeration. Mennonite markets. F=1741. D=RCC,ELCA.
7690	Youngstown-Warren, OH	542,000	66.00	358,000	95.62	C	685,000	Mahoning County seat on Mahoning River. Steel. Youngstown State U. (1908). F=1802. D=RCC.
7691	Warren, OH	55,900	68.00	38,000	97.62	C	70,600	Trumbull County on Mahoning River. Coal, iron, steel. F=1799 by E. Quinby. D=UMC.
7692	Youngstown, OH	105,000	65.50	69,000	95.12	C	133,000	Mahoning County seat on Mahoning River. Steel. Youngstown State U. (1908). F=1802. D=RCC.
7693	Yuba City, CA	135,000	68.50	92,500	98.12	C	171,000	Sutter County in Sacramento Valley. Steel. Beale Air Force Base. F=1849 during Gold Rush. D=LDS.
7694	Yuma, AZ	118,000	65.50	77,100	95.12	C	149,000	Yuma County seat on Colorado River. Irrigated desert, tourism. F=1854 as Colorado City. 'Smoke'. D=SBC.
7695	Zanesville, OH	74,600	69.00	51,500	98.62	C	94,300	Muskingum County at Muskingum & Licking rivers. Pottery (1890), coal, gas, tile. F=1797 by E. Zane. D=RCC.
	URUGUAY	**3,337,000**	**64.78**	**2,162,000**	**98.71**	**C**	**3,907,000**	**ROMAN CATHOLICS 78.1%, PROTESTANTS 3.3%. PENT-CHAR 9.1%, EVANGELICAL 1.9%, GCC 26.7%**
7696	rural areas	289,000	72.99	211,000	99.85	C	235,000	21.9% (1950), 17.9% (1970), 11.0% (1990), 8.6% (2000), 7.2% (2010), 6.0% (2025)
7697	urban areas	3,048,000	64.00	1,951,000	98.60	C	3,672,000	78.0% (1950), 82.1% (1970), 88.9% (1990), 91.3% (2000), 92.7% (2010), 93.9% (2025)
7698	non-metropolitan areas	1,329,000	63.87	849,000	98.62	C	1,796,342	*Sources of data:* Censuses of 1963, 1975, and 1985.
7699	metropolitan areas	1,718,000	64.10	1,101,000	98.58	C	1,876,000	*Definition:* Cities as officially defined.
7700	Melo	46,400	65.00	30,200	98.93	C	55,900	Capital of Cerro Largo on Arroyo de los Conventos. Distribution center for wool, hides, textiles. F=1795. D=RCC.
7701	Mercedes	39,900	66.00	26,400	99.93	C	48,100	On Negro River River. Noted for colonial architecture, beaches. Tourism. Television station. F=1783. D=RCC.
7702	Minas	37,700	65.00	24,500	98.93	C	45,500	Capital of Lavalleja. Hills & forest. Tourism, bottled mineral water, mining. F=1783. D=RCC.
7703	MONTEVIDEO	1,361,000	64.00	871,000	98.63	C	1,445,000	On north shore of Rio de la Plata Estuary. Wool, meat, hides. F=1726. D=RCC. University of the Republic.
7704	Las Piedras	63,400	65.00	41,200	98.93	C	76,400	North. Wine-growing district. Known for ostrich farming and horse racing. Decisive battle (1811). D=RCC.
7705	Paysandu	82,900	63.00	52,200	96.93	C	99,900	On Uruguay River. Tanneries, textile factories. F=1772 by priest & 12 Christian Indian families. D=RCC.
7706	Rivera	62,400	64.00	39,900	97.93	C	75,200	Capital of Rivera. Built on two hills. Manufacturing center for hinterlands. Grains, vegetables. D=RCC.
7707	Salto	88,000	65.00	57,200	98.93	C	106,000	Capital of Salto. On Uruguay River. Terminus for shallow-draft vessels. Wine, meats. Boat-building. D=RCC.
	UZBEKISTAN	**24,318,000**	**1.62**	**394,000**	**48.36**	**A**	**33,355,000**	**ORTHODOX 0.7%, INDEPENDENTS 0.4%. PENT-CHAR 0.6%, EVANGELICAL 0.05%, GCC 1.0%**
7708	rural areas	14,010,000	1.27	178,000	47.56	A	14,653,000	68.5% (1950), 63.2% (1970), 59.4% (1990), 57.6% (2000), 53.1% (2010), 43.9% (2025)
7709	urban areas	10,308,000	2.10	216,000	49.44	A	18,702,000	31.4% (1950), 36.7% (1970), 40.5% (1990), 42.3% (2000), 46.8% (2010), 56.0% (2025)
7710	non-metropolitan areas	3,837,000	2.24	86,100	49.63	A	6,965,385	*Sources of data:* Censuses of 1959, 1970, 1979, and 1989.
7711	metropolitan areas	6,472,000	2.01	130,000	49.33	A	11,737,000	*Definition:* Cities and urban-type localities, officially designated as such by each of the constituent republics.
7712	Almalyk	141,000	2.00	2,800	48.74	A	257,000	Tashkent on Akhangaran River. Nonferrous metallurgy, copper mining center, lead and zinc smelters.
7713	Andizan (Andizhan)	362,000	2.00	7,200	48.74	A	657,000	Andizhan in Ferghana Valley. Cotton. Uzbek theater of musical drama. F=9th century. Earthquake (1902).
7714	Angren	161,000	2.00	3,200	48.74	A	292,000	Tashkent on Akhangaran River. Coal industry, largest lignite mining center in Central Asia. F=1946.
7715	Bekabad	101,000	0.08	80	41.82	A	182,000	Tashkent on Syr River. Cement, cotton, steel, hydroelectric plant, Farkhad Dam. F=early 20th century.
7716	Buchara (Bukhara, Bokhara)	303,000	0.10	300	41.84	A	550,000	Bukharaon Shakhrud Canal. Lamb's fleece, natural gas, handicrafts. F=1st century AD. Mosques, Madaris.
7717	Chodzejli	74,300	0.05	37	41.79	A	135,000	Western Uzbekistan on Turkmenistan border near Nukus. Alfalfa, food processing, various light manufacturing.
7718	Denau	59,900	0.05	30	41.79	A	109,000	Surkhondaryo near Tajikistan border. Surkhan Darya River. Railroad, cotton ginning, sugarcane.
7719	Dzizak	135,000	0.10	140	41.84	A	244,000	Syrdarya on Sanzar River. Cotton, agriculture. Ancient settlement.
7720	Fergana (Skobelev, Ferghana)	275,000	2.00	5,500	48.74	A	499,000	Fergana at foot of Alay Mountains. Silk & cotton textiles. Numerous parks. F=1877 by Russians. D=ROC.
7721	Gulistan (Mirzachul)	69,100	0.07	48	41.81	A	125,000	Syrdarya on Golodnaya Steppe. Cotton, agricultural center, fiber plant processing, milk, butter, sewing. F=1920s.
7722	Jangijul' (Yangiyul)	69,100	0.08	55	41.82	A	125,000	Tashkent area. Food & oasis. Food & light industries. Ancient Kaunchi-Tepe Village.
7723	Kagan	60,500	0.05	30	41.79	A	110,000	Bukhoro near Bukhara. Residence of Russian political agent to Khan of Bukhara. Tobacco, wine processing.
7724	Karsi (Karshi)	204,000	2.00	4,100	48.74	A	370,000	Kashkadarya on Kashka River. Agriculture, pileless carpets, wheat, cotton, silk, fertile oasis. D=ROC.

Table 10-5–continued overleaf

Table 10-5–continued

Rec No 1	Country City 2	Pop 2000 3	AC% 4	Church Members 5	E% 6	W 7	Pop 2025 8	Notes 9
7725	Kattakurgan	72,400	0.05	36	41.79	A	131,000	Samarkand in Zaravshan Valley. Agricultural industry. Uzbek Theater of drama. F=18th century.
7726	Kokand (Khoqand)	213,000	2.00	4,300	48.74	A	386,000	Ferghana. Trade & handicrafts. Former religious center (300 mosques). F=10th century.
7727	Margilan (Margelan)	152,000	2.00	3,000	48.74	A	275,000	Ferghana. Most important silk center in ex-USSR. F=2nd century BC. Old Silk Road.
7728	Namangan	388,000	2.00	7,800	48.74	A	703,000	Namangan in Fergana Valley. Cotton, handicrafts. Sericulture, cattle, horses, sheep breeding. F=15th century.
7729	Navoi	136,000	0.10	140	41.84	A	246,000	Samarkand. Major chemical center, fertilizer. Large cement plant, world's fourth largest gold mine.
7730	Nukus	218,000	2.00	4,400	48.74	A	396,000	Capital of Kara-Kalpak ASSR near Amu Darya delta. Food processing. F=1932. Nukus State University (1979).
7731	Sachrisabz	64,600	0.10	65	41.84	A	117,000	South of Samarkand. Orchards, wheat, cotton, wine and tea production, leather goods, vegetables.
7732	Samarkand	450,000	2.00	9,000	48.74	A	817,000	Samarkand. One of oldest cities in Central Asia. Cotton, silk. Many old mosques. Tamerlane's capital.
7733	TASKENT (Tashkent)	2,495,000	3.00	74,900	53.74	B	4,522,000	Capital of Tashkent on canals from Chirchik River. Cultural center. F=7th century. Earthquake (1966). D=ROC.
7734	Circik (Chirchik)	192,000	1.00	1,900	47.74	A	349,000	On Chirchik River. Fertilizers, chemicals, machinery, ferro-alloys. F=1935 from several villages.
7735	Termez	110,000	0.10	110	41.84	A	199,000	Surkhandarya on Amu Darya near Afghanistan. Cotton. Hottest place in ex-USSR (122 degrees F). F=c100 BC.
7736	Urgenc (Urgench)	158,000	2.00	3,200	48.74	A	287,000	Khorezm on Amu Darya. Formerly center of trade. Light industries. Drama & music theater. F=mid 17th century.
	VANUATU	**190,000**	**89.31**	**170,000**	**99.32**	**C**	**319,000**	**PROTESTANTS 53.7%, ANGLICANS 18.1%. PENT-CHAR 24.7%, EVANGELICAL 27.9%, GCC 15.1%**
7737	rural areas	152,000	90.89	138,000	99.52	C	213,000	93.9% (1950), 86.8% (1970), 81.7% (1990), 79.9% (2000), 75.9% (2010), 66.6% (2025)
7738	urban areas	38,200	83.00	31,700	98.51	C	106,000	6.0% (1950), 13.1% (1970), 18.2% (1990), 20.0% (2000), 24.0% (2010), 33.3% (2025)
7739	non-metropolitan areas	7,900	83.00	6,600	98.52	C	22,147	*Sources of data:* Censuses of 1967, 1979, and 1989.
7740	metropolitan areas	30,200	83.00	25,100	98.51	C	84,400	*Definition:* Port Vila and Luganville.
7741	PORT VILA (Vila)	30,200	83.00	25,100	98.51	C	84,400	On Mele Bay, Efate Island. French character. British, Vietnamese. Meat cannery. D=Presbyterian.
	VENEZUELA	**24,170,000**	**94.07**	**22,736,000**	**99.38**	**C**	**34,775,000**	**ROMAN CATHOLICS 94.4%, PROTESTANTS 2.0%. PENT-CHAR 15.1%, EVANGELICAL 1.2%, GCC 7.7%**
7742	rural areas	3,057,000	97.30	2,975,000	99.94	C	2,952,000	53.1% (1950), 28.4% (1970), 16.0% (1990), 12.6% (2000), 10.4% (2010), 8.4% (2025)
7743	urban areas	21,112,000	93.60	19,761,000	99.30	C	31,823,000	46.8% (1950), 71.5% (1970), 83.9% (1990), 87.3% (2000), 89.5% (2010), 91.5% (2025)
7744	non-metropolitan areas	7,156,000	94.17	6,739,000	99.61	C	11,845,321	*Sources of data:* Censuses of 1950, 1961, 1971, 1981, and 1990.
7745	metropolitan areas	13,956,000	93.31	13,022,000	99.14	C	19,977,000	*Definition:* Centers with a population of 1,000 or more inhabitants.
7746	Acarigua-Araure	143,000	94.00	134,000	99.31	C	215,000	Portuguesa. Cattle, sugar cane, cotton, corn, rice, sawmilling, dairying. Former state capital. D=RCC.
7747	Barcelona-Puerto la Cruz	135,000	93.00	126,000	99.31	C	204,000	Capital of Anzoategui on Neveri River. Cattle shipment, coffee export, oil. Coalfields nearby. D=RCC.
7748	Barinas	189,000	94.00	178,000	99.31	C	286,000	Capital of Barinas on Santo Domingo River. Cattle, dairying, cacao, tobacco. D=RCC.
7749	Barquisimeto	914,000	92.00	841,000	98.81	C	1,280,000	Capital of Lara on Turbio River. Warm climate. Rope, cement, sisal, cacao. F=1552 by Spanish. D=RCC.
7750	Cabimas	219,000	93.00	203,000	99.31	C	330,000	Zulia on Lake Maracaibo. Important center in Ambrosio oil fields. D=RCC.
7751	Cagua	83,600	96.00	80,300	99.31	C	126,000	Aragua east of Maracay, Aragua River. Agricultural center, coffee, cacao, sugarcane, tobacco, fruit. D=RCC.
7752	Calabozo	96,600	95.00	91,700	99.31	C	146,000	On Guarico River. Cattle, rice. Irrigation & flood control center. F=1695. D=RCC.
7753	CARACAS	3,153,000	94.00	2,964,000	99.51	C	4,182,000	Seven miles from Caribbean Sea. Wood processing, sugar. Old cathedral. F=1567 by Spanish. D=RCC.
7754	Baruta	312,000	94.00	293,000	99.31	C	470,000	Miranda. Southern suburb. Formerly commercial center for agricultural area. Residential. D=RCC.
7755	Catia La Mar	137,000	94.00	129,000	99.31	C	206,000	Distrito Federal north of Caracas on Caribbean Sea. Aeropuerto Internacional Simon Bolivar. D=RCC.
7756	Chacao	113,000	93.00	105,000	98.31	C	171,000	Miranda. In a valley in central highlands. Eastern residential & commercial suburb. D=RCC.
7757	Los Dos Caminos	98,700	93.00	91,800	98.31	C	149,000	Miranda. Eastern suburb. Residential. Humboldt Planetarium. D=RCC.
7758	Los Teques	178,000	94.00	167,000	99.31	C	268,000	Capital of Miranda. Strategic pass in coastal range. Residential & resort. El Encanto Park train. D=RCC.
7759	Maiquetia	103,000	93.00	95,700	98.31	C	155,000	Distrito Federal on narrow strip of land. Leading port & popular beach resort. Glass factory. D=RCC.
7760	Petare	616,000	94.00	579,000	99.31	C	929,000	Miranda. Eastern residential suburb. Cardboard manufacturing. D=RCC.
7761	Carora	91,400	96.00	87,800	99.31	C	138,000	Western Lara in the mountains. Fertile cattle plains, sugarcane, bananas, coffee. D=RCC.
7762	Carupano	101,000	93.00	93,500	98.31	C	152,000	Sucre on Caribbean Sea. Port. Exports cacao, commercial nucleus, shipping, trading, fishing. D=RCC.
7763	Ciudad Bolivar	280,000	93.00	260,000	98.31	C	422,000	Capital of Bolivar on Orinoco River. Exports gold, diamonds, cattle. Fishing, tourism. F=1764. D=RCC.
7764	Ciudad Guayana(San Felix)	490,000	92.00	451,000	98.71	C	738,000	Bolivar at confluence of Caroni & Orinoco rivers. Industrial port complex. Iron, steel, gold. D=RCC.
7765	Ciudad Ojeda Lagunillas	130,000	93.00	121,000	98.31	C	196,000	Zulia on Lake Maracaibo. Near Lagunillas oil field, largest in Latin America. D=RCC.
7766	Coro	154,000	94.00	145,000	99.31	C	233,000	Capital of Falcon. Oil refining. Nation's first church and oldest bishopric (1531). F=1527. D=RCC.
7767	Cumana	263,000	93.00	245,000	98.31	C	397,000	Capital of Sucre on Manzanares River. Cotton, coffee. F=1523(oldest European settlement in SA). D=RCC.
7768	El Limon	101,000	95.00	96,400	99.31	C	153,000	Aragua, Buddhist center. Coffee, sugarcane, cacao, fruit, tobacco, agricultural center. D=RCC.
7769	El Tigre	115,000	94.00	108,000	99.31	C	173,000	Anzoategui east of Barcelona gap. Commercial center in Oficina oil fields. D=RCC.
7770	Guacara	113,000	95.00	108,000	99.31	C	171,000	Carabobo near Valencia, Lake Valencia. Agricultural center, cotton, sugarcane, cacao, corn, fruit. D=RCC.
7771	Guanare	103,000	96.00	99,200	99.11	C	156,000	Capital of Portuguesa on Portuguesa River. Cotton, coffee, corn. Shrine to Our Lady of Coromoto. D=RCC.
7772	Guarenas	158,000	94.00	149,000	99.31	C	239,000	Miranda east of Petare. Valley of coastal range, agricultural center, sugar milling, coffee, corn, fruit. D=RCC.
7773	La Victoria	110,000	95.00	105,000	99.31	C	166,000	Arogua east of Cagua. Trading and agricultural center, coffee, cacao, sugarcane, tobacco, vegetables. D=RCC.
7774	Maracaibo	1,857,000	93.00	1,727,000	99.01	C	2,606,000	Capital of Zulia. Gulf of Venezuela. Oil. F=1571 as Nuevo Zamora. 4,000 USA citizens. D=RCC.
7775	Maracay	1,077,000	92.00	991,000	98.91	C	1,532,000	Capital of Aragua. Cattle, textiles, sugar, paper. Bullring. Commercial center for agriculture. D=RCC.
7776	Mariara	73,600	96.00	70,600	99.11	C	111,000	Cotton, coffee, sugarcane, bananas, cassava, tobacco. D=RCC.
7777	Maturin	257,000	93.00	239,000	99.31	C	387,000	Capital of Monagas. On Guarapiche River. Center for cattle, cacao oil. F=1710 by Capuchins. D=RCC.
7778	Merida	208,000	93.00	194,000	99.31	C	314,000	Capital of Merida at 5,384 ft. Pleasant climate. Highest cable car in the world. Religious center. F=1558. D=RCC.
7779	Porlamar	79,600	94.00	74,800	99.31	C	120,000	Nueva Esparta on Isle de Margarita on Atlantic Ocean. Black pearls, resort. D=RCC.
7780	Pozuelos	125,000	95.00	119,000	99.31	C	189,000	Northern Anzoategui near Barcelona. Cotton, coffee, sugarcane, bananas, cassava, tobacco. D=RCC.
7781	Puerto Cabello	112,000	93.00	104,000	98.31	C	168,000	Carabobo on Caribbean Sea. Deepwater harbor with excellent port facilities. Petroleum. D=RCC.
7782	Puerto la Cruz	83,900	95.00	79,700	99.31	C	126,000	Northern Anzoategui on Atlantic Ocean near Barcelona. Petroleum, hotels, clubs. D=RCC.
7783	Punto Fijo	111,000	93.00	103,000	98.31	C	167,000	Falcon on Gulf of Venezuela. Large oil refineries. Deep draft tankers, fishing. D=RCC.
7784	San Carlos	62,400	94.00	58,600	99.31	C	94,000	Capital of Cojedes on San Carlos River. Corn, sugarcane, cassava, rice, cattle, dairying. F=1670. D=RCC.
7785	San Cristobal	274,000	92.00	252,000	99.31	C	412,000	Capital of Tachira near Torbes Rivers. Colonial atmosphere. Earthquake (1875). F=1561. D=RCC.
7786	San Felipe	81,500	95.00	77,500	99.31	C	123,000	Capital of Yaracuy in fertile Rio Yaracuy Valley. Sugarcane, cotton, cacao, corn, fruit. D=RCC.
7787	San Fernando	90,100	95.00	85,600	99.31	C	136,000	Capital of Apure on Apure River. Cattle, horse breeding, cassava, sugarcane, tobacco, cotton. D=RCC.
7788	San Juan de los Morros	83,800	96.00	80,500	99.11	C	126,000	Capital of Guarico south of Caracas. Health resort, warm sulfur springs, helium, argon, neon. D=RCC.
7789	Turmero	173,000	93.00	161,000	99.31	C	261,000	Aragua, BASF corp. Compressed natural gas, zoo park, coffee, cacao, sugarcane, corn, fruit, livestock. D=RCC.
7790	Valencia	1,817,000	93.00	1,690,000	99.21	C	2,633,000	Capital of Carabobo on Cabriales River. Animal feeds, fertilizers, auto assembly. F=1555. D=RCC.
7791	Valera	159,000	93.00	148,000	99.31	C	240,000	Trujillo on Motatan River. Agricultural commercial center. Flour milling. 1/4 of country's wheat. D=RCC.
7792	Valle de la Pascua	86,900	94.00	81,600	99.31	C	131,000	Guarico south of Tamanaco River. Livestock, some agriculture. D=RCC.
	VIET NAM	**79,832,000**	**8.23**	**6,568,000**	**66.78**	**B**	**108,037,000**	**ROMAN CATHOLICS 6.6%, INDEPENDENTS 0.8%. PENT-CHAR 1.0%, EVANGELICAL 0.7%, GCC 7.0%**
7793	rural areas	64,081,000	7.30	4,678,000	65.86	B	75,161,000	88.3% (1950), 81.7% (1970), 80.2% (1990), 80.2% (2000), 77.9% (2010), 69.5% (2025)
7794	urban areas	15,751,000	12.00	1,890,000	70.55	B	32,876,000	11.6% (1950), 18.3% (1970), 19.7% (1990), 19.7% (2000), 22.1% (2010), 30.4% (2025)
7795	non-metropolitan areas	3,041,000	11.91	362,000	70.32	B	7,377,834	*Sources of data:* Censuses of 1960, 1979, and 1989; estimates for 1948 and 1970.
7796	metropolitan areas	12,710,000	12.02	1,528,000	70.60	B	25,498,000	*Definition:* Urban centers.
7797	Bac Giang	64,400	9.00	5,800	67.55	B	135,000	Capital of Ha Bac. Northeast of Hanoi beyond Bac Ninh. Limestone, copper, coal, tea, mulberry. D=RCC.
7798	Bac Lieu	106,000	12.00	12,700	70.55	B	221,000	Far South on South China Sea. Marshes, swampland, wet rice cultivation, pineapples, shrimp, fishing. D=RCC.
7799	Bien Hoa	347,000	14.00	48,600	72.55	B	724,000	Dong Nai on Dong Nai River. Steel, refrigeration, paper pulp, pottery. Damaged in 1975. Town rebuilt. D=RCC.
7800	Buon Me Thuot	123,000	25.00	30,700	83.55	B	257,000	Capital of Dac Lac, Tay Nguyen. Tea, coffee, rubber plantations, tourism. D=RCC.
7801	Ca Mau	104,000	13.00	13,500	71.55	B	217,000	Capital of Minh Hai. Far south. Tanning, maritime industries, fisheries, shrimping, pineapples. D=RCC.
7802	Cam-pha	133,000	4.00	5,300	62.55	B	279,000	On Gulf of Tonkin. Exports coal, 90% of Vietnam's coal resources located in immediate hinterland. D=RCC.
7803	Cam-ranh	204,000	3.20	6,500	61.75	B	426,000	Phu Khanh on South China Sea. Strategic Soviet military port. 64% Buddhist. D=RCC,Evangelical,Baptist.
7804	Can-tho	335,000	20.00	66,900	78.55	B	698,000	Hau Giang on Hau Giang River. 38% Buddhist, 20% nonreligious, 10% Caodaist. D=RCC,Evangelical.
7805	Chau Doc	64,500	14.00	9,000	72.55	B	135,000	South on Cambodian border. Silk weaving, sericulture, quarries, boat building, rice, corn, kapok. D=RCC.
7806	Da-lat	130,000	26.70	34,700	80.25	B	271,000	Lam Dong on Cam Ly River. Rubber, vegetables, 5% Chinese. RC seminary. D=RCC.
7807	Da-nang (Da-Nhang)	468,000	15.60	73,100	74.15	B	978,000	Quang Nam-Da Nang. Textiles. Former U.S. military base. 25% nonreligious. D=RCC,Evangelical,Bible Society.
7808	Gia-dinh	291,000	4.00	11,700	62.55	B	608,000	Intensive rice cultivation. Three hospitals. Rubber tires, textiles. Ruined in 1968 but rebuilt. D=RCC.
7809	Hai Duong	67,600	10.00	6,800	68.55	B	141,000	Capital of Hai Hung east of Hanoi. Wet rice cultivation, tobacco, fruit, limestone, kaolin, clay. D=RCC.
7810	Hai-phong	1,834,000	4.90	89,800	63.45	B	3,827,000	Red River delta. Seaport since 1874. Glass, cement. 25% nonreligious, 5% atheist. D=RCC,Evangelical.
7811	HANOI	1,312,000	10.00	131,000	68.55	B	2,543,000	On Red River. Heavy bombing up to 1975. Chemicals. 3% Chinese. Pagoda (1049). D=RC Archdiocese.
7812	Hoa Binh	87,800	8.00	7,000	66.55	B	183,000	Capital of Hoa Binh west of Hanoi. Dam supplies electricity to entire nation, prehistoric caves. D=RCC.
7813	Hon-Gay (Hon Gai)	156,000	4.00	6,200	62.55	B	325,000	Quang Ninh on Gulf on Tonkin. Export center for coal. Rice farming, fishing. Notes for caves. D=RCC.
7814	Hue	268,000	11.50	30,800	70.05	B	560,000	On Huong River. Imperial citadel, Dai Noi. 10% Chinese, 4% Montagnard. 5% atheist. D=RCC.
7815	Long-xuyen	163,000	10.00	16,300	68.55	B	341,000	On Song Hau Giang River. Fishing, fish breeding, paddy-rice growing. D=RCC.
7816	Minh Hai	114,000	12.00	13,700	70.55	B	238,000	Minh Hai Melaleuca Forest. Rice, aquaculturing, industrial crops, coconut, fishing, shrimping. D=RCC.
7817	My-tho (Mytho)	133,000	16.70	22,200	75.25	B	277,000	Inland port on My Tho River. Coconut. 10% Caodaist & Hao Hoa, 10% nonreligious, 4% atheist. D=RCC.
7818	Nam-dinh	210,000	16.00	33,600	74.55	B	438,000	On canal linking Day & Red rivers. Textiles, distilling, salt. 3% Montagnard, 2% Chinese. D=RCC.
7819	Nha-trang	270,000	32.40	87,600	80.95	B	564,000	On Cai River. Resort, port city. F=c300. 78% Vietnamese, 10% Chinese. D=Evangelical Church(1 seminary).
7820	Phan Rang	90,100	28.00	25,200	81.55	B	188,000	Capital of Ninh Thuan on South China Sea south of Nha Trang. Rice, tobacco. D=RCC.
7821	Phan-thiet	145,000	4.00	5,800	62.55	B	302,000	South China seaport. Fishing, fish processing, brick and tile industry, fermented fish. D=RCC.
7822	Play Cu	97,500	13.00	12,700	71.55	B	204,000	Capital of Gia Lai on Plateau du Kontum. Agro-forestry products, coffee, tobacco, commercial center. D=RCC.
7823	Qui-nhon	202,000	8.40	17,000	66.95	B	423,000	Seat of Nghia Binh on South China Sea. Fishing. 10% Chinese. D=RCC, Evangelical Church.
7824	Rach-gia	175,000	11.50	20,100	70.05	B	364,000	Ca Mau Peninsula on Gulf of Thailand. 41% Vietnamese, 25% Chinese, 20% Cambodian. D=RCC,Evangelical.
7825	Sa Dec	64,300	18.00	11,600	76.55	B	134,000	Vinh Long on Mekong River. Major market and transportation complex, rice, vegetables, brickworks. D=RCC.
7826	Soc Trang	111,000	17.00	18,900	75.55	B	232,000	Capital of Soc Trang south of Can Tho. Administrative hub, marsh, swamp, forests, fisheries. D=RCC.
7827	Tan An	63,700	15.00	9,600	73.55	B	133,000	Capital of Long An west of Saigon. Jute, pineapples, food processing, aquaculture, coconuts. D=RCC.
7828	Thai Binh	73,000	7.00	5,100	65.55	B	152,000	Capital of Thai Binh near Gulf of Tonkin. Wet rice cultivation, vegetables, fruit, livestock, tobacco, cotton. D=RCC.
7829	Thai-nguyen	158,000	4.00	6,300	62.55	B	330,000	Iron ore. Metallurgical manufacturing center on Cau River. High proportion of Tai. D=RCC.
7830	Thanh-Pho Ho Chi Minh (Saigon)	3,678,000	13.00	478,000	73.55	B	6,841,000	On Saigon River. Textiles, fisheries. 20% Chinese. Buddhist pagodas. RC primary schools. D=RCC.
7831	Thanh-hoa	108,000	5.00	5,400	63.55	B	225,000	Seat of Thanh Hoa. Agricultural & forestry products. Phosphates. Sweet potatoes. Settled nomads. D=RCC.
7832	Tra Vinh	60,500	18.00	10,900	76.55	B	126,000	Capital of Tra Vinh on Mekong River at South China Sea. Mangroves, fisheries, aquaculture, distilling. D=RCC.
7833	Tuy Hoa	68,500	22.00	15,100	80.55	B	143,000	Capital of Phu Yen on South China Sea north of Nha Trang. 4th century Cham Towers. D=RCC.
7834	Uong Bi	62,800	10.00	6,300	68.55	B	131,000	Quang Nihn, near Yen Tu Mountain. Coal, rail station. Yen Tu Pagoda Festival, coal mining center. D=RCC.
7835	Viet Tri	92,900	7.00	6,500	65.55	B	194,000	Capital of Vinh Phu on Red Hong River northwest of Hanoi. Lumbering, auto assembly. D=RCC.
7836	Vinh	140,000	4.00	5,600	62.55	B	293,000	On Ca River delta. Focus of densely populated agricultural area. Chemical & textile industry. D=RCC.
7837	Vinh Long	103,000	20.00	20,700	78.55	B	216,000	Capital of Vinh Long on Mekong River west of Saigon. Marshland, mangroves, sawmilling, rice. D=RCC.
7838	Vung-tau	156,000	50.90	79,600	89.45	B	327,000	South China Sea port. Buddhist shrine. 15% Chinese. 10% syncretistic bodies. D=RCC,Evangelical Church.
7839	Yen Bai	74,300	5.00	3,700	63.55	B	155,000	Capital of Yen Bai on Red Hong River northwest of Hanoi. Market, gums, resins, tourism, coal. D=RCC.
	VIRGIN IS OF THE US	**93,000**	**92.69**	**86,200**	**99.58**	**C**	**83,600**	**PROTESTANTS 43.0%, ROMAN CATHOLICS 31.2%. PENT-CHAR 24.0%, EVANGELICAL 19.9%, GCC 12.8%**
7840	rural areas	49,800	93.29	46,500	99.75	C	33,800	55.5% (1950), 55.5% (1970), 55.5% (1990), 53.5% (2000), 49.1% (2010), 40.4% (2025)

Table 10-5–continued opposite

Table 10-5—concluded

Rec No 1	Country City 2	Pop 2000 3	AC% 4	Church Members 5	E% 6	W 7	Pop 2025 8	Notes 9
7841	urban areas	43,200	92.00	39,700	99.39	C	49,800	44.5% (1950), 44.5% (1970), 44.5% (1990), 46.4% (2000), 50.8% (2010), 59.5% (2025)
7842	non-metropolitan areas	9,100	92.00	8,400	99.39	C	10,513	*Sources of data:* Censuses of 1950, 1960, 1970, 1980, and 1990.
7843	metropolitan areas	34,000	92.00	31,300	99.39	C	39,300	*Definition:* Places of 2,500 or more inhabitants and urbanized areas.
7844	CHARLOTTE AMALIE (Saint Thomas)	34,000	92.00	31,300	99.39	C	39,300	On Saint Thomas Island. Built on three volcanic spurs. Tourism handicrafts. Predominately black. D=RCC.
	WALLIS & FUTUNA IS	**14,500**	**96.58**	**14,000**	**99.97**	**C**	**17,500**	**ROMAN CATHOLICS 96.0%, MARGINALS 0.3%. PENT-CHAR 2.2%, EVANGELICAL 0.1%, GCC 12.9%**
7845	rural areas	13,400	96.80	13,000	99.99	C	15,800	95.0% (1950), 94.0% (1970), 92.5% (1990), 92.3% (2000), 92.0% (2010), 90.0% (2025)
7846	urban areas	1,100	94.00	1,000	99.69	C	1,800	5.0% (1950), 6.0% (1970), 7.5% (1990), 7.6% (2000), 8.0% (2010), 10.0% (2025)
7847	non-metropolitan areas	–	–	–	–	–	–	*Sources of data:* Censuses of 1983 and 1990.
7848	metropolitan areas	1,100	93.97	1,000	99.73	C	1,800	*Definition:* No urban population.
7849	MATA-UTU	1,100	94.00	1,000	99.69	C	1,800	On Urea Island. Port facilities. Timber, volcanic. D=Virtually 100% Roman Catholic.
	YEMEN	**18,112,000**	**0.17**	**30,700**	**46.59**	**A**	**38,985,000**	**ORTHODOX 0.07%, INDEPENDENTS 0.04%. PENT-CHAR 0.05%, EVANGELICAL 0.01%, GCC 0.1%**
7850	rural areas	11,229,000	0.08	9,300	45.71	A	17,442,000	94.2% (1950), 86.7% (1970), 71.1% (1990), 62.0% (2000), 54.0% (2010), 44.7% (2025)
7851	urban areas	6,883,000	0.31	21,300	48.03	A	21,543,000	5.8% (1950), 13.3% (1970), 28.9% (1990), 38.0% (2000), 45.9% (2010), 55.2% (2025)
7852	non-metropolitan areas	4,882,000	0.31	15,100	48.03	A	15,281,667	*Sources of data:* Estimates through 1990 were based on censuses of 1973, 1975, and 1988.
7853	metropolitan areas	2,000,000	0.31	6,200	48.02	A	6,262,000	*Definition:* Entire former colony of Aden, excluding oil refinery and Al Burayqah and Bi'r Fuqum.
7854	ADAN (Aden, Asashaab)	582,000	0.30	1,700	48.72	A	1,822,000	On Gulf of Aden. Mentioned in Ezekiel. Commercial center, refueling stop. British crown colony (1937). D=COC.
7855	Al Mukalla	106,000	0.10	110	45.52	A	332,000	Capital of Hadramawt on Gulf of Aden. Market center, fishing, tobacco.
7856	Al-Hudaydah (Hodeida)	268,000	0.02	54	44.44	A	838,000	Chief Red Seaport. Imports food. Exports coffee, cotton. F=1454. Destroyed by fire (1961).
7857	SAN'A	737,000	0.50	3,700	49.92	A	2,307,000	Economic & religious center. At 7,226 ft. Cotton textiles. Mosques. F=Shem(Noah's son). D=RCC.
7858	Ta'izz (Taiz)	307,000	0.20	620	46.12	A	962,000	4,500 ft. Coffee. Thamad, 12th century mountain resort. F=7th century. Muslim madrasah. 'Bride of Yemen'.
	YUGOSLAVIA	**10,640,000**	**64.71**	**6,886,000**	**93.39**	**C**	**10,844,000**	**ORTHODOX 56.8%, ROMAN CATHOLICS 5.1%. PENT-CHAR 2.3%, EVANGELICAL 0.4%, GCC 13.1%**
7859	rural areas	4,272,000	62.79	2,683,000	88.05	C	3,021,000	81.0% (1950), 60.6% (1970), 46.8% (1990), 40.1% (2000), 34.4% (2010), 27.8% (2025)
7860	urban areas	6,368,000	66.00	4,203,000	96.98	C	7,823,000	18.9% (1950), 39.3% (1970), 53.1% (1990), 59.8% (2000), 65.6% (2010), 72.1% (2025)
7861	non-metropolitan areas	2,309,000	65.95	1,522,000	97.14	C	2,946,482	*Sources of data:* Censuses of 1953, 1961, 1971, and 1981.
7862	metropolitan areas	4,060,000	66.03	2,681,000	96.89	C	4,877,000	*Definition:* Urban centers.
7863	BEOGRAD (Belgrade)	1,232,000	65.00	801,000	97.68	C	1,403,000	Danube & Sava rivers. Tractors, University of Belgrade (1863). Stone Age settlements. D=SOC.
7864	Pancevo	67,400	65.00	43,800	98.68	C	82,800	Northeast of Beograd on Danube River. Oil refinery, chemicals, glass. Serb religious art. D=SOC.
7865	Cacak	124,000	70.00	86,700	98.68	C	152,000	Northwest of Kraljevo. Western Morava River. Plums, paper, apple orchards. D=SOC.
7866	Kragujevac	185,000	67.00	124,000	99.68	C	227,000	On Lepenica River. Autos, fruits & vegetables, livestock. 7,000 males massacred by Germans (1941). D=SOC.
7867	Kraljevo	136,000	69.00	93,900	97.68	C	167,000	On Ibar River. Heavy industry. Ecclesiastical center. Zica monastery (1207). Church of The Virgin (1190). D=SOC.
7868	Krusevac	149,000	68.00	101,000	96.68	C	183,000	On Rasina River. Commercial center, hydroelectric plant, chemical industry, medieval castle ruins. D=SOC.
7869	Leskovac	178,000	67.00	119,000	99.18	C	219,000	On Juzna River, Southern Morava River. Textiles, quince and hemp growing, vineyards, railroad. D=SOC.
7870	Nis	258,000	66.00	170,000	94.68	C	317,000	On Nisava River. Health spa. F=Roman Naissus(2nd century). Birthplace of Constantine (c280). D=SOC.
7871	Novi Sad	287,000	65.00	186,000	98.68	C	352,000	Vojvodina on Danube River. Annual agricultural fair. 1/5 Hungarian. F=18th century. D=SOC.
7872	Pec (Ipek, Pescium)	124,000	68.00	84,500	99.68	C	153,000	Kosovo on Beli Drim River. Oriental character. Leatherworking. Orthodox center (1253-1766). Mainly Albanian.
7873	Podgorica (Titograd)	158,000	55.00	86,700	83.68	B	194,000	Near confluence of Ribnica & Moraca. Aluminum. 1/7 parks & recreation facilities. F=Roman origins. D=SOC.
7874	Pristina	263,000	65.00	171,000	93.68	C	323,000	Capital of Kosovo. Oriental appearance. Market town. Albanians. Gracanica Monastery (1321). D=SOC.
7875	Prizren	151,000	70.00	106,000	98.68	C	185,000	Kosovo. Textiles, man-made fibers. Center for handicrafts. Bogorodica Ljeviska (1306) turned into mosque. D=SOC.
7876	Sabac	134,000	68.00	91,000	96.68	C	164,000	On Sava River. Trade center, plums, fishing, major agricultural, chemical industry, railroad terminus. D=SOC.
7877	Smederevo	120,000	68.00	81,800	96.68	C	148,000	Near Belgrade. 15th century Serbian fort. Oil refining, steel manufacturing, wine production, fortress. D=SOC.
7878	Subotica (Szabadka)	165,000	66.00	109,000	94.68	C	203,000	Vojvodina near Hungarian border. Market center, paprika, metal products. F=1491. Mainly Hungarian. D=SOC.
7879	Titova Mitrovica (Titova Uzice)	118,000	69.00	81,300	97.68	C	145,000	On Djetinja River. Nonferrous metals & machinery, livestock. Headquarters for partisan army (WWII). D=SOC.
7880	Urosevac	128,000	70.00	89,300	98.68	C	157,000	Kosovo. Railroad, 20 miles south of Pristina. Woodworking, textiles, food processing, mining. D=SOC.
7881	Zrenjanin	151,000	65.00	97,900	98.68	C	185,000	Near Novi Sad. Vojvodina. River port, foodstuffs, sugar, beer, liquor, railroad center. D=SOC.
	ZAMBIA	**9,169,000**	**76.91**	**7,052,000**	**98.76**	**C**	**15,616,000**	**ROMAN CATHOLICS 33.4%, PROTESTANTS 29.5%. PENT-CHAR 22.0%, EVANGELICAL 12.5%, GCC 16.4%**
7882	rural areas	5,086,000	82.47	4,194,000	98.29	C	6,651,000	91.1% (1950), 69.8% (1970), 58.0% (1990), 55.4% (2000), 51.2% (2010), 42.5% (2025)
7883	urban areas	4,083,000	70.00	2,858,000	99.35	C	8,965,000	8.8% (1950), 30.1% (1970), 41.9% (1990), 44.5% (2000), 48.8% (2010), 57.4% (2025)
7884	non-metropolitan areas	300,000	69.80	209,000	99.43	C	602,390	*Sources of data:* Censuses of 1963, 1969, and 1980; estimate for 1990.
7885	metropolitan areas	3,783,000	70.02	2,649,000	99.34	C	8,363,000	*Definition:* Localities of 5,000 or more inhabitants, the majority of whom depend upon non-agricultural activities.
7886	Chililabombwe (Bancroft)	101,000	73.00	74,000	99.85	C	223,000	At 4,459 ft. in highland copper belt. Copper mining. Bancroft mine (1957). D=RCC,UCZ.
7887	Chingola	222,000	72.00	160,000	99.35	C	487,000	At 5,000 ft. Purely civil & governmental township serving copper mining community. F=1943. D=RCC,UCZ.
7888	Kabwe (Broken Hill)	220,000	72.00	158,000	99.35	C	482,000	On Great North Road at 3,871 Ft. Mining center (Zinc, vanadium). Corn, tobacco. D=RCC,UCZ.
7889	Kalulushi	99,200	73.00	72,400	99.85	C	218,000	Copper mining, cobalt, selenium. food & beverages, wood products, plastics. D=RCC,UCZ.
7890	Kitwe	446,000	71.00	317,000	99.05	C	980,000	Copperbelt. Main industrial center in copper belt. F=1936. Main Europeans. D=RCC,UCZ.
7891	LUSAKA	1,695,000	69.20	1,173,000	99.55	C	3,778,000	On Great North & Great East roads in 4,198 ft. Corn, tobacco. University of Zambia (1966). D=RCC.
7892	Livingstone (Maramba)	108,000	69.00	74,900	99.15	C	238,000	On Zambezi River. Distribution point for agriculture & timber, tourism. F=1905. Livingstone museum. D=RCC,UCZ.
7893	Luanshya	193,000	72.00	139,000	99.35	C	424,000	Copperbelt south of Kitwe. Machine shops. Uranium and copper mining, tobacco. 'Garden town'. D=RCC,UCZ.
7894	Mufulira	202,000	71.00	143,000	99.05	C	443,000	Chief copper-mining center. Explosive-manufacturing. Near Zaire. Smelting, copper refining. D=RCC,UCZ.
7895	Ndola	497,000	68.00	338,000	98.85	C	1,090,000	Capital of Copperbelt on Zaire border. Copper refinery, sugar refinery, mine services. D=RCC,UCZ.
	ZIMBABWE	**11,669,000**	**59.28**	**6,917,000**	**98.22**	**B**	**15,092,000**	**INDEPENDENTS 40.2%, PROTESTANTS 12.3%. PENT-CHAR 42.2%, EVANGELICAL 4.5%, GCC 25.1%**
7896	rural areas	7,549,000	60.69	4,581,000	99.63	C	7,219,000	89.3% (1950), 83.0% (1970), 71.6% (1990), 64.6% (2000), 57.5% (2010), 47.8% (2025)
7897	urban areas	4,120,000	56.70	2,336,000	95.64	B	7,874,000	10.6% (1950), 16.9% (1970), 28.3% (1990), 35.3% (2000), 42.4% (2010), 52.1% (2025)
7898	non-metropolitan areas	1,247,000	56.67	707,000	95.61	B	1,864,146	*Sources of data:* Censuses of 1951, 1962, and 1982; estimate for 1972.
7899	metropolitan areas	2,873,000	56.71	1,630,000	95.65	B	6,010,000	*Definition:* Nineteen main towns.
7900	Bulawayo	816,000	53.00	433,000	91.94	B	1,560,000	Matabeleland on Matsheumlope River at 4,405 Ft. Rail & commercial center. Breweries. Tourism. F=1890. D=RCC.
7901	Gweru (Gwelo)	130,000	60.00	78,000	98.94	C	249,000	On Gweru River. Ferrochromium, textiles, dairy foods, mining. F=1894 as military outpost. D=AACJM.
7902	HARARE (Salisbury)	1,803,000	58.00	1,046,000	96.94	B	3,964,000	At 4,865 ft. Center of industry & commerce. Tobacco, gold. F=1890. Anglican & RC Cathedrals. D=RCC.
7903	Chitungwiza	322,000	58.00	187,000	96.94	B	616,000	Near Sambi & Umtar Rivers. Manyane River. Zimbabwe's third largest city, airport. D=AACJM,RCC.
7904	Mutare (Umtali)	124,000	59.00	73,300	97.94	B	237,000	Manicaland on border with Mozambique. Tobacco, gold, silver, oil refining, tourism (national parks). D=RCC.

Part 11

PROVINCESCAN

Major civil divisions (MCDs) in 238 countries: 3,030 profiles

It pleased Darius to appoint 120 satraps to rule throughout the kingdom, with three administrators over them, one of whom was Daniel.

—Daniel 6:1-2. New International Version

The globe's 238 nations and countries today are subdivided for administrative purposes into 3,030 MCDs (major civil divisions). The countries themselves term them by a variety of labels: provinces, states, regions, counties. Beneath these units at the first level of administration, every large country has one, 2, 3 or more lower levels (districts, areas). Part 11 lists all those at the first level with their populations and the status of Christianity within each.

Major civil divisions (MCDs) in 238 countries: 3,030 profiles

Major civil divisions (MCDs) in the world's 238 countries are alternately known as provinces, states, departments, districts, regions, territories, parishes, republics, islands, divisions, communes, prefectures, autonomous regions, municipalities, and a host of other names. In most cases, these divisions represent an attempt on the part of national governments to administrate their people in more manageable segments. MCDs tend to have capitals, or if not, some form of administration physically located within the MCD.

Some of these MCDs are heavily populated, such as Uttar Pradesh state in India with 167 million people in AD 2000, making it the world's sixth largest country after Brazil at 170 million and before Pakistan (see Table 11-1 below for the 10 largest MCDs in the world). Others have very few inhabitants such as Bikini in the Marshall Islands with only 12 people in AD 2000. MCDs also vary widely in size from the Northwest Territories in Canada at over one million square miles to the Biminis Islands in Bahamas at only nine square miles.

The living conditions in MCDs, as one would expect, are disparate. Tete in Mozambique is one of the poorest MCDs on the planet with a GNP per capita of less than $100 and very few resources. California in the USA, on the other hand, if it were a country, would be in the top ten economically.

Data are often available on MCDs through censuses, surveys, studies, polls, and other collection devices. In many cases, MCDs are considered the primary segment for data collection. This is true in the United States of America, where statistics of all kinds are available at the state level. These data are often used in a comparative fashion, e.g. Although 7.2% of all USA citizens over 25 years old have advanced degrees, this ranges from 17.2% in the District of Columbia to 4.5% in Arkansas (1990 census).

MCDs are strategic for Christian missions because of the significant administrative role of provincial governments. Permissions, rulings, permits, official documents, etc. are often granted at the MCD level. Christian research often focuses on MCDs. National surveys are often the sum of MCD research. In Nigeria, researchers are studying all of the peoples one state at a time. From the viewpoint of missions strategy note that Table 11-2 below enumerates the 10 largest World A major civil divisions. Each of these is as large as a medium-sized country.

LISTING OF 3,030 MAJOR CIVIL DIVISIONS

The listing of 3,030 major civil divisions in Table 11-3 is derived from the listing of major civil divisions in *Encyclopaedia Britannica's Book of the Year*. These are normally listed with square kilometers, square miles and population. However, a number of adjustments have been made. First of all, many smaller countries not listed in Britannica have been added. This includes many single line entries for very small countries that reflect the comparative nature of this listing. Although some of these countries have subdivisions, they are too small to report here. Second, the Britannica MCDs (and those from other sources) have populations relating to a wide variety

of dates (e.g. 1985-1999). These have been adjusted with the methodology explained below under column 6.

Meaning of columns

1. Rec. No. Record number. These are sequential beginning with Afghanistan. Each MCD receives a single line. Country names are not included in the sequence. Thus the last record number, 3,031, represents the total number of MCDs in this listing.

2. Country. Standard name of 238 countries. For more details on individual countries see Part 4 "Countries". The entire country line is in bold. All data on this line relates to the entire country, not to any individual MCD below.

Major civil division. In most cases the MCD name is the name of the MCD as it is known to its inhabitants. One example is Dogu Anadolu for East Anatolia, Turkey. Alternates are given in parentheses.

3. Capital. Name of capital city if MCD has one. Usually the administrative and governmental center of the MCD.

4. Sq. mi. Area covered by MCD in square miles.

5. Sq. km. Area covered by MCD in square kilometers.

6. Pop 2000. Population figures are for mid-2000 and are derived in the following fashion: A population figure is supplied by *Encyclopaedia Britannica* or another source for a particular date. To calculate the year 2000 population of an MCD, the following formula is used:

$$= \text{UN country population (AD 2000)} * \text{MCD population (Britannica)/UN country population (Britannica date)}$$

7. AC%. Percent affiliated church members. Totals for country are derived from Tables 1 in Part 4 "Countries". Certain guidelines were followed to determine the percentage of Christians within a particularly MCD. The 100% rule always applied. The total number of Christians in a country's MCDs always equals the total number of Christians in a country according to Table 1 for that country.

Apart from these overall guidelines, the following techniques were used

a. MCD surveys. For a number of MCDs a survey, usually filled out by missionaries or church workers in that MCD, was available. This often gave a detailed breakdown of Christians by denomination. Numbers were also often provided for other religions.

b. Country reports. The number of Christians could be determined for many MCDs by country reports done by missionaries and church workers. Often, detailed information on MCDs within these countries was included.

c. Censuses. For many countries, such as India, detailed census reports give figures for religions including Christianity by MCD.

d. Denominational reports. For many denominations, precise church membership figures are reported for MCDs. From this information a fuller picture of Christianity can often be constructed.

e. Ethnic affiliation. In many MCDs, the Christian situation can be derived from ethnic data. For exam-

ple, it may be known that an MCD is predominately one or two ethnic groups. Since the percentage Christian is known for all ethnic groups, the percentage of Christians in an MCD can be calculated using ethnic data.

8. Church members. Number of affiliated church members. Calculated by multiplying column 3 (Pop 2000) by column 4 (%AC) divided by 100. These figures are not meant to convey exactitude, i.e. 'There are exactly 75 Christians in Relizane, Algeria', but rather 'There are very few Christians in Relizane, perhaps as few as 0.01% of the population'.

9. E%. Percent evangelized. The percentage of this MCD who have received an adequate opportunity to become Christians. Evangelization of a MCD is measured by setting up a proportion related to the church members in the MCD and the evangelization of the country. The formula is as follows:

% evangelized of a MCD= church members (MCD)/church members (country)*% evangelized (country)

This result is then adjusted (figure available on companion CD *World Christian database*) to reconcile it with the total evangelized derived from Tables 1 in Part 4 "Countries".

10. W. Worlds. Using the church membership and evangelization data, one can determine where a MCD fits into the World A, B, C trichotomy. Worlds A, B, and C are defined in Part 2 "Glossary".

11. Notes. On the country line. The first data on this line are the two largest ecclesiastical megablocs in this country expressed as a percentage of the country's population. In some countries the title 'Marginal Christians' has been shortened to 'Marginals' in the interest of space. Following this are the three transmegabloc groupings. Pentecostals/ Charismatics is shortened to Pent-Char, followed by Evangelical and finally GCC, the short form for Great Commission Christians. Each of these it followed by the percentage they represent of the country's population. Fuller descriptions of these data can be found in Tables 1 in Part 4 "Countries".

On the MCD line. Here the reader is presented with a sequence of facts about a particular MCD. Normally the first word on this line refers to facts related to the geography or location. Often there are data on the main economic activity of each MCD. The code "F=" refers to the date in which the MCD was founded. The founding date refers to the earliest date of known settlement. This is usually followed with data on ethnic groups and religions, accompanied by percentages where these are known. Finally the code "D=" refers to denominations active in the city and the code "M=" to mission agencies working there. Abbreviations are listed in Part 15 "Indexes".

Table 11-1.	10 largest major civil divisions, AD 2000.			
Country	Name	Population	AC	Church members
India	1. Uttar Pradesh	166,915,000	3.1	5,175,000
Russia	2. Russia	123,457,000	60.9	75,186,000
China	3. Szechwan (Sichuan)	104,926,000	6.2	6,505,000
India	4. Bihar	103,655,000	5.2	5,390,000
China	5. Honan (Henan)	94,858,000	16.5	15,652,000
India	6. Maharashtra	94,542,000	5.0	4,727,000
China	7. Shantung (Shandong)	90,740,000	6.8	6,170,000
Pakistan	8. Punjab	88,000,000	3.0	2,640,000
India	9. West Bengal	81,617,000	2.5	2,040,000
India	10. Andhra Pradesh	79,663,000	7.0	5,576,000

Table 11-2.	10 largest World A major civil divisions, AD 2000.			
Country	Name	Population	AC	Unevangelized
Pakistan	1. Sindh	35,423,000	1.8	18,916,000
Pakistan	2. North-West Frontier	20,331,000	0.3	14,232,000
India	3. Haryana	19,590,000	1.1	9,990,000
China	4. Sinkiang Uighur	17,314,000	0.3	10,735,000
Turkey	5. ic Anadolu (Central Anatolia)	15,443,000	0.1	8,339,000
Iran	6. Tehran	11,172,000	1.0	5,809,000
India	7. Jammu and Kashmir	9,267,000	1.3	4,726,000
Turkey	8. Dogu Anadolu (East Anatolia)	8,098,000	0.1	4,535,000
Turkey	9. Karadeniz kiyisi (Black Sea Coast)	8,051,000	0.1	4,348,000
Pakistan	10. Balochistan	8,041,000	0.5	5,227,000

Table 11-3. 3,030 major civil divisions in 238 countries by Worlds A, B, and C in AD 2000.

Rec No 1	Country Major civil divisions 2	Capital 3	sq.mi. 4	sq.km. 5	Pop 2000 6	AC% 7	Church members 8	E% 9	W 10	Notes 11
	AFGHANISTAN		**251,825**	**652,225**	**22,720,416**	**0.03**	**6,897**	**29.58**	**A**	**Independents 0.01%, Protestants 0.01%. Pent-char 0.01%, Evangelical 0.00%, GCC 0.02%**
1	Badakhshan	Faizabad	18,418	47,703	856,596	0.01	85	28.56	A	NE region, Feyzabad. Panj River, border, military training camps. Rice, bread baking.
2	Badghis	Qala Nau	8,439	21,858	360,593	0.01	36	28.56	A	West, Turkmenistan border. Morghab River, Qal'eh-ye Now. Wheat.
3	Baghlan	Baghlan	6,606	17,109	851,052	0.01	85	28.56	A	Northeast. Qonduz River, E-Salang tunnel. Rice potatoes, peas, mung beans.
4	Balkh	Mazar-i-Sharif	4,862	12,593	1,007,298	0.01	101	28.56	A	North. Balkh River, Amu Darya River. Rice.
5	Bamian	Bamian	6,724	17,414	462,126	0.01	46	28.56	A	East central. Helmand River, Kuhe-Fuladi mountains. Potatoes, peas, mung beans chick peas.
6	Farah	Farah	18,451	47,788	404,008	0.01	40	28.56	A	West. Lake Dak, Harut River. Potatoes, peas, beans, mung beans.
7	Faryab	Maimana	8,602	22,279	932,971	0.01	93	28.56	A	North. Border, Shirin River, Selseleh-ye band-e Torkestan.
8	Ghazni	Ghazni	9,026	23,378	1,113,082	0.01	111	28.56	A	South region. Tarnak & Ghazni rivers. Oxen, potatoes, peas, mung beans, chick peas.
9	Ghowr	Qala Ahangaran	14,929	38,666	581,586	0.01	58	28.56	A	East central. Selseleh-ye Safed Kuh, Farah River.
10	Helmand	Lashkar Gah	23,872	61,828	891,099	0.01	89	28.56	A	Southwest. Band-ekajaki Lake, Helmand River. Beans, peas, chick peas, mung beans.
11	Herat	Herat	23,674	61,315	1,377,080	0.01	138	28.56	A	West, Harirud River. Wheat, rice, potatoes, mung beans.
12	Jowzjan	Shibarghan	9,866	25,553	1,084,252	0.01	108	28.56	A	North. Safid River, Torkestan range, border.
13	Kabul	Kabul	1,770	4,585	2,630,886	0.14	3,746	34.80	A	Central. Kabol River. Airport. Potatoes. M=IAM.
14	Kandahar	Kandahar	18,408	47,676	991,076	0.03	297	29.58	A	Southwest. Rigestan desert, Arghastan River. Peas, chick peas, beans.
15	Kapisa	Tagab	722	1,871	431,113	0.10	431	32.65	A	Central. Panjshor River, glacier. Rice, beans, mung beans, peas.
16	Konar	Chigha Sarai	4,046	10,479	430,406	0.01	43	28.56	A	East. Glaciers, Kovor River. Beans, peas, chick peas, mung beans.
17	Konduz	Kunduz	3,022	7,827	961,128	0.01	96	28.56	A	Northeast. Qonduz River, border, Amu Darya River. Rice
18	Laghman	Tigri	2,784	7,210	534,736	0.01	53	28.56	A	East. Kabol River, Hindu Kush Range, glaciers. Rice.
19	Lowgar	Baraki Barak	1,796	4,652	372,249	0.01	37	28.56	A	Central, Kalangar, Baraki. Potatoes.
20	Nangarhar	Jalalabad	2,941	7,616	1,288,136	0.05	689	31.60	A	East, Khyber Pass, Kabol River. Rice, maize, wheat, potatoes, beans, chick peas.
21	Nimruz	Zaranj	15,968	41,356	178,421	0.01	18	28.56	A	Southwest. Helmand River. Salt flats, desert, aqueducts.
22	Oruzgan	Tarin Kowt	11,311	29,295	764,340	0.01	76	28.56	A	Southwest. Varkhan River. Beans, peas.
23	Paktia	Gardez	3,699	9,581	832,987	0.01	83	28.56	A	South. Ghazni River. Maize, wheat, potatoes.
24	Paktika	Sharan	7,466	19,336	421,954	0.01	42	28.56	A	South. Gowmal River, Khumbur Khale Ghar mountains. Maize, wheat, potatoes.
25	Parvan	Charikar	3,629	9,400	868,836	0.01	87	28.56	A	Central. Hindu Kush Range, Panjshar River. Beans, peas, chick peas, mung beans.
26	Samangan	Haibak	5,971	15,465	393,752	0.01	39	28.56	A	North. Border, Amu Darya River.
27	Takhar	Taliqan	4,778	12,376	895,066	0.01	90	28.56	A	Northeast. Kowkcheh River border, Kuh-E Khvajeh Mohammad Range.
28	Vardak	Maidan	3,484	9,023	494,880	0.01	49	28.56	A	Central. Helmand River. Rice, potatoes.
29	Zabol	Qalat	6,677	17,293	308,705	0.01	31	28.56	A	Southwest. Tarnak River, Lurah River. Oxen, peas, beans, chick peas.
	ALBANIA		**11,100**	**28,748**	**3,113,434**	**34.38**	**1,070,390**	**85.41**	**B**	**Roman Catholics 16.7%, Orthodox 16.0%. Pent-char 3.2%, Evangelical 0.1%, GCC 19.7%**
30	Berat	Berat	396	1,027	172,592	34.00	58,681	85.03	B	Hilly terrain, Osum River. Oil fields. Former center of Albanian nationalist movement. D=AOC.
31	Dibër	Peshkopi	605	1,568	147,047	34.50	50,731	85.53	B	Eastern mountains. Drin Izi River, Luré National Park, Korab Mountains. Wheat, tobacco. D=AOC.
32	Durrës	Durrës	327	848	240,046	35.00	84,016	86.03	B	Adriatic coast. Ancient Illyricum. Tobacco, leather goods. D=AOC,RCC.
33	Elbasan	Elbasan	572	1,481	237,796	35.00	83,229	86.03	B	Fertile, well-watered plain. Olive, corn, tobacco, iron-nickel ore. Mainly Muslim. D=AOC.
34	Fier	Fier	454	1,175	240,128	34.00	81,644	85.03	B	Southwest. Seman River, Adriatic Coast. Railroad. D=AOC.
35	Gjirokastër	Gjirokastër	439	1,137	64,443	33.00	21,266	84.03	B	Drin River valley, Gjera mountains. Hoxha birthplace. Bektashiyah Muslims. 30% Greek. D=AOC.
36	Gramsh	Gramsh	268	695	42,831	33.00	14,134	84.03	B	Central. Devoll River. Cotton, tobacco, wheat. D=AOC.
37	Kolonjë	Ersekë	311	805	24,185	32.00	7,739	83.03	B	Southeast. Formerly known as Erseke. Mount Gramoz, Pindus mountains. D=AOC.
38	Korçë	Korçë	842	2,181	208,671	36.00	75,122	87.03	B	Fertile plateau (2,800 ft). Chief wheat-growing area. Sugar beets, apples, grapes, coal. D=AOC.
39	Krujë	Krujë	234	607	105,069	34.50	36,249	85.53	B	Western. Adriatic Sea. Brick, cement, fishing, hydroelectric power. D=AOC.
40	Kukës	Kukës	514	1,330	100,149	34.00	34,051	85.03	B	Northeast. Drin River. 25 miles east of Puke. Sugar beets, livestock, agriculture. D=AOC.
41	Lezhë	Lezhë	185	479	60,727	33.00	20,040	84.03	B	Northwest. Alessio. mouth of Drin River. F=385 BC by Dionysius of Syracuse. D=AOC,RCC.
42	Librazhd	Librazhd	391	1,013	70,639	33.00	23,311	84.03	B	Eastern. Shkumbin River. Railroad, sugar beets, tobacco, corn, potatoes. D=AOC.
43	Lushnjë	Lushnjë	275	712	131,799	35.00	46,130	86.03	B	Western. Adriatic Sea, Karavasta Lagoon. Navigable canals, trade, fishing. D=AOC.
44	Mat	Burrel	397	1,028	75,308	34.00	25,605	85.03	B	North central. Lake Ulëz, Mat plain. Wheat, corn railroad, potatoes, cotton. D=AOC.
45	Mirditë	Rrëshen	335	867	49,439	33.00	16,315	84.03	B	North central. Lake Ulëz. Railroad, coal, copper, chemicals, livestock, agricultural. D=AOC.
46	Pogradec	Pogradec	280	725	70,124	34.00	23,842	85.03	B	East. Capital 55 miles southeast of Tirane, Lake Ohrid, Shkumbin River. Corn, wheat. D=AOC.
47	Pukë	Pukë	399	1,034	48,086	33.00	15,868	84.03	B	North. Konan Reservoir, Drin Dam. Hydroelectric power. D=AOC.
48	Përmet	Përmet	359	929	38,650	33.00	12,755	84.03	B	Vljose River, southern region, Greek border. Nemercke mountains. Minerals, agricultural. D=AOC.
49	Sarandë	Sarandë	424	1,097	85,542	33.00	28,229	84.03	B	Southern. Adriatic coast, Corfu Straits. 41% Greek. Fashion, grains. D=AOC,GOC.
50	Shkodër	Shkodër	976	2,528	230,981	34.00	78,534	85.03	B	Lake Scutari, Buenë River, Drin River. Grains, tobacco, potatoes. D=RCC,AOC.
51	Skrapar	Çorovoda	299	775	45,522	33.00	15,022	84.03	B	South central. Osum River. Potatoes, sugar beets, deposits of coal, copper, chemicals.
52	Tepelenë	Tepelenë	315	817	48,790	34.00	16,589	85.03	B	Southern. Vijose River. 30 miles southeast of Vlore. Scene of fighting 1940-41.
53	Tiranë	Tiranë	478	1,238	358,098	37.00	132,496	88.07	B	Fertile plain, Ishm River. Coal mines, metalworking. Mainly Muslim. D=AOC,RCC.
54	Tropojë	Bajram	403	1,043	43,954	33.00	14,505	84.03	B	Northeast. Bajram Curri. North Albanian Alps, Koman Reservoir. Cotton, tobacco. D=AOC.
55	Vlorë	Vlorë	621	1,609	172,818	31.41	54,287	82.44	B	Mountainous Karaburun, Vlores Bay. Ancient Greek origin. Hilly olive groves. Muslim. D=AOC.
	ALGERIA		**919,595**	**2,381,741**	**31,471,278**	**0.29**	**90,877**	**49.55**	**A**	**Independents 0.2%, Roman Catholics 0.06%. Pent-char 0.1%, Evangelical 0.02%, GCC 0.2%**
56	Adrar	Adrar	163,127	422,498	298,776	0.01	30	41.27	A	Sand dune covered plains with palm-grove settlements. Strategic on trade routes. 'Mountain.'
57	Alger	Algiers	304	786	2,319,883	1.54	35,696	66.57	B	Sahel hills. Wine, vegetables, oranges. D=RCC.
58	Annaba	Annaba	1,347	3,489	625,731	1.00	6,257	65.26	B	Edough foothills. Cork tree, iron ore, phosphates. Site of Hippo Regius (Augustine).
59	Aïn Defla		–	–	737,413	0.01	74	41.27	A	North. Mediterranean Sea, Oneliff River. Railroad. Wheat, barley, grapes, olives, fishing.
60	Aïn Temouchent	Aïn Temouchent	–	–	377,438	0.01	38	41.27	A	Tessala mountains. Vineyards, orchards.
61	Batna	Batna	5,746	14,882	1,033,010	0.40	4,132	59.66	B	Waditilatou. Agriculture, forest products. Tourism (Roman ruins).
62	Bejaïa	Bejaïa	1,329	3,442	962,096	0.80	7,697	64.06	B	Fertile plain, Wadi Soummam. Oil, minerals, olive oil. Kabyle area.
63	Biskra	Biskra	42,366	109,728	590,477	0.01	59	41.27	A	Zab oases. Wadi Biskra. Winter resorts, dates, figs, apricots.
64	Blida	Blida	1,430	3,704	963,792	0.80	7,710	64.06	B	Mitidja plain, Tell Atlas mountains. Wheat, barley, vineyards, ski resorts.
65	Bordj Bou Arreridj	–	–	–	583,100	0.01	58	41.27	A	Monts du Hodna Range. Ancient ruins. Liquefied petroleum gases. Pulp and paper.
66	Bouira	Bouira	1,744	4,517	723,201	0.01	72	41.27	A	Tell Atlas ranges & valleys. Olive & cereals, vineyards. Horse, cattle, sheep. 'The Small Wells'.
67	Boumerdes	–	–	–	893,501	0.01	89	41.27	A	Institute of Petrol , Algerian Triathlon Association. Agriculture, citrus fruits, industry.
68	Béchar	Bechar	118,147	306,000	254,398	0.01	25	41.27	A	Mount Bechar, Wadi Bechar. Sand dunes, sandstone, oases. Dates, cereals.
69	Constantine	Constantine	1,375	3,562	911,792	0.80	7,294	64.06	B	Hauts Plateaux. Rhumel River & Gorge. Grain, leather goods. Prehistoric settlement. D=RCC.
70	Djelfa	Djelfa	8,844	22,905	678,722	0.01	68	41.27	A	Oulad Nail Mountains. Neolithic rock carvings. Meeting place of Oulad Nail people.
71	ech-Chleff	ech-Cheliff	3,350	8,677	939,093	0.20	1,878	54.46	B	Atlas Tellien mountains. Oued Zeddine River. Sand treatment plant. Railroad.
72	el-Bayadh	–	–	–	210,351	0.01	21	41.27	A	North central. Saharan Atlas mountains. Salt lakes. Citrus fruit, livestock, oil, wheat, barley.
73	el-Oued	–	–	–	517,328	0.01	52	41.27	A	Northeast. Grand Erg (sand dunes) Oriental. Souf Oases. Dates, carpets, cloth.
74	et-Tarf	–	–	–	364,160	0.01	36	41.27	A	Northeast. Wetlands. Salt, chemicals, textiles, industry, livestock.
75	Ghardaïa	–	–	–	296,664	0.01	30	41.27	A	Mzab Oasis. Female saint Dqia (11th century). Historic Jewish presence.
76	Guelma	Guelma	3,330	8,624	484,938	0.01	48	41.27	A	Atlas mountains, central valley (olives & cattle), farming (wheat & barley). Birth place of Augustine.
77	Illizi	–	–	–	25,983	0.02	4	41.28	A	Southeast. Tassili Najjer range, desert. Livestock, grains.
78	Jijel	Jijel	1,431	3,705	648,274	0.01	65	41.27	A	Mediterranean seacoast. Kabylie de Collo region. Cork-oak forest. Fishing, citrus fruits.
79	Khenchela	–	–	–	338,392	0.01	34	41.27	A	Northeast. Salt lakes. Tobacco, cotton, agriculture, livestock.
80	Laghouat	–	–	–	291,515	0.01	29	41.27	A	Southern edge of Saharan Atlas. Wadi Mzi. Date palms, woven wall hangings. D=RCC.
81	M' Sila	MSila	7,654	19,825	829,976	0.01	83	41.27	A	Plains of Hodna, salt lakes. Wheat & barley, semi-nomadic herding, dates.
82	Mascara	Mascara	2,257	5,846	778,105	0.01	78	41.27	A	Atlas mountains. Wadi Toudman. Wine production, grains. 'Mother of soldiers.'
83	Mila	–	–	–	702,206	0.01	70	41.27	A	North central. Citrus fruit, livestock, oil, barley grapes, olives, minerals, natural gas.
84	Mostaganem	Mostaganem	2,712	7,024	694,420	0.01	69	41.27	A	Wadi An Sefra. Port, beaches. Wheat & barley, citrus fruits, grapes, cotton.
85	Médéa	Medea	3,361	8,704	896,091	0.01	90	41.27	A	Atlas mountains. Mount Nador (3,693 ft.) Fertile, well-watered soil. Vineyards, cereals.
86	Naâma	–	–	–	156,060	0.01	16	41.27	A	Northwest. Salt flats, salt lakes. Livestock, iron ore, phosphates, railroad.
87	Oran	Oran	703	1,820	1,279,871	0.60	7,679	57.86	B	Mediterranean coast. Lake Sebkha d'Oran. Airport. Inedible meat processing. D=RCC.
88	Ouargla	Ouargla	215,921	559,234	390,430	0.01	39	41.27	A	Large enclosed basin in Sahara desert, Berbers. Oil, natural gas, date palms, fruits.
89	Oum el-Bouaghi	Oum el-Bouaghi	3,136	8,123	554,426	0.01	55	41.27	A	Atlas mountains high plains. Salt marshes, sheep pastures. Self-managed farms.
90	Relizane	–	–	–	747,874	0.01	75	41.27	A	Wadi, Mina. Cereals, grapes, cotton. Kaloa Oriental carpets.
91	Saïda	Saïda	41,227	106,777	323,229	0.01	32	41.27	A	Tell Atlas, high plateau. Fertile, well-watered. Sheep, wool, cereals, mineral water.
92	Sidi bel-Abbès	Sidi bel Abbès	4,497	11,648	612,541	0.50	3,063	57.76	B	Wadi Mekerra, Atlas mountains. Wheat, barley, grapes.
93	Skikda	Skikda	1,833	4,748	717,174	0.05	359	52.31	B	Gulf of Stora, Wadi Safsof. Oil fields, mineral products, sardine fishing.
94	Souk Ahras	–	–	–	406,382	0.01	41	41.27	A	Paint, varnish, lacquer industry, railroad, iron ore, phosphates, chemicals.
95	Sâtif	Setif	3,996	10,350	1,373,510	0.10	1,374	57.36	B	Wadi Bou Sellam. Cereal cultivation. High elevation (3,500 ft).
96	Tamanrasset	Tamanrasset	214,673	556,000	131,522	0.01	13	41.27	A	Mountainous Ahaggar region. Wadi Tamanrasset. Extremely dry climate. Tuaregs.
97	Tiaret	Tiaret	9,056	23,456	790,310	0.01	79	41.27	A	Atlas Mountains. Wadi Tiaret & Wadi Mina. Cereals, livestock. Arabian horses. 'The lioness'.
98	Tindouf	–	–	–	22,549	0.01	2	41.27	A	Saharan oasis. Iron ore. Regeibat nomads. Headquarters of Polisario Front.
99	Tipaza	–	–	–	851,191	0.01	85	41.27	A	North central, coastal. Railroad, chemicals, cosmetics, industry, cement, textiles.
100	Tissemsilt	–	–	–	313,108	0.01	31	41.27	A	Northwest. Railroad, wheat, barley, livestock, iron ore, minerals, chemicals.
101	Tizi Ouzou	Tizi Ouzou	1,450	3,756	1,286,014	0.20	2,572	57.46	B	Grand Kabylie, Wadi Tizi Ouzou. Flowering broom, olives, figs, basketry.
102	Tlemcen	Tlemcen	3,585	9,284	981,189	0.01	98	41.27	A	Well-watered Tiemcen Mountains, fertile Hennaya & Maghnia plains. Agriculture, silk. Hadars, Jews.
103	Tébessa	Tébessa	6,400	16,575	563,068	0.60	3,378	56.86	B	Ancient origins, Roman ruins. Phosphate mines. Sheep, grains, carpets.
	AMERICAN SAMOA		**77**	**199**	**68,089**	**81.13**	**55,240**	**99.63**	**C**	**Protestants 52.5%, Roman Catholics 13.9%. Pent-char 14.5%, Evangelical 8.0%, GCC 44.4%**
104	Eastern	–	–	–	30,824	81.04	24,981	99.76	C	Southwest central Pacific. Copra, fishing, canned tuna, pineapples. D=Congregational,RCC.
105	Manu'a	–	–	–	2,492	84.00	2,093	99.80	C	Southwest central Pacific. Copra, canned tuna, fishing, pineapples. D=Congregational,RCC.
106	Western	–	–	–	34,773	81.00	28,166	99.50	C	Southwest central Pacific Ocean. Copra, canned tuna, pineapples, fishing. D=Congregational,RCC.
	ANDORRA		**181**	**468**	**77,985**	**90.02**	**70,205**	**99.06**	**C**	**Roman Catholics 89.1%, Marginals 0.5%. Pent-char 1.0%, Evangelical 0.03%, GCC 34.0%**
107	Andorra la Vella	Andorra la Vella	49	127	29,240	90.00	26,316	99.65	C	Gran Valira valley. Valira & Valira del Norte rivers. Winter sports. 'Andorra the Old'. D=RCC.
108	Canillo	Canillo	74	191	2,165	92.00	1,992	99.69	C	21% Andorran, 31% Spanish. Palau Freezing. (Palate of Ice), skiing. D=RCC.
109	Encamp	Encamp	–	–	10,715	90.40	9,686	99.04	C	Pic des Pessoms (9,400 ft). Valira River. Agriculture, skiing. D=RCC.
110	La Massana	La Massana	25	65	6,275	91.00	5,710	99.64	C	15% Andorran, 32% Spanish. Skiing, tourism. D=RCC.
111	Les Escaldes-Engordany	–	–	–	18,594	89.61	16,662	98.34	C	19% Andorran, 50% Spanish. Cigars, cigarettes, tourism. D=RCC.

Continued opposite

Table 11-3 continued

Rec No 1	Country / Major civil divisions 2	Capital 3	sq.mi. 4	sq.km. 5	Pop 2000 6	AC% 7	Church members 8	E% 9	W 10	Notes 11
112	Ordino	Ordino	33	85	2,023	92.00	1,861	99.74	C	28% Andorran, 31% Spanish. Sheep, tourism. D=RCC.
113	Sant Julià de Lòria	Sant Julià de Lòria	–	–	8,974	88.90	7,978	97.94	C	49% Spanish, 23% Andorran. Sheep, cigars, tourism. D=RCC.
	ANGOLA		**481,354**	**1,246,700**	**12,878,188**	**84.91**	**10,934,238**	**99.29**	**C**	**Roman Catholics 62.1%, Protestants 14.9%. Pent-char 15.8%, Evangelical 9.5%, GCC 12.0%**
114	Bengo	Caxito	12,112	31,371	205,017	84.30	172,829	98.68	C	Northwest. Atlantic coast, Loge River, De Quicana National Park.
115	Benguela	Benguela	12,272	31,788	782,184	85.00	664,856	99.38	C	Coffee, corn, tobacco, sugarcane, manganese. D=RCC.
116	Bié	Kuito	27,148	70,314	1,388,321	86.00	1,193,956	99.98	C	Bie Plateau, Kwanza River. Upland savanna. Corn, rice, sisal, coffee.
117	Cabinda	Cabinda	2,807	7,270	206,131	85.00	175,211	99.38	C	Atlantic ocean coastline (56 miles). Offshore oil, timber, palm oil, cocoa. D=RCC.
118	Cunene	N'Giva	34,495	89,342	272,984	85.50	233,401	99.48	C	Cunene Dam, Ruacana Falls Dam, Cunene River. South, borders Namibia.
119	Huambo	Huambo	13,233	34,274	1,879,695	84.90	1,595,861	99.28	C	Bie Plateau. Banguela Railway. Coffee, wheat, corn. UNITA base of operations. D=RCC.
120	Huíla	Lubango	28,958	75,002	1,056,283	85.00	897,841	99.38	C	Mile-high plateau. Cunene River, Matala Dam, Mupa National Park. D=RCC.
121	Kuando Kubango	Menongue	76,853	199,049	152,649	86.00	131,278	99.43	C	Southeastern. Cuito and Cubango rivers. borders Caprivi Strip. D=RCC.
122	Kuanza Norte	N'Dalatando	9,340	24,190	459,060	85.50	392,496	99.58	C	Bono River. Railroad. D=RCC.
123	Kuanza Sul	Sumbe	21,490	55,660	766,586	85.00	651,598	99.38	C	Atlantic coast, Cuvo River, Serra Do Humbe.
124	Luanda	Luanda	934	2,418	2,251,846	84.00	1,891,551	99.17	C	Atlantic coast. Tropical coastal plain. Coffee, cotton. Cattle raising. D=RCC,Evangelical Church.
125	Lunda Norte	Lucapa	39,685	102,783	346,522	85.00	294,544	99.38	C	Northeast. Borders Congo Kinshasa, Luachimo River.
126	Lunda Sul	Saurimo	17,625	45,649	178,275	85.00	151,534	99.38	C	Chiumbe River, borders Congo Kinshasa. D=RCC.
127	Malanje	Malanje	37,684	94,602	1,061,854	84.50	897,267	98.88	C	Central plateau, (4,000+ ft.) Cotton, corn, goats. Game reserve. Mbundu peoples. D=RCC.
128	Moxico	Lwena	86,110	223,023	388,863	85.67	333,138	98.95	C	Eastern. DaCambeia National Park, Lungué-Bungo River, borders Zambia. D=RCC.
129	Namibe	Namibe	22,447	58,137	150,420	85.00	127,857	98.88	C	Namib Desert. Iron ore mines. Port. Fisheries.
130	Uíge	Uíge	22,663	58,698	1,056,283	85.00	897,841	99.38	C	Former center of coffee production. Headquarters for guerrilla movements. D=RCC,EJCSK(Congo).
131	Zaire	M'Banza Kongo	15,494	40,130	275,213	84.00	231,179	97.48	C	Northwest. Atlantic coast. Serra Do Congo, Zaire inlet, M'Bridge. D=RCC,EJCSK(Congo).
	ANGUILLA		**35**	**91**	**8,309**	**86.48**	**7,186**	**99.80**	**C**	**Protestants 49.6%, Anglicans 31.8%. Pent-char 12.5%, Evangelical 9.6%, GCC 13.2%**
132	Anguilla	The Valley	35	91	8,309	86.49	7,186	99.80	C	West Indies, Leeward Islands. Fishing, salt mining, stock raising, tourism. D=Anglican,Methodist.
	ANTARCTICA		**5,980,000**	**15,500,000**	**4,500**	**75.56**	**3,400**	**94.60**	**C**	**Roman Catholics 31.1%, Protestants 21.5%. Pent-char 0.00%, Evangelical 0.00%, GCC 0.00%**
133	Antarctica	–	5,980,000	15,500,000	4,500	75.56	3,400	94.60	C	Asymmetrically centered on the South Pole, less than 5% is free of ice and snow, lowest temperature ever recorded on earth at -126.9 degrees F. First landing in 1821.
	ANTIGUA		**171**	**442**	**67,560**	**79.50**	**53,713**	**99.77**	**C**	**Anglicans 33.4%, Protestants 31.0%. Pent-char 12.4%, Evangelical 10.3%, GCC 15.2%**
134	Barbuda	–	62	161	1,419	80.00	1,135	98.47	C	Resort area. Sugar, cotton, lumber, limestone. D=Anglican.
135	Saint George	–	10	26	5,087	80.00	4,070	99.47	C	North, northeast coast. Limestone, maris, sandstone. D=Anglican.
136	Saint John's	–	26	68	40,560	79.10	32,083	99.89	C	Resort area. Port handles sugar, cotton, lumber. Fort James. F=1703. D=RCC,Moravian,Anglican.
137	Saint Mary	–	25	65	6,036	80.00	4,829	99.77	C	Cities of Boland and Carlisle. Boggy Peak, volcanic cliffs. Limestone, railroad. D=Anglican.
138	Saint Paul	–	18	46	6,963	80.70	5,619	99.87	C	Southern peninsula. Cities of Sweets and English Harbortown, parks. Sugar. D=Anglican.
139	Saint Peter	–	13	33	4,123	79.50	3,278	99.47	C	Northwest region. City of Parham, port. Sugar, cotton, tourism, limestone. D=Anglican.
140	Saint Phillip	–	16	41	3,374	80.00	2,699	99.47	C	Eastern two peninsulas, towns of Willikies Village and Freetown. Sugar refinery. D=Anglican.
	ARGENTINA		**1,073,518**	**2,780,400**	**37,027,297**	**91.79**	**33,985,872**	**99.34**	**C**	**Roman Catholics 91.1%, Protestants 6.2%. Pent-char 22.6%, Evangelical 5.2%, GCC 7.4%**
141	Buenos Aires	La Plata	118,754	307,571	14,319,170	90.21	12,917,323	98.99	C	Humid Argentine Pampa, grass-covered plain. Cultural & economic center. Cattle, wheat. D=RCC.
142	Catamarca	Catamarca	39,615	102,602	302,576	91.04	275,466	98.59	C	Mountainous with tablelands & valleys. Scarcity of water. Traditional peoples. Tourism. D=RCC.
143	Chaco	Resistencia	38,469	99,633	912,852	92.00	839,824	99.55	C	Hardwood forest. Heavy rainfall. 17th century Jesuit reducciones. Cotton. D=RCC.
144	Chubut	Rawson	86,752	224,686	407,082	93.00	378,586	99.65	C	Patagonia. Mountain ranges, lakes. Los Alerces National Park. Sheep, wool, oil. D=RCC.
145	Corrientes	Corrientes	34,054	88,199	891,695	93.00	829,276	99.65	C	Subtropical plains, lakes, marshes. 16th century Jesuit reducciones. Rice, cotton, hunting. D=RCC.
146	Córdoba	Córdoba	63,831	165,321	3,156,858	92.00	2,904,309	99.55	C	Sierra Grande, Pampa grasslands. Cattle raising, wheat. Tourist resorts. D=RCC,AoG.
147	Distrito Federal	Buenos Aires	77	200	3,381,614	93.00	3,144,901	99.65	C	Capital, major port. Meat packing, auto manufacturing, flour mills, banking. F-1536. D=RCC,AoG.
148	Entre Ríos	Paraná	30,418	78,781	1,166,093	91.66	1,068,837	99.21	C	Undulating plain. Italian, Swiss, German immigrants. Cattle raising. 'Between rivers'. D=RCC.
149	Formosa	Formosa	27,825	72,066	414,609	94.00	389,732	99.75	C	Alluvial Plain. Forest, grassland, marshes. Rio Pilcomayo National Park. Indians. Wheat. D=RCC.
150	Jujuy	San Salvadore	20,548	53,219	586,120	95.00	556,814	99.85	C	Andes mountains, plateau. Inca empire. Important mineral mining. Sugarcane. D=RCC.
151	La Pampa	Santa Rosa	55,382	143,440	296,981	95.00	282,132	99.85	C	Dry Pampa & Patagonian Desert. Millet, sorghum, sunflowers. D=RCC.
152	La Rioja	La Rioja	34,626	89,680	252,293	94.00	237,155	99.75	C	Semiarid Plain, mountain ranges. Poor water supply. Cattle, sheep. Copper. D=RCC.
153	Mendoza	Mendoza	57,462	148,827	1,599,046	91.50	1,463,127	99.25	C	Andes Mountains, sandy plains. Wine grapes, apples, peaches, alfalfa. Petroleum, tourism. D=RCC.
154	Misiones	Posadas	11,506	29,801	899,389	97.00	872,407	99.85	C	Isolated plateau. 17th century Jesuit work among Guarani. Tea, lumber, tourism. D=RCC.
155	Neuquén	Neuquén	36,324	94,078	440,384	94.00	413,961	99.75	C	Andes Mountains, forest, plains. Colorado River. National parks. Apples. petroleum. D=RCC.
156	Rió Negro	Viedma	78,384	203,013	578,240	94.00	543,546	99.75	C	Andes Mountains, table lands. Negro River. Irrigated alfalfa, pears. Sheep. D=RCC.
157	Salta	Salta	60,034	155,488	986,385	82.00	808,836	97.55	C	Andean cordilleras, salt flats. Colla Indians. Oil, borax, salt, tobacco. D=RCC.
158	San Juan	San Juan	34,614	89,651	601,023	96.00	576,982	99.95	C	Mountains, semiarid marshlands. Wine, dried fruits. Copper. Food processing. D=RCC.
159	San Luis	San Luis	29,633	76,748	327,062	98.00	320,521	99.15	C	Dry Pampa, pre-Andean hills. Cattle raising, irrigated farming, lumbering. D=RCC.
160	Santa Cruz	Río Gallegos	94,187	243,943	180,134	97.00	174,730	99.85	C	Patagonia. Sparsely inhabited. constant winds, dust storm. Sheep ranching. D=RCC.
161	Santa Fe	Santa Fe	51,354	133,007	3,178,138	93.00	2,955,668	99.90	C	Lowland plains. Wheat, soy beans, dairy production. Four river ports. D=RCC,AoG.
162	Santiago del Estero	Santiago del Estero	52,645	136,351	765,625	96.00	735,000	99.95	C	Andean piedmont, lowland plains. Irrigated cotton, alfalfa. Cattle, mules. D=RCC.
163	Tierra del Fuego	Ushuaia	8,329	21,571	79,316	97.00	76,937	99.85	C	Archipelago. Mountains, plateau, plains. Ushuaia, southernmost city in the world. Fishing. D=RCC.
164	Tucumán	San Miguel	8,697	22,524	1,304,601	93.50	1,219,802	99.98	C	Andean ridges & piedmont. Irrigated sugarcane, beans, lemons. Prehistoric stones. D=RCC.
	ARMENIA		**11,500**	**29,800**	**3,519,569**	**83.92**	**2,953,693**	**97.79**	**C**	**Orthodox 78.2%, Roman Catholics 4.5%. Pent-char 2.1%, Evangelical 0.05%, GCC 11.2%**
165	Aragatsotn	Tsaghkahovit	1,064	2,755	151,368	84.00	127,149	97.87	C	West. Armenian highlands, Aragats Mountain. Cereal crops, wine, jewelry, food products. D=AAC.
166	Ararat	Vedi	812	2,104	282,797	83.00	234,722	96.87	C	West central. Avaks River, Hraedon River. Chemicals, food processing, fish, wine, forest. D=AAC.
167	Armavir	–	479	1,241	293,937	84.00	246,907	97.87	C	West. Akhuryon River, Armenian highlands. Dairy products, agriculture, cereals, wine. D=AAC.
168	Gegharkunik	–	1,573	4,073	239,456	85.00	203,538	98.87	C	East central. Lake Sevan. Fishing, minerals, wine, potatoes. D=AAC.
169	Kotayk	Kotayk	811	2,100	306,200	83.00	254,146	96.87	C	Central. Hrazdan River. Grapes, forests, potatoes, gourds, food processing, confectionery. D=AAC.
170	Lori	–	1,464	3,791	366,672	84.50	309,838	98.37	C	North. Bazum Range, Debed River. Cereal crops, livestock, minerals, dairy products. D=AAC.
171	Shirak	–	1,034	2,679	334,751	85.50	286,212	99.37	C	Northwest. Lesser Caucasus mountains, Akhunryan River. Wine, minerals, copper. D=AAC.
172	Syunik	–	1,739	4,505	151,087	84.00	126,913	97.87	C	South. Zangezur Range. Minerals, farming, grapes, forest, livestock, wine food processing. D=AAC.
173	Tavush	–	1,043	2,702	159,138	83.00	132,085	96.87	C	Northeast. Dilijan Nature Reserve, Lesser Caucasus mountains. Chemicals, leather. D=AAC.
174	Vayots-Dzor	–	891	2,308	65,246	85.00	55,459	98.87	C	South Arpa River. Vardenis Range. Cereal products, canned fruit, wine, livestock. D=AAC.
175	Yerevan	–	81	210	1,168,915	83.56	976,724	97.41	C	West central. Hrazdan River. State University (1919), Ruins of 16th century Turkish fort. D=AAC.
	ARUBA		**75**	**193**	**102,747**	**92.69**	**95,241**	**99.54**	**C**	**Roman Catholics 82.0%, Protestants 7.3%. Pent-char 8.2%, Evangelical 3.9%, GCC 5.2%**
176	Aruba	Oranjestad	75	193	102,747	92.69	95,241	99.54	C	South Caribbean Sea. Seaport, hotels, tourism, shipping, 7 mile long palm beach. D=RCC.
	AUSTRALIA		**2,966,200**	**7,682,300**	**18,879,524**	**66.68**	**12,587,959**	**98.37**	**C**	**Roman Catholics 28.6%, Anglicans 21.5%. Pent-char 13.0%, Evangelical 13.7%, GCC 34.3%**
177	Australian Capital Territory	Canberra	900	2,400	318,790	68.50	218,371	99.79	C	Rolling plain. Market gardening, dairy. Government jobs. 98% urban. D=Anglican,RCC,UCA.
178	New South Wales	Sydney	309,500	801,600	6,396,362	65.56	4,193,596	97.28	C	Coastal mountains, interior tableland. Farming, industry. 80% British. D=Anglican,RCC,UCA.
179	Northern Territory	Darwin	519,800	1,346,200	182,000	68.00	123,760	99.69	C	Coastland & plateau. 60% European, 27% Aborigine. Sorghum, minerals. D=RCC,Anglican.
180	Queensland	Brisbane	666,900	1,727,200	3,415,532	67.00	2,288,406	98.69	C	Coastal hills, inland plain. Cattle, sugarcane. Great variety of animals. D=Anglican,RCC,UCA.
181	South Australia	Adelaide	379,900	984,000	1,545,170	67.00	1,035,264	98.69	C	Dry, barren inland. Mining, quarrying. Major opal supply. 99% European. D=RCC,Anglican.
182	Tasmania	Hobart	26,200	67,800	496,384	68.20	338,535	99.89	C	Triangular island. Humid climate. Minerals. Original inhabitants extinct (1876). D=Anglican,RCC.
183	Victoria	Melbourne	87,900	227,600	4,716,604	67.00	3,160,125	98.69	C	Mountainous coastal region. Gas & oil fields. Wheat, sheep. Mainly European. D=RCC,Anglican.
184	Western Australia	Perth	975,100	2,525,500	1,808,679	68.00	1,229,902	99.69	C	Great Western Desert. 6,800 species of plants. Wool production, minerals. D=Anglican,RCC.
	AUSTRIA		**32,378**	**83,858**	**8,210,520**	**84.16**	**6,909,670**	**98.59**	**C**	**Roman Catholics 75.5%, Protestants 5.0%. Pent-char 3.6%, Evangelical 0.5%, GCC 20.9%**
185	Burgenland	Eisenstadt	1,531	3,966	280,604	88.00	246,932	99.93	C	East, bordering Hungary. Rosalien Mountains, Newsiedler Lake. Agriculture. German. D=RCC.
186	Kärnten	Klagenfurt	3,681	9,533	574,572	87.00	499,878	99.93	C	South, bordering Italy. Mountainous, Klagenfurt basin. Agriculture, forestry. 90% German. D=RCC.
187	Niederösterreich	Sankt Pölten	7,403	19,174	1,548,980	85.00	1,316,633	99.43	C	Northeast, bordering Czech Republic. Danube River. Grain, root crops. German. D=RCC.
188	Oberösterreich	Linz	4,626	11,980	1,411,249	82.00	1,157,224	97.33	C	North, bordering Germany. Granite plateau, forests, mountains. Lignite resorts. German. D=RCC.
189	Salzburg	Salzburg	2,762	7,154	514,956	86.00	442,862	99.93	C	West central, bordering Germany. Alps. Tourism, salt, copper. D=RCC (90%).
190	Steiermark	Graz	6,327	16,388	1,236,504	84.00	1,038,663	98.43	C	Southeastern, bordering Slovenia. Alps, hills, plains. Mineral resources. German D=RCC.
191	Tirol	Innsbruck	4,883	12,648	667,080	86.00	573,689	99.93	C	West, bordering Germany. Alpine. Health & winter-sports resorts, farming. D=RCC.
192	Vorarlberg	Bregenz	1,004	2,601	350,499	87.00	304,934	99.93	C	West, bordering Switzerland. Mountains, forests, valleys. Textiles, watches, tourism. D=RCC.
193	Wien (Vienna)	–	160	415	1,626,075	81.72	1,328,855	97.05	C	Capital. Danube River. Known for architecture & music. 30 museums. Industry. D=RCC,EKAR.
	AZERBAIJAN		**33,400**	**86,600**	**7,734,015**	**4.63**	**357,802**	**36.99**	**A**	**Orthodox 4.4%, Roman Catholics 0.1%. Pent-char 0.1%, Evangelical 0.01%, GCC 1.6%**
194	Baku	–	–	–	1,856,723	3.14	58,229	35.53	A	Caspian Sea border, Sihov Beach. Kobustan Museum. Reserve. Oil industry. F=c885 AD. D=ROC.
195	Nagorno Karabakh	Stepanakert	1,700	4,400	209,481	65.00	136,163	97.36	C	Karabakh Range, steppe, dense forest. Vineyards, orchards. 80% Armenian. D=AAC.
196	Nakhichevan	Nakhichevan	2,100	5,500	331,290	1.00	3,314	33.36	A	Transcaucasian plateau. Subject to earthquakes. Grains, cotton. Azerbaijanis.
197	Regions	–	29,600	76,700	5,336,520	3.00	160,096	35.36	A	Lezgians, Talish, Kurdish, Mingechau Reservoir. Cotton, rice, grain, oil production, wine. D=ROC.
	BAHAMAS		**5,382**	**13,939**	**306,529**	**87.06**	**266,851**	**99.72**	**C**	**Protestants 54.5%, Roman Catholics 15.6%. Pent-char 15.9%, Evangelical 29.5%, GCC 13.2%**
198	Abaco, Great and Little	Marsh Harbour	649	1,681	12,057	86.00	10,369	99.66	C	Caribbean pine. Crayfish, lumber, tomatoes, fruit. D=Baptist,Anglican.
199	Acklins	Pompey Bay	192	497	487	88.00	429	99.76	C	Adjoining Crook Island and West of Mayaguana Island. D=Baptist,Anglican.
200	Andros	Kemps Bay	2,300	5,957	9,830	88.00	8,650	99.76	C	Technically an archipelago. Barrier reef. Fruit, vegetables. 'The Big Yard.' D=Baptist.
201	Berry Islands	Nicolls Town	12	31	755	89.00	672	99.86	C	North of Andros Islands. Fruit, salt. D=Baptist,Anglican.
202	Biminis Islands	Alice Town	9	28	1,970	88.00	1,734	99.76	C	Elevation 20 ft. Named for mythical Bimini Islands supposed fountain of youth. Straits of Florida.
203	Cat Island	Arthur's Town	150	388	2,040	88.00	1,795	99.76	C	Leeward. Calm & sheltered. Southeast of Eleuthera Island. Fruit, crayfish.
204	Crooked and Long Cay	Colonel Hill	93	218	495	89.00	441	99.86	C	Highest point 206 ft. Crooked Island passage. Salt, lumber.
205	Eleuthera	Rock Sound	187	518	9,605	86.00	8,260	99.66	C	Early attempts at colonization (1647). US missile tracking station. D=RCC,Baptist.
206	Exuma	George Town	112	290	4,273	88.00	3,760	99.76	C	Southeast of New Providence, Exuma Sound. Salt, fruit.
207	Grand Bahama	Freeport	530	1,373	49,145	87.00	42,756	99.66	C	Caribbean pine. Tourism, forest products, fishing. Bunkering terminal. D=RCC,Baptist.
208	Harbour Island	–	3	8	1,465	89.00	1,304	99.86	C	Just off the north coast of Eleuthera Island.
209	Inagua, Great and Little	Matthew Town	599	1,551	1,184	89.00	1,054	99.86	C	Lake Rosa. Large lakes. Salt production. Lighthouse on Great Inogua.
210	Long Island	Clarence Town	230	596	3,550	88.00	3,124	99.76	C	Southwest of San Salvador. Hills. Fruit, salt.
211	Mayaguana	Abraham's Bay	110	285	375	90.00	338	98.36	C	East of Acklins Island, 25 miles long. Fruit fishing.

Continued overleaf

Table 11-3 continued

Rec No 1	Country Major civil divisions 2	Capital 3	sq.mi. 4	sq.km. 5	Pop 2000 6	AC% 7	Church members 8	E% 9	W 10	Notes 11
212	New Providence	Nassau	80	207	206,921	87.02	180,062	99.73	C	Settled in 1656. Large lakes. Caribbean pine. Agriculture, fishing, rum, tourism. D=Baptist,RCC.
213	Ragged Island	Duncan Town	14	36	107	90.00	96	99.96	C	West of Acklin Island. Fruit, fishing. D=Baptist.
214	Rum Cay	–	30	78	64	90.00	58	99.96	C	South southwest of San Salvador. Fruit, salt. D=Baptist.
215	San Salvador	–	63	163	559	89.00	498	99.86	C	Large lakes. Christopher Columbus landing (1492). 'Watling Island.'
216	Spanish Wells	–	10	26	1,649	88.00	1,451	99.76	C	Very small island off the north tip of Eleuthera Island. D=Baptist,Anglican.
	BAHRAIN		**268**	**694**	**617,217**	**10.16**	**62,698**	**57.21**	**B**	**Independents 4.3%, Roman Catholics 4.0%. Pent-char 4.6%, Evangelical 0.6%, GCC 3.4%**
217	al-Gharbiyah	–	60	156	26,769	5.50	1,472	52.55	B	Natural gas, aluminum, dates, fish, vegetables.
218	al-Hadd	–	2	6	10,460	4.00	418	46.05	A	al-Muharraq Island. Airport, vegetables, other produce, shipbuilding.
219	al-Manamah	–	10	26	166,441	17.33	28,850	64.81	B	Major port. Government offices, business district. Modern appearance. 'Place of Sleeping'. D=RCC.
220	al-Muharraq	–	6	15	90,201	11.00	9,922	58.05	B	al Muharraq Island. Densely-settled, narrow-winding streets. International airport.
221	al-Wusta	–	14	35	41,676	7.00	2,917	54.05	B	Off Al-Hasa coast. Dates, aluminum, fish, oilfields.
222	ar-Rifa	–	113	292	60,444	8.00	4,836	55.05	B	Central. Built-up area. Fish, aluminum, natural gas, oil fields, ship repair.
223	ash Sharquiyah	–	20	51	3,939	4.00	158	46.05	A	Few fishermen & quarry workers.
224	ash-Shamaliyah	–	14	37	41,019	6.00	2,461	53.05	B	Extensive oil fields, natural gas, aluminum, shipbuilding, ship repair, dates, fish, vegetables.
225	Hammad	–	5	13	35,299	6.00	2,118	53.05	B	Completed 1984. Fishing, vegetables, natural gas.
226	Jidd (Judd) Hafs	–	8	22	54,390	8.00	4,351	55.05	B	West of Manama. Aluminum, natural gas, fish, vegetables. D=RCC.
227	Madinat Isa	–	5	12	41,925	6.00	2,516	53.05	B	North-central, built-up area. Aluminum, vegetables, oil fields.
228	Sitrah	–	11	29	44,654	6.00	2,679	53.05	B	Bridge connects Sitra and Bahrain Island. Fish, vegetables, shipbuilding, ship repair. D=RCC.
	BANGLADESH		**56,977**	**147,570**	**129,155,152**	**0.72**	**931,740**	**57.21**	**B**	**Independents 0.4%, Roman Catholics 0.1%. Pent-char 0.3%, Evangelical 0.06%, GCC 0.4%**
229	Barisal	Barisal	5,134	13,297	8,989,199	0.50	44,946	54.69	B	Kirtan Khola River. Medical college, pharmaceuticals, textiles. Air Bengal, airport. D=RCC.
230	Chittagong	Chittagong	13,039	33,771	25,340,241	0.70	177,382	57.19	B	Bay of Bengal. Densely populated. Rice, tea, freshwater and salt water fish. D=RCC,Jamaat.
231	Dhaka	Dhaka	12,015	31,119	39,327,744	1.00	393,277	58.55	B	Level plain bounded by rivers. Rice, jute, sugarcane. Large industrial concentration. D=RCC.
232	Khulna	Khulna	8,600	22,274	15,343,632	0.60	92,062	57.09	B	Alluvial Plain in Gangetic Delta. Rice, jute, oilseeds, fish, farming. D=RCC.
233	Rajshahi	Rajshahi	13,326	34,513	31,862,576	0.60	191,175	57.09	B	Elevated Barind region. Well-drained Padma valley. Rice, jute, pulses. Weaving. D=RCC.
234	Sylhet	Sylhet	4,863	12,596	8,291,761	0.40	32,902	54.29	B	East in Surma Valley bounded by Assam. Rice, tea, oilseeds.
	BARBADOS		**166**	**430**	**270,449**	**72.79**	**196,858**	**99.20**	**C**	**Protestants 31.4%, Anglicans 28.5%. Pent-char 18.0%, Evangelical 29.7%, GCC 18.4%**
235	Christ Church	–	22	57	47,332	72.59	34,356	99.61	C	Southern tip. Oistins Bay, Southpoint. Sugar, molasses, rum, tourism. D=Anglican.
236	St. Andrew	–	14	36	6,760	75.00	5,070	99.91	C	Northeast coast. Mount Hilaby, Bruce Vale River. Tourism, rum. D=Anglican.
237	St. George	–	17	44	19,346	73.00	14,123	99.61	C	South-central, Constitution River. Belair, boarded hall. Sugar rum, molasses. D=Anglican.
238	St. James	–	12	31	21,910	73.00	15,994	99.61	C	West-central coast. Holetown, Westmoreland. Tourism, sugar. D=Anglican.
239	St. John	–	13	34	10,737	74.00	7,945	99.81	C	East coast. Coach Hill, Carter. Tourism, flat vegetation, sugar, molasses. D=Anglican.
240	St. Joseph	–	10	26	8,015	74.00	5,931	99.81	C	East central coast. Joes River. Bathsheba, Hillcrest. Fishing, sugar, tourism. D=Anglican.
241	St. Lucy	–	14	36	9,946	74.00	7,360	99.81	C	North tip of island. North Point, Harrison Point. Tourism, sugar. D=Anglican.
242	St. Michael	–	15	39	102,587	72.00	73,863	98.41	C	Southwestern coast, Constitution River, Carlisle Bay, Needhams Point. Sugar, tourism. D=Anglican.
243	St. Peter	–	13	34	10,928	74.00	8,087	99.81	C	Northwest and northeast coast. Sperghtstown, Portland. Sugar, rum, molasses. D=Anglican.
244	St. Philip	–	23	60	20,782	73.00	15,171	99.61	C	Southeastern tip. Ragged Point, Thicket, Six Cross roads. Tourism, molasses, sugar. D=Anglican.
245	St. Thomas	–	13	34	12,106	74.00	8,958	99.81	C	Central, landlocked. Sturges, Reeds hill, Bruce Vale River. Sugar, molasses. D=Anglican.
	BELGIUM		**11,787**	**30,528**	**10,161,164**	**83.84**	**8,518,696**	**97.84**	**C**	**Roman Catholics 80.9%, Protestants 1.2%. Pent-char 2.9%, Evangelical 0.2%, GCC 46.0%**
246	Antwerp	Antwerp	1,107	2,867	1,634,159	84.00	1,372,694	98.00	C	Kemperland plateau. Sand dunes, market gardening. Abbey of Premontre (1133). D=RCC.
247	Brussels	Brussels	62	161	949,815	80.00	759,852	94.00	C	Capital. World port, HQ of EEU & NATO. F=c200. 25% expatriate. D=RCC.
248	East Flanders	Ghent	1,151	2,982	1,354,188	85.00	1,151,060	99.00	C	Low hills. Intensive agriculture. Flowers, market gardening, cotton textiles. D=RCC.
249	Flemish Brabant	Leuven	813	2,106	1,000,976	82.74	828,206	96.74	C	Low plateau. Densely-populated. Wheat, sugar beets, pigs, poultry. Industrial centers. D=RCC.
250	Hainaut	Mons	1,462	3,786	1,287,054	83.50	1,074,690	97.50	C	Southwest. Wheat, oats, horses. 100 castles. Mainly French speaking. D=RCC.
251	Limburg	Hasselt	935	2,422	776,689	84.00	652,419	98.00	C	Northwest, bordering the Netherlands. Rich coal fields, dairy farms, fruit, grains. D=RCC.
252	Liège	Liège	1,491	3,862	1,015,537	85.00	863,206	99.00	C	East, bordering Germany. Cereals, orchards, dairies. Wool industry. Nature reserves. D=RCC.
253	Luxembourg	Arlon	1,714	4,440	241,775	86.00	207,927	99.60	C	Southeast, bordering Luxembourg. Ardennes highlands. Tourist industry, tobacco. D=RCC.
254	Namur	Namur	1,415	3,666	436,452	85.30	372,294	99.30	C	South, bordering France. Meuse River. Steel, chemicals. Resorts. 'Industrial crescent'. D=RCC.
255	Walloon Brabant	Wavre	421	1,091	339,667	82.50	280,225	96.92	C	Low plateau. Densely-populated. Wheat, sugar beets, pigs, poultry. Industrial centers. D=RCC.
256	West Flanders	Brugge	1,214	3,144	1,124,851	85.00	956,123	99.00	C	North Sea coast. Leading agricultural province. Potatoes, wheat. Seaside resorts. D=RCC.
	BELIZE		**8,867**	**22,965**	**240,709**	**81.90**	**197,139**	**97.86**	**C**	**Roman Catholics 56.8%, Protestants 16.4%. Pent-char 13.0%, Evangelical 7.1%, GCC 11.9%**
257	Belize	Belize City	1,663	4,307	72,485	80.00	57,988	96.28	C	Mangrove Swamps. Sugarcane, mahogany. Fisheries, sawmills. International airport. D=RCC.
258	Cayo	San Ignacio	2,006	5,196	47,907	81.90	39,236	97.86	C	Belize River, bordering Guatemala. Cattle, corn. Mayans, mestizos. D=Mennonite.
259	Corozal	Corozal	718	1,860	36,176	82.36	29,794	98.32	C	Chetumal Bay. Sugar refining, rum distilling, fish processing. Coconuts exported. D=RCC.
260	Orange Walk	Orange Walk	1,790	4,636	38,991	82.00	31,973	97.96	C	New River. Maya Indians, Creole. Sugarcane, rum. D=Mennonites,RCC.
261	Stann Creek	Dangriga	986	2,554	22,984	84.00	19,307	99.96	C	North Stann Creek. Founded 1823 by Black refugees from Honduras. Bananas, timber. D=RCC.
262	Toledo	Punta Gorda	1,704	4,413	22,166	85.00	18,841	99.91	C	Grande and Moho rivers, coastal plain. Sugarcane, bananas, livestock. Mainly Caribs. D=RCC.
	BELORUSSIA		**80,153**	**207,595**	**10,236,181**	**64.32**	**6,584,077**	**99.15**	**C**	**Orthodox 48.7%, Roman Catholics 13.1%. Pent-char 0.9%, Evangelical 0.3%, GCC 21.1%**
263	Brest	Brest	12,500	32,300	1,487,487	65.00	966,867	99.33	C	Pripyet River basin. Flat & swampy. Flax, hemp, dairying, forestry. F=1939. D=BOC.
264	Homel (Gomel)	Homel	15,600	40,400	1,603,977	66.00	1,058,625	99.43	C	Drepr River plain. Marsh & bog. Dairying, timber, petroleum. D=BOC.
265	Hrodno (Grodno)	Hrodno	9,700	25,000	1,193,773	66.00	787,895	99.43	C	West. Neman river. Swampy plain. Rye, oats, dairying, cattle. More than 50% urban. D=BOC,RCC.
266	Mahilyou (Mogilyov)	Mahilyou	11,200	29,000	1,261,476	65.00	819,959	99.33	C	Drepr River, lowland. Mixed forest. Timber, farm produce, vegetables, fruit. D=BOC.
267	Minsk (Mensk)	Minsk	15,700	40,800	3,257,736	61.57	2,005,788	98.64	C	Berezina plain. Dense pine forest. Potash production. Timber, rye, wheat. D=BOC,RCC.
268	Vitebsk	Vitebsk	15,500	40,100	1,431,732	66.00	944,943	99.43	C	Western Dvina River basin. Swamps, forest. Flax, rye, orchards. Peat for power. D=BOC.
	BENIN		**43,500**	**112,680**	**6,096,559**	**27.63**	**1,684,195**	**74.18**	**B**	**Roman Catholics 20.7%, Protestants 3.7%. Pent-char 5.6%, Evangelical 1.8%, GCC 16.4%**
269	Atacora	Natitingou	12,050	31,200	814,013	20.00	162,803	63.55	B	Atakora mountains. Somba people. De la Pendjari National Park. Iron ore, corn, capra. D=RCC.
270	Atlantique	Cotonou	1,250	3,200	1,331,367	34.00	452,665	83.08	B	South central. Atlantic coast. Bight of Benin. Railroad, port, capra, cotton, corn. D=RCC.
271	Borgou	Parakou	19,700	51,000	1,024,953	20.00	204,991	63.55	B	Eastern. Nigeria border, Alibori and Tassine rivers. Capra, corn. D=RCC.
272	Mono	Lokossa	1,450	3,800	812,306	26.50	215,261	73.05	B	Southwest. Atlantic coast, Kouffo River, Bight of Benin. Cotton, palm products. D=RCC.
273	Ouémé	Porto-Novo	1,800	4,700	1,091,772	35.05	382,715	83.60	B	Southeastern coast, Oueme River. Corn, ports, cassava, yams, marsh. D=RCC.
274	Zou	Abomey	7,200	18,700	1,022,149	26.00	265,759	72.55	B	Central. Oueme, Zoo and Kouffo rivers. Railroad, palm products, yams, cotton. D=RCC.
	BERMUDA		**21**	**54**	**64,590**	**86.20**	**55,675**	**99.81**	**C**	**Anglicans 37.4%, Protestants 30.1%. Pent-char 20.7%, Evangelical 11.9%, GCC 17.5%**
275	Devonshire	–	2	5	7,337	86.00	6,310	99.76	C	Edmund Gribbons Nature Reserve, Friendship Vale Park. Equestrian center. D=Anglican.
276	Hamilton	–	–	1	8,229	85.71	7,053	99.87	C	Northern shore. Deepwater harbor. Tourism. Clearview Art Gallery. D=Anglican,RCC.
277	Paget	–	2	5	5,845	87.00	5,085	99.91	C	Named for William Paget, Bermuda College, Hungry Bay. Nature reserve, Elbow Beach. D=Anglican.
278	Pembroke	–	2	5	17,258	86.00	14,842	99.76	C	Capital. Admiralty House Park, Fort Hamilton, St John's Church. D=Anglican.
279	Sandys	–	2	5	7,079	86.00	6,088	99.76	C	Named after Sir Edwin Sandys, founder of Virginia. Royal Navy, Scaur Hill Fort. D=Anglican.
280	Smith's	–	2	5	3,488	86.50	3,017	99.89	C	Named for Sir Thomas Smith, Harrington Sound, St. Mark's Church. D=Anglican.
281	Southampton	–	2	6	3,740	86.00	3,216	99.76	C	Bermuda Golf Academy, Giblo's Hill Lighthouse, St Anne's Church, Brewery. D=Anglican.
282	St. George's	–	2	4	3,165	87.00	2,754	99.91	C	Fort Cunningham, Biological Research. Fort Albert, NASA station. D=Anglican,RCC.
283	St. George	–	1	1	2,022	85.00	1,719	99.61	C	South on St George's Island. F=1612. St. Peter's Church (1612). Kings Square. D=Anglican,RCC.
284	Warwick	–	2	6	6,427	87.00	5,591	99.91	C	Astwood Cove and Park, Christ Church (1719), Warwick Academy. Golf. D=Anglican,RCC.
	BHUTAN		**18,150**	**47,000**	**2,123,970**	**0.45**	**9,649**	**20.76**	**A**	**Independents 0.2%, Protestants 0.1%. Pent-char 0.2%, Evangelical 0.05%, GCC 0.4%**
285	Bumthang	Jakar	1,150	2,990	45,425	0.01	5	12.32	A	Eastern hills. Bumthang River. Model village program. Potatoes, bulls, cross breeding farm.
286	Chirang	Damphu	310	800	206,790	0.33	682	22.64	A	Southern foothills. Kikhorthana, Sankosh River.
287	Dagana	Dagana	540	1,400	53,978	0.01	5	12.32	A	Western hills. Barley, wheat, buckwheat. D=CNI.
288	Gaylegphug	Gaylegphug	1,020	2,640	211,542	0.50	1,058	23.81	A	Southern foothills. India border.
289	Ha	Ha	830	2,140	31,741	0.01	3	12.32	A	Western hills. Wong River. Model village program. Barley, wheat. D=CNI.
290	Lhuntshi	Lhuntshi	1,120	2,910	75,265	0.01	8	12.32	A	Eastern hills. Kuru River.
291	Mongar	Mongar	710	1,830	139,127	0.50	696	25.81	A	Eastern hills. Manas River. Maize, paddy.
292	Paro	Paro	580	1,500	86,669	1.00	867	26.31	A	Western hills. Wong River, Paro-Chu River. Airport, potatoes, wheat, buckwheat. D=CNI.
293	Pema Gatsel	Pema Gatsel	150	380	70,514	0.01	7	12.32	A	Eastern hills. Dungsam Wildlife Reserve. Draname-chu River. Bamboo.
294	Punakha	Punakha	2,330	6,040	63,862	1.00	639	26.31	A	Western hills. Sankosh tributaries, Dechen Phodrang Dzong. Barley, buckwheat. D=CNI.
295	Samchi	Samchi	830	2,140	327,101	0.31	1,022	25.62	A	Southern foothills. Jaldakha River.
296	Samdrup Jongkhar	Samdrup Jongkhar	900	2,340	138,937	0.40	556	25.71	A	Southern foothills. Boda Chu River. India border. Market center.
297	Shemgang	Shemgang	980	2,540	84,579	0.01	8	12.32	A	Eastern hills. Manas River. Paddy, rice, orchids, bamboo, rattan, bananas, mangos.
298	Tashigang	Tashigang	1,640	4,260	337,745	0.02	68	12.33	A	Eastern hills. Manas River, Tasingana Dzong. Tropical fruits, apples, silk.
299	Thimphu	Thimphu	630	1,620	111,568	2.20	2,454	23.81	A	Capital. Thimpu River. Pangra Pamou Monastery, Monastic school. D=Assemblies.
300	Tongsa	Tongsa	570	1,470	49,417	1.00	494	26.31	A	Central. Black Mountains, largest Dzong in Bhutan, Manas River. Paddy.
301	Wangdi Phodrang	Wangdi Phodrang	1,160	3,000	89,710	1.20	1,077	25.51	A	Western hills. San Kosh River, Black Mountains. Handicrafts, wheat, barley. D=CNI.
	BOLIVIA		**424,164**	**1,098,581**	**8,328,665**	**93.49**	**7,786,232**	**99.71**	**C**	**Roman Catholics 88.2%, Protestants 6.3%. Pent-char 14.5%, Evangelical 4.5%, GCC 20.7%**
302	Beni	Trinidad	82,458	213,564	370,884	94.00	348,631	99.72	C	North. Siriono Indians. D=RCC.
303	Chuquisaca	Sucre	19,893	51,524	571,088	95.00	542,534	99.82	C	Southeast, bordering Paraguay. Livestock, cereals, corn, rice. Wet/dry extremes. D=RCC.
304	Cochabamba	Cochabamba	21,479	55,631	1,467,386	93.00	1,364,669	99.72	C	Central. fertile basin. Grains, potatoes, coffee. 'Granary of Bolivia.' D=RCC.
305	La Paz	La Paz	51,732	133,985	2,407,401	92.50	2,226,781	99.60	C	Northwest, bordering Peru & Chile. Peaks, plateau, rain forests. Mining, livestock, tin. D=RCC.
306	Oruro	Oruro	20,690	53,588	412,744	94.00	387,979	99.72	C	West-central. El. 12,000 ft. Tin mining. Tungsten, copper. D=RCC.
307	Pando	Cobija	24,644	63,827	46,299	95.00	43,984	99.82	C	North, bordering Brazil, Peru. Amazon Basin. Rubber, Brazil nuts. Poor communications. D=RCC.
308	Potosí	Potosí	45,644	118,218	762,231	95.00	724,119	99.82	C	Southwest, bordering Chile, Argentina. Andes mountains. Great mineral wealth. D=RCC.
309	Santa Cruz	Santa Cruz	143,098	370,621	1,904,399	93.50	1,780,613	99.72	C	East-central, hot, tropical lowlands. Sugar cane, rice, coffee, natural gas. D=RCC.
310	Tarija	Tarija	14,526	37,623	386,234	95.00	366,922	99.82	C	South. Corn, wheat. Known for outdoor religious processions. D=RCC.
	BOSNIA-HERZEGOVINA		**19,741**	**51,129**	**3,971,813**	**34.89**	**1,385,885**	**73.67**	**B**	**Orthodox 17.6%, Roman Catholics 17.1%. Pent-char 0.8%, Evangelical 0.01%, GCC 9.2%**
311	Banja Luka		476	1,232	178,732	55.00	98,303	94.78	B	Vrbas River. Turkish character. Leather goods, iron. F=c 200 AD as Roman fort. Mosque.
312	Mostar		502	1,300	115,183	15.00	17,277	48.78	A	Neretva River. Surrounded by vineyards. Wine, textiles, tobacco. F=1566 by Turks.

Continued opposite

Table 11-3 continued

Rec No 1	Country Major civil divisions 2	Capital 3	sq.mi. 4	sq.km. 5	Pop 2000 6	AC% 7	Church members 8	E% 9	W 10	Notes 11
313	Muslim-Croat Federation		9,039	23,412	1,815,119	34.80	631,661	75.58	B	Mainly Muslims and Croats. D=RCC.
314	Prijedor		322	834	103,267	17.82	18,406	51.60	B	North. Sana River. Kozara mountains. Wood pulp manufacturing, iron ore, coal deposits.
315	Sarajevo		405	1,049	476,618	16.00	76,259	49.78	A	Miljacka River. Muslim character. Metalware, carpets. F=14th century. Mosque (1530).
316	Serb Republic		8,685	22,494	1,032,671	50.00	516,336	89.78	B	Mainly Serbs. D=SOC.
317	Tuzla		119	307	119,154	10.00	11,915	42.78	A	Tuzla Basin. Salt deposits. Lignite mining, agriculture. F=10th century as Soli (salts).
318	Zenica		193	500	131,070	12.00	15,728	45.78	A	Central. Near Sarajevo. Bosna River. Railroad, Lignite mine, iron and steel works, paper mills.
	BOTSWANA		**224,607**	**581,730**	**1,622,220**	**46.30**	**751,073**	**94.86**	**B**	**Independents 30.7%, Protestants 10.9%. Pent-char 32.9%, Evangelical 3.1%, GCC 23.6%**
319	Barolong	–	425	1,100	22,497	46.00	10,349	94.56	B	Mining, livestock, agriculture, sorghum. D=RCC,Independents.
320	Central	Serowe	57,039	147,730	504,922	46.00	232,264	96.64	B	Salt flats, Makgadikgadipans game reserve, Shashe River, Lake Xau, desert. D=RCC,UCCSA.
321	Chobe	Kasane	8,031	20,800	17,272	46.00	7,945	94.56	B	Chobe National Park, desert, Linyanti Chobe River. Cattle, minerals. D=Independents.
322	Francistown	–	31	79	79,771	30.00	23,931	83.56	B	Northeast. Shashe River. Diamonds, minerals, agriculture, forestry, quarrying. D=Independents.
323	Gaborone	–	37	97	163,186	55.00	89,752	95.56	B	Southeast. Naptwane River, capital of Botswana. Airport, railroad. Agriculture. D=Independents.
324	Ghanzi	Ghanzi	45,525	117,910	30,224	45.00	13,601	93.56	B	Central. Okwa River, Qoxo River, central Kalahari Game Reserve. Salt flats, mining. D=Independents.
325	Jwaneng	–	39	100	13,679	50.00	6,840	95.56	B	Southern. Desert. Food products, sheep, mining, sorghum. D=Independents.
326	Kgalagadi	Tsabong	41,290	106,940	38,067	47.00	17,891	95.56	B	Southwest. Mabuasehube Game Reserve, Gremsbok National Park. Agriculture, livestock.
327	Kgatleng	Mochudi	3,073	7,960	70,633	46.00	32,491	94.56	B	Naotwane River, South African border. Sorghum, cereals, agriculture. D=Independents.
328	Kweneng	Molepolole	13,857	35,890	208,387	46.00	95,858	94.56	B	South central, desert, Quoxo River, Kutse Game Reserve. Livestock, mining. D=RCC,UCCSA.
329	Lobatse	–	12	30	31,852	45.00	14,333	93.56	B	Southeast. Railroad, agriculture, paper products. D=Independents.
330	Ngamiland	Maun	42,135	109,130	70,683	45.45	32,122	94.01	B	Aha Hills, Moremi Wildlife Preserve, Nxai National Park, Okavango Delta. Agriculture, livestock.
331	Ngwaketse	Kanye	10,568	27,370	157,709	48.00	75,700	96.56	B	Capital of Bangmaketsi tribe. Moselebe River. Named for Tswana tribe. D=Independents.
332	North East	Masunga	1,977	5,120	53,008	44.00	23,324	93.56	B	Shasne River. Minerals, agriculture, diamonds, forestry, quarrying, railroad. D=Independents.
333	Okavango	Orapa	8,776	22,730	44,900	43.00	19,307	91.56	B	Central. Salt Flats, sorghum, peanuts, sheep, mining quarry. D=Independents.
334	Orapa	–	4	10	10,791	43.00	4,640	92.56	B	Central. Salt Flats, sorghum, peanuts, sheep, mining quarry. D=Independents.
335	Selebi-Pikwe	–	19	50	48,628	47.00	22,855	95.56	B	Central. Motloutse River. Railroad, agriculture, livestock. D=Independents.
336	South East	Ramotswa	687	1,780	53,288	50.00	26,644	95.56	B	Capital of Botswana, Ngotwane River. Airport, railroad. Paper products, mining. D=RCC,UCCSA.
337	Sowa	–	61	159	2,724	45.00	1,226	93.56	B	Mining, diamonds, livestock, agriculture, sorghum. D=Independents.
	BOUGAINVILLE		**3,880**	**10,050**	**198,495**	**93.37**	**185,331**	**99.87**	**C**	**Roman Catholics 74.7%, Protestants 11.4%. Pent-char 4.6%, Evangelical 2.6%, GCC 8.1%**
338	Bougainville	Arawa	3,880	10,050	198,495	93.37	185,331	99.87	C	Southwest Pacific, Solomon Islands chain. Copra, ivory nuts, green snails, cacao. F=1768. D=RCC.
	BRAZIL		**3,300,171**	**8,547,404**	**170,115,463**	**91.39**	**155,475,609**	**99.75**	**C**	**Roman Catholics 90.1%, Protestants 17.7%. Pent-char 47.0%, Evangelical 16.3%, GCC 14.2%**
339	Acre	Rio Branco	49,343	153,698	485,867	94.00	456,715	99.76	C	Acre River, multiple rivers, Transamazonica highway. Forests, cattle, agriculture. D=RCC.
340	Alagoas	Maceió	11,238	29,107	2,924,421	94.00	2,748,956	99.76	C	Northeast. São Francisco River. Sugarcane, beans, palm, cattle raising, sugar refining. D=RCC.
341	Amapá	Macapá	54,965	142,359	336,437	96.57	324,913	99.93	C	North, bordering Suriname, French Guiana. Tropical rain forest. Manganese. F=1943. D=RCC.
342	Amazonas	Manaus	605,390	1,567,954	2,431,103	95.00	2,309,548	99.71	C	Northwest, bordering Colombia, Venezuela. Amazon Basin. Rubber. European/Indian mix. D=RCC.
343	Bahia	Salvador	218,912	566,979	13,736,637	91.00	12,500,340	99.66	C	East, bordering Atlantic Ocean. Cacao, tobacco, petroleum. Mulatto population. D=RCC,AoG.
344	Ceará	Fortaleza	56,253	145,694	7,394,936	94.00	6,951,240	99.76	C	Northeast. Atlantic Ocean, Highlands, coastal plain. Large producer of cotton, cattle. D=RCC.
345	Distrito Federal	Brasíia	2,237	5,794	1,857,848	89.00	1,653,485	99.66	C	Governmental center. Publishing printing, construction. 'City of the Sky'. D=RCC.
346	Espírito Santo	Vitória	17,658	45,733	3,024,194	95.00	2,872,984	99.71	C	East. Low mountain ranges, coastal plain. Coffee, cacao. Predominantly White. D=RCC.
347	Goiás	Goiânia	131,339	340,166	4,684,350	91.00	4,262,759	99.66	C	South-central. Brazilian Highlands. Rice, corn, cattle, pigs. Low standard of living. D=RCC.
348	Maranhão	São Luís	127,242	329,556	5,729,319	94.00	5,385,560	99.76	C	North. Atlantic Ocean. Plateau, delta region. Extraction of oils, cattle. Founded by Jesuits. D=RCC.
349	Mato Grosso do Sul	Campo Grande	138,021	357,472	2,070,067	93.00	1,925,162	99.66	C	West-central. Plateau, lowlands. Isolated. Iron ore, manganese, cattle. Mestizos. D=RCC.
350	Mato Grosso	Cuiabá	348,040	901,421	2,351,846	94.00	2,210,735	99.76	C	West-central. Frontier region. Plateau. Cattle raising. Mainly mestizos. 'Great Woods'. D=RCC.
351	Minas Gerais	Belo Horizonte	226,497	586,624	18,327,679	90.10	16,513,239	99.86	C	Inland. Brazilian Highlands. Mining, cattle raising, rice, beans. 'General mines.' D=RCC,AoG.
352	Paraná	Curitiba	76,959	199,324	9,795,350	94.00	9,207,629	99.76	C	South, bordering Argentina, Paraguay. Parana River. Main producer of coffee, corn. D=RCC.
353	Paraíba	João Pessao	20,833	53,958	3,725,342	93.00	3,464,568	99.84	C	Northeast. Atlantic Ocean. Cotton, sugar, sisal. Mining. 'Arm of the river'. D=RCC.
354	Pará	Belém	481,405	1,246,833	5,918,334	89.00	5,267,317	99.76	C	North, bordering Guyana, Suriname. Amazon River. Tropical rain forest. Brazil nuts, herbs. D=RCC.
355	Pernambuco	Recife	39,005	101,023	8,275,199	90.00	7,447,679	99.66	C	Northeast. Atlantic Ocean. Sugarcane, cotton, coffee, bananas. Blacks, mulattos. D=RCC.
356	Piauí	Teresina	97,017	251,273	3,004,205	94.00	2,823,953	99.76	C	Northeast. Parnaiba River. Livestock, palm seeds & oils. Isolated. Low standard of living. D=RCC.
357	Rio de Janeiro	Rio de Janeiro	16,855	43,653	14,647,180	90.00	13,182,462	99.86	C	Southeast. Atlantic Ocean. Plain, plateau. Coffee. Manufacturing. Mainly urban. D=RCC,AoG.
358	Rio Grande do Norte	Natal	20,528	53,167	2,809,321	94.00	2,640,762	99.76	C	Northeast. Atlantic Ocean. Salt production. Cotton, sugarcane. Few animal species. D=RCC.
359	Rio Grande do Sul	Pôrto Alegre	108,369	280,674	10,624,017	91.00	9,667,855	99.66	C	Southernmost, Atlantic Ocean. Plateau, tall-grass prairie. Wheat, corn, cattle. D=RCC,AoG.
360	Rondônia	Pôrto Velho	92,039	238,379	1,315,724	94.00	1,236,781	99.76	C	West-central, bordering Bolivia. Rain forest. Rubber exports, Brazil nuts. D=RCC.
361	Roraima	Boa Vista	86,880	225,017	251,175	95.00	238,616	99.71	C	North, bordering Venezuela, Guyana. Rain forest, wooded savanna. Cattle. Yanomano. D=RCC.
362	Santa Catarina	Florianópolis	36,803	95,318	5,280,146	94.00	4,963,337	99.76	C	South. Atlantic Ocean. Processed wood, furniture, charcoal, fishing, wheat. Mainly White. D=RCC.
363	Sergipe	Aracaju	8,441	21,863	1,737,066	92.00	1,598,101	99.86	C	East. Atlantic Ocean. Forested coastland. Cotton, rice, sugarcane. One half urban. D=RCC.
364	São Paulo	São Paulo	95,852	248,256	36,306,774	89.80	32,603,483	99.73	C	Southeast. Atlantic Ocean. One half of Brazil's manufacturing, one third of its coffee. D=RCC,AoG.
365	Tocantins	Palmas	107,075	277,322	1,070,979	95.00	1,017,430	99.86	C	North-central. Brazilian Highlands. Rain forest. Developing frontier area. Grain, cattle. D=RCC.
	BRITAIN		**94,251**	**244,110**	**58,830,160**	**66.38**	**39,053,151**	**98.10**	**C**	**Anglicans 44.6%, Roman Catholics 9.5%. Pent-char 9.8%, Evangelical 19.6%, GCC 35.9%**
366	Avon	Bristol	520	1,346	987,570	67.00	661,672	98.72	C	Bristol channel, Severn Tunnel, Abbey of St Augustine. Railroad, sugar. D=Anglican.
367	Bedfordshire	Bedford	477	1,235	548,627	68.50	375,809	99.82	C	Ivel River, John Bunyan museum. Center of large agricultural area. D=Anglican.
368	Berkshire	Reading	486	1,259	787,401	66.00	519,685	97.72	C	Lamboume River, Walbury Hill, Benedictine Abbey (1121). Biscuit making. D=Anglican.
369	Borders	Newton St Boswells	1,814	4,698	106,771	67.00	71,537	97.92	C	North Sea coast, Tweed River. Melrose Abbey, Dryburgh Abbey, Jedburgh Abbey. D=Anglican.
370	Buckinghamshire	Aylesbury	727	1,883	669,475	67.50	451,896	98.82	C	Great Ouse River, Chiltern Hills. Food processing, printing, canal. D=Anglican.
371	Cambridgeshire	Cambridge	1,316	3,409	697,626	67.00	467,409	98.72	C	University of Cambridge and related industry. Many old churches, Ely Cathedral. D=Anglican.
372	Central	Stirling	1,042	2,700	275,372	66.50	183,122	97.82	C	Forth River. Stirling Castle, Bannockborn battle site (1314), Doune Castle. Coal mining. D=Anglican.
373	Cheshire	Chester	899	2,329	983,346	67.50	663,759	98.82	C	Roman outpost for 20th legion, ecclesiastical center, Cheshire plain, Delamere Forest. D=Anglican.
374	Cleveland	Middlesbrough	225	583	562,199	67.50	379,484	98.82	C	North sea port. Tees Bay, Tees River. Heavy engineering. D=Anglican.
375	Clwyd	Mold	937	2,427	420,542	66.50	279,660	97.82	C	Valle Cruas Abbey, Wales, Clwydian Range, Irish Sea coast. D=Anglican.
376	Cornwall	Truro	1,376	3,564	485,290	67.00	325,144	98.72	C	Bodmin Moor, Black Moor, Tamar Vier, Penzance. D=Anglican.
377	Cumbria	Carlisle	2,629	6,810	492,932	67.50	332,729	98.82	C	Lake District National Park. Hadrian's Wall, Furness Abbey. Textiles, confectionery. D=Anglican.
378	Derbyshire	Matlock	1,016	2,631	963,038	68.00	654,866	98.92	C	Peak District National Park, Ladybower Reservoir, Chatsworth House. D=Anglican.
379	Devon	Exeter	2,591	6,711	1,064,479	67.50	718,523	98.82	C	Dartmoor National Park, St Peters (1133). Metal, leather, paper. D=Anglican.
380	Dorset	Dorchester	1,025	2,654	682,342	67.50	460,581	98.82	C	North Dorset Downs, Blackmoor Vale, Chesil Beach, Bournemouth. Railroad. D=Anglican.
381	Dumfries and Galloway	Dumfries	2,481	6,425	148,693	66.50	98,881	97.82	C	North channel coast. Solway Firth, Glenluce Abbey, Sweetheart Abbey. D=Anglican.
382	Durham	Durham	941	2,436	610,963	67.50	412,400	98.82	C	North sea coast. Egglestone Abbey, Stainmore Forest, Durham Cathedral. D=Anglican.
383	Dyfed	Carmarthen	2,227	5,768	355,193	66.00	234,427	97.72	C	Pembroke Castle. St David's Cathedral, Cambrian Mountains. D=Anglican.
384	East Sussex	Lewes	693	1,795	734,824	68.00	499,680	98.92	C	Ouse River, Hastings battle site (1066), The Weald. Railroad. D=Anglican.
385	Essex	Chelmsford	1,418	3,672	1,585,961	67.50	1,070,524	98.82	C	Foulness Point, The Naze, Southern Municipal Airport, Thames, Blackwater River. D=Anglican.
386	Fife	Glenrothes	509	1,319	353,487	66.00	233,301	97.72	C	St Andrews Bay, Firth of Forth Bridge, Black Devon River. D=Anglican.
387	Gloucestershire	Gloucester	1,020	2,643	555,663	68.00	377,851	98.92	C	Vale of Berkeley, Severn River. Fishing, railway, aircraft, agriculture. F=AD 96. D=Anglican.
388	Grampian	Aberdeen	3,379	8,752	535,660	67.00	358,892	97.92	C	Cairngorm mountains, Kildrummy, Balmoral and Dunnottar castles, Don River. D=Anglican.
389	Greater London	London	610	1,579	7,044,712	63.00	4,438,169	95.95	C	Thames River. International finance. F=AD 43 by Romans as Londinium. D=Anglican,RCC.
390	Greater Manchester	Manchester	497	1,287	2,592,133	64.00	1,658,965	96.72	C	Irwell River, 15th century cathedral. Printing, engineering. D=Anglican.
391	Gwent	Newport	531	1,376	455,028	66.50	302,594	98.22	C	Wye River, Severn Tunnel, Tintern Abbey. Railroad, port, fishing. D=Anglican.
392	Gwynedd	Caernarvon	1,494	3,869	241,692	66.00	159,517	97.72	C	NW Wales, Snowdonia National Park. Cambrian mountains, Lleyn peninsula. F=1974. D=Anglican.
393	Hampshire	Winchester	1,458	3,777	1,625,371	67.00	1,088,999	98.72	C	Winchester Cathedral. Airport, New Forest, Hampshire Downs. F=1974. D=Anglican.
394	Hereford & Worcester	Worcester	1,516	3,927	698,026	67.50	471,168	98.82	C	Wye River, Severn River, navigable waterways. Hereford Cathedral, golden valley. D=Anglican.
395	Hertfordshire	Hertford	631	1,634	1,016,626	67.50	686,223	98.82	C	Lea River, Colne River, Verulamium ruins. Railway, vegetables, barley, tourism. D=Anglican.
396	Highland	Inverness	10,092	26,137	209,418	66.50	139,263	97.82	C	North tip and peninsula of Scotland. Loch Ness, Dunegan Castle. D=Anglican.
397	Humberside	Hull	1,356	3,512	893,971	68.00	607,900	98.92	C	Humber Bridge, Bridlington Bay, Trent River, Humber Bay. F=974. D=Anglican.
398	Isle of Wight	Newport	147	381	125,773	67.50	84,897	98.82	C	English Channel, St. Catherine's Point, The Neatles. Fishing. F=1944. D=Anglican.
399	Kent	Maidstone	1,441	3,731	1,559,623	68.00	1,060,544	99.72	C	Channel Tunnel, Canterbury Cathedral, North Downs, Vale of Kent. Quarry, airport. D=Anglican.
400	Lancashire	Preston	1,183	3,064	1,433,650	67.00	960,546	98.72	C	Forest of Bowland, Ward's Stone. Coal, iron, lead, limestone, cotton, aircraft. D=Anglican.
401	Leicestershire	Leicester	986	2,553	927,952	66.00	612,448	97.72	C	Chamwood Forest, Bosworth Field (1485). Vegetables, airport, sugar beets, textiles. D=Anglican.
402	Lincolnshire	Lincoln	2,284	5,915	615,081	66.00	405,953	97.72	C	Holland Fen, The Wolds, Gibraltar Point, Lincoln Cathedral. Railroad. D=Anglican.
403	Lothian	Edinburgh	683	1,770	750,608	67.00	502,907	97.92	C	Holyrood Palace, Edinburgh Castle, Scottish capital, navigable canal. Tobacco, finance. D=Anglican.
404	Merseyside	Liverpool	252	652	1,434,856	65.50	939,831	97.22	C	Cathedral Church of Christ (1903). Airport. Flour milling, ships, fishing. F=1203. D=Anglican,RCC.
405	Mid Glamorgan	Cardiff	393	1,018	546,920	66.00	360,967	97.72	C	Caerphilly Castle, Tusker Rock, Brecon Beacons National Park. Coal mining, F=c75AD. D=Anglican.
406	Norfolk	Norwich	2,073	5,368	776,546	67.00	520,286	98.72	C	Sandringham House, Little Ouse River. Livestock, printing, footwear, mustard. D=Anglican.
407	North Yorkshire	Northallerton	3,208	8,309	734,518	67.50	495,800	98.82	C	Rockingham Forest, navigable canal. Shoes, leather, electronics, brewing. D=Anglican.
408	Northamptonshire	Northampton	914	2,367	602,515	67.50	406,698	98.02	C	York Minster, Marston Moor (1644), Whitby Abbey, Yorkshire Dales National Park. D=RCC.
409	Northern Ireland	Belfast	5,452	14,120	1,657,846	67.11	1,112,605	98.83	C	Lough Neagh, Mourne Mountains, Ulster Canal, Grants Causeway. Textiles, chemicals. D=Anglican.
410	Northumberland	Newcastle upon Tyne	1,943	5,032	308,947	65.00	200,816	96.72	C	North sea port. Flodden Field battle site (1513), national park. Engineering, coal, glass, iron. D=RCC.
411	Nottinghamshire	Nottinghamshire	836	2,164	1,037,435	66.00	684,707	97.72	C	Sherwood Forest, Vale of Belvoir, Robin Hood statue. Lace, pharmaceuticals, tobacco. D=Anglican.
412	Oxfordshire	Oxford	1,007	2,608	601,609	66.50	400,070	98.22	C	Oxford University. Cherwell River, Blenheim Palace. Vegetables, tourism. D=Anglican.
413	Powys	Llandrindod Wells	1,960	5,077	121,349	66.50	80,697	97.82	C	Wales, Brecon Beacons National Park, Black mountains. Livestock, vegetables. D=Anglican.
414	Shropshire	Shrewsbury	1,347	3,490	422,153	67.00	282,843	98.72	C	Severn River, Clun Forest, navigable canals. Dairy farming, livestock, vegetables. D=Anglican.
415	Somerset	Taunton	1,332	3,451	483,578	67.00	323,997	98.72	C	National park, Wells Cathedral, Bridgewater Bay. Railroad, fishing, livestock. D=Anglican.
416	South Glamorgan	Cardiff	161	416	419,541	66.50	278,995	98.22	C	Bristol Channel, capital of Wales, Llandaff Cathedral. Fishing, tourism, ships. D=Anglican,RCC.
417	South Yorkshire	Barnsley	602	1,560	1,310,895	67.50	884,854	99.22	C	Dearne River. Technical school. Coal mining, metallurgy, clothing, cutlery. D=Anglican.
418	Staffordshire	Stafford	1,049	2,716	1,062,067	67.50	716,895	98.82	C	Blithe River, navigable canals. Ceramics, coal mining, iron, steel, brick, tile, rubber. D=Anglican.
419	Strathclyde	Glasgow	5,318	13,773	2,295,953	67.00	1,538,289	98.72	C	Firth of Clyde, Clyde River. Prestwick Airport. Offshore oil rigs, tobacco. D=Anglican.
420	Suffolk	Ipswich	1,466	3,797	660,321	67.00	442,415	98.32	C	Port, Alde River, Blyth River. Fishing, ships, engineering, agriculture, railway. D=Anglican.
421	Surrey	Kingston upon Thames	648	1,679	1,050,001	67.00	703,501	97.92	C	University of Surrey, Albany Park, Loseley House, Basingstoke Canal. Tourism. D=Anglican.
422	Tayside	Dundee	2,951	7,643	397,721	67.50	268,462	97.72	C	Glamis Castle, Forest of Atholl, Tay River. Fishing, textiles. D=Anglican.
423	Tyne and Wear	Newcastle upon Tyne	208	540	1,137,069	66.50	756,151	97.82	C	Port. Shipbuilding, marine, coal, glass, food industries, fishing, steel, engineering. D=Anglican.
424	Warwickshire	Warwick	765	1,981	501,374	65.00	325,893	96.72	C	Avon River. Navigable canal, Kenilworth Castle, Warwick Castle. Agriculture, livestock. D=Anglican.
425	West Glamorgan	Swansea	316	817	372,189	67.00	249,367	98.72	C	Swansea Bay, Neath River, Port Eynon Pont. Fishing, coal, copper, steel. D=Anglican.
426	West Midlands	Birmingham	347	899	2,651,352	66.80	1,771,103	98.52	C	Coventry Cathedral, St Phillips Cathedral. Navigable canal, paints, textiles. D=Anglican,RCC.
427	West Sussex	Chichester	768	1,989	735,424	65.00	478,026	96.72	C	South Downs, Adur River, Vale of Sussex, English Channel. Fishing, livestock. D=Anglican.

Continued overleaf

Table 11-3 continued

Rec No 1	Country / Major civil divisions 2	Capital 3	sq.mi. 4	sq.km. 5	Pop 2000 6	AC% 7	Church members 8	E% 9	W 10	Notes 11
428	West Yorkshire	Wakefield	787	2,039	2,117,097	67.50	1,429,040	99.22	C	Kirkstall Abbey, Calder River. Clothing, wool, electronics, coal mining, livestock. D=Anglican.
429	Wiltshire	Trowbridge	1,344	3,480	593,767	65.50	388,917	97.22	C	Stonehenge, Longleat, Avebury Stone Circle, Salisbury Cathedral, Avon River. D=Anglican.
	BRITISH INDIAN OCEAN		**23**	**60**	**2,000**	**45.00**	**900**	**96.25**	**B**	**Roman Catholics 35.0%, Anglicans 10.0%. Pent-char 5.6%, Evangelical 0.5%, GCC 24.0%**
430	British Indian Ocean Ter	Diego Garcia	23	60	2,000	45.00	900	96.25	B	Chagos Archipelago, claimed by Mauritius. Leased to U.S. military since 1965. D=Anglican.
	BRITISH VIRGIN IS		**59**	**153**	**21,366**	**69.70**	**14,892**	**99.58**	**C**	**Protestants 45.8%, Anglicans 13.1%. Pent-char 12.5%, Evangelical 17.0%, GCC 29.1%**
431	British Virgin Islands	Road Town	59	153	21,366	69.70	14,892	99.58	C	West Indies, over 30 islands including Tortola, Anegada. Tourism, offshore banking. Acquired from Dutch in 1666. D=Anglican.
	BRUNEI		**2,226**	**5,765**	**328,080**	**7.50**	**24,592**	**45.13**	**A**	**Independents 2.5%, Protestants 1.8%. Pent-char 2.7%, Evangelical 1.9%, GCC 5.5%**
432	Belait	Kuala Belait	1,052	2,724	66,766	6.00	4,006	43.63	A	Belait River. Swampy terrain. Oil field. D=RCC,Anglican.
433	Brunei and Muara	Bandar Seri Begawan	220	571	214,253	8.66	18,562	46.66	A	Peat & mangrove swamps. Offshore oil wells. 18 hole golf course. D=RCC,Anglican.
434	Temburong	Bangar	504	1,304	9,678	1.60	155	31.23	A	Heart of the rain forest, Peradauan Forest Recreation Park. Batang Duri Park. Tourism, oil. D=RCC.
435	Tutong	Tutong	450	1,166	37,383	5.00	1,869	42.63	A	Sungai-Tutong River, port, central district. Forest, swampy plain at coast. D=RCC,Anglican.
	BULGARIA		**42,855**	**110,994**	**8,225,045**	**80.95**	**6,657,950**	**94.48**	**C**	**Orthodox 71.5%, Independents 7.0%. Pent-char 1.7%, Evangelical 1.4%, GCC 6.0%**
436	Burgas	Burgas	5,659	14,657	804,634	82.00	659,800	95.53	C	Gulf of Burgas. Black Sea trade. Fishing, food processing. Resorts. D=BOC.
437	Khaskovo	Khaskovo	5,364	13,892	965,927	83.00	801,719	96.53	C	Rhodope Mountains. Tobacco, cotton, silkworm breeding. Mineral spa. D=BOC.
438	Lovech	Lovech	5,849	15,150	960,429	81.00	777,947	94.53	C	North-central. Osum River. Prehistoric dwellings, caves. Bicycles, automobiles. D=BOC.
439	Mikhaylovgrad	Mikhaylovgrad	4,095	10,607	598,435	82.00	490,717	95.53	C	Northwest. Ogosta River. Fertile agricultural region. Grains, fruits. Game reserve. D=BOC.
440	Plovdiv	Plovdiv	5,262	13,628	1,182,207	82.00	969,410	95.53	C	South-central. Maritsa River. Tobacco, rice, vegetables, fruit. Food-processing. D=BOC.
441	Ruse (Razgrad)	Ruse	4,186	10,842	767,060	80.00	613,648	93.53	C	North. Danube River. Busy river port. Livestock farm, oil. Monk's settlement. D=BOC.
442	Sofiya (city)	Sofia (Sofiya)	506	1,311	1,118,056	79.00	883,264	92.54	C	Capital of Bulgaria. University of Sofia, National Opera House, Mount Vitosha. Airport. D=BOC,RCC.
443	Sofiya	Sofia (Sofiya)	7,328	18,978	920,105	79.87	734,892	93.40	C	Sofia Basin. Fruit, vegetables, dairy farming. Engineering, printing. D=BOC.
444	Varna	Varna	4,606	11,929	908,191	80.00	726,553	93.53	C	Varna Bay on Black Sea coast. Resorts. Livestock, grains. 4th century monastery. D=BOC.
	BURKINA FASO		**105,946**	**274,400**	**11,936,823**	**16.62**	**1,984,078**	**63.09**	**B**	**Roman Catholics 9.4%, Protestants 6.6%. Pent-char 7.0%, Evangelical 6.4%, GCC 12.7%**
445	Bam	Kongoussi	1,551	4,017	243,653	31.00	75,532	84.47	B	Small scale farms, sorghum, corn, rice, livestock raising, intermittent streams, savanna.
446	Bazéga	Kombissiri	2,051	5,313	455,521	32.00	145,767	87.47	B	Volte Rouge River. De PB National Park, Volte Blanch River.
447	Bougouriba	Diébougou	2,736	7,087	331,058	7.00	23,174	45.47	A	Bougouriba River. Volte Noire River. Rice sorghum, peanuts, minerals. D=RCC.
448	Boulgou	Tenkodogo	3,488	9,033	602,837	28.00	168,794	81.47	B	South. Sorghum, millet, livestock, raisins, small farms and villages.
449	Boulkiemde	Koudougou	1,598	4,138	547,365	10.00	54,737	56.47	B	3rd largest town. Peanuts, tobacco, cotton, textiles, handcrafted goods. D=RCC.
450	Comoé	Banfora	7,102	18,393	374,629	6.00	22,478	44.47	A	South. 5th largest town, Komoe River. Savanna. Railroad.
451	Ganzourgou	Zorgho	1,578	4,087	293,227	26.00	76,239	78.47	B	Sirba River, Blanche River. Millet, peanuts, cotton, child survival assistance program.
452	Gnagna	Bogandé	3,320	8,600	343,433	21.00	72,121	72.47	B	Expanded program on immunization. Intermittent stream. Rice millet, livestock, airport.
453	Gourma	Fada N'Gourma	10,275	26,613	440,975	18.00	79,376	69.47	B	Wooded savanna. Millet. Weaving, dyeing, pottery. Gourma people. D=RCC.
454	Houé	Bobo-Dioulasso	6,438	16,672	871,836	8.00	69,747	46.47	A	Chief trade center. Bicycles. Mainly Bobo Fing. D=CMA,AoG,RCC.
455	Kadiogo	Ouagadougou	451	1,169	689,149	36.00	248,094	91.47	B	Mainly Mossi. Capital. Sankara's grave. University. Textiles. F=c14th century AD. D=RCC,AoG.
456	Kossi	Nouna	5,088	13,177	499,012	10.00	49,901	56.47	B	Volte Noire River, Sourou River, savanna. Minerals, corn, rice, livestock. D=RCC.
457	Kouritenga	Koupéla	628	1,627	297,474	32.00	95,192	86.47	B	Banki Plains. Pottery, leather, weaving, rice, millet, livestock-raising. D=RCC.
458	Kénédougou	Orodara	3,207	8,307	209,780	6.00	12,587	44.47	A	Volte Noire, plateaus, savanna. Livestock, sorghum, minerals.
459	Mouhoun	Dédougou	4,032	10,442	432,731	9.00	38,946	55.47	B	Volte Noire. Savanna, rice, cotton, millet, leather goods. D=RCC.
460	Nahouri	Pô	1,484	3,843	158,128	6.89	10,895	45.36	A	De PT National Park, traditional Gourounsi capital, Volte Rouge River. Agriculture, elephants.
461	Namentenga	Boulsa	2,994	7,755	298,079	34.00	101,347	87.47	B	SIRBA and Bouli rivers. Pottery, leather goods, forest, livestock, agriculture.
462	Oubritenga	Ziniaré	1,812	4,693	456,007	35.00	159,602	88.57	B	Volta Blanche, Iodine deficiency test, Malaria research. Agriculture, livestock. D=AoG.
463	Oudalan	Gorom Gorom	3,879	10,046	159,155	10.00	15,916	56.47	B	Gorouol River. Forest, intermittent streams. Livestock, manganese, minerals.
464	Passoré	Yako	1,575	4,078	335,457	25.00	83,864	77.47	B	Volta Blanche. Cotton, textiles, leather goods, livestock.
465	Poni	Gaoua	4,000	10,361	352,917	6.00	21,175	44.47	A	Volta Noire. Intermittent streams. Traditional roots music. Livestock, sorghum, peanuts.
466	Sanguie	Réo	1,994	5,165	325,637	9.00	29,307	55.47	B	Central. Railroad, agriculture, livestock, pottery, small farms.
467	Sanmatenga	Kaya	3,557	9,213	551,114	11.00	60,623	57.47	B	Central. Volta Blanche, savanna. Zecko Mané Women's Center. Agriculture. D=RCC.
468	Sissili	Léo	5,303	13,736	367,063	6.00	22,024	44.47	A	South, Ghana border. Sissili River, De Po National Park, Djerma-Gourounsi ruins. Corn, agriculture.
469	Soum	Djibo	5,154	13,350	279,978	5.00	13,999	43.47	A	North. Airport, agriculture, minerals, livestock, sorghum.
470	Sourou	Tougan	3,663	9,487	401,817	6.00	24,109	44.47	A	West. Souray River, savanna. Integrated Development Program. Airport. Agriculture.
471	Sèno	Dori	5,202	13,473	343,063	8.00	27,445	46.47	A	East. Boult and Faga rivers, savanna. Agriculture, livestock.
472	Tapoa	Diapaga	5,707	14,780	238,085	6.00	14,285	44.47	A	Eastern tip. Tapoa River. National Park. Rice, millet, airport, agriculture, livestock.
473	Yatenga	Ouahigouya	4,746	12,292	804,178	19.00	152,794	67.47	B	North. White Volta River, plateau, savanna. Millet, sorghum, maize, cotton. F=1757. D=RCC.
474	Zoundwéogo	Manga	1,333	3,453	233,465	6.00	14,008	44.47	A	South. De Po National Park. Agriculture, gold prospect, minerals, manganese.
	BURUNDI		**10,740**	**27,816**	**6,695,001**	**76.97**	**5,152,841**	**99.18**	**C**	**Roman Catholics 57.1%, Protestants 11.9%. Pent-char 11.5%, Evangelical 12.7%, GCC 17.1%**
475	Bubanza	Bubanza	420	1,089	282,297	75.00	211,723	98.66	C	West. Kibira National Park, Ruzizi River. Electrical substation. Beans, bananas, corn, tea. D=RCC.
476	Bujumbura	Bujumbura	509	1,319	745,194	80.00	596,155	99.61	C	West. Lake Tanganyika, Ruzizi River, port. Huge electric power plant. Tea, cassava. D=RCC.
477	Bururi	Bururi	952	2,465	491,113	77.00	378,157	99.21	C	Lake Tanganyika, southwest. Thermal power plant. Beans, bananas, corn, sorghum. D=RCC.
478	Cankuzo	Cankuzo	759	1,965	177,734	77.60	137,919	99.11	C	East. Ruvubu National Park, Ruyubu River. Hydroelectric plant, cotton, sorghum, bananas.
479	Cibitoke	Cibitoke	631	1,636	353,264	78.00	275,546	99.51	C	Northwest, Ruzizi River, Kibira National Park. Power substation. Tea, sorghum, cassava, beans.
480	Gitega	Gitega	764	1,979	705,124	78.00	549,997	99.51	C	Central plateau. Livestock (cattle, goats, sheep), peanuts. Religious centers. D=RCC.
481	Karuzi	Karuzi	563	1,457	377,045	76.00	286,554	99.21	C	Central plateau. Ruvubu River. Cattle, goats, sheep, bananas, cassava, coffee.
482	Kayanza	Kayanza	476	1,233	554,569	78.00	432,564	99.51	C	Ruvubu River, North Kibira National Park, Kanuaru River. Tea, coffee, beans, cassava, livestock.
483	Kirundo	Kirundo	658	1,703	505,680	77.00	389,374	99.71	C	North. Lake Cohoha Sud, Oake Rworu, Kanyaru River. Airport, hydroelectric power plant. Livestock.
484	Makamba	Makamba	757	1,960	300,912	74.00	222,675	98.21	C	Southern tip. Lake Tanganyika. Cotton, livestock, sweet potatoes, corn, thermal power plants.
485	Muramvya	Muramvya	593	1,535	550,326	77.00	423,751	99.21	C	Central plateau. Ruvubu River. Hydroelectric plants, tea, coffee, livestock, corn, sorghum, beans.
486	Muyinga	Muyinga	709	1,836	481,873	75.00	361,405	98.61	C	Northeast. Ruvubu River, Rububu National Park. Beans, bananas, sorghum, corn, livestock. D=RCC.
487	Ngozi	Ngozi	569	1,474	604,737	77.00	465,647	99.21	C	North-central. Market center at 5,700 ft. Cattle raising, bananas, coffee. D=RCC.
488	Rutana	Rutana	756	1,959	247,501	74.00	183,151	98.21	C	Southeast. Muragarazi River. Cotton, livestock, beans, cassava, sweet potatoes, corn, thermal power.
489	Ruyigi	Ruyigi	903	2,339	317,630	75.00	238,223	98.59	C	East. Ruvubu National Park, Muragarazi River. Hydroelectric power, cotton, beans.
	CAMBODIA		**70,238**	**181,916**	**11,167,719**	**1.06**	**118,398**	**49.09**	**A**	**Independents 0.6%, Roman Catholics 0.2%. Pent-char 0.5%, Evangelical 0.1%, GCC 0.9%**
490	Batdambang	Batdambang	7,353	19,044	1,174,737	1.70	19,971	50.73	B	Sangke River. Textile & rice mills. Buddhist temple Wat Poveal. D=RCC.
491	Kaôh Kong	Krong Kaôh Kong	4,301	11,140	42,106	0.20	84	43.23	A	West. Gulf of Thailand, Chhak, Kamp-ng Saom Bay. Rubber, salt, timer.
492	Krâchéh	Krâchéh	4,283	11,094	255,438	0.30	766	46.33	A	Northeast. Mekong River. Slate, clay, rice, rubber, timber, bamboo. Khmer, Cham.
493	Kâmpóng Cham	Kâmpóng Cham	4,053	10,498	1,745,965	0.50	8,730	46.53	A	South-central. Mekong River. Timber, rubber, textiles, fishing. D=RCC,Khmer Evangelical Church.
494	Kâmpóng Chhnang	Kâmpóng Chhang	2,131	5,520	360,702	0.60	2,164	48.63	A	Central. Sab River. Clay deposits. Rice paddies, floating fishing villages.
495	Kâmpóng Saôm	Kâmpóng Saôm	27	69	85,614	2.60	2,226	51.63	B	South. On Gulf of Siam. Headquarters of maritime fishing industry. F=1956.
496	Kâmpóng Sp	Kâmpóng Spoe	2,709	7,016	555,789	0.40	2,223	46.43	A	South-central. Tnaot River. Rice, sugarcane, palm trees, silk spinning.
497	Kâmpóng Thum	Kâmpóng Thum	4,730	12,251	618,947	0.50	3,095	46.53	A	North-central. Sen River. Iron ore, rice, bananas. Rich in timber, bamboo.
498	Kâmpôt	Kâmpôt	3,808	9,862	578,246	0.40	2,313	46.43	A	South. Koh Sla River. Rice, pepper, durians. Salt marshes, rosewood, teak.
499	Kândal		1,472	3,813	1,176,141	1.80	21,171	50.83	B	South-central. Mekong River. Surrounds Phnom Penh. Rice, corn, jute. Fishing.
500	Môndôl Kiri	Senmonorom	5,517	14,288	25,264	2.80	707	51.83	B	East, Vietnam border. Slate, clay, bamboo, rubber, rice, timber.
501	Phnom Penh	Phnom Penh	18	46	791,579	3.70	29,321	60.68	B	South-central. Basak, Sab, MeKong Rivers. Education. M=CMA,YWAM. D=RCC,AoG.
502	Pouthisat	Pouthisat	4,900	12,692	286,316	1.30	3,722	50.33	B	West-central. Pouthisat River. Rich soil, important rice-growing center. Corn.
503	Preah Vihéar	Phnum Tbéng	5,541	14,350	112,280	0.90	1,011	48.93	A	North central. Stang Szn River. Livestock, rice, bamboo, minerals.
504	Prey Vêng	Prey Vêng	1,885	4,883	1,097,543	0.50	5,488	46.53	A	South. Mekong River. Former rubber plantations. Rice, corn, cotton.
505	Rôtânâkiri	Lumphat	4,163	10,782	72,982	1.40	1,022	50.43	B	Northeast. Tonle San. Rubber, minerals, rice, corn, manufacturing.
506	Siemréab	Siemréab	4,207	10,897	778,947	0.70	5,453	48.73	A	North West. Siamreab River. Pharmaceuticals, hogs. Angkor Wat temple complex.
507	Stoeng Trêng	Stoeng Trêng	4,328	11,209	64,562	0.60	387	48.63	A	North East. San, Kong, Mekong rivers. Rice, bamboo, minerals. Mon-Khmer, Lao-Thai. M=YWAM.
508	Svay Rieng	Svay Rieng	1,145	2,966	477,193	0.70	3,340	48.73	A	South East. Vai Kou River. Rice, corn, potatoes, bananas.
509	Takév	Takév	1,474	3,818	867,369	0.60	5,204	48.63	A	South. Tonlé Basak River. Pepper, rubber, sugar, rosewood, teak.
	CAMEROON		**183,569**	**475,442**	**15,084,969**	**51.45**	**7,761,501**	**79.93**	**B**	**Roman Catholics 26.4%, Protestants 20.6%. Pent-char 6.5%, Evangelical 4.1%, GCC 22.4%**
510	Adamoua	Ngaoundéré	24,591	63,691	711,727	41.00	291,808	64.48	B	Northwest, Adamou mountains. Railroad, timber, coffee, tea. D=RCC.
511	Centre	Yaoundé	26,613	68,926	2,373,766	55.00	1,305,571	86.51	B	Southwest central, Sanaga River. Railroad, falls, airport, plateau, timber, bananas. D=RCC.
512	Est	Bertoua	42,089	109,011	743,347	50.00	371,674	78.48	B	Southeast. Nyong River. Marsh, livestock, cocoa, coffee, timber. D=RCC.
513	Extrême-Nord	Maroua	13,223	34,246	2,667,109	58.00	1,546,923	86.48	B	North. De Waza National Park, Lake Chad. Coffee, tea, livestock. D=RCC,EEC,Presbyterian.
514	Littoral	Douala	7,814	20,239	1,947,189	54.00	1,051,482	82.48	B	West. Sanaga River, falls, airport, Douala-Edea Reserve. Gulf of Guinea. Marshes, port. D=RCC.
515	Nord	Garoua	25,319	65,576	1,196,081	53.00	633,923	81.48	B	North. Djerem River, Mbakaou Dam, La Benoue National Park. Railroad, minerals. D=RCC.
516	Nord-Ouest	Bamenda	6,877	17,810	1,778,456	48.00	853,659	76.48	B	West. Adamoua mountains. Timber, livestock, minerals, coffee, cocoa. D=RCC.
517	Ouest	Bafoussam	5,356	13,872	1,925,631	50.00	962,816	78.48	B	West, Noun River, Mbam River, Adamoua mountains. Timber, minerals, livestock. D=RCC.
518	Sud	Ebolowa	18,189	47,110	537,245	44.26	237,790	72.74	B	South. Ntem River, De Campo Reserve, marshes. Bananas, livestock. D=RCC.
519	Sud-Ouest	Buea	9,448	24,471	1,204,417	42.00	505,855	67.48	B	West, Nigerian border, Cameroon Mountain. Timber, minerals, coffee, bananas, peanuts. D=RCC.
	CANADA		**3,849,674**	**9,970,610**	**31,146,639**	**64.98**	**20,237,778**	**97.79**	**C**	**Roman Catholics 41.8%, Protestants 17.1%. Pent-char 14.2%, Evangelical 8.1%, GCC 40.4%**
520	Alberta	Edmonton	255,287	661,190	2,904,561	67.00	1,946,056	99.31	C	West. Canadian Rockies, undulating plateau. Oil, timber, tourism, wheat, cattle. D=RCC,UCC.
521	British Columbia	Victoria	365,947	947,800	3,744,941	67.00	2,509,110	99.31	C	West, on Pacific Ocean. Mountainous, offshore islands. Timber, mining, tourism. D=RCC,UCC.
522	Manitoba	Winnipeg	250,947	649,950	1,245,943	65.00	809,863	97.93	C	Central. Rocks, forests, rivers. Farming, lumbering, mining, fishing, wildlife. D=RCC,UCC.
523	New Brunswick	Fredericton	28,355	73,440	825,993	68.00	561,675	99.91	C	East on Gulf of St. Lawrence. 90% forest. Forestry, lumbering, pulp, paper, fishing. D=RCC,UCC.
524	Newfoundland	St. John's	156,649	405,720	648,647	67.50	437,837	99.81	C	East on Atlantic Ocean. 10,000 miles of coastland. Fishing. 95% British/Irish. D=Anglican,RCC.
525	Northwest Territories	Yellowknife	1,322,909	3,426,320	65,782	66.00	43,416	98.81	C	North. Arctic Circle. Thousands of islands. Gold, oil, fur trapping. 50% Eskimo/Indian. D=RCC,UCC.
526	Nova Scotia	Halifax	21,425	55,490	1,026,864	66.00	677,730	98.81	C	East on Atlantic Ocean. 3,000 lakes. Shipbuilding, fishing. Dairy farming, oil. D=RCC,UCC.
527	Ontario	Toronto	412,581	1,068,580	11,507,194	63.00	7,249,532	96.28	C	East-central. Hudson & James bays, St Lawrence seaway. Manufacturing, mining. D=RCC,UCC.
528	Prince Edward Island	Charlottetown	2,185	5,660	148,065	69.00	102,165	99.91	C	East on Gulf of St Lawrence. Dairying, fishing. Tourism. Few employment opportunities. D=RCC.
529	Quebec	Quebec	594,860	1,540,680	7,868,526	65.00	5,114,542	97.81	C	East. Majority are French descent. Mining, hydroelectric power, forestry. Sports. D=RCC.
530	Saskatchewan	Regina	251,866	652,330	1,128,399	67.76	764,602	99.87	C	Central. Great Plains. Oil, gas, potash, agriculture. 1/3 United Church of Canada. D=RCC,UCC.
531	Yukon Territory	Whitehorse	186,661	483,450	31,717	67.00	21,250	99.31	C	Northwest, bordering Alaska. Vast reserves of minerals. Unspoiled wilderness. D=RCC,UCC.

Continued opposite

Table 11-3 continued

Rec No 1	Country Major civil divisions 2	Capital 3	sq.mi. 4	sq.km. 5	Pop 2000 6	AC% 7	Church members 8	E% 9	W 10	Notes 11
	CAPE VERDE		**1,557**	**4,033**	**427,724**	**95.13**	**406,880**	**99.95**	**C**	**Roman Catholics 97.4%, Protestants 3.6%. Pent-char 7.4%, Evangelical 2.5%, GCC 13.0%**
532	Boa Vista	Sal Rei	239	620	4,324	96.00	4,151	99.97	C	Easternmost island. Salt, violet dye. D=RCC.
533	Brava	Nova Sintra	26	67	8,736	96.00	8,387	99.97	C	Southernmost island. Monte Fountain (3,201 ft.). Fishing, agriculture. D=RCC.
534	Fogo	Sao Filipe	184	476	42,464	95.00	40,341	99.95	C	Active volcano Pico (9,281 ft.). Peanuts, beans, coffee, oranges, tobacco. D=RCC.
535	Maio	Porto Inglês	104	269	6,223	96.00	5,974	99.97	C	High point 1,430 ft. Corn, beans, potatoes, salt extraction. D=RCC.
536	Sal	Santa Maria	83	216	9,667	96.00	9,280	99.97	C	Northeasternmost island. Noted for salt works. International airport. 'Salt.' D=RCC.
537	Santiago	–	383	991	220,055	95.00	209,052	99.95	C	Picoda Antonia (4,566 ft.). Corn, bananas, sugarcane, coffee, fishing. D=RCC.
538	Santo Antao	–	300	779	54,918	95.00	52,172	99.95	C	Northwesternmost island. Tope de Coroa (6,491 ft.). Coffee, bananas, horses, sheep. D=RCC.
539	São Nicolau	Ribeira Brava	150	388	17,109	96.00	16,425	99.97	C	Volcanic origin. Monte Gordo (4,277 ft.). Coffee, oranges, beans, horses. F=15th century. D=RCC.
540	São Vicente	Mindelo	88	227	64,227	95.13	61,098	99.96	C	Monte Verde (2,539 ft.). Corn, beans, potatoes, fishing. Oil refinery. D=RCC.
	CAYMAN ISLANDS		**100**	**259**	**38,371**	**67.29**	**25,820**	**98.05**	**C**	**Protestants 53.9%, Independents 10.5%. Pent-char 16.9%, Evangelical 14.5%, GCC 19.3%**
541	Cayman Islands	George Town	100	259	38,371	67.29	25,820	98.05	C	West Indies, Grand Cayman. Finance, tourism. Sighted by Columbus (1503). D=United Church.
	CENTRAL AFRICAN REP		**240,324**	**622,436**	**3,615,266**	**44.51**	**1,608,999**	**83.99**	**B**	**Roman Catholics 18.3%, Protestants 14.4%. Pent-char 13.4%, Evangelical 17.4%, GCC 22.4%**
542	Bamingui-Bangoran	Ndélé	22,471	58,200	38,518	30.00	11,555	65.48	B	Northern. Bamingui-Bangoon and Saint Floris National Parks. Livestock, agriculture. D=RCC.
543	Bangui	Banqui	26	67	607,411	50.00	303,706	90.43	B	Capital on Ubangi River. Commercial & administrative center. Soap making. D=RCC,EEF.
544	Basse-Kotto	Mobaye	6,797	17,604	261,891	39.00	102,137	78.48	B	South-central on Ubangi River. Cassava. Bororo-Fulani cattle-herders. Sango, Yakoma. D=RCC,EEF.
545	Haut-Mbomou	Obo	21,440	55,530	36,460	26.00	9,480	60.48	B	Southeastern, Sudan border. Econongo Wildlife Reserve, savanna, Ouhora River. D=RCC,EEF.
546	Haute-Kotto	Bria	33,456	86,650	79,123	36.00	28,484	75.48	B	North. Kotto River, Yata-Ngaua Wildlife Reserve, forest, savanna. Agriculture. D=RCC,EEF.
547	Kemo	Sibut	6,642	17,204	111,458	42.00	46,812	81.48	B	South central. Tomi River. Dense forest, agriculture, livestock, rubber. D=RCC,EEF.
548	Lobaye	Mbaïki	7,427	19,235	228,008	46.50	106,024	85.98	B	Southwest, Lobaye River, Congo border. Forest, rubber, agriculture. D=RCC,EEF.
549	Mambéré-Kadéï	Berbérati	11,661	30,203	309,782	46.00	142,500	85.48	B	West. Mambere River, Cameroon border. Agriculture, livestock. D=RCC,EEF.
550	Mbomou	Bangassou	23,610	61,150	160,365	41.00	65,750	80.48	B	Southeast. Mbomou River. Agriculture, cotton, coffee, rice, rubber. D=RCC,EEF.
551	Nana-Gribizi	Kaga-Bandoro	7,721	19,996	128,420	43.00	55,221	82.48	B	North. Grabingui-Bamirgui Wildlife Reserve. Dodo River, savanna. Agriculture. D=RCC,EEF.
552	Nana-Mambéré	Bouar	10,270	26,600	258,152	46.00	118,750	85.48	B	West. Nana River. Rubber, forest, livestock, agriculture. D=RCC,EEF.
553	Ombella-Mpoko	Boali	12,292	31,835	243,208	47.00	114,308	86.48	B	West. Mpoko River. Airports, cotton, coffee, livestock. D=RCC,EEF.
554	Ouaka	Bambari	19,266	49,900	280,155	44.00	123,268	83.48	B	Central south. Oubangui River. Cotton, rice, forest. D=RCC,EEF.
555	Ouham	Bossangoa	19,402	50,250	353,603	43.81	154,902	83.29	B	West. Ouham River. Nana Barya Wildlife Reserve, savanna. Rubber, livestock raising. D=RCC,EEF.
556	Ouham-Pendé	Bozoum	12,394	32,100	386,822	45.00	174,070	84.48	B	West. Ouham and Baba rivers, savanna. Agriculture, livestock. D=RCC,EEF.
557	Sangha-Mbaéré	Nola	7,495	19,412	88,701	46.00	40,802	85.48	B	Southwestern tip. Sangha River, forest, Congo border. Livestock, rubber. D=RCC,EEF.
558	Vakaga	Birao	17,954	46,500	43,191	26.00	11,230	60.48	B	North, bordering Chad, Sudan. Sorghum. Poor ground transport. D=RCC,EEF.
	CHAD		**495,755**	**1,284,000**	**7,650,982**	**18.80**	**1,438,014**	**50.09**	**B**	**Protestants 10.2%, Roman Catholics 6.5%. Pent-char 3.2%, Evangelical 8.5%, GCC 9.3%**
559	Batha	Ati	34,285	88,800	604,403	7.00	42,308	36.29	A	Central. Lake Fibri, desert, Batha River. Fishing.
560	Biltine	Biltine	18,090	46,850	305,988	5.00	15,299	34.29	A	North. Bedélé desert region, Tibestr mountains. Agoza ruins, intermittent streams.
561	Borkou-Ennedi-Tibesti	Faya Largeau	231,795	600,350	152,994	2.00	3,060	30.29	A	North. Arid desert. Arabs, Berbers, Tedas, Nakazas.
562	Chari-Baguirmi	N'Djamena	32,010	82,910	1,185,960	25.00	296,490	57.29	B	Southeast. Cattle raising, cotton, millet. Textiles, metalwork. Bagirmi people. D=RCC,EET,AdD.
563	Guéra	Mongo	22,760	58,950	359,638	22.00	79,120	53.29	B	South central. Siniaka-Minia Reserve. Millet, agriculture, cotton. D=EET,AdD,RCC.
564	Kanem	Mao	44,215	114,520	344,237	10.00	34,424	40.29	A	Northwest, several lakes in south central. Marsh area, desert.
565	Lac	Bol	8,620	22,320	229,491	21.00	48,193	52.29	B	West. Lake Chad, Bahr el Ghazal River, desert. Fish. D=EET,RCC.
566	Logone Occidental	Moundou	3,357	8,695	512,633	10.00	51,263	40.29	A	Southern. Chief town, Tandjile River. Agriculture, peanuts, millet, livestock. D=RCC.
567	Logone Oriental	Doba	10,825	28,035	535,607	20.00	107,121	51.29	B	Southern tip. Logone Occidental and Oriental rivers. Cotton, peanuts, millet, livestock. D=RCC,EET.
568	Mayo-Kebbi	Bongor	11,625	30,105	1,208,935	25.00	302,234	57.29	B	Southwest. Chari River. Agriculture, livestock. D=RCC,EET,AdD.
569	Moyen-Chari	Sarh	17,445	45,180	910,520	27.00	245,840	59.29	B	South. Ouham River, Siniaka-Minia Reserve. Marsh areas. Agriculture, millet. D=RCC,EET.
570	Ouaddaï	Abéché	29,436	76,240	596,830	10.00	59,683	40.29	A	East. Savanna grasslands. Cattle raising. Maba, Arabs, Fulani. Guerrilla warfare.
571	Salamat	Am Timan	24,325	63,000	183,542	19.00	34,873	50.29	B	East. Zakouma National Park, nearly all marshland. Millet.
572	Tandjilé	Laï	6,965	18,045	520,205	22.70	118,106	54.88	B	Southwest, Tanjile River. Agriculture, livestock, cotton. D=EET,AdD,RCC.
	CHANNEL ISLANDS		**75**	**194**	**152,898**	**65.91**	**100,781**	**99.53**	**C**	**Anglicans 44.1%, Roman Catholics 14.5%. Pent-char 5.4%, Evangelical 13.0%, GCC 26.5%**
573	Channel Islands	St. Helier	75	194	152,898	65.91	100,781	99.53	C	10 miles off Normandy. Chiefly agricultural, dairying, tourism. Christianization (6th cent). D=Anglican.
	CHILE		**292,135**	**756,626**	**15,211,294**	**87.82**	**13,358,340**	**99.60**	**C**	**Roman Catholics 77.5%, Independents 25.1%. Pent-char 36.4%, Evangelical 1.6%, GCC 14.6%**
574	Aisén del General	Coihaique	42,095	109,025	94,350	89.00	83,975	99.68	C	South, bordering Argentina. Andes Mountains. Potatoes, wheat, sheep, cattle. D=RCC.
575	Antofagasta	Antofagasta	48,820	126,444	468,357	88.00	412,154	99.67	C	North, bordering Bolivia, Argentina. Arid. Copper, borax, sulfur. D=RCC.
576	Araucanía	Temuco	12,300	31,858	890,894	87.00	775,078	99.48	C	South, bordering Argentina. Bio-Bio, Tolten rivers. Wheat, cattle, lumber. Mapuche Indians. D=RCC.
577	Atacama	Copiapó	29,179	75,573	265,312	89.00	236,128	99.68	C	North, bordering Argentina. Atacama Desert. Gold, silver, copper, iron. D=RCC.
578	Bío-Bío	Concepción	14,258	36,929	1,988,718	89.00	1,769,959	99.68	C	Central, bordering Argentina. Wheat, wine grapes, cattle. Mining. Coastal resorts. D=RCC.
579	Coquimbo	La Serena	15,697	40,656	577,629	86.00	496,761	99.48	C	North, bordering Argentina. Fruits, wine grapes, cereals. Goats, sheep, cattle. D=RCC.
580	Libertado General	Rancagua	6,319	16,365	791,368	86.00	680,576	99.48	C	Central, bordering Argentina. Named after first president. Wheat, rice, sheep, cattle. D=RCC.
581	Los Lagos	Puerto Montt	25,868	66,997	1,095,949	90.00	986,354	99.68	C	South, bordering Argentina. Potatoes, beef, dairy products. Tourism. Chiloe Island Indians. D=RCC.
582	Magallanes	Punta Arenas	50,979	132,034	164,460	86.00	141,436	99.48	C	Southernmost. Numerous islands. Named after Magellan. Mainly inhospitable. Oil. D=RCC.
583	Maule	Talca	11,700	30,302	958,829	88.00	843,770	99.67	C	Central, bordering Argentina. Mataquito & Maule rivers. Wheat, wine grapes, cattle. D=RCC.
584	Santiago	Santiago	5,926	15,349	5,943,774	86.71	5,153,846	99.55	C	On Mapocho River. Major industrial & agricultural region. Dairying, beef, copper. D=RCC.
585	Tarapacá	Iquique	22,663	58,698	392,143	95.00	372,536	99.68	C	Northernmost, bordering Peru & Bolivia. Atacama Desert. Fishing, sugarcane. D=RCC.
586	Valparaíso	Valparaíso	6,331	16,396	1,579,513	89.00	1,405,767	99.68	C	Central, bordering Argentina. Alfalfa, grapes. 'Christ of The Andes' statue. D=RCC.
	CHINA		**3,696,100**	**9,572,900**	**1,262,556,787**	**7.05**	**88,955,347**	**64.82**	**B**	**Independents 6.3%, Roman Catholics 0.5%. Pent-char 4.3%, Evangelical 0.2%, GCC 6.4%**
587	Anhwei (Anhui)	Ho-fei (Hefei)	54,000	139,900	62,679,127	8.50	5,327,726	66.27	B	Landlocked. North China Plain. Yangtze Valley. Wheat, rice. Famous for tea. Han Chinese.
588	Chekiang (Zhejiang)	Hang-cho	39,300	101,800	45,021,007	15.50	6,978,256	77.27	B	East China Sea. Yangtze River delta. Farm produce, tea. Porcelain, silk. Mainly Han Chinese.
589	Chungking (Chongqing)	–	8,900	23,000	15,218,986	8.00	1,217,519	65.77	B	Yangtze River. Textiles, hot springs. Christian Worship Church (TSPM), RCC.
590	Fukien (Fujian)	Fu-chou (Fuzhou)	47,500	123,100	33,742,209	12.80	4,319,003	72.57	B	East China Sea. Wooded hills, winding streams, orchards. 95% mountainous. Sugarcane. 99% Han.
591	Hainan (Hainan)	Hai-k'ou (Haikou)	13,200	34,300	7,546,933	2.60	196,220	60.37	B	Mountainous island. Tropical vegetation. Rubber, salt, tourism. Li, Hakka, Hungnese.
592	Heilungkiang	Harbin	179,000	463,600	38,578,938	1.30	501,526	54.07	B	Northeast, bordering Russia. Manchurian Plain. Manufacturing, paper. Manchus, Koreans.
593	Honan (Henan)	Cheng-chou	64,500	167,000	94,857,785	16.50	15,651,535	78.27	B	North central. Three River systems. Major wheat producers, cotton, silk. Northern Han.
594	Hong Kong	–	16	43	6,373,008	18.00	1,147,141	80.77	B	Container shipping terminal. Mainly Cantonese.
595	Hopeh (Hebei)	Shih-chia-chuang	78,200	202,700	67,098,833	2.90	1,945,866	60.67	B	North. Mountains & North China Plain. Heavy industry, coal mining. Minority Muslims, Mongols.
596	Hunan (Hunan)	Ch'ang-sha	81,300	210,500	66,629,793	3.00	1,998,894	60.77	B	Central. Yangtze River & Imperial Highway. Highlands. Major rice production.
597	Hupeh (Hubei)	Wu-han (Wuhan)	72,400	187,500	60,166,891	5.80	3,489,680	63.57	B	Yangtze River basin. Major flooding. Wheat, rice. Waterways, small villages.
598	Inner Mongolia	Hu-ho-hao-t'e	454,600	1,177,500	23,808,286	12.00	2,856,994	71.77	B	North, bordering Mongolia. Inland plateau. Harsh climate, little agriculture. Chinese & Mongols.
599	Kansu (Gansu)	Lan-chou	141,500	366,500	25,413,501	5.60	1,423,156	63.37	B	Northwest, bordering Mongolia. Plateaus. 1920 earthquake killed 200,000. Mongols, Turks, Tibetans.
600	Kiangsi (Jiangxi)	Nan-ch'ang	63,600	164,800	42,352,467	6.20	2,625,853	63.97	B	South-central. Kan River. Subtropical, rich agriculturally. Renowned porcelain industry. Mainly Han.
601	Kiangsu (Jiangsu)	Nanking (Nanjing)	39,600	102,600	73,655,543	10.30	7,586,521	70.31	B	East on Yellow Sea. Alluvial plain. Yangtze River. Silk, handicrafts. All Han Chinese.
602	Kirin (Jilin)	Ch'ang-ch'un	72,200	187,000	27,018,715	7.60	2,053,422	65.37	B	Northeast bordering Russia, North Korea. Sungali River. Most urbanized province.
603	Kwangsi Chuang	Nan-ning	85,100	220,400	47,355,854	1.10	520,914	54.87	B	South, bordering Vietnam. Rice, sugarcane, water buffalo, fishing. Chuang, Yio Miao, Tung.
604	Kwangtung (Guangdong)	Canton	76,100	197,100	71,591,515	4.70	3,364,801	62.47	B	Southernmost on South China Sea. Rice, sugarcane, fish. Water traffic, Cantonese dialect.
605	Kweichow (Guizhou)	Kuei-yang	67,200	174,000	36,567,180	9.40	3,437,315	67.17	B	Southwest, mild plateau climate. Many ethnic minorities. Rice, corn, wheat. Minerals.
606	Liaoning (Liaoning)	Shen-yang	58,300	151,000	42,654,597	2.60	1,109,020	60.37	B	Northeast, bordering North Korea. Mineral resources, heavy industry. Mainly Han Chinese.
607	Macau	Macau	3	7	476,994	14.50	69,168	77.27	B	Southeast on Pearl River. Hilly peninsula. Special admin. region (1999). Portuguese. D=RCC.
608	Ningsia Hui (Ningxia Hui)	Yin-ch'uan	25,600	66,400	5,347,433	1.60	85,559	55.37	B	North, mainly desert with canals. Wheat, mining. Handicrafts, Hui, Mongolians, Manchu.
609	Peking (Beijing)	–	6,500	16,800	13,040,318	1.30	169,524	55.07	B	On Yanyon River, capital since 1292. Steel, textiles, handicrafts. YWCA & YMCA active.
610	Shanghai (Shanghai)	–	2,400	6,200	14,749,820	16.00	2,359,971	76.77	B	East. Huangbu River. One of world's largest ports, heavy industry, finance and agriculture. D=TSPM.
611	Shansi (Shanxi)	T'ai-yüan (Taiyuan)	60,700	157,100	32,074,371	8.30	2,662,173	66.07	B	North, plateau surrounded by mountains, coal, iron, cotton. Mainly Han Chinese.
612	Shantung (Shandong)	Chi-nan (Jinan)	59,200	153,300	90,740,335	6.80	6,170,343	64.57	B	Northern Yellow sea. Cold winters, hot, dry summers. Wheat, cotton, peanuts. 90% rural.
613	Shensi (Shaanxi)	Sian (Xi'an)	75,600	195,800	36,629,676	4.90	1,794,854	62.67	B	Bordering Huang Ho river. 2 distinct climates. Corn, rice, coal. Nearly all Han Chinese.
614	Sinkiang Uighur	Wu-lu-mu-c'hi	635,900	1,646,900	17,314,199	0.30	51,943	38.07	A	Northwest. Mountains & deserts. Wheat, sheep, horses. Uighurs & 40 other groups.
615	Szechwan (Sichuan)	Ch'eng-tu	219,700	569,000	104,926,044	6.20	6,505,415	63.97	B	Southwest in Upper Yangtze Valley. Rice, corn, cattle, pigs. Great ethnic diversity.
616	Tibet (Xizang)	Lhasa	471,700	1,221,600	2,501,756	0.10	2,502	37.87	A	West. High plateau. Little economic development. Tibetans. 'roof of the world'. Buddhism 100%.
617	Tientsin (Tianjin)	–	4,400	11,300	9,819,283	1.20	117,831	54.97	B	Northeast, Hai River. Distribution center for north China plain. Textiles, chemicals, universities.
618	Tsinghai (Qinghai)	Hsi-ning (Xining)	278,400	721,000	5,013,866	1.00	50,139	53.77	B	West. Mountains & high plateau. Pasturelands for sheep, horses. Tibetan, Mongol, Hui.
619	Yunnan (Yunnan)	K'un-ming	168,400	436,200	41,591,524	2.80	1,164,563	60.57	B	Southwest. Tin mining, rice, fruit. Industrial complex. Many minorities.
	CHRISTMAS ISLAND		**52**	**135**	**3,424**	**12.91**	**442**	**64.87**	**B**	**Roman Catholics 7.3%, Protestants 3.5%. Pent-char 2.9%, Evangelical 1.9%, GCC 7.2%**
620	Christmas Island	Flying Fish Cove	52	135	3,424	12.91	442	64.87	B	Indian Ocean, south of Java. Ceded to Australia in 1958. National park, phosphate, papayas. D=RCC.
	COCOS (KEELING) IS		**5**	**14**	**726**	**16.94**	**123**	**49.59**	**A**	**Anglicans 11.4%, Roman Catholics 5.5%. Pent-char 2.0%, Evangelical 1.3%, GCC 8.6%**
621	Cocos Islands	West Island	5	14	726	16.94	123	49.59	A	Indian Ocean, Australian administration. Airport, coconuts, government facilities. F=1609. D=Anglican.
	COLOMBIA		**440,762**	**1,141,568**	**42,321,361**	**96.73**	**40,935,888**	**99.72**	**C**	**Roman Catholics 96.1%, Protestants 2.6%. Pent-char 29.7%, Evangelical 1.3%, GCC 6.3%**
622	Antioquia	Medellín	24,445	63,312	5,563,587	96.90	5,391,116	99.89	C	Northwest. Andes mountains. Gold & silver mining, asbestos, coffee, textiles. D=RCC.
623	Atlántico	Barranquilla	1,308	3,388	2,077,987	97.00	2,015,647	99.99	C	Northwest. Magdalena River. Strategic position for shipping. Cotton, sesame. F=1905. D=RCC.
624	Bolívar	Cartagena	10,030	25,978	1,925,000	97.00	1,867,250	99.99	C	Northwest. Magdalena River. Forested lowlands. Livestock, sugarcane, gold, textiles. D=RCC.
625	Boyacá	Tunja	8,953	23,189	1,487,786	97.50	1,450,591	99.99	C	East-central. Andean uplands, plains. Lake Tota. Grains, coffee, tobacco. Chiverdam. D=RCC.
626	Caldas	Manizales	3,046	7,888	1,164,895	97.00	1,129,948	99.99	C	West-central. Andes mountains. Coffee, mercury, gold, silver. F=1905. D=RCC.
627	Caquetá	Florencia	34,349	88,965	416,057	98.00	407,736	99.89	C	South. Caqueta River. Forested lowlands. Cedar, mahogany, rubber. Cattle raising. D=RCC.
628	Cauca	Popayán	11,316	29,308	1,275,291	97.00	1,237,032	99.99	C	Southwest. Cauca River. Minerals & forests. Poor transportation. Cattle raising, coffee. D=RCC.
629	Cesar	Valledupar	8,844	22,905	935,501	96.80	905,565	99.79	C	North, bordering Venezuela. Cesar River. Cotton, rice, corn, cattle raising. D=RCC.
630	Chocó	Quibdó	17,965	46,530	459,369	96.00	440,994	99.79	C	West, bordering Panama. Tropical rain forest. Gold, platinum. Descended from Slaves. D=RCC.
631	Cundinamarca	Santafé de Bogotá	8,735	22,623	2,120,817	97.00	2,057,192	99.99	C	Central. Andes mountains. Cool climate basin. Dairy cattle, fruits, cereals. Coal reserves. D=RCC.
632	Córdoba	Montería	9,660	25,020	1,442,600	97.00	1,399,322	99.99	C	Northwest. Caribbean lowlands. Important cattle-raising region. Cotton, rice, corn. D=RCC.
633	Huila	Neiva	7,680	19,890	954,249	96.50	920,850	99.49	C	Southwest. Andes Mountains. Livestock-raising, cotton. San Agustin archeological zone. D=RCC.
634	La Guajira	Riochacha	8,049	20,848	490,086	97.00	475,383	99.99	C	North, bordering Venezuela. Little rainfall. Sheep, goats, cotton, rice, salt, coal. 25% Indians. D=RCC.
635	Magdalena	Santa Marta	8,953	23,188	1,275,303	96.50	1,230,667	99.89	C	North. Magdalena River. Swamp, floodplain, mountains. Bananas, cattle. D=RCC.

Continued overleaf

Table 11-3 continued

Rec No 1	Country Major civil divisions 2	Capital 3	sq.mi. 4	sq.km. 5	Pop 2000 6	AC% 7	Church members 8	E% 9	W 10	Notes 11
636	Meta	Villavicencio	33,064	85,635	699,377	97.00	678,396	99.99	C	East. Meta River. Grains, oilseeds, coffee, cattle. Coal, salt. D=RCC.
637	Nariño	Pasto	12,845	33,268	1,632,644	96.00	1,567,338	99.79	C	Southwest, bordering Ecuador. Volcanic Andean highlands. Wheat, barley, beans, bananas. D=RCC.
638	Norte de Santander	Cúcuta	8,362	21,658	1,314,641	96.79	1,272,399	99.78	C	Northeast, bordering Venezuela. Cedar & pine forests. Oil, grains, potatoes. D=RCC.
639	Orinoquía-Amazonía	–	186,519	483,083	778,967	96.00	747,808	99.79	C	Amazon River basin. Mahogany, rubber, fishing. No good roads. Travel by river or air. D=RCC.
640	Quindío	Armenia	712	1,845	560,034	97.00	543,233	99.99	C	West-central. Andean mountains. Coffee, bananas, gold, silver, livestock. D=RCC.
641	Risaralda	Pereira	1,598	4,140	954,685	96.00	916,498	99.79	C	West-central. Cauca River. Coffee, sugarcane, beans, corn. Mining & hydroelectric. D=RCC.
642	San Andrés y Providencia	San Andrés	17	44	69,030	98.00	67,649	99.89	C	Caribbean islands. Coconuts, copra, tourism. F=1629 by English Puritans. D=RCC.
643	Santafé de Bogotá, D.C.	–	613	1,587	6,202,119	96.00	5,954,034	98.99	C	Capital district. El. 8,660 ft. Banks, commerce. F=1538. 6,000 USA expatriates. D=RCC.
644	Santander	Bucaramanga	11,790	30,537	2,048,896	98.00	2,007,918	99.89	C	North-central. Magdalena River valley. Petroleum, tobacco, coffee. D=RCC.
645	Sucre	Sincelejo	4,215	10,917	792,878	97.00	769,092	99.99	C	North on Caribbean coast. Lowlands. Cattle-raising, rice, corn, shrimp trawlers. D=RCC.
646	Tolima	Ibagué	9,097	23,562	1,454,424	96.60	1,404,974	99.59	C	Central. Andes mountains. First in rice & sesame. Cattle & pigs. F=1861. D=RCC.
647	Valle	Cali	8,548	22,140	4,225,136	96.50	4,077,256	99.49	C	West. Andes mountains, Cauca River. Leading in sugar, rice, tobacco & coffee. D=RCC.
	COMOROS		**719**	**1,862**	**592,749**	**1.19**	**7,061**	**37.35**	**A**	**Roman Catholics 0.9%, Protestants 0.1%. Pent-char 0.09%, Evangelical 0.04%, GCC 0.6%**
648	Anjouan (Nzwani)	Mutsamudu	164	424	244,926	1.00	2,449	37.16	A	Triangular island rising in a volcanic massif. No good natural harbors. D=RCC,EJCC.
649	Grande Comore (Njazidja)	Moroni	443	1,148	316,606	1.36	4,300	37.52	A	Largest island, Active volcano, Mount Karthala. Rocky surface. D=RCC,EJCC.
650	Mohéli (Mwali)	Fomboni	112	290	31,218	1.00	312	37.16	A	Smallest island, Plateau reaching 1,000 ft. Fertile valleys, thick forests. D=RCC,EJCC.
	CONGO-BRAZZAVILLE		**132,047**	**342,000**	**2,943,464**	**79.26**	**2,332,878**	**99.03**	**C**	**Roman Catholics 49.3%, Protestants 16.9%. Pent-char 20.0%, Evangelical 6.6%, GCC 19.2%**
651	Bouenza	Madingou	4,733	12,258	193,748	79.00	153,061	98.77	C	South. Niari River. Railroad. Livestock, agriculture, corn, avocado. D=EEC,EJCSK.
652	Brazzaville	–	39	100	1,024,228	80.20	821,431	99.97	C	Congo River, Batéké plateau, port. Airport, transit trade for central Africa. D=RCC,EEC.
653	Cuvette	Owando	28,900	74,850	165,872	78.00	129,380	97.77	C	North, bordering Gabon & Zaire. Swampland on Congo River. Coffee, rice, fish. 'Basin'. D=RCC.
654	Kouilou	Pointe-Noire	5,270	13,650	97,548	78.00	76,087	97.77	C	West. Kouilou River, coast, chief town. Railroad, minerals, agriculture. D=EEC.
655	Likouala	Impfondo	25,500	66,044	77,207	75.00	57,905	94.77	C	North. Likouala River, Oubongi River, marshlands. Sugarcane, plantains, bananas. D=EEC.
656	Loubomo	D	7	18	91,332	76.00	69,412	95.80	C	Gold and lead mining center, leather, Sisaland cattle center, Zaire transit center. D=ETCSK.
657	Lékoumou	Sibiti	8,089	20,950	81,298	79.00	64,225	98.77	C	South central. Niari River. Petroleum, products, forest, agriculture, minerals. D=EEC.
658	Mossendjo	–	2	5	17,921	80.00	14,337	99.77	C	Niari district. Railroad, agriculture, trade center. D=EEC,ETCSK.
659	Niari	Loubomo	10,007	25,918	131,174	79.00	103,627	98.77	C	South. Niari River. Agricultural research. copper, zinc, lead. D=EEC.
660	Nkayi	–	3	8	46,390	77.00	35,720	96.77	C	Major sugar producing center in the Niari Valley. Peanut oil, cattle feed, flour. D=RCC.
661	Ouesso	–	2	5	17,665	80.00	14,132	99.77	C	Cameroon border, Songha district, Songha River. Timber. D=RCC.
662	Plateaux	Djambala	14,826	38,400	130,786	78.00	102,013	97.77	C	East central. Congo River, La Lefini Hunting Reserve. Agriculture, peanuts, bananas. D=EJCSK.
663	Pointe-Noire	–	17	44	629,458	79.57	500,872	99.34	C	Principal Atlantic port for trade. Petroleum, light industries, mineral processing. D=RCC.
664	Pool	Kinkala	13,110	33,955	199,553	80.00	159,642	99.77	C	South. Brazzaville, Congo River. Airport, petroleum, agriculture. D=RCC,EEC.
665	Sangha	Ouesso	21,542	55,795	39,284	79.00	31,034	98.77	C	Northwest. Sangha River. Marsh regions. Agriculture, yams, avocados, peanut oil. D=RCC,EEC.
	CONGO-ZAIRE		**905,446**	**2,345,095**	**51,654,496**	**91.28**	**47,151,525**	**99.11**	**C**	**Roman Catholics 50.9%, Independents 23.3%. Pent-char 34.3%, Evangelical 8.6%, GCC 7.5%**
666	Bandundu	Bandundu	114,154	295,658	5,957,659	92.00	5,481,046	99.23	C	Southwest. Palm oil and kernels, peanuts, manioc. D=RCC,ECZ,EJCSK.
667	Bas-Zaïre	Matadi	20,880	54,078	3,129,989	88.00	2,754,390	99.33	C	West. Atlantic Ocean. Cristal Mountains. D=RCC,ECZ,EJCSK.
668	Equateur	Mbandaka	155,712	403,292	5,814,395	91.00	5,291,099	99.23	C	Northwest. Rubber, coffee, rice. D=RCC,ECZ,EJCSK.
669	Haute-Zaïre	Kisangani	194,302	503,239	6,595,070	92.00	6,067,464	99.03	C	Northeast. Palm, rice, cotton. D=RCC,ECZ,EJCSK.
670	Kasai Occidental	Kananga	60,605	156,967	3,784,394	93.00	3,519,486	99.63	C	South-central. Diamonds, coffee, cotton. Widespread revolt against Belgians (1895). D=RCC,ECZ.
671	Kasai Oriental	Mbuji-Mayi	64,949	168,216	4,586,924	90.00	4,128,232	99.43	C	South-central. Diamonds. D=RCC,ECZ,EJCSK.
672	Kinshasa	–	3,848	9,965	5,651,704	94.10	5,318,253	98.93	C	West. Congo River. Cassava, sugarcane, oil palms. D=RCC,ECZ,EJCSK.
673	Maniema	Kindu	50,916	131,871	1,272,390	94.00	1,196,101	99.53	C	East-central. Lualaba River. Coffee, rice. D=RCC,ECZ,EJCSK.
674	Nord-Kivu	Goma	23,188	60,057	4,305,247	91.00	3,917,775	98.86	C	East. Lake Kivu, Lake Edward, Virunga National Park. Tobacco, tea, agriculture, fishing. D=RCC,ECZ.
675	Shaba	Lubumbashi	191,845	496,877	6,801,466	88.00	5,985,290	98.29	C	Southeast. Lake Tanganyika. Borders Zambia, Angola. Mining: copper, cobalt, uranium. D=RCC,ECZ.
676	Sud-Kivu	Bukavu	25,048	64,875	3,755,256	93.00	3,492,388	99.63	C	East. Lake Kivu. Coffee, tea, tobacco. Virunga National Park. Refugees (1994). D=RCC,ECZ.
	COOK ISLANDS		**90**	**233**	**19,522**	**94.72**	**18,492**	**99.95**	**C**	**Protestants 72.7%, Roman Catholics 18.7%. Pent-char 15.8%, Evangelical 7.8%, GCC 12.9%**
677	Cook Islands	Avarua	90	233	19,522	94.73	18,492	99.95	C	South Pacific, free association state of New Zealand (1965). Fruit juices, citrus, clothing. D=CICC.
	COSTA RICA		**19,730**	**51,100**	**4,023,422**	**96.19**	**3,870,161**	**99.89**	**C**	**Roman Catholics 90.9%, Protestants 8.2%. Pent-char 12.2%, Evangelical 6.9%, GCC 12.7%**
678	Alajuela	Alajuela	3,766	9,753	716,276	95.90	686,934	99.90	C	Northwestern, bordering Nicaragua. San Juan River. Livestock, sugarcane, coffee, fruits. D=RCC.
679	Cartago	Cartago	1,206	3,125	451,907	96.20	434,735	99.90	C	East-central. Pilgrimage center. D=RCC.
680	Guanacaste	Liberia	3,915	10,141	322,274	96.50	310,994	99.80	C	Northwestern, bordering Nicaragua. Savanna grasslands. Cattle, corn, rice. D=RCC.
681	Heredia	Heredia	1,026	2,657	323,599	96.00	310,655	99.90	C	Central plateau. Important coffee-growing center. San Jose commuters. D=RCC.
682	Limón	Limón	3,548	9,188	291,470	97.00	282,726	99.82	C	East, bordering Nicaragua. Coastal lowlands. Heavy rainfall. Sugarcane, corn. Jamaicans. D=RCC.
683	Puntarenas	Puntarenas	4,354	11,277	449,365	96.00	431,390	99.90	C	West, on Gulf of Nicoya. Fishing. Shipping bananas, coffee. D=RCC.
684	San José	San José	1,915	4,959	1,468,531	96.20	1,412,727	99.90	C	Broad fertile valley. 19th century center of coffee production. Industry, government. D=RCC.
	CROATIA		**21,829**	**56,538**	**4,472,600**	**95.17**	**4,256,386**	**99.24**	**C**	**Roman Catholics 88.5%, Orthodox 5.5%. Pent-char 2.8%, Evangelical 0.1%, GCC 5.2%**
685	Bjelovar-Bilogora	Bjelovar	1,019	2,640	134,625	95.00	127,894	99.07	C	North central. Kupa River, Pannonian Plain. Railroad, livestock, fruits. D=RCC.
686	Dubrovnik-Neretva	Dubrovnikvn	689	1,784	118,077	94.00	110,992	99.07	C	Southern tip. Coast, Dinaric Alps, several islands, Gulf of Kotor. Ports, fishing. D=RCC.
687	Istria	Pazin	1,087	2,815	190,980	95.00	181,431	99.07	C	Northwestern tip. Rasa River. Airport, railroad, fruit, livestock. D=RCC.
688	Karlovac	Karlovac	1,278	3,311	162,803	94.00	153,035	99.07	C	Central. Kupa River, Medvednica mountains. Livestock, railroad, fruit, minerals. D=RCC.
689	Koprivnica-Krizevci	Koprimica	688	1,783	121,207	95.00	115,147	99.07	C	North-central. Zagorje Hills, Pannonian Plain, Deava River. Railroad, minerals, farming. D=RCC.
690	Krapina-Zagorje	Krapina	477	1,235	139,992	96.00	134,392	99.57	C	North-central. Zagorje Hills. Medieval castles, parks. Light industry, livestock. D=RCC.
691	Lika-Senj	Gospic	1,447	3,748	66,642	96.00	63,976	99.57	C	West-central. Coast. Mount Velebet (international natural biosphere reserve). D=RCC.
692	Medimurje	Cakovec	282	730	111,815	96.00	107,342	99.57	C	Northernmost, smallest county. Mura River. Fruit, livestock, agriculture, minerals. D=RCC.
693	Osijek-Baranja	Osijek	1,397	3,619	310,398	95.00	294,878	99.07	C	Northeastern. Drava River, 'The Tower on Bridge', settled by Romans. Fruit, livestock, ships. D=RCC.
694	Pozega-Slavonija	Pozega	917	2,374	125,680	96.00	120,653	99.57	C	East. Psunj mountains, one of the oldest counties. Fruit, dairy, livestock, minerals. D=RCC.
695	Primorje-Gorski Kotar	Rijeka	1,381	3,578	301,901	96.00	289,825	99.57	C	Southwest. Coastal, Krka River National Park, Dalmatia, Cetina River. Fruit, coal, livestock. D=RCC.
696	Sibenik	Sibenik	722	1,871	101,975	95.00	96,876	99.07	C	Northwest. Coastal, Velika Kopela mountains, Cres Island. Minerals, fishing, fruit, crafts. D=RCC.
697	Sisak-Moslavina	Sisak	1,976	5,117	268,356	94.00	252,255	98.65	C	Central. Site of concentration camp from WWII, Savanvier. Marshes. Heavy industry, textiles. D=RCC.
698	Slavonski Brod-Posavina	Slavonski Brod	782	2,026	163,697	93.00	152,238	98.07	C	East. Sava River, Bosnia-Herzegovina border, Psunj mountains. Fruit, minerals. D=RCC.
699	Split-Dalmatia	Split	1,745	4,520	442,787	96.00	425,076	99.57	C	Southwest coast. Krka River National Park, Cobina River. Tourism, fishing, port, textiles. D=RCC.
700	Varazdin	Varazdin	478	1,238	175,326	94.95	166,466	99.02	C	Central. Wine-growing country. Formerly lignite mining. Old churches and castles. D=RCC.
701	Virovitica-Podravina	Virovitica	798	2,068	97,950	96.00	94,032	99.57	C	East. Papuk mountains, Drava River. Minerals, textiles, agriculture, industry. D=RCC.
702	Vukovar-Srijem	Vukovar	943	2,442	216,027	94.00	203,065	99.07	C	East. Danube River. Rich county, heavily damaged during Croatian war. Dairy farms. D=RCC.
703	Zadar-Knin	Zadar	2,453	6,352	254,491	94.00	239,222	99.07	C	Central west coast. Velebit mountains, castles. Fishing, port, machinery, minerals, resort. D=RCC.
704	Zagreb	–	497	1,288	811,330	96.00	778,877	99.57	C	Central. Sava River. University (1699), world's longest concrete arch bridge, cathedral. D=RCC.
705	Zagreb	Zagreb	800	2,071	156,541	95.00	148,714	99.07	C	Central St. Mark's Church. Royal free market place (1292, King Bela IV). Minerals, textiles. D=RCC.
	CUBA		**42,804**	**110,861**	**11,200,684**	**43.06**	**4,822,909**	**99.10**	**B**	**Roman Catholics 39.0%, Protestants 1.7%. Pent-char 5.1%, Evangelical 1.2%, GCC 23.0%**
706	Camagüey	Camagüey	6,174	15,990	783,245	43.00	336,795	99.04	B	East-central on Atlantic Ocean. Cattle-raising area, sugar. F=1879 as Puerto Principe. D=RCC.
707	Ciego de Avila	Ciego de Avila	2,668	6,910	383,096	44.00	168,562	99.54	B	Central on Old Bahama Channel. Savanna, swamps. Sugarcane, tobacco, citrus, coffee. D=RCC.
708	Cienfuegos	Cienfuegos	1,613	4,178	383,664	45.00	172,649	99.89	B	South-central on Caribbean Sea. Fertile coastal plain. Sugarcane, rice, fishing. D=RCC.
709	Ciudad de la Habana	–	281	727	2,223,238	40.00	889,295	97.63	B	West-central on La Habana Bay. Shipping. Monasteries. D=RCC.
710	Granma	Bayamo	3,232	8,372	835,965	44.00	367,825	99.64	B	Southeastern on Gulf of Guacanayabo. Fertile plains, swamps. 1/3 of Cuba's rice. Mining. D=RCC.
711	Guantánamo	Guantánamo	2,388	6,186	525,785	45.00	236,603	99.89	B	Southeastern on Atlantic Ocean. Mountainous. Coffee, cacao, bananas, nickel, cobalt. D=RCC.
712	Holguín	Holguín	3,591	9,301	1,051,440	43.00	452,119	99.04	B	Southeastern on Atlantic Ocean. Maize beans. Iron ore, nickel. 'Granary of Cuba.' D=RCC.
713	Isla de la Juventud	Nueva Gerona	926	2,398	76,068	46.00	34,991	99.64	B	Formerly Islade Pinos. Undulating plain. Fishing, truck and citrus farming. D=RCC.
714	La Habana	Havana	2,213	5,731	681,424	45.00	306,641	99.89	B	West-central on Straits of Florida. Sugarcane, tobacco, fruit, shrimp trawling. D=RCC.
715	Las Tunas	Las Tunas	2,544	6,589	519,059	46.00	238,767	99.94	B	South-central on Caribbean Sea. Rolling plains, swamps. Cattle raising, sugarcane. D=RCC.
716	Matanzas	Matanzas	4,625	11,978	645,161	44.00	283,871	99.64	B	West-central on Straits of Florida. Fertile plains, Mangrove Swamps. Sugarcane, fruits. D=RCC.
717	Pinar del Río	Pinar del Río	4,218	10,925	732,604	45.00	329,672	99.89	B	West on Gulf of Mexico. Low mountain ranges. Sandy soils produce world's best tobacco. D=RCC.
718	Sancti Spíritus	Sancti Spíritus	2,604	6,744	453,908	45.00	204,259	99.89	B	South-central on Caribbean Sea. Tobacco, rice. Largest Cuban petroleum producer. D=RCC.
719	Santiago de Cuba	Santiago de Cuba	2,382	6,170	1,048,529	40.40	423,561	98.44	B	South on Caribbean Sea. Mountainous. Coffee, cacao. Shipping. D=RCC.
720	Villa Clara	Santa Clara	3,345	8,662	857,497	44.00	377,299	99.64	B	North-central on Nicholas Channel. Coastal marshes, plains. Sugarcane, tobacco, gold. D=RCC.
	CYPRUS		**2,284**	**5,916**	**600,506**	**91.85**	**551,594**	**99.82**	**C**	**Orthodox 87.4%, Roman Catholics 1.6%. Pent-char 0.5%, Evangelical 0.5%, GCC 11.0%**
721	Famagusta	Famagusta	766	1,984	30,316	94.00	28,497	99.64	C	Kyrenia Mountains. Wild flowers. Agriculture, dairy farming. 'Buried in the sand.' D=Orthodox.
722	Larnaca	Larnaca	433	1,121	99,715	92.00	91,738	99.62	C	Trosdos Mountains, 4,606 ft. Woodlands. Wheat, barley, salt, milled flour. D=Orthodox.
723	Limassol	Limassol	538	1,393	176,296	91.43	161,186	99.80	C	Akrotiri Bay. Chief tourist center. Wine exports. Lebanese Arabs. D=Orthodox.
724	Nicosia	Nicosia	–	–	243,794	91.60	223,315	99.98	C	Pedieos River. Wheat, barley, cotton yarns, textiles. D=Orthodox.
725	Paphos	Paphos	539	1,396	50,385	93.00	46,858	99.61	C	Southwest. Local fishing fleet, tourism, clothing. Djami Kebir Mosque. D=Orthodox.
	CZECH REPUBLIC		**30,450**	**78,864**	**10,244,177**	**47.04**	**4,819,136**	**99.42**	**B**	**Roman Catholics 40.3%, Protestants 3.1%. Pent-char 2.5%, Evangelical 1.2%, GCC 25.3%**
726	Jizní Cechy	Ceské Budejovice	4,380	11,345	693,807	49.00	339,965	99.88	B	South. Sumava Mountains. Corn, hay, pigs, dairying, forestry. Fishing. D=RCC.
727	Jizní Morava	Brno	5,802	15,028	2,039,441	46.00	938,143	99.27	B	Bohemian-Moravian highlands. Morava River. Wheat, barley, plums, apricots. D=RCC.
728	Prague	–	192	496	1,207,707	46.00	555,545	99.18	B	Vltava River, city of a hundred spires, Charles University. Precision equipment. D=RCC.
729	Severní Cechy	Ustí nad Labem	3,019	7,819	1,167,416	47.00	548,686	99.38	B	Northwest, bordering Germany & Poland. Elbe River. Corn, hops, apples, hogs. D=RCC.
730	Severní Morava	Ostrava	4,273	11,067	1,953,821	47.00	918,296	99.38	B	North, bordering Poland & Slovakia. Oder River. Sugar beets, hops. Cattle, steel. D=RCC.
731	Strední Cechy	Prague	4,245	10,994	1,101,351	46.42	511,257	99.13	B	North-central. Elbe River. Corn, sugar beets, hops, pigs. Coal mining. Steel. D=RCC.
732	Vychochí Cechy	Hradec Králové	4,340	11,240	1,226,607	48.00	588,771	99.68	B	North-central, bordering Poland. Krkonose Mountains. Elbe River. Corn, dairying. D=RCC.
733	Zapadní Cechy	Plzen	4,199	10,875	854,026	49.00	418,473	99.88	B	West, bordering Germany. Berouaka River. Corn, apples, hogs, coal. D=RCC.
	DENMARK		**16,639**	**43,094**	**5,293,239**	**89.76**	**4,751,110**	**99.22**	**C**	**Protestants 87.6%, Marginal Christians 0.6%. Pent-char 3.8%, Evangelical 4.9%, GCC 12.8%**
734	Bornholm	Rønne	227	588	46,697	92.40	43,148	99.96	C	Island in Baltic Sea. Granite, hilly wooded interior. Grains, dairy. 12th century churches. D=Lutheran.
735	Copenhagen (København)	–	34	88	476,366	86.00	409,675	98.01	C	Zealand and Amager islands, Shipbuilding, brewery, cannery. 'Paris of the North'. D=Lutheran.
736	Frederiksberg	–	3	9	88,566	91.00	80,595	99.96	C	Royal Porcelain Factory, Carlsberg breweries, cable, wireworks. F=1651. D=Lutheran.
737	Frederiksborg	Hillerød	520	1,347	353,310	90.00	317,979	99.46	C	Northeastern Zealand. Fertile loams. Mixed farming. National history museum. D=Lutheran.
738	Fyn	Odense	1,346	3,486	475,007	91.00	432,256	99.16	C	25 inhabited islands. Fertile agriculture, fruit-growing. D=Lutheran.

Continued opposite

Table 11-3 continued

Rec No 1	Country Major civil divisions 2	Capital 3	sq.mi. 4	sq.km. 5	Pop 2000 6	AC% 7	Church members 8	E% 9	W 10	Notes 11
739	København	–	203	526	618,499	87.00	538,094	98.86	C	Shipbuilding, agriculture, dressed meat, dairy products, fishing, farming. D=Lutheran.
740	Nordjylland	Ålborg	2,383	6,173	498,126	90.00	448,313	99.46	C	Northern Jutland. Poor soil, moorlands & dunes. Dairying, agriculture, fishing. D=Lutheran.
741	Ribe	Ribe	1,209	3,131	225,383	91.00	205,099	99.16	C	Southwestern Jutland. Ribe River. Agriculture & dairying. Medieval churches. D=Lutheran.
742	Ringkøbing	Ringkøbing	1,874	4,853	275,215	90.00	247,694	99.46	C	Western Jutland, Nissum Bay. Poor soil. Ports & resorts. D=Lutheran.
743	Roskilde	Roskilde	344	891	225,720	90.00	203,148	99.46	C	Eastern Zealand. Roskilde Fjord. Tanneries. University Center (1972). D=Lutheran.
744	Storstrøm	Nykøbing Falster	1,312	3,398	263,514	91.00	239,798	99.66	C	Baltic Sea, including Falster Island. Sugar beets, grain. D=Lutheran.
745	Sønderjyland	Åbenrå	1,520	3,938	257,125	90.00	231,413	99.46	C	Southern Jutland on North Sea. Agriculture, livestock, dairying. D=Moravian (1773),Lutheran.
746	Vejle	Vejle	1,157	2,997	341,157	93.00	317,276	99.26	C	Eastern Jutland. Vejle Fjord. Ships, dairy products, textile mills, shipbuilding. D=Lutheran.
747	Vestiæland	Sorø	1,152	2,984	292,339	91.00	266,028	99.66	C	West. Sjeland Island, Traelleborg ruins, Helsteinborg Castle. Railroad, dairy, grain. D=Lutheran.
748	Viborg	Viborg	1,592	4,122	235,390	90.00	211,851	99.06	C	Central, Jylland. Airport, dairy, farming, grains, machinery, textiles, brewery. D=Lutheran.
749	Århus	Århus	1,761	4,561	620,825	90.00	558,743	99.46	C	East. Jutland, Djursland Peninsula (castles & estates). Fertile lowland, agriculture. D=Lutheran.
	DJIBOUTI		**8,950**	**23,200**	**637,634**	**4.42**	**28,194**	**45.84**	**A**	**Orthodox 2.9%, Roman Catholics 1.3%. Pent-char 0.1%, Evangelical 0.01%, GCC 1.8%**
750	Ali Sabih (Ali-Sabieh)	Ali Sabih	925	2,400	32,981	2.50	825	42.92	A	East. Somali border. Many Somali refugees. Railroad, salt, livestock. D=Orthodox,RCC.
751	Dikhil	Dikhil	2,775	7,200	65,962	1.00	660	38.42	A	West. Lake Abhe Bad, Gulf of Tadjoura. Many Somali refugees. Salt lakes, salt.
752	Djibouti	Djibouti	225	600	439,748	5.70	25,060	48.47	A	Central East. Coral reefs (Gulf of Tadjoura). Extremely hot. Somali & Ethiopian refugees. D=Orthodox.
753	Obock	Obock	2,200	5,700	32,981	3.00	989	43.42	A	North. Barren desert. On Gulf of Tadjoura. Pastoral nomads. Many salt flats. D=Orthodox,RCC.
754	Tadjoura (Tadjourah)	Tadjoura	2,825	7,300	65,962	1.00	660	38.42	A	Central. Barren desert. On Gulf of Tadjoura. Pastoral nomads. Salt flats.
	DOMINICA		**290**	**750**	**70,714**	**94.40**	**66,757**	**99.91**	**C**	**Roman Catholics 79.6%, Protestants 15.8%. Pent-char 7.0%, Evangelical 6.6%, GCC 7.1%**
755	St. Andrew	–	69	179	11,033	94.00	10,371	99.91	C	Northeast. Toulaman River. Melville Hall Airport. Coconuts, cocoa. D=RCC.
756	St. David	–	49	127	6,931	96.00	6,654	99.94	C	East. Castle Bruce, Salibja, Morne Trois Piton National Park. Coconuts. D=RCC.
757	St. George	–	21	54	20,231	93.00	18,815	99.91	C	Southwest. Capital city of Roseau, Roseau River, Laudat. Coconuts, bananas. D=RCC.
758	St. John	–	23	60	4,957	95.00	4,709	99.92	C	Northwest. Prince Rupert Bay, Portsmouth, Glanville, Pointe Ronde. Bananas, cocoa. D=RCC.
759	St. Joseph	–	46	119	6,142	95.00	5,835	99.92	C	West. Salisbury, St. Joseph, Layou River, Morne Raquette. Bananas, coconuts. D=RCC.
760	St. Luke	–	4	10	1,542	96.00	1,480	99.94	C	Southwest coast. Point Michel town. Bananas, cocoa, coconuts. D=RCC.
761	St. Mark	–	4	10	1,930	95.00	1,834	99.92	C	Soufriere City, Soufriere Bay, Scotts Head, Point Des Fous. Bananas, limes. D=RCC.
762	St. Patrick	–	32	83	8,870	94.90	8,418	99.88	C	Southeast. Grand Bay, Berekua, Morne Trois Piton National Park. Bananas, limes. D=RCC.
763	St. Paul	–	26	67	7,446	95.00	7,074	99.92	C	West. Massacre, Pont Cassé. Bananas, limes, coconuts. D=RCC.
764	St. Peter	–	11	29	1,632	96.00	1,567	99.94	C	West. Colihaut, Morne Diablatins Mountain. Coconuts, lime, cocoa, bananas. D=RCC.
	DOMINICAN REPUBLIC		**18,704**	**48,443**	**8,495,338**	**94.48**	**8,026,705**	**99.93**	**C**	**Roman Catholics 88.5%, Protestants 4.2%. Pent-char 12.1%, Evangelical 3.1%, GCC 5.8%**
765	Azua	Azua	978	2,532	231,547	95.00	219,970	99.95	C	Southwest. Ocoa Mountains. Sugarcane, coffee, rice, corn. D=RCC.
766	Bahoruco (Baoruco)	Neiba	495	1,283	103,529	96.00	99,388	99.98	C	Southwest. Lake Enriquillo. Bananas, timber, other fruits, coffee. D=RCC.
767	Barahona	Barahona	671	1,739	180,580	95.00	171,551	99.95	C	Southwest. Neiba Bay. Fishing center. Sugar, molasses, coffee, fruit. D=RCC.
768	Dajabón	Dajabón	394	1,021	75,977	96.00	72,938	99.98	C	Northwest. Dajabon River. Hides, timber, bananas, coffee. D=RCC.
769	Duarte	San Francisco	620	1,605	310,110	95.50	296,155	99.95	C	North-central. Sugar, bananas, cocoa, coffee, tobacco. D=RCC.
770	El Seíbo	El Seíbo	690	1,786	115,632	95.00	109,850	99.95	C	East. Soco River, San Rafael Cape. Cocoa, coffee, wax, sugar. D=RCC.
771	Elías Piña	Elías Piña	550	1,424	86,082	95.00	81,778	99.95	C	West. Artibonita River. Sugar, bananas, livestock, minerals, tobacco. D=RCC.
772	Espaillat	Moca	324	838	215,940	95.50	206,223	99.95	C	North central. Cape Frances Viejo. Cigars, sugar, coffee, cocoa, livestock. D=RCC.
773	Hato Mayor	Hato Mayor	513	1,329	92,210	95.00	87,600	99.95	C	East-central. Cordillera Oriental. Trading, livestock, sugar, coffee, bananas. D=RCC.
774	Independencia	Jimaní	775	2,008	51,041	96.00	48,999	99.98	C	West. Lake Enriquillo. Cocoa, coffee, minerals, livestock, sugar, bananas. D=RCC.
775	La Altagracia	Higüey	1,162	3,010	131,806	95.00	125,216	99.95	C	Eastern tip. Cape Enga-o Del Este National Park, Saona Island. Fishing, trading. D=RCC.
776	La Romana	La Romana	253	654	200,507	95.00	190,482	99.95	C	Southeast on Caribbean Sea opposite Catalina Island. Sugar, fishing. Resorts. D=RCC.
777	La Vega	La Vega	883	2,286	359,072	94.50	339,323	99.95	C	West-central. Camu River. Cacao, coffee, tobacco, rice, fruits. D=RCC.
778	María Trinidad Sánchez	Nagua	491	1,271	148,284	95.00	140,870	99.95	C	North. Atlantic Ocean. Little development, very wet. Nagua River. Peanuts. D=RCC.
779	Monseñor Nouel	Bonao	383	992	147,865	95.50	141,211	99.95	C	Central. Primary highway, trade. Sugar, bananas, cocoa, coffee. D=RCC.
780	Monte Cristi	Monte Cristi	743	1,925	109,812	95.00	104,321	99.95	C	Northwest. Yaque del Norte River. Bay of Monte Cristi. Salt production, sugar, bananas. D=RCC.
781	Monte Plata	Monte Plata	1,017	2,633	207,114	94.50	195,723	99.95	C	Central. Sugar, bananas, cocoa, minerals, rice, livestock. D=RCC.
782	Pedermales	Pedermales	802	2,077	22,389	96.00	21,493	99.98	C	Southwestern tip. Beata Island, Cape Beata. Fishing, rice, livestock, fruits. D=RCC.
783	Peravia	Baní	636	1,648	221,346	95.00	210,279	99.95	C	South-central. Fishing, rice, cocoa, coffee, livestock, bananas. D=RCC.
784	Puerto Plata	Puerto Plata	717	1,857	272,210	94.28	256,639	99.73	C	Northwest. Atlantic Ocean. Leading coffee region. F=1503 by Christopher Columbus. D=RCC.
785	Salcedo	Salcedo	170	440	130,592	95.00	124,062	99.95	C	North Cibao Valley. Cacao, coffee, corn. D=RCC.
786	Samaná	Samaná	330	854	86,498	96.00	83,038	99.98	C	Northeast. Samang Peninsula. Timber, cacao, tanning. Founded by Spaniards. D=RCC.
787	San Cristóbal	San Cristóbal	616	1,265	380,250	94.50	359,336	99.92	C	South-central on Caribbean Sea. Rice, coffee, sugarcane. D=RCC.
788	San Juan	San Juan	1,379	3,571	315,920	95.00	300,124	99.95	C	West. Valle de Sun Juan. Rice, corn, coffee, bananas. D=RCC.
789	San Pedro de Macorís	San Pedro	485	1,255	234,441	95.00	222,719	99.95	C	Southeast. Macoris River. Sugar industry center. Clothing, soap. D=RCC.
790	Santiago Rodríguez	Sabaneta	429	1,112	72,953	96.00	70,035	99.97	C	Northwest. Cordillera Central. Yaque del Norte River. Livestock raising. D=RCC.
791	Santiago	Santiago	1,095	2,836	835,138	94.00	785,030	99.95	C	North. Yaque del Norte River. First European settlement (1494-95). D=RCC.
792	Santo Domingo	–	541	1,401	2,857,783	93.70	2,677,743	99.90	C	Southeast coast of Hispaniola island. Chief seaport. University (1538). F=1496. D=RCC.
793	Sánchez Ramírez	Cotuí	462	1,196	166,634	95.50	159,135	99.95	C	Central. Fertile La Vega Real region on Yuna River. F=1505 for mining. D=RCC.
794	Valverde	Mao	318	823	132,078	95.00	125,474	99.95	C	Northwest. Valle del Ciabo. Yaque del Norte River. Cacao, coffee, lumbering. D=RCC.
	ECUADOR		**105,037**	**272,045**	**12,646,068**	**97.33**	**12,307,787**	**99.44**	**C**	**Roman Catholics 94.1%, Protestants 1.9%. Pent-char 11.1%, Evangelical 2.3%, GCC 5.1%**
795	Azuay	Cuenca	2,973	7,701	668,233	98.00	654,868	99.81	C	South-central. Agriculture, cattle, hides, marble. D=RCC.
796	Bolívar	Guaranda	1,256	3,254	204,775	97.00	198,632	99.51	C	Central. Andes Mountains. Timber, cinchona, cereals, cattle. D=RCC.
797	Carchi	Tulcán	1,428	3,699	186,810	97.00	181,206	99.51	C	North, bordering Colombia. Wheat, barley, fruit. Sulfur mining. D=RCC.
798	Cañar	Azogues	1,509	3,908	250,010	97.50	243,760	99.61	C	Central. Câstle Incaico of Inga Pirca, Inca stone walls. Railroad, coffee, bananas. D=RCC.
799	Chimborazo	Riobamba	2,176	5,637	481,521	97.30	468,520	99.50	C	Central highlands. Mt. Chimborazo, highest Andean peak (20,702 ft.) Sheep. D=RCC.
800	Cotopaxi	Latacunga	2,041	5,287	364,854	97.00	353,908	99.51	C	North-central. World's highest active volcano, Cotopaxi. Cattle-raising. D=RCC.
801	El Oro	Machala	2,312	5,988	544,753	97.40	530,589	99.51	C	Southwest on Pacific Ocean. Bananas, cacao, coffee, hides. D=RCC.
802	Esmeraldas	Esmeraldas	5,875	15,216	404,866	97.00	392,720	99.51	C	Northwest on Pacific Ocean. Agriculture, lumber, bananas, oil. Tourism. D=RCC.
803	Galápagos	Puerto Baquerizo	3,093	8,010	12,920	95.00	12,274	98.11	C	Islands in Pacific Ocean. Volcanos. Unusual animal species. Natural wildlife park. D=RCC.
804	Guayas	Guayaquil	8,070	20,902	3,320,959	97.29	3,230,831	99.40	C	Guayas flood plain. Bananas, textiles. D=RCC.
805	Imbabura	Ibarra	1,925	4,986	350,560	97.00	340,043	99.51	C	North-central. Cotton, sugarcane, coffee, cereals. D=RCC.
806	Loja	Loja	4,167	10,793	507,950	97.30	494,235	99.41	C	South. Sugarcane, coffee, cereals. Tanning, textiles. D=RCC.
807	Los Ríos	Babahoyo	2,415	6,254	696,581	98.00	682,649	99.81	C	West-central. Densely forested lowland. Rio Guayas. Cotton, rice. D=RCC.
808	Manabí	Portoviejo	7,104	18,400	1,362,540	98.00	1,335,289	99.81	C	West. Fishing, tourism. Panama hats. D=RCC.
809	Morona-Santiago	Macas	11,164	28,915	111,197	97.50	108,417	99.61	C	East. Sangay National Park, Upano River. Coffee, textiles, bananas, corn. D=RCC.
810	Napo	Tena	12,899	33,409	136,511	97.30	132,825	99.41	C	Northeast. Yasuni National Park, Napo River, Yasuni River. Bananas, coffee. D=RCC.
811	Pastaza	Puyo	11,398	29,520	55,206	98.00	54,102	99.81	C	Central east. Rice, cotton, bananas, textiles, livestock, rural farming. D=RCC.
812	Pichincha	Quito	6,409	16,599	2,318,896	97.00	2,249,329	99.11	C	North-central highlands. Agriculture, cattle, textiles, tourism. D=RCC.
813	Sucumbíos	Nueva Loja	7,186	18,612	101,606	98.00	99,574	99.81	C	Northeast. Aguarico River. Corn, coffee, rice, bananas. D=RCC.
814	Tungurahua	Ambato	1,118	2,896	477,953	96.00	458,835	98.54	C	Central. Near Mt. Chimborazo. Fruits, sugarcane, tanning. D=RCC.
815	Zamora Chinchipe	Zamora	7,985	20,681	87,365	97.50	85,181	99.61	C	Andes mountains. Forested jungles. Mainly Indians. D=RCC.
	EGYPT		**385,229**	**997,739**	**68,469,695**	**15.07**	**10,320,466**	**77.65**	**B**	**Orthodox 13.6%, Protestants 0.8%. Pent-char 1.1%, Evangelical 0.6%, GCC 11.9%**
816	ad-Daqahliyah	al-Mansurah	1,340	3,471	4,931,085	8.00	394,487	65.58	B	Northeastern. Nile Delta on Mediterranean Sea. Primary rice-growing region, fishing.
817	al-Bahr al-Ahmar	al-Ghurdaqah	78,643	203,685	139,124	4.00	5,565	58.58	B	Eastern Desert. East of Nile River Valley. Minerals, oil. St Anthony monastery. 'Red Sea'.
818	al-Buhayrah	Damanhur	3,911	10,130	4,639,958	8.50	394,396	66.08	B	Nile Delta, Lower Egypt. Cotton, rice, natural gas. Rosetta stone.
819	al-Fayyum	al-Fayyum	705	1,827	2,215,638	17.00	376,658	81.58	B	Upper Egypt, desert. Lake Qarun. Commercial fishing. Historic Coptic Christian Center. D=COC.
820	al-Gharbiyah	Tanta	750	1,942	4,010,051	9.50	380,955	68.08	B	Middle Nile Delta. Cotton-growing center. Population density over 2,000 persons/sq. mile.
821	al-Iskandariyah	Alexandria	1,034	2,679	4,083,478	25.00	1,020,870	95.58	B	Chief sea port. Christian activities: music, radio, Bible sales. Cotton, trade. D=COC.
822	al-Ismailiyah (ismailia)	–	557	1,442	802,526	10.00	80,253	68.58	B	Northeastern Nile delta. On Suez Canal. Crops, cattle, fish. Military base.
823	al-Jizah	al-Jizah	32,878	85,153	5,494,015	17.50	961,453	82.08	B	Upper Egypt, west bank of the Nile. Corn, cotton, dates, iron ore. D=COC.
824	al-Minufiyah	Shibin al-Kawm	592	1,532	3,154,707	11.00	347,018	70.58	B	Western Nile delta. Very productive land. Corn. 2,500 persons/sq. mile.
825	al-Minya	al-Minya	873	2,262	3,756,282	28.66	1,076,426	99.74	B	Upper Egypt, Nile River and western desert. Cotton, corn, iron ore, limestone. D=COC.
826	al-Qahirah (Cairo)	–	83	214	8,311,221	16.00	1,329,795	80.58	B	Nile River, tombs of the Caliphs, Coptic Museum, Ain Shams University.
827	al-Qalyubiyah	Banha	387	1,001	3,694,447	5.20	192,111	59.78	B	North of Cairo. Corn, cotton, wheat, clover, Phosphates, basalt.
828	Al-Uqsur (Luxor)	–	30	78	157,480	12.00	18,898	72.58	B	On Nile River near Armant. Thebes nearby. Valley of the Kings. King Tut's tomb. D=COC.
829	al-Wadi al-Jadid	al-Kharijah	145,369	376,505	162,307	5.00	8,115	60.58	B	Southwest. Desert. 2/5 of Egypt. Some crops, sheep. Awlad Ali tribes. 'New Valley'.
830	as-Suways (Suez)	–	6,888	17,840	504,964	10.00	50,496	68.58	B	Capital on Suez Canal. Pilgrims to Mecca. Oil refinery, petroleum products.
831	ash-Sharqiyah	az-Zaqaziq	1,614	4,180	4,851,222	10.30	499,676	68.88	B	Eastern Nile delta. Lake Manzala. Cotton, corn rice. Ducks, chickens.
832	Aswan	Aswan	262	679	1,137,446	23.00	261,613	91.58	B	Upper Egypt, bordering Sudan. Aswan Dam. Sugarcane, lentils, corn. Tourism. D=COC.
833	Asyut	Asyut	600	1,553	3,163,724	28.60	904,825	99.75	B	Upper Egypt, Nile River. Cotton, grains, vegetables, chickens. Many Coptic Christians. D=COC.
834	Bani Suyayf	Bani Suwayf	510	1,322	2,043,026	20.00	408,605	87.58	B	Upper Egypt, Nile River. Cooperative farming. Cotton, grains, beans, alabaster. D=COC.
835	Bur Said (Port Said)	–	28	72	593,845	11.00	65,323	70.58	B	Suez Canal at Mediterranean Sea. Textiles, glass, fishing, salt.
836	Dumyat	Dumyat	227	589	1,040,835	9.00	93,675	66.58	B	Nile Delta, Lower Egypt. Bisected by Damietta branch. Fishing, agriculture.
837	Janub Sina'	al-Tur	12,796	33,140	42,506	5.00	2,125	60.58	B	Southern Sinai. Peninsula. Granite & sandstone mountains. Bedouins. St Catherine's monastery.
838	Kafr ash-Shaykh	Kafr ash-Shaykh	1,327	3,437	2,535,104	7.00	177,457	62.58	B	Central Nile delta. Cotton, rice, corn, wheat. Fish farming.
839	Matruh	Marsa Matruh	81,897	212,112	234,447	7.00	16,411	63.58	B	Northwest desert. 1% inhabited. Petroleum, natural gas. Roman ruins.
840	Qina	Qina	685	1,773	3,053,906	10.00	305,391	68.58	B	Upper Egypt, Nile River. Thebes. Valley of the Tombs of Kings. Sugar, phosphate. D=COC.
841	Sawhaj	Sawhaj	597	1,547	3,463,868	27.00	935,244	98.08	B	Upper Egypt, Nile River. Cotton, millet, wheat. Silk weaving. 5th century basilica church. D=COC.
842	Shamal Sina'	al-Arish	10,646	27,574	252,482	5.00	12,624	60.58	B	Northern Sinai Peninsula. Al Avish River, desert. Point in British advance to Palestine. D=COC.
	EL SALVADOR		**8,124**	**21,041**	**6,276,023**	**97.16**	**6,098,022**	**99.90**	**C**	**Roman Catholics 91.1%, Independents 11.3%. Pent-char 23.5%, Evangelical 6.7%, GCC 8.1%**
843	Ahuachapán	Ahuachapán	479	1,240	321,814	98.00	315,378	99.96	C	West. Molino River. La Laguita Volcano. Coffee, mineral baths. Geothermal power. D=RCC.
844	Cabañas	Sensuntepeque	426	1,104	233,452	98.00	228,783	99.96	C	North-central. Grain, sugar, dairy products, pottery. F=1873. D=RCC.
845	Chalatenango	Chalatenango	779	2,017	300,514	97.50	293,001	99.94	C	North. Tamulasco and Cholco rivers. Wheat, sugarcane. Agricultural fairs. D=RCC.
846	Cuscatlán	Cojutepeque	292	756	257,511	98.00	252,361	99.96	C	Central. Lake Ilopango. Sugar milling. Feast of St John (Aug. 29) pilgrimage. D=RCC.
847	La Libertad	Nueva San Salvador	638	1,653	522,664	97.50	509,597	99.94	C	West-central. San Salvador Volcano. Salvadorean Institute for Coffee Research. D=RCC.
848	La Paz	Zacatecoluca	473	1,224	328,415	97.50	320,205	99.94	C	South. Lempa River. San Vicente Volcano. Cotton goods, baskets, salt. Earthquake (1932). D=RCC.
849	La Unión	La Unión	801	2,074	406,837	97.50	396,666	99.94	C	East. Conchagua Volcano. Gulf of Fonseca. Tortoise shell industry, beaches. D=RCC.

Continued overleaf

Table 11-3 continued

Rec No 1	Country Major civil divisions 2	Capital 3	sq.mi. 4	sq.km. 5	Pop 2000 6	AC% 7	Church members 8	E% 9	W 10	Notes 11
850	Morazán	San Francisco	559	1,447	275,039	98.00	269,538	99.96	C	East. Rio Grande de San Miguel. Agriculture, livestock. Gold and silver mining. D=RCC.
851	San Miguel	San Miguel	802	2,077	564,714	97.10	548,337	99.94	C	East-central. San Miguel and Chinameca Volcanos. Textiles, rope. Earthquake (1917). D=RCC.
852	San Salvador	San Salvador	342	886	1,293,974	95.48	1,235,444	99.72	C	Central. Pacific Coast. San Salvador Volcano. Sugarcane, coffee, manufacturing. D=RCC.
853	San Vicente	San Vicente	457	1,184	254,766	98.00	249,671	99.96	C	South-central. Accihuapa River. San Vicente Volcano. Grain, sugar mills. D=RCC.
854	Santa Ana	Santa Ana	781	2,023	574,220	97.50	559,865	99.94	C	West. Santa Ana Volcano. Major coffee processing center. Summer resorts. D=RCC.
855	Sonsonate	Sonsonate	473	1,226	431,963	98.00	423,324	99.96	C	West. Rio Grande de Sonsonate. Livestock, tropical fruit, coffee. D=RCC.
856	Usulután	Usulután	822	2,130	510,137	97.20	495,853	99.94	C	Southeast. Pacific Coast. Usulutan Volcano. Grain, coffee. 'City of the Ocelots'. D=RCC.
	EQUATORIAL GUINEA		**10,831**	**28,051**	**452,661**	**87.20**	**394,698**	**98.57**	**C**	**Roman Catholics 86.3%, Independents 3.9%. Pent-char 5.5%, Evangelical 2.4%, GCC 14.0%**
857	Annobón	Palé	7	17	3,235	88.50	2,863	99.47	C	Volcanic island. Mainly fishermen speaking a Portuguese patois. D=RCC.
858	Bioko Norte	Malabo	300	776	77,584	88.00	68,274	99.17	C	Island in Gulf of Guinea. Originally Formosa. Cocoa, timber, coffee. Mainly Fang. D=RCC.
859	Bioko Sur	Luba	479	1,241	15,517	88.00	13,655	99.17	C	Isle de Bioko in Gulf of Guinea, Santiago Point, City of Riaba. Timber, fishing. D=RCC.
860	Centro-Sur	Evinayong	3,834	9,931	76,721	87.50	67,131	98.87	C	Central. Landlocked, Mbini River, Utamboni River. Cocoa, timber, crafts. D=RCC.
861	Kie-Ntem	Ebebiyin	1,522	3,943	101,504	86.16	87,455	97.76	C	Northeast. Abia River. Rapids, fishing, timber, coffee, palm oil. D=RCC.
862	Litoral	Bata	2,573	6,665	103,683	87.00	90,204	98.37	C	Western. Entire coast of Gulf of Guinea. Elobey Islands, Epote Point. Fishing, crafts, timber. D=RCC.
863	Wele-Nzas	Mongomo	2,115	5,478	74,418	87.50	65,116	98.87	C	Southeastern. Gabon border, Mbini River. Primary roads. Coffee, timber, cocoa, crafts. D=RCC.
	ERITREA		**45,300**	**117,400**	**3,850,388**	**50.24**	**1,934,358**	**73.57**	**B**	**Orthodox 46.0%, Roman Catholics 3.3%. Pent-char 0.9%, Evangelical 0.3%, GCC 7.4%**
864	Ameba	Keren	8,960	23,200	924,093	56.00	517,492	82.77	B	North central. Anseba River, primary highway junction. Cotton, railroad, salt. D=Orthodox.
865	Debub	Mendefera	3,090	8,000	423,543	55.00	232,949	81.33	B	Central. Mendefera Hospital. Pilgrimage and festival of Sheikh. Tobacco, leather. D=Orthodox.
866	Debubawi Keyh Bahri	Asseb (Aseb)	10,660	27,600	462,047	38.00	175,578	51.33	B	Southern tip, mouth of Red Sea. Cotton, salt, food products, market, fishing. D=Orthodox.
867	Gash Barka	Barentu	12,820	33,200	962,597	52.15	502,013	78.48	B	Southwest. Intermittent streams. Cotton, livestock, agriculture, leather, dairy processing. D=Orthodox.
868	Maekel	Asmara (Asmera)	500	1,300	577,558	53.00	306,106	80.33	B	Central. Capital. University (1967). Textiles, railroad, chemicals, dairy products. D=Orthodox.
869	Semenawi Keyh Bahri	Massawa (Mitsiwa)	10,730	27,800	500,550	40.00	200,220	53.33	B	East-central. Red Sea, Dahlak Archipelago. Railroad, livestock, agriculture. D=Orthodox.
	ESTONIA		**17,462**	**45,227**	**1,396,158**	**37.95**	**529,875**	**98.07**	**B**	**Protestants 17.1%, Orthodox 16.4%. Pent-char 4.3%, Evangelical 5.1%, GCC 20.9%**
870	Harju	Tallinn	1,601	4,147	525,186	36.26	190,435	97.35	B	Gulf of Finland. Kiek in die ksk tower fortress, St Olaf's Church. D=Orthodox,Evangelical Lutheran.
871	Hiiu	Kärdla	395	1,023	11,105	40.00	4,442	99.17	B	Island in Baltic Sea. Livestock herding, fishing. Founded by Brother of the Sword. D=Orthodox.
872	Ida-Viru	Jõhvi	1,233	3,194	194,403	37.00	71,929	97.12	B	Northeast. Nanva River, Nanva Reservoir, Lake Peipus. Dairy products, shipbuilding. D=Orthodox.
873	Järva (Paide)	Paide	1,013	2,624	40,530	39.00	15,807	99.12	B	North central. Ramport tower of Paide. Birthplace of author Anton Tammsaare. Farming. D=Orthodox
874	Jõgeva	Jõgeva	1,005	2,604	39,421	40.00	15,768	99.17	B	Northeast. Lake Peipus, Pedja River. Potatoes, rye, cement. D=Orthodox.
875	Lääne (Haapsalu)	Haapsalu	933	2,417	30,348	39.00	11,836	99.12	B	North. Birthplace of Prince Gorchakov (1798). Kyke Gallery. D=Orthodox,Evangelical Lutheran.
876	Lääne-Viru (Rakvere)	Rakvere	1,332	3,451	70,505	38.00	26,792	98.92	B	North-central. Kunda River, Loobu River. Seaport, fishing, shipbuilding. D=Orthodox.
877	Pärnu	Pärnu	1,842	4,771	92,528	39.00	36,086	99.12	B	Parnu River, Gulf of Riga. Holiday resort area, secondary schools. Shipbuilding. D=Orthodox.
878	Põlva	Põlva	836	2,164	33,858	41.00	13,882	99.19	B	Southeast, Russia border. Lake Pskov. Dairy products, rye, potatoes, textiles. D=Orthodox.
879	Rapla	Rapla	1,135	2,939	37,163	41.00	15,237	99.19	B	North-central. Marsh. Railroad, potatoes rye, livestock, port, shipbuilding. D=Orthodox.
880	Saare (Kingissepa)	Kuressaare	1,126	2,917	37,821	40.00	15,128	99.17	B	South of Hiiu, island in Baltic. Paper, pulp, plywood. D=Orthodox,Ev. Lutheran.
881	Tartu	Tartu	1,186	3,071	144,133	40.00	57,653	98.19	B	Emajogi River. Old university city. Observatory, art museum. 13th century cathedral. D=Orthodox.
882	Valga	Valga	789	2,044	37,377	40.00	14,951	99.17	B	Southeast. Emajogi River, Folk Art Days annually. Valga secondary school. D=Orthodox.
883	Viljandi	Viljandi	1,381	3,578	60,030	38.00	22,811	98.92	B	South-central. Birthplace of soldier Johan Laidoner (1884). Paper, pulp, plywood. D=Orthodox.
884	Võru	Võru	890	2,305	41,750	41.00	17,118	99.19	B	Residence of poet F. Reinhold Kreutzwald. Haanja Upland. Potatoes, rye. D=Orthodox.
	ETHIOPIA		**437,794**	**1,133,882**	**62,564,875**	**49.81**	**31,161,159**	**84.48**	**B**	**Orthodox 36.5%, Protestants 13.6%. Pent-char 6.5%, Evangelical 10.5%, GCC 15.5%**
885	Addis Ababa	–	–	–	2,626,599	48.00	1,260,768	88.67	B	Central. Capital since 1896. HQ of Organization of African Unity. Footwear, textiles. D=EOC.
886	Affar	–	–	–	1,375,489	41.00	563,950	85.67	B	Northeast. Arama. Agricultural industry, large deposits of potassium chloride salt (potash). D=EOC.
887	Amhara	–	66,409	172,000	17,199,147	81.50	14,017,305	99.17	C	Northeast. 81.5% Orthodox Christian, 18.1% Muslim. A top grain producer. D=EOC.
888	Benishangul Gumuz	Asosa	30,888	80,000	572,469	40.00	228,988	84.67	B	West. Extremely fertile lands, water for irrigation. Corn, sorghum, tea, millet, oilseeds. D=EOC.
889	Dire-Dawa	–	–	–	313,137	50.00	156,569	90.67	B	East. Agriculture, mining, tourism. Meat, coffee processing, textiles, cement, railroad. D=EOC.
890	Gambela	–	9,653	25,000	226,109	45.79	103,529	90.46	B	West tip. Agriculture, corn, sesame, cotton, rice, peanuts, home made gin. D=EOC.
891	Hariai	–	–	–	163,044	41.00	66,848	85.67	B	East. Tourism, historical sites. Agricultural exports, possible mining, fruits, vegetables. D=EOC.
892	Oromiya	–	138,996	360,000	23,288,774	33.00	7,685,295	80.82	B	Central and south, largest region. Produces 47% of cereals. D=EOC.
893	Southern Nations	–	–	–	12,901,002	26.00	3,354,261	65.67	B	Southwest. Lake Abaya, Lakes Natl. Park, Rift Valley. Agriculture, mining. Livestock, tourism. D=EOC.
894	Tigray	–	–	–	3,899,106	95.50	3,723,646	99.67	C	North. 95.5% Orthodox Christian, 4.1% Muslim, .4% Catholics. High plateau. Cereals, legume. D=EOC.
	FAEROE ISLANDS		**540**	**1,399**	**42,749**	**92.61**	**39,590**	**99.93**	**C**	**Protestants 90.9%, Independents 0.9%. Pent-char 6.9%, Evangelical 17.5%, GCC 27.5%**
895	Faeroe Islands	Thorshavn	540	1,399	42,749	92.61	39,590	99.93	C	North Atlantic, settled by Norsemen in 8th century. Fish processing. D=Ev. Lutheran.
	FALKLAND ISLANDS		**4,700**	**12,173**	**2,255**	**79.07**	**1,783**	**99.78**	**C**	**Anglicans 36.5%, Protestants 29.2%. Pent-char 13.3%, Evangelical 15.0%, GCC 33.5%**
896	Falkland Islands	Stanley	4,618	11,961	2,255	79.08	1,783	99.79	C	South Atlantic, discovered 1592, Argentine invasion in 1982. Fishing, gas and oil. D=Anglican.
	FIJI		**7,055**	**18,272**	**816,905**	**56.28**	**459,745**	**88.78**	**B**	**Protestants 45.9%, Independents 10.5%. Pent-char 22.6%, Evangelical 13.0%, GCC 12.8%**
897	Ba	–	1,017	2,634	225,682	59.66	134,646	92.16	B	West, mouth of Ba river. Technical Training Center. Agricultural service town, sugar. D=Methodist.
898	Bua	–	532	1,379	15,971	44.00	7,027	76.50	B	North. D=Methodist.
899	Cakaudrove	–	1,087	2,816	46,171	42.00	19,392	74.50	B	North. D=Methodist.
900	Kadavu	Vunisea	185	478	11,197	45.00	5,039	77.50	B	East. Island south of Vitu Levu. Timber, bananas, copra. Visited by W. Bligh (1792). D=Methodist.
901	Lau	–	188	487	16,219	44.00	7,136	76.50	B	East. 57 islands over 44,000 sq. miles. Copra. First Wesleyan missionary (1835). D=Methodist.
902	Lomaiviti	Levuka	159	411	18,346	46.00	8,439	78.50	B	East. Ovalua island. Tuna fishing for Japanese, South Korean, Taiwanese. F=1822. D=Methodist.
903	Macuata	–	774	2,004	85,342	55.00	46,938	87.55	B	North. D=Methodist.
904	Nadroga-Navosa	–	921	2,385	62,156	50.00	31,078	82.50	B	West. D=Methodist.
905	Naitasiri	–	643	1,666	114,452	63.00	72,105	95.50	C	Central. D=Methodist,RCC.
906	Namosi	–	220	570	5,522	55.00	3,037	87.50	B	Central. Copper deposits. D=Methodist.
907	Ra	–	518	1,341	35,725	48.00	17,148	80.50	B	West. D=Methodist,RCC.
908	Rewa	–	105	272	111,272	62.00	68,989	94.50	C	Central. Rewa River. Largest river and delta in Fiji. D=Methodist,RCC.
909	Rotuma	Ahau	18	46	3,070	40.00	1,228	72.50	B	East. Volcanic island. Formerly Grenville. Copra, woven mats. Polynesians. D=Methodist.
910	Serua	–	320	830	15,252	54.00	8,236	86.50	B	Central. D=Methodist.
911	Tailevu	–	369	955	50,529	58.00	29,307	90.50	B	Central. D=Methodist.
	FINLAND		**130,559**	**338,145**	**5,175,743**	**88.48**	**4,579,451**	**99.71**	**C**	**Protestants 89.5%, Independents 1.5%. Pent-char 12.8%, Evangelical 14.3%, GCC 19.9%**
912	Aland (Ahvenanmaa)	Mariehamn	590	1,527	25,538	91.00	23,240	99.93	C	Southwest. Archipelago at Gulf of Bothnia. 35 inhabited, 6,500 uninhabited islands. D=Lutheran.
913	Häme	Hämeenlinna	6,309	16,341	738,402	88.00	649,794	99.63	C	Southwest. Lake Paijanne. Lumber, rye, oats, livestock. Tavastians. D=Lutheran.
914	Keski-Suomi	Jyväskylä	6,266	16,230	261,607	89.00	232,830	99.73	C	South-central. Many lakes. Flat farming and timber lands. D=Lutheran.
915	Kuopio	Kuopio	6,374	16,509	262,708	90.00	236,437	99.83	C	South-central. Savo forest. Lakes. Wood products, tourism. D=Lutheran,Finnish Orthodox Church.
916	Kymi	Kouvola	4,163	10,783	338,445	91.00	307,985	99.93	C	Southeast on Gulf of Finland. Saimaa lake system. Timber, paper, textiles. D=Lutheran.
917	Lappi	Rovaniemi	35,930	93,057	205,380	90.00	184,842	99.83	C	North, bordering Norway. Sparsely populated, underdeveloped. Forestry, reindeer. D=Lutheran.
918	Mikkeli	Mikkeli	6,310	16,342	209,803	90.00	188,823	99.83	C	Southeast. Save forest. Forestry, wood products, metalworking. D=Lutheran.
919	Oulu	Oulu	21,957	56,868	456,499	91.00	415,414	99.93	C	Central, on Gulf of Bothnia. Lake Oulujarvi. Barley, forestry. F=1776. D=Lutheran.
920	Pohjois-Karjala	Joensuu	6,866	17,782	180,603	88.00	158,931	99.63	C	East-central, bordering Russia. Lake Pielinen. Lumbering, small-scale farming. D=Lutheran.
921	Turku ja Pori	Turku	8,818	22,839	711,283	88.00	625,929	99.63	C	Southwest on Gulf of Bothnia. Many lakes. Agriculture, dairying, timber. D=Lutheran.
922	Uusimaa	Helsinki	3,822	9,898	1,329,323	86.45	1,149,252	99.60	C	South on Gulf of Finland. Granite and limestone quarrying. Some Swedish areas. D=Lutheran.
923	Vaasa	Vaasa	10,199	26,416	456,151	89.00	405,974	99.73	C	West on Gulf of Bothnia. Timber industry, agriculture. D=Lutheran.
	FRANCE		**210,026**	**543,965**	**59,079,709**	**69.60**	**41,116,959**	**96.30**	**C**	**Roman Catholics 82.2%, Independents 2.2%. Pent-char 2.4%, Evangelical 0.4%, GCC 41.5%**
924	Ain	Bourg-en-Bresse	2,225	5,762	495,750	76.00	376,770	97.70	C	Rhone-Alpes. Rhone, Saone, and Ain rivers. Stock raising, cheese, tourism. D=RCC.
925	Aisne	Laon	2,845	7,369	558,262	78.00	435,444	99.20	C	Picardie. Aisne River. Rich grainlands. Beet sugar, gypsum, mirrors. D=RCC.
926	Allier	Moulins	2,834	7,340	370,619	72.00	266,846	98.70	C	Auvergne. Allier River. Livestock. Declining coal industry. Spas. D=RCC.
927	Alpes-de-Haute-Provence	Digne	2,674	6,925	137,490	67.00	92,118	93.70	C	Provence-Alpes-Cote-d'Azur. Mountainous. Cereals, sheep, tourism. D=RCC.
928	Alpes-Maritimes	Nice	1,660	4,299	1,021,376	64.00	653,681	92.70	C	Provence-Alpes-Cote-d'Azur. Mediterranean Sea. Resorts. D=RCC.
929	Ardennes	Charleville-Mézières	2,019	5,229	307,067	78.00	239,512	99.20	C	Champagne-Ardennes, bordering Belgium. Forest. Scene of major battles. D=RCC.
930	Ardèche	Privas	2,135	5,529	289,514	77.00	222,926	98.70	C	Rhone-Alpes. Ardeche River. Fruit, olives, textiles, cement. D=RCC.
931	Ariège	Foix	1,888	4,890	141,951	69.00	97,946	95.70	C	Midi-Pyrenees, bordering Spain. Pyrenees mountains. Corn, mining, tourism. D=RCC.
932	Aube	Troyes	2,318	6,004	300,521	74.00	222,386	97.70	C	Champagne-Ardennes. Chalk. Trade fairs, sheep breeding. D=RCC.
933	Aude	Carcassonne	2,370	6,139	312,567	78.00	243,802	99.20	C	Languedoc-Roussillon. Aude River. Inexpensive wines, plastics. D=RCC.
934	Aveyron	Rodez	3,373	8,736	279,648	69.00	192,957	95.70	C	Midi-Pyrenees. Cattle, sheep. Noteworthy castles and churches. D=RCC.
935	Bas-Rhin	Strasbourg	1,836	4,755	994,820	68.00	676,478	94.70	C	Alsace, Rhine River. Vosges Mountains. Corn, orchards, vineyards. D=RCC.
936	Bouches-du-Rhône	Marseille	1,964	5,087	1,831,896	58.49	1,071,476	93.19	B	Provence-Alpes-Cote-d'Azur. Rhone river. Rice, horses, wheat. D=RCC.
937	Calvados	Caen	2,142	5,548	645,180	74.00	477,433	97.20	C	Basse-Normandie. On English Channel. Stock-raising area. Dairying, tourism. D=RCC.
938	Cantal	Aurillac	2,211	5,726	164,383	72.00	118,356	98.70	C	Auvergne. Severe winters. Cheese, milk, uranium, thermal springs. D=RCC.
939	Charente	Angoulême	2,300	5,956	355,453	73.00	259,481	99.70	C	Poitou-Charentes. Fertile, arable land. Corn, fodder, vineyards, butter. D=RCC.
940	Charente-Maritime	La Rochelle	2,650	6,864	549,022	72.00	395,296	98.70	C	Poitou-Charentes, on Bay of Biscay. Oysters, cereals, cattle, tourism. D=RCC.
941	Cher	Bourges	2,793	7,235	334,373	77.00	257,467	98.70	C	Center. Cher River. Timber cutting, wheat, cattle, bee-keeping. D=RCC.
942	Corrèze	Tulle	2,261	5,857	246,628	70.00	172,640	96.70	C	Limousin. Chestnut forests. Correze River. Sheep, cattle, pigs, poultry. D=RCC.
943	Corse-du-Sud	Ajaccio	1,550	4,014	123,884	77.00	95,391	98.70	C	Corse, southern Corsica. High mountains. Olives, animal husbandry. Corse language. D=RCC.
944	Creuse	Guéret	2,149	5,565	135,724	70.00	95,007	96.70	C	Limousin. Creuse River. Stockbreeding, cereals, potatoes, chestnuts. D=RCC.
945	Côte-d'Or	Dijon	3,383	8,763	515,270	73.00	376,147	99.70	C	Bourgogne. Vine-growing hills. Vineyards. Cistercian houses. 'Golden ridge'. D=RCC.
946	Côtes-d'Armor	Saint-Brieuc	2,656	6,878	558,989	79.00	441,601	98.70	C	Bretagne. Noires Mountains. Cattle, horses wheat, oats. Seaside resorts. D=RCC.
947	Deux-Sèvres	Niort	2,316	5,999	359,606	79.00	284,089	98.70	C	Poitou-Charentes. Sevre Niortaise and Sevre Nantaise rivers. Cattle. D=RCC.
948	Dordogne	Périgueux	3,498	9,060	402,392	78.00	313,866	99.20	C	Aquitaine. Limestone plateaus. Seven rivers. Walnuts. Early human settlement. D=RCC.
949	Doubs	Besançon	2,021	5,234	503,849	73.00	367,810	99.70	C	Franche-Comte, on Swiss frontier. Doubs River. Severe winters. Cheese. D=RCC.
950	Drôme	Valence	2,521	6,530	433,131	76.00	329,180	97.70	C	Rhone-Alpes. Rhone River. Grain, fruit, silkworms, wines. D=RCC.
951	Essonne	Évry	696	1,804	1,138,431	61.00	694,443	95.70	C	Ile-de-France. Essonne River. Parisian suburbs. Grain, tourism. D=RCC.
952	Eure	Évreux	2,332	6,040	539,776	78.00	421,025	99.20	C	Haute-Normandie. Seine and Eure rivers. Rich agricultural region known for milk. D=RCC.
953	Eure-et-Loir	Chartres	2,270	5,880	415,059	78.00	323,746	99.20	C	Center. Paris Basin. Eure River. Corn, wheat. 12th century cathedral (Chartres). D=RCC.
954	Finistère	Quimper	2,600	6,733	872,076	80.00	697,661	99.70	C	Bretagne. Oceanic climate, forests. Fishing, agriculture. 'Lands end'. D=RCC.

Continued opposite

Table 11-3 continued

Rec No. 1	Country Major civil divisions 2	Capital 3	sq.mi. 4	sq.km. 5	Pop 2000 6	AC% 7	Church members 8	E% 9	W 10	Notes 11
955	Gard	Nîmes	2,260	5,853	614,441	72.00	442,398	98.70	C	Languedoc-Roussillon. Rhone River. Wines, cheese, steel, tourism. D=RCC.
956	Gers	Auch	2,416	6,257	181,416	71.00	128,805	97.70	C	Midi-Pyrenees. Gers River, vast plateau. Mixed farming, cattle raising. D=RCC.
957	Gironde	Bordeaux	3,861	10,000	1,270,627	67.00	851,320	93.70	C	Aquitaine, on Atlantic coast. Pine forest, seaside resorts. World-famous wines. D=RCC.
958	Haut-Rhin	Colmar	1,361	3,525	699,799	75.00	524,849	96.70	C	Alsace, east, bordering Switzerland. Rhine River. Noted for wine, asparagus, potash. D=RCC.
959	Haute-Corse	Bastia	1,802	4,666	136,764	77.00	105,308	98.70	C	Corse. northern Corsica. Mediterranean Sea. Grapes, olives. Corsu language. D=RCC.
960	Haute-Garonne	Toulouse	2,436	6,309	974,567	67.00	652,960	93.70	C	Midi-Pyrenees. Mountainous. Cereals, cattle, natural gas. Tourism. D=RCC.
961	Haute-Loire	Le Puy	1,922	4,977	214,749	72.00	154,619	98.70	C	Auvergne. Loire River. Cereals, potatoes, lace making. Pilgrimages. D=RCC.
962	Haute-Marne	Chaumont	2,398	6,211	211,216	70.00	147,851	96.70	C	Champagne-Ardennes. Marne River. Forests. Lumbering, cattle, cereals. D=RCC.
963	Haute-Pyrénées	Tarbes	1,724	4,464	233,442	78.00	182,085	99.20	C	Midi-Pyrenees. Mountainous. Sheep, corn, tourism. Pilgrimage (Lourdes). D=RCC.
964	Haute-Savoie	Annecy	1,694	4,388	599,801	75.00	449,851	96.70	C	Rhone-Alpes, bordering Lake Geneva. Dairy, cheese, tourism, sports. D=RCC.
965	Haute-Saône	Vesoul	2,070	5,360	238,115	68.00	161,918	94.70	C	Franche-Comte. Saone River. Forests, pasturelands. Dairy, spas, kirsch. D=RCC.
966	Haute-Vienne	Limoges	2,131	5,520	367,086	72.00	264,302	98.70	C	Limousin. Vienne River, mountainous. Fodder, potatoes, porcelain, leather. D=RCC.
967	Hautes-Alpes	Gap	2,142	5,549	118,591	67.00	79,456	93.70	C	Provence-Alpes-Cote-d'Azur. Durance River. Sheep, tourism. D=RCC.
968	Hauts-de-Seine	Nanterre	68	176	1,446,951	64.00	926,049	94.70	C	Ile-de-France, crescent shape around Paris. Woods, park, suburbs. Industry. D=RCC.
969	Hérault	Montpellier	2,356	6,101	836,456	69.00	577,155	95.70	C	Languedoc-Roussillon. On Mediterranean Sea. Wine, cheese, resorts. D=RCC.
970	Ille-et-Vilaine	Rennes	2,616	6,775	835,109	73.00	609,630	96.70	C	Bretagne. Rance and Vilaine rivers. Sheep raising, market gardening. D=RCC.
971	Indre	Châteauroux	2,622	6,791	246,421	78.00	192,208	99.70	C	Center. Indre River. Woods, lakes. Agriculture, tourism. D=RCC.
972	Indre-et-Loire	Tours	2,366	6,127	552,549	72.00	397,835	98.70	C	Center. Loire River. Orchards, vineyards. Known as 'Garden of France'. D=RCC.
973	Isère	Grenoble	2,869	7,431	1,064,705	67.00	713,352	93.70	C	Rhone-Alpes. Isere River. Winter and summer sports, tourism. D=RCC.
974	Jura	Lons-le-Saunier	1,930	4,999	259,194	69.00	178,844	95.70	C	Franche-Comte. Ognan River. Jura Mountains. Extensive forests. Cheese. D=RCC.
975	Landes	Mont-de-Marsan	3,569	9,243	325,133	74.00	240,598	97.70	C	Aquitaine. Sand dunes and sandy plain. Pate, asparagus. Missile base. D=RCC.
976	Loir-et-Cher	Blois	2,449	6,343	318,900	78.00	248,742	99.20	C	Center. Loire and Cher rivers. Historic chateaus. Vines, fruits, asparagus. D=RCC.
977	Loire	Saint-Étienne	1,846	4,781	775,811	70.00	543,068	96.70	C	Rhone-Alpes. Loire river. Forested mountains. Cereals, cattle. D=RCC.
978	Loire-Atlantique	Nantes	2,631	6,815	1,098,764	67.59	742,670	94.29	C	Pays de la Loire, on Bay of Biscay. Fishing, hunting. Resorts. D=RCC.
979	Loiret	Orléans	2,616	6,775	608,415	70.00	425,891	96.70	C	Center. Loire River. Farming, bee-keeping, vinegar. 9th century basilica. D=RCC.
980	Lot	Cahors	2,014	5,217	162,097	70.00	113,468	96.70	C	Midi-Pyrenees. Lot River. Vegetables, cattle, sheep, tourism. D=RCC.
981	Lot-et-Garonne	Agen	2,070	5,361	318,694	75.00	239,021	98.20	C	Aquitaine. Garonne River. Cereals, cattle, tobacco. D=RCC.
982	Lozère	Mende	1,995	5,167	75,492	69.00	52,089	95.70	C	Languedoc-Roussillon. Mountainous. National park. Sheep, cattle, tourism. D=RCC.
983	Maine-et-Loire	Angers	2,767	7,166	736,145	72.00	530,024	98.70	C	Pays de la Loire, . Loire and Maine rivers. Market gardens, orchards, vineyards. D=RCC.
984	Manche	Saint-Lô	2,293	5,938	499,383	75.00	374,537	98.20	C	Basse-Normandie. On English Channel. Horses, cows, oyster beds. D=RCC.
985	Marne	Châlons-sur-Marne	3,151	8,162	581,108	78.00	453,264	99.20	C	Champagne-Ardennes. Marne River. Woods, chalky plain. Champagne industry. D=RCC.
986	Mayenne	Laval	1,998	5,175	289,414	77.00	222,849	98.70	C	Pays de la Loire. Mayenne River. Wooded, hilly. Cattle-raising. D=RCC.
987	Meurthe-et-Moselle	Nancy	2,024	5,241	738,845	68.00	502,415	94.70	C	Lorraine. Forest, hills. Cereals, brewing, iron, steel. D=RCC.
988	Meuse	Bar-le-Duc	2,400	6,216	203,429	72.00	146,469	98.70	C	Lorraine. Meuse River. Forest. Cattle raising, cereals. D=RCC.
989	Morbihan	Vannes	2,634	6,823	647,047	79.00	511,167	98.70	C	Bretagne. Atlantic Ocean. Agriculture, fishing, oysters. 'Little Sea'. D=RCC.
990	Moselle	Metz	2,400	6,216	1,050,272	70.00	735,190	96.70	C	Lorraine. Moselle River. Heavy industry. Coal fields. D=RCC.
991	Nièvre	Nevers	2,632	6,817	241,541	79.00	190,817	98.70	C	Bourgogne. Forest, hilly plateau. Loire River. Cattle, sheep, cereals, white wine. D=RCC.
992	Nord	Lille	2,217	5,742	2,630,347	65.00	1,709,726	94.22	C	Nord-Pas-de-Calais, bordering Belgium. Productive agriculture and industry. D=RCC.
993	Oise	Beauvais	2,263	5,860	761,378	75.00	571,034	96.70	C	Picardie, north of Paris. Oise River. Cattle, cereals. Picturesque churches. D=RCC.
994	Orne	Alençon	2,356	6,103	304,154	75.00	228,116	98.20	C	Basse-Normandie. Hilly. Sarthe River. Horse and cattle breeding, butter. D=RCC.
995	Paris	Paris	40	105	2,234,914	60.00	1,340,948	95.66	C	North. Seine river. Financial, commercial center. Cathedral of Notre Dame. D=RCC.
996	Pas-de-Calais	Arras	2,576	6,671	1,490,150	75.00	1,117,613	96.70	C	Nord-Pas-de-Calais, on English Channel. Dairy farming, market gardening. D=RCC.
997	Puy-de-Dôme	Clermont-Ferrand	3,077	7,970	621,814	71.00	441,488	97.70	C	Auvergne. Three mountain ranges. Cereals, livestock, fruit. Spas. D=RCC.
998	Pyrénées-Atlantiques	Pau	2,952	7,645	603,641	74.00	446,694	97.20	C	Aquitaine. Pyrenees mountains. Sheep, cattle, natural gas. Tourism. D=RCC.
999	Pyrénées-Orientales	Perpignan	1,589	4,116	381,206	75.00	285,905	98.20	C	Languedoc-Roussillon. On Mediterranean Sea. Apricots, peaches, wines, tourism. D=RCC.
1000	Rhône	Lyon	1,254	3,249	1,574,781	65.00	1,023,608	91.70	C	Rhone-Alpes. Rhone River. Cereals, sugar beets, wines. Silk center. D=RCC.
1001	Sarthe	Le Mans	2,396	6,206	534,376	72.00	384,751	98.70	C	Pays de la Loire. Sarthe River. Cattle, cereals. Le Mans race track. D=RCC.
1002	Savoie	Chambéry	2,327	6,028	364,906	73.00	266,381	99.70	C	Rhone-Alpes. Rhone River. Forested mountains. Cattle, thermal springs. D=RCC.
1003	Saône-et-Loire	Mâcon	3,311	8,575	579,962	80.00	463,970	99.70	C	Bourgogne. Saone and Loire rivers. Cattle, cereals, wines. Coal mining. D=RCC.
1004	Seine-et-Marne	Melun	2,284	5,915	1,144,457	63.00	721,008	94.70	C	Ile-de-France. Outer suburbs of Paris. Marne and Seine rivers. Fruits, dairy. D=RCC.
1005	Seine-Maritime	Rouen	2,424	6,278	1,273,327	68.00	865,862	94.70	C	Haute-Normandie, on English Channel. Seine River. Dairy, cereal, petroleum. D=RCC.
1006	Seine-Saint-Denis	Bobigny	91	236	1,441,344	62.00	893,633	93.70	C	Ile-de-France, bordering Paris. Seine and Saint Denis rivers. Airports. D=RCC.
1007	Somme	Amiens	2,382	6,170	569,375	72.00	409,950	98.70	C	Picardie, on English Channel. Somme River. Cattle, market gardens, resorts. D=RCC.
1008	Tarn	Albi	2,223	5,758	356,599	78.00	278,147	99.20	C	Midi-Pyrenees. Tarn River plateau. Cereal, fruit, sparkling wine. D=RCC.
1009	Tarn-et-Garonne	Montauban	1,435	3,718	209,142	68.00	142,217	94.70	C	Midi-Pyrenees. Tarn River. Wheat, corn, cattle, vineyards. Ancient abbey. D=RCC.
1010	Territoire de Belfort	Belfort	235	609	139,564	78.00	108,860	99.20	C	Franche-Comte, bordering Switzerland, . Vosges Mountains. Strategic passageway. D=RCC.
1011	Val-d'Oise	Pontoise	481	1,246	1,105,824	63.00	696,669	94.70	C	Ile-de-France, outer suburbs of Paris. Oise River. Mushrooms, tourism. D=RCC.
1012	Val-de-Marne	Créteil	95	245	1,266,161	64.00	810,343	95.70	C	Ile-de-France, bordering Paris. Marne and Seine rivers. Residential, truck farms. D=RCC.
1013	Var	Toulon	2,306	5,973	860,136	68.00	584,892	94.70	C	Provence-Alpes-Cote-d'Azur. Mediterranean Sea. Seaside resorts. D=RCC.
1014	Vaucluse	Avignon	1,377	3,567	489,930	71.00	347,850	97.70	C	Provence-Alpes-Cote-d'Azur. Rhone River. Melons, vineyards, tourism. D=RCC.
1015	Vendée	La Roche-sur-Yon	2,595	6,720	531,676	68.00	361,540	94.70	C	Pays de la Loire. Atlantic Ocean. Fodder, apples. Seaside resorts. D=RCC.
1016	Vienne	Poitiers	2,699	6,990	395,539	73.00	288,743	99.70	C	Poitou-Charentes. Vienne River. Cereals, fruit, tobacco. D=RCC.
1017	Vosges	Epinal	2,268	5,874	400,005	78.00	312,004	99.20	C	Lorraine. Meuse and Moselle rivers. Heavily-wooded. Cereals, cattle. D=RCC.
1018	Yonne	Auxerre	2,868	7,427	337,073	75.00	252,805	98.20	C	Bourgogne. Yonne River. Woods and heath. Cereal, fodder, wines. D=RCC.
1019	Yvelines	Versailles	882	2,284	1,370,732	61.00	836,147	94.70	C	Ile-de-France, outer suburbs of Paris. Seine River, extensive forest. Residential. D=RCC.
	FRENCH GUIANA		**33,399**	**86,504**	**181,313**	**84.24**	**152,736**	**98.76**	**C**	**Roman Catholics 79.9%, Protestants 3.8%. Pent-char 5.7%, Evangelical 1.9%, GCC 13.1%**
1020	Cayenne	Cayenne	17,600	45,600	90,974	83.88	76,309	98.50	C	Hinterland and tropical coastal strip. Timber, rosewood essence, rum, sugarcane. D=RCC,JWs.
1021	Saint-Laurent-du Marconi	Saint-Laurent	15,800	40,900	90,339	84.60	76,427	99.03	C	Northwest. Formerly penal colonies. Maroni River. Sawmilling, boat repair. D=RCC,JWs.
	FRENCH POLYNESIA		**1,544**	**4,000**	**235,061**	**84.54**	**198,725**	**98.64**	**C**	**Protestants 46.8%, Roman Catholics 42.5%. Pent-char 10.5%, Evangelical 2.6%, GCC 13.7%**
1022	Archipelago Tuamotu	Rikitea	266	698	15,390	87.00	13,389	99.60	C	Two parallel ranges of 78 atolls. Sites of French nuclear testing, since 1966. Fisheries. D=EEPF.
1023	Iles Australes	Mataura	57	148	8,096	87.00	7,044	99.60	C	Southernmost. Tubuai Islands. Volcanic origin. Fish, coffee. Mainly Protestant. D=EEPF.
1024	Iles du Vent	Papeete	461	1,194	174,549	83.95	146,539	98.38	C	Windward Group. Coconuts, copra, tourism. D=EEPF,RCC.
1025	Iles Marquises	Taiohae	405	1,049	9,375	88.00	8,250	99.70	C	Pair of volcanic clusters. Copra, taros, breadfruit. Mainly Roman Catholic. D=RCC.
1026	Iles sous le Vent	Uturoa	156	404	27,651	85.00	23,503	99.10	C	Society Islands. Windward and Leeward Islands. Tahiti. D=RCC.
	GABON		**103,347**	**267,667**	**1,226,127**	**88.55**	**1,085,756**	**98.09**	**C**	**Roman Catholics 60.7%, Protestants 19.0%. Pent-char 7.3%, Evangelical 4.6%, GCC 8.3%**
1027	Estuaire	Libreville	8,008	20,740	338,860	85.94	291,208	97.61	C	West on Gulf of Guinea. Logging, hydroelectric power. D=EEG,RCC.
1028	Haut-Ogooué	Franceville	14,111	36,547	201,051	88.00	176,925	97.54	C	Ogooue River. Lumber, coffee, trade center. D=RCC,EEG.
1029	Moyen-Ogooué	Lambaréné	7,156	18,535	46,251	86.00	39,776	95.54	C	West-central. Lumber, rubber. Albert Schweitzer hospital (1913). D=RCC,EEG.
1030	Ngounié	Mouila	14,575	37,750	111,380	90.00	100,242	98.54	C	Southwest. Ngounie River. Cassava, bananas, coffee, diamonds. D=RCC,EEG.
1031	Nyanga	Tchibanga	8,218	21,285	92,502	88.00	81,402	97.54	C	Southwest. Nyanga River. Rice, peanuts, palm oil, lumber. D=RCC,EEG.
1032	Ogooué-Ivindo	Makokou	17,790	46,075	50,027	87.00	43,523	96.54	C	Northeast. Ivindo River. Major lumbering region. Pygmies. D=RCC,EEG.
1033	Ogooué-Lolo	Koulamoutou	9,799	25,380	46,251	90.00	41,626	98.54	C	South. Ogooue River. Timber, minerals, cassava, livestock, cocoa, coffee. D=RCC,EEG.
1034	Ogooué-Maritime	Port-Gentil	8,838	22,890	183,117	92.00	168,468	99.44	C	West. Lopez Island. Oil, petroleum. Port Gentil damaged in riots (1990). D=RCC,EEG.
1035	Woleu-Ntem	Oyem	14,851	38,465	156,688	91.00	142,586	99.34	C	North. Cameroon and Congo border. Woleu-Ntem River. Timber, livestock. D=RCC,EEG.
	GAMBIA		**4,127**	**10,689**	**1,305,363**	**3.62**	**47,198**	**44.07**	**A**	**Roman Catholics 2.3%, Independents 0.6%. Pent-char 0.8%, Evangelical 0.09%, GCC 2.3%**
1036	Banjul	–	5	12	83,861	6.60	5,535	51.05	B	On St Mary's Island. 30% Mandinka, 90% Muslim. Peanuts. F=1816. D=RCC.
1037	Kombo St. Mary	Kanifing	29	76	192,638	6.00	11,558	50.00	A	St Mary's Island near mouth of Gambia River. Peanuts, oil, tourism. Wolof, Aku. D=RCC.
1038	Lower River	Mansakonko	625	1,618	104,880	3.00	3,146	43.45	A	Central. Gambia River. Livestock, groundnuts, fisheries, minerals. D=RCC.
1039	MacCarthy Island	Kuntaur/Georgetown	1,117	2,894	239,135	2.50	5,978	40.95	A	Jangjangbure or Lemain Island. Gambia River. Peanuts. Malinke. D=RCC.
1040	North Bank	Kerewan	871	2,256	212,984	3.20	6,815	43.65	A	Gambia River. Mandinka villages. Schools, meteorological station. Minerals, livestock. D=RCC.
1041	Upper River	Basse	799	2,069	211,396	1.00	2,114	36.45	A	East on Gambia River. Peanuts, rice, cattle. Fulani, Malinke, Wolof. D=RCC,NAC.
1042	Western	Brikama	681	1,764	260,468	4.63	12,052	47.08	A	West. Agricultural trade center. Peanuts, palm oil. Forestry. Malinke, Dyola. D=RCC.
	GEORGIA		**26,900**	**69,700**	**4,967,561**	**60.57**	**3,008,814**	**88.61**	**C**	**Orthodox 58.1%, Roman Catholics 1.1%. Pent-char 0.6%, Evangelical 0.1%, GCC 14.9%**
1043	Abkhazia	Sokhumi (Sukhumi)	3,343	8,660	474,755	59.50	282,479	87.55	B	Black Sea, Caucasus Mountains. Tobacco, tea, silk. Georgians 46%, Abkhaz 18%. D=GOC.
1044	Adzharia Ajaria	Bat'umi	1,120	2,900	355,377	61.00	216,780	89.04	C	Southwest on Black Sea. Mountainous. Tea, citrus fruits, avocados. Georgians, Russians. D=GOC.
1045	Guria	–	785	2,033	147,775	61.00	90,143	89.04	C	West, on Black Sea. Political independence in 16th century. Tea, citrus fruits, tung oil. D=GOC.
1046	Imereti	–	2,452	6,349	725,001	61.00	442,251	89.04	C	Turkish invasion (1510). D=GOC.
1047	Kakheti	–	4,717	12,217	426,416	62.00	264,378	90.04	C	East, became part of Georgia in 1010 AD. D=GOC.
1048	Kvemo Kartli	–	2,615	6,772	552,778	61.75	341,321	89.79	C	Kura River. D=GOC.
1049	Racha-Lechkumi	–	1,245	3,224	41,723	61.00	25,451	89.04	C	South. Racha Mountains. Lachkumi Range. Tkibuli coal deposits. D=GOC.
1050	Samegrelo (Mingrelia)	–	1,697	4,395	384,142	60.00	230,485	88.04	C	West. Lowlands. Black Sea. Tea, grapes. D=GOC.
1051	Samtskhe-Javakheti	–	2,017	5,224	182,697	58.00	105,964	86.04	B	Southwest. Mountainous. Tea, citrus fruits. Georgians, Russians. D=GOC.
1052	Shida Kartli	–	3,043	7,882	446,542	61.00	272,391	89.04	C	Kura River. Hilly, central region. Grain, orchards. 'Heart of Georgia'. D=GOC.
1053	Svaneti	–	1,694	4,389	21,321	57.00	12,153	85.04	B	South. Mountainous region. Difficult access. Svan people. D=GOC.
1054	T'bilisi	–	534	1,384	1,168,784	60.00	701,270	88.04	C	Southeast. Kura River. Machine building. 1989 massacre of civilians. D=GOC.
1055	Tianeti	–	1,569	4,063	40,251	59.00	23,748	87.04	B	Northeast. Iora River. Parquet, lemonade, creamery. D=GOC.
	GERMANY		**137,828**	**356,974**	**82,220,490**	**71.49**	**58,783,222**	**97.64**	**C**	**Protestants 37.0%, Roman Catholics 34.9%. Pent-char 3.1%, Evangelical 1.6%, GCC 31.8%**
1056	Baden-Württemberg	Stuttgart	13,804	35,751	10,344,924	73.00	7,551,795	99.15	C	Southwest, bordering France. Danube River. Forests, meadows, lakes. Cattle, cheese. D=EKD,RCC.
1057	Bayern	Munich	27,241	70,554	11,991,998	72.00	8,634,239	98.15	C	Southeast bordering Austria. Bavaria. Mountains. Industrial and handcrafts products. D=RCC,EKD.
1058	Berlin	–	343	889	3,513,101	66.00	2,318,647	92.54	C	Capital of Germany, 1871-1945. Manufacturing and trade center. F=1237. D=EKD,RCC.
1059	Brandenburg	Potsdam	11,219	29,056	2,565,230	68.00	1,744,356	94.15	C	Recreated from East and West Germany in 1990. Sandy plain, lakes. Barley. D=EKD,RCC.
1060	Bremen	Bremen	156	404	690,512	71.00	490,264	97.15	C	Site of international conferences. Banking, insurance, cotton, tobacco. D=EKD,RCC.
1061	Hamburg	Hamburg	292	755	1,721,376	70.00	1,204,963	96.15	C	North on North Sea. Elbe River. Economic center of Germany. Major port. D=EKD,RCC.
1062	Hessen	Wiesbaden	8,152	21,114	6,032,032	73.50	4,433,544	99.65	C	West-central. Wooded uplands. Vogels mountains. Wheat, poultry. D=Protestant,RCC.
1063	Mecklenburg-Vorpommern	Schwerin	9,096	23,559	1,863,503	69.00	1,285,817	95.15	C	Northeast on Baltic Sea. Recreated from East and West Germany in 1990. Rye, wheat. D=EKD,RCC.
1064	Niedersachsen	Hannover	18,282	47,351	7,730,971	70.22	5,428,672	96.37	C	Lower Saxony. Sandy lowlands. Forests. Wheat, rye. 80% Protestant. D=EKD,RCC.
1065	Nordrhein-Westfalen	Düsseldorf	13,155	34,070	17,951,964	72.00	12,925,414	98.15	C	West, bordering Netherlands. Part of Rhine-Ruhr region. Heavy industry, wheat. D=EKD,RCC.

Continued overleaf

Table 11-3 continued

Rec No 1	Country Major civil divisions 2	Capital 3	sq.mi. 4	sq.km. 5	Pop 2000 6	AC% 7	Church members 8	E% 9	W 10	Notes 11
1066	Rheinland-Pfalz	Mainz	7,664	19,849	3,968,487	74.00	2,936,680	99.65	C	Southwest, bordering France. Woodlands. Manufacturing, services, wines, Stone Age. D=EKD,RCC.
1067	Saarland	Saarbrücken	992	2,570	1,096,262	72.00	789,309	98.15	C	Southwest, bordering France. Saar River. Thickly forested hills. Industry, mining. D=RCC,EKD.
1068	Sachsen	Dresden	7,081	18,341	4,657,684	69.00	3,213,802	95.15	C	East. Recreated from East and West Germany in 1990. Elbe River. Wheat, cattle. D=EKD,RCC.
1069	Sachsen-Anhalt	Magdeburg	7,956	20,607	2,808,035	71.00	1,993,705	97.15	C	East-central. Recreated from East and West Germany in 1990. Elbe River. Alfalfa. D=EKD,RCC.
1070	Schleswig Holstein	Kiel	6,074	15,731	2,724,137	73.00	1,988,620	99.15	C	Northwest on Baltic Sea. Shipbuilding, wheat, cattle, tourism. Mainly Protestant. D=EKD,RCC.
1071	Thüringen	Erfurt	6,275	16,251	2,560,272	72.00	1,843,396	98.15	C	Southwest. Recreated from East and West Germany in 1990. Forests. Glass. D=EKD,RCC.
	GHANA		**92,098**	**238,533**	**20,212,495**	**42.88**	**8,666,976**	**84.63**	**B**	**Protestants 16.6%, Independents 14.4%. Pent-char 22.1%, Evangelical 7.3%, GCC 19.4%**
1072	Ashanti	Kumasi	9,417	24,389	3,436,013	54.26	1,864,374	95.01	B	Former Ashanti empire. Plantains, bananas, cassava. Traditional religions. D=RCC,Presbyterian.
1073	Brong-Ahafo	Sunyani	15,273	39,557	1,983,214	27.00	535,468	71.16	B	Former Akan state. Gold-mining. Forests. Cocoa, Kola nuts. D=RCC,Independents.
1074	Central	Cape Coast	3,794	9,826	1,879,006	52.00	977,083	96.25	B	On Gulf of Guinea. fishing, trade, government, education. Anglicans (1865). D=RCC,Presbyterian.
1075	Eastern	Koforidua	7,461	19,323	2,762,684	48.00	1,326,088	92.25	B	Densu River. Cocoa production, granite. Accra-Kumasi railway (1923). D=RCC,Independents.
1076	Greater Accra	Accra	1,253	3,245	2,352,108	56.00	1,317,180	96.75	B	Gulf of Guinea. Portuguese settled in 1482. Administrative, economic, educational center. D=RCC.
1077	Northern	Tamale	27,175	70,384	1,914,289	16.00	306,286	55.75	B	North. White Volta River. Cotton milling, shea nuts. Education center. Muslims. D=RCC.
1078	Upper East	Bolgatanga	3,414	8,842	1,270,139	12.00	152,417	50.75	B	North. Great North Road. Staple crops, stock raising, basketry. D=RCC.
1079	Upper West	Wa	7,134	18,476	719,925	9.00	64,793	46.75	A	Northeast. Volta River. Wa Plateau. Grains, yams, stock-raising. D=RCC.
1080	Volta	Ho	7,942	20,570	1,992,146	55.00	1,095,680	96.75	B	Southeast. Volta River. Akwapim-Togo Range. Kola nuts, cocoa. D=RCC,Independents.
1081	Western	Sekondi-Takoradi	9,236	23,921	1,902,974	54.00	1,027,606	95.75	B	South on Gulf of Guinea. Fishing, bauxite, oil. Dutch and British origins. D=RCC,Presbyterian.
	GIBRALTAR		**2**	**6**	**25,082**	**85.19**	**21,368**	**94.58**	**C**	**Roman Catholics 84.5%, Anglicans 7.5%. Pent-char 15.5%, Evangelical 1.3%, GCC 9.1%**
1082	Gibraltar	Gibraltar	2	6	25,082	85.19	21,368	94.58	C	South of Spain in Mediterranean. British possession since 1704. Military installations. D=RCC.
	GREECE		**50,949**	**131,957**	**10,644,744**	**94.52**	**10,061,020**	**98.44**	**C**	**Orthodox 93.0%, Independents 2.1%. Pent-char 1.1%, Evangelical 0.1%, GCC 2.4%**
1083	Anatolik Makedhonia	Eastern Macedonia	5,466	14,157	591,407	96.00	567,751	99.92	C	Southeastern Balkans. Turkish tobacco, corn, rice, wine. Muslim minority. D=GOC.
1084	Attikí	Attica	1,470	3,808	3,653,391	92.00	3,361,120	96.48	C	East-central. Mediterranean Sea. Isthmus of Corinth. D=GOC.
1085	Dhytikí Ellás	Western Greece	4,382	11,350	728,058	97.00	706,216	99.92	C	Isolated by Pindus Mountains. Ionian Islands. Agriculture. D=GOC.
1086	Dhytikí Makedhonía	Western Macedonia	3,649	9,451	303,606	96.50	292,980	99.82	C	North central, bordered by Thessaly to the south. Central Macedonia to the East. D=Greek Orthodox.
1087	Iónioi Nísoi	Ionian Islands	891	2,307	198,085	97.50	193,133	99.92	C	Off western coast. Fertile lowlands. D=Greek Orthodox.
1088	Kedrikí Makedhonía	Central Macedonia	7,393	19,147	1,802,053	94.70	1,706,544	98.62	C	Balkans on NW shore of Aegean Sea, divided into 7 prefectures. D=Greek Orthodox.
1089	Kriti	Crete	3,218	8,336	556,890	96.00	534,614	99.92	C	Fifth largest island in Mediterranean Sea. Mountainous. Olives, olive oil. D=Greek Orthodox.
1090	Nótion Aiyaíon	Southern Aegean	2,041	5,286	267,070	96.50	257,723	99.82	C	Numerous islands. Wheat, wine, oil, tourism. Fishing. D=Greek Orthodox.
1091	Pelopónnisos	Peloponnesos	5,981	15,490	628,121	95.00	596,715	99.82	C	Peninsula south of Gulf of Corinth. Fertile coastal plain. D=Greek Orthodox.
1092	Watereá Ellás	Central Greece	6,004	15,549	600,340	96.46	579,075	99.88	C	Pindus mountains, between the Gulf of Corinth and Aegean Sea, divided in 5 prefectures. D=GOC.
1093	Thessalía	Thessaly	5,420	14,037	758,343	96.00	728,009	99.92	C	Trikala and Larissa lowlands. Ancient settlements. Horse breeding. D=Greek Orthodox.
1094	Vóreion Aiyaíon	Northern Aegean	1,481	3,836	205,592	97.00	199,424	99.42	C	Numerous islands. Wheat, wine, oil, tourism. Fishing. D=Greek Orthodox.
1095	Ípiros	Epirus	3,553	9,203	351,787	96.00	337,716	99.92	C	Gulf of Arta. Great limestone ridges. Sheep, goats, corn. Ancient oracles. D=GOC.
	GREENLAND		**840,000**	**2,175,600**	**56,156**	**70.07**	**39,350**	**99.70**	**C**	**Protestants 69.2%, Marginal Christians 0.4%. Pent-char 9.9%, Evangelical 3.7%, GCC 22.1%**
1096	East	–	–	–	2,650	75.00	1,988	99.88	C	Greenland Sea. Hunting. Seals, foxes, polar bears, large ice flows. D=Lutheran.
1097	North	Thule	41,200	106,700	608	74.00	450	99.83	C	North Peninsula (Peary land). Hunting. Seals, foxes, polar bears. D=Lutheran.
1098	Qaqortoq (Julianeha)	–	–	–	562	72.00	405	99.73	C	East Settlement, founded AD 986 by Eric the Red. D=Lutheran.
1099	Upernavik	–	–	–	449	73.00	328	99.78	C	Island in Baffin Bay. Whaling, sealing. Graphite. D=Lutheran.
1100	Uummannaq (Umana)	–	–	–	562	74.00	416	99.83	C	West. Baffin Bay. Hunting and fishing base. D=Lutheran.
1101	West	–	–	–	51,325	69.68	35,763	99.69	C	Disko Island. Fishing, cod, halibut, world's largest shrimp beds. D=Lutheran,Pentecostal.
	GRENADA		**133**	**344**	**93,717**	**96.83**	**90,745**	**99.97**	**C**	**Roman Catholics 56.2%, Protestants 20.3%. Pent-char 15.1%, Evangelical 10.7%, GCC 6.8%**
1102	Carriacou	Hillsborough	14	37	4,748	98.00	4,653	99.98	C	Sea Island. Cotton, resorts, hotels, yachting marinas. Airstrip. D=RCC.
1103	Petite Martinique	–	–	–	744	99.00	737	99.99	C	Northernmost island. Reefs. Cocoa, nutmeg, bananas, tourism. D=RCC.
1104	St. Andrew	Grenville	35	91	24,316	96.00	23,343	99.97	C	Eastern coast of main island. Marquis, cocoa, bananas. D=RCC,Anglican.
1105	St. David	–	18	47	11,060	96.83	10,709	99.97	C	Southeast. City of Corinth. Bananas, nutmeg, mace, cocoa. D=RCC.
1106	St. George's	–	25	65	25,544	97.00	24,778	99.97	C	On southwest coast. Picturesque pastel-colored houses. Yachting center. D=RCC,Anglican.
1107	St. George's	–	–	–	4,587	94.00	4,312	99.96	C	Capital city. Medical school, university. Tourism, fruits, port, fishing. D=RCC.
1108	St. John	Gouyave	15	39	8,832	98.00	8,655	99.98	C	Western coast. Port, fishing, tourism, fruits, crafts. D=RCC.
1109	St. Mark	Victoria	9	23	3,911	98.00	3,833	99.98	C	Northwestern. Nutmeg, bananas, other fruits, tourism. D=RCC.
1110	St. Patrick	Sauteurs	17	44	9,974	97.50	9,725	99.98	C	North tip. Tivoli, Laurant Point. Fishing, tourism, fruits, crafts. D=RCC,Anglican.
	GUADELOUPE		**687**	**1,780**	**455,687**	**95.01**	**432,948**	**99.90**	**C**	**Roman Catholics 95.0%, Protestants 4.9%. Pent-char 5.0%, Evangelical 3.0%, GCC 14.4%**
1111	Basse-Terre	Basse-Terre	332	861	183,128	95.30	174,521	99.95	C	Island. Soufriere Peak (4,868 ft.). Damaged by hurricanes (1979). F=1643. D=RCC.
1112	Pointe-à-Pitre	Pointe-à-Pitre	297	769	232,126	94.43	219,207	99.85	C	Grand-Terre island. Salee River. Handles most imports. D=RCC.
1113	Saint-Martin	Marigot	29	75	40,433	97.00	39,220	99.99	C	Creole, whites. D=RCC.
	GUAM		**571**	**1,478**	**167,556**	**93.49**	**156,656**	**98.98**	**C**	**Roman Catholics 83.2%, Protestants 10.4%. Pent-char 5.9%, Evangelical 5.0%, GCC 10.1%**
1114	Guam	Agana	571	1,478	167,556	93.49	156,656	98.98	C	West Pacific. University of Guam (1952). Reefs. U.S. military facilities, bananas. D=RCC.
	GUATEMALA		**42,042**	**108,889**	**11,385,295**	**93.84**	**10,684,153**	**99.93**	**C**	**Roman Catholics 84.3%, Protestants 12.7%. Pent-char 21.8%, Evangelical 10.3%, GCC 8.5%**
1115	Alta Verapaz	Cobán	3,354	8,686	713,538	94.96	677,567	99.93	C	North-central. Coffee, tea, cacao. Mayan ruins. August fiesta. 17th century church. D=RCC.
1116	Baja Verapaz	Salamá	1,206	3,124	221,417	95.00	210,346	99.95	C	Central. Chuacus and Minas mountains. Salama River. Agriculture. Earthquake (1976). D=RCC.
1117	Chimaltenango	Chimaltenango	764	1,979	413,458	94.00	388,651	99.94	C	Southwest. Mayan Indians. Coffee, sugarcane. 14,000 killed in earthquake (1976). D=RCC.
1118	Chiquimula	Chiquimula	917	2,376	300,685	94.00	282,644	99.94	C	Southeast. San Jose River. Corn, wheat, coffee, sugarcane. Earthquakes (1765,1773). D=RCC.
1119	El Progreso	Guastatoya	742	1,922	129,323	96.00	124,150	99.97	C	Central. Motagua River. Railroad, primary road. Bananas, livestock, coffee. D=RCC.
1120	Escuintla	Escuintla	1,693	4,384	652,529	94.00	613,377	99.94	C	Southwest. Guacalate River. Sugarcane, coffee, cotton. Popular winter resort. D=RCC.
1121	Guatemala	Guatemala City	821	2,126	2,423,731	92.50	2,241,951	99.90	C	Central. Kaminaljuyu ruins, Amatitlan Lake, capital city. Airport, major trade, university. D=RCC.
1122	Huehuetenango	Huehuetenango	2,857	7,400	865,025	95.00	821,774	99.95	C	West-central. Altos Cuchumatanes. Mayan Indians. Pottery, mining. 'Place of the Ancients'. D=RCC.
1123	Izabal	Puerto Barrios	3,490	9,038	393,706	96.00	377,958	99.97	C	Northeast. Lake Izabal, Gulf of Honduras, San Felipe Castle. Nickel mining. D=RCC.
1124	Jalapa	Jalapa	797	2,063	228,824	94.00	215,095	99.94	C	Southeast. Motagua and Ostva rivers. Amerindians. Corn, wheat, cheese, lumber. D=RCC.
1125	Jutiapa	Jutiapa	1,243	3,219	423,199	95.00	402,039	99.95	C	Southeast. Paz River, Pacific coast. Marsh, hot climate. Agriculture, rice, coffee. D=RCC.
1126	Petén	Flores	13,843	35,854	311,712	92.00	286,775	99.86	C	North, bordering Mexico. Limestone plateau. Tropical rain forest. Mayan ruins. D=RCC.
1127	Quetzaltenango	Quetzaltenango	753	1,951	670,234	94.00	630,020	99.94	C	Southwest, over 7,000 ft. Textiles, breweries. Education center. D=RCC.
1128	Quiché	Santa Cruz	3,235	8,378	693,026	93.00	644,514	99.93	C	Northwest, bordering Mexico. Mayan Indians. Livestock, corn, beans. D=RCC.
1129	Retalhuleu	Retalhuleu	717	1,856	287,497	94.00	270,247	99.94	C	Southwest on Pacific Ocean. Coffee, sugarcane, livestock, bees. D=RCC.
1130	Sacatepéquez	Antigua Guatemala	180	465	216,718	93.00	201,548	99.93	C	Southwest. Central highlands, volcanos. Chief coffee producing area. D=RCC.
1131	San Marcos	San Marcos	1,464	3,791	844,816	94.00	794,127	99.94	C	Southwest. Tajumulco volcano (13,845 ft.), highest peak in Central America. D=RCC.
1132	Santa Rosa	Cuilapa	1,141	2,955	319,570	94.00	300,396	99.94	C	South, on Pacific Ocean. Lake Ayarza. Corn, beans, coffee, sugarcane. D=RCC.
1133	Sololá	Sololá	410	1,061	291,812	95.00	277,221	99.95	C	Southwest. Central highlands. Lake Atitlan. Known for Friday markets. 16th century church. D=RCC.
1134	Suchitepéquez	Mazatenango	969	2,510	434,313	94.00	408,254	99.94	C	Southwest. Sis River. Cotton, coffee, sugarcane, rubber. D=RCC.
1135	Totonicapán	Totonicapán	410	1,061	357,688	93.00	332,650	99.93	C	West-central. Largely Mayan Indian. Corn, wheat, beans, flour-milling. D=RCC.
1136	Zacapa	Zacapa	1,039	2,690	192,473	95.00	182,849	99.95	C	East. San Jose and Motagua rivers. Sugarcane, corn, beans, cheese, cigars. D=RCC.
	GUINEA		**94,926**	**245,857**	**7,430,346**	**3.11**	**231,322**	**41.63**	**A**	**Roman Catholics 1.5%, Protestants 0.9%. Pent-char 0.8%, Evangelical 0.7%, GCC 2.2%**
1137	Beyla	Beyla	6,738	17,452	207,379	3.00	6,221	41.52	A	Southeast, bordering Ivory Coast. Guinea highlands. Rice, cattle, diamonds. Malinke. D=RCC.
1138	Boffa	Boffa	1,932	5,003	182,152	5.00	9,108	47.52	A	West, on Atlantic Ocean. Fish, bananas. Baga, Susu peoples. Holy Ghost Fathers (1877). D=RCC.
1139	Boké	Boké	3,881	10,053	289,459	3.20	9,263	41.72	A	West, on Atlantic Ocean. Nunez River. Bauxite, rice, fish. Landuma, Fulani, Nalu.
1140	Conakry	Conakry	119	308	906,498	8.76	79,405	51.54	B	West, on Tombo Island and Kaloum Peninsula. Commercial and education center. D=RCC,NAC.
1141	Coyah (Dubréka)	Coyah	2,153	5,576	172,475	4.50	7,761	47.02	A	West, on Atlantic Ocean. Railroad, primary roads, trade. Fruit, livestock, minerals. D=RCC.
1142	Dabola	Dabola	2,317	6,000	125,941	2.20	2,771	40.72	A	Central on Bouka River. Rice, peanuts, millet. Fulani and Malinke peoples. D=RCC.
1143	Dalaba	Dalaba	1,313	3,400	170,691	2.70	4,609	43.22	A	Central. Mount Kavendou. Coffee, bauxite, iron ore, diamonds, livestock, bananas. D=RCC.
1144	Dinguiraye	Dinguiraye	4,247	11,000	171,590	1.20	2,059	39.72	A	North-central. Fouta Djallon plateau. Rice, millet. Tukalor, Fulani, Dialonke. D=RCC.
1145	Faranah	Faranah	4,788	12,400	183,699	0.70	1,286	34.22	A	Central. Niger River. Rice, cattle, palm oil. Dialonke. RC mission (1948). D=RCC.
1146	Forécariah	Forécariah	1,647	4,265	149,691	4.00	5,988	46.52	A	West on Atlantic Ocean. Primary roads. Fishing, rice, pineapples, cassava, palm products. D=RCC.
1147	Fria	Fria	840	2,175	90,502	4.00	3,620	46.52	A	West. Konkoure River. Amaria Dam. Bauxite. Susu. RC mission (1959). D=RCC.
1148	Gaoual	Gaoual	4,440	11,500	174,360	0.80	1,395	34.32	A	Northwest. Fouta Djallon plateau. Tomine River. Cattle, peanuts. Fulani, Landuma, Tyapi. D=RCC.
1149	Guéckédou	Guéckédou	1,605	4,157	263,175	2.80	7,369	43.32	A	South. Guinea Highlands. Rice, coffee, kola nuts. Kissi. RC mission (1951). D=RCC.
1150	Kankan	Kankan	7,104	18,400	295,441	1.60	4,727	40.12	A	East. Milo River. Commercial center for savanna region. Malinke, Diula. D=RCC.
1151	Kindia	Kindia	3,409	8,828	277,692	3.00	8,331	43.52	A	West. Rice, cattle, bananas. Pasteur Institute (1925). Susu, Fulani. RC mission (1908). D=RCC.
1152	Kissidougou	Kissidougou	3,425	8,872	235,514	3.00	7,065	41.52	A	Southeast. Rice, cassava, livestock, coffee. Diamond mining. Kissi. RC mission. D=RCC.
1153	Koubia	Koubia	571	1,480	126,028	1.20	1,512	39.72	A	Central. Plains, cattle and other livestock, minerals, palm oil, corn, peanuts. D=RCC.
1154	Koundara	Koundara	2,124	5,500	121,096	0.30	363	31.82	A	Northwest. Cattle, chickens, rice. Konyagi, Bassari, Badiaranke, Fulani. D=RCC.
1155	Kouroussa	Kouroussa	4,647	12,035	175,991	0.50	880	34.02	A	East-central. Niger River. Savanna. Rice, onions, millet. Malinke, Dialonke. D=RCC.
1156	Kérouané	Kérouané	3,070	7,950	137,363	1.20	1,648	39.72	A	Southeast. Rice, millet, cattle. Alluvial diamonds iron ore. Malinke. D=RCC.
1157	Labé	Labé	973	2,520	325,457	5.00	16,273	43.52	A	West-central. Fouta Djallon plateau. Cattle, rice, oranges. Fulani. RC mission. D=RCC.
1158	Lola	Lola	1,629	4,219	137,082	3.50	4,798	46.02	A	Nimba Range, southeastern tip. Primary road. Cassava, pepper, coffee. Kpelle. D=RCC.
1159	Lélouma	Lélouma	830	2,150	177,972	0.60	1,068	34.12	A	North. Chutes de la Sala. Fouta Djallon plateau. D=RCC.
1160	Macenta	Macenta	3,363	8,710	248,203	2.60	6,453	43.12	A	Southeast. Guinea Highlands. Tea, coffee, rice. Loma, Malinke. D=RCC.
1161	Mali	Mali	3,398	8,800	271,056	0.50	1,355	34.02	A	North. Fouta Djallon plateau. Tantou River. Cattle, rice, millet. Fulani, Dialonke. D=RCC.
1162	Mamou	Mamou	2,378	6,160	244,882	3.00	7,346	43.52	A	West-central. Chief trading center for rice, cattle. Fulani, Dialonke, Limba RC mission (1948). D=RCC.
1163	Mandiana	Mandiana	5,000	12,950	175,208	0.70	1,226	34.22	A	East, bordering Mali. Sankaroni River. Secondary roads. Rice, cattle, peanuts. D=RCC.
1164	Nzérékoré	Nzérékoré	1,460	3,781	278,081	5.00	13,904	47.52	A	Southeast. Guinea Highlands. Rice, cassava, pepper. Kpelle, Mano, Kono. RC mission. D=RCC.
1165	Pita	Pita	1,544	4,000	292,935	0.60	1,758	34.12	A	Central. Fouta Djalon. Secondary roads. Minerals, livestock, coffee, corn, peanuts. D=RCC.
1166	Siguiri	Siguiri	7,626	19,750	268,839	0.30	807	31.82	A	Northeast. Niger River. Savanna. Cattle, corn. Malinke, Diula, Dialonke. RC mission (1924). D=RCC.
1167	Tougué	Tougué	2,394	6,200	145,589	0.60	874	34.12	A	North-central. Fouta Djallon plateau. Rice, millet, oranges, bauxite. Fulani. D=RCC.
1168	Télimélé	Télimélé	3,119	8,080	312,657	2.00	6,253	40.52	A	West. Fouta Djallon plateau. Cattle, rice, millet, livestock. Fulani. D=RCC.
1169	Yomou	Yomou	843	2,183	95,649	4.00	3,826	46.52	A	Southeast, bordering Liberia. Guinea Highlands. Rice, cassava, coffee. Kpelle, Mano. D=RCC.

Continued opposite

Table 11-3 continued

Rec No 1	Country Major civil divisions 2	Capital 3	sq.mi. 4	sq.km. 5	Pop 2000 6	AC% 7	Church members 8	E% 9	W 10	Notes 11
	GUINEA-BISSAU		**13,948**	**36,125**	**1,213,111**	**12.83**	**155,645**	**48.17**	**A**	**Roman Catholics 11.6%, Independents 2.5%. Pent-char 2.8%, Evangelical 0.7%, GCC 8.0%**
1170	Bafatá	Bafatá	2,309	5,981	186,251	16.00	29,800	51.34	B	East-central. Geba River. Peanuts, livestock. D=RCC.
1171	Biombo	Bissau	324	840	83,411	15.00	12,512	54.34	B	West on Atlantic Ocean, capital city. Livestock, coconuts, crafts. D=RCC,NAC.
1172	Bissau		30	78	172,764	18.00	31,098	59.17	B	Port city. 95% speak Crioule, 60% Muslim. Palm oil, fruits, trade. F=1687. D=RCC.
1173	Bolama	Bolama	1,013	2,624	40,983	12.50	5,123	47.84	A	West. Bolama Island. Former capital, before 1941. D=RCC.
1174	Cacheu	Cacheu	1,998	5,175	205,347	16.00	32,856	54.34	B	Northwest, on Atlantic Ocean. Cacheu River. Coconuts, palm oil, phosphates. D=RCC.
1175	Gabú	Gabú	3,533	9,150	166,970	9.00	15,027	40.34	A	East. Formerly Nova Lamego. Colufe River. Peanuts. Fulani. D=RCC.
1176	Oio	Farim	2,086	5,403	211,397	5.00	10,570	32.34	A	North-central. Cacheu River. Peanuts. Cattle, phosphates. D=RCC.
1177	Quinara	Fulacunda	1,212	3,138	57,277	13.00	7,446	52.34	B	Southwest on Atlantic Ocean. Rio Grande de Buba. Oil palms. Biafada, Balante, Malinke. D=RCC.
1178	Tombali	Catió	1,443	3,736	88,713	12.64	11,213	49.98	A	Southwest. Peanuts, beeswax, palm oil, timber, livestock. D=RCC.
	GUYANA		**83,044**	**215,083**	**861,334**	**43.43**	**374,036**	**81.25**	**B**	**Protestants 19.5%, Roman Catholics 10.0%. Pent-char 14.6%, Evangelical 12.1%, GCC 12.1%**
1179	Barima/Waini	Mabaruma	7,853	20,339	21,094	24.00	5,063	56.82	B	Northwest, coastal. Kaituma and Barama Rivers. Sugar, timber, rice, agriculture. D=RCC,Anglican.
1180	Cuyuni/Mazaruni	Bartica	18,229	47,213	20,439	33.00	6,745	68.82	B	North-central. Cuyuni River, Pakaraina Mountains. Tropical rain forests. Gold. D=RCC,AoG.
1181	Demerara/Mahaica	Paradise	862	2,233	354,022	47.82	169,304	86.60	B	North-central. Demerara River. Marsh, capital. Site of Jim Jones cult suicide. D=RCC,Anglican.
1182	East Berbice/Corentyne	New Amsterdam	13,998	36,255	169,706	45.00	76,368	82.82	B	Northeast. Atlantic Ocean. Bordering Suriname, Acarai Mountains. Sugarcane, rice. D=Anglican,RCC.
1183	Essequibo/West Demera	Vreed-en-Hoop	1,450	3,755	117,066	46.00	53,850	83.82	B	North-central. Essequibo River. Inland waterway. Fishing, shrimping. D=RCC,Anglican.
1184	Mahaica/Berbice	Fort Wellington	1,610	4,170	63,291	40.00	25,316	77.82	B	Northeast. Atlantic Ocean. Marsh. Berbice River. Rice, shrimping, agriculture. D=RCC,AoG.
1185	Pomeroon/Supenaam	Anna Regina	2,392	6,195	47,809	34.00	16,255	71.82	B	Pomeroon River, coastal. North-central. Rice, livestock, fishing. D=RCC,AoG.
1186	Potaro/Siparuni Mahdia	Mahdia	7,742	20,052	6,462	35.00	2,262	71.82	B	West-central. Dotaro River. Kaieteur Falls, Essequibo River. Tourism. Bauxite. D=RCC,Anglican.
1187	Upper Demerara/Berbice	Linden	6,595	17,081	43,972	31.00	13,631	65.82	B	Berbice River. Northeast. Demerara River. Bauxite mining. Marshes, shrimp. D=RCC,AoG.
1188	Upper Takutu/Esseququibo	Lethem	22,313	57,790	17,473	30.00	5,242	64.82	B	South. Kanuku mountains. D=RCC,Anglican,AoG.
	HAITI		**10,695**	**27,700**	**8,222,025**	**92.91**	**7,639,424**	**99.93**	**C**	**Roman Catholics 79.3%, Protestants 17.5%. Pent-char 18.2%, Evangelical 14.2%, GCC 6.5%**
1189	Artibonite	Gonaïves	1,924	4,984	1,168,737	94.00	1,098,613	99.97	C	West on Gulf of Gonaives. Coffee, cotton, sugar. Musee de Centenaire (1904). D=RCC.
1190	Centre	Hinche	1,419	3,675	568,311	93.00	528,529	99.95	C	Central. Livestock, coffee, cocoa, handcrafts, farming. D=RCC.
1191	Grande Anse	Jérémie	1,278	3,310	748,994	93.00	696,564	99.95	C	Southwest. Tiburon Peninsula. Gulf of Gonaives. Cacao, coffee, tourism, fishing. D=RCC.
1192	Nord	Cap-Haïtien	813	2,106	880,198	93.08	819,300	99.94	C	North. One of world's largest sisal plants. Bananas, pineapples. La Citadelle Laferriere. D=RCC.
1193	Nord-Est	Fort-Liberté	697	1,805	291,421	94.00	273,936	99.97	C	Northeast. Manzanillo Bay. Bananas, fruits, coffee, cocoa, fishing. D=RCC.
1194	Nord-Ouest	Port-de-Paix	840	2,176	480,700	93.00	447,051	99.95	C	Northwest. Atlantic Ocean. Coffee, bananas, sisal. First black slave revolt (1679). D=RCC.
1195	Ouest	Port-au-Prince	1,864	4,827	2,777,705	92.00	2,555,489	99.87	C	West on Gulf of Gonaives. Textiles, flour, sugar. F=1749 by French. Voodoo. D=RCC.
1196	Sud	Les Cayes	1,079	2,794	765,838	93.00	712,229	99.95	C	Southwest on Caribbean Sea. Exports sugar coffee, bananas. F=1786. D=RCC.
1197	Sud-Est	Jacmel	781	2,023	540,120	94.00	507,713	99.97	C	South on Jacmel Bay. Bananas, cacao, honey. Tourist resort. D=RCC.
	HOLY SEE		**0**	**1**	**1,000**	**98.00**	**980**	**100.00**	**C**	**Roman Catholics 98.0%. Pent-char 12.0%, Evangelical 2.0%, GCC 46.1%**
1198	Holy See	Vatican City	–	1	1,000	98.00	980	100.00	C	Enclave of Rome on Tibre River. Vatican library, Sistine Chapel, Pope's residence. D=RCC.
	HONDURAS		**43,433**	**112,492**	**6,485,445**	**93.40**	**6,057,600**	**99.90**	**C**	**Roman Catholics 86.1%, Protestants 6.5%. Pent-char 13.2%, Evangelical 4.7%, GCC 6.3%**
1199	Atlántida	La Ceiba	1,641	4,251	351,272	95.00	333,708	99.95	C	North. Gulf of Honduras. Mount Bonito (7,989 ft.). Bananas, citrus fruit, fishing. D=RCC.
1200	Choluteca	Choluteca	1,626	4,211	425,659	94.50	402,248	99.94	C	South. Pacific lowlands on Choluteca River. Coffee, cotton, bee-keeping. F=1522. D=RCC.
1201	Colón	Trujillo	3,427	8,875	225,916	96.00	216,879	99.96	C	Northeast. Trujillo Bay. Bananas, coconuts, mahogany, fishing. F=1524. D=RCC.
1202	Comayagua	Comayagua	2,006	5,196	354,027	95.00	336,326	99.95	C	West-central. Humuya River. Pharmaceuticals. 16th century churches. F=1537. D=RCC.
1203	Copán	Santa Rosa	1,237	3,203	311,323	94.33	293,668	99.93	C	Northwest. Highlands. Tobacco, sugar, mat weaving. F=18th century. D=RCC.
1204	Cortés	San Pedro Sula	1,527	3,954	972,541	93.00	904,463	99.90	C	Northwest. Gulf of Honduras. Bananas, coffee, coconuts. F=1520s. D=RCC.
1205	El Paraíso	Yuscarán	2,787	7,218	381,578	95.00	362,499	99.95	C	Southeast. Choluteca River. Timber, grains. F=1730s for gold and silver mining. D=RCC.
1206	Francisco Morazán	Tegucigalpa	3,068	7,946	1,209,478	90.00	1,088,530	99.78	C	Central. Hilly terrain. Capital. Textiles, education center. F=1578 as mining center. D=RCC.
1207	Gracias a Dios	Puerto Lempira	6,421	16,630	50,969	95.00	48,421	99.95	C	Northeast. Tansin Island, Colon Mountains, Patuca River, Caratasca Lagoon. Marsh, fishing. D=RCC.
1208	Intibucá	La Esperanza	1,186	3,072	179,080	94.00	168,335	99.94	C	Southwest bordering El Salvador. Lempa River. Wheat, hand-weaving. Mainly Indian. D=RCC.
1209	Islas de la Bahìa	Roatán	100	261	33,061	95.00	31,408	99.95	C	North. Islands. Coconuts, tourism. 17th century pirate forts. D=RCC.
1210	La Paz	La Paz	900	2,331	154,284	94.50	145,798	99.94	C	Southwest. Comayagua River. Henequen coffee, cattle. Mining. F=1792. D=RCC.
1211	Lempira	Gracias	1,658	4,290	247,957	95.00	235,559	99.95	C	Southwest. Mejocote River. Celaque Mountains. Corn, wheat. F=1536. D=RCC.
1212	Ocotepeque	Nueva Ocotepeque	649	1,680	106,070	95.00	100,767	99.95	C	West. Lempa River. Fertile agricultural region. D=RCC.
1213	Olancho	Juticalpa	9,402	24,351	425,659	93.00	395,863	99.90	C	East. Juticalpa River. Lumbering, livestock, coffee. F=1620. D=RCC.
1214	Santa Bárbara	Santa Bárbara	1,975	5,115	400,863	95.00	380,820	99.95	C	Northwest. Ulua River. Lake Yojoa. Livestock, sugarcane. F=1761. D=RCC.
1215	Valle	Nacaome	604	1,565	166,682	94.50	157,514	99.94	C	South. Nacaome River. Cement, tanneries. F=1535. Colonial church. D=RCC.
1216	Yoro	Yoro	3,065	7,939	489,026	93.00	454,794	99.90	C	Northwest. Aguan River. Highlands. Coffee, tobacco, livestock. F=17th century. D=RCC.
	HUNGARY		**35,920**	**93,033**	**10,035,568**	**87.19**	**8,749,732**	**99.35**	**C**	**Roman Catholics 63.0%, Protestants 25.5%. Pent-char 6.8%, Evangelical 4.5%, GCC 10.6%**
1217	Baranya	Pécs	1,732	4,487	405,136	84.00	340,314	99.16	C	South. Drava River, Mecsak Mountains. Peaches, pigs, wine. Coal mining. D=RCC,Reformed.
1218	Borsod-Abaúj-Zemplén	Miskolc	2,798	7,247	733,587	87.50	641,889	99.66	C	North. Tisza River. Peas, lentils, wines. Chemicals, oil. Mongol invasion (1241). D=RCC,Reformed.
1219	Budapest	–	203	525	1,955,813	84.67	1,656,071	99.07	C	Danube River. Heavy industry, trade. Mathias Church (13th century). F=3rd century BC. D=RCC.
1220	Bács-Kiskun	Kecskemét	3,229	8,362	526,451	86.00	452,748	99.16	C	South-central. Danube River. Wheat, corn, vegetables. Fishing, aquatic sports, folk art. D=RCC.
1221	Békés	Békéscsaba	2,175	5,632	396,609	88.00	349,016	99.66	C	Southeast. Great Hungarian Plain. Cereals, cattle. 'Stormy corner' (peasant uprisings). D=RCC.
1222	Csongrád	Szeged	1,646	4,263	424,801	86.50	367,453	99.26	C	Southeast. Great Hungarian Plain. Paprika, fishing, petroleum. D=RCC,Reformed.
1223	Fejér	Székesfehérvár	1,688	4,373	409,035	87.00	355,860	99.16	C	Central. Major producer of corn. Sunflower oil. Fishing, resorts. D=RCC,Reformed.
1224	Győr-Sopron	Győr	1,549	4,012	410,943	88.00	361,630	99.66	C	Northwest bordering Austria. Rich farmland. Pannonhalma Apatsaq (abbey, AD 969). D=RCC.
1225	Hajdú-Bihar	Debrecen	2,398	6,211	532,270	87.00	463,075	99.16	C	East. Great Hungarian Plain. Sandy soils. Herdsmen, cowboys. Churches (1480). D=RCC.
1226	Heves	Eger	1,404	3,637	323,098	90.00	290,788	99.76	C	North. Matra and Bukk mountains. Winter resorts, sanatoriums. Lentils, horses. D=RCC,Reformed.
1227	Jász-Nagykun-Szolnok	Szolnok	2,165	5,607	411,344	89.00	366,096	99.16	C	East-central. Great Hungarian Plain. Tisza River. Fruit, wheat, rice. D=RCC,Reformed.
1228	Komárom-Esztergom	Tatabánya	869	2,251	304,332	89.50	272,377	99.36	C	Northwest bordering Slovakia. Danube River. Sugar beets, peaches, lignite. D=RCC,Reformed.
1229	Nógrád	Salgótarján	982	2,544	218,777	93.00	203,463	99.66	C	Cserhat Hills. Nograd River. Poppy seeds, traditional weaving. Paloc. D=RCC,Reformed.
1230	Pest	Budapest	2,469	6,394	921,733	86.50	797,299	99.26	C	North-central. Principal industrial center. Resort area. D=RCC,Reformed.
1231	Somogy	Kaposvçr	2,331	6,036	332,729	87.00	289,474	99.16	C	Southwest. Lake Balaton. Rye, potatoes, pigs. Intricate wood carving. D=RCC,Reformed.
1232	Szabolcs-Szatmár-Bereg	Ny'regyháza	2,293	5,938	551,291	86.50	476,867	99.26	C	Northeast. Tisza River. Lowlands. Orchards, rye, cattle, pigs. D=RCC,Reformed.
1233	Tolna	Szekszçrd	1,430	3,704	245,076	88.00	215,667	99.66	C	South-central. Danube River. Corn, wheat, pigs. Embroidery. Wildlife sanctuary. D=RCC.
1234	Vas	Szombathely	1,288	3,337	266,976	90.00	240,278	99.76	C	West. Hill pasture, forest. Wheat, potatoes, winter cabbage. Church (1256). D=RCC.
1235	Veszprém	Veszprém	1,810	4,689	369,916	92.00	340,323	99.86	C	West. Lake Balaton. Bakony Mountains. Wines, tourism, mining. 12th century abbey. D=RCC.
1236	Zala	Zalaegerszeg	1,461	3,784	295,653	91.00	269,044	99.76	C	West. Drava River. Medicinal herbs. Racehorse breeding. Spas. D=RCC,Reformed.
	ICELAND		**39,699**	**102,819**	**280,969**	**94.41**	**265,259**	**99.95**	**C**	**Protestants 89.1%, Independents 3.9%. Pent-char 8.1%, Evangelical 2.3%, GCC 10.8%**
1237	Austurland	Egilsstadhir	8,491	21,991	13,595	96.50	13,119	99.98	C	East, Seydisfjsrdur. Primary road. Fishing, clothing, chemicals, greenhousing. D=Lutheran.
1238	Nordhurland eystra	Akureyri	8,636	22,368	28,207	95.00	26,797	99.95	C	North. Eyja Fjord. Fishing, agriculture, woolen goods. Ultra modern Lutheran church. D=Lutheran.
1239	Nordhurland vestra	Saudhçrkrókur	5,055	13,093	10,841	95.50	10,353	99.97	C	North, Skagafjord. Primary road. Agriculture, livestock, vegetables. D=Lutheran.
1240	Reykjanes	Reykjavík	765	1,982	181,353	93.89	170,266	99.94	C	On Faxa Bay. Cathedral. Major fishing port, ships, textiles. F=874 by Norsemen. D=Lutheran.
1241	Sudhurland	Selfoss	9,735	25,214	21,986	95.00	20,887	99.95	C	Southwest. Olfusa River. Agriculture, dairying center, resort. D=Lutheran.
1242	Vestfirdhir	Isafjördhur	3,657	9,470	9,950	96.00	9,552	99.97	C	Northwest. Vestfjarda Peninsula. Fishing, windows, boat-building. D=Lutheran.
1243	Vesturland	Borgarnes	3,360	8,701	15,037	95.00	14,285	99.95	C	Birthplace of Olafur Thors, prime minister (1942-1963). D=Lutheran.
	INDIA		**1,222,243**	**3,165,596**	**1,013,661,777**	**6.14**	**62,243,546**	**59.34**	**B**	**Independents 3.3%, Protestants 1.6%. Pent-char 3.3%, Evangelical 0.9%, GCC 4.9%**
1244	Andaman/Nicobar Islands	Port Blair	3,185	8,249	335,117	18.00	60,321	71.20	B	Bay of Bengal. Redwood, coconuts, copra. Many displaced persons. D=RCC.
1245	Andhra Pradesh	Hyderabad	106,204	275,068	79,662,665	7.00	5,576,387	60.20	B	Southeast on Bay of Bengal. Godavari & Krishna rivers. Rice, tobacco. 90% speak Telugu. D=CSI.
1246	Arunachal Pradesh	Itanagar	32,333	83,743	1,030,590	15.00	154,589	69.20	B	Northeast bordering Tibet. Dihang River. Himalayan Mountains. Rice, corn. Tibeto-Burmese. D=CNI.
1247	Assam	Dispur	30,285	78,438	26,765,942	8.00	2,141,275	61.20	B	Northeast bordering Bhutan. Brahmaputra River. Rice, tea. Hindus 66%. D=Baptist.
1248	Bihar	Patna	67,134	173,877	103,654,925	5.20	5,390,056	58.40	B	Northeast bordering Nepal. Ganges River. Rice. Urbanization 12%. Hindus 83%. D=CNI,RCC.
1249	Chandigarh	Chandigarh	44	114	769,268	2.55	19,615	52.75	B	Joint capital of Haryana and Punjab. Shiwalik Hills. Planned by Swiss architect.
1250	Dadra and Nagar Haveli	Silvassa	190	491	166,241	2.80	4,655	53.00	B	West. Forest. Rice, cereals, livestock. Adivasi tribals (80%). Hindus.
1251	Daman and Diu	Daman	43	112	121,741	3.30	4,017	56.50	B	West coast. Two widely separated districts. Damau, north of Bombay. Diu Island. Rice.
1252	Delhi	Delhi	572	1,483	11,249,821	4.60	517,492	57.80	B	North central. Yamura River. Delhi University, airport. Electronic, engineering, handicrafts. D=CNI.
1253	Goa	Panaji	1,429	3,702	1,403,009	40.00	561,204	98.20	B	West on Arabian Sea. Beaches. Rice. Portuguese India. Cathedral (1511). D=RCC.
1254	Gujarat	Gandhinagar	75,685	196,024	49,432,230	2.10	1,038,077	55.30	B	West on Arabian Sea. Wheat, millet. Most industrialized state. Hindus. D=CNI,RCC.
1255	Haryana	Chandigarh	17,070	44,212	19,590,433	1.10	215,495	49.30	A	North. Indo-Gangetic Plain. Sugarcane. Birthplace of Hinduism. 'The abode of God'. M=FMPB.
1256	Himachal Pradesh	Shimla	21,495	55,673	6,136,202	1.20	73,634	49.40	A	North bordering Tibet. Himalayan Mountains. Less than 10% urban. 'Snowy mountain' M=IEM.
1257	Jammu and Kashmir	Srinagar	38,830	100,569	9,266,795	1.30	120,468	49.50	A	Northwest, bordering Pakistan. 90% mountainous. Rice, orchards. Muslims 66%. M=KEF.
1258	Karnataka	Bangalore	74,051	191,791	53,792,800	4.00	2,151,712	57.20	B	Southwest on Arabian Sea. Formerly Mysore. Rice, gold, silver. Kannada. 'Lofty land'. D=RCC,CSI.
1259	Kerala	Trivandrum	15,005	38,863	34,855,672	32.00	11,153,815	93.20	B	Southwest on Malabar Coast. Plains. Cardamom, eggs, fish. Malayalam. Hindus. D=OSC,RCC.
1260	Lakshadweep	Kavaratti	12	32	62,036	1.30	806	49.50	A	Arabian Sea islands. Coral. Moplahs. Malayalam. Mainly Muslim.
1261	Madhya Pradesh	Bhopal	171,215	443,446	79,400,026	2.20	1,746,801	51.40	B	Central. Largest state. Deccan Plateau. Narmada River. Rice, minerals. Gonds. D=CNI. M=FMPB.
1262	Maharashtra	Mumbai (Bombay)	118,800	307,690	94,541,903	5.00	4,727,095	58.20	B	West-central. Deccan Plateau. Sorghum, fishing, cotton textiles. Marathi. Hindus 80%. D=RCC,CNI.
1263	Manipur	Imphal	8,621	22,327	2,193,057	40.00	877,223	93.20	B	Northeast. Manipur River. Corn, teak, bamboo. Meithei 50%. Literacy 40%. D=CNI,Baptist.
1264	Meghalaya	Shillong	8,660	22,429	2,113,688	60.50	1,278,781	99.70	C	Northeast bordering Bangladesh. Brahmaputra River. Rice, millet. Garos, Khasis. D=Presbyterian.
1265	Mizoram	Aizawl	8,140	21,081	823,803	88.00	724,947	98.80	C	Northeast bordering Myanmar. Hilly terrain. Rice, weaving. 'Highlanders'. D=CBCNEI.
1266	Nagaland	Kohima	6,401	16,579	1,459,369	89.00	1,298,838	99.20	C	Northeast bordering Myanmar. Himalayan hills. Rice, forestry. D=CBCNEI.
1267	Orissa	Bubaneswar	60,119	155,707	37,832,088	3.90	1,475,451	57.10	B	East on Bay of Bengal. Mahanadi River Delta. Rice, chromite. Oriya. Hindus 90%. D=RCC.
1268	Pondicherry	Pondicherry	190	492	968,858	20.00	193,772	73.20	B	Southeast coast (Coromandel Coast). Tourism, rice, peanuts. Tamil, Malayalam. Hindus. D=OSC.
1269	Punjab	Chandigarh	19,445	50,362	24,240,302	2.70	654,488	52.90	B	Northwest bordering Pakistan. Flat plain. Wheat, cotton. Sikhs 60%. 'Five waters'. D=CNI.
1270	Rajasthan	Jaipur	132,140	342,239	52,681,320	1.30	684,857	51.50	B	Northwest. Wool. Minas, Bhils. 1998 nuclear tests. 'The abode of the rajas'. D=RCC,CNI.
1271	Sikkim	Gangtok	2,740	7,096	486,862	4.40	21,422	57.60	B	Northeast. Himalayan Mountains. Corn, cardamom, minerals. Hindus, Buddhists. D=CNI.
1272	Tamil Nadu	Chennai (Madras)	50,216	130,058	66,797,169	17.95	11,990,092	79.68	B	Southeast on Indian Ocean. Cauvery River. Rice cotton. Tamil. 9,300 Hindu temples. D=CSI.
1273	Tripura	Agartala	4,049	10,486	3,295,313	5.20	171,356	58.40	B	East bordering Bangladesh. Hilly terrain. Rice. Bengali. Hindus 50%. D=RCC.
1274	Uttar Pradesh	Lucknow	113,673	294,411	166,915,225	3.10	5,174,372	56.30	B	North. Ganges River. Himalayan Mountains. Rice sugarcane. Little industry. Hindus 80%. D=CNI.
1275	West Bengal	Calcutta	34,267	88,752	81,617,309	2.50	2,040,433	55.70	B	East bordering Bangladesh. Gangetic Plain. Rice, tea. Bengali. Hindus 80%. D=RCC.

Continued overleaf

Table 11-3 continued

Rec No 1	Country Major civil divisions 2	Capital 3	sq.mi. 4	sq.km. 5	Pop 2000 6	AC% 7	Church members 8	E% 9	W 10	Notes 11
	INDONESIA		**741,052**	**1,919,317**	**212,107,385**	**12.43**	**26,364,858**	**62.85**	**B**	**Protestants 5.7%, Independents 3.9%. Pent-char 4.4%, Evangelical 1.9%, GCC 6.8%**
1276	Aceh	Banda Aceh	21,387	55,392	4,040,582	1.50	60,609	51.92	B	Extreme northern Sumatra. Rice, paper. Acehnese, Gajo. Muslims.
1277	Bali	Denpasar	2,147	5,561	3,285,883	1.00	32,859	51.42	B	Lesser Sunda island. Mountainous. Rice, wood carving. Mainly lower caste Hindus.
1278	Bengkulu	Bengkulu	8,173	21,168	1,394,542	1.80	25,102	52.22	B	Southwestern Sumatra. Bengkulu Mountains. Rice, tea, coffee. Minangkabau. Muslims.
1279	Irian Jaya	Jayapura	162,928	421,981	1,941,016	88.00	1,708,094	96.92	C	Western New Guinea. Maoke Mountains. Cacao, fish, copper. Melanesians. 'Glorious West'. D=GPI.
1280	Jakarta Raya	Jakarta	228	590	9,763,027	20.00	1,952,605	75.42	B	Western Java. Major center for trade, finance, industry, education, University of Indonesia.
1281	Jambi	Jambi	17,297	44,800	2,384,575	1.84	43,805	52.26	B	Southeastern Sumatra. Barisan Mountains. Rubber, tobacco. Minangkabau, Batak. D=RCC,HKBP.
1282	Jawa Barat	Bandung	17,877	46,300	42,734,208	6.20	2,649,521	57.02	B	Western Java. Chain of volcanoes. Rice, sugarcane, corn, textiles. Javanese. Sundanese. Muslim.
1283	Jawa Tengah	Semarang	13,207	34,206	33,736,486	11.00	3,711,013	63.82	B	Central Java. Volcanic mountains, tropical rain forest. Rice, tobacco. Javanese, Sundanese.
1284	Jawa Timur	Surabaya	18,502	47,921	38,446,479	4.00	1,537,859	54.82	B	Eastern Java. Volcanic cones. Teak, bamboo. Rice, tea. Javanese, Madurese. Muslims.
1285	Kalimantan Barat	Pontianak	56,664	146,760	3,831,168	41.00	1,570,779	96.42	B	Western Borneo. Java Sea. Swampy lowlands. Rice, corn, cassava. Mainly Dayak. D=RCC,GPI.
1286	Kalimantan Selatan	Banjarmasin	14,541	37,660	3,072,969	3.00	92,189	53.42	B	Southeastern Borneo. Makassar Strait. Meratus Mountains. Rice, rubber. Dayak.
1287	Kalimantan Tengah	Palangkaraya	58,919	152,600	1,651,214	20.00	330,243	74.42	B	South-central Borneo. Schwaner and Muller mountains. Rice, resin, rattan. Dayak.
1288	Kalimantan Timur	Samarinda	78,162	202,440	2,220,149	18.00	399,627	71.42	B	East-central Borneo. Celebes Sea. Iran Mountains. Rice, livestock. Iban, Kayar, Tidong.
1289	Lampung	Tanjung Karang	12,860	33,307	7,104,028	2.50	177,601	52.92	B	Southern Sumatra on Java Sea. Bengkulen Mountains. Rubber, tea. Lampungese.
1290	Maluku	Ambon	28,767	74,505	2,195,311	48.00	1,053,749	97.92	B	1,000 islands. Banda Sea. Rice, coconuts. Coastal Malay. Muslims. 'Spice islands'. D=RCC.
1291	Nusa Tenggara Barat	Mataram	7,790	20,177	3,986,113	2.00	79,722	52.42	B	Western Lesser Sunda Islands. Indian Ocean. Rice, coffee, fishing. Sasak.
1292	Nusa Tenggara Timur	Kupang	18,485	47,876	3,866,654	83.00	3,209,323	97.82	C	Eastern Lesser Sunda islands and West Timor. Savu Sea. Rice, horses. Papuan, Malay. D=RCC,GPI.
1293	Riau	Pakanbaru	36,510	94,561	3,910,412	4.00	156,416	54.42	B	East-central Sumatra islands. Rice, corn, tin, bauxite. Sakai, Laut, Hutan. Muslim.
1294	Sulawesi Selatan	Ujung Pandang	28,101	72,781	8,258,465	3.00	247,754	53.42	B	South Celebes. Flores Sea. Volcanic cones. Rice, fishing. Buginese, Makasarese.
1295	Sulawesi Tengah	Palu	26,921	69,726	2,023,801	27.00	546,426	82.42	B	Central Celebes. Celebes Sea. Mountainous. Rattan, resin. Buginese. D=RCC.
1296	Sulawesi Tenggara	Kendari	10,690	27,686	1,596,808	3.30	52,695	53.72	B	Southeast Celebes. Banda Sea. Rift valleys. Rice, sugarcane. Buginese.
1297	Sulawesi Utara	Menado	7,345	19,023	2,932,215	65.00	1,905,940	99.42	C	North Celebes. Celebes Sea. Mountainous. Rice, coffee. Menadoese. D=RCC,GPI.
1298	Sumatera Barat	Padang	19,219	49,778	4,730,101	2.00	94,602	52.42	B	West Sumatra. Indian Ocean. Barisan Mountains. Rice, corn. Minangkabau.
1299	Sumatera Selatan	Palembang	40,034	103,688	7,424,586	10.00	742,459	60.42	B	South Sumatra. Java Sea. Volcanic cones. Rubber, timber. Minangkabau, Batak. D=RCC,HKBP.
1300	Sumatera Utara	Medan	27,331	70,787	12,131,036	30.00	3,639,311	85.42	B	North Sumatra. Batak Plateau. Tropical rain forests. Rice. Acehnese, Batak. D=RCC,HKBP.
1301	Yogyakarta	Yogyakarta	1,224	3,169	3,445,557	10.00	344,556	60.42	B	South-central Java. Indian Ocean. Coastal plains. Rice, fishing, industry. Javanese.
	IRAN		**632,457**	**1,638,057**	**67,702,199**	**0.46**	**313,990**	**37.21**	**A**	**Orthodox 0.3%, Independents 0.1%. Pent-char 0.1%, Evangelical 0.03%, GCC 0.1%**
1302	Ardabil	Ardabil	6,878	17,814	1,384,239	0.01	138	26.76	A	Northwest. Agricultural market center. Carpets, rugs. Safavid shrine.
1303	Azarbaijan-e Gharbi	Orumiyeh	14,512	37,588	2,769,562	2.00	55,391	47.75	A	Extreme northwest. Large fertile plain. Grains, fruit, tobacco. 50% Christian in 1900. D=AAC.
1304	Azarbaijan-e Sharqi	Tabriz	19,030	49,287	3,975,405	1.00	39,754	37.75	A	Extreme northwest. Hilly. Earthquake zone. Resorts, carpet. Ancient Muslim ruins.
1305	Bushehr	Bushehr	9,792	25,357	841,809	0.01	84	26.76	A	Southwest on Persian Gulf. Zagros Mountains. Wheat, barley, oil fields.
1306	Chahar Mahall Bakhtiari	Shahr Kord	5,722	14,820	906,126	0.01	91	26.76	A	West. Bricks, mosaics, carpets.
1307	Esfahan (Isfahan)	Esfahan	40,405	104,650	4,464,960	1.00	44,650	42.75	A	West-central. Zayandeh River. Handicrafts, tiles, carpets.
1308	Fars	Shiraz	48,837	126,489	4,296,855	0.25	10,742	37.00	A	South-central. Zagros Mountains. Fruits, cereals, tobacco. Qashqa'i, Khomseh.
1309	Gilan	Rasht	5,722	14,811	2,672,409	0.35	9,353	37.10	A	Northwest on Caspian Sea. Elburz Mountains. Rice, tobacco, fish.
1310	Hamadan	Hamadan	7,508	19,445	2,002,225	0.50	10,011	37.25	A	West-central. Mount Alvand (11,716 ft.). Qareh Su River. Grain, fruit, resorts. Turkish minority.
1311	Hormozgan	Bandar Abbas	26,439	68,476	1,120,878	0.02	224	28.77	A	South on Persian Gulf. Zagros highlands. Barley, wheat, goats.
1312	Ilam	Ilam	7,369	19,086	534,306	0.01	53	26.76	A	West bordering Iraq. Barley, wheat, bricks. Curi, Kurds.
1313	Kerman	Kerman	71,978	186,422	2,258,342	0.03	678	36.78	A	Southeast. Sandy plain. Largest carpet-exporting center. Persians. Zoroastrians.
1314	Kermanshahan	Kermanshah	9,138	23,667	1,966,884	0.03	590	28.78	A	West. Zagros Mountains. Wheat, barley, pastureland. Oil refinery.
1315	Khorasan	Mashhad	120,979	313,335	7,290,985	0.17	12,395	36.92	A	Northeast. Elburz Mountains. Fruits, cereals, livestock. Turks, Kurds.
1316	Khuzestan	Ahvaz	25,920	67,132	3,850,698	0.25	9,627	37.00	A	Southwest on Persian Gulf. Desert climate. Known for oil fields. Arabs, Bakhtieris.
1317	Kohkiluyeh Buyer Ahmadi	Yasuj	5,506	14,261	602,279	0.10	602	26.85	A	Southwest. Sugar, bricks, mosaics, carpets. Thermoelectric power.
1318	Kordestan	Sanadaj	10,756	27,855	1,495,609	0.02	299	36.77	A	Northwest bordering Iraq. Wheat, barley, sugar. Sunni Muslim. 'Country of the Kurds'.
1319	Lorestan	Khorramabad	11,121	28,803	1,820,918	0.01	182	26.76	A	West. Oak forests. Rice, wheat, barley, iron ore. 'Land of the Lurs'.
1320	Markazi	Arak	11,402	29,530	1,433,933	0.13	1,795	36.88	A	North-central. Elburz Mountains, fertile plain. Known for carpets.
1321	Mazandaran	Sari	17,937	46,456	4,599,146	0.01	460	26.76	A	North on Caspian Sea. Known for horses. Rice, wheat. Mazandarani, Turkmen.
1322	Qazvin	–	4,633	12,000	677,022	0.01	68	26.76	A	Northwest. Textile and flour mills, F=by Shapur II in 4th century.
1323	Qom	–	4,220	10,930	918,042	0.10	918	34.85	A	West central. Semiarid. Textiles, glass, petroleum. Shiite Muslim center.
1324	Semnan	Semnan	35,345	91,538	555,497	0.01	56	26.76	A	North. Elburz Mountains. Corn, tobacco, sugar. Chromium mining.
1325	Sistan-va Baluchestan	Zahedan	70,066	181,471	1,764,319	0.02	353	36.77	A	East. Numerous rivers. Desert climate, 'wind of 120 days'. Wheat, barley. Tajiks.
1326	Tehran	Tehran	10,896	28,221	11,172,352	1.03	115,075	47.93	A	North central. Textiles, sugar, cement, chinaware. American hostage crisis 1980. F=c400. D=AAC.
1327	Yazd	Yazd	27,931	72,342	837,950	0.03	251	36.78	A	Central. Barren, sandy plain. Visited by Marco Polo. Famous for silk textiles. Religious center.
1328	Zanjan	Zanjan	9,266	24,000	1,489,448	0.01	149	26.76	A	Northwest. Uplands (8,200 ft.), Zanjan River. Rice, corn, poultry.
	IRAQ		**167,975**	**435,052**	**23,114,884**	**3.14**	**724,662**	**48.44**	**A**	**Independents 1.3%, Roman Catholics 1.1%. Pent-char 1.1%, Evangelical 0.3%, GCC 0.8%**
1329	Al-Anbar	ar-Ramadi	53,208	137,808	1,117,464	0.01	112	25.31	A	Central. Euphrates River. Dam (1955). British defeated Ottomans (1917). Dulaym tribes.
1330	al-Basrah	Basra	7,363	19,070	1,509,058	6.10	92,053	66.40	B	Southeast. Shatt al-Arab waterway. Ancient cultural center. Petroleum refining and exporting.
1331	al-Muthanna	as-Samawah	19,977	51,740	451,891	0.10	452	35.40	A	South. Euphrates River. Vineyards, orchards, cement.
1332	al-Qadisiyah	ad-Diwaniyah	3,148	8,153	768,991	0.01	77	25.31	A	South-central. Euphrates River. Palm trees, vineyards, orchards.
1333	an-Najaf	an-Najaf	11,129	28,824	860,401	0.50	4,302	40.80	A	Central. Euphrates River. Holy City. Ali ibn Abi Talib's tomb. Center of Shiite activity.
1334	as-Sulaymaniyah	as-Sulaymaniyah	6,573	17,023	1,451,474	5.70	82,734	61.00	B	Northeast. Tanjero River. Kurdish Autonomous Region. Tobacco, fruit, cereals. Tourism. D=RCC.
1335	at-Ta'mim	Kirkuk	3,737	9,679	782,293	5.50	43,026	60.70	B	Northeast. Tigris River. Zagros Mountains. Petroleum. Wheat, barley, sheep. D=RCC.
1336	Babil	al-Hillah	2,163	5,603	1,576,583	1.00	15,766	44.30	A	Central. Euphrates River. On Pilgrimage route. Grains.
1337	Baghdad	Baghdad	1,572	4,071	5,049,433	5.38	271,750	62.48	B	East. Tigris River. Center of finance, industry, oil trade. Two universities. D=RCC.
1338	Dahuk	Dahuk	2,530	6,553	399,342	0.10	399	35.40	A	North. Tigris River. Kurdish Autonomous Region. Fruit orchards, pastures. Tourism.
1339	Dhi Qar	an-Nasiriyah	4,981	12,900	1,331,013	0.01	133	25.31	A	Southeast. Euphrates River. Dates, boat-building. Ancient city of Ur (ruins). D=RCC.
1340	Diyala	Ba'qubah	6,828	17,685	1,339,665	0.01	134	25.31	A	East. Diyala River. Agricultural produce, livestock. Assyrian Christians.
1341	Irbil	Irbil	5,820	15,074	1,198,673	5.50	65,927	60.80	B	North. Ancient continuous habitation. Sesame, corn. Christians (2nd century). Kurds. D=RCC.
1342	Karbala	Karbala	1,944	5,034	732,839	1.00	7,328	44.30	A	Central. Foremost holy city. Battle of Karbala (AD 680). Husayn's tomb.
1343	Maysan	al-Amarah	6,205	16,072	676,804	0.01	68	25.31	A	Southeast. Tigris River. Agricultural produce, livestock, wool, hides, weaving, silverware.
1344	Ninawa	Mosul	14,410	37,323	2,089,932	6.50	135,846	61.80	B	Northwest. Tigris River. Oil fields, cement, textiles. Ancient Nineveh. Kurds, Christian Arabs. D=RCC.
1345	Salah ad-Din	Tikrit	9,407	24,363	997,000	0.30	2,991	37.60	A	North-central. Tigris River. Vineyards, orchards, palm trees. Bath Party leadership.
1346	Wasit	al-Kut	6,623	17,153	782,030	0.20	1,564	36.50	A	East. Tigris River. Agricultural produce. Notable British defeat in World War I.
	IRELAND		**27,137**	**70,285**	**3,730,239**	**89.95**	**3,355,446**	**99.72**	**C**	**Roman Catholics 84.7%, Anglicans 3.5%. Pent-char 13.1%, Evangelical 3.3%, GCC 48.4%**
1347	Connacht	–	6,611	17,122	447,554	92.00	411,750	99.91	C	West. Atlantic Ocean. Small farms. Sheep. Many Gaelic-speaking people. D=RCC.
1348	Leinster	–	7,580	19,633	1,968,895	89.08	1,753,913	99.63	C	Southeast. Ancient Kingdom of Meath. D=RCC,Anglican.
1349	Munster	–	9,315	24,127	1,068,117	90.00	961,305	99.77	C	Southwest. Sliabh Luaachra Mountains. D=RCC.
1350	Ulster	–	3,093	8,012	245,674	93.00	228,477	99.92	C	North. Great prominence in Irish literature. Many Protestants. D=RCC.
	ISLE OF MAN		**221**	**572**	**79,166**	**66.24**	**52,438**	**99.63**	**C**	**Anglicans 42.4%, Protestants 14.1%. Pent-char 7.5%, Evangelical 22.3%, GCC 32.3%**
1351	Isle of Man	Douglas	221	572	79,166	66.24	52,438	99.63	C	Irish British dependency. Oats, barley, turnips, potatoes, sheep, dairying, fishing. D=Anglican.
	ISRAEL		**7,876**	**20,400**	**5,121,683**	**5.74**	**294,078**	**56.02**	**B**	**Roman Catholics 2.7%, Independents 1.6%. Pent-char 2.0%, Evangelical 0.6%, GCC 3.7%**
1352	Central (Ha Merkaz)	Ramla	479	1,242	1,107,076	5.80	64,210	56.08	B	Coastal plain. Cement plywood. Ramla founded by Arabs (AD 716). Franciscan hospice. D=RCC.
1353	Haifa (Hefa)	Haifa	330	854	699,314	5.06	35,406	52.34	B	Northwest. Bay of Haifa. Mount Carmel. Major port, tourism. Baha'i headquarters. D=RCC.
1354	Jerusalem (Yerushalayim)	Jerusalem	215	557	634,703	7.50	47,603	59.78	B	Holy city of Jews, Christians and Muslims. Hebrew University (1925). F=1800 BC. D=RCC.
1355	Northern (Ha Zafon)	Tiberias	1,347	3,490	870,661	5.70	49,628	55.98	B	Northeast. Sea of Galilee. Most popular resort area. Tiberias founded AD 18. Fishing. D=RCC.
1356	Southern (Ha Darom)	Beersheba	5,555	14,387	618,607	3.20	19,795	46.48	A	South. Negev region. Formerly Bedouin nomads. Chemicals, porcelain, tiles. D=RCC.
1357	Tel Aviv	Tel Aviv-Yafo	66	170	1,191,323	6.50	77,436	61.08	B	West. Mediterranean Sea. Banking, tourism, botanical/zoological gardens. Textiles. F=1909. D=RCC.
	ITALY		**116,336**	**301,309**	**57,297,886**	**81.89**	**46,922,140**	**99.24**	**C**	**Roman Catholics 97.1%, Protestants 0.7%. Pent-char 7.3%, Evangelical 0.5%, GCC 42.2%**
1358	Abruzzi	L'Aquila	4,168	10,794	1,262,989	79.80	1,007,865	99.70	C	Central on Adriatic Sea. Mountainous. Wheat, grapes, fruit. Livestock raising. D=RCC.
1359	Basilicata	Potenza	3,858	9,992	614,440	84.40	518,587	99.95	C	South on Gulf of Taranto. Mountains. Poor soil. Wheat, rye. Disastrous earthquake. D=RCC.
1360	Calabria	Catanzaro	5,823	15,080	2,087,058	83.30	1,738,519	99.90	C	South. Citrus fruits, figs. Active Mafia. Albanians. 'Toe' of Italian 'boot'. D=RCC,Orthodox.
1361	Campania	Naples	5,249	13,595	5,702,492	82.50	4,704,556	99.20	C	South on Tyrrhenian Sea. Mountainous. Fruits, wines, fishing. Tourism. D=RCC.
1362	Emilia-Romagna	Bologna	8,542	22,123	3,943,458	84.10	3,316,448	99.97	C	North-central. Adriatic Sea. Great plain. Leading agricultural region. Natural gas, oil. D=RCC.
1363	Friuli-Venezia Giulia	Trieste	3,029	7,845	1,202,138	82.00	985,753	99.35	C	Northeast, bordering Austria and Slovenia. Adriatic Sea. Poor economy. Earthquakes. D=RCC.
1364	Lazio	Rome	6,642	17,203	5,192,667	82.50	4,283,950	99.85	C	West-central. Tyrrhenian Sea. Wheat, corn, olives, vineyards. Tourism. D=RCC.
1365	Liguria	Genoa	2,092	5,418	1,678,788	83.60	1,403,467	99.95	C	Northwest bordering Ligurian Sea. Flowers, olives, resorts. Shipyards. D=RCC.
1366	Lombardia	Milan	9,211	23,857	8,935,050	80.00	7,148,040	98.79	C	North, bordering Switzerland. Mountainous. Leading industrial region. Cereals, fruit. D=RCC.
1367	Marche	Ancona	3,743	9,693	1,442,491	82.40	1,188,613	99.75	C	Central on Adriatic Sea. Mountainous. Wheat, corn, olives, livestock. D=RCC.
1368	Molise	Campobasso	1,713	4,438	333,457	84.70	282,438	99.98	C	Southeast, central. Apennines Mountains. Wheat, potatoes. Mainly rural, slow growth. D=RCC.
1369	Piemonte	Turin	9,807	25,399	4,329,337	81.50	3,528,410	98.85	C	Northwest. Po River Valley. Hydroelectric plants. Dairy industry, wines, autos. D=RCC.
1370	Puglia	Bari	7,470	19,348	4,073,977	80.00	3,259,182	98.35	C	Southeast. Fortore River. Limestone, wheat, barley, tobacco. Fishing, wines. D=RCC.
1371	Sardegna	Cagliari	9,301	24,090	1,661,690	84.10	1,397,481	99.99	C	Sardinia Island. Nuraghi: prehistoric structures. Sheep, wheat, fishing, mining. Sards. D=RCC.
1372	Sicilia (Sicily)	Palermo	9,926	25,709	5,027,322	81.37	4,090,732	98.72	C	Sicily Island. 10,000 years of habitation. Wheat, barley. Oil refineries. Active Mafia. D=RCC.
1373	Toscana	Florence	8,877	22,992	3,549,650	81.50	2,892,965	99.85	C	West. Arno River. Marshes. Lead, zinc, mercury, copper, shipbuilding, olives, metallurgical. D=RCC.
1374	Trentino-Alto Adige	Bolzano	5,258	13,618	902,035	84.00	757,709	99.99	C	North. Mountainous. Heavily forested. Timber industry, fruit, wines. Tourism. D=RCC.
1375	Umbria	Perugia	3,265	8,456	819,623	84.40	691,724	99.95	C	Central. Tiber River. Wheat, corn, livestock. Roman and medieval architecture. D=RCC.
1376	Valle d'Aosta	Aosta	1,259	3,262	117,896	85.00	100,212	99.95	C	Northwest. Dora Baltea River. Dairy products, tourism. French character. D=RCC.
1377	Veneto	Venice	7,090	18,364	4,421,328	82.00	3,625,489	98.45	C	North, northeast. Adriatic Sea. Mountains, fertile plain. Corn, wheat. Textiles, silk. D=RCC.
	IVORY COAST		**124,504**	**322,463**	**14,785,832**	**29.45**	**4,353,882**	**72.75**	**B**	**Roman Catholics 14.7%, Independents 9.2%. Pent-char 8.2%, Evangelical 4.5%, GCC 13.7%**
1378	Abengourou	Abengourou	2,664	5,200	295,366	28.00	82,702	71.30	B	East. Productive forest region. Coffee, cocoa. Anyi paramount chief. D=RCC.
1379	Abidjan	Abidjan	3,301	8,550	3,398,331	34.64	1,177,175	80.79	B	Southeast, coastal. University (1963). Beer, lumber, soap, bananas, cocoa, coffee. D=RCC,Harrists.
1380	Aboisso	Aboisso	2,413	6,250	308,815	39.00	120,438	82.30	B	Southeast. Bia River. Aby Lagoon. Hydroelectric plants. Agriculture, timber.
1381	Adzopé	Adzopé	2,019	5,230	325,185	28.00	91,052	71.30	B	Southeast. Coffee, bananas, cocoa. Leprosy hospital. Attie people. D=RCC,Protestant.
1382	Agboville	Agboville	1,486	3,850	278,190	37.00	102,930	80.30	B	Southeast. Agneby River. Coffee, bananas, furniture. Abe people.
1383	Agnibilékrou	Agnibilékrou	656	1,700	115,312	31.00	35,747	74.30	B	East. Primary road. Bananas, rubber, timber, coffee, livestock.

Continued opposite

Table 11-3 continued

Rec No 1	Country Major civil divisions 2	Capital 3	sq.mi. 4	sq.km. 5	Pop 2000 6	AC% 7	Church members 8	E% 9	W 10	Notes 11
1384	Bangolo	Bangolo	795	2,060	109,337	29.00	31,708	72.30	B	West central. Near Du Mont Peka National Park. Coffee, timber.
1385	Biankouma	Biankouma	1,911	4,950	134,295	13.00	17,458	54.30	B	West. Nimba Range. Rice, cassava, coffee, cattle. Dan and Tura peoples. Known for dancers.
1386	Bondoukou	Bondoukou	3,876	10,040	238,213	18.00	42,878	61.30	B	East. Bouna Game Reserve. Tourism. Kulango and Brong peoples. Muslims. D=RCC.
1387	Bongouanou	Bongouanou	2,151	5,570	307,533	32.00	98,411	75.30	B	Central. Transcountry railroad. Manufacturing, textiles, crafts, industry, bananas, fruit.
1388	Bouaflé	Bouaflé	1,537	3,980	226,690	40.00	90,676	83.30	B	Central. Bandama Rouge River. Coffee, yams, cassava. Guro and Gagu peoples.
1389	Bouaké	Bouaké	1,815	4,700	615,994	39.00	240,238	82.30	B	Central. Cotton, tobacco, sisal. Handicrafts. Benedictine monastery. D=RCC. Protestants.
1390	Bouna	Bouna	8,290	21,470	185,666	2.50	4,642	40.80	A	Northeast. Komoe National Park. Wooded Savanna.
1391	Boundiali	Boundiali	3,048	7,895	174,776	5.00	8,739	43.30	A	Northwest. Livestock, corn, manioc. Senufo wood-carvers.
1392	Béoumi	Béoumi	1,088	2,820	123,484	22.00	27,166	65.30	B	Central. Kossou Lake. Secondary roads. Fishing, timber, textiles.
1393	Dabakala	Dabakala	3,734	9,670	111,853	26.00	29,082	69.30	B	Northeast. Komoe River, savanna. Cotton, corn, cattle, other livestock, sawmilling.
1394	Daloa	Daloa	2,104	5,450	491,808	35.00	172,133	78.30	B	West central. Coffee, Kola nuts, timber. Bete, Guro, Baule, Diula and Moss. D=RCC,Protestant.
1395	Danané	Danané	1,776	4,600	304,637	16.00	48,742	59.30	B	West. Boan River. Rice, coffee, kola nuts. Dan people.
1396	Daoukro	Daoukro	1,393	3,610	118,244	30.00	35,473	73.30	B	East. Timber, sawmilling, cocoa, coffee, palm kernels, rubber, textiles.
1397	Dimbokro	Dimbokro	1,900	4,920	194,080	40.00	77,632	83.30	B	South-central. Nzi River. Yams, bananas, coffee, textiles. Baule people.
1398	Divo	Divo	3,058	7,920	529,201	37.00	195,804	80.30	B	South-central. Bananas, pineapples, coffee, rubber. Dida people.
1399	Duékoué	Duékoué	1,131	2,930	139,671	34.00	47,488	77.30	B	North central. Transcountry railroad, savanna, Bandama. Millet, timber, livestock.
1400	Ferkessedougou	Ferkessedougou	6,845	17,728	236,357	8.00	18,909	46.30	A	North. Rice, millet, sugar, livestock. Muslim Senuto and Dyula. D=RCC.
1401	Gagnoa	Gagnoa	1,737	4,500	377,608	35.00	132,163	78.30	B	South. Coffee, cocoa, rice. Metalworking. Bete and Gagu peoples. D=RCC,Protestant.
1402	Grand-Lahou	Grand-Lahou	880	2,280	71,852	40.00	28,741	83.30	B	South central coast. Gulf of Guinea, Tadio Lagoon, inland waterways. Fishing, textiles.
1403	Guiglo	Guiglo	4,332	11,220	232,841	32.00	74,509	75.30	B	West. Nzo River. Rice, cassava, livestock. Guere, Yacouba, Mossi.
1404	Issia	Issia	1,386	3,590	267,486	37.00	98,970	80.30	B	Southwest. Lobo River. Kola nuts, coffee, cocoa, bananas, crafts, livestock.
1405	Katiola	Katiola	3,637	9,420	178,588	33.00	58,934	76.30	B	Central. Yams, tobacco, cattle. Mangoro known for pottery. Baule, Senufo, Diula. D=RCC.
1406	Korhogo	Korhogo	4,826	12,500	533,471	5.00	26,674	43.30	A	North-central. Corn, manioc, livestock. Senufo farmers. Muslim Fulani. D=RCC.
1407	Lakota	Lakota	1,054	2,730	159,634	30.00	47,890	73.30	B	South-central. Bananas, pineapples, rubber, timber, coffee, manufacturing.
1408	M'bahiakro	M'Bahiakro	2,108	5,460	140,167	30.00	42,050	73.30	B	Central. Nzi River. Cotton, tobacco, handicrafts, timer, bananas
1409	Man	Man	1,927	4,990	402,909	17.00	68,495	60.30	B	West. Nimba Range. Ko River. Iron ore, rice, coffee. Dan, Guereor Wobe, Diula. D=RCC.
1410	Mankono	Mankono	4,116	10,660	168,644	18.00	30,356	61.30	B	West-central. Bandama Rouge River. Cassava, corn, livestock, minerals.
1411	Odiénné	Odiénné	7,954	20,600	232,080	4.00	9,283	42.30	A	Northwest. Tienba River. Yams, rice, cattle. Manganese. Muslim Malinke. D=RCC.
1412	Oumé	Oumé	927	2,400	193,124	35.00	67,593	78.30	B	South-central. Bandama River, lake. Coffee, bananas, cocoa.
1413	Sakassou	Sakassou	725	1,880	81,152	33.00	26,780	76.30	B	Central. Nzi River, Lac de Kossou. Bananas, livestock, pineapples.
1414	San-Pédro	San-Pédro	2,664	6,900	233,317	40.00	93,327	83.30	B	Southwest coast, Gulf of Guinea. Primary road. Fishing, exporting, cocoa, bananas. D=RCC.
1415	Sassandra	Sassandra	2,004	5,190	147,767	38.00	56,151	81.30	B	South. Gulf of Guinea. Sassandra River. Exports timber, coffee, bananas.
1416	Sinfra	Sinfra	652	1,690	166,650	37.00	61,661	80.30	B	South-central. Bandama River. Livestock, yams, bananas, rubber, coffee, corn.
1417	Soubré	Soubré	3,193	8,270	424,872	40.00	169,949	83.30	B	South. Sassandra River. Primary road. Trading, handicrafts, fishing, rubber.
1418	Séguéla	Séguéla	4,340	11,240	165,737	13.00	21,546	56.30	B	West-central. Rice-processing, cassava, corn, yams, cattle. Diamonds. Muslim Malinke.
1419	Tabou	Tabou	2,100	5,440	79,492	34.00	27,027	77.30	B	Southwest corner, Gulf of Guinea. Growa Point. Fishing, lumber, bananas, cocoa, coffee.
1420	Tanda	Tanda	2,505	6,490	278,979	8.00	22,318	46.30	A	East. Secondary road. Timber, coffee, cocoa, bananas, rubber, livestock. D=RCC.
1421	Tengréla	Tengréla	849	2,200	74,980	2.00	1,500	39.30	A	North, bordering Mali. Wooded savanna. Cotton, corn, cattle. Senufo.
1422	Tiassalé	Tiassalé	1,301	3,370	182,788	30.00	54,836	73.30	B	South-central. Bandama River. Primary and secondary roads. Textiles, manufacturing.
1423	Touba	Touba	3,367	8,720	147,487	5.00	7,374	43.30	A	West, bordering Guinea. Sassandra River. Secondary roads. Iron ore, diamonds, livestock, fruit.
1424	Toumodi	Toumodi	1,073	2,780	110,462	40.00	44,185	83.30	B	Central. Secondary and primary roads. Cotton, bananas, livestock, handicrafts.
1425	Vavoua	Vavoua	2,378	6,160	230,068	30.00	69,020	73.30	B	West central. Secondary road. Timber, palm kernels, rubber, manufacturing, pineapples, bananas.
1426	Yamoussoukro	Yamoussoukro	2,378	6,160	384,751	43.00	165,443	86.30	B	Central. Manufacturing, textiles, cotton, tobacco, sisal, handicrafts, livestock.
1427	Zuénoula	Zuénoula	1,093	2,830	155,883	32.00	49,883	75.30	B	Central. Bandama Rouge River. Lac de Kossou. Secondary roads. Coffee, yams, cassava.
	JAMAICA		**4,244**	**10,991**	**2,582,577**	**43.43**	**1,121,713**	**98.93**	**B**	**Protestants 24.9%, Independents 8.9%. Pent-char 14.9%, Evangelical 11.7%, GCC 24.6%**
1428	Clarendon	May Pen	462	1,196	231,753	42.00	97,336	98.89	B	South-central. Primary and secondary roads. Railroad. Sugar, bananas, coffee, minerals, tourism.
1429	Hanover	Lucea	174	450	71,993	43.00	30,957	99.70	B	Northwest corner. Reefs, primary roads. Fishing, tourism, citrus fruit.
1430	Manchester	Mandeville	321	830	180,076	42.00	75,632	97.50	B	South central. Railroad, trade, primary roads. Rum, coffee, citrus fruit, cement, minerals.
1431	Portland	Port Antonio	314	814	83,028	42.00	34,872	97.50	B	Northeast. Bananas, coconuts, cacao. International Marlin Tournament. Tourism.
1432	Saint Andrew	Kingston	166	431	702,713	43.51	305,729	99.11	B	Southeast. Blue Mountains. Tourist resorts. Church of St Thomas (c1700). D=RCC,SDA.
1433	Saint Ann	Saint Ann's Bay	468	1,213	162,651	42.00	68,313	99.50	B	North-central, coastal. Tourism, fishing, snorkling, scuba diving, fruits, crafts.
1434	Saint Catherine	Spanish Town	460	1,192	394,618	47.00	185,470	99.50	B	Southeast. Railroad, industrial, tourism. Sugar, bananas, coffee, cocoa. D=RCC,SDA.
1435	Saint Elizabeth	Black River	468	1,212	157,306	40.00	62,922	99.50	B	Southwest. Swamp, Black River. Fishing, bananas, cocoa, fruit, marsh, reefs.
1436	Saint James	Montego Bay	230	595	170,441	46.00	78,403	97.30	B	Northwest. Business, industry, tourism. Snorkling, scuba, airport, rum, minerals.
1437	Saint Mary	Port Maria	236	611	117,875	42.00	49,508	98.50	B	North-central. Galina Point. Primary road. Sugar, fruit, industry.
1438	Saint Thomas	Morant Bay	287	743	91,977	43.00	39,550	99.70	B	Southeast coast. Minerals, agriculture, fruit, fishing. D=Baptist.
1439	Trelawny	Falmouth	338	875	78,202	42.00	32,845	98.50	B	Northwest central. Fishing, snorkling, cement, gypsum, industry.
1440	Westmoreland	Savanna-la-Mar	312	807	139,945	43.00	60,176	99.60	B	Southwest. Bluebeards Bay. Fishing, snorkling, scuba diving. Cocoa, citrus fruits. D=RCC,Baptist.
	JAPAN		**145,883**	**377,835**	**126,714,220**	**2.71**	**3,436,881**	**66.94**	**B**	**Independents 1.2%, Marginal Christians 0.5%. Pent-char 1.3%, Evangelical 0.3%, GCC 2.4%**
1441	Aichi	Nagoya	1,984	5,139	6,868,747	3.04	208,810	67.24	B	Central Honshu. Pacific Ocean. Cotton and silk textiles, ceramics, automobiles. D=RCC.
1442	Akita	Akita	4,484	11,613	1,249,301	2.10	26,235	66.33	B	Northwestern Honshu. Sea of Japan. Hachiman Plateau (volcanoes). Rice, lumber, wood products.
1443	Aomori	Aomori	3,714	9,619	1,508,799	1.70	25,650	65.93	B	Northern Honshu. Pacific Ocean, Tsugaru Strait, Sea of Japan. Rice, apples, dry grains.
1444	Chiba	Chiba	1,989	5,151	5,734,845	3.20	183,515	67.43	B	Honshu. Pacific Ocean. Rice, eggs, flowers, sake. Large natural-gas deposits.
1445	Ehime	Matsuyama	2,190	5,672	1,545,571	1.70	26,275	65.93	B	Northwestern Shikoku. Inland Sea, Bungo Strait. Rice, wheat, fertilizer.
1446	Fukui	Fukui	1,619	4,192	841,737	1.50	12,651	65.73	B	Central Honshu. Sea of Japan. Fukui Plain. Rice, silk textiles. Eihei temple (Zen).
1447	Fukuoka	Fukuoka	1,916	4,963	4,934,999	3.00	148,050	67.23	B	Northern Kyushu. Inland Sea, Shimonoseki Strait. Coal mines, industry. D=RCC.
1448	Fukushima	Fukushima	5,322	13,784	2,153,381	1.50	32,301	65.73	B	Northeastern Honshu. Pacific Ocean. Inawashiro Lake. Rice, tobacco, mulberry (silk).
1449	Gifu	Gifu	4,091	10,596	2,116,609	1.60	33,866	65.83	B	Central Honshu. Nobi Plain. Textiles, paper lanterns, fishing. Numerous spas.
1450	Gumma	Maebashi	2,454	6,356	2,016,492	1.60	32,264	65.83	B	Honshu. Western Kanto Plain. Volcanic mountains. Sericulture. Mineral deposits.
1451	Hiroshima	Hiroshima	3,269	8,467	2,919,521	2.30	67,149	66.53	B	Southwestern Honshu. Chugoku Mountains. Rice, chrysanthemums. Itsuku Island shrine. D=RCC.
1452	Hokkaido (Territory)	Sapporo	32,247	83,520	5,770,604	3.00	173,118	67.23	B	Northernmost of 4 main Japanese islands. Coal. Ainu people. Rice. D=RCC.
1453	Hyogo	Kobe	3,236	8,381	5,554,036	3.50	194,391	67.73	B	Western Honshu. Sea of Japan, Inland Sea. Iron, steel, textiles.
1454	Ibaraki	Mito	2,353	6,094	2,931,787	1.80	52,772	66.03	B	Central Honshu. Pacific Ocean. Suigo-Tsukuba Quasi-national Park. Cereals, tobacco.
1455	Ishikawa	Kanazawa	1,620	4,198	1,191,101	1.70	20,249	65.93	B	Western Honshu. Sea of Japan. Japanese Alps. Rice, machinery, silk, rayon.
1456	Iwate	Morioka	5,898	15,277	1,445,454	1.80	26,018	66.03	B	Northeastern Honshu. Pacific Ocean. Rikuchu Coast National Park. Rice, ironware, charcoal.
1457	Kagawa	Takamatsu	727	1,883	1,045,025	1.90	19,855	66.13	B	Shikoku. Inland Sea. Rice, barley, salt mines. Kotohira (Kompira) Shrine. D=RCC.
1458	Kagoshima	Kagoshima	3,539	9,167	1,830,577	2.80	51,256	67.03	B	Southernmost Kyushu. On-take volcano. Japan's only sub-tropical region. Tropical fruits, sugarcane.
1459	Kanagawa	Yokohoma	928	2,403	8,217,164	4.00	328,687	68.23	B	Honshu. Tokyo Bay, Pacific Ocean. Flowers, dairy products. Popular resort areas on coast. D=RCC.
1460	Kochi	Kochi	2,744	7,107	838,671	1.30	10,903	65.53	B	Southern Shikoku. Tosa Bay. Agricultural machinery, coral, processed seafood. Kochi castle.
1461	Kumamoto	Kumamoto	2,860	7,408	1,882,669	1.60	30,123	65.83	B	Central Kyushu. Amakusa Sea. Includes Amakusa Archipelago. Rice, forestry, tourism.
1462	Kyoto	Kyoto	1,781	4,613	2,660,061	3.50	93,102	67.73	B	South-central. Cultural center of Buddhism. Lake Biwako. Business, industry. F=794. D=RCC.
1463	Mie	Tsu	2,231	5,778	1,840,790	2.40	44,179	66.63	B	Central Honshu. Kii Peninsula. Cultured pearls, petroleum, porcelain, tourism.
1464	Miyagi	Sendai	2,815	7,292	2,312,737	1.40	32,378	65.63	B	Northern Honshu. Sendai Bay. Sendai Plain, Matsushima Bay. Rice, fishing industry, lumber.
1465	Miyazaki	Miyazaki	2,986	7,735	1,192,127	1.30	15,498	65.53	B	Southeastern Kyushu. Chemical fertilizers, cedar pulp, bamboo goods. Major honeymoon spot.
1466	Nagano	Nagano	5,245	13,585	2,206,500	1.90	41,924	66.13	B	Central Honshu. Volcanic peaks. Hydroelectricity. Sericuture, apples. Site of 1998 Winter Olympics.
1467	Nagasaki	Nagasaki	1,588	4,113	1,590,517	6.50	103,384	70.73	B	Northwestern Kyushu. East China Sea. Rice, sweet potatoes, fishing, shipbuilding. D=RCC.
1468	Nara	Nara	1,425	3,692	1,418,895	1.50	21,283	65.73	B	Southern Honshu. Central Kii Peninsula. Rice, wheat, flowers.
1469	Niigata	Niigata	4,857	12,579	2,527,252	1.40	35,382	65.63	B	North-central Honshu. Sea of Japan. One of Japan's largest rice producers. D=RCC.
1470	Oita	Oita	2,447	6,338	1,261,579	0.80	10,093	65.03	B	Northeastern Kyushu. Suo Sea. Forestry, tobacco, citrus fruits. Hot spring resorts. D=RCC.
1471	Okayama	Okayama	2,738	7,092	1,970,520	1.00	19,705	65.23	B	Western Honshu. Inland Sea. Rice, grapes. Oil refineries, automobile, steel factories.
1472	Okinawa	Naha	871	2,255	1,255,459	1.40	17,576	65.63	B	Island in East China Sea. Tuna fishing, sake. Semi-independent kingdom. World War II battle.
1473	Osaka	Osaka	722	1,869	8,925,078	3.80	339,153	68.03	B	Major commercial and industrial center. Northeast, Osaka Bay. Heavily damaged in WWII. D=RCC.
1474	Saga	Saga	942	2,440	895,882	1.50	13,438	65.73	B	Northern Kyushu. Sea of Japan, Ariake Sea. Rice, orange cultivation, dairy farming.
1475	Saitama	Urawa	1,467	3,799	6,622,554	3.00	198,677	67.23	B	Honshu. Bordering on Tokyo Metropolis. Fruits, vegetables, flowers, green tea. D=RCC.
1476	Shiga	Otsu	1,551	4,016	1,260,566	2.20	27,732	66.43	B	Southern Honshu. Lake Biwa (largest lake in Japan). Rice, beef.
1477	Shimane	Matsue	2,559	6,629	794,752	1.10	8,742	65.33	B	Southwestern Honshu. Oki Archipelago. Forestry. Izumo Taisha (oldest Shinto shrine in Japan).
1478	Shizuoka	Shizuoka	3,001	7,773	3,765,351	1.60	60,246	65.83	B	Central Honshu. Pacific Ocean. Volcanoes, hot springs. Mandarin Oranges, tea, ships.
1479	Tochigi	Utsunomiya	2,476	6,414	1,988,906	1.40	27,845	65.63	B	Honshu. Rice, tobacco, ceramics. Nikko National Park.
1480	Tokushima	Tokushima	1,601	4,146	847,870	1.30	11,022	65.53	B	Shikoku. Pacific Ocean. Salt, indigo, tobacco, rice, flowers.
1481	Tokyo	Tokyo	836	2,166	12,142,884	4.00	485,715	68.23	B	East central. Sumida River. Financial center, shipbuilding. D=RCC.
1482	Tottori	Tottori	1,349	3,494	629,263	1.50	9,439	65.73	B	Western Honshu. Sea of Japan. Tottori sand dunes. Rice, tobacco. Electrified railway.
1483	Toyama	Toyama	1,642	4,252	1,145,129	1.80	20,612	66.03	B	Central Honshu. Sea of Japan. Since 17th century chief center for patent medicines.
1484	Wakayama	Wakayama	1,824	4,725	1,099,157	1.80	19,785	66.03	B	South-central Honshu. Kii Peninsula. Typhoons. Fishing, tourism. Buddhist temple (9th cent).
1485	Yamagata	Yamagata	3,601	9,327	1,284,059	1.50	19,261	65.73	B	Northern Honshu. Sea of Japan. Dewa Sangan sacred mountains (Shugen-do sect of Buddhism).
1486	Yamaguchi	Yamaguchi	2,358	6,107	1,602,770	2.60	41,672	66.83	B	Extreme western Honshu. Shimonoseki Strait, Inland Sea. Rice, deep-sea fishing.
1487	Yamanashi	Kofu	1,723	4,463	876,470	1.70	14,900	65.93	B	Central Honshu. Mount Shirane (10,472 ft) and Mount Fuji (12,388 ft). Mulberries, peaches, apples.
	JORDAN		**34,458**	**89,246**	**6,669,341**	**4.10**	**273,522**	**54.25**	**B**	**Orthodox 1.9%, Independents 1.1%. Pent-char 1.3%, Evangelical 0.4%, GCC 3.4%**
1488	'Ajlun	'Ajlun	–	–	153,408	3.00	4,602	53.15	B	North. Ajlun Mountains. Wheat, millet, olives, vineyards. Biblical Gilead. D=GOC.
1489	Al-Aqabah	Al-Aqabah	–	–	129,859	2.50	3,246	52.65	B	Southwest. Gulf of Aqaba. Only sea outlet for Jordan. Phosphates. Resorts. D=GOC.
1490	al-Balqa'	as-Salt	425	1,100	445,359	3.10	13,806	53.25	B	West-central. Highlands (2,600-2,750 ft). Grapes, grain, pharmaceutical products. D=GOC.
1491	al-Karak	al-Karak	1,548	4,010	276,104	1.90	5,246	48.05	A	West-central. Dead Sea. Also spelled Kerak. Remains of several Byzantine churches.
1492	al-Mafraq	al-Mafraq	10,475	27,129	278,305	2.00	5,566	49.15	A	North, north of Az-Zarga, Syrian desert. Railroad, agriculture, wheat. D=GOC,RCC.
1493	at-Tafilah	at-Tafilah	850	2,202	99,587	1.60	1,593	47.75	A	East central, Israel border, Al-Ata-itah Mountain. Wheat, phosphates, vegetables.
1494	az-Zarqa'	az-Zarqa'	2,008	5,201	1,016,041	4.00	40,642	54.15	B	North of Amman, former Circassian center. Wetland reserve. Railroad, olives, potash. D=GOC.
1495	Irbid	Irbid	985	2,551	1,214,434	4.80	58,293	55.75	B	North. Agriculture. Many springs. Jordan River. Lake Tiberius. Wheat, textiles, fruits, olives. D=GOC.
1496	Jarash (Gerasa)	Jarash (Gerasa)	–	–	200,614	2.00	4,012	49.15	A	North. Tourism. Roman ruins. Ancient Decapolis. Circassians. D=GOC.
1497	Madaba	Madaba	–	–	173,116	2.20	3,809	52.35	B	South central. East of Dead Sea. Ancient Medeba. D=GOC.
1498	Ma`an	Ma`an	13,954	36,141	129,299	2.20	2,845	49.35	A	South. Bedouin tribes. Al Jafr depression, Mount Mabrak. Salt flats. D=GOC,RCC.
1499	`Amman	Amman	4,097	10,612	2,553,217	5.09	129,862	56.15	B	Eastern boundary of Ajlun Mountains. Biblical: Rabbah, ancient Greek: Philadelphia. D=GOC.

Continued overleaf

Table 11-3 continued

Rec No 1	Country Major civil divisions 2	Capital 3	sq.mi. 4	sq.km. 5	Pop 2000 6	AC% 7	Church members 8	E% 9	W 10	Notes 11
	KAZAKHSTAN		**1,049,200**	**2,717,300**	**16,222,563**	**15.98**	**2,591,803**	**64.25**	**B**	**Orthodox 8.6%, Independents 4.0%. Pent-char 0.5%, Evangelical 0.06%, GCC 8.9%**
1500	Almaty (Alma-Ata)	Almaty (Alma-Ata)	86,500	224,200	1,638,495	18.00	294,929	68.27	B	Southeast. Frequent earthquakes and mudslides. Food industry. D=ROC,RCC.
1501	Almaty city	–	–	–	1,140,300	21.11	240,697	71.57	B	Southeast. Frequent earthquakes and mudslides. Education center. D=Baptist,ROC.
1502	Aqmola (Akmola)	Aqmola (Akmola)	58,700	152,000	974,068	19.00	185,073	69.27	B	North. Ishim River, Lake Tengiz. Grain, dairy goods. Name means "white tomb". D=ROC.
1503	Aqtöbe (Aktyubinsk)	Aqtöbe	116,050	300,600	732,189	10.00	73,219	58.27	B	Northwest. Ilek River. Copper, chromium compounds, X-ray apparatus. D=ROC.
1504	Atyrau	Atyrau	45,800	118,600	447,013	5.00	22,351	45.27	A	West. Ural River. Until 1992: Guryev. Fishing, oil refineries, metalworking. D=ROC.
1505	Batys Qazaqstan	Oral	58,400	151,300	651,466	19.00	123,779	69.27	B	West. Ural River. Stock breeding, wheat, barley. Extensive hay lands. D=ROC.
1506	Baykonur (Leninsk)	–	–	–	66,723	20.00	13,345	68.27	B	South. Syrdarja River. Russian space launch complex (leased). D=ROC.
1507	Mangghysta-	Aqtau	63,950	165,600	315,513	22.00	69,413	70.27	B	Southwest. Caspian Sea. Marsh, railroad. Livestock, minerals, handicrafts. D=ROC.
1508	Ongtüstik Qazaqstan	Shymkent	45,300	117,300	1,933,389	5.00	96,669	43.97	A	South-central. Ugam mountain range. Chemical industry. D=ROC.
1509	Pavlodar	Pavlodar	48,200	124,800	917,775	17.00	156,022	65.27	B	North. Irtysh River. Tractor, aluminum, and chemical plants. D=ROC.
1510	Qaraghandy	Qaraghandy	165,250	428,000	1,706,484	18.00	307,167	68.27	B	Central. Steppe, Karkaraly Mountains. Coal mining. Dry, severe winters. D=ROC.
1511	Qostanay	Qostanay	64,000	165,800	1,172,421	19.00	222,760	70.27	B	North. Tobol River. Mining, grain, cattle raising. D=ROC.
1512	Qyzylorda	Kzyl-Orda	87,250	226,000	589,512	25.00	147,378	73.27	B	South. Aral Sea. Zankala ruins, Syrdarja River. Marsh, desert. Livestock. D=ROC.
1513	Shyghys Qazaqstan	Shyghys	109,400	283,300	1,702,590	12.00	204,311	60.27	B	East. Rudny Altay Mountains. Nonferrous metallurgy and associated research laboratories. D=ROC.
1514	Soltüstik Qazaqstan	Petropavl	47,500	123,300	1,223,473	19.00	232,460	70.27	B	North. Ishim River. Ishim Steppe. Several lakes, railroad, wheat, fruit tobacco, livestock. D=ROC.
1515	Zhambyl	Zhambyl	55,700	144,300	1,011,152	20.00	202,230	70.27	B	South. Cu River, Lake Balkhash. Marsh, desert. Textiles, livestock, farming. D=ROC.
	KENYA		**224,961**	**582,646**	**30,080,372**	**74.72**	**22,477,365**	**94.21**	**C**	**Roman Catholics 23.2%, Independents 21.9%. Pent-char 27.7%, Evangelical 22.4%, GCC 12.2%**
1516	Central	Nyeri	5,087	13,176	4,368,572	72.00	3,145,372	93.20	C	South-central. Elevation 5,750 ft. Leather goods, soap, wood and furniture. D=RCC,AIC.
1517	Coast	Mombasa	32,279	83,603	2,596,237	55.00	1,427,930	74.49	B	East. Indian Ocean. Sisal, cotton, sugar. D=RCC,AIC.
1518	Eastern	Embu	61,734	159,891	5,221,652	73.63	3,844,958	94.82	C	Central-east. Mount Kenya National Park. Food processing, clothing, furniture. D=RCC,AIC.
1519	Nairobi	–	264	684	2,021,702	74.20	1,500,103	95.69	C	South central. University of Kenya. National Park Game Reserve. D=RCC,AIC,Anglican.
1520	North Eastern	Garissa	48,997	126,902	491,513	66.00	324,400	85.49	C	East. Tana River. Food processing, tobacco products, plastics. D=RCC,AIC.
1521	Nyanza	Kisumu	6,240	16,162	4,868,508	78.00	3,797,436	97.49	C	Southwest. Lake Victoria. Cotton, coffee, tea. Luo and Gusii. D=RCC,AIC.
1522	Rift Valley	Nakuru	67,131	173,868	6,855,618	82.00	5,621,607	98.49	C	Northwest. Major branch of the East African Rift System. Kikuyu. D=RCC,AIC.
1523	Western	Kakamega	3,228	8,360	3,656,570	77.00	2,815,559	96.49	C	West. Food processing, clothing, footwear. D=RCC,AIC.
	KIRGHIZIA		**76,600**	**198,500**	**4,699,337**	**9.91**	**465,665**	**47.37**	**A**	**Orthodox 7.7%, Independents 1.5%. Pent-char 0.3%, Evangelical 0.06%, GCC 4.7%**
1524	Bishkek (Frunze)	–	–	–	681,581	14.04	95,706	52.02	B	Chu River Valley. Cultural center, museum, opera. Metallurgy, machine building. F=1878. D=ROC.
1525	Chüy (Chu)	Kara-Balta	7,200	18,700	840,765	9.80	82,395	47.26	A	North. Akso River, University (1951). Railroad, leather, textiles, meat packing. D=ROC.
1526	Jalal-Abad	Dzhalal-Abad	15,200	39,500	831,201	9.50	78,964	46.96	A	West. Food processing. Carycelekskij National Park, Catkalskj Mountains. Livestock, leather. D=ROC.
1527	Naryn	Naryn	18,300	47,300	276,181	6.00	16,571	41.46	A	Southeast. Separated from rest of country by mountain ranges. Sheep raising. D=ROC.
1528	Osh	Osh	14,700	38,100	1,405,455	11.00	154,600	49.26	A	Southwest. Cotton, tobacco, cereal grains, melons. D=ROC.
1529	Talas	Talas	4,400	11,400	211,042	7.00	14,773	44.46	A	Northwest. Talas River valley. Russians, Ukrainians, Germans, Hui. D=ROC.
1530	Ysyk-Köl	Issyk-Kul	16,800	43,500	453,112	5.00	22,656	40.46	A	Northeast. Victory Peak (24,406 ft.). Raw opium, grain, potatoes. Lake Ysyk-K"l resort. D=ROC.
	KIRIBATI		**313**	**811**	**83,387**	**92.74**	**77,331**	**99.93**	**C**	**Roman Catholics 52.8%, Protestants 44.3%. Pent-char 15.2%, Evangelical 7.1%, GCC 12.2%**
1531	Gilberts Group	Bairiki Islet	110	285	77,823	92.57	72,044	99.92	C	West-central. Pacific Ocean. 16 coral atolls. Phosphate, copra. D=RCC,GIPC.
1532	Line Group	Kiritimati	192	496	5,513	95.00	5,237	99.97	C	Southwest and west-central. Pacific Ocean. D=RCC,GIPC.
1533	Phoenix Group	Kanton	11	29	52	96.00	50	99.99	C	West-central. Pacific Ocean. 8 atolls, of which Kanton is the only inhabited one. D=RCC,GIPC.
	KUWAIT		**6,880**	**17,818**	**1,971,634**	**12.55**	**247,535**	**64.46**	**B**	**Roman Catholics 8.8%, Independents 3.2%. Pent-char 3.4%, Evangelical 0.9%, GCC 8.3%**
1534	al-Ahmadi	al-Ahmadi	1,984	5,138	331,037	9.83	32,554	61.65	B	South. Persian Gulf. Headquarters of Kuwait Oil Company. D=RCC.
1535	al-Farwaniyah	al-Farwaniyah	–	–	526,821	13.00	68,487	64.91	B	Southwest. Kuwait City. Construction materials, manufacturing, oil wells, pipelines. D=RCC.
1536	al-Jahra'	al-Jahra'	4,372	11,324	266,368	10.00	26,637	61.91	B	Central. Sparsely populated desert. Fruits, vegetables. Ali-Al Salem Airbase. D=RCC.
1537	Capital	Kuwait City	38	98	323,151	16.00	51,704	68.00	B	On Kuwait Bay and Persian Gulf. Commercial center, banking, financial districts. D=RCC.
1538	Hawalli	Hawalli	138	358	524,257	13.00	68,153	64.91	B	East of Kuwait City. Persian Gulf. 5 miles east of Al Kuwait. Fisheries, chemicals, oil. D=RCC.
	LAOS		**91,429**	**236,800**	**5,433,036**	**2.07**	**112,563**	**47.55**	**A**	**Independents 0.8%, Protestants 0.6%. Pent-char 0.9%, Evangelical 0.7%, GCC 1.8%**
1539	Attapu	Attapu	3,985	10,320	103,461	1.20	1,242	43.68	A	South. Kong River. Rice, corn.
1540	Bokèo	Houayxay	2,392	6,196	135,554	1.00	1,356	42.48	A	Northwest. Burma border, Thailand border. Tobacco, tea, livestock.
1541	Bolikhamxai	Pakxan	5,739	14,863	194,541	2.00	3,891	47.48	A	Central. Thailand and Vietnam border, Kading River. Rice, corn.
1542	Champasak	Pakxé	5,952	15,415	593,760	2.10	12,469	47.88	A	South. MeKong River. Rice, corn (maize), cotton.
1543	Houaphan	Xam Nua	6,371	16,500	291,749	2.00	5,835	47.48	A	Northeast. Vietnam border, Xam River. Cotton, agriculture. D=Gospel Church.
1544	Khammouan	Thakhek	6,299	16,315	324,901	1.50	4,874	46.98	A	Central. Mekong River. Rice, corn, livestock.
1545	Louangnamtha	Louangnamtha	3,600	9,325	135,907	2.00	2,718	47.48	A	Northwest. Tha River. Lamet, Lolo, Akha (Ko), Lu peoples.
1546	Louangphrabang	Louangphrabang	6,515	16,875	433,198	1.80	7,798	47.28	A	North. Corn (maize), rice, poultry. Khmu, Meo. D=RCC,Gospel Church.
1547	Oudomxay	Xay	5,934	15,370	249,279	2.00	4,986	47.48	A	Northwest. Mekong River. Rice, livestock.
1548	Phôngsali	Phôngsali	6,282	16,270	180,969	1.50	2,715	43.98	A	North. Nam On river. Rice, corn, tobacco, livestock, rural farming. D=Gospel Church.
1549	Salavan	Salavan	4,128	10,691	304,728	2.00	6,095	47.48	A	South. Don River, Vietnam and Thailand borders. Rice, livestock.
1550	Savannakhét	Savannakhét	8,407	21,774	796,206	2.20	17,517	48.18	A	South-central. Banghiang River, Mekong River. Fishing, crafts. Soft drinks, ice making. D=RCC.
1551	Special Region	–	2,743	7,105	63,941	2.00	1,279	47.48	A	South-central. Mekong River. Fishing, rice, livestock.
1552	Viangchan	Muang Phôn-Hông	6,149	15,927	338,348	2.00	6,767	48.48	A	West-central. Nam Ngum Reservoir. Lik River. Fishing, rice, cotton, corn, livestock.
1553	Viangchan	Vientiane	1,514	3,920	627,380	3.00	18,821	49.41	A	West-central. Thailand border. Airport, railroad, Mekong River. Fishing, industry.
1554	Xaignabouli	Xaignabouri	6,328	16,389	346,014	2.49	8,620	48.57	A	Northwest. Rattan, bamboo, rice, cotton. Meo, Khmu. D=Gospel Church.
1555	Xiangkhoang	Phônsavan	6,131	15,880	237,364	2.00	4,747	47.48	A	North-central. Corn, rice. Khmu, Meo. D=Gospel Church.
1556	Xékong	Thong	2,959	7,665	75,737	1.10	833	42.58	A	South. Kaman River. Rice, corn, cotton, tea, tobacco.
	LATVIA		**24,946**	**64,610**	**2,356,508**	**66.90**	**1,576,425**	**99.04**	**C**	**Protestants 23.7%, Orthodox 23.5%. Pent-char 3.8%, Evangelical 7.1%, GCC 20.0%**
1557	Aizkraukle	Aizkraukle	988	2,558	39,473	72.00	28,421	99.84	C	Southwest. Daugava River. Art school, theatre. Printing, publishing, woodworking. D=RCC.
1558	Aluksne	Aluksne	867	2,246	25,231	70.00	17,662	99.64	C	Northeast. Russia and Estonia border. Agriculture, livestock, textiles. D=Lutheran.
1559	Balvi	Balvi	920	2,384	29,451	72.00	21,205	97.14	C	Northeast. Balupe River, Russian border. Marsh. Rye, textiles. D=Orthodox.
1560	Bauska	Bauska	727	1,884	49,055	71.00	34,829	99.14	C	South-central. Musa and Memele Rivers, Bauskas Castle, Lutheran church (1705). D=Lutheran.
1561	Cesis	Cesis	1,182	3,062	56,616	72.00	40,764	98.64	C	North-central. Vidzeme highlands. Food processing, metalworking. German: Wenden. D=Lutheran.
1562	Daugavpils	–	28	72	113,408	65.00	73,715	98.64	C	Southeast. Cathedral of St Boris. Zoo, 2nd largest city. F=1582. D=Orthodox.
1563	Daugavpils	Daugavpils	975	2,526	40,440	65.00	26,286	98.64	C	Southeast. Cargo moving, industry, transit, chemicals, clothing, heavy equipment. D=Lutheran.
1564	Dobele	Dobele	649	1,680	39,737	72.00	28,611	98.64	C	West-central. Berze River. Railroad, agriculture, livestock, crafts. D=Lutheran.
1565	Gulbene	Gulbene	724	1,876	26,550	71.00	18,851	98.44	C	Northeast. Gauja River, Pededze River. Railroad, textiles, timber, farming. D=Lutheran.
1566	Jekabpils	Jekabpils	1,158	2,998	54,770	70.00	38,339	99.64	C	Southeast. Dougava River. Fishing, trade, railroad, lakes, marsh. D=Orthodox.
1567	Jelgava	–	23	60	65,495	63.00	41,262	99.14	C	South-central. Lielupe River. Inland maritime harbor. Jelgava Castle, Anna's Church=1570. F=c1264.
1568	Jelgava	Jelgava	623	1,613	34,374	62.00	21,312	99.14	C	South-central. Railroad, industry, shipping, trade, chemicals, textiles. D=Orthodox.
1569	Jurmala	–	39	100	58,462	70.00	40,923	99.64	C	West. Gulf of Riga. 'The Seaside' Fisherman's Museum. Resort, tourism. D=RCC.
1570	Kraslava	Kraslava	883	2,288	36,220	68.00	24,630	99.64	C	Southeast. Daugava River. Belarus border, Latgale, several lakes. Railroad, industry. D=Lutheran.
1571	Kuldiga	Kuldiga	966	2,503	35,868	70.00	25,108	99.64	C	West. Venta River, many lakes. Farming, barley, potatoes, rye, livestock. D=Orthodox.
1572	Liepaja	–	23	60	101,012	66.00	66,668	99.14	C	West on Baltic Sea, Kloval Port. Grain export, steel, deep sea fishing. F=1253. D=RCC,Lutheran.
1573	Liepaja	Liepaja	1,386	3,589	48,088	68.00	32,700	99.64	C	Southwest. Baltic Sea. Lake Liepaja. Fishing, commercial industry, railroad, trade. D=RCC,Lutheran.
1574	Limbazi	Limbazi	1,005	2,602	36,220	68.00	24,630	99.64	C	North-central. Salaca River, Bay of Riga. Flax, rye, potatoes, mining, agriculture. D=RCC.
1575	Ludza	Ludza	991	2,566	36,572	69.00	25,235	99.74	C	East. Several lakes, marsh. Potatoes, barley, livestock, agricultural. D=Orthodox.
1576	Madona	Madona	1,293	3,348	43,605	70.00	30,524	99.64	C	West-central. Teichi State Nature Reserve, Krust Kalns Nature Reserve. Railroad, farming. D=RCC.
1577	Ogre	Ogre	701	1,816	58,111	70.00	40,678	99.64	C	Central. Daugava River. Railroad, primary highways. Fishing, trading, textiles, industry. D=RCC.
1578	Preili	Preili	788	2,042	39,825	69.00	27,479	99.74	C	Southwest. 84 lakes, swamp. Dubna River. Dolomite, timber. D=RCC.
1579	Rezekne	–	7	17	38,005	65.00	24,703	98.64	C	Southeast. Rezekne River. Railroad, farming, trade, industry. D=Orthodox.
1580	Rezekne	Rezekne	1,025	2,654	37,952	65.00	24,669	98.64	C	Southeast. Malta River, Rezekne River. Agriculture, livestock, potatoes, barley, flax. D=Orthodox.
1581	Riga	–	114	295	800,184	65.10	520,935	98.70	C	Central. Dvina River. Shipping, electrical equipment, chemical, industry, tourism. F=1201. D=RCC.
1582	Riga	Riga	1,194	3,094	134,771	61.00	82,210	98.64	C	Central. Gulf of Riga, Dvina River, Latvian capital. Industry, farming, rye. D=Lutheran. D=RCC.
1583	Saldus	Saldus	824	2,134	34,902	70.00	24,431	99.64	C	Southwest. Railroad, farming villages. 'Kurzeme Switzerland' Lake Talsi, established 1231.
1584	Talsi	Talsi	1,061	2,748	43,869	69.00	30,270	99.74	C	Northwest. North Kurzeme, 'Switzerland'. D=RCC.
1585	Tukums	Tukums	949	2,457	52,044	68.00	35,390	99.64	C	West. Abava River, Engures Lake, Bay of Riga. Fishing, railroad, trade, textiles, agricultural. D=RCC.
1586	Valka	Valka	944	2,444	32,792	70.00	22,954	99.64	C	Northeast. Guada and Sedo Rivers, Estonia border. Railroad. Flax, potatoes, rye, livestock. D=RCC.
1587	Valmiera	Valmiera	918	2,377	55,561	68.00	37,781	99.64	C	Northeast. Gauga River, Lake Burtnieku. Hippodrome. Timber, potatoes, rye, livestock. D=RCC.
1588	Ventspils	–	18	46	44,308	75.00	33,231	99.92	C	West. Baltic Sea, coastal lowlands. Oil, chemical export. Fishing, canning. F=2000 BC. D=Orthodox.
1589	Ventspils	Ventspils	954	2,471	13,539	74.00	10,019	99.84	C	West. Lowlands. Radio astronomy center. Industry, chemicals. D=Lutheran.
	LEBANON		**3,950**	**10,230**	**3,281,787**	**52.86**	**1,734,821**	**91.87**	**B**	**Roman Catholics 42.5%, Orthodox 16.3%. Pent-char 5.0%, Evangelical 1.7%, GCC 21.9%**
1590	al-Biqa'	Zahlah	1,653	4,280	314,114	51.00	160,198	90.01	B	Northeast. Bekaa Valley, Orontes River, Mt. Hermon. Olives, tobacco. D=RCC,AAC.
1591	al-Janub	Sidon (Sayda)	772	2,001	385,767	55.00	212,172	94.01	B	Southwest. Mediterranean Sea, city of Tyre, Al-Utani River. Navigable canals. D=RCC.
1592	ash-Shamal	Tripoli (Tarabulus)	765	1,981	563,244	51.92	292,435	90.93	B	Northwest. Cedars of Lebanon, Mediterranean Sea. Fruit, vegetables, shipping. D=RCC,AAC.
1593	Bayrut	Beirut (Bayrut)	7	18	732,918	46.00	337,142	84.84	B	West-central. Mediterranean. Lebanon Mountains. Citrus fruit, bananas. D=RCC.
1594	Jabal Lubnan	B'abda	753	1,950	1,285,744	57.00	732,874	96.11	B	Central. Site of former Palestinian refugee camp Tall Za'tar. D=RCC,Orthodox.
	LESOTHO		**11,720**	**30,355**	**2,152,553**	**67.14**	**1,445,329**	**99.62**	**C**	**Roman Catholics 37.4%, Protestants 12.9%. Pent-char 15.8%, Evangelical 3.5%, GCC 23.7%**
1595	Berea	Tayateyaneng	858	2,222	265,593	67.00	177,947	99.98	C	Northwest. Little Caledon River. Mohair rugs, stoneware pottery. Beans, sorghum. D=RCC.
1596	Butha-Buthe	Butha-Buthe	682	1,767	137,054	69.00	94,567	99.53	C	North. Malibamatso River, Front Range. Corn, wheat, peas, sorghum, livestock. D=RCC,Evangelical.
1597	Leribe	Hlotse	1,092	2,828	352,084	67.00	235,896	99.98	C	North. Front Range, Mohokare River. Wheat, minerals, mohair. D=RCC,Evangelical.
1598	Mafeteng	Mafeteng	818	2,119	266,923	67.00	178,838	99.98	C	West. Makhaleng River. Secondary roads. Corn, wheat, peas, beans, agriculture. D=RCC.
1599	Maseru	Maseru	1,652	4,279	424,603	65.62	278,614	99.57	C	Northwest. Caledon River. Railroad, airport. Trade, crafts, mohair, diamonds. D=RCC.
1600	Mohale's Hoek	Mohale's Hoek	1,363	3,530	224,343	67.00	150,310	99.98	C	Southwest. Thaba-Putsoa Range, Le Bihan Falls. Wheat, corn (maize), sorghum. D=RCC.
1601	Mokhotlong	Mokhotlong	1,573	4,075	101,926	69.00	70,329	98.78	C	Northeast. Khubelu River, Orange River. Corn, peas, sorghum, crafts. D=RCC,Evangelical.
1602	Qacha's Nek	Qacha's Nek	907	2,349	87,289	70.00	61,102	98.48	C	Southeast. Drakensberg, Sehlaba Thebe National Park, Orange and Tsudibe Rivers. D=RCC.
1603	Quthing	Quthing	1,126	2,916	150,627	69.00	103,933	99.53	C	South. Drakensburg, Orange River. Wheat, maize, wool, mohair, sorghum, peas, livestock. D=RCC.
1604	Thaba-Tseka	Thaba-Tseka	1,649	4,270	142,111	66.00	93,793	98.48	C	Southeast-central, central range. Diamonds, minerals, livestock, mohair. D=RCC,Evangelical.

Continued opposite

Table 11-3 continued

Rec No 1	Country Major civil divisions 2	Capital 3	sq.mi. 4	sq.km. 5	Pop 2000 6	AC% 7	Church members 8	E% 9	W 10	Notes 11
	LIBERIA		**38,250**	**99,067**	**3,154,001**	**29.55**	**932,060**	**72.51**	**B**	**Independents 17.0%, Protestants 13.6%. Pent-char 16.4%, Evangelical 10.6%, GCC 17.2%**
1605	Bomi	Tubmanburg	755	1,955	95,991	33.00	31,677	75.96	B	Southwest. Lagoons, Saint Paul River. Railroad, rice, coffee, cassava. D=RCC,Baptist.
1606	Bong	Gbarnga	3,127	8,099	382,394	20.00	76,479	62.96	B	West-central. Saint John, Saint Paul rivers, Bong Range. Railroad, rubber, iron ore. D=RCC.
1607	Grand Bassa	Buchanan	3,382	8,759	238,051	35.00	83,318	77.96	B	Central. Atlantic Ocean. Coast, Saint John River. Railroad. Grain, trade, shipping, fruit. D=RCC.
1608	Grand Cape Mount	Robertsport	2,250	5,827	119,668	33.00	39,490	75.96	B	West. Atlantic Ocean. Lake Piso. Rubber, rice, palm kernels, food processing. D=RCC.
1609	Grand Gedeh	Zwedru	6,575	17,029	155,468	17.00	26,430	59.96	B	East. Putu Range, Sapo National Park, Dube River. Cassava, cocoa, timber. D=Baptist.
1610	Lofa	Voinjama	7,475	19,360	372,267	18.00	67,008	60.96	B	North. Largest region, Guinea border, Kpo Range. Rubber, agriculture, livestock. D=RCC,Baptist.
1611	Margibi	Kakata	1,260	3,263	148,336	21.00	31,151	63.96	B	West. Airport. Rubber, iron ore, diamonds, cocoa, palm kernels, rice, coffee. D=RCC,AoG.
1612	Maryland	Harper	2,066	5,351	196,403	33.00	64,813	75.96	B	Southeast. Cavally River. Secondary roads. Rubber, rice, fruit, livestock. D=RCC,Baptist.
1613	Montserrado	Bensonville	1,058	2,740	830,683	42.86	356,059	85.81	B	West. Capital city. Railroad, lagoons. Shipping, trade, industry, food processing. D=RCC,Baptist,AoG.
1614	Nimba	Sanniquellie	4,650	12,043	464,549	23.00	106,846	65.96	B	North. Nimba Range. Iron ore, diamonds, livestock, railroad, coffee, timber. D=RCC.
1615	Rivercress	Rivercress City	1,693	4,385	56,910	30.00	17,073	72.96	B	Central. Cestos River, lagoons. Rice, livestock, timber, cocoa, coffee. D=Baptist,AoG.
1616	Sinoe	Greenville	3,959	10,254	93,281	34.00	31,716	76.96	B	South. Atlantic Ocean. Putu Range, Sapo National Park. Rubber, coffee, timber. D=RCC,Baptist.
	LIBYA		**678,400**	**1,757,000**	**5,604,722**	**3.04**	**170,352**	**46.12**	**A**	**Orthodox 1.9%, Roman Catholics 0.8%. Pent-char 0.3%, Evangelical 0.1%, GCC 1.6%**
1617	al-Jabal al Akhdar	al-Bayda'	14,300	37,000	458,022	3.00	13,741	46.08	A	Northeast. Cyrene ruins, Appollonia ruins, Al-Akhdra mountains. Primary roads. D=Orthodox.
1618	al-Jabal al-Gharbi	Gharyan	33,600	87,000	303,516	2.80	8,498	45.88	A	Northeast. Tripolitania Tarabulus, south of Tripoli. Oil, barley, wheat. D=Orthodox.
1619	al-Kufrah	al-Kufrah	186,900	484,000	35,358	0.50	177	33.58	A	Southeast. Libyan desert. Gypsum, natural gas, oil.
1620	az-Zawiyah	za-Zawiyah	1,500	4,000	485,061	3.20	15,522	46.28	A	Northwest. Mediterranean. Potatoes, onions, tomatoes. D=Orthodox.
1621	Banghazi	Banghazi	5,800	1,500	760,946	3.20	24,350	47.08	A	Northeast. Gulf of Sidra. Great man-made river. Wheat, oil. D=RCC,Orthodox.
1622	Khalij Surt	Surt	145,200	376,000	567,662	3.00	17,030	46.08	A	North. Mediterranean. Great man-made river, Marble Arch. Tuna, salt. D=RCC,Orthodox.
1623	Margib	al-Khums	11,200	29,000	607,478	3.20	19,439	46.28	A	Northwest. East of Tripoli, Labdah Leptis Magna. Fishing, industry. D=Orthodox.
1624	Marzuq	Marzuq	135,100	350,000	67,151	0.50	336	33.58	A	Southwest. Desert oases. Olives, dates, gypsum.
1625	Nikat al-Khums	Zuwarah	39,000	101,000	291,185	3.22	9,390	46.30	A	Northwest. Tunisia border. Salt lakes. Fruit, livestock. D=Orthodox.
1626	Sabha	Sabha	31,700	82,000	180,802	1.50	2,712	39.58	A	Southwest central. Oil, dates, olives, desert.
1627	Tarabulus	Tripoli (Tarabulus)	1,200	3,000	1,609,096	3.50	56,318	48.39	A	Northwest. Mediterranean. Olives, citrus fruit, tobacco. D=RCC,Orthodox.
1628	Tubruq	Tubruq	32,400	84,000	164,758	1.50	2,471	39.58	A	Northeast. English, German, and French cemeteries. Scene of heavy fighting in WWII. D=RCC.
1629	Wadi al-Ha'it	Awbari	40,500	105,000	73,688	0.50	368	33.58	A	West. Desert. Oil, olives, barley, livestock.
	LIECHTENSTEIN		**62**	**160**	**32,843**	**82.36**	**27,051**	**98.36**	**C**	**Roman Catholics 74.2%, Protestants 7.6%. Pent-char 2.4%, Evangelical 0.3%, GCC 43.1%**
1630	Oberland	–	48	125	22,038	82.05	18,083	98.05	C	Western Europe. Rhine River. Dairy products, corn, tourism, pharmaceuticals, livestock. D=RCC.
1631	Unterland	–	13	35	10,805	83.00	8,968	99.00	C	Western Europe. Rhine River. Textiles, precision instruments, wine, ceramics, tourism. D=RCC.
	LITHUANIA		**25,213**	**65,301**	**3,670,269**	**87.55**	**3,213,397**	**99.60**	**C**	**Roman Catholics 84.6%, Orthodox 3.1%. Pent-char 1.4%, Evangelical 0.2%, GCC 11.7%**
1632	Alytus	Alytus	2,095	5,425	200,397	85.00	170,337	99.05	C	South. Nemanus River. Regional museum. Sawmilling, textile center, tanning, wool. D=RCC.
1633	Kaunas	Kaunas	3,154	8,170	747,634	89.00	665,394	99.85	C	South. Nemanus River. River port. 16th century town hall, 17th century monastery. D=RCC.
1634	Klaipeda	Klaipeda	2,219	5,746	411,070	88.00	361,742	99.75	C	West, on Baltic Sea. Ice-free seaport. Fishing, early 7th century settlement. Fertilizers. D=RCC.
1635	Marijampole	Marijampole	1,723	4,463	196,359	87.00	170,832	99.45	C	South. Sheshope River. Sugar, flour milling, breweries, cotton goods, leather. D=RCC.
1636	Panevezys	Panevezys	3,042	7,880	320,047	89.00	284,842	99.85	C	North-central. Nevezys River, Via Baltic highway. Major industrial center. F=16th century. D=RCC.
1637	Siauliai	Siauliai	3,379	8,751	397,123	88.00	349,468	99.75	C	North. Railroad repair shops. Site of 1236 victory over Livonian Knights. D=RCC.
1638	Taurage	Taurage	1,496	3,874	128,459	87.08	111,862	99.53	C	West. Yura River. Site of signing of Convention of Tauroggen. C=13th century. D=RCC.
1639	Telsiai	Telsiai	4,598	11,908	180,577	89.00	160,714	99.85	C	Northwest. Railroad, linen goods. Folk art museum, F=16th century. D=RCC.
1640	Utena	Utena	2,780	7,201	200,764	87.00	174,665	99.45	C	East. Roads, shoes, starches, brewery, textiles, flour, sawmilling. D=RCC.
1641	Vilnius	–	3,726	9,651	887,838	86.00	763,541	99.32	C	Southeast. Capital, Nevis River. Major industry and education. Ancient ruins. F=1323. D=RCC.
	LUXEMBOURG		**999**	**2,586**	**430,615**	**93.51**	**402,674**	**99.09**	**C**	**Roman Catholics 94.5%, Protestants 1.7%. Pent-char 4.6%, Evangelical 0.2%, GCC 17.5%**
1642	Diekirch	–	447	1,157	64,506	94.00	60,636	99.58	C	Northeast. Syre River, Our Nature Park, Grand duchy of Luxembourg. Potatoes, iron ore. D=RCC.
1643	Grevenmacher	–	203	525	49,478	94.00	46,509	99.58	C	Southeast. Syre River, Hou Forest, Sauer River. Iron ore, wheat, potatoes, minerals. D=RCC.
1644	Luxembourg	–	349	904	316,631	93.34	295,529	98.91	C	South. Grenge Forest. Center for finance, industry, tourism. Wine, airport. D=RCC.
	MACEDONIA		**9,928**	**25,713**	**2,023,580**	**63.61**	**1,287,192**	**88.05**	**C**	**Orthodox 59.3%, Roman Catholics 3.4%. Pent-char 0.3%, Evangelical 0.1%, GCC 10.5%**
1645	-	–	125	326	16,472	67.00	11,036	91.44	C	North-central. Foothills. Minerals, wheat, corn, livestock. D=MOC.
1646	Berovo	–	311	806	20,291	67.00	13,595	91.44	C	East. Turija River, Malesevske mountains. Wheat, corn, tobacco. D=MOC.
1647	Bitola	–	694	1,798	121,549	63.09	76,686	87.39	C	South. Bordering Greece. Turkish: Monastir. Cereals, tobacco, sugar refining. D=MOC.
1648	Brod	–	357	924	11,612	65.00	7,548	89.44	C	West-central. Sava River, Treska River. Wheat, corn, livestock, agriculture, handicrafts. D=MOC.
1649	Debar	–	106	274	26,132	64.00	16,724	88.44	C	West. Frequent earthquakes. Lake Spilsko Mavrovo National Park. Minerals, iron ore. D=MOC.
1650	Delcevo	–	227	589	25,401	66.00	16,765	90.44	C	Northeast. Osogovske mountains, Kalimanko Lake. Iron ore, fruit, tobacco, wheat. D=MOC.
1651	Demir Hisar	–	171	443	12,016	67.00	8,051	91.44	C	Central. Railroad, trade center for tobacco, cotton, silk. Sulfur springs nearby. D=MOC.
1652	Gevgelija	–	292	757	34,876	63.00	21,972	87.44	C	Southeast. Bordering Greece. Kozuf mountains. Railroad, Vardar River. Wheat, tobacco. D=MOC.
1653	Gostivar	–	517	1,341	115,514	64.00	73,929	88.44	C	Northwest. Foothills. Minerals, wheat, corn, livestock, rural farming. D=MOC.
1654	Kavadarci	–	437	1,132	41,638	66.00	27,481	90.44	C	South-central. Crna River, Vardar River, near Stobi ruins. Railroad, fishing, wheat. D=MOC.
1655	Kicevo	–	329	854	54,875	65.00	35,669	89.44	C	West. Near Mavroyo National Park, streams. Tobacco, wheat, corn. D=MOC.
1656	Kocani	–	220	570	49,866	65.00	32,413	89.44	C	Northeast. Bregalnica River, Osogovske and Malesevske mountains. Iron ore. D=MOC.
1657	Kratovo	–	145	376	11,271	67.00	7,552	91.44	C	Northeast. Osogovske mountains. Wheat, corn, tobacco, cereals, farming, livestock. D=MOC.
1658	Kriva Palanka	–	278	720	25,470	65.00	16,556	89.44	C	Northeast. Bulgaria border. Primary highway. Livestock, rural farming, cereals, trade. D=MOC.
1659	Krusevo	–	92	239	12,556	67.00	8,413	91.44	C	West-central. Rugged Terrain. Small rural farms, agriculture, minerals. D=MOC.
1660	Kumanovo	–	468	1,212	134,837	63.00	84,947	87.44	C	North. Primary highway junction, railroad. Trade, markets, fruit, handicrafts. D=MOC.
1661	Negotino	–	283	734	23,127	65.00	15,033	89.44	C	South, southeast of Skopje. Varar River. Railroad, trade center for wine growing. D=MOC.
1662	Ohrid	–	412	1,069	65,197	64.00	41,726	88.44	C	Southwest. Lake Ohrid. Borders Albania. Resort area. D=MOC.
1663	Prilep	–	646	1,675	97,825	65.00	63,586	89.44	C	South-central. Fruit, tobacco, leather, silica bricks. D=MOC.
1664	Radovis	–	284	735	30,817	64.00	19,723	88.44	C	East. Strumica River, Plackavica Mountain. Tobacco growing region. Handicrafts. D=MOC.
1665	Resen	–	285	739	23,085	64.00	14,774	88.44	C	Southwest. Trade center for apples, pears; pottery making. Roman ruins nearby. D=MOC.
1666	Skopje	–	702	1,818	560,425	61.70	345,782	86.18	C	North-central. Vardor River. Chemicals, steel, ceramics, beer. 15th century mosques. D=MOC.
1667	Stip	–	314	815	51,682	66.00	34,110	90.44	C	East-central. Mineral waters. Serb and Bulgarian empress, 14th century monastery. D=MOC.
1668	Struga	–	195	507	62,629	65.00	40,709	89.44	C	Southwest. Lake Ohrid, Black Drini River. Fish. Old Turkish style houses, museum. D=MOC.
1669	Strumica	–	367	952	94,035	64.00	60,182	88.44	C	Southeast. A nature center. Tobacco. Castle ruins built by Roman empire. Tiberius. D=MOC.
1670	Sveti Nikole	–	250	649	21,459	65.00	13,948	89.44	C	Central. Southeast of Skopie, in Ovce Polje valley. Local trade center. D=MOC.
1671	Tetovo	–	417	1,080	179,732	64.00	115,028	88.44	C	Northwest. Railroad. Pottery, apples. Site of former Albanian Dervish monastery. D=MOC.
1672	Titov Veles	–	593	1,536	67,190	63.00	42,330	87.44	C	Central. Vardar River. Market center for fruit and vegetables, chemicals. Roman ruins. D=MOC.
1673	Valandovo	–	128	331	12,201	66.00	8,053	90.44	C	Southeast. Near Vardar River. Local trade center in Sericulture region. Chromium mine. D=MOC.
1674	Vinica	–	166	432	19,801	65.00	12,871	89.44	C	Northeast. Kalimanko Lake. Iron ore, fruit, tobacco. D=MOC.
	MADAGASCAR		**226,658**	**587,041**	**15,941,727**	**47.86**	**7,629,263**	**82.99**	**B**	**Protestants 25.6%, Roman Catholics 22.9%. Pent-char 4.6%, Evangelical 5.9%, GCC 15.6%**
1675	Antananarivo	Antananarivo	22,503	58,283	5,309,481	54.89	2,914,502	91.25	B	Central. Tobacco, leather goods, clothing. D=RCC,FJKM,FLM.
1676	Antsiranana	Antsiranana	16,620	43,046	996,026	32.00	318,728	64.13	B	North. Ship construction and repair. Rice, cassava, sweet potatoes. Ankara caves. D=RCC,FJKM.
1677	Fianarantsoa	Fianarantsoa	39,526	102,373	3,371,879	53.00	1,787,096	89.13	B	East-central. 'Where one learns what is good'. D=RCC,FJKM,FLM.
1678	Mahajanga	Mahajanga	57,924	150,023	1,745,037	45.00	785,267	80.13	B	Northwest. Betsiboka River. Fishing, hardwood lumber, coffee, rice, sugar.
1679	Toamasina	Toamasina	27,765	71,911	2,208,522	47.00	1,038,005	82.13	B	East. Indian Ocean. Coffee, vanilla, pepper, cloves. D=RCC,FJKM,FLM.
1680	Toliara	Toliara	62,319	161,405	2,310,780	34.00	785,665	66.13	B	Southwest. Mozambique Channel. Mining, cattle, rice. D=RCC,FJKM,FLM.
	MALAWI		**45,747**	**118,484**	**10,925,238**	**64.37**	**7,032,260**	**96.05**	**C**	**Roman Catholics 24.6%, Protestants 19.5%. Pent-char 17.7%, Evangelical 8.6%, GCC 22.4%**
1681	Blantyre	Blantyre	777	2,012	806,245	71.00	572,434	98.68	C	South. Shire Highlands. Shoe manufacture, corn milling, brewing. D=RCC,CCAP.
1682	Chikwawa	Chikwawa	1,836	4,755	433,170	61.00	264,234	94.68	C	South. Shire River. Administrative center, cotton, tobacco, rice, corn. D=RCC,CCAP.
1683	Chiradzulu	Chiradzulu	296	767	288,447	60.00	173,068	94.68	C	South. Administrative and regional center. Agriculture, tobacco, tuna, cotton, rice, corn. D=CCAP.
1684	Chitipa	Chitipa	1,353	3,504	132,378	65.00	86,046	96.68	C	North. northernmost point, Zambia border. Corn, cassava, customs port, airfield. D=CCAP.
1685	Dedza	Dedza	1,399	3,624	563,168	63.00	354,796	95.68	C	Central. Dedza Mountain. Rice, potatoes, tobacco, cotton. Bushman cave dwellings. D=RCC.
1686	Dowa	Dowa	1,174	3,041	440,964	65.00	286,627	96.68	C	Central. Dowa Highlands. Tobacco, cotton, corn (maize). D=RCC,CCAP.
1687	Karonga	Karonga	1,141	2,955	202,427	63.00	127,529	95.68	C	North. Lake Nyasa. Cotton, rice, coffee, livestock. D=RCC,CCAP.
1688	Kasungu	Kasungu	3,042	7,878	442,361	62.00	274,264	95.68	C	Central. Tourism around Kasungu National Park. Tobacco. D=CCAP.
1689	Lilongwe	Lilongwe	2,378	6,159	1,335,654	70.00	934,958	97.88	C	Central. Capital of Malawi since 1973. International airport, railroad. D=RCC.
1690	Machinga	Machinga	2,303	5,964	704,687	64.00	451,000	96.73	C	Southern region. Administrative and region center, north of Zamba town. D=CCAP.
1691	Mangochi	Mangochi	2,422	6,272	679,130	63.38	430,454	95.06	C	South-central. Shire River. Tobacco, cotton, peanuts. Yao. D=RCC.
1692	Mchinji	Mchinji	1,296	3,356	341,690	65.00	222,099	96.68	C	West-central. Borders Zambia. Customs station, tobacco. Formerly called Fort Manning. D=RCC.
1693	Mulanje	Mulanje	1,332	3,450	872,626	62.00	541,028	94.68	C	South. Mulanje Peak. Borders Mozambique. Tea, pineapples, tung, tobacco. D=RCC,CCAP.
1694	Mwanza	Mwanza	886	2,295	166,184	61.00	101,372	95.18	C	Southwest. Administrative center. Police and customs stations, cotton, tobacco. D=CCAP.
1695	Mzimba	Mzimba	4,027	10,430	593,131	64.00	379,604	95.68	C	Northwest. Mount Hora (5,742 ft.). Administrative center, corn, cassava, mica deposits. D=RCC.
1696	Nkhata Bay	Nkhata Bay	1,579	4,090	189,252	60.00	113,551	94.68	C	North. Lake Nyasa. Administrative center, cassava, corn, fishing, tourist resort. D=CCAP.
1697	Nkhotakota	Nkhotakota	1,644	4,259	216,144	65.00	140,494	96.68	C	Central. Lake Nyasa. Rice, corn (maize), cotton. Tourist industry around hot springs. D=CCAP.
1698	Nsanje	Nsanje	750	1,942	279,506	65.00	181,679	96.68	C	South. Shire River. Borders Mozambique. Cotton, tobacco, rice. D=CCAP.
1699	Ntcheu	Ntcheu	1,322	3,424	490,657	62.00	304,207	94.68	C	South. Borders Mozambique. Administrative center. Tobacco processing, wheat, corn. D=RCC.
1700	Ntchisi	Ntchisi	639	1,655	165,290	61.00	100,827	95.18	C	South. Administrative center. Tobacco, cotton, corn, rice. D=RCC,CCAP.
1701	Rumphi	Rumphi	2,298	5,952	129,790	62.00	80,470	95.68	C	North. Administrative center, north northwest of Mzuzu town. D=RCC,CCAP.
1702	Salima	Salima	848	2,196	258,716	64.00	165,578	95.68	C	Central. Lake Nyasa. Railroad junction. Lake shore hotels, commercial port, tobacco. D=RCC.
1703	Thyolo	Thyolo	662	1,715	589,659	63.00	371,485	95.68	C	South. Shire Highlands. Tea, tobacco growing center, soybeans, tuna, sisal, corn, rice. D=CCAP.
1704	Zomba	Zomba	996	2,580	603,961	62.00	374,456	94.68	C	South. Shire Highlands. Tobacco, dairy. National capital until 1973, F=1880. D=RCC.
	MALAYSIA		**127,584**	**330,442**	**22,244,062**	**7.96**	**1,771,189**	**63.67**	**B**	**Roman Catholics 3.2%, Protestants 2.9%. Pent-char 2.4%, Evangelical 2.2%, GCC 6.0%**
1705	Johor	Johor Baharu	7,331	18,986	2,626,563	2.50	65,664	54.21	B	South West Malaysia. Strait of Malacca, South China Sea. Oil palms, coconut. F=1511. D=RCC.
1706	Kedah	Alor Setar	3,639	9,426	1,652,193	2.80	46,261	53.51	B	Northwest West Malaysia. Kedah River. Rice. D=RCC.
1707	Kelantan	Kota Baharu	5,769	14,943	1,496,294	3.00	44,889	53.71	B	West Malaysia. Colonized by Javanese in 14th century. Boat-building, sawmilling. D=RCC.
1708	Kuala Lumpur	–	94	243	1,449,944	3.40	49,298	63.11	B	Capital. Klang & Gombak Rivers. World's tallest building: Petronas Towers. F=1857. D=RCC.
1709	Labuan	–	35	91	68,763	2.80	1,925	53.51	B	Island off NW coast. Harbor, financial center. Botanical garden, coconuts, rubber, fishing. D=RCC.
1710	Melaka	Melaka	637	1,650	638,823	27.00	172,482	92.71	B	West Malaysia. Strait of Malacca. Portuguese and Dutch rule (16th-18th cent). Rubber. D=RCC.

Continued overleaf

Table 11-3 continued

Rec No 1	Country / Major civil divisions 2	Capital 3	sq.mi. 4	sq.km. 5	Pop 2000 6	AC% 7	Church members 8	E% 9	W 10	Notes 11
1711	Negeri Sembilan	Seremban	2,565	6,643	875,164	4.00	35,007	55.71	B	Southwestern West Malaysia. Strait of Malacca. Rice, rubber. 'Nine States'. D=RCC,Anglican.
1712	Pahang Darul Makmur	Kuantan	13,886	35,965	1,312,744	2.00	26,255	52.71	B	Eastern West Malaysia. South China Sea. Rubber, rice, coconuts, tobacco. D=RCC.
1713	Perak	Ipoh	8,110	21,005	2,380,557	3.00	71,417	58.71	B	Northwestern West Malaysia. Strait of Malacca. Rubber, rice, coconut, tin. D=RCC.
1714	Perlis	Kangar	307	795	233,078	2.50	5,827	53.21	B	Northwestern West Malaysia. Cement, sawmilling, rubber, paper. D=RCC.
1715	Pulau Pinang	Pinang	398	1,031	1,348,644	4.00	53,946	55.71	B	Island off northwest coast. Important tourist center. Rice, vegetables, fruit. D=RCC.
1716	Sabah	Kota Kinabalu	28,425	73,620	2,199,339	25.05	550,934	90.76	B	Borneo. South China Sea. Mount Kinabalu (13,455 ft.). Tobacco, coconuts. D=Ev Church.
1717	Sarawak	Kuching	48,050	124,449	2,087,042	26.00	542,631	91.71	B	Borneo. South China Sea. Joined Malaysia in 1963. Rubber, pepper, rice. D=Ev Church.
1718	Selangor Darul Ehsan	Shah Alam	3,072	7,965	2,898,728	2.60	75,367	55.89	B	West Malaysia. Strait of Malacca. Original Malaccan state. Tin, coconuts, rubber. D=RCC.
1719	Terengganu	Kuala Terengganu	5,002	12,955	976,185	3.00	29,286	53.71	B	Northeastern West Malaysia. South China Sea. Fishing, rice farming. D=RCC.
	MALDIVES		**115**	**298**	**286,223**	**0.13**	**358**	**19.60**	**A**	**Protestants 0.09%, Roman Catholics 0.03%. Pent-char 0.02%, Evangelical 0.02%, GCC 0.1%**
1720	Alifu	Mahibadhoo	–	–	12,395	0.15	19	19.62	A	West-central. Thoddu island. Buddhist temple remains. Ariyaddy channel, resorts.
1721	Baa	Eydhafushi	–	–	10,596	0.05	5	19.52	A	West-central. Moresby Channel. Coral reefs, south Malosmadul Atoll.
1722	Dhaalu	Kudahuvadhoo	–	–	5,766	0.05	3	19.52	A	West-central. South Nilandu Atoll. Resorts, snorkling, fishing, coral reefs.
1723	Faafu	Magoodhoo	–	–	3,590	0.05	2	19.52	A	Southwest. Second oldest mosque in Maldives. Hindu temple complex, resorts.
1724	Gaafu-Alifu	Viligili	–	–	10,018	0.12	12	19.59	A	Southeast. Suvadiva Atoll. Coral reefs, scuba diving, resorts, coconuts, fish.
1725	Gaafu-Dhaalu	Thinadhoo	–	–	14,305	0.10	14	19.57	A	Southwest. Large port, resorts, handicrafts, apparel, shipping, copra, coir, tourism.
1726	Gnyaviyani	Foah Mulah	–	–	8,459	0.06	5	19.53	A	Southeast. Consist of one island, tropical fruit. Kadeyre mosque, Buddhist stupa.
1727	Haa-Alifu	Dhidhdhoo	–	–	16,522	0.13	21	19.60	A	North. Gallandu Channel. Large port, tourism, fish, coconut products, handicraft.
1728	Haa-Dhaalu	Nolhivaranfaru	–	–	17,702	0.11	19	19.58	A	North. Laccadive Sea. Coral reefs, large anchorage port. Fruit, resorts, tourism, copra.
1729	Kaafu	Male	–	–	84,946	0.17	148	19.64	A	East-central. Male Atoll, South Male Atopp, capital. Tourism, fruit, coconut palms. D=CSI,RCC.
1730	Laamu	Hithadhoo	–	–	12,498	0.10	12	19.57	A	Southeast. Velmandu channel, 3 century old mosque, ancient ruins, limestone pyramid.
1731	Lhaviyani	Naifaru	–	–	9,921	0.08	8	19.55	A	Northeast. Fodiffolu Atoll. Tourism, fish, coconuts, products, handicrafts, apparel.
1732	Meemu	Muli	–	–	5,749	0.05	3	19.52	A	Southeast. Kudshuvadu Channel. Tourism, coral reefs, scuba diving, tropical fruits.
1733	Noonu	Manadhoo	–	–	11,586	0.13	15	19.60	A	Northeast. Laccadive Sea. Shipping, apparel, fruit, tourism, resorts.
1734	Raa	Ugoofaaru	–	–	15,522	0.12	19	19.59	A	Northwest. Moresby Channel. Tourism, fishing, scuba diving, tropical fruits, coconut products.
1735	Seenu	Hithadhoo	–	–	20,842	0.14	29	19.61	A	South. Resorts, one of the rarest naturally protested atolls. Koaganu cemetery.
1736	Shaviyani	Farukolhu Funadhoo	–	–	12,390	0.10	12	19.57	A	Northeast. Laccadive Sea. Shipping, tourism, oil tank station. Coral reefs, fruit, coconut.
1737	Thaa	Veymandhoo	–	–	11,246	0.10	11	19.57	A	Southwest. Velmandu Channel, Kolumadulu Atoll. Tourism, handicraft, markets, fruits.
1738	Vaavu	Felidhoo	–	–	2,168	0.05	1	19.52	A	Central East. Wataru reef, Fulidu Channel. Scuba diving, fishing, tourism, resorts.
	MALI		**482,077**	**1,248,574**	**11,233,821**	**2.00**	**224,365**	**43.56**	**A**	**Roman Catholics 1.1%, Protestants 0.7%. Pent-char 0.2%, Evangelical 0.7%, GCC 1.7%**
1739	Bamako	Bamako	97	252	1,087,018	3.43	37,237	49.76	A	On Niger River. Mud brick buildings. 50% Bambara. D=RCC,ECEM,EEPM.
1740	Gao	Gao	124,326	322,002	520,281	1.40	7,284	42.96	A	East. Niger River. Borders Algeria. Wheat, rice, sorghum. Phosphate mines. D=RCC.
1741	Kayes	Kayes	72,233	119,743	1,555,534	1.10	17,111	41.66	A	West. Senegal River. Peanuts. D=RCC,ECEM.
1742	Koulikoro	Koulikoro	37,007	95,848	1,802,401	2.20	39,653	43.76	A	Southwest. Niger River. Peanut oil, cottonseed oil, soap. Soninke, Bambara, Malinke. D=RCC.
1743	Mopti	Mopti	30,508	79,017	1,802,401	1.20	21,629	41.76	A	East. Niger and Bani Rivers. Rice, millet. Dogon, Fulani, Bambara, Bozo. D=RCC.
1744	Sikasso	Sikasso	27,135	70,280	1,900,618	2.80	53,217	44.36	A	South. Borders Burkina Faso. Sorghum, corn (maize). Cattle export. Bambara, Senufo. D=RCC.
1745	Ségou	Ségou	25,028	64,821	1,966,980	2.30	45,241	43.86	A	South-central. Niger River. Extensive irrigation system. Rice, cotton. Livestock raising. D=RCC.
1746	Tombouctou	Tombuktu	191,743	496,611	598,589	0.50	2,993	39.06	A	North. Borders Mauritania. Sahara desert. Salt mines. Tuaregs, Moors, Songhai. D=RCC.
	MALTA		**122**	**316**	**388,544**	**95.58**	**371,381**	**99.94**	**C**	**Roman Catholics 94.5%, Anglicans 0.2%. Pent-char 24.9%, Evangelical 0.1%, GCC 43.7%**
1747	Gozo and Comino	–	27	70	28,454	98.00	27,885	99.96	C	Northern Island, adjacent Maltese islands. Mediterranean. Beeswax, honey, grapes. D=RCC.
1748	Inner Harbour	–	6	15	111,079	94.49	104,959	99.95	C	Southern Island, East Valletta, capital. Manufacturing, tourism, shipbuilding. D=RCC.
1749	Northern	–	30	78	36,810	98.00	36,074	99.96	C	Southern Island, north. Processed food, tourism, clothing, paper, textiles. D=RCC.
1750	Outer Harbour	–	12	32	112,418	94.00	105,673	99.93	C	Southern Island, east central. Shipbuilding, ship repair, textiles, tourism. D=RCC.
1751	South Eastern	–	20	53	49,164	97.00	47,689	99.94	C	Southern Island, southeast. Clothing, tobacco products, grapes, wheat, barley, citrus fruits. D=RCC.
1752	Western	–	27	69	50,620	97.00	49,101	99.94	C	Southern Island, west central. Tourism, farming, fruit, vegetables, wheat, tobacco products. D=RCC.
	MARSHALL ISLANDS		**70**	**181**	**64,220**	**93.59**	**60,103**	**99.93**	**C**	**Protestants 105.0%, Independents 12.6%. Pent-char 47.0%, Evangelical 30.9%, GCC 11.3%**
1753	Ailinglaplap	–	6	15	2,550	93.00	2,372	99.89	C	Ralik chain. Triangular with 52 islets, formerly Odia island. Copra.
1754	Ailuk	–	2	5	706	94.00	664	99.97	C	Ratak chain. Kwajelain district, 20 miles long, 32 islets.
1755	Arno	–	5	13	2,505	93.00	2,330	99.89	C	Ratak chain. Majuro district. Main copra producer in area, 26 miles long, 83 islets.
1756	Aur	–	2	6	642	94.00	603	99.97	C	Ratak chain. Majuro district, 15 miles long, 42 islets. Formerly Calvert islands.
1757	Bikini	–	2	6	19	93.00	18	99.89	C	Atoll in Ralik chain. Testing ground for atomic weapons in late 1940's. D=UCCMI.
1758	Ebon	–	2	6	1,092	93.00	1,016	99.94	C	Southernmost atoll of Ralik chain. Copra, phosphate deposits, site of first mission station.
1759	Enewetak and Ujelang	–	3	8	1,028	94.00	966	99.97	C	Atoll. Ralik chain. 50 miles in circumference. Atomic testing 1948-1956. D=UCCMI.
1760	Jabat (Jabwot)	–	–	1	193	95.00	183	99.98	C	Ralik chain. West central. Pacific Ocean. Small coral island. Phosphorite.
1761	Jaluit	–	4	11	2,569	93.00	2,389	99.89	C	Atoll in the Ralik chain. First missionaries (1857). Copra export, fishing. D=UCCMI.
1762	Kili	–	–	1	899	94.00	845	99.97	C	Ralik (western) chain. West-central Pacific Ocean. Land area: 230 acres. Coconuts, fishing.
1763	Kwajalein	–	6	16	13,807	93.76	12,945	99.93	C	Ralik chain. US troops in World War II. World's largest lagoon (839 sq mi).
1764	Lae	–	1	1	450	94.00	423	99.97	C	Ralik chain. Kwajalein district, 5 miles long. Consists of 17 islets on lagoon.
1765	Lib	–	–	1	193	94.00	181	99.97	C	Ralik chain. Coral island, southwest of Kwajalein.
1766	Likiep	–	4	10	706	94.00	664	99.97	C	Ratak chain. Majuro district, 64 islets on lagoon 26 miles long.
1767	Majuro	–	4	10	29,092	93.50	27,201	99.93	C	Ratak (eastern) chain. Western Pacific Ocean. Comprises about 60 islets. D=AoG,UCCMI.
1768	Maloelap	–	4	10	1,156	94.00	1,087	99.97	C	Ratak chain. West central Pacific ocean, 71 islets. Japanese air base in World War II.
1769	Mejit	–	1	2	642	95.00	610	99.98	C	Ratak chain. Coral island, west central Pacific island. Formerly called Miadi.
1770	Mili	–	6	16	1,284	94.00	1,207	99.97	C	Southernmost atoll of Ratak chain. 30 miles long with 102 islets. Japanese airbase in WWII.
1771	Namorik	–	1	3	1,220	93.00	1,135	99.89	C	Ralik chain. Majuro district, west central Pacific, 5 miles long. Comprised of 2 islets.
1772	Namu	–	2	6	1,156	94.00	1,087	99.97	C	Ralik chain. West central Pacific, 35 miles long. Comprised of 51 islets.
1773	Ujae	–	1	2	642	94.00	603	99.97	C	Ralik chain. Kwajalein district, 30 miles long. Comprised of 14 islets.
1774	Utrik	–	1	2	578	95.00	549	99.98	C	Ralik chain. West-central Pacific Ocean. Triangular reef with base 10 miles wide.
1775	Wotho	–	2	4	128	94.00	120	99.97	C	Ralik chain. West central Pacific, 125 miles NW of Kwajalein. Comprised of 13 islets.
1776	Wotje	–	3	8	963	94.00	905	99.97	C	Ratak chain. Majuro district, Watje island is largest islet of Marshalls. Japanese airbase in WWII.
	MARTINIQUE		**436**	**1,128**	**395,362**	**94.44**	**373,372**	**99.87**	**C**	**Roman Catholics 92.5%, Protestants 5.9%. Pent-char 3.9%, Evangelical 4.0%, GCC 10.8%**
1777	Fort-de-France	Fort-de-France	147	381	205,911	92.00	189,438	99.85	C	West. Fort-de-France Bay, Madame River. Sugarcane, cacao, rum. Hot springs. D=RCC.
1778	La Trinité	La Trinité	131	338	86,744	97.19	84,308	99.92	C	North-central. Minor port. Sugar cane, pineapples, rum distilling, sugar milling. Parc Naturel. D=RCC.
1779	Le Marin	Le Marin	158	409	102,707	97.00	99,626	99.88	C	South. Caribbean Sea. Minor port, trading and processing alcohol, agriculture region. D=RCC.
	MAURITANIA		**398,000**	**1,030,700**	**2,669,547**	**0.24**	**6,526**	**31.89**	**A**	**Roman Catholics 0.1%, Independents 0.06%. Pent-char 0.08%, Evangelical 0.02%, GCC 0.1%**
1780	Adrar	Atar	83,100	215,300	87,412	0.10	87	27.75	A	Central. Arid terrain. Millet, sorghum, melons. Chinguetti: ancient center of learning and of Islam.
1781	Brakna	Aleg	14,000	37,100	275,165	0.28	776	31.93	A	Southwest. Senegal River, sufficient rainfall to support sedentary agriculture. 'Cherama'. D=RCC.
1782	Dakhlet Nouadhibou	Nouadhibou	11,600	30,000	90,258	0.10	90	31.75	A	Northwest. Atlantic Ocean. Fishing, Iron ore export.
1783	el-Açâba	Kiffa	13,900	36,000	239,317	0.30	718	32.45	A	South. Millet, gum arabic, sheep, goats, cattle, big game. Airport.
1784	Gorgol	Kaédi	5,400	14,000	263,998	0.10	264	31.75	A	South. Senegal and Gorgol Rivers. Zebu cattle, sheep, goats.
1785	Guidmaka	Sélibaby	4,000	10,000	166,734	0.10	167	31.75	A	South. Sedentary agriculture, millet, potatoes, rice sorghum, livestock (goats, cattle, sheep).
1786	Hodh ech-Chargui	Néma	64,000	166,000	303,870	0.30	912	31.95	A	Southeast in Sahara desert. Dates, livestock: camels, cattle, sheep, goats. Airport.
1787	Hodh el-Gharbi	Ayoûn el'-Atroûs	22,000	57,000	228,109	0.10	228	31.75	A	South-central. Sahara desert. Livestock raising: cattle, camels, sheep, goats.
1788	Inchiri	Akjoujt	19,000	49,000	20,926	0.10	21	27.75	A	West. Millet, melons, date palms, goats, cattle, sheep, copper mining nearby began in 1970. D=RCC.
1789	Nouakchott	Nouakchott	400	1,000	563,233	0.40	2,253	32.66	A	West. Atlantic Ocean. Petroleum and copper export, salt deposits.
1790	Tagant	Tidjikdja	36,000	93,000	92,947	0.10	93	31.75	A	South. Sand ravine, low plateau dissected by Wadis that support oases.
1791	Tiris Zemmour	Zouérate	98,600	255,300	47,466	0.10	47	27.75	A	West. Airport, terminus of RR, transport. Iron ore, salt works and iron deposits.
1792	Trarza	Rosso	26,000	67,000	290,113	0.30	870	32.45	A	Southwest. Atlantic Ocean. Borders Senegal. Savanna grasses and brushwood, Baobab trees.
	MAURITIUS		**788**	**2,040**	**1,156,498**	**31.94**	**369,432**	**74.86**	**B**	**Roman Catholics 26.8%, Protestants 9.5%. Pent-char 25.5%, Evangelical 8.8%, GCC 7.6%**
1793	Agalega/Cargados	–	27	71	180	20.00	36	52.92	B	North. No currency used. Airport. Coconut and vegetable plantations. F=1501. D=RCC.
1794	Black River	Tamarin	100	259	49,502	27.00	13,366	66.92	B	West. Black River gorge, Magenta Falls. Tourism, bird sanctuary, fishing, textiles. D=RCC,AoG.
1795	Flacq	Centre de Flacq	115	298	123,036	33.00	40,602	75.92	B	East. Flacq hospital. Sugarcane, livestock, deer and bear ranching. Tourist resort, distillery. D=RCC.
1796	Grand Port	Mahébourg	100	260	105,621	33.00	34,855	75.92	B	Southeast. Le Val Nature Park. Naval museum, Intl. airport. Sugarcane, livestock, fishing. D=RCC.
1797	Moka	Moka	89	231	71,760	28.00	20,093	70.92	B	Central. Mahatma Gandhi Inst., Moka Eye hospital. Vegetables, flowers, fruit, livestock. D=RCC,AoG.
1798	Pamplemousses	Pamplemousses	69	179	112,784	32.00	36,091	74.92	B	Northwest. Tobacco, vegetables, fruits, tourist resort. Natl. hospital, botanical garden. D=RCC.
1799	Plaines Wilhems	Plaines Wilhelmg	78	203	352,779	33.30	117,483	77.16	B	West. Most heavily populated district. Heavy industry, textiles, printing, tourism. D=RCC,AoG.
1800	Port Louis	Port Louis	17	43	142,539	33.00	47,038	77.92	B	Northwest. Capital. Economic center. Off-shore banking, Citadel=1838. D=RCC.
1801	Rivière du Rampart	Rivière du Rempant	57	148	95,443	32.00	30,542	71.92	B	Northeast. Poudre d'Or Chest hospital. Sugarcane, livestock, deer ranching, sand mining. D=RCC.
1802	Rodrigues	Rodrigues	40	104	36,550	24.00	8,772	61.92	B	Northeast. Mountainous. Coral reef, airport, handcrafts. F=1645 by Portuguese. D=RCC.
1803	Savanne	Savanne	95	245	66,303	31.00	20,554	73.92	B	South. Crocodile Park, Souillac hospital. Sugarcane, deer ranching, textiles, museum. D=RCC,AoG.
	MAYOTTE		**144**	**373**	**101,621**	**1.84**	**1,866**	**40.71**	**A**	**Roman Catholics 1.2%, Protestants 0.3%. Pent-char 0.2%, Evangelical 0.1%, GCC 0.9%**
1804	LaGrande Teree	Mamoudzou	140	362	86,581	1.98	1,716	40.86	A	Mozambique Channel, Kaoveni River, capital since 1962. Coffee, Ylang oil.
1805	Pamanzi	Dzaoudzi	4	11	15,040	1.00	150	39.87	A	Northwest promontory called 'the rock'. Meat processing, coffee, vanilla, coconuts, fish. D=RCC.
	MEXICO		**756,066**	**1,958,201**	**98,881,289**	**94.87**	**93,806,927**	**99.85**	**C**	**Roman Catholics 93.8%, Protestants 3.3%. Pent-char 13.2%, Evangelical 1.7%, GCC 5.1%**
1806	Aguascalientes	Aguascalientes	2,122	5,471	875,831	95.00	832,039	99.86	C	Central. Thermal springs. Corn (maize), cattle, horses, wine. 'Hot waters'. D=RCC.
1807	Baja California Norte	Mexicali	26,997	69,921	2,021,272	96.00	1,940,421	99.87	C	Northwest. Borders USA. Gulf of California. Cotton, wheat, grapes, olives. D=RCC.
1808	Baja California Sur	La Paz	28,369	73,475	386,725	95.00	367,389	99.86	C	Northwest. Gulf of California. Volcanoes. Cotton, fish-packing plants. Tourism. D=RCC.
1809	Campeche	Campeche	19,619	50,812	651,321	97.00	631,781	99.88	C	Southeast. Yucatan Peninsula. Gulf of Mexico. Borders Guatemala. Hardwoods, chicle. D=RCC.
1810	Chiapas	Tuxtla Gutiérrez	28,653	74,211	3,907,195	95.00	3,711,835	99.86	C	South. Gulf of Tehuantepec. Borders Guatemala. Coffee, rubber. Tourism around Maya ruins. D=RCC.
1811	Chihuahua	Chihuahua	94,571	244,938	2,971,778	94.00	2,793,471	99.78	C	North. Borders United States. Largest state in Mexico. Mining: iron, lead, zinc, gold, silver. D=RCC.
1812	Coahuila	Saltillo	57,908	149,982	2,400,353	96.00	2,304,339	99.87	C	North. Borders United States. Several mountain ranges. Cotton, corn (maize), wheat, beans. D=RCC.
1813	Colima	Colima	2,004	5,191	521,500	97.00	505,855	99.88	C	West-central. Pacific Ocean. Revillagigedo Islands. Sugarcane, rice, corn (maize), coffee. D=RCC.
1814	Distrito Federal	–	571	1,479	10,022,944	94.00	9,421,567	99.88	C	Central. Serious air pollution. One-third of Mexico's industrial production. D=RCC.
1815	Durango	Durango	47,560	123,181	1,642,201	95.00	1,560,091	99.86	C	North-central. Sierra Madre Occidental. Cotton, wheat, minerals. Europeans (1562). D=RCC.

Continued opposite

Table 11-3 continued

Rec No 1	Country Major civil divisions 2	Capital 3	sq.mi. 4	sq.km. 5	Pop 2000 6	AC% 7	Church members 8	E% 9	W 10	Notes 11
1816	Guanajuato	Guanajuato	11,773	30,491	4,846,834	94.00	4,556,024	99.78	C	Central. Corn (maize), beans, barley. Mining: gold, tin, lead, mercury. D=RCC.
1817	Guerrero	Chilpancingo	24,819	64,281	3,189,327	95.00	3,029,861	99.86	C	Southwest. Cotton, coffee, tobacco, forest products. Tourism around Acapulco. D=RCC.
1818	Hidalgo	Pachuca	8,036	20,813	2,298,149	96.00	2,206,223	99.87	C	East-central. Mountains. Lake Metztitlan. Corn, alfalfa, minerals. Indian Toltec civilization. D=RCC.
1819	Jalisco	Guadalajara	31,211	80,836	6,453,398	94.00	6,066,194	99.78	C	West-central. Corn (maize), wheat. Mineral mining. Tourism around Lake Chapala. D=RCC.
1820	Michoacán	Morelia	23,138	59,928	4,318,176	94.00	4,059,085	99.78	C	West-central. Sierra Madre Occidental. Volcanoes. Forest products, grains, minerals, oil. D=RCC.
1821	Morelos	Cuernavaca	1,911	4,950	1,454,395	95.00	1,381,675	99.86	C	Central. Rio Amacuzac. Birthplace of Emiliano Zapata. Sugarcane, rice, corn (maize). D=RCC.
1822	México	Toluca	8,245	21,355	11,945,878	94.10	11,241,071	99.88	C	Central. Highest population density. Corn (maize), maguey, coffee, mining. D=RCC.
1823	Nayarit	Tepic	10,417	26,979	1,003,596	97.00	973,488	99.88	C	West-central. Volcanoes. Corn (maize), tobacco, sugarcane, cotton, beans. D=RCC.
1824	Nuevo León	Monterrey	25,067	64,924	3,771,184	95.00	3,582,625	99.86	C	Northeast. Borders United States. Cotton, citrus fruits, sugarcane. D=RCC.
1825	Oaxaca	Oaxaca	36,275	93,952	3,674,824	95.00	3,491,083	99.86	C	South. Pacific Ocean. Corn (maize), wheat, coffee, cigarettes. Mineral mining. D=RCC.
1826	Puebla	Puebla	13,090	33,902	5,021,488	96.00	4,820,628	99.87	C	East-central. Elevation; 5,000-8,000 ft. Coffee, sugarcane, corn (maize). D=RCC.
1827	Querétaro	Querétaro	4,420	11,449	1,279,356	94.00	1,202,595	99.78	C	Central. Mountains, valleys, plains. Agriculture, livestock breeding. Opals. F=1824. D=RCC.
1828	Quintana Roo	Chetumal	19,387	50,212	600,318	97.00	582,308	99.88	C	Southeast. Yucatan Peninsula. Named for Andres Quintana Roo. Sponge and turtle fishing. D=RCC.
1829	San Luis Potosí	San Luis Potosí	24,351	63,068	2,437,889	94.00	2,291,616	99.78	C	Northeast. Mean elevation: 6,000 ft. Hides, tallow, wool. Silver mines. D=RCC.
1830	Sinaloa	Culiacán	22,521	58,328	2,682,343	95.00	2,548,226	99.86	C	Northwest. Gulf of California. Mining: salt, graphite, manganese, gold. D=RCC.
1831	Sonora	Hermosillo	70,291	182,052	2,219,341	96.00	2,130,567	99.87	C	Northwest. Gulf of California. Explored by Spaniards in 1530s. Cereals, cotton. D=RCC.
1832	Tabasco	Villahermosa	9,756	25,267	1,827,633	97.00	1,772,804	99.88	C	Southeast. Borders Guatemala. 'Damp earth'. D=RCC.
1833	Tamaulipas	Ciudad Victoria	30,650	79,384	2,737,756	95.00	2,600,868	99.86	C	Northeast. Gulf of Mexico. Sorghum. Produces a third of Mexico's natural gas. D=RCC.
1834	Tlaxcala	Tlaxcala	1,551	4,016	926,478	92.57	857,651	99.95	C	Central. Corn (maize), barley, livestock. D=RCC.
1835	Veracruz	Jalapa (Xalapa)	27,683	71,699	7,579,805	96.00	7,276,613	99.87	C	East central. Gulf of Mexico. Cotton, fishing. Half of Mexico's petroleum reserves. D=RCC.
1836	Yucatán	Mérida	14,827	38,402	1,658,704	95.00	1,575,769	99.86	C	Southeast. Gulf of Mexico. Tourism around old Mayan centers. D=RCC.
1837	Zacatecas	Zacatecas	28,283	73,252	1,553,297	96.00	1,491,165	99.87	C	North-central. Average elevation: 7,700 ft. Mining, meat processing, rubber. D=RCC.
	MICRONESIA		**271**	**701**	**118,689**	**91.55**	**108,662**	**99.63**	**C**	**Roman Catholics 62.8%, Protestants 39.6%. Pent-char 7.9%, Evangelical 11.7%, GCC 18.9%**
1838	Chuuk (Truk)	–	49	127	59,920	90.76	54,385	99.44	C	Western Pacific Ocean. Annexed by Japan:1914. Copra, fishing. D=RCC,Protestants.
1839	Kosrae	–	42	110	8,334	93.00	7,751	99.88	C	Easternmost of the Caroline Islands. Western Pacific Ocean. Taros, oranges, breadfruit. D=RCC.
1840	Pohnpei	–	133	345	37,823	92.00	34,797	99.88	C	Also: Ascension, Ponape. Volcanic island in eastern Caroline Islands. Western Pacific. D=RCC.
1841	Yap	–	46	119	12,612	93.00	11,729	99.88	C	Formerly: Guap. Western Caroline Islands. Western Pacific. Copra, bananas, coconuts. D=RCC.
	MOLDAVIA		**13,000**	**33,700**	**4,380,492**	**63.89**	**2,798,558**	**94.23**	**C**	**Orthodox 44.5%, Independents 15.3%. Pent-char 1.1%, Evangelical 0.4%, GCC 19.1%**
1842	Anenii Noi	–	320	830	78,091	65.00	50,759	95.34	C	Central. On Byk River. Grain, livestock, fruits, tobacco. D=MOC.
1843	Balti	–	–	–	160,703	63.00	101,243	93.32	C	On Reut River. Farm products, furniture, fur clothes. F=15th cent. D=MOC.
1844	Basarabeasca	–	255	660	44,116	66.00	29,117	96.34	C	South, Kohylnyk River, Ukraine border. Railroad junction, railroad shops, district center. D=MOC.
1845	Brinceni	–	313	810	84,009	64.00	53,766	94.34	C	North. Near Ukraine. Flour and oilseed milling. Before WWII many Jews. D=MOC.
1846	Cahul (Kachul)	–	–	–	43,608	66.00	28,781	96.34	C	South. Near Prut River. Flour milling, wine making. Passed to Russia in 1812. D=MOC.
1847	Cahul (Kachul)	–	309	800	44,847	66.00	29,599	96.34	C	South. Near Prut River. Flour milling, wines. Passed to Russia in 1812. D=MOC.
1848	Cainari	–	–	–	43,100	66.00	28,446	96.34	C	Southeast. Bohna River. Railroad, corn, wheat, stock, carpet weaving. D=MOC.
1849	Calaras	–	293	760	85,122	64.00	54,478	94.34	C	Central. Bacu River. Railroad, fruit and wine growing district, oilseed, milling. D=MOC.
1850	Camenca	–	317	820	59,833	66.00	39,490	96.34	C	Northeast. Dniester River. Transnistria region, grape-cure resort, wines, flour. D=MOC.
1851	Cantemir	–	332	860	61,616	66.00	40,667	96.34	C	Agriculture center producing corn, wheat. D=MOC.
1852	Causeni	–	432	1,120	73,584	65.00	47,830	95.34	C	Southeast. Botna River. Red wine production center, 18th century church with frescoes. D=MOC.
1853	Chisinau (Kishinyov)	–	62	160	741,135	60.00	444,681	90.34	C	South. Bacu River, capital. F=early 15th century as a monastery town. Plastics. D=MOC,ROC.
1854	Ciadâr-Lunga	–	278	720	69,251	65.00	45,013	95.34	C	South on railroad. Agriculture, livestock, corn, barley, sheep. D=MOC.
1855	Cimislia	–	452	1,170	61,581	64.00	39,412	94.34	C	South. Kohylnyk River, 35 miles south of Chisinau. Vineyards, wine, orchards. D=MOC.
1856	Comrat	–	324	840	71,844	65.00	46,699	95.34	C	South. Upper Yalpag River. Autonomous Gagauz district. Flour milling, wine making. D=MOC.
1857	Criuleni	–	328	850	92,520	64.00	59,213	94.34	C	East. on Dniester River, just below Rut River mouth. Fruit growing district. D=MOC.
1858	Donduseni	–	344	890	67,017	66.00	44,231	96.34	C	North. Flour and oilseed milling. Many Jews before WWII. D=MOC.
1859	Drochia	–	301	780	81,477	64.00	52,145	94.34	C	North on railroad. Orchards. Brick and soap manufacturing. D=MOC.
1860	Dubasari	–	–	–	24,439	67.00	16,374	97.34	C	East. Dniester River, Transnistria republic. Wine center, fruit canning, flour, dairying. D=MOC.
1861	Dubasari	–	259	670	54,397	66.00	35,902	96.34	C	East. Dniester River. Transnistria. Wine center, fruits, flour. D=MOC.
1862	Edinet	–	332	860	91,679	65.00	59,591	95.34	C	North. Road junction. Agriculture center, flour milling, limestone quarry. D=MOC.
1863	Falesti	–	413	1,070	95,788	64.83	62,101	95.17	C	West, in orchard district. Flour and oilseed milling, soap manufacturing, grain, fruit, livestock. D=MOC.
1864	Floresti	–	320	830	77,605	64.00	49,667	94.34	C	North. Railroad, tobacco and flour milling center, glass work, agriculture. D=MOC.
1865	Glodeni	–	293	760	66,308	65.00	43,100	95.34	C	Northwest. Agriculture center producing corn, wheat, sugar beets. D=MOC.
1866	Grigoriopol	–	317	820	52,746	67.00	35,340	97.34	C	East. Left bank of Dniester River, part of Transnistria. Wine center, flour milling. D=MOC.
1867	Hâncesti (Kotovsk)	–	521	1,350	119,206	63.00	75,100	93.34	C	South central, named for Bolshevik military leader. Agriculture center, flour, oilseeds. D=MOC.
1868	Ialoveni	–	–	–	88,455	65.00	57,496	95.34	C	Agricultural center producing corn, wheat. D=MOC.
1869	Leova	–	278	720	52,404	66.00	34,587	96.34	C	Southwest, Prut River, Romanian border. Agriculture center, flour and oilseed milling. D=MOC.
1870	Nisporeni	–	293	760	82,283	65.00	53,484	95.34	C	West. Corn, wheat, fruit, wine. D=MOC.
1871	Ocnita	–	259	660	63,578	66.00	41,961	96.34	C	North. Near Ukraine border. Flour and oilseed milling, phosphate deposits nearby. RR junction.
1872	Orhei	–	–	–	38,194	66.00	25,208	96.34	C	Central. Rut River. Rich agricultural district, orchards, vineyards.17th century church. D=MOC.
1873	Orhei	–	425	1,100	96,292	65.00	62,590	95.34	C	Central. Flour milling, fruit, tobacco processing, wine processing, food processing. D=MOC.
1874	Rezina	–	259	670	55,939	66.00	36,920	96.34	C	East. Eight bank of Dniester River. Agricultural center, oilseeds, tobacco, wine. D=MOC.
1875	Ribnita	–	–	–	62,321	65.00	40,509	95.34	C	East. Left bank of Dniester River. Cement, sugar milling, limestone. D=MOC.
1876	Riscani	–	386	1,000	84,127	65.00	54,683	95.34	C	North. Agricultural market, corn, wheat, sugar beets. D=MOC.
1877	Râbnita	–	328	850	33,055	67.00	22,147	97.34	C	East. Dniester River, bordering Ukraine. Cement, sugar milling, dairying. D=MOC.
1878	Slobozia	–	371	960	114,738	63.00	72,285	93.34	C	Southeast. Left bank of Dniester, in Transnistria region. Vineyards, orchards, distilling. D=MOC.
1879	Soldanesti	–	–	–	47,073	67.00	31,539	97.34	C	East on railroad. Northwest of Rezina. Tobacco center for trade and growth. D=MOC.
1880	Soroca	–	–	–	41,794	66.00	27,584	96.34	C	North. Dniester River. Orchards, flour and oilseed milling, brick and soap manufacturing. D=MOC.
1881	Soroca	–	336	870	58,563	66.00	38,652	96.34	C	North. Dniester River. Orchards, flour and oilseed milling. D=MOC.
1882	Stefan-Voda (Suvorova)	–	398	1,030	77,320	65.00	50,258	95.34	C	Agricultural center producing wheat, corn. D=MOC.
1883	Straseni	–	293	760	96,879	65.00	62,971	95.34	C	Central Bâcy River. Railroad, 13 miles northwest of Chisinau. Vineyard district, wine. D=MOC.
1884	Sângerei	–	–	–	92,420	65.00	60,073	95.34	C	North. Road junction. Agricultural center. Wheat, corn. D=MOC.
1885	Taraclia	–	–	–	46,280	67.00	31,008	97.34	C	South. Railroad. Agriculture, livestock, corn, barley, sheep. D=MOC.
1886	Telenesti	–	332	860	77,504	66.00	51,153	96.34	C	Central. Large Jewish population until WWII. Grain, livestock, cheese factory. D=MOC.
1887	Tighina (Bendery)	–	–	–	138,529	62.00	85,888	92.34	C	East. Port on Dniester River, gateway of Bessarabia. Timber, fruits, tobacco, footwear. D=MOC.
1888	Tiraspol	–	–	–	205,502	61.00	125,356	91.34	C	East. Dniester River. Capital of self-proclaimed Transnistria. Furniture. F=1792. D=MOC.
1889	Ungheni	–	–	–	38,772	67.00	25,977	97.34	C	West, on main Kiev-Bucharest railroad. Prut River. Formerly part of Romania. D=MOC.
1890	Ungheni	–	413	1,070	80,163	65.00	52,106	95.34	C	West. Prut River. Formerly part of Romania. D=MOC.
1891	Vulcanesti	–	359	930	62,694	66.00	41,378	96.34	C	South, on small Cahul River. 16 miles southeast of Cahul. Corn, barley, Karakul sheep. D=MOC.
	MONACO		**1**	**2**	**33,597**	**92.57**	**31,101**	**98.83**	**C**	**Roman Catholics 89.2%, Protestants 2.0%. Pent-char 3.1%, Evangelical 0.1%, GCC 26.1%**
1892	Monaco	Monaco	1	2	33,597	92.57	31,101	98.83	C	Resort on French Riviera. Boating, gambling. French language. D=RCC.
	MONGOLIA		**604,800**	**1,566,500**	**2,662,020**	**1.25**	**33,393**	**42.82**	**A**	**Protestants 0.8%, Independents 0.3%. Pent-char 0.3%, Evangelical 0.04%, GCC 1.1%**
1893	Arhangay	Tsetserleg	21,000	55,000	110,342	0.10	110	36.67	A	Central. Hangayn Nuruy mountains, Selenga River. Pastoral economy, livestock, wooded steppe.
1894	Bayan-Ölgiy	Ölgiy	18,000	46,000	118,419	0.20	237	38.77	A	West. Mongolian Altay mountain range, Kobdo River. Wooded steppe, hunting, agriculture.
1895	Bayanhongor	Bayanhongor	45,000	116,000	97,184	0.08	78	36.65	A	Southwest central. Khangai mountains, Gobi Altay mountains, Gobi desert. Pastoral.
1896	Bulgan	Bulgan	19,000	49,000	67,612	0.09	61	36.66	A	North central. Selenga River. Considerable agricultural land. Copper mining, livestock.
1897	Darhan	–	100	200	111,775	2.00	2,236	43.57	A	North. Sborin Gol coal-field, largest coal supplier. F=1961 as planned industrial area. D=Evangelical.
1898	Dornod	Choybalsan	47,700	123,500	105,261	0.20	211	38.77	A	East. Kerulen River. Largely a steppe plateau, formerly called Eastern Aymag.
1899	Dornogovi	Saynshand	43,000	111,000	74,256	0.10	74	36.67	A	Southeast, east part of Gobi desert. Crossed by Kalgan Ulaan Baatar highway. Railroad.
1900	Dundgovi	Mandalgovi	30,000	78,000	64,225	0.05	32	36.62	A	South-central. Steppe and semi-desert plateau with sparse population.
1901	Dzavhan	Uliastay	32,000	82,000	115,293	0.20	231	38.77	A	Northwest. Khargai mountains, Dzavhan Gol River. Alpine meadows, desert, Har Nuur Lake.
1902	Erdenet	–	300	800	73,084	1.30	950	42.87	A	North-central. 3rd largest city. Mining, copper and molybdenum ore. Trans-Mongolian railroad.
1903	Govi-Altay	Altay	55,000	142,000	81,682	0.02	16	36.59	A	Southwest. Gobi Altai mountain range, Gobi desert. Sheep, goats, camels.
1904	Hentiy	Ondörhaan	32,000	82,000	96,142	0.10	96	36.67	A	East central. Extends from wooded Kentei mountains to steppe, Kerulen River.
1905	Hovd	Hovd	29,000	76,000	99,660	0.10	100	36.67	A	West. Mongolian Altay mountains, Har Us Lake, Gobi desert. Stock grazing, some agriculture.
1906	Hövsgöl	Mörön	39,000	101,000	132,619	0.30	398	38.87	A	Northwest. Lake Khubsugal, Selenga River. Wooded steppe. Hunting and Yak raising, Graphite.
1907	Selenge	Sühbaatar	16,000	42,000	113,208	0.20	226	38.77	A	North. Largely wooded steppe drained by Selenda and Orhorn rivers. Leading agricultural areas.
1908	Suhbaatar	Baruun-Urt	32,000	82,000	66,310	0.15	99	36.72	A	East. Bounded by China's Inner Mongolian Autonomous Region. Largely a steppe plateau.
1909	Töv	Dzüünmod	31,000	81,000	130,274	0.20	261	38.77	A	Central. Situated in the steppe. Kentei mountains. Coal mining.
1910	Ulaanbaatar	–	800	2,000	714,423	3.84	27,452	55.09	B	East-central. Tuul River. Political, cultural, economic center, F=1639. D=Evangelical.
1911	Uvs	Ulaangom	27,000	69,000	109,300	0.20	219	38.77	A	Northwest. Highest point is Harhirra Uul peak, largest lake in Mongolia, Uvs Nuur.
1912	Ömnogovi	Dalandzadgad	64,000	165,000	55,236	0.10	55	36.67	A	South. Bounded by South China provinces, lies in the Gobi desert. Most sparsely settled.
1913	Övörhangay	Arvayheer	24,000	63,000	125,714	0.20	251	38.77	A	Central. On southeast slopes of Khangai mountains, Ongiyn Gal River, Gobi desert. Livestock.
	MONTSERRAT		**39**	**102**	**10,629**	**95.68**	**10,170**	**99.93**	**C**	**Protestants 51.7%, Anglicans 29.1%. Pent-char 33.3%, Evangelical 24.9%, GCC 18.3%**
1914	Montserrat	Plymouth	39	102	10,629	95.68	10,170	99.93	C	Leeward Islands, Eastern Caribbean. Flora. Destroyed by volcano (1997). D=Anglican.
	MOROCCO		**177,117**	**458,730**	**28,220,843**	**0.62**	**174,476**	**42.19**	**A**	**Independents 0.5%, Roman Catholics 0.08%. Pent-char 0.5%, Evangelical 0.1%, GCC 0.3%**
1915	Agadir	Agadir	2,282	5,910	898,605	0.20	1,797	38.77	A	Southwest. Atlantic Ocean. Barley, citrus fruits, olives. D=RCC.
1916	al-Hoceïma	al-Hoceïma	1,371	3,550	413,114	0.10	413	37.67	A	North. Fishing, food processing. Beach resort.
1917	Azilal	Azilal	3,880	10,050	466,561	0.10	467	37.67	A	Central. On north slope of the High Atlas mountains.
1918	Aïn Chok-Hay Hassani	–	–	–	503,307	0.60	3,020	42.17	A	West. Atlantic Ocean. Petroleum, fishing, vegetables.
1919	Aïn Sebaâ-Hay Moh.	–	–	–	653,631	0.50	3,268	43.07	A	West. On Atlantic Ocean, northeast of Casablanca. Truck-farming, zoological gardens.
1920	Ben Msik-Sidi Othmane	–	623	1,615	1,095,697	0.50	5,478	43.07	A	West. Atlantic Ocean. Refining, fishing, agriculture.
1921	Ben Slimane	Ben Slimane	1,066	2,760	227,155	0.10	227	37.67	A	North-central. Formerly: Boulhaut. Atlantic Ocean. Wheat, citrus fruits, grapes.
1922	Beni Mallal	Beni Mellal	2,732	7,075	1,042,247	0.30	3,127	42.87	A	Central. Middle Atlas Mountains. Oranges, olives, figs.
1923	Boulemane	Boulemane	5,558	14,395	173,708	0.10	174	37.67	A	North-central. Middle Atlas Mountains. Market center serving Berber nomads.
1924	Casablanca-Anfa	–	–	–	1,190,344	0.80	9,523	44.37	A	West. Atlantic Ocean. Largest city, economic center. Hassan II mosque with highest minaret in world.
1925	Chaouen (Chefchaouen)	Chaouen	1,680	4,350	404,204	0.20	808	37.77	A	West. Atlantic Ocean. Port, fishing, exports. National university.
1926	el-Jadida	el-Jadida	2,317	6,000	1,033,340	0.50	5,167	43.07	A	North-central. Atlantic Ocean. Portuguese settlement after 1502. Jews (1821). Cereals, grapes.

Continued overleaf

Table 11-3 continued

Rec No 1	Country / Major civil divisions 2	Capital 3	sq.mi. 4	sq.km. 5	Pop 2000 6	AC% 7	Church members 8	E% 9	W 10	Notes 11
1927	el-Kelaâ des Sraghna	el-Kelaâ	3,888	10,070	761,641	0.10	762	37.67	A	West. Olives, citrus fruits, cereals (wheat and barley). Phosphate deposits.
1928	er-Rachidia	er-Rachidia	23,006	59,585	560,096	0.20	1,120	38.77	A	Central. Borders Algeria. Citrus fruits, lead and zinc mines.
1929	Essaouira	Essaouira	2,446	6,335	476,582	0.10	477	37.67	A	West. Atlantic Ocean. Formerly: Mogador. Artisan industries. Resort area with beaches.
1930	Figuig	Figuig	21,618	55,990	120,260	0.08	96	36.65	A	Northeast. Sahara desert. 3,000 ft (900 m). Number of oases. Pottery, goatskin tanning.
1931	Fès	Fès	2,085	5,400	1,145,803	0.50	5,729	44.07	A	North-central. Leather works, carpet. 300 mosques, center of Islamic Morocco. F=808.
1932	Guelmim	Guelmim	11,100	28,750	187,070	0.20	374	38.77	A	Southwest. Southern Anti-Atlas Mountains. Annual camel-trading fair. Camel-herding.
1933	Ifrane	Ifrane	1,278	3,310	129,167	0.20	258	37.77	A	North-central. Middle Atlas Mountains. Elevation: 5,400 ft. (1,650 m)
1934	Kenitra	Kenitra	1,832	4,745	1,024,431	0.40	4,098	42.97	A	North. Atlantic Ocean. Fishing, citrus fruits, wheat, sheep. 'Little Bridge'.
1935	Khemisset	Khemisset	3,207	8,305	526,691	0.20	1,053	38.77	A	North-central. Cereals (wheat), citrus fruits, sheepherding. Zemmour Berbers.
1936	Khenifra	Khenifra	4,757	12,320	492,172	0.10	492	36.67	A	Central. Southern Middle Atlas Mountains. Zaian Berbers.
1937	Khouribga	Khouribga	1,641	4,250	609,090	0.10	609	36.67	A	Northwest. World's largest phosphate reserves. Cereals (wheat and barley), sheep and goats.
1938	Marrakech	Marrakech	5,697	14,755	1,698,105	1.00	16,981	48.57	A	West central. Haouz Plain. Renowned for leather goods, 16th century palace. F=1062.
1939	Meknès	Meknès	1,542	3,995	838,475	0.20	1,677	39.77	A	North-central. Market for fine embroidery and carpets. Ruins of the Roman Volubilis.
1940	Mohammadia-Znata	–	–	–	243,859	0.20	488	38.77	A	West. Atlantic Ocean. Chief petroleum importing and refining region. Fish, vegetables, cotton mill.
1941	Nador	Nador	2,367	6,130	886,355	2.30	20,386	49.87	A	Northeast. Mediterranean. Trading center for fish, fruits, livestock.
1942	Ouarzazate	Ouarzazate	16,043	41,550	722,668	0.30	2,168	38.87	A	South-central. Ouarzazate River. Military post during French occupation. Manganese, cobalt, copper.
1943	Oujda	Oujda	7,992	20,700	1,084,561	0.80	8,676	43.37	A	Northeast. Olives, grapes. Sidi Yahya oasis: legendary burial place of John the Baptist. F=944.
1944	Rabat	–	–	–	768,324	1.50	11,525	49.10	A	West. Atlantic Ocean, capital of Morocco. Political center, residence of king. Textile industry. D=RCC.
1945	Safi	Safi	2,813	7,285	944,258	0.20	1,889	38.77	A	West. Atlantic Ocean. Safi City originally settled by the Canaanites. Sardine canneries, pottery.
1946	Salé	–	492	1,275	730,463	0.90	6,574	45.47	A	Northwest. Harbor was a haven for pirates during early century. Flour, textiles, ceramics.
1947	Settat	Settat	3,764	9,750	879,675	0.30	2,639	38.87	A	Central. High-density rural population. Wheat, skins, leather, wool, grain, soap, textiles, chemicals.
1948	Sidi Kacem	Sidi Kacem	1,568	4,060	670,335	0.20	1,341	38.77	A	East edge of Ghob plain. Industrial and agricultural processing center. Oil refinery.
1949	Skhirate-Témara	–	–	–	221,590	0.10	222	38.67	A	West. On Casablanca-Rabat road. Coup attempt in 1971. Dairy, cattle, vegetables, grapes.
1950	Tan-Tan	Tan-Tan	6,678	17,295	61,242	0.20	122	37.77	A	Southwest. Atlantic Ocean. Site of warfare between Moroccan troops and Western Sahara guerrillas.
1951	Tangier	Tangier	461	1,195	630,248	3.23	20,370	54.80	B	North. Strait of Gibraltar. Dominated by capital. Major tourist center. D=RCC.
1952	Taounate	Taounate	2,156	5,585	671,447	0.40	2,686	41.97	A	North. Mountains. Cereals (wheat), cattle, figs, olives, cherries. Berbers. Idris I dam.
1953	Taroudannt	Taroudannt	6,355	16,460	732,692	0.20	1,465	38.77	A	Southwest. Fertile Sous valley. Fruits, vegetables, olive oil pressing, plaster manufacturing, tourism.
1954	Tata	Tata	10,010	25,925	119,146	0.20	238	38.77	A	Southwest. Oasis. Olives, lemons, oranges, almonds, carob. Shluh Berbers, Haratin.
1955	Taza	Taza	5,799	15,020	796,161	0.20	1,592	38.77	A	Northeast. Wool, grain, cork, palm fibers, footwear, carpets. F=11th century as a Berber fortress.
1956	Tiznit	Tiznit	2,687	6,960	424,247	0.20	848	38.77	A	South. Atlantic Ocean. Cereals, sheep, goats.
1957	Tétouan	Tétouan	2,326	6,025	962,074	2.50	24,052	49.07	A	North-central. Mediterranean. Early Roman settlement. Cereals (wheat), citrus fruits, tea, livestock.
	MOZAMBIQUE		**313,661**	**812,379**	**19,680,456**	**32.83**	**6,460,533**	**77.03**	**B**	**Roman Catholics 15.8%, Protestants 8.8%. Pent-char 11.8%, Evangelical 6.8%, GCC 18.0%**
1958	Cabo Delgado	Pemba	31,902	82,625	1,637,168	40.00	654,867	84.20	B	Northeast. Rio Rovuma. German occupation from 1894-World War I. D=RCC.
1959	Gaza	Xai-Xai	29,231	75,709	1,908,526	30.00	572,558	74.20	B	South, southernmost tip exposed to Indian Ocean. Limpopo River. Sugar, rice, corn. D=RCC.
1960	Inhambane	Inhambane	26,492	68,615	1,575,531	30.00	472,659	74.20	B	Southeast. Commercial agriculture. Sugar, coconuts. Musically gifted Chope and Bitonga. D=RCC.
1961	Manica	Chimoio	23,807	61,661	830,025	30.00	249,008	74.20	B	Central. Agriculture trade, cotton, bananas, sisal, tobacco, corn. Beira railroad. D=RCC.
1962	Maputo	Maputo	9,944	25,756	1,144,932	40.00	457,973	84.20	B	North bank of Espirito Santo Estuary of Delagoa Bay. Brewing, shipbuilding, fish canning. D=RCC.
1963	Maputo	–	232	602	1,268,630	40.00	507,452	84.20	B	Northeast. Port city, Moz. Administrative center, museums. F=late 18th century. D=RCC.
1964	Nampula	Nampula	31,508	81,606	3,869,406	28.09	1,086,746	72.28	B	Northeast. International airport. Cement, mangroves and swamps. Predominantly Muslim. D=RCC.
1965	Niassa	Lichinga	49,828	129,055	935,072	25.00	233,768	69.20	B	North. Rovuma River, Savanna hill country, railroad, airport. Cotton, corn, beans. D=RCC.
1966	Sofala	Beira	26,262	68,018	1,943,943	44.00	855,335	88.20	B	East-central, seaport. Save River, last Sultan of Sofala is buried here. Nature reserves. D=RCC.
1967	Tete	Tete	38,890	100,724	1,000,316	30.00	300,095	74.20	B	West-central. Zambezi River. Cattle raising, cassava, sorghum. D=RCC.
1968	Zambézia	Quelimane	40,544	105,008	3,566,906	30.00	1,070,072	74.20	B	East-central. Namuli mountains. Trade center, fishing, coconuts. Large Muslim culture. D=RCC.
	MYANMAR		**261,228**	**676,577**	**45,611,177**	**8.20**	**3,741,464**	**60.86**	**B**	**Protestants 5.5%, Roman Catholics 1.2%. Pent-char 2.1%, Evangelical 2.4%, GCC 4.9%**
1969	Chin	Hakha	13,907	36,019	476,719	16.00	76,275	68.48	B	West border with India and Bangladesh. Chin Hills mountain range. D=Baptist,RCC.
1970	Irrawaddy (Ayeyarwady)	Bassein (Pathein)	13,567	35,138	6,452,796	7.00	451,696	54.48	B	Northwest. Ayeyarwady river delta. Major rice growing region, fisheries, railroad. D=RCC.
1971	Kachin	Myitkyina	34,379	89,041	1,169,078	6.00	70,145	53.48	B	North. Mountainous. Rice, jade and amber mines. Mostly animists. D=RCC.
1972	Kayah	Loi-kaw	4,530	11,733	217,625	20.00	43,525	72.48	B	East. Tungsten mining, rice, maize, vegetables, teakwood forest. D=RCC,Baptist.
1973	Kayin	Pa-an (Hpa-an)	11,731	30,383	1,363,624	44.33	604,437	91.81	B	East. Heavily forested, rugged hills, Thanlwin River. Natural gas pipeline. D=Baptist.
1974	Magwe (Magway)	Magwe (Magway)	17,305	44,820	4,190,477	10.00	419,048	57.48	B	West. Ayeyarwady River. Rice, cotton, sesame, peanuts, beans, oil fields. D=Baptist.
1975	Mandalay	Mandalay	14,295	37,024	5,914,898	4.00	236,596	46.48	A	Central. Ayeyarwady River. Railroad, rice, sesame, sugarcane, teak forests. D=RCC.
1976	Mon	Moulmein	4,748	12,297	2,170,919	12.00	260,510	64.36	B	Southeast on Andaman Sea, contains 10 townships. Teak mills, rice, tea. D=Baptist.
1977	Pegu (Bago)	Pegu (Bago)	15,214	39,404	4,909,687	7.00	343,678	54.48	B	South, on Gulf of Martaban. Rice, sugarcane, teak forests, fisheries. D=RCC,Baptist.
1978	Rakhine (Arakan)	Sittwe (Akyab)	14,200	36,778	2,643,054	10.00	264,305	61.48	B	West. Arakan Yoma mountain range. Large minority of Bengali Muslims. Rice. D=RCC,Baptist.
1979	Sagaing	Sagaing	36,535	94,625	4,990,287	9.00	449,126	56.48	B	North. Ayeyarwady River. Rice, cotton, sesame, salt, fruit, railroad. D=Baptist.
1980	Shan	Taunggyi	60,155	155,801	4,802,506	5.00	240,125	52.48	B	East-central. Silver, lead, and zinc mines, teak forest. Golden triangle (opium and heroin). D=RCC.
1981	Tenasserim (Tanintharyi)	Tavoy (Dawei)	16,735	43,343	1,185,170	10.00	118,517	61.48	B	South. Includes many offshore islands. Rice, coconut, rubber, tea, tungsten, teak. D=RCC.
1982	Yangôn	Yangôn (Rangoon)	3,927	10,171	5,124,334	3.00	153,730	50.48	B	South-central. Rangoon River. Rice, teak. Arts and science university. D=RCC,Baptist.
	NAMIBIA		**318,580**	**825,118**	**1,725,868**	**78.18**	**1,349,211**	**97.73**	**C**	**Protestants 47.5%, Roman Catholics 17.7%. Pent-char 13.3%, Evangelical 9.2%, GCC 17.1%**
1983	Erongo	Omaruru	24,602	63,719	112,462	78.00	87,720	97.55	C	West central, from escarpments to Atlantic coast. Sparse population. Tin, tungsten. D=Lutheran.
1984	Hardap	Mariental	42,428	109,888	91,340	79.00	72,159	98.55	C	South-central. Processing of Karakul skins. Citrus fruits. Tourism at Hardap Dam. D=Lutheran.
1985	Karas	Keetmanshoop	62,288	161,324	83,348	80.00	66,678	99.15	C	Southeast. Karakul sheepskins, processed foods, leather. D=Lutheran.
1986	Khomas	Windhoek	14,210	36,804	183,822	79.00	145,219	98.55	C	Central. Hub of Namibian political and social life. Karakul sheepskins, livestock. D=Lutheran,RCC.
1987	Kunene	Opuwo	55,697	144,254	66,792	78.00	52,098	97.55	C	Northwest. Ualb River. Sparsely populated. Corn, beans. D=RCC.
1988	Liambezi	Katima Mulilo	7,541	19,532	105,040	77.00	80,881	97.55	C	Northeast. Karango River, Zambezi River. Education and tourism. Livestock. D=RCC.
1989	Ohangwena	Oshikango	4,086	10,582	203,231	77.00	156,488	96.55	C	North. Densely populated. Communal, livestock, raisins. D=Lutheran.
1990	Okavango	Rundu	16,763	43,417	155,278	79.00	122,670	98.55	C	Northeast. Political region centering around Rundu. Forest savanna, major timber area. D=RCC.
1991	Omaheke	Gobabis	32,714	84,731	63,481	77.00	48,880	97.55	C	East-central. Botswana border, Kalahari desert. Cattle country, game ranching. D=Lutheran.
1992	Omusati	Ongandjera	5,265	13,637	180,396	79.00	142,513	97.97	C	North. Etosha National Park, 3rd smallest political region, Mopane. Savannah grassland. D=Lutheran.
1993	Oshana	Oshakati	2,042	5,290	181,538	79.03	143,477	98.58	C	Central. Smallest, most densely populated area in the center of Ovamboland. D=Lutheran.
1994	Oshikoto	Tsumeb	10,273	26,607	200,948	77.00	154,730	96.55	C	North. Commercial, smelting, and distribution center for copper, zinc, and lead mines. D=Lutheran.
1995	Otjozondjupa	Grootfontein	40,667	105,327	97,049	78.00	75,698	97.55	C	Central. Copper, lead, zinc, vanadium, rich farmland. Site of largest known meteorite. D=Lutheran.
	NAURU		**8**	**21**	**11,519**	**72.41**	**8,341**	**96.44**	**C**	**Protestants 50.7%, Roman Catholics 25.3%. Pent-char 9.5%, Evangelical 2.6%, GCC 18.9%**
1996	Nauru	Yaran	8	21	11,519	72.41	8,341	96.44	C	Central Pacific. One of the smallest independent states. Imports food and water. High grade phosphate deposits. Discovered in 1798, mining has destroyed nearly 80% of the island. D=NCC,RCC.
	NEPAL		**56,827**	**147,181**	**23,930,490**	**2.41**	**576,061**	**46.23**	**A**	**Independents 2.3%, Protestants 0.06%. Pent-char 2.1%, Evangelical 0.7%, GCC 2.2%**
1997	Bagmati	Bhaktapur	3,640	9,428	2,912,908	3.17	92,368	47.08	A	Central. Capital city, Langtang National Park, Himalayas. Airport. Potatoes, millet, jute. D=NCF/N.
1998	Bheri	Nepalganj	4,071	10,545	1,427,518	1.40	19,985	45.22	A	West. Karnali River, India border. Wheat, potatoes, millet, oilseed.
1999	Dhawalagiri	Bagluri	3,146	8,148	635,276	2.10	13,341	45.92	A	Central. Himalayas, glaciers. Livestock, crafts, millet, potatoes.
2000	Gandaki	Chame	4,740	12,275	1,638,576	2.40	39,326	46.22	A	Central. Great Himalayas, glaciers. Livestock, millet, oilseed.
2001	Janakpur	Sindhulimadi	3,733	9,669	2,668,326	2.90	77,381	46.72	A	East. Railroad route. India and China borders. Potatoes, millet, jute.
2002	Karnali	Manma	8,244	21,351	337,166	1.30	4,383	45.02	A	Northwest. Himalayas, Rara National Park, Shey Phoksundo National Park. Glaciers, livestock.
2003	Koshi	Dharan	3,733	9,669	2,236,632	2.20	49,206	46.02	A	East. Arun River. China and India borders, glaciers. Railroad, rice, corn, wheat.
2004	Lumbini	Butawal	3,465	8,975	2,606,021	2.70	70,363	46.52	A	Central. India border, Kali Gandaki River. Potatoes, rice, livestock, rural farming.
2005	Mahakaii	Dadeldhura	2,698	6,989	860,557	1.20	10,327	44.92	A	Far west. India border, Mahakali River. Glaciers. Livestock, wheat, potatoes.
2006	Mechi	Ilam	3,165	8,196	1,447,146	1.30	18,813	45.12	A	East. India and China borders. Himalayas, glaciers. Wheat, corn, millet, livestock.
2007	Narayani	Hetauda	3,210	8,313	2,421,811	3.00	72,654	46.82	A	South central. Royal Chitum National Park, Harayani River. Railroad. Corn, jute. D=NCF/N.
2008	Rapti	Tulsipur	4,047	10,482	1,354,784	1.90	25,741	45.72	A	West. Duduwa Sringkla Range, Babat River. Potatoes, wheat, jute, millet, glaciers.
2009	Sagarmatha	Rajbiraj	4,089	10,591	2,071,038	2.70	55,918	46.52	A	East. Saptakosi River, Sagarmatha National Park, Mt. Everest. Potatoes, wheat. D=NCF/N.
2010	Seti	Silgadhi	4,846	12,550	1,312,731	2.00	26,255	45.82	A	West. Seti River, Dudwa National Park, Khapfad National Park. Glaciers. Wheat, corn.
	NETHERLANDS		**16,033**	**41,526**	**15,785,699**	**65.14**	**10,282,853**	**97.63**	**C**	**Roman Catholics 34.5%, Protestants 26.8%. Pent-char 6.5%, Evangelical 3.8%, GCC 41.2%**
2011	Drenthe	Assen	1,025	2,654	464,519	68.00	315,873	99.99	C	Northeast. Prehistoric settlement. Rye, potatoes, spinning, weaving, and rope making. D=RCC,NHK.
2012	Flevoland	Lelystad	549	1,422	261,067	66.00	172,304	98.49	C	Central. Lake Ijssel (Ijsselmeer). Apples, cereals, flowers. F=1986. D=RCC,NHK.
2013	Friesland	Leeuwarden	1,295	3,353	624,646	66.00	412,266	98.49	C	North. North Sea. Vast system of canals. Frisian language and literature. Potatoes. D=RCC,NHK.
2014	Gelderland	Arnhem	1,935	5,011	1,905,173	63.91	1,217,535	96.64	C	East-central. Rhine, Waal, Maas Rivers. Cherries, apples. F=11th century. D=RCC,NHK.
2015	Groningen	Groningen	906	2,346	572,773	65.00	372,302	97.49	C	North. Wadden Sea. Potato flour, paper, cardboard, engineering, shipbuilding. D=RCC,NHK.
2016	Limburg	Maastricht	838	2,170	1,157,867	65.00	752,614	97.49	C	South. Maas River. Dutch-Belgian treaty (1839). Wheat, rye, sugar beets. D=RCC,NHK.
2017	Noord-Brabant	's-Hertogenbosch	1,910	4,946	2,325,410	66.00	1,534,771	98.49	C	South. D=RCC,NHK.
2018	Noord-Holland	Haarlem	1,029	2,665	2,528,698	64.00	1,618,367	96.49	C	Northwest. North Sea. Bulb fields. Below sea level, reclaimed land. Cheese. D=RCC,NHK.
2019	Overijssel	Zwolle	1,289	3,339	1,074,989	64.00	687,993	96.49	C	Northeast. Borders Germany. Cattle, dairy, orchards. D=RCC,NHK.
2020	Utrecht	Utrecht	514	1,331	1,086,703	67.00	728,091	99.49	C	Central. Rhine, Lek, Vecht, and Eem Rivers. D=RCC,NHK.
2021	Zeeland	Middelburg	692	1,792	374,435	68.00	254,616	99.99	C	Southwest. North Sea. Disastrous flood (1953). Cereals, oysters. D=RCC,NHK.
2022	Zuid-Holland	The Hague	1,123	2,908	3,409,417	65.00	2,216,121	97.49	C	West. North Sea. Flowering bulbs, tomatoes, cucumbers. Reclaimed land (polders). D=RCC,NHK.
	NETHERLANDS ANTILLES		**308**	**800**	**216,775**	**85.30**	**184,912**	**99.29**	**C**	**Roman Catholics 69.5%, Protestants 10.6%. Pent-char 4.7%, Evangelical 3.2%, GCC 17.5%**
2023	Bonaire	Kralendijk	111	288	12,622	90.00	11,360	99.89	C	Second largest island. Caribbean Sea. Black slave descendants. Tourism. D=RCC.
2024	Curacao	Willemstad	171	444	162,958	84.00	136,885	99.10	C	Caribbean Sea. Oldest Jewish community in Western Hemisphere (1500s). Oranges. D=RCC.
2025	Saba	The Bottom	5	13	1,265	92.00	1,164	99.99	C	Caribbean Sea. Settled by the Dutch in 1632. Livestock, potatoes. D=RCC.
2026	Sint Eustatius or Statia	Oranjestad	8	21	2,018	92.00	1,857	99.99	C	Caribbean Sea. Two extinct volcanoes. Onions, yams, sweet potatoes, lobsters. D=RCC.
2027	Sint Maarten (Dutch)	Philipsburg	13	34	37,912	88.75	33,646	99.84	C	Caribbean Sea. Named by Christopher Columbus. Tourism. D=RCC.
	NEW CALEDONIA		**7,172**	**18,576**	**214,029**	**75.54**	**161,679**	**98.61**	**C**	**Roman Catholics 54.2%, Protestants 14.0%. Pent-char 5.5%, Evangelical 5.0%, GCC 18.8%**
2028	Loyaute	–	765	1,981	23,352	83.00	19,382	99.67	C	South Pacific Ocean. Nickel mining, tourism. F=1774. D=RCC.
2029	Nord	–	3,700	9,583	45,011	80.00	36,009	99.47	C	South Pacific Ocean. Mountainous, sub-tropical. Minerals. Tourism. D=RCC.
2030	Sud	–	2,707	7,012	145,667	72.97	106,288	98.18	C	South Pacific Ocean. 33% Melanesian, 45% European. D=RCC.

Continued opposite

Table 11-3 continued

Rec No 1	Country Major civil divisions 2	Capital 3	sq.mi. 4	sq.km. 5	Pop 2000 6	AC% 7	Church members 8	E% 9	W 10	Notes 11
	NEW ZEALAND		**104,454**	**270,534**	**3,861,905**	**66.35**	**2,562,219**	**99.07**	**C**	**Protestants 24.1%, Anglicans 21.3%. Pent-char 15.2%, Evangelical 17.0%, GCC 39.9%**
2031	Auckland	–	–	–	536,942	62.00	332,904	98.15	C	Northwest. North Island. Agriculture, dairy, sheep raising. D=Anglican,Baptist,RCC,Presbyterian.
2032	Bay of Plenty	–	–	–	117,203	73.98	86,711	99.90	C	Eastern North Island. Geysers, boiling mud. Dairy and sheep farming. D=Presbyterian.
2033	Canterbury	–	–	–	248,507	70.00	173,955	99.42	C	East-central South Island. Southern Alps. Sheep, mixed farming, salmon. Mount Hutt, resort. D=RCC.
2034	Gisborne	–	–	–	24,959	76.00	18,969	99.82	C	East-central North Island. First landing site of Europeans (Captain James Cook). D=Anglican.
2035	Hawkes Bay	–	–	–	78,370	76.50	59,953	99.82	C	Eastern North Island. Largest wool wholesale center. Resort area. D=RCC,Anglican.
2036	Manawatu-Wanganui	–	–	–	127,495	72.00	91,796	99.52	C	Southern North Island. Early center of Maori settlement. Dairy, sheep. D=Presbyterian,RCC.
2037	Nelson-Marlborough	–	–	–	63,704	74.00	47,141	99.72	C	Northeastern South Island. Cook Strait. Mixed farming, sheep, dairy farming. D=RCC,Anglican.
2038	North Island	–	44,702	115,777	1,436,485	63.00	904,986	98.72	C	South Pacific Ocean. Smaller of 2 principal islands. D=RCC,Presbyterian,Anglican.
2039	Northland	–	–	–	74,113	75.00	55,585	99.72	C	Northernmost region of North Island. Tasman Sea, Pacific Ocean. Maoris. Livestock. D=RCC.
2040	Otago	–	–	–	104,354	75.00	78,266	99.72	C	Southeastern South Island. Otago Mountains. Gold rush in 1861. Tourism, sheep. D=RCC.
2041	South Island	–	58,384	151,215	494,227	64.00	316,305	99.72	C	Southwest Pacific Ocean. Largest of 2 principal islands. D=Anglican,RCC.
2042	Southland	–	–	–	57,618	75.00	43,214	99.72	C	Southwestern South Island. Fiordland National Park. F=Dutch navigator Abel Tasman. D=RCC.
2043	Taranaki	–	–	–	60,346	76.00	45,863	99.82	C	West North Island. Tasman Sea. Taranaki volcano. Dairy. D=Anglican,RCC,Presbyterian.
2044	Waikato	–	–	–	190,655	70.00	133,459	99.42	C	Northern North Island. Tasman Sea. Sheep, dairy cattle. Resort area. D=Anglican.
2045	Wellington	–	–	–	226,400	70.00	158,480	99.42	C	South North Island. Fruits, vegetables, dairy, sheep, cattle farming. D=RCC,Presbyterian.
2046	West Coast	–	–	–	20,044	73.00	14,632	99.62	C	West-central South Island. Tasman Sea, Mount Cook: 12,349 ft (3,764 m). Sawmilling. D=RCC.
	NICARAGUA		**50,838**	**131,670**	**5,074,194**	**95.73**	**4,857,432**	**99.86**	**C**	**Roman Catholics 85.1%, Protestants 11.6%. Pent-char 14.1%, Evangelical 8.7%, GCC 6.0%**
2047	Boaco	Boaco	1,639	4,244	159,487	96.00	153,108	99.88	C	Central. Cattle, swine, hides and skins, dairy products. D=RCC.
2048	Carazo	Jinotepe	405	1,050	173,994	97.00	168,774	99.93	C	Southwest. Artesian wells, coffee, sugarcane, sesame, timber, limestone. D=RCC.
2049	Chinandega	Chinandega	1,902	4,926	407,848	95.50	389,495	99.85	C	Northwest. Cotton, sugarcane, bananas, furniture, perfume. D=RCC.
2050	Chontales	Juigalpa	2,463	6,378	168,438	96.00	161,700	99.88	C	Central, south. Lake Nicaragua. Sugarcane, beans, corn, coffee, silver mining. D=RCC.
2051	Estelí	Estelí	902	2,335	203,678	96.00	195,531	99.88	C	Northwest. Esteli River. Livestock, cotton, tobacco, sesame, cheese. D=RCC.
2052	Granada	Granada	359	929	181,306	95.00	172,241	99.83	C	Southwest. Mombacho Volcano. Furniture, soap, clothing, cottonseed oil, rum. D=RCC.
2053	Jinotega	Jinotega	3,766	9,755	300,382	95.50	286,865	99.85	C	North-central. Lake Apanas. Coffee, tobacco, corn (maize). Flour milling, tanning. D=RCC.
2054	León	León	1,972	5,107	392,342	96.00	376,648	99.88	C	West. Cotton, sugarcane. Heavy fighting between Sandinista and government (1978). D=RCC.
2055	Madriz	Somoto	619	1,602	125,272	96.00	120,261	99.88	C	North. Borders Honduras. Coco and Yali rivers. Coffee, grain, livestock, tobacco. D=RCC.
2056	Managua	Managua	1,418	3,672	1,273,770	94.71	1,206,384	99.79	C	South. History of earthquakes. Coffee, cotton, corn (maize). D=RCC.
2057	Masaya	Masaya	228	590	281,075	95.00	267,021	99.82	C	Southwest. Rope, hammocks. Heavy fighting between Sandinista and government (1978). D=RCC.
2058	Matagalpa	Matagalpa	3,291	8,523	446,940	97.00	433,532	99.93	C	West-central. Coffee, corn (maize), beans, rice. Gold and silver mining. D=RCC.
2059	North Atlantic	–	12,417	32,159	317,066	97.00	307,554	99.93	C	East. Atlantic Ocean. Coffee, corn, beans. D=RCC.
2060	Nueva Segovia	Ocotal	1,206	3,123	172,929	96.00	166,012	99.88	C	Northwest. Borders Honduras, Coco River. Gold and silver mining, tobacco, sugarcane. D=RCC.
2061	Rivas	Rivas	832	2,155	163,546	95.00	155,369	99.82	C	Southwest. Pacific Ocean. Livestock, sugarcane, coffee, cacao. D=RCC.
2062	R'o San Juan	San Carlos	2,885	7,473	81,689	97.00	79,238	99.93	C	Southeast. Rice, corn, coconuts, livestock. F=1949. D=RCC.
2063	South Atlantic	Bluefields	10,582	27,407	224,432	97.00	217,699	99.93	C	East. Tropical forest, gold mining, lumbering, bananas, coconuts, rice, corn. D=RCC.
	NIGER		**496,900**	**1,287,000**	**10,730,102**	**0.54**	**58,270**	**42.14**	**A**	**Independents 0.2%, Roman Catholics 0.1%. Pent-char 0.2%, Evangelical 0.1%, GCC 0.4%**
2064	Agadez	Agadez	244,869	634,209	304,648	0.10	305	33.70	A	Central. Air Massif. Tuareg, Fulani. Tin, coal, uranium mining. Livestock, hides, grains.
2065	Diffa	Diffa	54,138	140,216	277,926	0.05	139	31.65	A	East. Lake Chad. Desert. Livestock, uranium.
2066	Dosso	Dosso	11,970	31,002	1,511,210	0.20	3,022	36.80	A	Southwest. Multicrop subsistence farming, livestock. Zerma.
2067	Maradi	Maradi	14,896	38,581	2,058,201	0.50	10,291	42.10	A	South-central. Peanuts, cassava, cotton. Hausa. D=RCC. M=EMS.
2068	Tahoua	Tahoua	41,188	106,677	1,940,041	0.66	12,777	45.26	A	South. Desert, Mali border. Peanuts, cattle, goats, sheep. D=RCC.
2069	Tillabéri	Tillabéri	34,863	90,293	2,545,930	1.00	25,459	47.79	A	West. Niger River, Burkina Faso border. Airport. Peanuts, cotton, livestock. D=RCC.
2070	Zinder	Zinder	56,151	145,430	2,092,147	0.30	6,276	38.90	A	South-central. Peanut-processing, millet-flour mill, tannery. Hausa, Fulani. M=EMS.
	NIGERIA		**356,669**	**923,768**	**111,506,095**	**45.71**	**50,965,002**	**79.77**	**B**	**Independents 21.5%, Anglicans 18.0%. Pent-char 32.1%, Evangelical 20.0%, GCC 10.0%**
2071	Abia	Umuahia	10,516	27,237	2,894,877	70.00	2,026,414	98.06	C	East-central. Yams, taro, corn (maize), oil palm. D=Anglican,RCC,Independents.
2072	Abuja	Abuja	2,824	7,315	477,034	45.00	214,665	83.06	B	Central. Yams, millet, corn (maize). Gwari, Koro, Afo, Bassa, Hausa, Fulani. D=RCC.
2073	Adamawa	Yola	35,286	91,390	2,675,767	45.00	1,204,095	83.06	B	Northeast. Mandara and Shebshi Mountains. Peanuts, cotton. Fulani, Mumuye, Hausa. D=Anglican.
2074	Akwa Ibom	Uyo	2,734	7,081	2,972,674	68.00	2,021,418	97.56	C	Southeast. Bight of Biafra of Atlantic Ocean. Yams, rice, oil palms, rubber. Fishing. Ibibio. D=Anglican.
2075	Anambra	Awka	6,824	17,675	3,486,862	70.00	2,440,803	98.06	C	East-central. Yams, taro, oil palm products, rice, corn (maize). Igbos. D=Anglican,RCC.
2076	Bauchi	Bauchi	24,944	64,605	5,409,885	56.01	3,030,293	95.07	B	Northeast. Cotton, coffee. Fulani, Hausa. Yankari National Park. D=RCC,Anglican.
2077	Benue	Makurdi	17,442	45,174	3,502,607	58.00	2,031,512	95.06	B	East-central. Mining, lead, limestone, tin, Shea nuts. Tiv, Idoma. D=Anglican,RCC.
2078	Borno	Maiduguri	44,942	116,400	3,271,054	45.00	1,471,974	83.06	B	Northeast. Sorghum, millet, peanuts. Kanuri. 'Home of the Berbers'. D=RCC.
2079	Cross River	Calabar	7,782	20,156	2,350,192	71.00	1,668,636	98.26	C	Southeast. Cross River. Forests. Yams, cassava, rice. Fishing. Efik, Ekoi. D=RCC.
2080	Delta	Asaba	13,707	35,500	3,237,780	49.00	1,586,512	87.06	B	South. Yams, cassava, oil palm produce. Igbo, Edo (Bini), Itsekiri, Urhobo, Isoko, Ijaw. D=Anglican.
2081	Edo	Benin City	6,873	17,802	2,720,871	48.00	1,306,018	86.06	B	South. Yams, cassava, oil palm produce. D=Anglican,RCC,Independents.
2082	Enugu	Enugu	4,954	12,831	3,982,440	68.00	2,708,059	97.56	C	East-central. Yams, oil palm produce, taro. Coal mining. Igbo. D=Anglican.
2083	Imo	Owerri	4,575	11,850	3,131,102	72.00	2,254,393	98.36	C	South. Densely populated. Yams, taro, corn (maize), oil palm. Petroleum, coal. Igbo. D=RCC.
2084	Jigawa	Dutse	16,712	43,285	3,565,006	19.00	677,351	48.06	A	North. Borders Niger. Peanuts, sorghum, cotton. Hausa, Fulani. D=Anglican.
2085	Kaduna	Kaduna	27,122	70,245	5,000,268	38.00	1,900,102	75.34	B	North-central. Borders Niger. Cotton, peanuts, tobacco, textiles. Hausa, Fulani, Gbari. D=Anglican.
2086	Kano	Kano	7,773	20,131	7,094,954	20.00	1,418,991	49.06	A	North. Peanuts, cotton, onions, tobacco. Cattle, horses. Tin and columbite mining. D=RCC.
2087	Katsina	Katsina	9,341	24,192	4,885,740	19.00	928,291	48.06	A	North-central. Borders Niger. Peanuts, cotton, cattle. Hausa, Fulani. D=Anglican,RCC.
2088	Kebbi	Birnin Kebbi	39,589	102,535	2,597,891	16.00	415,663	45.06	A	Northwest. Peanuts, cotton, rice. Cattle, goats. Fulani, Hausa, Dakarki (Dakarawa). D=RCC.
2089	Kogi	Lokoja	11,519	29,833	2,644,267	50.00	1,322,134	89.06	B	Central. Yams, cassava, fishing, coal mining. Iglala, Igbira, Yoruba. D=Anglican,Independents.
2090	Kwara	Ilorin	25,818	66,869	1,973,357	39.00	769,609	76.06	B	West-central. Yams, corn (maize), rice, sugarcane. Yoruba, Nupe, Busa, Baatonun. D=RCC.
2091	Lagos	Ikeja	1,292	3,345	7,162,661	53.00	3,796,210	92.06	B	Southwest. Bight of Benin. Borders Benin. Cassava, palm oil, coconuts. Yoruba. D=Anglican.
2092	Niger	Minna	25,111	65,037	3,127,155	37.00	1,157,047	71.06	B	West-central. Niger River. Cotton, shea nuts, pottery, brass-work. Nupe, Gwari, Busa. D=RCC.
2093	Ogun	Abeokuta	6,472	16,762	2,946,013	35.00	1,031,105	69.06	B	West. Rice, corn (maize), cassava. Aro granite quarries. Tourism around Olumo rock. D=Anglican.
2094	Ondo	Akure	8,092	20,959	4,893,478	48.00	2,348,869	86.06	B	West. Bight of Benin (Atlantic Ocean). Cotton, tobacco, rubber, timber. D=Anglican,Independents.
2095	Osun	Oshogbo	14,558	37,705	2,775,253	35.00	971,339	72.06	B	West. Yams, cassava, corn (maize), brass work, woven cloth. D=Anglican,RCC.
2096	Oyo	Ibadan	10,986	28,454	4,395,002	34.00	1,494,301	71.06	B	West. Ogun River. Yams, corn (maize). Spinning, weaving, leatherworking. Tourism. D=Anglican.
2097	Plateau	Jos	22,405	58,030	4,136,642	55.00	2,275,153	94.06	B	Central. Groundnuts, soybeans, minerals, cotton, rubber, timber. D=Anglican,Independents.
2098	Rivers	Port Harcourt	8,436	21,850	5,018,666	71.00	3,563,253	98.26	C	South. Gulf of Guinea, Niger Delta, Nun River. Fishing, livestock. D=Anglican,RCC.
2099	Sokoto	Sokoto	25,380	65,735	5,533,312	23.00	1,272,662	57.06	B	Northwest. Jihad by Fulani in 1804. Peanuts, cotton, tobacco. Fulani, Hausa. D=RCC.
2100	Taraba	Jalingo	21,032	54,473	1,865,174	46.00	857,980	84.06	B	East. Borders Cameroon. Cassava, sorghum, millet, cattle. D=Anglican,RCC.
2101	Yobe	Damaturu	17,568	45,502	1,778,110	45.00	800,150	83.06	B	Northeast. Borders Niger. Sorghum, millet, peanuts. Kanuri. D=Anglican,Independents.
	NIUE ISLAND		**100**	**260**	**1,876**	**92.54**	**1,736**	**99.95**	**C**	**Protestants 57.3%, Marginal Christians 23.4%. Pent-char 11.7%, Evangelical 3.7%, GCC 17.5%**
2102	Niue Island	Alofi	100	260	1,876	92.53	1,736	99.94	C	World's largest coral island. Tropical fruits, sales of postage stamps. D=Niue Christian Church
	NORFOLK ISLAND		**15**	**40**	**2,075**	**65.20**	**1,353**	**99.66**	**C**	**Anglicans 29.4%, Protestants 22.8%. Pent-char 5.3%, Evangelical 20.4%, GCC 28.6%**
2103	Norfolk Island	Kingston	15	40	2,075	65.20	1,353	99.66	C	Pacific Ocean island. External territory of Australia. Y=1788. D=Anglican.
	NORTH KOREA		**47,399**	**122,762**	**24,039,193**	**2.08**	**500,213**	**49.97**	**A**	**Independents 1.8%, Roman Catholics 0.2%. Pent-char 1.8%, Evangelical 0.08%, GCC 1.9%**
2104	Chagang-do	Kanggye	6,551	16,968	1,436,438	1.20	17,237	39.09	A	North. Borders China. Timber, ceramics. Mining (copper, zinc, coal, graphite).
2105	Hamgyong-namdo	Hamhung	7,324	18,970	3,164,882	2.43	77,046	53.32	B	East-central. Synthetic textiles, machinery, oil refining. Scenic beaches. D=House churches.
2106	Hamgyong-pukto	Ch'ongjin	6,784	17,570	2,488,912	2.10	52,267	51.99	B	Northeast. Sea of Japan. Fishing, shipbuilding.
2107	Hwanghae-namdo	Haeju	3,090	8,002	2,378,322	2.50	59,458	53.39	B	Southwest. Yellow Sea. Cement, chemicals.
2108	Hwanghae-pukto	Sariwon	3,092	8,007	1,750,813	1.40	24,511	41.29	A	Southwest. Agricultural machinery, food processing, spinning mills.
2109	Hyangsan-chigu	–	–	–	34,792	0.80	278	33.69	A	In North Pyongan. Lumbering, coal, gold mining. Potatoes, soybeans.
2110	Kaesong-si	–	485	1,255	411,299	2.70	11,105	54.59	B	Near border with South Korea. Textiles, medicinal herbs, temples, tombs, palaces.
2111	Kangwon-do	Wonsan	4,306	11,152	1,524,662	2.50	38,117	53.39	B	Southeast. Sea of Japan. Grains, persimmons, fishing. Over 100 temples in Kumgang-san.
2112	Namp'o-si	–	291	753	888,453	2.80	24,877	54.69	B	Chief seaport on Taedong River. Market center for marine products, copper and gold refining.
2113	P'yongan-namdo	Pyongsan	4,470	11,577	3,296,598	1.50	49,449	44.39	A	Northwest. Lumber, chemical industry. Taedong River. Millet, fruit, rice, livestock, coal, gold.
2114	P'yongan-pukto	Sinuiju	4,707	12,191	2,957,369	1.70	50,275	51.59	B	Exclusive lumbering in the interior, gold and coal mining. Potatoes, soybeans, millet.
2115	P'yongyang-si	–	772	2,000	2,926,305	3.00	87,789	55.79	B	Taedong River. Textiles, food processing, iron, coal. F=1122 BC. D=100 House churches.
2116	Yanggang-do	Hyesan	5,528	14,317	780,348	1.00	7,803	40.89	A	North. Encompasses Kyema highlands. High quality anthracite, textiles, lumber, paper.
	NORTHERN CYPRUS		**1,288**	**3,335**	**185,045**	**8.70**	**16,106**	**56.02**	**B**	**Orthodox 7.5%, Independents 1.2%. Pent-char 1.1%, Evangelical 0.1%, GCC 2.4%**
2117	Northern Cyprus	Lefkose	1,288	3,335	185,045	8.70	16,106	56.02	B	Declared in 1983, recognized only by Turkey. Tobacco, fishing. D=GOC.
	NORTHERN MARIANA IS		**184**	**477**	**78,356**	**88.39**	**69,260**	**98.93**	**C**	**Roman Catholics 88.4%, Independents 8.5%. Pent-char 10.5%, Evangelical 4.2%, GCC 9.2%**
2118	Northern Mariana Is	Susupe	184	477	78,356	88.39	69,260	98.93	C	16 islands in Western Pacific Ocean. Sugar, coffee, coconuts. Chamorros. D=RCC.
	NORWAY		**125,050**	**323,878**	**4,461,033**	**94.18**	**4,201,262**	**98.63**	**C**	**Protestants 94.1%, Independents 3.0%. Pent-char 28.0%, Evangelical 10.8%, GCC 24.0%**
2119	Akershus	–	1,898	4,917	439,952	94.00	413,555	99.45	C	Southeast. Borders Sweden. Densely populated. Shipping, manufacturing, tourism. D=Lutheran.
2120	Aust-Agder	Arendal	3,557	9,212	102,108	96.00	98,024	99.65	C	South. Skagerrak. Burial mounds from Stone age. Mining, horticulture, forestry. D=Lutheran.
2121	Buskerud	Drammen	5,763	14,927	235,588	95.00	223,809	98.65	C	South-central. Paper, fruit, corn (maize). D=Lutheran.
2122	Finnmark	Vadsø	18,779	48,637	78,544	97.00	76,188	99.65	C	North. Above Arctic Circle. Borders Finland, Russia. Fishing. Lapps. D=Lutheran.
2123	Hedmark	Hamar	10,575	27,388	195,747	94.00	184,002	98.45	C	Southeast. Timber, agriculture. D=Lutheran.
2124	Hordaland	Bergen	6,036	15,634	432,154	93.00	401,903	97.45	C	Southwest. Hardangervidda. Grains, hay, cattle, fishing, tourism. D=Lutheran.
2125	Møre og Romsdal	Molde	5,832	15,104	249,259	94.00	234,303	98.45	C	West. Norwegian Sea. Fishing, tourism. D=Lutheran.
2126	Nord-Trondelag	Steinkjer	8,673	22,463	133,069	95.00	126,416	98.85	C	Central. Norwegian Sea. Borders Sweden. Fishing, grains, hay , potatoes. D=Lutheran.
2127	Nordland	Bodø	14,798	38,327	250,350	95.00	237,833	99.45	C	North. Norwegian Sea. Fishing, stock raising, rye, potatoes, mining. D=Lutheran.
2128	Oppland	Lillehammer	9,753	25,260	190,463	96.00	182,844	99.95	C	South-central. Livestock, grains, potatoes. Tourism around Gudbrand's valley. D=Lutheran.
2129	Oslo	Oslo	175	454	487,527	92.33	450,113	97.78	C	Southeast. Shipbuilding, graphic industries. Tourism, winter sports. D=Lutheran.
2130	Rogaland	Stavanger	3,529	9,141	356,795	93.00	331,819	97.45	C	Southwest. North Sea. Fishing. Copper mining. D=Lutheran.
2131	Sogn og Fjordane	Leikanger	7,195	18,634	111,508	96.00	107,048	99.65	C	West. North Sea. Tourism, grains, fruits, fishing. Vettisfossen, second highest waterfall. D=Lutheran.
2132	Sør-Trøndelag	Trondheim	7,271	18,831	263,936	94.00	248,100	98.45	C	Central. Norwegian Sea. Borders Sweden. Fishing, agriculture, shipping. D=Lutheran.
2133	Telemark	Skien	5,913	15,315	170,153	95.00	161,645	98.65	C	Southeast. Skagerrak. Lumber, fishing, paper products, farming. D=Lutheran.
2134	Troms	Tromsø	10,021	25,954	154,453	94.00	145,186	98.61	C	North. North of Arctic Circle. Norwegian Sea. Livestock, fishing. D=Lutheran.

Continued overleaf

Table 11-3 continued

Rec No 1	Country Major civil divisions 2	Capital 3	sq.mi. 4	sq.km. 5	Pop 2000 6	AC% 7	Church members 8	E% 9	W 10	Notes 11
2135	Vest-Agder	Kristiansand	2,811	7,281	152,340	95.50	145,485	99.15	C	South. North Sea. Fishing, lumbering, mixed farming, dairy. D=Lutheran.
2136	Vestfold	Tønsberg	856	2,216	208,284	95.00	197,870	99.45	C	Southeast. First royal dynasty in 10th century. Fishing, shipbuilding. D=Lutheran.
2137	Østfold	Moss	1,615	4,183	248,803	94.50	235,119	98.95	C	Southeast. Borders Sweden. Wood products, pulp. Popular resorts. D=Lutheran.
	OMAN		**119,500**	**309,500**	**2,541,739**	**4.80**	**121,916**	**46.97**	**A**	**Roman Catholics 2.0%, Independents 1.7%. Pent-char 1.8%, Evangelical 0.2%, GCC 2.1%**
2138	al-Batinah	ar-Rustaq; Suhar	4,850	12,500	711,204	5.84	41,565	49.01	A	Northeast. Gulf of Oman. Borders UAE. Dates, papaya, lime, livestock, fishing. Baluchi. D=RCC.
2139	al-Dakhiliyah	Nizwa; Sama'il	12,300	31,900	289,418	4.00	11,577	46.17	A	Highlands, center of opposition to the Sultan. Copper and brass works, leather, pottery, handicrafts.
2140	Al-Wusta	Hayma	30,750	79,700	21,495	0.50	107	32.67	A	Southwestern. Tourism, mild climate on coast. Cotton, wheat, tobacco, sugarcane.
2141	ash-Sharqiyah	Ibra; Sur	14,200	3,680	325,381	4.00	13,015	46.17	A	East. Persian Gulf, East Hajar Mountains. Famous for boat construction, chemicals, wood. 'Eastern'.
2142	az-Zahirah	al-Buraymi; `Ibri	17,000	44,000	228,248	2.00	4,565	42.17	A	West, bordering UAE. Dates, papaya, lime. Baluchi. D=RCC.
2143	Masqat	Muscat	1,350	3,500	691,650	7.00	48,416	53.09	B	Gulf of Oman, political heart of sultanate. Dates, dried fish, mother of pearl, frankincense. D=RCC.
2144	Musandam	Khasab	700	1,800	36,182	0.80	289	32.97	A	Northeast. Gulf of Oman. Borders United Arab Emirates. Dates, vegetables. Shihuh.
2145	Zufar (Dhofar)	Salalah	38,350	99,300	238,161	1.00	2,382	33.17	A	South. Indian Ocean. Dates, fishing.
	PAKISTAN		**307,374**	**796,095**	**156,483,155**	**2.44**	**3,812,245**	**46.76**	**A**	**Protestants 1.1%, Roman Catholics 0.7%. Pent-char 0.5%, Evangelical 0.4%, GCC 2.2%**
2146	Balochistan	Quetta	134,051	347,190	8,041,372	0.50	40,207	34.82	A	West. Borders Iran. Arabian Sea. Baluchi, Pashtun (Pathan). Wheat, sorghum, rice, fruit.
2147	Islamabad	–	350	906	626,073	1.40	8,765	45.72	A	North. Administrative center, large and prominent RC hospital. Airport, railroad.
2148	North-West Frontier	Peshawar	28,773	74,521	20,331,011	0.25	50,828	29.57	A	North. Muslim rule brought by Turks in 988. Afghan refugees. Wheat, tobacco. Pashtun.
2149	Punjab	Lahore	79,284	205,344	87,999,867	3.00	2,639,996	51.05	B	East. Borders India. Persian Empire, Darius I (c. 518 BC). Wheat, cotton, livestock. 'Five waters'.
2150	Sindh	Karachi	54,407	140,914	35,423,170	1.80	637,617	46.62	A	Southeast. Arabian Sea. Ancient Indus Valley Civilization. Islam (AD 711). Cotton, wheat.
2151	Tribal Areas	–	10,509	27,220	4,061,661	10.71	434,833	65.03	B	North. Many animists and Christians. Wheat, livestock. D=Church of Pakistan.
	PALAU		**630**	**1,632**	**19,426**	**94.57**	**18,371**	**99.94**	**C**	**Roman Catholics 44.2%, Protestants 28.8%. Pent-char 6.5%, Evangelical 10.0%, GCC 14.4%**
2152	Palau	Koror	630	1,632	19,426	94.57	18,371	99.94	C	Archipelago, over 200 islands. Independence (1003). D=RCC,Modekne.
	PALESTINE		**2,410**	**6,242**	**2,215,393**	**8.50**	**188,289**	**70.64**	**B**	**Independents 4.6%, Orthodox 2.1%. Pent-char 4.8%, Evangelical 0.6%, GCC 7.6%**
2153	Gaza Strip	–	140	363	894,429	10.71	95,822	77.29	B	Negev desert coast. Palestinian refugees, Jewish settlements. D=GOC,RCC.
2154	West Bank	–	2,270	5,879	1,320,964	7.00	92,467	66.14	B	Jordan River. 20% arable land. Olives, fruit. Palestinian Arabs. D=GOC,RCC.
	PANAMA		**29,157**	**75,517**	**2,855,683**	**86.04**	**2,457,064**	**98.35**	**C**	**Roman Catholics 77.3%, Protestants 11.9%. Pent-char 17.1%, Evangelical 9.2%, GCC 15.5%**
2155	Bocas del Toro	Bocas del Toro	3,376	8,745	132,033	90.30	119,229	99.71	C	Northwest. Archipelago de Bocas Del Toro, Laguna de Chariqui. Textiles, apparel, footwear. D=RCC.
2156	Chiriquí	David	3,341	8,653	440,960	88.00	388,045	99.31	C	Southwest. Highest elevation in country, Gulf of Chiriqui. Fishing, manufacturing, rice. D=RCC.
2157	Coclé	Penonomé	1,902	4,927	204,664	90.00	184,198	99.41	C	Southeast. Grande River, Chico River, marsh. Bananas, cocoa, timber, corn, fishing. D=RCC.
2158	Colón	Colón	1,888	4,890	203,616	89.00	181,218	99.41	C	Northeast. Lake Gratun, Caribbean Sea, entrance to Panama Canal. Bananas, timber. D=RCC.
2159	Darién	La Palma	4,823	12,491	50,243	91.00	45,721	99.51	C	Southeast central. Gulf of Panama. Bananas, timber, corn, rice, crafts. D=RCC.
2160	Emberá	–	1,614	4,180	11,166	90.00	10,049	99.41	C	Southeast bordering Colombia. Autonomous region. Choco Indians. D=RCC.
2161	Herrera	Chitré	904	2,341	108,670	90.00	97,803	99.41	C	South central. Gulf of Panama. Marsh. Bananas, cocoa, corn, rice, livestock, textiles. D=RCC.
2162	Kuna Yala (San Blas)	El Porvenir	910	2,357	40,859	92.00	37,590	99.61	C	Central. Peninsula De Azugro. Timber, agriculture, fruits, manufacturing. D=RCC.
2163	Los Santos	Las Tablas	1,470	3,806	85,259	91.00	77,586	99.51	C	South-central. Gulf of Panama. Manufacturing, textiles, apparel, footwear, food processing. D=RCC.
2164	Panamá	Panama City	4,590	11,887	1,343,190	82.90	1,113,505	97.34	C	East. Panama Canal. Commercial and transportation center. University of Panama (1935). D=RCC.
2165	Veraguas	Santiago	4,339	11,239	235,023	86.00	202,120	98.31	C	Central. Santa Maria River. Caribbean and Pacific coast. Bananas, agriculture. D=RCC.
	PAPUA NEW GUINEA		**178,704**	**462,840**	**4,608,145**	**82.15**	**3,785,528**	**97.53**	**C**	**Protestants 56.6%, Roman Catholics 29.9%. Pent-char 16.3%, Evangelical 17.5%, GCC 11.3%**
2166	Bougainville	Arawa (Buka)	3,600	9,300	199,239	88.00	175,330	97.98	C	East. Old copper mine, bananas, coconuts, rice, yams, fish. 19 separate languages. D=RCC.
2167	Central	Port Moresby	11,400	29,500	175,610	81.10	142,415	97.48	C	South-central. Slopes of Owen Stanley range. Variarata Natl. Park. Coconuts, cattle. D=RCC.
2168	East New Britain	Rabaul	6,000	15,500	230,352	82.00	188,889	97.38	C	East. Solomon Spa. Volcanic, commercial center. Coffee, cocoa, copra. D=RCC,Lutheran.
2169	East Sepik	Wewak	16,550	42,800	310,173	81.00	251,240	97.18	C	Northwest. Prince Alexander mountains. Coconuts, palm oil, bananas, sage, yams. D=RCC.
2170	Eastern Highlands	Goroka	4,300	11,200	374,268	81.00	303,157	97.18	C	North-central. Central highlands plateau. Mt. Gaharasuka Natl. Park. Coffee, fruit, tourism. D=RCC.
2171	Enga	Wabag	4,950	12,800	297,742	83.00	247,126	98.38	C	Northwest, central. Porgera gold mining district. Coffee, tea, sweet potatoes, timber. D=Lutheran.
2172	Gulf	Kerema	13,300	34,500	85,017	90.00	76,515	99.88	C	South-central. Heavily forested, Turama River. Fish, crocodile skins, timber, bananas, yams. D=RCC.
2173	Madang	Madang	11,200	29,000	337,643	81.00	273,491	97.18	C	North-central. Bismarck Sea. Copra, coconuts, coffee, fish, palm oil, lobster, prawns, tuna. D=RCC.
2174	Manus	Lorengau	800	2,100	41,009	90.00	36,908	99.88	C	North-central. Atolls, reefs, volcanic. Vegetables, coconuts, palm oil, fish, timber. D=Lutheran,RCC.
2175	Milne Bay	Alotau (Samarai)	5,400	14,000	196,476	82.00	161,110	97.38	C	Southeast. Hot springs, geysers, volcanos. Coconuts, bananas, trapping. D=RCC.
2176	Morobe	Lae	13,300	34,500	454,108	81.00	367,827	97.18	C	East-central. 2nd largest city, university of technology. Rice, sugarcane, coffee, lobster. D=RCC.
2177	National Capital District	Port Moresby	100	240	241,388	78.50	189,490	96.92	C	South-central. Administrative division, largest city. Main industrial, commercial center. D=Lutheran.
2178	New Ireland	Kavieng	3,700	9,600	108,918	83.00	90,402	98.38	C	East. Solomon Sea, Pacific Ocean. Copra, coconuts, palm oil, fish. D=RCC,Lutheran.
2179	Oro (Northern)	Popondetta	8,800	22,800	120,870	84.00	101,531	96.78	C	Southeast, Mambare River. Tapa cloth. Alexandra birdwing: largest butterfly in world. D=RCC.
2180	Sandaun (West Sepik)	Vanimo	14,000	36,300	168,866	83.00	140,159	98.38	C	North-central. Highest point in New Guinea. Coffee, tea, maize, sugarcane, sweet potatoes. D=RCC.
2181	Simba (Chimbu)	Kundiawa	2,350	6,100	229,594	82.00	188,267	97.38	C	East-central. Commercial center, airstrip. Coffee, tea, sweet potatoes, timber. D=Lutheran.
2182	Southern Highlands	Mendi	9,200	23,800	378,146	81.00	306,298	97.18	C	South central. Oil and natural gas development. Coffee, tea, sugarcane, timber. D=RCC.
2183	West New Britain	Kimbe	8,100	21,000	159,325	85.00	135,426	98.78	C	East. Kimbe Bay. Bananas, cocoa, coconuts, coffee, capra, palm oil, fish, prawns, tourism. D=RCC.
2184	Western Highlands	Mount Hagen	3,300	8,500	363,614	81.00	294,527	97.18	C	East-central. Commercial center. Coffee, vegetables, tea, sweet potatoes, timber, tourism. D=RCC.
2185	Western	Daru	38,350	99,300	135,788	85.00	115,420	97.78	C	Southwest. Torres Strait, Fly River. Crocodile skins, tourism. D=Lutheran.
	PARAGUAY		**157,048**	**406,752**	**5,496,453**	**94.13**	**5,173,602**	**99.82**	**C**	**Roman Catholics 90.0%, Protestants 3.6%. Pent-char 4.4%, Evangelical 2.8%, GCC 7.8%**
2186	Alto Paraguay	Fuerte Olimpio	17,754	45,982	15,750	97.00	15,278	99.99	C	North. Borders Brazil. Livestock, tanning, tile works. D=RCC.
2187	Alto Paraná	Ciudad del Este	5,751	14,895	538,319	94.00	506,020	99.85	C	East. Formerly: Puerto President Stroessner. Parana River. Ceramics. Itaipu Dam. D=RCC.
2188	Amambay	Pedro Juan Caballero	4,994	12,933	129,506	96.00	124,326	99.89	C	East. Borders Brazil. Livestock, coffee. D=RCC.
2189	Asunción	–	45	117	669,705	93.00	622,826	99.79	C	Capital, chief port. Botanical gardens, universities. Gudoi Museum. F=1536. D=RCC.
2190	Boquerón	Filadelfia	18,034	46,708	35,046	96.00	33,644	99.89	C	West. Borders Argentina, low grasslands, marshes. Cattle, cotton, dairy products. D=RCC.
2191	Caaguazú	Coronel Oviedo	4,430	11,474	510,942	95.00	485,395	99.85	C	East-central. Tobacco, oranges, sugarcane, livestock. D=RCC.
2192	Caazapá	Caazapá	3,666	9,496	171,350	96.00	164,496	99.89	C	South. Tebicuary River. Lumber, tanneries, maté, oranges, petitgrain, sugarcane, cattle. D=RCC.
2193	Canindiyú	Salto del Guaira	5,663	14,667	129,063	96.00	123,900	99.89	C	East. Borders Brazil. Paraguayan tea, hardwoods. D=RCC.
2194	Central	Asunción	952	2,465	1,152,382	91.33	1,052,492	99.68	C	Southwest. Paraguay River. Cotton, sugarcane, corn (maize), tobacco. D=RCC.
2195	Concepción	Concepción	6,970	18,051	222,529	96.00	213,628	99.89	C	North-central. Paraguay River. Flour, cotton, sugar. D=RCC.
2196	Cordillera	Caacupé	1,910	4,948	274,715	95.00	260,979	99.85	C	Central. Paraguay River, humid climate. Maté, tobacco, sugarcane, oranges. D=RCC.
2197	Guairá	Villarrica	1,485	3,846	216,262	95.50	206,530	99.88	C	South. Fertile lowlands. Lumbering, sugarcane, grapes, cotton, tobacco, livestock. D=RCC.
2198	Itapúa	Encarnación	6,380	16,525	500,851	95.00	475,808	99.85	C	Southeast. Paraná River. Copper deposits, lumbering, maté, cotton, soybeans, corn, rice. D=RCC.
2199	Misiones	San Juan Bautista	3,690	9,556	118,131	96.00	113,406	99.89	C	South. Paraná River. Jesuit missions (17th century). Hydroelectric dams, tungsten. D=RCC.
2200	Paraguarí	Paraguarí	3,361	8,705	270,603	95.00	257,073	99.85	C	South. Agriculture center. Franciscan churches, Santo Tomas grottoes, fisheries. D=RCC.
2201	Presidente Hayes	Pozo Colorado	28,150	72,907	78,777	96.00	75,626	99.89	C	West-central. Paraguay River. Livestock. Sugarcane, corn, cotton, alfalfa, tobacco, peanuts. D=RCC.
2202	San Pedro	San Pedro	7,723	20,002	369,372	95.50	352,750	99.88	C	Central. Paraguay River, subtropical climate. Maté, oranges, livestock, lumbering. D=RCC.
2203	Neembucú	Pilar	4,690	12,147	93,151	96.00	89,425	99.89	C	South. Lake Ypoá, Tebicuara River, humid climate. Oranges, sugarcane, cotton, corn. D=RCC.
	PERU		**496,225**	**1,285,216**	**25,661,669**	**96.26**	**24,702,049**	**99.73**	**C**	**Roman Catholics 95.6%, Protestants 5.7%. Pent-char 13.4%, Evangelical 4.4%, GCC 3.7%**
2204	Andres Avelino Cáceres	–	15,154	39,249	2,272,975	96.50	2,193,421	99.94	C	Central. Mantaro River. Tourism. Zinc, lead, silver, copper, rice, corn, wheat, beans. D=RCC.
2205	Arequipa	–	24,458	63,345	1,039,195	96.00	997,627	99.77	C	South. Pacific Ocean. Alpaca wool, cotton, rice, olives. Mining: gold, silver, copper, lead. D=RCC.
2206	Callao	Callao	57	147	725,129	95.00	688,873	99.77	C	West-central. Minerals, refined metals, fish oil. D=RCC.
2207	Chavín	–	27,758	71,892	1,105,302	97.00	1,072,143	99.97	C	West-central. Fishing, fish oils, potatoes, sugarcane, sheep, wool, cattle, lead, zinc, tourism. D=RCC.
2208	Grau	–	8,545	22,131	1,749,872	97.00	1,697,376	99.97	C	Northwest. Cotton, rice, citrus, tropical fruits, textiles, phosphate, hydrocarbon resources. D=RCC.
2209	Inca	–	8,235	21,328	1,474,558	97.00	1,430,321	99.57	C	Southeast. Corn, barley, quinine, yucca, rice, copper, iron, silver, gold, dairying, wool, cattle. D=RCC.
2210	José Carlos Mariátegui	–	17,147	44,410	1,617,437	97.50	1,577,001	99.97	C	Central. On Pacific Ocean. Sugarcane, rice. D=RCC.
2211	La Libertad	–	9,573	24,795	1,439,833	97.00	1,396,638	99.97	C	North. Andes Mountains. Inca empire. Sugarcane, cotton, rice, coffee. D=RCC.
2212	Lima	–	13,437	34,902	7,908,834	95.10	7,521,301	99.51	C	Central. Pacific Ocean. Andes Mountains. Nearly one-third of Peru's population. D=RCC.
2213	Loreto	–	142,414	368,852	779,029	98.00	763,448	99.97	C	East. Borders Colombia, Ecuador, Brazil. Rubber, Brazil nuts, rice. D=RCC.
2214	Los Libertadores-Wari	–	32,889	85,183	1,713,232	97.50	1,670,401	99.97	C	Southwest. Hot springs. Lead, zinc, gold, silver, rice, corn. D=RCC.
2215	Nor Oriental del Marañón	–	27,804	72,012	2,853,308	96.00	2,739,176	99.47	C	North. Borders Ecuador. Rainforest. Sugarcane, corn (maize), rice, potatoes. D=RCC.
2216	San Martín	–	19,789	51,253	626,127	96.85	606,406	99.99	C	Northeast. Named for liberator Jose de San Martin. Coffee, rice, cotton, rubber, vanilla. D=RCC.
2217	Ucayali	–	39,541	102,411	356,838	97.50	347,917	99.97	C	East. Ucayali River. Bananas, cassava, corn (maize), cattle and pigs. Shipibo Indians. D=RCC.
	PHILIPPINES		**115,860**	**300,076**	**75,966,500**	**87.67**	**66,600,057**	**94.44**	**C**	**Roman Catholics 82.3%, Independents 18.8%. Pent-char 26.3%, Evangelical 2.4%, GCC 5.1%**
2218	Bicol	–	6,808	17,633	4,789,004	95.00	4,549,554	98.77	C	Southeastern Luzon. Peninsula. Rice. Bicol. Rice, coconut, pineapple, gold, silver. D=RCC.
2219	Cagayan Valley	–	10,362	26,838	2,807,874	94.00	2,639,402	98.77	C	Northern Luzon. Undeveloped. Chromite, coal reserves, tobacco, rice. D=RCC.
2220	Caraga	–	7,277	18,847	2,150,915	75.00	1,613,186	92.00	C	Northeast Mindanao. Regional center is Surigao. Gold and silver mining. D=RCC.
2221	Central Luzon	–	7,039	18,231	7,675,731	93.00	7,138,430	98.77	C	Central. Rice, corn (maize), coconuts, sugarcane. Industry near Manila. D=RCC.
2222	Central Mindanao	–	5,549	14,373	2,612,792	65.00	1,698,315	75.77	C	West-central, region 12. Rice, corn, coconut, bananas, timber, fishing, livestock. D=RCC.
2223	Central Visayas	–	5,773	14,951	5,552,164	93.00	5,163,513	98.77	C	Negros and other islands between Visaya and Bohol seas. Mixed agricultural and industrial. D=RCC.
2224	Cordillera	–	7,063	18,294	1,389,351	94.00	1,305,990	98.77	C	North-central Luzon, created in 1987, region 13. Logging, mining, some agriculture. D=RCC.
2225	Eastern Visayas	–	8,275	21,432	3,727,828	93.00	3,466,880	98.77	C	Samar and Leyte islands, created 1975, one of poorest regions, region 8. Rice, corn, fishing. D=RCC.
2226	Ilocos	–	4,958	12,840	4,211,659	93.00	3,916,843	98.77	C	Northwest Luzon, region 1. Rice for food, tobacco as a cash crop, gold, copper. D=RCC.
2227	Muslim Mindanao	–	4,493	11,638	2,237,517	35.00	783,131	56.77	B	West-central. Includes Lamao del Sur, Maguindanao provinces. Rice, corn, coconut. D=RCC.
2228	National Capital Region	–	246	636	10,467,500	95.00	9,944,125	99.97	C	West-central Luzon. Consists of Manila, most populous region. Referred to as Metro Manila. D=RCC.
2229	Northern Mindanao	–	5,418	14,033	2,749,456	81.91	2,252,176	97.68	C	North-central Mindano, region 10. Corn, coconut, pineapple, chrome, manganese. D=RCC.
2230	Southern Mindanao	–	10,479	27,141	5,097,732	60.00	3,058,639	68.77	C	Southeast and South Mindanao, region 11. Corn, pineapple, bananas, coffee, gold, silver. D=RCC.
2231	Southern Tagalog	–	18,117	46,924	11,006,406	95.00	10,456,086	99.77	C	East-central coast and central Luzon, largest region. Rice, sugarcane, petrochemicals, coal. D=RCC.
2232	Western Mindanao	–	6,194	16,042	3,094,267	82.00	2,537,299	89.77	C	Zamboanga Peninsula, region 9. Rice, coconut, rubber, coal, chromite, smelting, wood. D=RCC.
2233	Western Visayas	–	7,808	20,223	6,396,303	95.00	6,076,488	98.77	C	West Negros, southwest Visayan Sea, region 6. Mixed agriculture and mining, fisheries. D=RCC.
	PITCAIRN ISLANDS		**0**	**4**	**47**	**89.36**	**42**	**100.00**	**C**	**Protestants 89.3%, Roman Catholics 92.2%. Pent-char 4.2%, Evangelical 10.6%, GCC 40.4%**
2234	Pitcairn Islands		–	–	47	89.36	42	100.00	C	Group of Volcanic South Pacific Ocean Islands. HMS Bounty mutineers. Fishing. D=SDA.
	POLAND		**120,728**	**312,685**	**38,765,085**	**96.73**	**37,498,059**	**99.96**	**C**	**Roman Catholics 92.2%, Orthodox 2.6%. Pent-char 5.2%, Evangelical 0.3%, GCC 7.6%**
2235	Biala Podlaska	Biala Podlaska	2,065	5,348	310,202	97.85	303,529	99.98	C	East. Borders Belarus. Wheat, rye, potatoes, textiles. D=RCC.

Continued opposite

Table 11-3 continued

Rec No 1	Country Major civil divisions 2	Capital 3	sq.mi. 4	sq.km. 5	Pop 2000 6	AC% 7	Church members 8	E% 9	W 10	Notes 11
2236	Bialystok	Bialystok	3,882	10,055	703,912	96.00	675,756	99.96	C	Northeast. Borders Belarus. Bialowieza Forest. D=RCC.
2237	Bielsko-Biala	Bielsko Biala	1,430	3,704	914,639	97.00	887,200	99.97	C	South. Carpathian Mountains. Borders Czech Republic. Textiles, machinery. D=RCC.
2238	Bydgoszcz	Bydgoszcz	3,996	10,349	1,128,614	97.00	1,094,756	99.97	C	Northwest-central. German: Bromberg. Vistula River. Paper, chemical processing. D=RCC.
2239	Chelm	Chelm	1,493	3,866	251,163	98.00	246,140	99.98	C	East. Borders Belarus, Ukraine. Potatoes, rye. Sobibor extermination camp WWII. D=RCC.
2240	Ciechanów	Ciechanów	2,456	6,362	435,270	97.00	422,212	99.97	C	Northeast-central. Rye, potatoes, sugar beets, wood pulp. D=RCC.
2241	Czestochowa	Czestochowa	2,387	6,182	789,156	96.00	757,590	99.96	C	South-central. Electrical machinery, paper. Large iron-ore deposits. Pilgrimage center. D=RCC.
2242	Elblag	Elblag	2,356	6,103	486,579	96.00	467,116	99.96	C	North. Baltic Sea. Chemicals, electrical machinery. F=Masury in Middle Ages. D=RCC.
2243	Gdansk	Gdansk	2,855	7,394	1,454,559	96.00	1,396,377	99.96	C	North-central. Baltic Sea. Shipyards, lumber mills, oil refineries, food processing. D=RCC.
2244	Gorzów	Gorzów Wielkopolski	3,276	8,484	508,730	96.00	488,381	99.96	C	West. Borders Germany. Rye, potatoes, wheat, wood pulp. Health spas in forests. D=RCC.
2245	Jelenia Góra	Jelenia Góra	1,690	4,378	526,205	97.00	510,419	99.97	C	Southwest. Western Sudeten Mountains. Synthetic fibers. Health spas. D=RCC.
2246	Kalisz	Kalisz	2,514	6,512	722,201	96.00	693,313	99.96	C	West-central. Textiles, chemicals. Wheat, rye. Ruins of Roman settlements. D=RCC.
2247	Katowice	Katowice	2,568	6,650	4,052,769	97.00	3,931,186	99.87	C	South-central. Densely populated. Large coal deposits. Textiles, plastics. D=RCC.
2248	Kielce	Kielce	3,556	9,211	1,144,768	96.00	1,098,977	99.96	C	Southeast. Glass, porcelain, wheat, rye. Metalworking, leather goods, oats, livestock. D=RCC.
2249	Konin	Konin	1,984	5,139	476,725	97.00	462,423	99.97	C	West-central. Wheat, sugar beets. Numerous health spas. D=RCC.
2250	Koszalin	Koszalin	3,270	8,470	516,351	97.00	500,860	99.97	C	Northwest. German: Koslin. Baltic Sea. Wheat, rye, potatoes. D=RCC.
2251	Kraków	Kraków	1,256	3,254	1,251,352	96.00	1,201,298	99.96	C	South. Pope John Paul II born here. Textiles, salt, limestone, heavy industries. D=RCC.
2252	Krosno	Krosno	2,202	5,702	502,938	97.00	487,850	99.97	C	Southeast. Borders Ukraine, Slovakia. Wheat, oats, oil. Numerous health spas. D=RCC.
2253	Legnica	Legnica	1,559	4,037	524,073	97.00	508,351	99.97	C	Southwest. German: Liegnitz. Copper, food processing, electrical machinery. D=RCC.
2254	Leszno	Leszno	1,604	4,154	393,004	97.00	381,214	99.97	C	West-central. German: Lissa. Grain, potatoes, electrical machinery. D=RCC.
2255	Lodz	Lodz	588	1,523	1,157,774	96.00	1,111,463	99.96	C	Central. Smallest province in Poland. Textiles, rye, potatoes. D=RCC.
2256	Lomza	Lomza	2,581	6,684	352,258	98.00	345,213	99.98	C	Northeast. Rye, potatoes, textiles. Numerous health spas. D=RCC.
2257	Lublin	Lublin	2,622	6,792	1,032,702	96.00	991,394	99.96	C	East. Livestock, wheat, rye. Cultural and industrial center of eastern Poland. D=RCC.
2258	Nowy Sacz	Nowy Sacz	2,153	5,576	709,091	97.00	687,818	99.97	C	South. Borders Slovakia. Wheat, oats. Tourism, national parks in Beskid Mountains. D=RCC.
2259	Olsztyn	Olsztyn	4,759	12,327	765,075	98.00	749,774	99.98	C	Northeast. Borders Russia. 2000 lakes. Tourism, food processing. Health spas. D=RCC.
2260	Opole	Opole	3,295	8,535	1,034,935	96.00	993,538	99.96	C	Southwest. Borders Czech Republic. Grain, sugar beets, lumber. D=RCC.
2261	Ostroleka	Ostroleka	2,509	6,498	403,672	98.00	395,599	99.98	C	Northeast. Cellulose. Treblinka labor and extermination camp WWII. D=RCC.
2262	Pila	Pila	3,168	8,205	488,409	97.00	473,757	99.97	C	West-central. Lumber, potatoes, building materials. Numerous health spas. D=RCC.
2263	Piotrków	Piotrków Trybunalski	2,419	6,266	652,905	96.00	626,789	99.96	C	Central. Castle ruins built by Casimir the Great. Rye, wheat, potatoes. D=RCC.
2264	Plock	Plock	1,976	5,117	524,682	97.00	508,942	99.97	C	Central. Wheat, rye, potatoes. Numerous health spas. D=RCC.
2265	Poznan	Poznan	3,147	8,151	1,355,495	96.00	1,301,275	99.96	C	West-central. Wheat, rye, metalworking. Health and recreational resorts. D=RCC.
2266	Przemysl	Przemysl	1,713	4,437	413,325	98.00	405,059	99.98	C	Southeast. Railroad junction, monastery, 15th century. Flour milling, distilling. D=RCC.
2267	Radom	Radom	2,816	7,294	763,145	96.00	732,619	99.96	C	East-central. Textiles, glass, grains. Numerous health spas. D=RCC.
2268	Rzeszów	Rzeszów	1,698	4,397	735,308	97.00	713,249	99.97	C	Southeast. Railroad, industrial center, airport, 17th century castle, 2 colleges. Wheat, rye. D=RCC.
2269	Siedlce	Siedlce	3,281	8,499	661,848	97.00	641,993	99.97	C	East-central. Agricultural machinery, textiles, food processing. D=RCC.
2270	Sieradz	Sieradz	1,880	4,869	414,748	98.00	406,453	99.98	C	South-central. Grains, potatoes, sugar beets. Numerous health and recreational spas. D=RCC.
2271	Skierniewice	Skieniewice	1,529	3,960	426,024	97.00	413,243	99.97	C	Central. Electrical goods, glass, ceramic, 17th century, Episcopal palace. Wheat, rye. D=RCC.
2272	Slupsk	Slupsk	2,878	7,453	420,434	97.00	407,821	99.97	C	North. Baltic Sea. Sparsely populated. Rye, potatoes, shipping industry. D=RCC.
2273	Suwalki	Suwalki	4,050	10,490	478,148	98.00	468,585	99.98	C	Northeast. Lumber, building materials. Numerous health spas. D=RCC.
2274	Szczecin	Szczecin	3,854	9,981	957,211	96.00	918,923	99.96	C	Northwest. Baltic Sea. Borders Germany. Wheat, potatoes, sugar beets. D=RCC.
2275	Tarnobrzeg	Tarnobrzeg	2,426	6,283	608,709	97.00	590,448	99.97	C	Southeast. Sulfur mining, textiles, timber. D=RCC.
2276	Tarnów	Tarnów	1,603	4,151	681,048	98.00	667,427	99.98	C	Southeast. Electrical machinery, chemicals. Natural gas wells, petroleum, salt mines. D=RCC.
2277	Torun	Torun	2,065	5,348	669,671	98.00	656,278	99.98	C	North-central. Chemicals, food processing, wheat, sugar beets. D=RCC.
2278	Walbrzych	Walbrzych	1,609	4,168	752,783	97.00	730,200	99.97	C	Southwest. Borders Czech Republic. Central Sudeten Mountains. Chemicals, textiles. D=RCC.
2279	Warszawa	Warszawa	1,463	3,788	2,460,435	97.00	2,386,622	99.97	C	East-central. Vistula River. Holy Cross Church, palaces, monuments. Intl. airport, steel. D=RCC.
2280	Wloclawek	Wloclawek	1,700	4,402	436,286	96.00	418,835	99.96	C	Central. Cellulose, chemicals, pottery. Vistula River. Port, cellulose, paper, salt, sulfur. D=RCC.
2281	Wroclaw	Wroclaw	2,427	6,287	1,146,904	96.00	1,101,028	99.96	C	Southwest. Metalworking, textiles, wheat, rye. Heavy machinery, electronics, airport. D=RCC.
2282	Zamosc	Zamosc	2,695	6,980	498,263	98.00	488,298	99.98	C	Southeast. Railroad, furniture, clothing, building materials, cattle, cathedrals. D=RCC.
2283	Zielona Góra	Zielona Góra	3,424	8,868	670,586	97.00	650,468	99.97	C	West-central. Borders Germany. Oder River. Rye, potatoes, textiles. Lignite mining. D=RCC.
	PORTUGAL		**35,574**	**92,135**	**9,874,853**	**91.95**	**9,080,231**	**99.64**	**C**	**Roman Catholics 90.8%, Independents 2.8%. Pent-char 6.5%, Evangelical 1.0%, GCC 36.1%**
2284	Aveiro	Aveiro	1,084	2,808	650,191	93.00	604,678	99.79	C	Northwest. Fishing, wine, salt. Mining: coal, lead. D=RCC.
2285	Azores (Acores)	Ponta Delgada	868	2,247	234,604	94.00	220,528	99.79	C	Archipelago of 9 major islands. Atlantic Ocean. Discovered: 1427. Hand embroideries. D=RCC.
2286	Beja	Beja	3,948	10,225	166,413	95.00	158,092	99.94	C	South. Grain, fruit, livestock. D=RCC.
2287	Braga	Braga	1,032	2,673	739,491	92.00	680,332	99.69	C	North. Capital city founded: 296 BC by Carthaginians. Firearms, jewelry, cutlery. D=RCC.
2288	Bragança	Bragança	2,551	6,608	156,898	95.00	149,053	99.94	C	Northeast. Borders Spain. Wine, olive oil. Tourism around Ash Wednesday celebration. D=RCC.
2289	Castelo Branco	Castelo Branco	2,577	6,675	212,798	94.00	200,030	99.79	C	Central. Livestock, cereals, mining (tin, zinc, titanium). D=RCC.
2290	Coimbra	Coimbra	1,524	3,947	423,813	92.00	389,908	99.69	C	North-central. Grain, olives, rice. D=RCC.
2291	Faro	Faro	1,915	4,960	337,088	94.00	316,863	99.79	C	South. Fish, wine, sumac (for tanning). Publishing industry since 1489. Tourism. D=RCC.
2292	Guarda	Guarda	2,131	5,518	186,137	96.00	178,692	99.96	C	North-central. Sheep raising, wine. Mining: tin, zinc, titanium. D=RCC.
2293	Leiria	Leiria	1,357	3,515	424,010	94.00	398,569	99.79	C	West-central. Atlantic Ocean. Wine, olives, corn (maize). D=RCC.
2294	Lisboa	Lisbon(Lisboa)	1,066	2,761	2,045,520	87.28	1,785,338	99.65	C	West-central. Atlantic Ocean. Agriculture, fishing, iron working. Disastrous flood in 1967. D=RCC.
2295	Madeira	Funchal	306	794	250,759	95.00	238,221	99.94	C	North Atlantic Ocean. Two inhabited islands. Sugar, wine, bananas. Tourism. D=RCC.
2296	Portalegre	Portalegre	2,342	6,065	133,110	96.00	127,786	99.96	C	East-central. Celtic and Roman artifacts at Medobriga (Aramenha) ruins. Olives, cork. D=RCC.
2297	Porto	Porto	925	2,395	1,607,930	91.00	1,463,216	99.19	C	North. Port wine, cereals, vegetables. D=RCC.
2298	Santarém	Santarém	2,605	6,747	438,779	94.00	412,452	99.79	C	Central. Food processing, china, pottery. Tourism. D=RCC.
2299	Setúbal	Setúbal	1,955	5,064	707,378	92.50	654,325	99.19	C	Southwest. Wheat, rye, corn (maize). D=RCC.
2300	Viana do Castelo	Viana do Castelo	871	2,255	246,497	96.00	236,637	99.96	C	Northwest. Wine, fishing. D=RCC.
2301	Vila Real	Vila Real	1,671	4,328	344,026	95.00	326,825	99.94	C	North. Borders Spain. Viticulture, cereals, livestock, tin mining. D=RCC.
2302	Viseu	Viseu	1,933	5,007	397,448	94.00	373,601	99.79	C	North. Corn (maize), cabbage, grapes. D=RCC.
2303	Évora	Évora	2,854	7,393	171,964	96.00	165,085	99.96	C	South-central. Ancient Roman military center. Corn (maize), apples, hay. D=RCC.
	PUERTO RICO		**3,515**	**9,104**	**3,868,602**	**96.22**	**3,722,291**	**99.90**	**C**	**Roman Catholics 74.9%, Protestants 13.0%. Pent-char 26.5%, Evangelical 9.0%, GCC 14.0%**
2304	Arecibo	–	–	–	102,518	96.50	98,930	99.88	C	North Atlantic port. Liquor, machinery. Largest radar/radio telescope in the world. D=RCC.
2305	Culebra	–	10	–	1,547	97.50	1,508	99.88	C	20 miles east of main island. Volcanic island. US Naval base, coconuts. D=RCC.
2306	Mayagüez	–	–	–	110,255	96.50	106,396	99.88	C	West. Port of entry. Shipping, manufacturing. Tourism, zoo. D=RCC.
2307	Ponce	–	–	–	206,196	96.50	198,979	99.88	C	South. Chief Caribbean port. Universities. Sugar, coffee. D=RCC.
2308	Puerto Rico	–	–	–	2,061,578	96.30	1,985,300	99.98	C	US overseas territory in Caribbean Sea. Central mountain range. Tropical. D=RCC.
2309	San Juan	–	–	–	1,377,222	96.00	1,322,133	99.79	C	Northeast. Chief port. Brewing, publishing. Bay named by Ponce de Leon. D=RCC.
2310	Vieques	–	52	–	9,285	97.42	9,045	99.90	C	East. Island. Holiday resort area. US Navy training. Fishing, tourism. D=RCC.
	QATAR		**4,412**	**11,427**	**599,065**	**9.95**	**59,635**	**56.37**	**B**	**Roman Catholics 6.0%, Independents 1.7%. Pent-char 2.4%, Evangelical 0.7%, GCC 5.0%**
2311	ad-Dawhah (Doha)	–	51	132	352,697	11.30	39,855	58.37	B	East-central. Persian Gulf, capital. Deepwater port. Oil, bazaars, University of Qatar. D=RCC.
2312	al-Ghuwayriyah	al-Ghuwayriyah	241	622	2,644	1.00	26	37.42	A	North. Limited agriculture. Oil and natural gas.
2313	al-Jumayliyah	al-Jumayliyah	990	2,565	11,714	4.00	469	48.42	A	North central. Oil and natural gas.
2314	al-Khawr	al-Khawr	385	996	14,597	5.00	730	49.42	A	Central. Persian Gulf. Tourism, oil and natural gas. D=RCC.
2315	al-Wakrah	al-Wakrah	430	1,114	38,439	5.00	1,922	49.42	A	East-central. Persian Gulf. Tourism, oil and natural gas. D=RCC.
2316	ar-Rayyan	ar-Rayyan	343	889	149,322	10.58	15,793	57.50	B	Central. Near Doha. Tourism, oil and natural gas. D=RCC.
2317	ash-Shamal	Madinat ash-Shamal	348	901	7,109	1.00	71	37.42	A	Far north. Tourism. Oil and natural gas.
2318	Jarayan al-Batinah	Jarayan al-Batinah	1,434	3,715	4,426	1.00	44	37.42	A	Persian Gulf. Oil and natural gas.
2319	Umm Salal	Umm Salal	190	493	18,116	4.00	725	48.42	A	Central. Tourism. Oil and natural gas.
	REUNION		**970**	**2,512**	**699,406**	**86.80**	**607,104**	**97.19**	**C**	**Roman Catholics 87.3%, Protestants 4.5%. Pent-char 7.8%, Evangelical 3.8%, GCC 8.0%**
2320	Saint-Benoît	Saint-Benoît	284	736	99,598	88.00	87,646	98.39	C	Northeast. 20 miles SE of Sainte-Denis, Cross Island Road. Sugar, alcohol, tapioca. D=RCC.
2321	Saint-Denis	Saint-Denis	164	423	242,359	86.00	208,429	96.38	C	North. St. Denis River. Sugar, rum, largest city, administrative center. F=Late 17th century. D=RCC.
2322	Saint-Paul	Saint-Paul	180	467	132,284	87.50	115,749	97.89	C	Northwest. Coastal. Railroad, sugar, alcohol, original settlements here, beach resort. D=RCC.
2323	Saint-Pierre	Saint-Pierre	339	878	225,165	86.73	195,280	97.12	C	South. Coastal. Seventh-day Adventists missions. Fishing port. Sugar, rum, vanilla. D=RCC.
	ROMANIA		**91,699**	**237,500**	**22,326,502**	**87.91**	**19,627,363**	**99.27**	**C**	**Orthodox 85.1%, Roman Catholics 14.5%. Pent-char 6.0%, Evangelical 6.2%, GCC 8.3%**
2324	Alba	Alba Iulia	2,406	6,231	406,300	87.50	355,513	98.86	C	West. Corn (maize), wheat. Mining: mercury, gold, silver. D=Orthodox.
2325	Arad	Arad	2,954	7,652	478,106	87.00	415,952	98.36	C	West. Borders Hungary. Cereals, livestock, wine. D=Orthodox.
2326	Arges	Pitesti	2,626	6,801	667,623	87.50	584,170	98.86	C	South. Transylvanian Alps. Wine, livestock. 13th century monastery in Cimpulung. D=Orthodox.
2327	Bacau	Bacau	2,551	6,606	722,064	88.30	637,583	99.66	C	East. Eastern Carpathians. Metal products, textiles, timber. D=Orthodox.
2328	Bihor	Oradea	2,909	7,535	622,010	88.40	549,857	99.76	C	West. Borders Hungary. Formerly feudal Transylvania. Machinery, wood products. D=Orthodox.
2329	Bistrita-Nasaud	Bistrita	2,048	5,305	320,961	88.00	282,446	99.36	C	North. Eastern Carpathian Mountains. Wine, livestock, wood and pulp products. D=Orthodox.
2330	Botosani	Botosani	1,917	4,965	450,149	88.50	398,382	99.86	C	Northeast. Textiles, cereals. Dragomina Monastery near Itcani village (1609). D=Orthodox.
2331	Braila	Braila	1,824	4,724	384,623	86.00	330,776	97.36	C	Southeast. Feudal Walachia. Danube River. Occupied by Turks (1554-1829). D=Orthodox.
2332	Brasov	Brasov	2,066	5,351	630,248	88.50	557,769	99.86	C	Central. Transylvanian Alps. Machinery, Persian carpets. D=Orthodox.
2333	Bucharest	Bucharest	703	1,820	2,306,171	87.41	2,015,923	99.97	C	Southeast. Seat of Romanian Orthodox Church. Several universities, libraries. F=1459.
2334	Buzau	Buzau	2,344	6,072	506,454	87.00	440,615	98.36	C	Southeast. Livestock, wheat, textiles. Monastery in Magura (1650). D=Orthodox.
2335	Calarasi	Calarasi	1,959	5,074	332,339	89.00	295,782	99.76	C	Southwest. Danube River. Paper, livestock. Dichiseni: former Roman settlement. D=Orthodox.
2336	Caras-Severin	Resita	3,283	8,503	368,635	87.00	320,712	98.36	C	Southwest. Danube River. Livestock, cereals, building materials. D=Orthodox.
2337	Cluj	Cluj-Napoka	2,568	6,650	721,084	88.50	638,159	99.86	C	Northwest. Western Carpathians. Machinery, metal products, chemicals. D=Orthodox.
2338	Constanta	Constanta	2,724	7,055	733,738	89.00	653,027	99.76	C	Southeast. Black Sea. Borders Bulgaria. Livestock, cereals, vineyards. D=Orthodox.
2339	Covasna	Sfântu Gheorghe	1,431	3,705	228,166	88.00	200,786	99.36	C	East-central. Eastern Carpathian Mountains. Timber, textiles, food processing. D=Orthodox.
2340	Dolj	Craiova	2,862	7,413	746,587	89.00	664,462	99.76	C	South, Walachia, flatland. Danube runs along south border. Farming, livestock. D=Orthodox.
2341	Dâmbovita	Târgoviste	1,559	4,036	549,223	87.50	480,570	98.86	C	South. Transylvanian Alps (Southern Carpathians). Oil, building materials, textiles. D=Orthodox.
2342	Galati	Galati	1,708	4,425	627,698	87.00	546,097	98.36	C	East. Borders Moldovia. Livestock, cereals, timber. Fishing resorts at Lake Brates. D=Orthodox.
2343	Giurgiu	Giurgiu	1,356	3,511	307,130	89.00	273,346	99.76	C	Southeast. Borders Bulgaria. Danube River. Livestock, cereals. D=Orthodox.
2344	Gorj	Târgu Jiu	2,178	5,641	392,471	87.00	341,450	98.36	C	Southwest. Transylvanian Alps. Wood products. Tismana Monastery (14th century). D=Orthodox.
2345	Harghita	Miercurea-Ciuc	2,552	6,610	341,071	89.00	303,553	99.76	C	North-central. Eastern Carpathian Mountains. Textiles, timber, livestock. D=Orthodox.
2346	Hunedoara	Deva	2,709	7,016	537,551	88.00	473,045	99.36	C	West. Transylvanian Alps (Southern Carpathians). Livestock, fruit, cereals. D=Orthodox.
2347	Ialomita	Slobozia	1,718	4,449	298,204	89.00	265,402	99.76	C	Southeast. Cereals, cattle. Walachia, flat plain, agricultural. D=Orthodox.
2348	Iasi	Iasi	2,112	5,469	791,416	89.00	704,360	99.76	C	Northeast. Borders Moldovia. Building materials, livestock, cereals. D=Orthodox.

Continued overleaf

Table 11-3 continued

Rec No 1	Country Major civil divisions 2	Capital 3	sq.mi. 4	sq.km. 5	Pop 2000 6	AC% 7	Church members 8	E% 9	W 10	Notes 11
2349	Maramures	Baia Mare	2,400	6,215	528,232	87.50	462,203	98.86	C	Northwest. Borders Ukraine. Eastern Carpathian Mountains. Timber, livestock, fruit. D=Orthodox.
2350	Mehedinti	Drobeta-Turnu	1,892	4,900	325,768	88.00	286,676	99.36	C	Southwest. Borders Serbia, Bulgaria. Timber, textiles, livestock. D=Orthodox.
2351	Mures	Târgu Mures	2,585	6,696	595,720	88.00	524,234	99.36	C	North-central. Eastern Carpathian Mountains. Vineyard and orchard cultivation. D=Orthodox.
2352	Neamt	Piatra Neamt	2,274	5,890	566,586	86.50	490,097	97.86	C	Northeast. Lake Rosu, Moldovia, Carpathian mountains. Livestock, fruit. D=Orthodox.
2353	Olt	Slatina	2,126	5,507	511,065	88.00	449,737	99.36	C	South-central. Borders Bulgaria. Livestock, cereals, orchard and vineyard cultivation. D=Orthodox.
2354	Prahova	Ploiesti	1,812	4,694	856,550	87.00	745,199	98.36	C	South-central. Cereals, livestock, vineyard and orchard cultivation, oil wells. D=Orthodox.
2355	Salaj	Zalau	1,486	3,850	261,222	89.00	232,488	99.76	C	Northwest. Western Carpathian Mountains. Livestock, cereals, viticulture. D=Orthodox.
2356	Satu Mare	Satu Mare	1,701	4,405	392,471	87.00	341,450	98.36	C	Northwest. Borders Ukraine, Hungary. Timber, orchard and vineyard cultivation. D=Orthodox.
2357	Sibiu	Sibiu	2,093	5,422	444,166	88.00	390,866	99.36	C	Central. Transylvanian Alps. Orchards. Historic churches in Cisnadie and Cisnadiora. D=Orthodox.
2358	Suceava	Suceava	3,303	8,555	687,437	88.00	604,945	99.36	C	Northeast. Eastern Carpathian Mountains. Timber, salt, barite. D=Orthodox.
2359	Teleorman	Alexandria	2,224	5,760	473,103	89.00	421,062	99.76	C	South-central. Borders Bulgaria. Danube River. Livestock, cereals, textiles. D=Orthodox.
2360	Timis	Timisoara	3,356	8,692	686,946	88.00	604,512	99.36	C	Southwest. Western Carpathian Mountains. Livestock, cereals, vineyard cultivation. D=Orthodox.
2361	Tulcea	Tulcea	3,255	8,430	265,047	88.00	233,241	99.36	C	Southeast. Danube River. Macin Massif. Cellulose, vineyard cultivation. D=Orthodox.
2362	Vaslui	Vaslui	2,045	5,297	449,071	89.00	399,673	99.76	C	East. Borders Moldovia. Livestock, cereals, vineyard cultivation. D=Orthodox.
2363	Vrancea	Focsani	1,878	4,863	385,114	88.00	338,900	99.36	C	East-central. Eastern Carpathian Mountains. Wine, livestock, cereals. D=Orthodox.
2364	Vâlcea	Râmnicu Vilcea	2,203	5,705	427,981	87.00	372,343	98.52	C	South-central. Transylvanian Alps. Hurez Monastery. Timber, health resorts. D=Orthodox.
	RUSSIA		**6,592,800**	**17,075,400**	**146,933,847**	**56.91**	**83,618,357**	**93.25**	**B**	**Orthodox 51.6%, Independents 5.3%. Pent-char 4.4%, Evangelical 0.3%, GCC 19.9%**
2365	Adygea	Maykop	2,900	7,600	446,826	40.00	178,730	76.34	B	Southwest. Corn (maize), wheat, sunflowers. Flowers: Crimean roses and lavender. D=ROC.
2366	Bashkortostan	Ufa	55,400	143,600	4,068,143	28.00	1,139,080	64.34	B	South-central. Ural Mountains. Petroleum. Russians, Tatars, Bashkirs, Chuvash. 65% urban. D=ROC.
2367	Buryatia	Ulan-Ude	135,600	351,300	1,045,581	45.00	470,511	81.34	B	Eastern Siberia. Lake Baikal. Gold. Horse breeding. D=ROC.
2368	Checheno-Ingushetia	Grozny	7,400	19,300	1,156,795	5.50	63,624	41.84	A	Southwest. Caucasus Mountains. D=ROC.
2369	Chuvashia	Cheboksary	7,100	18,300	1,351,409	45.00	608,134	81.34	B	East-central. Middle of Volga River valley, wooded steppe. Wood carving, mining. D=RCC.
2370	Dagestan	Makhachkala	19,400	50,300	2,083,213	7.00	145,825	43.34	A	Southwest. Caucasus Mountains. Avar, Russian, Dargin. 'Mountain country'. D=ROC.
2371	Gorno-Altay	Gorno-Altaisk	35,700	92,600	200,579	50.00	100,290	86.34	B	South. Altai Mountains. Borders Mongolia, China. Livestock, oats, grains. D=ROC.
2372	Kabardino-Balkaria	Nalchik	4,800	12,500	784,436	20.00	156,887	56.34	B	Southwest. Caucasus Mountains, many glaciers. Wheat, corn. Kabardin, Balkar. D=ROC.
2373	Kalmykia	Elista	29,400	76,100	316,760	23.00	72,855	59.34	B	Southwest. Caspian Sea, Volga River. Karakul sheep breeding, leather, wool. D=ROC.
2374	Karachay-Cherkessia	Cherkessk	5,400	14,100	432,926	26.00	112,561	62.34	B	Southwest. Livestock, produce. Russian, Karachay, Cherkess. D=ROC.
2375	Karelia	Petrozavodsk	66,600	172,400	779,469	60.00	467,681	96.34	C	Northwest. Gulf of Kandalaksha, White Sea. Mining, metallurgy, timber. D=ROC.
2376	Khakassia	Abakan	23,900	61,900	581,873	63.00	366,580	96.34	C	Central. Wheat, oats, millet. Mining: iron ore, gold, coal. Nearly 80% Russian. Khakass. D=ROC.
2377	Komi	Syktyvkar	160,600	415,900	1,176,661	50.00	588,331	86.34	B	Northwest. Ural Mountains. Partly within Arctic circle. Stock raising, fur trapping. D=ROC.
2378	Mari El	Ioshkar-Ola	9,000	23,200	760,603	68.00	517,210	96.84	C	West-central. Volga River. Machine building, timber processing, paper. Russian, Mari. D=ROC.
2379	Mordvinia	Saransk	10,100	26,200	949,266	58.00	550,574	94.34	B	West-central. Volga River Basin. Grains, bee-keeping. 60% Russian. Mordvin. D=ROC.
2380	North Ossetia	Vladikavkaz	3,100	8,000	658,337	51.00	335,752	87.34	B	Southwest. Borders Georgia. Wheat, corn (maize), potatoes. Ossetians, Russians, Ingush. D=ROC.
2381	Russia	Moscow	3,077,100	7,969,100	123,457,374	60.90	75,185,541	97.30	C	Central. Don River. Chief economic and commercial region. Ancient churches, ruins. D=ROC.
2382	Tatarstan	Kazan	26,300	68,100	3,733,516	26.55	991,103	62.89	B	West-central. Volga River Basin. Wheat, corn (maize), millet. 50% Tatar. D=ROC.
2383	Tuva	Kyzyl-Orda	65,800	170,500	306,827	25.00	76,707	61.34	B	South-central Siberia. Chinese empire (1757-1911). Cattle, leather. 60% Tuvan. D=ROC.
2384	Udmurtia	Izhevsk	16,300	42,100	1,627,454	56.00	911,374	92.34	B	East. Ural mountains, railroad, river valleys. Flax, hemp, sugar boots, handicrafts. D=ROC.
2385	Yakut-Sakha	Yakutsk	1,198,200	3,103,200	1,015,798	57.00	579,005	93.34	B	Extreme northeast. Lena River. Fish cannery. Institute of Permafrost studies. D=ROC.
	RWANDA		**10,169**	**26,338**	**7,733,127**	**81.94**	**6,336,822**	**98.86**	**C**	**Roman Catholics 50.9%, Protestants 20.9%. Pent-char 16.0%, Evangelical 19.4%, GCC 12.4%**
2386	Butare	Butare	709	1,837	827,644	82.00	678,668	98.92	C	South. Educational center, tree nurseries. Hospitals. F=1927. D=RCC,Anglican.
2387	Byumba	Byumba	1,838	4,761	845,464	83.00	701,735	99.92	C	North. Borders Uganda. Grazing, coffee, brick making. F=1931. D=RCC.
2388	Cyangugu	Cyangugu	712	1,845	555,975	83.00	461,459	98.02	C	Southwest. Borders Zaire. Lake Kivu. Coffee, cattle. D=RCC.
2389	Gikongoro	Gikongoro	794	2,057	501,423	83.00	416,181	98.47	C	Southwest. Borders Burundi. Sweet potatoes, bananas, sorghum. D=RCC,Anglican.
2390	Gisenyi	Gisenyi	791	2,050	792,953	82.72	655,930	98.64	C	Northwest. Borders Zaire. Lake Kivu. Beach resort. Tobacco, dairying. D=RCC.
2391	Gitarama	Gitarma	845	2,189	919,035	81.00	744,418	98.52	C	Northwest. Borders Zaire. Market and administrative center. F=1958. D=RCC.
2392	Kibungo	Kibungo	1,562	4,046	707,334	82.00	580,014	98.92	C	Southeast. Borders Tanzania. Administrative center. F=1933. D=RCC,Anglican.
2393	Kibuye	Kibuye	658	1,705	508,074	83.00	421,701	98.92	C	West. Lake Kivu. Tourism, hospital. 1994 massacre of Tutsis and Hutus. D=RCC.
2394	Kigali	Kigali	1,204	3,118	1,248,365	80.00	998,692	98.91	C	Central. Light industry, tanning, tin mining. International airport. F=1907. D=RCC,Anglican.
2395	Ruhengeri	Ruhengeri	642	1,663	826,859	82.00	678,024	98.92	C	North. Borders Zaire, Uganda. Potatoes, bananas, sorghum. Large hydro-electric plant. D=RCC.
	SAHARA		**102,680**	**266,769**	**293,357**	**0.17**	**487**	**24.62**	**A**	**Independents 0.1%, Roman Catholics 0.05%. Pent-char 0.1%, Evangelical 0.01%, GCC 0.1%**
2396	Sahara	El Aaiun	102,680	266,769	293,357	0.17	487	24.62	A	Sahara desert on Atlantic Ocean. Goats, sheep. Arabs, Berbers. D=RCC.
	SAINT HELENA		**47**	**122**	**6,293**	**84.73**	**5,332**	**99.86**	**C**	**Anglicans 70.1%, Protestants 8.2%. Pent-char 14.7%, Evangelical 2.4%, GCC 18.5%**
2397	Saint Helena	Jamestown	47	122	6,293	84.73	5,332	99.86	C	Three islands in South Atlantic Ocean. British dependency. Fishing, farming. D=Anglican.
	SAINT KITTS & NEVIS		**104**	**269**	**38,473**	**93.57**	**36,000**	**99.93**	**C**	**Protestants 57.8%, Anglicans 25.2%. Pent-char 18.5%, Evangelical 18.4%, GCC 5.4%**
2398	Nevis	Charlestown	36	93	7,109	95.00	6,754	99.94	C	Eastern Caribbean Sea. Nevis Peak. Cotton, vegetables, coconuts. D=Methodist,Anglican.
2399	St. Kitts	Basseterre	68	176	31,364	93.25	29,246	99.92	C	Eastern Caribbean Sea. Sugar, fruits, vegetables, tourism (seasonal). D=Methodist,Anglican.
	SAINT LUCIA		**238**	**617**	**154,366**	**93.50**	**144,339**	**98.98**	**C**	**Roman Catholics 75.1%, Protestants 13.2%. Pent-char 8.2%, Evangelical 6.7%, GCC 6.1%**
2400	Anse-la-Raye	Anse-la-Raye	10	26	5,830	95.00	5,539	99.38	C	West. Caribbean Sea. Fishing. D=RCC.
2401	Canaries	Canaries	8	21	2,083	94.00	1,958	99.48	C	West-central. Caribbean Sea. Bananas, coconuts. D=RCC.
2402	Castries	Castries	31	79	60,207	92.08	55,437	98.27	C	Northwest. Eastern Caribbean Sea. Bananas, sugarcane, rum. Cruise ships. D=RCC.
2403	Choiseul	Choiseul	12	31	7,417	95.00	7,046	99.38	C	Northeast. Caribbean Sea. Coconut, fruits, fishing, crafts. D=RCC.
2404	Dennery	Dennery	27	70	12,932	94.00	12,156	99.48	C	East-central. Eastern Caribbean Sea. Limes, bananas, fishing. D=RCC.
2405	Gros Islet	Gros Islet	39	101	15,639	94.00	14,701	99.48	C	North. Saint Lucia Channel. Rodney Bay. Fishing, limes, tourism. D=RCC.
2406	Laborie	Laborie	15	38	8,674	95.00	8,240	99.38	C	South. Caribbean Sea. Fishing. D=RCC.
2407	Micoud	Micoud	30	78	17,471	95.00	16,597	99.38	C	Southeast. Saint Vincent Passage. Bananas, fishing. D=RCC.
2408	Soufrière	Soufrière	19	51	8,897	94.00	8,363	99.48	C	Southwest. Eastern Caribbean Sea. Volcanic crater. Fishing, coconuts, limes. D=RCC.
2409	Vieux Fort	Vieux Fort	17	44	15,215	94.00	14,302	99.48	C	Southeast. Eastern Caribbean Sea. Sugar, coconuts. D=RCC.
	SAINT PIERRE & MIQUELON		**93**	**242**	**6,567**	**97.27**	**6,388**	**99.94**	**C**	**Roman Catholics 98.4%, Protestants 1.0%. Pent-char 2.4%, Evangelical 0.1%, GCC 34.2%**
2410	Saint Pierre & Miquelon	Saint Pierre	93	242	6,567	97.28	6,388	99.94	C	Barren islands in North Atlantic Ocean. World's richest fishing grounds. D=RCC.
	SAINT VINCENT		**150**	**389**	**113,954**	**68.83**	**78,439**	**98.78**	**C**	**Protestants 29.7%, Anglicans 17.3%. Pent-char 21.0%, Evangelical 13.2%, GCC 21.1%**
2411	Barrouallie	–	14	37	5,530	69.00	3,816	98.95	C	West. Eastern Caribbean Sea. Arrowroot, bananas, fishing, whaling. D=Methodist,Anglican.
2412	Bridgetown	–	7	19	7,973	70.00	5,581	99.55	C	Eastern Caribbean Sea. Bananas, fishing. D=Anglican,Methodist.
2413	Calliaqua	–	12	31	21,911	69.00	15,119	98.95	C	Southern tip of Saint Vincent. Eastern Caribbean Sea. Cotton, arrowroot. D=Methodist,Anglican.
2414	Chateaubelair	–	31	80	6,414	70.00	4,490	99.55	C	West. Eastern Caribbean Sea. Cotton, coconuts. D=Anglican,Methodist.
2415	Colonarie	–	13	35	8,329	69.00	5,747	98.95	C	East. Colonarie River. Hydroelectric plant. D=Anglican,Methodist.
2416	Georgetown	–	22	58	7,781	69.00	5,369	98.95	C	East. Eastern Caribbean Sea. Sugarcane, cotton, rum. D=Anglican,Methodist.
2417	Kingstown(city)	–	2	5	16,596	67.51	11,203	98.09	C	Exports bananas, arrowroot. Botanical gardens (1763). Very few tourists. D=Methodist,Anglican.
2418	Kingstown(suburbs)	–	6	17	11,514	68.00	7,830	97.95	C	South. Residential. Arnos Vale Airport. D=Anglican,Methodist.
2419	Layou	–	11	29	6,300	69.00	4,347	98.95	C	Southwest. Eastern Caribbean Sea. Cotton, arrowroot, fishing. D=Anglican,Methodist.
2420	Marriaqua	–	9	24	9,365	69.00	6,462	98.55	C	Eastern Caribbean Sea. Bananas, arrowroot. D=Anglican,Methodist.
2421	Northern Grenadines	–	9	23	6,174	69.00	4,260	98.95	C	Eastern Caribbean Sea. Separate island (Bequia). Admiralty Bay. Port Elizabeth. D=Anglican.
2422	Sandy Bay	–	5	14	2,967	70.00	2,077	99.55	C	Eastern Caribbean Sea. Carib settlement. Arrowroot. D=Anglican,Methodist.
2423	Southern Grenadines	–	8	19	3,099	69.00	2,138	98.95	C	Eastern Caribbean Sea. Separate islands (Isle a Quatre, Baliceaux). D=Anglican.
	SAMOA		**1,091**	**2,826**	**180,073**	**93.92**	**169,129**	**99.94**	**C**	**Protestants 71.0%, Roman Catholics 21.9%. Pent-char 15.7%, Evangelical 14.9%, GCC 47.4%**
2424	Savaii	–	659	1,707	51,481	95.00	48,907	99.97	C	Western island. Cape Mulinu'u. Mauga Silisili (1,858 m). D=Congregational,RCC,Methodist.
2425	Upolu	–	432	1,119	128,592	93.49	120,222	99.92	C	Eastern island. Apia. Robert Louis Stevenson's tomb. D=Congregational,RCC,Methodist.
	SAN MARINO		**24**	**61**	**26,514**	**89.68**	**23,779**	**99.88**	**C**	**Roman Catholics 88.6%, Marginals 1.0%. Pent-char 1.8%, Evangelical 0.00%, GCC 48.6%**
2426	Acquaviva	Acquaviva	2	5	1,348	91.00	1,227	99.90	C	West. Tourism. Wheat, corn (maize), barley. D=RCC.
2427	Borgo Maggiore	Borgo	3	9	5,472	89.41	4,893	99.91	C	Northeast. Mount Titano. Wine. D=RCC.
2428	Chiesanuova	Chiesanuova	2	5	861	92.00	792	99.92	C	Southwest. Tourism. 'New Church'. D=RCC.
2429	Città	San Marino	3	7	4,802	89.00	4,274	99.87	C	Mount Titano. Tourism, wine. Many Italians. D=RCC.
2430	Domagnano	Domagnano	3	7	2,319	90.00	2,087	99.90	C	Central. Fiumicello River. Tourism. D=RCC.
2431	Faetano	Faetano	3	8	844	92.00	776	99.92	C	Marano River. Tourism. D=RCC.
2432	Fiorentino	Fiorentino	3	7	1,808	91.00	1,645	99.90	C	South central. San Marino River. Tourism. D=RCC.
2433	Montegiardino	Montegiardino	1	3	725	92.00	667	99.92	C	Southeast. Marano River. Tourism. D=RCC.
2434	Serravalle/Dogano	Serravalle	4	11	8,335	89.00	7,418	99.86	C	Northeast. Bordering Forli, Italy. Ausa River. D=RCC.
	SAO TOME & PRINCIPE		**386**	**1,001**	**146,775**	**90.00**	**132,103**	**99.90**	**C**	**Roman Catholics 75.3%, Independents 10.5%. Pent-char 14.3%, Evangelical 3.1%, GCC 14.7%**
2435	Aqua Grande	São Tomé	7	17	53,044	90.00	47,740	99.90	C	São Tomé. Gulf of Guinea. Coffee, cocoa. D=RCC.
2436	Cantagalo	Santana	46	119	13,952	91.00	12,696	99.95	C	São Tomé. Gulf of Guinea. Coffee, cocoa. Working class residences. D=RCC.
2437	Caué	São João Angolares	103	267	6,769	89.35	6,048	99.82	C	São Tomé. Gulf of Guinea. Coffee, cocoa. D=RCC.
2438	Lemba	Neves	88	229	11,542	90.00	10,388	99.90	C	São Tomé. Gulf of Guinea. Coffee, cocoa. D=RCC.
2439	Lobata	Guadalupe	41	105	16,004	89.00	14,244	99.90	C	São Tomé. Gulf of Guinea. Coffee, cocoa. D=RCC.
2440	Mé-Zóchi	Trinidade	47	122	38,574	90.00	34,717	99.90	C	São Tomé. Gulf of Guinea. Coffee, cocoa. D=RCC.
2441	Príncipe	Santo António	55	142	6,890	91.00	6,270	99.95	C	Principe. Northeast. Gulf of Guinea. Fishing. D=RCC.
	SAUDI ARABIA		**868,000**	**2,248,000**	**21,606,691**	**3.64**	**786,985**	**54.94**	**B**	**Roman Catholics 2.9%, Independents 0.3%. Pent-char 0.5%, Evangelical 0.1%, GCC 1.9%**
2442	al-Gharbiyah (Western)	–	136,000	352,200	5,971,847	3.00	179,155	54.30	B	West. Date palms. Pilgrimage centers: Mecca & Medina. D=RCC.
2443	al-Janubiyah (Southern)	–	84,000	217,600	1,226,510	3.70	45,381	55.00	B	South. Red sea. Gardens, oil. Once important Christian region (AD 500-635). D=RCC.
2444	al-Wusta (Central)	–	232,000	600,900	7,127,488	4.00	285,100	55.30	B	Central. Includes market region & Riyadh. Oil, commerce. D=RCC.
2445	ash-Shamaliyah (Northern)	–	142,000	367,800	1,333,379	3.60	48,002	54.90	B	North. Bordering Jordan, Iraq. Date palms. D=RCC.
2446	ash-Sharqiyah (Eastern)	–	274,000	709,700	5,947,466	3.86	229,346	55.16	B	East. On Persian Gulf. Oil, dairying. Many Europeans & Americans. D=RCC.

Continued opposite

Table 11-3 continued

Rec No 1	Country Major civil divisions 2	Capital 3	sq.mi. 4	sq.km. 5	Pop 2000 6	AC% 7	Church members 8	E% 9	W 10	Notes 11
	SENEGAL		**75,951**	**196,712**	**9,481,161**	**4.93**	**467,291**	**46.01**	**A**	**Roman Catholics 4.6%, Independents 0.1%. Pent-char 0.3%, Evangelical 0.06%, GCC 3.1%**
2447	Dakar	Dakar	212	550	2,134,137	9.14	195,015	51.26	B	West. Atlantic Ocean. Peanut oil, fish, flour. D=RCC.
2448	Diourbel	Diourbel	1,683	4,359	842,182	2.00	16,844	42.58	A	West. Peanut oil, beverages, perfume.
2449	Fatick	Fatick	3,064	7,935	689,353	2.00	13,787	42.58	A	Southwest. Atlantic Ocean. Borders Gambia.
2450	Kaolack	Koalack	6,181	16,010	1,094,298	9.00	98,487	50.88	B	West-central. Borders Gambia. Center of Tijaniyah order of Islam in capital. D=RCC.
2451	Kolda	Kolda	8,112	21,011	805,521	1.00	8,055	41.08	A	Southwest. Atlantic Ocean. Borders Gambia, Guinea-Bissau, Guinea.
2452	Louga	Louga	11,270	29,188	689,245	1.00	6,892	41.08	A	Northwest. Atlantic Ocean. Peanuts. Fulani, Wolof.
2453	Saint-Louis	Saint-Louis	17,034	44,117	892,078	1.20	10,705	41.38	A	North. Atlantic Ocean. Borders Mauritania. Colonial settlement: 1659. D=RCC.
2454	Tambacounda	Tambacounda	23,012	59,602	520,863	1.00	5,209	41.08	A	Southeast. Millet, sorghum, cotton. Fulani, Malinke. Niokolo Koba National Park. D=RCC.
2455	Thiès	Thiès	2,549	6,601	1,272,937	5.00	63,647	46.08	A	West-central. Atlantic Ocean. Light industries. Aluminum phosphate. D=RCC.
2456	Ziguinchor	Ziguinchor	2,834	7,339	540,546	9.00	48,649	51.08	B	Southwest. Atlantic Ocean. Casamance River. D=RCC.
	SEYCHELLES		**176**	**455**	**77,435**	**92.72**	**71,795**	**99.55**	**C**	**Roman Catholics 90.4%, Anglicans 6.7%. Pent-char 5.2%, Evangelical 3.2%, GCC 11.9%**
2457	La Digue and satellites	–	6	15	2,174	94.00	2,044	99.64	C	East. Western Indian Ocean. Tourism. D=RCC.
2458	Mahé and satellites	Victoria	61	158	69,065	92.55	63,922	99.54	C	South. Western Indian Ocean. 40 central islands. Rocky with lush vegetation. Tourism D=RCC.
2459	Outer (Coralline) islands	–	83	214	334	95.00	317	99.74	C	Western Indian Ocean. Just above sea level. Coral reefs. Few residents. D=RCC.
2460	Praslin and satellites	–	16	42	5,646	94.00	5,307	99.64	C	North. Western Indian Ocean. Tourism. D=RCC.
2461	Silhouette	–	8	20	216	95.00	205	99.74	C	West. Western Indian Ocean. D=RCC.
	SIERRA LEONE		**27,699**	**71,740**	**4,854,383**	**10.52**	**510,494**	**59.18**	**B**	**Protestants 3.5%, Roman Catholics 3.4%. Pent-char 4.1%, Evangelical 1.7%, GCC 8.0%**
2462	Eastern Province	Kenema	6,005	15,553	1,326,217	12.00	159,146	63.66	B	Southeast. Diamonds, cocoa, coffee. D=RCC,NAC,Methodist.
2463	Northern Province	Makeni	13,875	35,936	1,739,228	5.00	86,961	45.66	A	Central. Gara tie-dyeing. D=RCC,NAC,Methodist.
2464	Southern Province	Bo	7,604	19,694	1,023,644	12.37	126,634	65.03	B	South-central. Palm oil, ginger, coffee. Educational center. D=RCC,NAC,Methodist.
2465	Western Area	Freetown	215	557	765,293	18.00	137,753	74.29	B	West. Palm oil, cocoa, coffee. Anglican St. George's Cathedral (1852) in capital. D=RCC,NAC.
	SINGAPORE		**247**	**641**	**3,566,614**	**11.30**	**402,936**	**72.69**	**B**	**Roman Catholics 4.0%, Protestants 3.5%. Pent-char 4.0%, Evangelical 3.3%, GCC 8.2%**
2466	Singapore	Singapore	247	641	3,566,614	11.30	402,936	72.69	B	Islands off southernmost tip of Malay peninsula. Financial center. D=RCC,Methodist.
	SLOVAKIA		**18,933**	**49,035**	**5,387,191**	**80.27**	**4,324,186**	**99.53**	**C**	**Roman Catholics 67.9%, Protestants 11.1%. Pent-char 4.5%, Evangelical 2.1%, GCC 14.1%**
2467	Bratislava	–	142	368	453,063	81.00	366,981	99.96	C	On Danube River. Cultural center, textiles, chemicals. F=Roman Posonium. D=RCC.
2468	Stredoslovensky	Bansk Bystrica	6,943	17,982	1,646,326	80.60	1,326,963	99.86	C	Central. Bordering Czech Republic & Poland. High Tatras mountains. Forestry, mining. D=RCC.
2469	Vychodoslovensky	Kosice	6,252	16,193	1,548,817	80.00	1,239,054	99.30	C	East. Bordering Poland & Ukraine. Bodrog River. Wheat, grapes, sheep. Copper. D=RCC.
2470	Zapadoslovensky	Bratislava	5,595	14,492	1,738,985	80.00	1,391,188	99.31	C	Southwest. Bordering Austria & Hungary. Wheat, rye, pigs, poultry. Glass sand. D=RCC.
	SLOVENIA		**7,821**	**20,256**	**1,985,557**	**87.47**	**1,736,806**	**99.80**	**C**	**Roman Catholics 83.5%, Protestants 1.6%. Pent-char 3.5%, Evangelical 0.7%, GCC 13.3%**
2471	Dolenjska	–	642	1,663	102,594	88.00	90,283	99.93	C	Southeast. Sava River. Ljubljana Valley. Thermal spas. D=RCC.
2472	Gorenjska	–	824	2,135	193,790	88.00	170,535	99.93	C	Northwest. Sava River. Savinja Alps. Ski resorts, tourism. D=RCC.
2473	Goriska	–	897	230	119,332	87.00	103,819	99.73	C	West. Bordering Italy. Furniture, textiles. D=RCC.
2474	Koroska	–	401	483	74,200	89.00	66,038	99.95	C	North. Karawanken Alps. Drava River. Zinc mining, tourism. D=RCC.
2475	Notranjsko-kraska	–	562	486	49,540	88.00	43,595	99.93	C	South. Pivka River. High plateaus, forest. Tourism (caverns). D=RCC.
2476	Obalno Krasko	–	403	240	100,866	89.00	89,771	99.95	C	Oil and coal mining. D=RCC.
2477	Osrednjeslovenska	–	1,369	105	510,864	86.49	441,857	99.74	C	Oil, lead. Dairy. D=RCC.
2478	Podravska	–	837	210	326,326	87.00	283,904	99.73	C	Coal mining. Hemp. D=RCC.
2479	Pomurska	–	516	421	129,776	89.00	115,501	99.95	C	Zinc mining. Potatoes, dairy. D=RCC.
2480	Savinjska	–	919	58	257,785	87.00	224,273	99.63	C	North. Savinja River. Hydroelectric plants, hops. D=RCC.
2481	Spodnjeposavska	–	349	425	74,260	89.00	66,091	99.95	C	Lead, mercury, tourism. D=RCC.
2482	Zasavska	–	102	480	46,224	89.00	41,139	99.95	C	Oil, coal, tourism. D=RCC.
	SOLOMON ISLANDS		**10,954**	**28,370**	**443,643**	**90.88**	**403,203**	**99.89**	**C**	**Anglicans 38.2%, Protestants 35.8%. Pent-char 13.9%, Evangelical 22.4%, GCC 13.5%**
2483	Central Islands	Tulagi	497	1,286	28,262	92.00	26,001	99.93	C	Southwestern Pacific Ocean. Includes Rennell and Bellona. D=Church of Melanesia,RCC.
2484	Guadalcanal	Honiara	2,060	5,336	82,015	91.00	74,634	99.91	C	Mount Makarakomburu (2,447 m). D=Church of Melanesia,RCC.
2485	Honiara	–	8	22	49,890	93.00	46,398	99.96	C	Capital. On Guadalcanal Island. D=Church of Melanesia,RCC.
2486	Isabel	Buala	1,597	4,136	22,332	92.00	20,545	99.93	C	Eastern chain. Hot & humid climate. D=Church of Melanesia,RCC.
2487	Makira	Kira Kira	1,231	3,188	34,198	91.00	31,120	99.91	C	Convergence of island chains. D=Church of Melanesia,RCC.
2488	Malaita	Auki	1,631	4,225	117,174	88.53	103,738	99.80	C	Eastern chain. Abundant rainfalls. D=Church of Melanesia,RCC.
2489	Temotu	Santa Cruz	334	865	22,297	91.00	20,290	99.91	C	Tinakula Volcano. Heavily wooded. D=Church of Melanesia,RCC.
2490	Western	Gizo	3,595	9,312	87,475	92.00	80,477	99.93	C	Southwestern Pacific Ocean. Includes Choiseul Island. D=Church of Melanesia,RCC.
	SOMALIA		**192,000**	**497,000**	**7,264,500**	**1.36**	**98,583**	**43.83**	**A**	**Orthodox 1.2%, Independents 0.08%. Pent-char 0.1%, Evangelical 0.01%, GCC 0.1%**
2491	Bakool	Xuddur	10,000	27,000	282,887	0.20	566	40.67	A	West central bordering Ethiopia.
2492	Banaadir	Mogadishu (Muqdisho)	400	1,000	989,437	2.40	23,704	48.14	A	East-central on Indian Ocean. Bananas, hides. F=10th cent. by Arabs. 96% Muslim. D=Orthodox.
2493	Bari	Boosaaso	27,000	70,000	422,904	0.20	846	40.67	A	Northeast on Gulf of Aden and Indian Ocean. Controlled by Somali Salvation Democratic Front.
2494	Bay	Baydhabo	15,000	39,000	857,982	1.80	15,444	44.77	A	South. Bohol Madagoi River. Rahanwayn clans. Granite formations.
2495	Galguduud	Dhuusamarreeb	17,000	43,000	486,824	0.40	1,947	41.87	A	Central bordering Indian Ocean and Ethiopia.
2496	Gedo	Gabahaarrey	12,000	32,000	447,064	0.20	894	40.67	A	Southwest bordering Kenya and Ethiopia. Jubba River.
2497	Hiiraan	Beledweyne	13,000	34,000	417,196	0.40	1,669	41.87	A	Central bordering Ethiopia. Snabeelle River. Beledweyne birthplace of Gen. Aydid (c1930).
2498	Jubbada Dhexe	Bu'aale	9,000	23,000	281,175	1.50	4,218	43.97	A	Southeast on Indian Ocean. Jubba River. Bananas.
2499	Jubbada Hoose	Kismaayo	24,000	61,000	518,214	2.00	10,364	44.47	A	South on Indian Ocean. Jubba River. Bananas. F=1872 by Sultan of Zanzibar. D=Orthodox.
2500	Mudug	Gaalkacyo	27,000	70,000	592,026	0.80	4,736	43.27	A	North central bordering Indian Ocean and Ethiopia. Majeerteen clans.
2501	Nugaal	Garoowe	19,000	50,000	213,449	0.20	427	40.67	A	North on Indian Ocean bordering Ethiopia and Somaliland. River flows in season.
2502	Shabeellaha Dhexe	Jawhar	8,000	22,000	669,645	1.80	12,054	44.27	A	Central on Indian Ocean. Shabeelle River. Sugar refinery, bananas, livestock.
2503	Shabeellaha Hoose	Marka	10,000	25,000	1,085,698	2.00	21,714	44.47	A	Southeast on Indian Ocean. Shabeelle River. Bananas, livestock. D=Orthodox.
	SOMALILAND		**54,000**	**140,000**	**2,832,677**	**0.30**	**8,381**	**44.69**	**A**	**Orthodox 0.1%, Independents 0.1%. Pent-char 0.1%, Evangelical 0.02%, GCC 0.1%**
2504	Sanaag	Ceerigaabo	21,000	54,000	488,495	0.20	977	42.59	A	East on Gulf of Aden. Galaodon Highlands. Surud Cad (2,408 m).
2505	Togdheer	Burao	16,000	41,000	866,233	0.10	866	42.49	A	South-central bordering Ethiopia. Sarar Plain. Seasonal rivers.
2506	Woqooyi Galbeed	Hargeysa	17,000	45,000	1,477,949	0.44	6,538	46.68	A	West bordering Ethiopia. On Gulf of Aden. Pastoral nomads, hides. 99% Muslim. D=Orthodox.
	SOUTH AFRICA		**472,281**	**1,223,201**	**40,376,579**	**78.76**	**31,800,789**	**98.06**	**C**	**Independents 45.8%, Protestants 30.7%. Pent-char 52.5%, Evangelical 11.2%, GCC 19.1%**
2507	Eastern	Bisho	65,483	169,600	6,451,483	80.00	5,161,186	97.30	C	South on Indian Ocean. Drakensberg. Mountains. 87% Black. 6% White. Xhosa. D=Anglican.
2508	Free State	Bloemfontein	49,992	129,480	2,733,062	76.00	2,077,127	98.36	C	Central bordering Lesotho. Gold mining. High veld plateau. 84% Black. South Sotho. D=RCC.
2509	Gauteng	Johannesburg	7,262	18,810	6,884,780	75.44	5,193,919	97.74	C	Formerly part of Transvaal. High veld plateau. Vaal River. 63% Black, 31% White. Bantu. D=RCC.
2510	KwaZulu/Natal	Ulundi	35,591	92,180	8,524,752	82.00	6,990,297	98.50	C	Southeastern on Indian Ocean. Formerly Natal. Drakensberg mountains. 82% Zulu. D=ZCC.
2511	Mpumalanga	Nelspruit	30,259	78,370	2,928,227	77.00	2,254,735	97.30	C	Northeast bordering Swaziland. Formerly part of Transvaal. High veld plateau (1,800 m). D=ZCC.
2512	North-West	Mafikeng	44,861	116,190	3,260,417	80.00	2,608,334	99.00	C	North central bordering Botswana. High veld plateau. Corn. Blacks 91%, Whites 8%. D=RCC.
2513	Northern Cape	Kimberley	139,692	361,800	738,992	83.00	613,363	99.30	C	West bordering Namibia & Botswana. Great Escarpment, Orange River. Mixed race 50%. D=RCC.
2514	Northern	Pietersburg	47,599	123,280	5,213,501	80.00	4,170,801	98.90	C	Northeast near Zimbabwe & Mozambique. Low veld plain. Corn, sorghum. Mainly Black. D=ZCC.
2515	Western Cape	Cape Town	49,950	129,370	3,641,366	75.00	2,731,025	97.11	C	Extreme south on Atlantic & Indian Oceans. Maritime climate. Mixed race 60%. Xhosa. D=Methodist.
	SOUTH KOREA		**38,330**	**99,274**	**46,843,989**	**39.88**	**18,681,876**	**98.80**	**B**	**Protestants 18.9%, Independents 16.4%. Pent-char 16.1%, Evangelical 19.5%, GCC 28.4%**
2516	Ch'ungch'ong-namdo	Taejon	3,211	8,317	2,182,897	39.00	851,330	98.92	B	West central on Yellow Sea. Rice, ginseng, tobacco. Mt. Gyeryong temples. Beaches. D=RCC.
2517	Ch'ungch'ong-pukto	Ch'ongju	2,872	7,437	1,521,999	50.00	761,000	99.62	B	Central. No seacoast, mostly mountainous. Rice, barley, gold. Pobjursa temple. D=Presbyterian.
2518	Cheju-do	Cheju	705	1,825	553,260	28.00	154,913	97.92	B	Island in South China Sea. Volcanic mountains. National park. Clams. D=Presbyterian,RCC.
2519	Cholla-namdo	Kwangju	4,561	11,812	2,715,701	42.00	1,140,594	99.42	B	Southwest on Yellow Sea. 2,000 islands. Seaweed and oysters. Rice, wheat. D=Presbyterian,RCC.
2520	Cholla-pukto	Chongju	3,109	8,053	2,228,102	29.00	646,150	97.92	B	Southwest on Yellow Sea. Noryong mountains. Rice, barley, cotton. Cattle. D=Presbyterian,RCC.
2521	Inch'on-si	Inch'on	121	313	1,956,856	40.00	782,742	98.92	B	Northwest on Yellow Sea. Chief seaport. Factories. D=Presbyterian,RCC.
2522	Kangwon-do	Ch'unch'on'	6,524	16,898	1,713,595	35.00	599,758	98.92	B	Northeast on Sea of Japan. 80% woodlands. Fishing. D=Presbyterian,RCC.
2523	Kwangju-si	Kwangju	193	501	1,232,451	45.00	554,603	99.52	B	South surrounded by Cholla-namdo. Textiles, breweries. Armed uprising (1980). D=Presbyterian.
2524	Kyonggi-do	Suwon	4,158	10,769	6,624,035	41.00	2,715,854	99.92	B	Northwest bordering North Korea and Yellow Sea. Rice, dairying, heavy industry. D=Presbyterian.
2525	Kyongsang-namdo	Masan	4,545	11,771	3,959,994	35.00	1,385,998	98.92	B	Southeast on Sea of Japan. Naktong River. Leading fishery. Rice. Haein Temple (802). D=RCC.
2526	Kyongsang-pukto	Taegu	7,507	19,443	3,084,902	28.00	863,773	97.42	B	East on Sea of Japan. Silla kingdom (57 BC-AD 935). Naktong River. Rice, barley. D=Presbyterian.
2527	Pusan-si	Pusan	203	526	4,088,084	46.00	1,880,519	99.52	B	Southeast on Korea Strait. Largest port. Foreign trade, universities. 'Kettle Mountain'. D=RCC.
2528	Soul-t' ukpyolsi	Seoul	234	605	11,439,752	45.80	5,239,601	99.12	B	North on Han River. Capital since 1394. Textiles, machinery. D=Presbyterian,RCC,Jesus Assembly.
2529	Taegu-si	Taegu	176	456	2,399,246	27.00	647,796	93.66	B	South-central on Kum River. Textiles, metals. Kyongbuk National University. D=Presbyterian,RCC.
2530	Taejon-si	Taejon	207	537	1,143,115	40.00	457,246	98.92	B	West-central. Cotton textiles, machines. 70% destroyed in WWII. D=Presbyterian,RCC.
	SPAIN		**194,898**	**504,783**	**39,629,775**	**93.55**	**37,073,672**	**99.68**	**C**	**Roman Catholics 96.0%, Independents 0.8%. Pent-char 2.7%, Evangelical 0.3%, GCC 43.2%**
2531	Andaluc'a	Seville	33,694	87,268	7,163,910	92.00	6,590,797	99.33	C	Southernmost on Mediterranean and Atlantic Ocean. Ancient Baetica. Agriculture. D=RCC.
2532	Aragón	Zaragoza	18,398	47,650	1,202,181	95.00	1,142,072	99.93	C	Northeast near France. Kingdom of Aragon (1035). Ebro River, Pyrenees. Wheat, sugar. D=RCC.
2533	Asturias	Oviedo	4,079	10,565	1,100,416	95.00	1,045,395	99.93	C	Northwest on Atlantic Ocean. Mountainous. Poorly developed. Steady emigration. Coal. D=RCC.
2534	Baleares	Palma de Mallorca	1,936	5,014	748,448	94.00	703,541	99.83	C	Archipelago in western Mediterranean. Seasonal tourism, wheat. D=RCC.
2535	Canarias (Canary Islands)	Santa Cruz	2,796	7,242	1,559,023	95.00	1,481,072	99.93	C	Archipelago in Atlantic Ocean. Bananas, tourism. D=RCC.
2536	Cantabria	Santander	2,042	5,289	534,360	95.00	507,642	99.93	C	North on Bay of Biscay. Mining. Cattle, sheep. Celtic origins. D=RCC.
2537	Castilla y Leon	Valladolid	36,368	94,193	2,543,736	95.00	2,416,549	99.93	C	North. Bordering Portugal. Douro River. Wheat, sheep. Heavy industry. D=RCC.
2538	Castilla-La Mancha	Toledo	30,591	79,230	1,682,213	95.81	1,611,701	99.94	C	Central. Toledo Mountains. Wheat, grapes, olives. Steady emigration. D=RCC.
2539	Cataluña	Barcelona	12,328	31,930	6,185,839	93.00	5,752,830	99.73	C	East on Mediterranean Sea. Roman origins. High-industrialized. Textiles, wines. D=RCC.
2540	Extremadura	Mérida	16,063	41,602	1,067,103	93.00	992,406	99.73	C	Southwest bordering Portugal. Sheep, pigs, wheat, flour mills. D=RCC.
2541	Galicia	Santiago	11,365	29,434	2,763,527	94.00	2,597,715	99.83	C	Northwest on Atlantic Ocean. Celtic origins. Animal husbandry, fishing. D=RCC.
2542	La Rioja	Logroño	1,944	5,034	267,576	95.00	254,197	99.93	C	North-central. Ebro River. Grapes, cereals. Annual festivals. D=RCC.
2543	Madrid	Madrid	3,087	7,995	5,113,687	92.00	4,704,592	99.29	C	Central. 2,100 ft. Publishing center, tourism, government. F=10th century. D=RCC.
2544	Murcia	Murcia	4,370	11,317	1,087,227	95.00	1,032,866	99.93	C	Southeast on Mediterranean Sea. Baetic Mountains. Barley, grapes. D=RCC.
2545	Navarra	Pamplona	4,023	10,421	531,843	95.00	505,251	99.93	C	North bordering France. Pyrenees. Ebro River. Milk, wheat, metal parts. D=RCC.
2546	País Vasco	Vitoria (Gasteiz)	2,803	7,261	2,108,185	95.00	2,002,776	99.93	C	North on Bay of Biscay. Pyrenees. Farming, metallurgy. Basque separatists. D=RCC.

Continued overleaf

Table 11-3 continued

Rec No 1	Country / Major civil divisions 2	Capital 3	sq.mi. 4	sq.km. 5	Pop 2000 6	AC% 7	Church members 8	E% 9	W 10	Notes 11
2547	Valencia	Valencia	8,998	23,305	3,970,499	94.00	3,732,269	99.83	C	East on Mediterranean Sea. Oranges, rice, tourism. Religious festivals. D=RCC.
	SPANISH NORTH AFRICA		**13**	**33**	**130,000**	**80.25**	**104,324**	**93.42**	**C**	**Roman Catholics 79.1%, Independents 0.6%. Pent-char 2.3%, Evangelical 0.2%, GCC 8.7%**
2548	Ceuta	–	7	19	70,538	80.10	56,501	93.27	C	Mediterranean port on Moroccan coast. Spanish character. Fishing, tourism. D=RCC.
2549	Melilla	–	5	14	59,462	80.43	47,823	93.60	C	Mediterranean walled town on Moroccan coast. Phoenician colony. Iron ore. D=RCC.
	SRI LANKA		**25,332**	**65,610**	**18,827,054**	**9.32**	**1,755,120**	**64.57**	**B**	**Roman Catholics 6.6%, Independents 1.7%. Pent-char 2.1%, Evangelical 0.4%, GCC 7.4%**
2550	Amparai (Ampara)	Amparai	1,705	4,415	525,162	1.93	10,131	52.18	B	East. Rice, timber, dairy products. Archaeological museum.
2551	Anuradhapura	Anuradhapura	2,772	7,179	781,089	5.00	39,054	57.25	B	North-central. Aruvi Aru River. Ancient kingdom. Buddhist pilgrimage center. D=RCC.
2552	Badulla	Badulla	1,104	2,861	776,661	7.00	54,366	62.25	B	Southeast on Badula River. Two large temples. Limestone, rice, tea. D=RCC.
2553	Batticaloa	Batticaloa	1,102	2,854	453,145	5.00	22,657	58.25	B	East on Indian Ocean. Trading central for rice and coconuts.
2554	Colombo	Colombo	270	699	2,143,842	20.00	428,768	80.25	B	West on Indian Ocean. Factories, exports. F=c AD 500. Dutch church (1749). D=RCC.
2555	Galle	Galle	638	1,652	1,032,590	14.00	144,563	72.25	B	South on Indian Ocean. Shipping, cement. F=13th century. Portuguese fort (1507-1640). D=RCC.
2556	Gampaha	Gampaha	536	1,387	1,681,838	9.00	151,365	64.25	B	Central highlands. Gampola dynasty (1340). Coconuts, rice. Botanical gardens.
2557	Hambantota	Hambantota	1,007	2,609	565,045	3.00	16,951	54.25	B	South on Indian Ocean. Coconut palms, salterns. Malays.
2558	Jaffna	Jaffna	396	1,025	956,143	13.00	124,299	70.30	B	North on Palk Strait across from India. Agricultural trade, fishing. Tamils. D=RCC.
2559	Kalutara	Kalutara	617	1,598	1,034,806	9.00	93,133	64.25	B	Southwest on Indian Ocean. Fishing and trade center. Dutch character.
2560	Kandy	Kandy	749	1,940	1,369,401	7.00	95,858	60.25	B	Kandy Plateau on Mahawel. River. Tea, rice. Buddhist Temple of the Tooth. D=SDA,RCC.
2561	Kegalle	Kegalle	654	1,693	823,192	6.00	49,392	61.25	B	West central. Graphite, rubber. Elephant orphanage.
2562	Kilinochchi	Kilinochchi	494	1,279	109,685	2.00	2,194	52.25	B	North. Under control of Liberation Tigers of Tamil. Eelam.
2563	Kurunegala	Kurunegala	1,859	4,816	1,562,180	9.00	140,596	64.25	B	West central. Sinhalese capital. Rice, coconuts. Silver monastery (100 BC). D=RCC.
2564	Mannar	Mannar	771	1,996	142,924	3.00	4,288	54.25	B	Northwest. Dry, barren island. Fishing. D=RCC.
2565	Matale	Matale	770	1,993	458,684	5.00	22,934	56.25	B	Central. Cattle, tea, rubber, cacao. Buddhist monastery & rock temple.
2566	Matara	Matara	495	1,283	847,566	8.00	67,805	63.25	B	South on Indian Ocean. Nilwala River. 'Great Ford'. Dutch influence.
2567	Monaragala	Monaragala	2,177	5,639	381,127	4.00	15,245	55.25	B	West. Rice, vegetables.
2568	Mullaitivu	Mullaitivu	1,010	2,617	100,821	1.00	1,008	51.25	B	Northeast. Sinhalese military base. Tamil insurgency. July 1996, 1,200 killed.
2569	Nuwara Eliya	Nuwara Eliya	672	1,741	587,203	7.00	41,104	62.25	B	South central near Pidurutalagala (8,281 ft). Former British hill station. Tea, health spa.
2570	Polonnaruwa	Polonnaruwa	1,271	3,293	347,890	4.00	13,916	55.25	B	North central. Mahaweli River. Ancient Ceylonese kingdom. Rice, tobacco. Buddhist temples.
2571	Puttalam	Puttalam	1,186	3,072	652,570	7.00	45,680	62.25	B	Northwest on Indian Ocean. Traditional landing point of Indo-Aryan tribes (c 500 BC).
2572	Ratnapura	Ratnapura	1,264	3,275	1,022,620	14.00	143,167	71.25	B	Southwest. Kalu River. Chief source of precious stones. 'City of Gems'.
2573	Trincomalee	Trincomalee	1,053	2,727	344,567	7.00	24,120	62.25	B	Northwest on Indian Ocean. Natural harbor. Early Indo-Aryan settlement. Resorts. D=RCC.
2574	Vavuniya	Vavuniya	759	1,967	126,303	2.00	2,526	52.25	B	North. Timber center, rice plantations.
	SUDAN		**966,757**	**2,503,890**	**29,489,719**	**16.53**	**4,874,391**	**53.81**	**B**	**Roman Catholics 10.6%, Anglicans 7.8%. Pent-char 2.2%, Evangelical 2.6%, GCC 6.4%**
2575	al-Istiwa'iyah (Equatoria)	Juba	76,436	197,969	2,016,507	72.03	1,452,553	99.31	C	Southernmost bordering Uganda & Zaire. Isolated by swamps. Wheat, lumber. Azande. D=RCC.
2576	al-Khartum (Khartoum)	Khartoum	10,875	28,165	2,584,479	22.00	568,585	64.83	B	Conurbation. Textiles, tanning. Mainly Arab. F=1823. D=Ethiopian Orthodox,RCC,Anglican.
2577	al-Wusta (Central)	Wad Madani	53,675	139,017	5,754,034	0.60	34,524	37.88	A	East central. Blue Nile River. Massive immigration project. Cotton. Arabs, Nubians. D=RCC.
2578	ash-Shamaliyah	ad-Damir	183,800	476,040	1,553,223	0.50	7,766	37.78	A	North. Nile River. Center of date production. Sheep trade.
2579	ash-Sharqiyah (Eastern)	Kassala	128,987	334,074	3,166,606	8.00	253,328	49.28	A	East central. Atbarah River. Cereals, oilseeds. Cattle, camels. Mainly Arabs, Beja, Nubians.
2580	A`ali an Nil (Upper Nile)	Malakal	92,198	238,792	2,293,710	3.00	68,811	42.28	A	East central bordering Ethiopia. White Nile River. Agricultural produce.
2581	Bahr al-Ghazal	Waw	77,566	200,894	3,248,882	65.00	2,111,773	98.78	C	South central. Jur River. Cotton, tobacco. Civil war (1983). D=RCC,Anglican.
2582	Darfur (Darfur)	al-Fashir	196,404	508,686	4,436,433	0.50	22,182	37.78	A	Westernmost. Marrah Mountains. Cereals, rice, handicrafts. 'House of the Fur'. Mainly Arabs.
2583	Kurdufan (Kordofan)	al-Ubayyid	146,817	380,255	4,435,844	8.00	354,868	45.28	A	Central. Desert. Camels, sheep, and goats. Traditional handicrafts. Mainly Arabs. D=RCC.
	SURINAME		**63,251**	**163,820**	**417,130**	**41.31**	**172,334**	**83.77**	**B**	**Roman Catholics 22.3%, Protestants 17.1%. Pent-char 2.6%, Evangelical 2.8%, GCC 17.0%**
2584	Brokopondo	Brokopondo	8,278	21,440	7,809	16.00	1,249	58.46	B	Central. Suriname River. Aluminum production. D=RCC,EBGS.
2585	Commewijne	Nieuw Amsterdam	1,587	4,110	23,664	32.00	7,572	76.46	B	North. Near mouth of Suriname River. D=RCC,EBGS.
2586	Coronie	Totness	626	1,620	3,275	19.00	622	61.46	B	North on Atlantic Ocean. Coconuts, rice. D=RCC,EBGS.
2587	Marowijne	Albina	17,753	45,980	19,019	30.00	5,706	74.46	B	East. Bordering French Guiana. Moroni River. D=RCC,EBGS.
2588	Nickerie	Nieuw Nickerie	24,946	64,610	38,557	31.00	11,953	75.46	B	Northwest. Atlantic Ocean. Rice, cocoa, lumber. D=RCC,EBGS.
2589	Para	Onverwacht	378	980	15,129	27.00	4,085	69.46	B	North. South of Paramaribo. Mining, forestry. D=RCC,EBGS.
2590	Paramaribo	Paramaribo	12	32	197,912	52.35	103,604	91.89	B	East. Atlantic Ocean. Suriname River. Tourism, paint, margarine. Dutch architecture. D=RCC,EBGS.
2591	Saramacca	Groningen	9,042	23,420	12,748	20.00	2,550	62.46	B	North, bordering Atlantic Ocean. Coppename River. D=RCC,EBGS.
2592	Sipaliwini	–	629	1,628	27,394	31.00	8,492	75.46	B	South, bordering Brazil, Guyana. Sipalwini River. D=RCC,EBGS.
2593	Wanica	Lelydorp	–	–	71,623	37.00	26,501	84.46	B	North. Urbanized and rural sections near Paramaribo. D=RCC,EBGS.
	SVALBARD & JAN MAYEN		**24,000**	**62,160**	**3,676**	**47.58**	**1,749**	**99.37**	**B**	**Protestants 27.2%, Orthodox 20.3%. Pent-char 2.5%, Evangelical 4.0%, GCC 29.0%**
2594	Svalbard & Jan Mayen Is	Longyearbyen	24,000	62,160	3,676	47.58	1,749	99.37	B	Nine ice-covered Arctic islands, north of Norway. Russian coal miners. D=ROC,CON.
	SWAZILAND		**6,704**	**17,364**	**1,007,895**	**67.55**	**680,841**	**99.36**	**C**	**Independents 45.6%, Protestants 15.2%. Pent-char 52.0%, Evangelical 12.2%, GCC 26.9%**
2595	Hhohho	Mbabane	1,378	3,569	264,806	70.00	185,364	99.41	C	West. Regional council. High veld. Cattle, iron ore. D=Independents.
2596	Lubombo	Siteki	2,296	5,947	227,842	64.46	146,863	99.19	C	South. Ingwavuma River. Lubombo Mountains. Rich flora. D=Independents.
2597	Manzini	Manzini	1,571	4,068	285,022	69.00	196,665	99.31	C	Central. Great Usutu River. Corn (maize), cotton, tobacco. D=Independents.
2598	Shiselweni	Nhlangano	1,459	3,780	230,226	66.00	151,949	99.51	C	South. Regional council (government). Tourism. First Swazi kingdom (1770). D=Independents.
	SWEDEN		**173,732**	**449,964**	**8,910,214**	**67.34**	**6,000,356**	**98.43**	**C**	**Protestants 94.5%, Roman Catholics 1.9%. Pent-char 6.9%, Evangelical 9.9%, GCC 28.0%**
2599	Blekinge	Karlskrona	1,136	2,941	153,104	72.00	110,235	99.69	C	South. Steel, textiles, industrial equipment. D=Church of Sweden.
2600	Dalarna	Falun	10,886	28,194	290,313	71.00	206,122	99.59	C	Central. Lumbering, sawmilling, woodworking. Mining: iron, gold. D=Church of Sweden.
2601	Gotland	Visby	1,212	3,140	58,398	72.00	42,047	99.74	C	Island in Baltic Sea. Grains, sugar beets, flower cultivation. D=Church of Sweden.
2602	Gävleborg	Gävle	7,024	18,191	288,923	70.00	202,246	99.49	C	East-central. Gulf of Bothnia. Paper, textiles, lumber. D=Church of Sweden.
2603	Göteborg och Bohus	Göteborg	1,985	5,141	781,399	66.00	515,723	97.93	C	Southwest. Skagerrak and Kattegat (straits). Fishing, boat-building. D=Church of Sweden.
2604	Halland	Halmstad	2,106	5,454	272,064	70.00	190,445	99.49	C	South. Rye, oats, sugar beets. D=Church of Sweden.
2605	Jämtland	Östersund	19,090	49,443	135,560	72.00	97,603	99.69	C	West. Borders Norway. Dairy, lumbering, quarrying. D=Church of Sweden.
2606	Jönköping	Jönköping	3,839	9,944	314,085	68.00	213,578	99.09	C	South. Rye, oats, timber. D=Church of Sweden.
2607	Kalmar	Kalmar	4,313	11,170	243,694	72.00	175,460	99.69	C	Southeast. Machinery, confectionery, glassworks. D=Church of Sweden.
2608	Kronoberg	Växjö	3,266	8,458	180,993	72.00	130,315	99.69	C	South. Rolling plateau of woods and marshland. Forest products, glass. D=Church of Sweden.
2609	Norrbotten	Luleå	38,191	98,913	266,282	69.00	183,735	99.39	C	North. Borders Finland, Norway. Gulf of Bothnia. Iron deposits. D=Church of Sweden.
2610	Skaraborg	Mariestad	3,065	7,937	280,333	71.00	199,036	99.59	C	South-central. Hilly. Agriculture, limestone, automobiles. D=Church of Sweden.
2611	Skåne	Malmo	4,257	11,025	1,122,651	64.00	718,497	97.09	C	South. Baltic Sea, Kattegat Strait. Sugar beets, grains, potatoes. D=Church of Sweden.
2612	Stockholm	Stockholm	2,505	6,488	1,757,290	62.81	1,103,715	97.01	C	East-central. Baltic Sea. Agriculture, metalworking, papermaking. D=Church of Sweden.
2613	Södermanland	Nyköping	2,340	6,060	259,296	69.00	178,914	99.39	C	East-central. Baltic Sea. Grains, fruit, livestock. D=Church of Sweden.
2614	Uppsala	Uppsala	2,698	6,989	291,302	68.00	198,085	99.09	C	East-central. Gulf of Bothnia. Grain, potatoes, livestock. Mining: iron. D=Church of Sweden.
2615	Värmland	Karlstad	6,789	17,584	284,245	70.00	198,972	99.49	C	West-central. Borders Norway. Iron mining, lumbering, paper making. D=Church of Sweden.
2616	Västerbotten	Umeå	21,390	55,401	261,827	71.00	185,897	99.59	C	North. Gulf of Bothnia. Borders Norway. Farming, lumbering, mining. D=Church of Sweden.
2617	Västernorrland	Härnösand	8,370	21,678	258,494	72.00	186,116	99.69	C	Northeast. Gulf of Bothnia. Timber, pulp. D=Church of Sweden.
2618	Västmanland	Västerås	2,433	6,302	261,916	68.00	178,103	99.09	C	Central. Dairy, market gardening, metalworking. Mining: iron, copper, lead. D=Church of Sweden.
2619	Älvsborg	Vänersborg	4,400	11,395	451,400	70.00	315,980	98.59	C	Southwest. Borders Norway. Wheat, rye, oats. D=Church of Sweden.
2620	Örebro	Örebro	3,289	8,519	277,901	68.00	188,973	99.09	C	South-central. Lumber, paper, steel. Mining: iron, zinc, copper. D=Church of Sweden.
2621	Östergötland	Linköping	4,078	10,562	418,744	67.00	280,558	98.09	C	Southeast. Textile weaving, stone quarrying. D=Church of Sweden.
	SWITZERLAND		**15,940**	**41,284**	**7,385,708**	**87.27**	**6,445,548**	**98.23**	**C**	**Roman Catholics 44.1%, Protestants 41.1%. Pent-char 6.4%, Evangelical 4.0%, GCC 34.4%**
2622	Aargau	Aarau	542	1,405	542,963	88.00	477,807	98.56	C	North. Dairy, fruit, cereal. D=RCC,FEPS.
2623	Appenzell Ausser-Rhoden	Herisau	94	243	56,312	90.00	50,681	98.96	C	Appenzell Ausser-Rhoden. D=RCC,FEPS.
2624	Appenzell Inner-Rhoden	Appenzell	66	172	14,850	90.00	13,365	98.96	C	Northeast. Cattle, dairy, hand embroidery. D=RCC,FEPS.
2625	Basel-Landschaft	Liestal	165	428	251,758	89.00	224,065	98.86	C	North. Fruit, dairy, cattle. D=RCC,FEPS.
2626	Basel-Stadt	Basel	14	37	209,828	86.00	180,452	97.46	C	North. Rhine River. Chemicals, pharmaceuticals. F=Celts. Bishopric since 5th century. D=RCC,FEPS.
2627	Bern	Bern	2,335	6,049	1,034,520	86.06	890,278	97.73	C	West-central. Cattle, cheese, pottery. D=RCC,FEPS.
2628	Fribourg	Fribourg	645	1,670	227,294	89.00	202,292	98.86	C	West. Cattle, dairy, cereals. D=RCC,FEPS.
2629	Genève	Geneva	109	282	411,322	85.00	349,624	96.86	C	Southwest. Jura Mountains, Alps. Wine, cattle, fruit. D=RCC,FEPS.
2630	Glarus	Glarus	264	684	41,189	89.00	36,658	98.86	C	East-central. Slate works, cattle, dairy. D=RCC,FEPS.
2631	Graubünden	Chur	2,744	7,106	186,441	88.00	164,068	98.56	C	East. Central Alps. Livestock, wine. Languages: German, Italian, Romansh and Ladin. D=RCC.
2632	Jura	Delémont	323	837	71,877	89.00	63,971	98.86	C	Northwest. Jura Mountains. Borders France. Agriculture, cattle, horse breeding. D=RCC,FEPS.
2633	Luzern	Luzern	576	1,492	349,582	86.00	300,641	97.46	C	Central. Foothills of the Alps. Field crops, fruit, cattle. D=RCC,FEPS.
2634	Neuchâtel	Neuchâtel	308	797	175,717	88.00	154,631	98.56	C	West. Borders France. Jura Mountains. Novum Castellum (1032). Wine, cattle, dairy. D=RCC,FEPS.
2635	Nidwalden	Stans	107	276	35,697	89.00	31,770	98.86	C	Central. 'Below the forest'. D=RCC,FEPS.
2636	Obwalden	Sarnen	189	491	31,524	90.00	28,372	98.96	C	Central. 'Above the forest'. Dairy. D=RCC,FEPS.
2637	Sankt Gallen	Sankt Gallen	778	2,014	459,801	87.00	400,027	98.46	C	Northeast. Borders Liechtenstein. Dairy, fruit, wine, health and winter sport resorts. D=RCC.
2638	Schaffhausen	Schaffhausen	115	298	78,441	88.00	69,028	98.56	C	North. Bodensee (Lake Constance). Two small German enclaves. Machinery, watches. D=RCC.
2639	Schwyz	Schwyz	351	908	120,923	89.00	107,621	98.86	C	Central. Lake Zurich, Lake Luzern. Rigi Massif. Cattle, textiles, furniture. D=RCC,FEPS.
2640	Solothurn	Solothurn	305	791	247,976	87.00	215,739	97.96	C	Northwest. Aare River. Borders France. Watches, jewelry, shoes. D=RCC,FEPS.
2641	Thurgau	Frauenfeld	391	1,013	225,319	88.00	198,281	98.56	C	Northeast. Bodensee (Lake Constance). Apples, pears, vineyards. D=RCC,FEPS.
2642	Ticino	Bellinzona	1,085	2,811	313,696	88.00	276,052	97.96	C	South. Lake Lugano, Lake Maggiore. Wheat, potatoes, tobacco. Italian. D=RCC.
2643	Uri	Altdorf	416	1,076	36,816	90.00	33,134	98.96	C	Central. Forestry, runner. Many glaciers. D=RCC,FEPS.
2644	Valais	Sion	2,018	5,226	271,671	90.00	244,504	98.96	C	South. Borders Italy, France. Dairy, orchards. D=RCC,FEPS.
2645	Vaud	Lausanne	1,243	3,219	638,525	88.00	561,902	98.56	C	Southwest. Lake Geneva (Lac Leman). Jura Mountains. Wine, wheat. Tourism. D=RCC,FEPS.
2646	Zug	Zug	92	239	92,892	88.00	81,745	98.56	C	Central. Smallest undivided canton. Fruit, metal goods, textiles. D=RCC,FEPS.
2647	Zürich	Zürich	668	1,729	1,258,774	86.50	1,088,840	98.36	C	Northeast. Lake Zurich. Linth Valley. Machinery, silk and cotton weaving. D=RCC,FEPS.
	SYRIA		**71,498**	**185,180**	**16,124,618**	**7.80**	**1,257,709**	**62.21**	**B**	**Orthodox 4.9%, Roman Catholics 2.0%. Pent-char 0.6%, Evangelical 0.2%, GCC 4.9%**
2648	al-Hasakah	al-Hasakah	9,009	23,334	1,199,680	1.00	11,997	40.41	A	Northeast. Kabur River. Extensive irrigated farming (wheat, rice). Tabuqah Dam.
2649	al-Ladhiqiyah	Latakia	887	2,297	971,391	13.00	126,281	73.41	B	Northwest on Mediterranean Sea. Principal port, agriculture. Ugaritic origins. D=GOC,RCC.
2650	al-Qunaytirah	al-Qunaytirah	719	1,861	52,413	0.50	262	34.91	A	Southwest bordering Sea of Galilee. Golan Heights. Occupied by Israel (1967-74).
2651	ar-Raqqah	ar-Raqqah	7,574	19,616	603,335	2.00	12,067	56.41	B	North. Euphrates River. Ancient Greek origins. Market center. Earthenware (9th century).

Continued opposite

Table 11-3 continued

Rec No 1	Country Major civil divisions 2	Capital 3	sq.mi. 4	sq.km. 5	Pop 2000 6	AC% 7	Church members 8	E% 9	W 10	Notes 11
2652	as-Suwayda	as-Suwayda	2,143	5,550	349,420	1.00	3,494	40.41	A	South, near Jordan. Ad-Duruz Mountains. 5th century bishopric. Byzantine church ruins. D=RCC.
2653	Damascus	–	41	105	1,807,671	10.00	180,767	67.63	B	Barada River. Inlaid wood, silk. Inhabited for 4,000 years. Great mosque. D=RCC,GOC.
2654	Dar`a	Dar`a	1,440	3,730	717,478	8.00	57,398	65.51	B	Southwest, bordering Jordan. Market center. Greco-Roman ruins. Mosque (1253).
2655	Dayr az-Zawr	Dayr as-Zawr	12,765	33,060	697,677	1.00	6,977	40.41	A	East, bordering Iraq. Euphrates River. Art, oil. 'Monastery of the Grove'.
2656	Dimashq	Damascus	6,962	18,032	1,690,032	9.46	159,938	67.37	B	Southwest bordering Lebanon. Qasiyun Mountains. Olives, grapes, handicrafts. 'The Northern'.
2657	Halab	Aleppo	7,143	18,500	3,326,489	10.00	332,649	67.51	B	Northwest bordering Turkey. Euphrates River. F=3000 BC. Massacre by Mongols (1200). Silk, cotton.
2658	Hamah	Hamah	3,430	8,883	1,299,846	6.00	77,991	60.41	B	Central. Orontes River. Prehistoric settlement. Agricultural market. Early Christian presence. D=RCC.
2659	Hims	Homs	16,302	42,223	1,515,322	9.00	136,379	66.51	B	Central. Orontes River. Ancient Emesa. Muslim conquest (636). Mass martyrdom of Christians (855).
2660	Idlib	Idlib	2,354	6,097	1,091,359	8.00	87,309	62.41	B	Northwest. Fertile basin. Textiles, cotton, cereals. Olive oil presses. D=RCC,GOC.
2661	Tartus	Tartus	730	1,892	802,505	8.00	64,200	62.41	B	West. Mediterranean Sea. Ancient Antaradus. Fishing, agriculture. 13th century cathedral. D=RCC.
	TAIWAN		**13,969**	**36,179**	**22,401,000**	**5.27**	**1,179,743**	**68.85**	**B**	**Independents 2.0%, Protestants 1.7%. Pent-char 1.6%, Evangelical 0.9%, GCC 3.6%**
2662	Chang-hua	Chang-hua	415	1,074	1,365,637	6.00	81,938	69.58	B	West-central on Formosa Strait. Paddy rice, sugarcane. Confucian & Buddhist temples. D=RCC.
2663	Chi-lung	–	51	133	387,820	5.60	21,718	69.18	B	North on East China Sea. Principal port. Coal, fertilizer, fishing. D=Presbyterian.
2664	Chia-i	Chia-i	734	1,902	603,066	5.00	30,153	68.58	B	West-central on Formosa Strait. A-li Mountains. Paddy rice, sugarcane. D=Presbyterian.
2665	Chia-i	–	23	60	280,965	5.00	14,048	68.58	B	West coastal plain at A-li Mountains. Lumber, rice trade center. D=RCC.
2666	Hsin-chu	Hsin-chu	551	1,428	413,890	5.50	22,764	69.08	B	Northwest on Taiwan Strait. HsYeh-shan Mountains. Tea, paddy rice. High tech park. D=Presbyterian.
2667	Hsin-chu	–	40	104	358,705	5.50	19,729	69.08	B	Northwest. Walled in 18th century. Rice, tea, and fruit market center. High tech park (1980). D=RCC.
2668	Hua-lien	Hua-lien	1,787	4,629	384,773	5.00	19,239	68.58	B	East-central on Pacific Ocean. Hua-lien & Wu rivers. Sugarcane. Taroko Gorge. D=RCC.
2669	I-lan	I-lan	825	2,137	493,895	3.00	14,817	63.58	B	Northeast on Philippine Sea. Chung-yang Mountains. Paddy rice, sulfur, tourism.
2670	Kao-hsiung	Feng-shan	1,078	2,793	1,234,409	5.00	61,720	68.58	B	Southwest on Taiwan Strait. YY Mountains. Rice, tobacco. Large Buddhist temple. D=Presbyterian.
2671	Kao-hsiung	–	59	154	1,520,860	5.40	82,126	68.98	B	Southwest. Major international port on Taiwan Strait. Heavy industry. Many colleges. D=RCC.
2672	Miao-li	Miao-li	703	1,820	599,652	5.00	29,983	68.58	B	Northwest on Taiwan Strait. Ta-an River. Rice, sweet potatoes. Coal, oil. D=Presbyterian.
2673	Nan-t'ou	Nan-t'ou	1,585	4,106	586,803	2.20	12,910	61.78	B	Central. Chung-yang Mountains. Paddy rice, coal, tourism.
2674	P'eng-hu	Ma-kung	49	127	103,450	5.70	5,897	69.28	B	64 islands west of coast in Taiwan Strait. Fishing, phosphates, naval base. D=Presbyterian.
2675	P'ing-tung	P'ing-tung	1,072	2,776	976,159	5.50	53,689	69.08	B	Southernmost on Luzon Strait. Central Range mountains. Sugarcane. Sugar refining industry.
2676	T'ai-chung	Feng-yuan	792	2,051	1,407,777	3.00	42,233	63.58	B	West-central on Taiwan Strait. Chung-yang Mountains. Paddy rice, cattle. Pilgrimage center.
2677	T'ai-chung	–	63	163	847,840	3.20	27,131	63.78	B	West-central. Export processing zone. Market center for rice sugarcane. Chinese refugees. D=RCC.
2678	T'ai-nan	Hsin-ying	778	2,016	1,128,966	4.00	45,159	67.58	B	Southwest on Taiwan Strait. Rice, sugarcane, food processing. Religious festivals.
2679	T'ai-nan	–	68	176	750,935	4.50	33,792	68.08	B	Southwest on Taiwan Strait. Former capital. Main market center for south. Handicrafts. D=RCC.
2680	T'ai-pei	Pan-ch'iao	792	2,052	3,394,697	6.50	220,655	71.38	B	Northernmost on East China Sea. Tan-shui River. Coal fields, Wu-Lai Forest. D=Presbyterian.
2681	T'ai-tung	T'ai-tung	1,357	3,515	278,626	5.00	13,931	68.58	B	Southeast on Philippine Sea. Chung-yang Mountains. Sugarcane. Sugar milling. Gold mining.
2682	T'ao-yuan	T'ao-yuan	471	1,221	1,512,677	5.50	83,197	69.08	B	North on Taiwan Strait. Tan-shui River. Paddy rice, sweet potatoes, oil, gas, tourism.
2683	Taipei	–	105	272	2,950,953	6.85	201,993	72.55	B	Northernmost on East China Sea. Foremost industrial area, electronics. National Palace. D=RCC.
2684	Yun-lin	Tou-liu	498	1,291	818,443	5.00	40,922	68.58	B	West-central on Taiwan Strait. A-li Mountains. Sugarcane, paddy rice, textiles. Many temples. D=RCC.
	TAJIKISTAN		**55,300**	**143,100**	**6,188,201**	**2.09**	**129,612**	**44.12**	**A**	**Orthodox 1.5%, Protestants 0.2%. Pent-char 0.05%, Evangelical 0.03%, GCC 0.8%**
2685	Badakhshoni Kuni	Khorugh	24,600	63,700	192,982	1.00	1,930	33.03	A	South-central. Pamir Mountains, Gunt River. Hydroelectric station, botanical gardens.
2686	Dushanbe	–	100	300	683,574	2.90	19,824	45.93	A	Southwest. On Varzob River. Textiles. Well-planned streets & parks. 60% Tajik. D=ROC.
2687	Khujand	Khujand	10,100	26,100	1,889,271	2.19	41,311	45.47	A	North on Syr Darya (river). Ancient Silk Road. Silk, cotton-processing. D=ROC.
2688	Kulob	Kulob	4,600	12,000	771,576	1.40	10,802	38.43	A	South on Afghan Border. Many Uzbeks.
2689	Other regions	–	11,000	28,400	1,364,839	2.20	30,026	46.23	A	Central and east. Mountainous. Tajiks, Uzbeks. D=ROC.
2690	Qurghonteppa	Qurghonteppa	4,900	12,600	1,285,960	2.00	25,719	44.03	A	South bordering Afghanistan and Uzbekistan. D=ROC.
	TANZANIA		**364,017**	**942,799**	**33,517,014**	**46.91**	**15,722,778**	**81.42**	**B**	**Roman Catholics 24.7%, Protestants 16.5%. Pent-char 10.2%, Evangelical 14.5%, GCC 16.7%**
2691	Arusha	Arusha	31,778	82,306	1,954,923	70.00	1,368,446	97.51	C	North. Coffee, grain. Tourism based on big game reserves. Arusha, Meru peoples. D=RCC.
2692	Coast	Dar es Salaam	12,512	32,407	922,760	36.00	332,194	73.01	B	East on Indian Ocean. Hot, humid. Agricultural & mineral exports. D=RCC,ELCT.
2693	Dar es Salaam	Dar es Salaam	538	1,393	1,968,196	40.00	787,278	77.01	B	East. Indian Ocean. Soap, paint. 'Haven of Peace'. F=1862 by Sultan of Zanzibar. D=RCC.
2694	Dodoma	Dodoma	15,950	41,311	1,790,258	66.00	1,181,570	99.51	C	Central. Capital since 1974. Market center for peanuts, wine. Gogo, Sanawe, Rangi peoples. D=RCC.
2695	Iringa	Iringa	21,955	56,864	1,748,452	55.00	961,649	93.51	B	South-central. Pyrethrum, wattle (Acacia) extract, tea. Hehe, Bena, Kinga, Nyakusa. D=RCC,ELCT.
2696	Kagera	Bukoba	10,961	28,388	1,918,058	47.03	902,107	85.54	B	North. Bordering Rwanda, Uganda & Lake Victoria. Lakes, swamps. D=RCC,ELCT.
2697	Kigoma	Kigoma	14,300	37,037	1,236,322	63.00	778,883	99.51	C	Northwest. Bordering Burundi and Lake Tanganyika. Rice, fishing. D=RCC,ELCT.
2698	Kilimanjaro	Moshi	5,139	13,309	1,603,511	72.00	1,154,528	99.51	C	Northeast. Borders Kenya. Coffee, barley, wheat. Chaga, Pare, Kahe, Mbugu. D=RCC,ELCT.
2699	Lindi	Lindi	25,501	66,046	935,105	40.00	374,042	74.51	B	Southeast. On Indian Ocean. Matandu River. Selous Game Reserve. Tsetse-infested. D=RCC,ELCT.
2700	Mara	Musoma	7,555	19,566	1,404,272	45.00	631,922	83.51	B	North. Bordering Kenya and Lake Victoria. Serengeti National Park. D=RCC,ELCT.
2701	Mbeya	Mbeya	23,301	60,350	2,135,024	60.00	1,281,014	96.51	C	South. Bordering Zambia & Malawi. Lake Rukwa. Nyakyusa peoples. Rice, coffee. D=RCC,ELCT.
2702	Morogoro	Morogoro	27,336	70,799	1,768,441	34.00	601,270	68.51	B	East-central. Great Ruaha River. Rich agriculture. D=RCC,ECLT.
2703	Mtwara	Mtwara	6,451	16,707	1,286,473	10.00	128,647	44.51	A	South. Bordering Mozambique. On Indian Ocean. Ruvuma River. Trade center. D=RCC,ELCT.
2704	Mwanza	Mwanza	7,564	19,592	2,716,541	68.00	1,847,248	98.51	C	North. On southern shore of Lake Victoria. Rail terminus, fishing. D=RCC,ELCT.
2705	Pemba North	Wete	222	574	198,719	20.00	39,744	54.51	B	Island in Indian Ocean. World's leader in clove production. 'Green Island'. D=RCC,ELCT.
2706	Pemba South	Chake Chake	128	332	184,605	20.00	36,921	54.51	B	Island in Indian Ocean. World's leader in clove production. 'Green Island'. D=RCC,ELCT.
2707	Rukwa	Sumbawanga	26,500	68,635	1,005,138	35.00	351,798	69.51	B	Southwest. Bordering Lake Tanganyika. Lake Rukwa. Fishing. Crocodiles. D=RCC,ELCT.
2708	Ruvuma	Songea	24,517	63,498	1,132,925	45.00	509,816	82.41	B	South. Bordering Mozambique. Ruvuma River. Fishing. D=RCC,ELCT.
2709	Shinyanga	Shinyanga	19,607	50,781	2,563,636	38.00	974,182	72.51	B	North. Swamps. D=RCC,ELCT.
2710	Singida	Singida	19,051	49,341	1,145,199	33.00	377,916	67.51	B	Central. Swamps. Extinct fishes. D=RCC,ELCT.
2711	Tabora	Tabora	29,402	76,151	1,498,790	45.00	674,456	79.51	B	West-central. Tobacco, vegetables, cassava. D=RCC,ELCT.
2712	Tanga	Tanga	10,351	26,808	1,856,521	22.00	408,435	56.51	B	Northeast. Indian Ocean. Sisal, cotton, millet. D=RCC,ELCT.
2713	Zanzibar North	Mkokotoni	182	470	140,332	3.00	4,210	37.51	A	Island in Indian Ocean. Limestone. Coconut palms. Tumbatu people. Swahili. D=RCC,ELCT.
2714	Zanzibar South/Central	Koani	330	854	101,506	3.60	3,654	38.11	A	Island in Indian Ocean. Limestone. Coconut palms. Hadimu people. Swahili. D=RCC,ELCT.
2715	Zanzibar West	Zanzibar	89	230	301,305	3.60	10,847	38.11	A	Island in Indian Ocean. Limestone. Coconut palms. Fishing. Swahili. D=RCC,ELCT.
	THAILAND		**198,115**	**513,115**	**61,399,249**	**2.19**	**1,345,167**	**56.82**	**B**	**Independents 1.2%, Protestants 0.4%. Pent-char 1.3%, Evangelical 0.3%, GCC 1.9%**
2716	Bangkok Metropolis	–	604	1,565	9,229,811	3.15	290,361	62.17	B	Central. Chao Phraya River port. Severe pollution. 93% Buddhist (687 temples). D=Hope of Bangkok.
2717	Central	–	39,512	102,336	2,984,562	1.90	56,707	53.53	B	Chao Phraya River basin. Core cultural region. Rice, sugarcane. Strong Buddhist character.
2718	Eastern	–	14,094	36,503	4,012,901	1.70	68,219	58.33	B	Borders Cambodia. Cambodian refugee camps. Rice, sugarcane. Mainly Thai. Buddhists.
2719	Northeastern	–	65,195	168,854	21,230,147	1.80	382,143	55.43	B	Borders Laos. Laotian dialect. Laotian refugee camps. Rice, sugarcane. Buddhists.
2720	Northern	–	65,500	169,644	12,434,699	2.90	360,606	59.53	B	Borders Myanmar and Laos. Many hill tribes. Rice, sugarcane. Buddhists.
2721	Southern	–	27,303	70,715	7,876,756	1.50	118,151	51.13	B	Borders Myanmar & Malaysia. Sugarcane, rice, tourism. Sino-Thai and Thai Muslims. Buddhists.
2722	Western	–	•16,621	43,047	3,630,372	1.90	68,977	55.53	B	Borders Myanmar. Mountainous. Sparsely-populated. Karen from Myanmar. Buddhists.
	TIMOR		**5,743**	**14,874**	**884,541**	**92.18**	**815,391**	**98.79**	**C**	**Roman Catholics 89.9%, Protestants 5.3%. Pent-char 5.2%, Evangelical 0.5%, GCC 4.4%**
2723	Timor Timur	Dili	5,743	14,874	884,541	92.18	815,391	98.79	C	East Timor Island. Timor Sea. Sandalwood forests, mountains. Copra, hides. Papuan. D=RCC.
	TOGO		**21,925**	**56,785**	**4,629,218**	**37.78**	**1,749,095**	**75.84**	**B**	**Roman Catholics 24.2%, Protestants 10.3%. Pent-char 8.1%, Evangelical 3.0%, GCC 19.8%**
2724	Centrale	Sokodé	5,090	13,183	462,717	37.00	171,205	75.06	B	Central. Togo Mountains. Cotton, sugar. Tem (Cotocoli). D=RCC.
2725	De la Kara	Kara	4,490	11,630	725,469	35.00	253,914	71.06	B	North. On Kara River. High density of villages on highway. D=RCC.
2726	Des Plateaux	Atakpamé	6,554	16,975	1,106,290	39.00	431,453	77.06	B	South Central. Cotton, cocoa, coffee. Settled by Ewe and Yoruba peoples. D=RCC.
2727	Des Savanes	Dapaong	3,321	8,602	560,311	35.00	196,109	71.06	B	North. Granite, gneiss. Cliffs. Oti River. Cattle, peanuts. Anoufe people. D=RCC.
2728	Maritime	Lomé	2,469	6,395	1,774,431	39.25	696,413	78.75	B	South. Gulf of Guinea. Oil palms, sugarcane, rice. Ewe, Ouatchi, Ane (Mina). D=RCC,JWs.
	TOKELAU ISLANDS		**4**	**10**	**1,500**	**91.20**	**1,368**	**99.93**	**C**	**Protestants 66.6%, Roman Catholics 37.3%. Pent-char 5.0%, Evangelical 6.0%, GCC 18.8%**
2729	Tokelau Islands	–	4	10	1,500	91.20	1,368	99.93	C	New Zealand dependency. South Pacific atolls. Tuna fishing, tourism. D=Congregational.
	TONGA		**290**	**750**	**98,546**	**91.01**	**89,688**	**99.91**	**C**	**Protestants 42.9%, Independents 21.1%. Pent-char 12.4%, Evangelical 7.4%, GCC 28.3%**
2730	'Eua	'Ohonua	34	87	4,574	94.50	4,322	99.98	C	East. Volcanic origins. Many trees. Tropical birds. D=FWCT,RCC,LDS.
2731	Ha'apai	Pangai	43	110	9,286	94.00	8,729	99.96	C	Central island cluster. South Pacific Ocean. 36 coral and volcanic islands. D=FWCT,RCC,LDS.
2732	Niuas	Hihifo	28	72	2,466	94.50	2,330	99.98	C	Northern island cluster. Vanilla beans. D=FWCT,RCC,LDS.
2733	Tongatapu	Nuku'alofa	101	261	66,421	89.51	59,455	99.88	C	Southernmost island cluster. Pacific Ocean. Copra, bananas. D=FWCT,RCC,LDS.
2734	Vava'u	Neiafu	46	119	15,800	94.00	14,852	99.96	C	Northernmost island cluster. Volcanic and coral. Corn, copra. D=FWCT,RCC,LDS.
	TRINIDAD & TOBAGO		**1,980**	**5,128**	**1,294,958**	**61.46**	**795,865**	**91.55**	**C**	**Roman Catholics 30.7%, Protestants 13.8%. Pent-char 10.5%, Evangelical 12.6%, GCC 22.2%**
2735	Arima	–	5	12	31,152	65.00	20,249	95.09	C	Northern Trinidad. Oldest Arawak Indian settlement. Sugarcane, oil. D=RCC.
2736	Caroni	Chaguanas	214	554	126,420	62.00	78,380	92.09	C	West-central Trinidad or Gulf of Paria, Caroni River. Bird sanctuary. Sugarcane, oil. D=RCC.
2737	Chaguanas	–	23	59	59,379	64.00	38,003	94.09	C	West-central Trinidad. Trade center. Sugarcane, oil. D=RCC.
2738	Nariva/Mayaro	Rio Claro	352	912	38,586	63.00	24,309	93.09	C	Southeast Trinidad. Ortoire River. Sugarcane, oil. D=RCC.
2739	Point Fortin	–	10	25	21,008	64.00	13,445	94.09	C	Southwest Trinidad. On Guapo Bay. Petroleum exports. D=RCC.
2740	Port-of-Spain	–	4	10	53,374	61.00	32,558	91.09	C	Northwest Trinidad. On Gulf of Paria. Petroleum, rum, beer. RC Archbishopric.
2741	San Fernando	–	3	7	31,568	64.00	20,204	94.09	C	Western Trinidad. On Guapo Bay. Petroleum exports. Horse racing. D=RCC.
2742	St. Andrew/St. David	Sangre Grande	362	937	66,032	64.00	42,260	94.09	C	East Trinidad. On Maturn Bay. Petroleum, sugarcane. D=RCC.
2743	St. George	Tunapuna	350	908	467,486	59.08	276,172	89.17	B	North Trinidad. Mountainous. Birthplace of C.L.R. James (political activist). D=RCC.
2744	St. Patrick	Siparia	251	650	126,024	63.00	79,395	93.09	C	South Trinidad. Oil, sugarcane. D=RCC.
2745	Tobago	Scarborough	116	301	52,749	64.00	33,759	94.09	C	Tobago Island. Main Ridge. Tropical climate. Carib Indians. Fishing, tourism. D=RCC.
2746	Victoria	Princes Town	314	814	221,179	62.00	137,131	92.09	C	Central Trinidad. Oil, sugarcane. D=RCC.
	TUNISIA		**63,378**	**164,150**	**9,585,611**	**0.53**	**50,503**	**48.91**	**A**	**Independents 0.3%, Roman Catholics 0.2%. Pent-char 0.1%, Evangelical 0.07%, GCC 0.3%**
2747	al-Kaf	al-Kaf	1,917	4,965	319,955	0.20	640	45.58	A	Northwest. Borders Algeria. Grains, cattle. Berbers.
2748	al-Mahdiyah	al-Mahdiyah	1,145	2,966	369,819	0.20	740	45.58	A	East. Mediterranean Sea. Olives, fishing, handicraft industries.
2749	al-Munastir	al-Munastir	393	1,019	388,458	0.30	1,165	48.68	A	East. Mediterranean Sea. Textiles, salt, soap. Beach resorts.
2750	al-Qasrayn	al-Qasrayn	3,114	8,066	421,225	0.40	1,685	48.78	A	West-central. Cattle, grains, olives.
2751	al-Qayrawan	al-Qayrawan	2,591	6,712	580,075	0.50	2,900	48.88	A	North-central. Grains, livestock, carpet. Tomb of one of Mohammed's companions.
2752	Aryanah	Aryanah	602	1,558	633,146	0.90	5,698	53.05	B	North-central. Low Steppes. Grain, livestock, carpets. F=670. Great Mosque.
2753	Bajah	Bajah	1,374	3,558	355,097	0.30	1,065	48.68	A	North. Wheat, livestock.
2754	Banzart	Banzart	1,423	3,685	531,043	0.50	2,655	48.88	A	North. Mediterranean Sea. Cork, wheat, cattle.

Continued overleaf

Table 11-3 continued

Rec No 1	Country Major civil divisions 2	Capital 3	sq.mi. 4	sq.km. 5	Pop 2000 6	AC% 7	Church members 8	E% 9	W 10	Notes 11
2755	Bin Arus	Bin Arus	294	761	364,001	0.20	728	45.58	A	Northeast. Administrative center and suburb of Tunis. D=RCC.
2756	Jundubah	Jundubah	1,198	3,102	478,568	0.50	2,393	48.88	A	Northwest. Grains.
2757	Madaniyin	Madaniyin	3,316	8,588	415,290	0.10	415	43.48	A	South. Jeffara Plain. Historical granaries. Trade center for dates, olives, cereals.
2758	Nabul	Nabul	1,076	2,788	629,583	0.50	3,148	50.88	B	Northeast. Hammamet Gulf. Pottery, ceramics, citrus fruit. Beach resorts.
2759	Qabis	Qabis	2,770	7,175	328,029	0.30	984	48.68	A	Southeast. Gulf of Gabes. Olives. Several oases.
2760	Qafsah	Qafsah	3,471	8,990	329,216	0.05	165	40.43	A	West-central. Esparto grass, cereals, dates. Phosphate mining.
2761	Qibili	Qibili	8,527	22,084	136,293	0.10	136	43.48	A	South. Bordering Algeria and Gulf of Gabes.
2762	Safaqis	Safaqis	2,913	7,545	789,857	0.80	6,319	53.18	B	East-central. Gulf of Gabes. Esparto grass, vegetables, olives.
2763	Sidi Bu Zayd	Sidi Bu Zayd	2,700	6,994	400,686	0.30	1,202	48.68	A	Northeast of Tunis on Bay of Tunis. Handicrafts, carpets. Religious festival (July).
2764	Silyanah	Silyanah	1,788	4,631	288,732	0.20	577	45.58	A	North-central. Agricultural trade center. Lead and zinc mines.
2765	Susah	Susah	1,012	2,621	462,303	0.50	2,312	49.88	A	Central-east. Sardines, olive oil, textiles.
2766	Tatawin	Tatawin	15,015	38,889	140,923	0.10	141	43.48	A	Southernmost. Bordering Libya & Algeria.
2767	Tawzar	Tawzar	1,822	4,719	91,178	0.10	91	43.48	A	West-central. Dates, hand-woven rugs, silver jewelry. Mirages.
2768	Tunis	Tunis (Tunis)	134	346	978,269	1.55	15,190	54.13	B	North. Mediterranean Sea. Olives, cereals, textiles. D=RCC.
2769	Zaghwan	Zaghwan	1,069	2,768	153,863	0.10	154	43.48	A	Northeast. Grapes, olives, vegetables.
	TURKEY		**300,948**	**779,452**	**66,590,940**	**0.56**	**373,155**	**48.58**	**A**	**Orthodox 0.3%, Independents 0.1%. Pent-char 0.1%, Evangelical 0.02%, GCC 0.3%**
2770	Akdeniz kiyisi (Mediterranean Coast)		22,933	59,395	6,419,207	0.15	9,629	46.17	A	South. Mediterranean Sea. Wheat, cotton. Many NT cities. Many Arabs.
2771	Bati Anadolu (West Anatolia)		29,742	77,031	4,557,064	0.90	41,014	52.92	B	West. Aegean Sea. 5,000 years of inhabitation. Many foreigners. M=DM.
2772	Dogu Anadolu (East Anatolia)		68,074	180,180	8,097,805	0.07	5,668	44.09	A	East. Mountainous. Sugar beets. 12th century mosque. Many Kurds.
2773	Guneydogu Anadolu (SE Anatolia		15,347	35,880	3,183,480	0.06	1,827	43.08	A	Southeast. Tigris River. Many Kurds. D=Armenian Orthodox,Syrian Orthodox.
2774	ic Anadolu (Central Anatolia)		91,254	236,347	15,442,539	0.11	16,987	46.13	A	Central. Cereals, livestock. Predominantly Turks.
2775	Karadeniz kiyisi (Black Sea Coast)		31,388	81,295	8,050,505	0.10	8,051	46.12	A	North. Black Sea. Tobacco, tourism, hazelnuts.
2776	Marmara ve Ege kiyilari (Marmara)		33,035	85,560	13,794,307	2.00	275,886	57.54	B	West. Sea of Marmara. Orchards, silk, baths, tourism. 90% Turks.
2777	Trakya (Thrace)		9,175	23,764	7,046,034	0.20	14,092	46.22	A	West. European Turkey. Gallipoli Peninsula.
	TURKMENISTAN		**188,500**	**488,100**	**4,459,293**	**2.22**	**98,883**	**34.54**	**A**	**Orthodox 1.6%, Independents 0.4%. Pent-char 0.2%, Evangelical 0.02%, GCC 1.0%**
2778	Ahal	Ashgabat	37,500	97,100	661,750	2.00	13,235	34.32	A	West. Near Iranian border. Caspian Sea. Orchards, wheat. Russians. D=ROC.
2779	Ashgabat (Ashkhabad)	–	–	–	535,588	3.00	16,068	39.35	A	South. Near Iranian border. Karakum desert. Glassworks, carpets. F=1881 by Russians. D=ROC.
2780	Balkan	Nebitdag	53,500	138,600	380,525	2.18	8,303	34.50	A	West. Bordering Caspian Sea. Oil, petroleum, ship repair.
2781	Dashhovuse	Dashhovuse	28,100	72,700	933,981	2.50	23,350	35.82	A	North. Bordering Uzbekistan. Sarygarnysh Koli. D=AAC,ROC.
2782	Leban	Leban	36,000	93,200	925,388	2.00	18,508	34.32	A	North. Bordering Uzbekistan. Amu Darya. D=ROC.
2783	Mary	Mary	33,400	86,400	1,022,061	1.90	19,419	31.22	A	Southeast. Cotton. Morghab River. Karakul sheep herding.
	TURKS & CAICOS IS		**192**	**497**	**16,760**	**79.13**	**13,262**	**99.79**	**C**	**Protestants 48.4%, Anglicans 11.9%. Pent-char 25.6%, Evangelical 17.9%, GCC 20.9%**
2784	Turks & Caicos Islands	Cockburn Town	192	497	16,760	79.13	13,262	99.79	C	30 low-lying islands, south of Bahamas in Caribbean Sea. Tourism. D=RCC.
	TUVALU		**9**	**24**	**11,719**	**83.16**	**9,745**	**99.83**	**C**	**Protestants 102.4%, Marginal Christians 2.4%. Pent-char 17.9%, Evangelical 4.7%, GCC 19.1%**
2785	Funafuti	–	1	3	4,025	81.00	3,260	99.77	C	30 islets in Pacific Ocean. Fongafale Village. Copra. U.S. Military Base (1943). D=Church of Tuvalu.
2786	Nanumaga	–	1	3	961	86.00	826	99.91	C	North. Polynesian. Fishing. D=Church of Tuvalu.
2787	Nanumea	–	1	4	1,259	82.00	1,032	99.82	C	Northernmost. Polynesian. Fishing. D=Church of Tuvalu.
2788	Niulakita	–	–	–	105	91.00	96	99.98	C	Southernmost. Polynesian. Fishing. D=Church of Tuvalu.
2789	Niutao	–	1	3	1,295	82.00	1,062	99.82	C	North. Polynesian. Fishing. D=Church of Tuvalu.
2790	Nui	–	1	3	865	88.00	761	99.95	C	North. Mainly Micronesian. Fishing. D=Church of Tuvalu.
2791	Nukufetau	–	1	3	994	87.00	865	99.92	C	Central. Polynesian. Fishing. D=Church of Tuvalu.
2792	Nukulaelae	–	1	2	451	90.00	406	99.97	C	South. Polynesian. Fishing. D=Church of Tuvalu.
2793	Vaitupu	–	2	6	1,764	81.47	1,437	99.69	C	North. Polynesian. Fishing. D=Church of Tuvalu.
	UGANDA		**93,070**	**241,040**	**21,778,450**	**86.99**	**18,944,173**	**99.10**	**C**	**Roman Catholics 41.9%, Anglicans 39.4%. Pent-char 23.0%, Evangelical 17.8%, GCC 13.8%**
2794	Apac	Apac	2,510	6,490	605,075	88.00	532,466	99.21	C	North. Cotton, tea. D=RCC,CURBZ.
2795	Arua	Olaki	3,020	7,830	820,338	87.00	713,694	99.11	C	Northwest. Borders Zaire. Coffee, cotton. D=RCC,CURBZ.
2796	Bundibugyo	Busaru	900	2,340	152,351	88.00	134,069	99.21	C	West. Borders Uganda. Ruwenzeri Mountains. Tea, cotton. D=RCC,CURBZ.
2797	Bushenyi	Bumbaire	2,080	5,400	965,071	87.00	839,612	99.11	C	West. Cotton, peanuts. D=RCC,CURBZ.
2798	Gulu	Bungatira	4,530	11,740	444,842	90.00	400,358	99.31	C	Northwest. Cotton, tea. Refugee camps. Birthplace of author Liyong and poet P'Bitek. D=RCC.
2799	Hoima	Hoima	3,820	9,900	259,786	90.00	233,807	99.31	C	West. Cotton, peanuts. D=RCC,CURBZ.
2800	Iganga	Bulamogi	5,060	13,110	1,239,830	85.00	1,053,856	99.11	C	East. Cotton, tobacco. D=RCC,CURBZ.
2801	Jinja	Jinja	280	730	374,182	88.00	329,280	99.21	C	Southeast. Lake Victoria. Owen Falls Dam. Tobacco, grains, sugar. Main industrial center. D=RCC.
2802	Kabale	Rubale	960	2,490	542,164	87.00	471,683	99.11	C	South. Tobacco, grains. D=RCC,CURBZ.
2803	Kabarole	Karambe	3,230	8,360	973,738	85.00	827,677	99.01	C	West. Tea, cotton, peanuts. D=RCC,CURBZ.
2804	Kalangala	–	2,207	5,716	21,539	88.00	18,954	99.21	C	Central. Cotton, tobacco. D=RCC,CURBZ.
2805	Kampala	Kampala	70	180	1,015,899	89.00	904,150	99.26	C	South. Lake Victoria. Coffee, cotton, tea. D=RCC,CURBZ.
2806	Kamuli	Namwenda	1,680	4,350	631,342	85.00	536,641	99.01	C	East. Coffee, cotton. D=RCC,CURBZ.
2807	Kapchorwa	Kaptanya	670	1,740	152,745	87.00	132,888	99.11	C	East. Tea, cotton. D=RCC,CURBZ.
2808	Kasese	Rukoki	1,240	3,200	450,489	87.00	391,925	99.11	C	Southwest. Peanuts, coffee. D=RCC,CURBZ.
2809	Kibaale	–	1,822	4,718	288,024	88.00	253,461	99.21	C	West. Cotton, peanuts. D=RCC,CURBZ.
2810	Kiboga	–	1,457	3,774	184,923	86.37	159,720	99.48	C	Central. Cotton, tea. D=RCC,CURBZ.
2811	Kisoro	–	256	662	242,843	88.00	213,702	99.21	C	West. Tea, cotton, peanuts. Virunga Mountains. D=RCC,CURBZ.
2812	Kitgum	Labongo	8,230	16,140	460,076	90.00	414,068	99.31	C	North. Coffee, peanuts. D=RCC,CURBZ.
2813	Kotido	Kotido	5,100	13,210	250,461	89.00	222,910	99.26	C	Northeast. Coffee. D=RCC,CURBZ.
2814	Kumi	Kumi	1,100	2,860	311,271	88.00	273,918	99.21	C	East. Tea peanuts. D=RCC,CURBZ.
2815	Lira	Lira	2,800	7,250	654,458	90.00	589,012	99.31	C	North. Coffee, tea. D=RCC,CURBZ.
2816	Luwero	Luwero	3,550	9,200	589,969	88.00	519,173	99.21	C	Central. Cotton, peanuts. D=RCC,CURBZ.
2817	Masaka	Kasawa Bukoto	6,310	16,330	1,091,813	85.00	928,041	98.38	C	South. Coffee, processed meat and fish, beverages. D=RCC,CURBZ.
2818	Masindi	Nyangeya	3,720	9,640	332,942	87.00	289,660	99.11	C	West-central. Cotton, tea. D=RCC,CURBZ.
2819	Mbale	Bunkoko	980	2,550	928,034	87.00	807,390	99.11	C	Southeast. Coffee, cotton, bananas. D=RCC,CURBZ.
2820	Mbarara	Kakika	4,190	10,840	1,220,917	84.00	1,025,570	98.81	C	Southwest. Textiles, soap, oils and fats. Historic Ankele kingdom. D=RCC,CURBZ.
2821	Moroto	Katikekile	5,450	14,110	225,244	90.00	202,720	99.31	C	Northeast. Cattle, corn (maize), cassava. D=RCC,CURBZ.
2822	Moyo	Moyo	1,930	5,010	234,438	89.00	208,650	99.26	C	North. Borders Sudan. Cross-border skirmishes. D=RCC,CURBZ.
2823	Mpigi	Mpigi	2,400	6,220	1,202,266	85.00	1,021,926	99.01	C	Central. Cotton, peanuts. D=RCC,CURBZ.
2824	Mubende	Bageza	3,980	10,310	653,406	86.00	561,929	99.11	C	Central. Historic Chuezi religious center. D=RCC,CURBZ.
2825	Mukono	Kawuga Mukono	5,500	14,240	1,071,979	86.00	921,902	99.11	C	Central. Cotton, tea. D=RCC,CURBZ.
2826	Nebbi	Nebbi	1,120	2,890	414,897	90.00	373,407	99.31	C	North. Coffee, tea. D=RCC,CURBZ.
2827	Pallisa	–	741	1,919	466,250	89.00	414,963	99.26	C	East. Peanuts, cotton. D=RCC,CURBZ.
2828	Rakai	Byakabanda	1,920	4,970	501,710	88.00	441,505	99.21	C	Central. Cotton, tea. D=RCC,CURBZ.
2829	Rukungiri	Kagunga	1,060	2,750	509,592	88.00	448,441	99.21	C	Southwest. Tea, cotton. D=RCC,CURBZ.
2830	Soroti	Soroti	3,880	10,060	565,935	88.00	498,023	99.21	C	East. Corn, cassava. Home of novelist Oculi. D=RCC,CURBZ.
2831	Tororo	Sukulu	1,780	4,550	727,611	87.00	633,022	99.11	C	East. Novelist Oculi educated here. Apatite mining. D=RCC,CURBZ.
	UKRAINE		**233,100**	**603,700**	**50,455,980**	**82.59**	**41,669,097**	**98.51**	**C**	**Orthodox 54.3%, Independents 16.8%. Pent-char 8.0%, Evangelical 2.0%, GCC 12.1%**
2832	Cherkasy	Cherkasy	8,100	20,900	1,487,029	82.50	1,226,799	98.42	C	Central. Dnieper River. Winter wheat, sugar beets. 50% rural. D=ROC.
2833	Chernihiv	Chernihiv	12,300	31,900	1,365,520	83.00	1,133,382	98.92	C	North-central. 17th century cathedrals in Novhorod-Siverskyy and Nizhyn. D=ROC.
2834	Chernivtsi	Chernivtsi	3,100	8,100	911,704	84.00	765,831	99.42	C	West. Prut River. Carpathian foothills. Wheat corn. 60% rural. 75% Ukrainian. D=ROC.
2835	Crimea (Krym)	Simferopol	10,400	27,000	2,476,738	83.00	2,055,693	98.92	C	South. Winter wheat, corn, sunflowers (north); tobacco, flowers, wine (south). Tourism. D=ROC.
2836	Dnipropetrovsk	Dnipropetrovsk	12,300	31,900	3,796,701	81.00	3,075,328	97.42	C	East-central. Dnieper River. Iron ore. Hydroelectric dams. D=ROC.
2837	Donetsk	Donetsk	10,200	26,500	5,193,495	83.00	4,310,601	99.16	C	Southeast. Formerly: Stalino. Sea of Azov. Steppe. Winter wheat, corn. Coal mining. D=ROC.
2838	Ivano-Frankivsk	Ivano-Frankivsk	5,400	13,900	1,401,556	84.00	1,177,307	99.42	C	West. Formerly: Stanislav. Densely populated. Wheat, rye, corn (maize). D=ROC.
2839	Kharkiv	Kharkiv	12,100	31,400	3,103,255	83.00	2,575,702	98.92	C	Northeast. Steppe. Grains, sugar beets, sunflowers. D=ROC.
2840	Kherson	Kherson	11,000	28,500	1,222,634	80.85	988,457	96.77	C	South. Black Sea. Steppe. Lowest population density of any oblast (province) in the Ukraine. D=ROC.
2841	Khmelnytsky	Khmelnytsky	8,000	20,600	1,477,028	83.00	1,225,933	98.92	C	Central. Dnieper River. Site of 1654 insurrection. D=ROC.
2842	Kirovohrad	Kirovohrad	9,500	24,600	1,209,617	84.00	1,016,078	99.42	C	South-central. Wheat, corn (maize), sunflowers. D=ROC.
2843	Kyyiv (Kiev)	Kiev	11,200	28,900	4,458,285	80.00	3,566,628	96.52	C	North-central. Flax, potatoes, dairy. D=ROC.
2844	Luhansk	Luhansk	10,300	26,700	2,788,833	84.20	2,348,197	99.42	C	Extreme east. Donets River. Grain, iron and steel production. Coal mining. D=ROC.
2845	Lviv	Lviv	8,400	21,800	2,685,187	83.00	2,228,705	98.92	C	West. Carpathian Mountains. Rye, wheat, corn (maize). D=ROC.
2846	Mykolayiv	Mykolayiv	9,500	24,600	1,303,934	82.00	1,069,226	97.92	C	South. Black Sea. Shipbuilding. D=ROC.
2847	Odessa	Odessa	12,900	33,300	2,559,788	84.00	2,150,222	99.42	C	Southwest. Black Sea. Borders Moldovia, Romania. Winter wheat, corn (maize), sunflowers. D=ROC.
2848	Poltava	Poltava	11,100	28,800	1,706,557	83.00	1,416,442	98.92	C	Dnieper River. Wheat, corn (maize), sugar beets. D=ROC.
2849	Rivne	Rivne	7,800	20,100	1,143,080	83.00	948,756	98.92	C	Northwest. Rye, flax, potatoes. D=ROC.
2850	Sumy	Sumy	9,200	23,800	1,389,220	84.00	1,166,945	99.42	C	Northeast. Grains, sugar beets, tobacco. D=ROC.
2851	Ternopil	Ternopil	5,300	13,800	1,141,430	82.00	935,973	97.92	C	West. Volyn-Podilsk Upland. Severe soil erosion. Grains, sugar beets. D=ROC.
2852	Vinnytsya	Vinnytsya	10,200	26,500	1,859,545	83.00	1,543,422	98.92	C	West-central. Volyn-Podilsk Upland. 70% under plow. Sugar beets, dairying. D=ROC.
2853	Volyn	Volodymyr-Volynsky	7,800	20,200	1,038,369	82.00	851,463	97.92	C	Northwest. Sugar beets, grain, rye. D=ROC.
2854	Zakarpatska	Uzhhorod	4,900	12,800	1,229,627	81.00	995,998	96.92	C	West. Bordering Slovakia & Hungary. Mount Hoverla (6,762 ft.). Timber. 60% rural. D=ROC.
2855	Zaporizhzhya	Zaporizhzhya	10,500	27,200	2,039,436	83.00	1,692,732	98.92	C	Southeast. Berdyansk Gulf. Oil processing, flour milling, fishing. Numerous health resorts. D=ROC.
2856	Zhytomyr	Zhytomyr	11,600	29,900	1,467,411	82.00	1,203,277	97.92	C	Northwest. Pripet Marshes. Wheat, sugar beets. China, glass. D=ROC.
	UNITED ARAB EMIRATES		**32,280**	**83,600**	**2,441,436**	**10.76**	**262,745**	**57.88**	**B**	**Roman Catholics 5.0%, Orthodox 2.8%. Pent-char 2.2%, Evangelical 0.5%, GCC 5.6%**
2857	Abu Dhabi (Abu Zaby)	Abu Dhabi	26,000	67,350	1,008,429	12.06	121,613	61.22	B	East-central. Persian Gulf. Oil production. One of the world's highest per capita incomes. D=RCC.
2858	Ajman (Ajman)	Ajman	100	250	96,788	2.00	1,936	41.12	A	Smallest state of the country. Poorest member of United Arab Emirates.
2859	Al-Fujayrah (Fujairah)	Al-Fujayrah	440	1,150	81,901	1.00	819	38.12	A	Northeast. Tobacco, fishing. One of the poorer states of the country.
2860	Ash-Shariqah (Sharjah)	Ash-Shariqah	1,000	2,600	404,383	10.00	40,438	56.12	B	Northeast. Persian Gulf. Oil, natural gas. Fishing. D=RCC.
2861	Dubayy (Dubai)	Dubayy	1,510	3,900	630,683	14.00	88,296	62.12	B	Northeast. Persian Gulf. Oil industry. International airport. D=RCC.
2862	Ra's al-Khaymah	Ra's al-Khaymah	660	1,700	175,268	5.00	8,763	50.12	B	Northeast. Persian Gulf. Borders Oman. Cabbages, onions, tomatoes. D=RCC.
2863	Umm al-Qaywayn	Umm al-Qaywayn	290	750	43,985	2.00	880	41.12	A	Northeast. Persian Gulf. Desert. Pearl diving, fishing. Sparsely populated.

Continued opposite

Table 11-3 continued

Rec No 1	Country Major civil divisions 2	Capital 3	sq.mi. 4	sq.km. 5	Pop 2000 6	AC% 7	Church members 8	E% 9	W 10	Notes 11
	USA		**3,679,192**	**9,529,063**	**278,357,141**	**68.91**	**191,827,627**	**98.53**	**C**	**Independents 28.2%, Protestants 23.2%. Pent-char 27.0%, Evangelical 14.6%, GCC 35.4%**
2864	Alabama	Montgomery	51,705	133,915	4,513,311	73.20	3,303,676	99.32	C	South-central. Gulf of Mexico. Cotton, soybeans, corn (maize). D=SBC,NBC,UMC.
2865	Alaska	Juneau	591,004	1,530,693	640,555	62.70	401,628	95.32	C	Extreme northwest. Bering Sea. Oil, natural gas, fishing. Eskimos (Inuit). D=RCC,SBC.
2866	Arizona	Phoenix	114,000	295,259	4,181,648	65.60	2,743,161	96.72	C	Southwest. Borders Mexico. Citrus fruits, cotton, coal. Grand Canyon National Park. D=RCC,SBC.
2867	Arkansas	Little Rock	53,187	137,754	2,617,893	70.70	1,850,850	99.42	C	South-central. Mississippi River, Arkansas River. Rice, soybeans, corn (maize). D=SBC,UMC.
2868	California	Sacramento	158,706	411,047	33,683,357	65.70	22,129,966	96.62	C	West. Pacific Ocean. Almonds, broccoli, dates. 91% urban. D=Independents,RCC,LDS.
2869	Colorado	Denver	104,091	269,594	3,786,604	64.60	2,446,146	97.22	C	West-central. Rocky Mountains. Gold discovered (1859). Alfalfa, wheat. Ski resorts. D=RCC,UMC.
2870	Connecticut	Hartford	5,018	12,997	3,580,369	70.90	2,538,482	99.42	C	Northeast. Colonized by Puritans in 1630s. Guns, ammunition. Yale University (1701). D=RCC,UCC.
2871	Delaware	Dover	2,045	5,294	751,870	66.40	499,242	97.52	C	East. Atlantic Ocean. First settlement by Swedes in 1638. Poultry, soybeans. D=RCC,UMC.
2872	District of Columbia	–	69	179	642,754	70.70	454,427	99.82	C	East. Potomac River. F=1790. Site of government for United States of America. Tourism. D=NBC.
2873	Florida	Tallahassee	58,664	151,939	14,718,663	65.80	9,684,880	97.62	C	Southeast. Gulf of Mexico. Low-lying plain. Citrus fruits. Fastest growing state. D=RCC,SBC.
2874	Georgia	Atlanta	58,910	152,576	7,366,972	69.60	5,127,413	99.22	C	Southeast. Atlantic Ocean. Last of 13 American colonies. Cotton, peanuts, tobacco. D=SBC,NBC.
2875	Hawaii	Honolulu	6,471	16,760	1,265,829	63.50	803,801	97.12	C	Central Pacific Ocean. Eight islands and 124 islets. Sugarcane. Pearl Harbor (1941). D=RCC,LDS.
2876	Idaho	Boise	83,564	216,430	1,164,368	67.60	787,113	97.22	C	Northwest. Rocky Mountains. Settled (1809). Gold (1860). Potatoes. D=Many Mormons,RCC.
2877	Illinois	Springfield	57,871	149,885	12,692,223	70.20	8,909,941	99.82	C	Mid-west. Lake Michigan. Flat prairie. Soybean, pork. Nuclear power stations. D=RCC,ELCA.
2878	Indiana	Indianapolis	36,413	94,309	6,178,610	66.80	4,127,311	97.42	C	North-central. Lake Michigan. Corn, soybeans, wheat. University of Notre Dame. D=RCC,UMC.
2879	Iowa	Des Moines	56,275	145,752	3,068,581	70.40	2,160,281	99.52	C	Midwest. Permanent settlement: 1830's. Livestock, corn (maize), soybeans. D=ELCA,RCC.
2880	Kansas	Topeka	82,277	213,096	2,753,203	68.80	1,894,204	98.42	C	Central. Cattle, wheat, sorghum. D=RCC,UMC,LCMS.
2881	Kentucky	Frankfort	40,410	104,659	4,097,612	70.30	2,880,621	99.92	C	East south-central. Tobacco, cattle, dairy products. D=SBC,RCC,UMC.
2882	Louisiana	Baton Rouge	47,752	123,677	4,678,154	73.10	3,419,731	99.72	C	South-central. Gulf of Mexico. Acquired from France (1803). Soybeans. Mardi Gras. D=RCC,SBC.
2883	Maine	Augusta	33,265	86,156	1,347,694	63.80	859,829	93.42	C	Northeast. Atlantic Ocean. Borders Canada. Potatoes, apples, . Acadia National Park. D=RCC.
2884	Maryland	Annapolis	10,460	27,091	5,355,814	67.00	3,588,395	96.62	C	East-central. Atlantic Ocean. Chesapeake Bay. Poultry, corn (maize), soybeans. D=RCC,NBC.
2885	Massachusetts	Boston	8,284	21,455	6,545,262	71.70	4,692,953	99.62	C	Northeast. First permanent European settlement (1620). Harvard University. D=RCC,UCC.
2886	Michigan	Lansing	97,102	251,493	10,298,045	67.60	6,961,478	98.22	C	North-central. Lake Michigan. Grains, potatoes. Automobile industry. D=RCC,NBC,LCMS.
2887	Minnesota	St. Paul	86,614	224,329	4,888,759	71.60	3,500,351	99.52	C	Northern Midwest. Borders Canada. Grains, meats, dairy products. D=ELCA,RCC.
2888	Mississippi	Jackson	47,689	123,514	2,852,493	73.00	2,082,320	99.72	C	South-central. Low-lying land. Mississippi Territory (1798). Soybeans, cotton, poultry. D=SBC,NBC.
2889	Missouri	Jefferson City	69,697	180,514	5,666,823	69.60	3,944,109	99.22	C	Midwest. Livestock, soybeans, corn (maize). Part of the Louisiana Purchase (1803). D=SBC,RCC.
2890	Montana	Helena	147,046	380,847	899,177	65.50	588,961	95.12	C	North. Rocky Mountains. Livestock, barley, wheat. American Indians. D=RCC,ELCA.
2891	Nebraska	Lincoln	77,355	200,349	1,752,537	71.30	1,249,559	99.62	C	West north-central. Rolling plains. Missouri River. Corn (maize), hay, wheat. D=RCC,UMC.
2892	Nevada	Carson City	110,561	286,352	1,448,070	62.60	906,492	95.22	C	West. Gold, silver. Tourism. Legal and state-regulated gambling. D=RCC,LDS.
2893	New Hampshire	Concord	9,279	24,032	1,212,357	64.60	783,183	96.22	C	Northeast. Atlantic Ocean. Dairy, lumber, paper. D=RCC,UCC.
2894	New Jersey	Trenton	7,787	20,168	8,499,691	70.60	6,000,782	99.62	C	Northeast. Atlantic Ocean. Chemicals, clothing, electrical machinery. D=RCC,NBC.
2895	New Mexico	Santa Fe	121,593	314,924	1,725,258	69.90	1,205,955	99.52	C	Southwest. First Spanish settlement: 1610. Cattle, milk, hay. Navajo, Pueblo, Ute. D=RCC,SBC.
2896	New York	Albany	52,735	136,583	19,772,209	71.80	14,196,446	99.62	C	Northeast. Atlantic Ocean, Lake Ontario. Borders Canada. Dairy, cattle, hay. D=RCC,NBC.
2897	North Carolina	Raleigh	52,669	136,412	7,467,376	70.20	5,242,098	99.82	C	Southeast. Atlantic Ocean. Tobacco, corn (maize), soybeans. D=SBC,NBC,UMC.
2898	North Dakota	Bismarck	70,702	183,117	696,199	74.60	519,364	99.62	C	West north-central. Barley, sunflower. Sioux, Ojibwa, Arikara, Hidatsa, Mandan. D=ELCA,RCC.
2899	Ohio	Columbus	44,787	115,998	12,021,104	67.50	8,114,245	98.12	C	Midwest. Lake Erie. Corn (maize), wheat, oats. D=RCC,UMC,NBC.
2900	Oklahoma	Oklahoma City	69,956	181,185	3,505,073	72.10	2,527,158	99.82	C	West south-central. Livestock, livestock products, wheat. D=SBC,UMC,AoG.
2901	Oregon	Salem	97,073	251,418	3,248,623	62.70	2,036,887	96.32	C	Northwest. Pacific Ocean. Livestock, wheat, vegetables. D=RCC,LDS,ELCA.
2902	Pennsylvania	Harrisburg	46,043	119,251	13,104,720	70.60	9,251,932	99.52	C	East. Lake Erie. Quaker colony (1682). Dairy, poultry. D=Quakers,Amish,RCC,ELCA.
2903	Rhode Island	Providence	1,212	3,139	1,096,699	74.80	820,331	99.62	C	Northeast. Atlantic Ocean. Smallest state in USA. Jewelry, textiles, fishing. D=RCC,ECUS.
2904	South Carolina	Columbia	31,113	80,582	3,931,739	70.80	2,783,671	99.52	C	South. Atlantic Ocean. Textiles, chemicals, paper. Tourism. D=SBC,NBC,UMC.
2905	South Dakota	Pierre	77,116	199,730	775,865	72.40	561,726	99.82	C	North-central. Missouri River. Cattle, wheat. Dakota Indians. Mount Rushmore. D=RCC,ELCA.
2906	Tennessee	Nashville	42,144	109,152	5,482,411	70.60	3,870,582	99.32	C	East south-central. Mississippi River. Great Smoky Mountains. Chemicals. D=SBC,UMC.
2907	Texas	Austin	266,807	691,027	19,266,963	71.40	13,756,612	99.32	C	South-central. Gulf of Mexico. Spanish explorations (1528). Cattle, cotton, oil. D=SBC,RCC.
2908	Utah	Salt Lake City	84,899	219,887	1,978,423	75.60	1,495,688	99.42	C	West-central. Pueblo Indians AD 400-1250. Mormons (70%) arrived in 1847. Livestock, hay. D=LDS.
2909	Vermont	Montpelier	9,614	24,900	622,017	65.40	406,799	98.02	C	Northeast. Green Mountains. Originally settled by Abnaki Indians. Dairy. Ski resorts. D=RCC,UCC.
2910	Virginia	Richmond	40,767	105,586	6,958,845	66.90	4,655,467	97.52	C	East. Atlantic Ocean. Great Britain's first American colony: 1607 (Jamestown). Tobacco. D=SBC,NBC.
2911	Washington	Olympia	68,139	176,479	5,604,610	62.90	3,525,300	97.52	C	Northwest. Pacific Ocean. Olympic Mountains. Lumber, paper. Aircraft industry. D=RCC,ELCA.
2912	West Virginia	Charleston	24,232	62,758	1,977,338	65.20	1,289,224	97.82	C	East-central. Appalachian Mountains. Adena Indians. Forests cover 75%. Coal mining. D=UMC,ARC.
2913	Wisconsin	Madison	66,215	171,496	5,463,844	71.50	3,906,648	99.82	C	North-central. Lake Superior, Lake Michigan. Milk, butter, cheese. D=RCC,ELCA,LCMS.
2914	Wyoming	Cheyenne	97,809	253,324	508,531	66.90	340,207	98.52	C	West. Rocky Mountains. Barley, wheat, wool. Coal mining. Yellowstone National Park. D=RCC,LDS.
	URUGUAY		**68,037**	**176,215**	**3,337,058**	**64.78**	**2,161,729**	**98.71**	**C**	**Roman Catholics 78.1%, Protestants 3.3%. Pent-char 9.1%, Evangelical 1.9%, GCC 26.7%**
2915	Artigas	Artigas	4,605	11,928	78,078	69.00	53,874	99.33	C	Northwest. Sugarcane, oranges, grapes. One of the least densely populated regions. D=RCC.
2916	Canelones	Canelones	1,751	4,536	411,309	66.00	271,464	98.13	C	South. Grains, grapes, sugar beets. Wine-processing school in capital. D=RCC.
2917	Cerro Largo	Melo	5,270	13,648	88,547	69.00	61,097	99.33	C	Northeast. Borders Brazil. Wool, hides, textiles. D=RCC.
2918	Colonia	Colonia	2,358	6,106	127,280	67.00	85,278	98.23	C	Southwest. Rio de la Plata. Tourism. F=1680 by Portuguese soldiers. D=RCC.
2919	Durazno	Durazno	4,495	11,643	62,193	69.00	42,913	98.43	C	Central. Yi River. Livestock, dairy, grains. D=RCC.
2920	Flores	Trinidad	1,986	5,144	27,935	70.00	19,555	98.43	C	South-central. Rolling hills. Livestock, wool, wheat. D=RCC.
2921	Florida	Florida	4,022	10,417	75,062	69.00	51,793	98.43	C	South-central. Wheat, corn (maize), oats. D=RCC.
2922	Lavalleja	Minas	3,867	10,016	69,407	68.00	47,197	98.33	C	Southeast. Livestock, milk, vegetables. D=RCC.
2923	Maldonado	Maldonado	1,851	4,793	106,499	68.00	72,419	99.23	C	Southeast. Atlantic Ocean. Grains, wool, fishing. Colonial buildings and Spanish ruins. D=RCC.
2924	Montevideo	Montevideo	205	530	1,481,483	62.09	919,882	98.66	C	South. On Rio de la Plata. Wool, meat, hides. University. D=RCC.
2925	Paysandú	Paysandú	5,375	13,922	117,169	65.00	76,160	98.96	C	West. Uruguay River. Textiles, flour, leather goods. D=RCC.
2926	Rivera	Rivera	3,618	9,370	101,035	67.00	67,693	99.13	C	North. Livestock, rice, sweet potatoes. D=RCC.
2927	Rocha	Rocha	4,074	10,551	75,206	66.00	49,636	99.03	C	Southeast. Atlantic Ocean. Wool, hides. D=RCC.
2928	Río Negro	Fray Bentos	3,584	9,282	54,929	69.00	37,901	99.33	C	West. Bordering Argentina. Rio Negro. Livestock. D=RCC.
2929	Salto	Salto	5,468	14,163	122,503	65.00	79,627	98.93	C	Northwest. Livestock, oranges and tangerines, corn (maize). D=RCC.
2930	San José	San José de Mayo	1,927	4,992	101,507	65.00	65,980	98.93	C	South. Meat and dairy products, leather goods, clothing. Baroque style Basilica Cathedral. D=RCC.
2931	Soriano	Mercedes	3,478	9,008	89,702	67.00	60,100	99.13	C	Southwest. Negro River. Tourism. D=RCC.
2932	Tacuarembó	Tacuarembó	5,961	15,438	94,286	67.00	63,172	99.13	C	North-central. Haedo Mountains. Orchids, hardwoods. D=RCC.
2933	Treinta y Tres	Trienta y Tres	3,679	9,529	52,923	68.00	35,988	99.13	C	East-central. Livestock, wheat, corn (maize). 'Thirty-three'. D=RCC.
	UZBEKISTAN		**172,700**	**447,400**	**24,317,851**	**1.62**	**394,334**	**48.36**	**A**	**Orthodox 0.7%, Independents 0.4%. Pent-char 0.6%, Evangelical 0.05%, GCC 1.0%**
2934	Andijon	Andijon	1,600	4,200	2,127,788	1.60	34,045	49.34	A	Eastern Fergana Valley. Cotton, grapes, silkworms. Most densely settled region in Uzbekistan.
2935	Bukhoro	Bukhara (Bukhoro)	15,200	39,400	1,414,059	0.60	8,484	42.34	A	Central. Kimirekkum Desert. Karakul sheep raising.
2936	Farghona	Fergana (Farghona)	2,700	7,100	2,619,689	1.80	47,154	49.54	A	East. Cotton, raw silk production. Oil fields at Chimion and Severny Sokh. D=ROC.
2937	Jizzakh	Jizzakh	7,900	20,500	931,131	0.30	2,793	41.04	A	East. Cotton, building materials.
2938	Khorazm	Urgench	2,400	6,300	1,271,751	1.40	17,805	49.14	A	South-central. Amu Darya. Ancient Persian empire.
2939	Namangan	Namangan	3,100	7,900	1,851,051	1.50	27,766	49.24	A	East. Fergana Valley. Cotton, grain, raw silk production. Uzbeks, Tajiks, Russians, Tatars, Kyrgyz.
2940	Nawoiy	Nawoiy	42,800	110,800	801,103	0.60	4,807	42.34	A	Central. Zeravshan River. World's 40 largest gold mine.
2941	Qashqadaryo	Qarshi (Karshi)	11,000	28,400	2,030,322	1.70	34,515	49.44	A	South. Karshi Steppe, Kashka River. Cotton, grains, sheep. 85% Uzbek.
2942	Qoraqalpoghiston	Nuqus	63,700	164,900	1,504,813	1.40	21,067	49.14	A	West. Aral Sea. Cotton, alfalfa, rice.
2943	Samarqand	Samarkand	6,300	16,400	2,601,767	1.40	36,425	49.14	A	Central. Cotton, grapes, tobacco. Uzbeks, Russians, Tatars, Tajiks. D=ROC.
2944	Sirdaryo	Guliston	2,000	5,100	672,291	0.40	2,689	42.14	A	Northeast. Golodnaya Steppe. Cotton.
2945	Surkhondaryo	Termiz	8,000	20,800	1,610,134	0.50	8,051	42.24	A	Southernmost on Amu Darya. Borders Afghanistan. Cotton. 80% rural, 70% Uzbek.
2946	Toshkent	Tashkent	6,000	15,600	4,881,954	3.05	148,734	52.64	B	Northeast. Cotton, wheat, rice. Uzbeks, Russians, Tatars, Jews, Ukrainians. D=RCC.
	VANUATU		**4,707**	**12,190**	**190,417**	**89.31**	**170,054**	**99.32**	**C**	**Protestants 53.7%, Anglicans 18.1%. Pent-char 24.7%, Evangelical 27.9%, GCC 15.1%**
2947	Ambae/Maéwo	Longana	270	699	14,686	90.00	13,217	99.41	C	Northeast. Highest rainfall (more than 100 inches). D=Presbyterian.
2948	Ambrym	Eas	257	666	9,345	91.00	8,504	99.51	C	East-central. Copra. Active volcanoes: Mt. Marum, Mt. Benbow.
2949	Banks/Torres	Sola	341	882	7,970	91.00	7,253	99.51	C	North. Coral reefs. Polynesians.
2950	Malekula	Lakatoro	793	2,053	25,699	88.00	22,615	99.01	C	West-central. Copra, coffee. D=Presbyterian,Church of Melanesia.
2951	Paama	Liro	23	60	2,256	91.00	2,053	99.51	C	Central. Copra, coffee.
2952	Pentecost	Loltong	193	499	15,006	90.00	13,505	99.41	C	East-central. Copra. Known for 'land divers'.
2953	Santo/Malo	Luganville	1,640	4,248	33,843	90.00	30,459	99.41	C	Northwest. Copra, cocoa. D=Presbyterian.
2954	Shepherd	Morua	33	86	5,313	90.00	4,782	99.41	C	South. Copra, coffee.
2955	Taféa	Isangel	629	1,628	29,972	89.00	26,675	99.31	C	South. Copra, cocoa. D=Presbyterian,Church of Melanesia.
2956	Éfaté	Vila	356	923	41,386	88.19	36,496	99.24	C	South. Copra, cocoa, coffee. D=Presbyterian,Church of Melanesia.
2957	Épi	Ringdove	172	446	4,940	91.00	4,495	99.51	C	Central. Copra.
	VENEZUELA		**352,144**	**912,050**	**24,169,722**	**94.07**	**22,735,834**	**99.38**	**C**	**Roman Catholics 94.4%, Protestants 2.0%. Pent-char 15.1%, Evangelical 1.2%, GCC 7.7%**
2958	Amazonas	Puerto Ayacucho	67,900	175,750	74,989	94.00	70,490	99.36	C	South. Borders Brazil, Colombia. Rubber, banana, vanilla. D=RCC.
2959	Anzoátegui	Barcelona	16,700	43,300	1,150,948	94.00	1,081,891	99.36	C	Northeast. Caribbean Sea. Cattle raising. Relatively little agriculture. Orinoco Heavy Oil Belt. D=RCC.
2960	Apure	San Fernando	29,500	76,500	380,047	95.00	361,045	99.51	C	Southwest. Borders Colombia. Cattle raising. D=RCC.
2961	Aragua	Maracay	2,700	7,014	1,488,367	94.00	1,399,056	99.36	C	North. Caribbean Sea. Sugarcane, potatoes, beans. Henri Pittier National Park. D=RCC.
2962	Barinas	Barinas	13,600	35,200	568,259	94.00	534,163	99.36	C	West. Beans, cotton, corn (maize). D=RCC.
2963	Bolívar	Ciudad Bolívar	91,900	238,000	1,206,528	95.00	1,146,202	99.51	C	Southeast. Borders Brazil, Guyana, Colombia. Caroni River. Hydroelectric power. D=RCC.
2964	Carabobo	Valencia	1,795	4,650	1,941,266	93.56	1,816,196	99.47	C	Northwest. Caribbean Sea. Rice, cotton, corn (maize). D=RCC.
2965	Cojedes	San Carlos	5,700	14,800	244,774	95.00	232,535	99.51	C	Northwest. Coffee, corn (maize), cotton. D=RCC.
2966	Delta Amacuro	Tucupita	15,500	40,200	113,445	95.00	107,773	99.51	C	Northeast. Atlantic Ocean. Borders Guyana. Bananas, cotton, peanuts. D=RCC.
2967	Distrito Federal	Caracas	745	1,930	2,824,969	94.00	2,655,471	99.36	C	North. Sugar, tobacco, clothing. D=RCC.
2968	Falcón	Coro	9,600	24,800	787,802	94.00	740,534	99.36	C	Northwest. Caribbean Sea, Gulf of Venezuela. Corn (maize), coconuts, sesame. D=RCC.
2969	Gu‡rico	San Juan	25,091	64,986	654,813	95.00	622,072	99.51	C	North-central. Orinoco River. Rice, cotton, corn (maize). D=RCC.
2970	Lara	Barquisimeto	7,600	19,800	1,582,046	95.00	1,502,944	99.51	C	Northwest. Segovia Highlands. Cacao, corn (maize), sisal. D=RCC.
2971	Miranda	Los Teques	3,070	7,950	2,523,696	93.00	2,347,037	99.21	C	North. Caribbean Sea. Cacao, coffee, sugarcane. D=RCC.
2972	Monagas	Maturín	11,200	28,900	626,714	95.00	595,378	99.51	C	Northeast. Gulf of Paria. Livestock, corn (maize), coffee. D=RCC.
2973	Mérida	Mérida	4,400	11,300	766,618	95.00	728,287	99.51	C	Northwest. Andes Mountains. Coffee, sugarcane, livestock, oil. D=RCC.
2974	Nueva Esparta	La Asunción	440	1,150	349,712	95.00	332,226	99.51	C	Northeast. Island state off the Peninsula de Araya. Fishing, tourism. D=RCC.
2975	Portuguesa	Guanare	5,900	15,200	779,164	94.00	732,414	99.36	C	Northwest. Livestock, rice, coffee. Shrine of Our Lady of Coromoto. D=RCC.
2976	Sucre	Cumaná	4,600	11,800	900,141	95.00	855,134	99.51	C	Northeast. Caribbean Sea, Gulf of Paria. Cacao, bananas, seafood industry. D=RCC.
2977	Trujillo	Trujillo	2,900	7,400	648,031	95.00	615,629	99.51	C	Northwest. Coffee, corn (maize), garlic. D=RCC.

Continued overleaf

Table 11-3 concluded

Rec No 1	Country Major civil divisions 2	Capital 3	sq.mi. 4	sq.km. 5	Pop 2000 6	AC% 7	Church members 8	E% 9	W 10	Notes 11
2978	Táchira	San Cristóbal	4,300	11,100	1,070,968	94.00	1,006,710	99.36	C	West. Borders Colombia. Coffee, sugarcane. Large coal deposits at Labatera. D=RCC.
2979	Yaracuy	San Felipe	2,700	7,100	513,126	95.00	487,470	99.51	C	Northwest. Peanuts, sugarcane, bananas. Mining: coal, copper, lead. D=RCC.
2980	Zulia	Maracaibo	24,400	63,100	2,973,299	93.00	2,765,168	99.19	C	Northwest. Gulf of Venezuela. Borders Colombia. Oil refineries. D=RCC.
	VIET NAM		**127,816**	**331,041**	**79,831,650**	**8.23**	**6,567,922**	**66.78**	**B**	**Roman Catholics 6.6%, Independents 0.8%. Pent-char 1.0%, Evangelical 0.7%, GCC 7.0%**
2981	Central Highlands	De Lat	21,455	55,569	3,314,259	15.00	497,159	73.55	B	South-central. Bordering Cambodia. Mekong River, densely forested. Lumber. D=RCC.
2982	Mekong River Delta	Long Xuyen	15,280	39,575	17,728,821	8.00	1,418,306	70.50	B	Southernmost. On South China Sea and Gulf of Thailand. Meking River. Fruits, rice. D=RCC.
2983	North Central Coast	Hue	19,760	51,178	10,863,235	5.20	564,888	59.75	B	North. Bordering Laos. Song Ma River. Marble, beeswax, coffee. D=RCC.
2984	North Mountains	Thai Nguyen	39,745	102,938	13,822,379	4.70	649,652	59.25	B	Northernmost. Bordering China. Limestone, copper, cement. D=RCC.
2985	Northeastern South region	Ho Chi Minh City	9,067	23,484	9,922,667	16.00	1,587,627	74.55	B	South. South China Sea. Sugarcane, tobacco, shipbuilding, tourism. D=RCC.
2986	Red River Delta	Hanoi	4,813	12,466	15,762,304	9.02	1,420,972	71.57	B	North of Gulf of Tonkin. Rice, livestock, vegetables, shipbuilding. D=RCC.
2987	South Central Coast	Da Nang	17,693	45,824	8,417,984	5.10	429,317	59.65	B	Central. On South China Sea. Saigon River. Textiles, fishing. Chinese. D=RCC.
	VIRGIN IS OF THE US		**136**	**352**	**92,954**	**92.69**	**86,159**	**99.58**	**C**	**Protestants 43.0%, Roman Catholics 31.2%. Pent-char 24.0%, Evangelical 19.9%, GCC 12.8%**
2988	St. Croix	Christiansted	84	217	48,029	92.34	44,350	99.29	C	Caribbean island. First settled (1625). Hurricane (1989). Tourism. D=RCC.
2989	St. John	*	20	52	2,965	94.00	2,787	99.94	C	Caribbean island. One half is US National Park. Wildlife, ecotourism. D=Anglican.
2990	St. Thomas	Charlotte Amalie	32	83	41,959	93.00	39,022	99.89	C	Caribbean island. Over 40 beaches. Settled 1666. Hurricane (1995). D=RCC.
	WALLIS & FUTUNA IS		**97**	**240**	**14,517**	**96.58**	**14,021**	**99.97**	**C**	**Roman Catholics 96.0%, Marginals 0.3%. Pent-char 2.2%, Evangelical 0.1%, GCC 12.9%**
2991	Wallis & Futuna Islands	Mata-utu	93	240	14,517	96.59	14,021	99.97	C	French oversees territory. Pacific Ocean islands. Subsistence crops. D=RCC.
	YEMEN		**182,278**	**472,099**	**18,112,066**	**0.17**	**30,656**	**46.59**	**A**	**Orthodox 0.07%, Independents 0.04%. Pent-char 0.05%, Evangelical 0.01%, GCC 0.1%**
2992	'Adan	Aden	2,695	6,980	697,068	0.50	3,485	59.92	B	South on Gulf of Aden. Mentioned in Ezekiel. Trade center, refueling. British crown colony (1937).
2993	Abyan	Zinjibar	8,297	21,489	745,545	0.05	373	38.47	A	South. Gulf of Aden. Cotton. Wadi Bana.
2994	al-Bayda'	al-Bayda'	4,310	11,170	533,216	0.05	267	38.47	A	South central. High plateau. Historic capital of Sultanate. Grains.
2995	al-Hadaydah	al-Hudaydah	5,240	13,580	1,817,910	0.10	1,818	41.52	A	West. Red Sea. Tihamah coastal plain. Port facilities, imports, exports.
2996	al-Jawf	al-Jawf	–	–	138,778	0.02	28	36.44	A	West. Desert. Ancient Ma'in kingdom. Camels, nomadic tribes.
2997	al-Mahrah	al-Ghaydah	25,618	66,350	145,429	0.02	29	36.44	A	Far east. Bordering Oman. Gulf of Aden. Fisheries, frankincense.
2998	al-Mahwit	al-Mahwit	830	2,160	495,155	0.05	248	38.47	A	North. Yemen Highlands. Desert nomads.
2999	Dhamar	Dhamar	3,430	8,870	1,327,622	0.10	1,328	41.52	A	Central. Yemen Highlands. Center for Zaydi sect of Islam. Grain, horses, handicrafts.
3000	Hadramawt	al-Mukalla	59,991	155,376	1,176,824	0.10	1,177	41.52	A	East. Gulf of Aden. Former Saudi Arabian kingdom.
3001	Hajjah	Hajjah	3,700	9,590	1,489,335	0.10	1,489	41.52	A	North. West edge of Yemen. Highlands. Trade center.
3002	Ibb	Ibb	2,480	6,430	2,221,023	0.15	3,332	46.57	A	Southwest. Yemen Highlands. Biblical origins. Fertile agricultural region. 60 mosques.
3003	Lahij	Lahij	4,928	12,766	655,276	0.05	328	38.47	A	Southwest. Wadi Tibban. Agriculture. Trade center.
3004	Ma'rib	Ma'rib	15,400	39,890	184,330	0.02	37	36.44	A	North-central. Ancient city. Principal caravan route. Ma'rib Dam. Bedouin tribes.
3005	Sa'dah	Sa'dah	4,950	12,810	562,503	0.05	281	38.47	A	Northwest. Yemen Highlands. Capital of Zaydi dynasty (AD 860-1962). Leather goods.
3006	San'a	San'a	7,840	20,310	2,936,996	0.30	8,811	57.26	B	North. Yemen Highlands. Chief economic & religious center. Cotton textiles.
3007	Shabwah	`Ataq	28,536	73,908	387,817	0.05	194	38.47	A	Central. Oil and natural gas deposits.
3008	Ta'izz	Ta'izz	4,020	10,420	2,597,238	0.29	7,431	54.71	B	Southwest. Former national capital. Coffee growing. Many mosques.
	YUGOSLAVIA		**39,449**	**102,173**	**10,640,150**	**64.71**	**6,885,557**	**93.39**	**C**	**Orthodox 56.8%, Roman Catholics 5.1%. Pent-char 2.3%, Evangelical 0.4%, GCC 13.1%**
3009	Kosovo	Pristina	4,203	10,887	2,164,457	15.00	324,669	71.33	B	Southeast. Wheat, barley. Albanian majority. Ethnic cleansing (1999).
3010	Montenegro	Podgorica	5,333	13,812	644,004	80.00	515,203	99.28	C	Southwest. Adriatic Sea. Dinaric Alps. Cereals, livestock. D=Serbian Orthodox.
3011	Serbia	Belgrade	21,609	55,968	5,836,284	76.24	4,449,361	98.92	C	Grain, sugar beets, dairy, coal, lead. D=Serbian Orthodox.
3012	Vojvodina	Novi Sad	8,304	21,506	1,995,406	80.00	1,596,325	99.28	C	East. Borders Hungary. Wheat, corn (maize), sugar. D=Serbian Orthodox.
	ZAMBIA		**290,586**	**752,614**	**9,168,700**	**76.91**	**7,052,080**	**98.76**	**C**	**Roman Catholics 33.4%, Protestants 29.5%. Pent-char 22.0%, Evangelical 12.5%, GCC 16.4%**
3013	Central	Kabwe	36,446	94,395	850,922	78.00	663,719	99.35	C	Central. Formerly: Broken Hill. Corn (maize), tobacco. D=RCC,NAC,UCZ.
3014	Copperbelt	Ndola	12,096	31,328	1,852,330	75.00	1,389,248	97.33	C	Central. Plateau. Corn, tobacco. Remains of Wilton culture (3,000 BC). Bemba, Lamba. D=RCC.
3015	Eastern	Chipata	26,682	69,106	1,141,997	76.00	867,918	97.85	C	Southeast. Tobacco, peanuts, cotton. Roman Catholic episcopal see. D=RCC.
3016	Luapula	Mansa	19,524	50,567	617,668	79.00	487,958	99.95	C	North. Livestock, agriculture. Seat of Roman Catholic bishopric. D=RCC,AACJM.
3017	Lusaka	Lusaka	8,454	21,896	1,416,599	76.00	1,076,615	98.35	C	South-central. Corn (maize), tobacco, hides. Nyanja, Soli. D=RCC,NAC,UCZ.
3018	North-Western	Solwezi	48,582	125,827	449,316	78.92	354,580	99.87	C	Northwest. Borders Zaire. Corn, pineapples, hardwood. D=RCC,NAC,UCZ.
3019	Northern	Kasama	57,076	147,826	1,017,664	77.00	783,601	99.25	C	North. Borders Tanzania, Zaire. Lake Tanganyika. Corn, coffee. D=RCC,NAC,UCZ.
3020	Southern	Livingstone	32,928	85,283	1,109,789	78.00	865,635	99.85	C	South. Borders Zimbabwe. Zambezi River. Cattle. D=RCC.
3021	Western	Mongu	48,798	126,386	712,413	79.00	562,806	99.95	C	West. Zambezi River. Lozi royal village. Cattle, timber. D=RCC,NAC,UCZ.
	ZIMBABWE		**150,872**	**390,757**	**11,669,029**	**59.28**	**6,917,360**	**98.22**	**B**	**Independents 40.2%, Protestants 12.3%. Pent-char 42.2%, Evangelical 4.5%, GCC 25.1%**
3022	Bulawayo	–	185	479	696,585	59.00	410,985	97.94	B	Matabeleland. Matsheumlope River. Principle industrial center. 'Place of Slaughter'. D=RCC,AACJM.
3023	Harare	–	337	872	1,658,975	59.76	991,468	98.70	B	North. Center of industry & commerce. Tobacco, gold. F=1890. D=Anglican,RCC,AACJM.
3024	Manicaland	Mutare	13,463	34,870	1,725,013	60.00	1,035,008	98.94	C	East. Borders Mozambique. Tea, tobacco, livestock. Tourism around national parks. D=RCC.
3025	Mashonaland Central	Bindura	10,534	27,284	961,766	58.00	557,824	96.94	B	Central. Middle Veld. Subsistence farming. Shona. D=RCC,AACJM.
3026	Mashonaland East	Marondera	9,627	24,934	1,159,229	59.00	683,945	97.94	B	Northeast. Timber, tobacco, corn (maize). D=RCC,AACJM.
3027	Mashonaland West	Chinhoyi	23,346	60,467	1,253,005	60.00	751,803	98.94	C	Northeast. Borders Zambia, Mozambique. Cattle. Shona. D=AACJM,RCC.
3028	Masvingo (Victoria)	Masvingo	17,108	44,310	1,370,704	58.00	795,008	96.94	B	South-central. Cattle, grain, cotton. Great Zimbabwe ruins (8th century). D=AACJM,RCC.
3029	Matabeleland North	Bulawayo	28,393	73,537	719,046	57.00	409,856	97.45	B	Northwest. Ndebele. Rhodes Matopos National Park. D=RCC,AACJM.
3030	Matabeleland South	Gwanda	25,633	66,390	663,841	61.00	404,943	99.44	C	Southwest. Corn (maize), peanuts, cattle. Mining: gold, coal, tin. Ndebele. D=RCC,AACJM.
3031	Midlands	Gweru	22,767	58,967	1,460,866	60.00	876,520	98.44	C	Central. Ferrochromium, textiles, dairy. Training section of Zimbabwe's airforce. D=AACJM,RCC.

Part 12

DICTIONARY

A survey dictionary of Christianity in the global context

Facts are the fingers of God.
—A. T. Pierson, *Missionary review of the world*, 1888

Part 12 takes the form of a topical survey dictionary. For any topic significant for global Christianity, it gives not simply definitions but also statistics and sufficient distinct survey information to adequately describe the topic's role on the world scene.

A survey dictionary of Christianity in the global context

A

abbess. A woman who is the superior of one of certain communities of nuns following the Benedictine rule, also of orders of canonesses or of the Second Franciscan order

abbey. A senior or superior monastery with a large number of monks ruled by an abbot or a convent ruled by an abbess, or an abbey church.

abbey nullius. (Latin, abbey of no diocese; symbol AN). An abbey whose abbot is exempt from diocesan control and under direct papal jurisdiction. Global statistics: (1995) 15

abbot. In the Western church, the superior of a large religious house of monks, either Benedictine (Cistercian, Trappist) or Canons Regular.

abbé. (French). A title applied in French to clerics in general.

ABORIGINAL. Worship service in Australia.

Aboriginal. Original indigenous inhabitant of country, of primitive culture.

Aboriginal indigenous churches. Churches indigenous to, because started by, Australian Aborigines.

accessibility. In evangelization, the quality or state or extent of a population's ability to be reached or accessible or approached or communicated with.

accumulated enrolment. See enrolment.

acolyte. In the Catholic Church, highest of the 4 minor orders conferred on candidates to the priesthood; also, a server who carries candles at mass.

acronym. A word formed from the initial letter or letters of each of the successive or major parts of a compound term.

active attenders. The most active among a group of practicing Christians (qv).

active enrolment. See enrolment.

active members. Church members who are practicing Christians (qv) or Great Commission Christians. Global statistics: (1970) 277.1 million; (1995) 603.0 million in 237 countries (137 significantly); largest, USA (93.4 million); (2000) 647.8 million; (2025) 887.5 million.

actual audience. Total persons who actually listen to or view a given radio/TV broadcast.

Addis Ababa. See city of Ethiopian Orthodox patriarchate and patriarch.

adelphoi. (NT Greek). Brothers, brethren; term in use by Christian Brethren (Plymouth Brethren) and other Protestants.

adept. An enthusiastic adherent, well-trained devotee.

adepte. (French). A follower, adherent.

adequately-evangelized. The state of evangelization or awareness of Christianity, Christ and the gospel in which persons may be described as having had an adequate opportunity to respond.

adherent. A follower of a particular religion, church or philosophy. As used here, the term adherents refers to followers of all kinds (professing, affiliated, practicing, non-practicing, etc.) men, women, children, infants, nationals and expatriates, native- and foreign-born, immigrants, armed forces, displaced persons, refugees, nomads, et alii.

Adivasis. Aboriginal tribesmen in India.

adjective of nationality. The adjective(s) describing a national (citizen) officially sanctioned by a state for United Nations' usage.

adult. In law a human male or female over a fixed age; collectively making up the working-age and old-age population. In church statistics, as often in civil law, a person over 14 years old. Global statistics: (1970) 2,310,543,000; (1995) 3,896,218,000; (2000) 4,254,647,000; (2025) 5,987,079,000.

adult baptisms. The administration of baptism to candidates over 14 years of age; in practice, the youngest age is as low as 6 years old (Anglicans, many Baptists and other Protestants, et alii).

adult Christians. Christians over 14 years of age. Global statistics: (1970) 4,393,194,000; (1995) 1,169,446,000; (2000) 897,471,000; (2010) 528,567,000.

adult literacy. See literacy.

adult members. Adult church members on average over 14 years of age and on the church's books or rolls, who are either communicants or full members, adult believers, probationary members, baptized adult non-communicants, sometimes also unbaptized attending adults.

Adventists. Protestant tradition begun 1844, emphasizing imminent Second Advent of Christ. Global statistics: (1970) 4.1 million; (1995) 10.4 million in 214 countries (2 significantly); largest, USA (1.0 million).

affiliated Christians. Church members; all persons belonging to or connected with organized churches; those whose names are inscribed, written or entered on the churches' books or records, or with whom the churches are in touch, usually known by name and address to the churches at grass-roots or local parish level; i.e. all distinct individuals attached to or claimed by the institutional churches or organized Christianity and hence part of their corporate life, community and fellowship; total church membership, or total Christian community, or inclusive membership; including full members, other attenders, their children and infants, members under discipline, and other adherents. Global statistics: (1970) 1.1 billion; (1995) 1.7 billion in 238 countries (186 significantly); largest, USA (184.2 million); (2000) 1.8 billion; (2025) 2.4 billion.

affiliation. Church membership, attachment to organized Christianity; usually begun by the inscribing, writing or entering of people's names on the churches' books or records.

affiliation, double. See doubly-affiliated Christians.

affiliation, legal. Church membership in countries where the bulk of the population belongs by law to the state church or established church.

affiliation, religious. Membership in, or attachment to a particular organized religion.

African. One of the 13 geographical races of mankind, excluding Middle Eastern (Semitic, Hamitic and Cushitic) and Early African (qv), speaking about 1,320 languages.

African independent churches. African indigenous churches (qv).

African indigenous Christianity. Type or style of Christianity evolved and practiced by African indigenous churches (qv).

African indigenous churches. Denominations indigenous to African peoples, begun without outside help; also termed African independent churches, African separatist churches.

Afro-American. One of the 13 geographical races of mankind, speaking over 60 languages.

Afro-American spiritists. Followers of Afro-Brazilian, Afro-Cuban and other African religious survivals in the Americas, low spiritists, syncretizing Catholicism with African and Amerindian animistic religions; low spiritists as opposed to high (non-Christian) spiritists; also Afro-American syncretistic cults with Christian elements. All varieties, including specifically Christian bodies, are detailed in G. E. Simpson, *Black religions in the New World* (New York: Columbia University Press, 1978). Global statistics: (1970) 1.7 million; (1995) 5.0 million; (2000) 5.6 million; (2025) 7.7 million.

aggiornamento. (Italian). Updating, renewal, bringing up-to-date, used by pope John XXIII to justify convening Vatican II in 1962.

agnosticism. The doctrine that the existence or nature of any ultimate reality or God is unknown and unknowable.

agnostics. Persons professing agnosticism. Global statistics: (1970) 532.1 million; (1995) 738.0 million in 236 countries (39 significantly); largest, China (509.5 million); (2000) 768.1 million; (2025) 875.1 million.

agricultural land. In FAO usage, arable land, land under permanent crops, permanent meadows and pastures.

agricultural missions. See rural missions.

ahimsa. (Sanskrit). In Hinduism, Jainism and Buddhism, the doctrine of non-violence, or refraining from harming others including animals and insects.

Ahmadis. Followers of the Ahmadiya movement (qv).

Ahmadiya. (Ahmadiyah, Ahmadiyya). Ex-Shia Muslim messianic movement, pronounced heretical by Pakistan, following 1889 founder Ghulam Ahmad. Global statistics: (1970) 2.6 million; (1995) 6.7 million; (2000) 7.9 million; (2025) 14.7 million.

aid and relief. At least 360 major Christian organizations are at work in this field.

Alabare. (Spanish: 'I will praise'). A theme song of Latin American Catholic charismatics.

Aladura. (Yoruba: People who pray). African indigenous tradition across West Africa, with 3 million adherents.

Alawites. Followers of Alawiya, a sect of Shia Islam in Latakia province, Syria, Lebanon and Cilicia (Turkey), also called Nusayris. Global statistics: (1970) 770,000; (1995) 1.4 million; (2000) 1.6 million; (2025) 2.6 million.

Albanian. A European ethnolinguistic family and people. Global statistics: (2000) 6.2 million in 19 peoples residing in 16 countries (3 significantly); largest, Albania (2.8 million).

Albanian/Greek. An Eastern Orthodox liturgical tradition dating back to the Apostolic era. Global statistics: (1970) 198,000; (1995) 537,000 in 6 countries (1 significantly); largest, Albania (400,000).

Alexandria. One of the 4 earliest patriarchates in the early Church, still the see city of 4 rival patriarchates and patriarchs: Coptic Orthodox, Coptic Catholic, Melkite and Greek Orthodox.

Alexandrian. The Alexandrian or Egyptian rite of the Roman Catholic Church consists of 2 sub-rites: Coptic, and Ethiopic (qv).

alien. A person of another family, race or place; stranger, foreigner.

Altaic. An Asian ethnolinguistic family. Global statistics: (2000) 163.9 million in 314 peoples residing in 60 countries (11 significantly); largest, Turkey (49.5 million).

altered states of consciousness. Religious experiences of a particular intensity, especially ecstatic states, trance, or dissociation; a category of psychobiological phenomena, amenable to observation and other objective methods of study; including spirit possession, soul loss, ecstatic religious behavior, faith-healing, mysticism, glossolalia, occult, shouting, visions, et alia.

alternative futures. Two or more alternative scenarios or possibilities or probable futures of a given present situation, based on current trends.

alternative media. In contrast to the mass media, small-scale participatory media, including drama, live theatre, dance, opera, ballet, wall newspapers (community-produced), etc.

alternative reality tradition. Term for the alternative view and experience of reality provided by modern Western cults of monistic/mystic/occult/shamanistic type (e.g. Theosophy, Rosicrucianism), as contrasted with the mainstream Western/European/Hebrew-Greek/normative scientific worldview of the Judeo-Christian tradition.

amateur radio. Operating of radio sets as a pastime rather than as a profession.

American Indian. One of the 13 geographical races of mankind, speaking 1,970 languages.

AMERICAN INDIAN. Gorotire tribal chief, Brazil.

Amerindian indigenous churches. Churches indigenous to Amerindian peoples.

amillennialists. Protestants who hold that the millennial reign of Christ will not be literal but occurs now in the hearts of believers.

amplitude modulation. (AM). Broadcasting termed (in Europe) medium-wave or (in USA) standard broadcasting (employing 540-1600 kilohertz).

Anabaptists. (from Greek: re-baptizers). Various groups in Continental Europe in the 16th century collectively termed the Left-Wing Reformation who refused to allow their children to be baptized and reinstituted the baptism of adult believers; represented today by Mennonites and Hutterites. Global statistics: (1970) 991,000; (1995) 1.7 million in 123 countries; largest, USA (546,000).

ancestor-veneration. A rite or cult in traditional African and other animistic religion, also in Confucianism, invoking the aid of departed ancestors; also termed ancestor-worship, and reverence for or remembrance of the living dead.
anchorite. One who renounces the world to live in seclusion for religious reasons; a hermit, recluse.
Ancient Church of the East. Also called Assyrians, Nestorians, Aramaean Christians, or East Syrians (Messihaye); Chaldean (Syriac)-speaking; the original Church of Mesopotamia, famed for its missionary expansion to 250 dioceses with 15 million adherents before its near extinction by Tamerlane around 1360. Global statistics: (1970) 121,000; (1995) 243,000 in 19 countries; largest, Iraq (58,000).
Anglican Communion. A worldwide family of 25 autonomous Churches and 6 other bodies in communion with the See of Canterbury and with each other, all of whom recognize the archbishop of Canterbury as the focus of unity within the Communion.
Anglican Consultative Council. (ACC). The major advisory body of the Anglican Communion, created by the Lambeth Conference in 1969.
Anglican Evangelicals. Evangelicals (qv) of Anglican persuasion both within and outside the Anglican Communion; sometimes termed either Conciliar or Conservative Evangelicals, and usually including all whose churchmanship is described as either Evangelical, Conservative Evangelical or Low Church, as distinct from High Church or sacramentalist persuasion, or Central or Broad Church.
Anglican pentecostals. Anglicans in the organized charismatic renewal, expressed in healings, tongues, prophesyings, etc.
Anglican religious orders. See religious orders in Anglicanism.
Anglicanism. The system of doctrine and practice upheld by those Christians in communion with the See of Canterbury.
Anglicans. Christians related to the Anglican Communion, tracing their origin back to the ancient British (Celtic) and English churches; including Anglican dissidents or schismatics in the Western world. Global statistics: (1970) 47.5 million; (1995) 74.5 million in 166 countries (27 significantly); largest, Britain (26.2 million); (2000) 79.6 million; (2025) 113.7 million.
anglicized. Spelt or written in a characteristically or recognizably English spelling and form.
Anglo-Catholics. Formerly called Tractarians or High Churchmen, that section of Anglicanism which emphasizes the dogmatic and sacramental aspects of the Catholic Faith.
Anglo-Romans. Adherents of recent schisms out of Anglicanism in a Roman Catholic direction, rejecting Anglican orders for some variant Roman succession.
animator. In Roman Catholic usage, an activist stimulating discussion or action groups.

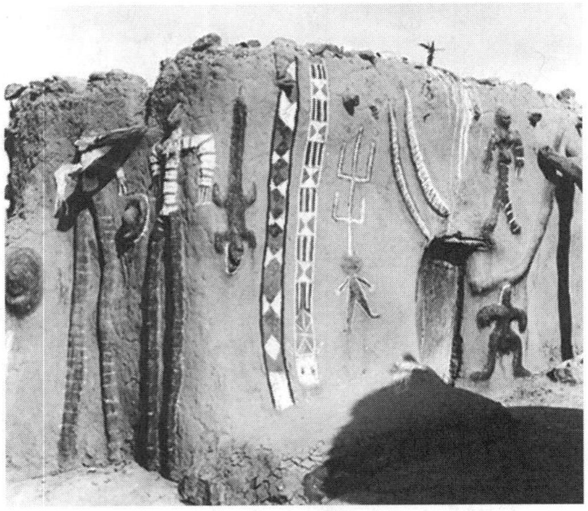
ANIMISM. Drawings on traditionalist fetish house in Mali.

animism. (animatism). The attribution of consciousness and personality to such natural phenomena as thunder and fire, and to objects such as rocks and trees.
animists. Adherents of animism; sometimes termed pagans, fetishists, traditional religionists, tribal religionists (qv). Global statistics: (1970) 143.5 million; (1995) 202.1 million; (2000) 216.1 million; (2025) 263.9 million.
Anno Domini. (AD 'In the Year of the Lord'). System of dating years after the birth of Christ
annual attenders. Practicing Christians who attend services of public worship only once a year (usually at Christmas or Easter).
annual baptisms. The total number of persons baptized in any year in a given diocese, denomination or country.
annual conference. In Methodism, the annual convocation of the church, and its basic governing body.
annual family income. The average annual income earned by a family in a country; derived by multiplying the national income per person by the average household size (average number of persons living in a household or family). Global statistics: (2000) $27,525.
annual letters. The total listeners' letters received in the course of a year by a radio/TV station or program.
anonymous Christians. Nominal Christians (qv); unaffiliated Christians unknown to the churches who nevertheless accept Christian beliefs and values. Global statistics: (1970) 106.2 million; (1995) 107.5 million in 236 countries (35 significantly); largest, USA (43.3 million); (2000) 111.1 million; (2025) 125.7 million.
Anthroposophy. A spiritual and mystical doctrine that grew out of Theosophy and derives mainly from the philosophy of Rudolf Steiner, an Austrian social philosopher.
anti-conciliar. Anti-ecumenical; opposed or hostile to the conciliar or ecumenical movements.
anti-religious. Opposed or militantly opposed to all religion; irreligious, hostile to religions and religious persons.
anti-religious quasi-religionists. Adherents of anti-religions quasi-religions (atheism, Communism, dialectical materialism, Leninism, Maoism, Marxism, scientific materialism, Stalinism, et alia). Global statistics: (1970) 697.5 million; (1995) 886.3 million in 397 countries (44 significantly); largest, China (509.5 million); (2000) 918.2 million; (2025) 1.0 billion.
anti-trinitarian. A Christian tradition openly repudiating the doctrine of the Trinity, hence unitarian.
Antioch. The third city in the ancient Roman empire where the disciples were first called Christians; in the 4th century, the 3rd patriarchal see of Christendom (after Rome and Alexandria); now the see of 5 rival patriarchs: Greek Orthodox, Syrian Orthodox, Melkite, Maronite, and Syrian Catholic (Uniate).
Antiochene. The Antiochene or Western Syrian rite of the Roman Catholic Church consists of 3 sub-rites: Malankarese, Maronite, and Syrian (qv).
Antiochian. Syro-Antiochian (qv).
apartheid. (Afrikaans). The policy of segregation and political and economic discrimination against Non-Whites in the republic of South Africa.
apartment ministry. A pastoral type of ministry to dwellers in high-rise apartment buildings in densely-populated city areas.
apocalyptic. Prophetic, revelatory, predicting ultimate destiny or doom.
apocrypha. Quasi-scriptural non-canonical or deutero-canonical books of doubtful authorship or authority; especially, 13 books attached to versions of the Old Testament.
apologetics. That branch of theology devoted to the defense of the Christian faith and addressed primarily to criticisms originating from outside.
apostasy. The renunciation or abandonment of one's previous religious profession of faith.
apostates. Former church members, especially Roman Catholics, who have renounced or forsaken the Christian faith; backsliders, lapsed, disaffiliated (qv), dechristianized, post-Christians.
apostle. A messenger, one sent forth, one of the 12 disciples of Christ; one of certain early Christian missionaries or (Eastern Orthodoxy) one of the 70 disciples of Jesus; first prominent Christian missionary in any part of the world; one who has extraordinary success in mission; high or highest ecclesiastical official in numerous denominations especially in African indigenous churches.
apostolate. In Roman Catholic usage, the service of souls and spread of the Faith, discharged by bishops, priests, religious and laity.
apostolate, persons dedicated to the. In Roman Catholic usage, also called the apostolic force, and consisting of all bishops, priests, permanent deacons, religious brothers, professed women religious, committed lay workers (catechists, etc.), but excluding the lay apostolate. World total (1995): 2.9 million.
apostolic administration. (symbol AA). Temporary operating of a diocese when normal operation is impossible, e.g. due to state hostility. Global statistics: (1995) 6.
apostolic delegate. An ecclesiastical plenipotentiary representing the Holy See (by means of an apostolic delegation) in a country without diplomatic relations with it.
apostolic exhortation. A papal document or letter published from the Vatican, hortative and pastoral in purpose rather than strictly dogmatic or legal; occasionally issued by popes since 1917.
Apostolic Fathers. Early Fathers who flourished and published writings in the times of the Apostles immediately following the New Testament period, and whose writings have survived: Barnabas, Clement of Rome, Hermas, Papias, Ignatius, Polycarp, et alii.
apostolic force. In Roman Catholic usage, the total full-time workers dedicated to the apostolate (bishops, priests, brothers, sisters, catechists, and other lay workers) available for mission in a particular situation.
apostolic region. One of several areas into which a Roman Catholic country has divided itself in order to provide more meaningful pastoral areas than the traditional ecclesiastical provinces.
apostolic succession. The dogma that uninterrupted succession or bishops from the Apostolic era is necessary for valid sacraments and transmission of orders.
apostolic work. A term in use in Catholic circles for pioneer or outstanding missionary work.
apostolicity. The quality or character of being apostolic.
Apostolics. Pentecostal Apostolics (qv).
appropriate technology. Intermediate technology (qv).
Arab. A Middle Eastern ethnolinguistic family. Global statistics: (2000) 228.5 million in 378 peoples residing in 130 countries (24 significantly); largest, Egypt (63.3 million).
Arabian Gulf. Also termed Persian Gulf.
Arabic/Greek. An Eastern Orthodox liturgical tradition dating back to the Apostolic era. Global statistics: (1970) 777,000; (1995) 1.3 million in 31 countries; largest, USA (350,000).
archbishop. (Greek: leading bishop). A metropolitan or primate having jurisdiction over an ecclesiastical province; occasionally an honorary title only.
archdeacon. In Anglican usage, a senior cleric with administrative charge over part of a diocese (archdeaconry). There are 103 archdeacons in the Church of England.
archdiocese. (symbol AD). A diocese presided over by an archbishop.
archetype. In Jungian psychology, an inherited idea or mode of thought derived from the experiences of the race and present in the unconscious of each.
archimandrite. In the Eastern Church, a high administrative official next in rank after bishop.

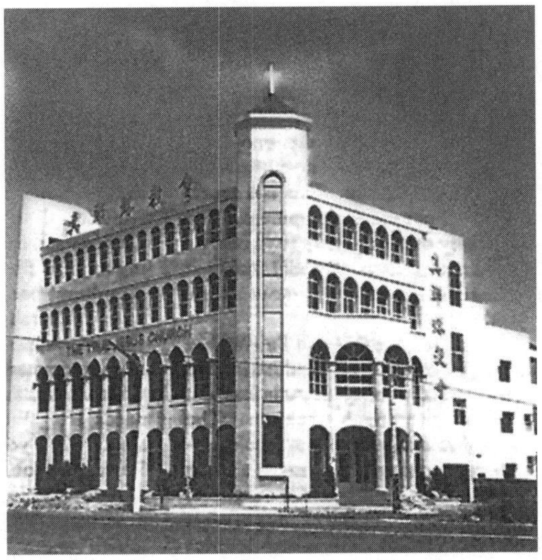
RELIGIOUS ARCHITECTURE. True Jesus Church, Taiwan.

architecture, religious. The art or practice of designing and building churches and temples to convey impressions and ideas basic to religion or Christianity.
archive. A repository for documents and other materials of historical value: diaries, photographs, correspondence, etc.
archpriest. In the eastern Church, the highest title of honor given a member of the secular clergy.
Arctic Mongoloid. One of the 13 geographical races of mankind. With 7 languages. Global statistics: (2000) 160,000 in 20 peoples residing in 5 countries (1 significantly); largest, USA (63,000).
areligious, a-religious. Noncommittal or professedly neutral concerning religious matters. Global statistics: (1970) 532.1 million; (1995) 738.0 million in 236 countries (39 significantly); largest, China (509.5 million); (2000) 768.1 million; (2025) 875.1 million.
argot, religious. A special vocabulary and idiom used by a religious group as a means of private communication within the group.
arithmetic mean. The sum of a number of quantities divided by their number.
armed forces. The combined military, naval and air forces of a nation or a group of nations; armed services.
Armenian. A European ethnolinguistic family. Global statistics: (2000) 7.4 million in 51 peoples residing in 48 countries (1 significantly); largest, Armenia (3.3 million).
Armenian Apostolic. An ancient Orthodox liturgical tradition dating back to the Apostolic era, also called Gregorians. Global statistics: (1970) 2.5 million; (1995) 5.5 million in 50 countries (1 significantly); largest, Armenia (2.6 million).
Armenian Catholicate of Cilicia (Sis). Oriental Orthodox. Global constituency in canonical relationship (1995) 1,364,000.
Armenian Catholicate of Echmiadzin. Oriental Orthodox. Global constituency in canonical relationship: (1995) 4,220,000.
Armenian Orthodox. Armenian Apostolic (qv).
Armenian rite. A rite of the Roman Catholic Church with 11 jurisdictions. Global statistics: (1970) 189,000; (1995) 151,000 in 17 countries; largest, USA (38,000).
Arminianism. The doctrine or teachings of Arminius who opposed the absolute predestination taught by Calvin and maintained the real possibility of salvation for all.
artificial languages. See constructed languages.
arts. In the field of religion and the arts, over 200 significant Christian organizations are at work.
Ashkenazis. The larger of the 2 great divisions of Jews comprising the eastern European Yiddish-speaking Jews, arising in the Rhineland in the 10th century, 5.7 million exterminated by Nazis, still 84% of all world's Jews today. Global statistics: (1970) 12.6 million; (1995) 10.6 million; (2000) 11.0 million; (2025) 12.3 million.
ashram, asrama. (Sanskrit). A religious retreat center for a colony of disciples, mainly in India.
Asian. One of the 13 geographical races of mankind; Asiatic; speaking over 840 languages. Global statistics: (2000) 2.1 billion in 2,207 peoples residing in 154 countries (52 significantly); largest, China (1.1 billion).
Asian indigenous churches. Non-White indigenous churches, indigenous to Asian peoples and begun since AD 1500. Global statistics: (1970) 6.7 million; (1995) 72.6 million in 80 countries; largest, China (35.7 million).
assembly. In some Protestant traditions (Pentecostal Brethren, et alii), the usual term for a congregation of believers.
assistant curate. In Anglican usage, an assistant or unbeneficed clergyman appointed to assist an incumbent in a parish.
assisted diocese. In the Anglican Church of Canada, a diocese not financially self-supported, hence assisted from outside.
Assyrian. A Middle Eastern ethnolinguistic family. Global statistics: (2000) 903,000 in 33 peoples residing in 22 countries; largest, Iraq (506,000).
Assyrians. Followers of the Ancient Church of the East, who for centuries called themselves Nestorians, followers of pa-

triarch Nestorius' theology. Global statistics: (1970) 121,000; (1995) 243,000 in 19 countries; largest, Iraq (58,000).
atheism. Disbelief in the existence of God or any other deity, the doctrine that there is no God; godlessness.
atheism, study of. A number of universities and research centers in the Communist world profess to study atheism; what in practice they study is religion, the survival of religion, and methods of eradicating it.
atheistic freedom. Freedom not to believe, and freedom to oppose religion.
atheistic states. In 1980 some 30 nations were atheistic, their regimes being either Communist or Marxist.
atheists. Persons professing atheism, skepticism, impiety, disbelief or irreligion, or Marxist-Leninist Communism regarded as a political faith, or other quasi-religions, and who abstain from religious activities and have severed all religious affiliation; and others opposed, hostile or militantly opposed to all religion (anti-religious); dialectical materialists, militant non-believers, anti-religious humanists, skeptics. Global statistics: (1970) 165.4 million; (1995) 148.3 million in 161 countries (5 significantly); largest, China (100.6 million); (2000) 150.0 million; (2025) 159.5 million.
attendance, church. See church attendance.
attending non-Christians. Non-Christians (Hindus, Muslims, pagans et alii) who, being interested in Christianity, attend church services regularly or occasionally.
attending non-members. Nominal Christians (unaffiliated to churches) who occasionally, or in some cases regularly, attend church services.
attribute. A quality, character or characteristic of a group.
audience, radio. See radio audience.
audio-visuals. Over 100 significant Christian organizations are at work in this field.
Australian Aborigine. An Austro-Asiatic ethnolinguistic family. Global statistics: (2000) 193,000 in 62 peoples residing in 1 country; largest, Australia (193,000).
Australoid. One of the 5 races of mankind; Archaic White, Classical Australoid, Proto-Caucasoid, speaking about 1,520 languages. Global statistics: (2000) 69.9 million in 1,842 peoples residing in 33 countries (11 significantly); largest, India (13.6 million).
Austro-Asiatic. One of the 13 geographical races of mankind, speaking 440 languages. Global statistics: (2000) 60.4 million in 422 peoples residing in 25 countries (2 significantly); largest, India (13.6 million).
authentic Christians. See committed Christians.
Authentic Orthodox. Paleohemerologites or Old Calendarists (qv).
auto-evangelization. Self-evangelization; the evangelization by the church of its own children and its younger generation.
autocephality. The state of ecclesiastical autonomy, of a church that appoints its own chief bishop without outside sanction.
autocephalous church. An independent, self-governing church appointing its own chief bishop.
autochthonous. Indigenous, native, aboriginal; the original population of an area.
automatic writing. See spirit writing.
autonomous church. In Eastern Orthodox usage a semi-independent and partially self-governing church; in Anglican usage, an independent and self-governing province or church.
auxiliary bishop. A titular bishop in the Roman Catholic Church who assists the ordinary of a diocese.
average. An arithmetical term derived by dividing the sum of a group of numbers by their total number, arithmetic mean.
average income. National income per person (qv). Global statistics: (2000) $4,767.
awakening, evangelical. A movement of the Holy Spirit in the church bringing about a revival of New Testament Christianity.
awareness. In evangelization, the quality or state or extent of realization or knowledge of the gospel; perception, understanding, cognizance, consciousness, comprehension, recognition of the facts of Christianity, Christ and the gospel.
awqaf. (Arabic: plural of *waqf*). Muslim trusts or foundations.
ayatollah. (Persian). Shia Muslim leader or cleric of great personal accomplishment, holiness, and renown.

B

baby. Infant (qv).
Babylon. See of Chaldean Catholic patriarchate.
back-calls. In Jehovah's Witnesses' terminology, return visits (qv) during house-to-house visiting work.
backsliders. Former church members who are falling away or have fallen away from the Christian faith; lapsed, disaffiliated, dechristianized, apostates.
Baha'i. The doctrine and practice of a sect founded in Iran in the 19th century that emphasizes the spiritual unity of mankind and advocates peace and universal education.
Baha'is. Followers of the Baha'i World Faith, founded by Baha'u'llah, since 1844. In government censuses Baha'is are usually counted as Muslims or Hindus and not shown separately. Global statistics: (1970) 2.6 million; (1995) 6.2 million in 218 countries; largest, India (1.4 million); (2000) 7.1 million; (2025) 12.0 million.
Baltic. A European ethnolinguistic family. Global statistics: (2000) 5.5 million in 35 peoples residing in 20 countries (2 significantly); largest, Lithuania (2.9 million).
banned churches. In many countries, a few, some, several, many or even all denominations and religions have been banned by decree of the regime in power. Such churches rarely dissolve themselves or cease Christian worship and other activity; they usually simply disappear from public view and operate underground.
Bantoid. An African ethnolinguistic family, with 205 languages. Global statistics: (2000) 74.5 million in 573 peoples residing in 24 countries (16 significantly); largest, Nigeria (28.4 million).
Bantu. An African ethnolinguistic family with 440 languages. Global statistics: (2000) 233.0 million in 955 peoples residing in 43 countries (23 significantly); largest, Congo-Zaire (43.0 million).
baptism. The sacramental rite which admits a candidate (adult or infant) to membership in the Christian church; usually by immersion (submersion), affusion (pouring), or aspersion (sprinkling) with water.

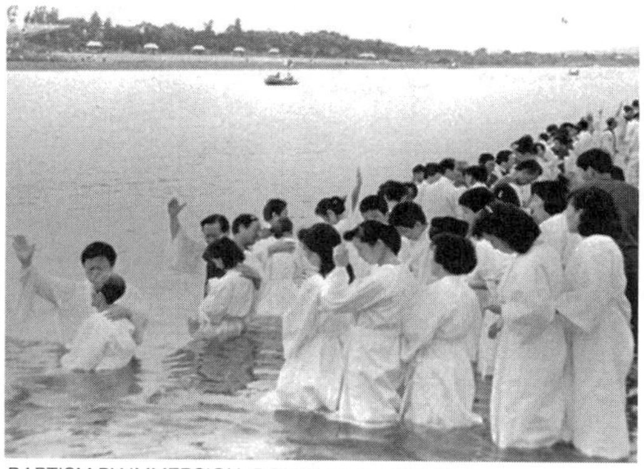

BAPTISM BY IMMERSION. 5,000 Koreans, Han River.

baptism by immersion. (1) The rite of adult baptism through submersion in water, practiced by Baptist, Pentecostal and other Protestant traditions; believer's baptism. (2) Baptism by total immersion is also universal for infant baptism among Eastern and Oriental Orthodox (e.g. Copts, at 40 days old for boys, 80 for girls).
baptism rate. The number of baptisms in a church or area in a given year, expressed as a percentage of the total baptized membership.
baptismal candidate. A catechumen (qv).
baptisms, annual. (1) The number of persons baptized in a given year. (2) The number of services of baptism held in a given year.
baptisms, annual Roman Catholic. (1996) 18,103,810 (15,867,550 children up to seven years old).
Baptist World Alliance. (BWA). The major Baptist communion. Global members: (1999) There are 192 Baptist unions and conventions in over 200 countries with a membership of more than 42 million baptized believers in a total community of 100 million Baptists.
Baptistic-Pentecostals. Also termed Keswick-Pentecostals, mainline Classical Pentecostals teaching 2-crisis experience (conversion, baptism of the Spirit). Global statistics: (1970) 11.4 million; (1995) 47.7 million in 380 countries (5 significantly); largest, Brazil (22.6 million).
Baptists. (1) In contrast to Pedobaptists (qv) who baptize infants, all Christian traditions which baptize adults only are termed Baptist, in its widest meaning. (2) The specific tradition of Protestants and Independents calling themselves Baptists. Global statistics: (1970) 26.7 million; (1995) 46.7 million in 313 countries (2 significantly); largest, USA (24.7 million).
baptized. Persons who have been admitted to churches through the rite of baptism.
basic communities. Small ecclesial communities or groups that have sprung up in the churches, stressing community, renewal, charismatic gifts, prayer, Bible study, evangelism, et alia; spontaneous communities, underground communities, et alia.
basic data. Raw data, crude data, primary data.
Basilians. Used of Eastern monks in general.

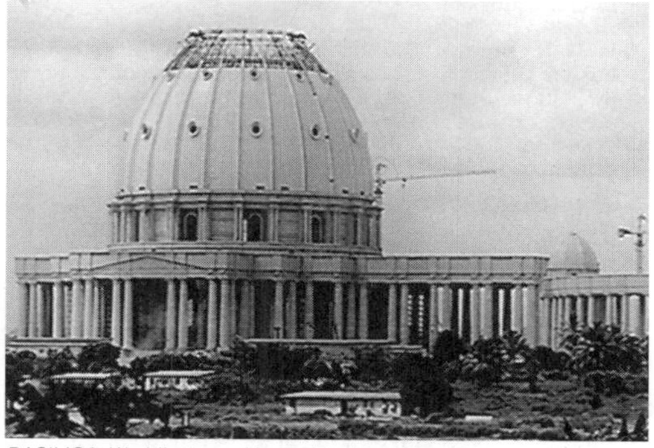

BASILICA. World's second largest, in Ivory Coast.

basilica. In Roman Catholic and Orthodox ecclesiology, a canonical title of honor with liturgical privileges given to churches distinguished either by their antiquity, dignity, historical significance, or by their role as international centers of worship and relation to a major saint, or historical event, or (in Orthodoxy) a national patriarch. In Catholicism, they are of 2 kinds (a) major basilicas (St Peter's, St John Lateran et alia in Rome), (b) minor basilicas (as in USA, Canada, et alia).
Basque. An isolated European ethnolinguistic family. Global statistics: (2000) 3.2 million in 15 peoples residing in 13 countries; largest, Spain (2.1 million).
Baster. A Eurafrican or Colored people in Namibia.
belief. Statistics of personal belief have been widely investigated in public-opinion polls and surveys. Typical questions, with nation-wide adult percentage of 'Yes' responses: 'Do you believe in a God? (1948) Brazil 96%, Australia 95%, Canada 95%, USA 94%, Norway 84%, UK 84%, Finland 83%, Netherlands 80%, Sweden 80%, Denmark 80%, France 66%; (1968) UK 74%; (1970) Netherlands 81%; (1973) Canada 67%, UK 77%; (1975) UK 72%; (1979) UK 73%. 'Do you believe Jesus Christ is the Son of God?' (1957) USA 90%, UK 71% , (1975) Spain 61%. 'Do you believe that Jesus Christ will ever return to earth?' (1960) USA 55%. 'Can a person be a Christian if he does not go to church?' (1957) UK 85%, USA 78%. 'Have you been born again through committing yourself to Christ?' (1976) USA 34%.
believer. One who believes or professes a religious faith; often used only of Christians, but sometimes of all religions.
believer's baptism. Adult baptism, by immersion, on profession of faith.
believing Christians. See committed Christians.
bell-ringing. Campanology (qv).
Belorussian. White-Ruthenian, a sub-rite of the Byzantine rite (qv); suppressed and with no jurisdictions (1980).
Berber. A Middle Eastern ethnolinguistic family, with 30 languages. Global statistics: (2000) 31.6 million in 103 peoples residing in 21 countries (5 significantly); largest, Morocco (15.4 million).
Bezirk. (German: District). An administrative region of the New Apostolic Church, which has 30 Districts across the world.
Bible. For Christians, the revealed Word of God, Holy Scriptures, with 66 Books (39 OT, 27 NT).
Bible correspondence courses. See correspondence courses.

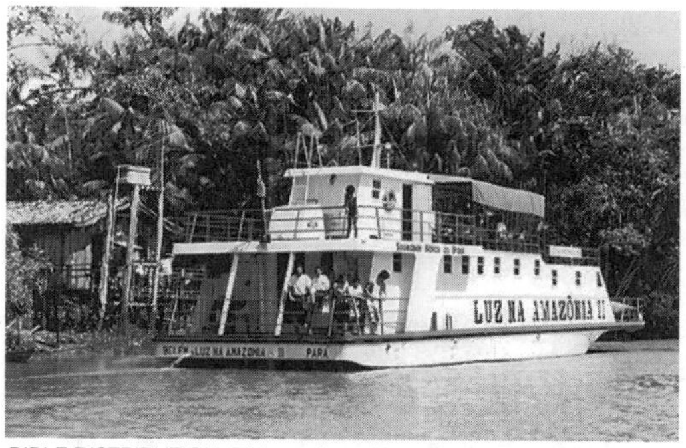

BIBLE DISTRIBUTION. Bible society ship on Amazon River, Brazil.

Bible distribution. Distribution (free, subsidized, commercial): copies of the whole Bible per year. Global statistics: 60 million (AD 2000).
Bible organizations. There are over 370 major Christian organizations at work in this field.
Bible schools. Centers for the training of Christian workers usually of less than secondary education, often for the ordained ministry in Third-World countries, more usually for lay ministries. In Latin American Protestantism the term tends to be synonymous with seminaries (qv).
Bible smuggler. A Western tourist or courier from Europe or North America who enters Communist or non-Christian lands with numerous copies of the Bible for illegal distribution
Bible Student movement. A schismatic movement out of Jehovah's Witnesses which has produced a number of new denominations.
Bible studies. In Jehovah's Witnesses' statistics, the number of Bible studies conducted each year by publishers in the course of house-to-house visiting. World total: (1959) 606,075, (1974) 1,351,404, (1998) 4,302,852.
Bible translations. World total among UBS-related societies (1999): complete Bibles in 378 languages, New Testaments alone in another 822 languages, portions in another 725 languages; total all languages with at least one book printed, 1,925.
Bible-reading. Surveys and polls have been taken in various countries. Typical questions, with nationwide adult percentages answering 'Yes': 'Do you own a Bible or NT?' Brazil 75% of young students and workers, Spain 64% (though only 42% read it); (1973) UK 76%, (1976) UK 71%. 'Have you a Bible in your home?' (1976) UK 84%. 'Have you read the Bible all the way through?' (1939) USA 26%. 'Have you read any part of the Bible at home within the last year?' (1944) USA 62% (10% every day); (1975) USA 63% (Protestants 75%, RCs 43%), UK 38% (7% every day, 16% every week, 24% every month).
bibliography. A catalog of writing and publications.
bilaterals, bilateral conversations. In ecumenical terminology, theological conversations undertaken by officially-appointed representatives of 2 churches, 2 traditions, or 2 confessional families, with purposes ranging from promoting mutual understanding to achieving full fellowship or eventual organic union.
bilingual. Used of a person knowing or speaking 2 languages.
billion. In British usage, a million millions; in American usage, 1,000 millions; the American billion is termed milliard in British, French, and German usage.
biological change. Demographic change in the population of a country or body due to natural causes properly so called, i.e. the annual net aggregate of births to members of the body minus deaths in it.
birth rate. The number of births per year in a population, expressed as a percentage or permillage of the total population.

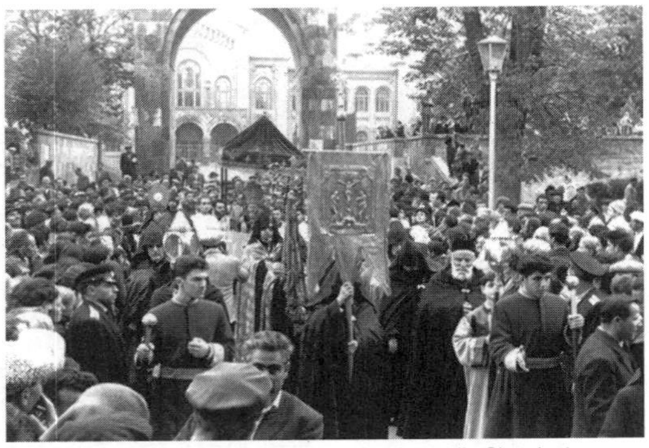

BISHOP. Consecration of four in Armenian Apostolic Church.

bishop. A clergyman of the highest rank or order in the Christian churches, with administrative and other duties, overseer, shepherd.
bishop in parlibus infidelium. (Latin: bishop in heathen land). A titular bishop (qv).
bishop's commissary. In Anglican usage, a clergyman appointed to represent his bishop in the latter's temporary absence abroad, or appointed by a bishop serving abroad to serve him in his home country.
bishopric. (1) The office of a bishop. 2) The administrative area under the jurisdiction of a bishop; a diocese.
bishops' conferences. Episcopal conferences (qv).
bishops, Roman Catholic. (1996) 4,375.
bishops-at-large. (in Latin, *episcopi vagantes*). Bishops founding or leading minuscule unrecognized autocephalous episcopal churches, with disputed apostolic succession. 130 such churches are described here in the table Episcopal Churches with Disputed Apostolic Succession, which also lists documentation of 760 bishops-at-large.
Black. Stylized skin color associated with the Negro (Negroid) race and the African and Afro-American geographical races. Global statistics: (2000) 637.8 million in 2,947 peoples residing in 115 countries (78 significantly); largest, Nigeria (109.1 million).
black magic. Magic (qv) used for evil purposes, with malevolent intent.
Black Muslims. Followers of unorthodox Nation of Islam (since 1977, World Community or Al-Islam in the West) in the USA. Total adherents: (1970) 200,000, (1980) 800,000, (1985) 1,100,000, (2000) 1,650,000.
Black neo-pentecostals. Regularly-active Black charismatics (more traditionally 'sanctified') in the non-pentecostal Black denominations in the USA.
Black theology. Christian theology as interpreted from the standpoint of the oppressed Black race.
Black/Third-World indigenous Christianity. Type or style of Christianity evolved and practiced by Non-White indigenous Christians (qv).
Black/Third-World indigenous councils of churches. Over 1,000 significant denominations of Non-White indigenous churches have banded themselves into national councils of churches, with 40 million church members.
Blanco (Spanish). A White, especially in Latin America.
blanketing. A term used in saturation evangelism for total coverage of a target population.
blind, the. Global total of totally blind persons: 16 million in 1973, rising to 32.6 million by AD 2000, a rate or density of 538 blind persons per 100,000 population.
bloc, ecclesiastical. De facto ecclesiastico-cultural grouping which has arisen during the course of Christian history. There are 6 major historico-cultural ecclesiastical blocs, coalitions or ongoing or enduring streams of Christianity: Roman Catholicism, Orthodoxy, Anglicanism, Protestantism, marginal Christians and Independent Christianity. Termed megablocs (qv).
body evangelism. Evangelism which results in visible, measurable growth of the church as the Body of Christ; extension growth, the planting of new congregations and churches.
body life. Life in the Body of Christ; the developing of spiritual gifts of the Body's members (fellow-Christians).
Bohras. Mustali Ismailis.
Bon. The pre-Buddhist animistic religion of Tibet.
book. (I) In UNESCO usage for statistical purposes any non-periodical publication of at least 49 pages excluding covers. (2) In UBS usage, the translation of a single portion, gospel or other book of the Bible when published separate.
book titles, annual new. The number of non-periodical commercial publications produced each year (books and pamphlets). Global statistics: 76,437 new Christian titles p.a., 1.0 million new book titles p.a.
bookshops. Global total of all Christian bookshops, bookstalls and outlets for Christian literature: (AD 2000) 73,500.
born-again Christians. Those who have had, or claim to have had, an experience of new birth in Christ; committed Christians (qv).
Botika. Digambara (qv).
brackets. In printing, square brackets [ ] as opposed to parentheses or curved marks ( ).
Braille. A system of writing for the blind using raised dots.
Branco (Portuguese). A White, especially in Brazil.
Branhamites. Followers of a marginal pentecostal evangelist, William Branham, and his End-Time Believers.
Brazilian indigenous churches. Denominations indigenous to Brazilians. Global statistics: (1970) 2.5 million; (1995) 19.6 million in 7 countries; largest, Brazil (15.2 million).
breakoff. A schism, secession (qv).
Brethren. A general term for Christians, used as a proper name by several traditions, especially Christian Brethren (qv). Global statistics: (1970) 465,000; (1995) 603,000 in 10 countries; largest, Central African Rep (290,000).
Britain. (I) A geographical term covering Great Britain, consisting of England, Wales and Scotland. (2) A political shorthand term for the United Kingdom of Great Britain and Northern Ireland.
British Isles. A geographical term covering England, Wales, Scotland, and Ireland (both Northern Ireland and the Republic of Ireland).
British-Israelites. A movement holding that the British and North American peoples are part of the 10 lost tribes of Israel; not a separate sect, since members belong to many British and American denominations. Some marginal Protestant denominations, however, retain British-Israel tenets.
Broad Church Anglicans. See Central or Broad Church Anglicans.
broadcast. A radio or TV program.
broadcasting station. See radio station.
broadcasting studio. Center for the production or compilation (but not transmission) of radio or TV programs, which are then sent elsewhere for broadcasting over stations.
broadcasting, Christian. There are over 500 organizations in this field significant at the national and wider levels.
broadcasting, religious. Often used as synonymous with Christian broadcasting, but incorrectly since Muslims, Hindus, Buddhists, and numerous New Religions and sects make extensive use of radio and TV in many countries.
brother. (I) A co-religionist, especially a fellow-member of a Christian church. (2) A member of a congregation of religious men not in holy orders.
brotherhood. An association of Christian men, e.g. a monastic society.
brothers. Members of men's religious institutes or congregations not in holy orders.
Brothers of Christ. Christadelphians (qv).
Brown. Stylized skin color associated with Dravidian, North Indian, Oceanic (Melanesian, Papuan) and other peoples. Global statistics: (2000) 1.4 billion in 2,293 peoples residing in 176 countries (49 significantly); largest, India (963.5 million).

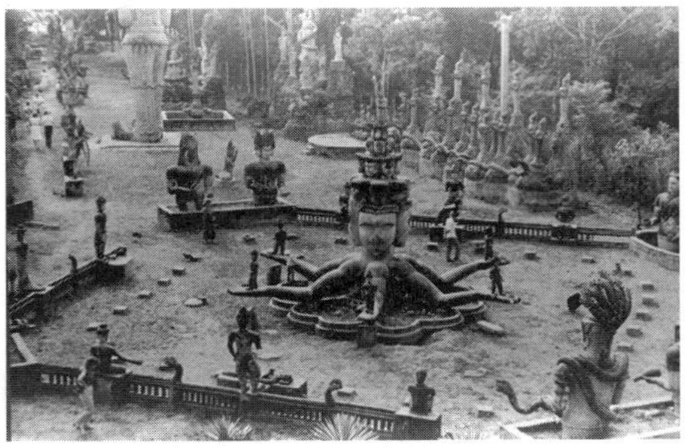

BUDDHISTS. A Buddhist memorial garden in Laos.

Buddhists. Followers of the Buddha, including: (a) Mahayana (Greater Vehicle) or Northern Buddhism; (b) Theravada (Teaching of the Elders) or Southern Buddhism, stigmatized by Mahayanists as Hinayana (Lesser Vehicle, i.e. available to fewer people), actually the older, purer form of Buddhism; (c) Vajrayana, Mantrayana, Guhyamantrayana, or Tantrayana (Esoteric Vehicle), known as Tantrism, Shingon or Lamaism; and (d) traditional Buddhist sects, but excluding neo-Buddhist new religions or religious movements. Global statistics: (1970) 233.4 million; (1995) 341.7 million in 126 countries (13 significantly); largest, China (99.9 million); (2000) 359.9 million; (2025) 418.3 million.
Bulgarian rite. A rite of the Roman Catholic Church. Global statistics: (1970) 7,000; (1995) 20,000 in 1 countries; largest, Bulgaria (20,000).
bull. See papal bull.
bush telegraph. The means whereby natives of a jungle or bush rapidly spread news from person to person, an informal but well-organized system of word-of-mouth communication.
Byzantine. The Byzantine or Constantinopolitan rite of the Roman Catholic Church consists of 13 sub-rites: Albanian, Bulgarian, Greek, Hungarian, Italo-Albanian, Melkite, Romanian, Russian, Ruthenian, Slovak, Ukrainian, White-Ruthenian (Belorussian), Yugoslavian (qv for separate statistics).

C

cadet. In Salvation Army usage, one undergoing training to become an officer.
Cafuso. The Portuguese-speaking issue of a Negro and an Amerindian; in Spanish, Zambo.
Calendar. In Orthodoxy, most churches follow the Old Calendar (qv), especially the Russian Orthodox Church, although a sizeable number follow the New Calendar (qv), notably Constantinople, Greece, Romania, Finland, Cyprus.
call sign. A combination of identifying letters, or letters and numbers, assigned to a radio/TV station or a radio operator for use in communication.
Calvinist. An adherent of Calvinism, the theological doctrines that emphasize the sovereignty of God in the bestowal of grace, election or predestination, limited atonement, total depravity, irresistibility of grace, and the perseverance of saints.
campaign. See evangelistic campaigns.
campanology. The art of bell ringing, or the science of making bells.
Campbellites. Disciples (qv).
campus. The grounds and buildings of a university, college or school; the university itself; the academic world.
candidate. In Salvationist usage, a soldier who offers to devote his or her life to being an officer.
canon. (I) A decree, decision, regulation, code or constitution made by ecclesiastical authority. (2) A relatively unchangeable part of the Catholic mass. (3) Books forming the accepted list of Holy Scripture. (4) A clergyman on the staff of a cathedral.
canonical relationship. In Eastern Orthodoxy, sanctioned, orthodox, authoritative relationship of one church with another, in accordance with Orthodox canons.
canonicity. Canonical acceptability, authority or genuineness, based on a church's history, tradition, apostolic succession, liturgy, canons and relationships with sister churches.
capitalism. An economic system characterized by private or corporate ownership or capital goods, by investments on private initiative, and by prices, production and distribution in a free market.
Capitalist world. Nations of the Western, free or First World that practice capitalism; sometimes used of the West together with similar nations in the Third World.
Capoid. One of the 5 races of mankind, Archaic African, Early African (qv), speaking about 60 languages. Global statistics: (2000) 1.1 million in 114 peoples residing in 21 countries; largest, Congo-Zaire (194,000).
captain. An officer in the Salvation Army, or Church Army (Anglican), or similar organizations with military terminology.
cardinals. In the Roman Catholic church, the highest ecclesiastical officials below papal rank, appointed to assist the pope in the College of Cardinals. Global statistics: Total: fixed at 70 from 1586-1959, then increased to 131 (1969), 145 (1973), falling to 132 (1977), rising to 151 (1997)..
cargo cults. Religio-political or nativistic (qv) movements among natives of various South Pacific islands, characterized by the messianic expectation of return of the ancestors in ships or planes carrying valuable modern cargoes.
cassette ministry. Evangelistic outreach through playing cassettes or tapes over recorders in outreach situations, especially in non-Christian languages in non-Christian areas.
caste. A social or socio-religious stratum or stratification, any hereditary and exclusive class based on socio-religious beliefs, in India, one of the 30,000 groupings, classified under 4 hereditary classes, into which society is divided in accordance with a system of rank and status fundamental to Hinduism.
catacomb church, church of the catacombs. See crypto-Christians.
catechesis. (1) The responsibility of every Christian to bear witness to the gospel and to communicate it. (2) A stage in evangelization. (3) The process of systematized instruction in the Christian faith.
catechetical center. A center for catechesis (teaching the Christian faith) and study of catechetical methods in the modern world.
catechetics. The technology or methodology of religious education.

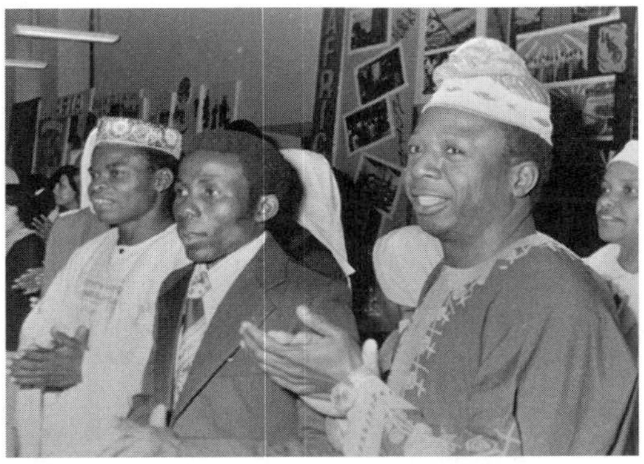

CATECHISTS. Nigerian catechists at conference in Rome.

catechists. Local teachers of catechumens. Roman Catholic totals (1996): 1,584,633.
catechumen. One receiving rudimentary instruction in church doctrines, discipline and morals prior to baptism; baptismal candidate.
cathedral. A church that contains a cathedra (bishop's throne) and that is officially the principal church of a diocese.
Catholic. (1) A person belonging to or attribute of the universal Christian church. (2) A member or attribute of a Catholic or Anglican church.
catholic. Related to the church universal, comprehensive, universal, general.
Catholic Apostolics. Followers of a tradition emerging from Protestantism in 1832 and stressing Catholic features, rejecting apostolic succession and substituting government by hierarchy of living apostles; also termed Irvingites (qv), Old Apostolics, and New Apostolics (qv). Global statistics: (1970) 1.7 million; (1995) 8.2 million in 176 countries; largest, India (1.4 million).
Catholic Charismatic. A Roman Catholic involved in the Catholic Charismatic Renewal.
Catholic Charismatic Renewal. Worldwide movement begun in 1967 in the USA and Colombia.
Catholic Charismatics. Catholic pentecostals. Roman Catholics active in the organized Catholic Charismatic Renewal, expressed in healings, tongues, prophesying, etc. Global statistics: 120 million (AD 2000).

Catholic Church. (1) The universal church begun by Christ. (2) The Church of Rome.
Catholic pentecostals. Catholic Charismatics (qv).
catholicate. The see of a catholicos.
Catholicism. Usually, Roman Catholicism (qv).

CATHOLICOS. Vasken I, Armenian Apostolic Church.

catholicos. The chief bishop of certain independent Oriental churches: Armenian, Assyrian, Georgian.
catholicossate. Catholicate (qv).
Catholics (non-Roman). Old Catholics and others in secessions from the Church of Rome since 1700 in the Western world, and other Catholic-type sacramentalist or hierarchical secessions from Protestantism or Anglicanism. Global statistics: (1970) 2.6 million; (1995) 4.5 million in 70 countries; largest, Brazil (3.0 million).
Caucasian. A European ethnolinguistic family, with 35 languages in the Caucasus (though also used for Caucasoid (qv) or White person). Global statistics: (2000) 8.5 million in 119 peoples residing in 26 countries (1 significantly); largest, Russia (3.4 million).
Caucasoid, Caucasian. One of the 5 major races of mankind, speaking 630 Indo-European languages. Global statistics: (2000) 3.0 billion in 3,738 peoples residing in 236 countries (196 significantly); largest, India (223.7 million).
celebration. An occasion or observance of public worship, especially (in Anglicanism) of Holy Communion.
celibacy. The state of a single, unmarried life, or the obligation (in Roman Catholicism and Orthodoxy) of bishops or priests and monks not to marry.
Celtic. A European ethnolinguistic family. Global statistics: (2000) 13.3 million in 21 peoples residing in 9 countries (2 significantly); largest, USA (5.0 million).
Celtic church. The ancient Church of Britain in the 1st-6th centuries AD.
cenobite. A member of a religious group living in common, as contrasted with hermits.
censorship, religious. The practice of censoring (deleting, banning, altering, excising) letters to and from a country, especially to intercept Christian material.
census. A term used here solely for an official government population census (qv) usually with complete (100%) enumeration of the whole population.
census schedule. A form or questionnaire used for collection of information in a census.
Central Amerindian. An American Indian ethnolinguistic family, with 220 languages. Global statistics: (2000) 32.5 million in 341 peoples residing in 11 countries (3 significantly); largest, Mexico (27.1 million).
central conference. See conference.
Central or Broad Church Anglicans. Prayer Book, Liberal or Comprehensive Anglicans, including (from 1976) the New Synod Group; attempting to provide a via media between Anglo-Catholics and Anglican Evangelicals. Global statistics: (1970) 9.8 million; (1995) 8.7 million in 12 countries (1 significantly); largest, Britain (8.7 million).
chaitya. A stupa (qv).
Chalcedonian. Eastern Orthodox (qv).
Chaldean. The Chaldean or Syro-Oriental or East Syrian rite of the Roman Catholic Church consists of 2 sub-rites: Chaldean, and Syro-Malabarese.
Chaldeans. Chaldean-rite Catholics subordinate to Rome. Global statistics: (1970) 281,000; (1995) 312,000 in 21 countries; largest, Iraq (214,000).
chapel. A Christian sanctuary other than a cathedral or parish church, sometimes private, sometimes in a school or other institution, or Nonconformist.
chaplain. A clergyman officially attached to a school college or other public institution, or to the armed forces or other bodies.
chaplaincy. The sphere of work and office of a chaplain (qv).

chapter. (1) The body of canons of a cathedral. (2) The regular assembly for business of the canons of a cathedral or collegiate church or religious order or congregation.
charisma, charismata. Spiritual gifts or talents divinely granted as exemplified in early Christianity by the power of healing, gift of tongues, or prophesying.
charismatic. Gifted, instructed; a person involved in the charismatic renewal.
charismatic communities. See basic communities.

CHARISMATIC RENEWAL. Exuberant worship service in Sydney, Australia.

Charismatic Renewal. The pentecostal or neo-pentecostal renewal or revival movement within the mainline Protestant, Anglican, Catholic and Orthodox churches, characterized by healings, tongues, prophesyings, et alia.
Chicano. A Latin American Mestizo (Spanish/Amerindian).
child, children. Persons who have not yet attained puberty; defined here as ages 5-14 years, i.e. the school-age population. Often used inclusively to cover infants (defined as under 5 years old, or the pre-school population).
children's organizations. In this field there are over 240 significant Christian organizations.
Chinese. An Asian ethnolinguistic family and people. Global statistics: (2000) 1.2 billion in 272 peoples residing in 114 countries (9 significantly); largest, China (1.1 billion).
Chinese folk-religionists. Followers of traditional Chinese religion (local deities including Taoist ones, ancestor veneration, Confucian ethics, Chinese universalism, divination and magic, some Buddhist elements). Global statistics: (1970) 231.8 million; (1995) 369.1 million in 89 countries (6 significantly); largest, China (345.4 million); (2000) 384.8 million; (2025) 448.8 million.
choirmaster. The director of a choir.
chorepiscopus. (Greek, Latin). (1) In the Early Church, bishop of a country district. (2) In the 20th century, sub-bishop in certain Orthodox and Uniate churches, especially the Coptic Orthodox Church.
chorten. A stupa (qv).
Christ Groups. A term coined by the World Literature Crusade for the large number of congregations of converts which have emerged through WLC ministry over the last 20 years in isolated areas or towns with no existing churches.
Christadelphians. A premillennial Protestant group rejecting the Trinity. Global statistics: (1970) 97,000; (1995) 71,000 in 21 countries; largest, USA (23,000).
Christendom. The traditional portion of the world in which Christianity prevails or which is governed principally under Christian institutions.
Christian. One who believes in, or professes or confesses Jesus Christ as Lord and Savior, or is assumed to believe in Jesus Christ; an adherent of Christianity.
Christian approaches to other faiths. There are over 100 significant organizations in this field worldwide.
Christian Brethren. Protestant tradition begun 1828; ex Church of England; also called Open Brethren; independent fundamentalist/dispensationalist. Global statistics: (1970) 1.4 million; (1995) 2.7 million in 124 countries (1 significantly); largest, Russia (400,000).
Christian cultures. A Christian culture is defined here as a culture related to a specific ethnolinguistic people or tribe among whom affiliated church members make up at least 60% of the population. Global statistics: (2000) 5,933 out of 12,583 (47.1%)..
Christian education. Organizations in this field, significant at the national or wider levels, number over 280.
Christian Era. (CE). Used by Jehovah's Witnesses, Muslims and other non-Christians to replace Anno Domini, The Year of Our Lord (AD).
Christian Greek Scriptures. The Jehovah's Witnesses' term for the New Testament.
Christian institutions. See institutions, Christian.
Christian literature. In this field organizations significant at the national or wider levels number over 300.
Christian political parties. In a number of countries, in West-

ern Europe in particular, certain political parties claim to have a Christian philosophy and basis and have long had close links with Catholics or Protestants.
Christian Scientist. A believer in Christian Science organized under the official name of the Church of Christ, Scientist.
Christian socialism. A political tradition in Europe with close links with the Roman Catholic Church.
Christian world communions. Official name since 1979 of what were previously termed world confessional families (WCFs), most of which are rooted primarily in Europe and North America, giving expression to the common heritages of worldwide groups of churches. Most have their own organized world confessional councils (confessional conciliarism). World total: (2000) 250.
Christian year. The year as it is observed by Christian churches marked by various festivals or commemorations at special seasons and on special days; the church year, church's year.
Christianity. The whole worldwide body of Christian believers and their religion.
christianization. The process of christianizing; the whole 3-fold process of church planting and growth (as outlined in the Great Commission in Matthew 28.19, qv), namely discipling, baptizing, and perfecting.
christianize. To make Christian, to convert to Christianity, to imbue with Christian principles.
Christians. Followers of Jesus Christ of all kinds: all traditions and confessions, and all degrees of commitment. Global statistics: (1970) 1.2 billion; (1995) 1.8 billion in 238 countries (187 significantly); largest, USA (227.5 million); (2000) 2.0 billion; (2025) 2.6 billion.
Christmas. The annual church festival kept on 25 December (Oriental Orthodox on 6 January) in memory of the birth of Christ.
Christmas attenders. The total of all persons who attend church at Christmas each year.
Christopaganism. A synthesis of popular Catholicism in Latin America with traditional pre-Columbian American Indian religion.
Christopagans. Amerindian Roman Catholics in Latin America who syncretize folk-Catholicism with organized traditional Amerindian pagan religion.
christocentric. Used of all thought, actions or theological systems in which Christ is placed at the center.

CHURCH. Constructing an Ethiopian Orthodox church, Addis Ababa.

church. (when used without a capital C). A building set apart for Christian worship, or the services which go on in it; the historical institution composed of believing members, or the body of Christian believers; a local congregation or worshipping body; the visible organization to which Christ committed his mission.
Church. (when used with a capital C). A particular denomination; or the universal Church
church attenders. These can be categorized under 8 mutually-exclusive types: daily attenders, weekly (or Sunday) attenders, fortnightly attenders, monthly attenders, radio/TV service listeners, festival attenders, occasional attenders, annual attenders.
church growth. The study of the growth of churches is usually divided into (a) quantitative (numerical) growth, and (b) qualitative growth, the latter including organic and spiritual growth as well as other less tangible aspects.
church in exile. See exiled church.
church invisible. The entire company of those on earth and in afterlife who whether members of the church visible or not belong to the faithful saved by Christ.
church members. Affiliated Christians (qv).
church militant. The Christian church on earth regarded as engaged in a constant warfare against its enemies, the powers of evil.
Church of Rome. The Roman Catholic Church, also officially termed 'the Holy Roman and Apostolic Faith' and 'the Roman, Catholic and Apostolic Religion'.
church of silence. See crypto-Christians.

church sendee. A missionary (term coined in 1977 by Indonesian churches).
Church Slavonic. (Old Slavic). The liturgical language of the Russian Orthodox and other churches for centuries up to the present. For global statistics of membership, see under Slavonic.
church triumphant. Members of the Church who have died and are regarded as enjoying eternal happiness through union with Christ.
church union negotiations. An attempt by 2 or more churches or denominations, through their officially-appointed representatives, to draw up a plan for organic union.
church visible. The whole body of professing or affiliated Christians on earth.
church year. See Christian year.
church-planting agencies. Missionary societies and other organizations existing specifically for the planting of new churches and worship centers.
church-state relations. Nations can be categorized into a 3-fold typology, in AD 2000 as follows: (a) 113 countries can be termed religious countries or states, this being how they define themselves in their constitutions or other official statements, (b) 102 are secular countries or states, defining themselves as completely separate from religion, and (c) 23 states or their regimes are atheistic or anti-religious (Communist or Marxist) officially hostile to all religion.
Churches of Christ. (Restoration Movement). Disciples (qv).
churches' statistics of membership. Statistics collected and published by the churches of their own membership are defined and termed here as affiliated Christians (qv).
churchgoer. One who habitually attends church.
churchmanship. The attitude, belief or practice of a churchman.
Cilicia, also known as Sis. See of 2 rival patriarchates and patriarchs: Armenian Apostolic (catholicate). Armenian Catholic.
cinema, religious. See religious drama.
circle. In Swedenborgian and other traditions, a local church congregation.
circuit. In Methodist and other traditions, a group of church congregations ministered to or under the supervision of one pastor. In Jehovah's Witnesses' usage, about 20 congregations; with several circuits making up a district, and several districts a country.
circulation, scripture. See scripture distribution.
circumscription. An ecclesiastical jurisdiction.
citadel. In Salvationist usage, a hall used for worship and as a base for corps operations.
cities. Global statistics: (2000) 4,049 over 100,000 population; 456 over 1 million population.
citizen. A member of a state or nation; subject, national.
civic attenders. Persons who attend church services only on civic occasions or state festivals.
civil servant. An employee of a country's central government.
civilian. A resident of a country who is not on active duty in the armed services.
clandestine Christians. See crypto-Christians.
Classical Pentecostals. Blanket term for traditional types of Pentecostal (Pentecostal Apostolic, Oneness-Pentecostal, Baptistic Pentecostal, Holiness-Pentecostal, Perfectionist-Pentecostal), as contrasted with Neo-pentecostal, Catholic pentecostal, Non-White pentecostal, etc.
classis. An ecclesiastical district, or the governing body of a district, in certain churches of Presbyterian polity (Dutch and German Reformed); presbytery.

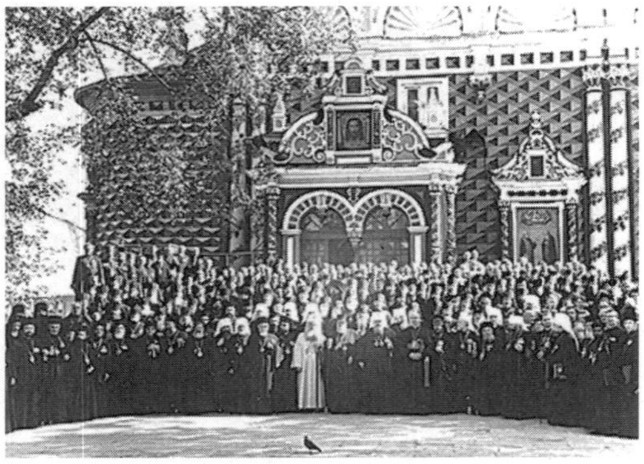

CLERGY. Bishops and priests of Russian Orthodox Church, Moscow.

clergy. The body of men and women duly ordained to the service of God in the Christian church: bishops, priests, deacons, ministers, deaconesses (in Anglican usage), and other ordained persons.
clergy organizations. There are over 200 significant bodies in this field.
clergyman. A member of the clergy, ordained minister, one in holy orders.
cleric. A clergyman.
clerk in holy orders. A clergyman of the Church of England.
clines. A number of hybrid races (Negroid-Caucasoid, Mongoloid-Caucasoid, etc.) existing between the 5 major races of mankind, but only distinguished from them by a series of almost imperceptible gradations of genetic character.
clinical theology. A psychiatric or psychological system of mental healing and mental health, derived in the Church of England in the 1950s-60s.
clinics. See medical centers.
Closed Brethren. Exclusive Brethren (qv).
closed communion. The offering of the sacrament of communion only to those who are full members of a particular church or denomination.
closed countries. 43 countries across the world which are completely closed to foreign mission (not necessarily to internal mission) by government policy.
closed dioceses. Dioceses which have been forcibly suppressed, destroyed or otherwise closed by state or other action.
cluster. A grouping of languages which all share in common 80% vocabulary of common human experience.
co-operative. (broader than credit union). An enterprise or organization owned by and operated for the benefit of those using its services.
co-religionist. A person having the same religion as another.
co-responsibility. In Roman Catholic usage, church government through all levels of the church, involving priests, religious personnel and laity in the whole process of consultation and decision-making.
co-responsible evangelization. In Roman Catholic usage, evangelization shared among the various ranks of clergy and laity.
coadjutor bishop. A bishop assisting another bishop nearing retirement, who usually has the right in due course to succeed him.
coenobite. See cenobite.
collegiality. The doctrine re-emphasized by Vatican II (1962-5) that government of the Roman Catholic Church is not by the pope alone but by the whole episcopate functioning as a college of bishops.
color. A term used loosely to refer to inherited apparent pigmentation.
Colored. Non-White, often of mixed blood (White/ Black).
colportage. The work of a colporteur.
colporteur. A peddler of Bibles, religious books and tracts.
commercial distribution of scriptures. Annual retail sales of scriptures published by commercial publishing houses, in which prices are not subsidized but are fixed on commercial considerations.
commissary. See bishop's commissary.
committed Christians. The inner nucleus of believing, active, practicing Christians of all traditions who have, or claim to have, personal and corporate commitment to Christ and to his church, also known as believing Christians, real Christians, converted Christians, nuclear Christians, authentic Christians, born-again Christians, etc.
Common Bible. A modern translation of the Bible into a major language in which Protestants, Catholics and others all co-operate.
communauté. (French community) The term used in Zaire for Protestant denominations within the sole legal Protestant church.
communautés de base. (French). Basic communities (qv).
communicant, communicant member. A church member in good standing who is entitled to partake of the sacrament of the Lord's Supper.
communication. The act or action of imparting or transmitting; interchange of thoughts and opinions.
communications. The means of communicating: equipment, systems, persons, channels, media, etc.
communion. (1) A body of Christians having one common faith and discipline; (2) the eucharist or Lord's Supper; (3) fellowship.
Communism. A system and theory advocating elimination of private ownership of property or capital; a totalitarian system of Marxist government.
communist. This term with a small 'c' is used in this Encyclopedia for individuals who hold Communist ideology.
Communist bloc. A term now in disfavor because the Communist world is, since the Sino-Soviet dispute, no longer a monolithic bloc.
Communist world. A term, based on political alignment, for some 30 nations in 1980 which were governed by Communist regimes, or Marxist or Marxist-Socialist regimes.
communists. Members of Communist Parties. Global membership: (1989) 88,700,000 members of 79 Parties (48 being illegal or semi-clandestine). 94% of these members live between the river Eloe and the Pacific in the 14 major nations governed by Communist Parties. Numbers greatly reduced after 1990 with collapse of Soviet Union.
community. (1) A body of individuals organized into a local unit, with its own culture; the maximal group of persons who normally reside together in face-to-face association, with moral responsibilities towards each other as well as to the community as a whole (up to 500 persons); the principal focus of associative life, the primary unit of social participation, the distinctive culture-bearing group; with internal divisions or factors usually 2 in number. (2) A monastic body or other unified religious group. (3) A variety of smaller Christian groups: basic communities (qv), spontaneous or charismatic communities, underground communities, et alia.
community church. An interdenominational or non-denominational church for community use in areas under North American influence.
comparative demographic evangelization. An index (%) of the extent of evangelization among a population.
comparative symbolics. See symbolics.
Comprehensive Anglicans. Central or Broad Church Anglicans (qv).
computer. An automatic electronic machine for storing, rearranging and retrieving information and for doing mathematical calculations, according to predesigned programs; widely used by churches and missions.
concelebration. A celebration of the eucharist, Lord's Supper, or mass, in which 2 or more clergy unite in saying the words of the liturgy.
concerts, religious. See religious drama.
conciliar. Relating to conciliarism.
conciliar Christianity. That portion of the Christian world which co-operates through Christian councils
Conciliar Evangelicals. Evangelicals in Protestant and Anglican churches that are affiliated to the Ecumenical Movement, and who generally work within and co-operate with that movement
conciliar fellowship. A model of unity embraced by part of the global ecumenical movement envisioning united local churches along primarily territorial lines, themselves united to other local churches so as to form a universal fellowship in such a way as to exclude the persistence of confessional differentiations and identities at least on the global level; in contrast to the model of 'reconciled diversity' (qv).
conciliar movement. The contemporary ecumenical movement, including Evangelical conciliarism.
conciliar region. In the Catholic Church of Italy, and other large national Catholic churches, one of a system of regions, each governed through an episcopal council, replacing the traditional but increasingly irrelevant system of dioceses attached to ecclesiastical provinces.
conciliarism. (1) The structuring of co-operation among differing Christian traditions into Christian councils and councils of churches at local, national, regional, continental and global levels (2) In Roman Catholicism, the theory of church government that places final ecclesiastical authority in representative church councils instead of in the papacy.
conciliarity. The principle of government found in Eastern Orthodox and other churches that places final authority in representative councils (Russian, *sobornost*, qu)
conclave. The assembly of cardinals in the Sistine Chapel, Vatican City, to elect a new pope for the Roman Catholic Church.
concord. Agreement by stipulation, compact, or covenant.
concordat. A compact between a national government and the Holy See establishing terms of agreement on matters of mutual interest.
conditional baptism. A Roman Catholic and Anglican baptismal rite given when it is doubtful whether the candidate has already previously been validly baptized.
conference. In Methodist, Mennonite and other churches, a stated meeting of preachers and others invested with authority to act on ecclesiastical matters. In Methodism, conferences can be annual, central or provisional.
Conference of Secretaries of Christian World Communions. Constituency: (2000) 1.5 billion, i.e. 80% of global church membership.
confessing Christians. Professing Christians (qv). Sometimes used in a narrower sense for Christians who confess the faith and suffer for it in times of severe testing or persecution.
confessing church. A church or denomination attacked by an anti-Christian state or regime but which nevertheless retains and publicizes a clear Christian confession in highly unfavorable circumstances.
confession. A world confessional family or body; a large family of distinct or different autonomous churches or denominations around the world which are linked by similar ecclesiastical tradition, history, polity and name and often by some informal or formal organization; officially known since 1979 as Christian world communions (qv).
confessional. (1) Denominational. (2) Adhering to a confession of faith. (3) Related to a world confessional family (qv).
confessional Christianity. The Christian faith as interpreted by a particular confession or Christian world communion, and emphasizing the superiority of its confessional tradition.
confessional conciliarism. See Christian world communions.
confessional identities. The recent trend emphasizing the distinctness and importance of world confessions (communions, confessional families) in contrast to the overall ecumenical movement.
confessional pluralism. The existence and continued persistence of some 45 Christian world communions (until 1979 termed world confessional families, WCFs) as distinct and separate identities in contrast to and hindering ecumenism and organic church union.
confessionalism. (1) The principle that a church should have a confession of faith. (2) Devotion or adherence to a confession of faith. (3) The contemporary movement towards reemphasizing confessional roots in contrast to ecumenicity.
confided. In Roman Catholic missionary usage, given into the care and charge of a missionary society or religious order or congregation.
confiding of a jurisdiction. The placing (by Propaganda in Rome) of a vicariate or prefecture (and, before 1969, of a diocese) in the charge of a missionary institute.
confirmation. A rite of various Christian churches supplemental to the rite of baptism, regarded as a sacrament and viewed as confirming a person in his religious faith.
confirmation, annual. (1) The number of persons confirmed in a given year. (2) The number of distinct services of confirmation held in a given year.
confirmed. Church members to whom the rite of confirmation has been administered.
confrontation. In evangelization, the bringing of people face-to-face with the gospel of Christ; challenging, facing, facing up to them, opposing them, forcing them to consider.
Confucians. Non-Chinese followers of Confucius and Confucianism; mostly Koreans and in Korea. Global statistics: (1970) 4.7 million; (1995) 6.0 million in 15 countries (1 significantly); largest, South Korea (5.0 million); (2000) 6.3 million; (2025) 6.8 million.
conglomerate. A large church or denomination composed of Christians from many different peoples (tribes, castes, races), each of whom has been converted virtually singly out of a largely non-Christian people.
congregation. (1) A distinct organized worship center (qv) or group of worshippers, usually quantified by church buildings, chapels, regular worship premises, sites, stations, centers, outposts, preaching points, or (Roman Catholics)

parishes and quasi-parishes. (2) In some Protestant usage, an organized self-supporting church or parish. (3) In Catholic usage, a religious institute (qv) for priests, monks, brothers or nuns living the religious life.
Congregation for the Evangelization of Peoples. See Sacred Congregation.
Congregation for the Oriental Churches. See Sacred Congregation.
Congregation of Bishops. Office in Roman Curia.
Congregational. Congregationalist (qv).
congregational publisher, congregation publisher. See publishers (Jehovah's Witnesses).
Congregationalism. A Protestant tradition with a system of church government in which the local congregation has full control and final authority over church matters within its own area.
Congregationalist. One who belongs to a Congregational church.
Congregationalists. Followers of Congregational tradition still so termed (many Congregational denominations have joined united churches since 1960).
congregations. For global statistics, see worship centers, also religious institutes.
congresses on evangelism. National or international conferences specifically on evangelism, organized by Conservative Evangelicals. Some 45 congresses have been organized since the first, the 1966 World Congress on Evangelism (Berlin).
conscientious objector. One who refuses to serve or is exempted from serving, in the armed forces, or to bear arms, as contrary to his moral or religious principles.
conscientization. (from the Portuguese, *conscientizai‹o*). Consciousness-raising; learning collectively to perceive social, political and economic contradictions and injustices and teaching the masses to take action against the oppressive elements of reality. The movement began in Brazil in the 1950s with the teaching of illiterates under Paulo Freire.

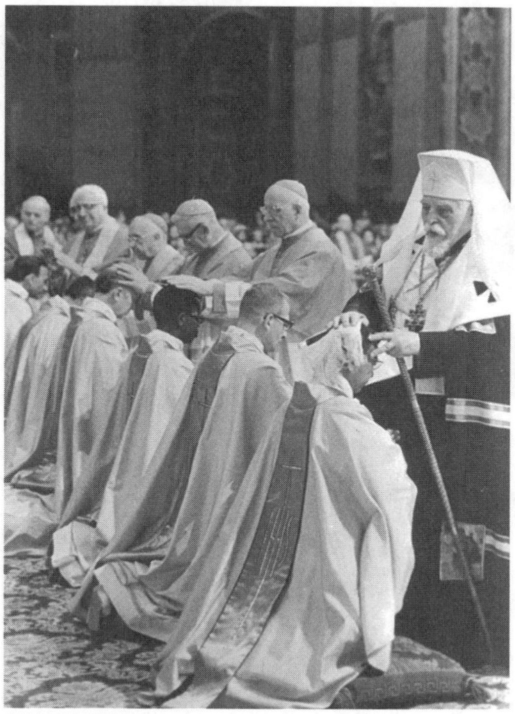
CONSECRATION. Seven become new Roman Catholic bishops.

consecration. The solemn dedication of a bishop or Christian monarch, or of the eucharistic elements.
conservatism. The tendency to accept an existing situation and to be cautious towards or suspicious of change.
Conservative Catholics. Followers of recent schisms ex Church of Rome in conservative or reactionary direction, rejecting authority of pope, protesting against up-dating or liberal trends; Tridentinists (qv), Traditional Catholics. Global statistics: (1970) 2.6 million; (1995) 4.5 million in 70 countries; largest, Brazil (3.0 million).
Conservative Evangelicals. Evangelicals in Protestant and Anglican churches who hold the theologically conservative doctrine of the verbal inspiration of the Bible, and all persons affiliated to denominations holding Conservative Evangelical doctrines.
Conservative Methodists. Holiness Christians (qv).
Constantinople. One of the 4 major patriarchates of the early Church, formally a patriarchate from AD 451; New Rome, or the 'Second Rome', seat of the Ecumenical Patriarchate (qv); now the see of 2 rival patriarchates and patriarchs, Eastern Orthodox and Armenian Apostolic.
Constantinopolitan. Byzantine (qv).
constituency. The body of supporters of followers of a specific church, denomination, tradition, council, confession, or religion.
constitution. A written instrument embodying the system of fundamental rules determining the powers and duties of official bodies and the people's guaranteed rights, and constituting the organic law of church or state. Most large churches and councils have formal constitutions for guiding procedure. Most states have constitutions which describe whether the state regards itself as religious, secular, or atheistic.
constructed languages. Artificial languages deliberately invented or constructed so as to provide a global universal language; total, over 500 attempts. The most successful is Esperanto (5 million speakers), a Romance/Germanic language, since 1887: Volapuk (1879; Germanic); and Interlingua (1920); primarily Romance). All have Scripture translations.
consultations. Discussions, conversations or bilateral or multilateral dialogues between churches of different confessions, with a view to better mutual understanding and eventual organic union.
consumer price index. An index showing changes over time in the price level of goods and services, relative usually to 1970 prices (= 100) in the country concerned; the principal means for calculating the inflation rate (qv).
contemplative. One who practices meditation on spiritual things as a private devotion.
contestation. (French). A method of disputation for confronting ecclesiastical authorities with the realities of a bad situation, developed in the 1970s by Roman Catholic priests in Latin Europe.
continental conciliarism. There are about 27 continent-wide multidenominational councils of churches excluding confessional continental councils.
Continental Pietists. Moravians (qv).
continuous evangelization. Evangelization implemented by a constant and continual complex of evangelistic activities.

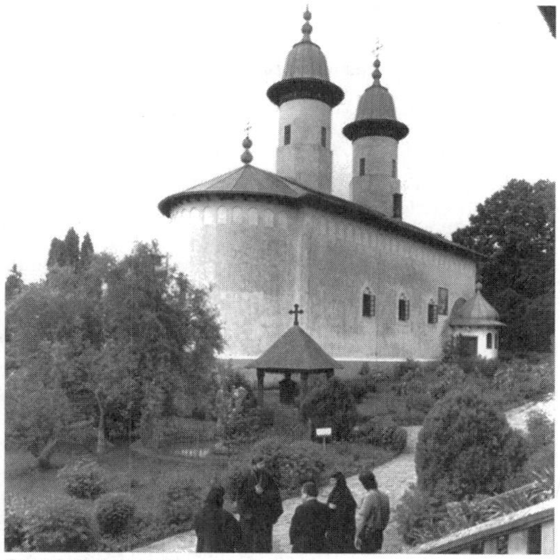
CONVENT. Varatec Convent in Moldavia.

convent. A house or association of female recluses devoted to the religious life under a superior; a nunnery.
conventual prior. A prior (qv).
conversations. In ecumenical terminology, discussions between churches or denominations where as yet no organic union is publicly envisaged nor constitutional questions discussed.
conversion. The change from one belief, faith or religion to another.
conversion change. Change in religious allegiance in a country or body, i.e. the annual net aggregate of conversions to the body of new adherents from other religions or religious bodies minus defections (sometimes termed apostasies) from it of former adherents leaving to join other religions or religious bodies.
Conversos. Marranos (qv).
convert. A person converted to a religious belief, faith or religion from another religion.
converted. The state of having been converted to faith in Christ.
converted Christians. Those who have had, or claim to have had, an experience of conversion to Christ committed Christians (qv).
conveyors. See decision-makers.
conviction. In evangelization, the state or extent of a population being convinced or persuaded or compelled to admit the truth of the gospel.
Coptic. Tradition dating back to Apostolic era, now referring to Egyptians in the Coptic Orthodox, Coptic Catholic, and Coptic Evangelical churches. Global statistics: (1970) 6.1 million; (1995) 9.2 million in 24 countries (1 significantly); largest, Egypt (8.6 million).
Coptic Calendar. Calendar of the Coptic Orthodox Church, and still used also by the government of Egypt for agricultural events (planting, harvesting); begun AD 284 at end of the age of martyrdom, 12 months each of 30 days each year; thus AD 2000 = Coptic 1716.
Coptic Orthodox Patriarchate of Alexandria. Oriental Orthodox. Global statistics: (1970) 6.1 million; (1995) 9.2 million in 24 countries (1 significantly); largest, Egypt (8.6 million).
Coptic rite. Catholic rite for Egyptian Copts under Rome. Global statistics: (1970) 107,000; (1995) 190,000 in 6 countries; largest, Egypt (190,000).
corporately-evangelized. A society or people who have been evangelized not individually but collectively, together with their traditions and institutions.
corps. In Salvation Army usage, a center for the propagation of the gospel under one or more officers.
correspondence courses. In this field, there are over 370 Christian centers and organizations significant at the national or wider levels.
council. An assembly of ecclesiastics or church representatives convened to discuss matters of doctrine, discipline, law, morals, etc.
Council for World Mission. Originated as London Missionary Society in 1795; 1955, renamed Congregational Council for World Mission; 1976, renamed Council for World Mission.
counseling. A professional service designed to guide an individual to a better understanding of his problems and potentialities by utilizing modern psychological principles
country. The land of a person's origin, birth, residence or citizenship; motherland; a term covering both sovereign nations and non-sovereign territories.
country's population. Defined here as the total present-in-area resident population of a country at a given date or mid-year date.
courier. A person carrying messages, news or information secretly or clandestinely to, within or from underground or illegal churches in anti-Christian lands.
credit unions. Co-operative savings and credit associations that make small loans to their members at low interest rates; widespread among Roman Catholics.
creeds. Brief authoritative doctrinal formulae beginning 'Credo' (Latin: I believe) intended to define what a Christian synod or church holds to be true and essential, and to exclude false doctrine.
Creole. In English usage, a Mulatto or person of mixed Black/White blood, or his language. In Spanish and French usage, a locally-born Spanish-speaking or French-speaking White (in the Antilles, Indian ocean, etc.), or his language.
creole. In linguistic terminology, a composite language or pidgin (qv) that has become the standard or native language of a community.
Criollo. A Spanish-speaking Creole or Mulatto.
crisis theology. Neo-orthodoxy (qv), especially in its pessimistic view of human nature.
cross-cultural missionaries. Full-time Christian workers sent by their churches to work among peoples of a different culture, either within their own nations or abroad.
crown colony. A colony of Britain over which the British crown through a governor retains some control.
crude birth rate. The unstandardized birth rate, not adjusted for influence of age or other variables.
crude death rate. The unstandardized death rate, not adjusted for influence of age or other variables.
crusade evangelism. Mass evangelism through organized city-wide campaigns with most denominations co-operating.
Crusades. Seven major military campaigns from AD 1096-1270 by the Western church to recover the Holy Land from Islam.

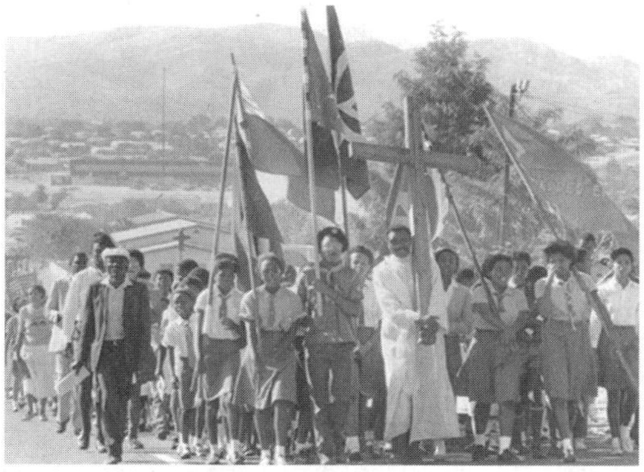
CRUSADES. Student-led march, Namibia.

crusades. Organized evangelistic mass campaigns in large cities a week or more in length.
crypto-Christians. Secret believers in Christ not professing publicly, nor publicly baptized, nor enumerated or known in government census or public-opinion poll, hence unknown to the state or the public or society (but usually affiliated and known to churches), of 7 distinct types: (1) unorganized individuals secretly affiliated to or attending legal churches, including persons who choose to identify themselves publicly as non-Christians; (2) individuals or congregations permanently exiled, deported or in prison or labor camps, treated as non-religious by the state but who remain believing Christians; (3) members of unregistered denominations, and unregistered congregations in legal denominations, which are forced to operate illegally by the state's refusal to grant registration (sometimes termed churches of silence, or catacomb churches); (4) members of organized deliberately-clandestine networks of illegal underground churches; (5) members of churches or marginal bodies in certain countries opposed to the state hence refusing to divulge their affiliation to census enumerators; (6) members of organized movements of believers in Christ who choose not to regard or identify themselves as Christians (but as Hindus, Muslims, non-religious, etc.); and (7) isolated radio believers (qv) in non-Christian or anti-Christian areas remote from existing legal churches. Global statistics: (1970) 59.2 million; (1995) 111.1 million in 85 countries (3 significantly); largest, China (67.0 million); (2000) 123.7 million; (2025) 190.4 million.

crypto-Communists. Secret sympathizers with Communism or secretly members of a Communist party.
crypto-Evangelicals. Secret Evangelicals or sympathizers with Evangelicalism in states or churches hostile to it.
crypto-Jews. Persons adhering secretly to Judaism though professedly Christians; including Marranos (qv).
crypto-Muslims. Persons adhering secretly to Islam, though professedly Christians.
cult. A religion or minority religious group holding beliefs regarded as unorthodox or spurious, a sect.
cultist. A devotee or practitioner of a cult; a sectarian.
cultural barrier. A cultural frontier (qv).
cultural distance. The number of cultural frontiers or barriers that exist between persons of one culture and those of another culture; up to a maximum of 6 frontiers.
cultural frontier. The line of demarcation between one culture and another. As defined in this Encyclopedia, there are up to 6 frontiers between any pair of the worlds' cultures.
culture. The patterned way in which a homogeneous people do things together; an integrated system of socially standardized actions, beliefs, thoughts, feelings, values, customs and institutions, all learned rather than inherited, and artifacts characteristic of a community; the total pattern of human behavior and its products embodied in thought, speech, action and artifacts and dependent upon man's capacity for learning and transmitting knowledge to succeeding generations, which bind a society together and give it a sense of identity, dignity, security and continuity; a worldview at the center together with values, standards of judgement and conduct, language (with proverbs, myths, folk-tales, arts), land and a common history.
culture area, culture province. A geographic unit in which are found similar cultures, i.e. similar patterns of cultural traits and similar modes of subsistence.
cultures. The exact total of cultures or peoples in particular areas depends on the exact definition used. On our definition here, the world has 12,600 constituent peoples or cultures, with 13,000 distinct languages.
cultures, Christian. See Christian cultures.
curate. In Anglicanism and Catholicism, (1) a clergyman who has the cure or care of souls, (2) a clergyman assisting a rector or vicar.
cure of souls. The spiritual charge of a parish.
Curia. The full body of organized congregations, tribunals and offices that aid the pope in the administration and government of the Roman Catholic Church.
cursillistas. Roman Catholics attending a cursillo (qv).
cursillo. (Spanish: short course). A worldwide Roman Catholic movement emphasizing devotion to Christ and spiritual formation of Christian leadership and apostolate, a cursillo can be made only once in one's lifetime, hence is not a retreat.
Cushitic. A Middle Eastern ethnolinguistic family. Global statistics: (2000) 50.7 million in 149 peoples residing in 17 countries (5 significantly); largest, Ethiopia (35.7 million).
Czech/Slavonic. Eastern Orthodox liturgical tradition using Czech and Slavonic in the liturgy. Global statistics: (1970) 60,000; (1995) 50,000 in 1 countries; largest, Czech Republic (50,000).

D

dagoba. A stupa (qv).
daily attenders. Affiliated Christians (church members) who attend church services daily or several times a week.
dancing. See trumping.
Darbyites. Exclusive Brethren (qv).
data. Detailed information of any kind; experientially encountered facts or principles, upon which inferences or arguments can be built or from which an intellectual system of any sort can be constructed.
data bank. A collection of data and information organized for retrieval by a recall scheme.
data-processing. The use of computers for storing, sorting, re-arranging, and retrieving information.
database. A description of the principles of organization of a data bank; the raw data from which a survey manuscript is compiled.
Dataria. An office of the Roman Curia where dates were added to papal letters, now charged with investigating the fitness of candidates for papal benefices.
de facto. (Latin). In fact, in reality, actually, existing in fact (in contrast to de jure).
de facto population. The actual population, enumerated population, or present-in-area population, i.e. physically-present whether residents or non-residents, based on exactly where people have slept or spent the night; made up of all persons actually in the area on a particular day or census date, covering residents, non-residents, visitors and transients, but excluding residents temporarily absent.
de jure. (Latin). By right, of right, by law, legal (in contrast to de facto).
de jure population. The population of a given area who normally inhabit and reside in the area, i.e. who are permanent, habitual, regular and legal residents or inhabitants, based on where people normally or regularly sleep or spend the night; consisting of all persons who habitually live or reside in the area, covering residents and temporarily-absent residents but excluding non-residents, visitors and transients.
deacon. A cleric in major orders ranking above a sub-deacon and below a priest, in Protestantism often a ruling lay elder.
deaconess. In Anglicanism, an ordained woman assigned to parish work; in Protestantism, a woman in an order or sisterhood serving the church in hospitals, schools or on the mission field.
deaf, the. About 365 million people (6% of the world) are deaf or have hearing problems. Many denominations and service agencies across the globe minister to the deaf (e.g. Assemblies of God, USA, has 111 all-deaf congregations with 70 pastors).
dean. The head of the chapter of a body of canons in an Anglican cathedral; head over 10 monks in a Roman Catholic monastery.
deanery. The jurisdiction of a dean.
death rate. The number of deaths per year in a population expressed as a percentage or per thousand of the total population.
dechristianization. The process or causing to turn from Christianity or to deprive of Christian characteristics.
dechristianized. See disaffiliated Christians.
decision cards. Printed cards filled in by enquirers or professing converts at evangelistic campaigns, giving name, address, age, and nature of decision being made.
decision-makers. Those individuals, classes, groups or elites in any society who take initiatives, act as censors, and make decisions particularly with regard to new situations or innovations arising during times of rapid social change. They are usually estimated to number from 5% to 15% of the total population.
decisions. During evangelistic campaigns, enquirers or seekers who make professions or faith in Christ often for the first time, and usually by public profession and the signing of decision cards.
declared Christians. Professing Christians (qv).
declericalization. The process of ridding a society of clerical influence deemed to involve dogmatic and authoritarian control of religious matters by clergy.
deconfessionalization. The process of ridding a society of excessive adherence to confessionalism (qv).
defections. Individuals lost from a religion or religious body either to other religions or religious bodies or to no religion (agnosticism, atheism).
defections from the priesthood. Roman Catholics leaving the priesthood: (1) secular: (1970) 1,848, (1991) 608, (1996) 714; (2) religious; (1975) 1,446, (1981) 359, (1996) 379.
degrees in religious studies. Academic degrees may be taken in over 2,500 departments of theology or religion in as many universities across the world.
deist. An adherent of deism, a rationalist movement based on natural religion, reason and morality, and belief in an otiose God.
Deliverance-Pentecostals. Perfectionist-Pentecostals (qv).
democratic rule. A measure of the extent to which all de facto political power is in the hands of the populace themselves.
demographer. A specialist in demography.
demographic. Relating to the dynamic balance of a population.
demographic audience. Total listening/viewing community including children, influenced regularly by Christian radio/TV broadcasts.
demographic commitment profile. A graphical presentation showing the commitment to Christianity of all sections of a particular population.
demographic evangelization. The extent of evangelization among a large or sizeable population, or the spreading of the gospel through all types of evangelizing activity including the church's evangelism.
demographic increase. An increase, or annual increase, in the size of a population due to secular or non-religious causes.
demographic inertia. The observable fact that large populations only change their basic characteristics, including religious characteristics, gradually or slowly over a period of years.
demographic statistics. The art of collecting and presenting statistical information about a population.
demographic time series. The values of a demographic variable over a period of time.
demography. The scientific and statistical study of human populations, primarily with respect to their size, structure, density, growth, distribution, development, migration and vital statistics.
demon. A pagan or unclean or evil spirit.
demonology. The systematized religious doctrine of evil spirits.
demonstration. In evangelization, the act of making the gospel known or evident by visible or tangible means; showing, manifesting, indicating, proving the merits of the gospel to others.
denomination. An organized Christian church or tradition or religious group or community of believers or aggregate of worship centers or congregations, usually within a specific country, whose component congregations and members are called by the same name in different areas, regarding themselves as an autonomous Christian church distinct from other denominations, churches and traditions. For totals, see under denominations.
denominational. Relating to, or controlled by, a denomination.
denominationalism. Devotion to denominational principles or interests; the emphasizing of denominational differences to the point of being narrowly exclusive.
denominationally-evangelized. Used of a people's evangelization seen only from the standpoint of a single denomination which does not acknowledge the work of other denominations.
denominations. For exact definition, see above under denomination. Global statistics: (1970) 16,075 denominations with 1,130 million members; (1995) 33,090 denominations with 1,769 million members..
dental mission. A foreign missionary society specializing in dentistry and dental services.
dependent. An economically inactive person dependent on others.
dependency. A territory politically dependent on another country or nation.
depopulation. Population decline in a specific area.
deprogramming. The process of forcibly changing or altering a person's religious beliefs; particularly, reversing the programmed indoctrination imparted by modern cultic organizations.
desacralization. The act of ceremonially divesting a taboo of supernatural qualities and rendering it non-sacred, also used for dechristianization (qv).
desertification. The process by which previously-valuable agricultural land or forest becomes a desert.
development. In Christian usage not only a techno-economic process but primarily a process by which both persons and societies come to realize the full potential of human life in a context of social justice with an emphasis on self-reliance (Montreux Conference Report), including a more equal distribution of wealth, including gross national product, in a just and human order. In this field, there are over 220 Christian organizations significant at the national or wider levels.
deviations, Christian. Marginal Christian movements regarded as departures from the established body of Christian beliefs.
devil. The personal supreme spirit of evil and unrighteousness in Jewish and Christian theology.
dharma. (Sanskrit). In Hinduism, social custom, the caste system, religion, the body of cosmic principles by which all things exist; in Buddhism, ideal truth element of existence.
diakonia. (Greek). Service to others; the witness of service.
dialect. A local or regional variety or variant of language.
dialectical materialism. The theory of reality advanced by Marx and Engels and adopted as official Soviet philosophy, maintaining the independent objective reality of matter and its priority both in time and logical importance over mind.
dialectical theology. Neo-orthodoxy (qv), holding that man's attempts to know God by his own reasoning must give way to faith.

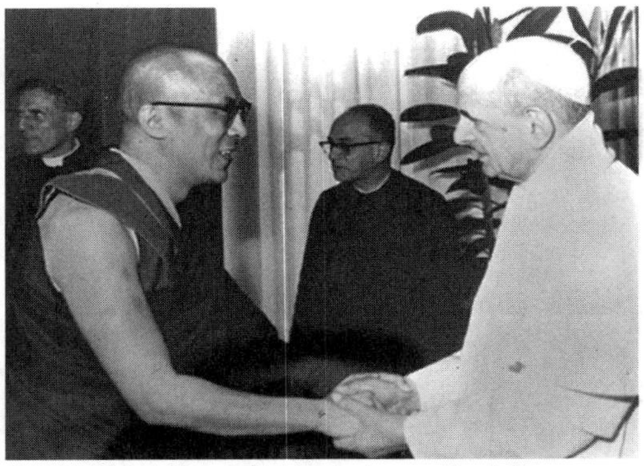

DIALOGUE. Buddhist and Christian leaders meet for dialogue.

dialogue. An exchange of ideas and opinions between a group of Christians and a group of non-Christians.
diaspora. A people of one country dispersed into other countries; the migration, spread, scattering, exile of a people abroad; especially the dispersion of Christians isolated from their own communions.
diaspora church. A church or denomination formerly strongly centralized but now dispersed thinly over a wide area including abroad.
diaspora missionaries. Full-time Christian workers who have usually themselves been emigrants, refugees, deportees or returnees, who now serve their own ethnic communities in diaspora as civilian or military chaplains, evangelists, religious educators, et alii.
dicastery. A department of the Roman Curia in Vatican City. The Curia has 28 principal dicasteries.
didache. (NT Greek). Teaching, the teaching of the Apostles.
differential fertility. The actual reproductive performance of one part of a population by comparison with that of another part.
Digambara. ('Sky-clad', or Naked, or Botika). A member of a major schism (AD 83) within Jainism originally abandoning all worldly possessions including clothes, and asserting that women cannot attain salvation.
digital computer. A computer that operates with numbers expressed directly as digits in a decimal, binary, or other system.
dignitaries. A collective term for clergy and hierarchs holding positions of dignity or honor in the church.
diocesan. (1) A bishop having jurisdiction over a diocese. (2) Relating to a diocese.
diocesan association. In Anglican terminology, a loose organization of church members in Britain who raise money to support one particular Anglican diocese in a developing country. Some 25 exist in Britain.
diocesan bishop. A bishop having jurisdiction over a diocese.
diocesan clergy. In Roman Catholic usage, secular clergy serving in a diocese, as contrasted with religious or regular clergy in religious houses or monasteries. World total (1996): 262,899.
diocesan synod. In Roman Catholic usage since Vatican II, a one-time occasion or assembly of the whole people of God (50% of whom must be priests).
dioceses. (symbol D). Areas over which bishops have ecclesiastical authority.
diplomatic representation. The Holy See, as a sovereign state, maintains diplomatic relations with 103 nations (in 1997) through 15 nunciatures with an apostolic nuncio, and 13 nunciatures headed by an apostolic pro-nuncio; and in addition maintains relations with nationwide Roman Catholic churches through 5 apostolic delegations.
directories. See yearbooks.
disaffiliated Christians. Dechristianized persons, or post-

Christians: baptized Roman Catholics (or other Christians) enumerated as affiliated by a majority or state-linked church but who have recently formally withdrawn or disaffiliated themselves completely from Christianity and now profess to be non-religious (agnostics) or atheists; i.e. recent withdrawals from state or majority churches still however regarded as members by those churches, although in fact now backsliders, lapsed, or apostates. Global statistics: (1970) 11.3 million; (1995) 24.1 million in 11 countries (5 significantly); largest, Italy (9.4 million); (2000) 22.6 million; (2025) 24.9 million.

disaster preparedness. Programs organized by churches and denominations, especially the Seventh-day Adventist Church, with relief, medical-aid centers and mobile disaster-aid units around the world ready to deal with either natural or man-made disasters as they arise.

disbelief. Refusal to believe; withholding or rejection of belief; atheism, skepticism, irreligion.

disciple. (verb). To give peoples the opportunity to become followers of Christ; to train individual believers extensively over a long period, with a view to them also becoming disciplers in multiplication evangelism (qv).

disciple. A committed follower; in biblical usage, any believer in Jesus Christ (not restricted only to mature or fully-committed or dedicated followers).

discipler. A Christian worker aiming to disciple a few believers with a view to making them also disciplers.

Disciples. (Churches of Christ) (Restoration Movement). Protestant tradition also known as Restorationist, Restoration Baptist, Campbellite, or simply 'Christian'. Global statistics: (1970) 1.8 million; (1995) 1.2 million in 17 countries; largest, USA (1.0 million).

discipline. One of the major areas of learning in the academic world.

discipline, church. A body of laws and practical rules relating to conduct and church government. Church members breaking or flouting such laws may be placed temporarily under discipline (usually exclusion from communion or the Lord's Table), or even, eventually be excommunicated (qv).

discipling. The first of the 3 stages in church planting and growth (discipling, baptizing, perfecting, based on the Great Commission in Matthew 28.19), involving the initial or preliminary bringing of a whole people to renounce idolatry or unbelief as a group, and to a group acknowledgement of Christ as Lord; measured as the total number of all professing Christians.

disestablishment. The act of a state in sundering the legal relationships between it and its established church or churches.

dispensary. A place where medicines are dispensed to ambulance patients; see medical centers

dispensationalism. Adherence to or advocacy of a futurist premillennialist system of interpreting history in terms of a series of God's dispensations, or 7 periods of history during which a particular divine revelation has predominated in the affairs of mankind; usually, futurist premillennialist and pretribulational.

displaced person. A person who has been moved by a public authority from his place of origin.

disputed episcopal churches. Autocephalous Catholic and other episcopal churches with disputed claim to apostolic succession of bishops.

dissent. Religious dissension or nonconformity.

dissenter. One who differs from an established church in the matter of doctrines, rites or government; a nonconformist.

dissertation. An extended systematic written treatment of a subject submitted for a doctoral degree, typically based on independent research and giving evidence of a candidate's mastery of both his own subject and of scholarly method.

district. An ecclesiastical division in larger denominations.

district superintendent. In Methodism, a minister with oversight of churches and workers in a district.

divine. A priest, clergyman, theologian, one skilled in divinity.

divine healing. Healing attributed to the direct agency of God, usually in response to faith.

Divine Science. See Religious Science.

divinity. The science of divine things; the science that deals with God, his laws and moral government, and the way of salvation; theology.

division. The act, process, or an instance of dividing into parts or portions; schism, breakoff, secession.

documentation center. A center for the collecting, assembling, coding and disseminating of recorded knowledge comprehensively treated, and for the processing of all kinds of documentation.

dogma. A doctrine or body of doctrines of theology and religion formally stated and authoritatively proclaimed by a church.

dogmatic constitution. The most solemn form of conciliar utterance emanating from a Roman Catholic ecumenical council. The most imposing achievement of Vatican II was 'Constitutio Dogmatica de Ecclesia', also called 'Lumen Gentium'.

domestic church. A term used in Roman Catholic circles for the family, or believers in a family.

dormant Christians. See non-practicing Christians.

double affiliation. See doubly-affiliated Christians.

doubling. The practice, in Africa and India, of having 2 preachers for a sermon: the first preaching a sentence at a time, the second repeating the sentence for emphasis and often (in the open air) louder or in a different direction.

doubly-affiliated Christians. Persons affiliated to or claimed by 2 denominations at once (especially by Evangelical and Catholic churches in Latin America and Latin Europe, and by state churches and free churches in Scandinavia). Global statistics: (1970) 29.7 million; (1995) 174.3 million in 253 countries (21 significantly); largest, Brazil (50.7 million); (2000) 194.7 million; (2025) 308.4 million.

doubter. An unbeliever, agnostic, skeptic.

drama, religious. See religious drama.

Dravidian. An Indo-Iranian ethnolinguistic family. Global statistics: (2000) 230.7 million in 121 peoples residing in 36 countries (5 significantly); largest, India (218.8 million).

Druzes. Members of an 11th-century Muslim Shia Ismaili schism with Christian and Jewish elements; strongest in Syria and Lebanon. Global statistics: (1970) 375,000; (1995) 744,000; (2000) 834,000; (2025) 1.4 million.

dual citizenship. Dual nationality, multiple nationality; the status of an individual who is a citizen of 2 or more states.

dual membership. Overlapping membership (qv).

Dunkers. Dippers; German Baptists practicing trine immersion, love feasts and simplicity of life. Global statistics: (1970) 465,000; (1995) 603,000 in 10 countries; largest, Central African Rep (290,000).

Dupka. Karma-pa or Red Hat (Unreformed) Lamaism (qv).

DXers. Amateur practitioners of long-distance radio transmission.

dynamic equivalence church. A local church, or denomination that has an equivalent impact on or in its own society and culture to that of the original New Testament church, with particular reference to indigeneity, degree of foreign dominance, relevance, vitality, scriptural quality, decision-making patterns, self-image, community-held image, et alia.

dynamic equivalence translation. A translation of Scripture, as developed by the United Bible Societies, designed to be the closest natural equivalent to the source-language message, i.e. to discover what the text meant at the time of writing in order to communicate its full equivalent meaning today (e.g. in English, the NEB, JB, GNB Bibles, with the NIV halfway between formal correspondence and dynamic equivalent). By contrast, a formal correspondence translation is an exact or literal or word-for-word translation of the original.

Dyophysites. Eastern Orthodox, Chalcedonian.

E

Early African. One of the 13 geographical races of mankind, speaking 57 languages. Global statistics: (2000) 1.1 million in 114 peoples residing in 21 countries; largest, Congo-Zaire (194,000).

Early Fathers. The Apostolic Fathers (qv).

East Syrians. Assyrians, Nestorians, Syro-Chaldeans.

Easter. Annual church celebration commemorating Christ's resurrection.

Easter attender. A church member who attends church at Easter.

Easter communicant. A church member who receives communion at Easter.

Eastern Church. A collective term for Eastern Orthodox, Oriental Orthodox, Assyrian (Nestorian) Eastern-rite Catholic and other churches east of the Mediterranean.

Eastern Orthodox. Chalcedonian Christians, sometimes collectively referred to as Greek Orthodox and excluding Oriental Orthodox (qv). Global statistics: (1970) 83.7 million; (1995) 132.4 million in 240 countries (13 significantly); largest, Russia (74.1 million).

Eastern rite. (Oriental-rite) Catholics. All Roman Catholics or Catholics in communion with the Church of Rome who follow rites other than the Latin rite (totaling 28 rites and sub-rites). A full listing is given in Table 1-5. Global statistics: (1970) 10.1 million; (1995) 16.8 million in 35 countries (2 significantly); largest, Ukraine (4.2 million).

Eastern Syrians. East Syrians (qv).

ecclesia. (NT Greek). A church; in particular, a local congregation of the Christadelphians.

ecclesial communion. In Roman Catholic usage, collegiality or co-responsibility (qv).

ecclesial community. A basic community (qv).

ecclesiarch. A high church official or ruling prelate.

ecclesiastic. A person in holy orders or consecrated to the service of the church: a clergyman

ecclesiastical. Relating to the church as a formal and established institution.

ecclesiastical crime. Term relating especially to embezzlements of church funds by top custodians. Global total (in 2000): $16 billion per year.

ecclesiastical name. A new Christian name taken on election by popes, patriarchs and other high ecclesiastics, usually one in a series down the centuries.

ecclesiastical province. A group of dioceses territorially contiguous, forming an ecclesiastical unit; so termed because originally coincident with the Provinces of the Roman empire. (See under province).

ecclesiastical territories. In Roman Catholic usage, circumscriptions or jurisdictions (qv).

ecclesiastical tradition. A church's or denomination's main tradition, family, rite, churchmanship, etc., with which it is most closely connected historically. Global total of all major traditions: 300, including 27 Roman Catholic rites and sub-rites.

ecclesiastical type. A descriptive typology combining ecclesiastico-cultural major bloc, and ecclesiastical tradition.

ecclesiastico-cultural major blocs. A global typology of 6 basic types of Christianity: Anglican, Marginal Christian, Independent, Orthodox, Protestant, Roman Catholic.

ecclesiography. Descriptive analyses of churches and denominations.

ecclesiola. A 'church within the church', or small group of Christians living a distinct and nearly separate existence, yet remaining within the institutional church without open schism.

ecclesiology. The science or study of the doctrine of the church, or church policy, or the study of ecclesiastical art and antiquities.

ecology. The study of the relation of social organization and culture to physical environment and technology.

ecumenical. Worldwide, general, universal, catholic; relating to the whole of a body of churches.

ecumenical centers. Centers operated by the churches primarily to sponsor ecumenical or interdenominational contacts and understanding. Total centers significant at national or wider levels number over 400.

ecumenical commission. (1) A Roman Catholic committee set up to deal with other separated churches in a particular diocese or country. (2) An organization serving the major denominations in an area. In this field some 200 significant commissions or agencies exist.

ecumenical council. Assemblies of bishops and other ecclesiastical representatives of the whole world's churches, whose decisions on doctrine, liturgy discipline, et alia, are binding on all Christians in those churches. Eastern Orthodox accept only the first 7 ecumenical councils, up to Nicea II (AD 787); Roman Catholics accept 21 councils including Vatican I and Vatican II (1962-5).

ecumenical Evangelicals. Conciliar Evangelicals (qv).

ecumenical movement. The movement to bring together all denominations and Christian bodies for fellowship, consultation, joint action, and eventually organic union.

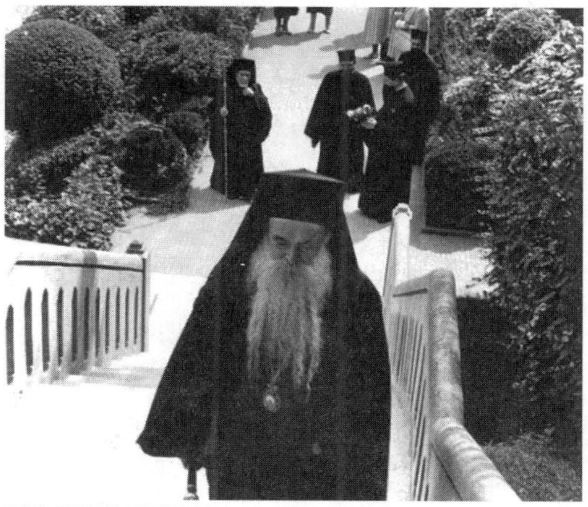

ECUMENICAL PATRIARCH. Athenagoras at meeting of Primates.

ecumenical patriarch. The patriarch of Constantinople, the acknowledged highest ecclesiastical office in the Eastern Orthodox Church by virtue of a primacy of honor.

Ecumenical Patriarchate of Constantinople. Leading patriarchate of the Eastern Orthodox world, since AD 451; New Rome, the 'Second Rome'. Global statistics: (1970) 83.7 million; (1995) 132.4 million in 240 countries (13 significantly); largest, Russia (74.1 million).

ecumenicity. The quality or state of being ecumenical.

ecumenics. The study of the nature, mission, problems and strategy of the Christian church from the perspective of its ecumenical character as a worldwide Christian fellowship.

ecumenism. Ecumenical principles and practices as exemplified in the ecumenical movement.

ecumenist. An advocate of ecumenism.

education rate. The percentage of the school-age population (aged 5-24) who are enrolled in schools.

ekistics. The science, art, study, and development of human habitation and dwellings.

electronic data processing. (EDP). The manipulation of data by means of a computer (qv).

eligible communicant. A church member in good standing who is eligible to partake of the sacrament of the Lord's Supper, whether in fact he does so or not.

emigrant. A person who leaves a country or region to establish permanent residence elsewhere.

emigration. The movement of migrants out of a particular territory.

emigre. A person forced to emigrate by political or other circumstances beyond his control.

encyclical. A letter sent by a bishop or high church official, especially the Roman Catholic pope, treating a matter of grave or timely importance and intended for extensive circulation.

encyclopedia. A work that treats comprehensively either all the various branches of knowledge, or a particular branch of knowledge, arranged either alphabetically or topically.

enquirers. See decisions.

enrolments. The term used to enumerate the total number of persons in an area or country who have registered for postal Bible correspondence courses, either active at present, or an accumulated total over the years since courses began there.

enumeration. Any operation which is designed to yield a population total using a list rather than a simple count.

enumeration, Christian. The spelling-out, describing in detail, listing in order, counting, or numbering of a Christian population or of some Christian entity or activity.

enumerator. A government employee who administers a census schedule of questions direct to the populace.

environment. The aggregate of social, cultural and ecological conditions (as customs, laws, language, religion, economic and political organization, climate, pollution, etc.) that influence the life of an individual or community.

eparchy. (1) In the Eastern Orthodox Church, a diocese or ecclesiastical province, especially in the early centuries AD. (2) In Roman Catholic usage a diocese of an Eastern rite, especially Malankara (India).

episcopacy. Government of the church by bishops or by a hierarchy.

Episcopal. Used of churches governed by bishops especially in North American Anglicanism.

episcopal. Hierarchical, related to a bishop, a diocese, or a denomination or tradition governed by bishops.
episcopal area. In Episcopalian (Anglican) usage, a subdivision of a diocese that is placed under the episcopal authority of a suffragan or assistant bishop.
episcopal commissariat. (symbol EC). A Roman Catholic diocese under a political regime not recognized by the Holy See, which attaches it to a diocese elsewhere.
episcopal conferences. Formally-constituted conferences of Roman Catholic bishops, totaling 108 national and 13 international conferences (1996).
Episcopalians. North American or USA usage for the term Anglicans (qv).

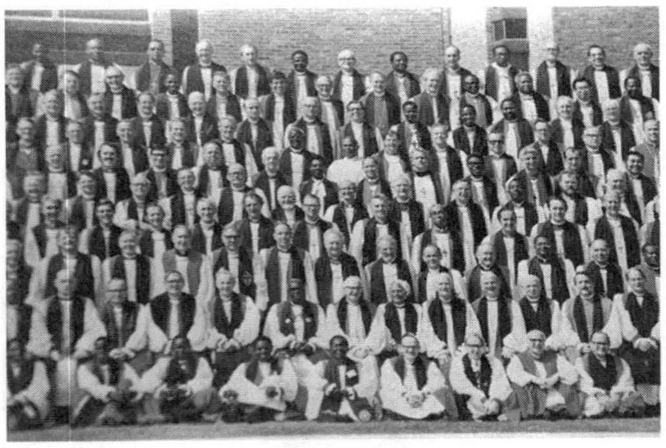

EPISCOPATE. 600 Anglican bishops attend Lambeth Conference.

episcopate. The whole body of bishops; office of a bishop, or the period over which a bishop is in office.
episcopi vagantes. (Latin). Bishops-at-large (qv).
erection. In Roman Catholic usage, the formal establishment of a new diocese.
eremite. A hermit; a Christian living for religious reasons in solitary confinement.
eschatological sign. The missionary preaching of the gospel among all nations as the sign of the imminence of the End (the Second Coming of Christ), given in Matthew 24.14 and Mark 13.10.
eschatology. The doctrine of the Last Things; Christian doctrine of the Second Coming of Christ and the ultimate destiny or purpose of mankind and of the world.
Eskimo-Aleut. An Arctic Mongoloid ethnolinguistic family. Global statistics: (2000) 160,000 in 20 peoples residing in 5 countries (1 significantly); largest, USA (69,000).
esoteric. Used of sects whose doctrines and rites guard a mystery known only to the initiated.
Esoteric Vehicle. Tantrayana, or Tantrism school of Buddhists (qv).
established church. A church that is recognized by law as the official church of a nation, supported by civil authority; state church, national church.
ethics, Christian. The discipline dealing with what is good and bad or right and wrong, or with moral duty and obligation, from the Christian standpoint; the principles of conduct governing an individual or a profession.
Ethiopian Calendar. Based on the Coptic Calendar (qv), this calendar (still used by church and state in AD 2000) is exactly 8 years behind the Gregorian Calendar (thus AD 2000 = Ethiopian 1992), begins its year on 11 or 12 September, and has 12 months each of 30 days each year, adjusted at leap years with a 13th month of 5 or 6 days.
Ethiopian rite. Rite for Ethiopian Catholics under Rome. Global statistics: (1970) 87,000; (1995) 141,000 in 3 countries; largest, Eritrea (74,000).
Ethiopian, Ethiopic. Oriental Orthodox liturgical tradition, using dead language Ge'ez in its liturgy. Global statistics: (1970) 11.9 million; (1995) 21.9 million in 15 countries (2 significantly); largest, Ethiopia (20.2 million).
Ethiopic. (1) A Middle Eastern ethnolinguistic family. Global statistics: (2000) 28.2 million in 31 peoples residing in 11 countries (2 significantly); largest, Ethiopia (25.2 million).
ethnic. Referring to a group distinguished by common cultural characteristics.
ethnic group. A group having common physical and mental traits, common heredity and cultural tradition.
ethnic Muslims. A term used to describe the 34 million persons (in 1970) belonging to traditionally Muslim nationalities in the USSR, of whom about 82% profess to be or regard themselves as religious Muslims.
ethnic origin. The racial, linguistic, tribal or cultural origin of a specific group.
ethnic religionists. Adherents of major world religions limited in theory or in practice to a particular ethnolinguistic group or groups; including Confucians, Hindus, Jains, Jews, Parsis, Shintoists, Sikhs, et alia.
ethnography. A branch of anthropology that describes the origin and filiation of races and cultures.
ethnolinguistic composition. The components parts of a population, with the percentage size of each, adding up to 100%.
ethnolinguistic families. A total of 71 micro-races or local races under which all peoples of the world can be described.
ethnolinguistic family. A large family of peoples, sometimes termed a local race or a micro-race.
ethnolinguistic people. An ethnic or racial group speaking its own language or mother tongue.
Ethnoreligionists. A collective term for primal or primitive religionists, animists, spirit-worshippers, shamanists (qv), ancestor-venerators, polytheists, pantheists, traditionalists (in Africa), local or tribal folk-religionists; including adherents of neo-paganism or non-Christian local or tribal syncretistic or nativistic movements, cargo cults, witchcraft eradication cults, possession healing movements, tribal messianic movements; still occasionally termed pagans, heathen, fetishists; usually confined each to a single tribe or people, hence tribal or local as opposed to 'universal' (open to any or all peoples). Global statistics: (1970) 160.2 million; (1995) 214.0 million in 142 countries (30 significantly); largest, China (53.5 million); (2000) 228.3 million; (2025) 277.2 million.
ethnology. The study of a culture on a comparative basis; cultural anthropology.
eucharist. (NT Greek: thanksgiving). The sacrament of the Lord's Supper.
eucharistic congress. A Roman Catholic series of congresses centered on the public celebration of the mass.
eugenics. Policies aimed at improving the quality of human populations.
Eurafrican. An African ethnolinguistic family; Colored Mulatto. Global statistics: (2000) 10.2 million in 83 peoples residing in 44 countries (11 significantly); largest, South Africa (4.1 million).
Eurasian. (1) The issue of a European and an Asian. (2) An Asian ethnolinguistic family. Global statistics: (2000) 1.8 million in 26 peoples residing in 16 countries; largest, China (669,000).
Euronesian. (1) The issue of a European and an Indonesian/Melanesian/Micronesian/Polynesian. (2) A Pacific ethnolinguistic family. Global statistics: (2000) 3.9 million in 35 peoples residing in 23 countries (8 significantly); largest, Philippines (2.7 million).
European. One of the 13 geographical races of mankind, with 180 languages. Global statistics: (2000) 923.1 million in 1,744 peoples residing in 235 countries (96 significantly); largest, Russia (117.8 million).
evangelical. (1) In Protestant and Anglican usage, of similar meaning to Evangelical. (2) In Roman Catholic usage, relating to the gospel.
evangelical academy. A German Protestant center to bring church and secular world into contact, some 17 such centers flourished in West Germany from 1945-75.
Evangelical Anglicans. Anglican Evangelicals (qv).
Evangelical Catholics. Roman Catholics who also call or regard themselves as Evangélicos, Evangéliques, or Evangelicals, or are also affiliated to churches which the state terms Evangelical (Protestant, Anglican, indigenous or marginal Protestant); in Latin America, Evangélicos who in a census are still regarded as, or profess to be, Roman Catholics. Global total: (AD 2000) 30 million.
evangelical counsels. The vows of the religious life: voluntary poverty, perpetual chastity, entire obedience.
Evangelicalism. The doctrines held by Evangelicals.
Evangelicals. A sub-division mainly of Protestants consisting of all affiliated church members calling themselves Evangelicals, or all persons belonging to Evangelical congregations, churches or denominations; characterized by commitment to personal religion (including new birth or personal conversion experience), reliance on Holy Scripture as the only basis for faith and Christian living, emphasis on preaching and evangelism, and usually on conservatism in theology; usually divided into the 3 groupings (qv) Conservative Evangelicals, Conciliar Evangelicals, and Fundamentalists. Global statistics: (1970) 93.4 million; (1995) 193.4 million in 237 countries (50 significantly); largest, USA (39.3 million); (2000) 210.6 million; (2025) 327.8 million.
evangelicals. The definition is based on 7 key components, as follows: evangelicals are believers centered on the person of Jesus and obedient to his Great Commission, committed to the evangel (the gospel), as set forth in the Bible, by means of their day-to-day personal witness to Christ, their organized evangelism, and their involvement in his mission to the world, looking and working toward his second and final Advent. Also termed Great Commission Christians. Global statistics: (1970) 277.1 million; (1995) 603.1 million in 237 countries (137 significantly); largest, USA (93.4 million); (2000) 647.8 million; (2025) 887.5 million.
evangelism. The activities involved in spreading the gospel.
Evangelism-in-Depth. A program and philosophy of mobilizing the total membership and resources of the churches of an area for proclamation of the gospel to non-Christians; initiated in 1960 in Latin America, later on other continents; keynote-'The expansion of any movement is in direct proportion to its success in mobilizing its total membership in continuous propagation of its beliefs'.

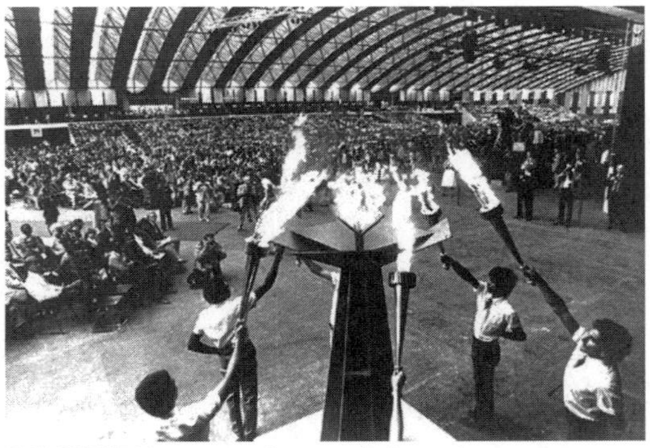

EVANGELIST. Itinerant preachers meet in Amsterdam.

evangelist. One who offers the good news through public preaching.
evangelistic. Concerned with offering the good news through public preaching.
evangelistic association. A para-church agency formed around the evangelistic ministry of a professional evangelist (mostly in the USA), which then tends to become virtually a separate denomination.
evangelistic campaigns. Each year several hundred campaigns of one to ten weeks' duration are held in cities across the world, usually co-operatively by most denominations in an area, specifically for evangelistic purposes.
evangelistic distance. The number of distinct religious and cultural frontiers or barriers that exist between a Christian worker, evangelist or missionary, or a group of such and their target population; measured by adding cultural distance and religious distance up to a maximum of 11 frontiers.
evangelistic frontier. From the standpoint of evangelism, a religious or cultural frontier (qv) which forms a barrier or obstacle to evangelists or other Christian workers.
evangelistic outreach. See outreach into the world.
evangelistic witness. An Orthodox term used in preference to evangelism or evangelization.
evangelistics. The science of the propagation of Christianity.
evangelization. (1) The whole process of spreading the good news of the Kingdom of God. (2) The extent to which the good news has been spread. (3) The extent of awareness of Christianity, Christ and the gospel.
evangelize. To spread the good news of Jesus Christ, with signs following, persuading and convincing people to obey him as Lord in the fellowship of his church, and to serve him responsibly in the world.
evangelized. The state of having had the good news spread or offered; the state of being aware of Christianity, Christ and the gospel.
evangelized non-Christians. Persons who are not believers in Christ but have nevertheless become sufficiently aware of Christianity, Christ and the gospel to be regarded as evangelized. Global statistics: (2000) 2,443,578,000.
evangelizer. One who spreads the good news; used of (1) Christ, (2) any Christian active in evangelism, and (3) any full-time worker involved in evangelism.
evangelizing. Actively involved in spreading the good news.
evangelizing Christians. Persons who contribute definitely and consciously to the ongoing process of the evangelization of their own people or country or the world; the effective evangelizing agency among a people or in a country; the force for evangelism; measured as all practicing Christians.
Evangélico. (Italian, Portuguese, Spanish). The term usually used for Protestant in Latin Europe and America; including also Anglican, marginal Christian, and Non-White indigenous (Christians).
examining chaplain. In Anglican usage, an archdeacon or other learned clergyman who examines candidates for holy orders, usually 3 or more to each diocese.
exarch. The primate of an independent Orthodox church, or a bishop with a special charge
exarchate. (symbol E). The jurisdiction of an exarch.
exarchate apostolic. (symbol EA). The jurisdiction of an exarch apostolic, the title for a bishop with a special mission or commission in some Eastern churches.
Exclusive Brethren. Followers of Protestant tradition begun 1848 ex Christian Brethren; also termed Closed, Strict, or Plymouth Brethren; exclusive fundamentalist/dispensationalist. Global statistics: (1970) 155,000; (1995) 186,000 in 20 countries; largest, Britain (79,000).
excommunicated. Persons placed under ecclesiastical censure by competent authority for infraction of church law or discipline, and then excluded from communion or the sacraments, often permanently. It remains relatively rare in most churches.
exegesis. In theology, the explanation of the original meaning of biblical texts.
exile church. A denomination that has largely left, or been expelled from, its original homeland by political circumstances and has begun permanent life in a foreign land; mainly from Russia, Estonia, Latvia and Eastern Europe.
exorcism. The act or practice of expelling evil spirits by means of prayer or set formulae and rituals; often practiced in larger denominations only by professionally competent and authorized clergy.
expatriate. A person who resides or lives in a foreign country.
experiential religions. Those which lay more emphasis on religious experience than on historical dogma (e.g. mysticism, faith-healing, charismatic renewal, Eastern religions, yoga, TM, etc.).
exposition. In preaching or Biblical teaching, the art of interpreting the original meaning (exegisis) and then applying it to contemporary life and issues.
exposure. In evangelization, the act or extent of subjecting a population to the influence of the gospel; explaining, laying open, making accessible, making known, setting forth, exhibiting, revealing, disclosing, bringing to light.
extension growth. Visible, measurable growth of the church, especially in the planting of new congregations and churches.
extrapolation. The estimation of values of a series beyond or outside the range of existing known values.

F

faith. Belief and trust in and loyalty to God in Christ; firm or unquestioning belief in something for which there is no proof; orthodox religious belief; also used for religion, creed, credo.
faith missions. A term generally applied to those non-denominational and interdenominational foreign missionary agencies since 1860 whose governing concept is to look to God alone for financial support.
faith-healing. A method or practice of treating diseases by prayer and exercise of faith in God.

faithful, the. The adherents of a system of religious belief, especially Eastern Orthodoxy; baptized Christians as opposed to catechumens.
family. Defined primarily by reference to relationships which pertain to or arise from reproductive processes and which are regulated by law or by custom.
family income, average. The total income of an average family or household in an area, computed by multiplying per capita income by average household size (qv).
fast. A time in the calendar of certain churches for abstaining from food as contrasted with a feast day.
fasting. Abstaining from food voluntarily for a time as a religious duty.
father. Used of ecclesiastics, i.e. of Catholic, Orthodox and some Anglican bishops, priests and monks, both in direct address and as title prefixed to the name.
feast. A religious festival of rejoicing as opposed to a fast; an annual holy day.
federation. A union of nations, states, societies, organizations, churches or denominations.
federations of religious communities. See religious institutes, federations of.
fellowship. A Christian group with intimate relationship, common purposefulness, brotherhood, partnership, and communion: in some denominations, used of a local worshipping congregation.
Ferrette succession churches. Autocephalous Catholic churches under bishops-at-large (qv) whose disputed episcopal orders pass through Mar Julius Ferrette (died 1889).
fertility. Capacity for reproducing, actual reproductive capacity, birthrate of a population.
festival. A Christian feast day: Christmas, Easter, Whitsuntide, Trinity Sunday, etc.
festival attenders. Affiliated Christians (church members) who attend church services of public worship only on the Christian festivals (Christmas, Easter, etc.).
fetishist. A believer in magical fetishes (objects believed by primitive peoples to have preternatural power).
field survey. An inquiry or survey in which information is obtained by personal interview.
Fijian. An Oceanic ethnolinguistic family. Global statistics: (2000) 352,000 in 10 peoples residing in 5 countries (1 significantly); largest, Fiji (338,000).
film. In the field of cinema and film, there are over 170 significant Christian organizations.
film libraries. Many denominations, councils and parachurch agencies own and operate libraries of 8mm, 16mm and 35mm movies which are hired out to churches on specific occasions.
films, religious. See religious drama.
financial member. A term used in some denominations in Africa for a full church member who has paid his annual dues.
Finnish/Slavonic. Eastern Orthodox liturgical tradition using Finnish and Slavonic in the liturgy. Global statistics: (1970) 58,000; (1995) 65,000 in 2 countries; largest, Finland (59,000).
first evangelization. A term used in Roman Catholic mission circles for the first preaching of the gospel in a newly-entered non-Christian area.
First World. The Western (or Capitalist) world, as loosely contrasted with the Second (Communist) world (qv) and Third World (qv).
fishing. A term used in evangelistic circles for street evangelism among passers-by.
fission. Splitting, breaking-up into pieces, schism, secession.
focused interview. In sociological research, an interview with a key individual, at a late stage in the research, in which key questions are asked focused on the origins and causes of phenomena under study.
folk media. Small-scale or local media, indigenous media, alternative media, participatory media, group media: traditional story-telling, wandering minstrels/storytellers, drama, traditional performing arts, live theatre, dance, poetry, recitation, mime, song, et al.
folk religion. Popular religion, popular religiosity (qv).
folk-Catholicism. Roman Catholic popular piety, religion, or religiosity (qv).
folk-religionists. Followers of traditional religion (qv), popular religion or religiosity (qv), or local or folk religion.
follow-through evangelism. Mass evangelistic campaigns in which converts or enquirers are systematically followed up, taught and trained in discipleship within local churches.
follow-up. A system of pursuing an initial evangelistic effort by following enquirers or converts to assist them joining churches.
force for evangelism. The total of all evangelizing persons and influences available in a given situation; the effective evangelizing nucleus, or the total community of all evangelizing Christians as measured by the total practicing Christians.
foreign. Alien; situated outside a place or country.
foreign chaplaincy. A chaplaincy, parish or mission ministering in a foreign country to expatriate residents who are members of the home church in its own land.
foreign evangelization. Evangelization by foreign persons outside a particular group, people or area.
foreign forces. Resident military forces from outside of a country.
foreign missionaries. Full-time long-term Christian workers sent abroad by parent foreign missionary societies, and regularly termed and terming themselves missionaries. Global statistics: 419,000 (AD 2000).
foreign missionaries and personnel. Full-time long-term foreign missionaries and similar personnel of all churches and from all countries now serving abroad.
foreign missionary councils. Consultative or executive councils of foreign mission organizations in sending countries, to facilitate co-operation and liaison. Over 60 such councils at the national level exist.
foreign missionary societies. Organizations founded for and dedicated to the purpose of extending Christianity to foreign countries and their populations. Total for all traditions: (2000) about 5,000.
foreign missionary training centers. These number over 500 worldwide.
foreign missions. The enterprise of taking a religion to foreign countries and planting it there through organized, full-time workers.
foreign personnel. Full-time long-term Christian workers serving in a foreign country, sent abroad on behalf of their churches, but who are not described as and do not use the term missionaries.
foreigner. An alien, stranger, expatriate; a person belonging to or owing allegiance to a foreign country.
formal correspondence translation. An exact or literal or word-for-word translation of Scripture preserving the form of the original from its original languages into contemporary languages (e.g. in English the AV (KJV), ASV, RV, NASB, RSV), in contrast to UBS policy of dynamic equivalence.
fortnightly attenders. Affiliated Christians (church members) who attend church services of public worship on average twice a month.
fraternal worker. A term in use in ecumenical Protestant circles, intended in the 1960s as a replacement for 'foreign missionary'.
Free Christians. Unitarians (qv).
Free churches. Minority churches not established or under state control, specially in countries with majority state churches.
free distribution of scriptures. Annual statistics of placements of scriptures, donated without cost to recipients.
Free Methodists. Holiness Christians (qv).
Free Pentecostals. Perfectionist-Pentecostals (qv).
Freemasons. Members of the secret fraternal order of Free and Accepted Masons, the largest worldwide secret society, spread by the advance of the British empire; 7,500,000 members worldwide (5 million in USA, 1.5 million in British Isles, 15,000 in France, 5,000 in Kenya also strong in Italy, Germany, Liberia, et alia. Strong hostility to the churches especially Roman Catholic Church) in France, Italy, Latin countries; banned in USSR, Hungary, Poland, Spain, Portugal, China, Indonesia, Egypt, et alia.
freethinkers. Agnostics, skeptics, unbelievers.
Friends. (quakers). A Protestant tradition dating from 1652. Global statistics: (1970) 348,000; (1995) 403,000 in 53 countries; largest, USA (132,000).
Friends World Committee for Consultation. (FWCC). The major Quaker world communion. Global statistics: (1970) 348,000; (1995) 403,000 in 53 countries; largest, USA (132,000).
fringe members. Persons who are church members on the rolls, but only in a marginal sense, being irregular or occasional or casual church attenders or rarely seen, or adherents only partly committed to church law and discipline or only partially accepting Christian faith and practice.
frontier. From a missionary point of view, the barrier or demarcation that exists between 2 distinct cultures or languages or types of religions, and which must be crossed before missionary contact and communication can be established.
fulfillment. Accomplishment, consummation, completion, e.g. of the Great Commission.
full communion. In Anglican usage, complete sacramental fellowship and mutual acceptance of ministries between 2 or more confessions or churches.
full member. An adult church member who is a baptized communicant in good standing within his church.
full-time ministry. Ordained persons whose primary occupation is in some form of ministry.
full-time workers. Persons whose primary occupation is in Christian or church work.
fully-evangelized. Used of an area or population in which the gospel has become universally known.
functional literacy. A higher level of competence than basic ability to read and write, qualifying a person to meet many of the practical needs of daily life in his culture or group
fund-raising. Over 1,000 organizations are devoted to direct raising of funds for Christian use. In many countries there are Christian para-church organizations, or branches of denominations, which specialize in fund-raising activities on behalf of local churches or development projects.
Fundamentalism. A militantly conservative movement in North American Protestantism originating around 1910 in opposition to modernist tendencies and emphasizing as fundamental to Christianity a group of 5 or 7 basic doctrines: inerrant verbal inspiration of the Bible, Virgin Birth, miracles of Christ, Resurrection, total depravity of man, substitutionary atonement, premillennial Second Coming.
fundamentalism, structural. A very conservative attitude to existing church structure regarded as of divine origin, or unchangeable, or otherwise sacrosanct.
fundamentalist. An adherent or proponent of Protestant Fundamentalism, often narrowed to premillennialism or dispensationalism.
Fundamentalists. Evangelicals (usually premillennialists or dispensationalists) holding the doctrine of the infallibility of the Bible, opposing modernism, liberalism and ecumenism, and stressing the 5 or 7 basic doctrines; all persons affiliated to denominations holding Fundamentalist doctrines; in the USA, estimated at 50 million persons: of whom 40% (20 million) are premillennialists.
furlough. A leave of absence granted to a foreign missionary to return to his home country for a time for leave.
fusion. The union, merging, blending of 2 or more denominations into one church.
future. The time or period or era that is still to come.
future research. Futurology (qv).
future studies. Research studies on the probable future development of a situation, involving the producing of alternative futures (qv) or possible scenarios.
futurist. Relating to futurology (qv).
futuristics. Futurology (qv).
futurology. The science of the systematic study of the future.
futurology of Christianity. Literature discussing possible futures of Christianity and the churches has been extensive for the last 100 years.

G

gallicanism. The movement, or body of doctrine, which asserted the complete freedom of the Roman Catholic Church (especially in France) from the ecclesiastical authority of the papacy. Vatican I (1870) signified the end of the movement within the Roman Church, but it survives in Old Catholic and other autocephalous Catholic churches.
gathered church. A denomination brought into being through the influx of individuals, families or small groups often through the mission station approach, rather than by means of a people movement (qv).

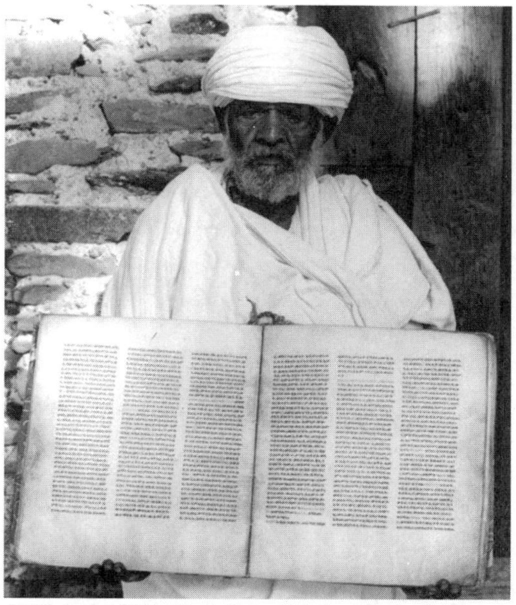

GE'EZ. Ancient Bible written in Ge'ez, Ethiopian Orthodox Church.

Ge'ez. Ethiopic, an extinct Semitic language still used as the liturgical language of the Ethiopian Orthodox Church.
Gelukpa. Yellow Hat (Reformed) Lamaism (qv).
general. The chief of a religious order or all houses or congregations under one religious rule; superior general of the Jesuit order; supreme commander of the Salvation Army.
general census. A population census in which all inhabitants of a country are counted simultaneously.
general order of magnitude. A number or statistic or set of statistics which establishes the broad area of size of a particular situation, whether local, denominational, tribal, national, regional, racial, continental or global.
general-order estimate. A number or statistic indicating approximately (rounded to the nearest 10, 100, 1000 or million) the broad area of size or magnitude of a particular category or variable.
generalate. The headquarters of a Roman Catholic religious institute headed by a general or superior general.
generation. (1) A group of persons born within a specified period of time, generally taken as a calendar year. (2) The average span of time, variously computed and varying according to cultural and other conditions, between the birth of parents and that of their children; usually taken as 30 years (sometimes as 25 or 33 years).
geographical race. One of 13 broad, geographically-delimited races of mankind; a collection of human populations usually rather similar physically, delimited by some natural boundary, such as an ocean, and tending to have similar heredity, skin color, hair type, languages, etc.
geography of religion. The description and analysis of religious phenomena in terms of the science of geography (spatial variations in human and physical phenomena).
geometric mean. The square root of the product of the 2 end figures or populations in a period.
geopolitical. Relating to or based on geopolitics.
geopolitico-religious. An overall term describing the major geographical, political, sociological, socio-economic demographic and religious characteristics of the world, or continents, or nations.
geopolitics. The study of the influence of physical factors such as geography, economics and demography upon the politics and foreign policy of a state; the political and geographical factors characterizing a particular state or region.
Georgian. Eastern Orthodox liturgical tradition (Georgian Orthodox Church). Global statistics: (1970) 1.2 million; (1995) 2.5 million in 9 countries (1 significantly); largest, Georgia (2.5 million).
German Baptists. Dunkers (qv).
Germanic. A European ethnolinguistic family, with about 15 major languages, Teutonic. Global statistics: (2000) 367.3 million in 556 peoples residing in 214 countries (35 significantly); largest, USA (138.8 million).
gethsemane. A mercy ground (qv).

glossolalia. (NT Greek). The gift of tongues; ecstatic speech unintelligible to hearers, uttered in worship services of contemporary charismatic churches.
Gnosticism. The thought and practice of various cults of late pre-Christian and early Christian centuries, declared heretical by the church, characterized chiefly by pretension to mystic and esoteric religious insights, by emphasis on knowledge (gnosis) rather than faith, and by the conviction that matter is evil.
Gnostics. Followers of a complex Jewish-Christian syncretistic movement in the 2nd century AD. The only surviving Gnostics today are the 39,000 Mandaeans (qv) of Iraq and Iran.
Goa. See of Latin Catholic patriarchate and patriarch, since 1886.
gospel. The good news of salvation and new life in Jesus Christ and the coming of the Kingdom of God.
gospelize. To instruct in the gospel, preach the gospel, evangelize.
Gospels. 4 New Testament books containing narratives of the life and death of Jesus Christ, ascribed to Matthew, Mark, Luke and John.
gospels. See portions.
government ministries of religion. See state departments for religious affairs.
government statistics of religion. Figures of adherents of religions and churches promulgated by governments, usually derived from government censuses of population.
graveyard evangelism. Preaching and evangelism engaged in on the occasion of funerals or burials, especially in anti-Christian countries where preaching outside church buildings is prohibited.
Great and Holy Council of the Orthodox Church. Major Eastern Orthodox ecumenical council to be held shortly, the first since Nicea II in AD 787. Eastern Orthodox in canonical relationship:. Global statistics: (1970) 83.7 million; (1995) 132.4 million in 240 countries (13 significantly); largest, Russia (74.1 million).
Great Britain. Geographically, the 3 countries England, Wales and Scotland; politically, often used for the whole United Kingdom of Great Britain and Northern Ireland.
Great Church. Official name of Santa Sophia, former cathedral church of Constantinople.
Great Commission. The universal or last commission delivered to his disciples by the Risen and Ascended Christ: 'Go throughout the whole world and preach the gospel to all mankind' (Mark 16.15, GNB).
Great Commission Christians. Believers in Jesus Christ who are aware of the implications of Christ's Great Commission, who have accepted its personal challenge in their lives and ministries, and who are seeking to influence the Body of christ to implement it. Global statistics: (1970) 277.1 million; (1995) 603.0 million in 237 countries (137 significantly); largest, USA (93.4 million); (2000) 647.8 million; (2025) 887.5 million.
Greater Vehicle. The Mahayana school of Buddhists.
Greek. A European ethnolinguistic family and people.
Greek Catholics. (1) Those using the Greek rite, under Rome: membership (1995) 2,350 total community. (2) Melkites (qv).
Greek Orthodox. (1) Christians related to the Church of Greece and the Ecumenical Patriarchate of Constantinople; often loosely used, instead of the more correct term Eastern Orthodox, to include Slavic Orthodoxy also. (2) Greek-speaking Orthodox using Greek rite. Global statistics: (1970) 12.2 million; (1995) 14.9 million in 78 countries (2 significantly); largest, Greece (9.7 million).
Gregorian Calendar. New Calendar (qv).
Gregorians. Armenian Apostolics, or Armenian Orthodox (qv).
Grey. Stylized skin color associated with the Australoid and Capoid races (Austro-Asiatic and Early African geographical races). Global statistics: (2000) 61.6 million in 536 peoples residing in 46 countries (3 significantly); largest, India (38.2 million).
gross national product. The total value of the goods and services produced in a nation during a specific period (usually a year), and also comprising the total of expenditures by consumers and government plus gross private investment.
gross national product per capita. National income per person (qv).
growth. In church and mission circles: development, rise, emergence, evolution, expansion, size.
growth rate. The annual increase in a population measured as a percentage per year.
guerrillas. Small military forces engaged in irregular warfare or in the rear of regular forces.
Guinean. An African ethnolinguistic family, with about 80 languages.
Gypsy. Itinerant Caucasoid people originally from India, and since the 14th century scattered throughout Europe.

H

hadith. In Islam, the collected traditions of Mohammed.
hajj. (hadj, haj). The pilgrimage to Mecca prescribed as a religious duty for Muslim.
hajj pilgrims to Mecca. Annual totals: (1912) 300,000, (1929) 90,000, (1941) 23,000, (1968) 692,784, (1975) 1,557,867, peaking at 2.5 million (1989); controlled thereafter at 2 million. Source of statistics: officially-released figures published in the Mecca newspapers soon after start of each Hajj.
hajji. (hadji, haji). A Muslim who has made the pilgrimage to Mecca, who may then add the term to his name as a title.
Half-Breed. A Half-Caste (qv).
Half-Caste. A person of mixed blood or race.
ham operators. Amateur radio operators (qv).
Hanafites. Followers of Hanafiya, the most liberal of the 4 schools or rites of Sunni Muslim law, and by far the most widespread. Global statistics: (1970) 236.4 million; (1995) 480.7 million; (2000) 0.5 billion; (2025) 0.7 billion.
Hanbalites. Followers of Hanabila, the most rigid of the 4 schools or rites of Sunni Muslim law; mainly in Central Arabia. Global statistics: (1970) 1.1 million; (1995) 2.0 million; (2000) 2.3 million; (2025) 3.3 million.
handicapped children. Of the world's 1.8 billion children under 15 years old, 100 million (5%) are severely handicapped and 240 million (13%) need special attention or rehabilitation services.
handicapped groups, ministry to. Special ministries exist, in most larger denominations and para-church agencies, to work with lepers, the blind, the crippled, and other groups.
hermeneutics. The study of the general principles of biblical interpretation and explanation.
hidden affiliation. The situation in which Christians affiliated to minority or illegal or anti-state or persecuted churches hide this affiliation in government censuses (or whose affiliation is ignored by enumerators) and profess another type of Christianity (usually that of the majority church).
hidden peoples. Non-Christian peoples among whom there is no culturally relevant organized Christian church able to evangelize them.
hierarch. A religious leader holding high office or vested with controlling authority; chief prelate, bishop, high priest.
hierarchical. Relating to or controlled by the hierarchy.

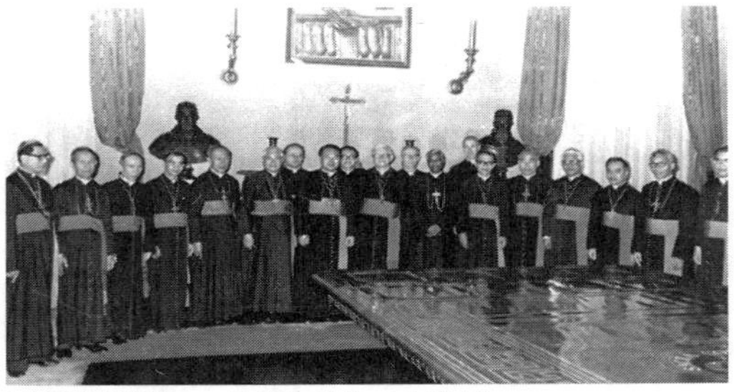

HIERARCHY. Roman Catholic bishops in Viet Nam.

hierarchy. In Roman Catholic usage, the episcopate or the whole body of bishops as an authoritarian body organized by rank and jurisdiction.
hierocracy. Government by ecclesiastics.
hieromonk. A monk of the Eastern Church who is also a priest.
High Church Anglicans. Also termed Prayer Book Catholics, or the High Church Party; Anglicans stressing the Catholic heritage. Global statistics: (1970) 2.9 million; (1995) 5.0 million in 31 countries (2 significantly); largest, South Africa (2.4 million).
high spiritism. Mediumistic cults or religions emphasizing a synthesis of science, philosophy and religion, as contrasted with low spiritism.
higher education. Tertiary education, education in universities.
higher schools. Church- or Christian-related junior and senior secondary schools, minor seminaries (secular and religious), technical schools, agricultural schools, vocational schools, teacher-training colleges, non-degree-granting colleges. Global statistics: 50,000 (AD 2000).
Hinayana. A school of Buddhists, Theravada (qv).
Hindu reformist movements. These include: Arya Samaj, Shanka Acharya, Ramakrishna Mission, et alia. Global statistics: (1970) 2.3 million; (1995) 4.0 million; (2000) 4.4 million; (2025) 5.8 million.
Hindus. Followers of the main Hindu traditions: (a) Vaishnavites (Vishnaivites) (qv) numbering 70% of all Hindus; (b) Saivites (qv) numbering 25% mostly in South India; (c) Saktists (qv) or other sects (3%); (d) neo-Hindu movements and modern sects arising out of Hinduism, about 1.5%; and (e) Arya Samaj and other reformist movements, 0.5% (Brahmo Samaj, Prarthana Samaj, Swami-Narayanis, Ramakrishna Mission, but excluding Jains and Sikhs). Global statistics: (1970) 462.6 million; (1995) 751.5 million in 114 countries (11 significantly); largest, India (700.5 million); (2000) 811.3 million; (2025) 1.0 billion.
historic churches. The major mainline or older churches or denominations with a long history in that part of the world under consideration.
historic succession of the episcopate. Apostolic succession (qv).
historical demography. The study of the history of population development.
holdings. The number of volumes and other discrete items held by a library.
Holiness, Holiness Christians. Protestant tradition originating in Methodism. Global statistics: (1970) 4.0 million; (1995) 7.2 million in 339 countries (1 significantly); largest, USA (1.9 million).
Holiness-Pentecostals. Pentecostals teaching 3-crisis experience (conversion, sanctification, baptism of the Spirit). Global statistics: (1970) 2.3 million; (1995) 5.6 million in 233 countries; largest, USA (1.2 million).
holistic church growth. The emphasis on church-planting combined with sociopolitical action.
holistic evangelism. Evangelism which involves sociopolitical action in some sense.
holy cities. Headquarters of Third-World Non-White indigenous churches, often regarded as New Jerusalem on earth. Global total: about 5,000.
holy day of obligation. One of the days on which Roman Catholics, Episcopalians et alii are obliged to hear mass and abstain from servile work.
Holy Land. Palestine; those areas of Israel and Jordan in which Christ lived and worked while on earth.
holy orders. Ordination; the state of being ordained.
Holy See. The supreme organ of the Roman Catholic Church, an international juridical entity, a sovereign state centered in Vatican City.
Holy Spirit. The Third Person of the Trinity.

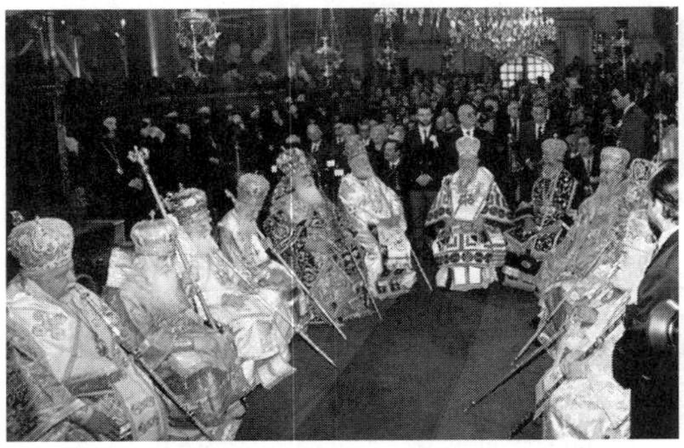

HOLY SYNOD. Eastern Orthodox Church in formal session, Turkey.

holy synod. The governing body in an autocephalous church, composed of bishops and primate.
holy war. See jihad, Crusades.
holy water. Water blessed by a priest and used as a purifying sacramental in church and home; especially by Roman Catholics and African indigenous churches.
holy writing. See spirit writing.
Holy Year. A jubilee year observed at Rome when proclaimed by the Holy See, in principle every 25 years. Total Holy Year pilgrims to Rome: (first Holy Year, in AD 1300) 200,000 (1950) 2.5 million (1975) 8,370,000, (2000) 15 million.
home missionaries. Full-time Christian workers sent by their churches to missionary areas within their own countries.
home missions and societies. Bodies significant at nation-wide or wider levels number over 500.
homiletics. A branch of theology that deals with homilies or sermons; the art of preaching.
Homo Sapiens. The entire human race; mankind sentient, conscious, thinking man.
homogeneous. Of the same kind or nature; alike, similar, congruous; of uniform nature or character throughout.
homogeneous unit. A population group, stratum society or segment of society within which a number of characteristics or interests or customs (geographical, ethnic, linguistic, social, educational, cultural, vocational, economic, etc.) are held in common by all members, with a common self-consciousness; a culture, sub-culture, people group, ethnolinguistic group.
hospitals. See medical centers.
hours. In Jehovah's Witnesses' statistics, the total number of hours devoted by its publishers to preaching and house-to-house literature distribution each year. Total (1959) 126,317,124 hours, rising to (1974) 371,132,570 hours and to (1998) 1,186,666,708.
house church. A group of Christians meeting as a worship center in a private house for regular Sunday worship.
household. A socioeconomic unit, consisting of individuals who live together sharing living quarters and principal meals.
household size. The average size of a household in a country or area, i.e. number of persons sharing the same unit, whether private or collective or institutional. Household size is slightly larger than average family size because it includes servants, maids, and lodgers, as well as hospitals, homes and other institutions where people live.
hovercraft. Land-water craft supported by cushion of air; used by Missionary Aviation Fellowship and other mission bodies.
Huguenots. A historical name, since 1560, for French Calvinists.
humanism. A philosophy based on agnosticism that rejects supernaturalism and revelation, regards man as a natural object only, and asserts the essential dignity and worth of man and his capacity to achieve self-realization and self-fulfillment through the use of reason and scientific method; naturalistic humanism, scientific humanism.
humanism, Christian. See religious humanism.
humanism, religious. See religious humanism.
humanist. A person who subscribes to humanism.
Hungarian rite. Roman Catholics following the Hungarian rite.
Hungarian/Slavonic. Eastern Orthodox liturgical tradition using Hungarian and Slavonic in the liturgy. Membership: (1970) 10 churches with 5,200 adult members, 40,400 total community. Global statistics: (1970) 40,000; (1995) 50,000 in 1 countries; largest, Hungary (50,000).
hybrid races. Clines (qv).
hymnody, hymnology. The study of hymns (songs of praise to God) and their composition; a body of hymns of a particular period or region.

I

'I found it' campaigns. A global series of evangelistic campaigns (Here's Life World) employing this deliberately-ambiguous slogan ('It' being New Life in Christ).
Ibadis, Ibadites. Kharijites (qv).
icon, ikon. A flat painted sacred picture.
iconoclasm. Anti-icon campaign at Constantinople, AD 726-842.
iconography. Art representing religious subjects by conventional images and symbols, the study of religious art and symbolism.

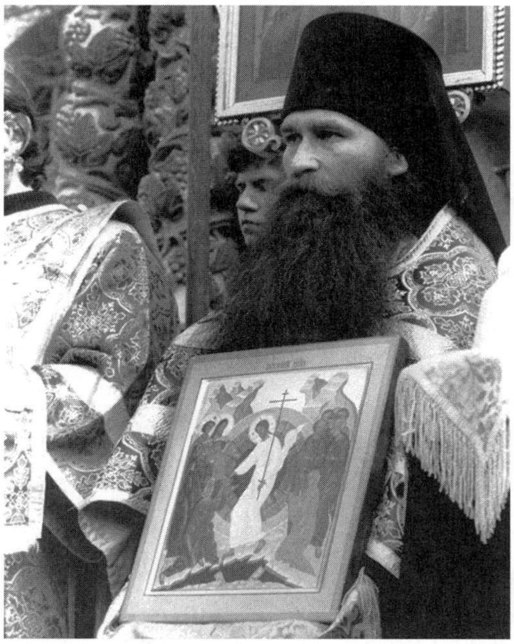

ICONOGRAPHY. Priest in Zagorsk, Russia, processing with icon.

iconostasis. Screen separating nave from sanctuary, adorned with icons, in Orthodox churches.
ideology. The science of ideas, their origin and nature; a particular sociopolitical set of theories.
illiterate. A person who can neither read nor write.
imam. (Arabic, divine guide). A Muslim religious practitioner or cleric.
Imamis, Imamites. Ithna-Asharis (qv), Ismailis (qv) and other Shias.
immediately subject. (Italian, *immediate soggette alla Santa Sede*). Used of Roman Catholic jurisdictions which are not attached to any ecclesiastical province in their own country but are immediately subject to the Holy See itself.
immigrant religion. A religion absent from a country until brought in by recent immigrants.
immigration. The movement of immigrants into a particular territory.
in-depth evangelism. The strategy of united programs of evangelism in a country or area; total mobilization evangelism, saturation evangelism, Evangelism-in-Depth, New Life for All, etc., stressing mobilization of all believers and their resources within the framework of church, reaching all unbelievers in the area, through every available means.
in-depth evangelism. See Evangelism-in-Depth.
inclusive membership. The total of a church's or denomination's affiliated Christians (qv) or church members, of all ages and varieties including children, infants and persons under instruction, also termed total Christian community.
income, average. See family income, national income per person.
incumbent. The holder of an ecclesiastical benefice (diocese, office, or, more usually, parish).
Independency. Congregationalism; A religious movement originating in England after AD 1600 asserting a congregation's independence of higher ecclesiastical authority.
independency, religious. A movement asserting independence of a previously recognized ecclesiastical authority, especially exemplified in the African indigenous churches (qv).
Independent. Congregationalist.
Independents. Christians independent of historic, organized, institutionalized, denominationalist Christianity. Global statistics: (1970) 95,605,000; (2000) 385,745,000; (2025) 581,642,000.
independent. Term for independent Evangelical churches with no denomination affiliation or ties.
Index Librorum Prohibitorum. List published at Rome of prohibited books judged dangerous to faith or morals; created 1557, abolished 1965.
Indian indigenous churches. Denominations indigenous to, and started by, Indians. Global statistics: (1970) 1.4 million; (1995) 14.0 million in 14 countries; largest, India (9.0 million).
indigenous. Originating or developing or produced naturally in a particular land or region or environment; not introduced directly or indirectly from the outside.
indigenous Christianity. In a particular region, that type of Christianity which, in contrast to imported or foreign types, is evolved or produced by populations indigenous to that region.
indigenous church. A locally-founded church, i.e. one originating within a country or race or people, or produced naturally by nationals of that country or members of that race or people, as opposed to a church of foreign or alien origin imported from abroad or introduced from outside.
indigenous churches. As classified here, there are 3 major groupings contemporary in the world: (1) Semitic Oriental Orthodox churches indigenous to the Middle East, (2) White churches (Roman Catholic, Eastern Orthodox, Anglican, Protestant, marginal Christian, Catholic (non-Roman)) indigenous to the White races of Europe and North America, and (3) Non-White indigenous churches begun since AD 1500.
indigenous evangelization. Spreading of the gospel among a non-Christian population by persons indigenous to that population.
indigenous media. See folk media.
indigenous religious institutes. In Roman Catholic usage, locally-founded religious congregations of men or women began in mission fields.
indigenous, Third-World. Churches and Christians indigenous to the Third World.
individual. A person; the fundamental statistical unit used in demography.
Indo-Iranian. One of the 13 geographical races of mankind, with over 230 languages. Global statistics: (2000) 1.2 billion in 749 peoples residing in 142 countries (17 significantly); largest, India (223.7 million).
Indo-Malay. An Asian ethnolinguistic family, with 300 languages. Global statistics: (2000) 306.4 million in 829 peoples residing in 53 countries (12 significantly); largest, Indonesia (198.6 million).
Indonesian indigenous churches. Denominations indigenous to, and started by, Indonesians. Global statistics: (1970) 2.6 million; (1995) 6.0 million in 3 countries; largest, Indonesia (4.9 million).
industrial mission. A Christian approach to industrial organizations in a particular region.
industrialization. The act or process of becoming industrial in a particular region or country.
ineligible member. An adult church member who is not eligible to take communion, usually being under discipline for some offense.

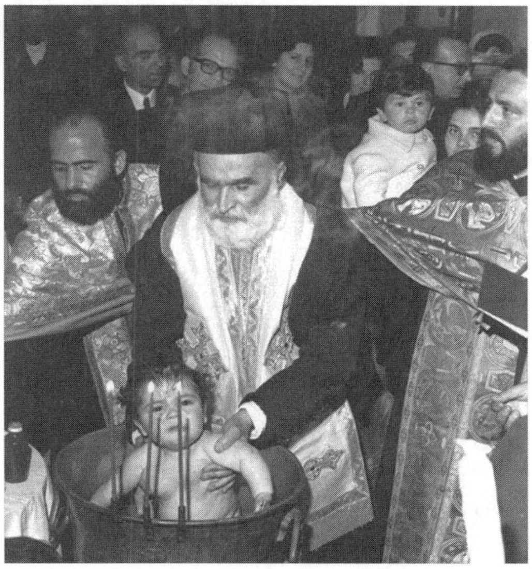

INFANT BAPTISM. Orthodox bishop performs ceremony in Cyprus.

infant baptism. In Catholic, Orthodox, Anglican, Lutheran, Methodist, Reformed and other pedobaptist (qv) traditions, the administration of baptism to children under 5 years old.
infants. Defined here as those under 5 years old, or the preschool population, including new-born babies; although the term is often restricted to children who have not reached their first birthday.
infilling by the Holy Spirit. Persons baptized in the Spirit each year are enumerated in the statistics of several Pentecostal denominations (e.g. Assemblies of God, US).
inflation. Annual percentage growth in consumer prices, as measured by the consumer price index (qv).
informant. A respondent (qv) in a census or survey; a person supplying information.
inhabitant. A person who dwells or resides permanently in a place as distinguished from a transient lodger or visitor, or a resident (who may be temporary or short-term).
Injerto. The issue of a Latin American White and a Chinese or Japanese.
inner-city ministry. The parish ministry adapted to inner-city dwellers in areas of urban blight.
inquirers. See enquirers.
inscriptions. A technical term in Bible correspondence course ministry for enrolments or the number of persons signing on, enrolling or writing in.
inspectorate. (French, *inspection*). In French Lutheran usage, a large area of ecclesiastical jurisdiction equivalent to a deanery or presbytery.
institutes, religious. See religious institutes.
institutional population. Persons in correctional schools, hospitals, prisons and other institutions, who are often separately enumerated in censuses.
institutions, Christian. Major Christian or church-operated or -related institutions of all kinds, i.e. fixed centers with premises, plant and permanent staff, excluding church buildings, worship centers, church headquarters or offices. For detailed statistics, see under: ecumenical centers, higher schools, medical centers, presses, radio stations, religious communities, research centers, seminaries, study centers, universities. Global statistics: 105,000 (AD 2000).
inter-censal period. The time elapsing between 2 censuses of population.
interchurch aid. Aid given by one church or denomination to another, usually as finance, personnel or other resources.
intercommunion. Mutual fellowship and limited sacramental and ministerial recognition between 2 or more churches or confessions, but falling short of full communion (qv).
interconfessional. Involving, supported by, or common to major Christian families or communions having different confessions of faith.
interdenominational. Occurring between or among or common to different denominations (qv).
intermediate technology. Technology that is sufficiently simple to directly benefit peasants and workers in developing nations.
internal province. In Anglicanism, a self-governing ecclesiastical province within an autonomous church.
international Christian radio stations. There are some 50 powerful radio stations under Christian auspices which beam programs worldwide in several hundred languages.
International Conference of Old Catholic Bishops. See International Old Catholic Bishops Conference.
International Congregational Council. (ICC). Confessional council begun 1891 linking all Congregationalist denominations. Merged in 1970 with World Alliance of Reformed Churches.
International Council of Christian Churches. (ICCC). The major global Fundamentalist, anti-Ecumenical, council. Global constituency: (AD 2000) 100 denominations with 3 million members.
international denominational bodies. See non-confessional international denominational bodies.
International New Thought Alliance. (INTA). World communion for metaphysical Christian bodies, begun 1914.
International Old Catholic Bishops Conference. Also known as the Union of Utrecht, begun 1889; the major Old Catholic world communion. Global statistics: (1970) 647,000; (1995) 866,000 in 26 countries; largest, USA (718,000).
international sharing of personnel. The sending and receiving, between and amongst all countries of the world, and between and amongst all churches of the world, of 420,000 full-time long-term foreign missionaries and personnel.
internuncio. A Vatican diplomat of lower rank than nuncio.
interpolation. The estimation of values of a series at points intermediate between known or given values.
interreligious. Existing between 2 or more religions; used of activities or relationships between Christianity and one or more of the major world religions (Judaism, Islam, Hinduism, Buddhism). Interreligious organizations significant at the national or wider levels number over 150.
invisible church. In reaction to excessive denominationalism and fragmentation of the visible Church many Christians profess to believe only in one undivided but invisible church, the Body of Christ, composed only of all true believers.
invitation. In evangelization, the act of inviting or challenging persons to accept Christ immediately often at the close of an evangelistic service or meeting.
Iranian. An Indo-Iranian ethnolinguistic family. Global statistics: (2000) 127.2 million in 237 peoples residing in 56 countries (11 significantly); largest, Iran (49.7 million).
irregular attenders. Persons affiliated to churches but who attend services only irregularly, infrequently or occasionally.
irreligion. Hostility to religion: impiety, skepticism, disbelief, atheism, anti-religious humanism.
Irvingites. Catholic Apostolics originating in Britain in 1832, also called Old Apostolics; marked decline since 1900 due to dying out of clergy originally ordained after 1836 by Apostles.

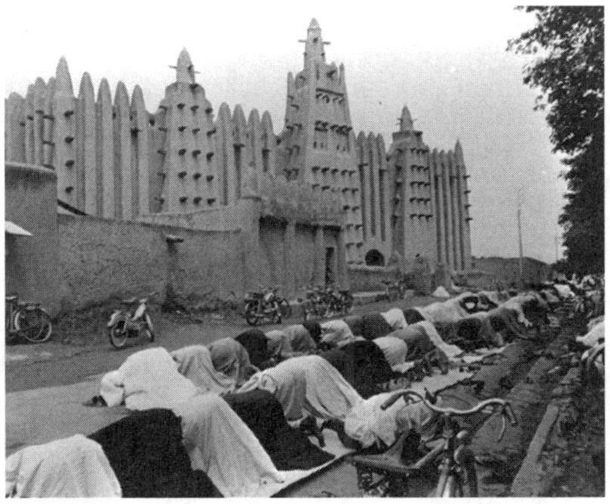

ISLAM. Friday afternoon prayers in front of mosque in Mali.

Islam. (Arabic: submission to the will of God). The religious faith of Muslims (qv) who profess belief in Allah as the sole deity and in Muhammad as the prophet of Allah.
Islamics. The academic study of Islam.
islamization. The act or process of converting people, or of being converted, to Islam.
Ismailis. Followers of Ismailiya (also known as Seveners). Second largest sect of Shia Islam and itself divided into Nizari Ismailis (Khojas) and Mustali Ismailis (Bohras). Global statistics: (1970) 9.7 million; (1995) 20.8 million; (2000) 23.7 million; (2025) 40.9 million.
isolated radio believers. The total community of those persons (with their dependent adults and children, and other adherents) who derive their ongoing corporate Christian life primarily from isolated radio churches or isolated Bible correspondence course student groupings. Global statistics: (1970) 2.8 million; (1995) 19.6 million in 72 countries; largest, India (9.0 million).

isolated radio churches. New indigenous house churches, cells or nuclei composed of isolated radio believers (qv) brought into being solely through Christian broadcasting and/or Bible correspondence courses by mail, who due to geographical remoteness or other reasons are isolated from existing Christian believers and are ignorant of the existence of organized denominations, hence group themselves into these new fellowships.
Issei. (Japanese: first-generation). A Japanese immigrant to the Americas.
Italo-Albanians. Roman Catholics following the Italo-Albanian rite. Global statistics: (1970) 68,000; (1995) 62,000 in 3 countries; largest, Italy (62,000).
Ithna-Asharis. Followers of Ithna-Ashariya (also known as Twelvers), largest sect of Shia Islam. Global statistics: (1970) 65.2 million; (1995) 122.3 million; (2000) 136.6 million; (2025) 229.1 million.

J

Jacobites. Syrian Orthodox (qv), so termed after Jacob Baradaeus, bishop of Edessa (died 578 AD).
Jains. Followers of the Jain reform movement from Hinduism, composed of the Svetambara and Digambara sects. Global statistics: (1970) 2.6 million; (1995) 3.8 million in 10 countries; largest, India (3.8 million); (2000) 4.2 million; (2025) 6.1 million.
Jansenists. Dissident Roman Catholics in Holland who in 1702,1724 et alia formed separatist churches and were later termed Old Catholics (qv).
Japanese. An Asian ethnolinguistic family and people. Global statistics: (2000) 130.0 million in 51 peoples residing in 36 countries (1 significantly); largest, Japan (125.2 million).
Japanese indigenous churches. Denominations indigenous to, and started by, Japanese. Global statistics: (1970) 299,000; (1995) 1.0 million in 2 countries; largest, Japan (983,000).
Jehovah's Christian witnesses. The preferred self-appellation of Jehovah's Witnesses (qv).
Jehovah's Witnesses. A marginal Protestant tradition begun in 1872 also called Russellites. Global statistics: (1970) 4.0 million; (1995) 11.3 million in 222 countries; largest, USA (2.2 million).
Jerusalem. One of the 4 original partriarchates of the Apostolic Church; now the see of 4 rival patriarchs: Greek Orthodox, Armenian Apostolic, Melkite and Latin.
Jerusalems. See holy cities.
Jesuits. Members of the Society of Jesus, Roman Catholicism's largest religious order; in 1975, 29,636 members (20,604 priests, the rest brothers), (1997) 22,580 in 1,931 houses.
Jesus Christ. Founder of Christianity, Son of God, acknowledged as Lord and Savior by 2 billion Christians and 33,000 denominations (AD 2000).
Jesus movement, people, generation. Terms covering the widespread revival of faith in Jesus, in the 1960s and 1970s, on the part of youth and students in the Western world.
Jesus-Only Pentecostals. Oneness-Pentecostals (qv).
Jew, Jews, Jewish. (1) The secular definition: A Middle Eastern (Semitic) ethnolinguistic family. (2) The religious definition: Followers of the Orthodox, Reformed or Liberal schools of Judaism; Ashkenazis (84% of all Jews), Orientals (10%), and Sefardis (Sephardis) (4%); and crypto-Jews. Global statistics: (2000) 16.0 million in 217 peoples residing in 131 countries (2 significantly); largest, USA (6.0 million).
Jewish-Christians. Also called Hebrew Christians, Messianic Christians, Messianic Jews, Jewish crypto-Christians. Total in 250 separate Jewish-Christian denominations. Global statistics: (1970) 50,000; (1995) 30,000 in 1 countries; largest, USA (30,000).
jihad. (Arabic). For Muslims, a holy war waged on behalf of Islam.
joint action for mission. An ecumenical program involving (a) a joint survey by all churches in an area, (b) joint planning to secure real and effective redeployment of resources in the light of agreed goals, and (c) joint action to implement this.
journalism, religious. See religious journalism.
Judaism. The religion of the Jews (qv) characterized by belief in one God and in the mission of Jews to teach the Fatherhood of God as revealed in the Hebrew Scriptures.
Julian Calendar. Old Calendar (qv).
jurisdiction. (1) Any territory within which a bishop or other church leader exercises his authority, such as an archdiocese, diocese, vicariate, prefecture, etc. (2) In some churches, a jurisdiction (symbol J) is a specific type of territory similar to a diocese.

K

Kanuri. An African ethnolinguistic family, with over 15 languages. Global statistics: (2000) 6.2 million in 29 peoples residing in 6 countries; largest, Nigeria (3.9 million).
Karaites. Readers of the Scriptures, followers of Qaraism (a Jewish sect). Global statistics: (1970) 16,000; (1995) 23,000; (2000) 24,000; (2025) 27,000.
Kardecism. High spiritism (qv) or spiritualism, notably in Brazil.
karma. (Sanskrit). In Buddhism and Hinduism, the force generated by a person's actions that is held to be the motive power for the round of rebirths and deaths endured by him until he has achieved spiritual liberation (nirvana).
Karmatians. See Qarmatians.
kerygma. (NT Greek). Preaching, the preaching of the gospel, the message preached.
Keswick-Pentecostals. Baptistic-Pentecostals (qv).
Kharijites. (Seceders). Followers of schism from Sunni and Shia Islam, mainly in Ibadite form. Global statistics: (1970) 780,000; (1995) 1.4 million; (2000) 1.6 million; (2025) 2.6 million.
Khoisan. An Early African ethnolinguistic family with about 50 languages. Global statistics: (2000) 602,000 in 81 peoples residing in 11 countries (1 significantly); largest, Namibia (199,000).
Khojas. Nizari Ismailis (qv), followers of the Aga Khan.
Kibei. A Japanese-American born of Issei parents but educated in Japan.
kingdom hall. In Jehovah's Witnesses' usage, a large central permanent church building and headquarters.
Kingdom of God. The central theme of Christ's teaching and of the New Testament, and of Christian theology subsequently.

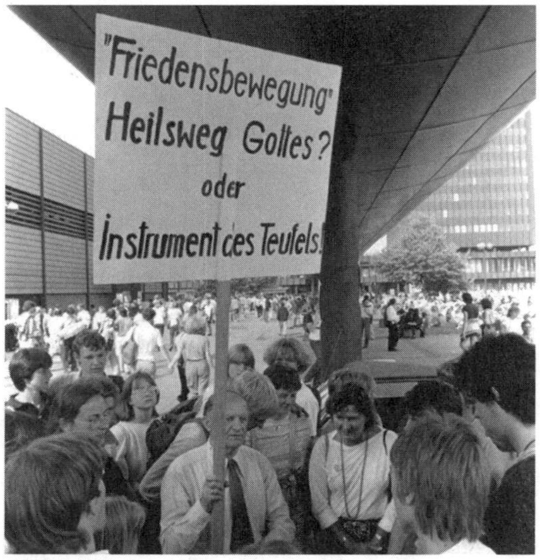

KIRCHENTAG. Church festival, Dusseldorf, Germany.

Kirchentag. (German: church congress). A series of annual mass Whitsun rallies or festivals of the German Churches (Protestant and Catholic), held approximately every 2 years since 1945; they last 4-7 days, with meetings, workshops, et alia.
koinonia. (NT Greek). Fellowship; the witness of fellowship.
Koran. See Quran.
Korean. An Asian ethnolinguistic family and people. Global statistics: (2000) 75.6 million in 36 peoples residing in 35 countries (2 significantly); largest, South Korea (45.7 million).
Korean indigenous churches. Denominations indigenous to, and started by, Koreans. Global statistics: (1970) 101,000; (1995) 2.8 million in 10 countries; largest, South Korea (1.1 million)
Krio. A Eurafrican or Colored person, in Sierra Leone.

L

labor force. In ILO usage, the economically-active population, both employed and unemployed, excluding students, women at home, retired persons, wholly-dependent persons, et alii.
labor-intensive. Methods of industrial or manufacturing organization which employ as many persons as possible, in developing countries.
laicization. The process or act of removing or nullifying priests' orders and returning clergy to the status of laity again, mainly among Roman Catholics.
laity. The great body of the people of a religious faith as distinguished from its clergy; in Christianity, laity number over 99.7% of the entire membership of the churches.
lama. (Tibetan: one who is superior). A priest or monk of Tibetan Buddhism (Lamaism).

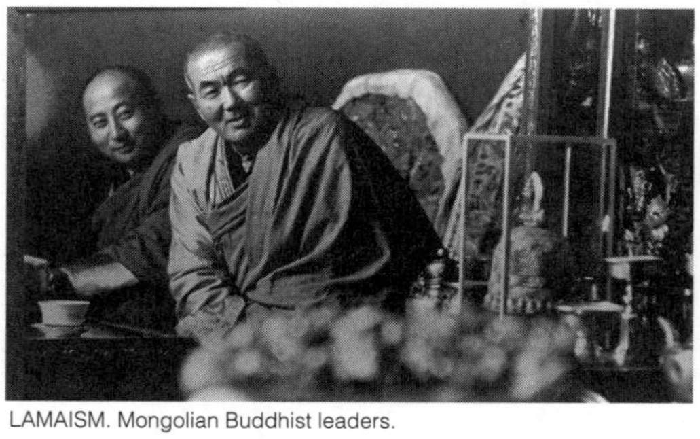
LAMAISM. Mongolian Buddhist leaders.

Lamaism. Tantrayana, or the Tantrism school of Buddhism (qv). Global statistics: (1970) 236.0 million; (1995) 348.0 million in 344 countries (13 significantly); largest, China (99.9 million); (2000) 0.3 billion; (2025) 0.4 billion.
Lambeth Conference. A conference of the bishops of the worldwide Anglican Communion called every 10 years or so by the archbishop of Canterbury; consultative only, not legislative.
land-line relay. In large evangelistic campaigns, a campaign meeting or service which is transmitted from the host city to another city by land cable, to be heard there by another audience.
Landeskirche. (German: territorial or state church). In West Germany, the Protestant state or established church of one of the 10 Lander (states).
language. The principal means of communicating culture (the entire way of life of a people); tongue, speech, idiom, dialect.
language, official state. See official state languages.
language, phyla. 24 major divisions under which the world's languages can be classified.
languages. On our classification, the world has 12, 900 distinct and separate languages, excluding dialects.
lapsed. Former church members who have abandoned churchgoing, or the practice of Christianity, or affiliation, or Christian profession, and have deserted the faith completely; backsliders, disaffiliated, dechristianized, post-Christians, apostates.
Last Commission. See Great Commission.
latent church. A theological term (coined by P. Tillich) for nominal Christians (qv) and others not part of the organized churches which assert that Jesus is the Christ.
latifundia. (Latin; Spanish, *latifundio*; Italian *latifondo*). A system of land concentration in vast rural estates; mainly in Latin America.
Latin. A European ethnolinguistic family; Romance. Global statistics: (2000) 207.4 million in 483 peoples residing in 176 countries (21 significantly); largest, Italy (54.5 million).
Latin American. One of the 13 geographical races of mankind, speaking Spanish and Portuguese. Global statistics: (2000) 362.2 million in 90 peoples residing in 42 countries (30 significantly); largest, Brazil (88.0 million).
Latin American indigenous churches. Non-White indigenous churches, indigenous to Latin American peoples. Global statistics: (1970) 2.9 million; (1995) 10.4 million in 24 countries (1 significantly); largest, Chile (2.5 million).
Latin Europe. A term for Belgium, France, Italy, Luxembourg, Monaco, Portugal, San Marino, and Spain.
Latin rite. Forms of Christian worship and liturgy utilizing or based on Latin; that part of the Roman Catholic Church that employs Latin liturgies. Global statistics: (1970) 345.0 million; (1995) 569.9 million in 202 countries (118 significantly); largest, Mexico (85.5 million).
Latter Rain. A type of Perfectionist-Pentecostals (qv) claiming to inaugurate the Latter or Springtime Rain cited by Old Testament prophets as immediate precursor to the Second Coming of Christ.
Latter-day Saints. Mormons; a generic term for followers of the Church of Jesus Christ of Latter-day Saints (Salt Lake City) or of its 85 schismatic breakoff bodies; a marginal Protestant movement. Global statistics: (1970) 3.1 million; (1995) 7.9 million in 116 countries (2 significantly); largest, USA (4.7 million).
laura. A monastery of the Eastern Church originally consisting of monks in community yet inhabiting separate cells grouped around a church.
lay. Belonging or relating to those church members not in holy orders, not of the clergy.
lay ministries. In this field, organizations significant at the national or wider levels number over 300.
lay missionaries, Roman Catholic. (1996) 9,554.
lay preachers. Unordained unpaid but officially-accredited spare-time preachers in Protestant churches.
lay readers. In Anglicanism, laypersons authorized by a bishop to read parts of the public service, to preach and to assist at Holy Communion.
lay training centers. Study centers and other specialized centers for training the laity in their role in church and mission in the modern world.
lay woman, laywomen. See laypersons.
lay workers, layworkers. Full-time unordained church workers.
layman, laymen. See laypersons.
laypersons. A contemporary term covering both laymen and laywomen, who together number over 99.7% of the entire membership of the churches.
Left-Wing Reformation. See Anabaptists.
legalism. The principles and practices characterizing the theological doctrine of strict conformity to a code of deeds and observances.
legate. An ecclesiastic representing the Roman Catholic pope and invested with the authority of the Holy See.
legislature. The organized body having the authority to make laws for a country or state.

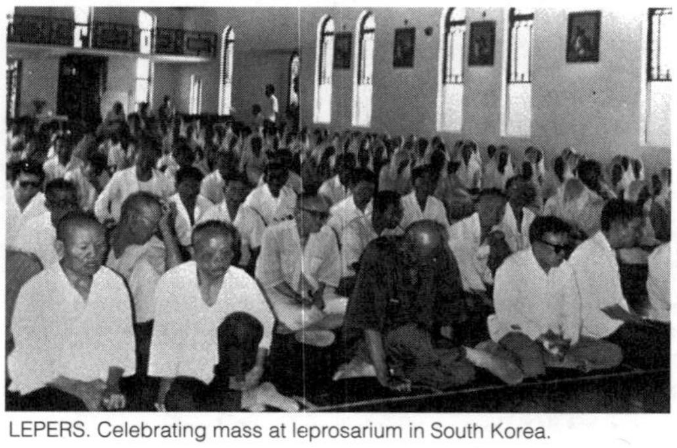
LEPERS. Celebrating mass at leprosarium in South Korea.

lepers. Sufferers from leprosy, still one of the most dreaded diseases and the greatest crippler of all diseases. Global statistics: 19.2 million (AD 2000).
leprosarium. A hospital for lepers; see medical centers.
Lesser Vehicle. The Theravada or Hinayana school of Buddhists (qv).
Liberal Anglicans. Central or Broad Church Anglicans.
Liberal Catholics. Followers of churches under bishops-at-

large (qv) holding liberal or deviant Catholic views usually including Theosophical, Masonic, Gnostic, magical or occult dogmas and practices. Global statistics: (1970) 87,000; (1995) 106,000 in 27 countries; largest, Philippines (77,000).
Liberal Christians. Unitarians (qv).
Liberal Protestants. See Unitarians.
liberation. The act of freeing from control or domination by a foreign party, or the state of being freed from such power.
libraries, religious. Major professional exclusively-theological or -religious library collections under church or Christian auspices, specializing primarily in Christianity and religion, a majority of each's holdings being religious. Global totals: (AD 2000) 16,000. Total large Christian libraries with over 35,000 volumes each: 2,100.
life expectancy. The expected number of years of life of individuals in a population, based on statistical probability. World average: (AD 2000) 67.6 years.
life span. The maximum possible length of human life.
life styles. Attitudes to money, property, discipline, moral imperatives, on the part of either denominations or individuals. During the 1970s there has been widespread discussion on what life styles (ways of living) are authentically Christian, focusing on subjects such as standard of living, waste, simplicity of dress and food, etc.
lingua franca. An auxiliary or compromise language used between groups having no other language in common.
linguistics. The study of human speech in its various aspects; linguistic science.
Lisbon. See of Latin Catholic patriarchate and patriarch, since 1716.
listeners' correspondence. Postal mail from listeners or viewers received by a broadcasting station or program.
listeners, radio. See radio listeners.
literacy. The ability to read and write, as measured by the percentage of the adult population who can read and write their own names and a simple statement. A higher level of competence is required for functional literacy (qv). Global literacy: (1900) 27.9%, (1950) 55.0%, (1975) 64.9%, (1980) 65.7%, (AD 2000) 76.7%.
literate. A person is defined as literate if he can, with understanding, both read and write a short, simple statement on his everyday life (United Nations).
literature, Christian. See Christian literature.
Liturgical blocs. A term for 3 of the 6 ecclesiastico-cultural major blocs (qv), which are Pedobaptist and whose worship centers on fixed or written liturgies: Roman Catholicism, Orthodoxy, Anglicanism, together with a few Protestant and indigenous Pedobaptist traditions (Lutheran, Methodist, Reformed, et alia). Global total: 74% of all church members. The other 3 blocs are partly Non-Liturgical (qv).
liturgical languages. Languages used in the liturgies of Catholic and Orthodox churches, of 2 main kinds: (1) ancient liturgical languages now no longer living (Latin, Coptic, Ge'ez, Syriac, Church Slavonic, etc.), and (2) contemporary living languages into which the liturgy has been translated.

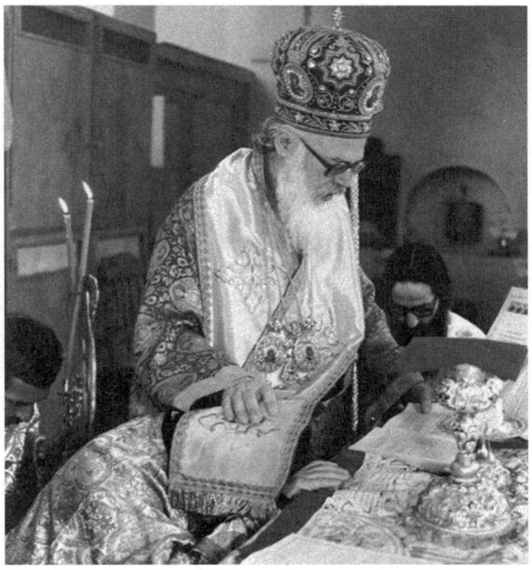

LITURGY. Ordination of clergy by archbishop in Tirana, Albania.

liturgy. A rite, series of rites, observances or procedures prescribed for public worship in Catholic, Orthodox, Anglican and other churches; the eucharist and its ceremonial and ritual. In the field of liturgy and worship, organizations significant at the national or wider levels number over 150.
local church. (1) In Protestant usage, the church in a particular restricted locality. (2) In Roman Catholic usage since Vatican II, either the nation-wide church, or the diocese, or the parish, or other well-defined (usually basic ecclesial) communities
local councils of churches. Councils of churches and denominations in a metropolis, city, district, province or other entity smaller than a country. Global statistics: 20,000 (AD 2000).
local personnel. Full-time church workers of local (not foreign) citizenship.
local preacher. An unordained unpaid but officially-accredited spare-time lay preacher.
local race. An ethnolinguistic family (qv) or micro-race.
local religionists. Adherents of local (as contrasted with universal) religions, such as tribal religionists (qv); usually restricted to a single tribe each, and with non-missionary aims.
locally-founded churches. Indigenous churches (qv).
logistics. The science or art of planning, handling and implementation of personnel, material, facilities and other related factors.
longitudinal study. The study of values of a variable over a period of time.
Lord's Supper. The Eucharist, Communion Service, Liturgy, Holy Communion, Breaking of Bread, Mass, Agape, Love-Feast.
Low Church Anglicans. Conservative Evangelicals and Fundamentalists within Anglicanism, stressing the Evangelical heritage. Global statistics: (1970) 3.7 million; (1995) 19.4 million in 15 countries (2 significantly); largest, Nigeria (17.5 million).
low spiritists. Afro-American spiritists (qv).
Lutheran World Federation. (LWF). The major Lutheran world communion. Global constituency: (1999) 124 member churches in 69 countries representing 57 million Lutherans.
Lutheran/Reformed united churches. Some 18 denominations, with most members being in East Germany, belong to united churches of Lutheran and Reformed composition. Global statistics: (1970) 4.6 million; (1995) 4.1 million in 24 countries (1 significantly); largest, Netherlands (3.5 million).
Lutherans. Followers of Martin Luther and the original German Protestant protesting tradition (16th century). Global statistics: (1970) 39.6 million; (1995) 46.2 million in 249 countries (12 significantly); largest, USA (8.3 million).

M

Macanese. Eurasians in Macao, of Portuguese-Chinese origin.
macro-ecclesiography. The descriptive and numerical analysis of the entire Christian church in the total world context.
macro-evangelistics. The scientific study, at the global level, of the propagation of Christianity.
macro-missiography. The descriptive and numerical analysis of the entire Christian world mission set in and related to the total global demographic, ecological, secular and world religious, non-religious and anti-religious contexts.
magic. The attempt of man to govern the forces of nature directly, by means of a special lore; white magic has benevolent intent, black magic has malevolent intent.
magisterium. In Roman Catholic usage, the church's teaching power, function or office.
magnetic healing. A ministry claimed by some charismatic leaders of marginal Protestant bodies, especially Religious Science.
magnitude, general order of. See general order of magnitude.
Mahayana. The Greater Vehicle school of Buddhists (qv), or Northern Buddhism (China, Japan, et alia). Global statistics: (1970) 131.8 million; (1995) 192.4 million; (2000) 202.2 million; (2025) 235.2 million.
mahdi. A Muslim leader who assumes a messianic role.
mail censorship. See censorship, religious.
mail evangelism. Postal evangelism (qv).
mail reliability. The proportion of Christian mail, expressed as a percentage, which gets through the postal systems of sending and receiving countries; the likelihood or probability of Christian mail getting through the postal services unhindered and uncensored.
mail survey. A postal survey (qv).
mail-order denomination. A body or organization claiming to be a church or denomination which is largely concerned with the sale by post of religious articles and or alleged academic degrees in theology and related subjects.
mainline churches. Mainstream, orthodox Christianity as manifested in its major churches and denominations, Catholic, Protestant, Orthodox, Anglican.
Maitreya. (Sanskrit). In Buddhism, the Buddha who is to be the next to appear on earth; a bodhisattva.
major orders. In Orthodox and Anglican usage: episcopate, priesthood, diaconate. In Roman Catholic usage: priesthood, diaconate, subdiaconate.
major races. The 5 races of mankind: Australoid, Capoid, Caucasian (Caucasoid), Mongolian (Mongoloid), Negro (Negroid).
major seminary. In Roman Catholic usage, a college for the training of future priests.
majority church. In a specific country, the dominant denomination, or largest church established in law.
Malankara. See Syro-Malankarese.
Malikites. Followers of Malikiya, one of the 4 schools or rites of Sunni Muslim law. Global statistics: (1970) 114.1 million; (1995) 201.0 million; (2000) 221.9 million; (2025) 346.6 million.
mallam. In West Africa, a Muslim religious practitioner or cleric.
Maltese. A Middle Eastern ethnolinguistic family. Global statistics: (2000) 563,000 in 7 peoples residing in 7 countries (1 significantly); largest, Malta (365,000).
Mandaeans. Gnostics (Mandaiia), followers of 2nd-century-AD syncretistic Jewish-Christian fertility religion (Christians of St John, Followers of John the Baptist, Dippers, Sabaeans, Nasoreans), regarding John the Baptist as the Messiah; found today only in Iraq and Iran. Global statistics: (1970) 23,000; (1995) 35,000 in 2 countries; largest, Iraq (27,000); (2000) 39,000; (2025) 58,000.
mandala. (Sanskrit: circle). A sacred design that represents the universe as an aid to meditation.
mandate. (Latin: mandarum). An agreement whereby Propaganda in Rome grants a missionary institute the care and charge of a missionary diocese (begun in 1969).
mandylion. In Christian art, (1) the Mandylion of Edessa, or Icon of Christ, the only alleged actual portrait painted of Jesus; eventually lost in the Crusades (2) the robe of Christ in glory.
manifest church. A theological term (coined by P. Tillich) for the organized churches who assert that Jesus is the Christ, i.e. for all affiliated Christians (qv).
manse. The residence of a Presbyterian clergyman.
Mantrayana. The Tantrism school of Buddhists; Tantrayana (qv).
Maoism. The teachings of Mao Tse-tung regarded as a secular quasi-religion.
maphrian. (Syriac). The primate or catholicos of the Syrian Orthodox, or his vicar general.
marabout. In West Africa, a charismatic Muslim practitioner.
marginal Catholics. Followers of recent schisms or movements ex Church of Rome which have embraced marginal, non-christocentric or non-Christian dogmas.
marginal Christians. Followers of para-Christian or quasi-Christian Western movements or deviations out of mainline Christianity (including pseudo-Christian 'New Age' cults), not professing mainstream Christian christocentric doctrine but claiming a second or supplementary or ongoing source of divine revelation in addition to the Bible (a new Book, angels, visions), but nevertheless centered on Jesus, Christ, the Cross, and other Christian features. Global statistics: (1970) 11.1 million; (1995) 23.8 million in 215 countries (5 significantly); largest, USA (9.5 million); (2000) 26.0 million; (2025) 45.5 million.
marginal churches. Churches with doctrines deviant from mainline Christian orthodoxy, usually claiming an additional source of ongoing divine revelation and offering or experiencing altered states of consciousness (qv), including trance, dissociation, ecstasy, spirit-possession, mysticism, glossolalia, visionary experiences, faith-healing, etc.; and usually drawn from the margins of society in age-distribution and in economic and social status.
market research. The gathering of factual information as to consumer preferences for goods and services.
marks of the church. The 4 characteristic marks or 'notes of the church': One, Holy, Catholic, and Apostolic; first enumerated in the Nicene Creed.
Maronites. Catholics of Antiochian rite, mainly in Lebanon. Global statistics: (1970) 1.0 million; (1995) 2.9 million in 23 countries (1 significantly); largest, Lebanon (1.4 million).
Maroon. A Mulatto (qv).
Marranos. Christianized Jews or Moors (Muslims) of medieval and contemporary Spain and Portugal who accepted forced conversion in the 15th century to escape persecution or death, but who still to this day secretly practice the Passover and other Jewish rites; also called Anusim, New Christians, Secret Jews, Crypto-Jews, Conversos. Total: 300,000.
marriage rate. The rate at which marriages or other types of liaison take place within a population, measured as marriages per year for every 1,000 population (on average, 8 per 1,000 per year).
marriages, church. The actual number of marriages or liaisons per year formally blessed in church or under Christian auspices, which can be expressed as a percentage of the local population's marriage rate (qv).
marriages, Roman Catholic. World totals (1996): 3,583,212 between Catholics, 302,630 (8.4%) mixed (between a Catholic and a non-Catholic).
martyr. A believer in Christ who has lost his or her life prematurely, in a situation of witness, as a result of human hostility.
martyrs, church of the. A popular term for a church undergoing heavy state persecution.
Marxist. An adherent of Marxism, the political, economic, and social principles and policies advocated by Marx, Engels and their followers.
Marxist-Leninist. Related to Communism as developed by Lenin from the doctrines of Marx.
Marxist-Leninist states. By 1980, some 30 countries of the world were ruled by regimes espousing Marxist-Leninist principles.
masjid. (Arabic). A mosque (qv).
mask. A representation of a face worn in dances and rituals among primitive peoples, especially for identification with supernatural powers or beings.
Masonic. Belonging to or connected with Freemasons (qv) or Freemasonry.
mass. A celebration of the eucharist or communion.
mass evangelism. In this field, organizations significant at the national or wider levels number over 300.
mass media. The media of communication designed to reach the masses and to set their ideals, standards and aims: newspapers, radio, motion pictures, television.
mass movement. A vast surge of non-Christians into the churches, both by group decision in people movements (qv) and also by individuals, for a variety of motives good and bad.
materialism. Preoccupation with material things rather than intellectual or spiritual things.
Matthew succession churches. Autonomous Catholic churches under bishops-at-large (qv) whose disputed episcopal orders pass through A.H. Mathew Archbishop of London (died 1919).
media. Channels, methods or systems of communication, information or entertainment.
median. That value of an element which divides a set of observations into 2 halves.
mediated training package. An instructional package based on the concept of teaching Christians how to disciple others, consisting of 16mm film, color slides, cassette tape, student manuals, and an instructor.
medical centers. Church- or Christian-sponsored hospitals, leprosaria, sanatoria, clinics, dispensaries, maternity centers, et alia, have long been widespread until superseded by government services. Global statistics: 30,000 (AD 2000).
medical missions. Foreign missionary societies whose primary purpose is medical mission, number some 400.

medicine. In the field of medicine and healing, Christian organizations significant at the national or wider levels number over 400.
medium. In spiritism, an individual through whom other persons seek to communicate with the spirits of the dead.
medium-religionists. Followers of medium-religions, low or high spiritism or spiritualism.
medium-wave broadcasting. Term used in Europe for (USA equivalents) AM or standard broadcasting, i.e. utilizing from 540-1600 kcs.
mediumistic. Having the qualities of a spiritualistic medium; postulated on the activities of mediums.
Melanesian. An Oceanic ethnolinguistic family, with 380 languages. Global statistics: (2000) 4.3 million in 520 peoples residing in 8 countries (6 significantly); largest, Indonesia (2.3 million).
Melkites. Byzantine Catholics of the Middle East using Greek or Arabic.
members, church. Affiliated Christians (qv).
membership turnover. A rapid flow of individuals into and out of church membership.
membership, total church. Affiliated Christians (qv).
Memorial. In Jehovah's Witnesses' usage, the major annual celebration of Christ's death, usually located on a single day worldwide at the beginning of Christendom's Holy Week; attenders number 100-150% more than baptized publishers; total attenders has risen from (1959) 1,283,603 persons to (1974) 4,550,457 to (1998) 13,896,312.
men, religious. Priests and brothers in religious orders and congregations.
Mennonite World Conference. (MWC). The major Mennonite world communion. Global constituency: (1999) 1.3 million.
Mennonites. A Protestant tradition dating back to 16th-century Anabaptists and Left-Wing or Radical Reformation. Global statistics: (1970) 991,000; (1995) 1.7 million in 123 countries; largest, USA (546,000).
mercy ground. In West African aladura and other indigenous churches, an open plot of ground near a church, often walled, where Christians may come for private prayer, often prostrate and for whole nights at a time; also called a gethsemane.
messiah. One accepted as, or claiming to be, a leader destined to bring about salvation.
messianic Jews. Jewish-Christians (qv).
messianic movement. A nativistic religious cult led by a prophet proclaiming salvation and the destruction of foreign culture and influence.
messianism. An ideological movement or system of ideas that teaches the salvation of mankind through a messiah.
Messihaye. (Assyrian, Syriac: Christians). East Syrian or Assyrian or Syro-Chaldean Christians.
Mestizo. (1) The issue of a European and an Amerindian. (2) A Latin American (Spanish-speaking) ethnolinguistic family. Global statistics: (2000) 166.4 million in 39 peoples residing in 25 countries (14 significantly); largest, Mexico (54.0 million).
Metaphysical. Term for movements dating back from the 19th-century New Thought movement in the USA, including spiritualism, Theosophy, Religious Science, et alia.
Methodists. A Protestant tradition ex Church of England in 1795. Global statistics: (bodies strictly Methodist in name) (1970) 21.6 million; (1995) 22.3 million in 121 countries (11 significantly); largest, USA (11.0 million). Many Methodist denominations are usually called, classified, or coded 'Wesleyan', 'Holiness', 'United', although most belong to the World Methodist Council. In addition to Protestant bodies, many Methodist bodies are here classified as Independents.
Métis. A Half-Breed of French and Amerindian ancestry.
metropolia. In Eastern Orthodoxy, a metropolitan archdiocese, or diocese.

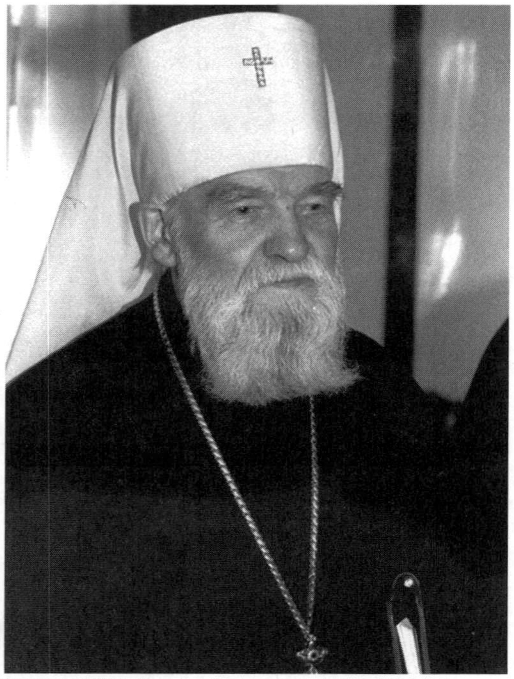

METROPOLITAN. Dorotej, Orthodox primate in Czech Republic.

metropolitan. The head of an ecclesiastical province in the Eastern Orthodox Church who has his headquarters in a large city; an Anglican archbishop: a Roman Catholic archbishop with suffragan dioceses.
metropolitan archdiocese. (symbol M). The senior diocese in an ecclesiastical province.
metropolitan French. French citizens born in France.
metropolitan see. A metropolitan archdiocese (qv).
metropolitanate. The see or office of a metropolitan bishop.
Miao-Yao. An Asian ethnolinguistic family. Global statistics: (2000) 12.8 million in 46 peoples residing in 9 countries; largest, China (11.3 million).
micro-church. A small, very small, miniscule or microcosmic church or fellowship.
micro-missiography. The descriptive analysis in detail of a single or a local missionary situation.
micro-race. An ethnolinguistic family (qv) or local race.
microfilm, microfiche, microform. An information-handling process involving photographically reducing documents to very small size on film.
Micronesian. A Pacific ethnolinguistic family, with 13 languages. Global statistics: (2000) 297,000 in 34 peoples residing in 12 countries (6 significantly); largest, Micronesia (106,000).
Middle Eastern. One of the 13 geographical races of mankind; Afro-Asiatic, Afrasian, Hamito-Semitic. Global statistics: (2000) 357.2 million in 917 peoples residing in 175 countries (41 significantly); largest, Egypt (63.3 million).
migrant church. A church made up largely or wholly of foreign immigrants from another country.
migration. Geographical or spatial mobility; the declared intention to reside in or leave a country for at least a year.
migration change, migration increase. The annual net aggregate of Christian or religious immigration into a country or other body (arrival or transfer of members or co-religionists from other countries or areas) minus emigration out of it (departure or transfer of members or co-religionists to other countries or areas); sometimes termed transfer change.
military chaplaincies. Organizations specializing in ministry to military forces number over 200.
military vicariates or ordinariates. (symbol MV). Roman Catholic jurisdictions each under a bishop serving the military forces of a particular country; vicariates castrensi. Total (1997) 32.
millenarian. One who believes in the millennium (the 1,000 years of Revelation 20 during which Christ will reign on earth); a chiliast.
millennialism. The doctrine that an earthly millennium of 1,000 years of universal peace and the triumph of righteousness will be fulfilled.
Millerites. Adventists (qv).
milliard. In British and French languages, 1,000 millions; equivalent to the American term billion.
Milliarde. (German). A milliard or one (American) billion; 1,000 millions.
million. 1,000 thousands; a very large or indefinite number; the mass of common people.
minifundia. (Latin; Spanish, *minifundio*; Italian *minifondo*). In Latin America, a subsistence farm, or sub-family farm (too small to sustain a family) employing 2 or less workers.
miniscule episcopal churches. Small or minute Catholic denominations operated by bishops-at-large (qv).
minister. One duly authorized by ordination to conduct Christian worship, preach the gospel, and administer the sacraments.
minister's fraternal. A regular but unofficial meeting for fellowship of clergy and ministers of different denominations working in the same city or area.
ministry. See apartment, full-time, group, part-time, team, telephone, tent-making, threefold.
minor. A person who has not yet attained his majority, generally a person under 21 years of age.
minor orders. Roman Catholic lower clerical grades: porter, lector, exorcist, acolyte.
minor seminary. In Roman Catholic usage, a school at secondary level for young men intending to enter the priesthood; junior seminary, preparatory seminary.
minority. An ethnic or linguistic group who live in a country but exhibit notable differences from the majority of the population.
missio Dei. (Latin, the mission of God). A theological term for God's purposes in the world.
missiography. The descriptive analysis of the Christian world mission.
missiology. The science of missions, missionary history, missionary thought and missionary methods.
mission. (sui juris). In Roman Catholic missionary usage, a small territory or station independent of any other jurisdiction or diocese. Total (1997) 7.
mission. The essence of mission is: Christian servants crossing the various boundaries which empirically separate men from one another, declaring to them that in Christ all the walls that divide men from each other are already broken down.
mission board. A denominational board implementing a denomination's policy with regard to missionary action.
mission church. (I) A denomination in a missionary area or land. (2) A church not locally self-supported. (3) A daughter church of a parish church or mother church.
mission field. The geographical region, country, or area in which foreign mission is undertaken
mission station. A place of missionary residence in or from which local missionary activity is carried on.
mission-receiving. Countries, areas or churches which regularly receive foreign missionaries in their midst.
mission-sending. Countries, areas or churches which regularly send foreign missionaries abroad.
mission-sharing. Countries, areas or churches which regularly both send and receive foreign missionaries.
missionaries on furlough. Foreign missionaries on leave in their home countries. Since, on average, missionaries serve for 4 years abroad and then proceed on 12 months' furlough, at any given time about 20% of the entire missionary force throughout the world (or 25% of the totals on the field) are at home.
missionary. A Christian worker sent to propagate the faith among non-believers usually of a different culture or nation to his own; also used of a non-Christian propagating another religion.
missionary congregation. In Roman Catholic usage, a religious institute or congregation whose main purpose is foreign missions.
missionary density. See missionary occupation.
missionary diocese. In Anglican usage, a diocese not fully self-supporting or autonomous, hence usually directed by a province or by the archbishop of Canterbury.
missionary district. An area presided over by an Episcopalian missionary bishop.
missionary institutes. Roman Catholic religious institutes (qv) which exist to further foreign missionary work.
missionary occupation. An older term meaning the density with which foreign missionaries had occupied a particular area; measured as missionaries per million population.
missionary proclamation. The preaching of the gospel with the clear intent to definitively notify people of the gospel and to win converts; first proclamation, first evangelization.
missionary religions. A name given to those religions which undertake deliberate and organized missionary work in order to win converts in other countries and cultures.
missionary societies. Local, denominational, national or international religious organizations dedicated to the opening of missionary work.
missionary training colleges. Foreign missionary training centers (qv).
missionary transportation. Service agencies specializing in transport of missionaries by land, sea, and air, are now numerous.
missioner. A home missionary, especially an evangelist in an Anglican diocese.
missionization. The act or process of conducting a mission.
missionize. To carry on missionary work.
missionizer. One carrying on missionary work.
mitra. Crown worn by Byzantine Catholic bishops.
mitre. Hat worn by cardinals, bishops, abbots and other prelates. Styles: precious, gold and simple.
mixed marriages. Marriages of a Roman Catholic to a non-Catholic. Total (1996): 302,630 (8.4% of all RC marriages).
mixed-economy states. States combining elements of free-enterprise competition with state ownership or direction of key industries.
mobilization evangelism. See total mobilization evangelism.
modality. Part of a missiological dichotomy; see under sodality.
moderator. The presiding officer of various denominations or church assemblies in Protestantism, mainly Presbyterian, Methodist, Reformed.
Modernism. A movement in Protestantism from 1870 onwards seeking to establish the meaning and validity of the Christian faith in relation to present human experience and to reconcile traditional theological concepts with the requirements of modern knowledge.
modernist. An adherent of Modernism in religion.
Mon-Khmer. An Austro-Asiatic ethnolinguistic family, with over 50 languages. Global statistics: (2000) 20.2 million in 185 peoples residing in 14 countries (2 significantly); largest, Cambodia (9.6 million).

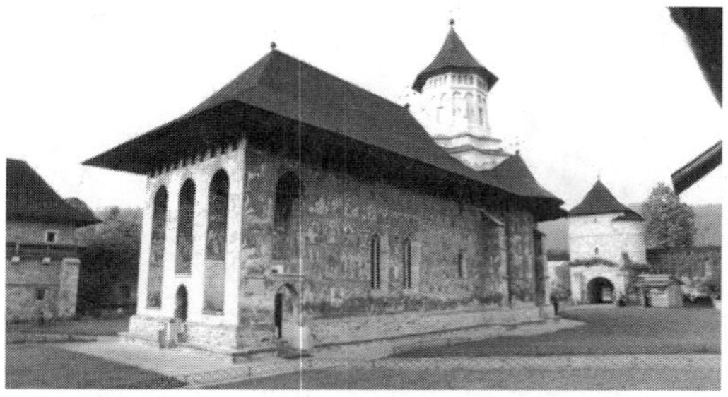

MONASTERY. Orthodox monastery in northern Moldavia, built 1532.

monastery. A house of religious retirement or seclusion from the world for persons under religious vows; in Roman Catholic usage a house operated by a religious monastic order for men or women and always dependent on an abbey.
monastic order. A religious institute dedicated to the monastic life.
monasticism. The monastic life, system or condition; organized asceticism as practiced in a monastery.
Mongolian, Mongoloid. One of the 5 major races of mankind; Asiatic, Oriental, speaking over 2,900 languages. Global statistics: (2000) 2.2 billion in 3,621 peoples residing in 167 countries (94 significantly); largest, China (1.1 billion).
monk. A man who is a member of a monastic order.
monocultural evangelism. Evangelistic activities that take place, from evangelist to audiences, within a single culture only.
monoethnic church. A church or denomination whose members are entirely, or mainly, from a single ethnic group, tribe, caste or people; a one-tribe or one-people church.
monolingual. A person or group knowing or speaking only their own language.
Monophysites. Pejorative term for Oriental Orthodox (qv).
monotheist. One who believes in monotheism, the doctrine or belief that there exists only one God.

monsignor, monseigneur. (mgr, msgr). A title of honor for a non-episcopal prelate of the Roman Catholic Church.
monthly attenders. Affiliated Christians (church members) who attend church services of public worship on average once a month.
monthly letters. The total regular monthly flow of listeners' letters received by a radio or TV station or program.
monthly radio audience. The average regular audience each month for a Christian radio or TV station or program.
Moravians. A Protestant tradition, also known as Unitas Fratrum (Unity of the Brethren), or Continental Pietists. Global statistics: (1970) 478,000; (1995) 582,000 in 29 countries (2 significantly); largest, Tanzania (230,000).

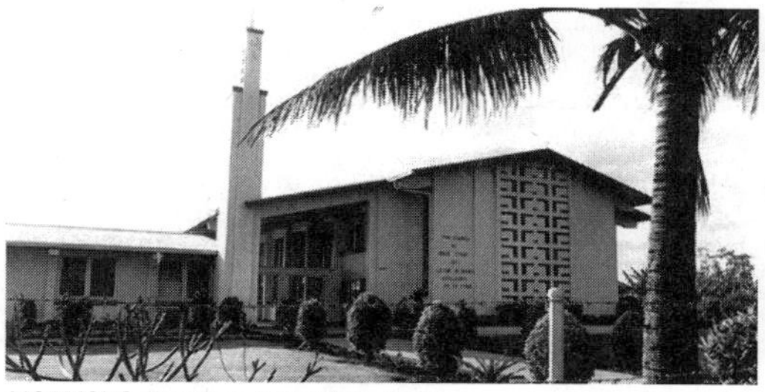
MORMONS. Temple in Nuku Alofa, Tonga.

Mormons. Followers of the Church of Jesus Christ of Latter-day Saints and its over 90 schismatic bodies.
mosque. (Arabic, *masjid*). A Muslim place of public religious worship.
mother. A rank or office in numerous Non-White indigenous churches.
mother church. Ecclesiastically (not theologically), a large central church (particularly in South American Protestantism) with a number of derived daughter churches.
mother house, motherhouse. The original monastery or convent of a religious community or the one where the superior general or provincial lives.
mother superior. A nun who is the head of a religious house.
mother tongue. The first language spoken in an individual's home in his early or earliest childhood; one's first language or native language.
motu propio. (Latin: by one's own impulse). A rescript initiated and issued by the Roman Catholic pope of his own accord and apart from the advice of others.
Mozarabs. Spanish Christians living under Arab rule in Spain. AD 711-1100.
Mulatto. The issue of a White and a Black (Negro).
mullah. Among Persians, Pakistanis and North Indians, a Muslim religious practitioner or cleric.
multi-individual conversion. (or decision). The entry of non-Christians into the church, not through one-by-one individual conversion or decision, but at a single point in time through a corporate collective decision of the whole family/village/clan/tribe/people/nation, as a result of evangelistic methods taking into account local village or extended-family decision-making patterns.
multi-party states. States in which more than one genuine political party are permitted, active, and alternating occasionally in government; often termed democracies.
multi-religious, multireligious. An organization or activity jointly operated by 2 or more religions.
multiethnic church. A church or denomination whose members come from a variety of distinct and different ethnic groups.
multilateral conversations. In ecumenical terminology, theological conversations undertaken by officially-appointed representatives of several churches, denominations, traditions, or confessional families.
multimedia campaign. An evangelistic or total mobilization campaign in which extensive, coordinated use is made of several of the mass media (radio, TV, film, audiovisuals, print media, et alia).
multinational corporation. A large centralized business organization with foreign branches whose activities outside its parent country represent a considerable percentage of its total sales, investments and profits, but whose decisions regarding production, forms of production, marketing, financing, opening of new factories, etc., are made by the parent company.
multiplication-evangelism. Evangelism and discipling of small numbers of believers with a view to them also becoming disciplers (qv) and multiplying exponentially.
Munda-Santal. An Austro-Asiatic ethnolinguistic family, with 70 languages. Global statistics: (2000) 11.7 million in 38 peoples residing in 4 countries; largest, India (11.2 million).

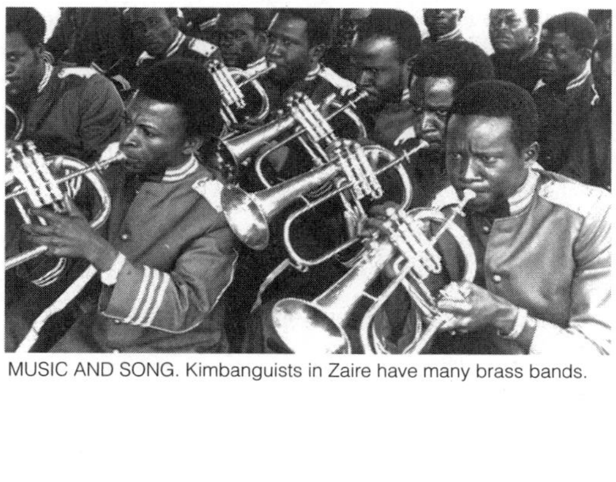
MUSIC AND SONG. Kimbanguists in Zaire have many brass bands.

music and song. In this field, Christian organizations significant at the national or wider levels number over 200.
musical groups. Amateur, semi-professional and professional groups specializing in Christian presentation through music and song have mushroomed in the Western world since 1960, and now number over 50,000.
musicals, religious. See religious drama.
Muslim religious orders. In Arabic, *tariqa* (qv).

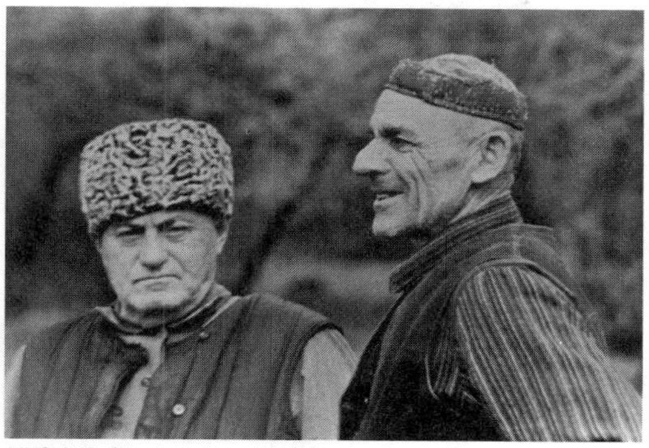
MUSLIMS. Chechens in national dress.

Muslims. Followers of Islam, in its 2 main branches (with schools of law, rites or sects): Sunnis or Sunnites (Hanafite, Hanbalite, Malikite, Shafiite), and Shias or Shiites (Ithna-Ashari, Ismaili, Alawite and Zaydi versions); also Kharijite and other orthodox sects; reform movements (Wahhabi, Sanusi, Mahdiya), also heterodox sects (Ahmadiya, Druzes, Yazidis), but excluding syncretistic religions with Muslim elements, and partially-islamized tribal religionists. Global statistics: (1970) 553.5 million; (1995) 1.0 billion in 204 countries (77 significantly); largest, Pakistan (130.9 million); (2000) 1.1 billion; (2025) 1.7 billion.
mutually-exclusive categories. A typology or series of categories each exclusive in its coverage.
mutually-unintelligible languages. A group of languages any 2 of which are each unintelligible to the other.
mysticism. The experience of mystical union or direct communion with God; the doctrine or belief that direct communion with God is attainable.
myth. A traditional story explaining some practice, belief, institution or natural phenomenon, parable, allegory, legend, saga, fable.
mythology. The myths dealing with gods and demigods of a particular people.

N

Nasoreans. Mandaeans (qv).
nation. A politically-organized nationality, ethno-linguistic group or family or people, usually with independent existence in a sovereign nation-state; state, country.
nation, sovereign. See sovereign territory.
national. (1) Relating to a nation. (2) One who owes permanent allegiance to a nation without regard to place of residence; often a citizen but not necessarily so.
national Christian councils. Councils of churches and denominations which also include para-church organizations as full members.
national church. The church of a nation; established church, state church, or occasionally a former state church now disestablished.
national clergy. Clergy who are nationals of the nation they work in.
national conciliarism. Nationwide councils of churches and Christian councils of all kinds number about 550.
national councils of churches. Councils of churches in which full membership is only open to denominations, but not to para-church organizations.
national income per person. The average per capita annual income in a country at a particular date, usually derived as gross national product (qv) per capita.
native. An individual born or raised in the territory in which he lives.
native speakers. Mother-tongue speakers of a specific language.
nativistic movement. Among tribal or primitive peoples, a movement advocating or advancing the perpetuation or reestablishment of native culture traits and a concomitant restriction or removal of foreign culture elements often accompanied by a strong messianic or ceremonial cult.
natural change. Demographic change as experienced by the whole population of a country or area including all its religious bodies, composed of biological change together with migration change. Global total: (1995) about 79 millions.
natural growth rate. The net sum of crude birth rate in the population minus crude death rate, plus net immigration rate.
natural increase. In United Nations usage, biological change or the excess of births over deaths in a population.
naturalization. The process by which aliens acquire the nationality of their country of residence.
naturalized persons. Former aliens who have now become citizens.
near-Bible. For any no-scripture language, a Bible in a near-language (qv) within its own cluster.
near-gospel. For any no-scripture language, a gospel in a near-language (qv) within its own cluster.
near-language. For any language, any other language within its cluster (outer language).
near-NT. For any no-scripture language, a NT in a near-language (qv) within its own cluster.
near-scripture. For any no-scripture language, a scripture in a near-language (qv) within its own cluster.
negotiations. In ecumenical terminology, church union discussions between 2 or more churches after a public commitment has been made towards eventual organic union.
Negrito. An Austro-Asiatic ethnolinguistic family; Asiatic Pygmy. Global statistics: (2000) 1.5 million in 69 peoples residing in 6 countries; largest, Philippines (1.1 million).
Negro. One of the 5 major races of mankind; Negroid, Equatorial, Black, speaking about 1,390 languages. Global statistics: (2000) 648.0 million in 3,028 peoples residing in 121 countries (144 significantly); largest, Brazil (56.1 million).
neo-Buddhist. Relating to a new or recent Buddhist sect or movement.
Neocharismatics. Followers of Third Wave of Pentecostal/Charismatic Renewal, experiencing the same gifts of the Holy Spirit but without accepting same terminology or polity. Global statistics: (1970) 53,490,000; (2000) 295,405,000.
Neo-Christianity. A reinterpretation of Christianity in terms of a current philosophy, as rationalism in the 19th century.
Neo-Evangelicals. A term used by Fundamentalists (qv) to describe Evangelicals willing to co-operate with non-Evangelicals and to re-examine basic Evangelical dogmas and positions.
Neo-Fundamentalists. A term used by extreme Fundamentalists to describe Fundamentals willing to work with other types of Evangelicals.
Neo-Hawaiian. The populace of the state of Hawaii, USA; Aboriginal Hawaiians (pure Polynesians) now number only 2%, the rest being Neo-Hawaiians, a highly-mixed population with (blood-group admixture) 78% Polynesian origin, 14% Mongoloid (Chinese/Japanese/Filipino/ Korean), 8% Caucasian (European).
neo-Hindus. Followers of new or recent Hindu sects offshoots or movements, including Divine Light Mission. Global statistics: (1970) 6.9 million; (1995) 15.2 million; (2000) 17.3 million; (2025) 23.2 million.
neo-orthodoxy. A 20th-century movement in Protestant theology characterized by a reaction against liberalism, re-emphasis on some orthodox Reformation doctrines, and renewed stress on classic Protestant formularies.
neo-paganism. Revived or new paganism, as in Iceland.
Neo-Protestants. A term sometimes applied to newer Protestant traditions, including Adventists, Brethren, Pentecostals, etc.
neologism. A new word, usage or expression; word coinage or redefinition.
neophyte. A recent convert, catechumen, proselyte; a newly-ordained Roman Catholic priest or novice in a convent.
Nestorians. Assyrians (qv).
New Apostolics. Christians of Catholic Apostolic origin (in 1863) and tradition, who belong to the New Apostolic Church (largely German in membership) or its offshoots. Global statistics: (1970) 1.7 million; (1995) 8.2 million in 176 countries; largest country, India (1.4 million).
new birth. A turning-point in life when a person commits himself or herself to Christ, experience claimed by 34% of the population in the USA.
New Calendar. The New Style or Gregorian Calendar, replacing the Old Style or Julian Calendar, introduced in 1582 by Pope Gregory XIII, adopted by England in 1752, and by most Orthodox in 1924 except the Churches of Jerusalem, Russia, Serbia and Bulgaria, and Old Calendarists (qv).
New Christian. (Spanish, *cristiano nuevo*). A Marrano (qv).
New Church. A major branch of the Swedenborgian movement (qv).

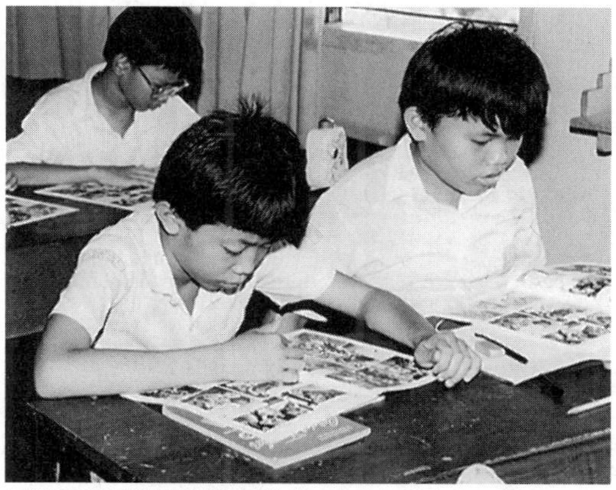
NEW READER SCRIPTURES. Children in Jakarta, Indonesia.

New Life for All. (NLFA). A saturation evangelism program, begun in Nigeria in 1964, involving total mobilization of Christians at the local church level.
New Reader Scriptures. UBS-sponsored program for producing versions of the Scriptures specially compiled for newly-literate persons. Global statistics: 30 million copies in 1,954 languages..
New Religions. The so-called Asiatic 20th-century New Religions, New Religious movements, or radical new crisis religions (new Far Eastern or Asiatic indigenous non-Christian syncretistic mass religions, founded since 1800 and mostly since 1945) including the Japanese neo-Buddhist and neo-Shinto new religious movements, and Korean, Chinese, Vietnamese and Indonesian syncretistic religions, et alia. See New-Religionists.
New Testament. The covenant of God with man embodied in the coming of Christ; the printed volume of 27 books.

New Testament distribution. Distribution (free subsidized, commercial): copies of the NT per year. Global statistics: 121.8 million (AD 2000).
New Thought. A mental healing movement embracing a number of small groups and organizations devoted to spiritual healing, the creative power of constructive thinking, and personal guidance from an inner presence.
New-Religionists. Followers of the so-called New Religions (qv) of Asia. Global statistics: (1970) 77.7 million; (1995) 97.7 million in 60 countries (5 significantly); largest, Indonesia (43.5 million); (2000) 102.3 million; (2025) 114.7 million.
newspapers, daily. In UNESCO usage, newspapers which are published at least 4 times a week.
newspapers, general-interest. In UNESCO terminology, publications devoted primarily to recording news of current events in public affairs, international affairs, politics, etc.
Nilotic. (Para-Nilotic). An African ethnolinguistic family, with about 90 languages. Global statistics: (2000) 24.7 million in 168 peoples residing in 8 countries (3 significantly); largest, Kenya (7.8 million).
nirvana. (Sanskrit). In Hinduism, Jainism and Buddhism, the state of freedom from karma, extinction of desire, passion and illusion.
Nisei. (Japanese: second-generation). A Japanese-American son or daughter of Issei (first-generation immigrants) parents, and born and educated in the Americas.
Nizaris. Nizari Ismailis, Khojas (qv).
no-church. See non-denominational.
no-party states. Independent nations ruled without a political party.
nomads. Peoples with no fixed residence but migrating seasonally.
nominal Christians. See unaffiliated Christians.
nominal fringe. In countries with a Christian majority, the fringe of nominal Christians around the churches who are not church members.
nomogram. A figure or diagram from which calculations can be made at sight.
non-adherents. Persons who are not adherents of any religion; non-religious, agnostics or atheists.
non-affiliated. Nominal Christians (qv).
non-attenders. Non-practicing Christians (qv).
non-attending Christians. Non-practicing Christians (qv).
non-belief. Unbelief (qv).
non-believers. Persons who are not adherents of or believers in any religion; non-religious, agnostics or atheists.
Non-Chalcedonian. Oriental Orthodox (qv).
non-Christian attenders. See attending non-Christians.
non-Christian religionists. Adherents of all religions in the world except Christianity. Global statistics: (2000) 3,137,237,000 (51.8%) (2000) 3.1 billion; (2025) 4.1 billion.
non-Christians. All persons who are not Christian adherents of any kind, including non-believers (agnostics, or atheists).
non-conciliar. Unconnected with the Ecumenical Movement or with Evangelical, Indigenous or any other form of councils or conciliarism.
Non-conciliar Evangelicals. Evangelicals rejecting contact or co-operation with the Ecumenical Movement.
non-confessional. Used of a denomination or Christian activity unaligned with any confessions.
non-confessional Christianity. Of the world's significant Christian denominations, those which have no confessional allegiance (membership in world confessional councils), or have no confessional allegiance but themselves form quasi-confessions (qv) or non-confessional international denominational bodies.
non-confessional international denominational body. (quasi-confessions). Denominations which do not belong to any of the recognized world confessional bodies or families, but which function, or regard themselves, or are often regarded, as themselves confessional bodies or world families of churches, each with organized branches and churches in 3 or more nations, although in fact each is a single worldwide or international denomination. Global membership: see quasi-confessions.
non-denominational. (no-church groups). Churches or movements which, in reaction to Western missionary work, reject all ecclesiastical labels even including 'Christian', and all ecclesiastical practices including baptism.
non-diocesan. A term describing clergy and other staff in a diocese who are not on the diocesan payroll but are employed by a province, other Christian body, or a secular agency.
non-evangelizing Christians. Nominal Christians and non-practicing Christians who although themselves evangelized, contribute nothing to the ongoing process of the evangelization of their own people or country or of the world.
non-historical Catholic. Churches or Christians who regard themselves as in the Catholic tradition but who have no historical continuity supporting their claim.
non-historical Orthodox. Churches or Christians who regard themselves as in the Orthodox tradition but who have no historical continuity supporting their claim.
Non-Liturgical blocs. A term used here for 3 of the 6 ecclesiastico-cultural major blocs (qv) which are largely Baptistic or Baptists (i.e. practicing adult or believer's baptism only) and whose worship is largely extempore without written liturgies: Protestantism (except for the Lutheran, Reformed, Methodist and a few other traditions), marginal Christians, and Independent Christianity. Numerically, Non-Liturgical Christians number only 26% of global church members. The other 3 blocs are termed Liturgical (qv).
non-participating member. A church member or affiliated Christian who does not practice regularly; a non-practicing Christian (qv).
non-practicing Christians. Christians who are affiliated to churches but are inactive, non-attending (sometimes called dormant Christians). Not Great Commission Christians. Global statistics: (1995) 1,167 million (2000) 1,240 million; (2025) 1,603 million.
non-receiving countries. From the standpoint of foreign mission, countries which prohibit the receiving of foreign missionaries from other countries.
non-religious. Persons professing no religion, or professing unbelief or non-belief, non-believers, agnostics, freethinkers, liberal thinkers, non-religious humanists, indifference to both religion and atheism, apathetic, opposed on principle neither to religion nor to atheism; sometimes termed secularists or materialists; also post-Christian, dechristianized or de-religionized populations. Global statistics: (1970) 532.1 million; (1995) 738.0 million in 236 countries (39 significantly); largest, China (509.5 million); (2000) 768.1 million; (2025) 875.1 million.
non-religious Buddhists. Persons whose family religion is Buddhism but who as individuals profess to have no personal religion.
non-religious quasi-religionists. Adherents of non-religious quasi-religions (some forms of agnosticism, fascism, humanism, liberal humanism, nationalism, Nazism, some forms of non-religion or secularism).
non-Roman Catholics. See Catholics (non-Roman).
non-sending. Countries, areas or churches which, for various reasons, never send, or are not permitted by the state to send, foreign missionaries abroad.
non-sovereign territory. A country listed in the United Nations' list of territories but not completely autonomous or independent or self-governing.
non-trinitarian. A Christian tradition not emphasizing the doctrine of the Trinity, hence often regarded as unitarian.
Non-White. A collective term referring to all races and ethnolinguistic groups distinct from the White races indigenous to Europe and North America. Global statistics: (2000) 5,106,867,000 (84.3%).
Non-White indigenous Christians. Black/Third-World indigenous Christians in denominations, churches or movements indigenous to Black or Non-White races originating in the Third World, locally-founded and not foreign-based or Western-imported, begun since AD 1500, Black/Non-White-founded, Black/Non-White-led, forming autonomous bodies independent of Western and Eastern churches, with no Western ties, often schismatic, separatist, anti-establishment, sometimes anti-Western, anti-White or anti-European in reaction to Western influences. Global statistics: (1970) 29.3 million; (1995) 174.7 million in 181 countries (9 significantly); largest, China (35.7 million).
Nonconformists. Dissenters, persons who do not conform to the doctrine or discipline of an established church, especially, members of religious bodies separated from the Church of England.
norm. A model, type, pattern; an authoritative rule or standard.
normative. Prescriptive, regulative, didactic.
North Indian. An Indo-Iranian ethnolinguistic family. Global statistics: (2000) 1.0 billion in 629 peoples residing in 138 countries (15 significantly); largest, India (744.8 million).
Northern Amerindian. An American Indian ethno-linguistic family, with 200 languages. Global statistics: (2000) 12.3 million in 213 peoples residing in 4 countries; largest, USA (11.2 million).
Northern Buddhism. Mahayana (qv).
notes of the church. Marks of the church (qv).
notice-boards. Since vast numbers of local church buildings carry their own detailed notice-boards, these are very useful in rapid surveys.
novice. One who has entered a religious house and is on probation.
nuclear Christianity. Active, practicing, committed Christianity.
nuclear Christians. See committed Christians.
Nuclear Mande. An African ethnolinguistic family with about 30 languages. Global statistics: (2000) 17.7 million in 108 peoples residing in 16 countries (8 significantly); largest, Mali (5.5 million).

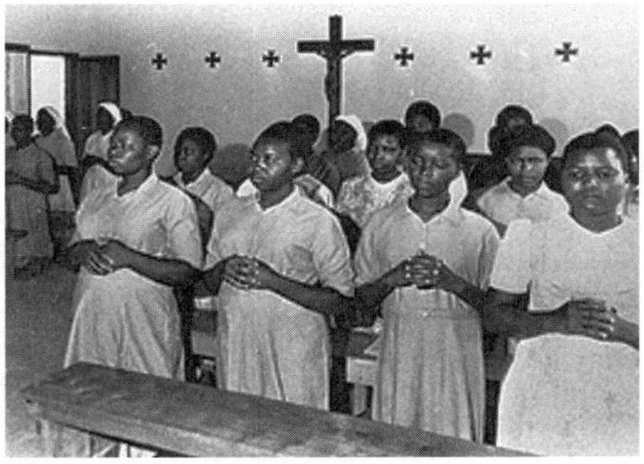

NUN. Religious Order of Mary, Kenya.

nun. A woman belonging to a religious institute or order of women with solemn vows (moniales), a woman religious in simple vows is more properly termed a sister.
nunciature. The diplomatic office of the Holy See in a foreign country. World total: (1997) 98.
nuncio. The diplomatic envoy of the Roman Catholic pope as Sovereign of the Holy See, accredited to a foreign government in a country where Catholics are a majority.
nuns, Roman Catholic. World total (1978) 946,398; declining to (1996) 828,660.
Nusayris. Alawites (qv).

O

obeah. Jamaican-African word for power.
obedience. A sphere of jurisdiction; control, rule, spiritual authority over others; conformity to the rule of a monastic order.
oblate. One offered or devoted to the monastic life or to some special religious service or work, sometimes a layman living at a monastery.
occasional attenders. Affiliated Christians (church members) who attend church services of public worship only occasionally or irregularly.
occult. The mysterious, supernatural, secret, esoteric in religion and magic.
Oceanic. One of the 13 geographical races of mankind speaking 1,083 languages. Global statistics: (2000) 9.5 million in 1,420 peoples residing in 12 countries (9 significantly); largest, Papua New Guinea (3.2 million).
offertory. A collection of money taken at a religious service.
office. In liturgy, a set form of prayer or worship drawn up by church authority, usually for daily recitation by clergy.
office-holders. (German, *Amtstragern*). Officials of the New Apostolic Church, mostly Germans, and totaling 50,000.
officer. In Salvation Army usage, a Salvationist who has left secular employment and is engaged in full-time commissioned Army service. Global total of SA officers: 25,449 in 101 countries.
official languages of the United Nations. In AD 2000, there were 6: Arabic, Chinese, English, French, Russian, Spanish.
official religion. See state religion.
official state languages. Languages proclaimed by states as their official or national means of communication number 114.
old age. Usually taken to begin at the age of retirement (60-65 years).
Old Apostolics. Catholic Apostolics (qv), Irvingites.

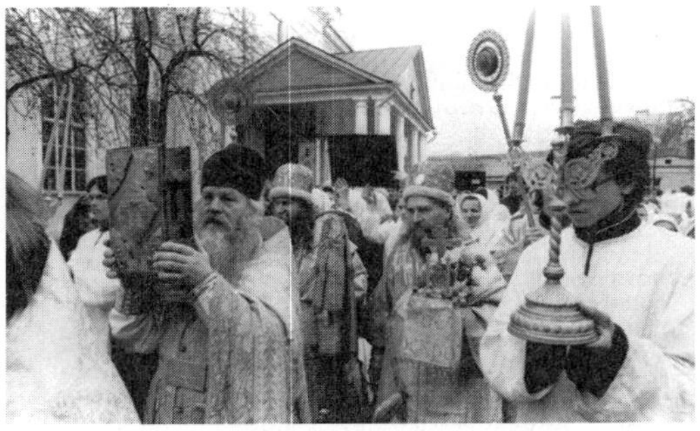

OLD BELIEVERS. Procession in Pokrovskaya church in Moscow.

Old Believers. Followers of AD 1666 schisms ex Russian Orthodox Church, retaining use of Old Slavonic; Old Ritualists. Global statistics: (1970) 2.6 million; (1995) 2.0 million in 24 countries; largest, Russia (1.2 million).
Old Calendar. The Old Style or Julian Calendar devised by Julius Caesar in BC 46, now 13 days behind the New or Gregorian Calendar followed by all Orthodox churches up to 1918 and still followed in AD 2000 by (a) the Churches of Jerusalem, Russia, Serbia, and Bulgaria, (b) most of the monasteries on Mount Athos, and (c) various groups of Old Calendarists (qv).
Old Calendarists. Also called Paleohemerologites (from Greek, Palaioimerologitai), or Authentic Orthodox; Greek Orthodox who reject the Ecumenical Patriarchate's change in 1924 from the Old (Julian) Calendar to the New (Gregorian) Calendar. Global statistics: (1970) 215,000; (1995) 261,000 in 8 countries; largest, Greece (212,000).
Old Catholics. Followers of schisms ex Church of Rome retaining Old Catholic apostolic succession of bishops; especially schisms of 1702, 1724, 1870, 1897. Global statistics: (1970) 647,000; (1995) 866,000 in 26 countries; largest, USA (718,000).
Old Ritualists. Old Believers (qv).
Old Slavic. Church Slavonic (qv).
Old Testament. The covenant of God with the Hebrews as set forth in the Bible; or, the 39 canonical books which form its record in the first part of the Bible; or a printed version or copy thereof.
old-age population. Persons over 65 years old.
older churches. A term sometimes used for the older or historical mainline denominations of Europe and North America, in contrast to the so-called younger churches of the Third World.
on trial. Used in Methodist and other circles for new members who are placed on trial for a period of months to demonstrate their commitment to becoming members.
on-demand publishing of books. Publication of material which cannot be economically handled conventionally; the production and distribution of copies of books, one or a few at a time, in response to orders rather than from a preprinted stock of copies; usually by photocopying author-prepared copy or production from microform; a recent technique for publishers with 'excess of material worthy of publication'.
on-line database. A large computerized data bank of information arranged for instant retrieval and in which all data can be immediately accessed.
Oneness-Pentecostals. Also termed Unitarian-Pentecostals, Jesus-Only Pentecostals (because of baptism in name of Jesus only). Global statistics: (1970) 939,000; (1995) 2.4 million in 80 countries; largest, USA (833,000).
Open Brethren. Christian Brethren (qv).
open communion. The practice of inviting all adults present at a service of worship, including those from other denom-

inations, to participate in communion at the Lord's Table.

operationalism. The view that the concepts or terms used in non-analytic scientific statements must be definable in terms of identifiable and repeatable operations.

operations research. The application of scientific and mathematical methods to the study and analysis of complex problems not traditionally considered to fall within the field of profitable scientific inquiry.

ophthalmic mission. A foreign missionary society specializing in eye services.

opinion-makers. See decision-makers.

opportunity. In evangelization, the occasion, chance, time, or combinations of circumstances, times and places suitable or favorable for persons to hear and understand the gospel.

ordained minister. See minister.

order, religious. See religious orders.

orders. The office and dignity of a person in the Christian ministry.

ordinand. A person in training for ordination.

ordinariates. (symbol O). In the Roman Catholic Church, 6 countries have country-wide jurisdictions for Eastern-rite Catholics, termed ordinariates.

ordinary. In canon law, an ecclesiastic in exercise of the jurisdiction permanently annexed to his office; in the RC Church, the pope and all diocesan bishops, abbots, apostolic administrators or vicars, prelates and prefects: in Anglican usage, the bishop or archdeacon.

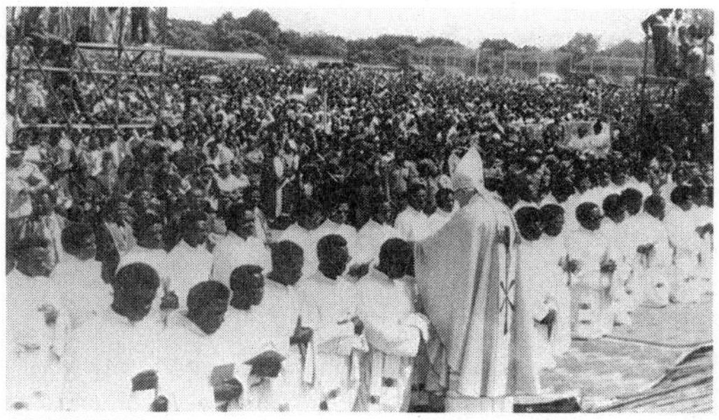

ORDINATION. Pope conducts mass ordination in Nigeria.

ordination. The act of admission into, or the status of being in, the Christian ministry.

ordination of women. See women, ordination of.

ordinations, annual. Total to the Roman Catholic priesthood: (1974) 4,380 secular, 2,551 religious; (1975) 4,140 secular, 2,488 religious; (1991) 6,600 secular, 2,403 religious; (1996) 6,800 secular, 2,509 religious.

organic union. The goal of church union negotiations whereby 2 previously separate denominations become a single organically-administered new denomination.

organized Christianity. Christianity as formally organized into blocs, traditions, denominations, and councils. Global statistics: (1970) 1.1 billion; (1995) 1.7 billion in 238 countries (186 significantly); largest, USA (184.2 million); (2000) 1.8 billion; (2025) 2.4 billion.

organized congregation. See congregation.

organized religion. A religion as formally organized by subdivisions, schools, sects, denominations or other bodies or groupings requiring membership.

Oriental Catholics. Eastern-rite Catholics (qv) in communion with the See of Rome.

Oriental Jews. The third major group of Diaspora Jews, after Ashkenazis (German-rite) and Sefardis (Spanish-rite); sometimes treated as a sub-division of Sefardis; Arabic-speaking Jews from North Africa and the Middle East. Global statistics: (1970) 1.5 million; (1995) 2.2 million; (2000) 2.3 million; (2025) 2.6 million.

Oriental Orthodox. Christians of Pre-Chalcedonian/ Non-Chalcedonian/Monophysite tradition, of 5 major types: Armenian, Coptic, Ethiopian, Syrian, Syro-Malabarese. Global statistics: (1970) 20.8 million; (1995) 37.7 million in 113 countries (4 significantly); largest, Ethiopia (20.2 million).

Oriental Orthodox Churches Conference. First conference of Syrian, Armenian, Coptic, Ethiopian and Syro-Malabarese Orthodox churches, held in Addis Ababa 1965. Global statistics: (1970) 20.8 million; (1995) 37.7 million in 113 countries (4 significantly); largest, Ethiopia (20.2 million).

Oriental-rite Catholics. Eastern-rite Catholics (qv).

Orthodox. In 4 traditions: Eastern (Chalcedonian), Oriental (Pre-Chalcedonian, Non-Chalcedonian, Monophysite), Nestorian (Assyrian), and non-historical Orthodox. Global statistics: (1970) 139.6 million; (1995) 209.6 million in 135 countries (22 significantly); largest, Russia (74.5 million); (2000) 215.1 million; (2025) 252.7 million.

Orthodox pentecostals. Orthodox in the organized charismatic renewal, expressed in healings, tongues, prophesying, etc. Global statistics: (2000) 2.9 million.

Orthodoxy. The systems of faith, practice and discipline of the Eastern Orthodox and Oriental Orthodox Churches.

orthodoxy. Right teaching in Christian theology, as contrasted with heresy and heterodoxy.

orthography. A method of representing the sounds of a language by written or printed symbols; the printed letter set used.

other religionists. A term used here in Tables 1 for total adherents of all other smaller non-Christian religious faiths, quasi-religions, pseudo-religions, para-religions, religious systems, religious philosophies and semi-religious brotherhoods (Gnostic, Occult, Masonic, Mystic, etc.).

otiose. Used of God in many pagan religions: remote, aloof, uninvolved, uninterested in the human race.

Outcastes. Persons in India considered outside caste society. See scheduled castes.

outer language. Also termed a language *cluster* (qv).

outreach. In evangelization, the extent or length or whole complex of all varieties of evangelistic reaching out to the non-Christian world on the part of the Christian community.

outreach into the world. The act or process of the church reaching out to the world's non-Christian populations, in evangelism and in service.

outsider. A non-Christian, or non-affiliated.

overlapping membership. Membership of an individual or group, or of congregations, in 2 distinct church areas or churches or denominations.

P

Pacific. One of the 13 geographical races of mankind, with 135 languages. Global statistics: (2000) 5.6 million in 145 peoples residing in 33 countries (27 significantly); largest, Philippines (2.7 million).

Pacific indigenous churches. Non-White indigenous churches in Oceania, indigenous to Pacific or Oceanic peoples. Global statistics: (1970) 26,000; (1995) 183,000 in 17 countries; largest, Fiji (50,000).

paedobaptist. See pedobaptist.

pagan religionists. See neo-paganism.

pagans. (Latin: country-dwellers). A somewhat outdated term for non-Christians, heathen, polytheists, animists, shamanists, et alii.

pagoda. A stupa (qv).

Paleoasiatic. An Asian ethnolinguistic family. Global statistics: (2000) 36,000 in 10 peoples residing in 1 country; largest, Russia (36,000).

Paleohemerologites. Authentic Orthodox or Old Calendarists (qv).

pantheism. A doctrine that the universe conceived of as a whole is God.

pantheist. A follower of pantheism.

papal bull. A formal letter from the Roman pope named after the lead seal (*bulla*) attached to it.

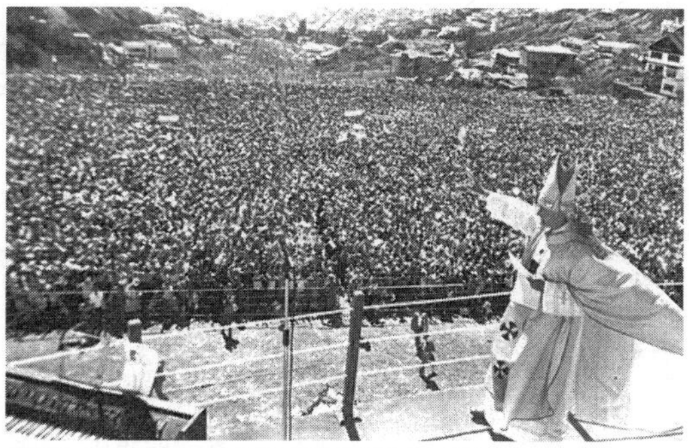

PAPAL JOURNEYS. John Paul II in Brazil: his total exceeds 100.

papal journeys. Official apostolic visits by Roman Catholic pope to various countries.

Papuan. An Oceanic ethnolinguistic family, with 700 languages. Global statistics: (2000) 4.8 million in 888 peoples residing in 6 countries (2 significantly); largest, Papua New Guinea (3.2 million).

para-Christians. See marginal Christians.

para-church. Almost a church, resembling a church.

para-church agencies. Service agencies (qv), especially those which develop a life distinct or separate from the organized churches.

para-denomination. A service agency which develops its own distinct and separate church life and resembles a new or separate denomination, offering its members worship facilities and other denominational perquisites.

parallel church. In Roman Catholic usage, suppressed but ongoing underground liberal or activist groups within the church, especially of priests (as in Portugal).

paraphrase. A loose translation of Scripture incorporating overt interpretation (e.g. NTME, LB).

parentheses. In printing, curved marks ( ) in contrast to square brackets [ ].

parish. An ecclesiastical unit of area committed to one pastor; a portion of a diocese committed to the pastoral care of one clergyman.

Parsis. (Parsees). Descendants of Zoroastrians of Persia, worshippers of Ahura Mazda. Sects: Kadmis and Shahanshahis. Global statistics: (1970) 122,000; (1995) 2.2 million in 24 countries; largest, Iran (1.7 million); (2000) 2.5 million; (2025) 4.4 million.

parson. A clergyman; rector or incumbent of a parochial church.

part-time worker. A recognized or accredited church worker whose main work is Christian ministry but who is also engaged in part-time secular work for his livelihood; in contrast to spare-time or full-time workers.

partially-closed countries. 43 countries in the world which are not fully closed to foreign mission, though strict control is exercised.

participating member. A practicing Christian (qv) or practicing church member. In Disciples (USA) usage, 'one who exercises a continuing interest in one or more of the following ways: attendance, giving, activity, spiritual concern for the fellowship of the congregation regardless of the place of residence'.

participatory media. See folk media.

particular church. In Roman Catholic usage (as e.g. in Vatican II documents), the universal church as organized in a particular diocese: the diocesan church; sometimes called the local church.

Partners in Mission. A scheme within the Anglican Communion whereby an autonomous church invites a number of sister churches or provinces to confer with it on discharging its mission in its own locality.

pasaka, pasika. (Shona and other African languages). Passover, Easter communion service in certain African indigenous churches, attracting scores of thousands of members.

pascalisants. (French). See Paschal communicants.

Paschal communicants. Roman Catholic Easter communicants (qv); all who actually take communion at Easter over a 4-week period.

passover. Annual Jewish religious festival commemorating deliverance from Egypt; for Christians, symbolic of Christ's atonement for sin.

pastor. A clergyman, priest or minister responsible for the cure of souls.

pastoral centers. In Roman Catholic usage, parishes, quasi-parishes, mission stations and a few other categories. World totals (1996): 423,064 centers (220,583 parishes and quasi-parishes, 112,224 mission stations, 90,257 other centers).

pastoral council. In Roman Catholic usage, a diocesan, or a nation-wide, council of bishops, priests, religious and laity.

pastoral region. See apostolic region.

pastoral reorganization. An updating or modernizing rearrangement of traditional jurisdictions in the Roman Catholic Church in a country, in the interests of more realism, better pastoral care, new urban situations, etc.

pastoralia. The study of pastoral work in the church.

pastors' conferences. Protestant conferences for pastors and clergy in developing countries, held frequently, under sponsorship of World Vision.

patriarch. The supreme bishop of an autocephalous church, especially Catholic or Orthodox.

patriarchal diocese. A diocese administered by a patriarch.

patriarchal exarchate. (symbol PE). The jurisdiction of an exarch under a patriarch.

patriarchal vicariate. (symbol VP). A vicariate, usually in another city, of one of the traditional patriarchates.

patriarchate. The office, dignity, jurisdiction, province, or see of a patriarch. Global total: (1999) 31 traditional Catholic (13) and Orthodox (18) patriarchates, and over 100 more of recent establishment and unsupported historical claim.

Patristics. Patrology (qv).

patrology. The science or scientific study of the teachings of the Fathers of the Church, defined as in the West all Christian writers up to Gregory the Great (died 604), and in the East to John Damascene (died 749).

peak publishers. In Jehovah's Witnesses' usage, the maximum number of publishers (qv) in action in any given year.

pedobaptist. Pedobaptist churches baptize children and infants of Christian families because they believe that in doing so they are faithful to the teaching and practice of Christ and his apostles and of the Church from the earliest times; they do not receive or give any second baptism, since baptism is by its very nature unrepeatable; they respect the convictions of fellow-Christians in the Baptist traditions (baptizing adults only) and desire fellowships and unity with them.

Pedobaptists. Christians in traditions that baptize infants. Global total: (1970) 1,041,265,000, (1980) 1,217,519,000, (1985) 1,311,851,000; i.e. 92% of global church membership. Some 3.3% of these are doubly-affiliated i.e. also members of non-Pedobaptist churches and traditions.

penetration. The extent of evangelization into a people's or region's culture and life, usually overcoming difficulties or resistance or opposition.

Pentecost. Christian festival on the 7th Sunday after Easter commemorating descent of the Holy Spirit; called Pentecost by Roman Catholics, Whitsunday by Anglicans and others.

Pentecostal. With a capital 'P', the noun or adjective refers here to charismatic Christians in separate or distinct Pentecostal denominations of White origin.

pentecostal. With a small 'p', the noun or adjective refers here to charismatic Christians (l) still within mainline non-Pentecostal denominations, and (2) those in Non-White indigenous pentecostal denominations.

Pentecostal Apostolics. Pentecostals differing from other Pentecostals in stress on complex hierarchy of living apostles, prophets and other charismatic officials. Global statistics: (1970) 706,000; (1995) 1.6 million in 31 countries; largest, Nigeria (844,000).

Pentecostal World Conference. (PWC). The major Pentecostal world communion, mainly a triennial conference (since 1947) with minimal continuity. Global statistics: (1970) 11.4 million; (1995) 47.7 million in 381 countries (5 significantly); largest, Brazil (22.6 million).

Pentecostal-charismatics. A blanket term for all Pentecostals, pentecostals, neo-pentecostals, and charismatics (qv). Global statistics: (1970) 72.2 million; (1995) 477.3 million in 237 countries (85 significantly); largest, Brazil (74.2 million); (2000) 523.7 million; (2025) 811.5 million.

Pentecostalism. A Christian confession or ecclesiastical tradition holding the distinctive teaching that all Christians should seek a post-conversion religious experience called the Baptism with the Holy Spirit, and that a Spirit-baptized believer may receive one or more of the supernatural gifts known in the Early Church: instantaneous sanctification, the ability to prophesy, practice divine healing, speak in tongues (glossolalia), or interpret tongues.

Pentecostals. Followers of Pentecostalism (qv), a major world tradition originating around 1900. Global statistics: (1970) 14.4 million; (1995) 54.9 million in 645 countries (6 significantly); largest, Brazil (22.7 million).

Pentecostals: 2-crisis-experience. See Baptistic-Pentecostals.

Pentecostals: 3-crisis-experience. See Holiness-Pentecostals.

Pentecostals: Oneness. (Jesus Only). See Oneness-Pentecostals.

people. (1) A collection of persons who are linked by a common past or a common culture, or who have a common affinity for one another. (2) An ethno-linguistic people (qv) or ethnolinguistic sub-family.
people distance. Cultural distance (qv).
people group. A people (qv).
people movement. A large-scale movement to Christ and into the church by a fair proportion of a people, acting as a group and with a group decision.
people's palace. In Salvation Army usage, a moderately-priced hotel in Australia, New Zealand or France.
per capita. Per head, per person; usually used of some national attribute (GNP, etc.) divided by the total population (men, women, children and infants).
per capita income. See national income per person.
percentage. A proportion in a hundred.
perfecting. The third of the 3 stages of church planting and growth (discipling, baptizing, perfecting, based on the Great Commission in Matthew 28.19), involving the bringing of individuals to conversion and commitment to Christ, the same for their children, teaching baptized individuals the full meaning of church membership and Christian maturity, and teaching about ethical change, holiness, witness, social justice, etc.
Perfectionist-Pentecostals. Also termed Free Pentecostal, Deliverance-Pentecostal, Radical-Pentecostal, Revivalist-Pentecostal; Pentecostals teaching crisis experience including deliverance/ecstatic confession/ascension/perfectionism/prophecy. Global statistics: (1970) 27,000; (1995) 63,000 in 4 countries; largest, Kenya (50,000).
Perfectionists. Holiness Christians (qv).
periodicals, Christian. Defined here as all Christian or church periodicals, journals, magazines, newspapers, bulletins, house organs; of popular, news, scholarly, professional or academic content; daily, semi-weekly, weekly, biweekly, monthly, quarterly, appearing at regular intervals each with 2 or more issues a year, excluding annuals and irregular serials; and in any language. Global statistics: 24,000 (AD 2000).
Peripheral Mande. An African ethnolinguistic family with about 30 languages. Global statistics: (2000) 5.1 million in 25 peoples residing in 5 countries (3 significantly); largest, Sierra Leone (1.6 million).
permanent deacon. A person ordained as a deacon in an episcopal church but who remains a deacon and does not seek or receive ordination as a priest.
permeation. In evangelization, the act or process or state or extent of a population or culture being pervaded or saturated or fully penetrated by the gospel.
permillage. The rate or proportion per thousand.
perpetual curate. A vicar, or minister of a new church or district.
persecuted Christians. Christians in nations where the churches experience severe persecution, obstruction, harassment, and repression.
persecution, religious. See religious persecution.
personal evangelism, personal work. Evangelistic witnessing and sharing by a Christian with other individuals. Global statistics: (1970) 27,000; (1995) 63,000 in 4 countries; largest, Kenya (50,000).
personnel. Officially-recognized, officially-accredited and officially-enumerated active full-time Christian workers of all varieties, salaried or tent-making, men and women, ordained and lay, national and foreign. Global statistics: 5.52 million (AD 2000).
persuasion. (1) A group, faction, sect or party adhering to a particular system of religious beliefs. 2) In evangelization, the act of persuading or influencing people to accept Christ by argument or reasoning.
Phanar. World headquarters (in Istanbul, Turkey) of the Ecumenical Patriarchate of Constantinople; the ecumenical patriarch and his curia.
philosophy of religion. The search for the underlying causes and principles of reality in religion through logical reasoning rather than revelation.
phylum, phyla. See language phyla.
pidgin. A contact language used for communication between groups having different native languages; when a pidgin becomes the native language of a community, it is customarily called a creole (qv).
Pietism. A 17th-century religious movement originating in Germany emphasizing the need for a revitalized evangelical Christianity over against an excessive formalism and intellectualism.
Pietists. (Continental). Moravians (qv).
pilgrim. One who travels to visit a shrine or holy place as a devotee.
pilgrims. Some 7.5% of all Christians (150 millions), of all traditions, are on the move as pilgrims every year, in most countries, visiting large numbers of local, national and international pilgrimage centers and shrines. In addition, there are annually over 30 million Hindu, Muslim, Buddhist and other non-Christian pilgrims.

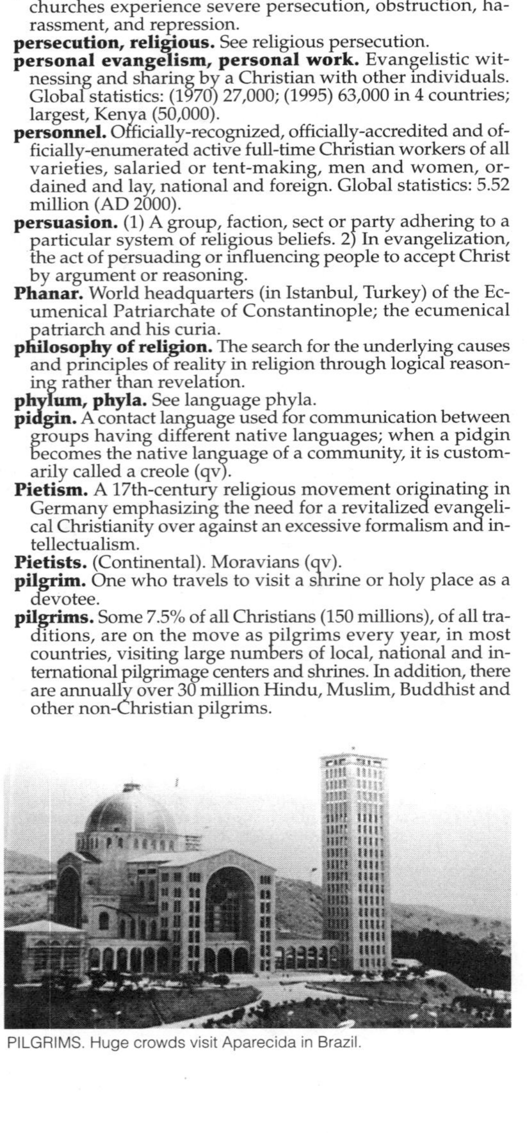
PILGRIMS. Huge crowds visit Aparecida in Brazil.

pioneer publishers. In Jehovah's Witnesses' terminology, unpaid part-time members who engage in pioneer preaching and house-to-house visiting, averaging 100 hours' work each per month. Total (1998): 698,781.
placements. Copies of the Bible or New Testament placed free of charge in a home, institution or in a recipient's hand, by free distribution agencies. Statistics of placements published by Gideons International give not annual totals but cumulative totals since the year 1908.
planning. The act or process of making or carrying out plans, especially the establishment of goals, policies and procedures for a social or economic unit.
plantatio ecclesiae. (Latin). The planting of the church; Catholic term for the aim of missions.
pluriform church. The contemporary church in which differences of doctrinal emphasis are accepted as inevitable but provide no basis for breaches in fellowship.
Plymouth Brethren. Exclusive Brethren (qv).
pneumatography. Spirit writing (qv).
Polish/Slavonic. Eastern Orthodox liturgical tradition using Polish and Slavonic in the liturgy. Global statistics: (1970) 547,000; (1995) 1.0 million in 2 countries; largest, Poland (1.0 million).
political parties. See Christian political parties.
political prisoners. Persons in custody or imprisoned for alleged political offenses; numbering in AD 2000 several millions across the world. See prisoners of conscience.
poll. An opinion inquiry taken at a single point in time, from a very small carefully-constructed sample (usually around 1,500-2,500 adults) representative of the entire adult population, to solicit answers to carefully-formulated questions, in order to derive information applicable to that entire population.
polyandry. Marriage of one wife to several husbands simultaneously.
polygamy. Marriage of one person to several persons simultaneously.
polyglot. (1) Multilingual. (2) An edition of the Bible containing parallel text in 2 or more languages.
polygyny. Marriage of one husband to several wives simultaneously.
Polynesian. A Pacific ethnolinguistic family, with over 100 languages. Global statistics: (2000) 1.4 million in 77 peoples residing in 22 countries (11 significantly); largest, New Zealand (531,000).
polytheism. Belief in or worship of a plurality of gods.
polytheist. One who believes in or worships a plurality of gods.
pope. The title of the spiritual head of each of several large Christian churches and non-Christian religions including: the Bishop of Rome as head of the Roman Catholic Church; the Eastern Orthodox and Coptic patriarchs of Alexandria; the heads of Maria Legio of Africa and other ex-Catholic African indigenous churches; the head of the Cao Daist Missionary Church; the head of Taoism; et alii.
popular piety. Popular expressions of Christian (especially Catholic) faith widely held by the masses, to some extent infiltrated by superstition and non-Christian values; including devotion to the Crucified Christ, devotion to the Madonna, cults of saints, etc.
popular religion. Term covering all widespread or popular expressions of religion held by the masses including non-Christian expressions and folk religion as well as christianized popular religiosity (qv) and popular piety (qv).
popular religiosity. Christianized but deviant popular expressions of religion widely espoused by the masses, especially by the poor in Latin American countries, the most widespread groupings being Christo-pagans (qv) and Spiritist Catholics (qv).
population. For an area, the total of all inhabitants or residents of that area; or occasionally, the total number of persons who spend or spent the night in the area.
population census. A government survey to obtain information about the state of the population at a given time.
population density. The average population to one square mile or kilometer.
population explosion. A popular term for the ultra-rapid expansion of population in Third-World countries since 1950.
population increase. See natural increase.
population parameter. Any numerical value that characterizes a population.
population projections. Calculations showing the future development of a population based on certain assumptions and present trends.
portions. In UBS usage, separately-bound single gospels or other complete single books of the Bible averaging over 48 pages in length. Global statistics: 323 million (AD 2000).
post-conciliar. In Roman Catholic usage, an event taking place after the Second Vatican Council of 1962-65.
post-religious. Persons or populations who have abandoned any form of religion or quasi-religion.
postal evangelism. Evangelism carried on by post or mail.
postal survey. An inquiry sending questionnaires by mail.
postmillennialists. Protestants who hold that Christ will return as King after the church has established the millennium on earth through its evangelization.
postulant. A candidate for admission to a religious order in the stage preliminary to the novitiate post-Christians. See disaffiliated Christians.
potential audience. In Christian broadcasting, all persons with access to receivers and thus able to receive and listen to or view Christian broadcasts if they wish to, and able to understand the languages employed.
practice, religious. See religious practice.
practicing. Actively engaged in, as a way of life.
practicing Anglican. An adult Anglican who fulfils the minimum obligation of attending communion 3 times each year.
practicing Christians. Great Commission Christians. Believers in Jesus Christ who are aware of the implications of Christ's Great Commission, who have accepted its personal challenge in their lives and ministries, and who are seeking to influence the Body of christ to implement it. Global statistics: (1970) 277.1 million; (1995) 603.0 million in 237 countries (137 significantly); largest, USA (93.4 million); (2000) 647.8 million; (2025) 887.5 million.
practicing Muslims. Muslims who, regularly or at least annually, practice all required Muslim duties
practitioner. In Christian Science usage, an authorized teacher and healer.
praeparatio evangelica. (Latin). Preparation for the gospel; used of any major factor in a people's life which prepares them for the message of Christ.
Prayer Book Anglicans. Central or Broad Church Anglicans (qv).
Prayer Book Catholics. High Church Anglicans (qv).
prayer group. A term used throughout Christianity for a group of Christians regularly meeting for prayer. Catholic charismatic prayer groups vary from 2 to 1,500 members, and average 50 persons.
prayer tower. (1) In Muslim usage, a minaret. (2) In Christian usage, a tower specially set aside for continuous prayer.
Pre-Chalcedonian. Oriental Orthodox (qv).
pre-Christian. Of, or being a time before, the beginning of the Christian era, or before the introduction of Christianity in a locality.
Pre-Dravidian. An Austro-Asiatic ethnolinguistic family. Global statistics: (2000) 26.3 million in 50 peoples residing in 5 countries; largest, India (25.8 million).
pre-school children. Infants, i.e. the population under 5 years old, including new-born babies.
preaching. The act, practice or art of delivering a sermon or exhortation.
prediction. An inference regarding a future event based on probability theory.
prefect. The supervising head of a prefecture apostolic (qv), not in episcopal orders.
prefectures apostolic. (symbol PA). In Roman Catholic usage, districts of a missionary territory in its initial stage of ecclesiastical organization. Total (1997) 44.
preference, religious. See religious preference.
prelacy. Episcopacy (qv); prelature (qv).
prelate. An ecclesiastic of superior rank and authority; a dignitary.
prelature (prelacy) nullius. (symbol PN). A prelatic benefice or bishopric held by a prelate exempt from diocesan control and directly under the pope. Total (1997) 53.
premillennialism. Doctrine expounded by premillennialists (qv); divisible into historicist and futurist premillennialism, and the later into pretribulationism, and posttribulationism.
premillennialists. Protestants, usually Fundamentalists or dispensationalists, who hold that Christ will return as King before the millennium in order to establish it by his own power; estimated at 60 million in the USA alone.
presbyter. (NT Greek). In episcopal churches, a priest. In the Presbyterian and Reformed churches, a lay elder.
presbyteral council. In the Roman Catholic Church, a senate or council of all priests in a diocese or area.
Presbyterians. See Reformed.
presbytery. In Presbyterian churches, (1) the ruling body of all ministers and representative lay elders, (2) the ecclesiastical district of all congregations under the ruling body. In the Roman Catholic Church, a parish clergy house.
present-in-area population. The de facto or actual population in the area, made up of all persons actually in the area on a particular day or census date, covering residents, visitors and transients, but excluding residents temporarily absent abroad.
presentation. A Protestant technical term used (l) in free scripture distribution by Gideons International for a formal, publicized gift of a Bible or Testament, (2) in Campus Crusade and other Protestant evangelism for a personal explanation of the gospel through exposition of 4 spiritual laws.
presidency, first. A council of 3 in the Church of Jesus Christ of Latter-day Saints (Mormons), consisting of a president and 2 counselors, and having jurisdiction in spiritual and temporal matters.
president. The presiding officer, chairman, or chief executive in a number of denominations, including the Mormon church.
presiding bishop. The president of the national council of the Episcopal Church in the USA who is elected by the General Convention; the chief member of the presiding bishopric of the Mormon church.
presiding bishopric. The chief office of the Aaronic priesthood in the Mormon church filled by 3 persons and supervised by the first presidency.
presiding elder. A district superintendent in Methodism, with oversight of churches and workers in a district.
presses. Printing presses owned and operated by churches or specifically Christian agencies number well over 3,000.

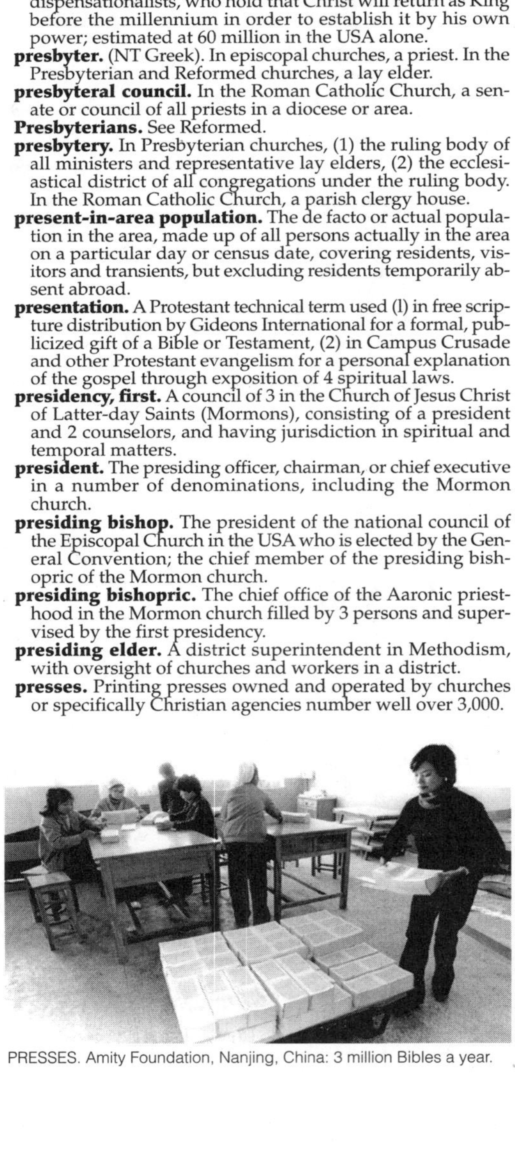
PRESSES. Amity Foundation, Nanjing, China: 3 million Bibles a year.

Preto. A Portuguese-speaking Black.
priest. (from NT Greek, *presbyteros*). A member of the second order of clergy in the Anglican communion, ranking below bishop and above deacon; a member of the highest order of clergy in the Roman Catholic and Eastern Orthodox churches; a professional clergyman of a religious denomination; a minister of religion.
priest-worker. See worker-priest.
priests' council. A presbyteral council (qv).
priests, Roman Catholic. World totals (1996) 404,336 (262,899 secular, 141,437 religious).
primal religionists. Original or primitive religionists in an area, animists, shamanists, spirit-worshippers, ancestor-venerators, polytheists, pantheists, tribal religionists, traditional religionists; sometimes called pagans, heathen, fetishists; usually exclusive to a particular tribe or people, hence non-missionary in emphasis; local as contrasted with universal religionists (qv).
primary education. Education given in primary or elementary schools.
primary evangelization. The first or initial or preliminary attempts at the evangelization of a people or area.
primary religious group. A sociological term for a denomination; defined as a social entity or group which claims the exclusive or primary religious affiliation or allegiance of its members, attempting to serve not specialized needs but the overall needs of its members, ministering to them on a regular, weekly or even daily basis.
primate. A bishop who has precedence in a province, group of provinces, or a nation; the ranking prelate.
primitive religionists. Tribal religionists (qv).
primus. The first in dignity of the bishops of the Episcopal Church in Scotland who has various privileges but no metropolitan authority.
primus inter pares. (Latin). The first among equals; often used of an archbishop with no jurisdiction over his fellow bishops.
print media. A term covering newspapers, magazines, books, comics, and other printed literature.
printing presses. See presses.
prior. The superior of a priory.
priory. A religious house that ranks immediately below an abbey; is either self-sustaining or dependent upon an abbey.
priory nullius. (Latin: priory of no diocese). A priory that is not dependent upon a diocese but on the pope.
prisoner of war. A person captured or interned by a belligerent power because of war with several exceptions provided by international law or agreement.
prisoners of conscience. Political prisoners undergoing torture, estimated at over one million across the world in over 100 countries.
private attenders. Persons who attend church services only for special private family occasions (baptisms, weddings, funerals).
pro-nuncio. The diplomatic envoy of the Roman Catholic pope to a foreign country where Catholics are in a minority. World total: (1997) 13.
probability. Something that is probable, statistically, logically or otherwise.
probationer. In Methodism, an intending new member who is put on probation for a period of time to demonstrate his commitment to full membership.
proclaim. To declare openly or publicly, make widely known in speech or in writing, announce, show, demonstrate, publish, extol; especially of the gospel and of Christ.
proclamation. The action of proclaiming, the condition of being proclaimed, something proclaimed; especially of the gospel.
professed. Monks or nuns who have taken the vows of a religious order.
professing. Declaring, stating, confessing, self-identifying.
professing Christians. Persons publicly professing (confessing, declaring, stating, self-identifying) their Christian preference or adherence in a government census or public-opinion poll, hence known as Christians to the state or society or the public. Global statistics: (1970) 1.1 billion; (1995) 1.7 billion in 236 countries (180 significantly); largest, USA (227.5 million); (2000) 1.8 billion; (2025) 2.4 billion.
profession, religious. See religious profession.
professional. One engaging in a particular pursuit, study, or science for gain or livelihood (as contrasted with an amateur); one with authority or practical experience in an area of knowledge.
professionals' associations. Christian organizations for workers or professionals, significant at the national or wider levels, number over 400.
professions. See decisions.
programmed learning. (PL), programmed instruction (PI). A teaching technique and device in which material to be taught is presented, the student providing his answers and immediately comparing them with correct answers; based on the concept of immediate reinforcement of correct answers as a way of impressing information on a learner.
progressivist. In Roman Catholicism, a progressive tendency or emphasis or attitude favoring reforms and activism, as opposed to more traditionalist attitudes.
projection. The carrying forward of a present trend into the future; an estimate of future possibilities based on current trends.
Propaganda. Sacred Congregation for the Evangelization of Peoples (qv).
prophecy. In modern usage in the charismatic renewal, an utterance in public by any Christian which purports to be direct speech by God concerning particular issues.
prophesying. Prophecy (qv).
prophet. (1) A Biblical, especially Old Testament, revealer, spokesman or seer. (2) An official or office-holder in some pentecostal churches. (3) A charismatic leader of a new religious movement of any sort.
prophet movement. An indigenous Christian movement led by a charismatic prophet figure, which usually results in a Non-White indigenous church (qv).
proselyte. One who has been converted from one religious faith to another, usually by questionable or dubious methods.
proselytism. A manner of behaving, contrary to the spirit of the gospel, using dishonest methods to attract men to a community, e.g. by exploiting their ignorance or poverty.
protest, movements of. See prophet movement, secession, schism.
Protestants. Christians in churches originating in, or reformulated at the time of, or in communion with, the Western world's 16th-century Protestant Reformation in European languages usually called Evangéliques (French), Evangelische (German), Evangélicos (Italian, Portuguese, Spanish), though not usually Evangelicals (in English). Global statistics: (1970) 210.7 million; (1995) 319.6 million in 233 countries (98 significantly); largest, USA (62.5 million); (2000) 342.0 million; (2025) 468.6 million.
province. In Roman Catholic usage, any of the principal ecclesiastical divisions of a country forming the jurisdiction of an archbishop or a metropolitan; a territorial division of a religious order. In Anglican usage, the term has 7 different meanings, including autonomous church, internal province within an autonomous church, or a group of dioceses which for some purposes act in association under a common constitution. Whilst provinces retain their full meaning in contemporary Anglicanism, in contemporary Roman Catholicism they have ceased to have meaning since the meaningful unit is now the nation-wide (local) church, or (in large nations) the newer apostolic regions.
provincial. A religious superior directing houses in a religious province.
provisional annual conference. A regional jurisdiction in North American Methodism.
provost. The head of a cathedral or cathedral chapter; in German Protestantism, a clergyman in charge of the chief church of a region.
pseudo-religions. See quasi-religions.
psychology of religion. The science of mind or of mental phenomena and activities with regard to religion: the psychology of religious phenomena.
psychoneurotics. Sufferers from psychoneuroses. Global statistics: 1 billion (AD 2000).
psychotics. The mentally ill, or mentally abnormal; sufferers from severe mental disorders (psychoses). Global statistics: 60 million (AD 2000).
public profession. (of religion). See professing Christians.
publishers. In Jehovah's Witnesses' terminology, ordinary members of congregations, who are expected to average 10-15 hours per month preaching, and in house-to-house visiting.
publishing houses. Organizations producing Christian literature member over 2,000.
puja, pooja. (Sanskrit). A Hindu rite, religious festival, or act of worship or propitiation.
pupil. A child or young person in school.
Pygmy. An Early African ethnolinguistic family; Negrillo. Global statistics: (2000) 592,000 in 33 peoples residing in 13 countries; largest, Congo-Zaire (194,000).

Q

Qadianis. Majority party among Ahmadis (qv).
Qaraism. See Karaites.
Qarmatians, Karmatians. A name for Muslims who are Shia Ismailis.
Quakers. Friends (qv).
quality of life. The effectiveness of social services in a country, measured by the HDI (human development index).
quantification. Measuring an item's quantity or number, or transforming qualitative data into quantitative.
quasi-Christian. Seemingly, partly, almost, in some sense, a Christian.
quasi-confessions. Non-confessional international denominational bodies (qv), which are partly or entirely de facto world confessional families, or world communions. Global membership: (1970) 56,908,200, (1980) 71,557,000, (1985) 79,522,100, (AD 2000) 120 million.
quasi-continent. Partly a continent; used of the Caribbean, Middle East and other regions.
quasi-parish. In Roman Catholic usage, partly or virtually a parish although not yet formally or canonically established.
quasi-religionists. Adherents of quasi-religions.
quasi-religions. Secular movements which are partly, or are virtually, religions; divided here into anti-religious quasi-religions (atheism, communism, dialectical materialism, Leninism, Maoism, Mantism, scientific materialism, Stalinism, et alia), and non-religious quasi-religions (some forms of agnosticism, fascism, humanism, liberal humanism, nationalism, Nazism, some forms of non-religion, some forms of secularism).

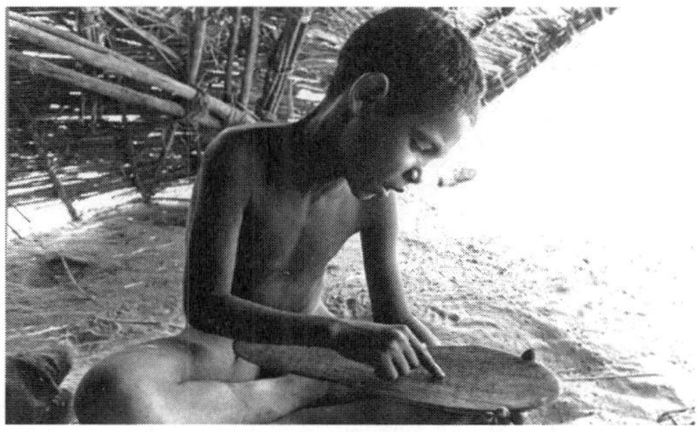

QURAN. Tuareg boy reading in Burkina Faso.

Quran. (Koran). The book of writings in Arabic accepted by Muslims as revelations made to Muhammad by Allah.
Quran translations. Languages into which the Quran has been translated: about 200 (25 European) by AD 2000 including Bengali, Chinese, Dutch, English Farsi, French, German, Gujarati, Hausa, Indonesian, Italian, Japanese, Javanese, Latin, Punjabi, Spanish, Swahili, Turkish, Urdu, Yoruba.
Quranic schools, Koranic schools. Elementary schools teaching only the Quran and memorizing passages.

R

race. A major division of mankind with certain inherited common distinctive physical characteristics (skin color, stature, head shape, hair type, genes, blood-group, etc.) which are hereditarily-transmittable; a breeding group with gene organization differing from that of other intraspecies groups; a physical type, a racial stock; one of the subspecies of Homo Sapiens.
racism. A belief in the inherent superiority of one's own race and its right to domination over others.
Radical Reformation. The Left-Wing Reformation; Anabaptists (qv).
Radical-Pentecostals. Perfectionist-Pentecostals (qv).
radio audiences. See radio listeners.

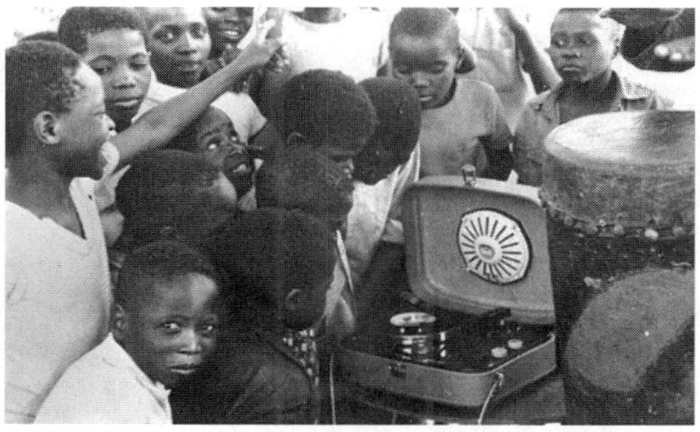

RADIO BELIEVERS. Listeners in Zimbabwe hear African preacher.

radio believers. See isolated radio believers.
radio churches. Groups or fellowships, meeting for Sunday worship, brought into being through hearing radio broadcasts.
radio converts. The number of converts to Christianity due to Christian broadcasting in the course of a month or a year.
radio letters. Annual listeners' letters or other communications received by international and national Christian radio and TV stations and programs. Global total per year: (1975) 4,230,360, (AD 2000) 10 million.
radio listeners. The regular listening or viewing audience in a country is made up of (a) listeners/viewers to Christian stations, and (b) listeners/viewers to Christian programs over secular, commercial or state radio/TV stations. Global statistics: 1.5 billion (AD 2000).
radio or TV denomination. A denomination (qv), or loosely-organized grouping of churches or believers, whose existence centers on regular radio or TV broadcasts of Sunday worship services.
radio stations. Broadcasting centers with transmitting plant and equipment. World total of Christian radio and TV stations:. Global statistics: 2,500 (AD 2000).
radio/TV-service listeners. Affiliated Christians who, for reasons of age, infirmity, sickness or absence of local churches, in place of physical church attendance instead regularly listen/view Sunday radio/TV services of worship once a week or once a month.
radiophonic school. A broadcasting network offering basic adult education in rural areas, with local teachers or postal feedback; mostly operated by Roman Catholic dioceses in Latin American countries.
Raskolniks. (Russian, Schismatics). Old Believers (qv).
rationalist. An advocate of rationalism, reliance on reason as the basis for the establishment of any ultimate truth including religious truth.
reached. The state of having had the gospel brought to one or to a people.
reactionary. Conservative.
real Christians. See committed Christians.
receiver. A receiving set for radio or TV broadcast programs.
reconciled diversity. A model for the unity of the church espoused by the confessional-identities part of the ecumenical movement, in opposition to the 'conciliar fellowship' model favored by the World Council of Churches: in order to live under the unity Christ wills, the world communions (confessions, world confessional families) must enter into a fully reconciled relationship, recognizing other confessions fully as churches of Jesus Christ, yet retaining their own confessional identities.
recording studios. Local broadcasting studios or sound-proofed rooms under church or Christian auspices where tapes are prepared for later release over radio or TV stations.
records, recording. See religious drama.
rector. A clergyman of the Church of England who has the charge and care of a parish and owns the tithes from it; in the Roman Catholic Church, the head priest of a church, university, school, or other religious institution.
Red. Stylized skin color associated with the American Indian geographical race. Global statistics: (2000) 77.6 million in 1,109 peoples residing in 27 countries (7 significantly); largest, Mexico (27.0 million).
Red Hat (Unreformed) Lamaism. (Dupka or Karmapa). That part of Tibetan Buddhism in which monasteries have

resisted the 14th-century reforms of the monk Tsong-kha-pa. Red Hat Lamaism is the official religion of Bhutan.

reduction. In South American Catholic history, the act or process of resettlement by missionaries of Amerindians in villages or compounds for purposes of acculturation or control; or the settlement itself.

Reformed. A major Protestant tradition originating in continental Europe, and including the term Presbyterian originating in English-speaking countries. Global statistics: (1970) 28.3 million; (1995) 38.7 million in 295 countries (11 significantly); largest, Indonesia (5.5 million).

Reformed Catholics. Followers of recent schisms ex Church of Rome in a Reformed or Protestant direction. Global statistics: (1970) 4.2 million; (1995) 5.1 million in 16 countries; largest, Philippines (4.8 million).

Reformed Ecumenical Synod. (RES). A conservative Reformed world communion. Global constituency (1980) 6,493,500 total community in 51 denominations.

Reformed Hindus. See Hindu reformist movements.

Reformed Orthodox. Uncanonical reform movements out of Orthodoxy, retaining Orthodox claims. Global statistics: (1970) 420,000; (1995) 1.0 million in 23 countries; largest, India (975,000).

refugee church. A local church or congregation formed entirely by or among refugees in a particular country.

refugees. Persons who have migrated due to persecution, fear of persecution, or other strong pressures endangering their continued stay in their countries of origin, and who are unable or unwilling to return; excluding labor and other migrants and also returnees.

regeneration. Spiritual rebirth, renewal, re-creation, revival, radical spiritual transformation.

region. (apostolic or conciliar). See apostolic region.

region. In United Nations terminology, one of 24 areas into which the whole world is divided for purposes of analysis.

regional conciliarism. There are about 55 international and regional (subcontinental) councils of churches of all kinds.

registration with government. Legalizing the existence and status of a denomination or church in countries where registration is compulsory in law.

regular attenders. Church members who attend Sunday worship weekly, monthly, or at the least once annually.

regular clergy. Religious clergy (qv) living under a monastic or similar rule.

regular communicant. A communicant (qv) who takes communion weekly, monthly, or at the least annually.

religio-political organizations. Bodies significant at the national or wider levels number over 200.

religion. A religious faith, creed, communion, sect, cult, persuasion; a system of faith and worship, centrally concerned with the means of ultimate transformation.

religion, comparative. Comparative study of the origin, development, and interrelations of the religious systems of mankind.

religion, organized. See organized religion.

religion, study of. See study of religion.

religionists. (1) Persons professing adherence to any religion, as contrasted with non-religious or antireligious persons or atheists. Global statistics: (2000) 5,136,801,000 (84.8%).

religionless Christianity. A term coined by German theologian D. Bonhoeffer for genuine, biblical Christianity without religious trappings.

religiosity. Intense, excessive, or affected religiousness.

religious. Monks, friars, clerks, regular, sisters or nuns who are bound by professed vows, sequestered from secular concerns, and devoted to lives of piety.

religious affiliation. See affiliation, religious.

religious architecture. See architecture, religious.

religious barrier. A religious frontier (qv).

religious books, new. Global total of new titles each year 32,000, of which 26,100 were on Christianity.

religious Buddhists. Buddhists who profess Buddhism as both a family religion and also a personal religion.

religious change. Demographic changes from one religion or religious system to another in the course of a year.

religious clergy. In Roman usage, clergy who are members of religious orders or institutes. World total (1975): 161,174 declining to (1996) 141,437.

religious communities. (1) Religious institutes (qv), orders, congregations, or societies of religious personnel for the religious life, total (for Roman Catholic Church) 1,530. (2) Religious communities in the sense of buildings and centers (large monasteries, abbeys, priories, including monasteries in anti-Christian countries where their presence as legitimate or tolerated institutions is significant, mother houses of religious institutes, ashrams, and the like) number over 5,000.

religious congregations. Religious institutes (qv).

religious distance. The number of religious frontiers or barriers that exist between a Christian worker, evangelist or missionary, or a group of such, and their target population; as defined here, up to a maximum of 5 frontiers.

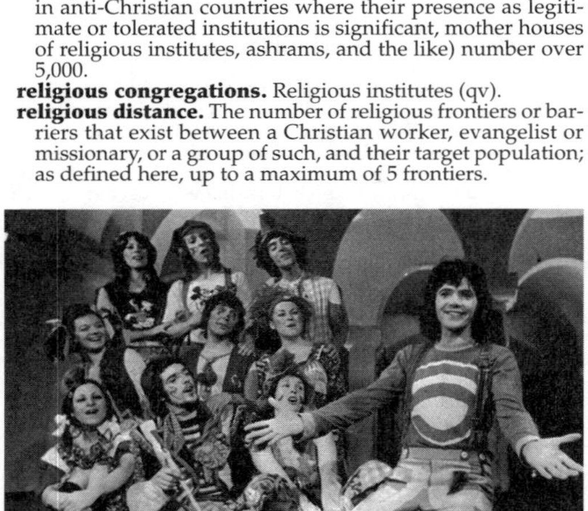

RELIGIOUS DRAMA. Famed rock musical 'Godspell' in London, U.K.

religious drama. The portrayal of Christian verities through art, literature, music, song, theatre, including live theatre, cinema, music concerts, broadcasting, recordings, etc. Worldwide annual statistical totals: each year, 10 million people attend live theatricals or musicals of this kind (e.g. Oberammergau Passion Play 500,000 every decadal year); 50 million see commercially-distributed films of Christian or biblical content; 50 million attend live concerts of Christian music; 100 million listen to religious drama by radio, and 300 million on television.

religious education. Instruction in the principles of a particular religious faith.

religious frontier. The line of demarcation between one category of religion and another, from the Christian standpoint; up to a maximum of 5 frontiers.

religious geography. See geography of religion.

religious house. A convent or monastery.

religious humanism. A modern North American movement composed chiefly of non-theistic humanist churches and dedicated to achieving the ethical goals of religion without beliefs and rites resting upon supernaturalism; sometimes called Christian humanism.

religious institutes. In Roman Catholic usage, religious orders, congregations and societies for the religious life. World totals (1997): for men (priests, monks, brothers), 80 orders, 90 clerical religious congregations, 30 societies of common life, 30 lay religious congregations, 6 secular institutes, totaling 230 religious institutes for men using a total of 740 distinct names; for women (nuns, sisters), 1,300 religious and 25 secular institutes or congregations.

religious institutes of perfection. Roman Catholic term for clerical and lay religious orders and congregations, societies without vows, and secular institutes.

religious institutes, federations of. Some 190 Roman Catholic national federations of male or female religious institutes exist (for clergy, monks, priests, brothers, sisters, nuns, with 3 international federations (CLAR, UISG, USG).

religious journalism. Organizations and centers significant at national and wider levels number over 300.

religious liberty. Defined here as encompassing the following 31 categories: freedom of inner belief and conscience, freedom of public worship indoors and outdoors, freedom of assembly, freedom of self-government, freedom of association, freedom to organize religious bodies, freedom to organize Bible study circles, freedom to run Christian libraries and bookshops, freedom to collect money and to disburse it, freedom to organize credit unions for the benefit of members, freedom to offer medical care where wanted, freedom to engage in mission at home and abroad, freedom to send abroad or receive from abroad foreign missionaries, freedom of Christian political expression, freedom to teach religion and to be taught, freedom for children to join religious associations and to receive Christian instruction, freedom to change one's religion or be converted, freedom of propagation, freedom to travel on religious business within the country and abroad and to return, freedom to listen to radio religious broadcasts from any country, freedom to send and receive religious mail and literature uncensored both inland and abroad, freedom to use national press and broadcasting (radio and TV) facilities; freedom to publish, mail, broadcast, circulate scriptures, buy and sell literature, evangelize, proselytize and baptize; and freedom for minority churches and religions as well as majority religions.

religious libraries. See libraries, religious.

religious life. The life of those who aspire to perfection by retirement from the world and practice of the evangelical counsels (qv).

religious movement. A movement swept along by its own momentum long before it becomes organized or institutionalized.

religious Muslims. Ethnic Muslims (qv) who practice or profess Islam.

religious orders. See religious institutes.

religious orders (communities), Protestant. Total about 100 orders, brotherhoods, sisterhoods or communities especially of deaconesses, mainly Lutheran, Reformed, Church of South India, et alii.

religious orders in Anglicanism. There are 150 distinct Anglican religious communities (in 1999), with 450 lay religious brothers, 2,700 nuns or lay religious sisters, and about 200 ordained monks in priest's or bishop's orders.

religious periodicals. See periodicals, Christian.

religious persecution. Persecution of believers specifically on religious grounds, though this is often denied.

religious personnel. See religious.

religious persuasion. A person's religious profession or preference.

religious pluralism. The peaceful co-existence of completely different religions or denominations within a particular community.

religious practice. The actual performing of religious duties.

religious preference. The religion or denominational tradition which a respondee professes to adhere to when asked in a public-opinion poll.

religious profession. (1) the religion or denominational tradition professed or preferred in a poll or census. (2) The taking of vows in a religious order.

religious research. Investigation, research and experiment on any religious subject or matter.

Religious Science. A marginal Protestant tradition emphasizing metaphysical science, Divine Science, Christian Science, New Thought, magnetic healing and the like. Global statistics: (1970) 1.2 million; (1995) 1.1 million in 59 countries; largest, USA (1.0 million).

religious sociology. The study of religion as it affects society.

religious state. The situation in life of the religious vocation (persons called to the religious life).

religious states. States, governments or ruling regimes which identify themselves as religious, or with religion and its promotion, numbered 113 out of the world total of 238 in AD 2000.

religious survival. A religious practice or belief dating back to an earlier, outmoded, religion, which has survived into the present.

religious toleration. The attitude of tolerance and acceptance, on the part of a state or a majority church, towards religious minorities.

religious zealots. Persons earnestly devoted to or attached to any religion. Global statistics: (1970) 353,000; (1995) 1.1 million in 23 countries (1 significantly); largest, Brazil (388,000).

renewal. A revival (qv) in personal zeal and commitment to Christ in the churches; the charismatic renewal (qv).

Renewal. Shorthand term for the worldwide Pentecostal/Charismatic/Neocharismatic Renewal in the Holy Spirit.

research. Studious inquiry or examination: critical and exhaustive investigation or experimentation having for its aim the discovery of new facts and their correct interpretation, the revision of accepted conclusions, theories or laws in the light of newly-discovered facts, or the practical applications of such new or revised conclusions, theories or laws.

research centers. Christian-related and church-related centers producing original research and significant at the national or wider levels numbered over 500 in AD 2000.

research, religious. See religious research.

resident. One who resides in a place for a time, often temporary or of short duration; usually distinguished from inhabitant which implies permanent or long-term habitation.

resident population. The de jure population (qv).

residential sees. Dioceses or other jurisdictions with a resident bishop each.

residual Christians. Nominal Christians (qv) or post-Christians (qv) in industrialized and secularized societies.

resistant. A term often used to describe peoples who have been exposed to the Christian message but have not accepted it. In most cases it can be shown that they have only been inadequately evangelized, or even faultily evangelized, and that because of the absence of a culturally-adequate message they have in fact been neglected.

respondent. A person who answers questions in a survey or government census, in the latter case usually under a legal obligation to answer.

Restoration Movement. (1) The Churches of Christ, or Disciples (qv), a major USA group of denominations. (2) A neocharismatic para-denomination splitting in 1974 from the Charismatic Renewal within the mainline Protestant and Anglican churches in UK and USA, also called Church of the Great Shepherd, Pyramid Church, House-Church Movement.

Restorationist Baptists. Disciples (qv).

restricted countries. 18 countries in the world which, although not closed or partially closed to foreign mission, restrict numbers of foreign missionaries considerably.

Resurrection. (1) The rising of Jesus Christ from the dead in AD 30. (2) The rising again to life of all the human dead throughout history before the Last Judgement.

retreat. A special center, or period, of group withdrawal to a place of seclusion for the purpose of deepening the spiritual life of participants through prayer, meditation and study under a retreat director.

returnee. An alien of long residence who is deported and forcibly repatriated to the country of his citizenship.

reunion. A union of churches or denominations after a period of separation or discord.

reunionist. An advocate of church reunion.

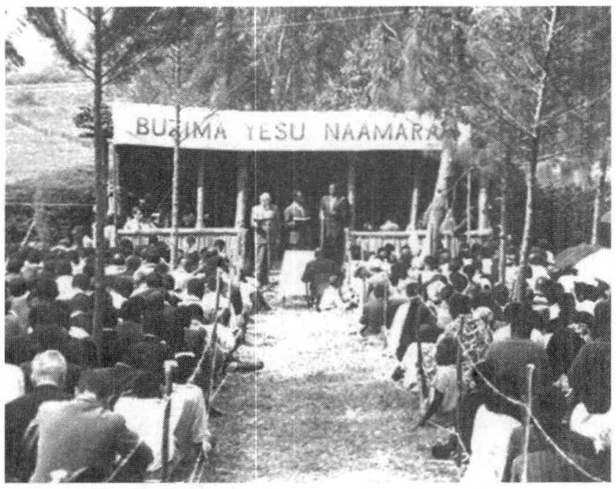

REVIVAL. 50,000 in Rwanda: text reads 'Jesus Satisfies'.

revival. A period of spontaneous religious awakening, or renewed interest in religion after indifference or decline; in some North American circles, a series of organized evangelistic meetings often characterized by emotional excitement; theologically, a great outpouring of the Spirit of God upon the churches.

Revivalist-Pentecostals. Perfectionist-Pentecostals (qv).

rice Christian. A convert to Christianity who accepts baptism not on the basis of personal conviction but out of a desire for food, medical services, or other material benefits

rite. One of the historical forms of the Christian eucharistic service; a division of the Christian church as determined by liturgy.

ritual. The prescribed order, words and actions of a religious ceremony.

roll-cleaning. The practice of regularly updating church membership rolls, in particular working through or over

rolls in order to remove former members who have now died, left the area, given up church membership, or otherwise ceased to be properly eligible for the rolls.
rolls. Written lists of names of church members of all varieties.
Roman. Of or relating to the Roman Catholic Church, or the Latin rite.
Roman Catholic jurisdictions. World totals in 1997 (followed by 1979 figures in parentheses): 2,606 (2,491) jurisdictions, consisting of 2,317 (2,142) residential sees, made up of 13 (11) patriarchates, 430 (397) metropolitan sees, 61 (62) archdioceses and 1,813 (1,672) dioceses; 1,988 (1,953) titular sees; 105 (101) prelatures, 21 (23) abbeys nullius, 9 (10) apostolic administrations, 18 (25) exarchates and ordinariates, 73 (81) vicariates apostolic, 59 (77) prefectures apostolic, 12 patriarchal vicariates, prefectures apostolic , 12 patriarchal vicariates, 4 (5) missions sui juris, 1 (1) priory, 27 (26) vicariates castrensi. Ecclesiastical territories by rite: 94% Latin-rite, 6% Oriental-rite.
Roman Catholicism. The faith, doctrine or polity of the Roman Catholic Church, or its entire system together with all its members.
Roman Catholics. All Christians in communion with the Church of Rome. Affiliated Roman Catholics are defined in this Encyclopedia as baptized Roman Catholics plus catechumens.
Roman Orthodox. The common Arabic designation for Christians related to the 4 Byzantine (Eastern Orthodox) patriarchates in the Middle East, including Constantinople as the 'New Rome'.
Romanian. Eastern Orthodox liturgical tradition (Romanian Orthodox Church). Global statistics: (1970) 16.1 million; (1995) 19.2 million in 23 countries (1 significantly); largest, Romania (19.0 million).
Romanian rite. Byzantine rite for Catholics under Rome, used in Romania; completely suppressed by state since 1948.
Romanism. Roman Catholicism (qv).
Rome. Roman Catholicism, or the capital city where its world headquarters are.
rounding. The expressing of a number with only a convenient degree of exactness, as by dropping decimals beyond a stated number of places or by substituting zeros for final integers or digits.
rural area. Defined in many countries as an administrative district with a population of under 2,000.
rural dean. In Anglicanism, an ecclesiastic ranking immediately under an archdeacon and appointed as a diocesan official to supervise the affairs of a group of parishes in the archdeaconry.
rural deanery. The area of jurisdiction under a rural dean.
rural missions. In the field of rural and agricultural missions, Christian organizations significant at the national or wider levels number over 250.
Russellites. A nickname for Jehovah's Witnesses (qv).
Russian rite. Byzantine rite used by Roman Catholics in USSR; only 3,000 faithful left. Global statistics: (1970) 3,000; (1995) 10,000 in 1 countries; largest, Russia (10,000).
Ruthenians. Roman Catholics using Byzantine rite of Ruthenian origin. Global statistics: (1970) 130,000; (1995) 391,000 in 4 countries; largest, Ukraine (300,000).

S

sabbatarian. A person or church which keeps the seventh day of the week (Saturday) as holy in conformity with the letter of the Decalogue (Ten Commandments), in contrast to Christians who observe Sunday instead.
Sabbath. The seventh day of the week (Saturday).
sabbath school. A school held on the Sabbath (Saturday) for purposes of religious education.
Sabras. Jews born in the post-l948 State of Israel.
sacrament. A religious act, ceremony, or practice that is considered specially sacred as a sign or symbol of a deeper reality; in many denominations 2 in number (baptism and the eucharist), in others 7 in number.
sacramentalist, sacramentarian. One placing great emphasis on religious ritual and the role and function of sacraments.
Sacred Congregation for the Eastern Churches. Founded in 1862, the branch of the Roman Curia dealing with Eastern-rite and Uniate Catholic Churches. Global statistics: (1970) 6.4 million; (1995) 10.7 million in 170 countries (1 significantly); largest, India (3.3 million).
Sacred Congregation for the Evangelization of Peoples. Founded in 1622 as SC for the Propagation of the Faith (Propaganda), the central Roman Catholic body with jurisdiction over foreign missions. Global constituency: (AD 2000) over 100 million.
sadhus. Hinduism's holy beggars. Total: 25 million.
saints. A theological and biblical term for the entire company of all baptized Christians; in a number of denominations, the usual term for all church members.
Saivites, Shaivites. Worshippers of Siva (Shiva), mainly in South India Hinduism; including these sects: Lingayats, Natha cult, Nayanars. Global statistics: (1970) 115.9 million; (1995) 198.7 million; (2000) 216.2 million; (2025) 278.9 million.
Saktists, Shaktites. Worshippers of the Hindu Supreme Goddess, Sakti (Sanskrit: power, energy) or Kali/Durga/Deva/Parvati consort of Siva; strong in Bengal and Assam. Global statistics: (1970) 13.9 million; (1995) 23.6 million; (2000) 25.7 million; (2025) 33.1 million.
salvation. The saving of man from the power and effects of sin; deliverance, redemption, restoration, reconciliation with God, liberation, healing, help, wholeness, preservation, etc.
Salvation Army. See Salvationists.
salvation religion. A religion offering its devotees salvation (e.g. Christianity, Omoto-kyo (Japan), etc.).
Salvationists. Soldiers or officers of the Salvation Army, a Protestant tradition begun ex Methodists in Britain, 1865. Global statistics: (1970) 2.9 million; (1995) 2.4 million in 85 countries; largest, USA (486,000).
salvific. In Roman Catholic usage, saving or with intent to save or impart salvation.

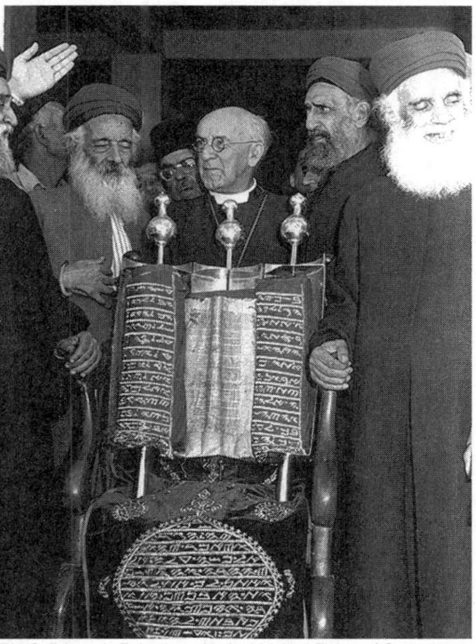
SAMARITANS. Priests in Palestine with Archbishop Fisher of Canterbury.

Samaritans. Children of Israel (Bene-Yisrael) or Shamerim (Observant Ones), a small Jewish sect. Total adherents: (AD 2000) 500.
samizdat. (Russian). Self-publishing (qv).
sample. A small segment or quantity taken as evidence of the quality or character of the whole; a very small part of the population used for purposes of investigation and comparing properties.
samsara. (Sanskrit). In Hinduism and Buddhism, successive reincarnations, the indefinitely-repeated cycles of birth, misery and death caused by karma.
Sanatanists. (Sanskrit: Old Ways; or Idol-Worshippers). The vast bulk (98%) of all Hindus, consisting of Vaishnavites, Saivites, and Saktists (qv). Global statistics: (1970) 453.3 million; (1995) 731.3 million; (2000) 791.5 million; (2025) 1.0 billion
sanatorium. A medical establishment for therapy, rest and recuperation, or for chronic illnesses; see medical centers.
Sansei. (Japanese: third-generation). A Japanese-American of Nisei or Kibei parents, and born and educated in the Americas.
saturated. In evangelization, used of a population completely penetrated by the gospel.
saturation evangelism. See in-depth evangelism.
saturation point. The situation in a country or area when the markets for copies of the scriptures have become saturated, or the point at which such saturation occurs.
scenario. A tool for studying the future: a series of events that we imagine happening in the future.
schedule. A census schedule (qv).
scheduled castes. Official term in India (after 1949) for low caste persons, or persons outside the traditional Indian caste system, previously called Outcastes, Untouchables, or Harijans (Children of God).
schism. A form of division or separation in the Christian church or from a church or religious body; a division, separation, secession, split, break-off faction, clique, etc.
schismatic. Used of a body or sect that has broken off or seceded from an existing Christian church denomination.
scholarly societies. Total of all societies important at international and national levels: 250.
school of evangelism. A local course in evangelistic method sponsored by a church or parish.
school-age children, school-age population. Those persons in the population who are ages 5-14 years old.
schools, Roman Catholic. World totals (1996): 84,027 elementary schools (25,020,462 pupils), 34,277 secondary schools (9,522,274 pupils), and over 1.5 million students in universities and colleges. Of all pupils, 16% are non-Catholics.
scripture distribution. See under Bible distribution, New Testament distribution, portions, selections.
scriptures. In United Bible Societies' statistical usage the sum total of all Bibles, NTs, portions and selections (qv) distributed through their auspices and agencies in a given year.
seamen's centers. Christian clubs or centers for seafarers exist in over 500 posts in 76 countries around the world; coordinated by ICMA.
seasonal assistants. Short-term Christian personnel serving abroad, for periods of 6 months or less.
seatings. A technical term for the seating capacity of a church or of all churches in a denomination; the actual number of seats available.
Seceders. Kharijites (qv).
secession. The formal withdrawal of a body of Christians from a larger denomination; a schism split, breakoff, separation, or faction.
Second Coming. The Second Advent of Christ as judge of the world on the Last Day.
Second Rome. Constantinople as New Rome, the successor to Rome as capital of the Christian world after the sack of Rome in AD 476 and the end of the Roman empire in the West; after 1453 replaced by Moscow claiming to be the Third Rome.
Second World. The 30 or so countries comprising the Communist (or Marxist Socialist) world, especially before 1990, loosely contrasted with the First (Western or Capitalist) bloc or world, and the so-called Third World or bloc.
secondary education. Education in secondary or high schools.
secret believers. Crypto-Christians (qv).
sect. A comparatively small recently-organized exclusive dissenting religious body, usually considered heretical.
sectarian. An adherent of a particular religious sect, a dissenter, often of bigoted views.
secular. Relating to the worldly or temporal in contrast to the spiritual or eternal; civil, non-religious.
secular clergy. Diocesan clergy (qv).
secular religions. See quasi-religions.
secular states. In AD 2000 some 102 nations and countries out of the world total of 238 regarded themselves as secular, promoting neither religion nor irreligion, and maintaining strict separation between church and state.
secularism. A view of life or of any particular matter holding that religion and religious considerations should be ignored or purposely excluded.
secularization. The act or process of transferring matters under ecclesiastical or religious control to secular or civil or lay control; the process whereby religious thinking, practice and institutions lose social significance.
see. The jurisdiction of a bishop, or his rank, office, power, authority, cathedral or diocesan center.
seekers. See decisions.
Sefardis. (Sephardis). The smaller of the two great divisions of Jews; often loosely used to include Oriental Jews; speaking Ladino, dating from medieval Spain, now scattered from North Africa to Afghanistan, speaking Arabic, Persian, Aramaic; 14% of world's Jews today. Global statistics: (1970) 607,000; (1995) 910,000; (2000) 952,000; (2025) 1.0 million.
selections. Small leaflets of 2 or 3 pages or so consisting of attractively-presented scripture passages printed in large numbers by Bible societies usually for special occasions or needs.
self-enumeration. A census or survey method in which the questionnaire employed is completed by the respondents themselves.
self-evangelization. Auto-evangelization (qv).
self-identifying Christians. Professing Christians (qv).
self-publishing. (in Russian, *samizdat*). Underground Christian literature (reports, descriptions, protests, et alia) typed, duplicated or handwritten, that is passed from reader to reader despite prohibition by the Soviet state; a major source of news of churches and persecution in the USSR.
semi-literate. A person who can read but not write, or read and write only with difficulty.
seminarian, seminarist. A student in a seminary, a candidate for ordination to the diaconate or priesthood.

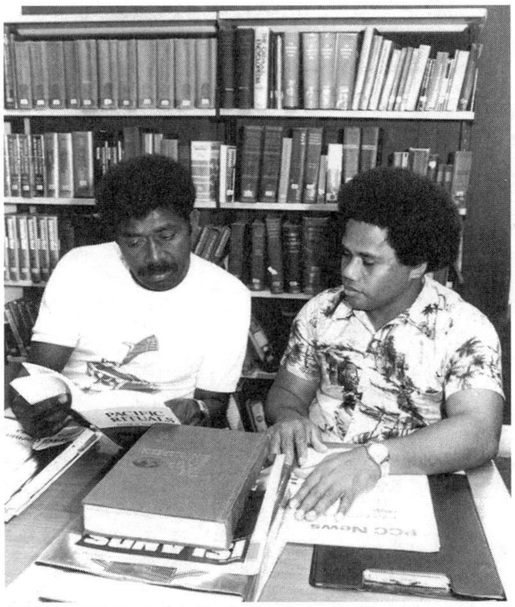
SEMINARIAN. Students in Pacific Theological College, Suva, Fiji.

seminaries. Centers for the training of the ordained ministry or priesthood, equipped with premises, plant and personnel; preparing persons of secondary or higher education for ordination; covering religious and secular major seminaries, theological colleges and advanced Bible schools of all churches and also independently-run; excluding smaller Bible schools and minor seminaries. Global total: (1975) 4,150 (1980) 4,500, (2000) 4,800.
seminary, major. See major seminary.
seminary, minor. See minor seminary.
seminary, united. See united seminary.
Semitic indigenous churches. Semitic initiatives or church traditions or Middle Eastern indigenous churches dating from the 1st century AD, and still completely Semitic in leadership and membership today, namely: Syrian Orthodox

(later Arab) Coptic Orthodox (later Arab), Ancient Church of the East (Assyrian, later Nestorian), Ethiopian Orthodox (Amharic). Global statistics: (1970) 18.2 million; (1995) 31.3 million in 58 countries (3 significantly); largest, Ethiopia (20.2 million).
sendee. See church sendee.
seniorate. An ecclesiastical geographical division within some Reformed denominations in Eastern Europe, corresponding to a presbytery.
separatism. A disposition towards secession or schism.
separatist. A dissenter or schismatic out of an established church; a nonconformist.
separatist church. A group of Christians who have separated from their parent church because of disagreement on some issue and who have formed themselves into a new and separate denomination.
Sephardis. See Sefardis.
Serbian/Slavonic. Eastern Orthodox liturgical tradition (Serbian Orthodox Church). Global statistics: (1970) 6.2 million; (1995) 7.2 million in 22 countries (2 significantly); largest, Yugoslavia (5.6 million).
sermon. A religious discourse delivered in public usually by a clergyman or minister, as part of a worship service.
serology. The science that treats of serums, their reactions and properties; necessary for the classification of races and peoples.
service. The performance of religious worship according to settled public forms or conventions.
service agencies. Major national, international or countrywide bodies, para-church organizations and agencies which assist or serve the churches but are not themselves denominations or church-planting missions. Global statistics: 23,000 (AD 2000).
session. The ruling body of a Presbyterian congregation consisting of the elders in active service moderated by the pastor; consistory, presbytery.
settler. A person who settles down in a new region or colony.
Seveners. Ismailis (qv).
Shaffiites. Followers of Shafiiya, one of the 4 schools or rites of Sunni Muslim law. Global statistics: (1970) 112.0 million; (1995) 215.2 million; (2000) 239.9 million; (2025) 393.5 million.
shakubuku. (Japanese). The aggressive-conversion process practiced by the New Religious movement, Soka Gakkai.
shaman. A priest-doctor who uses magic to cure the sick, to divine the hidden, and to control events that affect people's welfare.
shamanists. Followers of Ural-Altaic, Amerindian, Korean and other religions which believe that the unseen world of gods, demons, and ancestral spirits is responsive only to shamans. Global statistics: (1970) 16.7 million; (1995) 11.9 million in 12 countries (3 significantly); largest, South Korea (7.2 million); (2000) 12.3 million; (2025) 13.2 million.
sharia. (Arabic). Islamic law.
sharing countries. 12 countries across the world which both send and receive large numbers of foreign missionaries and personnel.
sheik, sheikh. A Muslim religious leader or cleric or scholar; an Arab chief.
shepherding. In the modern charismatic movement, the practice of a leader exercising strict or extensive authority over his flock of immediate followers.
shepherds. Apostles in charismatic bodies.
Shias. (Shi'is). Followers of the smaller of the 2 great divisions of Islam, rejecting the Sunna and holding that Mohammed's son-in-law Ali was the Prophet's successor and itself divided into the Ithna-Ashari Ismaili, Alawite and Zaydi sects. Global statistics: (1970) 79.5 million; (1995) 151.8 million; (2000) 170.1 million; (2025) 286.0 million.
Shintoists. Japanese who profess, or still profess, Shinto as their first or major religion. Global statistics: (1970) 4.1 million; (1995) 2.8 million in 8 countries; largest, Japan (2.7 million); (2000) 2.7 million; (2025) 2.1 million.

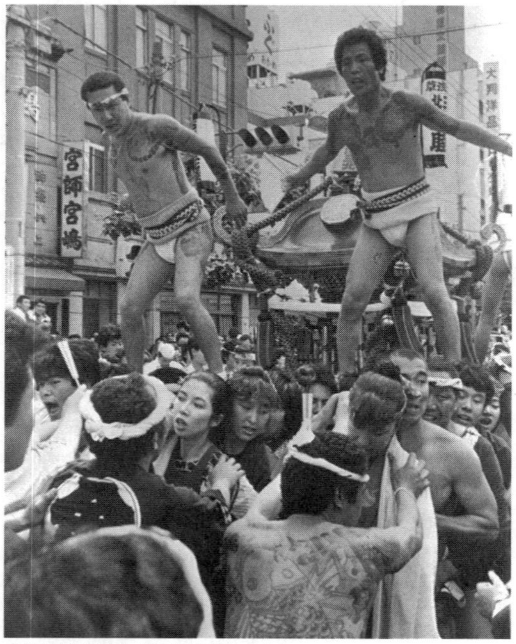
SHINTOISTS. Tokoi Festival, Tokyo, Japan.

short-service missionaries. Foreign missionary personnel serving abroad for a single period of from 6 to 24 months only.
short-term personnel. Short-service missionaries (qv).
short-wave broadcasting. Wireless communication, usually over long distances, using wavelengths of 60 meters or less (frequencies of 500 kilohertz or more).
Shroud of Christ. See sindonology.
sib, sibling. A brother or sister.
Sikhs. Followers of the Sikh reform movement out of Hinduism, who look to the Golden Temple in Amritsar, India (sects: Akali, Khalsa, Nanapanthi, Nirmali, Sewapanthi, Udasi). Global statistics: (1970) 10.6 million; (1995) 21.2 million in 34 countries; largest, India (20.2 million); (2000) 23.2 million; (2025) 31.3 million.
silence, churches of. See crypto-Christians.
simpatizante. (Spanish). A sympathizer, person interested in Protestantism in Latin America but unable to make public profession or seek church membership.
simultaneous audible prayer. Prayer in tongues (glossolalia) by a number of individuals, independently and on unrelated topics, aloud and at the same time during worship services.
sindonology. The science of the study of Christ's sindon (Holy Shroud) as preserved in Turin cathedral, Italy.
single congregation. A single autonomous worship center, completely independent and unaffiliated to any denomination, nor claiming to be a denomination. Global total: (AD 2000) over 200,000.
Sis. Cilicia (qv).
sister. A female church worker; a religious sister, nun; a female fellow-Christian.
sisterhood. A community or society of sisters.
skeptic. (skeptic). An unbeliever, agnostic.
skeptic. A skeptic (qv).
skepticism. The doctrine that any true knowledge is impossible or that all knowledge is uncertain especially in matters of religion; agnosticism.
Slav. A European ethnolinguistic family. Global statistics: (2000) 289.7 million in 356 peoples residing in 80 countries (19 significantly); largest, Russia (122.3 million).
Slavonic. Eastern Orthodox liturgical tradition followed in Russia, Bulgaria, et alia discontinued in the 1980s.
Slovak rite. Used by Byzantine Catholics in Czechoslovakia. Global statistics: (1970) 10,000; (1995) 239,000 in 2 countries; largest, Slovakia (209,000).
small communities. See basic communities.
small-group evangelism. Personal evangelism undertaken within the context of small study groups, house churches, et alia.
sobor. (Russian). A synod or council.
sobornost. (Russian). Conciliarity, ecumenicity, spiritual harmony based on freedom and unity in love.
social communication. Organizations coordinating social communications for the churches number over 200 with over 100 training centers.
social concern. Organizations significant at the national or wider levels number over 500.
Social Democratic states. States in which the party in power is of social democratic persuasion.
Socialist countries. States committed to the full implementation of political Socialism; often used of Marxist and Communist countries.
society. In several denominations, a local congregation of believers; in Christian Science.
socio-religious. Relating to social and religious factors.
sociology of religion. The study of religion from the standpoint of the science of society, social institutions, and social relationships.
sociology, religious. See religious sociology.
sodality. In missiological use, part of the sodality/modality dichotomy. (1) A sodality is an organized society, fellowship, community, fraternity or brotherhood based on mission as the common purpose (e.g. monastic pattern, or missionary society). (2) A modality is the more normal or typical pattern for mission, i.e. the diocesan pattern of Christianity following civil-governmental patterns, church-oriented missionary outreach, parish system, family involvement, etc.
soldier. In Salvationist usage, converted persons at least 14 years of age who have been enrolled as members of the Salvation Army after signing its Articles of War.
Songhai. An African ethnolinguistic family, with about 6 languages. Global statistics: (2000) 4.6 million in 17 peoples residing in 8 countries (1 significantly); largest, Niger (3.3 million).
sorcerer. A person who practices sorcery; a wizard, magician.
sorcery. The use of power gained from the assistance or control of evil spirits, especially for divining; necromancy, wizardry, black magic.
sound recordings. Christian organizations specializing mainly in this area and significant at the national or wider levels number over 200.
sous influence. (French). A statistical category enumerated in some Reformed denominations in Africa, covering the total membership plus non-members in the denomination's comity area or otherwise under its influence.
Southern Amerindian. An American Indian ethnolinguistic family, with over 1,500 languages. Global statistics: (2000) 32.8 million in 555 peoples residing in 23 countries (4 significantly); largest, Peru (13.7 million).
Southern Buddhism. Theravada or Hinayana (qv).
sovereign territory, sovereign nation. An independent, self-governing, autonomous state.
spare-time worker. A recognized or accredited church worker who nevertheless has a full-time secular job and is able to devote not part-time service but only his spare time out of work hours (e.g. Sundays or evenings) to church work; spare-time as contrasted with part-time or full time.
sparsely-evangelized. A people or area is defined as sparsely evangelized when less than 20% of its population have been evangelized.
speaking in tongues. Glossolalia (qv).
spirit possession. Possession or seizure by evil spirits.
spirit writing. Automatic writing held to be produced under the action of spirits; pneumatography.
Spirit, Spiritual. Adjectives widely used among African indigenous churches and in their official names, referring to the element of their control by the Holy Spirit.
spirit-worshippers. See tribal religionists.
spiritism. Belief in the action or agency of spirits of the dead producing mediumistic phenomena. See high spiritism, low spiritism.
Spiritist Catholics. Roman Catholics active in organized high or low spiritism, including syncretistic spirit-possession cults.
Spiritists. Non-Christian spiritists or spiritualists, or thaumaturgicalists; high spiritists, as opposed to low spiritists (Afro-American syncretists), followers of medium-religions, medium-religionists. Global statistics: (1970) 4.6 million; (1995) 11.1 million in 55 countries (2 significantly); largest, Brazil (7.3 million); (2000) 12.3 million; (2025) 16.2 million.
spiritual. Sacred, religious, ecclesiastical; influenced or controlled by the divine Spirit.
spiritual healing. Faith-healing (qv).
Spiritualists. Followers of a marginal Protestant tradition which holds that the word of God is constantly revealed to man via the mediumship of Spiritualist ministers, and which is nevertheless specifically Christian. Global statistics: (1970) 357,000; (1995) 145,000 in 20 countries; largest, USA (70,000).
spirituality. Sensitivity or attachment to religious values and things of the spirit rather than material or worldly interests.
split. A schism, secession (qv).
spontaneous communities. See basic communities.
spontaneous expansion of the church. See people movement.
spreading. In evangelization, the act or state or extent of the gospel being spread; reaching or thrusting out, expanding, extending, exposing, distributing, scattering, sowing, strewing, covering, overlaying, publishing, disseminating, making more widely known, diffusing, emitting, unfolding, circulating, propagating, radiating, et alia.
staff. (plural, staves). Wooden walking-sticks, symbols of discipleship and office in many African indigenous churches (qv).
stake. In Mormon usage, a territorial unit comprising a group of wards (qv) and governed by a stake presidency; equivalent to a diocese or jurisdiction.
state church. An established church (qv), national church (qv).
state departments of religious affairs. Over 75 countries operate government departments or ministries of religion, usually for purposes of control and surveillance of the churches.
state religion. An established religion, national religion recognized in law as the official religion of a country.
stateless persons. Persons who are citizens of no state at all.
stations, mission. See mission stations.
statistical compassion. The extending of the Christian attitude of *agape* (love, compassion) beyond one's immediate, visible circles of persons in need, to the demographically-vast but invisible multitudes beyond, and in particular to the entire world population in its totality.
statistics. (1) Numeral, numerical or quantitative data, or numerical facts systematically collected. (2) The science of collecting and classifying numerical data, or that branch of applied mathematics that actually arranges, describes and draws inferences from sets of numerical data. (3) A body of methods for making wise decisions in the face of uncertainty.
Sthanakavasis. Subsect of Svetambaras (qv) in western India.
stock. A racial stock, race (qv).
strategy. In war, the overall military and psychological plans that a general (in Greek, *strategos*) makes, or the science or art of employing all the resources of a nation or coalition of nations to achieve the objects of war. In missions, the overall plans guiding the long-term evangelization of a people or territory.
Strict Brethren. Exclusive Brethren (qv).
student organizations. Christian organizations for students, significant at the national or wider levels, number over 500.

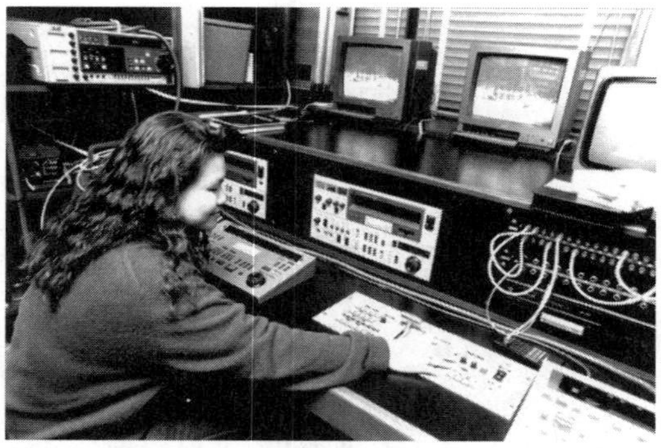
STUDIO. Editing Christian programs in Hong Kong, China.

studio. A room or center for the preparation (but not transmission) of Christian radio and TV programs.
study centers. Church- or Christian-operated study centers and other specialized lay training centers. Global total: (AD 2000) 10,000.
Stupa. A Buddhist hemispherical mound or tower, sur-

mounted by a spire or umbrella, forming a memorial shrine of the Buddha and often containing sacred relics; also known as chaitya, tope, chorten (Tibet), dagoba (Ceylon), pagoda (Burma).
style. The mode of address normally used for church dignitaries.
sub-culture. See homogeneous unit.
sub-deacon. A person in holy orders who ranks below a deacon, with duties including preparation of vessels for the eucharist.
sub-Orthodox sects. Formerly Russian Orthodox in the USSR who have split with their parent body to embark on total non-cooperation with the state yet retaining elements of Orthodox ritual, discontinued in 1990.
sub-population. In any population, part of the total inhabitants, e.g. schoolchildren, persons of marriageable age, etc.
subject. A citizen (qv), often of a colonial territory.
subsidized distribution of scriptures. Annual sales of scriptures produced by UBS-related and other Bible societies, which are subsidized to locally-realistic prices.
Sudanic. An African ethnolinguistic family; with over 255 languages. Global statistics: (2000) 20.7 million in 392 peoples residing in 8 countries (4 significantly); largest, Congo-Zaire (6.4 million).
suffragan bishop. In Anglican usage, (1) an assistant to the diocesan bishop, or (2) any bishop in relation to his archbishop or metropolitan. In Roman Catholic usage, a diocesan bishop in relation to his metropolitan.
suffragan diocese. In Roman Catholic usage, any diocese which is part of an ecclesiastical province and therefore to some extent dependent on its metropolitan see.
Sufism. Islamic mysticism, including scores of millions of Sunni Muslims in 70 orders: Ahmadiya, Bektashiya, Christiya, Dargawa, Dervishes, Fakirs, Malamatiya, Mawlawiya, Naqshbandiya, Qadriya, Qalandariya, Rifaiya, Shadhiliya, Shattariya, Suhrawardiya, Tijaniya.
Sunday attenders. Practicing Christians who attend church services of public worship on average every Sunday.
Sunday mass attenders. Practicing Roman Catholics who attend mass on average every Sunday.
Sunday schools. Christian or church classes held on Sundays for the purpose of religious education; with their pupils and teachers.
sunna. The body of hadith, traditions of Muhammed, i.e. of Islamic custom and practice.
Sunnis, Sunnites. Followers of the larger of the major branches of Islam, that adheres to the orthodox tradition of the sunna (qv), acknowledges the first 4 caliphs, and recognizes 4 schools of jurisprudence: Hanafite, Hanbalite, Malikite, Shafiite. Global statistics: (1970) 468.4 million; (1995) 905.5 million; (2000) 1.0 billion; (2025) 1.4 billion.
superintendent. A Protestant minister charged with the general supervision of churches within a certain district.

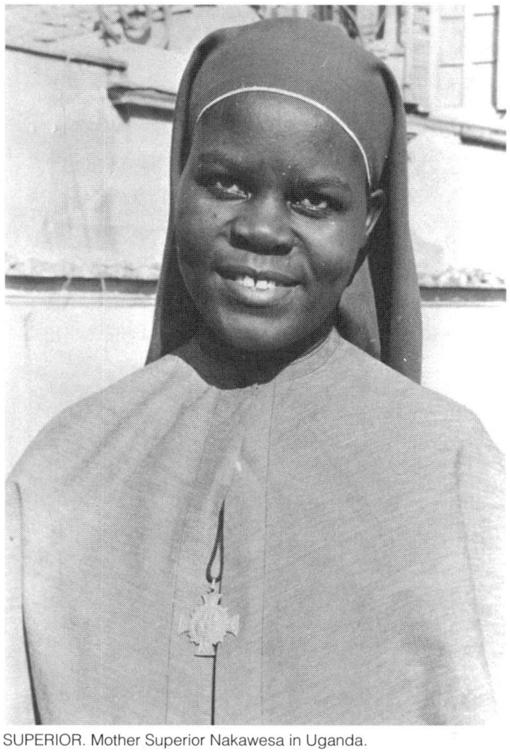
SUPERIOR. Mother Superior Nakawesa in Uganda.

superior. A head of a religious house, order or congregation.
superior general. The head of an entire religious order or congregation.
supernatural change, supranatural change. By contrast with natural change in a population (births minus deaths, plus immigrants minus emigrants), change in religious allegiance or adherence which from some points of view is unnatural, non-natural, supranatural or supernatural.
superstock. A language grouping or language phylum.
suppressed churches. Churches which have been forcibly suppressed, destroyed or otherwise permanently closed by state or other action.
suppressed dioceses. See closed dioceses.
surveillance. A recognized government tactic against churches in anti-Christian states; continuous close observation for purposes of obstruction, harassment and control.
survey. An inquiry or operation designed to furnish information on a special subject and which has limited aims.
suspended. Temporarily debarred from church membership, in particular from communicant status, because of some infringement of church law.
Svetambara. ('white-robed'). A major Jain sect whose members clothe themselves and their sacred images in white and in contrast to the Digambaras (qv) assert that women can attain salvation.
Swedenborgians. Followers of a marginal Protestant tradition, the Church of the New Jerusalem/New Church. Global statistics: (1970) 44,000; (1995) 31,000 in 18 countries; largest, USA (11,000).
switching. Used of church members who change from allegiance to one denomination to allegiance to another.
symbolics. Historical theology dealing with Christian creeds (Latin, *symbolae*) and confessions of faith; also termed symbolic theology. Comparative symbolics (German: Konfessionskunde) is the term traditionally applied to that branch of theology or ecclesiology which deals with the various Christian churches and confessions, their doctrines, their creeds, constitutions, ways of worship, devotional life and distinctive features studied as a whole.
synagogue. A Jewish local community or local assembly organized for public worship; or their building.

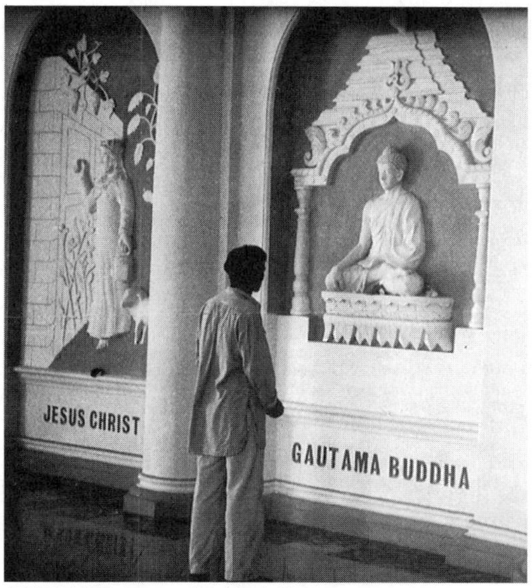

SYNCRETISM. Jesus and Buddha in Hindu temple, India.

syncretism. The developmental process of historical growth within a religion by accretion and coalescence of different and often conflicting forms of belief and practice; as understood by Christian theology, the religious attitude which holds that there is no unique revelation in history, that there are many different ways to reach the divine reality, that all formulations of religious truth or experience are inadequate expression of that truth, and that it is necessary to harmonize all religious ideas and experiences so as to create one universal religion for mankind.
syncretistic movement. A religious movement incorporating conflicting or divergent beliefs, principles or practices drawn from 2 or more religious systems.
synod. An ecclesiastical council or church governing or advisory body, including general synod diocesan synod (qv), holy synod (qv); either regularly meeting, or a one-time occasion.

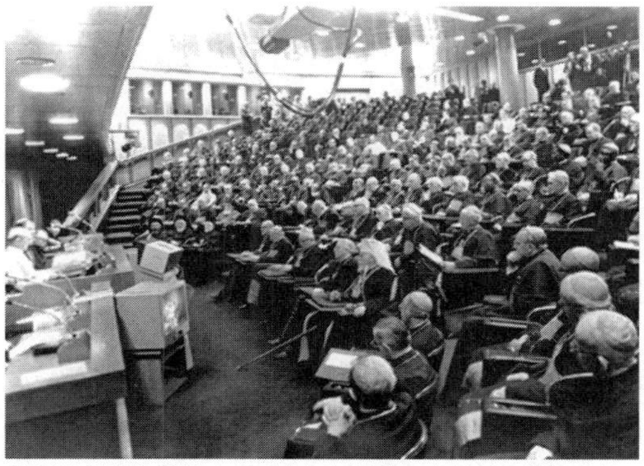
SYNOD OF BISHOPS. Assembly in the Vatican led by Paul VI at left.

Synod of Bishops. Since 1965 a permanent, central ecclesiastical institution assisting the Roman pope in the governing of the universal church. By AD 2000, 14 formal assemblies had been held.
Synodus Episcoporum. Synod of Bishops (qv).
synthesist, synthesizer. One who employs synthesis or follows synthetic methods with varying religious traditions.
Syriac. Oriental Orthodox liturgical tradition, dating back to New Testament era (Syrian Orthodox, West Syrian, Jacobite). Global statistics: (1970) 208,000; (1995) 1.0 million in 24 countries; largest, India (700,000).
Syriac/Malayalam. Oriental Orthodox liturgical tradition, using both languages in its liturgy, Syro-Malabarese (qv).
Syrian Orthodox Patriarchate of Antioch. Oriental Orthodox (Jacobite). Global statistics: (1970) 208,000; (1995) 1.0 million in 24 countries; largest, India (700,000).
Syrians. Roman Catholics using Antiochian rite. Global statistics: (1970) 75,000; (1995) 111,000 in 11 countries; largest, Iraq (52,000).
Syrians, Eastern. See Eastern Syrians.
Syrians, Western. See Western Syrians.
Syro-Chaldeans. Assyrians (qv).
Syro-Malabarese. (1) Orthodox St Thomas Christians of India who have remained independent of Rome but in communion with Jacobite Church (Damascus): global membership (1995) 2,197,000. (2) Catholic St Thomas Christians who submitted to Rome in 1599 and still use the East Syrian rite, with Malayalam; global membership (1995) 3,155,000.
Syro-Malankarese. Catholic St Thomas Christians who submitted to Rome in 1930, and who use the West Syrian rite. Global membership (1995) 311,000.
Syro-Oriental. A Roman Catholic rite (see Chaldean).
systematic theology. Constructive theology; a branch of theology that attempts to reduce all religious truth to statements forming a self-consistent and organized whole.
systems analysis. That approach which seeks to explain a situation or to solve a problem within the totality of its environment, seeing the situation and understanding how all of its parts are interrelated or affect one another.

T

tactics. In war, the science of disposing local resources to fight particular battles. In mission, the science or art of using available resources for the immediate evangelization of a people or territory.
Tai. An Asian ethnolinguistic family. Global statistics: (2000) 90.0 million in 111 peoples residing in 17 countries (2 significantly); largest, Thailand (49.4 million).
Tan. Stylized skin color (olive, light brown) associated with the Middle Eastern geographical race and the Iranian and some Latin American peoples. Global statistics: (2000) 659.8 million in 1,203 peoples residing in 177 countries (53 significantly); largest, Brazil (88.6 million).
Tantrayana. Tantrism, Vajrayana, Mantrayana, Esoteric Vehicle, or Lamaism; a school of Buddhists (qv), including Shingon in Japan.
Taoists. Followers of one of the 3 major religions of China, regarded as part of Chinese folk religion. Global statistics: (1970) 1.7 million; (1995) 2.5 million in 5 countries (1 significantly); largest, Taiwan (2.2 million); (2000) 2.6 million; (2025) 3.0 million.
tariqa. (Arabic). (1) A Muslim religious brotherhood or fraternity of mystics. (2) The Sufi path of spiritual development.
teacher. In Christian Science usage, one authorized to teach a class of not more than 30 pupils each calendar year.
telecast. A broadcast program over television.
telecenter. A church center equipped with a television receiver for use with classes and educational programs.
telephone ministries. Christian organizations in this area, significant at the national or wider levels, number over 200.
television. (TV). See under radio, broadcasting.
temple. An edifice dedicated to the worship of a deity in non-Christian religions, especially Hinduism and Buddhism; occasionally used of Christian buildings as in Mormon usage.
tent-making ministry. A self-supporting ministry in which a Christian worker, often an ordained minister earns his livelihood in some secular occupation.
tent-making missionary. A self-supporting foreign missionary who is not supported by a foreign missionary society or local church.
terminology, religious. The technical or special terms or expressions used in the descriptive study of religion.
territory. In Salvationist usage, a country or region in which Salvation Army work is organized under a territorial commander.
testimony. A brief personal account or narrative by an individual Christian concerning how Christ has worked in his life.
thaumaturgic. Connected with or dependent on thaumaturgy (performing of miracles or magic).
thaumaturgicalist, thaumaturgist. A performer of miracles, a magician.
theatre, religious. See religious drama.
theist. A believer in theism, belief in the existence of one God transcendent and immanent.
theocracy. Government of a state by allegedly the immediate direction or administration of God.
theological college associations. Associations at national or wider levels number over 80.
theological colleges. See seminaries.
theological education. An intensive and structured preparation of men and women for their participation in the ministry of Christ in the world.
theological education by extension. (TEE). Organization specializing in this area number over 200 worldwide.
theology. The study of God and his relation to man and the world: apologetics, dogmatic theology, natural theology, practical theology, systematic theology, et alia.
theophany. A physical presentation or personal manifestation of a deity to an individual.
Theosophists. Persons and bodies holding to Theosophy, or synthesist views combining philosophy and religions. A small number, including Liberal Catholics (qv), are specifically Christian.

Theosophy. A syncretistic system following chiefly Hindu philosophies originating in the USA in 1875.
Theravada. (Theraveda). The Teaching of the Elders or the Hinayana school of Buddhists (qv), or Southern Buddhism (in Sri Lanka, India, Burma Thailand, Cambodia, Laos). Global statistics: (1970) 87.7 million; (1995) 129.0 million; (2000) 136.2 million; (2025) 158.2 million.
thesis. Usually, a paper or essay submitted for a master's degree at a university.
Third Rome. Moscow; after the sack of Rome and the end of the Roman empire in the West in AD 476, Constantinople became known as the Second Rome but after its fall in 1453 its claim to be the capital of the Christian world passed to Moscow with its claim to be the Third Rome.
Third World. A term, based on political non-alignment, for those developing nations which are non-aligned with either the Western (Capitalist) world or the Communist (Marxist) world, and so form a third bloc. For an economic and social analysis see *The Third World: problems and perspectives*, ed. A. B. Mountjoy (London: Macmillan, 1978).
Third-World foreign missionaries. Citizens of Third-World nations who serve as foreign missionaries in other countries. Global statistics: 5,360 (AD 2000).
Third-World indigenous Christians. See Non-White indigenous Christians.
threefold ministry. In Anglicanism, the orders of bishop, priest and deacon.
Tibeto-Burmese. An Asian ethnolinguistic family, with over 300 languages. Global statistics: (2000) 82.2 million in 476 peoples residing in 18 countries (3 significantly); largest, Myanmar (37.0 million).
time lag. In church statistics, the delay incurred between the collecting of statistics at grass-roots level and their eventual publication at denominational or nationwide level; usually 2, 3, 4, 5 or even 6 years depending upon the size and complexity of the denomination concerned.
time level. The exact date, year or time to which particular data, especially statistical data, apply.
time series. The values of a variable over a period of time.
titular bishops. Roman Catholic bishops each with the title of, but without jurisdiction in, a defunct see; bishops in partibus infidelium. Totals: (1969) 1,953, (1977) 1,986, (1979) 1,988, (1996) 2,040.
toleration, religious. See religious toleration.
tongues. Glossolalia (qv).
total. Aggregate, sum, amount, whole.
total Christian community. The total of a church's or denomination's affiliated Christians (qv) or church members, who are part of the churches' corporate life, community and fellowship; of all ages and varieties including children, infants and persons under instruction; also called inclusive membership.
total church member community. Affiliated Christians (qv).
total church membership. Affiliated Christians (qv).
total community. The total of all persons affiliated to a particular denomination or religion, for the churches, affiliated Christians (qv).
total mobilization evangelism. See in-depth evangelism.
totalitarian. Authoritarian, dictatorial, despotic.
tourism. Travelling for recreation; touring. In this field, Christian ministries and organizations significant at the national or wider levels number over 150.
tourists. Persons travelling from place to place for pleasure or culture, defined as those who stay overnight usually at a hotel or inn.
tract. A pamphlet or leaflet containing a religious exhortation, doctrinal discussion or proselytizing appeal.
Tractarians. Anglo-Catholics (qv).
tradition. The totality of beliefs and practices (doctrine, dogmas, polity, ecclesiology, founding, origin characterizing a particular Christian school of thought, not derived directly from the Bible but arising and handed down within the Christian community.
tradition, ecclesiastical. See ecclesiastical tradition.
Traditional Catholics. Conservative Catholics (qv).
traditional religion. Often used of the dominant pre-Christian religion in a country, i.e. before the coming of Christianity.
traditionalist. One who adheres to tradition.
transconfessional. Church union negotiations between churches of 2 or more confessional families.
transient cults. Short-lived or ephemeral unorthodox or exotic religious movements.
transients. Impermanent, transitory, often homeless persons on the move.
translation projects. Member Bible Societies of the UBS were in AD 2000 engaged in a total of 685 translation projects (new translations of all or part of the scriptures).

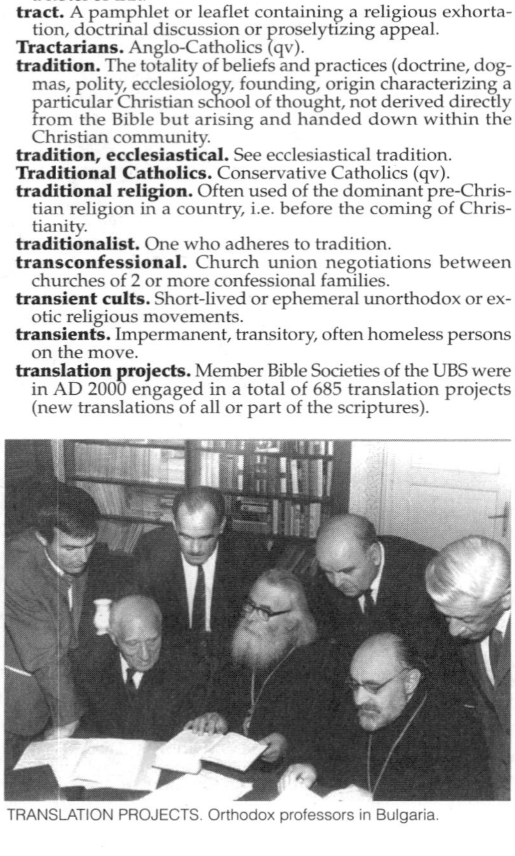
TRANSLATION PROJECTS. Orthodox professors in Bulgaria.

translations. Total scripture translations published or available. Global statistics: 392 with Bibles, 1,200 with New Testaments, 1,962 with Portions, 525 with Selections.
travel intensity. The ratio of annual international travelers to a country or area (including tourists) divided by the size of the total resident population or, within a country, the proportion of adults in the population who go away on holiday in a year.
trend. The general movement over a sufficiently long period of time of some statistical progressive change; tendency.
tribal religionists. A collective term for primal or primitive religionists, animists, spirit-worshippers, shamanists (qv), ancestor-venerators, polytheists, pantheists, traditionalists (in Africa), local or tribal folk-religionists; including adherents of neo-paganism or non-Christian local or tribal syncretistic or nativistic movements, cargo cults, witchcraft eradication cults, possession healing movements, tribal messianic movements; still occasionally termed pagans, heathen, fetishists; usually confined each to a single tribe or people, hence 'tribal or local as opposed to 'universal' (open to any or all peoples). Global statistics: (1970) 160.2 million; (1995) 214.0 million in 142 countries (30 significantly); largest, China (53.5 million); (2000) 228.3 million; (2025) 277.2 million.
tribe. A group of persons having a common character, occupation, avocation, interest, also common language, culture, territory and traditions.
tribunal. A court of church law at Rome; in particular the 3 senior courts, dating from the 13th and 14th centuries: Apostolic Penitentiary, Rota, and (the Catholic Church's supreme court) the Apostolic Signature.
Tridentine. Pertaining to or resulting from the Council of Trent (AD 1545-63).
Tridentinists. Roman Catholic traditionalists opposed to the reforms of Vatican II (1962-65) and upholding the Council of Trent (1545-63), including retention of the Latin mass and condemnation of Protestantism. In Europe, 20% of all RCs prefer the Tridentine mass.
trine. Threefold, triple.
trine immersion. The practice of immersing a candidate for baptism 3 times in the names in turn of the Trinity.
triumphalism. A theology of continuous success, namely that the church continually triumphs over evil, succeeds, grows numerically larger and larger. Once espoused by the Catholic Church and other large denominations, this is now rejected as unscriptural.
True Orthodox. Devoutly conservative Russian Orthodox in the USSR who have seceded from their parent body at various time (1900, 1927, 1944 1956, et alia) to embark on total non-cooperation with the Soviet state. Global statistics: (1970) 259,000; (1995) 358,000 in 6 countries; largest, Russia (330,000).
trumping. Black religious dance from the Caribbean (especially in Revival Zion and Pocomania) known as 'dancing, trumping and laboring for the Holy Ghost', being the means whereby the Spirit or spirits are invited to take possession. Worshippers form a dancing-trumping ring and dance counter-clockwise around a center post (symbolic of center of the world), in a shuffling 2-step dance done to 2-2 rhythm, bending forward and up in rhythmic sequence while sucking in breath and releasing with grunting sound.
Tukutendereza. (Luganda for 'We praise you, Jesus') A theme song of East African Revivalists (Balokole).
Twelvers. Ithna-Asharis (qv).

U

Ukrainian Orthodox Church of the Free World. The major Ukrainian Orthodox world communion. Global statistics: (1970) 24.6 million; (1995) 27.1 million in 10 countries (1 significantly); largest, Ukraine (26.9 million).
Ukrainians. Roman Catholics of the Byzantine rite using Ukrainian. Global statistics: (1970) 3.4 million; (1995) 5.0 million in 22 countries; largest, Ukraine (4.2 million).
ulema, ulama. (Arabic). The highest body of religious authorities in Islam; a group of Muslim theologians and scholars who are professionally occupied with the elaboration and interpretation of the Muslim legal system from a study of Quran and hadith.
ummah. (Arabic) The community of faith embracing all Muslims, adherents of Islam.
unaffiliated Christians. Persons professing publicly to be Christians but who are not affiliated to churches, i.e. not church members, unaffiliated or unchurched Christians not, no longer, or not yet attached to organized Christianity, or who have rejected the institutional churches whilst retaining Christian beliefs and values, who may be Christians individually but are not part of the churches' corporate life, community or fellowship. Global statistics: (1970) 106.2 million; (1995) 107.5 million in 236 countries (35 significantly); largest, USA (43.3 million); (2000) 111.1 million; (2025) 125.7 million.
unattached congregation. An independent single congregation or worship center with no denominational ties.
unbaptized Christian. A professing or believing Christian who has not, or not yet, undergone Christian baptism.
unbelief. Non-belief, doubt, incredulity, agnosticism, apathy in matters of religious faith.
unbelievers. Non-religious persons: doubters, non-believers, agnostics, freethinkers, liberal thinkers, non-religious humanists, persons indifferent to both religion and atheism.
uncanonical. Unsanctioned, unorthodox, not being in accord with church canons.
unchristen. To annul the baptism of a person.
unchristian. Not of the Christian faith, contrary to Christianity.
unchristianize. To turn people from Christianity, dechristianize.
unchurch. To excommunicate, expel, separate from the church, deprive of church membership.
unchurched. Christians unaffiliated to organized churches, not belonging to or connected with a church; nominal Christians (qv).
under discipline. See discipline.
under obligation. All baptized Roman Catholics of 7 years and older are obligated by canon law to attend Easter mass once a year.
underground churches, underground Christians. See crypto-Christians.
underground communities. See basic communities.
unevangelized. The state of not having had the gospel spread or offered.
Uniate. A Christian or a jurisdiction of an Eastern rite not belonging to a Latin patriarchate but in union with and submitting to the authority of the Roman papacy.
union congregations. Churches of English-speaking peoples abroad in which several denominations are present and hence an interdenominational ministry is required.
Union of Utrecht. International Old Catholic Bishops Conference (qv).
union, church. See church unions.
Unitarian-Pentecostals. Oneness-Pentecostals (qv).
Unitarians. Non-Trinitarians (denying the Trinity), Universalists, Free Christians, Liberal Christians: a marginal Protestant tradition in the direction of modernism. Global statistics: (1970) 469,000; (1995) 378,000 in 29 countries; largest, USA (190,000).
united churches. Protestant and Anglican denominations which in recent years have united to form new united denominations. Global statistics: (1970) 51.6 million; (1995) 60.7 million in 53 countries (10 significantly); largest, Germany (29.2 million).
united diocese, united dioceses. Dioceses which were large in the past but have now shrunk numerically (especially in Ireland), so are administered together as a single diocese.
united seminary. A theological college serving 2 or more denominations or confessions.
uniting churches. Churches or denominations that are in process of merging to form a united church.
unity. Oneness, singleness, accord among Christians of different traditions.
Unity of the Brethren. Moravians (qv).
unity undertaking. A Moravian jurisdiction.
universal church. The Christian church in its world-wide entirety down the ages; in Roman Catholic usage, the world-wide church as contrasted with local or particular churches (qv).
Universal Commission. The Great Commission (qv).
universal religion. Any religion which admits persons of any race or people; a world religion, usually missionary in emphasis.
universal religionists. Followers of universal religions as contrasted with primal religionists (qv).
universalism. The theological doctrine that all men will eventually be saved or restored to holiness and happiness.
Universalists. Unitarians (qv).
universe. In sampling and polls, the total population to which a sample survey refers.
universities, Christian. Degree-granting universities and colleges teaching secular subjects, operated by churches or under Christian auspices. Global statistics: 1,500 (AD 2000).
university departments of religion. Departments significant for the study of Christianity number over 1,500 in as many universities across to world.
unreached. The state of not having had the gospel brought.
unreached peoples. Ethnic, linguistic and other groups without previous contact with Christianity, who have not or not yet had the gospel brought to them.
unrecognized churches. Churches or denominations whom the state refuses to legalize.
Untouchables. A large hereditary group in India having, in traditional Hindu belief and practice, the quality of defiling by contact the person, food, or drink of members of higher castes, and formerly being strictly segregated and restricted to menial work; the term has been illegal in India since 1949 and in Pakistan since 1953, and is now replaced by Harijans (Children of God) or Scheduled Castes. Total (AD 2000): 150 million.
untouched. In evangelization, a population group that is not yet explored or traveled to or influenced or disturbed or reached by Christians, nor written about, but is still in its original (often primitive or aboriginal) intact state; non-evangelized
Uralian. An Asian ethnolinguistic family (Whites). Global statistics: (2000) 25.0 million in 139 peoples residing in 38 countries (5 significantly); largest, Hungary (8.4 million).
urban area. Defined in many countries as an administrative district with a population over 2,000.
urban dwellers. The population living in urban areas usually including cities and towns with over 5,000 inhabitants. Global statistics: 2.88 billion (AD 2000).
urban mission. In the field of urban industrial mission, Christian organizations significant at the national or wider levels number over 400.
urbanization. The state or extent of urban areas or the process of becoming urbanized, in a particular country.
usual language. The language customarily used by an individual, as distinct from his mother tongue (qv).

V

vagrants. Persons of no fixed abode.
Vaishnavites. Worshippers of Vishnu in any of his forms or incarnations; the predominant form of Hinduism outside South India; including these sects: Alvars, Caitanya, Kapalikas, Nimbarka, Ramanandis, Tenkalai, Vadakalai, Visnuvamins, et alia. Global statistics: (1970) 323.4 million; (1995) 508.9 million; (2000) 549.5 million; (2025) 708.1 million.
Vajrayana. The Tantrism school of Buddhists; Tantrayana (qv).

variable. A quantity that changes or varies in size; dependent variable, independent variable, etc.

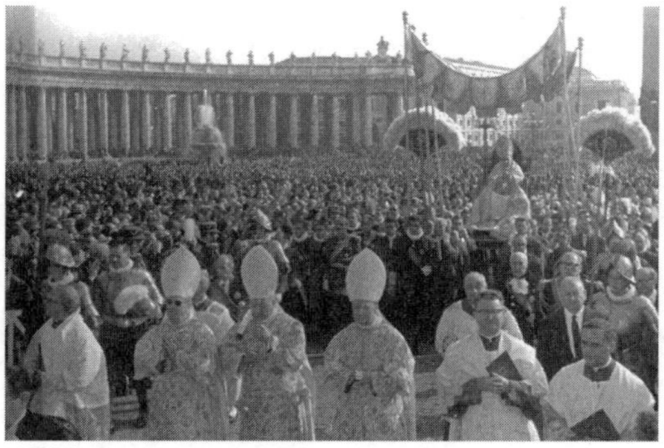

VATICAN. 2,500 bishops arrive for Vatican 2, 1962.

Vatican. Official headquarters and spiritual center of the Roman Catholic Church; in Rome.
Vaticanism. The dogma of absolute papal supremacy.
Vedas. The most ancient sacred writings of Hinduism; any of 4 Samhitas (Aranyaka, Brahmana, Sutra, Upanishad).
Venice. See of Latin Catholic patriarchate and patriarch, since 1451.
vicar. An Anglican incumbent who is not a rector; a Roman Catholic ecclesiastic who acts as the substitute or representative of another.
vicar-general. The deputy of a Roman Catholic or Anglican bishop assisting in the jurisdiction of the diocese.
vicariate. (symbol V). The office, authority, or jurisdiction of a vicar.

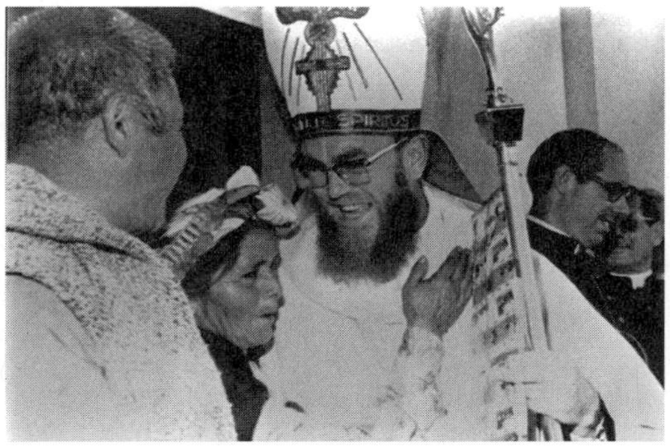

VICARIATES APOSTOLIC. New bishop in Chile greets Amerindians.

vicariates apostolic. (symbol VA). Roman Catholic missionary districts over each of which a vicar apostolic (a bishop) exercises jurisdiction. Total (1997) 76.
vicariates castrensi. Military vicariates (qv).
Viet-Muong. An Asian ethnolinguistic family. Global statistics: (2000) 71.9 million in 35 peoples residing in 22 countries (1 significantly); largest, Viet Nam (68.9 million).
village polytechnic. A Christian program in developing countries, offering local technical skills and intermediate technology at village level.
Villatte succession churches. Autocephalous Catholic churches under bishops-at-large (qv) whose disputed episcopal orders pass through J.R. Villatte, Mar Timotheus (died 1929).
Vishnavites. Vaishnavites (qv).
visible church. See church visible.
vital statistics. Registration statistics of births, deaths, marriages, divorces, etc.
vocation. A task or function to which one is called by God.

W

Wahhabites. Sunni Muslims reform movement of the most rigid school of law, Hanabila.
Waldensians. A Protestant tradition dating back in Italy to AD 1173, now loosely united with Methodism. Global statistics: (1970) 37,000; (1995) 41,000 in 2 countries; largest, Italy (29,000).
waqf, wakf. (Arabic; plural, *awkaf*). A Muslim religious or charitable foundation created by an endowed trust fund.
ward. In Mormon usage, a small territorial unit or division of a stake (qv) presided over by a bishopric and comprising branches of church auxiliary organizations and quorums of the Aaronic priesthood; equivalent to a parish.
Watchtower, Watch Tower. A name for Jehovah's Witnesses; part of their legal name, also of major publication.
weddings, church. See marriages, church.
weekly attenders. Affiliated Christians (church members) who attend church services of public worship at least once a week, i.e. regularly every Sunday (for sabbatarians, every Saturday).
Wesleyans. Holiness Christians (qv).
West Syrians. Syrian Orthodox (Jacobites), Orthodox Syrians (India).
Western Church. A collective term for the Christian Churches in the Western world, or western Europe, or the Patriarchate of the West (Rome).
Western Syrians. West Syrians (qv).
Western world. A term, based on political alignment, for the Western or Capitalist countries of Europe, North America, et alia, including capitalist and non-Marxist Socialist or Social Democratic countries.
White. Stylized skin color associated with the Caucasian race and the Uralian ethnolinguistic family. Global statistics: (2000) 948.1 million in 1,883 peoples residing in 235 countries (79 significantly); largest, USA (176.3 million).
White indigenous churches. Christian traditions indigenous to the White races, i.e. traditions which are predominantly White initiatives in origin. Global statistics: (1970) 7.4 million; (1995) 43.4 million in 163 countries; largest, USA (14.1 million).
white magic. Magic (qv) with benevolent intent, as opposed to black magic (qv).
Wider Episcopal Fellowship. An attempt to co-ordinate all churches and denominations with historic episcopacy and with some historical claim to apostolic succession.
witch. One supposed to possess supernatural powers in order to bewitch people inadvertently.
witchcraft. The inadvertent exercise of supernatural powers to harm others.
witchcraft eradication movement. A spontaneous movement, especially in Africa, attempting to eradicate witchcraft by offering holy water or other preventative magic and by denunciation of witches.
witchdoctor. A professional worker of magic in primitive society who by spells, charms, herbal remedies et alia seeks to cure illness, detect witches and counteract malevolent magical influences; a shaman, medicine man.
withdrawal from church membership. In West Germany and other European countries with state-established Protestant churches of which the whole population largely are members, legislation now provides for the possibility of persons making a formal legal withdrawal from membership, thereby avoiding church income tax.
witness. Public testimony by word or deed to one's religious or Christian faith.
Witness, a witness. A member of Jehovah's Witnesses (qv).
wizard. One devoted to black magic and the black arts in order deliberately to harm others; sorcerer, sorceress magician.
women lay workers. See under personnel.
women religious. Nuns, sisters, and other full-time female religious personnel. World total: 828,660 (1996).
women's organizations. Christian organizations serving lay women and girls, and significant at the national or wider levels number over 500.

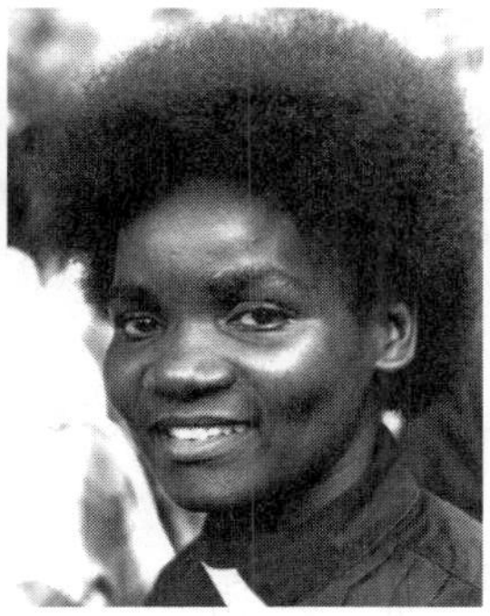

WOMEN, ORDAINED. Methodist pastor in Mozambique.

women, ordained. Organizations relating to women in the ordained ministry number over 200.
worker-priest. A French Roman Catholic priest who for missionary purposes spends part of each weekday as a worker in a secular job.
workers' organizations. Christian organizations for workers or professionals, significant at the national or wider levels, number over 400.
workers, church. See personnel.
working-age population. All persons of 15 years of age and older, up to 65 years.
World Alliance of Reformed Churches. (Presbyterian and Congregational) (WARC). The major Reformed world communion. Global constituency: (1999) 75 million Christians in 214 member churches in 105 countries.
world conciliarism. Councils linking, or offering to link, or attempting to link, all denominations in the world number only 3: World Council of Churches (WCC), World Evangelical Fellowship (WEF) International Council of Christian Churches (ICCC).
world confessional bodies or families. Known since 1979 as Christian world communions (qv).
World Council of Churches. (WCC). The major ecumenical body, founded 1948. Global constituency: (1999) 500 million in 336 churches and denominations in 120 countries.
World Evangelical Fellowship. (WEF). A loosely-organized global Conservative Evangelical alliance, which only accepts as members national alliances or councils or fellowship. Global constituency: (1999) 150 million.
world evangelization. The goal of the proclamation of the Gospel of Christ to all persons in the world; the professed goal of all Christian confessions and communions.
World Methodist Council. (WCM). The major Methodist world communion. Global constituency: (1997) 70,226,066.
world religion. A universal religion (qv).
world religions. The major religions of the world defined here as those with (in AD 2000) over 2% each of the world's population, as follows: Christianity (33.0%), Islam (19.6%), Hinduism (13.4%), Buddhism (5.9%), Chinese folk religion (6.4%), excluding (because local not universal) primal or tribal religion (3.8%), but including Asiatic New Religions (1.7%); also atheism (2.5%) and agnosticism (12.7%) regarded as worldwide quasi-religions.
world-religionists. Followers of the world's major religions (see definition under world religions). Global statistics: (2000) 5,136,801,000 (84.8%).
worldview. A general understanding of the nature of the universe and of one's place in it; outlook on the world, ideology, a cosmological conception of society and institutions.
worship centers. Distinct organized groups or congregations of Christian worshippers of any tradition or confession; usually measured by church buildings, chapels, regular worship premises, sites, stations, centers, outposts, preaching points, parishes and quasi-parishes. Global total: (1970) 1,506,400, (1975) 1,599,100, (1980) 1,718,400, (1985) 1,840,000, (2000) 2,800,000.

Y

Yazidis. Yezidis. Devil-Worshippers. Members of a 12th-century Muslim syncretistic religious sect in Iraq, also in Syria, USSR and Turkey. Global statistics: (1970) 102,000; (1995) 202,000; (2000) 226,000; (2025) 371,000.
yearbooks. Christian or church yearbooks, handbooks, directories, periodical lists, and other listings significant at national, international, denomination and confessional levels, number over 5,000.
Yearly Meeting. An organizational unit of the Religious Society of Friends composed of many Quarterly Meetings (local congregations), the most comprehensive Quaker administrative body.
Yellow. Stylized skin color associated with the Arctic Mongoloid, Asian and Pacific geographical races. Global statistics: (2000) 2.1 billion in 2,372 peoples residing in 161 countries (60 significantly); largest, China (1.2 billion).
Yellow Hat. (Reformed). Lamaism, or Yellow Church (in Tibetan, Dge-lugs-pa or Gelukpa, 'Model of Virtue'). That part of Tibetan Buddhism in which monasteries and monks have accepted the 14th-century reforms of the monk Tsong-Kha-pa. Its executive head is the Dalai Lama; The Panchen Lama also comes from this grouping.
younger churches. A term sometimes used for the newer or relatively-recent denominations of the Third World, in contrast to the older churches of Europe and North America.

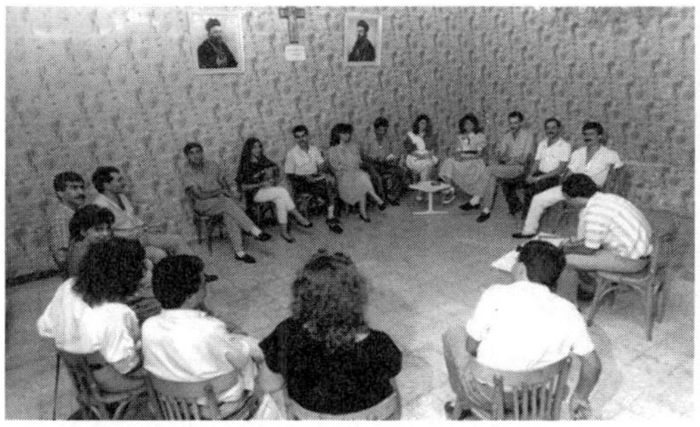

YOUTH ORGANIZATIONS. Syrian Orthodox in Aleppo.

youth organizations. Christian organizations serving youth, significant at the national or wider levels number over 500.
Yugoslav rite. A Byzantine rite for Catholics in Yugoslavia, discontinued in 1990.

Z

Zambo. (Sambo). A Spanish-speaking Latin American of mixed Negro and Amerindian origin; in Portuguese, a Cafuso.
Zaydis. (Zaidis). A Muslim sect in Yemen that constitutes one of the 4 major branches of Shia Islam recognizes a continuing line of imams descended through Zaid (the 5th imam), and is closest to sunna in its doctrine. Global statistics: (1970) 3.7 million; (1995) 7.1 million; (2000) 8.0 million; (2025) 13.1 million.
zionist. An African type of charismatic indigenous movement or church; also termed spirit, spiritual, Spirit dominated, pentecostal, aladura (qv), enthusiastic, faith-healing, etc.
Zionists. Southern Africa charismatic Christians in Black indigenous churches, numbering 12 million by AD 2000.
Zoroastrianism. A religion founded in Persia in BC 1200 by the prophet Zoroaster teaching the worship of Ahura Mazda, now followed by Parsis (qv) in India and a large underground presence in Iran, Afghanistan, et alia. Global total (AD 2000): 2.5 million.

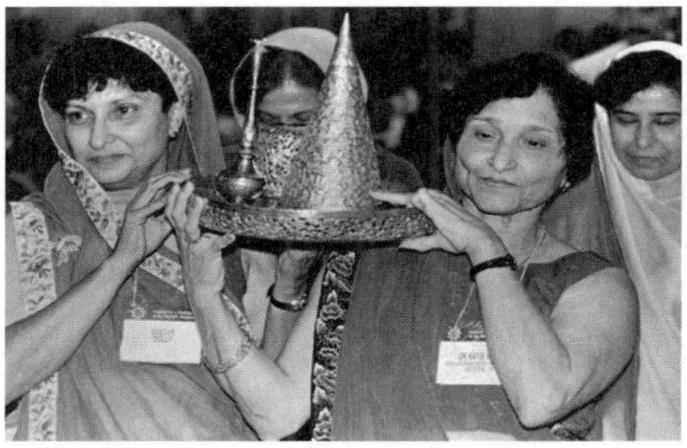

ZOROASTRIANISM. Procession under way in North America.

Part 13

BIBLIOGRAPHY

A world bibliography of Christianity and religions

There are also many other things which Jesus did; were every one of them to be written,
I suppose that the world itself could not contain the books that would be written.
—John 21:25, Revised Standard Version

Men of learning—whether you be theologians, exegetes or historians—
the work of evangelization needs your tireless work of research.
—Paul VI, *Evangelii Nuntiandi*, 1975

Bibliometrics is the science of measuring or counting books, authoring, publishing, librarianship, cataloging, and the like. Part 13 utilizes this approach to generate its own statistical variables. These include the total books available today on any country's Christian and religious situations, the total such new books published each year, and the global totals of books available on a range of 100 major Christian and religious subjects. This Encyclopedia also contains its own bibliographies listing 9,000 different titles. This Part ends with a Selective World Bibliography with 1,380 titles, mainly works in English, and half being on Christianity.

A world bibliography of Christianity and religions

The Fourth Evangelist, John, was so impressed by the magnitude of Jesus' impact on the world that he ended his narrative by saying:

> Jesus did many other things. If they were all written in books, I don't suppose there would be room enough in the whole world for all the books. (John 21:25, Contemporary English Version).

Today's facts and figures on the subject support John's vision.

To illustrate: the name of Jesus Christ is very widely known across the whole literate world and its cultures. Table 13-1 reveals that libraries contain over 60,000 distinct books whose main subject is Jesus and his significance. No one else has ever generated such an enormous and powerful impact on the human mind.

It is the same when the literature generated by the Christian religion that Jesus created is examined.

Table 13-2 shows how numerous books are on a whole range of terms mostly arising from Jesus' ministry.

The location of this vast amount of material is also worldwide. The literature described in these tables is found in libraries in every country of the world—even in countries hostile to the contemporary Christian enterprise. The whole phenomenon can best be studied in any of the world's largest libraries, all open to the public. Table 13-3 lists 130 of the largest specifically Christian libraries each of which has over 120,000 titles on its shelves and in its computerized catalogs. And Table 13-4 lists the total number of books describing empirical Christianity and religion in each country of today's world, together with totals in the bibliographies on every country in Part 4 "Countries".

Table 13-1. Book titles with Jesus Christ as main subject.

a. Total titles ever with these 3 terms as subject heading

Language	Jesus Christ	Jesus	Christ
English	46,268	47,169	60,215
German	6,613	6,681	6,783
French	3,348	3,636	3,395
Spanish	2,434	3,400	3,395
Italian	1,261	1,295	1,272
Dutch	700	718	706
Portuguese	397	481	416
Korean	262	263	26
Chinese	242	245	245
Polish	215	225	217
Arabic	195	195	197
Russian	189	197	191
Japanese	112	245	245
Hindi	4	4	4

b. Books with name in title

All languages	16,912	55,587	63,076

Table 13-2. Book titles on 135 major Christian and religious subjects and keywords.

The world's major English-language monitoring system for cataloguing, listing, locating, providing, and loaning the world's 40 million distinct and different book titles held in public and private libraries across the face of the globe is termed OCLC (Online Computer Library Catalog). Although it specializes in English-language books, its libraries include books in 360 other languages also. The table below accesses this Catalog to determine the magnitude of the world's current literature on Christianity, Christ, and the gospel, in the context of a few major secular or non-Christian terms. The latter are shown below in italics. All in medium type are Christian terms, or in practice are mainly Christian subjects. This survey was done in 1998, so columns 2, 3, 5 are all slightly larger in AD 2000 (utilize column 4 to estimate).

Column 1 lists terms by which the US Library of Congress classifies the main subject of each book; note that terms ending in a hyphen cover all subjects containing that root (thus 'martyr-' includes 'martyrs', 'martyrdom', 'martyred', etc). Column 2 enumerates the worldwide total of different titles on that subject, copies of which still exist today and therefore can, normally, for any enquirer anywhere on Earth, be seen on his screen, have its details printed out, or be loaned by mail for 2-3 weeks. Column 3 reduces each total to include only books published since 1970. Column 4 provides an estimate of the number of new titles on each subject being published every year in AD 2000. Column 5 enumerates all books which actually include the exact keyword (column 1) in their titles. Some of these may be larger than column 2 when their main subject is larger or more inclusive than column 1's term. Global grand total. Total of all titles whose main subject is Christianity or some aspect of it, excluding secular and non-Christian terms.

Search term(s) 1	Total titles ever 2	Titles since 1970 3	New per year 4	With term in title 5
Advent	7,127	2,483	95	4,578
Anglican-	10,422	4,561	175	6,201
apostasy	452	181	7	439
apostle-	12,670,	4,260	164	10,081
apostolic-	2,609	757	29	8,905
architecture, religio-	516	369	15	226
art, religio-	4,460	2,566	103	1,738
art, Christian	10,284	5,751	230	33
astrophysics	4,601	3,400	130	3,500
atheis-	3,226	1,444	58	2,217
Baha'i	1,095	797	32	678
bapti-	66,163	26,129	1,105	55,253
baptism	10,863	2,931	113	10,463
Bible	261,303	103,592	4,144	145,868
biblical	45,218	24,051	962	17,475
broadcasting	638	398	16	113
Buddh-	46,096	29,283	1,171	14,942
Buddhism	4,772	2,711	108	4,772
catechist, -m	15,061	1,958	75	16,334
Catholic-	198,678	76,293	2,934	54,383
Christ	80,327	31,172	1,247	63,076
Christian	192,339	105,301	4,212	111,318
Christian-	308,087	178,371	7,135	164,582
Christianity	105,554	67,578	2,703	21,414
church	563,393	210,816	8,433	273,284
church & state	30,100	9,130	365	6,099
church, growth	4,982	4,729	182	3,314
church, renewal	2,957	2,424	97	866
cities	58,067	39,614	1,524	44,210
city	174,511	110,712	4,258	312,804
clergy	46,129	20,693	796	9,444
Communism, -t	68,496	45,000	1,730	23,856
confession, Christian	3,899	1,251	50	18,000
conversion	13,171	7,420	285	18,981
cosmology	8,618	7,500	300	4,000
Creation (of universe)	13,272	8,000	320	7,500
creeds	9,975	3,100	119	4,771
Crucifixion	2,356	1,199	46	1,136
cults	3,891	2,821	113	1,375
Culture(s)	85,624	60,000	2,300	70,000
culture, religion	1,534	1,259	50	1,648
denomination-	116	30	1	4,296
drama, religio-	2,448	1,093	44	569
education, Christian	21,894	14,233	569	5,454
education, religious	24,244	11,597	464	7,017
Enlightenment	3,139	1,100	42	2,732
eschatolog-	6,583	3,032	121	1,972
ethnic-	34,568	31,142	1,198	20,104
Evangelical	8,079	2,668	107	12,623
Evangelicalism	3,001	2,179	87	360
evangelism	1,069	834	33	5,411
evangelist, -s	2,556	1,411	54	3,800
evangelistic work	12,881	8,716	349	152
faith-	15,941	8,538	328	54,845
finance	253,139	163,542	6,290	66,611
finance/Christ-/church	5,042	2,305	89	681
Fundamentalism, -t	3,895	3,248	127	2,588
futur-, Christian-	667	346	14	699
Genesis, Book of	9,664	4,200	160	7,000
geo-	539,616	284,579	10,945	1,500,000
geograph-	110,317	54,752	2,106	107,992
geolog-	183,824	106,607	4,023	208,569
geometr-	31,236	13,587	552	39,907
God	33,387	16,493	660	78,197
gospel-	36,903	23,642	946	42,849
Hindu-	27,873	16,545	662	8,788
Hinduism	8,851	5,444	218	1,285
holiness	3,154	1,123	45	3,976
Holy Spirit	8,875	4,503	173	5,761
human rights	37,016	28,000	1,100	26,000
independent church-	1,396	599	23	2,328
Islam	40,435	29,846	1,194	16,741
Islam-	71,300	51,383	2,055	30,775
Jainism	1,395	760	30	218
Jesus	68,391	26,647	1,066	55,587
Judaism	45,217	23,570	943	5,295
language-	780,544	470,346	18,090	161,950
language & culture	3,111	2,800	107	2,890
linguistic-	24,707	20,205	777	27,960
literacy	13,879	12,623	485	15,444
Lutheran	39,303	13,125	504	17,533
martyr-	4,849	1,448	58	11,843
martyr-, Christian	1,903	829	33	713
martyrdom	381	234	9	1,432
media, Christian-	335	274	10	128
messianism	305	195	8	106
Methodism, -t	46,486	15,670	602	36,982
missio-	93,431	1,264	51	83,976
missio-, Christian	7,588	4,416	177	4,056
missio-, Islam	628	376	15	134
missionary, -ies	19,468	8,533	341	25,560
missions	80,576	25,451	1,018	18,988
missions, theory	2,000	1,286	51	35
money	29,353	13,016	501	40,802
money/finance, church	3,881	1,398	54	458
Mormon, -s	19,789	5,996	230	9,783
Muhammad-	16,219	8,800	338	8,006
Muslim- (Moslem-)	15,164	11,415	457	6,683
New Testament	1,827	998	40	25,666
occultism	9,290	5,998	240	499
Old Testament	2,413	1,282	51	16,057
Orthodox-	18,261	9,596	369	8,486
Pentecostal-	4,551	3,164	126	1,953
persecution	10,138	8,200	320	6,000
pilgrim-	7,935	3,967	159	15,687
pilgrim-, Christian-	1,703	1,253	50	455
pilgrimage	4,875	3,022	121	4,833
pope-	21,228	6,227	240	14,683
pope or papacy	25,298	7,179	276	15,501
Postmodernism, -t	3,165	3,158	121	965
pray-	50,312	20,668	795	49,118
preach-	11,545	5,993	240	57,664
prophet, -ecy	15,697	7,299	280	17,836
Protestant-	20,647	5,510	212	30,861
race(s)	90,280	65,000	2,400	60,000
read-	214,192	144,689	5,564	284,364
reading	113,347	88,896	3,419	130,074
Reformation	14,533	3,565	137	15,919
Reformed	14,664	4,357	167	10,915
religion	114,658	56,434	2,200	72,466
religion & science	8,970	2,850	114	2,898
religion & state	4,766	2,496	100	1,792
religion-	129,978	64,108	2,257	93,918
religions	17,569	8,968	114	9,929
research-	237,623	182,254	7,010	610,953
science	359,531	177,850	7,100	458,073
science and religion	10,764	5,300	220	7,000
sect-	21,651	13,952	558	139,794
sect-, Christian	1,679	987	39	734
shamanism	1,436	1,253	50	369
Sikhism	1,043	780	31	223
Taoism	2,531	1,579	63	336
Trinity	8,346	3,332	133	11,462
union, Christian	7,894	2,674	107	1,445
urban-	83,356	69,137	2,659	137,913
Vatican	6,338	2,620	101	9,866
world, Christian-	6,582	1,738	67	5,180
worship	11,662	6,421	257	19,299
worship, Christian	990	768	31	2,523
writing	38,362	29,404	1,130	52,843
other Christian items	300,000	160,000	6,400	50,000
total Christian	3,239,000			
less duplicates	-230,000			
uncatalogued	1,500,000	900,000	36,000	500,000
Global grand total	4,510,000	2,700,000	110,000	1,900,000

Table 13-3. 130 of the world's largest Christian and/or theological libraries with over 120,000 books each, AD 2000.

Below are listed 130 of the world's largest Christian, theological, and/or religious libraries, ranked by size (number of bound or print volumes). The location of each within its country is either indicated by its city name being included in its title, or by adding the city or state name, anglicized, after the library's name, and a comma.

Name	*Country*	*Volumes*	*Name*	*Country*	*Volumes*
Biblioteca Apostolica Vaticana	Holy See	1,600,000	The Evangelical Library, London	Britain	250,000
Katholische Universitat Eichstatt	Germany	1,200,000	Pittsburgh Theological Seminary	USA	245,540
Trinity College/University of Dublin	Ireland	1,100,000	Reformed Academy of Theology, Budapest	Hungary	240,000
Urbe (Roman Network of Libraries), Rome	Italy	1,100,000	Kirchlichen Hochschule Berlin	Germany	240,000
Katholieke Universiteit Leuven	Belgium	920,000	Moravian Theological Seminary, Bethlehem, PA	USA	237,128
Tübingen University	Germany	900,000	Trinity Evangelical Divinity School, Deerfield, IL	USA	235,130
Institut Catholique de Paris	France	810,000	New Orleans Baptist Theological Seminary	USA	234,597
Pontificia Universita Gregoriana, Vatican City	Holy See	780,000	General Theological Seminary, New York	USA	234,510
Ludwig-Maximilians-Universitat, Munich	Germany	750,000	North Park Theological Seminary, Chicago	USA	229,685
University of St Andrews (Church of Scotland)	Britain	720,000	Congregational Library, Boston	USA	225,275
Union Theological Seminary, New York	USA	710,000	Luther Seminary Library, St. Paul, MN	USA	221,569
Catholic University of Gottingen	Germany	650,000	Free University of the Netherlands, Amsterdam	Netherlands	220,000
Regenstein Library, University of Chicago	USA	600,000	Fuller Theological Seminary (McAlister), Pasadena, CA	USA	220,000
Scarritt-Bennett Center, Nashville	USA	548,575	St Patrick's College, Maynooth	Ireland	220,000
Pontificia Universita Salesiana, Rome	Italy	510,000	Pontifical University of Santo Tomas, Manila	Philippines	220,000
Calvin Theological Seminary, Grand Rapids	USA	503,780	Bethel Theological Seminary, St Paul, MN	USA	215,000
Université Catholique de Louvain	Belgium	500,000	Concordia Seminary Library, St. Louis	USA	213,840
San Francisco de Borja Facultad Teologica, Barcelona	Spain	500,000	Asbury Theological Seminary, Wilmore, KY	USA	204,598
S. J. Saint-Albert, Louvain	Belgium	500,000	Caritasbibliothek, Freiburg im Breisgau	Germany	200,000
Andover-Harvard Theological Library, Cambridge, MA	USA	500,000	Groot Seminarie Mechelen-Brussel	Belgium	200,000
Pitts Theology Library, Emory University, Atlanta	USA	485,000	H. Orton Wiley (Nazarene) Library, Point Loma, CA	USA	200,000
Bibliotheek Canisianum (Jesuit), Maastricht	Netherlands	477,000	Jesuitenkollegs, Innsbruck	Austria	200,000
Princeton Theological Seminary	USA	475,000	Sion College (Anglican), London	Britain	200,000
Theologische Hogeschool (Jesuit), Amsterdam	Netherlands	460,000	Erskine College & Theological Seminary, Due West, SC	USA	199,487
Pontificia Universita Lateranense, Vatican City	Holy See	450,000	Anderson University, Anderson, IN	USA	197,752
Sint Jan Berchmanscollege, Heverlee	Belgium	450,000	Evangelical Lutheran Library, Budapest	Hungary	190,000
Drew University Theological School, Madison, NJ	USA	449,280	David Lipscomb University, Nashville, TN	USA	184,506
Jesuit-Krauss-McCormick Library, Chicago	USA	430,000	Reformed Theological Seminary, Jackson, MS	USA	181,964
Southwestern Baptist Theological Seminary, Fort Worth	USA	420,010	Iliff School of Theology, Denver, CO	USA	181,457
Yale University Divinity School, New Haven	USA	415,810	Biola/Talbot Theological Seminary, La Mirada, CA	USA	180,000
Facultés Dominicaines, Soissy-sur-Seine	France	400,000	Diozesanbibliothek Aachen	Germany	180,000
Pontificia Universita S Tommaso d'Aquino (Dominican), Rome	Italy	395,000	Makerere University, Kampala	Uganda	180,000
ITC Atlanta University Center	USA	384,350	Universidad Javeriana-Facultades Eclesiaticas, Bogota	Colombia	180,000
Graduate Theological Union, Berkeley	USA	382,530	Vanderbilt University Divinity School, Nashville	USA	168,729
Pontificio Ateneo Antonianum (OFM), Rome	Italy	380,000	Claremont School of Theology, Claremont, CA	USA	167,726
US Library of Congress (religion holdings), Washington, DC	USA	370,000	Grand Seminaire de Montreal	Canada	165,000
Southern Baptist Theological Seminary, Louisville	USA	361,710	Pontificia Facolta Teologica Marianum, Rome	Italy	165,000
St Johns University School of Theology, Collegeville	USA	359,710	Gordon-Conwell Theological Seminary, South Hamilton, MA	USA	163,588
Bischofliche-Theologische Hochschule, Eichstatt	Germany	350,000	Seminario Vescovile di Novara	Italy	160,000
Institut Catholique de Toulouse	France	350,000	Society of Friends Library, London	Britain	160,000
Pontificia Universita Urbaniana, Vatican City	Holy See	350,000	Chung Chi College, Shatin, Hong Kong	China	160,000
Andrews University (SDA), Berrien Springs, MI	USA	340,000	Dallas Theological Seminary, Texas	USA	158,023
Erzbischofliche Akademische, Paderborn	Germany	320,000	Christian Theological Seminary, Indianapolis	USA	151,126
Duke University Divinity School, Durham, NC	USA	308,030	Austin Presbyterian Theological Seminary, Austin, TX	USA	150,114
Catholic University of America, Washington, DC	USA	307,220	Grand Seminaire de Nancy	France	150,000
Garrett Evangelical/Seabury/United Library, Evanston	USA	303,410	Concordia Theological Seminary, Fort Wayne, IN	USA	149,769
Bollandists Library (saints, martyrs), Brussels	Belgium	300,000	Denver Conservative Baptist Seminary	USA	140,875
Union Theological Seminary, Richmond, VA	USA	295,630	Humboldt-Universitat Theologischer Institut, Berlin	Germany	140,000
Bischofliches Priesterseminars Mainz	Germany	290,000	Dr Williams' Library (Nonconformity), London	Britain	140,000
Colgate Rochester Divinity School, Rochester	USA	283,490	Christ the King Seminary, East Aurora, NY	USA	138,997
Jesuit Faculté de Théologie, Lyon	France	280,000	Collegio Alberoni (Vincentians), Piacenza	Italy	138,000
St Vincent College, Latrobe, PA	USA	280,000	Moore Theological College Library, Sydney	Australia	135,700
San Francisco Theological Seminary (PCUSA)	USA	280,000	Joint Theological Library, Parkville	Australia	135,000
Episcopal Divinity/Weston Jesuit Sch of Theology, Cambridge, MA	USA	277,174	Boston University School of Theology	USA	131,000
University of Notre Dame, IN	USA	273,907	Tokyo Union Theological Seminary	Japan	131,000
Perkins School of Theology, Dallas	USA	270,900	Doshisha University, Nishijin, Kyoto	Japan	130,000
Erzbischofliche Diozesan-Bibliothek, Cologne	Germany	270,000	Columbia Theological Seminary, Decatur, GA	USA	126,293
Facultés Catholiques de Lyon	France	270,000	Oral Roberts University, Tulsa, OK	USA	120,111
Pacific School of Religion, Berkeley, CA	USA	265,000			
Groot Seminarie 's-Hertogenbosch	Netherlands	250,000	Total USA & Canada libraries with over 50,000 volumes		**135**
Theologische Fakultat Trier	Germany	250,000	**Global total all Christian libraries with over 50,000 volumes**		**400**

4 MILLION BOOKS ABOUT CHRISTIANITY

Christian literature worldwide—books, encyclopedias, atlases, dictionaries, reports, surveys, articles, devotional material, and so forth—is vast and growing rapidly. A few examples will suffice to demonstrate this fact. The largest Christian library in the world is the Vatican Library (Biblioteca Apostolica Vaticana) in Vatican City, Rome. It contains 35% of the whole world's different books on Christianity—1,600,000 printed books, 150,000 manuscript volumes, 8,300 incunabula (ancient manuscripts), and also a database of 773,470 records accessible anywhere in the world via Telnet. Next come major theological libraries at universities and divinity schools. The largest in America is that of Union Theological Seminary, New York, with 700,000 books. The Regenstein Library at the University of Chicago has 600,000 in its theological holdings; Harvard University's Andover-Harvard Divinity Library holds 500,000 items; and Yale University's Divinity Library over 400,000 items. The holdings of several major free-standing seminary libraries approach similar levels: Princeton Theological Seminary's Speer Library holds 475,000 items, Union Theological Seminary (Richmond) and Presbyterian School of Christian Education's Morton Library 295,000 items, and Fuller Theological Seminary's McAlister Library has 220,000 items. This present survey estimates the grand total of all books primarily on Christianity and religion to have now reached 4,510,000 distinct and different titles in some 2,000 different languages. Each year sees an additional 110,000 new titles published. From all these, this Encyclopedia has selected and included here the bibliographical details listing the 8,500 most significant books for the main purpose of describing the whole phenomenon of empirical global Christianity.

Almost any attempt to grasp the full scope of this vast corpus of literature is bound to be incomplete, even if the attempt is simply to count titles. The researcher who sets out to accomplish even this most basic task quickly runs into at least 3 major obstacles. First, there exists to date no truly universal, international, comprehensive bibliographic database or catalogue on all subjects. Several very large computer databases do exist. Globally, the major one covering the sum total of all human knowledge on all subjects is OCLC (Online Computer Library Catalog or Center). Its Online Union Catalog lists 40 million titles growing by 2 million more each year. Begun in 1971, it now has 26,249 participating libraries in 64 countries around the world. It lists the physical locations of 652 million copies of books; and it has handled 79 million interlibrary loan requests. In addition to OCLC, several large universities run parallel but much smaller catalogues majoring on literature in either French, German, Spanish, Russian, Chinese, or Japanese.

While the number of titles immediately available through all of these is breathtaking, none encompasses all the literature in all the world on every subject. Moreover, they overlap to some extent, leaving the researcher the daunting task of correlating titles from the different major databases.

A second barrier to any attempt at a complete enumeration of world Christian literature is precisely this explosion of Christian literature around the world. In the past few decades Christian literature of all types—never in short supply—has begun to increase at a formidable rate, as indicated by title counts for all major Christian and religious themes in Table 13-2. It is reported that in the USA, in addition to the current 50,000 publishing houses utilizing the ISBN cataloging system, some 7,000 new publishers receive ISBN numbers each year. Of the books all these organizations publish, religious books form the single largest bloc with 11.3% of the total in 1997. Efforts have been made to track systematically the growth of this literature, though none is complete. The American Theological Library Association (ATLA) maintains a comprehensive bibliographic database, available in print and in electronic versions. The print versions appear as *Religion Index One: periodicals*, and *Religion Index Two: multi-author works*. The electronic version appears as *ATLA religion database on CD-ROM*. In addition, ATLA, through a consortium of member libraries, has compiled a two-volume index of non-Western Christian literature in North American libraries, the *International Christian literature documentation project*. This index, however, does not index literature in libraries in non-Western countries. Recently a group of ATLA member librarians has begun to explore the possibility of creating a more inclusive database of world Christian literature, to include literature from libraries outside North America. Meanwhile, the literature continues to outpace one's ability to track it. However, even the ATLA databases concentrate on academic works, leaving much devotional and evangelistic material unsurveyed and hence unquantified.

A third major problem, which would exist even if the first two could be overcome, is that a fair amount of Christian literature is published in some 5,000 languages remote from Western scholarship. Remote also from Western library networks, this vast literature is in the main locally catalogued but remains unknown in Europe and America. From tracts to translations, much literature for emerging Christian groups either does not find its way into libraries with wider circulation channels or it finds its way only into small libraries whose collections do not participate in larger cataloguing endeavors. In either case a sizable segment of the literature remains unreachable to all but the most persistent global bibliographer.

OVERVIEW OF BIBLIOGRAPHIES IN THIS ENCYCLOPEDIA

That said, it still remains possible to produce a meaningful overview of world Christian literature. In the present Encyclopedia, 5 types of literature selections are provided, as follows.

1. Global counts of titles

The first level of description is a simple count of titles. The figures in Tables 13-1, 13-2, and 13-4 provide this, derived from searches of the OCLC database. By entering discrete search terms from the Library of Congress subject index, exact indicators of the current scope of the literature emerged. The results of this inquiry, found in these 2 largest tables, contain many surprises. Important caveats remain, since OCLC does not yet catalog the contents of many major libraries outside the United States of America, especially those in the non-English speaking world. Nonetheless, it does provide a general idea of the immensity of Christian literature worldwide.

2. Country bibliographies

The second major description of world Christian literature lies in the bibliographies that follow all of the country surveys in Volume 1's Part 4 "Countries". Here the truly global nature of Christianity is illustrated through literature on Christianity and religion in every nation on the face of the globe.The grand total of all books in this category—those describing Christianity each in one single country—is 275,500. In the case of larger countries and countries whose populations are at least historically Christian, the literature dramatically outnumbers the space available for an adequate listing. Instead of attempting a complete cataloging, a selection of the most significant of the vast literature describing Christianity and religion in each country is provided here. In the case of smaller countries or those in which Christianity represents a small minority of the population, the bibliographies are more comprehensive, and in some cases are virtually complete. Indeed, there exists little or no Christian literature for several areas of the world, a clue to the still-great need for such descriptive writing.

Two aspects of the country bibliographies bear highlighting. First, the size of the bibliographic selection for each country corresponds very approximately to the population of the country, at least up to a point. A rule of thumb has been used of a minimum of one entry per 500,000 population, and/or its Christian population, resulting in a maximum for most countries of around 50 entries. Some countries have warranted exceptions to these rules. The bibliographies for many small countries, such as Brunei, with a population of about 285,000, exceed the minimum number of entries, since slavish adherence to the rule of thumb would result in unnecessarily brief bibliographies. Conversely, the bibliographies of many larger countries, in particular China and the United States of America, exceed the usual maximum since their literature is so vast. The second notable aspect of these bibliographies is that most contain works about the religious situation in general as well as about Christianity in each country, with emphasis on descriptive works. Here one finds studies utilizing history, sociology, anthropology, statistics, and other descriptive methodologies that provide a starting point for in depth study of the situation facing the church as it seeks to live out its calling.

3. Topical bibliographies

The third major type of selection of world Christian literature lies in the bibliographies that follow 9 of the 15 distinct Parts in the Encyclopedia. These bibliographies all deal with different areas of Christian activity and point the careful reader to other sources of similar information or to sources of methodology used in the sections. They help to substantiate both the present methodologies and the conclusions of this research.

Table 13-4. Bibliographical sources and resources by country: the number of significant books each describing a single country's empirical state of Christianity and related religion, for the world's 238 countries in AD 2000.

Among the main sources for the data on all countries in this Encyclopedia are the 4.5 million books on Christianity and related religion enumerated in Table 13-2 and the 275,500 books on Christianity and related religion in individual single countries enumerated below. The meanings of the columns are as follows. **Column 1.** Name of country. **Column 2.** Total of all books (including, occasionally, reports, manuscripts, dissertations, major articles, audio and video materials) whose main subject as assessed by the US Library of Congress is *Christianity* (including *church-* and related religious elements) *within the country* shown. **Column 3.** Total bibliographical items listed country by country in this Encyclopedia's Volume 1, being a small selection of the most significant books describing the broader subject of *Christianity, religion, and religions* in the *country* indicated, i.e. the role and place of Christianity and religion, or one of its components, in the country's history and present situation. These titles' names are given in full in each country's bibliography after its text in the standardized articles in Part 4 "Countries". Those bibliographies also contain a small number of journal articles. The reader wishing to consult the full bibliography on Christianity in a particular country (here enumerated in Column 2) can call up the complete titles on screen or in printout at any of the 28,000 OCLC-equipped major libraries across the world, using as here the search indicators 'country name' followed by 'Christian-' and/or 'church-'.

Country 1	Books 2	Part 4 3	Country 1	Books 2	Part 4 3	Country 1	Books 2	Part 4 3
Afghanistan	20	17	Germany	20,911	41	Oman	24	21
Albania	72	18	Ghana	373	57	Pakistan	258	54
Algeria	470	22	Gibraltar	12	10	Palau	22	5
American Samoa	10	5	Greece	3,186	25	Palestine	2,700	17
Andorra	9	6	Greenland	103	23	Panama	139	10
Angola	122	32	Grenada	20	13	Papua New Guinea	356	57
Anguilla	4	2	Guadeloupe	29	10	Paraguay	249	19
Antarctica	15	17	Guam	12	5	Peru	1,039	42
Antigua	10	9	Guatemala	628	50	Philippines	1,692	53
Argentina	1,001	46	Guinea	561	7	Pitcairn Islands	12	8
Armenia	501	31	Guinea-Bissau	40	20	Poland	3,716	57
Aruba	6	5	Guyana	63	16	Portugal	1,151	29
Australia	3,195	61	Haiti	325	37	Puerto Rico	381	40
Austria	2,185	25	Holy See	31,636	16	Qatar	10	7
Azerbaijan	18	6	Honduras	177	16	Reunion	18	14
Bahamas	45	17	Hungary	1,551	39	Romania	1,622	39
Bahrain	10	7	Iceland	141	17	Russia	3,421	83
Bangladesh	68	40	India	5,141	121	Rwanda	120	40
Barbados	62	21	Indonesia	1,262	73	Sahara	12	11
Belgium	1,594	17	Iran	212	40	St Helena	25	3
Belize	27	20	Iraq	271	24	St Kitts & Nevis	15	10
Belorussia	97	10	Ireland	6,604	35	St Lucia	13	12
Benin	60	17	Isle of Man	30	12	St Pierre & Miquelon	2	1
Bermuda	43	3	Israel	4,100	38	St Vincent & Grenadines	10	8
Bhutan	20	16	Italy	16,618	25	Samoa	54	20
Bolivia	392	32	Ivory Coast	40	25	San Marino	13	2
Bosnia-Herzegovina	50	37	Jamaica	276	36	Sao Tome & Principe	11	9
Botswana	52	34	Japan	3,157	72	Saudi Arabia	28	26
Bougainville	5	7	Jordan	138	8	Senegal	44	38
Brazil	3,280	57	Kazakhstan	20	9	Seychelles	12	9
Britain	18,527	88	Kenya	651	49	Sierra Leone	122	33
British Indian Oc Terr	3	2	Kirghizia	10	7	Singapore	180	49
British Virgin Islands	12	9	Kiribati	12	10	Slovakia	227	33
Brunei	12	10	Kuwait	20	12	Slovenia	267	36
Bulgaria	768	25	Laos	36	27	Solomon Islands	103	27
Burkina Faso	41	35	Latvia	130	18	Somalia	20	17
Burundi	55	23	Lebanon	560	41	Somaliland	6	8
Cambodia	29	12	Lesotho	72	22	South Africa	2,626	91
Cameroon	291	47	Liberia	248	24	South Korea	845	51
Canada	5,856	56	Libya	11	14	Spain	7,716	51
Cape Verde	28	15	Liechtenstein	6	5	Spanish North Africa	5	4
Cayman Islands	5	4	Lithuania	355	22	Sri Lanka	249	45
Central African Republic	40	14	Luxembourg	71	8	Sudan	230	49
Chad	24	8	Macedonia	218	34	Suriname	25	24
Channel Islands	30	2	Madagascar	212	36	Svalbard & Jan Mayen Is	2	2
Chile	1,160	40	Malawi	192	31	Swaziland	53	22
China	4,645	148	Malaysia	218	58	Sweden	2,025	24
Christmas Island	2	2	Maldives	8	7	Switzerland	2,738	33
Cocos (Keeling) Is	5	3	Mali	20	18	Syria	340	29
Colombia	910	44	Malta	137	16	Taiwan	404	46
Comoros	10	7	Marshall Islands	15	7	Tajikistan	8	7
Congo-Brazzaville	34	18	Martinique	18	10	Tanzania	341	43
Congo-Zaïre	1,011	52	Mauritania	17	14	Thailand	283	57
Cook Islands	9	7	Mauritius	58	26	Timor	29	27
Costa Rica	223	24	Mayotte	7	6	Togo	41	22
Croatia	512	41	Mexico	6,891	54	Tokelau Islands	8	7
Cuba	441	34	Micronesia	43	17	Tonga	121	22
Cyprus	212	19	Moldavia	45	3	Trinidad & Tobago	49	39
Czech Republic	708	31	Monaco	15	12	Tunisia	65	27
Denmark	1,773	24	Mongolia	29	25	Turkey	1,338	37
Djibouti	10	8	Montserrat	15	10	Turkmenistan	15	14
Dominica	14	6	Morocco	43	40	Turks & Caicos Islands	2	2
Dominican Republic	253	34	Mozambique	164	30	Tuvalu	10	9
Ecuador	1,021	22	Myanmar	241	48	Uganda	357	51
Egypt	1,211	51	Namibia	195	27	Ukraine	1,360	43
El Salvador	430	22	Nauru	3	3	United Arab Emirates	18	15
Equatorial Guinea	20	18	Nepal	45	70	USA	41,948	119
Eritrea	10	9	Netherlands	3,973	39	Uruguay	219	22
Estonia	105	21	Netherlands Antilles	17	14	Uzbekistan	15	14
Ethiopia	553	43	New Caledonia	30	16	Vanuatu	90	22
Faeroe Islands	20	14	New Zealand	658	35	Venezuela	498	34
Falkland Islands	16	12	Nicaragua	578	35	Viet Nam	110	35
Fiji	83	40	Niger	32	19	Virgin Islands of the US	17	16
Finland	662	32	Nigeria	1,403	85	Wallis & Futuna Islands	8	1
France	19,811	47	Niue Island	11	10	Yemen	26	24
French Guiana	10	4	Norfolk Island	8	7	Yugoslavia	769	38
French Polynesia	33	17	North Korea	150	19	Zambia	198	44
Gabon	38	27	Northern Cyprus	10	5	Zimbabwe	310	46
Gambia	18	14	Northern Mariana Is	2	1			
Georgia	11	9	Norway	1,213	34	**Total for all countries**	**275,506**	**6,286**

4. A world bibliography of Christian directories
This 500-title listing, in Part 14 "Directory", lists the various types of directories available to assist readers to navigate this immense resource.

5. A world bibliography of Christianity and religion
The last major type of selection of world Christian literature is the *Selective world bibliography of Christianity and religion* that immediately follows this essay. In this more comprehensive bibliography an attempt has been made to provide the reader with listings of significant works on several major areas of study of Christianity and religion. This bibliography consists, in the main, of multi-volume works such as commentaries, reference works, and so forth. In some cases single-volume works are listed, including dictionaries, lexicons, etymologies, biographies, chronologies, bibliographies, bibliographies of bibliographies, and other works that are both highly comprehensive and widely acclaimed as standard works in their field.

DESCRIBING THE WORLD BIBLIOGRAPHY

This largest bibliography of the 4 varieties of bibliograhpies is here divided into 3 main sections, as follows.

A. Christianity and Christian literature. The first main section of the world bibliography deals exclusively with Christianity and its literature. It is divided into 10 smaller lists. The first list includes works detailing the contemporary status of Christianity around the world. Here one will find works on topics such as major confessional groups, ethnolinguistics, and other areas that describe the state of Christianity today. These titles should guide the careful reader to consider the prospects and possibilities the church faces as it seeks to carry out its mission.

The second list includes major works in the field of biblical studies. Major commentaries, dictionaries, encyclopedias, and bibliographies make up the works here. Attention should be drawn to the vast resources devoted to serious research with regard to the Bible.

The third list includes major collections, encyclo-

World's largest Christian library. The Vatican Apostolic Library, in Rome, holds 1.6 million books (35% of all 4.5 million extant titles). *Top.* Main hall. *Left.* Reading room at related missions library. *Right.* Missions librarian Willi Henkel explains a research procedure to pope John Paul II.

Table 13-5. **Overview of major subjects, contents, and number of books listed as the 1,380 titles selected here for the Selective World Bibliography of Christianity and Religion.**

I. CHRISTIANITY (777)

1. Contemporary status of Christianity (86)
2. Biblical studies (123)
3. Church history (98)
4. History of doctrine (63)
5. Theology (133)
6. Theological ethics (38)
7. Missiology (53)
8. Ecumenism (24)
9. Esthetics (70)
   Architecture (5)
   Art (33)
   Liturgy (11)
   Spirituality (14)
10. Science and religion (37)
11. World religions (52)

II. NON-CHRISTIAN CONTEXT (249)

1. Islam (56)
2. Judaism (39)
3. Hinduism (16; Sikhism 6)
4. Buddhism (25)
5. Other religions (83; Baha'i 1, Confucianism 2, Jainism 10, Native American religion 2, New Religions 10, Occultism 4, Spiritism 1, Taoism 2, Zoroastrianism 1).
6. Interfaith dialogue (30)

III. APPROACHES TO THE STUDY OF RELIGION (122)

1. General methodologies (13)
2. Philosophy of religion (22)
3. History of religion (9)
4. Sociology of religion (35)
5. Anthropology of religion (5)
6. Psychology of religion (15)
7. Religious ethics (12)
8. Other approaches (11; Mythology 1, Numerology 2, Ritual 1, Semeiology 1).

IV. ELECTRONIC MEDIA (19)

V. BIBLIOGRAPHIES (215)

pedias, and dictionaries in church history. It includes studies and reference works in the field of church history, but not works that are themselves the subject of historical study.

The fourth list focuses on the history of doctrine. This list is distinct from the previous one in that it focuses on classical sources, rather than studies based on source materials The reader will find major works from the history of Christianity that have had the most significant impact on the development of Christian doctrine over the centuries through the post-World War II period. The placement of a number of 20th century works here does not imply that these works are out of date; rather, it represents a judgment that they are works of such enduring importance that theologians will have to take account of them for decades, perhaps even for centuries to come.

The fifth list includes major reference works and collections dealing with contemporary theology. Works included in this list concentrate on the major works in areas of theological work from approximately the past 30 to 40 years. Included in this list are works that could constitute a wide variety of bibliographies. Indeed, one would rarely expect to find Carl Henry's *God, revelation, and authority* on the same list as Rosemary Radford Reuther's *Sexism and God–talk*. However, to split this particular list into its half-dozen or so possible sub-lists would have been pedantic.

The sixth list highlights theological ethics. The seventh list deals with works related to the study of mission, missions, missiology, and mission work. Works here focus on major histories of mission, methodologies, and reference works. The eighth list treats ecumenism. This list includes the major documents of

ecumenical movements in the last hundred or so years, major studies of these movements, and reference works that focus on ecumenism.

The ninth list is perhaps the broadest in scope. It deals with major reference works related to Christianity and art, architecture, spirituality, liturgy, and so forth. This list focuses on what could be called the esthetic or experiential elements of Christianity. The final list of this Part deals with the relationship of science and religion, and in particular, of science and Christianity. This is a major development and a most illuminating one.

B. The non-Christian religious context. The second main section of the world bibliography highlights the non-Christian religious context in which Christianity is situated. This section is divided into 6 lists. Lists 1 through 4 deal with 4 other world religions: Islam, Hinduism, Buddhism, and also Judaism as the closest to Christianity through the shared Old Testament.

List 5 deals with other religions, and List 6 with interfaith dialogue. The aim here is to provide reading lists for non-specialists who wish to find definitive sources of information on religions with which Christianity interacts. In each list one will find not only major reference works about each religion, but also major works from within those religions, including historical and theological works by authors who practice them. The present attempt is to point the reader not only to descriptive works, but also to places where one may encounter devoted practitioners of these religions, and thus meet the religions on their own terms.

C. Approaches to the study of religion. The third main section of the world bibliography briefly examines a variety of methodological approaches to the study of religion and religions, including Christianity. Here the reader will find works describing or outlining methodologies used to study religion in general and Christianity in particular. This section attempts to provide a sense of the variety of methodological tools available to contemporary researchers and scholars. Inclusion of sources and methodologies does not imply either endorsement or indictment, but rather is an indication of the variety of tools that currently exists to study religion and religious phenomena, as well as the serious attention that religion receives. The range of approaches to the study of religion indicates, among other things, that the study of religion is not limited to one or two highly specialized disciplines, but can be profitably approached by almost any field of research. This range of approaches also points to the fact that religion can be—and is—studied from both the 'outside' as well as from 'within'. That is, some approaches lend themselves to a view of religion that does not assume the truth of any particular religion's claims. Other approaches, meanwhile, assume that the researcher believes the claims of the religion studied. Indeed, debate among scholars rages over the relationship between religious studies, as it exists primarily in Western colleges and universities, and theological studies. In general, religious studies indicate approaches that seek to apply scientific and social scientific methods to the study of religion as a phenomenon, while theological studies indicate approaches that seek to explicate the faith itself. Even this distinction does not do justice to the reality of the situation, however, for a number of prominent scholars disagree on the precise difference between the two. Suffice it to say that concern with methodology has occupied, and is likely to occupy for some time, the attention of serious students of religion and religions.

While a complete taxonomy of approaches to the study of religion is not necessary for this encyclopedia's purposes, some of the major contemporary and historic approaches to the study of religion have been placed in context. List 1 presents general works on methodology. Often these are general reference works or major textbooks that seek to orient students to the study of religion. List 2 presents works on the philosophy of religion. List 3 contains works that study religion from a historical perspective; List 4 highlights works in the sociology of religion; List 5 the anthropology of religion, List 6 the psychology of religion; and List 7 presents works that study religious ethics. Lastly, List 8 presents works that study other approaches to the study of religions and religious phenomena.

The last 2 sections of this world bibliography contain invaluable tools. First is a list that includes major resources found in electronic media, such as CD-ROM and online resources. This is perhaps the least definitive list of all, for not only is the number of resources on electronic media growing rapidly but also the variety of electronic media continues to proliferate. It is entirely possible that between the time the present work goes to press and its actual appearance in print, quite new media will have come to market. Given these possibilities, the purpose in this list is not to be even remotely complete, but simply to point the reader to a rapidly growing area of publication that will increasingly affect the study of Christianity and religion.

The final list here is a bibliography of bibliographies that touch on the previous 4 major listings. It is a formidable tool indeed.

THE IMPACT OF THESE MATERIALS

Doubtless many will be surprised at the findings of this bibliographical investigation. Agnostics or others who remain skeptical of the Christian movement—its size, its impact, its claims—will find it difficult to believe that such a 'minor' or 'outdated' religious movement could generate so many titles, let alone so much serious attention. And even if skeptics accept the size of the literature, they will question its quality and its scholarship. To these, the bibliographies in this Encyclopedia are an invitation to explore the world of Christian literature before attempting overall or definitive judgments. Even if un-

convinced by the normative claims of Christianity, one can at least begin to appreciate both the seriousness with which Christians approach the faith, as well as the quality of much of the work that grows out of it.

Others will no doubt simply feel overwhelmed by the extent of the literature. Even those who are already widely read may feel that they have barely touched upon the wealth of information on Christianity. To these, the bibliographies in the Encyclopedia are both a challenge and an aid. They challenge Christians to discover for themselves the rich variety of Christian literature beyond the comfortable limits of their accustomed reading. They aid Christians by providing some sense of how this vast collection may be organized and by pointing to some of the major works in the various fields. Hopefully readers of various stripes will think twice before dismissing persons and movements whose approaches and commitments are different from their own.

Still others may simply abandon any such efforts to expand their knowledge. Seeing that one person cannot possibly master even a portion of the works that may be relevant to their fields, they may deem it a waste of time to wade through the literature. Regrettably this is precisely the reaction that decision-makers are most likely to have. Christian mission executives are no exception at this point. Overwhelmed with the demands on their time, often lacking adequate human and financial resources, and facing a massive undertaking with endless deadlines, they simply do not have the time (so they would say) to engage all the literature relevant to the missionary enterprise. The unfortunate result is poorly focused efforts that waste valuable resources. To these, the bibliographies in the Encyclopedia are likewise a challenge. They challenge leaders to face boldly the vast horizons of Christian scholarship and to utilize the mass of research to provide them with invaluable guidance in fulfilling the Great Commission. Too much is at stake and too many resources are available to waste.

The problem, then, is how to make sense of the mass of resources available. Therein lies the key to understanding the purpose of these bibliographies in the Encyclopedia. In a word, they attempt to create order out of chaos.

ORGANIZING PRINCIPLES EMPLOYED

As has been mentioned, these bibliographies do not claim to be exhaustive. Nor do they claim to cover all the most important literature in its entirety. As bibliographies, they are selective. They are meant, above all, to be illustrative. That is, they seek to highlight the vastness of world Christian literature. Their purpose is to point the careful reader to other sources of similar information. They also serve to document and substantiate the data, events, statements, measurements, analysis, concepts, findings, conclusions, and claims described in the Encyclopedia's 15 Parts and especially in its country articles in Part 4.

Any single bibliographical entry in an English-language bibliography of books consists of up to 16 standard components: its title; a subtitle if present; sometimes a translation into English if a non-English title; additional explanatory title of any series or event or collection that explains the main title; names of authors, editors, and translators; year of publication; edition (if second, third, etc. is significant); number of volumes if more than one; titles and other details of component volumes; main title's number of pages if useful to substantiate length; name of publisher; city or place of publication, with country if necessary for clarity; and lastly, brief note or annotation in parentheses in cases where there is additional valuable information relevant for the purposes of the listing.

There are a number of different purposes varying from one type of bibliography to another. They can be organized on any one of the 16 different components based on which of them the author wants to put first.

The most common order used in presenting information begins with the author's name, organized alphabetically by surname and initials. This is useful for shorter bibliographies or for audiences who know the names of many or most of the significant authors on the subject. This method is less helpful in larger bibliographies or for those where most readers would

not be familiar with authors' names or significance. Other recognized forms are organized chronologically by year of publication, or by author with his or her works arranged chronologically. This is most helpful when most authors listed have multiple entries.

Another popular form is not to organize the entries into a list by any single component, but instead to write a reasonably short bibliographical essay mentioning the 10, 20, 30, or 40 major books on the subject being considered.

The procedure followed here is different in that most readers will not be familiar with authors' names, so lengthy listings of works by author mean little or nothing. For such readers, the most important component is the title, so it helps them most to make this the first item in every entry. This Encyclopedia therefore follows, in all its bibliographies, the practice of listing works alphabetically by title. Since these listings are computerized and automated, alphabetization follows strict rules including recognition of the definite and indefinite articles (The, A, An). Thus, *A Baptist bibliography* precedes *Acta sanctorum quotquot toto orbe coluntur.*

Another rule followed here throughout in English titles is to abandon the long-standing and widespread practice of artificially capitalizing all, or most, of the words in titles. Instead, we capitalize only names, titles, proper nouns, or adjectives referring to organizations. The most immediate beneficiary of this policy is the clearing up of ambiguities surrounding key words like 'church', 'gospel', 'evangelical', 'charismatic', and so on, which can employ either initial capitals or initial lowercase letters and thereby convey different meanings.

SUMMARY

These bibliographies, then, both complement and extend further the rest of the research in the Encyclopedia. They complement the other materials by providing the reader with further sources of information for verification and ongoing study. They extend the research to the extent that they represent a part of the data on world Christianity. In fact, they point beyond themselves to incredible wealth of accumulated knowledge on Christianity and religion in a whole variety of aspects. One can find other, more comprehensive bibliographies on almost any topic in the Encyclopedia; many of them are listed here. The overall bibliographies given here are unique in the range of topics covered under one cover. They aim to leave the reader without excuse for willful ignorance of the resources available for understanding the Christian phenomenon or the place of Christianity in the world. One need not become familiar with all of the 8,500 or so titles here to make good use of the knowledge they contain. Indeed, no one can. However, judicious use of these bibliographies can pay enormous dividends in terms of knowledge, as well as in terms of a more effective stewardship of resources in Christian mission and ministry. To the extent that these bibliographies assist the reader in developing greater understanding of Christianity in its world context, they achieve their purpose.

Selective world bibliography of Christianity and religion

I. CHRISTIANITY

1. CONTEMPORARY STATUS OF CHRISTIANITY

A critical guide to Catholic reference books. J. P. McCabe. 3rd ed. Englewood, CO: Libraries Unlimited, 1989. 337p.

A dictionary of Greek Orthodoxy. N. D. Patrinacos. Pleasantville, NY: Hellenic Heritage Publications, 1984. 391p.

A guide to the study of the Pentecostal movement. C. E. Jones. *ATLA Bibliographic Series,* 6. Metuchen, NJ and London: American Theological Library Association and Scarecrow Press, 1983. 1,245p in 2 vols. (Dated, but an important bibliography of the Pentecostal movement).

An international directory of theological schools 1997. A. Gilmore (ed). London: SCM Press; Geneva: WCC Publications, 1996. 512p.

Annuario pontificio 1997. Vatican City: Libreria Editrice Vaticana, 1997. 2,490p.

Annuarium statisticum ecclesiae 1994 (Statistical yearbook of the church 1994). Vatican City: Secretaria Status, 1994. 449p.

Atlas hierarchicus: descriptio geographica et statistica ecclesiae catholicae tum occidentis tum orientis. H. Emmerich. Mödling, Austria: St Gabriel–Verlag, 1968 (76p.), 1976, (107p. plus maps); 5th edition 1992 (118p. plus maps. ed. Z. Stezycki) 1976. 107p. (Contemporary survey of all Roman Catholic jurisdictions; in French, English, German, Italian, and Spanish).

Atlas of religious change in America, 1952–1990. P. L. Halvorson & W. M. Newman. Atlanta: Glenmary Research Center, 1994. 236p.

Atlas zur Kirchengeschichte: Die Christlichen in Geschichte und Gegenwart. H. Jedin, K. S. Latourette & J. Martin (eds). Freiburg im Breisgau: Herder, 1987. 190p.

Bilan du monde: encyclopédie catholique du monde chrétien. J. Frisque et al. (eds). 2nd ed. Louvain: Casterman, 1964. 2 vols.

Catholic encyclopedia. New York: McGraw-Hill, 1967–1989. 18 vols. (International reference work on the constitution, doctrine, discipline and history of the Catholic church).

Charismatic Christianity as a global culture. K. Poewe (ed). *Studies in comparative religion.* Columbia, SC: University of South Carolina Press, 1994. 316p.

Chinese churches handbook. G. Law. Hong Kong: Chinese Coordination Centre of World Evangelism, 1982. 378p.

Christianity and democracy: a theology for a just world order. J. W. de Gruchy. *Cambridge studies in ideology and religion,* 7. New York and Cambridge, UK: Cambridge University Press, 1995. 308p.

Constitutions of the countries of the world. A. P. Blaustein & G. H. Flanz. Dobbs Ferry, NY: Oceana Publications, 1971–. 17 vols; (Updated texts, chronologies, bibliographies; deals with constitutional status of Christianity and religion).

Corpus dictionary of Western Churches. T. C. O'Brien (ed). Washington, DC: Corpus Publications, 1970. 820p. (Primarily Roman Catholic).

Death of the church. M. Regele. Grand Rapids, MI: Zondervan, 1995.

Defenders of God: the fundamentalist revolt against the modern age. B. B. Lawrence. San Francisco: Harper & Row, 1989. 318p. (Fundamentalist movements in several religions, including Christianity, Judaism, and Islam.).

Enciclopedia cattolica. Città del Vaticano: Enciclopedia Cattolica, 1948–54. 12 vols.

Enciclopedia ecclesiastica. A. Bernareggi. Milan: F. Vallardi, 1942–63. 7 vols.

Encyclopedia of Methodism. M. Simpson. New York: Gordon Press, 1977. 2 vols.

Encyclopedia of modern Christian missions: the agencies. B. L. Goddard (ed). Camden, NJ: T. Nelson, 1967. 762p.

Encyclopedia of Southern Baptists. Nashville, TN: Broadman, 1958. 2 vols. (All Baptist denominations and movements).

Encyclopedia of the Lutheran Church. J. Bodensieck (ed). Minneapolis, MN: Augsburg, 1965. 3 vols.

Encyclopedia of the Reformed faith. D. F. McKim & D. F. Wright (eds). Louisville, KY: Westminster John Knox; Edinburgh: Saint Andrew, 1992. 438p.

Encyclopedia of world Methodism. N. B. Harmon (ed). Nashville, TN: United Methodist Publishing House, 1974. 2 vols.

Encyclopedic dictionary of religion. C. M. Aherne, T. C. O'Brien & P. K. Meagher (eds). Palatine, IL: Corpus, 1977. 3 vols. (Primarily Roman Catholic).

Encyclopédie du protestantisme. P. Gisel (ed). Paris: Cerf; Geneva: Labor et Fides, 1995. 1,700p.

Encyklopedia katolicka. F. Gryglewicz, R. Lukaszyk & Z. Sulowski (eds). Lublin, Poland: Catholic University, 1973–. (Polish; multivolume).

Ethnologue: languages of the world. B. F. Grimes (ed). 13th ed. Dallas: Summer Institute of Linguistics, 1996. 1,391p in 3 vols. (Current data on 6,703 languages, including status of scripture translation. Vols. 2 and 3 are indexes of language names and language families).

Fire from heaven: the rise of Pentecostal spirituality and the reshaping of religion in the twenty–first century. H. Cox. Reading, MA: Addison–Wesley, 1995. 339p.

Guida delle missioni cattoliche. Vatican City: SC Propaganda, 1975. 1,628p. (Earlier editions 1934, 1946, 1950, 1970).

Handbook of denominations in America. F. S. Mead & S. S. Hill. 10th ed. Nashville, TN: Abingdon, 1995. 352p.

Handbuch der Ostkirchenkunde. E. von Ivánka, J. Tyciak & P. Wiertz (eds). 2nd ed. Düsseldorf: Patmos, 1990–93. 3 vols. (Best overall reference work on Eastern churches).

Handbuch der Pfingstbewegung. W. J. Hollenweger. Geneva, 1965–67. 10 vols. (Duplicated; University Microfilms and ATLA Microtext Project).

Iglesias de Oriente (Churches of the East). A. S. Hernández. Santander: Editorial Sal Terrae, 1959–63. 2 vols. (Includes annotated bibliography of 2,250 items).

Kleines Wörterbuch des christlichen Orients. J. Assfalg & P. Krüger. Wiesbaden: Harrassowitz, 1975. 493p. (Translated into French as *Petit dictionnaire de l'Orient chrétien.* Turnhout: Brepols, 1991).

Les Ordres religieux: Guide historique. G. Duchet-Sachaux & M. Duchet-Sachaux. Paris: Flammarion, 1993. 320p.

Les Ordres religieux: La Vie et l'art. G. Le Bras (ed). Paris: Flammarion, 1979–80. 1,525p. in 2 vols.

Let the earth hear his voice: a comprehensive reference volume on world evangelization. J. D. Douglas. Minneapolis, MN: World Wide Publications, 1975. 1,471p. (International Congress on World Evangelization, Lausanne 1974).

Lexikon der christlicher Kirchen und Sekten. J. Gründler. Vienna: Herder, 1961. 2 vols. (History and description of all denominations).

Lexikon für Theologie und Kirche. W. Kasper (ed). 3rd ed. Freiburg: Herder, 1993–. 4 vols.; in progress to 10 vols.

Lutheran cyclopedia. E. L. Lueker (ed). St. Louis, MO: Concordia, 1954. 1,160p.

Modern American religion. M. E. Marty. Chicago: University of Chicago Press, 1986–1996. 3 vols.

New Catholic encyclopedia. Washington, DC: Catholic University of America, 1967. 15 vols.

Operation world: a handbook for world intercession. P. J. Johnstone. Grand Rapids, MI: Zondervan, 1993. 666p. (1st edition 1974, 208p).

Opus Dei: who, how, why. G. Romano. Trans., E. C. Lane. New York: Alba House, 1995. 207p.

Oriente cattolico: cenni storici e statistiche. 4th ed. Vatican City: S. C. per le Chiese Orientali, 1974. 857p.

Pentecostalism: origins and developments worldwide. W. J. Hollenweger. Peabody, USA: Hendrickson, 1997. 495p.

Prime–time religion: an encyclopedia of religious broadcasting. J. G. Melton, P. C. Lucas & J. R. Stone. Phoenix, AZ: Oryx, 1997. 432p.

Profiles in belief: the religious bodies of the United States and Canada. A. C. Piepkorn. New York: Harper & Row, 1977–79. 4 vols in 3.

Puebla and beyond: documentation and commentary. J. Eagleson & P. Scharper (eds). Trans., J. Drury. Maryknoll, NY: Orbis Books, 1979. 383p.

Reimagining denominationalism: interpretive essays. R. B. Mullin & R. E. Richey (eds). *Religion in America series.* New York: Oxford University Press, 1994. 336p.

'Religion,' in *Propaedia* of *New Encyclopaedia Britannica,* p.498–559. Chicago: Encyclopaedia Britannica, 1975.

Scriptures of the world: a compilation of the 2,018 languages in which at least one book of the Bible has been published since the Bible was first printed by Johann Gutenberg. L. Lupas & E. F. Rhodes (eds). New York and Reading, UK: United Bible Societies, 1992. 145p.

Sekai kirisuto–kyo hyakka–jiten (Encyclopedia of world Christianity). M. Takenaka et al. (eds). Tokyo: Kyobunkwan, 1986. (Japanese translation of the first edition of the *World Christian encyclopedia*).

Selective bibliography on evangelism and evangelization. D. B. Barrett. Nairobi: Centre for the Study of World Evangelization, 1980. (1,400 items).

Seventh–day Adventist encyclopedia. D. F. Neufeld (ed). Washington, DC: Review & Herald, 1966–76. 10 vols.

Six hundred ecumenical consultations 1948–1982. A. J. van der Bent. Geneva: World Council of Churches, 1983. 254p.

'The Anglican world in figures,' D. B. Barrett & T. de Bordenave III, London: Anglican Frontier Missions, 1998. 4p. (Prepared for Lambeth Conference 1998).

The book of a thousand tongues. E. A. Nida (ed). 2nd ed. London: United Bible Societies, 1972. 536p. (Catalogue of 1,399 languages with printed scriptures, giving a scripture passage for each).

The challenge of basic Christian communities. S. Torres & J. Eagleson (eds). Maryknoll, NY: Orbis, 1982.

The charismatic movement: a guide to the study of neo–pentecostalism with emphasis on Anglo–American sources. C. E. Jones. *ATLA Bibliographic Series,* 30. Metuchen, NJ and London: American Theological Library Association and Scarecrow Press, 1995. 1,266p in 2 vols. (A major bibliography of the charismatic movement).

The Christian churches of the East. D. Attwater. London: Geoffrey Chapman, 1961. 2 vols.

The Christian conspiracy: how the teachings of Christ have been altered by Christians. L. D. Moore. Atlanta: Pendulum Plus Press, 1994. 357p.

The Eastern Christian churches: a brief survey. R. G. Roberson. 3rd ed. Rome: Pontificum Studiorum Orientalium, 1990. 129p.

The fundamentalism project. M. E. Marty & R. S. Appleby (eds). Chicago: University of Chicago Press, 1991–96. 5 vols. (Vol. 1: *Fundamentalisms observed*; vol. 2: *Fundamentalisms and the state*; vol. 3: *Fundamentalisms and society*; vol. 4: *Accounting for fundamentalisms*; vol. 5: *Fundamentalisms comprehended.* A cross–religious study).

The gospel in a pluralist society. L. Newbigin. Grand Rapids, MI: Eerdmans, 1989.

The HarperCollins encyclopedia of Catholicism. R. P. McBrien (ed). San Francisco: Harper, 1995. 1,387p.

The index of leading spiritual indicators: trends in morality, beliefs, lifestyles, religious and spiritual thought, behavior, and church involvement. G. Barna. Dallas: Word, 1996. 160p.

The Latvian Orthodox church. Protopresbyter Alexander Cherney. Welshpool, Wales, UK: Stylite Publishing, 1985. 143p.

The Mennonite encyclopedia: a comprehensive reference work on the Anabaptist–Mennonite movement. Scottdale, PA: Mennonite Publishing House, 1955–59. 4 vols.

The modern Catholic encyclopedia. M. Glazier & M. Hellwig (eds). London: Gill & Macmillan; Collegeville, MN: Liturgical Press, 1994. 958p.

The new Catholic encyclopedia. W. J. McDonald (ed). New York: McGraw-Hill, 1967. 15 vols.

The Orthodox Church. T. Ware. 2nd ed. London: Penguin, 1983. 352p.

The Orthodox Church in the Ecumenical Movement: documents and statements 1902–1975. C. G. Patelos (ed). Geneva: World Council of Churches, 1978. 360p.

The revenge of God: the resurgence of Islam, Christianity and Judaism in the modern world. G. Kepel. University Park, PA: Pennsylvania State University Press, 1994. 215p. (Translated by A. Braley from *La Revanche de Dieu*).

The sociology of Protestantism. R. Mehl. Trans., J. H. Farley. London: SCM Press, 1970. 336p.

The world year book of religion: the religious situation. D. R. Cutler (ed). London: Evans Brothers, 1968–69.

Théo: L'Encyclopédie catholique pour tous. M. Dubost (ed). Paris: Droguet–Ardant/Fayard, 1993.

Turning over a new leaf: Protestant missions and the Orthodox churches of the Middle East: the final report of a multi–mission study group on Orthodoxy. London: Interserve, 1992. 134p. (Promotes Protestant and Orthodox cooperation).

Twentieth–century religious thought: the frontiers of philosophy and theology, 1900–1960. J. Macquarrie. New York: Harper & Row, 1963. 415p.

Weltkirchenlexikon. F. H. Littell & H. H. Walz (eds). *Handbuch der Ökumene im Auftrag des Deutschen Evangelischen.* Stuttgart: Kreuz–Verlag, 1960.

World Christian encyclopedia: a comparative survey of churches and religions in the modern world, AD 1900–2000. D. B. Barrett (ed). Nairobi: Oxford University Press, 1982. 1,025p.

World Christian handbook. E. J. Bingle, K. G. Grubb & H. W. Coxill (eds). 5th ed. London: Lutterworth, 1967. (Statistics).

Yearbook of the Orthodox Church, 1978. Munich: Verlag Alex Proc, 1978. 309p. (Annual on Eastern Orthodox jurisdictions worldwide, alternately published in English, French, and German).

2. BIBLICAL STUDIES

A bibliography of New Testament bibliographies. J. C. Hurd. New York: Seabury, 1966. (1,300 articles and books).

A concordance to the Greek Testament. W. F. Moulton & A. S. Geden. 5th ed. Edinburgh: T. & T. Clark, 1978. 1,126p.

A decade of Bible bibliography. Oxford, UK: Blackwell, 1967. (Covers 1957–66).

A dictionary of Biblical interpretation. R. J. Coggins & J. L. Houlden (eds). London: SCM; New York: Trinity Press International, 1990. 765p.

A dictionary of Biblical tradition in English literature. D. L. Jeffrey (ed). Grand Rapids, MI: Eerdmans, 1992. 992p.

A dictionary of the Bible. W. R. F. Browning. Oxford, UK and New York: Oxford University Press, 1996. 438p.

A Greek–English lexicon of the New Testament and other early Christian literature. W. Bauer, W. F. Arndt, F. W. Gingrich. 2nd ed. Chicago: University of Chicago Press, 1979. 940p.

Almanac of the Bible. G. Wigoder, S. M. Paul & B. T. Vivian (eds). Jerusalem: Jerusalem Publishing House; New York: Henry Holt, 1991. 448p.

An introduction to New Testament Christology. R. E. Brown. New York: Paulist Press, 1994. 238p.

Analytical concordance to the Bible. R. Young. 22nd ed. 1881; New York: Funk & Wagnalls, 1955. 1,257p. (Coded to dictionary of original Hebrew/Greek terms; 311,000 references).

Atlas of the Bible. L. H. Grollenberg. Trans., J. M. H. Reid & H. H. Rowley. New York and London: Nelson, 1956. 166p. (Originally published as *Atlas van de Bijbel,* Amsterdam: Elsevier).

Austieg und Niedergang der römischen Welt: Geschichte Roms im Spiegel der neueren Forschung. II. Principat. W. Haase & H. Temporini (eds). Berlin and New York: de Gruyter, 1982–1988. 4,794p. (Vols. 25.1 through 25.6 of 80 volumes).

Baker encyclopedia of Bible places. J. Bimson (ed). Grand Rapids, MI: Baker, 1995.

Bible bibliography, 1967–73. P. R. Ackroyd (ed). Oxford, UK: Blackwell, 1975. (Works in nearly 20 languages).

Biblia Patristica: index des citations et allusions bibliques dans la littérature patristique. Paris: CNRS, 1975–80. 3 vols. (27,000 references; computerized).

Biblical resources for ministry: a bibliography of works in biblical studies. D. R. Bauer. 2nd ed. Nappanee, IN: Evangel, 1995. 144p.

Biblical theology of the Old and New Testaments. B. Childs. Minneapolis, MN: Fortress, 1992.

Bibliographie de la Septante: (1970–1993). (Bibliography of the Septuagint). C. Dogniez. *Supplements to Vetus Testamentum,* 60. Leiden and New York: E. J. Brill, 1995. 361p.

Bibliographies for biblical research. W. E. Mills (ed). Lewiston, NY: E. Mellen Press, 1993–1996. 6 vols.

Bibliography of literature on First Peter. A. Casurella. *New Testament tools and studies,* 23. Leiden and New York: E. J. Brill, 1996. 178p.

Bibliography of New Testament literature, 1900–1950. T. Akaishi (ed). San Anselmo, CA: Seminary Cooperative Store, 1953. 312p. (2,400 annotated items).

Catalogue of English Bible translations: a classified bibliography of versions and editions including books, parts, and Old and New Testament Apocrypha and Apocryphal books. W. J. Chamberlin. *Bibliographies and indexes in religious stud-*

ies, 21. New York: Greenwood, 1991. 946p. (The best and most complete for its listing of English Bible translations, 9,000 titles and editions).

Comentario biblico de Collegeville. Collegeville, MN: The Liturgical Press.

Commentaries. J. Calvin. Grand Rapids, MI: Baker. 22 vols.

Das Alte Testament Deutsch. G. von Rad et al. (eds). Göttingen: Vandenhoeck & Ruprecht, 1949–66. 25 vols.

Das Neue Testament Deutsch. G. Friedrich (ed). Göttingen: Vandenhoeck & Ruprecht, 1960–68. 4 vols.

Dictionary of Christ and the Gospels. J. Hastings. New York: Scribner, 1906–1908. 2 vols.

Dictionary of Jesus and the Gospels. J. B. Green & S. McKnight (eds). Downers Grove, IL and Leicester, UK: InterVarsity, 1992. 959p.

Dictionary of Paul and his letters. G. Hawthorne & R. P. Martin (eds). Downers Grove, IL and Leicester, UK: InterVarsity, 1993. 1,067p.

Dictionary of the Bible. F. C. Grant & H. H. Rowley (eds). New York: Scribner, 1963. 1,059p.

Dictionary of the Bible. J. Hastings. Edinburgh: T. & T. Clark, 1898–1904. 5 vols.

Dictionnaire de la Bible: supplément. L. Pirot (ed). Paris: Letouzey et Ané, 1928–. 12 vols. to date.

Elenchus bibliographicus biblicus. P. Nober. Rome: Biblical Institute, 1970. (Annual).

Eleven years of Bible bibliography: the book lists of the Society for Old Testament study, 1946–56. H. H. Rowley (ed). Indian Hill, CO: Falcon's Wing, 1957. 804p.

Encyclopaedia biblica: thesaurus rerum biblicarum alphabetico ordine digestus. Hierosolymis: Instituti Bialik, 1950–.

Encyclopaedia of biblical theology. J. B. Bauer. London: Sheed & Ward, 1970. 3 vols. (Translation of 1959 *Bibeltheologisches Wörterbuch*).

Encyclopedia biblica. T. K. Cheyne & J. S. Black. New York: Gordon Press Publications, 1977. 4 vols.

Encyclopedia of archaeological excavations in the Holy Land. Stern. N.p., 1995. 4 vols.

Encyclopedia of Bible difficulties. G. J. Archer Jr. Grand Rapids, MI: Zondervan, 1982. 352p.

Encyclopedia of Biblical errancy. C. D. McKinsey. Buffalo, NY: Prometheus Books, 1995. 553p.

Encyclopedia of biblical interpretation: a millenial anthology. M. M. Kasher & H. Freedman (eds). New York: American Biblical Encyclopedia Society, 1953–79. 9 vols. (Jewish biblical interpretations from Talmudic–Midrashic literature).

Encyclopedia of Biblical personalities: Ishei haTanach. Y. Chasidah. Brooklyn, NY: Mesorah Publications, 1994.

Encyclopedia of Biblical prophecy: the complete guide to scriptural predictions and their fulfillment. J. B. Payne. Grand Rapids, MI: Baker, 1996. 779p.

Encyclopedic dictionary of the Bible. L. F. Hartman (ed). New York: McGraw–Hill, 1963. 2,600p.

Etudes bibliques. Paris: Lethielleux. (Commentary series).

Evangelical dictionary of biblical theology. W. A. Elwell (ed). Grand Rapids, MI: Baker, 1996.

Exhaustive concordance of the Bible. J. Strong. London: Hodder, 1894. 1,807p. (Every work of KJ (AV), RV Bibles).

Handbook of Biblical criticism. R. N. Soulen. 2nd ed. Atlanta: John Knox, 1981. 239p.

Harper's Bible commentary. J. L. Mays (ed). San Francisco: Harper, 1988. 1,344p. (2nd ed. in preparation).

Hermeneia: a critical and historical commentary on the Bible. Minneapolis, MN: Fortress Press. (Aims to present most complete surveys of research on each book of the Bible).

Hermeneutika BibleWorks 3.5 on CD–ROM.

Historical catalogue of printed editions of the English Bible, 1525–1961. A. S. Herbert. London: BFBS, 1968. (Lists 2,525 distinct editions of the Bible or parts of it).

Illustrated dictionary and concordance of the Bible. G. Wigoder (ed). Jerusalem: Jerusalem Publishing House; New York: Macmillan, 1986. 1,070p.

Index of articles on the New Testament and the early church. B. M. Metzger. Philadelphia: Society of Biblical Literature, 1951. 182p. (Indexes 2,350 articles).

International critical commentary on the Holy Scriptures. S. R. Driver, A. Plummer & C. A. Briggs (eds). Edinburgh: T. & T. Clark, 1896–1937. 45 vols. (Commentary series).

Internationale Zeitschriftenschau für Bibelwissenschaft und Grenzgebiete. Stuttgart: Verlag Katholisches Bibelwerk, bienniel since 1952. (Mostly German abstracts).

Interpretation: a Bible commentary for teaching and preaching. J. L. Mays et al. (eds). Louisville, KY: Westminster John Knox, 1986–. 36 vols. to date. (A series designed to bring scholarly work to bear on practical tasks of ministry).

Journal for the study of the Old Testament supplement series. Sheffield, UK: JSOT Press. 269 vols. to date.

Konkordanz zum hebräischen Alten Testament. G. Lisowsky. Stuttgart: Privilegierte Württembergische Bibelanstalt, 1958. 1,672p.

Kritisch–Exegetischer Kommentar über das Neue Testament. H. A. W. Meyer. Göttingen: Vandenhoeck & Ruprecht, 1856–1859. 7 vols.

La concordance de la Bible: concordantia polyglotta. Turnhout, Belgium: Brepols, 1980. 5 vols. (First complete Bible concordance in French with Hebrew, Greek, Latin, and English parallels).

Life applications Bible commentary. Wheaton, IL: Tyndale House.

Literary currents in Biblical interpretation. D. Fewell & D. M. Gunn (eds). Louisville, KY: Westminster John Knox, 1990–1995. 14 vols.

Mercer dictionary of the Bible. W. E. Mills (ed). Macon, GA: Mercer University Press, 1990. 1,023p. (Published in Britain as *The Lutterworth Dictionary of the Bible.* Cambridge, UK: Lutterworth, 1990).

Models for interpretation of scripture. J. Goldingay. Grand Rapids, MI: Eerdmans; Carlisle PA: Paternoster Press, 1995. 338p.

Modern New Testament concordance. M. Darton (ed). London: Darton, Longman & Todd, 1976. (Words and 341 themes, for all modern English versions).

Moffatt New Testament commentary. J. Moffatt (ed). New York: Harper, 1927–50. 17 vols.

Moody Gospel commentary. Chicago: Moody Press.

Multipurpose tools for Bible study. F. W. Danker. 4th ed. Minneapolis, MN: Fortress, 1993.

Nelson's complete concordance of the Revised Standard Version. J. W. Ellison (ed). New York: Thomas Nelson, 1957.

New American commentary. Nashville, TN: Broadman & Holman.

New Bible commentary: 21st century edition. D. A. Carson et al. (eds). 4th ed. Leicester, UK and Downers Grove, IL: InterVarsity, 1994. 1,468p.

New Bible dictionary. D. R. W. Wood (ed). 3rd ed. Downers Grove, IL: InterVarsity, 1996. 1,318p.

New international dictionary of New Testament theology. C. Brown (ed). Grand Rapids, MI: Zondervan, 1975–78. 3 vols. (Articles on NT Greek words).

New Testament abstracts. Weston, MA: Theological Faculty, Weston College, 1956–. (Issued 3 times a year; abstracts in English from articles in many languages).

New Testament tools and studies. B. M. Metzger (ed). Leiden: E. J. Brill, 1966–80. Vol I: *Index to periodical literature on the Apostle Paul.* Vol VI: *Index to periodical literature on Christ and the Gospels* (10,090 entries). Vol VII: *A classified bibligraphy of literature on the Acts of the Apostles* (6,645 entries). Vol X: *Philological, versional and patristic.*

NIV application commentary. Grand Rapids, MI: Zondervan.

Old testament abstracts on CD–ROM. Washington, DC: The Catholic Biblical Association; Evanston, IL: American Theological Library Association, annual since 1995.

Orbis biblicus et orientalis. Göttingen: Vandenhoeck & Ruprecht. 158 vols. to date.

Society of Biblical Literature dissertation series. Atlanta: Scholar's Press. 161 vols. to date.

Society of Biblical Literature monograph series. Atlanta: Scholar's Press. 49 vols. to date.

Society of Biblical Literature writings from the ancient world series. Atlanta: Scholar's Press. 5 vols. to date.

Soncino books of the Bible. London and New York: Soncino Press, 1945–51. 13 vols.

Supplements to "Vetus testamentum". Leiden: E. J. Brill. 70 vols. to date.

Table pastorale de la Bible. G. Passelecq & F. Poswick (eds). Paris: Lethielleux, 1974. 1,214p. (Over 9,000 articles on words and themes).

Thayer's Greek–English lexicon of the New Testament: a dictionary numerically coded to Strong's exhaustive concordance. J. H. Thayer. Nashville, TN: Broadman, 1977. 752p.

The Anchor Bible. Garden City, NY: Doubleday, 1964–. In progress to 38 vols. (Commentary series).

The Anchor Bible dictionary. D. N. Freedman et al. (eds). New York: Doubleday, 1992. 6 vols.

The Bible book: resources for reading the New Testament. E. Hort. New York: Crossroad, 1983. (A somewhat dated layperson's guide to the tools for biblical studies).

The book of Ephesians: an annotated bibliography. W. W. Klein. *Books of the Bible, 8; Garland reference library of the humanities*, 1,466. New York: Garland, 1996. 335p.

The book of Jeremiah: an annotated bibliography. H. O. Thompson. *ATLA bibliography series*, 41. Lanham, MD: Scarecrow Press, 1996. 777p.

The book of Psalms: an annotated bibliography. T. Wittstruck. *Books of the Bible, 5; Garland reference library of the humanities*, 1,413. New York: Garland, 1994. 2 vols.

The book of Revelation: an annotated bibliography. R. L. Muse. *Books of the Bible, 2; Garland reference library of the humanities*, 1,387. New York: Garland, 1996. 388p.

The books of the Bible. B. W. Anderson (ed). New York: Scribner, 1989. 2 vols., 879p.

The Cambridge companion to the Bible. H. C. Kee et al. Cambridge, UK: Cambridge University Press, 1997. 624p.

The Cambridge history of the Bible. P. R. Ackroyd and C. F. Evans (vol. 1), G. W. Lampe (vol. 2), S. L. Greenslade (vol. 3) (eds). Cambridge, UK: Cambridge University Press, 1963–70. 3 vols.

The computer Bible. J. A. Baird & D. N. Freedman (eds). Wooster, OH: Biblical Research Associates, Vols I–XV, 1975–78. (Word frequencies, concordances, indexes, using KWIC; computerization to make immediately available massive amounts of critical data).

The dictionary of Bible and religion. W. H. Gentz (ed). Nashville, TN: Abingdon Press, 1986. 1,147p.

The early versions of the New Testament. B. M. Metzger. Oxford, UK: Oxford University Press, 1977. (Origin, transmission, manuscripts, printed editions, for all versions up to AD 1000).

The Eerdmans Bible dictionary. A. C. Myers (ed). Grand Rapids, MI: Eerdmans, 1987. 1,103p. (Translated and updated from *Bijbelse encyclopedie.* W. H. Gispen (ed). Kampen: Kok, 1975).

The Englishman's Greek concordance of the New Testament numerically coded to Strong's exhaustive concordance. G. V. Wigram. Nashville, TN: Broadman, 1979. 1,174p.

The HarperCollins Bible dictionary. P. J. Achtemeier et al. (eds). 2nd ed. San Francisco: Harper, 1996. 1,280p.

The international standard Bible encyclopedia. G. W. Bromiley (ed). 3rd ed. Grand Rapids, MI: Eerdmans, 1979–1988. 4 vols., 4,466p.

The interpreter's Bible. G. A. Buttrick (ed). New York: Abingdon, 1951–57. 12 vols. (Exegesis and exposition of entire Bible).

The interpreter's dictionary of the Bible: an illustrated encyclopedia. G. A. Buttrick (ed). New York: Abingdon, 1962. 4 vols., with 1976 supplementary volume.

The IVP New Testament commentary series. Downers Grove, IL: InterVarsity.

The new international commentary on the New Testament. Grand Rapids, MI: Eerdmans, 1953–. 27 vols. to date.

The new international commentary on the Old Testament. Grand Rapids, MI: Eerdmans, 1965–. 15 vols. to date.

The new interpreter's Bible. Nashville, TN: Abingdon Press, 1994–. 6 vols. to date.

The new Jerome Biblical commentary. R. E. Brown S.S., J. A. Fitzmyer S.J. & R. E. Murphy O.Carm (eds). Englewood Cliffs, NJ: Prentice-Hall, 1990; London: Geoffrey Chapman, 1989; paperback, 1993.

The Old Testament library. P. R. Ackroyd et al. (eds). Louisville, KY: Westminster John Knox, 1961–. 48 vols.

The Oxford companion to the Bible. B. M. Metzger & M. D. Coogan (eds). New York and Oxford, UK: Oxford University Press, 1993. 933p.

The Schocken Bible, Vol. I: The five books of Moses. E. Fox. New York: Schocken, 1995. 1,056p.

Theological dictionary of the New Testament. G. Kittel et al. (eds). Trans., G. W. Bromiley. Grand Rapids, MI: Eerdmans, 1963–74. 9 vols. (Translation from German, *Theologisches Wörterbuch zum Neuen Testament*).

Theological dictionary of the New Testament: abridged in one volume. G. Kittel & G. Friedrich (eds). Trans., G. Bromiley. Grand Rapids, MI: Eerdmans; Devon, UK: Paternoster Press, 1985. 1392p.

Theologisches Wörterbuch zum Alten Testament. G. J. Botterweck & H. Ringgren. Stuttgart: W. Kohlhammer. (English edition by Eerdmans).

Tyndale Old Testament Commentaries. D. J. Wiseman (ed). Leicester, UK and Downers Grove, IL: InterVarsity, 1964–. 26 vols.

Understanding the Old Testament. B. W. Anderson. 4th ed. Englewood Cliffs, NJ: Prentice–Hall, 1986.

Westminster Bible companion. P. D. Miller & D. L. Bartlett (eds). Louisville, KY: Westminster John Knox, 1995–. 13 vols. to date. (A commentary for lay persons, designed as a replacement series to *The laymen's Bible commentary*).

What is postmodern biblical criticism? A. K. M. Adam. *Guides to biblical scholarship, New Testament series.* Minneapolis, MN: Fortress, 1995. 95p.

Who's who in the New Testament. R. Brownrigg. 1971; reprint, New York: Oxford University Press, 1993. 448p.

Who's who in the Old Testament together with Apocrypha. J. Comay. 1971; reprint, New York: Oxford University Press, 1993. 448p.

Word Biblical commentaries. D. A. Hubbard & G. W. Barker (eds). Waco, TX: Word, 1982–. 52 vols.

3. CHURCH HISTORY

A Baptist bibliography: being a register of printed material by and about Baptists, including works written against the Baptists. E. C. Starr. Rochester, NY: American Baptist Historical Society, 1947–76. 25 vols.

A dictionary of Christian biography. H. Wace & W. C. Piercy (eds). 1911; reprint, Peabody, MA: Hendrickson, 1994. 1,040p.

A documentary history of religion in America. E. S. Gaustad. Grand Rapids, MI: Eerdmans, 1982–83. 2 vols.

A history of Black Baptists. L. Fitts. Nashville, TN: Broadman, 1985. 368p.

A history of Christianity. K. S. Latourette. London: Eyre & Spottiswoode; New York: Harper & Row, 1953. 2 vols., 1,544p. (A classic of missions history.).

A history of Christianity in Asia. S. H. Moffett. New York: HarperCollins, 1991–. 2 vols. (Vol. 2 expected, 1999).

A history of the expansion of Christianity. K. S. Latourette. New York: Harper, 1937–45. 7 vols.

A religious history of the American people. S. E. Ahlstrom. New Haven, CT: Yale University Press, 1972. 1,174p. (A classic text on the history of Christianity and other religions in the United States).

A violent evangelism: the political and religious conquest of the Americas. L. N. Rivera. Louisville, KY: Westminster John Knox, 1992.

Acta sanctorum quotquot toto orbe coluntur. Paris: Palmé, 1863–1940. 85 vols. (The indispensable research work on the lives of the saints).

American Christianity: an historical interpretation with representative documents. H. S. Smith, R. T. Handy & L. A. Loetscher. New York: Scribner, 1960–63. 2 vols.

Analecta Bollandiana. Brussels: Société des Bollandistes, 1882–. (Quarterly; current bibliography on lives of saints).

Archiv für Reformationsgeschichte. N.p., 1903–.

Atlas of the crusades. J. Riley–Smith (ed). New York: Facts on File, 1990.

Atlas of the early Christian world. F. van der Meer & C. Mohrmann. Trans. and ed., M. F. Hedlund & H. H. Rowley. London: T. Nelson, 1958. 216p. (620 plates, 42 maps; first 6 centuries AD).

Backgrounds of early Christianity. E. Ferguson. 2nd ed. Grand Rapids, MI: Eerdmans, 1993. 631p.

Bibliographie de cartographie ecclésiastique. J. N. B. van den Brink et al. (eds). Leiden: E. J. Brill, Commission International d'Histoire Ecclésiastique Comparée, 1968–.

Bibliographie de la Réforme, 1450–1648. J. N. B. van den Brink et al. (eds). Leiden: E. J. Brill, 1958–70. 7 vols. (Covers 17 European countries plus U.S.).

Bibliography of published articles on American Presbyterianism, 1901–1980. H. M. Parker. *Bibliographies and indexes in religious studies*, 4. Westport, CT: Greenwood, 1985. 272p.

Bibliotheca Sanctorum. Rome: Città Nuova, 1987–91. 13 vols. (Dictionary of saints; originally published 1961–70).

Bishops at large: some autocephalous churches of the past hundred years and their founders. P. F. Anson. London: Faber and Faber, 1964. 593p.

Black evangelists: the spread of Christianity in Uganda, 1891–1914. M. L. Pirouet. London: Rex Collings, 1978. 269p.

Black religions in the New World. G. E. Simpson. New York: Columbia University Press, 1978. 429p.

Butler's lives of patron saints. M. Walsh (ed). San Francisco:

Harper & Row, 1987. 492p.

Butler's lives of the saints: complete edition. H. Thurston S.J. [1856–1939] & D. Attwater [1892–1977] (eds). London: Burns & Oates; Westminster, MD: Christian Classics, 1956; reprint, 1966. 2,900p.

Catholisme: hier—aujord'hui—demain. G. Jacquemet, G. Mathon & G. Baudry (eds). Paris: Letouzey & Ané, 1948–. 14 vols., 2 fasc. to date; in process to 15 vols. (Covers European Catholicism).

Christendom: the Christian churches, their doctrines, constitutional forms and ways of worship. E. Molland. London: A. R. Mowbray, 1959. 432p.

Christianity: the first two thousand years. D. L. Edwards. Maryknoll, NY: Orbis Books, 1997.

Church history: an introduction to research, reference works, and methods. J. E. Bradley & R. A. Muller. Grand Rapids, MI: Eerdmans, 1995. 252p.

Civilization of the ancient Mediterranean: Greece and Rome. M. Grant & R. Kitzinger (eds). New York: Scribner, 1988. 3 vols.

Coptic Egypt. B. Watterson. Edinburgh: Scotish Academy Press, 1988. 197p.

Cross and sword: an eyewitness history of Christianity in Latin America. H. M. Goodpasture (ed). Maryknoll, NY: Orbis, 1989.

Diccionario de historia eclesiástica. Madrid: Instituto Superior de Investigaciones Cientificas. 4 vols.

Dictionary of Catholic biography. J. J. Delaney & J. E. Tobin. Garden City, NY: Doubleday, 1961. 1,245p. (Biographies of 15,000 Catholics from beginning to 1961).

Dictionary of Christian biography, literature, sects, and doctrines. W. Smith & H. Wace. London: Murray, 1877–87. 4 vols. (Especially English, Scottish, and Irish church history; subjects to the end of the 8th century AD).

Dictionary of pentecostal and charismatic movements. S. M. Burgess & G. B. McGee (eds). Grand Rapids, MI: Zondervan, 1988. 927p. (A new edition, *The new international dictionary of Pentecostal and Charismatic movements*, Stanley Burgess, ed., forthcoming in AD 2000).

Dictionary of the Apostolic church. J. Hastings. New York: Scribner, 1916. 2 vols.

Dictionary of the Middle Ages. J. R. Strayer (ed). New York: Scribner, 1982–1989. 13 vols.

Dictionnaire de droit canonique, contant tous les termes du droit canonique. R. Nez (ed). Paris: Letouzey & Ané, 1935–65. 7 vols. (Canon law in the Catholic church).

Dictionnaire des ordres religieux. P. Hélyot. Paris: Migne, 1859–63. 4 vols.

Dictionnaire des philosophes antiques. R. Goulet (ed). Paris: CNRS, 1989–. 841p. in 1 vol. to date; in progress to 10 vols.

Dictionnaire d'histoire et de géographie ecclésiastiques. A. Baudrillart & R. Aubert (eds). Paris: Letouzey & Ané, 1912–. 24 vols. to date; fasc. 150, 1995.

Dictionnaire historique de la papauté. P. Levillain (ed). Paris: Fayard, 1994. 1,776p.

Die Religionen in Geschichte und Gegenwart: Handwörterbuch für Theologie und Religionswissenschaft. K. Galling (ed). 3rd ed. Tübingen: J. B. C. Mohr, 1986. 7 vols.

Dizionario patristico e di antichità cristiane. A. di Bernardino (ed). Casale Monferrato: Marietti, 1983. 2,320p. in 3 vols. (English and French translations appear under the respective titles, *Encyclopedia of the early church* and *Dictionnaire encyclopédique du christianisme ancien*).

Documents illustrative of the history of the church. B. J. Kidd. London: SPCK; New York: Macmillan, 1920–41. 3 vols. (From apostolic times to AD 1500).

Encyclopedia of African American religions. L. G. Murphy, J. G. Melton & G. L. Ward (eds). New York: Garland, 1993. 1,002p.

Encyclopedia of American Catholic history. M. Glazier. Ed., T. Shelly. Collegeville, MN: Liturgical Press, 1997.

Encyclopedia of American religions. J. G. Melton. 5th ed. Detroit, MI: Gale Research, 1996.

Encyclopedia of early Christianity. E. Ferguson (ed). 2nd ed. *Garland reference library of the humanities.* New York: Garland, 1997. 1,240p. in 2 vols.

Encyclopedia of German resistance to the Nazi movement. W. Benz & W. H. Pehle (eds). Del Mar, CA: Continuum, 1996. 360p.

Encyclopedia of heresies and heretics. C. S. Clifton. Santa Barbara, CA: ABC-CLIO, 1992.

Encyclopedia of the American religious experience. C. H. Lippy & P. W. Williams (eds). New York: Scribner, 1987. 1,888p. in 3 vols.

From federation to communion: the history of the Lutheran World Federation. J. H. Schørring et al. Minneapolis, MN: Fortress Press, 1997. 576p.

Fruit of the vine: a history of the Brethren, 1708–1995. D. F. Durnbaugh. N.p., 1996. 400p.

Great leaders of the Christian church. J. D. Woodbridge (ed). Chicago: Moody Press, 1988. 384p.

Handbook of denominations in America. F. S. Mead & S. S. Hill. 10th ed. Nashville, TN: Abingdon, 1995. 352p.

Histoire de l'Eglise depuis les origines jusqu'a nos jours. J. B. Duroselle & E. Jarry (eds). Paris: Bloud & Gay. 26 vols.

Histoire du Christianisme des origines à nos jours. J. M. Mayeur, L. Pietri, A. Vauchez & M. Venard. Paris: Desclée, 1995. 14 vols.

Historians of the Christian tradition: their methodology and influence on Western thought. M. Bauman & M. I. Klauber. Nashville, TN: Broadman & Holman, 1995. 637p.

Historical dictionary of Methodism. C. Yrigoyen Jr. & S. Warrick (eds). *Religions, philosophies, and movements series*, 8. N.p., 1996. 328p.

Historical dictionary of the Orthodox Church. M. Prokurat, A. Golitzin & M. D. Peterson. *Religions, philosophies, and movements series*, 9. N.p., 1996. 738p.

History of the Christian church. P. Schaff. New York: Scribner, 1889–1910. 7 vols.

Jehova's Witnesses: proclaimers of God's Kingdom. Brooklyn, NY: Watchtower Bible and Tract Society of New York and the International Bible Students Association, 1993. 750p.

Jesuiten–Lexikon: die Gesellschaft Jesu einst und jetzt. L. Koch S.J. (ed). 1934; Löwen: Bibliothek SJ, 1963. 939p.

Lexikon des Mittelalters. Munich and Zürich: Artemis, 1980–. 8 vols. to date; in progress to 10 vols.

Modern American Protestantism and its world. M. E. Marty (ed). Munich and New York: K. G. Sauer, 1992–1993. 14 vols.

New 20th–century encyclopedia of religious knowledge. J. D. Douglas (ed). Grand Rapids, MI: Baker, 1991. 912p.

Nouvelle histoire de l'Eglise. L. J. Rogier, R. Aubert & M. D. Knowles. Paris: Le Seuil, 1963–74. 5 vols.

Ostkirchliche Studien. Würzburg: Augustinus-Verlag, 1952–. (Quarterly. The best bibliographical source on the Eastern churches, with about 90 pages of bibliography each year).

Reallexikon für Antike und Christentum: Sachwörterbuch zur Auseinandersetzung des Christentums mit der antiken Welt. T. Klauser, E. Dassmann et al. (eds). Stuttgart: Hiersmann, 1941–. 17 vols. to date; in progress to 30 vols. (Relationship of the ancient world to Christianity to 6th century AD).

Revue d'histoire ecclésiastique. Louvain-la-Neuve: Université Catholique de Louvain. 1900-72, Vols 1-67; in progress.

Schaff–Herzog encyclopedia. S. M. Jackson. New York: Funk & Wagnalls, 1908 and 1912. 12 vols and index.

Taking the Word to the world: fifty years of the United Bible Societies. E. H. Robertson. Nashville, TN: T. Nelson, 1996. 350p.

The Archbishop Iakovos library of ecclesiastical and historical sources. Brookline, MA: Hellenic College Press.

The Blackwell dictionary of evangelical biography: 1730–1860. D. M. Lewis (ed). Oxford, UK and Cambridge, MA: Blackwell Reference, 1995. 2 vols., 1314p.

The Byzantine legacy in the Orthodox church. J. Meyendorff. Crestwood, NY: St. Vladimir's Seminary Press, 1982. 268p.

The Cambridge history of the Bible. P. R. Ackroyd and C. F. Evans (vol. 1), G. W. Lampe (vol. 2), S. L. Greenslade (vol. 3) (eds). Cambridge, UK: Cambridge University Press, 1963–70. 3 vols.

The concise dictionary of early Christianity. J. F. Kelly. Collegeville, MN: The Liturgical, 1992. 203p.

The concise dictionary of the Christian tradition: doctrine, liturgy, history. J. D. Douglas, W. A. Elwell & P. Toon (eds). Grand Rapids, MI: Zondervan, 1989. 419p.

The early church: an annotated bibliography of literature in English. T. A. Robinson & B. Shaw. *ATLA bibliography series*, 33. Metuchen, NJ: Scarecrow Press, 1993. 522p.

The encyclopedia of American religious history. E. Queen, S. R. Prothero & G. H. Shattuck. New York: Facts on File, 1996.

The encyclopedia of missions: descriptive, historical, biographical, statistical. O. Dwight, H. A. Tupper & E. M. Bliss (eds). 2nd ed. New York and London: Funk & Wagnalls, 1904; reprint, Detroit, MI: Gale Research, 1975. 865p.

The English Bible from KJV to NIV: a history and evaluation. J. P. Lewis. 2nd ed. Grand Rapids, MI: Baker, 1991. 512p.

The history of the popes, from the close of the Middle Ages. L. Pastor. Trans., F. I. Anthrobus et al. London: Hodges, 1891–1953. 40 vols. (Covers the period 1305–1799).

The Macmillan atlas history of Christianity. F. H. Littell. New York: Macmillan; London: Collier Macmillan, 1976. 196p.

The modern encyclopedia of religion in Russia and the Soviet Union. P. D. Steeves (ed). Gulf Breeze, FL: Academic International Press, 1988–. 5 vols.; in progress to 25 vols.

The new Cambridge medieval history. R. McKitterick (ed). Cambridge, UK: Cambridge University Press. 2 vols.

The new international dictionary of the Christian Church. J. D. Douglas (ed). Exeter, UK: Paternoster Press, 1978. 1,200p.; 5,000 articles.

The Oxford dictionary of Byzantium. A. P. Kashdan (ed). New York: Oxford University Press, 1991. 3 vols.

The Oxford dictionary of the Christian church. F. L. Cross & E. A. Livingstone (eds). 3rd ed. London: Oxford University Press, 1997. 1,823p. (Earlier editions, 1957, 1974, 1983; also an abridged version, *The Concise Oxford dictionary of the Christian Church*).

The Oxford dictionary of the Popes. J. N. D. Kelly. New York and Oxford, UK: Oxford University Press, 1986; paperback 1988. 361p.

The Oxford encyclopedia of the Reformation. H. J. Hillerbrand (ed). New York and Oxford, UK: Oxford University Press, 1996. 4 vols., 1,965p.

The Oxford illustrated history of Christianity. J. McManners (ed). Oxford, UK and New York: Oxford University Press, 1991; paperback, 1993. 736p.

The presence of God: a history of Western Christian mysticism. B. McGinn. New York: Crossroad, 1992–. 2 vols. to date; in planning to 4 vols.

The Westminster dictionary of church history. J. C. Brauer (ed). Philadelphia: Westminster Press, 1971. 899p.

Thriskeutiki kai Ithiki Egyklopaidia (Religious and ethical encyclopedia). Athens: A. Martinos, 1962–68. 12 vols. (Greece and Greek Orthodoxy).

Twentieth–century shapers of American popular religion. C. H. Lippy (ed). New York: Greenwood Press, 1989. 519p.

4. HISTORY OF DOCTRINE

A history of Christian doctrine. D. K. Bernard. Hazelwood, MO: Word Aflame Press, 1995–. 1 vol. to date. (Written from a Pentecostal perspective).

An essay on the development of Christian doctrine. John Henry Cardinal Newman. 6th ed. 1845; Notre Dame, IN: University of Notre Dame Press, 1989. 473p.

Ancient Christian writers: the works of the Fathers in translation. J. Quasten & W. J. Burghardt (eds). London: Longmans, Green, 1946–63. 31 vols.

Annotated bibliography of Luther studies, 1977–1983. K. Hagen. *Sixteenth century bibliography*, 24. St. Louis, MO: Center for Reformation Research, 1985. 91p.

Anselm of Canturbury. J. Hopkins & H. Richardson (eds). Toronto and New York: E. Mellen Press, 1974–76. 4 vols.

Ante–Nicene Fathers: translations of the writings of the Fathers down to AD 325. A. Roberts & J. Donaldson (eds). 1896–97; reprint, Grand Rapids: Eerdmans, 1956. 10 vols.

Archiv für Katholisches Kirchenrecht. 1857–1941; reprint, Leiden: E. J. Brill, 1973–75. 121 vols. (Germany, Austria, and Switzerland).

Archiv für Reformationsgeschichte. N.p., 1903–.

Augustinus–Lexikon. C. Mayer (ed). Basel: Schwabe, 1986–. 1 vol. to date; in progress to 7 vols. (Articles in German, French, and English discuss the life and thought of Augustine).

Bibliographia Calviniana, 1532–1899. D. A. Erichson. Nieuwkoop: De Graaf, 1950.

Bibliographia Patristica. W. Schneemelcher. Berlin: de Gruyter, 1959–65. 10 vols.

Brief introduction to the study of theology with reference to the scientific standpoint and the Catholic system (Kurze einleitung in das Studium der Theologie). J. S. Drey. Trans., M. J. Himes. 1819; Notre Dame, IN: University of Notre Dame Press, 1994. 220p.

Brief outline of the study of theology (Kurze Darstellung des theologischen Studiums). Friedrich Schleiermacher. 1811, 1830; Lewiston, NY: E. Mellen Press, 1990. 252p.

Bulletin de théologie ancienne et médiévale. Louvain: Abbey Mont César. in progress.

Calvin–Bibliographie, 1901–1959. W. Niesel. Munich: C. Kaiser, 1961. (Continuation of *Bibliographia Calviniana*).

Confessions. St. Augustine. Trans., H. Chadwick. Oxford, UK: Oxford University Press, 1991. 339p.

Creeds of the churches: a reader in Christian doctrine from the Bible to the present. J. H. Leith (ed). 3rd ed. Atlanta: John Knox Press, 1982. 746p.

De doctrina Christiana. St. Augustine. Trans. and ed., R. P. H. Greene. *Oxford early Christian texts.* Oxford, UK and New York: Clarendon, 1995.

Dialogues concerning natural religion. David Hume. *The Hafner library of classics.* 1779; New York: Hafner, Macmillan; London: Collier Macmillan, 1948. 113p.

Dictionnaire de théologie catholique. B. Loth & A. Michel (eds). Begun by Vacant & Mangenot, now E. Amann, 1909-50, 15 vols. Paris: Letouzey, 1951–72. 3 vols.

Dictionnaire de théologie catholique. A. Vacant, E. Mangenot & É. Amann (eds). Paris: Letouzey & Ané, 1909–50. 30 parts, 15 vols.

Dispensationalism. C. C. Ryrie. Rev. ed. 1965; Chicago: Moody, 1995. 224p.

Emil Brunner: a bibliography. M. G. McKim. *ATLA bibliographies*, 40. Lanham, MD: Scarecrow Press, 1996. 105p.

Encyclopaedia of religion and ethics. J. Hastings (ed). Edinburgh: T. & T. Clark; New York: Scribner, 1908–27. 12 vols.

Encyclopedia of heresies and heretics. C. S. Clifton. Santa Barbara, CA: ABC-CLIO, 1992.

Encyklopädie der katholischen Theologie und ihrer Hülfswissenschaften. H. J. Wertzer. Ed., F. Kaulen. Freiburg im Breisgau: Herder, 1882–1901. 12 vols. and index.

Fear and trembling; and sickness unto death. Søren Kierkegaard. Trans., W. Lowrie. 1843, 1849; Princeton, NJ: Princeton University Press, 1941, 1968. 278p.

Four anti-Pelagian writings: on nature and grace; on the procedings of Pelagius; on the predestination of the saints; on the gift of perseverence. St. Augustine. Trans., J. A. Mourant & W. J. Collinge. *The fathers of the church*, 86. Washington, DC: Catholic University Press, 1992. 370p.

God was in Christ: an essay on incarnation and atonement. D. M. Baillie. New York: Scribner, 1948. 230p.

Historians of the Christian tradition: their methodology and influence on Western thought. M. Bauman & M. I. Klauber. Nashville, TN: Broadman & Holman, 1995. 637p.

Institutes of the Christian religion. J. Calvin. Trans., F. L. Battles. *Library of Christian classics*, 20–21. Philadelphia: Westminster, 1960. 2 vols. (Annotated translation of the 1559 edition).

Library of early Christianity. W. A. Meeks (ed). Louisville, KY: Westminster John Knox, 1985–1987. 8 vols.

Loeb classical library. London: Heinemann, 1912–89. 488 vols. (Contains Greek and Latin texts and English translations on facing pages of the Greek and Latin classics).

Luther's works. J. Pelikan & H. T. Lehmann (eds). Philadelphia: Muhlenburg; St. Louis, MO: Concordia, 1971–. 56 vols. to date.

Medieval philosophers. J. Hackett (ed). Detroit, MI: Gale Research, 1992. 479p.

On religion: speeches to its cultured despisers. Friedrich Schleiermacher. Trans., R. Crouter. *Texts in German philosophy.* 1799; Cambridge, UK: Cambridge University Press, 1988. 243p. (Translation of *Über die Religion*).

On the unity of Christ. Saint Cyril, Patriarch of Alexandria. Trans., J. A. McGuckin. Crestwood, NY: St. Vladimir's Seminary Press, 1995.

On virginity. St. Ambrose. Toronto: Peregrinn, 1991. 65p.

Oxford early Christian texts. Oxford, UK and New York: Clarendon Press.

Patrologiae cursus completus, seu biblioteca universalis. J. P. Migne. Paris: Migne, 1844–80. 221 vols. (Latin and Greek fathers).

Protestant thought in the nineteenth century. C. Welch. New Haven, CT: Yale University Press, 1972–1985. 2 vols.

Realencyklopädie für protestantische Theologie und Kirche. J. J. Herzog. Leipzig, Hinrichs: Albert Hauck, 1896–1913. 24 vols.

Reformed dogmatics. L. Berkhof. Grand Rapids, MI: Eerdmans, 1932–37. 4 vols.

Religion within the limits of reason alone (Der Religion innerhalb der Grenzen der bloßen Vernunft). Immanuel Kant. Trans., T. M. Greene & H. H. Hudson. 1793; New York: Harper Torchbooks, 1960. 345p.

Saint Ambrose: theological and dogmatic works. St. Ambrose. Trans., R. J. Deferrari. *The fathers of the church*, 44. Washington, DC: Catholic University Press, 1963. 366p.

Sancti Ambrosii opera. St. Ambrose. Vindobonae, Pragae: F.

Tempsky, 1897–1990. 7 vols in 11 to date.
Select library of Nicene and post–Nicene Fathers of the Christian church. P. Schaff (ed). New York: Christian Literature Co., 1886–1900. 28 vols.
Sources chrétiennes. Paris: Éditions de Cerf, 1990–. 431 vols to date.
Systematic theology. L. Berkhof. 2nd ed. Grand Rapids, MI: Eerdmans, 1941. 759p.
Systematic theology. L. S. Chafer. Dallas, TX: Dallas Seminary Press, 1947–48. 8 vols.
The Christian faith (Glaubenslehre). Friedrich Schleiermacher. Ed., H. R. Mackintosh & J. S. Stewart. 1830; Edinburgh: T & T Clark, 1989. 772p.
The Christian tradition: a history of the development of doctrine. J. Pelikan. Chicago: University of Chicago Press, 1971–1989. 5 vols.
The complete works of John Wesley. T. Jackson (ed). Nashville, TN: Abingdon, 1856–62. 15 vols.
The creeds of Christendom: with a history and critical notes. 6th rev. ed. New York, London: Harper, 1919. 3 vols.
The fathers of the church. Washington, DC: Catholic University of America Press, 1947–. 96 vols to date.
The fundamentals: a testimony to the truth. A. C. Dixon, L. Meyer & R. A. Torrey (eds). Chicago: Testimony Publishing. 12 vols. of 128p. each. (These 12 little volumes were published as a reaction against the perceived threat of higher biblical criticism, and are the source of the term, "Fundamentalism").
The library of Christian classics. J. Baillie, J. T. McNeil & H. P. Van Dusen (eds). London: SCM Press; Philadelphia: Westminster, 1954–57. 26 vols. (A selection of important Christian treatises written before AD 1600).
The origins and development of African theology. G. H. Muzorewa. Maryknoll, NY: Orbis, 1985. 146p.
The summa theologica of St. Thomas Aquinas. London: Burns, Oates & Washbourne, 1964–72. 32 vols.
The works of Saint Augustine. St. Augustine. Ed., J. E. Rotelle. Brooklyn, NY: New City Press, 1990–. 16 vols to date.
What is Christianity? Adolph von Harnack. Trans., T. B. Saunders. *Fortress texts in modern theology.* 1900; Philadelphia: Fortress, 1957. 319p. (Translation of *Das Wesen des Christentums*).
Who's who in theology: from the first century to the present. J. Bowden. London: SCM Press, 1990; New York: Crossroad, 1992. 160p.
Women and religion: the original sourcebook of women in Christian thought. E. A. Clark & H. Richardson (eds). San Francisco: Harper, 1996. 399p.

5. THEOLOGY

A basic Christian theology. A. J. Conyers. Nashville, TN: Broadman & Holman, 1995.
A bibliography. K. Baago. *Library of Christian theology.* Madras: The Christian Literature Society, 1969. 110p. (A bibliography of theological works by Indian authors.).
A Black theology of liberation. J. Cone. 20th annniv. ed. 1970; Maryknoll, NY: Orbis, 1986, 1990. 236p.
A brief theology of revelation. C. Gunton. Edinburgh: T. & T. Clark, 1995. 144p.
A Catholic dictionary of theology. H. F. Davis et al. (eds). London: T. Nelson, 1962–1971. 3 vols. (A 4th volume was never published).
A handbook of Christian theologians. M. E. Marty & D. G. Peerman (eds). 2nd ed. Nashville: Abingdon, 1984. 735p.
A handbook of theological terms. V. A. Harvey. New York: Macmillan; London: Collier Macmillan, 1964. 253p.
A new handbook of Christian theology. D. W. Musser & J. L. Price (eds). Nashville, TN: Abingdon, 1992. 525p.
A preface to theology. W. C. Gilpin. Chicago: University of Chicago Press, 1996. 236p.
A theological book list. London: Theological Education Fund, 1960, 1965, 1968. (Comprehensive bibliographies on all subjects, with emphasis on works available for seminaries in developing countries; 3,000 entries).
A theology of liberation: history, politics and salvation. G. Gutiérrez. Trans. and ed., C. Inda & J. Eagleson. 15th anniv. ed. 1973; Maryknoll, NY: Orbis, 1988. 312p.
A theology of the Jewish–Christian reality. P. M. van Buren. 1980-87; Lanham, MD: University Press of America, 1995. 3 vols.
A theology primer. R. Neville. Albany, NY: State University of New York Press, 1991.
American religious creeds: an essential compendium of more than 450 statements of belief and doctrine. J. G. Melton (ed). 1988; New York: Triumph Books, 1991. 3 vols. (Texts of doctrinal documents of a wide variety of Christian and non–Christian religious groups in the U.S.).
Assurance of things hoped for: a theology of Christian faith. A. Dulles. New York: Oxford University Press, 1994.
Basic Christian doctrine. J. H. Leith. Louisville, KY: Westminster John Knox, 1993.
Beyond liberalism and fundamentalism: how modern and postmodern philosophy set the theological agenda. N. Murphy. Valley Forge, PA: Trinity Press International, 1996. 172p.
Bible doctrines: a Pentecostal perspective. W. W. Menzies & S. M. Horton. Springfield, MO: Logion Press, 1993.
Bibliography in contextual theology in Africa. J. R. Cochrane, I. W. Henderson & G. O. West (eds). Pietermaritzburg, South Africa: Cluster Publications, 1993–. 1 vol. to date.
Bilanz der Theology im 20 Jahrhundert. H. Vorgrimler & R. Van der Gucht (eds). Freiburg im Breisgau: Herder, 1970. 3 vols.
Blessed rage for order. D. Tracy. 1975; Chicago: University of Chicago Press, 1996.
Catholicism. R. McBrien. Rev. ed. Oak Grove, MN: Winston Press, 1994.
Christian doctrine. S. Guthrie. Rev. ed. Louisville, KY: Westminster John Knox, 1994. 448p.
Christian dogmatics. C. Braaten & R. Jenson (eds). Philadelphia: Fortress, 1984. 2 vols.
Christian faith: an introduction to the study of faith. H. Berkhof. Trans., S. Woudstra. Rev. ed. Grand Rapids, MI: Eerdmans, 1986.
Christian foundations. D. Bloesch. Downer's Gove, IL: InterVarsity, 1992–. 2 vols. to date; in progress to 7 vols.
Christian systematic theology in a world context. N. Smart & S. Konstantine. Minneapolis, MN: Fortress, 1991.
Christian theology. M. J. Erickson. Grand Rapids, MI: Eerdmans, 1983–85. 3 vols.
Christian theology: an eschatological approach. T. Finger. Scottdale, PA: Herald Press, 1985–87. 2 vols.
Christian theology: an introduction. A. McGrath. Oxford, UK: Basil Blackwell, 1993.
Christian theology: an introduction to its traditions and tasks. P. C. Hodgson & R. H. King (eds). 2nd ed. Minneapolis, MN: Fortress, 1994.
Christianity: essence, history, and future. H. Küng. New York: Continuum, 1995. 962p.
Christliche Philosophie im katholischen Denken des 19. und 20. Jahrhunderts. E. Coreth, W. M. Neidl & Pfligersdorfer (eds). Graz, Vienna, and Cologne: Styria Verlag, 1987–1989. 3 vols., 2,591p.
Christology: a Biblical, historical, and systematic study of Jesus. G. O'Collins S.J. Oxford, UK: Oxford University Press, 1995. 345p.
Church dogmatics (Die kirchliche Dogmatik). Karl Barth. Trans., G. T. Thompson. Edinburgh: T & T Clark, 1936–1968, 13 vols. in 4 parts.
Companion encyclopedia of theology. P. Byrne & L. Houlden (eds). London and New York: Routledge, 1995. 1,116p.
Concilium Vaticanum II: concordance, index verborum, liste de fréquence, tables comparatives. P. Delhaye, M. Gueret & P. Tombeur (eds). Leuven: CETEDOC, 1974. 978p.
Contours of Christian theology. Downers Grove, IL: InterVarsity, 1993–. 3 vols. to date.
Credible Christianity: the Gospel in contemporary society. H. Montefiore. Grand Rapids, MI: Eerdmans.
Dictionary of Christian theology. P. A. Angeles. San Francisco: Harper & Row, 1985. 221p.
Dictionary of ethics, theology, and society. P. B. Clarke & A. Linzey (eds). London and New York: Routledge, 1996. 960p.
Dictionary of feminist theologies. L. M. Russell & J. S. Clarkson (eds). Louisville, KY: Westminster John Knox, 1996.
Dietrich Bonhoeffer works. W. W. Floyd (ed). Minneapolis, MN: Fortress. 3 vols. to date; in progress to 17 vols.
Dizionario di teologia fondamentale (Dictionary of fundamental theology). R. Latourelle S.J. & R. Fisichelle (eds). Assissi: Cittadella, 1990. (Published in English, New York: Crossroad, 1994).
Doctrines of the Christian religion. W. W. Stevens. Nashville, TN: Broadman, 1967.
Doxology. G. Wainwright. Oxford, UK: Oxford University Press, 1980.
Ecclesia: a theological encyclopedia of the church. C. O'Donnell. Collegeville, MN: Liturgical Press, 1996. 542p.
Enciclopedia del pensiero sociale cristiano. R. Spiazzi (ed). Bologna: Edizioni Studio Dominicano, 1992.
Essentials of evangelical theology. D. Bloesch. San Francisco: Harper & Row, 1978–79. 2 vols.
Evangelical dictionary of theology. W. A. Elwell (ed). Grand Rapids, MI: Baker, 1984; Basingstoke, UK: Marshall–Pickering, 1985. 1,226p. (Also in a shorter version, *Concise evangelical dictionary of theology*).
Evangelical theology: a survey and review. R. Lightner. Grand Rapids, MI: Baker, 1990.
Evangelisches Kirchenlexikon: Internationale theologische Enzyklopädie. E. Fahlbusch et al. (eds). 3rd ed. Göttingen: Vandenhoeck & Ruprecht, 1986–. 3 vols., in progress to 4 vols.
Evangelisches Kirchenlexikon: kirchlich–theologisches Handwörterbuch. H. Brunotte & O. Weber (eds). Göttingen: Vandenhoeck & Ruprecht, 1955–61. 4 vols.
Faith seeking understanding: an introduction to systematic theology. D. Migliore. Grand Rapids, MI: Eerdmans, 1991.
Foundations of Christian faith: an introduction to the idea of Christianity. K. Rahner. New York: Seabury Press, 1978.
Foundations of dogmatics (Grundlagen der Dogmatik). O. Weber. Trans., D. L. Guder. Grand Rapids, MI: Eerdmans, 1981–83. 2 vols.
God Christ church: a practical guide to process theology. M. H. Suchocki. New York: Crossroad, 1982.
God, creation, and revelation: a neo–evangelical theology. P. Jewett. Grand Rapids, MI: Eerdmans, 1991. 554p. (Originally intended as the first of a multi–volume work before the author's death).
God encountered. F. J. van Beeck. Vol. I: New York: Harper & Row, 1988; vol. II: Collegeville, MN: Liturgical Press, 1993. 2 vols.
God, revelation, and authority. C. F. H. Henry. Waco, TX: Word, 1976–83. 6 vols.
God–walk: liberation shaping dogmatics. F. Herzog. Maryknoll, NY: Orbis, 1988.
God—the world's future: systematic theology for a postmodern era. T. Peters. Minneapolis, MN: Fortress, 1992.
Handbook of evangelical theologians. W. A. Elwell (ed). Grand Rapids, MI: Baker, 1993.
Handbuch der Pastoraltheologie. F. X. Arnold, K. Rahner et al. (eds). Freiburg im Breisgau: Herder. 1964–72, 6 vols.
Handwörterbuch religiöser Gegenwartsfragen. U. Ruh, D. Seeber & R. Walter (eds). Frieburg, Basel, and Vienna: Herder, 1986.
History and the theology of liberation: a Latin American perspective. E. Dussel. Maryknoll, NY: Orbis, 1976.
Images of Jesus. C. W. du Toit (ed). Pretoria, South Africa: University of South Africa, 1997.
In the face of mystery: a constructive theology. G. Kaufman. Cambridge, MA: Harvard University Press, 1993.
Integrative theology. G. R. Lewis & B. A. Demarest. Grand Rapids, MI: Zondervan, 1987–95. 3 vols.
Introduction to theology. O. Thomas. Cambridge, MA: Greeno, Hadden and Co., 1973.
Kleines Theologisches Wörterbuch. K. Rahner & H. Vorgrimler. 7th ed. Freiburg im Breisgau: Herder, 1969.
Lexikon der katholischen Dogmatik. W. Beinert (ed). Freiburg: Herder, 1987. (An English translation appears as *Handbook of Catholic theology.* W. Beinert and F. Schüssler Fiorenza (eds). New York: Crossroad, 1995).
Lexikon für Theologie und Kirche. J. Höfer & K. Rahner (eds). Freiburg: Herder, 1957–65. 10 vols; 3 vols on Vatican Council plus index (1967).
Lift every voice: constructing Christian theologies from the underside. S. B. Thistlewaite & M. P. Engel (eds). San Francisco: Harper & Row, 1990.
Message and existence. L. Gilkey. New York: Seabury, 1979.
Messianic theology. J. Moltmann. San Francisco: Harper, 1981–92. 5 vols.
Mysterium salutis. Dogmatic catholique de l'histoire du salut. J. Feiner and M. Löhrer (Ed). Paris: Le Cerf. 1969-. 12 vols. to date; in progress to 16 vols.
New dictionary of theology. S. B. Ferguson & D. F. Wright (eds). Downers Grove, IL and Leicester, UK: InterVarsity, 1988. 757p.
Not every spirit: a dogmatics of Christian unbelief. C. Morse. Valley Forge, PA: Trinity Press International, 1994.
One Christ—many religions: toward a revised christology. S. J. Samartha. *Faith meets faith series.* Maryknoll, NY: Orbis, 1991. 206p.
Orthodox dogmatic theology. M. Pomazansky. Trans., S. Rose. Wichita, KS: Eighth Day Books, 1994.
Orthodoxy and heterodoxy. J. Metz & E. Schillebeeckx (eds). Edinburgh: T. & T. Clark, 1987. 155p.
Principles of Christian theology. J. Macquarrie. 2nd ed. New York: Scribner, 1977. 557p.
Reconstructing Christian theology. R. S. Chopp & M. L. Taylor. Minneapolis, MN: Fortress, 1994.
Reformational theology: a new paradigm for doing theology. G. Spykman. Grand Rapids, MI: Eerdmans, 1992.
Religious and theological abstracts. Meyerstown, PA, 1958–. 41 vols. to date. (Quarterly).
Re–membering and Re–Imagining. N. J. Berneking & P. C. Joern. Cleveland, OH: Pilgrim Press, 1995. 263p. (Documents from the Re-Imagining conference, 1993).
Responsible faith: Christian theology in light of twentieth century questions. H. Schwarz. Minneapolis, MN: Augsburg, 1986.
Revisioning evangelical theology: a fresh agenda. S. J. Grenz. Downers Grove, IL: InterVarsity, 1993. 208p.
Sacramentum mundi: an encyclopedia of theology. K. Rahner et al. (eds). London: Burns & Oates, 1968–70. 6 vols.
Sexism and God–talk. R. R. Ruether. Boston: Beacon Press, 1983.
Studies in dogmatics. G. C. Berkouwer. Trans. and ed., G. W. Bromiley. Grand Rapids, MI: Eerdmans, 1962–76.
Systematic theology. J. W. McClendon. Nashville, TN: Abingdon Press, 1986. 2 vols.
Systematic theology. W. Pannenberg. Trans., G. Bromiley. Grand Rapids, MI: Eerdmans, 1991.
Systematic theology. R. J. Rushdoony. Vallecito, CA: Ross House, 1994. 2 vols.
Systematic theology. O. Thomas. San Francisco: Harper, 1987–92. 3 vols.
Systematic theology. P. Tillich. Chicago: University of Chicago Press, 1951–63. 3 vols.
Systematic theology: a historicist perspective. G. Kaufman. New York: Scribner, 1969. 565p.
Systematic theology: a modern Protestant approach. K. Cauthen. Lewistown, NY: E. Mellen Press, 1986.
Systematic theology: an introduction to biblical doctrine. W. Grudem. Grand Rapids, MI: Harper/Zondervan, 1994.
Systematic theology: biblical, historical, and systematic. J. L. Garrett Jr. Grand Rapids, MI: Eerdmans, 1990–95. 2 vols.
Systematic theology from a Charismatic perspective. W. Rodman. Grand Rapids, MI: Zondervan, 1988–92. 3 vols.
Systematic theology: Roman Catholic perspectives. F. S. Fiorenza & J. Galvin (eds). Minneapolis, MN: Fortress, 1991. 2 vols.
The Blackwell encyclopedia of modern Christian thought. A. E. McGrath (ed). Oxford, UK and Cambridge, MA: Blackwell Reference, 1993. 714p.
The challenge of basic Christian communities. S. Torres & J. Eagleson (eds). Maryknoll, NY: Orbis, 1982.
The Christian doctrine of God: one being, three persons. T. F. Torrance. Edinburgh: T. & T. Clark, 1996. 272p.
The Christian story. G. Fackre. Grand Rapids, MI: Eerdmans, 1978–87. 2 vols.
The cry of my people: out of captivity in Latin America. M. Arias & E. Arias. New York: Friendship Press, 1980.
The evangelical faith. H. Thielicke. Grand Rapids, MI: Eerdmans, 1974–82. 3 vols.
The faith we confess: an ecumenical dogmatics. J. M. Lochman. Trans., D. Lewis. Philadelphia: Fortress, 1984.
The Father's spirit of sonship: reconceiving the Trinity. T. G. Weinandy. Edinburgh: T. & T. Clark, 1995. 159p.
The Göttingen dogmatics: introduction to the Christian religion. K. Barth. Trans., G. W. Bromiley & H. R. ed. Grand Rapids, MI: Eerdmans, 1991.
The melody of theology: a philosophical dictionary. J. Pelikan. Cambridge, MA: Harvard University Press, 1988. 284p.
The modern theologians: an introduction to Christian theology in the twentieth century. D. F. Ford (ed). Oxford, UK and New York: Blackwell Reference, 1989. 2 vols., 699p.
The new dictionary of Catholic social thought. J. Dwyer (ed). Collegeville, MN: Liturgical Press, 1994. 1,050p.
The origins and development of African theology. G. H. Muzorewa. Maryknoll, NY: Orbis, 1985. 146p.
The reign of God: an introduction to Christian theology from a Seventh–day Adventist perspective. R. Rice. Berrien Springs, MI: Andrews University Press, 1985.
The Westminster dictionary of theological terms. D. K. McKim (ed). Louisville, KY: Westminster John Knox, 1996. (Contains over 5,000 theological terms.).

The word of truth: a summary of Christian doctrine based on biblical revelation. D. Moody. Grand Rapids, MI: Eerdmans, 1981. 640p.
Theological dictionary. K. Rahner & H. Vorgrimler. Trans., R. Strachan, ed., C. Ernst. New York: Seabury, 1965. 493p.
Theological questions: analysis and argument. O. Thomas. Wilton, CT: Morehouse–Barlow, 1983.
Theologische realenzyklopädie. G. Müller (ed). Berlin: de Gruyter, 1974–. 24 vols. and 20,000p to date.
Theology for the community of God. S. Grenz. Nashville, TN: Broadman & Holman, 1994.
Theology for the third millenium: an ecumenical view. H. Küng. Trans., P. Heinegg. New York: Doubleday, 1988. 324p.
Thinking about God: an introduction to theology. D. Soelle. London: SCM Press; Philadelphia: Trinity Press International, 1990.
Thinking the faith: Christian theology in a North American context; professing the faith: Christian theology in a North American context; confessing the faith: Christian theology in a North American context. D. J. Hall. Minneapolis, MN: Augsburg Fortress, 1989–96. 3 vols.
Tracking the maze: finding our way through modern theology from an evangelical perspective. C. H. Pinnock. San Francisco: Harper & Row, 1990.
Trinitas: a theological encyclopedia of the Holy Trinity. M. O. O'-Carroll. Wilmington, DE: Michael Glazier, 1987; Collegeville, MI: Michael Glazier/Liturgical, 1993.
Twentieth–century religious thought. J. Macquarrie. London: SCM Press; Philadelphia: Trinity Press International, 1988. 486p.
We have been believers: an African American systematic theology. J. H. Evans. Minneapolis, MN: Fortress, 1992.
What Christians believe: a biblical and historical summary. A. F. Johnson & R. E. Webber. Grand Rapids, MI: Zondervan, 1989.
Winds of the Spirit: a constructive Christian theology. P. C. Hodgson. Louisville, KY: Westminster John Knox, 1994.
Wörterbuch des Christentums. V. Drehsen et al. (eds). Gütersloh: Gerd Mohn, 1988. 1439p.

6. THEOLOGICAL ETHICS

A passion for the possible: a message to U.S. churches. W. S. Coffin. Louisville, KY: Westminster John Knox, 1993. 88p.
After virtue: a study in moral theory. A. MacIntyre. Notre Dame, IN: University of Notre Dame Press, 1981.
An interpretation of Christian ethics. R. Niebuhr. 1935; San Francisco: Harper & Row, 1963. 158p.
Authentic transformation: a new vision of Christ and culture. G. H. Stassen, D. M. Yeager & J. H. Yoder. Nashville, TN: Abingdon, 1996. 299p.
Beyond integrity: a Judeo–Christian approach to business ethics. S. B. Rae & K. L. Wong. Grand Rapids, MI: Zondervan, 1996. 656p.
Changing witness: Catholic bishops and public policy, 1917–1994. M. Warner. Grand Rapids, MI: Eerdmans, 1995. 220p.
Christ and Culture. H. R. Niebuhr. New York: Harper & Row, 1951. 217p.
Christian ethics. R. E. O. White. Macon, GA: Mercer University Press, 1994. 698p.
Competing gospels: public theology and economic theory. R. G. Simons. Alexandria, Australia: Dwyer, 1995. 253p.
Confusions in Christian social ethics: problems for Geneva and Rome. R. H. Preston. Grand Rapids, MI: Eerdmans, 1995. 215p.
Dictionary of ethics, theology, and society. P. B. Clarke & A. Linzey (eds). London and New York: Routledge, 1996. 960p.
Economic justice for all: pastoral letter on Catholic social teaching and the U.S. economy. Washington, DC: United States Catholic Conference, National Conference of Catholic Bishops, 1986.
Encyclopedia of ethics. L. C. Becker & C. Becker. New York: Garland, 1992. 2 vols, 1,462p.
Encyclopedia of morals. V. T. Ferm (ed). Repr. ed. Westport, CT: Greenwood, 1969. 682p.
Encyclopedia of war and ethics. D. A. Wells (ed). Westport, CT: Greenwood, 1996. 568p.
Ethics. D. Bonhoeffer. Ed., E. Bethge. 1949; New York: Collier/Macmillan, 1986. 382p. (Bonhoeffer, hanged in a Nazi concentration camp in 1945, never finished his *Ethics.* This volume is a compilation of early drafts and fragments written from 1940–1943).
Ethics from a theocentric perspective; vol. 1, theology and ethics; vol. 2, ethics and theology. J. Gustafson. Chicago: University of Chicago Press, 1981–84, 2 vols.
For the nations: evangelical and public. J. H. Yoder. Grand Rapids, MI: Eerdmans, 1997. 257p.
Ideology in America: challenges to faith. A. Geyer. Louisville, KY: Westminster John Knox, 1997. 149p.
In praise of virtue: an exploration of the biblical virtues in a Christian context. B. W. Farley. Grand Rapids, MI: Eerdmans, 1995. 191p.
Library of theological ethics. R. Lovin et al. (eds). Louisville, KY: Westminster John Knox, 1992–. 15 vols. to date. (Reprints, usually facsimile, of important older texts).
Postmodern times: a Christian guide to contemporary thought and culture. G. E. Veith Jr. Wheaton, IL: Crossway, 1994. 256p.
Protestant and Roman Catholic ethics. J. Gustafson. Chicago: University of Chicago Press, 1978. 204p.
Public theology and political economy: Christian stewardship in modern society. M. L. Stackhouse. 1987; Lanham, MD: University Press of America, 1991. 191p.
Religion and human rights. J. Kelsay & S. B. Twiss (eds). New York: The Project on Religion and Human Rights, 1994. 135p.
Religion in public life: a dilemma for democracy. R. E. Thiemann. Washington, DC: Georgetown University Press, 1996. 186p.
Religious human rights in global perspective: religious perspectives and legal perspectives. J. Witte Jr. & J. D. van der Vyer (eds). The Hague and Boston: M. Nijhoff, 1996. 2 vols.
Resident aliens: life in the Christian colony. S. Hauerwas & W. H. Willimon. Nashville, TN: Abingdon, 1989. 175p. (Written for laypersons by a pair of Duke University professors, this short book has been influential in promoting Christian communitarianism).
Sexual ethics: an evangelical perspective. S. J. Grenz. Louisville, KY: Westminster John Knox, 1997. 311p.
The encyclopedia of religion and ethics. J. Hastings (ed). Edinburgh: T. & T. Clark, 1926. 13 vols.
The ethical demand. K. E. Løgstrup. Ed., H. Fink & A. MacIntyre. Rev. ed. 1971; Notre Dame, IN: University of Notre Dame Press, 1997. 331p.
The family in theological perspective. S. C. Barton (ed). Edinburgh: T & T Clark, 1996. 367p.
The moral quest: foundations of Christian ethics. S. J. Grenz. Downers Grove, IL: InterVarsity, 1997. 379p.
The politics of Jesus. J. H. Yoder. Grand Rapids, MI: Eerdmans, 1972. 260p.
The sources of Christian ethics. S. Pinckaers. Trans., M. T. Noble. Washington, DC: Catholic University of America, 1995. 510p.
The Westminster dictionary of Christian ethics. J. Childress & J. Macquarrie (eds). 2nd ed. Philadelphia: Westminster, 1986. 687p. (Published in Britain as *A new dictionary of Christian ethics.* London: SCM Press, 1986, 1993).
Theology and biotechnology: implications for a new science. C. Deane–Drummond. London: Geoffrey Chapman, 1998.
Threskeutike kai ethike enkyklopaideia (Religious and ethical encyclopedia). Athens: Martinos, 1962–68. 12 vols.

7. MISSIOLOGY

A Church for all peoples: missionary issues in a world Church. E. LaVerdiere (ed). Collegeville, MN: Liturgical Press, 1993. 104p.
A history of the expansion of Christianity. K. S. Latourette. New York: Harper, 1937–45. 7 vols.
Anglican cycle of prayer: praying together for persons and places around the world—1996. London: Church House Publishing; Cincinnati, OH: Forward Movement Publications, 1995. 160p. (Annual publication of the Anglican Communion designed to focus attention on the world of Anglican missions worldwide).
Ateismo e dialogo: bolletino del Segretariato per i Non–Credenti. Rome, 1966–. (Christian dialogue with atheism and Marxism).
Atlas du monde chrétien: l'expansion du Christianisme à travers les siècles. A. Freitag et al. Paris and Brussels: Elsevier, 1959. 215p. (Maps and photographs. English edition under title, *The twentieth century atlas of the Christian world: the expansion of Christianity through the centuries.* New York: Hawthorn, 1964).
Believing in the future: toward a missiology of Western culture. D. J. Bosch. *Christian mission and modern culture.* Valley Forge, PA: Trinity Press International, 1995. 79p.
Bibliographia missionaria. 1935–74; Rome: Pontificia Università do Propagande Fide, 1986–. 50 vols. to date. (Annual review of previous year's literature; until 1971, some overlap with *Bibliotheca missionum,* but has now superseded it for current literature).
'Bibliography on world mission and evangelism,' *International review of mission,* (At end of all issues).
Bibliotheca missionum. R. Streit. Freiburg: Herder, 1916–71. 28 vols. (The major complete and retrospective Catholic bibliography of missions; discontinued 1971 and superseded by *Bibliographia missionaria*).
Called and empowered: global mission in Pentecostal perspective. M. Dempster, B. D. Klaus & D. Petersen (eds). Peabody, MA: Hendrickson, 1991.
Carrying the gospel to all the non-Christian world. Edinburgh: Oliphant/Revell, 1910. (World Missionary Conference, Report of Commission I).
Catholic mission history. J. Schmidlin. Techny, IL: Mission Press, 1933. 878p. (Translated from the German).
Catholic mission theory. J. Schmidlin. Techny, IL: Mission Press, 1931. 559p. (Translation of *Katolische Missionslehre im Grundriss*).
Christian mission in the twentieth century. T. Yates. Cambridge, UK: Cambridge University Press, 1994. 291p.
Christianity and missions, 1450–1800. J. S. Cummins (ed). *An expanding world: the European impact on world history, 1450–1800,* 28. Brookfield, VT: Ashgate, 1997. 350p.
Christianity and the religions: a biblical theology of world religions. E. Rommen & H. Netland (eds). *Evangelical Missiological Society series,* 2. Pasadena, CA: William Carey Library, 1995. 274p.
Classic texts in mission and world Christianity. N. E. Thomas (ed). *American Society of Missiology series,* 20. Maryknoll, NY: Orbis, 1995. 366p.
Concise dictionary of the Christian world mission. S. Neill, G. H. Anderson & J. Goodwin (eds). London: Lutterworth, 1970. 704p.
Contemporary missiology: an introduction. J. Verkuyl. Trans. & ed., D. Cooper. Grand Rapids, MI: Eerdmans, 1978. 428p.
Critical bibliography of missiology. L. Vriens. Nijmegen: VSKB Publ, 1960.
Dictionary catalog of the Missionary Research Library, New York. Boston: G.K. Hall, 1967. 17 vols., 13,039p. (273,000 entries).
Dictionary of mission: theology, history, perspectives. K. Müller et al. (eds). *American Society of Missiology series,* 24. Maryknoll, NY: Orbis, 1997. 544p.
Encyclopedia of missions: descriptive, historical, biographical, statistical. H. O. Dwight et al. (eds). 1904. Repr. ed. Detroit, MI: Omnigraphics, 1975.
Encyclopedia of modern Christian missions: the agencies. B. L. Goddard (ed). Camden, NJ: T. Nelson, 1967. 762p.
Errand to the world: American Protestant thought and foreign missions. W. R. Hutchison. Chicago: University of Chicago Press, 1987. 239p.
God's call to mission. D. W. Shenk. Scottdale, PA: Herald Press, 1994. 229p.
Gospel and mission in the writings of Paul: an exegetical and theological analysis. P. T. O'Brien. Grand Rapids, MI: Baker, 1993. 175p.
Histoire universelle des missions catholiques. S. Delacroix. Paris: Librarie Grund, 1956–58. 4 vols. (Profuse illustrations and maps).
International review of missions: index 1912–1966. O. G. Myklebust. Geneva: IRM, 1968. (Bibliography of 1,900 articles).
Lexikon missionstheologischer grundbegriffe. K. Müller & T. Sundermeier (eds). Berlin: Dietrich Reiner, 1987.
Media in church and mission: communicating the gospel. V. Søgaard. Pasadena, CA: William Carey Library, 1993. 301p.
Missiological abstracts, 25 years, 1966–1991. G. R. Grimes (ed). Rev. ed. Pasadena, CA: Fuller Theological Seminary, 1991. 336p. (Abstracts of 720 dissertations, theses, and projects produced at the School of World Mission at Fuller Theological Seminary).
Missiology: an ecumenical introduction: texts and contexts of global Christianity. F. J. Verstraelen (ed). Grand Rapids, MI: Eerdmans, 1995. 505p.
Mission trends. G. H. Anderson & T. F. Stransky C.S.P. (eds). New York: Paulist Press; Grand Rapids, MI: Eerdmans. 5 vols.
New directions in mission and evangelization; vol. 1: basic statements 1974–1991; vol. 2: theological foundations. J. A. Scherer & S. B. Bevans (eds). Maryknoll, NY: Orbis, 1992. 2 vols.
On the way to fuller koinonia. T. F. Best & G. Gassmann (eds). *Faith and Order paper,* 166. Geneva: World Council of Churches, 1994. 348p.
Pentecost, mission and ecumenism: essays on intercultural theology. J. A. B. Jongeneel et al. (eds). *Studies in the intercultural history of Christianity,* 75. Frankfurt am Main: Peter Lang, 1992. 386p.
Philosophy, science and theology of mission in the 19th and 20th centuries: a missiological encyclopedia. J. A. B. Jongeneel (ed). *Studies in the intercultural history of Christianity,* 92, 106. Frankfurt am Main: P. Lang, 1995–1997. 2 vols.
Portugal em Africa. Revista de Cultura Missionária. Lisbon: Editorial LIAM, 1894–1971. (Bi-monthly).
Re–visioning mission: the Catholic Church and culture in postmodern America. R. G. Cote. *Isaac Hecker studies in religion and American culture.* Mahwah, NJ: Paulist, 1996. 197p.
Roots of the great debate in mission: mission in historical and theological perspective. R. E. Hedlund. *Theological issues series,* 3. Bangalore, India: Theological Book Trust, 1993. 529p.
Sacrae Congregationis de Propaganda Fide Memoria Rerum. J. Metzler et al. (eds). Freiburg: Herder, 1972–76. 3 vols., 4,500p. (History of Catholic missions, 1622–1972).
Scripture and strategy: the use of the Bible in postmodern church and mission. D. J. Hesselgrave. *Evangelical Missiological Society series,* 1. Pasadena, CA: William Carey Library, 1994. 192p.
Spiritual power and missions: raising the issues. E. Rommen (ed). *Evangelical Missiological Society series,* 3. Pasadena, CA: William Carey Library, 1995. 163p.
Studies in missions: an index of theses on missions. Monrovia, CA: MARC, 1974. 73p. (200 theses and dissertations).
The Christian-Marxist dialogue: an annotated bibliography, 1959–1969. A. J. van der Bent. Geneva: World Council of Churches, 1969. 90p. (1,200 titles in 5 languages).
The evangelization of the world in this generation. J. R. Mott. New York: Student Volunteer Movement for Foreign Missions, 1900. 253p.
The good news of the kingdom: mission theology for the third millennium. C. Van Engen, D. S. Gilliland & P. Pierson (eds). Maryknoll, NY: Orbis Books, 1993. 336p.
The gospel and frontier peoples: a report of a consultation, December 1972. R. P. Beaver (ed). Pasadena, CA: William Carey Library, 1972. 413p.
The recovery of mission: beyond the pluralist paradigm. V. Ramachandra. Grand Rapids, MI: Eerdmans, 1996. 305p.
Transforming mission: paradigm shifts in theology of mission. D. J. Bosch. *American Society of Missiology series,* 16. Maryknoll, NY: Orbis, 1991. 597p.
Wichtige daten der Missionsgeschichte. T. Ohm. Münster: Aschendorffsche Verlagsbuchhandlung, 1956. (French: *Les principaux faits de l'histoire des missions,* 1961. 162p).
Write the vision: the Church renewed. W. R. Shenk. *Christian mission and modern culture.* Valley Forge, PA: Trinity Press International, 1995. 127p.

8. ECUMENISM

A history of the ecumenical movement, 1517–1948 (Vol 1). R. Rouse & S. C. Neill. London: SPCK; Philadelphia: Westminster, 1954. 822p.
Bibliografia tes Oikoumenikes Kineseos, 1960–1970 (Bibliography of the ecumenical movement). V. T. Istavridis. Athens: Theologia, 1978. 78p. (Orthodoxy and ecumenism; 1,500 titles).
Classified catalog of the Ecumenical Movement, World Council of Churches, Geneva. Boston: G. K. Hall, 1972. 2 vols., 967p. (20,300 entries).
Commentary of the documents of Vatican II. H. Vorgrimler (ed). New York: Herder & Herder, 1967–72. 5 vols.
Dictionary of the ecumenical movement. N. Lossky et al. (eds). Geneva: WCC Publications and Grand Rapids, MI: Eerdmans, 1991. 1,212p.
Documents on Christian unity. G. K. A. Bell. London and New York: Oxford University Press, 1929–58. 4 vols. (Illustrates the growth of the world ecumenical movement).
Ecumenical terminology. Geneva: World Council of Churches, 1975. 564p. (4 languages, 1,335 words, titles).

Ecumenism around the world: a directory of ecumenical institutes, centers, and organizations. 2nd ed. Rome: Centro pro Unione (Friars of the Atonement), 1974. 169p.
Forging a common future: Catholic, Judaic, and Protestant relations for a new millenium. A. Greeley et al. Ed., J. Neusner. Cleveland, OH: Pilgrim Press, 1997. 122p.
Historical dictionary of ecumenical Christianity. A. J. van der Bent. *Historical dictionaries of religions, philosophies, and movements,* 3. Metuchen, NJ and London: Scarecrow Press, 1994. 626p.
Internationale Ökumenische Bibliographie/International Ecumenical Bibliography/Bibliographie Oecuménique Internationale/Bibliografí Ecuménica Internacional. C. Graves et al. (eds). München: Chr Kaiser Verlag, 1962–75. 10 vols. (In English, French, German, and Spanish. 55,000 titles, over half articles, on contemporary dialogue between churches and with other religions).
Liberation and orthodoxy: the promise and failures of interconfessional dialogue. Y. Tesfai. Maryknoll, NY: Orbis, 1996. 208p.
Mission and evangelism: an ecumenical affirmation. E. Castro (ed). Geneva: CWME, 1982.
Oecumene 1 (1977) and 2 (1978). Strasbourg: CERDIC, 1977–78. (Ecumenical bibliography; abstracts of over 1,000 journals).
Ökumene Lexikon: Kirchen, Religionen, Bewegunen. H. Krüger, W. Löser & W. Müller-Römheld (eds). Frankfurt am Main: Verlag Otto Lembeck and Verlag Josef Knecht, 1983. 673p.
Reclaiming the great tradition: evangelicals, Catholics and Orthodox in dialogue. J. S. Custinger. Downers Grove, IL: InterVaristy, 1997. 214p.
'Selective bibliography of significant current ecumenical books and pamphlets,' *The ecumenical review,* (quarterly).
Sharing in one hope: Bangalore 1978, reports and documents from the meeting of the Faith and Order Commission. Faith and Order paper, 92. Geneva: World Council of Churches, Commission on Faith and Order, 1978. 304p.
Six hundred ecumenical consultations 1948–1982. A. J. van der Bent. Geneva: World Council of Churches, 1983. 254p.
The ecumenical advance: a history of the ecumenical movement, 1948–1968. H. E. Fey (ed). London: SPCK, 1970. 525p.
The ecumenical movement: an anthology of key texts and voices. M. Kinnamon & B. Cope (eds). Grand Rapids, MI: Eerdmans; Geneva: WCC Publications, 1996. 564p.
The Orthodox Church in the Ecumenical Movement: documents and statements 1902–1975. C. G. Patelos (ed). Geneva: World Council of Churches, 1978. 360p.
The reconciliation of peoples: challenge to the churches. G. Brown & H. Wells (eds). Geneva: WCC Publications; Maryknoll, NY: Orbis, 1997. 199p.
Toward a Christian theology of religious pluralism. J. Dupuis. Maryknoll, NY: Orbis, 1997. 447p.

9. ESTHETICS

20 centuries of great preaching: an encyclopedia of preaching. C. E. Fant Jr & W. M. Pinson Jr (eds). Waco, TX: Word, 1971. 13 vols.
A bibliography of Christian worship. B. Thompson (ed). *ATLA bibliography series,* 25. Philadelphia: American Theological Library Association; Metuchen, NJ, Scarecrow Press. 828p.
A bibliography of sources in Christianity and the arts. D. M. Kari. *Studies in art and religious interpretation,* 16. Lewiston, NY: E. Mellen Press, 1995. 774p.
A dictionary of hymnology. J. Julian (ed). 1907; New York: Dover, 1957. 2 vols.
A dictionary of liturgical terms. P. H. Pfatteicher. Philadelphia: Trinity Press International, 1991. 143p.
A dictionary of liturgy and worship. J. G. Davies (ed). London: SCM, 1972. 385p.
A feast of Anglican spirituality. R. Backhouse. Norwich, UK: Canterbury Press, 1998.
A pastoral liturgy bibliography. 2nd rev. ed. Notre Dame, IN: Notre Dame Center for Pastoral Liturgy, 1981. 28p.
A treasury of Russian spirituality. G. P. Fedotov (ed). London: Sheed & Ward, 1950. 501p.
Art and the Reformation: an annotated bibliography. L. B. Parshall & P. W. Parshall. *A Reference publication in art history.* Boston, MA: G. K. Hall, 1986. 328p.
Art in the Armenian Church: origins and teaching. G. Kochakian. New York: St. Vartan Press, 1995.
Art of the Christian world, A.D. 200–1500: a handbook of styles and forms. Y. Christe et al. New York: Rizzoli International Publications, 1982. 504p.
Asceticism. V. L. Wimbaugh & R. Valantasis (eds). New York: Oxford University Press, 1955.
Bibliographia internationalis spiritualitatis. Roma: Pontifical Institute of Spirituality, 1966–68. 3 vols. (6,487 titles in vol. 3).
Bulgarian monasteries: monuments of history, culture, and art. G. Chavrukov. Sofia: Naouka i Izkoustvo, 1974. 371p. (Photographic collection).
Christian art in Asia. M. Takenaka. Tokyo: Kyo Bun Kwan, 1975. 171p.
Christian art in India. J. F. Butler. Madras: Christian Literature Society, 1986. 199p.
Christian art of the 4th to 12th centuries. F. Abbate (ed). Trans., P. Swinglehurst. Milan: Fratelli Fabbri Editore; London and New York: Octopus Books, 1972. 158p.
Christian spirituality: the essential guide to the most influential spiritual writings of the Christian tradition. F. N. Magill & I. P. McGreal (eds). San Francisco: Harper & Row, 1988. 713p.
Christian symbols in a world community. D. J. Fleming. New York: Friendship Press, 1940. 160p.
Christianity, section 24 in *Iconography of religions.* Leiden: E. J. Brill, 1979-. 4 vols. to date.
Christianity and the arts in Russia. W. C. Brumfield & M. Velimirovich (eds). Cambridge, UK: Cambridge University Press, 1991. 172p.
Concise encyclopedia of preaching. W. H. Willimon & R. Lischer (eds). Louisville, KY: Westminster John Knox, 1995. 540p.
Dictionary of Catholic devotions. M. Walsh. London: Burnes & Oates; San Francisco: Harper, 1993. 366p.
Dictionnaire d'archéologie chrétienne et de liturgie. F. Cabrol, H. Leclerq & H. Marrou (eds). Paris: Letouzey & Ané, 1903–53. 30 parts, 15 vols.
Dictionnaire de la vie spirituelle. S. de Fiores & T. Goffi (eds). Paris: Le Cerf, 1987. 1,268p. (Adapted from the Italian, *Nuovo Dizionario di spiritualità.* Rome: Edizioni Paoline, 1983).
Dictionnaire de spiritualité, ascétique et mystique. M. Viller S.J. et al. (eds). Paris: Beachesne, 1937–1994. 20 vols.
Dictionnaire des église de France, Belgique, Luxembourg, Suisse. J. Brosse et al (eds). Paris: Robert Laffont, 1971. 5 vols. (History and architecture of church buildings).
Dictionnaire encyclopédique de la liturgie. D. Sartore & A. M. Triacca (eds). Turnhout: Brepols, 1992–. 1 vol.; in planning to 2 vols.
Dizionario francescano: Spiritualità. E. Caroli (ed). Padua: Edizioni Messagero, 1983.
Encyclopedia of medieval church art. E. G. Tasker and J. Beaumont. London: B. T. Batsford, 1993. 320p.
Encyclopédie des musiques sacrées. J. Porte (ed). Tours, France: Labergerie–Mame, 1968–71. 4 vols. (Vol. 4 consists of records).
Façades and festivals of Antigua: a guide to church fronts and celebrations. D. L. Jickling & E. Elliott. Antigua, Guatemala: Casa del Sol, 1989. 75p.
Historic churches of Barbados. B. Hill. Bridgetown, Barbados: Art Heritage Publications, 1984. 128p.
Iconography of Christian art. G. Schiller. New York: NY Graphic Society, 1971. 2 vols. (3 vols in German edition).
Icons: windows on eternity: theology and spirituality in colour. G. Limouris. *Faith and Order paper,* 147. Geneva: WCC Publications, 1990. 238p.
Images of religion in Australian art. R. Crumlin. Kensington, NSW: Bay Books, 1988. 204p.
Kirkjubøarstólarir og Kirkjubøur: brot úr søgu føroyska biskupssætisins. K. J. Krogh. Tórshavn: E. Thomsen, 1988. 133p. (Treats the history and art of the church on the Faeroe Islands).
La Bible et les saints: Guide iconographique. G. Duchet-Suchaux & M. Pastoreau. Paris: Flammarion, 1990. 319p. (English edition, *The Bible and the saints: Flammarion iconographic guides.* Paris and New York: Flammarion, 1994).
Lexikon der Christlichen Ikonographie. E. Kirschbaum et al. (eds). Freiburg im Breisgau: Herder, 1968–76. 8 vols.
Monasteries in Bulgaria. L. Prashkov, E. Bakalova & S. Boyadjiev. Sofia: Spectrum, 1990. 286p.
Orthodox saints: spiritual profiles for modern man. G. Poulos. 4th ed. Brookline, MA: Holy Cross Orthodox Press, 1990–1992. 4 vols.
Outward signs: the language of Christian symbolism. E. N. West. New York: Walker, 1989. 254p.
Reallexikon zur byzantinischen Kunst. K. Wessel & M. Restle (eds). Stuttgart: Hierseman, 1963–. 4 vols. (Explores interrelation of religion and art in Eastern Christianity).
Repertorium hymnologicum. C. U. J. Chevalier. Louvain and Brussels: Société des Bollandistes, 1892–1920. 6 vols.
Saints of the Roman calendar including feasts proper to the English–speaking world. E. Lodi. New York: Alba House, 1992. 444p.
Serima: towards an African expression of Christian belief = Ein Versuch in afrikanisch–christlicher Kunst. A. B. Plangger & M. Diethelm. Gwelo, Rhodesia: Mambo Press, 1974. 76p.
Shaker architecture. H. F. Schiffer. Exton, PA: Schiffer, 1979.
Spirituality and the secular quest. P. H. Van Ness (ed). *World spirituality: an encyclopedic history of the religious quest,* 26. New York: Crossroad, 1996.
'St. Lucian carnival: a Caribbean art form.' R. D. Dunstan. Ph.D. dissertation, State University of New York at Stony Brook, Stony Brook, NY, 1978. 373p. (A study of the preparations for and celebration of carnival, the pre–Lenten celebration. Includes consideration of the religious implications of carnival in St. Lucia).
The American Shakers and their furniture. J. G. Shea. New York: Van Nostrand, 1971.
The Bible in 20th century art. N. Usherwood & P. Holberton (eds). London: Pagoda Books, 1987. 111p.
The Bible through Asian eyes. M. Takenaka & R. O'Grady. Aukland, NZ: Pace Publishing, 1991. 199p.
The Christian oriental carpet: a presentation of its development, iconologically and iconographically, from its beginnings to the 18th century. V. Gantzhorn. Trans., C. Madsen. Köln: Benedikt Taschen, 1991. 532p. (A translation of the author's doctoral dissertation at the Eberhard-Karls-Univesität, Tübingen).
The dictionary of art. J. Turner (ed). New York: Grove, 1996. 34 vols.
"The habitation of thy house, Lord, I have loved well ...": Reformed ecclesiastical art in Hungary. J. Hapák & B. Takács. Budapest: Officina Nova, 1991. 79p.
The icon handbook: a guide to understanding icons and the liturgy, symbols and practices of the Russian Orthodox Church. D. Coomler. Springfield, IL: Templegate, 1995. 319p.
The liturgical dictionary of Eastern Christianity. P. D. Day. London: Burns & Oates; Collegeville, MN: Liturgical Press, 1993. 343p.
The new dictionary of sacramental worship. P. E. Fink S.J. (ed). Collegeville, MN: Liturgical Press, 1990. 1352p.
The new Westminster dictionary of liturgy and worship. J. G. Davies (ed). 2nd ed. Philadelphia: Westminster, 1986. 570p. (Published in Britain as *A new dictionary of liturgy and worship.* London: SCM Press, 1986, 1989).
The Oxford companion to Christian art and architecture. P. Murray & L. Murray. Oxford, UK and New York: Oxford University Press, 1996. 608p.
The painted churches of Cyprus: treasures of Byzantine art. A. Stylianou & J. Stylianou. London: Trigraph for the A. G. Leventis Foundation, 1985. 518p.
The painted churches of Romania: a visitor's impressions. J. Fletcher. London: New Knowledge Books, 1971. 103p.
The presense of God: a history of Western Christian mysticism. B. McGinn. New York: Crossroad, 1992–. 2 vols. to date; in planning to 4 vols.
The Sistine Chapel. F. Papava (ed). Vatican City: Monumenti, 1992.
The study of spirituality. C. Jones, G. Wainwright & E. Yarnold SJ (eds). New York and Oxford, UK: Oxford University Press, 1986.
The Westminster dictionary of Christian education. K. B. Cully (ed). Philadelphia: Westminster, 1962. 812p. (A second edition was published by Harper, *Harper's encyclopedia of religious knowledge.* San Francisco: Harper, 1990. 739p).
The Westminster dictionary of Christian spirituality. G. S. Wakefield (ed). Philadelphia: Westminster, 1983. 416p. (Published in Britain as *A dictionary of Christian spirituality.* London: SCM Press, 1983, 1988).
Vies des saints et des bienheureux selon l'ordre du calendrier, avec l'historique des fêtes. J. Baudot [1857-1929], L. Chaussin [1891–1945] & Bénédictins de Paris [to 1959] (eds). Paris: Letouzey et Ané, 1935–1959. 7,500p.
Zimbabwe Christian art: the first collected exhibition 28th November–13th December held at the Anglican Cathedral, Harare opened by H.E. the Rev Canaan Banana, president of the Republic of Zimbabwe. Harare: Anglican Cathedral, 1986. 24p.

10. SCIENCE AND RELIGION

A Christian view of modern science. R. L. Raymond. Nutley, NJ: Presbyterian and Reformed, 1977.
Belief in God in an age of science. J. Polkinghorne. New Haven: Yale University Press, 1999. 160p.
Beyond the cosmos: what recent discoveries in astronomy and physics reveal about the nature of God. H. Ross. Colorado Springs, CO: NavPress, 1996. 236p.
Chance and providence: God's action in a world governed by scientific law. W. Pollard. London: Faber, 1958.
Chaos and complexity: scientific perspectives on divine action. R. J. Russell, N. Murphy, and A. Peacocke, editors. Vatican City: Vatican Observatory Publications, 1995. 418p.
Creation and the world of science. A. Peacocke. Oxford: Clarendon Press, 1979.
Evolution and the Bible. E. G. Conklin. Chicago: American Institute of Sacred Literature, 1922. (Modernist defense of teaching evolution).
Faith and the physical world. D. Dye. Grand Rapids, MI: Eerdmans, 1966.
God and creation. P. J. Flamming. Nashville, TN: Broadman Press, 1984. 164p.
God and the astronomers. R. Jastrow. New York: W.W. Norton, 1992. 156p. (Evidence for the Big Bang).
God and the new physics. P. Davies. New York: Simon & Schuster, 1983.
In the beginning God: modern science and the Christian doctrine of creation. J.D. Weaver. Oxford: Regent's Park College, 1994. 218p.
Intelligent design: the bridge between science & theology. W. A. Dembski. Downers Grove, IL: InterVarsity Press, 1999. 242p.
Modern cosmology and the Christian idea of God. E.A. Milne. Oxford: Clarendon Press, 1952.
On the moral nature of the universe: theology, cosmology, and ethics. N. Murphy and G. F. R. Ellis. Minneapolis: Fortress Press, 1996. 270p.
Quantum cosmology and the laws of nature: scientific perspectives on divine action. R. J. Russell, N. Murphy, and C. J. Isham. Vatican City: Vatican Observatory Publications, 1993.
Quarks, chaos & Christianity. J. Polkinghorne. New York: Crossroad, 1995. 123p.
Religion and scientific naturalism: overcoming the conflicts. D. R. Griffen. State University of New York Press, 2000. 345p. (Draws on philosophy of A. N. Whitehead).
Religion in an age of science. I. Barbour. San Francisco: HarperSanFrancisco, 1990.
Science and creation: the search for understanding. J. Polkinghorne. London: SPCK, 1988.
Science and its limits: the natural sciences in Christian perspective. D. Ratzsch. Downers Grove, IL: InterVarsity Press, 2000. 192p.
Science and providence: God's interaction with the world. J. Polkinghorne. London: SPCK, 1989.
Science and religion: a critical survey. H. Rolston III. New York: Random House, 1987.
Science and the Christian experiment. A. Peacocke. London: Oxford University Press, 1971.
Science and theology: an introduction. J. Polkinghorne. Philadelphia: Fortress Press, 1999. 176p.
Stages of thought: the co-evolution of religious thought and science. M. H. Barnes. New York: Oxford University Press, 2000. 334p. (Utilizes cognitive theories of Piaget).
Summer for the gods: the Scopes trial and America's continuing debate over science and religion. E. J. Larson. New York: Basic Books, 1997. 318p.
The Christian view of science and scripture. B. Ramm. London: Paternoster, 1955.
The creator and the cosmos: how the greatest scientific discoveries of the century reveal God. H. Ross. Colorado Springs, CO: NavPress, 1993. 186p.
The creationists: the evolution of scientific creationism. R.L. Numbers. New York: Knopf, 1992.
The end of the world and the ends of God: science and theology on eschatology. J. Polkinghorne and M. Welker, editors. Trinity Press International, 2000.
The mind of God: science and the search for ultimate meaning. P. Davies. New York: Simon & Schuster, 1992.
The new consciousness in science and religion. H.K. Schilling.

London: SCM Press, 1973.
The new faith-science debate. J.M. Magnum, editor. Minneapolis: Fortress Press, 1989.
The sciences and theology in the twentieth century. A. Peacocke, editor. Notre Dame, IN: University of Notre Dame Press, 1981.
Theology for a scientific age: being and becoming—natural, divine, and human. A. Peacocke. Minneapolis: Fortress Press, 1993. 438p.
Theology in the age of scientific reasoning. N. Murphy. Ithaca, NY: Cornell University Press, 1990. 218p. (Draws on new historicist accounts of science, particularly Imre Lakatos).

11. WORLD RELIGIONS (including Christianity)

A dictionary of non-Christian religions. G. Parrinder. Philadelphia, PA: Westminster, 1971. 320p.
A handbook of living religions. J. R. Hinnells (ed). London and New York: Viking, 1984; London: Penguin, 1991. 528p.
A reader's guide to the great religions. C. J. Adams (ed). 2nd ed. New York: Free Press; London: Collier Macmillan, 1977. 539p.
A sourcebook for earth's community of religions. J. D. Beversluis (ed). Rev. ed. Grand Rapids, MI: CoNexus Press—Sourcebook Project; New York: Global Education Associates, 1995. 376p. (Contains statements from the Parliament of the World's Religions, Chicago, 1993).
Atlas of the world's religions. N.Smart (ed). New York: Oxford University Press, 1999. 240p.
Christian faith amidst religious pluralism: an introductory bibliography. D. G. Dawe et al. Richmond, VA: Union Theological Seminary in Virginia, 1980. 115p.
Christianity and the New Age religion: a bridge toward mutual understanding. L. D. Moore. Atlanta: Pendulum Plus Press, 1993. 244p.
Companions in consciousness: the Bible and the New Age movement. R. Quillo. Liguori, MO: Triumph Books, 1995. 191p.
Concise dictionary of religion. I. Hexham. Downers Grove, IL: InterVarsity Press, 1993. 245p.
Contemporary religions: a world guide. I. Harris et al (eds). Harlow, UK: Longman, 1992. 511p.
Defenders of God: the fundamentalist revolt against the modern age. B. B. Lawrence. San Francisco: Harper & Row, 1989. 318p. (An examination of fundamentalist movements in several religions, including Christianity, Judaism, and Islam.).
Dictionary of cults, sects, religions and the occult. G. A. Mather & L. A. Nichols. Grand Rapids, MI: Zondervan, 1993. 384p.
Dictionary of religion and philosophy. G. MacGregor. New York: Paragon House, 1989; paperback, 1991. 696p. (Published in Britain under the title, *The everyman dictionary of religion and philosophy,* London: Dent, 1990.).
Dictionnaire des religions. P. Poupard (ed). 3rd ed. Paris: Presses Universitaires de France, 1993. 2,218p in 2 vols.
Encyclopaedia of religion and ethics. J. Hastings (ed). Edinburgh: T. & T. Clark; New York: Scribner, 1908–27. 12 vols.
Geography of religions. D. E. Sopher. *Foundations of cultural geography series.* Englewood Cliffs, NJ: Prentice-Hall, 1967. 128p.
Great religions of the world. M. Severy (ed). *The Story of Man Library.* Washington, DC: National Geographic Society. 420p. (Examines Hinduism, Buddhism, Judaism, Islam, and Christianity).
Histoire des religions. H. Puech (ed). Paris: Gallimard, 1970–1976. 3 vols.
Historical atlas of the religions of the world. I. R. al Faruqi & D. E. Sopher (eds). New York: Macmillan; London: Collier Macmillan, 1974. 368p.
Interfaith directory. F. Clark (ed). New York: International Religious Foundation, 1987. 194p.
International directory of the world's religions. J. G. Melton et al (eds). Santa Barbara, CA: ABC CLIO, 2000. (Multivolume).
International directory of the world's religions. G. Ward. Carmel, CA: Apogee Press, 1991.
Japanese religion. H. Ichiro et al (eds). Tokyo: Kodensha, 1972. 272p.
Keyguide to information sources on world religions. J. Holm. London: Mansell Publishing, 1991. 271p.
Le grand atlas des religions. C. Baladier (ed). Paris: Encyclopaedia Universalis, 1990. 413p.
Longman guide to living religions. I. Harris et al. (eds). London: Longman Current Affairs, 1994. 294p.
New dictionary of religions. J. R. Hinnells (ed). Oxford, UK and Cambridge, MA: Blackwell Reference, 1995. 760p. (Enlarged edition of two earlier titles, *The Penguin dictionary of religions,* New York: Viking, 1984; and *The facts on file dictionary of religions,* New York and London: Facts on File, 1984.).
Our religions. A. Sharma (ed). San Francisco: Harper, 1993. 547p.
Religion in Europe: contemporary perspectives. S. Gill et al. (eds). Kampen, Netherlands: Kok Pharos Publishing, 1994.
Religions of America: ferment and faith in an age of crisis. L. Rosten (ed). Rev. ed. New York: Simon & Schuster, 1975. 672p.
Religions of Asia. J. Y. Fenton et al. 2nd ed. New York: St. Martin's Press, 1988. 336p.
Religions of the world. L. M. Hopfe, L. R. Hopfe & L. M. H. Hopfe (eds). 6th ed. Englewood Cliffs, NJ: Prentice-Hall, 1994. 454p.
Religious information sources: a worldwide guide. J. G. Melton & M. A. Köszegi. New York: Garland, 1992. 581p.
Religious traditions of the world: a journey through Africa, Mesoamerica, North America, Judaism, Christianity, Islam, Hinduism, Buddhism, China, and Japan. H. B. Earhart (ed). San Francisco: Harper, 1993. 1,224p.
Sacred worlds: an introduction to geography and religion. C. C. Park. London and New York: Routledge, 1994. 346p.
The concise encyclopedia of living faiths. R. C. Zaehner (ed). New York: Hawthorn Books, 1959. 431p.
The Continuum dictionary of religion. M. Pye (ed). New York: Crossroad/Continuum, 1994. 332p. (Published in Britain as *The Macmillan dictionary of religion.*).
The Eliade guide to world religions. M. Eliade, I. P. Couliano & H. S. Wiesner. San Francisco: Harper, 1991. 313p. (Later issued as *HarperCollins concise guide to world religions.* 2000. 320p).
The encyclopedia of religion. M. Eliade et al. (eds). 1986; New York: Macmillan, 1993. 16 vols.
The encyclopedia of world faiths: an illustrated survey of the world's living religions. P. Bishop & M. Darton (eds). New York: Facts on File, 1987. 352p.
The HarperCollins dictionary of religion. J. Z. Smith (ed). San Francisco: HarperCollins, 1995. 184p.
The Oxford dictionary of world religions. J. Bowker. Oxford: Oxford University Press, 1996. 1,111p.
The Penguin dictionary of religions. J. R. Hinnells (ed). New York and London: Penguin Books, 1984. 550p. (Includes brief articles on 1,150 terms, as well as an extensive section of bibliographies).
The perennial dictionary of world religions. K. Crim (ed). San Francisco: Harper & Row, 1989. 830p. (A reprint of *The Abingdon dictionary of living religions,* Nashville, TN: Abingdon, 1981).
The world's religions. N. Smart. New York: Cambridge University Press, 1995. 576p.
The world's religions. S. Sutherland et al. (eds). London: Routledge; Boston: G. K. Hall, 1988. 1,009p.
The world's religions: understanding the living faiths. P. B. Clarke (ed). Pleasantville, NY and London: Reader's Digest and Marshall Editions, 1993. 220p.
Twentieth century encyclopedia of religious knowledge. L. A. Loetscher (ed). Grand Rapids, MI: Baker, 1955. 2 vols.
Who's who of world religions. J. R. Hinnells (ed). New York: Simon & Schuster, 1992. 576p.
World religions: a sourcebook for students of Christian theology. R. Viladesau & M. Massa (eds). Mahwah, NJ: Paulist, 1994. 285p. (An anthology of selections from sacred texts of non-Christian world religions).
World religions and human liberation. D. Cohn-Sherbok. *Faith meets faith series.* Maryknoll, NY: Orbis, 1992. 151p.
World religions: the great faiths explored and explained. J. Bowker. London: DK Limited, 1997. 200p.

II. NON-CHRISTIAN CONTEXT

1. ISLAM

A bibliography of Islamic law, 1980–1993. L. Al-Zwaini & R. Peters. *Handbuch der Orientalistik. Erste Abteilung, der Nahe und Mittlere Osten (Handbook of Oriental studies, Near and Middle East),* 19. Leiden and New York: E. J. Brill, 1994. 248p.
A commentary on the Qur'an. R. Bell. Manchester, UK: University of Manchester Press, 1991. 630p. in 2 vols. (From a draft written by Richard Bell and edited by C. E. Bosworth and M. E. J. Richardson).
A concordance of the Qur'an. H. E. Kassis. Berkeley, CA: University of California Press, 1983. 1,483p.
A popular dictionary of Islam. I. R. Netton. London: Curzon, 1992. 279p. (For beginning students of Islam).
A reader on classical Islam. F. E. Peters. Princeton, NJ: Princeton University Press, 1994. 440.
An introduction to Islam. D. Waines. New York: Cambridge University Press, 1995. 344p.
Annuaire du monde musulman. L. Massignon. Paris: Presses Universitaires de France, 1954 (4th edition). 428p.
Deciphering the signs of God: a phenomenological approach to Islam. A. Scimmel. Albany, NY: State University of New York Press, 1994. 319p.
Der Koran: Kommentar und Konkordanz. R. Paret. 5th ed. Stuttgart: Kohlhammer, 1994. 555p.
Dictionnaire des symboles musulmans: ristes, mystique et civilisation. M. Chebel. Paris: Albin Michel, 1995. 501p.
Encyclopedia Iranica. E. Yarshater (ed). London and New York: Routledge & Kegan Paul, 1985–90 (vols. 1–4); Costa Mesa, CA: Mazda Publishing, 1992– (vols. 5–7). 7 vols. to date; in progress to at least 15 vols.
Encyclopédie philosophique universelle. A. Jacob (ed). Paris: Presses Universitaires de France, 1989–92. 5 vols. in 3. (51 articles on a variety of topics concerning Islam are scattered throughout).
Everyday life in the Muslim Middle East. D. L. Bowen & E. A. Early (eds). Bloomington, IN: Indiana University Press, 1993. (Describes life in World A).
Higher learning in Islam: the classical period 700 AD to 1300 AD. C. M. Stanton. Savage, MD: Rowman & Littlefield, 1990. 225p. (Scholarly look at the Golden Age of Islam).
Index Islamicus 1906–1955: a catalogue of articles on Islamic subjects in periodicals and other collective publications. J. D. Pearson et al. Cambridge, UK: Heffer, 1958. 807p. (Supplemental vols published in 1962, 1967, 1972, 1977).
Islam, section 22 in *Iconography of religions.* Leiden: E. J. Brill, 1974–. 3 vols. to date. (2 volumes on Muslim architecture and one volume on India and Pakistan).
Islam and Islamic groups: a worldwide reference guide. F. Shaikh (ed). Harlow, Essex, UK: Longman Group, 1992. 326p. (A political guide to Islam).
Islam in North America: a sourcebook. M. A. Köszegi & J. G. Melton (eds). New York: Garland, 1992. 392p.
Islam in tribal societies: from the Atlas to the Indus. A. S. Ahmed & D. M. Hart. London: Routledge & Kegan Paul, 1984. 350p.
Islamic Da'wah in the West: Muslim missionary activity and the dynamics of conversion to Islam. L. Poston. Oxford, UK: Oxford University Press, 1992. 224p.
Islamologie. F. M. Pareja (ed). Beyrouth: Imprimerie Catholique, 1957–64. 1,149p. (Though dated, still an excellent resource.).
Judaism, Christianity, and Islam: the classical texts and their interpretation. F. E. Peters. Princeton, NJ: Princeton University Press, 1990. 1248.
Lexikon religiöser Grundbegriffe: Judentum, Christentum, Islam. A. T. Khoury (ed). Graz: Styria, 1987. 637p. (A comparison of Judaism, Christianity, and Islam).
Muhammad and Jesus: a comparison of the prophets and their teachings. W. E. Phipps. New York: Continuum, 1996. 316p.
Muslim minorities in the West. S. Z. Abedin & Z. Sardar (eds). *Studies of Muslim minorities.* London: Grey Seal, 1995. 222p.
Muslim peoples: a world ethnographic survey. R. V. Weekes (ed). 2nd ed. Westport, CT: Greenwood, 1984. 2 vols.
Muslim women throughout the world: a bibliography. M. Kimball & B. R. von Schlegell. Sterling, VA: Lynne Reiner, 1997. 285p.
Piety and power: Muslims and Christians in West Africa. L. Sanneh. Maryknoll, NY: Orbis Books, 1996.
Political Islam: religion and politics in the Arab world. N. N. Ayubi. London: Routledge, 1991. 302p.
Qur'anic Christians: an analysis of classical and modern exegesis. J. D. McAuliffe. Cambridge, UK and New York: Cambridge University Press, 1991. 352p. (Examines the Islamic understanding of Christians. Studies passages in the Qur'an that make ostensibly positive remarks about Christians).
Religion and tradition in Islamic Central Asia. M. B. Olcott. Armonk, NY: M. E. Sharpe, 1992.
Shi'a Islam: from religion to revolution. H. Halm. 176p.
'The black Muslims as a new religious movement: their evolution and implications for the study of religion in a pluralistic context,' L. H. Mamiya, in *Conflict and cooperation between contemporary religious groups.* Chuo Academic Research Group. Tokyo: Nakamura, 1988.
The Cambridge history of Islam. P. M. Holt, A. K. S. Lambton & B. Lewis (eds). London: Cambridge University Press, 1970. 4 vols.
The Cambridge illustrated history of the Islamic world. F. Robinson (ed). Cambridge, UK: Cambridge University Press, 1996. 352p.
The concise encyclopedia of Islam. C. Glassé. San Francisco: Harper, 1989; paperback, 1991. 472p.
The contemporary Islamic revival: a critical survey and bibliography. Y. Y. Haddad, J. O. Voll & J. L. Esposito. Westport, CT: Greenwood, 1991. 230p.
The cultural atlas of Islam. I. R. al Faruqi & L. L. al Faruqi. New York: Macmillan, 1986. 528p. (Not a true atlas, this work examines a wide variety of aspects of Islam from the perspective of two devoted followers).
The encyclopædia of Islam. J. M. J. van Lent. 2nd ed. Leiden: E. J. Brill, 1997.
The encyclopedia of Islam: new edition. H. A. R. Gibb [1895-1971] and C. E. Bosworth et al. (eds). Leiden: E. J. Brill, 1960–. 9,000p. in 8 vols to date.
The hajj: the Muslim pilgrimage to Mecca and the holy places. F. E. Peters. Princeton, NJ: Princeton University Press, 1994. 452.
The influence of Islam upon Africa. J. S. Trimingham. 1968; London: Librairie du Liban, 1980. 182p.
The Iranians: Persia, Islam and the soul of a nation. S. Mackey. New York: Dutton, 1996. 448p.
The Islamic revival since 1988: a critical survey and bibliography. Y. Y. Haddad & J. L. Esposito. *Bibliographies and indexes in religious studies,* 45. Westport, CT: Greenwood, 1997. 317p.
The Isma'ilis: their history and doctrines. F. Daftary. Cambridge, UK: Cambridge University Press, 1990. 822p.
The Jews of Islam. B. Lewis. Princeton, NJ: Princeton University Press, 1984. 257p.
The lawful and the prohibited in Islam. Y. Al-Qaradawi. 20th ed. Plainfield, IN: American Trust, 1994.
The Muslim almanac. A. Nanji (ed). Detroit, MI: Gale Research, 1995.
The Oxford encyclopedia of the modern Islamic world. J. L. Esposito (ed). New York and Oxford, UK: Oxford University Press, 1995. 1,920p. in 4 vols.
The Prophet and the Pharoah: Muslim extremism in Egypt. G. Kepel. Trans., J. Rothschild. London: Al Saqi, 1985. 251p. (Translated from the French, *Le prophète et Pharaon.* Paris: La Découverte, 1984.).
The quarterly index Islamicus: current books, articles and papers on Islamic studies. J. D. Pearson (ed). London: Mansell, 1977–91; Bowker–Saur, 1992–93.
The revenge of God: the resurgence of Islam, Christianity and Judaism in the modern world. G. Kepel. University Park, PA: Pennsylvania State University Press, 1994. 215p. (Translated by A. Braley from *La Revanche de Dieu*).
The rumbling volcano: Islamic fundamentalism in Egypt. N. Jabbour. Pasadena, CA: Mandate Press, 1993. 311p.
The Shiites: ritual and popular piety in a Muslim community. D. Pinault. New York: St. Martin's Press, 1992. 240p.
The Sufis. I. Shah. New York: Doubleday, 1964. 429p.
The veil and the male elite: a feminist interpretation of women's rights in Islam. F. Mernissi. Reading, MA: Addison-Wesley, 1991. 240p.

2. JUDAISM

A book of Jewish concepts. P. Birnbaum. 2nd ed. New York: Hebrew Publishing, 1988. 732p.
Atlas of modern Jewish history. E. Friesel. New York: Oxford University Press, 1990. 159p.
Contemporary Jewish religious thought: original essays on critical concepts, movements and beliefs. A. A. Cohen & P. Mendes–Flohr (eds). New York: Scribner, 1987. 1,183p.
Encyclopaedia Judaica: das Judentum in Geschichte und Gegenwart. Berlin: Verlag Esckol, 1928–34. 10 vols.
Encyclopedia Judaica. C. Roth & G. Wigoder (eds). Jerusalem:

Keter Publishing House, 1972. 16 vols.

Encyclopedia of Hasidism. T. M. Rabinowicz (ed). Northvale, NJ: Jason Aronson, 1996.

Encyclopedia of Jewish history: events and eras of the Jewish people. J. Alpher (ed). New York: Facts on File, 1986. 288p.

Encyclopedia of Jewish prayer: Ashkenazic and Sephardic rites. M. Nulman. 1993; Arcade, NY: C. N. Aronson, 1996. 464p.

Encyclopedia of Talmudic sages. G. Bader. Arcade, NY: C. N. Aronson, 1993. 888p.

Encyclopedia of the holocaust. I. Guttman (ed). New York and London: Macmillan, 1990. 4 vols.

Encyclopedia of the Jewish religion. Z. Werblosky & G. Wigoder (eds). Bellmore, NY: Modan/Adama Books, 1986. 478p.

Encyclopedia Talmudica: a digest of Halachic Literature and Jewish law from the Tannaitic period to the present time alphabetically arranged. Rabbi Meyer Berlin. Jerusalem: Talmudic Encyclopedia Institute, 1969–. 2,900p. in 4 vols. to date. (Translated from the 18 vol. Hebrew edition).

Events and movements in modern Judaism. R. Patai & E. Goldsmith (eds). New York: Paragon House, 1995. 316p.

Holocaust literature: a handbook of critical, historical and literary writings. S. S. Friedman (ed). Westport, CT and London: Greenwood, 1994. 707p. (An essential handbook for anyone studying holocaust literature).

Jewish Encyclopedia. C. Adler et al. (eds). New York: Funk & Wagnalls, 1901–06. 12 vols. Rev. ed. I. Singer (ed), New York: Katy Publishers, 1964. 12 vols.

Jewish literacy: the most important things to know about the Jewish religion, its people and its history. Rabbi Joseph Telushkin. New York: Morrow, 1991. 688p.

Jewish–American history and culture: an encyclopedia. J. Fischel & S. Pinsker. New York: Garland, 1991.

Jews and Christians: a troubled family. W. Harrelson & R. M. Falk. Nashville, TN: Abingdon, 1990. 208p.

Judaism, section 23 in *Iconography of religions.* Leiden: E. J. Brill, 1975–. 4 vols. to date. (Covers Jewish sanctuary, Jewish year, Jewish life cycle, and Samaritans).

Judaism and Christianity: a guide to the reference literature. E. D. Starkey. *Reference sources in the humanities series.* Englewood, CO: Libraries Unlimited, 1991. 270p.

Judaism: between yesterday and tomorrow. H. Küng. New York: Continuum, 1992. 775p.

Judaism, Christianity, and Islam: the classical texts and their interpretation. F. E. Peters. Princeton, NJ: Princeton University Press, 1990. 1248.

Lexikon religiöser Grundbegriffe: Judentum, Christentum, Islam. A. T. Khoury (ed). Graz: Styria, 1987. 637p. (A comparison of Judaism, Christianity, and Islam).

Neues Lexikon des Judentums. J. H. Schoeps (ed). Frankfurt: Bertelsman, 1992.

New encyclopedia of Zionism and Israel. G. Wigoder (ed). 2nd ed. London and Toronto: Associated University Presses, 1994.

Perpetual dilemma: Jewish religion in the Jewish state. S. Z. Abramov. Cranbury, NJ: Associated University Presses, 1976. 432p.

Response to modernity: a history of the Reform Movement in Judaism. M. A. Meyere. New York: Oxford University Press, 1988.

The Blackwell dictionary of Judaica. D. Cohn–Sherbok. Oxford, UK and Cambridge, MA: Blackwell Reference, 1992. 642p.

The encyclopedia of Jewish symbols. E. Frankel & B. P. Teutsch. 1992; Arcade, NY: C. N. Aronson, 1995. 256p.

The encyclopedia of Judaism. G. Wigoder (ed). Jerusalem: Jerusalem Publishing House; New York: Macmillan, 1989. 800p.

The Jews of Islam. B. Lewis. Princeton, NJ: Princeton University Press, 1984. 257p.

The joys of Hebrew. L. Glinert. New York and Oxford, UK: Oxford University Press, 1992. 304p. (Explains the usage of more than six hundred (transliterated) Hebrew terms of particular importance to Jewish life).

The other Jews: the Sephardim today. D. J. Elazar. New York: Basic Books, 1989. 248p.

The Oxford dictionary of the Jewish religion. R. J. Z. Werblowsky & G. Wigoder (eds). New York and London: Oxford University Press, 1996. (An updated edition of *The encyclopedia of the Jewish religion.* Jerusalem: Masada, 1965; New York: Holt, Rinehart & Winston, 1966).

The revenge of God: the resurgence of Islam, Christianity and Judaism in the modern world. G. Kepel. University Park, PA: Pennsylvania State University Press, 1994. 215p. (Translated by A. Braley from *La Revanche de Dieu*).

The timetables of Jewish history: a chronology of the most important people and events in Jewish history. J. Gribetz et al. New York: Simon & Schuster, 1993. 752p.

The vocabulary of Jewish life. A. M. Heller. 2nd ed. New York: Hebrew Publishing, 1967. 367p.

Tradition, innovation, conflict: Jewishness and Judaism in contemporary Israel. Z. Sobel & B. Beit-Hallahmi (eds). *SUNY series in Israeli studies.* Albany, NY: State University of New York Press, 1991. 304p.

Vanishing diaspora: the Jews in Europe since 1945. B. Wasserstein. Cambridge, MA: Harvard University Press, 1996. 352p.

3. HINDUISM

A classical dictionary of Hindu mythology and religion, geography, history, and literature. J. Dowson. First edition 1879; 8th edition, London: Routledge & Kegen Paul, 1953. 411p.

A dictionary of Hinduism: its mythology, folklore and development, 1500 BC—AD 1500. M. Stutley & J. Stutley. London: Routledge & Kegan Paul, 1977. 390p. (Published in the U.S. as *Harper's dictionary of Hinduism: its mythology, folklore, philosophy, literature and history.*).

A primer of Hinduism. J. N. Farquhar. N.p., 1993. 208p.

A survey of Hinduism. K. R. Klostermeier. 2nd ed. Albany, NY: State University of New York Press, 1994. 734p.

An introduction to Hinduism. G. Flood. New York: Cambridge University Press, 1996. 350p.

Encyclopaedia of Puranic beliefs and practices. S. A. Dange. New Dehli: Narraing, 1986–90. 5 vols.

Encyclopaedia of Sikh religion and culture. R. C. Dogra & G. S. Mansukhani. Columbia, MO: South Asia Books, 1995.

Encyclopaedia of the Hindu world. G. R. Garg (ed). New Delhi: Concept Publishing, 1992–. 9 vols to date; in progress to 100 vols.

Encyclopaedia of Vedanta. R. M. Sharma. Columbia, MO: South Asia Books, 1993.

Encyclopedia of Sikhism. H. Singh (ed). Patiala, India: Punjabi University.

Historical dictionary of Sikhism. W. H. McLeod. *Religions, philosophies, and movements series,* 5. Metuchen, NJ: Scarecrow Press, 1995. 338p.

Sikhism and the Sikhs: an annotated bibliography. P. M. Rai. *Bibliographies and indexes in religious studies,* 13. New York: Greenwood, 1989. 272p.

The camphor flame: popular Hinduism and society in India. C. J. Fuller. Princeton, NJ: Princeton University Press, 1992. 328p.

The crown of Hinduism. J. N. Farquhar. 1913; reprint, 1971. 458p.

The Sikh diaspora: migration and the experience beyond Punjab. N. G. Barrier & V. A. Dusenbery (eds). Delhi: Chanakya Publications, 1989. 362p.

The Sikhs. No. 16 in section 13, *Indian religions,* in *Iconography of religions.* G. R. Thursby. Leiden: E. J. Brill, 1992. 42p.

4. BUDDHISM

A concise history of Buddhism. A. Skilton. 2nd ed. Birmingham, UK: Windhorse, 1997. 269p.

An encyclopedia of Buddhist deities. F. W. Bunce. New Delhi: D. K. Printworld, 1994.

An introduction to Buddhism. P. Harvey. New York: Cambridge University Press, 1990. 396p.

An introduction to Tantric Buddhism. S. B. Dargyay. Berkeley, CA: Shambhala, 1974. 211p.

Bibliographie bouddhique. Paris: Librarie d'Amérique et d'Orient, 1930–61 (fasc. 1–31). (Annual).

Bibliography on Buddhism. S. Hanayama. Tokyo: Hokuseido Press, 1961. 869p. (15,073 numbered entries).

Buddhism: art and faith. W. Zwalf (ed). London: British Museum Publications, 1985. 300p.

Buddhism in Afghanistan and Central Asia. No. 14 in section 13, *Indian religions,* in *Iconography of religions,* S. Gaulier, R. Jera-Bezard & M. Maillard. Leiden: E. J. Brill, 1976. 2 vols.

Buddhism of Tibet. Tenzin Gyatso, Fourteenth Dalai Lama. Trans. and ed., J. Hopkins. Ithaca, NY: Snow Lion, 1987. 219p.

Buddhism's contribution to the world culture and civilization. A. W. P. Guruge & D. C. Ahir (eds). New Delhi: Maha Bodhi Society of India, 1977. 219p. (Conference papers).

Buddhist iconography. L. Chandra. 3rd ed. New Delhi: Aditya Prakashan, 1988. 2 vols.

Buddhist spirituality: India, Southeast Asia, Tibet, China. T. Yoshinori. New York: Crossroad, 1993. 500p.

Cent Clés pour comprendre le zen. C. Durix. 2nd ed. 1976; Paris: Courrier du Livre, 1991. 367p.

Encyclopaedia of Buddhism. G. P. Malalasekera et al. (eds). Colombo, Sri Lanka: Government of Sri Lanka, 1961–. 5 vols. to date; in progress to 11 vols.

Encyclopaedia of Buddhist deities, demigods, godlings, saints and demons: with special focus on iconographic attributes. F. W. Bunce (ed). Columbia, MO: South Asia Books, 1994.

Handbook of Tibetan culture. G. Coleman (ed). London: Rider, 1993; Boston: Shambhala, 1994. 430p.

Historical dictionary of Buddhism. C. S. Prebish. *Religions, philosophies, and movements series,* 1. Metuchen, NJ and London: Scarecrow Press, 1993. 425p.

Les Dieux du bouddhisme: guide iconographique. L. Fréderic. Paris: Flammarion, 1992. 360p. (English translation, *Buddhism: Flammarion iconographic guides*).

Présence du bouddhisme. R. de Berval (ed). 2nd ed. Saigon: France–Asie, 1959; Paris: Gallimard, 1987. 816p.

The Buddhist handbook: a complete guide to Buddhist teaching, practice, history and schools. J. Snelling. Rochester, VT: Inner Traditions; London: Rider, 1992. 377p.

The Buddhist world of Southeast Asia. D. K. Swearer. *SUNY Series in religion.* Albany, NY: State University of New York Press, 1995. 272p.

The history of Buddhism in India and Tibet. Bu-ston. Trans., E. Obermiller. *Bibliotheca Indo-Buddhica,* 26. Delhi: Sri Satguru, 1986. 231p.

The iconography of Chinese Buddhism in traditional China. No. 5 of section 12, *East and Central Asia,* of *Iconography of religions.* H. A. van Oort. Leiden: E. J. Brill, 1986. 2 vols.

The iconography of Korean Buddhist painting. No. 9 of section 12, *East and Central Asia,* of *Iconography of religions.* H. H. Sorensen. Leiden: E. J. Brill, 1988. 21p.

The world of Buddhism: Buddhist monks and nuns in society. H. Bechert & R. Gombrich. London: Thames & Hudson, 1984. 198p. (Highly illustrated coffee-table style book).

5. OTHER RELIGIONS

A dictionary of comparative religion. S. G. F. Brandon (ed). London: Weidenfeld & Nicolson, 1970.

A dictionary of non–Christian religions. G. Parrinder. Amersham: Hulton; Philadelphia: Westminster, 1971; reprint, Hulton, 1981. 320p.

A dictionary of religious and spiritual quotations. G. Parrinder. London: Routledge; New York: Simon & Schuster, 1989. 228p.

America's alternative religions. T. Miller (ed). *SUNY series in religious studies.* Albany, NY: State University of New York Press, 1995. 484p. (Includes some Christian denominations and sects).

An introduction to Taiwanese folk religions. G. P. Kramer & G. Wu. Taipei, 1970. 89p.

Anthroposophy: a fragment. R. Steiner. Trans., C. E. Creeger. *Classics in anthroposophy.* Hudson, NY: Anthroposophic Press, 1996.

Approaches to Jaina studies: philosophy, logic, rituals and symbols. O. Qvarnström & N. K. Wagle (eds). Toronto: University of Toronto, Centre for South Asian Studies, 1997.

Atheism and theism. J. J. C. Smart. *Great debates in philosophy.* Oxford, UK and Cambridge, MA: Blackwell, 1996. 240p.

Bibliography of new religious movements in primal societies. H. W. Turner. Boston and New York: G. K. Hall, 1977–92. 6 vols.

Botswana handbook of churches: a handbook of churches, ecumenical organisations, theological institutions and other world religions in Botswana. J. N. Amanze. Gaborone, Botswana: Pula Press, 1994. 327p.

Defining Jainism: reform in the Jain tradition. J. E. Cort. Toronto: University of Toronto, Centre for South Asian Studies, 1995.

Dictionary of Celtic mythology. P. B. Ellis. New York: Oxford University Press, 1992; paperback, 1994. 232p.

Dictionary of cults, sects, religions and the occult. G. A. Mather & L. A. Nichols. Grand Rapids, MI: Zondervan, 1993. 396p.

Dictionary of deities and demons in the Bible. K. van der Toorn, B. Becking & P. van der Horst (eds). Leiden, Cologne, and New York: E. J. Brill, 1995. 923p.

Dictionary of Native American mythology. S. D. Gill & I. F. Sullivan (eds). Santa Barbara, CA: ABC-CLIO, 1992; New York: Oxford University Press, 1994. 455p.

Dictionary of Polynesian mythology. R. D. Craig. New York: Greenwood, 1989. 465p.

Dieux d'hommes: Dictionnaire des messianismes et millénarismes de l'Ere chrétienne. H. Desroche et al. Paris and The Hague: Mouton, 1969. 281p.

Encyclopaedia of occultism. L. Spence. 1960; New York: Carol Publishing, 1984. 464p.

Encyclopedia of eastern philosophy and religion. S. Schumacher & G. Woerner (eds). Boston: Shambhala, 1994. 482p.

Encyclopedia of gods: over 2,500 deities of the world. M. Jordan. New York: Facts on File, 1993. 351p.

Encyclopedia of Indian philosophies. K. H. Potter (ed). Delhi: Motilal Banarsidass; Princeton, NJ: Princeton University Press, 1970–1990. 5 vols.

Encyclopedia of Mormonism. D. H. Ludlow. New York: Macmillan, 1992. 5 vols.

Encyclopedia of mythology. A. Cotterell. Oxford, UK and New York: Oxford University Press, 1986.

Encyclopedia of mythology. E. Flaum. Philadelphia: Courage Books, 1993.

Encyclopedia of myths and legends. S. Gordon. North Pomfret, VT: Trafalgar, 1994. 799p.

Encyclopedia of Native American religions. A. Hirschfelder & P. Molin (eds). Reprint. 1996. 384p.

Encyclopedia of palmistry. E. O. Campbell. New York: Berkley Publishing, 1996. 320p.

Encyclopedia of parapsychology and psychical research. A. S. Berger & J. Berger. Champaign, IL: Marlowe, 1994. 554p.

Encyclopedia of signs, omens, and superstitions. Zolar. New York: Carol Publishing Group, 1995. 400p.

Encyclopedia of superstitions, folklore and the occult sciences of the world. C. L. Daniels & C. M. Stevans (eds). Repr. ed. Detroit, MI: Omnigraphics, 1997. 3 vols.

Encyclopedia of Tarot. S. R. Kaplan. Stamford, CT: US Games Systems, 1978–1990. 3 vols.

Encyclopedia of traditional epics. G. M. Jackson. Santa Barbara, CA: ABC-CLIO, 1994. 750p.

Encyclopedia of witchcraft and demonology. R. H. Robbins. New York: Random House, 1988.

Encyclopedia of witches and witchcraft. R. E. Guiley. New York: Facts on File, 1990. 432p.

Encyclopedia of women in world religions. Englewood Cliffs, NJ: Prentice-Hall, 1996.

Extraordinary groups: an examination of unconventional life–styles. W. M. Kephart & W. W. Zellner. 5th ed. New York: St. Martin's, 1994. 334p.

Fundamentalism as an ecumenical challenge. H. Küng & J. Moltmann (eds). London: SCM Press, 1992. 144p.

Goddesses in world mythology. M. Ann & D. M. Imel. Santa Barbara, CA: ABC-CLIO, 1993. 675p.

Guide to the gods. M. Leach. Santa Barbara, CA: ABC-CLIO, 1992. 1,007p.

Jain directory of North America. Boston: Jain Center of Greater Boston, 1992.

La voie Jaina: histoire, spiritualité, vie des ascètes pèlerines de l'Inde. N. Shântâ. Paris: O.E.I.L., 1985. 615p.

Lexikon der Götter und Dämonen. M. Lurker. Stuttgart: A. Krämer, 1984. 451p. (English edition, *Dictionary of gods and goddesses, devils and demons.* London and New York: Routledge, 1987–88).

Lexikon der östlichen Weisheitslehren. S. Shumacher & G. Woerner (eds). Bern and Munich: Otto Barth, 1986. (English translation, *The encyclopedia of Eastern philosophy and religion: Buddhism, Hinduism, Taoism, Zen*).

Lexikon der religionen: phänomene—geschichte—ideen. H. Waldenfels (ed). Freiburg: Herder, 1987; paperback, 1992. 751p.

Living without religion: eupraxophy. P. Kurtz. Amherst, NY: Prometheus, 1994. 159p. (Coins the term 'eupraxophy,' meaning 'good conduct and wisdom in living.' Advocates moral life apart from religion).

Money and power in the new religions. J. T. Richardson (ed). Lewiston, NY: E. Mellen Press, 1988.

Mythes et croyances du monde entier. A. Akoun (ed). Paris: Lidis-Brepols, 1985. 5 vols.

Mythologies. Y. Bonnefoy. Chicago: University of Chicago Press, 1991. 2 vols, 1,305p. (Translated and restructed under the direction of Wendy Doniger from the French, *Dictionnaire des mythologies et des religions, des sociétés traditionelles et du monde antique,* 1981. Translated by Gerald Honnigsblum, et al. A paperback edition in 4 vols. appeared in 1992.).

Myths, gods and fantasy. P. Allardica. Santa Barbara, CA: ABC-

CLIO, 1991. 232p.
Myths of the world: a thematic encyclopedia. M. Jordan. London: Kyle Cathie, 1993. 319p.
New religions and the new Europe. R. Towler (ed). Aarhus, Denmark: Aarhus University Press, 1995. 246p.
New religions as global cultures. I. Hexham & K. Poewe. Boulder, CO: Westview Press.
New religious movements and the churches. A. R. Brockway & J. P. Rajashekar (eds). Geneva: WCC Publications, 1987. 221p. (Report of a consultation sponsored by the Lutheran World Federation and the World Council of Churches held in Amsterdam, 1986).
New religious movements in the United States and Canada: a critical assessment and annotated bibliography. D. Choquette. *Bibliographies and indexes in religious studies,* 5. Westport, CT: Greenwood, 1985. 235p.
Pacific mythology: an encyclopedia of myth and legend. J. Knappert. London: Aquarian; San Francisco: Thorsons, 1992. 334p.
Puranic encyclopaedia: a comprehensive dictionary with special reference to the Epic and Puranic literature. V. Mani. 4th English ed. Delhi: Motilal Banarsidass, 1975. 930p.
Riches and renunciation: religion, economy, and society among the Jains. J. Laidlaw. Oxford, UK: Oxford University Press, 1995. 446p.
Scripture and community: collected essays on the Jains. K. W. Folkert. Ed., J. E. Cort. Atlanta: Scholars Press, 1993. 468p.
South Asian religions in the Americas: an annotated bibliography of immigrant religious traditions. J. Y. Fenton. *Bibliographies and indexes in religious studies.* Westport, CT: Greenwood.
Taoist ritual and popular cults of Southeast China. K. Dean. Princeton, NJ: Princeton University Press, 1993. 320p.
The advent of Sun Myung Moon: the origins, beliefs, and practices of the Unification Church. G. D. Chryssides. New York: St. Martin's, 1991. 242p.
The Aquarian guide to African mythology. J. Knappert. Wellingborough: Aquarian, 1990. 272p.
The Children of God/Family of Love: an annotated bibliography. W. D. Pritchett. *Sects and cults in America. Bibliographical guides,* 5; *Garland reference library of social science,* 209. New York: Garland, 1985. 209p.
The clever adulteress and other stories: a treasury of Jain literature. P. Grandoff (ed). London: Mosaic Press, 1990. 290p.
The dictionary of religious terms. D. T. Kauffman. London: Marshall, Morgan & Scott, 1967. 455p. (11,000 definitions).
The encyclopaedia of Middle Eastern mythology and religion. J. Knappert. Shaftesbury, UK, and Rockport, MA: Element, 1993. 309p.
The encyclopedia of native American religion: an introduction. A. Hirschfelder & P. Molin (eds). New York and Oxford, UK: Facts on File, 1992. 379p.
The Encyclopedia of unbelief. G. Stein (ed). Buffalo, NY: Prometheus, 1985. 835p.
The Facts on File encyclopedia of world mythology and legend. A. S. Mercatante. New York: Facts on File, 1988. 825p.
The fundamentalism project. M. E. Marty & R. S. Appleby (eds). Chicago: University of Chicago Press, 1991–96. 5 vols. (Vol. 1: *Fundamentalisms observed*; vol. 2: *Fundamentalisms and the state*; vol. 3: *Fundamentalisms and society*; vol. 4: *Accounting for fundamentalisms*; vol. 5: *Fundamentalisms comprehended.* A cross–religious study).
The future of religion: secularization, revival, and cult formation. R. Stark & W. Bainbridge. Berkeley, CA: University of California Press, 1985. 579p.
The Jaina path of purification. P. S. Jaini. Berkeley, CA: University of California Press, 1979.
The New Age movement in American culture. R. Kyle. Lanham, MD: University Press of America, 1995. 289p.
The new religions of Japan: a spotlight on the most significant development in postwar Japan. H. Thomsen. Rutland, VT and Tokyo: Tuttle, 1963. 269p.
The religions of the oppressed: a study of modern messianic cults. V. Lanternari. New York: Mentor, 1963. 286p. (Translated by L. Sergio from the Italian, *Movimenti religiosi di libertà e di salvezzi dei popoli oppressi*).
'The rise of Spiritism in North America,' M. Ortiz, *Urban mission,* 5, 4 (March 1988), 11–17.
The social dimensions of sectarianism: sects and new religious movements in contemporary society. B. R. Wilson. Oxford, UK and New York: Clarendon, 1992. 311p.
The social impact of new religious movements. B. R. Wilson (ed). *Conference series,* 9. Barrytown, NY: The Unification Theological Seminary, 1991. 256p. (A collection of essays by a diverse group of sociologists, including J. D. Hunter, examining the rise of the Unification Church.).
The way of heaven: an introduction to the Confucian religious life. No. 3 of section 12, *East and Central Asia,* of *Iconography of religions.* R. L. Taylor. Leiden: E. J. Brill, 1986. 37p.
The Zoroastrian faith: tradition and modern research. S. A. Nigosian. Cheektowaga, NY: McGill-Queen's University Press, 1993.
Trattato di antropologia del sacro. J. Ries (ed). Milan: Jaca Book, 1989–. 5 vols; in progress to 7 vols.
Wörterbuch der Mythologie. H. W. Haussig (ed). Stuttgart: Klett-Cotta, 1965–1984. 5 vols.
Zoroastrians: their religious beliefs and practices. M. Boyce. London and Boston: Routledge & Kegan Paul, 1979. 374p.

6. INTERFAITH DIALOGUE

A bibliography of interchurch and interconfessional theological dialogues. J. F. Puglisi & S. J. Voicu. Rome: Centro pro unione, 1984. 260p.
A bridge to Buddhist–Christian dialogue. S. Yagi & L. Swidler. Mahwah, NJ: Paulist, 1990. 162p.
A sourcebook for earth's community of religions. J. D. Beversluis (ed). Rev. ed. Grand Rapids, MI: CoNexus Press—Sourcebook Project; New York: Global Education Associates, 1995. 376p. (Contains statements from the Parliament of the World's Religions, Chicago, 1993).
A wider vision: a history of the World Congress of Faiths 1936–1996. M. Braybrooke. Oxford, UK: Oneworld, 1996. 192p.
Ateismo e dialogo: bolletino del Segretariato per i Non–Credenti. Rome, 1966–. (Christian dialogue with atheism and Marxism).
Atlas of the crusades. J. Riley–Smith (ed). New York: Facts on File, 1990.
Christ in Islam and Christianity. N. Robinson. Albany, NY: State University of New York Press, 1991. 246p.
Christianity and the encounter of the world religions. P. Tillich. New York and London: Columbia University Press, 1963. 107p. (1961 Bampton lectures at Columbia University).
Christianity and the world religions: paths to dialogue with Islam, Hinduism, and Buddhism. H. Küng et al. Garden City, NY: Doubleday, 1986. 480p.
Disinheriting the Jews: Abraham in early Christian controversy. J. S. Siker. Louisville, KY: Westminster John Knox, 1991. 296p.
Faith meets faith series. Maryknoll, NY: Orbis, 1990.
Hinduism and Christianity. J. L. Brockington. New York: St. Martin's Press, 1992. 229p. (Delineates contacts since the 3rd century).
Hindus and Christians: a century of Protestant ecumenical thought. S. W. Ariarajah. *Currents of encounter,* 5. Amsterdam: Editions Rodopi; Grand Rapids, MI: Eerdmans, 1991. 254p.
Interfaith directory. F. Clark (ed). New York: International Religious Foundation, 1987. 194p.
Jerusalem blessed, Jerusalem cursed: Jews, Christians, and Muslims in the Holy City from David's time to our own. T. A. Idinopulos. Chicago: Ivan R. Dee, 1991. 343p.
Jewish perspectives on Christianity: Leo Baeck, Martin Buber, Franz Rosenzweig, Will Herberg, and Abraham J. Heschel. F. A. Rothschild (ed). New York: Crossroad, 1990. 373p.
Jews and Christians: a troubled family. W. Harrelson & R. M. Falk. Nashville, TN: Abingdon, 1990. 208p.
Muhammad and Jesus: a comparison of the prophets and their teachings. W. E. Phipps. New York: Continuum, 1996. 316p.
Neely's history of the Parliament of Religions and Religious Congresses at the World's Columbian Exposition. W. R. Houghton. Chicago: Neely, 1893.
One Christ—many religions: toward a revised christology. S. J. Samartha. *Faith meets faith series.* Maryknoll, NY: Orbis, 1991. 206p.
One earth many religions: multifaith dialogue and global responsibility. P. F. Knitter. Maryknoll, NY: Orbis, 1995. 232p.
Piety and power: Muslims and Christians in West Africa. L. Sanneh. Maryknoll, NY: Orbis Books, 1996.
Qur'anic Christians: an analysis of classical and modern exegesis. J. D. McAuliffe. Cambridge, UK and New York: Cambridge University Press, 1991. 352p. (Islamic understanding of Christians. Studies passages in the Qur'an that make ostensibly positive remarks about Christians).
Religion in the Middle East: three religions in concord and conflict. A. J. Arberry. Cambridge, UK: Cambridge University Press, 1969. 2 vols. (Vol. 1: *Judaism and Christianity*; vol. 2: *Islam,* and *Concord and Conflict*).
The Christ and the faiths. K. Cragg. London: SCM; Philadelphia: Westminster, 1986. 372p.
The integration of Islam and Hinduism in Western Europe. W. A. R. Shadid & P. S. van Koningsveld. Kampen, Netherlands: Kok Pharos, 1991. 264p.
The Jews of Islam. B. Lewis. Princeton, NJ: Princeton University Press, 1984. 257p.
The World's Parliament of Religions. J. H. Barrows. Chicago: Parliament Publishing Company, 1893.
The World's Parliament of Religions: the east/west encounter, Chicago, 1893. R. H. Seager. *Religion in North America series.* Bloomington, IN: Indiana University Press, 1995. 239p.
World fellowship: addresses and messages by leading spokesmen of all faiths, races and countries. C. F. Weller (ed). New York: Liveright Publishing, 1935. 1,004p. (A collection of addresses of leaders of a number of faiths for the First International Congress of the World Fellowship of Faiths, held in Chicago in 1934).

III. APPROACHES TO THE STUDY OF RELIGION

1. GENERAL METHODOLOGIES

Dictionary of religion and philosophy. G. MacGregor. New York: Paragon House, 1989; paperback, 1991. 696p. (Published in Britain under the title, *The everyman dictionary of religion and philosophy,* London: Dent, 1990.).
Encyclopedia of contemporary literary theory: approaches, scholars, terms. I. R. Makaryk (ed). Toronto: University of Toronto Press, 1993. 576p.
Encyclopedia of the Enlightenment. P. H. Reill & E. J. Wilson. New York: Facts on File, 1996. 464p.
Encyclopédie des sciences religieuses. (A major French Catholic collection composed of 6 series).
Guides to theological inquiry. P. Lakeland & K. Tanner (eds). Minneapolis, MN: Fortress. 4 vols. to date; 4 more vols.).
Handbuch der Religionspädagogik. E. Feifel (ed). 1973–75, 3 vols.
Handbuch religionswissenschaftlicher grundbegriffe. H. Cancik, B. Gladigow & M. Laubscher (eds). Stuttgart: Kohlhammer, 1988–. 3 vols., 2 forthcoming.
Method and theory in the study and interpretation of religion. New York: Mouton.
Philosophical foundations of the social sciences: analyzing controversies in social research. H. Kincaid. Cambridge, UK, and New York: Cambridge University Press, 1996.
Social research methods and statistics. W. S. Bainbridge. Belmont, CA: Wadsworth, 1992.
Social scientific studies of religion. M. I. Berkowitz & J. Johnson. Pittsburgh: University of Pittsburgh Press, 1967.
The scientific study of religion. J. M. Yinger. New York: Macmillan, 1970.
Toronto studies in religion. D. Wiebe. New York: Peter Lang. 20 vols. to date.

2. PHILOSOPHY OF RELIGION

A companion to philosophy of religion. P. L. Quinn & C. Taliaferro (eds). *Blackwell companions to philosophy,* 8. Cambridge, MA: Blackwell, 1997. 655p. (A guide for nonspecialists).
A dictionary of philosophy. T. Mautner. Cambridge, MA: Blackwell, 1995.
Catalog of the Hoose Library of Philosophy, University of Southern California (Los Angeles). Boston: G. K. Hall, 1968. 6 vols. (96,000 entries, 4,577 pages).
Divine discourse: philosophical reflections on the claim that God speaks. N. Wolterstorff. Cambridge, UK and New York: Cambridge University Press, 1995. 336p.
Encyclopedia of philosophy. D. M. Borchert (ed). New York: Simon & Schuster, 1996.
Encyclopedia of philosophy. P. Edwards (ed). New York: Collier-Macmillan, 1967. 8 vols.
Encyclopedia of the philosophical sciences in outline. G. W. F. Hegel. Ed., E. Behler. Del Mar, CA: Continuum, 1990. 24 vols.
God, reason, and religions: new essays in the philosophy of religion. E. T. Long (ed). *Studies in philosophy and religion,* 18. Boston: Kluwer, 1996.
Ontological arguments and belief in God. G. Oppy. Cambridge, UK: Cambridge University Press, 1996. 394p.
Philosophy as a way of life: spiritual exercises from Socrates to Foucault. P. Hadot. Trans., M. Chase. Oxford, UK: Blackwell, 1995. 319p.
Philosophy in the 20th century: Catholic and Christian. G. McLean. Vol. I: *An annotated bibliography of philosophy in Catholic thought, 1900–64.* Vol. II: *A bibliography of Christian philosophy and contemporary issues.* New York: Ungar, 1967.
Philosophy of religion. J. Hick. Englewood Cliffs, NJ: Preutice-Hall, 1963.
Prolegomena to religious pluralism: reference and realism in religion. P. Byrne. New York: St. Martin's, 1995. 255p.
Répetoire bibliographique de la philosophie. Louvain: Editions de l'Institut Supérieure de Philosophie, 1948–70.
The beginning and the end of "religion". N. Lash. Cambridge, UK: Cambridge University Press, 1996. 296p.
The Blackwell companion to philosophy. N. Bunnin & E. P. Tsui-james (eds). Cambridge, MA: Blackwell, 1995.
The essence of Christianity (Das Wesen des Christentums). Ludwig Feuerbach. Trans., G. Eliot. 1841; New York: Harper, 1957. 383p.
The handbook of Western philosophy. G. H. R. Parkinson (ed). London and New York: Macmillan, 1988. 935p.
The naturalness of religious ideas: a cognitive theory of religion. P. Boyer. Berkeley, CA: University of California Press, 1994.
The Oxford dictionary of philosophy. S. Blackburn. Oxford, UK and New York: Oxford University Press, 1994. 416p.
Voprosy nauchnogo ateizma (Questions of scientific atheism). Moscow: Mysl. 1966–75
World philosophies: an historical introduction. D. E. Cooper. Oxford, UK and Cambridge, MA: Blackwell, 1996.

3. HISTORY OF RELIGION

Church history: an introduction to research, reference works, and methods. J. E. Bradley & R. A. Muller. Grand Rapids, MI: Eerdmans, 1995. 252p.
Essays in the history of religions. J. Kitagawa & G. Alles (eds). New York: Macmillan, 1988.
Handbuch der Religionsgeschichte. J. P. Asmussen, J. Laessoe & C. Colpe. Göttingen: Vandenhoeck & Ruprecht, 1971–72. 3 vols.
Histoire des religions. H. Puech (ed). Paris: Gallimard, 1970–1976. 3 vols.
Historians of the Christian tradition: their methodology and influence on Western thought. M. Bauman & M. I. Klauber. Nashville, TN: Broadman & Holman, 1995. 637p.
The history of religions: essays in methodology. M. Eliade & J. Kitagawa (eds). Chicago: University of Chicago Press, 1959.
The history of religions: essays on the problem of understanding. J. Kitagawa (ed). Chicago: University of Chicago Press, 1967.
The modern researcher. J. Barzun & H. F. Graff. 4th ed. New York: Harcourt Brace Jovanovich, 1985. 476p.
World historians and their goals: twentieth–century answers to modernism. P. Costello. DeKalb, IL: Northern Illinois University Press, 1993. 325p.

4. SOCIOLOGY OF RELIGION

Atlas narodov mira (Atlas of the peoples of the world). Moscow: Akademii Nauk SSSR, 1964. 184p. (Not concerned with religion per se, but its ethnic maps locate ethnic minorities of religious importance).
Dieux d'hommes: Dictionnaire des messianismes et millénarismes de l'Ere chrétienne. H. Desroche et al. Paris and The Hague: Mouton, 1969. 281p.
Encyclopedia of sociology. E. F. Borgatta & M. L. Borgatta (eds). New York: Macmillan, 1991. 4 vols.
Habits of the heart: individualism and commitment in American life. R. N. Bellah et al. Berkeley, CA: University of California Press, 1985. (An influential study of the loss of the 'second language' of piety in American culture).
Human values in a changing world: a dialogue on the social role of religion. B. Wilson & D. Ikeda. London: Macdonald, 1984; Secaucus, NJ: Lyle Stewart, 1987. 364p.

International bibliography of sociology of religion, in *Social compass* (International review of socio-religious studies), Louvain, 1958–1972.

International encyclopedia of the social sciences. D. L. Sills (ed). New York: Collier-Macmillan. 1968, 17 vols. (Reprinted, 1972, in 8 vols).

L'État des religions dans le monde. M. Clévenot (ed). Paris: La Découverte/Le Cerf, 1987. 640p.

'Marxist analysis and sociology of religions: an outline of international bibliography up to 1975,' O. Maduro, *Social compass,* XXII, 3–4 (1975), 401–479. (Lists 1,215 books, 730 articles, in 7 Western languages).

Millhands and preachers. L. Pope. New Haven, CT: Yale University Press, 1942.

Protestant, Catholic, Jew. W. Herberg. Garden City, NY: Doubleday, 1955.

Public religions in the modern world. J. Casanova. Chicago: University of Chicago Press, 1994. 330p.

Religion and the individual. C. D. Baatson, P. Schoenrade & W. L. Ventis. New York: Oxford University Press, 1993.

Religion in politics: a world guide. S. Mews (ed). Chicago and London: World Guide, 1989. 342p. (Examines religious political parties in over 200 countries).

Religion in sociological perspective: essays in the empirical study of religion. C. Y. Glock. *The Wadsworth series in sociology.* Belmont, CA: Wadsworth, 1973. 325p.

Religion: the social context. M. B. McGuire. Belmont, CA: Wadsworth, 1992.

Religious diversity and social change. K. J. Christiano. New York: Cambridge University Press, 1987.

Religious sects. B. R. Wilson. New York: McGraw–Hill, 1970.

Sects and society. B. R. Wilson. Berkeley, CA: University of California Press, 1961.

Sociology of Christianity: an international bibliography. H. Carrier & E. Pin (eds). Rome: Gregorian University Press, 1964. 313p.

Tables, signalétiques, Archives de sociologie des religions. Paris: CNRS, 1972. 300p. (Now *Archives des sciences sociales des religions:* reviews and abstracts of journal from 1956–70).

The churching of America 1776–1990. R. Fink & R. Stark. New Brunswick, NJ, 1992.

The good society. R. N. Bellah et al. New York: Knopf, 1991.

The Protestant ethic and the spirit of capitalism. M. Weber. Trans., T. Parsons. New York: Scribner, 1958. 313p.

The sacred canopy: elements of a sociological theory of religion. P. Berger. Garden City, NY: Anchor Books, Doubleday, 1967, 1969. 239p.

The social construction of reality: a treatise in the sociology of knowledge. P. Berger & T. Luckman. Garden City, NY: Doubleday, 1966. 231p.

The social impact of new religious movements. B. R. Wilson (ed). New York: Rose of Sharon Press, 1981.

The social impact of new religious movements. B. R. Wilson (ed). *Conference series,* 9. Barrytown, NY: The Unification Theological Seminary, 1991. 256p. (A collection of essays by a diverse and respected group of sociologists, including James Davison Hunter and others, examining the rise of the Unification Church.).

The social sources of denominationalism. H. R. Niebuhr. New York: Holt, 1929.

The social teaching of the Christian churches. E. Troeltsch. Trans., O. Wyon. *Library of theological ethics.* 1911; New York: Harper, 1960; Louisville, KY: Westminster John Knox Press, 1992. 2 vols.

The sociological study of religion. B. R. Scharf. New York: Harper, 1970. 190p.

'The sociology of conversion,' W. S. Bainbridge, in *Handbook of religious conversion,* p.178–91. H. N. Maloney & S. Southard (ed). Birmingham, AL: Religious Education Press, 1992.

The sociology of religion. T. F. O'Dea. Englewood Cliffs, NJ: Prentice–Hall, 1966.

The sociology of religious movements. W. S. Bainbridge. New York and London: Routlegde, 1997. 480p.

Wondrous events: foundations of religious belief. J. McClenon. Philadelphia: University of Pennsylvania Press, 1994.

5. ANTHROPOLOGY OF RELIGION

Anthropological studies of religion: an introductory text. B. Morris. Cambridge, UK and New York: Cambridge University Press, 1987, 1989. 379p.

Conceptualizing religion: immanent anthropologists, transcendent natives, and unbound categories. B. Saler. Leiden: E. J. Brill, 1993.

Religion: an anthropological view. A. F. C. Wallace. New York: Random House, 1966.

Religion, deviance, and social control. R. Stark & W. S. Bainbridge. New York: Routledge, 1997. 204p.

The pursuit of certainty: religious and cultural formulations. W. James (ed). London: Routledge, 1995. 328p.

6. PSYCHOLOGY OF RELIGION

Annotated bibliography in religion and psychology. W. W. Meissner. N.p.: Academy of Religion and Health, 1961.

Baker encyclopedia of psychology. D. G. Benner (ed). Grand Rapids, MI: Baker, 1985. 1246p.

Encyclopedia of psychiatry, psychology, and psychoanalysis. B. Wolman. New York: Henry Holt, 1996. 1,200p.

Encyclopedia of psychology. R. J. Corsini (ed). 2nd ed. New York: Wiley, 1994. 4 vols; 2,464p.

Encyclopedia of psychology. H. J. Eysenck, W. Arnold & R. Meili (eds). London: Search Press. 1972, 3 vols.

Handbook of religious experience. R. W. Hood Jr (ed). Birmingham, AL: Religious Education Press, 1995. 661p.

Is religion good for your health? H. G. Koenig. Binghamton, NY: Hayworth, 1997. 147p. (Examines empirical evidence and suggests religion's beneficial role in mental health).

Psychoanalytic studies in religion: a critical assessment and annotated bibliography. B. Beit-Hallahmi. *Bibliographies and indexes in religious studies.* Westport, CT: Greenwood.

Psychology of religion: classic and contemporary. D. M. Wulff. 2nd ed. New York: Wiley, 1997. 781p.

The collected works of C. G. Jung. H. Read, M. Fordham & G. Adler et al (eds). *Bollingen Series.* Princeton, NJ: Princeton University Press, 1953—72. 17 vols. (Vol 11: *Psychology and religion: east and west,* 1958).

The handbook of social psychology. G. Lindzey & E. Aronson (eds). 2nd ed. Reading, MA: Addison-Wesley, 1968-69. 5 vols. (Psychology of religion: vol 5, p. 602-659).

The innate capacity: mysticism, psychology, and philosophy. R. K. C. Forman (ed). New York: Oxford Univerity Press.

The psychology of religion: theoretical approaches. B. Spilka & D. N. McIntosh (eds). Boulder, CO: Westview Press, 1996.

The varieties of religious experience: a study in human nature. W. James. 1902; Cambridge, MA: Harvard University Press, 1985. 770p. (One of the classics in this field. Originally the Gifford Lectures on Natural Religion, 1901–02).

Young man Luther: a study in psychoanalysis and history. E. Erickson. New York: Norton. 288p.

7. RELIGIOUS ETHICS

After virtue: a study in moral theory. A. MacIntyre. Notre Dame, IN: University of Notre Dame Press, 1981.

Beyond integrity: a Judeo–Christian approach to business ethics. S. B. Rae & K. L. Wong. Grand Rapids, MI: Zondervan, 1996. 656p.

Competing gospels: public theology and economic theory. R. G. Simons. Alexandria, Australia: Dwyer, 1995. 253p.

Dictionary of ethics, theology, and society. P. B. Clarke & A. Linzey (eds). London and New York: Routledge, 1996. 960p.

Encyclopedia of ethics. L. C. Becker & C. Becker. New York: Garland, 1992. 2 vols, 1,462p.

Encyclopedia of morals. V. T. Ferm (ed). Repr. ed. Westport, CT: Greenwood, 1969. 682p.

Encyclopedia of war and ethics. D. A. Wells (ed). Westport, CT: Greenwood, 1996. 568p.

Religion and human rights. J. Kelsay & S. B. Twiss (eds). New York: The Project on Religion and Human Rights, 1994. 135p.

Religion in public life: a dilemma for democracy. R. E. Thiemann. Washington, DC: Georgetown University Press, 1996. 186p.

Religious human rights in global perspective: religious perspectives and legal perspectives. J. Witte Jr. & J. D. van der Vyer (eds). The Hague and Boston: M. Nijhoff, 1996. 2 vols.

The encyclopedia of religion and ethics. J. Hastings (ed). Edinburgh: T. & T. Clark, 1926. 13 vols.

The ethical demand. K. E. Løgstrup. Ed., H. Fink & A. MacIntyre. Rev. ed. 1971; Notre Dame, IN: University of Notre Dame Press, 1997. 331p.

8. OTHER APPROACHES

Biblical numerology: a basic study of the use of numbers in the Bible. J. J. Davis. Grand Rapids, MI: Baker, 1968. 174p.

Concise dictionary of religious quotations. W. Neill (ed). London: Mowbray, 1975. 224p. (2,500 quotations by topic; Christian, Muslim, Hindu, et al).

Cultures in conflict: a global survey of ethnic, racial, linguistic, religious and nationalist factors. E. M. Rhoodie. Jefferson, NC: McFarland, 1993. 976p.

Encyclopedia of cosmology: historical philosophical, and scientific foundations of modern cosmology. N. S. Hetherington (ed). Text ed. New York: Garland, 1993. 704p.

Encyclopedia of creation myths. D. A. Leeming & M. A. Leeming. Santa Barbara, CA: ABC-CLIO, 1994. 330p.

Mythologies. Y. Bonnefoy. Chicago: University of Chicago Press, 1991. 2 vols, 1,305p. (Translated and restructed under the direction of Wendy Doniger from the French, *Dictionnaire des mythologies et des religions, des sociétés traditionelles et du monde antique,* 1981. Translated by Gerald Honnigsblum, et al. A paperback edition in 4 vols. appeared in 1992.).

Number in Scripture: its supernatural design and spiritual significance. E. W. Bullinger. Grand Rapids, MI: Kregel Publications, 1967. 311p.

Religious and social ritual: interdisciplinary explorations. M. B. Aune & V. DeMarinis. Albany, NY: State University of New York Press, 1996.

Sacred worlds: an introduction to geography and religion. C. C. Park. London and New York: Routledge, 1994. 346p.

The philosophy of religious language: sign, symbol, and story. D. R. Stiver. Cambridge, MA: Blackwell, 1996.

The world treasury of religious quotations. R. L. Woods (ed). New York: Hawthorn Books, 1966. (15,000 quotations, arranged by subject).

IV. ELECTRONIC MEDIA

Academic index. Information Access Co., Foster City, CA. (Covers 950 scholarly journals; is available online and in CD-ROM).

Biblia Patristica: index des citations et allusions bibliques dans la littérature patristique. Paris: CNRS, 1975–80. 3 vols. (27,000 references; computerized).

Britannica online. Chicago: Encyclopaedia Britannica, 1994–. 44,000,000+ words.

CD–ROMs in print, 1996: an international guide to CD–ROM, CD–I, 3DO, MMDC, CD32, multimedia and electronic book products. M. Desmarais. New York: Gale Research, 1996. 1,243p.

Directory of electronic journals, newsletters, and scholarly discussion lists. Association of Research Libraries. Washington, DC: Association of Research Libraries, 1991. 173p.

Directory of online databases. New York. Cuadra/Elsevier Science Publishing Co., Inc.,

Directory of portable databases. New York. Cuadra/Elsevier Science Publishing.

Earthquest. Palo Alto, CA. Earthquest, Inc., (Hypercard stack which focuses upon global ecological, environmental, and historical issues).

Ethnic NewsWatch. Stamford, CT. SoftLine Information Company, (Selected articles from 100 top North American newspapers and magazines.)

Hermeneutika BibleWorks 3.5 on CD–ROM.

Judaism and Christianity: a guide to the reference literature. E. D. Starkey. *Reference sources in the humanities series.* Englewood, CO: Libraries Unlimited, 1991. 270p.

Old testament abstracts on CD–ROM. Washington, DC: The Catholic Biblical Association; Evanston, IL: American Theological Library Association, annual since 1995.

RIC: Répetoire bibliographique des institutiones chrétiennes. R. Metz & J. Schlick (eds). Strasbourg: Centre de Recherche et Documentation des Institutions Chrétiennes (CERDIC), annual since 1968. (Computer-produced indexes of Christian publications during the year; in 5 languages. 6,400 entries a year, increasing. Also RIC supplément, *Bibliographies thématiques*).

South African theological bibliography on CD–ROM. Pretroria: Research Institute for Theology and Religion, University of South Africa; Evanston, IL: American Theological Library Association, annual since 1995.

Statbase locator on disk: UNSTAT's guide to international computerized statistical databases. New York. United Nations Publications,

The Catholic periodical and literature index on CD–ROM. Catholic Library Association; Evanston, IL: American Theological Library Association, annual since 1996.

The CD–ROM directory. M. Finlay & J. Mitchell. 7th ed. Detroit, MI: Omnigraphics, 1992. 750p.

The computer Bible. J. A. Baird & D. N. Freedman (eds). Wooster, OH: Biblical Research Associates, Vols I–XV, 1975–78. (Word frequencies, concordances, indexes, using KWIC; computerization to make immediately available massive amounts of critical data).

The Sage digital library (CD-ROM). Albany, OR: Sage Software. Contains 220 books.

V. BIBLIOGRAPHIES

A biblical law bibliography: arranged by subject and by author. J. W. Welch. *Toronto studies in theology,* 51. Lewiston, NY: E. Mellen Press, 1990. 339p.

A bibliography. K. Baago. *Library of Christian theology.* Madras: The Christian Literature Society, 1969. 110p. (A bibliography of theological works by Indian authors.).

A bibliography of bibliographies in religion. J. G. Barrow. Ann Arbor, MI: Edwards Bros, 1930, 5th edition 1955. 489p. (1,945 titles with short evaluations).

A bibliography of Christian worship. B. Thompson (ed). *ATLA bibliography series,* 25. Philadelphia: American Theological Library Association; Metuchen, NJ, Scarecrow Press. 828p.

A bibliography of Greek New Testament manuscripts. J. K. Elliott. *Monographic series, Society for New Testament Studies,* 62. Cambridge, UK and New York: Cambridge University Press, 1988. 231p.

A bibliography of interchurch and interconfessional theological dialogues. J. F. Puglisi & S. J. Voicu. Rome: Centro pro unione, 1984. 260p.

A bibliography of Islamic law, 1980–1993. L. Al-Zwaini & R. Peters. *Handbuch der Orientalistik. Erste Abteilung, der Nahe und Mittlere Osten (Handbook of Oriental studies, Near and Middle East),* 19. Leiden and New York: E. J. Brill, 1994. 248p.

A bibliography of modern African religious movements. R. C. Mitchel & H. W. Turner. Evanston, IL: Northwestern University Press, 1966. 132p. (1,300 items; updated annually in *Journal of religion in Africa*).

A bibliography of New Testament bibliographies. J. C. Hurd. New York: Seabury, 1966. (1,300 articles and books).

A bibliography of Oman, 1900–1950. R. King & J. H. Stevens. *Occasional paper series,* 2. Durham, UK: University of Durham, Centre for Middle Eastern and Islamic Studies, 1973. 141p.

A bibliography of Salvation Army literature in English (1865–1987). R. G. Moyles. *Texts and studies in religion,* 38. Lewiston, NY: E. Mellen Press, 1988. 217p.

A bibliography of sources in Christianity and the arts. D. M. Kari. *Studies in art and religious interpretation,* 16. Lewiston, NY: E. Mellen Press, 1995. 774p.

A bibliography of the periodical literature on the Acts of the Apostles, 1962–1984. W. E. Mills. *Supplements to Novum Testamentum,* 58. Leiden: E. J. Brill, 1986. 145p.

A bibliography of the Samaritans. A. D. Crown. 2nd ed. *ATLA bibliography series,* 32. Philadelphia: American Theological Library Association; Metuchen, NJ: Scarecrow Press, 1993. 393p.

A bibliography on temples of the ancient Near East and Mediterranean world: arranged by subject and by author. D. W. Parry, S. D. Ricks & J. W. Welch. *Ancient Near Eastern texts and studies,* 9. Lewiston NY: E. Mellen Press, 1991. 320p.

A critical bibliography of writings on Judaism. D. B. Griffiths. *Jewish studies,* 2. Lewiston, NY: E. Mellen Press, 1988. 2 vols.

A critical guide to Catholic reference books. J. P. McCabe. 3rd ed. Englewood, CO: Libraries Unlimited, 1989. 337p.

A decade of Bible bibliography. Oxford, UK: Blackwell, 1967. (Covers 1957–66).

A guide to films about the Pacific islands. J. D. Hamnett. Honolulu, HI: University of Hawaii, Pacific Islands Studies Program, 1986. 148p.

A guide to the study of the Pentecostal movement. C. E. Jones. *ATLA Bibliographic Series,* 6. Metuchen, NJ and London:

American Theological Library Association and Scarecrow Press, 1983. 1,245p in 2 vols. (Though dated, remains an important bibliography of the Pentecostal movement).

A pastoral liturgy bibliography. 2nd rev. ed. Notre Dame, IN: Notre Dame Center for Pastoral Liturgy, 1981. 28p.

A theological book list. London: Theological Education Fund, 1960, 1965, 1968. (Comprehensive bibliographies on all subjects, with emphasis on works available for seminaries in developing countries; 3,000 entries).

African theology: a critical analysis and annotated bibliography. J. U. Young III. *Bibliographies and indexes in religious studies*, 26. Westport, CT: Greenwood, 1993. 269p.

AIDS—issues in religion, ethics, and care: a Park Ridge Center bibliography. K. A. Cahalan. Park Ridge, IL: Park Ridge Cente, 1988. 130p.

American Puritan studies: an annotated bibliography of dissertations, 1882–1981. M. S. Montgomery. *Bibliographies and indexes in American history*, 1. Westport, CT: Greenwood, 1984. 451p.

An annotated and classified bibliography of English literature pertaining to the Ethiopian Orthodox Church. J. Bonk. *ATLA bibliography series*, 11. Metuchen, NJ: American Theological Library Association and Scarecrow Press, 1984. 127p.

An annotated critical bibliography of feminist criticism. M. Humm. *Harvester annotated critical bibliographies*. Boston, MA: G. K. Hall, 1987. 251p.

An Aramaic bibliography. J. A. Fitzmyer et al. *Publications of the Comprehensive Aramaic Lexicon Project*. Baltimore, MD: Johns Hopkins University Press, 1992.

An introductory bibliography for the study of Scripture. J. A. Fitzmyer. 3rd ed. *Subsidia Biblica*, 3. Rome: Editrice pontificio istituto biblico, 1990. 231p. (Revised edition of *An introductory bibliography for the study of Scripture*, G. S. Glanzman).

Analytical guide to the bibliographies on the Arabian Peninsula. C. L. Geddes. *Bibliographic series*, 4. Denver, CO: American Institute of Islamic Studies, 1974.

Annotated bibliography in religion and psychology. W. W. Meissner. N.p.: Academy of Religion and Health, 1961.

Annotated bibliography of Luther studies, 1977–1983. K. Hagen. *Sixteenth century bibliography*, 24. St. Louis, MO: Center for Reformation Research, 1985. 91p.

Annotated bibliography of Mennonite writings on war and peace, 1930–1980. W. M. Swartley & C. J. Dyck (eds). Scottdale, PA: Herald, 1987. 740p. (Prepared by the Institute of Mennonite Studies, Elkhart, IN).

Apartheid: a selective annotated bibliography, 1979–1987. S. E. Pyatt. *Garland reference library of social science*, 587. New York: Garland, 1990. 188p.

Art and the Reformation: an annotated bibliography. L. B. Parshall & P. W. Parshall. *A Reference publication in art history*. Boston, MA: G. K. Hall, 1986. 328p.

Augustine's De civitate Dei: an annotated bibliography of modern criticism, 1960–1990. D. F. Donnelly & M. A. Sherman. New York: P. Lang, 1991. 119p.

Bible bibliography, 1967–73. P. R. Ackroyd (ed). Oxford, UK: Blackwell, 1975. (Works in nearly 20 languages).

Biblia Patristica: index des citations et allusions bibliques dans la littérature patristique. Paris: CNRS, 1975–80. 3 vols. (27,000 references; computerized).

Biblical resources for ministry: a bibliography. D. R. Bauer (ed). Wilmore, KY: Division of Biblical Studies, Asbury Theological Seminary, 1990. 95p.

Biblical resources for ministry: a bibliography of works in biblical studies. D. R. Bauer. 2nd ed. Nappanee, IN: Evangel, 1995. 144p.

Bibliografia tes Oikoumenikes Kineseos, 1960–1970 (Bibliography of the ecumenical movement). V. T. Istravridis. Athens: Theologia, 1978. 78p. (Orthodoxy and ecumenism; 1,500 titles).

Bibliographia Calviniana, 1532–1899. D. A. Erichson. Nieuwkoop: De Graaf, 1950.

Bibliographia internationalis spiritualitatis. Roma: Pontifical Institute of Spirituality, 1966–68. 3 vols. (6,487 titles in v.3).

Bibliographia missionaria. 1935–74; Rome: Pontificia Università de Propagande Fide, 1986–. 50 vols. to date. (Annual review of previous year's literature; until 1971, some overlap with *Bibliotheca missionum*, but has now superseded it for current literature).

Bibliographia Patristica. W. Schneemelcher. Berlin: de Gruyter, 1959–65. 10 vols.

Bibliographie bouddhique. Paris: Librarie d'Amérique et d'Orient, 1930–61 (fasc. 1–31). (Annual).

Bibliographie de cartographie ecclésiastique. J. N. B. van den Brink et al. (eds). Leiden: E. J. Brill, Commission Internationale d'Histoire Ecclésiastique Comparée, 1968–.

Bibliographie de la Réforme, 1450–1648. J. N. B. van den Brink et al. (eds). Leiden: E. J. Brill, 1958–70. 7 vols. (Covers 17 European countries plus U.S.).

Bibliographie de la Septante: (1970–1993). (Bibliography of the Septuagint). C. Dogniez. *Supplements to Vetus Testamentum*, 60. Leiden and New York: E. J. Brill, 1995.

Bibliographies for biblical research. W. E. Mills (ed). Lewiston, NY: E. Mellen Press, 1993–1996. 6 vols.

Bibliography in contextual theology in Africa. J. R. Cochrane, I. W. Henderson & G. O. West (eds). Pietermaritzburg, South Africa: Cluster Publications, 1993–. 1 vol. to date.

Bibliography of British theological literature, 1850–1940. D. Y. Hadidian. *Bibliographia tripotamopolitana*, 12. Pittsburgh, PA: Barbour Library, Pittsburgh Theological Seminary, 1985. 485p.

Bibliography of literature on First Peter. A. Casurella. *New Testament tools and studies*, 23. Leiden and New York: E. J. Brill, 1996. 178p.

Bibliography of new religions: movements in primal societies. H. W. Turner. Boston: G. K. Hall. Vol 2, Black Africa, 1977 (278, 1,900 entries); Vol 2, North America (280); Vols. 3-4, Latin America & Caribbean, Asia with Oceania.

Bibliography of new religious movements in primal societies. H. W. Turner. Boston and New York: G. K. Hall, 1977–92. 6 vols.

Bibliography of New Testament literature, 1900–1950. T. Akaishi (ed). San Anselmo, CA: Seminary Cooperative Store, 1953. 312p. (2,400 annotated items).

'Bibliography of original Christian writings in India in Tamil.' J. G. Muthuraj. Manuscript, Tamilnadu Theological Seminary, 161p.

Bibliography of published articles on American Presbyterianism, 1901–1980. H. M. Parker. *Bibliographies and indexes in religious studies*, 4. Westport, CT: Greenwood, 1985. 272p.

Bibliography of religion in the South. C. H. Lippy. Macon, GA: Mercer University Press, 1985. 514p.

Bibliography on Buddhism. S. Hanayama. Tokyo: Hokuseido Press, 1961. 869p. (15,073 numbered entries).

'Bibliography on world mission and evangelism,' *International review of mission*. (At end of all issues).

Bibliotheca missionum. R. Streit. Freiburg: Herder, 1916–71. 28 vols. (The major complete and retrospective Catholic bibliography of missions; discontinued 1971 and superseded by *Bibliographia missionaria*).

Black theology: a critical assessment and annotated bibliography. J. H. Evans. *Bibliographies and indexes in religious studies*, 10. New York: Greenwood, 1987. 217p.

Bonhoeffer bibliography: primary sources and secondary literature in English. W. W. Floyd & C. J. Green. Evanston, IL: American Theological Library Association, 1992. 159p.

Buletin signalétique: sciences religieuses. Paris: Centre de Documentation Sciences Humaines. 1947-74, vols 1-28; (8,000 periodical article abstracts a year).

Calvin bibliography 1991. P. De Klerk. p.389-411.

Calvin–Bibliographie, 1901–1959. W. Niesel. Munich: C. Kaiser, 1961. (Continuation of *Bibliographia Calviniana*).

Catalog of the Hoose Library of Philosophy, University of Southern California (Los Angeles). Boston: G. K. Hall, 1968. 6 vols. (96,000 entries, 4,577 pages).

Catalogue of English Bible translations: a classified bibliography of versions and editions including books, parts, and Old and New Testament Apocrypha and Apocryphal books. W. J. Chamberlin. *Bibliographies and indexes in religious studies*, 21. New York: Greenwood, 1991. 946p. (The best and most complete for its listing of English Bible translations, 9,000 titles and editions).

Catholic periodical and literature index. Haverford, PA: Catholic Library Association, 1930–72. vols 1-17.

Charismatic religion in modern research: a bibliography. W. E. Mills. *NABPR bibliographic series*, 1. Macon, GA: Mercer University Press, 1985. 17p

Chaucer and the Bible: a critical review of research, indexes, and bibliography. L. L. Besserman. *Garland reference library of the humanities*, 839. New York: Garland, 1988.

China bibliography: a research guide to reference works about China past and present. H. T. Zurndorfer. *Handbuch der Orientalistik*, Vierte Abteilung, China, 1. Leiden and New York: E. J. Brill, 1995. 394p.

Christian faith amidst religious pluralism: an introductory bibliography. D. G. Dawe et al. Richmond, VA: Union Theological Seminary in Virginia, 1980. 115p.

Christian periodical index. Buffalo, NY: Christian Librarians' Fellowship, Quarterly. (Covers a relatively small but important number of conservative Protestant periodicals from 1956 to the present).

Christian spirituality: the essential guide to the most influential spiritual writings of the Christian tradition. F. N. Magill & I. P. McGreal (eds). San Francisco: Harper & Row, 1988.

Christianity and Marxism worldwide: an annotated bibliography. M. R. Elliott (ed). Wheaton, IL: Institute for the Study of Christianity and Marxism, Wheaton College, 1988.

Cities and churches: an international bibliography. L. H. Hartley. *ATLA bibliography series*, 31. Metuchen, NJ: Scarecrow Press, 1992. 3 vols.

Cultural anthropology of the Middle East: a bibliography. R. Strijp. *Handbuch der Orientalistik. Erste Abteilung, Der Nahe und der Mittlere Osten*, 10. Leiden and New York: E. J. Brill, 1992–. 2 vols. to date.

Current bibliography on African affairs. P. Boesch (ed). Farmingdale, NY: Baywood Publishing Company, 1962–67. N.s. 1968—.

Das Evangelische Schrifttum. Gesamtausgabe 1975. Stuttgart: Vereinigung Evangelischer Buchhändler. 448p. (Protestant literature: 9,760 titles).

Der Katholische Schrifttum (Gesamtausgabe 1975). Stuttgart: Verbannd Katholischer Verleger & Buchhändler. 288p. (Catholic literature: 5,760 titles).

Dissertation Abstracts International: (1) *Comprehensive dissertation index, 1861–1975*, on all subjects, and (2) *Datrix II* computer retrieval system, by keywords in title, of over 500,000 North American and European university doctoral dissertations (300,000 on humanities and social sciences; about 8,000 on religion and Christianity; 950 with 'Catholic' in title, 490 with 'Protestant', 1,160 with 'Christian', 1,780 with 'church', 490 with 'God', 1,200 with 'theology' or 'theological', 2,400 with 'religion', etc). Annual and monthly editions and supplements, in volumes, printout or microfiche.

Elenchus bibliographicus biblicus. P. Nober. Rome: Biblical Institute, 1970. (Annual).

Eleven years of Bible bibliography: the book lists of the Society for Old Testament study, 1946–56. H. H. Rowley (ed). Indian Hill, CO: Falcon's Wing, 1957. 804p. (Annotated).

Emil Brunner: a bibliography. M. G. McKim. *ATLA bibliographies*, 40. Lanham, MD: Scarecrow Press, 1996. 105p.

Encyclopedia of library and information science. Kent. New York: Dekker, 1968–1996. 58 vols.

English religion, 1500–1540: a bibliography. D. D. Smeeton. *NABPR bibliographic series*, 2. Macon, GA: Mercer University Press, 1988. 114p.

Ethnographic bibliography of North America, 4th edition. Supplement 1973–1987. M. M. Martin & T. J. O'Leary. New Haven, CT: Human Relations Area Files Press, 1990. 3 vols. (Previously published as *Ethnographic bibliography of North America*. G. P. Murdock, 1960, 1975.).

Evangelical secularism in the Russian Empire and the USSR: a bibliographic guide. A. W. Wardin Jr. *ATLA bibliography series*, 36. Metuchen, NJ: Scarecrow Press, 1995. 906p.

Feminist spirituality and the feminine divine: an annotated bibliography. A. Carson. *The Crossing Press feminist series*. Trumansburg, NY: Crossing Press, 1986. 139p.

Glossolalia: a bibliography. W. E. Mills. *Studies in the Bible and early Christianity*, 6. New York: E. Mellen Press, 1985. 129p.

Guide to atlases: world, regional, national, thematic. G. L. Alexander. Metuchen, NJ: Scarecrow Press, 1971. (Listing of atlases published since 1950. 54 are listed under 'Bible and Christian history').

Guide to Catholic literature, 1888–1940. Detroit: Romig, 1940.

Guide to religious periodicals. (Provides an index to denominational publications, mainly American, post-1964).

Holiness works: a bibliography. W. C. Miller (ed). Kansas City, MO: Printed for Nazarene Theological Seminary by Nazarene Publishing House, 1986. 120p. (Revised edition of *The master bibliography of Holiness Works*, Beacon Hill Press, 1965).

Holocaust literature: a handbook of critical, historical and literary writings. S. S. Friedman (ed). Westport, CT and London: Greenwood, 1994. 707p. (An essential handbook for anyone studying holocaust literature).

Index Islamicus 1906–1955: a catalogue of articles on Islamic subjects in periodicals and other collective publications. J. D. Pearson et al. Cambridge, UK: Heffer, 1958. 807p. (Supplements published in 1962, 1967, 1972, 1977).

Index of articles on the New Testament and the early church. B. M. Metzger. Philadelphia: Society of Biblical Literature, 1951. 182p. (Indexes 2,350 articles).

Interfaith dialogue: an annotated bibliography. J. H. Berthrong. Wofford Heights, CA: Multifaith Resources, 1993. 32p.

International bibliography of sociology of religion, in *Social compass* (Intenational review of socio-religious studies), Louvain, 1958–1972.

International Christian literature documentation project. D. W. Geyer. Evanston, IL: American Theological Library Association, 1993. 2 vols, 1,730p. (Indexes nonwestern Christian literature in North American libraries.).

Irregular serials and annuals: an international directory. E. Koltay (ed). 1st ed. New York: R.R. Bowker, 1967. (350 items on religion out of 14,500).

Jerusalem, the Holy City: a bibliography. J. D. Purvis. *ATLA bibliography series*, 20. St. Meinrad, IN: American Theological Library Association; Metuchen, NJ: Scarecrow Press, 1988–1991. 2 vols.

Jesus the Christ: a bibliography. L. J. White. *Theological and Biblical resources*, 4. Wilmington, DE: Michael Glazier, 1988. 157p.

Jewish Christians in the United States: a bibliography. K. Pruter. *Sects and cults in America, Bibliographical guides*, 7; *Garland reference library of social science*, 306. New York: Garland, 1987. 203p.

Jewish–Christian relations: an annotated bibliography and resource guide. M. Shermis. Bloomington, IN: Indiana University Press, 1988. 306p.

Johannine bibliography, 1966–1985: a cumulative bibliography on the Fourth gospel. G. van Belle. *Bibliotheca Ephemeridum theologicarum Lovaniensium*, 82. Leuven: Leuven University Press, 1988. 580p. (Variant title: *Cumulative bibliography on the Fourth gospel*. Also published in series *Collectanea biblica et religiosa antiqua*).

John and Charles Wesley: a bibliography. B. Jarboe. *ATLA bibliography series*, 22. Metuchen, NJ: Scarecrow Press, 1987. 419p.

Jonathan Edwards: an annotated bibliography, 1979–1993. M. X. Lesser. *Bibliographies and indexes in religious studies*, 30. Westport, CT: Greenwood, 1994. 220p.

Judaism and Christianity: a guide to the reference literature. E. D. Starkey. *Reference sources in the humanities series*. Englewood, CO: Libraries Unlimited, 1991. 270p.

Katholische Zeitungen und Zeitschriften, in Streit-Dindinger, *Biblioteca missionum (Africa, vol XX*, p.716–742; India, vol XXVIII, p.484–506; China, vol XIV, p.378–408; Oceania, vol XXI, p.711–717).

Literary–critical approaches to the Bible: an annotated bibliography. M. Minor. West Cornwall, CT: Locust Hill, 1992. 551p.

Malcolm X: a comprehensive annotated bibliography. T. V. Johnson. *Garland reference library of social science*, 288. New York: Garland, 1986. 201p.

Martin Luther King, Jr.: an annotated bibliography. S. E. Pyatt. *Bibliographies and indexes in Afro-American and African studies*, 12. New York: Greenwood, 1986. 168p.

'Marxist analysis and sociology of religions: an outline of international bibliography up to 1975,' O. Maduro, *Social compass*, XXII, 3–4 (1975), 401–479. (Lists 1,215 books, 730 articles, in 7 Western languages).

Matrology: a bibliography of writings by Christian women from the first to the fifteenth centuries. A. Kadel. New York: Continuum, 1995. 191p.

Missiological abstracts, 25 years, 1966–1991. G. R. Grimes (ed). Rev. ed. Pasadena, CA: Fuller Theological Seminary, 1991. 336p. (Abstracts of 720 dissertations, theses, and projects produced at the School of World Mission at Fuller Theological Seminary).

Missions and evangelism: a bibliography selected from the ATLA religion database, January, 1985. A. E. Hurd & P. D. Petersen (eds). Rev. ed. Chicago: American Theological Library Association, Religion Indexes, 1985. 788p.

Modern American popular religion: a critical assessment and annotated bibliography. C. H. Lippy. *Bibliographies and indexes in religious studies*, 37. Westport, CT: Greenwood, 1996. 264p.

Muslim women throughout the world: a bibliography. M. Kimball & B. R. von Schlegell. Sterling, VA: Lynne Reiner, 1997. 285p.

Muslims in India: a bibliography of their religious, socio–economic and political literature. Satyaprakash. Haryana, India: Indian Documenation Service, 1985. 299p.

New Eden and new Babylon: religious thoughts of American authors: a bibliography. N. R. Burr. 11 vols.

New religious movements in the United States and Canada: a critical assessment and annotated bibliography. D. Choquette. *Bibliographies and indexes in religious studies,* 5. Westport, CT: Greenwood, 1985. 235p.

New Testament abstracts. Weston, MA: Theological Faculty, Weston College, 1956–. (Issued 3 times a year; abstracts in English from articles in many languages).

New Testament Christology: a critical assessment and annotated bibliography. A. J. Hultgren. *Bibliographies and indexes in religious studies,* 12. New York: Greenwood, 1988. 499p.

New Testament tools and studies. B. M. Metzger (ed). Leiden: E. J. Brill, 1966–80. Vol I: *Index to periodical literature on the Apostle Paul.* Vol VI: *Index to periodical literature on Christ and the Gospels* (10,090 entries). Vol VII: *A classified bibligraphy of literature on the Acts of the Apostles* (6,645 entries). Vol X: *Philological, versional and patristic.*

Old testament abstracts on CD–ROM. Washington, DC: The Catholic Biblical Association; Evanston, IL: American Theological Library Association, annual since 1995.

Oman and southeastern Arabia: a bibliographic survey. M. O. Shannon. Boston: G. K. Hall, 1978. 165p.

Ostkirchliche Studien. Würzburg: Augustinus-Verlag, 1952–. (Quarterly. The best bibliographical source on the Eastern churches, with about 90 pages of bibliography each year).

P. T. Forsyth bibliography and index. R. Benedetto. *Bibliographies and indexes in religious studies,* 27. Westport, CT: Greenwood, 1993. 187p.

Paul and his interpreters: an annotated bibliography. G. L. Borchert. *TSF-IBR bibliographic study guides.* Madison, WI: Theological Students Fellowship, 1985. 129p.

Peace, disarmament and war: a bibliography selected from the ATLA religion database. A. E. Hurd (ed). Rev. ed. Chicago: American Theological Library Association, 1985. 464p.

Periodicals from Africa: a bibliography and union list of periodicals published in Africa. C. Travis & M. Alman. *Bibliographies and guides in African studies.* Boston, MA: G. K. Hall, 1977. 619p.

Philo of Alexandria: an annotated bibliography, 1937–1986. R. Radice & D. T. Runia. *Supplements to Vigiliae Christianae,* 8. Leiden and New York: E. J. Brill, 1988. 510p.

Philosophy in the 20th century: Catholic and Christian. G. McLean. Vol. I: *An annotated bibliography of philosophy in Catholic thought, 1900–64.* Vol. II: *A bibliography of Christian philosophy and contemporary issues.* New York: Ungar, 1967.

Protestant theological education in America: a bibliography. H. F. Day. *ATLA bibliography series,* 15. Chicago: American Theological Library Association; Metuchen, NJ: Scarecrow Press, 1985. 521p.

Psychoanalytic studies in religion: a critical assessment and annotated bibliography. B. Beit-Hallahmi. *Bibliographies and indexes in religious studies.* Westport, CT: Greenwood.

Recent reference books in religion: a guide for students, scholars, researchers, buyers and readers. W. M. Johnston. Downers Grove, IL: InterVarsity, 1996. 318p. (Contains annotations on 318 major reference books on religion. The majority of books annotated are on Christianity, but it also contains other major religions.).

Religion and the American experience, the twentieth century: a bibliography of doctoral dissertations. A. P. Young & E. J. Holley. *Bibliographies and indexes in religious studies,* 31. Westport, CT: Greenwood, 1994. 426p.

'Religion', in *Guide to reference books,* 9th Edition, E. P. Sheehy (Chicago: American Library Association, 1976), p.252-283. (Details of 410 dictionaries, encyclopedias, directories, manuals, in English and other languages; 322 on Christianity).

Religion index one: periodicals (formerly *Index to religious periodical literature*), and *Religion index two: multi-author works* (essays, conferences, etc). Ed., G. F. Dickerson. Chicago: American Theological Library Association. 12 vols, 1949–77. (Vol 9, 1969–70, comprised 227p plus 75p of book reviews; since 1975, all articles are abstracted).

'Religions and theology' in *Ulrich's international periodicals directory,* Vol II (New York, London: R.R. Bowker, 14th edition, 1971), p.873–902. (Of the 35,000 periodicals currently published throughout the world, 1,000 deal with religion and theology).

Religious and theological abstracts. Meyerstown, PA, 1958–. 41 vols. to date. (Quarterly).

Religious books and serials in print, 1978–1979. New York: Bowker, 1978 (1st Edition). 1,259p. (Over 47,400 entries for titles available from 1,700 publishers, under 4,600 subject headings; classified by subject, author, title).

Religious books for children: an annotated bibliography. P. P. Dole. 3rd ed. *A CSLA bibliography.* Portland, OR: Church and Synagogue Library Association, 1993. 39p.

Religious books in print, 1974. Religious Books Publishers Group. London: Whitaker, 1975. (Nearly 10,000 titles under 18 headings).

Religious colleges and universities in America: a selected bibliography. T. C. Hunt & J. C. Carper. *Garland reference library of social science,* 422. New York: Garland, 1988. 374p.

Religious conflict in America: a bibliography. A. J. Menendez. *Garland reference library of social science,* 262. New York: Garland, 1985. 140p.

Religious schools in America: a selected bibliography. T. C. Hunt, J. C. Carper & C. R. Kniker. *Garland reference library of social science,* 338. New York: Garland, 1986. 402p.

Religious seminaries in America: a selected bibliography. T. C. Hunt & J. C. Carper. *Garland reference library of social science,* 539. New York: Garland, 1989. 240p.

Research in ritual studies: a programmatic essay and bibliography. R. L. Grimes. *ATLA bibliography series,* 14. Chicago: American Theological Library Association and Metuchen, NJ: Scarecrow Press, 1985. 174p.

Research on religion and aging: an annotated bibliography. H. G. Koenig. *Bibliographies and indexes in gerontology,* 27.

Westport, CT: Greenwood, 1995. 190p.

Resources for Buddhist–Christian encounter: an annotated bibliography. H. L. Wells. Wofford Heights, CA: Multifaith Resources, 1993. 30p. (Prepared by the Educational Resources Committee of the Society for Buddhist-Christian Studies).

Resources in sacred dance: annotated bibliography: books, booklets and pamphlets, articles and publications, organizations, non–print, and general dance resources. K. Troxell (ed). Peterborough, NH: Sacred Dance Guild, 1986. 40p.

Rhetorical criticism of the Bible: a comprehensive bibliography with notes on history and method. D. F. Watson & A. J. Hauser. *Biblical interpretation series,* 4. Leiden and New York: E. J. Brill, 1994. 226p.

RIC: Répetoire bibliographique des institutiones chrétiennes. R. Metz & J. Schlick (eds). Strasbourg: Centre de Recherche et Documentation des Institutions Chrétiennes (CERDIC), annual since 1968. (Computer-produced indexes of Christian publications during the year; in 5 languages. 6,400 entries a year, increasing. Also RIC supplément, *Bibliographies thématiques*).

School prayer and other religious issues in American public education: a bibliography. A. J. Menendez. *Garland reference library of social science,* 291. New York: Garland, 1985. 178p.

Selective bibliography on evangelism and evangelization. D. B. Barrett. Nairobi: Centre for the Study of World Evangelization, 1980. (1,400 items).

Seventh-day Adventist (SDA) periodical index. Riverside, CA: Loma Linda University Libraries, 1971—. (4,000 articles, book reviews, editorials from over 40 SDA periodicals).

Shelf list of the Union Theological Seminary Library, New York. Boston: G. K. Hall, 1960. 10 vols.

Sikhism and the Sikhs: an annotated bibliography. P. M. Rai. *Bibliographies and indexes in religious studies,* 13. New York: Greenwood, 1989. 272p.

Social scientific criticism of the New Testament: a bibliography. D. M. May. *NABPR bibliographic series,* 4. Macon, GA: Mercer University Press, 1991. 106p.

Sociology of Christianity: an international bibliography. H. Carrier & E. Pin (eds). Rome: Gregorian University Press, 1964. 313p.

Source book on Arabian Gulf States, Arabian Gulf in general, Kuwait, Bahrain, Qatar and Oman. S. Kabeel. Kuwait: Kuwait University, Libraries Department, 1975. 427p. (With over 3,000 item bibliography).

South African theological bibliography on CD–ROM. Pretroria: Research Institute for Theology and Religion, University of South Africa; Evanston, IL: American Theological Library Association, annual since 1995.

South Asian religions in the Americas: an annotated bibliography of immigrant religious traditions. J. Y. Fenton. *Bibliographies and indexes in religious studies.* Westport, CT: Greenwood.

The Bible and modern literary criticism: a critical assessment and annotated bibliography. M. A. Powell. *Bibliographies and indexes in religious studies,* 22. New York: Greenwood, 1992. 484p.

The book of Daniel: an annotated bibliography. H. O. Thompson. *Garland reference library of the humanities, 1,310; Books of the Bible,* 1. New York: Garland, 1993. 588p.

The book of Ephesians: an annotated bibliography. W. W. Klein. *Books of the Bible, 8; Garland reference library of the humanities,* 1,466. New York: Garland, 1996. 335p.

The book of Jeremiah: an annotated bibliography. H. O. Thompson. *ATLA bibliography series,* 41. Lanham, MD: Scarecrow Press, 1996. 777p.

The book of Psalms: an annotated bibliography. T. Wittstruck. *Books of the Bible, 5; Garland reference library of the humanities,* 1,413. New York: Garland, 1994. 2 vols.

The book of Revelation: an annotated bibliography. R. L. Muse. *Books of the Bible, 2; Garland reference library of the humanities,* 1,387. New York: Garland, 1996. 388p.

The book of Ruth: an annotated bibliography. M. Caspi. *Books of the Bible, 7; Garland reference library of the humanities,* 1,410. New York: Garland, 1994. 147p.

The Books of Chronicles: a classified bibliography. I. Kalimi. *Simor Bible bibliographies.* Jerusalem: Simor, 1990. 246p. (Entries in English, Hebrew, German, and French).

The Catholic novel: an annotated bibliography. A. J. Menendez. *Garland reference library of the humanities,* 690. New York: Garland, 1988. 342p.

The Catholic periodical and literature index on CD–ROM. N.p.: Catholic Library Association; Evanston, IL: American Theological Library Association, annual since 1996.

The charismatic movement: a guide to the study of neo–pentecostalism with emphasis on Anglo–American sources. C. E. Jones. *ATLA Bibliographic Series,* 30. Metuchen, NJ and London: American Theological Library Association and Scarecrow Press, 1995. 1,266p in 2 vols. (A major bibliography of the charismatic movement).

The Children of God/Family of Love: an annotated bibliography. W. D. Pritchett. *Sects and cults in America. Bibliographical guides, 5; Garland reference library of social science,* 209. New York: Garland, 1985. 209p.

The church: a bibliography. A. R. Dulles & P. Granfield. Wilmington, DE: Michael Glazier, 1985. 166p.

The Churches of God, Seventh–day: a bibliography. J. Bjorling. *Bibliographies on sects and cults in America, 8; Garland reference library of the humanities,* 362. New York: Garland, 1987. 315p.

The contemporary Islamic revival: a critical survey and bibliography. Y. Y. Haddad, J. O. Voll & J. L. Esposito. Westport, CT: Greenwood, 1991. 230p.

The Disciples and American culture: a bibliography of works by Disciples of Christ members, 1866–1984. L. R. Galbraith & H. F. Day. *ATLA bibliography series,* 26. Metuchen, NJ: Scarecrow Press, 1990. 390p.

The doctrine of the Holy Spirit: a bibliography showing its chronological development. E. D. Schandorff. *ATLA bibliography series,* 28. Lanham, MD: American Theological Library As-

sociation and Scarecrow Press, 1995. 2 vols.

The early church: an annotated bibliography of literature in English. T. A. Robinson & B. D. Shaw. *ATLA bibliography series,* 23. Philadelphia: American Theological Library Association; Metuchen, NJ: Scarecrow Press, 1993. 518p.

The early church: an annotated bibliography of literature in English. T. A. Robinson & B. Shaw. *ATLA bibliography series,* 33. Metuchen, NJ: Scarecrow Press, 1993. 522p.

The Gospel of Luke: a cumulative bibliography 1973–1988. F. van Segbroeck. *Bibliotheca Ephemeridum theologicarum Lovaniensium,* 88. Louvain: Leuven University Press, 1989. 243p.

The Gospel of Mark: a cumulative bibliography1950–1990. F. Neirynck. *Bibliotheca Ephemeridum theologicarum Lovaniensium,* 102. Leuven: Leuven University Press, 1992. 729p.

The Holy Spirit: a bibliography. W. E. Mills. Peabody, MA: Hendrickson Publishers, 1988. 181p.

The Islamic revival since 1988: a critical survey and bibliography. Y. Y. Haddad & J. L. Esposito. *Bibliographies and indexes in religious studies,* 45. Westport, CT: Greenwood, 1997. 317p.

The literary lives of Jesus: an international bibliography of poetry, drama, fiction, and criticism. A. L. Birney. *Garland reference library of the humanities,* 735. New York: Garland, 1989. 212p.

The lives of Jesus: a history and bibliography. W. S. Kissinger. *Garland reference library of the humanities,* 452. New York: Garland, 1985. 243p.

The New Testament: a bibliography. D. J. Harrington. *Theological and biblical resources,* 2. Wilmington, DE: Michael Glazier, 1985. 242p.

The Oxford movement and its leaders: a bibliography of secondary and lesser primary sources. L. N. Crumb. *ATLA bibliography series,* 24. Metuchen, NJ: American Theological Library Association and Scarecrow Press, 1988. 737p.

The Oxford movement and its leaders: a bibliography of secondary and lesser primary sources, supplement. L. N. Crumb. *ATLA bibliography series,* 24. Metuchen, NJ: Scarecrow Press, 1993. 312p.

The peace tradition in the Catholic Church: an annotated bibliography. R. G. Musto. *Garland reference library of social science,* 339. New York: Garland, 1987. 619p. (Companion volume to *The Catholic peace tradition*).

The quarterly index Islamicus: current books, articles and papers on Islamic studies. J. D. Pearson (ed). London: Mansell, 1977–91; Bowker–Saur, 1992–93.

The Society for Old Testament Studies book list 1995. L. L. Grabbe (ed). Atlanta: Scholar's Press, 1995. 203p. (Reviews of more than 500 titles).

The sociology of religion: an organizational bibliography. A. J. Blasi & M. W. Cuneo. *Garland library of sociology, 18; Garland reference library of social science,* 612. New York: Garland, 1990. 488p.

The synoptic problem: a bibliography, 1716–1988. T. R. W. Longstaff & P. A. Thomas (eds). *New gospel studies,* 4. Macon, GA: Mercer University Press, 1988. 263p.

The Unification Church in America: a bibliography and research guide. M. L. Mickler. *Sects and cults in America. Bibliographical guides, 9; Garland reference library of social science,* 211. New York: Garland, 1987. 238p.

The Yogacara school of Buddhism: a bibliography. J. Powers. *ATLA bibliography series,* 27. Philadelphia: American Theological Library Association; Metuchen, NJ: Scarecrow Press, 1991. 257p.

Theodicy: an annotated bibliography on the problem of evil, 1960–1990. B. L. Whitney. *Garland reference library of the humanities,* 1,111. New York: Garland, 1993. 659p.

Theodicy, suffering, and good and evil: a bibliography selected from the ATLA religion database. T. J. Davis (ed). Chicago: American Theological Library Association, 1987. 297p.

Theological education in Africa: an annotated bibliography. G. Lund. Wheaton, IL: Billy Graham Center, 1992. 48p.

'Theology and religion', in M. M. Reynolds, *A guide to theses and dissertations: an annotated, international bibliography of bibliographies* (Detroit, MI: Gale Research Company, 1975), p.499–511. (54 out of 2,200 bibliographies).

Tropical Africa and the Old Testament: a select and annotated bibliography. K. Holter. *Bibliography series,* University of Oslo, Faculty of Theology, 6. Oslo, Norway: University of Oslo, Faculty of Theology, 1996. 106p.

Western language literature on pre–Islamic central Arabia: an annotated bibliography. S. D. Ricks. *Bibliographic series,* American Institute of Islamic Studies, 10. Denver, CO: American Institute of Islamic Studies, 1991. 169p.

Women and religion in Britain and Ireland: an annotated bibliography from the Reformation to 1993. D. A. Johnson. *ATLA bibliography series,* 39. Lanham, MD: Scarecrow Press, 1995. 304p.

Women and religion in India: an annotated bibliography of sources in English, 1975–92. N. A. Falk. Kalamazoo, MI: New Issues Press, College of Arts and Sciences, Western Michigan University, 1994. 241p.

Women and women's issues in North American Lutheranism: a bibliography. B. A. DeBerg & E. Sherman. Minneapolis, MN: Augsburg Fortress, 1992. 52p. (Produced under the sponsorship of the Commission for Women of the ELCA).

Women in American religious history: an annotated bibliography and guide to sources. D. C. Bass & S. H. Boyd. *G. K. Hall women's studies publications.* Boston, MA: G. K. Hall, 1986. 169p.

Women in Christian history: a bibliography. C. D. Blevins. Macon, GA: Mercer University Press, 1995. 122p.

Women in the New Testament: a select bibliography. I. M. Lindboe. *Bibliography series,* no. 1. Oslo: University of Oslo, Faculty of Theology, 1990. 90p.

World guide to libraries/Internationales Biblioteks–handbuch. 4th ed. New York: Bowker. 1974, 2 vols. (Survey of 36,932 libraries in 157 countries, each with over 30,000 volumes; total religious and theological libraries, 2,100).

Part 14

DIRECTORY

Topical directory of Christianity, religions, and worldwide ministries

Almost incidentally the great world fellowship has arisen;
it is the great new fact of our era.
—Archbishop William Temple (1881-1944)

In the 1930s, archbishop of Canterbury William Temple marvelled at the mushrooming spread of Christianity across the 20th century and spoke of the 'great world fellowship' (see quotation on previous page). Part 14 illustrates this by listing the names, postal and street addresses, telephone and fax numbers, e-mail addresses, and websites of the major Christian organizations in the world's 238 countries, divided into 82 major subjects.

Directory of topics

Topical directory of Christianity, religions, and worldwide ministries

What this Directory is and is not. This survey directory of the Christian enterprise in the modern world is not offered here as, in the first instance, a carefully corrected or completely up-to-date address list suitable for immediate mass mailings. Those who try to use it for that purpose will possibly, depending on the topics or countries involved, be disappointed with a costly return rate. This list is a global survey of Christian activities, agencies, associations, centers, churches, denominations, facilities, functions, institutions, ministries, missions, networks, orders, organizations, programs, resources, ventures, and works for the 30-year period of 1970-2000. It is designed to reflect a historical interest as well as to provide for current practical tasks. For example, a few organizations known to not still exist appear here—because they did exist and they did play an important role in the 30-year period of this survey. Their inclusion is deliberate. Each one illustrates one more bit of the overall story of organized Christian activities in this period.

In this Part of the *Encyclopedia*, moreso than any other, the compilers were very much at the mercy of their sources. Names and contact information of these 15,000 entries (with 32,000 in the *World Christian database*) were drawn from hundreds of published directories and thousands of miscellaneous sources, and, by the nature of things, it was impossible to accurately determine which information was even then already out-of-date.

Not comprehensive. For each of the 82 topics of ministry, this listing is intended to include the largest or most significant organizations and agencies by country, to show the nature of their variety, and to illustrate the scope of their global distribution. In contrast to most other Parts of this *Encyclopedia*, here there is no pretension of comprehensiveness. Under the topic CHILDREN'S MINISTRIES, for example, the reader should not expect to find the name of every last Christian organization in the world devoted to this worthy area of work. The list need not be comprehensive for the reader to be able to learn a great deal about this area of Christian ministry during the period 1970-2000, and to draw upon this data for many practical purposes, despite its omissions. As it turns out, for many sections, the representation is nearly complete. For a few sections, the representation is very close indeed to being comprehensive. But for some others, only a scant, illustrative selection can be given.

This is a survey. This Directory provides a distinct way of looking at and understanding global Christianity. It is a picture of the extraordinary complexity of the total Christian enterprise, a selective, illustrative, suggestive report, and not exhaustive or definitive. It shows the great diversity of topics, causes, areas, and needs to which Christians in this period have devoted organized attention and resources. It shows the global spread of all kinds of Christian organizations, churches, ministries, orders, agencies, associations, etc., and which kinds of organizational structures Christians have felt the need to establish in every country, or nearly every country, of the world (e.g. national conciliar bodies). Here is shown, for example, the many ways in which Christians have enlisted modern technologies (computers, the Internet, satellites, electronic media, et alii) to their goals, and at the same time the many ways in which old or even ancient ways are still very much alive and in use (e.g. the arts, literature, music, street preaching, etc.). The reader is advised not simply to use this Directory for direct reference purposes, but to browse through it, to stroll reflectively among its columns, and thus widen one's general understanding of the organized efforts of the world Christian enterprise. Much can be learned; there are many surprises.

This is a specifically Christian listing. Though, for example, there are many organizations working in the field of AID AND RELIEF that are secular, or from various non-Christian religions, this directory lists only those that are church-based, church-supported, Christian in staff, Christian in origin, or Christian by formal or informal organizational link or association. As an other example, the listing of PERIODICALS is restricted to specifically-Christian periodicals. However, there are countless borderline cases of secular organizations just sufficiently Christian or pro-Christian to warrant their inclusion in this directory. In general such bodies have been included only if their name, objective, orientation, constitution or programs identify them as church or Christian organizations. This restriction must be remembered when searching for bodies in subjects where secular activity is much greater or better organized than specifically Christian activity.

The following topics are exceptions to this rule, but they are still included because of their relevance to the purposes and scope of this *Encyclopedia*:

2. ANTI-RELIGIOUS, ATHEIST, AND HUMANIST ORGANIZATIONS
44. INTERRELIGIOUS ORGANIZATIONS
56. NON-CHRISTIAN RELIGIONS
69. STATE DEPARTMENTS FOR RELIGIOUS AFFAIRS

Practical uses. Having noted all of the above, even an initial glance will prove that this is a significant practical tool. The reader seeking to contact a specific Christian organization will most likely be able to find here what is needed, or at least to find an organization close in place or purpose that can point the searcher to the destination. The reader interested in any specific topic of Christian work will be able to explore it fully, and globally. Those seeking to expand or enhance their own Christian work or ministry through cooperation, consultation, association, colleague interaction, or communication with others who share their area of ministry or concern will be greatly helped. Or, from a more theological or ethical direction, those Christians who value ecumenism, Christian unity, loving cooperation, or humble service will find here many new paths or opportunities for obedience. Christian ministries, in any part of the world, facing specific needs of many kinds will most likely be able to find specific help. Even those seeking to learn about a certain region or country, and organized Christian efforts of various kinds there, will find much of use here, though that may require a more demanding search through the various topics. Successful practical use of this Directory will require familiarization and facility with the Definitions of Topics and Subject Index that follow.

ORGANIZATION

Overall. Entries are organized first by topic, then by country, then by name. The topics are presented in alphabetical order by name. All entries are presented in a format that is frugal with space, not devoting a separate line to name, address, phone, and so on, as is common among directories of lesser scope. These items are separated by commas. Some topics require less than a page, while others span many pages. The layout is designed to allow the reader to easily find the countries within each topic. Country names are never repeated in the entries themselves, again for the sake of saving space. Actual organization names may be in various languages, even within a single country, but are all in Roman characters and are ordered according to the English alphabet.

Contents of each entry. The most complete entries will give the full, official name of the organization, possibly in more than one language, possibly also followed by a common or well-known acronym, then both a mailing address (PO Box or the equivalent) and a street location address, then one or several telephone numbers, then one or several fax numbers, then other contact information that may include a telex address, a cable address, an e-mail address, and a World Wide Web address. In fact, very few entries have such a complete array of contact information, though many have a great deal. Most have at least name, address, phone, and maybe fax. Many have only name and address. Some have only name and one point of other contact information, such as a Web address. Again, the compilers were at the mercy of their sources. Note that no personal names or even titles or designations of leaders, officers, officials, executives, or workers appear with any listed organizations. These tend to change even more often than the extremely volatile contact information that is included, and sources more often than not included no such information.

Name. Usually the full, official name of the organization, agency, church, or association is given, though not always. The reader should not expect the directory

---

Names are in bold (though not all alternative names).

Addresses directly follow names.

    T: precedes telephone numbers.
    F: precedes fax numbers.
    O: precedes other contact information, which might include cable, telex, E-mail, or World Wide Web addresses.

E-mail addresses and World Wide Web addresses may be divided between lines of text with a dash or dashes that *must not* be included when trying to use these addresses.

---

to be definitive on this point. The name may appear in English only, or in another language only, or in both, or several, and in some cases will be followed by an acronym. In a few cases, the name came in only its acronym form, and is thus presented. The reader seeking a specific organization by name should bear in mind these possibilities, which in some cases will carry the search to more than one place. Older city, country, ethnic, or regional names or terms are sometimes retained (by design or neglect) in the names of certain Christian bodies, and should not always be taken as a sure sign that the entry itself is outdated. The word 'The' is not included before names.

Address. The reader will quickly see here the complex and non-uniform variety of systems, codes, and abbreviations used by the postal systems of various countries around the world, operating in various languages, and should not expect standardization. The situation is made even more difficult by the historical nature of this directory. Many countries changed or introduced their national system of postal codes (or 'zip codes' or 'PIN codes', etc.) during the period 1970-2000, and some made such a change as many as 3 times (e.g. Singapore). Among the entries for a single country there may be a few with no code, others with an outdated code, and others yet with current codes, though this is not common. In almost all cases, a letter sent with an address that is out-of-date or incomplete on this point alone will still reach its intended destination, though large delays are possible. Mail forwarding policies and practices will also, similarly, help many pieces of personal mail to arrive successfully, even if outdated addresses are used. Such policies and practices are never so generous, however, with bulk or mass mailings, and the reader is again warned against applying this list to that use. For many entries, both a postal box address and a street location address are given. Some Christian organizations do not change their location for decades or even centuries; others (usually because of financial pressures) move often, even more often than annually. Many of the organizations and ministries here are well-established, well-funded, and operate at their address from a substantial, permanent campus or building, while many others are new, small, or even experimental or temporary. Thus some addresses will not be out-of-date 100 years from the publication of this *Encyclopedia*, but certainly not most. Some entire topics of ministry are so new that nearly all the entries in those categories can be expected to change their addresses many times before they become more firmly settled.

One helpful general rule is that postal box addresses

tend to be more permanent than street location or building addresses, so the reader is advised to address mail to PO Boxes whenever that option is offered, and in those cases to not put both addresses on the same envelope or package. In some countries there is no postal delivery to street addresses but only to boxes in central post offices. On the other hand, some package delivery services (e.g. UPS, United Parcel Service) do not deliver to post boxes but only to location addresses.

The reader should not be afraid to use mailing addresses that seem, at first glance, to be impossibly short or simple. Some addresses may have nothing more than, e.g., 'The Cathedral [name of city, name of country]' or 'Bishop's House [name of country]' or 'St. Joseph's School [name of country]'. In many cases such these, no further address is either needed or possible. City names change over time and from language to language, and it was not possible to standardize this, so the reader will at times find different orthography even in adjacent entries (e.g. Bayrut and Beirut). If possible, it is best to use city names as they appear in the country being written to (e.g. Roma over Rome, Moskva over Moscow, El Djezair/Alger over Algiers), and similarly with country names, which should be written in all capital letters.

Telephone. These numbers change as often as addresses and sometimes more often, as national telephone systems from time to time change their numbering systems or add digits to the entire scheme. In many places, local telephone systems allow an organization to carry its old phone number to a new physical location—in those cases, the phone number may prove more reliable than the address over time. It is very important for the reader to be aware that telephone numbers as presented here may differ greatly from each other in the presence or absence of nested codes and prefixes. Some numbers include country codes, region codes, city codes, area codes, and then local numbers; others are not so complete, giving only one level of prefix code, or none, or 2 of 3, or any number of other possibilities. One especially needs to be aware of country codes, which may or may not be present on any given number, and should never try to dial any of these without having at hand a listing of the world's country codes for telephone service, to refer to in the process. For international calls, carelessness on this point could be both frustrating and costly. The reader should also be aware that in some countries the telephone prefix number system differs between international and in-country calls in ways other than just the presence or absence of a country code. Not all of the numbers presented here are given in a form appropriate for international calls. Nor is there much consistency in the use of dashes or parentheses to separate numbers, to separate various prefixes, or to chop longer numbers into smaller pieces that are then supposedly easier to remember accurately. For some organizations, several alternative numbers are given, which may represent separate lines into one phone system, or separate phones, even in separate offices, departments, or locations. The telephone numbers that appear in the topic COMPUTER BULLETIN BOARD SYSTEMS should be dialed by computer modems with appropriate computer communications software.

Fax. All of the caveats, warnings, and points of guidance given above about telephone numbers apply equally to fax numbers. Readers familiar with the frustrating possibilities in fax temperament and behavior, especially internationally, need no further coaching.

Other. In some countries, cable and telex use is still common, extensive, reliable, and important, and has not at all been replaced by fax or e-mail, so they are included. As for the common computer-based means of communication:

E-mail. Readers unfamiliar with e-mail can simply ignore these addresses, while e-mail users will be indeed grateful for their inclusion. An enormous volume of e-mail communications is now moving around the Christian world, a trend that was born and has exploded many times in the 30-year period of this survey. Three unfortunate facts here: (1) The trend is still new enough that few sources included this information, so the representation is regrettably thin. A large and rapidly growing percentage of the entries here that show no e-mail address do in fact have such addresses. (2) Many users have changed their e-mail addresses even more often than their telephone numbers, as they have jumped from one ISP (Internet service provider) to another in these early years of this rapidly-moving technology. Message forwarding instructions, aids, or warnings are rare. (3) E-mail addresses tend to be connected more with individual users than with organizations, institutions, or offices. As noted above, this Directory is focused on organizations, agencies, churches,

and institutions, and not on individual Christian workers, clergy, or leaders of any kind. To repeat the important warning that appears above: some e-mail addresses are divided between lines of text, with a dash or dashes. *These dashes must be removed* before use is attempted, as e-mail addresses will only work successfully if every digit is exactly correct.

Web. Again, those readers unfamiliar with the World Wide Web will be baffled by these addresses. Their use requires a computer, a modem, web-browsing software, and an active account with an ISP. But, like e-mail, the Web is a vast and rapidly-expanding universe of Christian communication globally. Similar unfortunate realities apply: (1) Sources were thin with Web addresses, and so therefore is this directory. (2) Addresses have changed many times and often, and forwarding instructions are rare. And, in this case, (3) the reader needs to be alert to differences in format with these addresses. In most, the *http://* prefix is missing. In some the www prefix is missing. Thus a full address such as *http://www.bwanet.org* (for the Baptist World Alliance) most likely would appear as *www.bwanet.org* but might possibly appear as *bwanet.org*, though the full address is required for successful connection. The good news is that a printed directory of Web addresses is hardly necessary, except for the informative and illustrative purposes of this survey, thanks to the many excellent general and Christian search engines and constantly-updated directories that appear on the Web itself. Many of the Christian directory sites of this kind are noted under the topic INTERNET AND WORLD WIDE WEB MINISTRIES. Finally, the most important reminder: the dashes that appear when Web addresses are divided between two lines *must be removed* before connection is attempted, as Web addresses also require that every digit be exactly correct.

TOPICS

The list of 82 topics around which this survey is organized evolved during the process of compilation, emerging from the realities of the massive amount of source material scanned. No topic is watertight. These topics or categories are not, nor can they be, entirely logical and mutually exclusive. The wide variety of living activities and experiences they reflect are not so simple and straightforward. In the course of Christian activities of many kinds, in many places, over time, discrete categories related to a single word or phrase tend to arise and crystallize out by themselves to meet the working needs of the community. The directory therefore uses these latter natural clusters as its categories. Even at that, most topics tend to shade off into other topics in various directions. Thus the reader will do well to heed the 'see also …' notes appended to many topic definitions. The resulting list itself, with definitions, is instructive, showing the great diversity of organized Christian efforts.

Changes in the list of topics. Most topics appeared in the 1st edition of the *World Christian encyclopedia*, though several names and most definitions have been updated, and a few topics have been merged, all of which reflect changes in organized Christianity in the intervening years. The following 8 topics are new to this edition:

3. APPAREL, MERCHANDISE, AND GIFTS
9. BIBLE STUDY
18. COMPUTER BULLETIN BOARD SYSTEMS
19. COMPUTER SERVICES, SOFTWARE, AND RESOURCES
29. ECOLOGY
36. FOREIGN MISSIONARY FIELD CONTACTS
42. HOMOSEXUALITY (LESBIAN, GAY, AND BISEXUALITY)
43. INTERNET AND WORLD WIDE WEB MINISTRIES

Though Topics 9 and 36 were simply added to clarify and expand the earlier typology, the presence of the other 6 tells a story about new directions in global Christianity and its changing concerns and activities.

Assigning topics. It is often difficult to assign Christian organizations, institutions, and ministries to a single topic. Many, if not most, are active in more than one significant area of work or concern. It is the policy of this Directory though, with very few exceptions, to assign each entry to only one topic. The compilers determined for each entry the option that best reflected the most important, central, or significant single area of ministry or concern. Sometimes the organization's name was used for definitive guidance, though it is also true that for many organizations their name does not fit well with their primary mission. The reader seeking

contact information for a specific ministry might need to scan over several topics when more than one might pose valid options for assignment.

Selection. The database from which this printed Directory was drawn includes more than twice the number of entries as appear here. The entire 32,000 entries will appear on the *World Christian database* CD. The space constraints of this print version, despite the frugal format, forced difficult and painful decisions. Topics were not pared down in an equal or even way. The instructive survey purpose was one criterion that guided this process. The practical needs of users were also kept in view. For some topics, all entries appear in this printed report. For others, a selection of entries was assigned to appear here, usually on some basis of size, significance, or source. Unfortunately, the compilers were forced to the drastic measure of eliminating all entries for the following topics:

3. APPAREL, MERCHANDISE, AND GIFTS
8. BIBLE SCHOOLS AND COLLEGES
11. BROADCAST STATIONS
12. CAMPS, RETREAT CENTERS, AND LAY TRAINING CENTERS
23. CONCILIARISM: LOCAL (SUB-NATIONAL)
37. FOREIGN MISSIONARY SOCIETIES
51. MEDICAL CENTERS
53. MEN'S LAY ORGANIZATIONS
57. PERIODICALS
66. SCHOOLS AND COLLEGES
67. SOCIAL AND PASTORAL MINISTRIES
72. THEOLOGICAL COLLEGES AND SEMINARIES
76. UNIVERSITIES

The only encouraging note that can be offered in the face of this is that these topics will appear in their entirety in the *World Christian database* CD.

A special process was applied to the enormous topic of CHURCHES AND DENOMINATIONS. In Part 5 "CountryScan", Tables 2, certain denominations appear in a bolder typeface, those that represent 10% or more of the total number of Christians in that country. For the most part, it is only the contact information for these that appears in this Directory. Again, a large number of others will be included in the CD.

Coverage. The reader is again reminded that this survey is neither comprehensive nor even, across countries or topics. The varying availability and quality of sources deserves much of the blame. Some countries, ecclesiastical families, and topics of ministry or kinds of institutions are well served by one or many good directories, in various forms. But there remain many large gaps in this important ministry of directory compilation, gaps that to some extent are reflected here. Special mention should be made of the *India Christian Handbook*. This extensive research project, with coordinators in each state and broad participation across church and denominational lines, compiled massive, new, original data of many kinds on Indian Christianity. Unfortunately, for various reasons, the *Handbook* never came to print. Leaders of this project were gracious enough to allow directory data, of 1000s of entries across dozens of topics, to be included in this Directory, for which the editors are all most grateful. This data, which appears only here, stands as a generous gift to the Indian church as well as to all those who use this *Encyclopedia*.

Updating. The information here can be expected to go out of date at a rate of about 1% per year, on average. Some information is extremely stable, while some is not at all stable. However, often even an out-of-date address or phone number is useful in tracking down changed locations. The directory should remain useful as a working tool until after AD 2010. Updated versions of the directory will be issued from time to time from the *World Christian database*.

Definitions of topics

1. **AID AND RELIEF.** Christian organizations, service agencies, charities, charitable societies, and inter-church service agencies that help suffering people and populations faced with natural disaster, war, violence, famine, refugee situations, lack of water, lack of food, lack of shelter, epidemics, or disease. The emphasis here is on relatively short-term emergency situations, and situations of more extreme, immediate, or desperate crisis. See also: DEVELOPMENT, JUSTICE, AND PEACE and SOCIAL AND PASTORAL CONCERN.

2. **ANTI-RELIGIOUS, ATHEIST, AND HUMANIST ORGANIZATIONS.** Atheistic or non-religious humanist (or anti-supernaturalist) movements, organizations, and associations; freethinkers' organizations, societies, or groups; bodies committed to active or militant opposition to Christianity or to all religion; organizations for the promotion or propagation of atheism or non-theistic humanism, centers for the study of atheism, research centers dealing with religion from an anti-religious position.

3. **APPAREL, MERCHANDISE, AND GIFTS.** Companies, businesses, and organizations that design, manufacture, produce, sell, or distribute Christian T-shirts, clothing, hats, mugs, plaques, pictures, figurines, rosaries, objects of devotion, icons, toys, games, gifts for students or children, favors, craft items, or other merchandise — of a wide variety, on a range from costly to cheap, with Christian verses, slogans, symbols, saints, or uses. For items of greater artistic character, see ART (RELIGION AND THE ARTS). See also LITURGY AND WORSHIP.

4. **ART (RELIGION AND THE ARTS).** Christian involvement in the arts, including the visual arts, the fine arts, the performing arts, the literary arts; painting, sculpture, architecture, stained glass, drama, theater, opera, cinema, puppetry, mime, festivals, circus; renowned centers of Christian artistic presentation (e.g. Oberammergau, Forest Lawn, Einsiedein); mission and evangelization through the arts; expression of Christian and Biblical themes through the arts; notable Christian displays and exhibitions (e.g. the Holy Land museum, Nijmegen); major Christian museums; Christian art centers and centers for training in the arts; church architecture, historical monuments. See also CINEMA AND FILM, MEDIA AND COMMUNICATIONS, and MUSIC.

5. **AUDIO RECORDINGS.** Tape or cassette ministries, audio ministries; companies, centers or organizations which make, sell, or distribute records, tapes, audio cassettes, CDs, or recordings on other audio media; record, tape, cassette or disc libraries, or libraries of recorded music; ministries which produce or distribute records or cassettes in many languages for missionary or Christian training purposes.

6. **AUDIOVISUAL RESOURCES.** Agencies, programs, offices, and centers specializing in the production or distribution of all kinds of audiovisual aids: slides, filmstrips, transparencies, posters, pictures, flannel boards, drawings, presentation books, puppets, flip charts, cartoons, videos, tapes, records, recordings, compact discs, microfilm, microfiche, computer programs, CD-ROMs; audiovisual training centers oriented towards education, catechesis, evangelization, renewal, or development. For those organizations dedicated to film and video resources alone, see CINEMA, FILM AND VIDEO; similarly for SOUND RECORDINGS and for COMPUTER SERVICES, SOFTWARE, AND RESOURCES. See also MEDIA AND COMMUNICATIONS.

7. **BIBLE AND SCRIPTURE ORGANIZATIONS.** Bible societies; Bible and scripture publishing, Bible translation, translation training and assistance, Christian linguistic organizations and centers, Bible and scripture distribution and colportage (whether offered for free, at cost, or for profit), Bible text societies (literature, posters), Bible-reading organizations; the biblical apostolate. See also PUBLISHING for publishers specializing (but not exclusively) in Bible production, and BIBLE STUDY.

8. **BIBLE SCHOOLS AND COLLEGES.** Centers for the training of Christian workers, with (a) curricula especially centered on the Bible and basic Christian instruction, (b) programs both for the lay and ordained ministry, or especially for lay workers, (c) often less concern for academic accreditation, (d) courses of study that may result in the granting of degrees, but often of certificates or diplomas, (e) generally lower academic requirements for entry, (f) generally lower or simpler level of study than theological colleges or seminaries.

9. **BIBLE STUDY.** Ministries, agencies, organizations, and networks devoted to promoting, encouraging, guiding, and leading lay study of the Bible; organizations devoted to Bible-oriented basic Christian instruction; institutes for Biblical and theological study; Biblical and early Christian archeology; Bible teaching and Bible teacher training; Bible study aids, references, tools, techniques, methods, resources; home Bible studies, cell-group Bible studies, small-group Bible studies, and self-directed Bible studies; activism for the Bible or for the study of the Bible. See also RESEARCH CENTERS, and COMPUTER SERVICES, SOFTWARE, AND RESOURCES.

10. **BROADCASTING.** Organizations and centers (excluding radio/TV stations) specializing in Christian religious broadcasting, radio/TV programming, program production, production of related materials, spots; production studios, program distribution agencies (distributing to stations) or agents; radio/TV training schools and centers; educational or mass-education radio and TV; agencies specializing in radio/TV technology or technical services; satellite agencies, specialists, or organizations; listeners' and viewers' associations. See also BROADCAST STATIONS and MEDIA AND COMMUNICATIONS.

11. **BROADCAST STATIONS.** A brief selection of church- or Christian-owned, -operated, -controlled, or -sponsored radio, TV, or satellite broadcasting stations (organized centers with transmitting equipment).

12. **CAMPS, RETREAT CENTERS, AND LAY TRAINING CENTERS.** Places and programs dedicated to the training, education, instruction, spiritual refreshment, renewal, or spiritual growth of laypeople, almost always with a physical building, campus, or site; conference, fellowship, renewal, or retreat centers; camps for children, youth, or adults; study centers, Catholic pastoral centers and institutes, major Catholic catechetical centers, lay seminaries; leadership training or Christian service training sites; wilderness camps and programs; organizations for lay training through conferences, institutes, discipleship groups, or classes. Specialized training centers are listed under many of the other categories, by topic.

13. **CATECHESIS AND CHRISTIAN EDUCATION.** Organizations helping with Christian training and education for children, youth, and adults; Sunday schools, Sabbath schools, vacation Bible schools, Bible teaching, Bible classes, catechism classes, confirmation classes and courses; councils, organizations, and agencies of religious education; agencies producing or distributing curricula, books, media, and resources for all such education; catechetics.

14. **CHILDREN'S MINISTRIES.** Agencies specializing in work with or for children; children's missions, child evangelism ministries, child welfare agencies, children's homes, orphanages. For education and Sunday schools, see catechesis and christian education.

15. **CHRISTIAN APPROACHES TO OTHER FAITHS.** Christian research, activities, and initiatives directed primarily towards other major world religions (especially Judaism, Islam, Hinduism, Buddhism), including agnosticism and atheism, concerned with mission and evangelism, or with interfaith dialogue or mutual understanding; related activities, information and study centers. For joint activities involving Christians and non-Christians together, see INTERRELIGIOUS ORGANIZATIONS.

16. **CHURCHES AND DENOMINATIONS.** Headquarters, central offices, or main contact points for a selection of larger or more significant (in each country) of the world's Christian churches, denominations, or associations of churches. These can be paired with entries in Country Tables 2, Part 4 (where statistics, translations, alternate names, common acronyms, jurisdictions, and other information can be found). Thousands of smaller churches and denominations are excluded.

17. **CLERGY AND CLERGY-LAY ORGANIZATIONS.** Organizations of individuals for consultation and co-operation between clergy (priests, pastors, ministers), or clergy and laity, or clergy/laity/religious personnel, or missionary personnel; either within a single church or denomination, or interdenominational or ecumenical; priests' councils or senates, national priests' organizations, ministerial or clergy fellowships or associations, pastoral councils, pastoral consultative bodies, fellowships of foreign missionary personnel, Catholic national and diocesan synods; clergy recruitment organizations, clergy or lay employment bureaus. For women, see WOMEN IN THE ORDAINED MINISTRY. For religious personnel, see RELIGIOUS COMMUNITIES.

18. **COMPUTER BULLETIN BOARD SYSTEMS.** Modem-accessed sites for the posting or reading of messages, the uploading or downloading of files, and other computer-aided transmission of information or interaction, usually privately operated and serving a relatively small or localized community of netizens; BBS'. For those on the Internet see INTERNET AND WORLD WIDE WEB MINISTRIES; this category is for those on other network systems such as FidoNet, Free-Net, or FamilyNet. Note that rarely in history has an entire category of Christian ministry expanded and then contracted so rapidly. From almost zero in 1984, by the early 1990s there were many thousands of Christian BBS' in more than 100 countries (with the vast majority in the USA, Britain, and other English-speaking countries); as the World Wide Web grew in sites, users, and significance, many BBS' disappeared, though thousands remained active through AD2000.

19. **COMPUTER SERVICES, SOFTWARE, AND RESOURCES.** Companies, agencies, ministries, and organizations that provide computers, IT (information technology) services, software, network services, systems analysis, programming, or modem communications services especially to churches, mission agencies, or Christian organizations or institutions; web site construction, hosting, or maintenance; the designing, writing, publication, distribution, or installation of software for church, Christian, missionary, evangelization, or Biblical/theological study purposes; computer or software consultation or training. See also INTERNET AND WORLD WIDE WEB MINISTRIES.

20. **CONCILIARISM: CONFESSIONAL.** Councils of churches or denominations belonging to a world confessional family (world family of churches) of one particular ecclesiastical, historical, or theological tradition; international confessional councils, federations, associations, alliances, fellowships; similar groups organized on the continental, regional, or national level; confessional conciliarism, collegiality, and consultation.

21. **CONCILIARISM: CONTINENTAL OR REGIONAL.** Interdenominational or ecumenical councils of churches or denominations of different ecclesiastical traditions, for a single continent, sub-continent, or world region (of many countries); continental or regional Christian councils, federations, associations, alliances, fellowships; continental conciliarism, collegiality, and consultation.

22. **CONCILIARISM: GLOBAL.** Interdenominational or ecumenical councils of churches or denominations of different ecclesiastical traditions, at the international or world level; global Christian councils, federations, associations, alliances, fellowships; world conciliarism, collegiality, and consultation.

23. **CONCILIARISM: LOCAL (SUB-NATIONAL).** Interdenominational or ecumenical councils of churches or denominations of different ecclesiastical traditions, for a province, city, area of a city, or region within a single nation; local, provincial, or city-wide Christian councils, federations, associations, alliances, fellowships; local conciliarism, collegiality, and consultation.

24. **CONCILIARISM: NATIONAL.** Interdenominational or ecumenical councils of churches or denominations of different ecclesiastical traditions, at times including foreign missionary societies or other Christian organizations, for a single nation or a small grouping of a few adjacent nations; national Christian councils, federations, associations, alliances, fellowships; Roman Catholic national episcopal or bishops' conferences; national inter-rite ecumenical assemblies; national conciliarism, collegiality and consultation; including certain missionary councils (associations or fellowships of foreign missions or missionaries at work in a nation, especially in World A), but excluding interreligious national councils open to non-Christian bodies (for these, see INTERRELIGIOUS ORGANIZATIONS).

25. **CORRESPONDENCE SCHOOLS AND MINISTRIES.** Christian mass educational courses with curriculum and individual feedback sent by mail (post); instruction by radio/TV/satellite/video/computer with enrollment and local instructors or postal feedback; radio (radiophonic) schools, TV schools (teleschools, telecenters), video- or audio-cassette instruction or training by mail; radio literacy courses.

26. **DEVELOPMENT, JUSTICE, AND PEACE.** Economic development, community development, national development, international development, appropriate technology, poverty, underdevelopment, socio-economic development; empowerment of, or assistance to, or giving a voice to the poor, the marginalized, the oppressed, the needy, the neglected, minorities; political or social action on behalf of the poor, needy, or oppressed; social justice, community justice, human rights, human dignity, social or community activism; concern for injustice, racism, prejudice, or discrimination; pacifism, peace or anti-war groups, conscientious objection; Christian involvement in revolution, or liberation movements. For local development and community projects, see social and pastoral concern. See also AID AND RELIEF.

27. **DIPLOMATIC REPRESENTATION.** Diplomatic representation of the Holy See across the world, to nations and to major international organizations; diplomatic representation to the Holy See; diplomatic representation and offices to and from other major Christian bodies; Christian permanent observers or diplomatic representation in international bodies such as the United Nations; nunciatures, apostolic delegations.

28. **DIRECTORIES, YEARBOOKS, HANDBOOKS, AND ALMANACS.** Major directories, yearbooks, and reference handbooks (usually containing names, addresses, other contact information, statistics, listings, descriptive materials, but not extensive histories, surveys, or descriptive texts) of churches, denominations, councils, and Christian organizations, agencies, institutions, personnel, and periodicals; denominational, interdenominational, local, national, plurinational, international, and topical; with the addresses of the publishing or distributing agencies.

29. **ECOLOGY.** Christian stewardship of the natural world, God's creation; opposition to pollution, insensitive development, destruction of natural environments, misuse or waste of natural resources; advocacy for sustainable development and environmental responsibility; activist, educational, and advocacy organizations, agencies, and ministries; wilderness and wildlife conservation; theological reflection on earth, creation, or ecological themes; environmentalist or ecological activist resources, research, or training; appreciation and celebration of the beauty, glory, or goodness of nature. See also DEVELOPMENT, JUSTICE, AND PEACE.

30. **ECUMENICAL CENTERS.** Centers primarily for interdenominational or ecumenical meeting, study, dialogue, resources, and training, for both clergy and laity.

31. **ECUMENICAL COMMISSIONS AND AGENCIES.** Organizations for Christian unity, inter-church, inter-confessional, or multi-confessional dialogue or understanding; or functions organized for the fostering of relations between the churches, for ecumenical meeting, dialogue, study, fellowship, or joint action; faith and order commissions; church union negotiating bodies.

32. **EVANGELISM, EVANGELIZATION, AND CHURCH GROWTH.** International, national, or local evangelistic organizations, evangelistic societies, evangelistic associations, evangelistic missions, professional evangelists, revival campaigns, tent campaigns, crusades, missions, long-term campaigns (e.g. Evangelism-in-Depth, New Life for All), saturation evangelism programs (total mobilization evangelism); national or international organizations, cooperative ministries, or congresses on evangelism or evangelization; world evangelization agencies, councils, congresses, institutions, programs; Church Growth institutes, consultants, instruction, seminars, services, agencies, networks, or resources.

33. **FILM, VIDEO, AND CINEMA.** Christian involvement in the cinema, films, motion pictures, or videos; film or video-cassette production or distribution; film or video technology, services, casting, or equipment; movie theaters and associations; cinema, film, or video training schools and centers; film or video libraries, distributors, or rental facilities; film festivals, weeks, or seminars; Christian resources on videodisc, DVD, and other motion picture media.

34. **FINANCE, PROPERTY, AND STEWARDSHIP.** Church or Christian finance, giving, charitable giving, property, financial services, Christian stewardship, investment, taxes, accounting, or insurance; co-operatives, savings societies, credit unions, financial institutions; foundations, trusts, funds, funding agencies, fund-raising agencies, fund-transmitting agencies, pension programs, ministerial financial or insurance societies, insurance companies, credit unions; new church construction or building societies or funds; management consulting, business methods for churches or Christian organizations; agencies for fund-raising training, consultation, services, or activities; associations for financial or accounting integrity, standards, or accountability. See also AID AND RELIEF, and DEVELOPMENT, JUSTICE AND PEACE.

35. **FOREIGN MISSIONARY COUNCILS.** Councils, associations, commissions, committees, or fellowships of foreign missionary societies; organized councils of interdenominational or denominational or diocesan missionary societies, set up in sending countries for co-ordination, co-operation, joint discussion, joint projects, and missionary action to overseas or foreign countries (but that do not themselves generally serve as missionary-sending organizations).

36. **FOREIGN MISSIONARY FIELD CONTACTS.** A brief selection of contact information for the sites of missionary work, on the fields to which missionaries are sent; field offices, field contacts, field headquarters; bases, compounds, offices, centers, or central institutions for missionary efforts or teams.

37. **FOREIGN MISSIONARY SOCIETIES.** Societies and agencies primarily concerned with the sending of foreign missionary personnel and resources to another country or countries, including international missionary societies, denominational mission boards, orders which mainly or largely work in foreign missions, and Catholic missionary congregations or institutes. Thousands of smaller societies are not included.

38. **FOREIGN MISSIONARY TRAINING.** Training institutions or programs of various types and sizes, in sending countries or on mission fields, solely or primarily for the training of foreign missionaries or Christians proceeding overseas in secular employment; orientation schools and courses, programs for the continuing or advanced education of missionaries, refresher courses, post-field de-briefing courses, graduate schools of mission or missiology, missiological institutes; seminaries, schools, or colleges primarily for foreign missionaries. For the academic study of mission and missiology, see UNIVERSITY DEPARTMENTS OF RELIGION.

39. **FOREIGN MISSIONS SUPPORT ORGANIZATIONS.** Agencies that assist or promote foreign missionary work but that do not themselves generally send missionaries; service organizations, coordinating agencies, partnership ministries; fund-raising, support of national workers or indigenous missionaries or ministries overseas, fostering international inter-church relationships; mobilization, recruiting in sending countries; technical aid, missionary aviation and transport, missionary equipment services.

40. HOME AND FAMILY LIFE. Family ministries, family counseling, the family apostolate; marriage or parenting instruction, enrichment, guidance, and counseling; family planning, abortion, pregnancy counseling, adoption, orphans; ministries for the divorced or separated, marital introduction agencies. For advocacy and activism on abortion or other family issues, see RELIGIO-POLITICAL ORGANIZATIONS.

41. HOME MISSIONS AND RENEWAL MINISTRIES. Home or domestic missionary societies, agencies, congregations, or orders; mission organizations which work only or primarily within their own nation; evangelism among or ministry to ethnic or social minorities within a nation, evangelism among or ministry to certain classes, occupations, or social or financial classes; home evangelistic societies or ministries; renewal movements within the churches, inter- or non-denominational renewal or deeper life ministries; charismatic movements, services, networks, or communication centers. See also: RURAL AGRICULTURAL MISSION, URBAN INDUSTRIAL MISSION.

42. HOMOSEXUALITY (LESBIAN, GAY, AND BI SEXUALITY). Christian ministries, organizations, or groups for homosexuals, of homosexuals, or against homosexuality; gay, lesbian, or bi sexual conferences, commissions, committees, or agencies; advocacy or activist groups (those affirming the place of homosexuality or homosexuals in Christianity and the churches, and those opposing homosexuality as sin); ministries that evangelize homosexuals or that seek to help them to chastity or heterosexuality; theological or pastoral reflection on alternative sexuality. For ministry to AIDS sufferers, see MEDICINE AND HEALING.

43. INTERNET AND WORLD WIDE WEB MINISTRIES. Christian web sites, web site directories, Internet directories, evangelistic sites, devotional sites, news sites, educational sites, liturgical sites; e-mail forums, e-mail newsletters, e-mail list servers, e-mail services; companies, ministries, and organizations helping with the building or maintaining of web sites, or e-mail operations, or offering internet services; major internet networks or hosts. Note that World Wide Web site addresses and e-mail addresses for specific denominations, organizations, institutions, orders, and ministries are listed with those entries wherever they appear in their various topics. See also COMPUTER SERVICES, SOFTWARE, AND RESOURCES.

44. INTERRELIGIOUS ORGANIZATIONS. Commissions, councils, or organizations not primarily or exclusively Christian but run jointly by all or several major religions including Christianity, i.e. run by Christians and one or more non-Christian religions, for some joint non-missionary, inter-faith activities; including national councils of religious bodies open to Christians and non-Christians alike; inter-faith councils, agencies, organizations, and bodies of global, national, or local scope; inter-religious dialogue or study centers or agencies.

45. JOURNALISM, THE PRESS, AND INFORMATION. The religious press, newspapers, news periodicals, radio and TV religious news offices, news services, religion editors or religion departments of news media outlets; press agencies of major denominations or organizations, church or denominational or Christian information agencies and centers; religious press services, agencies publishing news bulletins, church publicity or public relations centers, church advertising; photographic libraries, agencies and services; journalism training centers, schools of journalism.

46. LAY MINISTRIES. Organizations for the laity only, specifically emphasizing the lay contribution in Christian life, mission, and work; lay associations, the lay apostolate, lay movements, lay preachers, lay readers, lay persons overseas, lay missionary societies; lay personal evangelism, small-group evangelism. See also WOMEN'S LAY ORGANIZATIONS and MEN'S LAY ORGANIZATIONS.

47. LIBRARIES. Major Christian and religious book library collections: theological, religious, missiological, biblical. Note that many major libraries are connected with UNIVERSITIES, RESEARCH CENTERS, THEOLOGICAL COLLEGES AND SEMINARIES, and UNIVERSITY DEPARTMENTS OF RELIGION. For non-book libraries (photographic libraries, film libraries, record libraries, recorded music libraries, tape libraries), see AUDIOVISUAL RESOURCES; FILM, VIDEO, AND CINEMA; JOURNALISM, THE PRESS, AND INFORMATION; MUSIC; MEDIA AND COMMUNICATIONS; and AUDIO RECORDINGS.

48. LITERATURE. Organizations for the printing and distribution of Christian literature; publications programs, major bookshops and bookshop chains and headquarters, booksellers associations; tract societies; religious book clubs; literacy materials, campaigns, courses, programs, agencies, or coordinating bodies. See also PERIODICALS and PUBLISHING.

49. LITURGY AND WORSHIP. Liturgical centers, organizations, movements; major supply agencies for liturgical equipment, literature, vestments; liturgical training centers; instruction or advocacy concerning ritual, rites, sacraments; wholesale and retail supply houses for religious articles. See also MUSIC.

50. MEDIA AND COMMUNICATIONS. Agencies, ministries, organizations, and centers working in the area of social communications, i.e. several or all types of mass and communications media (often including audiovisual, multimedia, cinema, recordings, radio, TV, literature, newspapers, public opinion media); Christian production of media and communications material, multimedia production centers and studios; the technical aspects of communication, mass communication, and instant communication; the production or distribution of media tools and resources for evangelism, discipleship, Christian education, catechesis, mission, or training; training centers or programs for media and communication arts and technologies.

51. MEDICAL CENTERS. Buildings, sites, campuses, or multi-site networks for medical ministry; Church- or Christian-sponsored or –owned hospitals, clinics, leprosaria, sanatoria, dispensaries, mobile units, maternity centers, et alia.

52. MEDICINE AND HEALING. Organizations, ministries, networks, missions, and movements dedicated to helping or healing the sick, dying, or handicapped; medical missions, associations of hospitals (or clinics or dispensaries), associations of medical ministries, medical missionary institutes, medical or nursing training centers or programs, dental missions, ophthalmic missions, leprosy missions, other specialist missions, medical supply agencies; public health, primary care, hospital chaplaincy, religion and health, theological reflection on health and healing; ministries to handicapped groups or specific diseased groups (the deaf, the blind, cripples, the mentally ill, incurables, lepers, et alia); Christian psychiatry and psychology, ministry to the depressed or suicidal, religion and psychiatry or psychology, clinical theology; spiritual or divine healing, faith-healing groups, ministries, and centers.

53. MEN'S LAY ORGANIZATIONS. Men's ministries, movements, missions, and agencies; organizations devoted to the evangelization, training, service, discipleship, teaching, or special needs of lay men; agencies, commissions, or ministries that assist, encourage, direct, or provide resources for men's fellowships in churches; men's rallies, conferences, crusades, missions, or events. See also LAY MINISTRIES.

54. MILITARY CHAPLAINCY. Organizations ministering to or providing chaplains for armed services at home or overseas (armies, navies, air forces, police forces, national guard groups, law enforcement agencies, government units, paramilitary units); chaplaincy training and support; chaplaincy associations.

55. MUSIC. Choirs, musical groups, singers and musical artists, evangelistic musical groups, singing groups, Christian musical groups of any genre of popular music; music publishers, producers, recording studios, record labels, promoters, agents; libraries of religious music, church or religious music training; orchestras, opera, festivals, evangelistic productions; music and theology, music and missions, ethnomusicology; campanology, bell-ringing, organs, music and worship. See also LITURGY AND WORSHIP.

56. NON-CHRISTIAN RELIGIONS. A selection of major headquarters, organizations, world federations, missionary organizations, and study centers operated by or for non-Christian religions; major non-Christian research centers, universities, periodicals, institutes, and institutions.

57. PERIODICALS. Christian or church periodicals, journals, magazines, newspapers, bulletins, house organs, newsletters, and other regular publications; of popular, news, scholarly, professional, devotional, instructive, or academic content; daily, semi-weekly, weekly, biweekly, monthly, quarterly – and certain annuals and irregular serials.

58. POLITICS AND SOCIETY. A selection of Christian political parties (e.g. Christian Democrats), activist groups, human rights organizations, religious rights groups, political action committees, political research centers, foreign or domestic policy think tanks, religio-political educational bodies; progressive or traditional groups, left-wing or right-wing groups, liberal or conservative groups; church or denominational committees, agencies, or commissions for political causes, representation, advocacy, activism or education; religio-political training, publications, or coordination; pressure groups or lobbies working on governments or the United Nations; single-issue groups or movements; public affairs offices and agencies; radical, non-violent, or liberation groups and movements.

59. PRAYER. A selection of major societies, ministries, movements, and fellowships devoted primarily to prayer, the prayer life, intercession, meditation, days of prayer, months of prayer, or prayer and evangelization; spiritual warfare, spiritual mapping, strategic prayer, prayer and deliverance or exorcism; church and denominational bodies as well as non- and inter-denominational bodies. Note that there are many thousands of other prayer groups, movements, fellowships and societies throughout the Christian world, of all sizes and many varieties and formats.

60. PUBLISHING. Publishing houses, agencies, and companies producing religious or Christian books and literature (usually church- or Christian-owned, -operated, or -linked), church or mission printing presses; including secular companies which give major importance to publishing books on religion, particularly Christian or Biblical subjects. See also BIBLE AND SCRIPTURE ORGANIZATIONS, LITERATURE, and PERIODICALS.

61. RELIGIOUS COMMUNITIES. Religious orders, institutes, congregations, societies, communities, brotherhoods, sisterhoods, and mixed communities, following a religious rule (regula) or the religious life, of any ecclesiastical traditions or families; with either ordained, religious, lay, or mixed personnel; usually or often with vows of poverty, chastity and obedience; Catholic congregations of pontifical status (directly under Rome); indigenous communities and local congregations (clerical or lay) begun in the Third World; federations, associations, or groupings of religious communities or congregations, or of religious personnel; agencies, institutions, organizations, structures of oversight, or commissions related to religious personnel, houses, or orders. For congregations primarily devoted to foreign missionary work, see FOREIGN MISSIONARY SOCIETIES.

62. RELIGIOUS HOUSES AND MONASTERIES. A scant selection of Catholic, Orthodox, Anglican, Protestant and other monasteries, abbeys, priories, convents, mother houses of religious orders or congregations; religious communities, organized communities or houses under formal religious rule, practice, or order.

63. RESEARCH CENTERS. Centers, institutes, and institutions undertaking original research related to Christianity and religions — religious, socio-religious, anthropological, historical, biblical, theological, communications, information, missiological, missiographical, missiometrical, futurological; ecumenical research centers and institutes at university level; experimental institutes, think tanks; documentation centers and services, resource centers, research or historical archives, public opinion polls, survey organizations, market research, radio/TV audience research centers or functions. Note that other research centers that specialize in specific topics, e.g. LITURGY AND WORSHIP, BROADCASTING, or ECOLOGY, are listed under those topics.

64. RURAL AND AGRICULTURAL MISSION. Agricultural missions, Christian rural or farming communities or centers, village polytechnics, farmers' trade unions; rural and agricultural training centers; agricultural assistance, rural transformation, rural development aid.

65. SCHOLARLY SOCIETIES. Associations of scholars and thinking practitioners who communicate with each other in their field of study, such as biblical studies, theology, missiology, church history, sociology of religion, anthropology, psychology, archeology, religion and science, religion and philosophy, religion and futurology, et alii; national and international associations, learned societies, and commissions (as contrasted with institutes or centers); Catholic pontifical commissions in scholarly disciplines.

66. SCHOOLS AND COLLEGES. Schools under church or Christian auspices or sponsorship: junior and senior secondary schools teaching secular anJ/or religious subjects, minor seminaries (secular or religious), technical schools, vocational schools, junior colleges, technical colleges, teacher-training colleges, and 4-year Christian colleges (emphasizing or only offering undergraduate baccalaureate degrees); organizations, institutions, and agencies that help or promote Christian home-schooling; schools for the children of foreign missionaries, MK schools and agencies. See also BIBLE SCHOOLS AND COLLEGES, CATECHESIS AND CHRISTIAN EDUCATION, THEOLOGICAL COLLEGES AND SEMINARIES, and UNIVERSITIES.

67. SOCIAL AND PASTORAL MINISTRIES. Local social, pastoral, compassionate, or community action and service; social welfare, moral welfare, community development; ministries dealing with unemployment, housing, population control, delinquency, alcoholism, temperance, addiction, drug addiction, gambling, pornography, crime, and other social, moral, or personal problems; community centers, rehabilitation centers, social ministry centers; prison ministries, prison chaplaincies, ministry to former prisoners; ministry to the poor, to inner cities, to the elderly, the underprivileged, the oppressed, the suffering.

68. SPIRITUAL LIFE CONVENTIONS, RALLIES, OR RETREATS. Annual or limited-duration movements or meetings not primarily for evangelism but for the deepening of the spiritual life; regular mass conventions, mass rallies, deeper life conventions, Keswick conventions, spiritual life conventions and conferences. Note that most such activities are not listed under RELIGIOUS COMMUNITIES and CAMPS, RETREAT CENTERS, AND LAY TRAINING CENTERS.

69. STATE DEPARTMENTS FOR RELIGIOUS AFFAIRS. State or government ministries or departments for religious or ecclesiastical affairs, or other government ministries whose responsibilities include the area of religious affairs, state religious organizations, state bodies for surveillance and control of churches or other religious organizations. Some are Christian in sympathies or activities, while others are hostile to Christianity and the churches.

70. STUDENT ORGANIZATIONS AND FEDERATIONS. Organizations of or for college and university students, for evangelism, instruction, fellowship, discipleship, and training; campus organizations, campus ministries, Inter-university Christian groups, major university chaplaincies and related national organizations, major student centers, student leadership training, scholarship-awarding bodies.

71. TELEPHONE MINISTRIES. Ministries that conduct evangelism, instruction or counseling by telephone; taped inspirational messages, sometimes in conjunction with radio programs; Christian or missionary news or prayer information services by telephone.

72. THEOLOGICAL COLLEGES AND SEMINARIES. Institutions for the training of the ordained ministry or priesthood, or for advanced theological, Biblical, or religious instruction, generally at the graduate (post-baccalaureate) level; major seminaries (religious or secular), theological colleges, advanced Bible schools.

73. THEOLOGICAL EDUCATION ASSOCIATIONS. Regional or international groupings of theological colleges, Bible Schools, seminaries, or other institutes for higher Christian education, for co-operation in accreditation, curricula, joint advanced programs of study, research, and conferences; international coordinating bodies.

74. THEOLOGICAL EDUCATION BY EXTENSION. Organized courses, programs, and centers of theological or Biblical instruction, or of ministry, pastoral, or leadership training using TEE principles; non-centralized theological education, conducted over broad geographical areas using centers, itinerating instructors, or the like; organizations producing or providing TEE curriculum, promoting or facilitating the TEE approach, or providing training for TEE trainers; TEE associations, agencies, seminars, or affiliations.

75. TOURISM, SPORTS, AND RECREATION. Christian tour organizations, travel agencies, cruises; pilgrimage organizations or ministries; ministries in the area of tourism, leisure, or recreation; Christian sports organizations, teams, or ministries; organizations of Christian athletes, ministries to athletes and spectators at sports events; sports evangelism, athlete evangelists. For missionary air travel, see FOREIGN MISSIONS SUPPORT ORGANIZATIONS.

76. UNIVERSITIES. Church- or Christian-operated, -owned, -controlled, -sponsored, or -linked universities granting academic degrees mainly in secular subjects.

77. UNIVERSITY DEPARTMENTS OF RELIGION. Academic faculties or departments within universities, offering advanced instruction, conducting research, and granting degrees in religious studies, divinity, theology, mission, missiology, church history, philosophy of religion, sociology or psychology of religion, or related subjects (but often not specifically training persons for the ordained ministry). See also RESEARCH CENTERS.

78. URBAN AND INDUSTRIAL MISSION. Ministry in and to large cities, inner cities, slums, or ghettoes; urban action, urban evangelism, urban theology, urban ministry; industrial missions and projects, evangelism of factory workers, ministry to urban workers; urban-industrial ecumenical parishes, inner-city parishes; ministries to urban structures and institutions; urban or industrial mission training.

79. WOMEN IN THE ORDAINED MINISTRY. Organizations for, or associations of women in the ordained ministry, diaconate, or priesthood; advocacy for the place of women in pastoral ministry or Christian leadership; education or training specifically for women looking toward serving in the ordained ministry, priesthood, or Christian leadership.

80. WOMEN'S LAY ORGANIZATIONS. Groups for lay women and girls emphasizing the role of women, the lay ministries of women, or the place of women in church and society; women's lay orders; women's rights, women's liberation agencies, feminist movements or organizations, women's caucuses or task forces; YWCA and organizations serving women and girls; and other movements either radical or conservative; rallies, conferences, retreats, and events for women. See also LAY MINISTRIES.

81. WORK AND THE PROFESSIONS. Organizations, ministries, agencies, and associations bringing together or serving Christians of specific occupational groups - workers (labor, industry, technical fields) or those in secular professions (the arts, journalism, law, medicine, science, engineering, education, business, social service, civil service, etc.); Christian (mainly Catholic) workers' movements and labor or trade unions; professional associations.

82. YOUTH ORGANIZATIONS AND MINISTRIES. Ministry to and by young people; youth evangelism, youth ministry, youth leadership training, youth discipleship, youth conferences, camps, rallies, and retreats; teen ministries, teen mission, youth work projects; youth counseling, at-risk youth, inner-city youth; recreation and activities for youth; YMCA and other facilities and organizations for young people.

Table 14-1.   Topical directory subject index.

This index lists 900 subjects, contained in the Directory (Part 14), relating to the Christian enterprise and its context in the secular and religious worlds. It then gives each a number or numbers, these being those of the Directory's 82 topics under which each subject may be found. The index enables the reader wanting a particular subject to find the number or numbers (1-82) of the topic or topics under which it is classified here. Usually, the bulk of the entries for a particular subject are found under one topic only.

1
Aid & relief

Christian organizations, service agencies, charities, charitable societies, and interchurch service agencies that help suffering people and populations faced with natural disaster, war, violence, famine, refugee situations, lack of water, lack of food, lack of shelter, epidemics, or disease. The emphasis here is on relatively short-term emergency situations, and situations of more extreme, immediate, or desperate crisis. See also: DEVELOPMENT, JUSTICE, AND PEACE and SOCIAL AND PASTORAL CONCERN.

ALGERIA

Christian Committee for Service in Algeria, 33 Av Ali-Khodja, Alger-El Biar.
Service Quaker, Arbaa des Ouacifs, Tizi Ouzou, T: Ouacif 19.

ARGENTINA

Comisión Católica Argentina de Inmigración (CCAI), Laprida 930, Buenos Aires, T: 842683.
Comisión Católica Argentina de la Lucha contra el Hambre, Montevideo 850, Piso 1, Buenos Aires.
Conferencias Vicentinas de Hombres, Combate de los Pozos 347, Buenos Aires.
Conferencias Vicentinas de Mujeres, Riobamba 258, Buenos Aires.
Emaus, Sarandi 1139, Buenos Aires.

AUSTRALIA

Australian Catholic Relief, P.O. Box C360, Clarence St., Sydney, NSW 2000, T: 297896.
Australian Council for Overseas Aid, 241 King St., Melbourne, Victoria 3000.
Bush Church Aid Society for Australia and Tasmania, BCA House, 135 Bathurst St., Syndey, T: 263164.
Compassion International, 1/60 Nerang Street, Nerang P.O. Box 2034, Nerang East, Queensland, Australia 4211.
Eastern European Aid Association, 34 Rigel St., Coorparoo, Brisbane 4151, Queensland, T: 61-7-397-9940.
Federal Catholic Immigration Committee (FCIC), 355 Kent St., Sydney, NSW 2000, T: 297884, 292441.
Interchurch Relief and Development Alliance (IRDA), P.O. Box 289, Hawthorn 3122, T: 3-9819-1900, F: 3-9818-3586, O: E-mail: tearaust@ozemail.com.au, Web site: www.ozemail.com.
Migrant and Refugee Services (Salvation Army), 69 Bourke St., Melbourne, Vic 3000, T: 03-9653-3213.
National Catholic Welfare Committee, 582 Victoria Rd., Ryde, NSW, T: 804022.
Quaker Service Council, Friends House, 631 Orrong Rd., Toorak, Victoria 3142, T: 243592.
World Vision of Australia, 343 Little Collins, 7th Floor, Melbourne, Victoria 3000, and Box 399-C, Melbourne, Victoria 3001.

AUSTRIA

Komitee zur Betreuung Serbisch-Orthodoxer Gastarbeiter in Österreich, Christian Coulinstr 24, A-4020 Linz.
Österpriesterhilfe, Nibelungengasse 1/4 Stg/III, A-1010 Wien, T: 571577.
Österreichische Caritas-Zentrale, Nibelungengasse 1/4, Postfach 114, A-1010 Wien, T: 0222-571577.

BANGLADESH

Bangladesh Ecumenical Relief & Rehabilitation Service (BERRS), 9 New Eskaton Road, Ramna, P.O. Box 220, Dacca 2, T: 282869.
Christian Organization for Relief and Rehabilitation (CORR), 23 New Eskaton Rd., P.O. Box 994, Dacca 2.

BELGIUM

Aide a l'Eglise en Detresse, Aide aux Croyants, rue Gal MacArthur, 48, Bruxelles 1180.
Aide aux Eglises Martyres, Rue de l'Enseignement 40, Braine-le-Comte 7490, T: 32-67-333995, F: 32-67-336345.
Entr'aide et Fraternité (Broederlijk Delen), Rue de Commerce 70-72, B-1040 Brussel, T: 02-5114255.
Entraide Educative et Sociale (EES), Rue Capouillet 10, Brussel 6, T: 02-374797.
Foyer Selah Salvation Army Home for Political Refugees, bd d'Ypres, 28, 1000 Brussels, T: 02-219-88-52.
Service National d'Emigration (SNE), Rue Guimard 5, B-1040 Brussel, T: 02-114255.

BOTSWANA

Adventist Development Relief Agency, P.O. Box 20975, Gaborone.
Kagisong Centre, PO Box 288, Mogoditshane, T: 373 624.
Lutheran World Federation, PO Box 1645, Gaborone, T: 312 371.

BRAZIL

Banco da Providência, Ladeira da Gloria 99, ZC-01 Rio de Janeiro, GB.
Federação de Orgãos para Assistência Social e Educacional (FASE), Rua Mena Barreto 161, Andar 3, Botafogo-Guanabara, Rio de Janeiro, T: 463230.
Secretariado Latinoamericano de Caritas, c/o Caritas Brasileira, Ladeira da Gloria 67, CP 16094, ZC-01 Rio de Janeiro, BG, T: 2454021.

BRITAIN (UK OF GB & NI)

Aid to European Refugees, 40 Windsor-House, 46 Victoria St., London SW1.
Aid to Russian Christians, P.O. Box 200, Bromley, Kent BR1 1QF, T: 44-081-460-6046.
Aid to the Church in Need (ACN), 3-5 North St., Chichester, West Sussex PO19 1LB.
Aid to the Russian Church, 25 Aldermay Rd., Bromley, Kent BR1 3PH.
British Council for Aid to Refugees, 35 Great Peter St., London SW1.
Christian Aid, Inter-Church Centre, 48 Elmwood Avenue, Belfast BT9 6AZ; P.O. Box 100, London, SE1 7RT, T: 08-0232 381204.
Churches Committee on Migrant Workers in Western Europe, 1 Rivercourt Rd., Hammersmith, London W6 9LD, T: 01-748-3575.
Churches Main Committee, Fielden House, Little College St., London SW1P 3JZ, T: 01-930-4984.
Committee on International Affairs and Migration, Church of England, Church House, Dean's Yard, Westminster, London SW1P 3NZ, T: 01-222-9011.
Compassion of Great Britain, 48 Kerr St., Kirkintilloch, Glasgow G66 1JZ, T: 041-776-6046.
Concern, 47 Frederick Street, Belfast BT1 2LW, T: 08-0232 23156.
Eastern European Aid Association, Weston Green Thames Dittion KT7 0JG, Surrey, T: 44-81-398-5161.
Forwarding Relief to Eastern Europe, 49 Chatsworth Dr., Mansfield NG18 4QS, Notts., T: 44-623-29367, F: 44-623-636-582.
Helps International Ministries, 44 Nickey Lane, Mellor, Blackburn, Lancashire, T: 44-254-812-816.
Indian Church Aid Association, 2 Eaton Gate, London SW1, T: 01-730-9611.
International Refugee Missionary Fellowship, Well House, Dean Row Rd., Wilmslow, Cheshire SK9 2BU, T: 22062.
International Associates of Co-Workers of Mother Teresa, Fernhurst, W Rd. St., George's Hill, Weybridge, Surrey KT13 0LZ, T: 44-09-323-84276.
International Needs, Clarence Court #D, Rushmore Hill, Orpington, Kent BR6 7LZ, T: 44-689-585-066, F: 44-689-853-353.
Jacob's Well Appeal, 2, Ladygate, Beverley, N. Humbs HU17 8HU, T: 44-0482-881162, F: 44-0482-865452.
Ladies of Charity and Companions of St Vincent, 39 Blakehall Rd., London E11 2QQ, T: 01-989-1336.
OXFAM, 274 Banbury Rd., Oxford OX2 7DZ.
Relief and Refugee Committee, Catholic Women's League, 21b Soho Square, London W1V 6NR, T: 01-437-4509.
Scottish Catholic International Aid Fund, St. Columbkille's, Rutherglen, Glasgow G73 2SL, Scotland.
Society of St Vincent de Paul, 2 Iddesleigh House, Caxton St., London SW1H 0PS, T: 01-799-1342.
Spanish and Portugese Church Aid Society, 4 Stone Bldgs, London WC2, T: Chancery 5716.
St Vincent de Paul Society, 546 Sauchiehall St., Glasgow C2, T: 041-332-7752.
Standing Conference of British Organizations for Aid to Refugees, 26 Bedford Square, London WC1.
TEAR Fund, 100 Church Road, Teddington TW11 8QE, Middlesex, T: 44-081-977-9144, F: 44-081-943-3594.
TEAR Fund (The Evangelical Alliance Relief Fund), 10 Wellington Place, Belfast BT1 6GE, T: 08-0232 324940.
Wales Romanian Aid, Plas Newydd, Blaenycoed Road, Carmarthen, Wales, T: 0267-87368.
War on Want, 3 Madeley Rd., Ealing, London W5.
World Vision, The Kings Building, 152 Albertbridge Road, Belfast BT5 4GS, T: 08-0232 739348.

BULGARIA

Feed the Hungary, Bl. 47, kb. 13, Sofia, T: 359-2-879-560.
Good Samaritan, A. Stamboliiski #4, Burgas, T: 359-56-239-15.

BURUNDI

ASSABU (Association des Services de Sante Adventistes au Burundi), Boite Postale 1710, T: 22-31-30.

CANADA

Adventist Development and Relief Agency (ADRA Canada), 1148 King St., E., Oshawa, ON L1H 1H8, T: 905-433-8004, F: 905-723-1903.
Aid to the Church in Need (ACN), 7575 Rt. Transcanadienne, #310, St. Laurent, QC H4T 1V6, T: 514-332-6333, F: 514-332-6555.
Anglican Church of Canada, Primates World Relief & Development Fund (PWRDF), 600 Jarvis St., Toronto, ON M4Y 2J6, T: 416-924-9192, F: 416-924-3483.
Bridgehead, Inc., 20 James St., Ottawa, ON K2P 0T6, T: 613-567-1455, F: 613-567-1468.
Canadian Feed the Children, 174 Bartley Dr., Toronto, ON M4A 1E1, T: 416-757-1220, F: 416-757-3318.
Canadian Food for the Hungry, 005-2580 Cedar Park Place, Abbotsford, BC V2T 3S5, T: 800-667-0605, F: 604-853-4332, O: E-mail: 657-3289@mci-mail.com.
Canadian Foodgrains Bank, Box 767, Winnipeg, MB R3C 2L4, T: 204-944-1993, O: 1-800-665-0377.
Canadian Friends Service Committee, 60 Lowther Ave., Toronto 180, Ontario, T: 920-5213.
Canadian Lutheran World Relief, 1080 Kingsburg Ave., R2P 1W5 Winnipeg, Manitoba, T: 204-694-5602, F: 1-204-694-5460.
Catholic Charities Council of Canada, 90 Av Parent, Ottawa, Ontario K1N 7B1.
Catholic Immigrant Services, 637 Craig Ouest, Montréal 101, Québec, T: 861-8581.
ChildCare Plus, The Pentecostal Assemblies of Canada, 6745 Century Ave., Mississauga, ON L5N 6P7, T: 905-542-7400, F: 905-542-7313.
Children's Health Education and Relief, Box 31012, 1300 King St., E., Oshawa, ON L1H 8N9, T: 905-434-7474, F: 905-434-1998.
Christian Children's Fund of Canada, 1027 McNicoll Ave., Scarborough, ON M1W 3X2, T: 416-495-1174, F: 416-495-9395.
Christian Indigenous Development Overseas, 142 Dalhousie Rd., N.W., Calgary, AB T3A 2H1, T: 403-286-0611.
Comité d'Accueil Interconfessionnel, 2000 Sherbrooke Ouest, Montréal 109, Québec, poste 224, T: 931-7311.
Compassion Canada, P.O. Box 5591, London, ON N6A 5G8, T: 519-668-0224, F: 519-685-1107, O: 1-800-563-KIDS.
Conseil des Oeuvres et du Bien-être du Diocèse de Québec, 625 Grande-Allée Est, CP 730, Québec 4, Québec.
Emergency Relief & Development Overseas (ERDO), The Pentecostal Assemblies of Canada, 6745 Century Ave., Mississauga, ON L5N 6P7, T: 905-542-7400, F: 905-542-7313.
Foundation for International Development Assistance (FIDA), 122 King St., S., Waterloo, ON N2J 1P5, T: 519-886-9520, F: 519-886-9740.
Global Relief Fund, Inc., #6 20306 Dewdney Trunk Rd., Maple Ridge, BC V2X 3E2, T: 604-465-2128, F: 604-465-2180.
Inter-Church Coalition on Africa, 129 Saint Clair Ave., West, Toronto, ON M4V 1N5, T: 416-927-1124, F: 416-927-7554.
International Christian Aid Canada, 4401 Harvester Rd., PO Box 5090, Burlington, ON L7R 4G5, T: 905-632-5703, F: 905-632-5176.
International Needs, 20210 84th Avenue, Langley, BC, T: 604-888-5558, F: 604-888-5919.
Office des Néo-Canadiens, 2000 Sherbrooke Ouest, Montréal 109, Québec, postes 126 et 110, T: 931-7311.
Office National du Bien-être et de la Santé, 1225 est, Boul Saint-Joseph, Montréal 176, Québec, T: 274-3658.
Samaritan's Purse - Canada, P.O. Box 20100, Calgary Place, Calgary, AB T2P 4J2, T: 403-250-6565, F: 403-250-6567, O: E-mail: Canada@samaritan.org, www.samaritan.org.
Service d'Accueil aux Voyageurs et aux Immigrants (SAVI), 750 Côte de la Place d'Armes, Montréal 126, Québec, T: jour 842-2971, soir 877-4291.
Siloam Childcare International, P.O. Box 3339, Langley, BC V3A 4R7, T: 604-532-2004.
World Relief Canada, 600 Alden Rd. Ste. 310, Markham, ON L3R 0E7, T: 905-415-8181, F: 905-415-0287, O: E-mail: 71102.1204.
World Vision Canada, 6630 Turner Valley Rd., Mississauga, ON L5N 2S4, T: 905-821-3030, F: 905-821-1825, O: E-mail: Info@worldvision.ca, www.worldvision.ca.

CENTRAL AFRICAN REPUBLIC

Secours Catholique Centrafricain, BP 710, Bangui.

CHAD

Secours Catholique National Tchadien, BP 654, N'Djamena.
World Vision International, P.O. Box 1108, N'Djamena.

CHILE

Ayuda Cristiana Evangélica, Bombero Salas 1351, Of 250, Casilla 14066, Correo 15, Santiago.
Instituto Católico Chileno de Migración (INCAMI), Erasmo Escala 1822, Piso 2, Casilla 468, Santiago, T: 89495.

CHINA

Asbury Village, Tai Wo Hau, Tsuen Wan, NT, Hong Kong, T: NT-201073.
Asian Migrant Centre (AMC), 4 Jordan Rd, Kowloon, Hong Kong, T: 852-2312-0031, F: 852-2367-7355.
Hong Kong Christian Service, Metropole Bldg., 57 Peking Rd. 4/f, Kowloon, Hong Kong, T: K-678031.
Hong Kong Christian Welfare and Relief Council, 23 Waterloo Rd., Kowloon, Hong Kong, T: K-55255.
Methodist Committee for Overseas Relief (CORE), 54 Waterloo Rd., Kowloon, Hong Kong, T: K-887174.
Secretariado dos Serviços Diocesanos de Assistência Social (USCC), Centro Católico, Rua da Praia Grande, Macau, T: 4486.

COLOMBIA

Minuto de Dios, c/o Padres Eudistas, Carrera 73 No 82A-05, Bogotá.
Sociedad de San Vincente de Paul, Calle 16 No 8-22, Bogotá.

CONGO-BRAZZAVILLE

Quaker Service, P.O. Box 7 Kyrenia, T: 08152591.
Secours Catholique, BP 117, Brazzaville, T: 3093.

CONGO-KINSHASA

Zaire Protestant Relief Agency, ECZ, BP 3094, Kinshasa-Gombe, T: 59829.

CROATIA

Bureau de Liaison entre la Conférence Episcopale Yougoslave et Caritas Internationalis (Ured Za Vezu Sa Caritas Internationalis), Biskupska Konferencija Yugoslavije, Archevêché, Kaptol 31, PB 02-406, 41000 Zagreb, T: 38446.

CZECH REPUBLIC

Caritas Catholique Tcheque, Vladislavova 12, 111 37 Praha 1, T: 249165.

DENMARK

DanChurchAid, Sankt Peders Straede 3, 1453 Copenhagen K, T: 45-33-15-28 00, F: 45-33-15-38 60.
Danish Committee for Algeria, Granbakken 13, Hillerod.
Danish Refugee Council, Frederiksborgvej 5, DK-2400 Kobenhavn NV.

ECUADOR

Conferencias de San Vicente de Paul, Quito.
Instituto Vivenda Caritas (INVICA), Quito.

EGYPT

Comité Conjoint pour la Coordination des Services et de l-Aide aux Personnes déplacées et Victimes de l'Agression, EACCS, Anba Rueis Bldg, Ramses St., Abbasiya, Al Qahirah.

ETHIOPIA

Christian Relief and Development Association, Adis Abeba.
Christian Relief Committee, P.O. Box 5674, Adis Abeba.
Ethiopian Catholic Welfare Organization, P.O. Box 2454, Adis Abeba.
Ethiopian Committee for Aid to Refugees, c/o Faculty of Law, Haile Selassie I University, P.O. Box 1176, Adis Abeba.
Inter-Church Aid Office, Ethiopian Orthodox Church, P.O. Box 503, Adis Abeba.

FINLAND

Finnchurchaid, Luotsikatu 1A, P.O. Box 185, SF-00161 Helskinki, T: 358-0-18-02-1, F: 358-0-180-22-07.

FRANCE

Action Chrétienne en Orient, 7 Rue général-Offenstein, Strasbourg-Meinau (B-Rhin), T: 341155.
Aid to Believers, 91 rue Olivier de Serres, Paris 75015, T: 42-50-53-66.
Chretiens de l'Est: Aide a l'Eglise en Detresse, B.P. 1 (29, rue du Louvre), Mareil-Marly 78750, T: 1-39-17-30-10, F: 1-39-17-30.
Comité de Liaison des Oeuvres Bénévoles travaillant pour les Réfugiés en France, 47-49 rue de la Glacière, F-75013 Paris.
Comité Inter-Mouvements auprès des Evacués (CIMADE), 176 rue de Grenelle, F-75007 Paris, T: 705-9399.
Commission Episcopale pour les Migrations, 106 rue du Bac, F-75341 Paris, T: 222-5708.
Entraide Protestante, 84 Av Niel, F-75017 Paris.
Faim et Soif, 6 rue du Faubourg Poissonnièere, F-75998 Paris.
International Missionary Benefit Society, 119 Rue du Président-Wilson, F-92 Levallois, T: 2708752, 2708753.
Oeuvre Apostolique, 8 Rue Daniel Lesueur, F-75007 Paris, T: 01-306-4437.
Orthodox Advisory Committee, 11 Rue Mongagne-Ste-Geneviève, F-75005 Paris, T: ODE 7446.
Société de Saint-Vincent de Paul, 5 Rue du Préaux-Clercs, F-75007 Paris, T: 01-548-6220.
World Conference of Christians for Palestine, 49 Rue du Faubourg Poissonnière, F-75009 Paris, T: 01-824-9764.

GABON

Secours Catholique Gabon, Maison des Oeuvres, BP 134, Libreville.

GAMBIA

ADRA/Gambia, Private Mail Bag 212, Serekunda, T: 220-394850, F: 220-392462.

GERMANY

Aid to the Church in Need, Postfach 1209, Konigstein im Taunus W-6240, T: 44-6174-291150, F: 44-6174-3423.
Arbeitsgemeinschaft Ev Auswandererfürsorge, Am Dobben 112, Postfach 450, D-28 Bremen.
Arbeitsstelle für Soziale Arbeit in Ubersee, International Social Services, Wintererstr 19, D-78 Freiburg im Breisgau, T: 0761-31497.
Bread for the World-Diaconal Association of Protestant Chs, Postfach 10 11 42, Stafflenbergstr. 76, 70010 Stuttgart, T: 49-711-21-59-0, F: 49-711-21-59-368.
Challenge Aid International, Frauenlobstrasse 39, Mainz 6500, T: 49-131-679535, F: 49-131-613602.
Christian Mission Service, Schulstr 17, D-7251 Hirschlanden.
Christian Relief—Work TABEA, Box 1246, Breniger Strasse 38, Swisstal 1 W-5357, T: 49-02254-5457, F: 49-02254-81197.
Christliche Osthilfe, Postfach 1380, 34497 Korbach, T: 05631-63011-14, F: 05631-63015.
Diakonisches Werk, Stefflenbergstrasse 76, Postfach 101142, Stuttgart 70010, T: 49-711-21-590, F: 49-711-2159-368.
Evangelische Zentralstelle Für Entwicklungshilfe E.V. (EZE), Mittelstrasse 37 D-5300 Bonn 2, Germany, T: 0228-81010, F: 0228-8101160, O: Telex: 8861 133 EZE d. Cable: Zentralstelle Bonn 2.
Feed the Hungry e.V., Postfach 450363, 12173 Berlin, T: 030-8138786.
Gustav-Adolf-Werk (West) der EKD, Zentrale, Kirchweg 68, Postfach 351, D-35 Kassel.
Help International, Wislader Weg 8, 58531 Lüdenscheid, T: 023-51-57-07-87, F: 023-51-57-01-95.
Hilfsaktion Märtyrerkirche (HMK), Pf. 1160, 88683 Uhldingen, T: 07556-6508.
Innere Mission und Hilfswerk der EKD (IMHEKD), Hauptgeschäftstelle, Alexanderstr 23, Postfach 476, D-7000 Stuttgart 1, T: 246951.
Kindernothilfe e.V., Pf. 2811, 47241 Duisburg, T: 0203-7789-0.
Kirchliches Aussenamt der EKD, Bochenheimer Landstr 109, Postfach 174025, D-6 Frankfurt/Main.
Konvent der Zerstreuten Evangelischen Ostkirchen, Geschäftsstelle, Andreastr 2A, D-3 Hannover.
Martin-Luther-Bund, Diasporawerk Evangelisch-Lutherischer Kirchen, Fahrstr 15, D-852 Erlangen.
Salvation Army Transit Camp for Emigrants, Wilhelmshavener Str 8, 30167 Hannover, T: 0511-15908, F: 0511-15512.
St. Raphaels-Verein, Grosse Allee 41, D-2000 Hamburg 1, T: 242239, 246155.
Verband Zur Förderung des Evangeliums in Spanien, Egidienplatz 37, D-85 Nürnberg.
World Vision, Am Hoiller Platz 4, 61381 Friedrichsdorf, T: 06172-763-0, F: 06172-763-270.

GREECE

Divine Providence, Greek Catholic Exarchate, 246 Acharnon St., Athinai 815, T: 870170, 872723.

GRENADA

Madonna Houses, Victoria (Grenada) and Carriacou (Grenadines).

GUATEMALA

Comité de Servicio de los Amigos, 38 Av 4-89, Zona 7, Ciudad de Guatemala, T: 45103.

Comité Evangélica Permanente Ayuda (CEPA), Ciudad de Guatemala.

HAITI

Secours Protestant/Service Chrétienne, Methodist Church, BP 6, Port-au-Prince.

HONDURAS

Comisión Cristiana de Desarrollo-CCD, Segunda calle, Av. Los Postal Dist. 21 Colonia Kennedy, Pinos, casa 4022, Colonia, Florencia Sur, Tegucigalpa, T: 504-320-792, F: 504-395-137.

Comité Evangélica (CEDEN), Tegucigalpa.

ICELAND

Icelandic Church Aid, Laugavegur 31, 150 Reykjavik, T: 354/-62-44-00, F: 354-562-44-95.

INDIA

Believers Relief Trust, 1-XLI/257, I. S. Press Road, Ernakulam, Kerala 682018.

Caritas India, CBCI Centre, Alexandra Place, New Delhi 1.

Cathedral Relief Service, St. Paul's Cathedral, Cathedral Road, Calcutta, West Bengal 700071.

Catholic Relief Services, 2, Community Centre, East Of Kailash, New Delhi 110065.

Central Relief Committee (India), Lok Kalyan Bhavan, 11A Rouse Av, New Delhi.

Christian Agency for Social Action, Relief and Development (CASA), 16 Ring Rd., Lajpat Nagar IV, New Delhi 24.

Christian Children's Fund, 5th Floor, Padma Palace, 86 Nehru Place, New Delhi 110019.

Committee on Relief and Gift Supplies, 4 Mathura Rd., Jungpura, Delhi, T: 618234.

EFICOR - Evangelical Fellowship of India Commission On Relief, 806/92 Deepali, New Delhi 110019.

India Evangelistic And Relief Fellowship, P. O. Box 28, Ongole, Andhra Pradesh 523001.

Indienhilfe, 3, 1st Cross, CSI Compound, Mission Road, Bangalore, Karnataka 560027.

Isua Krista Kohhran Relief Department, Bualpui (NG), Saiha, Mizoram 796901.

Lutheran World Service (India), 84, Dr. Suresh Sarkar Road, Calcutta, West Bengal 700014.

Missionaries of Charity, 54/A Acharya Jagadish ch, Bose Rd, Calcutta, India, T: Calcutta 247115.

Salvation Army Social Services Centre and Feeding Programme, 109 Gangadeswara Koll St., Madras 600084, T: 044-642-5311.

World Vision, St. No. 1, Tarnataka, Secunderabad, Andhra Pradesh 500017.

INDONESIA

Soegijapranata Social Foundation, Jalan Pandanaran 13, Semarang.

IRELAND

Catholic Social Service Conference, 75 Merrion Square, Dublin 2, T: 65608.

Catholic Social Welfare Bureau, 35 Harcourt St., Dublin 2, T: 780866.

Christian Aid, Rathgar Road, Rathgar, Dublin 6, T: 353-01 966184.

Concern, 1 Upper Camden Street, Dublin 2, T: 353-01 681237.

Emigrants Section, Catholic Social Welfare Bureau, 18 Westland Row, Dublin 2, T: 654189.

TEAR Fund (The Evangelical Alliance Relief Fund), 92 Landscape Park, Churchtown, Dublin 14, T: 353-01 298 4856.

World Vision of Ireland, 10 Main Street, Donnybrook, Dublin 4, T: 353-01 283 7800.

ISRAEL

Caritas Jerusalem, Social Centre, P.O. Box 19653, Jerusalem, T: 87574.

Catholic Relief Services-USCC, P.O. Box 19447, 91193 Jérusalem; 9 Bibers St., 91193 Jérusalem, T: 02-82-81-49, F: 02-82-92-80, O: Also tel: 02-82-81-75, 82-83-40.

International Christian Committee and Jerusalem Inter-Church Aid Committee, P.O. Box 19195, Jerusalem.

Near East Council of Churches Committee for Refugee Work, P.O. Box 49, Gaza, T: 972-51-860-146, 972-51-862-573, 972-51-864-170, F: 972-51-866-331.

Pontifical Mission for Palestine, P.O. Box 19642, East Jerusalem (Old City).

ITALY

Aide au Développement Intégral (AID), Via Nomentana 118, I-00161 Roma.

Aiuto all Chiesa che Soffre, Lungotevere Ripa 3/a, Rome 00153.

Caritas International, Piazza San Calisto, 16, I-00153 Roma, T: 39-6-698-7197, F: 39-6-698-7237.

Catholic Relief Services (UCSS), Regional Office, Via Boezio 21, I-00192 Roma, T: 318051.

Hands Extended, Via dei Carracci 2 (also Via Pagliano 2), I-20149 Milano, T: 4697188.

International Confederation of Catholic Charities (CICC), Piazza San Calisto 16, I-00153 Roma, T: 6984635, 6984695, 6984597, 6984578.

Opera Assistenza Spirituale Nomadi in Italia, Via della Scrofa 70, I-00186 Roma, T: 305794.

Pontificia Opera di Assistenza, Piazza Benedetto Cairoli 117, I-00146 Roma, T: 650563.

Società di S Vincenzo de Paoli, Via della Pigna 13/A, I-00186 Roma, T: 687393.

Unione Nazionale fra gli Enti di Beneficenza e di Assistenza (UNEBA), Piazza Missori 3, I-20123 Milano, T: 898657.

JAPAN

American Friends Service Committee, 12-7 4-chome, Minami Azabu, Minato-ku, Tokyo 106.

Japan Catholic Migration Commission (JCMC), 10 Rokubancho, Chiyoda-ku, Tokyo, T: 262-2663.

Japan ECLOF Committee (NCCJ), 22 Midorigaoka Shibuya-ku, Tokyo.

Japan Fellowship Deaconry Mission, 1-140 Megamiyama, Koyoen, Nishinomiya Shi, Hyogo Ken 662, T: 0798-71-5446.

Japan Friends Service Committee, Friends Center, 8-19 4-chome, Mita, Minato-ku, Tokyo 108.

Japan International Food for the Hungary, 7-26-304 Shinjuku, Shinjuku Ku, Tokyo 160, T: 03-203-0635.

JORDAN

Near East Council of Churches Committee for Refugee Work, P.O. Box 1295, Amman, T: 962-6-625-559, 962-6-623-658, F: 962-6-648-610, O: Tlx: 2355589 NECCRW JO.

KENYA

Joint Refugee Services of Kenya (JRSK), Diamond Trust Bldg, Ronald Ngala St., Moi Av, P.O. Box 45627, Nairobi, T: 26595.

LAOS

Quaker Service Laos, Box 11 18, Vietiane.

LEBANON

Association of the Aid Cross for Armenian, P.O. Box 80680, Beirut, T: 961-1-405-512, 961-1-491-169.

Conférence Mondiale des Chrétiens pour la Palestine, Rue Mak'houl (Abdel-Aziz), BP 1375, Bayrut, T: 341902/3.

Near East Ecumenical Committee for Palestinian Refugees (NEECPR), Bayrut, T: 223091.

Pontifical Mission for Palestine, Souheil Farah Bldg, Sidani St., P.O. Box 3264, Bayrut, T: 226928, 344508.

LIECHTENSTEIN

Association for the Study of the World Refugee Problem (AWR), Postfach 34706, FL-9490 Vaduz.

LITHUANIA

Caritas of Lithuania, Vilnius 29, Kaunas 23000, T: 20-54-27, 20-96-83, F: 20-55-49.

LUXEMBOURG

Bridderlech Delen, 23 Blvd du Prince Henri, Luxembourg-ville, T: 472172, 23698.

Caritas Luxembourg, 23 Blvd du Prince Henri, CP 138, Luxembourg-ville, T: 23698, 472172.

MADAGASCAR

Friends Service Council, Mission FFMA, Faravohitra, Tananarive.

MALAWI

Catholic Secretariat of Malawi, P.O. Box 5368, Limbe, T: Blantyre 50866.

Christian Service Committee, P.O. Box 949, Blantyre.

MALAYSIA

Sabah Catholic Welfare, P.O. Box 684, Jesselton, Sabah, T: 2038.

MALI

Secours Catholique Malien, BP 298, Bamako.

MALTA

Malta Emigrants' Commission, Palazzo Carafa, 94 Old Bakery St., Valletta, T: 22644.

National Caritas Council, Archbishop's Residence, Valletta, T: 27755.

MAURITANIA

Bureau Catholique d'Emigration, Centre Miséreor, Rue d'Estaing, Port-Louis, T: 22342.

MEXICO

Acción Católica Mexicana, Serapio Randon 43, México 4, DF.

Ayuda Social Católica de México, Liverpool 143-305, México 6, DF, T: 251307.

Comité de Servicio de los Amigos, Ignacio Mariscal 132, México 1, DF, T: 5352752.

MYANMAR

Burma National ECLOF Committee, State Commercial Bank, Rangoon.

NETHERLANDS

Aid for Algeria, Quaker Centrum, Vossiusstraat 20, Amsterdam Z, T: 020-794238.

Christelijke Emigratie Centrale, Heulstraat 3, 's-Gravenhage.

International Reformed Agency for Migration (IRAM), 42 Eperweg, 'tHarde, T: 05255550.

Katholiek Landelijk Centrum voor Maatschappelijke Dienstverlening, Luybenstraat 19, 's-Hertogenbosch, T: 04100-34134, 37513.

Katholieke Centrale Emigratiestichting (KCES), Laan van Meerdervoort 150, 's-Gravenhage, T: 070-333472.

Katholieke Stichting voor Vluchtelingen en Ontheemden, Jacob Catsstraat 19, 's-Hertogenbosch, T: 04100-31623.

Mensen in Nood-Caritas Neerlandica, Hekellaan 6, Postbus 1041, 's-Hertogenbosch, T: 073-144544.

Vincentius Vereniging, Westeinde 99, 's-Gravenhage, T: 070-392387.

NEW ZEALAND

Inter-Church Committee on Immigration, P.O. Box 297, Christchurch.

International Needs, P.O. Box 1165, Tauranga, T: 0-7-578-6198, F: 0-7-578-6198, O: E-mail: 1wainnz@enternet.co.nz.

New Zealand Catholic Overseas Aid Committee, Liston House, St. Patrick's Square, P.O. Box 780, Auckland 1.

New Zealand Friends Service Committee, 24 Turere Place, Wanganui, T: 6388.

NZ Council of Organizations for Relief Service Overseas (CORSO), 303 Willis St., P.O. Box 2500, Wellington.

St. Vincent de Paul Society, Catholic Immigration Committee, 181 High St., P.O. Box 30602, Lower Hutt, T: 699812.

TEAR Fund, P.O. Box 8315, Auckland, T: 0-9-629-1048, F: 0-9-629-1050.

World Vision of NZ, Private Bag 92-078, Auckland, T: 0-9-377-0879, F: 0-9-309-3166.

NICARAGUA

Evangelical Committee for Development (CEPAD), Managua.

NORWAY

Friends Service Committee, Meltzersgt 1, Oslo 2, T: 02-562518.

Norwegian Church Aid, P.O. Box 5868 Hegdehaugen, 0308 Oslo 3, T: 47-2-46-3970, F: 47-2-69-3910.

Norwegian Church Aid, P.O. Box 4544 Torshov, Sandakerveien 74, 0404 Oslo, T: 47-22-22-22-99, F: 47-22-22-24-20.

Norwegian Church Relief, Kirkegaten 5, Oslo 1.

Norwegian Refugee Council, Prof Dahls Gt 1, Oslo 3.

PANAMA

Fe y Alegria, Apdo B-3, Panamá, T: 235820.

PARAGUAY

Comité de Iglésias para Ayudas de Emergencia (CIPAE), General Diaz 429, C.P. 2085, Asunción, T: 59521-48559, F: 59521-443932, O: Also tel: 59521-96187 or 92397.

PERU

Comisión Católica Peruana de Migración (CCPM), Jiron Chancay 725, Lima 1.

PHILIPPINES

Catholic Charities of Archdiocese of Manila, Catholic Charities Bldg, 1499 Otis Pandacan, Manila, T: 505829, 505645.

Church World Service (CWS), c/o NCCP, 941, 941 Epifanio de los Santos Av, Quezon City.

POLAND

Caritas Committee, 62 ul Krakowskie Przedmiescie, Warszawa.

Christian Children's Fund, ul. Kredytowa 4, m. 18, Warsaw 00-062, T: 48-22-39-92-16, F: 48-22-49-73-75.

Secrétariat de Pastorale Charitable, ul Kanonicza 5, 31 002 Kraków.

PORTUGAL

União de Caridade Portuguesa (Caritas), Comissão Central, Av da Republica 84/2, Lisboa 1, T: 767736.

ROMANIA

Association Organizatie Crestina de Caritate, Str. Busuiocului 10, Oradea 3700.

Christian Children's Fund, P.O. Box 37-48, Arghezi 18, Apt 11, Bucharest 2, T: 40-0-11-11-55, F: 40-0-10-29-39.

RUSSIA

Catholic Relief Services, Shemov Street 56, Room 302, Khabarovsk, T: 338-566.

International Orthodox Christian Charities, Moscow, T: 7-095-952-8059, F: 7-095-955-6789.

World Vision—Russia, Prospekt Vernadskogo 41, Room 433, Moscow 117947, T: 7-095-437-6296, F: 7-095-437-6296.

RWANDA

Bureau Rwandais pour les Migrants, BP 124, Kigali.

SENEGAL

CIMADE, Centre de Bopp, Dispensaire Foyer, BP 5070, Dakar, T: 32607.

Secours Catholique du Sénégal, 3 Rue Paul Holle, BP 439, Dakar, T: 22077.

Seventh-day Adventist Senegal Mission, Boite Postale 1013, Dakar, T: 25 48 31.

SEYCHELLES

Union Chrétienne Seychelloise, P.O. Box 32, Victoria, Mahé.

SINGAPORE

World Vision International, 1 Sophia Road, #04-05 Peace Centre, Singapore 228149, T: 334-5835, F: 334-5848.

SLOVAKIA

Caritas Catholique Slovaque, Heydukova 20, 80000 Bratislava, T: 50566.

SOUTH AFRICA

Caritas South Africa, General Secreteriat, SACBC, Box 941, Pretoria 0001, Khanya House, 140 Visagie St, Pretoria, T: 012-323-6458, F: 012-326-6218.

World Vision of Southern Africa, PO Box 1101, Florida 1710, 5 Main Ave, Florida, Roodepoort, T: 011-674-2043, F: 011-472-4885.

SOUTH KOREA

Korean Catholic Migration Commission (KCMC), 1 Myong-Dong, 2-ka Chung Ku, c/o IPO Box 1035, Soul, T: 754381.

SPAIN

Campaña Contra el Hambre en el Mundo, Madrid.

Caritas Española, Cuesta de Santo Domingo 5, Madrid, T: 2489405.

Comisión Católica Española de Migración (CCEM), Guadiana 10—El Viso, Madrid 2, T: 2617200.

Edificio Migrans, San Roman del Valle s/n, Gran San Blas, Madrid 17, T: 2060241.

Manos Unidas, Barquillo 38, 2°. Izda., 28004 Madrid, T: 34-1-410-7500.

SUDAN

Sudanese Development and Relief Agency (ECS/SUDAN), P.O. Box 10502, Khartoum; Episcopal Church of the Sudan (ECS), Khartoum, T: 442533, F: 70898, O: Telex: 21990 ACROPSD.

SURINAME

Father Ahlbrinck Association, Marowijnestraat 2, Postbus 2075, Paramaribo.

Jepie Makandra, Aide Mutuelle, Paramaribo.

SWEDEN

Church of Sweden Aid/Lutherhjälpen, Sysslomansgatan 4, 75170 Uppsala, T: 46-18-16-95-00, F: 46-18-16-97-72.

Operation Mercy, Högtorp, Nybble, S-719 91 Vintrosa.

SWITZERLAND

American Friends Service Committee, 12 Rue Adrien Lachenal, CH-1207 Genève.

Bread for Brothers, Missionsstr 21, CH-4003 Basel, T: 061-243350.

Brethren Service Commission, 150 Route de Ferney, CH-1211 Genève 20.

Caritas Internationalis, 6 Rue du Conseil-Général, CH-1205 Genève.

Christian Children's Fund, P.O. Box 2100, Geneva 2 1211, T: 41-022-791-6462, F: 41-022-791-0361.

Commission Internationale catholique pour les migrations (CICM), 37-39, rue de Vermont, CP 96, 1211 Geneve 20, 022/7334150.

Eastern European Aid Association, Caisse Postale 36, Chavannes 1022.

Food for the Hungry, 108 route de Suisse, Versoix/Geneva 1290, T: 41-22-775-14-44, F: 41-22-755-16-86.

Inter-Church Aid, WCC, 150 Route de Ferney, CH-1211 Genève 20.

International Catholic Migration Commission (ICMC), 65 Rue de Lausanne, CH-1202 Genève, T: 022-314750.

Schweizerische Evangelische Freundeskreis für die Araber in Israel (SEFAI), Ref Pfarramt, CH-6260 Reiden, T: 062-811173.

Schweizerische Katholische Arbeitsgemeinschaft für Fremdarbeiter (SKAF), Löwenstr 3, CH-6002 Luzern, T: 041-222960.

Schweizerischer Caritasverband/Union Suisse de Charité/Unione Svizzera di Carità, Löwenstr 3, CH-6002 Luzern, T: 041-231144.

Swiss Aid to Tibetans, Kauffmannsweg 8, CP 234, CH-6000 Luzern 2; Geneva Ofc: 1228 Plan-les-Ouates, CP31.

Swiss Central Office for Aid to Refugees, Kinkelstr 2, CH-8035 Zürich.

Waldenserhilfe, Sempacherstr 41, CH-8032 Zürich.

SYRIA

Oeuvres Sociales Al Kalimat, BP 107, Halab, T: 10506, 13261, 13262.

TAIWAN

Taiwan Christian Service (Church World Service), Jen Ai Rd., Section 4, No. 6, Taipei, T: 773171.

THAILAND

Asian Christian Service, 14/2 Pramuan Rd., Bangkok.

Cama Services, 28/2 Pracha Utit Lane, Pradipa Rd., Bangkok 4, T: 279-7752.

YMCA for Northern Development Foundation, 11 Sersuk Rd, Mengrairasmi, Chiang Mai 5000, T: 66-53-221-819, F: 66-53-215-523.

TUNISIA

Service Social de la Prélature de Tunis, 4 Rue d'Alger, Tunis, T: 242235, 245832.

TURKEY

Association des Amis des Pauvres, Satirci Sok No 2, Pangalti, Istanbul.

UGANDA

Comboni Charity Fund, Kampala.

UKRAINE

Christian Charity Foundation 'Consensus', Michurina Street 64, Kiev 14 252014, T: 7-044-295-80-82, F: 7-044-295-50-82.

UNITED STATES OF AMERICA (USA)

Adventist Development and Relief Agency International, 12501 Old Columbia Pike, Silver Spring, MD 20904, T: 301-680-6380, F: 301-680-6370, O: telex: 440186 SDAY UI..

Albanian Humanitarian Aid, 492 East Broadway, Suite 181, South Boston, MA 02127, T: 617-268-1275, F: 617-268-3184.

All God's Children International, 4114 NE Fremont St. #1, Portland, OR 97212, T: 503-282-7652, F: 503-282-2582, O: E-mail: AGCI@aol.com.

American Council for Emigres in the Professions, Room 800, 345 East 46th St., New York, NY 10017.

American Friends Service Committee, 160 North 15th St., Philadelphia, PA 19102, T: 215-L03-9372.

American Waldensian Aid Society, Room 1850, 475 Riverside Drive, New York, NY 10027.

Arise & Build Ministries (Shelter Now International), 683 Monroe Street, Oshkosh, WI 54901-4646, T: 414-426-1207, F: 414-426-04321.

Armenian General Benevolent Union, 585 Saddle River Road, Saddle Brook, NJ 07662, T: 201-797-7600, F: 201-797-7338.

Blessings International, 5881 S. Garnett St., Tulsa,

OK 74146-6812, T: 918-250-8101, F: 918-250-1281.
Bread For the World, 1100 Wayne Ave., Ste. 1000, Silver Spring, MD 20910, T: 301-608-2400, F: 301-608-2401.
Brethren Service, Church of the Brethren, 1451 Dendee Ave., Elgin, IL 60120.
CARE, Inc., 660 First Ave., New York, NY 10016.
Catholic Near East Welfare Association (CNEWA), 330 Madison Ave., New York, NY 10017.
Catholic Relief Services, 209 West Fayette St., Baltimore, MD 21201-9349, T: 410-625-2220, F: 410-685-1635, O: Web; www.charity.com.
Chalcedon-Orphan Aid, 938 Calle Santa Cruz, Olivenhain, CA 92024, T: 619-436-1462, F: 619-944-9496.
Childcare International, P.O. Box W, Bellingham, WA 98227, T: 360-647-2283, F: 360-647-2392.
Children of Promise (COP), O: Web: www.gospelcom.net/promise.
Children's Fund, PO Box 26511, Richmond, VA 23261, T: 800-776-6767.
Christian Aid Ministries, P.O. Box 360, Berlin, OH 44610, T: 330-893-2428, F: 330-893-2305.
Christian Children's Fund, 2821 Emerywood Parkway, Richmond, VA 23294-3725, T: 804-756-2700, F: 804-756-2718.
Christian Reformed World Relief Committee, 2850 Kalamazoo Ave. S.E., Grand Rapids, MI 49560, T: 616-246-0740, F: 616-246-0806, O: CRWRC @crcnet.mhs.compuserve.com.
Christian Services Corps, 1501 11th St. N.W., Washington, DC 20001.
Christian Veterinary Mission, O: Web: www.vetmission.org/.
Christian World Mission, O: Web: www.jcwm.org/en_index.htm.
Church World Service, DOM-NCCCUSA, 475 Riverside Drive, New York, NY 10027, T: 212-870-2257.
Compassion International, Inc., P. O. Box 7000, Colorado Springs, CO 80933; 3955 Cragwood Dr., 80918-7860, T: 719-594-9900-800-336-7676, F: 719-594-6271, O: E-mail: CIInfo@us.ci.org, www.ci.org.
CROP, Box 968, Elkhart, IN 46515; 28606 Phillips St., Elkhart, IN 46515, T: 219-264-3102, F: 800-456-1310.
Cup of Cold Water Ministries, O: Web: www.ccwm.org/.
Direct Relief International, P.O. Box 30820, Santa Barbara, CA 93130-0820, T: 805-964-4767, F: 805-681-4838.
Eastern European Aid Association, P.O. Box 917, Waynesboro, PA 17268-0917, T: 717-762-1086.
Exodus World Service, P.O. Box 7000, West Chicago, IL 60185, T: 708-665-0004.
Feed the Children, Larry Jones International Ministries, Inc., P.O. Box 36, Oklahoma, OK 73101-0036, T: 405-942-0228, O: Web: www.feedthechildren.org/.
Food for the Hungry, Inc., 7729 E. Greenway Rd., Scottsdale, AZ 85260, T: 602-998-3100, F: 602-433-1420, O: E-mail: GaryS@fh.org, Web site: www.fh.org.
Foundation for His Ministry, Box 9803, North Hollywood, CA 91609, T: 818-766-6923.
Friends in the West, P.O. Box 250, Arlington, WA 98223, T: 360-435-8983, F: 360-435-6334, O: E-mail: Info@fitw.com, www.fitw.com/acc.
Global Outreach, Ltd., P.O. Box 1, Tupelo, MS 38802, T: 601-842-4615, F: 601-842-4620, O: E-mail: world@berean.net, www.globaloutreach.org.
Habitat for Humanity, 555 Tarpon Pond Road, John's Island, SC 29455.
Hand of Help, P.O. Box 3494, Fullerton, CA 92634, T: 714-447-1313, F: 714-447-1313.
Help for Romania Fund/Help the Children of Romania, 533 Oak Knoll Ave., N.E., Warren, OH 44483, T: 216-394-8575, F: 216-393-2581.
Helps International Ministries, Inc., P.O. Box 1209, Harlem, GA 30814, T: 706-556-3408, F: 706-556-9361.
Home of Onesiphorus, 3939 North Hamlin Ave., Chicago, IL 60618.
Hope for the Hungry, P.O. Box 786, Belton, TX 76513, T: 254-939-0124, F: 254-939-0882, O: E-mail: HHungry@sage.net, www.sage.net/~hhungry/index.htm.
Humanitarian Foundation for Russian Nations, 1106 S.E. 144th Ct., Vancouver, WA, T: 206-944-7813.
Int'l Aid, Inc, 17011 W Hickory, Spring Lake, MI 49456.
Inter-Lutheran Disaster Response, 4865 Hamilton Blvd., Wesconsville, PA 18106, T: 610-366-9141.
International Aid, Inc., 17011 W. Hickory, Spring Lake, MI 49456, T: 616-846-7490, F: 616-846-3842, O: E-mail: INTLAID@xc.org, IntlAid.
International Child Care, O: Web: www.gospelcom.net/icc.
International Christian Relief, 801 Haddon Ave., Collingswood, NJ 08108, T: 609-858-0700.
International Church Relief Fund, 182 Farmers Lane, Suite 200, Santa Rosa, CA 95405, T: 707-528-8000, F: 707-525-1310, O: E-mail: ICRF@sonic.net.
International Needs, Inc., Box 889, Scranton, PA 18501, T: 717-346-0455, F: 717-969-9838.
International Orthodox Christian Charities, 711 West 40th St., Suite 356, Baltimore, MD 21211, T: 410-243-9820, F: 410-243-9824.
Larry Jones International Ministries, P.O. Box 36, Oklahoma City, OK 73101, T: 405-942-0228, F: 405-945-4177, O: Web: www.feedthechildren.org.
Lifewater International, P.O. Box 3336, S. El Monte, CA 91733, T: 818-443-1787.
Love-N-Care Ministries, O: Web: www.sover.net/~djinno/.
Lutheran Immigration and Refugee Services, 390 Park Ave., South, New York, NY 10016-8803, T: 212-532-6350, F: 212-683-1329.
Lutheran World Relief, 390 Park Ave. S., New York, NY 10016-8803, T: 212-532-6350, F: 212-213-6081.
Meals for Millions Foundation, 1800 Olympic Blvd., P.O. Box 1666, Santa Monica, CA 90406.
Mennonite Church Board of Missions and Charities, 1711 Prairie St., Elkhart, IN 46514, T: 219-522-2630.
Mercy Medical Airlift, P.O. Box 1940, Manassas, VA 22110, T: 703-361-1191.
Mercy Ships, P.O. Box 2020, Lindale, TX 75771, T: 903-882-0887, F: 903-882-0336, O: E-mail: Indo@mercyships.org, www.mercyships.org.
Mission of Mercy, P.O. Box 62600, Colorado Springs, CO 80962, T: 719-593-0099, F: 719-531-6820.
Mission to the Migrants, 2007 West 78th Place, Los Angeles, CA 90047.
New England Albanian Relief Organization, 220 Barber Ave., Worcester, MA 01606, T: 508-852-5553, F: 508-853-7071.
Operation Blessing International, 977 Centerville Tnpk., Virginia Beach, VA 23463, T: 757-579-3400, F: 757-579-3411, O: Web: www.ob.org.
Pontifical Mission for Palestine, c/o Catholic Near East Welfare Association, 1011 First Ave., New York, NY 10022.
Project Mercy, Inc., 7011 Ardmore Ave., Fort Wayne, N 46809, T: 219-747-2559, F: 219-478-1361, O: E-mail: ProMer@gte.net.
Protestant Episcopal Church—Presiding Bishop's Fund World Relief, 815 Second Ave., New York, NY 10017-4594, T: 212-922-5129, F: 212-983-6377.
Relief Ministries, 3201 N. Seventh St., West Monroe, LA 71291, T: 318-396-6000, F: 318-396-1000.
Romanian Orthodox Episcopate of America-Help Romania Fund, 2522 Grey Tower Road, Jackson, MI 49201, T: 216-393-2581.
Samaritan's Purse, P.O. Box 3000, Boone, NC 28607, T: 704-262-1980, F: 704-262-1796, O: E-mail: USA@samaritan.org, www.samaritan.org.
Seventh-day Adventist Welfare Service, 6840 Eastern Ave., Washington, DC.
Society of St Vincent de Paul, 611 Olive St., St. Louis, MO 63101.
United Methodist Committee on Relief (Gen. Board of Global Min.), 475 Riverside Dr., Room 1374, New York, NY 10115, T: 212-870-3600, F: 212-870-3624.
United States Committee for Refugees, 20 West 40th St., New York, NY 10018.
Volunteers for International Technical Assistance Inc (VITA), College Campus, Schenectady, NY 12308.
World Concern, 19303 Fremont Ave., N., Seattle, WA 98133, T: 206-546-7201, F: 206-546-7269.
World Neighbors, 5116 North Portland Ave., Oklahoma City, OK 73112.
World Opportunities International, 1415 Cahuenga Blvd., Hollywood, CA 90028, T: 213-466-7187, F: 213-871-1546, O: E-mail: WorldOp@msn.com.
World Relief Corporation, P.O. Box WRC, Wheaton, IL 60189, T: 630-665-0235, F: 630-665-4473, O: E-mail: WorldRelief@xc.org, www.worldrelief.org.
World Vision International, P.O. Box 0, Pasadena, CA 91109; 919 W. Huntington Dr., Monrovia, CA 91016.
World Vision USA, P. O. Box 9716, Federal Way, WA 98063, T: 253-815-1000, F: 253-815-3447, O: Web: www.worldvision.org.

URUGUAY
Castores de Emmaus, Soriano 1472, Montevideo.
Emmaus, Soriano 1465, Montevideo.
Instituto Católico Uruguayo de Immigración (ICUI), Yaguarón 1448, Piso 6, Apdo 601, Montevideo.

VENEZUELA
Comisión Católica Venezolana de Migración (CCVM), Av Negrin, Calle El Apartado, La Florida, Apdo 2301, Caracas.
Instituto de Vivienda Cárita (INVICA), Edf América, Piso 4, Av Urdaneta Esq Veroes, Caracas 101, T: 812272.
Sociedad de San Vicente de Paul, Edf San Luis Ap 8, 2a Avda Santa Eduvigis, Caracas 107, T: 416542.

VIET NAM
Asian Christian Service of the East, 215/36/1A Chi-Lang, Phu-Nhuan, Saigon.

ZAMBIA
Socio-Economic Department, Zambia Catholic Secretariat, Unity House, Corner Stanley/Jameson Rds., P.O. Box 1965, Lusaka, T: 73467, 73470.
Zambia Christian Refugee Service, P.O. Box 2778, Lusa,a, T: 51358.

2
Antireligious, atheist, & humanist organizations

Atheistic or non-religious humanist (or anti-supernaturalist) movements, organizations, and associations; freethinkers' organizations, societies, or groups; bodies committed to active or militant opposition to Christianity or to all religion; organizations for the promotion or propagation of atheism or non-theistic humanism, centers for the study of atheism, research centers dealing with religion from an anti-religious position.

BRITAIN (UK OF GB & NI)
British Humanist Association, 13 Prince of Wales Terrace, London W8, T: 01-937-2341.
Communist Party (UK), National HQ, 16 King St, London WC2, T: 01-836-2151.
National Secular Society, 698 Holloway Rd, London N19; 103 Borough High St., London SE1, T: 01-272-1266, 01-407-2717.
Rationalist Press Association, 88 Islington High St, London N1 8EN; 40 Drury Lane, London WC2, T: 01-226-7251, Covent Garden 2077/8.

BULGARIA
Institute of Philosophy of the Academy of Sciences, 6 Rue P, Evtimi, Sofiya.

CHINA
Chinese Association for Atheism, Peking.
World Religion Research Institute (Institute of World Religions), Academy of Social Sciences, Peking.

CROATIA
Institut de Recherches Sociales, Section de Recherches sur l'Athéisme et les Religions, Jezuitski trg 4, Zagreb.

FRANCE
World Union of Freethinkers, 4 Rue Vitelu, F-94 Saint-Mandé.

GERMANY
Chair of Atheism, Jena University, Jena.

NETHERLANDS
International Humanist & Ethical Union (IHEU), Oudegracht 152, Utrecht, T: 312155.
International Humanist and Ethical Union, c/o IHEW Secretariat, Oudkerhof 11, Utrecht.

UNITED STATES OF AMERICA (USA)
American Association for the Advancement of Atheism, Box 2831, San Diego, CA 92110; 38 Park Row, New York, NY 10008.
Ethical Culture Movement, 2 West 64th St., New York, NY 10023, T: 212-873-6500.

3
Apparel, merchandise, & gifts

Companies, businesses, and organizations that design, manufacture, produce, sell, or distribute Christian T-shirts, clothing, hats, mugs, plaques, pictures, figurines, rosaries, objects of devotion, icons, toys, games, gifts for students or children, favors, craft items, or other merchandise — of a wide variety, on a range from costly to cheap, with Christian verses, slogans, symbols, saints, or uses. For items of greater artistic character, see ART (RELIGION AND THE ARTS). See also LITURGY AND WORSHIP.

4
Art (religion & the arts)

Christian involvement in the arts, including the visual arts, the fine arts, the performing arts, the literary arts; painting, sculpture, architecture, stained glass, drama, theater, opera, cinema, puppetry, mime, festivals, circus; renowned centers of Christian artistic presentation (e.g. Oberammergau, Forest Lawn, Einsiedein); mission and evangelization through the arts; expression of Christian and Biblical themes through the arts; notable Christian displays and exhibitions (e.g. the Holy Land museum, Nijmegen); major Christian museums; Christian art centers and centers for training in the arts; church architecture, historical monuments. See also CINEMA AND FILM, MEDIA AND COMMUNICATIONS, and MUSIC.

AUSTRALIA
International Creative Ministries, 3 Franklin Place, Caulinglord 2118.
True Colours Theatre and Video Works, 309 Waterworks Rd., Ashgrove 4060, T: 366 6126.

BELGIUM
Art Studio Slabbinck, L. Bauwensstraat 18, 8200 Brugge, T: 32-50-312557, F: 32-50-318-358.

BRAZIL
Associação Religiosa MILAD, Cx. Postal 10080, Goiânia-GO 74020-025, T: 62-225-6431, F: 62-225-2370.

BRITAIN (UK OF GB & NI)
Actors Church Union, St. Paul's Church, Covent Garden, London WC2.
Arts Centre Group, Batailes, Great Easton, near Dunmow, Essex.; 19 Draycot Place, London SW3 2SJ, T: Great Easton 246.
Arts Media Workshop, 35 Albany Rd., New Malden, Surrey, T: 01-949-4609.
Cathedrals Advisory Committee, 83 London Wall, London EC2M 5NA, T: 01-638-0971.
Catholic Stage Guild, c/o 29 St Peter's Road, Croydon CR0 1HN.
Chichester Diocesan Buildings Study Group, Diocesan Church House, 9 Brunswick Square, Hove, Sussex BN3 1EN, T: 0273-73571.
International Society of Christian Artists, Glasspools, Gillsman's Hill, St Leonards-on-Sea; Bologne 1967, Salzburg 1969.
New Christian Arts Centre Group, 17 Wansford Close, Brentwood, Essex.
New Churches Research Groups (NCRG), 11 Parkway, Wilmslow, Cheshire; 5a Lancaster Rd., Wimbledon, London SW10.
Religious Drama Society of Great Britain (RADIUS), George Bell House, Ayres St., London SE1 1ES, T: 01-407-4374.
Scottish Guild of Catholic Artists, 14 Newton Place, Glasgow C3.
Society of Catholic Artists, 19 Cranford Close, West Wimbledon, London SW20 0DP, T: 0181-947 6476.
Society of Church Craftsmen, 26 Conduit St, London W1, T: 01-629-629-8300.
Superstar Ventures Ltd., 118/120 Wardour St., London W1V 4BT, T: 01-437-3224, 5.

CANADA
Brookstone Performing Arts, 188 Lowther Ave., Toronto, ON M5R 1E8, T: 416-922-1238, F: 416-922-5124, O: E-mail: BRKSTN@io.org.
Bullas Glass Ltd., 15 Joseph St., Kitchener, ON N2G 1H9, T: 519-745-1124.
Canadian Art China Ltd., 18 Stewart Rd., Collingwood, ON L9Y 4K1, T: 705-445-1321.
Christian Drama Society of Canada, Toronto.
Covenant Players, 1061 Pinecrest Rd., Ottawa, ON K2B 6B7, T: 613-820-4714, F: 613-721-9848.
Desmarais & Robitaille, 60 Notre-Dame West, Montreal, QC H2Y 1S6, T: 514-845-3194, O: 1-800-363-1668.
Luxfer Studios Ltd., 8481 Keele St., Unit 6, Concord, ON L4K 1Z7, T: 905-669-4244, F: 905-669-4244.
Sacred Acts - The Canadian School of Performing Arts in Worship, c/o 78 Earl Grey Rd., Toronto, ON M4J 3L5, T: 416-463-5395.
Sunhound Glassworks Limited, Box 8452, Saint John's, NF A1B 3N9, T: 709-753-5097.

CHINA
Asian Christian Art Association (ACAA), 96, 2nd District, Pak Tin Village, Mei Tin Rd, Shatin, New Territories, Hong Kong, T: 852-2691-1068, F: 852-2692-4378.
Tao Fong Shan Christian Centre, 33, Toa Fong Shan Road, Shatin, NT., Hong Kong, T: 852-2605 083, F: 852-2694 0354.

FRANCE
Musée Calvin, Place Aristide-Briand, Noyon (Oise), T: 359.
Musée de la France Protestante de l'Ouest, Le Bois-Tiffrais, Monsireigne (Vendee).
Musée Huguenot de l'Eglise de la rochelle, 2 Rue Saint-Michel, La Rochelle, T: 348628.
Société d'Exportation d'Art Religieux (SEAR), 5 Faubourg St Honore, F-75008 Paris, T: 265-2260.

GERMANY
Oberammergau 1960, Ammergebirge, Bayerische Alpen.
Religionskundliche Sammlung der Universität Marburg, Schloss 1, Eingang Innenhof, D-3550 Marburg, T: 06421-6912480.

GREECE
Christian Drama Society of Greece, Athínai.

HOLY SEE
Pontificia Commissione Centrale per l'Arte Sacra in Italia, Segretario, Palazzo della Cancellaria Apostolica, Piazza della Cancellaria 1, I-00186 Roma, Italy, T: 6527226.

INDIA
Alpha Artistic Evangelism, Alpha Bhavan, Kuttapuzha P. O., Tiruvalla, Kerala.
Bethany Art Center, 58 Bhargava Lane, Civil Lines P. O. Box No. 8617, New Delhi 110054.
Bethany School of Arts and Theology, P. O. Box 2, Vennikulam P. O., Thiruvalla, Kerala 689544.
Beynon-Smith School of Fine Arts, Belgaum, Karnataka 590001.
Christian Art Service, Uthamapalayam, Tamil Nadu 626533.
Daiva Vani Twin Cities Christian Cultural Organisation, 1-11-571/16, Siyon Nivas, Golconda Cross Roads, Hyderabad, Andhra Pradesh 500020.
Indian Christian Art Association, J. J. School of Arts, Dr. D. N. Road, Bombay, Maharashtra 400001.
Indian Prasad Puppeteers, 654 Shaniwar Peth, Satara, Maharashtra 415002.
Salem Arts, CSI Compound, Pannerselvam Pathy Road, Erode, Tamil Nadu.
Sneha Sudarshan, 5-99. Church Street, Lingarajapuram, Bangalore, Karnataka 560084.
Talents for Christ, H.No 9-2-59, Regimental Bazar, Secunderabad, Andhra Pradesh 500025.

ITALY
Centro Cattolico Teatrale (CCT), Ente dello Spettacolo, Via della Conciliazione 2c, I-00193 Roma, T: 561775, 564132.
Museo Storico Valdese, Via Beckwith, Torre Pellice (To).

NETHERLANDS
Christian Artists Association, Postbus 81137, Rotterdam 3009 GC, T: 31-010456-8868, F: 31-010455-9022.

NORWAY
Institute for Christian Drama, Holsteinvn 22, Oslo.

POLAND

Centrum Kulturalne: OO.Barnabitów, Ul. Smoluchowskiego, 1, 02-679 Warszawa, T: 22-475-107-682-8560, F: 22-682-8556, O: E-mail: zaccaria@pol.pl.

SINGAPORE

Lu-Wei Performing Arts Fellowship, 6 Mount Sophia, Singapore 228457, T: 339-2571.

SOUTH AFRICA

CAM Trust, PO Box 72537, Lynnwood Ridge 0040, 209 Daffodil St, Lynnwoodridge, T: 012-47-5924, F: 012-47-7997.
Christian Artists SA, PO Box 35583, Menlo Park 0102, Pretoria, T: 012-47-4858, F: 012-47-5501.
Covenant Players, PO Box 1715, Roodepoort 1725, 14 Nel St, Roodepoort, T: 011-763-3407.

SOUTH KOREA

Catholic Academy for Korean Culture, 1, 2-ga, Myong-dong, Chung-gu, Seoul-shi, T: 02-774-5344.
Catholic Artists' Association, 566-4, Yonnam-dong, Map'o-gu, Seoul-shi, T: 02-324-5286.
Catholic Institute of Art, 54, 1-ga, Changch'ung-dong, Chung-gu, Seoul-shi, T: 02-273-6394.
Kangdong Catholic Cultural Center, 397-413, Ch'onho 3-dong, Kangdong-gu, Seoul-shi, T: 02-485-8204.
Society for the Promotion of Korean Catholic Culture, 1, 2-ga, Myong-dong, Chung-gu, Seoul-shi, T: 02-779-0753.

SWEDEN

Society for Liturgy and Drama (FLOD), Stockholm.

SWITZERLAND

Commission Suisse d'Art Religieux, CH-1041 Poliez-le-Grand, T: 021-811274.
International Society of Christian Artists, Hevelstr 21, CH-8032 Zürich.
Schweizerische Kommission für Biblische Wandbilder, General Guisan-Str 1 5, CH-4000 Basel.
Schweizerische Kommission für Gute Religiöse Bilder, 3123 Belp BE, T: 031-810142.

UNITED STATES OF AMERICA (USA)

Acadia Theatre Company, 924 E. Juneau Ave., #209, Milwaukee, WI 53202.
After Dinner Players, 2710 W. Alabama, Houston, TX 77098.
Agape Drama Press, Ltd., Box 1313, Englewood, CO 80110.
American Church Furnishings, 500 E St Charles Rd, Carol Stream, IL 60188, T: 800-359-3708.
American Society for Church Architecture, New York.
Archives of Modern Christian Art, 1500 Ralston Ave., Belmont, CA 94002.
Armenian Museum & Cultural Center, 630 2nd Ave., New York, NY 10016.
Artistic Fabrication Co., 15 E. 16th St., Paterson, NJ 07524, T: 201-523-8720.
Artists for Israel Institute, O: Web: www.afii.org/.
Artists In Christian Testimony, Box 395, Franklin, TN 37065, T: 615-591-2598, F: 615-591-2599, O: E-mail: 105222.3223@compuserve.com.
Arts and Religion Forum, Washington Theological Consort, 487 Michigan Ave., N.E., Washington, DC 20017.
Asbury College Theatre Arts, 201 N. Lexington Ave., Wilmore, KY 40390.
Associated Church Builders, P.O. Box 187, Palate, IL 60067.
Ballet Magnificate School & Studios, 4455 N. State, Jackson, MS 39206-5306.
Bible History Wax Museum, 3rd, 4th & E. Sts. S.W., Washington, DC 20001, T: 202-628-2994.
Bibletown USA, Box A, Boca Raton, FL 33432.
Botti Studio of Architectural Arts, Inc., 919 Grove St., Evanston, IL 60201, T: 708-869-5933, F: 708-869-5996.
Bovard Studio, Inc., 52 E. Briggs, Fairfield, IA 52556, T: 800-452-7796, O: 515-472-0974.
Bronner's Christmas Wonderland, 25 Christmas Lane, Frankenmuth, MI 48734, T: 517-652-8662.
Captain Ken's Marionette Ministries, P.O. Box 441, Phoenixville, PA 19460-0441.
Cartoonworks, 9818 Summit St., Kansas City, MO 64114, T: 816-941-9221, O: E-mail: cartoonworks@earthlink.net.
Casola Stained Glass Studio, Inc., 11000 Metro Pkwy. #11, Fort Myers, FL 33912, T: 800-330-4527, F: 813-939-0068.
Cathedral Art Metal Co., Inc., 25 Manton Ave., Providence, RI 02909, T: 800-493-GIFT, 401-273-7200, F: 800-47A-NGEL, 401-27, O: E-mail: camco@cathedralart.com, Web: www.cathedralart.com.
Catholic Actors' Guild of America, Inc., 1501 Broadway, Suite 510, New York, NY 10036.
Catholic Art Association, Washington, DC.
Catholic Fine Arts Society Inc., Maria Regina Hall/Molloy College, 1000 Hempstead Ave., Rockville Centre, NY 11570.
Catholic University Drama Dept., Catholic University of America, Washington, D.C. 20064.
Center for Performers & the Performing Arts, Inc., 484 W. 43rd St., #42A, New York, NY 10036.
Center for the Arts, Religion, and Education, c/o Pacific School of Religion, 1798 Scenic Ave., Berkeley, CA 94709.
Chicago Artists, 5255 N. Paulina, Chicago, IL 60640.
Christian Art League Ministry, 128 Westwood Dr., Visalia, CA 93277.
Christian Conjurer, 1705 Barbara Lane, Connersville, IN 47331.
Christian Costume Co, 4205 Pleasant Valley, Suite 242, Raleigh, NC 27612, T: 919-787-1415.
Christian Drama Consortium, O: Web: www.cadvision.com/Home_Pages/accounts/haynese/easter96.htm.
Christian Fiction Review, O: Web: members.aol.com/writewc/cfr.html.
Christian Performing Artists' Fellowship, 10523 Main St., Suite 31, Fairfax, VA 22030.
Christianity & the Arts, P. O. Box 118088, Chicago, IL 60611, T: 312-642-8606, F: 312-266-7719, O: Web: members.aol.com/chrarts/chrnarts.html.
Christianity and Literature, Dept. of English, Seattle Pacific Univ., Seattle, WA 98119.
Christians in the Arts Networking, Inc., P.O. Box 1941, Cambridge, MA 02238-1941.
Christians in the Visual Arts, P.O. Box 10247, Arlington, VA 22210.
Christians in Theatre Arts, c/o Malone College, 515 25th St., N.W., Canton, OH 44709.
Church Architectural Guild of America, Washington, DC.
Church Furnishings Manufacturing, 155 Jefferson, Box X, Carlisle, IA 50047, T: 800-383-1000.
Commission on Church Architecture, Lutheran Church in America, 231 Madison Ave., New York, NY 10016.
Committee on Religious Architecture, American Institute of Architects, Washington, DC.
Community Arts Foundation, 615 Wellington Ave., Chicago, IL 60657.
Continental Ministries (Jeremiah People), P.O. Box 1996, Thousand Oaks, CA 91360.
Cornerstone Festival, 4707 N. Malden, Chicago, IL 60640.
Covenant Players, 1741 Fiske Place, P.O. Box 2900, Oxnard, CA 93033.
Creative Arts Productions, Box 7008, Santa Cruz, CA 95061.
CrossCurrent Dance Theatre, 5724 Vincent Ave., S., Minneapolis, MN 55410.
Department of Church Building and Architecture, NCCCUSA, 475 Riverside Drive, New York, NY 10027.
Department of Speech and Drama, Catholic University of America, Washington, DC 20017.
Drama Store, 1442 E Lincoln Ave, #331. Orange, CA 92665, T: 714-282-2296.
Dramatic Publishing Co., 4150 N. Milwaukee Ave., Chicago, IL 60641.
Dramatic Word, P.O. Box 903, Salem, OR 97308.
Emmanuel Studios, Inc., 410 Maple Ave, Nashville, TN 37210, T: 615-255-5446.
Exaltation Dancers, c/o Briarwood Presbyterian, 2200 Briarwood Way, Birmingham, AL 35243.
Fellowship of Artists for Cultural Evangelism, 1605 Elizabeth St., Pasadena, CA 91104.
Fellowship of Christian Magicians, 5125 Larch Lane, Plymouth, MN 55442, O: E-mail: info@fcm.org.
Fellowship of Contemporary Christian Ministries, 24-B N. Belmont Ave., P.O. Box 1337, Arlington Heights, IL 60006.
First Presbyterian Theater, 300 W. Wayne St., Fort Wayne, IN 46802-3673.
Foundation for Religion and the Arts, P.O. Box 6482, FDR Station, New York, NY 10150.
Friends of John Wesley, 1716 1/4 Sierra Bonita, Pasadena, CA 91104.
Friends of the Groom, 909 Center St., Milford, OH 45150-1305.
Genesis Arts Phoenix, 2516 W. Curry St., Chandler, AZ 85224.
Great Passion Play Video T.M., P.O. Box 471, Eureka Springs, AR 72632, T: 501-253-8559.
Grunewald Guild, 19003 River Rd., Leavenworth, WA 98826.
Guild of Church Architects, Washington, DC.
Hosanna Sacred Dance, 1318 S. Reisner St., Indianapolis, IN 46221.
Hull-Stephens & Assoc Architects, 5023 Holland Dr, Swartz Creek, MI 48473, T: 313-635-4090.
II Chronicles Magazine, P.O. Box 42, Medford, OR 97501.
Ikon Studio, 3701 Fessenden St. NW, Washington, DC 20016, T: 202-363-5315.
Image: A Journal of the Arts and Religion, 526 Ziela Ave., Front Royal, VA 22630, T: 703-635-9217.
Index of Christian Art, Princeton University, McCormick Hall, Princeton, NJ, T: WA1-6600.
Institutional Statuary, 637 E. 132nd St., Bronx, NY 10450, T: 718-665-1125, F: 718-665-0956.
InterMission Thinkable Theatre, CBN University Performing Arts, Virginia Beach, VA 23464.
International Christian Cultural Center, 1300 Springwells, Fl 2, Detroit, MI 48209.
International Christian Media Commission, P.O. Box 70632, Seattle, WA 98107-0632.
John Cochran Repertory Company, 406 N. Raymond Ave., Pasadena, CA 91103-3705.
Kast & Company Liturgical Dancers, 5320 S. University Ave., Chicago, IL 60615.
Lamb's Players Theatre, 500 Plaza Blvd., P.O. Box 26, National City, CA 91951-0026; P.O. Box 26, National City, CA 92050.
Laws Stained Glass Studio, Inc., Rt 4, PO Box 377, Statesville, NC 28677, T: 704-876-3463.
Lion's Light Productions, 3280 S.W. 170th #1704, Beaverton, OR 97006.
Living Word Outdoor Drama, 6010 College Hill Rd., P.O. Box 1481, Cambridge, OH 43725.
Lynchburg Stained Glass Co., P.O. Box 4453, Lynchburg, VA 24502, T: 800-237-6161, F: 804-525-6168.
Master Arts Company, P.O. Box 9336, Grand Rapids, MI 49509.
Max Greiner Jr. Designs, P.O. Box 522, Kerrville, TX 78029, T: 210-896-7919, F: 210-367-4002.
Mecholah Yachad, 1202 Shelton Ave., Nashville, TN 37216.
Ministry of Music to All Churches, Kauai Evangelical Association, P.O. Box 636, Kalaheo, HI 96741.
New Life Drama Company, 45 Walden St., #G1, Concord, MA 01742-2504.
North American Academy of Liturgy, Room 120, Huegli Hall, Valparaiso University, Valparaiso, IN 46383.
Oil Tree Publishers, 14724 S. Yukon Ave., Glenpool, OK 74033, T: 918-322-3227, O: E-mail: lbclark@webzone.net.
Oliveart, 5990 Rear North Federal Hwy., Ft. Lauderdale, FL 33308, T: 800-813-4533, F: 954-771-3669.
On Stage, P.O. Box 25365, Chicago, IL 60625-0365.
Online Movie Reviews by Christian Pastor, O: Web: www.mcs.com/%7Esjvogel/wcrc/movies.html.
Opera/Music Theatre, 1755 W. End Ave., New Hyde Park, NY 11040.
Parable Players, c/o Church of the Ascension, 4729 Ellsworth Ave., Pittsburgh, PA 15213.
Performance Publishing Company, 978 McLean Blvd., N., Elgin, IL 60120.
Performing Arts, O: Web: www.dcez/com/~cpaf/cpaf.htm.
Phoenix Power & Light Company, Inc., 609 Chapelgate Dr., P.O. Box 60, Odenton, MD 21113.
Pioneer Drama Service, Inc., 2172 Colorado Blvd., S., P.O. Box 22555, Denver, CO 80222.
Potter's Place, 20 Beechwood Rd., Arnold, MD 21012, T: 410-647-2495.
Potters Cast, Green Acres Baptist Church, 1612 Leo Lynn, Tyler, TX 75701.
Praise Banners, P.O. Box 150849, Nashville, TN 37215, T: 615-298-3152, F: 615-298-9231, O: Web: www.praisebanners.com.
Rohlf's Stained Glass Studio, Inc., 783 S. 3rd Ave., Mount Vernon, NY 10550, T: 914-699-4848.
School of Speech, Marquette University, 625 North 15th St., Milwaukee, WI 53233.
Son Shine Puppet Co, P.O. Box 6203, Rockford, IL 61125, T: 815-965-8080.
South Jersey Black Theater Ensemble, Rd. #1, Lee Ave., Millville, NJ 08332.
St. Luke Productions, P.O. Box 761, Beaverton, OR 97075.
St. Mary's Museum & Cultural Center, 3256 Warren Rd., Cleveland, OH 44111.
Stained Glass Associates, P.O. Box 1531, Raleigh, NC 27602-1531, T: 919-266-2493.
Tapestry Theatre Company, P.O. Box 19844, Portland, OR 97280.
Taproot Theatre Company, 204 N. 85th St., P.O. Box 31116, Seattle, WA 98103.
Theatre of Involvement, UCCF Center, 331 17th Ave., S.E., Minneapolis, MN 55414.
Towne & Country Players, Inc., 55 E. Main, P.O. Box 551, Norwalk, OH 44857.
Unified Church Structures, 47925 North Gratiot Ave., Mt. Clemens, MI 48043.
United Church of Christ Fellowship in the Arts, Zion St. Paul UCC, Gen. Del. HCR 62, Hermann, MO 65041.
Universal Art Studio, 67 Mountain Spring Dr., Sparta, NJ 07871, T: 201-726-0835.
Vantage Theatre Ensemble, 18305 N.W. Tara St., Beaverton, OR 97006.
Vine Dance Theatre, P.O. Box 6482, FDR Station, New York, NY 10150.
Washington Arts Group, 2013 Q St., N.W., Washington, DC 20009.
Word Entertainment, Inc., 3319 West End Ave. Ste 200, Nashville, TN 37203, T: 800-876-WORD, F: 800-671-6601, O: Web: www.wordonline.com.

5
Audio recordings

Tape or cassette ministries, audio ministries; companies, centers or organizations which make, sell, or distribute records, tapes, audio cassettes, CDs, or recordings on other audio media; record, tape, cassette or disc libraries, or libraries of recorded music; ministries which produce or distribute records or cassettes in many languages for missionary or Christian training purposes.

AUSTRALIA

Gospel Extension Ministry (GEM), 144 Albany Rd, Petersham, NSW 2049, T: 594174.

AUSTRIA

Jona Cassette Service, Bahnhofstrasse 33, Postfach 197, 6800 Feldkirch, T: 05522/27 709.

BELGIUM

Centre Catholique d'Information Discographique (CCID), Rue Cornet de Grez 14, Brussel 3, T: 176815.

BRAZIL

Sonoviso do Brasil, Av Paulo de Frontin 568, ZC-10 Rio de Janeiro, GB.

BRITAIN (UK OF GB & NI)

Celebration Records, Yeldall Manor, Hare Hatch, Twyford, Berks RG10 9XR, T: (073522)2272.
Christadelphian Recordings Library Committee, Librarian for Tape Recordings, 159 Lazy Hill, Kings Norton, Birmingham 30.
Christian Recording Associates, 120 Chipstead Valley Rd, Coulsdon, Surrey.
Gospel Sound and Vision, 44 Georgia Rd, Thornton Heath, Surrey CR4 8DW, T: (01)764-1520.
International Christian Communications, ICC Studios, 4 Regency Mews, Silverdale Rd, Eastbourne, East Sussex BN20 7AB, T: (0323)26134.
Sacred Heart Publications, Southchurch Rd, Southend-on-Sea, Essex, T: 265238.

CANADA

Evangile sur Cassettes, C.P. 9, Succ. Montréal - Nord, Montréal–Nord, QC H1H 5L1, T: 514-324-7990.
Language Recordings International, #210 - 1059 Upper James St., Hamilton, ON L9C 3A6, T: 905-574-8220, F: 905-574-6843, O: http://www.netaccess.on.ca/fingertip/gallery/lri/display/display.html.
Lecture Biblique, C.P. 83015, Beloeil, QC J3G 6L7, T: 514-467-6831.

FRANCE

Evangélisation par la Chanson, BP 2002, F-68058 Mulhouse-Cédex (H-Rhin).
Jéricho, 31 Blvd de la Tour-Maubourg, F-75 Paris 7, T: (01)468-3053.
OCD (Pastorale & Musique, Unidisc-Clarté), 33 Rue de Fleurus, F-75 Paris 6, T: (01)548-4995.
Office Chrétien de l'Enregistrement Sonore (OCES), 193 Rue de l'Université, F-75 Paris 7, T: (01)705-4358, 551-9462.

GERMANY

Evangelische Arbeitskreis Schallplatte, Falkensteinstr 16, D-35 Kassel.
Gospel Recordings, Postfach 1211, Halver 1 5884, T: 49-2353-2120, F: 49-2359-137095.

INDIA

Amruthavani, Radio Department, Post Box 1558, Secunderabad, Andhra Pradesh 500003.
Arul Kalaingiyam, St. Mathew's Church, Thirutani, Tamil Nadu 631209.
Carnival Cassettes, Mulamoottil Thundiathu, Kozhencherry, Kerala 689641.
Cassette Library, P. O. Impur, Impur, Nagaland 798615.
Good News for All (GNFA), 188; St. John's Church Road, Bangalore, Karnataka 560005.
Gospel Recordings Association, 7/4, Commissariat Road, Bangalore, Karnataka 560025.
Grace To India, 31/6 Gurunanak Nagar, Shanker Shet Road, Pune, Maharashtra 411042.
World Cassette Outreach of India, 90, Osborne Road, Bangalore, Karnataka 560042.

ITALY

Angelicum, Piazza Sant'Angelo 2, I-20121 Milano.
Antomianum Centre, Via Guinizeli 3, I-40125 Bologna, T: 391484.
Edizioni Paoline Musicali e Discografiche, Via 4 Novembre, I-0041 Albano Laziale, T: 930396.
Pro Civitate Christiana, Cittadella Cristiana, CP 46, I-06081 Assisi, T: 812234, 812410.

LIBERIA

Bible Teaching Cassette Program, ELWA, Box 192, Monrovia.

NETHERLANDS

Gooi en Sticht, Vaartweg 51, Postbus 17, Hilversum.

NEW ZEALAND

Gospel Recordings, New Zealand Council, 19 Coates Av, Orakei, Auckland 5.

PAKISTAN

Language Recordings International, 6 Empress Road, Lahore.

PAPUA NEW GUINEA

Gospel Recordings, Banz.

SINGAPORE

CNEC Tape Inspiration Lending Library, 134-136 Braddell Road, Singapore 3599191, T: 280-0833, F: 280-0078.
Gospel Recording Singapore Ltd., #04-11 Upper Serangoon Shopping Centre, 756 Upper Serangoon Road, Singapore 534626, T: 288-3179, F: 282-7902.

SOUTH AFRICA

Christian Video Network, 288 25th Av, Villieria, Pretoria 0186.

SPAIN

Central Catequística Salesiana, Alcala 164, Madrid 2.
Enciclopedia Sonora de Enseñanza, Claudio Coelho 32, Madrid 1.

TANZANIA

Bible Courses on Cassette, Msalato Centre (DCT) PO Box 15 Dodoma.

THAILAND

Voice of Peace, P.O. Box 131, Chieng Mai, T: 235654.

UNITED STATES OF AMERICA (USA)

Argus Communications, 3505 North Ashland, Chicago, IL 60657.
Audio Bible Studies, 6430 Sunset Blvd., Hollywood, CA 90028, T: (213)466-6121.
Audio Scripture Ministries, 760 Waverly Rd., Holland, MI 49423, T: 616-396-5291 1-800-333-1616, F: 616-396-5294, O: ASM-MI@xc.org, www.goshen.net/AudioScriptures
Audio Scriptures International, P.O. Box 28417, San Diego, CA 92198-8417, T: (619)673-0867.
Audiotracts, P.O. Box 500, Grand River, OH 44045, T: 800-627-5937, F: 216-951-3929, O: proclaim@harborcom.net.
Bible Translations on Tape, Inc., P.O. Box 2500, Cedar Hill, TX 75104, T: 214-291-1555.
Creative Sound Productions, 911 Diamond St, Los Angeles, CA 90012.
Gospel Recordings, 1605 E. Elizabeth St., Pasadena, CA 91104, T: (818) 398-2380.
Hosanna, 2421 Aztec Rd., NE, Albuquerque, NM 87107, T: 505-881-3321, F: 505-881-1681, O: 74212.3202@compuserve.com.
Inspirational Media, PO Box 6046, San Bernardino, CA 92412, T: 714-886-5224.
Kingdom Tapes, US Rt 6 East, PO Box 506, Mansfield, PA 16933, T: 800-334-1456.
Missionary Tapes, 1721 North Lake Av, Pasadena, CA 91104; 173 West Mountain View, Altadena, CA 91102.
Truth on Tape, P.O. Box 776, Shawnee Mission, KS 66201, T: 913-764-TAPE, F: 913-764-0700.

6
Audiovisual resources

Agencies, programs, offices, and centers specializing in the production or distribution of all kinds of audiovisual aids: slides, filmstrips, transparencies, posters, pictures, flannel boards, drawings, presentation books, puppets, flip charts, cartoons, videos, tapes, records, recordings, compact discs, microfilm, microfiche, computer programs, CD-ROMs; audiovisual training centers oriented towards education, catechesis, evangelization, renewal, or development. For those organizations dedicated to film and video resources alone, see CINEMA, FILM AND VIDEO; similarly for SOUND RECORDINGS and for COMPUTER SERVICES, SOFTWARE, AND RESOURCES. See also MEDIA AND COMMUNICATIONS.

ARGENTINA
Centro Audio-Visual Evangélico de la Argentina (CAVEA), O'Higgins 3162/68, Buenos Aires 29.
Centro Audio-Visual Evangélico Rioplatense, Camacua 282, Buenos Aires 6.
Instituto Católico de Estudios Sociales (ICES), Dpto Audiovisuales, Junin 1063, 1113 Buenos Aires, T: 54-1-84-98-08.

AUSTRIA
AV-Media Centre of the the Archdiocese of Vienna, Stephansplatz 4, 1011 Wien, T: 0222-515 52 361.
Bild und Ton, Stephansplatz 6, A-1010 Wien.
Media Centre of the the Lutheran and Reformed Protestant Church, Ungargasse 9/10, 1030 Wien, T: 0222-75 59 26.
SHB Film, Bundestaatliche Haupstelle für Lichtbild und Bildungsfilm, Sensengasse 3, A-1090 Wien 9, T: 432147, 432148.

BANGLADESH
Christian Communications Centre, Audio-visual Dept., 61/1 Subhas Bose Avenue, Luxmibazar, Dhaka-1100, T: 880-2-233 885, F: 880-2-259 168, O: Telex: 780-642420 DTB BJ.

BELGIUM
Les Médias Communautaires du Hainaut, Rue de l'Eglise, 10, 7280 Quévy (Genly), T: 32-65-6-85-73.
Média Animation, Avenue Rogier, 32, 1030 Bruxelles, T: 32-2-242-57-93.
Organisation Catholique Internationale du Cinéma et de l'Audiovisuel (OCIC), 8, rue de l'Orme, 1040 Bruxelles, T: 32-2-734-42-94, F: 32-2-734 32 07.
Uitgeverscentrum Patmos, Kapelsestraat 222, B-2080 Kapellen, T: 03-654320.

BENIN
Centre Audio-Visuel, BP 714, Cotonou.

BRAZIL
Centro Audio-Visual Evangélico (CAVE), CP 943, Campinas, São Paulo, SP.
Federación de Organizaciones para la Asistencia Social y Educacional (FASE), Rua Mena Barréto 161, Piso 3, Botafogo, Rio de Janeiro, GB, T: 2464559, 2433230.
Instituto de Sistemas Audio-Visuais, Pontificia Universidade Católica de Pôrto Alegre, Pôrto Alegre, RS.

BRITAIN (UK OF GB & NI)
Audio Visual Ministries, P.O. Box 1, Newcastle, Co Down BT33 0EP, T: 08-0396 75388, F: 08-0396 75388.
Vigilanti Audio-Visual Library, 15 Victoria Crescent, Glasgow G12.
Vision Screen Services, Riversdale House, North Farmbridge, Chelmsford, Essex CM3 6NT, T: Maldon 740755.

CAMEROON
Audio-Visual Committee, Fédération Evangélique, BP 1133, Yaoundé.
Centre des Techniques Audio-Visuelles de l'Eglise Presbytérienne Camerounaise, BP 187, Yaoundé.
Multi Media Centre, P. Dany Desmet et P. Henri Boisschot, B.P. 11840, Yaoundé, O: Tel et Fax: 237-23-14 62.

CANADA
Novalis, Université Saint Paul, 1 Rue Stewart, Ottawa 2, Ontario, T: 613-2360807.
Novalis, 3826 Rue Saint Hubert, Montréal 132, Québec, T: 514-844-7996.
Praise A V Publishing, R.R. #2, Woodville, ON K0M 2T0, T: 705-439-2751, F: 705-439-2779.
Villagers Communications, 26 Linden St., Toronto, ON M4Y 1V6, T: 416-323-3228, F: 416-323-1201.

CHILE
Centre for Audio-Visual Instruction via Satellite (CAVISAT), Almirante Barroso 24, Casilla de Correos 10445, Santiago de Chile, T: 68442.
Centro Audio Visual Evangélico (CAVE-CHILE), Casilla 9558, Santiago.

CHINA
Audio Visual Evangelism Committee, Metropole Bldg, 57 Peking Rd., 3/F, Kowloon, Hong Kong; 373 Ma Tam Wei Rd., Kowloon, T: K-678031.
Diocesan Audio-Visual Centre, 16, Caine Road, Hong Kong, T: 852-525-8021.

COLOMBIA
CAVECOL (CAVE-Colombia), Apdo Aéreo 51092, Bogotá.
Departamento de Medios de Communicación Social (DEMECOS), Carrera 9a No 13-33, Apdo 6290, Bogotá, T: 414096, 466866.
Instituto de Sistemas Audiovisuales (ISAV), Instituto Colombiano de Desarrollo Social, Calle 16 No 4-75, Apdo Aéreo 11966, Bogotá.

CROATIA
Signs of the Times Audio-Visual, Prilaz Gjure Dezelica 77, 41000 Zagreb.

ECUADOR
Peliculas Y Audiovisuales, Villalengua No. 320, Casilla 691, Quito, T: 241-550.
Producciones Asoma, Villalengua No. 278 y 10 de Agosto, Casilla 691, Quito, T: 241-550.

EGYPT
Christian Centre for Audio-Visual Services, P.O. Box 1422, Al Qahirah, T: 913590.

FRANCE
Association Catéchétique Nationale pour l'Audio-Visuel (ACNAV), 6 Av Vavin, F-75006 Paris, T: 01-633-2160.
Bonne Presse Audio-Visuel, 22 Cours Albert-Ier, F-75008 Paris.
Centrale d'Editions et de Diffusion de Matériel Audio-Visuel (CEDIMA), 59 bis Rue Bonaparte, F-75006 Paris, T: 01-633-8076.
Centre Audiovisuel Recherche et Communication (CREC), 19 Rue de Chavril, F-69 Ste-Foy-lès-Lyon, T: 78-256817.
Centre International de Documentation Audio-Visuelle (CIDAL), Maison de la Radio-Télévision Catholique, Centre d'Etudes, L'Hôtellerie, Firfol, F-14100 Lisieux, T: Firfol 7.
Editions CEFAG, 153 Rue de Grenelle, F-75007 Paris.
Editions des Nouvelles Images, F-45 Lombreuil.
Editions du Berger, 4 rue Cassette, F-75006 Paris.
Editions du Chalet, 8 rue Madame, F-75006 Paris, T: 01)222-4121.
Editions du Sénevé, 34 rue Le Brun, F-75013 Paris.
Editions Internationales de Radio-Télévision, 121 Av de Villiers, F-75017 Paris, T: 01-380-3056.
Encyclopédie Oecuménique Audio-Visuelle, 121 Av de Villiers, F-75017 Paris.
Filmens, 8A rue des Heros-Nogentais, F-94 Nogent-sur-Marne.
Société pour l'Evangélisation par des Moyens Audio-Visuels (SEMA), BP 232, Vichy (Allier), T: 70-983721.

GABON
Service Audiovisuel Ste Marie, B.P. 2146, Libreville, T: 241-76 08 90.

GERMANY
Christophorus Verlag, Freiburg/Breisgau.
OCIC Audio-Visual Service, Sprollstr 20, D-7407 Rottenburg/Neckar, T: 07472-791.
Ton Bild (TB), Benediktiner Missionare, D-8711 Münsterscwarzach, T: 09324-217.

GUAM
St. Paul Book & Media Center, 285 Farenholt Ave., Ste. 308, Tamuning, GU 96911.

INDIA
Audio Visual Centre, Tindivanam, Tamil Nadu 604002.
Audio Visual Service, Catholic Centre, St. Thomas Town, Bangalore, Karnataka 560084.
Audio-Visual Service, Catholic Centre, St Mary's Town, Bangalore 5, T: 50369.
Christian Association for Radio and Audio-Visual Service (CARAVS), 15 Civil Lines, Jabalpur, MP, 482001.
St Paul's Audio Visual Centre, St Patrick's Church Compound, 21 Museum Road, Banglore, Karnataka 560025.
St. Paul Book and Audio Visual Center, 9-1 79 A, Sardar Patel, Secunderabad, Andhra Pradesh 500003.
St. Paul Book and Audio Visual Centre, 7A/41, WEA Karolbagh, New Delhi 110005.
Tamilnadu Audio-Visual Education Service (TAVES), Catholic Centre Tindivanam, PO Tindivanam, South Arcot, Tamil Nadu.

INDONESIA
Archdiocese of Semarang, Jl. Ahmad Jazuli 2, Yogyakarta 55151, T: 62-274 47 05.
Sanggar Bina Tama, Jl. Residen Sudirman 3 Surabaya 60136, T: 62-31 4 59 88.

ITALY
Editrice Elle Di Ci, Centro Catechistico Salesiano, I-10096 Torino-Leimann.
Editrice La Scuola di Brescia, Sede Centrale e Officine Grafiche, Via Luiji Cadorna 11, I-25100 Brescia.

JAPAN
Audio-Visual Aids Commission (AVACO), NCCJ, 4-13 Shibuya 4-chome, Shibuya-ku, Tokyo 150.
Audio-Visual Department, Sophia University, 7 Kioi-cho, Chiyoda-ku, Tokyo, T: 032659211.
Christian Audio-Visual Center, 4-13 Shibuya 4-chome, Shibyua-ku, Tokyo 150.
Evangelical Alliance Mission Audio-Visual Education Dept (TEAM-AVED), 10-8 3-chome, Umegaoka, Setagaya-ku, Tokyo 154.
Jiyu Christian Crusade Beyond The Sunset, 25-22 2-chome, Tahara, Fukui-shi 910.
Kinki Christian Audio-Visual Center, Osaka Christian Center, 5151 Niemon-cho, Higashi-ku, Osaka 540.

KENYA
Maturity Audio Visuals, P.O. Box 14740, Nairobi.

LEBANON
Beirut Audio-Visual Center, Artois St, Ras Beirut, T: 01-340933.
Paraboles et Symbôles pour Aujourd'hui (PSA), BP 7002, Bayrut.

MALTA
Media Centre, Dept. Audiovisuals, National Road, Blata L-Bajda, HMR 02, T: 356-24-74-60, F: 356-24 35 08.

MAURITIUS
Studio d'Art Sonore, c/o Paroisse N-D de Lourdes, Route Royale, Rose Hill, T: 41279.

MEXICO
Centro Audio-Visual Evangélico (CAVE de México), Gerente, Apdo M-9223 z1, 1 Liverpool 65-206 zl, México, DF, T: 148352.
Sociedad Audio-Visual Educative Sistema Todd, Apdo 23, Cuautla, Morelos.

MYANMAR
Christian Audio-Visual Centre (CAVE), 82nd St, Mandalay.

NEW ZEALAND
Christian Audio-Visual Society of NZ, P.O. Box 8727, Auckland.

NIGER
Centre Audio-Visuel Mission Catholique, B.P. 10270, Niamey, T: 227-73 49 78.

NIGERIA
Churches Audio-Visual Centre, P.O. Box 67, Ilesha.

PERU
Cine para el Desarrollo (CIDE/COC), Paseo de Colón 378, Apdo 44, Lima.
Sonoviso del Perú, Oficina Nacional de Catequesis Lima.

PHILIPPINES
National Office of Mass Media Production Centre, 2307 Herran, Sta Ana, P.O. Box 2722, Manila, T: 597081.

PORTUGAL
ERLE-VIDA, Produções e Audio Visuais, Ld., Rua Dr. Azevedo Neves, Lote 4, Bairro da Mina - 2700 Amadora, T: 01-494 69 40, F: 01-493 32 66.

SINGAPORE
Catholic Audio Visual Centre, 222 Queen St., #03-01, Singapore 0718, T: 65-338 0330, F: 65-339 0694.

SOUTH KOREA
Audio Visual Catechetical Center, 56-12, 1-ga, Changch'ung-dong, Chung-gu, Seoul-shi, T: 02-279-7429.
Korea Audio Visual Commission (KAVCO), 136-46 Yon Ji-Dong Chong Ro-ku, Seoul 110.

SPAIN
Centro de Communicación Aplicada, C Muntaner 270, IV B, Barcelona 6.
Centro de Documentación y Educación en Comunicación Audiovisual, c/ Castellana, s/n, E-09001 Burgos, T: 34-47-056-65.

SRI LANKA
Cetechetical and Audio-Visual Centre, Archbishop's House, Colombo 8.

SWITZERLAND
Centrale Protestante des Moyens Audio-Visuels, 8 Chemin des Crettets, CH-1211 Conches, Genéve, T: 470525.
Flanellbilder für Sonntagschulen, Verlag A Tobler, CH-8038 Zürich, T: 051-452050.
Graphoson, 7 Av de Crousaz, CH-1010 Lausanne.
Sonolux (Vita Series), Centre pour Audio-Visuelles, Prés, Grand-Rue 34, BP 45, CH-100 Fribourg 2.

TAIWAN
Taiwan Christian Audio-Visual Association, 105 Chung Shan Pei Rd., Section 2, Taipei, T: 556755.

THAILAND
National Catholic Office for Cinema and Audio Visual Aids, 251/1 Suranari Rd., Nakhon Ratchasima.

UGANDA
Developmental Education and Christian Communication Academy 'DECCA', P.O. Box 3617, Kampala, T: 256-41-245597.

UNITED STATES OF AMERICA (USA)
Associated Photo, P.O. Box 14270, Cincinnati, OH 45250, T: 800-727-2580.
Audio Communications Center, Inc., 1027 Superior Ave., Cleveland, OH 44114, T: 216-696-6525, F: 216-696-6519.
Audiovisual Resources, Inc., 1650 Elm Hill Pk. Ste. 11, Nashville, TN 37210, T: 615-871-9100, F: 615-871-0825.
Avcom Systems, Inc., P.O. Box 977, Cutchogue, NY 11935, T: 516-734-5080.
Bible True Audio Visuals, 1441 S. Busse Rd., Mount Prospect, IL 60056, T: 708-593-1454.
Burlington Audio/Video Media, Inc., 106 Mott St., Oceanside, NY 11572, T: 800-331-3191, F: 516-678-8959, O: E-mail: burl2@ix.netcom.com.
CAM Audio, Inc., 2210 Executive Dr., Garland, TX 75041, T: 800-527-3458, F: 972-271-1555, O: E-mail: rob@camaudio.com, Web: www.camaudio.com.
Capital Communications Industries, Box 481, Olympia, WA 98507, T: 800-562-6006.
Christian A-V Specialists, 115 W. Mepessing, Lapeer, MI 48446, T: 313-664-1600.
Credence Cassettes, 115 E. Armour Blvd, Kansas City, MO 64111, T: 816-531-0538, F: 816-931-5082.
Eastco Audio Visual Corp., 91 Haller Ave, Buffalo, NY 14211, T: 800-365-8273.
Ewert's Photo A/V & Productions, 2090 Duane Ave, Santa Clara, CA 95054, T: 408-727-3686.
Faith Venture Visuals, Inc, PO Box 423-R, Lititz, PA 17543, T: 717-626-8503.
Frazier Audio/Video Inc., 4295 Cromwell Rd. Ste. #412, Chattanooga, TN 37421, T: 423-855-1465, F: 423-855-1351.
Higher Standard Praise Systems, 2890 U.S. Hwy. 98 W., Santa Rosa Beach, FL 32459, T: 850-267-1111, F: 850-267-1103, O: E-mail: hismessinger@juno.com.
Ikonographics, 50 High St., Croton-on-Huston, NY 10520, T: 800-944-1505.
Int'l Christian Supply, 4600 San Dario, Laredo, TX 78041, T: 512-722-6832.
J-D Audio Visual, 1713 E. Walnut, Pasadena, CA 91106, T: 818-792-6682.
Longs Electronics, 2630 S. 5th Ave., Irondale, AL 35210, T: 205-956-9341, F: 205-951-2506.
Lutheran Film Associates, 390 Park Ave., S., 7th Fl., New York, NY 10016-8803, T: 212-532-6350.
OCIC (The International Catholic Organization for Cinema and Audio-Visual), O: Web: www.catholic.org/orgs/ocic/ocic.html.
Puppet Pals, 100 Belhaven Dr, Los Gatos, CA 95032, T: 408-265-7904.
Redemptorist Pastoral Communications, Liguori Publications, 1 Liguori Dr., Liguori, MO 63057, T: 314-464-2500.
S & S Films & Tapes, 20 W 38th St, Suite 402, New York, NY 10018, T: 212-768-2197.

7
Bible and Scripture organizations

Bible societies; Bible and scripture publishing, Bible translation, translation training and assistance, Christian linguistic organizations and centers, Bible and scripture distribution and colportage (whether offered for free, at cost, or for profit), Bible text societies (literature, posters), Bible-reading organizations; the biblical apostolate. See also PUBLISHING for publishers specializing (but not exclusively) in Bible production, and BIBLE STUDY.

ALGERIA
Société Biblique en Afrique du Nord, Chaplain's Apt, Villa Gardner, 64 Av Souidani Bou djemna, Alger, T: 633996.

ANGOLA
Sociedad Bíblica, Av Combatentes 114-A, 4 Andar, Apt 10, CP 10238 BG, Luanda, T: 45023.

ARGENTINA
Argentine Bible Society, Rodriguez Pena 3903, 1650 San Martin, Buenos Aires, T: 54-0-1-754-8040, 1, F: 54-0-1-754-8042, O: Telex: 21833 answerbackjudd ar, Cable: Biblehouse.
Sociedad Bíblica Argentina, Casa de la Biblia, Tucumán 352-358, 1049 Buenos Aires, T: 328558, 325787, 323400.

ARMENIA
Bible Society in Armenia, M Khorenatsi 43, Yerevan, 375018, T: 374-2-151-648, F: 374-2-151-729, O: Telex: 243326 Krest SU.

AUSTRALIA
Bible Society in Australia, Memorial Bible House, Garema Place, P.O Box 507, Canberra City, ACT 2601, T: 485118, F: 6249-6168.
Bible Union of Australia, 2 Swindon Grove, McKinnon, SE 14, Victoria.
Catholic Biblical Association of Australia, Holy Cross Retreat, Serpells Rd., Templestowe, Victoria 3106.
Gideons International in Australia, 511 Kent, Sydney, NSW, T: 616470.
Pocket Testament League of Australia (PTL), 24 Westminster Av, Dee Why, NSW 2099, T: 988854.
Scripture Union Anzea Council (SU), 1 Lee St., Sydney, NSW 2000, T: 612598.
Wycliffe Bible Translators, 315 Collins St., Melbourne C1.

AUSTRIA
Bible Literature Associates, Oehnhausnerstrasse 35, Tribuswinkel 2512, T: 43-2252-80-314.
Scripture Union, Fach 237, A-5021 Salzburg.
Österreichische Bibelgesellschaft, Bibelhaus, Breite Gasse 8, A-1070 Wien, T: 938240.
Österreichische Katholische Bibelwerk (OKB), Stiftsplatz 8, A-3400 Klosterneuburg.

BANGLADESH
Bangladesh Bible Society, 38 Hatkhola Rd., P.O. Box 360, Ramna, Dacca 2, T: 246442.

BARBADOS
Bible Society in the East Caribbean, P.O. Box 36B, Brittons Hill, St. Michael.

BELGIUM
Europe Regional Centre, United Bible Societies, Rue de Trône 160, B-1050 Brussel, T: 02-647-0102.

Flemish Biblical Association, Sint-Michielsstraat 2, B-3000 Leuven.
Société Biblique Belge, Rue de Trône 160, B-1050 Brussel, T: 02-640-1575.

BELORUSSIA
Bible Society of the Republic of Belarus, 19 Chikladze St., 220093 Minsk, T: 375-172-503-998, F: 375-172-502-284.
International Bible Society - Belorus, 2 Puthep-rovodny per 11, Minsk, 22009.

BENIN
Bible Society in Benin, 03 BP 1101, Cotonou; Place d' Aidjedo - Lot 293, Parcelle X - Porte 126., T: 229-32-11-68, 229-33-51-21, F: 229-32-14-83, O: Telex: 1121/1110 ansback-cablx ctnou.
Société Biblique du Benin, BP 34, Cotonou.

BOLIVIA
Sociedad Bíblica en Bolivia, Bolivar 3685, Casilla 329, Cochabamba, T: 1745.

BOTSWANA
Bible Society in Botswana, P.O. Box 251, Gaborone.
Bible Society of Botswana, P.O. Box 231, Gaborone, Independence Ave., Pt. No. 883/4, T: 352 030.
Living Bible International-Botswana, PO Box 1085, Gaborone, Tlokweng, T: 356 453.

BRAZIL
ALEM-Associação Lingüística Evangélica Missionária, Cx. Postal 6101, Brasília DF-70749-970, T: 61-349-9395.
Bible Society of Brazil, Caixa Postal 1070 - Tamboré, 06460-990 Barueri, Sao Paulo; Av. Ceci, 740 - Tamboré, Barueri - SP 06460-120, T: 55-0-11-7295-9590, F: 55-0-11-7295-9591.
International Bible Society - Brazil, Rua do Mar, 20, São Paulo -SP, CEP 04654-060, T: 011 55-11-246-7046, F: 011 5511-246-7046.
Liga de Estudio Bíblicos, Rua Pio XII 205, São Paulo, SP.
Liga do Testamento de Bolso, Cx. Postal 19068, São Paulo-SP 04505-970, T: 11-241-5706, F: 11-241-5706.
Memorizadores da Bíblia Internacional, CP 7966, 01.000 São Paulo, SP.
Scripture Union, CP 907, 01.000 São Paulo, SP.
Sociedade Bíblica do Brasil, Edificio da Biblia, CP 10-2371, 70.000 Brasília, DF.

BRITAIN (UK OF GB & NI)
Bible Fellowship Union, 11 Lyncroft Gardens, Hounslow, Middlesex.
Bible Reading Fellowship (BRF), 148 Buckingham Palace Rd., London SW1, T: 01-730-9181/2.
Bible Society, Stonehill Green, Westlea, Swindon, Wilshire SN5 7DG, T: 0793-617381.
Bible Society, 27 Howard Street, Belfast BT1 6NB, T: 08-0232 226577.
Bible Spreading Union, 1 Donald Way, Gloucester Av., Chelmsford, Essex.
Bible Text Publicity Mission, Metropolitan Tabernacle, Elephant & Castle, London SE1 6SD.
British and Foreign Bible Society, Stonehill Green Westlea Swindon, Wiltshire SN5709, T: 44-0793-513713, F: 44-0793-512539, O: Telex: 44283 answerback-bibles gg, Cable: Testaments.
Catholic Biblical Association of GB, 24 Golden Square, London W1R 3PA; St. Joseph's College, Mill Hill, London NW7.
Christian Colportage Association, 53 High St., Cobham, Surrey; 3 Grange Rd., Egham.
Gideons International, Western House, George St., Lutterworth, Leics, LE17 4EE, T: 04555-4241.
Hibernian Bible Society, 24, Howard St., Belfast BT1 6NB, Northern Ireland, T: 26577.
International Bible Reading Association (IBRA), Robert Denholm House, Nutfield, Surrey, T: Nutfield Ridge 2411.
International Bible Society - United Kingdom, 192-194 High St., 2nd floor, Guildford, Surrey, England GU1 3HW, T: 011 44-1-483-306869, F: 011 44-1-483-306874.
National Bible Society of Scotland, 7 Hampton Terrace, Edinburgh EH12 5XU, T: 44-131-337-9701, F: 44-131-337-0641.
Pocket Testament League, 11718 Cosmos House, 6, Homesdale Road, Bromley, Kent BR2 9LZ, T: 44-81-460-5317.
Scripture Gift Mission, Inc., Radstock House, 3 Eccleston St., London SW1W 9LZ, T: 44-071-730-2155, F: 44-071-730-0240.
Scripture Union (SU), 47 Marylebone Lane, London W1M 6AX, T: 01-486-2561.
Scripture Union Council for GB & NI, 5 Wigmore St., London W1H OAD, T: 01-486-2561.
Society for Distributing the Holy Scriptures to the Jews, 1 Rectory Lane, Edgware, Middlesex HA8 7LF, T: 01-952-9892.
Society for Distributing Hebrew Scriptures, 1 Rectory Lane, Edgware HA8 7LF, Middlesex, T: 44-081-952-9892.
Trinitarian Bible Society, 217 Kingston Road, London SW19 3NN, T: 44-081-543-7857, F: 44-081-543-6370.
UBS World Service Center, UBS World Service Center, 7th Fl., Reading Bridge House, Reading RG1 8PJ, T: 44-0-118-9500200, F: 44-0-118-9500857, O: Cable: Bibles Reading.
United Bible Societies, World Service Center, Reading Bridge House, 7th Fl., Reading RG1 8PJ, T: 44-0-118-9500200, F: 44-0-118-9500857.
United Bible Societies, 146 Queen Victoria St., London EC4V 4BX, T: 01-248-4751.
United Bible Societies—Europe, 3 Gleneagles Court, Brighton Road, Crawley West Sussex RH10 6AD, T: 44-293-553821, F: 44-293-553839, O: E-mail: 100655.543@compuserve.com, Telex: 848541 (Answer-back UBS G G), Telegraphic: BIBLES READING.
Wycliffe Bible Translators, 5 Glenkeen Avenue, Newtownabbey, Co Antrim BT37 0PH, T: 08-0232 866649.

BURUNDI
Bible Society in Burundi, BP 2100, Bujumbura; Avenue Industrie No 2, T: 257-0-2-226188, F: 257-0-2-218810, O: Cable: Bibles.
International Bible Society - Francophone Africa, B.P. 2560 Bujumbura, T: 011 257-21-4347, F: 011 257-21-2933.

CAMBODIA
Bible Society in Cambodia, 72 Moha Vithei 9, P.O. Box 2133, Phnom Penh, T: 24319.

CAMEROON
Société Biblique, Maison de la Bible, Av Foch, BP 1133, Yaoundé, T: 224276.

CANADA
Bible Club Movement, Box 4052, Station D, Hamilton, Ontario.
Bible League of Canada, P.O. Box 5037, Burlington, ON L7R 3Y8, T: 905-319-9500, F: 905-319-0484, O: BibLeag@worldchat.com.
Bibles International (LBI Canada), #8 - 2320 King George Hwy., Surrey, BC v4A 5A5, T: 604-531-3955, F: 604-531-9168.
Canadian Bible Society, 10 Camforth Rd., Toronto, ON M4A 2S4, T: 416-757-4171, F: 416-757-3376, O: 1-800-465-BIBL(2425).
Canadian Home Bible League, 734 Wilson Av, Downsview, Ontario.
Catholic Bible Society, 5221 De Gaspé Av, Montréal 151, Québec.
Evangel Bible Translators and Ministries, Box 583, Station U, Toronto M8Z 5Y9, Ontario, T: 416-236-1433, F: 416-236-1433.
Gideons International in Canada, P.O. Box 3619, Guelph, ON N1H 7A2, T: 519-823-1140, F: 519-767-1913.
International Bible Society - Canada, P.O. Box 40590, 1295 North Service Road (L7P 4W1), Burlington, ON L7P 3N8, T: 905-319-3800, 800 530-0223, F: 905-319-3888.
Lutheran Bible Translators of Canada, Inc., Box 934, Kitchener, ON N2G 4E3, T: 519-742-3361, F: 519-742-5989.
Pocket Testament League, 11717 Box 3020, Station F, Scarborough M1W 2K0, T: 416-391-2366.
Scripture Gift Mission (Canada), Inc., #32-300 Steelcase Rd., W., Markham, ON L3R 2W2, T: 905-475-0521, F: 905-475-8643, O: Order line: 1-800-989-6532.
Scripture Union, 2100 Lawrence Ave, East, Scarborough, Ontario M1R 2Z7, T: 759-4181.
SOCABI - Société Catholique de la Bible, 7400 blvd St.,-Laurent, #519, Montréal, QC H2R 2Y1, T: 514-274-4381.
Société Biblique Canadienne, 625 rue Ste-Catherine Ouest, Montréal, QC H3R 1B7, T: 514-848-9777.
Trinitarian Bible Society (Canada), 39 Caldwell Cres., Brampton, ON L6W 1A2, T: 905-454-4688, F: 905-454-1788, O: E-mail: TBSC@mail.ica.net, Web: www.trinitarian.com.
World Home Bible League, Box 524, Station A, Weston M9N 3N3, Ontario, T: 416-741-2140.
Wycliffe Bible Translators of Canada, P.O. Box 3068, Station B, Calgary, AB T2M 4L6, T: 403-250-5411, F: 403-250-2623, O: E-mail: general_CAD_delivery@wycliffe.org, Web: www.wbtc.org.

CENTRAL AFRICAN REPUBLIC
Société Biblique, Foyer de la Bible, BP 1127, Bangui, T: 3035.

CHAD
Bible Society in Tchad, BP 1291, N'Djamena, T: 235-51-47-47, F: 235-52-14-98, O: Telex: 5279 answerback-capub m kd.
Scripture Union, BP 127, Ndjamena (Fort Lamy).

CHILE
Sociedad Bíblica Chilena, San Francisco 54, Casilla 784, Santiago, T: 383139.

CHINA
Amity Printing Co. Ltd., 190 East Waigang Rd., Dongshan, Jiangning, Nanjing, 211100, T: 86-0-25-2282418, F: 86-0-25-2282132.
Bible Society in Hong Kong, 67-71 Chatham Rd., Oriental Centre (9th Floor), Kowloon, Hong Kong.
China Bible Society, Bible House, 58 Hong Kong Rd., Shanghai.
Hong Kong Bible Society, 9th Fl., Oriental Centre, 67-71 Chatham Road S., Kowloon, T: 852-2368-5147,8, 852-2368-5149/50, F: 852-2311-0167, O: Cable: Testaments.
International Bible Society - Hong Kong, 660 Castle Peak Road 1/F, Blk B, Mackenny Centre, Lai Chi Kok, Kowloon, Hong Kong, T: 011 852-23-709978, F: 011 852-23-709993, O: Cable: CHIN-LIVBBL.
Scripture Gift Mission (SGM), P.O. Box 9152, Kowloon, Hong Kong, T: K-829844.
United Bible Societies (UBS), Suite 1-4, 22 Floor, Universal Trade Centre, 3-5A Arbuthnot Rd, Hong Kong, T: 852-2868-4282, F: 852-2868-4737, O: E-mail: wscfap@asiaonline.net.
Upper Room Chinese Publication Committee, 57 Peking Rd., 7th Floor, Kowloon, Hong Kong.

COLOMBIA
Liga Bíblica, A.A. 076623, Santafé de Bogotá, T: 1-295-5753, F: 1-295-6195.
Movimiento Bíblico Católico, Calle 36, No 64/A 10, Medellín.
Sociedad Bíblica Colombiana, Carrera 5a, No 15-95, Apdo Aéreo 4931, Nacional 159, Bogotá 1, DE, T: 814671, 814635, 417427.

CONGO-ZAIRE
Bible Society of Congo, P.O. Box 8911, Kinshasa; 17 av. Haut-Congo, T: 243-12-21229, 243-12-26831, F: 243-12-21351, O: Cable: Testaments.
Centre pour l'Apostolat Biblique, BP 19, Bandundu.
International Bible Society - Zaire, c/o B.P. 8911, Kinshasa, 17 Haut Zaire Avenue, Kinshasa.
Société Biblique du Zaire, 17 Av Strauch, BP 8911, Kinshasa-Est.

COSTA RICA
Sociedad Bíblica de Costa Rica, Apartado 5672 (1.000), San Jose; Plaza Viquez, contiguo al Cine Plaza = Calle 13, Avenida 22, T: 506-233-8892, 506-255-1195, 506-222-5726, F: 506-222-9192, O: Cable: Biblehouse.

CROATIA
International Bible Society - Croatia, 54106 Osijek, T: 011 385/54-162272, F: 011 385-54-162272.

CUBA
Bible Society in Cuba, Neptuno 629, La Habana 2.

CYPRUS
Cyprus Bible House, Isaackiou Komninou St 12-14, P.O. Box 1066, Levkosia (Nicosia), T: 62876.

CZECH REPUBLIC
Bible Work of the Czech Ecumenical Council of Churches, Jungmannova 9, 11513 Praha 1, Nové Mesto 22, T: 247101-2.
International Bible Society - Czech Republic, Malirska 6, Prague, T: 011 42-2-371-520, F: 011 42-2-371-520.

DENMARK
Danish Bible Society, Kobmagergade 67, DK-1150 Kobenhavn K, T: 01-127835.

DOMINICAN REPUBLIC
Sociedad Bíblica en República Dominicana, Calle El Conde 29, Box 1767, Santo Domingo, T: 682-9528.

ECUADOR
Acción Béblica Católica, Av América 1886, Apdo de Correos 3008, Quito.
Distribuidores, Ave. America No. 2183 y Sosaya.
Sociedad Bíblica Ecuatoriana, Ave. America No. 2183 y Aozaya, Casilla 731A, Quito, T: 551-996.
Sociedad Bíblica en el Ecuador, Av Eloy Alfaro 171, Casilla 1030, Quito, T: 527912, 527942.
Traducciones, Rio Coca No. 1734, Casilla 579A, Quito, T: 246-690.
Traducciones, Voz Andes No. 186, Casilla 5185, Quito, T: 240-450.

EGYPT
Bible Society of Egypt, P.O. Box 724, Cairo 11511; 70 Gomhouria St., T: 20-0-2-588-5125, F: 20-0-2-588-5132, O: Cable: Biblehouse
E-mail: 74637.3655@compuserve.com.

EL SALVADOR
Bible Society in El Salvador, Apartado 1014, San Salvador; 41a Avenida Norte No 135, T: 503-260-6557, F: 503-260-6557, O: Cable: Biblehouse.

ETHIOPIA
Bible Society of Ethiopia, 39 Haile Selassie I Av, Box 30750, Adis Abeba, T: 122033.
International Bible Society - Northeast Africa, P.O. Box 100810, Adis Ababa, F: 011 251-1-513310.

FIJI
Bible Society in the South Pacific, P.O. Box 5173, Raiwaqa, Suva; 8-10 Luke St., Nabua, Suva, Fiji Islands, T: 679-383988, F: 679-370219.

FINLAND
Finnish Bible Society, Yliopistonkatu 29a, 20100 Turku 10, T: 921-17622.

FRANCE
Association Catholique Française Etude de la Bible (ACFEB), 21 Rue d'Assas, F-75006 Paris.
Equipes de Recherche Biblique, 47 Rue de Clichy, F-75009 Paris, T: 874-1508.
French Bible Society, BP 47, 95400 Villiers-le-Bel; Avenue des Erables, T: 33-1-3994-5051, F: 33-1-3990-5351.

GABON
Société Biblique au Caméroun-Gabon, Librarie Evangélique, BP 171, Oyem.

GERMANY
Bibel Mission: Slawische Evangeliums Vereinigung, Dirkenstrasse 2-5, Postfach 1173, Grosswallstadt W-8751, T: 49-6022-25271, F: 49-6022-25260.
Bibellesebund in Deutschland (Scripture Union), In der Fleute 33, Postfach 220152, D-5600 Wuppertal 22, T: 02121-602306.
Deutsche Bibelgesellschaft (German Bible Society), P.O. Box 81 03 40, 70520 Stuttgart; Balinger Str 31, Möhringen, 70567 Stuttgart, T: 49-0-711-7181-0, F: 49-0-711-7181-126, O: Cable: Bibelhaus.
Evangelisches Bibelwerk in der Bundesrepublik, Hauptstätterstr 51, Postfach 755, D-700 Stuttgart 1, T: 0711-247341.
Hungarian Scripture Mission, Ganzenstrasse 13, Stuttgart 80 W-7000, T: 49-711-717660, F: 49-711-712141.
International Bible Society - Germany, D-46284 Dorsten, T: 011 49-2362-68403, F: 011 49-2362-699233.
Katholisches Bibelwerk, Silberburgstr 121, D-7000 Stuttgart 1.
Ökumenische Arbeitsgemeinschaft für Bibellsen, Fröbelstr 26, D-843 Gütersloh.
United Bible Societies, 11787 Balingerstrasse 31, Stuttgart 80 W-7000; P.O. Box 810340, T: 49-711-72-00-30.
World Catholic Federation for the Biblical Apostolate (WCFBA), Silberburgstr 121A, D-700 Stuttgart 1.
Wycliff-Bibelübersetzer, Pf 603, 57295 Burbach; Deutscher Zweig, Siegenweg 32, D-5909 Burbach-Holzhausen, T: 02736-3027.

GHANA
Bible Society of Ghana, P.O. Box 761, Accra; High Street, James Town, T: 233-21-663803, F: 233-21-669613, O: Telex: 3033 answerback-bthó gh, Cable: Testaments.
International Bible Society - Ghana, P.O. Box 89, Legon; Scripture Union Centenary House, House No. C485/2, Castle Road Ridge Accra, T: 011 233-21-220698, F: 011 233-21-665555, O: Telex: 2390 ANM GH.

GREECE
Bible Society in Greece, 3 Nicodemou St., Athínai 118, T: 322800, 3241324.

GUAM
Bible Society in Micronesia, P.O. Box 338, Agaña, Guam 96910.

GUATEMALA
Sociedad Bíblica en Guatemala (Bible Society in Guatemala), Apartado Postal 1369 01901, Guatemala City, 01003; 3a Avenida 21-48, Zona 3, T: 502-0-251-1885, 502-0-221-2321/2, F: 502-0-221-2323, O: Cable: Biblehouse.

HAITI
La Chambre Haute, Office de l'Edition Française, Petit Goave.
Maison Haitïenne de la Bible/Haiti Bible House, 138 Rue du Centre, BP 253, Port-au-Prince, T: 22655.

HONDURAS
Sociedad Bíblica en Honduras, Av Jerez No 1011, Apdo Postal 747, Tegucigalpa, DF, T: 226555.

HUNGARY
Hungarian Bible Council, Abonyi utca 21, Pf 5, H-1440 Budapest XIV, T: 227870, 227879.

ICELAND
Icelandic Bible Society, P. O. Box 243, 121 Reykjavik; Hallgrímskirkja, Skólavörduhaed, T: 354-510-1040, F: 354-510-1045, O: Cable: Testaments.

INDIA
Bible and Tract Society of India, Watch Tower 458, Old Khandala Road, Lonavala, Maharashtra 410401.
Bible Center, 17'C' Govind Nagar, Ambala Cantt., Ambala, Haryana 134001.
Bible Centre Ministry, BCM 23/187, AZAD Apartment - 2, Settelite Road, Ahmedabad, Gujarat 380015.
Bible Friends Mission, Saikar, Hala Hali P. O., Kamalpur, Tripura 799286.
Bible Society of India, 206 Mahatma Gandhi Rd., Bangalore 560 001, T: 91-0-80-5584617-4336, F: 91-0-80-5584701, O: Cable: Testaments.
Bible Warehouse, A. 35-36 Commercial Complex, Dr. Mukerjee Nagar, Delhi 110009.
Bibles for India, 4221 Richmond NW, Grand Rapids, MI 49504, T: 616-453-8855.
Catholic Biblical Association of India (CBAI), St. Johns Regional Seminary, Ramanthapur Uppal P.O., Hyderabad 39 (AP).
Central India Bible Literature, KIV Group Industries, Sun Mill Compound, Lower Parel, Bombay, Maharashtra 400013.
Gideons International, Secunderabad Camp, 5-103, Post Office Road, Fathenagar, Hyderabad, Andhra Pradesh 500018.
India Bible League, Post Box 719, Greams Road P. O., Madras, Tamil Nadu 600006.
India Bible Literature, Nagarampalem, Guntur, Andhra Pradesh 522004.
India Bible Mission, 28-18-7, Sharon Office, Jampet, Near Market, Rajahmundry, Andhra Pradesh 533103.
India Bible Publishers, C-3/10, DDA Flats, East Of Kailash, New Delhi 110065.
Indian Bible Translators, Civil Aerodrome Road, Peelamedu, Coimbatore, Tamil Nadu 641014.
International Bible Society India, Logos Building, Kalathilpady, Kottayam 6866010, Kerala, T: 011 91-481-570269, F: 011 91-481-572269.
KJV Bible Society, P.B. No:4003, 24/25, 1st B. Main Road, Vijaynagar II Stage, Bangalore, Karnataka 560040.
Living Bible India, 4, Circus Market Place, Calcutta, West Bengal 700017.
National Biblical Centre of India (NBCLC), Mary Town, Post Bag No 577, Bangalore 560005.
Orient Bible Translators, Jeyaraj Illam, Checkanurani, Madurai, Tamil Nadu 625514.
Pearlcity Bible Centre, 77/2 A. V. E. Road, Opp. Holy Cross Convent, Tuticorin, Tamil Nadu 628002.
Peniel Bible Bhavan, Veloor P. O., Kottayam, Kerala 686003.
Pocket Testament League, 19 Raj Niwas Marg, New Delhi 110054.
Scripture Gift Mission, 18/1 Cubbon Road, Bangalore, Karnataka 560001.
United Bible Societies, 44, Logos Street, Kammanahalli Main Rd. , M. S. Nagar P. O., Bangalore, Karnataka 560033.
World Bible Translation Centre India, No:36, 3rd Cross, Hutchins Road, St. Thomas Town, Bangalore, Karnataka 560084.

INDONESIA
Bible Society, Kotak Pos 29, Jogjakarta.
Indonesian Bible Society, P.O. Box 1255/JKT, Jakarta 10012; Jalan Salemba Raya 12, T: 62-0-21-314-2890, F: 62-0-21-310-1061, O: Telex: 44376/46241 ansback-astra jkt, Cable: Aklitab.
Lembaga Alkitab Indonesia (LAI), Jl. Salemba Raya 12, Jakarta 10012, T: 021-332890, F: 021-3101061.

IRAN

Bible Society in Iran, 7/3-4 Av, Gharam-ol-Saltaneh, P.O. Box 1412, Tehran, T: 311987.

IRAQ

Bible Society in Iraq, 321/1 Rashid St., P.O. Box 337, Baghdad, T: 80969.

IRELAND

Hibernian Bible Society, 41 Dawson St., Dublin 2; Howard St., Belfast BT1 6NB.
Irish Catholic Biblical Association, Maynooth College.
National Bible Society of Ireland, 41 Dawson St., Dublin 2, T: 353-0-1-6773272, F: 353-0-1-6710040.

ISRAEL

Bible Society in Israel, Bible Society Bookshop, P.O. Box 19627, Jerusalem.
World Jewish Bible Society, P.O. Box 024, Jerusalem, T: 62536.

ITALY

Abbey of St Jerome for Revision of the Vulgate, Via di Torre Rossa 21, I-00165, T: 620173.
Bible Society in Italy, Via IV Novembre 107, 00187 Rome, T: 39-0-6-699-41416, F: 39-0-6-699-41702.
Bible Society in Italy, Libreria Sacre Scritture, Via Dell'Umilta 33, I-00187 Roma, T: 6794254.
Casa della Bibbia, Via Balbi 132r, Genova, T: 67948.
Commission for the New Vulgate, Palazzo San Calisto, Piazza San Calisto 16, I-00153 Roma.
Missione Evangelica per l'Europa (Gideons International), Via Terme di Traiano 5, Roma.
World Catholic Federation for the Biblical Apostolate, Via del Plebiscito 107-2, I-00186 Roma; 3 Piazza Madonna delle Salette, I-00152 Roma, T: 686675.

IVORY COAST

Maison de la Bible, BP 2559, Abidjan.
Société Biblique en Côte d'Ivoire, 30 Blvd Angoulevant, P.O. Box 1529, Abidjan, T: 229366.

JAMAICA

Bible Society of the West Indies, P.O. Box 146, Kingston 10; 24 Hagley Park Plaza, T: 1-809-926-2772, 1-809-960-3123, F: 1-809-926-0334, O: Cable: Biblehouse.

JAPAN

Gideons International in Japan, Toko Bldg., 12 Tomoe-cho, Shiba Nishikubo, Minato-ku, Tokyo 105.
Japan Bible Society, 5-1, 4-chome, Ginza, Chuoku, Kyobashi, P.O. Box 6, Tokyo, T: 03-567-1986.
Oriental Bible Study Fellowship, 3704 Karuizawa-machi, Nagano-ken 389-01.
Upper Room, 7-5, 4-chome, Sakai Mianami-cho, Musashino-shi, Tokyo 180.

JORDAN

Bible Society in Jordan, P.O. Box 627, Amman.

KAZAKHSTAN

Bible Society in Kazakhstan, Republic of Kazakhstan, 480018, Almaty, ul Raskova 35, T: 7-3272-34-93-15, 7-3272-44-63-86, F: 7-3272-34-93-15.

KENYA

Bible Society of Kenya, P. O. Box 72983, Nairobi; Mfangano St., T: 254-0-2-225587, 254-0-2-227338, F: 254-0-2-213226, O: Cable: Biblia.
Bible Translation and Literacy, Box 44456, Nairobi.
International Bible Society - Africa, Box 60595, Nairobi, T: 011 254-2-722681, F: 011 254-2-710583, O: Telex: 963-22018 LBIA.
International Bible Society - East Africa Anglophone, Box 60595, Nairobi, T: 011 254-2-711365/722919, F: 011 254-2-722943, O: Telex: 963-22018 LBIA.
Living Bibles International, East Africa Office, Box 60596, Nairobi, T: 722335, 722916, O: Telex: 22018 LBI-A.

LAOS

American Bible Society, P.O. Vientane.

LEBANON

Bible Society in Lebanon, P.O. Box 11-747, Beirut, T: 961-1-400-915, F: 961-1483-847.

LESOTHO

Bible Society in Lesotho, Machache House, P.O. Box 660, Maseru.

LIBERIA

Bible Society in Liberia, Bible House, Tubman Blvd, Sinkor, P.O. Box 39, Monrovia, T: 26175, 26024.

LUXEMBOURG

Swiss Bible Society, Av de la Liberté 6, Luxembourg, T: 22193.

MADAGASCAR

Malagasy Bible Society, BP 922, 12 Lalana Rabehevitra, Tananarive; 12 Lalana Rabehevitra, T: 261-0-2-25135, F: 33-1-5301-3234, O: Cable: Bible BP 922.

MALAWI

Bible Society in Malawi, Victoria Av, P.O. Box 740, Blantyre, T: 35443-4.

MALAYSIA

International Bible Society - (Malaysia) Publications Sdn Bhd, P.O. Box S-36, Sentul, 51700 Kuala Lumpur, T: 011 60-3-4410637, F: 011 60-3-4412795.

MALTA

Malta Bible Society, Dar il-Bibbja, 62 Triq il-Miratur, Floriana VLT 16, T: 356-220318, F: 356-236621.

MAURITIUS

Bible Society in Mauritius, 39b Royal Rd., Eau Coulée, Curepipe Rd., T: 42157.

MEXICO

Americas Regional Centre, United Bible Societies, Liverpool No 65, Apdo 61-281, México 6, DF, T: 905-592-1577.
Bible Society of Mexico, Apartado 6-820, Delegacón Cuauhtémoc, 06600 Mexico DF; Liverpool 65, Juárez, T: 52-0-5-533-5570, F: 52-0-5-525-0912, O: Cable: Biblehouse.
Gedeones (Gideons), México, DF, T: 242107.
Instituto de Santa Escritura, Universidad 1700, México 21, DF.
Instituto Penzotti, Liverpool 65, Apdo 6-820, México 6, DF, T: 288801.
International Bible Society - Mexico, Apartado M-9293, Mexico D.F. 06000; Calle Cusco #650, Colonia Linda Vista Mexico D.F. 07300, T: 011 52-5 586-0661, F: 011 52/5 586-0661.
Liga del Testamento de Bolsillo (PTL), Apdo 29, Cd Satélite, Edo de México, T: 602460.
Misión Biblica Católica, Apdo Postal 157, Naucalpan de Juarez.
Sociedad Biblica Católica de México, Mos, México.
Sociedad Biblica de México, Liverpool No 65, Apdo 6-820, México 6, DF, T: 905-533-5570.
Wycliffe Bible Translators, Apdo 22-067, México 22, DF.

MOLDAVIA

Bible Society in Moldova, 2059, Str Teodoroiu 33A, Chisinau, T: 373-2-49-80-85, 373-2-57-08-16, F: 373-2-57-07-35.

MOROCCO

Maison de la Bible, 5 bd Tahar el Alaoui, El-Dar-el-Beida (Casablanca).

MOZAMBIQUE

Casa da Biblia, Av Eduardo Mondlane 2678, Maputo, T: 28698.

MYANMAR

Bible Society of Myanmar, 262 Sule Pagoda Rd., PB 106, Rangoon, T: 14638.

NAMIBIA

Bible Society in Namibia, P.O. Box 1926, Windhoek 9000; Independence Ave 428, T: 09-264-0-61-235090, F: 09-264-0-61-228663, O: Cable: Evangelium.

NEPAL

International Bible Society Nepal, P.O. Box No. 907, Naxal Sanugaucher, Kathmandu, T: 011 977-1-470630, F: 011 977-1-220161.

NETHERLANDS

Bijbel Kiosk Vereniging, Hoofdstraat 55, Driebergen, T: 03438-3455.
Catholic Bible Society, Baroniestraat 43, Postbox 27, Boxtel.
Christian Esperanto International Association, Slijpkruikweg 17, Ede (Gld), T: 08380-11223.
International Bible Society - Holland, P.O. Box 41, NI-2760 AA Zevenhuizen; Nijverheidsstraat 13, NI-2751 GR Moerkapelle, T: 011 31-1793-3132, F: 011 31-1793-2975.
Netherlands Bible Society, P.O. Box 620, 2003 RP Haarlem; Zijlweg 198, 2015 CK Haarlem, T: 31-0-23-514-61-46, F: 31-0-23-534-20-95, O: Telex: 26401 answerback-intx nl, Cable: Bijbelhuis.
Society for Spreading the Holy Scriptures, NZ Kolk 19-21, Amsterdam.
Summer Institute of Linguistics, Postbus 195, Driebergen 3970 AD, T: 31-3405-672-79.
Wycliffe Bible Translators Europe Area, NL-Maanderpoort 45, 6711 AC Ede, T: 31-343-520-946, F: 31-318-653-445, O: E-mail: 100111.3306@compuserve.com.

NETHERLANDS ANTILLES

Antillean Bible Society, Maishiweg 39, P.O. Box 786, Willemstad, Curaçao, T: 93922.
Bible Society in Netherlands Antilles, Postbus 3466, Gaitoweg #3, Curacao; Gaitoweg #3, T: 599-0-9-7376711, 599-0-9-7376659, F: 599-0-9-7372387.

NEW ZEALAND

Bible Society in New Zealand, Private Bag 27901, Marion Square, Wellington 6037; Bible House, 144 Tory St., T: 64-0-4-384-4119, F: 64-0-4-385-4624, O: Cable: Testaments.
Scripture Gift Mission, NZ Council, 427 Queen St., Auckland 1.
Scripture Union (SU), P.O. Box 760, Wellington, T: 50782.
Summer Institute of Linguistics, P.O. Box 10, Featherston, T: 0-6-308-9555, F: 0-6-308-9257, O: E-mail: 100035.2014@compuserve.com.
Wycliffe Bible Translations, P.O. Box 10, Featherston, T: 0-6-308-9555, F: 0-6-308-9257, O: E-mail: 100035.2014@compuserve.com.

NICARAGUA

Sociedad Bíblica en Nicaragua, (**Bible Society in Nicaragua)**, Apartado 2597, Managua; Puente Larreynaga 25 mts. al Oeste, T: 505-2-442594, F: 505-2-498040.

NIGERIA

Bible Society of Nigeria, P.O. Box 68, Apapa, Lagos State; 18 Wharf Rd., T: 234-0-1-5876471, F: 234-0-1-873860, O: Telex: 23620 answerback-ng, Cable: Testaments.
International Bible Society - Nigeria, P.O. Box 1960, 110 Agbani Road, Enugu, T: 234/42-332317, O: Telex: 9005-51487 LBNIG NG.
Living Bibles International, Nigeria Regional Office, P.O. Box 1960, Enugu, T: 042-330648, O: Telex: 51487 LBINIG.
Scripture Union Africa Council, P.O. Box 643, Jos, T: 2109.

NORWAY

Norwegian Bible Society, Munchs Gate 2, P.O. Box 7062, Homansbyen, Oslo 3, T: 02-203477.

PAKISTAN

Pakistan Bible Society, Bible House, Anarkali, Lahore 54000, T: 92-42-7220978, 92-42-7238537, F: 92-42-7238587, O: Telex: 47513 answerback-murad pk, Cable: Testaments Lahore.

PANAMA

Sociedad Bíblica de Panamá, Calle Santa Rita, Urb Obarrio, Edif Valladolid, Apdo 3316, Panamá 4, T: 611510..

PAPUA NEW GUINEA

Bible Society of Papua New Guinea, Bible House, Hubert Murray Highway, Koke, P.O. Box 18, Port Moresby, T: 54668.

PARAGUAY

Sociedad Bíblica en el Paraguay, (**Paraguayan Bible Society)**, P. O. Box 167, Asunción; 15 de Agosto 652 casi Haedo, T: 595-0-21-448975, 595-0-21-494855, F: 595-0-21-448975, O: Cable: Bibliaroga.

PERU

Sociedad Bíblica Peruana, (**Peruvian Bible Society)**, Apartado 14-0295, Lima 14; Avda. Petit Thouars 991,, T: 51-0-14-336389, 51-0-14-335815, F: 51-0-14-336389, O: Cable: Biblehouse. Av Petit Thouars 991, Santa Beatriz, Apdo 448, Lima 1, T: 319555, 317247.

PHILIPPINES

Asia Pacific Regional Centre, United Bible Societies, P.O. Box 1730, Makati, Rizal 3117, T: 504470.
Christian Translators Fellowship, Box 4174, Manila.
International Bible Society - Philippines, P.O. Box 1079, QCPO Main, 1100 Quezon City, Metro Manila; #4-B Maningning St., Skatnua Village, Quezon City, T: 011 63-2921-5651, F: 011 63-2922-8363.
Philippine Bible Society, P.O. Box 755 or 2557, Manila; 890 United Nations Ave., Ernita, T: 63-0-2-525-94-01, 63-0-2-5215785/5215801, F: 63-0-2-521-5788, O: Telex: 27564 answerback-bible ph, Cable: Biblehouse.

POLAND

British and Foreign Bible Society, Nowy Swiat 40, 00-363 Warszawa, T: 264986.

PORTUGAL

Associação Wycliffe Para a Tradução da Bíblia, Travessa Francisco dos Santos, 2 - 6. Dt., 2745 Queluz; Apartado 59, 2746 Queluz Codex, T: 01-439 20 19, F: 01-439 20 21.
Liga do Testamento de Bolso, Praceta Filinto Elisio, 10 - 4. B, 2795 Carnaxide, T: 01-418 41 71.
OS Gideões Internacionais, Av. D. Pedro V, 13 - 2. Esq., 2795 Linda-a-Velha, T: 01-419 23 34.
Sociedade Bíblica de Portugal, Rua José Estêvão, 4-B, 1150 Lisboa, T: 01-54 55 34, F: 01-352 77 93.
União Bíblica, Vivenda A Candeia, Morelinho - 2710 Sintra; Apartado 167 Cova da Piedade, 2806 Alamada Codex, T: 01-924 23 40, F: 01-274 62 94.

PUERTO RICO

Bible Society of Puerto Rico, P.O. Box 2548, Bayamón PR 00960; Carrera #167 Km. 14.7, Barrio Buena Vista, T: 0-787-799-4460, F: 1-787-797-2065, O: Cable: Biblehouse.

RUSSIA

Bibel Mission: Slawische Evangeliums Vereinigung, Mitischi 101000, Moscowskaya Oblast, T: 7-095-582-95-18, F: 7-095-582-95-18.
Bible Society in Russia, P.O. Box 403, 51/14 Pyatnitskaya, 109017 Moscow, T: 7-095-233-1638, 7-095-953-4524, 7-095-232-2912, F: 7-095-230-2902, O: Web: www.bsr.ru.
Russian-German-American Bible Mission, 11737 P.O. Box 65, Mytischi 141000, Moskovskaya oblast, T: 7-095-582-9518.

RWANDA

Société Biblique au Rwanda, BP 788 Kigali.

SIERRA LEONE

Bible Society in Sierra Leone, 37a Westmoreland St., P.O. Box 1169, Freetown, T: 4644.

SINGAPORE

Bible Society of Singapore, Bible House, 7 Armenian St. #01-01, Singapore 179932, T: 65-337-3222, F: 65-337-3036, O: Cable: Testaments, Email: leesa@bible.org.sg.
Singapore Camp of Gideons International, c/o #02-03 Brightway Industrial Building, Singapore 348741; 3 Lorong Bakar Batu, T: 743-0555, 743-5000, F: 747-4022.
Wycliffe Bible Translators (S) Ltd., Block 507 #01-398 Upper Floor, Bishan Street 11, Singapore 470507, T: 258-1792, F: 353-8642.

SLOVAKIA

International Bible Society - Slovakia, P.O. Box 51, 81499 Bratislava I; Tovarenska 14, 81571 Bratislava, Slovenska republika, T: 011 42-7-383416, F: 011 42-7-383170.
Slovak Bible Society, Partizanska cesta 3, Banska Bystrica, 974 01, T: 421-0-88-45063, F: 421-0-88-45063.

SOUTH AFRICA

Bible Society of South Africa, P. O. Box 6215, Roggebaai, Cape Town 8012; 15 Anton Anreith Arcade, Cape Town 8001, T: 27-0-21-212040, F: 27-0-21-419-4846, O: Cable: Testaments.
Bibles for Africa, PO Box 72277, Lynwood Ridge 0040, Pretoria, T: 012-47-6122.
Gideons in South Africa, PO Box 11263, Hatfield 0028, 39 Nicholson St, Baileys, Muckleneuk, Pretoria, T: 012-46-7241, F: 012-46-8552.
SGM International, PO Box 1187, Johannesburg 2000, Merbrook Hse, 123, Commissioner St. Jhburg, T: 011-336-9563, F: 011-336-9564.
Word for the World, PO Box 2255, White River 1240, 12 Wm Lynn St, White River, T: 01311-3-3452.
Wycliffe Bible Translators, PO Box 548, Kempton Park 1620, 54 Pienaar Ave, 1619 Kempton Park Ext, T: 011-975-8631, F: 011-975-8632.

SOUTH KOREA

Korean Bible Society, 84-9, 2-Ka, Chongo, IPO Box 1030, Soul, T: 742792.
Korean Catholic Biblical Commission, 100 Kwa Seo Dong, P.O. Box 2, Suwon.

SPAIN

Bible Society of Spain, Calle Santa Engracia 133, 28003 Madrid, T: 34-1442-5898, F: 34-1858-3703.
Gedeones Internacionales, 28045 P° de Las Delicias, Madrid, T: 539-52-96.
Liga del Testamento de Bolsillo, **Pocket Testament League**, 08004 Elcano, 34 bis., Barcelona, T: 441-40-82, F: 329-85-03.
PROEL-Wycliffe España, Apdo. 472, Torrejón de Ardoz, 28850 Madrid, T: 1-656-0726, F: 1-675-6130, O: E-mail: 100272.151@compuserve.com.
Unión de Colportores, 08224 Galvani, 115, Terrassa, Barcelona.
Wycliffe Bible Translators, Wycliffe (Traductores de la Biblia), Apartado 472, Torrejón de Ardoz, 28850 Madrid, T: 91 6560726, F: 91 6756130.

SRI LANKA

Sri Lanka Bible Society, Bible House, 293 Galle Rd, Colombo 3, T: 24483.
International Bible Society Lanka Gte Ltd., 120 A. Dharmapala, Mawath, Colombo-7, T: 011 94-1-786851, F: 011 94-1-786851.

SUDAN

Bible Society in the Sudan, Bible House, Sharia Khalifia 15, P.O. Box 532, Al Khurtum, T: 80023.

SURINAME

Suriname Bible Society, P. O. Box 2154 Zd, Paramaribo Zuid; Gravenstraat 39,, T: 597-474338-476274, F: 597-476274, O: Cable: Biblehouse.

SWAZILAND

Bible Society, P.O. Box 550, Manzini.

SWEDEN

Institute for Bible Translation,(IBT) Box 20100, Stockholm S-10460, T: 08-93-07-10, F: 08-93-92-45.O: E-mail: gustafsson@ibtla.org.
International Bible Society - Sweden, Fabriksgatan 19, Box 205, S-524 23 Herrljunga, T: 011 46-513-11930, F: 011 46-513-11501, O: Telex: 854-35420 LIVING s.
Living Bibles International, P.O. Box 205, Herrljunga 524-23, T: 46-513-11930, F: 46-513-11501.
Russian Bible Society, Box 1801, Orebro 701 18.
Swedish Bible Society, Box 1235, SE - 751 41 Uppsala; Bangardsgatan 4, T: 46-0-18-186330, F: 46-0-18-186331.
Wycliffe Bible Translators, Anggatan 24, Box 394, Örebro.

SWITZERLAND

Bibellesebund (Scripture Union), Römerstr 151, CH-8404 Winterthur, T: 052-274801.
Geneva Bible Society, Le Roc, Cologny, Genève.
Heimstätte der Vereinigten Bibelgruppen, CH-6612 Moscia-Ascona/TI.
Ligue pour la Lecture de la Bible (Scripture Union), Route de Berne 90, CH-1010 Lausanne, T: 021-321538.
Portfolio for Biblical Studies, World Council of Churches, 150 Route de Ferney, CH-1211, Genève 20.
Scripture Union European Council, Talackerstr 15, CH-8404 Winterthur, T: 052-274801.
Scripture Union International Council, Talackerstr 15, CH-8404 Winterthur, T: 052-274801.
Swiss Bible Society, P. O. Box , 2501 Biel/Bienne; Waffengasse/Rue des Armes 20, T: 41-0-32322-3858, F: 41-0-32323-3957, O: Cable: Swissbible.
Swiss Catholic Biblical Works, Ch de Bethléem 76, CH-1700 Fribourg.
Vereinigte Bibelgruppen in Schule, Universität & Beruf (VBG), Angelrain 6, CH-5600 Lenzburg, T: 064-514440.
Wycliffe Bibelübersetzer, Postfach 2, Basel 1.

SYRIA

Bible Society in Syria, Pennsylvania St., P.O. Box 1305, Halab.

TAIWAN

Bible Society in the Republic of China, 116 Jen Ai Rd, Sec 3, P.O. Box 3401, Taipei, T: 02-7718445, 7719258.
Reformation Translation Fellowship, Nanking East Rd, Sec 4, Lane 144, Alley 8, No 1, Taipei, T: 711278.

TANZANIA

Bible Society of Tanzania, P.O. Box 175, Dodoma, T: 229.

THAILAND

Bible Society in Thailand and Laos, 150 North Sathorn Rd, Bangkok 5, T: 2342271.
Catholic Biblical Commission of Thailand, P.O. Box 4, Khon Kaen.
International Bible Society - East Asia, Box 4-58, 50/3 Soi Aree 4 (North), Paholyothin Road, Bangkok 10400, T: 011 66-2-279-3848, F: 011 66-2-617-0428.
Thailand Bible Society, P. O. Box 4-198, Bangkok

10400; 319/52-55 Vibhawadi Rangsit Rd., T: 66-0-2-279-8341-4, F: 66-0-2-616-0517.

TOGO

Bible Society in Togo (Biblia Habobo), BP 3014, Lomé; 38 Ave de la Libération, T: 228-210836-212864, F: 228-218042, O: Telex: 5300 answer-back-public tg, Cable: Socibible.

TURKEY

British and Foreign Bible Society, Istiklal Cad No 481, Geyoglu, P.O. Box 186 (Merkez), Istanbul, T: 278100.

UGANDA

Bible Society of Uganda, P. O. Box 3621, Kampala; Plot 38 Bombo Rd., T: 256-0-41-251165,66,67, O: Telex: 62050 answerback-ensure u, Cable: Baibuli.

UKRAINE

Ukrainian Bible Society, Baumana Str 18, 252190 Kyiv, T: 380-44-442-6544, F: 380-44-442-6544.

UNITED STATES OF AMERICA (USA)

American Bible Society, 1865 Broadway, New York, NY 10023, T: 212-408-1200, F: 212-408-1512, O: E-mail: mmaus@americanbible.org, Web: www.americanbible.org.
American Biblical Encyclopedia Society, 210 West 91st, New York, NY 10024, T: 212-SU7-4085.
American Scripture Gift Mission, 1211 Arch St., Philadelphia, PA 19107; 441 Bourse Bldg. 5th St. at Ludlow, T: 215-561-3232.
Association for Final Advance of Scripture Translation (FAST), 1740 Westminster Drive, Denton, TX 76201, T: 817-387-9531.
B. B. Kirkbridge Bible Co., K of P Bldg., Indianapolis, IN 46200.
Bethany Bible Collection, O: Web: www.cdrom.com/pub/bible.
Bible Gateway Online Bible and Concordance, O: Web: bible.gospelcom.net.
Bible League, 16801 Van Dam Rd., South Holland, IL 60473, T: 708-331-2094, F: 708-331-7172, O: E-mail: BibleLeague@xc.org, Web: www.bibleleague.org.
Bible Literature International (BLI), P.O. Box 477, Columbus, OH 43216-0477, T: 614-267-3116, F: 614-267-7110, O: E-mail: 70712.1412@compuserve.c, Web site: www.bli.org.
Bible Memory Association, 6341 Easton, Box 516, Wellston Station, St. Louis, MO 63112, T: 314-726-1323.
Bible Translations on Tape, P.O. Box 2500, Orange, CA 92669, T: 714-558-1027.
Bibles for All, 721 North Tejon, Colorado Springs, CO 80901, T: 719-473-8888.
Bibles for India, 4221 Richmond N.W., Grand Rapids, MI 49504.
Bibles for Russia, Inc., 15354 Old Hickory Blvd., Nashville, TN 37211, T: 615-834-6171, F: 615-834-4463.
Bibles for the World, P. O. Box 805, Wheaton, IL 60189; 116 N. Schmale Rd., Carol Stream, IL 60188, T: 630-668-7733, F: 630-668-6348.
Chicago Bible Society, 104 S. Michigan Ave., #520, Chicago, IL 60603, T: 312-236-2169.
Christian Literature and Bible Center, 1006 Oak Cliff Dr., Toccoa, GA 30577.
Church Bible Studies, 191 Mayhew Way, Walnut Creek, CA 94596, T: 415-937-7286.
Eastern European Bible Mission, P.O. Box 110, Colorado Springs, CO 80901; 721 N. Tejon, 80903, T: 719-577-4450, F: 719-577-4453.
Evangel Bible Translators, P.O. Box 669, Rockwal, TX 75087, T: 972-722-2140, F: 972-722-1721.
Foundation Publication/American Bible Sales, P. O. Box 5158, Fullerton, CA 92838, T: 800-535-5131, F: 714-535-2164, O: Web: www.gospelcom.net/lockman.
Gideons Int'l, 2900 Lebanon Rd, Nashville, TN 37214, T: 615-883-8533.
International Bible Society, 1820 Jet Stream Dr., Colorado Springs, CO 80921-3696; P.O. Box 62970, Colorado Springs, CO 80962, T: 719-488-9200, F: 719-488-3840, O: E-mail: IBS@gospelcom.net.
International Bible Society - Native American and Rural Communities Ministry, P.O. Box 205, Plummer, ID 883851; Route 1, Box 156 E, T: 208-686-1176, F: 208-686-1817.
International Bible Society - Promotion and Distribution Office, 609 Brickell Avenue, Miami, FL 33131, T: 305-372-8909.
International Conference of Evangelical Bible Societies (ICEBS), 172 Lexington Ave., New York, NY 10016, T: 212-213-5454, F: 212-779-1076.
Living Bibles International, P.O. Box 725, Wheaton, IL 60189, T: 708-510-9500.
Lockman Foundation, 900 S. Euclid St., La Habra, CA 90631, T: 714-879-3055, F: 714-879-3058, O: Web: www.gospelcom.net/lockman, E-mail: lockman@gospelcom.net.
Lutheran Bible Translators, P.O. Box 2050, Aurora, IL 60507-2050, T: 630-897-0660, F: 630-897-3567, O: E-mail: LBT@xc.org, Web: www.lbt.org.
Messengers of Christ-Lutheran Bible Translators, Inc., 303 N. Lake St., Box 2050, Aurora, IL 60507-2050, T: 708-897-0660.
Million Testaments Campaigns, 1505 Race St., Philadelphia, PA 19102, T: 215-567-1747.
Miniscriptures, 336 E. Forest Ave., Wheaton, IL 60187, T: 630-668-1293.
Miracle Press Bible Memory Association, P.O. Box 516, Wellston Station, St. Louis, MO 63112.
National Bible Translators (Unreached Peoples Missions, UPM), 8717 N. Dana, Portland, OR 97203, T: 503-289-6764.
National Center for the Catholic Biblical Apostolate, USCC, 1312 Massachusetts Ave., N.W., Washington, DC 20005.
New York Bible Society, 172 Lexington, New York, NY 10016, T: 212-213-5454, F: 212-779-1076.
Pioneer Bible Translators, 7500 W. Camp Wisdom Rd., Dallas, TX 75236; P.O. Box 381030, Duncanville, TX 75130-1030, T: 972-709-2460, F: 972-709-2463, O: E-mail: PBT@xc.org.
Pocket Testament League, P.O. Box 800, Lititz, PA 17543; 11 Toll Gate Road, T: 717-626-1919, F: 717-626-5553, O: E-mail: TPTL@prolog.net.
Reformation Translations Fellowship, 1031 Glenrose Ave., Phoenix, AZ 85014.
Russian Bible Society, Inc., P.O. Box 6068, Asheville, NC 28816, T: 704-252-8896, F: 704-252-8891.
Scripture Gift Mission—USA, 11746 P.O. Box 250, Willow Street, PA 17584, T: 717-464-3010, O: E-mail: SGMUS@Juno.com.
Scripture Union (SU), 1716 Spruce St., Philadelphia, PA 19103, T: K16-1160.
Summer Institute of Linguistics, 7500 W. Camp Wisdom Road, Dallas, TX 75236, T: 214-709-2400, O: Web: www.sil.org/.
United Bible Societies, World Service Center, 1865 Broadway, New York, NY 10023, T: 212-581-7400.
World Bible Translation Center, P.O. Box 820648, Fort Worth, TX 76182, T: 817-595-1664, F: 817-589-7013, O: Web: 71033.200@compuserve.com.
World Home Bible League, 16801 Van Dam Road, South Holland, IL 60473, T: 312-331-2094.
World Literature Crusade, 20232 Sunburst Ave., Chatsworth, CA 91311.
Wycliffe Bible Translators Int'l, 7500 W. Camp Wisdom Rd., Dallas, TX 75236, T: 972-709-2400, F: 972-709-3350, O: Web: www.wycliffe.org.
Wycliffe Bible Translators, P.O. Box 2727, Huntington Beach, CA 92647, T: 714-969-4600.

URUGUAY

Sociedad Bíblica del Uruguay,(Bible Society in Uruguay), Calle Constituyente 1540, Codigo Postal, 11200 Montevideo, T: 598-2-401-0034, 598-2-408-8985, F: 598-2-409-6915, O: Cable: Biblehouse.

VENEZUELA

Sociedad Bíblica de Venezuela, Av Jose A Páez, Qta Casa de la Biblia, El Paraiso, Apdo 222, Caracas 101, DF, T: 427784, 410928.

VIET NAM

Bible Society in Vietnam, 5 Suong nguyet Anh, P.O. Box 716, Saigon 2, T: 23802.

YUGOSLAVIA

British & Foreign Bible Society in Yugoslavia, Marsala Tita 26, 11000 Beograd, T: 011-656779.

ZAMBIA

Bible Society of Zambia, P. O. Box 31316, Lusaka; 1566 Freedom Way North-end, T: 260-0-1-229586, F: 260-0-1-229586, O: Telex: 40079 answerback-bsoz za, Cable: Testaments.

ZIMBABWE

Bible Society in Rhodesia, Bible House, 99 Victoria St., P.O. Box 1081, Salisbury C1, T: 24583.
International Bible Society - Central Africa Anglophone, P.O. Box 2219, 98, Victoria Street, Harare, T: 011 263/4-702942, F: 011 263/4-702942, O: Telex: 987-24786 WORVIS ZW.

8
Bible schools and colleges

Definitions: Centers for the training of Christian workers, with (a) curricula especially centered on the Bible and basic Christian instruction, (b) programs both for the lay and ordained ministry, or especially for lay workers, (c) often less concern for academic accreditation, (d) courses of study that may result in the granting of degrees, but often of certificates or diplomas, (e) generally lower academic requirements for entry, (f) generally lower or simpler level of study than theological colleges or seminaries.

9
Bible study

Centers for the training of Christian workers, with (a) curricula especially centered on the Bible and basic Christian instruction, (b) programs both for the lay and ordained ministry, or especially for lay workers, (c) often less concern for academic accreditation, (d) courses of study that may result in the granting of degrees, but often of certificates or diplomas, (e) generally lower academic requirements for entry, (f) generally lower or simpler level of study than theological colleges or seminaries.

BRITAIN (UK OF GB & NI)

Scriptural Knowledge Institute, 7 Cotham Park, Bristol, Avon B56 6DA.
Scripture Union, St. Lukes Church, Devereux Drive, Watford, Herts WD1 3DD, T: 44-923-819537, F: 44-923-819-537.
Scripture Union International Council, 207-209 Queensway, Bletchley, Milton Keynes, Bucks MK2 2EB, T: 1908-856188, F: 1908-856060, O: E-mail: emmanuelo@scriptureunion.
Scripture Union Online, O: Web: www.scripture.org.uk/.

CANADA

Ligue pour la Lecture de la Bible, 1701 rue Belleville, Lemoyne, QC J4P 3M2, T: 514-465-0445.
Navigators' Resource Centre, 490 Dutton Dr., Unit B-12, Waterloo, ON N2L 6H7, T: 519-747-9460, F: 519-747-9460, O: 1-800-839-4769.
On-Line Bible Bible Research Software, Timnathserah, Inc., R.R. 2, West Montrose, Ontario, N0B 2V0, T: 519-664-2266.
Precept Ministries, Inc., 3-236 Braneida Lane, PO Box 3717, Brantford, ON N3T 6H2, T: 519-751-7600, F: 519-751-7666.
Scripture Union, 1885 Clements Rd., Unit 226, Pickering, ON L1W 3V4, T: 905-427-4947, F: 905-427-0334.

COLOMBIA

Instituto Teológico-Pastoral-Itepal, Transversal 67 No. 173-71, Apartado Aéreo 253353, Santafé de Bogotá, T: 57-1-677-65-21 y 670-64-16, F: 57-1-671-40-04, O: E-mail: SITEPAL@ITECS5.TELECOM-CO.NET.

GERMANY

Scripture Union—Germany, Breslauerstrasse 2, Marienheide 3 5277, T: 49-2264-6236, F: 49-2264-7155.
World Catholic Federation for the Biblical Apostolate, Mittelstrasse 12, P.O. Box 601, D-7000, Stuttgart 1.

INDIA

Association for Biblical Studies, C/o. Allahabad Bible Seminary, 60/64, Stanley Road, , Uttar Pradesh 211002.
Bible Study Help, Takha, Shahganj P. O., Uttar Pradesh 222101.
Indian Biblical Students Association, Behind E. D. Hospital, Tilak Nagar, Mysore, Karnataka 570021.
Mysore Karnataka Bible Students Association, 1945/2 Akbar Road, Mandi Mohalla, Mysore, Karnataka 570021.

IRELAND

Bible Centred Ministries, Shalom, Roseberry, Newbridge, Co Kildare, T: 353-045 33166.

ISRAEL

Ecole Biblique et Archeologique Française, P.O. Box 19053, 91190 Jérusalem; 6 route de Naplouse, 91190 Jérusalem, T: 02-894468, F: 02-282567.
Institut Biblique Pontifical, P.O. Box 497, 91004 Jérusalem; Paul-Emile Botta str. 3, 91004 Jérusalem, T: 02-252843, F: 02-241203.
Instituto Español Bíblico y Arqueológico, P.O. Box 19030, 91190 Jérusalem; C/Sheyáh, 91190 Jérusalem, T: 02-28-27-82.
Jesuites (Institut biblique pontifical), P.O. Box 497, 91004 Jérusalem, T: 02-252843, F: 02-241203.
Studium Biblicum Franciscanum, P.O. Box 19424, 91193 Jérusalem, T: 02-282936, F: 02-894519, O: Also tel: 02-280271 or 894516,7,8.

JAPAN

Salvation Army Training College, 1-39-5 Wada Suginami-ku, Tokyo 166, T: 03-3381-9837/8.

PORTUGAL

Núcleo Interdenominacional de Fé Reformada, Rua Lucinda Simões, 7, 1900 Lisboa, T: 01-813 75 48.

SINGAPORE

Walk Thru the Bible Ministries, c/o 141 Middle Road, GSM Building #05-05, Singapore 188976, T: 334-3689, F: 566-3236.

SOUTH AFRICA

Bethel Series, 02 Denham Place, Westville 3630, T: 031-262-7623.
Protestant Association of SA, PO Box 13068, Mowbray 7705, Cape Town, T: 021-685-3015, F: 021-685-2618.
Scripture Union (SU), PO Box 291, Rondebosch, 7799, Cape Town, T: 021-686-8594, F: 021-685-5861.
Walk Thru the Bible, PO Box 48690, Roosevelt Park, 2129, 150 John Adamson Dr, Roosevelt Park, Johannesburg, T: 011-782-4222, F: 011-782-3977.

UNITED STATES OF AMERICA (USA)

AMG International, 6815 Shallowford Rd., Chattanooga, TN 37421, T: 1-800-251-7206, F: 1-800-267-7171, O: E-mail: vinces@amginternational.org.
Andrew Wommack Ministries, Inc., P.O. Box 3333, Colorado Springs, CO 80934; 1 Pawnee Avenue, 80829, Manitou Springs, CO, T: 719-685-5421.
Answers in Genesis, O: Web: www.christiananswers.net/.
Ask God Expert System Bible Software, Business Solutions, 15395 S.E. 30th Place, Suite 310, Bellevue, WA 98007, T: 206-644-2015.
Back to the Bible, O: Web: www.gospelcom.net/gcn-ministries.html.
Basic English Commentaries Project, O: Web: www.aiai.ed.ac.uk/-jkk/wycliffe-words.html.
Beacon Technology, Inc., P.O. Box 49788, Colorado Springs, CO 80949, T: 719-594-4884, F: 719-594-4271.
Bible Basics International, P.O. Box 340508, Tampa, FL 33694, T: 813-920-2264, F: 813-920-2265.
Bible Library on CD-ROM Software, Ellis Enterprises, Inc., 4205 McAuley Blvd., Suite 315, Oklahoma City, OK 73120, T: 405-749-0273.
Bible Memory Association, P.O. Box 12000, Ringgold, LA 71068, T: 318-894-9154.
Bible Pathway Ministries, P.O. Box 1515, Murfreesboro, TN 37129, T: 615-896-4243, F: 615-893-1744.
Bible Scholar Bible Research Software, Scholar Systems, Inc., 2313 Overland, Boise, ID 83705, T: 208-343-6262, F: 208-336-3844.
Bible Search Bible Study Software, SOGWAP Company, 115 Bellmont Road, Decature, IN 46733, T: 219-724-3900.
Bible Study Fellowship, 19001 Blanco Rd., San Antonio, TX 78258, T: 512-492-4676.
BookMaster Bible Study Software, Koala-T Software/BookMaster Bible, 3255 Wing St., Suite 220, San Diego, CA 92110, T: 800-642-1144.
Catholic Biblical Association of America, Catholic University of America, Washington, D.C. 20064.
CDWord Interactive Bible Library CD-ROM Bible Research Software, Two Lincoln Centre, 5420 LBJ Freeway LB7, Dallas, TX 75240-6215, T: 214-770-2414.
Christian Answers, O: Web: www.christiananswers.net/q-eden/edn-t004.html.
Christian Reconstruction, O: Web: www.geocities.com/Athens/6207.
Cross Line Ministries, O: Web: www.innerx.net/non-profit/crossline/ Also E-mail: crossline@innerx.net.
Diadem, T: 800-491-3820, F: 714-569-1471, O: Web: www.diadempro.com.
Discovery Interactive Bible Study, PO Box 3566, Grand Rapids, MI 49501, T: 800-283-8333.
Folow Up Ministries, Inc., P.O. Box 2514, Castro Valley, CA 94546, T: 415-881-1178.
Franklin KJV or RSV Handheld/Pocket Electronic Bible Hardware, Franklin Computer Corp. 122 Burrs Rd., Mt. Holly, NJ 08060, T: 609-261-4800, F: 609-261-1631.
Freedom in Christ, 491 E. Lambert Rd., La Habra, CA 90631, T: 310-691-9128, F: 310-691-4035.
GodSpeed Bible Research Software, Kingdom Age Software, 3368 Governor Dr., Suite F-197, San Diego, CA 92122, T: 619-586-1082.
GramCord Scholar, Greek NT Grammatical Research software plus Greek & Hebrew Multilingual Word Processor Software, GramCord Institute, 2065 Half Day Road, Deerfield, IL 60015, T: 312-223-3242.
Greek Literature from Homer through AD600 on CD-ROM, TLG Project-Thesaurus Linguae Graecae, 156 Humanities Hall, University of California, Irvine, CA 92717, T: 714-856-7031, F: 714-856-6404.
Int'l Video Bible Lessons, 3117 N Seventh St, W Monroe, LA 71291, T: 318-396-6265.
International Bible Institute, P.O. Box 2473, Santa Fe Springs, CA 90670, T: 562-907-5555, F: 562-907-5552.
International Institute for Christian Studies, P.O. Box 12147, Overland Park, KS 66282, T: 913-642-1166, F: 913-642-1280, O: E-mail: 73754.1132@compuserve.com, Web: www.goshen.net/iics.
LaserGreek, LaserHebrew, Fonts for over 200 other Languages in Postscript, Macintosh, Linguist's Software, Inc., P.O. Box 580, Edmunds, WA 98020-0580, T: 206-775-1130.
Laymen's National Bible Association, Inc., 1865 Broadway, New York, NY 10023, T: 212-408-1390, F: 212-408-1448.
Lexegete Lectionary Sermon Exegetical Helps Software, Tischrede Software, P.O. Box 9594, North Dartmouth, MA 02747, T: 617-994-7907.
Lightsource Online, O: Web: www.lightsource.net.
Ligonier Ministries, Inc., P.O. Box 547500, Orlando, FL 32854, T: 407-834-1633.
Living Water Teaching International, P.O. Box 1190, Caddo Mills, TX 75135, T: 903-527-4160, F: 903-527-2134, O: E-mail: LWTcaddo@aol.com.
Logos Biblical Training International, P.O. Box 409, Fresno, CA 93708-0409, T: 209-453-9377, F: 209-453-9379.
MegaWord Gold & MegaWord Silver Bible Research Software, Parachlete Software, 1000 E. 14th St., Suite 425, Plano, TX 75074, T: 214-578-8185, 800-825-6342.
Multi-Lingual Scholar Business/Academic Multilingual Word Processing Software, Gamma Productions, Inc., 710 Wilshire Blvd., Suite 609, Santa Monica, CA 90401, T: 213-394-8622, F: 213-395-4214.
NASB Computer Bible Study Software, Foundation Press Publications, Inc., 1121 N. Kraemer Place, P.O. Box 6439, Anaheim, CA 92806, T: 714-630-6450.
Nehemiah Ministries, O: Web: www.gospelcom.net/nehemiah/.
NIV On-Line Bible Research Software, ROCKware Publishing, 57 Bater Road, Coldwater, MI 49036, T: 517-369-6035.
Pastor's Story File & Parables, Auto-Illustrator, Saratoga Press, 14200 Victor Place, Saratoga, CA 95070, T: 408-867-4211.
Precept Ministries, Inc., P.O. Box 182218, Chattanooga, TN 37422, T: 423-892-6814, F: 423-499-0357.
Precepts International, 6201 S. Military Trail, Lake Worth, FL 33463-7288, O: E-mail: precepts@gospelcom.net.
Quaker Theological Discussion Group, Box 471-A, RD 4, Easton, PA 19042-9803.
Rainbow Studies International, P.O. Box 759, El Reno, OK 73036, T: 800-242-5348, F: 405-262-7599.
Reasons to Believe (RTB), O: Web: www.reasons.org/reasons.
Renewing Your Mind with R.C. Sproul, P.O. Box 547500, Orlando, FL 32854, T: 407-333-4244, F: 407-333-4233.
Scripture Union (USA), P.O. Box 6720, Wayne, PA 19087, T: 610-341-0830, F: 610-341-0836, O: E-mail: BlankSU@aol.com, Web: www.scripture.org.uk/.
Stephen Olford Center for Biblical Preaching, 3999 Germantown Rd., S., Memphis, TN 38125, T: 901-757-7977, F: 901-757-1372, O: E-mail: olford@memphisonline.cocom.
Theomatics, O: Web: www.theomatics.com/.
Village Schools of the Bible (VSB), O: Web: www.gospelcom.net/vsb/.

Walk Thru the Bible Ministries, 4201 N. Peachtree Rd., Atlanta, GA 30341; P.O. Box 80587, Atlanta, GA 30366, T: 770-458-9300, F: 770-454-9313, O: Web: 74721.1535@compuserve.com, www.walkthru.com.
Word of Grace Outreach, O: Web: www.gisco.net/ptp.wordgo.htm.
WORD Processor, VerseSearch Bible Research Software, Bible Research Systems, 2013 Wells Branch Parkway, #304, Austin, TX 78728, T: 512-251-7541.
WordSearch Bible Study Software & InfoSearch Sermon Illustration & Current Christian Abstracts & Music Hymnal DataBase Management & Quarterly Subscription Software, NavPress, P.O. Box 6000, Colorado Springs, CO 80934, T: 800-888-9898, 719-598-1212.

10
Broadcasting

Organizations and centers (excluding radio/TV stations) specializing in Christian religious broadcasting, radio/TV programming, program production, production of related materials, spots; production studios, program distribution agencies (distributing to stations) or agents; radio/TV training schools and centers; educational or mass-education radio and TV; agencies specializing in radio/TV technology or technical services; satellite agencies, specialists, or organizations; listeners' and viewers' associations. See also BROADCAST STATIONS and MEDIA AND COMMUNICATIONS.

ANDORRA
Emissions Catholiques, Radio Andorra, BP 1, Andorra, T: 61-20100, 20104.

ARGENTINA
Comisión de Radio y Televisión, Convención Evangélica Bautista, Tucuman 358, 6K, Buenos Aires.
Escuela de Radio y Televisión Educativa, Don Bosco 4002, Buenos Aires, T: 869352.
Escuela Superior de Periodismo, Dpto Radio y Television, Moreno 1921, 1094 Buenos Aires, T: 54-1-48-22-05.
Ministerio de la Canción, Sarandi 65, Buenos Aires.
Stacy Recording Studio, Venezuela 452, Buenos Aires.

AUSTRALIA
Adventist Media Centre, 150 Fox Valley Road, Wahroonga, N.S.W. 2076, T: 487-1844.
Australian Broadcasting Commission, Box 487, Sydney, NSW.
Back to the Bible Broadcast, P.O. Box 45, Stanmore, NSW 2048.
Bible Radio and Television Productions, Box 412F, GPO, Brisbane, Queensland.
Catholic Radio and TV, 143 A'Beckett St., Melbourne, Victoria 3000.
Christian Broadcasting Association, Managing Dir, 420 Lyons Rd., Five Dock, Sydney, NSW 2046.
Christian Radio Missionary Fellowship, Box 5271, GPO, Sydney, NSW, T: 417283.
Christian TV Association of South Australia, P.O. Box 518E, GPO, Adelaide, South Australia.
Gospel Broadcasters, 4 Verona St., Box Hill, Victoria.
Hillsongs Australia/Hills Christian Life Centre, P.O. Box 195, Castle Hill NSW 2154, Sydney, T: 011-62-2-96347633, F: 011-61-2-98994591.
National Catholic Radio/TV Centre, 50 Abbotsford Rd., Homebush, NSW 2140, T: 760459, 760450.

AUSTRIA
Gospel Radio, Sonnbergstrasse 3, 2380 Perchtoldsdorf, Postfach 150, 1235 Wien, T: 0222/86 25 20.
Katholische Funk- und Fernsehschau, Singerstr 7-IV-II, A-1010 Wien, T: 524386.
Trans World Radio—East European Office, P.O. Box 141, Vienna 1235, T: 43-222-865-2055, F: 43-222-865-2093.
World Satellite Communication, Markstrasse 24, Hard 6971, T: 43-055-78-39-93.

BAHAMAS
Bahamas Catholic Hour, P.O. Box 187, Nassau.
Bahamas Faith Ministries International, P.O. Box N 9583, Nassau, T: 809-341-6444, F: 809-361-2260.

BELGIUM
Catholic Radio and Television Network (CRTN), Rue de l'Association, 32, 1000 Bruxelles, T: 32-2-217-75-70, F: 32-2-219 83 72.
Centre de documentation pour la Télévision (CTV), Avenue des Nerviens, 3, 1040 Bruxelles, T: 32-2-735-22-77.
Emissions Missionnaires, Radio de Belgigue, Hemelaerstraat 58, Sint-Niklaas, Wass.
Global Gospel Broadcasters, 69 Av Devoer, Vilvorde.
Hoger Sint-Lucasinstituut, Paleizenstraat 70, B-1030 Brussels.
Katholiek Televisie en Radio Centrum (KTRC), De Vergniestraat 41, B-1050 Brussel, T: 02-489008.
Radio Télévision Catholique Belge, Rue au Bois, 365b, 150 Bruxelles, T: 32-2-762 82 51, F: 32-2-762 09 00.
TELEPRO (Magazine Catholique de Télévision), 31, rue Saint-Remacle, 4800 Verviers, T: 32-87-31-61-75, F: 32-87-31 35 37.
UNDA-Association Catholique Internationale pour la Radio et la Télévision (Intl,Catholic Association for Radio and TV), 12 rue de l'Orme, B-1040 Brussels, T: 32-2-734-97-08, F: 32-2-734-70-18, O: Cable: Undabrussels, 051-91-8023 GEONET G.

BENIN
Emissions Catholiques, Paroisse St-Michel, Cotonou.
La Voic de l'Esperance, BP 2153, Cotonou, R.P..

BOLIVIA
Southern Cross Studio, Cajon 1408, La Paz.

BOTSWANA
Catholic Broadcasting Secretary, P.O. Box 13, Gaberone.
Church Radio Council, P.O. Box 213, Gaborone, Radio Botswana, T: 352 541.

BRAZIL
CEPROL, Rua de Mocoa 3.758, São Paulo, SP.
Evangelical Studio, Missão Presbiteriana, CP 435, Recife, Pernambuco.
Fundação Centro Brasileiro de TV Educativa, Av NSenhora de Copacabana 928.10.0, Rio de Janeiro, GB.
Fundação Educativa Padre Landel de Moura, Av Bastian 285, Pôrto Alegre, RS.
HCJB-A Voz dos Andes, Cx. Postal 16050, Curitiba-PR 81611-970, T: 41-376-3553, F: 41-376-3553, O: E-mail: hcjb-br@kanopus.com.br.
Luz Para o Caminho, Cx. Postal 130, Campinas-SP 13001-970, T: 19-241-4133, F: 19-241-4133, O: E-mail: lpc@dglnet.com.br.
Movimento de Educação de Base (MEB), Rua São Clemente 385, Rio de Janeiro ZC-02-GB.
Pia Societá San Paolo, CP 7200, São Paulo, SP.
Radio-TV Difusora Portoalegrense, Rua Delfino Riet 183, Pôrto Alegre, Rio Grande do Sul.
Rádio Clube de Ribeirão Preto, Rua Barão do Amazonas 35, Riberão Preto, SP.
Rádio Trans Mundial, Cx. Postal 18300, São Paulo-SP 04699-970, T: 11-533-3533, F: 11-530-0857, O: E-mail: transmun@sp.dglnet.com.br.
VINDE-Visão Nacional de Evangelização, Cx. Postal 100.084, Niterói-RJ 24001-970, T: 21-611-0149, F: 21-611-0151, O: E-mail: vinde@ibm.net, WEB: www2.uol.com.br/vinde.

BRITAIN (UK OF GB & NI)
Assemblies of God Broadcasting Council, 106/114, Talbot St., Nottingham NG1 5GH, T: 44-0602-474525.
Back to the Bible Broadcast, 18 Upper Redlands Rd., Reading, Berkshire RG1 5JR, T: 64039.
Christian Communication, 646 Shore Road, Whiteabbey, Newtownabbey, Co Antrim BT37 0PR, T: 08-0232 853997.
Christian Newsletter, British Broadcasting Corporation, P.O. Box 76, Bush House, London.
Commission (Christian Programmers for Radio), 17 Millar Street, Belfast BT6 8JZ, T: 081-0232 830604.
Ecumenical Satellite Commission (ECUSAT), 7 St. James St., London SW1.
FEBA Radio, Ivy Arch Road, Worthing, West Sussex, BN14 8BX, T: 0903-237281, O: Prayer Line: 0903-237284.
Fellowship of European Broadcasters, 23 The Service Rd., Potters Bar, Hertfordshire EN6 1QA, T: 011-44-1707-649910, F: 011-44-1707-662653.
Gospel Broadcasting System, 67 Meadow Lane, Liverpool L12 5EB, T: 051-226-4212.
Gospel by Radio to Spain, c/o Temple Gothard & Co, 33/34 Chancery Lane, London SC2A 1EN, T: 01-836-7932.
HCJB, 131 Grattan Road, Bradford, West Yorkshire BD1 2H5, T: 44-274-721-810, F: 44-274-741-302.
Hour of Revival Association, 13 Lismore Rd, Eastbourne, East Sussex, T: 25231.
IBA Panel of Religious Advisors, Independent Broadcasting Authority, 70 Brompton Rd., London SW3 1EY.
IBRA Radio, The Haven, Barnfield Av., Luton, Bedfordshire.
Newbold College Production Studio, Bracknell, Berks RG12 5AN.
Radio Committee, Evangelical Missionary Alliance, 19 Draycott Place, London SW3 2SJ, T: 01-581-0051.
Radio ELWA (SIM), 84 Beulah Hill, London SE19, T: 01-653-3953.
Radio Worldwide (WEC), 13 Harold Rd., London SE19 3PU, T: 01-653-4753.
Religious Broadcasting Department, London W1A 1AA, T: 01-580-4468.
Television & Radio Dept, Church Information Office, Church House, Dean's Yard, London SW1.
Trans World Radio (TWR), 175 Tower Bridge Rd., London SE1 2AB, T: 01-407-3614.
UNDA (The International Catholic Association for Radio and Television), Catholic Comm. Centre, 39 Eccleston Square, London SW1V 1BX, T: 0171-233 8196, F: 0171-931 7497.
United Christian Broadcasters, P.O. Box 255, Stoke-on-Trent, Staffs ST4 2UE, T: 44-1782-642000, F: 44-1782-641121.
Voice of Prophecy, Stanborough Park, Watford, Herts. WD2 6JP.
World Association for Christian Communication (WACC), 357 Kennington Lane, London SE11 5QY, T: 44-71-582-9139, F: 44-71-735-0340, O: 8812669 WACC G, Cable: WACCLondonSE11.

BURKINA FASO
Emissions Catholiques, BP 149 Bobo-Dioulasso.

BURUNDI
Emissions Catholiques, Collège du Saint-Esprit, BP 825, Bujumbura.
La Voix de l'Esperance, B.P. 1710, Bujumbura.

CAMEROON
Emissions Catholiques Hebdomadaires, BP 75, Garoua.
Fédération Radio Studio (CENTAVEP), BP 187, Yaoundé.
La Voix de l'Eperance, BP 401, Yaounde.
Presbyterian Church in West Cameroon, Literature and Radio Department, P.O. Box 19, Buea.
Responsable des Emissions Catholiques, BP 4164, Yaoundé.
Studio Sawtu Linjiila, BP 2, Ngaoundere.

CANADA
Bridge 600 AM, Vancouver, BC V6H 1C9, T: 604-731-6111, F: 604-731-0493.
Canadian Broadcasting Corporation, 354 Jarvis St., Toronto, Ontario.
Canadian Perspective Christian Radio, Westport, ON K0G 1X0, T: 800-647-0921, F: 613-273-8483.
Christian Broadcasting Association, Inc. (The 700 Club in Canada), 680 Progress Ave., Unit 2, Scarborough, ON M1H 3A5, T: 416-439-6411, F: 416-439-1043.
Crossroads Christian Communications, Inc., P.O. Box 5100, Burlington, ON L7R 4M2, T: 905-845-5100, F: 905-332-0044.
Far East Broadcasting Associates of Canada, 6850 Antrim Ave., Burnaby, BC V5J 4V4, T: 604-430-8439, F: 604-430-5272.
HCJB World Radio Missionary Fellowship in Canada, 2476 Argentia Rd. Ste. 201, Mississauga, ON L5N 6M1, T: 905-821-6313, F: 905-821-6314, O: E-mail: HCJBcan@mhs.wrmf.org.
In Touch Ministries of Canada, P.O. Box 4900, Markham, ON L3R 6G9, T: 905-470-7870, F: 905-470-6269, O: Orders: 1-800-323-3747.
Insight for Living Ministries, Box 2510, Vancouver, BC V6B 3W7, T: 604-532-7172, F: 604-532-7173.
International Russian Radio and TV Ministry, P.O. Box 94234, Richmond BC V6Y 2A6, T: 604-241-8035, F: 604-241-8027, O: E-mail: irrtv@hsrtv.ppfi.
J. J. Show, 6061 Yonge St., Suite 504, Toronto, ON M2M 3W4, T: 416-733-1799.
L'Heure de la Bonne Nouvelle, C.P. 1054, Sherbrooke, QC J1H 5L3, T: 819-820-1693.
La Bonne Nouvelle Recording Studio, 249/253 St. George St., Moncton, NB.
La Voix de l'Evangile, C.P. 125, Chateauguay, QC J6J 4Z5, T: 514-699-7308.
Light of the World Ministries, P.O. Box 250, Station A, Downsview, ON M3M 3A6, T: 416-767-5152.
Mennonite Brethren Comm., 225 Riverton Ave., Winnipeg BC R2L 0N1, T: 204-667-9576, F: 204-669-6079, O: E-mail: 76173236@compuserve.com.
People's Gospel Hour, Box 1660, Halifax.
Radio Bible Class - Canada, P.O. Box 1622, Windsor, ON N9A 6Z7, T: 519-253-4742, F: 519-253-4743.
Religious Television Associates, 3250 Bloor St. W., Etobicoke, ON M8X 2Y4, T: 416-366-9221, F: 416-366-8204.
Sacred Heart Program, 2 Hawthorn Gardens, Toronto 287, Ontario.
Services des Emissions Religieuses, Radio-Canada, CP 6000, Montréal, Québec.
Shining Light Ministry, 286 Stonechurch Rd., E., Hamilton, ON L9B 1B2, T: 905-318-5929, F: 905-318-7041.
Spirit Alive, P.O. Box 280, Deseronto, ON K0K 1X0, T: 613-396-1435, F: 613-396-2555.
Terry Winter Christian Communications, 301 1600 West 6th Ave., Vancouver, BC V6J 1R3, T: 604-736-3677, F: 604-736-2597.
Trans World Radio Canada, O: Web: www.twr.org/.
Trinity Television, Inc., 1111 Chevrier Blvd., Winnipeg, MB R3T 1Y2, T: 204-949-3333, F: 204-949-3334.
Vision TV: Canada's Faith Network, 502-90 Eglington Ave., E., Toronto, ON M4P 2Y3, T: 416-480-2300, F: 416-480-2749.
Visit with Mrs. G Ministries, P.O. Box 150, Sta. O, Toronto ON M4A 2M8, T: 416-755-5918, F: 416-423-3895.

CHAD
UNDA/Centrafrique, Centre Jean XXIII, B.P. 855, Bangui, T: 236-61 22 78, F: 236-61 46 92.

CHILE
ARCA (Asociación de Radiodifusoras Católicas), Casilla 10227 - anexo 35, Phillips 56, of. 26 Santiago de Chile, T: 56-2-632-4101, F: 56-2-6 398 868.
Asociación de Radiodifusoras de Chile, Casilla 10476, Santiago.
Instituto Nacional de Acción Poblacional (INAP), Principe de Gales 87, Casilla 13508, Correo 15, Santiago.
Responsable TV, Universidad Católica de Santiago, Santiago.

CHINA
Catholic Broadcasting, Wah Yan College, Queen's Rd East, Hong Kong.
Chinese Provincial Broadcast, P.O. Box 13225, Hong Kong.
Far East Broadcasting Corp., P.O. Box 96789, Tsimhatsui, Kowloon, Hong Kong, T: 852-2744-2211, F: 852-2744-8800.
LWF Broadcasting Service, Room 408, Yu To Sang Bldg, Queen's Rd Central, Hong Kong.
Overseas Radio and Television, Inc. (ORTV), P.O. Box 37-3, Taipei 10098, T: 2-2533-8082, F: 2-2533-1009, O: E-mail: simon@ortv.com.tw.
UNDA/Hong Kong, 16, Caine Road, Hong Kong, T: 852-5-223 677, F: 852-5-845 3095.

COLOMBIA
Cine, Radio-TV Centro de Producción y Formación (CENPRO), Carrera 23, No 39-69, Bogotá, DE 1, T: 444675, 445154.
OSAL Centro, Técnicas de Comunicación para el Desarrollo, Calle 20 No 9-45, Apdo Aéreo 12-721 Bogotá, DE. (Regional branch, SEAPAL).

CONGO-BRAZZAVILLE
Emissions Catholiques, Séminaire Libermann, BP 210, Brazzaville.

CONGO-ZAIRE
RENAPEC, Service Technique Africain de Radio-TV (TELESTAR), BP 1698, Kinshasa, T: 25812.
Studiproka, BP 700, Luluabourg.

COSTA RICA
Adventist World Radio-Latin America, P.O. Box 1177, 4050 Alajuele, T: 506-42 12 83, F: 506-41 12 82.
Asociación de Radio Faro del Caribe, Apdo 2710, San José.
Catholic Broadcasting, Radio Fides, Calle ler, Av lla, San José.
Club Televideo Cristiano, Apdo 1082-1200, T: 255-4042.
Difusiones Inter Americanas (DIA), Apdo 2470, San José.
Radio Faro del Caribe, T: 226-2573.
Radio Nederland, Centro Regiónal de Latinoamérica, Sabana Sur, Apdo 880 Centro Colon, 1007 San José, T: 506-20-4141, F: 506-20 4302.
Radio Sendas de Vida, Apdo 648-1000, T: 233-8946.
Red de Radio Católica, Curia Metropolitana, 2 piso - Avda 4, Apdo 5079-1000 San José, T: 506-33-4546, F: 506-33 2387.

CYPRUS
SAT-7, P.O. Box 6760, Nicosia 1647, T: 011-357-2-361050, F: 011-357-2-361040, O: E-mail: mail@sat7.org.

DENMARK
Association Catholique des auditeurs, Teglbrandertoften 8, DK-2890 Hareskov, T: 987675.
Catholic Broadcasting, Askelkkevej 9, DK-2770 Kastrup, T: 513061.

DJIBOUTI
Emissions Catholiques, Paroisse de la Cathédrale, BP 94.

DOMINICAN REPUBLIC
Unión Dominicana de Emisoras Católicas (UDECA), Portes 871, 3er piso of. 40, Santo Domingo, T: 809-685-9619, F: 809-535-1535.

ECUADOR
All Ecuador Gospel Network, Vozandes, Establon del Guayas', Casilla 5383, Guayaquil.
Asistencia Medica, Shell, Casilla 6328, Quito.
Asociación Latinoamericana de Educación Radiofónica (ALER), Calle Valladolid 479 y Madrid, Casilla 4639-A, Quito, T: 593-2-524-358, F: 593-2-503 996.
Club 700, Telecentro, Canal 10, Casilla 4882, Quito, T: 554-545.
Club PTL, Canal 13, Casilla 5060, Quito, T: 545-835.
Cristo me Ama, Radio La Voz del Volante, Casilla 185, Portoviejo.
Ecos de Pentecostes, Radio Consular, Casilla 8782, Guayaquil, T: 368-831.
El Mensaje de Dios para Usted, Radio Voz de Portoviejo.
El Mensaje Eterno, Radio Universal, Casilla 860, Guayaquil, T: 390-380.
Escucha y Decide, Radio Presidents, Casilla 230, Quito, T: 542-875.
Getsemani, Radio Condor, Casilla 7592, Guayaquil, T: 330-018.
HCJB La Voz de Los Andes AM, Villalengua No. 320, Casilla 691, Quito, T: 241-550.
Impacto Evangelistico, Esmeraldas, Casilla 490, Quito, T: 634-964.
La Biblia Dice, Programa Internacional de Radio, Ave. 10 de Agosto No. 11635, Casilla 3715, Quito, T: 531-592.
La Voz de Pentecostes, Radio Condor, Casilla 8782, Guayaquil, T: 368-831.
Lugar Secreto, Canal 13, Casilla 4882, Quito, T: 554-545.
Luminares en el Mundo, Bolivia y 31, Casilla 4684, Guayaquil.
Mensajeros de Cristo, Radio Universal, Casilla 6367, Guayaquil.
Programas de Radio, Radio Condor, Casilla 7592, Guayaquil, T: 330-018.
Radio Católica Nacional, América 1830 y Mercadillo, Apartado 17-01-1081, Quito, T: 593-2-541-557, F: 593-2-501 429, O: 308-2427 CONFER ED.
Radio Interoceanica, Santa Rosa, Casilla 8283, Quito.
Radio La Voz de Ingapirca, Casilla 447, Canar.
Radio La Voz de la Asociacion, Illuchi, Casilla 208, Latacunga.
Radio Rio Amazonas, Macuma, Morona Santiago.
Radio y TV, Villalengua No. 278 y 10 de Agosto, Casilla 691, Quito, T: 241-550.
Teleproduccion Voz Andes, Villalengua No. 278 y 10 de Agosto, Casilla 691, Quito, T: 241-550.
Un Estudio en la Biblia con Jimmy Swaggart, Telecentro, Canal 10, Casilla 2475, Guayaquil, T: 513-984.
World Radio Missionary Fellowship, Villalengua 278, Casilla 691, Quito, T: 241550.

EGYPT
Catholic Broadcasting, Rue Adly Pasha 9, Ap 8, Al Qahirah.

EL SALVADOR
Latin American Radio Evangelism, San Salvador.

EQUATORIAL GUINEA
Catholic Broadcasting, Apdo 82, Bata, Rio Muni.

ETHIOPIA
Catholic Broadcasting, P.O. Box 21903, Adis Abeba.
Yemissrach Dimts Studio, P.O. Box 1153, Adis Abeba.

FINLAND
Finnish Broadcasting Company, Helsinki.

Helsingen Ev Lut Seurakuntien Elokuva—Ja TV-Palvelu, Helsinki.
International Russian Radio/TV, Box 71, Kerava 04251, T: 358-0-2945400, F: 358-0-244784.
Radio and Television Department, Catholic Information Centre (KATT), Kotipolku 18, Helsinki 60, T: 90-794197.

FRANCE
Association Evangélique de Radio, 109 Rue de l'Aiguillette, F-13012 Marseille, T: 488240.
Comission Education Religieuse Radio-TV, UNDA, Responsable, 121 Av de Villiers, F-75017 Paris.
Comité de Coordination Interorthodoxe, 4 rue de Ursuliness, F-75005 Paris, T: 633-9315.
Fédération Française des Radios Chrétiennes, (Radio Fourvière, F-69005 Lyon, T: 33-78-25-12-27, F: 33-72 38 20 57, O: Telex: 42-380835 EV LYON F.
L'Heure de la Décision, BP 345, F-75365 Paris-Cédex 08, T: 225-8051.
Le Jour du Seigneur, Comité Français de Radio-Télévision (CFRT), R.P. Bernard Marliangeas, 121 Rue de Villiers, T: 33-1-44-15-82-82, O: Telex: 33-1-44 15 82 99.
Les Amis de la Radio-Télévision Protestante, 47 Rue de Clichy, F-75009 Paris, T: 874-1508.
Lutheran Hour, BP 22, 67290 La Petite Pierre, T: 011-33-88-70-40-41.
Radio Vie et Sante, BP 200, 88005 Epinal Cedex, T: 29 82 30 30.
Radio Voix de l'Esperance, 132 Blvd. De l'Hopital, 74013 Paris, T: 1- 45 35 27 04.
Service de la Radio-Télévision, FPF, Responsable, 47 Rue de Clichy, F-75009 Paris, T: 874-1508.
Télérama, 10 Rue Laborde, F-75008 Paris; 4 Place de Breteuil, F-75006 Paris, T: 522-9185.
Voice of Orthodoxy, Boite Postale 416-08, Paris Cedex 08 75366.
Voix de l'Evangile, 109 Rue de l'Aiguillette, F-13012 Marseille, BP 45 Marseille RP (B-du-Rh), T: 488240.

FRENCH GUIANA
Emissions Catholiques, Evêché, BP 122, Cayenne.

FRENCH POLYNESIA
Episcopal Conference of the Pacific Commission for Social Communications, c/o Archevêque de Papeete, B.P. 94, Papeete, Tahiti, T: 689-42-02-51, F: 689-42-40-32.

GABON
Emissions Catholiques, Archevêché, BP 1146, Libreville.

GAMBIA
Catholic Radio Broadcasts, P.O. Box 165, Bathurst.

GERMANY
Adventist World Radio-Europe, Heidelberger Landstrasse 24, Darmstadt 64297, T: 49-6151-51123, F: 49-6151-52229.
Evangelische Radiomission 'Christus Lebt' (Christ Liveth), Box 140 380, Bielefeld 14 W-4800, T: 49-0521-448624, F: 49-0521-448681.
Evangelisches Rundfunk und Fernsehreferat der Norddeutschen Landeskirchen, Hamburg.
Evangeliums-Rundfunk, Box 1444, D-35573 Wetzlar, T: 49-6441-9570, F: 49-6441-957122.
Evangeliums-Rundfunk (ERF), Intl., Postfach 1444, Wetzlar 1 W-6330, T: 49-6441-5050, F: 49-6441-53603.
Internationaler Bibellehrdienst, Schwarzauerstr. 59, 83308 Trostberg, T: 08621-64146, F: 08621-61147.
Katholische Fernseharbeit in Deutschland (KFD), Grillparzerstr 30, D-6 Frankfurt 1, T: 0611-727097, 561088.
Katholische Rundfunk Arbeit in Deutschland, Wittelsbachering 9, Postfach 290, D-53 Bonn, T: 02221-51414.
Katholisches Rundfunkinstitut eV, Am Hof 28, 5 Köln, T: 0511-231600.
Kirchenfunk, Deutsche Welle, Hohenzollernring 62, D-5 K.
Konferenz für Evangelische Rundfunk- und Fernseharbeit, Haus der Ev Publizistik, Friedrichstr 34, D-6 Frankfurt am Main.
Lutherische Stunde, Wessenburger Str 36, D-28 Bremen.
M107, Gartenstr. 13, 60596 Frankfurt, T: 069-636404, F: 069-63153245, O: E-mail: 100700.762@Compuserve.com.
Radiodienst Vox Christiana, Bonner Platz 1/III, D-8 München 2.
Tellux-Film GmbH, Leopoldstr 20, D-8 München 23, T: 340724.
Trans World Radio, Postfach 1444, D-35573 Wetzlar; ERF Berliner Ring 62, Wetzlar, D-35576, T: 49-6441-957312, F: 49-6441-957-170, O: E-mail: 06441-9570-0001@t-online.de.
UNDA/Deutschland, Kaiserstrasse 163, D-5300 Bonn 1, T: 49-228-10-32-39, F: 49-228-10 33 29.

GHANA
Broadcasting and Audio-Visual Services (BRAVS), Box 919, Accra.
Department of Press & Broadcasting, National Catholic Secretariat, P.O. Box 7530, Accra, T: 22871.

GREECE
Catholic Broadcasting, 246 Rue Acharnon, Athínai 8.
Voice of Hope, Keramikou 18, 10437 Athens, T: 1-52-24-962, F: 1-52-33-013.

GUADELOUPE
Better Life Radio, P.O. Box 19, Pointe-a-Pitre, T: 83-25-73.
Emissions Catholiques, Maison des Oeuvres, 28 Rue Peynier, BP 414, Pointe à Pitre 971.

GUAM
Catholic Broadcasting, Chancery Office, Agaña.

GUATEMALA
Federación Guatemalteca de Escuelas Radiofonicas (FGER), 2da. calle 4-41, zona 1, T: 502-2-20-312, F: 502-2-942 467.
Radio Metropolitana, Palacio Arzobispol, Guatemala City.

GUINEA
Catholic Broadcasting, Prefecture Apostolic, CP 20 Bissau.

GUYANA
Christian Association of Broadcasters, 293 Oronoque St, Georgetown, T: 4893.

HAITI
Adventist Radio of Haiti, Diquihi, Port-au-Prince, Haiti, T: 4-42-48, 4-43-73.
Emissions Catholiques, Radio Manrè se, Poste 4 VM, CP 525, Port-au-Prince.

HOLY SEE
Radio Vatican, Radiovaticana, Production Studios, I-00120 Città del Vaticano, T: 06-6983045.
Radio Watch, Direzione Generale, 1-00120 Citta del Vaticano, Europe, T: 06-6983145.

HUNGARY
Voice of Hope, Studio, Szuret u. 19, 1118 Budapest, T: 185-3648.

INDIA
Adventist World Radio Asia, P.O. Box 15, Poona 411001.
Adventist World Radio Office, Post Box 2, HCF, Hosur 635110, Tamil Nadu.
Boro Christian Radio Ministry Vishwavani, Bongaigaon Mission Compound, Bongaigaon, Assam 783380.
Cephas Cine/Tele Communications India Pvt. Limited, 15, Vaibhav Buildings, Wadala (East), Bombay, Maharashtra 400037.
Dharshan Radio, Post Box 567, Bangalore, Karnataka 560005.
Far East Broadcasting Associates of India, FEBA House, A-42-44, Top Floor, Commercial Complex, Dr. Mukerjee Nagar, Delhi 110009.
FEBA Radio, 7, Commussarait Road, P.O. Box 2526, Bangalore, Karnataka 560025.
Good News Broadcasting Society, P.O. Box 2002, Secunderabad, Andhra Pradesh 500003.
International Bible Radio Associates, 61, Rajpur Road, Dehra Dun, Uttar Pradesh 248001.
Jeeva Vachanam Radio Ministry, 47, P. T. P. Nagar, Trivandrum, Kerala 695038.
Jeevanshanti Radio Ministry, 22, Kosha Society, Sion Nagar, Maninagar East, Ahmedabad, Gujarat 380008.
Living Waters Gospel Broadcast, Nav Bhavana, S. V. S. Road, Prabhadevi, Bombay, Maharashtra 400025.
Masihi Vandana (Good News Broadcasting Society), D-1, Virat Bhavan, Commercial Complex, Dr. Mukherjee Nagar, New Delhi 110009.
St. Xavier's Centre, Chaibasa, Singhbhum-District.
Trans World Radio - India, L-15, Green Park, New Delhi 110016.
UNDA/OCIC India, Diocesan Pastoral Centre, 4 Kane Rd., Bandra, Bombay 400050, T: 91-22-642 25 56.
Vishwa Vani, P. O. Box 3, Manjadi P. O., Tiruvalla, Kerala 689105.
Voice of the Second Coming, Tourist Road, Ukhrul P. O., Manipur 795142.

INDONESIA
Catholic Broadcasting, Jalan Kemiri 15, Jakarta 11/16.
DGI Broadcast Network, Production Studio, 10 Salemba Raya, Jakarta IV/3.
Educational Radio and TV Centre for Development, Jalan Kamiri 15/a, Jakarta 11/16.
Flambeau du Coeur, Sendia Ybu Cultural Center, 2-1-26 Kami-Sugi, Auba-ku, C.P.O. Box 114, Sendai 980-91, T: 81-22 261 5341, F: 81-22 221 9867.
UNDA-OCIC Indonesia, Jl. Bintaran Kidul 5, Yogyakarta 55151, T: 62-276-6 12 81.
Voice of Prophecy Correspondence School, P.O. Box 1303, Manado 95013, Sulawesi Utara.

IRAN
Near East Council of Churches Radio Program Centre for Iran, Box 2995, Tehran.

IRELAND
Let the Bible Speak, 55 Market Street, Dervock Road, Ballymoney, Co Antrim BT53 6ED, T: 08-026 56 62039.
Oblate Conference Library, Oblate Fathers, Inchicore, Dublin 8.
Radharc, 6 Rock Road, Blackrock, County Dublin, O: Tel/Fax: 353-1-288 1939.

ISRAEL
Jerusalem Capital Studios, P.O. Box 13172, JCS Bldg., 206 Jaffa Rd., Jerusalem 91131, T: 011-972-2-701-701, F: 011-972-2-370-629.

ITALY
Centro Cattolico Televisivo (CCTV), Ente dello Spettacolo, Via della Conciliazione 2c, I-00193 Roma, T: 561775, 564132.
Gospel Missionary Union, Voce della Biblia, CP 580, 41100 Modena.
Radio Réveil, 51 Via Tesserete, Lugano.
Radio Vatican, I-00120 Citta del Vaticano, T: 06-698-3145.
Radio Voce della Speranza, Lungotevere Michelangelo 7, 00192 Rome.
Studio Radio per L'Evangelo in Italia, Via Trieste 45, Florence.
Voce della Bibbia, C.P. 90, 41043 Formigine MO, T: 39-59 55-63-03, 55-79-10, F: 39 59 57-31-05, O: E-mail: vocedb@tin.it.

IVORY COAST
Adventist World Radio-Africa, 08 Boite Postale 1751, Abidjan 08, T: 225-44 00 97, F: 225-41 31 23.
Emissions Catholiques, BP 1287, Abidjan; BP 8016, Abidjan (TV).

JAPAN
Baptist Evangelical Broadcasting Center, Sapporo CPO Box 201, Sapporo-shi 060-91.
Baptist House, Japan Baptist Convention, 2-350 Nishi Okubo, Shinjuku-ku, Tokyo 160.
Broadcasting and Audio-Visual Aids Committee (BAVACO), 1-551 Totsuka-Machi, Shinjuku-ku, Tokyo 160.
Christian Broadcasting Association, 6-14 Nakamiya-cho, Asahi-ku, Osaka 535.
Far East Broadcasting Company (FEBC), CPO Box 55, Naha, Ryukyu Islands, T: 78208.
Hokkaido Radio Evangelism Mass Communications (HOREMCO), Box 202, Sapporo, Hokkaido.
Japan Lutheran Hour, Belvedere Kudan #201, 15-5 Fujimi 2 Chome, Tokyo 102, T: 011-81-3-3261-2288. O: Web: www.japan-lutheran-hour.org/index.html.
LWF Broadcasting Service, Tokyo Office, Room 624, Nikkatsu Hotel, 1-1 Yurakucho, Chiyoda-ku, Tokyo 100.
National Catholic Broadcasting Committee, Taishido-2 chome 15-3, Setagaya-ku, Tokyo.
Nazarene Hour, 8-589 Kami Meguro, Meguro-ku, Tokyo 153.
Pacific Broadcasting Association, 10-8 Umegaoka 3-chome, Setagaya-ku, CPO Box 1000, Tokyo 100-91, T: 4203166.
St. Paul Film and Radio Centre, 1-5 Wakaba, Shinjuku-ku, Tokyo 160.
Time for Christ, Minami Presbyterian Church Radio Evangelism Dept, 4-33 Chikara-cho, Higashi-ku, Nagoya-shi 461.
Voice of Life, Missions to Japan, 10-6 Hamadamachi, Kure-shi, Hiroshima-ken 737.
Voice of Prophecy Studio, 846 Kamikawai-cho, Asahi-ku, Yokohama 241.

KENYA
Afromedia, P.O. Box 21028, Nairobi, T: 25149.
Communications and Radio Centre, Baptist Convention of Kenya, P.O. Box 20312, Nairobi.
Department of Communications, Kenya Catholic Secretariat, P.O. Box 48062, Nairobi.
Kenya Christian Broadcasting Advisory Committee (KCBAC), P.O. Box 45009, Nairobi.
Religious Department, Voice of Kenya (VOK), Broadcasting House, Harry Thuku Rd., P.O. Box 30456, Nairobi, T: 34567 ext 209.

LEBANON
Baptist Recording Studio, P.O. Box 5232, Bayrut.
Catholic Broadcasting, Université St. Joseph, P.O. Box 293, Bayrut.
Christian Recording Society, Box 5269, Bayrut.
Division for Radio Broadcasting (DORBNECC), P.O. Box 5376, Bayrut.
Lissan-ul-Hal, Bayrut.
Path of Light (ELWA) Recording Studio, P.O. Box 5485, Bayrut; SIM, Liberia.
Trans World Radio, P.O. Box 6442 & 141, Bayrut.

LIBERIA
Catholic Broadcasting, Apostolic Internunciature, Monrovia.

MADAGASCAR
Radio Feon'Ny Filazantsara, BP 95, Antsirabe.

MALAWI
Catholic Broadcasting, Catholic Secretariat of Malawi, Zomba Rd., P.O. Box 5368, Limbe.
Gospel Broadcasting Committee, P.O. Box 162, Lilongwe.

MALI
Emissions Catholiques, Archevêché, BP 298, Bamako.

MALTA
Religious Broadcasting Advisor, 12 Old Treasury St, Valletta.

MARTINIQUE
Comité Diocésain de Radio-Télévision (CDRT), T: 596-78-80-50.
Emissions Catholiques, 1 Rue Le Cornu, Fort-de-France.

MAURITIUS
Voice of Prophecy, P.O. Box 18, Rose Hill.

MEXICO
Asociación Nacional de Radio-Escuchas, ACM, Serapio Rendon 43, México 4, DF.
Asociación National de Tele-clubs, Medellín 33, México 7, DF.
Audición Luz y Verdad, Apdo 30, México 1, DF, T: 496711.
Circulo Radiomundial, Apdo 12750, México 12, DF.
Hora de Hermandad Cristiana, Apdo 53-114, México 17, DF.

MICRONESIA
Catholic Nepukos Studio, Chuuk State, P.O. Box 202, Chuuk, 96942, T: 691-330-2456, F: 691-330-2399.
Catholic Studio, Palau, P.O. Box 128, Koror, Palau, T: 680-488-2226.
Catholic Studio, Pohnpei State, P.O. Box 160, Pohnpei, 96941, T: 691-320-2557, F: 691-320-2557.
UNDA/Oceania, P.O. Box 73, Kolonia, Pohnpei State-FMS 96941, T: 691-320-2557.

MONACO
Centre National Catholique Radio-TV, Evêché, Monte Carlo.
Eurofilm, Monte Carlo.
Trans World Radio (TWR), Field Dir, 5 Rue de la Poste, Box 141, Monte Carlo, T: 203233.

MONTSERRAT
Catholic Broadcasting, Bishop's House, Plymouth.

MOROCCO
IBRA, Tanger.
Trans World Radio (TWR), Box 92, Tanger.

MYANMAR
Broadcast Network, National Council of Churches, Production Studio, 82nd St., Mandalay.

NAMIBIA
Catholic Broadcasting, Vicariate Apostolic, Keetmanshoop.

NETHERLANDS
Evangelical Broadcasting Company, P.O. Box 565, AN Hilversum 1200, T: 31-35-882411, F: 31-35-882685.
Evangelische Omroep, P. O. Box 21000, 1202 BB Hilversum, T: 011-31-356474769, F: 011-31-356474544, O: E-mail: 100544.2515@compuserve.com.
Kabelvisie, Antwoordnummer 18, Culemborg.
KRO-schoolradio en-televisie, Emmastraat 52, NL Hilversum, T: 02150-491141.
NCRV-schoolradio en-televisie, Schuttersweg 8-10, Hilversum, T: 02150-13651.
NET, Box 75, Kampen.
Religious Dept KRO (Radio & Television), B.P. 9000, NL-1201 DH Hilversum, T: 31-35-71-33-57, F: 31-35-23 22 43.
Stichting de Evangelische Omroep, BP 565, Hilversum, T: 02150-12500.
Stichting Katholieke Radio-Omroep (KRO), Emmastraat 52, NL-Hilversum, T: 02150-49141.
Trans World Radio, Box 141, Baarn.
Trans World Radio-Europe, P.O. Box 2020, Hilversum 1200 CA, T: 31-352-17740, F: 31-352-34861.
Voice of Africa, Lieven de Keylaan 69, NL-1222 LD Hilversum, T: 31-35-853766.
Voice of Hope, Biltseweg 14, 3735 ME Bosch en Duin.
VPRO, Hilversum.

NETHERLANDS ANTILLES
Catholic Broadcasting, P.O. Box 220, Caraçao.
New Testament Baptist Enterprises, P.O. Box 147, St Maarten.

NEW CALEDONIA
Emissions Catholiques, Archevêché, BP 3, Nouméa.
Voice of Hope, Angle des rues Guynemer et Duquesne Quartier Latin, Noumea, T: 28-07.

NEW ZEALAND
Catholic Broadcasting Training Centre, National Catholic Broadcasting Committee, 154 Brougham St., Wellington C4, T: 50936, 76131.
Christian Radio Missionary Fellowship, P.O. Box 1154, Taupo, T: 0-7-378-9910, F: 0-7-378-2100.
Evangelical Radio Witness, Birkdale, Auckland.
Far East Broadcasting Co., P.O. Box 4140, Hamilton, T: 0-7-856-2427, F: 0-7-856-2427.
HCJB World Radio, P.O. Box 27-514, Mt. Roskill, Auckland, T: 0-9-625-7411, F: 0-9-625-7412, O: E-mail: hcjbnz@codeworks.gen.nz.
International Radio Crusades, P.O. Box 157, Paeroa, NI.
New Zealand Broadcasting Corporation, P.O. Box 98, Wellington.
New Zealand Churches TV Commission, P.O. Box 10000, Wellington CI.
Radio Rhema, Inc., 10635 Box 21, Christchurch, T: 64-3-338-3998.
TV Four Ltd., P.O. Box 108-111 Symonds St., Auckland, T: 011-64-9-3070526, F: 011-64-9-3024057, O: E-mail: 1074.1710@compuserve.com.

NIGERIA
Broadcasting and AV Services (BRAVS), Box 67, Ilesha.
Centre for Production of Radio & TV Programmes, Kaduna.
Christian Radio Studio, Box 795, Enugu, Eastern Nigeria.
Christian Radio Studio, Box 351, Jos.
ELWA Recording Studio, Igbaja via Ilorin.
Muryar Bishara, Box 287, Jos.
National Catholic Broadcasting Committee, Catholic Secretariat, P.O. Box 951, Lagos.
Nigerian Broadcasting Corporation, Broadcasting House, PMB 12504, Lagos.

NORWAY
Nordic Radio Evangelistic Association (NOREA), P.O. Box 4087, Kongsgard, Kristiansand 4602, T: 47-042-93-000, F: 47-042-94-100.
Norsk Rikskringkasting, Oslo.
Norwegian Christian Radio/TV Association, Thorvald Meyers Gate 48, Oslo 5.
Omega Radio, Akersgata 74, 0180 Oslo.
Radio Norea (Nordic Radio Evangelistic Association), Gransen 19, Oslo 1, T: 332525.
Television Mission, Grünersgt 6, Oslo 5.

PAKISTAN
Voice of Hope, P.O. Box 32, Lahore.

PAPUA NEW GUINEA
Catholic Broadcasting, Catholic Mission, Alexishafen-Madang.
Christian Radio Missionary Fellowship (CRMF), Rugli, P.O. Box 345, Mt. Hagen, WHD.
Voice of Prophecy, P.O. Box 631, Lae, T: 42-1488.

PARAGUAY

ACER (Asociación de Comunicación y Educación Radiofónica), Radio Cáritas, Avda. Kubitschek y Azara, Asunción, T: 595-21-21-35-70, F: 595-21-20 41 61.

PERU

Coordinadora Nacional de Radio (CNR), Garcilaso de la Vega 2170, Lima 14, Dirección postal: Apartado 2179, Lima 100, T: 51-14-708877, F: 51-14-717825.

PHILIPPINES

Back to the Bible Broadcast, P.O. Box 1750, Manila.
Call of the Orient, Box 2041, Manila.
Centre for Educational Television, Ateneo of Manila, P.O. Box 154, Loyola Heights, Quezon City, Manila.
Far East Broadcasting Co., Inc., Box 1, Valenzuela, Metro Manila 1405, T: 35-65-11, O: Telex: 40048 FEBCOM PM, Cable: FEBCOM.
Mascom Network Interchurch, 1648 Taft Av, Manila.
Mountain Province Broadcasting Corporation, St. Louis University Campus, Bonifacio St., P.O. Box 71, Baguio City, T: 2582, 2453, 3874.
National Council of Churches Broadcasting Network, Box 4147, Manila.
Philippine Federation of Catholic Broadcasters, P.O. Box 3169, Manila 2802; 2307 Pedro Gil Str., Santa Ana, Manila 2802, T: 63-58-4828, O: Cable: Reuter Jesuitas Manila.
Philippine Radio Education and Information Center, Radio Veritas, P.O. Box 132, Manila, T: 971158.
South East Asia Radio Voice (SEARV), Box 4148, Manila.
Tagum Community Development Radio Corporation, Davao del Norte.
UNDA/Philippines, 2307 Pedro Gil St., P.O. Box 3169, Santa Ana, Manila, T: 63-2-58 48 28, F: 63-2-521 8 125.
Visayan Educational Radio and TV Association (VERTA), Bishop's House, Bacolod City 70501.
Voice of Christian Brotherhood, Dumaguete City, Box 4148, Manila.
Voice of Prophecy Studio, P.O. Box 3,6000 Cebu City.

POLAND

Biuro do Spraw Srodków Oddzialywania Spolecznego, Aleja 1, Armii Wojska Polskiego 12, Warszawa, T: 212337.
Voice of Hope, 1 Maja 39 05-807 Podkowa Lesna.

PORTUGAL

Adventist World Radio (AWR), CP 2590, Lisboa 2.
Alfa-Tehillah, Rua Carvalho Araújo, 40-B, 2830 Lavradio, T: 01-204 37 89.
Açores para Cristo, Apartado 32, 9600 Ribeira Grande (S. Miguel-Açores).
Caminhos, Apartado 4113, 1504 Lisboa, T: 01-778 07 18.
Dabicor - da Bíblia para o Coração, Apartado 13, 9501 Ponta Delgada.
Dois Dedos de Conversa, Trav. do Alcaide, 12-A, 1200 Lisboa.
Hora do Milagre, Apartado 107, 2800 Cova da Piedade.
IBRA (Radio Trans-Europe), IFAP Secção 5, Rua, Braamcamp 84, 60, Esq. Lisboa.
Linda Manhã, Apartado 60256, 2701 Amadora.
Nova Vida, Rua General Humberto Delgado, 6, 8700 Olhão.
O Som do Evangelho, Rua Dr. José Saudade e Silva, 2500 Caldas da Rainha, T: 062-2 35 82, O: 062-84 23 19.
O Som e o Espírito, Rua D. José I, 11 e 15 - 3800 Aveiro, T: 034-2 05 81, F: 034-91 19 21 p.f..
Radio Renascença, Rua Capelo 5-2 Esq, Lisboa 2, T: 30172.
Tesouro Escondido, Rua Dr. Afonso Lopes Vieira, Apartado 225 - 2460 Alcobaça.
Vida Nova, Rua Vaz Monteiro, 63, 7400 Ponte de Sor.

PUERTO RICO

Calvary Evangelistic Mission, Inc., P.O. Box 367000, San Juan, PR 00936, T: 787-724-2727, F: 787-723-9633, O: E-mail: 104743.1413@compuserve.com.
La Cadena Del Milago TV, P. O. Box 949, Camuy, PR 00627, T: 809-262-5400.
Lutheran Church Mission—Puerto Rico, P.O. Box 3085, Mayaguez PR 00681, T: 809-833-5979, F: 809-831-2677.
Luz y Verdad (MBI), Apdo 25, Albonito.
Movimiento Defensores De La Fe Cristiana, Inc., Calle Comerio 125, Apartado 2816, Bayamon, PR 00621, T: 809-785-0220.
Radio Misionero WBMJ y WIVV, P.O. Box 367000, San Juan, P.R. 00907-4010, T: 787-724-1190, F: 787-722-5395, O: E-mail: 104743.1413@compuserve.com.

REUNION

Association Réunionnaise d'Education Populaire (AREP), Rue la Bourdonnais, St-Denis.
Emissions Catholiques, Cure du Tampon.

RUSSIA

Far East Broadcasting Co., P.O. Box 2128, Khabarovsk 680020.
Russian Christian Radio, Box 141, Moscow 125047, T: 7-095-138-9189.

RWANDA

Voice of Prophecy, BP 367, Kigali.

SAINT LUCIA

Catholic Broadcasting, Bishop's House, Castries.

SENEGAL

Emissions Catholiques, BP 5098, Dakar-Fann.
La Voix de l'Esperance, BP 1013, Dakar.

SEYCHELLES

Catholic Broadcasting, Evêché, Victoria.
Far East Broadcasting Association (FEBA), Box 234, Victoria, Mahé, T: 749.
Radio Religion Catholique, R.C. Mission, Box 12, T: 248-226 52, O: Telex: 965-52229NI.

SIERRA LEONE

American Wesleyan Mission Studio, Box 33, Bendumbu, via Makeni.
Catholic Broadcasting, Catholic Mission, St. Edward's Secondary School, P.O. Box 673, Freetown.

SINGAPORE

DXGN, Huna Subdivision, Davao City.
Singapore Recording Centre, Far East Broadcasting Company, 338 Jalan Minyek (York Hill), Singapore 3.
Trans World Radio, East Asia Office, 273 Thompson Road, #03-03 Novena Gardens, Singapore 307644, T: 251-4767, F: 251-4761.

SLOVENIA

Lutheran Hour Office, PO Box 104, 814 99 Bratislava 1, T: 011-427-5332-861.

SOUTH AFRICA

Andrew Timm Television, PO Box 2298, Randburg 2125, ATTV Hse, Bush Hill Office Park, Ostrich Rd, Bromhof, Randburg, T: 011-792-9140, F: 011-792-8231.
Associates of Christian Broadcasters, PO Box 404, Wapadrand 0050, 878 Wapadrand St, Wapadrand 0050, T: 012-807-0053, F: 012-807-1266.
Chrishande Productions, PO Box 98006, Sloane Park 2152, 17 Westminister Rd, Bryanston, T: 011-706-4606, F: 011-463-2323.
Christian Action in Radio in Africa (CARA), Box 269, Stellenbosch.
Christian Network Television, PO Box 8 Ferndale Farm 2194, Republic Rd/H Verwoerd Dr, Randburg, T: 011-789-5570, F: 011-789-5569.
Christian Radio Fellowship, PO Box 69, Roodepoort 1725, 16 Mare St, Roodepoort, T: 011-763-4215.
Far East Broadcasting (FEBA), PO Box 1276, Northcliff 2155, Johannesburg, T: 011-726-5981.
Go-Tell Communications, P. O. Box 1213, Gardenview 2047, T: 011-27-11-622-4608, F: 011-27-622-4142, O: E-mail: deith.strugnell@pixie.co.za.
Jimmy Swaggart Ministries, PO Box 10230, Johannesburg 2000, Sterling Hse, 131- Pritchard St, Johannesburg, T: 011-337-6920, F: 011-782-3977.
Oral Roberts Evangelical Ministries, P/B X45, Braamfontein 2107, Nedbank Cntr, 96 Jorissen St, Johannesburg, T: 011-339-2567, F: 011-403-3052.
Portuguese Radio Mission, PO Box 176, Linmeyer 2105, 172 Risi Ave, Linmeyer, Johannesburg, T: 011-435-3012.
Trans World Radio-South Africa, PO Box 36000, Menlo Park 0102, 878 Wapadrand St, Wapadrand, Pretoria, T: 012-807-0053, F: 012-807-1266.
Trinity Broadcasting Network, Easter Cape, PO Box 497, King William's Town 5600, Independence Blvd, Bisho, Eastern Cape, T: 0401-9-1179, F: 0401-956-4173.

SOUTH KOREA

Christian Broadcasting System of Korea, Christian Bldg., 136 Yun Chi Dong, Seoul.
KAVACO (Korea AV-TV Centre), 91 Chong No. 2, Ka, Soul.
Korean Christian Television System, 890-56 Dacchi-dong Kangnam-Ku, Seoul 135-280, T: 011-82-2-3469-4291, F: 011-82-2-3469-4286, O: E-mail: kcts7bpp@bora.dacom.co.kr.
National Office for Radio and Television Broadcasting, Catholic Conference of Korea, 52-15 2 Ka, Chung Mu Ro, Jung Ku, CPO Box 16, Soul, T: 23-8789.
P'yonghwa Broadcasting Corp. (PBC), 2-3, 1-ga, Cho-dong, Chung-gu, Seoul-shi, T: 02-2702-114.
UNDA/Korea, 2-3, 1 Ga Cho-Dong, Chung-Gu, Seoul 100-031, T: 81-2-270 22 41, F: 82-2-270 22 00.
Voice of Prophecy Studio, Chung Ryang P.O. Box 110, Seoul 130-650.

SPAIN

Asociación Evangélica de Radio y Televisión, San Eusebio, 54 1°, 08006 Barcelona, T: 202-34-36.
Cadena de Ondas Populares Españolas (COPE), Montesa 27, Madrid 6.
Evangelismo en Acción y Mecovan, Estudios de Grabación Radio y Casetes, Alonso de Palencia, 16, 29007 Málaga, T: 261-17-95, F: 227-47-13.
Ministerio Radial 'En Esto Pensad', Alamos, 1, 29012 Málaga, T: 32-65-21.
Pantalla 90 - Mensual, c/Añastro, 1, E-28033 Madrid.
Radio Génesis, Sevilla, 10, Castilleja de Guzmán, 41908 Sevilla, T: 572-05-04, F: 572-05-28.
Radio Impacto, 23770 20 de Octubre, 5-Apdo. 124, Marmolejo, Jaén, T: 50-36-70.
Transworld Radio, Mecovan, Ntra Stra de Guadelupe 11, Madrid 28, T: 91 2469604.

SRI LANKA

Back to the Bible Broadcast, 15 Melbourne Ave, Bambalapitiya, P.O. Box 1021, Colombo 4.
Catholic Broadcasting, St. Joseph's College, Colombo 10, T: 78491.
Catholic Radio and TV magazine, CINESITH-Quarterly, N 19, Balcombe Place, Colombo 8.
Technical Personnel for Broadcasting Stations, Radio and Electronics Ltd., 55 St Lucia's St, Colombo 13.

SUDAN

Catholic Broadcasting, Bishop's House, Al Khurtum.

SWAZILAND

Catholic Broadcasting, Bishop's House, P.O. Box 19, Manzini.
Christian Radio Fellowship, Box 244, Mbabane.
Trans World Radio, Box 64, Manzini.

SWEDEN

Catholic Broadcasting, Katolska Biskopämbetet, Fack S-102, 40 Stockholm 5.
Church of Sweden Mission, Uppsala.
IBR Radio, Box 733,52122 Falkoping, T: 46-515-81080.
IBRA Radio AB, S-105 36 Stockholm; HQ: Gammelgürdsvägen 38-42, Stora Essingen, T: 46-8-6192540, F: 46-8-6192539, O: Cable: Ibraradio.
IBRA Radio Mission, Box 396, S-101-25 Stockholm.

SWITZERLAND

Arbeitsgemeinschaft Radio-TV, Habsburgerstr 44, CH-6000 Luzern.
Association Catholique Internationale pour la Radiodiffusion et la Télévision (UNDA), 5 Rue de Romont, CP 211, CH-1701 Fribourg, T: 037-223012.
Baptist Recording Studio, Baptist Theological Seminary, Rüschlikon-ZH.
Catholic Broadcasting Secretary, Borghetto 2, CH-6901 Lugano, T: 091-21097.
Centre Catholique de Radio et Télévision, Dept Radio (RSR) et Télévision (TSR), Chemin des Abeilles 12, CH-1010 Lausanne, T: 41-21-653-50-22, F: 41-21-652 03 67.
Evangeliums-Rundfunk (ERF), Witzbachstrasse 23, Pfaffikon 8330, T: 41-1-915-0500.
Freedom in Christ Ministries, Hopoesche, Ruswil 6017, T: 41-41-732-957.
New Life Network, Swill Media, Erlenstr. 57, Oberglatt, CH 8154, T: 011-41-8505479, F: 011-41-850-4671, O: E-mail: ninnet.com.cserve:103763.1617.
Radio Messias, P.O. Box 1204, CH-6002 Luzern.
Radio Réveil et Paroles de Vie, Action Chrétienne par la Radio et la Presse, CH-2022 Bevaix (NE); BP 77, Genéva 6.
Radio-und Fernsehkommission, Christkatholische Kirche, Dufourstr 105, CH-2500 Biel, T: 032-42179.
Worte des Lebens (MBI), Bienenberg, CH-4410 Liestal.

TAIWAN

Churches Union Republic of China, 397-7, Section 4, Hsin Yi Rd, Taipei, T: 02-722-9354, F: 02-729-8736.
Kuangchi Program Service for Radio and TV, Tun-hua, South Rd, Lane 451, No 8, P.O. Box 24042, Taipei, T: 772136/37.
Lutheran Voice, Taipei.
Overseas Radio & Television Inc, Pei An Rd., Lane 501, No 55, P.O. Box 37003, Taipei, T: 559144.
Southern Baptist Mission Radio Studio, 47-1 Hwaining St, Taipei, T: 39887.
TEAM/Far East Broadcasting Company, P.O. Box 153, Taichung.
UNDA/Taiwan ROC, N 20, Lane 233, Tun Hua St. Rd., Sec 1, Taipei, T: 886-2-771 21 36, F: 886-2-771 22 46, O: Telex: 785-27944 CORIMAC.
Voice of Salvation, Box 44-80, Taipei 10098, T: 011-8862754-1144, F: 011-8862755-7822, O: E-mail: vosjh@ms1.hinet.net.
Wisdom Mass Media Center (FSP), 21 Chunghsiao W. Rd., Sect. 1, Taipei, T: 02-3710447.

TANZANIA

Catholic Broadcasting, Catholic Secretariat, PO Box 2133, Dar es Salaam.
Joint Christian Religious Broadcasting Committee, P.O. Box 2133 & 2537, Dar es Salaam.
Sauti ya Injili (Radio Voice of the Gospel)(RVOG), Lutheran Radio Centre, Dir, Box 777, Moshi.

THAILAND

Catholic Office MCS, Marivithaya School, Nakhornrajasima.
National Catholic Office for Radio and TV, 251/1 Surinari Rd., Nakhon Ratchasima.
Programme Production Center (B-RAVA), 14 Pramuan Rd, Bangkok.
Radio-TV and Visual Aids Dept, Southern Baptist Mission, GPO Box 832, Bangkok.
Voice of Peace, P.O. Box 131, Chiang Mai.
Voice of Prophecy Studio, P.O. Box 234, Prakanong, Bangkok 10110.

TOGO

Emissions Catholiques (Collège St Joseph), BP 63, Lomé.

TRINIDAD & TOBAGO

Caribbean Committee for Joint Christian Action (CCJCA), Trinidad and Tobago Television, Television House, Maraval Rd, Port of Spain.
Catholic Broadcasting, Catholic Centre, 52A Jerningham Ave., Port of Spain.

UGANDA

Catholic Association of Broadcasts & Cinematographers of Uganda (CABCU), c/o Social Communications Comm., P.O. Box 2886, Kampala, T: 256-41-26 77 99, F: 256-41-26 81 04.
Literature and Radio Centre, Church of Uganda, Box 4, Mukono, T: 644.

UKRAINE

Christian Broadcasting Network Intl., Oktoberskaya Revolutsija dom 1, Kiev 252001, T: 7-044-290-8982, F: 7-044-228-6593.

UNITED STATES OF AMERICA (USA)

Abundant Life Television, P.O. Box 7700, Lake Charles, LA 70606, T: 318-478-1112.
Accent International Radio, P.O. Box 610323, Dallas, TX 75261.
Accuracy in Media, 4455 Connecticut Ave., N.W. #330, Washington, DC 20008, T: 202-364-4401, F: 202-364-4098.
Adventist Broadcasting Service, Inc., 12501 Old Columbia Pike, Silver Spring, MD 20904-6600, T: 301-680-6302.
Adventist Media Center, 101 W. Cochran St., Simi Valley, CA 93065, T: 805-373-7777, F: 805-373-7702.
Alaska Radio Mission-Knom, P.O. Box 988, Nome, AK 99762, T: 907-443-5221, F: 907-443-5757.
Amateur Radio Missionary Service, 560 Main St., Chatham, NJ 07928.
American Family Radio, P.O. Box 2440, Tupelo, MS 38803, T: 601-844-8888.
American Religious Town Hall, 745 N. Buckner, Dallas, TX 75218, T: 214-328-9828, F: 214-328-3042.
Answers in Genesis, P.O. Box 6330, Florence, KY 41022, T: 606-647-2900, F: 606-371-4448, O: E-mail: cen@usa.
Antonio Orona Ministry, P.O. Box 370, Chesterfield, VA 23832, T: 804-230-0728, F: 804-674-1190.
Art of Family Living, P.O. Box 33000, Colorado Springs, CO 80933, T: 719-593-0200, F: 719-593-8761.
Association Evangelistica Misionera Alberto Espada-Matta, Inc., 20 Colton Rd., Edison, NJ 08817, T: 908-985-8509.
AWR-Adventist World Radio, 12501 Old Columbia Pike, Silver Spring, MD 20904-6600, T: 1-301-680-6304, F: 1-301-680-6303.
Back to God Hour, 6555 W. College Drive, Palos Heights, IL 60463, T: 708-371-8700, F: 708-371-1415.
Back to the Bible International, P.O. Box 82808, Lincoln, NE 68501, T: 402-464-7200, F: 402-464-7474, O: E-mail: Info@backtothebible.org, Web: www.backtothebible.org.
Beverly Exercise TV Corp., P.O. Box 5434, Anderson, SC 29623, T: 864-225-5799.
Bible-Science Association, Inc., P.O. Box 48220, Minneapolis, MN 55433, T: 800-422-4253, F: 612-856-2525.
Black Buffalo Trails, P.O. Box 2607, Hemet, CA 92546, T: 909-925-9083, F: 909-766-0043.
Black Catholic Televangelization Network, 5247 Sheridan Ave., Detroit, MI 48213.
Bob Larson Ministries, P.O. Box 36096, Denver, CO 80236, T: 303-980-1511, F: 303-986-1023, O: E-mail: bob@bob-larson.com.
Branches Communications, Inc., P.O. Box 6688, Orange, CA 92613, T: 714-997-8451, F: 714-997-8453, O: E-mail: 70506.1237@compuserve.com.
Briargate Media, Ltd., P. O. Box 998, Colorado Springs, CO 80901, T: 719-531-3300, F: 719-531-3302.
Broadcast & Film Commission, NCCCUSA, 475 Riverside Drive, New York, NY 10027, T: 212-870-2251.
Brooklyn Diocesan TV Centre, 500 19th St., Brooklyn, NY 11215.
Campmeeting Ministries, Inc., 3948 Hwy. 90, Pace, FL 32571, T: 904-994-7131, F: 904-994-9936.
Capitol Hill News, Inc., P.O. Box 5584, Washington, DC 20016, T: 202-462-3966.
Carolina Christian Broadcasting, P.O. Box 1616, Greenville, SC 29602, T: 864-244-1616, F: 864-292-8431.
Cathedral Caravan, Inc., 6550 Mango Ave. S., St. Petersburg, FL 33707, T: 813-347-2865, F: 813-381-4917.
Catholic Communications Office, 65 Elliot St., Springfield, MA 01101, T: 413-732-4546, F: 413-747-0273.
Catholic Perspective, O: Web: www.interpath.net/~toddwall/cathpers.html.
Catholic Telecommunications Network of America (CTNA), 3211 Fourth St., N.E., Fifth Fl., Washington, D.C. 20017-1194, O: E-mail: CATHOLICTV@connectinc.com.
CDR Communications, Inc., 9310-B Old Keene Mill Rd., Burke, VA 22015, T: 703-569-3400, F: 703-569-3448.
Center for Religious Telecommunications, University of Dayton, 102 Alumni Hall, Dayton, OH 45469, T: 513-229-3126, F: 513-229-4000.
Central Africa Broadcasting Company, 309 Laurel, Box A, Friendswood, TX 77546.
Challenger Films, Inc., 3361 Cardinal Lade Dr., Ste. A, Duluth, GA 30136, T: 404-476-3232, F: 404-476-2115.
Chapel of the Air Ministries, P.O. Box 30, Wheaton, IL 60189, T: 630-668-7292, F: 630-668-9660.
Children of the King Ministries, P.O. Box 92073, Elk Grove Village, IL 60009, T: 815-485-3792.
Children's Bible Hour, P.O. Box, Grand Rapids, MI 49501, T: 616-451-2009, F: 616-451-0032, O: E-mail: cbh@gospelcom.net.
Christ Truth Radio Crusade, 189 Wagner Drive, Claremont, CA 91711, T: 714-624-8875.
Christian Amateur Radio Fellowship (CARF), Route 3, Box 234. Worthington, MN 56187.
Christian Broadcasters Inc (KSEW), Box 258, Sitka, Alaska.
Christian Broadcasting Network, 1000 Centerville Tnpk., Virginia Beach, VA 23463; CBN Center, Virginia Beach, VA 23463, T: 757-579-7000, F: 757-579-2017, O: Web: www.cbn.org.
Christian Children'a Associates, Inc., P.O. Box 446, Toms River, NJ 08754, T: 201-240-3003.
Christian College Network, P.O. Box 250, Montreat, NC 28757, T: 704-669-9211, F: 704-669-6119, O: E-mail: 9695@aol.com.
Christian Film & TV Commission, 3079 Crossing Park Rd. St. 700, Norcross, GA 30071; Branch Off: P. O. Box 64, Camarillo, CA 93011, T: 770-825-0084, F: 770-825-0052, O: Branch Off: ph 805-383-2000, fax 805-383-4089.
Christian Radio Mission (Korea), 306 East Gerald, San Antonio, TX 78214.
Christian Reformed Church in North America, 6555 W. College Dr., Palos Heights, IL 60463, T: 708-371-8700, F: 708-371-1415.
Christian Research Institute, 17 Hughes Rd., Irvine, CA 92718, T: 714-855-9926, F: 714-951-6868.

Christian Television & Film Productions, 604 NE 20th Ave., Portland, OR 97232.
Christian Television Mission, P.O. Box 3411, Springfield, MO 658804, T: 417-881-6303.
Christian Television Network, P.O. Box 6922, Clearwater, FL 34618, T: 813-535-5622.
Christians United for Reformation (CURE), 2221 E. Winston Rd., Ste. K, Anaheim, CA 92806, T: 800-956-2644, F: 714-956-5111.
Christians' Hour, P.O. Box 1001, Cincinnati, OH 4520, T: 513-661-4240.
Christophers, 12 East 48th St., New York, NY 10017, T: 212-759-4050, F: 212-838-5073.
Church of Jesus Christ of Latter Day Saints, 15 East S. Temple St., Salt Lake City, UT 84150, T: 801-240-4397, F: 801-240-1167.
Columbia Union College Broadcasting, Inc., 7600 Flower Ave., Takoma Park, MD 20912.
Community Satellite Corp., P.O. Box 9060, Farmington Hills, MI 48018, T: 813-261-4703, O: Also: 813-262-1433.
Coral Ridge Ministries, c/o C.R. Adv. Associates, 5554 N. Federal Hwy., Fort Lauderdale, FL 33308, T: 954-771-7858, F: 954-491-7975.
Cornerstone Television, Rt. 48, Signal Hill Dr., Wall, PA 15148, T: 412-824-3930, F: 412-824-5442.
Covenant Marriages Ministry, 17301 W. Colfax Ave., #140, Golden, CO 80401, T: 303-277-9885, F: 303-277-1421.
Covenant Productions, 1100 E. 5th St., Anderson, IN 46012, T: 314-641-4348, F: 317-641-3825.
Creative Edge Communications, 9581 Business Ctr. Dr., Ste. A, Rancho Cucamnga, CA 91730, T: 909-980-8916, F: 909-980-8203, O: E-mail: 74047.227@compuserve.com.
Creative Juice Communications, 10120 Central Ave., Indianapolis, IN 46280, T: 317-844-6580, F: 317-844-7470.
Crystal Cathedral Ministries, 12141 Lewis St., Garden Grove, CA 92640, T: 714-971-4075.
Daystar, Inc., P.O. Box 6970, Springdale, AR 72766, T: 501-751-4523, F: 501-756-7109.
Derek Prince Ministries International, P. O. Box 19501, Charlotte, NC 28219, T: 704-357-3556, F: 704-357-1413.
Disciples Amateur Radio Fellowship, c/o A. Sharp, 67156 Joella, St. Clairsville, OH 43950.
Dominion Network/Video Satellite, PO Box 9060, Farmington Hills, MI 48018, USA, T: 813-262-1433, F: 813-261-1433.
Dove Broadcasting, Inc., P.O. Box 1616, 3409 Rutherford Rd., Greenville, SC 29602, T: 864-244-1616, F: 864-292-8481.
EBI Video, Inc., 5000 Tremont, #202, Davenport, IA 52807, T: 319-391-0619, F: 319-391-2568, O: E-mail: ebivideo@aol.com.
Ecumenical Communications, P.O. Box 270999, West Hartford, CT 06127, T: 860-585-0590.
Encounter Ministries, Inc., P.O. Box 757800, Memphis, TN 38175, T: 901-757-7977, F: 901-757-1372, O: E-mail: olford@memphisonline.com.
Endtime, Inc., 1214 S. 8th St., Richmond, IN 47375, T: 317-962-6344, F: 317-962-9417.
Episcopal Radio TV Foundation, 15 16th St., NE, Atlanta, GA 30309, T: 404-892-0141.
Eternal Word Television Network (EWTN), 5817 Old Leeds Rd., Birmingham, AL 35210, T: 205-956-9537, F: 205-956-0328, O: Web: www.catholic.org/ewtn/ewtn.htm..
Eurafilm, 21 E. 90th St., Ste. 8C, New York, NY 10128, T: 212-348-6926, F: 212-860-5725.
Evangelical Ministries, 1716 Spruce St., Philadelphia, PA 19103, T: 215-546-3696, F: 215-735-5133.
Excellence in Christian Broadcasting (EICB), P. O. Box 2528, Cedar Hill, TX 75106, T: 972-291-3750, F: 972-293-8506, O: E-mail: rwe352@airmail.net.
Family Life Radio, P. O. Box 35300, Tuscon, AZ 85740, T: 520-742-6976, F: 520-742-6979.
Family Radio, 290 Hegenberger Road, Oakland CA 94621, T: 510-568-6200, F: 510-562-1023.
Family Theater Productions, 7201 Sunset Blvd., Hollywood, CA 90046, T: 213-874-6633.
Familynet, 6350 W. Fwy., Fort Worth, TX 76150, T: 800-832-6638, F: 817-737-7853, O: E-mail: mail@familynet.org.
Far East Broadcasting Company, P. O. Box 1, La Mirada, CA 90637; 15700 E. Imperial Hwy., T: 562-947-4651, F: 562-943-0160, O: E-mail: FEBC@febc.org, www.febc.org.
Father Justin Rosary Hour, Station F - Box 217, Buffalo, NY 14212, T: 716-627-3861.
Four Winds Marketing, P.O. Box 3102, La Grange, GA 30240, T: 706-882-5368, F: 706-882-7999, O: E-mail: fwi@wp-lag.mindspring.com.
Franciscan Canticle, Inc., 13333 Palmdale Rd., Victorville, CA 92392, T: 619-241-2538.
Franciscan Communications Center (St. Francis Productions), 1229 South Santee St., Los Angeles, CA 90015, T: 213-748-2191.
Freedom in Christ Ministries, 491 E. Lambert Road, La Habra, CA 90631, T: 310-691-9128, F: 310-691-4035.
Galcom International, Box 16989, Tampa, FL 33687, T: 813-989-1755, F: 813-985-4816.
Gateway to Joy, O: Web: www.gatewaytojoy.org.
Gift of Encouragement Ministries/Loveland Communications, Box 8, Loveland, OH 45140, T: 513-575-4300, F: 513-575-2024, O: E-mail: encouragement@goodnews.net.
Good Friends, Inc., P.O. Box 2000, Goodyear, AZ, 85338, T: 602-932-2292, F: 602-932-1167.
Good News Productions International, P.O. Box 222, Joplin, MO 64802, T: 417-782-0060, F: 417-782-3999, O: E-mail: GNPI@xc.org.
Gospel Bandstand Ministries, P.O. Box 669, Fulton, TX 78358, T: 512-729-4249, F: 512-729-5338.
Gospel Music Television Network, P.O. Box 3428, Wilson, NC 27895, T: 919-237-3190, F: 919-237-1167.
Grace to You, 24900 Anza Dr., Valencia, CA 91355, T: 805-295-5777, F: 805-295-5779, O: E-mail: letters@gty.org.
Greek Orthodox Archdiocese of N&S America, 8-10 East 79th St., New York, NY 10021, T: 212-628-2500.
Growing in Grace Media Ministries/Church of the Open Door, 6421 45th Ave. N., Minneapolis, MN 55428, T: 612-522-3641, F: 612-522-8871, O: E-mail: 103215.3762@compuserve.com.
Guidelines International, 26076 Getty Dr., Laguna Niguel, CA 92677, T: 714-582-5001, F: 714-582-5026, O: E-mail: 74357.2751@compuserve.com.
HCCN Hispanic International Communications Network, P.O. Box 341700, Los Angeles, CA 90034, T: 310-837-8171, F: 310-837-8174.
HCJB World Radio Missionary Fellowship, P.O. Box 39800, Colorado Springs, CO 80949; 1065 Garden of the Gods Road, T: 719-590-9800, F: 719-590-9801, O: E-mail: PTolles@mhs.wrmf.org, Web: www.hcjb.org.ec.
Heaven & Home Hour, Inc., P. O. Box 100, Glendale, CA 91209, T: 818-241-3415, F: 818-241-1731.
Herald of Hope, Inc., P.O. Box 3, Breezewood, PA 15533, T: 717-485-4021.
Hermano Pablo Ministries, P.O. Box 100, Costa Mesa, CA 92628, T: 714-645-0676, F: 714-645-0374.
High Adventure Ministries/Voice of Hope Broadcasting Network, P.O. Box 100, Simi Valley, CA 93062, T: 805-520-9460, F: 805-520-7823, O: Web: www.highadventure.org.
Hispanic Telecommunications Network, 130 Lewis St., San Antonio, TX 78212, T: 210-227-5959, F: 210-554-0822.
Holy Archangel Broadcasting Center, 3770 39th St., N.W., Washington, DC 20016, T: 202-362-1775, F: 202-362-1775.
Home Education Radio Network, P.O. Box 3338, Idaho Springs, CO 80452, T: 303-567-4092.
Hour of Prophecy, P.O. Box 1417, Fort Worth, TX 76101; Highway 67, Keene, TX 76059, T: 817-641-9897.
Impact International, Inc., P.O. Box 2530, Boca Raton, FL 33427, T: 407-338-7515, F: 407-338-7516, O: E-mail: impactoint@aol.com.
Impact Productions, 3939 S. Harvard Ave., Tulsa, OK 74135, T: 800-422-7863, 918-746-0888, F: 918-746-0847, O: E-mail: kthompson@impactprod.org, Web: www.impactprod.org.
In Touch Ministries, 3836 DeKalb Technology Pkwy., Atlanta, GA 30340, T: 770-451-1001, F: 770-936-6399.
Insight for Living, 1065 Pacific Center Dr., Suite 400, Anaheim, CA 92806-2126, T: 714-575-5000, F: 714-575-5683.
Inspirational Network-INSP, 9700 Southern Pine Blvd., Charlotte, NC 28273, T: 704-525-9800, F: 704-525-9899.
Instructional Television, 215 Seminary Ave., Yonkers, NY 10704, T: 914-968-7800.
International Mission Radio Association (IMRA), WIHWK, Western Observatory, Weston, MA 02193.
International Russian Radio/TV, O: Web: www.serve.com/irr-tv.
International Television & Evangelism Center, P.O. Box 1681, Bellevie, WA 98009, T: 800-488-3153, F: 360-638-1625, O: E-mail: rtecpaul@sound-com.net, itecvideo.net.
International Mission Radio Association, c/o St. Anthony's Church, 250 Revere St., Revere, MA 02151, T: 617-289-1234.
Jack Van Impe Ministries, 1718 Northfield Dr., Rochester Hills, MI 48309, T: 810-852-2244, F: 810-852-2692, O: E-mail: jvimi@jvim.
Jimmy Swaggart Ministries, P.O. Box 262550, Baton Rouge, LA 70826, T: 504-768-8300.
John Ankerberg Show, P.O. Box 8977, Chattanooga, TN 37414, T: 423-892-7722, F: 423-892-8767, O: E-mail: 104665.2435@compuserve.com.
Jubilee Network, 1333 S. Sirkwood Rd., St. Louis, MO 63122, T: 800-325-6333, F: 314-965-3396, O: E-mail: ic_rassbajw@lcms.org.
Juventud Evangelica, Inc. (Evangelical Youth), 139 Macoma Ct., Fort Myers, FL 33908, T: 941-466-1194.
Kenneth Copeland Ministries, 14335 Morris Dido Rd., Newark, TX 76071, T: 817-489-3701.
Kenneth Hagin Ministries, P.O. Box 50126, Tulsa, OK 74150, T: 918-258-1588, F: 918-251-8016.
Key Life Network, Inc., 539 Versailles Dr., Maitland, FL 32751, T: 407-539-0001, F: 407-539-0121.
King is Coming World Wide Ministries, P.O. Box One, Washington, DC 20044, T: 703-979-7496, F: 703-271-8321.
Korean Christian Broadcasting Network, 1204 Broadway, Suite 400, New York, NY 10001, T: 212-447-0780.
Korean Christian Broadcasting Systems, 2839 W. Lawrence Ave., #1C, Chicago, IL 60625.
Lamb & Lion Ministries, P.O. Box 919, McKinney, TX 75070, T: 214-736-3567, F: 214-734-1054, O: E-mail: lamblion@lamblion.com.
Landmark Communications Group, P.O. Box 1444, Hendersonville, TN 37077, T: 615-452-3234, F: 615-868-0419.
Larry Lea Ministries, P.O. Box 600570, San Diego, CA 92160, T: 918-665-7729, F: 918-665-0090.
Laymen's Hour, Inc., P.O. Box 90066, Pasadena, CA 91109, T: 818-359-3869.
Leading the Way International, 3585 Northside Pkwy., Atlanta, GA 30327, T: 404-841-0100, F: 404-841-0117.
LESEA Broadcasting Network, P.O. Box 12, South Bend, IN 46624, T: 219-291-8200, F: 219-291-9043.
Let's Go Racing Productions, P.O. Box 853, Destin, FL 32540, T: 800-418-8971, F: 904-654-5453.
Liberty Broadcasting Network, 1971 University Blvd., Lynchburg, VA 24502-2269, T: 804-582-2607, F: 804-582-2918.
Lifeword Broadcast Ministries, 535 Enterprise Ave., Conway, AR 72032, T: 501-329-6891, F: 501-329-7951.
Ligonier Ministries, Inc., 400 Technology Pk., Lake Mary, FL 32746, T: 800-435-4343, F: 407-333-4233.
Living Way Ministries, 14820 Sherman Way, Van Nuys, CA 91405, T: 818-779-8400, F: 818-779-8411, O: E-mail: rmedall@livingway.org.
Lloyd Ogilvie Ministries, Inc., 6037 Hollywood Blvd., Hollywood, CA 90028, T: 213-464-7690.
Love Song to the Messiah, 7264 W. Oakland Park Blvd., Fort Lauderdale, FL 33313, T: 954-741-3160, F: 954-741-0794.
Love Worth Finding Ministries, P.O. Box 38-300, 2941 Kate Bond # 107, Memphis, TN 38133, T: 901-382-7900, F: 901-388-8346, O: Web: www.lwf.org, E-mail: lovwf@accessus.net.
Lumen School of Telecommunications, 4500 West Davis, P.O. Box 225008, Dallas, TX 75265, T: 214-333-2337, F: 214-333-2595.
Lutheran Church Television Production, 210 North Broadway, St. Louis, MO 63102, T: 314-231-6969.
Lutheran Hour Ministries, 2185 Hampton Ave., St. Louis, MO 63139-2983, T: 800-944-3450, F: 314-951-4295, O: E-mail: hm@gospelcom.net, Web: www.lhmint.org/.
Lutheran Ministries Media, Inc., 3425 Crescent Ave., Fort Wayne, IN 46805, T: 219-483-3173, F: 219-471-6141.
Marian Hour Radio Rosary Site, O: Web: net-page.bc.ca./marianhr.
Marienschwester (Darmstadt), Fairbanks, Alaska.
Marilyn Hickey Ministries, P.O. Box 17340, Denver, CO 80217, T: 303-770-0400, F: 303-796-1322.
Mars Hill Network, 4044 Makyes Rd., Syracuse, NY 13215, T: 315-469-5051, F: 315-469-4066, O: E-mail: mhnetwork@aol.com.
Maryknoll World Productions, Gonzaga Bldg., Maryknoll, NY 10545, T: 914-941-7590, F: 914-945-0670.
Media Ministries of the Assemblies of God, P.O. Box 70, Springfield, MO 65801, T: 417-869-8829, F: 417-862-5974, O: E-mail: media@ag.org.
Messianic Minutes, P.O. Box 4006, Frederick, MD 21705, T: 301-695-4496, F: 301-696-1879, O: E-mail: elshaddai@msn.com.
Methodist Bible Hour, International, 4078 Silver Lake Dr., Palatka, FL 32177, T: 904-328-4424, F: 904-328-6602, O: E-mail: cimcl@msn.com.
Morning Chapel Hour/Touchstone Ministries, Inc., P.O. Box 900, Paramount, CA 90723, T: 310-634-7988, F: 310-634-2195.
Musical Memories, Box 907, Oak Park, IL 60303, T: 708-771-9390, F: 708-771-9390.
National Interfaith Cable Coalition, Inc., 74 Trinity Pl., Ste. 1810, New York, NY 10016, T: 212-406-4121, F: 212-406-4105.
National Religious Broadcasters, 7839 Ashton Ave., Manassas, VA 20109, T: 703-330-7000, F: 703-330-7100, O: E-mail: mkisha@nrb.com, Web: www.nrb.com.
Northwestern Productions, 3003 N. Snelling Ave., St. Paul, MN 55113, T: 612-631-5040, F: 612-631-5010, O: E-mail: njp@nwc.edu.
Odyssey, 74 Trinity Pl., 9th Fl., New York, NY 10006, T: 212-964-1663, F: 212-964-5966.
Office for Film and Broadcasting (Catholic), 1011 First Avenue, Suite 1300, New York, NY 10022, T: 212-644-1880, F: 212-644-1886.
Old-Fashioned Revival Hour, 44 South Mentor Ave., Pasadena, CA 91101.
Overseas Radio & Television, Inc., P.O. Box 118, Seattle, WA 98118, T: 206-634-1919, F: 206-547-0400, O: Web: www.ortv.com.tw.
Pacific Garden Mission, 646 S. State St., Chicago, IL 60605, T: 312-922-1462, F: 312-922-7766, O: E-mail: unshackled@pgm.org.
Para Ti Mujer, P.O. Box 40, Irmo, SC 29063, T: 803-798-5771, F: 803-798-7575, O: E-mail: jcarlosm@aol.com.
Paragon Communications, 11 Spiral Dr., Ste. 3, Florence, KY 41042; Knoxville, TN (423-986-7777), T: 606-647-2800.
Parent Talk Radio, 7355 N. Oracle #200, Tucson, AZ 85704, T: 520-742-6976, F: 520-742-6979, O: E-mail: 75113.3340@compuserve.com.
Plain Truth Ministries Worldwide, 300 W. Green St., Pasadena, CA 91129, T: 818-304-6077, F: 818-795-0107.
Potter's Clay Group, P.O. Box 1051, Vero Beach, FL 32961, T: 407-337-9872.
Powerpoint Ministries, 15720 Hillcrest, Dallas, TX 75248, T: 214-387-4475, F: 214-991-9865.
Praise, Box 5331, Woodbridge, VA 22194, T: 703-590-0214, F: 703-670-6871.
Precept Ministries, Inc., P.O. Box 182218, Chattanooga, TN 37422, T: 423-892-6814, F: 423-499-0357.
Probe Ministries, 1900 Firman Dr., #100, Richardson, TX 75081, T: 214-480-0240, F: 214-644-9664.
Proclaiming the Message Ministries, 5061 Forest Rd., Mentor, OH 44060, T: 800-627-5937, F: 216-951-3929, O: E-mail: proclaim@harborcom.net.
Protestant Radio and Television Center, Inc., 1727 Clifton Rd., NE, Atlanta, GA 30329, T: 404-634-3324, F: 404-634-3326.
Pure Vision Ministries, 1615 N. El Camino Real #G, San Clemente, CA 92672, T: 714-492-4575, F: 714-492-0457, O: E-mail: brace@thegospel.com, Web: www.thegospel.com.
Quiet Hour, 630 Brooksire Ave., Box 3000, Redlands, CA 92373, T: 909-793-2588, F: 909-793-4754, O: E-mail: 74044.504@compuserve.
Radio Bible Class, Grand Rapids, MI 49555; P.O. Box 22, T: 616-942-6770, F: 616-957-5741, O: E-mail: RBC@rbc.net, Web: www.rbc.net.
Radio Voice of Christ, Inc., P.O. Box 7145, Beaverton, OR 97007, T: 503-649-0717.
Radio Worldwide, O: Web: ourworld.compuserve.com/homepages/rw.
RBC Ministries, P.O. Box 22, 3000 Kraft SE, Grand Rapids, MI 49555, T: 616-942-6770, F: 616-957-5741, O: E-mail: rbc@rbc.net.
Reach Satellite Network (RSN), 220 Great Circle Rd., Ste. 132, Nashville, TN 37228, T: 800-742-3969, F: 615-251-4094.
Reforma TV (La Hora De La Reforma), 6555 W. College Dr., Palos Heights, IL 60463, T: 708-371-8700, F: 708-371-1415, O: E-mail: eleanor@crc-net.mhs.compuserve.com.
Religious Broadcasting Magazine, P.O. Box 1926, Morristown, NJ 07962-1926.
Renewal Radio, P.O. Box 2400, Dallas, TX 75221, T: 800-736-3925, F: 214-578-9448, O: E-mail: renewal@airmail.net.
Robert H. Schuller Ministries, P.O. Box 100, Garden Grove, CA 92640, T: 714-971-4133, F: 714-971-2910.
Rock Solid Video Show, 201 Battle Ave., #4, Franklin, TN 37064, T: 615-591-9739.
Ron Hutchcraft Ministries, Inc., P.O. Box 1818, Wayne, NJ 07474-1818, T: 201-696-2161, F: 201-694-1182, O: E-mail: rhm@gospelcom.net.
Russian Christian Radio, P.O. Box 1667, Estes Park, CO 80517, T: 303-586-8638, F: 303-586-8713.
Russian Radio Bible Institute, 19 Summer St., Passaic, NJ 07055, T: 201-777-5173, F: 215-361-7994.
Russian-Ukrainian Radio Mission, P.O. Box 94, Millbrae, CA 94030, T: 415-697-3274.
Sacred Heart Program (Radio, TV), 3900 Westminster Place, St. Louis, MO 63108.
Salvation Army, 1424 Northeast Expwy., Atlanta, GA 30329, T: 404-728-6727, F: 404-728-6755.
SBC Radio & Television Commission, 6350 W. Fwy., Fort Worth, TX 76150, T: 817-737-4011, F: 817-377-4372, O: E-mail: mail@rtvc.org.
Seed Time Ministries, Inc., P.O. Box 580, Post Falls, ID 83854, T: 208-664-4883.
Select Religious Broadcasting Service, P.O. Box 1714, Spartanburg, SC 29304, T: 864-585-0470, F: 864-583-7946.
Seventh-day Adventist Radio, Television and Film Center (Adventist Media Center), 1100 Rancho Conejo Blvd., Newbury Park, CA 91320, T: 805-373-7777, F: 805-373-7702.
Shepherd Productions, 506 N. Garden St., Columbia, TN 38401, T: 615-388-9634, F: 615-381-2989, O: E-mail: dmlive@christianradio.com.
Slavic Gospel Association, 6151 Commonwealth Dr., Loves Park, IL 61111, T: 815-282-8900, F: 815-282-8901, O: E-mail: sga@sga.org.
Sounds of Joy, Inc., 362 N. 1350 E., Greentown, IN 46936, T: 317-628-3074.
Spacecom Systems Satellite, One Technology Plaza, 7140 S. Lewis Ave., Tulsa, OK 74136, T: 800-950-6690, 918-488-4800 (outside USA), F: 918-488-4848, O: E-mail: info@spacecom.com, Web: www.spacecom.com.
Spoken Word of God, 1712 Lee Rd., Orlando, FL 32810, T: 407-290-0121, F: 407-578-6665, O: E-mail: swog@worldramp.net.
Square 1 Production Co., 500 N. Dixieland, #4, Rogers, AR 72756, T: 501-631-1177, F: 501-631-1177.
Stephen Yake Productions, Inc., 237 French Landing Dr., Nashville, TN 37228, T: 615-254-500, F: 615-254-5705.
Successful Concepts, P.O. Box 222, Orlando, FL 32802, T: 407-886-4073, F: 407-886-4073, O: E-mail: 76603.17@compuserve.com.
Telicare, 1345 Admiral Lane, Uniondale, NY 11553, T: 516-538-8700.
That's the Spirit Productions, Inc., P.O. Box 7466, Greenwich, CT 06830, T: 203-348-7114, F: 203-324-6915.
Theovision Network, 1539 E. Howard St., #U-7, Pasadena, CA 91104, T: 818-398-2481, F: 818-398-2483.
Three Angels Broadcasting Network, P.O. Box 220, West Frankfort, IL 62896, T: 618-627-4651, F: 618-627-4155.
Trans World Radio, P.O. Box 8700, Cary, NC 27512; 300 Gregson Dr., T: 919-460-3700, F: 919-460-3702, O: E-mail: Info@twr.org, www.twr.org.
Tri State Christian TV, P.O. Box 1010, Marion, IL 62959, T: 618-997-9333, F: 618-997-1859.
Tri-State Catholic Committee for Radio and Television, 138 Waverly Place, New York, NY 10014-3845.
Trinity Broadcasting Network (TBN), 2442 Michelle Dr., Tustin, CA 92680, T: 714-832-2950, F: 714-730-0657, O: Web: www.tbn.org/home.html.
Truth for Life, P.O. Box 2300, Orange, CA 92859, T: 714-282-0466, F: 714-282-0171, O: E-mail: tflca@aol.com, Web: www.gospelcom.net/tfl.
Turning Point w/Dr. David Jeremiah, P.O. Box 3838, San Diego, CA 92163, T: 619-258-3600, F: 619-258-3636.
TV Radio Films, American Lutheran Church, 1568 Eustis St., St. Paul, MN 55113, T: 612-645-9173.
TVFirst, 505 S Beverly Dr. #1017, Beverly Hills, CA 90212, T: 310-772-0770, F: 310-772-0714.
UNDA-USA, 4400 Shakertown Rd., Dayton, Oh 45430-1075, T: 513-429-2663, F: 513-429-2664.
Under His Wing Ministries, Inc., 1500 Warren Ave., Williamsport, PA 17701, T: 717-326-9099, F: 717-326-3793.
USA Radio Network, 2290 Springlake Rd. #107, Dallas, TX 75234, T: 214-484-3900, F: 214-241-6826.
Victory Television Network, P.O. Box 22007, 701 Napa Valley Dr., Little Rock, AR 72211, T: 501-223-2525, F: 501-221-3837, O: E-mail: jgrant@aristotle.net.
Videolight, Rt. 1, Box 790, Thomasville, NC 27360, T: 910-472-1197, F: 910-472-1131.
Vidicomp: Church TV Specialists, 10998 Wilcrest, Houston, TX 77099, T: 888-232-8995, 281-575-7100, F: 281-943-4110, O: E-mail: guybills@vidicomp.com, Web: www.vidicomp.com.
Vine Communications, Inc. & Vine Alliance, 7003 Chadwick Dr. #289, Brentwood, TN 37027, T: 615-371-5178, F: 615-371-8489.
Vision Broadcasting Network, 1017 New York Ave., Alamogordo, NM 88310, T: 505-437-6363.
Vision Interfaith Satellite Network, P.O. Box 5630, Denver, CO 80217, T: 800-522-5131, F: 303-488-3209.
VISN: Interfaith Cable TV network, National Interfaith Cable Coalition, 9th Fl, 74 Trinity Place, New York, NY 10006.
Voice of Orthodoxy, P.O. Box 743, Hartsdale, NY 10536.
Voice of Prophecy, P.O. Box 2525, Newbury Park, CA 91319, T: 805-373-7611, F: 805-373-7703, O: E-mail: 74617.3107@compuserve.com.
WEWN Worldwide Catholic Radio, O: Web: www.catholic.org/wewn/wewn.html.

Wilshire Church of Christ Radio Preaching, 4105 1/2 S. Jordan Ave., Edmond, OK 73013, T: 405-340-0877.
Winning Walk Ministry, 6400 Woodway, Houston, TX 77057, T: 713-465-9331, F: 713-365-2353, O: E-mail: cdavis@win-walk.org.
Word Alive International Christian Worship, 1301 Sunview Terr., Jensen Beach, FL 34957, T: 407-334-9892, F: 407-334-9890.
Word for Today, 3000 W. MacArthur Blvd., Third Fl., Santa Ana, CA 92704, T: 714-546-9211, F: 714-549-8865.
Words of Hope, P.O. Box 1706, Grand Rapids, MI 49501-1706, T: 616-459-6181, F: 616-459-3830, O: E-mail: woh@gospelcom.net.
World by 2000-Radio, 1605 Elizabeth St., Pasadena, CA 91104, O: Web: www.febc.org/wb2000.html.
World Christian Broadcasting Corp., 605 Bradley Court, Franklin, TN 37064.
World International Broadcasters, P.O. Box 88, Red Lion, PA 17356, T: 717-244-5360, F: 717-244-9316.
World Missionary Evangelism, Inc., P.O. Box 660800, Dallas, TX 75266, T: 214-942-1564, F: 214-942-2466.
World Radio Bible Broadcasts, P.O. Box 2000, West Monroe, LA 71294-2000; 3201 N. Seventh, T: 318-396-2031, F: 318-396-1000.
World Radio Missionary Fellowship, 20201 NW 37th Ave., P.O. Box 553000, Opa Locka, FL 33055, T: 305-624-4252.
World Satellite Evangelism, P.O. Box 35045, Tulsa, OK 74153, T: 918-492-3431.
Worship Network, 14444 66th St. N., Clearwater, FL 34624, T: 813-536-0036, F: 813-530-0671.
Z Music Television, 2806 Opryland Dr., Nashville, TN 37214, T: 615-871-7858, F: 615-871-7853.

URUGUAY
Centro Nacional de MCS, Cerrito 475, Montevideo, T: 85903, 91905.
Servício de Radio y TV, Cerrito 485, Montevideo.
UNDA/Association Catholique Internationale pour la Radiodiffusion et la Télévision, Latin American Secretariat (UNDA-AL), Cerrito 475, Montevideo.

VANUATU
PIBA (Pacific Islands Broadcasting Association), Box 116, Port Vila, T: 678-24-250, F: 678-24-252.

VENEZUELA
TEAM Recording Studio, Apdo 355, San Cristobal, Tachira.

VIET NAM
Television Service Centre for Community Development (THDL), 161 Yen-do, P.O. Box 2094, Saigon, T: 98427.

US VIRGIN ISLANDS
Caribbean Catholic Network (CCN), Channel 7, St. Croix 00850, T: 809-779-3000.

WALLIS & FUTUNA ISLANDS
Komite Unda, B.P. 150, Mata-Utu, T: 681-72-26-82, F: 681-72-27-83.

YUGOSLAVIA
Voice of Hope, Bozidara Adzije 4, 11000 Belgrade.

ZAMBIA
Catholic Broadcasting, Zambia Catholic Secretariat, P.O. Box 1965, Lusaka.
Education TV Service, P.O. Box 1106, Kitwe.
Zambia Studio, Box 244, Lusaka.

ZIMBABWE
Radio and Television Apostolate, Zimbabwe Catholic Bishops' Conference, P.O. Box 1221, Salisbury.
Sound Studio Driefontein Mission, P Bag 9001, Gwelo.

11 Broadcast stations

A brief selection of church- or Christian-owned, -operated, -controlled, or -sponsored radio, TV, or satellite broadcasting stations (organized centers with transmitting equipment).

12 Camps, retreat centers, lay training centers

Places and programs dedicated to the training, education, instruction, spiritual refreshment, renewal, or spiritual growth of laypeople, almost always with a physical building, campus, or site; conference, fellowship, renewal, or retreat centers; camps for children, youth, or adults; study centers, Catholic pastoral centers and institutes, major Catholic catechetical centers, lay seminaries; leadership training or Christian service training sites; wilderness camps and programs; organizations for lay training through conferences, institutes, discipleship groups, or classes. Specialized training centers are listed under many of the other categories, by topic.

13 Catechesis & Christian education

Organizations helping with Christian training and education for children, youth, and adults; Sunday schools, Sabbath schools, vacation Bible schools, Bible teaching, Bible classes, catechism classes, confirmation classes and courses; councils, organizations, and agencies of religious education; agencies producing or distributing curricula, books, media, and resources for all such education; catechetics.

ALGERIA
Commission d'Enseignement Religieux d'Afrique du Nord, La Palmeraie, El-Biar, El Djezair.
Secrétariat National des Ecoles Diocésaines, 6 Rue Tagore, El Djezair.

ARGENTINA0
Consejo Superior de Educación Católica, Cordoba 1439, Buenos Aires.
Consejo Unido de Educación Cristiana (CUEC), Postal Dist. 161 Suc. 6, Juan Bautista Alberdi 2240, 1406 Buenos Aires, T: 541-613-6162, F: 541-613-4992.
Unión Cristiana Americana de Educadores (UCADE), Brasil 721, Buenos Aires.

AUSTRALIA
Catholic Education Office, 18 Brunswick St., Fitzroy, Victoria 3065, T: 416657.
Divison of Christian Education, Australian Council of Churches, 100 Flinders St., Melbourne C1, Victoria.
Federal Catholic Education Office, P.O. Box 1213, Canberra, ACT 2601.
Universities Catholic Federation of Australia, 36 Cochrane St., Brighton, Victoria 3186.

AUSTRIA
Erzbischöfliches Amt für Unterricht und Erziehung, Kathechetisches Institut, Stephanplatz 3/IV, A-1010 Wien, T: 526448, 526473.
European Federation for Catholic Adult Education, Kapuzinestrasse 84, A-4020 Linz.

BANGLADESH
Diocesan Board of Education, Bishop's House, P.O. Box 152, Chittagong.

BARBADOS
Catechetical Commission (Catholic), Catechetics Office, St. Patrick's Cathedral, Bridgetown, T: 427-8183.
Education (Renewal) Agency (ERA), Christian Action for Development in the Caribbean (CADEC), P.O. Box 616, Bridgetown.

BELGIUM
Centre International d'Etudes de la Formation Religiuses 'Lumen Vitae', Rue Washington 184-186, b-1050 Brussel, T: 02-3435023.
Office International de L'Enseignement Catholique (OIEC), rue des Eburons, 60, B 1040 Bruxelles.
OIEC Bureau de Recrutement de Professeurs, Rue des Ebucons 60, B-1040 Brussel, T: 02-7363041.
Secrétariat National de l'Enseignement Catholique (SNEC), Rue Guimard 5, B-1040 Brussel, T: 02-5136880.

BENIN
Direction National de l'Enseignement Catholique, BP 153, Cotonou, T: 4009.

BERMUDA
Catechetical Director (Catholic), Box HM1191, Hamilton; Diocesan Centre, Hamilton, T: 809-292-1981.

BOLIVIA
Alfalit Boliviano, Junin 6305, Casilla 1466, Cochabamba, T: 4953.
Asociación Boliviana de Educación Católica (ABEC), Colegio San Calixto, Casilla 283, La Paz.

BOTSWANA
Botswana Sunday School Association (BOSSA), P.O. Box 20179, Gaborone, T: 352 272.

BRAZIL
Alfabetizaçã de Adultos, Campinas, SP.
Associação Educação Católica (AEC), Rua Martins Ferreira 23, Rio de Janeiro.
Comision Evangélica LatinoAmericana de Educación Cristiana-CELADEC, Postal Dist. 16130, CEP. 81611-970-Curitiba-PR, T: 555041-2221505.
Evangelical Latin American Commission on Christian Education, Sala 1203, Av Campos Salles 890, CP 1440, Campinas, SP Apdo 3994; Apdo 3994, Lima.
Instituto Batista de Educacão Religiosa, Rua Uruguai 514, Tijuca, RJ-20510 Rio de Janeiro.
Secretariado Nacional de Educação e Cultura, Ladeira da Glória 99, ZC-01 Rio de Janeiro, GB, T: 2253290.

BRITAIN (UK OF GB & NI)
Association of Religious in Education, Wightman Road, Hornsey, London N8 0BB.
Association for Religious Education, Highcroft House, Crown Lane, Four Oaks, Sutton Colfield, Warwick, T: 021-353-5956.
Catholic Education Council for England and Wales, 41 Cromwell Rd., London SW7 2DJ, T: 01-584-7491-5.
Christian Education Fellowship, 39 Bedford Square, London WC1B 3EY.
Christian Education Movement, Annandale, North End Rd., London NW11 7QX, T: 01-458-4366.
Church Education Corporation, 100 Brook Green, London W6 (Also: 35 Denison House, London SW1, T: 01-834-3319.
Church in Wales Provincial Council of Education, 8 Hickman Rd., Penarth, South Glamorgan CF6 2YQ, T: 708234-8234.
Church Schools Company, 29 Euston Rd., London NW1 2SL, T: 01-837-2979.
Corporation of SS Mary and Nicolas (The Woodard Schools), The Manor House, Grinshill, near Shrewsbury, Salop, T: Clive 293.
National Institute of Religious Education, Corpus Christi College, 17 Denbigh Rd., London W11 2SL, T: 01-229-0725.
National Society for Promoting Religious Education, Church House, Dean's Yard, Westminster, London SW1P 3NP, T: 01-222-1672.
Our Lady's Catechists, 34 Woocote Road, Wanstead, London E11 2QA, T: 0181-989 4814.
Sabbath School Society for Ireland, The Manse, 19 Castlehill Rd., Belfast 4, NI.
Schools Lecturers' Association, 4 Banton Lodge Ave., Newcastle-upon-Tyne NE7 7LU.
Scottish Sunday School Union for Religious Education, 70 Bothwell St., Glasgow C2.
Vacation Bible School Fellowship, 14 Cherry Walk, Grays, Essex RM16 4UN, T: 0375-822602.
World Council of Christian Education (WCCE), Hillside, Merry Hill Rd., Bushey, Herts, T: 01-950-4488,9.

BURKINA FASO
Union Nationale des Etablissements Catholiques (UNEC), BP 90, Ouagadougou.

BURUNDI
Secrétariat National de l'Enseignement Catholique (SNEC), BP 690, Bujumbura, T: 2942.

CAMEROON
Direction Nationale de l'Enseignement Catholique, BP 297, Yaoundé, T: 3331.
Equipes Enseignantes Africaines et Malgaches, BP 815, Yaoundé.

CANADA
Canadian Christian Education Foundation, Inc., c/o 2621 Cavendish Dr., Burlington, ON L7P 3W6, T: 905-336-5619, F: 905-524-1203.
Canadian Sunday School Mission, Room 24, 177 Lombard Ave., Winnipeg, Manitoba.
Department of Christian Education, Canadian Council of Churches, 40 St. Clair Av East, Toronto 7, Ontario.
National Education Office, Canadian Catholic Conference, 90 Parent Av, Ottawa 2, Ontario, T: 613-236-9461.
Ontario Alliance of Christian Schools, 777 Hwy. 53 East, Ancaster, ON L9G 3L4, T: 905-648-2100.
Society of Christian Schools in B.C., 7600 Glover Rd., Langley, BC V3A 6H4, T: 604-888-6366, F: 604-888-2791.
Ukrainian Catholic Religious Education Centre, 1236 College Dr., Saskatoon, SK S7N 0W4, T: 306-652-1718, F: 306-244-7720.

CENTRAL AFRICAN REPUBLIC
Bureau National de l'Enseignement Catholique, B.P. 798, Bangui.

CHAD
Direction Nationale l'Enseignement Privé, Archevêché, BP 456, Ndjamena (Fort Lamy), T: 2711.

CHILE
Federación Nacional Colegios Católicos, Alonso Ovalle 1546, Casilla 13305, Santiago.
Oficio Central de Educación Católica (OCEC), Erasmo Escala 1822, 6 piso, Casilla 723, Santiago.

CHINA
China Sunday School Association, 6 Granville Rd, 3/F, Kowloon, Hong Kong, T: K-672099.
Hong Kong Catholic Education Council (HKCED), St. Francis Xavier's College, Maple St, Shum Shui Po, Kowloon, Hong Kong.
Hong Kong Council for Christian Education, c/o Hip Woh Primary School, 191B Prince Edward Rd., Kowloon, Hong Kong, T: K-801752.

COLOMBIA
Comité Latinoamericana de la Fe (CLAF), Sección Catequistica, Apdo Aéreo 20621, Bogotá, DE.
Confederación Colegios Cubanos Católicos (CCCC), Calle 36, No 13A-09, Bogotá.
Confederación Interamericana de Educación Católica (CIEC), Sec Ejecutivo, Calle 78, 12-16, Apdo Aéreo 7478, Apdo National 401, Bogotá, T: 411189.
Conferencia Nacional de Colegios Católicos, Carrera 13A No 23-80, Bogotá.
Departamento de Educación (DEC), Apdo 21437, Bogotá, DE.

CONGO-ZAIRE
Bureau National de l'Enseignement Catholique, Av Adjudant Cassart, BP 3258, Kalina-Kinshasa, T: 30082.
OIEC Secrétariat Régional pour l'Afrique et Madagascar (SRAM), BP 3258, Kinshasa-Kalina, T: 30082.

COSTA RICA
Asociación de Establecimientos Privados de Enseñanza (AEPE), Colegio Calasanz, Apdo 3187 (and 6141), San José.

CYPRUS
MECC Unit on Education and Renewal, P.O. Box 48, Ayia Napa, T: 357-37-21284, F: 357-37-22584, O: Tlx: 5323 ANCC CY.

DENMARK
Danish Free Church Sunday School Association, Pilealle 7, DK-9460 Brovst.
Danish Sunday School Committee, Radman Steinsalle 202, DK-2000 Kobenhavn F.

DJIBOUTI
Secrétariat Diocesain de l'Enseignement Catholique, c/o Evêché Djibouti.

DOMINICA
Diocesan Catechetical Centre, Case O'Reil, Turkey Lane, Roseau, T: 809-44-84505.

DOMINICAN REPUBLIC
Unión Nacional de Colegios Católicos (UNCC), Residencia Universitaria San José de Calasanz, Av Independencia, Santo Domingo.

ECUADOR
Confederación Ecuatoriana de Establecimientos de Educación Católica, Secretariado Nacional Educación Católica, Casilla de Correros A-126, Quito.

EGYPT
Board of Christian Education and Sunday Schools, Coptic Orthodox Church, 28 Khalifa-el-Mansour, Heliopolis, Al Qahirah.
Collège de la Sainte Famille, Al Qahirah, T: 900411, 900892.
Egypt and Sudan Sunday School Union, 4 Samuel Morcos St., Terra El Boulakia, Shubra, P.O. Box 1422, Al Qahirah.

EL SALVADOR
Federación Nacional de Colegios Católicos, Av Espana 312, alos, Apdo 1617, San Salvador, T: 215584.
Secretariado Nacional de Educación, Arzobispado, 1c Pte 3402, San Salvador, T: 234124.

ETHIOPIA
Catholic Education Office, P.O. Box 2454, Addis Abeba.
Christian Education Centre, Central Synod EC-MY, P.O. Box 24, Nakamte.

FIJI
Pacific Islands Christian Education Council (PICEC), P.O. Box 208, Suva.

FINLAND
Finnish Sunday School Association, Uudenmaankatu 4, Helsinki.
Swedish Sunday School Association in Finland, Lutherinstitutet, Helsinki 32.

FRANCE
Catholic International Federation for Physical and Sports Education, 5, rue Cernuschi, F-75017 Paris, T: 924-3112.
Centre National de l'Enseignement Religieux, 6 Av Vavin, F-75006 Paris, T: 01-633-2160.
Dialogue et Coopération/Equipes Enseignantes, 140 Av Daumesnil, F-75012 Paris, T: 01-344-0506.
Secrétariat Générale de l'Enseignement Catholique, 277 Rue Saint Jacques, F-75005 Paris, T: 01-633-9450.
Service Technique pour l'Education (STE), 19 bd Poissonnière, F-75002 Paris.
Société des Ecoles du Dimanche, 15 Rue de Buci, F-75006 Paris.
Syndicat National de l'Enseignement Chrétien (SNEC), 58 Rue Custine, F-75018 Paris.
World Organization of Former Students of Catholic Schools, 17 Rue Michel Charles, F-75012 Paris, T: 01-343-7629.

GABON
Direction de l'Enseignement Catholique, BP 1179, Libreville, T: 3054.

GAMBIA
Education Secretariat, Catholic Mission, Bathurst.

GERMANY
Arbeitsgemeinschaft Evangelischer Schulbünde, Paul-Gerhardt-Schule, D-3354 Dassel (Solling).
Arbeitsgemeinschaft für Evangelische Unterweisung, Karl-Ludwig-Str 18, D-6992 Weikersheim.
Bischöfliche Hauptstelle für Schule und Erziehung, Rubensstr 25-27, D-5000 Köln 1, T: 0221-230692.
Bund Katholischer Erzieher Deutschlands (BKED), Goldenbrunnengasse 4, D-65 Mainz.
Bundesarbeitsgemeinschaft für Katholische Erwachsenenbildung, Dransdorfer Weg 15, D-5300 Bonn, T: 02221-655969.
Commission on Education, National Council of the Lutheran Churches in Germany, Am alten Kirchof 10, D-235 Neumunster.
European Association for Catholic Adult Education, Dransdorfer Weg 15/IV, D-5300 Bonn, T: 02221-655969.
Evangelischer Schulbund in Bayern, Wilhilm-Löhe-Schule, Rollnerstr 15, D-85 Nürnberg.
Katholisches Schulkommissariat Bayern I und Bayern II, Maxburgstr 2, D-8000 München, T: 0811-213267/8.
Kirchliche Zentrale für Katholische Freie Schulen und Internate, Breite Str 106, D-5000 Köln 1, T: 0221-235480, 277771.

Verband Bildung und Erziehung (VBE), Theodor-Heuss-Ring 36, D-5 Köln.

GHANA

Catholic Schools Secretariat, P.O. Box 54, Accra, T: 22871.

GREECE

Comité des Ecoles Catholiques de Grèce, 10 Charilaou, Tricoupi, Athínai.

GUADELOUPE

Centre Diocesain de l'Enseignement Religieux (Catholic), B.P. 414, 17 rue de la Republique, 97163 Pointe-à-Pitre, T: 590-82-09-67.
Diocesan Director of Education (Catholic), Collège de Massabielle, 29 Fauborg Victor-Hugo, B.P. 245, Point-à-Pitre, T: 590-82-04-01.

GUAM

Office of Religious Education (Catholic), T: 671-472-6730.

GUATEMALA

Asociación Nacional Colegios Católicos, 12 Av 4-30, Zona 1, Guatemala.

GUYANA

Religious Education Department (Catholic), 293 Oronoque St., Georgetown, T: 592-2-64893.

HAITI

Association d'Enseignement Catholique, c/o Commission Nationale de Pastorale, Archevêché, Port-au-Prince, T: 22043.

HOLY SEE

Sacred Congregation for Catholic Instruction SC per l'Educazione Cattolica, Cardinal Prefect, Palazzo delle Congregazioni, Piazza Pio XII 3, I-00193 Roma, T: 6984569.

HONDURAS

Federación Colegios Católicos, Instituto San Francisco, Apdo Postal 367, Tegucigalpa.

INDIA

All India Sunday School Association, H. No. 12-2-826/C/1, Mehidipatnam, Hyderabad, Andhra Pradesh 500028.
Asia Institute of Christian Education, Shelter, Trivandrum, Kerala 695015.
Bethlehem Christian Educational Centre, Thamallackal P. O., Karuvatta, Kerala 690549.
Catechetical Centre, Bishop House, Raipur, Madhya Pradesh.
Catechetical Centre, Fort Cochin, Cochin, Kerala 682001.
Catechetics India, 52 A. Radhanath Chowdhury Road, Calcutta, West Bengal 700015.
Christian Education Department of EFI, Victoria Chambers, IInd Floor, 4-1-826, J. N. Road, Hyderabad, Andhra Pradesh 500001.
Church of South India Council for Education, 39 (Upstairs), II Cross Street, Ganga Nagar, Kodambakkam, Madras, Tamil Nadu 600024.
Diocesan Board of Education, Church of North India, 1, Church Lane, Delhi 110001.
Evangelical Sunday School Association of India, SHILOH, Charachira, Trivandrum, Kerala 695003.
Gnana Jyothi, Catholic Centre, Vijayawada, Andhra Pradesh 520010.
Green Pastures Christian Education Society, Ninappa Shetty Palaya Village, Bangargatta Road, Bangalore, Karnataka 560081.
India Sunday School Union, 'Keswick', Orange Grove Road, Coonoor, Tamil Nadu 643101.
Karnataka Christian Education Society, Karnataka Theological College, Balmatta, Mangalore 1, Mysore State.
National Evangelical and Educational Society, Modern Public School, 16/1 Khanpur Extn., New Delhi 110062.
Orthodox Syrian Sunday School Association of the East, Devalokam P. O., Kottayam, Kerala 686038.
Pastoral Training Centre and Regional Catechetical Centre, P. B. 41, Imphal, Manipur 795001.
Tamil Nadu Regional Catechists Training Centre, Tindivanam, Tamil Nadu 604002.
Tiruvalla Pastoral and Catechetical Centre, Santi Nilayam, Tiruvalla, Kerala 689101.
Vacational Bible School and Christian Education Ministries, Post Box 2581, 5, Norris Road, Richmond Town, Bangalore, Karnataka 560025.

INDONESIA

Catholic Education Association, Jalan Pos 2, Pakarta.
Department of Education, Kantor Waligeredja Indonesia (KWI), Taman Tiut Mutiah 10, Jakarta 11/14, T: 47548.
Department of Formation and Education of Communion of Churches in Indonesia, Jalan Kayu Jati III no. 2, Jakarta 13220, Jalan Salemba Raya 10, Jakarta 10430, T: 489-4540, F: 62-21-3150457, O: Telex: OIKOUMENE JAKARTA.

IRELAND

Catechetical Association of Ireland, The Pastoral Centre, Donamon, Roscommon, T: 353-0903 7277.
Catholic Schools Secretariat, Milltown Park, Dublin 6, T: 01-960343.
Council of Managers of Catholic Secondary Schools (CMCSS), Sacred Heart College, The Crescent, Limerick.
Sunday School Society for Ireland, Holy Trinity Church, Church Avenue, Rathmines, Dublin, T: 353-01 972821.

ITALY

Federazione Istituti Dipendenti della Autorità Ecclesiastica (FIDAE), Via della Pigna 13, I-00186 Roma, T: 6791341, 6791097.
Federazione Universitaria Catholica Italiana (FUCI), Via della Conciliazione 4d, I-00193 Roma, T: 655621, 581948.
Italian National Sunday School Council, Via della Signora 6, I-20122 Milano; Via T Grossi 17, I-22100 Como.
Katholischer Sudtirolere Lehrerbund (KLS), Haus der Kultur, Wlater v. da Vogelweide, Crispistrasse 4/3, I-39100 Bolzano.
Pontifical Faculty of Educational Science 'Auxilium', Via Cremolino, 141, 00166 Rome.
Pontificia Facoltà di Scienze dell Educazione, Via S Maria, Mazzarello 102, I-10142 Torino, T: 702911.

IVORY COAST

Direction Nationale de l'Enseignement Catholique, BP 4119, Abidjan, T: 22968.
Direction Nationale de l'Enseignement Protestant, BP 8840, Abidjan.

JAMAICA

Jamaica Catholic Education Association (JCEA), Archdiocesan Education Secretariat, 2 Emerald Rd, Kingston 4.

JAPAN

Catholic Education Council of Japan, 10-1 Rokubancho, Chiyoda-ku, Tokyo 102, T: 03-2622662.
Education Association of Christian Schools in Japan, 5-1 4-chome, Ginza, Chuo-ku, Tokyo 104.
Japan Sunday School Union, 21-3 5-chome, Mita, Minato-ku, Tokyo 108.

KENYA

Christian Churches' Educational Association (CCEA), Church House (3rd floor), Moi Av., P.O. Box 45009, Nairobi, T: 22312.
Christian Learning Materials Centre (CLMC), AEAM, Ralph Bunche Rd, PO Box 49332, Nairobi, T: 21894.
East Africa Religious Education Committee (EAREC), P.O. Box 45009, Nairobi, T: 22312.
Education Department, Kenya Catholic Secretariat, Westlands, P.O. Box 48062, Nairobi, T: 21613.
National Association of Religious Education Teachers (NARET), Alliance High School, PO Box 7, Kikuyu, T: 2026.
Nyanza Christian College, Church of Christ in Africa (CCA), Dala Hera (City of Love), Kibos Rd., P.O. Box 782, Kisumu. (Extensive African indigenous church schools), T: 2536.

LEBANON

Bible Lands Union for Christian Education, P.O. Box 235, Bayrut.
Commission Episcopale pour l'Ecole Catholique (CEEC), BP 4413, Bayrut, T: 241554.
Division of Christian Education, NECC, PO Box 5376, Bayrut.
Joint Catechesis, BP 7002, Bayrut.
OIEC, Secrétariat Régional pour le Proche et Moyen Orient, BP 4413, Bayrut, T: 241554.
Sunday Schools Directorate, Armenian Catholicossate of the Great House of Cilicia, Antelias.

LESOTHO

Catholic Education Secretariat, P.O. Box 80, Maseru.

LIBERIA

Centre de Pedagogie Catholique (CPC), Av Gaston Diderich 110 (et 243), Luxembourg, T: 25049.
National Secretariat of Catholic Education, Catholic Mission, P.O. Box 297, Monrovia.

MADAGASCAR

Direction Nationale de l'Enseignement, BP 667, Tananarive, T: 20478.

MALAWI

Education Department, Catholic Secretariat of Malawi, P.O. Box 5368, Limbe, T: Blantyre 50866.

MALAYSIA

Guild of Assisted Catholic Schools, Butik Nanas Convent, Kuala Lumpur, Selangor.

MALI

Direction Nationale de l'Enseignement Privé Catholique, Archevêché, BP 298, Bamako, T: 4439.

MALTA

Malta Private Secondary Schools' Association, De la Salle College, Cottonera.

MAURITIUS

Fédération des Enseignements Catholique (EEC), Morcellement Lamusse, Rue Malartic, Rose Hill.

MEXICO

Confederación Nacional Escuelas Particulares (CNEP), Madero 39-215, México 1, DF.

MOROCCO

Enseignement Catholique au Maroc (ECAM), BP 258, Rabat, T: 31430.

MOZAMBIQUE

Comissão Episcopal da Educação Cristã e do Ensino, Maputo (Lourenço Marques).

NETHERLANDS

Central Office for Catholic Education, Bezuidenhoutseweg 275, NL-2000 's-Gravenhage, T: 070-814491.
Netherlands Sunday School Union, Bloemgracht 65, Amsterdam C.
Reformed Sunday School Association (Jachin), Amsterdijk 85, Amsterdam 2.

NETHERLANDS ANTILLES

Catholic Teachers' Union, St. Thomas, Kashustraat 8, PO Box 582, Oranjestadt, Aruba.

NEW ZEALAND

Catholic Education Council, 152 Brougham St, Wellington 1.
New Zealand Council for Christian Education, P.O. Box 228, Wellington.
New Zealand Sunday School Union, 323 Queen St., P.O. Box 5166, Auckland E1.

NICARAGUA

Federación Nicaraguense Educación Católica (FENEC), 5a Calle No 614, Apdo 2934, Managua.

NIGERIA

Catholic Education Office, Federal District, P.O. Box 48, Abeokuta.
Centre for Applied Religion and Education, P.O. Box 9270, Ibadan.
Education Department, Catholic Secretariat, P.O. Box 951, Lagos, T: 25339.
Interdiocesan Religious Education Training Institute (IRETI), P.O. Box 11, Iperu-Remo.
National Institute of Moral and Religious Education, Project TIME, PMB 1140, Yaba, Lagos.

NORWAY

Norwegian Sunday-school Association, Kr Augusts gt 19, Oslo 1.
Norweigian Sunday School Council, Gronlandsleret, Oslo 1.

PAKISTAN

Adult Basic Education Office, Civil Lines, Gujranwala.
Catholic Board of Education, St. Patrick's Cathedral, Karachi 3.
Department of Christian Education, Pakistan Christian Council, Christian High School, Raja Bazar Rawalpindi.

PANAMA

Federación National Colegios Católicos, Apdo 6925, Panamá.

PAPUA NEW GUINEA

Churches' Education Council, P.O. Box 1323, Boroko.
National Catholic Education Office, Boroko.

PARAGUAY

Asociación Paraguaya Enseñanza Católica (APEC), Curia Vice-provincial, Casilla 346, Asunción.
Comité Lationoamericano de la Fe (CLAF), Eligio Ayala 907, Asunción, T: 47976.

PERU

Consorcio de Centros Educacionales de la Iglesia, Oficina Nacional de Educación Católica, Palacio Arzobispal, Oficina 22, Plaza de Armas, Lima, T: 75094.

PHILIPPINES

Catholic Educational Association of the Philippines (CEAP), Social Communications Center Bldg., R Magsaysay Blvd., corner Santol St, Santa Mesa, Manila, PO Box 1214, Manila, T: 612185, 605226, 605118.
Office of Education and Student Chaplains (FABC), P.O. Box EA-12, Manila.
OIEC Regional Secretariat for Asia, 2401 Taft Ave., Manila, T: 54592.
Philippine Assocation of Christian Education, P.O. Box 1417, Manila.

PORTUGAL

Centro de Orientação e Documentação do Ensino Particular (CODEPA), Duque de Loulé 75, 6D, Lisboa.
Liga Escolar Católica (LEC), Campo dos Martires de Patria 48, Lisboa.
Portugal (UEDNOP), Rua do Molhe 555, Foz do Douro, Porto.
Secretariado Nacional do Ensine Religioso Médie, Rua de Santa Catarina 428, Porto.

PUERTO RICO

Archdiocesan Office of Education, Box 1967, San Juan, PR 00903.

RWANDA

Secrétariat National de l'Enseignement Catholique (SNEC), BP 36, Kigali.

SAINT VINCENT & THE GRENADINES

Evangelical Institute of Christian Education, P.O. Box 143, Kingstown.

SENEGAL

Direction Nationale de L'Enseignement Catholique, 2 Rue Paul Holle, BP 3164, Dakar, T: 23478.

SIERRA LEONE

Catholic Education Office, P.O. Box 588, Freetown, T: 4011.

SOUTH AFRICA

Christian Education Movement, PO Box 11122, Johannesburg 2000, T: 011-333-5404, F: 011-337-1053.
Department of Education, South African Bishops' Conference, P.O. Box 941, Pretoria.
Foundation for Christ, Central Education, PO Box 3088, Coetzenburg 7602, T: 021-887-4948.
Methodist Christian Education Department, 14 Francis Rd, Pinelands 7405, Cape Town, T: 021-531-7064, F: 021-531-3367.
SANSSA Christian Education Ministries, PO Box 66109, Broadway 2020, 94 Kitchener St, Kensington, Johannesburg, T: 011-614-2329.
South African National Sunday School Association, Grace St., P.O. Box 17, Port Elizabeth.

SOUTH KOREA

Catholic Catechetica Institute, 90-12, Hyehwa-dong, Chongno-gu, Seoul-shi, T: 02-747-8501.
Korean Council of Christian Education, 136-46 Yunji-Dong Chongno-ku, Seoul.

SPAIN

Federación Española Comunidades Universitarias (FECUN), Hermosilla 20, Madrid 1.
FERE, Conde de Penalver 45, 4a Planta, Madrid 6.
Grupo de Educación Cristiana (GREC) (IEE), 08080 Apdo. 34030, Barcelona, T: 301-89-38.
Instituto Juan XXIII de Pedagogia Sacerdotal, Colegio Mayor Pio XI, Limite 3, Madrid 3, T: 2534007, 2335200.

SUDAN

Secretary for Catholic Schools, P.O. Box 356, Wad Medani, T: 2396.

SURINAME

Catholic Teachers' Union, Burenstraat 38, Paramaribo.
Co-ordinating Committee for Youth Catechetics, P.O. Box 489, Paramaribo; Gravenstraat 68, Paramaribo, T: 476-888, F: 471-602.

SWEDEN

Church of Sweden Sunday School Committee, P.O. Box 7034, S-10381 Stockholm 7.
Swedish Sunday School Council, P.O. Box 6302, S-11381 Stockholm.

SWITZERLAND

Aumônerie des Foyers d'Education, 124 Chemin de la Montagne, CH-1224 Chêne-Bougeries, T: 359571.
Education Renewal Fund (ERF), 150 route de Ferney, CH-1211 Genève 20.
Katholische Kommission für Erziehung und Unterricht der Schweiz, Löwenstr 5, CH-6000 Luzern.
Schweizerischer Sonntagsschulverband, Bahnofstr, CH-6460 Altdorf, UR.
Verband Freier Evangelischer Schulen der Schweiz, Muristr 8a, CH-3000 Bern, T: 031-447155.
World Council of Christian Education (WCCE), 150 Route de Ferney, CH-1211 Genève 20.

SYRIA

Commission Episcopale pour les Ecoles Catholiques, Archevêché des Arméniens Catholiques, Halab (Aleppo), T: 13946.
Société du Catechisme, Rue Al Tall, Halab.

TAIWAN

China Sunday School Association, Chung Shan North Rd, Section 2, No 105, Taipei, T: 545518.
Christian Education Commission, Catholic Central Bureau, 34 Lane 32, Kuang Fu Rd., P.O. Box 1723, Taipei, T: 771295.
United Board for Christian Higher Education in Asia, Tunghai University, Taichung.

TANZANIA

Education Secretary General, Tanzania Episcopal Conference, P.O. Box 2133, Dar es Salaam, T: 20477.

THAILAND

Catholic Education Council of Thailand, St. Gabriel's College, 565 Samsen Rd., Bangkok 3.
Office of Christian Education and Literature, Church of Christ in Thailand, 14 Pramuan Rd., Bangkok.

TRINIDAD & TOBAGO

Trinidad and Tobago Council of Christian Education, 20 Warner St., St. Augustine.

TUNISIA

Service de l'Enseignement, Prélature de Tunis, 4 Rue d'Alger, Tunis, T: 245831.

UGANDA

Interdiocesan Secretariat of Catholic Education, P.O. Box 2886, Kampala, T: 3042.

UNITED STATES OF AMERICA (USA)

American Baptist Education Association (ABEA), Valley Forge, PA 19481, T: 215-768-2065.
American Sunday School Union, 1816 Chestnut St., Philadelphia, PA 19103.
Catholic Religious Education on the World Wide Web, O: Web: www.microserve.net/~fabian/re.html.
Christian Education Publications, 9300 W 110th St #650, Overland Park, KS 66210, T: 800-628-6210.
Christian Education Today, P.O. Box 15337, Denver, CO 80215.
Christian Education Journal, P.O. Box 650, Glen Ellyn, IL 60138.
Christian Released Time Education Inc., 1346 North Highland Ave., Hollywood, CA 90028.
Church Society for College Work, 99 Brattle St, Cambridge, MA 02138, T: 617-491-3373.
Current Christian Abstracts Periodical, P.O. Box 7596, Columbia, MO 65205.
Friends Council on Education, 1507 Cherry St., Philadelphia, PA 19102, T: 215-241-7245.
Great Commission Publications, Inc., 7401 Old York Rd, Philadelphia, PA 19126, T: 215-635-6510.
Ministries in Education, National Council of Churches of Christ, 475 Riverside Dr., Room 8848, New York, NY 10115.
National Catholic Educational Association (NCEA), 1077 30th St., NW #100, Washington, DC 20007, T: 202-337-6232, F: 202-333-6707.
National Conference of Catechetical Leadership, 3021 4th St., N.E., Washington, D.C. 20017.
National Sunday School Association, P.O. Box 685, Wheaton, IL 90187, T: 312-653-3090.
National Union of Christian Schools, 865 25th St., SE, Grand Rapids, MI 49508, T: 616-245-8618.
North American Forum on the Catechumenate (Catholic), 7115 Leesburg Pike, Ste. 308, Falls Church, VA 22043-2301, T: 703-534-8082.
Program of Advanced Christian Education, 9405

N.E. Park Drive, Miami, FL 33138.
Religious Education Association, 545 West 111th St., New York, NY 10025, T: 212-865-7408.
Unitarian Sunday School Society, c/o First Parish, 3 Church St., Cambridge, MA 02138.
United Board for Christian Higher Education in Asia, 475 Riverside Dr., New York, NY 10027, T: 212-870-2601.
United Ministries in Higher Education, Witherspoon Bldg., Philadelphia, PA 19107, T: 215-735-6722.
Weekday Religious Education of Greater Indianapolis, 3544 Central Ave., Indianapolis, IN 46205.
World Association of Daily Vacation Bible Schools (VBS), Room 3202, 551 5th Ave., New York, NY 10017.
World Council of Christian Education and Sunday School Association, 475 Riverside Dr., New York, NY 10027.
Worldwide Christian Education Ministries, 5500 West Division St., Chicago, IL 60651, T: 312-626-5050.
Youth and Christian Ed. Leadership, 922 Montgomery Ave., NE, Cleveland, TN 37311.

URUGUAY
Consejo Metodista de Educación Cristiana, Constituyente 1462, Montevideo.
Unión Nacional Educación Católica (UNEC), Palacio Arzobispal, Treinta y tres 1360, Montevideo.

VENEZUELA
Asociación de Promoción de la Educación Popular (APEP), Av La Salle, frente a 4 Transversal, Sebucan, Apdo Postal 70045, Caracas 107, T: 340110.
Asociación Venezolana de Educación Católica (AVEC), Adif San Mauricio, Apdo 44, Mijares a Sta Capilla, Caracas, T: 828426.

VIET NAM
Office National de l'Enseignement Catholique (Institution Taberd), Box H-1, Saigon.

ZAMBIA
Education Department, P.O. Box 1965, Lusaka, T: 73467, 73470.

ZIMBABWE
General Secretariat for Catholic Education, Catholic Bishops' Conference, P.O. Box 2591, Salisbury.

14
Children's ministries

Agencies specializing in work with or for children; children's missions, child evangelism ministries, child welfare agencies, children's homes, orphanages. For education and Sunday schools, see catechesis and christian education.

ARGENTINA
Acción Católica de la Infancia, Montevideo 850, 1 piso, Buenos Aires.

AUSTRALIA
Algate House (Salvation Army), P.O. Box 477; 633 Lane St., Broken Hill, NSW 2880, T: 080-88-204-4.
Child Evangelism Fellowship (CEF), National Dir, 148 Ryde Rd, West Pymble, NSW 2073, T: 02-498-4775.
Kids' World, O: Web: www.tassie.net.au/~rclarke.

AUSTRIA
Children's Evangelism Fellowship, Hausmoning 45, Postfach 13, 5112 Lamprechtshausen, T: 06274/6331.
Katholische Jungschar Österreiches, Johannesgasse 16, A-1010 Wien.
Medienstelle der Kinder-Evangelisations-Bewegung, Hausmoning 45, Postfach 13, 5112 Lamprechtshausen, T: 06274/6331.
Österreichisches Nationalkomitee des BICE, Nibelungengasse 1 III/50, A-1010 Wien.

BELGIUM
Croisade Eucharistique, Service de Documentation et d'Action pour l'Enfance, Rue Brialmont 11, B-1030 Brussel.
Croisade Eucharistique Pie X, Abbaye d'Averbode, B-3281 Averbode.

BOTSWANA
Scripture Union of Botswana, PO Box 444, Gaborone.

BRAZIL
Associação de Educação de Brasil, Rua Martin Ferreira 23, Rio de Janeiro.

BRITAIN (UK OF GB & NI)
Aberlour Child Care Trust, 36 Park Terrace, Stirling FK8 2JR, T: 01786 450335.
Child Evangelism Fellowship (CEF), 31 Lampton Rd, Hounslow, Middx, T: 01-572-2656.
Child Welfare Office, 18 Park Circus, Glasgow G3.
Children's Council, Church of England Board of Education, Church House, Dean's Yard, London SWIP 3ZN, T: 01-222-9011.
Children's Relief International, Overstream House, Victoria Av., Cambridge, CB4 1EQ.
Children's Special Service Mission (CSSM), 5 Wigmore St., London W1, T: 01-486-2561.
Church of England Children's Society, Old Town Hall, Kennington, London SE11, T: 01-735-2441.
Commission for Social Welfare, BICE, 1A Stert St., Abingdon, Berkshire.
Girls Brigade International Council, 3 Burah Road, Aylsham, Norwich RN116AJ, Norfolk, T: 44-0263-734917, F: 44-0263-734917.
Our Lady's Catechists, 48 Lowndes Square, London SW1.
Shaftesbury Society, Shaftesbury House, 112 Regency St., London SW1P 4AX, T: 01-834-2656.
Society of the Holy Childhood, 23 Eccleston Square, London SW1V 1NU, T: 0171-821 9755, F: 0171-630 8466.
St. Dominic Savio Guild, 30 Orbel St., London SW11.
UK Band of Hope Union, 45 Great Peter St., London SW1, T: 01-222-6809.
Viva Network, P.O. Box 633, Oxford OX1 4YP, T: 44-1865-450-800, F: 44-1865-203-567, O: E-mail: 100423.2255@compuserve.com.

CANADA
Association Canadienne des Educateurs de Langue Française, 3 Place Jean Talon, Québec.
Association d-Education du Québec, Ste Foy, CP 518, Québec 10.
Association pour l'Evangélisation des Enfants, 31 Willowdale, Lennoxville, QC J1M 2A2, T: 819-569-2270.
Awana Youth Association Canada, P.O. Box 190, Fonthill, ON L0S 1E0, T: 905-892-5252, F: 905-892-1062, O: E-mail: awana@niagara.com.
Canadian Foundation for the Love of Children, Box 34002, 196A Kingsway Garden Mall, Edmonton, AB T5G 3G4, T: 403-448-1752.
Catholic Children's Aid Society of Metropolitan Toronto, 26 Maitland St., Toronto, ON M4Y 1C6, T: 416-395-1500, F: 416-395-1581.
Child Evangelism Fellowship of Canada, P.O. Box 165, Winnipeg, MB R3C 2G9, T: 204-943-2774, O: E-mail: 103442.1544@compuserve.com.
Children's Special Service Mission (CSSM), Scripture Union, 3 Rowanwood Av, Toronto 5, Ontario.
Children's Village (Salvation Army), 1731029 St., S.W., Calgary, AB T3C 1M6, T: 403-246-1124.
Christian Children's Fund of Canada (CCF), 1407 Yonge St., Toronto, Ontario, M4T 1Y8.
Christian Service Brigade, 1000 Stormont St., Ottawa, ON K2C 0M9, T: 613-225-3689, O: E-mail: au093@freenet.carleton.ca.
Conseil du Québec de l'Enfance Exceptionnelle, 2765 Chemin de la Côte Ste Catherine, Montréal 250, Québec.
Frank Wellington Children's Crusades, 298 Hillcrest Av, Willowdale, Ontario.
International Child Care (Canada), 2476 Argentia Rd. #113, Mississauga, ON L5N 6M1, T: 905-821-6317, F: 905-821-6319, O: E-mail: ICC.Canada@sympatico.ca, Web: www.intlchildcare.org.
Mission to Children, Box 3630, Station B, Calgary, AB T2M 4M4, T: 403-247-1060.
Mission to Orphans, Box 625, Three Hills, Alberta.
Odyssey, 518 Howard Ave., Burnaby, BC V5B 3R1, T: 604-299-6377, F: 604-299-4984.
Office Catéchistique Provincial, 1845 Blvd Pie IX, Montréal 4, Québec.
Patro le Prévôt, Inc., 7355 Christophe-Colomb, Montréal, QC H2R 2S5, T: 514-273-8535.
Pioneer Clubs Canada, Inc., Box 5447, Burlington, ON L7R 4L2, T: 905-681-2883, F: 905-681-3256.

CHILE
Federación Nacional de Instituciones Privadas de Protección de Menores, Erasmo Escala 1822, 2 piso, Santiago.

CHINA
Christian Children's Fund (CCF), 21 Chatham Rd., 6F, Kowloon, Hong Kong, T: K-667271/2.

COLOMBIA
Instituto Cristiano de San Pablo, Calle 13 No 12-42, Bogotá.

COSTA RICA
Asociación Roblealto Pro-Blenestar del Niño, Apdo 7966-1000, T: 227-3159.

DENMARK
Danish Organization for the Protection of Children, Nialsgade 19/2, Kobenhavn S.
Friends of Padre Pire in Denmark, Gronnevei 254, Virum.
YWA Girl Guides, Rosenborggade 3, 1130 Kobenhavn K, T: 33 12 95 38.

ECUADOR
Alianza Pro Evangelizacion Del Nino (APEN), 10 de Agosto No. 5070, Casilla 7356, Quito, T: 457-312.
Bienestar Social, Pedro Mon No. 141, Casilla 4988, Quito, T: 514-526.
Centros de Recreacion Infantil, Isla Isabela No. 221 y Bolanos, T: 247-079.
Centros Infantiles, Paris No. 633, Casilla 8043, Quito, T: 247-320.
Cuidado de Ninos, 6 de Diciembre y la Nina, Multicentro, T: 521-743, F: 547-062.
Promocion Estudiantil, Pedro Mon No. 141, Casilla 4988, Quito, T: 514-526.

EGYPT
Scouts Wadi El Nil, 15 Rue Emad El Dine, Al Qahirah.

FIJI
Child Evangelism Fellowship (CEF), 12 Matuku St, Samabula.

FINLAND
Salvation Army Children's Home, 16100 Porvoo, Aleksanterinkatu 24, T: 915-140-433.

FRANCE
Action Féminine pour une Pastorale de l'Enfance et de la Jeunesse, 43 Rue de Turbigo, F-75003 Paris, T: 01-887-0935.
Coeurs Vaillants Ames Vaillantes, 6 rue Duguay-Trouin, F-75006 Paris.
Comité Catholique de l'Enfance, 106 rue du Bac, F-75007 Paris.
Commission de la Presse et Littérature Enfantines, BICE, 31 rue de Fleurus, F-75006 Paris.
Commission des Institutions et Mouvements Internationaux Apostoliques des Enfants (CIMIADE), 8 rue Duguay-Trouin, F-75006 Paris.
Groupe des Ecoles d'Educateurs et d'Educatrices Spécialisés (Groupe AMCE), 145 Av Parmentier, F-75010 Paris.
International Association of Children of Mary, Secrétariat, 67 Rue de Sèvres, F-75006 Paris, T: 01-222-3390.
Le Foyer du Jeune Homme (Salvation Army), 42 ave Jean Jaurés, 67100 Strasbourg-Neudorf, T: 88-84-16-50.
Les Nids de Paris, 83 Av de St Mandé, F-75012 Paris.
Mouvement International D'Apostolat des Enfants (MIDADE), 8, rue Duguay-Trouin, F 75006 Paris.
Movement pour les Villages d'Enfants, 67 Rue Anatole France, F-92 Levallois-Perret.
Pontificia Opera della Santa Infanzia, 277 Rue Saint-Jacques, F-75005 Paris, T: 325-8028.
Secrétariat Catholique de l'Enfance et de la Jeunesse Inadaptées, 23 Av Bosquet, F-75007 Paris.
Union des Oeuvres Catholiques de France, 31 Rue de Fleurus, F-75006 Paris.
Union Nationale des Assistants et Educateurs de l'Enfance (UNAEDE), 47 Blvd Montparnasse, F-75006 Paris.

GERMANY
Arbeitsgemeinschaft für Ev Kinderpflege Deutschlands, Lenaustr 41, D-4 Düsseldorf.
Berufsgemeinschaft Katholischer Jugendleiterinnen und Kindergärtenerinnen, Karlstr 40, D-78 Freiburg im Breisgau.
Bonifatius der Kinder, Burgunder Weg 1, D-4790 Paderborn.
Bund Katholischer Erzieher Deutschlands, Goldenbrunnengasse 4, D-65 Mainz.
Evangelischer Verein für das Syrische Waisenhaus, Im Oberiddelsfeld 1, D-5000 Köln 80, T: 0221-682160.
Gesamtverband für Kindergottesdienst in der EKD, Am Alten Kirchhof 10, D-235 Neumünster.
Hilfsbund für das Lillian Trasher Waisenhaus Assiout, Im Stahlbühl 3, d-7100 Heilbronn, T: 07131-87860.
Katholische Diasporakinderhilfe, Burgunder Weg 1, D-4790 Paderborn.
Kindernothilfe (Aid for Children in Need), 28 Kufsteinerstr 100, D-4100 Duisburg, T: 02131-700064.
Kindernothilfe Duisburg-Rhurort, Kanalstr 5a, D-41 Duisburg-Meiderich.
Päpstliches Missionswerk der Kinder in Deutschland, Stephanstr 35, D-5100 Aachen.
Verband Ev Kinderpflegerinnen, Alsterdorfer Str 140, D-2 Hamburg 39.
Vereinigung Ev Kinderpflegeverbände Deutschlands, Reinsburgstr 50, D-7 Stuttgart-W.
Zentralverband Katholischer Kindergärten und Kinderhorte Deutschlands, Weissenburgstr 14, D-5000 Köln 1, T: 0221-732231.

GREECE
Oeuvre Charitable pour l'Enfance du Diocèse d'Athènes, 9 Rue Homere, Athinai 135.

GUADELOUPE
Action Catholique de l'Enfance, B.P. 414, 20 rue Paynier, Pointe-à-Pitre, T: 590-82-05-11.

HUNGARY
Child Evangelism Fellowship, Vasárnapi Iskolai Szövetség, 2119 Pécel, Nyirfa utca 1. Pf. 63.

INDIA
Bal Asha Dhan, King George Memorial Tulsi Pipe Road, Mahalaxmi, Bombay, Maharashtra 400011.
Child Evangelism Fellowship of India, 108, Gautam Nagar, New Delhi 110049.
Child Vision India, Gospel Center, Nedumparam P.O., Tiruvalla, Kerala.
Children's Lover - Group, C/o Jayesh Bible Centre, Jayesh Colony, Fatehganj, Baroda, Gujarat.
Children's Ministries of India, T. K. Road, Tiruvalla, Kerala 689101.
Childrens Home of Hope, 1, Sita Nagar Colony, Nungambakkam, Madras, Tamil Nadu 600034.
Christ for Every Child, 78, V. V. Koil Street, Choolai, Madras, Tamil Nadu 600112.
Christ for India's Children, P. O. Box 82, Pune, Maharashtra 411001.
Christian Education Department of Evangelical Fellowship Of India, No. 50, Viviani Road, Richards Town, Bangalore, Karnataka 560005.
Dohnavur Fellowship, Dohnavur, Tirunelveli, South India.
Dr Graham's Homes, Kalimpong, West Bengal.
Faith Children Ministries, Vijayanagar Colony, Hyderabad, Andhra Pradesh 500457.
God's Messengers for Children, Mogalrajpuram Road, Vijayawada, Andhra Pradesh 520010.
Gurukula Sarvajanik Anathashram (Boys), Taluka Bailhongal, Post Deshnur, Deshnur, Karnataka 591121.
Mennonite Boy's And Girl's Hostel, Jagdeeshpur, Madhya Pradesh 493555.
Nehru Home for Destitute Boys, Attalur P. O., Parastyallur, Andhra Pradesh 522436.
Nest, The, Jitpur, Gomoh P. O., Bihar 828401.
Prabhat Tara Boys Hostel, Post Sukhia Barhait, Bhagalpur, Bihar 812104.
Princess Indumati Boy's Hostel, Irwin Hostel Compound, Near Shahu Mill, 1244/45 'E' Ward, Rajaram Rd, Shahupuri, Kolhapur, Maharashtra 416008.
Salvation Army Home for Physically Handicapped Children, Joyland, Anand 388 011, Dist Kaira, Gujarat, T: 02692-21891.
Save the Children, Parsi Street, Sadar Bazar, Fatehganj, Baroda, Gujarat 390002.
Scripture Union And Children Special Service Mission, Hospital Road, Modipara (Opp. Lipi Gas), , Orissa.
St Joseph Convent Hostel (Girls), Belgaum, Karnataka 590001.
St. Mary's Girls' Hostel, Via Dalkhola, Altapur P. O., West Bengal 733201.
St. Mary's Sunday School and Evangelistic Associatiion, Kummamkulam P. O., Kerala 680503.
World Wide Faith Mission's Children's Home, Bhubaneswar, Orissa 751012.

ISRAEL
Child Evangelism Fellowship (CEF), P.O. Box 292, Nazareth.

ITALY
Azione Cattolica dei Ragazzi, Via della Conciliazione 1, I-00193 Roma.
Child Evangelism Fellowship (CEF), Via Picco dei Tre Signori 20, I-00141 Roma.
Comitato Nazionale Italiano del BICE, Via della Conciliazione 1, I-00193 Roma.
Opera Nazionale Città dei Ragazzi, Lungotevere Marzio 12, I-00186 Roma.
Unione Italiana Stampa Periodica Educativa per Ragazzi (UISPER), Via della Conciliazione 1, I-00193 Roma.

JAPAN
Child Care, 10-37 Kugenuma Kaigan, 2-chome, Fujisawa-shi, Kanagawa-ken 251.
Child Evangelism Fellowship of Japan, 1-37-1 Keyakidai Tokorozawa Shi, Saitama Ken 359, T: 0429-22-4076.
Christian Children's Fund, Shibuya Chiyoda Bldg 13, Nanpeidai, Shibuya-ku, Tokyo 150.
Christian Federation of Childhood Education, 17-11, 3-chome, Mejiro, Toshima-ku, Tokyo 171.
World Missions to Children, 850 Tenjin-cho, Sasebo-shi, Nagasaki-ken 857-11.

KENYA
Joytown, P.O. Box 326, Thika, T: 0151-21291.
Salvation Army Boys' Centre, P.O. Box 1625, Thika, T: 0151-21106.
Salvation Children's Home, P.O. Box 14454, Nairobi; Kabete, Nairobi, T: 02-442766.

LIBERIA
Child Evangelism Fellowship of Liberia (CEF), Box 50, Monrovia, T: 22059.

LUXEMBOURG
Action Catholique de L'Enfance, 105A Rue d'Eich, Luxembourg.

MALTA
Children's Homes, 84 Old Mint St., Valetta.

MEXICO
Centro Cultural Pro la Ninez, 16 de Septiembre 6-611, Zona 1, Apdo M 7571, México, DF, T: 102673.
Departamento Nacional de Infancia y Adolescencia de la Acción Católica Mexicana, Apdo Postal 1647, México 1, DF.

MYANMAR
Childrens' Home (Salvation Army), 50 Bago Rd., Pyu.

NETHERLANDS
Catholic Alliance for the Protection of Children, Buitenhaven 5, 's-Hertogenbosch, T: 04100-39661.
Catholic Parents Association, Woonark Oude Leideseweg t/o Zwembad, NL-Den Hommel (Oog in Al), T: 030-936823.
Dutch Federation of Institutions for Unmarried Mothers and Children, Nieuwe Schoolstraat 28, NL-'s-Gravenhage, T: 070-645848.

NEW ZEALAND
Child Evangelism Fellowship, New Zealand Council, 375 Cambridge Terrace, Lower Hutt.
Kids with a Destiny, P.O. Box 2223, Christchurch, T: 0-3-379-2781, F: 0-3-366-4445.

PAKISTAN
Child Evangelism Fellowship, 36 Ferozepur Rd., Lahore.

PHILIPPINES
Children's Mission, P.O. Box 3349, Manila.
International Child Evangelism Fellowship (CEF), P.O. Box 1205, Manila.
Joyville Rehabilitation Centre (Salvation Army), Km 52, Mla East Rd., Sitio Suyok Tanay, Rizal.
Philippine Children's Mission, P.O. Box 1897, Manila.

POLAND
Child and World Foundation, ul. Zagoma 10, Warsaw 00-441, T: 48-22-12-83-83.

PORTUGAL
Aliança Pró-Evangelização de Crianças de Portugal, Rua Marechal Craveiro Lopes, 41 Franqueiro, 2670 Loures, T: 01-983 09 44, F: 01-983 62 55.
Children's Summer Camp (Salvation Army), Rua das Marinhas, 13, Tomadia, Praia das Maçãs, 2710 Sintra, T: 929-0384.
Estudio Bíblico para Primários (Aluno e Professor) (Baptist), Rua do Conde Redondo, 31-A, 1150 Lisboa, T: 01-353 18 03, F: 01-352 50 37.
National Co-ordinating Commission of Children's Movements in Portugal, Av Duque de Loule 83/2, Lisboa.
Piparote, Rua do Roque, 14-A, Fogueteiro - 2840 Amora, T: 01-224 99 31.

PUERTO RICO
Un Niño Para Cristo, P.O. Box 2690, Vega Baja, P.R. 00694, T: 787-883-5059, F: 787-883-5059.

ROMANIA
Child and World Foundation, C.P. 337, Arad 2900, T: 40-66-65272.

SINGAPORE
Boys' Brigade in Singapore, BB Campus, 105 Ganges Avenue, Singapore 169695, T: 737-0377, F: 737-1676.
Child Evangelism Fellowship (S) Ltd., Bock 3 #03-27, Upper Pickering Street, Singapore 051003, T: 538-0430, F: 538-4252.
Gracehaven Children's Home (Salvation Army), 3 Lorong Napiri (off Yio Chu Kang Rd), singapore 1954, T: 382-3983.
Girls' Brigade, Singapore, 1 Sophia Road #05-38 Peace Centre, Singapore 228149, T: 336-0706, F: 336-0713.
Wesley Child Development Centre, 1 Block 29 #09-231, Telok Blangah Rise, Singapore 090029, T: 271-1216, F: 271-1918.

SOUTH AFRICA
Child & Youth Evangelism, PO Box 424, Sunninghill 2157, T: 011-803-2054.
Child Evangelism Fellowship, PO Box 1661, Somerset West 7129, Murray Chambers, Pickle St Strand 7140, T: 024-53-1043, F: 024-854-7118.
Child Evangelist Training Institute, P/B X9906, White River 1240, Petra Mountain, Numbi Rd, White River 1240, T: 013-751-1166, F: 013-750-0906.
Child Evangelization Fellowship of SA, PO Box 1661, Somerset West, 7129 Murray Chambers, Pickle St, Strand, T: 024-53-1043, F: 024-854-7118.
Royal Rangers of SA/Christian Veldwagters, PO Box 13842, Northmead, 1511, 2 Lakefield Ave, Lakefield, Benoni, T: 011-894-7693, F: 011-894-7694.
Society of the Precious Blood, c/o C P 120, Maputo, Mocambique.
St. Nicholas Home for Boys, PO Box 58138, Newville, 2114, T: 011-477-7324/5.
Target Timothy, PO Box 66109, Broadway 2020, 94 Kitchener Rd, Kensington, Johannesburg, T: 011-614-2329.

SPAIN
APEEN (Alianza Pro-Educación Espiritual del Niño), 28022 Gutiérrez Canales, 3, 1°, Madrid, T: 742-46-39.
Child Evangelism Fellowship, C C—rcega 568-1-2, Barcelona 08025, T: 93 2366837.
Colegio de Huérfanos de Ferroviarios, Atocha 83, Madrid 12.
Comisión Nacional Católica Española de la Infancia (Acción Católica), Calle Alfonso XI 4/4, Madrid 14.
Commission Juridique (BICE), Cea Bermúdez 46, Madrid 3.
Consejo Superior de Protección de Menores, Cea Bermúdez 48, Madrid 3.
Delegación Nacional de Juventudes, José Ortega y Gasset 71, Madrid 6.
Delegación Nacional de la Sección Femenina, BICE, Almagro 36, Madrid 4.
Escuelas Profesionales de la Sagrada Familia, Apdo 5, Ubeda, Jaén.
Instituto Municipal de Educación de Madrid, Mejia Lequerica 21, Madrid 4.
Mutualidad Nacional de Enseñanza Primaria, Fernández de la Hoz 64, Madrid 3.
Secretariado Categuístico Nacional, Alfonso XI 4/1, Madrid 14.
Servicio Español del Magesterio, Alcalá 44, Madrid 14.

SWITZERLAND
Bois-Soleil, Route du Signal 25-27, CH-1018 Lausanne.
Bureau International Catholique de L'Enfance (BICE), 65, rue de Lausanne, CH 1202 Genève.
Direktion des Seraphischen Liebeswerkes Pro-Infante et Familia, Antoniushaus, CH-4500 Solothurn.
European Child Evangelism Fellowship Center, Kilchzimmer, Langenbruck 4438, T: 41-62-601-405, F: 41-62-60566.
Home for Small Children (Salvation Army), Kinderheim Holee, Holeestrasse 62, 4054 Basel, T: 061-301-24-50.
International Catholic Child Bureau (ICCB), 65 Rue de Lausanne, CH-1202 Genève, T: 022-313248.
International Conference of Catholic Guiding, Postfach 60, CH-9004 Sankt Gallen.
Kinderdorf Pestalozzi, CH-9043 Trogen.
Komitee der Deutschsprahigen Länder im Internationalen Katholischen Büro des Kindes, Gurzelngasse 14, CH-4500 Solothurn.

TAIWAN
Child Evangelism Fellowship International, 1-7 Chin Hsi St, 2nd floor, Taipei.
Happy Children Center, 17 Lane 387, Wanta Road, Taipei, T: 02-3071201, F: 3058465.

UGANDA
Child Evangelism Fellowship (CEF), P.O. Box 2089, Kampala.

UNITED STATES OF AMERICA (USA)
21st Century Kids Connect, PMB 205, 7109 Staples Mill Road, Richmond,VA 23228-4110, T: 800-206-9431, O: E-mail 21stkidsconnect@xc.org, Web: www.21stCenturyKidsConnect.org
All Productions, 7025 Regner Rd., San Deigo, CA 92119, T: 619-460-4837, F: 619-460-6160, O: E-mail: allprod@connectnet.com.
Awana Youth Assoc, 3201 Tollview Dr, Arlington Heights, IL 60008, T: 312-394-5150, O: Web: www.awana.org.
Bible Lessons Int'l, P.O. Box 1289, Marshall, TX 75671, T: 214-935-2532.
Bibles for Children, Inc, RD 1, PO Box 820A, Afton, NY 13730.
Bronx Centre for Families (Salvation Army), 601 Crescent Ave., Bronx, NY 10458, T: 718-329-5410, F: 718-329-5409.
Bushwick Homes for Babies (Salvation Army), T: 718-574-0188/0193.
Cadet Corps, O: Web: www.gospelcom.net/cadets/.
Child Evangelism Fellowship, Inc., P.O. Box 348, Warrenton, MO 63383, T: 314-456-4321, F: 314-456-5000, O: Web: www.gospelcom.net/cef/, E-mail: cef@gospelcom.net.
Childcare International, P.O. Box W, Bellingham, WA 98225, T: 206-647-2283.
Children International, 2000 E. Red Bridge Rd., Kansas City, MO 64131, T: 816-942-2000, F: 816-942-3714, O: E-mail: Children@cikc.org.
Children of Promise, 4450 Outreach Dr., Hillsboro, MO 63050-2034, T: 1-888-6-ORPHAN, F: 314-797-2266, O: Also phone: 314-789-4368, E-mail: Sandy@Promise.org.
Children's Bible Hour, P.O. Box One, Grand Rapids, MI 49501, T: 616-451-2009, F: 616-451-0032, O: E-mail: cbh@gospelcom.net.
Children's Bible Mission, Box 1137, Lakeland, FL 33802.
Children's Haven International, 400 E. Minnesota Rd., Pharr, TX 78577, T: 956-787-7378, F: 956-783-4637.
Children's HopeChest, 459 Woodmen Road, Suite B, Colorado Springs, CO 80919, T: 719-598-9575, F: 719-598-3535, O: E-mail: chc@gospelcom.net, Web: www.gospelcom.net/chc.
Children's Media Promotions, PO Box 40400, Pasadena, CA 91114, T: 818-797-5462.
Children's Ministries, Inc., 250 N. Highland Ave., Pittsburgh, PA 15206, T: 412-363-0425.
Children's Sonshine Network, 1159 E. Beltline N.E., Grand Rapids, MI 49505, T: 800-530-9779, F: 616-942-7078, O: Web: www.gospelcom.net/csn/jstfrkids.html, E-mail: csn@gospelcom.net.
Christian Children's Fund (CCF), 203 East Carey St., P.O. Box 511, Richmond, VA 23204, T: 703-644-2375.
Christian Service Brigade, P.O. Box 150, Wheaton, IL 60189, T: 708-665-0630.
Department of Child Care, Catholic Charities of the Archdiocese of New York, 112 East 22nd St, New York, NY 10010. (Member, BICE).
Evangelizing Today's Child Magazine, PO Box 348, Warrenton, MO 63383, T: 314-456-4321.
Every Child Ministries Inc., P.O. Box 715, Crown Point, IN 46307, T: 219-996-4201.
Grace Place!, O: Web: www.bayou.com/~lou2247/.
Holy Childhood Association, 1720 Massachusetts Ave., N.W. Washington, D.C. 20036.
Holy Innocents Ministry, Inc., at Dayspring, P.O. Box 399, Chelsea, AL 35043, T: 205-678-8331.
International Child Care, 3620 North High St., Suite 110, Columbus, OH 43214, T: 1-800-72-CHILD, O: E-mail: icc-usa@gospelcom.net.
International Children's Care, P.O. Box 4406, Vancouver, WA 98662, T: 360-573-0429, F: 360-573-0491.
International Street Kids Outreach Ministries, P.O. Box 272446, Tampa, FL 33688, T: 800-265-1970.
Joy Ranch, Inc., P.O. Box 727, Hillsville, VA 24343, T: 703-236-5578.
K!DZweb Comics and Stories for Kids, O: Web: www.kidzweb.org.
Kids Alive International, 2507 Cumberland Dr., Valparaiso, IN 46383, T: 219-464-9035, F: 219-462-5611.
Kids' Quest: Adventures in the Rain Forest, O: Web: www.christiananswers.net/kids/kidshome.html.
Mailbox Club International, 404 Eager Rd., Valdosta, GA 31602, T: 912-244-6812, F: 912-245-8977.
Mission to Children, Box 1310, Glendale, CA 91209, T: 818-244-8497, F: 818-244-7073.
Missionary Kid Home Page, O: Web: www.xc.org/mk.
National Christ Child Society, Inc., 5101 Wisconsin Ave., N.W., Suite 304, Washington, D.C. 20016.
Noah's Ark Adventure Program, P.O. Box 850, Buena Vista, CO 81211, T: 719-395-2158.
One Way Street, Inc., P.O. Box 5077, Englewood, CO 80155, T: 303-790-1188, F: 303-790-2159, O: E-mail: onewayinc@aol.com.
Pioneer Clubs, P.O. Box 788, Wheaton, IL 60189, T: 630-293-1600, F: 630-293-3053, O: Web: www.pioneerclubs.org, www.pioneerclubs.org.
Project PATCH—Planned Assistance for Troubled Children, 13455 S.E. 97th Avenue., Clackamas, OR 97015, T: 503-653-8086.
Refugee Children, P.O. Box 106, Stamford, CT 06904.
Snowflake Mailbox Club, O: E-mail: pdamien@juno.com.
Trickster, O: Web: www2.csn.net/~esr.
WorldVillage Kidz, O: Web: www.worldvillage.com/kidz.

15

Christian approaches to other faiths

Christian research, activities, and initiatives directed primarily towards other major world religions (especially Judaism, Islam, Hinduism, Buddhism), including agnosticism and atheism, concerned with mission and evangelism, or with interfaith dialogue or mutual understanding; related activities, information and study centers. For joint activities involving Christians and non-Christians together, see INTERRELIGIOUS ORGANIZATIONS.

AUSTRALIA
Jewish Evangelical Witness (JEW), 4 David Court, 67 Murrumbeena Rd., Murrumbeena, Victoria 3163, T: 562961.

BOLIVIA
CMM-Comisión de Misiones a los Musulmanes, Casilla 1448, La Paz, T: 2-315918.

BRAZIL
Associação Internacional de Missões aos Israelitas, Cx. Postal 57055, São Paulo-SP 04093-970, T: 11-543-4122, F: 11-241-3312.
Centro Yoga Cristão, Av Lauro Sodré 83, ZC 82, Tunel Novo, Rio de Janeiro, GB.
Esperanca de Israel, Rua General Rondon 49, CP 9040, São Paulo, SP, T: 629055.
Projeto Amigos de Ismael, Caixa Postal 1573, CEP 13001-Campinas-SP, T: 0192-2-5175.

BRITAIN (UK OF GB & NI)
Centre for the Study of Christianity & Islam, Whitefield House, Kennington Park Road, London SE11 4BT.
Christian Mission to the Communist World (Jesus to the Communist World), P.O. Box 19, Bromley, Kent BR1 1DJ, T: 01-460-9319.
Christian Witness to Israel, 166 Main Road, Sundridge, Sevenoaks, Kent TN14 6EL, T: 44-1-959-56-59-55, F: 44-1-959-56-59-66.
Church's Ministry Among the Jews (CMJ), Vincent House, Vincent Square, London SW1P 2PX, T: 01-834-4527/8.
Fellowship of Faith for the Muslims Publications, 14 Tudor Close, Hove, East Sussex BN3 7NR.
Fellowship of Faith for the Muslims, The Manse, Hatch Beauchamp, Taunton, Somerset; The Manse, Great Sampford, Saffron Walden, Essex, T: 082348-335.
Hebrew Christian Testimony to Israel, 139 Whitechapel Rd., London E1 1DN, T: 01-247-5270.
Hebrew Evangelization Society, 92-94 Amhurst Park, London N16, T: 01-800-7315.
International Hebrew Christian Alliance (IHCA), Shalom, 8 Brockenhurst Rd., Ramsgate, Kent, T: 843-52669.
International Society for the Evangelization of the Jews, 45 Gildredge Rd, Eastbourne, East Sussex BN21 4RZ, T: 30617/8.
International Institute for the Study of Islam and Christianity, St. Andrew's Ctr., St., Andrew's Road, Plaistow, London E13 8QD, T: 44-071-474-0743, F: 44-071-511-4874.
Jerusalem and the East Mission (JEM), 12 Warwick Square, London SW1V 2AA, T: 01-834-9588.
Jews for Jesus, P.O. Box 1BE, London W1A 1BE, T: 44-81-343-7717.
Mildmay Mission to the Jews, Mildmay Hall, 214 Mile End Rd., Stepney, London E1 4LJ, T: 01-790-2079.
Pentecostal Jewish Mission, 23 John Campbell Rd., Stoke Newington, London N16, T: 01-254-3039.
Selly Oak Colleges, Centre for the Study of Islam and Christian-Muslim Relations, 996 Bristol Road, Selly Oak, Birmingham B29 6LQ.
Seventh-day Adventist Adventist Global Centre for Islamic Studies, Newbold College, Bracknell, Berkshire RG12 5AN, T: 344.
Study Centre for Christian-Jewish Relationships, 17 Chepstow Villas, GB-London W11 3DZ, T: 0171-727-3597.

CANADA
Bible Testimony Fellowship (Jews), 4249 Osler St., Vancouver, BC V6H 2X4, T: 604-731-1205, F: 604-736-7032.
Centre MI-CA-EI, 4661 Queen Mary Rd., Montréal 247, Québec, T: 7396048.
Chosen People Ministries (Canada), Box 897, Station B, North York, ON M2K 2R1, T: 416-250-0177, F: 416-250-9235.
Christian Research Institute of Canada, #240 - 1935 - 32nd Ave., N.E., Calgary, AB T2E 7C8, T: 403-277-7702.
Faith-in-Action Club, PO Box 275, Don Mills, ON M3C 2S2, T: 416-510-2443, F: 416-510-2664.
Fellowship of Faith for the Muslims, P.O. Box 65214, Toronto, ON M4K 3Z2, T: 416-778-6702, F: 416-466-3324.
Hebrew Evangelization Society, 55 East 18th Av, Vancouver 10, BC.
Jews for Jesus, 527A Mt. Pleasant Ave., Toronto, ON M4S 2M4, T: 416-481-5500.
Les Ministères du Peuple Choisi, 2566 boulevard Keller, St.-Laurent, QC H4K 2T3, T: 514-335-2543.
Messianic Times, 5334 Yonge St., Suite 1528, Toronto, ON M2, T: 416-635-7372.
Service Incroyance et Foi, 2930 Rue Lacombe, Montréal H3T 1LA, T: 514-735-1565/6.
Toronto Jewish Mission, 764 Sheppard Ave., W., Downsview, ON M3H 2S8, T: 416-636-1045.
United Messianic Jewish Outreach, 5334 Yonge St., Suite 140, Toronto, ON M2N 6M2, T: 416-635-7047.

CHINA
Catholic Commission for Non-Christian Religions, 13F 16 Caine Road, Hong Kong, T: 525-8021, F: 868-4118.
Christian Mission to Buddhists, Tao Fong Shan, Shating, Hong Kong, T: NT-61450.
Christian Study Centre on Chinese Religion & Culture, 6th floor Kiu Kin Mansion, no. 566 Nathan Road, Kowloon, Hong Kong, T: 852-2770-3310, F: 852-2782-6869.

DENMARK
Danish Israel Mission, P.O. Box 35, 6070 Christiansfeld, T: 45-74/56-22-33, F: 45-74/56-13-34.
Danish Mission to the Jews, Norregade 14, 6070 Christiansfeld, T: 74 56 22 33.
Danske Israelsmission, Lipkesgade 5, DK-2100 Kobenhavn O.
Den nordiske kristne Buddhist-mission, Dansk Afdeling, Isagervel 8, 6950 Ringkobing, T: 97 32 06 29.
Lausanne Consultation for Jewish Evangelism (LCJE), Ellebaek vej 5, DK- 8520 Lystrup Denmark, T: 45-86-2264-70, F: 45-86-2295-91, O: E-mail: lcje-int@post2.tele.dk.
Dialogue Centre (Witness to the New Religious Movement), Katrinebjergvej 46, 8200 Arhus N, T: 86 10 54 11.
Scandinavian Buddhist Mission, Bernstorffvej 65A, DK-2900 Hellerup, T: 01-HELrup 8405.

FINLAND
Friends of Israel, Pikku Robertinkatu 5/17, Helsinki.

FRANCE
Amitié Judéo-Chrétienne de France (AJCF), 68 Rue de Babylone, F-75007 Paris.
Chrétienne (SIDIC), 73 rue Notre Dame des Champs, F-75006 Paris, T: 325-5620.
Comité Episcopal pour les Relations avec les Juifs, Secrétariat Général de l'Episcopat, 106 Rue du Bac, F-75341 Paris, T: 222-5708.
Commission Inter-Africaine des Religions, Société Africaine de Culture, 25bis Rue des Ecoles, F-75005 Paris, T: 033-1374.
Eglise et Monde Juif, 13 Rue de Poissy, F-75005 Paris, T: 033-3241.
Encounter Today, 11 Rue Jules Guesde, F-92 Issy-les-Moulineaux, T: 6422170.
Foiet Cultures/Ad Lucem, 12 rue Guy de la Brosse, F-75005 Paris, T: 331-7955.
Rencontres entre Chrétiens et Juifs, 62 Blvd Montparnasse, F-75015 Paris.
Secrétariat pour la Rencontre avec les Musulmans, 24 Quai Fernand Saguet, F-94 Maisons-Alforet, T: 368-3464.
Service Incroyance-Foi (SIF), 127 Rue Notre Dame des Champs, F-75006 Paris, T: 633-5938.
SILOE, 61 Rue du Cherche-Midi, F-75006 Paris.

GERMANY
Arbeitsgemeinschaft für Dienst an Israel, Koblenzer Str 306, D-4972 Löhne 1, T: 05732-2258.
Evangelisch-lutherischer Zentralverein für Mission unter Israel, Motterstr 1, D-8500 Nürnberg, T: 0911-634774.
Jerusalemsverein, Handjerystr 19/20, D-1000 Berlin 41, T: 030-8513061.
Nazarethwerk, Hamburger Str 57, D-2057 Reinbek, T: 040-7226855.
Studienkommission Kirche und Judentum der EKD, Herrenhaüserstr 2A, Postfach 2, D-3000 Hannover 21.

HOLY SEE
Secretariat for Non-Believers, Piazza San Calisto 16, I-00120 Città del Vaticano, T: 6984393, 6984004, 6984773, 6984577.

INDIA
CBCI Commission for Dialogue, St. Mary's Cathedral Church, 66 Varanasi Cantt, UP.
Centre of Study of World Religions, Dharmaram College, Bangalore, Karnataka 560029.
Christian Literature for Muslims Committee, Henry Martyn Institute, 15 Nehru Rd, Lucknow 2, UP.
Gospel for Muslims, P. O. Box 3, Uravakonda, Andhra Pradesh 515812.
Gospel for Sons of Ishmael Fellowship, Sat Tal Ashram, Sat Tal, Uttar Pradesh.
Henry Martyn Institute of Islamic Studies, St. Luke's Compound, P.O. Box 153, Station Road, Hyderabad 500 001, T: 0842-23-11-34, O: E-mail: Henry.Martyn@HMI,SprintRpg.Sprint.Com.
Ishmaelite Salvation Association, P.O. Box 8431, St. Thomas Town, Bangalore 560 084; 14 Fourth East Cross Road, Vellore 632 006, T: 23156.
Pontifical Athenaeum of Poona, Institute of Philosophy and Religion, Pune 411 014.

INDONESIA
Sekolah Tinggi, Filsafat Driyarkara Teremolos 397/Jkt., Jakarta 10002, T: 024-411480.

ISRAEL
American Association for Jewish Evangelism, P.O. Box 376, Ramt Gan.
Maison St-Isaïe (Beit Yeshayaou), 20 Rue Gershon Agron, BP 1332, Jerusalem, T: 02-29763.
Oasis de Paix (Nevé Shalom), Rue Ha'nevlim, Jerusalem, T: 02-87250.

ITALY
Pontifical Council for Interreligious Dialogue, Via dell' Erba 1, 00193 Rome.
Pontificio Istituto di Studi Arabi e Islamalistica, Viale di Trastevere 89, I-00153 Rome, T: 39-6-588-2676.
Segretariato Per I Non Cristiani, Via dell'Erba 1, I-00193 Roma, T: 06-6984321 or 6983648.
Sidic. Service International De Documentation Judéo-Chrétienne, Via del Plebiscito 112/9, I-00186 Roma, T: 06-6786280.

JAPAN
Center for Christian Reponse to Asian Issues, 2-3-18 Nishi-Waseda, Hinjuku-ku, Tokyo 160, T: 202-0494.
Institute of Oriental Religions, Sophia University, 7 Kioi-cho, Chiyoda-ku, Tokyo 102, T: 03-3238-3540, F: 03-238-3855.
Nanzan Institute for Religion and Culture, Namzan University, 18 Yamazato-cho, Showa-ku, Nagoya 466, T: 52-832-3111, F: 52-833-6157.
NCC Center for the Study of Japanese Religions, Karasuma Shimotachiuri Kamikyo-ku, Kyoto 602, T: 81-75-432-1945.
Oriens Institute for Religious Research, Matsubara 2-28-5, Setagaya-ku, Tokyo 156, T: 03-3322-7601, F: 03-325-5322.

LAOS
Bureau du Bouddhisme, Mission Catholique, Vientiane, T: 3257.

LEBANON
Muslim World Evangelical Literature Service, Araya, Kehale PO.

MALAWI
Missionary Work Among the Islams, P.O. Nkhoma - c/o Nkhoma Synod Ofices.

NEW ZEALAND
International Jews Society, New Zealand Council, P.O. Box 6455, Auckland.

NIGERIA
Islam in Africa Project Council, 5 Awosika Av, Bodija, P.O. Box 4045, Ibadan, T: 23884.

NORWAY
Nordic Buddhist Mission Norwegian Department, Syrenveien 12, Postboks 74, TŒsen, 0801 Oslo 8, T: 02-23 28 63.
Norwegian Church Ministry to Israel, Colletsgt. 42 II, 0456 Oslo 4, T: 47-22/46-18-58, F: 47-22/56-58-03.
Norwegian Mission to Buddhists, Elisenbergveien 6, Oslo 2.
Norwegian Mission to Muslims, Haraldsgt. 81, 5500 Haugesund, Rogaland, T: 04-72 71 15.

PAKISTAN
Loyola Hall, 28 Warris Rd, Lahore.

PHILIPPINES
East Asian Pastoral Institute, P.O. Box 221, Quezon City; 1101 U.P. Campus, Quezon City, T: 924-0561, F: 924-4359.
Gowing Memorial Research Center, P.O. Box 5430, Iligan City 8801.
Love Your Neighbor, Inc., Don Alfaro Street, Tetuan (CAMACOP Compound), P.O. Box 281 Zamboangha City, T: 54-17.
Oriental Religions and Cultures Institute, University of Santo Tomas, Espana, Manila 2806.
Religious Study Center, Islam, c/o Adventist International Institute of Advanced Studies, PO Box 7682, Domestic Airport PO 1300 Pasay City, Metro Manila.
Tboli Study Center, P.O. Box 7878, Marbel, South Cotabato.

SOUTH AFRICA
Cape Town Diocesan Mission to Moslems, Rectory, Pinelands, CP.
Jesus to the Muslims, PO Box 1804, Benoni 1502, T: 011-849-6371.
Jews for Jesus/South Africa, Parklands 2121 Johannesburg, T: 27-11-880-7956, F: 27-11-880-7732, O: E-mail: jfjsa@iafrica.com.
Maayan Yeshuah Ministry, PO Box 98227, Houghton 2041, Johannesburg, T: 011-728-3841.
MERCSA (Muslim Evangelism Resource Centre of Southern Africa, PO Box 342, Mondeor 2110, Johannesburg, T: 011-433-3269.

SOUTH KOREA
Institute for the Study of Religion and Theology, Sogang University, Seoul, T: 2-701-8962, F: 2-701-8962.

SWAZILAND
Life Challenge (Africa), P.O. Box 3250, Manzine.

SWEDEN
Church and Judaism, Idungatan 4, Box 230 57, S-104 35 Stockholm, T: 08-339250.
Northern Christian Buddhist Mission, Box 297, S-751 05 Uppsala.
Swedish Jerusalem Society, Fredrikshovsgatan 3A, S-115 22 Stockholm.

SWITZERLAND
Church and the Jewish People, The, WCC, 150 Route de Ferney, CH-1211 Genève 20, T: 333400.
Schweizerische Evangelische Judenmission, Rötelstr 96, CH-8057 Zürich, T: 051-601310.

TAIWAN
Association of Friends for the Study of Chinese Culture, Chung-hua Rd, 2nd section, 404-1, Taipei.
Ricci Institute for Chinese Studies Hain Hai, Road, Section 1, No. 24 8F, Taipei 10718, T: 2-241-9968, F: 2-393-2050.

THAILAND
FABC Office of Ecumenical and Interreligious Affairs, 57 Oriental Ave., Bangkok 10500, T: 237-5275,8, F: 237-5227.
Religion and Culture Research Center, Saengtham College, 20 Petkasem Road, Sampran, Kakhon-Pathom 73110, T: 2-429-0819-22.
Thai Interreligious Commission for Development, 4753/5 Soi Wat Thongnoppakun, Somdejchaophya Road, Kiongsan, Bangkok 10600, T: 2-275-3953, F: 2-276-2171.

UKRAINE
Jews for Jesus, Odessa, T: 7-0482-240-948.

UNITED STATES OF AMERICA (USA)
American Association for Jewish Evangelism, 5860 North Lincoln Ave., Chicago, IL 60645.
American Board of Missions to the Jews, 236 West 72nd St., New York, NY 10023.
AMF International, P.O. Box 5470, Lansing, IL 60438-5470, T: 708-418-0020, F: 708-418-0132, O: E-mail: 76636.1350@compuserve.com.
Association of Hebrew Catholics, O: Web: www.panix.com/~mmoss/ahc.
Chosen People Ministries, 1300 Cross Beam Dr., Charlotte, NC 28217, T: 704-357-9000, F: 704-357-6359, O: E-mail: missiondirector@chosen-people.com, Web: www.chosen-people.com.
Christian Jew Foundation (CJF), O: Web: www.cjf.org.
Cleveland Hebrew Mission, P.O. Box 18056, Cleveland, OH 44118.
CMJ/USA, P.O. Box 429, Ambridge, PA 15003, T: 412-266-5991.
Evangelical Islamics Committee, IFMA, P.O. Box 395, Wheaton, IL 60187.
Evangelism to Communist Lands, P.O. Box 303, Glendale, CA 91209, T: 213-243-7973.
Fellowship of Christian Testimonies to the Jews, 7448 North Damen Ave., Chicago, IL 60645.
Friends of Israel Gospel Ministry, O: Web: www.fdoigm.org.
Graymoor Ecumenical and Interreligious Institute, 475 Riverside Dr., Rm. 1960, New York, NY 10115.
Hebraic Heritage Ministries International, O: Web: www.geocities.com/Heartland/2175/index.html.
Hinduism International Ministries, P.O. Box 602, Zion, IL 60099, T: 708-872-7022, F: 708-872-7022.
Institute of Japanese Studies, 1605 Elizabeth St., Pasadena, CA 91104, T: 626-794-4400.
Institute of Tribal Studies, 1605 Elizabeth St., Pasadena, CA 91104, T: 626-791-1491.
International Cult Research Institute, 7823 Lindley Ave., Reseda, CA 91335, T: 818-705-8572.
Jewish Christian Dialogue Project in the UCC, 250 Wellington Rd, Buffalo, NY 14216.
Jewish Christians Relations, O: Web: www.jcrelations.com/.
Jews for Jesus, 60 Haight St, San Francisco, CA 94102, T: 415-864-2600, F: 415-552-8325, O: Web: www.jews-for-jesus.org.
Message to Israel, P.O. Box 52, Brooklyn, NY 11210, T: 718-377-0744.
Messianic Jewish Movement International (MJMI), O: Web: www.messiah.net.
Messianic Jewish Resources International, 6204 Park Heights Ave., Baltimore, MD 21215, T: 410-358-6471, F: 410-764-1376, O: E-mail: ledmess-min@aol.com, Web: www.goshen.net//lederer.
Ministries to Muslims, P.O. Box 6400, Altadena, CA 91003, T: 818-794-9123, F: 818-794-8565.
Shalom, Box 500307, Atlanta, GA 31150.
Sonrise Center for Buddhist Studies, P.O. Box 116, Sierra Madre, CA 91025, T: 818 797-9008, F: 818 398-7485.
Spiritual Counterfeits Project, Inc., P.O. Box 4308, Berkeley, CA 94704, T: 510-540-0300.
Task Force on Christian-Muslim Relations of the NCC in the USA, 77 Sherman Street, Hartford, CT 06105, T: 203-232-4451.
Zwemer Institute of Muslim Studies, P.O. Box 41330, Pasadena, CA 91114-8330, T: 626-794-1121, F: 626-798-3469.

16 Churches & denominations

Headquarters, central offices, or main contact points for a selection of larger or more significant (in each country) of the world's Christian churches, denominations, or associations of churches. These can be paired with entries in Country Tables 2, Part 4 (where statistics, translations, alternate names, common acronyms, jurisdictions, and other information can be found). Thousands of smaller churches and denominations are excluded.

AFGHANISTAN
Catholic Church, Embassy of Italy, Kabul, T: 24247.
Community Christian Ch of Kabul, P.O. Box 0, Kabul, T: 42224.

ALBANIA
Archdiocese of Durrës-Tirana (Catholic), Kryeipeshkëvi, Durrës.
Autocephalous Orthodox Church of Albania, Kisha Ortodokse Autoqefale e Shqipërisë, Tiranë, T: 355-42-34117, F: 32109.

ALGERIA
Eglise Catholique en Algérie, Archevêché, 13 Rue Khelifa-Boukhalfa, El Djezair, T: 634244.
Protestant Church of Algeria, 31, rue Reda Houhou, 16000 Alger, T: 213-2-716238, F: 213-2-716238.

AMERICAN SAMOA
Assemblies of God in Samoa, Central Office, Mission House, P.O. Box 218, Pago Pago.
Congregational Christian Church in American Samoa, P.O. Box 1537, Pago Pago 96799, T: 684-699-9810, F: 684-699-1898.

ANGOLA
Archdiocese of Luanda (Catholic), Arcebispado, C.P. 87, Luanda, 1230-C, T: 244-02-334-640, F: 244-02-334-433.
Igreja Ev de Angola Central, CP 28, Bela Vista.
Seventh-day Adventist Angola Union Mission, Caixa Postal 3, Huambo; Rua Teixeira da Silva, T: 2150, O: cable: Adventista, Huambo, Angola.Luanda: 'Adventista,' Luanda, telex: 6033 (Ans. 6033 Advento AN).

ANTIGUA & BARBUDA
Diocese of Antigua (Anglican), Bishop's Lodge, P.O. Box 23, St. John's, T: 20151.
Moravian Church, Eastern West Indies Province, P.O. Box 504, Cashew Hill, St. John's.

ARGENTINA
Iglesia Armenia en la America del Sud Acevedo, 1369 Buenos Aires.
Testigos de Jehová, Calle Honduras 5646, Buenos Aires 14.
Unión Nacional de las Asambleas de Dios, Hidalgo 353, Casilla de Correo 4669, Buenos Aires.

ARMENIA
Armenian Apostolic Church, Katolikossaran Amenain Hayotz, 378310 Etchmiadzin, T: 374-6-271420, O: Also: 253434, 524747.
Union of Evan. Chr-Bapt. of Armenia, 90 Nar-Dos Str, Yerevan 375018.

AUSTRALIA
Anglican Church of Australia, Box Q190, Queen Victoria Post Office, St. Andrew's House, Sydney Square, Sydney NSW 2000, T: 61-2-265-1525, F: 61-2-264-6552.
Archdiocese of Canberra (Catholic), Archbishop's House, G.P.O. Box 89, Commonwealth Ave., Canberra, A.C.T., 2601, T: 61-062-248-64-11, F: 61-062-247-96-36.
Uniting Church in Australia, P.O. Box A2266, Sydey South, NSW 1235, T: 61-2-9287-0900, F: 61-2-9287-0999, O: E-mail: assysec@nat.uca.org.au.

AUSTRIA
Archdiocese of Wien (Catholic), Wollzeile 2, Wien, A-1010, T: 43-01-51-552.
Evangelische Kirche Augsburgischen Bekenntnisses in Osterreich, Severin Schreiber Gasse 3, 1180 Vienna, T: 43-1/479-15-23, F: 43-1/479-15-23/20.
Zeugen Jehovas, Gallgasse 44, A-1130 Wien.

BAHAMAS
Anglican Church in Bahamas, Addington Hse, Box N-7107, Nassau.
Bahamas Baptist Union, P.O. Box 516, Nassau.
Diocese of Nassau (Catholic), P.O. Box N 8187, Nassau; The Hermitage, Eastern Road, Nassau, T: 809-324-2010, F: 809-322-2599, O: Office tel: 809-322-4533.

BAHRAIN
Anglican Ch, P.O. Box 36, Al Manamah.
Catholic Ch, Sacred Heart Convent, Al Manamah.

BANGLADESH
(Catholic) Archdiocese of Dhaka, Archbishop's House, P.O. Box 3, 1 Kakrail Rd., Dhaka, 1000, T: 880-02-40-88-79, F: 880-02-41-80-95.
Bangladesh Baptist Sangha, 33 Senpara Parbata, Mirpur-10, P.O. Box 8018, Dhaka 1216, T: 880 2 802-967, F: 880 2 803-556.

BARBADOS
Anglican Church in Barbados, Bishopscourt, St. Michael.
New Testament Ch of God, Island Supervisor, River Rd., St. Michael.

BELGIUM
Eglise Catholique de Belgique, Aartsbisdom, Wollemarkt 15, B-2800 Mechelen, T: 015-16501.
Témoins de Jéhovah, Rue d'Argile 60, Kraainem, Brabant.

BELIZE
Diocese of Belize City & Belmopan (Catholic), P.O. Box 616, Belize City; 144 North Front St., Belize City, T: 02-72122, F: 02-31922, O: Cables: Bishop's House, Belize City.
Seventh-day Adventist Ch, 26 corner of Regent & Kings Sts, P.O. Box 90, Belize City, T: 2115.

BELORUSSIA
(Catholic) Archdiocese of Minsk-Mohilev, Belarus.
Union of Evangelical Christians-Baptists of Belarus, Box 108, Minsk 22093, T: 375-172 5392 67, F: 375172538249.

BENIN
(Catholic) Archdiocese of Cotonou, Archevêché, B.P. 491, Cotonou, T: 229-30-01-45, F: 229-30-07-07.
Eglise Protestante Méthodiste, Olodo, Boulevard E.H. Sekoutouré, B.P. 34, Cotonou, T: 229-32 29 32, F: 229-31 25 20.

BERMUDA
African Methodist Episcopal Ch, Harris Bay, Smith's Parish; St. Paul's, Hamilton, T: 20505.
Diocese of Hamilton-in-Bermuda (Catholic), Box HM 1191, Hamilton; Halcyon, 2 Astwood Rd., Paget, DV 04, T: 809-236-7740, F: 809-236-7724.

BOLIVIA
(Catholic) Archdiocese of La Paz, Calle Ballivián 1277, Casilla 259, La Paz, T: 591-02-341-920, F: 591-02-391-244.
Asambleas de Dios de Bolivia, Casilla 181, Santa Cruz; Super, Casilla 4462, La Paz.

BOSNIA & HERCEGOVINA
(Catholic) Archdiocese of Vrhbosna, Sarajevo, Nadbiskupski Ordinarijat, Radojke Lakic 7, Sarajevo, T: 387-071-663-512, F: 387-071-663-512.

BOTSWANA
Catholic Ch, Bishop's House, P.O. Box 218, Gaborone, T: 52928.
United Congregational Church of Southern Africa, PO Box 1263, Gaborone, T: 352 491.

BRAZIL
(Catholic) Archdiocese of Brasília, Cúria Metropolitana, C.P. 00561, Avenida L-2 Sul, Q. 601, Módulos 3-4, Brasília, DF, 70200-610, T: 55-061-223-3353.
Assembleias de Deus, CP 3274 (& CP 19), Rio de Janeiro, GB; Rua Henrique Fleiuss 4201, 20000 Tijuca, GB.

BRITAIN (UK OF GB & NI)
Catholic Ch in England and Wales, Archbishop's House, Westminster, London SW1P 1QJ, T: 01-834,4717.
Church of England, The, Lambeth Palace London SE1 7JU, T: 0171-928-8282.

BURKINA FASO
Assemblées de Dieu en Haute-Volta, BP 29 & 121, Ouagadougou.
Eglise Catholique en Haute-Volta, Archevêché, BP 1471, Ouagadougou, T: 35180.

BURUNDI
(Catholic) Archdiocese of Gitega, Archevêché, B.P. 118, Gitega, Burundi, T: 257-040-2160, F: 257-040-2547.
Eglise Protestante Episcopale du Burundi, Ibuye, BP 58, Ngozi; BP 17, Bujambura.

CAMBODIA
Eglise Catholique au Cambodge, Evêché, 69 Blvd Prachea Thippatei, Phnom-Penh, T: 24904.
Eglise Ev Khmère, 72 Preah Bat Norodom, BP 545, Phnom Penh, T: 24319.

CAMEROON
(Catholic) Archdiocese of Douala, Archevêché, B.P. 179, Douala, T: 237-423-714, F: 237-421-837.
Eglise Evangélique du Cameroun, B.P. 89, Douala, T: 237-423611/430620,431724, F: 237-432917.

CANADA
(Catholic) Archdiocese of Ottawa, Archevêché, 1247 place Kilborn, Ottawa, Ontario, K1H 6K9, T: 613-738-5025, F: 613-738-0130.
United Church of Canada, The United Church House, 3250 Bloor St. W, Etobicoke, ON M8X 2Y4, T: 416-231-5931, F: 416-231-3103.

CAPE VERDE
Associacão das Igrejas Adventistas do Setimo Dia de Cabo Verde, Caixa Postal 6, Praia, Santiago; Avenue Amilcar Cabral 61, Praia, T: 61-39-63.
Diocese of Santiago de Cabo Verde, CP 46, Av Amilcar Cabral, Largo 5 Outubro, Praia, T: 238-61-11-19, F: 238-61-45-99.

CAYMAN ISLANDS
United Church in Jamaica and the Cayman Islands, 12 Carlton Crescent, P.O. Box 359, Kingston 10.

CENTRAL AFRICAN REPUBLIC
(Catholic) Archdiocese of Bangui, Archeveche, B.P. 1518, Bangui, T: 236-61-31-48, F: 236-61-46-92.
Eglise Ev des Frères, Rue Languedoc et Missions, BP 240, Bangui.

CHAD
Assemblées Chrétiennes du Tchad, BP 116, N'Djamena (Fort Lamy); BP 10, Doba par Moundou.
N'Djaména (Catholic), Archevêche, B.P. 456, N'Djaména, T: 235-51-44-43, F: 235-51-2860.

CHILE
Iglesia Metodista Pentecostal de Chile (IMP), Jotabeche 36, Casilla 4581, Santiago.

COLOMBIA
(Catholic) Archdiocese of Bogotá, Arzobispado, Carrear 7a N. 10-20, Sanatefé de Bogotá, D.C. 1, T: 57-91-334-5500, F: 57-91-334-7867.

CONGO-BRAZZAVILLE
(Catholic) Archdiocese of Brazzaville, Archevêché, B.P. 2301, Brazzaville, Congo, T: 242-83-17-93.
Eglise Evangélique du Congo, B.P. 3205, Bacongo-Brazaville, T: 242-830263, F: 242-837733.

CONGO-ZAIRE
(Catholic) Archdiocese of Kinshasa, Avenue de l'Université, B.P. 8431, Kinshasa, 1, T: 243-12-78-762.
Eglise do Jésus Christ sur la Terre par le Prophète Simon Kimbangu, 87, Rue Monkoto, B.P. 7069, Kinshasa I, T: 68851, F: 243-12-27159, O: Telex: 21536 Lasco ZR.
Eglise du Christ au Zaire, B.P. 4938, Kinshasa-Gombe, T: 243-12-33077, 43826, F: 243-12-349-61.

COOK ISLANDS
Cook Islands Christian Church, P.O. Box 93, Avarua, Rarotonga.
Diocese of Rarotonga, Catholic Mission, PO Box 147, Rarotonga, T: 682-20-817, F: 682-26-174.

COSTA RICA
(Catholic) Archdiocese of San José de Costa Rica, Arzobispado, Apartado 497, San José, 1000, T: 506-33-60-29, F: 506-21-24-27.

Asambleas de Dios, Apdo 840, San José.

CROATIA

(Catholic) Zagreb, Zagabria, Nadbispupski Duhovni Stol, Kaptol 31, p.p. 553, Zabreb, 41000, T: 385-041-275-132, F: 385-041-271-936.

CUBA

(Catholic) Archdiocese of San Cristóbal de la Habana, Calle Habana 152, Apartado 594, La Habana, 10100, T: 53-0809-62-4000, F: 53-0809-33-8109.
Asambleas de Dios, Instituto Biblico, Manacas, Las Villas; 548, Camaguey.

CYPRUS

(Catholic) Archdiocese of Cipro, The Maronite Church, PO Box 2249, 8 Faviero St, Nicosia, T: 357-2-45-88-77, F: 357-2-36-82-60.
Orthodox Church of Cyprus, P.O. Box 1130, 1016 Nikosia, Cyprus, T: 357-2-430696, F: 474180.

CZECH REPUBLIC

(Catholic) Archdiocese of Praha, Arcibiskupská Kurie, Hradcanské nám. 56/16, Praha 1, 119 02, T: 42-02-35-62-15, F: 42-02-35-25-20.
Evangelical Church of Czech Brethren, 9, Jungmannova, P.O. Box 466, 111 21 Praha 1, T: 420-2-242-22217, F: 420-2-242-22218.

DENMARK

Diocese of Kobenhavn, Copenhagen, Katolsk Bispekontor, Bredgade 69 A, Kobenhavn K, DK-1260, T: 45-33-11-60-80, F: 45-33-14-60-86.
National Ch of Denmark, BP, Norregade 11, Kobenhavn K.

DJIBOUTI

Diocese of Djibouti, Evêché, Boulevard de la République, B.P. 94, T: 253-350140, F: 253-35-48-31.
Eglise Protestante Evangélique au Djibouti, Boulevard de la République, B.P. 416, T: 253-351820.

DOMINICAN REPUBLIC

(Catholic) Archdiocese of Santo Domingo, Arzobispado, Apartado 186, Calle Isabel la Católica 55, Santo Domingo, T: 809-685-3141, F: 809-685-0227.
Asociación Adventista del Séptimo Déa, Calle Juan Sanchez Ramirez 46, Apdo 1500, Santo Domingo, T: 682-2020, 2373.

ECUADOR

(Catholic) Archdiocese of Guayaquil, Arzobispado, Apartado 254, Calle Clemente Ballén 501 y Chimborazo, Guayaquil, T: 593-04-322-778, F: 593-04-329-695.
Iglesia Unión Misionera Ev en el Ecuador, Casilla 698, Guayaquil.

EGYPT

Coptic Orthodox Patriarchate of Alexandria, Anba Rueis, Ramses St., Abbasiya, P.O. Box 9035, Cairo, T: 20-2-821-274, F: 20-2-831-822, O: Tlx: 92333 OKINA UN, Cable: ELANBRUEIS.
Evangelical Church, P.O. Box 1304, Cairo, T: 00202-5-903905, F: 00202-5-904995, O: Also tel: 00202-2454062.

EL SALVADOR

(Catholic) Archdiocese of San Salvador, Arzobispado, Urbanización Isidro Menéndez, Calle San José y Avenida Los Américas, San Salvador, T: 503-26-05-01, F: 503-26-49-79.
Asambleas de Dios, Apdo 840, Santa Ana, T: 252064.

EQUATORIAL GUINEA

Iglesia Católica en la Guinea Ecuatorial, Obispado, Apdo 82 Mbini, T: 181.
Iglesia Ev en la Guinea Ecuatorial, Apdo 25, Ebebiyin, Rio Muni; Apdo 195, Bata.

ERITREA

Evangelical Church of Eritrea, (Wenghelawit Bete Kristian Be Ertra), P.O. Box 905, Asmara, T: 291-1/12-07-11, F: 291-1/12-00-62, O: Telex: 42088.

ETHIOPIA

Ethiopian Orthodox Church, P.O. Box 1283, Addis Ababa, T: 110099, 111989, F: 251-1-552211, O: Telex: 21489 EOC DD ET.
Word of Life Ev Ch, P.O. Box 127, Addis Abeba, T: 47679.

FAEROE ISLANDS

Evangelical Lutheran Church, P.O. Box 8, FO-110 Torshavn, T: 29-8/119-95.

FALKLAND ISLANDS

Catholic Ch, Port Stanley, T: Stanley 204.

FIJI

(Catholic) Archdiocese of Suva, Archdiocesan Office, Nicolas House, Pratt St, P.O. Box 109, Suva, T: 679-30-19-55, F: 679-30-15-65.
Assemblies of God of Fiji, Calvary Temple, 83 Robertson Rd., P.O. Box 3697, Samabula, Suva.

FINLAND

Evangelical Lutheran Church of Finland, P.O. Box 185, Satamakatu 11, SF-00161 Helsinki 16, T: 358-0/180-21.
Greek Catholic Orthodox Church, TiilimSki 25, 00330 Helsinki, T: 90-483 485.

FRANCE

(Catholic) Archdiocese of Paris, 8 rue de la Ville-l'Evêque, Paris CEDEX 08, 75384, T: 33-1-49-24-11-11, F: 33-1-49-24-10-80.
Eglise Réformée de France, 47 Rue de Clichy, F-75009 Paris, T: 874-9092.

FRENCH GUIANA

Eglise Adventiste du Septième Jour, 39 Rue Schoelcher, BP 169, Cayenne, T: 366.
Eglise Catholique, Evêché, BP 378, 97302 Cayenne, T: 310118.

GABON

Eglise Evangélique du Gabon, B.P. 10080, Libreville, Baraka, T: 241-724192/726177, O: Cable: EVANGAB Libreville.

GAMBIA

Anglican Diocese of the Gambia, Bishopscourt, P.O. Box 51, Banjul, T: 27405, F: 220-229495, O: Telex: 2203 GV.
Diocese of Banjul, Bishop's House, P.O. Box 165, Banjul, T: 220-93-437, F: 220-90-998.

GEORGIA

Baptist Union of Georgia, 4 Kakhovka Str, 380054 Tblisi, T: 7 8832 342910, F: 78832 985-017.
Georgian Orthodox Church, Erekle II, Moedani 1, 380005 Tbilisi, T: 995-32-989528, 990378, O: Also: 989539, 989542.

GERMANY

(Catholic) Archdiocese of München und Freising, Postfach 330360, Rochusstrasse 5-7, München, D-80333, T: 49-089-21371, F: 49-089-213-74-78.
Ev Kirche in Deutschland (EKD), Kirchliches Aussenamt, Bockenheimer Landstr 109, Postfach 174025, D-6 Frankfurt am Main 1.

GHANA

(Catholic) Archdiocese of Accra, Chancery Office, P.O. Box 247, Accra, Ghana, T: 233-21-222-728.
Presbyterian Church of Ghana, P.O. Box 1800, Accra, T: 662109/665594, F: 233-21-665594, O: Telex: 2525 PRESBY GH.

GIBRALTAR

Diocese of Gibraltar, 215 Main St., T: 350-76-688.
Gospel Hall-Capilla Evangélica, Queen's Way Quay, P.O. Box 891, T: 7-78656, O: Also tel: 7-71829.

GREECE

Ch of Crete, Archbp of Crete, Iráklion, T: 282632.
Church of Greece, Ag. Philotheis 21, 105 56 Athens, T: 30-1-3237-654, F: 3224673.

GREENLAND

Lutheran Ch of Greenland, Godthaab.
Pentecostal Chs, P.O. Box 320, Laxa, Julianehab.

GRENADA

Anglican Ch, Rectory, Church St., St. George's.
Diocese of Saint George's in Grenada, Bishop's House, Morne Jaloux, P.O. Box 375, St. George's, T: 809 443-5299, F: 809-443-5758.

GUADELOUPE

Diocese of Guadeloupe (Catholic), Place Saint-François, B.P. 50, 97101 Basse-Terre Cedes, T: 590-81-36-69.
SDA Guadeloupe Conference, Boite Postale 19, 97151 Pointe-a-Pitre Cedex; Morne Boissard, Pointe-a-Pitre, T: 19-590-82-79-76, F: 19-590-83-44-24, O: Cable: Adventiste, Pointe-a-Pitre, Guadeloupe.

GUAM

(Catholic) Archdiocese of Agana, Archbishop's Residence, Cuesta San Ramon, Agana, 96910, T: 671-472-6116.
Seventh-day Adventist Ch, P.O. Box EA, Agaña, T: 776618.

GUATEMALA

(Catholic) Archdiocese of Guatemala, Arzobispado, Apartado 723, 7 Avenida 6-21, Zona 1, Guatemala City, T: 502-02-707, F: 502-02-28-384.
Asambleas de Dios, Instituto Biblico, 28 Calle y Av Elena, Zona 3, Apdo 103, Ciudad Guatemala.

GUINEA

(Catholic) Archdiocese of Conakry, Konakry, Archevêché, B.P. 1006 Bis, Conakry, T: 224-44-32-70, F: 224-44-33-70.
Eglise Ev Protestante, BP 438, Conakry.

GUINEA-BISSAU

Diocese of Bissau, C.P. 20, Bissau CODEX, 1001, T: 245-25-10-57, F: 245-25-10-58.
Igreja Evangelica da Guinea-Bissau (IEGB), CP 326, Bissau Codex 1001, T: 20-1483.

GUYANA

Anglican Church, The Deanery, St. George's Cathedral, Georgetown, T: 65067.
Assemblies of God in Guyana, 330 Church and East Sts., Box 610, Georgetown.
Diocese of Georgetown, Bishop's House, P.O. Box 10720, 27 Brickdam, Georgetown, T: 592-2-64469, F: 592-2-64469.

HAITI

(Catholic) Archdiocese of Port-au-Prince, Archevêché, B.P. 538, rue Dr. Aubry, Port-au-Prince, T: 509-2-2043.
Eglise Adventiste du Septième Jour, Ruelle Ganot 78, BP 1325, Port-au-Prince, T: 23452.

HOLY SEE

Curia Romana (Roman Curia), Palazzo Apostolico Vaticano, I-00120 Città del Vaticano, T: 698-3954.
Vicariato della Città del Vaticano, Palazzo Apostolico Vaticano, I-00120 Città del Vaticano, T: 698-3145, O: Web: www.vatican.va.

HONDURAS

(Catholic) Archdiocese of Tegucigalpa, Arzobispado Apartado 106, 3 y 12 Av. 1113, Tegucigalpa, T: 504-37-03-53, F: 504-22-23-37.
Asambleas de Dios, Apdo 117, San Pedro Sula.

HUNGARY

(Catholic) Archdiocese of Esztergom-Budapest, Primási és Erseki Hivatal, Mindszenty Hercegprímás tér 2, Pf. 25, Esztergom, H-2501, T: 36-33-11-288, F: 36-33-11-085.
Reformed Church in Hungary, Abonyi Utca 21, P.O. Box 5, 1146 Budapest, T: 36-1-1227870, F: 36-1-218-0903.

ICELAND

National Ch of Iceland, Reykjavík.

INDIA

(Catholic) Archdiocese of Delhi, Archbishop's House, Ashok Place, New Delhi 110001, T: 91-011-31-20-58, F: 91-011-95-43-21.
Orthodox Syrian Church of the East, Catholicate Palace Devalokam, 686038 Kottayam Kerala, T: 91-481-570569, F: 570569.

INDONESIA

Batak Christian Protestant Ch (HKBP), Ephorus, Pearaja-Tarutung, Sumatera Utara.
Catholic Ch in Indonesia, Jalan Kathedraal 7, Jakarta V/6, T: 362392.
Protestant Church in Indonesia, Jln. Medan Merdeka Timur 10, Jakarta-Pusat 10110, T: 62-21-351-9003, F: 62-21-385-9250.

IRAN

(Catholic) Archdiocese of Teheran, Forsat Ave. 91, Teheran, 15819, T: 98-021-882-35-49.
Evangelical Presbyterian Church in Iran, P.O. Box 1505, Tehran, T: 98-21-674-095, O: Cable: INCULCATE.

IRAQ

(Catholic) Archdiocese of Bagdad (Babilonia), Archeveche Latin, PO Box 35130, Hay Al-Wahda-Mahalla 904, rue 8, Imm. 44, Baghdad, T: 964-01-719-95-37, F: 964-01-717-24-71.
Ancient Apostolic and Catholic Church of the East, P.O. Box 2363, Baghdad, T: 964-1-7198362, F: 7183919.

IRELAND

(Catholic) Archdiocese of Dublin, Archbishop's House, Drumcondra, Dublin, 9, T: 353-01-373732, F: 353-01-60-496.

ISRAEL

(Catholic) Archdiocese of Akka, San Giovanni D'acri, Tolemaide, Archevêché, Grec-Catholique, B.P. 279, rue Hagefen 33, Haifa, T: 972-04-523-114.
Greek Orthodox Patriarchate of Jerusalem, P.O. Box 19632, 91190 Jerusalem, T: 972-2-6285883, F: 6282048, O: 6271657, 6284917.

ITALY

Assemblee di Dio in Italia, Via dei Bruzi 11, I-00185 Roma.
Chiesa Cattolica in Italia, Conferenza Episcopal Italiana, Circonvallazione Aurelia 50, I-00165 Roma; Vicaiato di Roma, T: 6982 int 6197.

IVORY COAST

(Catholic) Archdiocese of Abidjan, Archevêché, av. Jean Paul II, 01 B.P. 1287, Abidjan, 01, IC, T: 225-21-12-46.
Eglise Harriste, Comité National Harris de Côte d'Ivoire, Sec Gén & Prédicateur-Episcopal, BP 20710, Abidjan. (Also: Bregbo, BP 25, Bingerville; Temple Biblique No 1 de Grand-Lahou).

JAMAICA

(Catholic) Archdiocese of Kingston in Jamaica, Archbishop's Residence, 21 Hopefield Ave., PO Box Box 43, Kingston, 6, T: 809-927-9915, F: 809-927-0140.
Jamaica Baptist Union, 6 Hope Rd., Kingston 10, T: 809-926-7820, F: 809 926-6580.
SDA West Indies Union Conference, P.O. Box 22, Mandeville, T: 809-962-2284, 962-2910, F: 809-962-3417, O: Cable: Adventist, Mandeville, Jamaica.

JAPAN

(Catholic) Archdiocese of Tokyo, Archbishop's House, 16-15 Sekiguchi, 3-chome, Bunkyo-ku, Tokyo, 112, T: 81-03-943-2301, F: 81-03-944-8511.
Spirit of Jesus Ch, 3-152 Ogikubo, Suginami-ku, Tokyo 167, T: 03-391-5925.
United Church of Christ in Japan, Room 31, Japan Christian Center, 3-18 Nishi-Waseda, 2-chome, Shinjuku-ku, Tokyo 169.

JORDAN

(Catholic) Archdiocese of Petra E Filadelfia, Archevêché Grec-Melkite Catholique, B.P. 2435, Jabal-Amman, Amman, T: 962-06-624-757.
Syrian Orthodox Church, P.O. Box 370, Amman 11118, T: 009626-771-751.

KAZAKHSTAN

Evangelical Lutheran Ministry (ELUMIN), 480091 Almaty Internationalnaya Str 57, Detsky Sod #115 'Teremok', T: 011-7-3272-39-94-52, F: 022-7-3272-39-15-21.
Intereparchial Orthodox Commission, Minina 10, 480013 Almaty, T: 7-3272-674032, F: 677975.

KENYA

(Catholic) Archdiocese of Nairobi, Archbishop's House, P.O. Box 14231, Nairobi, T: 254-02-441-919.
Church of the Province of Kenya, P.O. Box 40502, Nairobi, T: 714752/3/4 Direct. 714755, F: 714750.

KIRGHIZIA

Seventh-day Adventist Kyrgyzstan Conference, ul. Kulieva 128, Bishkek, 720030, T: 331-25-17-98.
Union of Evangelical Christians-Baptists of Kyrgyzstan, P.O. Box 807, Bishkek 720040.

KIRIBATI

Diocese of Tarawa and Nauru, Bishop's House, PO Box 79, Bairiki, Tarawa, T: 686-21-279, F: 686-21-401.
Kiribati Protestant Church, P.O. Box 80, Bairiki, Antebuka, Tarawa, T: 686-21195, F: 686-21453.

KUWAIT

Armenian Orthodox Church of Cilicia, PO Box 6641, Hawalli, T: 614392.
Catholic Ch, Bishop's House, PO Box 266,, T: 434637.

LATVIA

(Catholic) Archdiocese of Riga, Metropolijas Kurija, Maza Pils 2, Riga, 1050, T: 371-0132-227-266, F: 371-0132-220-775.
Evangelical Lutheran Church of Latvia, M. Pils iela, 4, 1050 Riga, T: 371-2/22-60-57, F: 371-8/82-00-41.

LEBANON

(Catholic) Archdiocese of Bairut, Beirut, Archeveche Grec-Melkite Catholique, Sabdeh-Firdaous, Beirut, T: 961-01-88-08-66, F: 961-01-88-44-60.
Armenian Apostolic Ch, Catholicos, Catholicate of Cilicia, Antelias; Summer address: Couvent Arménian Apostolique, Bikfaya (Amrieh), T: 410003, 980060.
Greek Orthodox Patriarchate of Antioch, Archevêché, Rue Sursock, P.O. Box 186, Bayrut; Summer address: Souk El-Gharb, T: 226281, 575013.

LESOTHO

(Catholic) Archdiocese of Maseru, Archbishop's House, P.O. Box 267, 19 Orpen Rd., Maseru, T: 266-0501-31-25-65.
Lesotho Evangelical Church, Casalis House, P.O. Box 260, Maseru 100, T: 266-313942, F: 266-310555.

LIBERIA

(Catholic) Archdiocese of Monrovia, Archbishop's Ofc, PO Box 2078, Monrovia, T: 231-221-389, F: 231-221-399.
Liberian Baptist Convention, P.O. Box 390 & 1416, Monrovia.

LIBYA

Catholic Ch in Libya, P.O. Box 365, Tarabulus, T: 31863.
Seventh-day Adventist Ch, P.O. Box 240, Banghazi.

LIECHTENSTEIN

Ev-Lutherische Kirche, Pastor, 9490 Vaduz-Bartegrosch, T: 075-22515.

LITHUANIA

(Catholic) Archdiocese of Vilnius, Sv. Mikalojaus 4, Vilnius, 2001, T: 370-22-62-70-98, F: 370-22-22-28-07.
Russian Orthodox Ch, Ausros Vartu 8-I, LT 2024, Vilnius, T: 370-261-3641.

LUXEMBOURG

(Catholic) Archdiocese of Luxembourg, Luxemburg, Archevêché, B.P. 419, 4 rue Génistre, L-2014, T: 352-02-46-20-23, F: 352-02-47-53-81.
Eglise Protestante du Grand-Duché de Luxembourg, Consistoire, Rue de la Congrégation, Luxembourg-ville, T: 29670.

MACEDONIA

(Catholic) Archdiocese of Skopje-Prizren, Scopia-Prisriana, Biskupski Ordinarijat, ul. Dimitrije Tucovic 31, Skopje, 91000, T: 389-091-234-123, F: 389-091-234-123.
Macedonian Orthodox Church, P.F. 69, Makedonska Arhiepiskopija ul. Partizanski Odredi 12, 91000 Skopje, T: 389-91-228042, F: 225546, O: Synod 223960.

MADAGASCAR

Eglise Catholique au Madagascar, Conférence Episcopale, 102 bis Av Maréchal Joffre, BP 667, Antanimena, Tananarive, T: 20726.
Eglise Luthérienne Malagasy, B.P. 1741, 54, Avenue du 26 JONA 1960, Antananarivo 101, T: 302-07, O: Telex: 22544- FLM MG.

MALAWI

(Catholic) Archdiocese of Blantyre, Archbishop's House, PO Box 385, Blantyre, T: 265-63-39-05, F: 265-60-61-07.
Ch of Central Africa Presbyterian, Blantyre Synod, P.O. Box 413, Blantyre, T: 30977.

MALAYSIA

Anglican Church of Malaysia, 9 Jalan Tengah, 50450 Kuala Lumpur, T: 60-3-242-7303, F: 60-3-241-6460, O: ANGLICAN, KUALA LUMPUR.
Ev Ch of Borneo, Lawas, Sarawak, via Labuan, East Malaysia.
Methodist Church Malaysia, 23 Jalan Mayang, Kuala Lumpur 50450, T: 60-3-262-2444, F: 60-3-2611-388.

MALI

(Catholic) Archdiocese of Bamako, Archevêché, B.P. 298, Bamako, T: 223-22-54-99, F: 223-22-52-14.
Eglise Chrétienne Ev du Mali, BP 19, Koutiala.
Eglise Ev Protestante au Mali, Mission Protestante, Av de la Nation, BP 158, Bamako.

MALTA

(Catholic) Archdiocese of Malta, Archbishop's Curia, P.O. Box 29, Valletta, T: 356-24-53-50, F: 356-24-21-73.
Ch of Scotland, St. Andrew's Church, South St, Valetta.

MARSHALL ISLANDS
Assemblies of God, Laura, Majuro.
United Ch of Christ in the Marshall Is, Ebeye, Kwajalein, Marshall Islands.

MARTINIQUE
SDA Martinique Conference, Boite Postale 580, 97207 Fort-de-France; Route de Schoelcher 2 Km. 100, Fort-de-France, T: 61-44-61, F: 61-04-21, O: Cable: Adventiste, Fort-de-France.

MAURITANIA
Eglise Catholique, Evêché, BP 353, Nouakchott, T: 2515.

MAURITIUS
Anglican Ch, Diocese of Mauritius, Bp, Bishop's House, Phoenix.
Catholic Ch, Evêché, Rue Mgr Gonin, Port-Louis, T: 23068.

MEXICO
(Catholic) Archdiocese of Mexico, Curia Arzobispal, Apartado Postal 24-433, México, D.F., 06700, T: 52-5-208-3200, F: 52-5-208-5350.
Asambleas de Dios de México, Calle Nicolas León No. 118, Colonia Jardín Balvuena, México 8, DF.

MICRONESIA
Diocese of The Caroline Islands, Bishop's Residence, PO Box 250, Chuuk, Caroline Islands, 96942, T: 691-330-2313, F: 691-330-4394.
Protestant Ch of East Truk, Dublon, Truk District.
United Ch of Christ in Ponape, Kolonia, Ponape District, P.O. Box 7, Caroline Islands.

MOLDAVIA
Moldavian Orthodox Church, ul. Tighina 3, 277061 Kisinev, T: 373-02-265444, F: 265401.

MONACO
(Catholic) Archdiocese of Monaco, Archevêché, B.P. 517, 6 rue de l'Abbaye, MC-98015, T: 33-93-30-88-10, F: 33-92-16-73-88.

MOROCCO
(Catholic) Archdiocese of Rabat, Archevêché, 1 rue Henri Dunant, BP 258 R.P., Rabat, T: 212-07-709-239, F: 212-07-706-282.
Eglise Evangélique au Maroc, 33 rue d'Azilal, Casablanca, T: 221-215564, F: 221-216337, 238579.

MOZAMBIQUE
(Catholic) Archdiocese of Maputo, Paço Arquiepiscopal, Avenida Eduardo Mondlane 1448, C.P. 258, Maputo, T: 258-01-42-62-40, F: 258-01-42-18-73.
Igrega Uniao Baptista de Moçambique, Caixa Postal 599, Maputo, T: 416787.

MYANMAR
(Catholic) Archdiocese of Yangon, Archbishop's House, 289 Theinbyu St, Botataund, Yangon, T: 95-72-752.
Myanmar Baptist Convention, P.O. Box 506, Yangon; 143, Minyekyawswa Rd, Yangon, T: 95 121465, F: 95 189702.

NAMIBIA
Catholic Ch in Namibia, P.O. Box 272, Windhoek 9100, T: 22220.
Evangelical Lutheran Church in Namibia (ELCIN), Private Bag 2018, Ondangwa, T: 264-6756/402-41, F: 264-6756/403-11.

NEPAL
Nepal Christian Fellowship (NCF), P.O. Box 4655, Kathmandu, T: 977-1-536-163.

NETHERLANDS
(Catholic) Archdiocese of Utrecht, Aartsbisdom, PB 14019, Maliebaan 40, Utrecht, 3508 SB, T: 31-030-316-956, F: 31-030-311-962.
Protestant Union of the Netherlands, Thorbeckegracht 11, 8011 VL Zwolle, T: 038-211333.

NETHERLANDS ANTILLES
Diocese of Willemstad (Catholic), Breedestraat 31, Otrobanda, Willemstad, Curaçao, N.A., T: 599-9-625876, F: 599-9-627-437, O: Home: 599-9-623347, Cables: Bisdom Willemstad, Curaçao.
United Protestant Church, Fortkerk, Fort Amsterdam, Williamstad, Curaçao.

NEW CALEDONIA
(Catholic) Archdiocese of Nouméa, Archevêché, B.P. 3, 4 rue Mgr-Fraysse, Nouméa, T: 687-273-149, F: 687-27-23-74.
Evangelical Ch in New Caledonia & Loyalty Islands, 8, rue Fernande Leriche, Vallée du Génie, B.P. 277, Nouméa, T: 687-283166, F: 687-263898.

NEW ZEALAND
(Catholic) Archdiocese of Wellington, Catholic Centre, PO Box 1937, Wellington, 6001, T: 64-04-496-1795, F: 64-04-499-2519.
Anglican Church, 114 E Queen St, PO Box 885, Hastings, T: 64-6-878-7902, F: 64-6-878-7905.
Presbyterian Church of Aotearoa New Zealand, 100 Tory St., P.O. Box 9049, Wellington, T: 64-4-801-6000, F: 64-4-801-6001, O: E-mail: aes@pcanz.org.nz.

NICARAGUA
(Catholic) Archdiocese of Managua, Arzobispado, Apartado 3058, Managua, T: 505-02-71-754, F: 505-02-67-01-30.
Asambleas de Dios, Apdo 1225, Managua.

NIGER
Eglise Catholique, Evêché, BP 10270, Niamey, T: 733079.
Eglises Ev du Niger, Sudan Interior Mission, BP 121, Maradi.

NIGERIA
(Catholic) Archdiocese of Lagos, Archdiocesan Secretariat, PO Box 8, 19 Catholic Mission St., Lagos, T: 234-01-263-38-41, F: 234-01-263-38-41.
Anglican Church of Nigeria, 29 Marian, P.O. Box 78, Lagos, T: 01-635681/01-633581, F: 01-631264.

NIUE ISLAND
Niue Christian Church, P.O. Box 25, Alofi, T: 683-4195, F: 683-4196.

NORTHERN MARIANA ISLANDS
Saipan Community Ch, P.O. Box 5, Saipan, Mariana Islands.

NORWAY
(Catholic) Archdiocese of Oslo, Oslo Katolske Bispedómme, Akersveien 5, Postboks 8270, Hammersborg, N-0177, Oslo, 1, T: 47-02-207-226, F: 47-02-204-857.
Church of Norway, P.O. Box 5816 Majorstua, N-0308 Oslo, T: 47-22/93-27-50, F: 47-22/93-28-28.

OMAN
Protestant Ch in Oman, P.O. Box 790, Masquat.

PAKISTAN
(Catholic) Archdiocese of Karachi, St. Patrick's Cathedral, Shahrah-Iraq, Karachi, 74400, T: 92-021-778-15-32.
Church of Pakistan, Synod Secretariat, Barah Patthar, Sialkot 2, Punjab, T: 92-432-264895.

PALAU
Protestant Ch in the Caroline Islands, Liebenzell Mission, Koror, Palau District, Western Caroline Islands, US Trust Territory 96940.

PALESTINE
Catholic Ch, Latin Patriarchate, Old City, P.O. Box 14152, Jerusalem, T: 02-282323.
Greek Orthodox Patriarchate of Jerusalem, Patriarch, David Hamelekh St., Old City, P.O. Box 190632, Jerusalem, T: 27846.

PANAMA
(Catholic) Archdiocese of Panamá, Arzobispado, Calle 20 y Av. México 24-45, Apartado 386, Panamá, 5, T: 507-62-7802, F: 507-62-6691.
Iglesia Adventista del Séptimo Día, 844 Gavilan Rd, P.O. Box 2006, Balboa, T: 525859, 526531, 526283.

PAPUA NEW GUINEA
(Catholic) Archdiocese of Port Moresby, Archbishop's House, PO Box 1032, Boroko, Natl Capital Dist., T: 675-25-1192, F: 675-25-6731.
Evangelical Lutheran Church of Papua New Guinea, P.O. Box 80, Lae, T: 675/42-37-11, F: 675/42-10-56.

PARAGUAY
(Catholic) Archdiocese of Asunción, Arzobispado, C.C. 654, Independencia Nacional y Col. Bogado 130, Asunción, T: 595-021-44-4150, F: 595-021-44-7510.
Asambleas de Dios en el Paraguay, Sede Central, Choferes del Chaco, Barrio Previsión Social, Casilla 514, Asunción.

PERU
(Catholic) Archdiocese of Lima, Arzobispado, Plaza de Armas, Apartado 1512, Lima, 100, T: 51-014-275-980, F: 51-014-636-125.
Iglesia Adventista del Séptimo Día, Av Comandante Espinar 610 & 730, Miraflores, Casilla 1002, Lima, T: 256639, 458297.

PHILIPPINES
(Catholic) Archdiocese of Manila, Arzobispado, 121 Arzobispado St., Intramuros, PO Box 132, Manila, 1099, T: 63-02-48-18-67, F: 63-02-48-15-48.
Philippine Independent Church, 1500 Taft Ave., Ermita, Box 2484, Manila.

PITCAIRN ISLANDS
SDA Pitcairn Island Mission, P.O. Box 24, Pitcairne Island, T: 872-144-5372, F: 582-144-5372.

POLAND
(Catholic) Archdiocese of Warszawa, Kuria Metropolitalna, ul. Miodown 17-19, Warszawa, 00-246, T: 48-022-31-52-31, F: 48-022-31-76-14.
Polish Orthodox Church, Al. Solidarnosci 52, 03402 Warszawa, T: 48-22-6190886.

PORTUGAL
(Catholic) Archdiocese of Braga, Cúria Arquiepiscopal, Rua de Santa Margarida 181, Braga, 181, T: 351-053-61-32-81, F: 351-053-61-20-06.
Assembleias de Deus em Portugal, Dirigente, Rua Neves Ferreira 13-3, Calcada do Poco dos Mouros, Lisboa 1.

PUERTO RICO
Iglesia Católica en Puerto Rico, Arzobispado, Apdo 1967, San Juan, PR 00903, T: 7277373.
Iglesia de Dios Pentecostal, Calle América 1473, Parada 22, Santurce.

QATAR
Diocese of Cyprus & the Gulf, British Embassy P.O. Box, Doha, T: 974-424-329.

REUNION
Diocese of Saint-Denis-de-La Réunion, Evêché, 36 rue de paris, BP 55, St.-Denis-de-La Réunion CEDEX, T: 262-212-849, F: 262-417-715.

ROMANIA
(Catholic) Archdiocese of Bucuresti, Bucarest, Arhiepiscopia Romano-Catolica, Str. Nuferilor 19, Bucuresti, 70749, T: 40-91-613-39-36, F: 40-91-312-12-07.
Romanian Orthodox Church, Aleesa Patriarhiei, 2, R-70526 Bucuresti 4, T: 40-1-6156772, 6130908, F: 3125086.

RUSSIA
Russian Orthodox Ch, Chisty Pereulok 5, Moskva G-34; Dept of External Affairs, Ryleev St 18/2, Moskva G34, T: 2022954, 2023043.
Union of Evangelical Christians-Baptists of the Russian Federation, Intl. P.O. Box 171, Moscow, T: 7095-958-1336, F: 7095-954-9231.

RWANDA
(Catholic) Archdiocese of Kigali, Archevêché, B.P. 715, Kigali, T: 250-75-769, F: 250-6371.
Eglise Anglicane du Rwanda (EAR), Evêqué, EAR Gahini, BP 61, Kigali.
Seventh-day Adventist Rwanda Union Mission, Boite Postale 367, Kigali; Avenue de la Paix, Kigali, T: 73228, F: 250-77232, O: Cable: Adventist, Kigali, telex: 596 RUM RW.

SAINT HELENA
SDA St. Helena Island Mission, S.D.A. Mission, P.O. Box 126, Jamestown, T: 290-3417.

SAINT KITTS & NEVIS
Methodist Ch in the Caribbean & the Americas, Basseterre.
St. Kitts Salvation Army, P.O. Box 56; Cayon Rd., Basseterre, T: 809-465-2106.

SAINT LUCIA
Archdiocese of Castries (Catholic), P.O. Box 267, Castries; Archbishop's House, Castries, T: 809-45-24949, F: 809-452-5040, O: Office: 809-45-2216, 25040.

SAINT PIERRE & MIQUELON
Eglise Catholique, Evêché, St-Pierre, via Newfoundland, T: 35.

SAINT VINCENT & THE GRENADINES
Anglican Church in the Province of the West Indies, Bishop's House, P.O. Box 128, T: 809-45-61895.
Province of Castries (Catholic), P.O. Box 862, Kingstown, T: 809-457-2363, F: 809-457-1903, O: Res. phone: 809-456-2427.

SAMOA
(Catholic) Archdiocese of Samoa-Apia, Archbishop's House, Fetuolemoana, PO Box 532, Apia, Western Somoa, T: 685-20400, F: 685-20402.
Ch of Jesus Christ of Latter-day Saints, Samoa Mission, P.O. Box 197, Apia.
Congregational Christian Church in Samoa, P.O. Box 468, Apia, T: 685-24414, F: 685-20429.
Methodist Church in Samoa, P.O. Box 1867, Apia.

SAO TOME & PRINCIPE
Diocese of São Tomé e Príncipe, Centro Diocesano, CP 104, Sao Tomé, T: 239-012-21-408, F: 239-012-21-365.

SENEGAL
(Catholic) Archdiocese of Dakar, Archevêché, B.P. 1908, Avenue Jean XXIII, Dakar, T: 221-23-69-18.
Assemblées de Dieu, BP 3130, Dakar.

SEYCHELLES
Anglican Church of Seychelles, Box 44, Victoria, Mahe, T: 24242.
Diocese of Port Victoria o Seychelles, Bishop's House, PO Box 43, Olivier maradan Str., Port Victoria, Mahé, T: 248-22152, F: 248-25545.

SIERRA LEONE
(Catholic) Archdiocese of Freetown and Bo, Santanno House, PO Box 893, Freetown, T: 232-224590, F: 232-224415.
United Methodist Church, U.M.C. House, P.O. Box 523, 31, Lightfoot Boston St., Freetown, T: 226652, O: Telex: Bremish.

SINGAPORE
(Catholic) Archdiocese of Singapore, Archbishop's House, 31 Victoria St, 0718, Singapore, T: 65-02-337-88-18, F: 65-02-337-88-18.
Methodist Church in Singapore, Methodist Centre, 10 Mount Sphia, Singapore 228459, T: 337-5155, F: 338-9575.

SLOVAKIA
Church of the Brethren in the Slovak Republic, Ul. 29 Augusta 27, 934 01 Levice, T: 421-813-23848, F: 421-813-23848, O: E-mail: cblv@uvt.uniag.sk.
Evangelical Ch of the Augsburg Confession in the Slovak Republic, (Evanjelická cirkev augsburgského vyznania na Slovensku), Palisady 46, 811 06 Bratislava, T: 42-7/533-08-27, F: 42-7/533-08-27.

SLOVENIA
(Catholic) Archdiocese of Ljubljana, Nadskofijski Ordinariat, Ciril-Metodov trg 4, p.p. 121/III, Ljubljana, T: 061-310-673, F: 061-314-169.

SOLOMON ISLANDS
(Catholic) Archdiocese of Honiara, Holy Cross, GPO Box 237, Honiara, T: 677-22-387, F: 677-22-869.
Church of Melanesia, P.O. Box 19, Honiara.
Seventh-day Adventist Ch, P.O. Box 63, Honiara.
South Sea Ev Ch (SSEC), Auki, Malaita.
United Church in the Solomon Islands, P.O. Box 82, Kokeqolo, Munda, T: 677-61125, F: 667-61265.

SOMALIA
Diocese of Mogadishu, C.P. 273, Ahmed Bin Idris, Mogadishu, T: 01-20-184.

SOUTH AFRICA
(Catholic) Archdiocese of Pretoria, Archbishop's House, PO Box 17245, 125 Main Str., Groenkloopf, 0027, T: 27-012-46-2048, F: 27-012-46-2452.
Zion Christian Ch (ZCC), Zion City, Morija, Boyne, Transvaal.

SOUTH KOREA
(Catholic) Archdiocese of Seoul, Archbishop's House, 2Ka-1 Myeong Dong, Jung Ku, Seoul, 100-022, T: 82-02-771-7600, F: 82-02-773-1947.
Presbyterian Church in the Republic of Korea (PROK), #1501 Korea Ecumenical Building, 136-56 Yunchi-Dong, Chongno-Ku, Seoul 110-470, T: 82-2-708-4021, F: 82-2-708-4027.

SPAIN
(Catholic) Archdiocese of Madrid, Arzobispado, Bailén 8, Madrid 28071, T: 34-91-541-48-02, F: 34-91-542-79-06.
Iglesia Ev Filadelfia, Chalet Ferrer, Av Paris, Puerto de Pollensa, Mallorca.

SRI LANKA
(Catholic) Archdiocese of Colombo, Archbishop's House, 976 Gnanartha Pradeepaya Mawatha, Colombo, 8, T: 94-01-695-471, F: 94-01-692-009.
Assemblies of God in Sri Lanka, 108 Rosemead Place, Colombo 7.

SUDAN
(Catholic) Archdiocese of Khartoum, Catholic Church, PO Box 49, Khartoum, T: 80-939.
Province of the Episcopal Church of Sudan, P.O. Box 110, Juba.

SURINAME
(Catholic) Archdiocese of Paramaribo, Bisschopshuis, Gravenstraat 12, PO Box 1230, Paramaribo, T: 597-47-33-06, F: 597-47-16-02.
Moravian Ch in Surinam, Provincial Board, P.O. Box 219, Paramaribo.

SWAZILAND
(Catholic) Archdiocese of Manzini, Bishop's House, PO Box 19, Sandlane St., Manzini, T: 268-52348, F: 268-54-876.
Swazi Christian Ch in Zion, BP, Boyane Tribal School, P.O. Box 42, Kwaluseni.

SWEDEN
Church of Sweden, The Archbishop's Office, Sysslomansgatan 4, 751-70 Uppsala, T: 46-18/16-95-00, F: 46-18/16-96-25.
Diocese of Stockholm, Katolska Biskopsämbetet, Götgatan 68, PO Box 4114, Stockholm, S-102 62, T: 46-08-643-80-26, F: 46-08-702-05-55.

SWITZERLAND
Schweizerischer Evangelischer Kirchenbund Fédération des Eglises protestantes de la Suisse, Federation of Swiss Protestant Churches, Sulgenauweg 26, Postfach 36, 3000 Bern 23, T: 41-31-370-25-25, F: 41-31-370-25-80, O: E-mail: sek@ref.ch or 106245.3462.

SYRIA
Greek Orthodox Patriarchate of Antioch, B.P. 0009, Damascus, T: 963-11-542440-0, F: 5424404, 5436211.
Syrian Orthodox Patriarchate of Antioch, P.O. Box 22260, Damascus Bab Touma, Damascus, T: 963-11-432-401, F: 963-11-432-400, O: 963-11-435-918 (Private).

TAIWAN
(Catholic) Archdiocese of Taipeh, PO Box 7-91, 94 Loli Road, Taipai, 10668, T: 886-02-737-1311, F: 885-02-737-1326.
Presbyterian Church in Taiwan, 3, Lane 269, Roosevelt Rd., Sec. 3, Taipei 106, T: 886-2-2362-5282, F: 886-2-2362-8096, O: E-mail: pctres@tpts1.seed.net.tw.

TANZANIA
(Catholic) Archdiocese of Mwanza, Archbishop's House, PO Box 1421, Mwanza, T: 255-068-41-616, F: 255-068-41-616.
Church of the Province of Tanzania, Mtingele, P.O. Box 899, Dodoma, T: 061-21437, F: 061-24565.
Evangelical Lutheran Church in Tanzania, P.O. Box 3033, Boma Rd., Arusha.

THAILAND
(Catholic) Archdiocese of Bangkok, Assumption Cathedral, Charoenkrung 40, Bangrak, Bangkok, 10500, T: 66-02-233-87-12, F: 66-02-237-10-33.

TIMOR
Christian Church in East Timor, P.O. Box 186, Dili, East Timor.
Diocese of Díli, Uskupan Lecidere (Bidau), K.P. 250, Díli, T: 0390-21-665.

TOGO
(Catholic) Archdiocese of Lomé, Archevêché, B.P. 348, 10 rue Maréchal-Foch, Lomé, T: 228-21-22-72.

TONGA
Ch of Jesus Christ of Latter-day Saints, P.O. Box 58, Nukualofa.
Diocese of Tonga, Toutaimana Catholic Centre, PO Box 1, Nuku'alofa, T: 676-23-822, F: 676-23-854.
Free Wesleyan Church, Box 57, Nuku'Alofa.

TRINIDAD & TOBAGO
(Catholic) Archdiocese of Port of Spain, 27 Maraval Road, Port of Spain, T: 809-622-1103, F: 809-662-1165.
Anglican Church in Trinidad, Hayes Ct, 21 Maraval Rd, Port of Spain.

TUNISIA
Eglise Catholique, Prèlature, 4 Rue d'Alger, Tunis, T: 245225.

TURKEY
Armenian Apostolic Patriarchate of Constantinople, Sirapnel sok 20-22, Kumkapi, Istanbul.
Ecumenical Patriarchate, Istanbul Rum Patrikligi, Haliç-Fener, 34220 Istanbul, T: 90-212-5255416, F: 5316533, 5349037.

TURKS & CAICOS ISLANDS
Anglican Church, Diocese of Nassau and the Bahamas, P.O. Box 24, Grand Turk.

TUVALU
Tuvalu Christian Church, P.O. Box 2, Funafuti, T: 688-20755, 20461, F: 688-20651.

UGANDA
(Catholic) Archdiocese of Kampala, Archbishop's House, PO Box 14125, Mengo, Kampala, T: 256-041-24-54-41, F: 256-041-24-54-41.
Church of Uganda, P.O. Box 14123, Kampala, T: 270218/9, F: 245597, O: Telex: 62014 KANISA UG.

UKRAINE
Catholic Archdiocese of Lviv, Kuria Metropolitalna Obrzadku Lacinskiego, pl. Katedralna 1, Lviv, 290008, T: 7-0322-79-70-92.
Ukranian Orthodox Ch, wl. Sicnerogo poustannia 25, Korp 49, Kiev 252015, T: 380-044-290150-8,-9, F: 294-9243.

UNITED STATES OF AMERICA (USA)
Catholic Ch in the USA, National Conference of Catholic Bishops, 1312 Massachusetts Ave., NW, Washington, DC 20005, T: 202-659-6600.
Southern Baptist Convention, 901 Commerce St., Suite 750, Nashville, TN 37203, T: 615-244-2355.

URUGUAY
(Catholic) Archdiocese of Montevideo, Arzobispado, Calle Treinta y Tres 1368, Casilla de Correo Central 356, Montevideo, 11000, T: 598-02-95-81-27, F: 598-02-95-89-26.
Waldensian Evangelical Church of the River Plate, Av. Armand Ugon 1488, 70-202 Valdense, Dpto Colonia, T: 598-552-8794, F: 598-552-8110, O: E-mail: mesaval@adinet.com.uy.

UZBEKISTAN
Seventh-day Adventist Asian-Caucasian Conference, ul. Volzhskaya 65, Tashkent, 700077, T: 3712-67-39-04.
Union of Evangelical Christians—Baptists of Middle East, P.O. Box 303, Tashkent 700015, T: 7 371 550 649, F: 7 371 550 967.

VANUATU
(Catholic) Archdiocese of Port-Vila, Evêché, BP 59, Port-Vila, T: 678-22640, F: 678-25342.
Presbyterian Church of Vanuatu, Box 150, Port-Vila, Efate, T: 678-26-480, F: 678-22-722.

VENEZUELA
(Catholic) Archdiocese of Caracas, Santiago de Venezuela, Arzobispado, Apartado 954, Plaza Bolívar, Caracas, 1010-A, T: 58-02-545-02-12, F: 58-02-545-17-55.
Iglesia Adventista del Séptimo Día, Carcel a Pilita 2, Apdo 986, Caracas, T: 413877.

VIET NAM
(Catholic) Archdiocese of Hanôi, Taà Tông Giám Muc, 40 Phô Nhà Chung, Ha Nôi, T: 84-254-424.
Ev Ch of Viet-Nam, 2 Su Van Hanh, Cholon District, P.O. Box 923, Saigon, T: 38136.

US VIRGIN ISLANDS
(Catholic) Archdiocese of St. Thomas in the Virgin Islands, Chancery Office, PO Box 1825, Charlotte Amalie, 00803, T: 809-774-3166, F: 809-774-5816.
(Episcopal) Diocese of the Virgin Islands, Box 7488, St. Thomas, Virgin Islands 00801, T: 809-776-1797, F: 809-777-8485.

WALLIS & FUTUNA ISLANDS
(Catholic) Archdiocese of Wallis et Futuna, Evêché, Lano, BP G6, Mata'Utu, T: 681-72-27-83, F: 681-72-27-83.

YEMEN
Catholic Ch, Vicariate of Arabia, Steamer Point, P.O. Box 1155, Aden, T: 22900.

YUGOSLAVIA
Serbian Orthodox Church, Kralja Petra br. 5, 11000 Beograd, T: 381-11-635699, F: 638161.
Slovak Evangelical Ch of the Augsburg Confession in Yugoslavia, Karadziceva 2, 21000 Novi Sad, T: 381-21/61-18-82, F: 381-21/254-43.

ZAMBIA
(Catholic) Archdiocese of Lusaka, Archdiocese, PO Box 32754, 41 Wamulwa Rd., Lusaka, T: 260-01-213-188, F: 260-01-290-631.
United Church of Zambia, P.O. Box 50122, 15101 Ridgeway, Lusaka, T: 260-1-250641.

ZIMBABWE
(Catholic) Archdiocese of Harare, P.O. Box 8060, Causeway, Harare, T: 263-14-727-386, F: 263-14-727-386.
African Apostolic Ch of Johane Maranke (AACJM), Maranke Reserve, P.O. Umtali.
Zion Christian Church, Stand 2705, Five Street, Mucheke Township, Fort Victoria.

17
Clergy & clergy-lay organizations

Organizations of individuals for consultation and co-operation between clergy (priests, pastors, ministers), or clergy and laity, or clergy/laity/religious personnel, or missionary personnel; either within a single church or denomination, or interdenominational or ecumenical; priests' councils or senates, national priests' organizations, ministerial or clergy fellowships or associations, pastoral councils, pastoral consultative bodies, fellowships of foreign missionary personnel, Catholic national and diocesan synods; clergy recruitment organizations, clergy or lay employment bureaus. For women, see WOMEN IN THE ORDAINED MINISTRY. For religious personnel, seeRELIGIOUS COMMUNITIES.

ARGENTINA
Consejo Pastoral Nacional (CPN), CEA, Paraguay 1867, Buenos Aires.
Cruzada Sacerdotal Argentina, Jujuy 1241, Buenos Aires.

AUSTRALIA
Priests' Forum, 10 Hamilton St, Bentheigh, Victoria 3204.

AUSTRIA
Arbeitsgemeinschaft Österreichischer Priesterräte, Stephansplatz 6, A-1010 Wien, T: 524644.
Pastoralkommission Österreichs, Stephansplatz 3, A-1010 Wien.

BAHAMAS
Diocesan Pastoral Council, P.O. Box 187, Nassau.
Senate of Priests, Our Lady of the Holy Souls, Deveaux St., South Youngtown.

BARBADOS
Barbados Evangelical Association, 41 Excel Rd., Elizabeth Park, Worthing P.O., Christ Church, T: 427-9746, F: 228-6855, O: E-mail: gaseale@caribsurf.com.

BELGIUM
Amitiés Sacerdotales, Ry de Brabant 5, B-6358 Manage-Longsart, T: 064-552268.
Bureau Européen des Délegués des Conseils Presbytéraux, c/o Abbé Dhanis, Rue Joseph II 34, B-1040 Brussel, T: 02-511-1259, 513-7796.
Centre National des Vocations, Rue Belliard 26, B-1040 Brussel, T: 02-512-1300.
Flemish Interdiocesan Pastoral Council Beraad, Guimardstraat 5, B-1040 Brussels, T: 02-511-0585, 512-3379.
Ghent Informal Priests Group, Maisstraat 12, B-9000 Gent.

BERMUDA
Bermuda Ministerial Association, The Manse, Paget.

BRITAIN (UK OF GB & NI)
Additional Curates Society, 14 Rothamsted Av, Harpenden, Herts, T: 3512.
Advisory Council for the Church's Ministry (ACCM), Church House, Dean's Yard, London SW1P 3NZ, T: 01-222-9011.
Association of Church Fellowships, ACF Office, 12 Abbey Square, Chester, T: 20711.
Catholic Priests' Association, St. George Presbytery, Eastbourne Rd, Polegate, East Sussex.
Church Patronage Trust, 3 Amen Court, London EC4M 7BU, T: 01-248-1817.
Evangelical Fellowship of the Anglican Communion (EFAC), 12 Weymouth St, London W1N 3FB, T: 01-580-1867.
Fellowship of Evangelical Churchman, St. John's Vicarage, London SE8, T: 01-692-2857.
Friends of The Holy Father, MBBS, Archbishop's House, Ambrosden Ave, London SW1P 1QJ, T: 01252-724924.
Islington Clerical Conference, St. Mary's Vicarage, Upper St, London N1.
National Conference of Priests, St. Therese's Presbytery, Southdown Rd, Port Talbot, Glamorgan, South Wales.
National Conference of Priests (England and Wales), St. Mary's Ford Green Road, Norton-le-Moors, Stoke on Trent ST6 8LT, T: 01782-535404.
Ordination Candidates' Exhibition Fund, 8 Victoria Rd, Chingfield, London E4.
Parochial Clergy Association, Minal Rectory, Marlborough, Wilts, T: 06725-2096.

BURUNDI
Union Apostolique et Culturelle des Prêtres Burundais (UACPB), Grand Séminaire, BP 850, Bujumbura.

CAMEROON
Association Interdiocésaine des Prêtres Indigènes (AIPI), BP 93, Deschang.

CANADA
Canadian Association of Clergy (CAC), P.O. Box 89070 (Westdale), Hamilton, ON L8S 4R5, T: 905-522-3775, O: 1-800-661-(PRAY) 7729.
National Federation of Senates of Priests, English Sector, P.O. Box 1689, Charlottetown, PEI.
Serra House, 226 St. George St., Toronto, ON M5R 2N5, T: 416-968-0997, F: 416-968-1227.

CHILE
Consejo Pastoral Nacional, CECH, Cienfuegos 47, Casilla 13191 Correo 21, Santiago, T: 717733.

CHINA
Macao Ministers' Fellowship, 89-100 Av Hortae Costa, Macau.
Pastoral Council, c/o Catholic Mission, 16 Caine Rd, Hong Kong, T: H-232487.
Senate of Priests, c/o Catholic Mission, 16 Caine Rd, Hong Kong, T: H-232487.

COLOMBIA
Asociación Ministerial de Bogotá, Calle 69 No 5-33, Apdo Aéreo 20236, Bogotá, T: 496997.
Departamento de Ministerios Jerárquicos, Av 39 No. 13-61 Apdo Aéreo 11086, Bogotá, DE, T: 453193.
Federation of Evangelical Ministries of Colombia, Apdo Aéreo 190, Sincelejo.
Secretaria del Clero, Depto de Ministerios Jerárquicos, Apdo Aéreo 51086, Bogotá, DE (RC).
Secretaria del Diaconado, Depto de Ministerios Jerárquicos, Apdo Aéreo 51086, Bogotá (RC).

CYPRUS
Arab World Evangelical Ministers Association (AWEMA), P.O. Box 2018, 1516 Nicosia, T: 2-317037.

CZECH REPUBLIC
Pacem in Terris Association of Catholic Priests, Czech Secretariat, Spálená 8, 110 00 Praha 1, T: 293985.

DENMARK
Pastoral Council, c/o Katolsk Bispekontor, Bredgade 69A, DK-1260 Kobenhavn K (RC), T: 01-116080.
Presbyteral Council, c/o Katolsk Bispekontor, Bredgade 69A, DK-1260 Kobenhavn K (RC), T: 01-116080.

ECUADOR
Asociacion De Pastores Evangelicos Del Ecuador (APEE), Casilla 8087, Quito.
Confraternidad De Pastores Evangelicos Del Guayas (COPEG), 18 y Capitan Najera, Casilla 239P, Guayaquil, T: 368-663.
Consejo Nacional de Presbiteros del Ecuador, Apdo 2876, Quito.
Cuerpo De Pastores De Quito, Casilla 8029, Quito, T: 247-235.

FIJI
Senate of Priests, c/o Catholic Presbytery, P.O. Box 160, Ba.

FRANCE
Association des Pasteurs de France (APF), 47 Rue de Clichy, F-75009 Paris.

FRENCH GUIANA
Conseil Presbytéral, c/o Evêché, BP 378, Cayenne.

GAMBIA
Pastoral Council, P.O. Box 165, Bathurst.

GERMANY
Arbeitsgemeinschaft der Priesterräten der Diözesen der BRD und West Berlins (AGPR), An der Stadtkirche 8, D-4440, T: 02531-3288.
Arbeitsgemeinschaft der Social-, Industrie- und Arbeiterpfarrer, Ev Sozialakademie, D-5241 Friedewald über Betzborf (Sieg).
Arbeitsgemeinschaft lutherischer Konferenzen und Konvente, Berlinstr 2, D-31 Celle.
Arbeitsgemeinschaft von Priester- und Solidaritätsgruppen in der BRD (AGP), Beethovenstr 28, D-6 Frankfurt.
Bekenntnisbewegung 'Kein anderes Evangelium', Worthstr 49, D-588 Lüdenscheid.
Bensheimer Kreis (Kreis ehemaliger röm-kath Priester, die heute im evang Pfarr-oder Lehramt stehen), Bahnhofstr 59, D-588 Lüdenscheid.
Bruderrat Evangelischer Kirchen, Geschäftsstelle, Marktplatz 8, D-714 Ludwigsburg.
Bund Evangelischer Missionare, (Vogelsangstr 62, D-7000 Stuttgart 1, T: 0711-638131.
Evangelische Michaelsbruderschaft, Koppel 55, D-2 Hamburg 1.
Evangelischer Bund, Hauptgeschäftsstelle und Konfessions-kindliches Institut, Eifelstr 35, D-614 Bensheim (Bergstrasse). (Mainly pastors. Conservative evangelical, anti Catholic).
Federation Internationale des Aides au Pretre, Prinz-Georg-Strasse 44, D 4000 Düsseldorf 30.
Kirchliche Sammlung um Bibel und Bekenntnis (Innerhalb der BDR), D-2418 Ratzeburg.
Notgemeinschaft Evangelischer Deutscher, Ludwigstr 8, Postfach 1107, D-7024 Bernhausen.
Pfarrer-Gebets-Bruderschaft, Postfach 80, D-3551 Wehrda bei Marburg.
Priester-Missionsbund, Hermannstr 14, D-5100 Aachen, T: 0241-35321.
Priesterkreise für Konziliare Erneuerung (PKE), Untergasse 27, D-6374 Steinbach.

GUADELOUPE
Conseil Pastoral, c/o Evêché, BP 50, F-97-1 Basse-Terre, T: 811169.
Conseil Presbytéral, c/o Evêché, BP 50, F-97-1 Basse-Terre, T: 811169.

GUATEMALA
Asociación Nacional de Pastores y Ministros Evangélicos, Iglesia Presbiteriana El Mesías, 15 Calle A 13-06, Zona 1.
Confederación de Sacerdotes y Seglares diocesanos en Guatemala (COSDEGUA), 15 Calle 34-24, Zona 5, Guatemala-Ciudad.

GUYANA
Pastoral Council, Bishop's House, 27 Brickdam, Georgetown (RC).
Pastoral Council (Catholic), B.P. 372, Cayenne, T: 594-31-10-28.
Senate of Priests, Bishop's House, 27 Brickdam, Georgetown.

HOLY SEE
Pontifical Missionary Union of the Clergy & Religious (MPU), International Secretariat, Propaganda Fide, 1 Via di Propaganda, I-00187 Roma.
Sacred Congregation for Priests, Cardinal Prefect, Palazzo delle Congregazioni, Piazza Pio XII 10, I-00193 Roma, T: 6982 int 4151.
Sacred Congregation for Religious and Secular Institutes, Cardinal Prefect, Palazzo Congregazioni, Piazzo Pio XII 10, I-00193 Roma, T: 6982 int 4128.

INDIA
Apostolic Union of the Clergy, Archbishop's House, 21 N. Parekh Marg, Fort, Bombay, Maharashtra 400039.
Full Gospel Ministers Fellowship, C/o Balvikas Primary School, Shiv Shrusti, Kurla (East), Bombay, Maharashtra 400024.
Missionary Union of Clergy, 44, Ulsoor Road, Bangalore, Karnataka 560042.
Vianney Home for Retired Priests, Jyothinagar, Hanuman Junction, Andhra Pradesh 521105.

INDONESIA
Komperensi Waligereja Indonesia (KWI), Jl. Cut Meutia 10, Jakarta 10002, T: 021-325374, F: 021-325757.

IRAQ
Alliance Sacerdotale Chaldéenne, Archevêché Chaldéen, Al Mawsil (Mosul).
Prêtres du Christ-Roi, Eglise Saint Thomas des Syriens Catholiques, Al Mawsil (Mosul).

IRELAND
Irish Missionary Fellowship, 95 Meadow Grove, Dundrum, Dublin 14.
Pontifical MIssionary Union of Priests and Religious, 64 Lower Rathmines Road, Dublin 6, T: 353-01 972035/972 422.
St. Joseph's Young Priest Society, 23 Merrion Square, Dublin 2.

ITALY
Congregation for Bishops, Piazza Io XII 10, 00193 Rome.
Congregation for the Clergy, Piazza Pio XII 3, 00193 Rome.

IVORY COAST
Secretariat Permanent du Clergé Africain (SPCA), Centre Mgr Chappoulie, Yopoungon, Abidjan.

JAMAICA
Pastoral Council, P.O. Box 43, Kingston 6.
Senate of Priests, P.O. Box 43, Kingston 6.

JAPAN
Fellowship of Christian Missionaries, Kyobunkwan, 2 4-chome, Ginza, Chuo-ku, Tokyo 104, T: 11357.
Japan Evangelical Missionary Association (JEMA), 1 2-chome, Surugadai, Kanda, Chiyoda-ku, Tokyo.
Tokyo Pastoral Synod, c/o Archbishop's House, 16-15 Sekiguchi 3-chome, Bunkyo-ku, Tokyo. (RC).

KENYA
Priests' Association of Kenya, Office: Jericho Parish, PO Box 48069, Nairobi.

LEBANON
Association Sacerdotale Interrituelle, Séminaire Mar Maroun, Ghazir, T: 955004.
Prêtres du Christ-Roi, Curé de la Paroisse St Jean-Baptiste, Broochyriyé, Bayrut.

LUXEMBOURG
Conseil Presbytéral, c/o Evêché, 4 Rue Génistre, BP 419, Luxembourg, T: 22069.

MALAWI
National Council of Priests, Archbishop's House, P.O. Box 385, Blantyre, T: 8523.

MALTA
Diocese of Gozo Presbyteral Council, Bishop's Curia, Rabat, Gozo.
Malta Presbyteral Council, Archbishop's Curia, Valletta.

MARTINIQUE
Conseil Presbytéral, c/o Archevêché, Route de Didier, Fort-de-France, T: 2070.

MAURITIUS
Conseil Presbyteral, c/o Evêché, Rue Mgr Gonin, Port-Louis, T: 23068, 23360.

MEXICO
Ministerios Jerárquicos, Secretaria de Seminarios, c/o Seminario Palafoxiano, 44 Nte y JM Morelos—Col El Porvenir, Puebla, T: 23707.
Sacerdotes para el Pueblo, Apdo Postal 61-128, México 6, DF.

MONACO
Conseil Presbytéral, c/o Evêché de Monaco, 1 Rue de l'Abbaye, Monte Carlo.

MOROCCO
Conseil Pastoral, Archevêché Rabat, BP 258, Rabat.
Conseil Presbytéral, Archevêché Rabat, BP 258, Rabat.

NETHERLANDS
Dutch Association for Religious Priests, van Alkemadelaan 1, 's-Gravenhage, T: 070-244594.
Hospitium Oecumenicum San Luchesio, Waldeck Pyrmontlaan 9, Amsterdam-Zuid, T: 020-716861.

Institute for Aid to Clergy in Europe, Stokstraat 47, Maastricht, T: 0400-14244.
Limburg Priests Group, Vrijthof 21, Echt, T: 04754-1659.
National Pastoral Conference, Biltstraat 121, Utrecht.

NEW ZEALAND
National Association of Priests, Catholic Presbytery, Nelson.

NICARAGUA
Consejo Nacional de Pastores Evangélicos de Nicaragua, Apdo Postal 3252, Managua, T: 2-79197, F: 2-42594.

PAPUA NEW GUINEA
Catholic Indigenous Priests' Conference, Catholic Mission, Wewak, New Guinea.
Conference of Indigenous Priests, Bomana Seminary, PO Box 1717, Boroko.
Missionary Association of Papua and New Guinea, P.O. Box 1627, Boroko.

PARAGUAY
Asociacion de Pastores del Paraguay, Casilla 167, Asuncion, T: 21-85524, F: 21-44-8975.

PERU
Comisión Episcopal del Clero (CEC), c/o Arzobispado, Plaza de Armas, Apdo Postal 1512, Lima, T: 271252.
Movimiento ONIS Sacerdotal/Oficina Nacional de Información Social (ONIS), c/o Parroquiá de San Juan Apostol, Aragón 280, Pueblo Libre, Lima.

PHILIPPINES
Philippine Priests Incorporated (PPI), Sta Mesa, Magsaysay Blvd, PO Box 1525, Manila, T: 618272.
Philippines Missionary Fellowship, P.O. Box 3349, Manila.

PUERTO RICO
Asociación Puertorriquena de Sacerdotes, Proyecto La Perla, Calle Hemetrio (Daly), Country Club, Rio Pedras.

REUNION
Conseil Presbytéral, c/o Evêché, 42 Rue de Paris, BP 55, St. Denis, T: 212849.

RWANDA
Conseil Pastoral, Université Nationale du Rwanda, BP 117, Butare.

SAINT LUCIA
Council of Priests, c/o Bishop's House, Castries.
Pastoral Council, c/o Bishop's House, Castries.

SAMOA
Senate of Priests, Diocese of Apia, P.O. Box 532, Apia.

SEYCHELLES
Conseil Presbytéral, c/o Evêché de Port-Victoria, PO Box 43, Port-Victoria, Mahé.

SINGAPORE
Senate of Priests, c/o Archbishop's House, 31 Victoria St, Singapore 7, T: 28818.

SLOVAKIA
Association of Officers of the Slovak Evangelical Church, Novi Sad.
Pacem in Terris Association of Catholic Priests (Cdruzení Katolickych Duchovních Pacem in Terris), Slovak Secretariat, Kapitulská 1, 886 10 Bratislava, T: 30266.

SOLOMON ISLANDS
National Presbyteral Council, P.O. Box 237, Honiara.
Pastoral Council of the Church in the Solomon Islands, P.O. Box 237, Honiara.

SOMALIA
Pastoral Council, c/o Vicariato Apostolico, CP 273, Mogadisho.
Presbyteral Council, c/o Vicariato Apostolico, CP 273, Mogadisho.

SOUTH AFRICA
Interdenominational African Ministers' Association of Southern Africa (IDAMASA), 165 Pietermarits St., Ubunye House, P.O. Box 2035, Pietermarizburg 200.
Southern African Council of Priests (SACP), PO Box 17054, Hillbrow, Transvaal, T: 419059.

SPAIN
AMEC (Asoc. Ministres de l'Evangeli de Catalunya), 08022 Ciutat de Balaguer, 40, Barcelona, T: 211-26-37.
Asamblea Conjunta de Obispos y Sacerdotes, Secretariado Nacional del Clero, Cuesta de Santo Domingo 5, Madrid 13.
Fraternidad de Ministerios Evangélicos, 14014 Don Teodomiro, 65-67, Córdoba, T: 26-52-95.
Hermandad Sacerdotal Española, San Marcos 3, Madrid, T: 2224572.
Obra de Cooperación Sacerdotal Hispanoamericana (OCSHA), Bosque 9, Apdo 14133, Madrid 3.
Spanish Conference of Ecclesiastics, Nuñez de Balboa 115 bis, 28006 Madrid, T: 91 2624612.
Synod of the Diocese of Seville, Palacio Arzobispal, Sevilla.

SURINAME
Presbyteral Council (Priesters Raad), c/o Bisschopshuis, Gravenstraat 12, POB 1230, Paramaribo, T: 73306.

SWEDEN
Presbyteral Council, Valhallavägen 132, Fack 102, 40 Stockholm 5, T: 08-618034.

SWITZERLAND
Fraternité Sacerdotale Saint Pie X, CH-1908 Econe-par-Riddes.
Schweizerische Verband Evangelischer Arbeiter und Angestellter (SVEA), Zentralsekretariat, Höhenring 29, CH-8052 Zürich-Seebach, T: 051-466424.
Schweizerischer Reformierter Pfarrverein, Zentralpräsident, CH-3645 Gwatt bei Thun, T: 033-363131.
Synode des Catholiques Suisses, Secrétariat Romand, rue des Alpes 49, CH-1700 Fribourg.
Vereinigung Reformierter Schweizer Auslandspfarrer, Aemtlerstr 23, CH-8003 Zürich, T: 051-334488.

TAIWAN
Taiwan Missionary Fellowship, 272 Nanking East Rd, Section 3, P.O. Box 555, Taipei, T: 772521/2.

TANZANIA
Association of Diocesan Priests of Tanzania (UMAWATA), PO Box 640, Morogoro.

TRINIDAD & TOBAGO
Council of Priests, 27 Maraval Rd, St Clair, Trinidad.

TUNISIA
Conseil Pastoral, Prélature de Tunis, 4 Rue d'Alger, Tunis.

UNITED STATES OF AMERICA (USA)
Academy of Parish Clergy (APC), PO Box 86, Princeton, NJ 08540.
Alaskan Native Brotherhood (ANB), c/o Mount Edgecumbe Hospital, Sitka, AL 99839.
American Ministerial Association, PO Box 1252, York, PA 17405.
Confraternity of Catholic Clergy, 4445 W. 64th St., Chicago, IL 60629.
Council of Black Clergy, 2200 Locust St, Philadelphia, PA 19103.
Evangelical Ministers Fellowship International, 105 West Madison St, Chicago, IL 60602.
International Ministerial Federation, 5290 North Sherman Av, Fresno, CA 93726; Box 8000, St. Petersburg, FL 33738, T: 209-222-9338, O: Web: www.i-m-f.org/.
Just Between Us (for clergy wives), 777 S Barker Rd, Brookfield, WI 53045, T: 800-260-3342.
Korean Pastors Association, 4324 Clairmont Mesa Bl., San Diego, CA 92117, T: 619-571-0445.
Nat'l Conference of Diocesan Vocation Directors, 1603 S Michigan Ave, Tuite 400, Chicago, IL 60616, T: 312-663-5456.
National Association of Priest Pilots, 660 Bush Ave., Garner, IA 50438.
National Conference of Black Churchmen (NCBC), Suite 1005, 200 West 57th St, New York, NY 10019; 671 Beckwich St., S.W., Atlanta, GA, T: 212-581-3860.
Online Resources for Pastors, O: Web: www.pastornet.com/.
Preacher's Study, O: Web: www.preacherstudy.simplenet.com.
Self-Supporting Priesthood Project, Idaho Lay Ministry Project, 107 East Fort St, Boise, ID 83702.
Serra International, 22 West Monroe St, Chicago, IL 60603.
Shephers Heart Ministries, P.O. Box 26064, Colorado Springs, CO 80936, T: 719-548-8588.
Southern California Korean Retired Pastors Association, Inc., 982 S. New Ham'e Ave., #102, Los Angeles, CA 90006, T: 213-380-6409.
Southern California Korean Ministers Association, 4949 York Bl., Los Angeles, CA 90042, T: 818-240-9204.
Union of Black Episcopalians, 729 8th SE, Washington, DC 20003.
United Indians of Nebraska, 11924 Popoleton Plaza, Omaha, NE 68114, T: 402-334-9477/8.
US Catholic Institutions for the Training of Candidates for the Priesthood, 1717 Massachusetts Av, NW, Washington, DC 20036.

URUGUAY
APEU-Asociación de Pastores Evangélicos del Uruguay, Mercedes 787 Piso 1, Constituyente 1540, Montevideo, T: 2-802594, F: 2-496915.
Mesa Nacional de Presbiteros, c/o Arzobispado, Treinta y Tres 1368, Montevideo.

WALLIS & FUTUNA ISLANDS
Conseil Presbytéral, c/o Evêché, Lano, via Nouméa.

18
Computer bulletin board systems

Modem-accessed sites for the posting or reading of messages, the uploading or downloading of files, and other computer-aided transmission of information or interaction, usually privately operated and serving a relatively small or localized community of netizens; BBS'. For those on the Internet see INTERNET AND WORLD WIDE WEB MINISTRIES; this category is for those on other network systems such as FidoNet, Free-Net, or FamilyNet. Note that rarely in history has an entire category of Christian ministry expanded and then contracted so rapidly. From almost zero in 1984, by the early 1990s there were many thousands of Christian BBS' in more than 100 countries (with the vast majority in the USA, Britain, and other English-speaking countries); as the World Wide Web grew in sites, users, and significance, many BBS' disappeared, though thousands remained active through AD2000.

AUSTRALIA
CRNET International Office, 3/41 Sherwood St., Revesby, NSW 2212.

UNITED STATES OF AMERICA (USA)
A.C.T.S. Network, T: 910-452-2914.
Across Christian Bulletin Board, O: Web: www.cybercore.net/taholo/htdocs/faith.
Agape Christian Network, T: 404-413-6579.
Agape Family Network, T: 317-664-3312.
All Nite Cafe, The, Phoenix, AZ, T: 602-938-6866.
American Christian Family Net, T: 619-582-2402.
AppleSeeds, Cary, NC, T: 919-469-5867.
CalvaryNet, T: 619-630-1364.
Canadian Christian Interchange, T: 403-481-4977.
Catholic Access Network, T: 210-423-1574.
Catholic Information Network-CIN, T: 619-258-0610, F: 619-449-6030, O: E-mail: sysop@catifo.cts.com.
Catholic Mail Box, Flint, MI, T: 313-631-6870.
Catholic Online (Compuserve) 'Go Catholic', P.O. Box 40188, Bakersfield, CA 93384, T: 805-833-9061, O: E-mail: 70007.4674@compuserve.com.
Catholic Resource Network (CRNET), P.O. Box 3610, Manassas, VA 22110; c/o Trinity Communications, Manassas, VA 22110, T: 703-2576, F: 703-791-4250, O: E-mail: sysop@ewtn.com.
Christ Connection, T: 310-398-7804.
Christian Apologetics Network, T: 205-808-0763.
Christian Distribution Network, T: 504-878-3023.
Christian Evangel Network, T: 318-397-2987.
Christian Fellowship Network, T: 504-878-3023.
Christian Information Network, T: 800-279-5673, O: Via Compuserve, Type GO CIN.
Christian Music Network, T: 718-893-7553.
Christianity Online (Via America Online), 465 Gunderson Dr., Carol Stream, IL 60188, T: 800-413-9747, O: E-mail: ccmaged@aol.com, Web: www.website.net/~ccmag.
ChristNET, T: 310-398-7804.
ChristNet Christian Fell. Network, T: 714-457-1019.
Computers for Christ, T: 708-0362-7875.
CRNET, O: Web: www.ewtn.com.
Ecclesia Place, Sewickley, PA, T: 412-741-5519.
ECUNET, T: 404-682-8888, O: E-mail: helper@ecunet.org.
FamilyNet International, T: 504-878-3023.
Fishnet, T: 502-569-8501, O: E-mail: Avatar@Ecunet.org., O: Web: www.fni.com/welcome.html.
Fr. John's BBS, West Haven, CT, T: 203-934-4641.
Freedom Information Net, T: 609-586-4847.
GraceNet, T: 612-474-0724.
Int'l Christian Discipleship, T: 206-866-3621.
Messianic Jewish Computer Network, T: 314-227-6885.
Nazarene Network, T: 403-472-8089.
Newlife Christian Network, T: 901-387-1768.
Opus Dei BBS, Portland, ME, T: 207-780-6567.
Pacific Northwest Christian Network, T: 206-823-1267.
PhileoNet, T: 301-870-0399.
SON-Net, T: 416-498-5259.
Spirit of Love, Grosse Pointe, MI, T: 313-886-1007.
Sprawl, The, Lexington, KY, T: 606-278-9709.
Steubenville Catholic, Steubenville, OH, T: 614-283-6409.
Theology Net, T: 408-229-0706.
Western Dominican, Eugene, OR, T: 503-343-3825.

19
Computer services, software & resources

Companies, agencies, ministries, and organizations that provide computers, IT (information technology) services, software, network services, systems analysis, programming, or modem communications services especially to churches, mission agencies, or Christian organizations or institutions; web site construction, hosting, or maintenance; the designing, writing, publication, distribution, or installation of software for church, Christian, missionary, evangelization, or Biblical/theological study purposes; computer or software consultation or training. See also INTERNET AND WORLD WIDE WEB MINISTRIES.

CANADA
Koinonia Data Systems, 98 Bechtel Dr., Kitchener, ON N2P 1S9, T: 518-895-0199, F: 519-748-1628.
State of the Flock, 18 Carle Cres., Ajax, ON L1T 3T8, T: 1-800-471-4912.

INDIA
Computer Centre, Main Road, Nellikuppam, Tamil Nadu.
Concordia Computer School, Pudur, Vaniyam badi, Tamil Nadu.

SOUTH AFRICA
Logos Bible Software, PO Box 48690, Roosevelt Park 2129, 150 John Adamson Dr, Roosevelt Park, Jhburg, T: 011-782-4222, F: 011-782-3977.
Logos Information Systems, PO Box 48993, Roosevelt Park 2129, 152 Oak Park, Oak/Dover Sts, Ferndale, Randburg, T: 011-886-6117, F: 011-886-6301.
Trinity Software SA, PO Box 36078, Glosderry 7702, T: 021-683-2035, F: 021-683-3411.

UNITED STATES OF AMERICA (USA)
Ages Software, P.O. Box 1926, Albany, OR 97321, T: 800-297-4307, F: 541-917-0839, O: E-mail: ages-library.com, Web: www.ageslibrary.com.
Alpha Omega Information Systems, 12604 Waterfowl Way, Ste. 100, Upper Marlboro, MD 20772, T: 301-390-1600, F: 301-390-1616, O: E-mail: church-wrks@aol.com.
Automated Church System, P.O. Box 3990, Florence, SC 29502, T: 800-736-7425, F: 800-227-5990, O: E-mail: info@acshome.com, Web: www.acshome.com.
Christian Computing Magazine, O: Web: www.cc-mag.com.
Christian Digital Library Foundation, O: E-mail: 76616.3452@compuserve.com.
Computer Aided Ministry Society, O: Web: bible.acu.edu/ctt/camsoc.htm.
Computing Today Magazine, O: Web: www.christianity.net/compt.
Cyberspace Ministry, O: Web: www.tagnet.org/cyberspace.
Dragonraid, O: Web: www.geocities.com/Heartland/5268/drinfo.html.
Epiphany Software, 15897 Alta Vista Way, San Jose, CA 95127, T: 408-251-9788, F: 408-251-9949, O: E-mail: fchannon@compuserve.com, Web: www.epiphanysofware.com.
Family Interactive/Nordic Software, P. O. Box 83499, Lincoln, NE 68501, T: 800-306-6502, 402-475-5300, F: 402-475-5310, O: E-mail: jlarsen@nordicsoftware.com, Web: www.nordicsoftware.com.
Free Christian Software Directory, O: Web: www.seriousd.com/freeware.htm.
Hermeneutika BibleWorks CD-ROM, P.O. Box 2200, Dept. MNET-98, Big Fork, MT 59911, T: 800-74-BIBLE, F: 406-837-4433, O: Web: www.bibleworks.com.
IM Concepts, Inc., 10050 Montgomery Rd. Ste. 351, Cincinnati, OH 45242, T: 513-247-0114, F: 513-247-0959, O: E-mail: info@imconcepts.com, Web: www.iamiam.com.
International Conference on Computing in Mission, O: Web: www.xc.org/iccm.
Kirkbride Bible & Technology, 335 W. 9th St., Indianapolis, IN 46202, T: 800-428-4385, 317-633-1900, F: 317-633-1444, O: E-mail: sales@kirkbride.com, Web: www.kirkbride.com.
KMS Software, Inc., 12001 N. Central Expwy., Ste. 730, Dallas, TX 75243, T: 972-383-7070, F: 972-383-7071, O: E-mail: fsmith@kma.com.
Logos Research Systems, 715 SE Finalgo Ave., Oak Harbor, WA 98277, T: 800-87-LOGOS, F: 360-675-8169, O: E-mail: Info@Logos.com, Web: www.Logos.com.
Mertes Internet Construction Co., 5517 Straub Rd., College Station, TX 77845, T: 409-690-0338, F: 409-690-9012, O: E-mail: phebc@web-ministries.org, Web: www.ministries.org.
Mission Computer Update, O: Web: www.xc.org/helpintl/computer/mcu-curh.htm.
NavPress Software, 5014 Lake View Dr., Austin, TX 78732, T: 512-266-2771, F: 512-266-2771, O: E-mail: jim@wordsearchbible.com.
Network of Single Adult Leaders, 7484 Carrie Ridge Way, San Diego, CA 92139-3936, T: 619-267-6226, F: 619-267-6226, O: E-mail: nsl@gospel-com.net.
Rainbow Studies International, 1900 S. Country Club Rd., El Reno, OK 73036, T: 800-242-5348, F: 405-262-7599, O: E-mail: rsimail@rainbow studies.com, Web: www.zondervan.com.
Serious Developments, O: Web: www.viper.net/clients/serious.

Shelby Systems, Inc., 65 Germantown Ct. #303, Cordova, TN 38108, F: 901-759-3682, O: E-mail: min@shelbyinc.com, Web: www.shelbyinc.com.
Software Library, 3300 Bass Lake Rd., Ste. 304, Brooklyn Center, MN 55429, T: 800-247-8044, F: 612-566-2250, O: E-mail: 70563.2140@compuserve.com.
Vision Software and Publishing, O: Web: www.wsnet.com/~alapadre/vision.html.
Winbible Software, O: Web: www.icis.on.ca/bible.

20 Conciliarism: confessional

Councils of churches or denominations belonging to a world confessional family (world family of churches) of one particular ecclesiastical, historical, or theological tradition; international confessional councils, federations, associations, alliances, fellowships; similar groups organized on the continental, regional, or national level; confessional conciliarism, collegiality, and consultation.

ARGENTINA
Lutheran Council of the River Plate, Esmeralda 162, Buenos Aires, T: 457520.
Union of Baptists in Latin America, Ramon L. Falcon, 4080, 1407 Buenos Aires, T: 541-636-1737, F: 541-636-1741.

BAHAMAS
Caribbean Baptist Fellowship, P.O. Box F44367, Freeport, T: 809-373-6213/6797, F: 809-352-3040.

BOTSWANA
Lutheran Communion in Southern Africa (LUCSA), P.O. BOX 1976, Independence Ave. 863/7, Gaborone, T: 267/35-22-27, F: 267/31-39-66.

BRITAIN (UK OF GB & NI)
Anglican Communion Secretariat, 157 Waterloo Rd., London SE1 8UT, T: 0171-620-1110, F: 0171-620-1070.
Anglican Consultative Council, Partnership House, 157 Waterloo Road, London SE1 8UT, T: 44-71-620-1110, F: 44-71-620-1070.
Baptist World Alliance (BWA), 4 Southampton Row, London WC1B 4AB.
Disciples Ecumenical Consultative Council, Fitzwilliam College, Cambridge CB3 0DG, England.
Friends World Committee for Consultation, 4 Byng Place, London WC2E 7JH, T: 44-071-388-0497, F: 071-388-3722.
Jerusalem Charismatic Leaders Meeting, 50 Wivelsfield Road, Haywards Heath, West sussex RH16 4EW, T: 0444-454531.
Lambeth Conference of Bishops of the Anglican Communion, Lambeth Palace, London SE1 7JU, England, T: 01-928-8282.

CANADA
Pentecostal/Charismatic Churches of North America, 10 Overlea Blvd., Toronto M4H 1A5, O: Web: www.iphc.org/iccna/unfinished.html.

EGYPT
Coptic Patriarchal Synod, 34 Rue Ibn Sandar, 14 Port de Koubbeh, Al Qahirah, T: 821740.

ETHIOPIA
Lutheran Communion in Central and Eastern Africa (LUCCEA), P.O. Box 2087, Addis Ababa, T: 25-11/55-32-80, F: 25-11/55-29-66, O: Telex: 21528 ecmy et.
Oriental Orthodox Churches Conference, P.O. Box 2717, Addis Abeba.

FINLAND
Friends Information Centers & Offices, Vassankatu 4 C 53, SF-00500 Helsinki, T: 90-728-4565.

FRANCE
Mennonite World Conference, 7, avenue de la Forêt-Noire, 67000 Strasbourg, T: 33-88-61-49-27, F: 33-88-61-57-17.

GERMANY
European Baptist Federation, Postfach 610340, D-22423 Hamburg, T: 49-40-550-9723, F: 49-40-550-9725.
Vereinigte Ev-Lutherische Kirche Deutschlands (VELKD), Postfach 1860, D-3 Hannover 1, T: 0511-623061/4.

HOLY SEE
Council for the Public Affairs of the Church, Palazzo Apostolico, I-00120 Città del Vaticano, T: 6983274.
Sacred Congregation for Bishops, Palazzo delle Congregazioni 10, Piazza Pio XII, I-00193 Roma, Italy, T: 6983311.
Sacred Congregation for the Oriental Churches, Palazzo dei Convertendi, Via della Conciliazione 34, I-00193 Roma, Italy. (Eastern-rite Catholics), T: 6982 int 4293.

IRAQ
Chaldean Patriarchal Synod, Chaldean Catholic Patriarchate, Baghdad, T: 8880689.

ITALY
Sacred Congregation for Bishops, Palazzo delle Congregazioni, Piazza Pio XII 10, 1-100193 Roma, T: 06-6984218.
Synod of Bishops, Segreteria Generale, Piazza Pio XII 3, I-00193 Roma, T: 06-698-4821, 6984324.

KENYA
All-Africa Baptist Fellowship, P.O. Box 17118, Nairobi, T: 254-2-55-8929.
Organisation of African Instituted Churches (OAIC), P.O. Box 21736, Nairobi, T: 254-567-849.

LEBANON
Armenian Patriarchal Synod, Jeitaoui, 2400 Bayrut, T: 329391.
Maronite Patriarchal Synod, Dimane, T: 675107.
Syrian Patriarchal Synod, Rue Damas, BP 118879, Bayrut, T: 381532.

LESOTHO
African Federal Council of Churches (Independent Churches), P.O. Box 126, Peka 340.

LIBERIA
Association of Independent Churches of Africa, P.O. Box 3604, Monrovia.

NETHERLANDS
Calvinistic World Association, 46 Potgieterweg, Heiloo 1851 CJ, T: 31-0723-30089.
International Association for Liberal Christianity and Religious Freedom (IARF), 40 Laan Copes Van Cattenburch, 's-Gravenhage.
International Old Catholic Bishops' Conference, Kon. Wilhelminalaan 3, 3818 HN Amersfoort, T: 31-33-62-0875, F: 31-851-42-3654.

NIGERIA
Lutheran Communion in Western Africa (LUCWA), P.O. Box 21, Numan, Adamawa State, T: 234-75/257-73, F: 234-735/63-70, O: TDS Box 11, Nitel, Jos.

PHILIPPINES
Asian Baptist Federation, #55 Dr. Pilapil St, Dagad Pasig City 1600, T: 63-2-641-2335.

SOUTH AFRICA
Council of Independent Churches, PO Box 189, Orlando 1804, T: 011-29-6822.
Lutheran Communion of Southern Africa, PO Box 7170, Bonaero Park 1622, 24 Geldenhuys Rd, Bonaero Park, Kempton Park, T: 011-973-1873, F: 011-395-1615.
United Evangelical Lutheran Ch in Southern Africa (UELCSA), P.O. Box 7095, 1622 Bonaero Park, T: 27-11/973-18-51, F: 27-11/395-18-62.

SOUTH KOREA
International Conference of Reformed Churches, Amman-Dong 34, Su-Koo, Pusan 602-030, T: 82-51-257-5131, F: 82-51-257-5133.

SWAZILAND
Federation of Zion Churches in Africa, Manzini.

SWEDEN
International Federation of Free Evangelical Churches, Tegnergatan 8, Box 6302, S-113 81 Stockholm, T: 08-349680.

SWITZERLAND
Bund Ev-Lutherischer Kirchen in der Schweiz und im Fürstentum Liechtenstein, Hirschwiesenstr 9, CH-8057 Zürich, T: 01-281162.
Conference des organisations internationales catholiques, 37-39, rue de Vermont,1202 Geneve 20, 022/7338392.
CWME Orthodox Advisory Group, Orthodox Centre of the Ecumenical Patriarchate, 37 Chemin de Chambésy, CH-1292 Chambésy, Genève.
Ecumenical Patriarchate of Constantinople, c/o Ecumenical Centre, 150 route de Ferney, P.O. Box 2100, 1211 Geneva 2, T: 41-22-791-6347, F: 41-22-791-0361.
International Conference of Old Catholic Bishops, Willadingweg 39, CH-3000 Bern.
Interorthodox Preparatory Commission, Great & Holy Council of the Orthodox Church, Orthodox Centre of the Ecumenical Patriarchate, 37 Chemin de Chambésy, CH-1292 Chambésy, Genève.
Lutheran World Federation, Ecumenical Centre, 150 route de Ferney, P.O. Box 2100, 1211 Geneva 2, T: 41-22-791-6363, F: 41-22-798-8618, O: Web: www.wcc-coe.org/lwf.
Moscow Patriarchate, c/o Ecumenical Centre, 150 route de Ferney, P.O. Box 2100, 1211 Geneva 2, T: 41-22-6327.
Pentecostal World Conference, c/o International Pentecostal Press Association, P.O. Box 98, CH-6376 Emmetten.
World Alliance of Reformed Churches, Ecumenical Centre, 150 route de Ferney, P.O. Box 2100, 1211 Geneva 2, T: 41-22-791-6237, F: 41-22-791-6505, O: E-mail: warc@info.wcc-coe.org.
World Methodist Council, 150 Route de Ferney, P.O. Box No. 2100, CH-1211 Geneva 2, T: 022-916-6231, F: 022-791-0361.

SYRIA
Greek-Melkite Patriarchal Synod, BP 22249, Bab-Charki, Dimashq, T: 223129.

TURKEY
Ecumenical Patriarchate of Constantinople, Rum Patrikhanesi, Fener-Halic, 34220 Istanbul.
Great and Holy Council of the Orthodox Church, Ecumenical Patriarchate, Rum Ortodoks Patrikhanesi, Sadrazam All Pasha Caddesi 35, Fener (Phanar), Istanbul, T: 239850.

UNITED STATES OF AMERICA (USA)
Alliance World Fellowship, 350 North Highland Ave., Nyack, NY 10960, T: 914-353-0750, O: Web: www.gospelcom.net/cmalliance/missions/worldfellow.htm
Anglican Church, Inc., Box 52702, Atlanta, GA 30355.
Anglican Orthodox Communion, 323 East Walnut St, P.O. Box 128, Statesville, NC 28677, T: 704-873-8365.
Apostolic World Christian Fellowship, 11 West Iowa St., Evansville, IN 47711, O: Web: www.awcj.org.
Baptist World Alliance, 6733 Curran St., McLean, VA 22101, T: 703-790-8980, F: 703-893-5160, O: Web: bwanet.org.
Bible Sabbath Association, HC 60, Box 8, Fairview, OK 73737-9504, T: 405-227-4494, F: 405-227-4495.
Charismatics United for World Evangelization, Singapore Consultation, PO Box 58, Northome, MN 56661, USA, T: 218-897-5794.
Christian Holiness Association, CHA Center, P.O. Box 100, Wilmore, KY 40390, T: 423-457-5978, F: 423-463-7280.
Christian Holiness Partnership, 263 Buffalo Rd., Clinton, TN 37716, T: 423-457-5978, F: 423-463-7280, O: Web: www.holiness.org.
Church of the Brethren, 1451 Dundee Ave., Elgin, IL 60120-1694, T: 708-742-5100, F: 1-708-742-6103.
Council of Christian Communions, 1836 Fairmont, Cincinnati, OH 45214.
Disciples Ecumenical Consultative Council, 130 East Washington St., P.O. Box 1986, Indianapolis, IN 46206-1986, T: 1-317-635-3100, F: 1-317-635-3700.
Federated Orthodox Catholic Churches Intl. (FOCUS), 407 Donovan Rd., Bruashton, NY 12916, T: 518-358-4168, F: 518-358-9667, O: Web: www.geocities.com/Athens/Acropolis/5835.
Free Methodist World Fellowship, Winona Lake, IN 46950, T: 615-256-1424.
Friends World Committee for Consultation Section of the Americas, 1506 Race St., Philadelphia, PA 19102, T: 215-241-7250, F: 215-241-7285.
General Conference of Seventh-day Adventists, Council on Interchurch Relations, 12501 Old Columbia Pike, Silver Spring, MD 20294-1608, T: 1-301-680-6680, F: 1-301-680-6090.
International Anglican Fellowship, 5712 Pommel Ct., West Des Moines, IA 50266-6355, T: 515-225-8863, F: 512-225-8870.
International Convention of Christian Churches, Box 19136, Indianapolis, IN 46219.
International Council of Unitarians and Universalists, 4 Kendal Common, Weston, MA 02193, T: 617-893-1058, F: 617-893-1058, O: E-mail: 73664.614@compuserve.com.
International Lutheran Council, 1333 South Kirkwood Rd., St. Louis, MO 63122-7295, T: 1-314-965-9000, F: 1-314-965-6108, O: Telex: 43-4452 stl.
International New Thought Alliance (INTA), 7015 Sunset Blvd, Hollywood, CA 90028.
International Federation of Free Evangelical Churches, 901 E. 78th St., Minneapolis, MN 55420-1300, T: 612-854-1300, F: 612-853-8488.
Mennonite World Conference, 3003 Benham Av, Elkart, IN 46514, T: 219-523-1385.
North American Baptist Fellowship, Baptist World Alliance Bldg., 6733 Curran St., McLean, VA 22101, T: 703-790-8980, F: 703-893-5160.
Pentecostal World Conference, 1445 Boonville Av, Springfield, MO 65802.
Pentecostal/Charismatic Churches of North America, 1001 E. Washington St., Greensboro, NC 27301, T: 910-272-6564.
Reformed Ecumenical Synod, 2017 Eastern Ave., S.E., Suite 201, Grand Rapids, MI 49507-3234, T: 1-616-241-4424.
Seventh Day Baptist World Federation, Seventh Day Baptist Center, 3120 Kennedy Rd., P.O. Box 1678, Janesville, WI 53547, T: 608-752-5055, F: 608-752-7711, O: Web: www.seventhdaybaptist.org.
Standing Conference of Canonical Orthodox Bishops in the Americas, 8-10 East 79th St., New York, NY 10021, T: 212-570-3500, F: 212-861-2183.
Traditional Anglican Communion, 4807 Aspen Dr., West Des Moines, IA 50265, T: 515-223-1591, F: 515-226-8987, O: Web: www.zeuter.com/~accc/tac.htm.
Wider Quaker Fellowship, 1506 Race Street, Philadelphia, PA 19102, T: 215-241-7293.
World Convention Churches of Christ, 1101 19th Ave., S., Nashville, TN 37212-2196, T: 1-615-321-3735, F: 1-615-327-1445.
World Methodist Council, World Methodist Bldg., 350 Lakeshore Dr., P.O. Box 518, Lake Junaluska, NC 28745, T: 704-456-9432, F: 704-456-9433.

21 Conciliarism: continental or regional

Interdenominational or ecumenical councils of churches or denominations of different ecclesiastical traditions, for a single continent, sub-continent, or world region (of many countries); continental or regional Christian councils, federations, associations, alliances, fellowships; continental conciliarism, collegiality, and consultation.

ALGERIA
Conference Episcopale Regionale du Nord de l'Afrique (CERNA), 13 rue Khelifa-Boukhalfa, Algiers.

ARGENTINA
Confraternidad Evangelica Latinoamericana (CONELA), Casilla de Correo (1636) Olivos, Buenos Aires 1636, T: 1-791-1065, F: 1-791-1065, O: E-mail: conela@sion.com.
Latin American Evangelical Fellowship (CONELA), Casilla de Correo 96, Sucursal 31, 1431 Buenos Aires, T: 54-1-572-1035, F: 54-1-572-1888.

AUSTRALIA
Australasian Alliance of Bible Believing Christian Churches, PO Box 8, St Agnes 5091.
Evangelical Fellowship of the South Pacific (EFSP), P.O. Box 1291, Fortitude Valley, Q 4006, T: 61-73-254-2615, F: 61-73-254-2615.

AUSTRIA
European Evangelical Alliance, Postfach 23, A-1037, Wien, T: 43-1-713-9151, F: 43-1-713-8382.

BARBADOS
Caribbean Conference of Churches, P.O. Box 616, Bridgetown, T: 809-427-2681, F: 1-809-429-2075.
Evangelical Association of the Caribbean (EAC), 41 Excel Rd., Elizabeth Park, Worthing P.O., Christ Church, T: 1246-427-9746, F: 228-6855, O: E-mail: gaseale@caribsurf.com.

BELGIUM
Commission of the Episcopates of the European Community (COMECE), 13 Avenue Pere Damien, B-1150 Brussels.

BOTSWANA
Organization of African Independent Churches (Southern Region), PO Box 40743, Gaborone.

BRITAIN (UK OF GB & NI)
Council of Churches for Britain & Ireland (CCBI), Inter-Church House, 35-41 Lower Marsh, London SE1 7RL, T: 44-171-620-4444, F: 44-171-928-0010.
European Baptist Federation, Baptist Church House, 4 Southampton Row, London WC1, T: Holborn 3939.
European Evangelical Alliance, 19 Draycott Place, London SW3 2SJ, T: 01-584-9333.
European Lausanne Committee, 64 Cricklade Road, Gorse Hill, Swindon, Wilts SN2 6AF, T: 44-1793-481444, F: 44-1793-435237.

BURKINA FASO
Conférence Episcopale Régionale de l'Afrique de l'Ouest Francophone (CERAO), BP 1471, Ouagadougou, T: 35180.

CENTRAL AFRICAN REPUBLIC
Association of Episcopal Conferences of the Region of Central Africa (ACERAC), Secretariat, B.P. 1518, Bangui.

CHILE
Latin American Alliance of Christian Churches, Arauco 890, Chillán.

CHINA
Chinese Coordination Centre of World Evangelism, P.O. Box 98435 Tsim Sha Tsui, Kowloon, Hong Kong, T: 3-910411.
Chinese Regional Episcopal Conference, 34 Lane 32, Kwang Fu South Rd., Taipeh 10552.
Christian Conference of Asia, Pak Tin Village, Mei Tin Rd., Shatin, N.T., Hong Kong, T: 852-2691-10-68, F: 852-2692-38-05, O: E-mail: cca_gs@hk.super.net.
Federation of Asian Bishops' Conferences (FABC), 16 Caine Rd, GPO Box 2984, Hong Kong, T: 852-2525-8021, F: 852-2521-3095.
Hong Kong Christian Council, Christian Ecumenical Bldg., 33 Granville Road, Tsimshatsui, Kowloon, Hong Kong, T: 852-2-368-7123, F: 852-2-724-2131.

COLOMBIA
Anglican Council of Latin America, Cra 13 63-39, Of 407, Apdo Aéreo 52964, Bogotá 2.
Commission for Presbyterian Co-operation in Latin America, Apdo Aéreo 14-650, Bototá.
Consejo Episcopal Latinoamericano (CELAM), Calle 78 No 11-17, Apdo Aéreo 5278, Bogotá, DE, T: 357041.
Latin American Bishops' Conference (CELAM), Carrera 5 No. 118-31, Usaquén, Bogota.

CONGO-ZAIRE
Africa Inter-Mennonite Mission, CIM Hostel, BP 4081, Kinshasa II.
Association of Episcopal Conferences of Central Africa, B.P. 20511, Kinshasa.

COSTA RICA
Communidad Latinoamericana de Ministerios Evangélicos, Apdo 1307, San José, T: 215622.

CYPRUS
Middle East Council of Churches, P.O. Box 4259, Limassol, T: 357-5-326-022, F: 357-5-324-496.

DENMARK
Nordic Bishops Conference, Bredgade 69A, DK-1260 Kobenhavn K, T: 01-116080.

ECUADOR
Asociacion de Iglesias Evangelicas de La Region Amazónica Ecuatóriana, Shell, Pastaza.
Consejo Latinoamericano do Iglesias, Casilla 85-22, Quito.
Latin American Council of Churches, Casilla 17-08-8522, Av. Patria y Amazonas 640, Edificio Banco Internacional, 11th Floor, Quito, T: 593-2-561-539, F: 593-2-504-377, O: E-mail: info@clai.org.

EL SALVADOR
Secretariado Episcopal de América Central y Panamá (SEDAC), Junto al Seminario, Apdo Postal 78, San Salvador, T: 236690.

FIJI
Episcopal Conference of the Pacific, P.O. Box 1200, Suva, T: 22851.

Pacific Conference of Churches, P.O. Box 208, Suva, T: 679-311-277, F: 679-303-205.

FINLAND
(Catholic) Episcopal Conference of Scandinavia, Rehbinderintie 21, SF-00150 Helsinki 15, Finland.

FRANCE
Commission des Eglises Evangéliques d'Expression Française à l'Exterieur (CEEEFE), 47 rue de Clichy, F-75009 Paris, T: 874-1508.

GERMANY
European Evangelical Alliance, Wilhelmshoeher Allee 258, D-34131 Kassel, T: 49-561-314-9711, F: 49-561-938-7520, O: Web: www.hfe.org/friends/eea.htm, E-mail: 100341,550.

GHANA
Symposium of Episcopal Conferences of Africa and Madagascar (SECAM), Secretariat, P.O. Box 9156 Airport, Accra, T: 27347.

GUATEMALA
Confraternidad Evangélica Latinoamericana (CONELA), Apartado 123, 01901 Guatemala.

INDIA
Asia Lausanne Committee, D4/4211 Vasant Kurj, New Delhi 110 070, T: 91-11-689-6658, O: E-mail: CONCERN@POBoxes.com.
Evangelical Fellowship of Asia (EFA), Victoria Chambers, 2nd Fl, 4-1-826 J N Rd., Hyderabad, Andhra Pradesh 500001, T: 40-590844, F: 40-473-4043, O: E-mail: francis@hd1.vsnl.net.in.
Syro-Malabar Bishops' Synod, Catholic Bishops' House, Kottayam-1, Kerala, T: 3527.

ISRAEL
Conference des Eveques Latins Dans les Regions Arabes (CELRA), P.O. Box 20531, 91204 Jérusalem; Notre Dame of Jerusalem Center, 91204 Jérusalem, T: 02-28-85-54, F: 02-28-85-55.

IVORY COAST
Regional Episcopal Conference of French-speaking West Africa (CERAO), B.P. 470, Abidjan 06.

KENYA
All Africa Conference of Churches, P.O. Box 14205, Westlands, (Waiyaki Way) Nairobi, T: 254-2-441-483, F: 254-2-443-241.
Association of Member Episcopal Conferences in Eastern Africa (AMECEA), P.O. Box 21191, Nairobi.
Association of Evangelicals in Africa (AEA), P.O. Box 49332, Nairobi, T: 2-720220, F: 2-710254, O: E-mail: AEA@MAF.org.
Central Africa Christian Council (CACC), Dala Hera, Kibos Rd, PO Box 782, Kisumu.
East Africa Christian Alliance (EACA), Mercury House, Tom Mboya St, PO Box 72681, Nairobi, T: 28280.
Ethiopian Orthodox Holy Spirit & United Churches of East Africa, P.O. Box 47909, Nairobi.
United Churches of Africa, Olympic House, Koinange St, PO Box 16362, Nairobi.

LEBANON
Middle East Bible Council, Box 2165, Bayrut.
Supreme Council of the Evangelical Community in Syria & Lebanon, PO Box 70890, Antelias, T: 961-1-411-179, F: 961-1-405-490.

LIBERIA
Association of Episcopal Conferences of Anglophone West Africa (AECAWA), P.O. Box 10-502, 1000 Monrovia.

MALAWI
Conference of the Anglican Provinces of Africa (CAPA), P.O. Box 19, Chilema.

MALAYSIA
Federation of Evangelical Lutheran Churches in Malaysia and Singapore, P.O. Box 11516, 88816 Kota Kinabalu, Sabah, T: 69-88/42-79-00, F: 60-88/42-85-95.

NEW ZEALAND
Federation of Catholic Bishops' Conferences of Oceania (FCBCO), P.O. Box 14-044, 112 Queen's Dr., Wellington 3.

NIGERIA
Association of the Episcopal Conferences of Anglophone West Africa (AECAWA), P.O. Box 951, Lagos.
West African Council of Christian Churches, P.O. Box 53, Abak, South Eastern State.

NORWAY
Conferentia Episcopalis Scandiae, Akersveien 5, P.B. 8270 Hammersborg, N-0129, Oslo 1.

PANAMA
Episcopal Secretariat of Central America and Panama, Calle 20 y Av., Mexico 24-45, Apartado 6386, Panama 5.
Secretariado Episcopal de América Central-SEDAC, c/o Arzobispo de Panamá, Calle 1a. Sur, Carrasquilla, Apartado 6386, Zona 5, T: 507-223-0075, F: 507-223-0042, O: 507-264-8238, 264-8539.

PERU
Anglican Council of South America, Apdo 10266, Correo Colmena, Lima.

PHILIPPINES
Asian Baptist Federation, F: 632-60-8151.

REUNION
Conference Episcopale de l'Ocean Indien (CE-

DOI), B.P. 55, 97462 St. Denis-de-La Reuinion.

SOLOMON ISLANDS
South Pacific Anglican Council (SPAC), Bishopdale, Mendana Av, PO Box C13, Honiara.

SOUTH AFRICA
Conference of Archbishops of Anglican Provinces in Africa (Anglican African Archbishops' Conference), Bishopscourt, Claremont, CP.
Inter-Regional Meeting of Bishops of Southern Africa (IMBISA), PO Box 17054, Hillbrow 2038, Johannesburg, T: 011-725-3244.
Southern African Catholic Bishops' Conference (SACBC), P.O. Box 941, Pretoria 0001.

SURINAME
Caribbean Council of Christian Churches, PO Box 478, Para aribo.

SWEDEN
Scandinavian Evangelical Council, Källparksgatan 10a, Uppsala; c/o Frederiksplein 24, Amsterdam 1002, Netherlands.

SWITZERLAND
Conference of European Churches, 150 route de Ferney, P.O. Box 2100, 1211 Geneva 2, T: 41-22-791-61-11, F: 41-22-91-62-27.
Council of European Bishops' Conferences (CCEE), Klosterhof 6b, CH-9000 Sankt Gallen.

TAIWAN
Regional Episcopal Conf. of China/Regional Conf. of Chinese Bishops, 34 Lane, 32 Kuangfu Rd, PO Box 1723, Taipei, T: 771295.

TOGO
Conférence des Eglises de Toute l'Afrique (CETA/AACC), Secrétariat Ouest-Africain, Rue Seth Harlley-Kodjoviakope, BP 2268, Lomé.

TRINIDAD & TOBAGO
Antilles Episcopal Conference of the Roman Catholic Church, 11 Mary St., St. Clair, Port-of-Spain.

UNITED STATES OF AMERICA (USA)
North American Commission of African Christians (NACAC), P.O. Box 1835, Tulsa, OK 74101, T: 918-747-7352.
Pentecostal Fellowship of North America (PFNA), 1445 Boonville, Springfield, MO 65802.
Standing Conference of Canonical Orthodox Bishops in the Americas, 8005 Ridge Blvd, Brooklyn, NY 11209, T: 212-745-8481.

ZIMBABWE
Inter-Regional Meeting of Bishops of Southern Africa (IMBISA), 4 Bayswater Rd., Highlands, Harare.

22
Conciliarism: global

Interdenominational or ecumenical councils of churches or denominations of different ecclesiastical traditions, at the international or world level; global Christian councils, federations, associations, alliances, fellowships; world conciliarism, collegiality, and consultation.

BRITAIN (UK OF GB & NI)
Lausanne Committee for World Evangelization, P.O. Box 300, Oxford OX2 9XB, T: 44-0865-749070, F: 44-0865-714324, O: Web: www.goshen.net/Lausanne.

CHINA
Chinese Coordination Centre of World Evangelism, P.O. Box 98435, TST, Hong Kong.

HOLY SEE
Synod of Bishops, Segreteria Generale, Piazza Pio XII 3, I-00193 Roma, Italy, T: 6984821, 6984324.

KENYA
Organization of African Independent Churches (OAIC), PO Box 21570, Nairobi, T: 567849, 23649.

NETHERLANDS
International Council of Christian Churches, Oud Milligenseweg 26, NL-3886 ZG Garderen.

PHILIPPINES
World Evangelical Fellowship (Manila Office)(WEF), P.O. Box 1294-1152 (Central), 62 Molave St., Project 3, 1100 Quezon City, T: 2-913-6605, F: 2-913-6503, O: E-mail: WEF-Phil@xc.org.

SINGAPORE
World Evangelical Fellowship (Intl. Ofc)(WEF), 141 Middle Road, #05-05 GSM Building, Singapore 188976, T: 339-7900, F: 338-3756, O: E-mail: WEF-Intl@xc.org, Web: www.worldevangeli.

SWITZERLAND
Conference of Secretaries of Christian World Communions (CWCs), 150 route de Ferney, CH-1211 Genève 20, T: 333400.
World Council of Churches, Ecumenical Centre, 150 route de Ferney, P.O. Box 2100, 1211 Geneva 2, T: 41-22-791-61-11, F: 41-22-791-0361, O: Web: www.coe.org/evanmiss.html, E-mail: info@wcc-coe.org.

UNITED STATES OF AMERICA (USA)
Lausanne International, P.O. Box 661029, Arcadia,

CA 91066-1029, T: 1-626-301-7714, F: 1-626-301-7786, O: E-mail: john_siewert@wvi.org.
World Council of Biblical Churches, P.O. Box 5455, Bethlehem, PA 18015.
World Evangelical Fellowship (N. America Office), P.O. Box WEF, Wheaton, IL 60189-8004, T: 630-668-0440, F: 630-668-0498, O: E-mail: WEF-NA@xc.org.

23
Conciliarism: local (sub-national)

Definitions: Interdenominational or ecumenical councils of churches or denominations of different ecclesiastical traditions, for a province, city, area of a city, or region within a single nation; local, provincial, or city-wide Christian councils, federations, associations, alliances, fellowships; local conciliarism, collegiality, and consultation.

24
Conciliarism: national

Interdenominational or ecumenical councils of churches or denominations of different ecclesiastical traditions, at times including foreign missionary societies or other Christian organizations, for a single nation or a small grouping of a few adjacent nations; national Christian councils, federations, associations, alliances, fellowships; Roman Catholic national episcopal or bishops' conferences; national inter-rite ecumenical assemblies; national conciliarism, collegiality and consultation; including certain missionary councils (associations or fellowships of foreign missions or missionaries at work in a nation, especially in World A), but excluding interreligious national councils open to non-Christian bodies (for these, see INTERRELIGIOUS ORGANIZATIONS).

ALBANIA
(Catholic) Episcopal Conference of Albania, Rruga Labinoti, Vilate, Gjermaneve Nr 3, Tirana.

ALGERIA
Association des Eglises et Oeuvres Protestantes en Algérie, c/o 78 Chemin Beaurepaire, El-Biar, El Djezair, T: 783291.

AMERICAN SAMOA
National Council of Churches in American Samoa, P.O. Box 921, Pago Pago 96799, T: 684-622-7715, 633-4493, F: 684-699-1898.

ANGOLA
Council of Christian Churches in Angola, C.P. 1659, Luanda, (Rua Amilcar Cabral no. 182, 1° andar, Luanda), T: 244-2-33-04-02, F: 244-2-39-37-46.
Evangelical Alliance of Angola, Caixa Postal 3715, Luanda, T: 2-338-629, F: 2-338-629.

ANTIGUA & BARBUDA
Antigua Christian Council, P.O. Box 23, St. John's, T: 1 809-462 01 51, F: 1 809-462 23 83.
United Evangelical Association of Antigua & Barbuda, P.O. Box 1583, St. John's, T: 462-1006, F: 462-1006.

ARGENTINA
Argentina Lausanne Committee, Juan B. Justo 1240, 2000 Rosario, S.F., T: 54-41-388-252, O: E-mail: forever1@satlink.com.
Argentine Alliance of Evangelical Churches (ACIERA), 22 Orientales, 1236 Capital Federal, Buenos Aires, T: 1-932-9599, F: 1-957-1577.
Argentine Federation of Evangelical Churches, José María Moreno 873, 1424 Buenos Aires, T: 54 1-922 5356, F: 54 1-922 5356.
Confederación de Iglesias Evangélicas del Rio de la Plata, Tucumán 358, 60L, Buenos Aires.
Conferencia Episcopal de Argentina, Calle Suipacha 1034, 1008 Buenos Aires, T: 54-1-328-2015, F: 54-1-328-9570, O: 328-0859, 328-0993.
Federación Argentina de Iglesias Evangélicas (FAIE), Tucumán 358, Piso 6 L, Buenos Aires 6, T: 317432.

AUSTRALIA
Australia Lausanne Committee, 12 Cornwall St., Turramurra, Sydney NSW 2074, T: 61-29-449-9252, F: 61-29-267-3626, O: E-mail: dclaydon@ozemail.com.au.
Australian Catholic Bishops' Conference, 63 Currong St., Braddon, A.C.T. 2601.
Australian Council of Churches (ACC), 401A Pitt St., Sydney, P.O. Box 111, Brickfield Hill, NSW 2001, T: 262901.
Australian Episcopal Conference (AEC), 12 Kennedy St., P.O. Box 297, Kingston, ACT 2604, T: 283539.
Australian Evangelical Alliance, Inc. (AEA), P.O. Box 175, 44 Rutland Rd., Box Hill, Victoria 3128, T: 3-9890-0633, F: 3-9890-0700, O: E-mail: evanall@ozemail.com.au.

National Council of Churches in Australia, 77 Capel Street, West Melbourne 3003; Private Bag 199, QVB Post Office, Sydney NSW 1230, T: 61-2-9299-2215, F: 61-2-9262-4514, O: Also: 370 Kent Street, Sydney NSW 2000.

AUSTRIA
(Catholic) Episcopal Conference of Austria, Sekretariat der Bischofxkonferenz, Wollzeile 2, A-1010 Wien.
Abeitsgemeinschaft Evangelikaler Gemeinden in ...sterreich (ARGEG), Felbigergasse 3/1/20, 1140 Wien, T: 0222-94 83 96.
Ecumenical Council of Churches in Austria, Severin-Schreiber-Gass 3, A-1180 Wien, T: 43-1-479-15-23-13, F: 43-1-479-15-23-DW 20.
LWF National Committee in Austria, c/o Evangelische Kirche Augsburgischen Bekenntnisses in Osterreich, Severin Schreiber Gasse 3, 1180 Vienna, T: 43-1-47-15-23, F: 43-1-47-15-23.
Oesterreichische Evangelische Allianz, Postfach 34, A-4046 Linz, T: 732-248-019, F: 732-248-019, O: E-mail: 113622.2445@compuserve...
Osterreichische Bischofskonferenz, Rotenturmstrasse 2, A1010 Vienna, T: 0222-515 52.

BAHAMAS
Bahamas Christian Council, P.O. Box 92, Shirley Street P.O., Nassau, T: 1 809-325-26-40, F: 1 809-293-16-57.

BANGLADESH
Bangladesh National Council of Churches, P.O. Box 220, Dhaka 1000, T: 880-2-402-869, F: 880-2-803-556, O: CHURCHSERV, DHAKA.
Catholic Bishops' Conference of Bangladesh (CBCB), P.O. Box 3, Dhaka-2.
National Christian Fellowship of Bangladesh, Plot 80, Block-B, Avenue-1, Section-12, Mirpur, Dhaka, 1221, T: 2-802-145, 2805-056, F: 2803-031, O: E-mail: koinonia@bdonline.com.
National Council of Churches, Bangladesh, G.P.O. Box 220, Dhaka 1000; Cable: CHURCHSERV, DHAKA, T: 880 2/402 869.

BARBADOS
Barbados Ministerial Association, Belmont Manse, Welches Territory.

BELGIUM
Alliance Evangelique Francophone de Belgique, 7 rue du Ponsart, B-7600 Peruwelz, T: 69-771469.
Episcopal Conference of Belgium, Sekretar der Bischofskonferenz, Guimardstraat 1, B-1040 Brussels.
Evangelische Alliantie Vlaanderen (Belgium), Boomlaarstraat 12, B-2500 Lier, T: 3-488-0430, F: 3-488-0430, O: E-mail: don.zeeman@ping.be, Web site: www.ping.be/erts.
Friends Information Centers & Offices, 50 Square Ambiorix, B-1040, Brussels, T: 02-230-4935.
Fédération des Eglises Protestantes de Belgique, Rue du Champs de Mars 5, B-1050 Brussels, T: 02-743154.

BELIZE
Belize Christian Council, P.O. Box 508, Belize City, T: 501 2-77-077, F: 501 2-78-825.

BELORUSSIA
(Catholic) Episcopal Conference of Belarus, ul. Shevtshenko 12, KW I, 225710 Minsk.

BENIN
Association des Eglises Chrétiennes, BP 532, Porto Novo.
Conference Episcopale du Benin, BP 491, Cotonou.
Federation des Eglises et Missions Evangeliques du Beni, B.P. 07-0596, Cotonou, T: 35-02-14.
Interconfessional Protestant Council of Benin, BP 2624, Cotonou.
Union of Evangelical Churches of Benin, B.P. 215, Parakou, T: 229-612-331.

BOLIVIA
Asociación Nacional de Evangélicos de Bolivia, Casilla de Correo 945, Cochabamba, T: 42-28280, F: 42-29902.
Confederation of Fundamental Evangelical Churches of Bolivia, Casilla 953, Cochabamba.
Conferencia Episcopal de Bolivia, Calle Potosí 814, Casilla Postal 2309, La Paz, T: 591-2-32-1254, F: 591-2-39-2326, O: 35-3658.

BOSNIA & HERCEGOVINA
(Catholic) Episcopal Conference of Bosnia, Puljic, Nadbiskup Sarajevo, Vikarijat ZA Prog. 1, Izbjeglice, Kaptol 29, 41000 Zagreb.

BOTSWANA
Botswana Association of Inter Spiritual Churches, P.O. Box 374, Gaberone.
Botswana Christian Council, P.O. Box 355, Gaborone, T: 267-351-981, F: 267-351-981, O: E-mail: BCC@wn.apc.org, Telex: c/o 2402 BD UN-HCR.
Botswana Spiritual Council of Churches, P.O. Box 40743, Gaborone.
Evangelical Fellowship of Botswana, P.O. Box 2055, Gaborone, T: 37-2948, F: 35-6150.

BRAZIL
Associacão Evangélica Brasileira, Caixa Postal 100.84 - Centro, Niteroi-RJ, CEP 24001-970, T: 21-717-6017, F: 21-620-2803, O: E-mail: aevb@aras.com.br.
Confederação das Igrejas Evangélicas Fundamentalistas (CIEF), Rua 14 de Julho 285, São Paulo, SP.
Conferência Nacional dos Bispos do Brasil, SE/Sul Quadra 801 - Conjunto B - CEP 70401-900 - Brasília-DF, T: 061-225-2955, F: 061-225-4361, O: E-mail: CNBB@EMBRATEL.NET.BR, Telex: 61-1104

e 61-4954.
Conselho Nacional de Igrejas Cristas do Brasil-CONIC, SCS-QUADRA 1, Bloco E, Edif. Ceará, sala 713, 70303 900-Brasilia-DF, T: 61-321-8341, F: 61-321-4034.
LWF National Committee in Brazil, c/o Evangelical Ch of the Lutheran Confession in Brazil, Caixa Postal 2876, Rua Senhor dos Passos 202.2 andar, 90001-970 Porto Alegre, RS, T: 55-51-221-34-33, F: 55-51-225-72-44.

BRITAIN (UK OF GB & NI)

(Catholic) Episcopal Conference of England and Wales, Archbishop's House, Westminster, London SW1P 1QJ.
(Catholic) Episcopal Conference of Scotland, Archdiocesan Offices, 196 Clyde Street, Glasgow, GI 4JY.
Action of Churches Together in Scotland, Scottish Churches House, Dunblaine, Perthshire FK15 0AJ, T: 44-786-82-35-88, F: 44-786-82-58-44.
Bishops' Conference of England and Wales, 39 Eccleston Square, London, SWIV IPD.
Bishops' Conference of Scotland, Archbishop's House, 196 Clyde St., Glasgow G1 4JY.
British Council of Protestant Christian Churches, 9 Milnthorpe Rd, Chiswick, London W4.
British Pentecostal Fellowship, 23 John Campbell Rd, Stoke Newington, London N17; 51 Newington Causeway, London SE1.
Churches Together in England (CTE), Inter-Church House, 35-41 Lower Marsh, London SE1 7RL, T: 44 171-620 4444, F: 44 171-928 5771.
Commission of the Covenanted Churches in Wales (ENFYS), Woodland Place, Penarth, South Glam. CF6 2EX, T: 44 1222-705 278, 708 234, F: 44 1222-387 835.
Council of African & Allied Churches in the UK, 99 Strathville Rd, London SW18 4QR.
Council of Churches for Britain & Ireland (CCBI), Inter-Church House, 35-41 Lower Marsh, London SE1 7RL, T: 44 171-620 4444, F: 44 171-928 0010.
Cytun-Churches Together in Wales, Ty John Penry, 11 St. Helen's Road, Swansea, West Glamorgan SA1 4AL, T: 44 1792-46 08 76, F: 44 1792-46 93 91.
Episcopal Conference of Ireland, Ara Coeli, Armagh, NI, T: 2045.
Evangelical Alliance of the United Kingdom, Whitefield House, 186 Kennington Park Road, London SE11 4BT, T: 171-207-2100, F: 171-207-2150, O: E-mail: sjones@eauk.org, Web site: www.eauk.org.
Evangelical Fellowship of Ireland, The Manse, 11 Waterloo Gardens, Belfast, NI BT15 4EX.
Free Church Federal Council (FCFC), 27 Tavistock Square, London WC1, T: 01-387-8413.
Friends Information Centers & Offices, 1 Byng Place, London, WC1E 7JH, T: 171-387-5648, F: 171-383-3722.
Irish Council of Churches, Inter-Church Centre, 48 Elmwood Ave., Belfast BT9 6AZ, T: 44 12332-66 31 45, F: 44-1232-38 17 37.
Lutheran Council of Great Britain, 8 Collingham Gardens, SW5 0HW London, T: 44-171-373-11-41.

BRITISH VIRGIN ISLANDS

Tortola Inter-Church Council, P.O. Box 33, Road Town, Tortola.

BULGARIA

(Catholic) Episcopal Conference of Bulgaria, Eparchialis, U1. Pashovi 10/B, Sofia, VI.
Bulgaria Lausanne Committee, Usta Gencho Str. BL 37B, ent. D Ap83, 1330 Sofia, T: 359-2-957-1115, F: 359-2-957-1555.
Bulgarian Evangelical Alliance, P.O. Box 13, Sofia 1330, T: 2-801855, F: 2-801855, O: E-mail be.alliance@mbox.cit.bg, Also: Nikolay e-mail: niknedelchev.

BURKINA FASO

Conférence des Evêques de la Haute-Volta et du Niger, BP 90, Ouagadougou, T: 2993.
Federation of Evangelical Churches and Missions of Burkina Faso, B.P. 108, Ouagadougou 01, T: 226-300-229, F: 226-300-405.

BURUNDI

Conference des Eveques Catholiques du Burundi (CECAB), B.P. 1390, 5 Blvd. de l'Uprona, Bujumbura.
Conférence des Ordinaires du Rwanda et du Burundi (COREB), 5 Av de l'Uprona, BP 690, Bujumbura, T: 3263.
Conseil National des Eglises du Burundi, B.P. 17, Bujumbura., Rue de la Science 14, Bujumbura, T: 257-22 42 16, F: 257-22 79 41.

CAMBODIA

Cambodia Christian Services, Fellowship of Cambodia, T: 855-23-362285.
Evangelical Fellowship of Cambodia, P.O. Box 543, Phnom Penh, T: 23-362-285, F: 23-362-285, O: E-mail: efc@forum.org.kh.

CAMEROON

Conference Episcopale Nationale du Cameroun (CENC), B.P. 807, Yaoundé.
Federation of Protestant Churches and Missions in Cameroon, B.P. 491, Yaoundé, T: 237-23-60-93, F: 237-23-60-91.
Union des Eglises Evangeliques au Nord Cameroun, B.P. 73, Maroua, T: 29-32-02.

CANADA

Alliance Francophone des Protestants Evangeliques du (AFPEQ), 455, rue St-Antoine Ouest, bureau 602, Montreal, Quebec H2Z 1J1, T: 514-878-3035, F: 514-878-8048.
Canada Lausanne Committee, 5 Riverhead Drive, Rexdale, Ont. M9W 4G3, T: 1-416-741-2205, F: 1-416-741-1175.
Canadian Anglican Evangelical Fellowship, Box 731, Station F, Toronto, Ontario.
Canadian Conference of Catholic Bishops, 90 Parent Ave., Ottawa, K1N 7B1.
Canadian Council of Evangelical Protestant Churches, 130 Gerrard St East, Toronto 2, Ontario.
Canadian Council of Churches, 40 St. Clair Ave., East, Suite 201, Toronto, Ontario M4T 1M9, T: 1-416-921-7759, F: 1-416-921-7478.
Canadian Unitarian Council, 175 St Clair Av, W Toronto 195, Ontario.
Evangelical Fellowship of Canada (EFC), M.I.P. Box 3745, Markham, ON L3R 0Y4, T: 905-479-5885, F: 905-479-4742, O: E-mail: efc@-canada.com, Web site: www.efc-canada.co.
Friends Information Centers & Offices, 60 Lowther Ave, Toronto, Ontario M5R 1C7, T: 416-921-0368.
Lutheran Council in Canada, 500-365 Hargrave St, Winnipeg, Manitoba R3B 2K3, T: 204-942-0096.
LWF National Committee in Canada, c/o Evangelical Lutheran Church in Canada, 1512 St. James T., R3H 0L2 Winnipeg, Manitoba, T: 1-204-786-67-07, F: 1-204-783-83-7548.
Ukrainian Catholic Metropolitan Conference, Archbishop's House, 235 Scotie St, Winnipeg 17, Manitoba R2V IVZ, T: 204-339-7457.

CENTRAL AFRICAN REPUBLIC

Association des Eglises Evangeliques Centrafricaines (AEEC), B.P. 342, Bangui, T: 61-3330, F: 61-3330.
Conference Episcopale Centrafricaine (CECA), B.P. 798, Bangui.

CHAD

Conference Episcopale du Tchad, B.P. 456, N'Djamena.
Entente des Eglises et Missions Evangeliques au Tchad (EEMET), B.P. 2006, N'Djamena, T: 51-5393, F: 51-6161.

CHILE

Christian Fellowship of Churches in Chile, Casilla 52928, Correo Central, Santiago; Av. Blanco Encalada 1943 - 2° piso, Santiago, T: 56-2-695 89 23.
Confederación Fundamentalista de Iglesias Evangélicas de Chile (CFEC, or CIEF), Aranco 890, Chillán.
Conferencia Episcopal de Chile, Cienfuegos 47, Casilla 517-V, Correo 21, Santiago de Chile, T: 56-2-671-7733, F: 56-2-698-1416, O: Telex: 343066 CONSEC CK.
Confraternidad Evangélica de Chile, Ariosto 7351, La Reina-Santiago, T: 2-226-8125, F: 2-226-8125.
Unión de Misiones Pentecostales Libres, Obispo Presidente, Casilla 14727, Correo 21, Santiago, T: 375680.

CHINA

Catholic Diocesan Centre, 16 Caine Rd., Hong Kong, T: 5-258021 ext.478.
Catholic Patriotic Association, Beijing.
Chinese Bishop's Conference, Beijing West District, Liu Yin St. No. 14.
Hong Kong Chinese Christian Churches Union, 6th Floor, Metropole Bldg, 57 Peking Rd, Kowloon, Hong Kong, T: 666467.
Hong Kong Christian Council, 33 Granville Road, 9th Fl., Tsim Sha Tsui, Kowloon, Hong Kong, T: 852-2-368-7141, F: 852-2-724-2131.
Hong Kong Evangelical Fellowship, P.O. Box 96605, Tsimshatsui, Kowloon, Hong Kong.
National Christian Council of China, Missions Bldg, 169 Yuan Ming Yuan Rd, Shanghai.
Protestant Three-Self Movement, Beijing.

COLOMBIA

Confederacion Evangélica de Colombia, Apartado Aereo 85130, Bogota, T: 1-613-3352, F: 1-226-9572.
Conferencia Episcopal de Colombia, Carrera 47 No. 84-85, Apartado Aéreo 7448, Santafé de Bogota, T: 57-91-240-0864, 311-5630, O: Telex: 44740 CEC CO.

CONGO-BRAZZAVILLE

Conference Episcopale du Congo, B.P. 200, Brazzaville.
Fédération des Eglises Chrétiennes du Congo, BP 3205, Bacongo-Brazzaville.

CONGO-ZAIRE

Church of Christ in Zaire, 1A Av Pumbu, BP 3094, Kinshasat Gombe, T: 30493.
Conférence Episcopale du Congo, B.P. 3258, Kinshasa-Gombe.
Conseil Supérieur des Sacrificateurs pour l'Unité des Eglises Indépendantes du Congo, BP 985, Kananga (Luluabourg).
Eglise du Christ au Congo, BP 4938, Kinshasa-Gombe.

COOK ISLANDS

Religious Advisory Council of the Cook Islands, P.O. Box 886, Avarua, Rarotonga.

COSTA RICA

Alianza Evangélica Costarricense, Apartado postal 5481-1000, 1002 San Jose, T: 236-2171, F: 236-5921, O: E-mail: semlfp@sol.com.
Conferencia Episcopal de Costa Rica, c/o Arzobispado, Apartado 3187, 1000 San Jose, T: 506-221-0941, 221-3053, F: 506-221-6662.

CROATIA

Hrvatska Biskupska Konferencija, Kaptol 22, 4100 Zagreb.
Protestant Evangelical Council in Croatia, Severinska 16, 10000 Zagreb, T: 1-336-257, F: 1-336-257, O: E-mail: pev@zg.tel.hr.

CUBA

Conferencia Episcopal de Cuba, Calle 26 No 314 entre 3ra. y 5a Avenidas, Miramar Municipio Playa, Apartado 623, Ciudad de la Habana, T: 53-7-33-2468, 33-2001, F: 53-7-33-2168.
Consejo de Iglesias Evangélicas de Cuba, Calle 6 No 273 E/11 y 13, Vedado, Apdo 4179, La Habana 4.
Council of Churches of Cuba, Calle 14 #304 e/3 y 5, Miramar, Playa, 11 300 Cindad de la Habana, T: 53-7-33-17-92, F: 53-7-33-17-88.

CYPRUS

Cyprus Evangelical Alliance, P.O. Box 5083, 1306 Nicosia, T: 2-466-498, F: 2-466-493, O: E-mail: cogopn@spidernet.com.cy.

CZECH REPUBLIC

Czech Bishop's Conference, Thakurova 3, 160 00 Prah 6, T: 2-3315201, F: 2-24310144.
Czech Evangelical Alliance, Korunni 60, CZ-120 00 Praha 2, T: 2-255-681, O: E-mail: ealiance@mbox.vol.cz.
Ecumenical Council of Churches in Czech Republic, Donska 5/370, CZ-101 00 Praha, T: 42-2-74-62-47.

DENMARK

Council of Free Churches, Toftefaeksvej 15, DK-2800, Lyngby.
Danish Lausanne Committee, übjergvej 8B, DK-2720 Vanlose, T: 45-3961-2777, F: 45-3940-1954, O: E-mail: bn@dmr.org.
Ecumenical Council of Denmark, Dag Hammarskjölds Alle 17/3, DK-2100 Købebgavb Ø, T: 35 43 29 43, F: 35 43 29 44.
Evangelical Alliance of Denmark, Ledojetoften 10, Ledoje, DK-2765 Smorum, T: 44-973728, F: 44-973417.
LWF National Committee in Denmark, c/o Church of Denmark, Council on Inter-Church Relations, Vestergade 8/1, 1456 Copenhagen K., T: 45-33-11-44-88, F: 45-33-11-95-88.

DOMINICA

Dominica Association of Evangelical Churches, P.O. Box 1820, Roseau, T: 448-8767, O: E-mail: goodwillsch@tod.dm.
Dominica Christian Council, P.O. Box 92, Roseau.

DOMINICAN REPUBLIC

Conferencia Episcopal de Republica Dominicana, Calle Isabel la Católica No 55, Esquina Pellerano Alfau 3, Apartado 186, Santa Domingo, T: 1-809-685-3141, F: 1-809-689-9454, O: Also tel: 685-3142.
Dominican Evangelical Fraternity, Apdo 1897, Santo Domingo, T: 537-5297, 537-5858, F: 530-7975.

ECUADOR

Conferencia Episcopal de Ecuador, Avenida América 1805 y La Gasca, Apartado 17-01-1081, Quito, T: 593-2-22-3140, F: 593-2-50-1429, O: Also tel: 22-3144, 22-3138, 22-3139, 22-3142, Telex: 2427 CONFER ED.
Confraternidad Evangelica Ecuatoriana, Casilla 691, Quito, T: 2-241-550, F: 2-447-263.

EGYPT

Catholic Inter-Rite Assembly, Apostolic Nunciature, Safarat Al-Vatican, 5 Sharia Mohamed Mazhar, Zamalek, Al Qahirah, T: 805152.
Ecumenical Advisory Council for Church Services in Egypt, Amba Rueis Bldg, Ramses St, Abbasiya, Al Qahirah.
Fellowship of Evangelicals in Egypt, P.O. Box 162-11811 El Panorama, Cairo, T: 2-297-5901, F: 2-297-5878, O: E-mail: gm@ceoss.org.eg.

EL SALVADOR

Conferencia Episcopal de El Salvador, 15 Avenida Norte 1420, Colonia Layco, Apartado 1310, San Salvador, T: 503-25-8997, F: 503-26-5330, O: Telex: 20420 CEDES.
Confraternidad Evangélica Salvadoreña, Apdo. Postal 884, San Salvador, T: 226-7244, F: 226-2482, O: E-mail: aaob@es.com.sv.

EQUATORIAL GUINEA

Conferencia Episcopal de Guinea Ecuatorial, Apartado 106, Malabo.

ERITREA

Evangelical Fellowship of Eritrea, P.O. Box 1784, Asmara, T: 1-161403, F: 1-162582.

ESTONIA

Estonian Evangelical Alliance, Siili 21-72, EE-0034 Tallinn, T: 6-311501, F: 6-311501, O: E-mail: logos@logos.kirik.ee.
Estonian Lausanne Committee, Adamsoni 32-10, Tallinn EE0001, T: 372-2-452-302, O: E-mail: meego@kalju.kirik.ee.

ETHIOPIA

Council for Co-operation of Churches in Ethiopia (CCCE), P.O. Box 1283, Addis Abeba.
Ethiopian Episcopal Conference, P.O. Box 2454, Addis Ababa.
Evangelical Churches Fellowship of Ethiopia (ECFE), P.O. Box 8773, Addis Ababa, T: 1-51-1498, 1-51-13-27, F: 1-51-7429, 1-51-1327, O: E-mail: ecfe@telecom.net.et.
Union of Evangelical Churches of Ethiopia, P.O. Box 70367, Addis Ababa.

FIJI

Conferentia Episcopalis Pacifici (CEPAC), P.O. Box 289, Suva.
Evangelical Fellowship of Fiji, P.O. Box 3842, Samabula, Suva, T: 393-250, F: 340-468.
Fiji Council of Churches, P.O. Box 2300, Government Bldgs., Suva, T: 679-31 37 98, F: 679-302-152.

FINLAND

Council of Free Christians and Churches in Finland (Association of Free Evangelical Congregations in Finland), Nynasg 4, 68620 Jakobstad 20; Also: Hämeenkatu 4 A 1, 20500 Turku 50.
Finland Lausanne Committee, Keskikuja 2, FIN-12310 Ryttlä, T: 358-19-75821, F: 358-19-757055, O: E-mail: ssvaisanen@online.tietokone.fi.
Finnish Ecumenical Council, Luotsikatu 1 a, PB 185, FIN-00161 Helsinki; P.O. Box 185, T: 358 0-180 21, F: 358 0-174 313.
LWF National Committee in Finland, c/o Evangelical Lutheran Church of Finland, Council for Foreign Affairs, P.O. Box 185, Satamakatu 11, 00161 Helsinki, T: 358-0-180-21, F: 358-0-180-22-30.
Suomen Ekumeeninen Neuvosto, POB 185, SF-00161 Helsinki 16, T: 358-0-18021.

FRANCE

(Catholic) Episcopal Conference of France, 2 Rue des Bonnetiers, B.P. 886, F-76001 Rouen Cedex.
Alliance Evangelique Francaise, 30 bis, rue de la Tour Magne, F-30000 Nimes, T: 4-66-67-22-95, 4-66-21-69-75, F: 4-66-21-69-75.
Conference des Evêques de France, 106 rue du Bac, 75341 Paris CEDEX 07.
Conférence Episcopale de France (CEF), 106 rue du Bac, F-75341 Paris Cedex 07, T: 01-222-5708.
Evangelical Community for Apostolic Action, 12 rue de Miromesnil, F75008 Paris, T: 33-4265-2458,9.
France Lausanne Committee, Comite Francais Lausanne, 3 rue Germain Dardon, F-92130 Montrouge, T: 33-1-4657-3809, F: 33-1-4735-0648, O: E-mail: claudebaty@compuserve.com.
Friends Information Centers & Offices, 114 rue de Vaugirard, F-75006, Paris, T: 01-454-87423.
Fédération Protestante de France (FPF), 47 Rue de Clinchy, F-75009 Paris, T: 33 1-44 53 47 00, F: 33 1-42 81 40 01.
LWF National Committee in France, c/o Alliance Nationale des Eglises Luthériennes de France, 1b Quai Saint-Thomas, 67081 Strasboruge Cedex, T: 33-88-25-90-05, F: 33-88-25-90-99.

GABON

Conference Episcopale du Gabon, B.P. 209, Oyem.

GAMBIA

Evangelical Fellowship of the Gambia (EFG), P.O. Box 428, Banjul, T: 37-3105, F: 37-3104.
Gambia Christian Council, P.O. Box 27, Banjul, T: 220-92092, O: Telex: 2290 Gamtel GV.

GERMANY

(Catholic) Episcopal Conference of Germany, Bischofsplatz 2a, D-6500 Mainz.
Arbeitsgemeinschaft Christlicher Kirchen in Deutschland, Ökumenische Centrale, Friedrichstr 2-4, Postfach 174025, D-6000 Frankfurt/Main.
Bund Evangelisch-Reformierter Kirchen Deutschlands, Untere Karspüle 11a, D-34 Göttingen.
Council of Christian Churches in Germany, Postfach 900617, D-60446 Frankfurt am Main, BRD; Ludolfusstrasse 2-4, D-60487 Frankfurt am Main, T: 49-69-24-70-27-0, F: 49-69-24-70-27-30.
Deutsche Bischofskonferenz, Kaiserstrasse 163, D-53113 Bonn 1.
Deutsche Evangelische Allianz, Stitzenburgstr. 7, D-70182 Stuttgart, T: 711-241010, F: 711-23644600, O: E-mail: info@ead.de, Web site: www.ead.de.
Deutsches Nationalkomitee des Lutherischen Weltbundes, Richard-Wagner-Str 26, D-3 Hannover.
Evangelische Kirche des Union (EKU), Kirchenkanzlei, Jebensstr 3, D-1, Berlin 12.
Evangelisches Missionswerk in Deutschland (EMW), Normannenweg 17-21, 20537 Hamburg, T: 49-40-41-17-40, F: 49-40-45-84-79.
Friends Information Centers & Offices, Planckstrasse 20, D-10117 Berlin, T: 30-208-2284.
German Lausanne Committee, Postfach 1444, D-35573 Wetzlar, T: 49-6441-957312, 915200, F: 49-6441-957-170, O: E-mail: horst.marquardt@erf.de.
Lutherischer Weltbund, Deutscher Hauptausschuss, Diemershaldenstr 45, D-7 Stuttgart-0.
LWF National Committee in Germany, c/o Vereinigte Evangelisch-Lutherische Kirche Deutschlands (VELKD), Postfach 51 04 09, Richard-Wagner-Str. 26, 30634 Hannover, T: 49-511-626-12-23, F: 49-511-626-12-11.
Reformierter Bund, Generalsekretariat, Bleichstr 40, D-6 Frankfurt/Main; Bockenheimer Landstr 109.
Vereinigte Ev-Lutherische Kirche Deutschlands (VELKD), Lutherisches Kirchenamt, Richard-Wagner-Str 26, Postfach 1860, D-3 Hannover.

GHANA

Christian Council of Ghana, P.O. Box 919, Lokko Road, Christiansborg, Accra, T: 233-21-776-678, F: 233-21-776-725.
Ghana Bishops' Conference, National Catholic Secretariat, P.O. Box 9712, Airport, Accra.
Ghana Evangelical Fellowship, P.O. Box 3110, Kumasi.
National Association of Evangelicals of Ghana (NAEG), P.O. Box 30, Achimoto, T: 21-225-554, F: 21-220-271.
National Council of Spiritual Churches, Bikhazi House, Liberty Av, P.O. Box 446, Accra.
National Pentecostal Council of Spiritual Churches of Ghana, Bikhazi House, Liberty Av, P.O. Box X-118 or 446, James Town, Accra.
Pentecostal Association of Ghana, P.O. Box 2546, Accra.
Supreme Council for Ghana Pentecostal Churches, Tunisia House, Liberty Ave., P.O. Box 446, Accra.

GREECE

Conferentia Episcopalis Graeciae, Odos Homirou 9, 106 72 Athens.
Panhellenic Evangelical Alliance, G. Souri 14, GR-185 47, Pireas, T: 1-483-4001, F: 1-483-4000, O: E-mail: amglogos@hol.gr.

GRENADA

Grenada Christian Council, Lucas St, Box 104, St. George's.

GUATEMALA

Alianza Evangélica de Guatemala, Apartado Postal 2862, Guatemala City, T: 2-71-0778, F: 2-26782.

Conferencia Episcopal de Guatemala, Kra. 15 Calzada Roosevelt 4-54, Zona 7 de Mexco, Apartado Postal 1698, 01901 Ciudad de Guatemala, T: 502-2-93-1931, F: 502-2-93-1834, O: Also tel: 93-1832, 93-1833.

GUINEA

Association of Evangelical Churches and Missions of Guinea, B.P. 438, Conakry, T: 2240-4-482-522.

Conference Episcopale de la Guinee, B.P. 1006 Bis, Conakry.

GUYANA

Guyana Council of Churches, P.O. Box 10864, 71 Quamina Str., Georgetown, T: 592 266-610, F: 592 2-61-789.

Guyana Evangelical Fellowship, P.O. Box 10967, Georgetown, T: 63888, F: 2-76892.

LWF National Committee in Guyana, c/o Lutheran Ch in Guyana, Lutheran Courts, New Amsterdam, Berbice, T: 592-3-38-96, F: 592-3-38-96.

HAITI

Concile des Eglises Evangelique d'Haiti, B.P. 2475, Port-au-Prince, T: 22-5755, F: 23-4628.

Conference Episcopale de Haiti (CEH), B.P. 1572, Angle rues Piquant et Lammarre, Port-au-Prince, T: 509-24-855, F: 509-88-2163.

HONDURAS

Conferencia Episcopal de Honduras, Barrio Morazán Boulevar Estadio Suyapa, Apartado 847, Tegucigalpa, M.D.C., T: 504-39-1900, F: 504-32-7838, O: Also tel: 32-4043, Telex: 1633 CONFEP HO.

Confraternidad Evangélica de Honduras, Apartado Postal 909, San Pedro Sula, T: 57-4727, F: 57-5846.

HUNGARY

(Catholic) Episcopal Conference of Hungary, Szechenyi-u. 1, Pf. 80, H-3301 Eger.

Ecumenical Council of Churches in Hungary, Bimbo ut 127, H-1026 Budapest, T: 36-1-176-4847, F: 36-1-176-1210.

Hungarian Bishops Conference, Ferenciek tere 7-8, H-1053 Budapest.

Hungarian Episcopal Assembly, Erseki Szekhaz, Szabadság-tér 1, Kalocsa.(Also: Berenyi Zsigmond u.2, Pf 25, H-2501 Esztergom).

Hungarian Evangelical Fellowship, Felso Erdosor u.5, H-1068 Budapest, T: 1-122-4723, F: 1-122-4723, O: E-mail: 100262.11@compuserve.co.

LWF National Committee in Hungary, c/o Lutheran Church in Hungary, P.O. Box 500, Puskin utca 12, 1447 Budapest, T: 36-1-138-23-02, F: 36-1-138-23-02.

ICELAND

LWF National Committee in Iceland, c/o Evangelical Lutheran Ch-The National Ch of Iceland, Laugavegur 31, 150 Reykjavik, T: 354-562-15-00, F: 354-562-44-95.

INDIA

Catholic Bishops' Conference of India (CBCI), CBCI Center, Ashok Place, Goldakkhana, New Delhi 110001.

Council of Christian Churches of India, 32, Medavakkam, 2nd Street, Kilpauk, Madras, Tamil Nadu 600010.

Evangelical Fellowship of India (EFI), 803/92 Deepali, Nehru Place, New Delhi, Bharat 110 019, T: 11-643-1133, F: 11-689-0246, O: E-mail: efiindia@del2.vsnl.net.in.

Federation of Evangelical Churches of India, 7/A, P. And T. Colony , P. O. Box 274, Amravati Road, Nagpur, Maharashtra 440010.

LWF National Committee in India, c/o United Evangelical Lutheran Chs in India, 1, First St., Haddows Rd., Nungambakkam, 600 006 Madras, T: 91-44-827-16-76, F: 91-44-827-45-57.

National Council of Churches in India, Christian Council Lodge, Post Bag 205, Civil Lines, Nagpur 440001 M.S., T: 91 712-531 312, F: 91 712-532 939.

INDONESIA

Communion of Churches in Indonesia, Jalan Salemba Raya 10, Jakarta Pusat 10430, T: 62-21-315-0451, F: 62-21-315-0457.

Council of Churches in Indonesia, Jalan Salemba Raya 10, Jakarta IV/3, T: 82317.

Konperensi Waligereja Indonesia (KWI), Taman Cut Mutiah 10, Tromolpos 3044, Jakarta 10002.

Persekutuan Injili Indonesia, Kotak Pos 1799, Jakarta 10017, T: 21-567-3452, F: 21-570-8296, O: E-mail: gbi@cbn.net.id.

IRAN

Inter-Rite Episcopal Conference, c/o Arquidiocèse de Isfahan, Khibane Djamshid Abad 100, Tehran, T: 69203.

Iran Council of Churches (ICC), P.O. Box 1505, Tehran, T: 311868.

IRAQ

Inter-Rite Bishops' Meeting of Iraq, Baghdad.

IRELAND

(Catholic) Episcopal Conference of Ireland, Ara Coeli, Armagh BT61 7QY.

Irish Council of Churches, 48 Elmwood Ave., Belfast, BT9 6AZ, T: 44-1232-66-31-45, F: 44-1232-38-17-37.

Irish Lausanne Council for Evangelization, The Manse, Brannockstown, Naas, County Kildare, T: 353-45-483629, F: 353-45-483629.

ISLE OF MAN

Churches Together in Man, The Rectory, Village Road, Andreas 1M7 4HH, T: 44 1624-842 388.

ISRAEL

Assemblee des Ordinaires Catholiques de Terre Sainte, P.O. Box 20531, 91294 Jérusalem; Notre Dame of Jerusalem Center, 91204 Jérusalem, T: 02-28-85-54, F: 02-28-85-55.

International Christian Committee and Jerusalem Inter-Church Aid Committee, P.O. Box 19195, Jerusalem.

International Christian Committee in Israel, P.O. Box 304, Nazareth 16102.

United Christian Council in Israel, P.O. Box 2773, Tel Aviv 61027, T: 3-682-1459, F: 3-682-9817, O: E-mail: beitimm@netvision.net.il.

ITALY

(Catholic) Episcopal Conference of Italy, P. San Giovanni in Laterano 4, I-00184 Rome.

Consultation of Evangelical Ministers, c/o I.P.C., Casella Postale No. 58, 00044 Frascati, Rome, T: 39-6-94-10236, F: 39-6-94-11823, O: E-mail: i.p.c.@interbusiness.it.

Federation of the Protestant Churches in Italy, Via Firenze 38, I-00184 Rome, T: 39 6-482 51 20, F: 39 6-482 87 28.

Italy Lausanne Committee (Consultation of Evangelical Ministers), c/o I.P.C., Casella Postale No. 58, 00044 Frascati, Rome, T: 39-6-94-10-126, F: 39-6-94-11-823, O: E-mail: i.p.c.@interbusiness.it.

LWF National Committee in Italy, c/o Evangelical Lutheran Ch in Italy, Via Toscana 7, 00187 Rome, T: 39-6-488-03-94, F: 39-6-487-45-06.

IVORY COAST

Conférence Episcopale de la Côte d'Ivoire, BP 1287, Abidjan 01, T: 312041.

Federation Evangelique de la Cote d'Ivoire, 08 B.P. 50, Abidjan 08, T: 44-2902, F: 44-1123.

JAMAICA

Friends Information Centers & Offices, 11 Caledonia Ave, Kingston 5,, T: 808-926-7371.

Jamaica Association of Evangelicals, P.O. Box 123, Kingston 8, T: 922-6764, F: 967-2789.

Jamaica Council of Churches, 14 South Ave., Kingston 10, Jamaica, T: 1-809-926-09-74, F: 1-809-926-69-90.

JAPAN

Catholic Bishops' Conference of Japan, Shiomi 2-10-10, Koto-Ku, Tokyo 135.

Japan Bible Christian Council, 4-5 15 Azuma-cho, Iruma-shi, Saitama-ken 358.

Japan Evangelical Association (JEA), OCC Bldg., 2-1 Kanda Surugadai, Chiyoda-ku, Tokyo 101-0062, T: 3-3295-1765, F: 3-3295-1933, O: E-mail: jea@air.linkclub.or.jp.

National Christian Council in Japan, Japan Christian Center, 24, 2-3-18 Nishiwaseda, Shinjuku-ku, Tokyo 169, T: 81-3-3203-0372, F: 81-3-3204-9495.

KENYA

East African United Churches (Eastern Orthodox Churches and the Coptic Communion), PO Box 9217, Nairobi.

Evangelical Fellowship of Kenya (EFK), P.O. Box 56596, Nairobi, T: 2-725-259, F: 2-724-832.

Kenya African United Christian Churches, PO Box 521, Kisumu.

Kenya Episcopal Conference (KEC), The Kenya Catholic Secretariat, P.O. Box 48062, Nairobi.

Kenya Independent Churches Fellowship, HQ, AICN Nineveh, PO Box 701, Kisumu.

Kenya Lausanne Committee, P.O. Box 53665, Nairobi, T: 254-15-441965.

National Council of Churches of Kenya, P.O. Box 45009, Nairobi; Church House, Moi Avenue, Nairobi, T: 254 2-338 211, F: 254 2-224 463.

United Orthodox Independent Churches of East Africa, Penguin House, Tom Mboya St, PO Box 28919, Nairobi.

United Orthodox Independent (Zion) Churches of Kenya, PO Box 28159, Nairobi.

KUWAIT

Council of Churches in Kuwait, Bishop's House, PO Box 266, T: 434637.

LAOS

Conference Episcopale du Laos et du Cambodge, Centre Catholique, Thakhek, Khammouane.

LATVIA

Conferentia Episcopalis Lettoniae, Maza Pils, 2, Riga 226050.

LEBANON

Assembly of Catholic Patriarchs and Bishops of Lebanon, Archevêché Grec-Catholique, Rue de Damas, BP 901, Bayrut.

LESOTHO

Christian Council of Lesotho, P.O. Box 547, Maseru 100, T: 266-259 93, F: 266-310 310.

Episcopal Conference of Lesotho, Archbishop's House, P.O. Box 267, Maseru, T: 22565.

Federation of African Independent Churches, Maseru.

Lesotho Catholic Bishops Conference, Catholic Secretariat, P.O. Box 200, Maseru 100.

LIBERIA

Association of Evangelicals of Liberia (AEL), P.O. Box 393, Monrovia, T: 22-2026.

Liberian Council of Churches, P.O. Box 2191, 1000 Monrovia 10; 182 Tubman Blvd., Monrovia, T: 231-262 820, F: 231-22 61 26.

United Pentecostal Assemblies of the World in Liberia & Sierra Leone, P.O. Box 9038, Monrovia.

LITHUANIA

Conferentia Episcopalis Lituaniae, Sv. Mikalojanus, 4, 22001 Vilnius.

LUXEMBOURG

(Catholic) Episcopal Conference of Luxemburg, B.P. 419, L-2014 Luxemburg.

MADAGASCAR

Fédération des Eglises Protestantes à Madagascar (FJKM), VK 2 vohipiraisana, Ambohijatovo-Atsimo, 101 Antananarivo, T: 201-44, F: 010-261-2345-34.

Fédération des Eglises Indépendantes de Madagascar, Foyer Chrétien des Jeunes Filles, IV-D 18A Behoririka, Tananarive.

LWF National Committee in Madagascar, c/o Malagasy Lutheran Ch, Boîte Postale 1741, 54, Ave. du 26 juin 1960, 101 Antananarivo, T: 261-2-223-47, F: 261-2-337-67.

MALAWI

Christian Council of Malawi, P.O. Box 30068, Capital City, Lilongwe 3, T: 265-783 499, F: 265-634 452.

Episcopal Conference of Malawi, Catholic Secretariat of Malawi, P.O. Box 30384, Lilongwe 3.

Evangelical Fellowship of Malawi (EFM), P.O. Box 30296, Lilongwe 3, T: 730-373, F: 730-281.

LWF National Committee in Malawi, c/o Evangelical Lutheran Ch in Malawi, P.O. Box 650, 1 Lilongwe, T: 265-74-20-71, F: 265-74-26-72.

Reformed Independent Churches Association of Malawi, P.O. Box 28, Namadzi.

MALAYSIA

Catholic Bishops' Conference of Malaysia, Singapore and Brunei (BCMSB), Archbishop's House, 31 Victoria St., Singapore 0718.

Council of Churches of Malaysia, 26 Jalan University, 46200 Petaling Jaya, Selangor DE, T: 60 3-756 7092, F: 60 3-756 0353.

National Evangelical Christian Fellowship Malaysia (NECF), 32A Jalan SS 2/103, 47300 Petaling Jaya, Selangor, T: 3-717-8227, F: 3-719-1139, O: E-mail: necf@po.jaring.my, Web site: www.unityonline.co.

MALI

Association des Groupements des Eglises et Missions P (AGEMPEM), B.P. 158, Bamako, T: 22-7073, F: 22-6905.

Association of Evangelical Protestant Church and Missions in Mali, B.P. 158, Barnako, T: 223-223-072, F: 223-228-695.

Conference Episcopale du Mali, B.P. 298, Bamako.

MALTA

(Catholic) Episcopal Conference of Malta, Archbishop's Curia, P.O. Box 29, Valletta.

MEXICO

Asociación Fraternal de Iglesias Pentecostales en la República de México, Calle Nicolás León 118, Colonia Jardín Balbuena, México 8, DF, T: 5716531.

Conferencia Episcopal de México, Prolongación Misterios No. 24, Col. Tepeyac-Insurgentes, Apartado Postal 118-055, C.P. 07020, Mexico, D.F., T: 52-5-781-8462, F: 52-5-577-5489, O: Also tel: 577-5401, 577-5431.

Confraternidad Evangelica Mexicana (CONEMEX), Liverpool 65 - Col. Juaréz 06600 México D.F., T: 5-525-2720, F: 5-525-2720.

Evangelical Federation of Mexico, Apartado 1830, México 06.001, D.F.; Motolinia no. 8-107, México 06.002, D.F., T: 52 5-585.05.94.

MONTSERRAT

Montserrat Council for Social Action, P.O. Box 226, Plymouth.

MOROCCO

Conseil des Eglises du Maroc, 33 rue d/Azilal, Casablanca.

MOZAMBIQUE

Christian Council of Mozambique, C.P. 108, Maputo; Ave. Ahmed Sekou Touré 1822, Maputo, T: 258 1-42 28 36, 42 51 03, F: 258 1-42 19 68.

Conferencia Episcopal de Mocambique (CEM), C.P. 286, Maputo.

MYANMAR

Evangelical Fellowship of Myanmar, P.O. Box 1301, No. 8, 8th Street, A.F.P.F.L. Quarter, Yangon.

Myanmar Catholic Bishops' Conference (MCBC), 292 Pyi Rd., Sanchaung P.O., Yangon.

Myanmar Evangelical Christian Fellowship (MECF), P.O. Box 534 G.P.O., Yangon, T: 1-22-3745, F: 1-227-068.

NAMIBIA

Council of Churches in Namibia, P.O. Box 41, Windhoek 9000; Mashego Street 8521, Windhoek, T: 264 61-217621, F: 264 61-262786.

LWF National Committee in Namibia, c/o Evangelical Lutheran Ch in Namibia (ELCIN), Private Bag 2018, Ondangwa, T: 264-6756-402-41, F: 264-6756-402-11.

Namibia Evangelical Fellowship, P.O. Box 40300, Windhoek 9000, T: 61-22204, F: 61-36661.

NEPAL

National Churches Fellowship of Nepal, P.O. Box 4689, Kathmandu, T: 1-536519, F: 1-536519, O: E-mail: sp@ncfn.mos.com.np.

NETHERLANDS

(Catholic) Episcopal Conference of the Netherlands, Maliebaan 40, P.B. 14019, NL-3508 SB Utrecht.

Council of Churches in the Netherlands, Kon. Wilhelminalaan 5, NL-3818 Amersfoort, T: 31 33-4633 844, F: 31 33-4613 995.

Dutch Lausanne Committee, P.O. Box 47, NL-3840 AA Harderwijk, T: 31-3414-32203, F: 31-3414-31299-12825, O: E-mail: 101335.510@compuserve.com.

Evangelische Alliantie, Hoofdstraat 51a, 3971 KB, Driebergen, T: 343-513-693, F: 343-531-488, O: E-mail: ea@lifenet.nl.

Friends Information Centers & Offices, Vossiusstraat 20, 1071 AD, Amsterdam Zuid, T: 020-6794238.

LWF National Committee in the Netherlands, Charlotte van Montpensierlaan 12, 1181 RR Amstelveen; c/o Evangelical Lutheran Ch in the Kingdom of the Netherlands, T: 31-20-641-62-67.

Netherlands Bishops' Conference, Postbus 13049, NL-3507 LA, Utrecth.

NETHERLANDS ANTILLES

Curacao Council of Churches, Fortkerk - Fort Amsterdam, Willemstad, Curaçao, T: 599 -0461-11-39, F: 599 9-465-74-81.

NEW ZEALAND

Conference of Churches in Aotearoa New Zealand, Private Bag 11903, Ellerslie, Auckland, Aotearoa; 409 Great South Road, Penrose, Auckland, T: 64 9-525 4179, F: 64 9-525 4346.

Evangelical Fellowship of New Zealand, P.O. Box 27-548, Mount Roskill, Auckland 4, T: 9-828-7728, F: 9-625-7412, O: E-mail: 100354.1143@compuserve..

Maori Council of Churches in Aotearoa, Private Bag 11903, (409 Great South Road, Penrose) Ellerslie, Auckland, Aotearoa, T: 64-9-525-4179, F: 64-9-525-4346.

New Zealand Episcopal Conference, Private Bag 1937, Wellington 1.

NICARAGUA

Conferencia Episcopal de Nicaragua, Ferretería Lang. 1 c. al Norte, 1 c. al Este, Apartado Postal 2407, Managua, T: 505-2-66-6292, F: 505-2-66-8069, O: Also tel: 66-8103.

Consejo Nacional Evangelico de Nicaragua (CNPEN), Apartado postal 1692, Managua, T: 2-66-6915, F: 2-66-6915.

NIGERIA

Catholic Bishops Conference of Nigeria, P.O. Box 951, 6 Force Rd., Lagos.

Christian Council of Nigeria, P.O. Box 2838, Marina, Lagos; 139 Ogunluna Drive, Surulere, T: 23 41-83 60 19, F: 23 41-63 23 86.

Communion of Aladura Churches of Nigeria, HQ Office, PO Box 1693, Ibadan.

Nigeria Evangelical Fellowship, P.O. Box 634, No. 40B, Stadium Road, Ilorin, Kwara State, T: 31-223-204, F: 31-221-463, O: E-mail: facts@skannet.com.

Nigeria Lausanne Committee, 24 Moremi Rd., Bodija, P.O. Box 9565, Ibadan Oyo State, T: 234-22-416-428.

NORWAY

Baptist Union of Norway, F: 472-53-9286.

Evangeliske Allianse i norge, Alf Andersens veg 33, N-3670 Notodden, T: 350-11679, F: 350-11679.

Friends Information Centers & Offices, Skovveien 20, N 0257 Oslo, T: 22-440187.

LWF National Committee in Norway, c/o Church of Norway, Council on Ecumenical & International Relations, P.O. Box 5816 Majorstua, 0308 Oslo, T: 47-22-93-27-50, F: 47-22-93-28-29.

Norway Lausanne Committee, c/o Misjonshogskolen, Misjonsveien 34, N-1024 Stavanger, T: 47-51-51-62-10, F: 47-51-51-62-25, O: E-mail: jmb@misjonshs.no.

Norwegian Free Church Council, c/o St Olavsgt 28, Oslo 1.

PAKISTAN

Evangelical Fellowship of Pakistan, P.O. Box 1722, Rawalpindi 46000, T: 703-81889, F: 731-72126, O: E-mail: peof@efp.isb.erum.com.pk.

National Council of Churches in Pakistan, P.O. Box 357, Lahore 4; 32-B Sharah-e-Fatima Jinnah, Lahore 4, T: 92 42-357 307, F: 92 42-63 69 745.

Pakistan Episcopal Conference, St. Patrick's Cathedral, Shahrah-Iraq, Karachi 74400.

PALESTINE

International Christian Committee and Jerusalem Inter-Church Aid Committee, P.O. Box 19195, Jerusalem.

PANAMA

Conferencia Episcopal de Panama (CEP), Apartado 870033, Panama 7, T: 507-262-6691, F: 507-223-0042, O: E-mail: FTORRES@NS.SINFO.NET.

Confraternidad Evangelica Panamena (CONEPA), Apartado 6-6809, El Dorado, T: 223-1270, F: 221-2773.

PAPUA NEW GUINEA

Catholic Bishops' Conference of Papua New Guinea and Solomon Islands, Archbishop's Office, P.O. Box 179, Aitape, Sandam Province.

Evangelical Alliance of Papua New Guinea, P.O. Box 382, Mt. Hagen, WHP, T: 546-2311, F: 546-2204.

Papua New Guinea Council of Churches, P.O. Box 1015, Boroko, T: 675-259-961, F: 675-251-206.

PARAGUAY

Conferencia Episcopal de Paraguay, Calle Alberdi 782, Casilla Correo 1436, Asuncion, T: 595-21-49-0920, F: 595-21-49-5115, O: Also tel: 49-2670.

PERU

Concilio Nacional Evangelico del Peru, Apdo 2566, Lima 100, T: 14-323972, F: 14-329067.

Conferencia Episcopal de Peru, Rio de Janeiro 488, Jesús María, Apartado 310, Lima 100, T: 51-

14-63-1010, F: 51-14-63-6125, O: Also tel: 62-2134.

PHILIPPINES

Catholic Bishops' Conference of the Philippines (CBCP), P.O. Box 3601, 470 General Luna St., 1099 Manila.

National Council of Churches in the Philippines, P.O. Box 1767, 1099 Manila; 879 Epifanio de los Santos Ave., Quezon City, T: 63 2-99 8636, F: 63 2-926 7076.

Philippine Council of Fundamental Evangelical Churches, P.O. Box 1886, Manila.

Philippine Council of Evangelical Churches (PCEC), P.O. Box 1294-1152 (Central), 1100 Quezon City, T: 2-913-7004, F: 2-913-6660, O: E-mail: pcec@amanet.net.

POLAND

(Catholic) Episcopal Conference of Poland, ul. Miodowa 17-19, 00-246 Warsaw.

LWF National Committee in Poland, c/o Evangelical Ch of the Augsburg Confession in Poland, Al. 3 Maja 41, 00-401 Warsaw, T: 48-22/21-26-83.

Polish Ecumenical Council, ul Willowa 1, PL-00-790 Warsaw, T: 48-22-49-96-79, F: 48-22-49-65-01.

PORTUGAL

(Catholic) Episcopal Conference of Portugal, Casa Episcopal, Rua do Brasil, P-3049 Coimbra Codes.

Alianca Evangelica Portuguesa, Apartado 4113, P-1503 Lisboa Codex, T: 1-771-05-30, F: 1-771-06-13, O: E-mail: geral@aliancaevang.pt.

Comissão Inter-eclesiástica Portuguesa, Pres, Praça Coronel Pacheco, Porto.

Portuguese Council of Christian Churches, Rua da Lapa 9, sala 1, 2°, P-3080 Figueira da Foz, T: 351-33-2-82-79, F: 351-33-2-26-03.

PUERTO RICO

Comite Ad Hoc pro Unida Evangélico, Apdo 6445, Caguas 00626, T: 744-1444.

Conferencia Episcopal de Puerto Rico, Calle Pumarada 1706, P.O. Box 40682, Santurci, 00940-0682 San Juan, T: 1-809-728-1654, F: 1-809-728-1654, O: Also tel: 728-1654.

Evangelical Council of Puerto Rico, Calle El Roble 54 (altos), Rio Piedras, 00928, T: 1 809-765 6030, F: 809-765 5977.

ROMANIA

(Catholic) Episcopal Conference of Romania, Palatul Archiepiscopiei, Str. P.P. Aroni 2, RO-3175 Blaj.

Alianta Evangelica din Romania, Tihertului 29, 19/A/10/42, Bucharest 4 76 162.

RUSSIA

(Catholic) Episcopal Conference of Russia, ul. Malaja Lubianka 2, 101000 Moscow.

RWANDA

Alliance Evangelique du Rwanda, P.O. Box 2579, Kilgali, T: 87306, F: 87306.

Conference Episcopale du Rwanda C. Ep. R), B.P. 357, Kigali.

Conseil Protestant du Rwanda (Protestant Council of Rwanda), B.P. 79, Kigali; 20, Rue de Bugesera, Kicukiro, T: 250-85 825, 83 553, F: 250-83 554.

SAINT KITTS & NEVIS

St. Kitts Christian Council, P.O. Box 48, Basseterre, T: 809-465-2504, F: 809-465-7812.

St. Kitts Evangelical Association, P.O. Box 773, Basseterre, T: 465-7284, F: 465-4279.

SAINT LUCIA

Fellowship of Gospel Preaching Churches, P.O. Box 603, Castries, St. Lucia, T: 452-5621.

SAINT VINCENT & THE GRENADINES

Association of Evangelical Churches of St. Vincent & the Grenadines, P.O. Box 143, Kingstown, T: 457-0033, F: 457-9103.

Saint Vincent and the Grenadines Christian Council, P.O. Box 26, Kingstown; Melville Street, Kingstown, T: 1-809-457-19-89.

SAMOA

Samoa Council of Churches, P.O. Box 1867, Apia, T: 685-22-283, F: 685-205 73.

Samoan Evangelical Fellowship (SEF), P.O. Box 3957, Apia, T: 20343, F: 25539.

SENEGAL

Conference Episcopale du Senegal, de la Mauritanie, du Cap-Vert et de Guinée Bissau, B.P. 941, Dakar.

Fraternite Evangelique du Senegal, B.P. 2961, Dakar, T: 217-903.

SIERRA LEONE

Council of Churches in Sierra Leone, P.O. Box 404, Freetown; 4A Kingharman Road, Freetown, T: 232 22-240568, F: 232 22-241109.

Evangelical Fellowship of Sierra Leone, P.O. Box 207, Freetown, T: 22-272700, F: 22-4429, O: E-mail: EFSL@sierratel.sl.

Inter-Territorial Catholic Bishops' Conference of the Gambia, Liberia and Sierra Leone (ITCABIC), Santanno House, P.O. Box 893, Freetown.

SINGAPORE

Chinese Church Union (Singapore), 140 Mackenzie Road, Singapore 228720, T: 338-2482, F: 338-2482.

Evangelical Fellowship of Singapore (EFOS), 6 Mount Sophia, Singapore 228457, T: 466-9675, F: 468-4456, O: E-mail: btefc@cyberway.com.sg.

National Council of Churches, Singapore, 6D Mount Sophia, Singapore 0922, T: 65-337 2150, F: 65-336 0368.

SLOVAKIA

(Catholic) Episcopal Conference of Slovakia, Nám. SNP 19, 97590 Banská Bystrica/Slowakei.

Ecumenical Council of Churches Slovak Republic, Palisady 46, 811 06 Bratislava, T: 42-7-53-33-238, F: 42-7-53-33-235.

Evangelical Alliance Slovakia, Sulovska str. 2, 82105 Bratislava, T: 7-598-7203, F: 7-598-7203.

SLOVENIA

(Catholic) Episcopal Conference of Slovenia, PP 121-III, Ciril Metodov Trg 4, 61001 Ljubljana.

SOLOMON ISLANDS

Solomon Islands Christian Association (SICA), P.O. Box 1335, Honiara, T: 677-23350, F: 677-20955, O: Fax: 61258 (hospital) or 453/61265 (project).

South Sea Evangelical Church, P.O. Box 16, Honiara, T: 22388, 22398, F: 20302.

SOUTH AFRICA

African Independent Churches Association (AICA), 35 Jorissen St, PO Box 31190, Braamfontein, Transvaal.

African Independent Churches' Ecumenical Movement, Johnson Rd, Veeplaats, Port Elizabeth.

African Independent Churches' Movement (AICM), V560 Umlazi Township, 4066 Ntokozweni, near Durban, Natal.

African Independent Churches of Southern Africa, P.O. Box 189, Orlando 1804.

Apostolic and Zionist Assembly of South Africa, P.O. Box 97, Johannesburg.

Assembly of Zionist and Apostolic Churches, Box 97, Johannesburg.

Association of Independent Ministers & Churches in Africa, PO Box 23420, Gezine 0031, 1245 Ben Swart St, Moregloed, Pretoria, T: 012-333-0258.

Bureau of African Churches, PO Box 11, Rossburgh, Durban, Natal.

Evangelical Alliance of South Africa (TEASA), P.O. Box 1751, Johannesburg 2000, T: 11-331-6761, F: 11-331-6783, O: E-mail: ntlharo@icon.co.za.

Federal Council of African Indigenous Churches, PO Box 30938, Braamfontein 2017, 37 Jorissen St, Braamfontein, Johannes, T: 011-403-2664.

Federation of Non-White Pentecostal and Apostolic Missionary Churches, Dreifontein, P.O. Box 114, Groot Marico, Transvaal.

Reformed Independent Churches Association, P.O. Box 19, Iketlo, Johannesburg.

South African Council of Churches, P.O. Box 4921, Johannesburg 2000; Khotso House, 62 Marshall St., Johannesburg 2001, T: 27 11-492 1380, F: 27 11-492 1448.

Southern African Catholic Bishops' Conference (SACBC), P.O. Box 941, Pretoria 0001, Khanya House, 140 Visagie St 0002, Pretoria, T: 012-323-6458, F: 012-326-6218.

United Apostolic Ministers' Council in Africa, PO Box 2392 0001, Pretoria, 337 Central House, 278 Pretoria St 0002, Pretoria, T: 012-323-8585.

Zion Combination Churches of South Africa, P.O. Box 99, Gingindlovu, Zululand.

SOUTH KOREA

Catholic Bishops' Conference of Korea, 85-12, Nung-dong, Kwangjin-gu, Seoul-shi, T: 02-466-0123, F: 02-465-7978.

Korea Evangelical Fellowship (KEF), Kangnam, P.O. Box 1279, Seoul, T: 2-3463-0815, F: 2-573-9865, O: E-mail: mhkim7@unitel.co.kr.

Korea Lausanne Committee, c/o Seoul Presbyterian Church, 737-3 Banpo Dong, Seocho-Ku, Seoul 137-040, T: 82-2-517-7651, 5, F: 82-2-517-9480, O: E-mail: seljyl@unitel.co.kr.

National Council of Churches in Korea, Kwang Wha Moon, P.O. Box 134, Seoul; Christian Bldg., 136-46 Yun-chi-do-dong, Chong-no=ku, Seoul 110-701, T: 82-2-763-8427, F: 82-2-744-6189.

SPAIN

(Catholic) Episcopal Conference of Spain, Plaza de La Seo 5, E-50001 Zaragoza.

Alianza Evangelica Espanola, Apdo. 99023, E-08080 Barcelona, T: 93-431-62-27, F: 93-431-62-27, O: Web site: www.lander.es/-ae.

Spain Lausanne Committee, c/o Bible Society of Spain, Calle Santa Engracia 133, 28003 Madrid, T: 34-1442-5898, F: 34-1442-5855.

Spanish Committee of Cooperation between the Churches, c/. Sol - 210 08201 Sabadell, Espagne.

Spanish Federation of Religious Organizations, c/ Princesa, 3 Dpdo. No 1308, E-28008 Madrid.

SRI LANKA

Bishops' Conference of Sri Lanka, Archbishop's House, Borella, Colombo 8.

Catholic Bishops' Conference of Sri Lanka, 19 Balcombe Place, Cotta Rd., Borella, Colombo 8.

Evangelical Alliance of Sri Lanka, 25 Hospital Road, Dehiwela, Colombo 4, T: 1-724-793, F: 1-735-674, O: E-mail: easl@systec.lk.

National Christian Council of Sri Lanka, 368/6 Bauddhaloka Mawatha, Colombo 7, T: 94 1-69 37 60, F: 94 1-69 78 79.

SUDAN

Sudan Catholic Bishops' Conference (SCBC), P.O. Box 6011, Khartoum.

Sudan Council of Churches, P.O. Box 469, Khartour; Inter-Church House, Street 35, Amarat New Extension, Khartoum, T: 249 11-45-25-44, F: 249 11-45-25-45.

SWAZILAND

Council of Swaziland Churches, P.O. Box 1095, Manzini, T: 268-53-628, 53-931, O: Telex: 2398 WD.

League of African Churches in Swaziland, P.O. Box 122, Manzini.

Swaziland Conference of Churches, P.O. Box 1157, 175 Newane Street, Manzini, T: 55259, F: 53338.

SWEDEN

Christian Council of Sweden, Lästmakargatan 18, Box 1764, S-111 87 Stockholm, T: 46-8-453-6800, F: 46-8-453-6829.

Friends Information Centers & Offices, PO Box 9166, S-102 72 Stockholm, T: 8-66868128, F: 8-6689494.

LWF National Committee in Sweden, c/o Ch of Sweden Secretariat for Intl and Ecumenical Affairs, 751 70 Uppsala, T: 46-18-16-95-00, F: 46-18-16-96-40.

Svenska Evangeliska Alliansen, c/o Lausanne Committee, Box 1623, S-70116 Orebro, T: 19-307753, F: 19-307779, O: E-mail: goran.janzon@nybygget.se.

Sweden Lausanne Committee, Box 1623, S-701 16 Ørebro, T: 46-19-307-753, F: 46-19-307-759, O: E-mail: goran.janzon@nybygget.se.

Swedish Free Church Council, Box 1205, 111 82 Stockholm.

SWITZERLAND

Commission de Travail des Eglises Chrétiennes en Suisse, Sulgenauweg 26, CH-3007 Bern (Arbeitsgemeinschaft Christlicher Kirchen in der Schweiz), T: 031-462511.

Conference des Vicaires generaux et episcopaux de Suisse, 58, Baselstr, 4500 Soleure, 069/232811.

Federation des Eglises protestantes de la Suisse (FEPS), 26, Sulgenauweg, CP 36, 3000 Berne 23, 031/372 25 11.

Schweizerische Evangelische Allianz (SEA), Josefstr. 32, CH-8005 Zurich, T: 1-273-0044, F: 1-273-0066, O: E-mail: info@each.ch, Web site: www.each.ch.

SYRIA

Assemblée de la Hiérarchie Catholique en Syrie, Archeêché Maronite, Rue Azizié, Halab.

National Evangelical Synod of Syria & Lebanon, P.O. Box 2024, Damascus, T: 00963-11-5431766, F: 00963-11-2246262, O: Tlx: 411463 FAMBOK SY.

TAIWAN

Association of Lutheran Churches, Taiwan, 15 Hang Chow South Rd., Section 2, 10608 Taipei, T: 886-2-351-93-17, F: 886-2-391-39-93.

China Evangelical Fellowship, No. 1, Alley 10, Lane 26, Chao An Street, Taipei, T: 2-922-3204.

Chinese Catholic Bishops Conference, 34 Lane 32, Kuangfu S. Rd., Taipei, T: 02-5782355, F: 02-5773874.

National Council of Churches of Taiwan, 7 Lane 183, Ho-Ping E Rd, Section 1, Taipei 106, T: 886-2-351-0087, F: 886-2-351-0118.

TANZANIA

Christian Council of Tanzania, P.O. Box 1454, Dodoma, T: 255 61-21 204, F: 255 61-24 352.

LWF National Committee in Tanzania, c/o Evangelical Lutheran Ch in Tanzania, P.O. Box 3033, Boma Rd., Arusha, T: 255-57-88-55, F: 255-57-88-58.

Tanzania Episcopal Conference (TEC), P.O. Box 2133, Mansfield St., Dar-es-Salaam.

Tanzania Evangelical Fellowship, P.O. Box 1822, Mwanza, T: 68-40334, F: 68-41726.

THAILAND

Bishops' Conference of Thailand, 57 Oriental Ave., Praetham Bldg., Bangrak, Bangkok 10500.

Church of Christ in Thailand, 14 Pramuan Rd, Bangkok, T: 37976,7.

Evangelical Fellowship of Thailand (EFT), 485/20 Silom Road, Bangkok 10500, T: 2-235-2667, F: 2-237-8264, O: E-mail: swkm@samart.co.th.

TOGO

Association des Eglises Chrétiennes, BP 1997, Lomé.

Conference Episcopale du Togo, B.P. 348, Lomé.

TONGA

Tonga Evangelical Union, P.O. Box 367, Nuku'alofa.

Tonga National Council of Churches, P.O. Box 1205, Nuku'alofa, T: 676-21 177, F: 676-22 988.

TRINIDAD & TOBAGO

Christian Council of Trinidad and Tobago, Hayes Court, Hayes Street, Port-of-Spain, T: 1 809-627 0856.

Trinidad and Tobago Council of Evangelical Churches, c/o 52 Frederick St., Port-of-Spain, T: 652-3410, F: 652-5384.

TURKEY

(Catholic) Episcopal Conference of Turkey, Olcek Sokak No 83, TR-80230 Harbiye, Istanbul.

Union of Evangelical Churches, Box 142, Istanbul.

TURKS & CAICOS ISLANDS

Turks and Caicos Inter-Church Committee, The Rectory, Grand Turk.

UGANDA

Evangelical Fellowship of Uganda, P.O. Box 16704, Kampala, T: 41-232561, F: 41-243757.

Uganda Episcopal Conference, P.O. Box 2886, Kampala.

Uganda Jont Christian Council (UJCC), P.O. Box 30154, Nakiivubo-Kampala, T: 256-41-24-42-49, F: 256-41-24-42-51.

UKRAINE

Catholic Episcopal Conference of Ukraine (Byzantine), Sobor Sviatoho Jura, Ploshcha Bohd. Khmelnyckoho 5, 290000 Lviv.

Catholic Episcopal Conference of Ukraine (Latin), c/o Mickiewicza 85, PL-37-600 Lubaczów.

UNITED STATES OF AMERICA (USA)

American Association of Lutheran Churches, c/o Dr. Duane Lindberg, PO Box 17097, Minneapolis, MN 55417.

American Council of Christian Churches, P.O. Box 19, Wallingford, PA 19086, T: 610-566-8154.

Friends Contact Information, PO Box 2326, Richmond, IN 47375, T: 317-874-1991.

LWF National Committee in USA, c/o Evangelical Lutheran Ch in America, Dept. for Ecumenical Affairs, 8765 West Higgins Rd., Chicago, IL 60631-4192, T: 1-312/380-2615, F: 1-312-380-2977.

National Association of State Catholic Conferences, 1312 Massachusetts Av, NW, Washington, DC 20005.

National Association of Evangelicals (NAE), 450 E. Gundersen Dr., Carol Stream, IL 60189, T: 630-665-0500, F: 630-665-8575, O: E-mail: nae@nae.net, Web. site: www.nae.net.

National Black Evangelical Association (NBAE), P.O. Box 193, Pasadena, CA 91101.

National Committee of the Lutheran World Federation, 315 Park Ave., South, New York, NY 10010, T: 212-677-3950.

National Conference of Catholic Bishops (NCCB), 1312 Massachusetts Ave., N.W., Washington, DC 20005, T: 202-659-6600.

National Council of the Churches of Christ in the USA, 475 Riverside Dr., Room 880, New York, NY 10115-0050, T: 1-212/870 2141, F: 1-212/870 2817.

National Office for Black Catholics, 3025 Fourth St., N.E., Washington, D.C. 20017.

United States Catholic Conference, 3211 Fourth St., N.E., Washington, D.C. 20017.

United States Lausanne Committee, c/o Mission America, 901 East 78th St., Minneapolis, MN 55420, T: 760-324-5889, F: 1-760-836-9481, O: E-mail: 105020.3522@compuserve.com.

Willow Creek Association, P.O. Box 3188, Oklahoma City, OK 73157, T: 847-765-0070, F: 847-765-5046.

URUGUAY

Asociación Cristiana de Iglésias Evangélicas de la Rep. (ACIERU), Estero Bellaco 2580, 11600 Montevideo, T: 2-80-2594, F: 2-92-8155.

Conferencia Episcopal de Uruguay, Avenida Uruguay 1319, 11100 Montevideo, T: 598-2-98-1975, F: 598-2-91-1802, O: Also tel: 90-2642.

Federation of Evangelical Churches of Uruguay, Av. 8 de Octubre 3324, 11.600 Montevideo, T: 598 2-47 3316, F: 598 2-472 181.

VANUATU

Vanuatu Christian Council, P.O. Box 150, Port Vila, T: 678/26.480.

VENEZUELA

Conferencia Episcopal de Venezuela, Prolongación Av. Páez a 200 mts. antes de UCAB-Frente Igl. J.P. II, Urbanización Montalbán, Apartado 4897-Zona Postal 1010-A, Caracas, T: 58-2-442-2250, F: 58-2-442-3562, O: Also tel: 442-9322, 442-3562.

Consejo Evangélico de Venezuela, Apartado Postal 61152, Caracas 1060-A, T: 2-263-9156, F: 2-264-1268.

VIET NAM

Conference Episcopale du Viêtnam, Toa Giam Muc, B.P. 11, 70 Hung Vuong, Xuân Lôc, Dong Noi.

Evangelical Fellowship of Viet-Nam, 30 Huynh Quang Tien, HO Chi Minh Ville.

US VIRGIN ISLANDS

St. Croix Evangelical Ministerial Association, P.O. Box 4280, Kingshill P.O., St. Croix, T: 778-7942, F: 773-5728.

YUGOSLAVIA

Ecumenical Council of Churches in Yugoslavia, 7 Juli No. 5, Fah 182, 110 01 Beograd, T: 381-11-635-699.

Serbian Evangelical Alliance (SEA), Simina 8, YU-11000 Beograd, T: 11-622-642, F: 11-104-831, O: E-mail: chreview@eunet.yu.

ZAMBIA

Apostles Council of Churches, P.O. Box 2147, Ndola.

Association of Independent Churches, c/o Holy Gospel Church, P.O. Box 2116, Lusaka.

Christian Council of Zambia, P.O. Box 30315, Lusaka; Church House, Cairo Road, Lusaka, T: 260 1-229 551, F: 260 1-224 308.

Evangelical Fellowship of Zambia (EFZ), P.O. Box 33862, Lusaka 10101, T: 1-233-243, F: 1-281-115, O: E-mail: evafeza@zamnet.zm.

United Spiritual Independent Churches Council of Zambia, P.O. Box 90147, Luanshya.

Zambian Anglican Council, P.O. Box 8100, Lusaka.

ZIMBABWE

African Independent Churches' Conference (AICC), 22 Fitzgerald Av, P.O. Box 127, Fort Victoria, T: 2787.

Evangelical Fellowship of Zimbabwe, EFZ, P.O. Box 2803, Bulawayo, T: 9-74922, F: 9-68179, O: E-mail: evanfel@acacia.samara.co.z.

Friends Information Centers & Offices, 3 Vincent Ave, Belvedere, Harare, T: 25883, O: 302219.

Zimbabwe Catholic Bishops' Conference (ZCBC), P.O. Box 8135, Causeway, Harare.

Zimbabwe Council of Churches, 128 Victoria St., P.O. Box 3566, Harare, T: 263-4-791208, F: 263-4-790100, O: Telex: 6243 OIK ZW.

25

Correspondence schools & ministries

Christian mass educational courses with curriculum and individual feedback sent by mail (post); instruction by radio/TV/satellite/video/computer with enrollment and local instructors or postal feedback; radio (radiophonic) schools, TV schools (teleschools, telecentres), video- or audio-cassette instruction or training by mail; radio literacy courses.

ALGERIA
Cercles Bibliques, Centre Diocésain, Section Théologie, 5 Chemin des Glycines, El Djezair.

ANGOLA
Escola Biblica de Emaus (Emmaus BCC Centre), CP 107, Luso.
Voice of Prophecy, Caixa Postal 611, Huambo.

ARGENTINA
Argentina, Paraguay and Uruguay Bible Correspondence School, Echeverria 1452, 1602 Florida, Buenos Aires.
Asociación Latinoamericana de Educación Radiofónica (ALER), Buenos Aires.
Centro de Promoción Humana del Nordeste (CEPRHU), Reconquista, Prov de Santa Fe.
Instituto de Cultura Popular (INCUPO), Casilla 30, Reconquista, Prov de Santa Fe.

AUSTRALIA
Living Word Correspondence Courses, World Outreach, P.O. Box 10, Tabulam, NSW 2470; P.O. Box 105, Carlingford, NSW 2118.
Postal Sunday School, 6 Orchid St, Guildford, NSW.
Voice of Melody and Bible School of the Air, 25 Ray Rd., Epping, NSW.

AUSTRIA
Biblische Ausbildlung am Ort (BAO), Hauersteigstrasse 61, 3003 Gablitz, T: 02231-23 25.
Institut Fernkur für theologische Bildung (Institute for Theological Education by Correspondence), Stephansplatz 3/III, 1010 Wien, T: 0222-515 52 0.
Light of Life BCC Centre, Beckmanngasse 66/48, Wien 15.
Voice of Hope, Nussdorferstrasse 5, 1090 Vienna, T: 02 22-3199300.

BAHAMAS
Emmaus BCC Center, P.O. Box 436, Marsh Harbour, Abaco.
Radio Bible School, P.O. Box N-356, Nassau.

BANGLADESH
Bangladesh BCC Centre, Principal, P.O. Manikganj, Dacca District.
Voice of Prophecy Correspondence School, B.P.O. Box 80, Khaka 1000.

BARBADOS
Light of Life BCC Centre, Ebenezer Manse, St Philip 2.
Radio Bible School, P.O. Box 223, Bridgetown.

BELGIUM
Le Monde à Venir, BP 31, B-6000 Charleroi.
Voice of Hope, Dreef 1, 3600 Genk,, T: 089-35-60-08.

BELIZE
Radio Bible School, P.O. Box 90, Belize City.

BERMUDA
Emmaus BCC Centre, P.O. Box 659, Hamilton.

BOLIVIA
Acción Cultural Loyola (ACLO), Casilla 155, Sucre, T: 2230.
Centro Teórico de Capacitación de Adultos (CETCAR), Emisoras Bolivia, Calle Potosí 421, Casilla 525, Oruro, T: 52110.
Departamento de Investigación y Promoción Social San Rafael, Radio San Rafael, Casilla 546, Cochabamba, T: 4495.
Escuelas Radiofónicas de Bolivia (ERBOL), Oficina de MCS, Casilla 4064, La Paz, T: 41920.
Escuelas Radiofónicas de Radioemisoras Juan XXIII, Vicariato de Chiquitos, Correo Central, San Ignacio de Velasco.
Escuelas Radiofónicas Fides, Radio Fides, Casilla 5782, La Paz, T: 24422.
Escuelas Radiofónicas Pío XII, Radio Pío XII, Casillo 434, Oruro.
Escuelas Radiofónicas San Gabriel, Radio San Gabriel, Casilla 4792, Peñas, La Paz.
Escuelas Radiofónicas San Miguel, Radio San Miguel, Casilla 9, Riberalta-Beni.
Estudios Biblicos per Correspondencia, Cajón 514, Cochabamba.

BRAZIL
Brazil Bible Correspondence School, Rua da Matriz RJ.
Escolas Radiofônicas, Uruguaiana, RS.
Movimento de Educação de Base (MEB), Rua São Clemente 385, ZC-02 Rio de Janeiro, GB.
Sistema Educativo Radiofônico de Bragança (SERB), Av Barão do Rio Branco s/n, Bragança (Guamá), PA.
Sistema Radioeducativo de Santarém (SIRESEME), Trav dos Mártires s/n, Santarém, PA.

BRITAIN (UK OF GB & NI)
BCC Department, Bientôt (Soon Magazine), 49 Offington Av, Worthing, West Sussex.
Christian Witness, Slough Gospel Tabernacle, Pitts Rd, Slough, Bucks.
Sunday School by Post, Sleepy Hollow, Swinmore, Ledbury, Herefordshire, T: Trumpet 313.
Voice of Prophecy, Stanborough Park, Watford, Herts. WD2 6JP.
World Outreach, Living Word Correspondence Courses, 13 Wollaston Rd, Dorchester, Dorset DT1 1EH.

BURUNDI
Light of Life BCC Centre, PO Box 122, Bujumbura.

CANADA
Canadian Pentecostal Correspondence College, P.O. Box 700, Abbotsford, BC V2S 6R7, T: 604-853-5352.
Latin American Mission, BCC Dept., Box 33, Station F, Toronto 5, Ontario.
Light of Life, Ukrainian Missionary & Bible Society, P.O. Box 126, Saskatoon, Saskatchewan.
Link School of Ministry, 3 Robert Speck Pkwy., Suite 900, Mississauga, ON L4Z 2G5, T: 905-452-7058, O: 905-452-1151 or 905-279-7528.
Salvation Army Bible Studies, Education Dept, 37 Dundas St E, Toronto 2, Ontario.

CAYMAN ISLANDS
Radio Bible School, P.O. Box 515, Georgetown.

CHAD
Emmaus BCC Centre, Mission Evangélique, Doba, par Moundou.

CHILE
Escuelas Radiofónicas Santa Clara, Radio La Voz de la Costa, Casilla 5, Osorno.
Fundación Radio Escuela para el Desarrollo Rural (La Voz de la Costa), Misión de Rahue, Casilla Postal 5-0, Osorno, T: 3518.
Instituto Nacional de Acción Poblacional (INAP), Príncipe de Gales 87, Casilla 13508, Correo 15, Santiago.
Pontificia Universidad de Chile, Avda Bernardo O'Higgins 340, Casilla 114D, Santiago de Chile.
Secretariado de Communicación Social (SEDECOS), Cienfuegos 15, CP 9990, Santiago 1, T: 713217.

CHINA
Living Word BCC, World Outreach, Dir, 9th Floor, 102 Macdonnell Rd, PO Box 13448, GPO, Hong Kong.
Voice of Prophecy Correspondence School, P.O. Box 95186, Kowloon, Hong Kong.

COLOMBIA
Acción Cultural Popular (ACPO), Calle 20, No 9-45, Apdo Aéreo 7170, Bogotá, DE, T: 420543.
Cursos de Correspondencia, Emmaus BCC Centre, Apdo Aéreo 14818, Bogotá 1, DE.
Escuela Radiopostal, Apartado 37815, Bogota.

CONGO-ZAIRE
Ndinga ya Moto Ecole Biblique Emmaus, AMBM, BP 4714, Kinshasa II.

COSTA RICA
Curso de Correspondencia, Apdo 1307, San José.
Escuela Radiopostal, Apartado 1946, San Jose.

CROATIA
Dopisna Biblijska Skola, P.P. 925, 41001 Zagreb.

CYPRUS
SDA Bible Correspondence School, 42 Gladstone Street, Nicosia; P.O. Box 1984 and 2043, Nicosia, T: 2-455008.
SDA Middle East Centre for Correspondence Studies, P.O. Box 1984, Nicosia.

DENMARK
Korrespondanceskolen, Fuglebakkevej 1A, 8210 Aarhus V, T: 86-159200.

DOMINICA
Emmaus BCC Centre, P.O. Box 103, Roseau.

DOMINICAN REPUBLIC
Escuela Radiopostal, Apartado 1500, Santo Domingo.
Radio ABC Radio Schools, Arzobispado de Santo Domingo, Casilla 186, Santo Domingo, T: 99203.
Radio Santa María, Casa Curial, Santo Cerro, La Vega.

ECUADOR
Academia Christiana del Aire, Casilla 691, Quito.
Curso Bíblico por Correspondencia Emmaus, Boyaca No. 1104 y P. Icaza, Casilla 7824, Guayaquil, T: 385-353.
Curso por Correspondencia para Ninos, Ave. 10 de Agosto No. 50-70, Quito.
Cursos Biblico-Teologicos por Correspondencia, Villalengua No. 320, Casilla 691, Quito, T: 241-550.
Cursos por Correspondencia La Biblia Dice, Ave. 10 de Agosto No. 11635, Quito, T: 531-592.
Educacion Teologica, Ave. 10 de Agosto No. 50-70, Quito.
Seminario Biblico por Correspondencia (Quichua), Illuchi, Casilla 208, Quito.

EL SALVADOR
Escuela Radiopostal, Apartado 2150 CG, San Salvador.
Escuelas Radiofónicas de El Salvador, Radio YSAX, 2a Av Sur 102, Altos, San Salvador, T: 218011,2.

ETHIOPIA
Light of Life BCC Centre, Emmaus Centre, SIM, Box 127, Addis Abeba.

FAEROE ISLANDS
Emmaus BCC Centre, Tórshavn.

FIJI
Living Word Correspondence Courses, World Outreach, P.O. Box 29, Tavua, Fiji.

FINLAND
Kirjeopisto Codex, Jalkarannantie 2 A 10, 15110 Lahti, T: 358-18-826-375.

FRANCE
Bible Correspondence School, BP 7, 77350 Le Mee sur Seine, France, T: 1-64-09-48-92, F: 1-64-52-60-03.
Cours Bibliques par Correspondance, Centre de Formation Chrétienne, 8 Villa du Parc Montsouris F-75 Paris. (Evangelical Alliance).
Etudes Agricoles par Correspondance, 271 Av de Grande-Bretagne, F-31 Toulouse 03 (Haute Garonne), T: 61423387.
Formation Oecuménique Interconfessionelle (FOI), 2 Place Gailleton, F-69002 Lyon.
L'Eau Vive BCC Department, Principal, 63 Rue St Gabriel, 51 Lille.
La Chaine (Association Radiophonique pour l'Eglise du Silence), BP 79, F-92405 Courbevoie.
Les Cours Legendre, 5 Blvd Morland, Paris 4 (Correspondence), T: 272-3365, 3147.
Voice of Prophecy, 63 Rue du Faubourg Poissonniere 75009 Paris, T: 1-45 23 31 36.

FRENCH GUIANA
Emmaus BCC Centre, BP 127, Cayenne.
Radio Bible School, Boite Postal 169, Cayenne.

GERMANY
International Institute for Bible Studies, An der Ihle 19, 39291 Friedensau bei Burg/Sachse-Anhalt, T: 3921-78122 (Burg).
Servicio Radiofónico para Latina América (SERPAL), Bonner Platz 1/III, D-8000 München 23, T: 3001316.

GHANA
BCC Department, WEC Mission, PO Box 5, Kpandai, via Yendi.
Radio Bible School, Emmaus BCC Centre, P.O. Box 1958, Kumasi.

GREECE
Bible Correspondence School, Keramikou 18, 10437 Athens, T: 1-52-24-962, F: 1-52-33-013.
Voice of Hope, Keramikou 18, 10437 Athens.

GRENADA
Emmaus BCC Centre, P.O. Box 68, St George's.

GUADELOUPE
Radio Bible School, P.O. Box 19, Pointe-a-Pitre.

GUATEMALA
Escuela Radiopostal, Apartado 355, Guatemala City.
Escuelas Radiofónicas, Radio Chortis, Jocotan, Dpto Chiquimula.
Escuelas Radiofónicas La Voz del Hogar, 13 Calle 2-52, Zona 1, Guatemala City, T: 85592.
Federación Guatemalteca de Escuelas Radiofónicas (FGER), Edificio Recinos, 8a Calle 11-13, Z 1 of 303; 2a Calle, 4-80, Zona 9, Apdo Postal 13-29 Guatemala City, T: 20650 ext 50, 67982.

GUYANA
Radio Bible School, Box 10191, Georgetown.

HAITI
Radio Bible School, P.O. Box 1325, Port-au-Prince.

HONDURAS
Escuela Radiopostal, Apartado 121, Tegucigalpa.
Escuelas Radiofónicas Suyapa y Acción Cultural Popular Hondureña, Av República de Chile 516, Barrio San Rafaél, Apdo Postal C-24, Tegucigalpa, DC. (RC), T: 21401.

HUNGARY
Levelezo Biblia Iskola, Szekely Bertalan u. 13, 1062 Budapest.

ICELAND
Bible Correspondence School, P.O. Box 60, 230 Keflavik, T: 354-2-15220.
Light of Life BCC Centre, Asvallagata 13, Box 243, Reykjavik.

INDIA
Al-Bashir Bible Correspondence School, P.O. Box 13, Patel Nagar, New Delhi 110008.
Amar Jyoti India, P. O. Box 27, Makerbag, Cuttack, Orissa 753001.
Bible Correspondence School, 62, Akbar Sahib Street, Triplicane, Madras, Tamil Nadu 600005.
CACS Bible Correspondence Course, 21, Eldam Road, Teynampet, Madras, Tamil Nadu 600018.
Christu Jeevita Charitra, Catholic Centre, Vijayawada, Andhra Pradesh 520010.
Emmanuel Bible Institute, Tarikere Tk., Lakkavalli, Karnataka 577128.
Good News Correspondence School, 'Good News', Akkulam Road, Trivandrum, Kerala 695031.
Gurmukhi Bible Correspondence Course Centre, Dhariwal, Gurdaspur, Punjab 143521.
International Correspondence Institute, 15, Cockburn Road, Bangalore, Karnataka 560051.
International Correspondence Centre, Christian Faith Centre, 610 Sion-Koliwada, Chembur, Bombay, Maharashtra 400071.
International Correspondence Institute University, L-16, South Extension-II, New Delhi 110049.
Jeevan Deepika, The Bible Correspondence Institute, C/o. Balasore Tech. School, Mission Boy's Compound, Balasore, Orissa 756001.
Jiwan Jyoti Bible Correspondence Centre, A-28, Rajouri Garden, P. O. Box 6521, New Delhi 110027.
Light of Life Bible Correspondence School, P. O. Box 2, Mission Compound, Nasrapur, Maharashtra 412213.
Nepali BCC Centre, PO Box 39, Ranchi 1, Bihar.
Quickly Ministries, 11/5, H. A. U. Campus, Hissar, Haryana 125004.
Soon Bible Correspondence, C/o The Editor, Soon, P. O. Box 701, Bangalore, Karnataka 560001.
TEAM Jiwan Jyoti (Correspondence Course), 65, Lalitpur Road, Jhansi, Uttar Pradesh 284001.
Vishwa Vani (Bible Correspondence Course), Good News Centre, Arts College P. O., Calicut, Kerala 673018.
Voice of Prophecy, Mizo Conference Of Seventh-Day Adventists, Seventh Day Tlang, Aizawl, Mizoram 796009.
Voice of Prophecy Correspondence School, Maninagar, Ahmedabad 380008.
Way of Truth Bible Correspondence School, P. O. Box 26, Baramati, Maharashtra 413102.

INDONESIA
Voice of Prophecy Bible Correspondence School, Kotak Pos 2120, Jakarta 10002.
Voice of Prophecy Bible Correspondence School, P.O. Box 1303, Manado 95013, Sulawesi Utara.

IRAN
SDA Bible Correspondence School, Tehran Adventist Center, 501 Mossadegh Avenue, Tehran, T: 64-4525.

IRAQ
SDA Bible Correspondence School, P.O. Box 1290, Baghdad, T: 8878865.

IRELAND
Emmaus BCC Centre, 6 Ashdale Park, South Douglas Rd, Cork.
ICI (International Correspondence Institute), 6 Queens Park, Monkstown, Blackrock, Co Dublin, T: 353-01 280 3227.
National Bible Study Club, Lower Glenageary Road, Dun Laoghaire, Co Dublin.

ISRAEL
Bible Correspondence School, P.O. Box 19329, Jerusalem.

ITALY
Centro Cattolico Radiofonico (CCR), Ente dello Spettacolo, Via della Conciliazione 2c, I-00193 Roma, T: 561775, 564132.
Corso Biblico per Corrispondenza, Centro di Cultura Biblica 'La Voce della Speranza' (The Voice of Hope), Lungotevere Michelangelo 7, I-00192 Roma.
Corso Biblico Superiore 'La Via della Salvezza', (The Way of Salvation), Ecumenical Centre 'Ut unum sint', Via Antonino Pio 75, I-00145 Roma. (RC; Sisters of St Paul).
Corso Quadriennale, Istituto di Teologia per Corrispondenza, Ecumenical Centre 'Ut unum sint', Via Antonio Pio 75, I-00145 Roma.
Voice of Hope, Lungotevere Michelangelo 7, 00192 Rome.
Way of Life, Crociata dell'Evangelo per Ogni Casa, Via Palestro 30, I-00185 Roma.

IVORY COAST
Light of Life BCC Centre, Mission Protestante, BP 585, Bouaké.

JAMAICA
Emmaus BCC Centre, Jamaica Bible School, Box 141, Manelville.
Radio Bible School, P.O. Box 22, Mandeville.

JAPAN
Good Shepherd Movement, Kawaramchi-Sanjo, Kyoto 604 (Correspondence courses in religion on national radio/TV; Maryknoll).
Voice of Prophecy Bible Correspondence School, 846 Kamikawai-cho, Asahi-ku, Yokohama 241.

JORDAN
SDA Bible Correspondence School, P.O. Box 2404, Amman, T: 625345.

KENYA
Correspondence Course Department, Nairobi Pentecostal Bible College, Garden Estate, Thika Rd, PO Box 30202, Nairobi. (Pentecostal; 7,400 enrolled), T: Ruaraka 2391.
Kenya: Voice of Prophecy Correspondence School, P.O. Box 43224, Nairobi; Karua, Redhill Road, Nairobi.
Living Word Correspondence Courses, World Outreach, PO Box 30791, Nairobi.

LEBANON
BCC, Middle East Lutheran Ministry, PO 2496, Bayrut.
Light of Life BCC Centre, PO Box 3276, Bayrut.
SDA Bible Correspondence School, Sabtieh Jdeidet El Matn, P.O. Box 91028.

LIBERIA
Emmaus BCC Centre, ELWA, PO Box 192, Monrovia.

MACEDONIA
Dopisna Biblijska Skola, P.P. 215, 91001 Skopie.

MADAGASCAR
Emmaus BCC Centre, BP 351, Tananarive.

MALAWI
Emmaus BCC Centre, P.O. Box 688, Blantyre.
Malawi: Voice of Prophecy Bible School, P.O. Box

444, Blantyre.

MALAYSIA
Light of Life BCC Centre, North Borneo Mission, Principal, Box 108, Kuching, Sarawak.

MARTINIQUE
Radio Bible School, P.O. Box 580, Fort-de-France.

MEXICO
Asociación Nacional de Radio-escuelas, ACM, Serapio Rendon 43, México 4, DF.
El Camino de la Vida Cursos por Correspondencia, Apdo 1608, Guadalajara, Jalisco.
Escuela Radiopostal, Apartado 12-750, Mexico D.F. 03020.
Escuelas Radiofónicas de la Tarahumara, Sisoguichi, Chita.
Estudios Biblicos por Correspondencia, Aniceto Ortega No 841-1, z12, México, DF, T: 750407.
Instituto Bíblico por Correspondencia, Apdo 3, Pob Anahuac, Tamps.
Sistema Educativo Radiofónico de México (SER), México, DF.

MOROCCO
BCC Department, Gospel Missionary Union, Principal, BP 10, Khemisset.

MOZAMBIQUE
Bible Correspondence School, Caixa Postal 1541, Maputo.

MYANMAR
Voice of Prophecy Corressppondence School, Post Box 681, Yangon 11191.

NEPAL
Voice of Prophecy Correspondence School, P.O. Box 4373, Kathmandu.

NETHERLANDS
Esda Instituut, Pr. Alexanderweg 1c, Huis ter Heide (Gem. Zeist), T: 3404-31509.

NETHERLANDS ANTILLES
Radio Bible School, P.O. Box 300, Curacao.

NEW ZEALAND
Asociación Cultural Nicaraguense, Box 607, Managua, DN.
Bible Correspondence School, P.O. Box 76-281, Manukau City.
Escuelas Radiofónicas de Nicaragua, c/o Radio Católica, Apdo 11.30, Managua, T: 72260.
Light of Life BCC Centre, United Maori Mission, 32 Shackleton Rd, Mt Eden, Auckland SE.

NICARAGUA
Asociación Cultural Nicaraguense, Box 607, Managua, DN.
Escuela Radiopostal, Apartado 92, Managua.
Escuelas Radiofónicas de Nicaragua, c/o Radio Católica, Apdo 11.30, Managua, T: 72260.

NIGER
Emmaus BCC Centre, BP 620, Niamey.

NIGERIA
Islam in Africa Project Council, Study Centre for Islam and Christianity, 5 Awosika Av, Bodija, Ibadan.
Light of Life BCC School, Principal, UMS, Jebba.

NORWAY
Norsk Bibelinstitutt, Akersgata 74, 0180 Oslo, T: 22-20-81-05.

PAKISTAN
BCC School, Principal, 214-B Chandni Chowk, Satellite Town, P.O. Box 104, Rawalpindi.
Bible Correspondence School, Principal, c/o Indus Christian Fellowship, Baker Bldg., Larkana.
Pakistan BCC School, Principal, Jail Rd, Campbellpur.
Pakistan Bible Correspondence School (PBCS), 33-A People's Colony, PO Box 117, Lyallpur.
Voice of Prophecy Correspondence School, P.O. Box 32, Lahore.

PANAMA
Escuela Radiopostal, Apartado 3244, Panama City 3.

PAPUA NEW GUINEA
Living Word Correspondence Courses, World Outreach, P.O. Box 67, Goroka.

PARAGUAY
Centro Experimental de TV Educativa (CETE), Universidad Católica, Asunción.

PERU
Argentina, Paraguay and Uruguay Bible Correspondence School, Casilla 560, Lima 100.
Escuelas Radiofónicas del Perú, Radio Onda Azul, Casilla 112, Puno.
Radio San José, Apdo 216, Iquitos.
Tele-Escuela Popular Americana (TEPA), Calle Don Bosco 129, Casilla 891, Arequipa, T: 4786.

PHILIPPINES
Back to the Bible, Light of Life BCC Center, Box 1750, Manila.
Good News BCC Centre, P.O. Box 1417, Manila.
Voice of Prophecy Bible Correspondence School, P.O. Box 8, 1099 Manila.

POLAND
Korespondencyiny Kurs Biblijny, Kochanowskiego 2, 43-300 Bielsko-Biala, T: 239-32.
Miedzynarodowny Instytut Korespondencyjny, Oddzial na Polske, ul Olgierda 31, PL-81-534 Gydnia.

PORTUGAL
A Nova Pessoa (Baptista), Centro Baptista de Comunicções, Rua Marechal Gomes da Costa, 3 - 2., 2745 Queluz, T: 01-436 49 70.
Centro Bíblico 'O Caminho da Vida', Apartado 512, Carcavelos, 2777 Parede Codex.
Crescendo Com Deus (Interdenominacional), Rua Fontainhas das Pias, Lote 83, 1675 Caneças, T: 01-981 16 31, F: 01-981 14 31.
Curso Bíblico por Correspondência Elementar (Interdenominacional), Apartado 1028 Areosa, 4437 Rio Tinto Codex, T: 02-902 23 99.
Cursos Bíblicos por Correspondência (Acção Bíblica), Rua Pé da Cruz, 10, 8000 Faro, T: 089-82 23 87.
Ensinamentos Básicos da Bíblia (Baptista), Centro Baptista de Comunicações, Rua Marechal Gomes da Costa, 3 - 2., 2745 Queluz; Apartado 85-2746 Queluz Codex, T: 01-436 49 70.
Escola Bíblica por Correspondência (Interdenominacional), Apartado 4003, 2700 Amadora, T: 01-492 25 72.
O Caminho Para a Vida (Interdenominacional), Rua D. Frei Caetano Brandão, 200-202, 4700 Braga; Apartado 2294-4700 Braga Codex, T: 053-2 97 85.
Voice of Hope, Rua Ilha Terceira 3, 3ß, 1000 Lisbon.

PUERTO RICO
Emmaus BCC Centre, P.O. Box 10913, Caparra Heights, Puerto Rico 00922.
Escuela Radiopostal, P.O. Box 1629, Mayaguez 00709.
Estudios Béblicos del Caribe, 1409 Ponce de Leon, 4o Andar, San Juan, P.R. 00907, T: 787-724-2727, F: 787-722-5395, O: E-mail: 104743.1413@compuserve.com.

RUSSIA
ECB Correspondence Courses, AUCECB, P.O. Box 520, Moskva.

RWANDA
Université Radiophonique de Gitarama, BP 13, Gitarama.

SIERRA LEONE
Emmaus BCC Centre, c/o Christian Literature Crusade, PO Box 1465, Freetown.

SINGAPORE
Living Word BCC, Christian Literature Centre, PO Box 3038, Singapore 1.
Voice of Prophecy Bible Correspondence School, P.O. Box 123, Singapore 9134.

SLOVENIA
Dopisna Biblijska Skola, P.P. 22, 61105 Ljubjana.

SOUTH AFRICA
AICA Theological Correspondence Course, 603 Pharmacy House, 80 Jorissen St, Braamfontein, Johannesburg.
Bible Way Correspondence School, PO Box 50, Roodepoort 1725.
Byelkor, PO Box 5, Wellington 7655, Bybel-gebou, Kerk St, Wellington, T: 02211-3-3851, F: 02211-3-3864.
Christ Gospel Bible Institute, PO Box 15492, Lynn East, Pretoria 0039.
Emmaus Bible School, PO Box 1999, Northcliff 2115, T: 011-781-2035.
ICI University, PO Box 952, Roodepoort, 1725, T: 011-760-1549, F: 011-760-1560.
International Theological Institute, PO Box X45, Halfway House 1685, T: 011-315-0648, F: 011-805-1806.
Johannesburg Correspondence Bible Studies, PO Box 97, Roodepoort 1725, 16 Mare St. Roodepoort, T: 011-763-4216, F: 011-763-6187.
Light for Life Correspondence Bible Courses, PO Box 73, Parow 7500, 111 Chamberlain St, Parow, Cape Town, T: 021-92-7569.
Nehemiah Bible Institute, PO Box 841, Wellington 7655, 69 Church St, Wellington, T: 02211-3-4033, F: 02211-3-3864.
RICCOR, PO Box 37, Grootviel2420, T: 01506-9-0051.
University of South Africa, Faculty of Theology & Religious Studies, PO Box 392, Pretoria 0001, Muckleneuk Ridge, Pretoria, T: 012-429-4567, F: 012-429-3332.
Vista University, Dept for Biblical Studies, P/Bag X641, Pretoria 0001, T: 021-322-1303, F: 021-322-3243.
Voice of Prophecy Bible School, P.O. Box 88, Cape Town 8000.
Word of God Christian College, PO Box 337, Winburg 9420, 51b Voortrekker St, Winburg.

SOUTH KOREA
Living Word Correspondence Courses, World Outreach, IPO Box 1442, Soul.
Voice of Prophecy Bible Correspondence School, Chung Ryang P.O. Box 110, Seoul 130-650.

SPAIN
Cursos Bíblicos por Corresp. Multilingües, 12005 Apdo 1.022, Castellón de La Plana, T: 20-76-07.
Cursos Bíblicos Por Correspondencia, 46017 Augustina de Aragón, 53, 1°, Valencia, T: 378-42-62.
Cursos Cristianos Por Correspondencia, Apdo 2137 Suc 2ª, 03500 Benidorm, Alicante.
Evang. por Correo, B. de los Rios, s/n. 'Al Andalus', Bl. 1 -1° C., La Línea, 11300 Cádiz, T: 10-42-67.
Gospel Missionary Union, Apdo 570, Malaga.
Voice of Hope, Cuevas, 23, 28039 Madrid.

SRI LANKA
Voice of Prophecy Bible Correspondence School, Post Box 905, Colombo 3.

SUDAN
Emmaus BCC Centre, American Mission, PO Box 112, Was Mendani.

SURINAME
Radio Bible School, Box 1909, Paramaribo.

SWAZILAND
BCC Department, Every Home Crusade, Principal, Box 379, Mbabane.

SWEDEN
Brevskolan, Hoppets Rost, Box 10042, 80010 Gavle, T: 46-26-112860, 112870.
Emmaus BCC Centre, Kindbovagen 16, Mölnlycke.

SWITZERLAND
Bible Correspondence School, Case Postale 453, 1020 Renens 1.
Biblischer Fernkurs (Ev Reformed Church), Apollos Verlag, Teufen/AR.
Cours Bibliques par Correspondance, Evangile et Culture, 7 Chemin des Cedres, Lausanne.

TAIWAN
Living World Bible Correspondence School, c/o Overseas Radio & Television, Inc, P.O. Box 37003, Taipei.
Voice of Prophecy Bible Correspondence School, 195 Chung Hwa Road, Section 2, Taichung, Taiwan 404.

TANZANIA
Acts of the Apostles, Diocese of Central Tanzania, St Philip's College, Kongwa.
Life of Jesus (Swahili), Mennonite Church, PO Box 7, Musoma.
Read the New Testament, Tarime Bible School, PO Box 26, Tarime.
Word of Life BCC, PO Box 2572, Dar es Salaam.

THAILAND
Lamp of Thailand (CCT), PO Box 111, Chieng Mai.
Light of Life BCC Centres, 201 Hicks Lane, North Sathorn Rd, Bangkok.
Living Word BCC School, World Outreach Literature Centre, New Life Centre, GPO Box 1864, Bangkok.
Voice of Prophecy Bible Correspondence School, P.O. Box 234, Prakanong, Bangkok 10110.

TRINIDAD & TOBAGO
BCC Centre, Principal, 28 Av Bap Djebid, Tunis.
Radio Bible School, Box 66, Port-of-Spain.
TEAM, Bible Correspondence Department, PO Box 77, Port of Spain, Trinidad.

TURKEY
SDA Bible Correspondence School, 14 Saray Arkasi, Ayazpasa, Taksim, Istanbul, T: 149-14-48.

UGANDA
Emmaus BCC Centre, PO Box 14180, Mengo, Kampala.

UNITED STATES OF AMERICA (USA)
Alaska Radio Mission of Northern Alaska, Box 101, Nome, AK 99762.
Bethel Series, Adult Christian Education Foundation, 313 Price Place, Box 5305, Madison, WI 53705.
Bible Study Hour Cassettes, 1617 Spruce St, Philadelphia, PA 19103.
Capuchin Correspondence Course, 4121 Harewood Rd, NE, Washington, DC 20017.
CCD Correspondence Courses for Catechists and Parent-Educators, 424 N Broadway, Wichita, KS 67202.
Christian Outreach BCC Centre, Box 115, Huntingdon Valley, PA 19006.
Confraternity of Christian Doctrine Course, PO Box 179, Aledo, IL 61231.
Emmaus BCC Center, PO Box 2244, Charlotte Amalie, St. Thomas, VI 00802.
Emmaus Bible School, Home Study Division, 156 North Oak Park Av, Oak Park, IL 60301.
Good Shepherd Ministries, O: E-mail: goodshepherdmin@compuserve.com.
Home Bible Studies, Mennonite Broadcasting, Harrisonburg, VA 22801.
Home Study Service, Religious Information Bureau, 3473 South Grand, St Louis, MO.
ICI University, 6300 N. Belt Line Road, Irving, TX 75063, T: 972-751-1111, F: 972-714-8185, O: E-mail: info@ici.edu, Web site: www.ici.edu.
International Correspondence Institute, 1445 Boonville Av, Springfield, MO 65802.
International Institute, 5661 N Northcott Av, Chicago, IL 60631; P.O. Box 66053, Chicago, IL 60666, T: 312-823-1852.
International Institute for Christian Studies (IICS), P.O. Box 12147, Overland Park, KS 66282, T: 913-962-4422, F: 913-962-1912, O: E-mail: IICS@compuserve.com, Web site: www.iics.com.
St. Stephen's Course of Studies in Orthodox Theology, 358 Mountain Road, Englewood, NJ 07631.
University Correspondence Study, Tennessee School of Religion, University of Tennessee, Knoxville, TN 37916.
Voice of Prophecy, 1500 East Chevy Chase Drive, PO Box 1519, Glendale, CA 91206, T: 213-245-2349.
World to Come, Ambassador College, PO Box 111, Pasadena, CA 91123.

URUGUAY
Asociación pro Emisiones Culturales (APEC), Agraciada 2974, Montevideo, T: 593778.

VENEZUELA
Acción Cultural Popular Venezolana (ACPOVEN), Edificio Don Miguel, 7 piso, Ap 71 Esquina de Cipreses, Casilla 13437, Caracas, T: 454216.
Escuela Radiopostal, Apartado 986, Caracas.

VIET NAM
Living Word BCC School, Christian Literature Distribution Centre, P.O. Box 1262, Saigon.

YUGOSLAVIA
Dopisna Biblijska Skola, P.P. 20, YU-11091 Beograd.
Voice of Hope, P.O. Box 20, 11091 Belgrade-Rakovica, T: 4461-887.

ZIMBABWE
BCC Department, Source of Light Mission, 19 Alexandra Drive, Hatfield, Salisbury.
Light of Life BCC Centre, P.O. Box 2, PO Karoi.
Zimbabwe: Voice of Prophecy Bible School, P.O. Box 1092, Bulawayo.

26 Development, justice, & peace

Economic development, community development, national development, international development, appropriate technology, poverty, underdevelopment, socio-economic development; empowerment of, or assistance to, or giving a voice to the poor, the marginalized, the oppressed, the needy, the neglected, minorities; political or social action on behalf of the poor, needy, or oppressed; social justice, community justice, human rights, human dignity, social or community activism; concern for injustice, racism, prejudice, or discrimination; pacifism, peace or anti-war groups, conscientious objection; Christian involvement in revolution, or liberation movements. For local development and community projects, see social and pastoral concern. See also AID AND RELIEF.

ALGERIA
COPRODEV, 5 Rue Cne Mennani, El Djezair.

ARGENTINA
Centro Ecuménico de Acción Solidaria (CEASOL), Avda. Corrientes 1485, Fl. 1, Apt A, 1042 Buenos Aires, T: 54-1-40-5077, F: 54-1-503-0631.
Movimiento Ecuménico por los Derechos Humanos (MEDH), Av. Jose Maria Moreno 873, Planta Baja, 31 (1435) Suc. 35, 1424 Buenos Aires, T: 541-4240769, F: 541-9225101.

AUSTRALIA
Action for World Development, CIDSE, P.O. Box 124, Brickfield Hill, NSW 2000.
Christian Solidarity International Australian Office, P.O. Box 519, Blackwood, South Australia 5051; Box 670, Kuranda North Queensland 4872.
Joint Secretariat on Action for World Development in Australia, ACC, PO Box 111, Brickfield Hill, NSW 2001, T: 262901.
Quaker Service Australia, P.O. Box 119, North Hobart, Tasmania 7002; 20 Carr St., North Hobart, Tasmania 7002, T: 002-34-3240.

AUSTRIA
CIDSE, Türkenstr 3, Wien 9.
Evangelische Akademie Wien, Schwarzspanierstr. 13, Postfach 15, A-1096 Wien, T: 0043-1-4080695, F: 0043-1-4080695-33.
Institut für Internationale Zusammenarbeit, Osterreichische Stetkion, Pax Christi, Annagasse 20, Wien 1.

BANGLADESH
Christian Commission for Development in Bangladesh (CCDB), 88, Senpara Parbatta, Mirpur-10, Dhaka, T: 801971-72, F: 880-2-803556.

BARBADOS
Christian Action for Development in the Caribbean (CADEC), PO Box 616, Bridgetown.
Jubilee Research Centre, Diocesan Office, Mandeville House, Henry's Lane, St. Michael, T: 809-428-8707, F: 809-426-0871.

BELGIUM
Centre de Recherche des Pays en Développement, E Van Evenstraat 2A, B-3000 Leuven, T: 016-228597.
International Cooperation for Development and Solidarity (CIDSE), rue Stévin 16, R-1040 Brussels.
Pax Christi Intl., 11713 Oude Graan Markt, 21, Brussels 1000.

BENIN
Comité pour le Développement des Investissements Intellectuels en Afrique et à Madagascar (CODIAM), BP 249, Cotonou, T: 3888.
Développement et Culture, BP 262, Cotonou, T: 2604.

BOLIVIA
Acción Cultural Loyola (ACLO), Casilla 155, Sucre, T: 1885, 1677.
Comisión Boliviana de Acción Social Evangélica (COMBASE), Av 9 de Abril, Casilla 869, Cochabamba.
Departamento de Investigación y Promoción Social San Rafael, Casilla 546, Cochabamba, T: 4495.
Equipo Chapare, Villa Tunari, Chapare, Casilla 770, Cochabamba.

BOTSWANA

Mennonite Ministries, PO Box 33, Gaborone, T: 373 247-351 090.

BRAZIL

Academia Evangélica, Rua Senhor dos Passos 202, Porto Alegre R.S..

Comissão de Desenvolvimento da Mata Sul de Pernambuco (CODEMAS), c/o Arcebispado, Residência Episcopal, Palmares, PE.

Comissão Ecumenica de Serviço, Rua Artur Azevedo 32, Apt 8, 05404 São Paulo, SP.

Institute for Religious Studies (ISER), Ladeira da Gloria, 98, 22211-120 Rio de Janeiro, R.J., T: 55-21-265-5747, F: 55-21-205-4796.

BRITAIN (UK OF GB & NI)

Ammerdown Centre, Radstock, GB-Bath BA3 5SW, T: 44-761-33-709.

Anglican Pacifist Fellowship, 11 Weavers End, Hanslope, Milton Keynes MK19 7PA, T: 0666 825249.

Catholic Association for Racial Justice, St. Vincent's Comm. Centre, Talma Road, Brixton, London SW2 1AS, T: 0171-274 0024.

Centre for Black and White Christian Partnership, Westhill College, GB-Selly Oak, Birmingham B29 6LL, T: 44-21-472-7952.

Cornerstone Community, 443 Springfield Road, Belfast BT12 7DL, T: 08-232 321649.

Corrymeela Centre, 5, Drumaroan Road, Ballycastle, Co. Antrim BT54 6QU, Northern Ireland, T: 44-2657-626-26.

Corrymeela Community, 8 Upper Crescent, Belfast BY7 1NT, T: 44232-325008, F: 44232-315-385, O: Also Tel: 44232-328606.

Interface Academy, Hamling House, Bull Road, GB-Pakenham, Suffolk IP31 2LW, T: 44-359-30934, F: 44-359-32298.

Intermediate Technology Development Group, 9 King St, Covent Garden, London WC2E 8 HN.

Jubilee Campaign, P.O. Box 80, Cobham KT11 2BQ, Surrey, T: 44-081944-7280, F: 44-081944-7230.

National Liaison Comm. of Diocesan Justice and Peace Groups, 39 Eccleston Square, London SW1V 1BX, T: 0171-834 5138.

Pax Christi, 9 Henry Road, Manor House, London N4 2LH, T: 0181-800 4612, F: 0181-802 3223.

Quaker Peace and Service, Friends House, Euston Road, London NW1 28J, T: 44-071-387-3601, F: 44-071-388-1977.

Scottish Churches Action for World Development, 41 George IV Bridge, Edinburgh EH1 1EI.

TEAR Fund, 100 Church Road, Teddington, Middlesex TW11 8QE.

War on Want, 9 Madeley Rd, London W5, T: 01-567-1429.

CAMEROON

Commission pour le Développement, FEMEC, BP 491, Yaoundé, T: 222821.

CANADA

Aboriginal Rights Coalition (Project North), 153 Laurier E., Ottawa ON K1N 6N8, T: 613-235-9956, F: 613-235-1302.

Canada Asia Working Group, 11 Madison Ave., Toronto, Ontario M4R 2S2, Canada, T: 416-924-9351.

Canadian Catholic Organization for Development and Peace, 3028 Danforth Ave., Toronto, ON M4C 1N2, T: 416-698-7770, F: 416-698-8269, O: E-mail: CCODP@WEB.APC.ORG.

Canadian Centre for Victims of Torture, 25 Merton St., Toronto, ON M4S 1A7, T: 416-480-0489.

Canadian Food for the Hungry, 005-2580 Cedar Park Place, Abbotsford, BC V2T 3S5, T: 604-853-4262, F: 604-853-4332, O: E-mail: CFH@mindlink.bc.ca, www.cfh.ca.

Canadian Jesuits International, Canadian Jesuit Missions (CJM), 1190 Danforth Ave., Toronto, ON M4J 1M6, T: 416-465-1824, F: 416-465-1825.

Daybreak Refugee Ministry, Diocese of Calgary Anglican Ch, 3015 Glencoe Rd., S.W., Calgary, AB T2S 2L9, T: 403-243-3673, F: 403-243-2182.

Développement et Paix, 5633 rue Sherbrooke Est, Montréal, QC H1N 1A3, T: 514-257-8711, F: 514-257-8497.

Ecumenical Coalition for Economic Justice (ECEJ), 77 Charles St. W., Ste. 402, Toronto, ON M5S 1K5, T: 416-921-4615, F: 416-922-1419.

Emmanuel International of Canada, Box 4050, 3967 Stouffville, Rd., Stouffville, ON L4A 8B6, T: 905-640-2111, F: 905-640-2186.

HOPE International Development Agency, P.O. Box 608, New Westminster, BC V3L 4Z3, T: 604-525-5481, F: 604-525-3471, O: E-mail: Hope@web.apc.org, web: www.idirect.com/~hope/index.html.

Inter-Church Association to Promote Justice in Canada, c/o Vancouver & District Council of Christian Churches, 1708 West 16th Av, Vancouver, BC VLJ 2M1, T: 733-3131.

Lighthouse Community Centre, 1008 Bathurst St., Toronto, ON M5R 3G7, T: 416-535-6262, F: 416-535-3293.

Mennonite Central Committee Canada, 134 Plaza Dr., Winnipeg, MB R3T 5K9, T: 204-261-6381, F: 204-269-9875, O: E-mail: MCC@mennonitecc.ca, Web: www.mennonitecc.ca/mcc.

Mennonite Economic Development Association, 402-280 Smith St., Winnipeg R3C 1K2, Manitoba, T: 204-944-1995, F: 204-942-4001.

Mennonite Self Help, PO Box 869, New Hamburg, ON N0B 2G0, T: 519-662-1879.

Montreal House of Friendship, 120 Duluth Ave., Montreal, QC H2W 1H1, T: 514-843-4356.

New Home Immigration and Settlement Centre, 572 Hermitage Rd., Edmonton, AB T5A 4N2, T: 403-456-4663, F: 403-456-6040.

Presbyterian World Service and Development, 50 Wynford Dr., North York, ON M3C 1J7, T: 416-441-1111, F: 416-441-2825.

Project Ploughshares, Conrad Grebel College, Waterloo, ON N2L 3G6, T: 519-888-6541, F: 519-885-0806.

Ten Days for Global Justice, 77 Charles St. W. Ste. 401, Toronto, ON M5S 1K5, T: 416-922-0591, F: 416-922-1419.

Working Group on Refugee Resettlement, Suite 3, 1339 King St., W., Toronto, ON M6K 1H2, T: 416-588-1612.

World Vision Canada, 6630 Turner Valley Rd., Mississauga, ON L5N 2S4, T: 905-821-3030, F: 905-821-1356.

CHAD

Centre d'Etudes et de Formation pour le Développement (CEFOD), BP 456, Ndjamena (Fort-Lamy), T: 3916.

CHILE

Centro Evangélico Misión Urbano Rural de la Iglesia (CEMURI), Serrano 535, Casilla 2705, Concepción, T: 56-041-230012, F: 56-041-230012.

Centro para el Desarrollo Económico y Social de América Latina (DESAL), Carmen Silva 2542, Casilla 9990, Santiago, T: 499269.

Hogar de Cristo Viviendas, Chorrillos 3808, Santiago.

Instituto de Viviendas Populares (INVICA), Erasmo Escala 1835, Santiago.

CHINA

Hong Kong Sodepax Committee, c/o 57 Peking Rd, 5/f, Kowloon, Hong Kong.

Joint Development Committee, HKCC/Catholic Church, 57 Peking Rd, 5/f, Kowloon, Hong Kong.

COLOMBIA

Acción Cultural Popular (ACOP), Calle 20 No 9-45, Bogotá.

Centro para el Desarrollo Económico y Social de América Latina (DESAL), Carrera 10 No 65-48, Bogatá.

Fundación Populorum Progressio Sede Para América Latina y el Caribe, Carrera 9A No. 124-78, Santafé de Bogotá, T: 57-1-213-40-43, F: 57-1-620-42-97.

CONGO-ZAIRE

Bureau pour le Développement, BP 3258, Kinshasa, T: 30082.

COSTA RICA

Centro Ecuménico de Formación Pastoral y Acción Social (CEFPAS), 231, 2120 San Jose, T: 506-277105, F: 506-267261.

Comunidad Negra Centro Americana, Apdo 901, 1000 San José, T: 506-333830, F: 506-337531.

Exodo, Calle 9, Av 14 bis, Apdo Postal 3771, San José.

Visión Mundial Internacional, Apdo 133-2300, T: 234-1419.

CROATIA

Christian Information Service, P.P. 152, Ilica 44, 41001 Zagreb, O: E-mail: [1007005.3303@compuserve.com].

CUBA

Acción Social Ecuménica Latinoamericana, C.P. 205, Matanzas, T: 4150-4250, O: 52350 CIEMTCU.

CZECH REPUBLIC

Christian Peace Conference (CPC), P.O. Box 136, Prokopova 4, 130 00 Praha 3, T: 42-2-279-722, F: 42-2-276-853.

DENMARK

Nordisk Katolsk Utviklingshjelp, Griffenfeldsgade 44, 2200 Copenhagen, T: 01-353085.

DOMINICAN REPUBLIC

Caribbean Organisation for Indigenous People (COIP), Carib Territory, Dominica, T: 4482308, F: 4482308.

ECUADOR

Centro de Prducción Pequeña Industria, 22 entre Capitán Najera y Febres Cordero, Guayaquil, T: 461-583.

Desarrollo Agricola Y/O Comunal, 22 entre Capitan Najera y Febres Cordero, Guayaquil, T: 461-583.

Pastoral de Consolación y Solidaridad, Ave. Patria No. 640 y Amazonas, T: 238-220.

Saneamiento Ambiental, Illuchi, Casilla 208, Latacunga.

EGYPT

Middle East Council of Churches, P.O. Box 2237, Al Horriya, Cairo, T: 20-2-666-122, F: 20-2-247-8837.

ETHIOPIA

Ethiopia Orthodox Church Development Commission, Haile Selassie Av, PO Box 503 Addis Abeba, T: 119661, 123642.

FINLAND

Viittakivi International Centre, Hauho, SF-14700, T: 35-358-17-44911, F: 35-358-17-44930.

FRANCE

Association Internationale de Développement, 7 Av de Jena, F-75016 Paris.

Centre Animation Rencontre Tourisme (CART), 31 rue Emilien Dumas, F-30250 Sommires, T: 33-66-80-0302.

Centre Catholique pour l'UNESCO, 9 rue Cler, F-75007 Paris, T: 551-1759.

Centre d'Information sur le Développement (CIDEV), 47 Quai des Grands-Augustins, F-75006 Paris, T: 01-325-3102.

Centre de Coopération pour Développement Economique et Humain, 82 rue Sain-Lazare, F-75009 Paris.

Centre de Formation des Experts de la Coopération Technique Internationale, 27 rue Saint-Guillaume, F-75007 Paris.

Centre de Formation pour le Développement, 3 rue St-Léon, F-67082 Strasbourg.

Centre de Reflexion et d'Information sur la Coopération (CRIC), 30 rue Voltaire, Grenoble 12.

Centre LJ Lebret/Foi et Développement, 9 rue Guénégaud, F-75006 Paris, T: 01-033-2502.

Comite Catholique Contre la Faim et Pour le Developpement, 4 rue Jean Lantier, 75001 Paris, T: 33-1-44-82-8000.

Comité Catholique National contre la Faim et pour le Développement (CCFD), 47 Quai des Grands-Augustins, F-75262 Paris, T: 01-325-3102.

Délégation Catholique pour la Coopération (DCC), 277 rue St Jacques, F-75005 Paris, T: 01-326-1250.

Economique et Humain, 82 rue Sain-Lazare, F-75009 Paris.

Ecumenical Institute for the Development of Peoples, 34 Av Reille, F-75014 Paris, T: 01-589-1321.

Entraide pour le Développement Intégral, 6 Rue Boissac, F-69002 Lyon.

GERMANY

Aktion Sühnezeichen Friedensdienste, Jebensstr 1, D-1000 Berlin 12, T: 030-316701.

Arbeitsgemeinschaft Ev Seminare für Gemeindedienst, Graf-Recke-Str 209, D-4 Düsseldorf.

Arbeitsgemeinschaft für Entwicklungshilfe (AGEH), Franzstr 107/109, Postfach 23, D-5100 Aachen; Mittelstr 16, D-5100 Aachen, T: 0241-29894/5.

Ecumenical Society for Justice, Peace and the Integrity of Creation, Rendeler-Strasse 9-11, Frankfurt 60; Office: Mittelstrasse 4, Wethen, T: 49-5694-1417.

Evangelische Zentralstelle für Entwicklungshilfe e.V., Mittelstr. 37, 53175 Bonn/Bad Godesberg, T: 49-228/810-11-28, F: 49-228/810-11-60.

Institut für Entwicklungshilfe, Theodor Hurth Str 2-6, D-5 Köln-Deutz.

Institut für Vorbereitung von Akademischen Mitarbeitern für Entwicklungsländer, Overathers Str 21/23, D-506 Bensberg-Köln.

Institut St. Michel/Vorbereittungsstätte für Entwicklungshelfer, Kuhlendalh 63, D-433 Mülheim/Ruhr.

Kirchenrechtliches Institut der EKD, Prof-Huber-Platz 1/III, D-8 München 22.

Konferenz der Ev Pfarrer an den Justizvollzugsanstalten der BDR und in West-Berlin, Postfach 600, D-325 Hameln.

Mennonite Central Committee, Langendorferstrasse 29, Neuwied 1 5450, T: 49-2631-21690, F: 49-2631-25808.

Misereor, Mozartstr 9, D-51 Aachen.

MISSIO, Hirtenstr 26, D-8 München 2, T: 555981,2.

Seminar für Socialarbeit in Ubersee, 19 Winterstr, D-78 Freiburg/Breisgau.

Weltbund für Religiöse Freiheit/Association Internationale pour la Liberté Religieuse, Frankfurt/Main.

Wirtschtsgilde Ev Arbeitskreis für Wirtschaftsethik und sozialgestaltung, Blumenstr 7, D-75 Karlsruhe 1.

GHANA

Department of Socio-Economic Development, National Catholic Secretariat, P.O. Box 7530, Accra North.

GRENADA

Grenada Community Development Agency (GRENCODA), Depradine St., Gouyave, St. John's, T: 809-444-8430, F: 809-444-8111.

GUADELOUPE

Comite Chretien pour le Development en Guadeloupe (CCDG), B.P. 414, Pointe-à-Pitre, T: 590-82-09-67.

GUATEMALA

Centro de Desarrollo Integral, Apdo 6, Huehuetenango.

Instituto para el Desarrollo Económico Social de América Central (IDESAC), 1a Av 8-16, Zona 1, Apdo Postal 10-A Reforma, Ciudad de Guatemala, T: 29991.

Proyecto de Colonización Juan XXIII, San Juan Acul, Sayaxche, Petén.

GUYANA

Faith, Justice and Social Action Group of the Catholic Church, 59 Brickdam, Stabroek, Georgetown, T: 592-2-63314, F: 592-2-67461.

University of Guyana Workers Union, University of Guyana, Georgetown, T: 592-2-67461, F: 592-2-67461.

HAITI

Centre Haitien d'Investigation en Sciences sociales (CHISS), P.O. Box 2479, Port-au-Prince; Rue Bonne Foi 23, Port-au-Prince.

Commission Haïtienne des Eglises pour le Développement (CHED), Angle Rue Camp-de-Mars et Magasin de l'Etat, BP 285, Port-au-Prince.

HOLY SEE

Pontifical Commission for Preparation of the Code of Oriental Canon Law, Palazzo dei Convertendi, Via della Conciliazione 34, I-00193 Roma, Italy, T: 698-4295.

Pontifical Commission for the Revision of the Code of Canon Law, Palazzo dei Convertendi, Via dell'Erba 1, I-00193 Roma, Italy, T: 6982 int 3933.

Pontificia Commissione Iustitia et Pax, Palazzo San Calisto, Piazza San Calisto 16, Roma, I-00120 Città del Vaticano, T: 698-4776, 4491.

Pontificio Consiglio Cor Unum, Palazzo Apostolico, I-00120 Città del Vaticano, T: 6984556, 6984831.

INDIA

ACISCA (Association of Christian Institutes for Social Concern in Asia), Ecumenical Christian Centre, Whitefield, Bangalore 560 066, T: 91-80-8452270, F: 91-80-8452653, O: Also tel: 8452653.

Action Research Institute for Socio-economic Studies (ARISES), Gospel House, 83, Civil Lines, Bareilly, Uttar Pradesh 243001.

Adventists Development and Relief Agency, Chingmeirong West, P. O. Box 26, Imphal, Manipur 795001.

AEM Mission Vocational Training, C/o. Mr. T. Singh, REO Road, Umerkote, Orissa.

All India Christian Peoples Forum, 15, Raj Niwas Marg, New Delhi 110054.

Auto Skills - Industrial Training Institute, Sharanpur, Nashik, Maharashtra 422005.

Banjara Development Trust, 6-1-140, Tank Bund Road, Hanamkonda, Andhra Pradesh 506001.

Bellary Diocesan Development Society, St Antony's Cathedral, Cowl Bazaar, , Karnataka 583104.

Burden & Love for the Economically and Socially Suppressed- BLESS, 12-5-55 Vijayapuri, C/O Baptist Church, South Lallaguda, Secunderabad, Andhra Pradesh 500017.

Caritas India, CBCI Centre, Goldakkhana, New Delhi 110001.

Catholic Housing Society, C/o Catholic Church Mochi Bazar, Rajkot, Gujarat 360001.

CBCI Commission for Justice Peace and Development, CBCI Centre, Ashok Place, New Delhi 110001.

Centre for Social Action, 849, Ramdev Gardens, Kacharakanahalli, Bangalore, Karnataka 560084.

Christian Social Development Project Association, Lower Chopra, Pauri Garhwal, Uttar Pradesh 246001.

Church's Auxiliary for Social Action, Methodist Centre, 21, YMCA Road, Bombay, Maharashtra 400008.

Community Development Society, Y. M. C. A. Complex, Maharaj Bag Road, Nagpur, Maharashtra 440001.

Community Service Centre, 17, Balfour Road, Kilpauk, Madras 600 010, T: 612684, O: Also tel: 611619.

Comprehensive Health and Community Development Programme, Christian Hospital, Dhar, Madhya Pradesh 454001.

Ecumenical Development Centre of India (EDCI), Dhadiwal Building, Katol Road, Chaoni, Nagpur-13, T: 525786, F: 91-0712-525786.

Ecumenical Social & Industrial Institute, Collins Path, Bidhan Nagar, Durgapur 12, W.B., T: Durgapur 6388, O: Cable: ECUMENICAL.

Education and Development Services - India, ICSA Centre, 93, Pantheon Road, Egmore, Madras, Tamil Nadu 600008.

Grihini School(Home Science), c/o Catholic Church, P. O. Haddo, Port Blair, Andaman & Nicobar Is 744102.

Grihini Training Centre, Mariamban Koath P. O., Bihar.

Holy Cross Grihini School, Rajibpur P. O., West Bengal 733124.

Inter-Mission Industrial Development Association (West), Elim, 19. August Kranti Marg, Nana Chowk, Bombay, Maharashtra 400007.

Kattunilathu Fellowship Enterprises Society, Tholicode P. O., Punalur, Kerala 691333.

Liberation Education and Development (LEAD), Christian Street, Jeypore, Orissa 764001.

Lievens Vocation Centre, Post Torpa, , Bihar 835227.

Light and Salt Group, Changtongya, Nagaland 798613.

M. M. Sisal Handicraft Centre, Rose Cottage, Station Road, Ahmednagar, Maharashtra 414001.

Mar Gregorios Garments Ltd., Nalamchira, Trivandrum, Kerala.

Mar Thoma Development Society, Hermon Aramana, Adoor P.O., Kerala 691523.

Medico-Health and Socio-Economic Community Development, Woodstock School, Mussoorie Hills, Uttar Pradesh 248179.

National Evangelical Christian Development Society, P. B. No. 1543, Dharvera Chowk, Rewari, Haryana 123401.

Social Action, Indian Social Institute, 10 Institutional Area, Lodi Road, New Delhi 110003.

Social Justice Cell, C/o St. Jude's Church, M. Vassanji Road, Jeri Meri, Bombay, Maharashtra 400072.

St. Joseph's Brick Cooperative Society, C/o Catholic Church, Umreth, Gujarat 388220.

St. Mary's Industrial Training Centre, Village Kadapra, Tiruvalla Taluk, Niranam P. O., Kerala 689621.

St. Mary's Lace Making Centre, Vadakangulam, Tamil Nadu 627116.

TUSHAR Community Health, Education and Development Project, Manduwala, Premnagar, Uttar Pradesh 248007.

Vijoya Industries, Berhampur, Orissa 760010.

INDONESIA

Episcopal Commission for Socio-Economic Development, Jalan Kemiri 15 (Belakang), Jakarta.

Inspiration and Reflection Centre (Inri Centre) Social Welfare Guidance Foundation, P.O. Box 84, Solo 57101; Gang Jeruk No. 2 Semanggi, Solo 57117, Solo 57101, T: 0271-37342, O: Cable: INRI SOLO.

Social Welfare Guidance Foundation (YBKS), P.O. Box 284, Surakarta 57102; Gang Jeruk 2, Semanaggi, Surakarta 57101, Surakarta 57102, T: 062-271-53342, F: 062-271-47645.

SODEPAXI (Sodepax Indonesia), DGI, Jalan Salemba Raya 10, Jakarta IV/3.

IRELAND

Aid to the Church in Need, 151 St Mobhi Road, Glasnevin, Dublin 9, T: 353-01 377516.

Dublin Mennonite Community, 4 Clonmore Villas,

92 Ballybough Road, Dublin 3, T: 353-01 309384.
Muintir Na Tire, Canon Hayes House, Tipperary, T: 353-062 51163.

ISRAEL
Commission 'Justice et Paix', P.O. Box 20459, 91204 Jérusalem; Notre Dame of Jerusalem Center, 91204 Jérusalem, T: 02-28-77-19.

ITALY
Comitato per Gli Interventi Caritativi a Fa Vore del Terzo Mondo, Circonvalazione Aurelia, 50, 00165 Roma, T: 39-6-663-7141, F: 39-6-662-3037.
Commission for Justice and Peace, Piazza San Calisto 16, I-00153 Roma, T: 6984697, 6984521.
Comunione E Liberazione, Via Mosè Bianchi, 94, I 20149 Milano.
Coordinamento dei Gruppi di Volontariato della Castellana, c/o Maria De Marzi, Via Platani no. 18, 31033 Castelfranco, Veneto (Treviso), T: 39-423-496832.
MIVA, St. Joseph's Missionshaus, Postfach 185, I-39042 Brixen, BZ.
Movement for a Better World, Centro Internationale Pio XII, Via dei Laghi Km 10, I-00040 Rocca di Papa, T: 949010, 949122.
Movimento Internazionale della Riconciliazione (MIR), Via Rasella 155, Roma, T: 463206.
Pontifical Council for Justice and Peace, Piazza S. Calisto 16, 00153 Rome.

IVORY COAST
Commission du Synode Eglise et Développement, c/o Archevêché, 23 Blvd Clozel, BP 1287, Abidjan, T: 222007.
Institut Africain pour le Développement Economique et Social (INADES), 15 Av Jean-Mermoz, Cocody, BP 8008, Abidjan-Cocody, T: 49292.

JAPAN
Asia Conference on Religion and Peace (ACRP), Fumon-Kan, 2-6-1, Wada, Suginami-Ku, Tokya 166, T: 81-3-3383-7944, F: 81-3-3383-7993.
Keiyo Culture and Industrial Center, 3-11 Tatsumidai Higashi, Ichihara-shi, Chiba-ken, T: 81-436-742151, F: 81-436-742152.
Sodepax Japan, 24 Japan Christian Center, 551 Totsuka-cho, 1-chome, Shinjuku-ku, Tokyo 160; 10-1 Rokubancho, Chiyoda-ku, Tokyo 102.
Tomisaka Christian Center, 2-9-4 Koishikawa, Bunkyo-ku, Tokyo 112, T: 03-3812-3852, F: 03-3817-0860.

KENYA
African Independent Churches Service (AICS), P.O. Box 59969, Nairobi, T: 26894, 23649.
Socio-Economic Development Department, Kenya Catholic Secretariat, PO Box 48062, Nairobi, T: 21613.

LEBANON
Ecumenical Commission for Development, Justice & Peace, PO Box 1375, Bayrut.
Middle East Council of Churches, PO Box 5376, Beirut, T: 01-353938.

LESOTHO
LESODEPAX (Lesotho Sodepax Commission), P.O. Box 929, Maseru.
Transformation Resource Centre, P.O. Box 1388, Maseru 100.

MADAGASCAR
Centre d'Etudes et d'Animation du Développement, Lot IV-G 199, Antanimena, Tananarive.

MALAWI
Christian Service Committee of the Churches of Malawi (CSC), Chileka Rd, PO Box 949, Blantyre, T: 30671.
Movement for Ecumenical Action in National Development (MEND), P.O. Box 949, Blantyre.

MAURITIUS
Institut pour le Développement et le Progrès, 42 Rue Pope Hennessy, Port-Louis, T: 20975.

MEXICO
CCIDD-Cucrnavaca Center for Intercultural Dialog on Development, Apartado 580, Cuernavaca, Morelos, T: 52-731-265-64.
Friends Information Centers & Offices, Ignacio Mariscal 143, Mexico D.F. 06030, T: 5-705-0646.

NETHERLANDS
Apostolate of Reconciliation, Prins Hendrikstraat 47, Boxtel, T: 04116-3040.
Dominican Activity Center, Stadsdam 1, P.O. Box 5g, 6850 AB Huissen, T: 085-259006, F: 085-254694.
Ecumenical Development Co-operative Society (EDSC), UA Utreschtseweg 91, 3818 EB Amersfoot, Nederland, T: 033-633-22, F: 31-33-650336, O: Telex: 200 10 PMS NL-EDSC.
European Quaker Peace Consultation, P.O. Box 808, 2300 AV Leiden, T: 071-156097, F: 071-156097.
Interchurch Council for Peace, Celebesstraat 60, 's-Gravenhage, T: 070-656823.
Interkerkelijke Adventsactie voor Latijns Amerika, Laan van Meerdervoort 148, 's-Gravenhage, T: 070-655207.
Kerk en Wereld, De Horst 7, P.O. Box 19, NL-3970 AA Driebergen, T: 03438-12241, F: 03438-17503.

NEW ZEALAND
Amnesty International (NZ), P.O. Box 3597, Wellington.
Christian Pacifist Society of New Zealand, 19 Head St, Christchurch 8.
Citizen's Association for Racial Equality (CARE), P.O. Box 2794, Auckland.

NICARAGUA
Centro Intereclesial de Estudios Teológicos y Sociales (CIEETS), RP-082, Las Lomas, Manaqua, T: 5052-71434, F: 5052-671010.
Comisión Evangélica de Promoción de la Responsabilidad Social (CEPRES), De la Shell El Calvario 2 Cuadras al Lago, Media Cuadra Abajo, C.P. 706, Managua, T: 5052-24332, 22074.
Comité Evangélico pro Ayuda al Desarrollo (CEPAD), Apdo Postal 3091, Managua.

NIGERIA
Institute of Church and Society Arochukwu Nigeria, P.O. Box 110, Abia State; Ibom Village G.R.A., Arochukuw, Abia State, T: 088-721118, F: 088-221777.
Institute of Church and Society, P.O. Box 4020, Ibadan; off Sango/U.I. Road, behind Immanuel College of Theology, Samonda, Ibadan, T: 022-411418.

NORWAY
Christian Institute for Project Aid, Munchsgate 2, Oslo 1.
Council of Church Academies in Norway, Postboks 5913, Hegdehaugen, N-0308 Oslo 3, T: 47-2-60-46-90, F: 47-2-69-72-80.

PAPUA NEW GUINEA
Sodepang (Sodepax Papua New Guinea), c/o Box 1015, Boroko, Port Moresby.

PERU
Centro Cristiano de Promoción y Servícios (CEPS), Calle Santa Marta NRO. 176, Urbanización Colmenares, C.P. 10291, Lima 100, T: 5114-712550.

PHILIPPINES
Federation of Asian Bishops' Conferences (FABC), 2325 Agno St (off Taft Av, near La Salle), Malate, PO Box EA-12 Ermita, Manila.
Integrated Church & Community Development Center, Banhigan, Badian, Cebu City.
Kapatiran Kaunlaran Foundation, Inc., P.O. Box 1600, Manila; 937 P. Paredes St., Sampaloc, Metro Manila, T: 63-731-0111 to 14, F: 632-732-0917.
National Christian Peace Federation, 1519 Craig St, Sampaloc, Manila.
Philippine Peace Federation of Christian Churches, 1908 Taft Av, Pasay City.
Socio-Pastoral Institute, P.O. Box 439, 1099 Manila; 2/f Jacinto Apts., 380 Quezon Ave., Quezon City, 1099 Manila, T: 924-3205, F: 924-3205.

POLAND
Pax Association, Ul Mokotowska 43, Warszawa.

PORTUGAL
Centro de Desenvolvimento Cristão, Rua João Dias Correia Pimenta, 22, 2830 Barreiro, T: 01-206 01 12.

PUERTO RICO
Caribbean Project for Justice and Peace, Condominio Condendo 607, Oficina 601, Ave Condendo, Samurce P.R. 00907, T: 809-722-1640, F: 809-754-6462.

SAINT LUCIA
Archdiocesan Integral Human Development Office, Archdiocese of Castries, P.O. Box 267, Castries, T: 452-3379, F: 452-3697.

SAINT VINCENT & THE GRENADINES
Caribbean Peoples Development Agency (CARIPEDA), P.O. Box 1132, Kingstown, T: 457-2953, F: 457-2445.

SOUTH AFRICA
ACAT - Africa Co-operative Action Trust, PO Box 1743, Pietermarizburg 3200, 215 Burger St, Pietermaritzburg, T: 033-45-2302, F: 0331-42-7589.
Care, PO Box 61341, Bishop's Gate 4008, Ecumenical Centre, 20 St, Andrew's St, Durban, T: 031-305-6001, F: 031-305-2486.
Catholic Action for Racial Education (CARE), PO Box 31135, Braamfontein, Transvaal.
Catholic Justice & Peace Commission, PO Box 2910, Cape Town 8000, 12 Bouquet St, Cape Town, T: 021-462-2417, F: 021-461-9330.
Catholic Welfare & Development, 37a Somerset Rd, Cape Town 8001, T: 021-25-2095, F: 021-25-4295.
College of the Transfiguration, PO Box 77, Grahamstown, 6140, T: 0461-2-3332, F: 0461-2-3817.
HELP Ministries International, PO Box 38256, Gatesville 7764, T: 021-637-1350, F: 021-637-1818.
Mfesane 1975, P/Bag 2, Cape Town Int Airport 7525, 5 Old Klipfontein Rd, Phillipi, Cape Town, T: 021-31-7173, F: 021-34-3461.
Mfesane Transkei, PO Box 42, Umtata 5100, Efata, Melville Farm, Engcobo, Transkei, T: 0471-36-0535, F: 0471-36-0551.
Trust for Christian Outreach & Education, PO Box 2980, Pietermaritzburg 3200, 236 Pine St, Pietermaritzburg, T: 0331-45-5760.

SOUTH KOREA
Christian Institute of Social Studies, Soong Sil University, Sang Do Dong 1-1, Seoul, T: 2-813-5060, F: 2-824-2314.
Christian Institute for the Study of Justice and Development, 35 Choongjeungno 2 Ga, Sodaemun-ku, Seoul 120-012, T: 82-2-312-2217-9, F: 82-2-313-0261.
Justice & Peace Committee Archdiocese of Seoul, 1, 2-ga, Myong-dong, Chung-gu, Seoul-shi, T: 02-771-7600.
Justice and Peace Commission of Korea, c/o CPO Box 16, Soul 100, T: 238789.
Sodepax Korea Committee, 52-15, 2KA, Chung Mu Ro Jung-ku, Seoul.

SPAIN
Secretariado de Cooperación al Desarrollo, Paseo de Juan XXIII 3, Madrid-3, T: 01-2534007.

SRI LANKA
Interfaith Fellowship for Peace and Development, Interfaith Centre, 218/4 Tewatta Road, Ragama, F: 94-1-538044.
Social and Economic Development Centre, 976 Gnanartha Pradipaya Mawata, Colombo 8.
Sodepax Sri Lanka Committee, 61 Sir James Peiris Mawata, Colombo 2.

SURINAME
Centre for Community Development of the Moravian Church in Suriname, Domineestraat 46 Boven, Paramaribo, T: 597-410-855, F: 597-475-794.

SWEDEN
Swedish Ecumenical Committee for Development (SEKURF), Justice and Peace, Bellmansgatan 100, S-75428 Uppsala.

SWITZERLAND
International Nepal Fellowship (INF), Schweizerfreunde, Kehrstr. 3, CH-Bäretswil, T: 01-939-1939, O: PC 80-31841-4.
International Social Service, 24 Blvd des Philosophes, Genève.
Interteam (Entwicklungsdienst durch Freiwilligen Einsatz), Zürichstr 68, CH-6000 Luzern, T: 041-366768.
Mennonite Central Committee, Grand Rue 114, Caisse Postale 52, Trmelan 2720, T: 41-3297-5335.
MIVA, Catholic Parish, CH-9499 Altenrhein.
Programme Unit of Justice and Service, WCC 150 Route de Ferney, CH-1211 Genève 20.
Sodepax (Commission de Recherche du COE et de l'Eglise Catholique sur la Société, le Développement et la Paix), 150 Route de Ferney, CH-1211 Genève 20, T: 22-333400.
Swiss Bishops Lenten Fund, CP 40, CH-1700 Fribourg 3, T: 037-244794.
Swiss Lenten Projects, Zentralstelle, Habsburgerstr 44, Postfach 754, CH-6000 Luzern, T: 041-227538.
Theologische Konkordatsprüfungsbehörde, Sandackerstr 1, CH-8200 Schaffhausen.

TAIWAN
Christian Institute for Social Transformation (CIST), 117, Sec. 1, East Gate Road, Tainan 70 1, T: 886-6-2353670, F: 886-6-2353673, O: Cable: THEOCOL TAINAN.

THAILAND
Baptist Church Development Division, 84 Soi 2, Sukhumvit Rd, Bangkok, T: 2525057.
Catholic Council of Thailand for Development (CCTD), National Catholic Centre, 25/2 Soi Sunklangtheva, Prachasongkhroh St, Bangkok 10, T: 770108.

TRINIDAD & TOBAGO
CEPAC (Collaboration for Ecumenical Planning and Action in the Caribbean, 12, Harris Promenade, San Fernando, Trinidad, T: 809-652-4489, F: 809-652-4489, O: Cable: GLOMIN.

UNITED STATES OF AMERICA (USA)
Action for Interracial Understanding (AIU), 575 Neponset St, Norwood, MA 02062, T: 617-762-4139.
Africa Faith and Justice Network, PO Box 29378, Washington DC 20017; 1233 Lawrence Avenue., NE, T: 202-832-3112.
American Friends Service Committee, 1501 Cherry St., Philadelphia, PA 19102, T: 215-241-7000, F: 215-864-0104.
Arise & Build Ministries, 683 Monroe Street, Oshkosh, WI 54901.
Baptist Peace Fellowship of North America, 499 S. Patterson St., Memphis, TN 38111, T: 901-324-7675, F: 901-526-1320.
Bread for the World, 1100 Wayne Ave., Ste. 1000, Silver Spring, MD 20910, T: 301-608-2400, F: 301-608-2401, O: E-mail: Bread@igc.apc.org, www.bread.org.
Bright Hope International, 1000 Brown St. #207, Wavconda, IL 60084, T: 847-526-5566, F: 847-526-0073, O: E-mail: BrightHipe@aol.com.
Christian Community Development Association, 3827 W. Ogden Avenue, Chicago, IL 60623, T: 773-762-0994, F: 773-762-5772.
Christian Freedom Foundation, 7960 Cresent Av, Buena Park, CA 90602.
Christian Peacemaker Teams, Box 1245, Elkhart, IN 46515-1245, T: 219-294-7536.
Church Coalition for Human Rights in the Philippines, PO 70, 110 Maryland Ave., NE Washington, DC 2002, T: 202-543-1094.
Church Committee on Human Rights in Asia, 5253 N. Kenmore, Chicago, IL 60640, T: 312-561-4953.
Church World Service & Witness, Unit of the National Council of the Churches of Christ in the USA, 475 Riverside Dr., Rm. 678, New York, NY 10015, T: 212-870-3004, F: 212-870-3523, O: Web: www.ncccusa.org.
CODEL-Coordination in Development, 79 Madison Ave, New York, NY 10016, T: 212-685-2030.
Commission for Racial Justice, 700 Prospect Ave., Cleveland, OH 44115.
Cooperation in Development (CODEL), 79 Madison Av, New York, NY 10016.
Development Companions Intl., 1250 W. Pioneer Way, Oak Harbor, WA 98277, T: 206-679-3723, F: 206-679-3723.
Educational Concerns for Hunger Organization (ECHO), 17430 Durance Rd., N. Ft. Myers, FL 33917, T: 941-543-3246, F: 941-543-5317, O: E-mail: ECHO@xc.org, Web: www.xc.org/echo.
Enterprise Development International, 1730 N. Lynn St. Ste. 500, Arlington, VA 22209, T: 703-243-9500, F: 703-243-1681, O: E-mail: EDI1@ix.netcom.com, logos.ghn.org/ENTERPRISE.
Fellowship of Reconciliation, Box 271, Nyack, NY 10960, T: 914-358-4601, F: 914-358-4924.
Friends Committee on National Legislation, 245 2nd St, NE, Washington, DC 20002, T: 202-547-6000.
Habitat for Humanity International, 121 Habitat St., Americus, GA 31709, T: 912-924-6935, F: 912-924-6541, O: E-mail: Info@habitat.org, Web: www.habitat.org.
Heifer Project Int'l, O: E-mail: www.intellinet.com/Heifer.
Institute for Peace and Justice, 4144 Lindell Blvd. #122, St. Louis, MO 63108, T: 314-533-4445.
Inter-American Technical Assistance Foundation, P.O. Box 3146, Mansfield, Ohio.
Interfaith Impact for Justice and Peace, 100 Maryland Ave. N.E., Ste. 200, Washington, DC 20002, T: 202-543-2800, F: 202-547-8107.
International Justice Mission, 615 Slaters Lane, Alexandria, VA 22313, T: 703-379-1980, F: 703-379-1992, O: E-mail: IJM@NETCOM.COM, Web: www.IJM.ORG.
Interreligious Foundation for Community Organization (IFCO), 402 W. 145th St., New York, NY 10031, T: 212-926-5757, F: 212-926-5842.
John M. Perkins Foundation for Reconciliation & Developement, P.O. Box 40125, 1581 Navarro Ave., Pasadena, CA 91103, T: 818-798-7431, F: 818-791-7451.
Jubilee Campaign, 7002-C Little River Turnpike, Annandale, VA 22003, T: 703-750-0318, F: 703-658-0077.
Jubilee Crafts, 300 W. Apsley, Philadelphia, PA 19144, T: 215-849-0808.
Jubilee Foundation, 175 W. Jackson Blvd., Chicago, IL 60604.
Lifewater International, 15854 Business Center Dr., Irwindale, CA 91706, T: 626-962-4187, F: 626-962-6786, O: E-mail: Lifewater@xc.org, Web: www.lifewater.org.
Lutheran Peace Fellowship, 1710 11th Ave., Seattle, WA 98122-2420, T: 206-720-0313.
Lutheran World Relief, 390 Park Ave. S., New York, NY 10016-8803, T: 212-532-6350, F: 212-213-6081, O: E-mail: LWR@lwr.org, Web: www.lwr.org.
Mennonite Central Committee International, P.O. Box M, Akron, PA 17501, T: 717-859-1151, F: 717-859-2171, O: E-mail: MailBox@mcc.org, Web: www.mennonitecc.ca/mcc.
Mennonite Voluntary Service, 722 Main St, P.O. Box 347, Newton, KS 67114, T: 316-283-5100, F: 316-283-0454.
Mision: Moving Mountains, 10800 Lyndale Ave., S. #100, Bloomington, MN 55420, T: 612-884-8450, F: 612-884-8456, O: E-mail: MMM@xc.org, www.movingmountains.org.
MIVA, South Rd., Wurtsboro, NY 12790.
National Catholic Conference for Interracial Justice (NCCIJ), 1307 South Wabash Ave., Chicago, IL 69605.
New Call to Peacemaking, 38 W. 691 Ridgewood Lane, Elgin, IL 60123, T: 708-697-1741, F: 708-742-6103.
Opportunity International, P.O. Box 3695, Oak Brook, IL 60522, T: 800-793-9455, F: 630-279-3107, O: Web: www.opportunity.org.
Orthodox Peace Fellowship (OPF), 132 West 4th St, New York, NY 10012.
Pax Christi USA, 348 E Tenth St, Erie, PA 16503, T: 814-453-4955.
Peace Doves, O: Web: www/lookup.com/Homepages/102301/home.html.
People Against Racism, 212 McKerchy Bldg., 2361 Woodward Av, Detroit, MI 48201.
Secretariat for World Justice and Peace, National Conference of Catholic Bishops, 1312 Massachusetts Av, Washington, DC 20005.
Shelter Now International, Inc., P.O. Box 1306, Oshkosh, WI 54902, T: 920-426-1207, F: 920-426-4321, O: E-mail: Thor@shelter.org, Web: www.shelter.org.
Sojourners Magazine, 2401 15th St, NW, Washington, DC 20009, T: 800-714-7474.
United States Interreligious Committee on Peace (USICOP), 100 Maryland Av, NE, Washington, DC 20002.
VITA-Volunteers in Technical Assistance, 1815 N Lynn St, Suite 200, Arlington, VA 22209, T: 703-276-1800.
World Concern, P.O. Box 33000, Seattle, WA 98133, T: 206-546-7201, F: 206-546-7317, O: Web: www.worldconcern.org.
YokeFellows, O: Web: www.donet.com/~brandyjc/p6main.htm.

URUGUAY
Instituto de Promoción Económico-Socio del Uruguay (IPRU), Cerrito 475, 1 piso, Montevideo.
Servicio Ecuménico Para la Dignidad Humana (SEDHU), Colonia 1569, C.P. 201, 11200 Montevideo RO, T: 598-2480934.
Sodepax-Uruguay, c/o Arzobispado, Treinta y Tres 1368, Montevideo.

VENEZUELA
Centro de Servicios CEVEJ, Urbanizacion Urdaneta, Vereda 7 con 1a Avenida, El Parque No. 15, Catia, Caracas, T: 58-2-8710113, F: 58-2-895868.
Presencia Cristiana Popular, Apdo. 517, Maracaibo, T: 061-543345, F: 061-543345.

27
Diplomatic representation

Diplomatic representation of the Holy See across the world, to nations and to major international organizations; diplomatic representation to the Holy See; diplomatic representation and offices to and from other major Christian bodies; Christian permanent observers or diplomatic representation in international bodies such as the United Nations; nunciatures, apostolic delegations.

ALGERIA
Délégation Apostolique de l'Afrique Septentrionale, Délégué, 1 Rue de la Basilique, Bologhine-Alger, T: 578430.
Nonciature Apostolique, Pro-Nonce, 1 Rue de la Basilique, Bologhine-Alger, T: 623430.

ANGOLA
Apostolic Delegation, Irmas NS de Muxima 29, CP 1030, Luanda, T: 30532.

ARGENTINA
Nuncio Apostólico, Avenida Alvear 1605, 1014 Buenos Aires, T: 54-1-813-9697, F: 54-1-815-4097, O: Also tel: 813-9698, Telex: (0033)17406 NUNAP AR.

AUSTRALIA
Apostolic Nunciature, Pro-Nuncio, 2 Vancouver St, Red Hill, ACT 2603, T: 062-953876.

AUSTRIA
Agence Internationale de l'Energie Atomique (AIEA), Délégué Apostolique, Theresianumgasse 31, A-1040 Wien IV, T: 651327.
Apostolische Nunziatur, Nunzius, Theresianumgasse 31, A-1040 Wien IV, T: 651327.

BANGLADESH
Apostolic Nunciature, Pro-Nuncio, House No 9, Rd 50, PB 361, Gulhsan, Dacca 12, T: 300218, 302446.

BELGIUM
Comitato Internazionale di Medicina e Farmacia Militare, Delegate, Rue de Louvain 84, Tirlemont.
Communauté Européenne (CECA, CEE, Euratom), Nonce, Av des Franciscains 5-9, B-1150 Brussel, T: 7622005.
Nonciature Apostolique de Belgique, Nonce, Av des Franciscains 5-9, B-1150 Brussel, T: 7622005.

BELIZE
Belize Mission to the Holy See, Chancery, 15 Thayer Street, London W1, T: 01-44-1-486-8381.

BOLIVIA
Nuncio Apostólico, Avenida Arce 2990, Casilla Postal 136, La Paz, T: 591-2-43-1007, 02-375007, F: 591-2-43-2120.

BRAZIL
Nuncio Apostólico, Avenida das Nações, lote n. 1, C.P. 07-0153, Brasília-DF, T: 55-61-223-0794, F: 55-61-224-9365, O: Telex: (0038)61-21-25 NUAP BR.

BRITAIN (UK OF GB & NI)
Apostolic Delegation to Great Britain, 54 Parkside, Wimbledon, London SW19 5NF, T: 01946-1410.
Apostolic Nunciature, 54 Parkside, London SW19 5NE, T: 0181-946 1410, F: 0181-947 2494.

BURUNDI
Nonciature Apostolique, Nonce, BP 1068, Bujumbura, T: 2326.

CAMEROON
Nonciature Apostolique, Pro-Nonce, Rue du Vatican, BP 210, Yaoundé, T: 220475.

CANADA
Apostolic Nunciature, Pro-Nuncio, 724 Manor Av, Ottawa K1M OE3, T: 613-746-4914.

CENTRAL AFRICAN REPUBLIC
Nonciature Apostolique, Pro-Nonce, Av Boganda, angle Av Bokassa, BP 1447, Bangui, T: 612654.

CHILE
Nuncio Apostólico, Calle Nuncio Sótero Sanz 200, Casilla 16183 Correo 9, Santiago, T: 56-2-231-7240, F: 56-2-231-0868, O: Telex: 0034 241035 APOST CL.

CHINA
Apostolic Nunciature of China, Hong Kong Office, 133 Waterloo Rd, Kowloon, Hong Kong, T: 821566.

COLOMBIA
Nuncio Apostólico, Carrera 15 No 36-33, Apartado Aéreo 3740, Santafé de Bogota, D.C., T: 57-91-2880705, F: 57-91-2851817, O: Also tel: 3200289.

CONGO-ZAIRE
Nonciature Apostolique, Pro-Nonce, Av Goma 81, BP 3091, Kinshasa-Gombe, T: 31419.

COSTA RICA
Nuncio Apostólico, Centro Colón, Apartado Postal 992, San Jose, T: 506-232-2128, O: Also tel: 231-2557.

CUBA
Nuncio Apostólico, Calle 12 No 514, Miramar Mariano 13, La Habana, T: 53-7-33-2700, O: Also tel: 33-2296.

CYPRUS
Nonciature Apostolique a Chypre, P.O. Box 1964, Nicosie 1515; Nonciature Apostolique, Holy Cross Church, Paphos Gate, Nicosie 1515, T: 00-357-2-46-21-32, F: 00-357-2-46-67-67.

DENMARK
Apostolic Delegation to Scandinavia, Delegate, Immortellevej 11, DK-2950 Vedbaek, Kobenhavn, T: 891550.

DOMINICAN REPUBLIC
Nuncio Apostólico, Avenida Máximo Gómez 27, Apartado Postal 312, Santo Domingo, T: 1-809-682-3773, F: 1-809-687-0287.

ECUADOR
Nuncio Apostólico, Avenida Orellana 692 entre Coruã y 6 de Diciembre, Apartado Postal 17-07-8980, T: 593-2-50-5200, F: 593-2-56-4810, O: Also tel: 50-5201, Telex: 00308-2053 NUNQ ED.

EGYPT
Apostolic Nunciature, Pro-Nuncio, Safarat Al-Vatican, 5 Sharia Mohamed Mazhar, Azmalek, Al Qahirah, T: 805152.

EL SALVADOR
Nuncio Apostólico, 87 Avenida Norte y 7 Calle Poniente, Colonia Escalón, Apartado Postal 01-95, San Salvador, T: 503-223-2454, F: 503-223-7607, O: Also tel: 279-3335.

ETHIOPIA
Apostolic Nunciature, Pro-Nuncio, Makanissa Rd, PO Box 588, Addis Abeba, T: 448095.

FINLAND
Apostolic Nunciature, Pro-Nuncio, Bulevardi 5 as 12, Helsinki 12, T: 644664.

FRANCE
Conseil de l'Europe, 2 rue le-Nôtre, F-67000 Strasbourg, T: 88-350244.
Nonciature Apostolique, Nonce, 10 Av du Président Wilson, F-75116 Paris, T: 72358834.
UNESCO, Observateur Permanent, 10 Av du Président Wilson, F-75116 Paris, T: 7236229.

GERMANY
Apostolic Nunciature, Nuncio, Turmstr 29, Plittersdorf, D-5300 Bonn-Bad Godesberg, T: 00492221-376901.

GHANA
Apostolic Nunciature, Nuncio, 2 Akosombo St, Airport Residential Area, PO Box 9675, Accra, T: 75972.

GUATEMALA
Nuncio Apostólico, 10a Calle 4-47, Zona 9, Ciudad de Guatemala, T: 502-2-32-4274, F: 502-2-34-1918.

HAITI
Nonce Apostolique, Morne Calvaire, Pétion-ville, B.P. 326, Port-au-Prince, T: 509-57-3411, F: 509-57-3411, O: Also: 57-6308.

HOLY SEE
Consilium pro Publicis Ecclesiae Negotiis, Palazzo Apostolico Vaticano, I-00120 Città del Vaticano.
Istituto Internazionale per l'Unificazione del Diritto Privato, Delegate I-001200 Città del Vaticano, T: 6983068.
Secretariat of State (Papal Secretariat), Cardinal Prefect, Palazzo Apostolico, I-00120 Città del Vaticano, T: 6983126.
World Tourist Organization, Permanent Observer, I-00120 Città del Vaticano, T: 6984663.

HONDURAS
Nuncio Apostólico, Apartado Postal 324, Tegucigalpa, M.D.C., T: 504-31-4381, F: 504-32-8280.

INDIA
Apostolic Nunciature, Pro-Nuncio, 50-C Niti Marg, Chanakyapuri, New Delhi 110021, T: 616522.

INDONESIA
Apostolic Nunciature, Pro-Nuncio, Jalan Merdeka Timur 18, PO Box 4227, Jakarta, T: 341142/3.

IRAN
Apostolic Nunciature, Pro-Nuncio, Carrefour Av de France 97, BP 47, Tehran, T: 643574.

IRAQ
Apostolic Nunciature, Pro-Nuncio, Abu Nawas St 207/1, PO Box 2090, Alwyiah, Baghdad, T: 92426.

IRELAND
Apostolic Nunciature, Nuncio 183 Navan Rd, Dublin 7, T: 309344.

ISRAEL
Delegation Apostolique à Jérusalem et en Palestine, P.O. Box 19199, Jérusalem 91191; Mont des Oliviers, Rue Shmuel Ben Adaya, Jérusalem 91191, T: 02-28-22-98, F: 02-28-18-80, O: Also tel: 02-28-86-30.
Nonciature Apostolique en Israel, P.O. Box 150, Jaffa, Tel Aviv; Netiv Hamazalot, 1, Jaffa, Tel Aviv, T: 03-683-56-58, F: 03-683-56-59.

ITALY
British Embassy to the Holy See, Via Condotti 91, 00187 Rome, T: 678-9462, F: 679-7479.
Food & Agriculture Organization (FAO), Permanent Observer, Piazza San Calisto 16, I-00153, Roma, T: 6984634.
Nunziatura Apostolica, Nunzio, Via PO 27-29, I-00198 Roma, T: 866287, 862092.

IVORY COAST
Nonciature Apostolique, Pro-Nonce, BP 1347, Abidjan 08, T: 443835.

JAMAICA
Jamaica Mission to the Holy See, Sebastianusweg 14, D-5300 Bonn 2, T: 01-49-228-31-48-28.

JAPAN
Apostolic Nunciature, Pro-Nuncio, 9-2 Sanban-Cho, Chiyoda-ku, Tokyo, T: 2636851.

JORDAN
Nonciature Apostolique en Jordanie, P.O. Box 5634, Amman, T: 00-962-6-69-25-01, F: 00-692-6-69-25-02.

KENYA
Apostolic Nunciature, Pro-Nuncio, Manyani Rd, P.O. Box 14326, Nairobi, T: 48468, 48583.

LEBANON
Nonciature Apostolique, Nonce, Rue Georges Picot, BP 1882, Bayrut, T: 361766/7.

LIBERIA
Apostolic Nunciature, Pro-Nuncio, P.O. Box 297, Monrovi.

MADAGASCAR
Nonciature Apostolique, Pro-Nonce, Villa Roma II, Route d'Ivandry, BP 650, Tananarive-Amboniloha, T: 42376.

MALTA
Apostolic Nunciature, Nuncio, Villa Cor Jesu, Pitkali Rd, Attard, T: 41543.

MEXICO
Nuncio Apostólico, Mixcoac. Deleg. Benito Juárez (C.P. 01020), Apartado Postal 19-106.

MOZAMBIQUE
Délégation Apostolique, Av Julius Nyerere 882, Maputo, T: 741144.

NETHERLANDS
Apostolic Nunciature, Pro-Nuncio, Carnegielaan 5, 's-Gravenhage, T: 070-468966,7.

NEW ZEALAND
Apostolic Delegation to the Pacific Ocean, Delegate, 112 Queen's Drive, Wellington 3, T: 873470.
Apostolic Nunciature, Pro-Nuncio, 112 Queen's Drive, Wellington 3, T: 873470.

NICARAGUA
Nuncio Apostólico, Carretera Sur, Km 10.8, Apartado Postal 506, Managua, T: 505-2-65-8657, F: 505-2-65-7416, O: Also tel: 65-8052.

NIGERIA
Apostolic Delegation to Nigeria, Delegate, 9 Anifowoshe St, Victoria Island, P.O. Box 2470, Lagos, T: 21411, 22984.

PAKISTAN
Apostolic Nunciature, Pro-Nuncio, Diplomatic Enclave N.1, 5th, P.O. Box 1106, Islamabad, T: 28287/8.

PANAMA
Nuncio Apostólico, Punta Paitilla, Apartado 4251, T: 507-69-3138, F: 507-64-2116, O: Also tel: 69-2102.

PAPUA NEW GUINEA
Apostolic Nunciature, Pro-Nuncio, PO Box 98, Port Moresby, T: 256021.

PARAGUAY
Nuncio Apostólico, Calle Ciudad del Vaticano, Casilla Correo 83, Asuncion, T: 595-21-20-0750, F: 595-21-21-2590, O: Also tel: 21-2590.

PERU
Nuncio Apostólico, Avenida Salaverry y Nazca s/n, Apartado 397-Lima 100, Jesus Maria, T: 51-14-431-9473, F: 51-14-432-3236, O: Also tel: 431-9436, 431-9474.

PHILIPPINES
Apostolic Nunciature, Nuncio, 2140 Taft Av, P.O. Box 3604, Manila, T: 593515, 583072.

PORTUGAL
Nunciatura Apostólica, Nuncio, Av Luis Bivar 18, Lisboa 1, T: 547186.

RWANDA
Nonciature Apostolique, Nonce, BP 261, Kigali, T: 5293.

SAINT LUCIA
St. Lucia Mission to the Holy See, Manoel Street, Castries, T: 809-45-22153.

SENEGAL
Nonciature Apostolique, Pro-Nonce, BP 5076, Dakar, T: 212674.

SOUTH AFRICA
Apostolic Delegation to Southern Africa, Delegate, 800 Pretorius St, Pretoria 0002, T: 742489.

SOUTH KOREA
Apostolic Nunciature, 2, Kungjong,-dong, Chongno-gu, Seoul-shi, T: 02-736-5725, F: 02-736-5738.

SPAIN
Nunciatura Apostólica, Nuncio, Av Pio XII 46, Apdo 19041, Madrid 16, T: 2020840.

SRI LANKA
Apostolic Delegation, 1 Gower St, Colombo 5, T: 82554, 86099.

SUDAN
Apostolic Delegation for the Red Sea, PO Box 623, Al Khurtum.
Apostolic Nunciature, Pro-Nuncio, New Bridge St, Al Safia City, Shambat, PO Box 623, Al Khurtum, T: 32792.

SWITZERLAND
Nonciature Apostolique en Suisse, 60, Thunstrasse, 3000 Berne 16, 031/352 60 40.
United Nations (ONU, OMS, OIT), Observateur Permanent, Chemin Colladon 24, CH-1209 Genève, T: 985111,2.

SYRIA
Nonciature Apostolique, Pro-Nonce, 82 Rue Masr, BP 2271, Dimashq, T: 332601.

TAIWAN
Apostolic Nunciature in China, 87 Aikuo East Rd., Taipei 106, T: 02-3216847, F: 02 3911926.

TANZANIA
Apostolic Nunciature, Pro-Nuncio, Plot No 462, Msasani Peninsula, PO Box 480, Dar es Salaam, T: 68403.

THAILAND
Apostolic Delegation to Laos, Malaysia & Singapore, Delegate, 217-1 Sathorn Tai Rd, Bangkok, T: 31804.
Apostolic Nunciature, Pro-Nuncio, 217 Sathorn Tai Rd, Bangkok, T: 2339109.

TRINIDAD & TOBAGO
Apostolic Nunciature & Apostolic Delegation, P.O. Box 854, Port of Spain; 11 Mary Street, St. Clair, Port of Spain, T: 809-622-5009, F: 809-628-5457, O: Cables: Nuntius Port of Spain.

TURKEY
Apostolic Nunciature (Vatikan Sefareti), Pro-Nuncio, Koroglu Sokak 6, Gazi Osman Pasa, Ankara, T: 275188.

UGANDA
Apostolic Nunciature, Pro-Nuncio, PO Box 7177, Kampala, T: 61167.

UNITED STATES OF AMERICA (USA)
Apostolic Delegation to the United States, 3339 Massachusetts Av, NW, Washington, DC 10008, T: 202)333-7121.
Christian Embassy at the United Nations, P.O. Box 20145, New York, NY 10017.
Holy See Mission to the United Nations, O: E-mail: info@catholic.net.
Lutheran Office for World Community, 777 United Nations Plaza, New York, NY 10017-3521, T: 212-808-5360, F: 1-212-808-5480.
Organization of American States (OAS), Permanent Observer, 3339 Massachusetts Ave., NW, Washington, DC 20008, T: 202-333-7121.
Quaker Office at the United Nations, Room 206, 345 East 46th St, New York, NY 10017, T: 212-682-2745.
United Nations (UN, ONU), Permanent Observer, 20 East 72nd St, New York, NY 10021, T: 212-734-2900.

URUGUAY
Nuncio Apostólico, Bulevar Artigas 1270, C.P. 1503, 11300 Montevideo, T: 598-2-77-2016, F: 598-2-77-2209, O: Also tel: 77-2051, Telex: 032-26670 NUNTIUS UY.

VENEZUELA
Nuncio Apostólico, Avenida la Salle, Urbanización Los Caobos, Apartado 29, Plaza Venezuela, Caracas 1050-A, T: 58-2-781-8939, F: 58-2-793-2403, O: Also tel: 781-3101.

VIET NAM
Délégation Apostolique au Vietnam et Cambodge, Délégué, 173 Hai Bà Trung, P.O. Box 592, Saigon, T: 96876.

YUGOSLAVIA
Apostolic Nunciature, Pro-Nuncio, Svetog Save 24, Beograd, T: 432822.

28
Directories, yearbooks, handbooks, & almanacs

Major directories, yearbooks, and reference handbooks (usually containing names, addresses, other contact information, statistics, listings, descriptive materials, but not extensive histories, surveys, or descriptive texts) of churches, denominations, councils, and Christian organizations, agencies, institutions, personnel, and periodicals; denominational, interdenominational, local, national, plurinational, international, and topical; with the addresses of the publishing or distributing agencies.

ANTIGUA & BARBUDA

Caribbean Catholic Directory 1994.

ARGENTINA

BWA 1995 Yearbook, Directory & General Council Meetings Minutes, Buenos Aires, Argentina.
Evangelical Methodist Church, 1205 Buenos Aires, Argentina.

AUSTRALIA

Jahrbuch 1996 der Altkatholischen Kirche Osterreichts, 1010 Wien, Schottenring 17/1/3/12.

BARBADOS

Handbook of Churches in the Caribbean, The Cedar Press, Bridgetown.

BELGIUM

Katholiek Jaarboek Van België 1994-95, Annuaire Catholique de Belgique, s.c.r.l. LICAP c.v.b.a., rue Guimardstraat 1, 1040 Brussel-Bruxelles.
UNDA Directory 1993, International Catholic Association for Radio and Television, Brussels.

BOTSWANA

Botswana Handbook of Churches, P.O. Box 91, Gaborone.

BRAZIL

Catálogo de Juntas e Agências Missionárias Atunantes no Brasil 1992, Sepal, C.P. 7540, 01064 São Paulo, SP, T: 011-523-2544.
Entidades Cristãs de Comunicação Social no Brasil, Ediçoes Paulinas, Rua Dr. Pinto Ferraz, 183, 04117-São Paulo-SP.

BRITAIN (UK OF GB & NI)

1995 Directory, St. Joseph's Missionary Society, St. Joseph College, Lawrence Street, Mill Hill, London NW7 4JX.
Assemblies of God in Great Britain and Ireland Inc. 1996/7 Year Book, 16 Bridgeford Road, West Bridgford, Nottingham NG2 6AF, T: 0115-981-1188, F: 0115-981-3377.
Catholic Directory of England and Wales, The, Gabriel Communications Limited, St James's Court, Oxford St., Manchester M1 6FP.
Communications Directory 1996-97 WEC International, Bulstrode, Oxford Road, Gerrards Cross, Bucks, SL9 8SZ.
Daily Watchwords (The Moravian Text Book)/Being the Scripture 'Watchwords' and Doctrinal Texts for the Year 1996 (and Almanac), Moravian Book Room, 5 Muswell Hill, London N10 3TJ.
Directory of Orthodox Parishes & Clergy in the British Isles 1994-95, 26 Denton Close, Botley, Oxon OX2 9BW.
Elim Pentecostal Church, P.O. Box 38, Cheltenham Glos. GL 50 3HN, T: 01242-519904, F: 01242-222279.
European Churches Handbook Part 2, Austria, Netherlands, Northern Ireland, Republic of Ireland, Spain, MARC Europe, Vision Building, 4 Footscray Road, Eltham, London SE9 2TZ.
European Churches Handbook Part 1, MARC Europe, Vision Building, 4 Footscray Road, Eltham, London SE9 2TZ.
Free Church of Scotland, The, Yearbook 1996, Knox Press (Edinburgh), 15 North Bank St., Edinburgh EH1 2LS, T: 0131-220-0669.
Friends World Committee for Consultation, 4 Byng Place, London WC1E 7JH, T: 44-171-388-0497, F: 44-171-383-4644.
ICMA Directory, Christian Centres, Chaplaincies and other Seamen's Welfare Agencies throughout the maritime world, Fifth Edition 1989, Intl. Christian Maritime Association, 2/3 Orchard Place, Southampton S01 1BR.
Intercontinental Church Society, 175 Tower Bridge Road, London SE1 2AQ, T: 0171 407 4588, F: 0171 378 0541.
Methodist Church in Ireland (Minutes of Conference, Belfast, Northern Ireland, Britain, 1995).
Quakers around the World (Friends World Committee for Consultation), 4 Byng Place, London WC1E 7JH.
Scottish Baptist Year Book for 1996, The/Council of the Baptist Union of Scotland, 14 Aytoun Road, Glasgow G41 5RT, T: 0141-423-6169, F: 0141-424-1422.
Scottish Episcopal Church Directory 1996/97, 21 Grosvenor Crescent, Edinburgh EH12 5EE.
Year Book of the Congregational Union of Scotland 1990, P.O. Box 189, Glasgow G1 2BX, T: 041-332-7667, F: 041-332-8463.

CANADA

Anglican Church Directory 1996, The Anglican Church of Canada, The Anglican Book Centre, 600 Jarvis St., Toronto, Ontario M4Y 2J6.
Bottin 1994/Société des Missions-Etrangères, 180, place Juge-Desnoyers, Laval (Québec), T: 514-667-4190.
Canadian Christian Sourcebook, The-4th Annual (1996), Genesis Publications, 5803 Cornell Crescent, Mississauga, ON L5M 5R5, T: 1-800-285-6399, F: 905-858-3560, O: E-mail: genesis@surf-sup.net.
Redeemer's Voice Press, 165 Catherine St., P.O. Box 220, Yorkton, Sask., S3N 2V7, T: 306-783-4487, F: 306-783-4487.
United Church of Canada, The Year Book and Directory 1995, 3250 Bloor St., West, Etobiocoke, Ont. M8X 2Y4.
Yearbook of American & Canadian Churches, 475 Riverside Dr., New York, NY 10115.

CHINA

Christian Conference of Asia Directory, 96, 2nd District, Pak Tin Village, Mei Tin Rd, Shatin, New Territories, Hong Kong, T: 852-2691-1068, F: 852-2692-4378, O: CHRISCONAS, HONG KONG (cable).
Hong Kong Catholic Church Directory 1996, Catholic Truth Society, 16, Caine Road, Hong Kong.
Hong Kong Christian Council, the Annual Report 1993-94/40th Anniversary Special Issue, Christian Ecumenical Bldg., 33 Granville Rd., Tsimshatsui, Kowloon, Hong Kong, T: 368-7123, F: 724-2131.

COLOMBIA

Directorio de la Iglesia de América Latina y el Caribe 1996, Carrera 5a. No. 118-31, Apartado Aéreo 51086, Santafé de Bogotá, T: 612-16-20, F: 612-19-29.

COSTA RICA

Alianza Evangélica Costarricense, Apdo 2265-1002, San José, T: 286-1103, F: 286-1104.
Latin American Socio-Religious Studies Program (PROLADES), Apartado Postal 181-2350, San Francisco de Dios Rios, T: 506-227-9579, 283-8300, F: 506-234-7682, O: E-mail: prolades@racsa.co.cr.

CYPRUS

MECC Communications, P.O. Box 4259, Limassol.
MECC, The Directory 1994.
Middle East Council of Churches, 1, Petrarchi St, Limassol, T: 051-26022, F: 051-24613.

DOMINICAN REPUBLIC

Directorio Católico Dominicano 1993, Conferencia del Episcopado Dominicano Instituto Nacional de Pastoral, Apartado 1715, Santo Domingo, D.N., T: 685-3141, 687-2307.

ECUADOR

Directorio de la Iglesia Evangólica del Ecuador, Casilla 8559, Suc. 8, Quito.

FINLAND

1994 Ekumenisk ũrsbok (Ecumenical Yearbook), Helsinki Helsingfors.

FRANCE

Annuaire de la France Protestante 1987, Imprimerie Lormand, Boite Postale n , 62, avenue Gambetta, 82003 Montauban347, T: 63-03 40 70 (France).

GERMANY

Adreßbuch für das Katholische Deutschland, Bonifatius Druck, Buch, Verlag Paderborn.
Christian Communication Directory Africa, Verlag Ferdinand Schöningh, Postfach 2540, D-4790 Paderborn.
Christian Communication Directory ASIA, Verlag Ferdinand Schöningh, Postfach 2540, D-4790 Paderborn.
Jahrbuch für die Erzdiözese Wien 1996, Dein Wille geschehe, wie im Himmel so auf Erden, Stiftsplatz 8, A-3400 Klosterneuburg (im Stift Klosterneuburg), T: 02243-53 77-0.
Katholisches Bistum der Alt-Katholiken in Deutschland/Liturgischer Kalender und Adressenverzeichnis 1996, Gregor-Mendel-Straße 28, 53115 Bonn, T: 02-28-23-22-85.
Ostkirchliches Institut, Ostengasse 29-31, D-93047 Regensburg.

GUATEMALA

Directorio de la Arquidiócesis de Guatemala 1997, Palacio Arzobispal, 7a. Av. 6-21, Zona 1, Ciudad de Guatemala, T: 232-9601, 232-9707, 232-1071.

HOLY SEE

Lay Associations, Summary Data, Pontificium, Consilium, Pro Laicis.

HONDURAS

Anuario de la Iglesia Católica de Honduras, Secretaría de la Conferencia Episcopal de Honduras, Apdo. 847, Tegucigalpa, T: 504-39-1900, F: 504-32-7838.

INDIA

AD 2000 Plans for the Evangelisation of India: A Directory, Draft Edition, AD 2000 and Beyond Movement, 1-1-385/28/A P&T Colony New Bakaram Hyderabad 500 380.
Golden Jubilee Edition, The Catholic Directory of India 1994, C.B.C.I. Centre, 1, Ashok Place, Goldakkhana, New Delhi 110 001.
Indian Missionary Training Centres, Directory 1995, India Missions Association, 48, First Main Rd., East Shenoy Nagar, Chennai 600 030, T: 617596, F: 611859.
Languages of India: Present status of Christian work in every Indian language, P.O. Box 2529, 48, First Main Rd., East Shenoy Nagar, Chennai 600 030, T: 044-6444602, 6444603, F: 044-6442859, O: E-mail: ima@pobox.com, Website: http://www.inmissions.org.
Madurai Christian Directory/Church Growth Association of India, Post Bag 512, 13/2, Aravamuthan Garden St., (behind Hotel Dasaprakash), Egmore, Chennai 600 008, T: 8255372.
Nilgiris Christian Directory/Church Growth Association of India, Post Bag 512, 13/2, Aravamuthan Garden St., (behind Hotel Dasaprakash), Egmore, Chennai, T: 8255372.
Peoples of India: Christian presence and works among them, P.O. Box 2529, 48, First Main Rd., East Shenoy Nagar, Chennai 600 030, T: 044-6444602, 6444603, F: 044-6442859, O: E-mail: ima@pobox.com, Website: http://www.ad2000.org/ima.

INDONESIA

Almanak Kristen Indonesia 1996, Persekutuan Gereja-Gereja Di Indonesia, Jl. Salemba Raya 10 Jakarta 10430, T: 315-0451, F: 62-21-315-0457.

IRELAND

Directory of the Gen Asmbly of the Presby. Ch in Ireland, Church House, Belfast, BT1 6DW, T: 01232-322284, F: 01232-236609.

ISRAEL

Annuaire de L'Eglise Catholique en Terre Sainte 1995, Franciscan Printing Press, Jerusalem.

ITALY

Calendario delle Chiese Valdesi e Metodiste Waldensian and Methodist Calendar Waldenser und Methodisten Kalender, Casa Valdese, Via Beckwith 2-10066 Torre Pellice (To), T: 0121-9-12-96, F: 0121-9-16-04.
Catalogus Monasteriorum O.S.B. (Benedictines), Editio XVIII, Centro Studi S. Anselmo-00153 Roma-Piazza Cavalieri di Malta, 5.
Congregatio Immaculati Cordis Mariæ (C.I.C.M.)/Elenchus 1996, Casa Generalizia C.I.C.M., Via S. Giovanni Eudes, 95, 00163 Roma.
Evangelization 2000, Directory 1993, Rome.
International Directory of Ecumenical Research Centers and Publications, Centro Pro Unione, Via S.M. dell'Anima, 30, 00186 Roma, T: 687-9552.
Istituto Missioni Consolata, Annuario 1996, Direzione Generale, Viale delle Mura Aurelie, 11-13, 00165 Roma, T: 06-638-4241, F: 06-638-2879.
Missionari Comboniani del Cuore di Gesù, Annuario 1996, Missionari Comboniani, C.P. 10733, Via Luigi Lilio, 80, 00142 Roma, T: 39-6-51-91-224, F: 51-91-333.
Missionari Saveriani (Xavierian Missionaries), Casa Generalizia, Missionari Saveriani, Viale Vaticano 40, 00165 Roma, T: 06-393-754-21, F: 06-393-665-71, O: E-mail: xaverian.dg.roma@rm.nettuno.it.
OCD Direcciones 1995, Casa Generalizia dei Carmelitani Scalzi, Corso d'Italia, 38, 00198 Roma, T: 39-0-6-85-44-31, F: 39-0-6-85-35-02-06.
Personnel O.M.I. 1993, Casa Generalizia O.M.I., C.P. 9061, 00100 Roma-Aurelio; Oblataurelia, 00165 Roma, T: 06-63-70-251, F: 39-6-39-37-53-22.
Xaverian Missionaries, 100 years:, Our home-the world. 1995, Viale Vaticano 40-00165-Rome.
Yearbook of the Society of Jesus 1997, General Curia of the Society of Jesus, Borgo S. Spirito 4, 00193 Rome, F: 39-6-687-9283, O: E-mail: infosj@sjcuria.org.

IVORY COAST

Annuaire de L'Eglise Catholique de Cote-D'Ivoire 1996, Procure des Missions Catholiques, 01 BP 1826 Abidjan 01, T: 37-13-82, 37-60-43, F: 37-11-89.

KENYA

ACTEA Director of Theological Schools in Africa, P.O. Box 60875, Nairobi.
All Africa Conference of Churches, P.O. Box 14205, Nairobi.
Catholic Directory of Eastern Africa, Amecea Documentation Service, PO Box 21400, Nairobi, Kenya.

LEBANON

Almanac of the Melkite-Greek Catholic Church 1986, P.O. Box 50076 Beirut, T: 280-826.

LUXEMBOURG

Archidiocèse de Luxembourg, Annuaire 1995, 3, avenue Marie-Thérèse, B.P. 419, L-2014 Luxembourg, T: 451603, F: 455680.

MAURITIUS

Annuaire du Diocese de Port-Louis pour l'Année Commune 1996, Diocèse de Port-Louis, Ile Maurice, Evêché, Port-Louis, T: 208-3068, 2081360, 208-5663.

MOROCCO

Anuario de las Archidiocesis de Tanger y de Rabat, Arzobispado, Sidi Bouabid, 55, Tangier.

MYANMAR

Catholic Directory of Myanmar, The 1995, 289, Thein Byu St., Yangon.

NETHERLANDS

Satellite Broadcasting Guide, P.O. Box 9027, 1006 AA Amsterdam, F: 31-20-4875120.
SVD Word in the World, Steyler Verlag, 4054 Nettetal 2.
World Radio/TV Handbook, P.O. Box 9027, 1006 AA Amsterdam.

NEW ZEALAND

New Zealand Assembly Missionary Prayer Handbook 1993, G.P.H. Society, Ltd., 154 King St., Palmerston North.

PAPUA NEW GUINEA

Directory of the Catholic Churches in Papua New Guinea and Solomon Islands 1985, Catholic Book Centre, P.O. Box 1501, Port Moresby.

PORTUGAL

Anuário Católico de Portugal, Rei dos Livros, Rua dos Fanqueiros, 77 a 79, 1100 Lisboa, T: 8-88-47-55, 8-88-31-88, F: 8-86-22-43.
Prontuário Evangélico 1995, NUCLEO-Centro de Publicações Cristãs, Lda, Apartado 1, 2746 Quelus Codex.

SINGAPORE

Guide to the Catholic Church in China, A. Queen St., Singapore 0718, T: 3387715.
Official Catholic Church Directory, Catholic Bishops' Conf. of Malaysia-Singapore-Brunei, 222 Queen St., #01, Singapore 0718.
Singapore Church Directory 1996-1997, Singapore Every Home Crusade Co. Ltd., No. 8, Lorong 27A Geylang, #02-04, Guilin Building, Singapore 388106, T: 744-7355, F: 744-7266.

SOUTH AFRICA

Afrikaanse Protestante Kerk Jaarboek, PO Box 1188, Brooklyn 0011, Pretoria.
Almanak en Bybelse Dagboek, PO Box 5777, Pretoria 0001, T: 012-322-8885, F: 012-322-7907.
Almanak van die GKSA, PO Box 20004, Noordbrug 2522, T: 0148-297-3986, F: 0148-293-1042.
Church of the Province of Southern Africa, 7 Forest Hill Ave., Oranjezicht, Cape Town, 8001, T: 021-461-4519.
Clerical Directory, Church of the Province of SA, PO Box 61394, Marshalltown 2107, Johnnesburg.
Die Almanak van die Gereformeerde Kerke in Suid-Afrika vir die jaar 1996, Admin. Buro, Posbus 20004, Noordbrug 2522, Potchefstroom, T: 0148-297-3986, F: 0148-293-1042.
Jaarboek (NGK), PO Box 1444, Cape Town 8000, T: 021-23-9233, F: 021-23-5522.
Jaarboek 1996 van die Nederduitse Gereformeerde Kerke, Posbus 1444, Kaapstad 8000, T: 021-23-9233, F: 021-23-5522.
Jaarboek van die Nederduitse Gereformeerde Kerke (Moeder-, Sending- en Bantoekerke). 124 Jaargang, 1973, 119 de Korte St, Braamfontein, Johannesburg, T: 442037.
Journal of Theology for Southern Africa, Dept of Rel Stud UCT, Rondebosch 7700, Cape Town, T: 021-650-3453, F: 021-650-3761.
Minutes of Methodist Church of SA, PO Box 708, Capetown 8000, T: 021-461-8214, F: 021-461-8249.
Minutes of the One Hundred-and-twelth Annual Conf. of the Methodist Church of Southern Africa: 1994, Methodist Publishing House and Book Depot, Cape Town.
SA Baptist Journal of Theology, Cape Town Baptist Theo College, PO Box 82, Crawford 7770, Cape Town, T: 021-637-9020, F: 021-633-2626.
South African Christian Handbook, Christian Info., PO Box 2540, Welkom 9460, T: 057-353-2018.
The Directory of Christian, Camps & Conference Centres, Christian Camping International, PO Box 13, Simon's Town 7995.

SOUTH KOREA

Catholic Address Book, Conference of Korea.
Directory of Korean Missionaries and Mission Societies, Korea Research Institute for Missions and Communication, Seoul.

SPAIN

Guia de la Iglésia Católica en España/Nomenclator 1996, Editorial de la Conferencia Episcopal Española, Don Ramón de la Cruz, 57 - 1°B, 28001 Madrid; Oficina de Estadística y Sociología de la Iglésia (OESI), Secretariado General de la Conferencia Episcopal Española.
Vademecum Evangélico 1999, Libreria Calatrava, c/. Calatrava, 34, 28005 Madrid, T: 91-365-36-26, F: 534-54-92.

SRI LANKA

Catholic Directory of Sri Lanka 1989-90, Catholic Church in Sri Lanka, Cardinal's Residence, Tewatta, Ragama.

SUDAN

Catholic Directory of Sudan, 1995, The Sudan Catholic Bishops' Conf. Secretariat, P.O. Box 6011, Khartoum.

SWAZILAND

Hand Book of Member Churches, World Alliance of Reformed Church (Presbyterian and Congregational), 150, route de Ferney, 1211 Geneva 2, Switzerland.

SWITZERLAND

An International Directory of Theological Colleges 1997, WCC Publications, World Council of Churches, 150 route de Ferney, 1211 Geneva 2.
Directory Liste D'Adresses Guia de Direcciones 1996, 16 Ancienne Route, 1218 Grand Saconnex, Geneva, T: 41-22-929-6040, F: 41-22-929-6044, O: E-mail: worldywca@gn.apc.org.
Directory of Ecumenical Conference Centres (1994), B.P. 2100, 1211 Geneva 2, T: 41-22-7916331, F: 41-22-7910361, O: E-mail: 31domain.wcc1.app@wccxsmtp.wcc.coe.org.
Jahrbuch 1997 der Christkatholischen Kirche der Schweiz, Der ganzen Folge 107 Jahrgang, Des Hauskalenders 93, Jahrgang Preis Fr. 10.
Lutheran World Federation, P.O. Box 2100, 150, route de Ferney, CH-1211 Geneva 2, T: 41-22-791-61-11.
Sacred Heart General Hospital, Editions Saint-Paul, Fribourg.
World Alliance of Reformed Churches: List of Member Churches, 1995, Route de Ferney 150, PO Box 2100, 1211 Geneva 2, T: 22-791 62 38, F: 22-791 65 05, O: E-mail: vm@wcc-coe.org.
World Student Christian Federation (WSCF) Directory/Quadrennium 1995-1999, Ecumenical Centre, route des Morillons 5, 1218 Grand Saconnex, Geneva, T: 4122-798-89-52/53, F: 4122-798-23-70, O: Telex. 415-730 OIK CH, Cables FUACE.
YMCA Directory/World Alliance of YMCAs, 12 Clos-Belmont, 1208 Geneva, T: 41-22-849-51-00, F: 41-22-849-51-10.

TAIWAN

Secetariate of Chinese Bishops Conference, 34, Lane 32, Kuang-Fu South Rd., Taipei, 105, T: 02-578-2355, F: 02-577-3874.

THAILAND

Catholic Directory of Thailand: 1996, Catholic Social Communications Centre of Thailand, 122-122/1 Soi Naaksuwan, Nonsi Rd., Chong Nonsi, Bangkok 10120, T: 662-681-5401-8, F: 662-682-5409.

UNITED STATES OF AMERICA (USA)

1995 Catholic Almanac, Our Sunday Visitor Publishing Div., Huntington, IN 46750.
1995-1996 Church Almanac (The Church of Jesus Christ of Latter-day Saints), Deseret News, P.O. Box 1257, Salt Lake City, UT 84110.
1996 Catholic Internet Directory, O: E-mail: listmaster@catholic.net.
1996 Free Will Baptist Yearbook/National Associ-

ation of Free Will Baptists, Inc., P.O. Box 5002, Antioch, TN 37011-5002; 5233 Mt. View Road, Antioch, TN 37013-2306, T: 615-731-6812, F: 615-731-0771.
1997 Directory of Religious Media, 7839 Ashton Ave., Manassas, VA 20109, T: 703-330-7000, F: 703-330-6996.
1998 Charisma MinistriesToday Networking Directory, 600 Rinehart Rd., Lake Mary, FL 32746, T: 407-333-0600, O: E-mail: harnden@strang.com, Web: www.ministriestoday.com.
A Guide to Religious Ministries for Catholic Men and Women, 210 North Avenue, New Rochelle, NY 10801, T: 914-632-1220.
A Source Book for Earth's Community of Religions, Revised Edition, CoNexus Press-Source-Book Project, P.O. Box 6902, Grand Rapids, MI 49516; Global Education Associates, 475 Riverside Dr., Suite 1848, New York, NY 10115.
Acts of the Council Athens 1992, The Reformed Ecumenical Council, 2017 Eastern Ave., Grand Rapids, MI 49507-3234.
Africa: A Directory of Resources, Orbis Books, Maryknoll, New York 10545.
Almanac of the Christian World, 1993-1994 Edition, Tyndale House Publishers, Inc., Wheaton, IL.
American Society for Church Growth: Membership Directory 1998, P.O. Box 145, 1230 U.S. Highway Six, Corunna, IN 46730, T: 219-436-1565, F: 219-436-1565, O: E-mail: christyascg@fwi.com.
Annual of the Southern Baptist Convention 1996, Exec. Comm., Southern Baptist Convention, 901 Commerece St., Nashville, TN 37203.
Baptist General Conference, 2002 S. Arlington Heights, Arlington Heights, IL 60005-4193, T: 708-228-0200, F: 708-228-5376, O: 1-800-323-4215.
Christian Reformed Church in North America, Year Book 1987, 2850 Kalamazoo Ave SE, Grand Rapids, MI 49560.
Christian Reformed Church in North America Yearbook 1996, Ofc. of the Gen. Sec., 2850 Kalamazoo Ave., S.E., Grand Rapids, MI 49560, T: 616-246-0833, F: 616-247-5895.
Church of the Brethren 1994 Statistical Report, General Board, 1451 Dundee Ave., Elgin, IL 60120, T: 708-742-5100, F: 708-742-6103, O: Also: 800-323-8039.
Conservative Congregational Christian Conference, 1990 Yearbook, 7582 Currell Blvd., Suite 108, St. Paul, MN 55125.
Council of Societies for the Study of Religion/Directory of Departments and Programs of Religious Studies in N. America, Valparaiso University, Valparaiso, IN 46383-6493.
Covenant Yearbook 1995, Evangelical Covenant Church, The, 5101 N. Francisco Ave., Chicago, IL 60625, T: 312-784-3000, F: 312-784-4366.
Diocese of the Armenian Church of America (Directory) 1992, St. Vartan Armenian Cathedral, 630 Second Ave., New York, NY 10016-4885, T: 212-686-0710, F: 212-779-3558.
Directory and Statistics, Moravian Church, Northern and Southern Provinces 1996, The Moravian Church in America, 1021 Center St., Bethlehem, PA 18018; 500 S. Church St., Winston-Salem, NC 27101.
Directory of African American Religious Bodies, a Compendium by the Howard University School of Divinity, Research Center on Black Religious Bodies, Howard Univ. School of Divinity, Washington, DC.
Directory of Cult Research Organizations, The 1993, American Religions Center, Trenton, MI.
Directory of Intentional Communities: a guide to cooperative living, 1992 edition, Fellowship for Intentional Community, Evansville, IN.
Directory of Inter-Religious and Ecumenical Organizations (Pre-publication edition), Chicago, IL.
Directory of Schools and Professors of Mission in the USA and Canada, MARC, 121 E. Huntington Dr., Monrovia, CA 91016.
Directory of the American Baptist Churches in the USA, 1996, P.O. Box 851, Valley Forge, PA 19482-0851, T: 610-768-2000, O: Also: 1-800-ABC-3USA.
Directory of Traveling Friends, 1994-95, 1216 Arch St. 2B, Philadelphia, PA 19107, T: 800-966-4556, F: 215-561-0759, O: 215-561-1700.
Encyclopedia of African American Religions, Religious Info. Systems, Garland Publishing, Inc., New York, NY.
Episcopal Church Annual 1995, 5480 Linglestown Rd., PO Box 1321, Harrisburg, PA 17105, T: 717-541-8130, F: 717-541-8128.
Evangelical Lutheran Church in America, Augsburg Fortress.
Friends Directory, FWCC Section of the Americas, 1506 Race St., Philadelphia, PA 19102.
Futures Research Directory, The: Individuals, World Future Society, 4916 St. Elmo Ave., Bethesda, MD 20814, T: 301-656-8274.
Global Interfaith Directory 1993, Temple of Understanding, 1047 Amsterdam Ave., New York, NY 10025.
Handbook 1997, The Reformed Ecumenical Council, 2050 Breton Rd., SE, Suite 102, Grand Rapids, MI 49546-5547, T: 616-949-2910, O: E-mail: RVHREC@aol.com.
Handbook of Information 1996, Gen. Conf. Mennonite Church, 722 Main St., P.O.f Box 347, Newton, KS 67114-0347.
In Mission 1996/97: Calendar of prayer for the United Church of Christ, 700 Prospect Ave, Cleveland, OH 44115, T: 216-736-3200.
Interdenominational Foriegn Mission Association of North America, Inc., P.O. Box 395, Wheaton, IL 60189-0395, T: 312-682-9270.
ISS Directory of Overseas Schools, The, 1987/88 Edition, Intl. Schools Services, Inc., P.O. Box 5910, Princeton, NJ 08543, T: 800-336-4776, F: 609-452-2690, O: Cable: SCHOOLSERV PRINCETON, Telex: SCHOLSERV PRIN 843 308.
Lausanne Committee Task Force on Jewish Evangelism, P.O. Box 11250, San Francisco, CA 94101.
Lausanne Directory 1998, O: Web: www.lausanne.org.
Lutheran Church, Missouri Synod, 1333 S. Kirkwood Rd., St. Louis, MO 63122-7295.
Mennonite yearbook & Directory, 1996, Mennonite Publishing House, Scottdale, PA 15683-1999.
Mission Handbook 1998-2000 U.S. and Canadian Christian Ministries Overseas, 800 W. Chestnut Ave., Monrovia, CA 91016.
Official Catholic Directory Anno Domini 1994, The, P.J. Kenedy & Sons, 121 Chanlon Road, New Providence, NJ 07974, T: 908-665-6680.
Official guide to Catholic educational institutions and religious communities in the US, 1972-73, Ed Doris B. Gray, US Catholic Conference, Washington, DC.
Orthodox Church in America, 1995 Yearbook & Church Directory, P.O. Box 675, Syosset, NY 11791-0675.
Pilgrimage of Hope: One Hundred Years of Global Interfaith Dialogue, 370 Lexington Ave., New York, NY 10017.
Prayer Group Directory, 1992, Catholic Charismatic Prayer Groups, Renewal Centers, and Liaisons in the US, P.O. Box 628, Locust Grove, VA 22508-0628.
Prison Fellowship International, Membership Handbook & Directory 1994-95, P.O. Box 1734, Washington, DC 20041, T: 01-703-481-0000, F: 01-703-481-0003.
Quaker Information Center, 1501 Cherry St., Philadelphia, PA 19102, T: 215-241-7024, F: 215-864-0104.
Seventh-day Adventist Yearbook 1994, Office of Archives and Statistics, General Conference of Seventh-day Adventist, 12501 Old Columbia Pike, Silver Spring, Maryland 20904.
To All Peoples, Camp Hill, PA.
U.S. Nonprofit Organizations in Development Assistance Abroad, Taich Directory 1983, Technical Assistance Info., Clearing House of the American Council of Voluntary Agencies for Foreign Service, 200 Park Ave., New York, NY 10003.
Wisconsin Evangelical Lutheran Synod, 1996 Yearbook, 2929 N. Mayfair Rd., Milwaukee, WI 53222-4398, T: 414-256-3888, F: 414-256-3899.
World Directory of Missionary Training Programmes, Second Edition, William Carey Library, P.O. Box 40129, Pasadena, CA 91114, T: 818-798-0819.
World Directory of Pentecostal Periodicals, an unofficial listing compiled by the International Pentecostal Press Assoc, 1993, Box 12609, Oklahoma City, OK 73157.
World Methodist Council (Handbook of Information, 1992-1996), Lake Junaluska, NC 28745.
Year Book & Directory 1995 of the Christian Church (Disciples of Christ), 130 E. Washington St., P.O. Box 1986, Indianapolis, IN 46206-1986, T: 317-635-3100, F: 317-635-3700.
Yearbook 1995, Official Personnel, Organization and Statistics of The Free Methodist Church around the World, Free Methodist World Ministries Center, P.O. Box 535002, Indianapolis, IN 46253-5002.
Yearbook of Christian Churches and Churches of Christ, 1996, 1525 Cherry Road, Springfield, IL 62704, T: 217-546-7338, 546-3566.
Yearbook of the Church of God 1996, Leadership Council of the Church of God, P.O. Box 2420, Anderson, IN 46018.

29
Ecology

Christian stewardship of the natural world, God's creation; opposition to pollution, insensitive development, destruction of natural environments, misuse or waste of natural resources; advocacy for sustainable development and environmental responsibility; activist, educational, and advocacy organizations, agencies, and ministries; wilderness and wildlife conservation; theological reflection on earth, creation, or ecological themes; environmentalist or ecological activist resources, research, or training; appreciation and celebration of the beauty, glory, or goodness of nature. See also DEVELOPMENT, JUSTICE, AND PEACE.

BRITAIN (UK OF GB & NI)
Catholic Study Circle for Animal Welfare, 39 Onslow Gardens, London E18 1ND, T: 0181-989 0478.

CANADA
Earthkeeping (Food & Agriculture in Christian Perspective), #205 - 10711 107th Ave., Edmonton, AB T5H 0W6, T: 403-428-6981, F: 403-428-1581.

INDIA
Taru-Mitra 'Friends of Trees', St. Xavier's School, West Gandhi Maidan, Patna, Bihar 800001.

UNITED STATES OF AMERICA (USA)
Friends Committee on Unity with Nature, 7700 Clarks Lake Rd., Chelsea, MI 48118, T: 313-475-9976.
Friends Contact Information, PO Box 2117, Des Moines, IA 50326, T: 515-274-5718.
Green Cross, 10 Lancaster Ave, Wynnewood, PA 19096, T: 800-650-6600.
Network for Environmental & Economic Responsibility, 12 Terrence Ave., Nutley, NJ 07110.
North American Conference on Christianity and Ecology, P.O. Box 14305, San Francisco, CA 94114, T: 415-626-6064.

30
Ecumenical centers

Centers primarily for interdenominational or ecumenical meeting, study, dialogue, resources, and training, for both clergy and laity.

ARGENTINA
Centro De Estudios Cristianos, Paran† 489,2ß/of. 9., Ra-1017 Buenos Aires, T: 1-49-4996.
Centro Ecuménico de Cordoba, Lima 266, 5000 Cordoba, T: 5451-210-251.

AUSTRIA
Insitut Für Patrologie Und Ostkirchenkunde, Schottenring 21, A-1010 WIEN, T: 0222-31 25 44-235.
Insitut Für ôkumenische Theologie Und Patrologie, Universitatsplatz 3, A-8010 GRAZ, T: 0316-380-3180.
Pro Orient Centres, In der Burg, Saulenstiege II-54, A-1010 Wien.

BELGIUM
Centre d'éaction (Ecuméeniques), rue do la Reine, 19, B-5200 HUY, T: 085-21-26-71.
Centre International d'Action Culturelle (CIAC), avenue du Hockey 52, B-1150 Bruxelles, T: 02-771-78-92.
Foyer Oriental Chrétien, Av de la Couronne 206, B-1050 Brussels, T: 02-477106.
Les Eaux Vives, Rue Grétry, 213, B-4020 Liege, T: 041-41-29-08.
Monastère Bénédictin, Dom Olivier Rousseau, B-5395 Chevetogne.

BRAZIL
Casa da Reconciliação, Rua Afonso de Preitas, 704, Paraíso, 04006 São Paulo SP, T: 884-1544.
Cedi-Centro Ecuménico de Documentação, Av. Higienápolis, 983, T: 01283-Sao Paulo-SP, F: 66-7273.
Centro de Ecumenismo do Rio de Janeiro (CERJ), Rua Cosme Velho 98, Laranjeiras, Rio de Janeiro, GB, T: 2251547.

BRITAIN (UK OF GB & NI)
Association of Interchurch Families, The Old Bakery, Danehill, GB-Haywards Heath, Sussex RH17 7ET, T: 0825-790 296.
Ecumenical Soceity of the Blessed Virgin Mary, 11 Belmont Road, GB-Wallington Surrey SM6 8TE, T: 647-5992.
Farnecombe Community, 5 Wolseley Rd, Farnecombe, Godalming, Surrey, T: Godalming 7255.
Iona Community, Community House, 214 Clyde St, Glasgow C1, Scotland; Summer address: Isle of Iona, by Oban, Argyll.
Irish School of Ecumenics, 20 Pembroke Park, SE-Dublin 20, T: 01-684960.684914.
London Ecumenical Centre, 35 Jermyn St, London SW1, T: 01-437-0235.
NACCAN - The National Centre for Christian Communities and Networks, Westhill College, Weoley Park Road, Selly Oak, GB-Birmingham B29 6LL, T: 021-472-8079.
Scottish Churches House, Kirk Street, Dunblane, Perthshire FK15 0AJ Scotland, T: 0786-823588, F: 0786-82544.
St. Basil's House (Fellowship of Sts. Alban & Sergius), 52 Ladbroke Grove, GB-London W11 2PB, T: 01-727-7713.
St. Colm's Education Centre and College, 20 Inverleith Terrace, GB-Edinburgh EH3 5NS, T: 44-31-332-0343.
Vita et Pax Foundation for Unity, Turvey Abbey, GB-Turvey, Bedordshire MK43 8DE, T: 023-064-432.
World Association for Christian Communication, 122 King's Road, GB-London SW3 4TR, T: 01-589-1484.

CANADA
Canadian Centre for Ecumenism, 2065 Sherbrooke St., W., Montreal, QC H3H 1G6, T: 514-937-9176, F: 514-931-3432.
Christian Info. Resource Centre, 63 King St., E., Oshawa, ON L1H 1B4, T: 905-434-7977, F: 905-434-2933.
Dialogue Centre, 25 Jarry O., 113, Montréal Québec H2P 1Sy, T: 514-382-8197.
Ecumenical Forum of Canada, 22 Madison Ave., Toronto, Ontario M5R 2S2, T: 1-416-924-9351, F: 1-416-924-5356.
Saskatoon Centre for Ecumenism, 1006 Broadway Ave., Saskatoon, SK S7N 1B9, T: 306-653-1633.

CHINA
Hong Kong Christian Institute, 11 Mongkok Road, 10F, Kowloon, Hong Kong, T: 398-1699, F: 398-787-4765.
Tao Fong Shan Ecumenical Centre, Tao Fong Shan Road, Shatin, NT, Hong Kong, T: 0-6050839.

CYPRUS
Ayia Napa Conference Center, P.O. 48, Ayia Napa, T: 037-21284-88, F: 037-21229, O: Telex: 5323 ANCC-CY, Cable: AYIANAPA OIKOUMENE NICOSIA.

CZECH REPUBLIC
Joannis Hus Facultas Theological Pragae, Sectiom Oecumenica, V.V. Kujbyseva 5, CS-166 26 Praha 6 - Dejvice, T: 320569.
Oekumenisches Institut der Comenius-Fakultt, Dr. Z. Wintra 15, Praha 6, SC 160 00.

DENMARK
Det Okumeniske Center, V. Bo Torppedersen, Ronnevangshusene 51, 2. m.p., DK-2630 Taastrup, T: 02-52 83 60.
Dialogue Center, Katrinebjergvej 46, DK-8200 Aahus N., T: 06-105411.
Ecumenical Centre, Klovermarksvej 4, DK-8200 Arhus N., T: 06-162655.
Institut for Systematisk Teologi, Afdeling for Ekumenisk Teologi, Kobmagergade 44-46, DK-1150 Kopenhagen, T: 01-15-28-11, Loc. 279.

DOMINICAN REPUBLIC
Centro de Planificación Acción Ecuménica (CEPAE), P.O. Box 252-2, Gazcue, Santo Domingo; c/o Elvira de Mendoza 253, Gazcue, Santo Domingo, T: 809-687-5255, F: 809-687-5255.

ETHIOPIA
Saint Frumentius Ecumenical Centre, P.O. Box 3, Adi-Ugri.

FIJI
Ecumenical Institute Renewal and Resource Centre, Suva, T: 00679-39-39-36.

FINLAND
Ecumenical Centre of Myllyjärvi, Myllyjärvi, 00950 Kunnarla, T: 90-857148.
Orthodox Institute, Helsingin Yliopiston Ekumeeninen Arkisto, Helsinki.
University of Helsinki. Division of Ecumenical Studies, Neitsytpolku 1B, SF-00140 Helsinki, T: 90-661791-258.

FRANCE
Amitié- Rencontre Entre Chrétiens, 13, rue des Pleins Champs, F-76000 Rouen, T: 16-35-70-55-26.
Centre d'Etudes Oecuméniques, 8 rue Gustave Klotz, F-67 Strasbourg, T: 88-362926.
Centre d'êtudes Istina, 45, rue de la Glaciäre, F-75013 Paris, T: 1-45-35-37-04.
Centre de Villemétrie, Orgemont, 91 La Ferte Alais.
Centre do Recherche et de Documentation des Institutions Chrétiennes, 9, place de l'Universitè, F-67084 Strasbourge, T: 16-88-35-59-40.
Centre Ocuménique Unité Chrétienne, 2, rue Jean-Carriäs, F-6900 Lyon, T: 16-78-42-11-67.
Centre Oecuménique, 12 rue Fénélon, 36 Lyon.
Centre Oecuménique de Liaisons Internationales (COELI), 68 rue de Babylone, F-75007 Paris, T: 555-2554.
Centre Saint-Irènèe, 2, Place Gailleton, F-69002 Lyon, T: 78-374982.
Formation Oecuménique Interconfessionnelle (FOI), 2 Place Gailleton, F-69002 Lyon, T: 78-374982.
Groupe Ocumènique des Dombes, Abbaya Notre-Dame des Dombes, F-01240 Marlieux par St Paul-de-Varay, T: 16-74-98-14-40.
Institue Franâais d'ètudes Byzantines, 14, rue Sèguier, F-75006 Paris, T: 1-43-26-12-36.
Monastère Invisible de l'Unité Chrétienne, 6 Rue Jean-Ferrandi, F-75006 Paris.

GERMANY
Bund Für Evangelisch-Katholische Wiedervereinigung e.v., Gichenbacher Str.9, D-6412 Gersfeld-Dalherda, T: 06656-8566.
Institut Für missionswissenschaft und ôkumenische Theologies der Universitat Tübingen, Kauberstr. 43, D-7400 Türbingen, T: 07071-292592.
Institut Für ôkumenische Theologies der Universitat München, Geschwister-Schol-Platz 1, D-8000 München 22.
Johann-Adam-Hîhler-Institut Für ôkumenik, Leostra·e 19a, D-4790 Paderborn, T: 05251-26059.
Katholisch-ôkumenisches Institue der Westfalisches Wilhelms Universitat, Bogenstra·e 6/abt 2, D-4400 Münster i.W..
Konfessionskundliches Institut des Evangelischen Bundes, Eifelstra·e 35, D-6140 Bensheim, T: 06251-3800 & 6632.
Ostkirchliches Institut der Deutschen Augustiner, Steinbachtal 2a, D-8700 Würzburg, T: 0931-71085.
Philosophisch-Theologisches Studium Erfurt, Dozentur für îkumenische Theologies, Domstra·e 10, Erfurt, T: 26577.
Stiftung ôkumenisches Instuitut e.v., Annabergstr. 46, D-5880 Ludenscheid, T: 02351-83225.
Westalische Wilhelmsuniversitat, Institut für îkumenische Theologie, Am Stadtgraben 13/15, D-4400 Münster i.W..
ôkumenisch Arbeitsstelle Dresden, Am Hochwal 2, Dresden, T: 37073.
ôkumenisch-Mission arisches Zentrum, Georgenkirchstr. 70, Berlin, T: 43830.
ôkumenische Centrale, Postfach f10 17 62, Neue Schllesingergasse 22-24, D-6000 Frankfurt Am Main1, T: 069-20335.
ôkumenisches Institut der Benediktinerabtei Niederaltaich, D-8351 Niederaltaich bei Deggendorf, T: 09901-6318 or 6124.
ôkumenisches Seminar der Universitat Hamburg, Sedanstra·e 19, D-2000 Hamburg 13, T: 0909-4123 3770.

GUYANA
David Rose Centre, 274 Front Rd, West Ruimveldt, South Georgetown, T: 71209, 68899.

HUNGARY
House of Reconciliation, A Berekfurdoi Megbekeles Haza, Berek ter 19, H-5309 Berekfurdo.
Magyarorszagi Reformatus, Egyhaz Balatonszarszoi, Soli Deo Gloria Konferenciatelepe, Abonyi u. 21, H-1146 Budapest.
Sion Hegye, Reformatus Konferenciatelep, H-2022 Tahi, Abony u. 21, H-1146 Budapest.

INDIA
Christian Ecumenical Centre, 20 Ramakrishnappa Rd, Whitefield PO, Bangalore 5, T: Bangalore 50113.
Christian Retreat and Study Centre, Rajpur P.O.,

Dehra Dun, U.P. 248 009, T: Rajpur 258.
Ecumenical Biblical and Oriental Study Centre, Kottayam, Kerala 686 001.
Ecumenical Centre, Sneha Sena Office, P.O. Box 1774, Cochin-16, Kerala, T: 32056.
Ecumenical Christian Centre, Post Bag 11, Whitefield, Bangalore 560 066, Karnataka, T: 91-80-8452-270, F: 91-80-8452-653.
Theology Centre, Kottayam, Kerala 687 017, T: 0481-7430.

INDONESIA
Akademi Leimena, Jln Salemba Raya 10, Jakarta 10430, T: 62-8581321.
Christian Ecumenical Centre, Jalan Teuku Umar 17, Jakarta.
Wisma Oikumene, 13-B Jalan Gudang, Sukabumi.

IRELAND
Irish School of Ecumenics, Bea House, Milltown Park, Dublin 6, T: 01-2698607.

ISRAEL
Centro Delle Chiese Orientali, Vacariat Patriarcal Grec-Melkite Catholique, B.P. 14130, 91141 Jerusalem, T: 02-282023.
Ecumenical Institute of Jerusalem, c/o St George's Close, Jerusalem.
Ecumenical Institute for Theological Research, P.O. Box 19556, Jerusalem, T: 02-713451,2,3,4.
Ecumenical Theological Research Fraternity in Israel, P.O. Box 249, Jerusalem 91002, T: 02-824645.
St. Isaiah's House, 20 Rehov, Gershon Agron, P.O. Box 1332, Jerusalem, T: 02-29763.
Tantur Ecumenical Institute for Theological Research, P.O. Box 19556, Jerusalem.

ITALY
Abazia Greza di Grottaferrata, I-00046 Roma.
Agape Ecumenical Centre, Borgata Agape 1, 10060 Prali (Torino), T: 121-807514, F: 121-807690.
Anglican Centre in Rome, Palazzo Doria, Via del Corso 303, 00186 Rome, T: 39 6-678 0302, F: 39 6-678 0674, O: E-mail: anglican_centre@ecunet.org.
Associazione Unitas, Via del Corse 306, I-00186 Roma, T: 06-689052.
Centro di Orientamento Ecumenico e Missionario, Corso Ticinese 15, Milano.
Centro Ecumenico Cremonese, Via Cavallotti 25, I-26100 Cremona.
Centro Ecumenico Eugenio IV, Piazza Duomo 12, I-36100 Vicenza, T: 0444-543-422.
Centro Ecumenico Nordico, US Pietro Campagna 154, I-06081 Assis (Perugia), T: 821379.
Centro Ecumenico Russo Vladimir Solov'ev, Via Roma 17, I-35010 Compadoro (PD), T: 049-5008182.
Centro Ecumenico S.Nicola, Padri Domenicani, Largo Abate Elia 13, I-70122 Bari, T: 080-2112-69, 2112-05.
Centro Evangelico, Via Provinciale 17, San Fedele d'Intelvi (Como).
Centro Evangelico di Cultura, Via Pietro Cossa 42, Roma.
Centro Francescano d'Azione Ecumenica, Chiesa Nouvá, I-06081 Assisi (Perugia).
Centro Pro Unione, Via S. Maria dell'Anima 30, I-00186 Roma, T: 06-687-9552.
Centro Uno, Piazza Tor Sanguigna 13/2, I-00186 Roma, T: 06-6569598.
Centro Ut Unum Sint, Via Antonino Pio 75, I-00145 Roma, T: 06-5138898, 5132941.
Comunità Ecumenica di Rose, I-13050 Magnano (VC), T: 015-679185.
Comunità Evangelica Ecumica di Ispra-Varese, Chiesa Evangelica di San Giovanni, I-21034 Cocquio-Caldana (Varese), T: 79371.
Ecumenical Institute of the Pontifical University St. Thomas, Largo Angelicum 1, I-00184 Roma, T: 06-67021.
IDOC (International Documentation of the Contemporary Church), Via S. Maria dell'Anima 30, I-00186 Roma, T: 06-6568332.
Instituto Internazionale di Studi Theologici Ecumenci e Religiosi, Via Principe Amedeo 75, I-00185 Roma, T: 06-737228.
Istituto Distudiecumenici S. Bernardino, Via A. Provolo 28, I-37123 Verona, T: 045-59-10-68.
Segretariato AttivitÒ Ecumeniche, Via della Cava Aurelia 8, I-00165 Roma, T: 06-637-40-33.
Sezione Ecumenico-Patristica Greco-Bizantina S. Nicola, Via Bisanzio e Rainaldo 15, I-70122 Bari, T: 235252.
St. Anthony's Ecumenical Hospice, Suore dell'-Atonement, Via Galeazzo Alessi 10, I-06081 Assisi (Perugia).
Studi Ecumenici/Centro Internazionale della Pace, Via Goffredo Casalis 35, I-10143 Torino, T: 745819.

JAPAN
Japan Christian Center, Rm. 51, 2-3-18 Nishi Waseda, Shinjuku Ku, Tokyo 169, T: 033-203-0101.

KENYA
Peace Foundation (Africa), Diakonia House, P.O. Box 24252, Nairobi, T: 569493, F: 569493.

LEBANON
Monastère Notre-Dame de l'Unité, Yarzé-Baabda, BP 4077, Bayrut, T: 420095.

LESOTHO
Thaba-Khupa Ecumenical Centre, P.O. Box 929, Maseru 100, T: 350284.

MALAWI
Chilema Ecumenical Training and Conference Centre, Private Bag 2, Chilema Zomba, T: 531234-227.

MEXICO
Centro de Estudios Ecuménicos, Fresnos 45, San Angel Inn. T.F..
Centro Regional de Informacion Ecumenica, Yosemite 45, Col. N†poles, 03810 México 18 D.F., T: 536-9321.

MYANMAR
Myanmar Ecumenical Sharing Centre (MESC), P.O. Box 1400, Yangon; c/o Myanmar Council of Churches, 263 Naha Bandoola St., Yangon, T: 73290, O: Also tel: 82295 or 72110 and Cable: OIK-OUMENE.

NETHERLANDS
Ecumenical Research Exchange, Oostmaaslaan 950, NL-3063 DM Rotterdam, T: 010-139485.
Ecumenical Training Centre, Oegstgeest.
Hospitium Oecumenicum, Waldeck Pyrmontlaan 9, Amsterdam Zuid, T: 020-716861, 717631.
Instituut Voor Byzantijnse en Oecumenische Studies, Louiseweg 12, NL-6523 NB Nijmegen, T: 080-224061.
Interuniversitair Instituut Voor Missiologie en Oecumenica, Afdeling oecumenica, Heidelberglaan 2, NL-3584 CS Utrecht, T: 030-532079, F: 31-30-531357.
OSACI (Stichting Oecumenisch Studie en Actie Centrum Voor Investeringen), Prins Hendrikkade 48, NL-1012 AC Amsterdam, T: 020-241149.
Provincial Training Centre, Natteweg 9, Bergen.
St. Willibrord Vereniging, Walpoort 10, NL-5211 DK 'S-Hertogenbosch, T: 073-13 64 71.

NICARAGUA
Centro Ecuménico Antonio Valdivieso, Apartado 3205, Managua.

NORWAY
Centre for Ecumenical Theology, P.O. Box 1046, N-5001 Bergen.
Institute for Ecumenical Meeting, Gemlevn 17, Oslo.
Norwegian Ecumenical Press Bureau, Postboks 114\53, N-5001 Bergen, T: 05-320416.

PHILIPPINES
John XXIII Ecumenical Center (JEC), Loyola House of Students, PO Box 4082, Manila, T: 991561.

POLAND
Ecumenical Institute, Catholic University of Lublin, Al. Raclawickie 14, skr. Poczt 279, PL-20 950 Lublin, T: 30426.

PORTUGAL
Centro Ecumenico Reconciliaçao, Apartado 2088, Vais, Buarcos, P-3081 Figueira da Foz, T: 0035-33-32-617, F: 0035-33-22-603.

ROMANIA
Evangelical Academy Transylvania, Str. Gen. Magheru, RO-2400 Sibiu, T: 0040-69-433-850, F: 0040-69-433-850.

SOUTH AFRICA
Bureau of African Churches, Christ the King Theological School, Durban.
Edendale Lay Ecumenical Centre, P.O. Box 63, Piessislaer 4500, T: 0331-81018.
Stellenbosch Ecumenical Centre, 81 Brich St, Stellenbosch, CP.
Wilgespruit Ecumenical Centre, P.O. Box 81, Roodepoort, Transvaal, T: 763-1270, 2650.

SPAIN
Asociacion Ecuménica Juan XXIII, Colegio Mayor Oriental (Univer. Pont), Ramón y Cajal 15, E-37007 Salamanca, T: 923-21 24 20.
Centro de Estudios Orientales y Ecuménicos Juan XXIII, Universidad Pontificia, Comassia 5, E-37008 Salamanca, T: 923-21-59-80.
Centro Ecuménico, Delegación Diocesana de Ecumenismo, Palacio Episcopal, Córdoba.
Centro Ecuménico a la Unidad Por María, Plaza Santo Domingo el Real 1, E-45080 Toledo, T: 925-223324.
Centro Ecuménico de Los Rubios, 29730 (Chilches), Los Rubios, Málaga, T: 240-11-99.
Centro Ecuménico El Salvador, Playa del Inglés, Gran Canaria.
Centro Ecuménico Interconfessional de Valencia, Cirilo Amoros 54, E-46004 Valencia, T: 96-351-77-50.
Centro Ecuménico Misioneras de la Unidad, Plaza Conde Barajas 1-2a, E-28005 Madrid, T: 2661741.
Hogar Ecuménico de Ancianos, 41002 Teodosio, 57, Sevilla, T: 438-34-44.
Instituto Ecuménico Juan XXIII, Ramon y Cajal 7, Salamanca.

SRI LANKA
Centre for Society and Religion, 281 Deans Road, Colombo 10, T: 94-69-54-25, F: 695602, O: Also fax: 698315 (attn. CSR), Telex: 696715.
Ecumenical Institute for Study and Dialogue, 490/5 Havelock Road, Colombo 6, T: 586998.

SWEDEN
Fîrbundet Fîr Kristen Enhet, Box 277, S-721 06 Vasterus, T: 021-12-15-13.
Ljungskile Folkshögskola, Box 111, S-459 00 Ljungskile, T: 46-522-20111.
Nordic Ecumenical Institute, Box 438, S-751 06 Uppsala, T: 46-18-169550.
Sigtunastiftelsen, Manfred BJörkquists allé 2-4, Box 57, S-193 00 Sigtuna, T: 46-502-16.
Svenska Institut Fîr Missionsforskning, Gîtgatan 3, S-752 22 Uppsala, T: 018-10 53 50, 13 75 25.

SWITZERLAND
Centre oecumenique de catechese du canton de Geneve, 14, rue du Village-Suisse, 1205 Geneve, 022/3280458.
Centre International Réformé John Knox, 27, Chemin des Crêts de Prégny, CH-1218 Grand Saconnex/Geneva, T: 41-22-989161.
Commission oecumenique de l'Episcopat catholique-romain en Suisse, Albertinum, 2, Square des Places, 1700 Fribourg, 037/221802.
Commission de dialogue Eglise reformee - Eglise catholique-romaine, Institut d'etudes oecumeniques, Universite Misericorde, 1700 Fribourg, 037/29 74 29.
Commission de dialogue des Eglises orthodoxe et catholiqque-romaine, Centre orthodoxe, 37, ch. de Chambesy, 1292 Chambesy, 022/758 1629.
Ecumenical Center, P.O. Box 2100, 150 Route De Ferney, 1211 Geneva 2, T: 41-22-7916-222, F: 41-22-7910-361, O: Tlx: 415730 OIK CH.
Ecumenical Institute, Château de Bossey, CH-1298 Céligny, Genève, T: 41-22-776-25-31, F: 41-22-776-09-69, O: Cable: INSTITUTCELIGNY.
Evangelische Arbeitsstelle ôkumeneschez, Sulgenauweg 26, Postfach, CH-3000 Bern 23, T: 031-46 26 85.
Insitut Oumènique, Chéteau de Bossey, CH-1298 èligny, T: 021-76531.
Institut d'etudes oecumeniques de l'Universite de Fribourg, Universite Misericorde, 1700 Fribourg, 037/29 74 29.

TRINIDAD & TOBAGO
Ecumenical Centre, Deane St, St Augustine.

UKRAINE
Ukrainian Center for Christian Cooperation, 16, Kiev 252042, T: 7-044-2-269-4655, F: 7-044-2-269-7697.

UNITED STATES OF AMERICA (USA)
Boston Ecumenical Institute, Box 171, Merrimac, MA 01860.
CHARIS Ecumenical Centre for Church and Community and Fargo/Moorhead, Communiversity, Concordia College, Moorhead, MN 56560, T: 218-299-3566.
Graymoor Ecumenical & Interreligious Institute, 475 Riverside Dr., Room 1960, New York, NY 10115-1999, T: 212-870-2330, F: 212-870-2001.
Institute for Ecumenical and Cultural Research, PO Box 6188, Collegeville, MN 56321, T: 612-363-3366.
Interdonominational Theological Center, 671 Beckwith Street., SW, Atlanta, GA 30314, T: 404-522-1772 ext. 107.
National Council of Churches, Faith and Order, Room 872, 475 Riverside Drive, New York, NY 10115, T: 212-870-2569.
North American Academy of Ecumenists, c/o New York Theological Seminary, 235 East 49 St, New York, NY 10017.
Pacific and Asian American Center for Theology and Strategies (PACTS), 1798 Scenic Ave., Berkeley, CA 94709, T: 510-849-0653.
Packard Manse Ecumenical Center, Stoughton, MA 02072.
Parishfield, Brighton, Michigan.
Training for Ecumenical Action in Mission (TEAM), Kansas City, Kansas.
Washington Theological Consortium, 487 Michigan Avenue, NE, Washington, DC 20017, T: 202-832-2675.
Wilton Ecumenical Center, Box 74, Wilton, CT 06897.

URUGUAY
Instituto Ecuménico, 8 de Octubre 3324, Casilla de Correo 2123, Distrito 5, Montevideo, T: 586818.

VENEZUELA
Acción Ecuménica, calle Norte 10, San Vicente Medina 139, La Pastora-Caracas, Apartado 6314, Carmelitas, Caracas 1010-A, T: 58-2-811548, O: Also tel: 8611196.

ZAMBIA
Makeni Ecumenical Centre, P.O. Box 50255, Lusaka, T: 01-217853.
Mindolo Ecumenical Centre (Foundation), Box 1192; P.O. Box 1493, T: 84712/3.

ZIMBABWE
Bureau of African Churches, Lobengula St, Bulawayo.

31 Ecumenical commissions & agencies

Organizations for Christian unity, interchurch, inter-confessional, or multi-confessional dialogue or understanding; or functions organized for the fostering of relations between the churches, for ecumenical meeting, dialogue, study, fellowship, or joint action; faith and order commissions; church union negotiating bodies.

ALGERIA
Commission pour l'Oecuménisme, c/o Archêveché, 13 Rue Khelifa-Boukhalfa, El Djezair, T: 634244.

ARGENTINA
Catholica Unio, Abadia de Niño Dios, Victoria, ER.
Comisión Episcopal de Fe y Ecumenismo, CEA, Paraguay 1867, Buenos Aires.
Departmento de Ecumenismo, Arzobispado de Buenos Aires, Suipacha 1034, Buenos Aires.
Secretariado Nacional de Ecumenismo, CEA, Paraguay 1867, Buenos Aires.

AUSTRALIA
Committee for Ecumenism, Australian Episcopal Conference, GPO Box 42, Canberra, ACT 2600.
Ecumenical Office, Archdiocese of Melbourne, Sacred Heart Presbytery, 199 Rathdowne St, Carlton 3053, T: 3471644.
Joint Secretariat RCEC-ACC, c/o 401A Pitt St, P.O. Box 111, Brickfield Hill, NSW 20001.

AUSTRIA
Altkatholisch-römisch-katholische Konsultationen, Sek der Österreichischen Bischofskonferenz, Rotenturmstr 2, A-1010 Wien.
Catholica Unio, Zentrale fur Österreich, Landessekretär, p/A Dreifaltigkeitsgasse 14, Postfach 66, A-5024 Salzburg.
Diözesankommission für Ökumenische Fragen, Wollzeille 3, A-1010 Wien.
Katholischer Arbeitskreis für die Weltgebetswoche in Deutschland, Österreich und der Schweiz, Catholica Unio, Maria Plain, A-5028 Salzburg-Kasern.
Katholischer Ökumenischer Arbeitskreis in Österreich, CM v Weber-Grasse 3, Graz.

BAHAMAS
Ecumenical Commission, Diocese of Nassau, P.O. Box 187, Nassau.

BELGIUM
Commission pour l'Oecuménisme, Rue Guimard 5, B-1040 Brussel, T: 02-5118256.

BELIZE
Planning Commission of Churches, Regent St, Belize City.

BENIN
Commission Episcopale pour l'Islam et l'Oecumenisme, BP 491, Cotonou.

BRAZIL
Catholica Unio, National Sec, Priorado San Ana, Jundiaí, SP.
Coordenadoria Ecuménica de Servicios, Rua da Graça, 164, 40080-410-Salvador-ba, T: 5571-336-5457, F: 5571-336-0733.
Equipe Fraterna, CP 2013, Recife, PE.
Fraternidade de Reconciliação, Rua São Bento 44, CP 975 Recife, PE.
Presenca Ecuménica e Servico-Koinonia, Rua Santo Amaro 129, Gloria 22211-230-Rio de Janeiro-RJ, T: 5521-221-3016, F: 5521-224-6713.
Secretaria de Ecumenismo da CNBB e Regionais, Ladeira da Glória 99, Rio de Janeiro GB.
Servico Interconfessional de Aconselhamento (SICA), AV Alberto Bins 1008, Pôrto Alegre, Rio Grande do Sul, T: 247877.

BRITAIN (UK OF GB & NI)
Amitié, 67 Cranford Av, London, N13.
Anglican and Eastern Churches Association, 85 Mortimer Rd, London NI; 88 Farlington Av, Drayton, Portsmouth, T: 01-254-7945.
Catholic Episcopal Commission for Ecumenism, Ara Coeli, Armagh, NI.
Church 2000, Committee for Christian Unity, 39 Eccleston Square, London SWIV 1PD, T: 01-834-5612.
Columbanus Community of Reconciliation, 683 Antrim Road, Belfast BT15 4EG, T: 08-0232 778009.
Community of the Peace People, Peace House, 224 Lisburn Road, Belfast BT9 6GE, T: 08-0232 663465.
Consultative Committee for Local Ecumenical Projects England & Wales (CCLEPE), 10 Eaton Gate, London SW1.
Ecumenical Society of the Blessed Virgin Mary, 237 Fulham Palace Rd, London SW6 6UB, T: 01-381-1615.
English Catholic-Methodist Committee, c/o RC Bishops Conference and Methodist Headquarters, London.
One for Christian Renewal, 300 Granville Rd, Sheffield S2 2RT, T: 0742-21020.
Order of Christian Unity, 39 Victoria St, London SW1, T: 01-222-6331.
Roman Catholic Ecumenical Commissions of England and Wales, Sacred Heart Convent, Woldingham, Nr Caterham, Surrey CR3 7YA, T: Caterham 46703.
Roman Catholic Ecumenical Commission of Scotland, Convent of Notre Dame, 7 Victoria Circus, Dowanhill, Glasgow G12 9LA.
Society of St. John Chrysostom, 14 Macduff Road, London SW11 4DA.
Vita et Pax Foundation for Unity, For Monks: Christus Rex Priory, 29 Bramly Rd, London N14; 1 Priory Close, Southgate, London N14 4AT, T: 01-449-8336, 01-449-6648.
World Association for Christian Communication (WACC), Edinburg House, 2 Eaton Gate, London SW1.

CAMEROON
Comité de l'Union des Eglises au Cameroun, Bibia, BP 10, Lolodorf.
Oeuvre Sociale Oecuménique, BP 913, Douala.

CANADA
Canadian Centre for Ecumenism, 2065 Ouest, rue Sherbrooke, Montreal, Quebec H3H 1G6, T: 514-935-5497.
Ecumenical Forum of Canada, 11 Madison Ave., Toronto, Ontario M5R 2S2, T: 416-924-9351.
General Commission on Church Union, Room 312, 85 St. Clair Av East, Toronto 290, Ontario, T: 416-920-4030.
Global March for Jesus, Box 65130, Toronto, ON M4K 3Z2, T: 905-848-7080, F: 905-272-2100.
Joint Working Group of Montreal Churches, Montréal, Québec.
Office National d'Oecuménisme, CCC, 1444/1452

Rue Drummond, ch 214, Montréal 107, Québec, T: 514-845-7141.
People's Opportunities in Ecumenical Mission (POEM), 1708 West 16th Av, Vancouver, BC, V6J 2M1, T: 733-3131.

CHANNEL ISLANDS
St Brelade Group of Churches, Rectory, La Marquanderie, St Brelade, Jersey, T: 0534-42302.

CHILE
Departamento Nacional de Ecumenismo, Las Ramadas 716, Dpto 23, Classificador 11, Casilla 9194 (& 13861), Santiago.

CHINA
Tao Fong Shan Ecumenical Centre, P.O. Box 33, Shatin, N.T., Hong Kong, T: 0-6050839.

COLOMBIA
Comité Nacional de Ecumenismo del Secretariado Permanente del Episcopado, Carrera 10 No 19-42, of 410, Bogotá, T: 414642.

CONGO-ZAIRE
Secrétariat pour l'Unité, Conférence Episcopale du Zaire, BP 3258, Kinshasa-Gombe.

CROATIA
Commission for Ecumenism, Biskupska Konferencija Jugoslavije, Kaptol 31, YU-41000 Zagreb.

CUBA
Comisión Episcopal Nacional de Ecumenismo, Apdo 594, La Habana 1, T: 68463.

CZECH REPUBLIC
Catholic Diocesan Ecumenical Commission, c/o Archdiocese of Prague, Hradcanské nám 16, 119 02 Praha 1, T: 536022.

DOMINICAN REPUBLIC
Centro de Planificación y Acción Ecuménica-CEPAE, Elvira de Mendoza No. 253-Zona Universitaria-Santo Domingo, T: 687-5820, F: 687-5255.

EGYPT
Bishopric of Public, Ecumenical and Social Services, Coptic Orthodox Church, P.O. Box 9035, Nasr City, Cairo, T: 20-2-2822-215, F: 20-2-2825-983.

FINLAND
Ecumenical Secretariat of the Diocese of Helsinki, Stadium Catholicum, Helsinki.
Ecumenical Society in Finland, Temppelikatu 21 C 13, 00100 Helsinki 10.

FRANCE
Association Oecuménique (BOSEB), 67 Rue St. Dominique 75, F-75007 Paris.
Comité Mixte Catholique-Protestant, 8 Villa du Parc Montsouris, F-75014 Paris (Also: 17 Rue de l'Assomption, F-75016 Paris, T: 01-589-5569, 01-647-7357.
Groupe Interconfessionnel des Dombes, Côté Catholique, 6 Rue Jean Ferrandi, F-75006 Paris.
Groupe Mixte Anglican-Catholique Romain, 17 Rue de l'Assomption F-75016 Paris, T: 01-288-2185.
Recherche Theologique et Relations Oecuméniques, FPF, 47 Rue de Clichy, F-75009 Paris, T: 874-1508.
Secrétariat Français pour l'Unité des Chrétiens, 17 Rue de l'Assomption, F-75016 Paris, T: 01-647-7357.
Unité Chrétienne (Association Interconfessionnelle), 2 Rue Jean-Carries, F-69005 Lyon, T: 78-421167.

GERMANY
Ausschuss der EKD für des Gespräch mit der Russischen Orthodoxen Kirche, Bockenheimer Landstr 109, D-6 Frankfurt/Main.
Bund für Evangelisch-Katholische Wiedervereinigung, Postfach 15, D-6393 Wehreheim (Taunus).
Catholica Unio, Zentrale für Deutschland, Nationalsek, Dominikanerplatz 4, D-87 Wurzburg.
Catholica-Ausschuss der EKD, Meiserstr 13, D-8 München 37.
EUKUMINDO (EuropSische Arbeitsgemeinschaft für Okumenische Beziehunge mit Indonesien E.V.), Vogelsangastr 62, 7000 Stuttgart 1, Germany.
Evang Kath Okumenischer Arbeitkreis, Herzog-Wilhelm Str 24, D-8000 München 2.
Evangelische Arbeitsgruppe für die Ökumenische Gebetswoche in Deutschland, Österreich und der Schweiz, Ökumenische Centrale, Bockenheimer Landstr 109, D-6 Frankfurt/M.
Gemeinsame Kommission der Konferenz der Katholischen Bischofe Deutschlands und der Alt-katholischen Kirche in Deutschland, Arndtstr 23, D-53 Bonn (Also: Abtei St Mathias, D-55 Trier).
Institute for Ecumenical Research, 8, rue Gustave Klotz, 67000 Strasbourg, T: 33-88-36-10-57, F: 33-88/52-17-40.
Kommission für Ökumenische Fragen der Katholischen Bischöf Deutschland, Beringstr 30, D-5300 Bonn, T: 02221-631661/65.
Ökumenischer Arbeitskreis der Evangelischen Michaels-brüderschaft, Wiesenstr 26, D-477 Soest.
Ökumenischer Leiterkreis der Akademien und Laieninstitute in Europa, Ev Akademie, D-7325 Bad Boll über Göppingen, T: 07164-351.
Ökumenisches Referat des Kirchlichen Aussenamites der EKD, Bochenheimer Landstr 109, D-6000 Frankfurt/Main.

GHANA
Committee of Co-operation, c/o National Catholic Secretariat, P.O. Box 5730, Accra, T: 22871.
Ghana Church Union Committee, P.O. Box 1434, Accra.

HAITI
Groupe Oecuménique de Recherches, BP 117, Port-au-Prince.

HOLY SEE
Pontifical Council for Promoting Christian Unity, 00120 Vatican City, T: 39-6-6988-4384, F: 39-6-6988-5365.
Secretariat for Christian Unity, I-00120 Città del Vaticano; Via-dell-'Erba 1, I-00193 Roma.

HUNGARY
Ecumenical Council, 1026 Budapest, Bimbo utca 127, T: 36-1-115-0031.

INDIA
All India Liaison Body, c/o CBCI, Ashok Place, New Delhi 110001.
Commission for Ecumenism, CBCI, Ashok Place, New Delhi 110001.
Fellowship of St. Thomas and St. Paul, Adur P.O., Travancore.
Joint Faith and Order Study Project, Catholic Bishop of Poona, Poona 411001, Maharashtra; CSI Bishop of Madras, San Thome, Mylapore, Madras 600004.
United Christmas Celebration Committee in Trivandrum Area, Syro-Malankara Archbishop's House, Trivandrum 4, Kerala.

INDONESIA
Ecumenical Commission, MAWI PWI Ekumene, Jalan Jend Achmad Yani 25, Bogor.

IRELAND
Inter-Church Relations Board, Clones Road, Ballybay, Co Monaghan, T: (353) 42 41051.
Irish School of Ecumenics, Milltown Park, Dublin 6, T: (353) 01 269 8607 or 8819.

ISRAEL
Ecumenical Commission, Latin Patriachate, Old City, POB 14152, Jerusalem, T: 0282323.
Fraternite Oecumenique de Bose, P.O. Box 51937, 91190 Jérusalem, T: 02-28-18-01.
Institut Oecumenique de Recherches Theologiques, P.O. Box 19556, 91194 Jérusalem, T: 02-76-09-11, F: 02-76-09-14.

ITALY
Associazione Cattolica Italiana per l'Oriente Cristiano (ACIOC), Piazza Bellini 3, I-90133 Palermo.
Associazione Internazionale Unitas, Via del Corso 306, I-00186 Roma.
Azione Ecumenica Europea, Largo Chigi 19, I-00187 Roma.
Centro Ecumenico di Preghiera e d'Accoglienza, 38010 Sanzeno (Trento), T: (0463) 434-011.
Circolo Ecumenico Koinonia, Via dei Greci 3, I-00187 Roma.
Gruppo Ecumenico Genovese, Gall Mazzini 7/5A, I-16121 Genova.
Interconfessional Ecumenical Training, Via Statuto 4, I-20121 Milano.
Pontifical Council for Promoting Christian Unity, Via dell' Erba 1, 00193 Rome.
Segretariato Attivita Ecumeniche, Via della Cava Aurelia 8, I-00165 Roma; Via A De Gasperi 2, I-00165 Roma, T: 635049.
Segretariato Per L'Unione Dei Cristiani, Via del-l'Erba 1, I-00193 Roma, T: (06) 6983071 or 6984271.

JAMAICA
Commission on Ecumenism, Archbishop's Residence, 21 Hopefield Av, P.O. Box 43, Kingston 6.

JAPAN
Episcopal Commission for Ecumenism, c/o National Catholic Committee of Japan, 10-1 Rokubancho, Chiyoda-ku, Tokyo 102, T: 26236913.
Japan Ecumenical Association (JEA), 2-28-5 Matsubara, Setagaya-ku, Tokyo 156, T: 3227601.

KENYA
Inter-Christian Churches Denomination, Nyeri Parish PCEA, Hospital Rd, Po Box 182, Nyeri, T: 251.

LEBANON
Comité de Coordination des Mouvements Chrétiens, BP 1375, Bayrut, T: 341902.
Commission du Catholicossat Arménien de Cilicie pour les Relations Ecuméniques, Catholicossat Arménien, Antélias.
Groupe Oecuménique de Pastorale (GOP), BP 7002 or 1375, Bayrut, T: 300425, 341902.
MECC on Faith and Unity, Makhoul St., Deeb Building, P.O. Box 5376, Beirut, T: 961-1-353-938, 961-1-344-896, F: 961-1-353-938, O: Tlx: 22662 OIK LE.

LIBERIA
United Ecumenical Organization (UEO), Monrovia.

LUXEMBOURG
Oekumenische Heimstätte, Lorochette, T: 87081.

MADAGASCAR
Commission pour l'Oecuménisme, Conférence Episcopale de Madagascar, BP 3846, Tananarive, T: 20763.

MALAWI
National Catholic Commission for Ecumenism, P.O. Box 385, Blantyre.

MALTA
Ecumenical Commission, Episcopal Conference, Archbishop's House, Valletta.
Ecumenical Group, 1 Victory St, Valletta.

MEXICO
Coordinadora Popular Ecuménica-COPEC, Postal Dist. 713343, 06900-M'exico-DF.
Secretariado Nacional de Ecumenismo, Av Universidad 1700, Apdo Postal 21-984, México 21, DF, T: 5348245.

MOZAMBIQUE
Comissão Episcopal do Ecumenismo, CP 21, Maputo (Lourenço Marques).

NAMIBIA
Christian Foundation of South West Africa, P.O. Box 8090, Bachbrecht, Windhoek.

NETHERLANDS
Ecumenical Action Centre, Di Horst 1, Driebergen.
Ecumenical Research Exchange (ERE), Oostmaaslaan 950, NL-3063 DM Rotterdam.

NEW ZEALAND
Ecumenical Affairs Committee, Convenor, 272a Te Atatu Rd, Auckland 8.
Joint Commission on Church Union in NZ, P.O. Box 87, Wellington.
Joint Working Committee (NCCNZ-RCC), P.O. Box 297, Christchurch.
National Commission of Ecumenism, 140 Austin St, Wellington 1, T: 58518.
Negotiating Churches Unity Council, P.O. Box 6133, Te Aro, Wellington, Aotearoa, T: 64-4-385-0351, F: 64-4-385-0165.

NORWAY
Church of Norway Council on Foreign Relations, Geitmyrsveien 7D, Oslo 1, T: 463416.
Contact Circle for Churches, Kragsvei 1, Oslo 3.

PAKISTAN
Commission for Ecumenism, Catholic Bishops' Conference, St Patrick's Cathedral, Karachi 3.

PANAMA
Departamento Arquidiocesano de Ecumenismo, Apdo 6386, Panamá 5, T: 627400 ext 13.

PARAGUAY
Departamento de Ecumenismo, CEP Coronel Bogado 884, Casilla de Correo 654, Asunción, T: 41946.

PERU
Secretariado para la Unión de los Cristianos, Malecon Armendarriz 211, Dpto 142, Miraflores, Lima.

PHILIPPINES
Bishops' Commission for Promoting Christian Unity (BCPCU), Loyola House of Studies, PO Box 4082, Manila, T: 981441, 991561/4.

POLAND
Episcopal Ecumenical Commission, ul Miodowa 17, Warszawa.
Secion Oecuménique, Université Catholique de Lublin, 7 ul Nowotki, Lublin.

PUERTO RICO
Movimiento Ecumenico Nacional, Apdo. 2448, Bayamon, 00621USA, T: 883-4284, F: 785-0102.

RUSSIA
Department of International Church Relations, Moscow Patriarchate, Ryleev St 18/2, Moskva G-34, T: 467405.

RWANDA
Fraternité Oecuménique, BP 528, Kigali.
Secrétariat pour l'Unité des Chrétiens, BP 405, Kigali.

SEYCHELLES
Comité Oecuménique, Evêché, PO Box 43, Port Victoria, Mahé, T: 2152.

SOUTH AFRICA
Church Unity Commission, PO Box 990508, Kibler Park 2053, Johannesburg; P.O. Box 31083, Braamfontein, Transvaal, T: 011-943-2351, F: 011-432-2896.
Commission for Ecumenism and Afrikaans Affairs, PO Box 941, Pretoria, T: 36230, 30322.

SOUTH KOREA
Ecumenical Commission, 90-2 Hye Hwa Dong, Jong Ro Ku, Soul, T: 736781.

SPAIN
Episcopal Commission of Interconfessional Relations, Anastro 1, 28033 Madrid, T: 91 7665500.
Misioneras de la Unidad, Los Arfe 43, Madrid 17, T: 4073798.
Secretariado Nacional de Ecumenismo, CEE, Calle Alfonso XI 4-1, Madrid 14.
Spanish Committee of Cooperation between the Churches, c/. Sol-210, 08201 Sabadell, Espagne.

SRI LANKA
Ecumenical Commission, Archbishop's House, Colombo 8.
Secretariat for Christian Unity, 976 Marandana Rd, Colombo 8.

SWEDEN
Nordiska Ekumeniska Inst, P.O. Box 438, S-751 06 Uppsala.
Swedish Ecumenical Association, Box 6302, 113 81 Stockholm 6.

SWITZERLAND
Catholica Unio Internationalis, Generalsek, Charrière, CH-1700 Fribourg.
Commission de Dialogue entre les Eglises Réformées et l'Eglise Catholique Romaine, Rue de Morat 262, CH-1700 Fribourg, T: (037)234744.
Commission de Dialogue entre l'Englise Catholique Romaine et l'Eglise Vieille Catholique, Fellenbergstr 1, CH-3012 Bern, T: (031)238144.
Commission pour l'Oecuménisme, Conférence des Evêques Suisses, Chemin Eaux-Vives 21, CP 40, CH-1700 Fribourg 3, T: (037)2444794.
Okumenische Kommission der Christkatholischen Kirche der Schweiz, Bumelochstrasse 7, 4656 Starrkirch, Bern, T: 062 295 43 66.
Schweizerische Ostkirchenwerk Catholica Unio, Adligenswilerstr 13, CH-6000 Luzern, T: (041)226657.
Solidaritätsgruppen Schweiz, Postfach 613, CH-8050 Zürich.
Ökumenische Kommission des Schweizerischen Evangelischen Kirchenbundes, Zeltweg, CH-8032 Zürich.

TANZANIA
Commission for Ecumenism, Tanzania Episcopal Conference, Mission Bldg, Mansfield St, PO Box 2133, Dar es Salaam, T: 20430, 20477.

TRINIDAD & TOBAGO
Collaboration for Ecumenical Planning and Action in the Caribbean (CEPAC), 12, Harris Promenade, San Fernando, T: 809-652-4489, F: 809-652-4489, O: Cable: GLOMIN.

TUNISIA
Service Oecuménique en Tunisie, 10 Rue Eve Nohelle, Tunis, T: 245592.

TURKEY
Commission pour les Affairs Oecuméniques, Vicariat Apostolique, Satirci Sok 2, Pangalti, Istanbul.

UNITED STATES OF AMERICA (USA)
Consultation on Church Union, 151 Wall St., Princeton, NJ 08540, T: 609-921-7866, F: 609-921-0471.
Ecumenical Office of the Episcopal Church, Ctr 815, Second Ave., New York, NY 10017.
Ecumenical Partnership Committee, 700 Prospect Ave., Cleveland, OH 44115.
Episcopal Russian Orthodox Joint Coordinating Committee, 815 Second Ave., New York, NY 10017, T: 212-922-5344, F: 212-867-7652.
March for Jesus USA, P.O. Box 3216, Austin, TX 78764, T: 512-416-0066, F: 512-445-5393.
National Association of Ecumenical Staff, c/o National Council of Churches, 475 Riverside Dr., New York, NY 10115-0050, T: 212-870-2155, F: 212-870-2690.
National Association of Diocesan Ecumenical Officers (NADEO), 462 North Taylor St., St. Louis, MO 63108, T: 314-531-9700.
Packard Manse, 583 Plain St, Stoughton, MA 02072; 41 Winthrop St., Roxbury, MA.
Society for the Study of Eastern Orthodoxy and Evangelicalism, c/o 88 Tierra Montanosa, Rancho Santa Margarita, CA 92688.
Standing Conference of Canonical Orthodox Bishops in the Americas, 8th East 79th, New York, NY 10021.

VENEZUELA
Comisión Arquidiocesana de Ecumenismo, Apdo 954, Caracas 101, T: 811189.
Comisión de la Fe, Moral y Ecumenismo, Edf Juan XXIII, piso 6, Torre a Madrices, Caracas 101.

ZAMBIA
Mindolo Ecumenical Foundation, P.O. Box 21493, Kitwe, T: 02-214572, O: Also tel: 211269, 215198, 211488.
National Ecumenical Commission, ZEC, Unity House, Stanley Rd., Jameson St, P.O. Box 1965, Lusaka, T: 73470.

ZIMBABWE
Episcopal Commission for Ecumenism, P.O. Box 2591, Harare.

32
Evangelism, evangelization & church growth

International, national, or local evangelistic organizations, evangelistic societies, evangelistic associations, evangelistic missions, professional evangelists, revival campaigns, tent campaigns, crusades, missions, long-term campaigns (e.g. Evangelism-in-Depth, New Life for All), saturation evangelism programs (total mobilization evangelism); national or international organizations, cooperative ministries, or congresses on evangelism or evangelization; world evangelization agencies, councils, congresses, institutions, programs; Church Growth institutes, consultants, instruction, seminars, services, agencies, networks, or resources.

AUSTRALIA
Asia Evangelical Fellowship, P.O. Box 122, Epping, NSW2121
Asian Minorities Outreach - Australia, 67 Andrew Thomson Drive, NSW 2756, T: (045) 774-917.
Bill Newman Crusades, P.O. Box 195, Toowong, Qld. 4066, T: 07-371-0750, F: 07-870-1664.

Campaigners for Christ, 379 Kent St., P.O. Box A87, Sydney South, NSW 2000, T: 2901592.
Church Army in Australia, Wyatt Av, Belrose, Sydney, T: 4518395.
Cult Awareness & Information Centre, O: Web: www.student.up.edu.au/~py101663/zentry1.htm.
Institute for Evangelism and Church Development, Wernhardstr 5, A-4522, Sierning, T: 010 43-7259-2872.
Open Air Campaigners, National Office and Training Department, 20 Minnie St., Belmore, NSW 2192, T: 7508646.
Oral Roberts Evangelistic Association, P.O. Box 17, Rockdale, NSW 2216.
Servants of the King Ministries, 92 Springwood Road, Springwood 4127, Queensland, T: 07-8411006, F: 61-7-8411006.
United Churches Evangelistic Crusades, CENEF Memorial Centre, Bathurst & Kent Sts, Sydney, T: 617788.
World Evangelism, World Evangelism Centre, Wingello Hse, 1 Angel Pl, Sydney 2000, Australia, T: 02-2328244.

AUSTRIA

Agape-Osterreich (Agape Austria), F Fischer-Strasse 15, 6020 Innsbruck, T: 0512/62 618.
Amt für Evangelisation und Gemeindeaufbau (Ministry for Evangelism and Church Renewal), Mitterweg 4, 4522 Sierning1, T: 07259/31 46.
Institute for Evangelism and Church Development, Wernhardst 5, A-4522, Sierning, T: 010 43-7259-2872.
Operation Mobilisation (OM), Getreidemarkt 17/2, 1060 Wien, T: 0222/587 94 60.
Project CARE (Coordinating All Resources for Evangelism), Postfach 37, Vienna A-1184, T: 43-222-442701, F: 43-222-442078.

BOTSWANA

Campus Crusade for Christ, P.O. Box 25052, Gaborone.

BRAZIL

ABUB-Aliança Bíblica Universitária do Brasil, Cx. Postal 2216, São Paulo-SP 01064-970, T: 11-530-7785, F: 11-240-6278, O: E-mail: ziel@opus.com.br e/ou abub.
AMAI-Associação Missionária de Alcance Internacional, Rua Afonso Pena, 3384, Gov Valadares-MG 35010-001, T: 33-271-3447, F: 33-271-3447, O: E-mail: ieadgv@brasilnet.com.br.
Assoc. Religiosa Cruzada Estudantil e Profissional Para Cristo, Cx. Postal 41582, São Paulo-SP 05422-970, T: 11-287-4520, F: 11-289-6561.
Centro Ecuménico de Servicio a Evangelizacão-CESEP, Av. Brigadeiro Luis Antonio 993-sala 205, 01317-001-São Paulo-SP, T: 11-605-1680, F: 11-239-1169.
Evangelismo Explosivo III Internacional no Brasil, Cx. Postal 21.265, São Paulo-SP 04620-970, T: 11-535-5129, F: 11-535-5129.
Janz Team Associação Brasileira de Evangelização, Cx. Postal 80, Gramado-RS 95670-000, T: 54-286-1006, F: 54-286-3170.
Rio Evangelistic Center, Rua da Matriz 16, 3° Andar, Botafogo 22260-100 Rio de Janeiro, T: 266-3022, F: 266-2612.
T. L. Osborn Evangelistic Association, CP 2, Penha, ZC-22, 20.000 Rio de Janeiro, GB.

BRITAIN (UK OF GB & NI)

26.3 Trust, 12 Derryvolgie Avenue, Belfast BT9 6FL, T: (08) 0232 669833.
Ambassadors for Christ Britain, 63 Ivybridge Rd, Coventry CU3 5PF, T: 411577.
Archbishops' Council on Evangelism, Diocesan House, Quarry St, Guildford, Surrey GU1 3XG, T: (0483)32237.
Association for the Propagation of the Faith (APF), 23 Eccleston Square, London SW1V 1NU, T: 0171-821 9755, F: 0171-630 8466.
Belfast City Mission, Church House, Fisherwick Place, Belfast BT 1 6DW, T: (08) 0232 320557.
Billy Graham Evangelistic Association, 23 Carisbrooke Road, Hucclecote, Gloucester GL3 3QR, T: 44-452-611505.
British Church Growth Association, 3A Newnham Street, Bedord MK40 2JR, T: 0234-327905.
Cambrian Outreach, 10, Penvel Close, Loughor, Swansea, Wales SA4 2PU, T: 0792-894045, F: 0792-890427.
Catholic Enquiry Centre, 120 West Heath Rd, London NW3 7TY, T: 0181-455 9871.
Catholic Truth Society, 192 Vauxhall Bridge Rd, London SW1V 1PD, T: 0171-834 4392, F: 0171-630 1124.
Eurovangelism, P.O. Box 50, Kingswood, Bristol, B5151EX, T: 272-615-161, F: 272-352-127.
Evangelization Society, 64 Cricklade Road, Gorse Hill, Swindon, Wilts SN2 6AF, T: 44-1793-481444, F: 44-1793-435237.
Faith Mission, The, 43a Upper Lisburn Road, Belfast BT10 0GX, T: (08) 0232 613316.
International Charismatic Consultation on World Evangelization (ICCOWE), P.O. Box 2000, Haywards Heath, West Sussex RH16 4YP, T: 0444-413321, F: 0444-457524.
International Gospel Outreach, 47 Bleary Road, Portadown, Craigavon, Co Armagh BT63 5NE.
Irish Evangelistic Band, 39 Belmore Street, Enniskillen, Co Fermanagh BT74 6HH, T: (08) 0365 322400.
Irish Mission, Church House, Gisherwick Place, Belfast BT1 6DW, T: (08) 0232 320598, F: (08) 0232 248377.
Kingdom Come Trust, O: Web: www.gpl.net/customers/kingdom-com.
Luis Palau Evangelistic Association, 36 Sycamore Rd., Amersham, Buckinghamshire HP6 5DR, T: 44-494-431-567, F: 44-494-431-128.
Morris Cerullo World Evangelism, P.O. Box 277, Hemel Hempstead HP2 TDH, Hertz, T: 44-0442-219525, F: 44-0442-219049.
Nationwide Initiative in Evangelism (NIE), 146 Queen victoria St., London EC4V 4BX, T: 01-248-4616.
Office for Evangelisation (Catholic), 114 West Heath Road, London NW3 7TX, T: 0181-458 3316, F: 0181 905 5780.
Project Evangelism, Project House, 38 Mark Street, Portrush, Co Antrim BT56 8BT, T: (08) 0265 822775.
Sion Catholic Community for Evangelism, Sion House, Greenland Rd, Selly Park, Birmingham B29 7PP, T: 0121-414 1648, F: 0121-414 1076.
Training for Evangelism, 5 Alpins Close, Harpenden, Herts.
Underground Evangelism, Box BM 7001, London WC1V 6KX.

BURKINA FASO

New Life for All, BP 128, Bobo-Dioulasso.

BURUNDI

New Life for All, BP 120, Gitega.

CAMEROON

New Life for All, BP 4092, Yaoundé.

CANADA

Action International Ministries, P.O. Box 280, Three Hills, AB T0M 2AQ, T: 403-443-2221, F: 403-443-7455.
Ambassadors for Christ Canada, 1217 Scottsburg Cres., Mississauga, ON L4W 2Z9, T: 905624-3605, F: 905-566-0049.
Barry Moore Ministries, P.O. Box 9100, Sub Station 40, London, ON N6E 1V0, T: 519-661-0205, F: 519-661-0206.
Billy Graham Evangelistic Association of Canada, P.O. Box 841, Station Main, Winnipeg, MB R3C 2R3, T: 204-943-0529, F: 204-943-7407.
Campbell Reese Evangelistic Association, Box 10, Milton, Ontario.
Campus Crusade for Christ, Canada, P.O. Box 300, Vancouver, BC V6C 2X3, T: 604-582-3100, F: 604-588-7582, O: Web: www.crusade.org.
Canada for Christ Crusade, P.O. Box 36, Ivujivik, QC J0M 1H0, T: 819-922-3038.
Catholic Church Extension Society of Canada, 1155 Yonge St., Toronto, ON M4T 1W2, T: 416-977-1500.
Centre for Evangelism & World Mission (Every Home Intl./Canada), 2146 Robinson St., Suite 1B, Regina, SK S4T 2P7, T: 306-569-8999, F: 306-569-1536.
Centre for Evangelism, Canadian Bible College/Theological Seminary, 4400 Fourth Ave., Regina, Saskatchewan S4T 0H8, T: 306-545-1515.
Chinese Coordinating Committee on World Evangelization (CCCOWE), Rev. Hay-Him Chan, 675 Sheppard Ave., E., Willowdale, Ont. M2K 1B6, F: 416-223-6617.
Christ Alive International Ministries, 40 Abergale Close, N.E., Calgary, AB T2A 6J1, T: 403-273-9563.
Church Army in Canada, 397 Brunswick Ave., Toronto, ON M5R 2Z2, T: 416-924-9279, F: 416-924-2931.
Church Growth Resources, 128 Yellow Birch Dr., Kitchener, ON N2N 2N3; 36 Hiscott St., Catharines, ON, T: 519-742-8347, O: (tel #: 905-704-0875).
Eurovangelism, 2476 Argentia, Suite 207, Mississauga, ON L5N 6M1, T: 905-858-8140, F: 905-821-8400.
Evangelism Canada Association, 1453 Henderson Hwy., Box 28059, Winnipeg, MB R2G 4E9, T: 204-654-2539, F: 204-338-8846.
Golden Age Society, 2825 Clearbrook Rd., Clearbrook, BC V2T 2Z3, T: 604-853-5532.
Invitation to Live Crusades, 7716 Yonge St., Thornhill, ON L4J 1W2, T: 905-881-2245.
Janz Team Ministries, Inc., 2121B Henderson Hwy., Winnipeg R2G 1P8, Manitoba, T: 204-334-0055, F: 204-339-3321.
LIFE Outreach Intl./James Robison Evangelistic Association, PO Box 4000, Langley, BC V3A 8J,, T: 604-574-1060, F: 604-574-3177.
Navigators of Canada, Box 27070, London, ON N5X 3X5, T: 519-666-0301, F: 519-666-2004, O: E-mail: 71744.755@compuserve.com.
New Life Evangelistic Association, #210 - 8860 Beckwith Rd., Richmond, BC V6X 1V5, T: 604-276-0119, F: 604-276-0119.
Oeuvre pontificiale de la Propagation de la Foi, 175 rue Sherbrooke E., Montréal, QC H2X 1C7, T: 514-845-1342.
Outreach Canada, #16 - 12240 Horseshoe Way, Richmond, BC V7A 4X9, T: 604-272-0732, F: 604-272-2744, O: Web: www.outreach.ca.
Parole à l'Evangile, C.P. 717, Ste-Julie, QC J0L 2C0, T: 514-649-5128.
Terry Winter Evangelistic Association, 416 West 28th Av, Box 7307, Vancouver, BC.
Village Missions, P.O. Box 1200, Postal Station A, Willowdale, ON M2N 5T5, T: 416-222-0548.
Vision 2000 Canada, P.O. Box 154, Waterloo, ON N2J 3Z9, T: 519-725-2000, F: 519-725-2001.
World Harvest Outreach Ministries, P.O. Box 724, Kelowna, BC V1Y 7P4, T: 604-860-4775, F: 604-861-8744, O: E-mail: World_Harvest@Cyberstore.CA.
World Impact Ministries, P.O. Box 968, St. Catharines, ON L2R 6L4, T: 905-646-0970, F: 905-646-0834.

CENTRAL AFRICAN REPUBLIC

New Life for All, Life in Christ, BP 240, Bangui.

CHINA

Chinese Coordination Center of World Evangelism (CCCOWE), P.O. Box 98435, Tsim Sha Tsui, Kowloon, Hong Kong, T: 2-391-0411, F: 2-789-4740, O: E-mail: adm@cccowe.org, Web: www.cccowe.org.
Sowers Ministry, 154 Prince Edward Road, 4/F, Kowloon, Hong Kong, T: 671-0460, F: 397-2576.

CONGO-ZAIRE

Christ Pour Tous, BP 3691, Kinshasa-Kalina.
New Life for All, BP 3366, Kinshasa.

COSTA RICA

Asociación Instituto Internacional de Evangelización a Fondo, Apartado Postal 168-2350, San Francisco de Dos Rios, San José, T: 227-9385, F: 227-8598.
Communidad Latinoamericana de Ministerios Evangélicos (CLAME), Apdo 1307, San José, T: 215622.
Instituto Internacional de Evangelización a Fondo-IINDEF, T: 227-9385.

CZECH REPUBLIC

AD 2000 and Beyond Movement, ul. Selcanska 512, Banask Bystrica 97405, T: 42-008-305089, F: 42-088-87420.

ECUADOR

Asociación Evangelística Cristo Vive, Eloy Alfaro y Portete, Guayaquil, T: 372-180.
Carpas, Luis Cordero No. 410 y 6 de Diciembre, T: 521-150.
Evangelismo, 6 de Dic. y la Nina, Multicentro, Casilla 40, Quito, T: 521-743, F: 547-062.
Evangelismo Explosivo Internacional, Casilla 7451, Guayaquil, T: 384-065.
Evangelismo y Oración, Eloy Alfaro y Portete, Guayaquil, T: 372-180.
Misión y Evangelización, Patria No. 640, Casilla 8522, Quito, T: 238-220.
Movimiento Alfa y Omega, Pasaje Chiriboga No. 433 y Ave. America, Casilla 4990, Quito, T: 237-725.
Quito al Encuentro con Dios, Luis Cordero No. 410 y 6 de Diciembre, Casilla 137, Quito.

ETHIOPIA

New Life for All, Sudan Interior Mission, PO Box 127, Addis Abeba.

FINLAND

Church Growth, Soukankuja 9.D.25, SF-02360, Espoo, T: 010 358-90-8023732.
Lutheran Evangelical Association of Finland, P.O. Box 184, Lastenkodinkuja 1, 00181 Helsinki, T: 358-0/69-39-01, F: 358-0/6939-02-0-.

FRANCE

France Evangelization, Caleseraignes 14 rue de la Verdiere, Aix-en-Provence 13090, T: 33-4259-5503.

GERMANY

Christus für alle Nationen (CfaN), Missionszentrale, Pf. 60 05 74, 60335 Frankfurt a.M..
Church Growth Association, Postfach 1309, D-7928 Giengen, T: 010 49-7322-13650.
Euro Vision, Speckertsweg 80, 97209 Veitshöchleim, T: 07244-5320.
Friendship Evangelism International, Hinter den Garten, 24, Augsburg 8900, T: 49-821-520-393, F: 49-821-432-379.
Janz Team, Postfach 1710, Loerrach 7850, T: 49-7621-86043, F: 49-7621-12713.
Josh McDowell Ministry, Brombacherstrasse 1, Loermach 7850, T: 49-7621-88058.
Mission Europe e.V., Postfach 1180, 79396 Kandern.
Mission International, P.O. Box 1162, 27341 Rothenburg, T: 04266-325.

GHANA

New Life for All, Box 919, Accra.
Resurrection Faith Ministry, P.O. Box 24, Ashaiman, Tema.
Task, The, Ghana Evangelism Committee, Box 8699, Accra.

GUATEMALA

Centro Misionológico 'El Calvario' (CEMCA), Oficinas Generales: 33 Calle 'A' 2-19, Zona 8, Apdo. Postal 2-B, Ciudad, T: 711195.
Equipo SEPAL, Guatemala, Apartado Postal 2961, Av. Simeón Cañas 10-61 Z. 2, T: 20834-537229.

GUINEA

Africa for Christ Evangelistic Association, Mission Philafricaine, B.P. 2125, Conakry I.

HOLY SEE

Decade of Universal Evangelization, Segreteria di Stato, Palazzo Apostolico Vaticano, 1-00120 Citta del Vaticano, Europe, T: 06-6984826.
Evangelization 2000, Central, Palazzo Belvedere, 1-00120 Citta del Vaticano, Europe, T: 06-6873288, F: 06-3595639.
Mouvement International d'Apostolat des Milieux Sociaux Indépendants (MIAMSI), Piazza San Calisto 16, I-00120 Città del Vaticano, T: 6894683.
Sacred Congregation for the Evangelization of Peoples, Palazzo di Propaganda Fide, Piazza di Spagna 48, I-00187 Roma, T: 686941.

HUNGARY

A Song for the Nations, 1399 Budapest, Pf. 701/1050, T: 36-1-141-3852, F: 36-1-141-7929.
Alliance for Saturation Church Planting, Budafoki ut 34/B 3/3m, H-1111 Budapest, T: 361-165-6406, O: E-mail: 100324,34@Compuserve.Com.
Ambassador Ministries, Moses Vegh, Budapest, T: 36-1-689-6041.
Campus Crusade for Christ, Timóteus Társág, Hungary Office, 1116 Budapest, Zsurió utca 6; Mail: 1464 Bp., 94 Pf. 1341, T: 36-1-228-0682, F: 36-1-277-5862, O: E-mail: CCC.HUNGARY@MAGNET.HU.
Ellel Ministries East, 2112 Veresegyház, Pf. 17., T: 36-27-387-106, F: 36-27-387-106.
Evangeliumi Kiado, Outca 16, Budapest 1066, T: 36-1-115-860.
Friendship International, Fegyvemek U. 11, Budapest 1116, T: 36-1-181-2729, F: 36-1-181-2729.
Harvest International, 2045 Törökbálint, Pf. 32, T: 36-23-336-515.
International Messengers, 1148 Budapest, Lengyel Utca 16. IV/24, T: 36-1-251-4192.

INDIA

Action in Crisis, Happy Valley, Narsapur-534 275, West Godavari District, Andhra Pradesh.
Aeropagus Fellowship, P. O. Box 8474, Bombay, Maharashtra 400103.
All Kerala United Evangelistic Movement, Convenor, P.O. Box 16, Tiruvalla, Kerala.
Almighty God Evangelistic Prayer Association, Avaranthalai, Dhonavur (Via), Tamil Nadu 627102.
Ambassadors for Christ India, No. 18, VI Cross, Hutchins Road, P. O. Box 8402, St. Thomas Town, Bangalore, Karnataka 560084.
Asia Evangelistic Fellowship India, No. 10, Bhavna, 422, V. S. Marg, Prabhadevi, Bombay, Maharashtra 400025.
Calvary Evangelical Crusade for India, Cantonment Post, Vizianagram, Andhra Pradesh 531003.
Catholic Enquiry Centre, Bishop's House, Tanjore, Tamil Nadu 613007.
Catholic Info and Dialogue Centre, 12, Kangalpura, Fawara Chowk, Ujjain, Madhya Pradesh 456001.
Christ Ambassadors, 108, Mahavir Apts, Narayan Nagar, Chunabhati, Bombay, Maharashtra 400012.
Christian Sushrusha Sangham, Kunnackal P. O., Valakam, Muvattupuzha, Kerala.
Church Growth Association of India, P. B. 512,, 13/2 Aravamuthan Garden Street,Egmore, Madras, Tamil Nadu 600008.
Cornerstone School of Evangelism, P. O. Box 5219, Bangalore, Karnataka 560001.
David Evangelistic Outreach, P.O. Box 110, Kathmandu.
Echo of His Call Evangelistic Programme, 18, Mohammed Abdullah Sahib Street, Chepauk, Madras, Tamil Nadu 600005.
Episcopal Jubilee Institute of Evangelism, Kompady, Manjadi P.O., Tiruvalla, Kerala 689105.
Evangelical Crusade of India, Post Box 7, Kachari Road, Siliguri, West Bengal 734401.
Evangelise India Fellowship, P. O. Box 16, Tiruvalla, Kerala 689101.
Evangelise India Ministries, 99 Railway Layout, Pillana Garden, 3rd Stage, Bangalore, Karnataka 560045.
Evangelism Explosion III, Vishal Apartments, G/001, Andheri East, Bombay, Maharashtra 400069.
Evangelistic Companions of India, P. O. Box 9532, Koramangala, Bangalore, Karnataka 560095.
Evangelistic Crusade for Asia, Jaigaon P.O., West Bengal 735208.
Evangelists' Training Centre, TELC Gurusala, Tranquebar, Thanjavur, Tamil Nadu 613001.
Evangelize India Vision, SRT 92, Municipal Qrs., Malakpet, Hyderabad, Andhra Pradesh 500036.
Good News Messengers, P. O. Box 306, Kannavarithota 4th Lane, Guntur, Andhra Pradesh 522004.
Good News Ministry, 11-A, Rajiraj Society, Station Road, Vyara, Gujarat 394650.
Gospel Carrier's Evangelistic Team, P. O. Box 11., Damoh, Madhya Pradesh 470661.
Gospel for Asia - Native Missionary Training Institute, P. O. Box 82, 3rd Mile, Dimapur, Nagaland 797112.
Gospel Outreach Ministries, 8th Ward, Repalle, Andhra Pradesh 522265.
Gospel Penetration Ministries, House No. : 1444, Sector 6, P. O. Box 139, Karnal, Haryana 132001.
Grace School of Evangelism, Agathethara, Engineering College P. O., Palakkad, Kerala.
Heavenly Gospel Ministry, 4, Kakkanji Street, Gandhi Nagar, Pattabiram, Madras, Tamil Nadu 600072.
Hospital Evangelism Fellowship, D-8, Royal Apartments, 3rd Floor, Khanpur, Ahmedabad, Gujarat 380001.
India Association of Evangelists, 11/8A, Krishna Nagar, Kurnool, Andhra Pradesh 518004.
India Campus Crusade for Christ, 2, Elim Apartment, Maninagar (East), Ahmedabad, Gujarat 380008.
India Church Growth Mission, Pasumalai, Madurai-625 004, Tamil Nadu.
India Evangelistic Association, P. O. Box 96, 785/A, Tulsipur, Cuttack, Orissa 753008.
India Evangelistic Crusade, 60-C, Ritchie Road, Calcutta, West Bengal 700019.
India Good News Associates, Prarthana Bhawan Building, 186/1 Tagore Town, Allahabad, Uttar Pradesh 211002.
India Gospel Outreach, Rangasamuthiram Post, Sathiyamangalam, Tamil Nadu 638402.
India Nationals Evangelism Fellowship, Trinity Bible Church, Yacharam (Mandal), Andhra Pradesh 501509.
Indian Christian Outreach, No. 1, 4th Vediappan Koil Street, Tiruvannamalai, Tamil Nadu 606602.
Indian Gospel Service, Alli Nagar, Orakkadu, Sholavaram, Madras, Tamil Nadu 600067.
Inter Denominational Gospel Ministry, Box 668, Haddo, Port Blair, Andaman & Nicobar Is 744102.
ISPCK, P.O. Box 1585, 1654, Madarsa Road, Kashmere Gate, Delhi 110006.
Jesus Christ Prayer & Evangelistic Ministries, 50-53-8, MIG 241, Sithammadhara NE Layout, Visakhapatnam, Andhra Pradesh 530013.
Jesus Lives Evangelistic Ministry, 3A/Alagar Nagar, K. Pudar, Madurai, Tamil Nadu 625007.
Karnataka Evangelistic Association, No. 1519/1 Oil Mill Road, Aravindha Nagar, Sait Palaya, Bangalore, Karnataka 560084.
Kashmir Evangelical Fellowship, Mission House, Udampur, Jammu & Kashmir.
Kerala Evanglistic and Missionary Fund, C/o Manager G. L. S. , C. M. C., Vellore, Tamil Nadu.
Last Day Harvest Ministries, 10, Ritherdon Road, Vepery, Madras, Tamil Nadu 600007.
Laymen's Evangelical Fellowship, 9-B Nungambakkam High Road, Nungambakkam, Madras, Tamil Nadu 600034.
Living Water for Dying Souls in India, 91-A/13, Munirka, Post Box No. 10529, New Delhi 110067.
Love India Evangelistic Trust, 26, Laxman Nagar, Agra, Uttar Pradesh 282001.

Lumen 2000, No. 4 Wheeler Road, 1st Cross (First Floor), Bangalore, Karnataka 560005.
Madras College of Evangelism, W-83, North Main Road, Anna Nagar West Extension, Madras, Tamil Nadu 600101.
Malabar Mar Thoma Syrian Christian Evangelistic Association, M. T. E. A. Office, Tiruvalla, Kerala 689101.
Mar Thoma Evangelistic Association, Mar Thoma Sabha Office, Tiruvalla, Kerala 689101.
Maranatha Full Gospel Association, 254, Kilpauk Garden Road, Madras, Tamil Nadu 600010.
McGavran Institute, P. B. 512, 13/2 Aravamuthan Garden St., Egmore, Madras, Tamil Nadu 600008.
Mission to Asia, P.O. Box 16, Tiruvalla, Kerala 689101.
National Training Institute for Village Evangelism, 11-2-881, Habib Nagar, Hyderabad, Andhra Pradesh 500001.
New India Evangelistic Association, H-5, Jawahar Nagar, Trivandrum, Kerala 695 041, T: 64618.
New Life Miracle Team, Dr. Ambrose Street, Vettoornimadam P. O., Nagercoil, Tamil Nadu 629003.
Outreach Leadership Training Center, P. O. Box 150, 6th Mile, Dimapur, Nagaland 797112.
Outreach Training Institute, Attur Road, Mugalapally Gate, Thumanapally, B. P. O., Berikai, Tamil Nadu 635105.
Passiton, Passiton Centre, Maruthoor, Vattappara PO, Trivandrum, Kerala 695028.
Power Evangelism Mission (India), Mulamootil Buildings, Tholaserry, Tiruvalla, Kerala 689101.
Propagation of Faith Society, 10, Ulsoor Road, Bangalore, Karnataka 560042.
Ravi Zacharias International Ministries, 673, East Main Road, Anna Nagar Western Extention, Madras, Tamil Nadu 600101.
Rays of Love Evangelical Association, B-35, Mansarovar Park, G. T. Road, Sahdara, Delhi 110032.
Red Man Gospel Team, 1-1-18 Pillaimar Street, Surandai P.O., Tamil Nadu 627859.
Rose of Sharon Evangelistic Team, 26 Annanagar NGO 'B' Colony, Tirunelveli, Palayamkottai, Tamil Nadu 627007.
Sadhu Sundar Selvaraj, Jesus Ministries, Kalimpong - 734301, West Bengal.
Sadhu Sundar Singh Evangelical Association, 8, Millers Road, P.O. Box 763, Kilpauk, Madras, Tamil Nadu 600010.
South India Soul Winner's Association, P. B. 645, Haddo Post, Port Blair, Andaman & Nicobar Is 744102.
Speed-the-Good News Crusade, 3327, Christian Colony, Karol Bagh, New Delhi 110005.
St. Thomas Evangelical Church Board for Evangelistic Work, Manjadi, Tiruvalla, Kerala 689105.
Street Preaching Ministry, Changtongya, Nagaland 798613.
Thlarau Bo Zawngtute (Seekers of the Spiritually Lost), Lushai Trading Co. Building, Top Floor, Bara Bazar, Aizwal, Mizoram 796001.
West Bengal Evangelistic Society, 91, Ramkrishna Road, Ashrampara, Siliguri P. O., West Bengal 734401.
Youth With A Mission - Training Centre, P. O. Box 127, Pune, Maharashtra 411001.
Zoram Evangelical Fellowship, Chanmari P.O., Aizwl, Mizoram 796007.

INDONESIA
Malachi Evangelistic Foundation, Martadinata 75, Bandung.
Masirey Evangelism Fellowship, P.O. Box 723, Jauapura: 99000, Irian Jaya.

IRELAND
Agape (Ireland), 264 Merrion Road, Dublin 4, T: (353) 01 2695611.
Church Army, The Rectory, Glencarse, Perth PH2 7LX, T: (0738) 86386.
Faith Mission, Oakvale, Stradbally, Portlaoise, Co Laois, T: (08) 0232 613316.
Irish Church Missions, 28 Bachelor's Walk, Dublin 1, T: (353) 01 730829.
Knights of St Columbanus, Ely House, 8 Ely Place, Dublin 2, T: (353) 01 298 7184.
Legion of Mary, De Montfort House, Dublin 7.

ITALY
Center for Decade of World Evangelization, Via del Mascherino 75 (Pizaaz Risorgimento), Roma.
Crociata dell'Evangelo per Ogni Casa, Via Curtatone 10, Roma.
Evangelization 2000, Via Boezio 21, I-00192, Roma, T: 06-687-3288.
Pontifical Council for Culture, Piazza S. Calisto 16, 00153 Rome.
Propaganda Fide, Sacred Congregation for the Evangelization of Peoples or for the Propagation of the Faith, Pallazo Propaganda Fide, Piazza de Spagna 48, 00187 Roma, T: 39-699-42-192, O: Cables: Propaganda Vaticancity.

IVORY COAST
New Life for All, BP 585, Bouaké.

JAPAN
Christian in Action, P.O. Box 13, Kadena Cho, Okinawa Ken 904-02, T: 09895-6-3697.
Japan Campus Crusade for Christ, #201 Hasegawa Bldg., 3-11-9 Yato Cho, Tanashi Shi, Tokyo 188, T: 0424-21-8990.
Japan Evangelistic Band, 6-32-4 Shioya Cho, Tarumi Ku, Kobe Shi 655, T: 078-752-3979/07912-3-2047.
Japan Good News Evangelistic Association, P.O. Box 18, Niiza; 1-2-3 Hatanaka, Niiza Shi, Saitama Ken 352, T: 0484-79-4552.
LIFE Ministries, 6-16 Enoki Cho, Tokorozawa Shi, Saitama Ken 359, T: 0429-25-4101.
Navigators, The, OSCC Bldg., Rm. 402, 2-1 Kanda Surugadai, Chiyoda Ku, Tokyo 101, T: 03-295-0146.
New Life League, 1-9-34 Ishigami, Niiza Shi, Saitama Ken 352, T: 0427-74-2212.
Tokyo Evangelistic Center, 2-30 6-chome, Higashi Fushimi, Hoya-shi, Tokyo.

KENYA
African Evangelistic Enterprise (AEE), Convenor, Bible House, Mfangano St, P.O. Box 47596, Nairobi, T: 28023.
Every Home Evangelism, National Dir, Leslander House, Haile Selassie Av, PO Box 72933, Nairobi, T: 25702.

LEBANON
Equipes d'Evangélisation, BP 7002, Bayrut.

LIBERIA
Christian Institute of Personal Evangelism, P.O. Box 3604, Monrovia.
Full Gospel Evangelistic Association Inc., P.O. Box 20-4377, 1000 Monrovia 20.

MALAWI
Evangelist M. Dimba, P.O. Box 60083, Ndirande, Blantyre 6.
New Life for All, P.O. Box 450, Lilongwe.

MALAYSIA
Asia World Mission, 95B, Lorong SS 21/1A, Damansara Utama, 47400 Petaling Jaya, T: 7180859, O: Also: 7187317.
Campaign for Christ, 151 Jalan Pasar, 55100 Kuala Lumpur, T: 03-9845318.
Malaysia Evangelistic Fellowship (MEF), 35 Jalan Munshi Abdullah, Melaka (Malacca).
Noble Vision (M) SDN. BHD., 3rd Floor Bangunan Jee Hin, 91 Jalan Sultan, 50000 Kuala Lumpur, P.O. Box 12075, 50766.

MALI
New Life for All, BP 158, Bamako.

MEXICO
Asociación Billy Graham, Bucareli No 42-303, Zona 1, México, DF, T: 133014.

NETHERLANDS
Navigators, 11698 Hoofdstraat 53, Driebergen 3980 AA.

NEW ZEALAND
Asian Minorities Outreach - New Zealand, 100 Adrers Read, R.D. 5, Palmerston North, T: (06) 354-9909, F: (06) 354-9909.
N.Z. Evangelical Apologetic Society, P.O. Box 48027, Auckland 7.
Navigators, 19 Homewood Crescent, Karori, Wellington 6005, T: 0-4-476-2731, F: 0-4-476-2731, O: E-mail: 100355.3624@compuserve.com.
Open Air Campaigners (NZ), P.O. Box 2160 Auckland 1.
Oral Roberts Evangelistic Association, New Zealand Rep, PO Box 6288, Te Aro, Wellington.

NIGER
New Life for All, Sudan Interior Mission, Maradi.

NIGERIA
Gabriel Olasoji World Evangelism (GOWE), P.O. Box 9351, University of Ibadan, Ibadan, T: 022-412121, 410252.
Koma Hills Mission, P.O. Box 748 Yola, Gongola State.
Messiah is Coming Ministry, P.O. Box 22288, University of Ibadan Post Office, Ibadan Oyo State.
National Congress on Evangelisation, P.O. Box 500, Jos.
New Life for All, P.O. Box 77, Jos, Northern Nigeria.

NORWAY
Anskar Institue for Mission and Church Growth, Nedre Brattbakken 14, N-4635 Kristiansand, T: 010 47-42-43900.
DAWN Network, Norway, Ungdom i Oppdrag, N-2312 Ottestad, T: 47-62-57-23-33, F: 47-62-57-29-72.
Norwegian Church Growth Forum, Salhusvegen, Stopp 4. N-5090, Nyborg, T: 010 47-2-601143.

PERU
Evangelismo a Fondo, Jr Unión 521, Of 205, Apdo 3997, Lima, T: 31888.

PHILIPPINES
A. A. Allen Revivals, Lauan and Molave Sts, Quirnio District, Project III, Quezon City.
Asian Evangelists Commission, P.O. Box 2799, Manila.
Christ for Greater Manila, 989 Fermin St, Malate, Manila.
Christian Laymen's Evangelistic Crusade, 949 East de los Santos Av, Quezon City.
Church Growth Institute, P.O. Box 401, 1099 Manila.
Gospel Harvestors Evangelistic Association, P.O. Box 2002, Manila.
National Fellowship for Philippines Evangelism (NAFE), P.O. Box 2557, Manila.
Philippine Crusades, Inc., 41 Cordillera St., Mandaluyong, M.M., P.O. Box 1416, Manila, T: 721-2920/79-6923.

PORTUGAL
A Outra Face!, Rua Cap. Mor Lopes de Sequeira, Lote A 2. C, 1900 Lisboa, T: 01-859 34 13.
Acção Missionária de Evangelização, Rua Palmira Bastos, Lote 10 - 2 E, 2835 Baixa da Banheira; Apartado 1450, 1012 Lisboa Codex, T: 01-204 37 51.
Associação Evangelística Batalhão de Cristo, Chão da Silva - (Apartado 12 - Carregosa), 3730 Vale de Cambra, T: 056-85 12 48, F: 056-41 23 16, O: 056-41 23 12.
BEST - Brigada Evangelista de Salvação e Trabalho, Rua Padre José Feliciano, 55, 2830 Baixa da Banheira.
EEA/Missão Evangélica Europeia, Courela da Ponte Velha, 7050 Lavre, T: 065-8 44 05.
Evangelismo Explosivo de Portugal, Rua D. Manuel I, Lote 44 - Loja B, Paivas - Fogueteiro, 2840 Seixal, T: 01-268 74 08.
Luz Nas Trevas, Rua do Ibo, 1 - 3. Dt., 1800 Lisboa, T: 01-851 46 61.
Missão Evangélica Portuguesa Janz Team, Rua José Branquinho, 95 - 4. Dt., 3510 Viseu, T: 032-42 16 29, F: 42 20 54.
Vida Nova - Associação Evangélica e Missionária de Portugal, Rua Fontainhas das Pias, Lote 83, 1675 Canecas, T: 01-981 16 31.

PUERTO RICO
Calvary Evangelistic Mission, Inc., P.O. Box 367000, San Juan, P.R. 00936-7000, T: 787-724-2727, F: 787-723-9633, O: E-mail: 104743.1413@compuserve.com.

ROMANIA
Organizatia Crestina Ecce Homo, Plata Uniril Nr. 1, Cluj Napoca 3400, T: 40-5-17-17-64.

RUSSIA
Friendship and Good News, Stankostroytelnaya 18, kv. 109, Krasnodar 350007, T: 8612-520391.
Khabarovsk Grace Mission, Chomemorskaya 33/51/73, Khabarovsk 680022.
New Life Eurasia, ul. Ostravityanova, dom 36, kv. 113, Moscow 117647, T: 7-095-420-4781, F: 7-095-420-4781.

SIERRA LEONE
New Life for All, P.O. Box 86, Bo.

SINGAPORE
Ambassadors for Christ Singapore, 57 Duxon Road, Singapore 089521, T: 227-7800.
Asia Evangelistic Fellowship, Balestier Estate, PO Box 485, Singapore 913203; 68, Lorong 16 Geyland, #05-07 Association Building, T: 538-8355, F: 533-5117.
Asian Ministry Teams, 109-A, Lorong G, Telok Kurau, Singapore, T: 65/346-0795/65/344-9582.
Campus Crusade Asia Ltd, Singapore Campus Crusade for Christ, 2 Jurong East St 21, #04-31 IMM Building, Singapore 609601, T: 560-7656, F: 560-8867.
Christian Asian Outreach Ltd., 1 Sophia Road, #03-46 Peace Centre, Singapore 228149, T: 334-7774, F: 334-7862.
Christian Nationals Evangelism Commission, Toa Payoh North PO Box 771, Singapore 913133; 134-136 Braddell Road, Singapore 359919, T: 280-0312,280-0833, F: 280-0078.
Eagles Communications, Marine Parade PO Box 581, Singapore 914403, T: 748-5056, F: 746-0452.
Living Word, Ltd., Maxwell Road, P.O. Box 3038, Singapore 9050.
Navigators, The, 117 Lorong K, Telok Kurau Road, Singapore 425758, T: 344-4133, F: 344-0975.
Worldwide Victories, Bukit Panjan PO Box 156, Singapore 916806.

SOUTH AFRICA
AFNET, PO Box 11128, Queenswood, 0121 Pretoria, T: 012-3323824, O: E-mail: 100076,2414@compuserve.com.
Africa Alliance for Church Planting, PO Box 21535, Helderkruin, Roodepoort 1733, T: 012-663-7324, F: 012-663-7325, O: E-mail: 100076,743@compuserve.com.
Africa Enterprise, PO Box 13140, Cascades, 3202 Pietermaritzburg, 1 Nonsuch Rd, Town Bush Valley, Pietemaritzburg, T: 0331-47-1911.
Africa Evangelistic Band, PO Box 782, Parow 7500, 219 Toplin House, Voortrekker Rd, Parow, Cape Town, T: 021-92-7372.
Africa for Christ (Christelike Lektuursentrum), PO Box 13447, Sinoville 0129, Melt Marais/Erras Sts, Wonderboom, Pretoria, T: 012-57-1105, F: 012-57-1106.
Africa for Christ Evangelistic Association, 19 Meyer Rd, Newlands, Johannesburg 2092, T: 011-477-1673, F: 011-477-8471.
Ampelon Ministries, PO Box 5857, 114 Newville, 515 Prince George St, 1540 Brakpan.
Bet-el Evangelistic Action, PO Box 23227, Innesdale 0031, 385 Voortrekker Rd, Capital Park 0084, Pretoria, T: 011-329-4507, F: 011-329-4510.
Bethel Evangelistic Band, PO Box 402, Wellington 7655, T: 02211-3-3455.
Campus Crusade for Christ SA, PO Box 4078, Halfway House 1685, T: 011-315-2340, F: 012-315-2350.
Christ for All Nations, PO Box 13010, Witfield 1467, T: 011-826-6246, F: 011-823-1607.
Crusade for Christ, PO Box 16, Uvonga 4370, 63 Edward Ave, Uvango, T: 03931-7-1221.
Cult Awareness Project, PO Box 82644, Southdale 2135, T: 011-433-8116.
Cult Information & Evangelistic Centre, PO Box 8009, Edleen 1625, Pretoria, T: 012-976-3294.
Dove Ministries, PO Box 680, Kloof 3460, T: 031-764-2492.
Evangelical Christian Outreach, PO Box 118, Thohoyandou NIP, T: 0159-3-1306.
Evangelism Action, PO Box 447, Milnerton 7435, T: 021-45-2740.
Evangelism Explosion III SA, PO Box 2945 0001, Pretoria 0001, Patterson Place, Mitchell/Maltzen Sts, Pretoria West, T: 012-327-2062, F: 012-327-2072.
Evangelism International, PO Box 17088, Hillbrow 2038, 58 Kotze St, Hillbrow, Johannesburg, T: 011-725-5128.
Gospel Ambassadors for Christ, PO Box 5789, Pretoria 0001, 1143F West Soshanguve.
Gospel Fire Ministries, P/B X104, Vereeniging 1930, Merriman St, Vereeniging, T: 016-22-1144.
Gospel Outreach, PO Box 61885, Marshalltown 2017, Glencairn Bldg, 73 Market St, Johannesburg, T: 011-336-3624, F: 011-336-3919.
Hope for Southern Africa, 339 Block U, 0100 Mabopane.
Institute for Church Growth in Africa, PO Box 1134 , Kempton Park 1620Fernandes Rd, Bredell, T: 011-967-1455, F: 011-967-1400.
Jesus Alive Ministries, PO Box 1502, Honeydue 2040, Port 123 Nooitgedacht, District Krugrsdorp, T: 011-708-1721, F: 011-708-1990, O: Telex: 4-23212.
Kingdom Advancement Ministries, PO Box 1785, Glenvista 2058 Tehore Rd, Mulbarton, Johannesburg, T: 011-682-1344, F: 011-682-2079.
Mission Southern Africa, PO Box 751257, Gardenview 2047, The Cornerstone, Bernard Rd, East, Bedfordview, T: 011-615-7655, F: 011-622-4142.
Revival Challenge Ministry, PO Box 125, Uvongo 4270, 14 Nice Dr., Uvongo 4270, T: 03931-1448.
Rudi van Heerden Ministries, PO BOx 2266, Helderkruin 1733, 116 Nicolas Smit St, Monument Krugersdorp, T: 011-660-2590.
Sowers International Southern Africa, PO Box 6293, Parow East 7501, Cape Town, T: 021-92-7448.
Touch International (South Africa), PO Box 1223, Newcastle 2940 Memel/Gemsbok Rds, Newcastle, T: 03431-2-8126, F: 03431-2-4211.
Word of Life World Outreach, PO Box 1678 Northriding, 2162 Gauteng, T: 011-708-2000, F: 011-708-2006.

SOUTH KOREA
Church Growth International, Yoido P.O. Box 7, Seoul 150.
International Fellowship for World Evangelization, OMS International, CPO Box 1261, Soul 100.
Korean Union Soul-Winning Institute, Chung Ryang P.O. Box 110, Seoul 130-650; 66 Hoegidong, Dongdaemun-ku, Seoul 130-650, T: 966-0071.

SPAIN
Betel, Jacinto Verdaguer, 16, Reus, 43205Tarragona, T: 32-25-10.
Campus Crusade for Christ, Agape, Diputación 113-115, ESC D-enthlo 3a, 08015 Barcelona.
Conferencia de Evangelistas de España, 28017 Trav. Vázquez de Mella, 3 Ap. 2192, Madrid, T: 742-79-11.
Encuentro con Jesús Minist. Evangel., Avda. Villajoyosa, 1, El Campello, 03560 Alicante, T: 563-32-04.
Escuela de Evangelismo (EDEN), 28180 Apdo. 8, Torrelaguña, Madrid, T: 949-85-7614.
Evangelismo en Acción, Nª Srª de Guadalupe, 11 bj, 28028 Madrid, T: 356-9604, F: 726-74-19.
Instituto Esp. de Evangelización A Fondo (IESEF), Antonio Susillo, 36-38, 41002 Sevilla, T: 490-34-70, F: 490-09-74.
Juventud con Una Misión, Apdo. 133, Torrejón de Ardoz, 28850 Madrid, T: 91-676-43-71, F: 91-675-61-30.
Juventud Para Cristo, Gran vía, 576 pral. 2, 08011 Barcelona, T: 454-52-11, F: 665-56-90, O: Also tel: 665-41-26.
Misión Evangélica Holandesa Para España, 28029 Mondariz (pl) 6, 5°, Madrid, T: 378-02-79.
Navigators, The, C/Urzaiz 35-1B, 36201 Vigo, T: 986 433731.
Open Air Campaigners, Castrillo do Aza 19, ESC 1z, Bajo D, Santa Eugenia, 28031 Madrid, T: 91 3311033.
Operación Movilización España, 08330 Apdo. 120, Premiá de Mar, 08330 Barcelona, T: 752-07-52, F: 752-52-12.

SWEDEN
Institute of Church Growth, c/o Linöping University, Dept of Management and Economics, S-58) 883 Linköping, T: 010 46-13028 15 03.

SWITZERLAND
Commission on World Mission and Evangelism (CWME), World Council of Churches, 150 route de Ferney, CH-1211 Genève 20, T: (0104122)333400.
Eurovangelism, 30 Ch des Passereaux, CH-1225 Chêne-Bourg, Genève.
International Congress on World Evangelization, Continuation Committee, Palais de Beaulieu, Av de Jomini, CP 225, CH-1001 Lausanne, T: (021)213270.
National Swiss Church Growth Association, Pfarrhaus, CH-3452, Grunematt, T: 010 41-34-71-1426.
New Life for All, PO Box 333, Mbabane.
Schweizerische Zeltmission, Gossetstr 64, CH-3084 Wabern, T: (031)543672.

TAIWAN
Commission for Evangelization (Catholic), 124, 2nd Sect., Chung Yang West Rd., Chungli, Taoyuan Hsiln, T: 03-4933548, F: 03-4914533.
Every Home Crusade, Hsin Sheng S Rd., Sec 1, Lane 146, No 7-1, Box 4020, Taipei, T: 20084.
Overseas Crusades, Nanking East Rd, Sec 3, No 272, Box 555, Taipei; Nanking East Rd., Lane 405, No. 6, Taipei, T: 772522, 42122/3.
Taiwan Church Growth Society, P.O. Box 30-525 Taipei, Taiwan ROC 107.
Yeon 2000 Gospel Movement on Taiwan, F 3,4, No.1, Lin-Yi-Street, Taipei,.

TANZANIA
New Life for All, Diocese of Morogoro, Berega, PO Kilosa.

THAILAND
Asian Minorities Outreach - Thailand, Box 17, Chang Klan P.O., Chiang Mai, 50100, T: (66 53) 281-778, F: (66 53) 281-778.
Thailand Church Growth Comm., B.P.O. Box 432 Bangkok.

UGANDA
African Enterprise, PO Box 114, Kabale.

UNITED STATES OF AMERICA (USA)
Adleta Ministries, P.O. Box 722401, Houston, TX 77272.
Advance Ministries, 2421 Willow Street Pike, Suite

D, P.O. Box 427, Willow Street, PA 17584, T: 717-464-9639.

African Enterprise, 465 East Union, PO Box 988, Pasadena, CA 91102, T: (213)796-5830.

Agape Europe, O: Web: www.webcom.com/-ninnet/agape.html.

Alberto Mottesi Evangelistic Association, Inc., P.O. Box 2478, Huntington Beach, CA 92647, T: 714-436-1000, F: 714-375-0137.

Alliance of Saturation Church Planting (SCP), P.O. Box 248, Marble Hill, GA 30148-0248, T: 706-268-3888, F: 706-268-3810, O: E-mail: 74217.3427@compuserve.c.

Alpenland Ministries, P.O. Box 9491, Fountain Valley, CA 92728, T: (714) 995-0707, F: (714) 995-0223.

Ambassador Speakers Bureau, P.O. Box 50358, Nashville, TN 37205, T: 615-370-4700, F: 615-661-4344, O: E-mail: 76135.3421@compuserve.com.

Ambassadors for Christ, Inc., P.O. Box 0280, Paradise, PA 17562-0280, T: 717-687-8564, F: 717-687-8891, O: E-mail: AFC@afcinc.org, Web: www.idsonline.com/afc.

American Society for Church Growth, Inc., Box 145 1230 US Highway Six, Corunna, IN 46730.

Andre' Kole Ministry, 325 W Southern Ave, Tempe, AZ 85282, T: 602-968-8625.

Anis Shorrosh Evangelistic Association, Inc., P.O. Box 7577, Spanish Fort, AL 36577, T: 334-626-1124, F: 334-621-0507.

Answers of Action—Christian Apologetics, O: Web: orlando.power.net/users/aia.

Apologia Report, P.O. Box 552, Crestline, CA 92325, T: 909-338-4873, O: E-mail: apologia@xc.org.

Apostle Rodrick Owensby Ministry International, P.O. Box 39064, Chicago, IL 60639, T: 773-622-7879.

Asian Minorities Outreach - United States, P.O. Box 132232, Tyler, TX 75713, T: (903) 509-1479, F: (903) 509-1479.

Barry Evangelistic Association, Brownsburg, IN 46112.

Bill Glass Evangelistic Association, P.O. Box 1105, Cedar Hill, TX 75104, T: 214-291-7895.

Billy Graham Evangelistic Association, P.O. Box 779, Minneapolis, MN 55440, T: 612-3338-0500, F: 612-335-1289, O: Web: www.graham-assn.org.

Billy Ottereyes Ministries, Box 368, Senneterre, Quebec, J0Y 2M0, T: (819) 737-8272.

Billy Walker Evangelistic Association, Southgate, MI 48192.

Bluefield College of Evangelism, Christian Acres, P.O. Box 1601, Bluefield, VA 24701, T: (304)589-6223.

Bob & Rose Weiner Ministries, P.O. Box 1799, Gainesville, FL 32602, T: (908) 375-4455, F: (908) 375-6000.

Bob Watters Evangelistic Association, P.O. Box 1330, Minneapolis, MN 55440.

California Evangelistic Association, 1800 East Anaheim, Long Beach, CA 90813.

Campus Crusade for Christ International, 100 Sunport Ln., Orlando, FL 32809, T: 407-826-2000, F: 407-826-2120, O: E-mail: DCASE@CCCI.org, Web: www.crusade.org, www.ccci.org/.

Carwile Center for Evangelism, O: Web: www.traveller.com/-jparkes/cce/.

Catholic Answers, O: Web: www.catholic.com/~answers.

Celebration 2000, P.O. Box 1777, Colorado Springs, CO 80901-1777, T: 719-636-2000, F: 719-636-2000.

Center for Illiterate Outreach, 6300 N. Beltline Road, Irving, TX 74063.

Center for Parish Development, 5407 S. University Ave., Chicago, IL 60615, T: 773-752-1596.

Charles Correl Evangelistic Association, Somerset, KY 42501.

China Outreach Ministries, P.O. Box 310, Fairfax, VA 22030, T: 703-273-3500, F: 703-273-3500.

Christ for All Nations, P.O. Box 3851, Laguna Hills, CA 92654, T: 714-586-2440, F: 714-586-1176.

Christ for the Nations, 3404 Conway, Dallas, TX 75224, T: 214-376-1711, F: 214-302-6228, O: E-mail: info@cfni.org, www.cfni.org.

Christ is the Answer Crusades, P.O. Box 12863, El Paso, TX 79913-0863, T: 915-581-8179.

Christ Related Ministries, 104 Berkeley Sq. Ln., Suite 203, Goose Greek, SC 29445, T: (803) 728-2463.

Christian Layman's Missionary Evangelistic Association, 826 Ford St., Prosser, WA 99350, T: 509-786-3178.

Christian Outreach International, 12480 Wayzata Blvd., Minnetonka, MN 55305-1936, T: 800-451-3643, F: 612-541-9620.

Christian Tent Ministries, O: Web: www.projectpartner.com/ctm.htm.

Christopher Sun Evangelistic Association, 1201 W. Hungtington Drive, Ste. 200, Arcadia, CA 91007, T: (818) 793-1100, F: (818) 793-2600.

Church Army, P.O. Box 1425, Pittsburgh, PA 15230, T: (412)263-0533.

Church Growth Center, P.O. Box 145, Corunna, IN 46730; 1230 U.S. Highway Six, Corunna, IN 46730.

Church Growth Consulting Network, 1513 Grady Ln., Cedar Hills, TX 75104, T: 214-291-3663, F: 214-291-7319, O: E-mail: cdcnetwork@aol.com.

Church Growth Group - Sunday School Board, 127 Ninth Ave. N., Nashville, TN 37234, T: 800-458-2772, F: 615-251-5933, O: E-mail: customerservice@bssb.com, Web: www.bssb.com.

Church Growth Ministries, P. O. Box 371026, Omaha, NE 68137, T: 402-333-7869, F: 402-697-0366, O: E-mail: cgmshow@aol.com.

Church Resource Ministries, P.O. Box 5189, Fullerton, CA 92635-0189, T: 714-879-5540, F: 714-879-6076.

Churches Alive!, PO Box 3800, San Bernardino, CA 92413, T: 714-886-5361.

Dann Divine Ministries, 2489 Tiebout Ave. #43, Bronx, NY 10458.

Dave Roever Evangelistic Associates, P.O. Box 136130, Fort Worth, TX 76136, T: 817-237-8491.

DAWN Ministries, 5775 N. Union Blvd., Colorado Springs, CO 80918, T: 719-548-7460, F: 719-548-7475, O: E-mail: 73143.1211@compuserve.c.

End Times Ministries, O: Web: www.etm.org.

Eridard Mukasa Ministries, P.O. Box 40078, Pasadena, CA 91114-7078, T: (818) 791-0032.

Evangel Fellowship International, 200 Evangel Road, Spartanburg, SC 29301, T: 803-576-8170, F: 803-5447.

Evangelism Explosion III International, P. O. Box 23820, Ft. Lauderdale, FL 33307, T: 954-491-6100, F: 954-771-2256, O: E-mail: 102336.426@compuserve.com.

EvanTell, Inc., 9212 Markville Dr., Dallas, TX 75243, T: 214-690-3624.

Final Harvest Ministries, Inc., P.O. Box 520, Wheaton, IL 60189, T: 708-682-0400, F: 708-682-0660.

Flaming Fire Ministries, Inc., P.O. Box 227456, Dallas, TX 75222, T: 972-258-1485, O: E-mail: ffmi@msb/com.

Florida Evangelistic Association, Hobe Sound, FL 33455.

Ford Philpot Evangelistic Association, Inc., P.O. Box 3000, Lexington, KY 40533.

Friends of Israel Gospel Ministry, P.O. Box 908, Bellmawr, NJ 08099, T: 609-853-5590, F: 609-853-9565, O: E-mail: Daniel_n_p@msn.com, www.foigm.org.

Friendship Evangelism International, P.O. Box 7023, Ventura, CA 93006.

Friendship Ministries, Totem Lake, Box 8387, Kirkland, WA 98034, T: 206-820-2167.

Gandzasar Theological Center (Armenian), O: Web: www.arminco.com/ganzasar.

Gary Case Evangelistic Ministries, Inc., P.O. Box 70-114, Louisville, KY 40270, T: 812-969-2888.

Gathering/USA, Inc., 106 E. Church St., Orlando, FL 32801, T: 407-422-9200.

Gimeniz Evangelistic Association, P.O. Box 61777, Virginia Beach, VA 23466, T: (804) 495-5282.

Global Ministries, P.O. Box 1842, Waynesboro, VA 22980.

Globe Missionary Evangelism, P.O. Box 3040, Pensacola, FL 32516-3040, T: 904-453-3453, F: 904-456-6001.

Gospel Communicators Network, O: Web: www.gospelcom.net.

Gospel Outreach & Verbo Ministries, O: Web: www.verbo.org.

Guido Evangelistic Association, Inc., P.O. Box 508, 600 N. Lewis St., Metter, GA 30439, T: 912-685-2222, F: 912-685-3502.

Haggai Evangelistic Association, PO Box 13, Atlanta, GA 30301.

Harbor Evangelism Mobilisation Society, 1705 S. 49th St., Tacoma, WA 98408, T: 206-472-3712, F: 206-535-2240.

Harvest Crusades Online, O: Web: www.harvest.org.

Harvest Evangelism, O: Web: www.harvestevan.org.

Harvest Share Ministries, O: Web: netministries.org/see/chamin/cm00203.

High Flight Foundation, P.O. Box 1387, Colorado Springs, CO 80901; 4615 Northpark, 80918, T: 719-594-4489, F: 719-594-4453.

Int'l Tent, Inc., P.O. Box 248, Valdosta, GA 31603, T: 912-242-0730.

International Crusades, Inc., 500 S. Ervay St. #409, Dallas, TX 75201, T: 214-747-1444, F: 214-747-1417, O: E-mail: IntCrusade@aol.com, members.aol.com/intcrusade/ichome/htm.

International Ministries Fellowship, 134 Miramar Drive, Colorado Springs, CO 80906, T: 719-576-7756, F: 719-576-7756.

International Outreach, Inc., P.O. Box 219, Rialto, CA 92377-0219, T: 714-386-7511, F: 714-386-7513.

Iranian Christians International, Inc., P.O. Box 25607, Colorado Springs, CO 80936; 4720 Wood Sorrel Drive, T: 719-596-0010, F: 719-574-1141.

Jerry B. Walker Evangelistic Association, 2718 Raintree Street, Sugar Land, TX 77478, T: (713) 980-2718.

Jim Matthews Revivals & Crusades, 808 N. Hickory, Broken Arrow, OK 74012, T: 918-259-8132.

Jimmy Swaggart Ministries, P.O. Box 2550, Baton Rouge, LA 70821, T: 504-769-9620.

Joe Purcell Ministries, P.O. Box 875271, Wasilla, AK 99687, T: 907-376-2053, F: 907-274-3342.

John Guest Evangelistic Team, P.O. Box 581, Sewickley, PA 15143, T: 412-741-0581, F: 412-741-0595.

Josh McDowell Ministries, 660 International Pkwy. Ste. 100, Richardson, TX 75081, T: 972-907-1000, F: 972-669-4053.

Juanita Ross Evangelistic Ministries Inc., 1406 Old Taylor Trail, Louisville (Goshen), KY 40026, T: (502) 228-5847, F: (502) 499-9132.

Korean Campus Crusade for Christ, 1504 S. Wilton Pl., Los Angeles, CA 90019, T: 213-737-5694.

Korean Harvest Mission, P.O. Box 741863, Los Angeles, CA 90004, T: 213-383-8885.

Korean Mission to America, 1124 S. Oxford Ave., Los Angeles, CA 90006, T: 213-737-8122.

Larry Ramsour Evangelistic Association, P.O. Box 68, Winnsboro, TX 75494-0068, T: 903/342-3089/342-6959, F: 903-342-3075.

Legion of Mary, P.O. Box 1313, St. Louis, MO 63188.

Leighton Ford Ministries, 6230 Fairview Rd., #300, Charlotte, NC 28210, T: 704-366-8020.

Lester Sumrall Evangelistic Association, 530 E. Ireland Road, South Bend, IN 46614.

LeTourneau Ministries International, 1101 Ridge Road, Suite 201, P.O. Box 736, Rockwall, TX 75087, T: 214-722-8325.

Light Newsletter/Personal Testimony Resources, P.O. Box 801, Cadillac, Mi 49601, T: 800-937-5995.

Love Mission, The, 1722 Crenshaw Bl., Los Angeles, CA 90019, T: 213-732-9189.

Luis Palau Evangelistic Association, P.O. Box 1173, Portland, OR 97207-1173, T: 503-614-1500, F: 503-614-1599, O: E-mail: LPEA@palau.org, www.gospelcom.net/lpea.

Lutheran Evangelism Association, P.O. Box 10021, Phoenix, AZ 85064, T: 602-949-5325.

Mahesh Chavda Ministries Int'l, P.O. Box 24113, Ft. Lauderdale, FL 33307-4113, T: 305-462-3778, F: 305-462-7313.

Mercy Seat Ministries, 3713 Choctaw Dr. SE., Decatur, AL 35603, T: 205-351-9197, F: 205-355-7440, O: E-mail: msm@annanet.com.

Miami Missionary Tent Co, Inc., Rt. 5, Box 187, Miami, OK 74354, T: 918-540-2435.

Mike Porter Ministries, P.O. Box 702424, Tulsa, OK 74170, T: (918) 492-4212.

Ministry Services (Bus Ministry), P.O. Box 432, Pleasant Grove, AL 35127, T: 205-744-6395.

Mission America, 901 East 78th St., Minneapolis, MN 55420, T: 1-760-836-9481, F: 760-324-5889, O: E-mail: 105020.3522@compuserve.com.

Missionary Crusader, Inc., 2451 34th St., Lubbock, TX 79411-1689, T: 806-799-1040, F: 806-799-0092.

Missionary Revival Crusade, 102 E. Lyon St., Laredo, TX 78040, T: 512-722-2646, F: 512-722-6365.

Mizpah Gospel Mission, 18700 Sherman Way Reseda, CA 91335, T: 818-345-0943.

Music Evangelism Foundation, P.O. Box 6617, Colorado Springs, CO 80934; 411 Lakewood Circle, Suite C, 80934, T: 719-591-7481.

National Council for Catholic Evangelization, 215 E. 10th St., Houston, TX 77008.

National Evangelization Teams (NET), O: Web: www.powerup.com.au/~netaust.

Navigators, 3820 N. 30th St., Colorado Springs, CO 80904, T: 719-594-2200, F: 719-598-4063, O: E-mail: 72667.2150@compuserve.c, Web: www.navigators.org.

Network of Biblical Storytellers, O: Web: www.nobs.org.

New Focus, Vanir Tower, 6th Fl., San Bernardino, CA 92401, T: 714-885-2622.

Nicky Cruz Outreach, P.O. Box 25070, Colorado Springs, CO 80936; 6295 Lehman Dr., Suite 101B, 80918, T: 719-598-2600, F: 719-598-2811.

Nora Lam Ministries Int'l, P.O. Box 24466, San Jose, CA 95154, T: 408-629-5000.

On the Go Ministries/Keith Cook Evangelistic Association, P.O. Box 963, Springfield, TN 37172, T: 615-382-7929, F: 615-382-1344.

Open Air Campaigners, P.O. Box 2542, Stuart, FL 34995, T: 561-692-4283, F: 561-692-4712, O: Web: www.u-net.com/~oac.

ORA International, P.O. Box 64154, Virginia Beach, VA 23467, T: 757-497-9320, F: 757-497-9352, O: Web: ora@infi.net, Web: www.orainternational.org.

Oral Roberts Evangelistic Assoc, 7777 S Lewis, Tulsa, OK 74171, T: 918-495-6161.

Outreach Unlimited, O: Web: www.u-net.com/-oum/out.htm.

P & R Schenck Assoc in Evangelism, P.O. Box 26, Buffalo, NY 14223, T: 716-877-0694, F: 716-877-1335.

Parish Resource Center, Inc., 633 Community Way, Lancaster, PA 17603, T: 717-299-2223, F: 717-299-7229.

Paulist Nat'l Catholic Evangelization Assoc, 3031 4th St., N.E., Washington, DC 20017, T: 202-832-5022.

Pentecostal Knight, 17002 Palda Dr., Cleveland, OH 44128.

Ravi Zacharias International Ministries (RZIM), 4725 Peachtree Comers Circle, Suite 250, Norcross, GA 30092, T: 770-449-6766, F: 770-729-1729, O: E-mail: rzim@rzim.com, Web: www.rzim.com.

Reinhard Bonnke Ministries, Inc., P.O. Box 277440, Sacramento, CA 95827, T: 800-434-3257, 916-856-5300, F: 916-856-5311, O: E-mail: sales@rbmi.org, Web: www.rbmi.org.

Religion in American Life, Inc., 2 Queenston Place, Rm. 200, Princeton, NJ 08540, T: 609-921-3639, F: 609-921-0551.

Rock of Israel Inc., P.O. Box 18038, Fairfield, OH 45018, T: (800) 7722-7625.

Roloff Evangelistic Enterprises, Inc., P.O. Box 1177, 410 S. Padre Island Dr., #201, Corpus Christi, TX 78403, T: 519-289-9215, F: 512-289-7719, O: E-mail: familyaltar@juno.com.

Ron Hutchcraft Ministries, Inc., P.O. Box 1818, Wayne, NJ 07474-1818, T: 201-696-2161, F: 201-694-1182, O: E-mail: rhm@gospelcom.net, Web: www: gospelcom.net/fhm.

Scott Hinkle Outreach Ministries Inc., P.O. Box 30642, Phoenix, AZ 54606, T: (602) 661-6406.

Serve International, P.O. Box 723846, Atlanta, GA 30339, T: 1-800-832-9991, O: In GA: 404-952-3434.

SONShine Ministries, O: Web: www.gulf.net/~johnweidert/sonframe.htm.

Sound the Trumpet Ministries, 325 Pennsylvania Ave., S.E., Washington, D.C. 20003.

Sowers International, 22631 Hickory Ave., Torrance, CA 90505, T: (310) 325-9580.

Taking Christ to the Millions (TCM International, Inc.), P.O. Box 24560, Indianapolis, IN 46224, T: 317-299-0333, F: 317-290-8607.

Teaching Ministry of Chuck Singleton, 13053 Baseline Rd., Rancho Cucamonga, CA 91739, T: (909) 899-0777.

Terry Law Ministries, P.O. Box 92, Tulsa, OK 74101, T: 918-492-2858.

Transnational Institute—East-West Bridges for Peace, P.O. Box 710, Norwich, VT 05055, T: 802-649-1000, F: 802-649-2003.

Triumphant Living-The Ministry of Mike Shreve, P.O. Box 4260, Cleveland, TN 37320, T: 423-478-2843, F: 423-479-2980, O: E-mail: triumph4us@aol.

Trust the Truth Association, O: Web: www.members.aol.com/PeterElias/thetruth.htm, E-mail: peterelias@aol.com.

Voice of the Truth, P.O. Box 15013, Colorado Springs, CO 80935, T: 719-574-5900.

Wayne Parks Ministries, 2201 NE 19 Street, F. Lauderdale, FL 33305, T: (305) 761-7729.

Westside Ministries, 322 W. Madison Ave., Ashburn, GA 31714, T: 912-567-4700, F: 912-567-4736, O: E-mail: wministries@juno.com.

World Evangelism (World Methodist Council, WMC), 1008 19th Ave., S., Scarritt-Bennett Center, Nashville, TN 37212-2166, T: 615-340-7541.

World Harvest Now, Inc., P.O. Box 911, 300 No. Carroll Blvd., Ste. A, Denton, TX 76202, T: (817) 891-440, F: (817) 484-6097, O: E-mail: 73312.2011@compuserve.com.

World Methodist Council, World Evangelism, Scarritt-Bennett Center, 1008 19th Ave., South, Nashville, TN 37212-2166, T: 615-340-7541, F: 615-340-7463.

World Methodist Evangelism Institute, Candler School of Theology, Emory University, Atlanta, GA 30322, T: 404-727-6344, F: 404-727-2915.

World of Faith Christian Center, 7616 East Nevada, Detroit, MI 48234, T: (810) 927-4953.

VENEZUELA

Iglesia Centro de Orientación Evangelístico 'El Shadai', Carrera 23 Entre Calles 55-56, #55-16. Urban. El Obelisco, Barquisimeto Estado Lara, T: 51-425527, F: 51-413820.

Sociedad Luterana de Evangelizacion en Venezuela (SLEV), Coninas de Bello Monte, Avenida Cuarimare Quinta Lutero, Caracas, T: 011-58-2-752-6031, F: 011-58-2-752-4683.

VIET NAM

Inter-Evangelistic Movement, 88/1 LeLdi - Ben Thanh -District 1 - HCM City, T: 8299755.

US VIRGIN ISLANDS

Lumen 2000/Caribbean Region, P.O. Box 1767, St. Thomas 00803, T: 809-774-0201, F: 809-776-9586.

Office of Evangelization, P.O. Box 7338, St. Thomas 00801.

ZAMBIA

Every Home Crusade, P.O. Box 2211, Lusaka.

New Life for All, Box 172, Ndola.

ZIMBABWE

New Life for All, 99 Victoria St (& 68 Third Av, Parktown), P.O. Box 925, Salisbury.

33
Film, video & cinema

Christian involvement in the cinema, films, motion pictures, or videos; film or video-cassette production or distribution; film or video technology, services, casting, or equipment; movie theaters and associations; cinema, film, or video training schools and centers; film or video libraries, distributors, or rental facilities; film festivals, weeks, or seminars; Christian resources on videodisc, DVD, and other motion picture media.

ARGENTINA

Comisión Episcopal del Cine, Departmento de CEA, Rodriguez Pena 834, Buenos Aires.

Festival de Cine Experimental y Documental, Calle Obispo Trejo 323, Cordoba, T: 48080, 26671.

AUSTRALIA

Australian Religious Film Society (ARTS), 162 Russell St., Melbourne, Victoria 3000, T: 6632061, 296134.

Fact and Faith Films, Lido House, 400 Kent St., Sydney, NSW 2000, T: 2901600.

AUSTRIA

Katholische Filmkommission fur Österreich, Goldschmiedgasse 6, A-1010 Wien, T: 639100.

Word and Image, Ungargasse 9/11, 1030 Wien, T: 0222/72 54 75-0.

BELGIUM

Africa Films, PB, Rue Guillaume Leke 13, B-4802 Heusy, Verviers.

Cedoc-Film (Cinéma Educatif, Documentaire et Culturel), Rue Cornet de Grez 14, B-1030 Brussel, T: 02-172498.

Centre Catholique d'Action Cinématographique (CCAC), Rue de l'Orme 10, B-1040 Brussel, T: 02-340880, 343438.

Films and Youth Service, OCIC, Rue de l'Orme 10, B-1040 Brussels.

Organisation Catholique Internationale du Cinéma et de l'Audiovisuel (OCIC), 8, rue de l'Orme, 1040 Bruxelles, T: 32-2-734-42-94, F: 32-2-734 32 07.

BOLIVIA

Centro de Orientación Cinematográfica, Av Ecuador 595, Casilla 2283, La Paz, T: 24797.

BRAZIL

Central Católica do Cinema, Rua do Russel 76, CP 16085, Rio de Janeiro, GB, T: 523541.

Cineduc, Rua do Russel 76, 5 andar, CP 16085, Rio de Janeiro, GB, T: 523541.

Escola Superior de Cinema, Universidade Católica de Minas Gerais, Av Brasil 2023, 6 andar, Belo Horizonte, MG, T: 40486.

BRITAIN (UK OF GB & NI)

Callister Communications Ltd., 88 Causeway End Road, Lisburn, Co Antrim BT28 2ED, T: 08-0846 673717.

Catholic Video Education, Our Lady of Muswell, 1 Colney Hatch Lane, Muswell Hill, London N10 1PN, T: 0181-883 5607.

Evangelical Outreach Ltd., 11 Old Ballybracken Road, Doagh, Ballyclare, Co Antrim BT39 0SF, T: 08-09603 52470.
Fact & Faith Films, Falcon Court, 32 Fleet St, London EC4Y 1NA, T: 01-351-6147.
His Paper Film Department, P.O. Box 166, London SE19 3TG.
International Christian Films, 545 Harrow Rd, London W10 4RH, T: 01-969-3000.
International Films, 253, Shaftesbury Avenue, London, WC2H 8EL, T: 71-836-2255, F: 071-240-0005.
Light and Life Films, 4 Pandora Street, Donegall Road, Belfast BT12 5PR, T: 08-0232 241550.
Midlands Evangelistic Film Unit, 22 Westfield Rd, Hurst Green, Halesowen, Hereford and Worcester, T: 021-422-6158.
Vision Screen Services, Riverside House, N. Farmbridge, Chelmsford, Essex.

CANADA
Growth Seasons Series, Crossroads Centre, P.O. Box 5100, Burlington, Ontario L7R 4M2, T: 416-332-6400.
Paragon Productions (Campus Crusade for Christ), Box 300, Vancouver, BC V6C 2X3, T: 604-582-3100, F: 604-588-7582.

CHILE
Centro de Educación Cinemagográfica, Depto 42, de la Olleria 966, Santiago, T: 34470.
Instituto Filmico, Universidad Católica de Chile, Bernardo O'Higgins 1801, Casilla 10445, Santiago, T: 36958.

CHINA
Chinese Gospel Film International, 1/F, 167 Tung Choi Street, Kowloon, Hong Kong, T: 3-7898965, 3-7870082.

COLOMBIA
Centro Católico de Orientación Cinematográfica, Oficina 402, Carrera 10, No 19-64, Bogotá, T: 494985.

CONGO-ZAIRE
Centre Catholique d'Action Cinématographique Zairois (CCACZ), BP 936, Kinshasa, T: 2248.
Luluafilm, BP 21, Kananga, Luluabourg.
Service d'Images Chrétiennes Africaines (SICA), Av des Huileries 478, BP 936, Kinshasa, T: 22248.

COSTA RICA
Ministerio Preparación de Líderes y Película Jesús, T: 240-4025.
Video Cristiano Sepecri, 100 este, 50 sur de La Cunica Biblica, Edificio #1455, San José, T: 222-8954, F: 221-5622.

CUBA
Centro Católico de Orientación Cinematográfica (CCOC), Apdo 594, La Habana.

DENMARK
Catholic Film Group, 9 HC Orstedvej, DK Kobenhavn V.

DOMINICAN REPUBLIC
Centro Católico de Orientación Cinematográfica, Apdo Postal 841, Santo Domingo, T: 27665.

ECUADOR
Alquiler de Películas, Lorenzo de Garaicoa No. 739, III Piso, Casilla 860, Guayaquil, T: 301-655.
Alquiler de Películas Alianza, Luis Cordero No. 410 y 6 de Diciembre, Casilla 137, Quito, T: 521-150.
Centro de Orientación Cinematográfica (COC), Apdo 2296, Quito.
Instituto de Antropologia Filmica, Centro de Educación Cinematográfica (CEDUCI), Calle Benalcazar 615, Tercer piso, Oficina 3, Casilla 2296, Quito, T: 513070.
Películas, Delores Veintimilla de Galindo No. 1-51, Casilla 710, Cuenca.
Películas Evangelísticas para Niños, Ave. 10 de Agosto No. 50-70, Casilla 7356, Quito.

EGYPT
Centrale Catholique Egyptienne du Cinéma, 9 Rue Adly Pacha, Al Qahirah, T: 59892, 74568.

EL SALVADOR
Oficina Católica de Cine, Av España 312, Altos, Apdo Postal 1236, San Salvador, T: 215584.

FRANCE
Cinéma et Télécinéma, 129 Fg St-Honore, F-75008 Paris.
Decision (Films de l'Association d'Evangélisation Billy Graham), BP 345, F-75365 Paris, T: 225-8051.
Expression, Association Culturelle de Diffusion Cinematographique, 10 Place de la Libération, Dijon. (Production), T: 80-303430.
Films et Vie, 24 rue de Milan, F-75009 Paris.
Missions par le Cinéma et la Radio-Télévision, 222 Rue du Faubourg St-Honoré, F-75008 Paris.
OCIC Service Scolaire, 21 Rue de la Paix, F-42 Saint-Etienne, Loire, T: 77-322640.
Office Catholique Français du Cinéma (OCFC), 193 Rue de l'Université, F-75007 Paris, T: 01-705-4358, 551-9462.
Organisation Internationale Catholique du Cinéma (OCIC), Service Scolaire, 10 Place de l'Abbaye, F-42 St Etienne.
Production du Parvis, 121 Av de Villiers, F-75017 Paris, T: 01-380-3056.

GERMANY
Deutscher Katecheten-Verein, Preysingstr 83c, D-8000 München 2.
Eikon Gemeinnützige Gesellschaft für Fernsehen und Film, Lachnerstr 20, D-8 Müchen 19.
Evangelische Filmgilde, Gottfried-Keller-Str, D-6 Frankfurt (Main) 50.
Evangelischer Arbeitskreis Lichtbild (EAL), Geschädtsstelle, Querallee 50-52, D-35 Kassel.
Evangelisches Filmwerk, Haus der Ev Publizistik, Friedrichstr 34, 6 Frankfurt am Main.
Film und Bildverlag, Renatastr 71, Postfach 146, D-8000 München 19, T: 0811-5163476.
Ichtys-Film, Goethestr 24, D-8 München.
Katholisches Filmwerk (KFW), Ludwigstrasse 33, Postfach 11 11 52, D-6000 Frankfurt/Main 11, T: 49-69-75-20-88, F: 49-69-74 89 94.
Tellux, Leopoldstr 20, D-8000 München 2.
Werner Junger Verlag, Eppstreiner Str 36, D-6 Frankfurt am Main.

GREECE
OCIC Middle East Service, Eglise Catholique, Saint-François, Rhodes.

HOLY SEE
OCIC Filmis, Secretariat for Africa, Asia and Oceania, Piazza San Calisto 16, Scala 4, Piano 3, I-00120 Città del Vaticano, T: 5806216, 6984755.
Vatican Film Library, Palazzo San Carlo, I-00120 Città del Vaticano, T: 6983197, 6983597.

HONDURAS
Oficina Nacional de Cine, Gimnasio de Choluteca, Choluteca.

INDIA
Arunodaya Ministries, 10-5-7/6/1, 1st Lancer Road, Masab Tank, Hyderabad, Andhra Pradesh 500028.
Christ's Disciples' Films, 127 Manicktala Street, Calcutta, West Bengal 700006.
Christian Film Ministry, E-9, Panchshila Park, New Delhi 110017.
Corner Stones, 2, Hutchins Road, Bangalore, Karnataka 560084.
Creative Routes, J2, Green Park Extension, New Delhi 110016.
Galilean International Films and Television Service (GIFTS) India, 15 Vaibhav Buildings, Wadala (East), Bombay, Maharashtra 400037.
Good News Film Evangelical Ministries, 9-2-451, Regimental Bazaar, Secunderabad, Andhra Pradesh 500025.
Good News Films International, P. O. Box 6819, 3-Vishwajit Apartments, 35 Nehru Road, Santa Cruz East, Bombay, Maharashtra 400055.
Gospel Video Outreach, 2. Saraswati Co-op Housing Society, Pantnagar, Plot 285, Ghatkopar (E), Bombay, Maharashtra 400075.
Institute of Film Technology, Adyar, Madras, Tamil Nadu 600020.
Samuel Video Production, A-2B/152, Paschim Vihar, New Delhi 110063.
Sharon Video Ministry and Library, Sharon 29/614, Vyttila P. O., Ernakulam, Kerala 19.
Sunil Studio, Manvila, Kulathur, Trivandrum.
Vision India, 11/2 Semmonpet, 1 Street, (Upstairs) Kellys Corner, Kilpauk, Madras, Tamil Nadu.
World Video Bible School, 13 Sai Nagar, Periyar Nagar, Madras, Tamil Nadu 600082.

IRELAND
National Film Institute of Ireland, 65 Harcourt St., Dublin, T: 53638.
Redharc Films, Booterstown Av, Blackrock, County Dublin, T: 881939.

ITALY
Centro Cattolico Cinematografico (CCC), Ente dello Spettacolo, Via dello Conciliazione 2c, I-00193 Roma, T: 561775, 564132.
Oltremare Film, Centro Saveriano d'Azione Missionario, Viale Vaticano 90, I-00165 Roma, T: 315949.
Pontificio Istituto Missioni Estere, Via S Teresa 12, I-00198 Roma.
San Paolo Films, Via Portuense 746, CP 5033, I-00148 Roma, T: 5230292, 5230207.
Vita-Film, Via Briosco 3, I-35100 Padova.

JAMAICA
Catholic Film Centre, St. George's College, Winchester Park, Kingston.

JAPAN
Saint Paul Film and Radio Centre, 1-5 Wakapa, Shinjuku-ku, Tokyo.

KENYA
East African Religious Films Library, NCCK Film Library, PO Box 45009, Nairobi, T: 22264.
NCCK Film Library, Librarian, Church House (1st floor), Moi Av, P.O. Box 45009, Nairobi, T: 22264.

LEBANON
Centrale Catholique Libanaise du Cinéma, Université St-Joseph, BP 293, Bayrut, T: 249766.

LUXEMBOURG
Office Catholique du Cinéma, de la Radio et de la Télévision, 5 Rue Bourbon, Luxembourg, T: 485181.

MALAYSIA
LCMS (Lutheran Church of Malaysia & Singapore) Film Library, Audiovisual Centre, Jalan Semangat, P.O. Box 1068, Petaling Jaya, Selangor.

MALTA
Film Section, Catholic Institute, Floriana.

MAURITIUS
Comité Catholique du Cinéma, 20 Rue Rope Hennessy, Port-Louis.

MEXICO
Cinematográfica Interamericana, Porfirio Diaz 195, Zona 12, México, DF.
Instituto de Cultura Cinematográfica, Universidad Iberoamericana, Cerro de las Torres 395, Churubusco-Campestre, México 21, DF.
Oficina Nacional de Cine, Apdo Postal 61-166, México 6, DF.
Películas Científicas, Sara 4508, Col Guadaloupe Tepeyac, Zona 14, México, DF, T: 340755.
Películas Rodríguez, México 13, DF.

NETHERLANDS
International Inter-Church Film Centre (INTERFILM), Steynlaan 8, Postbus 515, Hilversum, T: 42222.
Katholieke Film Actie, Nieuwe Schoolstraat 85, 's-Gravenhage, T: 112211.
Office National Catholique du Cinema en Hollande, Amersfoortsestraat 10, His Ter Heide.

NICARAGUA
Oficina Nacional de Cine, Apdo 2183, Managua.

NORWAY
Christian Film Society, Munchsgate 2, Oslo 1.

PANAMA
Oficina Nacional de Cine (CENCOS), Apdo 386, Panamá 1.

PARAGUAY
Oficina Nacional de Cine, Casilla de Correos 587, Asunción, T: 8422.

PERU
Centro de Orientación Cinematográfica (CEOC), Av 9 de Diciembre 378, Paseo Colón, Apdo 44, Lima, T: 312339.
Imágenes para el Desarrollo, Jirón Chancay 716, Apdo 10226, Lima, T: 238944.
OCIC Centro Latinoamericano de Lenguaje Total (SAL), Av 9 de Diciembre 378, Paseo Colón, Apdo 44, Lima, T: 312339.
Servicio de Educación Cinematográfica (SEC), Av 9 de Diciembre 378, Paseo Colón, Apdo 44, Lima, T: 312339.

POLAND
Catholic Episcopal Commission for Film, Radio, TV and Theatre, Aleja I Armii Wojska Polskiego 12, Warszawa X.

PORTUGAL
Secretariado do Cinema, Rua de Serpa Pinto 10D, Lisboa 2, T: 30172.

PUERTO RICO
Sección de Cine, Centro de MCS, Barro Obrero Station, Apdo 14125, Santurce, PR 00916, T: 7246471.

RUSSIA
Jesus Film New Life, 11655 ul. Ostravityanova, dom 36, kv. 177, Moscow 117647, T: 7-095-420-4104.

SOUTH AFRICA
Campus Crusade for Christ Deo Video, P/B X07, Lynnwood Ridge 0040, Perseus Park, Camelia Ave, Lynnwood Ridge, T: 012-348-9511, F: 012-47-7871.
Visual International, PO Box 3163, Tiger Park 7536, T: 021-919-0909, F: 021-99-7563.
World Wide Pictures, 835 Maritime House, 26 Loveday St, P.O. Box 4134, Johannesburg, T: 8382859, 8366326.

SPAIN
Audifilm, Albareda 15, Gerona, T: 203297.
Bosco Films, Fuencarral 13, Madrid 4.
Catéfilms, Condal 27, Barcelona 02.
Decisión: Películas Evangélicas, 28022 Mequinenza, 20, Madrid, T: 742-7911.
Departamento de Cine, Secretariado de MCS, 4 Alfonso XI, Madrid 14, T: 2315400.
Estudios de Vídeo (A. de Dios), 11403 Campana, 20, Jerez de la Frontera, Cádiz, T: 33-29-49.
Películas Evangélicas, 08080 Apdo. 27199, Barcelona, T: 308-82-60.
Sallem-Films, Victor Pradera, Madrid.
San Pablo Films (PSSP), Mayor 11, Madrid 13.
Semana Internacional de Cine Religioso y de Valores Humanos (SEMINCI), Edif Caja de Ahorros Provincial, Plaza de Madrid 1, Valladolid, T: 229493.
Video, Proyecciones, Películas Evangélicas, 29080 Apdo. 5144, Málaga, T: 223-51-25.
Visión Video Edificación, 29004 Camino del Pato, 21 3° 2a C., Málaga, T: 223-51-25.

SWITZERLAND
Schweizer Film-Mission, Leitung, CH-7299 Valzeina, T: 081-521166.
Schweizerischer Protestant Film- und Radio-Verband, Saatweisenstr 22, CH-8600 Dübendorf, T: 051-852070.
Schweizerisches Katholisches Filmburo, Wilfriedstr 15, Zürich 7, T: 051-320208.
Vereinigung Ev-ref Kirchen der deutschsprachigen Schweiz fur kirchl Film-Radio- und Fernseharbeit, Sulgenauweg 26, CH-3000 Bern 7, T: 031-461676/7.

SYRIA
Office Catholique Syrien du Cinéma, 10 Haret el Bagdadi, Kassaa, Dimashq.

THAILAND
Catholic Film Office, MCS Catholic National Committee, 251/1 Suranari Rd, Nakhon Ratchasima.

UGANDA
Catholic Association of Broadcasts & Cinematographers of Uganda (CABCU), c/o Social Communications Comm., P.O. Box 2886, Kampala, T: 256-41-26 77 99, F: 256-41-26 81 04.

UNITED STATES OF AMERICA (USA)
Allied Film & Video, 370 J.D. Yarnell Industrial Pkwy., Clinton, TN 37716, T: 615-457-7772, F: 615-457-7799.
Asian Screen, P.O. Box 1432, Hollywood, CA 90028, T: 213-466-7187.
Association Films, 347 Madison Av, New York, NY 10017.
Bob Harrison Films & Videos, 203 Ashford Ave, Greenville, SC 29609, T: 803-233-5479.
Broadman Press & Films, 127 Ninth Ave., N., Nashville, TN 37203.
Cathedral Films, Inc, PO Box 4029, Westlake Village, CA 91359, T: 818-991-3290.
Catholic Video Club, O: Web: www.inetbiz.com/cvc.
Catholic Video Company, O: Web: www.connect.net/ccca.
Century Gospel Film & Video, 810 Rt. 113 E., P.O. Box 707, Soudertonk PA 18964, T: 800-523-6748, F: 215-723-1414.
Challenger Films, Inc., 2951 Flowers Rd., S. Suite 243, Atlanta, GA 30341, T: 404-458-6632.
Child Evangelism Press, P.O. Box 348, Warrenton, MO 63383, T: 314-456-4321, F: 314-456-5000.
Christian Cinema, Inc., 108 Butler Pike, Ambler, PA 19002, T: 800-777-0244.
Christian Film Service, 2015 S. Orange Ave., Orlando, FL 32806, T: 407-423-4567.
Christian Films, 415 W. Imperial Hwy., La Habra, CA 90631, T: 714-871-5670.
Christian Films Interstate, 7915 Bib Bend Blvd., St Louis, MO 63116, T: 314-968-9330.
Church-Craft Pictures, 4222 Utah St., St. Louis, MO 63116.
Columbia Video, PO Box 3122, Columbia, SC 29230, T: 800-845-2721.
Concordia Publishing House & Films, 3558 South Jefferson Av, St. Louis, MO 63118.
Covenant Productions, 1100 E. 5th St., Anderson, IN 46012, T: 317-641-4348.
Crosroads Church Films, 3817 S. Western, Sioux Falls, SD 57105, T: 800-843-3715.
Crown Ministries International, 9 Winstone Ln., Bella Vista, AR 72714, T: 800-433-4685, F: 501-855-6997.
Day Star Productions, 326 S Wille Ave, Wheeling, IL 60090, T: 708-541-3547.
Dayspring Enterprises International, 1062 Laskin Rd. #21A, Virginia Beach, VA 23451, T: 757-428-1092, F: 757-428-0257.
Dove Foundation, 4521 Broadmoor, SE, Grand Rapids, MI 49512, T: 616-554-9993, F: 616-554-9997, O: E-mail: movies@dove.org.
Endtime, Inc., 1214 S. 8th St., Richmond, IN 47375, T: 317-962-6344, F: 317-962-9417.
Evangelical Films, 1750 Northwest Hwy, Garland, TX 75041, T: 214-270-6675.
Family Films, 582 Santa Monica Blvd, Hollywood, CA 90038.
Family Theater Productions, 7201 Sunset Blvd., Hollywood, CA 90046, T: 213-874-6633.
Films Afield, P.O. Box 3022, Boise, ID 83703, T: 208-344-5145.
Films Department, Augsburg Publishing House, 425 South Fourth St., Minneapolis 15, Minnesota. (Lutheran tradition).
Films for Christ Association, 1204 North Elmwood Ave., Peoria, IL 61606.
Gateway films, Inc., P.O. Box 540, 2030 Wentz Church Rd., Worcester, PA 19490, T: 610-584-1893, F: 610-584-4610.
Glenray Communications, PO Box 40400, Pasadena, CA 91114, T: 818-797-5462.
Good News Production, Chester Springs, PA 19425.
Gospel Film, Inc., Box 455, Muskegon, MI 49442-0455, T: 616/773-3361, F: 616-777-1847, O: Web: www.gospelcom.net/gf, E-mail: gf@gospelcom.net, 1-800-253-0413.
Gospel Music Network, 6068 Whitlers Creek Ct., Springfield, VA 22152, T: 703-451-5010, F: 703-451-5010, O: E-mail: bcrook@juno.com.
Gospel Thru Films, 701 Decatur #110, Minneapolis, MN 55427, T: 800-333-5344.
Gospel Witmess Films, 1699 Tullie Cir. NE, Ste. 108, Atlanta, GA 30329, T: 800-241-1755.
Great Passion Play Video T.M., P.O. Box 471, Eureka Springs, AR 72632, T: 501-253-8559.
Harvest Productions (EBM), Box 2225, Kokomo, IN 46904, T: 317-455-2112, F: 317-455-0889, O: E-mail: 75053.3553@compuserve.com.
Heritage Films and Video, P.O. Box 365, Bilivar, NY 14715, T: 800-528-5683.
Inspiration Fellowship Films, 110 Pleasant Valley Dr., Midland City, AL 36350, T: 800-232-4283.
Inspirational Films Distributors, 2508 Hayes Ct., Burnsville, MN 55337, T: 612-890-1969.
Inspirational Media, PO Box 6046, San Bernardino, CA 92412, T: 714-886-5224.
INTERCOMM, 1520 E. Winona Ave., Warsaw, IN 46580, T: 219-267-5834, O: E-mail: 71430.3002@compuserve.com.
International Films, Inc., P. O. Box 40400, Pasadena, CA 91114, T: 626-797-5462, F: 626-797-7524.
Jeremiah Films, P.O. Box 1710, Hemet, CA 92546, T: 909-652-1006, F: 909-652-5848, O: E-mail: jeremiah@pe.net.
Jesus Project, The ('Jesus' Film), 30012 Ivy Glen Dr., Suite 200, Laguna Niguel, CA 92677; P.O. Box 7690, Laguna Niguel, CA 92677, T: 714-495-7383, F: 714-495-0760, O: E-mail: 199.107.73.1/JESUS-project, jsstarr@aol.org.
Ken Anderson Films, P.O. Box 618, Winona Lake, IN 46590, T: 219-267-5774, F: 219-267-5876.
Klausmeier Video Productions, 8515 Cedarplace Dr., Ste. 103B, Indianapolis, IN 46240, T: 317-251-9896, F: 317-251-9947.
Lewis Film Service, 1425 E. Central, Wichita, KS 67214, T: 800-362-0040.
Majestic Media, 7201 I-40W #301, Amarillo, TX 79106, T: 806-354-2990, F: 806-354-8180.
Mark IV Film & Video, 5907 Meredith Dr, Des Moines, IA 50322, T: 515-278-4737.
McDouglas Films, 350 Adams Ave, Glencoe, IL 60022, T: 708-835-5333.
Mercy Foundation, O: Web: www.xroads.com/~jbperry/Mercy.html.

Mid America Films, 411 5th St, West Des Moines, IA 50265, T: 515-279-9679.
Moody Institute of Science Division of Moody Bible Institute, 820 N. LaSalle Dr., Chicago, IL 60610, T: 800-647-6909, F: 800-647-6910.
Mustard Seed International, 5907 Meredith Dr., Des Moines, IA 50322, T: 515-270-2080, F: 515-278-4738, O: E-mail: rdfilms_msi@dsmnet.com.
Office for Film and Broadcasting (Catholic), 1011 First Avenue, Suite 1300, New York, NY 10022, T: 212-644-1880, F: 212-644-1886.
Olive's Film Productions, P.O. Box 9, Madison, AL 35758, T: 203-837-4166.
Omega Films, 13582 Glen Ln., Valley Center, GA 92082, T: 619-942-8672.
Our Master's Video, 1019 N. Lincoln Ave., Fullerton, CA 92631, T: 714-879-9482.
Paraclete Video Productions, 39 Eldridge Rd., Brewster, MA 02631, T: 508-240-1563, F: 508-240-3675, O: E-mail: pvp@paraclete-press.com.
Paulist Communications, Roeder Rd., Suite 600, Silver Spring, MD 20910.
Paulist Productions, P.O. Box 1057, Pacific Palisades, CA 90272.
Rainbow Film Ministries, P.O. Box 70192, Houston, TX 77270, T: 713-861-1390.
Religious Film Corporation, P.O. Box 4029, Westlake Village, CA 91359, T: 800-338-3456.
Religious Film Library, 17 Park Place, New York.
Roa's Films, 1696 North Astor St, Milwaukee, WI 53202, T: 414-271-0861.
Russ Doughten Films, Inc., 5907 Meredith Dr., Des Moines, IA 50322, T: 800-247-3456, 515-278-4737, F: 515-278-4738, O: E-mail: doughten@mustardseed-rdfilms.com.
Sacred Cinema/Valley Forge Films, Chester Springs, PA 19425.
Sacred Film Library, 309 Fairview Ave., Newtown Square, PA 19073, T: 800-345-8106.
Sacred Films, P.O. Box 144, Coatesville, IN 46121, T: 800-678-2343.
Sacred Films, 8583 Zionsville Rd, Indianapolis, IN 46268, T: 317-876-3031.
Spirit & Truth Films, 155 Filmore Ave., Deer Park, NY 11729, T: 516-242-4234.
Spoken Word of God, 1712 Lee Rd., Orlando, FL 32810, T: 407-290-0121, F: 407-578-6665, O: E-mail: swog@worldramp.net.
Tabernacle and Cumming Films, 11718 Barrington Ct. #111, Los Angeles, CA 90049, T: 818-509-7880, F: 818-509-7880.
Technical Animations, Inc., 2860 River Rd. Ste. 130, Des Plaines, IL 60018, T: 847-297-1000, F: 847-297-4820, O: E-mail: techanim@theramp.net.
Timeless Video, Chatsworth, CA 91311, T: 805-773-0284.
Trinity Pictures, 139 Old Stone Hill Rd., Pound Ridge, NY 10576, T: 914-764-8396.
Vision Video/Gateway Films, 2030 Wentz Church Rd, Worcester, PA 19490, T: 800-453-4488.
Wolfram Video, 1700 S. 60th St., West Allis, WI 53214, T: 414-546-1379, F: 414-546-4654.
World Horizon Films, Maryknoll, Walsh Bldg, New York, NY 10545.
World Trust Films/World Film Crusade, P.O. Box 20888, Tampa, FL 33622, T: 813-677-2242, F: 813-671-0550.
World Wide Pictures, 1201 Hennepin Ave., Minneapolis, MN 55403, T: 800-745-4318, F: 612-338-3029, O: E-mail: thetchler@bgea.org, Web: www.wwp.org.
World, Inc., 1501 Lyndon B. Johnson Fwy. #650, Dallas, TX 75234, T: 800-933-9673, F: 214-488-1312.

URUGUAY
Centro Católico del Espectaculo, Cerrito 475, Montevideo, T: 85903.
Centro de Cultura Filmica (CCF), Torre a Madrices, Edf Juan XXIII, Apdo del Este 4310, Caracas, T: 815208.

34
Finance, property & stewardship

Church or Christian finance, giving, charitable giving, property, financial services, Christian stewardship, investment, taxes, accounting, or insurance; co-operatives, savings societies, credit unions, financial institutions; foundations, trusts, funds, funding agencies, fund-raising agencies, fund-transmitting agencies, pension programs, ministerial financial or insurance societies, insurance companies, credit unions; new church construction or building societies or funds; management consulting, business methods for churches or Christian organizations; agencies for fund-raising training, consultation, services, or activities; associations for financial or accounting integrity, standards, or accountability. See also AID AND RELIEF, and DEVELOPMENT, JUSTICE AND PEACE.

AUSTRALIA
Wells Organization Pty, Box A248, PO Sydney South, T: 618569.

BRAZIL
Movimento Cooperativista, Barra, BA.

BRITAIN (UK OF GB & NI)
Aged Pilgrims' Friendly Society, 26-30 Holborn Viaduct, London EC1, T: (01)583-8116/1.
Apprenticeship Society, Livingstone House, 11 Carteret St, London SW1.
Baptist Building Fund, 4 Southampton Row, London WC1B 4AB.
Came's Charity for Clergymen's Widows, 7 New Square, Lincoln's Inn, London WC2, T: (01)405-6789.
Catholic National Building Office, 3 Great James St, London WC1, T: (01)242-5096.
Central Finance Board of the Methodist Church, Iddesleigh House, Caxton St, London SW1.
Christian Witness Fund, 120 Leamington Rd, Coventry CV3 6JY.
Church Commissioners for England, 1 Millbank, Westminster, London SW1P 3JZ, T: (01)930-5444.
Church Extensions Association, St. Michael's Convent, Ham Common, Richmond, Surrey.
Church Finance Supplies, Ltd., Radley Rd Industrial Estate, Abingdon-on-Thames, Berks, T: 4488.
Church of England Pensions Board, 53 Tufton St, London SW1, T: (01)222-1568.
Community Counselling Service, 27 Grosvenor St, London W1, T: (01)629-1715.
Congregational Fund Board, Livingstone House, 11 Carteret St, London SW1.
Congregational Ministers' Friendly Society, 11 Carteret St, London SW1.
Congregational Pastors' Insurance Aid Society, 11 Carteret St, London SW1.
Congregational Welfare Fund, Welfare Dept, 11 Carteret St, London SW1.
Curates' Augmentation Fund, East Wing, Fulham Palace, London SW6, T: (01)736-7141.
Fidelity Trust, 41 Tothill St, London SW1H 9LG, T: (01)930-6524/7203.
Incorporated Church Building Society, 7 Queen Anne's Gate, London SW1H 9BX, T: (01)930-8889.
Martyrs' Memorial and Church of England Trust, CPAS, Falcon Court, 32 Fleet St, London EC4Y 1DB, T: (01)353-4821.
Methodist Insurance Company, 51 Spring Gardens, Manchester M60 2AR, T: (061)236-1818/6801.
Milton Mount College, Livingstone House, 11 Carteret St, London SW1.
New Life Foundation Trust, P.O. Box 20, Bromley BR1 1DW, Kent.
Planned Giving, Ltd., Boardman House, Chestergate, Stockport, Cheshire.
Protestant Union, Livingstone House, 11 Carteret St, London SW1.
Robinson's Relief Fund, 22 St. Andrew St, Holborn Circus, London EC4.
Salvation Army General Insurance Corp. Ltd., 117-121 Judd St., King's Cross, London WC1H 9NN, T: 0171-383-4804.
Salvation Army Trustee Company, 101 Queen Victoria St., London EC4P 4EP, T: (01)236-5222.
SBJ Stephenson Ltd., Ins. Brokers to Catholic Religions, 7-10 The Grove, Gravesend, Kent DA12 1DU, T: 01474-537777.
Southwark Christian Stewardship Department, 112 Kennington Rd, London SE11 6RE.
Wells International Advisory Services/Wells Management Consultants, 1-11 Hay Hill, London W1, T: (01)629-1061.
Widows' Fund for Widows of Protestant Dissenting Ministers of the Three Denominations, 92 Great North Way, Hendon, London NW4, T: (01)203-3282.

CANADA
Aaron Communications, P.O. Box 5000, Niagara-on-the-Lake, L0S 1J0, T: 905-468-1880, F: 905-468-1994.
Best Fundraising Products, 7050 Telford Way, Unit 14, Mississauga, ON L5S 1V7, T: 905-672-5315, F: 905-677-8998, O: 1-800-563-1049.
C. Reimer Advertising, Ltd., 2265 Pembina Hwy., #104, Winnipeg MB R3T 5J3, T: 204-269-8093, F: 204-275-1246.
Canadian Association on Charitable Gift Annuities, 10 Carnforth Rd., Toronto, ON M4A 2S4, T: 416-598-2181.
Canadian Council of Christian Charities, 28 Arthur St., Elmira, ON N3B 2M5, T: 519-669-5137, F: 519-669-3291.
Christian Aid Mission, 201 Stanton St., Fort Erie, Ontario L2A 3N8.
Christian Stewardship Services, #210 - 455 Spadina Ave., Toronto, ON M5S 2G8, T: 416-598-2181.
Planned Giving Associates, c/o Executive Financial Services, 3700 Griffith, Suite 339, St. Laurent, QC H4T 1A7, T: 800-731-2438, F: 514-735-1419.
ShareLife, 355 Church St., Toronto, ON M5B 1Z8, T: 416-977-6217, F: 416-977-6063.
Thompson McJarrow Stewardship & Planned Giving Ministries, 211 Hazelglen Dr., Kitchener, ON N2M 2E6, T: 519-743-3043.

CHINA
Cedar Fund, Ltd., Suite 504, Rightful Centre, 12 Tak Hing St., Kowloon, Hong Kong, T: 2381-9627, F: 2392-2777, O: E-mail: sharing@cedarfund.org.hk, Web: www.cedarfund.org.

EL SALVADOR
Fundación Promotora de Cooperativas, Av España 312, 3 piso, San Salvador, T: 216468, 217200.

FRANCE
Caisse Auxiliaire de Retraites des Ministres du Culte Protestant (CARP), 47 rue de Clichy, F-75009 Paris.
International Missionary Benefit Society, 119 Rue du Président-Wilson, F-92 Levallois, T: 2708752, 2708753.

GERMANY
Education Fund Committee for Young Christian Asia & Africa, Wilhelmshoher Alee 330, Postfach 410 260, 3500 Kassel Wilhelmshoher, Germany.
Evangelisches Studienwerk, D-5845 Haus Villigst, bei Schwete (Ruhr).
Kirchenkanzlei der EKD, Harrenhaüser Str 2A, Postfach 210220, D-3 Hannover-Herrenhausen.

GREECE
Organization for Finances and Property of the Church of Greece, Holy Synod, I Grennadiou 14, Athínai 140.

HOLY SEE
Administration of the Patrimony of the Apostolic See, I-00120 Città del Vaticano, T: 6982 int 4306.
Prefecture of the Economy of the Holy See, Palazzo delle Congregazioni, Largo del Colonnato 3, I-00193 Roma, T: 69282 int 4263.

INDIA
Bishop Benziger Saving Scheme, Puthenthurai, Keezhkulam, Tamil Nadu 629193.
Catholic Suprian Bank Pvt. Ltd., Subara Nagar, Nellore, Andhra Pradesh 524001.
Christian Council for Financial Accountability, 427, I. Cross, VII Block, Koramangala, Bangalore, Karnataka 560095.
East India Charitable Trust, 51, Chowringhee Road, Calcutta, West Bengal 700071.
Ecumenical Church Loan Fund of India (ECLOF), C. L. S. Building, Madras, Tamil Nadu 600003.
Gujarat Catholic Co-operative Credit Society, C/o Catholic Church, Anand, Gujarat 388001.
India Financial Association of Seventh-Day Adventist, H. Q. Gujarat Regional, Near Rly Station, Maninagar (East), Ahmedabad, Gujarat 380008.
Indian Evangelical Trust, XLI/257, I. S. Press Road, Ernakulam, Kerala 682018.
J. Sikile Foundation, Manor House, 2nd. Floor, 100 Harrington Road, Madras, Tamil Nadu 600031.
Lott Carey Baptist Mission Charitable Trust, 5, Ansari Road, Daryaganj, New Delhi 110002.
Parimala Mar Gregorios Memorial Charitable Trust, Thalakkode, Ernakulam, Kerala 682314.
Stewards Association in India, 7 (4), John Armstrong Road, Richards Town, Bangalore, Karnataka 560005.
Stewards Fund of India, Manor House, Second Floor, 100, Harrington Road, Madras, Tamil Nadu 600031.
Suvishesha Pravarthaka Sahaya Fund, Thadiyoor, Sabri Mankal P.O., Kerala 689653.
Xavier Inst of Management, Mahapalika Magr, Fort, Maharashtra 400001.

INDONESIA
Institute for the Education and Counselling of Credit Union Leaders, Biro Sosial, Jalan Jend A Yan 13, Semarang, Surabaja.

ITALY
Prefecture for the Economic Affairs of the Holy See, Largo del Colonnato 3, 00193 Rome.

JAMAICA
Church Credit Union, Moravian Church in Jamaica, 3 Hector St, Kingston 5.

KENYA
Church Commissioners for Kenya (CPK), Church House (5th floor), Moi Av, PO Box 30422, Nairobi, T: 25004.
Co-operative Savings and Credit Society, enya House, Koinange St, PO Box 49539, Nairobi, T: 23455 ext 2.

LESOTHO
Lesotho Credit Union League, c/o PO Box 267, Maseru.

MALAWI
Faith Christian Services, Box 5436, Limbe.

NEW ZEALAND
Zealandia Associates, Brandon House, Corner of Featherston & Brandon Sts, GPO Box 2808, Wellington, T: 51794.

NORWAY
Christian Institute for Project Aid, Munchsgate 2, Oslo 1.

PANAMA
Fondo de Apostolado Arquidiocesano, Apdo 6386, Panamá 5, T: 627400 ext 17.

SOUTH AFRICA
Christian Foundation, PO box 132, Roodepoort 1725, 5 Timotheus St, Helderkruin 1724, T: 011-768-1307, F: 011-7681334.
Christian Ministry Resource Centre, PO Box 556, Muldersdrift 1747, T: 011-662-1977, F: 011-662-1316.
ClergyPlan, PO Box 41074, Craighall 2024, T: 011-789-3580, F: 011-789-1481.
Foundation Beersheba, 184 Lyndhurst Rd, Lyndhurst, 2192 Johannesburg, T: 011-477-2919, F: 011-882-6697.

SOUTH KOREA
Catholic Myong-Dong Credit Union, 1, 2-ga, Myong-dong, Chung-gu, Seoul-shi, T: (02) 776-0011.

SWITZERLAND
Ecumenical Church Loan Fund (ECLOF), 150 Route de Ferney, CH-1211 Genève 20.
Stiftungsrat der Schweizerischen Reformationsstiftung, CH-3000 Bern.

TANZANIA
New Life Crusade, M. P. Nyagwaswa, PO Box 2679, Dar es Salaam.

UNITED STATES OF AMERICA (USA)
A.B. Culbertson & Company, 1250 Continental Plaza, 777 Main St., Fort Worth, TX 76102, T: 817-335-2371, F: 817-335-2379.
Ambassador Advertising Agency, 515 E. Commonwealth Ave., Fullerton, CA 92832, T: 714-738-1501, F: 714-738-4625.
American Church Lists, Inc., P.O. Box 1544, Arlington, TX 76004, T: 800-433-5301, 817-261-6233, F: 817-861-0167, O: E-mail: amchlist@ix.netcom.com, Web: www.americanchurchlists.com.
American Investors Group Inc., 10237 Yellow Circle Dr., Minnetonka, MN 55343, T: 800-815-1175, 615-945-9455, F: 612-945-9433, O: E-mail: brett@amerinvest.com.
Aurora Foundation, P.O. Box 1848, Bradenton, FL 34206, T: 813-748-4100.
Believers Foundation, 1570 Dutch Hollow Rd., P.O. Box 3175, Elida, OH 45807, T: 419-339-4441.
Ben Wood & Associates, Inc., 400 W. Roosevelt Rd. #2E, Wheaton, IL 60187, T: 630-665-6633, F: 630-665-6659.
Benefits Administration, 8057 Arlington Expressway, Jacksonville, FL 32211, T: 904-721-4199, F: 904-725-9660.
Berry, Lowell, Foundation, 315 Washington Ave., Waco, TX 76701, T: 817-752-5551.
Brotherhood Mutual Insurance Co, P.O. Box 2227, Fort Wayne, IN 46801, T: 219-482-8666.
Caddock Foundation, Inc., 1717 Chicago Ave., Riverside, CA 92507, T: 714-788-1700.
Capital Dynamics Corp., P.O. Box 1404, Dallas, TX 75221, T: 800-396-2729, F: 214-881-2723, O: E-mail: capdyn@aol.com.
Cargill Associates, PO Box 330339, Fort Worth, TX 76163, T: 817-292-9374.
Catholic Knights Insurance Society, O: Web: www.execpc.com/~lamphear/ckis.html.
Christian Financial Services, Inc, P.O. Box 265, Brundidge, AL 36010, T: 205-735-5007.
Christian Financial Concepts, 601 Broad St., SE, Gainesville, GA 30501, T: 404-534-1000.
Christian Fundraising, P.O. Box 84, Seagoville, TX 75159, T: 214-287-1205.
Christian Purchasing Network, Inc., 3231 Gulf Gate Dr. # 204, Sarasota, FL 34231, T: 800-927-6775, 941-927-3377, F: 941-927-3378, O: E-mail: 104032.3073@compuserve.com, Web: www.cwd.com/cpn.
Christian Stewardship Association, 3195 S. Superior Ave., #303, Milwaukee, WI 53207, T: 414-483-1945, F: 414-483-4844.
Church Extension Plan, P.O. Box 12629, Salem, OR 97309-0629, T: 503-399-0552.
Church Mutual Insurance Co, 3000 Schuster Ln, Merrill, WI 54452, T: 715-536-5577.
Church Program Services, PO Box 471229, Tulsa, OK 74147, T: 918-664-6330.
CIOS, 4 Orinda Way, #140B, Orinda, CA 94563-2513, T: 415-254-1944.
Class Promotional Services LLC, 5201 Via Pauma, Oceanside, CA 92057, T: 619-630-2677, F: 619-630-9355, O: E-mail: bookintrvw@aol.com.
Clergycard Int'l, 950 W Norton, Suite 200, Muskegon, MI 49441, T: 616-733-4154.
Cookbooks by Morris Press, PO Box 1681, #1 Cookbook Ln, Kearney, NE 68848, T: 800-445-6621.
D. M. Stearns Missionary Fund, 147 West School House Lane, Philadelphia, PA 19144.
Del Rey Communications, Box 5274, Oak Brook, IL 60522, T: 630-655-0020, F: 630-655-1886, O: E-mail: 75051.1262@compuserve.com.
DeMoss Group, Inc., 3473 Satellite Blvd., #211, Duluth, GA 30136, T: 770-813-0000, F: 770-813-8887.
DeMoss, Arthur S., Foundation, St. Davids Center, Suite A-300, St. Davids, PA 19087, T: 215-254-5500.
Development Direction, Inc., 1539 Franklin Ave, Mineola, NY 11501, T: 516-747-0100, F: 516-747-0103.
Donor Automation, Inc., 912 New York St. #B, Redlands, CA 92374, T: 909-793-1230, F: 909-793-4434, O: E-mail: dasales@donor.com.
ELCA Foundation, 8765 West Higgins Road, Chicago, IL 60631.
Evangelical Christian Credit Union, 1150 N. Magnolia Ave., P.O. Box 3068, Anaheim, CA 92803-3068, T: 714-828-3228, O: Also: 1-800-634-ECCU.
Evangelical Council for Financial Accountability, P. O. Box 17456, Washington, DC 20041, T: 703-713-1414, F: 703-713-1133, O: E-mail: ecfa@aol.com.
Evangelical Scholarship Initiative, G151 Hesburgh Lib., Univ. Notre Dame, Notre Dame, IN 46556, T: 219-239-8347, F: 219-239-6630.
Exodus Real Estate Network, 2244 Ravine Rd., Kalamazoo, MI 49004, T: 800-395-2556, 616-349-0647, F: 616-349-9178, O: E-mail: info@exodusnetwork.net, exodusnetwork.net.
Exodus, Inc., P. O. Box 894, Greenwood, IN 46142, T: 317-887-1618, F: 317-882-3799.
Family Resources, 1318 E. Mission Rd. #371, San Marcos, CA 96069, T: 619-737-6872, F: 619-741-5791.
First Fruit, Inc., 7400 W. 20th Ave., Lakewood, CO 80215, T: 303-232-4084.
Focus Direct, Inc., 9707 Broadway, San Antonio, TX 78217, T: 800-299-9185, F: 210-804-1071.
Foundation Center, 888 Seventh Ave., New York, NY 10106.
Fundcraft Cookbook Publishing, 410 High 72 W, Collierville, TN 38017, T: 901-853-7070.
Fundraising Consultants, 519 Normal Rd, Dekalb, IL 60115, T: 815-756-6925.
General Conference Insurance Service, 6930 Carroll Av, Takoma Park, MD 20012, T: (202)723-0800.
Globalink Ministries, P.O. Box 1842, Waynesboro, VA 22980, T: 703-943-6721.
Indiana Christian Benevolent Association, 7860 Lafayette Rd, Indianapolis, IN 46278.
Interfaith Committee on Social Responsibility in Investments, New York, NY.
Intermedia Communications, 19689 7th Ave., NE, #174, Poulsbo, WA 98370, T: 360-779-1709, F: 360-779-6695.
Jubilee Foundation, 175 W. Jackson, Suite 800, Chicago, IL 60604, T: 312-922-2494.
Kelley-Professional Fund Raising Consultants, 203 W. Seventh St, Traverse City, MI 49684, T: 616-947-9636, F: 616-922-8120.

Killion McCabe & Associates, 900 Coit Central Tower, 12001 N. Central Expy., Dallas, TX 75243, T: 972-239-6000, F: 972-383-1985, O: Web: www.kma.com/kma.html, E-mail: jmccabe@kma.com.
Kirby Smith Association, Inc., 5 Fawn Dr., Quarryville, PA 17566, T: 800-762-3996, F: 717-284-3659.
Kresge Foundation, P.O. Box 3151, Troy, MI 48007, T: 313-643-9630.
LeTourneau Foundation, P.O. Box 26200, Colorado Springs, CO 80936; 5373 N. Union, Suite 100, T: 719-528-6000, F: 719-528-6001.
Lockman Foundation, The, 900 S. Euclid St., La Habra, CA 90631, T: 714-879-3055, F: 714-773-0627.
Luce, Henry, Foundation, 111 W. 50th St., New York, NY 10020, T: 212-489-7700.
Lutheran Brotherhood, 625 Fourth Ave., South, Minneapolis, MN 55415.
Lutheran Church Extension Fund, 1333 S. Kirkwood Rd., St. Louis, MO 63122-7295.
Maclellan Foundation, Provident Bldg., Suite 501, Chattanooga, TN 37402, T: 615-755-1366.
Marketing Solutions, 345 W. Foothill Blvd., Ste. D, Glendora, CA 91741, T: 818-914-5399, F: 818-914-1070, O: E-mail: marketings@aol.com.
Massachusetts Congregational Charitable Society, 10 Broad St, Salem, MA 01970.
Mom's Publishing Fundraisers, R.R. 1 Box 88A, Larned, KS 67550, T: 800-725-5772.
Mostyn Foundation, Inc., c/o James C. Edwards and Co., Inc., 805 Third Ave., New York, NY 10022, T: 212-319-8490.
National Catholic Stewardship Council, 1275 K St., N.W., Suite 980, Washington, D.C. 2005.
National Church Purchasing Group, 1018 Edgeworth Rd, Mechanicsville, VA 23111, T: 800-795-6274, F: 800-795-6275.
Nelson Word Ministry Services, P.O. Box 141000, Nashville, TN 37214, T: 615-902-2158, F: 615-902-2507, O: Web: www.ThomasNelsonGifts.com.
Outreach, Inc., 3140 Mile Rd. NE, Grand Rapids, MI 49505, T: 616-363-7817, F: 616-363-7880, O: E-mail: Outreachin@aol.com.
Overseas Council for Theological Education & Missions, Inc., P.O. Box 751, Greenwood, IN 46142, T: 317-882-4174.
Partners International, 1470 North Fourth St., San Jose, CA 95112, T: 408-453-3800.
Peer Neusken, Shepherd's Mrktg, 1201 N Sheridan, Peoria, IL 61606, T: 309-674-7337.
Pension Trust (Church of Christ), Box 851, Mount Vernon, IL 62864, T: (618)244-1636.
Potter's Clay Ad Agency, P.O. Box 1052, Vero Beach, FL 32961, T: 407-337-9872, F: 407-337-9872.
Preferred Risk Insurance Group, 1111 Ashworth Rd., West Des Moines, IA 50265, T: 515-225-5000.
Puckett Group, Inc. The, 2970 Clairmont Rd., #130, Atlanta, GA 30359, T: 404-248-1500, F: 404-248-0700.
Resource Services, Inc, 12770 Merit Dr, Suite 900, Dallas, TX 75238, T: 800-527-6824.
Response Unlimited, c/o The Old Plantation, Rt. 5, Box 251, Waynesboro, VA 22980, T: 540-943-6721, F: 540-943-0841.
Right Sharing of World Resources Office (Quakers), 3960 Winding Way, Cincinnati, OH 45229-1250.
Russ Reid Company, 2 N. Lake Ave., Ste. 600, Pasadena, CA 91101, T: 818-449-6100, F: 818-449-6190.
Sabbath Stewardship Ministries, P.O. Box 121407, Arlington, TX 76012, T: 817-633-4552.
Security Church Finance, Inc., 14615 Benfer Rd., Houston, TX 77069, T: 800-231-0373, 281-893-1390, F: 281-444-9797, O: E-mail: fpoc@churchbonds.com, Web: www.churchbonds.com.
Share Incorporated, 5153 E 51, Suite 111, Tulsa, OK 74135, T: 918-663-2663.
Sheer Joy! Press/Promotions, Box 608, Pink Hill, NC 28572, T: 919-568-6101, F: 919-568-4171, O: E-mail: sheerjoy@juno.com.
Soma Communications, Inc., 19927 Wittenburg Dr., San Antonio, TX 78256, T: 210-698-0207, F: 210-698-0208.
Stewardship Growth Associates, P.O. Box 640, Grapevine, TX 76051, T: 817-481-5904.
Stewardship Ministries, Inc, Church Div. Adv. Resource Dev, 9550 Skillman LB121 #506, Dallas, TX 75243, T: 214-349-3232.
Storehouse Foundation, P.O. Box 1532, Camden, SC 29020, T: 803-432-8677.
Sunday International, 5672 Buckingham Dr., Huntington Beach, CA 92649, T: 714-901-2455, F: 714-901-2466, O: E-mail: info@sundayint.com, Web: www.sundayint.com.
TELL Foundation, 4010 N. 38th Ave., Phoenix, AZ 85019, T: 602-278-6209.
Transamerica Marketing Services, Inc., 8130 Boone Blvd., Ste. 350, Vienna, VA 22182, T: 703-903-9500, F: 703-903-9511.

ZIMBABWE
National Co-ordinating Council for the Credit Union Movement in Zimbabwe, P.O. Box 8409, Causeway, Salisbury.

35
Foreign missionary councils

Councils, associations, commissions, committees, or fellowships of foreign missionary societies; organized councils of interdenominational or denominational or diocesan missionary societies, set up in sending countries for co-ordination, co-operation, joint discussion, joint projects, and missionary action to overseas or foreign countries (but that do not themselves generally serve as missionary-sending organizations).

ARGENTINA
COMIBAM, P.O. Box 711, Junin 2966, 3000 Santa Fe, T: 54-42-55-2189, F: 54-42-55-2189.
Misiones Mundiales, Casilla 711-3000 Santa Fe, República Argentina, T: 042-27684, O: Telex: 48222 PCOSF AR.

AUSTRALIA
Australian Evangelical Alliance, Inc., Missions Commission, P.O. Box 536, Camberwell Vic 3124; 1a Wills Street Hawthorn East, T: 03-882-7475, F: 03-882-7498.
Evangelical Missionary Alliance (NSW), 9 Carramarr Rd, Castle Hill, 2154.
National Council of Churches in Australia: Commission on Mission, Private Bag 199, QVB Post Office, Sydney NSW 1230; 379 Kent Street, Sydney, T: 61 2/9299 2215, F: 61 2/9262 4514.

AUSTRIA
Austrian Missionary Council, Martinstrasse 25/10, A-1180 Wien, Oesterreich.

BELGIUM
Comité des Instituts Missionnaires (CIM), Rue François Gay 276, B-1150 Brussel, T: (02)7704869.
Conseil Missionnaire National (CMI), Blvd du Souverian 199, B-1160 Brussel, T: (02)6736040.
Missionary Commission of the United Protestant Church of Belgium, 5, rue du Champ de Mars, B-1050 Bruxelles, T: 32 2/511 44 71, F: 32 2/511 28 90.

BOSNIA & HERCEGOVINA
Missions Office (Misijska Centrala), R Lacic 7, pp 155, YU-71001 Sarajevo.

BRAZIL
AMTB-Associação de Missões Transculturais Brasileiras, Cx. Postal 7001, Campinas-SP 13090-990, T: 19-255-3524, F: 19-255-3524, O: E-mail: amtb@bestway.com.br.

BRITAIN (UK OF GB & NI)
Churches' Commission on Mission, Inter-Church House, 35-41 Lower Marsh, GB-London SE1 7RL, T: 44-171-620-4444, F: 44-171-928-0010.
Council for World Mission, Livingstone House, 11 Carteret Street, London SW1H 9DL, T: 44 171/222 4214, F: 44 171/233 1747.
Evangelical Missionary Alliance, Whitefield House, 186 Kennington Park Road, London SE11 4BT, T: 44-171-207-2156, F: 44-171-207-2159, O: E-mail: 44-171-207-2159.
National Missionary Council of England and Wales, St. Joseph's College, Lawrence St, London NW7 4JX, T: (01)959-8125.

CANADA
Commission on World Concerns (CCC-CWC), Canadian Council of Churches, Chairman, 40 St Clair Av East, Toronto, Ontario M4T 1M9, T: (416)921-4152.
Conseil National Missionnaire (CNM), 1145 Chemin de la Canardirèe, Québec 3, Québec, T: (418)529-4924. (RC).
Interdenominational Foreign Mission Association, 10 Huntingdale Blvd., Scarborough, Ontario M1W 2S5.
National Missionary Council (NMC), 2661 Kingston Rd, Scarboro 713, Ontario, T: (416)266-9704. (RC).

CHINA
Evangelical Missions Fellowship, PO Box 6605, Kowloon, Hong Kong.
Hong Kong Association of Christian Missions, P.O. Box 71728, Kowloon C.P.P, Hong Kong, T: (852) 2392-8223, F: (852) 2787-4299.

COLOMBIA
COMIBAM Colombia, Apartado Aéreo 32408, Santafé de Bogotá 2, T: 1-255-2536, F: 1-235-4036.

COSTA RICA
COMIBAM, Apartado 289-1000, San Jose, T: 506-2215-522, F: 506-2550-257.
Federación Misionera Evangélica Costarricense (FEDEMEC), Apartado Postal 1307-1000, San José, T: 221-5522, F: 233-4389, O: E-mail: Fedemec@intercentro.com.

CROATIA
National Missionary Council, Biskupska Konferencija, Kaptol 31, YU-41000 Zagreb.

DENMARK
Danish Missionary Council, Skt Lukas Vej 13, DK-2900 Hellerup, T: 45 39/61 27 77, F: 45 39/40 19 54.
Missionsvennen, Kobenhavensvej 8, 3400, Hillerod.

ETHIOPIA
Ethiopian Inter-Mission Council, P.O. Box 2642, Addis Abeba.

FINLAND
Finnish Ecumenical Council, P.O. Box 185, SF-00161 Helsinki; Luotsikatu la, Helsinki, T: 358-0-180-21, F: 358-0-174-313.

FRANCE
Evangelical Community for Apostolic Action, 12 rue de Miromesnil, F-75008 Paris, T: 33 1/42 65 24 58, F: 33 1/40 07 09 91.
French Evangelical Department for Apostolic Action, 102 boulevard Arago, F-75014 Paris, T: 33 1/43.20.70.95, F: 33 1/43.35.00.55.
Fédération de Missions Evangéliques Francophones, O: Web: www.paroles.ch/index/FMEFInd.htm.

GERMANY
Association of Evangelical Missions, Hindenburgstrasse 36, 715 Korntal, Munchingen 1.
Conference of Evangelical Missions, Ganzenstr 13, D-7 Stuttgart-Mohringer.
Deutscher Katholischer Missionsrat, Kieler Str 35, D-5000 Köln 80; Hermannstr 14, D-5100 Aachen.
Evangelisches Missionswerk in Südwestdeutschland e V, Vogelsangstr 62, D-7000 Stuttgart 1; (ELK Württenburg, EK Baden, Moravian Ch, Basel Mission, et alia), T: (0711)638131.
Katholisches Auslandssekretariat, Kaiser-Friedrich-Str 9, D-5300 Bonn 3, T: (02221)225991.
Protestant Association for World Mission, Normannenweg 17-21, D-20537 Hamburg, BRD, T: 49 40/254 56-0, F: 49 40/25 29 87.
Verband Evangelischer Missionskonferenzen, Peiner Weg 57, D-2080 Pinneberg, T: (04101)22625.

GREECE
Hellenic Missionary Union, Lydias 12, 115 27, Athens.
Inter-Orthodox Missionary Centre, 30 Sina St, Athínai 135.

GUATEMALA
Cooperation of Mission from Latin America (COMIBAM), Apartado 27-1, CP 01907, T: 289-0040, F: 254-2951, O: E-mail: lilian@comibam.org.gt, Web: comibam.org.

HONDURAS
FEMEH-Federación Misionera Evangélica de Honduras, Apdo 5323, Tegucigalpa, MDC, T: 230-8779, F: 230-8263, O: E-mail: dhouston@hondudata.hn.

INDIA
India Missions Association, 48, First Main Road, East Shenoy Nagar, Madras 600 030; P.O. Box 2529, Madras 6000 030, T: 044-617596, F: 044-6442859, O: E-mail: ima@pobox.com, Web: www.ad2000.org/ima.

INDONESIA
Indonesian Missionary Fellowship, The (IMF), Jalan Trunojoyo 2 Kotak Pos No. 4-Batu 65301, Malang, Jawa Timur, T: Batu 99-283-65, O: Cable: YPPII Batu-Malang, Indonesia.

IRELAND
Association of Irish Missionary Societies, 35 Molesworth St, Dublin, T: 790939.
Irish Missionary Union, Orwell Park, Rathgar, Dublin 6, T: (353) 01 965433.
National Mission Council of Ireland, 54 Wellington Road, Dublin 4, T: (353) 01 689674.
Pontifical Mission Aid Societies, 64 Lower Rathmines Road, Dublin 6, T: (353) 01 972035.

ITALY
Commissione Episcopale de la Cooperazione tra le Chiese, Via della Conciliazione 1, I-00193 Roma.
Conférence des Supérieurs Majeurs des Instituts Missionnaires d'Origine Italienne, Via Luigi Lilio 80, I-00143 Roma.
Consiglio Missionario Nazionale, Segreteria Generale, Via Levico 14, I-00198 Roma, T: 867080.
Secrétariat Unitaire des Instituts Missionnaires, Via Guerrazzi 11, I-00152 Roma.

JAPAN
Asia Missions Association (MTC), P.O. Box 1, Takaku, Nasu 325-03, T: 287-781585, F: 287-78-2532, O: E-mail: mtc-jp@sa2.so-net.o.jp.

NETHERLANDS
Central Missions Commissariat, van Alkemadelaan 1, 's-Gravenhage, T: (070)244594.
Evangelical Missionary Alliance, Eendrachtstraat 29A, NL-3784 KA Terschuur, T: 31-432-462198, F: 31-342-461492.
Netherlands Missionary Council, 37 Prins Hendriklaan, NL-1075 BA Amsterdam, T: 31 20/4671 76 54, F: 31 20/4675 57 36.
SEZA, Mereveldlaan 89, 3454 CC De Meern.

NEW ZEALAND
Centre for Mission Direction, P.O. Box 31-146 Ilam, Christchurch 8004, T: (64-3) 388-4845.
Commission Overseas Missions and Inter-Church Aid, National Council of Churches of New Zealand, P.O. Box 291, Christchurch.
Council for Mission and Ecumenical Co-operation, P.O. Box 21 395, Christchurch, T: 64-3-355-1370, F: 64-3-355-1371.
New Zealand Evangelical Missionary Alliance, 427 Queen St, PO Box 8140, Auckland.

NIGERIA
Nigeria Evangelical Missions Association (NEMA), P.O. Box 6001, Jos, T: Jos 54481.

NORWAY
European Evangelical Missionary Alliance, c/o Norwegian Santal Mission, P.O. Box 9219, Waterland N-0134 Oslo 1.
Norwegian Missionary Council, Geitmyrsvn 7 D, Oslo 1.

PANAMA
Departamento de Misiones, Apdo 18, Bocas del Toro, T: 59258.

PHILIPPINES
Philippine Mission Association, P.O. Box 005, Mailman Outlet, Mandaluyong City, 1554, T: (63-2) 5310713, F: (63-2) 5310713, O: E-mail: rcorpuz@jmf.org.ph.
Philippine Missions Association, Inc., P.O. Box 1416, Manila; 41 Cordillera St., Mandaluyong, Metro Manila, T: 77-44-79, 79-69-23.

POLAND
Commission Missionnaire de l'Episcopat de Pologne, Secrétariat de la Commission (Komisja Episkopatu Polski do Spraw Misji, Sekretariat (Komisji), Ul Dziekania 1, 00 279 Warszawa, T: 319662.

PORTUGAL
Liga Evangélica de Accão Missionaria, Alameda das Linhas de Torres, 122, Lisboa 5, T: 790039.

SINGAPORE
Singapore Centre for Evangelism & Missions, Raffles City P.O. Box 1052, Singapore 911736, T: 65-299-4377, F: 291-8919.

SOUTH KOREA
Asian Missionary Association, C.P.P. Box 2732, Seoul.
Korean Center for Adopt-A-People Program, Munjung-dong 77-3, Somngpa-ka, Seoul 138-200, T: (82-2) 402-4967, F: (82-2) 402-4968.
Korean Christian Mission Association, 443, Shinmoon - Rou 1-Ga, Chongro, Seoul.
Third World Missions Association (TWMA), Korea International Mission, C.P.O. Box 3476, Seoul, T: 82-33921301.

SPAIN
Association of Foreign Missions, Apartado, 48, 08880 Castelldefels (Barcelona), T: 93 6655690.
Comisión Episcopal de Misiones y Cooperación entre las Iglesias, Calle del Bosque 9, Madrid 3, T: 2332003.

SWEDEN
Swedish Missionary Council, Kungsgatan 28, S-751 05 Uppsala, T: (018)20240.

SWITZERLAND
Alliance Missionnaire Evangélique (AME), Siège Central, 7 Av de Cour, CH-1007 Lausanne.
Centre Missionnaire, 10, pl. Notre-Dame, 1700 Fribourg, 037/22 19 31.
Commission on World Mission and Evangelism (CWME), World Council of Churches, Ecumenical Centre, 150 Route de Ferney, CH-1211 Genève 20, T: (0104122)333400.
Conseil missionnaire catholique suisse, 2, ch. Cardinal-Journet, 1762 Villars-sur-Glane, 037/24 42 81.
Département Missionnaire des Eglises Protestantes de la Suisse Romande, Chemin des Cèdres 5, CP 136, CH-1000 Lausanne 9.
Federation de Mission Evangeliques, Francophones, Chemin de Rechoz, 1027 Lonay.
Groupe de cooperation missionnaire en Suisse romande, 1891 Verossaz, 025/65 23 62.
Kooperation Evangelischer Kirchen und Missionen in der Deutschsprachigen Schweiz (KEM), Missionsstr 21, CH-4003 Basel, T: (061)253725.
Schweizerischer Katholischer Missionsrat, Grandrue 34, CH-1700 Fribourg 2.
Swiss Protestant Missionary Council, Florastr. 21, CH-4600 Olten, T: 062/266 268, F: 062/263 069.

TAIWAN
Taiwan Missionary Fellowship, P.O. Box 555, Taipei 100.

UNITED STATES OF AMERICA (USA)
Accelerating International Mission Strategies (AIMS), P.O. Box 64534, Virginia Beach, VA 23464, T: 804-523-7979, F: 757-579-5851, O: Web: www.aims.org.
Associated Missions, International Council of Christian Churches (TAM-ICCC), 756 Haddon Av, Collingswood, NJ 08108, T: (609)858-0700.
Association of International Mission Services (AIMS), 2901 W. Taft, Wichita, KS 67213, T: 316-942-8293, 316-945-7636, F: 316-942-9861, O: E-mail: steveaims@aol.com.
Committee on the Missions-National Conference of Catholic Bishops, 3211 Fourth St, NE, Washington, DC 20017.
Division of Overseas Ministries (DOMNCCCUSA), 475 Riverside Drive, New York, NY 10027, T: (212)870-2175.
Evangelical Fellowship of Mission Agencies, The, 4201 North Peachtree Road, Suite 300, Atlanta, GA 30341, T: 770-457-6677, F: 770-457-0037, O: E-mail:EFMA@XC.XC.Org.
Fellowship of Missions (FOM), 4205 Chester Av, Cleveland, OH 44103, T: (216)431-5222.
Interdenominational Foreign Mission Association (IFMA), P.O. Box 0398, Wheaton, IL 60189, T: 630-682-9270, F: 630-682-9278, O: E-mail: IFMA@aol.com.
U.S. Catholic Mission Association, 3029 4th St., N.E., Washington, DC 20017-1102, T: 202-832-3112, O: E-mail: uscma@igc.org.
World Evangelical Fellowship Missions Commission (MC), 4807 Palisade Dr., Austin, TX 78731, T: 512-467-8431, F: 512-467-2849, O: E-mail: BillTaylor@xc.org.

36

Foreign missionary field contacts

A brief selection of contact information for the sites of missionary work, on the fields to which missionaries are sent; field offices, field contacts, field headquarters; bases, compounds, offices, centers, or central institutions for missionary efforts or teams.

ALBANIA

Virginia Mennonite Board of Missions, Rruge Kouf Peres, Pall 136, Shul, Apt 7, Tirana, T: 352-42-25297, F: 352-42-25297.

AUSTRIA

Assemblies of God—Europe, Staackmann Gasse 23, Vienna 1210, T: 43-222-278-0732, F: 32-222-278-0732.
Bethany Missions—Eastern Europe Team, Untere Haupt 13/2/13, Lanzendorf MO 2326, T: 43-22-35-7192.
Church Resource Ministries, Meister Kliegergasse 35, Perchtoldsdorf 2380, T: 43-1-864-595.
Eastern European Mission and Bible Foundation, Heizwerkstrasse #12, Vienna 1232, T: 43-1-515-5710, F: 43-1-616-7375.
TEAM-Austria, Wumbstrasse 34111, Vienna A-1120, T: 43-1-83-53-53, F: 43-1-83-53-55.
United World Mission, 11790 Postfach 176, Vienna 1051, T: 43-1-649-6713.
Youth with a Mission—Slavic Ministries, Grossharras 1, Grossharras 2034, T: 43-2526-336, F: 43-2526-6146.

BELGIUM

Greater Europe Mission, Ave. du Renard Argente 4, Wezembuk Oppem 1970, T: 32-2-731-66-44, F: 32-2-782-03-94.

BOLIVIA

Norwegian Lutheran Mission in Bolivia, Casilla 1519 Pasaje Zoologico 1220, 1519 Cochabamba, T: 591-42/495-51, F: 591-42/806-12.

BOTSWANA

Love Botswana Outreach, P.O. Box 448, Maun.

CAMEROON

Lutheran Brethren World Mission, BP 25, Kaele.

CANADA

Greater Europe Mission, P.O. Box 984, Oshawa L1H 7N2, Ontario.

CHINA

Norwegian Lutheran Mission, 8 Dianthus Road, G/F, Yau Yat Chuen, Kowloon, Hong Kong.

CZECH REPUBLIC

Greater Europe Mission, Kurimska 15, Brno 62100, T: 42-577-1535.

ECUADOR

Alianza Cristiana Y Misionera, Luis Cordero No. 410 y 6 de Dic, Casilla 137, Quito, T: 521-150.
Cristianos En Acción, Dolores Veintimilla de Galindo 151, Casilla 710, Cuenca.
Cristo Al Mundo, Francisco de Nates No. 134, Casilla 11137, Quito, T: 454-571.
Cruzada Cristiana, Lizardo Garcia No. 321 y F. Segura, Guayaquil.
Cruzada Estudiantil Y Profesional Para Cristo Alfa Y Omega, Pasaje Chiriboga No. 443 y America, Casilla 4990, Quito, T: 237-725.
Iglesia Misionera Del Ecuador, Ave. Kennedy, Casilla 187, Esmeraldas, T: 710-534.
Iglesia Cristiana 'Cuerpo De Cristo', Esmeraldas No. 1012 y Velez, Guayaquil, T: 341-059.
Iglesia Cristiana Verbo, 9 de Octubre No. 923, Casilla 34A, Quito, T: 523-960.
Iglesia de Dios, La Tierra No. 392 y Los Shyris, Casilla 8030, Quito, T: 246-831.
Iglesia del Nazareno, Manzana 46 Lote 4 Carcelen, Casilla 4964, Quito, T: 539-461.
Iglesia del Pacto Evangelico (Switzerland), Isla Isabela No. 221, Casilla 8283, Quito, T: 247-079.
Iglesia del Pacto Evangélico (USA), Isla Isabela No. 221, Casilla 6068, Quito, T: 453-921.
Junta Misionera Foranea de la Convención Bautista Del Sur (USA), Marchena No. 425 y Ave. América, Casilla 4725, Quito, T: 527-470.
Mision Bautista del Companerismo, Casilla 4789, Quito, T: 455-554.
Misión Evangélica Bereana del Ecuador, Ignacio f. Salvador No. 314, Casilla 8241, Quito, T: 237-777.
Misión Evangélica Luterana, Luis Cordero No. 1185 y Sangurima, Casilla 1334, Cuenca, T: 822-516.
Misión Evangélica Menonita en Ecuador, Ciudadela FAE Maz. 35, Villa 4, Casilla 10936, Guayaquil, T: 391-005.
Misión Luterana Sudamericana de Noruega, Panamericana Sur, Casilla 178, Cuenca, T: 810-637.
Movimiento Misionero Mundia (from Puerto Rico), Eloisa, Casilla 490, Quito, T: 534-964.
OMS Internacional, Inc., Lorenzo de Garaicoa No. 739, Casilla 860, Guayaquil, T: 301-655.
Unión Misionera Evangélica, Voz Andes No. 186, Casilla 5185, Quito, T: 240-450.

GAMBIA

West African Association of Seventh-day Adventists (Gambia), P.O. Box 2828, Serekunda; 3, 24th Street South, Fajara 'F' Section, T: (220) 293347, F: (220) 392462, O: Cable: Adventist, Banjul, Gambia.

GERMANY

Church of God World Missions, Postfach 91, Obersulm 7104, T: 49-07134-3036, F: 49-07134-10231.
Church of the Nazarene, Kerkelbornstrasse 3, Biebergemuend 3 6465, T: 49-6050-2840, F: 49-6050-2849.
SEND International, Hammersteinerstrasse, Kandem 7842.

GUINEA

Seventh-day Adventist Guinea Mission Stationa, Boite Postale 1530, Conakry, T: 224-443276.

HUNGARY

ABWE, 2030 Érd, Törkoly utca 34, T: 36-23-366-024, F: 36-23-366-024.
Christian & Missionary Alliance, 4028 Debrecen, Vasvári Pál utca 4 fz. 2, T: 36-52-446-605.
Church Resource Ministries, Brasso U. 102/A, Budapest 1118, T: 36-1-185-9878, F: 36-1-201-4953.
Friendship International Hungary, 1025 Budapest, Gábor Áron 80., T: 36-1-393-0696, F: 36-1-393-0697.
Grace Ministries International - Christian Counseling, 1118 Budapest, Beregszász utca 43, T: 36-1-185-8875.
Greater Europe Mission, 2049 Diósd, Rákóczi utca 36, T: 36-23-38-1126, F: 36-23-381-126.
International Teams, 1037 Budapest, Laborc köz 32, T: 36-1-250-2685, F: 36-1-250-2685.
OMS International, 1118 Budapest, Sümegvár köz 10, T: 36-1-209-2308, F: 36-1-209-2308.
Operation Mobilisation, 2030 Érd, Gyula út 64, T: 36-23-367-348, F: 36-23-367-348.
Reach Out Ministries, 2030 Érd Kővirózsa utca 14, T: 36-23-374-886, F: 36-23-374-886.
Southern Baptist Convention, 1037 Budapest, Rozália utca 38-42. D/3, T: 36-1-173-0627.
World Gospel Mission, 1013 Budapest, Attila út 23, T: 36-1-175-7476, F: 36-1-175-7476.
Youth With A Mission, 1149 Budapest, Rona utca 106. III/12, T: 36-1-163-2773.

INDIA

American Advent Mission, 42, Velachery Road, Madras, Tamil Nadu 600032.
BCM International (India), Karnataka Branch, No. 56, Benson Cross Road, Bangalore, Karnataka 560056.
Evangelical Alliance Mission, At Jamine, PO Mirkot, TA Fort Songhadh, Songhadh, Gujarat.
Evangelize Every Muslim in India, P. B. 420, Vellore, Tamil Nadu 632004.
Fellowship for Neighbours India, House Of Hope, Gopalapuram, Post Box 611, Gandhinagar, Vellore, Tamil Nadu 632006.
Francen World Outreach, Sharon Gardens, Venugopal Nagar, Guntur, Andhra Pradesh 522004.
Free Church of Finland Mission, Baksaduar, Chunabhati, West Bengal 731001.
Friends Missionary Prayer Band, Church Street, Khergam P.O., Valsad, Gujarat 394730.
Ichthus Fellowship, Ichthus House, Nima Sahi, Peyton Street, Cuttack, Orissa 753001.
India Field Council Of Baptist Mid Mission, Court Road, Silchar, Assam 788001.
Interserve, C-20 Community Centre, 1st Floor, Janakpuri, New Delhi 110058.
Norwegian Free Evangelical Mission, Karvi, Banda, Uttar Pradesh 210205.
OMS International, 60/64, Stanley Road, Allahabad, Uttar Pradesh 211002.
Pioneers - India, Plot 114, Rajeevnagar, Behind A. G. 's Colony, Hyderabad, Andhra Pradesh 500045.
United Christian Missionary Society of India, Pattanam P.O., Ondipudur (Via), Coimbatore, Tamil Nadu 641016.
WEC International, 'Farley', Ddhagamandalam, Octamundu, Tamil Nadu 643001.

INDONESIA

Navigators, Cisitu Indah IV/9, Bandung.
WEC International/Indonesia Mission Fellowship, Jalan Rereng Wulung 34, Bundung 40R3.

JAPAN

American Baptist Foreign Mission Society, Japan Christian Center, Rm. 71, 2-3-18 Nishi Waseda, Shinjuku Ku, Tokyo 169, T: 03-202-0051.
Apostolic Christian Church of America, 699-2 Shioda, Ichinomiya Cho, Higashi Yatsushiro Gun, Yamanashi Ken 409-14, T: 05534-7-1177.
Assemblies of God Evangelistic Association, 3-15-20 Komagome, Toshima Ku, Tokyo 170, T: 03-915-1551.
Association of Baptists for World Evangelism, Inc., 814 Shimoishiki Cho, Kagoshima Shi 890, T: 0992-29-2353.
Baptist General Conference, Japan Mission, 13-3 Toride, Narumi Cho, Midori Ku, Nagoya Shi 458, T: 052-621-1221.
Baptist International Missions, Inc., R2, 1170 Kawasaki, Hamura Machi, Nishitama Gun, Tokyo 190-11, T: 0425-53-2577.
Baptist Mid-Missions in Japan, 122-5 Kotakakura Aza, Tamanoi, Otama Mura, Adachi Gun, Fukushima Ken 969-13, T: 0243-48-2731.
Baptist World Mission, 6231 Tokorozawa Heights, Tokorozawa Shi, Saitama Ken 359, T: 0429-98-2364.
Brethren in Christ Missions, c/o Slaymaker, 4-309-15 Hanakoganei, Kodaira Shi, Tokyo 187, T: 0424-66-0372.
Christian and Missionary Alliance, Japan Mission, Mezon Kosumosu #205, 3-31-4 Kotesashi, Tokorozawa Shi, Saitama Ken 359, T: 0429-49-8262.
Christian Missions in Many Lands (Japan Fellowship), 2-1-30 Showa, Kurashiki Shi, Okayama Ken 710, T: 0864-21-9448.
Christian Reformed Japan Mission, CRJM Office, #304 OSCC Bldg., 2-1 Kanda Surugadai, Chiyoda Ku, Tokyo 101, T: 03-292-7604.
Church of God Mission, 3-26-12 Hagiyama Machi, Higashi Murayama Shi, Tokyo 189, T: 0423-91-6131.
Church of the Nazarene, Japan Mission, 101 Kobuke Cho, Chiba Shi 281, T: 0434-23-4602.
Evangelical Alliance Mission, 3-15-15 Daizawa, Setagaya Ku, Tokyo 155, T: 03-413-2345.
Evangelical East Asia Mission, 11-1 Sannodai, Numazu Shi, Shizuoka Ken 410, T: 0559-63-2065.
Evangelical Orient Mission, 27-5 Aza Maekawada Minami Shirado, Taira, Iwaki Shi, Fukushima Ken 970, T: 0246-23-5490.
Finish Lutheran Mission, 2-16-41 Sen Cho, Otsu Shi, Shiga Ken 520, T: 0775-34-3210.
Finnish Free Foreign Mission, 101 Kamihate Cho, Kitashirakawa, Sakyo Ku, Kyoto Shi 606, T: 075-501-1077.
Free Christian Mission, 1-4-21 Zenshoji Cho, Suma Ku, Kobe 654, T: 078-732-2175.
General Conference Mennonite Mission, 1-6-35-703 Funairi Minami, Naka Ku, Hiroshima Shi 730, T: 082-232-4849.
German Alliance Mission, 361 One Cho, Tenpaku Ku, Nagoya Shi 468, T: 052-804-1589.
German Midnight Mission, 617-14 Futtsu, Futtsu Shi, Chiba Ken 299-13, T: 0439-87-5044.
GFAM Gospel Fellowship Association Missions, 5-115 Tsuchihara, Tenpaku Ku, Nagoya Shi 468, T: 052-801-8064.
Grace Brethren Foreign Mission, Miyazaki Bldg., 2F, 3-7-8 Hibarigaoka Kita, Hoya Shi, Tokyo 202, T: 0424-23-2002.
Grace Evangelistic Mission, 1-16-9 Nishi Nippori, Arakawa Ku, Tokyo 116, T: 03-806-5686.
International Missions, Inc., P.O. Box 50, Yamaguchi Shi, Yamaguchi Ken 753-91, T: 0839-23-2877.
Japan Advent Christian Mission, 5-3-37 Okayama Higashi, Shijonawate Shi, Osaka Fu 575, T: 0720-76-0580.
Japan Conservative Baptist Mission, 4-19-20 Koyodai, Sendai Shi, Miyagi Ken 981-31, T: 022-373-5342.
Japan Evangelical Free Church Mission, 5-11-24 Takakura, Iruma Shi, Saitama Ken 358, T: 0429-64-4557.
Japan Evangelical Lutheran Missionary Association of Evangelical Lutheran Church in America, 1-1 Ichigaya Sadohara Cho, Shinjuku Ku, Tokyo 162, T: 03-260-8637.
Japan Faith Mission, 2-24-60 Itsukaichi Iwate Cho, Iwate Gun, Iwate Ken 028-43, T: 0195-62-8470.
Japan Free Methodist Mission, 12-3-1 Maruyama Dori, Abeno Ku, Osaka Shi 545, T: 0798-74-7984.
Japan Free Will Baptist Mission, 48-1 Higashi Machi, Nopporo, Ebetsu Shi, Hokkaido 069, T: 011-385-2690.
Japan Mission, 1-6-1 Hibikino, Habikino Shi, Osaka Fu 583, T: 0729-39-6600.
Japan Mission of the International Mission Board of Southern Baptist Convention, Kamiyama Ambassador #209, 18-6 Kamiyama Cho, Shibuya Ku, Tokyo 150, T: 03-481-6641, F: 481-6637.
Japan Missionary Fellowship, Nikka Bldg., B-1, 7-9-7 Nishi Shinjuku, Shinjuku Ku, Tokyo 160, T: 03-371-7558.
Japan Presbyterian Mission (Mission to the World), 21-149 Aza Yamagoe, Oaza Nagakute, Nagakute Cho, Aichi Gun, Aichi Ken 480-11, T: 0561-63-1361.
Liebenzeller Mission Japan, 1-32-14 Kugahara, Ota Ku, Tokyo 146, T: 03-751-0211.
Lutheran Brethren Japan Mission, 1-8 Kita Machi, Tegata Yama, Akita Shi 010, T: 0188-35-7470.
Lutheran Free Church of Norway, Japan Mission, 2-2-18 Isoji, Minato Ku, Osaka Shi 552, T: 06-573-5921.
Maranatha Baptist Mission, Inc., 6226 Tokorozawa Heights, Tokorozawa Shi, Saitama Ken 359, T: 0429-95-5175.
Mennonite Brethren Mission, 3-10-12 Ishibashi, Ikeda Shi, Osaka Fu 563, T: 0727-62-7123.
New Tribes Mission, 214 Asahigaoka, Uchinada Machi, Kahoku Gun, Ishikawa Ken 920-02, T: 0762-38-0409.
North American Baptist General Mission in Japan, 706-83 Mitsugarasu Cho, Nar Shi 631, T: 0742-43-7361.
Norwegian Lutheran Mission, 2-2-11 Nakajima Dori, Chuo Ku, Kobe Shi 651, T: 078-221-8366.
Norwegian Mission Alliance, 2-19-20 Shinden, Ichikawa Shi, Chiba Ken 272, T: 0473-78-7553.
Norwegian Missionary Society, 2-2-18 Isoji, Minato Ku, Osaka Shi 552, T: 06-573-5921.
O.C. Ministries, Inc., 101 Musashino San Heights, 2-2-19 Hon Cho, Higashi Kurume Shi, Tokyo 203, T: 0424-75-0440.
Orthodox Presbyterian Church, Japan Mission, 7-18-6 Nakayama, Sendai Shi, Miyagi Ken 981, T: 0222-78-0127.
Overseas Missionary Fellowship, 3-1 Kita 38 Higashi 10 Chome, Higashi Ku, Sapporo Shi, Hokkaido 065, T: 011-753-4444.
Reformed Presbyterian Mission of Japan, 7-3-711-101 Gakuen Nishi Machi, Nishi Ku, Kobe Shi 673, T: 078-791-0644.
Reinforcing Evangelists & Aiding Pastors Mission, Inc., REAP Mission, Inc., 7-39-6 Higashi Oizumi, Nerima Ku, Tokyo 177, T: 03-922-6402.
Scandinavian East Asia Mission, 4-13-26 Shinohara Kita Machi, Nada Ku, Kobe 657, T: 078-861-3243.
SEND International, 111 Hakuraku, Kanagawa Ku, Yokohama 221, T: 045-432-3221.
Swedish Alliance Mission in Japan, 4-34-44 Kamoe Cho, Hamamatsu Shi, Shizouoka Ken 432, T: 0534-53-5051.
Swedish Free Missionaries, 2-122 Iwama-cho, Hodo-gaya-ku, Yokohama 240, T: 045-333-8965.
Swiss Alliance Mission, 4-26-13 Narashinodai, Funabashi Shi, Chiba Ken 274, T: 0474-62-3034.
Swiss East Asia Mission, 35 Betto Cho, Kitashirakawa, Sakyo Ku, Kyoto Shi 606, T: 075-781-3456.
WEC International (Worldwide Evangelization for Christ Intl.), 569 Kondo, Gokasho Cho, Kanzaki Gun, Shiga Ken 529-14, T: 0748-48-2047.
Wesleyan Mission in Japan, 2135-1 Kita Hassaku Cho, Midori Ku, Yokohama 227, T: 045-932-5655.
World Gospel Mission, 20-11 Nakamaru Cho, Itabashi Ku, Tokyo 173, T: 03-959-7242.
World Opportunities Intl., c/o Osaka Christian Center, 2-26-47 Tamatsukuri, Higashi Ku, Osaka 540, T: 06-768-4385.
World Outreach, 1-26-2 Minami Sakurazuka, Toyonaka Shi, Osaka Fu 560, T: 06-841-0504.

KENYA

Pentecostal Assemblies of Canada, P.O. Box 44091, Nairobi.

NIGER

Seventh-day Adventist Niger Mission Station, Boite Postale 11506, Niamey.

PAKISTAN

Campus Crusade for Christ, 36-B/6, Pechs, Karachi -29.

PHILIPPINES

East-West Center for Missions, A.C.P.O., Box 128, Quezon City.
Navigators, Tritech, Bricktown Gammens, Metrop Manila.
YWAM, P.O. Box 2725, Manila 1099.

POLAND

Youth with a Mission—Slavic Ministries, SKR, Poczt 35, Krakow 23 30-093, T: 48-12211153, F: 48-122223606.

PORTUGAL

A Missão dos Irmãos da Graça Abundante (AMIGA), Av. Santos Leite, 157 - 1. Dt., 4470 Maia; Apartado 325-4471 Maia Codex, T: 02-948 22 30.
BCM Internacional, Rua General Norton de Matos, Lote F - 2 D, 2640 Mafra, T: 061-81 10 74.
Missão Europa Maior (Greater Europe Mission), Rua Dr. Jaime Cortesão, 13 - 5. Esq, 2675 Póvoa de Santo Adrião, T: 01-937 41 80.

RUSSIA

Assemblies of God—Russia, Mozhaiskoye Shosse 39, kv. 62, Moscow 121354, T: 7-095-448-5779, F: 7-095-292-6511.

SINGAPORE

Baptist Mission of the International Mission Board, S.B.C., 1 Goldhill Plaza #03-19, Singapore 308899, T: 253-7423, F: 251-4028.
Pentecostal Evangelical Mission, Finnish Free Foreign Mission, Thomson Road PO Box 26, Singapore 915701, T: 456-4891, F: 756-3527.

SOUTH AFRICA

Baptist Southern Africa Region (International Mission Board, SBC USA), PO Box 861, Edenvale 1610, 1 Bethia St, Harmelia, 1600 Edenvale, T: 011-974-8828, F: 011-974-1002.
Biblical Ministries Worldwide (WEF Ministries formerly), PO Box 2881, Rivonia 2128.
Christian Missions in Many Lands (USA), Echoes of Service (UK), PO Box 6203, Weltevreden Park 1725, Randburg, T: 011-781-2035.
Evangelical Alliance Mission, The (TEAM), PO Box 190, Florida 1710, 54 Barkly Ave Ave, Dicovery, Roodepoort, T: 011-674-1876, F: 011-472-4816, O: E-mail: 100100, 2450 @compuserve.com.
Mission of Lutheran Churches (Bleckmar Mission), PO Box 73377, Fairland 2030, Johannesburg, T: 011-678-0522.
Swedish Alliance Mission, P/Bag X 9303, White River 1240, 20 Van Riebeeck St, White Rivet, T: 013-788-4093.
World Outreach, PO Box 180, Halfway House 1685, T: 011-8052381, F: 011-805-2382.

SOUTH KOREA

Youth With A Mission, K.P.O. Box 1709, Seoul.

SPAIN

Assemblies of God (USA), Apartado 29.152, 28080 Madrid, T: 91 2565604.
Association of Baptist for World Evangelism, Alardel Roy S/N E4-3D, Urbanización Las Villas, Madrid 28042.
Baptist International Mission, C/Pozo de la Nieve 11, Piso 6B Derecha, 38850 Torrejón de Ardóz, Madrid.
Baptist Mid-Missions, Calle Hilados, 16, ESC Centro 11c, Torrejón de Ardoz, Madrid 28850, T: 91 6563408.
BCM International UK, Misión Bíblica Betel, Los Guardas 13, 40100 La Granja (Segovia).
Bible Christian Union, Camino de Los Nolales, 19, 33429 La Fresneda, Oviedo.
CAM International, Calle Federico Mompoul, 2B, Alcalá de Henares, Madrid 28806, T: 91 8822469.
Christ for the Nations, Cabelleros 22, Arico C, 13003B Ciudad Reál, T: 926 222121.
Christian and Missionary Alliance, Villarroel 205, Pisco 4, Apt 1, 08036 Barcelona, T: 93 3223170.
Church of God of Prophecy, Maestro Albenez 5-3, 03202 Elche, Alicante.
Church of the Nazarene, Calle Pelícano 26, Madrid 28025, T: 91 4715919.
Elim Fellowship, Ctra de Vicalvaro 131, la Esc 8-A, 28022 Madrid, T: 91 2137056.
European Missionary Fellowship, Juan Ramon Jiménez 30, 13600 Alcazar de San Juan (Ciudad Reál), T: 926 544390.
Finnish Free Foreign Missions, c/ Juntas Generales 30-2D, 01011 Vitoria (Alava), T: 945 275282.
Global Outreach Mission, Libreria Biblica, Pasage Aranzazu 9, Málaga.
Gospel Missionary Union, Calle República Argentina 28,2A, 29016 Málaga, T: 952 227518.
Grace Baptist Mission, C/San Eusebio 54, 08006 Barcelona.
Horizons/Mission Without Bounds, AP de Correos 89, 11360 San Roque, Cádiz, T: 956 781268.
Latin American Mission, c/Montelirio, 8, 41908 Castilleja de Guzman (Seville), T: 95-572-0503.

Maranatha Baptist Mission, Apartado 116, 33080 Oviedo, Asturias.
Mennonite Board of Missions, C/Madrid 12, 3 Iz, 09002 Burgos.
Mennonite Brethren (USA), Foresta 17, 5G, 28760 Tres Cantos, Madrid.
Misión Bautista A.B.E.M.E., Avda. Floréncia, 8, 3° A., Coslada, 28820 Madrid, T: 329-55-27, O: Also tel: 672-97-08.
Missionary Church, Apartado 35, Godella, Valencia, T: 96 3642356.
National Association of Free Will Baptists, Board of Foreign Missions, C/Pintor Salvador Dali 4, 2D (izda), 28933 Mostoles, Madrid, T: 91 6179070.
OMS International, Apartado 3071, 28080 Madrid, T: 91 7330904.
Open Bible Standard Missions, Sta Teresa 23, Entlo la, San Justo Desvern, Barcelona, T: 93 3719259.
Operation Mobilization, Apartado 120, 98330 Premia de Mar, Barcelona, T: 93 5557692.
Project Magreb, Apartado 573, 18080 Granada.
Send International, Cantabria 33, 7A, 28042 Madrid, T: 91 7475365.
Southern Baptist Convention, Crta Rota KM.1, Chatlet Isabel, 11500 Peurto Sant Maria, Cadiz, T: 96 856874.
Spanish Gospel Mission, Monescillo 15, 13300 Valdepeñas, C Reál, T: 926 322824.
TEAM (The Evangelical Alliance Mission), Apartado 695, Seville 41080.
World Team, C/Zazuar 2 10D, 28031 Madrid, T: 91 3310580.
Worldwide Evangelization Crusade (WEC), Local 6, Madrid 28022, T: 91 2137489.

SWEDEN
Finnish Lutheran Overseas Mission, Harjunreuna 27 B, 01230 Vantaa.
Wycliffe Bible Translators, Walling 3A, 11160 Stockholm.

TAIWAN
Norwegian Lutheran Mission, Lung Chiang Rd., No 135, Taipei 104.

THAILAND
Assemblies of God, P.O. Box 202, Phrakhanong, Bangkok 10110.

UKRAINE
Bethany Mission of Ivanofrankovisk, ul. Sovietskaya 33, kv. 5, Ivanofrankovisk 284000.

UZBEKISTAN
Central Asian Christian Mission, ul. Panchenko, 35, Tashkent 700100, T: 55-06-49.

ZAMBIA
Dorthea Mission, P.O. Box 32696 - Lusaka.

ZIMBABWE
Maryknoll Sisters in Zimbabwe, P.O. Box 298, Harare.

37
Foreign missionary societies

Societies and agencies primarily concerned with the sending of foreign missionary personnel and resources to another country or countries, including international missionary societies, denominational mission boards, orders which mainly or largely work in foreign missions, and Catholic missionary congregations or institutes. Thousands of smaller societies are not included.

38
Foreign missionary training

Training institutions or programs of various types and sizes, in sending countries or on mission fields, solely or primarily for the training of foreign missionaries or Christians proceeding overseas in secular employment; orientation schools and courses, programs for the continuing or advanced education of missionaries, refresher courses, post-field debriefing courses, graduate schools of mission or missiology, missiological institutes; seminaries, schools, or colleges primarily for foreign missionaries. For the academic study of mission and missiology, see UNIVERSITY DEPARTMENTS OF RELIGION.

ALGERIA
Centre de Langues et de Pastorale, Grand Séminaire, Komba.

AUSTRALIA
Missionary Training College, St. Leonards, Tasmania.
Summer Institute of Linguistics (SIL), Gumbalanya, Barnawarth South, Victoria.

AUSTRIA
Missiologisches Institut der Päpstlichen Missionswerke, Seilerstätte 12, A-1010 Wien, T: 523275.
Salzburger Missionsschule, Brauhausstr 22, Salzburg-Maxglan.

BELGIUM
CIM Service de Formation, Chaussée de Mont-Saint-Jean 95, B-3030 Heverlee.
Collège pour l'Amérique Latine (COPAL), Tervursestraat 56, B-3000 Leuven, T: (016)225845, 226415.
Compagni Costruttori, Naamsesteenweg 537, Haverlee, T: (016)279, 20523.
Semaine de Missiologie de Louvain, Chaussée de Mont-Saint-Jean 95, B-3030 Heverlee.

BOLIVIA
Bolivia A Las Misiones, Casilla 3327, Cochabamba, T: 42-68434.
Instituto de Misionologia, Facultad de Filosofia y Teologia/Universidad Católica Boliviana, C. Oruro E3-0492, Casilla 2118, Cochabamba, T: 591-42-57153/57086, F: 591-42-57086.

BRAZIL
Centro de Treinamento Missionário, C.P. 14139, São Paulo-SP 02799-970, T: 11-875-3320, F: 11-875-3320, O: E-mail: ctmsp@ibm.net.
Centro Evangélico de Missões, Cx. Postal 53, Viçosa-MG 36570-000, T: 31-891-3030, F: 31-891-3030, O: E-mail: cem@homenet.com.br.
Kairós - Associação para Treinamento Transcultural, Cx. Postal 12.762, São Paulo-SP 04798-970, T: 11-541-9953, F: 11-246-5908, O: E-mail: 102702.1237@compuserve.com.
Missionary Training Centre, CP 14.139, SP-02799-970 São Paulo, T: 55-11-875-3320, F: 55-11-875-3320.
Missão Transcultural: Treinamento Transcultural E. Lingüístico, C.P. 1324, Belo Horizonte-MG 30161-970, T: 31-494-6518, F: 31-494-6518.
WEC Missionary Training College, CP 289, Sitio Aguas Vivas, Vila Oliveira, MG-39400 Montes Claros, T: 55-38-221-0790, F: 55-38-221-4922.

BRITAIN (UK OF GB & NI)
Ad Lucem, c/o CIIR, Hinsley House, 38 King St, London WC2.
All Nations Christian College, Easneye, Ware, Hertfordshire SG12 8LX, T: Ware 0920-61243.
Catholic Institute for International Relations (CIIR), 38 King St, London WC2E 8JT.
Catholic Overseas Appointments Bureau, 38 King St, London WC2E 8JT.
Centre for International Briefing, The Castel, Farnham, Surrey, T: (02513)21194.
Centre for the Study of Christianity in the Non-Western World, University of Edinburgh, Edinburgh, Scotland.
Lebanon Missionary Bible College, Castle Terrace, Berwick-on-Tweed, T: 6190.
Missionary Education Centre, 23 Eccleston Square, London SW1.
Missionary Horticultural Training College, Arkley Manor, Arkley, Nr Barnet, Herts, T: (01)449-3131.
Missionary Institute London, Hocombe House, The Ridgeway, Mill Hill, London NW7 4HY, T: 44-181-906-1893, F: 44-181-906-4937, O: Also tel: 44-181-441-7091 or 181-449-0041.
Missionary Orientation Centre, WEC, Bulstrode, Gerrards Cross, Bucks SL9 8SZ.
Missionary Training Service, 18 Aston Way, Oswestry, Shropshire SY11 2XY, T: 44-1691-65361, O: Web: www.btinternet.com\~ajg\mtshome.htm.
National Lay Missionary Centre, All Saints Pastoral Centre, Colney, Herts.
OCMS, P.O. Box 70, Oxford, OX2 6HB.
Overdale College, Bristol Rd, Selly Oak, Birmingham B29 6LE.
Oxford Centre for Mission Studies, P.O. Box 70, Oxford OX2 6HB, T: 44-1865-58741, F: 44-1865-510823, O: E-mail: 100413.1026 compuserve.com.
Redcliffe Missionary Training College, 66 Grove Park Road, Chiswick, London W4 3QB, T: 44-181-994-3408, F: 44-181-994-9125.
School of Mission and World Christianity, Central House, Bristol Road, Birmingham B29 6LR, T: 44-121-472-4231, F: 44-121-472-8852.
Scottish Institute of Missionary Studies, University of Aberdeen, King's College, Aberdeen AB9 2UB.
Selly Oaks Colleges, Training in Mission Program, Birmingham B29 6LQ, T: (021)472-4231.
Seventh-day Adventist European Insitute of World Mission, Newbold College, Berkshire RG12 5AN, T: (344) 867359, F: (344) 861692.

CANADA
Canadian School of Missions and Ecumenical Institute, 97 St George St, Toronto 5, Ontario.
Institute of Mission Studies, Saint Paul University, 223 Main St., Ottawa, ON K1S 1C4, T: 613-236-1393, F: 613-782-3005.
Missionary Internship, 6507 Panton, Kilbride LOP 1GO, Ontario.
Saint Paul University, Institute of Mission Studies, 223 Main St., Ottawa, K1S 1C4; Institut des Sciences de la Mission, 223, Rue Main.
Spiritan Mission Institute, 2475 Queen St., East, Ontario M4E 1H8, T: 416-691-0792.
Venture Teams International, #3A, 3023 21 St., N.E., Calgary, AB T2E 7T1, T: 403-772-2970, F: 403-777-2973, O: 1-800-565-3818.

CHINA
Hong Kong Christian Short-term Mission Training Centre, 2A, 85 Wo Tong Tsui Street, Kwai Wo Bldg., Kwai Chung, N.T., Hong Kong, T: 0-4892982, F: 852-0-4899133.

COLOMBIA
Instituto Linguístico de Verano, Apdo Nac 5787, Bogotá.

COSTA RICA
Federación Misionera Evangélica Costarricense (FEDEMEC), Apartado Postal 1307-1000, San José, T: 221-5522, F: 233-4389, O: E-mail: Fedemec@intercentro.com.
Instituto Bautista Misionero, T: 224-4258.
Instituto Misionológico de las Américas (IMDELA), Apartado Postal 232-1011, San José, T: 233-7298, F: 255-0257, O: E-mail: imdela@sol.racsa.co.cr.
Spanish Language Institute, Apdo 2240, San José.

DENMARK
Berkop Højskole, Indre Missions Bibelskole, Aagbade 3, DK-7080 Berkop.

ECUADOR
Instituto Linguístico de Verano, Casilla 1007, Quito.

EL SALVADOR
Centro de Animación Misionera, c/o Hogar Santa Teresita, Apulo.
Seminario de Misiones San Carlos de Borromeo, Apartado #82, Santa Tecla 04101, T: 503-228-0879, F: 503-229-3337.

FINLAND
Finnish Evangelical Lutheran Mission, Missionary Training Institute, Tähtitorninkatu 18, P.O. Box 154, SF-00140 Helsinki.

FRANCE
Centre de Formation Missionnaire, 50 rue des Galibouds, Albertville (Savoie); 5 Rue Monsieur, Paris 7 and 24 Rue du Maréchal-Joffre, F-78000 Versailles, T: 950-2771.
Centro di Formazione e Scambi Internazionali, 73 rue des Heros Nogentais, F-94 Nogent-sur-Marne, T: 871-2320.
Ecole Technique d'Outre-Mer, 1 rue Dume d'Aplemont, Le Havre.
Missionary Orientation Centre, 156 Rue de Longchamp, Paris 16.
Prévoyance des Techniciens Missionnaires de la Coopération Internationale (PRETEMIC), 77 Rue du Président Herriot, Lyon 2.

GERMANY
Arbeitsgemeinschaft für Entwicklungshilfe, Leonhardstr 4, Aachen.
Arbeitskreis für Mission und Ökumeinische Beziehungen in der Evangelischen Studentengemeinde, Mercedesstr 5-7, D-7 Stuttgart 50, T: 562303/04.
Freie Hochschule für Mission der AEM/Evangelische Missiologie, Hindenburgstrasse 36, D-7015 Korntal-Munchingen 1, T: 49-711-83308, F: 49-711-833-087.
Freie Hochschule für Mission, Evang. Kreditgenossenschaft EG, Stuttgart, Konto 405 531 BLZ 600 606 06, T: 07-11-83-30-87.
Institut für Missionswissenschaft und Ökumenische Theologie der Universität Tübingen, Hausserstr. 43, D-7400 Tübingen.
Marienhoehe Missionary Seminary, Auf der Marienhoehe 32, D-61 Darmstadt, T: 55055/6.
Miss. Wiss. Institut, Hüfferstr.27, 48149 Münster, T: 02582/586.
Missionsakademie an der Universität Hamburg, Rupertistr 67, Hamburg-Nienstedten; Mittelweng 143, D-2 Hamburg 13.
Missionshaus Bibelschule Wiedenest, Olperstr 10, D-5275 Bergneustadt 2, Wiedenest, T: (02261)4777.
Missionspädagogische Arbeitsgemeinschaft, Mittelweg 143, D-2000 Hamburg 13, T: (040)417021.
Missionsw. Inst. Missio e.V., Postfach 1110, 5100 Aachen.
Nordelbisches Zentrum für Weltmission und Kirchlichen Weltdienst, Agathe-Lasch-Weg 16, D-2000 Hamburg 52, T: (0411)880183.
Theologisches Seminar der Liebenzeller Mission, Postfach 1240, Schiessbrain 9, D-75375 Bad Liebenzell, T: 49-7052-17291, F: 49-7052-17304, O: Also tel: 49-7052-17299.

GHANA
Akrofi-Christaller Memorial Centre, P.O. Box 76, Akropong-Akuapem.
Summer Institute of Linguistics (SIL), P.O. Box 47, Achimota.
Tamale Institute of Cross Cultural Studies, P.O. Box 5563, Tamale.

GUATEMALA
CEMCA, Apartado Postal 129, T: 276-7583, F: 276-7862.
ILV-Instituto Linguístico de Verano, Apartado Postal 1949, 01901, T: 476-2446, F: 477-0622.
Instituto de Capacitación Misionera (ICM), 4a Calle 5-52, Zona 1, Guatemala.

INDIA
Catholic Mission Seminary, Pilar, Goa 403203.
Christian Leadership Training Center, Luthergiri, Rajahmundry, Andhra Pradesh 533105.
Faith Missionary Institute, P.O. Box 2, Narsapur, Andhra Pradesh 534275.
India Full Gospel Missionary Institute, 23, Ashoka Garden, Govindpura P. O., Bhopal, Madhya Pradesh 462023.
Indian Institute for Cross Cultural Communication (IICCC), Ananthagiri S.P.O., Visak Dt., A.P. 531150.
Indian Institute for Cross Cultural Training, P. O. Box 376, Andhra University P. O., Vishakhapatnam, Andhra Pradesh 530003.
Missionary Training Institute, Serkawn, P.O. Zotland, Lunglei District 796 691.
Outreach Training Institute, c/o IEM, 7 (old 38) Langford Road, Bangalore 560 025.
Pentecostal Mission Training Centre, 45-A, V. Street, Padmanaba Nagar, Adayar, Madras, Tamil Nadu 600020.
Shiloh Missionary Training Center, 24, Paramount Apartments, 1/39, North Parade Road, St. Thomas Mount, Madras, Tamil Nadu 600016.
St. Paul's Mission Training Centre, Marvelikara, Kerala 690103.
United Missionary Training College, 1, Ballygunge Circular Road, Calcutta, West Bengal 700019.
Vikas Maitri, (Miss. Orientation Centre For Sisters), Via Narsinghgarh, Kotra, Madhya Pradesh 465679.

ITALY
Centro Assistenza Laici Missionari (CALM), Via Vittorio Veneto 197, I-19100 La Spezia.
Centro Collegamenti Tecnici per le Missioni (CCTM), Via Belvedere 11, I-80127 Napoli.
Centro Educazione Missionario (CEM), Via San Martino 8, Parma.
Centro Laici Italiani per le Missioni (CLIM), Piazza Fontana 2, I-20122 Milano, T: 806184.
Instituto Italo Cinese, Via Uffici del Vicario, 35-00186 Roma, T: 6785613.
International Centre for Missionary Animation, St. Peter's College, Viale delle Mura Aurelie 4, I-00152 Roma, T: 582228.
Piccoli Operai Missionari Ecumenici, Città della Ecumenica, Via Taddeide 24, I-00060 Riano (Roma).
Pontificio Instituto Missioni Estere (PIME), Via Santa Terese 12, I-00198 Roma.

JAPAN
Hayama Missionary Seminar, Lacy-kan, Hayama, Kanagawa-ken.
Japan Missionary Language Institute, Tokyo.
Missionary Training Center, 600-12 Takakuotsu Nasumachi, Nasugun Tochigi-Pref. 325-03; P.O. Box 1, Takaku, Nasu 325-03, T: 81-287-78-1585, F: 81-287-78-2532.

KENYA
Baptist Language School, Brackenhurst Baptist Assembly, Tigoni, PO Box 137, Limuru, T: Tigoni 256.
CPK Language & Orientation School, Bishops Rd, PO Box 49849, Nairobi, T: 20992.
St. John's School of Mission, P.O. Box 87, Nylima, Via Kisumu; P.O. Box 87, Nylima, Via Kisumu.

MALAWI
Katete Language Centre, P.O. Box 7, Champira.
Language Centre, P.O. Box 274, Lilongwe.

MEXICO
Instituto Linguístico de Verano, Apdo 2975, México 1, DF.
Instituto Mexicano de Misiones Mundiales, Apdo. Postal 7-114, Morelia, MI 58282, T: 43-24-25-31, F: 43-24-18-81, O: E-mail: 104576.541@compuserve.com.
Seminario de Misiones Extranjeras, Apdo 22009, México 22, DF.
Spanish Language School, 12 de Diciembre 25, Apdo 1616, Guadalajara, Jalisco, T: 57663.

NETHERLANDS
Contact Training School, Amersfoortsestraat 20, Soesterberg.
Hendrik Kraemer Institute, Postbus 12, 2340AA Oegstgeest.
Mission School of the Netherlands Reformed Church, Leidsestraatweg 11, Oegstgeest.
Missionary Seminary of the Reformed Churches in the Netherlands, Wilhelminalaan 3, Baarn.
Missionary Training Centre, Ubbergen-bij Nijmegen.

NEW ZEALAND
Advance Ministry Training Centre, P.O. Box 19-208, Avondale, Auckland, T: 0-9-828-9456, F: 0-9-828-9456.
NZ Missionary Training College, P.O. Box 15, Gordonton, T: 0-7-824-3611, F: 0-7-854-7848.

NICARAGUA
CENIEE-Centro Nicaraguense de Estudios Etnolingüísticos, Apartado Postal 3592, Managua, T: 2-78-3949, F: 2-28-4004.

NIGERIA
Christian Leadership and Missions Institute, P.O. Box 2449, Warri.
Nigeria Evangelical Missionary Institute, P.O. Box 5878, JOS, Plateau State.

NORWAY
Bible and Missionary Training School, Gá Ut Senteret, N-2090 Hurdal, T: 47-639-87777.
Fjellhaug Mission Seminary, Sinsenveien 15, N-0572 Oslo 5, T: 47-2-3770-90.
Misjonshogskolcn, Misjonsveien 34, N-4024 Stavanger, T: 47-5151-6210, F: 47-5151-6225.
Missionary College of the Norwegian Mission Society, Stavanger.
Missionshogskolen, N-4000 Stavanger.
Troens Bevis Bibel og Misjons Institut, P.O. Box 8, Sarons Dal, N-4480 Kvinesdal, T: 47-383-50711.

PAPUA NEW GUINEA
Melanesian Institute for Pastors and Socio-Economic Service, P.O. Box 571, Goroka, EHD.
Summer Institute of Linguistics (SIL), P.O Ukarumpa, EHD.

PERU
CEFMA-Centro de Formación Misiológica Andina, Apartado Postal 077, Huanuco, T: 064-51-2498.
Centro Latinoamericano de Lenguaje Total, Av 9 de Diciembre (Paseo Colón) 378, Lima, T: 312339.
Instituto Linguistico de Verano, Casilla 2492, Lima.

PHILIPPINES

Central Institute of Missions, P.O. Box 403, Iloilo City, 5000.
China Studies Program, De La Salle Univ. 2401 Taft Ave. D-406 Manila.
Unreached Peoples Missionary Training Center, Asian Theological Seminary, Q.C.C., P.O. Box 1454, Quezon City, 1154.

POLAND

Missionary Centre of the Verbist Priests, ul Kolonia 19, 14 500 Pieniezno.

PORTUGAL

Centro de Estudos Missionários, Lisboa.

PUERTO RICO

College of World Mission (Churches of Christ USA), Box 66, Catano, PR 00632.
Escuela de Misiones Betania, Calle 13 S.O. 824, Caparra Terrace, San Juan, P.R., T: 787-782-5152, F: 787-782-5152.

SAMOA

Fatuoaiga Missiological Institute, Pastoral & Cultural Centre, P.O. Box 596, Pagopago 96799.

SINGAPORE

Asian Cross-Cultural Training Institute, Simpang Bedok PO Box 0157, Singapore 914806, T: 870-0955, F: 522-8130.
Bethany School of Missions, Singapore, Raffles City PO Box 143, Singapore 911705, T: 339-5722, F: 339-0337.

SOUTH AFRICA

Africa School of Missions, P.O. Box 439, White River 1240, Peebles Valley Rd (off Numbi Gate Rd), White River, T: 01311-3-2341, F: 013-750-1340.
Lumko Missiological Institute, P.O. Box 5058, 1403 Delmenville, T: 011-827-8924.
Miss. Inst. at Lutheran Theol. College, P.O. Private Bag 206, Mapumulo, Natal 4470.
Msinga Society, % Univ of Stellenbosch, Faculty of Medicine, PO Box 19063, Stellenbosch 7505, T: 021-932-2850, F: 021-931-7810.

SOUTH KOREA

Center for the Study of World Mission, 353, Kwangjang-Dong, Sungdong-Ku, Seoul 133, T: 453-3101/7.
East-West Centre for Missions Research and Development, 110-1 Wolmoon, Paltan, Hwasung, Kyunggi-do 445-910, T: 860-339-353-1301, F: 860-339-52-5234, O: E-mail: hec ewc @bora,dacom,co,kr.
International School of Missions, 238 Hooam-dong, Yonsaku, PO Box 3476, Seoul.
World Missionary Training Institute, 1370 Soon-gin-Dong, Jongro-Ku, Seoul 110.

SPAIN

Centro Missionero de Adaptación Pastoral, Colegio Vasco de Quiroga, Ciudad Universitaria, Madrid 3.

SWEDEN

Missionsskolan Gōtabro, Gōtabro PL 6370, S-692 93 Kumla.

SWITZERLAND

Frères sans Frontières, Grand Rue 34, CH-1700 Fribourg, T: (037)231432.

TAIWAN

Taichung Language Institute, Wei Tao Rd., Lane Chiu Tso No 69, Taichung, T: 8842.
Taipei Language Institute, Chunghsiao Rd., Section 1 No 5, Taipei; 1559 Chung Cheng Rd., Taipei.

TANZANIA

Maryknoll Language School, PO Box 298.

UGANDA

Mushanga Language Centre, PO Box 187, Mbarara.

UKRAINE

Jahresbibelkolleg der Mission 'Licht des Evangeliums', ul Moscowskaja 64, oblast g Makejewka, 339051 Donezkaja, CIS.

UNITED STATES OF AMERICA (USA)

Asbury Theological Seminary, E. Stanley Jones School of World Mission & Evangelism, 204 N. Lexington Ave., Wilmore, KY 40390, T: 606-858-2261, F: 606-858-2375.
Bethany College of Missions, 6820 Auto Club Rd., Minneapolis, MN 55438, T: 612-944-2121, F: 612-829-2535.
Calvin Institute of World Mission (Korean), 355 P.O. Box 6008, Cerritos, CA 90701, T: 310-431-4900.
Campos Indígenas, P.O. Box 2, Bisbee, AZ 85603, T: 520-432-4171, F: 520-432-4171, O: E-mail: ScripturesinUse.siu@sil.org.
Central American Mission Practical Missionary Training, 216 East Commonwealth Av, PO Box 628, Fullerton, CA 92631, T: (714)526-5139.
Chicago Center for Global Ministries, 5420 S. Cornell Ave., Chicago, IL 60615, T: 312-363-1342, F: 312-324-4360.
Christ for the Nations Inst., P.O. Box 769000, Dallas, TX 75376-9000, T: (214) 376-1711, F: (214) 372-4529.
Church Planting International, P.O. Box 1002, Cucamonga, CA 91730, T: (714) 987-3274.
Frontier Internship in Mission, O: Web: www.wcc-coe.org/fim/fim.html.
Global Education Associates, 552 Park Ave, Orange, NJ 07017, T: 201-675-1409.
Habakkuk International Min Inc., 5957, Bufkin Drive, San Jose, CA95123, U. S. A..
Harvest International Ministries School of Missions, O: Web: VEHQ78A@Prodigy.com.
Institute for World Evangelism, WE, Candler School of Theology, Emory University, Atlanta, GA 30322, T: 404-727-6322.
Institute of International Studies, US Center for World Mission, 1605 Elizabeth St., Pasadena, CA 91104, T: 818-797-2106, F: 818-398-2111.
Institute on Sub-Saharan Africa, University of Notre Dame, Notre Dame, IN 46556, T: 219-239-6155.
Life Mission Training Center, O: Web: www.life-mission.org/index.html.
Maryknoll Center for Mission Studies, Maryknoll Post Office, Maryknoll, NY 10545, T: 914-942-7590.
Maryknoll Mission Institute, P.O. Box 529, Maryknoll, NY 10545.
Mission Training and Resource Center, 3800 Canon Blvd., Altadena, CA 91001, T: 626-797-7903, F: 626-797-7906, O: E-mail: PhilElkins@aol.com.
Mission Training International, P.O. Box 50110, Colorado Springs, CO 80949, T: 719-594-0687, F: 719-594-4682, O: E-mail: MIntern@aol.com, www.mti.org.
Missionary Orientation Center, Crickettown Rd., Stony Point, NY 10980, T: (914)886-2752.
Overseas Ministries Study Center, 490 Prospect St., New Haven, CT 06511, T: 203-624-6672, F: 203-865-2857, O: E-mail: mailbox@omsc.org, www.omsc.org.
Peoples Mission International, P.O. Box 66, Fremont, CA 94537, T: 510-793-6919, F: 510-793-6919, O: 74404.447@compuserve.com.
Perspectives Study Program, 1605 Elizabeth St., Pasadena, CA 91104, T: 818-398-2125.
Seventh-day Adventist Institute of World Mission, Sutherland House, Andrews University, Berrien Springs, MI 49104, T: (616) 471-2522, F: (616) 471-6252.
Stony Point Centre, Education for Mission, Stony Point, NY 10980, T: 914-786-5674.
Summer Institute of Missions, Wheaton College, Wheaton, IL 60188.
Summer Mission Institute, University of San Francisco, 2131 Fulton St, San Francisco, CA 95053.
United Presbyterian Center for Mission Studies, P.O. Box 2613, Fullerton, CA 92633, T: (714)870-4481.
Washington Mission Seminar, 1233 Lawrence St., N.E., Washington, DC 20017, T: 202-832-3112.

ZAMBIA

Language Training Centre, Ilondola, PO Chinsali (Bemba).

39
Foreign missions support organizations

Agencies that assist or promote foreign missionary work but that do not themselves generally send missionaries; service organizations, coordinating agencies, partnership ministries; fund-raising, support of national workers or indigenous missionaries or ministries overseas, fostering international interchurch relationships; mobilization, recruiting in sending countries; technical aid, missionary aviation and transport, missionary equipment services.

ARGENTINA

Agencia de Promoción Misiologica (APOYO), Casilla 3, 1602 Suc, Puente Saavedra, Buenos Aires.
Centro Cristiano de Educación y Difusión, Volta 766, 9200 Esquel, Chubut, T: 945 50661, F: 945 50661.
Iniciativa 10/40, Presidente Perón 164, 3100 Paraná, Pvncia Entre Rios, T: 43-31-7948, F: 43-31-7948.
Junta Unida de Misiones, Posal Dist. 34, 3705-J.J. Castelli-Chaco, T: 54732-71090.
SEPAL, Habana 4804, 1419 Buenos Aires, T: 1-502-8150, F: 1-502-8150, O: E-mail: bruce@sepal.satlink.net.

AUSTRALIA

Brisbane Centre for World Mission, P.O. Box 175, Annerby, Q.4103, Brisbane.
Centre for World Mission, Bible College of Victoria, P.O. Box 380, Lilydale, Victoria 3180.
Sydney Centre for World Mission,P.O. Box 217, Eastwood, NSW, 2122, T: 02-9874-2485, F: 02-9804-7978, O: E-mail: scwm@pastornet.net.au,web: www.pastornet.net.au/scwm/
Target 2000 Frontier Missions Office, P.O. Box 8501, Stirling Street, Perth WA 6849, T: 221 1217, F: 325 1830.

AUSTRIA

Evangelischer Arbeitskreis fürWeltmission (Protestant Workg Group for World Mission), Zierefeldstrasse 50, 4033 Linz, T: 0732/30 53 67.
Gruppo Austriaco di Lavoro per i Transporti nelle Missioni (MIVA), Gmundnerstr 21, A-4651 Stadl-Paura.
Institut für Internationale Zusammenarbeit (IZA), Singerstr 7, A-1010 Wien.
MIVA, Zentrale Österreichs, Mivagasse 2, A-4651 Stadi-Paura, T: (07245)545.
Päpstliche Missionswerk in Österreich, Seilerstätte 12, A-1010 Wien, T: (0222)523275.

BELGIUM

Amis du Père Damien, Rue Stévin 16, B-1040 Brussel, T: (02)2192996.
RAPTIM-Belgium, Rue Rouale 179, Brussel 3, T: 193235.
Sending of Technicians (CCET), Rue de la Limite 6, B-1030 Brussel.

BELORUSSIA

Slavic Missionary Service, P.O. Box 200, Minsk 220071.

BOTSWANA

Flying Mission, PO Box 1022, Gaborone, T: 312 981.

BRAZIL

ACMI-Associação de Conselhos Missionários de Igrejas, Cx. Postal 7540, São Paulo-SP 01064-970, T: 11-523-2544, F: 11-523-2201, O: E-mail: acmi@ibm.net, Web: www.infobrasil.org/acmi.
AMIDE-Associação Missionária de Difusão do Evangelho, SEPA 705/905-Bl C Sala 315, Ed. Mont Blanc, 70390-055 Brasília-DF, T: 61-242-3774, F: 61-242-3774.
APMB-Associaçõ de Professores de Missões no Brasil, Caixa Postal 8381, 01065-970 São Paulo, SP, T: 11-605-5845, O: E-mail: betel@sti.com.br.
Asas de Socorro, Cx. Postal 184, Anápolis-GO 75001-970, T: 62-314-1133, F: 62-314-1450, O: E-mail: AsasDeSocorro@maf.org.
COMIBAM-Cooperação Missionária Ibero Americana, Cx. Postal 7001, Campinas-SP 13090-990, T: 19-255-3524, F: 19-255-3524, O: E-mail: interact@bestway.com.br.
Convenção das Igrejas Batistas Independentes, Cx. Postal 61, Campinas-SP 13001-970, T: 19-254-1346, F: 19-254-1346, O: E-mail: lejon@bestway.com.br.
MEM-Ministério de Estratégia e Mobilização Missionária, Av. Rio Branco, 2231 Sala 20, Centro, Juiz de Fora-MG 36010-010, T: 32-211-6746, F: 32-211-6746.
Missão A Voz dos Mártires, Cx. Postal 3356, Curitiba-PR 80001-970, T: 41-223-4438, F: 41-224-3716.
Missão Portas Abertas, Cx. Postal 45371, São Paulo-SP 04010-970, T: 11-5181-3330, F: 11-5181-7525, O: E-mail: PortasAbertas@compuserve.com, Web: www.solcon.nl/od_fo.
SEPAL-Serviço de Evangelização Para A América Latina, Caixa Postal 7540, São Paulo, SP 01064-970, T: 11-523-2544, F: 11-523-2201, O: E-mail: sepal@xc.org, WEB: www.infobrasil.org.
UMBET-União Missionária Brasileira O Evangelho Por Telefone, Cx. Postal 3205, São Paulo-SP 01065-970, T: 11-221-2435, F: 11-221-2435.

BRITAIN (UK OF GB & NI)

Aid to the Church in Need, 124 Carshalton Road, Sutton, Surrey SM1 4RL, T: 0181 642 8668, F: 0181-661 6293.
Albanian Evangelical Trust, P.O. Box 388, Wrexham, Clwyd LL11 2TW, Wales, T: 44-0978-354006.
Capernwray Missionary Fellowship, O: Web: www.capernwray.co.uk.
Christian Cargo, 7 Braithwaite Dr., Great Walding-field CO10 OUD, Suffolk, T: 44-0787-79329, F: 44-0787-880488.
Christian Mission to the Communist World, Glenbur House, Glenburn Road South, Dunmurry, Belfast BT17 9JP, T: (08) 232 301697.
Churches Commission on Mission, Inter-Church House, 35 Lower Marsh, London SE1 7RL, T: (0044) 071 620 4444.
Evangelize China Fellowship, 72a Ballymacormick Road, Bangor, Co Down BT19 2AB, T: (08) 0247 465783.
Global Care, P.O. Box 61, Coventry CV5 6RQ, T: 44-203-632203, F: 44-203-632203.
Linking Up Enterprises, Ltd., 27 Blackfriars Road, Manchester M3 7AQ, T: 44-061-839-3500, F: 44-061-839-3500.
MAF (Mission Aviation Fellowship), Ingles Manor, Castle Hill Avenue, Folkstone, Kent CT20 2TN, T: 01303, 850950.
Mission Supplies Limited, Alpha Place, Garth Rd., Morden SM4 4LX, Surrey, T: 44-81-337-0161, F: 44-81-337-7220.
Pontifical Missionary Union, 23 Eccleston Square, London SW1V 1NU, T: 0171-821 9755, F: 0171-630 8466.
Resourcing Christian Outreach, 12 York Road, Woking GU22 7XH, Surrey, T: 44-483-714-734, F: 44-483-714-734.
Sharing of Ministries Abroad, 50 Wivetsfield Rd, PO Box 200, Haywards Heath, West Sussex RH16 4EW, T: 0444-454531.
South Asia Church Aid Association, 2 Eaton Gate, London SW1W 9BL, T: (01)730-9611.
Worldwide Missionary Convention, 15 Ranfurly Avenue, Bangor, Co Down BT20 2SN, T: (08) 0247 460868.

CANADA

African Enterprise Association of Canada, 4509 West 11th Ave., Vancouver, BA V6R 2M5, T: 604-228-0930, F: 604-228-0936, O: E-mail: 74667.3105@compuserve.com.
Alberta Centre for World Mission, 11302 58 St., Edmonton, AB T5W 3W5, T: 403-474-2296.
Calcutta Mission of Mercy, P.O. Box 65599, Vancouver, BC V5N 5K5, T: 604-929-1330, F: 604-253-6167.
Canada China Programme, c/o Council of Churches, 40, St. Clair East, Toronto, ON M4T 1M9, T: 416-921-4152.
Canadian Centre for World Mission (CCWM), 52 Carondale Crescent, Agincourt, Ontario M1W 2B1, T: 416-499-8339.
Canadian Churches' Forum for Global Ministries, 230 St. Clair Ave., W., Toronto, ON M4V 1R5, T: 416-924-9351, F: 416-924-5356, O: E-mail: CCForum@web.net.
Centre for World Mission, Box 2436, Clearbrook BC V2T 4X3, T: (604) 854-3818.
Christian Aid Ministries, Route 3, Wallenstein N0B 2S0, Ontario, T: 519-664-2440.
Christian Aid Mission, 201 Stanton St., Fort Erie, ON L2A 3N8, T: 905-871-1773, F: 905-871-5165.
Council of USSR Ministries (CUM), 134 Plaza Dr., Winnipeg R3T 5K9, Manitoba, T: 204-261-6381, F: 204-269-9875.
Emmanuel International, P.O. Box 4050, Stouffville, ON L4A 8B6, T: 905-640-2111, F: 605-640-2186, O: E-mail: Info@e-i.org, Web: www.e-i.org.
Gospel for Asia, 120 Lancing Dr., #6, Hamilton, ON L8W 3A1, T: 905-574-8800, F: 905-574-1849.
International Christian Aid Canada, P.O. Box 5090, Burlington, ON L7R 4G5, T: 905-632-5703, F: 905-632-5176.
International Needs - Canada, 52 Harvey Close, Red Deer, AB T4N 6C4, T: 403-340-0882, F: 403-340-0882, O: Web: www.ualberta.ca/~dharapnu/intlneed.
Jesus to the Communist World, P.O. Box 117, Port Credit, Mississauga L5G 4L5, Ontario, T: 416-276-6210, F: 416-276-0228.
Lutheran Association of Missionaries and Pilots, 9335 47th St., Edmonton, AB T6B 2R7, T: 403-466-8507.
Master's Foundation, 1295 Eglinton Ave., E., Unit 28, Mississauga, ON L4W 3E6, T: 905-602-1350, F: 905-602-1352.
Missionary Ventures of Canada, 336 Speedvale Ave. W., Guelph, ON N1H 7M7, T: 519-824-5311, F: 519-824-9452, O: E-mail: Javco@in.on.ca.
Missions Fest Vancouver, 7200 Cariboo Rd., Burnaby, BC V3N 4A7, T: 604-524-9944, F: 604-524-4690.
MSC Canada, 27 Charles St. E., Toronto, ON M4Y 1R9, T: 416-920-4391, F: 416-920-7793, O: E-mail: MSCCan@ican.net.
Open Doors With Brother Andrew, P.O. Box 597, Streetsville, ON L5M 2C1, T: 905-567-1303, F: 905-567-9398.
Partners International Canada, 8500 Torbram Rd. #48, Brampton, ON L6T 5C6, T: 905-458-1202, F: 905-458-4339.
PCF Missionary Society (Persecuted Church Fellowship), 15620 Westminster Hwy., Richmond, BC V6V 1A6, T: 604-278-0692, F: 604-279-9080.
RAPTIM-Canada, 1652 Rue St Hubert, Montréal 132, Québec, T: 849-5323.
Shining Light Ministry, 286 Stonechurch Rd., E., Hamilton, ON L9B 1B2, T: 905-318-5929, F: 905-318-7041.
Society of Saint Peter the Apostle, 3329 Danforth Ave., Scarborough, ON M1L 4T3, T: 416-699-7077, F: 416-699-9019.
Voice of the Martyrs, Box 117, Port Credit, Mississauga, ON L5G 4L5, T: 905-602-4832, F: 905-602-4833, O: E-mail: VOM@planeteer.com.
White Fields Mission, 123 Strathbury Bay, S.W., Calgary, AB T3H 1N3, T: 403-246-0932.
World Missionary Assistance Plan (World MAP), 16073 12th Ave., Surrey V4R 6V7, British Columbia, T: 604-538-9627, F: 604-538-4480.

CHAD

Missionary Aviation Fellowship, BP 275, Ndjamena (Fort-Lamy).

CONGO-ZAIRE

Missionary Aviation Fellowship (MAF), BP 393 & 3160, Kinshasa.

COSTA RICA

FEDEMEC/COMIBAM, Apartado 1307, San Jose 1000, T: (506) 21-5522, F: (506) 21-5622, O: E-mail: rsperger@ucrvm2.bitnet.
Instituto de Lengua Española, T: 227-7366.
Misiones Costarricenses(FEDEMEC), T: 221-5522.

DENMARK

Lay Movement for World, Risvangen 1, 5210 Odense NV, T: 66 16 34 23.
Society of Aid to the Church of Pakistan, v/Gelstedvej 58, 5591 Gelsted, T: 64 49 10 96.

ECUADOR

Alas de Socorro del Ecuador, Casilla 17-11-06228, Quito, T: 2-441-593, F: 2-441-593.
Asociacion Misionera Evangelica Ecuatoriana (AMEE), Shell, Pastaza.
Puente, Casilla 8559, Quito, T: 593-2-246-934.

FRANCE

Aide aux Missions d'Afrique, 82 Rue Dutot, F-75015 Paris, T: (01)532-8749.
Centre de Formation pour la Coopération Internationale, BP 14, Saint-Ilan, F-22120 Yffiniac.
Cercle St-Jean-Baptiste, 3 rue de l'Abbaye, F-75006 Paris, T: 633-2414.
European Student Missionary Association (ESMA), European Bible Institute, Paris.
Foi et Cultures Ad Lucem, 12 rue Guy-de-la-Brosse, F-75005 Paris, T: (01)331-7955.
Groupe d'Organismes de Coopération Missionnaire (OCM), 128 Rue du Bac, F-75007 Paris, T: (01)222-8123.
Interdev France, 18 Bis, Rue Violet 75015 Paris.
International Missionary Benefit Society, Paris.
Oeuvre Apostolique, 8 Rue Daniel Lesuer, F-75007 Paris, T: (01)306-4437.

GERMANY

Deutsche Evang. Missionshilfe, Normannenweg 17-21, 20537.
Evangelisches Missionswerk im Bereich der BRD und Berlin (West), Berlin.
German Center for World Mission, Breite Str. 16, D-5300 Bonn 1, T: 0228-63-87-84.
Glaubenszentrum Bad, Gandersheim, Dr.-Heinrich-Jasper-Str. 20, D-37581 Bad Gandersheim, T: 05382-9300, F: 05382-930100.
Gospel for Asia, Karsauer Str. 15a, 79618 Rheinfelden, T: 07623-5834, F: 07623-59335.
Inter Mission e.V., Kestner Str. 20 A, 30159 Hannover, T: 0511-28-374-0, F: 0511-28374-30.
MBK Mission, Mission der Evangelischen Schü-

lerinnen- und Frauen- Bibelkreise, Hermann-Lons-Str 14, D-4902 Bad Salzuflen. (Mission of Protestant Girl Students' and Women's Bible Circles; 1925), T: (05222)50088.
MISSIO Internationales Katholisches Missionswerk, Hermannstr 14, Postfach 1110, D-5100 Aachen, T: (0241)32441.
RAPTIM-Deutschland, Hermannstr 14, D-51 Aachen, T: 32757.
Vereinigte Deutsche Missionshilfe, Postfach 93, D-7016 Gerlingen, T: (07156)22890.
Vereinigte Missionsfreunde, Bismarckstr 44, D-5930 Hüttental-Weidenau; Oranienstr 18, D-5905 Freudenberg, T: (0271)44122, (02734)7930).
Wirtschaftsstelle Ev Missionsgesellschaften Ubersee-Warenversorgung und Passagen GmbH, Mittelweg 143, D-2000 Hamburg 13.

GUATEMALA
CONEMM-Comisión Nacional Evangélica de Misiones al Mundo, Apdo. Postal 28, T: 288-4330, F: 254-0945.
SETECA, Apartado Postal 213, T: 471-5160, F: 473-5957.

HUNGARY
Alliance for Saturation Church Planting, 1111 Budapest, Budafoki út 34/B. III/3, T: 36-1-371-0710, F: 36-1-165-6406.
Church Resource Ministries, 1022 Budapest, Lóránttfy Zs. utca 3/A, T: 36-1-342-7144.
Eastern European Resource Center, 4028 Debrecen, Samsoni utca 4/B, T: 36-52-347-850, F: 36-52-347-487.
Educational Services International (ESI), 1091 Budapest, ullői út 157. 3. 1h. 1/4, T: 36-1-158-9641.
Protestant Institute for Mission Studies (PIMS), Budapest, O: Web: ourworld/compuserve.com/homepages/anne_marie_kool.

INDIA
Assistance to Indian Ministries Mission Society, M. R. D. Cottage, Balaclava, Coonoor, Tamil Nadu 643102.
Borgaon Mission Centre, Rupohi P. O., Surupeta, Assam 781318.
Ceylon and India Gospel Mission, II Pottery Road, Bangalore, Karnataka 560005.
Christ for India Mission and Education Centre, Palakotta Valiyaparampil, Kuttappuzha P. O., Tiruvalla, Kerala 689103.
Christian Aid Mission, Hill Patna, Berhampur, Ganjam, Orissa 760005.
Indian Christian Mission Centre, St. Basil School, Behind Housing Board, Chinna-Thirupathy (Post), Salem, Tamil Nadu 636008.
Inter-Mission Business Office, 3rd Floor, Lawrence And Mayo House, 276, Dr. D. N. Road, Bombay, Maharashtra 400001.
Native Missionary Movement, Vill. Lamdon, P. O. Pojenga, Gumla, Bihar 835220.
St. Thomas Orthodox Mission Centre, Haripad, Kerala 690514.
Strategic World Evangelism, Post Box 1023, 1, New Avadi Road, Kilpauk P. O., Madras, Tamil Nadu 600010.

INDONESIA
Adventist Aviation Indonesia, P.O. Box 1079, Jayapura 99011, Irian Jaya.

IRELAND
Survive-MIVA, The Grove, Celbridge, Co Kildare.

ITALY
Associazione di Laici in Aiuto alle Missioni, Via Kramer 5, Milano.
Associazione Laici Pro-Missioni, c/o Scuola del Cristo, Cannaregio 1723, I-30121 Venezia.
Centro di Collegamento Tecnica-Missioni, Via Belvedere 11, Napoli.
Centro Internazionale per l'Aviazione e la Motorizzazione Missionaria (CIAMM), Via Magenta 12 bis, I-10128 Torino; Via Francesco Duodo 49/12, I-00136 Roma, T: 531441.
Cooperatori Salesiani, Ufficio Centrale Cooperatori Salesiani, Via Maria Ausiliatrice 32, I-10152 Torino; Via della Pisana III, I-00163 Roma.
Gruppi Appoggio Missionario (GAM), Piazza Tripoli 22, Milano.
Oeuvres Pontificales Missionnaires, Via di Propaganda 1c, I-00187 Roma, T: 6795183, 6780508, 6795007, 681568.
Opera Apostolica per il Corredo Missionario, Via Levico 14, Roma.
Servizio Missionario per l'Africa e l'Asia, Consiglio Missionario Nazionale, Via Levico 14, I-00198 Roma.
Società Tecnica Aiuto Missioni (STAM), Ufficio Missionario Diocesano, Via Arcivescovado 12, Torino.

KENYA
African Coordination Center for World Missions (ACCWM), P.O. Box 53012, Nairobi.

MEXICO
Alas de Socorro, Apdo 17, San Cristobal las Casas, Chiapas (MAF), T: 470.
COMIMEX, APDP 6-55, Toluca 50091, T: 52-72-16-20-11, F: 52-72-71-09-56, O: E-mail: moiseslo@vm-tectol.tol.itesm.mx.
Mexico Missionary Services, Suc K, 12 de Diciembre No 365, Col Chapalita, Apdo 3115, Guadalajara, Jalisco.

NETHERLANDS
Aid to Dutch Missions, Van Alkemadelaan 1, 's-Gravenhage, T: (070)244594.
Carosi, Groot Haesebroekseweg 12, Wassenaar.
Continents Contact Centre, Amersfoortsestraat 20, Soesterberg, T: (03463)1755.
DAWN Ministries Europe, 49, Epe 8161 BL, T: 31-5780-16322, F: 31-5780-16369.
Group for Mission Support Agencies, Amersfoortsestraat 20a, Soesterberg, T: (03463)1536.
MIVA (Stichting Missie Verkeersmiddelen Actie), Keizergracht 252, Amsterdam.
Pontifical Missionary Works, Laan Copes van Cattenburgh 127, 's-Gravenhage, T: (070)112343.
RAPTIM-Nederland, Anna Paulownastraat 45A, 's-Gravenhage; Heuvelring 31, Tilburg, T: (04250)35085.
SIAMAS-Societies for the Interests of Active Missionaries, 105 Gerard Brandstraat, Box 664f, Leidan, T: 071-76.09.51.
Youth With A Mission, Prins Hendrikkade 50, 1012 AC Amsterdam, T: 31-20-269-233.

NEW ZEALAND
Centre for Mission Direction, P.O. Box 31-146, Christchurch 8030, T: 0-3-342-8410, F: 0-3-342-8410, O: Web: www.cmd.org.nz, E-mail: 100354.3311@compuserve.com.
Consiglio Neozelandese delle Organizzazioni di Assistenza d'Oltremare (CORSO), 63 Abel Smith St, PO Box 2500, Wellington.
Majestic House, 122-126 Manchester St., New Life Centre, P.O. Box 2223, Christchurch, T: 792-781.
Mission Aviation Fellowship, P.O. Box 774, Papakura 1730, T: 0-9-297-7375, F: 0-9-297-7375.
Mobile Mission Maintenance, 27 Rangataua St., Tauranga, T: 0-7-544-3932.
Music for Missions, 294 Massey Rd., Mangere East, Auckland.
North West Frontier Fellowship, 89 Masters Ave., Hamilton, T: 0-7-856-2060.

NIGERIA
African Coordination Center for World Missions (ACCWM), 186 Awolowo Rd., Ikoyi, Lagos.
Association of Evangelicals, P.O. Box 1933, Jos Plateau State, T: (234) 73-53110, F: (234) 73-53110, O: E-mail: postmaster@simjos.sim.org.

PAPUA NEW GUINEA
Missionary Aviation Fellowship (MAF), Operations Manager, Wewak 82, New Guinea.

PHILIPPINES
Missionary Aviation Fellowship (MAF), 1300 M De Comillas, PO Box 4198, Manila.

PORTUGAL
Acção Cristã, Rua dos Açores, 29-A, 2830 Barreiro; Apartado 20, 2831 Barreiro Codex, T: 01-204 65 72.
Assistência da Acção Bíblica à Igreja Evangélica de S. Tomé e Príncipe, Av. Dr. Bernardino da Silva, 84-A, 8700 Olhão, T: 089-70 27 77.
TEMA - A Associação Missionária Europeia (Grupo de Trabalho Português), Apartado 35 - 2746 Queluz Codex, T: 01-437 57 37.

PUERTO RICO
Escuela de Misiones Bethania, Calle 13 SO #824, Caparra Terrace 00921.

SINGAPORE
Asia Evangelistic Fellowship, 68 Lorong 16 Geylang Rd., #05-07 Association Bldg., Singapore, T: 398889.
Church in Missions Association, Block 808 French Road #07-173 Kitchener Complex, Singapore 200808, T: 294-5166, F: 294-5766.
International Christian Mission (Singapore), 2 Handy Road, #10-02 Cathay Building, Singapore 229233, T: 338-4769, F: 338-3679.
Mission Aviation Fellowship (Singapore), 20 Jalan Insaf, Singapore 578014, T: 259-5990, F: 259-5990.
Open Doors (S) Company Limited, 1 Sophia Road, #03-28 Peace Centre, Singapore 228149, T: 338-9144, F: 338-8196.
Overseas Crusade Ministries (Asia), Bras Basah, P.O. Box 0311, Singapore 911811, T: 339-8598, F: 334-0405.
Singapore Centre for Evangelism and Missions, Raffles City P.O. Box 1052, Singapore 911736, T: 65-299-4377, F: 65-291-8919.
World Outreach Singapore, Taman Warna PO Box 199, Singapore 912737, T: 827-9019, F: 474-7529.

SOUTH AFRICA
Africa Centre for World Mission, Private Bag, Walkerville 1876, T: 011-9489651.
Andrew Murray Centre, PO Box 263, Wellington 7655, 6 Market St, Wellington, T: 02211-3-4380, F: 02211-64-3571.
Christian Mission International, PO Box 7157, Primrose Hill, 1417 Germiston, T: 011-873-2604, F: 011-873-3859.
Frontline Fellowship—Vegters vir Christus, P.O. Box 74, Newlands, Cape Town 7725, T: 27-21-619672, F: 27-21-619672.
Hofmeyr Mission Centre, PO Box 6058, Uniedal 7612, 39 Church St, Stellenbosch, T: 021-887-5453, F: 021-883-2158.
Japan Evangelistic Band, PO Box 40224, Cleveland 2022, Johannesburg, T: 011-626-2510.
Light to the Nations Mission Network, PO Box 296, Retreat 7945, Cape Town, T: 021-510-2843, F: 021-511-9226.
Love Southern Africa (LSA), PO Box 30233, Sunnyside 0132, Pretoria, T: 012-343-1165, F: 012-343-1167.
Mercy Air (YWAM), PO Box 1735, White River 1240, T: 01311-750-1221.
Mission India, PO Box 30262, Sunnyside 0132, Taaibos Bldg, Tuinhof Comp, 265 West St., Verwoerdburg, T: 012-663-7323, F: 012-663-7325.
Missionary Aviation Fellowship, PO Box 1688, Edenvale 1610, T: 011-609-2807, F: 011-609-4644.
SAAWE (South African Action for World Evangelisation), PO Box 709, Kempton Park 1620, 34 Vila Vilencia, Anemoon St, Kempton Pk, T: 011-396-1225, F: 011-396-1302.
Society of St Nicholas of Japan, PO Box 56303, Arcadia 0083, Pretoria, T: 012-333-6727.
World Mission Centre, PO Box 36147, Mento Park 0102, 669 Church St, Pretoria, T: 012-343-1165, F: 012-343-1167.
World Thrust SA, PO Box 3170, Benoni 1500, 34 Villa Valencia, Anemoon St, Glen Marais, Kempton Park, T: 011-979-2686, F: 011-396-1302.
Zululand Mission Air Transport, c/o Bethesda Hospital, PO Box 5, Ubombo 3970, T: 035-595-1024, F: 035-595-1004.
Zululand Networking Ministries, PO Box 237, Umhlali, 4390, T: 0322-7-1136, F: 0332-7-1559.

SOUTH KOREA
Center for World Mission, 353 Kwangjang Dong, Kwangjin Ku, Seoul 143-756, F: 822-201-6953.
Inter-Mission Intl., 110-1 Wolmoon Paltau, Hwasung, Kyunggi, T: 82-339-2-1301, F: 82-339-52-5234.
Korean World Mission Council for Christ (KWMC), 135-25 Northern Blvd. Flushing, NY 11354, T: 718-762-2055, 2711, F: 718-762-1716, O: E-mail: kwmcc@aol.com.

SWITZERLAND
Associazione Internazionale dei Soci Costruttori (IBO), Postfach 28, CH-9658 Vildhaus.
Associazione Svizzera di Assistenza Tecnica (HELVETIAS), CH-1950 Sion.
Comité Auxilliaire Suisse de l'Eglise Chrétienne Missionnaire Belge, Rue de St-Jean 86, CH-1201 Genève.
Commission on World Mission & Evangelism, Ecumenical Centre, 150 route de Ferney, PO Box 66, CH-1211 Geneva 20, Switzerland, T: 022-916111.
Groupes Missionnaires, 2 Av des Pléiades, CH-1800 Vevey.
Heli Mission, CH-9043 Trogen.

UNITED STATES OF AMERICA (USA)
ACTS International Ministries, P.O. Box 62725, Colorado Springs, CO 80962, T: 719-282-1247, F: 719-282-1139, O: E-mail: 73524.1100@compuserve.com.
AD 2000 and Beyond Movement, 2860 South Circle Dr., Suite 2112, Colorado Springs, CO 80906, T: 719-576-2000, F: 719-576-2685, O: E-mail: info@Ad2000.org, Web: www.AD2000. org.
Adopt-A-Church International, O: Web: www.adoptachurch.org.
Adopt-A-People Clearinghouse, P.O. Box 17490, Colorado Springs, CO 80935, T: 719-574-7001, F: 719-574-7005, O: E-mail: AAPC@xc.org.
Advancing Churches in Missions Commitment (ACMC), P.O. Box 3929, Peachtree City, GA 30269, T: 770-631-9900, F: 770-631-9470, O: E-mail: 76331.2051@compuserve.com.
Advancing Indigenous Missions, P.O. Box 690042, San Antonio, TX 78269, T: 830-367-3513, F: 210-734-7620.
Advancing Native Missions, P.O. Box 5036, Charlottesville, VA 22905, T: 804-293-8829, F: 804-293-7586, O: E-mail: ANM@adnamis.org, Web: www.cstone.net/~adnamis.
Advancing Renewal Ministries, 11616 Sir Francis Drake Dr., Charlotte, NC 28277, T: 704-846-9355, F: 704-846-9356, O: E-mail: 104273.3130@compuserve.com.
Africa Missions Resource Center, O: Web: www.genesis.acu.edu/chowning/africa/africa5.htm.
African Coordination Center for World Missions (ACCWM), P.O. Box 1835, Tulsa, OK 74101.
African Leadership, P.O. Box 977, Greenwood, IN 46142, T: 317-889-0456, F: 317-882-8854, O: E-mail: MHAfrica@aol.com.
Agape Gospel Mission, P.O. Box 11785, Roanoke, VA 24022, T: 540-562-0322, O: E-mail: 104072.747@compuserve.com.
Aid to Special Saints in Strategic Times (ASSIST), P.O. Box 2126, Garden Grove, CA 92642, T: 714-530-6598, F: 714-636-7351, O: E-mail: 74152.337@compuserve.com.
Aid to the Church in Need, P.O. Box 576, Deer Park, NY 11729.
Air Serv, O: Web: www.airserv.xc.org.
Air Team, P.O. Box 304, Lexington, MA 02173.
Albanian Evangelical Trust, 1032 South 18th St., Harrisburg, PA 17104, T: 717-233-5899, F: 717-236-3099.
Alliance, The, P.O. Box 248, Marble Hill, GA 30148-0248.
ALM International, 1 Alm Way, Greenville, SC 29601, T: 864-271-7040, F: 864-271-7062, O: E-mail: AmLep@leprosy.org, Web: www.leprosy.org.
Amazing Grace Missions, 600 Richmond Av, San Antonio, TX 78215.
Ambassadors for Christ International, 1355 Terrell Mill Rd., Bldg. 1484, Marietta, GA 30067-5494, T: 770-980-2020, F: 980-956-8144, O: E-mail: 73440.127@compuserve.com.
American Council of Voluntary Agencies for Foreign Service, 9th Floor, 44 East 23 St, New York, NY 10010.
American Waldensian Society, 183 Shiloh Ct., Whitehall, PA 18052, T: 610-432-9569, F: 610-432-9518, O: E-mail: Waldensi@ptd.net.
Antioch Network, 5060 N. 19th Ave., Suite 312, Phoenix, AZ 85015, T: 602-242-4414, F: 602-242-0416.
Armenian Missionary Association of America, Inc., 140 Forest Ave., Paramus, NJ 07652, T: 201-265-2607, F: 201-265-6015.
Asian Outreach USA, 3941 S. Bristol St. #67, Santa Ana, CA 92704, T: 714-557-2742, F: 714-557-2742, O: E-mail: JR2135@aol.com.
Assistance in Missions (AIM), 9003 Terhune Av., Sun Valley, CA 91352, T: (213)767-9767.
Association for Native Evangelism, T.L. Osborn Evangelistic Association, 1400 East Skelly Dr., Box 10, Tulsa, OK 74102, T: 918-743-6231, F: 918-492-6237.
Bethany World Prayer Center, O: Web: www.bethany-wpc.org.
Bezalel World Outreach/Galcom International, Box 270956, Tampa, FL 33688, T: 813-933-8111, F: 813-933-8886, O: E-mail: GalcomUSA@aol.com.
Big World Ventures Inc., P.O. Box 703203, Tulsa, OK 74170, T: 800-599-8778, F: 918-481-5257, O: E-mail: Venture@galaxt.galstar.com.
Billy Graham Center, 500 College Ave., Wheaton, IL 60187, T: 630-752-5157, F: 630-752-5916, O: E-mail: BGCadm@wheaton.edu, Web: www.wheaton.edu/bgc/bgc.html.
Brigada, O: Web: www.brigada.org.
Caleb Project, 10 W. Dry Creek Cir., Littleton, CO 80120-4413, T: 303-730-4170, F: 303-730-4177, O: E-mail: Info@cproject.com, Web: www.calebproject.org.
Catholic Coordinating Center for Lay Volunteer Ministries, 1234 Massachusetts Ave, NW, Washington DC 20005, T: 202-638-4197.
Catholic Medical Mission Board, 10 W. 17th St., New York, NY 10011.
Catholics in America Concerned with China (CACC), Maryknoll, New York, NY 10545, T: 914-941-7590.
Central Missionary Clearing House, O: Web: ccn-web.com/cmc/cmc.htm.
China Harvest/Weiner Ministries, P.O. Box 64474, Virginia Beach, VA 23467, T: 757-579-5858, 800-715-3292, F: 757-579-5889.
China Ministries International, P.O. Box 40489, Pasadena, CA 91104, T: 626-398-0145, F: 626-398-2361, O: E-mail: 104435.2547@compuserve.com.
China Service Coordinating Office, Institute for China Studies, Wheaton College, Wheaton, IL 60187, T: 630-752-5951, F: 630-752-5916, O: E-mail: China@xc.org.
Christ for India Ministries, P. O. Box 210765, Columbia, SC 29221, T: 803-794-5504, F: 803-794-5504, O: E-mail: CFI@csrnet.org.
Christ for the Nations, Inc., P. O. Box 769000, Dallas, TX 75376, T: 214-376-1711, F: 214-302-6228, O: E-mail: Info@cfni.org, Web: www.cfni.org.
Christian Aid Mission, 3045 Ivy Rd., Charlottesville, VA 22903; P.O. Box 4488, Charlottesville, VA 22905, T: 804-977-5650, F: 804-295-6814, O: E-mail: CAidInfo@christianaid.org, Web: www.christianaid.org.
Christian Missions in Many Lands, P.O. Box 13, Spring Lake, NJ 07762, T: 732-449-8880, F: 732-974-0888.
Christian Service Int'l, P.O. B. 16044, Colorado Springs, CO 80935, T: 719-633-0755.
Christian Tent Ministries, O: Web: www.projectpartner.com/ctm.htm.
Church Ministries International, 500 Turtle Cove Blvd. #101, Rockwall, TX 75087, T: 972-772-3406, F: 972-722-0012, O: E-mail: Church_Ministries@compuserve.com.
CSI Ministries, 804 W. McGalliard Rd., Muncie, IN 47303, T: 765-286-0711, F: 765-286-5773.
David Livingstone Missionary Foundation, P.O. Box 232, Tulsa, OK 74102, T: 918-494-9902, F: 918-496-2873.
DAWN Ministries, 7899 Lexington Dr. Ste. 200B, Colorado Springs, CO 80920; P.O. Box 40969, Pasadena, CA 91114, T: 719-548-7460, F: 719-548-7475, O: Web: www.tecc.co.uk/jesusa/dawnindx.html.
DELTA Ministries, O: Web: www.teleport.com/-pmagee/delta.html.
Door of Hope International, P.O. Box 10460, Glendale, CA 91209, T: 818-500-3939, F: 818-500-9933.
East West Missionary Service, P. O. Box 2191, La Habra, CA 90632, T: 562-697-7143, F: 562-691-3468, O: E-mail: 74553.546@compuserve.com.
Eastern European Bible Mission, P. O. Box 110, Colorado Springs, CO 80901, T: 719-577-4450, F: 719-577-4453.
Emmaus Road, International, 7150 Tanner Ct., San Deigo, CA 92111, T: 619-292-7020, F: 619-292-7020, O: E-mail: Emmaus-Road@eri.org, Web: www.eri.org.
Engineering Ministries International, 110 S. Wever St. Ste 104, Colorado Springs, CO 80903, T: 719-633-2078, F: 719-633-2970, O: Web: members.aol.com/emiusa/website/emipage.htm, E-mail: EMusa@aoi.com,.
Evangelical Missions Information Service, Box 794, Wheaton, IL 60189, T: 312-653-2158.
Exodus World Service, P.O. Box 620, Itasca, IL 60143, T: 708-775-1500, F: 708-773-1916.
FingerTip Data-base, O: Web: www.netaccess.on.ca/fingertip.
Foreign Missions Foundation, 10875 S.W. 89th St., Tigard, OR 97223, T: 503-246-5862, F: 503-977-9343, O: E-mail: 76101.176@compuserve.com.
Foundation For His Ministry, P. O. Box 9803, N. Hollywood, CA 91609, T: 818-834-4734, F: 818-834-4724.
Global Advance, P.O. Box 742077, Dallas, TX 75374-2077, T: 972-771-9042, F: 972-771-3315, O: E-mail: GlobalAdv@earthlink.net.
Global Mapping International, 7899 Lexington Dr., Suite 200A, Colorado Springs, CO 80920-4279, T: 719-531-3599, F: 1-719-548-7459, O: Web: www.gmi.org/index/html, E-mail: 70172.1002@compuserve.com.
Go International, P.O. Box 123, Wilmore, KY 40390, T: 606-858-3171, F: 606-858-4324.
Gospel for Asia, 1932 Walnut Plaza, Carrollton, TX 75006, T: 972-416-0340, F: 972-416-6131, O: E-mail: info@gfa.org, Web: www.gfa.org.
Gospel Recordings USA, 122 Glendale Blvd., Los Angeles, CA 90026, T: 213-250-0207.
Great Commission Center, 769 Orchid Lane, Copper Canyon, TX 76226, T: 001-214-219-7921, F: 001-817-455-2205, O: Also tel: 001-817-455-2205.
Greater Grace World Outreach, P. O. Box 18715, Baltimore, MD 21206, T: 410-483-3700, F: 410-483-3708, O: E-mail: missions@ggwo.smart.net, Web: www.ggwo.org.
HBI Gospel Partners, P. O. Box 245, Union Mills, NC 28167, T: 704-286-8317, F: 704-287-0580, O: E-mail: 103207.2556@compuserve.com.
Help for Christian Nationals, Inc., P.O. Box 381006, Duncanville, TX 75137, T: 972-780-5909.
Helps International Ministries, O: Web: www.xc.org/helpintl.

ILS/People Partnership Project, Box 806, Apple Valley, CA 92307, T: 619-247-3645, F: 619-247-4862.
Impact International, P.O. Box 2530, Boca Raton, FL 33427, T: 561-338-7515, F: 561-338-7516.
Independent Board for Presbyterian Foreign Missions, 246 W. Walnut Lane, Philadelphia, PA 19144-3299, T: 215-438-0511, F: 215-438-0560.
Independent Gospel Missions, 327 Stambaugh Ave., Sharon, PA 16146-4123, T: 412-342-1090, F: 412-342-1371.
India Gospel Outreach, P.O. Box 550, Rancho Cucamonga, CA 91729-0550, T: 909-948-2404, F: 909-948-2406, O: Web: 103417.3401@compuserve.com, igo.ncsa.com/igo.
India Mission for Evangelism, 995 Elm Dr., Apple Valley, MN 55124-9106.
India National Inland Mission, P.O. Box 652, Verdugo City, CA 91046, T: 818-241-4010.
Institute for East-West Christian Studies, Billy Graham Ctr. Wheaton College, Wheaton, IL 60187-5593, T: 708-752-5917, F: 708-752-5555.
Institute of Latin American Studies, 1605 Elizabeth Street, Pasadean, CA 91104, T: (818) 398-2316.
Institute of Technology and Theology (IITT), O: Web: www.iitt.org.
Int'l Institute for Christian Studies, P.O. Box 12147, Overland Park, KS 66282, T: 913-642-1166, F: 913-642-1280.
INTERDEV, P. O. Box 3883, Seattle, WA 98124, T: 425-775-8330, F: 425-775-8326, O: E-mail: INTER-DEV-US@xc.org.
International Cooperating Ministries, 606 Aberdeen Rd., Hampton, VA 23661, T: 757-827-6704, F: 757-838-6486.
International Needs - USA, P.O. Box 977, Lynden, WA 98264, T: 360-354-1991, F: 360-354-1991, O: E-mail: 102006.2256@compuserve.com, ualberta.ca/~dharapnu/intlneed.
International Partnership Ministries, Inc, P. O. Box 41, Hanover, PA 17331, T: 717-637-7388, F: 717-637-1618, O: E-mail: IPM@sun-link.com.
InterVarsity Mission, P.O. Box 7895, Madison, WI 53707, T: 608-274-9001, F: 608-274-9680, O: E-mail: LINK@ivcf.org, Web: www.ivcf.org/missions.
Issachar Frontier Missions, 3906A S. 74th St. Ste.103, Tacoma, WA 98409; P.O. Box 6788, Lynnwood, WA 98036, T: 253-318-8777, F: 253-474-0317, O: E-mail: IssacharHQ@aol.com.
JAARS, Inc, P.O. Box 248, Waxhaw, NC 28173, T: 704-843-6000, F: 704-843-6200.
Japan - North American Commission on Cooperative Mission, 475 Riverside Dr. Rm. 618, New York, NY 10115, T: 212-870-2021, F: 212-870-2055.
Japanese Evangelical Missionary Society, 948 E. Second St., Los Angeles, CA 90012, T: 213-613-0022, F: 213-613-0211.
Joshua Generation, 4748 White Tail Lane, New Port Richey, FL 34653, T: 813-376-2098, F: 813-376-5347.
Korean American CWM, 1605 Elizabeth St., Pasadena, CA 91104, T: (818) 398-2405, F: (818) 398-2410.
Korean World Mission, Billy Graham Center, Wheaton, IL 60187.
List of Mission Agency Links, O: Web: www.netaccess.on.ca/~sma/gallery/gallery.htm.
Logos Missionary Foundation (Korean), 4761 Round Top Dr., Los Angeles, CA 90065, T: 213-258-7700.
Love the Parsee People, Inc., O: Web: web2.airmail.net/babbitt/parsee/messages/Msg0001.html.
MAP International, P.O. Box 50, Brunswick, GA 31521, T: 912-265-6010, F: 912-265-6170, O: Web: www.map.org.
Mercy Flight Int'l, P.O. Box 115, Sierra Madre, CA 91024, T: 800-456-0843.
Middle East Christian Outreach, P.O. Box 1008, Moorhead, MN 56561, T: 218-236-5963, F: 218-236-5963, O: E-mail: 75227.633@compuserve.com.
Ministries in Action, P O. Box 140325, Coral Gables, FL 33114, T: 305-234-7855, F: 305-234-7825.
Mission 21 India, P.O. Box 141312, Grand Rapids, MI 49514, T: 616-453-8855, F: 616-791-9926, O: E-mail: M21India@alliance.net, Web: www.missionindia.org.
Mission Aviation Fellowship, P.O. Box 3202, Redlands, CA 92374, T: 909-794-1151, F: 909-794-3016, O: E-mail: MAF-US@maf.org, Web: www.maf.org.
Mission Center International, P.O. Box 190226, St. Louis, MO 63119, T: 314-843-0096, F: 314-843-4311.
Mission Link, The, 15930 S.W. 96th Ave., Miami, FL 33157, T: 305-251-8308.
Mission Network News, O: Web: www.gospelcom.net/mnn.
Mission Opportunity Database, O: Web: www.pneumasoft.com/fingertip/search.htm.
Mission Possible, P.O. Box 520, Fort Pierce, FL 34954, T: 561-465-0373, F: 561-465-0639, O: E-mail: 103167.2325@compuserve.com, Web: www.odyssey.on.ca/~missionpossible.
Mission Possible Foundation, Inc., P.O. Box 2014, Denton, TX 76202-2014, T: 940-382-1508, F: 940-566-1875, O: E-mail: MP@xc.org, www.mp.org.
Mission Services Association, P.O. Box 2427, Knoxville, TN 37901, T: 423-577-9740, F: 423-577-9743, O: E-mail: 102774.1772@compuserve.com.
MissionAir, O: Web: www.missionair.org.
Missionary Aviation Fellowship, P.O. Box 3202, Redlands, CA 92373.
Missionary Flights International, P.O. Box 15665, West Palm Beach, FL 33406, T: 561-686-2488, F: 561-697-4882.
Missionary Kid Home Page, O: Web: www.xc.org/mk.
Missionary Supply Lines, Inc., P.O. Box 536, Woodlake, CA 93286, T: 209-564-3546.
Missionary TECH Team, 25 FRJ Dr., Longview, TX 75602, T: 903-757-4530, F: 903-758-2799, O: E-mail: MTTEAM@aol.com.
Missions Hotline, The, O: Web: www.webguy-prod.com/hotline.
Missions Resource Center (Christian Churches/Churches of Christ), 9452 Winton Rd., Cincinnati, OH 45231, T: 800-827-5663, F: 513-522-2847.
Missions Without Borders, T: (818) 345-1494.
MissionWeb, O: Web: www.iclnet.org/pub/resources/text/mnet/mweb-home.html.
MIVA-Missionary Vehicle Association, P.O. Box 29184, 1326 Perry St., NE, Washington DC 20017, T: 202-635-3444.
MNet - Computers for Missions International, 520 Okanogan Ave., Wenatchee, WA 98801.
Morning Star Technical Services, O: Web: www.morningstar.org.
Mustard Seed, Inc., P.O. Box 400, Pasadena, CA 91114, T: 626-791-5123, F: 626-398-2392, O: E-mail: mseedinc@wavenet.com.
National Baptist Convention of America, Foreign Mission Board, P.O. Box 223665, Dallas, TX 75222, T: 214-942-3311, F: 214-943-4924.
Network International, 126 S. Jackson, San Angelo, TX 76901, T: (915) 655-9044.
New Life League International, P.O. Box 16030, Phoenix, AZ 85011, T: 602-650-2203, F: 602-650-2215, O: E-mail: NLLI@ix.netcom.com.
New Missions Systems, P.O. Box 4548, West Hills, CA 91308, T: 818-888-3180, F: 818-888-3180.
Nora Lam Ministries, 5442 Thornwood Dr. #200, San Jose, CA 95123, T: 408-629-5000, F: 408-629-4846.
North American Council (NAC), P.O. Box Wheaton, Wheaton, IL 60189-9963, T: 630-668-0440, F: 630-668-0498, O: E-mail: DwightGibson@xc.org.
Outreach Foundation of the Presbyterian Church, O: Web: www.isdn.net/outreach.
Outreach To Asia Nationals, P.O. Box 1909, Winchester, VA 22604, T: 540-665-6418, F: 540-665-0793, O: E-mail: 102045.2310@compuserve.com.
Overseas Council for Theological Education & Missions, Inc., P.O. Box 17368, Indianapolis, IN 46217, T: 317-788-7250, F: 317-788-7257, O: E-mail: OCTEAM@ocmhs.mhs.com, Web: www.octeam.org.
Pacific Southwest Conference on World Christian Mission, O: Web: www.gbgm-umc.org/conference/PSConWCM.
Paraclete Mission Group, Inc., P.O. Box 49367, Colorado Springs, CO 80949, T: 719-590-7777, F: 719-590-7902, O: E-mail: 74262.3071@compuserve.com.
Partners in Christ International, P.O. Box 1715, Chandler, AZ 85244-1715, T: 602-821-9321.
Partners International, P.O. Box 15025, San Jose, CA 95115, T: 408-453-3800, F: 408-437-9708, O: E-mail: Info@partnersintl.org, Web: www.partnersintl.org.
Peter Deyneka Russian Ministries, P.O. Box 496, Wheaton, IL 60189, T: 630-462-1739, F: 630-690-2976, O: E-mail: RMUSA@mcimail.com, shoga.wwa.com/~strtegy.
Pontifical Missionary Union, 366 Fifth Ave., New York, NY 10001.
Praxis Resources, 11720 P.O. Box 708, Ventura, CA 93002, T: 805-647-0214, F: 805-647-8514.
Praying through the 10/40 Window, O: Web: www.ad2000.org/1040ovr.htm.
Presbyterian Frontier Fellowship (PCUSA), 6146 N. Kerby Ave., Portland, OR 97217, T: (503) 289-1865.
Priority One International, 555 Republic Dr. # 510, Plano, TX 75074, T: 972-423-3800, F: 972-422-7535, O: E-mail: TotalTV@gte.net, www.total-tv.com.
Project Partner with Christ, P.O. Box 610, Springboro, OH 45066, T: 513-425-0938, F: 513-425-6628, O: E-mail: partner@projectpartner.com, Web site: www.projectpartner.
Quaker US/CIS Committee, 5419 N. Umberland St., Pittsburgh, PA 15217, T: 412-681-7760, F: 412-661-7763.
Ramesh Richard Evangelism and Church Helps—RREACH, 16250 Dallas Parkway, Suite 110, Dallas, TX 75248.
RREACH International, 6350 LBJ Freeway #250, Dallas, TX 75240, T: 972-702-0303, O: RREACHint@aol.com.
Seed Company, The, P.O. Box 2727, Huntington Beach, CA 92647, T: 714-969-4697, F: 714-969-4661, O: Seed_Co@wycliffe.org, www.wycliffe.org/seedco.
Servants in Faith & Technology, 2944 County Rd. 113, Lineville, AL 36266, T: 205-396-2017, F: 205-396-2501, O: Info@sifat.org, www.sifat.org.
Slavic Gospel Association, 6151 Commonwealth Dr., Loves Park, IL 61111, T: 815-282-8900, F: 815-282-8901, O: SGA@sga.org, www.goshen.net/sga/sga.html.
Speed the Need, O: http://www.netnet.net/~dhatch/speed/.
Spiritual Overseers Service International Corporation, P.O. Box 2756, Vacaville, CA 95696, T: 707-451-9830, F: 707-451-2827, O: SOSIntl@commu-nity.net.
TAOCJ-Technical Assistance Info Clearing Hse, 200 Park Ave, So, New York, NY 10003, T: 212-777-8210.
TECHNOSERVE-Technology and Service, 11 Belden Ave, Norwalk, CT 06850, T: 2203-846-3231.
Tentmakers International Exchange (TIE), P.O. Box 45880, Seattle, WA 98145-0880.
TOUCH Outreach Ministries, Box 19888, Houston, TX 77224, T: (281) 497-7901, F: (281) 497-0904, O: www.touchusa.org.
Trans World Missions, P.O. Box 10, Glendale, CA 91209, T: 818-762-4231, F: 818-762-5872.
U.S. Catholic Mission Association, 1233 Lawrence St NE, Washington, DC 20017, T: 202-832-3112.
U.S. Center for World Mission Adopt-A-People Campaign, 1605 Elizabeth St., Pasadena, CA 91104, T: 818-398-2200, F: (818) 398-2206, O: E-mail: aap.campaign@wciu.edu.
United Board for Christian Higher Education in Asia, 475 Riverside Dr., Rm. 1221, New York, NY 10115, T: 212-870-2609, F: 212-870-2322, O: staff@ubchea.org.
United Missionary Services, 5114 Beechnut, Houston, TX 77035.
United States Center for World Mission (USCWM), 1605 E. Elizabeth St., Pasadena, CA 91104-2721, T: 626-797-1111, F: 626-398-2240, O: E-mail: greg.parsons@uscwm.org, Web site: www.uscwm.org.
University Language Services, P.O. Box 701984, Tulsa, OK 74170, T: 918-495-7045.
Urbana Missions Conference, O: http://www.urbana.org/.
Venture Middle East, P.O. Box 15313, Seattle, WA 98115, T: 800-421-2159, F: 206-729-8011, O: 74512.3725@compuserve.com.
Voice of China and Asia Missionary Society, Inc., P.O. Box 15, Pasadena, CA 91102, T: 626-441-0640, F: 626-441-8124.
Voice of the Martyrs, P.O. Box 443, Bartlesville, OK 74005, T: 918-337-8015, F: 918-337-9287, O: VOMUSA@ix.netcom.com, www.icinet.org/pub/resources/text/vom/vom.html.
Wheaton College Missions, O: http://www.wheaton.edu/Missions/MissionsHome.html.
Witnessing Ministries of Christ, 4717 N. Barton Ave., Fresno, CA 93726-1119, T: 209-226-7349, F: 209-226-0558.
World Evangelical Fellowship Missions Commission, 2 Lands End North, Russelville, AR 72801, T: 501-967-8623.
World Help, P.O. Box 501, Forrest, VA 24551, T: 804-525-4657, F: 804-525-4727, O: WorldHp@aol.com.
World Indigenous Missions, Inc., P.O. Box 310627, New Braunfels, TX 78131, T: 512-629-0863, F: 512-629-0357.
World Outreach Ministries, P.O. Box B, Marietta, GA 30061, T: 770-424-1545, F: 770-424-1545.
World Servants, 7130 Portland Ave. S., Richfield, MN 55423, T: 612-866-0010, F: 612-866-0078, O: WorldServant@worldservants.org.
World Thrust International, Inc., 3545 Cruse Road, Suite 309-B, Lawrenceville, GA 30044, T: 770-923-5215, F: 770-923-3933, O: E-mail: wthrustint@aol.com.
WorldWide Frontier Mission Crusade, Inc., 463 Fensalir Ave., Pleasant Hill, CA 94523, T: 510-680-7294, F: 510-080-0400.
Wycliffe Associates, Inc, P.O. Box 2000, Orange, CA 92669, T: 714-639-9950, F: 714-771-5262.

ZIMBABWE
African Coordination Center for World Missions (ACCWM), P.O. Box 2219, Harare.

40
Home & family life

Family ministries, family counseling, the family apostolate; marriage or parenting instruction, enrichment, guidance, and counseling; family planning, abortion, pregnancy counseling, adoption, orphans; ministries for the divorced or separated, marital introduction agencies. For advocacy and activism on abortion or other family issues, see RELIGIO-POLITICAL ORGANIZATIONS.

ARGENTINA
Fundación Hogares Argentinos, Av Antártida Argentina y Ramos Mejia, Buenos Aires.
Liga de Madres de Familia, Aráoz 2972, Buenos Aires.

ARUBA
Marriage and Family Life, P.O. Centro Pastoral, Sta Cruz, Aruba, T: 297-8-28378.

AUSTRALIA
Australian Federation of Christian Family and Social Apostolate Organizations (AFCFSAO), 222 Victoria Square, Adelaide, SA 500.
Salvation Army Adoption Service, Principal Officer, 140 Elizabeth St, Sydney, T: (02)261711.

AUSTRIA
International Family/Church Growth Institute (IFCI), Stall 35-A-9832 Stall/Moelltal, T: 43-48-23 315, F: 43-48-23 315, O: E-mail: 100611,1632.
Katholische Familienverband Österreichs, Wollzeile 2, A-1010 Wien.
Katholische Familienwerk Österreichs, Stephansplatz 6, A-1010 Wien.

BARBADOS
Home and Family Life Programme, CADEC, Coordinator, P.O. Box 616, Bridgetown.

BELGIUM
Centre d'Education à la Famille et à l'Amour (CEFA), Rue de la Prévoyance 58, B-1000 Brussels, T: (02)5131749.
Groupe International 'Femmes et Hommes dans l'Eglise', Rue de la Prévoyance 58, B-1000 Brussels, T: (02)5131749.
Worldwide Marriage Encounter, 26, rue Belliard, B 1040 Bruxelles.

BENIN
Action Catholique des Familles (ACF), BP 1590, Cotonou.

BRAZIL
Movimento Familiar Cristiano (MFC), Secretariado para Latino America, CP 480, Belo Horizonte, MG.

BRITAIN (UK OF GB & NI)
Association of Separated and Divorced Catholics (ASDC), c/o Cathedral House, 250 Chapel St, Salford M3 5LL, T: 01706 352 925.
Catholic Centre for Healing in Marriage, Oasis of Peace, Penamser Road, Porthmadog, Gwynedd LL49 9NY, T: 01766-514300.
Catholic Marriage Care, Clitherow House, 1 Blythe Mews, Blythe Road, London W14 0NW, T: 0171-371 1341, F: 0171 371 4921.
National Association of Catholic Families, 2 Belstead Ave, Ipswich, Suffolk, IP2 8NP.
Salvation Army Family Tracing Service, 105 Judd St., King's Cross, WC1H 9TS, T: 0171-387-2772.
Union of Catholic Mothers, 1 Petersfinger Cottages, Clarendon Park, Salisbury, Wilts SP5 3DA, T: 01722-331449.
Worldwide Marriage Encounter England and Wales, 15a Abbey Lane, Sheffield, S8 0BJ, T: 0114-274 6992.

BURUNDI
Mouvement d'Action Catholique des Familles, BP 690, Bujumbura.

CAMEROON
Association Chrétienne des Foyers (ACF), BP 550, Yaoundé.

CANADA
Alliance for Life, B1-90 Garry St., Winnipeg, MB R3C 4H1, T: 204-942-4772, F: 204-943-9283.
Beginnings Counselling and Adoption Services of Ontario, Inc., 1 Young St., Suite 308, Hamilton, ON L8N 1T8, T: 905-528-6665.
Beginnings Guelph, 20 Douglas St., Guelph, ON N1H 2S9, T: 519-763-7980.
Bethany Home and Day Care Centre (Salvation Army), 450 Pape Ave., Toronto, ON M4K 3P7, T: 416-461-0217/8.
Bethel Home, 115 Bonis Avenue, Agincourt, Ontario M1T 3S4, T: (416) 293-2074.
Calgary Pregnancy Care Centre, #315, 1035 - 7 Ave., S.W., Calgary, AB T2P 3E9, T: 403-269-3110.
Campaign Life Coalition, 53 Dundas St., East, Suite 305, Toronto, ON M5B 1C6, T: 416-368-8479, F: 416-368-8575.
Catholic Children's Aid Society of Metropolitan Toronto, 26 Maitland St., Toronto, ON M4Y 1C6, T: 416-395-1500, F: 416-395-1581.
Catholic Family Services of Toronto-Central Office, 1155 Yonge St., Toronto, ON M4T 1W2, T: 416-977-1500.
Christian Adoption Services and Licensed Adoption Search, #221, 276 Midpark Way, S.E., Calgary, AB T2X 2B5, T: 403-256-3224.
Christians Concerned for Life, Box 42141, Acadia Postal Outlet, Calgary, AB T2J 7A6, T: 403-252-3343.
Christians for Life, 777 Shetland Crt., Oshawa, ON L1J 7R3, T: 905-434-7977, F: 905571-0021.
Community Pregnancy Care Society, 2512 Arundel Lane, Coquitlam, BC V3K 5R8, T: 604-939-4525.
Crisis Pregnancy Centre, 7487 Edmonds St., Suite F, Burnaby, BC V3N 1B3, T: 604-525-0999.
Family Life Ministries, 2020 Cleaver Ave., Suite 201, Burlington, ON L7M 4C3, T: 905-319-1798.
Family Seminars of Canada, Box 1409, Grand Bend, ON N0M 1T0, T: 519-236-7375, F: 519-236-7182.
Focus on the Family (Canada) Association, P.O. Box 9800, Vancouver, BC V6B 4G3, T: 604-8333, F: 604-684-8653.
Institute of Family Living, 188 Eglinton Ave., E., Suite 700, Toronto, ON M4P 2X7, T: 416-487-3613, F: 416-487-2096.
International Confederation of Christian Family Movements (ICCFM), 151 Bay Street, Apartment 1409, Ottawa, Ontario K1R7T2.
Life is for Everyone, 38 Prospect St., Newmarket, ON L3Y 3S9, T: 905-836-5433.
Maywood Home (Salvation Army), 7250 Oak St., Vancouver, BC V6P 3Z9, T: 604-266-6931.
Pregnancy Counselling Centre, 455 St. Antoine West, Montreal, QC H2Z 1J1, T: 514-876-4564.
Pro-Life Society of British Columbia, #202 - 5658 176th St., Surrey, BC V3S 4C6, T: 604-574-0225.
Promise Partners Family Institute, RR #2, Woodville, ON K0M 2T0, T: 705-439-1173, F: 705-439-2779.
Right to Life Association of Toronto & Area, 120 Eglinton Ave., E., Suite 700, Toronto, ON M4P 1E2, T: 416-483-7869, F: 416-483-7052.
Salvation Army Family & Community Services, 26 Howden Rd., Scarborough, ON M1R 3E4, T: 416-285-0080, F: 416-285-4677.
Straight Talk of Ontario, Box 60072, Oakville, ON L6M 2S0, T: 905-338-8581, F: 905-338-9618.

CENTRAL AFRICAN REPUBLIC
Action Catholique des Familles, BP 855, Bangui.

CHILE
Federación de Asociaciones de Padres de Familia de Establecimentos Educacionales Particulares (FEDAP), Bellavista 67, Santiago.
Hogar de Cristo, Calle Alonso Ovalle 1479, Casilla 4594 Correo 2, Santiago.

CHINA
Christian Family Service Centre, 3 Tsui Ping Rd, Kwun Tong, Kowloon, Hong Kong, T: K-891242.

COLOMBIA
Movimiento Familiar Cristiano, Carrera 17 n. 4671, Bogota, D.E..

CONGO-ZAIRE
Mouvement Familial Chrétien (MFC), BP 7213, Kinshasa.

COSTA RICA
Federación Centro-Americana de Centros de Integración Familiar, Av 7 No 358, San José.

ECUADOR
Asesoramiento Familiar, Ave. America No. 4569 y Manosca, Casilla 8556, Quito, T: 455-770.
Consejeria Pre-matrimonial, Ave. 10 de Agosto No. 3429 y Murgeon, Casilla 8556, Quito, T: 538-144.
Dinamica Familiar, Pasaje Chiriboga No. 433 y Ave. America, T: 237-725.
Terapia Familiar, Ave. America No. 4569 y Manosca, Casilla 8556, Quito, T: 246-0774.

FIJI
Family Care Centre (Salvation Army), 21 Spring St., Toorak, Suva, T: 679-305-518.

FRANCE
Centre de Preparation au Mariage (CPM), 4, avenue Vavin, F 75006 Paris.
International Family/Church Growth Institute (IFCI), 13b, rue Principale - 68610 Lautenbach, T: 33-89-76 31 59, F: 33-89-76 31 59, O: E-mail: 102234,2563.

GERMANY
Bundesvereinigung Evangelischer Eltern und Erzieher, Goldlackstr 6, D-56 Wuppertal-Ronsdorf.
Evangelische Aktionsgemeinschaft fur Familienfragen, Bundesgeschäftsstelle, Meckenheimer Allee 162, D-53 Bonn.
Evangelische Konferenz fur Familien- und Lebensberatung, Stafflenbergstr 78, Postfach 476, D-7 Stuttgart 1.
Katholisches Zentralinstitut für Ehe- und Familienfragen, Hohenzollernring 38-40, T: (0221)210931.

GHANA
Christian Marriage and Family Life Committee, Christian Council of Ghana, P.O. Box 919, Accra.

HOLY SEE
Commissione Speciale di Dispensa dal Matrimonio, Palazzo delle Congregazioni, Piazza Pio XII 10, I-10093 Roma, T: 6982 int 4005,4416.
Secretariat for Family Life, Concilium de Laicis, Piazza San Calisto 16, I-00153 Roma; I-00129 Città del Vaticano, T: 698-4322, 4441, 4843.

HUNGARY
International Family/Church Growth Institute (IFCI), ICSB, Diosd 2049, Budapest, O: E-mail: 102452,2132.

INDIA
Christian Marriage Bureau, 3/350, Dr. Ambedkar Chowk, Rajatalab, Raipur, Madhya Pradesh 492001.
Christian Marriage Bureau, 3/1-Welcome Colony, Anna Nagar West, Madras, Tamil Nadu 600101.
Christian Marriage Information Centre, 36, Trivandrum Road, Palayankottai, Tamil Nadu 627002.
Engaged Encounter, 1B Catholic Colony, Santa Cruz, Bombay, Maharashtra 400054.
Family Apostolate Centre, Santhome Centre, 297 Vidyanagari Marg, Kalina, Bombay, Maharashtra 400098.
Family Welfare Centre, 1B Prince Of Wales Drive, Pune, Maharashtra 411001.
Holy Childhood Association, Arch. Board Of Education, 5 Convent Street, Fort, Bombay, Maharashtra 400039.
Marriage Information Centre, Vandikara Street, Tanjore, Tamil Nadu 613001.
National Marriage Bureau, HIG 17, Shankar Nagar, Raipur, Madhya Pradesh.
Prema Mandira Dispensary and Family Planning Centre, 4 Harris Road, Banglore, Karnataka 560046.
Regional Marriage Tribunal, Bishop's House, Varanasi, Uttar Pradesh 221002.
World Wide Marriage Centre, 1/1 Twinkle Star Society, Ghatla Road, Chembur, Bombay, Maharashtra 400071.

IRELAND
Central Council of Catholic Adoption Societies, O'Connell Street, Ennis, Co Clare, T: (353) 065 28178.
Christian Family Movement, 14 Rossmore Drive, Templeogue, Dublin 6, T: (353) 01 902284.
Cura, 30 South Anne Street, Dublin 2, T: (353) 01 710598.
Protestant Adoption Society, 71 Brighton Road, Rathgar, Dublin 6, T: (353) 01 906438.
Protestant Orphan Society, 28 Molesworth Street, Dublin 2, T: (353) 01 762168.

ITALY
Pontifical Council for the Family, Piazza S. Calisto 16, 00153 Rome.
Pro Sanctity Movement, Piazza S. Andrea della Valle 3, 00166 Rome.

IVORY COAST
Action Catholique des Familles (ACF), BP 1993, Abidjan.

JAMAICA
Family Life Centre, P.O. Box 36, Kingston 10; Holy Cross Rectory, Kingston 10, T: 809-926-7579.
Marriage & Family Life, P.O. Box 197, Montego Bay; c/o Blessed Sacrament Rectory, Montego Bay, T: 809-952-2481.
Marriage Counselling Services, P.O. Box 8, Mandeville, Manchester, T: 809-962-1269, F: 809-962-1297.

LATVIA
Maternity Centre (Salvation Army), Bruninieku iela 10A, LV 1001 Riga, T: 371-22-71-384.
Whole Family Ministries, ul. Vidzemes 12, kv. 117, Rizdski R-N 229036, T: 7-013-995-556.

LUXEMBOURG
Action Catholique des Hommes et Pères de Famille (ACHPF), 3 Rue Bourbon, Luxembourg.

MALAYSIA
Christian Family and Social Movement, 528 Bukit Nanas, Kuala Lumpur.

MALI
Action Catholique des Familles, BP 298, Bamako.

MARTINIQUE
Association des Centres de Préparation au Mariage (ACPM), C 15 Lotissement 'Les Flamboyants', Cité Dillon 97200, Fort-de-France, T: 596-73-64-08.

MAURITIUS
Action Familiale, Route Royale, Rose Hill, T: 43512.

NETHERLANDS
Family Ministries, O: www.webcom.com/-nlnnet/agadutch/family.html.
National Catholic Association for Family Social Service, Fred Hendrikstraat 77, Utrecht, T: (030)514471.
National Catholic Organization for Family and Youth, Niewe Gracht 85, Utrecht, T: (030)10649.

NORWAY
Church Families Association, Mollergt 43, Oslo 1.

RWANDA
Mouvement Familial Chrétien, BP 425, Kigali.

SAINT LUCIA
Nazareth Family Apostolate, Esperance Estate, Monchy, T: 809-45-28653/28319.

SINGAPORE
Bukit Panjang Family Services Centre (Salvation Army), Block 404, Fajar Rd., Singapore 2367, T: 763-0837.
Christian Family and Social Movement (CFSM), 73 Bras Basah Rd, Singapore 15.
Fei Yue Family Service Centre, 185 Bukit Batok West Avenue 6 #01-187, Singapore 650185, T: 569-0381, F: 569-5868.
Kallang Bahru Family Services Centre (Salvation Army), Block 65, Kallang Bahru, Singapore 1233, T: 291-6303.
Methodist Family Service Centre, Block 106 #01-217, Bukit Batok Central, Singapore 650106, T: 562-2211, F: 569-8038.

SOUTH AFRICA
Birthright, National Office, 15 Essen Park, 314 Essenwood Rd, Durban4001, T: 031-202-6528.
Focus on the Family Southern Africa, PO Box X1023, Hillcrest 3650, 8 Old Main Rd, Hillcrest, T: 031-75-1200, F: 031-75-1228.

SOUTH KOREA
Catholic Matrimonial Introduction Agency, 1, 2-ga, Myong-dong, Chung-gu, Seoul-shi, T: (02) 755-9726.
Happy Family Movement, 1, 2-ga, Myong-dong, Chung-gu, Seoul-shi, T: (02) 756-1045.
Marriage Encounter, 263, Nonhyon-dong, Kangnam-gu, Seoul-shi, T: (02) 511-9901.
Seoul City Dong Bu Child Guidance Clinic, 329-1, Chnag-an 2-dong, Tongdaemun-gu, T: (02) 248-4567.

SPAIN
Asoc. de Separados y Divorciados Evangélicos, Tiziano, 2 y 4, 08023 Barcelona, T: 212-38-73, O: Also tel: 2110706.
Centro de Recursos, Aragó, 429, prl. 1ª, 08013 Barcelona.
Confederación Católica Nacional de Padres de Familia, Relatores 22, Madrid 12.
De Familia a Familia, Ganduxer, 5-15, local int. 4, 08021 Barcelona, T: 201-0341, F: 453-09-15.
Movimiento Familiar Cristiano (MFC), Velásquez 92, Madrid 6.

SRI LANKA
Dias Place Family Welfare Centre (Salvation Army), 1 Dias Place, Colombo 11, T: 423-912.
Hope House Family Welfare Centre (Salvation Army), 11 Sir James Peiris Mawatha, Colombo, T: 324-655.
Weerasoriya Family Welfare Centre (Salvation Army), 88 Weerasoriya Watta, Patuwatha, Dodanduwa.

SWEDEN
Mothers' and Babies' Home (Salvation Army), Borüs: 'FAM-huset', Teknologgatan 4, 502 30 Borüs, T: 033-11-12-09.

SWITZERLAND
Evangelische Eheanbahnungsstellen, Kinkelstr 28, CH-8006 Zürich, T: (051)280185.
International Catholic Child Bureau, 63, rue de Lausanne, CH-1202 Geneva.
Mutter- und Familienerholungsheime, CH-1823 Glion.
Offices de consultations conjugales, Couple et famille, 20, rue du Marche, 1204 Geneve, 022/3213168.

SYRIA
Middle East Council of Churches, PO Box 3678, Aleppo, T: 969+21+444-466.

TAIWAN
Taipei Central Corps Baby Centre (Salvation Army), 2F, 273 Sec 2, Tun Hwa S Rd., Taipei 106, T: 737-2985.

TRINIDAD & TOBAGO
Encounter, 17 Alacazar Street, St. Clair, T: 809-622-5852.
Family Life, Catholic Marriage Advisory Council, Catholic Centre, 31 Independence Square, Port of Spain, T: 809-623-7141.

UNITED STATES OF AMERICA (USA)
Adventist Adoption and Family Services, 6040 S.E. Belmont St., Portland, OR 97215, T: 503-232-1211.
Agape Social Services, Inc., 3200 Maple, #400, Dallas, TX 75201.
All About Families Newsletter, O: Web: www.mindchurch.org/family.
Apostolate for Family Consecration, Pope John Paul II Holy Family Center, Rt. 2, Box 700, Bloomingdale, OH 43910.
Art of Family Living, P.O. Box 33000, Colorado Springs, CO 80933, T: 719-593-0200, F: 719-593-8761, O: E-mail: JohnNieder@aol.com.
Beginning Experience, 305 Michigan Ave., Detroit, MI 48226.
Bethany Christian Services, 901 Eastern Ave., NE, Grand Rapids 49503.
Booth Memorial Home Youth and Family Services, Box 31427, Los Angeles, CA 90031; 2670 Griffin Ave., Los Angeles, CA 90031, T: 213-225-1586.
Born Again Marriages, P.O. Box 385, Sonora, CA 95370, T: 800-BORN AGAIN, 209-928-3000, F: 209-928-3061.
Capitol Hill Crisis Pregnancy Center, 323 8th St., NE, Washington, DC 20002, T: 202-546-1018.
Catholic Family Services, 4206 Chamberlayne Ave., Richmond, VA 23227.
Catholic Parent Magazine, 200 Noll Plaza, Huntington, IN 46750, T: 800-348-2440.
Choices, Inc., 775 Second Street Pike, Southampton, PA 18966, T: 215-322-8520.
Christian Family Care Agency, 1121 E. Missouri, Phoenix, AZ 85014, T: 602-234-1935.
Christian Family Movement (CFM), Box 272, Ames, IA 50010.
Christian Hope Indian Eskimo Fellowship (CHIEF), 1644 E. Campo Bello Dr., Phoenix, AR 85022.
Christian Parenting Today Magazine, 4050 Lee Vance View, Colorado Springs, CO 80918, T: 800-708-5550, F: 719-535-0172, O: gfm.pcisys.net, www.cookministries.com.
Christian Singles Magazine, 127 Ninth Ave North, Nashville, TN 37234-0140, T: 800-458-2772.
Couple to Couple League, O: Web: www.mission-net.com/~mission/cathlic/ccl.
Covenant Children, P.O. Box 2344, Bismark, ND 58502.
Dad the Family Shepherd, Inc., P.O. Box 21445, Little Rock, AR 72212, T: 501-221-1102.
Deaconess Home, 5401 N. Portland Ave., Oklahoma City, OK 73112.
Dillon's Children's Services, Inc., 7615 E. 63rd Place S., #215, Tulsa, OK 74133.
Evangelical Adoption and Family Service, Inc., 119 Church St., North Syracuse, NY 13212.
Evangelical Child and Family Agency, 1530 N. Main St., Wheaton, IL 60187, T: 708-653-6400.
Face to Face Ministries, O: www.gospelcom.net/ftf.
Family Life Services, 1880 S. Cascade, Colorado Springs, CO 80906, T: 719-632-4661.
Family Walk, PO Box 37060, Boone, IA 50037-0060, T: 800-627-4942.
FamilyLife Today, 3900 N. Rodney Parham, Little Rock, AR 72212, T: 501-228-2330, F: 501-228-2394, O: blepine@fltoday.org.
Focus on the Family, 102 N. Cascade, Colorado Springs, CO 80903, T: 719-531-4300, F: 719-531-3359, O: Web: www.fotf.org.
Friends Contact Information, 2025 Nicoliet Ave #203, Minneapolis, MN 55404, T: 612-870-1501.
Hand in Hand International, 4695 Barnes Rd., Colorado Springs, CO 80917.
Hannah's Prayer, O: Web: www.quiknet.com/~hannahs.
Hearts At Home Ministries, 708 Point of the Pines, Colorado Springs, CO 80919, T: 719-260-8151.
Highlands Child Placement Services, 1445 Boonville Ave., Springfield, MO 65802.
Holston United Methodist Home for Children, P.O. Box 188, Greenville, TN 37744.
Holt International Children's Services, Inc., P.O. Box 2880, Eugene, OR 97402, T: 541-687-2202, F: 541-683-6175, O: Info@holtintl.attmail.com.
Institute of Singles Dynamics, P.O. Box 11394, Kansas City, MO 64112, T: 816-763-9401.
International Christian Adoption Agency, 60 W. River Rd., Waterville, ME 04901.
Korean American Family Institute, 3360 W. 7th St., #303, Los Angeles, CA 90005, T: 213-487-0620.
Korean Christian Martyrs Family Association, USA, 18700 Sherman Way, Reseda, CA 91335, T: 818-345-0943.
Korean School of Family Life, 3319 W. Lincoln Ave., #206, Anaheim, CA 92801, T: 714-828-0280.
Love Life Adoption Agency, P.O. Box 247, Florence, SC 29503.
Lutheran Family Association, O: Web: http://tcm-net.com/~famconn/.
Lutheran Social Services, 2414 Park Ave., S., Minneapolis, MN 55404.
Marriage Ministries International, P.O. Box 1040, Littleton, CO 80160, T: (303) 740-3333.
Marriage Partnership Magazine, P.O. Box 37060, Boone, IA 50037-0060, T: 800-627-4942.
Moms of Preschoolers International, Inc. (MOPS), 1311 S. Clarkson St., Denver, CO 80210, T: 303-733-5353, F: 303-733-5770, O: Web: www.gospelcom.net/mops.
Movimiento Familiar Cristiano-USA, 3727 View Ct., Santa Rosa, CA 95403.
National Association of Catholic Families, O: Web: http://homepage.interaccess.com/~dfroula/nacf.html.
National Catholic Rural Life Conference, 4625 Beaver Ave., Des Moines, IA 50310.
National Center for Fathering, 10200 W. 75th St. Ste. 267, Shawnee Mission, KS 66204, T: 913-384-4661, F: 913-384-4665, O: ncf@aol.com.
New Hope Child and Family Agency, 2611 N.E. 125th St., Suite 146, Seattle, WA 98125, T: 206-363-1800.
New Moms, Inc., 3600 W. Fullerton, Chicago, IL 60647, T: 312-252-3253.
North American Conference of Separated and Divorced Catholics, 80 St. Mary's Dr., Cranston, R.I. 02920.
Open Arms, 1100 Lake City Way, NE, Seattle, WA 98125.
Orthodox Christian Adoption Referral Service, P.O. Box 396, Tuckahoe, NY 10707, T: 914-961-1811.
Parents of Teenagers Magazine, 309 E. Hitt St., Mt Morris, IL 61054-0482, T: 800-238-2221.
Respect Life Office, P.O. Box 2000, Dallas, TX 75221, T: 214-437-4377.
SafeHaven, O: Web: www.worldvillage.com/wv/square/chapel/safe-haven/.
Shepherd Care Ministries, Inc., 5935 Taft St., Suite B, Hollywood, FL 33021.
Single Adult Ministries Journal, P.O. Box 3010, Colorado Springs, CO 80934.
Single-Parent Family Magazine, Focus on the Family, Colorado Springs, CO 80995, T: 800-A-FAMILY.
Singles Ministry Resources, 4050 Lee Vance View, Colorado Springs, CO 80918; P.O. Box 62056, Colorado Springs, CO 80906, T: 888-888-4726, F: 800-430-0726, O: www.cookministries.com.
Singles News, Christian Singles International, Box 543, Harrison, OH 45030.
Singles Scene, P.O. Box 310, Allardt, TN 38504, T: 615-879-4625.
Sunny Ridge Family Center, 2S426 Orchard Rd., Wheaton 60187.
Today's Christian Woman, 465 Gundersen Dr., Carol Stream, IL 60188.
Ukrainian Family Bible Association, P.O. Box 3723, Palm Desert, CA 92261-3723, T: 619-345-4913.

URUGUAY
Centro de Investigationes y Estudios Familiares (CIEF), Calle Lavalleja 2115, Montevideo, T: 400681.
Movimiento Familiar Cristiano (MFC), Juan Benito Blanco 614, Montevideo, T: 793616.

41
Home missions & renewal ministries

Home or domestic missionary societies, agencies, congregations, or orders; mission organizations which work only or primarily within their own nation; evangelism among or ministry to ethnic or social minorities within a nation, evangelism among or ministry to certain classes, occupations, or social or financial classes; home evangelistic societies or ministries; renewal movements within the churches, inter- or non-denominational renewal or deeper life ministries; charismatic movements, services, networks, or communication centers. See also: RURAL AGRICULTURAL MISSION, URBAN INDUSTRIAL MISSION.

ARGENTINA
Comisión Misionera (Hermanos), El Salvador 4570, 1414 Capital Federal, T: 1-833-0064, F: 1-833-0064.
Junta Unida de Misiones, C.P. 34, 3705 J.J. Castelli, Chaco, T: 541-592778.

AUSTRALIA
Aborigines Inland Mission Fellowship, 9 Carramarr Rd., Castle Hill 2154.
Asiana Centre, 38 Chandos St., Ashfield N. S. W. 2131, T: 02-799-2423.
Eremos Institute, P.O. Box 131, Newtown, NSW 2042, T: 02-5165786.
Evangelization Society of Australia (ESA), Box 122, East Bentleigh, Victoria 3165, T: 573456.
United Aborigines Mission, 262 Flinders Lane, Melbourne C1, Victoria, T: 632506.

AUSTRIA
Charismatic Renewal in the Catholic Church, St Bartholomaüs-Platz 3, 1170 Wien, T: 0222/42 63 92.
Cursillo Movement, Bennogasse 21, 1080 Wien, T: 0222/42 53 18.
Focolare Movement, MSnner-Zentrum: Breitenfurterstrasse 432a, 1235 Wien, T: 0222/889 17 01.
Geistiche Gemeindeerneuerung, 7432 Oberschützen, T: 03353/232.
Pallotti Fellowship, Evangelistionszentrum, Raiffeisenstrasse 1, 5061 Elsbethen, T: 0662/28 897.
Repentance to the Lord, Portheimgasse 1/70, 1220 Wien, T: 0222/224 38 85.
Rhema-Fellowship, Aumühlstrasse 28, 4050 Traun, T: 07229/610 41-21.
Youth with a Mission, Herklotzgasse 14/2, 1150 Wien, T: 0222/83 02 71.

BAHAMAS
Universal Household of Faith, Inc., P.O. Box F-41688, Freeport, Grand Bahama, T: 242-351-2244.

BELGIUM
International Communication Office, Boulevard de Smet de Naeyer 570A, B-1020 Brussels, T: (02)4798565.
Missions Catholiques Chinoises, Rue del Hotel

des Monnaies 65, B-1060 Bruxelles.

BOLIVIA

Misioneras Cruzadas de la Iglesia, Cala-Cala, Casilla 698, Cochabamba, T: 2763.

Misioneras de María Madre de la Iglesia, Av Final 20 Octobre 2656, La Paz, T: 24137.

Misión Antioquía, Casilla 5293, Cochabamba, T: 42-44081, F: 42-44081, O: E-mail: antiokia@llajt.nrc.bolnet.bo.

BOTSWANA

Independent Order of True Templers, PO Box 366, Lobatse, T: 330 793.

Living Waters Christian Fellowship, PO Box 788, Gaborone, T: 356 453.

BRAZIL

ATE-Associação Transcultural Evangélica, Cx. Postal 554, Valinhos-SP 13270-970, T: 19-881-1457.

Junta de Missões Nacionais/Convenção Batista Brasileira, Cx. Postal 2844, Rio de Janeiro-RJ 20001-970, T: 21-570-2570, F: 21-288-2650, O: E-mail: jmn@jmn.org.br.

MEAP-Missão Evangélica de Assistência aos Pescadores, R. Marechal Pego Júnior, 21, Santos-SP 11013-500, T: 13-222-6556, F: 13-222-6556.

MEIB-Missão Evangélica aos Indios do Brasil, Cx. Postal 13030, Belém-PA 66040-970, T: 91-241-3293, F: 91-235-0945.

MEVA-Missão Evangélica da Amazônia, Cx. Postal 154, Boa Vista-RR 69301-970, T: 95-224-1621, F: 95-224-1135.

Missao Catolica Chinesa no Brasil, Rua Santa Justina, 290, Vila Olimpia, Sao Paulo 04545.

Missão Edificando, Cx. Postal 672, Centro, São Paulo-SP 01060-970, T: 11-6179-0617 Ram 27.

Missão Evangélica Caiuá, Cx. Postal 04, Dourados-MS 79804-970, T: 67-421-4197, F: 67-421-4197.

Missão Evangélica dos Irmãos Armênios, Rua Maria Curupaiti, 117, São Paulo-SP 02452-000, T: 11-267-1856.

Missão Filadélfia, Cx. Postal 5101-Venda Nova-, Belo Horizonte-MG 31611-970, F: 31-441-2549.

Missão Hora Final, Rua Joaquim Coelho Júnior 48, Pouso Alegre-MG 37550-000, T: 35-422-1223.

Missão Novas Tribos do Brasil, Cx. Postal 221, Anápolis-GO 75001-970, T: 62-318-1234, F: 62-318-2000.

Missão Renascer, Rua Florianópolis, 1265, Cerejeiras-RO 78997-000.

PAZ-Missão Projeto Amazonas, Cx. 232, Santarém-PA 68005-080, T: 91-522-7314, F: 91-522-3325.

Secretaria de Missões da Ig Presbiteriana Independente do Brasil, Cx. Postal 7050, Londrina-PR 86047-990, T: 43-339-1331, F: 43-339-6165, O: E-mail: smiipib@inbrapenet.com.br.

UNIEDAS-União das Igrejas Evangélicas, Cx. Postal 81, Aquidauana-MS 79200-000.

Visão Mundial, Cx. Postal 848, Belo Horizonte-MG 30190-060, T: 31-273-5944, F: 31-273-3949, O: E-mail: vmbrasil@br.homeshopping.com.

BRITAIN (UK OF GB & NI)

Agape Fellowship, 22 Everton Drive, Belfast BT6 0LJ, T: (08) 0232 796368.

Anglican Society, 1 Harcourt Villas, London Rd, Sittingbourne, Kent.

Capenwray Missionary Fellowship, Capernwray Hall, Carnforth, Lancashire, T: 2785.

Catholic Biblical Association of Great Britain, 6 St Helier House, Melville Rd, Edgbaston, Birmingham B16 9HG.

Catholic Charismatic Renewal, National Serv. Committee, Allen Hall, 28 Beaufort St, London, SW3 5AA, T: 0171-352 5298.

Catholic Missionary Society, The Chase Centre, 114 West Heath Road, London NW3 7TX, T: 0181-458 3316, F: 0181-455 9871, O: 0181 905 5780.

Chinese Overseas Christian Mission (COCM), 4 Earlsfield Road, London SW18 3DW, T: 01-870-2251.

Christian Life Communities, 31 Dalton Drive, Swinton Manchester M27 8UK, T: 0161-743 9295.

Christian Renewal Centre, Shore Road, Rostrevor, Newry, Co. Down BT34 3ET, T: (08) 069 37 38492.

Churchyard, Manchester 2.

Community of Celebration Christian Trust, Yeldall Manor, Hare Hatch, Twyford, Berks RG10 9XR, T: Wargrave 2272.

Community of the Risen Christ, P.O. Box 422, 20 Belleisle Street, Glasgow G42 8LW, T: 041-644-1267.

Congregational Evangelical Revival Fellowship, The Manse, Hoestock Rd, Sawbridgeworth, Herts, T: 2373.

Dar El Aman (House of Refreshment), 3 Bromley Street, GB-London E1 ON.

Derek Prince Ministries, P.O. Box 169, Enfield EN3 6PL, Middlesex, T: 44-081-804-0601, F: 44-081-443-3775.

Episcopal Cursillo in Scotland, 47 Lennel Mount, Coldstream TD12 4NS, T: 01890 882479.

Gaelic Society of the Scottish Episcopal Church, St. Margaret's Clergy House, Gallowgate, Aberdeen AB1 1EA, T: 01224 644969.

Iona Abbey, GB-Isle of Iona, Argyil, Scotland PA76 6SN, T: 44-6817-404.

Irish Evangelistic Band, 39 Belmore St, Enniskillen, Country Fermanagh, NI, T: 2400.

Irish Evangelistic Treks, Woodlands Conference Centre, Wellington St, Matlock, Derby DE4 3GU, T: 2258.

Jesus Family, The Living Room, 41 Westow St, Upper Norwood, London SE19; Commune: 56 Beulah Hill Rd., Upper Norwood, T: (01)653-6413.

Jesus Liberation Front, Sunnyhill, Hemel Hempstead, Herts, T: 59817.

Lord's Day Observance Society (LDOS), 55 Fleet St, London EC4Y 1DR.

Mersey Mission to Seamen, Kingston House, James St, Liverpool 2, T: (051)236-2432.

Mission House, 175 Tower Bridge Rd, London SE1 4TR, T: (01)407-7585.

One for Christian Renewal, 300 Granville Rd, Sheffield S2 2RT, T: 21020.

Open-Air Mission, 19 John St, Bedford Row, London WC1, T: (01)405-6135.

Protestant Truth Society (PTS), 194 Fleet St, London EC4.

Revival Movement Association, 43 Oakland Ave., Belfast BT4 3BW, T: 44-0232-455026, F: 44-0232-455026.

Romans One Eleven Trust, 9 Colonsay Road, Broadfield, Crawley, Sussex RH11 9DF, T: 02930-53-0194.

Royal National Mission to Deep Sea Fishermen (RNMDSF), 43 Nottingham Place, London W1M 4BX, T: (01)935-6823/4.

Scottish Episcopal Renewal Fellowship, Rose Court, Fortnose IV10 8TN.

Seamen's Christian Friend Society, 87 Brigstock Rd, Thornton Heath, Surrey CR4 7JL, T: (01)684-2244/5.

Society of Our Lady of Lourdes, 21a Soho Square, London W1V 6NR, T: 0171-434 9966, F: 0171-434 9965.

Society of St David, 22 Park Av, Porthcawl, Mid Glamorgan, Wales.

Southwark Diocesan Charismatic Fellowship, 17 Stradella Rd, Herne Hill SE24 9HN, T: (01)274-6677.

World Revival Crusade, 10 Clarence Av, London SW4.

CANADA

Archdiocesan Charismatic Service Team (ACST), 71 Gough Ave., Toronto, ON M4K 3N9, T: 416-466-0776, F: 416-466-0214.

BCM International (Canada), Inc., 798 Main St., E., Hamilton, ON L8M 1L4, T: 905-549-9810.

Calgary Catholic Charismatic Renewal Society, 480E - 36 Ave., S.E., Calgary, AB T2G 1W4, T: 403-691-2912.

Calgary Chinese Catholic Mission, 202. 28 Ave. & 1 St. S.E., Calgary, AB T2L 0A3, T: 403-282-4991.

Canadian Revival Fellowship, Box 584, Regina, Saskatchewan, T: 584-0999.

Chinese Catholic Mission, Mt. Carmel Church, 101 St. Patrick St., Toronto 130, ON M5T 1V4, T: 416-598-3920.

Church Alive, R.R. #2, 7L97 Lakeshore Rd., Port Colborne, ON L3K 5V4, T: 905-835-2884.

Community of Concern, 69 Pearl St., N., Hamilton, ON L8R 2Z1, T: 905-318-9244, F: 905-318-0311, O: WATTS 1-800-465-7186.

Continental Mission, Inc., P.O. Box 98, Thompson, MB R8N 1M9, T: 204-778-4491.

Cursillos - Secteur de langue française, Diocèse de Montréal, 7400 boulevard Saint-Laurent, bureau 614, Montréal, QC H2R 2Y1, T: 514-495-2404.

Dynamic Churches International, 1436 Big Springs Way, Airdrie, AB T4A 1N3, T: 403-948-6758.

Edmonton Native Healing Centre, 11435-107 Ave., Edmonton, AB T5H 0Y6, T: 403-424-8885.

End Time Reapers, Apt. 115, 1575 London Rd., Sarnia, ON N7T 7H2, T: 519-542-3423.

Esk-Omi Missions, Inc., P.O. Box 159, St. Norbert, MB R3V 1L6, T: 204-269-0474.

Freedom in Christ Ministries - Canada, Box 328, Lumsden, SK S0G 3C0, T: 306-731-3565, F: 306-731-3013.

Growth Ministries Canada, Box 54053, Village Square Postal Outlet, Calgary, AB T1Y 6S6, T: 403-293-7150, F: 403-280-6894.

Heart to Heart Family Ministries, P.O. Box 32241, Hamilton, ON L8W 3L3, T: 905-574-4718, F: 905-574-9219.

InterAct Ministries of Canada, 202 110 11th Ave., S.W., Calgary, AB T2R 0B8, T: 403-265-8383, F: 403-265-7737.

Intertribal Christian Communications (Canada), P.O. Box 3765, RPO Redwood Centre, Winnipeg, MB R2W 3R6, T: 204-661-9333, F: 204-661-3982.

Ligonier Ministries of Canada, P.O. Box 1870, Guelph, ON N1H 7M7, T: 519-763-0339, F: 519-837-2883.

Mission Chinoise, 979 Rue Cote, Montreal, QB H2Z 1LL, T: 514-843-3339.

NAIM Ministries, P.O. Box 39, Delta, BC V4K 3N5, T: 604-946-1227, O: E-mail: Compuserve 102216,2755.

National Alliance of Covenanting Congregations, 5300 Drenkelly Court, Mississauga, ON L5M 2H4, T: 905-826-2104, F: 905-826-1816.

Outreach Canada, O: www.outreach.ca/.

Philoxenia/Hospitality Ministry, 3081 Grenville Dr., Mississauga, ON L5A 2P6, T: 905-279-1020.

Renewal Fellowship within the Presbyterian Church in Canada, 3819 Bloor St., W., Etobicoke, ON M9B 1K7, T: 416-233-6581.

Saints Alive Ministry Association, 1511 Mayor McGrath Dr., S., Lethbridge, AB T1K 2R4, T: 403-329-6502.

Shantymen International, 2476 Argentia Rd., Suite 213, Mississauga, ON L5N 6M1, T: 905-821-1175, F: 905-821-8400.

Société des Saints-Apôtres, 3719-est Blvd Gouin, Montréal 459, Québec, T: (514)322-0560.

Spirit Alive, P.O. Box 280, Deseronto, ON K0K 1X0, T: 613-396-1435, F: 613-396-2555.

United Church of Canada Renewal Fellowship, P.O. Box 188, Newburgh, ON K0K 2S0, T: 613-378-2511.

CHILE

Departamento de Misiones de la Alianza Cristiana y Misionera Chilena, Casilla 5, Correo 22, Santiago, T: 2-222-9120, F: 2-222-9120.

CHINA

Breakthrough, Breakthrough Centre, 191 Woo Sung Street, Kowloon, Hong Kong 3-7224411.

Hong Kong Church Renewal Movement Committee, 5/F Breakthrough Centre, 191 Woosung St., Kowloon, Hong Kong, T: 3-7224411.

COLOMBIA

Asociación Cristiana Nuevos Horizontes, Apartado Aéreo 385, Santafé de Bogotá, D.C., T: 1-295-3542, F: 1-295-6253.

CRISALINCO, Apartado Aéreo 30898, Santafé de Bogotá, T: 1-263-1661, F: 1-263-1661.

Departmento de Misiones (DMC), Calle 37 No 13-A-09, Apdo 5258, Bogotá, DE, T: 455992.

Escuela de Servidores, Centro Carismatico El Minuto de Dios, Apdo Aéreo 56437, Bogotá, DE.

ETNAI-Equipo Técnico Nacional de Apoyo a Indígenas, Apartado Aéreo 70287, Santafé de Bogotá, T: 1-366-1132, F: 1-337-1032.

Federación Colombiana de Ministerios Evangélicos, Apdo Aéreo 190, Sincelejo.

Organización Misiones en Colombia, Apartado Aéreo 32408, Santafé de Bogotá, T: 1-263-0071.

COSTA RICA

Asociación de Iglesias Evangélicas Nacionales (ACIENA), Apartado 265-2100, Guadalupe, San José, T: 221-6664.

ETNO, Apartado Postal 47-6151, Santa Ana 2000, San José, T: 282-6143, F: 282-6143, O: E-mail: pkjetno@sol.racsa.co.cr.

CZECH REPUBLIC

Faith in Action Intl., Santraziny 3312, Zlin 760011, T: 42-67-444-98, F: 42-67-444-98.

ECUADOR

Asamblea de Dios Americana-Distrito Indígena, Casilla 06-01-1446, Riobamba, T: 9-727-766.

Convención Bautista Ecuatoriana, Casilla 17-16-221, CEQ, Quito, T: 2-527-639.

Evangelical Ecuadorian Missionary Association, Casilla 3787, Quito.

Pastoral Aborigen, Ave. Patria No. 640, Casilla 8522, Quito, T: 238-220.

EGYPT

Souls Salvation, 12 Kotta Street, Shoubra, Cairo.

FINLAND

Lutheran Evangelical Association of Finland, Malminkatu 12, 00100 Helsinki 10.

FRANCE

Aumonerie des Chinois Eglise Sainte Elizabeth, 195, rue du Temple, 75003 Paris, T: 548-1544.

Centre France Asie, 16, rue Rover-Collard, 75005 Paris.

La Franernite de la Mission Populaire, 45 Rue Jacques Henry, 17000 La Rochelle.

Mission Populaire Evangélique de France, 47 Rue de Clichy, F-75009 Paris, T: 874-9858.

GERMANY

Arbeitsgemeinschaft Evangelischer Stadtmissionen, Stafflenbergstr 78, Postfach 476, D-7 Stuttgart 1.

Berliner Missionswerk, Handjerystr. 19/20, 12159 Berlin.

Evang. Missionswerk in Deutschland, Normannenweg 17-21, 20537 Hamburg.

Evangelisches Missionswerk, Vogelsangstr. 62, 70197 Stuttgart.

Innere Mission und Hilfswerk der EKD, Hauptgeschäftsstelle, Stafflenbergstr 78, Postfach 476, D-7 Stuttgart 1.

Lebenszentrum für die Einheit der Christen, Begegnungsstatte Schlo· Craheim, Post Stadtlauringen, D8721 Wetzhausen, T: (09724) 741.

Spiritual Parish Renewal, Speersort 10, 2000 Hamburg 1, T: 040-336-43, F: 040-32-24-03.

World Catholic Federation for the Biblical Apostolate, WCFBA General Secretariat, Mittelstrasse 12, P.O. Box 601, D-7000 Stuttgart, T: 0711-609274.

World Catholic Federation for the Biblical Apostolate (WCFBA), Mittelstrasse 12, P.O. Box 601, D-7000 Stuttgart, T: 0711-609274.

GHANA

Christian Outreach Fellowship, c/o Christian Service College, P.O. Box 3110.

Christians United in Action, P.O. Box 319 - Akim Oda.

Divine Redeemers Society, P.O. Box 243 - Accra.

Outreach Mission Center, c/o J. Frauseh Frank, Buduburam Reception Center, Box 46, State House, Accra.

GREECE

Hellenic Missionary Union, 12 Lydias St., Athens 11527, T: 01-777-9845, F: 301-770-4964.

Orthodox Missionary Society of Crete, Chania.

HOLY SEE

Int'l Catholic Charismatic Renewal Office, Piazza della Cancellaria 1, Paliazzo della Cancelleria, 1-00120 Citta del Vaticano, Europe, T: 06-6985392, F: 06-6985374.

HONDURAS

Iglesia Episcopal Hondureña, Apartado 586, San Pedro Sula CP 21105, T: 556-6155, F: 556-6467.

HUNGARY

Bridge Mission Society, Hid Missziós Tásaság, 1161 Budapest, Mária utca 31, T: 36-1-271-5161, F: 36-1-271-5161.

Navigators, 1631 Budapest, Pf. 128; Ofc: 1027 Budapest, Bem J. u. 6.II.1, T: 36-1-201-3837, F: 36-1-202-3837.

School of Tomorrow Foundation, 2022 Tahi, Fészty 'Árpád út 12, T: 36-26-385-171.

INDIA

Abundant Life Ministries Associates, Podnalavari Street, Pathenkhanpet, Nellore, Andhra Pradesh 524001.

Adivasi Christiya Samaj, Tauscher Bungalow, Mission Compound, Koraput, Orissa 764020.

Advancing the Ministries of the Gospel, AMG India International, Post Box 12, Chilakaluripet, Andhra Pradesh 522616.

All India Bodo Christian Revival Church Association, Bamungaon Christian Revival Church, Dattapur P.O., Assam 783373.

All India Christian Mission, Chattupara, Adimali P. O., Kerala 685561.

Alpha and Omega Bethel Shem Care Mission, 198, Subhana Palaya, Jai Jawan Nagar, Bangalore, Karnataka 560043.

Alpha Omega Bethel Full Gospel Mission, 56, Govinda Chetty Colony, Near Queen's Road, Bangalore, Karnataka 560051.

Asia for Christ, 1813, R. T. Prakashnagar, Secunderabad, Andhra Pradesh 500016.

Association for Christian Thoughtfulness, A1/1 Rajat Rekha, 142/6 J. P. Road, Andheri West, Bombay, Maharashtra 400058.

At Any Cost Jesus Movement, Bethel, T.C. 13/553 (3), Kunnukuzhy P.O., Trivandrum, Kerala 695037.

Baptist General Conference North Bank Mission, Baptist Christian Hospital, Post Box 14, Tezpur, Assam 784001.

BCM International (India), 1-1-385/28/A, P. And T. Colony, New Bakaram, Hyderabad, Andhra Pradesh 500380.

Better Life Movement, Aloor, Kalletumkara, Kerala 680683.

Bible Faith Mission, Mount Sinai, Parasuvaikal P.O., Parassala, Thiruvananthapuram, Kerala 695502.

Blessed Peniel Mission, Opp. Old Post Office, Rangat, Middle Andaman, Andaman & Nicobar Is 744205.

Bombay Revival and Prayer Band, 17/199, Smruti Building, Sion (E), Bombay, Maharashtra 400022.

Calvary Gospel Mission, 'Zion', Aramada P.O., Kerala 695032.

Calvary Malai Mission, Kattur, Thiruppathur, Tamil Nadu 620006.

Catholic Charismatic Renewal, C/o OL Of Salvation Ch. Gokhale Road, Dadar, Bombay, Maharashtra 400028.

Christ for India Movement, 3,Barde Layout, Borgaon, Nagpur, Maharashtra 440013.

Christ for the World Movement, 7, St. Thomas Street, South Subramaniyapuram, Arumuganeri, Tamil Nadu 628202.

Christ is the Answer, B-2 Ashish Society, Near Efforts Factory, Nadiad, Gujarat 387001.

Christ Lover's Team, Post Box 47, P. O. Bhilai, Madhya Pradesh 490001.

Christ Mission Ashram, 144 Santoshpur Ave., Calcutta, West Bengal 700075.

Christ the Hope Ministries, 13, Sindhi Colony, P. O. Box 6, Upanagar, Nasik Road, Nasik, Maharashtra 422101.

Christer Agradut Samity, Mahatma Gandhi Road (Adhikary Para), Thakurpukur Post, Calcutta, West Bengal 700063.

Christian Ministries India, Manikandeswaram P. O., El Shalom, Trivandrum, Kerala 695013.

Christian Revival Movement, Chittilappilly House, Kalathode, Ollukkara, Kerala 680655.

Church of the Living God Ministries, P. O. Box 6, Chintalapet, Gannavaram, Andhra Pradesh 521101.

Compassion of Agape, Post Box 6, Nedumkandam, Kerala 685553.

Cross Bearers, Chelikere, Banaswadi P. O., Bangalore, Karnataka 560043.

Cross Fellowship, 8-2-23 Nizampet, Khammam, Andhra Pradesh 507001.

Crusaders for Christ in India, P. B. 172, B-4, Nandpuri Colony, Hawa Sarak, Jaipur, Rajasthan 302001.

Deeper Life Ministries, Irrigation Colony, Jeypore, Orissa 764004.

Dying Seed Ministries, Post Box 487, 21 Murugappa Street, Vepery, Madras, Tamil Nadu 600007.

Echoes of Angels, North Street, Near Kanya Tyres - Branch Office, Martandam, Tamil Nadu 629165.

Eternal Light Ministries, 1/2, Setlur Street, Langford Town, Bangalore, Karnataka 560025.

Evangelical Action Team of India, 4A, 2nd Street, Mullainagar, P. N. Pudur, Coimbatore, Tamil Nadu 641041.

Evangelical Lambadi Inland Ministries, Gypsy Gospel Centre, Ragulapadu Post, Uravakonda, Andhra Pradesh 515832.

Evangelize India Fellowship, P.O. Box 16, Tiruvalla, Kerala.

Faith and Work Mission India, Thoppippala P. O., Lebbakkada, Kerala 685511.

Final Call India, Kudamalloor P. O., Kottayam, Kerala 686017.

Followers of Christ, Post Box 414, H-21, Housing Unit, Periyar Nagar, Erode, Tamil Nadu 638009.

Friends Missionary Prayer Band, 110 Berach Road, Kilpauk, Madras 60001.

Full Gospel Business Mens Fellowship International, 70-A Hill Road, Bandra (West), Bombay, Maharashtra 400050.

Gideon Jeba Veedu, Puthu Thullakka Street, Thiruvannamalai, Tamil Nadu.

Go Ye Missions, 29, Water Tank Road, Nagercoil, Tamil Nadu 629001.

Gospel in Action Movement, Office 50'494, E. W. S., Doogara Piyo, Vapi, Vapi, Gujarat.

Gospel Team for Christ, St. Kiran Girl's High School, Hazirbagh, Bihar 825301.

Gubbi Mission, CSI,KCD, Diocesan Office, 20, 3rd Cross, CSI Compound, Bangalore, Karnataka 560027.

Harvest Mission for Christ in India, Junagaon Devjipura, Songadh P. O., Gujarat 394670.

Himalaya Needs Ministry, 2 Anand Vihar, Jakhan, Dehra Dun, Uttar Pradesh 248001.

Home Missionary Movement, Box Takou P. O., Tamei, Manipur 795125.

Home Missionary Society- South Kerala Diocese, C. S. I. Bishop's House L. M. S., Trivandrum, Kerala 695033.

India Church Growth Mission, Pasumalai, Madurai 625 004.

India Every Home Crusade, All India Dir, L-2 Green Park, New Delhi, 110016.

India for Christ Ministries, 713 Ex-Servicemen's Colony, Dodda Banaswadi, Bangalore 560-043.

India Frontiers Mission, Post Box 176, Kohima 797001, Nagaland.
India Gospel Ministries, Gospel Centre, Ashokapuram P. O., Alwaye, Kerala 683101.
India Gospel Mission, Chullimannur P. O., Mannur Koram, Nedumagadu, Kerala.
India Gospel Outreach Mission, 33 Dispensary Road, Bangalore, Karnataka 560001.
India Gospel Team, Plot No. 37, Rajivnagar, Hyderabad-500 890. AP.
Indian Christian Revival Movement, Wisdom School, Manjoor, Kundah (Bridge) P. O., Ooty, Tamil Nadu 643219.
Indian Evangelical Lutheran Mission, No. 2, 15th East Cross Road, Gandhi Nagar, Vellore, Tamil Nadu 632006.
Indian Evangelical Mission, 7 Langford Road, Post Bag 2557, Bangalore 560 025.
Indian Evangelical Team, P. O. Box 6, Jagdalpur, Madhya Pradesh 494001.
Indian Gospel Team, St. Thomas Town P. O., Bangalore, Karnataka 560084.
International Needs-India, P.O. Box 3408, Bangalore 560034.
Jesus Calls, No 16, Greenways Road, Madras, Tamil Nadu 600028.
Jesus Comes International, 48-B, Ambai Road, Melapalayam, Tirunelveli, Tamil Nadu 627005.
Jesus for All, No. 59, Bhiuli Colony, Mandi, Himachal Pradesh 175001.
Jesus for India, Vakathanam P. O., Kerala 686538.
Jesus is Alive Ministries, 11A, Ayikulam Road, Kumbakonam, Tamil Nadu 612001.
Jesus Lives Gospel Team, 123-A, Dohnavur Road, Mavadi, Tamil Nadu 627107.
Kaizypa Hawti Py, No Py Thyutlia Py - E. C. M., Saiha, Mizoram 796901.
Karnataka Baptist Sabhegala Samaikya, 3, Ananda Nagar Road, Hebbal, Bangalore, Karnataka 560024.
Karnataka Shubhasamachara Mandali, 84, MIG. KHB Colony, Koramangala Extension, Bangalore, Karnataka 560095.
Kizs Karbi Anglong Mission, P. O. Diphu Karbi, Anglong, Assam.
Laymen's Home Missionary Movement, 7, Main Raod, Siruvallur Road, Perambur, Madras, Tamil Nadu 600011.
Ling Liang Chinese Church Trust, P-7, Hide Lane, Calcutta, West Bengal 700012.
Living Hope Ministries, B-189, Lok Vihar, Pitampura, Delhi 110034.
Manipur Missionary Society, C/o Manipur Theological College, Kangpokpi P.O., Manipur 795129.
Manna Full Gospel Ministries, Post Box 4., Amalapuram, Andhra Pradesh 533202.
Maranatha Full Gospel Association, 254, Kilpauk Garden Road, Kilpauk, Madras, Tamil Nadu 600010.
Maranatha Revival Crusade, No. 1. Pratibha Apartments, Sebastian Road, Secunderabad, Andhra Pradesh 500003.
Messiah Evangelical Team, 13, Bersheba Society, Vitthalnagar Tekro, P.O. Vatva G.I.D.C., Ahmadabad, Gujarat 382445.
Metropolitan Mission, Gunadala P.O., Vijayawada, Andhra Pradesh 520005.
Miracle Ministry, 2054, 2nd Avenue, Anna Nagar, Madras, Tamil Nadu 600040.
Missionary Society of St. Thomas the Apostle (SST), Deeptinagar, Melampara, Bharananganam.
Mizoram Danial Pawl Chhantu, SDA Church, Chanmari II, Lunglei, Mizoram 796701.
Mount Tabor Dayara, Pathanapuram, Kerala 689642.
National Missionary Fellowship, Nalini Kutir, Peyton Sahi, Cuttack, Orissa 753001.
National Missionary Society of India, 206 Peters Road,, Royapettah, Madras, Tamil Nadu 600014.
Native Missionary Movement, Filadelfia Campus, Opp. Sanjay Park, Rani Road, Udaipur, Rajasthan 313001.
New India Evangelistic Association, H.5. Jawahar Nagar, Trivandrum 695 041.
New Life Crusaders, Box 12, Imphal, Manipur 795001.
New Life League, P.O. Box 2013, 12 Bungalow, Varanasi Cantonment, Uttar Pradesh 221002.
Newman Association, Silvan Shades 16 Sebastian Road, Bandra, Bombay, Maharashtra 400050.
Nur Ul Alam Ministry, P. O. Box 15, Manjeri, Kerala 676121.
Operation Mobilisation India, Prem kunj, Christian Society, Ahmedabad, Gujarat 380022.
Peniel Gospel Team, Bagdogra P. O., West Bengal 734422.
Pentecost Fellowship in India, Kanamala P.O., Kerala 686510.
Priority One India, P. O. Box 7, Udipi, Brahmavar P. O., Karnataka 576213.
Quiet Corner India, 3, Ramakrishnappa Road, Cox Town, Bangalore - 560 005.
Rashtriya Susamachar Parishad, P.O. Box No. 1, Izatnagar, Uttar Pradesh 243122.
Rava for Christ, Kalanbari Village, P. O. Debitola, Assam 783339.
Rehoboth Evangelical Ablaze Prayer-Wheel Trust, Post Bag 5552, Choolaimedu P. O., Madras, Tamil Nadu 600094.
Revival Gospel Mission, Chellackadu P. O., Kerala 689677.
Revival Ministries, Post Box 7, Mannargudi, Tamil Nadu 614001.
Salem Gospel Ministries India, Gospel Centre, Anchumaramkala, Vellarada P. O., Trivandrum, Kerala 695505.
Salt and Sunshine, P. O. Box 802, Ulsoor, Site 40, Abbya Reddy Layout, 1st A, Main, 5th Cross, Dodda, Banaswadi, Bangalore, Karnataka 560043.
Saviour Jesus Christ Mission, 7, N.G.O. Colony, Chromepet, Madras, Tamil Nadu 600044.
Send the Light, 15, Christ Folk Society, Behind Sindhvai Mandir, Ramol Road, Ahmedabad, Gujarat 380026.
Shalom Kendra, Paranwadi, Talegaon Dabhade Tamaval, Pune, Maharashtra.
Shiloh Evangelistic Mission, 24, Paramount Apartments, 1/39, North Parade Road, St. Thomas Mount, Madras, Tamil Nadu 600016.
Siloam India Gospel Mission, 17, Hutchins Road, 5th Cross, Bangalore, Karnataka 560084.
Soldiers for Christ, 724, 2nd B. Cross, 8th Block, Koramangala, Bangalore, Karnataka 560095.
Spirituality Centre, Irinjalakuda, Kerala 680121.
Thlarau Bo Zawng Pawl - Seekers of Lost Souls, Zarkawt, Aizawl, Mizoram 796001.
United Team Action Internation, No. 1426, Lawrence Villa, Sait Palya, Hennur Road Cross, Bangalore, Karnataka.
Village Revival Mission, 65, Vishwanatha Puram, Madurai-625 014, Tamin Nadu.
Vimukti Christian Ministries, Plot No. 15, Sapthagiri Colony, Sainikpuri Post, Secunderabad, Andhra Pradesh 500594.
Vishwa Vani, 235 Unit III, Kharvel Nagar, Bhubaneswar, Orissa 751001.
Yesuvin Thiruupani Senai, Muthu Madaliyar House, Somangalam, Tamil Nadu 602109.
Yesuvirke Puhal, Prarthanai Illam, Kalayar Koil Street, Tamil Nadu.

INDONESIA

Indonesian Missionary Fellowship (JPPII), Institut Indjil Indonesia, Batu Malang, East Java.

IRELAND

Charismatic Renewal Movement, 'Emmanuel' House of Prayer, 3 Pembroke Road, Dublin 4, T: (353) 01 685223.
Christian Renewal Centre, Shore Road, Rostrevor, T: 06937, 38492, F: 06937, 38996.
Irish Missionary Fellowship, 95 Meadow Grove, Dundrum, Dublin 16, T: (353) 01 298 7184.
National Service Committee for Catholic Charismatic Renewal in Ireland, 2 Saval Park Gardens, Dalkey, County Dublin, T: 602622.

ITALY

'Focolare Movement' or 'Work for Mary', Via di Frascati, 304, I-00040 Rocca di Papu, Rome.
Catholic Charismatic Renewal, Via Ferruccio, 19, I 00185 Rome.
Communione e Liberazione Fraternity, Via Marcello Malpighi 2, 00161 Rome.
ICCRS, Palazzo della Cancelleria, 00120 Vatican City; Piazza della Cancelleria, 1 00186 Rome.
Int'l Bishops Retreat 2000, Piazza Pio XII 3, 1-00193 Roma, Italy, T: 06-6984821, F: 06-6984324.
National Service Committee, Via Pasubio 94, 70124 Bari, T: 0039-80-5223806, F: 0039-80-5221250.
Overseas Chinese Apostolate, Sacred Congregation for the Evangelization of Peoples, Via Urbano VIII, 16, 00165 Roma, T: 656-7851.
Risorse Per La Crescita Spirituale, Casella Postale 94, San Salvo 66050, T: 873-34-31-88, F: 873-34-31-94.
Union of Adorers of the Blessed Sacrament, Largo dei Monti Parioli 3, I-00197, Rome.

JAPAN

Korean Christian Centre, 2-6-10 Nakagawanishi, ilkuno-ku, Osaka 544, T: 81-6-731-6801, F: 81-6-718-0988.

KAZAKHSTAN

Revival Mission for Kazakhstan, Aksaiskaya 30, Almaty 480061 Kazakhstan.

KENYA

Africa Inland Church Missionary Society, AIC Mukaa, PO Kilome, Machakos.
Christian Churches/Churches of Christ, Outreach Ministries, P.O. Box 44400, Nairobi, T: 724317.
Church Army in Eastern Africa (CA), Jogoo Rd (opposite St Stephen's Church), PO Box 72584, Nairobi, T: 558253.
Maseno South Diocesan Missionary Association (DMA), Church House, Dhanwant Singh Rd, PO Box 380, Kisumu, T: 2131.
Mount Kenya Diocesan Missionary Association (DMA), Martyrs' Memorial Cathedral, PO Box 121, Murang'a, T: 53.
Nairobi Diocesan Missionary Association (DMA), PO Box 40502, Nairobi, T: 28146.
Nakuru Diocesan Missionary Association (DMA), PO Box 56, Nakuru.
Trinity Fellowship (TF), Siriba Teachers College, PO Box 192, Maseno, T: 4.

LATVIA

DVIM Mission-Latvia, Prospekt Bulduru 124, Jumala 10 229070, T: 7-013-2-75-49-49, F: 7-013-2-75-24-52.
Latvian Christian Mission, Veidenbauma Str. 13, Riga 226050, T: 7-013-226-189-287721.

MADAGASCAR

Centre Catholique Chinois, B. P. 508 Tamatave, 5 rue Ile de France, Tamatave.
Malagasy Missionary Society, Tranon'd Rasalama, Andravoahangy, Tananarive.

MALAYSIA

Malaysia Renewal Fellowship, 11 Jalan Padang Midah, Taman Midah, Kuala Lumpur 20-17.

MALTA

Communications Office of the Charismatic Renewal in Malta, 'Maranatha', Triq Dun M. Zammit, Siggiewi Qrmoiz, T: 468223, F: 244968.

MAURITIUS

Ming Tek Centre, 25 Eugene Laurent St., Port Louis.

MEXICO

Buenas Nuevas, Apdo. 6-17, C.P. 68020 Oaxaca, OA,, T: 951-3-27-13, F: 951-3-27-13, O: E-mail: 74174.1051@compuserve.com.
Centro de Vida Cristiana, Apdo. 13-145, C.P. 03400 México D.F., T: 5-579-93-11, F: 5-590-49-18.
HALUSA (Hasta Lo Ultimo de la Sierra), Apdo. 42, C.P. 58000 Morelia, MICH, T: 43-15-23-04, F: 43-24-42-35.
Horizonte de Esperanza, Lomas de Zoquipan 2186, Lomas de Atemajal, C.P. 45170, Zapopan, JAL, T: 913-656-0130, F: 913-659-2996.
Iglesia Cristiana Casa del Alfarero A.R., Calle Puebla 292, Col. Roma C.P. 06700, T: 525-74-90, F: 208-13-29.
Iglesia Cristiana Evangélica de México, A.R., Dalias 145 Lt. 40, Hacienda Ojo de Auga, C.P. 55770, Tecámac, Edo. MEX, T: 8-79-53-49, F: 915-9-38-47-38.
Junta de Misiones Mundiales de la Convención Nacional Bautista, Vizcainas 16 Ote., México 1, D.F., Col Centro 06080, T: 5-518-26-91, F: 5-521-01-18.
Misioneros Josefinos de México, Zempoala 496, México 13, DF, T: 5391987.
Sociedad Misionera de México, Apdo. 1067, C.P. 31000 Chihuahua, CHIC., T: 14-35-45-80, F: 14-35-45-79, O: E-mail: 105334.364@compuserve.com.
Vela, Reg. Fed. Caus., Vel-860703, Apartado Postal, M-9293 C.P., Mexico City, DF, CO 06000, Mexico.
Vision Evangelizadora Latinoamericana, Apartado Postal M-9293, C.P. 06000, México, D.F., T: 395-06-25.

MOROCCO

Groupe du Renouveau, 29, Derb Aïn, Sefli-Rouamzine-50120 Meknes (Médina), T: (07)726794.

NETHERLANDS

Dutch Pentecostal Charismatic Action Community, Abeelweg 238, Box 286.41.71, Rotterdam 3012, T: (010)182908, (05270)4488.
National Service Committee for Catholic Charismatic Renewal in the Netherlands, Tuurkesweg 5, Weert 6006 SG, T: 04956-1979.

NEW ZEALAND

Christian Advance Ministries, P.O. Box 6549, Wellington, T: 46698.
United Maori Mission, 358 Hillsborough Rd, Auckland 4.

NIGERIA

African Reform Group, P.O. Box 5025K, Ikega HO; No. 11, Adebawale Street, Mende-Maryland, Lagos.
Apostles Missions, Inc., No 5, Basorun Road, Idi-Ape P.O. Box 36238 Agodi Post Office, Ibadan 714942, T: 02-710651.
Calvary Ministries, P.O. Box 6001, Jos.
Christ Church Mission, P.O. Box 162 - Uyo, C.R.S..
Continental Ministry of Reconciliation, P.O. Box 117, Enugu, T: 042-770264, O: Telex: (CMOR NIG.).
Good News Inter-Fellowship International, P.O. Box 36 Ajawa, Ogo Oluwa L. G. A. Oyo State.
GOTAV 2000 (Global Outreach to All Villages by 2000 AD), Rural Evangelism Programme, P.O. Box 7662, Ibadan, Oyo State.
Universal Missions, Inc., Eka Nto-Obo - P.M.B. 43, Abak, S.E..
West African Episcopal Church Mission, St. Stephen's Cathedral, 76 Adeniji Adele Road - Lagos.

NORWAY

Mission to the Lapps, Kongensg 14b, 7011 Trondheim, T: 07-52 48 10.
Norwegian Lutheran Inner Mission, Staffeldtsg. 4, Postboks 6830, St Olavs Plass, 0130 Oslo 1, T: 02-11 13 15.
OASE (OASIS), Damtrakka 6, 1300 Sandvika, T: 47-237-88-20, F: 47-238-44-33.
West Coast Inner Mission, C Sundtsgt. 33, 5000 Bergen, T: 05-32 21 90.
Youth With A Mission, 2312 Ottestad (4 andre sentre i norge), T: 065-72 333.

PANAMA

Departamento de Misiones, Apdo 18, Bocas del Toro, T: 59258.
Fondo de Apostolado Arquidiocesano, Apdo 6386, Panamá 5, T: 627400 ext 17.
Junta Americana de Misiones a Israel (JAMI), Entrega General, Panamá 1, T: 228-1640.

PARAGUAY

Friendship Mission, Casilla de Correo 255, Asunción.
La Misión Alemana Entre Los Nativos Del Paraguay, Casilla de Correo 1828, Asunción, T: 21-600-216, F: 21-602-144, O: E-mail: mision-alemana@supernet.com.py.

PERU

ETAE—Entrenamiento Transcultural Alcanzando las Etnias, Apartado 1710, Lima 100, T: 1-349-2648, F: 1-348-7974.
Iglesia Alianza Cristiana y Misionera, Jr. Heros 110, Bellavista, Callao, T: 429-0979.
MEPTAL-Misión Evangélica Peruana Transcultural Para América Lat, Apartado 02, Pucallpa-Ucuyali, T: 064-57-3046.
MEVI-Misión Evangelística Internacional, Manuel Zelaya 449, Urb Pamplona Baja, Lima 29, T: 1-276-7759, F: 1-423-2382.
Segadores, Apartado 1710, Lima 100, T: 1-348-2648, F: 1-348-7974.
Sociedad Misionera Autoctona, Apartado 771, Cuzco, T: 84-27-2143.

PHILIPPINES

DAWN 2000 (Disciple a Whole Nation), P.O. Box 1416, Manila.
Faith Venture in Missions, Tay Tay, Cainta, Rizal, Box 4530, Manila.
Mission Society of the Philippines (FIL Mission), Patria de Cebu, Cebu City.
Partners for World Mission-Philippines, ACPO Box 128 Cubao, 1109 Quezon City.
Philippine Crusades, 41 Cordillera St., Mandaluyong, P.O. Box 1416, Metro Manila.

POLAND

Dominican Missionary Sisters of Jesus and Mary, ul Sienkiewicza 27, 05 220 Zielonka k/Warszawa.
Sisters of the BVM of the Immaculate Conception, woj Rzeszowskie, 23 104 Stara Wies, pt Brzozów.

PORTUGAL

A Missão de Evangelizaçõ Mundial (AMEM), Rua do Caires, 283 4. Esq., Maximinos - 4710 Braga; Apartado 2294-4700 Braga Codex, T: 053-61 05 90.
Associação Evangélica Luso-Africana (AEL-A), Rua Luís Camões, 48-A - 2., 1495 Algées, T: 01-410 43 58.
JOCUM - Jovens Com Uma Missão, Apartado 46 - 2726 Mem Martins Codex.
Liga Evangélica de Acção Missionária e Educacional, Alameda das Linhas de Torres, 122, 1750 Lisboa, T: 01-759 13 39, O: 01-759 00 39.
Missão Antioquia, Rua da Tapadinha, 320, 4630 Rio de Galinhas, T: 055-52 27 82.

ROMANIA

Fides, B-dul 1 Decembrie 1918, Cluj-Napoca 3400, T: 40-989-64021, F: 40-989-62554.
Heartland International Ministries, Str. Rovimari nr 11, Tirgu Mures 4300, T: 40-54-24502.
Societatea Misionara Romana, Strada Romana NR5, Oradea 3700, T: 40-91-15078, F: 40-91-14149.

RUSSIA

Murmansk Christian Mission, g. Murmansk, ul. Kropskoj 22-138.

SINGAPORE

Chinese Christian Mission Ltd., P.O. Box 3999, Robinson Road, Singapore 905999; 153 Bukit Batok Street 11, #03-288, T: 569-7966, F: 569-0346.
Full Gospel Business Men's Fellowship International (Singapore), 2 Finlayson Green, #19-00 Asia Insurance Building, Singapore 049247, T: 223-4529, F: 221-7606.
Singapore Catholic Central Bureau, 225-B Queen St., Singapore 0718, T: 3377489.

SOUTH AFRICA

Afmin-Network, PO Box 594, Kempton Park 1620, 2 Green Ave., Edleen, Kempton Park, T: 011-975-8858, F: 011-975-8819.
Andrew Murray Centre for Prayer, Revival and Missions, 6 Market St., Wellington 7655.
Chinese Catholic Mission, P. O. Box 3303, Port Elizabeth 6056, T: 041-22958.
Christian Gospel Outreach, Suite 177, Net X9307, Pietersburg 0700, T: 0152-291-2496.
Christian Ministry to Miners, PO Box 1888, Rustenburg 0300, 227 Klopper St, Rustenburg, T: 0142-96-1211.
Church of the Province of Southern Africa, CPSA, 4th floor, Khotso House, 62 Marshall St, Marshalltown, 2107, T: (011) 836-7197, F: (011) 836-5782.
Emmanuel Mission, PO Box 1710, East London 5200, 9 Jacob Nanini Place, North End, East London, T: 0431-43-7385, F: 0431-43-5882.
Global Victory Ministries Inc, PO Box 411, Constantia, 7848 Capetown, T: 021-72-7911, F: 021-75-2502.
International Prophetic Ministries, PO Box 2298, Trekker Brakpan 1547, 30 Springs Rd, Sallies, Village, Brakpan, T: 011-743-2446.
Nederduitse Gereformeerde Kerk, Committee for Mission & Evangelism General Synod, PO Box 433, Pretoria 0001, Sinodale Sent, 234 Visagie St, Pretoria, T: 012-322-6588, F: 012-322-3803.
Project Ismael, PO Box 990066, Kibler Park 2053, T: 011-934-4111.
Samaria Mission, PO Box 1687, Potgietersrus 0600, 21 Bonsmara St, Potgietersrus, T: 0154-5741, F: 0154-491-4296.
St. Joseph Children's Home, PO Box 20, Westhoven, 2142, T: (011) 673-5126.
Tshwana Christian Ministries, P/Bag X20, Rosslyn 0200, T: 012-561-1247.

SOUTH KOREA

Association of Perpetual Eucharistic Adoration Societies, 100, Hwaso-dong, Chang-an-gu, Suwon-shi, Kyonggi-do, T: (0331) 44-5001.
Center of Catholic Bible Life Movement, 177-8, Huksok-dong, Tongjak-gu, Seoul-shi, T: (02) 914-3968.
Charismatic Renewal, 1, 2-ga, Myong-dong, Chung-gu, Seoul-shi, T: (02) 777-1538.
National Catholic Charismatic Service Association, 1, 2-ga, Myong-dong, Chung-gu, Seoul-shi, T: (02) 771-2199.
National Council for One Nation Evangelization, 1, 2-ga, Myong-dong, Chung-gu, Seoul-shi, T: (02) 755-1434.
Secretariate of Cursillo Movement, 97-1, Hapchong-dong, Map'o-gu, Seoul-shi, T: (02) 337-8588.

SPAIN

Charismatic Catholics, Almagro 6, 28004 Madrid, T: 91 4990700.
Cristo en Casa, Secretariado Nacional Fe Católica, C Maldonado 1, Madrid 6.
Juventud con una Misión, Apdo. 4042, 41080 Sevilla, T: 490-79-55, F: 490-08-05.
Popular Christian Communities, Plaza de la Hispanidad s/n, 03600 Elda (Alicante).
Youth with a Mission, Apdo 133, 28850 Torrejon do Ardoz, Madrid, T: 91 6764371.

SWEDEN

Alliance for the Service of the Church to Finnish-speaking People in Sweden, Humlegardsgatan 17, S102 40 Stockholm, T: (08)601393.
Eastern Smaland Missionary Society, c/o E Ek-

lund, Bestorp, S-590 54 Sturefors.
Movement of L. L. Laestadius, Hugleiksvägen 6, S-161 54 Bromma.
National Evangelical Association, Tegnérgatan 34, S-113 59 Stockholm.
OAS, P1 110, 440 06 Grabo, T: 0-302-40-844, F: 0-302-415-07.

SWITZERLAND
Association Biblique Catholique (ABC), 17, rte du Jura, 1700 Fribourg, 037/263722.
Basileia Bern, Allmendstr. 7, 3014 Bern, T: 41-31-400430, F: 41-31-401519.
Evangelische Gesellschaft des Kantons Zürich, Augustinerhof 2, CH-8001 Zürich; Brauerstr 60, CH-8004 Zürich.
Evangelische Stadtmission Basel, St. Alban-Ring 176, CH-4000 Basel.
Focolari, Mouvement des, Centre international de rencountre et de formation, 1483 Montet, 037/65 1695.
Freunde der Erweckung, Chalet Ebenezer, Biel.
Inländische Mission (IM)/Missions Intérieures, Zug.
Internationale Vereinigung Christlicher Geschaftsleute, Box 110, CH-8024 Zürich.
Mission Intérieure de l'Eglise Nationale Protestante de Genève, Rue de la Madeleine 10, 2 étage, CH-1204 Genève.
Missionswerk Strassen- und Haus-Mission, H Federer-Str 5, CH-8038 Zürich, T: (051)452059.
Schweizerische Erweckungsgemeinschaft, Viktoriastr 32, Zürich.
Schweizerische Zigeuner-Mission (SZM), Kleiner Adlergarten, CH-8400 Winterthur, T: (052)232279.
Schweizerischer Verband für Innere Mission und Evangelische Liebestätigkeit, Sihlstr 33, Postfach 384, CH-8021 Zürich, T: (051)238899.
Union pour le Réveil, Allées 34, La Chaux-de-Fonds.
Vereinigung für Evangelisation und Erweckung, Zürich.

TAIWAN
Taiwan 2000, Taipei Ling Liang Church, 24 Ho Ping Road, East, Section 2, Taipei, T: 7003427.

THAILAND
Lamp of Thailand, 57/3 Tung Hotel Road, Soi 3/1, PO Box 111, Chiang Mai 50000.

TRINIDAD & TOBAGO
Bible Institute, Catholic Charismatic Centre, Frederick Settlement, Caroni, T: 809-645-2902.

UNITED STATES OF AMERICA (USA)
AD 2000 Together, North American Renewal Service Committee, 5601 NW 72nd St, Suite 242, OKlahoma City, OK 73132, USA, T: 405-728-2277.
Adoremus: The Society for the Renewal of the Sacred Liturgy, O: Web: www.erinet.com/aquinas/arch/adoremus.html.
Advancing Renewal Ministries, 9929 Manchester Road, Suite 258, St. Louis, MO 63122, T: 314-962-6558, F: 314-962-0532.
AIM (Agnesians in Mission), 475 Gllett St, Fond du Lac, WI 54935, T: 414-923-1978, F: 414-923-3194.
Alban Institute, Inc., The, 4550 Montgomery Ave., Ste. 443N, Bethesda, MD 20814-3341, T: 800-486-1318.
Aldersgate Renewal Ministries, P.O. Box 1205, Goodlettsville, TN 37070, T: 615-851-9192, F: 615-851-9372.
ALIVE (A Lay Invitation to a Visitation Experience), 223 W Mountain Rd, Ridgefiled, CT 06877, T: 203-438-5282, F: 203-438-3150.
American Missionary Fellowship, P.O. Box 368, Villanova, PA 19085, T: 610-527-4439, F: 610-527-4720, O: AMFGerhart@aol.com, www.sonic.net/~mfergie/amf.
AmeriTribes, P.O. Box 3717, Flagstaff, AZ 86003-3717, T: 520-526-0875, F: 520-526-0872, O: E-mail: challeng@ameritribes.org, www.primenet.com/ask.
Appalachian Bible Fellowship, P.O. Box ABC, Bradley, WV 25818.
Association Committee of Friends on Indian Affairs, 17012 Hoover Rd., Hagerstown, IN 47346, T: 317-489-4834, F: 317-489-5842.
Associate Missionaries of the Assumption, 227 N. Bowman Ave., Merion, PA 19066, T: 610-664-1284, F: 610-664-7328.
Black Evangelistic Enterprise, 777 South R.L. Thornton Freeway, Suite 115, P.O. Box 4539, Dallas, TX 75208, T: 214-941-3108.
BONA (Benedictine Outreach to the Native Americans), Queen of Peace Monastery, P.O. Box 370, Belcourt, ND 58316, T: 701-477-6167, F: 701-477-5575.
Bureau of Catholic Indian Missions, 2021 H St., Washington, D.C. 20006.
Catholic Charities Volunteer Corps, 286 Marshall Ave, St Paul, MN 55102, T: 612-298-0959.
Catholic Negro-American Mission Board, 2021 H St., N.W., Washington, DC 20005.
Catholic Network of Volunteer Service, 4121 Harewood Rd, NE, Washington, DC 20017, T: 202-529-1100, F: 202-526-1094.
Center for Student Missions (CSM), O: Web: www.gospelcom.net/csm.
Center for the Renewal of the Churches, c/o Northern Baptist Theological Seminary, 660 East Butterfield Road, Lombard (Chicago), IL 60148, T: 708-620-2193.
Charles and Frances Hunter, 201 McClellan Road, Kingwood, TX 77339-2710, T: (713) 358-7575, (800) 683-3024, F: (713) 358-4130.
Chinese Catholic Information Centre, 86 Riverside Dr., New York, NY 10024.
Christian and Missionary Alliance, P.O. Box 35000, Colorado Springs, CO 80935-3500, T: (719) 599-5999.
Christian Appalachian Project, 322 Crab Orchard Rd, Lancaster, KY 40446, T: 606-792-2219, F: 606-792-6625.
Christian Hope Indian Eskimo Fellowship (CHIEF), 1644 E. Campo Bello Dr., Phoenix, AZ 85022, T: 602-482-0828.
Christian Reformed Home Missions, 2850 Kalamazoo Ave., S.E., Grand Rapids, MI 49560, T: 616-241-1691.
Christian Renewal Ministries, Inc., 200 N. Main St., Milltown, NJ 08850, T: 908-828-4545.
Church Resource Ministries, P.O. Box 5189, Fullerton, CA 92635, T: 714-879-5540, O: http://www.crmnet.org/.
Churches Alive International, P.O. Box 3800, San Bernardino, CA 92413, T: 714-886-5361.
Commission for Catholic Missions among the Colored People and the Indians, Black and Indian Mission Office, 2021 H St., N.W., Washington, D.C. 20006.
Continental Baptist Missions, O: http://ourworld.compuserve.com/homepages/cbm/.
Council for American Indian Ministry, 122 Franklin Ave., Minneapolis, MN 55404.
Council for Hispanic Ministries, 705 Northwest 20th, Portland, OR 97209.
Council of Religious Volunteer Agencies (CRVA), 100 Witherspoon St, Louisville, KY 40202, T: 502-569-5286.
Cursillo Movement, National Cursillo Center, P.O. Box 210226, Dallas, TX 75211.
David du Plessis Center for Christian Spirituality, Pasadena, CA 91182.
Dean Clark Revivals, 20520 Plummer St., Chatsworth, CA 91311, T: (818) 341-2951.
Desiring God Ministries, O: Web site: www.desiringgod.org.
Episcopalians United, 30325 Bainbridge Rd., Bldg A, Suite 1, Solon, OH 44139, T: 216-248-7176.
Evangelical Friends Mission, Box 525, Arvada, CO 80001, T: 303-421-8100, F: 303-431-6455.
Fellowship of Friends of African Descent, 1515 Cherry St., Philadelphia, PA 19102, T: 610-874-5860.
Flagstaff Mission to the Navajos, PO Box AA, Flagstaff, AZ 86002, O: http://www.primenet.com/~navajo/.
Forum for Scriptural Christianity, Inc., P.O. Box 150, Wilmore, KY 40390, T: 606-858-4661.
Franciscan Volunteer Ministry, PO Box 29276, Philadelphia, PA 19125, T: 215-427-3070, F: 215-427-3059.
Friendship Crisis Pregnancy Center, Inc., P.O. Box 1491, Morristown, NJ 07962, T: 201-538-0967.
Full Gospel Business Men's Fellowship Intl., P.O. Box 5050, Costa Mesa, CA 92628.
Glenmary Home Missioners, 4119 Glenmary Trace, Fairfield, Ohio; P.O. Box 465618, Cincinnati, OH 45246.
Gospel and Our Culture Network, 86 E. 12th St., Holland, MI 49423.
Greeks for Christ International (Greek Assembly of God), P. O. Box 6536, Oakland, CA 94603, T: 510-536-1033, F: 510-534-6024.
Hispanic Christian Comm. Network, P.O. Box 70070, Los Angeles, CA 90070.
Holy Cross Associates, P.O. Box 668, Notre Dame, IN 46556, T: 219-631-5521, F: 219-631-6813.
Home Missions Baptist General Conference, 2002 S. Arlington Heights Rd., Arlington Heights, IL 60005-4193, T: (800) 323-4215, in IL (708) 228-0200.
Inner City Impact, 2704 W. North Ave, Chicago, IL 60647.
Insight International, P.O. Box 162002, Altamonte Springs, FA 32716, T: (407) 884-6628.
Institute of Native American Studies, P.O. Box 1441, Solvang, CA 93463, T: 805-688-9790.
Inter-Religious Foundation, 475 Riverside Drive, New York, NY 10027.
International Lutheran Renewal Center, 2701 Rice St., St. Paul, MN 55113.
International Pentecostal Holiness Church, World Missions & Evangelism USA, P.O. Box 12609, Oklahoma City, OK 73157-2609.
Iranian Christians International, P.O. Box 25607, Colorado Springs, CO 80936, T: 719-596-0010, F: 719-574-1141, O: ICI@farisnet.com, www.farsinet.com/ici.
Jews for Jesus, 60 Haight St., San Francisco, CA 94102, T: 415-864-2600.
Lay Mission-Helpers Association, 1531 W. Ninth St., Los Angeles, CA 90015, T: 213-388-8101.
Lord's Day Alliance of the United States, 2930 Flowers Rd. S., Ste. 16, Atlanta, GA 30341, T: 770-936-5376, F: 770-454-6081.
Lutheran Volunteer Corp, 1226 Vermont Ave NW, Washington, DC 20005, T: 202-387-3222, F: 202-667-0037.
Lutherans in Jewish Evangelism, 7207 Monetary Dr., Orlando, FL 32809, T: 407-857-5556, F: 407-857-5665.
Messianic Jews, O: www.mjaa.org.
Ministry Renewal Network, 2661 Riva Rd., Suite 1042, Annapolis, MD 21401, T: 410-266-6462.
Mission America, 901 East 78th St., Minneapolis, MN 55420.
Mission to the Americas (MTTA), P.O. Box 828, Wheaton, IL 60189, T: 630-260-3800, F: 630-653-4936.
Missionary Gospel Fellowship (CBAMS), 264 West Main St., Turlock, CA 95380, T: 209-634-8575.
Mountain T.O.P., 2704 12th Ave., South, Nashville, TN 37204, T: 615-298-1575, O: E-mail: ontheM-TOP@aol.com.
Nat'l Cursillo Movement, P.O. Box 210226, Dallas, TX 75211, T: 214-339-6321.
National Service Committee of the Catholic Charismatic Renewal, Inc., Chariscenter USA, P.O. Box 628, Locust Grove, VA 22508-0628, T: 703-972-0225.
Navajo Gospel Mission, P.O. Box 3717, Flagstaff, AZ 86003, T: (602) 526-0875.
Navajoland Area Mission (Episcopal), Box 720, Farmington, NM 87499-0720, T: (505)327-7549, F: (505)327-6904.
North American Renewal Service Committee (NARSC), 5601 NW 72nd St., Suite 242, Oklahoma City, Ok 73132, T: 405-728-2277, F: 405-728-2280.
Old Foundations: a newsletter for Jewish Friends, 20 Jenkins St., Islip, NY 11751.
Open Church Ministries, 1284 Mica Lane, Colorado Springs, CO 80906, T: 719-471-9191.
Our Lady of China Mission, 510 Educonsior Dr., Rockville, MD 20853, T: 301-279-7013.
Outreach Fellowship Inc., Box 69, Dinuba, CA 93618.
Pacific Islander & Asian American Ministries (PAAM), 2055 Makiki St, Honolulu, HI 96822.
Power Ministries, Rt. 3, Box 23, Warrenton, VA 22186, T: (703) 349-0178.
Pro Sanctity Movement, 205 S. Pine Dr., Fullerton, CA 92633.
Race and Reconciliation WWW site, O: www.net-door.com/com/rronline/.
Red Cloud Volunteers, Holy Rosary Mission, Pine Ridge, SD 57770, T: 605-867-5888.
Scott & Kim Anderson Ministries, World Harvest Church, 615 N. Riverview Dr., Kalamazoo, MI 49004, T: (616) 343-5683.
Sharing of Ministries Abroad, P.O. Box 2306, Fairfax, VA 22031, T: (703) 591-1974.
Small Group Network, O: http://smallgroup.com.
Spiritual Life Harvest Center, 5950 S. Platte Canyon Rd., Littleton, CO 80123, T: (800) 888-SLHC.
Spiritual Life Institute of America, Box 219, Crestone, CO 81131.
St Bonaventure Indian Mission & School, Lay Missionary Program, PO Box 610, Thoreau, NM 87323, T: 505-862-7847, F: 505-862-7709.
St. Theresa Chinese Mission, 218 W. Alexander St., Chicago, IL 60616, T: 312-842-6777.
Third-Wave Renewal in the Holy Spirit, 135 North Oakland Ave., Pasadena, CA 91182, T: 818-584-5284.
Transfiguration Church Chinese Catholic Association, 29 Mott St., New York, NY 10013, T: 212-619-0875.
United Church Board for Homeland Ministries, 700 Prospect, Ave, Cleveland, OH 44115, T: (216) 736-3800.
United Indian Missions, Inc, P.O. Box 3600, Flagstaff, AZ 86003.
Voice of the Armenian Church, P.O. Box 333, Waltham, MA 02254.
Wesley Mission, O: Web: www.wesleymission.org.au.
Western Indian Ministries, P.O. Drawer F, Window Rock, AZ 86515, T: 505-371-5749.
Works Ministry, 68 Church St., Montclair, NJ 07042, T: (201) 746-1098.
World Apostolate of Fatima (The Blue Army USA), Mountain View Rd., P.O. Box 976, Washington, NJ 07882.
World Charismatic Renewal Fellowship, 342 West Pearl St., Coldwater, MI 49036, T: (517)278-5244.
World Messianic Fellowships, Inc., P.O. Box 449, Lynbrook, NY 11563, T: 516-593-1724.

URUGUAY
AVANCE-Misión Evangélica Transcultural, Casilla de Correo 48032, C.P. 94000 Florida, T: 352-7019, F: 352-2144, O: E-mail: nuevaman@chasque.apc.org.

VENEZUELA
Iglesia Emmanuel, Apartado 52, San Fernando, Edo. Apure, T: 47-23427, F: 47-23427.
Iglesia Hay Paz con Dios, Apdo. 4750, Maracay 2101-A Araqua, T: 43-417769.
Iglesia Luz del Mundo, Carrera 10 #160, Maturin, Edo Monagas, T: 91-426-186, F: 91-426-186.
Iglesia Manantial de Vida, Apartado 1.109, Puerto Ordaz, Ciudad Guayana, T: 86-522596, F: 86-522568.
Misión Nuevas Tribus de Venezuela, Apartado 6373, Carmelitas, Caracas 1010-A, T: 48-213-217, F: 02-443-4918, O: E-mail: field-committee_ven@ntm.org.

US VIRGIN ISLANDS
Catholic Charismatic Renewal Services, P.O. Box 1160, St. Croix 00851; Charismatic Regional Service Team, Kingshill, St. Croix 00851, T: 809-774-0484.

42
Homosexuality (lesbian, gay & bisexuality)

Christian ministries, organizations, or groups for homosexuals, of homosexuals, or against homosexuality; gay, lesbian, or bi sexual conferences, commissions, committees, or agencies; advocacy or activist groups (those affirming the place of homosexuality or homosexuals in Christianity and the churches, and those opposing homosexuality as sin); ministries that evangelize homosexuals or that seek to help them to chastity or heterosexuality; theological or pastoral reflection on alternative sexuality. For ministry to AIDS sufferers, see MEDICINE AND HEALING.

BRITAIN (UK OF GB & NI)
EnCourage, P.O. Box 3745, London N2 8LW.
Pilot Trust, 116 Shankill Road, Belfast BT12 2BD, T: (08) 0232 230743.
Quest, B.M Box 2585, London, WC1N 3XX, T: 0171-792 0234.

CANADA
Courage, 412 Queen St., E., Toronto, ON M5A 1T3, T: 416-439-3070.
New Directions for Life Ministries of Canada, PO Box 1078, Station F, Toronto, ON M4Y 2T7, T: 416-921-6557, F: 416-921-0052.
Rivers of Grace, 915 - 9 Ave., S.E., Calgary, AB T2G 0S5, T: 403-258-2696, F: 403-264-8465.

UNITED STATES OF AMERICA (USA)
ALERT, 8704 Santa Monica Blvd. 2nd Fl., West Hollywood, CA 90069, T: 310-360-8640, F: 310-360-8680.
Courage: Ministry for Gay and Lesbian Catholics, O: E.mail: CourageCP@aol.com, or www.allencol.edu/pastoral/Courage.html.
Desert Stream, 12488 Venice Blvd., Los Angeles, CA 90066, T: 213-572-0140.
Exodus International, P.O. Box 2121, San Rafael, CA 94912, T: 415-454-1017.
Friends Contact Information, 1216 Arch St., 2-B, Philadelphia, PA 19107, T: 215-561-1700, F: 215-561-0759.
Friends for Lesbian & Gay Concerns, Box 222, Sumneytown, PA 18084, T: 215-234-8424.
Homosexuals Anonymous Fellowship Services, Box 7881, Reading, PA 19603, T: 800-253-3000.
Love in Action, P.O. Box 2655, San Rafael, CA 94912, T: 415-454-0960.
New Life Treatment Center, Inc., 570 Glenneyre Ave., Suite 107, Laguna Beach, CA 92651, T: 714-494-8383.
Outpost, 3044 Chicago Ave., S., P.O. Box 7067, Minneapolis, MN 55407, T: 612-827-1419.
Spatula Ministries, P.O. Box 444, LaHabra, CA 90631, T: 213-691-7369.
UCC Parents of Lesbians/Gays, 3530 Damien Ave., Sp 266, La Verne, CA 91750.
United Church Coalition for Lesbian/Gay Concerns, 18 N. College, Athens, OH 45701.

43
Internet & world wide web ministries

Christian web sites, web site directories, Internet directories, evangelistic sites, devotional sites, news sites, educational sites, liturgical sites; e-mail forums, e-mail newsletters, e-mail list servers, e-mail services; companies, ministries, and organizations helping with the building or maintaining of web sites, or e-mail operations, or offering internet services; major internet networks or hosts. Note that World Wide Web site addresses and e-mail addresses for specific denominations, organizations, institutions, orders, and ministries are listed with those entries wherever they appear in their various topics. See also COMPUTER SERVICES, SOFTWARE, AND RESOURCES.

ARGENTINA
Research on Sects, O: Web: www.civila.com/argentina/fapes/investigacion.html.

AUSTRIA
KathWeb, O: Web: www.kathpress.co.at/kathweb.

BRITAIN (UK OF GB & NI)
Christiannet Scotland, O: E-mail: ChristianNet@ccis.org.uk.
Edinburgh Christian WWW Server, O: www.dcs.ed.ac.uk/misc/local/ecwww/.
International Christian Internet Conference (ICIC), O: Web: http://ecic.ucsm.ac.uk/icic/.
Jesus Army, O: Web: www.jesus.org.uk.
Minerav–History of Ideas Online, O: Web: www.browncat.demon.co.uk/hoi.

CANADA
Anglicans Online!, O: www.anglican.ca/anglican.
Christmas Page: Canada, O: www.kanservu.ca/~fairchild/sermons/christmas-page.html.
Church Online!, R.R. #1, Canning, NS B0P 1H0, T: 902-582-3058.
Cults, Sects and New Religions Bibliography: Part I - to 1983 (32 pages), O: Web: www.acs.ucalgary.ca/!nurelweb/.
Fingertip, Missions on the Internet, O: http://www.netaccess.on.ca/~sma/.
FuturLinque Internet Publishing Services, 3266 Yonge St., Suite 1714, Toronto, ON M5N 3P6, T: 800-446-8894, F: 416-322-4852.
Life & Faith Network, 100 Bell Blvd., Suite 355, Belleville, ON K8P 4Y7, T: 613-962-5776, F: 613-962-5703.
Momentum (Campus Crusade for Christ), Box 300, Vancouver, BC V6C 2X3, T: 604-582-3100, F: 604-588-7582.
Show Me Internet, O: Web: www.interlog.com/~smi/showme/christ.html#seminars.
University of Calgary, Cults, Sects and New Religions, O: Web: www.acs.ucalgary.ca/~nurelweb/.

CHINA
ABCD-A Born Again Christian Doctor, O: www.hkstar.com/~doctor/home/html.
Research Institute of the Humanities, Chinese University of Hong Kong, O: Web: www.arts.cuhk.hk/rel.html.

COSTA RICA
Latin American Socio-Religious Studies Program (PROLADES), O: Web:

www.geocities.com/athens/aegean/4170.

GERMANY

German Christian E-mail Directory, O: www.bibel.com/email/data/germany.htm.
German Devotionals Online, O: http://home.pages.de/~wellen/.

HUNGARY

Pastoral Care Internet in Hungary & in Hungarian, O: www.elender.hu/-sifr/lelkgond.htm.

ITALY

Center for Studies on New Religions (CESNUR), O: Web www.cesnur.org.
Congregación para el Clero, O: Web: www2.chiesacattolica.it/clerus/.
Directorio de Páginas Católicas (DIPAC), O: Web: www.aciprensa.com/dipac/.

MEXICO

Centro de Investigación Religiosa, O: Web: www.angelfire.com/id/cir.
Red de Investigadores de Iglesias, Movimientos y Religiones (REDIMIR), O: Web: www.redimir.org.mx/.

NEW ZEALAND

Mission Internet NZ, P.O. Box 27-548, Mt. Roskill, Auckland, T: 0-9-625-0030, F: 0-9-625-7412.

SOUTH AFRICA

TACIV -Transformal Africa Christian Information Village, PO Box 14343, Verwoerburg 0140, T: 012-664-5513, F: 012-664-3730.

SPAIN

La Piedra Lisa, O: http://web.jet.es/~caza/.

UNITED STATES OF AMERICA (USA)

711 Christian White/Yellow Pages, O: Web: www.711.net.
Alapadre's Catholic Directory, O: Web: www.ws-net.com/~alapadre/index.html.
All in One Christian Website Index, O: Web: www.interlog.com/~mkoehler/allinone/.
Archive of Catholic Documents, O: http://listserv.american.edu/catholic.
Ask the Pastor, O: Web: http://members.aol.com/walts9/askthepastor/home/.
Association for the Development of Religious Information Systems (ADRIS), P.O. Box 210735, Nashville, TN 37221-0735, T: 615-662-5189, F: 615-662-5251.
BibleNet, O: www.isstb.com/biblenet/index.html.
Billy Graham Center's Institute of Evangelism, O: Web: www.christcom.net/iec/.
Catechism of the Catholic Church, O: Web: www.christusrex.org/wwwl/CDHN/ccc.html.
Catholic Calendar Page, O: Web: www.mainelink.net/~easter/calendar/index.html.
Catholic Commentary, O: Web: www.veritas.org.sg/.
Catholic Connect!, P.O. Box 369, Durand, IL 61024, T: 815-248-4407, F: 815-963-2808, O: E-mail: tobserver@aol.com.
Catholic E-mail Directory, O: Web: http://pwa.acusd.edu/~rpgordon/pages/yellow-pages.html.
Catholic Information Center, O: E-mail: Cath.Info.Center@ewtn.com.
Catholic Information Network, O: Web: www.cin.org/cin.
Catholic Information Center on the Internet, O: Web: http://www.catholic.net.
Catholic Online, O: E-mail: 70007.4674@compuserve.com.
Catholic Resource Network, O: E-mail: Sysop@ewtn.com.
Catholic Resources, O: Web: http://wizard.spry.com/cgi-bin/wizard.cgi?search+catholic&hotlist=on.
Catholic Resources on the World Wide Web, O: Web: www.cs.cmu.edu/Web/People/spok/catholic/html.
Catholic Saints Information Page, O: Web: http://web.sau.edu/~cmiller/saints.html.
Catholic Theological Databanks, O: Web: http://www.theol.kfunigraz.ac.at.
Catholicism Page, O: Web: http://web.sau.edu/~cmiller/religion.html.
Charity Website Design, O: Web: www.churchoffice.com.
Christian Classics Ethereal Library, O: http://ccel.wheaton.edu/.
Christian Clipart, O: Web: http://www2.netdoor.com/~timojaak/clipart/clipart.html.
Christian Interactive Network, O: http://www.gocin.com/.
Christian Internet Directory, O: Web: www.bakerbooks.com/ccc/appcmain.html.
Christian Internet Ministries, O: http://www.oz.net/~bconklin/index.html.
Christian Internet Resources, O: Web: http://saturn.colorado.edu:8080/Christian/list.html.
Christian Missions Home Page, O: www.sim.org/.
Christians in Recovery, O: http://www.goshen.net/cir.
ChurchNet, O: www.parklawn.toronto.on.ca/churchnet.htm.
College of Cardinals Online, O: Web: www.er-inet.com/aquinas/arch/cardinals.html.
Comparative Study of Religion at University of Washington, O: Web: weber.u.washington.edu/~madin.
CrossSearch, O: http://www.crosssearch.com.
Crosswords Electronic Magazine, O: Web: www.mtgroup.com/crosswords/.
Cults and New Religious Movements: A Bibliography (54 pages), O: Web: www.clas.ufl.edu/users/gthrusby/rel/nanninga/htm.
Daily Guideposts, O: Web: www.guideposts.org/daily/daily.shtml.
DataRealm Internet Services, O: Web: www.serve.com/pages/non-profit.html.
DeoLira Telecommunications Network (DTN), O: Web: www.dtnhome.com/.
Devotional Web Pages, O: Web: www.nd.edu/~jvanderw/stations.html.
Distinctive Church Collection, O: Web: www.rwf2000.com/church.html.
Easter in Cyberspace: A Christian Perspective, O: http://members.aol.com/REMinistry/devotionals/easter.html.
Ecclesia Web Service, O: Web: www.catholic-church.com.
Ecclesiastical Calendar Calculator, O: Web: http://cssa.standford.edu/~marcos/ec-cal.html.
Ecunet, O: E-mail: helper@ecunet.org, and http://164.109.10.6/~cpforbes/workshop.html.
Facts on Religion, O: Web: www.christusrex.org.
Fatima Homepage, O: Web: www.cais.com/hpacheco/fatima/fatfaq/html.
FingerTip-Missions on the Internet, O: http://www.netaccess.on.ca/fingertip/.
Franciscan Calendar of Saints, O: Web: http://listserv.american.edu/catholic/other/irish.calendar.
Free Catholics Web, O: Web: http://listserv.american.edu/catholic.
FreeTel, 1000 Airport Rd., Destin, FL 32541, O: E-mail: healing@gnt.net.
Galaxy–Religion, O: Web: www.einet.net/galaxy/community/religion.html.
Global Christian Network Chat Page, O: www.gcnhome.com/chat.htm.
Global Online Service Helping Evangelize Nations, O: http://www.goshen.net/.
God on the Internet, O: www.reston.com/kellner/kellner.html.
Gospel Com Net, O: www.gospelcom.net (directory of www addresses of Christian organizations).
Graduate Theological Union (San Francisco, CA), O: Web: www.gtu.edu/library/libraryNRLinks.html.
Guide to Early Church Documents, O: Web: www.iclnet.org/pub/resources/christian-history.html.
Holy Spirit Outpourings E-mail List, O: Web: www.wave.net/upg/sharlow/hsp.html.
In Christ Ministries, O: www.inchrist.inter.net.
In Touch Ministries, O: Web: www.intouch.org.
InterAmerica InterFaith, O: www.milknhoney.co.il/interamerica.
Internet Family Fun: A Parent's Guide to Safe Surfing, O: Web: www.worldvillage.com/familyfun/index.html.
Internet for Christians: An Internet Newsletter, O: www.gospelcom.net/ifc.
King's Info. Highway Ministries, O: http://www.common.net/~jdreedy/kihmenul.html.
Links to Religion Megasites, O: Web: cti.itc.virginia.edu/~kjh8x/soc257/genlinx.html.
MAF Cross Connect, O: http://www.xc.org/.
Mary: Frequently Asked Questions, O: Web: www.udayton.edu/mary/questions.html.
Mike Croghan's Religion Page, O: Web: www.servtech.com/public/mcroghan/re12.html#intro.
Mining Company, The–Society/Culture–Religion, O: Web: www.miningco.org.
Missions Forum, O: http://www.eramp.net/~britt/mission/index.html.
Old Catholic Network, O: Web: www.maths.tcd.ie/hyplan/thomas/oldcath.html.
Omnilist of Christian Links, O: Web: members.aol.com/karthurs/omnmain.htm.
Orthodox Catholic Page, O: Web: www.nikon.ssl.berkeley.edu/~dv/orthodox/orthodox.html.
Ourchurch.com, O: Web: www.ourchurch.com.
Papal Encyclicals, O: Web: www.knight.org/advent/docs.
Patron Saints, O: Web: http://listserv.american.edu/catholic/franciscan/francisc.calendar.html.
Pope John Paul II Page, O: Web: www.zpub.com/un/pope.
Poptel USA, 1839 Fifteenth St., #354, San Francisco, CA 94103, T: 415-255-7827.
Profiles of New Religious Movements, University of Virginia, O: Web: cit.itc.virginia.edu/~jkh8x/soc257/profiles.htm.
Prophecy Central, O: Web: www.Bible-prophecy.com.
Reformed Network, O: Web: www.reformednet.org.
Religious Resources, O: Web: www.aphids.com/relres/.
Religium Religion Index, O: Web: www.teleport.com.
Rosary Homepage, O: Web: www.cs.cmu.edu/Web/People/spok/catholic/rosary.html.
Saint's Biographies, O: Web: http://listserv.american.edu/catholic/other/patron.saints.
SAMUEL (Scripture & Mission—United Church of Christ Electronic Library), O: BORKOD@UCC.ORG.
Search Electric Library–Religion, O: Web: www.elibrary.com.
Sermon Source, O: www2.linknet.net/djp/.
Speed the Need, O: http://www.netnet.net/~dhatch/speed/.
Speed the Need-Cyberfaith, O: http://www.iclnet.org/pub/resources/text/stn/cfaith/cfaith-home.html.
Spiritual Counterfeits Project, O: Web: www.scp-inc.org.
Spirituality for Today, O: Web: www.spirituality.org.
Stations of the Cross, O: Web: http://www.nd.edu/~jvanderw/stations/open.html.
Sword of the Lord Ministries, O: Web: www.post1.com/~sword.
This Week in Biblical Prophecy, O: www.twibp.com/-twibp/.
TradeNet–Religion, O: Web: www.tradenet.it/links/arsocu/religion.html.
Undernet Christian Chatroom, O: www.christian.email.net/chat.html.
University of Florida, Religion Studies, O: Web: www.clas.ufl.edu/users/gthursby/rel/.
University of Washington–Religion, O: Web: weber.u.washington.edu/~madin.
Virtual Religion Index–Rutgers University Religion Dept., O: Web: religion.rutgers.edu.
WEB Evangelism, O: www.brigada.org/today/articles/web-evangelism.html.
Web Pages for Mainline Protestant Denominations, O: Web: http//193.73/243.3/resources.html.
WebWatch E-mail Newsletter, O: Web: www.pe.net/mcj/webwatch.htm.
White Pages, Christian, O: Web: www.cs.odu.edu/~eisen_j/ccn/list.html.
World Council of Churches Directories, O: Web: http://193.73.243.3/oikumene.html.
World Internet Directory–Religion, O: Web: www.tradenet.it:80/links/arsocu/religion.html.
WorldConnect, O: www.familyville.com.

44 Interreligious organizations

Commissions, councils, or organizations not primarily or exclusively Christian but run jointly by all or several major religions including Christianity, i.e. run by Christians and one or more non-Christian religions, for some joint non-missionary, inter-faith activities; including national councils of religious bodies open to Christians and non-Christians alike; interfaith councils, agencies, organizations, and bodies of global, national, or local scope; inter-religious dialogue or study centers or agencies.

ARGENTINA

Argentina Temple of Understanding, c/o CEDIN, Echeverria 2146 1 A, 1428 Buenos Aires, T: 54-1-781-0563, 0726.
Confraternidad Judeo-Cristiana, Florida 681, 7 piso, of 63, Buenos Aires, T: 3929135.
SERPAJ-Argentina, Mexico 479, 1097 Buenos Aires, T: 54-30-7036, O: Also tel: 34-8206.

AUSTRALIA

Australia Fellowship of Reconciliation, P.O. Box 63, O'Connor, A.C.T. 2601, T: 61-62-57-1050.
Australian & New Zealand Unit. Association (International Association for Religious Freedom), 135 Leicester St., Parkside 5063 S.A..
Council of Christians and Jews, 179 Cotham Road, AUS-Kew, Victoria 3101.
World Conference on Religion and Peace/Australia, 5 Barkly Ave., Armadale, Victoria 3143, T: 61-3-412-6213, F: 61-3-412-6205.

AUSTRIA

Aktion gegen den Antisemitismus in Österreich, Bachenbrümgasse 7, Postfach 458, A-1011 Wien, T: 4725662.
Informationszentrum im Dienste der Christliche-Jüdischen Verständigung (IDCIV), Burggasse 37, A-1070 Wien; Bibliothek: Lassingleithnerplatz 3/6, A-1020 Wien, T: 246235.
Internationaler Versohnungsbund Osterreichischer Zweig, Lederergasse 12/III/27, 1080 Wien, T: 43-1-485332.
Koordinierungsausschuss für Christlich-Jüdische Zusammenarbeit, Stephansplatz 6/VI/51, A-1010 Wien, T: 524646.
World Conference on Religion and Peace/Austria, AAI, Turkenstr. 3, A-1090 Wien, T: 43-222-310-5145.

BANGLADESH

Association for Social Development, Md. Nurul Huda Choudhury, Bldg. No. 14, Flat No. 4, Sobhanbag Officers Qtr, Dhaka.
Bangladesh Chapter International Association for Religious Freedom, Dayemi C., Chotto Dayera Sharif, 42/2 Azimpur Road, Dhaka 1203.
Bangladesh Inter-Religious Council for Peace and Justice (BICPAJ), 4/10, Iqbal Road, Dhaka 1207, T: 328707.
Society for Peace and Development, 77, Monipuripara, 1215 Tejgaon, Dhaka.
World Conference on Religion and Peace/Bangladesh, 24 Larmini St., Wari, Dhaka 3, T: 88-02-230-453.

BELGIUM

Bureau de Documentation sur les Relations Judéo-Chrétiennes, Rue Felix Delharse 2, B-1060 Brussel.
MIR-IRG, Maison de la Paiz, 35 Rue van Eleweyck, 1050 Bruxelles, T: 32-2-6485220.
OCJB, Trevierenstraat 18, B-1040 Bruxelles.
Wereldconferentie van de Godsdiensten Voor de Vrede/Belgie, Rue Loui Hap 214, B-1040 Brussels, T: 32-2-734-2096.

BOLIVIA

Bolivia Temple of Understanding, c/o Conferencia Episcopal Bolivia, T: Calle Potosi 814, La Paz, F: 591-2-39-23-26.
SERPAJ-Bolivia, Casilla 5807, La Paz, T: 36-5685, O: Also tel 36-3564.

BRAZIL

Conselho de Fraternidade Cristao-Judaica, Casa 01, 01226 V. Buarque, Rua Martim Francisco, 748-C.01, BR-São Paulo.
ISER, Ladeira da Gloria, 98 Gloria, CEP 2211, Rio de Janeiro, T: 55-21-265-5747.
National Commission for Catholic-Jewish Dialogue, Rua Rio de Janeiro, 182 - Conj. S-2/S-3, 01240 Sao Paulo, T: 55-11-66-2715.
SERPAJ-Brazil, SDS/Edificio Venancio V. 1097, Sala 313, 70300 Brasilia D.F., T: 55-229-7448.
SERPAJ-Latin America, Caixa Postal 2321, 20001 Rio de Janeiro, T: 55-21-229-9697.

BRITAIN (UK OF GB & NI)

Brahma Kumaris World Spiritual University, 65 Pound Lane, London NW10 2HH, T: 81-459-1400.
British Members' Group International Association for Religious Freedom, 21 Clissold Court, Greenway Close, Green Lanes, LondonN4 2EZ.
Centre for the Study of Islam and Christian-Muslim Relations, Selly Oak Colleges, Birmingham B29 6LQ.
Council for the World's Religions, 5 Alexander Godley Close, Ashtead, Surrey KT21 1DF.
Council of Christians and Jews, West End Lane, 1, Dennington Park Road, London NW6 1AX.
Cymdeithas y Cymod yng Nghymru/FOR Wales, 2 Oak Mews, Heol-y-Dderwen, Llangollen LL20 8RP, Clwyd, Wales, T: 44-978-860835.
Fellowship of Reconciliation in England, 40 Harleyford Road, Vauxhall, London SE11 5AY, T: 44-1-582-9052.
Fellowship of Reconciliation in Scotland, 10 Thomson Road, Currie, Midlothian EH14 5GHP.
Inter-Faith Network for the United Kingdom, 5-7, Tavistock Place, London WC1H 9SS, T: 071-388-0008, O: Also tel: 071-387-7968.
International Association for Religious Freedom (IARF), 2 Market St., Oxford, OX1 3EF, T: 44-1865-202-744, F: 44-1865-202-746, O: www.geocities.com/~iarf/.
Manchester College Oxford, Mansfield Road, Oxford OX1 3TD.
Modern Churchpeople's Union, The Recotry, Church Square, Shepperton, Middlesex TW17 9JY.
Multi-Faith Centre, Harborne Hall, Old Church Rd., Birmingham B17 OBD.
Spiritual Unity of Nations Association (SUN), International Pres, Sun House, 49 Portland Rd, Hove, East Sussex.
Standing Conference of Jews, Christians and Muslims in Europe (JCM), British Branch, 17 Chepstow Villas, London W11 3DZ, T: (01)727-3597.
Study Centre for Christian-Jewish Relations, 17 Chepstow Villas, London W11 3DZ, T: (01)727-3597.
Temple of Understanding, U.K. Chapter, 18 Fairlawn Mansions, New Cross Road, London SE14 5PH.
World Congress of Faiths, 28, Powis Gardens, London W11 1JG, T: 01-727-2607.
World Spiritual Council, Monks Horton, Sellindge, Ashford, Kent, T: Sellindge 2138.

CANADA

Alberta Inter-Faith Community Action Committee, 9901-107 St, Edmonton, Alberta T5K 1G4.
Canada Fellowship of Reconciliation, 4536 West 8th Ave., Vancouver, B.C. W6N 3B9, T: 604-261-0351.
Canadian Chapter IARF, 3234 West 21st Ave., Vancouver, BC V6L 1L2.
Canadian Coalition for Ecology, Ethics and Religion, 22 Carriage Bay, Winnipeg MMB R2Y OM5, T: 204-832-1882.
Canadian Council of Christians and Jews, 49 Front St., East, CDN-Toronto, Ontario M5E 1B3.
Canadian Council of Churches, 40 St. Clair Ave., E., Toronto, Ontario M4T 1M9, T: 1-416-921-7478, F: 416-921-7478.
Canadian Ecumenical Action, 2040 West 12th Ave., Vancouver, BC V6J 2G2, T: 604-736-1613, O: Also tel: 604-875-1433.
Multi-Faith Saskatoon, Inc., 533-750 Spadina Crescent East, Saskatoon, Saskatchewan S7K 3H3, T: 306-242-4243.
Multifaith Calendar Canadian Ecumenical Action, c/o Arrowwood Place, Port Moody, BC V3H 4J1, T: 604-469-1164.
Ontario Provincial Interfaith Committee on Chaplaincy, 880 Bay St., 4th Floor, Toronto, Ontario M7A 1E9.
United Church of Canada, The, 85 St. Clair Ave., E., Toronto, Ontario M4T 1M8, T: 416-925-5931, F: 416-925-3394.
World Conference on Religion and Peace/Canada, 73 St. George St., #286, Toronto, Ontario M5S 2E5, T: 416-340-8586, F: 416-971-2029.
World Inter-Faith Education Association (Canada), P.O. Box 7384, Station D, Victoria, BC V9B 5B7, T: 604-360-1259.

CHILE

Confraternidad Judeo-Cristiana de Chile, Casilla 4106, Santiago.
SERPAJ-Chile, Casilla 139, Santiago-3, T: 56-22-56872, O: Also tel: 49-8150.

CHINA

Center for the Progress of People, 48 Princess Margaret Road, Homantin, Kowloon, Hong Kong.

CONGO-ZAIRE

GUR Kinshasa, c/o BP 897 Limete, Kinshasa.

COSTA RICA

Instituto Interamericano de Derechos Humanos, Apartado Postal 10.081, 1000 San Jose, T: 506-34-04-04.

CROATIA

World Conference on Religion and Peace/Croatia, Lonjscina 1a, 41000 Zagreb, T: 38-41-420013, F: 38-41-411622.

CZECH REPUBLIC

Spolecnost Krestanu a Zidu, V CSFR, Saská 3, CR-11800 Praha 1.

DENMARK

Dialog Centre International, Katrinebjergve 46, 8200 Aarhus, N. Denmark, Denmark.

Forsoningsforbundet, Aavendingen 6a, 2700 Bronshoj, T: 45-71-6882.

ECUADOR

SERPAJ-Ecuador, Casilla 3280, Guayaquil, T: 593-20-1536, O: Also tel: 20-1855.

FINLAND

Sovintolitto/Forsoningsforbundet, Laehteenkatu 7-9 G 50, 33500 Tampere, T: 358-931-50802.

FRANCE

Amitié Judéo-Chrétienne, de France, 10 rue de Rocroy, F-75010 Paris.

Conference Mondiale des Religions pour la Paix/Section Francaise, 78 rue d'Assas, 75006 Paris, T: 33-16-45-48-23-017, F: 33-16-45-48-26-34.

Mouvement International de la Reconciliation, MIR, 18, rue Bayard, 38000 Grenoble, T: 33-76-511601.

Partage avec les Enfants du Tiers Monde, 6, rue d'Humieres, Boite Potale no 311, 60203 Compiegne Cedex, T: 33-44-402040, F: 33-44-400034.

Versohnungsbund, Kuhlenstr. 5a-7, 2082 Uetersen, T: 49-4122-3663.

GERMANY

ANISA Interkulturelle Projekte, c/o Jorg Weispfenning, Konigstraße 51, D-4432 Gronau/Wesf., T: 02562-20250.

Deutsche Mitgliedergruppe der International Association of Religious Freedom, c/o IARF Sekretariat, Dreieichstrasse 59, D-6000 Frankfurt 70.

Deutscher Koordinierungsratder Gesellschaften für Christlich-Jüdische Zusammenarbeit, Otto Weiß-Str. 2, 6350-Bad Nauheim.

International Association for Religious Freedom (IARF), Dreieichstrasse 59, 6000 Frankfurt 70, T: 69-62-87-72, F: 69-18-20, O: Also tel 62-16-11.

International Council of Christians and Jews, P.O. Box 11 29, D-64629 Heppenheim; Martin Buber House, D-64629 Heppenheim, T: 49-6252-5041, F: 49-6252-68331.

International Religious Fellowship, Buchenweg 20, 6052 Muhlheim.

Interreligiose Arbeitsstelle (INTR'A), P.O. Box 1201, D-5992 Nachrodt; Am Hardtkopf 17, D-5992 Nachrodt, T: 02352 or 30483, 02371, 023795, 36, 37, 29, F: 02371 or 79557.

International Council of Christians and Jews, Martin Buber House, Werlestrasse 2, Postfach 1129, D-64629 Heppenheim, T: 49-6252-5041, F: 49-6252-68331, O: www.jcrelations.com/icci/.

Standing Conference of European Jews, Christians, and Muslims (JCM), Postfach 1260, D-5413 Bendorf-am-Rhein, T: 02622 3006.

Theologische Studienabteilung, Auguststrasse 80, 1040 Berlin.

World Conference on Religion and Peace, Nollenstr. 50, D-7000 Stuttgart 1, T: 49-711-24-43-81, F: 49-711-262-49-10.

GHANA

Ghana Fellowship Group, P.O. Box 1443, Accra.

GUATEMALA

Confregua, Conferencia de Religiosos de Guatemala, 10a Calle 1-40, Zona 1, Apartado 793, 01901 Guatemala, T: 502-2-25243.

HUNGARY

Magyaroszagi Keresztények, Zsidok Tanacsa, Abonyi u. 21, H-1146 Budapest XIV.

INDIA

Bhai Vir Singh Sahitya Sadan, Bhai Vir Singh Marg, New Delhi 110 001.

Bombay Sarvodaya Friendship Center, 2 Kajupada Pipe Line Road, Kurla W, Bombay, 400072.

Donyi-Polo Mission, P.O. Itanagar, Arunachal Pradesh 791 111.

India Fellowship of Reconciliation, c/o CSI Redeemer Church, Anna Nagar East, 600 102, Madras.

International Association for Religious Freedom, India Steering Committee, Ladthalaboh, P.O. Jowai 793 150.

New Delhi Chapter, The Organization for Universal Communal Harmony (TOUCH), c/o 4A, Mathura Road, Jangpura 'A', New Delhi, 110 014.

Sarva Dharma Nilaya, Delhi Orthodox Centre, 2 Tughlakabad Institution Area, New Delhi 110062, T: 011-643-6417, O: Also tel: 641-3527.

Temple of Understanding India Chapter, 3, Nyaya Marg, Chanakyapuri, New Delhi 110021.

United of Man, 361 Mall Road, Amritsar.

World Conference of Religion for Peace/India, C-191 Defence Colony, New Delhi 110-024, T: 91-11-22-15654, F: 91-11-22-43087.

World Fellowship of Inter-Religious Councils, c/o CBCI Centre, Ashok Place, New Delhi 110001, T: 344470, O: Also tel: 344453.

World Fellowship of Religions, c-599, Chetna Marg, New Delhi.

INDONESIA

Indonesian Committee on Religion and Peace, Jalan Sukabumi 11, Jakarta Pusat 10310, T: 62-21-384-7696, F: 62-21-321-582.

IRELAND

Fellowship of Reconciliation in Ireland, 224 Lisburn Road, Belfast BT9 2GE.

Irish Council of Christians and Jews, Herzog House, 3 Zion Road, Dublin 6.

Peace People, Fredheim, 224 Lisburn Road, Belfast BT9 6GE, T: 44-232-663465.

World Conference on Religion and Peace/UK-Ireland, c/o The Vicarage, 93 Pelham Rd., Barnehurst, Bexleyheath DA7 4LY, T: 44-322-523-344, F: 44-322-557-384.

ISRAEL

Clergy for Peace, P.O. Box 8343, 91083 Jerusalem, T: 972-2-710-892.

Ecumenical Theological Research Fraternity, P.O. Box 249, 91002 Jerusalem.

Interreligious Coordinating Council in Israel, P.O. Box 7855, Jerusalem, T: 02-669865, F: 02-666675.

Israel Interfaith Association, 14 Radak Street, P.O. Box 7739, Jerusalem 91077, T: (02)635212

Palestinians and Israelis for Nonviolence, Fellowship and Peace, P.O. Box 8343, Jerusalem.

ITALY

Amicizia Ebraico-Cristiana di Firenze, CP 282, I-50100 Firenze.

Associazione Amicizia Ebraico-Cristiana di Roma, Via Ulpiano 29, I-00193, T: (06) 343267.

Federazione delle Amizicie Ebraico-Cristiane in Italia, vai A. Gramsci 7, I-00197 Roma.

Movimento Internationale della Riconciliazione, MIR, via Pavaglione 65, 35030 Galzignano (PD).

Pontifical Council for Interreligious Dialogue, 001200 Citta del Vaticano, T: 39-6-698-4321, F: 39-6-698-4494.

Sezione Italiana Della Conferenza Mondiale Delle Religioni Per la Pace, Via Acciaioli 7, I-00186 Rome, T: 39-6-630-434.

JAPAN

Asian Conference on Religion and Peace, Wada 2-6-1, Suginami-ku, Tokyo T166, T: 81-3-383-7944, F: 81-3-383-7993.

Japan Chapter International Association for Religious Freedom, c/o Japan Yoga Association, I-31-8-607 Takadanobaba Shinju, Tokyo 160.

Japan Free Religious Association, 400 Oaza Shimoochiai, Yono-shi, Saitama-ku.

Japan Religions League, c/o Nishihongan-ji Betsuin, 3-15-1 Tsukiji, Chuo-ku, Tokyo 104.

Japan Temple of Understanding, 16-1 Kishinoue, Nakayada, Kameoka-shi, Kyoto-Fu 621, T: 08812-2-0410.

Japanese Committee of the World Conference on Religion and Peace, WCRP Fumon Hall, 2-6-1 Wada, Suginami-ku, Tokyo 166, T: 81-3-33-84-2337, F: 81-3-33-83-7993.

Nihon Yuwa Kai/FOR Japan, Schinkohjimachi 854-10, Machida, Tokyo 194-01, T: 81-427-35-7921.

Organization for Industrial, Spiritual and Cultural Advancement International (OISCA), 105-1 Yochomachi, Shinjuku-ku, Tokyo, T: 3598555.

Rissho Kosei-kai, 2-11-1 Wada, Suginami-ku, Tokyo 166.

World Conference on Religion and Peace, Japan Committee, Sec, 2-7 Motoyoyogi-machi, Shibuya-ku, Tokyo 151.

KENYA

World Conference on Religion and Peace/Kenya, P.O. Box 24668, Nairobi, T: 25-42-229-104, F: 25-42-332-711.

World Conference on Religion and Peace/Africa, P.O. Box 45009, Nairobi; c/o National Christian Council of Kenya, T: 254-2-338-211, F: 254-2-330-170.

LEBANON

Christian-Muslim Dialogue Group, Ibn Roshd-Zaidania, Bayrut.

LUXEMBOURG

Association Interconfessionnelle du Luxembourg, c/o Rue Jules Wilhelm 1, Luxembourg, T: 431619.

Comité Interconfessionel Luxembourgeois, 32 bld. de la Fraternité, 1541.

MAURITIUS

Inter-Religious Committee of Mauritius, c/o Evêché, Rue Mgr Gonin, Port Louis, T: 23068.

Interfaith Forum, 23, Boundary Road, Rose-Hill, T: 4643247.

Solidarité Fraternelle Mondiale, 20 Rue Pope Hennessy, BP 278, Port-Louis, T: 43420, 23318.

MEXICO

SERPAJ-Mexico, Apartado 66, Los Reyes, La Paz, Estados de Mexico, 56400, T: 52-587-0534.

NAMIBIA

Namibia International Fellowship of Reconciliation, Box 33, 9000Grootfontein.

NEPAL

Religion and Peace Academy/Nepal, G.P.O. Box 2685, Kathmandu, T: 977-1-226-743, F: 977-1-226-702.

NETHERLANDS

Cent. Comm. v. het Vrijz. Protestantisme, Nieuwe Gracht 27, NL-3512 LC Utrecht.

Doopsgezinde Vredesgroep, Singel 450-454, 1017 AV Amsterdam.

International Fellowship of Reconciliation, Spoorstraat 38, 1815 BK Alkmaar, T: 31-72-12-30-14, F: 31-72-12-30-14.

Kerk en Vrede, Utrechtseweg 159, 3818 ED Amersfoort, T: 31-33-610445.

Nederlandse Ledengroep International Association for Religious Freedom, Gele Brem 31, NL-3068 TJ Rotterdam.

Overlegorgaan van Joden en Christenen in Nederland, OJEC, Keizersgracht 104 B, NL-Amsterdam 1015 CV.

Remonstrantse Broederschap, CoZa, Nieuwe Gracht 27, NL-3512 LC Utrecht.

Vrijzinnige Geloofsgemeenschap NPB, Algemeen Secretaris, 'Thorbeckehuis', Thorbechegracht 11, NL-8011 VL Zwolle.

Wereldconferentie van Reigies voor Vrede, Helmkruidstraat 35, NL-6602CZ Wijchen, T: 31-20-625-8294, F: 31-20-622-4825.

World Congress of Faiths, Interreligio, Boerhavelaan 99 B I, NL-3112 LE Schiedam.

NEW ZEALAND

Auckland Council of Christians and Jews, 6d 'The Pines Epsom', 75 Owens Road, Auckland 3.

Mission Internet NZ, P.O. Box 27-548, Mt. Roskill, Auckland, T: 0-9-625-0030, F: 0-9-625-7412.

World Conference on Religion and Peace/Aotearoa New Zealand, 161 Seaton Heights Road, Wellington 6003, T: 64-4-495-7316.

NICARAGUA

SERPAJ-Nicaragua, Apartado 3373, J. Arce Navisco Crist., 2 Cuadras al Sur, Barrio Santa Rosa, Managua, T: 25-174, O: Also tel: 22-544.

NIGERIA

Akwa Kbom Group, P.O. Box 269, Abak L. G. Area, Cross River State.

Society for the Promotion of Peace in Nigeria, P.O. Box 140, Nworieubi, Mbaitoli, Imo State.

NORTH KOREA

World Conference on Religion and Peace, Otandong, Central District, Pyongyang.

NORWAY

Kristent Fredslag, Uranienborg Terrasse 8, 0351 Oslo 3, T: 47-2-468344.

PAKISTAN

Karachi Chapter, The Organization for Universal Communal Harmony (TOUCH), c/o Block 68, GF2, Seaview Township, Karachi, T: 538-276.

World Conference on Religion and Peace/Pakistan, 240 Garden East, Kashanai Hafiz, Karachi 74550, T: 92-21-721-1426, F: 92-21-466-878.

PANAMA

SERPAJ-Panama, Apartado 861, Panama 1, T: 507-22-8180.

PERU

SERPAJ-Peru, Apartado 5602, Lima 100, T: 51-27-7303.

PHILIPPINES

AKKAPKA, c/o La Ignaciana Apostolic Center, 2215 Pedro Gil St., Santa Ana, Manila, 1009.

Philippine Chapter International Association for Religious Freedom, San Felipe, Zambales.

Silliman University, Extension Dept., Negros Oriental, Dumaguete 6501.

World Conference on Religion and Peace/Philippines, Lot 2, Block 8, Maharik Vill., Taguig, Metro Manila.

POLAND

Polska Rada Chrzescijan i Zydow, Prof. Dr. Waldemar Chrostowski, ul. Dickensa 5, 02107 Warszawa.

RUSSIA

Logos Society of Christian Culture and Education, pr Wernadskogo, d.97, kor.1, kw.8, 117526 Moscow.

RWANDA

Groupe Islamo-Chrétien, c/o Université Nationale, Butare.

SINGAPORE

Inter-Religious Organization, 5001 Beach Road, 07-24 Golden Mile Complex, 0719 Singapore, T: 65-292-2510, F: 65-293-1105.

SOUTH AFRICA

South Africa Fellowship of Reconciliation, Box 2861, Durban 4000, T: 27-31-3015663, F: 27-31-4032823.

World Conference on Religion and Peace/South Africa, 08 Piet Meyer St., Mindalore, Krugersdorp 1740, T: 27-11-762-2938, F: 27-12-429-2925.

SOUTH KOREA

Korea Fellowship of Reconciliation, c/o Seoul Friends Meeting, 2-87 Shinchon-dong, Seodaemoon-Ku, Seoul.

Won Buddhist Committee for the United Religious Movement, 344-2 Sin-yong-dong, Irl-si, Chonbuk, T: 653-50-3271, F: 653-50-3270.

World Conference on Religion and Peace/South Korea, Academy House, Tobong P.O. Box 37, 132-600 Seoul, T: 82-2-900-3944, F: 82-2-907-9089.

SPAIN

Amistad Judeo-Cristiana, Residencia de Nuestra Señora de Sion, Calle Hilarion Eslava 50, Madrid 15.

Centro de Estudios, Judeo-Cristianos, Hilarion Eslave 50, E-28015 Madrid.

Communidad del Arca, 39697 Soto Iruz, Cantabria.

SRI LANKA

Communication for Peace and Reconciliation (COMPAR), 61, Issipathana Mawatha, Colombo 5, T: 585186, O: Also tel: 581514.

Congress of Religions, 118 Rosmead Place, Colombo 7.

Interfaith Fellowship for Peace and Development, 76, Thimbirigasyaya, Weliamuna Rd., Hendala, Wattala.

National Conference on Religion and Peace (WCRP/Sri Lanka), c/o Marga Institute, 61 Isipathana Mawatha, Colombo 5, T: 94-1-585-186, F: 94-1-580-585.

SWEDEN

Samarbetsradet för Judar och Kristna, Gamla Uppsalagatan 37, 753 34 Uppsala.

Sweden Fellowship of Reconciliation, Gotgatan 3, 752 22 Uppsala, T: 46-18-127505, F: 46-18-150042.

SWITZERLAND

Christlich-Jüdische Arbeitsgemeinschaft in der Schweiz (CJA), Amselstr 25, CH-4000 Basel, T: (061)344234.

Christlich-Jüdische, Arbeitsgemeinschaft in der Schweiz, Hirzenstraße 10, CH-4125 Riehen.

Mouvement International de la Reconciliation, MIR, Secretariat Romand, College 9, 1400 Yverdon, T: 41-24-211595.

Office on Interreligious Relations, The World Council of Churches, P.O. Box 2100, Ch-1211 Geneva 2; 150 route de Ferney, Geneva 2, T: 22-791-61-11, F: 22-791-03-61.

Project for Joint Standing Committee of Christians and the World Muslim Congress, c/o World Council of Churches, 150 route de Ferney, P.O. Box 66, 1211 Geneva.

Schweizer Versohnungsbund, Kreuzbleichestrasse 7, 9000 St. Gallen, T: 41-71-282657.

Schweizer, Verein fur Freies Christentum, Bellerivestr. 59, Ch-8008 Zurich.

World Assembly for Moral Re-armament (MRA), Mountain House, CH-1824 Caux; Winkerlriedstr 14, CH-6000 Luzern, T: 614241.

World Conference on Religion and Peace, Intl., Chemin Auguste-Vilbert 14, 1218 Grand Saconnex, Genève, T: 31-22-985-162, F: 41-22-791-0034.

TAIWAN

Fo Kuang Shan Temple, The Comm. of Religious Affairs, Ta Shu, Kaohsiung 84010.

Office of Ecumenical and Inter-religious Affairs (FABC), P.O. Box 7-91, Taipei.

TANZANIA

Tanzania Fellowship of Reconciliation, P.O. Box 70193, Dar-Es-Salaam.

THAILAND

ACFOD, GPO BOX 2930, Bangkok 10501, T: 66-2-236-7783.

World/Asian Conference on Religion and Peace/Thailand Chapter, 40/4 Village No. 1, Bangkrang, Nonthanburi 11000, T: 66-2-465-4443, F: 66-2-428-1943.

TRINIDAD & TOBAGO

Inter-Religious Organization of Trinidad and Tobago (IRO), Archbishop's House, 27 Maraval Rd, Port-of-Spain, T: 21103.

UGANDA

Uganda Fellowship of Reconciliation, P.O. Box 14123, Kampala.

UNITED STATES OF AMERICA (USA)

AIDS National Interfaith Network, 110 Maryland Ave., N.E., Washington, D.C. 20002, T: 202-546-0807, F: 202-546-5103.

Association of Religious Communities, 213 Main St., Danbury, CT 06810, T: 203-792-9450.

Center for Muslim-Christian Understanding, E. A. Walsh School of Foreign Service, Georgetown University, 37 & O Streets, N.W., Washington, D.C. 20057.

Chicago Chapter, The Organization for Universal Communal Harmony (TOUCH), c/o 2620 West Pratt Blvd., Chicago, IL 60645, T: 312-274-4134.

Council for a Parliament of the World's Religions, P.O. Box 1630, Chicago, IL 60690, T: 312-629-2990, F: 312-629-2991.

Council of Churches and Synagogues, The, 628 Main St., Stamford, CT 06901, T: 203-348-2800.

CrossSearch: Online Forums, O: Web: www.crosssearch.com/Online_Forums/.

Dutchess Interfaith Council, 9 Vassar St., Poughkeepsie, NY 12601, T: 914-471-7333.

Faith Organizations in Covenant for Understanding and Service (FOCUS), P.O. Box 22397, Nashville, TN 37202-2397, T: 615-256-3639, F: 615-255-3077.

Fellowship in Prayer, 291 Witherspoon St., Princeton, NJ 08542, T: 609-924-6863, F: 609-924-6910.

Global Cooperative Focus, 414 North K St., Apt. 7, Tacoma, WA 98403.

Graymoor Ecumenical & Interreligious Institute, 475 Riverside Dr., Room 1960, New York, NY 10115-1999, T: 212-870-2330, F: 212-870-2001.

Institute for Dialogue among Religious Traditions, Boston Univ., School of Theology, Suite 110, 745 Commonwealth Ave., Boston, MA 02215, T: 617-353-3050, F: 617-353-3061.

Institute for World Spirituality, P.O. Box 91611, Santa Barbara, CA 93190-1611.

Inter-Religious Federation for World Peace, 4 West 43rd St., New York, NY 10036, T: 212-869-6023, F: 212-869-6424, O: www.ifwp.org.

Interfaith Conference of Metropolitan Washington, D.C., 1419 V Street, N.W., Washington, D.C. 20009, T: 202-234-6300, F: 202-234-6303.

Interfaith IMPACT for Justice and Peace, 110 Maryland Ave., N.E., Suite 509, Washington, D.C. 20002, T: 202-543-2800, F: 202-547-8107.

International Religious Foundation, 4 West 43rd St., New York, NY 10036, T: 212-869-6023, F: 212-869-6424.

Listen (Interfaith Ministry), 6620 Arlesworth, Lincoln, NE 68505.

Monastic Interreligious Dialogue, 104 Chapel Lane, St. Joseph, MN 56374-0277, T: 612-363-5084, F: 612-363-5203.

National Conference of Christians and Jews, 71 Fifth Ave., Suite 1100, New York, NY 10003, T: 212-206-0006.

National Council of Churches of Christ in the USA Office on Interfaith Relations, 475 Riverside Dr., New York, NY 10115, T: 212-870-2560.

New York, The Organization for Universal Communal Harmony (TOUCH), c/o 243 Palisade Ave., Dobbs Ferry, NY 10522, T: 914-693-4219.

Pacific Interfaith Network, 2340 Durant Ave., Berkeley, CA 94709, T: 510-540-0150.

Religion in American Life, 2 Queenston Place, Rm. 200, Princeton, NJ 08540, T: 609-921-3639, F: 609-921-0551.

Society for Interreligious Intercultural Dialogue (SIID), 218 Martroy Lane, Wallingford, PA 19086-

6314, T: 215-566-1033.
Temple of Understanding, 1047 Amsterdam Ave., New York, NY 10025, T: 212-865-9117, O: Also tel: 353-0001.
United Religions Initiative, P.O. Box 29242, San Francisco, CA 94129, O: www.united-religions.org.
Universal Third Order, 1029 Pomfret Rd., Hampton, CT 06247, T: 203-455-9143.
Washington, D.C., The Organization for Universal Communal Harmony (TOUCH), c/o 10029 Mosby Woods Dr., #326, Fairfax, VA 22030, T: 703-273-5879.
World Conference on Religion and Peace, 777 United Nations Plaza, New York, NY 10017, T: 212-687-2163, F: 212-983-0566.
World Conference on Religion and Peace/Youth, P.O. Box 2159, Cambridge, MA 02238, T: 617-489-4012, F: 617-489-4012.
World Faiths Center for Religious Experience and Study (CRES), P.O. Box 4165, Overland Park, KS 66204, T: 913-649-5114.

URUGUAY
Confraternidad Judeo-Cristiana del Uruguay, Av. 8 de Octubré 3324, Montevideo.
SERPAJ-Uruguay, Joaquin Requena 1642, Montevideo, T: 598-45-701.

VENEZUELA
Comite de Relaciones entre Iglesias y Sinagogas, Establecidas en Venezuela C.R.I.S.E.V., Apartado 5506 Caracas 1010A.

ZAMBIA
Zambia Fellowship of Reconciliation, King George Memorial, P.O. Box 81521, Kabwe.

ZIMBABWE
People-to-People Congress of Zimbabwe, c/o Dept of Theology, P.O. Box MP 167, Mount Pleasant, Salisbury; Affiliated to World Congress of Faiths founded in 1936.
Zimbabwe Fellowship of Reconciliation, P.O. Box 4979, Harare, T: 263-56608.

45 Journalism, the press, & information

The religious press, newspapers, news periodicals, radio and TV religious news offices, news services, religion editors or religion departments of news media outlets; press agencies of major denominations or organizations, church or denominational or Christian information agencies and centers; religious press services, agencies publishing news bulletins, church publicity or public relations centers, church advertising; photographic libraries, agencies and services; journalism training centers, schools of journalism.

AMERICAN SAMOA
Catholic Communications Media Relations Office, P.O. Box 596, Pago Pago, AS 96799, T: 684-699-1923, F: 684-699-1459.

ARGENTINA
Agencia Informative Católica Argentian (AICA), Rodréguez Peña 846, Buenos Aires, T: Central 2886.
Escuela de Periodismo y Ciencias de la Información, Facultad Católica de Humanidades, Maipú 1369, Rosario, Santa Fe.

AUSTRALIA
Anglican Media Council, P.O. Box Q190, QVB Post Office, Sydney, NSW 2000, T: 61-2-265-1507, F: 61-2-261-2864.
National Catholic Press Association Standard Publishing Company, Box 393 D, Hobart, Tasmania.
Worldwide Photos Ltd., O: E-mail: rigmedia@ozemail.com.au.

AUSTRIA
Katholische Presse-Agentur (Kathpress), Singerstrasse 7/6/2, 1010 Vienna 1.
Verband Katholischer Publizisten Österreichs, Wollzeile 2, Wien 1.

BELGIUM
Association des Journalistes Catholiques de Belgique, Blvd de Smet de Naeyer 613, B-1020 Brussel.
Centre d'Information de Presse (CIP), 38 Av des Arts, Brussel, T: 100636, 119243.
Centre d'Information et d'Education Populaire, Rue de la Loi 121, B-1040 Brussel, T: (02)735-6050.
Institut Robert Schuman, Institut de Journalisme, European Media Studies, 32, rue de l'Association, 1000 Bruxelles, T: 32-2-217-23-55, F: 32-2-219 57 64.
Union des Journaux Catholiques de Belgique, Av des Arts 38, B-1000 Brussel.

BOLIVIA
Agencia de Noticias Fides (ANF), CP 5782, La Paz, T: 24422.
Latin American Meetings, Casilla 11083, La Paz, Bolivia.
Secciėn Periodismo, Escuela Normal Católica, Cochabamba.

BRAZIL
Centro Ecumênico de Informações (CEI), Av Princesa Isabel 323/1012, Copacabana, Rio de Janeiro, GB, T: 2367088.
Centro Informativo Católico (CIC), CP 23, Petropólis, RJ.
Curso de Jornalismo, Universidade Católica de Pernambuco, Rua do Principe 526, Recife, Pernambuco.
Departmento de Jornalismo, Pontificia Universidade Católica, Rua Marquês de São Vicente 209/223, Rio de Janerio, ZC-20, GB.
Missionary Information Bureau (MIB), C.P. 1498, 01 000 São Paulo, SP.

BRITAIN (UK OF GB & NI)
Catholic Information Office for England and Wales (CIOEW), Avante House, 9 Bridge St, Pinner, Middx; 14 Howick Place, London SW1, T: (01)866-2278, (01)834-8700.
Catholic Media Office, 39 Eccleston Square, London SW1V 1PD, T: 0171-828 8709, F: 0171-931 7678.
Catholic Media Trust, Catholic Comm. Centre, 39 Eccleston Square, London SW1V 1PD, T: 0171-233 8196.
Catholic Press Office, 86 St. Vincent St, Glasgow C2, Scotland, T: (041)221-7600.
Catholic Writers' Guild (The Keys), 60 Julian Ave, London, W3 9JF, T: 0181-248 6328, F: 0181-723 2910.
Christian Intelligence Service, Evangelical Alliance, 19 Draycott Place, London SW3 2SJ, T: (01)584-9333/4.
Christian Publicity Organization, Ivy Arch Rd., Worthing, West Sussex BN14 8BU, T: 30852.
Christian Weekly Newspapers (CWN), 146 Queen Victoria St, London EC4V 4BX, T: (01)248-4751.
Church News Service, 11 Ludgate Square, London EC4, T: (01)248-2872.
DAWN Friday Fax, O: Web: www.jesus.org.uk/dawn.
Keston News Service (British news agency for Eastern Europe), F: 44689-5-3662.
Methodist Press and Information Service, 1 Central Bldgs, Westminster, London SW1, T: (01)930-1751.
Overseas Christian Communication Centre, Denholm House, Nutfield, near Redhill, Surrey.
Overseas Information Service, Graduates' Fellowship, 39 Bedford Square, London WC1B 3EY, T: (01)636-5113.
Sociology of Religion in Britain Information Service, Department of Sociology, University of York, York, T: 59861.
World Assc for Christian Communication (WACC), 357 Kennington Ln, London SE11 5QY, T: 44-71-582-939, F: 44-71-735-0340.

CAMEROON
Serv. des Informations Cath. Conférence Episcopale Nationale, B.P. 185 ou 807, Yaoundé, T: 237-22-31 14 62, F: 237-22-31 29 77.

CANADA
Association Canadienne des Périodiques Catholiques (ACPC), 5875 Est Rue Sherbrooke, Montréal, Québec.
Christian Info. News, #200 - 20316 56th Ave., Langley, BC V3A 3Y7, T: 604-534-1444.
International Free Press Agency in Canada, The, P.O. Box 359, Mansonville, QC J0E 1X0.
Office of Public Information Canadian, Conference of Catholic Bishops (CCCB), 90 Parent Ave., Ottawa, Ontario K1N 7B1, T: 613-236-9461, O: Telex: 21-053-3311.
Salvation Army Editorial Dept., 2 Overlea Blvd., Toronto, ON M4H 1P4, T: 416-425-2111.

CHILE
Agencia informativa y de comunicaciones (AIC Chile), Brasil 94, Santiago.
Escuela de Periodismo, Universidad Católica de Chile, Calle San Isidro 560, Casilla 114-D, Santiago, T: 383018, 31913.

CHINA
Catholic Centre Press Bureau, PO Box 2964, Hong Kong.
China News Analysis, Wise Mansion, 52 Robinson Rd, PO Box 13225, Hong Kong.
UCA-News, P.O. Box 69626, Kwun Tong.

CONGO-ZAIRE
Agence de Presse DIA (Documentation et Information Africaine), BP 2598, Kinshasa, T: 3805.

CROATIA
Christian Information Service, Marulicev 14, PP 434, 410001 Zagreb.
Comité Episcopal de la Presse Catholique, Nadbiskupski Ordinarijat, 51000 Rijeka, T: 38-51-37-999.

FINLAND
Catholic Information Centre, PL 133, SF-00141 Helsinki 14, T: 358-0-650751, F: 358-0-650715, O: Telex: 57-19101415 VDX SF.
Information Centre of the Church of Finland, Mannerheimintie 18A, Helsinki 10.

FRANCE
Agence Française d'Articles et de Reportages (AFAR), 153 Rue de Granelle, F-75007 Paris, T: 705-9875.
Association Française des Journalistes Catholiques, 14 Rue St Benoît, F-75006 Paris, T: 548-6916.
Bureau d'Information Missionnaire (BIM), 5 rue Monsieur, F-75007 Paris, T: (01)783-6795.
Bureau d'Information Protestant (BIP), 47 rue de Clichy, F-75009 Paris, T: 744-7126.
Centrale Technique d'Information Catholique (CTIC), 31 rue Croulebarbe, F-75013 Paris, T: 535-8860.
International Catholic Press Union (ICPU), 43 Rue St Augustin, F-75002 Paris, T: (01)742-9216.
International Federation of Directors of Catholic Publications, 22 Cours Albert I, F-75008 Paris, T: (01)359-9111.
International Federation of Catholic Journalists, 43 Rue St. Augustin, F-75002, Paris, T: (01)742-9216.
International Federation of Catholic Dailies & Periodicals, 43 Rue St Augustin, F-75002 Paris, T: 742-9216.
Oeuvre d'Orient, 20 Rue du Regard, F-75006 Paris.
Office Catholique d'Information sur les Problèmes Européens (OCIPE), 6 Rue Wencker, Strasbourg, T: 366325.

GERMANY
Altkatholischer Internationaler Informationsdienst (AKID), Vater-Jahn-Str 11, D-4150 Krefeld, T: (02151)61941.
Evangelischer Pressedienst, Zentralredaktion, Friedrichstr 34, D-6 Frankfurt am Main.
Evangelischer Presseverband für Deutschland, Haus der Ev Publizistik, Friedrichstr 34, D-6 Frankfurt am Main.
Gemeinschaftswerk der Ev Presse, Haus der Ev Publizistik, Friedrichstr 34, D-6 Frankfurt am Main.
Gesellschaft Katholischer Publizisten Deutschlands, Breitestr 110, D-Köln.
Institut zur Forderung Publizistischen Nachwuchses, Koniginstr 29, D-8000 München 2, T: 285811.
Katholische Nachrichten Agentur (KNA), Pressebild, Eyssenneckstr 25, D-6 Frankfurt am Main, T: 551252.
Kommission für Publizistik der Deutschen Bischofskonferenz, Beringstr 30, D-53 Bonn.

GHANA
Guild of Catholic Journalists, c/o DEPSOCOM, P.O. Box 9712, Airport Accra, T: 233-21-776-491, F: 233-21-772 753, O: Telex: 94-2587 SECAM GH or 2471 NCS.

GREECE
Agence TYPOS, Rue Acharnon 246, Athens 815.
Typos-Bonne Presse, Agence Catholique d'Information, 246 Rue Acharnon, Athinai 815, T: 626091, 878363.

HOLY SEE
Photo-TV-Radio-Film Service, Palazzo San Carlo, 00120 Vatican City, T: 39-6-69-88-3197, F: 39-6-69 88 5373, O: Telex: 504-PCCS VA.

HUNGARY
Magyar Kurir, Milkszath ter 1, 1088, Budapest.
Press Department, Reformed Church in Hungary, Synodal Office, Abonyi u 21, Budapest XIV.

ICELAND
Centre for Information and Ecumenism, Stigahlio 63, Reykjavik, T: 9184740.

INDIA
Catholic Charismatic Information Centre (CCIC), St. Mary's High School (ISC), Nesbit Rd, Mazagon, Bombay 400 010, T: 378294.
Catholic Information Centre, P.O. Box 1588, Secunderabad 3, AP.
Catholic News Services of India (CNI), 4 Raj Niwas Marg, Delhi 6.
Christian Information Centre, Thoburn Methodist Church, 151 Dharamtalla St, Calcutta 13, Bengal.
Hornuman College of Journalism, Matunga, P. O. Box 6606, Bombay, Maharashtra 400019.
Indian Catholic Press Association, 4 Ludlow Castle Rd, Delhi 6.
South Asian Religious News (SAR-News), PB 6236, Mazagaon, Bombay 400 010.
Union of Catholic Asian News (UCAN), India, 74 Shanti Vihar, Delhi 110092.

INDONESIA
Agence Pax, Jalan Kramat Raya 134, Jakarta IV/5.
Documentation and Information Dept., Taman Tjut Mutiah 10, Jakarta II/14.

IRELAND
Catholic Press and Information Office, 169 Booterstown Road, Blackrock, Co Dublin, T: (353) 01 288 5043.
Information Office, Catholic Church in Ireland, St Dominics, 130 Booters Town Av, Blackrock, County Dublin.
Religious Press Association, 27 Upper Sherrard Street, Dublin 1, T: (353) 01 749464.

ISRAEL
Christian Information Centre (CIC), Omar Ibn el-Khattab Square, Jaffa Gate, PO Box 14308, Jerusalem, T: 287647.
Christian News from Israel, 23 Shlomo Hamelech, PO Box 1167, Jerusalem.

ITALY
Agencia Stampa Cattolica Associata (ASCA), Via Uffici del Vicario 30, I-00186 Roma, T: 6794442/3/4/5.
Agenzia Internationale FIDES (AIF), Palazzo di Propagande Fide, Via di Propaganda I-c, 00187 Rome.
Centrum Informationis Catolicae (CIC-Roma), via Delmonte de la Farina, 30/4, 00186 Roma.
CSEO Documentazione, CP 210, I-40100 Bologna.
Pontificia Fotografia Felici, Via del Babuina 75, I-00187 Roma, T: 6790836.
Servizio Informazioni per le Chiese Orientali (SICO), Via della Conciliazione 34, I-00193 Roma.
Servizio Informazioni Romano Cattolico (SIRC), Piazza San Silvestro 13, I-00165 Roma.
Servizio Informazioni Stampa Evangelica, Via Curtatone 10, Roma.
Servizio Informazioni Religiosa (SIR), Via di Porta Cavalleggeri 143, I-00165 Rome.
SJ Press and Information Office, Borgho Santo Spirito 8, I-00193 Roma, T: 659283, 657032.
Unione Cattolica della Stampa Italiana (UCSI), Piazza Montecitorio 115 int 6, I-00186 Roma; Via Uffici del Vicario 30, Roma, T: 6790847, 673344.
Unione Cattolica Pubblicità (UCP), Corso Vittorio Emanuele II 326, I-00186 Roma.

JAPAN
Catholic Press Center, Yotsuya 1-5, Shinjuku-ku, Tokyo, T: 3595427.
Journalism and Education Department, Sophia University, 7 Kioicho, Chiyoda-ku, Tokyo.
To-Sei News, 10 6-Brancho, Chiyoda-ku, Tokyo, T: 331323, 334874, 334763.

KENYA
Africa Acts Feature Service, AACC, Waiyaki Way, P.O. Box 20390, Nairobi, T: 33510.
Africa Church Information Service (ACIS), AACC, Waiyaki Way, P.O. Box 14205, Nairobi, T: 62601.

LEBANON
Documentation Service, PO Box 5376, Beirut, T: 01-353938.
Near East Ecumenical Bureau Information Interpretation (NEEBII), Immeuble Anis Daouk, Rue Abdel Aziz, BP 5376, Bayrut, T: 349584.

LUXEMBOURG
Association des Journalistes Catholiques du Luxembourg, 5 Rue Bourbon, Luxembourg.

MADAGASCAR
Bureau de Liaison de'Information Religieuse dans l'Océan Indien (BLIROI), BP 3920, Tananarive.

MALAWI
CAPA Information Service, P/A Chilema, Zomba.

MARTINIQUE
Press 'Eglise en Martinique', Archevêché - B.P. 586, 97207 Fort-de-Granier, T: 596-63-70-70.

MEXICO
Comité Nacional de Publicidad Evangélica, Priv de Agustin Gutierrez 67, Zona 1, México, DF, T: 346603.
Documentación e Información Católica, Aristoteles 239, México 1.
Escuela de Periodismo, Instituto de Humanidades Pio XII, Av La Paz 275, Guadalajara, Jalisco.
Escuela de Periodismo Carlos Septién García, Durando 341, México 7, DF, T: 286679.
Facultad de Ciencias y Técnicas de la Información, Universidad Iberoamericana, Cerro de las Torres 395, México 21, DF, T: 493500.

NETHERLANDS
Netherlands Catholic Journalists' Association, Koninginstraat 22b, Hilversum; van Alphenstraat 18, Utrecht.
Press and Publicity Commission, Biltstraat 119, Utrecht.

NEW ZEALAND
Catholic Enquiry Centre, 140 Austin St, Wellington.

NIGERIA
Catholic News and Photo Service, Press Department, National Catholic Secretariat, PO Box 951, Lagos.

NORWAY
Christian Press Office, Holbergs Plass 4, Oslo 1.
Church Information Office, Munchsgt 2, Oslo 1.

PAKISTAN
Catholic News Service of Pakistan (CNSP), III Depot Lines, Karachi 3.

PERU
ACI-PRENSA, A.P. 040062, Lima.
Centro de Información Católica, Ucayali 259, 8 piso, Casilla 5594, Lima, T: 272839.
Escuela de Periodismo, Pontificia Universidad Católica del Perú, Plaza Francis 1164, Apdo 1761, Lima, T: 41716.

PHILIPPINES
Institute of Journalism and Communication Arts, University of Santo Tomas, Espana, Manila, T: 32231.

RUSSIA
Information Service of the Pentecostal Movement in Russia, P.O. Box 520, Moskva, T: 2278947.

SAINT LUCIA
Catholic TV News, T: 809-45-27050.

SENEGAL
Centre Catholique d'Information, Rue de Neuville 1, B.P. 160, St. Louis, T: 221-61 10 27.

SINGAPORE
Malaysian Catholic News, Kingsmead Hall, 8 Victoria Park Rd, Singapore 10.

SOUTH AFRICA
Catholic Newspaper & Publishing Co., Ltd., PO Box 2372, Cape Town 8000, The Grimley, Tuin Plein, Cape Town 8001, T: 021-45-5007, F: 011-45-3850.
Ecumenical Press Agency, South Africa Council of Churches, PO Box 21190, Braamfontein, Transvaal.
Information Bureau of the Dutch Reformed Church, 119 De Korte St, Braamfontein, Transvaal, T: 7245158, 442037.

SOUTH KOREA
Catholic Journalist Club, 85-12, Nung-dong, Kwangjin-gu, Seoul-shi, T: (02) 466-7918.
Catholic Pharmacists Association, 441, Chungnim-dong, Chung-gu, Seoul-shi, T: (02) 360-4124.

SPAIN

Centro de Información y Orientación (CIO), Paseo de la Habana 44, Madrid 16, T: 2595381.
Escuela de Periodismo de la Iglesia, Paseo Juan XXIII 3, Ciudad Universitaria, Madrid 3, T: 2534007, 2335200.
Información Católica Ibero-americana (ICIA), OC-SHA Centro de Información y Sociologia, Ciudad Universitaria, Madrid 3.
Instituto de Periodismo, Universidad de Navarra, Ciudad Universitaria, Pamplona, T: 221650.
LOGOS, Mateo Inurria 15, Madrid 16.
Officina General de Información y Estatistica de la Iglesia en España, Alfonso XI 4, Madrid 14.
Prensa Asociada (PA), Alfonso XI 4, Apdo 14530 Madrid 14, T: 221090.
Servicio de Información Prensa y Espetáculos (SIPE), Calle Pintor J Pinazo 15, Apdo 1677, Valencia 10, T: 693700.

SWITZERLAND

APD (Swiss Adventist Press Service, Basel), F: 4161-25-6118.
APIC, Agence de presse internationale catholique, 40, bd de Perolles, Fribourg, CP 1054, 1701 Fribourg, 037/864811.
Ecumenical Press Service (EPS), Geneva, F: 4122-798-1346.
European Baptist Press Service, Gheistrasse 31, Ruschlikon 8803, F: 411-724-3148.
idea schweiz (Swiss edition of Idea), F: 4141-23-2904.
Informationsbeauftragte, Zinggstrasse 33, 3007 Bern, T: 031 372 20 19, F: 031 372 50 04.
Institut de Journalisme et de Communication Sociate de l'Universite de Fribourg, 1700 Fribourg 037/29 83 80.
Katholische Internationale Presse-Agentur (KIPA), Case Postale 1054 CH 1701, Fribourg.
LWI (Lutheran World News Service), Geneva, F: 4122-798-8616.
Service de Presse Protestant, Evole 2, CH-2000 Neuchâtel.
Union Catholique International de la Presse, 37-39 rue de Vermont, Case Postale 197, CH-1211 Genève 20, T: 41-22-734 00 17, F: 41-22-733 10 51, O: Telex: 45-412 946 UCIP CH.

TAIWAN

Catholic I-Shi News Agency, 120 Yun-Ho St, Taipei.

TANZANIA

All-Africa Lutheran Information & Coordination Centre (ALICE), ELCT Building, PO Box 3033, Arusha.

THAILAND

Catholic Information Bureau, National Catholic Committee for the Mass Media, 251/1 Suranari Rd, Nakhon Ratchasima.
Christian Information Service, PO Box 1405, Bangkok.

UGANDA

Uganda Catholic Press Association, Catholic Secretariat, PO Box 2886, Kampala.

UNITED STATES OF AMERICA (USA)

American Lutheran Publicity Bureau, 155 East 22nd St, New York, NY 10010.
Associated Church Press, 875 North Dearborn St, Chicago, IL 60610; 27 East 39th St, New York, NY 10016.
Catholic Information Society, 310 Westfield St, Middletown, CT 06457.
Catholic Institute of the Press, 315 East 47th St, New York, NY 10017.
Catholic News Service (CNS), 3211 Fourth St., N.E., Washington, D.C. 20017, F: 202-541-3279, O: E-mail: CNSInfo@aol.com.
Catholic Press Association of the U.S. and Canada, Inc., 3555 Veterans Memorial Hwy., Unit O, Ronkonkoma, NY 11779.
Christian Daily News, O: Web: www.christiandailynews.org.
Christian Information Service, 1712 West Greenleaf, Chicago, IL 60626, T: (312)763-6374.
Christian News Insitute, P.O. Box 2340, Cheasapeake, VA 23327, T: (800) 659-NEWS.
DAWN Friday Fax, O: http://www.tecc.co.uk/jesusa/dawnindx.html.
Ecumedia News Service, 475 Riverside Dr., Room 850, New York, NY 10115.
Ecumenical News International, O: E-mail: eni@wcc-coe.org, and www.wcc-coe.org/eni.html.
Evangelical Press Association, 485 Panorama Rd., Earlysville, VA 22936, T: 804-973-5941, F: 804-973-2710.
Evangelism and Missions Information Service, P.O. Box 794, Wheaton, IL 60189, T: 630-653-2158, F: 630-653-0520, O: PulseNews@aol.com.
Friends Contact Information, C/O FUM. 101 Quaker Hill Dr, Richmond, IN 47374, T: 910-727-1063.
Friends Information Centers & Offices, 101 Quaker Hill Dr., Richmond, IN 47374, T: 317-962-5741.
Knights of Columbus, Dir. of Public Info., 1275 Pennsylvania Ave., N.W., Washington, DC 20004-2404, T: 202-628-2355, F: 202-628-1243.
Mission Network News, 1159 E. Beltline N.E., Grand Rapids, MI 49505, T: 800-530-9779, F: 616-942-7078, O: E-mail: mnn@gospelcom.net.
National & Int'l Religion Report, O: www.cs.moravian.edu/NIRR.
Newsservice 2000, Suite 269, P.O. Box 16400, Mesa, AZ 85201, T: 602-844-1930.
O Theopilus, O: Web: www.cbl.org/otheo/.
Office for Media Relations, U.S. Catholic Conference, 3211 Fourth St., N.E., Washington, D.C. 20017, T: 202-541-3320, F: 202-832-1520.
Press & Media Services, Youth With A Mission, P.O. Box 26479, Colorado Springs, CO 80936.
Public Religion Project, O: prp-info@publicreligionproj.org.
Religion News Service, 1101 Connecticut Ave., N.W., Suite 350, Washington, DC 20036, T: 202-463-8777, F: 202-463-0033, O: Web: www.religionnews.com.
Religion Newswriters Association, 88 West Plum St., Westerville, OH 43081, T: 614-891-9001.
Religious News Service, 43 West 57th St, New York, NY 10019, O: Web: www.nj.com/rns.
UCC News, Office of Communication, 700 Prospect Ave., Cleveland, OH 44115.
Western Rite Information Center, 333 Reed St, Philadelphia, PA 19147.

URUGUAY

Unión Latinoamericana de Prensa Católica (UCLAP), 25 de Mayo 617, Casilla de Correo 1052 Sub-Central, Montevideo.

VENEZUELA

Escuela de Periodismo y Ciencias de la Communicación Social, Universidad Católica Andres Bello, Esquina de Jesuitas a Tienda Honda 37, Apdo 422, Caracas, T: 817731.

VIET NAM

Centre de Presse et d'Information Catholique du Viêt-Nam, 72/12 Nguyên-dinh-Chiêu, Saigon, T: 41366.
Office of Missionary Information, P.O. Box 410 Saigon.

US VIRGIN ISLANDS

Catholic Islander, P.O. Box 301825-V.D.S., St. Thomas 00803, T: 809-774-3166, F: 809-774-5816.

ZAMBIA

Africa Literature Centre, Art Studio and Journalism Courses, P.O. Box 1319, Kitwe.

46
Lay ministries

Organizations for the laity only, specifically emphasizing the lay contribution in Christian life, mission, and work; lay associations, the lay apostolate, lay movements, lay preachers, lay readers, lay persons overseas, lay missionary societies; lay personal evangelism, small-group evangelism. See also WOMEN'S LAY ORGANIZATIONS and MEN'S LAY ORGANIZATIONS.

ALGERIA

Union des Croyants, BP 5, Boufarik, El Djezair.

ARGENTINA

Acción Misionera Argentina (AMA), Rodríguez Peña 881, Buenos Aires.
Subsecretariado de Apostolado de los Laicos, CEA, Paraguay 1867, Buenos Aires.

AUSTRALIA

Navigators, Box 17, Haberfield, NSW 2045.
Paulian Association Lay Missionary Secretariat (PALMS), 175 Elisabeth St, Sidney, NSW 2000.

AUSTRIA

Arbeitsgemeinschaft der Katholischen Aktion Österreichs, Türkenstr 3/II/225, A-1090 Wien IX, T: 340321/2.
Arbeitsgemeinschaft Katholischer Verbände, Postgasse 4a, A-1010 Wien.
Cursillo-Europäischen Arbeitsgemeinschaft, Wickenburggasse 16/18, Postfach 52, A-1081 Wien, T: 428358.
Institut für Internationale Zusammenarbeit (IZA), Singerstr 7, A-1010 Wien.
Kanaa-Gemeinschaft, Viriotgasse 4, A-1090 Wien.
Kartellverband Katholischer Nichtfarbentragen der Akademischer/Vereiniging Österreichs, Ebendorferstr 6, A-1010 Wien.
Katholischer Männerbewegung Österreichs, Türkenstr 3, A-1090 Wien.
Katholischer Märiae, Rennweg 10, A-1030 Wien.
Salzburger Hochschulwochen, Mönchsberg 2, Postfach 219 (5010), A-5020 Salzburg.
Österreichischer Laiensrat, Türkenstr 3, A-1090 Wien.

BELGIUM

Aide Educative et Sociale, Capouilletstraat 10, B-1060 Brussel.
Association Internationale des Compagnons Bâtisseurs, Internationale Bouworde Naamsesteenweg 573, B-3030 Heverlee, T: (016)227979, 220523.
Bureau de Recruitement de l'Office International de l'Enseignement Catholique, Rue Guimard 5, B-1040 Brussel.
Centre International de Formation des compagnons Bâtisseurs, Kapelstraat 71, Heusden, Limburg.
Collaboration des Laïcas en Amérique Latine, Tervuuresestraat 56, B-3000 Leuven.
Compagnons Bâtisseurs Internationaux, Internationale Bouworde, Naamsesteenweg 573, B-3030 Heverlee, T: (016)227979.
Conférence des Organisations Internationales Catholiques (OIC), Av Molière 248, B-1060 Brussel, T: (02)345-4848.
Conseil Général de l'Apostolat des Laïcs (CGAL), Rue Guimard 5, B-1040 Brussel.
Coopération des Laïcs en Amérique Latine, Tervuursestraat 56, B-3000 Leuven, T: (016)226415.
Coopération Technique Internationale (ITECO), Rue du Moulin 32, B-1030 Brussel.
European Forum of National Committees of the Laity, Mutsaerstraat 32, B-2000 Antwerpen, T: (031)317835.
Fraternite Seculiere Charles de Foucauld, Katharinenweg, 4, B 4700 Eupen.
Volontaires de l'Enseignement, Rue Guimard 5, B-1040 Brussel, T: (02)513-6880.

BENIN

Union Dahoméenne d'Apostolat des Laïcs (UDAL), c/o Centrale des Oeuvres Catholiques, BP 519, Cotonou, T: 3592.

BRAZIL

Navegadores, CP 2925, Curitiba, Paraná, T: 227769.

BRITAIN (UK OF GB & NI)

Catholic Overseas Appointments, 38 King St, London WC2E 8JS, T: (01)836-1701.
Catholic People's Weeks, 66 Orchard Av, Parkstone, Poole, BH14 9AJ.
Central Readers Conference, Church of England, Church House, Dean's Yard, London SW1P 3NZ, T: (01)222-9011.
Christian Action, 2 Amen Court, London EC4, T: (01)606-6123.
Church of England Guild of Vergers, The Verger's Lodge, Coventry Cathedral, Warwickshire CV1 5ES, T: (0203)27597.
Knights of St Columba, 54 Berkeley St, Glasgow C3.
National Council for Lay Apostolate in Scotland, 17 Marlborough Av, Glasgow G11.
National Council for the Lay Assoc., 103 Leopold Road, Liverpool L7 8SR.
Navigators, 88a Coombe Rd, New Malden, Surrey, T: (01)942-2211, 7788.
One By One Band, Evangelical Publications, 56 Orchard st, Weston-super-Mare, Somerset.
Serra Club, 14 Sheldon Av, London N6 4JT, T: (01)340-5642.
St. Louise de Marillac Association, 24 Blandford St, London WI.
Sword of the Spirit, 38 King St, London WC2, T: Temple 1973.
Toc H, 42 Crutched Friars, London EC3, T: (01)709-0472.
Volunteer Missionary Movement, 1 Victoria Rd, Mill Hill, London NW7 4SA, T: (01)959-2491.
William Temple Association, Liddon House, 24 South Audley St, London W1Y 5DL, T: (01)493-2782.

BURKINA FASO

Secrétariat de l'Apostolat des Laïcs, BP 90, Ouagadougou, T: 2993.

BURUNDI

Coordination des Mouvements d'Apostolat Laïcs, BP 2010, Bujumbura.

CAMEROON

Conseil National de l'Apostolat des Laïcs, c/o Archevêché, BP 207, Yaoundé, T: 222478.

CANADA

Canadian Lay Missioners, Box 200, Wawa, Ontario.
Centre d'Etudes et de Coopération International (CECI), 1961 Est Rue Rachel, Montréal.
Latin American Institute, Box 310, St Mary's Ontario.
Madonna House, Combermere, via Berry's Bay, Ontario.
Missionnaries Laïques de Notre-Dame, 150 Ouest Blvd Gouin, Montréal, Québec.
Office of Lay Apostolate, 90 Av Parent, Ottawa, T: 236-9461.

CENTRAL AFRICAN REPUBLIC

Direction Nationale des Oeuvres, Centre Jean XXIII, BP 855, Bangui, T: 2984.

CHILE

Secretariado Nacional de Acción Católica Especializada, Carrera 94, Santiago.

CHINA

Lay Apostolate Central Council Diocesan Office, Grand Bldg, 16th Floor, 15-18 Connaught Rd, Hong Kong.

COLOMBIA

Acción Católica Colombiana, Carrera 13 No 68-50, Bogotá.

COSTA RICA

Instituto de Teología para Seglares, Apdo 4562, San José.
Navegantos, Apdo 2927, San José.

CROATIA

Commission pour l'Apostolat des Laïcs, Biskupska Konferencija, Kaptol 31, YU-41000 Zagreb.

CUBA

Apostolado Seglar Organizado (ASO), Apdo 594, La Habana 1.

EGYPT

Action Catholique, Assemblée Interrituelle Catholique, 5 Sharia Mohamed Mazhar, Zamalek, Al Qahirah.

ETHIOPIA

Christian Business Men's Association, P.O. Box 6, Addis Abeba.

FINLAND

Navigators, Haapasaarentie 9B 318, Helsinki 96.

FRANCE

Ad Lucem, Association Catholique de Coopération Internationale, 12 Rue Guy-de-la-Brósse, F-75005 Paris.
Auxiliaires Missionnaires de l'Assomption (AMA), 17 rue de l'Assomption, F-75016 Paris.
Centre Chrétien de Formation pour Laïcs au Service des Pays en Dévelopement, 5 rue St-Léon, F-69 Strasbourg.
Centre de Formation et d'Echanges Internationaux, 73 rue des Héros-Nogentais, F-94130 Nogent/Marine.
Chrétienne/Latiy and Christian Community, 98 rue de l'Université, F-75007 Paris.
Conférence des OIC, Centre Catholique pour l'UNESCO, 9 Rue Cler, F-75007 Paris, T: 551-1759.
Délégation Catholique pour la Coopération, 277 rue St Jacques, F-75005 Paris.
Equipes Notre-Dame, 49 Rue de la Glacière, F-75013 Paris, T: (01)587-0588.
Foi et Lumiere, 8, rue Serret, F 75015 Paris.
Fédération Internationale Catholique d'Education Physique, 5 Rue Cernuschi, F-75017 Paris, T: 924-3112.
Fédération Internationale des Associations d'Enfants de Marie Immaculée, 67 Rue de Sèvres, F-75006 Paris, T: (01)222-3390.
Grail, The, Secrétariat International, 222 Rue du Dr Germain Sée, F-75015 Paris.
Institut International de Recherche et de Formation en Vue du Dévelopement Harmonisé (IRFED), 47 Rue de la Glacière, F-75013 Paris.
Secrétariat Général pour l'Apostolat des Laïcs, 106 Rue du Bac, F-75341 Paris, T: (01)222-5639.
Service du Laïcat Missionnaire, 12 Rue Sala, Lyon 2.
Societe Saint François de Sales, 57-59, rue Léon-Frot, F 75011 Paris.
World Organization of Lay Missionaries, 17 Rue de l'Assomption, F-75016 Paris.

FRENCH GUIANA

Association des Hommes Indiens de la Guyane, c/o Evêché, BP 378, Cayenne.

GAMBIA

Lay Apostolate Council, P.O. Box 165, Banjul (Bathurst).

GERMANY

Action 365, Ökumenische Laienbewegung, Kennedy-allee 111a, D-6000 Frankfurt 70.
Apostolic Movement of Schönstatt, Hans Sonneck Postfach 180, D 5414 Vallendar (GFR).
Arbeitsgemeinschaft für Volksmission, Alexanderstr 23, 7 Stuttgart 1.
International Kolping Society, Postfach 100 428, Kolpingplatz 5-11, D 5000 Köln 1.
Männerarbeit der EKD, Hauptgeschäftsstelle, Kanstr 9, D-605 Offenbach (Main).
Navigators, Am Bahnhof 70, D-6541 Niederschren; Hohe St 18, D-46 Dortmund, T: (06543)2141.
Sozialdienst Katholischer Männer, Ulmesnst 32, D-4000 Düsseldorf-Nord, T: (0211)441592.
Unio Internationalis Laicorum in Servitio Ecclesiae, Secretariat, Breite Str 106-110 Postfach 102068, D-5 Köln, T: (0221)218817.
Zentralkomitee der Deutschen Katholiken (ZDK), Hochkreuzalle 246, D-5300 Bonn-Bad Godesberg, T: (02221)738190.

GREECE

Zoe Brotherhood of Theologians (Zoe Movement), Hippocratus St 189, Athinai 708.

GUADELOUPE

Direction des Oeuvres et des Mouvements, 28 Rue Peynier, BP 414, F-97-1 Pointe-à-Pitre, T: 820967.

HOLY SEE

Consilium de Laicis/Council for the Laity, Palazzo San Calisto, Piazza San Callisto 16, I-00120 Città del Vaticano, T: 5890141, 5890851, 4322.
Fédération Internationales des Hommes Catholiques (FIHC) (Unum Omnes), Piazza San Calisto 16, I-00153 Roma, Italy, I-00120 Città del Vaticano.

HONDURAS

Fomento Cooperativo (Educación de Adultos por Acción en Grupo), Centro Loyola, Apdo 676, Colonia Palmira, Tegucigalpa, T: 25467.

INDIA

Cherupusha (Little Flower) Mission League, League Central Office, Bharananganam PO, Kerala.
Quaker International Affairs Program in South Asia, Quaker House, 224 Jor Bagh, New Delhi 3, T: 617657.
Teaching Teams, Regional Secretariat for Asia, 69 Perumal Koil St, Karaikal, Madres State.

INDONESIA

Navigators, Jalan Rangga Malela 22, Bandung, T: 50957.

IRELAND

European Forum of National Committees of the Laity, 12, Brookwood Lawn Artane, Dublin 5.
Legion of Mary, De Montfort House, North Brunswick St, Dublin 7, T: 776011/2.
National Council for the Apostolate of the Laity, 7 Lower Abbey St, Dublin 1, T: 48750, 48759.

ITALY

Apostolado de la Oración, Borgo S. Spirito, 5, I 00195 Roma.
Association des Cooperateurs de L'Opus Dei, Viale Bruno Buozzi, 73 I 000197 Rome.
Association Laïque Pro-Missions, c/o Scuola del Cristo, Cannaregio 1723, I-30121 Venezia.
Associazione Italiana Volontarie per l'Africa e il Sud-America, Via e Filiberto 8, I-12100 Cueno.
Ausilarii Laichi della Missioni, Via Trullo 300, Roma.
Azione Cattolica Italiana (ACI), Via della Conciliazione 1, I-00193 Roma, T: 6568751.
Centro Laici Italiani per le Missioni (CELIM), Via Garibaldi 10, I-24100 Bergamo.

Christian Life Community (CVX), Borgo Santo Spirito 8, C.P. 6139, I-00195 Rome.
Comunità di S. Egidio, Piazza S. Egidio, 3 A, I 00153 Roma.
Conférence des OIC, Permanence de Rome, Piazza San Calisto 16, I-00153 Roma, T: 6984842.
Cooperazione Internationale, CP 977, I-20100 Milano.
Federation Internationale des Hommes Catholiques—Unum Omnes (FIHC), Piazza S. Calisto, 16, I 00153 Rome.
International Pen Friend Service, Bellavista, I-10015 Ivrea.
Legio Mariae, Via Ruggero Bonghi 11/B, I-00184 Roma.
Milizia Dell'Immacolata (MI), Via S. Teodoro, 42, I 00186 Roma.
Mouvement International D'Apostolat des Milieux Sociaux Independants (MIAMSI), Piazza San Calisto, 16, I 00153 Rome.
Movement for a Better World, The, Via Vinova, 58, I 00166 Rome.
Movimento 'Pro Sanctitate', Piazza S. Andrea della Valle, 3, I 00186 Roma.
Movimento dei Focolari (Opera di Maria), Via di Frascati, 302, I 00040 Rocca di Papa, Roma.
Movimiento Teresiano de Apostolado, Via Valcannuta, 130, I 00166 Roma.
Orden Franciscana Seglar, Via Piemonte, 70, I 00187 Roma.
Pia Unione Santa Caterina de Genova, Sol San Bartelomeo del Carmine 4-1, Genova.
Pontifical Council for the Laity, Piazza S. Calisto 16, 00153 Rome.
Segretario Triveneto Laici Missionari, Fundamenta Nuova 4885, Venezia.
Tecnici Volontari Cristiani, Via Roentgen 20, I-20136 Milano.
Tercera Orden Dominicana, Convento Santa Sabina, Piazza Pietro d'Illiria, 1, I 00153 Roma.
World Federation of Christian Life Communities, Borgo Santo Spirito 8, CP 9048, I-00193 Rome.

IVORY COAST
Conseil National de l'Apostolat des Laïcs, BP 1287, Abidjan.
Direction Nationale des Oeuvres, BP 1287, Abidjan, T: 222968.

JAPAN
Navigators, 1-31 Higashi-Kiebukuro, P.O. Box 121, Toshima-ku, Tokyo 170-91; Box 73, Koza, Okinawa, T: 9828649, (077)4709).
Quaker International Affairs Program in East Asia, Sendagaya Apts, Room 606, 9-9 Sendagaya 1-chome, Shibuya-ku, Tokyo 151, T: (402)4656.

KENYA
Catholic Lay Council of Kenya, Catholic Secretariat, Westlands, PO Box 48062, Nairobi, T: 21613.

LEBANON
Comité de Coordination des Mouvements d'Apostolat des Laïcs, BP 5690, Bayrut, T: 252054.
Navigators, BP 235, Bayrut, T: 253940.

LUXEMBOURG
Conseil National pour l'Apostolat des Laïcs, 5 Rue Bourbon, Luxembourg-ville.

MALAWI
National Council of the Laity, P.O. Box 5368, Limbe.

MALAYSIA
Navigators, 10 Jalan 3, Petaling Jaya, Selangor, T: 59046, 563549.

MALTA
Archdiocese of Malta Council for the Lay Apostolate, Archbishop's Curia, Valletta.
Diocese of Gozo Commission for the Lay Apostolate, 37 Racecourse St, Nadur, Gozo.

MARTINIQUE
Direction de l'Apostolat des Laïcs, Rue Martin Luther, Voie 7, F-97200 Fort-de-France, T: 716268.

MAURITIUS
Centrale des Oeuvres, 42 Rue Pope Hennessy, Port-Louis, T: 20975.

MEXICO
Comisión Episcopal de Apostolado de los Laicos, Apdo 331, Guadalajara, Jalisco.
Navegantes, Apdo 805, Guadalajara, Jalisco.

MONACO
Direction desf Oeuvres Diocésaines, Paroisse St Charles, 8 Av St-Charles, Monaco, T: 300345.

NETHERLANDS
Academic Lay Missionary Action, Raamweg 32, 's-Gravenhage.
Centrum Kontakt der Kontinenten, Amersfontsestraat 20, Soesterberg.
Navigators, 4 Van Limburg Stirumstraat, Utrecht, T: (030)14125.
Sekulier Instituut Unitas, Priorij Gods Werkhof, Hollende Wagenweg 16, Werkhoven.
St. John Crusades, Vogelenzangseweg 77, Vogelzang.
Werkgroep Landen in Ontwikkeling, Laan van Meerdervoort 150, 's-Gravenhage.

NEW ZEALAND
Navigators, P.O. Box 1951, Christchurch, T: 67156.

NORWAY
Navigators, Postboks 122, Sentrum, Oslo 1, T: 604183.
Oslo Diocese Lay Council (Legmannsradet), Akersveien 5, N-Oslo 1, T: 207268.

PARAGUAY
Consejo Nacional de Coordinación de los Movimientos Laicos, Independencia Nacional y Communeros, Asunción.
Departmento de Laicos, Coronel Bogado 884, Casilla Correo 1170, Asunción, T: 47130.

PERU
Acción Católica Peruana, Junta Nacional, Maximo Abril 608, Lima, T: 33392.

PHILIPPINES
Asian Working Group on Cursillos de Cristiandad, Pius XII Catholic Center, United Nations Av, Manila.
Chinese Catholic Apostolate in the Philippines, P.O. Box 113, Manila.
National Catholic Action, Pius XII Catholic Center, United Nations Av, Manila.
Navigators, 65 West Av, P.O. Box 63, Quezon City.

PORTUGAL
Junta Central da Acção Católica Portuguesa, Campo de Santana 43, Lisboa 1, T: 536108.
Liga Evangélica de Acção Missionária e Educacional, Alameda das Linhas de Torres 122, Lisboa 5, T: 790039.

SENEGAL
Direction Nationale des Oeuvres Catholiques, 4 Rue Sandiniéry, BP 1354, Dakar, T: 26005.

SINGAPORE
Quaker International Seminars in South East Asia, 203-B Thomson Rd, Singapore 11, T: 530288.

SOUTH AFRICA
Commission for the Lay Apostolate, Standard Bank Bldgs, Paul Kruger St, PO Box 941, Pretoria, T: 36230, 30322.
Executive Ministry Seminar, Campus Crusade for Christ, PO Box 91015, Auckland Park, Johannesburg 2006.
Southern Africa Council of Catholic Laity, PO Box 3336, Pretoria.

SOUTH KOREA
Catholic Lay Apostolate Council of Archdiocese of Seoul, 1, 2-ga, Myong-dong, Chung-gu, Seoulshi, T: (02) 777-2013.
Korean Association of Voluntary Agencies (KAVA), IPO Box 1641, Soul, T: 233797.
National Council for the Lay Apostolate, 52-15, 2 Ka, Chung Mu Ro, Jung Ku, Seoul, T: 271161/3, 267951.
Navigators, IPO Box 1952, Seoul.

SPAIN
Asociación de Misionerismo Seglar (AMS), Ercilla 48, Apdo 623, Madrid 5.
Junta Nacional de AC Española, Alfonso XI 4, Madrid 14.
Misiones de las Dioceses Vascongadas, Sancho el Sabio 15, Vitoria.
Navigators, Joaquin Garcia Morato 147, 7-C, Madrid 3, T: 2545510.
Obra de Cooperción Apostólica Seglar Hispanoamericana (OCASHA), Belisana 2, Madrid 17, T: 2000146.
Seglares Missioneros de San Pablo, Avda de los Toreros 9, Madrid 2.
Unión Nacional de Apostolado Seglar (UNAS), Cuesta Santo Domingo 5/1, Madrid 13, T: 2489405.
Voluntarias del Sagrado Corazón, Santa Magdalena Sofia 12, Madrid 16, T: 2021943.

SWEDEN
Navigators (Navigatorerna), Box 433, S-751 06 Uppsala.

SWITZERLAND
Comité National de l'Apostolat des Laïcs, Chemin Eaux-Vives 21, CP 40, CH-1700 Fribourg 3, T: (037)244794.
Communauté Romande de l'Apostolat des Laïcs (CRAL), CP 836, CH-1000 Lausanne.
Conférence des OIC, Secretariat Permanent. 1 Route du Jura, BP 365, CH-1700 Fribourg, T: (037)26782.
Deutscheschweizerisches Katolisches Lainhelferwerk, 34 Grand Rue, Fribourg.
Fraternite romande des Laics du Carmel, 28, rue Marterey, 1005 Lausanne, 021/323 5483.
Informations Missionnaires pour Laïcs (IMPL), 34 Grand Rue, CH-1700 Fribourg.
International Catholic Migration Commission (ICMC), 65 Rue de Lausanne, CH-1202 Genève.
International Conferences and Seminars, Centre Quaker International, 12 Rue Adrien-Lachenal, CH-1207 Genève, T: 368876/7.
Internationales Altkatholisches Laienforum (Schweiz), Neumattstrasse 23, 4450 Sissach, T: 061 971 45 70.
MFL Mouvement Franciscain Laic, 1135 Denens, 021/8019578.
Mouvement International des Intellectuels Catholiques (MIIC-Pax Romana), 37-39, rue de Vermont, CH 1211 Genève 20-CIC.
Oeuvres des Missionnaires Laïques de Fribourg, Villa Beata, 8 Rue Fries, Fribourg.
Schweizerisches Katholisches Laienhelferwerk (SKLW), Reichengasse 34, CH-1700 Fribourg.

TANZANIA
Council of Catholic Laity in Tanzania, PO Box 9361, Dar es Salaam, T: 20430, 20477.

TOGO
Dialogues Internationaux en Afrique Occidentale, BP 971, Lomé, T: 5329.

TRINIDAD & TOBAGO
Catholic Action, 27 Maraval Rd, St Clair, Trinidad.

UGANDA
National Council of the Lay Apostolate, UEC, PO Box 2886, Kampala.

UNITED STATES OF AMERICA (USA)
American Laymen Overseas, NCCCUSA, 475 Riverside Drive, New York, NY 10027, T: (212)870-2200.
Amigos Internacionales, Box 1068, Athens, TX 75751.
Catholic Central Union of America, 3835 Westminster Pl., St. Louis, MO 63108.
Catholic Movement for Intellectual and Cultural Affairs of Pax Romana, 31 Chesterfield Rd., Stamford, CT 06902.
Chaminade's Auxillaries from North America (CANA), Front Line, University of Dayton, Dayton, OH.
Christian Lay Ministries, P.O. Box 1027, Lake Junaluska, NC 28745, T: 704-456-3960.
Christian Life Communities, 3601 Lindell Blvd., Rm 421, St. Louis, MO 63108.
Churchmen Overseas Program, NCCCUSA, 475 Riverside Drive, New York, NY 10027, T: (212)870-2200.
Friends in the Orient Committee, Friends Meeting House, 2151 Vine St, Berkeley, CA 94709.
Interamerican Cooperative Institute (ICI), Room 803, 21 East van Buren St, Chicago, IL 60605.
International Christian Leadership, Suite 614, 1028 Connecticut Av, NW, Washington, DC 20036, T: (202)296-5830.
International Lutheran Laymen's League, 2185 Hampton Ave., St. Louis, MO 63139-2983, T: (314)647-4900, F: 314-951-4295.
Jesuit Volunteer Corps, PO Box 4408, Portland, OR 97208.
Knights of Columbus, Supreme Council, New Haven, Connecticut.
Layman's Home Missionary Movement, Chester Springs, PA 19455.
Laymen's Christian Council, 312 Woodlawn Drive, Lexington, NC 27292.
Laymen's League, 7908 Orchid St, NW, Washington, DC 20012.
Laymen's Movement, International HQ, Wainwright House, 250 Stuyvesant Ave., Milton Point, Rye, NY 10580.
Nat'l Center for the Laity (NCL), 10 E Pearson St #101, Chicago, IL 60611.
National Association for Lay Ministry, 5420 S. Cornell Ave., Chicago, IL 60615, T: 773-241-6050.
National Council of Catholic Men, 1312 Massachusetts Av, NW, Washington, DC 20005.
National Council of the Catholic Laity (NCCL), 1312 Massachusetts Av, NW, Washington, DC 20005.
Papal Volunteers for Latin America (PAVLA), Tower Bldg Mezzanine, 1410 K St, NW, Washington, DC 20005.
Techo Foundation, Scarborough Rd, P.O. Box 1200, Briarcliff Manor, NY 10510.
United Methodists for Methodism, Box 17, Bellwood, IL 60104.
World Brotherhood Exchange, 315 Park Av South, New York, NY 10010.

VENEZUELA
Junta Nacional de Apostolado Seglar, CEV, Edif Juan XXIII, piso 2, Torre a Madrices, Apdo 954, Caracas 101, DF, T: 815922.
Latin American Office of the International Council of Catholic Men, Edificio Juan XXIII, 4 Piso, Torre a Madrices, Apdo de Correos 1352, Caracas, T: 818716/7.
Oficina Latinoamericana de Cursillos de Cristiandad, Mosen Sol, Av Sorocaina, El Marques, Apdo 70489, Caracas 107, T: 217722.

ZAMBIA
Association of Christian Lay Centres in Africa (ACLCA), Mindolo Ecumenical Centre, P.O. Box 1192 or 1493, Kitwe, T: 3389, 84712/3.
National Council for the Lay Apostolate, ZEC, Stanley Rd., P.O. Box 1965, Lusaka, T: 73467, 73470.

ZIMBABWE
Roman Catholic Council of the Laity, P.O. Box 512, Que Que.

47 Libraries

Major Christian and religious book library collections: theological, religious, missiological, biblical. Note that many major libraries are connected with UNIVERSITIES, RESEARCH CENTERS, THEOLOGICAL COLLEGES AND SEMINARIES, and UNIVERSITY DEPARTMENTS OF RELIGION. For non-book libraries (photographic libraries, film libraries, record libraries, recorded music libraries, tape libraries), see AUDIOVISUAL RESOURCES; FILM, VIDEO, AND CINEMA; JOURNALISM, THE PRESS, AND INFORMATION; MUSIC; MEDIA AND COMMUNICATIONS; and AUDIO RECORDINGS.

ARGENTINA
Pontificia Universidad Católica Argentian Santa Maria de los Buenos Aires, Facultad de Teología, José Cubas 3543, Buenos Aires 19.

AUSTRALIA
Society of the Sacred Mission, Australian Province, St Michael's House, Crafers, South Australia.
St. Mark's Library & Inst. of Theology, P.O. Box 67, Canberra, Act. 2600.
St. Patrick's Ecclesiastical College, Manly, NSW.

AUSTRIA
Jesuitenkollegs, Sillgasse 6, Postfach 569, A-6021 Innsbruck.

BELGIUM
Groot Seminarie Mechelen-Brussel, 18 de Merodestraat, Mechelen.
Ruusbroec-Genootschap, Printsstraat 17, Antwerpen 1.
Saint-Albert, 95 St Jansbergsteenweg, Leuven.
Sint Jan Berchmanscollege, Waversebaan 220, Heverlee.
Séminaire Episcopal, Rue des Jésuites 28, Tournai.

BRAZIL
Alfonsianum, Via Raposo Tavares KN 20, CP 11.170, São Paulo 9.
Colegio Cristo Rei, São Leopoldo, Rio Grande do Sul.

BRITAIN (UK OF GB & NI)
Catholic Archives Society, Innyngs House, Hatfield Park, Hatfield, Hertfordshire AL9 5PL.
Catholic Central Library, Franciscan Friars of the Atonement, 47 Francis St, London SW1P 1QR, T: 0171-834 6128.
Chapter Library, Archivist, The Precincts, Canterbury, Kent, T: (0227)63510.
Durham Cathedral Library, Durham.
Friends House, Euston Rd, London NWI.
Friends Reference Libraries, Friends House, Euston Rd, London NW1 2BJ, T: 171-387-3601, F: 171-388-1977.
House of the Sacred Mission (SSM), Kelham, Newark, Notts.
Oscott College, Sutton Coldfield, Warwick.
Sion College Library, Victoria Embankment, Blackfriars, London EC4Y 0DN, T: (01)799-7983.
St. Deiniol's Library, Warden, Hawarden, Deeside, Clwyd CH5 3DF, T: (0244)523350.
Woodbrooke Library, Woodbrooke, 1046 Bristol Rd., Birmingham B29 6LJ, T: 021-472-5171, F: 021-472-5173.

CANADA
Abbaye Saint-Benoît du Lac, Province de Québec.
Anglican General Synod Archives, 600 Jarvis St., Toronto, ON M4Y 2J6, T: 416-924-9192.
Canadian Baptist Archives, McMaster Divinity College, Hamilton, ON L8S 4K1, T: 416-525-9140.
Canadian Council of Churches Archives, 395 Wellington, Ottawa, ON K1A 0N3.
Canadian Disciples Archives, 39 Arkell Rd., R.R. 2, Guelph, ON N1H 6H8, T: 519-824-5190.
Holy Redeemer College, Windsor, Ontario.
Librairie Chrétienne, 1148 rue Des Cascades, St.-Hyacinthe, QC J2S 3G8, T: 514-774-8086.
McGill University, Faculty of Divinity, 3520 University St, Montréal 2, Québec.
Mennonite Heritage Centre, 600 Shaftesbury Blvd., Winnipeg, MB R3P 0M4, T: 204-888-6781.
Presbyterian Archives, 59 St. George St., Toronto, ON M5S 2E6, T: 416-595-1277.
Scholasticate St. Joseph, Av des Oblates, Ottawa 1, Ontario.
St. Basil's Seminary, 95 St. Joseph St, Toronto 5, Ontario.
United Church of Canada Central Archives, Victoria Univ., Toronto, ON M5S 1K7.

CHINA
Chung Chi College, Shatin, NT, Hong Kong.

COLOMBIA
Universidad Javeriana, Faculdades Eclesiasticas, Carrera 10, No 65-48, Bogotá 2.

ECUADOR
Entrenamiento Ministerial, Ave. 10 de Agosto No. 11635, Casilla 3715, Quito.
Materiales Impresos, Ave. 10 de Agosto No. 11635, Casilla 3515, Quito, T: 531-572.

EGYPT
Library of the Greek Orthodox Patriarchate of Alexandria, 166 Rue Port Said, Al-Iskandariyah (Alexandria).

FRANCE
Collegium Wilhelmitanum, Séminaire Protestant, 1 bis Quai St-Thomas, Strasbourg 67, Bas-Rhin.
Faculté Théologie Protestante, rue Louis Perrier, Montpellier, Herault.
Facultés Dominicaines, Le Saulchoir-Etoilles, Soissy-sur-Seine.
Grand Séminaire de Besançon, 20 Rue Megevand, F-25 Besançon.
Grand Séminaire de Nancy, 54 Villars-les-Nancy.
Institut Catholique, 31 Rue de la Fonderie, F-31 Toulouse.
Institut Catholique de Paris, 21 rue d'Assas, Paris 6.

GERMANY
Bischofliche-Philosophie-Theologische Hochschule, Am Hofgarten 1, D-8833 Eichstatt/Bayern.
Bischofliches Priesterseminars Mainz, Augustinerstr 34, D-6500 Mainz.
Caritasbibliothek, Werthmannplatz 4, D-78 Freiburg im Breisgau.
Diozesanbibliothek, Mozarstr 7, Postfach 233, D-5100 Aachen.
Erzbischofliche Diozesan-Bibliothek Köln, Gereonstr 2-4, D-5 Köln.
Katholisch-Theologisches Seminar, Liebermeisterstr 12, D-74 Tübingen.
Priesterseminars Trier, Jesuits-str 13, Postfach 320, D-55 Trier.
Seminar der Abteilung für Ev Theologie,

Buscheystr, Gebäude 1A 1/40, D-463 Bochum-Querenburg.
Universität Bochum, Im Lottental, Zeche Klosterbusch, D-4630 Bochum-Querenburg.
Universität Marburg, Theologischen Seminare, Lahntor 3, Marburg/Lahn.
Universität Wurzburg, Theologischen Facultät, Sanderring 2, D-8700 Wurzburg.
Vereinigte Theologische Seminare, Nikolausberger Weg 5v, D-34 Göttingen.
Westfallischen-Wilhelms-Universität, Seminare und Institute der Ev-Theologischen Facultät, Universitätsstr 13-17, D-4400 Münster.

HOLY SEE
Pontificia Biblioteca Missionaria della SC per l'Evangelizzazione dei Popoli (Biblioteca Missionum), Pontificia Università Urbaniana, I-00120 Città del Vaticano.
Vatican Library, I-00120 Città del Vaticano.

HUNGARY
Library of the Lutheran Church in Hungary, Ulloi ut 24, Budapest VIII.
Reformed Academy of Theology, Raday-utca 28, sz, Budapest.

INDIA
Central Christian Library, Elluvila P. O., Karakkonam, Kerala 695504.
Himalaya Christian Library, Prayer House, Talli Tal Post, Naini Tal, Uttar Pradesh 263002.
India Full Gospel Mission Library, 23, Ashoka Gardens, Govindpura P. O., Bhopal, Madhya Pradesh 462023.
Macleod Memorial Reading Room, Mission Compound, Chhapara, Madhya Pradesh 480884.
Manipur State Christian Library, Deulahland, Imphal, Manipur 795001.
Martin Luther Library, Arcot Lutheran Church, Thiruvannamalai, Tamil Nadu.
Nazarene Lending Library, P. O. Box 10, Hope Farm, Whitefield, Bangalore, Karnataka 560066.
United Theological College Library, 63, Millers Road, P. O. Box 4163, Bensontown, Karnataka 560046.

IRELAND
Central Catholic Library, 74 Merrion Square, Dublin 2, T: (353) 01 761264.
Community Lending Library, Mask Road, Artane, Dublin 5, T: (353) 01 316912.
Friends Historical Library, Swanbrook House, Bloomfield Ave., Dublin 4, T: 01-683684.
Representative Church Body Library, Braemor Park, Dublin 14, T: (353) 01 979979.
St. Patrick's College, Maynooth, County Kildare.
Trinity College, University of Dublin, Dublin.

ITALY
Collegio Alberoni, Via Emilia Parmense 77, Piacenza.
Facultà Valdese di Teologia, Via Pietro Cossa 42, I-00193 Roma.
Libreria Leoniana, via dei Corridori, 16-28 - 00193 Roma, T: (06) 6869113, F: (06) 6833854.
Pontificia Facultà Teologica Marianum, Viale Trenta, Aprile 6, I-00153 Roma, T: 5890441.
Pontificia Università Gregoriana, Piazza della Pilotta 4, I-00187 Roma, T: 6701.
Pontificia Università Lateranense, Piazza San Giovanni in Laterano 4, I-00184 Roma, T: 754385.
Pontificia Università Salesiana, Piazza dell'Ateneo Salesiano 1, I-00139 Roma, T: 884641.
Pontificia Università Urbaniana de Propaganda Fide, Via Urbano VIII, 16, I-00165 Roma, T: 655992.
Pontificio Ateneo Antonianum, Via Merulana 124/B, I-00185 Roma, T: 7574551.
Pontificio Ateneo San Anselmo, Piazza dei Cavalieri di Malta 5, I-00153 Roma, T: 570073.
Pontificio Istituto di Studi Orientali, Piazza Maria Maggiore 7, I-00185 Roma, T: 7312254.
Pontificium Institutum Archeologia Christiana, Via Napoleone III 1, I-00185 Roma, T: 735824.
Seminario Maggiore della Diocesi de Faenza, Stradone 30, Faenza.
Seminario Vescovile di Novara, Via Monte San Gabriele 60, Novara.

JAPAN
Doshisha University, School of Theology, Nishijin, Kyoto.
Tokyo Union Theological Seminary, 264 Iguchi, Mitaka-shi, Tokyo (UCCJ).

LEBANON
Université Saint-Joseph, Bibliothèque Orientale, PO Box 293, Bayrut.

NETHERLANDS
Bibliotheek Canisianum, Tongersestraat 53, Maastricht.
Doopsgezinde Gemeente, Singel 452, Amsterdam.
Free University, De Boelelaan 1115, Amsterdam-Buitenveldert.
Groot Seminarie, Ryksweg 9, Haaren, NB.
Theologische Hogeschool, Keizersgracht 105, Amsterdam.

PALESTINE
Armenian Patriarchal Library, Old City, Jerusalem.

PHILIPPINES
University of Santo Tomas, Espana, Manila.

SOUTH AFRICA
Documentation & Resource Centre, PO Box 941, Pretoria 0001, Khanya House, 140 Visagie St 0002, Pretoria, T: 012-323-6458, F: 012-326-6218.
Ecumenical Resource Centre, PO Box 1128, Durban 4000, 20 St Andrew's St, Durban, T: 031-301-8614, F: 031-301-6611.

SOUTH KOREA
Presbyterian Theological Seminary, Kwangiang-dong, Sungdong-ku, Seoul.

SPAIN
Abodia de Montserrat, Catalonia.
Facultad de Filosofía, Apdo 10, Alcala de Henares, Madrid.
Facultad de Teología, Apdo 32, Paseo de Cartuja, Granada.
San Francisco de Borja Facultad Teologica, San Cugat del Valles, Barcelona.

SWITZERLAND
Priesterseminar St. Luzi, CH-700 Chur.
World Council of Churches, 150 Route de Ferney, CH-1211 Genève 20.

UGANDA
Makerere University, Department of Religion and Philosophy, PO Box 7062, Kampala.

UNITED STATES OF AMERICA (USA)
Alma College, P.O. Box 1258, Los Gatos, CA 95030.
American Baptist Archives Center, P.O. Box 851, Valley Forge, PA 19482-0851, T: 215-768-2000.
American Bible Society Library, 1865 Broadway, New York, NY 10023-9980, T: 212-408-1495, F: 212-408-1512.
American Theological Library Association, Inc., 820 Church St., Ste. 400, Evanston, IL 60201, T: 847-869-7788, F: 847-869-8513.
Andover Newton Theological School, 169 Herrick Rd., Newton Center, MA 02159, T: 617-964-1100.
Antiochian Village Library, Route 711 North, POB 638, Ligonier, PA 15658-0638, T: 412-238-3677.
Archives of the American Catholic Historical Society of Philadelphia, St. Charles Boromeo Seminary, 1000 E. Wynnewood Rd., Overbrook, Philadelphia, PA 19096-3012, T: 215-667-3394, F: 215-664-7913.
Archives of the Episcopal Church, P.O. Box 2247, 606 Rathervue Pl., Austin, TX 78768, T: 512-472-6816.
Billy Graham Center Library, Wheaton College, Wheaton, IL 60187.
Bloomfield College, Bloomfield, NJ 07003.
Brethren Historical Library and Archives, 1451 Dundee Ave., Elgin, IL 60120, T: 708-742-5100.
Burke Library, Union Theological Seminary, 3041 Broadway At Reinhold Niebuhr Place, NY 10027, U. S. A..
Catholic Library Association, Box 26, St. Mary's College of Minnesota, 700 Terrace Hts, Winona, MN 55987.
Catholic University of America, Washington, DC 20017.
Central Baptist Theological Seminary, 2915 Minnesota Av, Kansas City, KS 66102.
Christian Theological Seminary, 1000 West 42nd St, Box 88267, Indianapolis, IN 46208.
Church of Jesus Christ of the Latter-day Saints Library-Archives, Historical Dept., 50 E. North Temple St., Salt Lake City, UT 84150, T: 801-240-2745.
Columbia Theological Seminary, Decatur, GA 30031.
Conception Seminary, Conception, MO 64433.
Concordia Historical Institute, 801 De Mun Ave., St. Louis, MO 63105-3199, T: 314-721-5934.
Concordia Theological Seminary, Springfield, IL 62702.
Congregational Library, 14 Beacon St, Boston, MA 02108.
Dept. of History and Records Management Services, 425 Lombard St., Philadelphia, PA 19147-1516, T: 215-627-1852, F: 215-627-0509.
Divinity Library, 3655 West Pine Bluff, St. Louis, Mo 63108.
Eastern Mennonite College, Eastern Mennonite College, Harrisonburg, VA 22801, T: 703-433-2771.
Emory University, Petts Theological Library, Atlanta, GA 30322.
Episcopal Theological Seminary of the Southwest, PO 2247, Austin, TX 78767.
Evangelical Lutheran Theological Seminary, 2199 East Main St, Columbus, OH 43209.
Evangelical Lutheran Church in American Archives, 8765 W. Higgins Road, Chicago, IL 60631-4198, T: 800-NET-ELCA, 312-380-2818.
Family History Library (LDS), 35 North West Temple St., Salt Lake City, UT 84150, T: 801-240-2331, F: 801-240-5551.
Friends Historical Collection, Guildford College Library, 5800 W. Friendly Ave., Greensboro, NC 27410, T: 919-316-2264, F: 919-316-2950.
Friends' Historical Library, Swarthmore College, 500 College Ave., Swarthmore, PA 19081, T: 215-328-8557, F: 215-328-8673.
Goshen College Biblical Seminary, Goshen, IN 46526.
Hamma School of Theology, Springfield, OH 45504.
Hartford Divinity School, 45 Francis Ave., Cambridge, MA 02138, T: 617-495-5770.
Hill Monastic Manuscript Library, Collegeville, MN 56321-7300, O: www.csbsju.edu/hmml.
Holy Name College, 14th and Shepherd Sts, NE, Washington, DC 20017.
Iliff School of Theology, Denver, CO 80210.
Lancaster Theological Seminary, 555 W. James St., Lancaster, PA 17603-2897, T: 717-393-0654.
Lexington Theological Seminary, South Limestone, Lexington, KY 40508.
Luther Theological Seminary, 2375 Como Ave., West, St. Paul, MN 55108.
Lutheran School of Theology at Chicago, 1100 E. 55th St, Chicago, IL 60615.
Meadville Theological School, 5701 Woodlawn Av, Chicago, IL 60637.
Mennonite Historians of Eastern Pennsylvania Library and Archives, P.O. Box 82, 656 Yoder Rd., Harleysville, PA 19438, T: 215-256-3020.
Moody Bible Institute, 820 N. LaSalle Blvd., Chicago, IL 60610.
Mount Saint Mary's Seminary, 5440 Moeller Ave., Norwood, OH 45212.
National Council of Churches Archives, 425 Lombard St., Philadelphia, PA 19147, T: 215-627-0509, F: 215-627-0509.
Nazarene Archives, Int'l Hdqtrs., Church of the Nazarene, 6401 Teh Paseo, Kansas City, MO 64131, T: 816-333-7000.
New Orleans Baptist Theological Seminary, 4110 Seminary Place, New Orleans, LA 70126.
Northwestern Lutheran Theological Seminary, 1501 Fulham St., St. Paul, MN 55108.
Pacific School of Religion, 1798 Scenic Av, Berkeley, CA 94709.
Pendle Hill Library, Pendle Hill, 338 Plush Mill Rd., Wallingford, PA 19086-6099, T: 215-566-4507.
Pentecostal Research Center, Church of God, P.O. Box 3448, Cleveland, TN 37320, T: 615-472-3361, F: 615-478-7052.
Perkins School of Theology, Southern Methodist University, Dallas, TX 75222.
Petts Theological Library, Emory University, Atlanta, GA 30322.
Princeton Theological Seminary, Mercer St. at Library Place, Box 111, Princeton, NJ 08540.
Quaker Collection-Haverford College Library, Haverford College, Haverford, PA 19041, T: 215-896-1161, F: 215-896-1224.
Quaker Room, Edmund Stanley Library, Friends University, 2100 University Ave., Wichita, KS 67213, T: 316-261-5800.
Salvation Army Archives and Research Center, 615 Slaters Lane, Alexandria, VA 22313, T: 703-684-5500.
Southern Baptist Historical Library & Archives, 901 Commerce St. Ste. 400, Nashville, TN 37203-3620, T: 615-244-0344, F: 615-242-2153.
Southern Baptist Theological Seminary, 2825 Lexington Rd., Louisville, KY 40206.
St. Albert's College, 6172 Chabot Rd., Oakland, CA 94618.
St. Bernard's Seminary, 2260 Lake Av, Rochester, NY 14612.
St. Francis Seminary, 3257 South Lake Drive, Milwaukee, WI 53207.
St. John's Seminary, 5012 East Seminary Rd., Camarillo, CA 93010.
St. Leonard College, 8100 Clyo Rd, Dayton, OH 45459.
St. Mary's Seminary and University, 5400 Roland Ave., Roland Park, Baltimore, MD 21210.
St. Paul's College, 3015 Fourth St, NE, Washington, DC 20017.
St. Vincent College, Latrobe, PA 15650.
Union Theological Seminary, 3041 Broadway, New York, NY 10027, T: 212-280-1505, F: 212-280-1416.
Union Theological Seminary at Virginia, 3400 Brook Rd., Richmond, VA 23229.
United Methodist Historical Library, Ohio Wesleyan Univ., 43 University Ave., Delaware, OH 43015, T: 614-369-4431, F: 614-363-0079.
University of Chicago Divinity School, 5801 South Ellis Ave., Chicago, IL 60637.
University of Notre Dame Archives, Box 513, Notre Dame, IN 46556, T: 219-239-5252.
University of the South School of Theology, Sewanee, TN 37375.
Virginia Theological Seminary, 3737 Seminary Rd., Alexandria, VA 22304.
Wadhams Hall Seminary, Riverside Drive, Ogdensburg, NY 13669.
Wesley Theological Seminary, 4400 Massachusetts Ave., NW, Washington, DC 20016.
Wesleyan Church Archives & Historical Library, P.O. Box 50434, Indianapolis, IN 46250-0434, T: 317-842-0444.
Western Theological Seminary, 86 East 12th St, Holland, MI 49423.
Wilmington College Archives and Quaker Collection, Wilmington College, Wilmington, OH 45177, T: 513-382-6661.
Yale University Divinity School Library, Box 1603 A, Yale Station, New Haven, CT 06520.

VENEZUELA
Acción Ecuménica-Biblioteca/Documentación, C.P. 6314, Caracas, 1010-A Carmelitas, T: 582-811548, F: 861-11-96.

48
Literature

Organizations for the printing and distribution of Christian literature; publications programs, major bookshops and bookshop chains and headquarters, booksellers associations; tract societies; religious book clubs; literacy materials, campaigns, courses, programs, agencies, or coordinating bodies. See also PERIODICALS and PUBLISHING.

AUSTRALIA
Canterbury Book Depot, 22 Leigh St, Adelaide, SA 5000.
Church of England Book Depot, Mayfair Arcade, 124 Adelaide St, Brisbane, Queensland 4000.
Diocesan Book Depot, 27 Murray St, Hobart, Tasmania 7001.
Friends Book Supplies, Friends Meeting House, 10 Hampson St., Kelvin Grove, Queensland 4059, T: 07-356-4185.
Methodist Book Depot, Box 2036-S, GPO, Melbourne, Victoria 3001.
Pacific Christian Literature Society, 511 Kent St, Sydney, NSW.

AUSTRIA
Gospel to Every Home, Püstling 3, 4844 Regau, T: 077672/62 372.
Licht des Lebens, P.O. Box 13, A-9503 Villach.
Literature Information Service, Kerngasse 4, Guntramsdorf A-2353, T: 43-2236-53750, F: 43-2236-52390.

BOLIVIA
Alfalit Boliviano, Junín 6305, Casilla 1466, Cochabamba, T: 4953.

BOTSWANA
Every Home Crusade, PO Box 1538, Gaborone.
Lesedi Christian Centre, PO Box 1465, Pt. 402, Independence Ave., Gaborone, T: 372 328.

BRAZIL
Camara de Literatura Evangélica do, CP 1061-ZC-00, Rio de Janeiro, GB.
Cruzada Mundial de Literatura, Cx. Postal 301, S. José dos Campos-SP 12201-970, T: 12-344-1277, F: 12-344-1277.
Periodicos da Igreja Metodista, CP 8816, 01000 São Paulo, SP.

BRITAIN (UK OF GB & NI)
Agency for Christian Literature Development (ACLD), 7 St. James's St., London SW1A 1EF, T: (01)839-5776.
Associates of the Late Dr. Bray (Dr. Bray's Libraries), SPCK, Holy Trinity Church, Marylebone Rd, London NW1 4DU, T: (01)387-5282.
Blythswood Tract Society, Lochcarron, Ross-shire IV54 8YD Scotland, T: 44-05202-337, F: 44-5202-338.
Catholic Truth Society (CTS), 40 Eccleston Square, London SW1, T: (01)834-4392.
Christian Literature Development Agency, 20 Warwick St, London W1.
Christian Literature Crusade, 201 Church Road, London SE19 2PT, T: 44-081771-4616, F: 44-081653-0851.
Church House Bookshop, Great Smith St., London SW1P 3BN, T: (01)222-9011.
Cornerstone Bookshop, St. John's Church, Princes Street, Edinburgh EHs 4BJ, T: 0131 229 3776, F: 0131 0284.
Crusade Book Club, 19 Draycott Place, London SW3 3SJ.
East European Literature Advisory Committee, 3 Florence Road, Bromley BR1 3NU, Kent, T: 44-081-464-0460, F: 44-081-313-1373.
Eurolit, 320 Robertson House, Leas Road, Guildford, Surrey GU1 4QW.
Evangelical Literature Trust, The Church House, Stoke Park Dr., Ipswich, Suffolk IP2 9TH, T: 44-473-687513, F: 44-473-690881.
Every Home Crusade, 52 Redcar Street, Belfast BT6 9BP, T: (08) 0232 455026, F: (08) 0232 455026.
Feed the Minds, Edinburgh House, 2 Eaton Gate, PO Box 461, London SW1W 9BL, T: (01)730-9611.
Friends Book Centre, Friends House, Euston Rd., London NW1 2BJ, T: 071-387-3601, F: 071-388-1977.
Overcomer Literature Trust, 3 Munster Rd, Parkstone, Poole, Dorset BH14 9PS, T: Parkstone 744551.
Scripture Gift Mission, Inc., Scottish Provident Building, 7 Donegall Square West, Belfast BT1 6JB, T: (08) 0232 321923.
Society for Promoting Christian Knowledge (SPCK), Holy Trinity Church, Marylebone Rd, London NW1 4DU, T: (01)387-5282.
SOON Gospel Literature Worldwide, 44 Twyford Rd., Willington, Derby DE65 6BN, T: 01283 702334, O: E-mail: tony@soon.org.uk.
Stirling Tract Enterprise (Drummond Press) and Drummond Tract Depot, 41 The Craigs, Sterling, T: 3384.
Tufton Books, 7 Tufton St., London SW1P 3QN.
United Society for Christian Literature (USCL), Luke House, Farnham Rd, Guildford, Surrey GU1 4XD, T: (0483)77536.
Victory Tract Club, 189 Brighton Rd, South Croydon, Surrey, T: (01)688-4986.

BURKINA FASO
Adventist Book Center, ADRA/Burkina Faso, 01, Boite Postale, 4273, Ouagadougou 01, T: 30 09 38, F: 226-300938.

BURUNDI
Burundi Literature Fellowship, BP 76, Gitega.
Christian Literature, P.O. Box 2260, Bujumbura.

CAMEROON
Centre de Littérature Evangélique, BP 4048, Yaoundé.

CANADA
Anglican Book Centre, 600 Jarvis St., Toronto, ON M4Y 2J6.
Canadian Tract Society, 26 Hale Rd., P.O. Box 2156, Brampton, ON L6T 3S4, T: 905-457-4559, F: 905-457-4559.
Christian Booksellers Association, Canadian Chapter, 679 Southgate Dr., Guelph, ON N1G 4S2, T: 519-766-1683, F: 519-763-8184.
Christian Literature Crusade, 4257 ouest Ste-Catherine, Montreal, PQ H3Z 1P7, T: 514-933-9466, F: 514-933-7629.
Colporteur's House, 293 Kingswood Rd., Toronto, ON M4E 3N8, T: 416-690-3538, F: 416-694-6101.
Divine Mercy Centre of Canada, R.R. #1, Clarksburg, ON N0H 1J0, T: 519-599-7318, F: 519-599-7019, O: 1-800-461-9254.
Evangelical Tract Distributors, P.O. Box 146, Edmonton, AB T5J 2G9, T: 403-477-1538, F: 403-474-4744.
Every Home International/Canada, P.O. Box 3636, Guelph, ON N1H 7S2, T: 519-837-2010, F: 519-837-3280, O: 1-800-265-7326.
Maranatha Communications Network, Inc., 700-55 Town Centre Court, Scarborough, ON M1P 4X4, T: 416-609-3163, F: 416-609-3066.
Northern Tract Ministries, P.O. Box 1314, Iroquois Falls A, ON P0K 1G0, T: 705-232-6062.

Quaker Book Service, Box 4652, Station E, Ottawa, Ontario K1S 5H8.
Therapeutic Bibliotheca, 35 Richard Ave., Toronto, ON M4L 1W8, T: 416-466-6610, O: Web: http://www.cybervision.sk.ca/hoff/books.html Also: Internet: hoff@inforamp.net.
Valaam Bookstore and Icon Gallery, 4883 MacKensie St., Vancouver V6L 2R7, British Columbia, T: 604-264-1454.
Western Tract Mission, Inc., 104-33rd St. W., Saskatoon, SK S7L 0V5, T: 306-244-0446.

CENTRAL AFRICAN REPUBLIC
Ligue Evangélique de Littérature de l'Afrique Centrale, BP 13, Bozoum.

CHANNEL ISLANDS
Christian Bookshop Mission, 78 Central Market, St Helier, Jersey, T: Central 33380.

CHINA
Catholic Centre, Grand Bldg., 15-18, 2nd Fl., Connaught Rd. C, Hong Kong, T: 5-221071.
Christian Communications Limited, P.O. Box 95364, TST, Kowloon, 3rd Fl., Yan Yee Mansion, 29-33 Soares Ave., Homantin, T: 7139131, F: 7604158.
Lutheran Literature Society, 50 Waterloo Rd, Kowloon, Hong Kong, T: K-844806, 887061.

COSTA RICA
Alfalit Internacional, Postal Dist. 292-Presidente, 4050 Alajuela, T: 506-441-5526, F: 506-442-1152.
Alfalit Latinoamericano, C.P. 292, 4050 Alajuela, T: 506-4415526, F: 506-4421152.
Librería Biblica de Desamparados, Apdo 3332-1000, T: 250-2424.
Librería Vida, T: 225-5502.
Literature Evangélica para América Latina, Apdo 3813, San José.
Ministerio de Alfabetización y Literatura, T: 227-1686.

CYPRUS
Family Bookshop Group, Themis Tower, 2nd Fl, P.O. Box 4259, Olympiou St., Limassol, T: 051-69221.
Middle East Council of Churches/Family Bookshop, P.O. Box, Limassol, T: 357+5+369-221, F: 357-5-353-580.

ECUADOR
Alfabetizacion y Literatura, Ave. America No. 4445, Casilla 634 A, Quito, T: 450-476.
Distribuidores, Godin No. 433, Casilla 230A, Quito, T: 542-875.
Entrenamiento Ministerial, Manuel Larrea No. 433, Casilla 2990, Quito, T: 525-694.
Fundación Para la Alfabetización, Literatura, Educación y Desarrollo (FALED), Ayacucho 1305 y Av. Quito of 04, 2do. Piso; C.P. 10612, Guayaquil, T: 438785, 398578.
Imprentas, Ave. Primera No. 437 y Calle 6, Urdesa Norte, T: 387-377.
Literatura Cristiana, Villalengua No. 320, Casilla 691, Quito, T: 241-550.

EGYPT
Literature and Sunday School Centre, Shubra, Al Qahirah.
SPCK Depot, CMS Bldg, Boulac, Al Qahirah.

ETHIOPIA
Ethiopia Literature Fellowship, P.O. Box 1087, Addis Abeba.
Light & Life Book Fellowship, P.O. Box 131, Addis Abeba.
Lutheran Publications, P.O. Box 658, Addis Abeba.
Yemissrach Dimts Literature Programme, P.O. Box 658, Addis Abeba.

FIJI
Lotu Pasifika Productions (LPP), P.O. Box 208, Suva.

FRANCE
Office Chrétien du Livre (OCL), 193 Rue de l'Université, F-75007 Paris, T: (01)705-4358, 551-9462.

GERMANY
Evangelische Buchhilfe, Geschäftstelle, Falkensteinstr 5A, D-35 Kassel-Oberzwehren.
Martin Luther Federation Literature Dist. Agency, Fahrstr. 15, 91054 D-Erlangen, T: 49-9131/290-39.

GHANA
Sudan Interior Bookshops (SIM), P.O. Box 402, Accra.

GREECE
O Logos Publications, Athínai.

HUNGARY
Christian Bookhouse, OMS, Keresztyén Könyvesház, 1086 Budapest, Bankó utca 9, T: 36-1-209-2308, F: 36-1-209-2308.

INDIA
Alpha Literature Society, D. No. 47-9-26, 3rd Lane, Dwarakanagar, Vishakapatnam, Andhra Pradesh 530016.
Angami Christian Literature Society, ABCC Mission Centre, Kohima, Nagaland 797001.
Association of Christian Publishers and Booksellers, ISPCK, P. Box1585, 1654, Madarsa Road, Kashmere Gate, New Delhi 110006.
Bangalore Tract Book Society, 16 St. Mark's Road, Bangalore, Karnataka 560001.
Beschi Writer's Association, Beschi College, Dindigul, Tamil Nadu 624004.
Bible and Literacy League (India), 10, Venkatamma, Samati Street, Madras, Tamil Nadu 600007.
Bible World - Bible Showroom, International Bible Society India, 2, Gol Market, P. O. Box 154, Port Blair, Andaman & Nicobar Is 744101.
Bombay Tract & Book Society, 21, Hazarimal Somani Marg, Fort, Bombay, Maharashtra 400001.
Book World, Examiner Bookshop, 35 Dalal Street, Fort, Bombay, Maharashtra 400001.
Calcutta Christian Tract and Book Society, 65A, Mahatma Gandhi Road, Calcutta, West Bengal 700009.
Christi Sahitya Prasarak Bookshop, Clover Centre, Shop No. 14, 7, Moledina Road, Pune, Maharashtra 411001.
Christian Digest Society of India, 21 YMCA Road, Bombay, Maharashtra 400008.
Christian Information Service, Hnialum House Saikah, P. O. Lawngtlai, , Mizoram 796891.
Christian Literature Centre, Darrang Baptist Christian Association, Chok Village, Harisinga P. O., Assam 784510.
Christian Literature Depot, Impur P.O., Nagaland 798615.
Christian Literature Distributors, 21, Waudby Road, (Hazarimal Somnai Marg), Bombay, Maharashtra 400001.
Christian Literature Service Bookshop, 110, Avanashi Road, Coimbatore, Tamil Nadu 641018.
Christian Literature Society, Main Police Point, Mokokchung, Nagaland 798601.
Christian Literature Society Bookshop, C. L. S. Bookshop, M. G. Road, Ernakulam, Kerala 682011.
Christian Literature Centre, Church Road, Dimapur, Nagaland 797112.
Christian Literature Society, Trivandrum, Kerala 695001.
Church of South India Diocesan Book Centre, Diocesan Office, Madras, Tamil Nadu 600086.
Council of Communication and Literature, 37, Cantonment Road, Lucknow, Uttar Pradesh 226001.
Dharmaram Publications and Book Centre, Dharmaram Publicatings, Dharmaram College Post, Banglore, Karnataka 560029.
Eastern Book Department, High School Road P. O. Mokokchung, Mokokchung, Nagaland 798601.
Evangelical Literature Fellowship of India (ELFI), 9-2-763, St. Francis Street, Secunderabad, Andhra Pradesh 500025.
Evangelical Literature Service, 73, Maker Arcade, Cuffe Parade, Bombay, Maharashtra.
Evangelical Literature Service Book Depot, C/o Ambassador Book Centre, 12, Mount Road, Madras, Tamil Nadu 600002.
Faith Prayer and Tract League, 23 Outer Circular Road, Kilpauk Garden Colony, Madras, Tamil Nadu 600010.
Free Gospel and Tract Distribution, Paderoo, Vizag, Andhra Pradesh 531024.
Good Pastor International Book Centre, 63, Armenian Street, Madras, Tamil Nadu 600001.
Gospel Literature Worldwide, Vere Lodge, 44 Twyford Road, Willington, Derby DE65 6BN, U. K..
Gospel Tract Society, Minlapra P. O., Quilon, Kerala 691013.
Gospel Tracts, 23 Outer Circular Rd, Kilpauk Garden Colony, Madras, Tamil Nadu 600007.
Grace Book House, Sahitya Seva Sadan, Near Gujarat College, Ahmedabad, Gujarat 380006.
Gujarat Christian Literature Board, Ellis Bridge, Sahitya Seva Sadan, Ahmedabad, Gujarat 380001.
Gujarat Tract and Book Society, Opposite Gujarat College, Ellisbridge, Ahmedabad, Gujarat 380006.
Hindi Theological Literature Committee, 968, North Civil Lines, Jabalpur, Madhya Pradesh 482001.
Hindustan Bible Literature, Madavakkam Tank Road, Madras, Tamil Nadu 600010.
India Every Home Crusade, P. O. Box 4830, A-2/63 Safdarjung Enclave, New Delhi 110029.
Indian Promotion of Christian Knowledge Bookshop, Opp. Liberty Cinema, Sadar, Nagpur, Maharashtra.
Indian Society for Promoting Christian Knowledge, Post Box - 1585, Kashmere Gate, 1654 Madrasa Road, New Delhi 110006.
Jeevadhara Literature Service, 16-4-226/1, Vidya Nagar, Warangal, Andhra Pradesh 506002.
Jeevan Dhara Book Centre, Nirmala Convent Road, Vijayawada, Andhra Pradesh 520010.
Kannada Christian Literature Society, The Methodist Church Compound, Belgaum, Karnataka 590016.
London Mission Book Depot, C/o London Mission Press, Nagercoil, Kanyakumari, Tamil Nadu 629001.
Marathi Mission Station Road Book Shop, Clara Bruce High School Compound, Station Road, Ahmednagar, Maharashtra 414001.
Methodist Church Mobile Bookshop, 4A, Bengal Christian Literature Centre, 6, Riverside Road, Barrackpore, West Bengal 743101.
Nepali Christian Literature Society, Gandhi Road, Darjeeling, West Bengal 734101.
North India Bible Literature, House No. 812 Sector 15, P. Box No. 713, Faridabad, Haryana 121007.
North India Christian Tract and Book Society, 18, Clive Road, Allahabad, Uttar Pradesh 211001.
Operation Mobilisation India Logos Book Room, 20, Cama's Cold Storage, Sun Mill Compound, Lower Parel (W), Bombay, Maharashtra 400013.
Revival Literature Fellowship, P. O. Box 513, 51/1, Kenchappa Road, Fraser Town, Bangalore, Karnataka 560005.
Salem Tract Society, Vakathanam P. O., Kerala 686538.
Scripture Union Book Shop, 138-A Trivandrum Road, Palayamkottai, Tamil Nadu 627002.
St. Paul International Book Centre, H-30, Connaught Place, New Delhi 110001.
Tamil Literature Society, Bharathi Road, Tiruchy, Tamil Nadu 620001.
Tamil Theological Book Club, Tamilnadu Theological Seminary, Arasaradi, Madurai, Tamil Nadu 625010.
Theological Literature Council, C. L. S. Buildings, M. C. Road, Tiruvalla, Kerala 689101.
Zion Book Depot, Kumbanad, Kerala 689547.

IRAN
Literature Committee, Iran Council of Churches, P.O. Box 1505, Tehran.

IRELAND
Fallon (CJ), 77 Marlboro St, Dublin 1, T: 46191.

ITALY
Crociata del Libro Cristiano (CLC), Via Ricasoli 97r, Firenze, T: 283205.
Libreria Editrice Claudiana, Via Principe Tommaso 1D, Torino, T: 682458.
Pontificia Universita Urbaniana, 00165 Roma - Via Urbano VIII, 16, T: 06/6833314, F: 06/6833314.

IVORY COAST
Centre de Publications Evangéliques, BP 8900, Abidjan.
Croisade du Livre Chrétien, BP 4494, Abidjan.
Editions Africains, BP 4142, Abidjan.

JAPAN
Christian Literature Crusade, 4-13-34 Hon Cho, Higashi Kurume Shi, Tokyo 203, T: 0424-71-1527.
Concordia-Sha, 2-32 1-chome, Fujimi-cho, Chiyoda-ku, Tokyo 102.
Japan Assemblies of God Literature Dept, 3-430 Komagome, Toshima-ku, Tokyo 170.
Nippon Seikokai Publications Division, 4-21 1-chome, Higashi, Shibuya-ku, Tokyo 150.
Omi Brotherhood Kosei-Sha, Moto Uoyamachi, Omi Hachiman-shi, Shiga-ken 523.
United Church of Christ in Japan Board of Publications, 5-1 4-chome, Ginza, Chuo-ku, Tokyo 104.

KENYA
Baptist Publications, Likoni Rd, PO Box 30370, Nairobi, T: 558744.
Catholic Bookshop, Manager, Kaunda St (behind Holy Family Cathedral), PO Box 30249, Nairobi, T: 25172.
Evangelical Literature Fellowship of East Africa (ELFEA), PO Box 36351, Nairobi.
Kenya Pastors' Book Club, PO Box 665, Nakuru.

LEBANON
Arabic Literature Mission, PO Box 5039, Bayrut.
Christian Arabic Literature League, PO Box 166, Bayrut.
Family Bookshop Group, PO Box 113-5007, Rubeiz Bldg, Makdessi St., Beirut, T: 01-345797.
Gospel Lietrature Service, PO Box 5269, Bayrut.
Muslim World Evangelical Literature Service (MWELS), Kehale PO.

LESOTHO
Lesotho Book Centre, P.O. Box 608, Maseru.
Sesuto Book Depot, P.O. Box 4, Morija.

LIBERIA
Christian Literature Crusade, Mission Dir, Box 26, Monrovia, T: 22728.

MALAWI
Christian Literature Association in Malawi (CLAIM), P.O. Box 503, Blantyre.
Emmanuel Tract Fellowship, P.O. Box 135, Zomba, T: 2465.

MEXICO
Alfalit, Comite Nacional en México, Calz México-Coyoacan 349, Zona 13, México, DF, T: 244792.
Cruzada de Literatura, Anicerto Ortego 845-1, Zona 12, México, DF, 750407.

MYANMAR
Burma Christian Literature Society, Rangoon.

NETHERLANDS
Quaker Literatuur (Miep Lieftinck), Stadhouderslaan 8, 2517 HW Den Haag, T: 070-3632132.

NEW ZEALAND
Anglican Book Centre, P.O. Box 800, Christchurch.
Arabic Literature Mission, New Zealand Council, PO Box 380, Auckland 1.
Christian Literature Crusade, 10 MacArthur St., Feilding, T: 0-6-323-0290, F: 0-6-323-0290.
Every Home for Christ, P.O. Box 31-260, Milford, Auckland, T: 0-9-520-2179, F: 0-9-520-2179.
Evidence Book Depot, P.O. Box 6288, Te Aro, Wellington.
Kell's Christian Book Centre, P.O. Box 994, Hastings.
Quaker Book Sales, 50 Ruahine St., Dannevirke, T: 06-3749148, F: 06-3746884.

NIGERIA
Baptist Publications and Bookstore, PM Bag 5070, Ibadan.
Baraka Publications, PM Bag 2086 (and Box 171), Kaduna.
Daystar Publications, P.O. Box 1261, Ibadan.
Niger Challenge Publications, Editor, PM Bag 12067, Lagos.
SUM/EKAS Publications, P.O. Box 643, Jos.

NORWAY
Andaktsbokselskapet, Munchs Gate 2, Oslo 1.

PAKISTAN
Christian Literature Crusade (CLC), Christian Bookshop, Bonus Rd, Karachi.
Punjab Religious Book Society, Anarkali, Lahore.

PANAMA
Publicaciones El Escudo, Apdo 808, Panamá.

PAPUA NEW GUINEA
Christian Literature Crusade (CLC), Okari St, Port Moresby; Box 1136, Boroko, T: 53059.
NAMASU Bookshop, 4th St, P.O. Box 615, Lae, T: 53732.

PHILIPPINES
Christian Literature Crusade, 104 Karuhatan, P.O. Box 513, Valenzuela, Manila.
Literature Crusades, P.O. Box 3627, Manila.
Philippines Every Home Crusade, P.O. Box 2650, Manila.

PORTUGAL
Campanha de Literatura de Casa em Casa, Rua Alvaro de Castelões, 656 r/c, 4200 Porto; Apartado 4246, 4004 Porto Codex, T: 02-550 05 80.
Centro de Literatura Ev do Norte, Av Afonso Henriques, Fontainhas, S João de Madeira.
Depósito de Literatura Cristã, Rua de Infantaria 16, 77-r/c-Esq, Lisboa 3.
Junta Presbiteriana de Publicações, RD Vasco da Câmara Belmonte 8, Carcavelos.
Nucleo de Distribuição de Literatura Cristã, Rua Higino de Sousa 6-3 Dt, Apdo 1, Queluz.

PUERTO RICO
La Reforma Retail Store, 54 El Roble St., PO Box 21402, Rio Piedras, T: 809-765-1635, F: 800-628-4842.

RUSSIA
Every Home for Christ, Street 64, kv. 315 Moscoe 113534, T: 7-095-386-6532.
Religious Books for Russia, Starokonushennii Pereulok 37-27, Moscow.
Valaam Monastery Bookstore, 11792 Nevsky Prospekt 1/29, St. Petersburg 198020.

SINGAPORE
Bethesda Book Centre, Marine Parade, 80 #01-784 Marine Parade Central, Singapore 440080, T: 348-3775.
Christian Literature Evangelism Ltd., Block 37 #01-401, Circuit Road, Singapore 370037, T: 746-0258.
Crest Christian Book Corner, 14 Scotts Road, Far East Plaza #05-58, Singapore 228213, T: 235-8593, F: 737-5545.
Life Book Shop, 9A Gillstead Road, Singapore 309063, T: 254-1223.
Living Word Ltd., 132-A Sophia Road, Singapore 228186, T: 336-1922, F: 344-2600.
Scripture Union Singapore, 7 Armenian Street, #03-07 Bible House, Singapore 179932, T: 337-1437, F: 338-0983.
Singapore Every Home Crusade Co Ltd., No. 8, Lorong 27-A Geylang, #02-04/05 Guilin Building, Singapore 388106.
SKS Books Warehouse, 315 Outram Road, #10-05 Tan Boon Liat Building, Singapore 169074, T: 227-9700, F: 221-4595.
SU Bookshop, Peace Centre, 1 Sophia Road, #02-21/25 Peace Center, Singapore 048622, T: 337-3682.

SOUTH AFRICA
Abundant Life Bookshop & Publishers, PO Box 825, Roodepoort 1725 Lindhaven Shopping Centre, 91 Progress Rd, Lindhaven, Roodepoort, T: 011-763-2512.
ACLA (Africa Christian Literature Advanced), PO Box 332 Roodepoort 1725, 16 Mare St, Roodepoort, T: 011-763-6187.
AEB Bookroom - Pretoria, PO Box 1376, Pretoria 0001, 169 Andries St, Pretoria 0002, T: 012-21-9400, F: 012-323-4636.
AGLO (African Gospel Literature Outreach), PO Box 627, Krugersdorp 1740, 39 Rory St, Krugersdorp, T: 011-953-3738, F: 011-953-1981.
All Nations Gospel Publishers, P.O. Box 2191, Pretoria 0001, 228 Christoffel St, Pretoria West, T: 012-327-4441, F: 012-3272478.
Bible Centre Boeke, PO Box 2119, Pietermaritzburg 3200, 141 Longmarket St, Pietermaritzburg, T: 0331-42-2333, F: 0331-94-6931.
Boekwinkel van die APK, PO Box 11488, Hatfield 0028, 109 Brook St, Brooklyn, Pretoria, T: 012-43-4461, F: 012-342-3946.
Central Book Depot, P.O. Box Roodepoort 1725, Van Wyk St, Roodepoort, T: 011-760-2666.
Christelike Boek-en Geskenkwinkel, PO Box 88, Parow 7500, 223 Voortrekker Rd, Parow, T: 012-930-2807, F: 021-92-2472.
Christian Book Centre, Robinson Blvd, Robinson St, Port Shepstone 4240, T: 0291-2-0669.
Christian Booksellers Association, 229 Nicolson Rd, Durban, Natal.
Christian Centre Bookroom, PO Box 18249, Dalbridge 4014, 9 Galway Rd, Mayville, Durban, T: 031-207-5030, F: 031-301-3549.
Christian Literature & Bible Centre, PO Box 3698, Durban 4000, 141 Woodford Gr, Morningside, Durban, T: 031-23-4034, F: 031-23-1473.
Christian's Writer's Circle, PO Box 2298, Trekker, Brakpan, 30 Springs Rd, Sallies Village, Brakpan, T: 011-743-2446.
Cornerstone Books & Music Centre, PO Box 1978, Cape Town 8000, 22 Lower Burg St, Cape Town, T: 021-25-3888.
CUM Boeke - Port Elizabeth, PO Box 27395, Greenacres 6057, B16, The Bridge Greenacres Cent, Cape Re, Port Elizabeth, T: 041-33-4426, F: 041-34-5826.
Dibukeng, PO Box 97013, Presas, Pretoria 0114, 512 Bosman St, Pretoria, T: 012-326-8737, F: 012-323-5825.
Die Boeke Depot Bk, PO Box 182, Aberdeen 6270, 21 Cathart St, Aberdeen, T: 049212-1.
Every Home for Christ SA/World Literature Crusade, PO Box 7256, Hennopsmeer 0046, 265 West Ave, Verwoerburg City, T: 021-663-4587, F: 021-663-4589.
HAUM Boekhandel, PO Box 460, Pretoria 0001, Nedbank Forum Gebou, Festival St, Hatfield, Pretoria, T: 012-43-7051, F: 012-342-2495.
Impact Menlyn, PO Box 33626, Glenstantia 0010, Hatfield Christian Christian Church, Corobay Ave, Waterkloof Glen, Pretoria, T: 012-348-9372, F: 012-348-3212.
Lewensvreugde Boekwinkel, PO Box 641, Volk-

srust 2370, 16 Vrede St, Volksrust, T: 01773-4444.
Literacy for Africa, PO Box 809, Paulshot 2056, Sandton, T: 011-803-8823.
Living Way Bookshop, White River, PO Box 1018, White River 1240, 41 Kruger Park St, White River, T: 013-751-1540, F: 0131-751-3242.
Lus Boekhandel & Winkel, Private Bag X1, Belhar 7507, Cnr Suikerbossie & Watsonia Sts, Belhar, T: 021-952-5806.
Methodist Bookshop - Cape Town, P.O. Box 708, Cape Town 8000, 33 Parliament St, Cape Town, T: 021-461-8212, F: 021-461-8249.
Moravian Book Depot, PO Box 24493, Lansdowne 7780, 63 Albert Rd, Lansdowne, T: 021-762-8430, F: 021-761-4046.
NG Kerk-Jeughoekhandel, PO Box 396, Bloemfontein 9300, 154 Maitand St, Bloemfontein, T: 051-47-7778, F: 051-47-1560.
Oasis Christian Bookshop & Coffee Shop, Suite 308, Postnet X10039, Randburg 2125, Randburg Baptist Church, 263 Oak Ave, Ferndale, Randburg, T: 011-787-1702, F: 011-787-7111.
Ons Klyntjie Christian Book Shop, 49e Van Riebeeck Rd, Kuils River 7580, T: 021-903-1311, F: 021-903-2839.
Operation Upgrade of Southern Africa, PO Box 314, Durban 4000, 74 NMR Ave, Durban 4001, T: 031-32-9591, F: 031-37-2759.
Protestant Book Centre, PO Box 13068, Mowbray 7705, T: 021-685-3015, F: 021-685-2618.
Psalm 99 Bybelwinkel, Wamakersplein, Fabriek St, Paarl 7646, T: 02211-2-9565.
Salt Institute, PO Box 104, Mondeor, 2110 Enterprise House, Shamrock St, Unified, Roodepoort, T: 011-674-5282, F: 011-672-2102.
Scipture Union Bookshop Cape Town, 14 Park Rd, Rondebosh 7700 Cape Town, T: 021-689-8283, F: 021-689-8283.
Sunday School Centre Bookshop, PO Box 3020, Cape Town, CP.
TEAM Bookstore, PO Box 1038, Empangeni 3880, 7 NBS Cntr, Commercial Rd, Empangeni, T: 0351-2-4409.
The Cathedral Bookshop, PO Box 425, Port Elizabeth 6000, 2 Prospect Hill, Port Elizabeth, T: 041-55-3935.
The Catholic Bookshop, PO Box 379, Cape Town 8000, 12 Tuin Plein, Cape Town, T: 021-45-5904, F: 021-46-1087.
The Grapevine Bookshop, PO Box 992, Northlands, 2116 Shop 9 The Village, 60 Tyrone Ave, Parkview, Johannesburg, T: 011-646-9675.
The Salvation Army Bookroom, PO Box 1018, Johannesburg 2000, PO Box 1018, Johannesburg 2000, 121 Rissik St, Wanderers View, Jhburg, T: 011-403-3614, F: 011-648-4278.
Umtata Christian Books, Private Bag X5131, Umtata, 5100, Zanmed Centre, 58 Madeira St, Umtata, T: 0471-31-1380, F: 0471-31-1255.
Vibrant Life Bookshop, PO Box 14800, Kenwyn 7790, Old Ottery Rd/Clifford St, Sunset Park, Ottery, Cape Town, T: 021-739-490, F: 021-739-496.
Vida Bookshop, PO Box 49066, Rosettenville 2130, 239 Johnannesburg Rd, La Rochelle, Jhb, T: 011-435-3452.
Word of Faith Bookshop, PO Box 200, Welkom 9460, 114 Constantia Rd, Dagbreek, Welkom, T: 057-5-6262, F: 057-396-4313.
Wycliffe Booksellers, PO Box 2130, Pretoria, Transvaal.
Zera Mobile Books, PO Box 10001, Drusana 9311, 54 Rose Ave, Wilgehof, Bloemfontein, T: 051-22-6935, F: 051-22-4369.

SOUTH KOREA

Christian Literature Society of Korea, PO Box 170, Seoul.

SPAIN

Centro de Literatura Cristiana, Cristo de la Sed, 117, 41005 Sevilla, T: 457-86-30.
Centro de Literatura Cristiana, Dr. Marín Lago, 24, bajo, Apdo. 3050, Vigo, 36205 Pontevedra, T: 27-17-36.
Centro Derecursos-Bibliotecas Creativas, Aragó, 429, prl. 1ª, 08013 Barcelona, T: 232-65-56.
CLC (Centro de Literatura Cristiana), Pl. América Española, 3, 28028 Madrid, T: 725-78-53.
Editorial Logos, Valverde, 45, 1°, 28004 Madrid, T: 532-55-52, F: 532-91-96.
Librería Evangélica, Camelias, 19, 08024 Barcelona, T: 213-66-99, F: 213-16-84, O: Also tel: 213-35-15.
Librería Evangélica, Apdo. 353, Roquetas de Mar, 04740 Almería, T: 32-17-67.
Librería Marantha, Tao, s/n, Apdo. 28, Vecindario, 35110 Las Palmas, T: 75-44-24, F: 75-50-43.
Sociedad Bíblica, 11701 Velarde, 2, Ceuta, T: 51-77-00.

SWEDEN

Christian Science Committee on Publications, Stenbackstigen 5, S-181 62 Lidingö, T: (08)766-3937.

SYRIA

Damascus MECC Liaison/Family Bookshop, Sahat-al-Najme - Doctors' Syndicate Bldg, PO Box 4889, Damascus, T: 963+11+222-7006, F: 932-11-444-7328.

TAIWAN

Hua Ming Press (Catholic), P. O. Box 8-121, 5th Fl., 2 Chungshan N. Rd., Sect. 1, Taipei (100), T: 02-3119489, 3119481.
Kuangchi Press and Bookstore, 24 Hsin Hai Rd., Sect. 1, Taipei (107), T: 02-3414922, 3416024.

TANZANIA

Christian Literature Distribution, PO Box 113, Morogoro.
Literature & Christian Education Centre, PO Box 15, Dodoma.
Msalato Literature Centre, PO Box 15, Dodoma.
Swedish Free Tract Centre, PO Box 838, Dar es Salaam.

THAILAND

Alliance Literature Department, 28/2 Soi Pracha Utit, Pradipat Rd, Bangkok 4, T: 2791523.

UGANDA

Evangelical Literature Centre, 9 Bambo Rd, PO Box 4607, Kampala.

UNITED STATES OF AMERICA (USA)

All Nations Literature, P.O. Box 26300, Colorado Springs, CO 80936-6300; 4291 Austin Bluffs Parkway, 80918, Ste 104, T: 719-528-1944, F: 719-528-8010, O: E-mail: stearns@cscns.com.
American Friends Service Committee Bookstore, 980 N. Fair Oaks Ave., Pasadena CA 91103, T: 818-791-1978, F: 818-791-2205.
American Tract Society, P.O. Box 462008, Garland, TX 75046, T: 972-276-9408, 1-800-548-7228, F: 972-272-9642, O: E-mail: amtract@aol.com, Web: www.goshen.net/AmericanTractSociety.
Ball World Missions (Bible & Literacy League), 8955 Old Lemay Ferry Rd, Hillsboro, MNO 63050, T: 314-789-4368, F: 314-789-5735.
Bible Literature International, P O. Box 477, Columbus, OH 43216, T: 614-267-3116, F: 614-267-7110, O: E-mail: 70712.141@compuserve.com, Web: www.bli.org/home.htm.
Biblical Literature Fellowship, P.O. Box 629, Wheaton, IL 60189, T: 630-858-0348, F: 630-858-1946, O: E-mail: BiblicalLF@aol.com.
Board of Publications, Lutheran Church in America, 2900 Queen Lane, Philadelphia, PA 19129.
Bookmates International, 3905 Rolling Hills Rd, St Paul, MN 55112, T: (612)633-6948.
Books, Inc., 1250 Connecticut Av, NW, Washington, DC 20036.
Candytrax, 3225 W. Shaw Ave. Ste. 123, Fresno, CA 93711, T: 800-984-9625, 209-224-6723, F: 209-226-0680, O: E-mail: candytrax@aol.com.
Catholic Book Club, 106 W. 56th St., New York, NY 10019.
Catholic Digest Book Club, 475 Riverside Dr., Suite 1268, New York, NY 10115.
Chick Publications, Inc, PO Box 662, Chino, CA 91708, T: 714-987-0771.
Chinese Evangelical Literature Committee, 199 Bridge St, South Hamilton, MA 01982.
Christian Booksellers Association (CBA), 2031 West Cheyenne Rd, Colorado Springs, CO 80906.
Christian Life Missions—Christian Writers Institute, 177 E. Crystal Lake Ave., Lake Mary, FL 32746, T: 407-324-5465, F: 407-324-0209.
Christian Life Publications, Gundersen Drive/Schmale Rd, Wheaton, IL 60187, T: (312)653-4200.
Christian Literacy Associates, 541 Perry Hwy., Pittsburg, PA 15229, T: 412-364-3777.
Christian Literature, P.O. Box 388, Midway City, CA 92655.
Christian Literature and Bible Center, 3840 Oakley Av, Memphis, TN 38111.
Christian Literature Crusade, 701 Pennsylvania Ave., P.O. Box 356, Ft. Washington, PA 19034, T: 215-542-1244, F: 215-542-7580, O: E-mail: 76043.3053@compuserve.com, Web: www.hkstar.com/~clchk.
Christian Printing Mission, 8115 Mahoet Rd., Minerva, OH 44657, T: 216-895-3801, F: 216-895-3656.
Christian Publications, Third & Reily Sts, Harrisburg, PA 17102.
Committee on Publication, Christian Science Center, Boston, MA 02115.
Committee on World Literacy and Christian Literature, 475 Riverside Drive, New York, NY 10027.
Concordia Tract Mission, PO Box 201, St Louis, MO 63166, T: (314)664-7000.
Cook Communications Ministries International, 850 N. Grove Ave., Elgin, IL 60120, T: 847-741-2400, F: 847-741-2444, O: Web: www.cookministries.com/internat.htm.
Distrib Int'l de Materiales Evangelicos, 10353 Imperial Ave, PO Box 480, Cupertino, CA 95014, T: 408-253-9096.
Encouraging Words Bookstore, O: Web: www.ewbooks.com.
Evangelical Literature League, 941 Wealthy St, PO Box 6219, Grand Rapids, MI 49506, T: (616)454-3196.
Evangelical Literature Overseas (ELO), 491 Gundersen Drive, PO Box 725, Wheaton, IL 60187, T: (312)668-4747.
Evangelical Reprint Library, College Press, Box 1132, Joplin, MO 64801.
Every Home for Christ, P. O. Box 35930, Colorado Springs, CO 80935; 7899 Lexington Dr., Colorado Springs, CO 80920, T: 719-260-8888, F: 719-260-7408, O: E-mail: Wes@ehc.org, Web: www.sni.net/ehc.
Forward Movement Publications, 412 Sycamore St, Cincinnati, OH 45202.
Good News Hungarian Literature Mission, Inc., P.O. Box 602, Center Harbor, NH 03226, T: 603-253-4298, F: 617-861-1134.
Gospel Literature International, Inc. (GLINT), 2910 Inland Empire Blvd. #104, Ontario, CA 91764, T: 909-481-5222, F: 909-481-5216, O: E-mail: GLINT@glint.org, Web: www.glint.org.
International Christian Literature Distributors, Inc., P.O. Box 8295, Minneapolis, MN 55408, T: 612-920-4687.
Korean American Christian Literature Association, 3171 W. Olympic Bl. #533, Los Angeles, CA 90006.
Last Days Ministries, Box 40, Lindale, TX 75771-0040.
Literacy & Evangelism International, 1800 S. Jackson Ave., Tulsa OK 74107, T: 918-585-3826, F: 918-585-3224, O: E-mail: 75313.2613@compuserve.
LOGOI/FLET, 14540 S.W. 136th St., Ste. 200, Miami, FL 333186, T: 305-232-5880, F: 305-232-3592, O: E-mail: LOGOI@aol.com.
Mailbox Club Intl., 404 Eager Road, Valdosta, GA 31602, T: 912-244-6812, F: 912-245-8977.
Media Associates International, Inc., 130 N. Bloomingdale Rd., Bloomingdale, IL 60108, T: 708-893-1977, F: 708-893-1141.
Message of Life, Inc., 58607 Rd. 601, Ahwahnee, CA 93601, T: 209-683-7028, F: 209-683-7028, O: E-mail: mensjevida@aol.com.
Middle East Media, P.O. Box 359, Lynnwood, WA 98046, T: 206-778-0752.
Missionary Literature Foundation, P.O. Box 374, Burbank, CA 91503, T: (213)845-7931.
Moody Literature Mission, 820 N. LaSalle St, Chicago, IL 60610, T: (312)642-1570.
Multnomah Literature Ministries, 10209 S.E. Division St., Portland, OR 97266, T: 503-257-0526, F: 503-255-7690.
Osborn Foundation International (OSFO), Box 7572, Tulsa, OK 74105.
Pan American Literature Mission, 5215 East Fort Lowell Rd, Tucson, AZ 85716, T: (602)326-1787.
Religious Book Discount House, P.O. Box 2455, Grand Rapids, MI 49501, T: (616)949-9500.
Religious Books for Russia, P.O. Box 522, Glen Cove, NY 11542, T: 516-671-7716, F: 516-671-1012.
Rusthoi Soul Winning Publications, Box 595, Montrose, CA 91020.
Saint Gabriel's Book Nook, O: Web: www.stgabriel.com/gabriel.
Scripture Press Ministries, Box 513, Glen Ellyn, IL 60137, T: (312)668-6002.
Seeds Christian Tracts, O: Web: www.tracts.com.
Society for Promoting Christian Knowledge, P.O. Box 879, Sewanee, TN 37375-0879.
Thomas More Book Club, Thomas More Association, 205 W. Monroe St., Sixth Fl., Chicago, IL 60606.
Trinity Zone, O: Web: www.trinityzone.com.
Watch Tower Bible & Tract Society, 25 Columbia Heights, Brooklyn, NY 11201, T: 212-625-1240.
World Literature Crusade, 20232 Sunburst Ave, Chatsworth, P.O. Box 7139, Canoga Park, CA 91304, T: 818-341-7870.
World Missionary Press, Inc., P.O. Box 120, New Paris, IN 46553, T: 219-831-2111, F: 219-831-2161, O: E-mail: 74357.3222@compuserve.com, Web: www.WMPress.org.
World Wide Tract Ministry, West End, P.O. Box 3625, Birmingham, AL 35211.
World-Wide Missionary Crusader, 4606 Av H, Lubbock, TX 79404, T: (806)747-5417.

ZAMBIA

Africa Literature Centre, P.O. Box 21319, Kitwe, T: 260-02-210765, F: 260-02-211001.
Copperbelt Christian Publications, P.O. Box 959, Ndola.
Lunda Ndembu Publications, CMML, PO Ikelenge.
Message of Victory Evangelism (Zambian Christian Book Crusade), P.O. Box 783, Luanshya.

49

Liturgy & worship

Liturgical centers, organizations, movements; major supply agencies for liturgical equipment, literature, vestments; liturgical training centers; instruction or advocacy concerning ritual, rites, sacraments; wholesale and retail supply houses for religious articles. See also MUSIC.

ARGENTINA

Centro Litúrgico Nacional, CEA, Paraguay 1867, Buenos Aires, T: 425708.
Una Voce Argentina, Reconquista 165, Oficina 622, Buenos Aires.

AUSTRALIA

Australian Episcopal Liturgical Commission, c/o Catholic Presbytery, 33 Howard St, West Melbourne, Victoria 3033, T: 303474.
Institute of Pastoral Liturgy, St. Patrick's College, Manly, NSW 2095, T: 974870.
Latin Mass Society, GPO Box 2773, Sydney, NSW.

AUSTRIA

Liturgisches Institut, Erzabtei St Peters, Postfach 113, A-5010 Salzburg, T: (06222)42166.
Una Voce Austria, An der Furt 2, A-6020 Innsbruck.

BELGIUM

Apostolate for Church Life, Norbertijneabdij, B-3190 Tongerlo, T: (014)55041.
Commission Interdiocésaine de Pastorale Liturgique (CIPL), Av Reine Astrid 10, B-7000 Mons, T: (065)331278.
Interdiocesan Commission for Pastoral Liturgy, ICLZ, Guimardstraat 5, B-1040 Brussels; Hoogstraat 41, B-9000 Gent, T: (02)123379, 125203.
Liturgical Institute, Abdij Keizersberg, Mechelsestraat 202, B-3000 Leuven, T: (016)224174.
Liturgisch Centrum De Wijngaard, Begijnhof, B-8000 Brugge, T: (050)330011.
Madrigal, Herestraat 51, B-3000 Leuven, T: (016)33967.
Una Voce Belgique, Rue de la Montagne 52a, B-1000 Brussel.

BRAZIL

Centro Catequético e Litúrgico Lumen Christi, c/o Secretariado Arquidiocesano de Pastoral, Rua Ir Serafina 88, Campinas, SP, T: 25316, 89784, 92742.
Centro Litúrgico Nacional, Comissão Nacional de Litúrgia, Rua do Russel 76, 5 andra, CP 16085, 20000 Rio de Janeiro, GB, ZC-01-Gloria, T: 2252761.
Instituto Nacional de Pastoral, Rua Cosme Velho 120, 20000 Rio de Janeiro, GB, ZC-01-Cosme Velho.

BRITAIN (UK OF GB & NI)

Association for English Worship, 123 Marsham Court, Westminster SW1, T: 0171 828 1072.
Association for Latin Liturgy, 16 Brean Down Ave., Bristol BS9 4JF, T: 0117-962 3558.
Church of England Liturgical Commission, Church House, Dean's Yard, Westminster, London SW1P 3NZ, T: (01)222-9011.
Gregorian Association, Rosedale, Petersham Rd, Richmond, Surrey TW10 7AD.
Latin Mass Society of England & Wales, 43 Blandford St, London W1.
Liturgy Commission, General Synod of the Church of England, Church House, Dean's Yard, London SW1P 3NZ, T: (01)222-9011.
Society of St. Gregory, 'Mair Wen', 8 Hampton Fields, Oswestry, Shropshire SY11 1TJ, T: 01691-652720.
Una Voce Scottish Branch, 6 Belford Park, Edinburgh 4.

CANADA

Canadian Council on Liturgy, 1070 Waterloo St, London 11, Ontario, T: (519)433-0658.
D. Shuter Robes Ltd., 26 Duncan St., Toronto, ON M5V 2B0, T: 416-977-3857, F: 416-977-1777.
Dominion Regalia, 1550 O'Connor Dr., Toronto, ON M4B 2V3, T: 416-752-2382, F: 416-752-4615.
Harcourts Limited, 26-28 Duncan St., Toronto, ON M5V 2B9, T: 416-977-4408, F: 416-977-3856.
Luxfer Studios Ltd., 8481 Keele St., Unit 6, Concord, ON L4K 1Z7, T: 905-669-4244, F: 905-669-4244.
National Liturgical Office, 90 Parent Av, Ottawa 2, Ontario K1N 7B1, T: (613)236-9461.
Office National de Liturgie, 1215 est, Blvd Saint-Joseph, Montréal 176, Québec, T: (204)247-9851.
Una Voce Canada, Box 5093, Station F, Ottawa 5.
Universal Church Supplies (1988) Ltd., 11105 - 102 Ave., Edmonton, AB T5K 2P4; #160-3803 Calgary Tr. S., Edmonton, AB T6J 5M8, T: 403-429-3153, F: 403-425-0585, O: (tel: 403-435-8605).
Will & Baumer Canada, Inc., 1200 Aerowood Dr., Unit 31 Mississauga, ON L4W 2S7, T: 905-602-4444, F: 905-629-9181.

CHILE

Magnificat, Morandé 322, Of 210, Santiago.

COLOMBIA

Departmento de Litúrgia, CELAM, Apdo Aéreo 1931, Medellín, Ant.
Departmento de Litúrgia, Secretariado Permenente del Episcopado Colombiano, Calle 26 No 27-48, Apdo Aéreo 7448, Apdo Nacional 4553, Bogotá, T: 414186, 414642.
Instituto Latinoamericano de Litúrgia Pastoral (ILP), Calle 19, No 81-83, Apdo Aéreo 1931, Medellín, Ant, T: 381626, 381728.

CROATIA

Centre Présent Chrétien, Zagreb.

DENMARK

Una Voce Dacia, Maglekildevej 6, DK-1853 Kobenhavn V.

EL SALVADOR

Comisión Nacional de Litúrgia, Equipo de Reflexión, Arzobispado, San Salvador, T: 257041, 257042, 257082.

FRANCE

Association des Amis de Kuer-Moussa, Abbaye Saint-Pierre de Solesmes, F-72 Sablé-sur-Sarthe.
Association Una Voce, BP 174, F-75017 Paris.
Centre National de Pastorale Liturgique (CNPL), Institut Supérieur de Liturgie, 4 Av Vavin, F-75006 Paris, T: (01)325-4000.
Editions Ouvrières, Disques DMO, 12 Av Soeur Rosalie, F-75013 Paris.
Institut Supérieur de Liturgie, 4 Av Vavin, F-75006 Paris, T: (01)325-4000.

GERMANY

Berneuchener Dienst, Geschäftsstelle, über Hob aN, D-7241 Kloster Kirchberg.
Liturgisches Institut, Jesuitenstr 13c, Postfach 371, D-5500 Trier, T: (0651)48106/7.
Lutherische Liturgische Konferenz Deutschlands, Am Markt 7, D-2418 Ratzeburg.
Una Voce in Deutschland, Akazienhof 1, D-414 Rheinhausen.

HOLY SEE

Sacred Congregation for the Causes of Saints, Cardinal Prefect, Palazzo delle Congregazioni, Piazza Pio XII 10, I-00193 Roma, T: (6982)4247.
Sacred Congregation for the Discipline of the Sacraments, Cardinal Prefect, Palazzo delle Congregazioni, Piazza Pio XII 10, I-00193, Roma, T: (6982)4005, 4416.
Sacred Congregation for the Divine Worship, Cardinal Prefect, Palazzo delle Congregazioni, Piazza Pio XII 10, I-00193 Roma, T: (6982)4316/8.
Sacred Congregation for the Doctrine of the Faith, Palazzo della stessa S, Congregazione, Piazza del S. Uffizio 11, I-00193 Roma, T: (6982)3357.

INDIA

National Biblical Catechetical and Liturgical Centre (NBCLC), St. Mary's Town, PB 577, Bangalore 560005, T: 52369.
Pastoral, Catechetical, and Liturgical Centre, Subedarpet, Andhra Pradesh 524001.
Tamil Nadu Biblical, Catechetical and Liturgical Centre (TNBCLC), Tindivanam PO, Tamil Nadu.

INDONESIA

Pastoral Research and Service Centre, Jalan Jendral Sundirman 3, Surakarta, Central Java, T: 3904.

IRAQ

Latin Church, Karadat Mariam, Baghdad, T: 33643.

IRELAND

Coetus Consultorum Commissionis Liturgicae, St. Patrick's College, Maynooth, Country Kildare, T: 286261.

International Society for Liturgical Study and Renewal, The Deanery, Lismore, County Waterford.

Irish Institue of Pastoral Liturgy, College Street, Carlow, T: (353) 0503 42942.

ITALY

Centro di Azione Liturgica, Via Liberiana 17, I-00185 Roma, T: 481870.

Congregation for Divine Worship and the Discipline of the Sacraments, Piazza Pio XII 10, 00193 Rome.

Istituto di Liturgia Pastorale per le Tre Venezie, Via Giuseppe Ferrari 2A, I-35100 Padova.

Pontificio Istituto Liturgico di San Anselmo, Via di Porta Lavernale 19, I-00153 Roma, T: 5745127.

Standing Committee for International Eucharistic Congresses, Via del Pozzetto 160, Roma, T: 6790310.

Una Voce Italia, Corso Vittorio Emanuele 21, I-00186 Roma.

Union of Adorers of the Blessed Sacrament, Largo dei Monti Parioli 3, I-00197, Roma.

JAPAN

Liturgical Institute, Sophia University, 1-710 Kamishakujii, Nerima-ku, Tokyo 102, T: (03)264-0875.

KENYA

Kenya Association for Liturgical Music (KALM), St. Thomas Aquinas Seminary, Langata, PO Box 30517, Nairobi, T: Langata 405.

LEBANON

Institut Supérieur de Liturgie, Université St-Esprit, Kaslik.

LITHUANIA

Episcopal Liturgical Commission of Lithuania, Kretingos 16, 232024 Vilnius, T: 26455.

NETHERLANDS

Ecumenical Liturgical Centre, Mathenesserlaan 301c, NL-3003 Rotterdam, T: (010)252759.

National Liturgical Council, Biltstraat 119, Utrecht, T: (030)334244.

Netherlands Liturgical Centre, Biltstraat 119, Utrecht, T: (030)12950.

Netherlands Society for Religious Articles, Haarlemmerstraat 123, Leiden, T: (01710)22889.

Society for the Study of Liturgy, Biltstraat 119, Utrecht, T: (030)12950.

St Gregory Association of the Netherlands, Biltstraat 119, Utrecht, T: (030)334244.

NEW ZEALAND

National Liturgical Commission, St. Joseph's Parish House, 7 Paterson St, Wellington 1, T: 50914.

NIGERIA

Pastoral Department, Catholic Secretariat of Nigeria, 6 Force Rd, PO Box 951, Lagos, T: 25339.

Pastoral Institute, Bodija, PO Box 1784, Ibadan, T: 24328.

NORWAY

Una Voce Norvegia, Majorstuveien 8, Oslo 3.

PAPUA NEW GUINEA

National Liturgical Centre, P.O. Box 1101, Port Moresby, Boroko, T: 81347.

National Subcommission for Christian Initiation, Catholic Mission Yobai, P.O. Gumine via Goroka.

National Subcommission for General Liturgy, Catholic Mission Mapua, Tabar Island, PO Kavieng, New Ireland.

PARAGUAY

Departamento Nacional de Litúrgia, Coronel Bogado 884, Casi Tucuari, CP 1436, Asunción, T: 41122.

PERU

Officina Nacional de Litúrgia, Azangaro 260, Oficina 309, Apdo 1512, Lima, T: 280137.

PHILIPPINES

Asian Institute for Liturgy and Music, P.O. Box 3176, Manila.

East Asian Pastoral Institute, Ateneo de Manila Campus, Loyola Heights, Quezon City, P.O. Box 1815, Manila, T: 903182.

POLAND

Catholic Univ. of Lublin, Dept. of Liturgics, Katedra Liturgiki, Instytut Teologii Pastoralnej, Katolicki Uniwersytet Lubelski, Aleje Raclawickie 14, skr p 279, 20 950 Lublin 1, T: 30426.

Liturgical Institute, ul sw Marka 10, Kraków.

Pastoral Institute, Liturgical Section, Papieski Instytut Pastoralny, Sekcja Liturgi zna, KUL, Aleje Raclawickie 14, Lublin.

PORTUGAL

Grémio Concelho dos Comerciantes de Antiguidades, Artigos Religiosos e Funerários de Lisboa.

Liga dos Amigos do Canto Gregoriano, Campo Martires da Patria 96-2, Lisboa.

RWANDA

Centre de Pastorale Liturgique et Catéchétique, BP 49, Butare, T: 3032.

SAMOA

Liturgical Translations Committee, Catholic Cathedral, Apia, T: 58.

SENEGAL

Monastère de Keur-Moussa, Keur-Moussa, par Pout.

SOMALIA

Commissione Liturgica del Vicariato, Centro Laicato Cattolico, Via Tomaso Carletti, P.O. Box 273, Mogadisho.

SOUTH AFRICA

Catholic Centre Liturgical Arts, PO Box 166, Pietersburg 0700, 68 Landdros Mare St 0699, Pietersburg, T: 0152-295-5013.

SOUTH KOREA

Liturgical Vestment Store, 85-12, Nung-dong, Kwangjin-gu, Seoul-shi, T: (02) 464-0934.

SPAIN

Centro de Pastoral Litúrgica, Canuda 45, Barcelona 2.

Departamento de Litúrgia, Instituto Superior de Pastoral, Instituto León XIII, Límite 3, Madrid 3.

Secretariado Nacional de Litúrgia, Plaza del Conde Barajas 1, Madrid 12, T: 2664834.

Una Voce España, Fundación Pastor, Serrano 107, Madrid.

SRI LANKA

National Liturgy Centre, Archbishop's House, Colombo 8, T: 95471.

SWEDEN

Una Voce Suecia, Skomakarg 13 III, S-111 29 Stockholm.

SWITZERLAND

Centre de liturgie (Liturgisches Institut), 72, Hirschengraben, 8001 Zurich, 01/252 16 30.

Centre Romand de Liturgie, Petit Séminaire du St-Sacrement, CH-1723 Marly-le-Petit, T: (037)221666.

Centro di Liturgia, CP 26, CH-6901 Lugano, T: (093)334762.

Commission suisse de liturgie, 8840 Einsiedeln 055/53 44 31.

Fédération Internationale Una Voce, St. Georges 18, CH-1815 Clarens.

Liturgische Konsultativkommission, Christkatholische Kirche der Schweiz, Willadingweg 39, CH-3000 Bern.

Liturgisches Institut, Gartenstr 36, CH-8002 Zürich, T: (05)361146.

UNITED STATES OF AMERICA (USA)

A & O Church Furniture, P.O. Box 1053, Jamestown, NC 27282, T: 919-454-5145.

Academic Choir Apparel, 9747 Independence Ave., Chatsworth, CA 91311, T: 800-626-5000, F: 818-886-8743, O: E-mail: academicapparel.com.

Acrylic Creations/Hoosier Craft, PO Box 2824, South Bend, IN 46680, T: 219-674-7636.

American Clergy Shirts, P.O. Box 1267, Douglasville, GA 30133, T: 770-489-1785.

Arnold's Industries, A Trust, 828 W 4th Ave, Holdrege, NE 68949, T: 308-995-5471.

Art Needle Gown Co., 500 First Ave., N, Minneapolis, MN 55401, T: 612-333-7949.

Autom Church Supply Co, 2226 N 7th St, Phoenix, AZ 85006, T: 602-258-8481.

C M Almy & Son, Inc, P.O. Box 2628, Greenwich, CT 06836, T: 203-531-7600.

Cathshop, O: Web: http://transporter.com/cathshop.

Celebration: An Ecumenical Worship Resource, P.O. Box 419493, Kansas City, MO 64141-6493, T: 816-531-0538, F: 816-968-2280.

Church Furnishing Manufacturers, 155 Jefferson, Box X, Carlisle, IA 50047, T: 800-383-1000.

Church Pews, Inc., Rt 2, Box 328, Grove Hill, AL 36451, T: 800-522-5014.

Coalition Ecclesia Dei, P. O. Box 2071, Glenview, IL 60025-6071, T: 847-724-7151, F: 847-724-7158, O: www.ecclesiadei.org.

Cokesbury, 201 8th Ave S, Nashville, TN 37202, T: 800-672-1789.

Evangelical Purchasing Service, 646 Roosevelt Rd, Glen Ellyn, IL 60137, T: 800-837-7373.

F. C. Ziegler, Co., 415 East 12th St., Tulsa, OK 74120, T: 800-331-4117, F: 800-863-4356.

Glass Place, The, 14 Oakland Blvd, Elliot Lake, ON, Canada P5A 2T1.

Gregorian Institute of America, 7404 South Madison Av, Chicago, IL 60638.

Holy Rood Guild, The, St. Joseph's Abbey, 167 N. Spencer Rd., Spencer, MA 01562-1233, T: 508-885-8750, F: 508-885-8701.

Imperial Woodworks, Inc., P.O. Box 7835, Waco, TX 76714, T: 800-234-6624.

J P Redington & Co, PO Box 954, Scranton, PA 18501, T: 800-233-4281.

Kanel Brothers, PO Box 2286, Canton, OH 44720, T: 216-499-4802.

Kay Barry Originals-Robes, 3450 Rosemont Dr, Sacramento, CA 95826, T: 800-258-3444.

Latin Liturgy Association, 740 Carriage Way, Baton Rouge, LA 70808.

Liturgical Conference, 8750 Georgia Ave., Ste., 123, Silver Spring, MD 20910-3621, T: 301-495-0885.

Liturgical Design, P.O. Box 103-106, Houston, TX 77219-0106, T: 800-758-2099, F: 713-464-9013.

Liturgical Press, P.O. Box 7500, Collegeville, MN 56321, T: 800-858-5450, F: 800-445-5899, O: E-mail: sales@litpress.org, Web: www.litpress.org.

Lyric Choir Gown Co., P.O. Box 16954-RS, Jackson, FL 32245, T: 904-725-7977.

Martin Yale Industries, 500 N. Spauding Ave, Chicago, IL 60624, T: 312-826-4444.

Mission Service Supply, Inc., P.O. Drawer 2957, W Monroe, LA 71294, T: 800-352-7222.

Murphy Cap & Gown Co., 4200 31st St. N., St. Petersburg, FL 33714, T: 800-237-8951, F: 813-526-3528, O: E-mail: murphyrb@gte.net, Web: www.murphyrobes.com.

National Church Purchasing Group, 8108 Virginia Manor Dr., Mechanicsville, VA 23111, T: 800-795-6274, F: 804-730-9255.

New Covenant Communion Supply, P.O. Box 161909, Ft Worth, TX 76161, T: 817-232-5661.

North American Academy of Liturgy, Valparaiso Univ., Valparaiso, IN 46383.

North American Liturgy Resources, 10802 N 23rd Ave, Phoenix, AZ 85209, T: 602-864-1980.

Oak Hall/Bently & Simon Robe Co., 840 Union St., Salem, VA 24153, T: 703-387-0000.

Overholtzer Church Furniture, Inc., 626 Kearney Ave, PO Box 4039, Modesto, CA 95352, T: 800-366-1716.

Professional Brass Refinishing, P.O. Box 603, Merrill, WI 54452, T: 800-843-0617.

Rainsville Church Pew Mfg Co, 434 Main St. E., Rainsville, AL 35986, T: 800-828-8140.

Regency Cap & Gown Co, P.O. Box 10557, Jacksonville, FL 32207, T: 800-826-8612.

Sofpew, Inc, 14441 State Rt 93 S, Jackson, OH 45640, T: 800-535-3876.

St. Gregory Foundation for Latin Liturgy, 15 E. 26th St., Bayonne, NJ 07002.

St. Michael Altar Bread-Meyer-Vogelpohl, 717 Race St., Cincinnati, OH 45202, T: 800-543-0264, F: 513-241-4454.

Superior Church Furnishings, P.O. Box 1334, Dublin, GA 31021, T: 912-275-2129.

Taylor-Ramsey Furniture Corp, P.O. Box 11988, Lynchburg, VA 24506, T: 804-239-2671.

Thomas Creativity Apparel, Inc., One Harmony Place, New London, OH 44851, T: 800-537-2575.

United Church Products, P.O. Box 667, Hartselle, AL 35640, T: 205-773-2585.

Virginia Church Furniture, 190 First St NW, Pulaski, VA 24301, T: 703-980-5388.

Woodstock Center for Religion and Worship, Room 240, 475 Riverside Drive, New York, NY 10027, T: (212)866-7646.

World Center for Liturgical Studies, P.O. Box DD, Boyton Beach, FL 33435.

Worship Institute, The, P.O. Box 130, Bedford, TX 76095, T: 800-627-0923, 817-498-9717, F: 817-788-1663, O: E-mail: worshipint@aol.com, Web: www.worshipinstitute.com.

URUGUAY

Instituto Nacional de Estudios Litúrgicos (INEL), Secretariado Nacional de Litúrgia, Rio Branco 1430, Montevideo, T: 84404.

Una Voce Uruguay, Casilla 12, Montevideo.

YEMEN

Liturgical Commission, Catholic Mission, Steamer Point, P.O. Box 1155, Aden, T: 22900.

50 Media & communications

Agencies, ministries, organizations, and centers working in the area of social communications, i.e. several or all types of mass and communications media (often including audiovisual, multimedia, cinema, recordings, radio, TV, literature, newspapers, public opinion media); Christian production of media and communications material, multimedia production centers and studios; the technical aspects of communication, mass communication, and instant communication; the production or distribution of media tools and resources for evangelism, discipleship, Christian education, catechesis, mission, or training; training centers or programs for media and communication arts and technologies.

AMERICAN SAMOA

Catholic Communications Office, 18 Brunswick St., Fitzroy VIC 3065, T: 61-3-417-7800, F: 61-3-419-8959.

ARGENTINA

Centro de Comunicación Educativa La Crujia, Av. Eva Pero 3059, Tucumán 1993, 1050 Buenos Aires, T: 54-1-40-2509, F: 54-1-814 3656.

Centro de Comunicaciones Salesianas (COSAL), Dpto Locución, Don Bosco 4002, 1206 Buenos Aires, T: 54-1-981-26-19.

Oficina Coordinadora de los Medios de Comunicación Social (OCMCS), Paraguay 1867, Buenos Aires, T: 869352.

Pontificia Universidad Católica Argentina, Santa Maria de los Buenos Aires, Dpto Comunicación Social, Juncal 1912, 1116 Buenos Aires, T: 54-1-44-10-36.

Universidad del Salvador, Dpto Comunicación Social, Rodriguez Peña 640, 1020 Buenos Aires, T: 54-1-40-89-06.

AUSTRALIA

Good Views Media, O: http://www.goodviews.com.au/.

South Pacific Adventist Media Centre, P.O. Box 15, Wahroonga, N.S.W. 2076, G.P.O. Box 4112, Sydney, N.S.W. 2001, T: 02-487-1844, F: 02-487-1659, O: Cable: 'Adventist', Sydney, Telex: 22064.

AUSTRIA

Katholisches Zentrum für Film, Funk und Fernsehen in Österreich, Singerstr 7, A-1010 Wien, T: 524386.

UNDA/Austria, Katholisches Zentrum für Massenkommunikation, Singerstr. 7/IV/2, A-1010 Wien, T: 43-222-51-55-27-30, F: 43-222-51 55 27 39.

BAHAMAS

Templeton Foundation, New Providence.

BANGLADESH

Christian Communications Centre, 61/1 Subhas Bose Avenue, Luxmibazar, Khaka 1100, T: 880-2-23 38 85, F: 880-2-25 91 68, O: Telex: 780-642420 DTB BJ.

BARBADOS

CADEC Communications Network (CCN), P.O. Box 616, Bridgetown.

Caribbean Christian Communications Network, Diocesan House, St Michael's Row, Bridgetown.

BELGIUM

ACG - Médialogue, 32, avenue Rogier, 1030 Bruxelles, T: 32-2-242-92-75.

Centre des Techniques de Diffusion et Relations Publiques (CETEDI), Université Catholique de Louvain, Van Evenstraat 2A, B-3000 Leuven, T: (016)28751.

Centre for Social Communications, Katholieke Universiteit Leuven, Van Evenstraat 2A, B-3000 Leuven, T: (016)21070.

Conseil Interdiocésain des Moyens de Communication Sociale, Rue Guimard 5, B-1040 Brussel.

Département de Communications Sociales, Université Catholique de Louvain, Van Evenstraat 2A, B-3000 Leuven, T: (016)28751.

Institut des Arts de Diffusion, Rue des Wallons, 77, 1348 Louvain-la-Neuve, T: 32-10-45 06 85.

Institut des Hautes Etudes de Communications Sociales (IHECS), Rue de L'Etuve 58-60, 1000 Bruxelles, T: 32-2-512 90 93.

K.U. Leuven, Faculteit der Sociale Wetenschappen, Dept. Communicatiewetenschappen, E. Van Evenstraat 2A, B-3000 Leuven, T: 32-16-28-30-20, F: 32-16-28 32 53.

Média Forum, Rue de l'Ermitage, 21, 1300 Wavre, T: 32-10-22-49-37, F: 32-10-24 23 84.

TELECOM-UNIO, Centre Informatique et Bible, Rue de l'Abbaye, 11, 5198 Denée, T: 32-82-9-96-47.

BOLIVIA

Educación Radiofónica de Bolivia ERBOL, Calle Ballivián 1323, 4to. piso, Casilla 5946, La Paz, T: 591-2-354-142, F: 591-2-391 985.

Instituto Superior de Ciencias y Técnicas de la Opinión Pública, Universidad Católica Boliviana, Casilla 892, La Paz.

Oficina de Medios de Comunicación Social, Casilla 4064, La Paz, T: 41920.

Universidad Católica Boliviana, Carrera de Comunicación Social, Av. 14 de Septiembre 4807, Casilla 4805, La Paz, T: 591-2-783-283.

BRAZIL

Brazil Voice of Prophecy Media Center, Caixa Postal 1189, 20001-970 Rio de Janeiro; Office: Rua da Matriz 16, 3/Andar, Botafogo, 22260-100 Rio de Janeiro, T: 266-3022, 266-2612, F: 266-3790.

Centro Educativo de Comunicações do Nordeste (CECOSNE), Av Conde da Boa Vista 921, Recife, PE, T: 234029.

Conferência Nacional dos Bispos do Brasil, Setor de Comunição Social, Caixa Postal 13-2067, 70.401 Brasilia D.F., T: 55-61-225-2955, F: 55-61-225 4361.

Departamento de Comunicação Social, Centro de Ciências Sociais da Pontificia Universidade Católica, Rua Marquês de São Vicente 209/223, Rio de Janeiro, GB, ZC-20.

Departamento de Comunicação Social, Universidade Católica de Minas Gerais, Av do Contorno 7919, Belo Horizonte, MG.

Departamento de Comunicação Social, Universidade Católica de Paraná, Rua 15 de Novembro 1004, CP 670, Curitiba, Paraná.

Faculdade dos Meios de Comunicação Social, Pontifícia Universidade Católica do Rio Grande do Sul, Av Ipiranga 6681, CP 1429, Pôrto Alegre, Rio Grande do Sul.

Secretariado Nacional de Opinião Publica, Rua do Russel 76, 5 andar, CP 16085, Rio de Janeiro, ZC-01, GB, T: 2252761.

SEPAC - Serviço à Pastoral da Comunicaçao, Rua Joaquim Távora 756, 04015-11-Sao Paulo-SP, T: 55-11-571-9762.

BRITAIN (UK OF GB & NI)

Catholic Communications Centre, 39 Eccleston Square, London SW1V 1PD, T: 44-71-233-81-96, F: 44-71-630 51 66.

Centre for Overseas Communications Students, Westbourne Park Baptist Church, Bayswater, London.

Centre for the Study of Communication and Culture (CSCC), 221 Goldhurst Terrace, GB-London NW6 3EP, T: 44-71-328-28-68, F: 44-71-372 11 93.

International Christian Media Commission (ICMC), P.O. Box 100, Witney, Oxford, OX8 7TD, T: 1993-776-249, F: 1993-776-259, O: E-mail: adams@xc.org, Web site: www.icmc.org.

Middle East Media (MEM), P.O. Box 118, London SE9 2UB, T: 0181-8594035.

Network, 26 Tresco Gardens, Seven Kings, Ilford, Essex, T: (01)599-0506.

Overseas Christian Communication Centre, Reeth, Langley Marsh, Wiveliscombe, near Taunton, Somerset, T: (09842)793.

Overseas Communication Courses (COVAT), Selly Oak Colleges, Birmingham B29 6LE, T: (021)472-4231.

St. Paul Multimedia Productions UK, Middle Green, Slough SL3 6BS, T: 01753-577629.

Wire, The, O: Web: www.roehampton.ac.uk/link/wire.

World Association for Christian Communication (WACC), 357 Kennington Lane, London SE11 5QY, T: 44-71-5829-139, F: 44-71-7350-340, O: Tlx: 8812669 WACC G.

CANADA

Centre Saint-Pierre, Département des Communi-

cations1212 rue Panet, Montréal, Québec H2L 2Y7, T: 514-524-3561, F: 514-524 5663.
Communications Centre, 9761-47 Avenue, Edmonton, AB T6E 5M7, T: 403-437-0830.
Cornerstone Communications, 2206-10 Avenue S.W., Calgary, Alberta T3C 0K6, T: 403-246-3590.
Department of Communication Arts, Loyola College, 7141 Sherbrooke St North, Montréal 262, Québec, T: (514)482-0320.
Ecumenical Satellite Commission (ECUSAT), Toronto.
Escuela de Comunicación Social de la Universidad del Norte, Av Angamos 6010, Casilla 1282, Antofagasta, T: 22686, 23077.
Institut des communications sociales Université Saint-Paul, 223 rue Main, Ottawa, Ontario K1S 1C4, T: 613-236-1393, F: 613-782 3005.
Interchurch Communications, 3250 Bloor St. W., Etobicoke, ON M8X 2Y4.
Mennonite Brethren Communications, Box 2, Station F, Winnipeg R2L ON1, Manitoba, T: 204-667-9576, F: 204-669-6079.
Office National des Communications Sociales, 1340, boul. Saint-Joseph est, Montréal, Québec H2J 1M3, T: 514-524 -8223, F: 514-524 8522.

CHILE
Departamento de Opinión Publica del Arzobispado de Santiago (DOPAS), Erasmo Escala 1822, Oficina 401, Casilla 1540, Santiago, T: 85581.

CHINA
Asia Christian Communications Fellowship (ACCF), CCL Box 5364, Tsim Sha Tsui PO, Hong Kong.
Centro de Comunicaçáo 'Shalom, Rua do Campo, 1A, Macau, T: 853-323 209, F: 853-346 167.
Christian Communications Foundations, 144 Boundary St, Kowloon, Hong Kong.
Communications Department, Hong Kong Baptist College, 224 Waterloo Rd, Kowloon, Hong Kong.
Hong Kong Catholic Social, Catholic Social Comm. Ofc., 11/F Catholic Diocese Centre, 16, Caine Road , Hong Kong, T: 852-5-223-677, F: 852-845 3095.

COLOMBIA
Centro Nacional de MCS, Carrera 10 No 19-64, Oficina 402, Apdo Aéreo 14453, Bogotá, DE, T: 428008.
Escuela de Ciencias de la Comunicación Social, Pontificia Universidad Javariana, Carrera 7a No 40-62, of 307, Apdo Aéreo 5315, Bogotá, DE.
Escuela de Humanidades y Ciencias de la Comunicación Social, Pontificia Universidad Bolivariana, Calle 48 No 27.05, Apdo 14-16, Medellín, Antioquia.
Servicio Colombiano de Communicación Social, Apdo Aéreo 24910, Bogotá, DE 1.
Técnicas de Comunicación Social para el Desarrollo (OSAL), CAlle 20 No 9-45, Apdo Aéreo 12721, Bogotá, DE.

CONGO-BRAZZAVILLE
COMAFRIQUE, B.P. 2080, Brazzaville, T: 83 03 28.

CONGO-ZAIRE
Département de Communications Sociales, Université de Kinshasa, BP 832, Kinshasa XI.

COSTA RICA
Co-ordination Offices for Press, Radio, TV and Cinema, c/o Av 2-4 Calle I, Apdo 10-64, San José, T: 225903.
Interamerican Gospel Communication, Apdo 2470, San José.

CYPRUS
Adventist Media Centre-Middle East, P.O. Box 1984, Nicosia, T: 02-316065, 317063, F: 02-317168, O: Telex: 4808 ADVENT CY.
Middle East Media (MEM), P.O. Box 3545, CY-1684 Nicosia, T: 2-377435, F: 2-377436, O: E-mail: 100116.1170@compuserve.

DENMARK
Asian Institute of Christian Communication, c/o Amosevej 7, 7200 Grindsted, T: 05-321140.

DOMINICAN REPUBLIC
Centro Nacional de MCS (CENICOS), Calle Mercedes 17, Altos, Apdo 841, Santo Domingo, T: 23848.

ECUADOR
Entrenamiento Ministerial, Villalengua No. 320, Casilla 691, Quito, T: 241-550.
Oficina Nacional de Medios de Comunicación Sociale (OMECO), Av América 1866 y la Gasca, Casilla 1081, Quito, T: 520926.

EGYPT
MECC Dept. on Communication, P.O. Box 2238, Horriya, Heliopolis, Cairo, T: 20-2-2483 616, F: 20-2-2478-837, O: Tlx: 23309 OIK UN.
Office Catholique Egyptien pour les MCS, Rue Adly Pacha 9 (app. 8), Le Caire, T: 20-2-391 1568, F: 20-2-66 28 39.

ETHIOPIA
Communications Dept., Ethiopian Catholic Secretariat, P.O. Box 2454, Addis Ababa, T: 251-1-55 03 00, F: 251-1-55 31 13, O: Telex: 980-21381 ET.
SIM Communications Centre, P.O. Box 127, Addis Abeba.
Voice of Good News, P.O. Box 658, Addis Abeba.

FIJI
CEPAC, CEPAC House, P.O. Box 289, Suva.
Lotu Pasifika, PCC, PO Box 357, Suva.

FINLAND
Cross Curtain Communications, Box 18, 00661, Helsinki, T: 358-0539-109, F: 358-0538-152.

FRANCE
Chrétiens-Médias Fédération, 47, quai des Grands Augustins, F-75006 Paris.
CREC-AVEX (Centre Intl. de Formation pour les Comm. Chrétiens des Jeunes Eglises), 12, rue de Chalin, F-69132 Ecully Cédex, T: 33-78-33-42-20, F: 33-78 43 33 65.
Fédération des Organismes de Communication Sociale (FOCS), 193 rue de l'Université, F-75007 Paris, T: (01)705-4358, 551-9462.
Institut Catholique de Lyon, Dpt. de Communication, 10, 12 rue Forhier, F-69002 Lyon, T: 33-72-32-50-50.
Secrétariat National de l'Opinion Publique et des Moyens de Communications Sociales, 106 Rue du Bac, F-75007 Paris, T: (01)222-6170.
SISCOMS (Secrétariat Intl. Spiritain de Communications Sociales par l'audio-visuel), 30, rue Lhomond, F-75005 Paris, T: 33-1-43-31-88-62, F: 33-1-45 35 29 01.
Studio Media Production, 130 Blvd. De l'Hopital, 75013 Paris, T: (01) 45-34-27-04.

GABON
Service National des Médias Catholiques, B.P. 2146, Libreville, T: 241-76 08 90.

GERMANY
CAMECO (Catholic Media Council), Anton-Kurze-Allee, Postfach 1912, D-5100 Aachen, T: 49-241-7-30-81, F: 49-241-7-34-62, O: Telex: 41-832 719 MIRA D.
Christliche Medien Corporation, Herborner Str. 25, Asslar 35614, T: 011-49-64418722, F: 011-49-644188122.
Evangelische Konferenz für Kommunikation, Geschäftsstelle, Friedrichstr 34, D-6 Frankfurt/Main.
Gemeinschaftswerk der Evangelischen Publizistik e.V. (GEP), (Protestant Association for Media Comm.), Postfach 50 05 50, Emil-von-Behring Str. 3, 60394 Frankfurt A. Main, T: 49-69/580-98/183, F: 49-69/580-98/242.
Hochschule für Philosophie, Institut für Kommunikationsforschung und Medienarbeit, Kaulbachstr, 22a, D-8000 München 22, T: 49-89-23-86-24-00, F: 49-89-23 86 24 02.
Institut Zur Förderung publizistischen Nachwuchses e.V., Studio Ludwigshafen, Frankenthaler Str. 229, D-6700 Ludwigshagen, T: 49-621-51-10-91.
Kath. Institut für Medieninformation, Am Hof 38, D-5000 Köln 1.
PROA, Am Kiefernwald 21, D-8000 München 45, T: 49-89-311-73-31.
Vereinigung für Christliche Publizistik, Frankfurt-am-Main.

GHANA
CEPACS, Comité Episcopal Panafricain pour les Communications Sociales, 4 Senchi St., P.O. Box 9156 Airport, Accra, T: 233-21-776-491, O: Telex: 94-2471 NCS GH.
Department of Social Communications, P.O. Box 1989, Accra.

GUADELOUPE
Eglise de Guadeloupe-Communications (Catholic), B.P. 369, Evêché, 97101 Basse-Terre Cedex, T: 590-81-36-69.

GUAM
Office of Social Communication (Catholic), P.O. Box 2553, Agana, Guam 96910, T: 671-472-6427, F: 671-477-3519.

GUATEMALA
Departamento de Communicaciones Sociales, Secretariado Católico Nacional, 4a Av 9-35, Zona 1, Apdo 1698, T: 26831.

HOLY SEE
Pontifical Council for Social Communications, Palazzo S. Carlo, 00120 Vatican City State, T: 39-6-698-83197, F: 39-6-698-85373, O: 2019 PCCS VA.

INDIA
A. R. Communication Centre, House No. 43/66, Narasingarao Peta, Kurnool, Andhra Pradesh 518004.
Amruthavani, P. O. Box 1588, 50 Sebastian Road, Secunderabad, Andhra Pradesh 500003.
Assemblies of God Studio, 18, Royd Street, Calcutta, West Bengal 700016.
Bible Media Ministries, 1/36 North Parade Road, St. Thomas Mount, Madras, Tamil Nadu 600016.
Chitrabani, 76 Rafi Ahmed Kidwai Road, Calcutta, West Bengal 700016.
Christian Arts and Communication Service, 21, Eldams Road, Teynampet, Madras, Tamil Nadu 600018.
Christian Institute of Media and Management, Clara Swain Hospital Campus, P. O. Box 126, Bareilly, Uttar Pradesh 243001.
C'ristian Media Centre - India, 21 Eldams Road, Teynampet, Madras, Tamil Nadu 600018.
Christian Media Consultancy, 15, 7th Main, II stage, Indiranagar, Bangalore, Karnataka 560038.
Church of South India Department of Communications, Vellore Diocese, 4-12, Anna Salai, P. O. Box 16, Thiruvannamalai, Tamil Nadu 606601.
Communications Co-ordination Centre, CBCI Centre, Alexandra Place, New Delhi 1, T: 43176.
Communications Co-ordination Centre, Golmuri PO, Jamshedpur 3, Bihar.
Communications Department of Evangelical Fellowship Of India, EFICOM, 804/92 Deepali, New Delhi 110019.
Deepika, INS Rafi Marg, New Delhi 110001.
India Communications Institute, 15 Vaibhav Buildings, Wadala (East), Bombay, Maharashtra 400037.
Institute of Communication Arts, St. Xavier's College, Bombay 1, T: 266661.
Jesuits In Social Communication, C/o Xavier Institute Of Communications, St. Xavier's College, Bombay, Maharashtra 400001.
Kalai Kaviri (Communication Centre), 18 Benwells Road, Tiruchy, Tamil Nadu 620001.
Karnataka Christian Communications Service, Balmatta, Mangalore, Karnataka 575001.
Lumen Institute, Tamil Nadu Catholic Centre, PO Tindivanam, South Arcot, Tamil Nadu.
Madhyam Communications, 59, Millers Road, P. B. 4610, Benson Town, Bangalore, Karnataka 560046.
Media Centre, 96, Lavelle Road, Bangalore, Karnataka 560001.
Media Production and Training Centre, Mid India Christian Services, Civil Lines, Damoh, Madhya Pradesh 470661.
Multi Media Ministries, P. O. Box 179, Dehra Dun, Uttar Pradesh 248001.
New Life Mass Media Ministries, Burli Peta, Vizianagaram, Andhra Pradesh 531201.
Presbyterian Church of India -Synod Communications Department, Mission Veng, Aizawl, Mizoram 796001.
Ravi Bharati Institute of Communication, Sadaquat Ashram Post, Patna, Bihar 800010.
Social Communications Service (SCS), St. Xavier's College, 30 Park St, Calcutta 16.
St. Mary's Media Centre, St. Agnes Church, Guntur, Andhra Pradesh 522004.
St. Paul Communications, W-128, Greater Kailash -2, New Delhi 110048.
Star of the East, Orthodox Centre, 2, Tuglakabad Institute Area, New Delhi 110062.
Synod Electronic Communications, Mission Veng, Aizawl, Mizoram 796001.
Theological Research and Communication Institute (TRACI), E-537, Greater Kailash-II, New Delhi 110048.
Xavier Institute of Communications, Saint Xavier's College, Mahapalika Marg, Bombay, Maharashtra 400001.

INDONESIA
Bishop's Conference of Indonesia, Comm. of Social Communication, Jl Cut Mutiah 10, Tromolpos 3044, Jakarta 10002, T: 62-21-310 04 79, F: 62-21-37 77 01, O: Telex: 78 61522 RAPTIM IA.
DGI Communications Commission, Jalan Salemba Raya 10, Jakarta IV/3.

IRELAND
Catholic Communications Institute of Ireland, Veritas House, 7/8 Lower Abbey St, Dublin 1, T: 886144, 48502.
Catholic Communications Institute, 169 Booterstown Road, Blackrock, Co Dublin, T: (353) 01 288 7311.

ITALY
Department of Social Communications, SVD Generalate, 1 Via dei Verbiti, CP 5080, I-00154 Roma, T: 570059, 575000.
Ente dello Spettacolo, Via della Conciliazione 2c, I-00193 Roma, T: 561775, 564132.
International Jesuit Centre for Social Communication (JESCOM), Borgo Santo Spirito 4, C.P. 6139, I-00195 Roma, T: 39-6-689-77-395, F: 39-6-687 92 83, O: Telex: 43-504-2018 GISAROMA VA.
ISCOS - UPS, Piazza dell' Ateneo Salesiano 1, I-00139 Roma, T: 39-6-37-13-10-78, F: 39-6-37 29 05 36.
Istituto Superiore di Scienze e Techiche del'Opinione Pubblica, Università Internazionale degli Studi Sociali Pro Deo, Vilae Pola 12, I-00198 Roma.
Multimedia International, Borgho Santo Spirito 5, CP 9048, I-00100 Roma.
Multimedia International, Fratelli Cristiani, Via della Moglianella, 375, I-00166 Roma, T: 39-6-696-0253, F: 39-6-696 4545.
Office of Social Communication, White Fathers, General Secretariat, Via Aurelia 269, I-00165 Roma, T: 632314, 632318.
Scuola Superiore delle Communicazioni Sociali, Università Cattolica del S Cuore, Piazza Vecchia 8, Palazzo del Podestà, Bergamo; Via Sant' Agnese 2, I-20123 Milano.
Secretariat for Social Communications, Missionary Oblates of Mary Immaculate (OMI), Via Aurelia 290, I-00165 Roma, T: 6370251.
Social Communications Office, Casa Generalizia della Pia Società Figlie di San Paolo, Via Antonino Pio 75, I-00145 Roma.
Ufficio Nazionale Comunicazioni Sociali, Circonvallazione Aurelia 50, I-00165 Roma, T: 39-6-663-71-41, F: 39-6-662 30 37.
Università Cattolica del Sacro Cuore, Scuola di Specializzazione Comunicazioni Sociali, Largo Gemelli 1, I-20123 Milano, T: 39-2-885-68-14, F: 39-2-885 65 08.

IVORY COAST
ISACOM (Institut Supérieur Africain de Communication), 20 B.P. 234 Abidjan 20, T: 225-42 46 95 (CERAO), F: 225-42 51 76 (ISACO).

JAMAICA
National Office of Cinema, Radio and Television, 126 Red Hills Rd, Kingston 8, T: 9242337.

JAPAN
Catholic Bishops' Conference of Japan, Dept. Social Comm., 10-1 Rokuban-Cho, Chiyoda-Ku, Tokyo 102, T: 81-3-3262 3691, F: 81-3-3262 3699.
Episcopal Commission for Social Communications, 10-1 Rokuban-cho, Chiyoda-ku, Tokyo 102.

KENYA
AACC Communications Training Centre, Waiyaki Rd, P.O. Box 14206, Nairobi, T: 61166.
AMECEA Office of Social Communications, P.O. Box 21191, Nairobi, T: 66506.
Baptist Communications Centre, Likoni Rd, PO Box 30370, Nairobi, T: 557392, 559076.
Communications Department, Kenya Catholic Secretariat, Westlands, PO Box 48062, Nairobi, T: 21613/4.
Daystar Communications, Valley Rd & Ngong Rd, PO Box 44400, Nairobi.
Department of Christian Communications, NCCK, PO Box 45009, Nairobi, T: 22264.

KIRIBATI
St. Paul's Communication Centre, P.O. Box 79, Bairiki, Tarawa, T: 686-21-219, F: 686-21-401.

LEBANON
Commission Episcopale pour les MCS, Centre Catholique d'Information, P.O. Box 60019, Jal Edbib (Beyrouth), T: 961-1-414 950-414 955, F: 961-1-414 955, O: Telex: 494-42214 CENCA LE.

LESOTHO
Catholic Social Communications, Box 200, Maseru 100, T: 266-32 30 92, F: 266 31 02 94.
Lesotho Communications Centre, Box 80, Maseru, T: 2525.

LUXEMBOURG
Office Catholique du Cinéma, de la Radio et de la Télévision, 5 Rue de Bourbon, Luxembourg, T: 485181.

MALAWI
Mass Media Office, Catholic Secretariat of Malawi, P.O. Box 5368, Limbe, T: 50866.

MALAYSIA
Cahayasuara Communications Centre, Training and Research, St. Anthony's, Jalan Robertson, 50150 Kuala Lumpur, T: 60-3-238 0912, F: 60-3-238 8010.
Commission for Mass Media, 5 Jalan Bukit Nanas, Kuala Lumpur.

MALTA
Media Centre Complex (Catholic), National Road, Blata L-Bajda, HMRO2, T: 356-24-90-05, F: 356-24 35 08.
National Commission for Means of Social Communications, Catholic Institute, Floriana.

MEXICO
Centro de Comunicaciones, Puente de Alvarado 14, México 1, DF.
Centro de Comunicación Javier, A.C., Serapio Redón 57 B, Colegio San Rafael, C.P. 06470, T: 52-5-535-68-92, F: 52-5-705 66 21.
Centro Nacional de Comunicación Social (CENCOS), Medellín 33, México 7, DF, T: 286898, 256541.
Communications Institute of the Americas (CITA), Hacienda Vista Hermosa, Apdo Postal 127, Cuernavaca, Morelos.
Escuela de Ciencias de la Communicación, Instituto Tecnológico y Estudios Superiore de Occidente (ITESO), Av Lopez Mateos 2352, Cd del Sol, Guadalajara, Jalisco, T: 152334/5/6.
Universidad Anahuac, Escuela de Ciencas de la Comunicación, Centro de Estudios Analisis y Critica de las Comunicaciones, A.P. 1100, Mexico 10 D.F., T: 52-5-589-22-00, F: 52-5-589 97 96.
Universidad del Tepeyac, Esc. de Ciencias y Tecs. de la Comunicación, Callao 802 Lindavista, 07300 Mexico, D.F., T: 52-5-781-40-33, F: 52-5-750 01 65.
Universidad Iberoamericana, Plantel Golfo-Centro de Comunicación, Km. 3.5 Carretera Federal Puebla Atlixco, A.P. 1436, 72430 Puebla, Pue., T: 52-22-30-44-60, F: 52-22-30 44 57.

MYANMAR
Catholic Social Communications (CBCM), 292 (A) Pyi Road, Sanchaung P.O., Yangon, T: 95-1-30268.

NETHERLANDS
Catholic Mass Media Institute, Universiteit Nijmegen, Verlengde Grone Straat 43, Nijmegen.
Convent van Kerken, Hilversum.
Proclama Communications & Video, Jachtlaan 22, P.O. Box 91, 3958 ZV Amerongen, T: 03434.
Stem van Afrika, Wassenaar.
Stichting Koinonoyntes Communicantes, Kanunnik Faberstraat 7, Nymegen 6525 T.P., T: 31-0805-53900.

NEW ZEALAND
Catholic Communications, 24 Hill St., P.O. Box 12-367, Wellington, T: 64-4-496-1745, F: 64-4-499-2519.

NIGERIA
Catholic Secretariat of Nigeria, Social Comm. Dept., P.O. Box 951, Lagos, T: 234-1-63 58 49, O: Telex: 905-22 592 CATHOLISEC NG.
Media Service Center, Attn: Media Service Center, P.O. Box 200, Kaduna, Kaduna State, T: 234-62-215229, F: 234-62-214383.

NORWAY
Mass Media Commission, Oslo Katolske Bispedömme, Liavn, 7 Lysaker.

PAKISTAN
National Catholic Commission for Social Communications, 9A Warris Rd., Lahore 54000, P.O. Box 909, Lahore, T: 92-42-476 281, F: 92-42-869 654.

PANAMA
Comisión Nacional de MCS y Centro de Comunicaciones Sociales del Arzobispado, Av México y Calle 20, Apdo 386, Panamá City, T: 255270.

PAPUA NEW GUINEA
Communication Institute (Catholic), P.O. Box 448, Goroka E.H.P., T: 675-721-388, F: 675-721-117.

PARAGUAY
Departmento de Ciencias de la Comunicación, Universidad Católica de Asunción, Av 25 de Diciembre, Casilla 346, Asunción.

PERU

Consejo Nacional de Medios de Comunicación Social (CONAMCOS), Río de Janeiro No. 488, Lima 11, T: 51-14-631010, F: 51-14-636125.
Departamento de Comunicación Social (DECOS), CELAM, Av 9 de Diciembre, Pasco Colón 378, Apdo 44, Lima 1.
Facultad de Ciencias de la Comunicación Social, Universidad Católica Santa Maria, Casilla 491, Arequipa.
Universidad Católica del Perú, Centro de Teleducación CETUC, Av. Universitaria s/n, Lima 21, Apartado 12514, Lima 4, T: 51-14-622540.

PHILIPPINES

Communication Foundation for Asia (CFA), 4427 Int. Old Sta. Mesa, P.O. Box 434, Manila 2806, T: 63-2-607 411/15, F: 63-2-721 7760, O: Telex: 75-27854 CFA PH.
National Catholic Office of Mass Media, 2307 Pedro Gil St., P.O. Box 3169, Santa Ana, Manila, T: 63-2-58 48 28, F: 63-2-521 8 125.
National Office of Mass Media, P.O. Box 2061, Manila.
Philippines Association for Media Education (PAME), Ateneo de Manila University, Mass Comm. Dept., Loyola Heights, Quezon City, T: 63-2-98 50 06, F: 63-2-56 59 31.
Programmes in Communication, Ateneo de Manila University, Loyola Heights, Quezon City, PO Box 154, Manila, T: 998721.
Social Communications Centre, Ramon Magsaysay Blvd Corner Santol Rd, PO Box 2156, Santa Mesa, Manila, T: 608917.

POLAND

Episcopal Commission for Film, Radio, TV & Theatre, Aleja I Armii Wojska Polskeigo 12, Warszawa X.

PORTUGAL

Radio Renascença, Lda, Rua Ivens, 14, P-1294 Lisboa Codex, T: 351-1-347-52-70.
Secretariado do Cinema e da Radio, 5 Rua Capelo, 2 Esq, Lisboa 2, T: 30172.

PUERTO RICO

Centro Nacional de MCS, Obrero Station, Apdo 14125, Santurce, PR.
Intercultural Communication Institute, Universidad Católica de Puerto Rico, Ponce, PR 00731, T: (809)842-4150.

RUSSIA

Voice of Hope Media Center, Box 170, Tula, 300000; ul. Stanislavskogo 48, Tula 300018, T: 0872-25-56-57, F: 0872-25-49-64.

RWANDA

Office National Catholique des Moyens de Communication Sociale (ONCMCS), BP 69, Butare.

SIERRA LEONE

National Catholic Comm. Centre, 10 Howe St., Santanno House, P.O. Box 893, Freetown, T: 232-22 45 90.

SINGAPORE

Christian Life Media Ministries, Raffles City PO Box 1275, Singapore 9111743, T: 250-6955.
Christian Voice Educational Resource Centre, 37 Goodman Road, Singapore 439003, T: 344-0216.
Good News Productions International (Singapore), 84 St. Francis Road, Singapore 328069, T: 292-2225.
Great Joy Media Centre/Baptist Media, 54 Blair Road, Singapore 089954, T: 227-7611, 227-6733 (Flim), F: 227-6162.

SLOVENIA

Gospel Media, P.P. 53, Ljubljana 61107, T: 061-559-655, F: 061-553-260.

SOMALIA

Archdiocesan Social Communications Commission, P.O. Box 532, Apia, T: 685-20-400, F: 685-20-402.

SOUTH AFRICA

Bet-eL Media Ministries, PO Box 23227, Innesdale 0031, 385 Voortrekker Rd, Capital Park, Pretoria, T: 012-329-4507, F: 012-329-4510.
Bible-Media, PO Box 5, Wellington 7655, T: 02211-3-3851, F: 02211-3-3864.
Christian Outreach Med (COM), PO Box 588, Botha's Hill 3660, 164 Old Main Rd, Botha's Hill, T: 031-777-1010, F: 031-777-1798.
Derek Prince Ministries SA, PO Box 33367, Glenstantia 0010, 191 Corobay St, Waterloof Glen, Pretoria, T: 012-348-9537, F: 012-348-9538.
Director of Communications and Studies, SACC, PO Box 31190, Braamfontein, Transvaal.
FOCCISA Fellowship of Christian Communicators in South Africa, PO Box 3026, Pretoria 0182, T: 012-57-1485, F: 012-567-1485.
Go-Tell Communications, PO Box 1213, 2047 Gardenview 2047, The Cornerstone, 43 Boeing Rd, Bedfordview, T: 011-622-4608, F: 011-455-3946.
Lutheran Productions, P.O. Box 59, Roodepoort, Transvaal.
Radio and Cinema Department, SABC, PO Box 941, Pretoria, Transvaal.

SOUTH KOREA

Catholic Mass Communications Committee, 85-12, Nung-Dong, Seongdong-Gu, Seoul 133-180, T: 82-2-466 79 18, F: 82-2-465 79 18.
Department of Mass Communications, Sogang University, CPO Box 1142, Soul, T: (73)5201/2/3/4.

SPAIN

Colegio Universitario San Pablo, Ciencas de la Información, Edificio Seminario, E-46113 Moncada (Valencia, T: 34-6-139-16-66, F: 34-6-139 52 72.
Forum-Comcrea (Asoc. de Comunicadores y Creativos Cristianos), Apdo. 23022, 08080 Barcelona, T: 232-65-56.
Impacto (Comunicaciones), Apdo. 192, 15780 Lugo, T: 58-29-19.
Secretariado Nacional de Medios de Communicaciones Sociales, Alfonso XI 4-2, Madrid 14, T: 2320446, 2213508.
Universidad del Navarra, Faculdad de Ciencias de la Información, Campus Universitario, E-31080 Pamplona (Navarra), T: 34-48-25-27-00, F: 34-48 17 36 50.
Universidad Pontificia de Salamanca, Facultad de Ciencas de la Información, Compañía, 5, E-37008 Salamanca, T: 34-23-21-65-81, F: 34-23-21 34 50.

SRI LANKA

Office of Social Communications, Archbishop's House, Colombo 8.
Social Communications Centre (Catholic), No. 45, Kinsey Road, Colombo 8, T: 94-69 70 62.

SUDAN

Sudan Catholic Bishops' Conference, Comm. Dept., S.C.B.C., P.O. Box 6011, Khartoum, T: 249-22 50 75, O: Telex: 984-24261 SCBC SD or 22190 ACROP SD.

SURINAME

Diocese Paramaribo Communication Commission-UNDA, P.O. Box 1802, Paramaribo, T: 5-97-47-25-21, F: 5-97 47 16 02.

SWEDEN

Catholic Bishop's Commission, Valhallavägen 132, S-102 40 Stockholm 5.
World Association for Christian Communication, 357 Kennington Lane, SE11 5QY London, T: 44-171/582-91-30, F: 44-171/735-03-40.

SWITZERLAND

Department of Communication, World Council of Churches, 150 Route de Ferney, CH-1211 Genève 20.
Gospel Media, Postfach 95, 6376 Emmetten, T: 41-41-620-5530, F: 41-41-620-2052.
Institut de Journalisme et des Communications Sociales, Université de Fribourg, Miséricorde, CH-1700 Fribourg, T: 41-37-21-93-49, F: 41-37-21 97 02.
World Council of Churches, Communications Dpt., 150 Route de Ferney, P.O. Box 2100, CH-1211 Geneva 2, T: 41-22-791 61 11, F: 41-22-798 13 46.

TAIWAN

Christian Cosmic Light Media Center, P.O. Box 7-3, Taipei; 8th Fl., No. 24, Hoping East Rd., Sec.2, Taipei, T: (02) 3627278, F: (02) 3639764.
Fu Jen University, Mass Media, 242 Taipei Hsien, Hsinchuang, T: 886-2-903 11 11, F: 886-2-901 64 44.
Kuangchi Program Service, 8, Lane 451 Tun Hua So. Rd., P.O. Box 24-42, Taipei 106-27, T: 886-2-771 2136, F: 886-2-771 2246, O: Telex: 785-27944 CORIMAC.

TANZANIA

Comm. Dept., Tanzania Episcopal Conference, P.O. Box 2133, Dar es Salaam, T: 255-51-51075, F: 255-51-51133, O: Telex: 41877/41989 TEC TZ.
Publicity Media Institute, Social Training Centre, PO Box 307, Mwanza, T: 2218.

THAILAND

Baptist Mass Communications, PO Box 11-1007, Bangkok 11, T: 2528473.
Catholic Social Communications Centre of Thailand, 57 Oriental Ave., Chareon Krung Road, Bangrak, Bangkok 10500, T: 66-2-233 29 77, F: 66-2-237 73 17.
Department of Mass Communications, Church of Christ in Thailand, 14 Pramuan Rd, Bangkok 5.
ECCE (Encouraging Contemporary Communications Enterprises), GPO Box 127, Bangkok.
Thailand Full Gospel Mass Communication, 10-12 Soi 6, Sukhumvit Rd, GPO Box 1825, Bangkok, T: 2525418.

TRINIDAD & TOBAGO

Catholic Communications Studios, St. Finbar's Church, Four Roads, Diego Martin, T: 809-637-0651, F: 809-622 1165.

UNITED STATES OF AMERICA (USA)

Abba Communications Arts, 7435 Mount Hope Rd., Grass Lake, MI 49240, T: 517-522-6202, F: 517-522-6202.
Alba House Communications, A Ministry of the Society of St. Paul, Rt. 224, Box 595, Canfield, OH 44406, T: 216-533-5503.
American Sound & Video Corporation, 7300 Miller Dr., Warren, MI 48092, T: 800-238-3873, F: 810-268-1708, O: www.asvc.com.
Arrowhead Productions International, 100 Sunport Ln. #1500, Orlando, FL 32809, T: 407-826-2350, F: 407-826-2367, O: api@cci.org.
Aurora Communication Intl., Inc., P.O. Box 1300, Belmont, CA 94002, T: 415-595-1180, F: 415-595-0221.
Banner Media Services, 6215 S. 107th E. Ave., Tulsa, OK 74133, T: 800-976-3342, F: 918-252-0014, O: mike@bannerinc.com, www.bannerinc.com.
Catholic Communications Foundation (CCF), Chrysler Bldg, 405 Lexington Av, New York, NY 10017, T: (212)867-8460.
Catholic Communication Campaign, U.S. Catholic Conference, 3211 Fourth St., N.E., Washington, D.C. 20017, T: 202-541-3237.
Center for Media and Values, 1962 S. Shenandoah St., Los Angeles, CA 90034, T: 310-202-7652, F: 310-559-0396, O: E-mail: Mediavalue@igc.org, Telex: 54205417.
Center for Religious Communication, Univ. of Dayton, 300 College Park Dr., Dayton, OH 45469-0314, T: 513-229-4000, O: Web: www.udayton.edu/~relcomm.
Christian Communication Specialities, 6944 Indianapolis Blvd, Hammond, IN 46324, T: (219)845-1700.
Christian Communications Council, 491 Gundersen Drive, Carol Stream, IL 60187.
Christian Communicator, Joy Publishing, Biola Writers Institute, LaMirada, CA 90639, T: 310-903-4805.
Christian Communication Technology (CCT), P.O. Box 64188, Virginia Beach, VA 23464, T: 804-420-0489.
Christian Media Alliance (CMA), O: Web: www.christmedia.com.
Christian Media Fellowship, P.O. Box 6511, Charlottesville, VA 22906, T: 804-973-8439.
Christian Media Foundation, P.O. Box 4111, Helena, MT 59064, T: 406-449-4251, F: 406-449-3553.
Communication Arts Department, Fordham University, Bronx, New York, NY 10458.
Communication Arts Department, Loyola University, 7101 West 80th St, Los Angeles, CA 90045.
Communication Arts Department, Xavier University, Victory Parkway, Cincinnati, OH 45207.
Communication Arts Division, Creighton University, 2500 California St, Omaha, NE 68131, T: (402)536-2817.
Community Now (New Life Communications Foundation), 2045 Main St, Kansas City, MO 64108.
Conference of Major Superiors of Men, 8808 Cameron St., Silver Spring, MD 20910, T: 301-588-4030, F: 301-587-4575.
Cross & Quill, 590 W. Mercers Fernery Rd., DeLand, FL 32720.
Daystar Media, Inc, 2090 Duane Ave, Santa Clara, CA 95054.
Department of Arts and Communication, Detroit University, 4001 West McNichols Rd, Detroit, MI 48221.
Department of Communications, Maryknoll Fathers, Maryknoll, NY 10545, T: (914)WI1-7590.
Department of Communication Art, University of Notre-Dame, Indiana, T: 284-7316.
Department of Communications, Loyola University, 6363 St Charles Av, New Orleans, LA 70118.
Department of Communications Arts and Instructional Aids, Loyola University, 6525 Sheridan Rd, Chicago, IL 60626.
Derek Prince Ministries, International, P. O. Box 19501, Charlotte, NC 28219, T: 704-357-3556, F: 704-357-1413, O: 76520.3105@compuserve.com, www.derekprince.com.
Dominican Central Productions, 7200 W. Division St., River Forest, IL 60305, T: 708-771-3030, F: 708-771-4510.
Doug Ross Communications, Inc., 1969 E. Broadway, Ste. #4, Tempe, AZ 85282, T: 602-966-1744, F: 602-894-1770, O: drc@primenet.com.
Franciscan Communications, 1229 South Santee St., Los Angeles, CA 90015, T: 213-746-2916, F: 213-747-9126.
Gospel Communications Network, O: http://www.gospelcom.net.
Heavy Light Productions, R 3, Dept CRD-9091, Howe, IN 46746, T: 708-665-3190.
Hispanic Telecommunications Network, Inc., 130 Lewis St., San Antonio, TX 78212, T: 512-227-5959, F: 512-227-6122.
IMPACT Productions, 807 S. Xanthus Place, Tulsa, OK 74104-3620, T: 918-582-4464.
Instutute for International Christian Communication, 6012 S.E. Yamhill St., Portland. OR 97215, T: 503-234-1639, F: 503-234-1639, O: 73143.2050@compuserve.com.
Integrity Communications, 251 O'Connor Ridge Blvd., #285, Irving, TX 75028, T: 214-650-8200, F: 214-650-9491.
Interamerican Gospel Communications, P.O. Box 6050, Philadelphia, PA 19114.
Intercommunity Telecommunications Project, 818 Roeder Rd., Suite 705, Silver Spring, MD 20910, T: 301-588-0505.
Intermedia, National Council of Chs., 475 Riverside Dr., Rm. 670, New York, NY 10115, T: 212-870-2376.
International Christian Media Commission, P.O. Box 70632, Seattle, WA 98107-0632, T: 206-781-0461, O: www.icmc.org/who.htm.
International School of Christian Communications, 13280 Chapman Ave., Garden Grove, CA 92640, T: 714-971-4238, F: 714-971-4204.
Jesuit Media Literacy Project, O: Web: http://interact.uoregon.edu/MediaLit/HomePage.
Jesuits in Communication in North America (JESCOM), Suite 300, 1424 16th St., N.W., Washington, DC 20036, T: 202-462-0400.
Lord & Spirit Media, 3976 Versailles Dr., Orlando, FL 32808, T: 407-292-0966, F: 407-292-9066.
Maryknoll Media Relations and Productions, Maryknoll, NY 10545, T: 914-941-7590.
Mass Communications Board-Church of God, 1303 E. Fifth St., P.O. Box 2007, Anderson, IN 46018, T: 317-642-0255, F: 317-642-0255.
Mass Media Newsletter, 2116 N. Charles St, Baltimore, MD 21218.
Master's Communication, P.O. Box 4000, Panorama City, CA 91412, T: 805-295-5777.
Media Associates International, P.O. Box 218, Bloomingdale, IL 60108, T: 630-893-1977, F: 630-893-1141.
Media Ministries, General Council of the Assemblies of God, 1506 Boonville Ave., Springfield, MO 65803, T: 417-869-8829, F: 417-862-5974, O: media@ag.org.
Mennonite Media Services, Box 1018, 1251 Edom Rd, Harrisonburg, VA 22801, T: (703)434-2026.
Middle East Media - USA, P.O. Box 359, Lynnwood, WA 98046, T: 425-778-0752, F: 425-778-0752, O: 73004.645@compuserve.com.
Mission Media Productions, Inc., O: http://www.seidata.com/~mmpi/.
Multi-Language Media, P.O. Box 301-C, Ephrata, PA 17522, T: 717-738-0582.
Multimedia Ministries Int'l, 18221 Torrence Ave, Lansing, IL 60438, T: 302-895-7000.
National Franciscan Comm. Conf., 138 Waverly Place, New York, NY 10014-3845, T: 212-255-6731.
Nazarene Communications Network, 6401 The Paseo, Kansas City, MO 64131, T: 816-333-7000, F: 816-333-1748, O: ncn@nazarene.org.
Oblate Media and Communications Corp., 1944 Innerbelt Business Center Dr., St. Louis, MO 63114-5718, T: 314-427-0403, F: 314-427-2868.
Office of Communication, United Church of Christ, 289 Park Av South, New York, NY 10010, T: (212)475-2121.
Passionist Communications, Inc., P.O. Box 440, Pelham, NY 10803, T: 914-738-3344, F: 914-738-7652.
Paulist Communications, 818 Roeder Rd., Suite 705, Silver Spring, MD 20910, T: 301-588-0505.
Paulist Productions, P.O. Box 1057, 17575 Pacific Coast Highway, Pacific Palisades, CA 90272, T: 213-454-0688.
Prelature of Opus Dei, Ofc. of Comm., 330 Riverside Dr., New York, NY 10025, T: 915-235-1201.
Salvation Army Office of Media Ministries, 6500 Harry Hines Blvd., Dallas, TX 75235, T: 800-527-4691.
Secretary for Communications, U.S. Catholic Conference, 3211 Fourth St., N.E., Washfington, D.C. 20017, T: 202-541-3320, F: 202-541-3129.
Share the Word Television, 3031 Fourth St., N.E., Washington, DC 20017, T: 202-832-5022.
Sound Words Communications, Inc., 1000 S. 84th St., Lincoln, NE 68510, T: 402-488-5949.
St. Joseph Catholic Communications, O: Web: www.imsweb.net/stjoe/comp.
Strang Communications, 600 Rinehart Rd., Lake Mary, FL 32746, T: 407-333-0600, F: 407-333-7100.
Tele-Missions International, Inc., P.O. Drawer J, Valley Cottage, NY 10989, T: 914-268-9222.
TRAFCO, United Methodist Church, 1908 Grand Av, P.O. Box 840, Nashville, TN 37202, T: (615)327-2727.
TRAV, Presbyterian Church in the US, 341 Ponce de Leon Av NE, Atlanta, GA 30308, T: (404)875-8921.
UNDA-National Catholic Association for Communicators, O: Web: www.catholic.org/orgs/unda.
United Communications Mission, Route 3, Box 399, Orlando, FL 32811, T: (305)241-9632.
Vision Media International, 5437 Parker Rd., Modesto, CA 95357, T: 209-526-6500, F: 209-522-2100.
WACC Los Angeles Group, Los Angeles, California.
Windsent, Inc., P.O. Box 101, Madison, MN 56256, T: 612-598-3330.

URUGUAY

Conferencia Episcopal Uruguayana, Departemento de Medios de Comunicaciones Sociales, Calle Uruguay 1319, 11100 Montevideo, T: 598-2-98-1975.

VENEZUELA

Dpto. Comunicación Social Camejo a Colón, Avenida Este 6, Torre 'La Oficina', piso 7, Oficina 7, Apartado Postal 3445, Caracas 1010-A, T: 58-2-563 2632, F: 58-2-5634625, O: Telex: 31-26476 SEPV VE.
Secretariado de Opinión Publica, Torre a Madrices, Edf Juan XXIII Apdo 954, Caracas, T: 818715.
Servicio de Communicación Social (SERCOS), Jesuitas a Tierra Honda 37, Apdo 422, Caracas, T: 817731/35.

WALLIS & FUTUNA ISLANDS

RFO Wallis et Futuna, B.P. 27, Brigave, Futuna, T: 681-72-33-08.

ZAMBIA

Multimedia Zambia (and Multimedia Publications), Woodlands, P.O. Box 1965, 8199 & 1373, Lusaka, T: 73467, 73470.

ZIMBABWE

IMBISA, Inter-Regional Meeting of Bishops of Southern Africa, P.O. Box BE 139, Harare (Belvedere), T: 263-4-79 10 53, F: 263-4-52 979, O: Telex: 907-22 390 GENSEC ZW.
Zimbabwe Catholic Media Workers Assoc, P.O. Box 8135, Causeway, Harare, T: 263-0-705569, F: 263-0-732735.

51
Medical centers

Definitions: Buildings, sites, campuses, or multi-site networks for medical ministry; Church- or Christian-sponsored or -owned hospitals, clinics, leprosaria, sanatoria, dispensaries, mobile units, maternity centers, et alia.

52
Medicine & healing

Organizations, ministries, networks, missions, and movements dedicated to helping or healing the sick, dying, or handicapped; medical missions, associations of hospitals (or clinics or dispensaries), associations of medical ministries, medical missionary institutes, medical or nursing training centers or programs, dental missions, ophthalmic missions, leprosy missions, other specialist missions, medical supply agencies; public health, primary care, hospital chaplaincy, religion and health, theological reflection on health and healing; ministries to handicapped groups or specific diseased groups (the deaf, the blind, cripples, the mentally ill, incurables, lepers, et alia); Christian psychiatry and psychology, ministry to the depressed or suicidal, religion and psychiatry or psychology, clinical theology; spiritual or divine healing, faith-healing groups, ministries, and centers.

AFGHANISTAN

International Afghan Mission, Medical Assistance Program (MAP), Box 625, Kabul.

National Organization for Ophthalmic Rehabilitation (NOOR), Box 625, Kabul.

ALGERIA

Union Nationale des Religieuses d'Action Hospitalière et Sociale, El-Djezair.

AUSTRALIA

Christian Medical Fellowships, 7a Drummoyne Av, Drummoyne, NSW 2047.

Nurses' Christian Fellowship (NCF), 63 Orchard St, P.O. Box 168, Chatswood, NSW 2067, T: 412-1197.

Sheltered Hostels for Handicapped Persons (Salvation Army), The Anchorage, 73 Victoria Cres., Abbotsford, Vic 3067, T: 03-9419-7833.

BAHAMAS

School for the Blind (Salvation Army), P.O. Box N-205, Nassau; 33 Mackay St., Nassau NP.

Visually Handicapped Workshop (Salvation Army), P.O. Box N 1980; Ivanhoe Lane, Nassau NP, T: 809-393-2745.

BANGLADESH

Community Health Care Project (CHCP), GPO Box 2013, Dhaka-1000; Plot 1, Road 4, Section-2, Block-B, Mirpur, Dhaka-1216, T: 80510-02, F: 880-2-831965, O: Also tel: 801914 or 815930.

Salvation Army Health Services, P.O. Box 3; Jessore, T: 0421-3438-3430.

Salvation Army Home for Blind Boys, Dhaka.

BELGIUM

Aid for Maternity Hospitals and Dispensaries in Central Africa, Rue Brialmont 11, B-1030 Brussel, T: (02)2170497.

Fédération des Institutions Hospitalières (FIH), Rue Guimard 5, B-1040 Brussels.

International Committee of Catholic Nurses, Square Vergote 43, B-1040 Brussel, T: (02)2170631.

International Federation of the Catholic Associations of the Blind, Avenue Dailly 90, B-1030, Brussels.

JAF Ministries Europe, Pagoodenlaan 69, B-1020 Brussels; 1 er trimestre '95-Bureau de dépot, 1000 Bruxelles 1, T: 322-245-5402, F: 322-245-5186, O: E-mail: jafmin@jafministries.com, WEB: http://www.jafministries.com.

Medical Aid to Central Africa, Blvd. Louis Schmidt 111, B-1040 Brussel, T: (02)7347377.

BENIN

Rehabilitation Centre for Physically Handicapped Children (Salvation Army), P.O. Box 108, Benin City, Edo State.

BOTSWANA

Association of Medical Missions of Botswana, Private Bag 0038, Gaborone, T: 312 582.

Medical Missionary Association of Botswana, Scottish Livingstone Hospital, Molepolole.

BRAZIL

Centro Evangélico Hokma, R. Itália, 531, Campinas-SP 13070-350, O: E-mail: hokma@juno.com.

Christian Psychology/Psychiatry Corps, Caixa Postal 127, 13100 Campinas, SP.

Corpo de Psicólogos e Psiquiatras Cristãos, Cx. Postal 900, Curitiba-PR 80001-970, T: 41-223-5415, F: 41-223-5415.

Eirene do Brasil, Caixa Postal 10-2449, 70.849 - Brasllia-DF.

UNES-União Nacional Evangélica da Saúde, R. Princesa Isabel, 605, Nova Petrólis, S Bern do, Campo-SP 09771-110, T: 11-458-5904, F: 11-458-5904.

BRITAIN (UK OF GB & NI)

AIDS Care Education and Training, P.O. Box 1323, Ealing, London W5 5TF, T: 44-81-840-7879, F: 44-81-8480.

Apostolate of the Sick, St. Mary of the Angels, Moorhouse Road, London W2 5DJ, T: 0171-229 0487.

Association of Blind Catholics, 58 Oakwood Road, Horley, Surrey RH6 7BU, T: 01293-772104.

Bible and Medical Missionary Fellowship (BMMF), 352 Kennington Rd, London SE11 4LF, T: (01)735-8228.

Calix Society, 60 Lamington Rd, Glasgow SW2, T: (041)882-1941.

Catholic AIDS (CAL), PO Box 646, London, E9 6QP, T: 0171-485 7298.

Catholic Handicapped Fellowship, 56 Stockwood Road, Seabridge, Newcastle, Staffordshire ST5 3LG.

Catholic Nursing Institute, 80 Lambeth Rd, London SE1, T: (01)928-6526.

Christian Medical Fellowship, 157 Waterloo Road, London SE1 8XN, T: 44-071-928-4694, F: 44-071-620-2453.

Church's Ministry of Healing, 11 The Mount, Belfast BT5 4NA, T: (08) 0232 457853.

Churches' Council for Health and Healing, St. Peter's Vestry, Eaton Square, London SW1W 0HH, T: (01)235-3305.

ECHO (The Joint Mission Hospital Equipment Board Limited), Ullswater Crescent, Coulsdon CR5 2HR, Surrey, T: 44-081-660-2220, F: 44-081-0751, 924507.

Edinburgh Medical Missionary Society, 7 Washington Lane, Edinburgh, EH112HA, T: 44-031313-3828, F: 44-013313-4662.

Emmanuel Hospital Association (EHA), European Fellowship, P.O. Box 43, Sutton SM2 5WL, T: 0818-770-9717, F: 0181-770-9747.

Equipment to Charity Hospitals Overseas, Ullswater Crescent, Coulsdon Surrey CR5 2HR, T: 44-81-660-2220, F: 44-81-668-0751.

Euro MediBus, 7 Mount Pleasant, Ayrlang, Stives, Cornwall TR26 JW, T: 44-0136-794751, F: 44-0872-561194.

Federation of Catholic Hospitals and Health Care Institutions in England and Wales, 60 Grove End Road, London NW8 9HN, T: 0171-286 5126.

Guild of Our Lady of Ransom (The Catholic Ch Extension Society), 31 Southdown Road, London SW20 8QJ, T: 0181-947 2598.

Leprosy Mission International, Northern Ireland Office, 44 Ulsterville Avenue, Belfast BT9 7AQ, T: (08) 0232 381937, F: (08) 0232 381842.

Leprosy Mission Intl., 80 Windmill Road, Brentford, Middlesex, TW8 9LW.

Lingfield Hospital School, Lingfield, Surrey RH7 6PN.

London Healing Mission, 20 Dawson Place, London W2, T: (01)229-3349.

Medical Missionary Association (MMA), 6 Canonbury Place, London N1 2NJ, T: (01)359-1313.

Medical Service Ministries, 2, Powis Place, Great Ormond St., London WC1N 3HT, T: 44-071-837-5832.

Mental After Care Association, 110 Jermyn St, London SW1Y 6HB, T: (01)839-5953.

Nurses Christian Fellowship International, 157 Waterloo Rd, London SE1 8UU.

Richmond Fellowship, 8 Addison Rd, Kensington, London W14 8DL, T: (01)603-6373/4/5.

Royal Association in Aid of the Deaf and Dumb, 7/11 Armstrong Rd, Acton, London W3 7JL, T: (01)743-6187.

St. John's Guild for the Blind, 44 Abingdon Rd, Luton, Beds, T: (0582)57824.

St. Joseph's Hospice Association, Ince Road, Thornton, Liverpool L23 4UE, T: 0151-924 7871.

Torch Trust for the Blind, 10258 Market Harborough, Hallaton LE16 8UJ, Leicestershire, T: 44-085-889301, F: 44-085-889371.

CANADA

Barrett House, 412 Queen St., E., Toronto, ON M5A 1T3, T: 416-869-3619, F: 416-869-0510.

Bethesda Christian Association, 201-31667 S. Fraser Way, Clearbrook, BC V2T 1T9, T: 604-850-6604, F: 604-850-7242.

Burden Bearers of Canada, 303-32555 Simon Avenue, Abbotsfor, B.C. V2T 4Y2, T: (604) 852-2370.

Canadian Hearing Society, 271 Spadina Rd., Toronto, ON M5R 2V3, T: 416-964-9595.

Cardinal Leger Institute Against Leprosy, 130 Ave., De L'Epee, Outrement, QC H2V 3T2, T: 514-495-2409.

Christian Blind Mission Intl., P.O. Box 800, Stouffville, ON L4A 7Z9, T: 905-640-6464, F: 905-640-4332, O: 1-800-567-CBMI.

Christian Counselling Services, 20 Eglinton Ave., W., Suite 1901, Toronto, Ontario M4R 1K8, T: (416) 489-3350.

Christian Horizons, 384 Arthur St., S., Elmira, ON N3B 2P4, T: 519-669-1571, F: 519-669-1574.

Christian Record Services, National Camps for the Blind, 1300 King St., E., Ste. 119, Oshawa, ON L1H 8N9, T: 905-436-6938, F: 905-436-7102.

Dayspring Counselling Service, Weston, Ontario, T: (416) 748-8583.

DeSales Chaplaincy, 71 Gough Ave., Toronto, ON M4K 3N9, T: 416-469-9993.

EMAS Evangelical Medical Aid Society, Box 160, Warkworth, ON K0K 3K0, T: 705-924-3246, F: 705-924-3384.

Friendship Groups Canada, Box 220, Simcoe, ON N3Y 4L1, T: 519-426-5152, F: 519-426-1536.

Global Medical Ministries, Box 1210, St. Catharines, Ontario L2R 7A7.

Gold Cross, The, 130 Avenue De L'Epee, Outrement, QC H2V, T: 514-495-2409.

Good Samaritan Society, 9405 - 50 St., Edmonton, AB T6B 2T4, T: 403-431-3600, F: 403-431-3795.

Homestead Residential and Support Services, 326 Locke St., S., Hamilton, ON L8P 4C6, T: 905-529-0454.

John Milton Society for the Blind in Canada, 40 St. Clair Ave., E., Suite. 202, Toronto, ON M4T 1M9, T: 416-960-3953.

L'Arche Western Prairie Region (Calgary-Edmonton-Lethbridge, AB; Winnipeg, MB), 307-57 Ave., S.W., Calgary, AB T2H 2T6, T: 403-571-1051, F: 403-255-1354.

Leprosy Mission Canada, 75 The Donway W. Ste 1410, North York, ON M3C 2E9, T: 416-441-3618, F: 416-441-0203, O: E-mail: TLM@timcanada.org, Web: www.tlmcanada.org.

Meadowbrook Counselling Associates, 4591 Highway 7 East, Suite 220, Unionville, ON L3R 1M6.

Medical Ambassadors of Canada, Ladner Postal Outlet, PO Box 18558, Delta, BC V4K 4V7, T: 406-245-2654, F: 406-245-8745.

Operation Eyesight Universal (OEU), P.O. Box 123, Station M, Calgary, AB T2P 2H6, T: 403-283-6323, F: 403-270-1899.

Raphah Clinics, Christian Counselling Centre, 160 George St., Sarnia, ON N7T 7V4, T: 519-344-1700.

Rehoboth Christian Association for the Mentally Handicapped, Box 1089, Stony Plain, AB T0E 2G0, T: 403-963-4044, F: 403-963-3075.

Salem Christian Mental Health Association, 512-1 Young Street, Hamilton, Ontario L8N 1T8, T: (416) 528-0353.

Salvation Army Community Mental Health Services, 143 Lakeshore Blvd., E., Toronto, ON M5A 1B7, T: 416-862-9880, F: 416-862-2696.

Shalom - L'Arche Association of Edmonton, 7708 - 83 St., Edmonton, AB T6C 2Y8, T: 403-465-0618, F: 403-465-8091.

Southdown (Emmanuel Convalescent Foundation), 1335 St. John's Sdrd. E., Aurora, ON L4G 3G8, T: 905-727-4214.

Special Needs Ministries, Box 892, Valleyview, AB T0H 2N0, T: 403-539-5852, F: 403-524-3249.

Tobias House Attendant Care, Inc., Suite 611 - 695 Coxwell Ave., Toronto, ON M4C 5R6, T: 416-690-3185, F: 416-690-5487.

World Mission to the Deaf (WMD), 39 Meadow Cres., Whitby, ON L1N 3J2, T: 905-723-1278, F: 905-404-2577.

CHINA

Junk Bay Medical Relief Council, Po Lam Rd, Junk Bay, NT, PO Box 9072, Kowloon, Hong Kong.

CONGO-BRAZZAVILLE

Dispensary and Maternity (Salvation Army), BP 10, Yangui, Kinkala.

Institute for the Blind (Salvation Army), BP 20, Brazzaville.

CONGO-ZAIRE

Bureau des Oeuvres Médicales, BP 3258, Kinshasa-Gombe, T: 30082 ext 57.

DENMARK

Den danske Hjlpekomitå for Spedaiskhedsmission, Pile Alle 3, 2000 Frederiksberg C, T: 31 22 86 16.

Missionary Association of Nurses, Lyshojgardsvej 43, Valdy.

ECUADOR

Asistencia Medica, Ave. America No. 1574 y Marchena, Casilla 4725, Quito, T: 235-702.

Caravanas Medicas, Ave. America No. 1574 y Marchena, Casilla 4725, Quito, T: 330-018.

Caravanas Medicas Voz Andes, Villalengua No. 278 y 10 de Agosto, Casilla 691, Quito, T: 241-550.

Dispensario Medico Filadelfia, 42 y Bolivia, Casilla 8729, Guayaquil, T: 371-721.

Servicio Medico, Manuel Larrea No. 224, Quito, T: 525-694.

Servicio Odontologico Comunitario, Rio Coca No. 1734, Casilla 579 A, Quito, T: 242-690.

EGYPT

Adventist Health Education Foundation (Egypt Food Factory), P.O. Box 12, Heliopolis, Cairo.

ETHIOPIA

All-Africa Leprosy & Rehabilitation Training Centre, P.O. Box 165, Addis Abeba.

FRANCE

International Crusade for the Blind, 15 Rue Mayet, F-75006 Paris, T: (01)734-9732.

L'Arche, BP 35, F 60350 Trosly-Breuil.

Salvation Army Rehabilitation Centre for Handicapped, 45410 Artenay, Château d'Auvilliers, T: 38-80-00-14.

Secrétariat National des Oeuvres Catholiques Sanitaires et Sociales, 103 Faubourg St-Honoré, F-75008 Paris, T: (01)225-1676.

Union Evangélique Médicale et Para-Médicale, 463 Rue de l'Eglise, Bois-Guillaume (Seine-Mar), T: Rouen 705003.

Union Nationale Interfédérale des Oeuvres et Organismes Privés Sanitaires et Sociaux (UNIOPSS), 103 Faubourg St-Honoré, F-75008 Paris, T: (01)225-1676.

GERMANY

AIDS Counselling (Salvation Army), Talstrasse 11, 20359 Hamburg, T: 040-31-95-571.

Arbeitsgemeinschaft Deutscher Evangelischer Seelsorger für Gemüts- und Nervenkranke, D-4813 Bethel.

Arbeitsgemeinschaft Ev Gehörlosenseelsorger Deutschlands, D-68 Mannheim.

Christliche Fachkräfte International, Wächterstr. 3, 70182 Stuttgart, T: 0711-210-66-0, F: 0711-210-66-33.

Christlicher Blindendienst, Postfach 630, D-355 Marburg/Lahn.

Christoffel-Blindenmission im Orient, Nibelungenstr 124, D-6140 Bensheim-Schönberg, T: (06251)6043.

Deutsches Institut Für ärztliche Mission, Paul-Lechler-Str.24, 72076 Tübingen.

Evangelische Arbeitsgemeinschaft für Müttergenesung, Deutenbacher Str 1, D-8504 Stein Bei Nurnberg.

German Health Food Factory, Luener Rennbahn 18, 21339 Lueneburg.

GHANA

Catholic Nurses Guide of Ghana, St. Patrick's Hospital, PO Box 17, Maase-Offinso.

Christian Health Association of Ghana, P.O. Box 7316, Accra.

Christian Medical Workers' Fellowship (CMWF), P.O. Box M-77, Accra.

Ghana Society for Sick, Destitutes & Deviants, P.O. Box 846, Kumasi.

GUADELOUPE

Centre Hospitalier, Abymes, Point-à-Pitre, T: 590-82-88-88.

GUATEMALA

Cristo Rey Nutritional Center, zona 6 of the city, San Antonio suburb.

El Buen Pastor Nutritional Center, village of Chumanzana.

El Buen Samaritano Clinic, Cristo Rey Church.

HAITI

Dispensary and Under-Fives Clinic (Salvation Army), Port-au-Prince.

HOLY SEE

Comite Intl. Catholique des Infirmieres et des Assistantes Medico-Sociales (CICIAMS), Palazzo S. Calisto, I 00120 Cité du Vatican.

International Federation of Catholic Medical Associations, Palazzo San Calisto, I-00120 Vatican City.

HUNGARY

Leprosy Mission, Alagi Tgr 13, Budapest 1151.

INDIA

Agape Leprosy Ministries India, Mangananm P. O., Kottayam, Kerala 686018.

Agape Mental Health and Research Institute, Mundukottackal P.O., Kerala 689649.

Alexis' School for the Blind, Bethany Convent, Inaciarpuram, Tuticorin, Tamil Nadu 628002.

Anne's Rehabilitation Centre for Handicapped, Tamil Nadu 627011.

Arpana CSI School for Special Education, All Saints Church Compound, 1, Hosur Road, Bangalore, Karnataka 560025.

Asha Niketan, Nandi Bazar, Katalur P. O., Kerala 673531.

Asha Nilayam, Ponkunnam, Kerala 686506.

Ashalaya, Home for the Welfare Of Mentally Retarded, 56, Lazar Road Lay-out, Fraser Town, Bangalore, Karnataka 560005.

Assisi Home for the Deaf and Dumb, Karunapuram, P. Pendial, Andhra Pradesh 506151.

B. C. M. Nursing School, Serkawn, Zotlang P. O., Mizoram 796691.

Baldwin Opportunity School, Inter-Mission Business Office, 3rd Floor, Lawrence And Mayo House, 276 Dr. D. N., Bombay, Maharashtra 400001.

Baramasia Rehabilitation Training Centre, C/o D. S. W. C. Gandhi Bhavan, Polytechnic Road, P. B. 47, Dhanbad, Bihar 826001.

Bishop Sargent School for the Mentally Retarded, Palayamkottai, Tamil Nadu 627002.

Blind People Rehabilitation Centre, 201 Mettur Road, Erode, Tamil Nadu 638052.

Blind Working Mens Hostel, Wellingdon Compound, Sheikh Hafizuddin Marg, Byculla, Bombay, Maharashtra 400008.

Bombay Centre for the Deaf, C/o St. Stanislaus High School, Bandra, Bombay, Maharashtra 400050.

Bombay Institute for the Deaf, 33 Nesbit Road, Mazagaon, Bombay, Maharashtra 400010.

C. S. I. Rehabilitation Centre, Home for Handicapped Children, CSI Compound, Woodville Road, Kodaikanal, Tamil Nadu 624101.

Canossa School for Mentally Handicapped, Canossa Annexe, Pitamber Lane, Mahim, Bombay, Maharashtra 400016.

Catholic Hospital Association (CHA), CBCI Centre, Ashok Place, New Delhi 1.

Chandkhuri Leprosy Hospital and Homes, P. O. Baitalpur, Madhya Pradesh 495222.

Christian Counselling Center, P. B. No. 110, Sainathapuram, Vellore, Tamil Nadu 632001.

Christian Foundation for the Blind, Via Pampady, Velloor P. O., Kerala 686501.

Christian Guardians Association, Lamka, Churachandpur, Manipur 795128.

Christian Medical Association of India, Plot 2, A-3 Local Shopping Center, Janakpuri, New Delhi 110058.

Christian Medical College, Ludhiana, Punjab 141008.

Christian Medical Journal of India, Plot No. 2, A-3 Local Shopping Center, Janakpuri, New Delhi 110058.

Christian Public Health Centre, Macherla, Andhra Pradesh 522426.

Church of South India School for the Deaf, Kottaram, Tamil Nadu 629703.

Clara Olive CSI Polio Home, CSI Church Compound, Melur, Tamil Nadu 625106.

Community Health Centre, Holy Family Hospital , Okhla Road, Jamia Nagar P. O., New Delhi 110025.

Cottolengo Special School for the Mentally Handicapped, Fort Cochin, Cochin, Kerala 682001.

Counselling Centre, Alempang Ward, P. O. Mokokchung Town, Mokokchung, Nagaland 798601.

Damien Rehabilitation Centre for Cured Hansenites, Mathakottai Road, Tamil Nadu 613005.

Deaf Girls Project, Perumalpuram, Kottaram, Tamil Nadu 629702.

Dhanbad Blind School, C/o De Nobili School, Digwadih, F. R. I., Bihar 828108.

Emmanuel Blind Relief Society, 7 E, Woodcote Road, Post Box No. 47, Coonoor, Tamil Nadu 643102.

Evangelical Medical Fellowship of India, Montauban Christian Guest House, Ettines Road, Ootaccamund, Tamil Nadu 643001.

German Leprosy Relief Association, 4, Gajapathy Street, Shenoy Nagar, Madras, Tamil Nadu 600020.

Good Shepheard School for the Deaf, 3rd Street, Bryant Nagar, Tuticorin, Tamil Nadu 628008.

Grace Counseling India, P. O. Box 29, Muvattupuzha, Kerala 686661.

Hamsalaya, 106, Church Street, Lingaraja Puram, Bangalore, Karnataka 560005.

Haythornthwaite Memorial Leprosy Services, C/o Mary Wanless Hospital, Tararani Chowk, Kavala Naka, Kolhapur, Maharashtra 416003.

HEAL India, Pottakuzhi, Pattom P.O., Trivandrum, Kerala 695004.

Home for Blind Boys and Girls (Salvation Army),

Kalimpong West Bengal.
Home for Handicapped (Polio) Children, L. M. S. Compound, Trivandrum, Kerala 695033.
Home for Mentally Handicapped, C/o Missionary Brothers of Charity, AndulRoad, Howrah, West Bengal.
Home for Sick and Dying Destitutes, Missionaries Of Charity, Brodipet, 6th Line, Guntur, Andhra Pradesh 522002.
Home for the Deaf and Dumb (Salvation Army), Erin House, 3 Colinton Rd., Darjeeling, W. Bengal.
Home for the Disabled and Destitute, New Pochamma Temple, Kashibugga, Warangal, Andhra Pradesh 506002.
Hospital Christian Fellowship of India, 155 Mahendra Hills, East Marredpally, Secunderabad, Andhra Pradesh 500026.
Hospital Ministries India, P.O. Box 27217, Chembur P. O., Bombay, Maharashtra 400071.
Hostel for Blind Men (Salvation Army), 172 Acharya Jagdish Chandra Rd., Calcutta 700014.
Hostel for Blind Working Men (Salvation Army), Railwaypura, Raipur-Hirpur, Ahmedabad, Gujarat, T: 0272-368217.
IELC High School for the Deaf, 78 M. C. Road, Ambur, Tamil Nadu 635802.
IELC Polio Home (Children), IELC Mission Compound, Krishnagiri, Tamil Nadu.
IEM Medical Ministry, 38, Langford Road, Bangalore, Karnataka 560025.
India Evangelical Lutheran Church School for the Blind, Barugur, Tamil Nadu 635104.
India Fellowship for the Visually Handicapped, Anna Nagar, House No. 22, Near Passport Office, Worli Bombay, Maharashtra 400025.
Jeevan Jyothy Computer Centre for Disabled, ICSA Complex, 94 Pantheon Road, Egmore, Madras, Tamil Nadu 600008.
Leprosy Mission, Bankura Leprosy Control Prog., P. O. 27, Bankura, West Bengal 722101.
Leprosy Mission India, Vocational Training Centre, Hirawadi Road Corner, Panchavti P. O., Nashik, Maharashtra 422003.
Light to the Blind, Sivagiry P. O., Varkala, Kerala 695141.
Mairan School for the Hearing Impaired, E-6, Private Sector, Bhopal, Madhya Pradesh 462016.
Mar Gregorios Rehabilitation Centre for the Blind, Maonammoodu, Kodunganoor P. O., Kerala 695013.
Mary Scott Home for the Blind, 23-24 Marquis Street, Calcutta, West Bengal 700016.
Medico-Pastoral Association, 47, Pottery Rd., Fraser Town, Bangalore, Karnataka 560005.
Mentally Retarded Home & School, Peranampet, Tamil Nadu.
Methodist School of Nursing, Mission Road, Nadiad, Gujarat 387001.
Mission to the Blind, 3B Hebron Apts, Maninagar (East), Ahmedabad, Gujarat 380008.
Missionaries of Charity, Ludhiana, Punjab 141008.
National Fellowship for the Blind, P.O. Box 1709, Past Akurdi, Pune, Maharashtra 411035.
National Home and Health Services, Seventh-Day Tlang, Aizawl, Mizoram 796009.
National Training Centre for the Handicapped, Nagamangalam, Via Ramjeenagar, Tiruchy, Tamil Nadu 620009.
Nav Vani School (Deaf And Dumb School), Bojubir, Varanasi, Uttar Pradesh 221001.
Navajivan Dermatological Centre, C/o Modest II Row House, Block No 4 Subhashsnagar, Bhavnagar, Gujarat 364001.
Nirmal Hriday Home for the Dying and Destitutes, Bethany Home, Ramanathapuram P. O., Coimbatore, Tamil Nadu 641045.
Nirmal Kennedy Centre, C/o M. C. Sisters Green Park, Post Michaelnagar, New Barrackpore, West Bengal.
Nur Manzil Psychiatric Centre, Lalbagh, Lucknow, Uttar Pradesh 226001.
Rehabilitation Centre for Blind Women, Medical Mission Hospital, Kolencherry P. O., Kerala 682311.
Salvation Army Health Services Advisory Council, Post Bag No. 6 Ahmednagar-414 001, Maharastra State, T: 91-241-27796.
Sandarshan - Institute for Counseling and Personal Growth, 15, Rajniwas Marg, New Delhi 110054.
Schieffelin Leprosy Research and Training Centre, S. L. R. Sanatorium P. O., Karigiri, N. Arcot, Tamil Nadu 632106.
School for the Handicapped, C/o Gloria Church, Byculla, Bombay, Maharashtra 400027.
Scudder Memorial Polio Home, Ranipet, Tamil Nadu 632401.
Sevadaan Special School, 243 St. Anthony's Road, Chembur, Bombay, Maharashtra 400071.
Sophia Opportunity School, 70 Palace Road, Bangalore, Karnataka 560001.
St John's Medical College, Robert Koch Bhavan, Sarjapura Road St John's Medical College, Bangalore, Karnataka 560034.
St. Ann's Home for Physically Handicapped Children, Mayer's Home, Mangalagiri, Andhra Pradesh 522503.
St. John's Medical College and Hospital, Sajrapur Road, Bangalore, Karnataka 560034.
St. Lucia's School for the Blind, Silverpuram, Tuticorin, Tamil Nadu 628002.
St. Mary's School for Deaf and Dumb, Maha Lakshmipuram-Post, Via Stone Housepet, Chennapallipalem, Andhra Pradesh 524002.
St. Philomena's Hospital, Campbell Road, Bangalore, Karnataka 560047.
Steves Fitness Incorporated, 35, Harris Road, Benson Town, Bangalore, Karnataka 560046.
Thomas Mar Athanesius Counselling Centre, Near Medical College, Amalagiri P.O., Kerala 686036.
Tropical Health Foundation of India, Guruvayoor Road, Kunnamkulam, Kerala 680503.
Vianney Home (for the handicapped), Vengalrao Nagar, Andhra Pradesh 524004.
Vijaya Mary Integrated School for the Blind, Carmelnagar, Vijayawada, Andhra Pradesh 520005.
Vocational Training Centre for Disabled Persons, Maulpui, Aizawl, Mizoram 796001.
Word and Deed India, Miryalaguda, Andhra Pradesh 508207.
Xavier Inst of Counselling, Mahapalika Marg, Fort, Fort, Maharashtra 400001.
Zion Blind Home and School, Gunadala, Vijayawada, Andhra Pradesh 520004.

INDONESIA
Indonesian Christian Medical Workers' Association, DGI, Jalan Salemba Raya 10, Jakarta IV/3.

IRELAND
Church's Ministry of Healing, St. Andrews Church, Suffolk Street, Dublin 2, T: (353) 01 776078.
Leprosy Mission International, Republic of Ireland Office, 5 St James Terrace, Clonskeagh Road, Dublin 6, T: (353) 01 269 8804.
National Catholic Chaplaincy for the Deaf, 40 Lower Drumcondra Road, Dublin 9, T: (353) 01 305744/301057.

ISRAEL
Centre Catholique de Rehabilitation pour Handicapes, P.O. Box 20531, 91204 Jérusalem; Mont des Oliviers, 91204, Jérusalem, T: 02-28-18-01.
Health Education Center, P.O. Box 2012, 16000 Nazareth, T: 6-559103.

ITALY
Centro Italiano di Sessuologia, Instituto di Psicologia, Città Universitaria, I-00100 Roma, T: (4991)550212.
Ente Nazionale per la Protezione e d'Assistenza di Sordomuti, Via Gregorio VII 120, I-00165 Roma, T: 6377041.
Istituto Internazionale di Teologia Pastorale Sanitaria Camillianum, Largo Ottorino Respighi 6, I-00135 Rome, T: 39-6-3297-495, F: 39-6-3296-352.
Medical Mission Sisters/Society of Catholic Medical Missionaries, Via di Villa Troili 32, I-00163 Roma.
Medico-Missionary Association for Women, Via delle Terme Deciane 5/A, I-00153 Roma, T: 573482.
Order of Malta, Via Condotti, 68, Palazzo Malta, 00187 Rome.
Pontifical Council for Pastoral Assistance to Health Care Workers, Via della Conciliazione 3, 00193 Rome.
Unione Medici Missionaria Italian (UMMI), Ospedale San Cuore/Civile, I-37024 Negrar (Verona), T: 650044.
University College for Medical Missionary Aspirants, Via Galileo Galilei 18, I-35100 Padova; Via Acquetta 12, Padova, and Via Napoleone III 1, I-00185 Roma, T: 735824.

JAMAICA
Francis Ham Residence (Salvation Army), 57 Mannings Hill Rd., Kingston 8, T: 924-1308.
Rae Town Clinic (Salvation Army), 24 Tower St., Kingston, T: 928-1489.
School for Blind and Visually Handicapped (Salvation Army), P.O. Box 562; 57 Mannings Hill Rd., Kingston 8, T: 925-1362.

JAPAN
Association for the Relief of Leprosy in Asia, No. 7 Yuraka-cho 1-chome, Chiyoda-ku, Tokyo.
Japan Christian Medical Association (JCMA), National YMCA Bldg, 1-2 Nishi Kanda, Chiyoda-ku, Tokyo.
Japan Mission for Hospital Evangelism, 242-3 Hanyuno, Habikino, Osaka-fu 583.
Japan Overseas Christian Medical Cooperative Service, National YMCA Bldg, 1-2 Nishi Kanda, Chiyoda-ku, Tokyo; Also: 551-23 1-chome Tetsukache, Shinjuku-ku, Tokyo.

JORDAN
Society of the Mission to the Blind in Bible Lands, P.O. Box 265, Jerusalem.

KENYA
Hospitals Chaplaincy of Kenya, Westlands, PO Box 14424, Nairobi, T: 60803.
Kenya Hospitals Christian Fellowship (KHCF), PO Box 30024, Nairobi.
Salvation Army Health Centre, P.O. Box 88; Kolanya, Malakisi, via Bungoma.
Salvation Army Hostel for Physically Handicapped Children, P.O. Box 7231; Mji wa Amani, Nakuru, T: 41595.

LEBANON
Christian Medical Association of the Near East, CMC Hospital, Bayrut.

LIBERIA
Gospel Witness to the Deaf, Mail Bay 9038, Monrovia.

MALAWI
Private Hospital Association of Malawi (PHAM), P.O. Box 948, Blantyre, T: 8581.

MALAYSIA
Centre for Mentally Handicapped (Salvation Army), Melaka Day Care Centre, 321 Jalan Parameswara, 75000 Melaka, T: 23-2101.

MARTINIQUE
Fraternite Catholique des Malades et Handicapes (FCMH), Enclos - 97233 Schoelcher, T: 596-61-24-97.

MEXICO
Centro Psiquiatrico Infantil, 437 Col Del Valle, Zona 12, Mexico, DF, T: 231412.
Clinica Dental/International Dental Institute, Calle 4a No 1524, Tijuana, BC.

NETHERLANDS
Forensic Psychiatric Clinic (Probation Community) (Salvation Army), 6741 MK Lunteren, Postweg 249, T: 03420-15241.
Medicus Mundi Internationalis, P.O. Box 1547, 6501 BM Nijmegen.
Nursing Home for Homeless and AIDS Patients (Salvation Army), 1217 EC Hilversum, Nimrodlaan 12, T: 035-247624.

NEW ZEALAND
Bible & Medical Missionary Fellowship (BMMF), New Zealand Council, 427 Queen St, Auckland 1.
Christian Blind Mission International (NZ), P.O. Box 99-820, Newmarket, Auckland, T: 0-9-522-0902, F: 0-9-522-0923.
Inter-Church Advisory Council on Hospital Chaplaincy, P.O. Box 800, Christchurch.
Leprosy Mission, P.O. Box 10-227, Dominion Road, Auckland, T: 0-9-630-2818, F: 0-9-630-0784, O: E-mail: 100246-2617@compuserve.com.

NIGERIA
HIV/AIDS Action Centre (Salvation Army), Box 125, Lagos; 11 Odunlami St., Lagos, T: 2633556.
Rehabilitation Centre for Physically Handicapped Children (Salvation Army), Oji River, via Enugu, Anambra State.

NORWAY
Christian Medical Association, Theresesgt 51 B, Oslo 3.
Nurses' Missionary Association, PA Munchs vei 3, Oslo 8.

PAKISTAN
Karachi Adventist Hospital, Post Box 7289, Karachi 3.
Seventh-day Adventist Dental Services, 269 Mahd Hussain Road, Rawalpindi.

PALESTINE
Pontifical Mission Centre for the Blind, Gaza City, Gaza Strip.

PANAMA
School for the Blind (Salvation Army), La Boca Rd., Apartado Postal N, Balboa, Rep de Panamá.

PHILIPPINES
AIDS Programme (Salvation Army), 1815 Velasquez St., 1012 Tondo.

PORTUGAL
Assistência Evangélica a Doentes da Lepra, Travessa Actor Alvaro, 2425 Vieira de Leiria, T: 044-69 51 57.
Luz da Vida, Rua Magalhães Lima, 8 - 1. Esq., Paivas - 2840 Seixal, T: 01-222 84 82.
União Médica Hospitalar Cristã Evangélica, Av. Gomes Pereira, 63 - 3. Esq., 1500 Lisboa, T: 01-715 54 71.

ROMANIA
AIDS Care Education and Training—Romania, 11472 Str. Amurgului Nr. 54, Constanta 8700, T: 40-91-680452.
Christian Medical Association, Str. Manastur N.R. 50, Cluj-Napoca 3400, T: 40-51-62380.

RUSSIA
Christian Medical Association, Moscow 113209, T: 7-095-121-23-33.

SINGAPORE
Christian Outreach to the Handicapped, 155 Own Road, Sinapore 218950, T: 295-2007, F: 299-9073.
Gospel Mission to the Blind Ltd., No 8, Lorong 27A Geylang, #02-06 Guilin Building, Singapore 388106, T: 741-4490.
Leprosy Mission Corporation, 6001 Beach Road, Golden Mile Tower #08-6, Singapore 199589, T: 294-0137, F: 294-7663.

SOUTH AFRICA
Adventist Professional Health Services, P.O. Box 337, Bethlehem 9700, Orange Free State, T: 58-3032530, 3035561, F: 58-3038265.
Athlone School for the Blind, P/B X1, Kasselsviei 7533, Athlone St, Bellville, South Cape Town, T: 021-951-2234, F: 021-951-5118.
Bet-el School for Epilepsy, PO Box 105, Kuils River 7580, T: 021-903-5146.
Catholic Psychological Services, PO Box 5305, Troyville 2139, 36 Terrace Rd, Bertrams 2094, Johannesburg, T: 011-614-2931.
Christian Counseling Centre, PO Box 414, Middelburg 1050, 42 Hospital Rd, Clubville, Middelburg, T: 0132-282-6833.
Churches AIDS Programme, PO Box 32610, Braamfontein, Johnannesburg, T: 011-403-3243, F: 011-339-3528.
Efata School for the Deaf & Blind, PO Box 177, Umtata 5100, T: 0471-36-0527, F: 0471-36-0525.
FAMSA, National Council, PO Box 2800, Kempton Park 1620, T: 011-975-7106, F: 011-975-7108.
Good Shepherd Hospice, PO Box 570, Middleburg 5900, T: 04924-2-1331.
Leprosy Mission (Southern Africa), P/B X06, Lyndhurst 2106, Tempo Bldg, 148 Jhburg Rd, Lyndhurst, Jhburg, T: 011-882-6156, F: 011-882-0441.
Nuwe Hoop Sentrum, P/B X3047, Worcester 6850, Leipoldt Ave, Worcester, T: 0231-7-2791, F: 0231-7-4607.
Phomolong Chronic Care Unit, PO Box 1117, East Rand 1462, T: 011-917-2571.
Regionald Orsmond Counselling Services, PO Box 58051, Newville 2114, 21 Annandale St, Martindale, Johannesburg.
Thiboloha Skool vir Dowes en Blindes, P/B 829, Witsieshoek 9870, T: 058-713-0048, F: 058-713-1800.

SOUTH KOREA
Catholic Association for Deaf & Dumb, 10-3, Suyu 3-dong, Kangbuk-gu, Seoul-shi, T: (02) 995-7394.
Catholic Hospital Association, 505, Panp'o-dong, Soch'o-gu, Seoul-shi, T: (02) 590-1334.
Catholic Leprosy Workers' Association, 17, Chong-dong, Chung-gu, Seoul-shi, T: (02) 755-6311.
Catholic Nurses Association, 1, Hoegi-dong, Tongdaemun-gu, Seoul-shi, T: (02) 961-0307.

SPAIN
Escuela Española de Medicina para Misioneros, Raimundo Lulio, Colegio Vasco de Quiroga, Ciudad Universitaria, Madrid 3.
Misión Evang. Contra la Lepra, Beneficencia, 18 Bis, 1°, 28004 Madrid, T: 594-51-05.

SWAZILAND
Swazi Eye Services, P.O. Box 2346, Manzini.

SWEDEN
African Mission of the Deaf, c/o Evangeliska Fosterlands-Stiftelsen, Tegnergatan 34, Stockholm VA.
Catholic Nurses' Association, Framnasgatan 14, Goteborg S.
Deaf and Blind Ministry (Salvation Army), Femte Tvärgatan 18, tr, 802 84 Gävle, T: 026-12-03-13.
Healthy Kitchen Food Co., The, (AB Halsans kok), 762 91 Rimbo.
Hultafors Health Centre and Hospital, 517 00 Bollebygd 1.

SWITZERLAND
Adventist Foundation for the Blind, Naefelserstrasse 34, 4055 Basel, T: 061-302-66-50.
Albania Health Projects, 39, Rupperswil 5102, T: 41-47-2053, F: 41-64-2691.
Annuaire du diocese de Lausanne, Geneve et Fribourg (Catholic), 38, av. Montoie, 1007 Lausanne, 021/624 3538.
Christian Fraternity of the Sick and Handicapped, 9, Avenue de la Gare, CH-1630, Bulle.
Federation Internationale des Associations Catholiques D'Aveugles (FIDACA), Mme. Helga Gruber, Secrétaire, Chamblioux 18, CH 1700 Fribourg.
Fraternite Chretienne des Malades et Handicapes, 9, Avenue de la gare, CH 1630 Bulle.
Lausanne Health and Healing Network, 6, chemin de la Tourelle, 1209 Geneva, T: 41-22-798-41-83, F: 41-22-798-65-47.

TAIWAN
Fu Yo Handicapped Children's Centre (Salvation Army), No. 12, Alley 2, Lane 217, Section 2, Hsing Lung Rd., Taipei, T: 933-4188.
Intercontinental Christian Brotherhood of Sick and Handicapped People, 3, Lane 85, Lin Sen N. Rd., Taipei, T: 02-5676846, F: 02-5676846.

TANZANIA
Adventist Seminary of Health Evangelism, Heri Mission Hospital, SLP Kogoma.

THAILAND
Mission Health Food Co., Ltd., PO Box 12, Klong Ton, Bangkok 10116.

UGANDA
Home of Joy (Salvation Army), P.O. Box 16178; Kampala, T: 041-532517.

UKRAINE
Christian Medical Association of Western Ukraine, Yakivna Malorivnenska 59, Rivne.

UNITED STATES OF AMERICA (USA)
Adventist Health System/West, 2100 Douglas Blvd., Roseville, CA 95661-9002.
American Institute for Teen AIDS Prevention, P.O. Box 136116, Fort Worth, TX 76136, T: 817-237-0230.
American Leprosy Missions, Inc., 1 Alm Way, Greenville, SC 29601, T: 803-271-7040.
Blanton-Peale Institute, 3 W. 29th St., New York, NY 10001, T: 212-725-7850, F: 212-689-3212.
Blessings International, 5881 S. Garnett St., Tulsa, OK 74146, T: 918-250-8101, F: 918-250-1281, O: E-mail: 75554.3572@compuserve.com.
Bronx Family AIDS Centre (Salvation Army), 425 East 159 St., Bronx, NY 10451, T: 718-665-8472.
Carroll Center for the Blind, 770 Centre St., Newton, MA 02158.
Catholic Medical Mission Board, 10 W 17th St, New York, NY 10011, T: 212-242-7757, F: 212-242-0930.
Children's Medical Ministries, P. O. Box 3382, Crofton, MD 21114, T: 301-261-3211, F: 301-888-2533, O: E-mail: ChildMedMinistries@charitiesusa.com.
CHOSEN, Inc., 3642 W. 26th St., Erie, PA 16506, T: 814-833-3023, F: 814-833-4091.
Christian Blind Mission International, P.O. Box 19000, Greenville, SC 29602-9000, T: 864-239-0065, F: 864-239-0069, O: E-mail: 102070.3266@compuserve.com.
Christian Counseling Center (CCC), O: Web: www.gospelcom.net/counsel.
Christian Dental Society, Box 177, Sumner, IA 50674, T: 800-237-7368, F: 319-578-8843.
Christian Medical & Dental Society, P.O. Box 5, Bristol, TN 37621, T: 423-844-1000, F: 423-844-1005, O: E-mail: 75364.331@compuserve.com, www.gocin.com/CMDS.
Christian Medical Missions, O: Web: www.iag.net/~toporkov/.
Christian Psychology for Today, 2100 N. Collins Blvd., Richardson, TX 75080.
Conference of Diocesan Coordinators of Health Affairs (Catholic), 1031 Superior Ave., Cleveland, OH 44114, T: 216-696-6525.
Deaconess College of Nursing, St. Louis, MO.
Dr. Fred Gross, Christian Theraphy Program, 570 Glenneyre Ave., Suite 107, Laguna Beach, CA

92651, T: (800) HELP-4-ME, (800) 435-7463.
Episcopal Conference of the Deaf of the Episc. Ch in the USA, Box 27459, Philadelphia, PA.
Fellowship of Associates of Medical Evangelism, P. O. Box 688, Columbus, IN 47202, T: 812-379-4351, F: 812-379-1105.
Flying Doctors of America, 1951 Airport Rd. Ste. 203, Atlanta, GA 30341, T: 770-451-3068, F: 770-457-6302, O: E-mail: FDOAmerica@aol.com, home.navisoft.com/vip/flyingdoctorsofamerica.htm.
Friends Contact Information, 1501 Cherry St, Philadelphia, PA 19102, T: 215-241-7024.
Global Medical Ministries, Box 711, Buffalo, NY 14240, T: 716-688-5048, F: 716-688-5049.
Health Talents International, O: Web: www.the-matrix.com/hti/.
Health Teams International, Inc., 7518 S. Evanston Ave., Tulsa, OK 74136-5615, T: (918) 481-1115, F: (918) 481-1115, O: E-mail: 76265.3374@compuserve.com.
Hospital Chaplains' Ministry of America, O: Web: www.hcmachaplains.org.
Inter-American Health Food Company, P.O. Box 140760, Miami, FL 33114-0760.
Interchurch Medical Assistance, P.O. Box 429, New Windsor, MD 21776, T: 410-635-8720, F: 410-635-8726, O: E-mail: IMA@ecunet.org, Web: www.interchurch.org.
International Catholic Deaf Association, 8002 S. Sawyer Rd., Darien, IL 60561.
International Child Care, P.O. Box 14485, Columbus, OH 43214, T: 614-447-9952, F: 614-447-1123, O: E-mail: 103220.473@compuserve.com.
International Health Services Foundation, P.O. Box 49536, Colorado Springs, CO 80945, T: 719-481-1379, F: 719-481-1376, O: E-mail: Drsneu@aol.com.
ISOH/Impact, 905 Farnsworth Rd., Waterville, OH 43566, T: 419-878-8546, F: 419-878-2869.
JAF Ministries, P.O. Box 3333, Agoura Hills, CA 91301, T: 1-818-707-5664, F: 1-818-707-2391, O: E-mail: 102704.3130@compuserve.com.
John Milton Society for the Blind, 475 Riverside Dr., Rm. 455, New York, NY 10115, T: 212-870-3335, F: 212-870-3229.
Journal of Christian Nursing, P.O. Box 1650, Downers Grove, IL 60515-0780, T: 708-887-2500.
Kathleen Ministries, 626 N. Garfield Ave., Ste. 187, Alhambra, CA 91801, T: (818) 458-8708.
Kettering College of Medical Arts (Educational Division of the Kettering Medical Center), 373 Southern Blvd., Kettering, OH 45429, T: 513-296-7201, F: 513-296-4238.
Korean American Handicap Mission, 10221 White Oak Ave., #1 Northridge, CA 91325, T: 818-360-5322.
L'Arche Central US Region, 151-A S Ann St, Mobile, AL 36604, T: 334-438-2094.
Lalmba Assoc, 7685 Quartz St, Arvada, CO 80007, T: 303-420-1810, F: 303-467-1232.
Link Care Center, 1734 W. Shaw Ave., Fresno, CA 93711, T: 209-439-5920, F: 209-439-2214, O: E-mail: 75027.2265@compuserve.com.
Love & Action (AIDS), 3 Church Circle, Annapolis, MD 21401, T: 301-268-3442.
Ludhiana Christian Medical College Board, USA, Inc., 900 S. Arlington Ave., Rm. 221, Harrisburg, PA 17109, T: 717-561-0990.
Luke Society, The, P.O. Box 349, Vicksburg, MS 39181, T: 601-638-1629, F: 601-636-6711, O: E-mail: LukeSoc@juno.com.
MAP International, P.O. Box 215000, Brunswick, GA 31521, T: 912-265-6010, F: 912-265-6170, O: E-mail: MAPUS@map.org, Web: www.map.org.
Martin Luther Home Society, Inc., Resource Center Library, 650 J St., Suite 305, Lincoln, NE 68508-2961.
Mastering Life Ministries (MLM), O: Web: www.goshen.net/xpsexualityxp.
Medical Ambassadors International, P.O. Box 576645, Modesto, CA 95357, T: 209-524-0600, F: 209-571-3538, O: E-mail: MedAmb@ix.netcom.com, Web: www.med-amb.org.
Medical Clinic on Wheels, 7029 Applewood Dr., Madison, WI 53719, T: 608-833-1953, F: 608-829-1937.
Minirth Meier New Life Clinic, 2100 N. Collins Blvd., Ste. 300, Richardson, TX 75080, T: 972-907-1972, F: 972-699-9516.
Mission Doctors Assoc, 3424 Wilshire Blvd, Los Angeles, CA 90010, T: 818-285-8868, F: 818-309-1716.
Missionary Dentists, P.O. Box 7002, Seattle, WA 98133, T: 425-771-3241, F: 425-775-5155.
Narramore Christian Foundation, P.O. Box 661900, Arcadia, CA 91066, T: 626-821-8400, F: 626-821-8409.
National Apostolate with People with Mental Retardation, 4516 30th St., N.W., Washington, D.C. 20008.
National Catholic Office for the Deaf, 814 Thayer Ave., Silver Spring, MD 20910.
National Catholic Office for Persons with Disabilities (NCPD), P.O. Box 29113, Washington, D.C. 20009.
National Woman's Christian Temperance Union, 1730 Chicago Ave., Evanston, IL 60201, T: 708-864-1396.
Natural Christian, O: Web: www.livrite.com/nc.
NCCC Committee on Deaf Ministries, 475 Riverside Dr, New York, NY 10115.
Northwest Medical Teams, P.O. Box 10, Portland, OR 97207, T: 503-644-6000, F: 503-644-9000, O: Web: www.nwmti.org.
Operation Sound, P.O. Box 60309, Colorado Springs, CO 80906, T: 800-659-3656/ask for 540-8390.
REAP International (Radiological Equipment Assistance Program), 992 W. Ninth St., Upland, CA 91786-4542, T: 714-981-5777, F: 714-949-2447.
Share Foundation with the Handicapped, 1001 W 8th St, Michigan City, IN 46360, T: 219-872-2866, F: 219-874-3491.
Supervised Group Home for Developmentally Disabled (Salvation Army), Box 2037, Wichita, KS 67201; Wichita Booth Memorial Residence, 2050 W. Eleventh St., Wichita, KS 67201, T: 316-263-6174.
Total Health, Inc., P.O. Box 592, Kailua-Kona, HI 96734, T: 808-261-8400, F: 808-261-0220.
UCC Chaplains in Health Care, 13829 S 85th St., Orland Park, IL 60462.
Welfare of the Blind, 4706 Bethesda Ave., Bethesda, MD 20014; 4813 Woodway Lane, N.W., Washington, DC 20016.
World Medical Mission, Inc., P.O. Box 3000, Boone, NC 28607-3000, T: 704-262-1980, F: 704-262-0175.
Xavier Society for the Blind, 154 E. 23rd St., New York, NY 10010.

53
Men's lay organizations

Definitions: Men's ministries, movements, missions, and agencies; organizations devoted to the evangelization, training, service, discipleship, teaching, or special needs of lay men; agencies, commissions, or ministries that assist, encourage, direct, or provide resources for men's fellowships in churches; men's rallies, conferences, crusades, missions, or events. See also LAY MINISTRIES.

54
Military chaplaincies

Organizations ministering to or providing chaplains for armed services at home or overseas (armies, navies, air forces, police forces, national guard groups, law enforcement agencies, government units, paramilitary units); chaplaincy training and support; chaplaincy associations.

ARGENTINA
Military Vicariate of Argentina, Arzobispado, Suipacha 1034, Buenos Aires.

AUSTRALIA
Catholic Military Vicariate of Australia, 3 Coral Place, Campbell, Canberra, ACT 2601.

AUSTRIA
International Military Apostolate, Kaiseralle 23, A-2100 Korneuburg; Militärvikariat, Mariahilferstr 24, A-1070 Wien, T: (0222)939666.

BELGIUM
Military Vicariate of Belgium, Place de Jamblinne de Meux 38, B-1040 Brussel, T: (02)343498.

BOLIVIA
Military Vicariate of Bolivia, Calle Ingavi 44, Casilla 25, La Paz.

BRAZIL
Military Vicariate of Brazil, CP 07-561, Brasília, DF.

BRITAIN (UK OF GB & NI)
Bishopric of the Forces, 26 The Crescent, Farnborough, Hants GU14 7AS, T: 01252-373699, F: 01252-517910.
Catholic Military Vicariate of Great Britain, 54 Ennismore Gardens, London SW7.
Church of England Soldiers', Sailors, & Airmen's Clubs (CESSAC), Central Office, 1 Shakespeare Terrace, High St, Portsmouth, Hants PO1 2RH, T: (0705)29319.
Mission to Military Garrisons, Ashfield House, 402 Sauchiehall St, Glasgow G2 3JH, Scotland, T: (041)332-2438.
Officer's Christian Union (OCU), 35 Catherine Place, London SW1.
Royal Naval Lay Readers' Society, Ministry of Defence, Lacon House, Theobalds Rd, London WCIX 8RY, T: (01)242-0222 ext 847.
Royal Navy Chaplain of the Fleet, Ministry of Defence, Lacon House, Theobalds Rd, London WC1X 8RY, T: (01)242-0222.
Sanders Soldiers' & Airmens' Homes, 508 Scottish Provident Bldg, 7 Donegall Square West, Belfast BT1 6JG, NI; 30a Belmont Road, Belfast BT4 2AN, T: 25724.
Soldiers and Airmen's Scripture Readers' Association (SASRA), Havelock House, 35 Catherine Place, London SW1E 6ER, T: (01)834-1314/5.
United Services Catholic Association, Duke of York's HQ, King's Road, London SW3 4RY.

CANADA
Catholic Military Vicariate of Canada, Quartiers Généraux des Forces Canadiennes, Ottowa K1A 0K2, T: (612)992-6025.
Officers Christian Union (OCU), Royal Military College, Kingston, Ontario.

CHILE
Military Vicariate of Chile, Vicaría Castrense, Correo 8, Santiago.

COLOMBIA
Military Vicariate of Colombia, Arzobispado, Correo 7 N 10-20, Bogotá, DE.

DOMINICAN REPUBLIC
Military Vicariate of the Dominican Republic, Arzobispado, Apdo 186, Santo Domingo.

EL SALVADOR
Military Vicariate of El Salvador, Obispado, Apdo Postal 43, San Miguel.

FRANCE
Aumônerie Militarie, Aumônier Général, FPF, 47 Rue de Clichy, F-75009 Paris, T: 874-7742.
Military Vicariate of France, 20 Rue Notre-Dame-des-Champs, F-75006 Paris, T: 222-4130.

GERMANY
Catholic Military Vicariate of Germany, Zwölfling 16, Postfach 1428, D-4300 Essen.
Evangelisches Kirchenamt (EKD) für die Bundeswehr, Kölner Str 107a, D-53 Bonn-Bad Godesberg.
Seventh-day Adventist Servicemen's Center (Germany), Johann Klotz Strasse 13, 6000 Frankfurt/Main 71, T: (69) 67-38-87.

GUADELOUPE
Military Chaplain (Catholic), Camp Dugomemier, Baie-Mahault, T: 590-26-22-50.

INDIA
Red Shield Guest House (Salvation Army), 2 Shaddar St., Calcutta 700 016, T: 28-41-824.

INDONESIA
Catholic Military Vicariate of Indonesia, Jalan Pandanaran 13, Semarang, Java.

ITALY
Accademia Allievi Cappellani Militari (Castrense Collegio), Vicario Generale Militare, Rettore, Salita del Grillo 37, I-00184 Roma, T: 675100.
Military Vicariate of Italy, Salita del Grillo 37, I-000184 Roma, T: (06)6795100.

JAPAN
Overseas Christian Servicemen's Centers, 34-2 Wakamatsu Cho, Yokoshuka Shi, Kanagawa Ken 238, T: 0468-27-0020.
Seventh-day Adventist Servicemen's Center (Okinawa), 1035 Adaniya, Kitanakagusuku-son, Okinawa 901-23, T: (988) 935-2004.

KENYA
Catholic Military Vicariate of Kenya, PO Box 14231, Nairobi.
Officers' Christian Fellowship (OCU), PO Box 40668, Nairobi, T: 27411.

MADAGASCAR
Aumônerie Protestante de l'Armée Nationale, College Soamiandry, Ampasampito, Tananarive.

NETHERLANDS
Catholic Military Vicariate of the Netherlands, Aartbisdom, Maliedaan 40, Utrecht.

OMAN
Mission to Military Garrisons, Royal Air Force, Mazirah.

PARAGUAY
Military Vicariate of Paraguay, Av Mariscal López y Pai Pérez 410, Asunción, T: 23329.

PERU
Military Vicariate of Peru, Tacna 482, Lima, T: 249395.

PHILIPPINES
Military Vicariate of the Philippines, 1000 General Solano St, San Miguel, Manila.
Overseas Christian Servicemen's Centers, Subic Service Center, Olongapo City, Zambales.

PORTUGAL
Military Vicariate of Portugal, Rua da Cova da Moura 1, Lisboa 3.

SOUTH AFRICA
Catholic Military Vicariate of South Africa, Archbishop's House, Main St, Pretoria.
Chaplain's Commission for Pentecostal Churches, PO Box 16, Voortrekkerhoogte 0143, T: 012-314-3911.

SOUTH KOREA
Seventh-day Adventist Servicemen's Center, c/o Korean Union Conference, Chug Ryang PO Box 110, Seoul 130-650; 66 Hoegi-dong, Dongdaemunku, Seoul 130-650, T: 82 (2) 964-6124.
World Military Missions Crusade, Armed Forces Service Center, 35 Hwa-Chung Dong, Chinhae.

SPAIN
Military Vicariate of Spain, Calle Nuncio 13, Madrid 5, T: 2653654.

SWITZERLAND
Armeeseelsorge, Feldpredigerchef, Herrengasse 22, CH-3000 Bern.

TAIWAN
Overseas Christian Servicemen's Centres, P.O. Box 332, Taichung, T: 91603.
World Military Missions Crusade, 91 Chien Yeh Village, Tsoying.

UGANDA
Catholic Military Vicariate of Uganda, Bishop's House, PO Box 200, Gulu.

UNITED STATES OF AMERICA (USA)
Chaplaincy Endorsement Commission, Christian Churches & Churches of Christ, Box 637, Johnson City, TN 37601.
Chaplains Commission, Natl Assoc of Evangelicals, 33625 Wapiti Circle, Buena Vista, CO 81211, T: 719-395-8585.
Chaplains' Aid Association, Inc., 962 Wayne Ave., Silver Spring, MD 20910.
Christian Military Fellowship, P.O. Box 1207, Englewood, CO 80150, T: 303-761-1959, O: Web: www.cmf.com.
Evangelical Lutheran Ch in America, 224 E. Capitol St., Washington, DC 20003-1006, T: 202-783-7503.
General Commission on Chaplains and Armed Forces Personnel, 122 Maryland Av, NE, Washington, DC 20002, T: (202)617-8310.
Island Memorial Chapel, Kwajalein, Marshall Islands, Protestant Chaplain, Box 1711, APO San Francisco, CA 96555.
Ministry to the Armed Forces, 815 2nd Ave., New York, NY 10017.
Missions to Military, O: Web: www.exis.net/mtm.
National Conference on Ministry to the Armed Forces, 4141 N. Henderson Rd., Ste. 13, Arlington, VA 22203, T: 703-276-7905, F: 703-276-7906.
Officers' Christian Fellowship of the USA, P.O. Box 1177, Englewood, CO 80150-1177, T: 303-761-1984.
Overseas Christian Servicemen's Centers, P.O. Box 1268, Englewood, CO 80150, T: 303-762-1400.
Travis International Hospitality (TIHI), PO Box 1223, Travis Air Force Base, CA 94535, T: (707)422-8600.
UCC Military Chaplains Association, 1528 E Elgin Way, Bolling Air Force Base, Washington, D.C. 20336.
World Military Missions Crusade, 846 Fifth Av, PO Box 2001, San Diego, CA 91212, T: (714)234-1300.

55
Music

Choirs, musical groups, singers and musical artists, evangelistic musical groups, singing groups, Christian musical groups of any genre of popular music; music publishers, producers, recording studios, record labels, promoters, agents; libraries of religious music, church or religious music training; orchestras, opera, festivals, evangelistic productions; music and theology, music and missions, ethnomusicology; campanology, bell-ringing, organs, music and worship. See also LITURGY AND WORSHIP.

AUSTRALIA
Celebrate the Feasts Inc., P.O. Box 1135, Wangara 6065.

BRITAIN (UK OF GB & NI)
Archbishop of Canterbury's Certificate in Church Music, IGCM, 16 The Cloisters, Windsor Castle, Berks.
Cathedral Organists' Association, Addington Palace, Croydon CR9 5AD, T: (01)654-7676.
Central Council of Church Bell-Ringers, 19 Ravensgate Rd, Charlton Kings, Cheltenham, Glos GL53 8NR, T: (0242)32454.
Choir Schools Association, Cathedral Choir School, Ripon, Yorks, T: (0765)2134.
Church Music Association (CMA), 171 Victoria St, London SW1E 5LR; 24 Ashley Place, London SW1, T: (01)828-5775.
Festivals of Male Voice Praise, 82 Lismurn Park, Ahoghill, Ballymena, Co Antrim BT42 1JW, T: (08) 0266 871643.
Friends of Cathedral Music, The Wardenry, Farley, Salisbury; 7 Tufton St., London SW1.
Global March for Jesus, Wellington House, New Zeland Ave., Walton on Thames, Surrey, KT12 1PY, T: 1932-232345, F: 1932-232398, O: E-mail: 100572.323@compuserve.c, Web: www.gmfj.com.
Gregorian Association, 67 Grange Crescent, Grange Hill, Chigwell, Essex, T: (01)500-3457.
Humming Birds, SAMS, 157 Waterloo Rd, London SE1, T: (01)928-3188.
Irish Church Music Association, Irish Institute of Pastoral Liturgy, T: (353) 0503 42942.
Lay-Clerks E-mail List, O: Web: www.ncl.ac.uk/~n211552/lay-clerks.html.
Livingston Organs & Church Furnishings Ltd., Greycaines House, Greycaines Rd, North Watford, Herts, T: 27378.
Methodist Church Music Society, 1 Central Bldgs, Westminster, London SW1, T: (01)930-7608.
Musical Gospel Outreach, 10 Seaforth Av, New Malden, Surrey KT3 6JP, T: (01)942-8847.
Other Hand Music, 21 Tandragee Road, Portadown, Craigavon, Co Armagh BT62 3BQ, T: (08) 0762 337668.
Pueri Cantores, Cathedral House, Ingrave Road, Brentwood, Essex, CM 15 8AT, T: 01277-232046, F: 01277-234103.
Royal School of Church Music, Cathedral House, 60 York Place, Edinburgh EH1 3JD, T: 0131 556 1798.
Scottish Association of Change-Ringers, 39a Titchfield Road, Troon KA10 6AN, T: 01292 312398.

CANADA
Christian Musician Management, 275 Ormond Dr., Unit #65, Oshawa, ON L1K 1S1, T: 905-725-0655, F: 905-725-5071.
Morning Star Recording Studios, T: 416-261-8131, F: 416-261-0906.
Music Group, Inc., 190 Hwy. 7 W., #5, Brampton, ON L7A 1A2, T: 905-455-0797.
Viscount Ministries, Inc., 92 Hillcrest Dr., Newmarket, ON L3Y 4V8, T: 905-830-0857.

COSTA RICA
Escuela de la Música Cristiana, Avenida 10,

Calles 8 y 10, Frente a la Bomba La Castellana, T: 223-4619, O: Also tel: 232-1814.
Instituto de Capacitacion Musical, Costado sur de La Plaza de Deportes, Barrio Las Américas, Moravia, San José, T: 235-6240, F: 240-4615.

CYPRUS
Music Center, 1127 Corniche el Nil, PO Box 1422, Cairo, T: 747063.

ECUADOR
Asociacion de Musicos Evangelicos del Guayas (AMEG), 17 y Capitan Najera, Guayaquil.

FRANCE
Association des Choeurs d'Eglise Protestantes d'Alsace-Lorraine, 4 Cem de la Holzmatt, Strasbourg 3, T: 300088.

GERMANY
Verband Evangelischer Kirchenmusikere Deutschlands, Domplatz 5, D-672 Speyer.
Zentralstelle für Evangelische Kirchenmusik, Jebensstr 1, D-1 Berlin 12.

HOLY SEE
Pontificio Instituto di Musica Sacra, Piazza San Agostino 20A, I-00186 Roma, T: 6540422.

HUNGARY
School of Music Ministries International, 1012 Budapest, Déli Pu. Kerengő Quickinfo 60, T: 36-1-185-8086, F: 36-1-133-7327.
Viakukt Recording Studio, 2051 Biatorbágy, Nagy utca 10, T: 36-23-310-890, F: 36-23-310-885.

INDIA
Baptist Music Committee, Bazar Veng, Lunglei, Mizoram 796701.
Christian Melodies Singing Group, Jeeva Transport Corporation, Erode, Tamil Nadu 638102.
Christian Melody Singers: Khasi - Jaintia, Melody Home, Lum Balang, Malki, Shillong, Meghalaya 793001.
Gospel Tuners International, Valanjavattom P. O., Kerala 689104.
Indian Gospel Singers, Shpoorti Niketan, Mangalam, Karwar Road, Hubli, Karnataka 580028.
Jerusalem Singers, WZ/A-113 Ram Dutt Enclve, Uttam Nagar, New Delhi 110059.
Kingsley Music Team, Ganthan Illam, No. 4/11, Annasalai, Tiruvannamalai, Tamil Nadu 606601.
Living Gospel Band, Mission Compound, Mokokchung Town P. O, Nagaland 798601.
Marthandam Music Association, Panbivilai, Main Street, Marthanadam, Tamil Nadu 629165.
Priya Orchestra, 21, Vaniyambadi Road, Upper Room Prayer House, Bargur, Tamil Nadu 635104.
Rajan Musicals, Annanda Nagar, Chenimalai Road, Perundurai, Tamil Nadu 638052.
Sruti (School of Liturgical Music), Orthodox Seminary, Post Box 98, Kottayam, Kerala 686001.
Swarani School of Music, H. No:11-26-137, Opp. Arka Hospital, Kothawada (Street), Warangal, Andhra Pradesh 506012.
Tarapada College of Music, 33, Gariahata Road (South), Calcutta, West Bengal 700031.

INDONESIA
Yayasan Musik Gerejawi (YAMUGER), d/a STT Jakarta, Jl. Proklamasi 27, Jakarta 10320, T:)021) 3155750.

ITALY
Consociatio Internationalis Musicae Sacrae (CIMS), Piazza San Agostino 20A, I-00139 Roma, T: 6540422.
Pontifical Institute of Sacred Music, Via di Torre Rossa, 21, 00165 Rome.

JAPAN
Japan Church Music Publishing Society, 2-193 Ogikubo, Suginami-ku, Tokyo 167.

KENYA
Kenya Church Music Society (KCMS), PO Box 41482, Nairobi.

MEXICO
Comisión Episcopal de Litúrgia, Música y Arte de México, Apdo M-2181, México, T: 5355589.
Conjunto Bethel, Pesos No 32, Zona 9, México, DF, T: 346303.

NEW ZEALAND
Contemporary Hymns (NZ), P.O. Box 2437, Christchurch.

NORWAY
Norwegian Society of Organists, Bleikerfaret 63, Asker.

PHILIPPINES
Asian Institute for Liturgy and Music (AILM), P.O. Box 3167, 1099 Manila; 275 E. Rodriguez Sr. Blvd., Quezon City, Metro Manila 1099, T: 63-707591 to 94, F: 63-707591, O: Cable: SATSEM, Manila.

PORTUGAL
Centro Fonográfico Evangélico, Urb. Queimada, Lote 48 - 2 F, Madalena - 4600 Amarante, T: 055-42 56 75.
Missão Evangélica Pedras Vivas, Rua das Teixugueiras, 28, 3860 Pardilhó; Apartado 5-3860 Pardilho, T: 034-85 51 46.

SINGAPORE
Hallelujah Ortorio Society, No 111 North Bridge Road, #08-09 Pennisular Plaza, Singapore 179098, T: 339-2822, F: 789-2481.
Life Strings Musical Outreach, Toa Payoh Central PO box 69, Singapore 913103, T: 552-3918, F: 552-3918.
Singapore Church Music Association, c/o 586 Balestier Road #02-01, Singapore 329898, T: 255-0913.

SOUTH AFRICA
Affordable Christian Music, PO Box 1458, Ladysmith 3370, T: 0361-2-8177.
Charis Music, PO Box 90, Florida 1710, 130 Goldman St, 1710 Florida, Roodepoort, T: 011-674-2079, F: 011-472-1660.
Cooper, Gill & Tomkins (Pty) Ltd (pipe organs), PO Box 3329, Cape Town 8000, 2 Prieska St, Sybrand Park, Cape Town, T: 021-697-1799.
Eietydse Musiekbediening/Contemporary Christian Music Ministry, PO Box 977, Rant & Dal 1751, 36 Swallow St, Rant & Dal, Krugersdorp, T: 011-953-2481.
Frontline Music, PO Box 67290, 2021 Bryanston, T: 011-704-1068, F: 011-462-1962.
Gloria Singers, c/o Box 40, Irene 1675, Jan Smuts Ave, Irene, T: 012-667-1072.
Grace Music (Pty) Ltd., PO Box 997, Florida 1710, 130 Goldman St, Florida, Roodepoort, T: 011-674-2030, F: 011-472-1660.
Maranatha Record co, PO Box 32823, Glenstantia 0010, T: 012-346-2138, F: 012-346-2519.
Password International, PO Box 387, Pinegowrie 2123, T: 011-463-6097, F: 011-463-6099.
Royal School of Church Music, 15 10th St, Parkhurst, 2193 Johannesburg, T: 011-682-1867.
Sarepta Music, PO Box 833, Kloof 3640, 20 Village Rd, Kloof, T: 031-764-5503, F: 031-764-4975.

SPAIN
Sela-Música, 03700 Patricio Ferrándiz, 40B, Denia, Alicante, T: 642-03-09.

UNITED STATES OF AMERICA (USA)
Acappella Company, P. O. Box 15, Paris, TN 38242, T: 901-644-1771, F: 901-644-7171, O: Web: www.acappella@acapella.org.
Allen Organ Co., P.O. Box 36, Macungie, PA 18062-0036, T: 610-966-2202, F: 610-965-3098.
American Choral Directors Association, 2834 W. Kingsley Road, Garland, TX 75041.
American Guild of Organists, P.O. Box 26811, Richmond, VA 23261.
Amersom Music Ministries, 11846 Balboa Blvd., #337, Granada Hills, CA 91344, T: 818-368-0749, F: 818-360-0445, O: E-mail: troubadr@aol.
Andover Organ Co., Inc., P.O. Box 36, Methuen, MA 01844-0036, T: 508-686-9600, F: 508-685-8208.
Ascencion Recordings, Inc., P.O. Box 1406, 1908 Rivershore Rd., Elizabeth City, NC 27906, T: 919-331-5898, F: 919-331-5898, O: E-mail: ascencion.recordings@internetmci.com.
Assoc of Lutheran Church Musicians, P.O. Box 16575, Worcester, MA 01601, T: 508-799-7924.
Ben Radtke Ministries, P.O. Box 1132, La Mesa, CA 91944, T: (619) 462-2730.
Benson Music Group, Inc., 365 Great Circle Rd., Nashville, TN 37228, T: 615-742-6800, F: 615-742-6911.
Brentwood Music, One Maryland Farms, Brentwood, TN 37027, T: 800-333-9000, F: 615-373-0386.
Brosamer's Bells, 207 Irwin St., Brooklyn, MI 49230, T: 517-592-9030.
C-Music Online, O: Web: www.cm-online.net/cmusic.
Carman Ministries, Inc., O: Web: www.carman.org/car1h.html.
Celebrant Singers, P.O. Box 1416, Visalia, CA 93279, T: 209-740-4000, 800-321-2500, F: 209-740-4040, O: E-mail: Celebrants@celebrants.com, Web: www.celebrants.com.
Chime Master Systems, 2669 Sawbury Blvd., Columbus, OH 43235, T: 800-344-7464.
Choral Club Services, 1418 Robinson Rd SE, Grand Rapids, MI 49506, T: 800-444-4012.
Choral Conductors Guild, 519 N. Halifax, Daytona Beach, FL 32018.
Choristers Guild, 2834 W Kingsley Rd, Garland, TX 75041, T: 214-271-1521.
Christian Artists' Songship, c/o Christian Artists Corp., P.O. Box 1984, Thousand Oaks, CA 91358, T: 800-827-0099.
Christian Booking Directory, P.O. Box 730, Ojai, CA 93023, T: 805-646-4382.
Christian Music X-Change, O: Web: www.users.aol.com/cmx1/cmx1.htm.
Church Music in the Smokies, 234 N. Craft Highway, Chickasaw, AL 36611, T: 800-456-4966.
Church Music Publishers Association, P.O. Box 158992, Nashville, TN 37215.
Church Music Service, 3201 E Court St, Iowa City, IA 52240, T: 319-337-7041.
Church Organ Systems, 422 Wards Corner Rd., Loveland, OH 45140, T: 513-576-4660, F: 513-576-4546.
Contemporary Christian Music, 25231 Paseo De Alicia, Ste. 201, Laguna Hills, CA 92653.
Creation Festival, P.O. Box 86, Medford, NJ 08055, T: 800-327-6921.
Creative Music, 127411 Research, Suite 403, Austin, TX 78759, T: 800-531-2525.
Curb Records, 47 Music Sq. E., Nashville, TN 37203, T: 615-321-5080, F: 615-327-1964, O: Web: www.curb.com.
Cyber Hymnal, O: Web: www.accessone.com/~rwadams/h.
Davidsons Music, 6727 W Metcalf, Shawnee Mission, KS 66204, T: 800-782-7664.
Daywond Music Group, 128 Shivel Dr., Hendersonville, TN 37075, T: 800-635-9581, F: 615-264-1499, O: E-mail: daywind@viponline.
Diamante Music Group, 1000 Quail St., # 110, Newport Beach, CA 92660, T: 800-766-4364, F: 714-442-7531, O: E-mail: diamantemg@aol.com.
Discovery Music, PO Box 3566, Grand Rapids, MI 49501, T: 800-283-8333.
Doxology Music, P.O. Box M, Aiken, SC 29802, T: 803-649-1733, F: 803-642-9901.
Eddie Crook Co., O: Web: www.eddiecrookco.com, E-mail: ecrookco@usit.net.
Elders Choir of Southern California (Korean), 4761 Round Top Dr., Los Angeles, CA 90065, T: 213-254-8964.
Eternal Song Agency, 6326 E. Livingston Ave., #I-53, Reynoldsburg, OH 43068, T: 614-868-9162.
Firstcom Music, 13747 Montfort Dr., #220, Dallas, TX 75240, T: 800-858-8880, F: 214-404-9656, O: E-mail: info@firstcom.com.
Forefront Records, O: Web: www.forefrontrecords.com.
Fred Bock Music Company, P. O. Box 570567, Tarzana, CA 91357, T: 818-996-6181, F: 818-996-2043.
Genevox Music Group, 127 Ninth Ave. N., Nashville, TN 37234, T: 800-436-3869, F: 615-251-5933, O: E-mail: customerservice@bssb.com, Web: www.bssb.com.
Gospel Music Association, 1205 Division St., Nashville, TN 37203, T: 615-242-0303, F: 615-254-9755, O: E-mail: gmatoday@aol.com.
Gospel Music E-mail List, O: Web: copper.ucs.indiana.edu/~stephenl.
Gregorian Chant, O: Web: www.music.princeton.edu:80/chant_html.
Halal Ministries, M611 Birch, Marshfield, WI 54449.
Higher Standard Praise Systems, 2890 U.S. Hwy. 98 W., Santa Rosa Beach, FL 32459, T: 850-267-1111, F: 850-267-1103, O: E-mail: hismessinger@juno.com.
Hinshaw Music, Inc, P.O. Box 470, Chapel Hill, NC 27514, T: 919-933-1691.
Homeland Recording & Publishing Co, 1011 16th Ave S, Nashville, TN 37212.
Hosanna '90, 8225 Worthington, Galena Road, Westerville, OH 43081, T: 614-431-8221.
Hymn Society of America, Texas Christian University, Fort Worth, TX 76129.
Integrity Music, 1000 Cody Rd., Mobile, AL 36695, T: 334-633-9000, F: 334-633-0882.
Jesus Northwest, People's Church, P.O. Box 7718, Salem, OR 97303, T: 503-393-1616.
Johannus of America, Inc, 2602 SE Bella Vista Loop, Vancouver, WA 98684, T: 503-640-4950.
Joyful Heart Music/Li'l Folks Music/Rejoice Music, 16 Crockett, Irvine, CA 92620, T: 714-559-0894, F: 714-857-1798, O: E-mail: Hanneke@aol.com.
Kempke's Music Service, Inc, 2005 Tree Fork Lane, Suite 105, Longwood, FL 32750, T: 305-831-0333.
Keynote Music Productions, O: Web: www.keynotemusic.com.
Kingdom '90 Youth Conference, Regal Ventures, P.O. Box 1010, Kings Mountain, NC 28086, T: 704-739-3838.
Korean Church Music Association of SO. CA., 717 W. 9th St., San Bernardino, CA 92410, T: 909-885-7782.
L.A. Pilgrim Men's Chorus (Korean), 17441 Hiawatha St., Granada Hills, CA 91344, T: 818-360-3430.
Landmark Communications Group, P.O. Box 1444, Hendersonville, TN 37077, T: 615-452-3234, F: 615-868-0417.
Leach Piano Course, P.O. Box 742, Valley Forge, PA 19481, T: 215-983-9144.
Ludwig Music, 557 E 140th St, Cleveland, OH 44110, T: 216-851-1151.
Lyon & Healy (Harps), 168 N Ogden Ave, Chicago, IL 60607, T: 312-786-1881.
Malmark, Inc. Bellcraftsmen, P.O. Box 1200, Plumsteadville, PA 18949, T: 215-766-7200.
Maranatha! Music, P.O. Box 31050, Laguna Hills, CA 92654, T: 714-248-4000, F: 714-248-4001.
McShane Bell Foundry Co., Inc., 400 C Arundel Corp. Rd., Glen Burnie, MD 21060, T: 410-636-4390, F: 410-636-7533.
Music Country Audio, 230 E, Cumberland Bend, Nashville, TN 37228, T: 615-248-6224.
Music Educators National Association, 1902 Association Dr., Reston, VA 22091.
Music Mansion, the Midi Store, 433 Union Ave., Providence, RI 02909, T: 800-880-6434, F: 401-946-1234, O: E-mail: midi@edgenet.net, Web: www.musicmansion.com.
Music Ministry of Campus Crusade, 22912 Mill Creek Rd, Suite A, Laguna Hills, CA 92653, T: 714-587-8900.
Music Texas, c/o Kempke's Music, 2005 Tree Fork Lane, Suite 105, Longwood, FL 32750, T: 407-831-0333.
Myrrh Records, 3319 West End Ave., Ste. 200, Nashville, TN 37203, T: 615-385-9673, F: 615-385-9696, O: Web: www.myrrh.com.
Nash Productions, 700 Paloma Ave., Oakland, CA 94610.
National Association of Pastoral Musicians, 225 Sheridan St., N.W., Washington, D.C. 20011.
National Quartet Convention, National Quartet Convention, 54 Music Square West, Nashville, TN 37203, T: 615-320-7000.
New Hope Publications, O: Web: www.members.aol.com/newhopepub/index.html.
New Jerusalem Music, P.O. Box 225, Clarksboro, NJ 08020, T: 609-423-8844.
Organ Clearing House, P.O. Box 104, Harrisville, NH 03450-0104, T: 603-827-3055, F: 603-827-3750.
Promusic, 941-A Clint Moore Rd., Boca Raton, FL 33487, T: 800-322-7879, F: 561-995-8434, O: E-mail: promuse@aol.com.
Quasimodo Bells by JPH Systems, Inc., 14 S. Chestnut St., Palmyra, PA 17078, T: 800-521-9838, F: 717-838-7017.
Reunion Records, 2908 Poston Ave., Nashville, TN 37203, T: 615-320-9200, F: 615-320-1734.
Rhythm City, 287 E. Paces Ferry Rd., NE, Atlanta, GA 30305, T: 404-237-9552.
Rodgers Instrument Corp, 1300 NE 25th Ave., Hillsboro, OR 97124, T: 503-648-4181.
Schulmerich Carillons, Inc, Dept. A06, Carillon Hill, Sellersville, PA 18960, T: 215-257-2771, F: 215-257-1910.
Seek First His Kingdom/Music Pub, P.O. Box 811143, Dallas, TX 75381, T: 214-517-1674.
Shattinger Music Co, 1810 South Broadway, St. Louis, MO 63104, T: 314-621-2408.
Shining Star Publications, P.O. Box 299, Carthage, IL 62321, T: 800-435-7234.
Singing Machine Co., Inc., 6350 E Rogers Circle, Boca Raton, FL 33487, T: 800-451-3692.
Solid Rock Christian Music Dist, 682 Milwaukee Ave, Prospect Heights, IL 60070, T: 800-798-SING.
Sparrow Corp., 9255 Deering Ave, Chatsworth, CA 91311, T: 818-709-6900.
Star Song Communications, 2325 Crestmoor, Nashville, TN 37215, T: 615-269-0196, F: 615-385-6920.
Tabernacle Publishing Co, 380 S Main Place, Carol Stream, IL 60188, T: 708-665-3200.
Tempo Music-Computer Div, 3773 W 95th St, Leawood, KS 66206, T: 913-381-5088.
United Methodist Publishing House, P.O. Box 801, Nashville, TN 37202, T: 615-749-6181, F: 615-749-6512.
University Music Service, 731 Cherry Dr, Hershey, PA 17033, T: 717-533-8900.
Vineyard Music Group, P.O. Box 68025, Anaheim, CA 92817, T: 714-777-7733, F: 714-777-8119.
Westminster Choir College, Hamilton at Walnut, Princeton, NJ 08540.
Wicks Pipe Organ Co, 1100 Fifth St, Highland, IL 62249, T: 618-654-2191.
William D Miller Pipe Organ Co, 210 Main, Cleveland, MO 64734, T: 816-658-3519.
Word Entertainment, Inc., 3319 West End Ave., Nashville, TN 37203.
Word Music, 5221 N O'Conner Blvd, Suite 1000, Irving, TX 75039, T: 214-556-1900.
Word Records, O: Web: www.wordrecords.com.
Worship Seminars International, Box 922020, Sylmar, CA 93290.
Worship to the Nations (Pioneers), P.O. Box 8188, Rolling Meadows, IL 60008-8188, T: (708) 776-1851, 800-735-PRAY, F: (708) 776-9364, O: E-mail: 76543,1405.

56 Non-Christian religions

A selection of major headquarters, organizations, world federations, missionary organizations, and study centers operated by or for non-Christian religions; major non-Christian research centers, universities, periodicals, institutes, and institutions.

ALGERIA
Institut al-Hayat (La Vie), Guerara (Oasis).

ARGENTINA
Arab Islamic Society, San Nigel 1650, La Heras, Mendoza.
Centro de Estudios Islamicos, Rojas 6, Piso 2, Of 1, Buenos Aires.
Centro Islamico, San Juan 3053, Buenos Aires.
Confederación Espíritista Argentina (CEA), Buenos Aires.
Seminario Rabinico Latinoamericano, 11 de Setiembre 1669, Buenos Aires.
World Jewish Congress, Casilla 20, Suc. 53, Buenos Aires, T: 54-1-962-5028.
World Union of Jewish Students, Luca 2280, Buenos Aires 23.

AUSTRALIA
'I Am' Religious Sanctuary of Sydney, 55 Manson Rd, Strathfield, T: 769109.
Australian Federation of Islamic Societies, 90 Cramer St., Preston, Victoria 3072; 11 Thomas St., Thomastown, Victoria, 3074, T: 472424.
Baha'i National Spiritual Assembly, 2 Lang Rd, Paddington, T: 313696.
Buddhist Peace Fellowship, Box 368, Lismore, NSW 2480.
L. A. Falk Library and F. L. Cohen Memorial Library, 69 Cook Rd, Centennial Park, Syndey, NSW.

AUSTRIA
Institut für Judaistik, Universität Wien, Landesgerichtsstr 18, A-1010 Wien.
Verband der Österreichischen Israelitischen Kultusgemeinden, Bauernfeldgasse 4, Wien 19.
Verein Österreichisches Jüdisches Museum Eisenstadt, Universität Wien, Landesgerichtsstr 18, A-1010 Wien.

BANGLADESH
Bangladesh Bouddha Kristi Prachar Sangha, Dhamarajika Buddhist Monastary, Atish Dipankar Sarak, Kamalapu, Dhaka 1214.
Bangladesh Brahmo Samaj, 19 Larmini St., P.O. Wari, Dhaka 1203.
Bangladesh Buddhist Missionary Society, GPO Box 1168, Chittagong 4000.

BELGIUM
Centre Islamique, Imam, Av Damien 17, B-1150 Brussel.
Centre National des Hautes Etudes Juives, Av Jeanne 14, B-1050 Brussel, T: (02)6488158.
Service Social Juif, Av Ducpétiaux 68, St Gilels, Brussel 6.

BERMUDA
Baha'i World Faith, Court St., Hamilton, T: 21141.

BOSNIA & HERCEGOVINA
Muslim Religious Union, Reis-ul-Ulema, Sarajevo.
Supreme Council of Islam, Mufti, Sarajevo.

BOTSWANA
Bahai Faith National Centre, P.O. Box 466, Gaborone, T: 352 532.

Botswana Buddhist Society, P.O. Box 272, Gaborone.

Botswana Hindu Society, P.O. Box 1843, Gaborone, T: 352 933.

Botswana Muslim Association, P.O. Box 40310, Gaborone.

Sikh Council of Botswana, PO Box 43001, Gaborone, T: 356 785.

BRAZIL

Centro Budista Theravada, Rua Princesa Leopoldina 8, Rio de Janeiro, GB.

Centro Hinduista Samadhi, Rua Visconde de Pirajá, Rio de Janeiro, GB.

Tenda de Umbanda, Caboclo Inco, Av Pacaembó, São Paulo SP.

BRITAIN (UK OF GB & NI)

Baha'i Centre, 27 Rutland Gate, London SW7.

Belfast Hebrew Synagogue, 49 Somerton Rd, Belfast 15.

Bhagawan Soaham World Peace Meditation Centre, Soaham Yogashram, 90 Alma Rd, London SW18, T: (01)870-3602.

British-Israel World Federation, 6 Buckingham Gate, London SW1.

Buddhist Peace Fellowship, 16 Upper Park Road, London NW3, T: 44-1-586-7641.

Buddhist Society, 58 Eccleston Square, London SW1V 1PH, T: (01)828-1313.

Conference of European Rabbis, 735 High Rd., London, N12 0US, T: 44-181-343-8989.

European Council of Hindu Organizations (ECHO), Radha Kishan Temple, 10 Soho St., London W1 5DA.

Federation of Islamic Organizations in Europe, P.O. Box 5, Markfield, Leicester, LE67 9RY, T: 44-1530-245919, F: 44-1530-245-913.

Institute of Ismaili Studies, 14-15 Great James St, London WC1, T: (01)405-5328/9.

International Society for Krishna Consciousness, 7 Bury Place, London WC1A 2LA.

Islamic Council of Europe, 38 Mapesbury Rd, London NW2 4JD.

Islamic Cultural Centre, Regent's Lodge, 146 Park Rd, London NW8.

Islamic Foundation, 223 London Rd, Leicester LE2 1ZE.

Jewish Chronicle Publications, 25 Furnival St, London EC4, T: (01)405-9252.

Jewish Historical Society of England, 33 Seymour Place, London W1, T: PAD 4404.

Muslim World League, 46 Goodge St., London W1P.

Pagan Federation International, c/o The Wiccan, BM Box 7097, London WC1N 3XX, T: 44-1691-671-066.

Reform Synagogues of Great Britain, 33 Seymour Place, London W1, T: (01)723-8118.

Standing Conferences of Organization in the Welfare of the Falashas of Ethiopia, Woburn House, Upper Woburn Place, London WC1, T: (01)387-5849.

Theosophical Society in England, 50 Gloucester Place, London W1, T: WEL 9261.

Theosophical Society in Europe, 2 Tekels Park, Camberley, Surrey.

Union of Muslim Organizations of UK and Eire, 30 Baker St, London W1M 2DS.

World Jewish Congress, British Section, 55 New Cavendish St, London W1.

World Sephardi Federation, EC1N 8JY, T: (01)242-4556.

World Union for Progressive Judaism, 34 Upper Berkeley St, London W1, T: (01)262-0999.

World Union of Jewish Students, 247 Gray's Inn Rd, London WC1, T: (01)837-3070.

World Zionist Organization, 4 Regent St, London SW1, T: (01)930-5152.

BURKINA FASO

Communauté Musulmane, Ouagadougou.

CAMEROON

Association Culturelle Islamique, BP 594, Yaoundé.

CANADA

Buddhist Center, 5250 Saint-Urbain, Montéal 14, Québec.

Canadian Bahá'í Community, 7200 Leslie St., Thornhill, Ontario L3T 6L8, T: 416-889-8168, F: 416-889-8184.

Canadian Jewish Congress, 1590 McGregor Av, Montréal 109, Québec.

Council of Muslim Communities of Canada, 1250 Ramsey View Ct. Ste. 504, Sudbury, ON P3E 2E7, T: 705-522-2948.

Islamic Foundation of Toronto, 182 Rhodes Av, Toronto, Ontario, T: (416)465-2525.

National Spiritual Assembly of Baha'is in Canada, 7290 Leslie St, Willowdale, Ontario.

Native Spiritual Voices, 1818 Lorne Ave., Sasakatoon, SK S7H 0Y0, T: 306-664-3753.

Sound of India, 3702 Mountain, Montréal 7, Québec.

World Union of Progressive Judaism, 1950 Bathurst St at Ava Rd, Toronto 10, Ontario.

CHILE

Comunidad Israelita, Calle Canada Strongest 1846, Santiago, T: 28052.

Departamento de Cultura Judaica, Instituto Pedagogico, Universidad de Chile, Av Bernardo O'Higgins 1058, Casilla 10-D, Santiago.

CHINA

Buddhist Centre: China Association, Temple of Vast Succour No. 25, Xi Si Fu Nei Dajie (West of Beihai Park), China Guoji Shudian, Beijing P. O. Box 2820.

China Islamic Association, Nan Heng West St. No. 03 (South of Nantang Church), Guoji Shudian, P.O. Box 399, Beijing.

CZECH REPUBLIC

Council of Jewish Religious Communities in Bohemia and Moravia, Maislova 18, Staré Mesto, Praha 1.

Jewish State Museum, Jachmova 3, Praha.

DENMARK

Ahmadiya Mosque, Eriksmunde Alle 2, Hvidovre, Koberhavn.

Islamic Cultural Centre, Norre Sogade 43, DK-1370 Kobenhavn.

EGYPT

Académie des Recherches Islamiques, Administration Générale de l'Azhar, Al Qahirah, T: 909922.

Al Azhar Islamic University, Rector, Administration General, Al-Azhar, Al Qahirah, T: 905914.

Cairo Radio, Box 325, Al Qahirah.

City of Muslim Missions, Al Qahirah.

Council for Islamic Studies, Al Qahirah.

Halabi Press, 5 Khan Jaafar, Al Hussein, Al Qahirah, T: 905871.

Higher Council of Islamic Affairs, 11 Rue Hassan Sabri, Zemalek, Al Qahirah, T: 802665.

House of the Qu'ran, Midan el Azhar, Al Qahirah.

FIJI

Ahmadiyya Islamic Centre, 82 Kings Rd, Samabula.

Baha'i World Faith, 68 Pender St, Suva.

Hindu Temple (Shree Sanatan Dharm Ramayan Mandali), Mandir St, Samabula.

Sikh Temple, Samabula.

Suva Muslim League, Jame Mosque, Amy St, Suva.

FRANCE

Alliance Israélite Universelle (AIU), 45 Rue La Bruyère, F-75425 Paris, T: 7447584.

Bureau d'Animation des Centres Communautaires (BACC), 19 rue de Téhéren, F-75008 Paris.

Centre Universitaire d'Etudes Juives (CUEJ), 30 Blvd du Port-Royal, F-75005 Paris.

Consistoire Israélite de France, 17 Rue Saint-Georges, F-75009 Paris.

European Council of Jewish Community Services, 14 Rue Georges Berger, F-75017 Paris, T: 6225351.

Fonds Social Juif Unifié (FSJU), 19 rue de Téhéran, F-75008 Paris.

Fraternité d'Abraham, 20 blvd Poissonière, F-75009 Paris, T: 770-2369.

Grande Famille Amana, 123 Rue Pelleport, Paris 20, T: 636-8456.

Union Musulmane Internationale, Institut Musulman de Paris, Grande Mosquée de Paris, Place du Puits-de-l'Ermite, F-75005 Paris.

World Union of Jewish Students, HQ, 17 Rue Fortuny, F-75017 Paris.

GHANA

African Herbalist Healing Union, P.O. Box 1380, Kumasi.

Akonnedi's Healing Shrine, Nana, P.O. Box 37, Larteh.

Spiritual Assembly of the Baha'is of Ghana, P.O. Box 2582, Accra.

Theosophical Society in Ghana, P.O. Box 720, Accra.

GREECE

Central Board of the Jewish Communities of Greece, 8 Melidoni St, Athénai.

Organization for Muslim Unity in Greece (Itihad Islam), 35 Antigonou St, Komotiny.

HUNGARY

Jewish Theological Seminary of Hungary, Jozsef-Korut 17, Budapest.

INDIA

Aligarh Muslim University, Aligarh, UP, T: 20.

Anjuman Tanzim-ul-Muslamin, Calcutta.

Benaras Hindu University, Varanasi 5, UP, T: 64491.

Bharat Sevak Samaj, 9-A Theatre Communication Bldg, Con Place, New Delhi 1.

Bharatiya Vidya Bhavan, Chowpatty Rd, Bombay 7.

Chief Khalsa Diwan, GT Rd., Amritsar, Punjab.

Dar ul 'ulum Seminary, Deoband, UP.

Darul-Musannifin, Shibly Academy, Azamgarh, UP.

Department of Adi Granth Studies, Punjabi University, Patiala.

Department of Religious Studies, Punjabi University, Patiala.

Guru Nank Foundation, 15-16 Institutional Area, near J.N.U. & Quitab Hotel, New Delhi 110 067.

HH Shankaracharya Ashrams, Dwarka/Badrinath/Mysore/Puri/Bhanpur. There are in India 5 Shankaracharyas.

Indian Institute of Islamic Studies, Panchkuin Rd, New Delhi 110001; Kalka Tughlaq Rd., Tughlaqabad, New Delhi.

Indo-Muslim Cultural Institute, Hyderabad.

Institute of Islamic Studies, Muslim University of Aligarh, Aligarh.

Islam and Modern Age Society, Jamia Nagar, New Delhi 110025.

Islamic Cultural Centre, 317/321, Prospect Chambers Dr., Dadabhoy Naoroji Road, Fort, Bombay 400 001, T: 2042493, F: 2872945, O: Also tel: 2874502, fax: 2044821.

Islamic Research Association, 8 Shephard Rd, Bombay 8.

Islamic Research Circle, Islamic Library, Shamshad Bldg, Aligarh.

Kerala Philosophical Congress, 66 Varanasi Cantt, UP, Kerala.

Lumen Institute, Davis Rd., Cochin 682016, Kerala, T: 32056.

Maha Bodhi Society, 14, Kalidasa Road, Bangalore 560 009.

Mahabodhi Society of India, Kalimpong; 4A Bankim Chatterjee St, Calcutta 12.

Masih Vidya Bhavan, 87 Municipal Office Rd., Indore 452003.

Muslim Community of India, Chitli Qabar, Jama Masjid, Delhi 6.

Nadwa Arabic College, Lucknow (Nadwat-ul-Ulama).

Osmania Oriental Publication Bureau, Osmania University, Hyderabad, AP.

Quran Foundation, 128 Dr Ambadkar Rd, Meerut, UP.

Ramakrishna Institute of Culture, Gol Park, Calcutta 29.

Ramakrishna Mission Lokasiksha Parishad, 24 Parganas, DT Soutyh P.O., Narendrapur 743 508.

Sadharan Brahmo Samaj, 211 Bidhan Sarani, Calcutta 700 006.

Shanti-Bhavan, 1/32B Prince Golam Mohamed Rd, Calcutta 26, T: 467300.

Shriomani Gurdwara Prabandhak Committee (SGPC), Golden Temple, Amritsar, Punjab.

Signasu Kendra, Kamala Nehru Rd, Allahabad 1, UP.

Sufi Hamsaya, Bara Bazar Rd, Shillong 1.

Theosophical Society, Adyar, Madras 20, T: 73915, 71904.

United Lodge of Theosophists, Theosophy Hall, 40 New Marine Lines, Bombay 20, T: 299024.

Urdu University (Jami's Millia), Delhi.

INDONESIA

International Islamic Organization, Jakarta.

Perisada Hindu Dharma, Jakarta.

IRAN

Faculty of Islamic Theology, Tehran University, Tehran.

Radio Naft-E Melli Shoru Mishavad, National Iranian Oil Company, Abadan.

Zoroastrian Anjuman, Bimeh Iran, Saadi Av, Tehran.

IRAQ

Institute of Higher Learning in Iraq, Shari'ah College, Baghdad.

Shari'ah College, Baghdad.

Shi'ah Theological Academy, Najaf.

ISRAEL

Agudas Israel World Organization, POB 326, Jerusalem.

Department of Arabic Language & Literature, and History of the Islamic Peoples, University of Haifa, Hefa.

Universal House of Justice, Supreme Administrative Body, Baha'i World Centre, Hefa.

World Jewish Congress, P.O. Box 4293, Jerusalem 91042, T: 972-635-261/4, O: Web: www.virtual.co/orgs/wjc.

World Union of Jewish Students, NUIS, POB 1184, Jerusalem.

ITALY

Assemblea Spirituale Nazionale, La Fede Baha'i, vai Astoppani 10, Roma.

Centro di Documentazione Ebraica Contemporanea, Via Guastalla 19, Milano.

Centro Islamico Culturale d'Italia, Via Sebastiano Conca 6, Roma; Via Salaria 290, I-00199 Roma.

Unione delle Communità Israelitiche Italiane, Lungotevere Sanzio 9, Roma.

Unione Islamica in Occidente, Via Poggio Moiano 55, I-00199 Roma.

JAPAN

Church of Perfect Liberty, Patriarch, PO Box 1, Tondabayashi-shi, Osaka 584.

Committee of Shinto Shrines, Ashihara Shrine, 28 Yusaka, Askasak-machi, Tottori-ken 628-25.

Federation of Sectarian Shinto, 7-18-5 Roppongi, Minato-ku, Tokyo.

Institute of Theology and Applied Education, Church of Perfect Liberty, 1-14-1 Ebisu, Shibuya-ku, Tokyo 150.

Itto-en, 8 Yanagiyama-cho, Shinomiya, Yamashina-ku, Kyoto 607.

Japan (Shin Nippon Religious Organizations in Japan), 2-1 Nishi Kanda, Chiyoda-ku, Tokyo; 2-7 Moto Yoyogimachi, Shibuya-ku, Tokyo, T: (291)4231.

Japan Buddhist Council for World Federation, c/o Engakuji Temple, Yamanouchi, Kamakura-shi, Kanagawa-ken 247.

Japan Buddhist Federation (Zen-Nihon Bukkyo-kai), c/o Tsukiji Honganji Temple, Chuo-ku, Tokyo, T: 5422969.

Japan Free Religious Association, 26 Shiba Nishikubo Hiro-machi, Minato-ku, Tokyo 105.

Japan Muslim Association, 1-24-4 Yoyogi Shibuya-ku, Tokyo.

Shinto University (Kokugakuin Daigaku), 10-28 Higashi 4-chome, Shibuya-ku, Tokyo.

Shrine Work Department, Association of Shinto Shrines, Yutenji Apartment House, 4-31-11 Kamimeguro, Meguro-ku, Tokyo 153.

World Peace Prayer Society, 3-20-17 Yawata, Ichikawa-shi, Chiba-ken 272.

JORDAN

Al-Albait Foundation, The Royal Academy for Islamic Civilization Research, P.O. Box 950361, Amman, T: 962-6-815-471.

Grand Mufti of Jordan, Amman.

KENYA

Arya Samaj (Vedic Churches of East Africa), Vedic House, Mama Ngina St, P.O. Box 40243, Nairobi, T: 21573.

HH The Aga Khan Ismailia Supreme Council for Africa, Jamatkhana Bldg, Moi Av, PO Box 40555, Nairobi, T: 25114.

Hindu Council of Kenya (HCK), PO Box 49012, Nairobi, T: 27054.

Khoja Shia Ithnasheri Jamaats of Africa, Supreme Council of the Federation, Nehru Rd, PO Box 81085, Mombasa, T: 5856.

Medicine Men's Society, Plot 909/123, PO Box 334, Machakos.

Sanatan Dharma Sabha, Chairman, PO Box 40032, Nairobi.

Shree Sthanakvasi Jain Mandal, Chairman, Keekorok Rd, PO Box 46469, Nairobi, T: 25831.

Siri Guru Sinhg Sabba, Uyoma Rd, PO Box 40496, Nairobi, T: 25340.

Wakf Commissioners for Kenya, White Fathers Rd, PO Box 80272, Mombasa.

LEBANON

Grand Mufti of the Lebanon, Bayrut.

World Muslim Congress, Bureaux Régionaus Moyen Orient, PB 883, Bayrut.

LESOTHO

Basotho Medicine Men and Herbalist Association (Unification of Basotho Medicine Men), P.O. Box 320, Maseru.

Lesotho Muslim Congregation, Mosque, Butha Buthe.

LIBERIA

Ahmadiyya Muslim Mission, 116 Carey St, Monrovia.

Muslim Community of Liberia, Vai Town, Bushrod Island.

LIBYA

Association de la Vocation Islamique, Tarabulus.

MALAWI

Nuru Muslim Association, Islamic Education HQ, P.O. Box 5742, Limbe.

Shree Hindu Seva Mandal, P.O. Box 676, Blantyre.

Wochiritsa African Traditional Medicine, Proprietor, Blantyre.

MALAYSIA

Malayan Muslim Welfare Association, Kuala Lumpur.

Penang Chinese Muslim Association, Penang.

MOROCCO

Université al Qarawiyin, Rabat.

Université Ben Youssef, Cité Universitaire, Marrakech.

MYANMAR

All Burma Council of Young Monks Association, Rangoon.

International Institute of Advanced Buddhistic Studies, Rangoon.

Pāli Buddhist University, Rangoon.

NETHERLANDS

Dutch Muslim Association, BP 9070 Utrecht.

Islam Foundation Holland, Nierkerkstraat 87 II, Amsterdam.

Islamic Centre Foundation, Ottersstraat 82, Utrecht.

Islamic Society, Oostduinlaan 79, 's-Gravenhage.

Netherlands Islamic Society, Actsveld 30, Vinkeveen.

Portuguese Israelite Community of Amsterdam (Es Hain), Rapenburger St 197, Amsterdam.

NETHERLANDS ANTILLES

Association of Curaçao Muslims, Curaçao.

NIGERIA

Grand Qadi, Sharia Court of Appeal, Kaduna, Northern Nigeria.

Muslim International Relief Organization (MIRO), 60a Campbell St, Lagos.

United Muslim Council of Nigeria, Lagos.

PAKISTAN

Ahimia Institute of Islamic Studies, Islamic Centre, B Block, North Nazimabad, Karachi.

Ahmadiyya Muslim Mission, Headquarters, Rabwah, Lyallpur District, T: 573.

Al-Ahibba (Friends of the Muslim World), 92 Gulberg, Lahore.

Begum Aisha Bawany Wakf, P.O. Box 4178, Karachi 2.

Central Institute of Islamic Research, P.O. Box 1035, Islamabad.

Holy Quran Society of Karachi, Karachi.

Iqbal Academy, Karachi.

Islamic Publications, Sha Alam Market, Lahore.

Muslim World, P.O. Box 5030, Karachi 2.

Muslimnews International, 3 Bonus Rd, PO Box 3955, Karachi 4.

Shah Wali Ullah Academy, Hyderabad, Sind.

Society for the Protection of Islam, Islamiya High School, Islamiya College, Lahore.

Umma Publication House, Bahadurabad Commercial Area, Karachi 5.

United Islamic Organization, 140 E Bloack 7, Gulshan Iqbal, Karachi, T: 91-497-3818.

World Federation of Islamic Missions, Islamic Centre, B Block, North Nazimabad, Karachi 5.

World Muslim Congress, 171-B Block 3, Pechs, PO Box 5030, Karachi 29, T: 412822, 414047.

PHILIPPINES

Agama Islamic Society, Majliso Shoora Pacasum St, Marawi City.

Muslim Association of the Philippines, Headquarters, BP 4221, Manila.

Sulu Muslim Association, Sarentes St, Jolo, Sulu.

PORTUGAL

Comunidade Islâmica de Lisboa, Rua Luis de Camões 100, 3 Esq, Lisboa 3, T: 635203.

RWANDA

Association Islamique du Rwanda, BP 594, Kigali.

Ismaili Community, BP 31, Kigali.

SAUDI ARABIA

Grand Mufti of Saudi Arabia, Riyadh.

Hajj Research Centre, King Abdulaziz University,

POB 1540, Jeddah.
Islamic University of Medina, Vice Chancellor, Medina.
Muslim World League, P.O. Box 537, Makkah al Mukarramah, O: Web: www.arab.net/mwl.
Organization of the Islamic Conference, Kilo 6 Mecca Rd., P.O.B. 178, Jeddah 21411, T: 2-680-0800, F: 2-687-3568, O: Web: www.oic.ir.
World Muslim Secretariat, Islamic Secretariat, Sec Gen, Kilo 6, Mecca Rd, PO Box 178, Jeddah, T: 23880, 25848, 24848.

SENEGAL
Shaikhul Islam, P.O. Box 1, Madina, Kaolack.
Union Culturelle Musulmane, Dakar.

SIERRA LEONE
Supreme Islamic Council, 62 Kissy Rd, Freetown.

SINGAPORE
Islamic World, Semenanjog Press Ltd, Singapore.
Jamiat al-dawah, c/o Room AD, 14th Floor, Asia Insurance Bldg, Finlayson Green, Singapore.
Muslim Religious Council, Singapore.
Ramakrishna Mission, 9 Norris Rd, Singapore 8.
Sikh Missionary Society (Malaya), 35 Medeiros Bldg, 18 Cecil St, Singapore.
Singapore Buddhist Federation, Yan Kit Rd, Singapore.
Singapore Buddhist Sangha Organization, Pho Kark See, Bright Hill Drive, Thomson Rd, Singapore 20.
Singapore Regional Centre of World Fellowship of Buddhists, 387 Guillemard Rd, Singapore.
World Red Swastika Society, Singapore Branch Association HQ, Hill St, Singapore.

SLOVAKIA
Union of Jewish Religious Communities in Slovakia, Smeralova 29, Bratislava.

SOMALIA
Islamic Assembly, P.O. Box 179, Mogadisho.

SOUTH AFRICA
Al Jihaad Propagation Department, 72 Aspeling St, Cape Town.
Islamic Bureau, PO Box 17, Athlone, Cape.
Islamic Propagation Centre, 47-48 Madressa Arcade, PO Box 2349, Durban, Natal.
South African Jewish Board of Deputies, POB 1180, Johannesburg.
World Union of Jewish Students, Sixth Av, Lower Houghton, Johannesburg, Transvaal.

SOUTH KOREA
Headquarters of Won Buddhism, 344-2 Shin Yong-Dong, Iri City 570-754.
Korea Muslim Federation, IPO Box 2865, Soul.
Won Buddhism Gangnam Branch, 609 Yangjaedong, Seocho-gu, Seoul 137-130, T: 82-2-574-6282.

SPAIN
Asociación Musulmana en España, Calle Aguilar de Campoo 25/5D, Madrid.
Centro Islamico, Apdo de Correos 2024, Granada.
Congress of Arab and Islamic Studies, Ciudad Universitaria, Madrid 3.
Instituto de Estudios Sephardies, Duque de Medinaceli 4, Madrid.
Instituto Egipcio de Estudios Islamicos, Mendez Casariego 10, Madrid.
Islamic Institute, Arriza 3, 5 dch, Madrid.
Islamic Spanish Institute, Hous Bacquer 4, Madrid 6.
Misión Ahmadia del Islam en España, Calle Cuidad Real 12 1 izda, Madrid.

SPANISH NORTH AFRICA
Asociación Musulmana de Melilla, Calle García Cabrelles 31, Melilla (Málaga).
Zauia Musulmana de Mohamadia Mahoma (CEUTA), Arroyo Paneque A, Cádiz, Spain.

SRI LANKA
Al-Ilm, 211 Dematagoda Rd, Maradana, Colombo 9.
All Sri Lanka Buddhist Congress, 380 Bullers Rd, Colombo 7, T: 91695.
All Sri Lanka Muslim League, Colombo.
Buddhist Publication Society, PO Box 61, Kandy.
Buddhist Theosophical Society, Colombo.
Buddhist Training Centre for Missionaries, Maharagama; Buddhist Academy of Ceylon, 29 Rosmead Place, Colombo 7.
Islamic Study Circle, Khalafat House, 1 Poonagala Rd, Bandarawela.
Maha Bodhi Society of Sri Lanka, 130 Maligakande Rd, Maradana, Colombo 10.
Muslim Ladies' Arabic College, Colombo.
Ramakrishna Mission, Colombo.
Sri Lanka Assembly of Muslim Youth, 41 Dematagode Rd, Colombo 9.
World Buddhist Sangha Council, Pirivena Teachers Training College, Pirivena Rd, Mount Lavinia.

SUDAN
African Islamic Institute, Wadmedani Rd, Al Khurtum.
College for Arabic and Islamic Studies, PO Box 238, Umm Durman.
Islamic University, Morada, Umm Durman.
Republic of the Sudan, PO Box 572, Umm Durman.

SURINAME
Arya Dewaker, Wanicastraat 210, Paramaribo.
Islamic Movement of Surinam, Keizerstraat 88A, Paramaribo.
Surinam Muslim Association, PO Box 912, Jadenbreestraat 51, Paramaribo.

SWEDEN
Baha'i Center, Matilda Jungstedts Väg 27, S-122 35 Stockholm-Enskede.
Jewish Congregation in Stockholm, Box 7057, S-103 82 Stockholm.
Theosophical Society, (Teosofiska Samfundet), Östermalmsgatan 12, S-114 26 Stockholm.

SWITZERLAND
Ahmadiyya Mission des Islams, Imam Mushtag Bajwa, Mahumud Moschee, Forchstr 323, CH-8008 Zürich, T: (01)325577.
B'nai B'rith International Council, 94 Rue des Eaux-Vives, CH-1207 Genève.
Bahai-Sekretariat, Dufourstr 13, CH-3000 Bern.
Buddhistische Informationsstelle der Schweiz, Postfach 681, CH-8021 Zürich.
Centre Védantique, Swami Nityabodhânanda, Av Peschier 20, CH-1200 Genève, T: (022)461248.
Co-ordinating Board of Jewish Organizations for Consultation with ECOSOC, 94 Rue des Eaux-Vives, CH-1207 Genève.
Divine Light Zentrum, Anton-Graff-Str 65, CH-8400 Winterthur, T: (052)221903.
European Council of Jewish Community Services, 75 Rue de Lyon, CH-1211 Genève 13.
Groupement Bouddhique, Place Pépinet 4, CH-1000 Lausanne, T: (021)227136.
International Association for the Advancement of the Science of Creative Intelligence (IAASCI), Hotel Seeblick, CH-6353 Weggis.
International Council on Jewish Social and Welfare Services, 75 Rue de Lyon, CH-1211 Genève 13, T: 449000.
International Islamic Publications, Genève-Cornavin 253.
Jewish Agency for Israel, 26 Route de Malagnou, CH-1211 Genève 17.
Krishnamurti-Freunde der Schweiz, Herrn Edgar Graff, CH-6986 Novaggio-TI.
Maharishi European Research University (MERU), World Plan Administrative Centre, Seelisberg.
Tibet-Institut, Herrn P Lindegger-Stauffer, CH-8486 Rikon/ZH, T: (052)351729.
World Jewish Congress (WJC), 1 Rue de Varembé, CH-1211 Genève 20, T: 341325.

SYRIA
Abu Nour Islamic Foundation, P.O. Box 4656, Damascus, T: 963-11-776-653, O: Also tel: 963-11-772-032.

TAIWAN
Chinese Muslim Association, 62 Sin Sheng S Rd., Sec 2, Taipei.
Chinese Muslim Youth League, Taipei.
National Taoist Association of the Republic of China, Taipei.

TANZANIA
Ahmadiyya Muslim Association, PO Box 376, Dar es Salaam.
Comorian Mosque, PO Box 181, Dar es Salaam.
National Spiritual Assembly of Baha'is, PO Box 585, Dar es Salaam.
Shia Imami Ismaili Provincial Council, PO Box 460, Dar es Salaam.

THAILAND
Buddhist University, Bangkok.
World Fellowship of Buddhists, 33 Sukhumvit Rd., Bangkok, T: 66-25-111-8890, O: Web: www.buddhanet.net/wfb.htm.

TOGO
Conseil Suprême pour les Affairs Islamiques du Togo, BP 64, Lomé.

TRINIDAD & TOBAGO
Anjuman Sunnatul Jamat Association, 16 Farah St, PO Box 97, San Fernando.
Islamic Missionaries Guild of the Caribbean and South America, 1 Mucurapo Rd, PO Box 800, Port of Spain.

TUNISIA
Grand Mufti, Tunis.
Quranic Zaitunah University, Tunis.

TURKEY
Higher Institute for Islamic Studies, Baglarbasi, Istanbul.
Imam ve Hatip School, Istanbul.
Islamic Institute, Imam ve Haliji School, Istanbul.
Université d'Ankara, Faculté de Théologie (Ankara Universitesi, Ilâhiyat Falkütesi), Yldirim Beyazit Meydani, Ankara, T: 113176.

UGANDA
National Association for the Advancement of Muslims (NAAM), Kampala.
National Muslim Secretariat, Kadhi of Uganda, PO Box 30380, Kampala.

UNITED STATES OF AMERICA (USA)
American Buddhist Association, 1151 West Leland Av, Chicago, IL 60640, T: (312)334-4461.
American Humanist Association, P.O. Box 146, Amherst, NY 14226-0146; 7 Harwood Dr., Amherst, NY 14226-0146.
American Jewish Committee, Interreligious Affairs Department, 165 East 56th St, New York, NY 10022.
American Jewish History Center, Jewish Theological Seminary of America, 3080 Broadway, New York, NY 10027, T: (212R19-8000.
American Muslim Council, 1212 New York Ave., N.W., Suite, 525, Washington, D. C 20005, T: 202-789-2262, F: 202-789-2550.
Anti-Defamation League of B'nai B'rith, 315 Lexington Av, New York, NY 10016.
B'nai B'rith International Council, 1640 Rhode Island Av, NW, Washington, DC 20036, T: EX3-5284.
Baha'i International Community (BIC), 866 United Nations Plaza, New York, NY 10017, T: (212)752-0510.
Baha'is of the United States, 1320 19th St., N.W., Suite 701, Washington, D.C. 20036, T: 202-833-8999, F: 202-833-8988.
Buddhist Center of the USA, P.O. Box 193, Fredericksburg, VA 22401.
Buddhist Churches of America, HQ, 1710 Octaiva St, San Francisco, CA 94109.
Buddhist Peace Fellowship, P.O. Box 4650, Berkeley, CA 94704; National Office, Berkeley, CA 94704.
Church of All Worlds, PO Box 2953, St Louis, MO 63130.
Church of Light, PO Box 1525, Los Angeles, CA 90053.
Church of Satan, 6114 California St, San Francisco, CA 94121.
Church of the Eternal Source, PO Box 7091, Burbank, CA 91505.
College of Jewish Studies, 72 East 11th St, Chicago, IL 60605.
Conference on Jewish Social Studies (CJSS), 1814 Broadway, New York, NY 10023, T: (212)C15-7826.
Consultative Council of Jewish Organizations, Suite 1711, 61 Broadway, New York, NY 10006.
Federation of Reconstructionist Congregations, Church Rd. and Greenwood Ave., Wyncote, PA 19095, T: 215-887-1988, F: 215-887-5348.
Federation of Zoroastrian Association of North America, 626 West 56th St., Hinsdale, IL 60521, T: 514-656-2067.
Fellowship of Religious Humanists, P.O. Box 597396, Chicago, IL 60659-7396.
Hebrew Theological College, 7135 Carpenter Rd, Skokie, IL 60076.
Hebrew Union College, Jewish Institute of Religion, 40 West 68th St, New York, NY 10023.
Hongwanji Buddhist Mission of Hawaii, 1727 Fort St, Honolulu, Hawaii.
International Mahavir Jain Mission Siddhachalam, 65 Mud Pond Road, Blairstown, NJ 07825, T: 908-362-9793, F: 908-362-9649.
International New Thought Alliance, 5003 E. Broadway Road, Mesa, AZ 85206, T: 602-830-2461, F: 602-830-2561, O: Web: webstyle.com/alan/inta.htm.
International Society for Krishna Consciousness (ISKCON), 61 Second Av, New York, NY 10003.
Islamic Centers in USA, East 97th St, New York, NY.
Islamic World Review, Islamic Press Agency, P.O. Box 8139, Ann Arbor, MI 48107.
Jewish Chautauqua Society of the Union of American Hebrew Congregations, 538 Fifth Av, New York, NY 10021.
Jewish Theological Seminary, 3080 Broadway, New York, NY 10027.
Muslim Brotherhood, 5312 West Girard Av, Philadelphia, PA; 2618 , MI.
Muslim Students Association of the USA and Canada, University Station, Minneapolis, MN 55414; 3702 W. 11th Ave., Gary, IN 46404.
National Federation of Buddhist Women's Associations, Buddhist Churches of America, 1710 Octavia St, San Francisco, CA 94109.
National Spiritual Assembly Bahá'í, 536 Sheridan Rd., Wilmette, IL 60091, T: 708-869-9039, F: 708-869-0247.
National Young Buddhist Association (NYBA), Buddhist Churches of America, 1710 Octavia St, San Francisco, CA 94109.
New Religious Movements web-site, O: Web: www.cti.itc.virginia.edu/~jkh8x/soc257/profiles.html.
Nichiren Shoshu of American (NSA), 1351 Ocean Front, Santa Monica, CA 90401.
Overseas Buddhist Association, c/o Fellowship of Reconciliation, Box 271, Nyack, NY 10960.
Rosicrucian Order (AMORC), Rosicrucian Park, San José, CA 95114.
Sikh Council of North America,, 95-30 118th St., Richmond Hill, NY 11419.
Sikh Dharma International, Rte 3 Box 132D, Espenola, NM 87532, T: 310-552-3416, F: 505-557-8414.
Subud North American Inquiry Section, P.O. Box 453, Cooper Station, New York, NY 10003.
Synagogue Council of America, 432 Park Av South, New York, NY 10016.
Theosophical Society in America, Box 270, Wheaton, IL 60187.
Union of Orthodox Jewish Congregations in America, 333 Seventh Ave., New York, NY 10001, T: 212-563-4000, F: 212-564-9058.
United Lodge of Theosophists, 245 West 33rd St, Los Angeles, CA 90007.
United Synagogue of Conservative Judaism, 155 Fifth Ave., New York, NY 10010, T: 212-533-7800, F: 212-353-9439.
Universal Federation of Pagans, c/o Association of Cymmry Wicca, P.O. Box 674884, Marietta, GA 300667, O: Web: www.tylwythteg.com/ufp.html.
World Conference of Jewish Organizations (COJO), 515 Park Av, New York, NY 10022.
World Union for Progressive Judaism, 838 Fifth Av, New York, NY 10021, T: (212)249-0100.
World Vaisnava Association, 4138 N.W. 23rd Ave., Miami, FL 33142, T: 305-638-2503, F: 305-638-4055, O: Web: www.wva-vvrs.org.

UZBEKISTAN
Mir-i-Arab Medresseh, Bokhara.

VENEZUELA
Culto Aborigen de Maria Lionza, Apdo 10980, Caracas 101.

VIET NAM
Cao Daist Missionary Church (Dai Dao Tam Ky Pho Do Doctrine of the Third Revelation of God), Sa Saintété Pham-Cong-Tac, Gaio-Tong (Pope), Saint-Siège de Tayninh.
Cham and Vietnam Muslim Association, 23 TK 10 Ben Choung Doung, Saigon.
Unified Buddhist Association of Viet-Nam, Hanoi.
Unified Buddhist Church (UBC), HQ, Vietnam Quoc Tu (National Pagoda of Vietnam), 243 Su Van Hanh, Ho Chi Minh City/Saigon 10.

YUGOSLAVIA
League of Jewish Communities of Yugoslavia, 7 Jula 71 a/III, Beograd.

57
Periodicals

Definitions: Christian or church periodicals, journals, magazines, newspapers, bulletins, house organs, newsletters, and other regular publications; of popular, news, scholarly, professional, devotional, instructive, or academic content; daily, semi-weekly, weekly, biweekly, monthly, quarterly – and certain annuals and irregular serials.

58
Politics & society

A selection of Christian political parties (e.g. Christian Democrats), activist groups, human rights organizations, religious rights groups, political action committees, political research centers, foreign or domestic policy think tanks, religio-political educational bodies; progressive or traditional groups, left-wing or right-wing groups, liberal or conservative groups; church or denominational committees, agencies, or commissions for political causes, representation, advocacy, activism or education; religio-political training, publications, or coordination; pressure groups or lobbies working on governments or the United Nations; single-issue groups or movements; public affairs offices and agencies; radical, non-violent, or liberation groups and movements.

ARGENTINA
Ciudad Católica, Córdova 679, 5 piso, of 504, Buenos Aires.
Macabeos Siglo XX, José Hernández 2535, Buenos Aires.
Movimiento de Sacerdotes para el Tercer Mundo (MSTM), P Genesio 630, Santa Fe.
Movimiento Ecumenico por los Derechos Humanos (MEDH), Av. José María Moreno 873, Planta Baja, 1424-Buenos Aires, T: 541-424-0769, F: 541-922-5101.
Sociedad Argentina de Defensa de la Tradición, Familia y Propiedad (TPF), Avda Figueroa Alcorta 3260, Suc 25, Buenos Aires.

AUSTRALIA
Catholic Lay Association of Melbourne, Alfred St, Kew, Victoria.
Catholic Worker, c/o Dept of Mathematics, University of Melbourne, Parkville, Victoria.
Latin Mass Society, Box 2773, GPO, Sydney, NSW.
Non-Violent Power, c/o Catholic Presbytery, Harbord, Sydney, NSW.
Pax/Catholics for Peace, Dept. of Philosophy, University of Melbourne, Parkville, Victoria.

AUSTRIA
Arbeitskreis Kritisches Christentum (AKC), Kärtnerstr 25, A-1010 Wien, T: (02222)521681.

BELGIUM
Alternative Ecclésiastique Eliker-Ik/Kerkelijk Alternatief Eliker-Ik, Hoogstraat 9, B-9000 Gent.
Assemblée pour un Concile des Wallons et des Bruxellois (ACWB), Rue Agimont 5, B-4000 Liège, T: (041)230486.
Chrétien pour le Socialisme, Rue Agimont 5, B-4000 Liège; Consciencestraat 46, B-2000 Antwerpen, T: (041)230486.
European Christian Democratic Union, Rue de Deux Eglises 41, B-1040 Brussel.
Groupe d'Action, Co-responsabitité Diocèses de Gand, Chaussée de Gand 85, B-9411 Erondegem.
Inspraak, Voornitgangstraat 245, B-1000 Brussels.
Les Fraternités Jean XXIII, Les Rameaux, B-1340 Ottignies, T: (010)416225.
Pax Christi, Rue de la Poste 111, B-1030 Brussel, T: 190589.
Présence et Témoignage, Rue des Frères Taymans 202, B-1360 tubize.
Quaker Council for European Affairs, Quaker House, 50 Square Ambiorix, B-1040, Brussels, T: 02-230-49-35, F: 02-230-6370.
Rassemblement des Silencieux de l'Eglise, Clos des Peuplieurs 58, B-1200 Brussel.
Thomas More Genootschap, O. I. Vrouwdrey 8, B-9040 Oostakker.

BOLIVIA
Legión Boliviana Social Nacionalista, Cochabamba.

BRAZIL
Hora Presente, Rua Sete de Abril 125, 3 andar, conj 307, São Paulo, SP.
Permanência, Rua da Laranjeiras 540, CP 88, Rio de Janeiro, GB.
Sociedade Brasileira de Defesa da Tradição, Familia e Propiedade (TFP), Rua Alagoas 344, São Paulo, SP.

BRITAIN (UK OF GB & NI)
Catholic Institute for International Relations (CIIR), 22 Coleman Fields, London N1 7AF, T: (01)

354-0883.

Catholic Union of Great Britain, 63 Jeddo Rd, London W12 9EE, T: 0181-749 1321.

Christian Solidarity Intl., 49b Leigh Hall Road, Leigh on Sea, Essex SS9 1RL, T: 44-702-74066, F: 44-702-480103.

Co-operation North, 7 Botanic Avenue, Belfast BT7 1JJ, T: (08) 0232 321462.

Evangelical Contribution on Northern Ireland (ECONI), City of Belfast YMCA, 12 Wellington Place, Belfast BT1 6GE, T: (08) 0232 327231, F: (08) 0232 235826.

Lord's Day Obervance Society, 29 Howard Street, Belfast BT1 6ND, T: (08) 0232 238224.

Protestant & Catholic Encounter, 103 University Street, Belfast BT7 1HP, T: (08) 232 232864.

CANADA

Aboriginal Rights Coalition, 151 Laurier Ave., E., Ottawa, ON K1N 6N8, T: 613-235-9956, F: 613-235-1302.

Alberta Coalition Against Pornography, #312, 223 - 12 Ave., S.W., Calgary, AB T2R 0G9, T: 403-264-6778, F: 403-269-2012.

Canadians for Decency, P.O. Box 637, Station B, Willowdale, ON M2K 2P9, T: 416-438-2374, F: 416-438-2723.

Christian Embassy (Campus Crusade for Christ), 1420 Youville Dr., Unit 5A, Gloucester, ON K1C 7B3, T: 613-830-9187, F: 613-830-1751.

Christian Heritage Party of Canada, 156 Walts St., Welland, ON L3C LG5, T: 905-788-2238, F: 905-788-2943.

Church Council on Justice and Corrections, 507 Bank St., Ottawa, ON V2P 1Z5, T: 613-563-1688.

Citizens for Public Justice, 229 College St., Suite 311, Toronto, ON M5T 1R4, T: 416-979-2443.

Family Action Council, 63 King St., E., Oshawa, ON L1H 1B4, T: 905-434-7977, F: 905-434-2933.

Family Coalition Party of Ontario, 4736A Yonge St., Toronto, ON M2N 5M6, T: 416-224-1168, F: 416-733-8816.

ICCHRLA Inter-Church Committee on Human Rights in Latin America, 129 St. Clair Ave., W., Toronto, ON M4V 1N5, T: 416-921-0801, F: 416-921-3843.

International Free Press Agency in Canada, P.O. Box 359, Mansonville, QC J0E 1X0.

Jesuit Centre for Social Faith and Justice, 947 Queen St., E., Toronto, ON M4M 1J9, T: 416-469-1123, F: 416-469-3579.

Ontario Consultants on Religious Tolerance, O: Web: web.canlink.com/ocrt.

Prayer Canada, P.O. Box 237, Surrey, BC V3T 4W8, T: 604-589-1110, F: 604-589-4383.

Project Plough Shares, c/o Conrad Grebel College, Waterloo, ON N2L 3G6, T: 519-888-6541, F: 519-885-0014.

Torch, Jericho House, R.R. #8, Mono Mills, Orangeville, ON L9W 3T5, T: 519-941-1747.

Traditional Value Advocates, 627 - 104 Ave., S.W., Calgary, AB T2W 0A4, T: 403-252-3343.

CHILE

Christian Democratic Organization of America, Av Bernardo O'Higgins 1460, Casilla 1448, Santiago.

Sociedad Chilena para la Defensa de la Tradición y Propiedad (Fiducia), Casilla 85-12 Correo 12, Santiago.

CHINA

Documentation for Action Groups in Asia (DAGA), CCA Centre, 96, 2nd District, Pak Tin Village, Mei-Tin Rd, Shatin, New Territories, Hong Kong, T: 852-2691-6391, F: 852-2697-1912, O: E-mail daga@asiaonline.net.

COLOMBIA

Grupo Tradicionalista de Jóvenes Cristianos de Colombia, Apdo Aéreo 51918, Medellín.

Juventud de Colombia Pro-Civilización Cristiana, Apdo Aéreo 52885, Bogotá.

COSTA RICA

Exodo, Calle 9, Av 14 bis, Apdo Postal 3771, San José.

Juventud Obrera Cristiana, Apdo Postal 5271, San José.

Juventud Universitaria Cristiana, Centro Universitario Cultural, San Pedro de Montes de Oca.

Movimiento Estudiantil Cristiano, Apdo Postal 5271, San José.

Movimiento Iglesia Joven, Apdo Postal 5271, San José.

Movimiento Juvenil Cristiano, Departamento de Vida Estudiantil, Universidad Nacional, Heredia.

ECUADOR

Entrenamiento Ministerial, Villalengua No. 278 y 10 de Agosto, Casilla 691, Quito, T: 241-550.

FINLAND

World Evangelical Fellowship Religious Liberty Commission (RLC), Katarinantori 1, FIN-67100 Kokkola, T: 6-831-4805, F: 6-831-6495, O: E-mail: Candelin@pp.kolumbus.fi.

FRANCE

Cercle Jean XIII, 51 Route de St-Joseph, F-44 Nantes, T: (40)748848.

Chrétiens pour le Socialisme, Comité International, Centre Oecuménique de Liaisons Internationales (COELI), 68 rue de Babylone, F-75007 Paris; Also for the Spanish diaspora, 6 Rue St-Severin, F-75007 Paris, T: 5552554.

Cité Nouvelle Midi, 26 Blvd des Dames, F-13001 Marseille.

Cité Nouvelle/Chrétiens Marxistes, 46 Rue Vaugirard, F-75006, Paris, T: 0333149.

Collectif 'Pour une Société Nouvelle'/Collectif St-VBenoît, 14 rue St Benoît, F-75006 Paris.

Concertation, 25 Quai de Bondy, F-69005 Lyon.

Echanges, Centre International d'Echanges Religieux, Culturels et Sociaux (CIDERCS), 72 Rue de Sèvres, F-75007 Paris, T: (01)566-9166.

L'Homme Nouveau, Place Saint Sulpice 1, F-75006 Paris.

La Lettre, 68 Rue de Babylone, F-75007 Paris, T: (01)551-5713.

Ligue de la Contre-Réforme Catholique, Maison St-Joseph, F-10 Parres-les-Vaudes.

Notre Combat (Chrétiens pour le Socialisme), 49 Rue du Faubourg-Poissonnière, F-75009 Paris, T: 8249764.

Pax Christi, 5 Rue de l'Abbaye, F-75006 Paris.

Rassemblement des Silencieux de l'Eglise (Pro Fide et Ecclesia), 43 Rue de Turbigo, F-75003 Paris, T: (01)887-0935.

Témoignage Chrétien (TC), 49 Rue du Faubourg-Poissonnière, F-75009 Paris, T: (01)824-9764. -

Vie Nouvelle, 73 Rue Ste-Anne, F-75002 Paris, T: (01)742-7367.

World Conference of Christians for Palestine, Secretariat Général, 49 Rue du Faubourg Poissonnière, F-75009 Paris, T: (01)824-9764.

GERMANY

Christen für des Sozialismus, Wiesbadenstr 98, Konigstein TS, T: (06174)3234.

Pax Christi, Windmühlstr 2, D-6 Frankfurt/Main, T: 252398.

GRENADA

Bretton Woods Reform Organisation (BWRO), Cnr. Green St., Bain Alley, St. George's, T: 809-440-0834, F: 809-440-6651.

GUATEMALA

Confederación de Sacerdotes y Seglares Diocesanos en Guatemala (COSDEGUA), 15 Calle 34-24, Zona 5, Ciudad de Guatemala.

HUNGARY

International Christian Embassy, 1022 Budapest, Filler u. 67, T: 36-1-212-4803.

Opus Pacis, Dezsö u 3, Budapest I.

Rutherford Institute of Central and Eastern Europe, Vinceller u. 42, Budapest 1113, T: 36-1-166-9948.

INDIA

All India United Christian Movement for Equal Rights, St. Alfonsus Campus, Rashtrapathi Rd., Nalgonda, Andhra Pradesh 508001.

Blue Army of Our Lady of Fatima, Indian National Secretariat, 92 Acharya Jagadish Bose Rd, Calcutta 70014.

Moral Ministry of India, Vazhimuttathu House, Pallippad P. O., Haripad, Kerala 690512.

IRELAND

Christian Concern for Freedom of Conscience, 28 South Lotts Road, Dublin 4, T: (353) 01 688781.

Clencree Centre for Reconciliation, Glencree, Co Wicklow, T: (353) 01 896802.

Co-operation North, 37 Upper Fitzwilliam Street, Dublin 2, T: (353) 01 610588.

Pax Christi, 11 Sandymount Castle Drive, Dublin 4.

ISRAEL

International Christian Embassy Jerusalem (ICEJ), P.O. Box 1192, Brenner Street 10, Jerusalem 91010, T: 02-669823, F: 972-2-669970, O: Telex: 25378 ICEJIL.

Liberation Theology Center, P.O. Box 1248, Jerusalem.

Messianic Action Committee, P.O. Box 75 Rishon LeTsion 75100, T: 972 3 966 1898, O: E-mail: 100320.1324@compuserve.com.

ITALY

Christian Democratic Union of Central Europe (CDUCE), Piazza del Gesu 46, Roma, T: 684541.

Christian Democratic World Union, Palazzo Doria, Via del Plebiscito 107, I-00186 Roma, T: 688583.

Comitato Civico Nazionale, Via della Conciliazione 1, I-00198 Roma, T: 6569551.

Movimento Nazionale 7 Novembre, Via Allessandro Severo 105/A, I-00145 Roma, T: (06)5139694.

Pax Christi, Piazza Adriana 21, Roma.

JAPAN

Centre for Christian Response to Asian Issues NCC Japan, 2-3-18-25 Nichi-Waseda, Shinjuku-ku, Tokyo 169, T: 81-3-3202-0494, F: 81-3-3204-9495.

LEBANON

Conférence Mondiale des Chrétiens pour la Palestine, Secrétariat pour les Pays Arabes, Rue Mak'houl (Abdel-Aziz), Immeuble Tanios Rebeiz, BP 1375, Bayrut, T: 341902/3.

Eglise pour Notre Temps (Maronite), BP 1145 Bayrut.

LUXEMBOURG

Pax Christi, 5 Rue Bourbon, Luxembourg.

MALTA

Ghaqda Christus Rex, c/o Archbishop's Seminary, Florina.

MEXICO

Cristianos para el Socialismo, Apdo Postal 27-533, México, DF, T: 5743982.

NETHERLANDS

Action Committee for Pope and Church, Haydnlaan 21, Enschede, T: (05420)20108.

Association for the Preservation of Roman Catholic Life in the Netherlands, Röntgenstraat 11, Tilburg, T: (013)422831.

Catholic Life Association, Postbus 214, Heerlen.

Christians for Socialism, Woudschoten, Zeist, T: (03439)226.

Confrontation, Ververstraat 10, Heerlen, T: (045)714703.

Michael Legioen, Le van Swindenstraat 31, Amsterdam, T: (020)356094.

Open Kerk, Postbus 2, Heemstede.

Pax Christi International, Celebesstraat 60, 's-Gravenhage, T: (070)656823, 65356, 110536.

Rooms Katholiek Partij Nederland (RKPN), Agippinastraat 7, Postbus 100, NL-2119 Voorburg, T: (070)909275.

Septuagint, De Wetstein Pfisterlaan 55, Driebergen, T: (03438)3204.

NEW ZEALAND

Christian Pacifist Society, 29 Halswell Road, Christchurch 3, T: 64-3-895075.

New Zealand Inter-Church Council on Public Affairs, 1 Randwick St, Northland, Wellington 5.

POLAND

Catholic Intellectuals' Club, Secretariat of Co-ordination of Clubs, Rue Kopernika 34, Warszawa.

Christian and Social Association, Marszalkowska 4, 00 590 Warszawa, T: 299251.

Social Publishing Institute 'The Sign', Rue Wislna 12, Kraków.

PORTUGAL

Christians for Socialism, Rua Rodriguez Sampaio 79/3, Lisboa 5, T: 763097.

Embaixada Cristã Internacional Jerusalém, Bairro S. Francisco, Lote 28 r/c Esq., 2685 Camarate, T: 01-947 23 02.

SINGAPORE

International Christian Chamber of Commerce, Singapore, 14 Balmoral Road, Garden Hotel Basement, Singapore 259800, T: 235-6119, F: 733-2909.

SOUTH AFRICA

Africa Christian Action (Salt Shakers), PO Box 36129, Glosderry 7702, T: 012-689-4481, F: 021-685-5884.

Christians for the Truth, P/Bag 250, Kranskop 3550, T: 03344-4-1512, F: 03344-4-1050.

Institute for Multi-Party Democracy, PO Box 2811, Durban 4000.

Institute of World Concerns, PO Box 4739, Halfway House 1685, T: 011-315-2323, F: 011-805-1211.

National Initiative for Reconciliation, PO Box 3053, Pretoria 0001, T: 012-320-2230, F: 012-322-9411.

Pietermaritzburg Agency for Christian Social Awareness (PACSA), PO Box 2238, 3200 Pietermaritzburg, 174 Berg St, Pietermaritzburg, T: 0331-42-0052, F: 0331-42-0303.

Truth and Reconciliation Commission, 106 Adderley St., P.O. Box 3162, Cape Town 8000.

Watchman Ministries, PO Box 3200, Edenvale 1610, T: 011-453-3928.

SPAIN

ICCC (Intern. Christian Chamber Commerce), 28920 Apdo. 169., Alcorcón, Madrid, T: 641-11-82.

Iglesia Mundo, Santa Teresa 6, Madrid 4, T: 4199465.

Iglesia Viva, c/o Desclée de Brower, Henao 6, Bilbao 9.

Pax Christi, Duque de Mandas 43/4 centro, San Sebastian.

Qué pasa?, Lagasca 121, Madrid 6, T: 2613797.

SRI LANKA

Nonviolent Direct Action Group, P.O. Box 2, Chavakachcheri.

SWEDEN

Christian Group, Swedish Parliament, Stockholm.

Pax Christi, Valhallavägen 132, Stockholm.

Thursday Group (Parliament Bible Class), Swedish Parliament, Stockholm.

SWITZERLAND

Armée Bleue de N-D de Fatima, Secrétariat Mondial, 25 Beim Buremichelskopf, CP 9, CH-4024 Basel, T: (061)345919.

Christian Solidarity Intl., Forchstrasse 280, Postfach 52, Zurich 8029.

Chrétiens du Mouvement, Rue Rothschild 52, CP 25, CH-1211 Genève, T: (022)327977.

Commission of the Churches on International Affairs (CCIA), Ecumenical Centre, 150 route de Ferney, CH-1211 Genève 20.

Communione et Liberazione, Chemin de Béthléem 3, CH-1700 Fribourg.

Dialoghi, Via del Tiglio, CH-6605 Locarno.

Union Protestante Libérale, 11 Chemin Monplaisir, Chêne-Bougeries, T: 351411.

TRINIDAD & TOBAGO

In Defence of Human Dignity (Pro-Life), Emmanuel Community, 46 Rosalino St., Woodbrook, Port of Spain, T: 809-628-1586, O: 809-628-8181.

UNITED STATES OF AMERICA (USA)

'One Nation under God' E-Newsletter, O: Web: www.webcom.com/bba/onug.

Accuracy in Media, 4455 Connecticut Ave. NW #330, Washington, DC 20008, T: 202-364-4401, F: 202-364-4098.

Acton Institute for the Study of Religion and Liberty, 161 Ottawa St., N.W., Suite 405 K, Grand Rapids, MI 49503, T: 616-454-3080, F: 616-454-9454, O: Web: www.acton.org.

Alliance Defense Fund, Inc., 7819 E. Greenway Rd. #8, Scottsdale, AZ 85260, T: 602-953-1200, F: 602-953-5630.

American Center for Law & Justice, P.O. Box 64429, Virginia Beach, VA 23467, T: 757-579-2489, F: 757-579-2835.

American Family Association, P.O. Drawer 2440, Tupelo, MS 38803, T: 601-844-5036, F: 1-800-FAMILIE.

American Life League, Inc, P.O. Box 490, Statford, VA 22554, T: 703-659-4171.

Americans United for the Separation of Church and State, 1816 Jefferson Pl, NW, Washington, DC 20036.

Amnesty International USA, 304 West 58th St., New York, NY 10019.

Baptist Joint Committee on Public Affairs, 200 Maryland Ave., N.E., Washington, D.C. 20002, T: 202-544-4226.

Campaign for Refugee Protection, c/o Church World Service, 110 Maryland Ave., NE, Suite 108, Washington, DC 20002.

Catholic Civil Rights League, O: Web: www.io.org/~ccrl.

Catholic League for Religious and Civil Rights, 1011 First Ave., Room 1670, New York, NY 10022.

Center of Concern, 3700 13th St., N.E., Washington, D.C. 20017.

Children's Legal Foundation, P.O. Box 10050, Phoenix, AZ 85064-0050, T: 602-381-1322.

Christian Action Council, 701 W Broad St., #405, Falls Church, VA 22046, T: 703-237-2100.

Christian Legal Society, 4208 Evergreen Lane, Suite 222, Annandale, VA 22003-3264, T: 703-642-1070, F: 703-642-1075.

Christian Research Forum Foundation, O: Web: members.gnn.com/infinet/crisis.htm.

Christian Solidarity International, P.O. Box 16367, Washington, DC 20041-6367, T: 540-636-8907, O: Also: 800-323-CARE, E-mail: csiusa@rma.edu.

Citizens for Community Values (CCV), O: Web: www.ccv.org/.

Concerned Women for America, 370 L'Enfant Promenade, S.W., Ste. 800, Washington, DC 20024, T: 202-488-7000, F: 202-488-0806.

Council on Religion and International Affairs, Press, 170 East 64th St, New York, NY 10021, T: (212)TE8-4120.

Eagle Forum, 78 Bonhomme Ave., St. Louis, MO 63105, T: 314-721-1213, F: 314-721-3373.

Evangelicals for Social Action (ESA), O: Web: www.libertynet.org/~esa/.

Faith and Freedom Forum, P.O. Box 608392, Chicago, IL 60660, T: 312-465-9004, F: 312-761-2920.

Family Research Council, 801 G Street, NW, Washington, DC 20001, T: 202-393-2100, F: 202-393-2134.

Free the Fathers, 1120 Applewood Circle, Signal Mountain, TN 37377.

Friends Committee on Unity with Nature, 179 N Prospect St, Burlington, VT 05401, T: 802-658-0308.

Friends Committee on National Legislation, 245 Second St., NE, Washington, DC 20002, T: 202-547-6000, F: 202-547-6019.

Gospel and Our Culture Network, O: Web: www.gocn.org.

Government Liaison, US Catholic Conference, 3211 Fourth St NE, Washington, DC 20017.

Institute on Religion and Democracy, 1331 H Street, N.W., #900, Washington, DC 20005-4706, T: 202-393-3200, F: 202-638-4948.

Interfaith Center on Corporate Responsibility, 475 Riverside Drive, New York, NY 10115, T: (212) 870-2294.

International Christian Concern, 2020 Pennsylvania Ave., NW, #941, Washington, DC 20006, T: 301-989-1708, O: E-mail: icc@idsonline.com, Web:www.persecution.org.

International Christian Chamber of Commerce, O: Web: www.iccc.net/home.

Jubilee Campaign, 9689-C Main St., Fairfax, VA 22031, T: 703-503-0791, O: E-mail: justlaw@tidalwave.net.

Liberty Counsel, P.O. Box 540774, Orlando, FL 32854, T: 407-875-2100, F: 407-875-0770, O: E-mail: liberty@ic.org.

Lutherans Alert, 409 North Tacoma Ave., Tacoma, WA 98403.

Lutherans for Life, P.O. Box 819, Benton, AR 72018-0819, T: 602-949-5325.

Morality in Media, Inc., 475 Riverside Rd., New York, NY 10115, T: 212-870-3222, F: 212-870-2765, O: E-mail: mimnyc@ix.netcom.com.

National Association for Christian Political Action, Box 185, Sioux Centre, IA 51250, T: (712)722-8641.

National Coalition Against Pornography, 800 Compton Rd., #9224, Cincinnati, OH 45231, T: 513-521-6227.

National Interreligious Service Board for Conscientious Objectors, 1830 Connecticut Ave. NW, Washington, DC 20009-5732, T: 202-483-2220, F: 202-483-1246.

NETWORK: A National Catholic Social Justice Lobby, 801 Pennsylvania Ave SE, Suite 460, Washington, DC 20003, T: 202-547-5556, F: 202-547-5510.

Peoples Christian Coalition, Editor, Box 132, Deerfield, IL 60015.

Prayer for the Persecuted Church, 2025 S. Arlington Heights Rd., Suite 113, Arlington Heights, IL 60005, T: 847-718-0560, F: 847-718-0564, O: E-mail: IDOP@XC.ORG, Web: www.persecuted-church.org.

Priests for Life, O: Web: www.catholic.org.

Prism Magazine, 10 Lancaster Ave, Wynnewood, PA 19096, T: 800-650-6600.

Protestants and Other Americans United for Separation of Church and State, 1633 Massachusetts Ave., NW, Washington, DC 20036.

Religion and Politics Digest, O: Web: home.aol.com/RPDigest.

Religion in American Life, 2 Queenston Place, Rm. 200, Princeton, NJ 08540, T: 609-921-3639.

Religious Coalition for Reproductive Choice, 1025 Vermont Ave. N.W., Suite 1130, Washington DC 20005.

Religious Coalition for Equality for Women, 8765 West Higgins Rd., Chicago, IL 60631.

Resistance Intl., P.O. Box 70265 S.W., Washington, DC 20024, T: 202-488-7453, F: 202-863-2058.

Rutherford Institute, P.O. Box 7482, Charlottesville, VA 22906-7482, T: 804-978-3888, F: 804-978-1789, O: E-mail: rutherford@fni.com.

Sojourners, Box 29272, Washington, DC 20017.

Southern Christian Leadership Conference, PO Box 89128, Atlanta, GA 30312, T: (404) 522-1420.

United Society of Friends Women International,

c/o FUM, 101 Quaker Hille, Richmond, IN 47374, T: 317-896-3380.
Voice of the Martyrs, P.O. Box 443, Bartlesville, OK 74005, T: 918-337-8014, O: E-mail: vomusa@aol.com, Web: www.vom.org.
William Penn House, 515 E. Capital St., Washington, DC 20003, T: 202-543-5560.

59
Prayer

A selection of major societies, ministries, movements, and fellowships devoted primarily to prayer, the prayer life, intercession, meditation, days of prayer, months of prayer, or prayer and evangelization; spiritual warfare, spiritual mapping, strategic prayer, prayer and deliverance or exorcism; church and denominational bodies as well as non- and inter-denominational bodies. Note that there are many thousands of other prayer groups, movements, fellowships and societies throughout the Christian world, of all sizes and many varieties and formats.

AUSTRALIA
Intercessors for Australia, P.O. Box 95, Gordon, N.S.W. 2072.

BELGIUM
European Prayer Link, O: Web: www.ontonet.be/~ont002/epl.html.

BOLIVIA
Liga de Oración en Misión Mundial, ANDEB, Casilla 266, La Paz.

BRAZIL
Dia Mundial Da Oracão-DMO, Rua Pascoal Simone, 471-Coqueiros, Florianopolis-SC, CEP 80080-350.

BRITAIN (UK OF GB & NI)
Guild of Prayer and Spiritual Healing, Addington Park, Near Maidstone, Kent, T: West Mailing 3589.
Intercessors for Britain, 100 Broadwater St West, Worthing, West Sussex.
LIFE (Love Intercedes for Europe), Upper Brimmon House, Brimmon Lane, Newtown SY16 3AE, Powys., T: 44-0686-625682, F: 44-0686-625682.
Prayer for the Persecuted, 163 Hunter's Square, Dagenham, Essex RM10 8, T: 44-081-595-2648.
PrayerWatch, 713 Virginia Heights, Dublin 24, T: (353) 01 517920.
Society for Spreading the Knowledge of True Prayer, 14a Eccleston St, London SW1, T: (01)730-4635.
Southwest England European Prayer and Support Group (SWEEPS), 59 Banneson Road, Nether Stowey, Bridgwater, Somerset, T: 44-0278-733033, F: 44-0278-424329.
World Eastern Europe Prayer Fellowship (WEEP), 44 Headowpark, Ayr., Scotland KA7 2LR, T: 44-0292-287918.
World Movement for United Prayer, Glen Rossal House, Nash Court, Marnhull, Dorset.

CANADA
Canadian Prayer Alert (Campus Crusade for Christ), Box 300, Vancouver, BC V6C 2X3, T: 604-582-3100, F: 604-588-7582.
Centre for Prayer Mobilization, Every Home Intl./Canada, P.O. Box 3636, Guelph, ON N1H 7S2, T: 519-837-2010, F: 519-837-3280, O: 1-800-265-7326.
Intercessors for Canada, P.O. Box 125, Niagara Falls, ON L2E 6S8, T: 905-357-5143.
Mothers Who Care (Campus Crusade for Christ), Box 300, Vancouver, BC V6C 2X3, T: 604-582-3100, F: 604-588-7582.

COLOMBIA
Intercesores Por Las Naciones, A.A. 32408, Santafé de Bogotá, T: 1-411-4114.

GERMANY
European Prayer Link, Postfach 706, 57296 Burbach, T: 49-2736-2223, F: 49-2736-2150.
Evangelische Arbeitsgruppe für die Ökumenische Gebetswoche, Bockemheimer Landstr 109, D-6000 Frankfurt/Main 1.
Katholischer Arbeitskreis für die Veltgebetswoche, D-8351 Niederaltaich b Deggendorf/Ndb, T: (09901)318, 224.

GHANA
Intercessors Prayer Network for Africa, Labourers, Box 0654, Christiansborg, Accra.

HOLY SEE
Apostleship of Prayer, Borgo Santo Spirito 5, I-00193 Roma, T: 650933.
Worldwide Prayer Crusade, Evangelization 2000, Palazzo Belvedere, I-00120 Citta del Vaticano, T: 06-6873288.

INDIA
All India All Night Prayer Fellowship, 642, Annanagar, Madurai, Tamil Nadu 625020.
All India Prayer Fellowship, Bible Bhavan, Nr. Ganesh Guest House, Vallabhvidhyanagar, Anand, Gujarat.
All Night Prayer Warrior, 642, Annanagar, Madurai, Tamil Nadu 625020.
Almighty God Evangelistic Prayer Association, Avaranthalai, Dohnavur (Via), Tamil Nadu 627102.
Apostleship of Prayer, Archbishop's House, 21 N. Parekh Marg, Fort, Bombay, Maharashtra 400039.
Arpana Prayer Fellowship - Operation Mobilisation, P.O. Box 8414, St. Thomas Town P.O., Bangalore, Karnataka 560084.
Christian Young Men Prayer Band, 46/AA Santhi Nagar, Hosur, Tamil Nadu 635109.
Evangelical Prayer Fellowship, 58-5-13, Rangarao Street, Patamata, Vijayawada, Andhra Pradesh 520006.
Faith Prayer Fellowship of India, Kotananduru, Andhra Pradesh 533407.
Good Shepherd Prayer Fellowship, 43 D; Dr. William Nurses Quaters, Zahariah Street, Nagercoil, Tamil Nadu 629001.
Gospel Echoing Missionary Society Prayer House, 13th Cross Street, Chrompet, Madras, Tamil Nadu 600044.
Greater Cochin Prayer Fellowship, C/o. K. M. Chacko, G. 170, Panampally Nagar, Cochin, Kerala 682016.
Halleluiah Prayer Tower, Basel Mission Compound, P.O.Box 415, Hubli, Karnataka 580029.
Hebron Prayer House, Ashok Nagar, Kudiyatham, Tamil Nadu.
Immanuel Village Gospel Prayer Team, No. 9-A Pattamangalem Pulion Street, Mayiladuthurai, Tamil Nadu 609001.
Inter Collegiate Prayer Fellowship, Doctor's Tower, Changanasser, Kerala 686101.
Intercession Working Group, 180 Jal Vayu Vihar, Bangalore 560 080, T: 91-80-546-7238, F: 91-80-547-7782, O: E-mail: juliet.thomas@gems.vsnl.net.in.
International Christians Charitable Blessings Prayer Mission, Blessings Prayer House, P. O. Box 103, Madras, Tamil Nadu 600053.
Jesus Prayer Fellowship of India, Post Box No. 3010, Lodhi Road, New Delhi 110003.
Madras Intercessory Chain of Prayer Fellowship, 28, Thommayapan Street, Royapettah, Madras, Tamil Nadu 600014.
Prayer Partners Fellowship, Grace College, Kesavadasapuram, Pattom, Trivandrum, Kerala 695004.
Prayer-Life Seminars India, 393, 1 Block, II Main, Bangalore, Karnataka 560032.
Revival for Every Nation Prayer Fellowship, 11-A Ayikulam Road, Kumbadonam, Tamil Nadu 612001.
Shalom Prayer Fellowship for Women International, House of Prayer, 18/3 R.T. Prakash Nagar, Secunderabad, Andhra Pradesh 500016.
Upper Room Prayer and Evangelistic Fellowship, P. O. Box 419, Waltair R. S., Vishakapatnam, Andhra Pradesh 530004.

ITALY
Apostleship of Prayer, Borgo Santo Spirito 5, I-00193 Rome.

JAPAN
Kyoto Overseas Missionary Intercessory Prayer Fellowship, c/o CLC, Teramachi Imadegawa Sagaru, Kamigyoku, Kyoto-shi.

KENYA
Kenya Christian Teachers' Prayer Fellowship (KCTPF), PO Box 21352, Nairobi, T: 22312.

LEBANON
Prière Commune, BP 7002, Bayrut.

NEW ZEALAND
Latin American Prayer Fellowship (LAPF), 1719 Great North Rd, Auckland 7.

PHILIPPINES
World-Wide Christian Prayer Fellowship, 544-546 Asuncion, San Nicolas, Manila.

SINGAPORE
House of Intercession, Ang Mo Kie Central PO 0932, Singapore 915615, T: 298-1703, F: 297-4395.
Singapore Christian Prayer House, 69 Tanjong Rhu Road, Singapore 436902, T: 345-3794, 447-2393, F: 344-1630.

SOUTH AFRICA
Herald Ministry, PO Box 72163 Lynnwood Ridge 0040, 294 Edna St, Lynnwood Park 0018, Pretoria, T: 012-47-6077, F: 012-348-1377.
Hillandale House of Prayer, PO Box 72, Grahamstown 6140, Situ 7 km from Grahamstown, T: 0461-2-8111.
NUPSA - Network for United Prayer in Southern Africa, PO BOx 30221, Sunnyside 0132, 1238 Webb St, Queenswood, Pretoria, T: 012-333-2180, F: 012-333-2169.

SPAIN
Día Mundial de Oración, Mariano Supervía, 52, 50006 Zaragoza, T: 35-35-68.

UNITED STATES OF AMERICA (USA)
AD 2000 US Prayer Track, 7710-T Cherry Park Dr., #224, Houston, TX 77095, T: 1-713-398-9673, F: 1-713-492-7554.
All Nations Prayer Mountain (Korean), 8383 Swarthout Cyn Rd., San Bernardino, CA 92407, T: 909-883-7145.
Apostleship of Prayer, 3 Stephen Ave., New Hyde Park, NY 11040.
Breakthrough Intercessor Magazine, PO Box 121, Lincoln, VA 22078, T: 540-338-5522.
Concerts of Prayer International, P.O. Box 770, New Providence, NJ 07974, O: Web: www.goshen.net/COPI/COPI.
E-Prayer Internet Services, O: Web: www.eprayer.org.
Esther Network Int'l, 854 Conniston Road, West Palm Beach, FL 33405, T: (407) 832-6490.
Fellowship of the Burning Bush, P.O. Box 31136, Amarillo, TX 79120.
Full Gospel International Fasting Prayer Mountain Camp (Korean), 30250 Gunther Rd., Romoland, CA 92380, T: 909-928-4415.
Global Harvest Ministries, P.O. Box 63060, Colorado Springs, CO 80962, T: 719-262-9922, F: 818-262-9920, O: E-mail: 74114.570@compuserve.com, Web: www.globalharvest.org.
Harvest Evangelism, Inc., P.O. Box 20310, San Jose, CA 95160-0310, T: 408-927-9052, F: 408-927-9830.
Intercesors for America, P.O. Box 2639, Reston, VA 22090, T: 703-471-0913.
Intercessors for Africa Foundation, P.O. Box 671, Falls Church, VA 2204.
International Reconciliation Coalition, Intl. Operations Office, P.O. 3278, Ventura, CA 93006-3278, T: 805-642-5327, F: 805-642-2588, O: E-mail: ircio@pacbell.net, Web: www.reconcile.org.
Internet Prayer Center, O: Web: www.nccn.net/~clc/needpray.htm.
Kum Ran Prayer Home Center (Korean), 956 Menlo Ave., Los Angeles, CA 90006, T: 213-382-0011.
Larry Lea Ministries, P.O. Box 9000, Rockwall, TX 75087.
Latin American Prayer Fellowship (LAPF), PO Box 323 M, Pasadena, CA 91102.
Los Angeles Prayer Mountain (Korean), 24100 Pine Canyon Rd., Lake Hughes, CA 93532, T: 805-724-2126.
National Day of Prayer, O: Web: www.lesea.com/ndp.
Prayer Room, O: Web: www.dnw.com/pray/pray.htm.
Praying through the 10/40 Window, O: Web: www.ad2000.org/1040ovr.htm.
Round the World Prayer Event, World Evangelism World Methodist Council, Lake Junaluska, NC 28745, T: 704-456-9432.
Watchment National Prayer Alert, 7710-T Cherry Park Drive, Suite 224, Houston, TX 77095, T: 800-569-4824.
World Day of Prayer, 475 Riverside Dr., Rm. 560, New York, NY 10115, T: 212-870-3049, F: 212-870-3587.
World Mission Prayer League, 232 Clifton Avenue, Minneapolis, MN 55403, T: (612) 871-6843.
World Prayer Force, P.O. Box 2000, St. Petersburg, FL 33731, T: 813-527-5205.
World Prayer Guide, O: Web: www.believers.org/wpg.htm.
World Prayer Network, Box 92.2020, Sylmar, CA 91393.

60
Publishing

Publishing houses, agencies, and companies producing religious or Christian books and literature (usually church- or Christian-owned, -operated, or -linked), church or mission printing presses; including secular companies which give major importance to publishing books on religion, particularly Christian or Biblical subjects. See also BIBLE AND SCRIPTURE ORGANIZATIONS, LITERATURE, and PERIODICALS.

ANGOLA
Angola Publishing House, CP 3, Nova Lisboa.
Angola Publishing House (SDA), Caixa Postal 24 27, Huambo.

ARGENTINA
Buenos Aires Publishing House (SDA), Avenida San Martin 4555, 1602 Florida, Buenos Aires, T: 541-760-2426, 761-4802, F: 541-760-0416.

AUSTRALIA
Open Book Publishers, 205 Halifax St., Adelaide, South Australia 5000, GPO Box 1368 5001, T: 011-61-08/223-5468, F: 011-61-08/223-4552.
Signs Publishing Company, Warburton, Victoria 3799, T: 059-66-9111, F: 61-059-66-9019.

AUSTRIA
Austrian Publishing House (SDA), Nussdorferstrasse 5, 1090 Vienna, T: 43-222-34-52-97.

BANGLADESH
Bangladesh Adventist Publishing House, G.P.O. Box 80, Dhaka 1000; Adventpur, 149 Mirpur Road No. 1, Shah Ali Bagh, Mirpur, Dhaka 1216, T: 802340.

BRAZIL
Brazil Publishing House (SDA), Caixa Postal 34, 18270-000 Tatui, SP; Rodovia SP-127, KM 106, 18270-000 Tatui, SP, T: 152-51-2710, F: 152-51-2810, O: Cable: 'Atalaia', Tatui, Sao Paulo, Brazil, Telex: 0152-343 (CPUB BR).

BRITAIN (UK OF GB & NI)
Ambassador Production Ltd., 16 Hilliview Avenue, Belfast BT5 6JR, T: (08) 0232 658462, F: (08) 0232 659518.
Aquin Press, Bloomsbury Publishing Co, Woodchester Lodge, Woodchester, Stroud, Gloucs GL5 5PB, T: Amberley 2591/2.
Arthur James, 70 Cross Oak Road, Berkhamsted, Hertfordshire HP4 3HZ.
Canterbury Press Norwich, St. Mary's Works, St. Mary's Plain, Norwich NR3 3BH.
Dovewell Communication, 10th Floor, Newcombe House, 45 Notting Hill Gate, London W11 3JB.
Ellel Ministries Ltd., Ellel Grange, Ellel, Lancaster, LA2 0HN.
Gabriel Communications Ltd., First Floor, St. James's Buildings, Oxford Street, Manchester M1 6FP, T: 0161-236 8856, F: 0161-236 8530.
Hodder and Stoughton, 338 Euston Rd., London SW1 3BH.
Hymns Ancient & Modern, Ltd., St. Mary's Works, St. Mary's Plain, Norwich NR3 3BH, T: 01603-612914, F: 01603-624483.
Inter-Varsity Press (IVP), 39 Bedford Square, London WC1B 3EY, T: (01)737-5113.
James (Arthur), The Drift, Evesham, Worcs WR11 4NW, T: 6566.
Lutterworth Press, Albion House, Woking, Surrey, T: 64765/8.
Marshall Pickering, 34-42 Cleveland St, London, W1P 5FB.
Marshall, Morgan & Scott Publications, 1-5 Portpool Lane, Holborn, London EC1, T: (01)405-7011/6.
Modern Churchpeople's Union, MCU Office, 25 Birch Grove, London W3 9SP.
Mowbray (AR) & Company, Alden Press, Osney Mead, Oxford OX2 0EG, T: (0865)42507.
Saint Andrew Press, 121 George St, Edinburgh EH2 4YN, T: (031)225-5722.
Salvationist Publishing and Supplies, 117-121 Judd St, London WC1H 9NN, T: (01)387-1656.
SCM, St. Alban's Place, London N1 0NX, T: 0171-359-8033, F: 0171-359-0049.
Sheed and Ward, 33 Maiden Lane, London WC2E 7LA, T: (01)240-1777/8.
Society for Promoting Christian Knowledge (SPCK), Holy Trinity Church, Marylebone Rd, London NW1 4DU, T: (01)387-5282.
Stanborough Press Limited (SDA), Alma Park, Grantham, Lincs NG31 9SL, T: 476-591700, F: 476-77144, O: Cable: 'Stanpress', Grantham, Lincs, Telex: 265283 (SDAGB G).

BULGARIA
Bulgarian Adventist Publishing House, Solunska 10, 1000 Sofia, T: 88-12-18, F: 46-34-08.

BURUNDI
Grace Memorial Press, WGM, PB 59, Gitega.

CAMEROON
Central African Publishing House (SDA), Boite Postale 61, Yaounde, T: 20-43-23, O: Telex: WCAUMSDA 8550 KN.
Centre de Littérature Evangélique, Editions CLE, BP 1501 (& 4048), Yaoundé, T: 4673.
Equatorial African Publishing House, BP 61, Yaoundé, T: 4437.

CANADA
Abingdon and Broadman: Distributed in Canada by R.G. Mitchell Family Books, Inc., 565 Gordon Baker Rd., Willowdale, ON M2H 2W2, T: 416-499-4615, F: 416-499-6340.
Augsburg Fortress Canada, 500 Trillium Dr., PO Box 940, Kitchener, ON N2G 4E3, T: 519-748-2200, F: 519-748-9835.
Beacon Distributing/Cook Communications - Canada, PO Box 98, Paris, ON N3L 3E5, T: 800-263-2664, F: 800-461-8575.
Canadian Christian Publications, 612-30 Harding Blvd., W., Richmond Hills, ON L4C 9M3, T: 905-770-5999.
Canadian Conference of Catholic Bishops-Publications Service, 90 Parent Ave., Ottawa, ON K1N 7B1, T: 613-241-9461, F: 613-241-5090.
Choice Books, 50 Kent Ave., Kitchener, ON N2G 3R1, T: 519-579-2270.
Editions Impact, 230 rue Lupien, Cap-de-la-Madeleine, QC G8T 7W1, T: 819-378-4023.
Faith & Life Press Canada, 600 Shaftesbury Blvd., Winnipeg, MB R3P 0M4, T: 204-888-6781, F: 204-831-5675.
Frontier Research Publications, Box 129, Station U, Toronto, ON M8Z 5M4, T: 905-271-6960, F: 905-271-3830, O: E-mail: paul.r.g@sympattco.ca, Web: www.grantjeffrey.com.
Genesis Publications, 5803 Cornell Cres., Mississauga, ON L5M 5R5, T: 905-858-3784, F: 905-858-3560, O: 1-800-285-6399.
Gospel Publishing House, 6745 Century Ave., Mississauga, ON L5N 6P7, T: 905-542-7514, F: 905-542-1624.
Harmony Printing Limited, 123 Eastside Dr., Toronto M8Z 5S5, Ontario, T: 416-232-1472, F: 416-232-2862.
Harper Collins Canada Ltd., 1995 Markham Rd., Scarborough, ON M1B 5M8, T: 800-387-0117, F: 800-668-5788.
Light & Life Press Canada, 4315 Village Centre Court, Mississauga, ON L4Z 1S2, T: 800-563-3363, F: 905-848-2603.
Mennonite Publishing House, Inc./Herald Press, 490 Dutton Dr., Waterloo, ON N2L 6H7, T: 519-747-5722, F: 519-747-5721, O: 519-747-0161.
Novalis, PO Box 990, Outremont, QC H2V 4S7, T: 514-278-3020, O: Telecopie: 514-278-3030.
Oxford University Press, 70 Wynford Dr., Don Mills, ON M3C 1J9, T: 416-441-2941, F: 800-665-1771, O: 1-800-387-8020.
Shepherd's Guide, 8515 - 86 Ave., Edmonton, AB T6C 1J4, T: 800-563-4276.
Standard Publishing, c/o Lawson Falle Ltd., Box 940, 1245 Franklin Blvd., Cambridge, ON N1R 5X9, T: 800-265-8673, F: 800-565-2755.
Windflower Communications, 844-K McLeod Ave., Winnipeg, MB R2G 2T7, T: 204-668-7475, F: 204-661-8530.
Wood Lake Books, Inc., 10162 Newene Rd., Winfield, BC V4V 1R2, T: 604-766-2778, F: 604-766-2736.
World Missionary Press of Canada, Inc., Box 10, Poole, ON N0K 1S0, T: 519-595-4732.

CENTRAL AFRICAN REPUBLIC
Presse Biblique Baptiste, BP 6, Fort Sibut.

CHINA
Assemblies of God Press, 102 East Argyle St, Victory Av, Kowloon, Hong Kong, T: K-846691.
Christian Witness Press, 144 Boundary St, Kowloon, Hong Kong, T: K=822205.
Evangel Press & Bookstore, 110 Prince Edward Rd, Kowloon, Hong Kong, T: K-801106.
Morning Light Press, 17 Cumberland Rd, Kowloon, Hong Kong, T: K-823002.

Rock House Publishers, PO Box 6138, Kowloon, Hong Kong.
Sheng Tao Press, 893 King's Rd, 2/F, North Point, Hong Kong, T: H-612538.
Taosheng Publishing House, 50A Waterloo Rd, Kowloon, Hong Kong, T: K-844806, 887061.

COLOMBIA
Centro de Publicaciones-CELAM, Transversal 67 No. 173-71, San José de Bavaria, Apartado Aéreo 5278-51086, Santafé de Bogotá, T: 57-1-671-47-89, F: 57-1-612-19-29.

CONGO-ZAIRE
Editions du Léopard, BP 2244, Kinshasa 1.
Editions Evangéliques, Nyanbkunde par Bunia, Province Orientale.
Librairie Evangélique au Zaire (LEZA), BP 123, Kinshasa 1.

COSTA RICA
Centro de Publicaciones Cristianas, Apdo 2773, San José.

CROATIA
Croatian-Slovenian Publishing House (SDA), Klaiceva 40, 41000 Zagreb, T: 41-174-196, 174-283, F: 41-174-861.
Duhovna Stvamost Publishing House, Basaricerova 2, Zagreb 41000, T: 041-428-559, F: 041-426-558.

CYPRUS
Middle East Press (SDA), P.O. Box 2042, Nicosia; P.O. Box 90484, Jdeidet El Matn, Beirut, T: 2-476265, O: Cable: 'Adventist', Nicosia, Telex: ADVENT 4804 CY.

CZECH REPUBLIC
Czech Publishing House, Londynska 30, Vinohrady, Praha 2, T: 257863.
Czecho-Slovakian Publishing House, Roztocka 5/44, 160 00 Praha 6-Sedlec, T: 2-32-51-65, 32-55-28.
Society of St. Adalbert, Divadelná 4, 917 85 Trnava, T: 21745.

DENMARK
Danish Publishing House, Borstenbindervej 4, PB 550, DK-5100 Odense, T: (09)139843.
Danish Publishing House (SDA), P.O. Box 8, DK-2850, Naerum; Concordiavej 16, 2850 Naerum, T: 42804300, F: 42807075.

ETHIOPIA
Ethiopian Advent Press, P.O. Box 145, Adis Abeba, T: 113718.
Globe Publishing House, P.O. Box 4798, Adis Abeba.
Tenzae Zugubae Printing Press, P.O. Box 1563, Adis Abeba, T: 12296.

FIJI
Rarama Publishing House, Queen's Rd., P.O. Box 3083, Lami, Suva, T: 361727.

FINLAND
Finland Publishing House (SDA), P.O. Box 94, 33101, Tampere; Ketarantie 4, 33680 Tampere, T: 931-600 000, 358-31-600000, F: 358-31-600454, O: Cable: 'Kirjatoimi', Tampere.
St. Michel Print, Iso Roobertinkatu 20-A, Helsinki 00120, T: 358-680-1772, F: 358-680-1776.

FRANCE
French Publishing House, 60 Av Emile-Zola, F-77 Dammarie-les-Lys, T: (437)0521.
Life and Health Publishing House (France), 60 Avenue Emile Zola, 77192 Dammarie-les-Lys Cedex, T: 1-64-39-38-26, F: 1-64-87-00-66, O: Cable: 'Signes', Dammarie-les-Lys, France, Telex: 690587 (Ans. SANTE 690587F).
Société Nouvelle de Publications Protestantes, 33 Rue Puits-Gaillot, Lyon 1.
United Publishers, 11 Rue de la Montagne-Ste Genevieve, Paris F75005, T: 01-033-74-46.
YMCA Press, 11, rue de la Montagne St Genevieve, Paris 75005, T: 331-43-54-74-46, F: 331-43-25-34-79.

GERMANY
Christliches Verlagshaus, Senefelderstr 109, D-7 Stuttgart 1.
Hamburg Publishing House (SDA), Grindelberg 13-17, 20144 Hamburg, T: 40-441871-0, F: 40-418441, O: Cable: 'Advent', Hamburg.
Oncken Press (West German Baptist publications), Kassel, F: 49561-200-9950.
Vereinigung Evangelischer Buchhändler, Silberburgstr 58/1, Postfach 721, D-7 Stuttgart-W.
Verlag Herder, D 79080 Freiburg im Breisgau.

GHANA
Advent Press, P.O. Box 0102, Osu, Accra, T: 777861, O: Telex: 2119 ADVENT GH.
Africa Christian Press, P.O. Box 30, Achimota.

GREECE
Bureau de la Bonne Presse, 246 Acharnon, 815 Athínai.
Greek Publishing House, Keramikou 18, Athínai 107, T: 520796.

HOLY SEE
Tipografia Poliglotta Vaticana, I-00120 Città del Vaticano, T: 6982 int 4649.

HUNGARY
Advent Publishing House, Borsfa u. 55, 1171 Budapest, T: 163-8165.
Ecclesia Szövetkezet, Károlyi Mihály u 4/8, 1053 Budapest.
Omega Publishing, Ltd., Postfach 197, Debrecen 4002.
St. Stephen's Society, Kossuth Lajos u 1, 1053 Budapest.

ICELAND
Iceland Publishing House (SDA), Sudurhlid 36, 105 Reykjavik, T: 354-1-679270, F: 354-1-689460, O: Cable: 'Adventistar', Reykjavik, Iceland.

INDIA
Amar Jyothi Printing Press, P. B. 4012, Vijaya Nagar, Bangalore, Karnataka 560040.
Assemblies of God Press, 18, Royd Street, Calcutta, West Bengal 700016.
Assisi Press, Bharananganam, Kerala 686578.
Benagaria Mission Press, Benagaria Mission, Santal Parganas, Bihar 816103.
Bengal Christian Literature Centre, 65A, Mahatma Gandhi Road, Calcutta, West Bengal 700009.
Bethany Printing House, Psot Kumily, Kerala 685509.
Bethel Printers, Cellar No.14 &15, Lakshmi Engineer. Ind. Complex, Shapurnagar, Phase I, IDA, Jeedimetla, Hyderabad, Andhra Pradesh 500855.
Bethel Printers and Publishers, Gomathi Buildings, Chingavanam, Kottayam, Kerala 686531.
Bible Mission Publications, Kranthi Nagar, Nellore, Andhra Pradesh 524003.
Catholic Press Ranchi, , P.O. Box 8, Ranchi, Bihar 834001.
Catholic Mission Press, Surada, Orissa 761108.
Catholic Press, Fatima Road, Quilon, Kerala 691013.
Catholic Vani, Catholic Centre, Labbipeta, Vijayawada, Andhra Pradesh 520010.
Centenary Printing Press (Salvation Army), P.O. Aizawl, Mizoram, T: 796-001.
Christian Literature Society Press, 1 Dickenson Rd, Bangalore 42.
Christian Literature Centre India, F-58 Green Park, New Delhi 110016.
Christian Publishing House, 7/182 Court Road, Anantapur, Andhra Pradesh 515001.
CLC International, TC. 2/74, Kakanad Lane, Kesavadasapuram, Pattom, Trivandrum, Kerala 695004.
CMS Press Publications, P. B. No. 11, Kottayam, Kerala 686001.
Compassion Publications, 32. Neetaji Road, Bangalore, Karnataka 560005.
Diocesan Press, 69 W. C. College Road, Nagercoil, Tamil Nadu 629001.
Evangelical Book & Tract Depot, Post Box 719, Salem, Tamil Nadu 636007.
Evangelical Literature Service, 95 A, Vepery High Road, Madras, Tamil Nadu 600007.
GDM Press and Book Depot, Mission High School Road, Narsapur, Andhra Pradesh 534313.
Gospel Literature Service, Udyog Bhavan, 250 D, Worli, Bombay, Maharashtra 400025.
Gujarat Sahitya Prakash, Post Box 70, Anand, Gujarat 388001.
Holy Spirit Printing Press, Old Goa, Goa 403402.
Life and Worship, St. Albert' College, Post Box 5, Bihar 834001.
Little Flower Press, Manjummel, Kerala 683501.
Maranatha Printing Press, 91 Dr. Alagappa Road, Purasawalkam, Madras, Tamil Nadu 600084.
Narcheythi Printers, 4, Association Road, Madhavaram, Madras, Tamil Nadu 600060.
Nishkalanka, Xavier Publications, Post Box 2, Bihar 834001.
Oriental Institute of Religious Studies India Publications, Vadavathoor, Kerala 686010.
Orissa Mission Press, Mission Road, Cuttack, Orissa 753001.
Oxford University Press, 2/11, Ansari Road, Dayaganj Post Box 7035, New Delhi 110002.
Pentecost Press Trust, 45-A, 5th Street, Padmanaba Nagar, Adayar, Madras, Tamil Nadu 600020.
SAGE Publications India Pvt., Post Box 4215, New Delhi 110048.
Sevartham, St. Albert' College, Post Box 5, Bihar 834001.
Shalom Baptist Publications, 317/3, 8th Cross, 8th Block, Koramangala Village, Bangalore, Karnataka 560095.
St. Paul Publications, P.O. Box 9814, Bandra West, Bombay 4000050.
Steward Press, 71 Aspiran Garden Colony, Kilpauk, Madras, Tamil Nadu 600010.
Synod Publication Board, Mission Veng, Aizawl, Mizoram 796001.
Theological Publications in India, St. Peter's Seminary, P. B. 5553, Malleswaram West P. O., Bangalore, Karnataka 560055.
Thomas Athanasius Memorial Press, Saji Mathew Thottakad, Tiruvalla, Kerala 689101.
Thomson Press, Corporate Sales Office, K-13 Connaught Circus, New Delhi 110001.
Tranquebar Printing & Publishing House, 11 Abirami Street, Vepery, Madras, Tamil Nadu 600007.
Tribal Documentation Centre and Xavier Ho Publications, C/o St. Xavier's Lupungutu, P. B. 30, Chaibasa, Bihar 833201.
Tripura Christian Literature Society, Arundhuti Nagar, Tripura 799003.
Vailankanni Calling, Don Bosco Press, Pookara Street, Tamil Nadu 613001.
Vani Tharangini, 2/3 Sikh Village, Secunderabad, Andhra Pradesh 500003.
Wesley Press, P. O. Box 37, Mysore, Karnataka 570001.
Xaverian Press, Training School, Pilar, Goa 403203.
Xavier Press, St. Vincent's Industrials, P. B. 1107, Calicut, Kerala 673032.
YMCA Publishing House, Massey Hall, Jai Singh Rd, New Delhi 1.
YWAM Publishing, P.O. Box 127, Pune, Maharashtra 411037.

INDONESIA
Indonesia Publishing House (SDA), Post Bos 1188, Bandung 40011, Java, T: 62-22-630-392, F: 62-22-441-229, O: Cable: 'Indopub', Bandung, Java.

IRELAND
Columba Pess, 93 The Rise, Mount Merrion, Blackrock, Co Dublin, T: (353) 01 283 2954, F: (353) 01 288 3770.
Gill and Macmillan, Goldenbridge, Inchicore, Dublin 8, T: (353) 01 531005, F: (353) 01 541688.
Veritas Publication, 7 Lower Abbey Street, Dublin 1, T: (353) 01 786507, F: (353) 01 786507.

ISRAEL
Franciscan Printing Press, P.O. Box 14064, 91140 Jérusalem; New Gate, 91140 Jérusalem, T: 02-28-65-94, F: 972-2-27-22-74.

ITALY
Centro Editoriale Studi Islamici (CESI), Via Riboty 1, I-00195 Roma, T: 373306.
Editrice Missionaria Italiana (EMI), Via Meloncello 3/3, Bologna; Also: Corso Ferrucci 14, Torino; Via Mosè Bianchi 94, Milano; Via S Matrino 8, Parma.
IRADES Edizioni Pastorali, Centro Stampa IRADES, Via Paisiello 6, I-00198 Roma.
Italian Publishing House, Via Chiantigiana 30, Falciani 50023, Impruneta, Florence.
Libreria Editrice Claudiana, Via S Pio Quinto 18 bis, I-10125 Torin.
Unione Editori Cattolici Italiani, Via Doménico Silveri 9, I-00165 Roma.

IVORY COAST
Centre d'Edition et Diffusion Africaine (CEDA), BP 4541, Abidjan.

JAPAN
Evangelical Publishing Depot, 1-15 Kagurazaka, Shinjuku-ku, Tokyo 162.
Fukuin Dendo Kyodan Publishing Department, 4-4 2-chome, Hiyoshi-cho, Maebashi-shi, Gunmaken 371.
Japan Alliance Church Publishing Department, 12-2 5-chome, Sanban-cho, Matusyama-shi, Ehimeken 790.
Japan Publishing House (SDA), 1966 Kamikawaicho, Asahi-ku, Yokohama 241, T: 81-45-921-1414, F: 81-45-921-4349, O: Cable: 'Adventist', Yokohama, Japan, Telex: 03823586 (Ans. SDAJPN).
Jordan Press, 2-350 Nishi Okubo, Shinjuku-ku, Tokyo 160.
Protestant Publishing Company, 3-1 Shin Ogawamachi, Shinjuku-ku, Tokyo 162.
Salesian Press (Shinjiko-ku), Wakaba, Tokyo 122.
Salvationist Publishing and Supplies, 2-17 Kanda Jinbo-cho, Chiyoda-ku, Tokyo 101.
Tamagawa University Press, 1-1 6-chome, Tamagawa Gakuen, Machida-shi, Tokyo 194.
Word of Life Press, 6 Shinano-machi, Shinjuku-ku, Tokyo 160.
YMCA Press, 2nd Kosuga Bldg, 6/F, 30 Ryogoku, Nihonbashi, Chuo-ku, Tokyo 103.

KENYA
Africa Herald Publishing House, P.O. Box 95, Kendu Bay, T: 22, O: Cable: AHPH, Kendu Bay, Kenya.
Church of God Press, Editor, Kima Mission, PO Box 160, Maseno.
Evangel Publishing House (EPH), PO Box 969, Kisumu, T: Nyang'ori 1Y5.
Uzima Press, Imani House, PO Box 48127, Nairobi, T: 20239.

LEBANON
Middle East Press, P.O. Box 2042, Nicosia; P.O. Box 90484, Jdeidet El Matn, Beirut, Lebanon.

LESOTHO
Morija Printing Works, P.O. Box 5, Morija.

MADAGASCAR
Adventist Printing House, Boite Postale 1134, Antananarivo 101, T: 261-2-40365, F: 261-2-40134, O: Cable: 'Adventiste', Antananarivo, Madagascar, Telex: 22259 ZODIAC MG.
Imprimerie Luthérienne, BP 538, Tananarive.
Malagasy Publishing House, BP 1134, Tananarive, T: 40365.

MALAWI
Assemblies of God Press, P.O. Box 5749, Limbe.
Malamulo Publishing House (SDA), P.O. Box 11, Makwasa, T: 474206, 474229, O: Telex: 43483 and 44216.
Petro Printing Press, Nkhoma.

MOZAMBIQUE
Mozambique Publishing House, Av 24 de Julho 453, CP 1468, Maputo.
Mozambique Publishing House (SDA), Caixa Postal 1468, Maputo; Avenida Maguiguana No. 300, Maputo.

MYANMAR
Kinsaung Publishing House, Post Box 997, Yangon 11191.

NAMIBIA
Angelus Printing Press, P.O. Box 8315, Windhoek 9000, T: 264-61-64 261.

NETHERLANDS
Boekencentrum Publishing House, P.O. Box 29, 2700 AA Zoetermeer, T: 0031-79-362-82-82, F: 0031-79-361-55-89, O: E-mail: boekencentrum@wxs.nl.
E. J. Brill Publishers, P.O.B. 9000, 2300 PA Leiden.
Netherlands Publishing House (SDA), Postbus 29, 3720 AA Bilthoven; Biltseweg 14, 3735 ME Bosch en Duin, T: 30-783214.

NORWAY
Norwegian Publishing House (SDA), Olaf Helsets vei 8, 0694 Oslo, T: 22285220, F: 22298511, O: Cable: 'Sunnhetsbladet', Oslo,.
Unges Forlag, NKRO, Hausmannsgate 22, Oslo.

PAKISTAN
Christian Publishing House (MIK Press), 36 Ferozepur Rd., Lahore 4.
Qasid Publishing House of Seventh-day Adventists, Post Box 32, Lahore; Adventpura, Multan Road, Lahore, T: 92-42-5839497, F: 92-42-5839559, O: Cable: 'Adventist', Lahore, Pakistan.

PAPUA NEW GUINEA
Salvationist Press (Trades as 'SalPress'), P.O. Box 3003, Boroko; Pascal Ave., BBadili, Boroko, National Capital Dist, T: 675-321-7151.

PHILIPPINES
Philippine Publishing House (SDA), P.O. Box 813, 1099 Manila; 1401 Baesa, Caloocan City, T: 63-2-35-54-85, 35-52-05, F: 63-2-34-42-44, O: Cable: 'Filpub', Manila.

POLAND
Polish Publishing House, Foksal 8, Warszawa, T: 277611/3, 262506.
Reconciliation Publications, Rycerska 6/57, Lublin 20-552, T: 48-81-56-34-42, F: 48-81-214-75.

PORTUGAL
(CLC) Centro de Literatura Cristá, Av. Emidio Navarro, 90 - 4. Esq., 3000 Coimbra, T: 039-3 33 91, F: 039-3 61 55.
APECP - Centro Nacional de Literatura, Rua Marechal Craveiro Lopes, 41, Fanqueiro, 2670 Loures; Apartado 144, 2670 Loures, T: 01-983 09 44, F: 01-983 26 55.
Casa Publicadora das Assembleias de Deus (Edições Novas de Alegria), Av. Almirante Gago Coutinho, 158, 1700 Lisboa, T: 01-849 28 69, O: 01-849 34 73.
Centro Baptista de Publicações, Rua Marechal Gomes da Costa 2-3, Dt, Apdo 8, Queluz.
Edições Palavras de Vida (TEAM), Rua da Prata 156, Lisboa-2.
Edições Vida Nova, Apdo 10, Marinha Grande.
Núcleo - Centro de Publicações Cristas, Rua das Fontainhas das Pias, Lote 83, Casal Novo - 1675 Caneças, T: 01-981 16 31, F: 01-981 14 31, O: 01-981 16 39.
Portuguese Publishing House (SDA), Rua Salvador Allende, Jote 18-1° and 2°, 2686 Sacavem Codex, T: 11-941-08-44, 942-59-10, F: 11-942-57-64, O: Telex: 65114 (Ans. 65114 PUBATL).

ROMANIA
Romanian Adventist Publishing House, Strada Plantelor 12, 70308 Bucharest 2, T: 01-312-92-53, F: 01-312-92-55.

RUSSIA
Logos Publishing, Prospekt Kosmonavtov, dom. 96, kv 2, St. Petersburg 196233, T: 7-812-127-86-46, F: 7-812-315-17-01.
Source of Life Publishing House, ul. Rudeneva 43-A, p. Zaoski, Tula Region 301000.

SINGAPORE
Southeast Asia Publishing House (SDA), 251 Upper Serangoon Road, Singapore 1334, T: 65-280-4684, F: 65-382-3510, O: Cable: 'Adventist', Singapore.

SOUTH AFRICA
Baptist Publishing House, PO Box 50, Roodepoort 1725, T: 011-764-1000.
Bible Media, PO Box 5, Wellington 7655 Kerk St, Wellington, T: 02211-3-3851, F: 02211-3-3864.
Christelike-Uitgewers-maatskappy (CUM Boeke), PO Box 1599, Vereeniging 1930, 20 Smuts Ave, Vereeniging, T: 016-55-2147, F: 016-21-1748.
Christian Publication International, 409 Buitenkloof Centre, 8 Kloof St, Cape Town 8001, T: 021-22-2202, F: 021-22-2221.
Countdown Publishing, PO Box 4780, Randburg 2195, T: 011-792-8036, F: 011-792-7348.
Emmanuel Press, P/Bag, White River 1240, T: 01311-751-2395, F: 013-750-1487.
Evangelie Uitgewers/Gospel Publishers, PO Box 1, Westhoven 2142, Perth Rd/3rd Ave, Westdene, Johannesburg, T: 011-673-2623, F: 011-673-2644.
Lux Verbi (NG Kerk Uitgewers), PO Box 1822, Cape Town 8000, 30 Waterkant St, Cape Town, T: 021-21-5540, F: 021-419-1865.
Methodist Publishing House, PO Box 708, Cape Town 8000, 31 Parliament St, Cape Town, T: 021-461-8214, F: 021-461-8249.
Orion, PO Box 3068, Halfway House 1685, 17-49 Richards Dr, Halfway House, T: 011-315-3647, F: 011-315-2729.
Pre Christo Publications (NG Sending Uitgewers), PO Box 19, Bloemfontein 9300, 39 Blignaut St, Bloemfontein, T: 051-30-3174, F: 051-47-0596.
Redemption Pastoral Publications, PO Box 341, Merrivale, 3291, T: 0332-30-2527.
Scripture Union Publishing Agency, PO Box 291, Rondebosch, 7700 Cape Town, T: 021-689-1083, F: 011-685-5861.
Southern Publishing Association (SDA), P.O. Box 14800, Kenwyn 7790, Cape Town; Corner Old Ottery Road and Clifford St., Ottery 7800, Cape Town, T: 27-21-739-490, F: 27-21-739-496, O: Cable: 'ADPRINT', Cape Town, South Africa.
Struik Christians Books, PO Box 193, Mailand 7405, Graph Ave, Montague Gdns, Capetown, T: 021-551-5900, F: 021-551-1124.
Successful Christian Living, PO Box 1613, Capetown, 8000, 92 Bree St, Capetown, T: 021-23-6254, F: 021-22-1381.
Verenigde Gereformeerde Utigewars, PO Box 40, Springs 1560, 26 Plantation Rd, Springs, T: 021-362-4060, F: 011-815-3524.

SOUTH KOREA
Benedict Press, 54, 1-ga, Changch'ung-dong, Chung-gu, Seoul-shi, T: (02) 279-9581.
Bible & Life Publishing Co., 670-28, Mia 6-dong,

Kanbuk-gu, Seoul-shi, T: (02) 945-5983.
Catholic Publishing House, 149-2, Chungnimdong, Chung-gu, Seoul-shi, T: (02)3609-110.
Korean Publishing House (SDA), c/o Korean Union Conference, Chung Ryang P.O. Box 110, Seoul 130-650; Chung Ryang Ri, Seoul, T: 82-2-966-0071, 966-0075, F: 82-2-960-0848, O: Cable: 'Adventist" Seoul, Telex: K25329 (KUMSDA).
Publishing Department, 85-12, Nung-dong, Kwangjin-gu, Seoul-shi, T: (02) 466-0123.
St. Paul Publishing Co., 103, Mia 9-dong, Kangbuk-gu, Seoul-shi, T: (02) 984-1611.

SPAIN
Ediciones Bíblicas, Apdo. 15, Palafrugell, 172000 Gerona.
Ediciones Don Bosco, Paseo San Juan Bosco 62, Barcelona 17.
Safeliz Publishing House (SDA), C/Aravaca 8, 28040 Madrid, T: 34-1-533-42-38, 534-86-61, F: 34-1-533-16-85.
Spanish Publishing House, Paseo San Francisco de Sales 11, Madrid 3, T: 2436544, 2438832.

SRI LANKA
Lakpahana Press of Seventh-day Adventists, 8 Dewala Road, Pagoda, Nugegoda, T: 94-1-856166, F: 94-1-585851.

SWEDEN
Swedish Publishing House (SDA), P.O. Box 10036, S-80010 Gavle, T: 46-26-187298, F: 46-26-141978.

SWITZERLAND
Advent Publishers (Switzerland), Wylerhalde, 3704 Krattigen, T: 33-54-10-65, F: 33-54-44-31.
CVN Buch & Druck, Badenerstr 69, CH-8026 Zürich.
Schweizerische Evangelische Verlagsgesellschaft, CH-3177 Laupen.
Swiss Publishing House, Wylerhalde, CH-3704 Krattigen, T: (033)5410065.

TAIWAN
Christian Witness Press, 63 Chung Shan Rd, P.O. Box 210, Taipei.
Signs of the Times Publishing Association, 424 Pa Te Road, Section 2, Taipei 105, T: 886-2-752-1322, 752-0387, F: 886-2-740-1448.
Wisdom Publications (FSP), 21 Chunghsiao W. Road, Sect. 1, Taipei, T: 02-3710447.

TANZANIA
Central Tanganyika Press, Msalato, PO Box 15, Dodoma.
Evangelical Press (CMML), PO Box 524, Mtwara.
Inland Publishers, PO Box 125, Mwanza.
Mennonite Press, PO Box 7, Musoma.
Ndanda Mission Press, PO Ndanda via Lindi.
Tanzania Adventist Press, P.O. Box 635, Morogoro, T: 056-3338, O: Cable: 'Advent Press'.
Vuga Press (ELCT, PO Box 25, Soni.

THAILAND
Assumption Printing Press, 51 Oriental Ave., Bangrak, Bangkok 10500, T: 233-0523.
Gospel Printing Press, Mass Communication Building, 1st Floor, PO Box 11/1293. Bangkok.
Kingdom Development (Gospel Press), 10 Soi 6, Sukhumvit Rd, Bangkok 11, T: 2525418, 3920756.
OMF Publishers, 111/0 Pan Rd, Silom, Bangkok 5, T: 2348258.
Suriyaban Publishers (Church of Christ in Thailand), 14 Pramuan Rd, Bangkok 5, T: 2347991/2.
Thailand Publishing House (SDA), P.O. Box 14, Klongtan, Bangkok 10116; P.O. Box 152, Prakanong, Bangkok 10110, Also: 12 Soi Kasempanichakarn, Klongtan, Prakanong, Bangkok, T: 66-2-391-3594, 381-1811, F: 66-2-381-1928, O: Cable: 'Adventist', Bangkok.

TURKEY
Redhouse Press, PK 142, 34432 Sirkeci, Istanbul.

UGANDA
Uganda Church Press, Georgiadis Chambers, 6A Kampala Rd, PO Box 2776, Kampala, T: 41599.
Upper Nile Press, P.O. Box 10740, Kampala; 6 miles east on Jinja Road, Kireka Hill, Kampala, T: 256-41-542455, 285031, F: 256-41-245597, O: Telex: 0988-61143 UG DEV BANK, attn: Mr. Kiwanuka.

UNITED STATES OF AMERICA (USA)
Abbey Press, P.O. Box 128, St. Meinrad, IN 47577, T: 800-621-1588, F: 800-222-3995, O: E-mail: abytrade@abbeypress.com.
Abilene Christian University Press, 1634 Campus Court, Abilene, TX 79601, T: 800-444-4228.
Abingdon Press, 201 - 8th Avenue S., Nashville, TN 37202.
Accent Books, P.O. Box 15337, 12100 W. 6th Ave., Denver, CO 80215.
Advocate Press, P.O. Box 98, Franklin Springs, GA 30639.
Aglow Publications, P.O. Box 1548, Lynnwood, WA 98046, T: 206-775-7282.
American Catholic Press, 16565 S. State St., South Holland, IN 60473, T: 708-331-5485, F: 708-331-5484.
American Christian Press (The Way Inc.), New Knoxville, OH 45871.
Associated Church Press, 343 South Dearborn St, Chicago, IL 60604, T: (312)922-5444.
Augsburg Fortress Publishers, P.O. Box 1209, Minneapolis, MN 55440, T: 800-328-4648, F: 800-722-7766, O: E-mail: afp_bookstore.topic@ecunet.org, Web: www.elca.org/afp/afphome.html.
Ave Maria Press, Notre Dame, IN 46556, T: 800-282-1865, F: 800-282-5681.
B.B. Kirkbride Co., Inc., P.O. Box 606, Indianapolis, IN 46206.
Baker Book House, P.O. Box 6287, Grand Rapids, MI 49506.
Balcony Publishing, 3011 Hwy 620 North, Austin, TX 78734, T: 512-266-3777.
Ballantine/Epiphany Books, 201 East 50 Street, New York, NY 10022.
Banner of Truth, P.O. Box 621, Carlisle, PA 17013, T: 717-249-5747.
Baptist Press, Nashville, TN 37102.
Baptist Publishing House, 1319 Magnolia St., Texarkana, TX 75501.
Baptist Spanish Publishing House, 7000 Alabama St., El Paso, TX 79904, T: 800-755-5958, 915-566-9656, F: 915-565-9008, O: E-mail: 70423.771@compuserve.com.
Barclay Press, 600 E. Third St., Newberg, OR 97132; P.O. Box 232, Newberg, OR 97132.
Beacon Press, 25 Beacon St, Boston, MA 02108, T: (617)742-2100.
Benetvision, 355 East Ninth St., Erie, PA 16503-1107, T: 814-459-5994, F: 814-459-8066, O: E-mail: 71231.3115@compuserve.com.
Berean Publishers, P.O. Box 1091, Indianapolis, IN 46206.
Berry Publishing Services, 701 Main St., Evanston, IL 60202.
Bethany House Publishers, 11300 Hampshire Ave. S., Minneapolis, MN 55438, T: 800-328-6109, F: 612-829-2503, O: E-mail: cs@bethanyhouse.com.
Bethany Press, Box 179, St Louis, MO 63166.
Bethel Publishing, 1819 S. Main St., Elkhart, IN 46516, T: 800-348-7657, 219-293-8585, F: 800-230-8271, 219-52.
Bob Jones University Press, Greenville, SC 29614.
Brethren Press, 1451 Dundee Ave., Elgin, IL 60120.
Bridge-Logos Publishers, 1300 Airport Rd. Ste E, North Brunswick, NJ 08902, T: 800-631-5802, 732-435-8700, F: 800-935-6467, 732-43, O: E-mail: bridgelogos@worldnet.att.net, Web: www.bridgelogos.com.
Broadman & Holman Publishers, 127 Ninth Ave., N., Nashville, TN 37234, T: 615-251-2644, F: 615-251-2701.
Casa Editorial Nueva Albanza, P.O. Box 9944, El Paso, TX 79990.
Casa Nazarene de Publicaciones, 6401 The Paseo, Kansas City, MO 64131.
Catholic Book Publishers Association, Inc., 333 Glen Head Rd., Old Brookville, NY 11545.
Catholic Book Publishing Co., 77 West End Road, Totowa, NJ 07512, T: 973-890-2400, F: 800-890-1844, O: E-mail: cbpcl@bellatlantic.net, Web: www.catholicbkpub.com.
Chariot Victor Publishing, 4050 Lee Vance View, Colorado Springs, CO 80918, T: 800-437-4337, F: 800-664-7167.
Child Evangelism Press, P.O. Box 348, Warrenton, MO 63383, T: 314-456-4321, F: 314-456-5000.
Christian Booksellers Association, P.O. Box 200, Colorado Springs, CO 80901, T: 719-576-7880, F: 719-576-0795.
Christian Heritage Publishing, P.O. Box 5010, Lake Wylie, SC 29710.
Christian Publications, 3825 Hartzdale Dr., Camp Hill, PA 17011, T: 800-233-4443, F: 717-761-7273, O: E-mail: salemktg@cpi-horizon.com, Web: www.cpi-horizon.com.
Church Publishing, Inc., 445 Fifth Ave., New York, NY 10016.
Clarion Books, 52 Vanderbilt Ave., New York, NY 10017.
Complete Biblical Library, 2274 E Sunshine, Springfield, MO 65804, T: 800-446-6238.
Conciliar Press, P.O. Box 76, Ben Lomond, CA 95005-0076.
Concordia Publishing House, 3558 S Jefferson, St. Louis, MO 63118, T: 800-325-3040.
Congregational Holiness Publishing House, Griffin, GA 30223.
Covenant Press, 5101 North Francisco Av, Chicago, IL 60625.
Creation House Publishers, 600 Rinehart Rd., Lake Mary, FL 32746, T: 407-333-0600, F: 407-333-7129, O: E-mail: creationhouse.com.
Cross Publishing Company, 290 Monroe Av, Kenilworth, NJ 07033.
Crossway Books, 9825 W Roosevelt Rd, Maywood, IL 60153, T: 708-345-7474.
David C. Cook Church Ministries, 4050 Lee Vance View, Colorado Springs, CO 80918, T: 719-536-0100, F: 719-536-3266, O: Web: www.cookministries.com.
Dayspring Greeting Cards, PO Box 1010, Siloam Springs, AR 72761, T: 501-524-9301.
Deeper Revelation Books, 9825 Fifeshire Dr, Winter Park, FL 32792.
Derek Prince Ministries, P.O. Box 300, Ft. Lauderdale, FL 33302.
Editorial Betania, 5541 N.W. 82nd Ave., Miami, FL 33166.
Editorial Caribe, 3934 S.W. 8th St., Suite 303, Miami, FL 33134.
Eerdmans Publishing Co, 255 Jefferson SE, Grand Rapids, MI 49503, T: 616-459-4591.
Episcopal Book Resource Center, 815 Second Ave., New York, NY 10017, T: 212-922-5106, F: 212-661-1706.
Essence Publishing, O: Web: www.essence.on.ca/.
Evangelical Christian Publishers Association, 1969 E. Broadway Rd. #2, Tempe, AZ 85282, T: 602-966-3998, F: 602-966-1944, O: E-mail: dross@ecpa.org.
Faith Library Publications/Kenneth Hagin Ministries, P. O. Box 50126, Tulsa, OK 74150, T: 888-258-0999, 918-258-1588, F: 918-251-8016.
Fleming H. Revell Co., 120 White Plains Rd., Tarrytown, NY 10591.
Focus on the Family Publishing, 420 N. Cascade Ave., Colorado Springs, CO 80903.
Forward Movement Publications, 412 Sycamore St., Cincinnati, OH 45202, T: 800-543-1813.
Foundation Press, PO Box 6439, Anaheim, CA 92816, T: 714-630-6450.
Fresh Wind Ministries, 18603 E. Saratoga Pl., Aurora, CO 80015.
Gessler Publishing Co, Inc, 55 W 13th St, New York, NY 10011, T: 212-627-0099.
Good News Publishers, 1300 Crescent St., Wheaton, IL 60187, T: 708-682-4300, F: 708-682-4785.
Gospel Light/Regal Books, 2300 Knoll Dr., Ventura, CA 93003, T: 800-4-GOSPEL, F: 800-860-3109, O: Web: www.gospellight.com.
Gospel Publishing House, 1445 Boonville Ave., Springfield, MO 65802, T: 417-831-8000, F: 417-862-7566.
Grace Publications, 23740 Hawthorne Blvd., Torrance, CA 90505, T: 800-421-5565, F: 800-837-7260.
Gramcord Institute, 2065 Half Day Rd, Trinity Ev Divinity Sch, Deerfield, IL 60015, T: 800-445-8337.
Harold Shaw Publishers, Box 567, Wheaton, IL 60189, T: 800-742-9782, 630-665-6700, F: 630-665-6793, O: E-mail: shaw.pub@compuserve.com.
Harper Collins, Evangelical Books, 151 Union St., Icehouse One–401, San Francisco, CA 94111.
Harrison House, PO Box 35035, Tulsa, OK 74135, T: 800-331-3647.
Harvest House Publishers, 1075 Arrowsmith, Eugene, OR 97402, T: 541-343-0123, F: 541-342-6410.
Hendrickson Publishers, Inc., 137 Summit St., P.O. Box 3473, Peabody, MA 01961, T: 800-358-3111, 978-532-6546, F: 978-573-8111, O: E-mail: orders@hendrickson.com.
Herald Press, 616 Walnut Ave, Scottdale, PA 15683, T: 412-887-8500.
Here's Life Publishers, Inc., P.O. Box 1576, 2700 Little Mountain Dr., Bldg. F, San Bernardino, CA 92405, T: 714-886-7981.
Hope Publishing Company, 5707 West Lake St, Chicago, IL 60644.
Howard Publishing, 3117 North 7th St., W. Monroe, LA 71291, T: 800-858-4109, F: 800-342-2067, O: E-mail: ryan@howardpublishing.com.
Ignatius Press, P.O. Box 1339, Ft. Collins, CO 80522, T: 970-221-3920, F: 800-278-3566, O: Web: www.ignatius.com.
Impact Books, Inc., 137 W. Jefferson, Kirkwood, MO 63122.
Information Resource Technologies, Inc., 3120 Highland Rd., Hermitage, PA 16148, T: 800-458-1996, 412-347-7100, F: 412-347-1315, O: E-mail: dyanck@irtnet.com, Web: www.nauticom.net/www/irt.
Inter-American Publishing Association, P.O. Box 520627, Miami, FL 33126; 1890 N.W. 95th Ave., Miami, FL 33172, T: 305-599-0037, F: 305-592-8999, O: Cable: 'Adventist', Miami, Florida, U.S.A., Telex: 51-9306 (Ans. GEN CONF CGBL).
InterVarsity Press, P.O. Box 1400, 5206 Main St., Downers Grove, IL 60515, T: 630-887-2500, F: 630-964-1251, O: Web: www.ivpress.com.
John Knox Press, 341 Ponce De Leon Ave., NE, Atlanta, GA 30308.
Josh McDowell Ministry, Box 1330, Wheaton, IL 60189.
Judson Press, P. O. Box 851, Valley Forge, PA 19482, T: 800-331-1053, F: 610-768-2107, O: E-mail: 74531.1171@judsonpress.com.
Kenneth Copeland Publications, Fort Worth, TX 76192, T: 800-998-3971, 817-489-3701, F: 817-489-2903, O: Web: www.kcm.org.
Kenneth Hagin Ministries, P.O. Box 50126, Tulsa, OK 74150, T: 918-258-1588.
Korean Christian Press, 4055 Wilshire Bl., #512, Los Angeles, CA 90010, T: 213-380-5947.
Kregel, Inc., P.O. Box 2607, Grand Rapids, MI 49501, T: 1-800-733-2607, F: 616-451-9330, O: E-mail: kregelbooks@kregel.com.
Leaflet Missal, 976 W. Minnehaha Ave., St. Paul, MN 55104, T: 612-487-2818.
Lederer Messianic Publications, 6204 Park Heights Ave., Baltimore, MD 21215, T: 410-358-6471, F: 410-764-1376, O: E-mail: ledmessmin@aol.com, Web: www.goshen.net/lederer.
Life Publishers, Intl., 3333 S.W. 15th St., Deerfield, FL 33442-8134, T: 305-570-8765, F: 305-570-8900.
Lillenas Publishing Company, 2923 Troost Ave., Kansas City, MO 64109, T: 800-877-0700, F: 816-753-4071, O: E-mail: music@lillenas.com.
Lion Publishing Corp., 1705 Hubbard Ave., Batavia, IL 60510.
Liturgical Press, St. John's Abbey, P.O. Box 7500, Collegeville, MN 56321-7500, T: 800-858-5450, F: 800-445-5899.
Liturgical Publications (Catholic), O: Web: www.execpc.com/~1pi.
Loizeaux Brothers, Inc., P.O. Box 277, 1238 Corlies Ave., Neptune, NJ 07753, T: 201-774-8144.
Macmillan Publishing Company, 866 Third Ave., New York, NY 10022.
Maranatha Publications, P.O. Box 1799, Gainesville, FL 32602, T: 352-375-4455, F: 352-335-0080, O: E-mail: youthnow@aol.com.
Masterplanning Group International, Box 6128, Laguna Niguel, CA 92677-9990.
Methodist Publishing House, 201 Eight Ave., South, Nashville 2, Tennessee.
Moody Press, 820 N. LaSalle Blvd., Chicago, IL 60610, T: 800-678-8812, 312-329-2102, F: 800-678-3329, 312-32, O: Web: www.moodypress.org.
Morehouse Publishing, P.O. Box 1321, Harrisburg, PA 17105-9763, T: (800)877-0012, F: (717)541-8128.
Morehouse-Barlow Company, 14 East 41st St, New York, NY 10017, T: (212)532-4370.
Morning Star Publications & Ministries, 16000 Lancaster Hwy., Charlotte, NC 28277, T: 800-542-0278, F: 704-542-0280, O: Web: www.eaglestar.org.
Multnomah Publishers, Inc., P.O. Box 1720, 204 W. Adams Ave., Sisters, OR 97759, T: 800-929-0910, 541-549-1144, F: 541-549-2044.
Navpress, P.O. Box 35001, Colorado Springs, CO 80935; 7899 Lexington, Dr., 80920, T: 719-548-9222, 800-366-7788, F: 719-260-7223, 800-860-3109, O: Web: www.navpress.com.
Nazarene Publishing (Beacon Hill), P.O. Box 527, Kansas City, MO 64141.
New Hope Publishers, P.O. Box 12065, Birmingham, AL 35202-2065.
Office for Publishing and Promotion Services, U.S. Catholic Conf., 3211 Fourth St., N.E., Washington, D.C. 20017, T: 202-541-3090.
Omega Publications, P.O. Box 4130, Medford, OR 97501, T: 503-826-1030.
Overcomer Press, Inc., P.O. Box 248, Owosso, MI 48867, T: 517-723-8277, F: 517-725-3103.
Oxford University Press, 198 Madison Ave., New York, NY 10016, T: 212-726-6000.
Pacific Press Publishing Association, 1350 North Kings Road, Nampa, ID 83651.
Pathway Press, 1080 Montgomery Av, Cleveland, TN 37311.
Paulist Press, 997 Macarthur Blvd., Mahwah, NJ 07430, T: 201-825-7300.
Pilgrim Press, 700 Prospect Ave., Cleveland, OH 44115.
Practical Press, Box 111, Bible School Park, NY 13737.
Presbyterian & Reformed Publishing Company, Box 185, Nutley, NJ 07110.
Quakers Uniting in Publications, The Clerk, 343 West St., Amherst, MA 01002.
Questar Publishers, P.O. Box 1734, Sisters, OR 97759, T: 503-549-1144.
Rapids Christian Press, P.O. Box 467, Wisconsin Rapids, WI 54494.
Regular Baptist Press, 1300 N. Meacham Rd., Schaumburg, IL 60173, T: 800-727-4440, 847-843-1600, F: 847-843-3757, O: E-mail: rbporders@garbc.org, Web: www.garbc.org/rbp.
Religious Herald Publishing Association, P.O. Box 8377, Richmond, VA 23226.
Review & Herald Publishing Association, 6800 Eastern Av NE, Washington, DC 20012, T: (202)723-3700.
Roper Press, Inc., 4737 A Gretna, Dallas, TX 75207, T: 214-630-4808, F: 214-630-4822.
Russian Christian Publishing, Inc., P.O. Box 364, Wheaton, IL 60189, T: 708-510-1581, F: 708-510-1582.
Scripture Press/Victor Books, 4050 Lee Vance View, Colorado Springs, CO 80918, T: 800-323-9409, F: 719-533-3045.
Seabury Press, 815 Second Av, New York, NY 10017, T: (212)TN7-8282.
Servant Publications, P.O. Box 8617, Ann Arbor, MI 48107, T: 313-761-8505.
Shaw Publishers, 388 Gundersen Dr, Wheaton, IL 60189, T: 708-665-6700.
Shawnee Press, Inc., 49 Waring Dr., Delaware Water Gap, PA 18327, T: 800-962-8584, 717-476-0550, F: 717-476-5247, O: E-mail: shawneepress@noln.com, Web: www.shawneepress.com.
Sheed & Ward, 64 University Place, New York, NY, T: (212)OR4-8807.
Society for Promoting & Encouraging Arts & Knowledge, 100 Skyline Dr., Eureka Springs, Ark 72632-9705, T: 501-253-9701.
Spire Books, 184 Central Ave., Old Tappan, NJ 07675.
St. Bede's Publications, P.O. Box 545, Petersham, MA 01366-0545, O: Web: www.stbedes.org.
St. Columba Press (Orthodox), O: Web: www.stmichael.org/exhome.html.
St. Thomas Publishing Co., 16902 Bolsa Chica Road, Huntington Beach, CA 92649, T: 714-840-4848.
St. Vladimir's Seminary Press, 575 Scarsdale Rd., Crestwood, NY 10707, T: 914-961-8313, F: 914-961-5456.
Standard Publishing, 8121 Hamilton Ave., Cincinnati, OH 45231, T: 800-543-1353, F: 513-931-0904.
STL Books, #2 Industrial Park Rd., Waynesboro, GA 30830.
Strang Communications Co., 600 Rinehart Rd., Lake Mary, FL 32746.
Sword of the Lord Publishers, 224 Bridge Ave., Murfreesboro, TN 37130.
Tabor Publishing, 200 E. Bethany Dr., Allen, TX 75002.
Thomas Nelson Publishers, P.O. Box 141000, Nashville, TN 37214, T: 800-251-4000, F: 615-883-3287, O: Web: www.tommynelson.com.
Triad Christian Publishing, O: Web: www.dnc.net/users/triad.
Tyndale House Publishers, Inc., 351 Executive Dr., Carol Stream, IL 60188, T: 800-323-9400, 630-668-8300, F: 630-668-8905, O: Web: www.tyndale.com.
Victory House Publishers, P.O. Box 700238, Tulsa, OK 74170, T: 918-747-5009, F: 918-747-1970, O: E-mail: vhi@msn.com.
Warner Press, 1200 E. Fifth St., Anderson, IN 46012, T: 800-741-7721, 765-644-7721, F: 765-640-8005.
WaterBrook Press, 5446 N. Academy Blvd., Ste. 200, Colorado Springs, CO 80918, T: 800-603-7051, 719-590-4999, F: 800-294-5686, 719-59.
Westminister/John Knox Press, 100 Witherspoon St, Louisville, KY 40202, T: 502-569-5043.
William Carey Library, Publishers and Distributors, P.O. Box 40129, Pasadena, CA 91114; 1705 N. Sierra Bonita Ave., Pasadena, CA 91104, T: 626-798-0819, F: 626-794-0477.
Winepress Publishing, 12108 Mukilteo Speedway, Mukilteo, WA 98275, T: 800-326-4467, 425-513-0769, F: 425-353-4402, O: E-mail: bbooks4him@aol.com, Web: www.winepresspub.com.
Wolgemuth & Hyatt Publishers, P.O. Box 1941, Brentwood, TN 37027, T: 615-371-1210.
Word Books, 5221 N O'Conner Rd #1000, Irving, TX 75039, T: 214-556-1900.
Wordpress Intl., P.O. Box 216, Alhambra, CA 91802, T: 818-281-4740, F: 818-458-0677.
World Library Press, 2274 E Sunshine, Springfield, MO 65804, T: 800-446-6238.
World Missionary Press, Inc., P.O. Box 120, New

Paris, IN 46553, T: 219-831-2111, F: 219-831-2161.
World Publishing Company, 2231 West 110th St, Cleveland, OH 44102.
World Wide Publications, 1303 Hennepin Ave., Minneapolis, MN 55403, T: 612-333-0940.
Write Christianity, O: Web: www.geocities.com/Athens/9359/index.html.
Youth Specialities, Inc., 1224 Greenfield Dr., El Cajon, CA 92021.
Zondervan Publishing House, 5300 Patterson Ave., S.E., Grand Rapids, MI 49530, T: 800-727-3480, 616-698-6900, F: 610-532-9001, O: E-mail: zpub@zph.com, Web: www.zondervan.com.

VENEZUELA
Tipografía Evangélica Asociada, Apdo 402, Maracaibo.

VIET NAM
Vietnam Signs Press, 373 Dai-lo Vo di Nguy, PO Box 453, Phu-Nhuan, Saigon, T: 41604.

YUGOSLAVIA
Yugoslavian Publishing House (SDA), Bozidara Adzije 4, 11000 Belgrade, T: 38-11-453-842, F: 38-11-458-694, O: Telex: ADVENT YU 72645.

ZAMBIA
African Christian Books, P.O. Box 376, Luanshya.
Baptist Publishing House, P.O. Box 1995, Lusaka.
Zambia Adventist Press, P.O. Box 31309, Lusaka; 4013 Burma Road, Lusada, T: 260-1-229688, 229689, F: 260-1-229689.

ZIMBABWE
Mambo Press, P.O. Box 779, Gwelo, T: 2293.
Rhodesian Christian Press, P.O. Box 2146, Bulawayo.

61 Religious communities

Religious orders, institutes, congregations, societies, communities, brotherhoods, sisterhoods, and mixed communities, following a religious rule (regula) or the religious life, of any ecclesiastical traditions or families; with either ordained, religious, lay, or mixed personnel; usually or often with vows of poverty, chastity and obedience; Catholic congregations of pontifical status (directly under Rome); indigenous communities and local congregations (clerical or lay) begun in the Third World; federations, associations, or groupings of religious communities or congregations, or of religious personnel; agencies, institutions, organizations, structures of oversight, or commissions related to religious personnel, houses, or orders. For congregations primarily devoted to foreign missionary work, see FOREIGN MISSIONARY SOCIETIES.

ALGERIA
Union des Supérieures Majeures Diocèsaines, Maison Provinciale des Soeurs Blanches, BP 29, Birmandreis, El Djezair.

ANGOLA
Conferenza dei Superiori Maggiori (CIRMA), CP 1230, Luanda.

ARGENTINA
Conferencia Argentina de Religiosos (CAR), Callao 289, 3 Piso, Buenos Aires, T: 408615, 464393.

AUSTRALIA
Association of Major Clerical Religious Superiors, Sacred Heart Monastery, Kensington, NSW 2033.
Conference of Major Religious Superiors of Women's Institutes (CMRSWI), St. Vincent's Convent, Potts Point, NSW 2011.
Provincials Conference of Religious Brothers, Holy Cross College, Victoria Rd, Ryde 2112.

AUSTRIA
Superiorenkonferenz der Männlichen Ordensgemeinschaften Österreichs, Schotternabtei, Freyung 6, A-1010 Wien.
Vereinigung der Frauenorden und Kongregationen Österreichs (VFKO), Stephansplatz 6, A-1010 Wien.

BELGIUM
Concile des Frères Enseignants de Belgique, Rue du Strop 125, Gand.
Union des Supérieures Majeures de Belgique, Rue de la Senne 20, B-1000 Brussel, T: (02)5111440.

BOLIVIA
Conferencia Nacional de Religiosos de Bolivia (CONFER), Arzobispado, Casilla 283, La Paz, T: 41920.

BRAZIL
Conferência dos Religiosos do Brasil (CRB), Rua Alcindo Guanabara 24/4, 20.000 Rio de Janeiro, RJ, T: (021)224-3004.

BRITAIN (UK OF GB & NI)
Council of Major Religious Superiors of England and Wales (CMRS), 114 Mount St, London W1Y 6AH.
Council of Major Superiors of Scotland, St. David's, Glasgow.

BURKINA FASO
Association des Supérieurs Majeurs des Instituts Masculin en Haute-Volta, BP 630, Ouagadougou.
Union des Supérieures Majeures en Haute-Volta (USMHV), BP 630, Ouagadougou.

BURUNDI
Conférence des Supérieurs Majeurs du Burundi et du Rwanda (COSUMA), BP 825, Bujumbura.
Union des Supérieurs Majeures, BP 1390, Bujumbura.

CAMEROON
Conférence des Supérieurs Majeurs du Cameroon, BP 185, Yaoundé.
Union des Supérieures Majeures et Déléguées du Cameroun (USMDC), BP 185, Yaoundé.

CANADA
Canadian Religious Conference, 324-est Av Laurier, Ottawa K1N 6P6.
Fédération des Frères Enseignants du Canada, Cap Rouge, Québec.

CHILE
Conferencia de Superiores Mayores Religiosos de Chile (CONFERRE), Erasmo Escala 822, of 302, Casilla 9501, Santiago, T: 87832.

CHINA
Association of Major Religious Superiors of Men in Hong Kong, c/o Ricci Hall, 93 Polnfulam Rd, Hong Kong.
Association of Major Religious Superiors of Women in Hong Kong, c/o Maryknoll Convent, Boundary St, Kowloon Tong, Hong Kong.

COLOMBIA
Confederación Latino Americana de Religiosos (CLAR), Calle 78 No 12-16, Apto 101, Apdo Aéreo 90710, Bogotá 2. DE, T: 550504.
Conferencia Costarricense de Religiosos (CONCOR), Apdo 6377, San José.
Conferencia de Religiosas de Costa Rica (CONFEREC), Apdo 2819, San José.
Conferencia de Superiores Mayores, Calle 71A No. 11-20, Apdo Aéreo 52332, Chapinero, Bogotá 2, T: 498674.

CONGO-ZAIRE
Assemblée des Supérieurs Majeurs (ASUMA), BP 180, Kinshasa 1.
Union des Supérieures Majeures du Zaïre (USUMA), BP 3276, Kinshasa-Gombe.

CROATIA
Higher Council of Religious, Palmoticeva 33, YU-41001 Zagreb, T: (041)441604.

CUBA
Confederación Cubana de Religiosas (CONCUR), Reina 463, La Habana 2, T: 622480.

DENMARK
Catholic Council of Religious Women, Jens Jessensvej 7, DK-2000 Kobenhavn F, T: (01)714872.
Union of Superiors of Women Religious of Denmark, Collegievej 2, Charlottenlund, Kobenhavn.

DOMINICAN REPUBLIC
Confederación Dominicana de Religiosos (CONDOR), Calle Ramón Santana 16, Apart 76, Santo Domingo, T: 682820.

ECUADOR
Conferencia Ecuatoriana de Religiosos (CER), Av América 1866, Apdo 3904, Quito, T: 522436.

EGYPT
Assemblée des Supérieurs Majeurs des Instituts, Sekket El Daher 29, Al Qahirah.
Union des Supérieures Majeures, 194 Rue Ramsés Ghamra, Al Qahirah.

EL SALVADOR
Confederación de Religiosos de El Salvador (CONFRES), Apdo 06971, San Salvador.
Secretariado para Religiosos de Centroamérica y Panamá (SERCAP), 1a C Poniente 1148, Apdo 1095, San Salvador, T: 221070.

ETHIOPIA
Conference of Religious Superiors of North Ethiopia, Strada 317, Campo Polo, Asmera.
Conference of Religious Superiors of Southern Ethiopia, P.O. Box 30220, Addis Abeba.

FRANCE
Religieuses dans les Professions de Santé (REPSE), 106 Rue du Bac, F-75007 Paris.
Union des Frères Enseignants (UFE), 277 Rue St Jacques, F-75005 Paris.
Union des Religieuses Educatrices Paroissiales (UREP), 106 Rue Jean-Bart, F-75006 Paris.
Union des Religiouses Enseignantes (URE), 10 Rue Jean-Bart, F-75006 Paris.
Union des Supérieures Majeures de France (USMF), 10 Rue Jean-Bart, F-75006 Paris, T: (01)548-1832/3.
Union des Supérieurs Majeurs de France, 95 Rue de Sèvres, F-75006 Paris, T: 222-7784.

GERMANY
Arbeitskreis Kirchlicher Brüderschaften, An der Thomaskirche, D-4 Düsseldorf-Nord.
Frankfurter Gespräche, Arbeitskreis Verschiedener Kreise und Brüderschaften, Geleitstr 104, D-605 Offenbach (Main).
Vereinigung Deutscher Ordensoberen (VDO), Kielstr 35, D-5000 Köln 80.
Vereinigung Höherer Ordensoberen der Brüderorden und Kongregationen Deutschlands (VHOB), Rütscherstr 182, D-5100 Aachen, T: 32033.
Vereinigung Höherer Ordensoberinnen Deutschlands (VHOD), Bonner Talweg 135, D-53 Bonn.

GHANA
Conference of Major Superiors of Religious Men of Ghana, POB 492, Sekondi.
Conference of Major Superiors of Religious Women, P.O. Box 306, Nsawam.

GREECE
Union des Religieux de Grèce (URG), 28 Rue Michel Voda, Athinai.

GUATEMALA
Conferencia de Religiosos y Religiosas de Guatemala (CONFREGUA), 4a Calle 5.52, Zona 1, Apdo 1698, T: 29816.

HAITI
Conférence Haïtienne des Religieux (CHR), Angle Rue Lamarre et Champ-de-Mars, Port-au-Prince.

HONDURAS
Conferencia de Institutos Religiosos de Honduras (CIRH), Calle 25 de Enero, Bo Morazón, Apdo 307, Tegucigalpa, T: 221765.

INDIA
Ceylon Conference of Major Religious Superiors, Brother's Subsection, St Andrew's House, 24 Palmgrove, Bangalore 7.
Conference of Religious India, 13 Ashiana Apartments, Pitampura, Delhi 110034.
Conference of Religious, Sophia College, Bulabhai Desai Road, Cumballa Hill, Bombay, Maharashtra 400026.
National Assembly of Religious Brothers, India (NARBI), 128/1 Ulsoor Road, Bangalore, Karnataka 560042.

INDONESIA
Association of Sisters of All Indoneisa, Jalan Supratman 1, Bandung.
National Association of Brothers Institutes, Jalan Dr Sutomo 4, Semarang.
National Association of Clerical Institutes, Kolese Kanisius, Jalan Menteng Raya 64, Jakarta-Pusat.

IRELAND
Conference of Major Religious Superiours, Milltown Park, Dublin 6 (Men and women.

ISRAEL
Union des Religieuses d'Israël (URI), Pensionnat St-Joseph, Rehov Yafo 25, Yafo.
Union des Superieures Religieuses de Terre Sainte (USRTS), P.O. Box 20531, 91204 Jérusalem; Notre Dame Center of Jerusalem, 91294 Jérusalem, T: 02-28-85-54, F: 02-28-85-55.

ITALY
Conferenza Italiana dei Superiori Maggiori (CISM), Via degli Scipioni 256/B, I-00192 Roma, T: (06)314254.
Conferenza Mondiale degli Istituti Secolari (CMIS), Via Florida 20, I-00186 Roma, T: (06)657489.
Federazione Nazionale delle Congregazioni Mariane (CCMM), Via Serchio 7, I-00198 Roma, T: 864578.
Holy Ghost Fathers (Congregation of the Holy Spirit), Clivo di Cinna 195, I-00136 Roma, T: 06-348247.
Unione dei Superiori Generali (USG), Via dei Penitenzieri 19, I-00193 Roma, T: (06)6568229.
Unione Internazionale delle Superiore Generali (UISG), Piazza Ponte San Angelo 28, I-00186 Roma, T: (06)655921.
Unione Superiore Maggiori d'Italia (USMI), Via Zanardelli 32, I-00186, Roma.
World Federation of Christian Life Communities, Borgo Santo Spirito 8, CP 9048, I-00198 Roma, T: 6568079.

JAMAICA
Conference of Major Superiors of the Antilles, Mount Alvernia, PO Box 124, Montego Bay.

JAPAN
Association of Religious Congregations of Sisters in Japan, 1966-chome, Gotanda Shinagawa-ku, Tokyo.
National Conference of Major Superiors of Women Religious, 10-1 Rokuban-cho, Chiyoda-ku, Tokyo 102.
Superiors Conference of Japan, National Catholic Committee of Japan, 10-1 Rokuban-cho, Chiyoda-ku, Tokyo 102, T: (03)2623691.

KENYA
Association of Sisterhoods of Kenya (AOSK), P.O. Box 48062, Nairobi.
Religious Superiors' Association of Kenya (RSAK), PO Box 1913, Kisumu.

LEBANON
Assemblée des Supérieures Majeures, BP 3744, Bayrut.
Assemblée des Supérieurs Majeurs, Couvent St-Roch, Decouané près de Bayrut.
Union Interrituelle des Religieuses Enseignantes, BP 472, Bayrut.

LESOTHO
Lesotho Conference of Major Religious Superiors, P.O. Box MH 134, Mohale's Hoek.

LUXEMBOURG
Union des Instituts Religieux Féminins, 50 Av Gaston Diderich, BP 1181, Luxembourg.

MADAGASCAR
Union des Supérieures Majeures Féminines de Madagascar, ND du Cénacle, Rue Albert Picquié 33, Tananarive.
Union des Supérieurs Majeurs de Madagascar (USMM), BP 34, Maintirano.

MALAWI
Association of Men Religious Institutes in Malawi (AMRIM), P.O. Box 133, Lilongwe.
Association of Religious Institutes of Malawi (ARIMA), P.O. Box 477, Lilongwe.

MALAYSIA
Association of Major Superiors of Women, c/o Convent of the Infant Jesus, Bukit Nanas, Kuala Lumpur.
Superiors' Conference of Malaysia and Singapore, Montfort Boys Town, PO Box 211, Batutiga, Subang Salangor.

MALI
Union des Supérieures Majeures des Congrégations Autochtones d'Afrique de l'Ouest Francophone, BP 298, Bamako.

MALTA
Consilium Nationale Religiosorum Melitensium, St. Benild School, Church St, Sliema.
Malta Sisters Conference (KSSM), Catholic Institute, Floriana.

MARTINIQUE
Conseil des Religieuses, Cité Godissard Z5 C16, 97-2 Fort-de-France, T: 2070.

MAURITIUS
Union des Supérieures Majeures, Couvent de Marie Réparatrice, Route Royale 232, Rose-Hill, T: 43723.

MEXICO
Conferencia de Institutos Religiosos de México (CIRM), Av Amores 13-18, Apdo Postal 44-051 (ZP 12), México 12, DF, T: 5752700.
Federación de Religiosas Enfermeras Mexicanas (FREM), Av Ejército Nacional 613, México 17, DF.

MOROCCO
Conseil des Religieuses, c/o Archevêché, BP 258, Rabat.

MOZAMBIQUE
Federação dos Institutos Religiosos Maculinos de Moçambique, Paroquia NS de Fátima, CP 1233, Beira.
Federação Nacional dos Institutos Religiosos Femininos, Casa de Maria Imaculada, CP 39, Matola, Maputo (Lourenço Marques).

MYANMAR
Conference of Religious Sisters of Burma (CRSB), 133 Kyaikasan Rd, Tamwe, Rangoon.

NETHERLANDS
Association Council for Monks, Hollende Wagenweg 20, Werkhoven, T: (03437)330.
Association of Dutch Congregations of Brothers, Zwanenveld 25-40, Nijmegen, T: (08800)32918.
Association of Dutch Religious Priests, Postbus 3170, 5003 DD Tilburg.
Association of Dutch Sisters, Carmelweg 1, Nijmegen, T: (08800)32642.
Central Missionary Council for Brothers and Sisters, van Alkemadelaan 1, Den Haag, T: (070)244594.
Union des Congrégations des Religieuses Infirmières (St. Canisiusbond), Curaçaoweg 1, Nijmegen.

NEW ZEALAND
Conference of Major Superiors of Women Religious, St. Mary's Convent, P.O. Box 7025, Auckland 1.
New Zealand Conference of Major Superiors of Men, 30 Bassett Rd, Remuera, Auckland 5.

NICARAGUA
Conferencia Nacional Nicarajüense de Institutos Religiosos (CONFER), Apdo 3796, Managua, T: 25168.

NIGER
Comité des Religieuses, c/o Evêché, BP 208, Niamey.

NIGERIA
Conference of Major Women Religious Superiors, PO Box 5245, Ibadan.
Nigerian National Conference of Major Superiors, 6 Awolowo Av, PO Box 1784, Ibadan.

PAKISTAN
Association of Major Religious Superiors of Men in Pakistan, c/o St. Patrick's Cathedral, Karachi 3, Sind.
Association of Major Religious Superiors of Women, St. Joseph's Convent, PO Box 7260, Karachi.

PALESTINE
Union des Religeuses de Jordanie (URJ), P.O. Box 11, Bethlehem.

PANAMA
Federación de Religiosos y Religiosas de Panamá (FEDEPAR), Parroquia del Carmen-Pasadena, Apdo 4980, Panamá 5, T: 230360, 238204.

PAPUA NEW GUINEA
Association of Religious Superiors, Catholic Mission, PO Alexishafen, Madang.
Conference of Religious Brothers, P.O. Box 760, Goroka, EHD.

National Conference of Major Women Superiors, P.O. Box 1321, Boroko.

PARAGUAY
Federación de Religiosos del Paraguay (FERELPAR), Calle Alberdi 782, CC 1847, Asunción, T: 41122.

PERU
Conferencia Peruana de Religiosos (CPR), Jirón Cuzco 376, Apdo Postal 5016, Lima 100, T: 273485.

PHILIPPINES
Association of Major Religious Superiors of Men in the Philippines (AMRSMP), 214 N. Domingo St, PO Box 2156, Quezon City, Manila.
Association of Major Religious Superiors of Women in the Philippines (AMRSWP), PO Box 3553, Manila.

POLAND
Conference of Major Superiors of Religious Women of Poland, ul Dziekania 1, 00-279 Warszawa 40.

PORTUGAL
Conferência Nacional dos Institutos Religiosos (CNIR), Praça Prof. Santos Andrea 18, 1 Dto, Lisboa 4, T: 707987.
Federação Nacional dos Institutos Religiosos Femininos (FNIRF), Praça Prof. Santos Andrea 18, 1 Dto, Lisboa 4.

PUERTO RICO
Conferencia de Religiosas de Puerto Rico (CORPORI), Apdo 2204 or 4201, San Juan, PR 00903, T: 7257053, 7230476.
Conferencia de Religiosos de Puerto Rico (COR de Puerto Rico), Avda. Ponce de León 265, Aparada 5, San Juan, PR 00906, T: 7224289.

RWANDA
Conférence des Supérieurs Majeurs du Burundi et du Rwanda (COSUMA), BP 69, Kigali.
Union des Supérieures Majeures du Rwanda, BP 130, Butare.

SENEGAL
Conférence des Supérieures Majeures, BP 5082, Dakar.
Conférence des Supérieurs Majeurs des Instituts Masculins du Sénégal, Monastère Bénédictin, Keur-Moussa.

SINGAPORE
Superiors' Conference of Malaysia and Singapore, 300 Thomson Rd, Singapore 11.

SOUTH AFRICA
Association of Religious Women, Cathedral Place, PO Box 32, Johannesburg 2000.
Association of Teaching Brothers, Corner 3 Av & 3 Rd, Victory Park, Johannesburg 2001.
Conference of Clerical Major Superiors in Southern Africa, St. John Vianney Seminary, 191 Main St, Waterkloof, Pretoria.

SOUTH KOREA
Association of Major Superiors of Religious Women in Korea, CPO Box 16, Soul, T: 271161/3.
Conference of Major Superiors of Men in Korea, CPO Box 16, Soul, T: 271161/3.
Conference of Major Superiors of Men Religious, 17, Chong-dong, Chung-gu, Seoul-shi, T: (02) 776-3189.

SPAIN
Conferencia Española de Religiosos (CONFER), Calle Núñez de Balboa 115 bis, Madrid 6, T: 2624612.
Federación Española de Religiosos de Enseñanza (FERE), Conde de Peñalver 45, Madrid 6.
Federación Española de Religiosas Sanitarias (FERS), Martínez Campos 18, Madrid 10.

SRI LANKA
Conference of Major Religious Superiors of Sri Lanka, 130 de la Salle St, Colombo 15.

SWITZERLAND
Union des Supérieures Majeures de Suisse Romande (USMSR), Av de la Tour, CH-1950 Sion, T: (027)21448.
Vereinigung Christikatholischer Schwestern und Fürsorgerinnen, Leiterin, Taubblindenheim, Sudstr 10, CH-8008 Zürich.
Vereinigung der Höhern Ordensobern der Schweiz, Grand'rue 34, CP 20, CH-1702 Fribourg.
Vereinigung Höherer Oberinnen Ordensgemeinschaften der Deutschsprachigen Schweiz, CH-6440 Ingenbohl.

TAIWAN
Association of Major Superiours of Religious Men, 25 Mingsheng Rd, Taipei.
Association of Major Superiours of Religious Women, Regina Mundi Convent, 121 Hsinsheng St, RD Section 1, Taipei.

TANZANIA
Association of Religious Superiors in Tanzania, PO Box 5124, Dar es Salaam.
Association of Women Religious Superiors of Tanzania, PO Box 2133, Dar es Salaam.

THAILAND
Association of Major Religious Superiors of Men in Thailand, 123/19 Ruam Rudi Lane, Wireless Rd, Bangkok 5.
Association of Major Religious Superiors of Women in Thailand, c/o St Joseph's Convent, 7 Convent Rd, Bangkok 5.

TUNISIA
Union des Congrégations (Féminines) en Tunisie (UDTC), c/o Maison Provinciale des Soeurs Blanches, 9 Rue Raspail, Tunis.

TURKEY
Union des Religieux et des Religieuses de Turquie (URT), Eglise St Louis, PK 280, Beyoglu.

UGANDA
Association of Religious Women of Uganda, PO Box 1587, Kampala, T: 64251, 46251.
Conference of Major Superiors of Men's Institutes in Uganda (COMSIU), PO Box 2912, Kampala.

UNITED STATES OF AMERICA (USA)
Association of Contemplative Sisters, Esopus, NY 12429.
Conference of Major Superiors of Men's Institutes (CMSM), 1302 18th St, NW, Suite 601, Washington, DC 20036, T: (202)785-1343.
Conference of Major Superiors of Women's Institutes, 1302 18th St, NW, Suite 601, Washington, DC 20036.
Leadership Conference of Women Religious in the USA (LCWR), 1325 Massachusetts Av, NW, Washington, DC 20005.
National Association of Religious Brothers, 11601 Georgia Av, Wheaton, MD 20902.
National Association of Women Religious (NAWR), 720 North Rush St, Chicago, IL 60611.
National Black Sisters' Conference (NBSC), 3508 Fifth Ave., Pittsburgh, PA 15213.
National Coalition of American Nuns (NCAN), 1307 South Wabash Av, Chicago, IL 60605.
National Sister Formation Conference (NSFC), 1325 Massachusetts Av, NW, Washington, DC 20005.
National Sisters Vocation Conference (NSVC), 1307 South Wabash Av, Chicago, Il 60605.
Sisters Uniting, 700 North Seventh St Memphis, TN 38107.

URUGUAY
Federación de Religiosos del Uruguay (FRU), Canelones, 1164 Montevideo, T: 44157.

VENEZUELA
Conferencia Venezolana de Religiosos (CONVER), Torre a Madrices, Apdo 4582, Caracas 101, T: 814437.
Federación de Religiosas de Venezuela (FERVE), Torre a Madrices, Apdo 4582, Caracas 101.

VIET NAM
Comité Permanent des Religieux du Vietnam, 38 Ky-Dông, Saigon.
Union des Supérieures Majeures, 4 Cu'o'ng-Dê, Saigon, T: 20455.
Union des Supérieurs Majeurs, 4 Cuong-De, Ho Chi Minh Ville.

ZAMBIA
Association of Religious Superiors in Zambia, P.O. Box 2494, Lusaka.
Association of Sisterhoods of Zambia, P.O. Box 162, Kitwe.

ZIMBABWE
Conference of Major Religious Superiors of Zimbabwe, 1 Sawley Close, Marlborough, Salisbury.
Conference of Major Superiors of Women Religious of Zimbabwe, PB 804, Marandellas.

62
Religious houses & monasteries

A scant selection of Catholic, Orthodox, Anglican, Protestant and other monasteries, abbeys, priories, convents, mother houses of religious orders or congregations; religious communities, organized communities or houses under formal religious rule, practice, or order.

BRITAIN (UK OF GB & NI)
Ampleforth Abbey, York YO6 4EN, T: +01439 766000, F: +01439 788770, O: Web: www.ampleforth.org.uk.
Douai Abbey, Upper Woolhampton, Reading, Berks, RG7 5TQ, T: 188 971 5300, F: 118 971 5203, O: E-mail: douaiabby@aol.com, Web: www.members.aol.com/douaiweb.

FRANCE
Taizé, 71250, O: E-mail: taize@cpe.ipl.fr, Web: www.almac.co.uk/taize/taize.html.

GERMANY
Benediktinerabtei Koenigmünster, Postfach 1161, D-59851, Meschede, O: Web: members.aol.com/monasteriu.
Benediktinerinnenabtei St. Hildegard, Postfach 1320, D-65378 Ruedesheim am Rhein, T: 49-6722-499-0, F: +49-6722-499-185, O: Web: www.uni-mainz.d/~horst/hildegard/eibingen/abtei.html.

GHANA
Kristo Buase Abbey, P.O.Box 291, Techiman Brong Ahafo, O: Web: www.ukonline.co.uk/david.w34/davidw/_pnash14.html.

GUADELOUPE
Sisters of the Third Order of St. Dominic, (of Saint-Catherine of Sienne of Albi), Basse-Terre, T: 590-98-70-28.

HUNGARY
Pannonholma, H-9090 Pannonhalma, Var 1, T: (36) (96) 470-022, F: (36) (96) 470-0111, O: Web: www.osb.hu/english.

IRELAND
Glenstal Abbey, Murroe, Co. Limerick, T: 353-61386103, F: +353-61-386328, O: E-mail: Glenstal@iol.ie, www.iol.ie/~glenstal.

ITALY
Sacrum Archicoenobium S.P.N. Benedicti, Arcibadia I-03043 Montecassino (FR), O: Web: www.officine.it/montecassion/main_e.htm.

SOUTH AFRICA
Anglican Diocese of Lesotho, PO Box 43, Leribe 300, T: (09266) 40-0249.
Anglican Diocese of Namibia, PO Box 12183, Jacobs, 4026, T: (031) 47-4279.

63
Research centers

Centers, institutes, and institutions undertaking original research related to Christianity and religions — religious, socio-religious, anthropological, historical, biblical, theological, communications, information, missiological, missiographical, missiometrical, futurological; ecumenical research centers and institutes at university level; experimental institutes, think tanks; documentation centers and services, resource centers, research or historical archives, public opinion polls, survey organizations, market research, radio/TV audience research centers or functions. Note that other research centers that specialize in specific topics, e.g. LITURGY AND WORSHIP, BROADCASTING, or ECOLOGY, are listed under those topics.

ALGERIA
Centre Chrétien d'Etudes Maghrébines, 36 Chemin Cheikh Bachir Brahimi (Beaurepaire), El-Biar, El Djezair.
Centre d'Etudes Berbères (CEB), 20 Rue des Fusillés, El Djezair.
Centre d'Etudes Interdiocésaïn, 5 Chemin des Glycines, El Djezair.
Centre de Langues et de Pastorale d'El Biar, El Djezair.
Centre Pédagogique Arabe, 70 Av Souidàni Boudjemaa, El Djezair.

ANGOLA
Centre for the Study of Theology and Culture, P.O. Box 1659, Luanda; c/o Angolan Council of Churches, Luanda.

ARGENTINA
Centro de Estudios Cristianos (CEC), Paraná 489, piso 2, Of 9, Buenos Aires, T: 494996.
Centro de Investigación y Acción Social (CIAS), O'Higgins 1331 (also Palpa 2440), Buenos Aires 26.
Centro de Investigación y Estudio (CIE), Centro Eclesiástico de Documentación y Estadística (CEDE), Av La Plata 50, Buenos Aires.
Centro de Investigaciones Sociales, Lavalle 106, 5 piso, Buenos Aires.
Centro de Investigaciones Sociales y Religiosas, 1054 Rodriguez Pena, Buenos Aires, T: 418393.
Centro de Investigaciones y Estudio de Servicio Social, Sarandi 65, Buenos Aires.
Instituto de Ciencias Sagradas, Colegio Champagnat, Montevideo 1050, Buenos Aires.
Instituto de Teologia, Junta Catequistica Central, La Plata 15-51 y 53, Buenos Aires, T: 26672.
Secretaria Tecnica del Arzobispado de Santa Fe, Gral López 2720, Santa Fe.

AUSTRALIA
Australian Frontier, 10 Floor, Room 18, 422 Collins St, Melbourne, Victoria 3000.
Division of Studies and Communication, Australian Council of Churches, 511 Kent St, Sydney, NSW 2000.
Worldview Research Tool-Kit, O: Web: www.iinet.net.au/~createit/ResearchLinks.html.

AUSTRIA
Erstes Philosophisches Institut der Universität, Liebiggasse 5, Wien 1.
Institut für Dogmengeschichte und Ökumenische Theologie, Universität Graz, Universitätsplatz 3, A-8010 Graz, T: (03122)31581/338.
Institut für Kirchliche Sozialforschung (IKS), Grillparzerstr 5, A-1010 Wien, T: 434284.
Institut für Kirchliche Zeitgeschichte (IKZ), Mönchsberg 2a, A-5020 Salzburg.
Institut für Ökumenische Theologie, Universität Salzburg, Sigmund-Haffnergasse 20, A-5020 Salzburg, T: (06222)86111247.
Katholische Sozialakademie, Schottenring 35, A-1010 Wien.
Philosophisches Institut, Universität Salzburg, St-Peter-Bezirk 8/9, I Stock, Z20, A-5020 Salzburg, T: (06222)84285.
Wiener Katholische Akademie, Freyung 6, 1 Stiege, A-1010 Wien, T: 6374927.
Ökumensiches Institut der Universität Graz, A-8010 Graz.

BANGLADESH
Henry Martin Institute of Islamic Studies, Baptist Mission House, Sadarghat, Dacca 1.

BARBADOS
Department of Documentation and Research, Christian Action for Development in the Caribbean (CADEC), P.O. Box 616, Bridgetown.

BELGIUM
Académie Internationale des Sciences Religieuses, Av de Tervuren 221, B-1150 Brussel, T: (02)733-2311.
Bureau de Documentation Pastorale, Chaussée de Wavre 216, B-1040 Brussel.
Centre Chrétien Flamand d'Etude et de Documentation, St-Pietersnieunstraat 79, B-9000 Gent.
Centre d'Etudes des Problèms du Monde Musulman, Université de Bruxelles, Brussel.
Centre d'Etudes des Religions, Université Libre de Bruxelles, Av Franklin Roosevelt 50, Brussel.
Centre de Recherches Socio-Religieuses, Université Catholique de Louvain, Place Montesquieu, 1-Bte 21, B 1348-Ottignies-Louvain-la-Neuve, T: 010-43-42-51.
Centre de Traitement Electronique des Documents (CETEDOC), Université Catholique de Louvain, Tiensevest 156, B-3000 Leuven, T: (016)235375.
Centre des Techniques de diffusion et Relations Publiques (CETEDI), Université Catholique de Louvain, Van Evenstraat 2a, B-3000 Leuven, T: (016)28751.
Centre for Socio-Religious Research, de Beriotstraat 34, B-3000 Leuven, T: (016)225244.
Centre for Sociological Research, Afdeling Godsdienstsociologie, Van Evenstraat 2a, B-3000 Leuven, T: (016)25601.
Centre International d'Etudes de la Formation Religieuse (Lumen Vitae), Rue Washington 186, B-1050 Brussel, T: (02)343-5023.
CMN Centre de Documentation, Blvd du Souverain 199, B-1160 Brussel.
Institut des Hautes Etudes des Communiciations Sociales (IHECS), Chaussée de Tournai 26b, B-7721 Ramegnies-Chin.
Institut Supérieur de Sciences Religieuses, Redingenstraat 16, B-3000 Leuven; B-1348 Louvain-la-Neuve, T: (016)224915.
International Association Pro Mundi Vita, rue de las Schience 7, B-1040 Brussels.
International Centre for Studies in Religious Education, Rue Washington 186, B-1050 Brussels, T: 435023.
Pro Mundi Vita, Rue de la Limite 6, Brussel 3, T: (02)25136880.
Prospective (Centre Internationale de Recherche et de Communication pour l'Eglise à Venir), Av Armand Huysmans 77, B-1050 Brussel; Rue E Cattoir 16, B-1050 Brussel, T: (02)648-2766.

BELIZE
Society for the Promotion of Education and Research (SPEAR), P.O. Box 1766, Belize City; 126 North Front St., Belize City, T: 501-2-31668, F: 501-2-32367, O: Also tel: 45641.

BOLIVIA
Centro de Investigación Socio-Religiosa, Yanacacha 545, Casilla 3077, La Paz.
Centro de Investigación y Acción Social (CIAS), Av Buenos Aires 588, Casilla 283, La Paz.
Centro de Investigación y Promoción del Campesinado (CIPCA), Illampu 733, Casilla 5458, La Paz, T: 21176.
Iglesia y Sociedad en America Latina (ISAL), c/o Icthus, Casilla 356, La Paz.
Instituto Boliviano de Estudio y Acción Social, Depto de Estudios Socio-Religiosos, Casilla 3277, La Paz, T: 25667.
Instituto de Investigación Cultural para Educación Popular (INDICEP), Calle Potsi 421, Casilla 525, Oruro, T: 52110.
Instituto Superior de Estudios Teológicos (ISET), Av Peru 3901, Casilla 2118, Cochabamba.

BRAZIL
Centre for Advanced Studies in Evangelism (CASE), CP 30.548, 01000 São Paulo, SP.
Centro Brasileiro de Informação Missionária (CEBIMI), Rua Dr Gradim 365 fundos, 24400 São Goncalo, RJ.
Centro de Estatística Religiosa e Investigações Sociais (CERIS), Rua Dr Julio Ottoni 571, Santa Tereza, 20,000 Rio de Janeiro, ZC 45, GB, T: (245)1464.
Centro de Estudos Bíblicos e Ecumênicos, Rua Almirante Alexandrino 3286, Sta Tereza, Rio de Janeiro, GB, T: (245)2780.
Centro Latinoamericano de Parapsicologia (CLAP), Via Anhanguera Km 26, CP 11587, São Paulo, SP.
Instituto Brasiliero de Desenvolvimento (IBRADES), Rua Bambina 115, Botafogo, 20 000 Rio de Janeiro, ZC 02, GB, T: (226)8137, 5866, 6335.
Instituto de Teologia do Recife (ITER), Faculdade de Filosofia do Recife, Conde da Boa Vista s/n, Recife, PE.
Instituto Evangélico de Pesquisas, Rua Rêgo Freitas 530, Apto F 13, São Paulo, SP.
Missionary Information Bureau, C.P. 1498, 01051 São Paulo, S.P., T: 011-223-5097, 223-0292.
Operação Anchieta, Av Alberto Bins 1026, 90 000 Porto Alegre, RS.
Sepal do Brasil, Rua Princesa Isabel 109, 2 Andar, CP 30.548, São Paulo, SP, T: (61)9084.
Serviço de Cooperaçõ Apostólica Internacional (SCAI), CP 133, 20 000 Rio de Janeiro, GB.
Voluntários Internacionais e Brasileiros para a Amazôniz, Rua Dr Assis 834, Arsenal, 66 000 Belém, Pará.

BRITAIN (UK OF GB & NI)
British Church Growth Association, St. Mark's Chambers, Kennington Park Road, London SE11 4PW, T: 01-793-0264.
Catholic Institute for International Relations (CIIR), 41 Holland Park, London W11, T: (01)727-3195.
Catholic Missionary Education Centre, Holcombe

House, The Ridgeway, London NW7 4HY, T: 0181-906 1642, F: 0121-329 2058.

Centre for New Religious Movements, Selly Oak Colleges, Birmingham B29 6LQ.

Christian Studies Unit, 94 Kennington Av, Bishopston, Bristol 7.

Christian Study Centre, St. Margaret Pattens Church, Eastcheap, London EC3, T: (01)623-6630.

Gallup, 211 Regent St, London W1A 3AU, T: (01)734-3671.

Grubb Institute of Behavioural Studies, 1 Whitehall Place, London SW1 2HD, T: (01)930-6364.

Institute for Strategic Studies, 18 Adam St, London WC2.

Keston College/Keston Research, 33a Canal Street, Oxford OX2 6BQ, T: 44-0865-311022, F: 44-0865-311280.

Koinonia Information Service, 10 Parkfield Rd., Worthing, Sussex BN13 1EL, T: (0903) 208169.

Library for Charismatic Studies, Fountain Trust, Central Hall, Durnsford Rd, London SW19 8ED, T: (01)947-4314.

Liverpool Institute of Social-Religious Studies, Christ's College, Woolton Rd, Liverpool L16 8DN, T: Childwall 3121.

Oxford Institute of Methodist Theological Studies, 2 College House, Richmond College, Surrey.

Pastoral Research Centre (PRC), 16 Osborne Gardens, Malone, Belfast 9, NI, T: 667127.

Project for the Study of New Religious Movements (PRONERM), Department of Religious Studies, King's College, Aberdeen AB9 2UB.

Religious Experience Research Unit (RERU), Manchester College, Holywell St/Mansfield Rd, Oxford.

Research Department, Worldwide Evangelization Crusade, Bulstrode, Gerrards Cross, Bucks, T: 84631.

Rutherford House, 17 Claremont Park, GB-Edinburgh EH6 7PJ, T: 44-31-669-5227.

Southwark Diocesan Department of Religious Sociology, 94 Lambeth Rd, London SE1.

SSRC Data Bank, University of Essex, Wivenhoe Park, Colchester, Essex.

Statistical Unit, Church House, Dean's Yard, Westminster, London SW1, T: (01)222-9011.

University Centre for the Study of Christianity in the Non-Western World, New College, Mound Place, Edinburgh EH1 2LU, T: 031-225-8400, O: Telex: 727442 (UNIVED G).

Urban Theology Unit (UTU), 210 Abbeyfield Rd, Sheffield S4 7AZ.

WEC International Research Office, Bulstrode, Oxford Road, Gerrards Cross, Bucks SL9 8SZ, T: 0753-884631.

BULGARIA

Institute of Christian Culture, Sophia University, Sofia.

BURKINA FASO

Centre d'Etudes Economiques et Sociales d'Afrique Occidentale (CESAO), BP 305, Bobo-Dioulasso, T: 9551.

Centre de Recherche et d'Action Sociale (CERAS), BP 90, Ouagadougou, T: 2674.

BURUNDI

Centre de Coopération au Développement et de Recherches Sociologiques, BP 1390, Bujumbura, T: 3263.

Centre de Recherches et d'Animation Sociale (CERAS), BP Bujumbura, T: 3236.

Centre de Recherches Socio-Religieuses (CERES), BP 1390, Bujumbura.

CANADA

Biblical Museum of Canada at Regent College, U.B.C., Collingwood PO Box 27090, Vancouver, BC V5R 6A8, T: 604-432-6122, F: 604-432-1286.

Canadian Church Growth Centre, 4400-4th Av, Regina S4T 0H8, T: (306)545-1515.

Centre de Recherches en Sociologie Religieuse (CRSR), Grand Séminaire, Université Laval, Cité Universitaire, Québec G1K 7P4, T: 656-3207.

Centre Diocésain de Recherches Pastorales, 725 Rue Brassard, CP 1268, Nicolet, PQ.

Centre for Ecumenical Studies, St. Michael's College, University of Toronto, Toronto, Ontario.

Centre for Mennonite Brethren Studies in Canada, 1-169 Riverton Ave., Winnipeg, MB R2L 2E5, T: 204-669-6575.

Centre for the Study of Institutions and Theology, 215 Cottingham St, Toronto 7, Ontario.

Creation Science Association, of Ontario, P.O. Box 821, Station A, Scarborough, ON M1K 5C8, T: 519-822-5601, F: 519-822-0800.

Expo - Bible, 491 Dorion St., Granby, QC J2G 1A4, T: 514-375-1140.

Institute for Behavioural Research, York University, 4700 Keele St, Downsview 463, Ontario.

Institute of Christian Studies, Regent College, Vancouver, BC.

Institute of Islamic Studies, McGill University, 1345 Redpath Crescent, Montréal, Québec; 805 West Sherbrooke, Montréal 25, T: VI4-6311.

Institute of Mediaeval Studies, 59 Queen's Park Crescent, Toronto, Ontario.

Institute of Mission Studies, 233 Rue Main, Ottawa, Ontario K1S 1C4, T: (613)235-1421 local 37.

Lutheran Historical Institute, 7100 Ada Blvd., Edmonton, AB T5B 4E4, T: 403-474-8156, F: 403-477-9829.

MARC Canada, 6630 Turner Valley Rd., Mississauga, ON L5N 2S4, T: 905-821-3030.

McMaster Divinity College, Hamilton, Ontario L8S 4K1.

Office National des Techniques de Diffusion, 4635 de Lorimier, Montréal 34, Québec.

Outreach Canada, #16 - 12240 Horseshoe Way, Richmond, BC V7A 4X9, T: 604-272-0732, F: 604-272-2744, O: E-mail: outreach@universe.com.

Parousia Christian Info. Services, 453A Deslauriers, Montréal, QC H4N 1W2, T: 514-856-3032.

Research Center in Religious History in Canada, St. Paul Univ., 223 Main St., Ottawa, ON K1S 1C4, T: 613-236-1393.

Research Committee of the Sociology of Religion, International Sociological Association, 60 Oak Av, Dundas, Ontario.

School of Communication, St. Paul University, 223 Main St, Ottawa 1, Ontario.

Sermons from Science, P.O. Box 602, Station B, Montréal 2, Québec.

Toronto Institute of Linguistics, 16 Spadina Rd, Toronto, Ontario M5R 2S8, T: (416)924-7167.

Vancouver School of Theology Chaimers' Institute, 6000 Iona Dr., Vancouver, BC V6T 1L4, T: 604-228-9031, F: 604-228-0189.

CHILE

Centro de Investigación y Acción Social (CIAS), Centro Bellarmino, Casilla 10445, Santiago, T: 68442.

CIDE, Almirante Barroso 22, Santiago.

DEC, Sección Planeamiento, Erasmo Escala 1822, Oficina 415, Casilla 13383, Santiago.

Oficina de Sociologia Religiosa, Cienfuegos 47, Clas 197, Santiago, T: 713126.

CHINA

Centre for the Study of Religion, Nanjing University, Nanjing.

Chinese Church Research Center, P.O. Box 312, Shatin Central P.O., N.T., Hong Kong, T: 0-6044456, O: Cable: 'CCRCENTER' H.K.

Christian Study Center on Chinese Religion & Culture, Tao Fong Shan, PO Box 33, Shatin, NT, Hong Kong, T: 061490.

Cooperative Services, 908 Star House, 3 Salisbury Road, Kowloon, Hong Kong.

FEBC Communication Research Centre, 423-427 J Hotung House, Hankow Rd, Box 6789, Kowloon, Hong Kong.

Holy Spirit Study Centre, 6 Welfare Rd., Aberdeen, Hong Kong, T: 5-530141/2.

Hongkong Catholic Church Directory, Catholic Truth Society, 16 Caine Rd., Hong Kong.

COLOMBIA

Centro Antropológico de Misiones (ETHNIA), Carrera 10 No 9-64, Bogotá.

Centro de Investigación y Acción Social (CIAS), Carrera 5a No 11-43, Bogotá, T: 435581.

Escuelo de Ciencias de la Comunicación, Pontificia Universidad Bolivariana, Calle 48, No 27.05, Apdo 14-16, Medellín, Antioqiua.

Instituto Colombiano de Desarollo Social (ICODES), Calle 37 No 13A-09, Apdo Aéreo 11966, Bogotá, T: 435581.

Instituto de Doctrina y Estudios Sociales (IDES), Calle 26 No 27-48, 6 piso, Apdo Aéreo 12309, Bogotá, T: 328821, 328841.

CONGO-ZAIRE

Centre d'Etudes Bibliques et de Réflexion Chrétienne, Centre St Irenée, Dir, BP 144, Kikwit.

Centre d'Etudes de Sciences Humaines (CESH), Université Nationale du Zaire, Kinsagani.

Centre d'Etudes des Religions Africaines (CERA), Faculté de Théologie, Université Nationale du Zaire, BP 756, Kinshasa XI.

Centre d'Etudes Ethnologiques de Bandundu (CEEB), Collège St-Paul, Bandundu.

Centre d'Etudes Pastorales, BP 724, Limete-Kinshasa, T: 77418.

Centre de Communications Sociales, Université Nationale du Zaire, BP 832, Kinshasa XI.

Centre de Recherches Socio-Religieuses, c/o Conférence Episcopale, BP 3258, Kinshasa-Gombe, T: 5457 ext 40.

Institut Supérieur des Sciences Religieuses, Université Nationale du Zaire (ex-Lovanium), Campus de Kinshasa, BP 832, Kinshasa XI.

COSTA RICA

Institute of In-Depth Evangelism (INDEPTH), Secretariado, Apdo 1307, San José, T: 227188.

Instituto Misionológico de las Américas (IMDELA), Apdo 232-1011 Y Griega, San José, T: 233-7298.

Latin American Evangelical Center for Pastoral Studies, San José.

CUBA

Centro de Estudios Ecumenicos (CENDESEC), Seminario San Carlos y San Ambrosio, Av del Puerto Esquina a Chacón, Apdo 594, La Habana 1, T: 613735.

Study Centre, Apdo 4179, La Habana 4.

CZECH REPUBLIC

Ecumenical Section, VV kujbyseva 5, Dejvice, Praha 6, T: 320569.

DENMARK

Academy of Futures Research, Society for Futures Research, Skovfaldet 2S, DK-8200 Arhus N.

Church History Institute, Kobmagergade 44-46, DK-1150 Kobenhavn K.

Ecumenical Institute, Copenhagen University, Kobenhavn.

IDOC, Cathrinebjergvej 95, DK-8200 Arhus N.

Institut for Kirkehistorie, Kobmagergade 44-46, DK-1150 Kopenhagen K.

Institute of Church and Mission History, University of Copenhagen, Lille Kirkestraede 1, DK-10072 Kobenhavn K; Also: Kobmagergade 44-46, DK-1150 Kobenhavn K.

Institute of Ecumenical Theology and Missionary Science, Faculty of Theology, Arhus Universitet, DK-8000 Arhus C, T: (06)136711.

New Religious Movements in Western Societies Study Centre, Ecumenical Centre, Arhus Universitet, DK-8000 Arhus C.

DOMINICAN REPUBLIC

Centre for Ecumenical Planning and Action (CEPAE), Benigno F Rojas 67 (Altos), Santo Domingo.

Centro de Investigación y Acción Social (CIAS), Apdo 1004, Santo Domingo, DN.

ECUADOR

Centro de Investigación y Acción Social (CIAS), Benalcázar 562, Apdo 2876, Quito.

Instituto de Ciencias Sagradas, Pontificia Universidad Católica del Ecuador, 12 de Octubro No 1076, Apdo 2184, Quito.

EGYPT

Centre d'Etudes Arabes, Collège La Salle, 6 Rue Sekket el Bechnine, Daher, Al Qahirah, T: 904322, 904740.

Centre d'Etudes Dar El-Salam, 4 Midan Cheikh Youssef, Garden City, Al Qahirah.

Franciscan Centre of Christian Oriental Studies, 12 Bendâqah St, POB 381, Muski, Al Qahirah, T: 909906.

Institut Dominicain d'Etudes Orientales (IDEO), 1 Rue Masna Al-Tarabich, Abassiyah, Al Qahirah, T: 825509.

Institute for Coptic Studies, St. Peter's Church, Abbassiyah, Al Qahirah.

Institute for Oriental Studies of the Library of the Greek Orthodox Patriarchate of Alexandria, Al Iskandariyah (Alexandria).

EL SALVADOR

Centro de Estudios Sociales y Promoción Popular (CESPROP), Centro Universitario Católico, Apdo Postal 723, San Salvador, T: 258979.

ETHIOPIA

Department of Audience Research & Planning, RVOG, P.O. Box 654, Addis Abeba, T: 448190.

Department of History, Research, Mission and Publications, Ethiopian Orthodox Church, Miazia 27, PO Box 30066, Addis Abeba.

FINLAND

Ecumenical Institute of the University of Helsinki, Fabianinkatu 33, Helsinki 17; Aleksanterinkatu 15 B4, 00100 Helsinki 10.

Institute for Ecumenics and Social Ethics, Biskopsgatan 16, Abo 2, T: 18968.

Research Institute of the Lutheran Church in Finland (Kirkon Tutkimuslaitor), PL 239, SF-33101 Tampere 10, T: (9) 31-31783.

Research Institute of the Lutheran Church of Finland, Satakunnankatu 11 B 21, Box 239, SF-33100 Tampere 10, T: 931-31212.

Studium Catholicum, Dominikaainien Kulttuurikeskus, Ritarikatu 3bA, Helsinki 17, T: 634221.

FRANCE

Action Populaire, Centre de Recherche et d'Action Sociales (CERAS), 15 Rue Raymond Marcheron, 92 Vanves.

Association Internationale Futuribles, 52 Rue des Saints-Pères, Paris 7.

Centre Catholique de Socialogie Religieuse, 99 Qui Clémenceau, F-69 Caluire, Rhône.

Centre d'Etudes Africaines, 31, rue de Fonderie, F-31068.

Centre d'Etudes et de Recherches Interdisciplinaires en Théologie (CERIT), Palais Universitaire, F-67084 Strasbourg.

Centre d'Etudes et de Recherches Missionnaires (CRTM), 128 rue du Bac, F-75341 Paris.

Centre d'Etudes Istina, 45 rue de la Glacière, F-75013 Paris, T: 587-3735.

Centre d'Etudes Orthodoxes, Institut de Théologie Orthodoxe St-Serge, 93 Rue de Crimée, Paris, T: 208-1293.

Centre de Documentation Oecuménique et Judéo-Chrétienne, 43 bis Rue du Port, F-59 Lille.

Centre de Recherche Théol. Missionaire, 5, rue Monsieur, F-75007 Paris.

Centre de Recherche et de Documentation des Institutions Chrétiennes (CERDIC), Palais Universitaire, Place de l'Université, F-67084 Strasbourg, T: (88)355940.

Centre pour l'Intelligence de la Foi (CIF), 76 rue des Saints-Pères, F-75007 Paris.

Centre Régional d'Etudes Socio-Religieuses, 39 rue de la Monnaie, F-59042 Lille, T: (20)553026.

Centre Régional Protestant de Recherche et de Formation, 15 rue Jeanne-d'Arc, Lille.

Centre Saint-Irénée, 2, Place Gailleton, F-69002 Lyon, T: (78)374982.

Centre Thomas More, La Tourette-Eveux, F-69210 L'Arbresle, T: (78)019111.

Commission de Sociologie de la Fédération Protestante de France, 47 rue de Clichy, F-75009 Paris.

Documentation et Information sur l'Amérique Latine (DIAL), 170 Blvd du Montparnasse, F-75014 Paris.

Economie et Humanisme, 99 Quai Clémenceau, F-69300 Caluire, T: (78)232178.

Ecumenical Research Institute, 8 rue Gustav Klotz, F-67 Strasbourg, T: (88)362926.

Groupe de Sociologie des Religions, 82 Rue Cardinet, Paris, T: (01)924-2624.

Institut d'Etudes Sémitiques (IES), 16 Rue de la Sorbonne, F-75005 Paris, T: ODE-2413 ext 287.

Institut de Langage Total, Recherches Educatives et Culturelle (REC), 21 Rue de la Paix, F-42 Saint-Etienne, T: (77)331621.

Institut de Science et de Théologie des Religions (ISTR), Institut Catholique, 5 Rue Roger Verlomme, F-75003 Paris; 128 rue du Bac, F-75007 Paris, T: (01)548-1992.

Institut de Sciences Sociales des Religions (ISSR), c/o Groupe de Sociologie des Religions (CNRS), 22 Rue d'Athènes, F-75009 Paris, T: (01)526-1512.

Institut de Théologie Orthodoxe, Saint Serge, 93 Rue de Crimée, F-75019 Paris.

Institut des Sciences Religieuses de Nancy, 35 Cours Léopold, F-54000 Nancy.

Maison des Science de l'Homme, 54 Blvd Raspail, F-75006 Paris.

Semaines Sociales de France, 9 Rue Guénégaud, F-75006 Paris, T: (01)033-2501.

Service Documentation Sectes, Lique Catholique de l'Evangile, 2 Rue de la Planche, F-75007 Paris.

GERMANY

Academy of Mission at the University of Hamburg, Rupertistrasse 67, Hamburg 52, T: 49-828642.

Agency for Church Growth and Journalism, Altkönigstr. 4, D-6239 Kriftel, bei Frankfurt, T: 0-61-92-26882.

Bysantinisches Institut der Abtei Scheyern, D-8069 Scheyern, T: (08441)2244.

Bysantinisches Institut Ettal, D-8101 Ettal.

Detusches Inst. für rür Arztl. Mission, Paul-Lechler-Str. 24, 7400 Tübingen.

Deutsche Ges. f. Missionswissensch, Vogelsangstr. 62, 7000 Stuttgart 1.

Forschungsstätte der Evangelischen Studiengemeinschaft Christiphorus Stift (FEST), Schmeilweg 5, D-6900 Heidelberg, T: (06221)25317.

German Church Growth Movement, Postfach 1309, 7928 Giengen/Brenz, T: 0-73-22-136-50, F: 0-73-22-136-15, O: Telex: 7-14-831 dribod.

Gesellschaft für Zukunftsfragen, c/o Hamburgisches Weltwirtschaftsarchiv, Karl-Muck-Platz 1, D-2 Hamburg 36.

Institut der Orden für missionarisches Seelsorge und Spiritualität (IMS), Waldschmidstr 42a, D-6 Frankfurt I.

Institut für Christliche Gesellschaftslehre, Universität Tübingen, Olgastr 8, D-7400 Tübingen.

Institut für Christliche Gesellschaftwissenschaften, Universität Münster, Universitätsstr 13-17, D-44 Münster, T: (0251)4902550.

Institut für Christliche Sozialwissenschaften der Universität Münster, Pferdegasse 3, D-4400 Münster.

Institut für Christliche Weltanschauung und Religionsphilosophie der Universität München, Kaulbachstr 31/I, D-8000 München 22.

Institut für Konfessionskunde der Orthodoxie, Evangelisch-Theologische Fakultät, Grosse Steinstr 16, 401 Halle/Salle.

Institut für Missionswissenschaft und Ökumenische Theologie der Universität, Hausserstr 43, D-74 Tübingen, T: 712592.

Institut für Staatskirchenrecht der Diözesen Deutschlands, Lennistr 25, D-5300 Bonn 1, T: (02221)633633.

Institut für Ökumenische Forschung, Universität Tübingen, Nauklerstr 37a, D-7400 Tübingen, T: (07122)712871.

Institut für Ökumenische Theologie an der Evtheologische Fakultät, Münster.

Institut für Ökumenische Theologie an der Katholisch-Theologische Fakultät, Leopoldstr 101, D-8000 München 23.

Institut Kirche und Judentum, Kirchlichen Hochschule Berlin, Teltower Damm 120-122, D-1000 Berlin 37 (Zehlendorf), T: (0311)8151067.

Institutum Judaicum Delitzschianum, Wilmergasse 1-4, D-4400 Münster, T: (0251)49014400.

Institutum Judaicum der Universität, Liebermeisterstr 12, D-7400 Tübingen, T: (07122)292590.

International Institute f. Missionsw. Forsch., P.O. Box 20 04 43, 5300 Bonn.

Konfessionskundliches Seminar, Evangelisch-Theologische Fakultät, Universität Heidelberg, Plock 66, D-69 Heidelberg.

Korean New Religions Research Centre, Hamburg.

Lenenszentrum für Einheit der Christen, Schloss Craheim, D-8721 Wetzhausen.

Missionsv. d. Ev.-Luth. Kirche, Postfach 68, 8806 Neuendettelsau.

Missionsw. Inst. Missio e.v., Bergoriesch 27, 5100 Aachen.

Missionswissensch Institut, Arnold Jannsen Str. 24, 5205 St. Augustin.

Missionswissenschaftliches Institut Missio, Hermannstr 14, Postfach 1110, D-5100 Aachen.

Ostkirchliches Institut, Ostengasse 31, D-93047 Regensburg, T: (49) 09 41/570 09, F: 5 25 51.

Religionssoziologisches Institut an der Kirchlichen Hochschule Berlin, Teltower Damm 120-122, D-1000 Berlin 37 (Zehlendorf), T: (0311)8151067/9.

Religionswissenschaftliches Institut der Freien Universität Berlin, Boltzmannstr 4, D-1000 Berlin 33.

Seminar für Geschichte und Theologie des Christlichen Ostens, Evangelisch-Theologische Fakultät, Universität Erlangen, Kochstr 6, D-852 Erlangen.

Seminar für Missionstheologie und Religionswissenschaft, Johs Gutenberg Universität, Saarstr 21, D-6500 Mainz.

Seminar für Ostkirchenkunde, Katholisch-Theologische Fakultät, Universität Würzburg, Sanderring 2, D-87 Würzburg.

Seminar für Theologie des Christlichen Ostens, Evangelisch-theologische Fakultät, Universität Erlangen-Nürnberg, Kochstr 6, Erlangen.

Südasien-Institut der Universität Heidelberg, Im Neuerheimer Feld 13, D-6900 Heidelberg.

Theological Information and Documentation Centre (THEODOK), Universitätsbibliothek, D-7400 Tübingen 1.

Ungarisches Kirchensocialogischen Institut (ULI), Rosenheimerstr 141, D-8 München, T: 448610.

Ökumenisches Archiv der EKD, Jebensstr 3, D-1000 Berlin 12, T: (030)310491.

Ökumenisches Institut, Abteilung fur Evangelische Theologie, Universität Bochum, Overbergstr 16, D-463 Bochum-Querenburg.

Ökumenisches Institut, Katholisch-theologische Fakultät, Universität Münster, Johannisstr 8-10, D-44 Münster.

Ökumenisches Seminar, Theologische Fakultät, Universität Marburg, Lahntor 3, D-355 Marburg.

Ökumenisches Seminar, Universität Hamburg, Dir, Von-Melle-Park 6, 2 Hamburg 13, T: 441972560.

GHANA

Akrofi-Christaller Memorial Centre for Mission Research and Applied Theology, P.O. Box 1588, Accra, T: 222879.

Ghana Evangelism Committee, Box 8699, Accra North.

GREECE

Athens Centre of Ekistics, Athens Technological Organization, 24 Strat Syadesmou St, Athínai 136.

Inter-Orthodox Missionary Centre' Porefthendes', 30 Sina St, Athínai 135.

National Centre of Social Research, Athénai.

Patriarchal Institute for Patristic Studies, Hiera Patriarchiki Moni Vlatadon, Thessaloniki.

Scientific Conference Centre of Denys the Areopagite, Michael Voda St 28, Athínai, T: 813570.

GUADELOUPE

Centre d'Etude et d'Action Sociale (CEAS), 28 Rue Peynier, BP 414, F-97-1 Pointe-à-Pitre, T: 820967.

GUYANA

Guyana Institute for Social Research and Action (GISRA), 1 Brickdam, P.O. Box 528, Georgetown, T: 61789.

HAITI

Centre d'Information et de Statistique Evangélique (CISE), BP 458, Port-au-Prince.

Haitian Research Centre in Social Sciences (CHISS), Rue Bonne Foi 23, BP 1294, Port-au-Prince.

HOLY SEE

Archivio del Concilio Vaticano II, Via P Pancrazio Pfeiffer 10, I-00193 Roma, T: 69282 int 4236.

Archivio Secreto Vaticano, I-00120 Città del Vaticano, T: 6982 int 3314.

Central Office of Statistics of the Church, Palazzo Apostolico, I-00120 Città del Vaticano, T: 6983046.

Istituto Superiore di Scienze Religiose'Ecclesia Mater', Piazza San Giovanni in Laterano 4, I-00184 Roma, T: 750892.

Pontificia Commissione per gli Archivi Ecclesiastici d'Italia, Palazzo Apostolico, I-00120 Città del Vaticano, T: 6982 int 3314.

Scuola Vaticana di Biblioteconomia, Palazzo Apostolico, I-00120, Città del Vaticano, T: 6983323.

Superior Institute for the Study of Atheism, Pontifical Urbanian University, Città del Vaticano.

INDIA

Catholic Family Social Welfare Centre, Indian Social Institute, South Ext 11d-25-D, New Delhi 49, T: 622379.

Christian Association for Socio-Religious Research of India, 17 Miller's Rd, PO Box 1504, Bangalore 6, T: 75181.

Christian Institute for Sikh Studies, Baring Union Christian College, Batala, District Gurdaspur, Punjab.

Christian Institute for the Study of Religion and Society (CISRS), Devanandan House, 17 Miller's Rd, PO Box 604, Bangalore 6, T: 75181.

Christian Institute for the Study of Religion and Society, 14, Jangpura B., Mathura Road, New Delhi 110014.

Church Growth Research Centre (CGRC), 109 6th Street, Secretariat Colony, Post Bag 768, Kilpauk, Madras 600 010, T: 663972.

Gurukul Lutheran Theological College and Research Institute, 94 Purasawalkam High Road, Kilpauk, Madras 600 010.

Henry Martyn Institute, 5-8-660/B-1, Chirag Ali Lane, P.O. Box No. 153, Hyderabad-500 001. A.P..

Indian Social Institute, South Ext 11d-25-D, New Delhi 49, T: 622379.

Institute for Social Studies and Community Development (Seva Sadan), Department of Socio-Religious Studies, 1250 Quarters, TT Nagar South, Bhopal, MP, T: 432.

Institute for Social Sciences And Research, Greenwoods, Jabberpet, West Of Gandhi Nagar, Vellore, Tamil Nadu 632006.

Missions Research Centre, C/o.IIMCS , 204 P. L. Banerjee Road, Lalgarh, Madhupur, Bihar 834001.

Snehasadan Institute for the Study of Religion, 250 Shaniwar Peth, Pune, Maharashtra 411014.

Theological Research and Communication Institute (TRACI), Union Biblical Seminary, Dir, Yeotmal, Maharashtra 445 001.

Tribal Research and Training Centre, C/o St. Xavier Church, P. B. 10, Chaibasa, Bihar 833201.

Xavier Centre of Historical Research, Goa.

INDONESIA

Atma Jaya Research Centre, Jalan Jenderal Sudirman 49A, PO Box 2639, Jakarta, T: 586491.

Drijarkara Philosophical Institute, Jalan Menteng Raya 64, Jarkarta, T: 47278.

Institute for Research and Study, Council of Churches in Indonesia, Jalan Salemba Raya 10, Jakarta-Pusat, T: 82317.

Institute of Social Research and Development, Jalan Kemiri 15 pav, Jakarta; Jalan Kramat Raya 134, Jakarta IV/5.

LINK, Jl. Garuda 31 M, Jakarta 10610, T: 62-21-411341, F: 62-21-4201058, O: Telex: 49486 KJIA.

Pastoral Research and Service Centre, Jalan Jendral Sudirnam 3, Surakarta, Central Java, T: 3904.

Research Centre, Satya Wacana Christian University, Salatiga, Central Java.

Research Institute (HKBP), Nommensen University, P Siantar, North Sumatra.

IRELAND

Mater Dei Institute, Clonliffe Road, Dublin 3, T: 40854.

Research and Development Unit/Commission, Catholic Communications Institute of Ireland, Veritas House, 7/8 Lower Abbey St, Dublin 1, T: 48502.

ISRAEL

American Institute of Holy Land Studies, P.O. Box 1276, Mt Zion, Jerusalem.

CARTA, Beit Hadar, Mazie St, Jerusalem.

Centre of Jewish Studies and Jewish-Christian Dialogue, Dominican Fathers, Jerusalem.

Ecole Biblique et Ecole Archéologique Française, Couvent Dominicain St-Etienne, P.O. Box 19055, Jerusalem, T: 82213.

Ecumenical Institute for Advanced Theological Studies in Jerusalem (EIATS), P.O. Box 19556, Tantur (on the main road to Bethlehem), Jerusalem.

Ecumenical Theological Research Fraternity in Israel, PO Box 249, Jerusalem, T: (02)66308.

German Evangelical Institution for Archaeology of the Holy Land, Sheikh Jarah, Jerusalem, T: 84792.

Institut Biblique Franciscain, P.O. Box 190 & 424, Old City Jerusalem.

Institute of Contemporary Jewry, Hebrew University of Jerusalem, Jerusalem.

Near East Christian Centre, Saint Anne, P.O. Box 19079, Jerusalem, T: (02)83285.

Pontifical Biblical Institute, 3 Paul Emil Botta St, P.O. Box 497, Jerusalem, T: 22843.

ITALY

Centro di Previsione Sociale, Via Carlo Alberto 57, I-10123 Turin.

Centro di Studi Ecumenici Giovanni XXIII, Priorato di Santo Egidio, I-24039 Sotto il Monte (Bergamo).

Centro Studi Asiatici, Centro Missionario PIME, Via Mosè Bianchi 94, I-20149 Milano.

Centro Studi Emigrazione Roma (CSER), Via della Pisana 1301, I-00163 Roma, T: 6740074.

Ente dello Spettacolo, Via della Conciliazione 2c, I-00193 Roma, T: 561775, 564132.

IDOC International (International Documentation on the Contemporary Church), Via Santa Maria dell'Anima 30, I-00186 Roma, T: 6568332.

International Centre of Sindonology, Archdiocese of Turin, Torino.

Istituto Superiore di Scienze Religiose 'Mater Ecclesiae', Largo Angelicum 1, I-00184 Roma, T: 673400.

Laboratorio di Sociologia Religiosa, Facoltà di Scienze Politiche, Università di Padova, Padova.

Pontifical Institute of Arab Studies (PIAS), Rector, Piazza di San Apollinare 49, I-00186 Roma, T: 561131, 561592.

Pontificio Seminario per gli Studi Giuridici, Piazza Santo Apollinare 49, I-00186 Roma, T: 561103.

Pontificium Institutum Biblicum de Urge, Via della Pilotta 25, I-00187 Roma, T: 672778.

Scuola Superiore delle Communicazioni Sociali, Università Cattolica del S Cuore, Via Sant'Agnese 2, I-20123 Milano.

Servizio di Documentazione e Studi (SEDOS), Via dei Verbiti 1, CP 5080, I-00100 Roma, T: 571350.

IVORY COAST

Centre des Sciences Humaines, Abidjan.

Institut Supérieur de Culture Religieuse (ISCR), BP 8022, Abidjan-Cocody, T: 340325.

JAPAN

Catholic Social Research Institute, Tokyo-to, Shijuku-ku, Kita, Shinjuku 1-33-20.

Christian Center for the Study of Japanese Religions, Shugakuin (10 Daido-cho), Sakya-ku, Kyoto.

Church Information Service, OSCC Bldg., 1 Kanda Surugadai 2-chome, Chiyoda-ku, Tokyo 101, T: 03-295-0935.

Department of Communications, Sophia (Jochi) University, Chiyoda-ku 7, Kioicho, Tokyo.

Institute for Taoistic Research, Tokyo, T: (203)4111.

Institute of Oriental Culture, University of Tokyo, Hongo Bunkyo-ku, Tokyo, T: (812)2111.

International Institute for the Study of Religions, Sophia University, 7 Kioicho, Chyoda-ku, Tokyo, T: 2636267.

Japan Church Growth Institute, Nukui Bldg., Apt. 203, 16-5 Higashi Honcho, Higashi, Kurume City, 203.

Japan Society of Christian Studies, College of Theology, Kanto-Gaskuin University, Kanagawa-ku, Mutsuura-cho 4834.

Japanese Institute of Religious Sociology, Shinseikaikan, 33 Shinano machi Shinjuku-ku, Tokyo.

Kansai Missionary Research Center, 3-5-2 Chome Nakajima-dori, Kobe 651.

Nanzan Institute for Religion and Culture, Nanzan University, Nagoya.

NCCJ Center for the Study of Japanese Religions, School of Theology, Doshisha University, Karasuma-Shimotachiuri, Kamikyo-ku, Kyoto, T: 4321945.

Oriens Institute for Religious Research, Chitose, PO Box 14, Tokyo 156, T: 3227601/2.

Oriental Institute for Religious Research, 28-5 Matsubara 2, chome, Setagaya-ku, Tokio 156.

Research Institute on Mission, United Church of Christ in Japan, 551 Totsukamachi 1-chome, Shinjuku-ku, Tokyo 160, T: 2020541.

St. Thomas Aquinas Institute, Research Center for Christian Philosophy, Kyoto-fu, Kyoto-shi, Kami-kyo-kui, Kawara-machi, Hirokogi, Kajil-cho 461.

Studium Biblicum Franciscanum, 4-16-1 Seta, Setagaya-ku, Tokyo 158.

KENYA

AMECEA Research Department, Gaba Pastoral Institute, Kisumu Rd, PO Box 908, Eldoret, T: 2634.

Daystar Communications, Valley Rd & Ngong Rd, PO Box 44400, Nairobi, T: 26894, 337600.

Daystar Nairobi, P.O. Box 44400, Nairobi, T: 254-2-723002.

Great Commission Research & Strategy Centre, PO Box 21417, Nairobi, T: 336110.

Kenya Beliefs Systems Project, Institute of African Studies (near National Museum), University of Nairobi, PO Box 30197, Nairobi, T: 28631/2.

Kenya Church History Archives, Librarian, St Paul's United Theological College, Redhill Rd, Private Bag, Limuru, T: Tigoni 338.

LAOS

Bureau d'Etudes Buddhiques, Mission Catholique, BP 130, Vientiane.

LEBANON

Centre d'Etudes pour le Monde Arabe Moderne (CEMAM), St. Joseph's University, BP 8664, Bayrut.

Centre de Recherches et d'Etudes Arabes, Université St-Joseph, BP 293, Bayrut, T: 3226636.

Centre de Sociologie Religieuse, Archevêché Grec-Catholique, Rue de Damas, BP 901, Bayrut, T: 231612, 222375, 236066.

Centre for Religious Studies, PO Box 90f, Bayrut.

Institut Supérieur de Formation Religieuse (ISFR), c/o Université St-Joseph, Bayrut.

Institute for Oriental Studies, St. Joseph's University, Bayrut.

MALAWI

Pastoral Service, Catholic Secretariat, P.O. Box 368, Limbe, T: 5866.

MALTA

Catholic Institute, Floriana, T: 239.

Pastoral Research Services, 65 Old Mint St, Valletta, T: 22360.

MEXICO

Center for the Study of Protestantism in Mexico, Apartado 84/Centro/06000 México, D.F., T: 355-8820.

Centro Intercultural de Documentación (CIDOC), 7 Calle Principal, Rancho Tetela, Apdo Postal 479, Cuernavaca, Morelos, T: 24590.

Comisión de Estudios de la Iglesia en América Latina (CEHILA), Celaya 21, Dep. 402, Colonia Hipodromo, 06100, T: 525-5745661, F: 525-5745661.

Escuela de Ciencias y Tecnicas de Información, Universidad Iberoamericana, Cerro de las Torres 395, México 21, DF, T: 493500.

Iglesia y Sociedad en América Latina (ISAL), Apdo 71-343, México 3, DF.

Instituto Mexicano de Estudios Sociales (IMES), Av Cuauhtémoc 1486-501, Piso 5, Apdo Postal 549, México 13, DF, T: 5242448, 5244941.

Instituto Superior de Estudios Eclesiásticos, Seminario Conciliar de México, Tlalpan, Calle Victoria 21, México 22, DF, T: 5732222, 5732225, 5732918.

Secretariado Regional para América Latina (FERES), c/o IMES, Av Cuauhtémoc 1486, Piso 5, México 13, DF, T: 5242448, 5244941.

Vela, Reg. Fed. Caus., Vel-860703, Apartado Postal, M-9293 C.P., Mexico City, DF, CO 06000, Mexico.

MOROCCO

Centre Diocesain D'Etudes et de Documentation 'La Source', 24, Av. du Chellah, Rabat 74-07B, T: (07)726652, F: (07)205114.

MYANMAR

Centre for the Study of Buddhism, Commission on Buddhism, 104c Inya Rd, University P.O., Rangoon.

NETHERLANDS

Catholic Documentation Centre, Erasmuslaan 36, 6525GG Nijmegen, T: (08800)58711.

Catholic Institute for Mass Media, Universiteit Nijmegen, Verlengde Grone Straat, Nijmegen.

Catholic Institute for Socio-Ecclesiastical Research, Paul Gabriëlstraat 28-30, 's-Gravenhage, T: (070)245415.

De Horstink, Koningin Wilhelminalaan 17, Amersfoort, T: (03490)17958.

Hendrik Kraemer Institut, Leidsestraat 11, Oegstgeest 2311 GR.

Institute for Byzantine and Ecumenical Studies, Louisweg 12, Nijmegen, T: (08800)24061.

Institute of Applied Sociology, Verlengde Groenestraat 55, Nijmegen, T: (080)512460.

Institute of Religious Iconography, State University, Groningen.

Instituut voor Godsdiensthistorische Beelddokumentatie (IGB), Niewe Kujk in 't Jantstraat 104, Groningen, T: (050)114791.

Interuniversity Institute for Missiological and Ecumenical Research, Boehaavelaan 43, Leiden (Dept of Ecumenics: Heidelberglaan 2, Utrecht), T: (01710)51925, (030)539111).

Labour Institute (Instituut voor Arbeidsvraagstukken, IVA), Prof Verbernelaan 121a, Tilburg, T: (04250)70960.

Nederlandse Missieraad, Halva Maanstraat 7, S-Hertogenbosch 5211 VV.

Netherlands Institute for Public Opinion, Westerdokhuis, Barentzplein 7, Amsterdam, T: 248844.

Peshitta Institute, Leiden University, Leiden.

Sociology of Religion Working Group, Prins Hendriklaan 27-29, Amsterdam, T: (020)723677.

Titus Brandsma Instituut, Groesbeekseweg 147, Nijmegen, T: (08800)58711 toestel 2162.

NEW ZEALAND

Keston College/Keston Research, P.O. Box 30-254, Lower Hutt, Wellington, T: 64-456-967-37, F: 64-456-964-05.

NICARAGUA

Instituto de Cultura Religiosa Mater Ecclesiae, Colegio de la Asunción, Managua, T: 4801.

NIGERIA

Capro Research and Information Centre, P.O. Box 6001, Jos, Nigeria.

Catholic Institute of West Africa, P.O. Box 499, Port Harcourt.

Institute of Church and Society, Oyo Rd, PO Box 4020, Ibadan, T: 22078.

National Institute for Religious Studies, Lagos.

NEMA Research Function, P.O. Box 10008, Kaduna.

Pastoral Institute, Bodija, PO Box 1784, Ibadan, T: 24328.

Religious Studies Unit, Polytechnic University, Ibadan.

Study Centre for Islam and Christianity, Islam in Africa Project Council, General Advisor, 5 Awosika Av, Bodija, PO Box 4045, Ibadan, T: 23884.

NORWAY

Centre for Development Research, Herman Foss gate 9, PO Box 1046, N-5001 Bergen, T: 30994.

Centre for the Study of Ideologies, Christiesgate 16, Bergen.

Ecumenical Institute, Oslo University, Krags Vei 1, Oslo 3.

Egede Institute for Missionary Study and Research, Theresesgt 51 B, Oslo 3, T: 466800.

PAKISTAN

Christian Study Centre, 126B Murree Rd., Rawalpindi, Cantt; 128 Saifullah Lodhi Rd., Burton Rd..

Institute for Religious and Social Studies (IRSS), Franciscan Friary, St. Patrick's Cathedral, Karachi 0328, T: 417978.

Islamic Research Institute, 692-E, G-VI-4, P.O. Box 1035, Islamabad.

PANAMA

Centro de Investigaciones Socio-Religiosas de la Arquidiócesis de Panamá (CISRAP), Apdo 6386, Panamá 5.

Instituto de Estudios Religiosos Avanzados (IDERA), Apdo 6386, Panamá 5, T: 625693.

PAPUA NEW GUINEA

Institute of Social Order, Box 1897, Boroko.

Melanesian Institute, P.O. Box 571, Goroka EHP.

PARAGUAY

Centro de Estudios Antropológicos de la Universidad Católica (CEADUC), Universidad Católica, Independencia Nacional y Comuneros, Asunción.

Centro de Estudios Socio-Religiosos (CESR), Coronel Bogado 367, Asunción, T: 45598, 41009.

Instituto Superior de Teologia y Ciencias Religiosas, Universidad Católica Nuestra Señora de la Asunción, Independencia Nacional y Comuneros, Asunción, T: 41044.

PERU

Centro de Investigaciones Sociales, Economicas, Políticas y Antropológicas, Sección de Investigaciones Socio-Religiosas, Pontificia Universidad Católica del Perú, Camaná 459, Apdo 1761, Lima, T: 39824.

Centro Latinoamericano de Lenguaje Total (SEC-SAL-OCIC), Av 9 de Diciembre, Paseo Colon 378, Apdo 44, Lima, T: 312339.

Departamento de Investigación y Planeamento Parroquial, c/o Arzobispado, Apdo 1512, Lima.

MAC Research, Apartado 18-0872, Miraflores Lima 18.

Oficina Arquidiocesana de Investigación y Planeamiento, Arzbispado de Lima, Plaza de Armas, Apdo 1512, Lima.

PHILIPPINES

Christian Institute for Ethnic Studies in Asia, P.O. Box 1767/3167, Manila, T: 72907.

Dansalan Research Center, Dansalan College, PO Box 5430, Iligan City 8801.

Department of Communication, Ateneo de Manila University, Loyola Heights, Quezon City, PO Box 154, Manila, T: 998721.

Gowing Memorial Research Center, Dansalan College Foundation, Inc., P.O. Box 5430, Iligan City 9200; Islamic City of Marawi, 9700 Lanao del Sur, Iligan City 9200, O: Cable: DANSALAN COLLEGE MARAWI CITY.

Institute of Philippine Culture, Ateneo de Manila University, Loyola Heights, Quezon City, T: 91721.

Institute of Religion and Culture, 12-C Bayanihan St., West Triangle, Quezon City, T: 632-924-0215, F: 632-924-0207, O: Also tel: 954-0219.

Research Department, Far East Broadcasting Company (FEBC), Box 2041, Manila, T: 233357.

Research Institute on Sulu Culture, Ateneo University, Loyola Heights, Quezon City, PO Box 154, Manila, T: 998721.

Target 2-2-2, Center for Research and Statistics, CAMACOP, 3rd Fl., API Building, 13 West Capital Dr., Pasig, Metro Manila 3130.

POLAND

Catholic Faculty of Theology, Missiology Department, Akademia Teologii Katolickiej Warszawie, ATK, ul Dewajtis 3, 01 653 Warszawa.

Catholic Univ. of Lublin, Inst. of Pastoral Theology, Dept. of Religious Sociology, Katedra Socjologii Religii, Instytut Teologii Pastoralnej, Katolicki Uniwersytet Lubelski, Aleje Raclawickie 14, skr p 279, 20 950 Lublin, T: 30426.

Centre for Religious Documentation and Studies, Ul Mokotowska 43, Skr poctz 79, Warszawa, T: 291758.

Centre for Social Documentation and Studies, Ul Mokotowska 45, Skr poctz 79, Warszawa, T: 291758.

Institute for Socio-Religious Research, Oftzerzew, Kilingskiego 20, Ozanow Mazowiecki.

PORTUGAL

Centro de Cultural Católica (CCC), Casa da Torre da Marca, Rua D Manuel II 286, Porto, T: 29691.

Centro de Estudos Missionários, Rua de Junqueira 86, Lisboa.

Escola de Ciencias Socio-Empresariais, Universidade Católica, Lisboa.

Instituto Superior de Psicologia Aplicada, Rua da Emenda 40, Lisboa.

Liga Intensificadora de Acção Missionária (LIAM), Rua Santo Amaro à Estrela 51, Lisboa 2, T: 661424.

SAINT LUCIA

Folk Research Centre, P.O. Box 514, Castries, T: 452-2279, F: 451-7444.

SINGAPORE

China Catholic Communication, 'A' Queen St., Singapore 0718, T: 3387715.

Singapore Every Home Crusade Co Ltd., No. 8, Lorong 27-A Geylang, #02-04/05 Guilin Building, Singapore 388106, T: 744-7355, F: 744-7266.

SLOVENIA

Episcopal Centre for Socio-Pastoral Research (KRSOL), Cirkulane Pri Ptuju, Slomskov trg 19, Maribor, T: 21341.

SOLOMON ISLANDS

Pacific Research Unit, Pacific Conference of Churches (PCC), P.O. Box 19, Honiara.

SOUTH AFRICA

Association for the Study of Religion, c/o Dept of Phil & Rel Studies, Universal of Natal, P/B X01 Scottsville 3209, Pietermaritzburg, T: 0331-260-5111, F: 0331-260-5858.

Bureau of African Churches Information and Research Institute, Christ the King Theological School, Durban.

Christian Info, PO Box 2540, Welkom 9460, T: 057-353-2018.

Christian Institute of Southern Africa, 305 Dunwell, 35 Jorissen St, PO Box 31134, Braamfontein, Transvaal, T: 7240346/7.

Church of the Province of Southern Africa, Bishopscourt, Claremont, 7700, T: (021) 797-6451, F: (021) 761-4193.

Ecumenical Research Unit, St. John Vianney Seminary, 1911 Main St, Waterkloof, PO Box 17128, Groenkloof, Pretoria, T: 789011.

Institute for Missiological Research (ISWEN), Theological Faculty, University of Pretoria, Pretoria 0002, T: 012-420-2789, F: 012-43-2189.

Institute for Social Research, King George V Av, Durban.

Institute for Theological Research, University of South Africa (UNISA), PO Box 392, Pretoria 0001, T: 4402171.

NERMIC (New Religious Movements and Indigenous/Independent Churches), University of Zululand, P/Bag X1001, Kua Diangezwa 3886, T: 0351-9-3911, F: 0351-9-3159.

Research Centre for Church and Industry, UNISA, PO Box 392, Pretoria 0001.

Research Institute for Theology & Religion, Faculty of Theology, UNISA, PO Box 392, Pretoria 0001, T: 012-429-4369, F: 012-429-3525.

SOUTH KOREA

East/West Center for Missions, Research & Development, C.P.O. Box 2732, Seoul, T: 827-1129, O: Cable Address: EWCENTER.

Institute for Church Growth, Seoul.

Institute for Ecumenical and Inter-Religious Studies, Hanguk Jongkyo Munje Yonku-so, International PO Box 3251, Seoul, T: 746712.

Institute of Korean Culture, CPO 206, Soul.

Institute of Socio-Religious Research, Korean Union College (Sam Yuk Tai Hak), IPO Box 1243, Seoul, T: 964287.

Korea Research Institute for Missions, Kang Nam P.O. Box 1667, Seoul, 135-616, T: (02) 569-0716, F: (02) 563-6950.

Korea World Mission Research and Development Center, 512-6 Shinsa-Dong, Kangnam-Gu, Seoul 135, T: 546-7912/3.

Korean Christian Mission Center, 55 Yang Jae-Dong, Suh Cho-Ku, Seoul, T: 570-7080, F: 5770-7011.

Korean Church History Institute, 187, 1 Ka, Han Kang Ro, Yong San Ku, Seoul, T: 422821.

New Religious Research Institute, c/o NCCK, PO Box 143, Seoul.

Research Institute for Life and Culture, 1-1, Shinsu-dong, Map'o-gu, Seoul-shi, T: (02) 706-6907.

Social Research Institute, Sogang University, IPO Box 1142, Seoul.

SPAIN

Barriada y Vida, Centro de Investigaciones Sociales y Religiosas, Calle Claudio Coello 141, Madrid 6.

Centro de Estudios Orientales, Calle Claudio Coello 129, Madrid 6, T: 275-0698.

Centro de Pastoral Litúrgica, Canuda 45, Barcelona.

Centro Investigaciones Bíblicas, Apdo 967, 38080 Santa Cruz de Tenerife, T: 64-30-60.

Departamento de Misionología Española, Serrano 123, Madrid 6, T: 2619800.

Instituto Católico de Estudios Sociales de Barcelona, Rivadeneyra 6, 3, Barcelona 2, T: 2315220, 2222110.

Instituto de Ciencias Sociales, Universidad de Deusto, Av Dr Morcillo 28, Apdo 1, Bilboa.

Instituto de Cultura Religiosa Superior, Cuesta de Santo Domingo 5, Madrid 13.

Instituto Fe y Secularidad (FEYSEC), Diego de Leon 33, 3 Dcha, Madrid 6.

Oficina General de Sociología Religiosa y Estadistica de la Iglesia, Alfonso XI 4, 2, Madrid 14, T: 2324887.

SEDI (Serv. Evang. de Documentación e Inform.), Apdo. 2002, Sabadell, 08200 Barcelona.

SRI LANKA

Centre for Social and Economic Development, 916 Gnartha Pradipaya Mawata, Colombo 8.

Centre for Society & Religion, 281, Deans Road, Colombo 10.

Christian Institute for the Study of Religion and Society (CISRS), Christa Seva Ashram, Chunnakam, Jaffna.

Study Centre for Religion and Society, 490/5 Havelock Rd, Colombo 6, T: 86998.

SWEDEN

Institute for Ethnics and Work, Mälartorget 15, Stockholm C.

Nordic International Institute of Missionary and Ecumenical Research (NIME), Ostra Agatan 9, PO Box 297, S-75105 Uppsala.

Stockholm Institute of Sociology of Religion, Blasieholmasgatan 4B, 111 48 Stockholm, T: 215464, 212290.

Stockholm Theological Institute, Värdshusbacken 1, 11265 Stockholm K.

Svenska Inst. Missionsforskning, Ostra Agatan 9, 5 TR, S-753-22 Uppsala.

Swedish Institute of Missionary Research, Domkyrkoplan 1/2, S-75220 Uppsala.

SWITZERLAND

Apologetisches Institut, Scheideggstr 45, CH-Zürich 2.

Centre de Recherches et d'Etudes des Institutions Religieuses, 3 Route de Suisse, CH-1290 Versoix, Genève.

Centre Protestant d'Etudes, 7 Rue Tabazan, CH-1204, Genève, T: 255660.

Glaube in der 2 Welt, Zürichstr 155, CH-8700 Kusnacht.

Humanum Studies, World Council of Churches, 150 Route de Ferney, CH-1211 Genève 20.

Institut d'Ethique Social, Fédération des Eglises Protestantes de la Suisse, Sulgenauweg 26, CH-3007 Bern.

Institut d'Etudes Missionnaires, Faculté de Théologie, Salle 1019, Université de Fribourg, CH-1700 Fribourg.

Institut de Missiologie et de science des religions, Universite Misericorde, 1700 Fribourg, 037/29 74 38.

Kirchensoziologische Forschung und Beratung (KFB), Ackerstr 57, CH-8005 Zürich; Hadlaubstr 121, CH-80006 Zürich, T: (051)428466, 443380.

Schweizerisches Pastoralsoziologisches Institut (SPI), Webergasse 5, CH-9001 St. Gallen.

Study on Christians in Changing Institutions, WCC, 150 Route de Ferney, CH-1211 Genève 20.

Swiss Society for Futures Research, Ecole Polytechnique Fédérale Léonhardstr 27, Zürich.

Zentralarchiv/Archiv des Synodalrates, Pavillonweg 10, 3012 Bern, T: 031 971 66 80.

TAIWAN

Taiwan Church Growth Society, 11 Lane 241, No 16, Ta-ya Rd, Taichung 400.

TANZANIA

Tanzania Pastoral and Research Institute (TAPRI), PO Box 325, Tabora, T: 2532.

THAILAND

Thailand Church Growth Committee, 120 Kasemkit Building, Room 702, 7th Floor, Silom Rd, GPO Box 432, Bangkok, T: 2339560.

TOGO

Groupe de Recherches Culturelles et Religieuses dans le Sud Togo (GREST), c/o Père Prieur, Monastère de Dzogbégan, Par Palimé.

TUNISIA

Centre Protestant d'Etudes, 39 Av des Felibres, Tunis.

Institut des Belles Lettres Arabes (IBLA), 12 Rue Djemaa-el-Haoua, Tunis, T: 260133.

UGANDA

Archives Kampala Archdiocese, P.O. Box 14125, Mengo (Kla).

Church of Uganda Research Unit, Planning/Development Advisory Ofc, Provincial Secretariat, Bishop Willis Rd, Namirembe, PO Box 14123, Kampala.

UNITED STATES OF AMERICA (USA)

Adventist Information Ministry, O: Web: www.andrews.edu/homes/Staff/aims/shared/www/aim.org/index.html.

Alverno Research Center on Women, Alverno College, 3401 South 39th St, Milwaukee, WI 53215.

American Institute of Holy Land Studies, 460 Central Av, PO Box 456, Highland Park, IL 60035, T: (315)433-4060.

American Institute of Public Opinion, Gallup International, 53 Bank St, Princeton, NJ 08540, T: (609)924-9600.

Amistad Research Center, Fisk University, Nashville, TN.

Archives of the Episcopal Church USA, P.O. Box 2247 Austin, TX, 78768, T: (512)472-6816.

Archives of the United Church of Christ, Philip Schaff Library, 555 W. James St., Lancaster, PA 17603.

Association of Catholic Diocesan Archivists, 5150 Northwest Highway, Chicago, IL 60630.

Associates for Biblical Research, O: Web: www.christiananswers.net/abr/abrhome/html.

Association of Statisticians of American Religious Bodies, c/o Evangelical Lutheran Church in America, 8765 W. Higgins Rd., Chicago, IL 60631-4198, T: 773-380-2803, F: 773-380-2977.

BARNA Research, 1225 N. Pacific Ave., Suite C, Glendale, CA 91202, T: 818-500-8481.

Biblical Research Associates, College of Wooster, Wooster, OH 44691.

Billy Graham Center, Wheaton College, 510 College Ave., Wheaton, IL 60187-5593, T: 708-752-5910, O: Web: www.wheaton.edu/bgc.

Bureau of Community Research, Pacific School of Religion, Berkeley, California.

Bureau of Research and Survey, NCCCUSA, 475 Riverside Drive, New York, NY 10027.

Center for Advanced Study in Theology and the Sciences, Meadville Theological School, Lombard College, 5750 Ellis Av, Chicago, IL 60637.

Center for Applied Research in the Apostolate (CARA), c/o Georgetown University, Washington, DC 20057-1033, T: 202-687-8080, F: 202-687-8083.

Center for Eastern Christian Studies, University of Scranton, Scranton, PA 18510, T: 717-941-7400, F: 717-941-6369.

Center for the Study of the Future, 4110 NE Alameda, Portland, OR 97212.

Center for the Study of World Religions, Harvard University, 42 Francis Av, Cambridge, MA 02138.

Center for Theology and the Natural Sciences, O: Web: www.ctns.org.

Center for Urban Church Studies, 127 Ninth Av North, Nashville, TN 37234, T: (615)251-2920.

Center of Interreligious Research, 105 West Adams St, Chicago, IL 60603.

Christian Forum Research Foundation, 1111 Fairgrounds Road, Grand Rapids, MN 55744, T: 218-326-2688.

Christian Information Ministries Intl., 2050 N. Collins St., #100, Richardson, TX 75080, T: 214-690-1975.

Christian Research Inc., 2624 First Av South, Minneapolis, MN 55408, T: (612)822-4428.

Christian Research Institute, Inc., P.O. Box 500, San Juan Capistrano, CA 92693, T: 714-855-9926, F: 714-855-4428.

Christian Resource Associates (CRA), PO Box 2100, Orange, CA 92669.

Christian Theological Seminary Program in Church Research and Planning, Box 88257, Indianapolis, IN 46208, T: (317)924-1331.

Church Data Systems, 6705 NE 38th Av, Portland, OR 97211.

Church Growth Center, Corunna, IN 46730, T: 219-281-2452.

Church Surveys, Department of Sociology and Social Ethics, Boston University, 745 Commonwealth Av, Boston, MA 02215, T: 353-3064.

Cities for Christ Worldwide, P.O. Box 300340, Escondido, CA 92030.

Conference on Religion and the Future, Crozer Theological Seminary, Chester, PA 19031.

Cooperation in Documentation and Communication (CoDoC), 1500 Farragut St, NW, Washington, DC 20011.

Council of Societies for the Study of Religion, CSSR Executive Offices, Mercer University, Macon, GA 31207.

Creation Science Research Center, 2716 Madison Av, San Diego, CA 92116, T: (714)283-2164.

Department of Research, Office of Planning and Program, NCCCUSA, 475 Riverside Drive, New York, NY 10027, T: (212)870-2562.

Dynasty Church Systems, 1011 N Broadway, Los Angeles, CA 90052.

Ecumenical Center of Renewal and Planning, Merom Institute, Merom, IN 47861; Also: PO Box 88377, Indianapolis, IN 46208, T: (317)924-1331.

Ecumenical Consultants, 1829 Post Rd, Darien, CT 06820, T: (203)655-2307.

Ecumenical Institute of Religious Studies, Assumption College, 500 Salisbury St, Worcester, MA 01609.

Ecumenism Research Agency, 11040 Windsor Drive, Sun City, AR 83551.

Evangelical Communications Research Foundation, Box 28539, Dallas, TX 75228, T: (214)279-6995.

FEBC Research Department, Far East Broadcasting Company, Box 1, Whittier, CA 90608, T: (213)698-0438.

Foundation for Reformation Research, 6477 San Bonita Av, St Louis, MO 63105, T: PA7-6655.

Gallup Organization, Inc., 53 Bank St., P.O. Box 310, Princeton, NJ 08542, T: 609-924-9600.

Geoscience Institute, 600 College Av, PO Box 161, Andrews Rural Station, Berrien Springs, MI 49104, T: (616)471-7751.

Glenmary Research Center, 235 E. Ponce De Leon Ave., Ste. 226, Decatur, GA 30030, T: 404-377-7010.

Global Church Growth, Church Growth Center, Corunna, IN 46730.

Global Evangelization Movement: Research and Planning Office, P.O. Box 6628, Richmond, VA 23230, T: 804-355-1646, F: 804-355-2016, O: E-mail: GEM@xc.org, www.gem-werc.org.

Globel Mapping International (GMI), 7899 Lexington Dr., Suite 200-A, Colorado Springs, CO 80920, T: 719-531-3599, F: 719-548-7459, O: E-mail: info@gmi.org, Web: www.gmi.org.

Historical Society of the Episcopal Church, Box 2247, Austin, TX 78768.

IDEA/PROLADES, P.O. Box 3406, Orange, CA 92857, T: 714-666-1906, F: 714-666-1906, O: E-mail: CLHolland@xc.org.

IDOC North America, 637 West 125 St, New York, NY 10027.

Institute for Advanced Pastoral Studies, 380 Lone Pine Rd, Bloomfield Hills, MI 48013.

Institute for Advanced Religious Studies, University of Notre Dame, Notre Dame, IN 46556.

Institute for American Church Growth, 1857 Highland Oaks, Arcadia, CA.

Institute for Antiquity and Christianity, Claremont Graduate School, 880 North College Av, Claremont, CA 91711.

Institute for Chinese Studies, Billy Graham Center, Wheaton College, Wheaton, IL 60187-5593, T: 312-260-2528.

Institute for Creation Research, P.O. Box 2667, El Cajon, CA 92021, T: 619-448-0900, O: Web: www.icr.org.

Institute for Cross-Cultural Research, 4000 Albermarle St NW, Washington, DC 20016, T: (202)362-6668.

Institute for Ecumenical and Cultural Research, St. John's University, Collegeville, MN 56321, T: (612)363-7761.

Institute for the Study of American Religion, P.O. Box 90709, Santa Barbara, CA 93190-0709, T: 805-967-7721, F: 805-683-4876, O: E-mail: jgordon@rain.org.

Institute for the Study of American Evangelicals, Billy Graham Center, Wheaton College, Wheaton, IL 60187, T: 312-260-5917.

Institute for Thomistic and Ecumenical Studies, 2570 Asbury St, Dubuque, IA 52002.

Institute of Christian Oriental Research, Washington, DC 20017.

Institute of Church Growth (ICG), Fuller Theological Seminary, 135 North Oakland Av, Pasadena, CA 91101, T: (213)449-1745.

Int'l Research Center, World Radio Missionary Fellowship, P.O. Box 62577, Colorado Springs, CO 80962-2577.

International Research Associate, 1270 Av of the Americas, New York, NY 10020, T: (212)581-2010.

International Workshop on Mass Media and Religious Education, 6815 South Zarzamora St, PO Box 28240, San Antonio, TX 78228.

International Lutheran Society for Church Growth, P.O. Box 633, Kendallville, IN 46755, T: 219-281-2706.

John XXIII Center for Eastern Christian Studies, Fordham University, 2546 Belmont Av, Bronx, NY 10458; Fordham Rd. and 3rd Ave., New York, NY 10458.

Light International, Box 368, Etna, CA 96027, F: 916-467-3686.

Maryknoll Center for Mission Research, Maryknoll P.O., NY 10545, T: 914-941-7590.

Maryknoll China Historical Project, Maryknoll Fathers & Brothers, Maryknoll, NY 10545.

Maryknoll Mission Institute, P.O. Box 529, Maryknoll, NY 10545.

Mediaeval Institute, University of Notre Dame, Notre Dame, IN, T: (219)284-6604.

Membership Information Systems for Churches, 608 N St. Paul, Dallas, TX 75210.

Ministry Studies Board, 608 Dupont Circle Bldg., 1717 Massachusetts Ave., NW, Washington, DC 20036, T: (202)232-3432.

Mission Advanced Research & Communications Center (MARC), 800 W. Chestnut Ave., Monrovia, CA 91016, T: 626-303-8811, F: 626-301-7786, O: E-mail: MARC@wvi.org, www.wvi.org/marc.

Mission Aviation Fellowship/Research Department, Box 202, Redlands, CA 92373-0065, T: 714-794-1151, O: Telex: 676-483.

Mission Research Network, O: http://members.aol.com/missionres/mrn.htm.

Mission Research Web Sties, O: http://www.gmi.org/research/websites.htm.

Missions Resource Center, 9452 Winton Rd., Cincinnati, OH 45231, T: 513-522-2847, F: 513-522-2846, O: 71005.1031.1031@compuserve.com, www.ccmrc.org.

Moody Institute of Science, Moody Bible Institute, 12000 E Washington Blvd, Whittier, CA 90606, T: (213)698-8256.

National Church Growth Research Center, P.O. Box 17575, Washington, DC 20041.

Office of Pastoral Research, Archdiocese of New York, 1011 First Av, New York, NY 10022.

Pentecostal Research Center, Oral Roberts University Library, 7777 South Lewis, PO Box 2187, Tulsa, OK 74102.

Peoples Group Consultants Research Assistant, O: Web: www.xc.org/brigada/pgcra.

Percept, 151 Kalmus Dr., Ste. A104, Costa Mesa, CA 92626, T: 714-957-1282, F: 714-957-1924.

Population Crisis Committee, 1120 19th Street, N.W., Suite 550, Washington, DC 20036, T: 202-659-1833, O: Cable: CRISIS WASHINGTON, Telex: 440450.

Princeton Religion Research Center, P.O. Box 310, Princeton, NJ 08542.

Regional Church Planning Office, 2230 Euclid Av, Cleveland, OH 44115.

Religion Analysis Service, Minneapolis, MN 55440.

Religious Heritage of the Black World, 671 Beckwith St SW, Atlanta, Georgia.

Religious Research Center, Candler School of Theology, Emory University, Atlanta, GA 30303, T: (414)377-2411 ext 7633.

Research Center for Religion and Human Rights in Closed Societies, 475 Riverside Dr., Suite 448, New York, NY 10115, T: 212-870-2481.

Research Enablement Program, Overseas Ministries Study Center, 490 Prospect St., New Haven, CT 06511-2196, T: 203-865-1827, F: 203-865-2857.

Research Office, Episcopal Church in the USA, 815 Second Av, New York, NY 10017, T: (212)867-8400.

Research Office of the Presbytery of Chicago, 800 W Belden Av, Chicago, IL 60614, T: (312)549-3700 ext 35.

Research Publications, P.O. Box 3903, Amity Station, New Haven, CT 06525.

Resources for the Future Inc., 1755 Massachusetts Av, NW, Washington, DC 20036.

Roper Public Opinion Research Center, Williams College, Box 624, Williamstown, MA 01267.

Samuel Zwemer Institute (SZI), Box 365, Altadena, CA 91001, T: (213)794-1121/2.

Sentinel Group, The, P.O. Box 6334, Lynnwood, WA 98036, T: 425-672-2989, F: 425-672-3028, O: E-mail: sentinelgp@aol.com.

Society for the Study of Religion under Communism, P.O. Box 171, Wheaton, IL 60187.

Spiritual Counterfeits Project, P.O. Box 4308, Berkeley, CA 94704, T: 510-540-0300, F: 510-540-1107.

St. Sophia Religious Research Institute, 2615 30th St., N.W., Washington, DC 20008, T: 202-234-2330.

Studies in Church and State, Box 380, Baylor University, Waco, TX 76703.

Study Centre on Religion and Society, 2880 Oahu Av, Honolulu, Hawaii 96822.

Survey Research Centre, University of California, 2220 Piedmont Av, Berkeley, CA 94720, T: 845-6000 ext 4044.

Toward 2000, Issachar Frontier Missions Research,

P.O. Box 30727, Seattle, WA 98013, T: 206-789-2806.

Unitarian Universalist Futures Program, Dept. of Development, Unitarian Universalist Association, 25 Beacon St., Boston St, Boston, MA 02108.

United States Center for World Mission (USCWM), 1605 E. Elizabeth St., Pasadena, CA 91104, T: (626)794-7155.

Western Church Records Management Inc., 2034 Glenview Terrace, Altadena, CA 91001, T: (213)798-4616.

World by 2000 International Radio Research Center, 1605 E. Elizabeth Street, Pasadena, CA 91104, T: (818) 398-2489, F: (818) 398-2490.

World Christian Encyclopedia, Web: www.gem-werc.org.

World Evangelization Research Center, P.O. Box 6628, Richmond, VA 23230, T: 804-355-1646, F: 804-355-2016, O: E-mail: GEM@xc.org, Web: www.gem-werc.org

World Future Society, 5501 Lincoln St, Bethesda, PO Box 19285, 20th St Station, Washington, DC 20036.

Xerox University Microfilms, 300 North Zeeb Rd., Ann Arbor, MI 48106.

YWAM Int'l Operation Office, Research & Information, P.O. Box 26479, Colorado Springs, CO 80936-6479, T: 719-380-0505, F: 719-380-0936.

URUGUAY

Centro de Estudios Cristianos del Rio de la Plata, Casillo Correo 445, Montevideo.

Centro de Estudios Religiosos (CER), Av Agraciada 2974, Montevideo.

Centro Nacional de Sociologia Religiosa, Treinta y Tres 1368, Montevideo.

Iglesia y Sociedad en América Latina (ISAL), Pza Cagancha 1342, 1 Piso, Of 6, Casilla Correo 179, Montevideo.

Instituto Teológico del Uruguay, Av 8 de Octubre 3060, Montevideo.

VANUATU

Pacific Churches Research Centre, Box 551, Port Vila.

VENEZUELA

Centro de Desarrollo Indigena (CEDI), Apdo 8150, Caracas 101.

Centro de Estudios del Futuro de Venezuela, Universidad Católica Andrés Bello, Urb Montalban, Apdo 13228, Caracas.

Centro de Investigaciones en Ciencias Sociales (CISOR), Apdo 1283, Caracas 101.

Centro de Investigación y Acción Social (CIAS), Apdo 638, Esquina de Pajaritos, Caracas.

Centro Gumilla, Av Berrizbeitia 14, El Paraiso, Apdo Postal 29056, Caracas 102, T: 423482.

Fundación La Salle de Ciencias Naturales, CAS, Apdo 8150, Caracas 101.

Instituto Caribe de Antropología y Sociología (ICAS), Apdo 8150, Caracas 101, T: 729612.

Instituto de Estudios Teológicos, Universidad Católica Andrés Bello, Caracas.

Instituto Venezolano de Lenguas Indígenas, UCAB, Apdo 13228, Caracas 101, T: 496721.

ZAMBIA

Institute for Social Research, University of Zambia, P.O. Box 900, Lusaka, T: 74721.

Pastoral Service, Catholic Secretariat, P.O. Box 8002, Lusaka, T: 62180.

ZIMBABWE

Pastoral Service, Catholic Secretariat, Salisbury.

64

Rural & agricultural mission

Agricultural missions, Christian rural or farming communities or centers, village polytechnics, farmers' trade unions; rural and agricultural training centers; agricultural assistance, rural transformation, rural development aid.

ARGENTINA

Misiones Rurales Argentinas, Santa Fe 1005, Buenos Aires.

Movimiento Rural de Acción Católica, Montevideo 850, Buenos Aires.

Secretariado del Movimiento Rural, Rodriguez Pena 846, 1 Piso, Buenos Aires.

AUSTRALIA

National Catholic Rural Movement, P.O. Box 125, Camberwell.

Steer, Inc., P.O. Box 21, Armadale, Victoria 3143.

AUSTRIA

KLJ/O und KLJM/O, Generalsekretariat, Johannesgasse 16, A-1010 Wien 1.

BELGIUM

Alliance Agricole Belge, Rue Joseph II 82, B-1040 Brussel, T: (02)2186979.

Catholic International Union for Social Service, Rue de la Poste 111, B-1030 Brussel, T: (02)172858.

Federation Internationale des Mouvements D'Adultes Ruraux Catholiques (FIMARC), Rue Africaine, 92, B 1050 Bruxelles.

International Federation of Catholic Rural Movements, Rue Africaine 92, B-1050 Brussel, T: (02)5187842.

International Federation of Rural Adult Catholic Movements, Rue Jaumain 15, B-5330 Assesse.

International Movement of Catholic Agricultural & Rural Youth, Diestsevest 24, B-3000 Leuven, T: (016)228312.

KLJ Centrale, Diestsevest 26, B-3000 Leuven.

KLJM, Diestsevest 18, B-3000 Leuven.

Mouvement International de la Jeunesse Agricole et Rurale Catholique (MIJARC), 68, Tiensevest, B 3000 Leuven.

Secrétariat de la JRC et JRCF, Rue du Sémanaire 11, B-5000 Namur.

BELIZE

Lynam Agricultural College, Belize.

BENIN

JAC/F, Mission Catholique, Dangbo via Porto-Novo.

BOLIVIA

Departmento de Fomento Cooperativo, Yanococha 545, Casilla Correo 3077, La Paz.

Hermanas Franciscanas Misioneras Rurales, Casilla 3848, La Paz, T: 43049.

Instituto de Educación Rural (IER), Casilla 731, Cochabamba, T: 9084.

Secretariado JAC y JACF, Casilla 731, Cochabamba.

BRAZIL

Centro de Formação de Líderes Rurais (CFLR), Casa Sagrada Familia, Av João XIII s/n, CP 37, São Mateus, ES.

Cooperativa de Colonização Agro-Pecuária de Pindorama, Penedo, AL.

Cooperativa Mista Agricola do Araguaia, São Felix, MT.

Frente Agrária Paranaense, Residência Episcopal, CP 152, 87 100 Maringá, PR, T: 21700.

Servico de Orientação Rural de Pernambuco (SORPE), Rua do Giriquiti 48, 50 000 Recife, PE.

BRITAIN (UK OF GB & NI)

Agricultural Christian Fellowship, 39 Bedford Square, London WC1B 3EY.

Institute of Rural Life at Home and Overseas, 3 Hendon Av, Finchley, London N3; 27 Northumberland Rd., New Barnet.

BURKINA FASO

Bazega Horticultural Training Center, BP 592, Ouagadougou.

CAMEROON

JAC et JACF, BP 4272, Yaoundé.

MIJARC, Sécretariat Panafricain, BP 859, Yaoundé.

CANADA

Fédération des Caisses Populaires des Jardins, 59 Av Bégin, Levis, Québec.

JRC, Apt 1, 1225 Jean Talon Est, Montréal 328, Québec.

Jubilee Centre for Agricultural Research, 115 Woolwich St., Guelph, ON N1H 3V1, T: 519-837-1620, F: 519-824-1835.

Rural Life Mission, 41 Main St N, Hagersville, Ontario.

CENTRAL AFRICAN REPUBLIC

Animation Rurale Féminine (ARF), Central Jean XXIII, Bangui.

CHAD

Société Chrétienne Agricole, BP 2162, Ndjamena (Fort-Lamy).

CHILE

ACR, Secretariado, Classificador 515, Santiago.

Instituto de Educación Rural, Casilla 10397, Santiago.

COLOMBIA

Acción Cultural Popular (ACPO), Escuelas Radiofónicas, Calle 20 No 9-45, Bogotá.

Granjas del Padre Luna, Carrera 7 No 26-37, Bogotá.

JAC y JACF, Secretariado, Calle 8 No 23-20, Ocana, Norte de Santander.

ECUADOR

Central Ecuatoriana de Servicios Agrícolas (CESA), c/o Apdo 36, Riobamba, Chimborazo.

Centro de Producción Agrícola, Catarama, Los Rios, T: 383-005.

Cooperativa de Ahorro, Illuchi, Casilla 208, Latacunga.

Desarrollo Agrícola Y/O Comunal, Rumipamba No. 815 y Republica, Casilla 8184, Quito, T: 457-166.

Desarrollo de la Comunidad, Illuchi, Casilla 208, Latacunga.

Entrenamiento Ministerial, Rumipamba No. 815 y Republica, Casilla 8184, Quito, T: 457-166.

JAC/F, Apdo 36, Riobamba, Chimborazo.

Mejoramiento Agropecuario, Rumipamba No. 915, Casilla 4829, Quito, T: 456-714.

Pastoral Rural Ecuatoriana, Vasco de Contreras 113-Barrio Granda Centeno-Quito, T: 444-035.

Promocion de Salud Comunitaria, Rumipamba No. 815, y Republica, Casilla 8184, Quito, T: 457-166.

Proyecto Agropecuario Luterano, Chuchum, Casilla 178, Cuenca, T: 27-27.

EL SALVADOR

Coordinación Centroamericana de Centros Campesinos Cristianos, Centro La Providencia, Apdo 1941, Santa Ana, T: 413110.

Juventud Agrária Católica 9JAC) & JACF, Secretariado, Colegio Pio X, Cujutepeque, Dpto Cuscatlan, T: 320308.

ETHIOPIA

Agri-Service Ethiopia, P.O. Box 3406, Soddo-Wolloam.

FIJI

Farm and Rural Rehabilitation Unit (Salvation Army), Lomaivuna, Farm 80, Viti Levu.

FRANCE

Centri d'Istruzione Agricola Nord-Africana, 33 rue Rabelais, Angers.

Donation Rurale, F-59232 Vieux-Berquin.

Ecole Supérieure d'Agriculture de Purpan, 271 Av de Grande-Bretagne, F-31300 Toulouse.

Institut Social d'Action Populaire, 15 Rue Raymond Marcheron, F-92170 Vanves.

GABON

JAC et JACF, Secrétariat, BP 100, Oyem.

GAMBIA

Agricultural, Technical & Community Development Centre, P.O. Box 165, Bathurst.

GERMANY

Arbeitsgemeinschaft für Dorfkirchlichen Dienst innerhalb der EKD, In Weidergarten 12, D-35 Kassel-K.

Bauernschule Gamburg, Ländliche Heimvolkshochschule, D-6981 Gamburg (Tauber).

Ev-Lutherische Ländvolk-Hochschule, D-2321 Koppelsberg über Plön.

Internationale Föderation Katholische Ländlicher Heimvolkschochschulen, Adrianstr 141, D-5300 Bonn-Oberkassel, T: (02221)440323.

Katholische Landvolkbewegung Deutschlands, Kriemhildenstr 14, D-8000 München 38.

KLJB, Bundestelle, Klausenhofstr 38, D-4203 Dingden, Westfalen.

Ländliche Heimvolkshochschule, D-7112 Hohebuch-Waldenburg.

Ländvolkshochschule Rheinland, Diepersbergweg 13-17, D-523 Altenkirchen (Westerwald).

Ostfriesische Evangelische Ländvolkshochschule, D-2919 Potshausen (Ostfriesland).

Schwäbische Bauernschule Bad Waldsee, Döchbuhl, D-7967 Waldsee.

GREECE

Union des Cooperatives Agricoles de Syra, Place Hérouu 7, Hermoupolis, Syra.

HOLY SEE

Agrimission, Secretariat, Piazza San Calisto 16, I-00120 Città del Vaticano, T: 6984443.

HONDURAS

Agricultural Production and Community Development Program (NCS), Apdo 586, San Pedro Sula, Cortés.

INDIA

Action for Food Production Office (AFPRO), C-52, ND South Extension II, New Delhi 49, T: 621651.

Action for Integrated Rural Development Society, Goshen 3-6-195/1, Himayatnagar, Hyderabad, Andhra Pradesh 500029.

Agricultural Institute, Kasam, Katpadi, Tamil Nadu 632007.

Agriculture Centre, Hemgir P. O., Orissa 770013.

Agriculture Development Centre, Archbishop's House, Trivandrum, Kerala.

Allahabad Agricultural Institute, Agricultural Institute P. O., Allahabad, Uttar Pradesh 211007.

Allahabad Farmer Quarterly, P. O. Allahabad Agricultural Institute, Allahabad, Uttar Pradesh 211007.

Bedona Village Mission, Sarni, , Madhya Pradesh.

Bellary Area Comprehensive Rural Development Project, C. S. I. Nava Jeevana Kendra, (Mandalam), Kavutalam, Andhra Pradesh 518344.

Bethel Agricultural Fellowship, Danishpet, Tamil Nadu 636354.

Biate Tribal Social Welfare Organisation (B.T.S.W.O.), Jowai Ladthaladboh, Jaintia Hills, Jowai P. O., Meghalaya 793150.

Centre for Promotion of Rural Development, Sharan, 12-2-826/C/1, Mehdipatnam, Hyderabad, Andhra Pradesh 500028.

Centre for Rural Development, Raghopur, Via Rasra, Athilapura, Uttar Pradesh 221712.

Centre for Rural Employment and Education for Development, Azhagiamandapam, Mulagumoodu P. O., Tamil Nadu 629167.

Christ for the Rural Mission, 4, Mullai Ave, First Cross, Periyar Nagar, Irumbuliyur, West Tambaram, Madras, Tamil Nadu 600045.

Christ Village Gospel Team, Holy Spirit Kudil, Ramagiri (PO), Guziliampari, Tamil Nadu 624703.

Comprehensive Rural Development Services, Silver Oak Avenue, Darogapathar Area, P. O. Box 49, Dimapur, Nagaland 797112.

Dairy Unit, D. M. Convent, Assisi Farm, Thadikarakonam, Tamil Nadu.

Don Bosco Agricultural Training School, Via Takkolam, Sagayathottam, Tamil Nadu 631151.

Evangelical Lambadi Inland Ministries (ELIM), Venkatam Palli, Via Vazra Karur, Rayalaseema, Andhra Pradesh 515832.

Every Village Evangelism, 5, 4th Street, Camp Road, Selaiyur, Sri Ram Nagar, East Tambaram, Madras, Tamil Nadu 600073.

FARMS India, No. 5, Indira Gandhi III Street, Avvai Nagar, Madras, Tamil Nadu 600094.

Fish-Farming Project, St. Joseph's Church, Chirakal, Cochin, Kerala 682006.

Friends Rural Centre, Rasulia, Hoshangabad 461001.

Hill Gospel Fellowship, Thumbal (Via), Pappanaikan Patty PO, Tamil Nadu 636114.

India Rural Evangelical Fellowship, Gold Fields, Repalle (P. O.), Andhra Pradesh 522265.

Indian Christian Society for Rural Development and Welfare, 30/370 Malakapatam, P. B. No. 64, Machilipatnam, Andhra Pradesh 521001.

King's Village Gospel Ministry, Kazathil Zone House, Cheriyakolla P. O., Kerala 695504.

Maharashtra Village Ministries, Plot No. 89, Kukdey Layout, Parvatinagar P. O., Nagpur, Maharashtra 440027.

Malankara Fisheries, Kunnam, Thottappally, Kerala.

Mission for the Interior, Post Box 1355, Humayun Nagar, Hyderabad, Andhra Pradesh 500028.

Rural Aids Service Organisation (RASO), Lake View Colony, Podalakur Road, A. K. Nagar, Nellore, Andhra Pradesh 524004.

Rural Development Centre, Lillipur, Via Palmakole, Dubbacherla P. O., Andhra Pradesh 509359.

Rural Development Project for Girls, Mission Compound, Mahasamund, Madhya Pradesh 493445.

Rural Development Training Centre, Ambakkam Village, Sathyavedu 517 588.

Rural Life Programme, Opp. Circuit House, Civil Lines, Raipur, Madhya Pradesh 492001.

Rural Technical School, Asha Niketan, Kapa P. O., Madhya Pradesh 492005.

Satyaniketan Dharmvigyan Mahavidyalaya, Indalpur Road, P. O. Agricultural Institute, Allahabad, Uttar Pradesh 211007.

SHARE (Share for Health and Rural Education), Firs Estate, Landour Cantonment, Mussoorie, Uttar Pradesh 248179.

Society for Comprehensive Rural Health Projects in India, Karmala Road, Jamkhed, Maharashtra 413201.

St. Joseph's Agricultural Training Centre, Umran-Sohbatnong, Via Naya, Bunfalow, Meghalaya 793105.

SWORD (Society For Women, Orphan and Rural Development), Post Box 99, St. Peter's Church Compound, Hubli, Karnataka 580020.

Tamil Nadu Agricultural University, Coimbatore, Tamil Nadu 641033.

Tamil Villages Gospel Mission, Post Box 612, 5, Kuaran Nagar, Puthur, Trichy, Tamil Nadu 620017.

Village Evangelism And Revival Crusade, 8/B, Nirmal Society, Mission Area, Nadiad, Gujarat 387001.

Village Gospel Ministry, 1. Thanthai Periyar Nagar, Jayanagaram, Velacheri, Madras, Tamil Nadu 600042.

Village Revival Mission, 65 Viswanathapuram, Madurai, Tamil Nadu 625014.

Xavier Institute of Rural Development, Mohitnagar P. O., West Bengal 735101.

Xavier's Research Farm and Agricultural School, C/o St Xavier's High School, Mogar, Anand, Gujarat 388001.

INDONESIA

Ikatan Petani Pancasila, Jalan Gunung Sahari III/7, Jakarta.

IRELAND

Ferns Diocesan Youth Service, Bunclody, Wexford.

Irish Creamery Milk Suppliers' Association, John Feely House, 15 Upper Mallow St, Limerick.

National Farmers' Association, 27 Earlscourt Terrace, Dublin 2.

People of the Country, Tipperary.

ITALY

Centro Sociale e Cooperativa Agricola di Villa S Sebastiano, Via S Barbara 23, Villa S Sebastiano (Aq).

Communità dei Braccianti, Viale Ferdinando Baldelli 41, I-00146 Roma, T: 552251.

Confederazione Cooperative Italiana, 78 Borgo S Spirito, Roma.

Confederazione Nazionale Coltivatori Diretti, Via XXIV Maggio 43, Roma.

Federazione Italiana Clubs 3P, Via XXIV Maggio 43, Roma.

International Catholic Rural Association, Piazza San Calisto, 00153, Rome.

Teleradio Agricoltura Informazione, Via Tor Pisana 98, I-72100 Brindisi.

IVORY COAST

JAC/F, Secretariat, BP 4119, Abidjan.

JAPAN

Asian Rural Institute, 442-1 Tsukinokizawa, Nishinasuno, Nasu-gun, Tochigi-ken 329-27.

HELP Asian Women's Shelter, Japan Women's Christian Temperance Union, 2-23-5 Hyakunincho, Shinjuku-ku, Tokyo.

Japan Rural Evangelism Fellowship, Tachi West Court W-145, Nakagami-Machi, Akishima-shi, Tokyo 196.

Japan Rural Mission, C.P.O. Box 142, Oita 870-91; 517-4 Shimo Munakata, Oita Shi 870-11, T: 0975-41-4739.

KEEP Seisenryo, Kiyosato, Takane-cho, Kita-Koma-gun, Yamanashi-ken 407-03, T: 81-551-48-2111, F: 81-551-482099.

Rural and Printing Evangelism in Japan, 1014 Kuge/Yana Cho, Ono City, Hyogo-ken.

Tsurukawa Rural Institute, 2024 Nozuta-cho, Machida-shi, Tokyo, T: (0427)35-2430.

KENYA

Christian Rural Fellowship of East Africa (CR-FEA), Lugari Farmers Training Centre, PO Box 30, Turbo.

Christian Rural Service (CRS), PO Box 79, Eldoret, T: 2051.

Kataboi Fishing Village, Kataboi Catholic Mission, Private Bag, Kitale.

Loarengak Fishing Village, Catholic Mission, PO Box Lokitaung, Kitale.

Maasai Rural Training Centre (CPK), Isinya, PO Box 24, Kajiado.

LESOTHO

Machobane Rural Training Centre, Machobane.

Roma Valley Agricultural Project, Archbishop's House, PO Box 267, Maseru, T: 2565.

LUXEMBOURG

JACF, Secrétariat, 3 Place du Théâtre, Luxembourg-ville.

JBJW, Secrétariat, 3 Rue Borgen, Luxembourg.

MADAGASCAR
Centre Artisanal de Promotion Rurale, BP 1170, Fianarantsoa.
Centre d'Apprentissage Agricole, Bevalala, Tananarive.
Centre d'Education Familiale et Rurale, BP 98, Antsiramandroso, Tamatave.
Centre Ménager Rural, PB 1782, Tananarive.
Ferme-Ecole, Betomba par Belo-sur-Tsirbihina.
Madagascar Catholic Rural Youth Movement, Evêché, BP 100, Antsirabe.

MEXICO
Acción Católica Mexicana, Consejo Nacional de Campesinos, Minerva 104, 5 piso, México 20, DF.
ACJM, Secretariado, Jalapa 35-c, México 7, DF.
Heifer Project, Apdo 390, Celaya, Gto.
Ingenieros Agrónomos, Antonio Vélez 24, Apdo 15, Atlacomulco.
JAC, Secretariado, 20 de Noviembre 9, Morelia Mich.

NETHERLANDS
Agromisa (Bureau voor Landvouwkindige Adviezen aan Missionarissen), Postbus 41, Wageningen.
KPJM, Sekretariat, Scheveningseweg 46, 's-Gravenhage.

NIGERIA
COCIN Agricultural and Bible Training Institute, Church of Christ in Nigeria, PMB 2127, JOS, Plateau State.

PAKISTAN
Rural Health Education Center, Pakistan Adventist Seminary, Farooqabad Mandi, Sheikhpura District.
Rural Rehabilitation Centre (Salvation Army), P.O. Box 10735, Karachi; Manzil-e-Umead, Site Metroville, Karachi, T: 21-6650513.

PAPUA NEW GUINEA
Mount Diamond Adventist High School and Agriculture Centre, Magi Highway, Central Province.

PARAGUAY
Instituto de Educación Rural (IDER), Mariscal Estigarribia 629, Tavá Arroyo.
JAC y JACF, Secretariado, Oliva 476, Asunción.
Ligas Agrarias Cristianas, c/o Oliva 476, Asunción.

PERU
Movimiento Sindical Cristiano del Perú, Jiron Ucayali 332, Apdo 1321, Lima.

PHILIPPINES
Agricultural Missions, 941 Epifanio de los Santos Av, Quezon City.
College of Agriculture, Xavier University, Cagayan de Oro City.
Farm Workers for an Enlightened Republic, P.O. Box 1767, Manila, T: 998636.
Free Farmers' Federation (FFF), 39 Highland Drive, Blue Ridge, Quezon City D504.
Junior Free Farmers, 39 Highland Drive, Blue Ridge, Quezon City D504.
Rehabilitaion Hog-raising and Fishing (Salvation Army), La Union Sto. Tomas, Balaoc 2505, La Union.
South East Asian Rural Social Leadership Institute (SEARSOLIN), c/o Xavier University, Cagayan de Oro City L-305.

PORTUGAL
JARC, Secretariado, Campo Martires da Patria 43, Lisboa 1.
JARCF, Secretariado, Av Duque de Loulé 90, r-c dto, Lisboa 1.

RWANDA
JAC et JACF, Sécretariat, BP 87, Gisenyi.

SENEGAL
Union des Jeunesses Catholiques Rurales du Sénégal, BP 24, Thies.

SOUTH AFRICA
Church Agricultural Projects, Manager, Maria Ratschitz, North Natal.
Tshwane Christian Ministries, P/Bab X20, Rosslyn 0200, T: 012-561-1247, F: 012-561-1201.

SOUTH KOREA
Catholic Farmers' Movement, 1-170, Songnam 2-dong, Tong-gu, Taejon-shi, T: (02) 673-4040.
Catholic Rural Youth, 6 Ku Wonpyung Kumi, Kyongbuk.
Isidore Development Association, PO Box 50, Cheju Do, T: Cheju City 4635.
Kuokmal Agricultural Worker's Council, 481 Wonsan-Ri, Sapkyo-Eup, Yesan-Kun, Chungnam-Do, 340-900, T: 82-458-33-0564, O: Also tel: 33-0474.
Yesan Association for Rural Development, Yesan Agricultural Technical College, Yesan-eup, Yesankun, 340 Choongchungnam-do, T: 82-458-2-3544.

SPAIN
Comisión Nacional JARCF, República Argentina 72-20, Benicarlo, Castellon.

SWAZILAND
Lutheran Farmers Training Centre, Pigg's Peak.

SWITZERLAND
JRC et JRCF, Grand Rue 48, CH-1680 Romont.

TAIWAN
Association for Social-Economic Development in China (ASEDROC), 279-1 3rd Floor, Roosevelt Rd, Section 3, Taipei.

THAILAND
Co-Operative Farm, Chiengmai.

TOGO
JAC et JACF, Secrétariat, BP 55, Sokode.
Société Civile et Agricole de Dzoghégan (SCAD), Dzoghégan.

TUNISIA
Association pour le Développement et l'Animation Rurale poursuivant les Activités du Service Oecuménique en Tunisie (ASDEAR), 10 Rue Eve Nohelle, Tunis, T: 245592.

UGANDA
Agricultural and Animal Husbandry School, Diocesan Development Department, PO Box 1103, Mbale, T: 2570.
Buswale Agricultural Scheme, PO Box 673, Jinja.
Christian Rural Service (CRS), PO Box 7046, Kampala.
Mugalibe Tea and Dairy Scheme, PO Box 34 Hoima.

UNITED STATES OF AMERICA (USA)
Agricultural Missions Foundation, O: Web: www.xmission.com/~ip/AMF/.
Agropolitan Ministries, P.O. Box 145, Merom, IN 47861, T: (812)356-4681.
Christian Rural Fellowship (CRF), 475 Riverside Drive, New York, NY 10027.
Christian Rural Overseas Program (CROP), 117 West Lexington Av, Box 227, Elkhart, IN 46514; 475 Riverside Drive, New York, NY 10027.
Commission on Agricultural Missions, NCC-CUSA, 475 Riverside Drive, New York, NY 10027.
Commission on Religion in Appalachia, 864 Weisgarber Rd, NW, Knoxville, TN 37919, T: (615)584-6133.
Farms International, Inc., P. O. Box 270, Knife River, MN 55609, T: 218-834-2676, F: 218-834-2676, O: E-mail: 102554.3305@compuserve.com, Web: www.gospelcom.net/mnn/media/farms.html.
Farms, Inc., 123 West 57th St, New York, NY 10019, T: (212)246-9692.
Floresta USA, 1015 Chesnut Ave., Suite F2, Carlsbad, CA 92008, T: 619-434-6311.
Friends Information Centers & Offices, 515 E Capitol St., Washington, DC 20003, T: 202-543-5560.
Good Shepherd Agricultural Mission, 822 Main St, Box 116, Fontanelle, IA 50846, T: (515)745-4041.
Harvesters International, 3409 Gumwood, Box 1986, McAllen, TX 78501.
Heifer Project International, 1015 Louisiana St., Little Rock, AR 72202, T: 501-376-6836, F: 501-376-8906, O: E-mail: 74222.1542@compuserve.com, Web: www.intellinet.com/Heifer.
Hinton Rural Life Centre, P.O. Box 27, Hayesville, NC 28904.
National Catholic Rural Life Conference, 3801 Grand Ave., Des Moines, IA 50312.
National Farm Worker Ministry, Suite 511, 1411 West Olympic Blvd, Los Angeles, CA 90015, T: (213)286-8130.
Rural Church Resource Center, O: Web: www.digitmaster.com/hp/ohf/church/newsletter/index.html.
Self-Help Foundation, 805 W. Bremer Ave., Waverly, IA 50677, T: 319-352-4040, F: 319-352-4040, O: E-mail: selfhelp@sbt.net, Web: www.sbt.net/self-help.
STEER, Inc., P.O. Box 1236, Bismarch, ND 58502, T: 701-258-4911, F: 701-258-7684.
Unitarian Universalist Ministry to Migrant Farm Workers, 1148 Cragmont Ave., Berkeley, CA 94708, T: (415)848-6304.
World Neighbors, 4127 N.W. 122nd St., Oklahoma City, OK 73120, T: 405-752-9700, F: 405-752-9393.

URUGUAY
JAC y JACF, Secretariado, 25 de Mayo 493, Casilla 61, San José.
MIJARC, Secretariado Latinoamericano, Cerrito 475, Casilla Postal 1811 (Correo Central), Montevideo.

VENEZUELA
Instituto Venezolano de Acción Comunitaria, Av Libertado, Edif La Línea, 3er piso No 34-A, Caracas.

VIET NAM
Secrétariat Social, 86 Nguyen Du, Ho Chi Minh Ville; In ICRA.

ZAMBIA
Agriculture Training Center (Salvation Army), P.O. Box 34352, Lusaka 10101; Ibbwe Munyama, Lusaka 10101.
Chikankata Community Development Programme (Salvation Army), PB S2, Mazabuka.

ZIMBABWE
Friends Rural Service Centre, (Hlekweni), P.O. Box 708, Bulawayo, T: 79888.

65
Scholarly societies

Associations of scholars and thinking practitioners who communicate with each other in their field of study, such as biblical studies, theology, missiology, church history, sociology of religion, anthropology, psychology, archeology, religion and science, religion and philosophy, religion and futurology, et alii; national and international associations, learned societies, and commissions (as contrasted with institutes or centers); Catholic pontifical commissions in scholarly disciplines.

AUSTRIA
Société du Droit de Eglises Orientales, Karl Luerger Ring I, A-1010 Wien.
World Union of Catholic Philosophical Societies, Secretariat, Aignerstr 25, A-5026 Salzburg.

BELGIUM
International Association for the History of Religions, Rue Ducale 1, Brussel.

BRAZIL
Administração Central Sociedade Brasiliense de Belas Letrase d Ciências, Rua Barão da Guaratiba, 44 - Glória, 22.220-000 Rio de Janerio -RJ, T: (021) 265-1312, F: (021) 265-4174.

BRITAIN (UK OF GB & NI)
Alcuin Club, c/o Canon Gate House, Chichester.
Archivists of England and Wales, Assoc. of Diocesan, 1 Milton Road, Portsmouth PO3 6AN, T: 01705-822166.
Bampton Lectures (Oxford University), University Registry, Clarendon Bldgs, Broad St, Oxford, T: 48491.
Baptist Historical Society, Baptist Church House, 4 Southampton Row, London WC1.
Congregational Historical Society, 9 Priory Way, Hitchin, Herts, T: 3580.
Ecclesiastical History Society, Westfield College, London NW3, T: (01)435-7601.
Ecclesiological Society, 1 Burghley Rd, Wimbledon, London SW19, T: (01)946-4340.
English Catholic History Group, 4 Lower Chilton, Chilton Cantelo, Nr Yeovil, Somerset BA22 8BD, T: 01935-850821.
English Church History, 68 Irby Rd, Heswell, Liverpool, T: (051)342-4476.
Evangelical Fellowship for Missionary Studies, 19 Draycott Place, London SW3 2SJ.
Friends Historical Society, Library, Friends House, Euston Rd, London NW1, T: Euston 3601.
Historical Society of the Church in Wales, Trinity College, Carmarthen, T: (0267)7971.
Hulsean Lectures (Cambridge University), University Marshal, 1a Rose Crescent, Cambridge, T: 58933/296.
Hymn Society of Great Britain and Ireland, 85 Lord Haddon Rd, Ilkeston, Derbyshire, T: 5850.
Royal Institute of Philosophy, 14 Gordon Square, London WC1, T: Euston 4130.
Scottish Catholic Historical Association, c/o John S Burns & Sons, 25 Finlas St, Glasgow G22.
Scottish Ecclesiological Society, 16 Heriot Row, Edinburgh 3, T: 26188.
Society for African Church History, Dept. of Religious Studies, University of Aberdeen AB9 2UB.
Society for Physical Research, 1 Adam and Eve Mews, London W8, T: Western 8984.
Society for the Christian Religion in Publications and Transmission, All Souls College, Oxford.
Society for the Study of Medical Ethics, 103 Gower St, London WC1.
Society for the Study of the New Testament, King's College, Old Aberdeen AB9 2UB, T: (0224)40241 ext 308.
Studiorum Nove Testamenti Societas (SNTS), The University, Nottingham.
Unitarian Historical Society, Unitarian College, Victoria Park, Manchester 14, T: Rusholme 2849.
Victoria Institute (Philosophical Society of Great Britain), 38 Jennings Rd, St Albans, Herts.
Wesley Historical Society, The Manse, St Keverne, Helston, Cornwall, T: 399.

CANADA
Canadian Catholic Historical Association, 355 Church St., Toronto, ON M5B 1Z8, T: 416-977-1500.
Canadian Church History Society, c/o Scarborough College, 1265 Military Trail, West Hill, Ontario.
Canadian Society of Biblical Studies, Dept. of Religious Studies, Memorial Univ. of Newfoundland, St. John's, NF A1C 5S7, T: 709-737-8166, F: 709-737-4569.
Evangelical Theological Society of Canada, Ontario Bible College, 16 Spadina Rd, Toronto 4, Ontario.
Salvation Army Archives, Research and Museum, George Scott Railton Heritage Centre, 2130 Bayview Ave., Toronto ON, M4N 3K6, T: 416-481-4441.

CHINA
Programme for Theology and Cultures in Asia (PTCA), PO Box 1423, Shatin, Hong Kong, T: 852-2609-6497, F: 852-2603-5280.

COLOMBIA
Comision de Estudios de Historia de la Iglesia en America Latina-CEHILA, Calle 56, No. 3-54-Santa Fe de Bogota, T: 571-345-5363, F: 571-345-7876.

DENMARK
Nordic Society for Studies in Church History, Nordic Missionary Council, Strandagervej 24, Hellerup.

FRANCE
Association Française de Sociologie Religieuse, 32 bis Rue du Bois, F-75019 Paris, T: 2037414.
International Association for Patristic Studies, IC Quai Saint Thomas, F-67000 Strasbourg.
International Conference for the Sociology of Religion, Rue de la Monnaie 39, F-59042 Lille, T: (20)553026.
Société Calviniste de France, 10 Rue de Villars, St-Germain-en-Laye (Yvelines).
Société de Histoire du Protestantisme Français (SHPF), 54 Rue des Saints-Pères, F-75007 Paris, T: LIT 7845, 6207.

GERMANY
German Society for the Study of Missions, Finkenstr. 5, 91564 Neuendettelsou, T: 09874/5 09 51, F: 09874/5 09 95.
Gesellschaft für Geistegeschichte, Kuchstr 4, D-8520 Erlangen.
Görres-Gesellschaft zur Pflege der Wissenschaft, Postfach 100905, D-5000 Köln 1, T: (0221)237774.
International Association for Mission Studies, Mittelweg 143, D-2000 Hamburg 13.
Internationale Gesellschaft für Religionsychologie, Hiltenspergerstr 107/I, D-8000 München 40, T: (089)3002800.
Konvent Ev Theologinnen in der BDR und Westberlin, Goethestr 26-30, D-1 Berlin 12.
Luther-Gesellschaft, Geschäftsstelle, Grindel-Allee 7, D-2 Hamburg 13.

HOLY SEE
Pontifical Academy of Sciences, Cancelleria, Casina di Pio IV, Città del Vaticano, T: 6982 int 3195, 3451.
Pontifical Commission for Biblical Studies, Palazzo della SCDF, Piazza del Santo Uffizio 11, I-00193 Roma, T: 6983357.
Pontificia Commissione di Archeologia Sacra, Palazzo del PIA, Via Napoleone III 1, I-00185 Roma, Italy, T: 735824.
Pontificia Commissione per gli Archivi Ecclesiastici d'Italia, Palazzo Apostolico, I-00120 Città del Vaticano, T: 6982 int 3314.

INDIA
Christian Society for Oriental Culture & Social Study, 1,1 Street Haddows Road, Nungambakkam, Madras, Tamil Nadu 600034.
Church Growth Society of India.
Church History Association of India, Vidyajyothi 23, Raj Niwas Mg., New Delhi 110054.
Ecumenical Association of Third World Theologians (EATWT), 63 Miller's Rd, P.O. Box 4635, Bangalore 560 046, T: 91-80-3334-385, F: 91-80-563-249.

ITALY
Commission for Latin America, Palazzo delle Congregazioni, Piazza Pio XII 10, I-00193 Roma, T: 6982 int 3311, 4465, 4738.
Commission for the Revision of Canon Law, Palazzo dei Convertendi, Via dell'Erba, I-00193 Roma, T: 6982 int 3933, 3934, 3994.
Commission for the Revision of Oriental Canon Law, Palazzo dei Convertendi, Via della Conciliazione 34, Roma, T: 698 int 4295.
Congregation for the Doctrine of the Faith, Piazza del S. Uffizio 11, 00193 Rome.
Consociatio Internationalis Studio Iuris Canonici Promovendo, Prof Cesare Mirabelli, Via Cicerone 49, I-00193 Roma.
International Society for the Study of Prehistoric and Ethnological Religions, Roma.
Pontificio Istituto di Archeologia Cristiana, Via Napoleone III, 1, I-00185 Rome, T: 39-6-446-5574, F: 39-6-446-9197.
Società di Studi Valdesi, Via Massimo d'Azeglio, I-10066 Torre Pellice (To).

LUXEMBOURG
Association Catholique Internationale d'Etudes Médico-Psychologiques (ACIEMP), 31 Blvd Jacquemart, Luxembourg, T: 483860.

MEXICO
Commission of Studies for Latin American Church History (CEHILA), Apdo 22-278, México 22, DF.

NETHERLANDS ANTILLES
FESSKA, Pastorie Jandoret, Curaçao, T: 599-9-681655, F: 599-9-681655.

NIGERIA
Ecumenical Association of African Theologians (EAAT), Catholic Higher Institute of West Africa, P.O. Box 499, Port Harcourt.
Nigerian Association for the Study of Religions, Department of Religious Studies, University of Ibadan, Ibadan.

SOUTH AFRICA
South African Academy of Religion, c/o Research Institute for Theology & Religion, Unisa, PO 392, Pretoria, 0001; Unisa, Samuel Pauw Building, Room 3-31, T: (012) 429-4369, F: (012)429-3535, O: E-mail: saarsc@alpha.unisa.ac.za.
South African Society for the Study of Mission, PO Box 213, Umtata, Transkei.
Southern Africa Missiological Society, c/o Dept of Missiology, PO Box 392, 0001 Pretoria, T: 012-429-4477, F: 012-429-3332.

SOUTH KOREA
Research Institute for Korean Church History, 1, 2-ga, Myong-dong, Chung-gu, Seoul-shi, T: (02) 756-1691.

SWEDEN
International Association for the Study of the Old Testament (IASOT), Dekanhuset, The University, Uppsala.

SWITZERLAND
Verband Schweizerischer Theologinnen, CH-4125 Riehen/BS.

TAIWAN
Ricci Institute for Chinese Studies, 8th Fl., 24 Hsinhai Rd., Sect. 1, Taipei, T: 02-3689968, F: 886-2-3654508.

UNITED STATES OF AMERICA (USA)
Academy of Religion and Mental Health, 16 East 34th St, New York, NY 10016.
American Academy of Religion (AAR), Dept. of Religious Thought, University of Pennsylvania, Philadelphia, PA 19104; AAR National Office, Wilson College, Chambersburg, PA 17201.
American Baptist Historical Society, P.O. Box 851, Valley Forge, PA 19481.
American Catholic Historical Association, Catholic University of America, Washington, D.C. 20064.
American Catholic Historical Society, 263 S. Fourth St., Philadelphia, PA 19106.
American Catholic Philosophical Association, Catholic University of America, Washington, DC 20017.
American Society of Christian Ethics (ASCE), Candler School of Theology, Emory University, Atlanta, GA 30322; Bucknell University, Lewisburg, PA 17837.
American Society of Missiology, 616 Walnut Ave., Scottdale, PA. 15683-1999
Association for Social-Economics (ASE), 2323 North Seminary Av, Chicago, IL 60614.
Association for the Development of Religious Information Systems (ADRIS), Dept of Sociology & Anthropology, Marquette University, Milwaukee, WI 53233, T: (414)224-6838.
Association for the Sociology of Religion, 1403 North St Mary's St, San Antonio, TX 78215; Loyola Marymount University, Los Angeles, CA 90045.
Association of Statisticians of American Religious Bodies (ASARB), 120 West 14th St, New York, NY 10011, T: (212)243-8700.
Biblical Research Society, 4005 Verdugo Rd, Los Angeles, CA 90065.
Canon Law Society of America (CLSA), 134 Farmington Av, Hartford, CT 06105, T: (203)527-4201.
Catholic Biblical Association (CBA), Catholic University of America, Washington, DC 20017.
Catholic Commission on Intellectual and Cultural Affairs (CCICA), 620 Michigan Av, Washington, DC 20017.
Catholic Theological Society of America (CTSA), St. Mary of the Lake Seminary, Mundelein, IL 60060.
Catholic Theological Society of America, LaSalle University, Philadelphia, PA 19141.
Christian Association for Psychological Studies, 746 East Chapman Ave., Orange, CA 92660, T: 714-532-6761.
Christian History Institute, P.O. Box 540, Worcester, PA 19490, T: 610-584-1893, F: 610-584-4610, O: E-mail: chglilmpses@aol.com.
College Theology Society (CTS), Manhattan College, Bronx, NY 10471.
Conference on Science and Religion, 1090 South La Brea Av, Los Angeles, CA.
Congregational Christian Historical Society, 14 Beacon St., Boston, MA 02108.
Council of Societies for the Study of Religion, Valparaiso University, Valparaiso, IN 46383-6493, T: (219)464-5515, F: (219)464-6714, e-mail: cssr@valpo.edu.
Evangelical Missiological Society, (EMS) P.O. Box 794, Wheaton, IL 60189, 630-752-7158; O: E-mail: EMS@wheaton.edu
Evangelical Theological Society (ETS), c/o RTS, 5422 Clinton Blvd. Jackson, MS 39202.
Fellowship of Catholic Scholars, 714 Hesburgh Library, Notre Dame, IN 46556.
Friends Historical Association, c/o Quaker Collection, Magill Library, Haverford College, Haverford, PA 19041, T: 215-896-1161.
Gospel and Our Culture Network, O: Web: www.gocn.org.
Historical Commission, 901 Commerce St., Suite 400, Nashville, TN 31203-3620.
Institute for Advanced Christian Studies, P.O. Box 241, Wheaton, IL 60189, T: 708-665-3417.
Institute for the Study of American Evangelicals, O: Web: www.wheaton.edu/bgc/isae.
International Society for Frontier Missiology, 1605 Elizabeth St., Pasadena, CA 91104, T: 818-797-1111, F: 818-398-2263.
Mexican Theological Society, Montezuma Seminary, Montezuma, NM 87731.
Mormon History Association (MHA), Brigham Young University, Provo, UT 84601.
North American Society for Church Growth, P.O. Box 90910, Pasadena, CA 91109-0910, T: 818-449-0425.
Pope John Center on Biomedical Ethics, O: Web: www.pjcenter.org/pjc.
Presbyterian Historical Society, 425 Lombard St, Philadelphia, PA 19147.
Religious Research Association, P.O. Box 228, Cathedral Station, New York, NY 10025.
Seventh Day Baptist Historical Society, 510 Watchung Av, P.O. Box 868, Plainfield, NJ 07061, T: (201)754-3404.
Society for Pentecostal Studies, Lee College, Cleveland, TN 37311.
Society for Religion in Higher Education, 400 Prospect St, New Haven, CT 06511, T: (203)865-8839.
Society for the Integration of Faith and Thought, O: http://www.sift.org.au/.
Society for the Scientific Study of Religion (SSSR), 1200 17th St NW, Washington, DC 20036; Dept. of Sociology, Univ. of Notre Dame, Notre Dame, IN 46556.
Society of Biblical Literature (SBL), Dept. of Religious Studies, University of Montana, Missoula, MT 59801, T: (406)243-2632.
Society of Biblical Literature and Exegesis, (SBLE), Divinity Quadrangle, Vanderbilt University, Nashville, TN.
Unitarian Historical Society, First Church of Boston, 66 Marlborough St, Boston, MA 02116.
United States Catholic Historical Society, O: Web: www.catholic.org/uschs/index.html.
Universalist Historical Society, 2425 Sierra Blvd, Sacramento, CA 95825.
World Association for Public Opinion Research, Roper Public Opinion Research Centre, Williams College, Williamstown, MA.
World Future Society, 4916 St. Elmo Ave., Bethesda, MD 20814-5089, T: 301-656-8274, O: Cable: WORLDFUTUR.
World Methodist Historical Society, Cambridge Apartment, 402 Alden Park, PA 19144.
World Union of Catholic Philosophical Societies, Catholic University of America, Washington, D.C. 20017.
Zygon, 5700 South Woodlawn Av, Chcago, IL 60637, T: (312)643-0800 ext 3163.

66
Schools and colleges

Definitions: Schools under church or Christian auspices or sponsorship: junior and senior secondary schools teaching secular and/or religious subjects, minor seminaries (secular or religious), technical schools, vocational schools, junior colleges, technical colleges, teacher-training colleges, and 4-year Christian colleges (emphasizing or only offering undergraduate baccalaureate degrees); organizations, institutions, and agencies that help or promote Christian home-schooling; schools for the children of foreign missionaries, MK schools and agencies. See also BIBLE SCHOOLS AND COLLEGES, CATECHESIS AND CHRISTIAN EDUCATION, THEOLOGICAL COLLEGES AND SEMINARIES, and UNIVERSITIES.

67
Social and pastoral ministries

Definitions: Local social, pastoral, compassionate, or community action and service; social welfare, moral welfare, community development; ministries dealing with unemployment, housing, population control, delinquency, alcoholism, temperance, addiction, drug addiction, gambling, pornography, crime, and other social, moral, or personal problems; community centers, rehabilitation centers, social ministry centers; prison ministries, prison chaplaincies, ministry to former prisoners; ministry to the poor, to inner cities, to the elderly, the underprivileged, the oppressed, the suffering.

68
Spiritual life conventions, rallies or retreats

Annual or limited-duration movements or meetings not primarily for evangelism but for the deepening of the spiritual life; regular mass conventions, mass rallies, deeper life conventions, Keswick conventions, spiritual life conventions and conferences. Note that most such activities are not listed under RELIGIOUS COMMUNITIES and CAMPS, RETREAT CENTERS, AND LAY TRAINING CENTERS.

AUSTRALIA
Belgrave Heights Convention, 237 Flinders Lane, Melbourne, Victoria 3000, T: 635955.

BRITAIN (UK OF GB & NI)
Association for Promoting Retreats, Aldwych House, Aldwych, London WC2, T: (01)242-9790 ext 28.
Keswick Convention, 12 Skiddaw St, Keswick, Cumbria; 231 Mereside Way North, Solihull, Warwick, T: (021706)7536.
Society of Retreat Conductors, Stacklands Retreat House, West Kingsdown, Sevenoaks, Kent, T: (04)7485-2247.
SPRE-E 73 (Spiritual Re-Emphasis), Shirley House, 27 Camden Rd, London NW1 9YG, T: (01)267-0065.

GERMANY
Arbeitsgemeinschaft Lutherischer Konferenzen und Konvente, Berlinstr 2, D-31 Celle, T: (05141)7730.
Deutscher Evangelischer Kirchentag, Leitung, Magdeburgerstr 59, D-64 Fulda, T: 891.

INDIA
Maramon Convention, Diocese of Maramon, Mar Thoma Syrian Church, Maramon, Kerala.

ITALY
Better World Movement, Pope John XIII Centre, Roma.

KENYA
Kenya Keswick Convention, PO Box 45942, Nairobi.

MEXICO
Annual Spiritual Life Conference, Apdo 1114, Puebla, Puebla, T: 11601.

SOUTH KOREA
Passionist House of Meditation, 245-4, Ui-dong, Tobong-gu, Seoul-shi, T: (02) 990-1004.
Religious Consulation Center, 1, 2ga, Myong-dong, Chung-gu, Seoul-shi, T: (02) 776-8405.
Seton Retreat House, 120-3, 1-ga, Songbuk-dong, Songbuk-gu, Seoul-shi, T: (02) 744-9825.

SWITZERLAND
Association des Retriates Spirituelles de Presinge, CH-1253 Vandoeuvres.

UNITED STATES OF AMERICA (USA)
Americas' Keswick Inc, Route 530, Whiting, NJ 08759.
Cornerstone Christian Music and Arts Festival, O: Web: http://cornerstone.jesusfreak.com/index.html.
Creation Festival, Box 86, Medford, NJ 08055, T: 717-394-9466, F: 717-394-6593, O: E-mail: creation@gospelcom.net, Web: www.gospelcom.net/creation.
Friends Information Centers & Offices, 1501 Cherry St, Philadelphia, PA 19102, T: 215-241-7000.
Inter-Church Holiness Convention, 375 West State St, Salem, OH 44460, T: (216)337-7377.

69
State departments for religious affairs

State or government ministries or departments for religious or ecclesiastical affairs, or other government ministries whose responsibilities include the area of religious affairs, state religious organizations, state bodies for surveillance and control of churches or other religious organizations. Some are Christian in sympathies or activities, while others are hostile to Christianity and the churches.

ALGERIA
Ministère de l'Enseignement Original et des Affaires Religieuses, 4 Rue de Timgad, Hydra, El Djezair, T: 600290, 600293, 600936.

ANGOLA
Direcção dos Serviços de Educação, Repartição de Cultos, Luanda.

ARGENTINA
Subsecretaria de Culto, Ministerio de Relaciones Exteriores y Culto, Calle Arenales 761, Buenos Aires.

AUSTRIA
Kultursektion der Bundesministeriums für Unterreicht und Kunst, Minoriterplatz 5, A-1010 Wien.

BARBADOS
Ministry of Ecclesiastical Affairs, Ministry of Education, Hon Minister, Bridgetown.

BELGIUM
Administration des Cultes, Ministère de la Justice, 58 Rue aux Laines, B-1000 Brussel, T: (02)51142000.

BENIN
Ministère des Affaires Intérieures, Cotonou.

BOLIVIA
Ministerio de Relaciones Exteriores y Culto, Calle Ingavi Esq, Plaza Murillo 1099, La Paz, T: 2428.

BOTSWANA
Ministry of Health, Labour and Home Affairs, Private Bag 2, Gaborone.

BRAZIL
Serviço de Estatistica Demográfica, Moral e Politica, 128 Rua Mexico, 2 Floor, Rio de Janeiro, Guanabara.

BURKINA FASO
Ministère de l'Intérieur et de la Sécurité, Ouagadougou.

CAMBODIA
Ministry of Religious Affairs, Terak vithei Phaatarak Pheap (ex Preap Sisovath), Phnom Penh, T: 25151.

CHAD
Ministère de l'Intérieur, BP 742, Ndjamena.

CHINA
Bureau of Religious Affairs, Xi'anmen Ave., Beijing.
Religious Affairs Commision, Beijing West District, Liu Yin St. No. 14.

COMOROS
Chargé de l'Intérieur et de la Justice Musulmane, Prés Moroni.

CONGO-ZAIRE
Direction des Cultes et Associations, Ministère de la Justice, Palais de la Justice, BP 3137, Kinshasa 1, T: 30850.

CROATIA
Commission for Relations with Religious Communities, Jezuitski Trg 4, 41000 Zagreb.

CZECH REPUBLIC
Federal State Office for Ecclesiastical Affairs, Nábr kpt Jarose 4, 125 09 Praha 1, T: 2102.

DENMARK
Ministry for Church Affairs (Kirkeministeriet), Staldmestergarden, Frederiksholms Kanal 21, DK-1220 Kobenhavn K, T: (01)146263.

DOMINICAN REPUBLIC
Secretaría de Estado de Educación, Bellas Artes y Culto, Av Máximo Gómez, Santo Domingo, DN.

ECUADOR
Ministerio de Gobierno y Cultos, Quito.

EGYPT
Ministry for Azhar and Waqfs, Bab-el-Louk, Al Qahirah.

ETHIOPIA
Department of Security, Ministry of Interior, Ethiopian Government, Addis Abeba.

FINLAND
Ministry of Education, Rauhankatu 4, Helsinki 17.

FRANCE
Bureau des Cultes, Ministère de l'Intérieur, 1 Place des Saussaies, Paris 8, T: 2652830.

GERMANY
Ministry of Religious Affairs, Wiesbaden.

GREECE
Ministry of National Instruction and Religions, Office for Religions (Geniki Dievthynsis Thriskevmaton), Hodos Mitropoleos, Athinai, T: 32079.

GREENLAND
Greenland Ecclesiastical Commission, P.O. Box 63, DK-3900 Godthab, T: 1134.

HAITI
Département des Affairs Etrangères et des Cultes, Cité de l'Exposition, Port-au-Prince.

HOLY SEE
Segretaria di Stato/Secretaria Status seu Papalis, Segretario di Stato, Palazza Apostolico Vaticano, I-00120 Città del Vaticano, T: 6983126.

HUNGARY
State Office for Church Affairs, Sec of State for Church Affairs, Lendvay u 28, 1062 Budapest VI.

ICELAND
Ministry of Justice and Ecclesiastical Affairs, Arnarhvoli, Reykjavik.

INDONESIA
Directorate for Christian Religious Affairs, Departemen Agama RI, Jl Siah 6, Jakarta, T: 49962 ext 54.

IRAQ
Ministry of Waqfs, Baghdad.

ISRAEL
Department of Christian Affairs, Ministry of Religious Affairs, 23 Rue Shlomo Hamelekh, Jerusalem.
Ministry of Religious Affairs, 30 Rue Yafo, Jerusalem, T: 25206.

ITALY
Camera dei Deputati, Affari Interni e di Culto, Pres, Piazza di Montecitorio, Roma, T: Centr 6760.
General Department of Religious Affairs, Ministero dell'Interno, Palazzo Viminale, Roma, T: Centr 4667.

JAPAN
Department of Religious Affairs, Bureau of Culture, Ministry of Education (Shukyo-Hojin Bunkacho, Mombusho), 3-2-2 Kasumigaseki, Chiyoda-ku, Tokyo 100.

KUWAIT
Ministry of Waqfs and Islamic Affairs, PO Box 13.

LAOS
Département de l'Administration Religieuse, Ministère des Cultes (Kom Pokkhong Satsana), Vientiane.

LIBERIA
Department of Education, Monrovia.

LIBYA
Ministry of Unity and Foreign Affairs, Tripoli, T: 41302, 34060.

LUXEMBOURG
Ministère Affaires Culturelles et des Cultes, 19 Côte d'Eich, Luxembourg-ville.

MADAGASCAR
Ministère de l'Intérieur, Tananarive.

MALAYSIA
National Council for Islamic Affairs, Religious Affairs Department (Jabatan Hal Ehwal Ugama Islam), Prime Minister's Office, Kuala Lumpur.

MAURITIUS
Prime Minister's Office, Government House, Port-Louis.

MEXICO
Comité Nacional Evangélico de Defensa, Isabel la Católica No 13-308, Zona 1, Apdo 7665, México, DF, T: 215553.

MONACO
Ministère d'Etat, Département de l'Intérieur, Monaco-Ville.

MOROCCO
Ministère des Habbous, Ministre des Habbous, Palais Royal, Rabat.

MYANMAR
Ministry of Religious Affairs, Old Secretariat, Rangoon.

NETHERLANDS
Ministerie van Justitie, Secretaris-Generaal, 's-Gravenhage.

NICARAGUA
Ministerio de Gobernación, Palacio Nacional, Managua, DN.

NORWAY
Royal Ministry of Church Affairs and Education, Akersgaten 42, Oslo 1.

PARAGUAY
Ministerio de Educación y Culto, Chile, el Humasta y Piribeby, Asunción.

PERU
Sub-Dirección de Culto, Palacio de Gobierno, Calle Pescaderia, Lima 1.

POLAND
Office for Religious Affairs, Al Ujardowskie 5, Warszawa.

ROMANIA
Department of Cults/Religious Affairs, Str Snagov 40, Buçuresti 6.

SAUDI ARABIA
Ministry of Pilgrimage and Religious Foundations, Riyadh.

SOMALIA
Ministerio di Grazia, Giustizia ed Affari Religiosi, Central Government Offices (Governo), Mogadisho.

SOUTH KOREA
Ministry of Education, Seoul.

SPAIN
Comisión de Libertad Religiosa, Ministerio de Justicia, San Bernardo 47, Madrid 8.

SRI LANKA
Ministry of Cultural and Religious Affairs, 212 Bauddhaloka Mawatha, Colombo 7.

SUDAN
Office for Christian Education, Ministry of Education, Al Khurtum.

SWAZILAND
Ministry of Education, PO Box 39, Mbabane.

SWEDEN
Office for Religious Affairs, Ministry of Education (Utbildningsdepartementat), Mynttorget 1, Fack, 103 10 Stockholm 2. (Handles affairs of the free churches).

SYRIA
Ministère des Biens-Dédiés, Charch Al-Nassr, Dimashq.

TAIWAN
Bureau of Social Affairs, Ministry of Interior (Min-Cheng-Sse, Nei-Cheng-Pu), 107 Roosevelt Rd, Sec IV, Taipei.

THAILAND
Department of Religious Affairs, Ministry of Education (Kromkarn Satsana), Ratchadamnoen Av, Bangkok, T: 46411.

TUNISIA
Ministry of Foreign Affairs, Place du Gouvernement, Tunis.

TURKEY
Presidency/Office of Religious Affairs, Olgunlar Sok, Kocatepe, Ankara.

UGANDA
Department of Religious Affairs, Office of the President, PO Box 7168, Kampala.

VENEZUELA
Dirección de Cultos y Asuntos Indígenas, Ministerio de Justicia, Edf Lincoln, piso 11, Av Lincoln, Sabana Grande, Caracas 105, T: 724461, 723018, 726500, 727013.

VIET NAM
Comité pour les Questions Religieuses auprès du Bureau de la Présidence du Conseil, Hanoi.

70 Student organizations & federations

Organizations of or for college and university students, for evangelism, instruction, fellowship, discipleship, and training; campus organizations, campus ministries, Inter-university Christian groups, major university chaplaincies and related national organizations, major student centers, student leadership training, scholarship-awarding bodies.

ARGENTINA
Christian Student Center, Parana 489, 2nd Fl., Room 9, 1017 Buenos Aires, T: 54-494996.

AUSTRIA
Österreichische Studentenmission (Astrian Student Mission), Ksstlergasse 10/4, 1060 Wien, T: 0222/56 81 08.

BELGIUM
Fondation Catholique des Bourses pour Etudiants Africains (FONCABA), Rue du Mulin 29, B-1030, Brussels; Rue de la Prévoyance 60, B-1000 Brussel, T: (02)5116943.

BRITAIN (UK OF GB & NI)
Catholic Chaplaincy for Overseas Students, 2 Chiswick Lane, W4 2JS, T: 0181-742 0232.
International Fellowship of Evangelical Students, 55 Palmerston Rd., Wealdstone, Harrow, Middlesex HA3 7RR, T: 44-081-863-8688, F: 44-081-863-8229.

CANADA
Campus Ministries (Campus Crusade for Christ), National Campus Office, Box 300, Vancouver, BC V6C 2X3.
Inter-Varsity Christian Fellowship of Canada, 40 Vogell Rd. #17, Richmond Hill, ON L4B 3N6, T: 905-884-6880, F: 905-884-6550, O: National@ivcf.dar.com, www.dar.com/ivcf.

CHINA
World Student Christian Federation Asia-Pacific (WSCF-AP), Kiu Kin Mansion, 12 floor, 568 Nathan Rd, Kowloon, Hong Kong, T: 852-2385-2550, F: 852-2782-3980.

COSTA RICA
Alfa y Omega (Estudiantes Universitarios), T: 227-9951.
Estudiantes Cristianos Universitarios (ECU), T: 253-3137.

ECUADOR
Comunidad Estudiantil Cristiana Del Ecuador (CECE), Ave. América No. 4569 y Manosca, Casilla 8559, Quito, T: 246-934.

FRANCE
International Movement of Catholic Students, 171, rue de Rennes, F-75006, Paris.
International Young Catholic Students, 171 rue de Rennes, F-75006 Paris.

INDIA
Evangelical Students Union, DFO Tura, Forest Tilla, W. Garo Hills, Tura, Meghalaya 794002.
Missionary Settlement for University Women, L. Melville Rd. , Near YMCA Int. House, Byculla, Bombay, Maharashtra 400008.

INDONESIA
Gerakan Mahasiswa Kristen Indonesia (GMKI), Jl. Salemba Raya 10, Jakarta 10430.

ITALY
Associazione Studentesca Euro-Afro-Asiatica, S Marcuola 1723, I-30121 Venezia.

JAPAN
Waseda Hoshien Christian Student, 2-3-1 Nishi-waseda, Shinjuku-ku, Tokyo 160, T: 81-3-203-5411, F: 81-3-2034186.

KENYA
Christian Student Leadership Centre (Ufungamano House), P.O. Box 48802, Nairobi, T: 02-725921,2,3.

LEBANON
Ecumenical Youth and Students Office for the Middle East, Rue Mak'houl (Abdel-Aziz), Immeuble Tanios Rebeiz, 1375, Bayrut, T: 341902/3.

MOROCCO
Aumonerie des Etudiants Chretiens, 40, Rue Jaâfar Es Sadik-10000 Rabat-Agdal, T: (07)670250.

NETHERLANDS
Liberal Christian Student Movement, Nieuwe Gracht 27, Utrecht.

NORWAY
Forbundssenteret Haugtun, N-2884 Aust-Torpa, T: 47-61-18044.

PANAMA
Comunidad de Estudiantes Cristianos, Apartado Postal 873533, Panamá 7, T: 223-0803, F: 223-0803, O: E-mail: EVasquez@ancon.up.ac.pa.

PORTUGAL
COMACEP - Comissão Para a Acção Educativa Evangélica nas Escolas Públicas, Av. Conselheiro Barjona de Freitas, 16 B/C, 1500 Lisboa, T: 01-778 07 18, F: 01-778 90 25.

SINGAPORE
Student Christian Movement of Singapore, 7 Armenian Street, #04-07 Bible House, Singapore 179932, T: 334-0831.

SOUTH AFRICA
Campus Crusade for Christ, University Ministry, PO Box 4078, Halfway House 4078, T: 011-679-2983.
Interaction Ministries, PO Box 903, Melville 2109, Johannesburg, T: 011-726-7113, F: 011-726-7093.

SOUTH KOREA
Catholic University Students Association, 1, 2-ga, Myong-dong, Chung-gu, Seoul-shi, T: (02) 777-8249.

SPAIN
International Fellowship of Evangelical Students, C/Mallorca 99, 1, 2a, 08029 Barcelona, T: 93 2546863.

SWITZERLAND
Studentenheim-Kommission, Rabbentalstrasse 55, 3013 Bern, T: 031 332 12 18.
World Student Christian Federation, O: www.wcc-coe.org/wscf.

THAILAND
Student Christian Centre, 328 Phyathai Road, Bangkok 10400, T: 66-2150628/9.

UNITED STATES OF AMERICA (USA)
Campus Crusade for Christ, 100 Sunport Ln, Orlando, FL 32809, T:407-826-2000, 407-826-2851. O: www.ccci.org.
Catholic Campus Ministry Assoc, 300 College Park Ave, Dayton, OH 45469, T: 513-229-4648.
Inter-Varsity Christian Fellowship of the U.S.A., 6400 Schroeder Rd., P.O. Box 7895, Madison, WI 53707, T: 608-274-9001, F: 608-274-7882, O: E-mail: iv@gospelcom.net, www.gospelcom.net/iv/index.html.
International Students, Inc., P.O. Box C, Colorado Springs, CO 80901, T: 719-576-2700, F: 719-576-5363, O: ISIteam@aol.com, www.isionline.org.
Navigators, 3820 N. 30th St., Colorado Springs, CO 80904, T:719-598-1212; F: 719-260-0479. E-mail: navs@gospelcom.net.

71 Telephone ministries

Ministries that conduct evangelism, instruction or counseling by telephone; taped inspirational messages, sometimes in conjunction with radio programs; Christian or missionary news or prayer information services by telephone.

AUSTRALIA
Life Line International, Welsey Centre, 210 Pitt St., Sydney, NSW 2000.
Oasis Youth Care Centre (Salvation Army), T: 02-360-9000.

BRITAIN (UK OF GB & NI)
Bristol Telephone Ministry, 1 Unity St, Bristol 1, T: 298787.
Christian Counsel Telephone Service, 102 Bramshot Av, London SE7, T: (01)858-1212.
Christian Message, Barnet, Redbridge, Merton, Eltham, T: (01)440-7277, (01)553-0828, (01)648-8639, (01)850-5511.
Lifeline Birmingham, 47 Newhall St, Birmingham B3 3RB, T: (021)233-1641.
Message, 47 The Drive, Sevenoaks, Kent, T: (0732)53164.
Samaritans Incorporated, 17 Uxbridge Rd, Slough, Bucks, T: 32713.
Samaritans, The, 17 Hungate, Lincoln, Grantham 67616, T: (0522).

CANADA
Telecare Distress Centre Etobicoke, P.O. Box 39069, 235 Dixon Rd., Etobicoke, ON M9P 3V2, T: 416-247-2528, O: Crisis line 416-247-5426.
Today's Watch Telephone Hotline, T: 805-822-0202.

ECUADOR
Evangelismo y Discipulado, Villalengua No. 320, Casilla 691, Quito, T: 243-670.

FRANCE
Eglise du Tabernacle Bonne Nouvelle par Téléphone, 163 bis Rue Belliard, F-75018 Paris, T: 627-4719.
SOS Amitié France, 5 Rue de Laborde, F-75008 Paris, T: 825-7050.

GERMANY
Evangelische Konferenz für Telefonseelsorge, Stafflenbergstr 78, Postfach 476, D-7 Stuttgart 1.
Tu Teléfono Amigo, Remscheid, T: 021-91-255-15.

ITALY
La Voce Amica, Roma, T: 7310354/5.
Tele-Soccorso Spirituale, (Under different names, in Bologna, Cagliari, Firenze, Genova, Mestre, Milano, Napoli, Palermo, Roma, Torino, Verona).
Telefono Amico, Angelicum, Piazza Sant 'Angelo 2, I-20121 Milano, T: 6882153.

JAPAN
Life Phone, Phone Center, Lutheran Center, Tokyo, T: (03)264-4343.
Tokyo English Life Line (TELL-a-phone), Tokyo, T: 264-4347.

NORWAY
Lutheran Telegraph and Telephone Mission, Televerket, 5500 Haugesund.
Telephone Mission, Grunersgt 6, Oslo 5.

SOUTH AFRICA
Telefriend Ministries, PO Box 74089, Lynwood Ridge 0040, Pretoria, T: 012-348-8325, F: 012-47-3166.

SPAIN
Teléfono de Dios, Radio Nacional de España, Madrid.

SWITZERLAND
Schweizerische Verband Für Telephonseelsorge, Schützengasse 19, CH-2500 Biel, T: (032)28733.

UNITED STATES OF AMERICA (USA)
New Hope Korean Telephone Counselling, 12141 Lewis St., Garden Grove, CA 92640, T: 714-971-4261.
Tele-Soul, 3567 Grand Ave, San Marcos, CA 92069, T: 619-727-4408.
Telephone Bible Reading, New York Bible Society, New York, NY, T: (212)PL5-5500.

72 Thelogical colleges and seminaries

Definitions: Institutions for the training of the ordained ministry or priesthood, or for advanced theological, Biblical, or religious instruction, generally at the graduate (post-baccalaureate) level; major seminaries (religious or secular), theological colleges, advanced Bible schools.

73 Theological education associations

Regional or international groupings of theological colleges, Bible Schools, seminaries, or other institutes for higher Christian education, for co-operation in accreditation, curricula, joint advanced programs of study, research, and conferences; international coordinating bodies.

ARGENTINA
Asociación de Seminarios e Instituciones Teológicos (ASIT), CC 129, Sucursal 24, Buenos Aires 1424.
Asociación Subamericana de Instituciones Teológicas (ASIT), Camacua 282, Buenos Aires.

AUSTRALIA
Australian and New Zealand Association of Theological Schools (ANZATS), Queen's College, University of Melbourne, Parkville, Victoria 3052.
International Council of Accrediting Agencies for Evangelical Theological Education (ICAA), 4A Paterson Road, Springwood, NSW 2777.
South Pacific Association of Bible Colleges (SPABC), 176 Wattle St., Malvern SA 5061.

BARBADOS
Caribbean Association of Theological Schools (CATS), Codrington College, Bridgetown.

BOLIVIA
Asociación Andina de Educación Teólogica (AADET), CP 266 La Paz.

BRAZIL
Evangelical Assoc for Theological Education in Latin America (AETAL), Rua Vergueiro 3051, Vila Mariana 04101-300, Sao Paulo SP, T: 11572-8824, F: 1150844099, O: E-mail: aetal@usa.net, Web site: www.centralsbc.co.

CAMEROON
Association des Institutions d'Enseignement Théologique en Afrique Occidentale (ASTHEOL), Faculté de Théologie Protestante, BP 4011, Yaoundé.
Ecumenical Association of African Theologians (EAAT), BP 1539, Yaoundé.

CANADA
Associated Canadian Theological Schools (ACTS), 7600 Glover Rd., Langley, BC V2Y 1Y1, T: 604-888-6158, F: 604-888-5729, O: 604-888-7511, e-mail: raske@twu.ca.
Churches' Council on Theological Education in Canada, 60 St. Clair Ave. E., Ste. 302, Toronto, ON M4T 1N5, T: 416-928-3223, F: 416-928-3563.

CHINA
Association for the Promotion of Chinese Theological Education (APCTE), Room 604, 310 King's Rd, 6/f, Hong Kong.

COLOMBIA
Union of Bible Institutions of Colombia (UNICO), Apdo Aéreo 5945, Cali.

CONGO-ZAIRE
Association des Institutions d'Enseignement Théologique en Afrique Central (ASTHEOL), Faculté de Théologie, BP 4745, Kinshasa 2.

COSTA RICA
Asociación Latinoamericana de Instituciones de Educación Teológica (ALIET), Apdo 3977-1000, San José 1000.

CYPRUS
Association of Theological Institutes in the Middle East (ATIME), MECC, P.O. Box 4259, Limassol.

EGYPT
Association for Theological Education in the Near East (ATENE), Faculté de Théologie Copte Orthodoxe, Terrains Anba Roueiss, Rue Ramsés, Al Qahirah, T: 827954.

FIJI
South Pacific Association of Theological Schools (SPATS), P.O. Box 2426, Suva.

GERMANY
World Evangelical Fellowship Theological Commission, Albrecht Bengel Haus, Ludwig Krapf Strasse 5, Tubingen D72072, T: 7071-700514, F: 7071-700540, O: E-mail: ABH-Tuebingen@t-online.de.

HOLY SEE
Sacra Congregazione per l'Educazione Cattolica, Palazzo delle Congregazioni, Piazza Pio XII 3, I-00193 Roma, T: 6984569.

INDIA
All India Association for Christian Higher Education, 39, Institutional Area, D-Block, Janakpuri, New Delhi 110058.
Association for Evangelical Theological Education in India, P. B. No. 9522, Koramangala, Bangalore, Karnataka 560095.
Board of Theological Education of the Senate of Serampore College (BTESSC), P.O. Box 4635, 63 Miller's Rd, Bangalore 560 046 Karnataka, T: 91-80-3334-385, F: 91-80-563-249.

INDONESIA
Majelis Pusat Pendidikan Kristen di Indonesia (MPPK), Jl. Salemba Raya 10, Jakarta 10430, T: (021) 331928.

ITALY
Congregation for Catholic Education, Piazza Pio XII 3, 00193 Rome.
Protestant Theological Schools of Latin Europe (PTSLE), Waldensian Faculty of Theology, Via Petro Corsa 42, Rome I-00193.

JAMAICA
Caribbean Evangelical Theological Association (CETA), P.O. Box 121, 14 West Ave., Constant Spring, Kingston 8.

JAPAN
Japan Association of Theological Education (JATE), c/o Lutheran Theological College and Seminary, 3-1-20 Osawa, Mitaka-shi, Tokyo 181.

KENYA
Association of Theological Institutions in Eastern Africa (ATIEA), AACC, PO Box 50784, Nairobi, T: 62601.

LEBANON
Association of the Theological Institutes in the Middle East (ATIME), PO Box 5376, Beirut, T: 01-813121.

MADAGASCAR
Association of Theological Teachers of Madagascar (ATTM), 29 Rue George V, Tananarive.

MEXICO
Asociacíon LatinoAmericana de Instituciones de Educacíon Teológica-ALIET, Calle Arenal No. 36, Esquina-Av, Universidad, T: 661-1010.
Organización de Seminarios Latinoamericanos (OSLAM), Departamento de Ministerios, CELAM, Apdo Postal M-8877, México 1, DF, T: 5331520.

NIGERIA
Accrediting Council for Theological Education in Africa (ACTEA), PMB 2009, Jos.
West African Association of Theological Institutes (WAATI), Department of Religion, University of Nigeria, Nsukka.

PAPUA NEW GUINEA
Melanesian Association of Theological Schools (MATS), Holy Spirit Regional Seminary, P.O. Box 1101 and 5768, Boroko.

PERU
Asociación Evangélica de Educación Teológica, Apdo 664, Lima.

PHILIPPINES
Philippine Association of Bible and Theological Schools (PABATS), P.O. Box 1416, Manila; P.O. Box 99, Davao City.

SINGAPORE
Association for Theological Education in South East Asia, 324 Onan Road, Singapore 424716, T: 344-7316, F: 344-7316.

SOUTH AFRICA
Association of Southern African Theological Institutions (ASATI), P.O. Box 2839, Randberg 2125.

SOUTH KOREA
Korean Association of Accredited Theological Schools (KAATS), College of Theology, Yonsei University, 134 Shinchondong, Sudaemoon-ku, Seoul 120-749.
North East Asia Association of Theological Schools (NEAATS), College of Theology, Yonsei University, Seoul 120-749.

SWITZERLAND
Internationale Altkatholische Theologenkonferenz, A. van Nieuwenaarlaan 3a, NL-6824 AM Arnhem, T: 0031-26-442 36 54.

TAIWAN
Asia Theological Association (WEF)(ATA), P.O. Box 1477, Taichung 400.

TANZANIA
Eastern Africa Association for Theological Education (EAATE), P.O. Box 32, Njombe.

UNITED STATES OF AMERICA (USA)
Accrediting Association of Bible Colleges, The, P.O. Box 1523 or 130 F North College, Fayeteville, AK 72702, T: 501-521-8164, F: 501-521-9202.
Association of Theological Schools in the United States and Canada, The, 10 Summit Park Dr., Pittsburgh, PA 15275-1103, T: 412-788-6505, F: 412-788-6510.
Chicago Cluster of Theological Schools, 1100 E Fifty-fifth St, Chicago, IL 60615, T: 312-667-3500.
Coalition for Christian Colleges & Universities, 329 Eight St., N.E., Washington, D.C. 20002, T: 202-546-8713, F: 202-546-8913, O: E-mail: coalition@cccu.org.

ZAMBIA
Association of Evangelical Bible Institutes and Colleges of Africa and Madagascar (AEBICAM), P.O. Box 131, Choma.

ZIMBABWE
Association of Theological Institutions in Southern and Central Afdrica (ATISCA), The Regional Seminary, P.O. Box 1139, Harare.

74
Theological education by extension

Organized courses, programs, and centers of theological or Biblical instruction, or of ministry, pastoral, or leadership training using TEE principles; non-centralized theological education, conducted over broad geographical areas using centers, intinerating instructors, or the like; organizations producing or providing TEE curriculum, promoting or facilitating the TEE approach, or providing training for TEE trainers; TEE associations, agencies, seminars, or affiliations.

ARGENTINA
Seminario por Extensión Anglicano, Santiago 1862, San Migueld e Tucumán.

AUSTRALIA
ITE, GBRE, P.O. Box 535, Boronia, VIC 3155, T: 61-3-762-6055.

AUSTRIA
Biblical Education by Extension, Strehlgasse 13, Vienna 1190, T: 43-222-44-27-91, F: 43-222-44-20-78.

BANGLADESH
St. Andrew's Theological College, St. Thomas's Church, 54 Johnson Road, Dhaka 1100, T: 880-2-236-546, F: 880-2-832-915.

BELGIUM
International Correspondence Institute, Chausse de Waterloo 45, Rhode St., Genese 1640, T: 32-2358-3510, F: 32-2358-5695.

BOTSWANA
Kgolagano College of Theological Education by Extension in Botswana, P.O. Box 318, Gaborone, T: 352 196.

BRAZIL
Seminário Teológico de Fortaleza, Avenida João Pessao 5570/80, CE-60435-682 Fortaleza.

BRITAIN (UK OF GB & NI)
St. John's Extension Studies, Chilwell Lane, Bramcote, Nottingham NG9 3DS, T: 44-115-251-117, F: 44-115-220-134.

CHILE
Seminary by Extension to All Nations, Casilla 561, Vitna del Mar,, T: 661484.

COLOMBIA
Latin American Association of Institutions and Theological Seminaries by Extension (ALISTE), Apdo Aéreo 3041, Medellín.

CONGO-ZAIRE
Goma Literature Ministry Seminary, BP 797, Goma; 6225 Avenue du Lac, Goma, T: 477.

ECUADOR
Educacion Teologica, Ave. America No. 2183 y Sosaya, Casilla 8504, Quito, T: 551-996.
Seminario Luterano de Extensión, Casilla 1334, Cuenca.

FRANCE
Centre d'Enseignement Théologique à Distance (CETAD), 22 rue Cassette, F-75006 Paris.

GHANA
Ghana Literature Ministry Seminary, P.O. Box 1016, Accra, T: 223720, O: telex: 2119 ADVENT GH..

GUATEMALA
Extension Seminary, Apdo 1881, Guatemala.

HAITI
Extension Bible School of Eastern Haiti, BP 1096, Port-au-Prince.

HONDURAS
Instituto Bíblico de Extensión, Apdo 164, La Ceiba.

HUNGARY
Biblical Education by Extension, Keresztyén Ismeretterjesztö Alapitvány, 1133 Budapest, Vág u. 5. VI. 32., T: 36-1-120-3767.

INDIA
Association for Theological Education by Extension, Madapattil House, Kuttapuzha P. O., Tiruvalla, Kerala 689103.

INDONESIA
Western Indonesia Theological Education, 10 Medan Merdeka Timur, Jakarta.

IRAN
Iran Extension of the Near East School of Theology, P.O. Box 1505, Tehran.

ITALY
Instituto Biblico Evangelico, Via Cimone 100, I-00141 Roma.

KENYA
Eastern Africa Association for Theological Education by Extension (EAATEE), P.O. Box 61070, Nairobi.

LEBANON
TEE, PO Box 126, Tarabulus (Tripoli).

MALAWI
Theological Education by Extension in Malawi, Private Bag 25, Zomba.

MEXICO
Departamento de Extensión, Seminario Lutereno Augsburgo, Apdo Postal 20-416, México 20, DF.
Seminario Teológico por Extensión del Sureste, Calle 61/529, Mérida, Yucatán.

PAKISTAN
Open Theological Seminary, 8-FC College, Lahore 54600, T: 92-42-575-5490, F: 92-42-759-0797.

PERU
Seminario de Extensión Teológico, Iglesia del Nazareno, Apdo 85, Chiclayo.

PHILIPPINES
Conservative Baptist Bible College, Extension Dept, PO Box 1882, Manila.

RWANDA
Rwanda Literature Ministry Seminary, BP 367, Kigali, T: 7328/73239, O: telex: 596 RUM RW.

SOUTH AFRICA
Bless the Nation School of World Mission, PO Box 7526, Newton Park 6055, T: 041-73-3780.
Great Commission College, Africa Ablaze Ministries, PO Box 110, Northriding 2162, Campus Judah, # Rietvallei Rd, Millgate, T: 011-708-1059, F: 011-708-1058.

SPAIN
Radio Amistad, Pza. España, 4 Alfocea, 50120 Zaragoza, T: 93-723-24-25.

SRI LANKA
TAFEE, 36 Moor Road, Dehiwela.

THAILAND
Tahi CoCo TEE, 422/3 Suan Plu Bangkok.
Thailand Theological Education by Extension Committee, 7th Floor, Sirinee Building, Pleonchit Rd, Bangkok, T: 2527703.

UNITED STATES OF AMERICA (USA)
Biblical Education by Extension, Intl., 6730 L.B.J. Freeway, Suite 2195, Dallas, TX 75240, T: 214-404-8077, F: 214-991-0684.
International Correspondence Institute, 6300 North Belt Line Road, Irving TX 75063, T: 214-751-1111, F: 214-714-8185, O: Toll free: 800-444-0424.
Los Angeles Christian Training Center, 8219 Florence Av, Downey, CA 90240.
Melodyland Schools, P.O. Box 6000, Anaheim, CA 92806.

ZIMBABWE
Rusitu Bible Institute, Extension Dept, P.O. Box 576, Umtali.

75
Tourism, sports & recreation

Christian tour organizations, travel agencies, cruises; pilgrimage organizations or ministries; ministries in the area of tourism, leisure, or recreation; Christian sports organizations, teams, or ministries; organizations of Christian athletes, ministries to athletes and spectators at sports events; sports evangelism, athlete evangelists. For missionary air travel, see FOREIGN MISSIONS SUPPORT ORGANIZATIONS.

AUSTRALIA
Centenary Travel Service, 213 Victoria Rd, Gladesville, NSW 2111.

AUSTRIA
Österreichische Turn-und Sport-Union, Falkestr 1, A-1010 Wien.

BELGIUM
Commission du Plein Air et des Loisirs, Av Zénobe Gramme 58, B-1050 Brussel.
Mouvement Mondial des Travailleurs Chretiens (MMTC), Rue des Palais, 90, B 1030 Bruxelles.

BRAZIL
Atletas de Cristo no Brasil, Cx. Postal 55011, São Paulo-SP 04733-970, T: 11-246-6538, F: 11-524-9444, O: E-mail: atletas@ibm.net.

BRITAIN (UK OF GB & NI)
Baptist Holiday Fellowship, 4 Southampton Row, London WC1B 4AF.
Catholic Association Pilgrimage Trust, 29 Chestnut Grove, Owl End, Great Stukeley, Huntingdon, Cambs. PE17 5AT.
Catholic Travel Association, 21 Fleet St, London EC4, T: (01)353-2428.
CE Holiday Homes, Dept O, 24 Berwick Av, Heaton Mersey, Stockport SK4 3AA.
Christian Holiday Crusade, 10 Cuthbert Rd, Croydon, CR0 3RB, T: (01)688-7458.
Christian International Travel Club (CITC), 31 Oxford St, Barnsley, South Yorkshire; Gelderd Rd., Leeds LS12 6DH, T: (0532)636181.
Christian Mountain Centre (Snowdonia), Warden, Gorffwysfa, Tremadoc, Gwynedd.
Christian Travel International, 111 Oxford St, Box 4RH London W1A, T: (01)437-9151, 4136.
Good News Travels, Freetown Way, Hull, Horth Humberside HU2 8ES, T: 44-0482-26755, F: 44-0482-216565.
Rosary Pilgrimage Apostolate, 12 Farleigh Crescent The Lawns, Swindon, Wiltshire SN3 1JY, T: 01793-422714, F: 01793-422715.
Timeline Heritage Tours, 1 Schofield Gardens, Witney, Oxfordshire, England, OX8 5JY, T: 01993 779651, F: 01993 779651, O: IDD: +44 1993 779861, www.oxlink.co.uk/business/timeline.html.

CANADA
Aide Olympique Chrétienne, Room 600, 455 Craig St West, Montréal, Québec H2Z 1JL, T: (514)866-2787.
Athletes in Action (Campus Crusade for Christ), Box 300, Vancouver, BC V6C 2X3, T: 604-582-3100, F: 604-588-7582.
Canadian Churchman Tours, 600 Jarvis St, Toronto, Ontario M4Y 2J6.
Hockey Ministries International, P.O. Box 36, Beaconsfield, QC, H9W 5T6, T: 514-694-6440, F: 514-694-9673.
In-Church Travel Tours, Suite 214, 6 Lansing Square, Willowdale, Ontario M2J 1T8.
Transport for Christ, Box 371, Rexdale, Ontario.

CHINA
Booth Lodge, 7/F, 11 Wing Sing Lane, Yaumatei, Kowloon, Hong Kong, T: 2771-9266, F: 2385-1140, O: Telex: 57091 SALVO HX.
Holy Carpenter Church Hostel, No. 1 Dyer Avenue, Hung Hom, Kowloon, Hong Kong, T: 3620301, F: 3622193.

CONGO-ZAIRE
Zaire Travel Service, 11 Blvd du 30 Juin, BP 15812, Kinshasa, T: 23288, 24875.

COSTA RICA
Atletas en Acción, T: 257-5866.

EGYPT
Commission du Tourisme Religieux Chrétien, EACCS, Anba Rueis Bldg, Ramses St, Abbasiya, Al Qahirah.

FRANCE
Catholic International Federation for Physical and Sports Education, 5, rue Cernuschi, F-75017 Paris.
Federation Internationale Catholique D'Education Physique et Sportive (FICEP), 5, rue Cernuschi, F 75017 Paris.

GERMANY
Power Management Team, Albania Tours,

Haydnstr. 38, 44145 Dortmund, T: 0231-83-43-63.

GREECE
Commission de Tourisme, 246 Acharnon, 815 Athínai.

HOLY SEE
Pontificia Commissione per la Pastorale delle Migrazioni e del Turismo (Apostolatus Maris), Palazzo San Calisto, Piazza San Calisto 16, I-00153 Roma, T: (698)4693-4775.

HONDURAS
Centro de Capacitacíon La Santa Cruz, Apdo 586, San Pedro Sula.

INDIA
Fellowship Travel and Tour, 8246, Sector-B, Pocket XI, Nelson Mandela Road, Vasant Kunj, New Delhi 110030.
Methodist Sports Services, M-3, Lajpat Nagar - III, New Delhi 110024.

INDONESIA
Dhyana Pura Centre (Dhyana Pura Beach Hotel), P.O. Box 1010, Interport Ngurah Rai, Bali, T: 0361-2290, F: 0361-51463.

ISRAEL
Christian Information Centre, P.O. Box 14308, 91140 Jérusalem; Omar Ibn el Khatib Square, Jaffa Gate, 91140 Jérusalem, T: 02-272692, F: 02-286417.
Franciscan Pilgrims Office, P.O. Box 186, 91001 Jérusalem; Omar Ibn El-Khattab Square, Jaffa Gate, 91001 Jérusalem, T: 02-27-26-97.
Stella Maris Centre pour pélerinages et retraites, P.O. Box 9047, 31090 Haifa, T: 04-33-20-84, F: 04-33-15-93, O: Also tel: 04-33-25-29.
Vatican Pilgrims Liaison Office 'Commission des Pèlerinages Chrétiens', P.O. Box 20531, 91204 Jérusalem; Notre Dame of Jerusalem Center, (en face de la Porte neuve), 91204 Jérusalem, T: 02-27-91-09, F: 02-27-19-95, O: Telex: 265-26-NDC IL.

ITALY
Centro Sportivo Italiano (CSI), Via Conciliazione 3, I-00193 Roma, T: 6567941.

KENYA
Menno Travel Service, Lullington House, Kaunda Lane, PO Box 40444, Nairobi, T: 33051, 29487.

NETHERLANDS
Commission for Recreation, PO Box 38, Driebergen.
National Catholic Secretariat for Church and Recreation, Brinkstraat 85, Putten (Geld).

SINGAPORE
Christian Sports Club, 3 Jalan Kayu, Singapore 799434, T: 483-5348, F: 483-4071.

SOUTH AFRICA
Athletes in Action, 760 Windsurf St, Weltevreden Park 1709, T: 011-475-6778.
Christian Motorcyclists Association, PO Box 72475, Lynwood Ridge 0040, Pretoria, T: 012-803-7333, F: 012-83-3916.

SWEDEN
Church of Sweden Committee for Tourist & Church Activities in Foreign Countries, Kyrkoherde i St Petri, Själbodgatan 4B, Malmö C.

THAILAND
Ecumenical Coalition on Third World Tourism (ECTWT), PO Box 35, Senanikhom P.O. Bangkok 10902, T: 66-2-51070-287, F: 66-2-5107-287.

UNITED STATES OF AMERICA (USA)
Athletes International Ministries, 13613 N. Cave Creek Rd., Phoenix, AZ 85022.
Athletic Ministries International, Inc., P.O. Box 241076, Memphis, TN 38124, T: 901-345-0258.
Basketball Travelers Inc., 9233 Holman Road N.W., Seattle, WA 98117, T: 206-781-0557.
CBN Travel, 700 CBN Center. Ste. CSB112, Virginia Beach, VA 23463, T: 804-579-3470.
Champions for Christ, P.O. 1799, Gainesville, FL 32602.
Christian Camping International, Box 400, Somonauk, IL 60552.
Christian Ministry in the National Parks, 745 Riverside Drive, New York, NY 10027, T: (212)870-2155.
Christian Team Ministries, Inc., 1025 Grange Rd., Meadow Vista, CA 95722.
Embrace Israel, P.O. Box 10077, Cedar Rapids, IA 52410, T: 319-390-4780, F: 319-393-2912, O: Embracelsrael@msn.com, www.Embracelsrael.org.
Episcopal Camps and Conference Centers, Inc. (ECCC), 2702 W. Old State Rd 34, Lizton, IN 46149-9375.
Fellowship of Christian Athletes, 8701 Leeds Rd., Kansas City, MO 64129-1680, T: 800-289-0909, F: 816-921-8755, O: E-mail: fca@gospelcom.net.
Friendship International Tours - Lion of Judah, 5955 DeSota Ave., Ste. 206, Woodland Hills, CA 91367, T: 818-999-4434, F: 818-347-4315.
Friendship Sports Intl., P.O. Box 221, Upland, IN 46989.
Global Tours, Inc., P.O. Box 4503, Burlingame, CA 94011-4503.
Hockey Ministries International (HMI), P.O. Box 36, Beaconsfield, PQ H9W 5T6, O: Web: www.gospelcom.net/hmi/.
International Sports Coalition, 579 Peachtree St., N.E., Atlanta, GA 30308.
International Sports Ministries, 1212 East Prairie Avenue, Wheaton, IL 60187, T: 708-653-3023.
Lo Debar Race Track Ministry, P.O. Box 4822, Hollywood, FL 33083.
Maranatha Tours, Inc., 13825 N. 32nd St., Ste. 24, Phoenix, AR 85032, T: 602-788-8864, F: 602-788-6182.
Ministry to Golfers, 1904 N. Adams St., Arlington, VA 22201.
Missionary Athletes International, P.O. Box 25010, Colorado Springs, CO 80936, T: 719-528-1636, F: 719-528-1638, O: 103016.1115@compuserve.com.
Modern Pilgrimages, Inc., 31882 Camino Capistrano Ste. #102, San Juan Capistrano, CA 92675, T: 800-662-3700, F: 714-248-7626.
Motor Racing Outreach, Smith Suite 336, Highway 20 North, Harrisburg, NC 28075.
Motorsports Ministries, P.O. Box 2737, Rohnert Park, CA 94927.
New World Tours and Travel, 100690 Elm Ave., Loma Linda, CA 92354, T: 714-799-1356.
Overwhelming Victory Ministries, 2130 31st St., N.W., Canton, OH 44709.
PASS Ministry, 9 Meadowrue Dr., Mt. Laurel, NJ 08054.
Pro Athletes for Christ, P.O. Box 271073, Tampa, FL 33688.
Pro Basketball Fellowship, P.O. Box 792, Salida, CA 95368.
Professional Skiers Fellowship, 401 Ute Lane, Gunnison, CO 81230.
Royal Travel & Tours, 19742 MacArthur Blvd., Ste. 235, Irvine, CA 92612, T: 800-626-6280, F: 714-752-4929, O: royalrtt@aol.com.
Spiritual Wrestling Federation, 3212 NY 150, Box 185, East Greenbush, NY 12061, T: 518-477-2385, F: 518-477-2388, O: fredbayeco@aol.com.
Sports and Cultural Exchange International, P.O. Box 777, Chula Vista, CA 92012, T: 619-421-9828.
Sports Outreach Institute, P.O. Box 119, Monroe, VA 24574, T: 804-929-5015.
Sports Spectrum Magazine, Box 3566, Grand Rapids, MI 49501-3566, T: 616-942-9218, F: 616-957-5741.
Sports World Ministries, Inc., P.O. Box 500, New Tazewell, TN 37825, T: 615-626-8291.
Tennis Ministry, 135 Fir Hill, Akron, OH 44304.
Unlimited Potential, Inc., P.O. Box 1355, Warsaw, IN 46580, T: 219-267-7988, F: 219-267-6190.
Victory Ministry, 7420 Stone Creek Ave., Anaheim, CA 92808.
Wheaton Tours, Box 468, Wheaton, IL 60187.
Winning Women, 1010 Eckles Dr., Tampa, FL 33612.
Women's Tennis Ministry, 3417 Worth Hills Dr., Fort Worth, TX 76109.
World Mission Taekwondo Association, 3750 W. 6th St., #107, Los Angeles, CA 90020, T: 213-487-5959.
World Sports, 160 Harbor Dr., Key Biscayne, FL 33149, T: 305-361-2058.
Youth Enterprises Sports & Cultural Exchange, Intl., P.O. Box 777, Chula Vista, CA 92010.

76 Universities

Definitions: Church- or Christian-operated, -owned, -controlled, -sponsored, or -linked universities granting academic degrees mainly in secular subjects.

77 University departments of religion

Academic faculties or departments within universities, offering advanced instruction, conducting research, and granting degrees in religious studies, divinity, theology, mission, missiology, church history, philosophy of religion, sociology or psychology of religion, or related subjects (but often not specifically training persons for the ordained ministry). See also RESEARCH CENTERS.

ARGENTINA
Departamento de Pastoral, Facultad de Teología, Universidad Católica Argentina, José Cubas 3543, Buenos Aires.
Escuela de Teología, Universidad del Norte Santo Tomás de Aquino, Casilla de Correo 32, San Miguel de Tucuman.
Facultad de Teología, Pontificia Universidad Católica Argentina Santa Maria de los Buenos Aires, Rio Bamba 1227, Buenos Aires.
Facultad de Teología, Universidad del Salvador, Calle 542, Buenos Aires.
Facultad de Teología y Filosofía San Miguel, Mitre 3236, Casilla 10, San Miguel, B7.

AUSTRALIA
Department of Religion Studies, Australian National University, Canberra.
Faculty of Theology, St. Patrick's College, Manly, Syndey, NSW 2095.
University of Syndey, Dept of Religious Studies, Sydney NSW 2006.

AUSTRIA
Evangelisch-Theologische Fakultät, Universtät Wien, Wien.
Evangelisch-Theologische Fakultät der Universität Wien, Rooseveltplatz 10, A-1090 Vienna, T: 43-406 SP 81.
Katholisch-Theologische Fakultät, Universität Wien, Dr-Karl-Lueger-Ring 1, A-1010 Wien, T: (427611)244/5.
Katholisch-Theologische Fakultät der Leopold-Franzens-Universität, Karl-Rahner-Platz 1, A-6020 Innsbruck, T: 43-5222-7240.
Katholische-Theologische Fakultät der Universität Wien, 1 Dr Karl Lüger-Ring 1, A-1010 Vienna.
Philosophische-Theologische Hochschule, Wienerstrasse 38, A-3100 St. Polten, T: 43-2742-52792.
University of Graz: Faculty for Catholic Theology, O: Web: http://143.50.50.11.
University of Innsbruck: Faculty for Catholic Theology, O: Web: http://info.uibk.ac.at.

BELGIUM
Faculté de Théologie, Université Catholique de Louvain, Place Croix du Sud 1, B-1348 Louvain-la-Neuve, T: (010)416201.
Faculté de Théologie Protestante, Bollandistenstraat 40, Brussel 4.
Faculté Universitaire de Théologie Protestante, Rue de Bollandistes 40, B-1040 Brussels.
Facultés Universitaires N-D de la Paix, Rue de Bruxelles 61, B-5000 Namur, T: (081)229061.
Religious Sociology Dept, Katholieke Universiteit te Leuven, E Van Evenstraat 2B, B-3000 Leuven, T: (016)226335.
Universitaire Faculteiten St. Ignacius, Prinsstraat 13, B-2000 Antwerpen, T: (031)316660.

BELORUSSIA
European Humanities University, Faculty of Theology, Skorina Avenue 24, 220030 Minsk, T: 7-172-76-81-61.

BOTSWANA
University of Botswana, Dept. of Theology and Religious Studies, Private Bag 0022, Gabarone.

BRAZIL
Departamento de Ciências Religiosas, Universidade Federal de Juiz de Fora, Juiz de Fora, MG.
High Course of Theology Universidad de Santa Ursula, Rua Fernando Ferrarri 75, RJ-22231-040 Rio de Janeiro, T: 55-21-551-5542, F: 55-551-6446.
Instituto Central de Filosofia e Teologia, UCMG, Av Augusto de Lima 1705, Belo Horizonte, MG, T: 355873, 355899.
Instituto de Teologia, Universidade Católica de Salvador, Pça Pe Anchieta 1, Salvador, BA.
Instituto de Teologia, Filosofia e Ciências Humanas, Universidade Católica de Petrópolis, Petrópolis.
Instituto Superior de Teologia Pastoral (ISTEP), Pça Sta Helena, CP 174, Goiânia, GO, T: 61854.

BRITAIN (UK OF GB & NI)
Blackfriars, Oxford, T: 44-1865-278-400, F: 44-1865-278-403.
Christ's College Aberdeen, 25 High St., Aberdeen AB9 2UB, T: 44-1224-272-380, F: 44-1224-273-750.
Department of Theology, University of Birmingham, Birmingham 15.
Faculty of Divinity, New College, University of Edinburgh, The Mound, Edinburgh.
Faculty of Theology, Christ's College, University of Aberdeen, Aberdeen.
Greenwich School of Theology, Greenwich University (USA), 29 Howbeck Lane, Clareborough, Retford DN22 9LW, T: 44-777-703-058.
Greyfriars, Oxford.
King's College, University of Aberdeen, Dept. of Religious Studies, Aberdeen AB9 2UB.
Kings College, Dept. of Theology and Religious Studies, Strand, London WC2R 2LS, T: 44-171-836-5454, F: 44-171-873-2339.
Manchester College, Mansfield Road, Oxford OX1 3TD, T: 44-1865-271-006, F: 44-1865-271-012.
Mansfield College, Oxford OX1 3TF, T: 44-1865-270-999, F: 44-1865-270-970, O: E-mail: @Oxford.ac.uk.
North Atlantic Missiology Project, O: www.divinity.cam.ac.uk/carts/namp/.
Regent's Park College, Pusey Street, Oxford OX1 2LB, T: 44-1865-288-120.
Ripon College, Cuddesdon, Oxford OX44 9EX, T: 44-1865-874-427, O: E-mail: ripo0001@SABLE.OX.AC.UK.
School of Theology, St. David's University College, University of Wales, Lampeter.
School of Theology, University College, University of Wales, Bangor.
Scottish Institute of Missionary Studies, Univ. Aberdeen, King's College, Aberdeen AB9 2UB.
University of Aberdeen, Dept. of Divinity with Religious Studies, Kings College, Old Aberdeen AB9 2VB, T: 44-124-272-383.
University of Edinburgh Faculty of Divinity, New College, Mound Place, Edinburgh EH1 2LX, T: 44-131-650-8959, F: 44-131-650-6579, O: Also tel: 44-131-650-8900.
University of Glasgow Faculty of Divinity and Trinity College, Glasgow G12 8QQ, T: 44-141-339-8855.
University of St. Andrews Faculty of Divinity, St. Mary's College, South Street, St. Andrews KY16 9JU, T: 44-1334-76161, F: 44-1334-462-852, O: E-mail: rap@st.andrews.ac.uk.
Westminster College, Madingley Road, Cambridge CB3 OAA, T: 44-1223-353-997, F: 44-1223-300-765, O: Also tel: 44-1223-354-720.
Wycliffe Hall, 54 Banbury Road, Oxford OX2 6PW, T: 44-1865-274-200, F: 44-1865-274-215.

BULGARIA
Theological Academy of St Clement of Ochrida, Lenin Square 19, Sofia.

CAMEROON
Faculté de Théologie Protestante, BP 4011, Yaoundé.

CANADA
Acadia Divinity College, The Graduate School of Theology of Acadia University, Wolfville, NS B0P 1X0, T: 902-542-2285, F: 902-542-7527, O: E-mail: Dorey@acadiau.ca.
St. Paul University Faculty of Theology, 223 Main St., Ottawa, OT K1S 1C4, T: 613-236-1393, F: 1-613-782-3033.
Univeristy of Manitoba, Winnipeg R3T 2N2.
University of St. Michael's College, Faculty of Theology, 81 St. Mary's St., Toronto, OT M5S 1J4, T: 416-926-7140, F: 1-416-926-7276.
University of Winnipeg, Faculty of Theology, 515 Portage Ave., Winnipeg, MB R3B 2E9, T: 204-786-9390, F: 204-775-1942.
Université de Montréal Faculté de Théologie, C.P. 6128, Succ. Centre Ville, Montreal, QU H3C 3J7, T: 514-343-7160, F: 1-514-343-5738.
Université de Sherbrooke, Faculté de Théologie, 2500 boul Université, Sherbrooke, QC J1K 2R1, T: 819-821-7600.
Université Laval, Faculté de Théologie, Cité Universitaire Ste-Foy, Ste-Foy, QU G1K 7P4, T: 418-656-7823, F: 1-418-656-2809, O: E-mail: Rene-Michel.Roberge@ft.ulaval.ca.
Université Saint-Paul, 223 rue main, Ottawa, ON K1S 1C4, T: 613-236-1393, O: Telecopie: 613-782-3033.

CHILE
Facultad de Teología, Universidad Católica de Chile, Av Bernardo O'Higgins 340, Casilla 114-D, Santiago, T: 224450.

CHINA
Christian Study Centre, 6/F Kiu Kin Masion, 566 Nathan Rd., Kowloon, Hong Kong.
Chung Chi College Theology Division, Chinese Univ. of Hong Kong, Shatin NT, Hong Kong, T: 852-2609-6705, F: 852-2603-5224, O: Also tel: 852-2609-6710 or 2609-6708.
Dept of Religious Knowledge and Philosophy, Chung Chi College, Chinese University of Hong Kong, Shatin, NT, Hong Kong, T: 61431.

COLOMBIA
Facultad de Ciencias Religiosas, Universidad Social Católica de La Salle, Calle 11 No 47, Apdo Aéreo 28638, Bogotá, DE.
Facultad de Teología, Pontificia Universidad Javeriana, Carrera 10 No 65-48, Apdo Aéreo 5315, Bogotá, DE.
Instituto de Teología, Colegio Mayor de San Buenaventura, Calle 72 No 10-88, Bogotá.

CONGO-ZAIRE
Faculté de Théologie Protestante au Congo, Université National du Zaire, BP 2012, Kisangani.

CROATIA
Catholic Theological Faculty, Kaptol 29, 4100 Zagreb.

CZECH REPUBLIC
Bohoslovecká Fakulta University Karlovy, ul Komenského 4, Litomerice, CZ-48282 Prague.
Evangelical Theological Faculty of Charles University, Jungmannova 9, Postfach 466, SK-111 21 Prague 1.
Protestant Theological Faculty Karl's University, Cerná 9/646, CZ-11000 Prague, T: 42-2-2422-1425, F: 42-2-2422-6566.

DENMARK
Inst. Missionsteol. og Ökumenisk T., Aarhus University, DK-8000 Aarhus C.
University of Copenhagen Faculty of Theology, Kobmagergabe 46, DK-1150 Copenhagen K, T: 45-3532-3605, F: 45-3532-3603.
üarhus Universitet det Teologiske Fakultet, Bygning 410, DK-8000 Aarhus C.

DOMINICAN REPUBLIC
Universidad Nacional, Escuela Evangélica de Teología, Av Duarte No 110, Santiago.

EGYPT
Coptic Orthodox Theological and Clerical University College, Anba Rueis Bldg, Ramses St, Abbasiah, Al Qahirah.

ETHIOPIA
Theological College of the Holy Trinity, Haile Selassie University, PO Box 665, Addis Abeba.

FINLAND
Abo Akademi University Faculty of Theology, Biskopsgatan 10, SF-20500 Turku, T: 358-21-265-4281, O: Also tel: 358-21-265-4289, E-mail: hkan.nasman@abo.fi.
University of Helsinki, Faculty of Theology, Neitsytpolku 1B, SF-00140 Helsinki.
University of Joensuu, Institute of Orthodox Theology, Tulliportinkatu 1a, P.O. Box 111, SF-80 100 Joensuu.

FRANCE
Centre de Rech. Théol. Missionaire, 5, rue Monsieur, F-75007 Paris.
Comité International de Liaison des Facultés Catholiques de Théologie, 21 rue D'Assas, F-75006 Paris, T: (01)222-4180.
Faculté de Théologie Catholique de Strasbourg, Palais Universitaire, 9 Place de l'Université, F-67084 Strasbourg, T: (88)355940.
Faculté de Théologie Protestante de Montpellier, 26 Blvd Berthelot, Rue Louis-Perrier, F-34 Montpellier (Hérault), T: 67926128.
Faculté de Théologie Protestante de Strasbourg, Palais de l'Université, F-67 Strasbourg (B-Rhin), T: 355940.
Faculté Libre de Théologie Evangélique de Vaux-sur-Seine, 85 av de Cherbourg, Vaux-sur-Seine (Yvelines), T: 4740986.
Faculté Libre de Théologie Protestante d'Aix-en-

Provence, 33 Av Jules-Ferry, F-13 Aix-en-Provence (B-du-Rh), T: 261355.

Inst. de Science et de Théologie, 128 Rue du Bac, Paris VII.

Institut de Théologie Orthodoxe St Serge, 93 Rue de Crimée, F-75019 Paris.

GERMANY

Abteilung für Katholische Theologie der Ruhr-Universität, Universitätsstrasse 150, Postfach 102148, D-44801, Bochem-Querenburg.

Alt-Katholisches Seminar der Universität Bonn, Hauptgebäude, Am Hof 3-5, D-53 Bonn.

Alttestamentliches Seminar der Universität Heidelberg, Klingenteichstr 2, D-6900 Heidelberg, T: (06221)541270.

Alttestamentliches Seminar der Universität Mainz, Saarstr 21, Forum Universitatis 5, D-6500 Mainz, T: (06131)1712652.

Alttestamentliches Seminar der Universität München, Veterinärstr 1/III (Geschäftszimmer), D-8000 München 22, T: (0811)218013479.

Anerkannter Sonderforschungsbereich (DFG-SFB Nr 1) Patristik an der Universität Bonn, Am Hof 1, D-5300 Bonn, T: (02221)7314414.

Arbeitsstelle der Historischen Kommission zur Erforschung des Pietismus an der Universität Münster, Universitätsstr 13-17, D-4400 Münster, T: (0251)49012572.

Biblisch-Archäologisches Institut an der Universität Tübingen, Liebermeisterstr 12 und Gartenstr 18, D-7400 Tübingen, T: (07122)7112879.

Christlich-Archäologisches Seminar der Universität Bonn, Liebfrauenweg 3, D-5300 Bonn, T: (02221)7314454.

Deutsche Ges. F. Missionswissensch, Vogelsangstr. 62, 7000 Stuttgart 1.

Deutsches Ev Institut für Altertumswissenschaft des Heiligen Landes, Bockenheimer Landstr 109, Postfach 4025, D-6000 Frankfurt/Main, T: (0611)770521.

Deutsches Inst. für ArzH Mission, Paul-Lechler-Str. 24, 7400 Tübingen.

Diakoniewissenschaftliches Institut der Universität Heidelberg, Haupstr 126, D-6000 Heidelberg, T: (06221)541267.

Ev-Theologische Facultät der Eberhard-Karls-Universität, Wilhelmstr 7, D-74 Tübingen.

Ev-Theologische Facultät der Johannes-Gutenberg-Universität, Saarstr 21, D-65 Mainz.

Ev-Theologische Facultät der Rheinischen Friedrich-Wilhelm-Universität, Am Hof 1, D-53 Bonn.

Ev-Theologische Facultät der Universität Hamburg, Edmund-Siemers-Allee 1, D-2 Hamburg 13.

Ev-Theologische Facultät der Universität München, Veterinärstr 1, D-8 München 22.

Ev-Theologische Facultät der Westfälischen Wilhelms-Universität, Universitätsstr 13-17, D-44 Münster/Westfalen.

Ev-Theologisches Seminar der Universität Bonn, Am Hof 1, D-5300 Bonn, T: (02221)7314414.

Evangelisch-Theologische Fakultät Ruhr-Universität, Gebäude GA, Stockwerk 7/8, Univeersitätsstrasse 150, D-44780 Bochum, T: 49-234-700-2500, F: 49-234-700-2620.

Evangelisch-Theologische Fakultät München-Universität, Schellingstrasse 3, D-80799 München, T: 49-892-180-3478.

Evangelisch-Theologische Fakultät Eberhard-Karis-Universität, Liebermeisterstrasse 12, D-72076 Tübingen, T: 49-7071-292-538.

Evangelisch-Theologische Fakultät Bonn-Universität, An der Schlosskirche 1, D-53123 Bonn.

Fachbereich Ev Theologie Alttestamentlisches Seminar der Universität Marburg, Lahntor 3, D-3550 Marburg, T: (06421)6912451.

Fachbereich Evangelische Theologie Hamburg-Universitat, Sedanstrasse 19, D-20146 Hamburg 13, T: 49-4123-4011.

Fachbereich Katholische Theologie Johannes Gutenberg-Universität, (Prüfungsamt/Studienberatung), Saarstrasse 21, D-55099 Mainz, T: 49-613-139-2215, F: 49-613-139-3501.

Fachbereich Theologie Georg-August-Universität Göttingen, Platz der Göttinger Sieben 2, D-37073 Gottingen, T: 49-551-397-100, F: 49-551-397-108, O: Also tel: 49-551-397-101.

Fakultät für Theologie Bielefeld-Universität, Universitätsstrasse 1, D-33615 Bielefeld 1.

Gerhard-Mercator-Universität Gesamthochschule Duisburg, Fachbereich Evangelische Theologie, Lotharstrasse 65, D-47057 Duisburg.

Institum Judaicum der Universität Tübingen, Liebermeisterstr 12, D-7400 Tübingen, T: (07122)7112590.

Institut für Biblische Archäologie der Universität Mainz, Saarstr 21, Forum Universitatis 4, D-6500 Mainz, T: (06131)1712685.

Institut für Christliche Gesellschaftslehre der Universität Tübingen, Olgastr 8, D-7400 Tübingen, T: (07122)7112591.

Institut für Christliche Sozialethik der Universität Erlangen-Nürnberg, Kochstr 6, D-8520 Erlangen, T: (09131)8512216.

Institut für Evangelische Theologie Westfälische, Wilhelms-Universität, Scharnhorstrasse 103-109, D-440 Münster.

Institut für Hermeneutik der Universität tübingen, Wildermutstr 10, D-7400 Tübingen, T: (07122)7112066.

Institut für Missionswissenschaft und Ökumenische Theologie der Universität Tübingen, Hausserstr 43, D-7400 Tübingen, T: (06122)7112592.

Institut für Neutestamentliche Textforschung der Universität Münster, Am Stadtgraben 13-15, D-4400 Münster, T: (0251)49012581/2.

Institut für Spätmittelalter und Reformation der Universität Tübingen, Hölderlinstr 17, D-7400 Tübingen, T: (07122)7112886.

Institut für Wissenschaftliche Irenik der Universität Frankfurt, Mertonstr 17, D-6000 Frankfurt, T: (0611)79813179.

Institut für Ökumenische Theologie der Universität Münster, Am Stadtgraben 13-15, D-4400 Münster, T: (0251)49012576.

Institutum Judaicum Delitzschianum an der Universität Münster, Wilmergasse 1-4, D-4400 Münster, T: (0251)49012561.

Intern. Inst. f. Missionsw. Forsch, P.O. Box 20 04 43, 5300 Bonn.

Johann Wolfgang-Universität Fachbereich Evan Theologie, Hausener Weg 120, D-60489 Frankfurt/Main 90.

Katholisch-Theologische Fakultät Westfälischen Wilhelms-Universität, Johannisstrasse 8-10, D-48143 Münster, T: 49-251-832-610, F: 49-251-832-611.

Katholisch-Theologische Fakultät Regensburg-Universität, Universitätsstrasse 31, D-93040 Regensburg, T: 49-941-943-3748, F: 49-941-943-4944, O: Also tel: 49-941-943-3747 or 941-943-3746.

Katholisch-Theologische Seminar, Liebermeisterstrasse 12, D-72076 Tübingen, T: 49-7071-292-544, F: 49-7071-292-866, O: Also tel: 49-7071-296-414 or 7071-292-543.

Katholisch-Theologische Fakultät Augsburg-Universität, Universitätsstrasse 10, D-86159 Augsburg.

Katholisch-Theologische Fakultät, Universitätsstrasse 150, D-44801 Bochum.

Katholisch-Theologische Fakultät Ludwig-Maximillan-Universität, Geschw-Scholl-Platz 1, D-8000 Munich 22.

Katholisch-Theologische Fakultät Eberhard-Karls-Universität, Keplerstrasse 17, D-7400 Tubingen.

Katholisch-Theologische Fakultät Julius-Maximilians-Universität, Sanderring 2, D-8700 Wurzburg.

Katholische-Theologie Fakultät Bamberg-Universität, An der Universität 2, Postfach 1543, D-36047 Bamberg.

Kirchen- und Dogmengeschichtliches Seminar der Universität Hamburg, Sedanstr 19, D-2000 Hamburg 13, T: (0411)4419713818.

Kirchengeschichtliches Seminar der Universität Heidelberg, Karlstr 2, D-6900 Heidelberg, T: (06221)541486/7.

Kirchengeschichtliches Seminar der Universität Mainz, Saarstr 21, Forum Universitatis 5, D-6500 Mainz, T: (06131)1712686 bzw 2749.

Kirchengeschichtliches Seminar der Universität München, Gorgenstr 7, D-8000 München 13, T: (0811)218013481.

Kirchlich-Archäologisches Institut der Universität Kiel, Neue Universität Haus 14, Olshausenstr 40-60, D-2300 Kiel, T: (0431)53112394.

Konfessionskundliches Institut des Evangelischen Bundes, Eifelstr 35, D-6140 Bensheim/Bergstrasse, T: (06251)270077732.

Konfessionskundliches Seminar der Universität Heidelberg, Karlstr 2, D-6900 Heidelberg, T: (06221)541486/7.

Lehrstuhl für Grundfragen der Ev Theologie der Universität Regensburg, Universitätsstr 31, D-8400 Regensburg, T: (0941)94312325.

Missionsakademie an der Universität Hamburg, Rupertistr 67, D-2000 Hamburg 52, T: (040)828642.

Missionsw. d. Ev. Luth. Kirche i. B., Postfach 68, 8806 Neuendettelsau.

Missionsw. Inst. Missio e. V., Bergdriesch 27, 5100 Aachen.

Missionswissensch. Institut, Arnold Jannsen Str. 24, 5205 St. Augustin.

Neutestamentliches Seminar der Universität Mainz, Saarstr 21, Forum Universitatis 5, D-6500 Mainz, T: (06131)1712603 bzw 2285.

Neutestamentliches Seminar der Universität Marburg, Lahntor 23, D-3550 Marburg, T: (06421)6912443.

Neutestamentliches Seminar der Universität München (Ev-Theol Fakultät), Veterinärstr 1/III, D-8000 München 22, T: (0811)218013480.

Neutestamentliches Seminar der Universität Münster, Universitätsstr 13-17, D-4400 Münster, T: (0251)49012542/43.

Neutestamentliches Seminar und Jüdisch-Hellenistsche Abteilung der Universität Heidelberg, Klingenteichstr 2, D-6900 Heidelberg, T: (06221)541270.

Patristisches Arbeitsstelle an der Universität Münster, Universitätsstr 13-17, D-4400 Münster, T: (0251)49012572.

Patristisches Seminar der Universität Marburg, Lahntor 3, D-3550 Marburg, T: (06421)6912446.

Praktisch-Theologisches Seminar der Universität Kiel, Neue Universität Olshausenstr 40-60, D-2300 Kiel, T: (0431)59312389.

Praktisch-Theologisches Seminar (mit Abteilung Ev Kirchenmusik) der Universität Main, Saarstr 21, Forum Universitatis 5, D-6500 Mainz, T: (06131)1712653.

Religions Kundliche Sammlung der Universität Marburg, Schloss 1, D-3550 Marburg.

Religionswissenschaftliches Seminar der Universität Bonn, Am Hof 34, D-5300 Bonn.

Seminar für Alte Kirchengeschichte der Universität Münster, Universitätsstr 13-17, D-4400 Münster, T: (0251)4912536.

Seminar für Christliche Religionsphilosophie der Universität Freiburg, Belfortstr 11, D-7800 Freiburg.

Seminar für Christliche Soziallehre und Allgemeine Religionssoziologie der Universität München, Geschwister-School-Platz 1, D-8000 München 22.

Seminar für Ev Theologie der Freien Universität Berlin, Ihnestr 56, D-1000 Berlin 33, T: (0311)769013669.

Seminar für Ev Theologie der Universität Frankfurt, Fachbereich Religionswissenschaften' Gräfstr 69, D-6000 Frankfurt/M, T: (0611)79813179.

Seminar für Ev Theologie und Didaktik der Glaubenslehre Fachbereich Religionswissenschaften der Universität Frankfurt, Farrentrappstr 47, D-6000 Frankfurt/M, T: (0611)79813538.

Seminar für Ev Theologie (Aussenstelle der Ev-Theol Fakultät der Universität Bonn), Repgowstr 9, D-5000 Köln-Lindenthal, T: (0221)47012511.

Seminar für Geschichte und Exegese des Alten Testaments der Universität Erlangen-Nürnberg, Kochstr 6, D-8520 Erlangen, T: (09131)8512206.

Seminar für Katholische Religionsphilosophie der Universitüt Frankfurt, Geog-Viogt-Str 8, D-6000 Frankfurt/M.

Seminar für Missionswissenschaft, Sanderring 2, D-8700 Würzburg, T: (0931)31258.

Seminar für Missions- und Religionswissenschaft der Universität München, Veterinärstr 1, D-8000 München 22, T: (0811)218013484.

Seminar für Mittlere und Neuere Kirchengeschichte der Universität Münster, Universitätsstr 13-17, D-4400 Münster, T: (0251)49012539.

Seminar für Neutestamentliche Theologie der Universität Erlangen-Nürnberg, Kochstr 6, D-8520 Erlangen, T: (09131)8512207.

Seminar für Praktische Theologie, Fachbereich Ev Theologie der Universität Marburg, Lahntor 3, D-3550 Marburg, T: (06421)6914284 bzw 4282.

Seminar für Praktische Theologie der Universität Hamburg, Sedanstr 19, D-2000 Hamburg 13, T: (0411)4419713797.

Seminar für Praktische Theologie der Universität Heidelberg, Schulgasse 2, D-6900 Heidelberg, T: (06221)541272.

Seminar für Praktische Theologie und Religionspädagogik der Universität Münster, Universitätsstr 13-17, D-4400 Münster, T: (0251)49012551.

Seminar für Reformationsgeschichte der Universität Erlangen-Nürnberg, Kochstr 6, D-8520 Erlangen, T: (09131)85187071.

Seminar für Reformierte Theologie der Universität Erlangen-Nürnberg, Kochstr 6, D-8520 Erlangen, T: (09131)8512202.

Seminar für Religionsgeschichte der Universität Freiburg, Belfortstr 11, D-7800 Freiburg.

Seminar für Religionsgeschichte der Universität Marburg, Lahntor 3, D-3550 Marburg, T: (06421)6914287.

Seminar für Religionspädagogik der Universität Erlangen-Nürnberg, Kochstr 6, D-8520 Erlangen, T: (09131)8512221.

Seminar für Religionsphilosophie und Geschichte der Theologie der Universität Marburg, Lahntor 3, D-3550 Marburg, T: (06421)6914288.

Seminar für Religionswissenschaft, Pferdegasse 3, D-4400 Münster.

Seminar für Religions -und Geistsgeschichte der Universität Erlangen-Nürnberg, Kochstr 6, D-8520 Erlangen.

Seminar für Religions- und Missionswissenschaft der Universität Münster, Universitätsstr 17-17, D-4400 Münster, T: (0251)49012531.

Seminar für Sozialethik der Universität Marburg, Lahntor 3, D-3550 Marburg, T: (06421)6914276.

Seminar für Systematische Theologie der Universität Erlangen-Nürnberg, Kochstr 6, D-8520 Erlangen, T: (09131)8512215.

Seminar für Systematische Theologie der Universität Hamburg, Sedanstr 19, D-2000 Hamburg 13, T: (0411)4419713801.

Seminar für Systematische Theologie und Apologetik der Universität Marburg, Lahntor 3, D-3550 Marburg, T: (06421)6912444.

Seminar für Territorialkirchengeschichte der Universität Mainz, Saarstr 21, Forum Universitatis 5, D-6500 Mainz, T: (06131)1713284.

Seminar für Theologie der Christlichen Ostens an der Ev-Theologische Fakultät, Kochstr 6, D-8520 Erlangen.

Seminar für Wissenschaft vom Judentum der Universität Mainz, Saarstr 31, Forum Universitatis 5, D-6500 Mainz, T: (06131)1712545.

Socialethisches Institut der Universität Kiel, Neue Universität, Haus 14, Olshausenstr 40-60, D-2300 Kiel, T: (0431)59312395.

Systematisches Seminar der Universität Heidelberg, Karlstr 4, D-6900 Heidelberg, T: (06221)541.

Theologische Fakultät der Christian-Albrechts-Universität, Neue Universität, Olshausenstr 40-60, D-2300 Kiel.

Theologische Fakultät der Friedrich-Alexander-Universität, Kochstr 6, D-8520 Erlangen.

Theologische Fakultät der Ruprecht-Karl-Universität, Schulgasse 2 und 4, D-6900 Heidelberg.

Theologische Fakultät Paderborn, Kamp 6, D-4790 Paderborn, T: (05251)25619.

Theologische Fakultät Trier, Jesuitenstr 13, D-5500 Trier, T: (0651)75011.

Theologische Fakultät Humboldt-Berlin-Universität, Burgstrasse 25, Unter den Linden 6, D-10099 Berlin, T: 49-30-2468-376, O: Also tel: 49-30-2468-393 or 30-2468-378.

Theologische Fakultät Albert-Ludwigs-Universität, Erbprinzenstrasse 13, D-79085 Freiburg, T: 49-761-203-2001.

Theologische Fakultät Ernst-Moritz-Arndt-Universität, Domstrasse 11/IV, D-17487 Greifswald, T: 49-3834-63296, O: Also tel: 49-3834-898-213.

Theologische Fakultät Friedrich-Schiller-Universität, Ibrahim-Strasse 24, D-07745 Jena, T: 49-3641-23947.

Theologische Fakultät Universität, Schröderplatz 3/4, D-18051 Rostock, T: 49-381-369-622.

Theologische Fakultät Trier, Universitätsring 19, D-54296 Trier, T: 49-51-201-3520.

Theologische Fakultät Martin-Luther-Universität, Universitätsplatz 8/9, (Melanchthonianum), D-06099 Halle (Salle).

Theologische Fakultät Christian-Albrechts-Universität, Olshausenstrasse 40-60, D-24098 Kiel.

Theologisches Institut (im Aufbau) der Universität Bielefeld (Arbeitsstelle Theologie), Schulstr 9, D-4400 Münster, T: (0251)23022.

Theologisches Seminar der Universität Kiel, Neue Universität, Haus 14/16, Olshausenstr 40-60, D-2300 Kiel, T: (0431)59312352.

University of Passau: Faculty for Catholic Theology, O: Web: www.unipassau.de/ktf.

Universität Mannheim Theologisches Institut, L 13, 17/I, 68161 Mannheim-Quadrate.

Universität zu Köln Seminar für Theologie, Gronewaldstrasse 2, Postfach 41 07 20, D-5000 Köln 41.

Vereinigte Theologische Seminar der Universität Göttingen, Nikolausberger Weg 5b, D-3400 Göttingen, T: (0551)5241.

GHANA

Department for the Study of Religions, University of Ghana, P.O. Box 66, Legon, Accra.

Tamale Institute of Cross Cultural St., P.O. Box 5563, Tamale.

GREECE

Faculty of Theology, University of Athens, Odos Ivannou Gennadiou 14, Athinai 140, T: (021)7795177.

Faculty of Theology, University of Salonica, Thessaloniki, T: (031)23922260.

University of Thessalonika, Faculty of Theology, GR-54006 Thessalonika.

GUATEMALA

Facultad de Teologia, Universidad Mariano Galvez de Guatemala, Apartado 1811, Guatemala CA.

HUNGARY

Academy of Theology, Eötvös Lorand u 7, 1053 Budapest.

Reformatus Theologiai Akademia, Kalvin tér 16, Debrecen.

Reformatus Theologiai Akademia, Rakay u 28, Budapest.

Theological Academy, Ullöi u 24, Budapest VIII.

INDIA

Pontifical Athenaeum (Papal Seminary), Poona 6.

Pontifical Theological Institute, St. Joseph's Pontifical Seminary, Alwaye 683103, Kerala.

Serampore College Department of Theology, Serampore, Hooghly, West Bengal 712 201.

INDONESIA

Fakultas Theologia, Universitas HKBP Nommensen, Jalan Asahan 4, Pematangsiantar, Sumatera.

Fakultas Theologia Satya Watjana, Satya Watjana Christian University, Jl Diponagosla 54-58, Salatiga, Jateng.

Fakultas Theologia UKIT, Tomohon, Sultara, Sulawesi.

IRELAND

Faculty of Divinity, Trinity College, Dublin University, Dublin 2.

Faculty of Theology, College of St Joseph, Milltown Park, Dublin 6.

Faculty of Theology, St. Patrick's College, Maynooth, County Kildare, T: Celbridge 286261.

Milltown Institute of Theology and Philosophy, Milltown Park, Dublin 6, T: (01)976731.

ITALY

Facoltà di Missionologia, Pontificia Università Gregoriana, Piazza della Pilotta 4, I-00187 Roma.

Facoltà Teologica Napoletana, Viale Colli Aminei Capodimonte, I-80131 Napoli; Via Petrarca 115.

Facoltà Valdese di Teologia, Via Pietro Cossa 42, I-00193 Roma, T: 374266.

Instituto Missionario Scientifica, Pontificia Università Urbaniana, Via Urbano VIII 16, I-00165 Roma, T: 655992.

Istituto Internazionale Don Bosco Università Pontificia Salesiana, Facolta di Teologia, Sezione di Torino, Via Caboto 27, I-10129 Torino, T: 39-11-58111, F: 39-11-581-1396.

Pontifical Gregorian University, Piazza della Pilotta, 4, 00187 Rome.

Pontifical Lateran University, Piazza S. Giovanni in Laterano, 4, 00184 Rome.

Pontificia Facoltà Teologica dei Santi di Gesù e Giovanni della Crose, Piazza San Pancrazio 5-A, 1-00152 Roma.

Pontificia Facoltà Teologica del SS Cuore di Gesù, Pontificio Seminario Regionale Sardo, I-08100 Cuglieri, Nuoro.

Pontificia Università S Tommaso Facoltà di Teologia, Largo Angelicum 1, I-00184 Rome, T: 39-6-670-2350, F: 39-6-679-0407, O: Also tel: 39-6-670-2291 or 60670-2292.

Pontificio Ateneo Antonianum, Via Merulana 124, I-00184 Roma.

Pontificio Ateneo San Anselmo, Piazza de, Cavalieri di Malta 5, I-00153 Roma.

Pontificio Facoltà Teologica San Bonaventura, Via dei Serafico 1, I-00142 Roma, T: 5911651.

JAPAN

College of Theology, Kanto Gakuin University, 4834 Mutsuura-cho, Kanazawa-ku, Yokohama 236.

Department of Theology, Aoyama Gakuin University, 4-4-25 Shibuya, Shibuya-ku, Tokyo.

Department of Theology, Kwansei Gakuin University, 1-155 Ichiban-cho, Uegahara Nishinomiya-shi 662.

Department of Theology, Seinan Gakuin University, 420 Hoshiguma, Oaza, Nishi-ku, Fukuoka City 814.

Faculty of Theology, Sophia University, 1-710 Kamishakujii, Nerima-ku, Tokyo 177.

School of Theology, Doshisha University, Karasuma-Imadegawa, Kamikyo-ku, Kyoto.

St. Paul's (Rikkyo) University, Christian Studies Department, Nishi-Ikebukuru 3-chome, Toshima-ku, Tokyo.

Tohoku Gakuin University, Tsuchidoi 3-1, Sendai City Miyagi Pref 982.

KENYA

Department of Philosophy and Religious Studies, University of Nairobi, Harry Thuku Rd, PO Box 30197, Nairobi, T: 34244.

Department of Religious Studies, Kenyatta University College, PO Box 43844, Nairobi, T: Templer 356.

LATVIA

University of Latvia Faculty of Theology, Raina Blvd 19, LV-1586 Riga, T: 371-211-288, O: Also tel: 371-212-019 or 213-117.

LEBANON

Department of Religious Studies, American University of Beirut, PO Box 1428, Bayrut.
Faculté de Théologie, Université St Joseph en Beirut, Rue de l'Université St Joseph, BP 293, Bayrut.
Facultés de Théologie et de Philosophie de l'Université Saint-Esprit, Kaslik-Jounieh.

LESOTHO

Department of Theology, University of Botswana, Lesotho and Swaziland (UBLS), P.O. Box Roma, vai Maseru.
National University of Lesotho Department of Theology, P.O. Roma, Maseru, T: 266-340-601, F: 266-340-000.

LIBERIA

Cuttington College and Divinity School, PO Box 277, Monrovia.

MADAGASCAR

Institut Supérieur de Théologie, Ambatoroka, Tananarive, T: 20763.

MALAWI

Department of Religious Studies, Chancellor College, University of Malawi, P.O. Box 280, Zomba.

MALTA

Faculty of Theology, Royal University of Malta, Msida, Valletta, T: 36451.

NAMIBIA

University of Namibia Department of Religion and Theology, Private Bag 13301, Windhoek 9000, T: 264-61-242-421, F: 264-61-207-2444.

NETHERLANDS

Faculteit der Godgeleerdheid aan de Rüksuniversiteit te Leiden, Matthias de Vrieshof 1, Postbus 9515, NL-2300 RA Leiden, T: 31-71-27-2570.
Faculty of Religion, Gemeentelijke Universiteit, Kloveniersburgwal 89, Amsterdam.
Faculty of Theology, Vrije Universiteit, De Boelelaan 1105, NL-1081 HV Amsterdam.
Hogeschool voor Theologie en Pastoraat te Heerlen, Oliemolenstraat 60, Heerlen, T: (045)717851.
Katholieke Theologische Hogeschool te Amsterdam, Keizergracht 105, Amsterdam, T: (020)242752.
Katholieke Theologische Hogeschool Utrecht, Rijksuniversiteit Utrecht, Heidelberglaan 2, Utrecht, T: (030)539111 toestel 2149.
Nederlandse Missieraad, Halve Maanstraat 7, S-Hertogenbosch 5211 VV.
Sektie Missiologie van de Theologische Faculteit van de RK Universiteit te Nijmegen, Nijmegen.
Theologische Akademie, Johannes Calvin Stiching, Oudestraat 5, Kampen.
Theologische Faculteit te Tilburg, Hoteschoollaan 225, Tilburg, T: (013)669111.
Theologische Faculteit van de Katholieke Universiteit te Nijmegen, Erasmuslaan 4, Nijmegen, T: (08800)58711.

NEW ZEALAND

Department of Religion, University of Otago.
Department of Religion, University of Wellington.

NIGERIA

Catholic Inst. of West Africa, P.O. Box 499, Port Harcourt.
Department of Religion, University of Nigeria, Nsukka, East Central State.
Department of Religious Studies, University of Ibadan, Ibadan.
Department of Religious Studies and Philosophy, University of Ife, PMB 27, Ile-Ife.
Department of Religion, Bendel State University, Ekpoma.
University of Jos, Dept. of Religion, Jos, Palteau State ,P.O. Box 2984.

NORWAY

Faculty of Theology, University of Oslo, Niels Treschow's House (6th Floor), PB 1023 Blindern, N-0315 Oslo 3.
Teologiske Menighedsfakultet, St. Olavsgatan 29, Oslo.

PAKISTAN

Christian Study Centre, 126 B Murree Rd., Rawalpindi, Cantt..
Institute for Religious & Social Studies, St. Patricks Cathedral, Karachi.

PAPUA NEW GUINEA

Department of Religious Studies, University of Papua New Guinea, P.O. Box 1144, Boroko.

PERU

Facultad de Teología Pontificia y Civil, Av Sucre 1200, Pueblo Libre, Apdo 1838, Lima 21, T: 618531.

PHILIPPINES

College of Theology, Central Philippine University, P.O. Box 231, Jaro, Iloilo City 5000.
College of Theology, Northern Christian College, PO Box 105, Laoag, Ilocos Norte, Luzon.
Department of Theology, Ateneo de Manila Loyola Heights, Quezon City, PO Box 4082, Manila.
Divinity School, Silliman University, Dumaguete City 6200, T: 63-225-2410, F: 63-225-4768.
Faculty of Theology, Pontifical University of Santo Tomás, Espana St, Manila.
Faculty of Theology, University of San Carlos, PO Box 182, Cebu City, T: 72419.

POLAND

Christian Theological Academy, Ul Miodowa 21, Warszawa.
Faculty of Theology, Katolicki Uniwersytet Lubelski, Aleje Raclawickie 14, Lublin.
Faculty of Theology and Law, ul Podzamcze 8, 31-003 Kraków.
Faculty of Theology, Law and Christian Philosophy, Catholic Theological Academy, Akademia Teologii Katolockiej, ATK, Gwiazdzista 81, Warszawa 45.
Higher School of Theology, 52/54 ul Krakowskie Przedmiéscie, 00-322 Warszawa.
Pontifical Faculty of Theology, 2 ul Wiezowa, Poznan.
Pontifical Faculty of Theology, 14 Plac Katedralny, 50-329 Wroclaw.

PORTUGAL

Facultad de Teología, Campus Universitario Cartuja, Apartado 2002, E-18080 Granada, T: 34-958-160-202.
Universidad de Deusto Facultad de Teologia, Apartado 1, E-48080 Bilbao, T: 34-4-445-3100.

PUERTO RICO

Facultad de Teología, Universidad Católica de Porto Rico, Ponce, PR 00731, T: (809)842-4150.

ROMANIA

Institutul Teologic de Grad Universitar, Piata 1848, 1, RO-3175 Blaj, T: 40-710-838, F: 40-712-895.
Institutul Teologic Adventist de Grad Universitar, Str Romulus Nr 59, RO-74124 Bucharest.
Institutul Teologic Penticostal de Grad Universitar, Str Carol Davila 81, Sector 5, RO-76252 Bucharest, T: 40-90-38-44-25.
Institutul Teologic Baptist de Grad Universitar, Nicolae Titulescu No 56a, Str Berzei 29, RO-70159 Bucharest.
Institutul Teologic Protestant de Grad Universitar, Piatar Victoriel 13, RO-3400 Cluj-Napoca.

RUSSIA

Moscow Theological Academy, Zagorsk, Moskva.

SIERRA LEONE

University of Sierra Leone, Department of Theology, Fourah Bay College, Mount Aureol, Freetown.

SLOVAKIA

Ecumenical Institute of the Protestant Theological Faculty, Konventna 11, Bratislava.
Evangelical Theological Faculty of the Comenius University, Svoradova 1, SK-81103 Bratislava.
Orthodox Theological Faculty, Sladkovicova 23, Presov.
Pravoslavna Bohoslovecká Fakulta Univ P J Safrika, ul Masarykova 15, SK-08080 Presov.

SLOVENIA

Orthodox Theological Faculty in Presov, University of Pavol Josef Safarik in Kosice, Masarykova 15, SK-080-80 Presov, T: 42-91-724-729, F: 42-91-732-677.
Theological Faculty, Dolnicargeva 5, 61001 Ljubljana.
Univerze v Ljubljana Teoloska Fakulteta, Z Oddelkom v Mariborn, Poljanska 4, Ljubljana 61000.

SOUTH AFRICA

Dept of Missiology, Faculty of Divinity, University of South Africa (UNISA), Pretoria.
Faculty and Department of Divinity, Rhodes University, PO Box 94, Grahamstown, CP.
Faculty of Theology, University of Natal, Pietermaritzburg.
Potchetstroom University Faculty of Theology, Private Bag X6001, Potchefstroom 2520, T: 27-148-299-1844, F: 27-148-299-1562.
University of Durban-Westville, Faculty of Theology, P/Bag X54001, Durban 4000, T: 031-820-2234, F: 031-820-2286.
University of Fort Hare, Faculty of Theology, Private Bag X1314, Alice 5700, T: 0404-2-2011.
University of Natal, Dept of Theo Studies, P/Bag X01, Scottsville 3209, New Arts Block, Golf Rd, Scottsville Pietemaritzburg, T: 0331-260-5540, F: 0331-2605858.
University of Pretoria, Faculty of Theology, Lynn Rd, Hillcrest, Pretoria 0083, T: 012-420-2322, F: 012-43-2185.
University of South Africa, Faculty of Theology, P.O. Box 392, Pretoria 0001, T: 27-12-429-4567, F: 27-12-429-4647, O: Also tel: 27-12-429-3332.
University of Stellenbosch, Faculty of Theology, P/Bag X1, Matieland 7602, 1 Dorp St, Stellenbosch 7600, T: 021-808-3255, F: 021-808-3251.
University of the North Faculty of Theology, Qua Qua Branch, Private Bag X812, Witsieshoek 9870.
University of the Orange Free State, Faculty of Theology, PO Box 339, Bloemfontein 9300, T: 051-401-2667, F: 051-48-9203.
University of the Western Cape, Faculty of Religion and Theology, P/Bag X17, Bellville 7535, Modderdam Rd, Bellville South, T: 021-959-2206, F: 021-959-3355.
University of the Witwatersrand, Dept of Religious Studies, P/Bag 3, Wits 2050, 1 Jan Smuts Ave, Johannesburg 2001, T: 011-716-3505, F: 011-403-7299.
University of Zululand, Faculty of Theology, P/Bag X1001, Kwa-Diangezwa, 38886 K/N, T: 0351-9-3911, F: 0351-9-3159.

SOUTH KOREA

Chongsin University and Presbyterian Theological Seminary, 31-3 Sadang Dong, Dongiak Ku, Seoul, T: 860-2-537-5101-6, F: 860-2-536-2602, O: Also tel: 335-38-3285-7 or 335-38-2475.
College of Theology, Yonsei University, 134 Shinchen-dong, Sudaemoon-ku, Soul.
Department of Christian Studies, College of Liberal Arts, Ewha Womans University, Soul.
Hoshin University and Theological Seminary, 108 Yanrim-dong Nam-gu, Kwangju 502-756.
Sung Kong Hoe University, Dept. of Theology, 1-1 Hang Dong, Kuro-Ku, Seoul 152-140, T: 860-2-618-0888, F: 860-2-683-8858, O: Also tel: 860-2-610-4114 or 2-610-4100.
Sungkyul Christian University, 147-2 Anyang-Dong, Anyang City 430-742.
United Graduate School of Theology, Yonsei University, 134 Shin-Chong Dong, Seoul.

SPAIN

Canónico, Universidad de Navarra, Ciudad Universitaria, Pamplona.
Facultad de Sagrada Teología, de Derecho Canónico y de Filosofía, Universidad Pontificia Comillas, Maldonado 1-B, Madrid 6.
Facultad de Sagrada Teología, Universidad de Deusto, Av de las Universidades, Apdo 1, Bilbao.
Facultad de Teología y de Derecho Canónico, Universidad Pontificia de Salamanca, Compañia 1, Apdo 23, Salamanca.
Facultad Teológica de Barcelona, Sección San Paciano, Seminario Conciliar, Calle Disputación 231, Barcelona 7.
Facultad Teológica del Norte, Seminario Metropolitano, Calle 5 Tomas de Zumarraga, Apdo 48, Burgos.

SRI LANKA

Centre for Society & Religion, 281, Deans Road, Colombo 10.

SWAZILAND

University of Swaziland, Department of Theology and Religious Studies, Private Bag 4, Kwaluseni.

SWEDEN

Svenska Inst. Missionsforskning, Ostra Agatan 9, 5 TR, S-753-22 Uppsala.
University of Lund, Dept. of Theology, Allhelgona Kyrkogata 8, S-223 62 Lund.
Uppsala Universitet Teologiska Institutionem, Slottsgrand 3, PB 1604, S-751 46 Uppsala, T: 46-18-182-195.

SWITZERLAND

Christkatholisch-Theologische Fakultät, Universität Bern, Hochschulstr 4, CH-3000 Bern.
Evangelisch-Theologische Fakultät der Universität Bern, Gesellschaftsstr. 15, CH-3012 Bern, T: 41-31-631-8061.
Faculté Autonome de Théologie Protestante, Univ de Genève, 3 Place de l'Université, CH-1211 Geneva.
Faculté de Théologie Catholique, Université de Fribourg, Rue du Botzet 8, CH-1700 Fribourg, T: (037)221124.
Faculté de Théologie de l'Université de Lausanne, BFSH 2, CH-1015 Lausanne.
Inst. de Missiol. et de Sc. des Rel., Universite/Misericorde, CH-1701 Fribourg.
Neue Zeitschr. I. Missionswissenson, CH-6405 Immensee.
Theologische Fakultät der Univrsität Basel, Nadelberg 10, CH-4051 Basel, T: 41-61-267-2900, F: 41-61-267-3111.
Theologische Fakultät der Universität Zürich, Kirchgasse 9, CH-8001 Zürich, T: 41-1-257-6721.
Université Neuchâtel Faculté de Théologie, Faubourg de l'Hôpital 41, CH-2000 Neuchâtel, T: 41-38-243-040.

THAILAND

Payap University McGillvary Faculty of Theology, Ampher Muang, Chiang Mai 50000.

TURKEY

Faculty of Theology, University of Ankara, Ankara Universitesi, Ilâhiyat Falkütesi, Yldirim Beyazit Meydani, T: 113176.

UGANDA

Department of Religious Studies and Philosophy, Makerere University, PO Box 7062, Kampala.

UNITED STATES OF AMERICA (USA)

Baylor University, Department of Religion, P.O. Box 97284, Waco, TX 76798-7284, T: 817-755-3735, F: 817-755-3740.
Boston University School of Theology, 745 Commonwealth Ave., Boston, MA 02215, T: 617-353-3064, F: 617-353-3061.
Brite Divinity School, Texas Christian University, Fort Worth, TX 76129.
Candler School of Theology, Emory University, Atlanta, GA 30322.
Center for the Study of World Religions, c/o Dept. of Religion, Temple University, Philadelphia, PA 19122, T: 215/546-4789.
Council on the Study of Religion, Department of Religious Thought, University of Pennsylvania, Philadelphia, PA 19104.
Department of Religion, Columbia University, New York, NY 10027.
Department of Religion, University of Hawaii, 2560 Campus Rd, Honolulu, HA 96822.
Department of Theology, Fordham University, Fordham Rd & Third Av, New York, NY 10458.
Department of Theology, Marquette University, 615 North 11th St, Milwaukee, WI 53233.
Division of Religion and Philosophy, Bishop College, 3837 Simpson Stuart Rd, Dallas, TX 75241.
Division of Religion and Philosophy, Marion College, 4301 S Selby, Marion, IN 46952.
Division of Theology and Christian Education, Houghton College, Houghton, NY 14744, T: (716)567-8776.
Drew University Theology School, 36 Madison Ave., Madison, NJ 07940, T: 1-201-408-3266, F: 1-201-408-3808.
Duke University Divinity School, P.O. Box 90972, Durham, NC 27706, T: 1-919-684-3691.
George W. Truett Seminary Baylor University, P.O. Box 97126, Waco, TX 76798, T: 817-755-3755, F: 1-817-755-3753, O: E-mail: Russell_Dilday@baylor.edu.
Graduate School of Theology, Oberlin College, Oberlin, OH 44074.
Hamma School of Theology, Wittenberg University, Springfield, OH 45501, T: (513)327-6121.
Harding University Graduate School of Religion, 1000 Cherry Rd., Memphis, TN 38117, T: 1-901-761-1352, F: 1-901-761-1358, O: Also tel: 1-901-761-1350.
Harvard Divinity School, Harvard University, 45 Francis Av, Cambridge, MA 02138.
Howard University School of Religion, Washington, DC 20001.
Institute for World Evangelism of the World Methodist Council, Candler School of Theology, Emory University, Atlanta, GA 30322, T: (404) 329-6344.
Lampon School of Religion, J. P. Cambell College, PO Box 1526, Jackson, MS 39205.
Meadville Theological School, Lombard College, 5701 Woodlawn Av, Chicago, IL 60637, T: (312)493-7531.
Perkins School of Theology, Southern Methodist University, Dallas, TX 75222, T: 214-363-5611.
Phillips University Graduate Seminary, University Station, Enid, OK 73701.
School of Theology at Claremont, 1325 N. College Ave., Claremont, CA 91711, T: 909-626-3521.
Southern Wesleyan University Division of Religion and Philosophy, One Wesleyan Dr., P.O. Box 1020, Central, SC 29630-1020, T: 1-803-639-2453, F: 1-803-639-0826.
St. John's School of Divinity, St. John's University, Collegeville, MN 56321.
St. Louis University, Dept. of Theological Studies, 3634 Lindell Blvd., St. Louis, MO 63108-3395, T: 1-314-977-2881, F: 1-314-977-2947.
St. Paul Seminary School of Divinity, Univ. of St. Thomas, 2260 Summit Ave., St. Paul, MN 55105-1094, T: 612-962-5500, F: 1-612-962-5790.
University of Notre Dame, Dept. of Theology, University of Notre Dame, Dept. of Theology, Notre Dame, IN 46556, T: 219-631-7811, F: 219-631-4268.
University of the South School of Theology, 335 Tennessee Ave., Sewanee, TN 37383-1000, T: 615-598-1288, F: 615-598-1165.
Virginia Union University School of Theology, 1601 West Leigh St., Richmond, VA 23220, T: 1-804-257-5600.
Yale University Divinity School, 409 Prospect St., New Haven, CT 06511, T: 1-203-432-5307, F: 1-203-432-5356.

VIET NAM

Faculté de Théologie Université de Dalat, Collège Pontifical St Pie X, BP 88, Dalat.
Faculté de Théologie Université Minh Duc, Ho Chi Minh Ville.

ZIMBABWE

Africa University Faculty of Theology, P.O. Box 1320, Mutare.
University of Zimbabwe, Dept. of Religious Studies, Classics and Philosophy, P.O. Box MP 167, Mount Pleasant, Harare, T: 263-4-303-211, F: 263-4-732828.

78
Urban & industrial mission

Ministry in and to large cities, inner cities, slums, or ghettoes; urban action, urban evangelism, urban theology, urban ministry; industrial missions and projects, evangelism of factory workers, ministry to urban workers; urban-industrial ecumenical parishes, inner-city parishes; ministries to urban structures and institutions; urban or industrial mission training.

ARGENTINA

Centro de Estudios Urbanos y Regionales, Virrey del Pino 3230, Buenos Aires.
Centro Urbano Nueva Parroquia, Viamonte 3445, 1822 Valentin Alsina, Provincia de Buenos Aires.

AUSTRALIA

Inter-Church Trade & Industry Mission, ACC, GPO Box 3582, NSW 2001, T: 278889.
Servants to Asia's Urban Poor, P.O. Box 394, Upper Mt. Gravatt, Queensland 4122, T: 07-34990233.

BOTSWANA

Shashi Complex Urban and Industrial Mission, c/o Botswana Christian Council, PO Box 94, Francistown.

BRITAIN (UK OF GB & NI)

Christian Teamwork Trust, Grubb Institute of Behavioural Studies, 1 Whitehall Place, London SW1A 2HD, T: (01)930-6364.
Church of England Industrial Committee, Church House, Dean's Yard, Westminster, London SW1P 3NZ, T: (01)222-9011.
Coventry Industrial Mission, Cathedral Offices, Priory Row, Coventry.
Deanery of Priest-Workers, Diocese of Southwark, Dean, 73 Woodbrook Rd, London SE2 0PB, T: (01)854-4509.
Evangelical Urban Training Project, St. John's Church, Everton, Liverpool.
French Protestant Industrial Mission (British Committee), 22 The Gallop, Sutton, Surrey.

Gateshead Team Ministry, St. Mary's Rectory, 347 Durham Rd, Gateshead, Tyne and Wear NE9 5AJ.
Industrial Christian Fellowship (ICF), St. Katharine Cree Church, Leadenhall St, London EC3, T: (01)283-5733/4.
Sheffield Industrial Mission, 2 Old Vicarage, Highgate, Sheffield S9 1WN; 19 Division St., Sheffield, T: 42879, 79452.
South London Industrial Mission (SLIM), Industrial Centre, Christ Church, 27 Blackfriars Rd, London SE1.
Urban Theology Unit, 210 Abbeyfield Road, Sheffield S4 7AZ, T: 0742-435-342, F: 0742-435342.
William Temple Foundation, Manchester Business School, Manchester M15 6PB, T: 44-61-275-6533/4, F: 44-61-272-8663.

CAMEROON
Evangélisation Urbaine et Industrielle Edéa, BP 4, Edéa.
Western Africa Urban Industrial Mission Committee, AACC/Comité Ouest-Africain pour les Villes et l'Industrie, CETA, BP, 4 Edéa.

CANADA
Canadian Urban Training Project for Christian Service, 51 Bond St (& 875 Queen St East), Toronto, Ontario M5B 1X1.

CHINA
Caritas Urban Community Development, Caritas House, PO Box 13522, Kowloon, Hong Kong, T: H-242071.
Hong Kong Christian Industrial Committee, HKCC, Metropole Bldg, 57 Peking Rd, Kowloon, Hong Kong, T: K-678031.
Tao Fong Shan Porcelain Workshop, Tao Fong Shan, Shatin, NT, Hong Kong, T: NT-61450.

COSTA RICA
Cristo Para la Ciudad, Apartado Postal 509-2350, Sn Frn 2 Rios, San José, T: 227-6805, 223-4204, F: 226-9726, O: E-mail: cpcinter@sol.racsa.co.cr.

DENMARK
Industrial Mission in Armenia, Mejlgade 101, 8000 Arhus C, T: (06)122240.

FRANCE
Mission dans l'Industrie de la Région Parisienne (MIRP), Groupe de Coordination des Enterprises d'Evangélisation, Conseiller, 47 Rue de Clichy, F-75009 Paris, T: 874-9092.

GERMANY
Ev Aktionsgemeinschaft für Arbeitnehmerfragen in Deutschland, Blumenstr 1, Postfach 4, D-7325 Bad Boll (Wttbg).
Sozialamt der Evangelischen Kirche von Westfalen, Industrial Mission, Haus Villigst, P.O. Box 5020, Schwerte, T: 49-2304-755-140, F: 49-2304-755-249.

GHANA
Tema Industrial Mission, P.O. Box 25, Tema.

INDIA
Bombay Urban Fellowship, St. Mary's Church, Parel, Bombay, Maharashtra 400012.
Bombay Urban Industrial League for Development, 11, Sujata Nivas, P. O. Box No. 16695, S. V. Rd. B., Bombay, Maharashtra 400050.
Calcutta Urban Service, 16, Sudder Street, Calcutta, West Bengal 700016.
Chowpatta Agricultural & Industrial Mission, PO Berenag, vai Almora, Kumaon, UP.
Christian Service to Industrial Society, 17 Balfour Road, Kilpauk, Madras, Tamil Nadu 600010.
Coimbatore Industrial Service, 100 Race Course, Coimbatore 641018, South India.
CSI Industrial Training Centre, Kodiannoorkonam, Nellimood PO, Trivandrum, Kerala.
CSI School of Industries, PB 1, Station Rd, Tumkur.
Durgapur Industrial Service (ESII), Bidhan Nagar, Durgapur 1.
Ecumenical Social & Industrial Institute (ESII), St. Michael's Centre, Bidhan Nagar, Durgapur 1, West Bengal, T: 5817.
India Industrial Mission, 5A, Seal's Garden Lane, Cossipore, Calcutta, West Bengal 700002.
Industrial Service Institute, 1840 Church Hall, Kingway, Nagpur 1, Maharashtra, T: 33455.
Mar Baselios Industrial Training Centre, Mavelikara P.O., Alleppey District, Kerala.
Mar Thoma Industrial Training Centre, Kozhencherry, Kerala.
National Commission on Urban Industrial Mission, 1 Mahatma Gandhi Rd, Bangalore 560001.
NCCI Urban Industrial Mission Committee, N-21, Greater Kailash, New Delhi.
Sharan Society for Serving the Urban Poor, 42 Gautam Nagar, New Delhi 110049.
United Christian Institute, Suranussi, Jullundur City, Punjab.
Urban Ministry Centre, C-13, Cozi Home, 251 Pali Hill, Bandra, Bombay, Maharashtra 400050.

INDONESIA
Industrial Evangelism Institute, Jalan Guntur 43, Jakarta III/10.
UIM Committee, DGI, Jalan Salemba Raya 10, Jakarta IV/3, T: 82317.

IVORY COAST
Abibjan Industrial Mission, BP 1282, Abidjan.

JAPAN
Ikoi no le Labour Centre, 79-1 Sakura-machi, Toyota-shi, Aichi Prefecture.
Kansai Industrial Mission Committee, Japan Institute for International Study, 2nd Ashike Bldg, 3-40 Andojibashi-dori, Minami-ku, Osaka, T: (06)252-8236.
Kansai Labour Evangelism, c/o Naniwa Church, 3-20 Koraibashi, Higashi-ku, Osaka, T: 2314951.
Kitakyushu Urban Industrial Mission, 1-2-35 Saburomaru-cho, Kokura-ku, Kitakyushu-shi 802.
Mining Mission in Northern Kyushu, c/o Miyata Church, 73 Miyata, Miyata-cho, Kurate-gun, Fukuoka Prefecture, T: Miyata 20733.
Poor Little Church in the Day Labourers District, Tmahime Hotel, 2-21-20 Kiyokawa, Daito-ku, Tokyo.
Tokyo Labour School (Tokyo Industrial Mission Committee), 4-5 Ginza, Chuoku, Tokyo, T: 5679069.
Traffic Workers' Welfare Centre, 115 Takaha-take, Hiraoka-cho, Kakogawa-shi, T: 26768.
UIM Committee, NCCJ, 1-551-24 Totsuka, Shinjuku-ku, Tokyo 160, T: (03)203-0372.
Urban Mission for Slum Area, c/o Nishinari Church, 6-14 Nankai, Nishinari-ku, Osaka, T: 5621450.

KENYA
Christian Industrial Training Centre (CITC), Principal, Meru Rd, Pumwani, PO Box 72935, Nairobi, T: 24763.
CITC Secretarial College, Principal, Bonyo Rd, PO Box 1437, Kisumu, T: 3046.
Eastern Africa Committee for Urban Industrial & Rural Mission, AACC, Pioneer House, PO Box 20301, Nairobi, T: 33510.

LIBERIA
Bendoo Industrial Mission, Lake Piso, Grand Cape Mount Country, T: 26008.
Bong Mining Parish, P.O. Box 1538, Monrovia.

MADAGASCAR
Centre d'Initiation Technique, Frères de la Doctrien Chrétienne, Mananjary.

MALAYSIA
Committee for Selangor UIM, 6 Jalan 11/4A, Petaling Jaya, Selangor.

MEXICO
Christ for the City, Apartado 61-002, Mexico, D.F. 06600, T: 533-5570.

MYANMAR
UIM Initiatives, Burma Christian Council, 20 Signal Pagoda Rd, Rangoon, T: 13290.

NETHERLANDS
Churches Industrial Service, Noordermarkt 26, Amsterdam-C.
Europe Urban Industrial Mission, De Horst 1, Driebergen.
SBI Slotemaker de Bruine-Institut Centrum voor studie en vorming, Amersfoortseweg 98, NL-3941 EP Doorn, T: 31-3430-14544, F: 31-3430-13218.
X-Y Action Groups, Van Blankenburgstr 6, 's-Gravenhage.

NEW ZEALAND
Inter-church Trade & Industry Mission, 26 Charles Upham Av, PO Box 297 Christchurch, T: 69274.
Urban Leadership Foundation, 83/2 Glendale Road, Glen Eden, Auckland, T: 0-9-813-1440, F: 0-9-813-1440.

NIGERIA
Lagos Industrial Mission, P.O. Box 78, Lagos.

PAKISTAN
Pakistan Christian Industrial Service, 74 Garden Rd, Karachi 3, T: 74607.
Technical Services Association, 3 Empress Rd, Lahore.

PHILIPPINES
Committee on Industrial Life and Vocations, P.O. Box 718, Manila, T: 96241.
Division of UIM, NCCP, PO Box 1767, Manila, T: 998636.
Interchurch Committee on Urban Squatter Resettlement (ICUSR), NCCP, PO Box 1767, Manila, T: 998636.
Workers' Institute for Social Enlightenment, NCCP, PO Box 1767, Manilla, T: 998636.

PUERTO RICO
Puerto Rico Industrial Mission Project, Apdo 9002, Santurce, PR 00908.

SIERRA LEONE
Industrial Ministry, UCCSL, PO Box 404, Freetown, T: 3268.

SINGAPORE
Jurong Industrial Mission, Jurong Christian Church and Civic Centre, 4-J Block 111, Ho Ching Rd, Jurong Town, T: 21539.

SOUTH AFRICA
Agency for Industrial Mission, Khotso House, Marshall St, Johannesburg, T: 011-833-1938, F: 011-764-1468.
D'Urban Network, 21 St Andrews St, Durban 3001, T: 031-301-0904, F: 031-301-6611.
ICIM (interdenominational Committee for Industrial Mission), PO Box 4928, Jhburg 2000, 602 Khotso House, 62 Marshall St, Jhburg, T: 011-833-1938, F: 011-836-5776.
South African Intermediate Technology Group, PO Box 31190, Braamfontein, Transvaal.
Urban Mission, PO Box 2098, Bloemfontein 9300, T: 051-31-4271.
Witwatersrand Committee for Industrial Mission, PO Box 81, Roodepoort, Transvaal.

SOUTH KOREA
Catholic Urban Poor Pastoral Committee, 1, 2-ga, Myong-dong, Chung-gu, Seoul-shi, T: (02) 777-7261.
Dong Inchon Labour Centre, 72-11 Mansuk Dong, Dong-ku, Inchon, T: 20181.
Industrial Welfare Centre, 58-76 Moonraedong 3-ka, Yongdongpo, Seoul, T: 623436.
Institute of Urban Studies and Development, Yonsei University, Sudaemoon-ku, Soul, T: 330131/41.
Korea Christian Action Organizations for UIM, IPO Box 3668, Soul, T: 746076.
Mission to Labour & Industry, 183 Wha Soo Dong, Dong-ku, Inchon.

SPAIN
Misión Evangélica Urbana, La Jordana, 44, 46003 Valencia.
Misión Urbana, Hinojosa del Duque, 11/Fco Iñiguez Alme, 28022 Madrid, T: 320-45-43.

SWITZERLAND
Advisory Committee on Technical Services (ACTS), WCC, 150 Route de Ferney, CH-1211 Genève 20.
Arbeiterseelsorger, Kapuzinerhospiz, Rebbergstr 16, CH-5400 Ennetbaden, T: (056)24130.
Foi et Citè, 5 Route des Acacias, CH-1227 Genève, T: 429952.
Institut Kirche und Industrie, Zeltweg 21, CH-8032 Zürich.
Ministère Protestant dans l'Industrie, 5 Route des Acacias, CH-1227 Genève, T: 429952.
Schweizerische Katholische Arbeitsgemeinschaft Kirche und Industrie, Ackerstr 57, CH-8005 Zürich, T: (01)429582.
Schweizerische Reformierte Arbeitsgemeinschaft Kirche und Industrie, Vorsitzender, Guggenbühlstr 41, CH-8404 Winterthur.
Urban Industrial Mission Desk, WCC, 150 Route de Ferney, CH-1211 Genève 20.

TAIWAN
Taiwan Ecumenical Industrial Ministry, 26 Shanhsia Lane, Kaohsiung 800, T: 554994.
YMCA Industrial Projects, 19 Hsu-chuan St, Taipei, T: 24431.

TANZANIA
Urban Project, Christian Council of Tanzania, PO Box 2537, Dar es Salaam.

THAILAND
Urban Industrial Life Division, Church of Christ in Thailand, 14/2 Pramuan Rd, Bangkok, T: 37976/7.

UNITED STATES OF AMERICA (USA)
Action Ministries International, P.O.Box 490, Bothell, WA 98041.
Apartment House Ministry, 163-47 103rd Ave., Queens, New York, NY.
Board of Metropolitan Strategy and Christian Social Relations, 105 West Monument St, Baltimore, MD 21201.
Boston Industrial Mission, 56 Boylston St, Cambridge, MA 02138.
Business Industrial Ministry, Suite 301, 6804 Windsor Av, Berwyn, IL 60402.
Catholic Committee on Urban Ministry, PO Box 606, Notre Dame, IN 46556.
Catholic Council on Working Life (CCWL), 1307 South Wabash Av, Chicago, IL 60605.
Center for Urban Encounter, 2200 University Av, St Paul, MN 55114.
Center of Metropolitan Mission in Service Training (COMMIT), 817 West 34th St, Los Angeles, CA 90007.
Christian Associates of Metropolitan Erie (CAME), Room 200, YMCA Bldg., Erie, PA 16501.
Church and Industry Institute, Wake Forest University, Box 7223, Winston-Salem, NC 27109.
Church on the Dyke Ministry to Fishermen, Box 2188, Texas City, TX 77591.
Church on the East Side for Social Action (CESSA), 3840 Fairview Av, Detroit, MI 48214.
Cities of Christ Worldwide, P.O. Box 301032, Escondido, CA 92030, T: 760-489-1812, F: 760-489-1813, O: 76132.170@compuserve.com.
City Hope, Intl., P.O. Box 38, New York, NY 13731, T: 914-676-4400, F: 914-676-3332.
Commission for Metropolitan Mission, Northern California Council of Churches, San Francisco, CA; Oakland-Berkeley, San José.
Comprehensive Suburban Training Program, 778 Sherman St, Denver, CO 80203.
Cooperating Churches of East Harlem, 2050 Second Av, New York, NY 10029.
Core City Ministries, 861 Galapago St, Denver, CO 80204.
Department of Urban Ministries, United Methodist Church, 475 Riverside Drive, New York, NY 10027.
Hawaii Interfaith Urban Coalition, Catholic Social Services Bldg, Honolulu, Hawaii.
House-Church Structure in Congregation, Trinity Presbyterian Church, South High and Maryland Av, Harrisburg, PA.
Institute on the Church in Urban-Industrial Society (ICUIS), 800 West Belden Av, Chicago, IL 60614.
International Urban Associates, 5151 N. Clark St., 2nd Fl., Chicago, IL 60640, T: 773-275-9260, F: 773-275-9969, O: IUA1@ais.net, www.ci.ais.net:80/iua1.
Internship for Clergymen in Urban Ministry, 9606 Euclid, Cleveland, OH 44106.
Joint Office of Urban & Industrial Ministries, UP-USA, 475 Riverside Drive, New York, NY 10027.
Joint Urban Ministry (JUM), 1213 Delaware Av, Wilmington, DE 19806.
Lutheran Inner City Ministry, 322 Ohio St, Racine, WI 53405.
Market Place Ministries, 5725 Duke St., Alexandria, VA.
Metropolitan Community Action Corporation, Syracuse Area Council of Churches, 3049 E. Genesee St., Syracuse, NY 13224.
Metropolitan Ecumenical Consultation on Christian Action (MECCA), 601 Fifth Av, Watervliet, NY 12189.
Metropolitan Interchurch Ministries, 282 West Bowery St., Akron, OH 44307, T: (216)535-3112.
Metropolitan Urban Service Training Facility (MUST), 235 East 49th St, New York, NY 10017.
Ministry of the Protestant Chapel to the Christian Transient, JFK International Airport, Jamaica, NY 11430.
Ministry to Low Income Areas, 120 Sigourney St., Hartford, CT 06105.
Ministry to Night Workers, 130 East Oak St., Chicago, IL 60611.
Ministry to Single Women on Manhattan, Ten Eyck Troughton, 145 East 39th St., New York, NY 10016.
Mobile Home Ministry, Box 15066, Broadview Station, Baton Rouge, LA 70815.
National Center for Urban Ethnic Affairs, 702 Lawrence St., NE, Washington, DC 20017.
National Committee on Industrial Missions, 10600 Puritan Av, Detroit, MI 48238.
Native American Urban Transition Program, 548 South Lincoln, Denver, CO 80209.
Night Ministry Project, United Community Church, 4690 Weiss Rd, Saginaw, MI 48602.
Protestant Community Services, 304 North Church St, Rockford, IL 61101, T: (815)965-8769.
St. Paul's Urban Center, 15th and J Sts., Sacramento, CA.
Street Ministry, 715 West State St, Rockford, IL 61101.
United Methodist Church Night Ministry, 485 Appleton St, Holyoke, MA 01040.
Urban Leadership Foundation, 727 South Brady, East Los Angeles, CA 90022, T: 213-726-2817, F: 213-726-1735.
Urban Training Centre for Christian Mission, 21 East Van Buren St, Chicago, IL 60605; 40 North Ashland Ave., T: (312)939-2762.
Urban Training Organization of Atlanta, 1026 Ponce de Leon Ave., NE, Atlanta, GA.
Urban Young Adult Action, 74 Trinity Place, New York, NY 10006.
Value Analysis Linkage with Urban Educational Systems (VALUES), Center for Urban Affairs, 740 DeMun, St. Louis, MO 63105.
Wall Street Ministry, 55 Liberty St, New York, NY 10005.
Watertown Urban Mission, 327 Franklin St, Watertown, NY 13601.
Yokefellow Institute, 920 Earlham Drive, Richmond, IN 47374.

ZAMBIA
Church and Industry on the Copperbelt, Christian Council of Zambia, PO Box 555, Kitwe.
Commerce and Industry Programme, Mindolo Ecumenical Foundation, P.O. Box 4093, Kitwe.

ZIMBABWE
Christian Urban Programme, Christian Council of Rhodesia, P.O. Box 3566, Salisbury, T: 28500.

79
Women in the ordained ministry

Organizations for, or associations of women in the ordained ministry, diaconate, or priesthood; advocacy for the place of women in pastoral ministry or Christian leadership; education or training specifically for women looking toward serving in the ordained ministry, priesthood, or Christian leadership.

AUSTRALIA
All Australia Anglican Deaconess Conference, Deaconess House, 28 Carillon Av, Newton, NSW 2042, T: 511172.
Methodist Deaconess Association, Wesley House, Box 674 GPO, Brisbane, Q-4001.
Presbyterian Deaconess Association of NSW, Pittwood Home for Aged Ladies, 23 Charlotte St, Ashfield, NSW 2131.
Presbyterian Deaconess Association of Victoria, 130 Belford Rd, North Kew, Victoria 3102.

AUSTRIA
Evangelische Diakonissenanstalt Gallneukirchen, Ev Diakoniewerk, Haupstr 3, A-4210 Gallneukirchen/Linz.

BAHAMAS
Deaconess Order of the Methodist Church in the Caribbean & the Americas, Box 497, Nassau.

BRAZIL
Núcleo de Estados Teológicos de la Mujer en Américano Latina (NETMAL), Rua do Sacramento 230, Caixa Postal 5150, Cep 09731-970, Rudge Ramos.

BRITAIN (UK OF GB & NI)
Anglican Group for the Ordination of Women to the Historic Ministry of the Church, 29 Thurlow Court, Fulham Rd, London SW3; Guillard's Oak House, Midhurst, West Sussex.
Church of Scotland Deaconess Board, Room 306, 121 George St, Edinburgh 2.
Church Sisters of the Presbyterian Church in Ireland, Women's Home Mission, Church House, Belfast 1, NI.
Council for Women's Ministry in the Church, Church House, Dean's Yard, Westminster, London SW1, T: (01)222-9011.
Deaconess Association of the United Reformed Church of England, 373 Andover St, Sheffield S3 9ER, South Yorkshire.
Deaconess Community of St Andrew, St Andrew's House, 12 Tavistock Crescent, London W11, T: (01)229-2662.

Deaconess Order of Anglican Accredited Lay Workers Federation, Church of England, St Wilfreds' House, Brayton, Selby, North Yorkshire.
Deaconess Order of the United Reformed Church of England, Church Cottage, Manaton, Newton Abbot, Devon.
Society for the Ministry of Women in the Church, 93 Hatherley Court, Hatherley Grove, London W2, T: (01)229-3197.
Welsey Deaconess Order of the Methodist Church, Ilkley House, 7 Pritchatts Rd, Birmingham B15 2QU.

CANADA
Fellowship of Deaconesses and Other Professional Women Workers, United Church of Canada, 6060 Côte Saint Luc Rd., Apt. 206, Montrál 253, Québec.
Order of Deaconesses of the Presbyterian Church in Canada, Box 400, Harriston, Ontario.

COSTA RICA
Asociación de Mujeres Teologas y Pastoras de América Latina y el Caribe, Apartado 901-1000, San José.

DENMARK
Association of Danish Deaconess Houses, Danske Diakonissestiftelse, Kobenhavn F.

FIJI
WEAVERS (Women and Theological Education—SPATS), P.O. Box 2426, Government Buildings, Suva.

FINLAND
Association of Deaconess Houses in Finland, Büro, Diakonissalaitos, Alppikatu 2, Helsinki 53.

FRANCE
Communauté des Diaconesses de Reuilly, 95 rue de Reuilly, F-75571 Paris, T: 343-5433, 345-7000.
Fédération Nationale des Communautés de Diaconesses de France, 10 Rue Porte de Buc, F-5800 Versailles.

GERMANY
Bund Deutscher Gemeinschafts-Diakonissen-Mutterhäuser, Hildesheimer Str 8, Postfach 226, D-3353 Bad Gandersheim.
Diakonia (World Federation of Deaconess Associations), Glockenstr 8, D-1000 Berlin 37 (Zehlendorf), T: 846707.
Diakonissen-Mutterhaus Aidlingen, D-7031 Aidlingen (1951; overseas sisters), T: (07034)651.
Kaiserwerther Verband Deutscher Diakonissen-Mutterhäuser, Hofstr 3, D-532 Bad Godesberg.
Verband der Ev-Freikirchlichen Diakonissen-Mutterhäuser in Deutschland, der Schwiez und Frankreich, Martinistr 41-49, D-2 Hamburg 20.
Zehlendorfer Verband für Evangelische Diakonie, Glockenstr 8, D-1000 Berlin 37 (Zehlendorf), T: 846707.

GHANA
Deaconess Order of the Methodist Church, Ghana, PO Box 522, Kumasi.

INDIA
Association of Theologically Trained Women of India, H-No. 107, 4th Cross, 19th Main, 2nd Block, Koramangala, Bangalore, Karnataka 560034.
Order for Women in the Church of South India, P.O. Box 3, Erode, South India.
Tamil Evangelical Lutheran Church Deaconesses, Bethania Deaconess Home, 1084 Mission Church Rd, Thanjavur-613001.

ITALY
Casa Valdese delle Diaconesse, I-10066 Torre Pellice, Torino.

JAMAICA
Deaconess Order of the Methodist Church in the Caribbean and the Americas, UTCWC, Kingston.

JAPAN
Bethsda Deaconess Mother House, UCCJ, 526 Oizumigakuen-cho, Nerima-ku, Tokyo 177.
Deaconess House, Hamamatsu-Shi, Nikatabaracho 3015, Juji No Sono.

LEBANON
Deaconesses of Hülfsbund (Germany), Armenian Evangelical High School, Bayrut, T: Anjar 4.
Deaconesses of Richen (Switzerland), Institute for the Deaf, PO Box 4623, Bayrut, T: 420735.

MALAYSIA
Deaconesses of the Evangelical Lutheran Church in Malaysia, 21 Djalan Abdul Samad, Kuala Lumpur.

MEXICO
Escuela Metodista para Diaconisas, Sedi Carnot 73, México 4, DF, T: 356570.

NETHERLANDS
Verband Christlicher Krankernhäuser und Diakonissenmutterhäuser, Ziekenhuiscentrum, Oudlaan 4, Utrecht.

NEW ZEALAND
Anglican Deaconesses, Diocese of Christchurch, 124 Elisabeth St, Christchurch 4.
Presbyterian Deaconess Association, 23a Frederick St, Lower Hutt.

NIGERIA
Church sisters of the Presbyterian Church of Nigeria, Nigerian Deaconesses, Creektown, Calabar, SE State.

NORWAY
Norwegian Deaconesses Association of the Methodist Church, Sosterhjemmet Betanien, Akersbakken 35, Oslo 1.
Norwegian Lutheran Deaconesses Association, Loviesnberggt 15, Oslo.

PAKISTAN
United Biblical Training Centre, Gujranwala.

PHILIPPINES
Central Conference Commission on Deaconess Work of the United Methodist Church, Harris Memorial College, PO Box 1174, Manila D-406.

SOUTH AFRICA
Deaconess Order of the Methodist Church of South Africa, 120 de Korte St, Clifton, Johannesburg.

SPAIN
Spanish Conference of Nuns, Nuñez de Balboa 99-3 C, 28006 Madrid, T: 91 2627696.

SURINAME
Surinam Deaconess Order, Madeliefjesstraat 32, Paramaribo.

SWEDEN
Church of Sweden Deaconess Board, Erstagatan 1, S-11636 Stockholm SO.

SWITZERLAND
Arbeitsgemeinschaft für den Diakonischen Einsatz, Sihlstr 33, Postfach 384, CH-8021 Zürich, T: (051)238899.
Deaconess Community of Bern, Schanzlistr 43, Bern.
Schweizerische Reformierte Diakonenhaus, CH-8606 Greifensee, T: (051)871682.

UNITED STATES OF AMERICA (USA)
Deaconess Home Missionary Service of the United Methodist Church, Room 326, 475 Riverside Drive, New York, NY 10027.
Deaconesses of the Episcopal Church in the USA, Central Home for Deaconesses, 1914 Orrington Av, Evanston, IL 60201.
Deaconesses of the United Church of Christ, 6150 Oakland Av, St Louis, MO 63139.
LCA Deaconess Community, Lutheran Church in America, Exec Sec, 2900 Queen Lane, Philadelphia, PA 19129.
Women in Mission & Ministry, Episcopal Church Center, 815 Second Ave., New York, NY 10017.

80
Women's lay organizations

Groups for lay women and girls emphasizing the role of women, the lay ministries of women, or the place of women in church and society; women's lay orders; women's rights, women's liberation agencies, feminist movements or organizations, women's caucuses or task forces; YWCA and organizations serving women and girls; and other movements either radical or conservative; rallies, conferences, retreats, and events for women. See also LAY MINISTRIES.

ARGENTINA
Liga Misional De Damas Luteranas, CC5, 1655 Jose L Suarez, Buenos Aires, T: 1-766-8991.
Organismo Latinoamericano de la Unión Mundial de Organizaicones Femeninas Católicas (UMOFC), Gelly y Obes 2213, Buenos Aires.
Orientación para la Joven, Montevideo 1440, Buenos Aires.

AUSTRALIA
Katholische Frauenwerk Österreichenentwicklungshilfe, Stephansplatz 6, A-1010 Wien, T: 525531, 524646/48.
Seminar für Kirchliche Frauen Berufe, Seminar für Wolfrathplatz 2, Wien 13.
Vocational Centre for Girls, 15 Jephson St., Toowong, Queensland 4066, T: Brisbane (072)217526.
Ökumenischer Arbeitkreis der Frauen, Schwegelerstr 39, A-1150 Wien.

AUSTRIA
ACISJF, Katholische Frauenwerk in Österriech, Stephansplatz 6, A-1010 Wien.
Austrian Catholic Women's Movement, Stephansplatz 6/V, A-1010 Wien.

BARBADOS
Caribbean Church Women (CCW), CADEC, P.O. Box 616, Bridgetown.

BELGIUM
ACISJF, Accueil et Orientation, Av des Ormeaux 26, B-1100 Brussel.
Auxilaires Féminines Internationales (AFI), Rue Gachard 13 & 84, Brussel 5, T: (02)472039.
Fédération des Foyer Belges de l'YWCA, Rue St Bernard 43, B-1060 Brussels, T: 372876.
Fédération Nationale des Patros de Jeunes Filles (FNPF), Chausée de Châtelet 48, B-6060 Gilly, T: (071)412026.
Groupe International 'Femmes et Hommes dans l'Eglise', Rue de la Prévoyance 58, B-1000 Brussels, T: (02)131749.
St. Joan's International Alliance, Quai Churchill 19-Boite 061, B-4020 Liege.
Vie Féminine (VF), Rue de la Poste 111, B-1030 Brussel, T: (02)2172952.

BOLIVIA
Orientación para la Joven, Casilla 2573, La Paz.

BOTSWANA
Christian Women's Fellowship, P.O. Box 20784, Gaborone, T: 313 427.
Young Women's Christian Association, PO Box 35, Gaborone, T: 353 681.

BRAZIL
ACISJF, Orientação da Joven, Rua Pereira da Silva 251, Laranjeiras, Rio de Janeiro, GB.
Associaçã Feminina do Rio de Janeiro, Av Franklin Roosevelt 84, 10 andar, Rio de Janeiro, GB, T: 2425358, 2426786.
Confédération Internationale du Guidisme (GISC), Av Maréchal Camara 186, 20000 Rio de Janeiro.

BRITAIN (UK OF GB & NI)
Association of Catholic Women, 22 Surbiton Hill Park, Surbiton, Surrey KT5 8ET, T: 0181-399 1459.
British League of Unitarian & Other Liberal Christian Women, Essex Hall, 1/6 Essex St, London, WC2R 3HY.
Catholic Association of Widows, c/o 83 Watford Road, Croxley Green, Rickmansworth, Herts WD3 3DT.
Catholic Guide Advisory Council, 17 Buckingham Palace Rd, London SW1.
Catholic Women's League, National Headquarters, CWL, 164 Stockwell Road, London, SW9 9TQ, T: 0171-738 4894.
Catholic Womens Network, Walbottle House, Walbottle, Newcastle, NE15 8JD, T: 0191-264 1108.
Girls' Brigade, International Council, Brigade House, 8 Parsons Green, London SW6 4TH, T: (01)736-8481.
Girls' Friendly Society and Townsend Fellowship, Townsend House, Greycoat Place, London SW1, T: (01)834-3524.
International Catholic Girls' Society (ACISJF), Rooms 16-17, 1st Floor, 39 Victoria St, London SW1H 0EE, T: (01)799-4588.
International Union of Liberal Christian Women (IULCW), 86 Chatsworth Rd, Croydon CR0 1HB, Surrey, T: 7803.
Ladies of Charity and Companions of St Vincent, 39 Blakehall Rd, London E11 2QQ, T: (01)989-1336.
Mothers' Union, Mary Sumner House, 24 Tufton St, London SW1P 3RB, T: (01)222-5533.
National Board of Catholic Women, 67 Bodley Rd, New Malden, Surrey KT3 5QJ, T: (01)942-3738.
Scottish Catholic Guiders' Advisory Committee, 16 Coates Crescent, Edinburgh 3, T: (031)225-3455.
St. Joan's International Alliance, Newman House, 15 Carlisle St, London W1, T: (01)437-4564.
Union of Catholic Mothers, 47 Oakdene Drive, Surbiton, Surrey KT5 9NH, T: (01)337-2196.
Women Together, 1 Claremont St, Belfast BT9 9AP, N Ireland, T: 26446.
Womens' Missionary Association, 86 Tavistock Place, London WC1.
Womens' Social Services in Gt Britain & Ireland (Salvation Army), 280 Mare St, Hackney, London E8 1HE, T: (01)985-1181, 1801.
World Women's Christian Temperance Union (WWCTU), 62 Becmead Av, London SW16 1UP, T: (01)769-6649.

CANADA
Aid to Women, 300 Gerrard St., E., Toronto, ON M5A 2G7, T: 416-921-6016.
Baptist Women's Missionary Society of Ontario and Quebec, 188-190 St George St, Toronto 5, Ontario.
Catholic Women's League of Canada, 1-160 Murray Park Rd., Winnipeg, MB R3J 3X5, T: 204-885-4856.
Christian Women's Club, 121 Willowdale Ave., Suite 305, Willowdale, ON M2N 6A3, T: 416-222-0548, F: 416-226-0540.
Ecumenical Decade: Churches in Solidarity with Women, 40 St. Clair Ave., E., Suite 201, Toronto, ON M4T 1M9, T: 416-921-7759, F: 416-921-7478.
LEAD International, 2-391 Masson St., Oshawa, ON L1G 4Z7, T: 905-433-4616.
National Council of the YWCA, 571 Jarvis St., Toronto 285, Ontario, T: 921-2117.
Pioneer Girls, 2320 Fairview St, Burlington, Ontario.
Promise Partners International, RR #2, Woodville, ON K0M 2T0, T: 705-439-1173, F: 705-439-2779, O: 705-439-2751.
REAL Women of Canada (Realistic, Equal, Active for Life), Box 8813, Station T, Ottawa, ON K1G 3J1, T: 819-682-3937, F: 819-682-3938.
Servants Anonymous Society of Calgary, 1032 5 Ave., S.W., Box 21066, Dominion Postal Outlet, Calgary, AB T2P 0V0, T: 403-237-8477.
Women Aglow Fellowship of Canada, 6245 136 St., Suite 100, Surrey, BC V3X 1H3, T: 604-532-8100.
Women Missionary Society Regular Baptists of Canada, 75 Lowther Av, Toronto 5, Ontario.
Women Today, Box 300, Vancouver, BC V6C 2X3, T: 604-582-3100, F: 604-588-7582.
Women's Inter-Church Council of Canada, 815 Danforth Ave., Suite 402, Toronto, ON M4J 1L2, T: 416-462-2528, F: 416-462-3915.
Young Women's Christian Association of/du Canada, 80 Gerrard St. E., Toronto, ON M5B 1G6, T: 416-593-9886, F: 416-971-8084.

CHILE
Orientación para la Joven, Erasmo Escala 1822, Santiago.

CHINA
Asian Women's Resource Centre for Culture and Theology, 6/f Kiu Kin Mansion, No. 566 Nathan Road, Kowloon, Hong Kong.
Committee for Asian Women (CAW), Metropole Bldg, 4th floor, Rm 403, 57 Peking Rd, Kowloon, Hong Kong, T: 852-2722-6150, F: 852-2369-9895.
YWCA, 1 Mcdonnell Rd, Hong Kong, T: 852-2522-3101, F: 852-2524-4237.

COLOMBIA
Orientación para la Joven, Carrera 15 No 42-45, Bogotá.

COSTA RICA
AGLOW, T: 223-5414.

DOMINICAN REPUBLIC
Comité de Orientación a la Joven, Santomé 94, Santo Domingo.

ECUADOR
Capcitacion de la Mujer Campesina, Rumipamba No. 815 y Republica, T: 457-166.
Programa de Becas para la Mujer, Isla Isabela No. 221 y Bolanos, Casilla 11294, Guayaquil, T: 247-079.
Union De Mujeres Evangélicas Ecuatorianas, Casilla 221B, Quito, T: 535-329.

FRANCE
Auxiliaires Missionnaires de l'Assomption (AMA), 17 rue de l'Assomption, F-75016 Paris.
Groupe International 'Femmes et Hommes dans l'Eglise', Section Parisienne, 72 Rue de Sèvres, F-75006 Paris.
International Grail Movement, Secretariat, 22 Rue du Dr Germain Sée, F-75016 Paris.
Services de la Jeunesse Féminine, 70 Av Denfert-Rochereau, F-75014 Paris.
World Union of Catholic Women's Organizations (WUCWO), Secretariat, 20 Rue Notre-Dame-des-Champs, F-75006 Paris; 98 rue de l'Université, Paris 7.

GERMANY
Arbeitsgemeinschaft für Ev Schülerinnen- und Frauen-Bibel-Kreise (MBK Mission), Hermann-Löns-Str 14, D-4902 Bad Salzuflen.
Bayerischer Mutterdienst der Ev-Lutherischen Kirche, Deutenbacherstr 1, D-8504 Stein über Nürnberg.
Deutscher Evangelischer Frauenbund, Bodekerstr 59, D-3 Hannover; Unterlindau 80, D-6 Frankfurt.
Deutscher Frauen-Missions-Gebetsbund-Arbeitsgruppe West, Heisterkamp 18 (and Kleekamd 3), D-2000 Hamburg 63, T: (040)5385478.
Deutscher Verband Katholischer Mädchensozialarbeit, Werthmannhaus, Karlstr 40, Postfach 420, D-78 Freiburg, T: (0761)2001.
Evangelische Frauenhilfe in Deutschland, Geschäftsstelle, Bahnhofstr 24, D-44 Münster; Unterlindau 80, D-6 Frankfurt.
Evangelische Weibliche Jugend Deutschlands (YWCA), Burckhardthaus, Herzbachweg 3, D-6460 Gelnhausen, T: (06051)5021/3.
Frauenmission Malche, Portastr 8, D-4954 Barkhausen a.d. Porta, T: (0571)7552.
Frauenstudien- und -bildungszentrum der Evangelischen Kirche in Deutschland, Anna-Paulsen-Haus, Herzbachweg 2, D 6371 Gelnhausen, T: 06051-89290, F: 06051-89290, O: Also fax: 89240.
Haus der Katholischen Frauen, Prinz Georgstr 44, D-4 Düsseldorf.
International Grail Movement, German Centre, 470 Duisburgstr, D-Mülheim.
Katholischer Deutscher Frauenbund, Kaessenstr 18, D-5 Köln.
Mission der Ev Schulerinnen- und Frauen-Bibelkreise (MBK), Hermann-Löns-Str 14, Postfach 560, D-4902 Bad Salzuflen, T: 50088/9.
Pfarrfrauenbund, Melittastr 10, D-7 Stuttgart-Degerloch.
Päpstliches Werk der Missionsvereinigung Katholischen Frauen und Jungfrauen, Raven-steynstr 26, D-5400 Koblenz-Pfarrendorf.
Sozialdienst Katholischer Frauen, Agnes-Neuhaus-Str 5, D-4600 Dortmund, T: (0231)528126/7.

GHANA
Presbyterian Women's Training Centre, P.O. Box 138, Legon.

GREECE
Foyer International Divine Providence, 52 Rue Capodistriou, Athínai 102.

HOLY SEE
Ecumenical Women's Liaison Group, Consilium de Laicis, Piazza San Callisto 16, I-00120 Città del Vaticano.

INDIA
Agape Association of Presbyterian Women, C/o.Synod Women Worker, Synod Office, Aizawl, Mizoram 796001.
Baptist Hmeichhe Pawl, L. B. K. Office, Lawngtlai, Mizoram 796891.
Bombay YWCA Head Office, 75, Motlibai St., Byculla, Bombay, Maharashtra 400008.
Comforter Ministries, Shalome, Plot No. 21, Door 5, Rajaji Avenue, Valasarawakkam, Madras, Tamil Nadu 600087.
Council of Women's Work, Hudson School, 14/18 Civil Lines, Kanpur, Uttar Pradesh 208001.
Diocesan Council of Catholic Women, Villa Rosa, 75 TPS III, Bandra, Bombay, Maharashtra 400050.
Focolare Community, 3 Pali Village, Pali Hill, Bandra, Bombay, Maharashtra 400050.
Manipur North Naga Women Union, Tadubi, Manipur 795104.
Mount Carmel Home for the Poor Women, 21 Palace Road, Banglore, Karnataka 560052.
New Woman, Fair Mount, Laitumkhrah Main Road, Shillong, Meghalaya 793003.
Vanitha Mandiram, Mar Thoma Suvisesha Sevika Sangam, Manjady P. O., Kerala 689105.
Women's Aglow Fellowship International, 19/4

Marigold, Church Road, Kalina, Bombay, Maharashtra 400029.
Women's Development Unit, 75, Motlibai Street, Byculla, Bombay, Maharashtra 400008.
Women's Training Centre, Canossa Convent, Dhule, Maharashtra 424001.
Yesu Karuna Prarthanalaya Sister's Order Project, Heggada Devanakote, Karnataka 571114.
Young Women's Christian Association of India, 10, Parliament Street, New Delhi 110001, T: 45294, 43561.

INDONESIA
HKBP Women's Bible School, Laguboti, Tapanuli Utara.
Persatuan Wanita Kristen Indonesia (PWKI), Jl. Menteng Pal Batu II/12 Tebet, Pasar Minggu, Jakarta Selatan.

IRELAND
Catholic Women's Federation, 4 Lower Abbey Street, Dublin 1, T: (353) 01 761594.
International Catholic Girls' Society (ACISJF), 91 Lower Baggot St, Dublin.

ISRAEL
YWCA of Jerusalem, Sheikh Jarrah Quarter, Wadil Joz St, Jerusalem, T: 82593.

ITALY
Associazione Guida Italiane, Via Alpi 30, I-00198 Roma.
Ausiliarie Femminili Internazionali (AFI), Via Filipo Lippi 45, I-20131 Milano; Via di Villa Albani 20, I-00198 Roma.
Centro Italiano Femminile (CIF), Via Carlo Zucchi 25, I-00165 Roma, T: 6221167, 6221436, 6221507.
Collegio Universitario Missionario Internazionale Femminile (CUMIF), Via Santa Brigida 8, I-35100 Padova; Via Acquetta 12, Padova.
Comitato Nazionale Italiano AC Servizio della Giovane, Via Urbana 158, I-00184 Roma.
Gruppo Femminile Missionaire, Via Trino 24, I-15033 Casale Monferrato (Alessandria).
Scuola Biblica Femminile/Istituto Betania, Via Antelao 14, Monte Sacro, Roma, T: 890941.
Unione Cristiana delle Giovani (YWCA), Via Balbo 4, I-00184 Roma, T: 474525.

JAMAICA
Sistren Research, 20, Kensington Crescent, Kingston 5, T: 809-977-1107, F: 809-926-6990.

JAPAN
Woman's Union Missionary Society, 221 Yamate, Naka-ku, Yokohama-shi 231.

KENYA
Association of Sisterhoods, P.O. Box 48062, Nairobi.
National Council of Catholic Women, PO Box 48437 or 48062, T: 21613.

MALAWI
Chigodi Women's Training Centre Synod of Blantyre, P.O. Box 5584, Limbe.

MEXICO
Asociación Cristiana Femenina (ACF) (YWCA), Humboldt 62, México 1, DF, T: 5850655.
Association Catholique Internationale des Services de la Jeunesse Féminine, Secrétariat Latino-Américain, 89 Av Oaxaca, México 7, DF.
Bolletin Documental sobre la Mujer, CIDAL, Rio Fuerte 3, Cuernevaca, Morelos.
Federación Mundial de la Juventud Femenina Católica (FMJFC), Secretariado Regional para América Latina, Apdo Postal 1143, México 1, DF.
Juventud Católica Femenina Mexicana, Tabasco 264, México.
Orientación a la Joven, International Catholic Girls' Society (ACISJF), Latin American Secretariat, Av Oaxaca 89, México 7, DF.
Union Nacional Interdenominacional de Sociedades Femeniles Cristianas, Apdo 1415, Zona 1, México, DF.

MYANMAR
Burmese Women's Bible School, Seminary Hill, Insein.
Karen Women Bible School, Seminary Hill, Insein.

NETHERLANDS
Catholic Women's Guild, Heusdenhoutseweg 13, Breda.
Catholic Women's Society, Kameelstraat 6, Nijmegen.
Co-operation of Men and Women in the Church, de Horst 1, Driebergen, T: (03438)2241.
International Grail Movement (De Graal), International Secretariat, Koningslaan 30, Amsterdam.
International Union of Liberal Christian Women (IULCW), 40 Laan Copes van Cattenburch, 's-Gravenhage, T: 558360.
Netherlands Union of Reformed Women's Movements, Steynlaan 8, Baarn.
Reformed Women's Service, Oude Arnhemseqweg 281, Zeist.
YWCA, FC Dondersstraat 23, Utrecht, T: (030)715525.

NEW ZEALAND
Girl's Brigade (NZ), P.O. Box 5141, Wellesley St, Auckland.
YWCA, 33 Tory St, Courtenay Place, PO Box 9315, Wellington C1, T: 558363.

NORWAY
Norwegian Catholic Women's Federation, P.O. Box 281, N-1371 Asker.
Sisters Missionary Guild, Johs Brungst 12c, Oppgang B, Oslo.
St Catherine's, Dominican Sisters, 8 Gjorstads Gate, N-Oslo.
Women Missionary Workers, Storgt 38, Oslo 1.
YWCA, Holbergspl 1, Oslo 1, T: 204475.

PAKISTAN
Women's Union Missionary Society, Women's Christian Hospital, 85 Nusrat Rd, Multan.

PANAMA
Federación Nacional de Mujeres Católicas, Apdo 8714, Panamá.

PARAGUAY
Orientación para la Joven, Independencia Nacional 1060, Asunción.

PERU
Asociación de Orientación para la Joven, Calle Roma 452, San Isidro, Lima.

PHILIPPINES
Asian Church Women's Conference (ACWC), 21 V Luciano St, Project 4, Quezon City 1109, T: 63-2-911-8543, F: 63-2-924-0207.

PORTUGAL
ACISJF, Travessa do Ferragial 1, Lisboa.
Comunhão Lídia Internacional, Av. do M.F.A., 108 r/c Dt., 2710 Sintra, T: 01-923 05 56.
Senhoras Evangélicas Unidas de Portugal, Rua da Bela Vista 5-1, Cascais.
União Cristã da Mocidade Feminina, Rua Santana a Lapa 157/2D, Lisboa-3.
União Cristã Feminina, Rua do Arco a S Mamede 9/3D, Lisboa-2.

SINGAPORE
Women's Algow Fellowship Singapore, Block 4 Lew Lian Vale, #02-04 Jade Towers, Singapore 537015, T: 289-2498, F: 289-2498.
Young Women's Christian Association of Singapore, 150 Orchard Road, #08-08 Orchard Plaza, Singapore 238841, T: 235-8822, F: 737-3804.

SOUTH AFRICA
National Council of the Catholic Women's League, 2 Canal Dr., Westville 3630, T: 031-86-2571.
Pan African Christian Women's Alliance, 3 Wyehill Way, Retreat 7945, Cape Town, T: 021-72-0512, F: 021-797-2651.
Women for South Africa, PO Box 75334, Lydiane 0184, Pretoria, T: 012-804-5397, F: 012-86-1819.
Young Womens' Christian Association of SA (YWCA), PO Box 31746, Braamfontein, 2017, 128 de Korte St., Braamfontein, Jhburg, T: 011-403-2423.

SOUTH KOREA
AWRC Asian Women's Resource Centre for Culture and Theology, 134-5 Nokbun Dong, Eunpyong-ku, Seoul 122-020, T: 389-2833, F: 358-8284.
Catholic Women's Organization, 1, 2-ga, Myongdong, Chung-gu, Seoul-shi, T: (02) 778-7543.
Hanil Women's Seminary, Wha San Dong 149, Chulla Pukto, Chonju.
National Organisation of the Korean Presbyterian Women, PCK, #805, Presbyterian Women's Bldg., 1-1, Yeon J I Dong, Chong ˝o Ku, Seoul 110 470.
Seoul Catholic Womens Organization, 1, 2-ga, Myong-dong, Chung-gu, Seoul-shi, T: (02) 778-7543.
Taejon Women's Biblical Seminary, 347 Sunwha Dong, Taejon-shi.

SPAIN
Unión Femenina Evangélica Española, Apdo. 2548, 28080 Madird.

SRI LANKA
Asian Church Women's Conference, 28 Hotel Rd, Mt. Lavinia, Colombo.

SWEDEN
Girls' Association, Dominican Sisters, 21 Villagatan, S-Stockholm.
Missionary Society of Swedish Women, Kungsgatan 28, S-751 05 Uppsala, T: (018)120240.
Swedish Ecumenical Women's Council, Kungsholms Kyrkoplan 4, S-111 24 Stockholm, T: (08)522142.
Women Missionary Workers, Birger Jarlsgatan 67, S-113 56 Stockholm, T: (08)304884.
Women Teachers' Missionary Association, Vasaplatsen 4, S-411 34 Göteborg, T: (031)112440.

SWITZERLAND
Alliance Mondiale des Unions Chrétiennes Féminine (YWCA), 37 Quai Wilson, CH-1201 Genève, T: 323100.
Alliance Nationale Suisse des Unions Chrétiennes Féminines (UCF), 15 Av Virgile-Rossel, CH-1012 Lausanne, T: (021)324334.
Association des Femmes de Pasteurs de Genève, 9 Rue des Alpes, CH-1201 Genève, T: (022)324898.
Auxilaires Femінines Internationales (AFI), 31/91 Rue de la Servette, CH-1202 Genève, T: 330907.
Co-operation of Men and Women in Church, Family and Society, WCC, 150 Route de Ferney, CH-1211 Genève 20.
Evangelischer Frauenbund der Schweiz, Schönaustr 27, CH-5430 Wettingen, T: (056)66668.
International Catholic Girls Society, International Secretariat, 1 Route du Jura, CH-1700 Fribourg, T: (037)223727.
Schweizerische Evangelische Verband Frauenhilfe, Gryphenhübeliweg 45, CH-3000 Bern, T: (031)447782.
Schweizerische Pfarrfrauenvereiniqung, CH-8303 Bassersdorf/ZH.

TAIWAN
Good Shepherd for Women & Girls Service Group, 3rd Fl., 11 Alley 1, Lane 82, Fushing Rd., Wenshan, Taipei; Box 93-187, T: 02-9325710.
Tribal Girls Bible School, 1-3 Tieh Shan Rd, Puli, Hantou Hsien.

TANZANIA
Bishop Kisanji Women's Training Centre, Christian Council of Tanzania, P.O. Box 696, Morogoro, T: 056-2830.

UNITED STATES OF AMERICA (USA)
Aglow International, 9055 Chetwood Dr., Colorado Springs, CO 80920.
Board of American Lutheran Church Women, 422 South 5th St, Minneapolis, MN 55415.
Board of Missions Women's Division, United Methodist Church, 475 Riverside Dr, New York, NY 10027, T: (212)749-0700.
Board of Women's Work, Baptist General Conference, 5750 North Ashland Av, Chicago, IL 60626.
Christian Federation of Korean Women in U.S.A., 748 S. Kingsley Dr., Los Angeles, CA 90005, T: 213-385-5604.
Christian Women's Benevolent Association, 6600 Washington Av, St. Louis, MO 63130.
Christian Working Woman, Inc., P. O. Box 1210, Wheaton, IL 60189, T: 630-462-0552, F: 630-462-1613.
Church Women United in the U.S.A., 475 Riverside Dr., Ste. 500, New York, NY 10115, T: 212-870-2347, F: 212-870-2338.
Coordinating Center for Women, 700 Prospect Ave. Cleveland, OH 44115.
Grail, The, Grailville, 932 O'Bannonville Rd., Loveland, OH 45140.
Healing Love Outreach Ministries, O: Web: http://hlom.org/index2.html.
International Lutheran Women's Missionary League, Gen Ofc 3558, S. Jefferson Ave., St. Louis, MO 63118-3910, T: 314-268-1530, F: 314-268-1532.
Korean Christian Women Federation, Inc., 857 S. Wilton Pl., Los Angeles, CA 90005, T: 213-385-5513.
National Council of American Baptist Women, Valley Forge, PA 19481.
National Council of Catholic Women, 1275 K St., N.W., Suite 975, Washington, D.C. 20005.
National Women's Christian Temperance Union, 1730 Chicago Ave., Evanston, IL 60201.
National Women's Missionary Society, Church of God (Anderson), 1303 East 5th St, P.O. Box 2328, Anderson, IN 46011.
Nazarene World Missionary Society, 6401 The Paseo, Kansas City, MO 64131, T: (816)333-7000.
New York Task Force on Women in Changing Institutions, 99 Claremont Ave., New York, NY 10027.
Office of Women's Affairs, Graduate Theological Union, 2465 LeConte Av, Berkeley, CA 94709.
Philadelphia Task Force on Women in Religion (PTFWR), P.O. Box 24003, Philadelphia, PA 19139.
United Foursquare Women, Angelus Temple, 1100 Glendale Blvd, Los Angeles, CA 90026.
United Society of Friends Women, Friends United Meeting, RR 2, Marshalltown, IA 50158.
United Society of Friends Women-International, c/o FUM, 101 Quaker Hill Dr., Richmond, IN 47374.
Virtue Magazine, 4050 Lee Vance View, Colorado Springs, CO 80918, T: 800-708-5550, F: 719-535-0172, O: gfm@pcisys.net, www.cookministries.com.
Woman Volunteers Association, 1671 Madison St, NW, Washington, DC 20011.
Women in Christ Ministries, P.O. Box 2253, New Smyrna Beach, FL 32170-2253, T: (904) 788-5591.
Women of the Promise, O: Web: www.cross-plaza.com/wotp/main.asp.
Women's Aglow Fellowship International, P.O. Box 1548, Lynwood, WA 98046, T: 425-775-7282.
Women's Auxiliary, National Baptist Convention of USA, 584 Arden Park, Detroit, MI 48202.
Women's Auxiliary Church of God, Keith St at 25th, NW, Cleveland, TN 37311, T: (615)472-3361.
Women's Auxiliary Convention Free-Will Baptists, 1134 Murfreesbord Rd, Nashville, TN 37217.
Women's Commission, P.O. Box 850, Joplin, MO 64802, T: 417-624-7050, F: 417-624-7102.
Women's Congress National Primitive Baptist Convention, 2112 Russell St, Charlotte, NC 28208.
Women's Home & Foreign Mission Society, AME Zion Church, 7405 Monticello St, Pittsburgh, PA 15208.
Women's Home and Foreign Mission Society, Advent Christian Church, Box 117, Arlington, MA 02174.
Women's Missionary Council, Assemblies of God, 1445 Boonville Av, Springfield, MO 65802.
Women's Missionary Union, Southern Baptist Convention, 600 North 20th St, Birmingham, AL 35203.
Women's Rights Committee, National Association of the Laity, 2303 Canterbury Rd, University Heights, OH 44118.
World Evangelical Fellowship Commission on Women's Concerns (CWC), 270 Elm St., Shafter, CA 93263, T: 805-746-3035, F: 805-746-4748, O: E-mail: ewbartel@lightspeed.net.
World Federation of Methodist Women (WFMW), 475 Riverside Drive, New York, NY 10027.
Young Women's Christian Association of the United States, 726 Broadway, New York, NY 10003, T: 212-614-2700, F: 212-677-9716.

URUGUAY
Orientación para la Joven, Palmar 2519, Montevideo.

ZAMBIA
Women's Training Centre, Mindolo Ecumenical Centre, P.O. Box 1493, Kitwe.

81 Work & the professions

Organizations, ministries, agencies, and associations bringing together or serving Christians of specific occupational groups - workers (labor, industry, technical fields) or those in secular professions (the arts, journalism, law, medicine, science, engineering, education, business, social service, civil service, etc.); Christian (mainly Catholic) workers' movements and labor or trade unions; professional associations.

ARGENTINA
Confederación Argentina Católica de Educadores (CACE), Brasil 721, Buenos Aires.
Federación de Circulos Católicos de Obreros, Junin 1063, Buenos Aires.

AUSTRALIA
AZTEM (Tent-makers for Christ), 641 Whitehorse Road, Mont Albert, Vic 3127, T: 03-7350011, O: 03-8985493, 03-8743658, E-mail: 100244.2110@compuserve.com.

AUSTRIA
Berufsgruppe Fürsorgerinnen in der Katholische Frauenbewegung, Stephansplatz 6, A-1010 Wien.
Christian Businessmen of the Full Gospel, Friedhofgasse 36, 2380 Perchtoldsdorf, T: 0222/86 41 82.
Katholische Arbeiterbewegung Österreichs (KAB), Stephansplatz 6/5, A-1010 Wien.
Katholische Lehrerschaft Österreichs (KLO), Stephansplatz 5, II Stiege, IV Stock, A-1010 Wien 1.
Katholischer Akademikerverbard, Währingerstr 2-4, A-1090 Wien IX, T: 346165.

BAHAMAS
Mission to Seamen, The Deanery Cumberland, Box 653, T: (809)322-1523.

BARBADOS
Mission to Seamen, St. Mary Vicarage, Cave Hill, Bridgetown 8.

BELGIUM
Association des Dirigeants et Cadres Chrétiens (ADIC), Blvd Lambermont 140, B-1030 Brussel, T: (02)2418677.
Equipes Populaires (EP), Rue de la Loi 127, B-1040 Brussel.
Federation Internationale des Pharmaciens Catholiques (FIPC), 59, Bergstrasse, B 4700 Eupen.
Fédération des Instituteurs Chrétiens de Belgique (FIC), Rue Belliard 159, B-1040 Brussels.
International Catholic Committee of Nurses and Medico-Social Assistants (ICCN), Square Vergote, 43, B-1040 Brussels.
International Christian Union of Business Executives/Christian Managers and Businessmen's Union, Av d'Auderghem 49, B-1040 Brussels, T: (02)354178.
International Federation of Christian Agricultural Workers Unions (FISCOA), Rue Joseph II 50, B-1040 Brussel, T: 176387.
International Federation of Christian Metalworkers Unions, Av Julien Hanssens 23, B-1020 Brussel, T: 258141.
International Federation of Catholic Pharmacists, Rue Berckmans 92, B-1060 Brussels.
Mouvement Ouvrier Chrétien (MOC)/Algemeen Christelijk Werkeraverbond (ACW), Rue de la Loi 121, B-1040 Brussel, T: (02)7356050.
National Teachers Service, Biekorfstraat 46, B-1030 Brussel.
Union Internationale Chrétienne des Dirigeants d'Enterprise (UNIAPAC), Av d'Auderghem 49, B-1040 Brussel, T: (02)7354178.
World Movement of Christian Workers, 90, rue des Palais, 1210 Brussels.

BERMUDA
Mission to Seamen, The Rectory, Warwick, T: (809)236-5744.

BRAZIL
Associação Brasileira de Assistentes Sociais, Av F Roosevelt 137, 5 andar, Rio de Janeiro, GB.
Movimento Sindical, Barra, BA.
Sindicatos de Trabalhadores Rurais, R Jaime Coelho 444, Campo Mourão, PR.

BRITAIN (UK OF GB & NI)
Accountants' Christian Fellowship, 53 Downsview Drive, Wivelsfield Green, Haywards Heath, West Sussex RH17 7RN.
Apostleship of the Sea, Stella Maris, 66 Dock Road, Tilbury, Essex RM18 7BX, T: 01375-845641, F: 01375-843736.
Association of Nursing Religious, Pield Heath House School, Pield Heath Road, Uxbrdge, Middlesex UB8 3NW, T: 01895-233092.
Association of Christian Teachers, 47 Marylebone Lane, London W1M 6AX.
British Sailors' Society, 680 Commercial Rd, London E14 7HF, T: (01)987-4191.
Catholic Nurses Guild of England and Wales, 46 Fowberry Crescent, Fenham, Newcastle upon Tyne NE4 9XJ.
Catholic Police Guild, Francis St, London SW1P 1QW.
Catholic Social Workers' Guild, 12 Barr Beacon, Canonbie Road, London SE23 3AH, T: 0181-699 8438.
Catholic Teachers Federation, 24 Knowlands Rd, Monkspath, Solihull, W Midlands B90 4UE, T: 0121-

745 4265.
Christian Businessmen's Committe of Great Britain and Ireland, 9 Newforge Grange, Belfast BT9 5BQ, T: (08) 0232 667187.
Fair Trade Links, Ranworth House, Osborne Road, Crowborough TN6 2HN, T: 44-0892-667485, F: 44-0892-668048.
Guild of Catholic Doctors, Brampton House, 60, Grove End Road, London NW8 9NH, T: 0171-266-4246.
International Hospital Christian Fellowship in Ireland and Scotland, 349 Beersbridge Road, Belfast BT5 5DS, T: (08) 0232 453595.
International Society of Christian Artists, Glasspools, Gillsman's Hill, St Leonards-on-Sea; World Congresses: Bologna 1967, Salzburg 1969.
Mission to Seamen, College Hill, London EC4R 2RL, T: (071)248-5202, O: Also: 071-248-7442.
Missions to Seamen, Scotland, Containerbase, Gartsherrie Road, Coatbridge ML5 2DS, T: 01236 440132.
National Union of Funeral Service Operatives, 16 Woolwich New Rd, London SE18 6DH, T: (01)854-5870.
Nurses Christian Fellowship Intl. (NCF Intl), 18 Buckland Road, Maidstone, Kent ME16 0SL, T: 1622-753111, F: 1622-754111, O: E-mail: ncfi@compuserve.com, Web site: http://ourworld.com.
Seamen's Christian Friend Society, 58 Orangefield Road, Belfast 5, T: (08) 232 654272.
Teachers' Prayer Fellowship, 45 Old Bisley Rd, Frimley, Surrey.
Young Christian Workers (YCW), 106 Clapham Rd, London SW9 0JX, T: (01)735-7031.

CAMEROON
Ecumenical Association of African Theologians (EAAT), BP 1539, Yaoundé.
Syndicat des Enseignants Catholiques du Diocèse de Douala (SECDD), BP 1138, Douala.

CANADA
(ELIC) English Language Institute in China Society, 41 - 13320 78 Ave., Surrey, BC V3W 0H6, T: 604-572-0329, F: 604-572-0387, O: 1-800-663-0372.
Apostleship of the Sea, 150 Robson St., VAncouver, BC V6B 2A7, T: 604-683-0281.
Canadian Tentmaker Network, 10 Huntingdale Blvd., Scarborough, ON M1W 2S5, T: 416-499-7511, F: 416-499-4472, O: E-mail: CompuServe 74140,3626.
Christian Business and Professional Association (Campus Crusade for Christ), Box 300, Vancouver, BC V6C 2X3, T: 604-582-3100, F: 604-588-7582.
Christian Business Men's Committee of Canada, 1001 191 Lombard Ave., Winnipeg, MB R3B 0X1, T: 204-942-2148, F: 204-957-7647.
Christian Farmers Federation of Ontario, 115 Woolwich St., 2nd Floor, Guelph, ON N1H 3V1, T: 519-837-1620, F: 519-824-1835.
Christian Labour Association of Canada, 5920 Atlantic Dr., Mississauga, ON L4W 1N6, T: 905-670-7383, F: 905-670-8416, O: 1-800-268-5281.
Christian Legal Fellowship, Box 1, Group 14, Oakbank, MB R0E 1J1, T: 204-228-3445, F: 800-442-8850.
Christian Medical Dental Society of Canada/EMAS Evangelical Medical Aid Society, Box 160, Warkworth, ON K0K 3K0, T: 705-924-3246, F: 705-924-3384.
Fellowship of Christian Firefighters, 11 Gilmer Pl., S.W., Calgary, AB T3E 5B5, T: 403-249-0742.
God's Disciples M.C., 442 rue Lessard, St.-Nicéphore, QC J2A 2C9, T: 819-477-2568.
Homeland Harbour Ministries in Vancouver Harbour, P.O. Box 2475, Vancouver, BC V6B 3W7, T: 604-437-8142.
International Seamen's Centre, 201 de la Commune St., W., Montreal, QC H2Y 2C9, T: 514-844-1476.
Interplace, P.O. Box 129, Winnipeg, MB R3C 2G1, T: 204-944-1400, F: 204-475-2992.
Lighthouse Harbour Ministries, P.O. Box 87020, North VAncouver, BC V7L 4P6, T: 604-988-5084.
Mennonite Economic Development Associates, #302 - 280 Smith St., Winnipeg, MB R3C 1K2, T: 204-956-6430, F: 204-942-4001, O: E-mail: 74260,125CompuServe.
Ministry to Seafarers, P.O. Box 76721, Station A, Vancouver, BC V5R 5S7, T: 604-434-3012.
Nexus, P.O. Box 42026, Mississauga, ON L5M 4Z4, T: 905-821-6300, F: 905-821-6325.
Nurses Christian Fellowship of Canada, #17 - 40 Vogell Rd., Richmond Hill, ON L4B 3N6, T: 905-884-6880, F: 905-884-6550.
Open Road Chapels, P.O. Box 5, S.S. #3, Stroud, ON L0L 2M0, T: 705-436-3733.
Operation Bootstrap, Box 175, Toronto Dominion Centre, Suite 2707, T.D. Bank Tower, Toronto, ON M5K 1H6, T: 416-947-9220, F: 416-366-0818.
Taskforce on the Churches and Corporate Responsibility, 129 St. Clair Ave. W., Toronto, ON M4V IN5, T: 416-923-1758, F: 416-927-7554.
Teachers' Christian Fellowship, #17 - 40 Vogell Rd., Richmond Hill, ON L4B 3N6, T: 905-884-6880, F: 905-884-6550.

CHILE
Academia de Asistentas Sociales San Vicente de Paul, Villavicencio 337.
Movimiento de Profesores de Acción Católica (MOPAC), 2 Sur No 870, Talca.

CHINA
Christian Workers' Association, Caritas House, 2 Caine Rd, Hong Kong.

COLOMBIA
Federación Nacional de Trabajadores Sociales, Apdo Aéreo 16434, Bogotá, DE.

CONGO-ZAIRE
Jeunesse Ouvrière Chrétienne Internationale, Panafricain, BP 8314, Kinshasa.

COSTA RICA
Confederación de Obreros y Campesinos Cristianos (COCC), Calle 6, 4 y 6 No 449, Apdo 4137, San José, T: 217701.

DENMARK
Nurses Missionary Fellowship, Frejasvej 6, 6070 Christiansfeld, T: 74 56 23 00.
Women Teachers' Missionary Association, V Ostensgade, DK-2791 Dragor.

DOMINICAN REPUBLIC
Confederación Autonoma de Sindicatos Cristianos (CASC), Juan Pablo Pina, 27 altos, Apdo 309, Santo Domingo, T: 28454.

ECUADOR
Evangelismo y Discipulado, Pasaje Chiriboga No. 433 y Ave. America, Casilla 4990, Quito, T: 237-725.

EGYPT
Soeurs Scolaires Franciscaines, 9 Rue el Haras, Garden City, Al Qahirah.

EL SALVADOR
Movimiento Obrero de Acción Católica, Iglesia El Rosario, San Salvador.

FINLAND
Salvation Army Harbour-Light Corps, Inarintie 8, 000550 Helsinki, T: 90-714-013.

FRANCE
Action Catholique Ouvrième (ACO), 7 Rue Paul Lelong, F-75002 Paris.
Confédération Française des Travailleurs Chrétiens (CFTC), 13 rue des Ecluses St-Martin, F-75010 Paris, T: 205-7966.
Fédération des Syndicats Chrétiens des Finances et des Affairs Economiques et Assimilés, 13 Rue des Ecluses St-Martin, F-75010 Paris, T: 205-7966.
Fédération Générale des Syndicats Chrétiens des Fonctionnaires de l'Etat, des Collectivit´s Locales et Assimilés, 56 Rue du Faubourg Poissonnière, F-75010 Paris, T: 523-3022.
Fédération Syndicale Chrétienne des Travailleurs des PTT, 56 Rue du Faubourg Poissonnière, F-7510 Paris, T: 523-3377.
Organisation Mondiale des Anciens et Anciennes, Eleves de l'Enseignement Catholique, 17 Rue Michel Charles, F-75012 Paris, T: (01)343-7629.
Section des Assistantes Sociales de l'UCSS, 16 Rue Tiphaine, F-75015 Paris.
Syndicat National de l'Enseignement Chrétien, Siège, 359 Rue Herbeuse, F-76230 Bois-Guillaume, T: 709923.
Union Departmentale des Syndicats Chrétiens de Moselle, 38 Rue Mazelle, F-5700 Metz, T: 742857.
Union des Religieuses Educatrices Paroissiales, 10 bis Rue Jean Bart, F-75006 Paris.
Verband der Renaissance (Gesellschaften Katholischer Akademiker an Schweizerischen Hochschulen), 10 Rue du Centre, F-1723 Marly le Petit.

FRENCH GUIANA
Centrale des Travailleurs Chrétiens de la Guyane (CTCG), 113 Rue Christophe Colomb, BP 383, F-973 Cayenne, T: 232.

GERMANY
Arbeitgemeinschaft für Ev Schulerinnen und Frauen-Bibel-Kreise, PO Box 560, D-4902 Bad Salzuflen, T: 50088.
Daniel Consulting, Srukturaufbau Ost, Nagolder Str. 27, 71083 Herrenberg b. Stuttgart, T: 07032-9283-0, F: 07032-9283-11.
Deutsche Seemannmission, W 2800, Faulen Strasse 110, Germany.
Evangelische Arbeiterbewegung, Geschäftsstelle, Brunostr 12, D-43 Essen.
Junge Christliche Arbeitnehmer (CAJ), Hüttmannstr 52, D-4300 Essen, T: (02141)671065.
Katholische Arbeiterbewegung (KAB), Bernhard Letterhausstr 26, Köln.
Verband Evangelischen Sozialpädagogen, Bismarckstr 140, D-662 Völklinger.
Werkvolk, Pettenkoferstr 8, München 15.

GREECE
Christian Union of Professional Men, Athínai.

GRENADA
Grenada Catholic Teachers Association, Calvigny Rd, Woburn P.O., St George's.

GUADELOUPE
Centrale Démocratique des Travailleurs Chrétiens de Guadeloupe (CDTGG), 15 Rue Victor Hugo, BP 369, Pointe-à-Pitre, T: 821168.

HAITI
Action Catholique Ouvrière (ACO), BP 160B, Port-au-Prince.
Mission to Seamen, S Esprit Rue 13a Cap Hatian BP 1309, Port-au-Prince.

HONDURAS
Mission to Seamen, Santisima Trin, Apdo 28 Av Morazan, 1175 La Ceiba Atlantida, T: (011)504422641.

HUNGARY
Actio Catholica, Kàrolyi u 4-8 III I-8, Budapest V.

INDIA
Apostleship of the Sea, C/o Stella Maris Church, 4 Nimak Mahal Road Garden Reach, Calcutta, West Bengal 700043.
Christian Business Men, 1A/1, 3rd Street West Bryantnager, Tuticorin, Tamil Nadu 628008.
Christian Businessmen's Committee India, Box 2050, Kadavanthara, Kerala 682020.
Christian Workers Movement, 5, Nandidurg Road, Bangalore, Karnataka 560046.
Evangel Engineers (India) Consortium, 2/90 N-8, Bharathidasan Street, Kamalakshipuram, Vellore, Tamil Nadu 632002.
Evangelical Nurses Fellowship of India, 7, Tank Bund Street, 1st Floor, Ottery, Madras, Tamil Nadu 600012.
Industrial Employees Prayer Fellowship, Plot 12 A. N. Sastri Square, Korattur, Madras, Tamil Nadu 600080.
Interserve, Tentmaker Center, C-20/164, Janakpuri, New Delhi 110 058, O: E-mail: isvindia@del2.vsnl.net.in.
Nurses' Link, ENFI Office, 7, Tank Bund Street, First Floor, Otteri, Madras, Tamil Nadu 600012.
St. Antony's Institute of Commerce, Chengamaned, Kerala 683578.
Tentmaker Centre, P.O. Box 8630, Delhi 110054.

INDONESIA
Federation of Pancasila Unions, c/o Taman Cut Mutiali 10, Jakarta II/14.
Indonesian Federation of Christian Workers' Associations (KESPEKRI), Jalan Jenderal Sudirman 1, Jakarta.

IRELAND
Apostleship of the Sea (Ireland), Anchor House, Penrose Quay, Cork, T: (353) 021 505833.
International Hospital Christian Fellowship in Ireland and Scotland, 149 Meadow Grove, Dundrum, Dublin 16, T: (343) 01 298 69870.

ITALY
Apostolatus Maris, Pontifical Council for Migrants and Itinerant People, Piazza San Calisto 16, 00153 Rome.
Federazione Italiana Religiose Assistenza Sociale (FIRAS), Via Zanardelli 32, I-00186 Roma.
Mouvement International des Intellectuels Catholiques (MIIC), Secrétariat Professionnel SIJC (Juristes), Via della Conciliazione 4d, I-00193 Roma.
Union Mondiale des Enseignants Catholiques (UMEC), Piazza S. Calisto, 16 I 00153 Rome.
World Union of Catholic Teachers (WUCT), Piazza San Calisto 16, I-00153 Roma; Via della Conciliazione 3-4d, I-00193 Roma, T: 6984786, 564978.

JAMAICA
Jamaica Catholic Education Association, P.O. Box 124, Montego Bay; Mt. Alvernia Convent, Montego Bay, T: 809-952-2391.
Mission to Seamen, Trin, Box 998, Montego Bay 1.

JAPAN
Fellowship of Small and Middle-sized Industry Workers, 473 Kita-hosoe, Shikama-ku, Himeji-shi, T: 354718.
Fellowship of Young Workers, St. Messiah Church, 6 Fuyuki-cho, Fukagawa, Koto-ku, Tokyo, T: 6413886.

KENYA
Kenya Christian Graduates' Fellowship (KCGF), PO Box 48789, Nairobi.

LESOTHO
Lesotho Catholic Teachers Federation (LCTF), Sacred Heart High School, St Monica, PO Leribe.

LUXEMBOURG
Union Catholique Luxembourgeoise des Infirmières et Assistantes Sociales, 23 Blvd du Prince, Luxembourg-ville.

MADAGASCAR
Confédération Chrétienne des Syndicats Malgaches (CCSM), Route de Majunga, BP 1035, Tananarive, T: 23174.
Mouvement d'Adultes, 6 Rue Rainizanabololona, Antanimena, Tananarive.

MALTA
Malta Catholic Action Teachers' Movement (MCATM), Catholic Institute, Floriana.
Malta Union of Teachers (MUT), Teachers Institute, 7/3 Merchants St., P.O. Box 525, Valletta.
Social Action Movement Azjoni Socjali, 15 Old Mint St, Valletta.
YCW Adults, Piazza Filippo Sciberras, Floriana.

MAURITIUS
Ligue Ouvrère d'Action Catholique (LOAC), 42 Rue Pope Hennessy, Port-Louis.

MEXICO
Acción Cristiana Obrera (ACO), Patricio Sanz 449, México 12, DF.
Mission to Seamen, Apdo 1034, Tampico.
Unión Mexicana de Trabajadores Sociales, Liverpool 69-102, México 6, DF.

MOROCCO
Action Catholique, Monde Du Travail, Eglise St. François-Av. Mohammed Slaoui-3000 FES, T: (05)622347.

NETHERLANDS
Good Time Management, Postbus 108, Woudenberg 3930 EC, T: 31-03498-1771, F: 31-0333498-4694.
Netherlands Protestants Union of Civil Servants, Postbus 1804, 's-Gravenhage, T: (070)514051.
Netherlands Union of Catholic Teachers, Koninginnergracht 70-71, 's-Gravenhage, T: (070)557193.
Norwegian Seaman's Mission, Drooglever Fortuynplein 2-6, 3016 GK Rotterdam, T: 010-365123.

NETHERLANDS ANTILLES
Catholic Teachers' Council (RK Onderwijsraad), Juliana Plein 5, Willemstad, Curaçao.
Christian Trade Union of Curaçao, Emmastraat esp Ijserstraat 2, PO Box 154, Willemstad, Curaçao, T: 24405.

NEW ZEALAND
Marketplacers International, P.O. Box 97-543, South Auckland, T: 0-9-266-1101, F: 0-9-266-1095.

NICARAGUA
Central de Trabajadores Nicaragüenses, Apdo Postal 1863, Managua.

NIGERIA
Catholic Teachers' Association, Lagos Branch, P.O. Box 262, Surrulere, Lagos.
Nigerian Movement of Christian Workers, 45 Ikorodu Rd, Yaba, Lagos.

NORWAY
Norwegian Brethren on the Seas, Saltod, 4815 Arendal, T: 041-30 464.
Norwegian Fishermen's Mission, Domkirkegaten 4, 5017 Bergen, T: 05-31 16 10.
Norwegian Seamen's Mission, Strandgaten 198, Postboks 2007 Nordnes, 5024 Bergen, T: 05-32 76 30.
Tentmakers International Exchange, Mäkeberget 6, N-4048 Hafrsfjord, T: 47-51-521-744, F: 47-51-591-9-01, O: E-mail: ekloster@online.no.

PANAMA
Federación Istmena de Trabajadores Cristianos, Via España 16, Of 3, Apdo 6308, Panamá 5, T: 235813.

PARAGUAY
Confederación Cristiana de Trabajadores (CTC), Calle John F. Kennedy 1038, Asunción, T: 235813.
Movimiento International de Intelectuales Católicos (MIIC), Secretariado Latinoamericano, Quinta Ykuá Barrio Isla de Francia, Asunción, T: 60058.
Movimiento Obrero Católica, Oliva 472, Asunción.

PERU
Juventud Obrero Católica Internacional, Secretariado para Latina América, Apdo de Correo 1494, Lima.
Mission to Seamen, Apdo 5152 Lima 18.

PHILIPPINES
Catholic Teachers' Guild of the Philippines, Pius XII Catholic Center, United Nations Av, Manila.
Ozanam Guild, P.O. Box 1329, Manila.
Young Christian Socialists (YCS), Manila.

PORTUGAL
Associação dos Homens de Negócios do Evangelho Completo, Alameda Eça de Queirós, N. 242 - 4. Dt., 4200 Porto; Apartado 4562, 4009 Porto Codex, T: 02-52 22 59.
Associação Portuguesa de Professores Cristãos Evangélicos, Rua Francisco José Vitorino, 13 - 6. Esq., 2795 Linda-a-Velha, T: 01-419 32 91.
MHCN - Cristãos Profissionais e Empresarios, Trav. Francisco dos Santos, 2 - 6. Dt., 2745 Queluz, T: 01-439 18 66, F: 01-439 20 21.

PUERTO RICO
Mission to Seamen, Box 9262 Santurce, PR 00908, T: (809)722-3254.

RUSSIA
Association of Christians in Business, ul Profsouiznaya 43, korp 2, kv 699, Moscow 113209, T: 7095-233-4524, F: 7095-230-2903.

SAINT LUCIA
St. Lucia Catholic Teachers' Association, 36 Coral St, Castries.

SAINT VINCENT & THE GRENADINES
Catholic Teachers' Association, New Montrose.

SEYCHELLES
Union Seychelloise des Travailleurs Chrétiens (USTC), Victoria, Mahé.

SINGAPORE
Christian Business Men's Committe (Singapore) Ltd., 7 Armenian Street #04-12 Bible House, Singapore 179932, T: 344-3838, F: 344-4546.
Christian Seamen Mission, 277 Upper East Coast Road, Singapore 466423, T: 242-5187.
Singapore Nurses Christian Fellowship, 417 New Bridge Road, Singapore 088761, T: 222-3309.

SOUTH AFRICA
Apostleship of the Sea, PO Box 30145, Mayville 4058, 171 Bulwer Rd, Durban, T: 021-81-2207.
Biblia Harbour Mission, PO Box 433, Pretoria 0001, T: 021-21-2328.
Christian Businessmen's Association in Southern Africa, PO Box 977, Rand-en-Dal 1751, 36 Swallow St., Rand-en-Dal, Krugersdorp, T: 011-953-2481.
Christian Lawyers Association, PO Box 7090, Primrose Hill, 1417, T: 011-822-2831, F: 011-822-2147.
Christian Medical Fellowship of South Africa, PO Box 36365, Menlo Park 0102, 54 Daphne Rd, Maroelana, Pretoria, T: 012-46-7148, F: 012-346-1586.
Die Christelike Seemansorganisasie/The Christian Seamen's Organisation, P/B X09, Milnerton 7435, 303 Milpark, Koeberg/Ixia Sts, Milnerton, T: 021-551-2694, F: 021-52-5201.
Dosente vir Christus, c/o Dept of Electrical Engineering, University of Pretoria 0002, Pretoria, T: 012-420-3082, F: 012-43-3254.
Healthcare Christian Fellowship, PO Box 353, Kempton Park 1620, T: 011-975-2934, F: 011-970-4153.

International Sailors' Society (Southern Africa), PO Box 18148, Dalbridge 4014, 113 Umbilo Rd, Durban, T: 031-301-4380.
Natal Teachers' Christian Fellowship, PO Box 100943, Scottsville 3209, 15 Pine St, Pietermaritzburg, T: 0331-42-5373.
Praxis: Journal for Christian Business Management, PO Box 436, Bedfordview 2008, T: 011-455-5146, F: 011-455-2626.

SOUTH KOREA
Catholic Merchant & Industrialist, 1-5, 4-ga, Tangsan-dong, Yongdungp'o-gu, Seoul-shi, T: (02) 632-7419.
Catholic Middle & High School Students Association, 90-7, Hyewhwa-dong, Chongno-gu, Seoul-shi, T: (02) 742-4151.
Catholic Oriental Medical Doctors Association, 434-8, Yonhul 1-dong, Sodaemun-gu, Seoul-shi, T: (02) 324-1004.
Catholic Workers' Movement, 167, Inui-dong, Chongno-gu, Seoul-shi, T: (02) 765-6105.
Christian Society for the Projects of Industrial Development, 2-1, Ewha-dong, Chongro-ku, Seoul 110-500, T: 82-2-742-2520, O: Also tel: 742-2809 or 744-8471 or 744-8472.
Franciscan Association of Market-Traders, 167, Inui-dong, Chongno-gu, Seoul-shi, T: (02) 272-4318.
National Association of the Catholic Taxi-Drivers Apostolate, 24/2, 440-14, Yonghwa-dong, Changan-gu, Suwon-shi, Kyonggi-do, T: (0331) 254-9486.
National Federation of Catholic Physicians' Guilds, 505, Panp'o-dong, Soch'o-gu, Seoul-shi, T: (02) 590-1320.
Seoul Catholic Professsors Association, 1-1, Sinsu-dong Map'o-gu, Seoul-shi, T: (02) 705-8559.
Young Christian Workers, 4491, Shin-gil 6-dong, Yongdungp'o-gu, Seoul-shi, T: (02) 843-6967.

SPAIN
Asociación Cultural de Asistentes Sociales Españolas (ACASE), Lagasca 79, Madrid 6.
Hermandad Obrera de Acción Católica Femenina (HOACF), Alfonso XI 4, Madrid 14.
Hermandades del Trabajo, 1 Juan de Austria 6, Madrid 10.
Movimiento de Apostolado Seglar Maestros de Acción Católica, Alfonso XI 4-6, Madrid 14.
Unión de Graduados de la ACE (Juristas, Farmaceuticos, Tacnicos, Medicos, Cientificos), Luchana 21, Madrid.

SRI LANKA
Christian Workers' Fellowship, YMCA Bldg, PO Box 381, Colombo 1, T: 25252.
Christian Workers' Movement (CWM), 108 Minuwangoda, Negombo.

SURINAME
Catholic Teachers (Katholiek Onderwijs), Gravenstraat 21, Paramaribo.

SWEDEN
Christian Workers (Kristna Arbetare), Järnvägsgatan 35/IV, Landskrona.
United Christian Teachers' Association of Sweden, Box 5, S-610 60 Tystberga, T: (0155)60500.

SWITZERLAND
International Catholic Movement for Intellectual and Cultural Affairs, rue de Alpes 7, C.P. 1062, CH-1701 Fribourg.
Mouvement International des Intellectuels Catholiques (MIIC) (Pax Romana), 1 Route de Jura, Fribourg, T: (037)222649, 222653.
Schweizerischer Verband Evangelischer Arbeiter und Angestelltar (SVEA), Höhenring 29, Zürich 52, T: 466424.

TAIWAN
Adult Movement, Pei Ta Lu 263, Hsinchu.

THAILAND
Catholic Teachers' Association of Thailand, St. Gabriel's College, 565 Samsen Rd, Bangkok 3.

TOGO
Association Togolaise des Volontaires Chrétiens au Travail (ASTOVOCT), Eglise Evangélique, BP 97, Palime.

TRINIDAD & TOBAGO
Catholic Teachers' Association of Trinidad and Tobago, Busby St, Marabella, Trinidad.
Mission to Seamen, Box 561, Port of Spain, T: (809)625-4826.

UNITED STATES OF AMERICA (USA)
America Association of Christians in Behavioral Sciences, P.O. Box 14188, Oklahoma City.
Apostleship of the Sea, 3211 Fourth St., N.E., Washington, D.C. 20017.
Biblical Business Council, P.O. Box 448, Sewell, NJ 08080, T: 609-228-6353, F: 609-216-1403.
Business for Christ International, 1036 Baydon Ln., Chesapeake, VA 23322, T: 757-546-9632, 757-546-8155, F: 757-546-1354, O: seeberger@earthlink.net.
Business Institutes Intl., Inc., 1012 Cliff Dr., Laguna Beach, CA 92681, T: 714-497-7164, F: 714-497-2418.
Business Resource Group, 26W 110 Durfee Road, Wheaton, IL 60187, T: 708-260-0323, F: 708-668-5876.
Catholic Order of Foresters, 355 Shuman Blvd., P.O. Box 3012, Naperville, IL 60566.
Catholic Yellow Pages, O: Web: http://acusd.edu/~rpgordon/pages/yellowpages.html.
Center for Org. & Min. Dev., 120 E. La Habra Blvd., #203, La Habra, CA 90631.
Central Asian Free Exchange (CAFE), P.O. Box 17903, Indianapolis, IN 46217-0903, T: 317-889-1899, F: 317-889-1891.
Christian Architects' Fellowship, 115-25 84th Ave., Kew Gardens, NY 11418.
Christian Business Men's Committee of USA, P.O. Box 3308, Chattanooga, TN 37404, T: 423-698-4444, F: 423-629-4434, O: dferrel@voyageonline.net, www.cmbc.com.
Christian Business Online Magazine, O: Web: www.praiseGodscribes.com/e-zine.shtml.
Christian Educators Association Intl., P.O. Box 50025, Pasadena, CA 91115, T: 818-795-1983.
Christian Labor Association, 260 Gordon Ave., W., P.O. Box 65, Zeeland, MI 49464, T: 616-772-9164, F: 616-772-9830, O: E-mail: chrlabor@eagledesign.com.
Christian Management Association, P.O. Box 4638, Diamond Bar, CA 91765, T: 909-861-8861, F: 909-860-8246.
Christian Medical and Dental Society, P.O. Box 830689, 1616 Gateway, Richardson, TX 75083-0689, T: 214-783-8384, F: 214-783-0921.
Christian Mission for the United Nations Community, P.O. Box 159, Monroe, CT 06468, T: 203-261-1277.
Educational Resources and Referrals-China, 2606 Dwight Way, Berkeley, CA 94704-3000, T: 415-548-7519, F: 415-524-5062, O: Telex: 4941476 PRINZUI.
Educational Services Intl., O: http://osfl.gmu.edu/~dgreene2/esi.html.
Embassy/Executive Ministries Intl., PO Box 545, St. Charles, IL 60174-2590, T: 708-377-2590.
Enterprises for Emmanuel, P.O. Box 2450, Elkhart, IN 46515, T: 219-262-3440, F: 219-262-3440.
Fellowship of Christian Cowboys, P.O. Box 3010, Colorado Springs, CO 80934-3010; Penrose Stadium 1045 W. Rio Grande, 80906, T: 719-630-7636, F: 719-630-7611.
Fellowship of Companies for Christ, 2920 Brandywine Rd., #150, Atlanta, GA 30341, T: 404-457-9700.
Friends Medical Society, 125 W. Walnut Lane, Philadelphia, PA 19144.
Guild of St. Barnabas for Nurses, 68 Adelaide Rd., Manchester, CT 06040.
Houston International Seamen's Center, PO Box 9506, Houston, TX 77261, T: 713-672-0511, F: 713-672-2444.
Institute for Christian Organizational Development, Pasadena, CA 91182, T: 1-800-235-2222, O: Also: 818-584-5342.
Intercristo, 19303 Fremont Ave., N., Seattle, WA 98133-3800, T: 800-251-7740, F: 206-546-7375, O: DHL@crista.org, www.halcyon.com/ico.
International Council of Seamen's Agencies, 2513-162nd Ave. N.E., Bellevue, WA 98008, T: (206) 885-9201.
International Leadership Group, 11590 W. Bernardo Court, Suite 230, San Diego, CA 92127, T: 619-487-2766.
Journal of Christian Nursing, P.O. Box 1650, Downers Grove, IL 60515-0780.
Korean American Christian Business Men's Com. of SC, 4761 Round Top Dr., Los Angeles, CA 90065, T: 213-620-0000.
Marketplace 2000, P.O. Box 234, Pleasanton, CA 94566.
Mastermedia International, Inc., 409 E. Palm Ave., Suite E., Redlands, CA 92373-6135, T: 714-335-7353.
Media Fellowship, P.O. Box 82685, Kenmore, WA 98028, T: 206-488-3965, F: 206-488-8531, O: mfi@usa.net.
Namma, 237 Thompson Street, New York, NY 10012.
National Association of Christian Educators, P.O. Box 3200, Costa Mesa, CA 92628, T: 714-251-9333, F: 714-251-9466.
National Catholic Conference for Seafarers, 545 Savannah Ave., Port Arthur, TX 77640.
National Catholic Society of Foresters, 446 E. Ontario St., Chicago, IL 60611.
National Christian Fellowship, P.O. Box 516, Carlsbad, CA 92008, T: 619-431-9890.
National Institute of Business and Industrial Chaplains, 2650 Fountainview, Ste. 444, Houston, TX 77057, T: 713-266-2456, F: 713-266-0845.
Priority Living, Inc., 17240 E. 17th St., Suite 200, Tustin, CA 92680, T: 714-544-8903.
Religious Conference Management Association, Inc., One RCA Dome, Ste. 120, Indianapolis, IN 46225, T: 317-632-1888, F: 317-632-7909.
Religious Public Relations Council, 475 Riverside Dr., Rm. 1948-A, New York, NY 10115, T: 212-870-2985.
Russian-American Christian Professional Institute, P.O. Box 725500, Orlando, FL 32872-5500, T: 407-859-3388, F: 407-859-8661.
Spiritual Fitness in Business, 1900 Firman Dr., Ste. 100, Richardson, TX 75081.
Strategic Ventures Network, P.O. Box 220, Woodland Park, CO 80866, T: 719-687-6818, F: 719-687-3694, O: 74211.2162@compuserve.com.
Tentmakers International, P.O. Box 33836, Seattle, WA, T: 206-546-8411.
Transport for Christ Intl., P.O. Box 303, Denver, PA 17517, T: 215-267-2444.
University Language Services, P.O. Box 701984, Tulsa, OK 74170, T: 918-495-7045.
Writers Information Network, Box 11337, Bainbridge Island, WA 98110, T: 206-842-9103.

URUGUAY
ACUPS-Asociación Cristiana Uruguaya de Profesionales de la Salud, Casilla de Correo, 23034, Distrito 10, Montevideo, T: 2-356830, F: 2-320621, O: E-mail: acups@chasque.apc.org.
Asociación de Asistentes Sociales del Uruguay, Lavalleja 1824, Montevideo.
Movimiento Obrero de Acción Católica (MOAC), Arenal Grande 2564, Montevideo.

VENEZUELA
Asociación de Ex-Alumnas de la Escuela de SS, Calle de la Iglesia 6, Sabana Grande, Caracas.
Association Catholique Internationale des Enseignants et des Chercheurs en Sciences et Techniques de l'Information, Apdo 422, Caracas.
Comité Unitario de los Sindicalistas Cristianos (CUSIC), Av Paez, Quinta Granada, Apdo 6058, El Paraiso, Caracas, T: 425981.
Movimiento Obrero de Acción Católica, Casa Parroquial, Urbanización Gil Fortoul, Barquisimeto.

VIET NAM
Association des Professionnelles du Servide Social, 38 Rue Tu'Xuong, Saigon.
Association Enseignants Catholiques du Viet Nam, 53 Nguyen-Du, Saigon.
Mouvement des Travailleurs Chrétiens, 370 La Van Duyêt, Saigon.

ZIMBABWE
Christian Writers' Club, Bulawayo.

82
Youth organizations & ministries

Ministry to and by young people; youth evangelism, youth ministry, youth leadership training, youth discipleship, youth conferences, camps, rallies, and retreats; teen ministries, teen mission, youth work projects; youth counseling, at-risk youth, inner-city youth; recreation and activities for youth; YMCA and other facilities and organizations for young people.

AMERICAN SAMOA
Youth for Christ/American Samoa, Box 4235, Pago Pago 96799, T: 684-699-9424.

ANTIGUA & BARBUDA
Youth for Christ/Antigua, P.O. Box 1001, St. John's, Antigua.

ARGENTINA
Youth for Christ/Argentina, Marmol 2, 1655 Chilavert, Buenos Aires; Esmeralda 1065, 1653 Chilavert, Buenos Aires, T: 54-1-729-0073.

AUSTRALIA
Youth for Christ/Australia, 85 Burwood Hwy., Burwood, V1C 3125, T: 61-3-9888-7228, F: 61-3-9888-7221, O: CompuServe IDI: 100036,2244.

AUSTRIA
Christlicher Verein junger MSnner und Frauen (CVJM u. F), Giessaufgasse 27/10, 1050 Wien, T: 0222/54 25 42.
Young Life, Peter Jordan Strasse 72-2, Vienna 190, T: 43-1-368-693.

BANGLADESH
Youth for Christ/Bangladesh, 5/1 Sir Syed Road, Ground Floor, Mohammad Pur, Dhaka 1207, T: 88-02-310-504, F: 88-02-817-280.

BARBADOS
Youth for Christ/Barbados, P.O. Box 660 C, Bridgetown, T: 809-429-4136, F: 809-426-9254.

BELGIUM
Conseil de la Jeunesse Catholique (CJC), Rue Guimard 5, B-1040 Brussel.
Festival Audiovisuel des Jeunes Chrétiens, Rue de l'Ermitage, 21, 1300 WAVRE, T: 32-10-22-49-37.
International Young Christian Workers, 11, rue Plantin, B-1070 Brussels.
Mouvement International de la Jeunesse Agricole et Rurale Catholique (MIJARC), 68, Tiensevest, B 3000 Leuven.
World Federation of Catholic Youth, Av de l'Hôpital Français 31, B-1080 Brussel, T: (02)4280682.

BENIN
Youth for Christ/Benin, Jeunese Pour Christ Benin, BP 1253, Cotonou, T: 229-30-1137.

BOLIVIA
Youth for Christ/Bolivia, Casilla 9096, La Paz, T: 591-278-5458, F: 591-811-9125.

BOTSWANA
Jesus Generation Movement, PO Box 719, Gaborone.
Youth for Christ/Botswana, P.O. Box 686, Gaborone.

BRAZIL
MPC-Mocidade Para Cristo do Brasil, Cx. Postal 1508, Belo Horizonte-MG 30161-970, T: 31-444-5078, F: 31-443-6723.

BRITAIN (UK OF GB & NI)
Baptist Youth (Baptist Union of Ireland), 117 Lisburn Road, Belfast BT 9 7AF, T: (08) 0232 663108, F: (08) 0232 663616.
Belfast City YMCA, 12 Wellington Place, Belfast BT1 6GE, T: (08) 0232 327231, F: (08) 0232 235826.
Catholic Youth Council, Catholic Youth Office, 14 Newton Place, Glasgow C3, T: (041)332-6103.
Catholic Youth Services, 39 Fitzjohn's Ave, London, NW3 5JT, T: 0171-435 3596.
CAYA Catholic Association of Young Adults, 6 Brownsville Road, Heaton Moor, Stockport SK4 4PE.
Church Lads' and Church Girls' Brigade, Nation HQ, Claude Hardy House, 15 Etchinglam Park Rd, Finchley, London N3 2DU, T: (01)349-2616.
Church of Ireland Youth Council, 217 Holywood Road, Belfast BT4 2DH, T: (08) 0232 671659.
Congregational Youth, Livingstone House, 11 Carteret St, London SW1.
Evangelical Youth Movement, Inch Abbey House, Downpatrick, Country Down, NI, T: 2392.
EYM Minitries, 285 Newtownards Road, Belfast BT4 1AG, T: (08) 0232 455158.
Frontier Youth Turst, 183 Albertbridge Road, Belfast BT5 4PS, T: (08) 0232 454806.
IMPACT!, YCW HQ, 120a West Heath Road, London NW3 7TY, T: 0181-458 8416.
International Catholic Society for Girls, c/o St Patrick's Intl. Centre, 24 Gt. Chapel St, London W1V 3AF, T: 0171-734 2156, F: 0171 287 6282.
Irish Methodist Youth Department and Irish Methodist Association of Youth Clubs, Aldersgate House, University Road, Belfast BT7 1NA, T: (08) 0232 327191.
National Catholic Youth Association, 41 Cromwell Rd, London SW7.
National Council of the YMCAs of Ireland, St George's Buildings, 37 High Street, Belfast BT1 2AB, T: (08) 0232 327757.
National Youth Council of Assemblies of God in GB & I, 2 Thornridge, Brentwood, Essex.
Salvation Army Centre for Adolescents, Raisdale, 605 Parkhouse Rd., Barrhead G78 1TE Glasgow, T: 0141-881-1130.
Scripture Union Online, O: www.scripture.org.uk/.
Teen Challenge in Great Britain and Ireland, 4 York Rd, Tunbridge Wells, Kent.
Young Christian Workers, 120A West Heath Road, London NW3 7TY, T: 0181-458 8416, F: 0181-458 7485.
Young Quaker, Friends Meeting House, Meeting House Lane, Lancaster LA1 1TX.
Youth for Christ/Britain, Cleobury Place, Cleobury Mortimer, Kidderminster, Worcs DY14 8JG, T: 44-1299-270-260, F: 44-1299-271-158.

BURKINA FASO
Youth for Christ/Burkina Faso, B.P. 8057, Ouagadougou 04, T: 226-34-5156.

CAMEROON
Presbyterian Youth Centres in Cameroon (PYCs), P.O. Box 57, Bamenda; National Youth Secretary 1/c PYCs, Bamenda, T: 237-36-23-07, F: 237-36-12-81, O: Telex: 5952 KN.

CANADA
Awana Youth Association of Canada, P.O. Box 190, Fonthill, ON L0S 1E0, T: 905-892-5252, F: 905-892-1062, O: E-mail: awana@niagara.com.
Christian Endeavour, R.R. #1, Elora, ON N0B 1S0, T: 519-744-1108, F: 519-744-3546.
Covenant House Toronto, 20 Gerrard St., E., Toronto, ON M5B 2P3, T: 416-598-4898, F: 416-204-7030, O: Intake & admission: 416-593-4849.
Exodus Program, P.O. Box 3280, Langley, BC V3A 4R6, T: 604-888-7348.
Langley Youth Resource Centre, 8393 - 200 St., Langley, BC V3A 4R6, T: 604-888-1717, F: 604-888-7121.
Living Rock Ministries, P.O Box 83015, Hamilton, ON L8L 8E8, T: 905-528-ROCK, F: 905-528-7625.
New Life Girls' Home (Canada), P.O. Box 149, Consecon, ON K0K 1T0, T: 613-394-3341, F: 613-394-0940.
Salvation Army Broadview Village, 1132 Broadview Ave., Toronto, ON M4K 2S5, T: 416-425-1052, F: 416-425-6579.
Straight Talk of Ontario, Box 60072, Oakville, ON L6M 2S0, T: 905-338-8581, F: 905-338-9618.
Turning Point Girl's Home, R.R. #1 Nigh Rd., Ridgeway, ON L0S 1N0, T: 905-894-0671.
Young Life of Canada, 1155 W. Pender #610, Vancouver, BC V6E 2P4, T: 604-688-7622, F: 604-688-3125, O: YLife@alternatives.com, www.alternatives.com/groups/ylife/index.htm.
Young Men's Christian Association in Canada, 2160 Yonge St., Toronto, ON M4S 2A9, T: 416-485-9447, F: 416-485-8228.
Youth for Christ - Canada, 1212-31 Ave. N.E., #540, Calgary, AB T2E 7S8, T: 403-291-1197, F: 403-291-1197, O: YFCCan@cadvision.com.

CAYMAN ISLANDS
Youth for Christ/Cayman Islands, P.O. Box 427W, West Bay, Grand Cayman, T: 809-949-5399, F: 809-949-7602.

CHILE
Salvation Army Youth Camp, Complejo Angostura, Panamericana Sur Km 55, T: 02-824-2398.

CHINA
Youth for Christ/Hong Kong, P.O. Box 78823, Mongkok, Kowloon, Hong Kong; 3 F. Winfield Bldg., 847-861 Canton Road, Yaumatei, Kowloon, T: 852-2385-5900, F: 852-2782-3693, O: Also fax: 852-2782-6490.

COLOMBIA
Youth for Christ/Colombia, Apatado Aereo 38804, Bogota 1, T: 57-1-683-7175.

CONGO-ZAIRE
Fédération Nationale de la Jeunesse Protestante, BP 3094, Kinshasa-Kalina.

COSTA RICA
Asociación Cristiana de Jóvenes, Apdo 701-1007, T: 233-5394.

CROATIA
Youth for Christ/Croatia, c/o The Life Centre, Set. V. Nazora 55, 51260 Crikevenica, T: 385-51-542930.

DENMARK
KFUM og KFUK's Ydre Mission (YMCA and YWCA in Denmark), Valby Langgade 19, 2500 Valby, T: 31 16 60 33.
Youth for Christ/Denmark, P.O. Box 1248, Noerre Alle 44, DK-8000 Aarhus C, T: 45-86-209-855, F: 45-86-209-866.

DOMINICAN REPUBLIC
Union LatinoAmericana de Juventudes Ecuménicas-ULAJE, Postal Dist. 45-2 Sto. Domingo.

ECUADOR
Bienestar Social, 9 de Octubre No. 923, Casilla 34 A, Quito, T: 523-960.
Carceles: Ministerio Carcelario, Casilla 1735, Cuenca, T: 830-277.
Entrenamiento Ministerial, Ave. 10 de Agosto No. 3429 y Murgeon, Casilla 6078, Quito, T: 538-144.
Youth for Christ/Ecuador, Casilla 17-08-8029, Quito, T: 593-2-539-803, F: 593-2-247-235.

EGYPT
Bishopric of Youth, Anba Rueiss, Ramses St, Abbassiya, Cairo, T: 820681.

ESTONIA
Youth for Christ/Estonia, Box 3045, Tallinn 90, EE 0090, T: 372-5-449-257.

ETHIOPIA
Youth for Christ/Ethiopia, P.O. Box 5390, Addis Ababa, T: 251-1-153-190, F: 251-1-515-310.

FIJI
Youth for Christ/Fiji, P.O. Box 16663, Suva, T: 679-361-124.

FINLAND
Salvation Army Youth Centre, Antaverkka, 33480 Yiöjävi, T: 931-81-510.

FRANCE
International Independent Christian Youth (IICY), 11, rue Martin Bernard, F-75013, Paris.
Les Barandons (Salvation Army), 43400 Le Chambon-sur-Lignon, T: 71-59-74-79.
Mission Française de la Jeunesse Orthodoxe auprès des Disséminés, 14 Rue Victor-Hugo, F-92400 Courbevoie.
SYNDESMOS, B.P. 44, 92333 Sceaux, T: 33-1-46-601-774, F: 33-1-46-604-554.
Youth for Christ/France, 9 Rue de l'Industrie, 26000 Valence, T: 33-75-440-309, F: 33-75-811-292.
Youth for Christ—Europe, 13B rue Marechal Ney, Valence 26000, T: 33-75-441-310.

GABON
Jeunesse Chrétienne, Eglise Evangélique du Gabon, BP 80, Libreville.

GAMBIA
Youth for Christ/Gambia, P.O. Box 2562, Serekunda, Banjul; Ofc: 7 MacCarthy Square, Banjul, T: 220-224-752, F: 220-226-962.

GERMANY
Christliche Pfadfinderschaft Deutschlands, Herzbachweg 2, D-646 Gelnhausen.
Eurasia Teen Challenge, Postfach 1246, 6204 Taunusstein 1, T: 06128-5249, F: 06128-5249.
Internationales Katholisches Jugendwerk für Ost- und Mitteleuropa, Beichstr 1, Postfach 149, D-8000 München 44, T: (0811)398160.
Salvation Army Youth Colony, 24306 Plön, Seehof, Steinberg 3-4, T: 04522-9605.
Youth for Christ/Germany, P.O. Box 1180, D-64355 Mühltal; Ofc: Am Klingenteich 16, D-64355 Mühltal, T: 49-6151-145-194, F: 49-6151-144-399.

GHANA
Youth for Christ/Ghana, P.O. Box 11150, Accra North, T: 233-21-226-300.

GRENADA
Youth for Christ/Grenada, Good Hope, St. Pauls, c/o Box 362, St. George's.

GUADELOUPE
Jeunesse Ouvriere Chretienne (JOC), B.P. 414, 28, Peynier, Pointe-à-Pitre, T: 590-83-44-78.

GUATEMALA
Youth for Christ/Guatemala, Juventud Para Cristo, Apartado 736-A, Ciudad de Guatemala 09019, T: 502-492-071.

HONDURAS
Youth for Christ/Honduras, P.O. Box 4055, San Pedro Sula, T: 504-57-3511.

HUNGARY
Youth for Christ/Hungary, 1026 Budapest, Gabor Aron u. 80, T: 36-1-393-0696, F: 36-1-393-0697.

INDIA
Adventist Youth Federation, Southern Flower School, Chanmari II, Lunglei, Mizoram 796701.
Association of Christian Endeavour in India, 8246, Sector - B, Pocket-XI, Nelson Mandela Road, Vasant Kunj, New Delhi 110030.
Blessing Youth Mission, Jadiger Building, Mission Compound, Bijapur, Karnataka 586101.
CBCI Commission for Youth, CBCI Centre, Ashok Place, New Delhi.
Christian Youth Fellowship, Saiha P. O., Mizoram 796901.
Council of Youth Work, Sat-Tal Estate, P. O. Mehragaon, Nainital, Uttar Pradesh 263132.
Full Gospel Christian Youth Fellowship, 8A, Chinnakkadai Street, Papanasam, Tamil Nadu 614205.
India Youth for Christ, Z-64, Anna Nagar, Madras, Tamil Nadu 600040.
National Council of YMCAs of India, Bharat Yuvak Bhavan, Jaisingh Road, New Delhi 110001.
Orthodox Christian Youth Movement of the East, St. Paul's Mission Training Centre, Pulimood P. O., Mavelikara, Kerala 690103.
Pentecostal Youth Department (UPE), Bazar Veng, Lunglei, Mizoram 796701.
Young Life, Peace Cottage, Thottumugham P. O., Kuttamassery, Kerala 683105.

INDONESIA
Youth for Christ/Indonesia, P.O. Box 4089, Jakarta 12040, T: 62-21-740-2105.

IRELAND
Catholic Young Men's Society, 29 North Frederick Street, Dublin 1, T: (353) 01 744264.
Youth for Christ/Ireland, 3 Fitzwilliam St., Belfast BT9 6AW, T: 44-1232-332277, F: 44-1232-230-024.

ISRAEL
YMCA, P.O. Box 19023, Nablus Road, Jerusalem, T: 972-2-894-271, 972-2-894-272, F: 972-2-276-301.

ITALY
Associationes Juventutis Salesianae, Via della Pisana, 1111, 00163 Rome.
General Union of Pastoral Work for Youth, Secretariat, Via Palestro 26, I-00185 Roma.
International Coordination of Young Christian Workers (YCYCW), via dei Barbieri 22, 100186 Rome.
International Federation of Catholic Paorchial Youth Communities, Kipdorp 30, B-2000 Antwerp.
Movimento Oasi, Via dei Laghi, 3 - km. 8,500, I 00040 Castelgandolfo.

IVORY COAST
Youth for Christ/Ivory Coast, 18 B.P. 832 Abidjan 18, T: 225-217-483, F: 225-221-236.

JAMAICA
Youth for Christ/Jamaica, 2 Acacia Avenue, Kingston 5, T: 809-929-7809, F: 809-960-4830, O: Also tel: 809-926-8073.

JAPAN
Kobe Student Youth Center, 3-1-1- Yamada-cho, Nada-ku, Kobe 657, T: 81-78-851-2760, F: 81-78-821-5878.
Osaka YMCA Rokko Center, 875 Kitarokko, Rokkozan-cho, Kobe 657-01, T: 81-78-891-0050, F: 81-78-891-0054.
Youth for Christ/Japan, Ikoma P.O. Box 46, Ikoma Shi, Nara Ken, T: 81-7437-4-4697.

KENYA
Youth for Christ/Crisis Pregnancy Ministry, P.O. Box 66633, Nairobi, T: 254-2-445-997.
Youth for Christ/Kenya, P.O. Box 14880, Nairobi, T: 254-2-781-755, F: 254-2-440-825.

LEBANON
Ecumenical Youth and Student Secretariat of the Middle East, Rue Makhoul, Imm Tanios Rubeiz, BP 1375, Bayrut, T: 341902, 341903.
Youth for Christ/Lebanon, P.O. Box 90-1624, Jdeidet el-Metn, Beirut, T: 961-1-502-596.

LESOTHO
Evangelize Youth, Lesotho Ecumenical Youth Centre, PO Box 6, Morija.

MALAWI
Youth for Christ/Malaysia, P.O. Box 6612, Kg. Tunku, 47308 Petaling Jaya, Selangor Darul Ehsan; No. 4B Tingkat 2, Jalan SS 2/61, 47300 P.J. Selangor 2/6, Darul Ehsan, T: 603-774-6746.

MAURITIUS
Youth for Christ/Mauritius, Allee Brillant Rd., Castel - Phoenix, T: 230-686-7150, F: 230-212-6197.

MEXICO
Adelante Juventud, Apdo 45-641, Argentina No 29, Zona 1, México, DF, T: 212003.
Clubes Bíblicos Juveniles, 21 Pte No 1501-A, Apdo 1011, Puebla, T: 28536.

MOZAMBIQUE
Youth for Christ/Mozambique, Caixa Postal 4539, Maputo.

MYANMAR
Youth for Christ/Myanmar, University P.O. 11041, Yangon; Judson Church Centre, 601 Pyay Road, Yangon, T: 95-1-33957.

NAMIBIA
Youth for Christ/Namibia, P.O. Box 800, Okahandja, T: 264-6221-503748, F: 264-6221-50-1959, O: Also tel: 264-6221-501834.

NEPAL
Youth for Christ/Nepal, P.O. Box 9529, Kathmandu, T: 977-1-524-443, F: 977-1-521-773.

NETHERLANDS
Youth for Christ/Netherlands, Postbus 73, 3970 AB Driebergen; Ofc: Hoofdstraat 260, Driebergen, T: 31-343-515-744, F: 31-343-515-674.

NETHERLANDS ANTILLES
Jeugd Centrale, c/o Bisdom, Willemstad, Curaçao.

NEW ZEALAND
Youth for Christ/New Zealand, P.O. Box 8013, Symonds St., Auckland 1035; 8-10 Dundonald St., Eden Tce, Auckland, T: 64-9-302-7693, F: 64-9-302-7696.

NICARAGUA
Consejo de la Pastoral Juvenil, Av del Centenario 502, Apdo 2008, Managua.

NIGERIA
Youth for Christ/Nigeria, P.O. Box 2532, Akure, Ondo State; Ofc: 39 Oba Adesida Road, Akure, Ondo State, T: 234-34-230-083, F: 234-34-231-633.

NORWAY
Norwegian YWCA/YMCA, Pilestredet 38, Postboks 6814, St Olavs Plass, 0130 Oslo 1, T: 02-20 44 75.

PAKISTAN
Youth for Christ/Pakistan, P.O. Box 1829, Rawalpindi 46000; Fauji Foundation Hospital, Rawalpindi 46000, T: 92-51-486-816, F: 92-61-513-213.

PERU
Youth for Christ/Peru, P.O. Box 3801, Lima 100, T: 51-1-224-8795.

POLAND
Youth for Christ/Poland, Ul Raclawicka 20m 52, 53-145 Wroclaw, T: 48-71-614-500.

PORTUGAL
Ajuda Cristã à Juventude, Quinta Omega, Bairro do Pinheiro, 2640 Mafra, T: 061-5 21 82, F: 061-5 23 72.
Youth for Christ/Portugal, Mocidade Para Cristo, Apartado 10204, 1017 Lisbon-Codex, T: 351-1-887-9051.

REUNION
Youth for Christ/Reunion, Youth in Action, BP 241, 97835 Tampon Cedex.

ROMANIA
Youth for Christ/Romania, Tineret Pentru Cristos, Of.P 7, C.P. ARAD, T: 40-57-259-759.

RUSSIA
YMCA of Moscow, Angels Street 7-21/73, Moscow 107005, T: 7-095-267-9490.

RWANDA
Youth for Christ/Rwanda, B.P. 2140, Kigali, T: 250-84102, F: 250-72045, 76504.

SAINT VINCENT & THE GRENADINES
Youth for Christ/St. Vincent & the Genadines, P.O. Box 818, Kingstown, T: 809-456-2437, F: 809-456-1648.

SAMOA
Youth for Christ/Western Samoa, P.O. Box 511, Matafele, Apia; Forsgren Building, Matafele, T: 685-22665, F: 685-22852, O: Also tel: 685-26888.

SENEGAL
Youth for Christ/Senegal, B.P. 40, Dakar.

SIERRA LEONE
Youth for Christ/Sierra Leone, P.O. Box 1465, Freetown; 33 Garrison St., Freetown, T: 232-22-224-915, F: 232-22-224-439, O: Telex: 3210 BOOTH SL.

SINGAPORE
Metropolitan YMCA, Singapore, 60 Stevens Road, Singapore 257854, T: 737-7755, F: 737-2297.
Youth for Christ Int'l, Raffles City P.O. Box 214, Singapore 911708; 1 Colombo Court #04-18, Singapore 179742, T: 338-7944, F: 336-8776, O: http://www.supernet.ab.ca/yfci, E-mail: 104541.1217@compuserve.com, Web site: www.gospelcom.ne.

SOUTH AFRICA
Africa Youth Evangelism, PO Box 31004, Toriusdal 0134, 1343 Starkey Ave, Waverley, Pretoria, T: 0123-5-1766.
National Youth Leadership Training Programme, PO Box 286, Betha's Hill, 3600 Tanglewood, Wooton ave, Botha's Hill 3600.
Youth Alive Ministries & Foundation, PO Box 344, Dube 1800, 34 Eloff St Ext, Johannesburg, T: 011-331-2228, F: 011-331-2229.
Youth for Christ/South Africa, P.O. Box 75558, Gardenview 2047; Benard Road East, Bedfordview 2008, T: 27-11-615-8970, F: 27-11-622-9909.

SOUTH KOREA
Youth for Christ/Korea, P.O. Box 647, Pusan 600-606, T: 82-51-463-5221, F: 82-51-463-5220.

SPAIN
Asociación Crist. de Asistencia al Joven, Greco, 6. Apdo 306, Roses, 17480 Gerona, T: 25-71-59, F: 15-23-64, O: Also tel: 15-08-97.
Youth for Christ/Spain, Gran Via 576 pral. 2A, 08011 Barcelona, T: 34-3-454-5211, F: 34-3-665-5690.

SRI LANKA
Youth for Christ/Sri Lanka, P.O. Box 1311, Colombo; 129/1B High Level Road, Kirillapone, Colombo 6, T: 94-1-853-242-825, F: 94-1-823-808.

SWAZILAND
Youth for Christ/Swaziland, P.O. Box 384, Manzini, T: 268-5-55-295, F: 268-5-53-338.

SWEDEN
Swedish Christian Youth Council, Regeringsgatan 80, S-111 39 Stockholm, T: (08)115721.

SWITZERLAND
Assoc. Catholique Internationale des Services de la Jeunesse Feminine (ACISJF), 37-39, rue de Vermont, CH 1211 Genève.
European Alliance of YMCAs, Teufenerstrasse 94, St. Galler 9000.
World Alliance of YMCAs, 37 Quai Wilson, 1201 Geneva, T: 41-22-323-100.

TAIWAN
Youth for Christ/Taiwan, 7/Flr 24 Sec. 2 Ho-Ping E. Rd., Taipei, T: 886-2-363-2565, F: 886-2-362-0131, O: Also tel: 886-2-363-7596.

THAILAND
Youth for Christ/Thailand, P.O. Box 1263 NANA, Bangkok 10112; 102/22 Soi Hawgaanka Vipawadee-Rangsit Rd., Dindang, Bangkok 10400, T: 66-2-692-1825, F: 66-2-275-4467, O: Also tel: 66-2-692-1826, 27.

TOGO
Youth for Christ/Togo, B.P. 20091, Lome, F: 228-21-215-836.

TRINIDAD & TOBAGO
Youth for Christ/Trinidad, Corner Cocorite & Farfan Sts, Arima, T: 809-667-1711.

UGANDA
Youth for Christ/Uganda, P.O. Box 6249, Kampala, T: 256-41-273-107.

UKRAINE
Youth of Christ/Ukraine, P.O. Box 42, 252133, Kiev 133, T: 380-44-294-8541.

UNITED STATES OF AMERICA (USA)
Booth House and Host Home, 264 Furman St., Syracuse, NY 13205, T: 315-471-7628.
Cadence International, P.O. Box 1268, Englewood, CO 80150, T: 303-762-1400, F: 303-788-0661, O: Admin@cadence.mhs.compuserve.com.
Christian Endeavor International, 3575 Valley Rd., P. O. Box 820, Liberty Corner, NJ 07938-0820, T: 908-604-9440, F: 908-604-6075.
Evangelical Youth, 139 Macoma Ct., Fort Myers, FL 33908, T: 941-466-1194.
Exodus Youth Services, Inc, PO Box 2398, Gaithersburg, MD 20886, T: 301-590-0155, F: 301-590-0396.
Glacier View Camp, 8748 Overland Rd., Ward, CO 80481, T: 303-459-3244, F: 303-459-3325.
High School Evangelism Fellowship, Inc., P.O. Box 7, Bergenfield, NJ 07621, T: 201-387-1750, F: 201-387-1348, O: HIBA@carroll.com.
Interim Home for Youth (Salvation Army), Box 5085, Hilo, HI 96720; 1786 Kinoole St., Hilo, HI 96720, T: 808-959-5855.
Life Teen Program, O: Web: www.mindspring.com/~jtreanor/.
Mahattan East Group Home, 241 East 116th St., New York, NY 10031, T: 212-534-5455.
Nat'l Catholic Young Adult Ministry Assoc (NCYAMA), 2121 Commonwealth Ave, Brighton, MA 02135, T: 617-746-5850.
National Federation for Catholic Youth Ministry, Inc., 3700-A Oakview Terr., N.E., Washington, D.C. 20017.
New Horizons Youth Ministries, 1002 S. 350 E., Marion, IN 46953-9562, T: 800-333-4009.
Summit Ministries, P.O. Box 207, Manitou Springs, CO 80829, T: 719-685-9203.
Teen Missions International, 885 East Hall Rd., Merritt Island, FL 32953, T: 407-453-0350, F: 407-452-7988, O: TMI@cape.net, www.teenmissions.goshen.net.
VanGuard Mission Teens, Inc., P.O. Box 52, Norma, NJ 08347, T: 609-691-9855.
World Evangelical Fellowship Youth Commission, 1 Minute Man Lane, Lexington, MA 02173, T: 617-862-6499, F: 617-674-2824, O: E-mail: 73314.3240@compuserve.c.
YMCA of the USA, 101 N. Wacker Dr., Chicago, IL 60606, T: 312-977-0031, F: 312-977-9063.
Young Life, P.O. Box 520, Colorado Springs, CO 80901, T: 719-381-1800, F: 719-381-1750, O: www.YoungLife.com.
Young Women's Christian Association of the USA, 726 Broadway, New York, NY 10003, T: 212-614-2700.
Youth Enterprises, Box 95, Chula Vista (Box 1001), Imperial Beach, CA 92032.
Youth for Christ/USA, U.S. Headquarters, P. O. Box 228822, Denver, CO 80222, T: 303-843-9000, F: 303-843-9002, O: www.gospelcom.net/yfc/, E-mail: yfc@gospelcom.net.
Youth Guidance, Inc., R.D. 2, Duff Rd., Sewickley, PA 15143, T: 412-741-8550.
Youth Ministry International, 3366 Burton St., S.E., Grand Rapids, MI 49546, T: 616-949-7030, F: 616-949-1066, O: E-mail: ymi@gospelcom.net, www.gospelcom.net/ymi/.

URUGUAY
Youth for Christ/Uruguay, Casilla De Correo, 875 Montevideo; Ciudad de Bahia Blanca 2464, Montevideo, T: 598-2-470-540.

VENEZUELA
Youth for Christ/Venezuela, Apartado 89875, Zona Postal 1083-A, El Hatillo, Caracas, T: 58-2-963-5714.

US VIRGIN ISLANDS
Diocesan Youth Coordinator, P.O. Box 1918-Kingshill, St. Croix 00851, T: 809-774-0484, F: 809-778-5773.

ZAMBIA
Youth for Christ/Zambia, P.O. Box 72105, Ndola, T: 260-2615-246.

ZIMBABWE
Youth for Christ/Zimbabwe, P.O. Box FM34, Famona, Bulawayo, T: 263-9-74689, F: 263-9-76854.

Part 15

INDEXES

Topics, abbreviations, acronyms,
initials, and photographs

The end of the survey is the beginning of action.
—Samuel Marinus Zwemer, Apostle to Islam (1867-1952)

These indexes assist the reader to navigate in situations of poor information visibility and to find whatever instrumentation or measurement is needed at the moment.

Table 15-1. Polyglot glossary of religious terminology.

The Christian world worships, preaches, teaches, communicates, and functions in more than 10,000 languages, large and small, around the globe. Christians of 6,665 different languages have at least portions of Scripture they can understand. All of this requires the use of very important theological, ecclesiastical, liturgical, religious, and missiological terms. As Christian faith has spread from language to language through 2 millennia, missionaries have faced the challenge of what words to use in each new language to convey Christian truth or to employ in Christian life, service, and worship. Should one (1) find a word that already exists in the new language and put it to new use, or (2) introduce a foreign word as a new term in the new language, or (3) invent a new word by taking one from another language and changing the sounds or orthography to make it fit comfortably in the new language? Each approach has been used many times, and important debates in mission theology have centered on this process, the most notable being the choice of the word for 'God' in Chinese. Some terms have migrated from the words used by the prophets, the apostles, and Jesus himself into thousands of present-day languages. Other terms have been transformed through long chains of transliteration to hundreds of similar, but different, forms.

This list demonstrates the results of this process for 8 of the world's greatest Christian languages. Note that none of these terms began in any of these languages, but in the Greek, Aramaic, and Hebrew of biblical times. This list provides a resource that may help the reader understand many of the non-English names and terms that appear throughout this Encyclopedia. It stands as a reminder that the training of missionaries and world Christian workers of all kinds requires instruction in key Christian terms among many languages. Finally, it is a helpful tool for the large number of international and intercultural Christian churches, denominations, and ministries that must function in many languages.

English	Chinese	French	German	Italian	Portuguese	Russian	Spanish
apostle	shitu	apôtre	Apostel	apostolo	apóstolo	apostol	apóstol
baptism	jinli	baptême	Taufe	battesimo	baptismo	kreshchenie	bautismo
baptize, to	shoujin	baptizer	taufen	battezzare	baptizar	krestit	bautizar
Bible	Shengjing	Bible	Bibel	Bibbia	Bíblia	Biblia	Biblia
bishop	zhujiao	evêque	Bischof	vescovo	bispo	episkop	obispo
blessing	zhufu	bénédiction	Segen	benedizione	bênção	blagoslovenie	bendición
Christ	Jidu	Christ	Christus	Cristo	Cristo	Khristos	Cristo
Christian	jidujiaotu	Chrétien/Chrétienne	Christ/Christin	Cristiano	Cristão	khristianin	Cristiano
Christianity	Jidujiao	Christianisme	Christentum	Cristianesimo	Cristianismo	Khristianstvo	Cristianismo
church	jiaotang	église	Kirche	chiesa	igreja	tserkov	iglesia
commandment	jielü	commandement	Gebot	comandamento	mandamento	zapoved	mandamiento
communion	shengcan	communion	Kommunion	communione	comunhão	prichastie	comunión
community	shequ	communauté	Gemeinschaft	communità	comunidad	soobshchestvo	comunidad
confession	renzui	confession	Bekenntnis	confessione	confissão	ispoved	confesión
congregation	huizhong	congrégation	Kongregation	congregazione	congregação	sobranie	congregación
conversion	zhuanbian	conversion	Bekehrung	conversione	conversação	obrashchenie	conversión
council	juhui	conseil	Rat	concilio	concelho	soviet	consejo
cross	shizijia	croix	Kreuz	croce	cruz	krest	cruz
denomination	jiaopai	dénomination	Denomination	denominazione	denominação	veroispovedanie	denominación
devil	mogui	diable	Teufel	diavolo	diablo	dyavol	diablo
evangelist	chuanjiaoshi	évangéliste	evangelist	evangelista	evangelista	evangelist	evangelista
faith	xinxin	foi	Glaube	fede	religião	vera	fe
fasting	zhaijie	jeûne	Fasten	digiuno	jejum	post	vigilia
fellowship	zhunei	communauté	Gemeinschaft	compagnia	comunhão	bratstvo	comunidad
God	Shen	Dieu	Gott	Dio	Deus	Bog	Dios
gospel	fuyin	évangile	Evangelium	Vangelo	evangelho	evangelie	evangelio
grace	renci	grâce	Gnade	grazia	graçia	milost	gracia
heaven	tiantang	ciel	Himmel	cielo	céu	nebesa	cielo
hell	diyu	enfer	Hölle	inferno	inferno	ad	infierno
Holy Spirit	shengling	Saint-Esprit	Heilige Geist	Spirito Santo	Espírito Santo	svyatoy dukh	Santo Espíritu
hymn	zanmeishi	hymne	Hymne	inno	hino	tserkovny gimn	himno
independent	zizhude	indépendant	selbstandig	indipendente	independente	nezavisimy	indipendiente
Jesus	Yesu	Jésus	Jesus	Gesù	Jesus	Iisus	Jesús
Lord	Zhu	Seigneur	der Herr	Signore	Senhor	Gospod	Señor
love	ci ai	aimer	Liebe	amore	amor	lyubov	amor
man/men	ren	homme/hommes	Mann	uomo/uomini	homen	chelovek	hombre
minister, a	mushi	pasteur	Pfarrer	pastore	pastor	svyashchennik	pastor
missionary	chuanjiaoshi	missionnaire	Missionar	missionario	missionário	missioner	misionario
New Testament	Xinyuequanshu	Nouveau Testament	Neue Testament	Nuovo Testamento	Novo Testamento	Novy Zavet	Nuevo Testamento
offering	fengxian	offrande	Opfer	offerta	offrenda	pozhertvovanie	oblación
Old Testament	Jiuyuequanshu	Ancien Testament	Alte Testament	Antico Testamento	Antigo Testamento	Vetkhy Zavet	Antiguo Testamento
prayer	daogao	prière	Gebet	preghiera	oração	molitva	rezo
preacher	mushi	prédicateur	Prediger	predicatore	pregador	propovednik	predicador
preaching	jiangdao	prédication	Predigt	predicatione	pregar	propovedovanie	predicación
priest	shenfu	prêtre	Priester	prete	sacerdote	svyashchennik	sacerdote
prophet	xianzhi	prophète	Prophet	profeta	profeta	prorok	profeta
religion	zongjiao	religion	Religion	religione	religião	religia	religión
repentance	chanhui	repentir	Reue	pentimento	arrependimento	raskayanie	arrepentimiento
resurrection	fuhuo	résurrection	Auferstehung	risurrezione	ressurreição	voskresenie	resurrección
sacrament	shengcan	sacrement	Sakrament	sacramento	sacramento	prichastie	sacramento
sacrifice	xisheng	sacrifice	Opfer	sacrificio	sacrifício	zhertva	sacrificio
saint	shengren	saint	Sankt	santo	santo	svatoy	santo
salvation	jiushi	salut	Heil	salvazione	salvação	spacenie	salvación
sermon	jiangdao	sermon	Predigt	predica	sermão	propved	sermón
service (worship)	zhurichongbai	office divin	Gottsdienst	servizio	cerimonia	sluzhba	servicio
sin	zui-e	péché	Sünde	peccato	pecado	grekh	pecado
soul	linghun	âme	Seele	anima	alma	dusha	alma
spirit	shengling	esprit	Geist	spirito	espírito	dukh	espíritu
testimony	jiansheng	témoignage	Zeugnis	attestazione	testamunho	svidetelstvo	testimonio
traditions	chuantong	traditions	Traditions	tradizioni	tradição	traditsii	tradicións
Trinity	Sanweiyiti	Trinité	Dreieinigkeit	Trinità	Trinidade	Troitsa	Trinidad
witness, a	jianzhengren	témoin	Zeuge	teste	testamunha	svidetel	testigo
worship	chongbai	adoration	Anbeten	adorare	adoração	poklonenie	adorar

Table 15-2.   Names of countries in 6 major languages.

Hundreds of millions of Christian workers have to live their lives and do their work, including their Christian service, in multilingual situations. Tens of thousands of Christian denominations, churches, organizations, missions, and orders must communicate and function in many languages. They all must remember that the names of countries change from language to language. This list presents standard short names of all the countries of the world in 6 major Christian languages. Not all of the official UN languages are here (Russian, Chinese, and Arabic are excluded). German, for example, is not an official language for the UN, though it is for the WCC, a fact that shows its special importance in international Christian communication. This entire Encyclopedia seeks to present Christianity in the global, international context, though it must be written in one language. With this list, those many Christians interested and involved in the global context will be able to refer to the nations of the world in more than one language, which can prove not only useful but important.

English	French	German	Italian	Portuguese	Spanish
Afghanistan	Afghanistan	Afghanistan	Afghanistan	Afeganistão	Afganistán
Albania	Albanie	Albanien	Albania	Albania	Albania
Algeria	Algéria	Algerian	Algeria	Algélia	Argelia
American Samoa	Samoa Américaine	Amerikanisch-Samoa	Samoa Americane	Samoa Americana	Samoa Americana
Andorra	Andorre	Andorra	Andorra	Andorra	Andorra
Angola	Angola	Angolo	Angola	Angola	Angola
Anguilla	Anguilla	Anguilla	Anguilla	Anguilla	Anguila
Antarctica	Antarctique	Antarkis	Anartide	Antártico	Antártico
Antigua & Barbuda	Antigua	Antigua	Antigua	Antigua	Antigua
Argentina	Argentine	Argentinien	Argentina	Argentina	Argentina
Armenia	Arménie	Armenian	Armenia	Armenia	Armenia
Aruba	Aruba	Aruba	Aruba	Aruba	Aruba
Australia	Australie	Australien	Australia	Austrália	Australia
Austria	Autriche	Osterreich	Austria	Austria	Austria
Azerbaijan	Azerbaïdjan	Azerbaijien	Azerbaijan	Azerbaijan	Azerbaiyan
Bahamas	Bahamas	Bahamainseln	Bahama	Baamas	Bahamas
Bahrain	Bahrein	Bahrein	Bahrein	Barhein	Bahrain
Bangladesh	Bangladesh	Bangladesch	Bangladesh	Bangladesh	Bangladesh
Barbados	Barbade	Barbados	Barbados	Barbados	Barbados
Belgium	Belgique	Belgien	Belgio	Bélgica	Bélgica
Belize	Belize	Belize	Belize	Blize	Belice
Belorussia	Bélarus	Belarußland	Belarus	Belarús	Belarús
Benin	Bénin	Benin	Benin	Benin	Benin
Bermuda	Bermudes	Bermudsinsein	Bermuda	Bermudas	Bermudas
Bhutan	Bhoutan	Bhutan	Bhutan	Bhután	Bután (Bhután)
Bolivia	Bolivie	Bolivien	Bolivia	Bolivia	Bolivia
Bosnia-Herzegovina	Bosnie-Herzégovine	Bosnien-Hertzegovinien	Bosnia-Herzegovina	Bosnia-Herzegovina	Bosnia-Herzegovina
Botswana	Botswana	Botswana	Botswana	Botswana	Botswana
Bougainville	Bougainville	Bougainville	Bougainville	Bougainville	Bougainville
Brazil	Brésil	Brasilien	Brasile	Brasil	Brasil
Britain (UK of GB & NI)	Royaume Uni (Grande-Brétagne)	Grossbritannien	Regno Unita (Gran Bretagna)	Reino Unido	Reino Unido
British Indian OceanTerritory	Territoire Britannique de l'Océan Indien	Britisches Indischer Ozean Territorium	Territorio Britannico dell'Oceano Indiano	Território Británico do Oceano Indico	Territorio Británico del Océano Indico
British Virgin Islands	Iles Vierges Britanniques	Britisch Jungferninseln	Vergini Isole (GB)	Ilhas Virgens Británicas	Islas Vírgenes Británicas
Brunei	Brunéi	Brunei	Brunei	Brunei	Brunei
Bulgaria	Bulgarie	Bulgarien	Bulgaria	Bulgaria	Bulgaria
Burkina Faso	Burkina Faso	Burkina Faso	Burkina Faso	Burkina Faso	Burkina Faso
Burundi	Burundi	Burundi	Burundi	Burundi	Burundi
Cambodia	Cambodge	Kambodscha	Cambodia	Comboja	Camboya
Cameroon	Cameroun	Kamerun	Camerun	Camarões	Camerú
Canada	Canada	Kanada	Canadá	Canadá	Canadá
Cape Verde	Cap-Vert	Kap-verdische Inseln	Isole del Capo Verde	Cabo Verde	Cabo Verde
Cayman Islands	Iles Caimanes	Kaiman Inseln	Isole Caiman	Ilhas Caiman	Islas Caimán
Central African Republic	République Centrafricaine	Zentralafrikanisches Republik	Repubblica Centrafricana	República Centro-Africana	República Centroafricana
Chad	Tchad	Tschad	Ciad	Chade	Chad
Channel Islands	Iles Anglo-Normandes	Kanal Inseln	Isole del Canel	Ilhas Canal	Islas del Canal
Chile	Chili	Chile	Cile	Chile	Chile
China	Chine	China	Cina	China	China
Christmas Island	Ile Christmas	Weihnachtinsel	Isola Christmas	Ilha Natal	Isla Christmas
Cocos (Keeling) Islands	Iles des Cocos (Keeling)	Kokos-Inseln	Isole Cocos (Keeling)	Ilhas Cocos (Keeling)	Islas Cocos (Keeling)
Colombia	Colombie	Kolombien	Colombia	Colômbia	Colombia
Comoros	Comores	Komoren	Comore	Comores	Comores
Congo-Brazzaville	Congo Brazzaville	Congo Brazzaville	Kongo Brazzaville	Congo Brazzaville	Congo Brazzaville
Congo-Zaire	Congo-Zaïre	Congo-Zaire	Kongo Zaire	Congo-Zaire	Congo-Zaire
Cook Islands	Iles Cook	Cook-Inseln	Isole Cook	Ilhas Cook	Islas Cook
Costa Rica	Costa Rica	Costerica	Costa Rica	Costa Rica	Costa Rica
Croatia	Croatie	Croatien	Croatia	Croacia	Croacia
Cuba	Cuba	Cuba	Cuba	Cuba	Cuba
Cyprus	Chypre	Zypern	Cipro	Chipre	Chipre
Czech Republic	République tchèque	Tschechisch Republik	Repubblica Ceca	República Checa	República Checa
Denmark	Danemark	Dänemark	Danimarca	Danamarca	Dinamarca
Djibouti	Djibouti	Dschibuti	Djibouti	Djibouti	Djibouti
Dominica	Dominique	Dominica	Dominica	Dominica	Dominica
Dominican Republic	République Dominicaine	Dominikanische Republik	Repubblica Dominicana	República Dominicana	República Dominicana
Ecuador	Equateur	Equador	Ecuador	Ecuador	Ecuador
Egypt	Egypte	Agypten	Egitto	Egito	Egipto
El Salvador	El Salvador	El Salvador	El Salvador	El Salvador	El Salvador
Equatorial Guinea	Guinée Equatoriale	Aquatorial-Guinea	Guinea Equatoriale	Guiné Equatorial	Guinea Ecuatorial
Eritrea	Erythrée	Eritreien	Eritrea	Eritrea	Eritrea
Estonia	Estonie	Estonien	Estonia	Estonia	Estonia
Ethiopia	Ethiopie	Athiopien	Etiopia	Etiopia	Etiopía
Faeroe Islands	Iles Féroé	Fäöer Inseln	Isole Faroë	Ilhas Feroe	Islas Feroe
Falkland Islands	Iles Falkland	Falklandinseln	Isole Falkland	Ilhas Malvinas	Islas Malvinas
Fiji	Fidji	Fidschi	Figi	Fiji	Fiji
Finland	Finlande	Finnland	Finlandia	Finlândia	Finlandia
France	France	Frankreich	Francia	França	Francia
French Guiana	Guyane Française	Französisch-Guayana	Guyana Francese	Guyana Francesa	Guayana Francesa
French Polynesia	Polynésie Française	Französisch-Polynesien	Polinesia Francese	Polinésia Francesa	Polinesia Francesa
Gabon	Gabon	Gabun	Gabon	Gabão	Gabón
Gambia	Gambie	Gambia	Gambia	Gambia	Gambia
Germany	Allemagne	Deutschland	Germania	Alemanha	Alemania
Ghana	Ghana	Ghana	Ghana	Gana	Ghana
Gibraltar	Gibraltar	Gibraltar	Gibilterra	Gibraltar	Gibraltar
Greece	Grèce	Griechenland	Grecia	Grécia	Grecia
Greenland	Groenland	Grönland	Groenlandia	Gronelândia	Groenlandia
Grenada	Grenade	Grenada	Grenada	Grenada	Granada
Guadeloupe	Guadeloupe	Guadeloupe	Guadalupa	Guadalupe	Guadalupe
Guam	Guam	Guam	Guam	Guam	Guam
Guatemala	Guatemala	Guatemala	Guatemala	Guatemala	Guatemala
Guinea	Guinée	Guinea	Guinea	Guiné	Guinea
Guinea-Bissau	Guinée-Bissau	Guinea-Bissau	Guinea-Bissau	Guiné-Bissau	Guinea-Bissau
Guyana	Guyane	Guayana	Guyana	Guiana	Guayana
Haiti	Haiti	Haiti	Haiti	Haití	Haití
Holy See	Saint-Siège	Heilige Stuhl	Santa Sede	Santa Sé	Santa Sede
Honduras	Honduras	Honduras	Honduras	Honduras	Honduras
Hungary	Hongrie	Ungarn	Ungheria	Hungria	Hungría
Iceland	Islande	Island	Islanda	Islândia	Islandia
India	Inde	Indien	India	India	India
Indonesia	Indonésie	Indonesien	Indonesia	Indonésia	Indonesia
Iran	Iran	Iran	Iran	Irã	Irán
Iraq	Irak	Irak	Iraq	Iraque	Iraq
Ireland	Irlande	Irland	Irlanda	Irlanda	Irlanda
Isle of Man	Ile de Man	Insel Man	Isola Man	Ilha de Man	Isla de Man
Israel	Israël	Israel	Israele	Israel	Israel
Italy	Italie	Italien	Italia	Itália	Italia
Ivory Coast	Côte d'Ivoire	Elfenbeinküste	Costa d'Avorio	Costa do Marfim	Costa de Marfil
Jamaica	Jamaïque	Jamaika	Giamaica	Jamaica	Jamaica
Japan	Japon	Japan	Giappone	Japão	Japón
Jordan	Jordanie	Jordanien	Giordania	Jordania	Jordania
Kazakhstan	Kazakhstan	Kazakstan	Kazakstan	Kazajstán	Kazajstán
Kenya	Kenya	Kenia	Kenya	Quênia	Kenia (Kenya)
Kirghizia	Kirghizistan	Kirgiztan	Kirgiztan	Kirguistán	Kirguistán
Kiribati	Iles Gilbert	Gilbert Inseln	Isole Gilbert	Ilhas Gilbert	Islas Gilbert

Table 15-3. Index of Christian abbreviations, acronyms, and initials.

Some 2,400 sets of initials, most being abbreviations of the names of organizations, are widely used by Christians around the world, or are used in their extensive literature across the 20th century. This index lists, alphabetically by initials, a representative selection of them. First are all recognized and widely-used abbreviations used in this Encyclopedia (excluding codes designed only for this Encyclopedia, which are given in Part 3 "Codebook"); second are acronyms (names as words formed from the initial letters of other words); third are initials of Christian and religious bodies in widespread or international use; fourth are a select few other abbreviations, not of organizations, but commonly used by Christians or in this Encyclopedia (e.g. KJV). The vast majority relate to Christian organizations, with a few widely-used secular abbreviations.

As this is a simple quick-reference tool, translations into other languages are not usually given, nor additional identification, description, or explanation. Most bodies may be identified further from various other resources in this Encyclopedia, in particular Part 14 "Directory". In some cases, the initials do not match the name given, because the commonly-used initials come from one language while the commonly-used name comes from another. This is especially true for Roman Catholic religious orders and congregations, whose initials are usually taken from Latin. Although this index deals predominantly with the abbreviations of names and titles in the main European language they are used in, in a number of cases their counterpart initials in other international languages are also given, with equivalents (e.g. WCC=COE=OKR). In cases where the same initials are used by 2 different bodies, both usages are given. Most of the organizations listed here are still in existence under the names shown, but a small proportion no longer exist or have changed their names; they are given here for historical interest and ease of identification. In many cases, both older and newer names are given (e.g. CIM and OMF, same body, name changed 50 years ago).

An interesting trend of recent decades is that many mission organizations have jettisoned outdated names without departing from well-known initials, resulting in new names that are curious cross-breeds of form. Thus, e.g. Bible Churchmen's Missionary Society became BCMS Crosslinks, Central American Mission became CAM International, Overseas Crusades became OC International, Oriental Missionary Society became OMS International, Regions Beyond Missionary Union became RBMU International, Sudan Interior Mission became SIM International, Unevangelized Fields Mission became UFM International, Worldwide Evangelization Crusade became WEC International, and the Conservative Baptist Foreign Mission Society became CBInternational. These new names are, in fact, names, and not still acronyms—the organizations have deliberately departed from earlier implied geographical restrictions or unpleasant terms (e.g. 'crusade'). That they have deliberately adopted new names with such awkward forms shows the power and importance of initials and acronyms.

Many thousands of initials and abbreviations used in the Christian world are not included here. This listing emphasizes global organizations and organizations of international influence, thus excluding (1) initials of churches and denominations within a country, except major plurinational or global ones, (2) most organizations at the subnational level, and (3) a number at the national level, too. For these, see the individual country articles and tables in Part 4 "Countries". National denominations and organizations whose influence spreads over many nations are more likely to be included.

A

AA	apostolic administration
AA	Assumptionists (Augustinians of the Assumption)
AABF	All Africa Baptist Fellowship
AACC	All Africa Conference of Churches
AACJM	African Apostolic Church of Johane Maranka
AAM	American Advent Mission
AAPC	Adopt-a-People Clearinghouse
AB	Augsburg Bekenntnis/Confession
ABC	African Brotherhood Church
ABCFM	American Board of Commissioners for Foreign Missions
ABCIM	American Baptist Churches in the USA, International Ministries
ABCUSA	American Baptist Churches in the USA
ABFMS	American Baptist Foreign Mission Society
ABHMS	American Baptist Home Mission Societies
ABM	Australian Board of Missions
ABMS	Australian Baptist Missionary Society
ABS	American Bible Society
ABWE	Association of Baptists for World Evangelism
AC	Apostolic Church (Great Britain)
ACAC	American Christian Action Council
ACC	Advent Christian Church
ACC	Anglican Consultative Council
ACC	Australian Council of Churches
ACCC	American Council of Christian Churches
ACE	Ayuda Cristiana Evangélica (Christian Aid)
ACE	Action Catholique de l'Enfance
ACEACCAM	Association des Conférences Episcopales de l'Afrique Centrale et du Cameroun
ACECCT	Association des Conférences Episcopales du Congo/RCA/Tchad
ACF	Action Catholique Familiale
ACF	Asociación Cristiana Femenina (YWCA)
ACGF	Action Catholique Générale des Femmes
ACGH	Action Catholique Générale des Hommes
ACI	Action Catholique des Milieux Indépendants
ACISJF	Association Catholique Internationale des Services de la Jeunesse Féminine
ACJ	Asociación Cristiana de Jovenes (YMCA)
ACKD	Arbeitsgemeinschaft Christlicher Kirchen in der BRD
ACKDDR	Arbeitsgemeinschaft Christlicher Kirchen in der DDR
ACKS	Arbeitsgemeinschaft Christlicher Kirchen in der Schweiz
ACM	Alliance Chrétienne Missionnaire
ACMC	Advancing Churches in Missions Commitment
ACMC	Association of Church Missions Committees
ACMM	Apostolic Church Missionary Movement
ACNAC	Anglican Council of North America & the Caribbean
ACO	Action Catholique Ouvrière
ACP	Apostolic Church of Pentecost
ACROSS	Africa Committee for the Rehabilitation of the Southern Sudan
ACTS	Asia Center for Theological Studies and Mission
ACU	Action Catholique Universitaire
AD	archdiocese
AD	Anno Domini (In the Year of Our Lord)
AdD	Asambleas de Dios
AdD	Assemblées de Dieu
ADEOPA	Association des Eglises et Oeuvres Protestants en Algérie
AE	African Enterprise
AEA	Australian Evangelical Alliance
AEAM	Association of Evangelicals of Africa and Madagascar
AEBET	Asociación Evangélica Boliviana de Educación Teológica
AEBG	Asociación Evangelistica de Billy Graham
AEC	Alianza Evangélica Costarricense
AEC	Antilles Episcopal Conference
AEC	Association des Eglises Chrétiennes
AECEWA	Association of Episcopal Conferences of English-speaking West Africa
AEE	African Evangelistic Enterprise
AEEC	Association des Eglises Evangéliques Centrafricaines
AEET	Asociación Evangélica de Educación Teológica
AEF	Africa Evangelical Fellowship
AEF	Asia Evangelistic Fellowship
AEGM	Anglican Evangelical Group Movement
AEH	Alianza Evangélica Hondureña
AELC	Association of Evangelical Lutheran Churches
AEM	Arbeitsgemeinschaft Evangelikaler Missionen
AEP	Alianza Evangélica de Panamá
AEP	Aliança Evangélica Portuguesa
AEPB	Alliance des Eglises Protestantes du Burundi
AERDO	Association of Evangelical Relief and Development Organizations
AETTE	Associação Evangélica Teológica para Treinamonto por Extensão
AFI	Auxiliaires Féminines Internationales
AFM	Apostolic Faith Mission
AFM	Anglican Frontier Missions
AFMSA	Apostolic Faith Mission of South Africa
AFPRO	Action for Food Production Office
AFREC	Africa Regional Center, UBS
AI	artificial intelligence
AIC	Africa Inland Church
AICA	African Independent Churches Association
AICA	Agencia Informativa Católica Argentina
AICC	Aboriginal and Islander Catholic Council
AICM	African Independent Churches Movement
AICN	African Israel Church Nineveh
AICOME	All-India Congress on Missions & Evangelism
AICS	African Independent Churches Service
AICs	African Indigenous/Independent Churches
AIDS	acquired immune deficiency syndrome
AIM	Africa Inland Mission
AIMI	Africa Inland Mission International
AIMS	Association of International Mission Services
AIMS	Accelerating International Mission Strategies
AIPF	All-India Pentecostal Fellowship
AJI	Amar Jyoti India
AKC	Arbeitskreis Kritisches Christentum
ALC	American Lutheran Church
ALCOE	Asian Leadership Conference on Evangelism
ALER	Asociación Latinoamericana de Educación Radiofónica
ALET	Asociación Latinoamericana de Escuelas Teológicas
ALFALIT	Alfabetización y Literatura
AM	audio modulation, amplitude modulation
AM	Antioch Mission
AMA	Asia Missions Association
AMAA	Armenian Missionary Association of America
AMAC	Medical Aid to Central Africa
AMDAC	Aid to Maternity Dispensaries of Central Africa
AMEC	African Methodist Episcopal Church
AMECEA	Association of Member Episcopal Conferences in Eastern Africa
AMEN	American Military Evangelizing Nations
AMEN	Asociacíón Misionera Evangélica a Las Naciones
AMEZC	African Methodist Episcopal Zion Church
AMG	American Mission to Greeks
AMORC	Ancient Mystical Order Rosae Crucis
AMREC	Americas Regional Center, UBS
AMTB	Associação de Missoes Transculturais Brazileiras
AN	abbey nullius
ANDEB	Asociación Nacional de Evangélicos de Bolivia
AO	autonomous oblast
AOC	African Orthodox Church
AoG	Assemblies of God
AOI	Asian Outreach International
AP	Annuario Pontificio
APCA	Association of Pentecostal Churches in America
APCM	Asia Pacific Christian Mission
APCTE	Association for the Promotion of Chinese Theological Education
ARCIC	Anglican/Roman Catholic International Commission
ARENSA	Asociación Regional Episcopal del Norte del Sud América
ARM	Anglican Renewal Ministries
ARMS	Amateur Radio Missionary Service
ARPC	Associate Reformed Presbyterian Church
ASGM	American Scripture Gift Mission
ASIT	Asociación Sudamericana de Instituciones Teológicas
ASO	Apostolado Seglar Organizado
ASPREC	Asia Pacific Regional Center, UBS
ASSR	autonomous soviet socialist republic
ASTE	Associação de Seminarios Teológicos Evangélicos
ASV	American Standard Version (of the Bible)
ATENE	Association for Theological Education in the Near East
AUCECB	All-Union Council of Evangelical Christians-Baptists
AV	Augsburg Confession
AV	Authorized Version (of the Bible)
AVC	Association of Vineyard Churches
AWCF	Apostolic World Christian Fellowship
AWE	Association for World Evangelism
AWE	Associates for World Evangelization
AWM	Arab World Ministries
AZASA	Assembly of Zionist & Apostolic Churches of South Africa

B

B	Barnabites (Clerics Regular of St Paul)
BAM	Brazilian Association of Missions
BAVACO	Broadcasting and Audio-Visual Aids Committee
BB	Boys' Brigade
BB	Bush Brotherhood
BBC	British Broadcasting Corporation
BBFI	Baptist Bible Fellowship International
BBS	bulletin board system
BC	Before Christ
BCAS	Bush Church Aid Society
BCC	Bible correspondence course
BCC	Botswana Christian Council
BCC	British Council of Churches
BCE	Before Christian Era, or Before Common Era
BCEC	Barbados Council of Evangelical Churches
BCEOM	Bureau Central d'Etude pour les Equipements d'Outre Mer
BCF	Bangladesh Christian Fellowship
BCMC	Belgian Christian Missionary Church
BCMS	Bible Churchmen's Missionary Society
BCMS	BCMS Crosslinks
BCMS	Bible Churchmen's Missionary Society
BCOQ	Baptist Churches of Ontario and Quebec
BCPCU	Bishops' Commission for Promoting Christian Unity
BCSC	Belize Christian Social Council
BCSL	Bishops' Conference of Sri Lanka
BCU	Bible Christian Union
BCWM	Brethren in Christ World Missions
BD	bachelor of divinity
BDKJ	Bund der Deutschen Katholischen Jugend
BEC	British Evangelical Council
BECs	basic ecclesial communities
BEM	Borneo Evangelical Mission
BEM	Belgian Evangelical Mission
BERRS	Bangladesh Ecumenical Relief & Rehabilitation Service
BFBS	British & Foreign Bible Society
BFM	Bethany Fellowship Missions
BFM	Board of Foreign Missions
BFTW	Bibles For The World
BGC	Baptist General Conference
BGEA	Billy Graham Evangelistic Association
BGM	Board of Global Ministries
BiCC	Brethren in Christ Church
BICE	Bureau International Catholique de l'Enfance
BIM	Baptist International Missions
BIM	Bureau d'Information Missionnaire
BIP	Bureau d'Information Protestant
BKED	Bund Katholischer Erzieher Deutschlands
BLASC	Bureau de Liaison d'Action Sociale et Caritative
BLI	Bible Literature International
BLIROI	Bureau de Liaison de l'Information Religieuse dans l'Océan Indien
BLUCE	Bible Lands Union for Christian Education
BM	Basel Mission

806 INDEXES

CFTC Confédération Française des Travailleurs Chrétiens
CFX Brothers of St Francis Xavier
CGAL Conseil Général de l'Apostolat des Laïcs
CGBD Christlicher Gewerkschaftsbund Deutschlands
CGEA Church of God in East Africa
CGH Church of God Holiness
CGI Church Growth International
CGM Church Growth Movement
CGNA Churches of God in North America (General Eldership)
CGP Church of God of Prophecy
CHA Catholic Hospital Association
CHA Christian Holiness Association
CHAG Christian Hospital Association of Ghana
CHC Calvary Holiness Church
CHC Christian Holiday Crusade
CHEF Christian Hope Indian Eskimo Fellowship
CHFD Commission Haitienne des Eglises pour le Développement
CHR Conférence Haitienne des Religieux
CHSFM Committee on the Holy Spirit and Frontier Missions
CIAC Centro Italiano Addestramento Cinematografico
CIAE Conselho das Igrejas Angolanas Evangélicas
CIC Centrum Informationis Catholicum
CIC Christian Information Center
CICC Cook Islands Christian Church
CICM Commission Internationale Catholique pour les Migrations
CICM Missionaries of Scheut (Immaculate Heart of Mary Mission Society) (Scheutists)
CICOP Catholic Inter-American Cooperation Program
CIDAL Centre International de Documentation Audio-Visuelle
CIDER Centro Italiano Documentari Educativi Religiosi
CIDEV Centre d'Information sur le Développement
CIDSE Coopération Internationale pour le Développement Socio Economique
CIEC Confederación Interamericana de Educación Católica
CIEF Centro de Investigaciones y Estudios Familiares
CIEF Confederação das Igrejas Evangélicas Fundamentalistas
CIEMAL Council of Evangelical Methodist Churches in Latin America
CIIC Concilio Internacional de Iglesias Cristianas (ICCC)
CIIR Catholic Institute for International Relations
CIM China Inland Mission
CIM Comité des Instituts Missionnaires
CIMADE Comité Inter-Mouvements aupès des Evacués
CIMIADE Commission des Institutions et Mouvements Internationaux Aposoliques des Enfants
CIMS Consociatio Internationalis Musicae Sacrae
CIO Centro de Información y Orientación
CIO Church Information Office
CIOEW Catholic Information Office for England and Wales
CIP Centre d'Information de Presse
CIPBC Church of India, Pakistan, Burma, and Ceylon
CIPL Commission Interdiocésaine de Pastorale Liturgique
CIRH Conferencia de Institutos Religiosos de Honduras
CIRIC Centre International de Reportages et d'Information Culturelle
CIRMA Conferencia de Institutos Religiosos de México
CIS Catholic Immigrant Service
CISL Confederazione Italiana Sindacati Lavoratori
CISM Conferenza Italiana dei Superiori Maggiori
CISR Conférence Internationale de Sociologie Religieuse
CITA Communications Institute of the Americas
CITC Christian Industrial Training Center
CITC Christian International Travel Club
CJ Josephite Fathers (Congregation of St Joseph)
CJA Christlich-Judische Arbeitsgemeinschaft in der Schweiz
CJC Conseil de la Jeunesse Catholique
CJCLdS Church of Jesus Christ of Latter-day Saints (Mormons)
CJM Eudists (Congregation of Jesus and Mary)
CJPM Central Japan Pioneer Mission
CJSS Conference on Jewish Social Studies
CLA Church of the Lord Aladura
CLADE Congreso Latinoamericano de Evangelización
CLAF Comité Latinoamericano de la Fé
CLAI Concilio Latinoamericano de Iglesias
CLAIM Christian Literature Association in Malawi
CLAL Coopération des Laiques en Amérique Latine
CLAME Comunidad Latinoamericana de Ministerios Evangélicos
CLAR Confederación Latino Americana de Religiosos
CLAST Latin American Federation of Christian Trade Unions
CLAT Latin American Federation of Workers
CLATT Comité Latinoamericano de Textos Teológicos
CLB Church of the Lutheran Brethren
CLC Christian Literature Crusade/Crociata del Libro Cristiano
CLIM Centro Laici Italiani per le Missioni
CLS Christian Literature Society
CLSA Canon Law Society of America
CLSA Christian Literature Service Association
CM Lazzarists (Congregation of the Mission), Vincentians
CM Calvary Ministries (Nigeria)
CMA Church Music Association
CMA Christian and Missionary Alliance
CMC Catholic Media Council
CMC Central Missions Commissariat
CMC Christian Medical Commission
CMCSS Council of Managers of Catholic Secondary Schools
CMCW Christian Mission to the Communist World
CMEC Christian Methodist Episcopal Church
CMF Christian Family Movement
CMF Christian Missionary Fellowship
CMF Claretians (Missionary Sons of the Immaculate Heart of Mary)
CMF Christian Missionary Foundation (Nigeria)
CMI Carmeliani della BV Maria Immacolata
CMI Consejo Mundial de Iglesias (WCC)
CMJ Church's Ministry among the Jews
CMM Congregation of Mariannhill Missionaries
CMML Christian Missions in Many Lands
CMN Conseil Missionnaire National
CMRSWI Conference of Major Religious Superiors of Women's Institutes
CMS Catholic Mission Society
CMS Christian Medical Society
CMS Church Missionary Society (Church Mission Society)
CMSF Missionary Congregation of St Francis of Assisi
CMSM Conference of Major Superiors of Men's Institutes
CMT Confédération Mondiale du Travail
CMWF Christian Medical Workers' Fellowship
CNBB Conferência Nacional dos Bispos do Brasil
CNEC Christian Nationals Evangelism Commission
CNEP Concilio Nacional Evangélico del Peru
CNEP Confederación Nacional Escuelas Particulares
CNEWA Catholic Near East Welfare Association
CNG Christlich Nationaler Gewerkschaftsbund der Schweiz
CNI Catholic News Service of India
CNI Church of North India
CNIR Conferencia Nacional dos Institutos Religiosos
CNM Conseil National Missionnaire
CNPC Centre National de Presse Catholique
CNPL Centre National de Pastorale Liturgique
CNSP Catholic News Service of Pakistan
CoB Church of the Brethren
COC Centro de Orientación Cinematográfica
CoC Church of Christ
COC Coptic Orthodox Church
COCC Confederación de Obreros y Campesinos Cristianos
COCDYC Conservative & Christian Democratic Youth Community
COCU Church of Christ Uniting
COCU Consultation on Church Union
COCU Council on Christian Unity
CODEL Cooperation in Development
CODEPA Centro de Orieniação e Documentação do Ensino Particular
CODIAM Committee for the Development of Intellectual Investments in Africa & Madagascar
COE Church of England
COE Conseil Oecuménique des Eglises (WCC)
COEM Comité Oecuménique d'Entr'aide au Maroc
COEMAR Commission on Ecumenical Mission and Relations
COEMAS Congress on Evangelism for Malaysia and Singapore
COFAE Co-ordinating Office for Asian Evangelism
CofE Church of England
CoG Church of God
COG Church of God
CoGiC Church of God in Christ
CoGWM Church of God World Missions
COJO World Conference of Jewish Organizations
COLJCB Church of Our Lord Jesus Christ (Bickertonites)
COM Centro de Orientacáo Missionária
COMBASE Comisión Bolivianä de Acción Social Evangélica
COMIBAM Ibero-American Missions Congress
COMIBAM Ibero-American Missions Committee
COMINA Conselho Missionário Nacional
CoN Church of the Nazarene
CON Church of the Nazarene
CONCUR Confederación Cubana de Religiosos
CONDOR Confederación Dominicana de Religiosos
CONELA Confraternidad Evangélica Latinoamericana
CONELCO Conseil des Eglises Libres du Congo
Conf conference
CONFER Conferencia Argentina de Religiosas
CONFER Conferencia de Religiosos
CONFER Conferencia Española de Religiosos
CONFER Conferencia Nacional Nicaraguense de Institutos Religiosos
CONFERRE Conferencia de Religiosos de Chile
CONFREGUA Conferencia de Religiosos y Religiosas de Guatemala
CONFRES Confederación de Religiosos de El Salvador
CONVER Conferencia Venezolana de Religiosos
COp Calasantini (Congregation of St Joseph Calasanctius for Christian Works)
COPAL Collège pour l'Amérique Latine
COPE Cadena de Ondas Populares Españolas
COPIC Conselho Português de Igrejas Cristãs
CORDAC Central Africa Broadcasting Company
CORE Committee for Overseas Relief
COREB Conférence des Ordinaires du Rwanda et du Burundi
CORPORI Conferencia de Religiosas de Puerto Rico
CORR Christian Organization for Relief and Rehabilitation
CORSO Council of Organizations for Relief Services Overseas
COSEI Consiglio degli Organismi per Studenti Esteri in Italia
COSIM Coalition for the Support of Indigenous Ministries
COSSEUJCA Conseil Supérieur des Sacrificateurs pour les Eglises Unies de Jésus-Christ en Afrique
COSUMA Conférence des Supérieurs Majeurs du Burundi et du Rwanda
COTE Commission of Theological Education in Taiwan
COTLA Church of the Lord Aladura
COWE Consultation on World Evangelization
CP casella postale/caixa postal/post box
CP Passionists (Congregation of the Passion)
CPA Catholic Press Association
CPAS Church Pastoral-Aid Society
CPB Confederação Pentecostal do Brasil
CPC Centre de Pédagogia Catholique
CPC Christian Peace Conference
CPCV Comité Protestant des Centres de Vacances
CPG Centro Salesiano di Pastorale Giovanile
CPM Ceylon Pentecostal Mission
CPM Congregation of Priests of Mercy
CPN Consejo Pastoral Nacional
CPPS Precious Blood Fathers (Society of the Precious Blood)
CPR Conseil Protestant du Rwanda
CPS Canada Presbyterian Synod
CPSA Church of the Province of Southern Africa
CPSS Catholic Prisoners' Social Service
CPU Church Peace Union
CPWA Church of the Province of West Africa
CPWI Church of the Province of the West Indies
CR(1) Resurrectionists (Congregation of the Resurrection)
CR(2) Theatine Fathers (Order of Regular Clerics)
CRAC Central Religious Advisory Committee
CRAL Communauté Romande de l'Apostolat des Laics
CRB Conferência dos Religiosos do Brasil
CRC Christian Revival Crusade
CRC Conferencia de Religiosos de Colombia
CRC Canadian Religious Conference
CREC Centre Audiovisuel Recherche et Communication
CRFEA Christian Rural Fellowship of East Africa
CRI Conference of Religious of India
CRIC Congregation of Canons Regular of the Immaculate Conception
CRIF Conseil Représentatif des Israelites de France
CRL Congregation of Canons Regular of the Lateran (Augustinian)
CRMF Christian Radio Missionary Fellowship
CRP Conferencia de Religiosos del Peru
CRP Premonstratensians (Order of Canons Regular of Prémontré), Norbertines (O Praem)
CRS Catholic Relief Services
CRS Christian Rural Service
CRS Order of Clerks Regular of Somascha
CRSA Canonesses of St Augustine
CRSB Conference of Religious Sisters, Burma
CRSL Christian Road Safety League
CRU Centre Religieux Universitaire
CRWM Christian Reformed World Missions
CS Scalabrinians (Congregation of the Missionary Fathers of St. Charles)
CSB Basilians (Congregation of St Basil)
CSC Christian Service Committee of the Churches of Malawi
CSC Christian Students Council
CSC Confédération des Syndicats Chrétiens de Belgique
CSC Council of Swaziland Churches
CSC Holy Cross Fathers (Congregation of the Holy Cross)
CSCU Civil Service Christian Union
CSCW Church Society for College Work
CSF Congregazione della Sacra Famiglia di Bergamo
CSI Centro Sportivo Italiano
CSI Christian Safety Index
CSI Church of South India
CSJ Josephites of Murialdo (Congregation of St Joseph)
CSM Christian Socialist Movement
CSM Church of Scotland Mission
CSM Charles Simpson Ministries
CSP Centre Social Protestant
CSP Paulists (Congregation of Missionary Priests of St Paul the Apostle)
CSS Stigmatines (Congregation of the Sacred Stigmata)
CSSM Children's Special Service Mission
CSSp Spiritans (Congregation of the Holy Ghost and the Immaculate Heart ot Mary)
CSsR Redemptorists (Congregation of the Most Holy Redeemer)
CSSR Redemptorists
CSsS Brigittines (Congregation of the Most Holy Savior)
CSV Clerics of St Viator
CSWE Centre for the Study of World Evangelization
CT Christusträger
CT Christianity Today
CTCG Centrale des Travailleurs Chrétiens de la Guyane
CTCH Centro de Teología e Ciencias Humanas
CTEN Council for Theological Education in Nigeria
CTF Catholic Teachers' Federation of England and Wales
CTIC Centrale Technique d'Information Catholique

CTS	Catholic Truth Society
CTS	College Theology Society
CTSA	Catholic Theological Society of America
CTV	Centro Televisivo Vaticano
CUAMM	Collegio Universitario Aspiranti Medici Missionaria
CUC	Church Unity Commission
CUC	Churches' Unity Commission
CUEJ	Centre Universitaire d'Etudes Juives
CUF	Citizens United for Faith
CUFF	Catholics United for the Faith
CUMIF	Collegio Universitario Missionario Internazionale Femminile
CURBZ	Church of Uganda, Rwanda, Burundi, and Zaire
CUSIC	Comité Unitario de los Sindicalistas Cristianos
CUWE	Charismatics United for World Evangelization
CV/AV	Coeurs Vaillants (boys)/Ames Vaillantes (girls)
CVM	Vincentian Congregation of Malabar (Congregazione Vincenziana Malabarese)
CVUOSB	Congregazione Benedettina Vallombrosana
CWA	Concerned Women for America
CWC	Commission on World Concerns
CWCs	Christian World Communions
CWI	Christian Witness to Israel
CWM	Christian Workers' Movement
CWM	Council for World Mission
CWM	Commission on World Missions
CWME	Commission on World Mission and Evangelism
CWN	Christian Weekly Newspapers
CWR	Crusade for World Revival
CWS	Church World Service
CYFA	Church Youth Fellowship Association

D

D	diocese, eparchy
DAWN	Discipling a Whole Nation
DCC	Délégation Catholique pour la Coopération
DCG	Deutsche Christentumsgesellschaft
DCL	doctor of canon law
DD	doctor of divinity
DEA	Deutsche Evangelische Allianz
DEC	Departamento de Educación
DECOS	Departamento de Communicación Social
DEFAP	Départment Evangélique Français d'Action Apostolique
DEMECOS	Departamento de Medios de Comunicación Social
DESAL	Centro para la Desarrollo Económico y Social de América Latina
DFI	Dialogue with People of Living Faiths and Ideologies
DFM	Division of Foreign Missions
DGI	Council of Churches in Indonesia
DIA	Difusiones Interamericanas
DIAL	Documentation et Information sur l'Amérique Latine
DICARWS	Division of Inter-Church Aid, Refugee, and World Service
DKR	Deutscher Koordinierungsrat der Gesellschaften für Christlich-Jüdische Zusammenarbeit
DLBC	Deeper Life Bible Church (Nigeria)
DLM	Danish Lutheran Mission
DM	Dorothea Mission
DMA	Diocesan Missionary Association
DMC	Departamento de Misiones
DMin	doctor of ministry
DMiss	doctor of missiology
DMS	Danish Missionary Society
DNR	David Nunn Revivals, USA
DOM	Division of Overseas Ministries, NCCCUSA
DOPAS	Departamento de Opinión Publica del Arzobispado de Santiago
DRC	Dutch Reformed Church
DRCM	Dutch Reformed Church Mission
DSS	doctor of sacred scripture
DTLM	Door to Life Ministries
DU	Dienste in Ubersee
DVS	Dominion Video Satellite
DW	Diakonisches Werk
DWME	Division of World Mission and Evangelism
DZINTARS	Latvian Catholic Student Association

E

E	east, eastern
E	exarchate
E-2000	Evangelization 2000
EA	exarchate apostolic
EA	Evangelical Alliance
EAB	Evangelische Arbeitnehmerbewegung in Deutschland
EAC	Evangelical Association of the Caribbean
EACA	East Africa Christian Alliance
EACC	East Asia Christian Conference
EACCSE	Ecumenical Advisory Council for Church Service in Egypt
EAD	Evangelical Alliance of Denmark
EAF	Evangelismo a Fondo (Evangelism-in-Depth)
EAFJ	Evangelischer Arbeitskreis für Jugendführung
EAGB	Evangelical Alliance of Great Britain
EAGWM	Evangelische Arbeitsgemeinschaft für Weltmission
EAL	Evangelischer Arbeitskreis Lichtbild
EAM	Evangelical Association of Malawi
EAREC	East Africa Religious Education Committee
EASPI	Evangelical Alliance of the South Pacific Islands
EBF	European Baptist Federation
EBM	Evangelical Baptist Mission
ECAM	Enseignement Catholique au Maroc
ECC	Evangelical Covenant Church
ECCA	Evangelical Covenant Church of America
ECCLA	Latin American Catholic Charismatic Renewal
ECCY	Ecumenical Council of Churches in Yugoslavia
ECD	Ecumenical Council of Denmark
ECF	Episcopal Charismatic Fellowship
ECF	Evangelize China Fellowship
ECFA	Evangelical Council for Financial Accountability
ECHL	Ecumenical Council of Hungarian Churches
ECI	Evangelical Church of India
ECI	Episcopal Conference of Ireland
ECJME	Episcopal Church in Jerusalem & the Middle East
ECL	Episcopal Conference of Lesotho
ECLA	Evangelical Committee for Latin America
ECLOF	Ecumenical Church Loan Fund
ECM	Episcopal Conference of Malawi
ECM	European Christian Mission
ECMY	Evangelical Church Mekane Yesus
ECOC	Evangelical Churchmen's Ordination Council
ECUMEDIA	Ecumenical Media Services
ECUSA	Episcopal Church in the USA
ECUSAT	Ecumenical Satellite Commission
ECWA	Evangelical Church of West Africa
ECZ	Eglise du Christ au Zaire
ed	editor, edited by
EEA	European Evangelical Alliance
EES	Entr'aide Educative et Sociale
EES	European Evangelistic Society
EF	Elim Fellowship/Elim Pentecostal Churches
EFA	Evangelical Fellowship of Asia
EFAC	Evangelical Fellowship of the Anglican Communion
EFB	Evangelical Fellowship of Botswana
EFCA	Evangelical Free Church of America
EFE	Evangelical Fellowship of Egypt
EFGA	Elim Foursquare Gospel Alliance
EFI	Evangelical Fellowship of India
EFK	Evangelical Fellowship of Kenya
EFL	Economic Freedom Level
EFMA	Evangelical Foreign Missions Association
EFMA	Evangelical Fellowship of Mission Agencies
EFOS	Evangelical Fellowship of Singapore
EFP	Evangelical Fellowship of Pakistan
EFR	Evangelical Fellowship of Rhodesia
EFS	Swedish Evangelical Mission
EFSA	Evangelical Fellowship of South Africa
EFSP	Evangelical Fellowship of the South Pacific
EFT	Evangelical Fellowship of Thailand
EFV	Evangelical Fellowship of Viet Nam
EFZ	Evangelical Fellowship of Zambia
EHC	Every Home Crusade
EHC	Every Home for Christ
EID	Evangelism-in-Depth
EIRENE	International Christian Service for Peace
EJCSK	Eglise de Jésus-Christ sur la Terre par le Prophète Simon Kimbangu
EKD	Evangelische Kirche in Deutschland
EKU	Evangelische Kirche der Union
El.	elevation (above sea level)
ELC	Evangelical Lutheran Church
ELCA	Evangelical Lutheran Church of America
ELCE	Evangelical Lutheran Church of Estonia
ELCL	Evangelical Lutheran Church of Latvia
ELCT	Evangelical Lutheran Church in Tanzania
ELFEA	Evangelical Literature Fellowship of East Africa
ELFI	Evangelical Literature Fellowship of India
ELK	Evangelish Lutherische Kirche
ELO	Evangelical Literature Overseas
ELWA	Eternal Love Winning Africa
EMA	Elim Missionary Assemblies
EMA	Evangelical Missionary Alliance
EMB	Evangelical Missions Board
EMBMC	Eastern Mennonite Board of Missions and Charities
EMC	Evangelical Mennonite Church
EMI	Editrice Missionaria Italiana
EMI	Edizioni Missionaire Italiane
EMI	Ent'raide Missionnaire Internationale
EMIS	Evangelical Missions Information Service
EMQ	Evangelical Missions Quarterly
EMS	Evangelical Missionary Society
EMS	Evangelical Missiological Society
ENA	Evangelischer Nachrichtendienst in der DDR
EOC	Ethiopian Orthodox Church
EP	Ecumenical Patriarchate
EP	Equipes Populaires
EPC	Elim Pentecostal Churches
EPC	Ecumenical Patriarchate of Constantinople
EPF	European Pentecostal Fellowship
EPIS	Enseignment par l'Image et par le Son
EPS	Ecumenical Press Service
ERA	Educational (Renewal) Agency
ERBOL	Escuelas Radiofónicas de Bolivia
ERF	Educational Renewal Fund
ERV	English Revised Version (of the Bible)
ESA	Evangelization Society of Australia
ESCEAL	Estudios Sociológicos dul Cristianismo Evangélico en America Latina
ESG	Evangelische Studentengemeinde in Osterreich
ESII	Ecumenical Social & Industrial Institute
ESP	Ecumenical Sharing of Personnel
ESP	extra-sensory perception (telepathy)
esp	especially
ESYSME	Ecumenical Secretariat for Youth and Students of the Middle East
et al	& others
et alia	& other things
et alii	& other people
ETS	Evangelical Theological Society
EUB	Evangelical United Brethren
EUREC	Europe Regional Center, UBS
EUSA	Evangelical Union of South America
eV	eingetragener Verein (registered society) (Germany)
Ev-l	Evangelisch-lutherische
Ev-L	Evanglelsch-Luthensche
EVAF	Evangelismo a Fondo (Evangelism-in-Depth)
EWIBM	East & West Indies Bible Mission
ex	out of, from (used in this Encyclopedia exclusively of schisms or secessions)
EYCE	Ecumenical Youth Council in Europe
EYS	Ecumenical Youth Service
EZA	Evangelische Alliantie (Netherlands)
EZE	Evangelische Zentralstelle für Entwicklungshilfe

F

FABC	Federation of Asian Bishops' Conferences
FAIE	Federación Argentina de Iglesias Evangélicas
FALMI	Francescane Ausiliarie Laiche Missionairie Immacolata
FAO	Food and Agriculture Organization
FASE	Federação de Orgãos para Assistencia Social e Educacional
FAST	Association for Final Advance of Scripture Translation
FBC	Freewill Baptist Church
FBF	see OH
FBM	French Bible Mission
FC	Figli della Carità
FCA	Fellowship of Christian Athletes
FCAC	Federal Council of African Churches
FCC	Fiji Council of Churches
FCCS	Fellowship of Christian Churches in Samoa
FCEI	Federazione delle Chiese Evangeliche in Italia
FCFC	Free Church Federal Council
FCIC	Federal Catholic Immigration Committee
FCME	Federación Católica de los Maestros Españoles
FdCC	Canossians (Congregation of Sons of Charity)
FDM	Brothers of Mercy
FDP	Brothers of Divine Providence
FDPMM	Father Divine Peace Mission Movement
FEAM	Far East Apostolic Mission
FEB	Féderação Espírita Brasileira
FEBA	Far East Broadcasting Association
FEBC	Far East Broadcasting Company
FEBC	Fellowship of Evangelical Baptist Churches
FEBEC	Federación Boliviana de Educación Católica
FEC	Fédération des Enseignements Catholiques
FECC	Fédération des Eglises Chrétiennes du Congo
FECCC	Far Eastern Council of Christian Churches
FECI	Fédération Evangélique de Côte d'Ivoire
FECI	Federation of Evangelical Churches of India
FECOR	Federación Costarricense de Religiosos
FECUN	Federación Española Comunidades Universitarias
FEDAAS	Federación Española de Asociaciones de Asistentes Sociales
FEDAE	Federazione Instituti Dipendenti della Autorita Ecclesiastica
FEDEMEC	Federación Misionera Evangélica Costarricense
FEDEPAR	Federación de Religiosos y Religiosas de Panamá
FEECA	Europäische Foderation für Katholische Erwachsensbildung
FEET	Fédération des Eglises Evangéliques du Tchad
FEGC	Far Eastern Gospel Crusade
FELCSA	Federation of Evangelical Lutheran Churches in Southern Africa
FEM	Federación Evangélica de México
FEME	Fédération des Eglises et Missions Evangéliques en Haute-Volta
FEMEC	Fédération des Eglises et Missions Evangéliques du Cameroun
FENEC	Federación Nicaraguense Educación Católica
FEPS	Fédération des Eglises Protestantes de la Suisse
FERE	Federación Española de Religiosos de Enseñanza
FEREC	Federación de Religiosas de Costa Rica
FERELPAR	Federación de Religiosos del Paraguay
FERES	Fédération Internationale des Instituts de Recherches Socio-Religieuses
FERVE	Federación de Religiosas de Venezuela
FES	Fraternité Evangélique du Sénégal
FFF	Free Farmers' Federation
FFFM	Finnish Free Foreign Mission
FFKM	Fédération Chrétien de Madagascar
FFM	Fellowship of Faith for the Muslim
FFNI	Fellowship for Neighbors India
FFPM	Christian Council of Madagascar
FFSC	Fratelli Francescani della Santa Croce (Treviri)
FFSI	Fratelli Figli di San Giuseppe del Rwanda (Bayozefiti)
FFW	Federation of Free Workers
FGBMFI	Full Gospel Business Men's Fellowship International
FGC	Friends General Conference
FGER	Federación Guatemalteca de Escuelas Radiofónicas
FHSC	Fédération Haitienne des Syndicats Chrétiens
FI	Frontiers International
FIAC	Fédération Internationale des Agences Catholiques de Presse

MMS	Methodist Missionary Society
MMTC	Mouvement Mondial des Travailleurs Chrétiens
MNS	Missionary News Service
MO	Missionari degli Operai
MOAC	Movimento Obrero de Acción Católica
MOC	Mouvement Ouvrier Chrétien
MOPAC	Movimiento de Profesores de Acción Católica
MOSICP	Movimiento Sindical Cristiano de Peru
MRA	World Assembly for Moral Re-armament
MS	Missionaries of Our Lady of La Salette
MSC(1)	Missionaries of the Sacred Heart of Jesus (Issoudun Missionaries)
MSC(2)	Guadelupe (Missionaries of the Sacred Heart and of St Mary of Guadelupe, Mexico)
MSF	Congregation of Missionaries of the Holy Family (Missionari della Sacra Famiglia)
MSFS	Missionaries of St Francis de Sales (Annecy) (Fransalians)
MSG	Management Study Group
msgr	monsignor, monseigneur
MSP	Missionari Servi dei Poveri (Boccone del Povero)
MSpS	Missionaries of the Holy Ghost
MSsCc	Congregation of Missionaries of the Sacred Hearts of Jesus and Mary
MSSP	Società Missionaria di San Paolo
MSSST	Congregation of Missionary Servants of the Most Holy Trinity
MSTM	Movimento de Sacerdotes para el Tercer Mundo
MT	Messianic Testimony
MTC	Mouvement des Travailleurs Chrétiens
MTh	master of theology
MTS	Menno Travel Service
MTW	Mission to the World (Presbyterian Ch in America
MU	Mothers' Union
MUP	Mission to Unreached Peoples
MUST	Metropolitan Urban Service Training Facility
MUT	Malta Union of Teachers
mv	motor vessel
MW	medium-wave
MWC	Mennonite World Conference
MWE	Movement for World Evangelization
MXY	Foreign Missions Institute of Yarumal (Xaverian Missionaries of Yarumal)

N

N	north, northern
N-D	Notre-Dame
n.d.	no date (undated book or publication)
NAAC	Nigeria Association of Aladura Churches
NAAM	National Association for the Advancement of Muslims
NAC	New Apostolic Church
NACLA	National Christian Leadership Assembly
NAE	National Association of Evangelicals
NAES	National Association of Ecumenical Staff
NAFWB	National Association of Free Will Baptists
NAK	Neuapostolische Kirche
NAL	National Association of Laity
NAM	North Africa Mission
NAMB	North American Mission Board (Southern Baptist)
NAPARC	North American Presbyterian and Reformed Council
NARET	National Association of Religious Education Teachers
NARSC	North American Renewal Service Committee
NASB	New American Standard Bible
NASSA	National Secretariat for Social Action
NAWR	National Association of Women Religious
NBBC	non-baptized believers in Christ
NBCLC	National Biblical Catechetical and Liturgical Center
NBEA	National Black Evangelical Association
NBSC	National Black Sisters' Conference
NCAN	National Coalition of American Nuns
NCBC	National Conference of Black Churchmen
NCC	National Christian Council
NCC	National Council of Churches
NCCB	National Conference of Catholic Bishops
NCCC	National Catholic Communications Center
NCCC	National Conference of Catholic Charities
NCCCUSA	National Council of Churches of Christ in the USA
NCCI	National Christian Council of India
NCCIJ	National Catholic Conference for Interracial Justice
NCCJ	National Christian Council of Japan
NCCJ	National Conference of Christians and Jews
NCCK	National Christian Council of Kenya
NCCK	National Council of Churches in Korea
NCCL	National Council of Catholic Laity
NCCNZ	National Council of Churches in New Zealand
NCCP	National Council of Churches in Pakistan
NCCP	National Council of Churches in the Philippines
NCCSL	National Christian Council of Sri Lanka
NCEA	National Catholic Educational Association
NCF	Nurses Christian Fellowship
NCORT	National Catholic Office for Radio and Television
NCRG	New Churches Research Groups
NCRMA	Netherlands Christian Reformed Missionary Association
NCRMS	Netherlands Christian Reformed Missionary Society
NCRV	Netherlands Christian Broadcasting Corporation
NCW	Nederlands Christlijk Wekgeversverbond
NE	northeast, northeastern
NE-2000	New Evangelization 2000
NEA	Norwegian Evangelical Alliance
NEAATS	North East Asia Association of Theological Schools
NEB	New English Bible
NECC	Near East Council of Churches
NEEBII	Near East Ecumenical Bureau Information Interpretation
NEECPR	Near East Ecumenical Committee for Palestinian Refugees
NEFM	National Evangelical Fellowship of Malaysia
NELC	Northern Evangelical Lutheran Church
NEMA	Nigeria Evangelical Missions Association
NEOM	Norwegian Evangelical Orient Mission
NF	National Fellowship
NFCC	Norwegian Free Church Council
NFCC	National Fraternal Council of Churches
NFPC	National Federation of Priests' Councils
NGGM	New Guinea Gospel Mission
NGK	Dutch Reformed Church (South Africa)
NGO	nongovernmental organization
NHA	National Holiness Association
NHK	Netherlands Reformed Church (Nederduits Hervormde Kerk)
NIV	New International Version (of the Bible)
NKJV	New King James Version (of the Bible)
NKV	Nederlandse Christlijke Bond van Overheidspersoneel
NLFA	New Life for All
NLI	New Life International
NLL	New Life League
NLM	Norwegian Lutheran Mission
NMA	Norwegian Missionary Alliance
NMC	National Missionary Council
NMM	Native Missionary Movement
NMR	Nederlandse Missieraad
NMS	National Missionary Society
NMS	Norwegian Missionary Society
NMZ	Nordelbisches Zentrum für Weltmission und Kirchlichen Weltdienst
NNAE	National Negro Evangelical Association
NOBC	National Office for Black Catholics
NOOR	National Organization for Ophthalmic Rehabilitation
NOW	National Organization for Women
NPY	Norwegian Pentecostal Mission
NRB	National Religious Broadcasters
NRC	Netherlands Reformed Church
NRGP	Nationaale Raad voor Gezinspastoraal
NRP	New Reader Scripture Portions
NRS	New Reader Scripture Selections
NRSV	New Revised Standard Version (of the Bible)
NS	Nossa Senhora, Nuestra Señora
NSFC	National Sister Formation Conference
NSS	Navjeevan Susamachar Samiti
NSVC	National Sisters Vocation Conference
NT	New Testament
NTM	New Tribes Mission
NTME	New Testament in Modern English
NTMU	New Testament Missionary Union
NW	northwest, northwestern
NWEF	North West Frontier Fellowship
NYBA	National Young Buddhist Association
NYLC	National Young Life Campaign
NZBFMS	New Zealand Baptist Foreign Mission Society
NZEC	New Zealand Episcopal Conference
NZG	Netherlands Missionary Society (Nederlandsch Zendeling-Genootschap)

O

O	ordinarite
OAIC	Organization of African Instituted (Independent) Churches
OAR	Order of Recollect Augustinians
OBNOVA	Federation of Associations of Ukrainian Catholic Students
OBSC	Open Bible Standard Churches
OC	Carmelites (Order of Our Lady of Mt Carmel)
OCart	Carthusian Order
OCASEI	Obra Católica de Asistencia a Estudiantes Iberoamericano
OCASHA	Obra de Cooperación Apostólica Seglar Hispano-americana
OCD	Order of Discalced Carmelites
OCEC	Oficio Central de Educación Católica
OCES	Office Chrétien de l'Enregistrement Sonore
OCFC	Office Catholique Français du Cinéma
OCFRT	Office Catholique Francais de Radio-Télévision
OCI	OC International (formerly Overseas Crusades)
OCIC	Office Catholique International Cinéma
OCIPE	Office Catholique d'Information sur les Problèmes Européens
OCist	Cistercians
OCL	Office Chrétien du Livre
OCLC	Online Computer Library Catalog
OCM	Grupe d'Organismes de Coopération Missionnaire
OCMCS	Oficina Coordinadora de los Medios de Comunicación Social
OCR	Cistercian Order, Reformed (Trappists)
OCSHA	Obra de Cooperación Sacerdotal Hispanoamericana
OCSO	Trappists (Order of Cistercians of the Strict Observance)
OCU	Officers Christian Union
OCYAK	Orthodox Christian Youth Association of Kenya
OD	Open Doors with Brother Andrew
OdeM	Mercedarians (Order of Our Lady of Mercy for the Ransom of Captives)
ODUCAL	Organización de Universidades Católicas de América Latina
OESA	Hermit Augustinians (Order of Hermits of St Augustine)
OFM	Franciscan (Order of Friars Minor)
OFMCap	Capuchins (Order of Friars Minor Capuchin)
OFMConv	Conventuals (Order of Friars Minor Conventual)
OH	Order of Brothers Hospitallers of St John of God
OHC	Order of the Holy Cross
OIC	Organisations Internationales Catholiques
OIEC	Office International de l'Enseignement Catholique
OJD	Okumentscher Jugenddienste
OJRiO	Okumenischer Jugendrat in Osterreich
OKB	Osterreichische Katholische Bibelwerk
OKR	Okumenischer Rat der Kirchen (WCC)
OM	Operation Mobilization
OM	Minim Hermits of St Francis of Paola
OMECO	Oficina Nacional de Medios de Communicación Social
OMF	Overseas Missionary Fellowship
OMI	Missionaries Oblates of Mary Immaculate
OMS	Oriental Missionary Society
OMSI	OMS International
OMSC	Overseas Ministries Study Center
OMV	Oblates of the Blessed Virgin Mary
ONCS	Office National des Communications Sociales
OOCC	Oriental Orthodox Churches Conference
OP	Dominicans (Order of Preachers)
OPC	Orthodox Presbyterian Church
OPraem	Premonstratensians, or Norbertines (Canons Regular of Prémontré)
ORSA	Recollect Augustinians (Order of Augustinian Recollects)
ORU	Oral Roberts University
OSA	Augustinian Friars (Order of St Augustine)
OSB	Confederate Benedictines (Order of St Benedict)
OSBM	Basilians (Order of St Basil the Great)
OSC	Crosier Fathers (Canons Regular of the Order of the Holy Cross)
OSC	Orthodox Syrian Church
OSCam	Camillians (Ministers of the Sick, Clerics Regular)
OSCE	Orthodox Syrian Catholicossate of the East
OSCO	Overseas Students Coordination
OSFO	Osborn Foundation International
OSFS	Oblates of St Francis of Sales
OSLAM	Organización de Seminanos Latinoamericanos
OSM	Servites (Order of the Servants of Mary)
OSsT	Trinitarian Fathers (Order of the Most Holy Trinity)
OSU	Ursuline Sisters of the Roman Union
OT	Old Testament
OW	Operation World
OYM	Orthodox Youth Movement

P

P	patriarchate, patriarchal diocese
p	number of pages in book, article, or periodical
p.a.	per annum/year
p.d.	per diem/daily
PA	Patres Albi, Pères d'Afrique (WF)
PA	prefecture apostolic
PABATS	Philippine Association of Bible and Theological Schools
PACLA	Pan-African Christian Leadership Assembly
PACTEE	Pakistan Committee on Theological Education by Extension
PAFES	Pan African Fellowship of Evangelical Students
PAFTEE	Philippine Committee on Theological Education by Extension
PAG	Pentecostal Assemblies of God
PALMS	Paulian Association Lay Missionary Secretariat
PAO	Professional Athletes Outreach
PAoC	Pentecostal Assemblies of Canada
PAoW	Pentecostal Assemblies of the World
PAoWI	Pentecostal Assemblies of the West Indies
PAS	Pater Ahlbrinckstrichting
PATS	Philippines Association of Theological Schools
PAVLA	Papal Volunteers for Latin America
PAW	Pentecostal Assemblies of the World
PBCS	Pakistan Bible Correspondence School
PCA	Presbyterian Church of Australia
PCA	Presbyterian Church in America
PCC	Pacific Conference of Churches
PCC	Pentecostal Church of Christ
PCE	Presbyterian Church of England
PCEA	Presbyterian Church of East Africa
PCEC	Philippine Council of Evangelical Churches
PCG	Pentecostal Church of God
PCI	Pentecostal Church Incorporated
PCJ	Prêtres du Sacré-Coeur de Jésus de Bétharram
PCMA	Protestant Churches Medical Association
PCR	Programme to Combat Racism
PCSA	Presbyterian Church of South Africa
PCUS	Presbyterian Church in the US
PCUSA	Presbyterian Church of the USA
PCW	Presbyterian Church of Wales
PDC	Partido Democrata Cristiano
PDG	Pastoral Development Group
PE	patriarchal exarchate
PECUSA	Protestant Episcopal Church in the USA
PEFA	Pentecostal Evangelical Fellowship of Africa
PEMS	Paris Evangelical Missionary Society
PERSETHIA	Association of Theological Schools in Indonesia

Table 15-4. Photographic index.

Listed here are all subjects and topics illustrated in the photographs contained in this Encyclopedia, or described in their accompanying captions. In particular, the index lists their countries, places, occasions, events, persons, peoples, languages, cultures, ethnolinguistic groups, religions, types of Christian, ecclesiastical blocs and traditions, types of denomination, types of Christian organization, councils, activities, evangelism, religious practices, resources, buildings, projects, rituals, liturgies, uniforms, vestments, robes, representations (images, icons, paintings, statues, art), and

the range of phenomena of religion and Christianity in general. It also lists illustrations of the methods of description, enumeration and analysis evolved in this Encyclopedia. On the other hand, the index does not record the smaller details of all photographs. In general, it omits names of small towns and villages, also names of smaller denominations and individual churches or congregations.

The index omits certain widely-applicable terms that would otherwise occur too frequently. 'Roman Catholics' and 'Protestants', for instance, occur in every other illustration.

Terms thus omitted include: cathedrals, Christian, Christians, church, churches, church buildings, Protestants, Roman Catholics, Catholics, Evangelicals (partially included), priests, ministers, clergy, preachers.

Christianity is noted in greater detail than other religions. For 'processions', for example, the listing is of Christian processions, even though processions of other religions may appear in the Encyclopedia. So also with many other listings.

Table 15-5. Standard and definitive locations index.

This is primarily an index of general subjects, major categories of data, and types of information.

KEY
1. Numbers standing alone (1–999) = page numbers of major or definitive locations, always preceded by Part number.
2. Entries without page numbers = standard locations, repeated for all countries.
3. The world 'total' = global total of category shown.

There is no need in this Encyclopedia for a general subject index because (a) most significant material has already been presented throughout under several alphabetical listings (countries, denominations, service agencies, directory entries), and (b) most specific categories of data or information are placed in standardized locations within the overall framework. As a result, comparative data from one country to the next can rapidly be found. This final index attempts to facilitate the whole process of locating specific data.

There are 2 types of entry below: those with page numbers, and those with Part numbers. These will now be described.

(1) All numbers (1–999) standing alone below are *page numbers* unless otherwise clearly stated. These, located by preceding Part number, give the definitive or major or unique location or locations of specific categories—items of data or information or definition, or directory of addresses; they also indicate pages with global maps where relevant. Hence, if you wish to find the total number of Methodists, or Maronites, in the world for a particular year, this index refers you to its definitive location. Sometimes 2 or more locations are given, placing the required total in different contexts. This represents the quickest way of finding herein an exact total or figure or definition that you require for any clearly-defined category.

(2) Locations with *Part numbers* (e.g. 'Part 4, SECULAR DATA') give the regular or standardized or repeated location or locations in which may be found information on any category existing in a large number of countries. The locations are repeated in exactly the same position and sequence from one country to the next, especially throughout Part 4. Hence, in cases where a specific statistical category or other item of data occurs frequently for a large number of countries, or denominations, or religions, the index refers the reader to any standard position or location that it occupies in a country's survey article or other position, at which the data may immediately be found. These locations are given here mainly by Parts (Part 1, Part 2, etc), with further internal position where simple to describe. Thus the reference 'Part 4, SECULAR DATA, STATE' tells the reader that the items he or she wants will be found throughout Part 4 for all countries under the heading SECULAR DATA, and under the sub-heading STATE at that location.

INDEX TO MAJOR SUBJECTS IN THE 15 PARTS

Volume 1 contains Parts 1-6
Volume 2 contains Parts 7-15

atlas, Part 6
bibliography, Part 13
Christianity, by country, Part 4
Christianity, global status of, Part 1
cities, Part 10
codebook, Part 3
countries, Part 4
countries, statistics of, Part 5
cultures, Part 8
dictionary, Part 12
directory, Part 14
glossary, Part 2
indexes, Part 15
languages, Part 9
maps, Part 6
organizations, Christian, Part 14
peoples, Part 8
provinces, Part 11
religion, by country, Part 4
religions, Part 7
statistics, by country, Part 5
world summary, Part 1

10/40 Window, map, Part 6, Global Map 4

A

abbreviations, Christian, Part 15, Table 15-3
academies, Bible, Part 4, Tables 2, column 10
acronyms, Christian, Part 15, Table 15-3
activities, global Christian, Part 5, Table 5-1
additional smaller denominations, Part 4, Tables 2, NOTES, OTHER DENOMINATIONS/CHURCHES
adherents of all religions in countries, Part 4, Tables 1
adherents of all religions by continents, Table 1-4
adherents of all religions, global, Part 1, Table 1-1
adjectives of nationality, Part 4, SECULAR DATA, STATE
adult church members, Part 4, Tables 2, column 6
adult church members, total, Table 1-5
adult literacy, Part 4, SECULAR DATA, EDUCATION
Adventists, global statistics, Table 1-5
affiliated Christians, by country, Part 4, Country Tables 1
affiliated Christians, total, Part 1, Table 1-1
affluence, Part 1, Global Diagram 1
Afghanistan, Part 4, 49f
Africa, adherents of all religions in, Table 1-4
African Independent Christians/churches, global statistics, Table 1-5
Africans, total, Table 1-4
Afro-American spiritists, Part 4, Tables 1
Afro-Americans, total, Part 8, Table 8-1
agricultural & rural mission, organizations, directory, Part 14, 786
Ahmadis, Part 4, Tables 1, NOTES
Ahmadis, total, Part 1, Table 1-1
aid & relief organizations, directory, Part 14, 709
Alawites, Part 4, Tables 1, NOTES
Alawites, total, Part 1, Table 1-1
Albania, Part 4, 51f
Albanian/Greek, total, Part 12, 651
Albanians, total, Part 8, Table 8-1
Algeria, Part 4, 55f
aliens received from abroad as missionaries, Part 5, Table 5-1, columns 111-112
Altaic, total, Part 8, Table 8-1
alternative ethnolinguistic names, Part 8, Table 8-2
American Indians, total, Part 8, Table 8-1
American Samoa, Part 4, 58f
Amerindians, total, Part 8, Table 8-1
Anabaptists/Mennonites, global statistics, Table 1-5
Andorra, Part 4, 60f
Anglican Charismatics, Table 1-6b
Anglican Evangelicals, global statistics, Table 1-5
Anglican pentecostals/charismatics, Table 1-6b
Anglican religious orders, Part 12, 672
Anglicans, by continent, AD 1900-AD 2025, Table 1-4
Anglicans, by country, AD 1900-AD 2025, Part 4, Country Tables 1
Anglicans, High Church, global statistics, Table 1-5
Anglicans, Low Church, global statistics, Table 1-5
Anglicans, total, Part 1, Table 1-1
Anglo-Catholics, global statistics, Table 1-5
Angola, Part 4, 61f
Anguilla, Part 4, 66f
animists, Part 12, 652
annual change in religious adherents, Part 4, Tables 1
annual family income, Part 4, SECULAR DATA, ECONOMY
annual rate of increase, all religions, Part 1, Table 1-1
Antarctica, Part 4, 68f
Antigua & Barbuda, Part 4, 69f
anti-religious, atheist, & humanist organizations, directory, Part 14, 711
apostolate, persons dedicated to the, Part 12, 652
apostolic force, Part 12, 652
Apostolic Pentecostals, global statistics, Table 1-5
apparel, merchandise, & gifts, Part 14, 711
Arabic/Greek, total, Part 12, 652
Arabic-speaking Orthodox, global statistics, Table 1-5
Arabs, total, Part 8, Table 8-1
architecture, by country, Part 4, (text), Christianity
Arctic Mongoloids, total, Part 8, Table 8-1
area, by country, Part 4, SECULAR DATA, State
Argentina, Part 4, 71f
armed forces, by country, Part 4, SECULAR DATA, State
Armenia, Part 4, 76f
Armenian Apostolics, total, Table 1-5
Armenian Orthodox, global statistics, Table 1-5
Armenians, total, Part 8, Table 8-1
art & architecture, by country, Part 4, (text), Christianity
art (religion & the arts) organizations, directory, Part 14, 711
Aruba, Part 4, 79f
Ashkenazis, Part 4, Tables 1, NOTES, JEWS
Ashkenazis, total, Part 1, Table 1-1
Asian Indigenous churches, total, Table 1-5
Asians, total, Table 1-4
assemblies, local spiritual, Part 4, Tables 1, NOTES, BAHA'IS
Assyrians, total, Part 12, 652
atheist, anti-religious, & humanist organizations, directory, Part 14, 711
atheistic states, Part 5, Table 5-1, columns 60-63
atheists, Part 12, 653
atheists, by continent, AD 1900-AD 2025, Table 1-4
atheists, by country, AD 1900-AD 2025, Part 4, Country Tables 1
atlas, Part 6
atlases, Part 13
audiences, radio/TV, Part 5, Table 5-1, columns 147-149
audio recordings, organizations, directory, Part 14, 712
audio scriptures, availability by language, Part 9, Table 9-13
audiovisual resources, directory, Part 14, 713
Australia, Part 4, 81f
Australian Aborigines, total, Part 8, Table 8-1
Australoid, Part 8, Table 8-1
Australoids, total, Part 8, Table 8-1
Austria, Part 4, 86f
Austro-Asiatics, total, Part 8, Table 8-1
autonomy, year of church's, Part 4, Tables 2, column 10
availability of scriptures, in all countries, Part 5, Table 5-1, columns 120-146
Azerbaijan, Part 4, 90f

B

Baha'is, Part 12, 653, Part 7
Baha'is, by continent, AD 1900-AD 2025, Table 1-4
Baha'is, by country, AD 1900-AD 2025, Part 4, Country Tables 1
Baha'is, total, Part 1, Table 1-1, Part 7
Bahamas, Part 4, 93f
Bahrain, Part 4, 95f
Baltics, total, Part 12, 653
Bangladesh, Part 4, 97f
banned churches, Part 4, Tables 1, footnotes, CRYPTO-CHRISTIANS
Bantoid, total, Part 8, Table 8-1
Bantu, total, Part 8, Table 8-1
baptismal candidates, Part 4, Tables 2, column 10
baptisms, annual adult, Part 4, Tables 2, column 10
baptisms, annual infant, Part 4, Tables 2, column 10
baptisms, total annual, Part 1, GD 3
Baptistic-Pentecostals, global statistics, Table 1-5
Baptistic-Pentecostals, total, Part 12, 653
Baptists, global statistics, Table 1-5
Baptists, total, Part 12, 653
Barbados, Part 4, 101f
Basques, total, Part 12, 653
beds, hospital, Part 4, SECULAR DATA, HEALTH
Belgium, Part 4, 103f
Belize, Part 4, 107f
Belorussia, Part 4, 110f
Belorussian Orthodox, global statistics, Table 1-5
Belorussians (Eastern-rite), Part 12, 653
Benin, Part 4, 112f
Berbers, total, Part 12, 653
Bermuda, Part 4, 115f
Bhutan, Part 4, 117f
Bible & scripture organizations, directory, Part 14, 713
Bible academies, Part 4, Tables 2, column 10
Bible distribution, by country, Part 5, Table 5-1, 843-846
Bible institutes, Part 4, Tables 2, column 10
Bible schools & colleges, Part 14, 716
Bible study organizations, directory, Part 14, 716
Bibles distributed, for all countries, Part 5, Table 5-1, columns 120, 125
biblical studies, bibliography, Part 13, 686-687
bibliographic resources, by country, Part 13, Table 13-4
bibliographies in this Encyclopedia, Part 13, 683-685
bibliography, Part 13
bibliography, biblical studies, Part 13, 686-687
bibliography, bibliographies, Part 13, 695-697
bibliography, Buddhism, Part 13, 693
bibliography, by country, Part 4, (text), Bibliography
bibliography, Christianity & religions, Part 13, 692
bibliography, Christianity, contemporary status, Part 13, 686
bibliography, church history, Part 13, 687-688
bibliography, cities, Part 10, 544-547
bibliography, directories, yearbooks, handbooks, & almanacs, Part 14, 739
bibliography, ecumenism, Part 13, 690-691
bibliography, electronic media, Part 13, 695
bibliography, esthetics (Christian), Part 13, 691
bibliography, Hinduism, Part 13, 693
bibliography, history of doctrine, Part 13, 688-689
bibliography, interfaith dialogue, Part 13, 694
bibliography, Islam, Part 13, 692
bibliography, Judaism, Part 13, 692-693
bibliography, missiology, Part 13, 690
bibliography, non-Christian religions, Part 13, 692-694
bibliography, peoples, Part 8, 20-25
bibliography, religion, study of, Part 13, 694-695
bibliography, theological ethics, Part 13, 690
bibliography, theology, Part 13, 689-690
birth rate, by country, Part 4, SECULAR DATA, Demography
bishops-at-large, total, Part 12, 654
Black indigenous Christians, Part 12, 654
Black Muslims, total, Part 12, 654
Black neo-pentecostals, Part 12, 654
Black population, total, Part 12, 654
Black/Third-World indigenous councils, total, Part 12, 654
blind population, by country, Part 4, SECULAR DATA, Health
Bolivia, Part 4, 119f
book titles on Christian & religious subjects, Part 13, Table 13-2
book titles with 'Jesus Christ', by language, Part 13, Table 13-1
books about Christianity, Part 13, 682-683
books, new titles p.a., by country, Part 4, SECULAR DATA, Literature
Bosnia-Herzegovina, Part 4, 123f
Botswana, Part 4, 126f
Bougainville, Part 4, 129f
Braille scriptures, availability by language, Part 9, Table 9-13
Brazil, Part 4, 130f
Brethren (Christian Brethren), global statistics, Table 1-5
Britain (UK of GD & NI), Part 4, 138f
British Indian Ocean Territory, Part 4, 148f
British Virgin Islands, Part 4, 149f
British-Israelites, Part 12, 654
broadcast stations, Part 14, 721
broadcasting organizations, directory, Part 14, 717
broadcasting, Christian, by country, Part 4, (text), Broadcasting & media
broadcasting, Christian, by country, map, Part 6, Global Map 9
broadcasting, Christian, by language, Part 9, Table 9-13
broadcasting, Christian, by region & peoples, map, Part 6, Global Map 9
Brown population, total, Part 12, 654
Brunei, Part 4, 151f
Buddhism, bibliography, Part 13, 692
Buddhist believers in Christ (hidden), global statistics, Table 1-5
Buddhists, by continent, AD 1900-AD 2025, Table 1-4
Buddhists, by country, AD 1900-AD 2025, Part 4, Country Tables 1
Bulgaria, Part 4, 153f
Bulgarian Orthodox, global statistics, Table 1-5
Bulgarian-rite, Part 12, 654
Burkina Faso, Part 4, 157f
Burundi, Part 4, 159f
Byzantine, Part 12, 654

C

Cambodia, Part 4, 162f
Cameroon, Part 4, 165f
camps, retreat centers, & lay training centers, Part 14, 721
Canada, Part 4, 169f
canonical relationships, Part 4, Tables 2, column 4
Cape Verde, Part 4, 175f
capital city, Part 10, Table 10-5
Capoids, total, Part 12, 654
cardinals, total, Part 12, 654
cargo cults, Part 12, 654
catechesis & Christian education, directory, Part 14, 721
catechist training schools, Part 4, Tables 2, column 10
catechists, Part 4, Tables 2, column 10
catechists, total, Part 12, 654
catechumens, Part 4, Tables 2, column 10
Catholic (non-Roman) churches, in a country, Part 4, Tables 2
Catholic Apostolics, total, Table 1-5
Catholic Charismatic Renewal, by continent, AD 1970-AD 2000, Part 6, Global Map 5-2
Catholic Church, in a country, Part 4, Tables 2
Catholics (non-Roman), Part 4, Tables 2
Catholics (non-Roman), total, Table 1-5
Catholics, Latin-rite, global statistics, Table 1-5
Catholics, Roman, by continent, AD 1900-AD 2025, Table 1-4

Volume 1 contains Parts 1-6
Volume 2 contains Parts 7-15

Acknowledgements

The authors and editors wish to acknowledge their indebtedness not only to the contributors, collaborators, and consultants listed at the beginning of the First and Second Editions of this Encyclopedia, but also to the very large number of other persons and organizations who supplied information each about their own activities. Many of the denominations listed in each country, and many other agencies and bodies mentioned or described, supplied this information to us either directly by mail, e-mail, or in person in interviews.

We also express gratitude to a number of church-related organizations which contributed grants towards the compiling either of one of the two Editions or of both. Grants and assistance small or large were received from the following: Adveniat (Germany), American Baptist Churches, Anglican Church of Canada, Anglican Consultative Council (UK), Anglican Frontier Missions, Apostolic Nunciature of Kenya, Bethany World Prayer Center, Bishops' Conference of Germany, William R. Bright, Campus Crusade for Christ International, Caleb Project, CBInternational, Christian Church (Disciples of Christ), Church Missionary Society (UK), Church of the Province of Kenya, Church of the Savior Philadelphia, John & Pam Cobb, Commission on World Mission and Evangelism/WCC, Cooperative Baptist Fellowship, Des Plaines Trust, Division of Overseas Ministries/NCCCUSA, Mark & Beth Dubis, Dunwoody Foundation, Episcopal Church in the USA, FERES (Belgium), Field Ministry Internships, First Foursquare Church on the Way Los Angeles, Global Center Samford University, Global Strategy Mission Association, Humanum (Germany), the 'Jesus' Film Project, Kempsville Presbyterian Church Virginia Beach, John & Beth Labonty, Lausanne Committee for World Evangelization, Lonnie & Ramona Long, Lutheran Church Missouri Synod, Lutheran World Federation, Maryknoll Mission, Missio (Germany), Mission Training and Resource Center (Pasadena), Missions Advanced Research and Communication Center (Monrovia, USA), National Council of Churches of Christ in the USA, William R. O'Brien, Operation World, Jerry & Deana Parker, Charles Price, Sacred Congregation for the Evangelization of Peoples, Short-term Evangelical Mission, Southern Baptist Convention, St. Giles Endowment Fund, St. Giles Presbyterian Church Richmond, Strang Communications, Survey Application Trust (Grubb Institute for World Studies, UK), Vinson Synan, Third Presbyterian Church Richmond, United Bible Societies, United Church of Christ (USA), United Methodist Church (World Division, Board of Global Ministries), United Presbyterian Church in the USA, Virginia Baptist Resource Center, World Council of Churches, World Mission Prayer League, World Reach, World Vision International. Among donors of smaller grants were: Abbaye d'Orval (Belgium), American Baptist Foreign Missionary Society, Assemblies of God (USA), Christian Reformed Church, Conservative Baptist Association of America, Department of Philosophy & Religious Studies/University of Nairobi, Lutheran Church in America, The Navigators, Netherlands Reformed Church, Reformed Church in America, Sudan Interior Mission, United Church Board for World Mission, United Reformed Church (UK), West Indies Mission, World Radio Missionary Fellowship, et alia.

Maps
The authors are grateful also to Oxford Cartographers for designing and producing the 16 Global Maps in Part 6 "Atlas", and also to Oxford University Press who permitted us to reproduce in our Part 6 their 18 Human Environment maps from the Oxford World Atlas/Penguin World Atlas, suitably updated by Oxford Cartographers.

Photographs
We further acknowledge with gratitude the assistance of a number of photographic libraries and agencies, as well as individual experts and specialists, in the assembling of a collection of illustrations which would do justice to the complexity of contemporary global Christianity and its context in the modern world. Half of the photographs in the First Edition were the editor's own. Half in the Second Edition were taken and supplied by Maurice Harvey, photojournalist of the United Bible Societies for many years. The other photographs in both Editions were supplied by the organizations and persons listed alphabetically below (with individuals included alphabetically by surname), whose cooperation and permission to reproduce has been much appreciated. In a number of cases, the denominations illustrated in photographs sent us copies waiving credit or charges. Their illustrations have made our survey that much more complete. Lastly, a few professional photographic libraries searched their collections for our more unusual categories.

Every effort has been made to trace and contact copyright owners. If there are any inadvertent omissions in these acknowledgements, we apologize to those concerned and will remedy this when possible.

Photo credits
Joy Adamson, Aegte Foto, Africapix, Agenzia Informazioni Missionarie, Hamilton Aikin, Air France, AMECEA, American Bible Society, Anglican Consultative Council, AREPI, Argus Group, Asia Theological Association, Associated Newspapers Ltd, Associated Press Ltd, Association Culturelle Orthodoxe Russe, Association of Evangelicals of Africa & Madagascar, Audiovisie NZR Baarn, Australian Inland Mission, Dr K. Baago, L. Balterman, Baptist Missionary Society, Carlo Bavagnoli, BBC Photographic Library, Bernhard Johnson, British & Foreign Bible Society, British Airways, British Museum, Brunner & C., Camera Hawaii, Camera Press Ltd, Camerapix, Campus Crusade for Christ, Candida Photos, Central Office of Information, Central Press Photos Ltd, Ceylon Pictorials, Christian Mission to the Communist World, Christian Weekly Newspapers Ltd, Christianity Today, Church Information Office, Church Missionary Society, Church Times, Church of Jesus Christ of Latter-day Saints, Church World Service, Collection Iris, Council for World Mission, Create International, Gerald Cubitt, Dagen, Daily News, M. L. Daneel, P. V. de Decker, Die Burger, Jesper Dijohn, Gregory Duriniak, East African Standard, East African Venture Co, Editions de Luxe Estel Lavelle, Editions Greff, Editions Hoa-qui, Editions Jaeger, Edizioni Angeli Terni, Evangelical Union of South America, Eveche de Basse-Terre, Fides-Foto, Foto Felici, Foto Simon, Gibraltar Tourist Office, Dr Roswith Gerloff, Lydon Giles, V. G. Greisen, Hal Herman, Dr Norman Horner, Iglesia Anglicana en el Norte Argentina, Indonesia Council of Churches, Info (Botswana), International Baha'i Audio-Visual Center, Michael Irwin, Carl Iwasaki, Harold D. Jantz, Jeremy Grayson, Jersey Evening Post, John Piercy Ltd, D. Kalaba, Otis Keener, Keston College, Leon V. Kofod, Edouard Kutter Jr, Hans Lachmann, RWJV, Lamontfoto, Lausanne Committee for World Evangelization, Life Picture Service, Logos Ministry for Orthodox Renewal, London Daily Mail, Luis Palau Evangelistic Team Inc, K. Lyons, L'Osservatore Romano, Michael McCann, D. A. McGavran, Kalevi A. Mäkinen, Malaysian Airline System, Malaysian Information Service, Ted Marriott, K. Martens, Maryknoll, Dr John Mbiti, Methodist Church in Tonga, Methodist Church Nigeria, Methodist Missionary Society, Methodist Missions, Methodist Prints, Robert Miles, Missionary Aviation Fellowship, Missions to Seamen, J. H. Moore, Nationfoto, New Covenant Magazine, Newsweek International, Nordisk Pressefoto, Operation Mobilization, T. J. Padwick, Paris-Match, May Park, C. D. Paulme, Photo Almassy, Photo COE, Photo Lamont, Pilgrim Films, Paul Popper Ltd, Porter's Photo News, Press Association Ltd, Pressefoto, Johann Gürer, Pressfoto, Pretoria News, Qantas, Radio Times Hulton Picture Library, M. T. Ramakatane, Revista Mundo, Rex Studio Garbis Semerdjian, Ross Photo, Royal Norwegian Ministry of Foreign Affairs, Salvation Army Information, Ernest Satow, Frank Scherschel, Walter Scott, Max Seifert, Seventh-day Adventists, Calvin Shenk, SIM Publications, S. Skulina, Sky-foto Möller, Lester Sloan, Peter Solbjerghoj, South American Missionary Society, Southern Baptist Convention, Sport & General Press Agency, State Museum Berlin, Swazi Times, Sygma, George Talanos, John Taylor, The News/New York, Pat Thomas, Time, Inc, Trans World Radio, Dr Gary Trompf, Y. Tourigny, Dr Harold W. Turner, UNESCO, Unification Church, United Bible Societies, United Church of Canada/Berkeley Studio, Unitedf Methodist Communications, United Methodist Global Ministries, United Methodist Missions, United Nations, United Press International, United Society for the Propagation of the Gospel, Rein Välme, J. -F. Vincent, Vivante Afrique, Harold Wenger, West Indies Mission, Wide World Photos Inc, World Council of Churches, World Outlook, World Pentecost Magazine, World Vision International, Worldwide Evangelization Crusade

Technical description
The authors and editors also acknowledge their indebtedness to the large number of persons and organizations who supplied information, data, and programs about their own activities in electronic form.

Computers played an essential role in the formation and presentation of this work. The following lists the major areas of development, the programs and the equipment used.

The GEM file server/workstation was custom built from Tailored Data Solutions in Chester, Virginia. It is a dual Pentium™ 350 MHz with 256 MB of RAM running Windows NT™ 4.0 SP4 with two 10 GB Quantum™ hard drives. The 'Great Commission Instrument Panel' graphics were developed using Microsoft Visual FoxPro™ 5.0, Microsoft Excel™ 97 with SP2, and Corel Draw™ 7. Regional Maps were created using Atlas GIS™ 3.01 and Corel Draw™ 7. Databases were developed on Microsoft Visual FoxPro™ 5.0 and Microsoft Access™ 97 with SP2.

The bulk of data entry was undertaken on five machines: an Apple Macintosh PowerPC™ 6100/60AV with a Sonnett Crescendo™ G3 NuBus card, 40 MB RAM and 250 MB hard drive; an Apple Power Macintosh™ G3 233 MHz with 64 MB RAM and a 4 GB hard drive; an Apple iMac™ 233 MHz with 64 MB of RAM and a 4 GB hard drive; a Dell Dimension XPS™ P133c Pentium 133 MHz, 32 MB RAM, and a 3 GB hard drive; and a Compaq Presario™ 4712 Pentium 166 MHz with 72 MB RAM and a 3 GB hard drive.

Desktop publishing was done on the three Apple machines listed above and a primary machine: an Apple Power Macintosh™ G3 233 MHz with 96 MB RAM, 4 GB hard drive, and a Hitachi SuperScan™ Pro 21 inch screen. The manuscript was published using QuarkXPress™ 4.04 with Em Software XData™ 4.0 and MarkzWare MarkzTools™ III 7.9. Photos were produced using an Epson® ES-1000C scanner with Second Glance Scantastic™ software 4.0 and Adobe Photoshop™ 4.0.1. Graphics were developed using Macromedia Freehand™ 5.02 and Ready, Set, Go™. Prepress preparations were processed with MarkzWare Flightcheck™ 3.61, and Adobe Acrobat™ 4.0.

The manuscript was printed on our Apple LaserWriter™ 8500 with 48 MB of RAM.